Contemporary Authors®

Cumulative Index

Contemporary Authors

Cumulative Index

Contemporary Authors Volumes 1-168
Contemporary Authors New Revision Series Volumes 1-72

Citations to entries in *Contemporary Authors* are identified as follows:

R after number • *Contemporary Authors* First Revision Volumes 1-44
Volume number only • *Contemporary Authors* Original Volumes 45-168
CANR • *Contemporary Authors New Revision Series*, Volumes 1-72
CAP • *Contemporary Authors Permanent Series*, Volumes 1-2
CAAS • *Contemporary Authors Autobiography Series*, Volumes 1-30
CABS • *Contemporary Authors Bibliographical Series*, Volumes 1-2

Citations to entries in other reference works are identified as follows:

AAYA • *Authors and Artists for Young Adults*, Volumes 1-27
AITN • *Authors in the News*, Volumes 1-2
BEST • *Bestsellers* (quarterly; citations appear as Year: Issue number)
BLC • *Black Literature Criticism*
BW • *Black Writers*, Volumes 1-2
CDALB • *Concise Dictionary of American Literary Biography*, 1640-1865, 1865-1917, 1917-1929, 1929-1941, 1941-1968, 1968-1988
CDBLB • *Concise Dictionary of British Literary Biography*, Before 1660, 1660-1789, 1789-1832, 1832-1890, 1890-1914, 1914-1945, 1945-1960, 1960 to Present
CLC • *Contemporary Literary Criticism*, Volumes 1-112
CLR • *Children's Literature Review*, Volumes 1-52
DA • *DISCovering Authors*
DAB • *DISCovering Authors: British*
DAC • *DISCovering Authors: Canadian*
DAM • *DISCovering Authors: Modules*
    DRAM: *Dramatists Module;* **MST:** *Most-studied Authors Module;*
    MULT: *Multicultural Authors Module;* **NOV:** *Novelists Module;*
    POET: *Poets Module;* **POP:** *Popular Fiction and Genre Authors Module*
DC • *Drama Criticism*, Volumes 1-8
DLB • *Dictionary of Literary Biography*, Volumes 1-202
DLBD • *Dictionary of Literary Biography Documentary Series*, Volumes 1-18
DLBY • *Dictionary of Literary Biography Yearbook*, 1980-1997
HLC • *Hispanic Literature Criticism*
HW • *Hispanic Writers*
JRDA • *Junior DISCovering Authors*
MAICYA • *Major Authors and Illustrators for Children and Young Adults*
MTCW • *Major 20th-Century Writers*
NNAL • *Native North American Literature*
PC • *Poetry Criticism*, Volumes 1-23
SAAS • *Something about the Author Autobiography Series*, Volumes 1-26
SATA • *Something about the Author*, Volumes 1-102
SSC • *Short Story Criticism*, Volumes 1-31
TCLC • *Twentieth-Century Literary Criticism*, Volumes 1-84
WLC • *World Literature Criticism*; **WLCS:** *World Literature Criticism Supplement*
YABC • *Yesterday's Authors of Books for Children*, Volumes 1-2

Note: This cumulative index supersedes all lower-numbered *CA* indexes and is not bound in any *CA* volume.

Staff

Index Coordinators
Catherine Donaldson
Joshua Kondek

Printed in the United States of America

Contemporary Authors®

Cumulative Index
Contemporary Authors Volumes 1-168
Contemporary Authors New Revision Series Volumes 1-72

This Index Includes References to All Entries in the *Contemporary Authors* Series

Contemporary Authors--Volume 168 brings the total coverage to approximately 101,000 writers, both living and deceased, a large portion of whom cannot be found in other reference works. Writers in fiction, general nonfiction, poetry, journalism, drama, motion pictures, television, and other fields are all included in *CA*. Each new volume contains sketches on authors not previously listed in the series. Cumulative index published separately and distributed with even-numbered original volumes. All volumes in the series are in print.

***Contemporary Authors New Revision Series*--** Provides completely updated information on authors listed in previous volumes of *CA*. Sketches from a number of volumes are assessed, and only entries requiring significant change are revised and published in the *CA New Revision Series*. Volumes 1-72 are in print.

(All volumes published under the former revision system, 1-4 through 41-44 First Revision, will remain in print.)

***Contemporary Authors Permanent Series*--**Consists of updated listings for deceased and inactive authors removed from original volumes 9-36 when these volumes were revised. Two volumes only; both are in print.

***Contemporary Authors Autobiography Series*--** Presents specially commissioned autobiographies by leading writers. Volumes 1-30 are in print.

***Contemporary Authors Bibliographical Series*--** Contains primary and secondary bibliographies as well as analytical bibliographical essays. Volumes 1-2 are in print.

A Sample Index Entry:

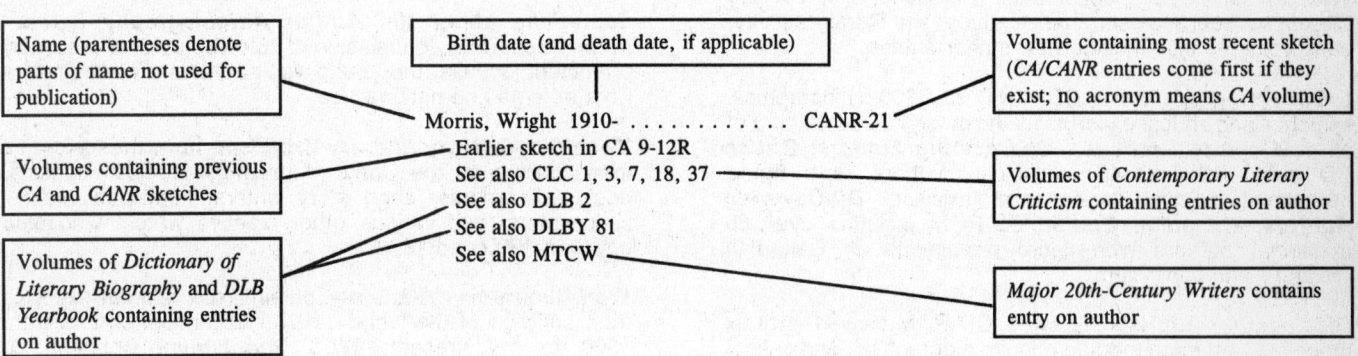

| Name (parentheses denote parts of name not used for publication) | Birth date (and death date, if applicable) | Volume containing most recent sketch (*CA/CANR* entries come first if they exist; no acronym means *CA* volume) |

Morris, Wright 1910- CANR-21
Earlier sketch in CA 9-12R
See also CLC 1, 3, 7, 18, 37
See also DLB 2
See also DLBY 81
See also MTCW

Volumes containing previous *CA* and *CANR* sketches

Volumes of *Dictionary of Literary Biography* and *DLB Yearbook* containing entries on author

Volumes of *Contemporary Literary Criticism* containing entries on author

Major 20th-Century Writers contains entry on author

The *CA* Index Also Includes References to All Entries in These Gale Reference Works

Authors and Artists for Young Adults--Provides sketches on young adult authors and creative artists of all nationalities.

Authors in the News--Reprints articles from American periodicals covering authors and members of the communications media. Two volumes, 1976-77.

Bestsellers--Furnishes information about best-selling books and their authors for the years 1989-90.

Black Literature Criticism--Contains excerpts from criticism of the most significant works of major black writers from the past 200 years.

Black Writers--Compiles selected *CA* sketches on prominent 20th-century black writers.

Children's Literature Review--Includes excerpts from reviews, criticism, and commentary on works of children's authors and illustrators.

Concise Dictionary of American Literary Biography--Contains selected entries on major American authors from the *Dictionary of Literary Biography*.

Concise Dictionary of British Literary Biography--Provides selected entries on major British authors from the *Dictionary of Literary Biography*.

Contemporary Literary Criticism--Presents excerpts from current criticism of the works of today's novelists, poets, playwrights, short story writers, scriptwriters, and other creative writers.

Dictionary of Literary Biography--Encompasses three series. *Dictionary of Literary Biography* furnishes overviews of authors and their work in the larger context of literary history. *Dictionary of Literary Biography Documentary Series* illuminates the careers of major figures through a selection of literary documents. *Dictionary of Literary Biography Yearbook* summarizes the year's literary activity; early volumes also include new author entries.

DISCovering Authors--CD-ROM of 300 biographical sketches and critical excerpts for the most-studied authors of all eras and nationalities. **DISCovering Authors: British** CD-ROM includes 46 additional authors who figure prominently in British literature and curriculum. **DISCovering Authors: Canadian Edition** CD-ROM includes over 50 additional authors who figure prominently in Canadian literature and curriculum.

DISCovering Authors Modules--CD-ROM divided into six modules, with each module offering biographical and critical information on authors within a specific genre: *DISCovering Most-Studied Authors, DISCovering Novelists, DISCovering Multicultural Authors, DISCovering Poets, DISCovering Dramatists,* and *DISCovering Popular Fiction and Genre Authors.*

Drama Criticism--Furnishes excerpts from criticism of the works of most-studied dramatists of all eras and nationalities.

Hispanic Literature Criticism--Compiles excerpts from criticism of the works of Hispanic writers of the late 19th and 20th centuries.

Hispanic Writers--Contains selected *CA* sketches on over 400 prominent 20th-century Hispanic writers.

Junior DISCovering Authors--CD-ROM product containing biographical sketches and critical excerpts for over 300 authors, from all eras, nationalities and genres, most-studied by middle-school students.

Major Authors and Illustrators for Children and Young Adults--Contains in six volumes both newly written and completely updated *SATA* sketches on nearly 800 authors and illustrators for young people.

Major 20th-Century Writers--Presents in four volumes selected *CA* sketches on over 1,000 of the most influential novelists, poets, playwrights, and other creative writers of our time.

Native North American Literature--Features sketches on prominent Native North American writers.

Poetry Criticism--Furnishes excerpts from criticism of the works of the most-studied poets of all eras and all nationalities.

Short Story Criticism--Provides excerpts from criticism of the works of the most-studied short story writers of all eras and nationalities.

Something about the Author--Contains heavily illustrated sketches on juvenile and young adult authors and illustrators of all eras and nationalities.

Something about the Author Autobiography Series--Presents specially commissioned autobiographical essays by prominent juvenile and young adult authors and illustrators from all eras and nationalities.

Twentieth-Century Literary Criticism--Furnishes excerpts from criticism of the works of the most-studied novelists, poets, playwrights, short story writers, nonfiction writers, scriptwriters, and various other creative writers who died between 1900 and 1960.

World Literature Criticism--Contains in six volumes excerpts from criticism of the works of over 200 major writers from 1500 to the present. **WLC Supplement**--Contains 50 additional writers of all eras.

Yesterday's Authors of Books for Children--Consists of heavily illustrated sketches on children's authors who died before 1961. Two volumes only.

Contemporary Authors®

Cumulative Index

20/1631
See Upward, Allen
A/C Cross
See Lawrence, T(homas) E(dward)
Aach, Herb(ert) 1923-1985 Obituary 118
Aaker, David A(llen) 1938- CANR-31
Earlier sketch in CA 49-52
Aalben, Patrick
See Jones, Noel
Aallyn, Alysse
See Clark, Melissa
Aalto, (Hugo) Alvar (Henrik)
1898-1976 Obituary 65-68
Aamodt, Donald 166
Aardema, Verna
See Vugteveen, Verna Aardema
See also CLR 17
See also MAICYA
See also SAAS 8
See also SATA 4, 68
Aaron, Benjamin 1915- 21-24R
Aaron, Betsy 1938- 139
Aaron, Chester 1923- CANR-38
Earlier sketches in CA 21-24R, CANR-8
See also MAICYA
See also SAAS 12
See also SATA 9, 74
Aaron, Daniel 1912- CANR-7
Earlier sketch in CA 13-16R
Aaron, David (Laurence) 1938- 126
Aaron, Hank 1934- 147
Brief entry 104
See also Aaron, Henry Louis
Aaron, Henry (Jacob) 1936- 129
Aaron, Henry Louis 147
See also Aaron, Hank
Aaron, James Ethridge 1927- 21-24R
Aaron, R. I.
See Aaron, Richard Ithamar
Aaron, Richard Ithamar 1901-1987 Obituary 122
Aaron, Shirley L. 1941- 123
Aaron, Sidney
See Chayefsky, Sidney
Aaron, Stephen 1936- 124
Aaronovitch, Sam 1919- 13-16R
Aarons, Edward S(idney) 1916-1975 .... CANR-58
Obituary 57-60
Earlier sketch in CA 93-96
Aarons, Leroy 1933- 150
Aarons, Slim 1916- Brief entry 106
Aaronson, Bernard S(eymour) 1924- 29-32R
Aarsleff, Hans 1925- 21-24R
Aaseng, Nate
See Aaseng, Nathan
Aaseng, Nathan 1953- CANR-36
Earlier sketch in CA 106
See also AAYA 27
See also JRDA
See also MAICYA
See also SAAS 12
See also SATA 51, 88
See also SATA-Brief 38
Aaseng, Rolf E(dward) 1923- CANR-27
Earlier sketch in CA 49-52
Aasheim, Ashley 1942- 115
Abadinsky, Howard 1941- 110
Abagnale, Frank W., Jr. 1948- 112
Abajian, James De Tar 1914- 65-68
Abarbanel, Karin 1950- 65-68
Abarbanel, Sam X. 1914- Brief entry 106
Abas, Syed Jan 1936- 154
Abasiyanik, Sait Faik 1906-1954 Brief entry 123
See also Sait Faik
Abata, Russell M(ary) 1930- 113
Abate, Frank R(obert) 1951- 118
Abayakoon, Cyrus D. F. 1912- Brief entry 115
Abbagnano, Nicola 1901- 33-36R
Abbas 1934- 149
Abbas, Jailan 1952- 155
See also SATA 91
Abbas, Khwaja Ahmad 1914-1987 .... CANR-69
Earlier sketch in CA 57-60
Abbazia, Patrick 1937- 57-60
Abbe, Elfriede (Martha) 1919- 13-16R
Abbe, George (Bancroft) 1911- CANR-10
Earlier sketch in CA 25-28R
Abbe, Kathryn McLaughlin 1919- 142
Abbensetts, Michael 1938- CANR-67
Earlier sketches in CA 104, CANR-37
Abberley, Aldwyn
See Cowie, Donald
Abbey, Edward 1927-1989 .... CANR-41
Obituary 128
Earlier sketches in CA 45-48, CANR-2
See also CLC 36, 59
Abbey, Edwin Austin 1852-1911 .... DLB 188
Abbey, Lloyd (Robert) 1943- 125
Brief entry 104
Abbey, Lynn
See Abbey, Marilyn Lorraine
Abbey, Maj. J. R. 1894-1969 .... DLB 201
Abbey, Margaret
See York, Margaret Elizabeth
Abbey, Marilyn Lorraine 1948- CANR-62
Earlier sketch in CA 119
Abbey, Merrill R. 1905- CANR-3
Earlier sketch in CA 1-4R
Abbington, John
See Gibson, Walter B(rown)
Abbot, Anthony
See Oursler, (Charles) Fulton
Abbot, Charles G(reeley) 1872-1973 77-80
Obituary 45-48
Abbot, Rick
See Sharkey, John Michael
Abbot, W(illiam) W(right) 1922- Brief entry 110
Abbot, Willis J(ohn) 1863-1934 Brief entry 119
See also DLB 29
Abbott, Alice
See Borland, Kathryn Kilby
and Speicher, Helen Ross S(mith)
Abbott, Anthony S. 1935- 17-20R
Abbott, Berenice 1898-1991 106
Obituary 136
Abbott, Carl (John) 1944- CANR-11
Earlier sketch in CA 65-68
Abbott, Claude Colleer 1889-1971 .... 5-8R
Obituary 89-92
Abbott, Edwin A. 1838-1926 .... DLB 178
Abbott, Eric Symes 1906-1983 Obituary 110
Abbott, Freeland K(night) 1919-1971 .... CAP-2
Earlier sketch in CA 25-28
Abbott, George (Francis) 1887-1995 .... CANR-72
Obituary 147
Earlier sketch in CA 93-96
Abbott, H(orace) Porter 1940- 45-48
Abbott, Jack Henry
See Abbott, Rufus Henry
Abbott, Jacob 1803-1879 .... DLB 1, 42
See also SATA 22
Abbott, James H(amilton) 1924- 77-80
Abbott, Jerry (Lynn) 1938- 45-48
Abbott, John J(amison) 1930- 17-20R
Abbott, Keith 1944- CANR-47
Earlier sketch in CA 121
Abbott, L(enwood) B(allard)
1908-1985 Obituary 117
Abbott, Lee K(ittredge) 1947- CANR-51
Earlier sketch in CA 124
See also CLC 48
See also DLB 130
Abbott, Lyman 1835-1922 .... DLB 79
Abbott, Manager Henry
See Stratemeyer, Edward L.
Abbott, Margaret Evans 1896-1976 Obituary 110
Abbott, Martin 1922-1977 .... 33-36R
Abbott, May L(aura) 1916- 9-12R
Abbott, Pamela 1947- 135
Abbott, Philip (R.) 1944- 126
Brief entry 106
Abbott, R(obert) Tucker 1919-1995 .... CANR-37
Obituary 150
Earlier sketches in CA 9-12R, CANR-4
See also SATA 61
See also SATA-Obit 87
Abbott, Raymond H(erbert) 1942- 57-60
Abbott, Richard H(enry) 1936- 33-36R
Abbott, Robert S. 1868-1940 .... DLB 29, 91
Abbott, Rowland A(ubrey) S(amuel) 1909- 53-56
Abbott, Rufus Henry 1944- 107
Abbott, Sarah
See Zolotow, Charlotte S(hapiro)
Abbott, Scott 1949- 138
Abbott, Shirley 1934- 113
Abbott, Sidney 1937- 41-44R
Abbott, Walter M(atthew) 1923- 9-12R
Abbotts, John 1947- 73-76
Abboushi, W(asif) F(ahmi) 1931- 29-32R
Abbs, Peter 1942- 93-96
ABC
See Caddick, Arthur
Abcarian, Richard 1929- 33-36R
'Abd Al-Khaliq, Jabir
See Herbert, Nick
Abdallah, Omar
See Humbaraci, D(emir) Arslan
Abdel-Magid, Isam Mohammed 1952- 152
Abdel-Malek, Anouar 1924- CANR-44
Earlier sketch in CA 29-32R
Abdel-Quddous, Ihsan (Mohammad)
1920(?)-1990 Obituary 130
Abdelsamad, Moustafa H(assan) 1941- 53-56
Abdul, Raoul 1929- 29-32R
See also SATA 12
Abdul-Jabbar, Kareem 1947- 139
See also BW 2
Abdullah, Achmed 1881-1945 Brief entry 115
Abdullahi, Guda 1946- 93-96
Abdul-Rauf, Muhammad 1917- 101
Abe, Kobo 1924-1993 .... CANR-60
Obituary 140
Earlier sketches in CA 65-68, CANR-24
See also CLC 8, 22, 53, 81
See also DAM NOV
See also DLB 182
See also MTCW 1
Abeel, Erica (Hennefeld) 1937- 113
Brief entry 109
Abel, Alan (Irwin) 1928- CANR-12
Earlier sketch in CA 17-20R
Abel, Bob
See Abel, Robert
Abel, Christopher (Graham) 1946- 127
Abel, Elie 1920- CANR-36
Earlier sketches in CA 61-64, CANR-8
Abel, Emily K. 1942- 153
Abel, Ernest L(awrence) 1943- CANR-14
Earlier sketch in CA 41-44R
Abel, I(orwith) W(ilbur) 1908-1987 Obituary 123
Brief entry 105
Abel, Jeanne 1937- 17-20R
Abel, Lionel 1910- 61-64
Abel, Raymond 1911- .... SATA 12
Abel, Reuben 1911-1997 .... 37-40R
Obituary 160
Abel, Richard (Owen) 1941- 129
Abel, Richard L. 1941- 131
Abel, Robert 1913(?)-1987 Obituary 122
Abel, Robert 1931-1981 .... CANR-11
Obituary 105
Earlier sketch in CA 65-68
Abel, Robert H(alsall) 1941- CANR-37
Earlier sketch in CA 102
Abel, Sam 1957- 156
Abel, Theodora M(ead) 1899- 57-60
Abel, Theodore 1896- 21-24R
Abel, Wilhelm 1904- Brief entry 119
Abelard, Peter c. 1079-c. 1142 .... DLB 115
Abeles, Elvin 1907- 104
Abell, Arunah S. 1806-1888 .... DLB 43
Abell, George O(gden) 1927-1983 .... CANR-3
Obituary 111
Earlier sketch in CA 9-12R
Abell, Kathleen 1938- 49-52
See also SATA 9
Abell, Kjeld 1901-1961 Obituary 111
See also CLC 15
Abell, Ron(ald F.) 1932- 119
Abella, Alex 1950- 93-96
Abella, Irving (Martin) 1940- CANR-28
Earlier sketch in CA 49-52
Abels, Harriette S(heffer) 1926- 121
See also SATA 50
Abels, Jules 1913- 61-64
Abel-Smith, Brian 1926- CANR-9
Earlier sketch in CA 21-24R
Abelson, Alan 1925- 136
Abelson, Philip Hauge 1913- 155
Brief entry 107
Abelson, Raziel A(lter) 1921- CANR-6
Earlier sketch in CA 9-12R
Abelson, Robert P(aul) 1928- 41-44R
Abend, Norman A(nchel) 1931- 33-36R
Aber, William M(cKee) 1929- 57-60
Aberbach, David 1953- 135
Aberbach, Joel D(avid) 1940- CANR-20
Earlier sketch in CA 45-48
Abercrombie, Barbara (Mattes) 1939- 81-84
See also SATA 16
Abercrombie, Lascelles 1881-1938 Brief entry 112
See also DLB 19
Abercrombie, M(innie) L(ouie) J(ohnson)
1909(?)-1984 Obituary 115
Abercrombie, M. L. Johnson
See Abercrombie, M(innie) L(ouie) J(ohnson)
Abercrombie, Michael 1912-1979 Obituary 115
Abercrombie, Nicholas 1944- CANR-59
Earlier sketch in CA 128
Abercrombie, Nigel J(ames) 1908-1986 101
Obituary 118
Abercrombie, Stanley 1935- 117
Aberg, Sherrill E. 1924- 21-24R
Aberle, David F(riend) 1918- 21-24R
Aberle, John Wayne 1919- 1-4R
Aberle, Kathleen Gough 1925- CANR-5
Earlier sketch in CA 13-16R
Abernathy, David M(yles) 1933- CANR-37
Earlier sketch in CA 53-56
Abernathy, (M.) Elton 1913- 17-20R
Abernathy, M(abra) Glenn 1921-1990 .... 13-16R
Obituary 131
Abernathy, Ralph David 1926-1990 133
Obituary 131
Abernathy, William J(ackson) 1933-1983 .... CANR-37
Obituary 111
Earlier sketch in CA 93-96
Abernethy, Francis Edward 1925- CANR-8
Earlier sketch in CA 21-24R
Abernethy, George Lawrence 1910- 1-4R
Abernethy, Peter L(ink) 1935- 69-72
Abernethy, Robert G(ordon) 1927- 21-24R
See also SATA 5
Abernethy, Thomas Perkins 1890-1975 .... CAP-1
Obituary 111
Earlier sketch in CA 19-20
Abernethy, Virginia 1934- 93-96
Abert, Donald B. 1907-1985 Obituary 116
ab Hugh, Dafydd 1960- 154
Abisch, Roslyn Kroop 1927- CANR-10
Earlier sketch in CA 21-24R
See also SATA 9
Abisch, Roz
See Abisch, Roslyn Kroop
Abish, Walter 1931- CANR-37
Earlier sketch in CA 101
See also CLC 22
See also DLB 130
Able, James A(ugustus), Jr. 1928- 93-96
Able, Mark
See Krooth, Richard
Ableman, Paul 1927- CANR-67
Earlier sketches in CA 61-64, CANR-12
Abler, Ronald F. 1939- CANR-4
Earlier sketch in CA 53-56
Abler, Thomas S(truthers) 1941- 101
Ablesimov, Aleksandr Onisimovich 1742-1783. DLB 150
Abley, Mark 1955- CANR-50
Earlier sketch in CA 120
Ablow, Keith Russell 1961- 141
Abodaher, David J. (Naiph) 1919- CANR-10
Earlier sketch in CA 17-20R
See also SATA 17
Abolafia, Yossi 1944- 142
See also SATA 60
See also SATA-Brief 46
Abourezk, James G(eorge) 1931- 135
Abou-Saif, Laila 1941- 147
Abrahall, Clare Hoskyns
See Hoskyns-Abrahall, Clare (Constance Drury)
Abraham, Claude K(urt) 1931- CANR-36
Earlier sketch in CA 21-24R
Abraham, David 1946- 129
Abraham, George 1915- 110
Abraham, Gerald Ernest Heal 1904-1988 89-92
Obituary 125
Abraham, Henry Julian 1921- CANR-18
Earlier sketches in CA 5-8R, CANR-2
Abraham, Katherine 1922- 110
Abraham, Katy
See Abraham, Katherine
Abraham, Louis Arnold 1893-1983 Obituary 108
Abraham, M(annamplakkal) Francis 1939- 110
Abraham, Pearl 152
Abraham, Willard 1916- CANR-5
Earlier sketch in CA 13-16R
Abraham, William E. 1934- 13-16R
Abraham, William I(srael) 1919- 25-28R
Abraham a Sancta Clara 1644-1709 .... DLB 168
Abrahami, Izzy 1930- Brief entry 110
Abrahamian, Ervand 1940- 110
Abrahams, Doris Caroline 1901(?)-1982(?) 129
Obituary 108
Abrahams, Edward 1949- 122
Abrahams, Gerald 1907-1980 102
Obituary 97-100
Abrahams, Hilary (Ruth) 1938- .... SATA 29
Abrahams, Howard Phineas 1904- 57-60
Abrahams, Jim 1944- 138
Abrahams, Lionel (Isaac) 1928- 145
Abrahams, Peter (Henry) 1919- CANR-26
Earlier sketch in CA 57-60
See also BW 1
See also CLC 4
See also DLB 117
See also MTCW 1
Abrahams, Peter 1947- 152
Abrahams, R(aphael) G(arvin) 1934- 25-28R
Abrahams, Robert David 1905- CAP-2
Earlier sketch in CA 33-36
See also SATA 4
Abrahams, Roger D(avid) 1933- CANR-49
Earlier sketches in CA 9-12R, CANR-5, 24
Abrahams, William Miller 1919- CANR-43
Earlier sketch in CA 61-64
Abrahamsen, Christine Elizabeth 1916- 101
Abrahamsen, David 1903- 65-68
Abrahamson, Irving 1925- CANR-65
Earlier sketch in CA 129
Abrahamson, Mark J. 1939- 101
Abrahamsson, Bengt 1937- 97-100
Abrahms, Sally (Ellen) 1953- 113
Abram, H(arry) S(hore) 1931-1977 .... 29-32R
Abram, Morris Berthold 1918- 108

Abramov, Emil
  See Draitser, Emil
Abramov, Fyodor Aleksandrovich 1920-1983 ... 133
  Obituary ... 109
Abramov, S(hene'ur) Zalman 1908- ... 134
  Brief entry ... 108
Abramovitz, Anita (Zeltner Brooks) 1914- ... 97-100
  See also Brooks, Anita
Abramowitz, Jack 1918- ... CANR-6
  Earlier sketch in CA 5-8R
Abramowitz, Shalom Jacob 1835(?)-1917 Brief entry ... 118
Abrams, Alan E(dwin) 1941- ... 89-92
Abrams, Charles 1901-1970 ... CAP-2
  Earlier sketch in CA 23-24
Abrams, Douglas Carl 1950- ... 143
Abrams, Elliott 1948- ... 140
Abrams, George J(oseph) 1918-1978 ... CANR-12
  Earlier sketch in CA 61-64
Abrams, Harry N(athan) 1904-1979 Obituary . 93-96
Abrams, Joy 1941- ... 77-80
  See also SATA 16
Abrams, Lawrence F. ... 124
  See also SATA 58
  See also SATA-Brief 47
Abrams, Linsey 1951- ... CANR-18
  Earlier sketch in CA 102
Abrams, M(eyer) H(oward) 1912- ... CANR-33
  Earlier sketches in CA 57-60, CANR-13
  See also CLC 24
  See also DLB 67
Abrams, Mark 1906- ... 124
Abrams, Peter D(avid) 1936- ... 33-36R
Abrams, Philip 1933(?)-1981 ... 129
  Obituary ... 105
Abrams, Richard M. 1932- ... 13-16R
Abrams, Sam(uel) 1935- ... 21-24R
Abramsky, Chimen 1916- Brief entry ... 109
Abramson, Albert 1922- ... 155
Abramson, Doris E. 1925- ... 25-28R
Abramson, Edward A. 1944- ... 143
Abramson, Harold Alexander 1889-1980 Obituary ... 102
Abramson, Harold J(ulian) 1934- ... 45-48
Abramson, Jesse P. 1904-1979 Obituary ... 89-92
Abramson, Jill 1954- ... 156
Abramson, Joan 1932- ... CANR-37
  Earlier sketch in CA 25-28R
Abramson, Leslie W. ... 166
Abramson, Martin 1921- ... 49-52
Abramson, Michael 1944- ... 69-72
Abramson, Paul R(obert) 1937- ... CANR-37
  Earlier sketches in CA 61-64, CANR-8
Abramson, Rudy 1937- ... 152
Abrash, Merritt 1930- ... 21-24R
Abrashkin, Raymond 1911-1960 ... 115
  See also SATA 50
Abravanel, Elizabeth 1944- ... 112
Abravanel, Elliot D(on) 1942- ... 112
Abrecht, Mary Ellen (Benson) 1945- ... 69-72
Abreu, Maria Isabel 1919- ... 45-48
Abruzzo, Ben(jamine Lawrence) 1930-1985 Obituary ... 115
Absalom, Roger Neil Lewis 1929- ... CANR-57
  Earlier sketches in CA 111, CANR-31
Abse, Dannie 1923- ... CANR-46
  Earlier sketches in CA 53-56, CANR-4
  See also CAAS 1
  See also CLC 7, 29
  See also DAB
  See also DAM POET
  See also DLB 27
Abse, David Wilfred 1915- ... 49-52
Abse, Joan 1926- ... 108
Abse, Leo 1917- ... 137
Abshire, David M. 1926- ... CANR-37
  Earlier sketches in CA 21-24R, CANR-8
Abt, Clark C(laus) 1929- ... CANR-21
  Earlier sketch in CA 69-72
Abt, Lawrence Edwin 1915- ... CANR-13
  Earlier sketch in CA 33-36R
Abt, Vicki 1942- ... 120
Abuba, Ernest Hawkins 1947- ... 133
Abu-Jaber, Diana 1959- ... 142
Abu Jaber, Kamel S(aleh) 1932- ... CANR-14
  Earlier sketch in CA 21-24R
Abu-Jamal, Mumia 1954(?)- ... 154
Abu-Lughod, Ibrahim Ali 1929- ... CANR-10
  Earlier sketch in CA 5-8R
Abu-Lughod, Janet L(ouise) 1928- ... CANR-10
  Earlier sketch in CA 65-68
Abu-Lughod, Lila 1952- ... 150
Abun-Nasr, Jamil Miri 1932- ... 69-72
Aburdene, Patricia 1947(?)- ... 140
Aburish, Said K. 1935- ... 140
Aby, Stephen H. 1949- ... 123
Abzug, Bella S(avitsky) 1920-1998 ... 137
  Obituary ... 165
  Brief entry ... 104
Abzug, Martin 1916-1986 Obituary ... 119
Abzug, Robert H(enry) 1945- ... CANR-21
  Earlier sketch in CA 104
Academicas Mentor
  See Montagu, Ashley
Academic Investor
  See Reddaway, W(illiam) Brian
Accad, Evelyne 1943- ... 162
Accinelli, Robert 1939- ... 160
Accola, Louis W(ayne) 1937- ... CANR-12
  Earlier sketch in CA 29-32R
Accomando, Claire Hsu 1937- ... 142
Accrocca, Elio Filippo 1923- ... DLB 128
Ace, Goodman 1899-1982 ... 61-64
  Obituary ... 106
Aceto, Vincent J(ohn) 1932- ... 106
Achard, George
  See Torres-Levin, Tereska (Szwarc)
Achard, Marcel
  See Ferreol, Marcel Auguste
Achebe, (Albert) Chinua(lumogu) 1930- ... CANR-47
  Earlier sketches in CA 1-4R, CANR-6, 26
  See also AAYA 15
  See also BLC 1
  See also BW 2
  See also CLC 1, 3, 5, 7, 11, 26, 51, 75
  See also CLR 20
  See also DA
  See also DAB
  See also DAC
  See also DAM MST, MULT, NOV
  See also DLB 117
  See also MAICYA
  See also MTCW 1
  See also SATA 40
  See also SATA-Brief 38
  See also WLC
Achenbaum, W(ilbert) Andrew 1947- ... CANR-34
  Earlier sketches in CA 89-92, CANR-15
Acheson, David C(ampion) 1921- ... 132
Acheson, Dean (Gooderham) 1893-1971 ... CAP-2
  Obituary ... 33-36R
  Earlier sketch in CA 25-28
Acheson, Patricia Castles 1924- ... 1-4R
Achilles
  See Lamb, Charles Bentall
Achinstein, Peter Jacob 1935- ... 111
Achtemeier, Elizabeth (Rice) 1926- ... CANR-8
  Earlier sketch in CA 17-20R
Achtemeier, Paul J(ohn) 1927- ... CANR-8
  Earlier sketch in CA 17-20R
Achternbusch, Herbert 1938- ... DLB 124
Achyut
  See Birla, Lakshminiwas N.
Ackart, Robert 1921- ... 109
Ackelsberg, Martha A. 1946- ... 139
Acker, Alison 1928- ... 125
Acker, Bertie (Wilcox Naylor) 1922- ... 147
Acker, Duane Calvin 1931- ... 33-36R
Acker, Helen ... 73-76
Acker, Kathy 1948-1997 ... CANR-55
  Obituary ... 162
  Brief entry ... 117
  Earlier sketch in CA 122
  See also CLC 45, 111
Acker, Robert Flint 1920- ... 89-92
Acker, William R. B. 1910(?)-1974 Obituary ... 49-52
Ackerley, Chris(topher John) 1947- ... 129
Ackerley, J(oe) R(andolph) 1896-1967 ... 102
  Obituary ... 89-92
Ackerman, Bruce A. 1943- ... CANR-4
  Earlier sketch in CA 53-56
Ackerman, Carl W(illiam) 1890-1970 ... 73-76
  Obituary ... 29-32R
Ackerman, Diane 1948- ... CANR-54
  Earlier sketches in CA 57-60, CANR-31
  See also CAAS 20
  See also DLB 120
  See also SATA 102
Ackerman, Edward A. 1911-1973 Obituary . 41-44R
Ackerman, Eugene (Francis) 1888-1974 ... SATA 10
Ackerman, Forrest J(ames) 1916- ... 102
  Interview in ... 102
Ackerman, Gerald M(artin) 1928- ... CANR-1
  Earlier sketch in CA 45-48
Ackerman, J. Mark 1939- ... 53-56
Ackerman, James D. 1950- ... 153
Ackerman, James S(loss) 1919- ... 9-12R
Ackerman, Nathan W(ard) 1908-1971 ... CAP-2
  Earlier sketch in CA 29-32
Ackerman, Robert E(dwin) 1928- ... CANR-43
  Earlier sketches in CA 45-48, CANR-20
Ackerman, Robert K. 1933- ... 123
Ackerman, Robert W(illiam) 1910-1980 ... 103
Ackerman, Susan Rose
  See Rose-Ackerman, Susan
Ackerman, Susan Yoder 1945- ... 156
  See also SATA 92
Ackermann, Paul Kurt 1919- Brief entry ... 104
Ackermann, Robert John 1933- Brief entry ... 108
Ackerson, Duane (Wright), Jr. 1942- ... 33-36R
Ackland, Rodney 1908- ... 57-60
Ackley, Charles Walton 1913-1975 ... 41-44R
Ackley, Hugh Gardner 1915-1998 ... 61-64
  Obituary ... 164
Ackley, Peggy Jo 1955- ... SATA 58
Ackley, Randall William 1931- ... CANR-6
  Earlier sketch in CA 53-56
Ackoff, Russell L(incoln) 1919- ... CANR-32
  Earlier sketches in CA 41-44R, CANR-15
Ackroyd, Joyce Irene ... 103
Ackroyd, Peter 1949- ... CANR-51
  Brief entry ... 123
  Earlier sketch in CA 127
  Interview in ... 127
  See also CLC 34, 52
  See also DLB 155
Ackroyd, Peter R(unham) 1917- ... CANR-31
  Earlier sketch in CA 25-28R
Ackworth, Robert Charles 1923- ... 5-8R
Acland, Alice
  See Wignall, Anne
Acland, James H. 1917-1976 ... 41-44R
Acocella, Marisa 1960(?)- ... 156
Acomb, Evelyn Martha
  See Acomb-Walker, Evelyn
Acomb, Frances (Dorothy) 1907- Brief entry ... 109
Acomb-Walker, Evelyn 1910- ... 85-88
Acorn, John (Harrison) 1958- ... SATA 79
Acorn, Milton 1923- ... 103
  Interview in ... 103
  See also CLC 15
  See also DAC
  See also DLB 53
Acosta, Juvenal 1961- ... CAAS 27
Acosta, Oscar Zeta 1935(?)- ... 131
  See also DLB 82
  See also HW
Acquaviva, Sabino Samele 1927- ... 101
Acquaye, Alfred Allotey 1939- ... 25-28R
Acre, Stephen
  See Gruber, Frank
Acred, Arthur 1926- ... 25-28R
Acs, Laszlo (Bela) 1931- ... SATA 42
  See also SATA-Brief 32
Acton, Edward J. 1949- ... CANR-2
  Earlier sketch in CA 45-48
Acton, Harold Mario Mitchell 1904-1994 ... CANR-3
  Obituary ... 144
  Earlier sketch in CA 1-4R
Acton, Jay
  See Acton, Edward J.
Acton, Thomas (Alan) 1948- ... 57-60
Acuff, Frederick Gene 1931- Brief entry ... 110
Acuff, Selma Boyd 1924- ... 111
  See also SATA 45
Acuna, Rodolfo
  See Acuna, Rodolfo F(rancis)
Acuna, Rodolfo F(rancis) 1932- ... CANR-72
  Brief entry ... 108
  Earlier sketch in CA 131
  See also HW
Acuna, Rudy
  See Acuna, Rodolfo F(rancis)
Aczel, Amir D. 1950- ... 164
Aczel, Tamas 1921- ... CANR-29
  Earlier sketch in CA 49-52
Ada, Alma Flor 1938- ... 123
  See also SATA 43, 84
Adachi, Barbara (Curtis) 1924- ... CANR-27
  Earlier sketch in CA 49-52
Adachi, Ken 1929(?)-1989 Obituary ... 128
Adair, Cecil
  See Everett-Green, Evelyn
Adair, Christy 1949- ... 147
Adair, Dennis 1945- ... 107
Adair, Gilbert 1944- ... 157
  See also DLB 194
  See also SATA 98
Adair, Ian 1942- ... CANR-11
  Earlier sketch in CA 69-72
  See also SATA 53
Adair, Jack
  See Pavey, Don
Adair, James 1709(?)-1783(?) ... DLB 30
Adair, James R. 1923- ... 17-20R
Adair, John G(lenn) 1933- ... 49-52
Adair, Margaret Weeks (?)-1971 ... CAP-1
  Earlier sketch in CA 13-14
  See also SATA 10
Adair, Robert Kemp 1924- ... 136
Adair, Virginia Hamilton 1913- ... 156
Adam, Ben
  See Drachman, Julian M(oses)
Adam, Cornel
  See Lengyel, Cornel Adam
Adam, Graeme Mercer 1839-1912 ... DLB 99
Adam, Hans Christian 1948- ... 131
Adam, Helen (Douglas) 1909-1993 ... CANR-7
  Obituary ... 143
  Earlier sketch in CA 17-20R
Adam, Heribert 1936- ... 105
Adam, Jan 1920- ... CANR-38
  Earlier sketch in CA 115
Adam, Michael 1919- ... CANR-37
  Earlier sketch in CA 53-56
Adam, Paul 1951- ... 145
Adam, Peter 1929- ... CANR-51
  Earlier sketch in CA 127
Adam, Robert 1948- ... 158
  See also SATA 93
Adam, Robert Borthwick II 1863-1940 ... DLB 187
Adam, Ruth (Augusta) 1907- ... 21-24R
Adam, Thomas R(itchie) 1900- ... CAP-1
  Earlier sketch in CA 19-20
Adamczewski, Zygmunt 1921- ... 13-16R
Adame, Leonard 1947- ... 131
  See also DLB 82
  See also HW
Adamec, Christine 1949- ... 141
Adamec, Ludwig W(arren) 1924- ... CANR-49
  Earlier sketches in CA 21-24R, CANR-9, 24
Adamic, Alojzij 1899(?)-1951 Brief entry ... 109
  See also Adamic, Louis
Adamic, Louis
  See Adamic, Alojzij
  See also DLB 9
Adamov, Arthur 1908-1970 ... CAP-2
  Obituary ... 25-28R
  Earlier sketch in CA 17-18
  See also CLC 4, 25
  See also DAM DRAM
  See also MTCW 1
Adams, A. Don
  See Cleveland, Philip Jerome
Adams, A. John 1931- ... 33-36R
Adams, Abby 1939- ... 154
Adams, Abigail 1744-1818 ... DLB 183, 200
Adams, Adrienne 1906- ... CANR-35
  Earlier sketches in CA 49-52, CANR-1
  See also SATA 8, 90
Adams, Alexander B. 1917(?)-1984 Obituary ... 112
Adams, Alice (Boyd) 1926- ... CANR-53
  Earlier sketches in CA 81-84, CANR-26
  Interview in ... CANR-26
  See also CLC 6, 13, 46
  See also DLBY 86
  See also MTCW 1
  See also SSC 24
Adams, Andy
  See Gibson, Walter B(rown)
Adams, Andy 1859-1935 ... TCLC 56
  See also YABC 1
Adams, Anne H(utchinson) 1935-1980 ... CANR-27
  Earlier sketch in CA 41-44R
Adams, Annette
  See Rowland, D(onald) S(ydney)
Adams, Ansel (Easton) 1902-1984 ... CANR-10
  Obituary ... 112
  Earlier sketch in CA 21-24R
  Interview in ... CANR-10
  See also AAYA 14
  See also AITN 1
Adams, Arthur E(ugene) 1917- ... CANR-4
  Earlier sketch in CA 5-8R
Adams, Arthur Gray, (Jr.) 1935- ... CANR-46
  Earlier sketches in CA 107, CANR-23
Adams, Arthur Merrihew 1908- ... 53-56
Adams, Arthur Stanton 1896-1980 Obituary ... 102
Adams, Barbara
  See Gardner, Virginia (Marberry)
Adams, Barbara Johnston 1943- ... SATA 60
Adams, Bart
  See Bingley, David Ernest
Adams, Bernard (Paul Fornaro) 1915- ... 128
Adams, Betsy
  See Pitcher, Gladys
Adams, Bronte (Jane) 1963- ... 140
Adams, Brooks 1848-1927 Brief entry ... 123
  See also DLB 47
  See also TCLC 80
Adams, Bruin
  See Ellis, Edward S(ylvester)
Adams, Captain Bruin
  See Ellis, Edward S(ylvester)
Adams, Captain J. F. C.
  See Ellis, Edward S(ylvester)
Adams, Caren 1946- ... 135
Adams, Carol J. 1951- ... 134
Adams, Cedric M. 1902-1961 Obituary ... 89-92
Adams, Charles 1930- ... 150
Adams, Charles Francis, Jr. 1835-1915 Brief entry ... 113
  See also DLB 47
Adams, Charles J. III 1947- ... 150
Adams, Charles J(oseph) 1924- ... CANR-24
  Earlier sketches in CA 17-20R, CANR-8
Adams, Charles Lynford 1929- ... 113
Adams, Charlotte 1899- Brief entry ... 107
Adams, Chuck
  See Tubb, E(dwin) C(harles)
Adams, Cindy ... CANR-17
  Earlier sketch in CA 21-24R
Adams, Cleve F(ranklin) 1895-1949 Brief entry . 112
Adams, Clifton 1919-1971 ... CANR-63
  Earlier sketches in CA 13-16R, CANR-21
Adams, Clinton 1918- ... 33-36R
Adams, Colin C. 1956- ... 152
Adams, Dale
  See Quinn, Elisabeth
Adams, Daniel
  See Nicole, Christopher (Robin)
Adams, Debra
  See Speregen, Devra Newberger
Adams, Don(ald Kendrick) 1925- ... 33-36R
Adams, Donald K(napp) 1924-1987 Obituary ... 123
  Brief entry ... 111
Adams, Donald R., Jr. 1940- Brief entry ... 113
Adams, Douglas (Noel) 1952- ... CANR-64
  Earlier sketches in CA 106, CANR-34
  See also AAYA 4
  See also BEST 89:3
  See also CLC 27, 60
  See also DAM POP
  See also DLBY 83
  See also JRDA
Adams, E(lie) M(aynard) 1919- ... 1-4R
Adams, Edith
  See Shine, Deborah
Adams, Edward E. 1921- ... 155
Adams, Elsie B(onita) 1932- ... 69-72
Adams, Eugenia
  See Owens, Virginia Stem
Adams, Evangeline (Smith) 1872(?)-1932 Brief entry ... 121
Adams, F(rank) Ramsay 1883-1963 ... CANR-61
  Earlier sketch in CA 5-8R
Adams, Faith 1960- ... 121
Adams, Florence 1932- ... 49-52
  See also SATA 61
Adams, Francis A(lexandre) 1874-1975 Obituary ... 61-64
Adams, Frank C(lyde) 1916- ... 69-72
Adams, Franklin P(ierce) 1881-1960 Obituary ... 93-96
  See also DLB 29
Adams, Frederick C(harles) 1941- Brief entry ... 105
Adams, Gail Galloway 1943- ... 128
Adams, George Matthew 1878-1962 Obituary ... 93-96
Adams, George Worthington 1905- ... 41-44R
Adams, Georgia Sachs 1913- ... 37-40R
Adams, Gerald R. 1946- ... 144
Adams, Glenda 1939- ... CANR-62
  Earlier sketch in CA 104
Adams, Graham, Jr. 1928- ... 17-20R
Adams, Hannah 1755-1832 ... DLB 200

Adams, Harlen M(artin) 1904-1997 .... CAP-1
Obituary 164
Earlier sketch in CA 13-14
Adams, Harold 1923- CANR-58
Earlier sketch in CA 126
Adams, Harriet S(tratemeyer) 1892(?)-1982 ....
CANR-27
Obituary 106
Earlier sketch in CA 17-20R
See also AITN 2
See also MAICYA
See also SATA 1
See also SATA-Obit 29
Adams, Harrison CANR-26
Earlier sketches in CAP-2, CA 19-20
Adams, Harry Baker 1924- Brief entry 106
Adams, Hazard 1926- 9-12R
See also SATA 6
Adams, Henry (Brooks) 1838-1918 133
Brief entry 104
See also DA
See also DAB
See also DAC
See also DAM MST
See also DLB 12, 47, 189
See also TCLC 4, 52
Adams, Henry 1949- 132
Adams, Henry H(itch) 1917- CANR-13
Earlier sketch in CA 21-24R
Adams, Henry Mason 1907- CAP-1
Earlier sketch in CA 17-18
Adams, Henry T.
See Ransom, Jay Ellis
Adams, Herbert Baxter 1850-1901 Obituary ... 162
See also DLB 47
Adams, Herbert Mayow 1893-1985 .... CAP-2
Obituary 115
Earlier sketch in CA 25-28
Adams, Howard (Joseph) 1928- 89-92
Adams, J(ames) Donald 1891-1968 ...... CANR-1
Earlier sketch in CA 1-4R
Adams, J(ames) Mack 1933- 85-88
Adams, Jad 1954- 142
Adams, James (Macgregor David) 1951- 138
Adams, James E(dward) 1941- 73-76
Adams, James F(rederick) 1927- 17-20R
Adams, James Luther 1901- 41-44R
Adams, James R(owe) 1934- 41-44R
Adams, James Truslow 1878-1949 Brief entry . 115
See also DLB 17
See also DLBD 17
Adams, Jane (Ellen) 1940- 116
Adams, Jay Edward 1929- 126
Brief entry 108
Adams, Jerome R(obertson) 1938- 139
Adams, Joanna Z.
See Koch, Joanne
Adams, Joey 1911- CANR-1
Earlier sketch in CA 49-52
Adams, John 1734-1826 .... DLB 31
Adams, John 1938- 111
Adams, John Anthony 1944- 134
See also SATA 67
Adams, John Clarke 1910- 1-4R
Adams, John Coldwell 1927- 121
Adams, John Cranford 1903-1986 Obituary 121
Adams, John D(avid) 1942- 115
Adams, John F(estus) 1930- 33-36R
Adams, John M(ilton) 1905-1981 107
Adams, John P. 1923(?)-1983 122
Obituary 111
Adams, John Paul
See Kinnaird, Clark
Adams, John Quincy 1767-1848 .... DLB 37
Adams, John R. 1900- 25-28R
Adams, Jonathan S(eth) 1961- 141
Adams, Julian 1919- CANR-11
Earlier sketch in CA 25-28R
Adams, Julius J. 1901(?)-1989 Obituary 130
Adams, Justin
See Cameron, Lou
Adams, Kenneth Menzies 1922- 103
Adams, Kramer A. 1920- 9-12R
Adams, L(ouis) Jerold 1939- 49-52
Adams, Laura 1943- 53-56
Adams, Laurie 1941- 53-56
See also SATA 33
Adams, Lee (Richard) 1924- Brief entry 111
Adams, Leon D(avid) 1905-1995 45-48
Obituary 149
Adams, Leonie (Fuller) 1899-1988 .... CAP-1
Obituary 125
Earlier sketch in CA 9-10
See also DLB 48
Adams, Les 1934- 97-100
Adams, Levi 1802(?)-1832 .... DLB 99
Adams, Lowell
See Joseph, James (Herz)
Adams, Marilyn Jager 1948- 136
Adams, Marion 1932- 41-44R
Adams, Mary (Grace Agnes)
1898-1984 Obituary 113
Adams, Maurice 1915(?)-1965 Obituary 116
Adams, Michael (Evelyn) 1920- 33-36R
Adams, Michael C(harles) C(orringham)
1945- 89-92
Adams, Mildred
See Kenyon, Mildred Adams
Adams, Nancy 1943(?)-1987 Obituary 123
Adams, Nathan Miller 1934- 45-48
Adams, Nicholas
See Smith, Sherwood
Adams, Nicholas
See Macdonald, James D.
Adams, Nicholas
See Pine, Nicholas
Adams, Nicholas 1947- 127
Adams, Norman (Edward Albert) 1927- 114
Adams, Orvill 1950- 144
Adams, Paul L(ieber) 1924- 61-64
Adams, Percy G(uy) 1914- CANR-4
Earlier sketch in CA 1-4R
Adams, Perseus 1933- 107
Adams, Philip R. 1908- 85-88
Adams, Phoebe-Lou 1918- 125
Brief entry 121
Adams, R(alph) J(ames) Q(uincy) 1943- 128
Adams, Rachel Leona White
1905(?)-1979 Obituary 93-96
Adams, Ramon Frederick
1889-1976 Obituary 65-68
Adams, Ramona Shepherd 1921- 106
Adams, Richard (George) 1920- CANR-35
Earlier sketches in CA 49-52, CANR-3
See also AAYA 16
See also AITN 1, 2
See also CLC 4, 5, 18
See also CLR 20
See also DAM NOV
See also JRDA
See also MAICYA
See also MTCW 1
See also SATA 7, 69
Adams, Richard E(dward) W(ood) 1931- 106
Adams, Richard N(ewbold) 1924- CANR-12
Earlier sketch in CA 29-32R
Adams, Richard P(errill) 1917-1977 .... CAP-2
Obituary 69-72
Earlier sketch in CA 33-36
Adams, (Franklin) Robert 1932-1990 .... CANR-66
Earlier sketch in CA 69-72
Adams, Robert H(ickman) 1937- CANR-22
Earlier sketch in CA 105
Adams, Robert Martin 1915-1996 .... CANR-4
Obituary 155
Earlier sketch in CA 5-8R
Adams, Robert McCormick 1926- CANR-39
Earlier sketches in CA 61-64, CANR-12
Adams, Robert Merrihew 1937- 135
Adams, Robert P. 1910- 13-16R
Adams, Rolland Leroy
1905(?)-1979 Obituary 89-92
Adams, Roy J(oseph) 1940- 154
Adams, Russell B(aird), Jr. 1937- 69-72
Adams, Russell L. 1930- 53-56
Adams, Ruth Joyce .... SATA 14
Adams, Sally Pepper (?)-197(?) 41-44R
Adams, Sam 1934- 57-60
Adams, Samuel 1722-1803 .... DLB 31, 43
Adams, Samuel A. 1933(?)-1988 Obituary 126
Adams, Sarah Fuller Flower 1805-1848 ... DLB 199
Adams, Scott
See Adams, Charles
Adams, Scott 1957- 168
See also AAYA 27
Adams, Sexton 1936- CANR-37
Earlier sketch in CA 25-28R
Adams, Sheila Kay 1953- 150
Adams, (Llewellyn) Sherman
1899-1986 Obituary 120
Adams, Stanley 1927- 135
Adams, Stephen J(on) 1945- 111
Adams, T(homas) W(illiam) 1933- 25-28R
Adams, Terrence Dean 1935- 33-36R
Adams, Theodore Floyd 1898-1980 .... CAP-1
Obituary 97-100
Earlier sketch in CA 11-12
Adams, Thomas 1582(?)-c. 1652 .... DLB 151
Adams, Thomas Boylston 1910-1997 114
Obituary 158
Adams, Thomas F. 1927- 13-16R
Adams, Thomas Randolph 1921- 107
Adams, Timothy Dow 1943- 133
Adams, Tricia
See Kite, Pat
Adams, Tricia
See Kite, (L.) Patricia
Adams, Val 1917(?)-1983 Obituary 109
Adams, Walter 1922- CANR-37
Earlier sketches in CA 1-4R, CANR-3
Adams, Willi Paul 1940- 105
Adams, William Howard 129
Brief entry 105
Adams, William James 1947- 148
Adams, William Taylor 1822-1897 .... DLB 42
See also SATA 28
Adams, William Yewdale 1927- Brief entry 104
Adamski, George 1891-1965 Obituary 112
Adam Smith, Janet (Buchanan) 1905- ... CANR-35
Earlier sketch in CA 113
See also SATA 63
Adam-Smith, Patricia Jean 1926- 105
Adam-Smith, Patsy
See Adam-Smith, Patricia Jean
Adamson, Alan (Herbert) 1919- 81-84
Adamson, David Grant 1927- 13-16R
Adamson, Donald 1939- CANR-39
Earlier sketch in CA 53-56
Adamson, Ed(ward Joseph)
1915(?)-1972 Obituary 37-40R
Adamson, Frank
See Adams, (Franklin) Robert
Adamson, Gareth 1925-1982(?) CANR-11
Obituary 106
Earlier sketch in CA 13-16R
See also SATA 46
See also SATA-Obit 30
Adamson, George 1906-1989 129
See also SATA-Obit 63
Adamson, George Worsley 1913- 107
See also SATA 30
Adamson, Graham
See Groom, Arthur William
Adamson, Hans Christian 1890-1968 .... 5-8R
Adamson, Joe
See Adamson, Joseph III
Adamson, Joseph III 1945- CANR-21
Earlier sketches in CA 45-48, CANR-1
Adamson, Joy(-Friederike Victoria) 1910-1980 .....
CANR-22
Obituary 93-96
Earlier sketch in CA 69-72
See also CLC 17
See also MTCW 1
See also SATA 11
See also SATA-Obit 22
Adamson, Lesley
See Grant-Adamson, Lesley
Adamson, M. J.
See Adamson, Mary Jo
Adamson, Mary Jo 1935- 134
Adamson, Robert 1943- 153
Adamson, Sir John (Ernest) 1867-1950 162
See also DLB 98
Adamson, Walter L(uiz) 1946- 107
Adamson, Wendy Writson 1942- 53-56
See also SATA 22
Adamson, William Robert 1927- 21-24R
Adas, Michael 1943- 53-56
Adastra
See Mirepoix, Camille
Adatto, Kiku 1947- 153
Adburgham, Alison Haig 1912- CAP-1
Earlier sketch in CA 9-10
Adcock, Almey St. John 1894- 65-68
Adcock, Arthur St. John 1864-1930 ...... DLB 135
Adcock, Betty
See Adcock, Elizabeth S(harp)
See also DLB 105
Adcock, C(yril) John 1904- CAP-1
Earlier sketch in CA 19-20
Adcock, Elizabeth S(harp) 1938- 57-60
See also Adcock, Betty
Adcock, Fleur 1934- CANR-69
Earlier sketches in CA 25-28R, CANR-11, 34
See also CAAS 23
See also CLC 41
See also DLB 40
Adcock, Frank Ezra 1886-1968 Obituary 106
Adcock, Thomas 1947- CANR-59
Earlier sketch in CA 138
Addae, Akili
See Obika, Akili Addae
Addams, Charles (Samuel) 1912-1988 ... CANR-12
Obituary 126
Earlier sketch in CA 61-64
See also CLC 30
Addams, Jane 1860-1945 .... TCLC 76
Addanki, Sam 1932- 109
Adde, Leo 1927(?)-1975 Obituary 57-60
Addeo, Jovita A. 1939- 103
Adderson, Caroline 1963- 146
Addie, Bob 1911(?)-1982 Obituary 105
Addie, Pauline Betz 1919(?)- Brief entry 105
Addinall, Peter 1932- 141
Addington, Arthur Charles 1939- 105
Addington, Larry H(olbrook) 1932- 33-36R
Addison, Gwen
See Harris, Alf(red)
Addison, Herbert 1889-1982 Obituary 108
Addison, Jan
See Foster, Jeannette Howard
Addison, Joseph 1672-1719 .... CDBLB 1660-1789
See also DLB 101
Addison, Lloyd 1937- 45-48
Addison, William Wilkinson 1905- CANR-5
Earlier sketch in CA 13-16R
Addiss, Stephen 1935- 120
Addleshaw, George William Outram
1907(?)-1982 Obituary 107
Addleton, Jonathan S. 1957- 164
Addona, Angelo F. 1925- 25-28R
See also SATA 14
Addonizio, Kim 1954- .... CAAS 28
Addy, George M(ilton) 1927- 21-24R
Addy, John 1915- 69-72
Addy, Ted
See Winterbotham, R(ussell) R(obert)
Ade, George 1866-1944 Brief entry 110
See also DLB 11, 25
Ade, Walter Frank Charles 1910- 53-56
Adelberg, Doris
See Orgel, Doris
Adelberg, Roy P. 1928- 17-20R
Adeler, Max
See Clark, Charles Heber
Adell, Sandra 1946- 150
Adelman, Bob 1930- 69-72
Adelman, Clifford 1942- 41-44R
Adelman, Deborah 1958- 141
Adelman, Gary 1935- 33-36R
Adelman, Howard 1938- 25-28R
Adelman, Irma Glicman CANR-3
Earlier sketch in CA 5-8R
Adelman, Irving 1926- 21-24R
Adelman, Janet (Ann) 1941- 61-64
Adelman, M(orris) A(lbert) 1917- 126
Brief entry 104
Adelman, Saul J(oseph) 1944- 104
Adelmann, Frederick J(oseph) 1915- CANR-27
Earlier sketch in CA 49-52
Adelsberger, Lucie 1895-1971 Obituary 33-36R
Adelson, Alan 1943- 145
Adelson, Daniel 1918- 69-72
Adelson, Joseph (Bernard) 1925- 17-20R
Adelson, Leone 1908- 61-64
See also SATA 11
Adelson, Roger 1942- 150
Adelson, Sandra 1934- 105
Adelstein, Michael E. 1922- CANR-15
Earlier sketch in CA 33-36R
Aden, John M(ichael) 1918- 97-100
Adenauer, Konrad 1876-1967 Obituary 112
Adeney, David Howard 1911- 53-56
Adeney, Martin 1942- 128
Adepoju, Aderanti 1945- 154
Ader, Paul (Fassett) 1919- 65-68
Aderman, Ralph M(erl) 1919- 5-8R
Ades, Dawn 1943- 103
Adey, Lionel 1925- 132
Adickes, Sandra 1933- 139
Adiseshiah, Malcolm S(athianathan)
1910-1994 81-84
Obituary 147
Adizes, Ichak 1937- 33-36R
Adkin, Mark 1936- 139
Adkins, Arthur W(illiam) H(ope) 1929- 111
Brief entry 104
Adkins, Cecil (Dale) 1932- 115
Adkins, Dorothy C.
See Wood, Dorothy Adkins
Adkins, Jan 1944- 33-36R
See also CLR 7
See also MAICYA
See also SAAS 19
See also SATA 8, 69
Adkins, Nelson F(rederick) 1897-1976 73-76
Obituary 65-68
Adkins, Patrick H. 1948- 126
Adlard, John 1929- CANR-21
Earlier sketches in CA 57-60, CANR-6
Adlard, (Peter) Mark 1932- CANR-57
Earlier sketch in CA 65-68
Adleman, Robert H. 1919- CANR-55
Obituary 150
Earlier sketch in CA 25-28R
Adler, Alfred (F.) 1870-1937 159
Brief entry 119
See also TCLC 61
Adler, B.
See Adler, William
Adler, Betty 1918-1973 .... CAP-1
Earlier sketch in CA 13-14
Adler, Bill
See Adler, William
Adler, C(arole) S(chwerdtfeger) 1932- ... CANR-40
Earlier sketches in CA 89-92, CANR-19
See also AAYA 4
See also CLC 35
See also JRDA
See also MAICYA
See also SAAS 15
See also SATA 26, 63, 102
Adler, Carol 1938- 61-64
Adler, Christopher Edward
1954(?)-1984 Obituary 114
Adler, Cyrus 1863-1940 Brief entry 122
Adler, David A. 1947- CANR-23
Earlier sketches in CA 57-60, CANR-7
See also MAICYA
See also SATA 14, 70
Adler, Denise Rinker 1908- 102
Adler, Elizabeth 144
Adler, Elmer 1884-1962 Obituary 89-92
Adler, France-Michele 1942- 105
Adler, Freda 1934- CANR-56
Earlier sketches in CA 69-72, CANR-11, 27
Adler, Gerhard 1904-1989(?) Obituary 128
Adler, H. G. 1910- CANR-10
Earlier sketch in CA 25-28R
Adler, Hans A(rnold) 1921- 49-52
Adler, Helmut E(rnest) 1920- 33-36R
Adler, Irene
See Penzler, Otto
and Storr, Catherine (Cole)
Adler, Irving 1913- CANR-47
Earlier sketches in CA 5-8R, CANR-2
See also CLR 27
See also MAICYA
See also SAAS 15
See also SATA 1, 29
Adler, Isidore 1925(?)-1990 Obituary 131
Adler, Jack 73-76
Adler, Jacob 1873(?)-1974 Obituary 53-56
Adler, Jacob 1913- 17-20R
Adler, Jacob H(enry) 1919- 13-16R
Adler, Jeffrey S(cott) 1957- 141
Adler, John Hans 1912-1980 Obituary 97-100
Adler, Joyce
See Adler, Joyce Sparer
Adler, Joyce Sparer 1915- 128
Adler, Kathleen
See Jones, Kathleen Eve
Adler, Larissa 1932- 150
Adler, Larry 1939- 105
See also SATA 36
Adler, Lucile 1922- 105
Adler, Lulla
See Rosenfeld, Lulla
Adler, Manfred 1936- 49-52
Adler, Margot 1946- 107
Adler, Max K(urt) 1905- CANR-3
Earlier sketch in CA 9-12R
Adler, Mortimer J(erome) 1902- CANR-33
Earlier sketches in CA 65-68, CANR-7
Interview in CANR-7
See also MTCW 1
Adler, Norman Tenner 1941- CANR-20
Earlier sketch in CA 69-72
Adler, Peggy .... SATA 22

Adler, Renata 1938- ... CANR-52
Earlier sketches in CA 49-52, CANR-5, 22
See also CLC 8, 31
See also MTCW 1
Adler, Ruth 1915-1968 ... CANR-4
Obituary ... 25-28R
Earlier sketch in CA 5-8R
See also SATA 1
Adler, Selig 1909-1984 ... 5-8R
Obituary ... 114
Adler, Sol 1925- ... CANR-22
Earlier sketches in CA 17-20R, CANR-7
Adler, Warren 1927- ... CANR-11
Earlier sketch in CA 69-72
Adler, William 1929- ... CANR-49
Earlier sketches in CA 9-12R, CANR-7
Adler, William 1951- ... 124
Adlerblum, Nina H. 1882-1974 Obituary ... 49-52
Adlerman, Daniel 1963- ... 161
See also SATA 96
Adlerman, Kimberly M. 1964- ... 161
See also SATA 96
Adloff, Virginia Thompson 1903-1990 Obituary . 130
Adnan, Etel 1925- ... 154
Adoff, Arnold 1935- ... CANR-67
Earlier sketches in CA 41-44R, CANR-20, 37
See also AAYA 3
See also AITN 1
See also CLR 7
See also JRDA
See also MAICYA
See also SAAS 15
See also SATA 5, 57, 96
Adolph, E. F.
See Adolph, Edward F(rederick)
Adolph, Edward F(rederick)
1895-1986 Obituary ... 121
Adomeit, Ruth E(lizabeth) 1910- ... 111
Adon, Aaron Bar
See Bar-Adon, Aaron
Adonias Filho 1915-1990 ... DLB 145
Adony, Raoul
See Launay, Andre (Joseph)
Adorjan, Carol (Madden) 1934- ... CANR-56
Earlier sketches in CA 41-44R, CANR-14, 31
See also SATA 10, 71
Adorno, Theodor W(iesengrund) 1903-1969 .. 89-92
Obituary ... 25-28R
Adoum, Jorge Enrique 1926- ... 152
See also HW
Adrian, Arthur A(llen) 1906- ... CAP-2
Earlier sketch in CA 19-20
Adrian, Charles R. 1922- ... CANR-3
Earlier sketch in CA 1-4R
Adrian, Edgar Douglas 1889-1977 ... 159
Obituary ... 73-76
Adrian, Frances
See Polland, Madeleine A(ngela Cahill)
Adrian, Mary
See Jorgensen, Mary Venn
Adrian, Rhys Brief entry ... 106
Adshead, Gladys L(ucy) 1896- ... 29-32R
See also SATA 3
Adshead, S(amuel) A(drian) M(iles) ... 167
Advani, Rukun 1955- ... 119
Ady, Endre 1877-1919 Brief entry ... 107
See also TCLC 11
Ady, Ronald W(illiam) 1934- ... 117
Adytum
See Curl, James Stevens
Adzigian, Denise Allard 1952- ... 97-100
A.E. 1867-1935
See Russell, George William
See also TCLC 3, 10
Aebi, Ormond 1916- ... 89-92
Aeby, Jacquelyn ... CANR-24
Earlier sketch in CA 29-32R
Aelfric c. 955-c. 1010 ... DLB 146
Aero, Rita ... 112
Aers, David 1946- ... CANR-8
Earlier sketch in CA 61-64
Aeschines c. 390B.C.-c. 320B.C. ... DLB 176
Aeschliman, Michael D(avid) 1948- ... 113
Aeschylus 525B.C.-456B.C. ... DA
See also DAB
See also DAC
See also DAM DRAM, MST
See also DC 8
See also DLB 176
See also WLCS
Aesop 620(?)B.C.-564(?)B.C. ... CLR 14
See also MAICYA
See also SATA 64
Aesop, Abraham
See Newbery, John
Affabee, Eric
See Stine, R(obert) L(awrence)
Affable Hawk
See MacCarthy, Sir(Charles Otto) Desmond
Affleck, Ben(jamin G.) 1972- ... 168
Affron, Charles 1935- ... 21-24R
Afkhami, Mahnaz 1941- ... 146
Afnan, Ruhi Muhsen 1899-1971 ... CAP-2
Earlier sketch in CA 29-32
Africa, Ben
See Bosman, Herman Charles
Africa, Thomas Wilson 1927- ... 17-20R
Africano, Lillian 1935- ... CANR-29
Earlier sketches in CA 69-72, CANR-11
Aftel, Mandy 1948- ... 108
Afterman, Allen 1941- ... 103
Afton, Effie
See Harper, Frances Ellen Watkins
Afzal, Omar 1939- ... 159
Agan, Patrick 1943- ... CANR-10
Earlier sketch in CA 65-68
Agan, Raymond J(ohn) 1919- ... 33-36R
Agan, (Anna) Tessie 1897- ... CAP-1
Earlier sketch in CA 17-18
Agapida, Fray Antonio
See Irving, Washington
Agar, Brian
See Ballard, (Willis) Todhunter
Agar, Herbert (Sebastian) 1897-1980 ... 65-68
Obituary ... 102
Agar, Michael H(enry) 1945- ... CANR-2
Earlier sketch in CA 45-48
Agar, William (Macdonough)
1894-1972 Obituary ... 37-40R
Agard, H. E.
See Evans, Hilary
Agard, Nadema 1948- ... SATA 18
Agarossi, Elena 1940- ... CANR-20
Earlier sketch in CA 97-100
Agarwala, Amar N. 1917- ... CANR-13
Earlier sketch in CA 21-24R
Agassi, Joseph 1927- ... CANR-41
Earlier sketches in CA 41-44R, CANR-15
Agassiz, Elizabeth Cary 1822-1907 ... DLB 189
Agassiz, Jean Louis Rodolphe 1807-1873 ... DLB 1
Agawa, Hiroyuki 1920- ... 134
Agay, Denes 1911- ... 69-72
Agbodeka, Francis 1931- ... CANR-4
Earlier sketch in CA 53-56
Agee, James (Rufus) 1909-1955 ... 148
Brief entry ... 108
See also AITN 1
See also CDALB 1941-1968
See also DAM NOV
See also DLB 2, 26, 152
See also TCLC 1, 19
Agee, Joel 1940- Brief entry ... 105
Agee, Jonis 1943- ... 139
Agee, Philip 1935- ... 135
Brief entry ... 104
Agee, Warren Kendall 1916- ... 17-20R
Agell, Charlotte 1959- ... 167
See also SATA 99
Ager, Cecelia 1902-1981 Obituary ... 103
Ager, Derek Victor 1923-1993 ... 107
Obituary ... 140
Ageton, Arthur Ainsley 1900-1971 ... CANR-1
Obituary ... 29-32R
Earlier sketch in CA 1-4R
Aggeler, Geoffrey D(onovan) 1939- ... 97-100
Aggertt, Otis J. 1916-1973 ... 33-36R
Aghill, Gordon
See Garrett, (Gordon) Randall (Phillip)
and Silverberg, Robert
Agich, George J. 1947- ... 146
Aginsky, Bernard W(illard) 1905- ... 85-88
Aginsky, Burt W.
See Aginsky, Bernard W(illard)
Aginsky, Ethel G(oldberg) 1910- ... 41-44R
Agle, Nan Hayden 1905- ... CANR-3
Earlier sketch in CA 1-4R
See also SAAS 10
See also SATA 3
Agnelli, Susanna 1922- ... CANR-28
Earlier sketch in CA 109
Agnew, Edith J(osephine) 1897- ... CAP-1
Earlier sketch in CA 17-18
See also SATA 11
Agnew, Eleanor 1948- ... 168
Agnew, James Barron 1930- ... 89-92
Agnew, Patience McCormick-Goodhart
1913(?)-1976 Obituary ... 69-72
Agnew, Peter L(awrence) 1901-1969 ... CAP-2
Earlier sketch in CA 21-22
Agnew, Spiro T(heodore) 1918-1996 ... 135
Obituary ... 153
Brief entry ... 110
Agniel, Lucien D. 1919- ... 29-32R
Agnon, S(hmuel) Y(osef Halevi) 1888-1970 ...
CANR-60
Obituary ... 25-28R
Earlier sketches in CAP-2, CA 17-18
See also CLC 4, 8, 14
See also MTCW 1
See also SSC 30
Agonito, Rosemary (Giambattista) 1937- ... 122
Brief entry ... 112
Agoos, Julie 1956- ... CANR-55
Earlier sketch in CA 127
Agor, Weston H(arris) 1939- ... CANR-29
Earlier sketch in CA 49-52
Agosin, Marjorie 1955- ... CANR-53
Earlier sketch in CA 131
See also HW
Agostinelli, Maria Enrica 1929- ... 33-36R
Agovi, Kofi Ermeleh 1944- ... 168
Agranoff, Robert 1936- ... CANR-14
Earlier sketch in CA 37-40R
Agree, Rose H. 1913- ... 21-24R
Agress, Hyman 1931- ... 89-92
Agress, Lynne 1941- ... 112
Agresto, John 1946- ... 115
Agronsky, Martin (Zama) 1915- ... 109
Interview in ... 109
See also AITN 2
Aguero, Kathleen 1949- ... 73-76
Aguila, Pancho 1945- ... 105
See also HW
Aguilar, Luis E. 1926- ... 21-24R
Aguilar, Ricardo
See Aguilar Melantzon, Ricardo
Aguilar, Rodolfo J(esus) 1936- ... 53-56
Aguilar, Rosario 1938- ... 160
Aguilar Melantzon, Ricardo 1947- ... 152
See also HW
Aguilera, Donna Conant ... 37-40R
Aguilera, Jaime Roldos
See Roldos Aguilera, Jaime
Aguilera Malta, Demetrio 1909-1981 ... 124
Brief entry ... 111
See also DAM MULT, NOV
See also DLB 145
See also HW
Aguolu, Christian Chukwunedu 1940- ... CANR-42
Earlier sketches in CA 101, CANR-19
Agus, Irving A(braham) 1910-1984 ... CAP-2
Obituary ... 113
Earlier sketch in CA 33-36
Agus, Jacob Bernard 1911-1986 ... CANR-2
Obituary ... 120
Earlier sketch in CA 5-8R
Agustini, Delmira 1886-1914 ... 166
See also HW
Agutter, Jennifer Ann 1952- ... 133
Agutter, Jenny
See Agutter, Jennifer Ann
Aguzzi-Barbagli, Danilo 1924- ... 49-52
Agwani, Mohammed Shafi 1928- ... CANR-7
Earlier sketch in CA 17-20R
Agyeman, Opoku 1942- ... 145
Agyeya
See Vatsyayan, Sachchidanand Hiranand
Aharoni, Reuben 1943- ... 151
Aharoni, Yohanan 1919-1976 ... CANR-15
Earlier sketch in CA 25-28R
Ahearn, (Edward) Allen 1937- ... 151
Ahearn, Barry 1950- ... 110
Ahearn, Catherine 1949- ... 114
Ahearn, Patricia 1937- ... 151
Ahern, Barnabas M. 1915- ... CANR-3
Earlier sketch in CA 5-8R
Ahern, Emily M(artin)
See Martin, Emily
Ahern, Emily M.
See Martin, Emily
Ahern, James F(rancis) 1932-1986 ... 41-44R
Obituary ... 118
Ahern, John F(rancis) 1936- ... 61-64
Ahern, Margaret McCrohan 1921- ... 13-16R
See also SATA 10
Ahern, Thomas Francis 1947- ... CANR-21
Earlier sketches in CA 45-48, CANR-1
Ahern, Tim(othy James) 1952- ... 115
Ahern, Tom
See Ahern, Thomas Francis
Aherne, Brian (de Lacy) 1902-1986 ... 135
Obituary ... 118
Brief entry ... 117
Aherne, Owen
See Cassill, R(onald) V(erlin)
Ahern Emily M(artin)
See Martin, Emily
Ahituv, Niv 1943- ... 117
Ahl, Anna Maria 1926- ... SATA 32
Ahl, Frederick Michael 1941- ... CANR-30
Earlier sketch in CA 111
Ahlberg, Allan 1938- ... CANR-70
Brief entry ... 111
Earlier sketches in CA 114, CANR-38
See also CLR 18
See also MAICYA
See also SATA 68
See also SATA-Brief 35
Ahlberg, Janet 1944-1994 ... 114
Obituary ... 147
Brief entry ... 111
See also CLR 18
See also MAICYA
See also SATA 68
See also SATA-Brief 32
See also SATA-Obit 83
Ahlberg, William A. 1922(?)-1985 Obituary ... 116
Ahlborn, Richard Eighme 1933- ... 108
Ahlers, John C(larke) 1927-1983 Obituary ... 110
Ahlert, Richard 1921-1985 Obituary ... 117
Ahlfors, Lars V(alerian) 1907- ... 155
Ahlgren, Gillian T. W. 1910- ... 157
Ahlin, Janne 1942- ... 136
Ahlstroem, G(oesta) W(erner) 1918-1992 ...
CANR-21
Obituary ... 136
Earlier sketch in CA 45-48
Ahlstrom, G(osta) W(erner)
See Ahlstroem, G(oesta) W(erner)
Ahlstrom, Sydney E(ckman) 1919-1984 ... 21-24R
Obituary ... 113
Ahmad, Ishtiaq 1937- ... 53-56
Ahmad, Nafis 1913- ... 17-20R
Ahmad, Suleiman M(uhammad) 1943- ... 110
Ahmad, Zakaria Haji
See Zakaria, Haji Ahmad
Ahmann, Mathew H(all) 1931- ... 9-12R
Ahmed, Akbar S(alahudin) 1943- ... 141
Ahmed, Leila 1940- ... 140
Ahnebrink, Lars 1915- ... 5-8R
Ahnstrom, D(oris) N. 1915- ... 5-8R
Aho, James (Alfred) 1942- ... 107
Ahokas, Jaakko (Alfred) 1923- ... 65-68
Ahrari, Mohammed E. 1945- ... 120
Ahsen, Akhter 1931- ... CANR-25
Earlier sketches in CA 61-64, CANR-10
Ahuja, Savitri 1924- ... 112
Ai 1947- ... CANR-70
Earlier sketch in CA 85-88
See also CAAS 13
See also CLC 4, 14, 69
See also DLB 120
Aichinger, Helga 1937- ... CANR-19
Earlier sketch in CA 25-28R
See also SATA 4
Aichinger, Ilse 1921- ... 85-88
See also DLB 85
Aichinger, Peter 1933- ... CANR-11
Earlier sketch in CA 61-64
Aickman, Robert (Fordyce) 1914-1981 ... CANR-72
Earlier sketches in CA 5-8R, CANR-3
See also CLC 57
Aidala, Thomas R(ichard) 1933- Brief entry ... 112
Aidells, Bruce 1944- ... 138
Aidenoff, Abraham 1913-1976 ... 37-40R
Obituary ... 61-64
Aidoo, (Christina) Ama Ata 1942- ... CANR-62
Earlier sketch in CA 101
See also BLCS
See also BW 1
See also DLB 117
Aiguillette
See Hargreaves, Reginald (Charles)
Aiken, Clarissa Lorenz 1899- ... CAP-2
Earlier sketch in CA 21-22
See also SATA 12
Aiken, Conrad (Potter) 1889-1973 ... CANR-60
Obituary ... 45-48
Earlier sketches in CA 5-8R, CANR-4
See also CDALB 1929-1941
See also CLC 1, 3, 5, 10, 52
See also DAM NOV, POET
See also DLB 9, 45, 102
See also MTCW 1
See also SATA 3, 30
See also SSC 9
Aiken, George D(avid) 1892-1984 Obituary ... 114
Brief entry ... 111
Aiken, Henry David 1912-1982 ... CANR-1
Obituary ... 106
Earlier sketch in CA 1-4R
Aiken, Irene (Nixon) ... 93-96
Aiken, Joan (Delano) 1924- ... CANR-64
Earlier sketches in CA 9-12R, CANR-4, 23, 34
See also AAYA 1, 25
See also CLC 35
See also CLR 1, 19
See also DLB 161
See also JRDA
See also MAICYA
See also MTCW 1
See also SAAS 1
See also SATA 2, 30, 73
Aiken, John (Kempton) 1913- ... 101
Aiken, John R(obert) 1927- ... 33-36R
Aiken, Lewis R(oscoe), Jr. 1931- ... CANR-10
Earlier sketch in CA 25-28R
Aiken, Maurice C. 1909(?)-1983 Obituary ... 109
Aiken, Michael Thomas 1932- ... CANR-9
Earlier sketch in CA 21-24R
Aikens, Tom Pitt
See Pitt-Aikens, Tom
Aikin, Charles 1901- ... 5-8R
Aikin, Lucy 1781-1864 ... DLB 144, 163
Aikman, Ann
See McQuade, Ann Aikman
Aikman, David (B. T.) 1944- ... 65-68
Aikman, Lonnelle (Davison)
1901(?)-1986 Obituary ... 121
Aimes, Angelica 1943- ... CANR-14
Earlier sketch in CA 81-84
Ainsbury, Ray
See Paine, Lauran (Bosworth)
Ainsbury, Roy
See Paine, Lauran (Bosworth)
Ainsley, Alix
See Steiner, Barbara A(nnette)
Ainslie, Rosalynde 1932- ... 25-28R
Ainslie, Tom
See Carter, Richard
Ainsworth, Catherine Harris 1910- ... SATA 56
Ainsworth, Charles H(arold) 1935- ... 49-52
Ainsworth, Dorothy Sears
1894-1976 Obituary ... 69-72
Ainsworth, Ed(ward Maddin) 1902-1968 ... CANR-4
Earlier sketch in CA 5-8R
Ainsworth, G(eoffrey) C(lough) 1905- ... 73-76
Ainsworth, Harriet
See Cadell, (Violet) Elizabeth
Ainsworth, Katherine 1908- ... 29-32R
Ainsworth, Mary D(insmore) Salter 1913- .. CANR-8
Earlier sketch in CA 21-24R
Ainsworth, Norma ... CANR-5
Earlier sketch in CA 13-16R
See also SATA 9
Ainsworth, Patricia
See Bigg, Patricia Nina
Ainsworth, Ray
See Paine, Lauran (Bosworth)
Ainsworth, Roy
See Paine, Lauran (Bosworth)
Ainsworth, Ruth (Gallard) 1908- ... CANR-37
See also MAICYA
See also SATA 7, 73
Ainsworth, Thomas Hargraves, Jr. 1920- ... 123
Ainsworth, William Harrison 1805-1882 ... DLB 21
See also SATA 24
Ainsworthy, Roy
See Paine, Lauran (Bosworth)
Ainsztein, Reuben 1917-1981 ... 110
Obituary ... 108
Air Chief Marshal Lord Dowding
See Dowding, Hugh Caswell Tremenheere
Aird, Catherine
See McIntosh, Kinn Hamilton
Aird, Eileen M(argaret) 1945- ... 49-52
Airlie, Catherine
See MacLeod, Jean Sutherland
Airola, Paavo (Olavi) 1915- ... 81-84
Aisenberg, Nadya 1928- ... 135
Aislin
See Mosher, (Christopher) Terry
Aistis, Jonas 1908(?)-1973 Obituary ... 41-44R

Aistrop, Jack 1916- CANR-3
Earlier sketch in CA 1-4R
See also SATA 14
Aitchison, James 1938- 137
Aitchison, Janet 1962- 57-60
Aitken, A(dam) J(ack) 1921- CANR-7
Earlier sketch in CA 13-16R
Aitken, Amy 1952- 108
See also SATA 54
See also SATA-Brief 40
Aitken, Dorothy 1916- CANR-2
Earlier sketch in CA 49-52
See also SATA 10
Aitken, Douglas 1933- 115
Aitken, George A. 1860-1917 .... DLB 149
Aitken, Hugh G(eorge) J(effrey) 1922- CANR-3
Earlier sketch in CA 1-4R
Aitken, Jonathan (William Patrick) 1942- 21-24R
Aitken, (John William) Max(well) 1910-1985 Obituary 116
Aitken, Robert (Baker) 1917- 130
Aitken, Thomas, Jr. 1910- 1-4R
Aitken, W(illiam) R(ussell) 1913- 41-44R
Aitken, William Maxwell
See Beaverbrook, William Maxwell Aitken
Aitkin, Don(ald Alexander) 1937- CANR-15
Earlier sketch in CA 93-96
Aitmatov, Chingiz (Torekulovich) 1928- .. CANR-38
Earlier sketch in CA 103
See also CLC 71
See also MTCW 1
See also SATA 56
Ai Wu 1904- 168
Ajami, Alfred M(ichel) 1948- Brief entry 110
Ajami, Fouad 1946- 167
Ajar, Emile
See Kacew, Romain
Ajay, Betty 1918- 69-72
Ajayi, J(acob) F(estus) Ade(niyi) 1929- CANR-40
Earlier sketches in CA 61-64, CANR-18
Ajegbo, Keith 1946- 122
Ajilvsgi, Geyata 1933- 124
Akaba, Suekichi 1910- .... SATA 46
Akaha, Tsuneo 1949- 120
Akalaitis, JoAnne 1937- 138
Akanji, Sangodare
See Beier, Ulli
Akar, John J(oseph) 1927-1975 153
See also BW 2
Akare, Thomas 1950- 109
Akarli, Engin Deniz 1945- 146
Akashi, Yoji 1928- 33-36R
Akass, John Ewart 1933-1990 Obituary 131
Akass, Jon
See Akass, John Ewart
Ake, Claude 1939-1996 .... CANR-10
Obituary 154
Earlier sketch in CA 21-24R
Akehurst, M(ichael) B(arton) 1940- 25-28R
Akens, David S. 1921- CANR-12
Earlier sketch in CA 25-28R
Akenside, Mark 1721-1770 .... DLB 109
Akenson, Donald Harman 1941- CANR-45
Earlier sketches in CA 57-60, CANR-7, 22
Aker, George F(rederick) 1927- CANR-15
Earlier sketch in CA 41-44R
Akeret, Robert U(lrich) 1928- 45-48
Akerman, Chantal (Anne) 1950- 127
Akerman, Susanna (Kristina) 1959- 139
Akers, Alan Burt
See Bulmer, (Henry) Kenneth
Akers, Charles W(esley) 1920- 13-16R
Akers, Floyd
See Baum, L(yman) Frank
Akers, Keith 1949- 112
Akers, Ronald L(ouis) 1939- CANR-1
Earlier sketch in CA 45-48
Akers, Susan Grey 1889-1984 Obituary 112
Akhmadulina, Bella Akhatovna 1937- 65-68
See also CLC 53
See also DAM POET
Akhmatova, Anna 1888-1966 .... CANR-35
Obituary 25-28R
Earlier sketches in CAP-1, CA 19-20
See also CLC 11, 25, 64
See also DAM POET
See also MTCW 1
See also PC 2
Akhnaton, Askia
See Eckels, Jon
Akhtar, Shabbir 1960- 139
Akhurst, Bertram A. 1928- 45-48
Akiba Sullivan Harper, Donna
See Sullivan Harper, Donna Akiba
Akin, Wallace E(lmus) 1923- 25-28R
Akin, William E(rnest) 1936- CANR-39
Earlier sketch in CA 116
Akinjogbin, I(saac) A(deagbo) 1930- CANR-29
Earlier sketches in CA 21-24R, CANR-12
Akins, Ellen 135
Akins, Zoe 1886-1958 Brief entry 115
See also DLB 26
Akinsha, Konstantin 1960- 155
Akita, George 1926- 17-20R
Akmakjian, Hiag 1926- 57-60
Akpabot, Samuel Ekpe 1932- 101
Akrigg, G(eorge) P(hillip) V(ernon) 1913- 25-28R
Aks, Patricia 1926- 136
See also SATA 68
Aksakov, Sergei Timofeyvich 1791-1859 .. DLB 198
Aksenov, Vassily
See Aksyonov, Vassily (Pavlovich)
Akst, Daniel 1956- 161
See also CLC 109
Aksyonov, Vassily (Pavlovich) 1932- CANR-48
Earlier sketches in CA 53-56, CANR-12
See also CLC 22, 37, 101
Akurgal, Ekrem 1911- 130
Akutagawa, Ryunosuke 1892-1927 154
Brief entry 117
See also TCLC 16
Akutagawa Ryunosuke 1892-1927 .... DLB 180
Akyeampong, Emmanuel K(waku) 1962- 166
Alabaster, William 1568-1640 .... DLB 132
Aladjem, Henrietta H. 1917- 105
Alagoa, Ebiegberi Joe 1933- 167
Alailima, Fay C. 1921- 33-36R
Alain
See Brustlein, Daniel
Alain 1868-1951 163
See also TCLC 41
Alain-Fournier
See Fournier, Henri Alban
See also DLB 65
See also TCLC 6
Alajalov, Constantin 1900-1987 Obituary 123
See also SATA-Obit 53
Alali, A. Odasuo 1957- 140
Al-Amin, Jamil Abdullah 1943- 125
Brief entry 112
See also BLC 1
See also BW 1
See also DAM MULT
Alan, Jack
See Green, Alan (Baer)
Alan, Sandy
See Ullman, Allan
Aland, Kurt 1915- CANR-12
Earlier sketch in CA 25-28R
Alarcon, Francisco X(avier) 1954- 147
See also DLB 122
Alas (y Urena), Leopoldo (Enrique Garcia) 1852-1901 131
Brief entry 113
See also HW
See also TCLC 29
Alaya, Flavia (M.) 1935- 33-36R
al-Azm, Sadik J. 1934- CANR-9
Earlier sketch in CA 21-24R
Alazraki, Jaime 1934- CANR-21
Earlier sketch in CA 33-36R
Alba, Nanina 1915-1968 141
See also BW 2
See also DLB 41
Alba, Richard D(enis) 1942- 109
Alba, Victor 1916- CANR-25
Earlier sketches in CA 21-24R, CANR-10
Alba de Gamez, Cielo Cayetana 1920- 93-96
Albanese, Catherine L(ouise) 1940- CANR-24
Earlier sketches in CA 65-68, CANR-9
Albany, James
See Rae, Hugh C(rauford)
Albaret, Celeste (Gineste) 1891-1984 73-76
Obituary 112
Albarn, Keith 1939- 135
Albaugh, Edwin (Doll, Jr.) 1935- 89-92
Albaugh, Ralph M. 1909- CAP-1
Earlier sketch in CA 13-14
Albaum, Gerald (Sherwin) 1933- CANR-38
Earlier sketches in CA 37-40R, CANR-14
Albaum, Melvin 1936- 53-56
Albee, Edward (Franklin III) 1928- CANR-54
Earlier sketches in CA 5-8R, CANR-8
Interview in CANR-8
See also CABS 3
See also AITN 1
See also CDALB 1941-1968
See also CLC 1, 2, 3, 5, 9, 11, 13, 25, 53, 86, 113
See also DA
See also DAB
See also DAC
See also DAM DRAM, MST
See also DLB 7
See also MTCW 1
See also WLC
Albee, George Sumner 1905-1964 .... 1-4R
Alber, Mike 1938- 25-28R
Alberoni, Francesco (Saverio) 1929- 130
Albers, Anni 1899-1994 .... CANR-2
Obituary 145
Earlier sketch in CA 1-4R
Albers, Henry H. 1919- CANR-6
Earlier sketch in CA 1-4R
Albers, Josef 1888-1976 .... CANR-3
Obituary 65-68
Earlier sketch in CA 1-4R
Albert, A(braham) Adrian 1905-1972 Obituary 37-40R
Albert, Allan (Praigrod) 1945- Brief entry 116
Albert, Bill 1942- 164
Albert, Burton 1936- CANR-46
Earlier sketches in CA 61-64, CANR-8, 23
See also SATA 22
Albert, Carl (Bert) 1908- 132
Albert, Ethel M(ary) 1918- 21-24R
Albert, Fred 1957- 140
Albert, Gail 1942- 108
Albert, Hans 1921- 141
Albert, Harold A. 1909-1997 .... 29-32R
Obituary 162
See also Cathcart, Helen
Albert, Linda 1939- CANR-27
Earlier sketch in CA 110
Albert, Louise 1928- 69-72
Albert, Marv 1943- 101
Albert, Marvin H(ubert) 1924-1996 .... CANR-58
Obituary 151
Earlier sketches in CA 73-76, CANR-30
Albert, Mimi (Abriel) 1940- 73-76
See also CAAS 30
Albert, Neil 1950- 160
Albert, Peter J(oseph) 1946- 114
Albert, Richard E. 1909- 149
See also SATA 82
Albert, Stephen P.
See Albert, Steve
Albert, Steve 1950- 147
Albert, Susan Wittig 1940- 167
Albert, Walter E. 1930- 21-24R
Albertazzie, Ralph 1923- 101
Alberti, Johanna 1940- 136
Alberti, Rafael 1902- 85-88
See also CLC 7
See also DLB 108
Alberti, Robert E(dward) 1938- CANR-7
Earlier sketch in CA 61-64
Albertinus, Aegidius c. 1560-1620 .... DLB 164
Alberts, David Stephen 1942- 29-32R
Alberts, Frances Jacobs 1907- 5-8R
See also SATA 14
Alberts, Robert C(arman) 1907-1996 .... 33-36R
Obituary 154
Alberts, William W. 1925- 21-24R
Albertson, Chris 1931- 57-60
Albertson, Dean 1920-1989 .... CANR-3
Obituary 128
Earlier sketch in CA 1-4R
Albertson, Susan
See Wojciechowski, Susan
Albert the Great 1200(?)-1280 .... DLB 115
Albertyn, Dorothy
See Black, Dorothy
Albery, Nobuko 81-84
Albin, Peter S(teigman) 1934- 85-88
Albini, Joseph L(ouis) 1930- 61-64
Albinski, Henry Stephen 1931- CANR-23
Earlier sketches in CA 21-24R, CANR-8
Albinson, Jack
See Albinson, James P.
Albinson, James P. 1932- 57-60
Albion, Lee Smith .... SATA 29
Albion, Robert Greenhalgh 1896-1983 .... CANR-3
Obituary 110
Earlier sketch in CA 1-4R
Albom, Mitch (David) 1958- 140
Albornoz, Claudio Sanchez
See Sanchez Albornoz (y Mediuna), Claudio
Alborough, Jez 1959- 131
See also SATA 86
Albran, Kehlog
See Shacket, Sheldon R(ubin)
Albrand, Martha (a pseudonym) 1914-1981 .... CANR-11
Obituary 108
Earlier sketch in CA 13-16R
Albrecht, Ernest (Jacob) 1937- 152
Albrecht, Gary L(ouis) 1937- 147
Albrecht, Lillie (Vanderveer) 1894- 5-8R
See also SATA 12
Albrecht, Milton C(harles) 1904- CANR-13
Earlier sketch in CA 33-36R
Albrecht, Robert C(harles) 1933- 21-24R
Albrecht, Ruth E. 1910- 17-20R
Albrecht, Steve 1963- 146
Albrecht, William P(rice) 1907- 73-76
Albrecht-Carrie, Rene 1904-1978 .... CANR-1
Earlier sketch in CA 1-4R
Albright, Bets Parker
See Albright, Elizabeth A.
Albright, Bliss (James F.) 1903- 33-36R
Albright, Daniel 1945- 125
Albright, Elizabeth A. 1920- 108
Albright, Horace M(arden) 1890-1987 124
Obituary 122
Albright, John Brannon 1930- 65-68
Albright, Joseph (Medill Patterson) 1937- 97-100
Albright, Madeleine Korbel 1937- 158
Albright, Peter 1926- 108
Albright, Raymond W(olf) 1901-1965 .... CAP-1
Earlier sketch in CA 9-10
Albright, Roger (Lynch) 1922- 106
Albright, Thomas 1935-1984 Obituary 112
Albright, William F(oxwell) 1891-1971 Obituary 33-36R
Albrow, Martin 1937- 33-36R
Albus, James Sacra 1935- 124
Albyn, Carole Lisa 1955- 150
See also SATA 83
Alcaeus c. 620B.C.- .... DLB 176
Alcala, Kathleen 1954- 158
Alcala-Galiano, Juan Valera y
See Valera y Alcala-Galiano, Juan
Alcalde, E. L.
See Chaij, Fernando
Alcalde, Miguel
See Burgess, Michael (Roy)
Alcantara, Ruben R(eyes) 1940- 105
Alcayaga, Lucila Godoy
See Godoy Alcayaga, Lucila
Alchemy, Jack
See Gershator, David
Alchian, Armen A(lbert) 1914- 127
Brief entry 110
Alcibiade
See Praz, Mario
Alcindor, (Ferdinand) Lew(is)
See Abdul-Jabbar, Kareem
Alcock, Gudrun 1908- .... SATA 56
See also SATA-Brief 33
Alcock, John 1942- CANR-52
Earlier sketch in CA 125
Alcock, Vivien 1924- CANR-41
Earlier sketch in CA 110
See also AAYA 8
See also CLR 26
See also JRDA
See also MAICYA
See also SATA 45, 76
See also SATA-Brief 38
Alcorn, Alfred 1941- 122
Alcorn, John 1935- .... SATA 31
See also SATA-Brief 30
Alcorn, Marvin D. 1902- 13-16R
Alcorn, Pat B(arker) 1948- 107
Alcorn, Robert Hayden 1909- 5-8R
Alcosser, Sandra (B.) 1944- 142
Brief entry 124
Alcott, Amos Bronson 1799-1888 .... DLB 1
Alcott, Julia
See Cudlipp, Edythe
Alcott, Louisa May 1832-1888 .... AAYA 20
See also CDALB 1865-1917
See also CLR 1, 38
See also DA
See also DAB
See also DAC
See also DAM MST, NOV
See also DLB 1, 42, 79
See also DLBD 14
See also JRDA
See also MAICYA
See also SATA 100
See also SSC 27
See also WLC
See also YABC 1
Alcott, William Andrus 1789-1859 .... DLB 1
Alcuin c. 732-804 .... DLB 148
Alcyone
See Krishnamurti, Jiddu
Ald, Roy A(llison) CANR-24
Earlier sketch in CA 73-76
Alda, Alan 1936- 103
Alda, Arlene 1933- 114
See also SATA 44
See also SATA-Brief 36
Aldan, Daisy 1923- CANR-25
Earlier sketches in CA 13-16R, CANR-8
Aldanov, M. A.
See Aldanov, Mark (Alexandrovich)
Aldanov, Mark (Alexandrovich) 1886(?)-1957 Brief entry 118
See also TCLC 23
Aldcroft, Derek H. 1936- CANR-55
Earlier sketches in CA 25-28R, CANR-12, 29
Alden, Carella
See Remington, Ella-Carrie
Alden, Dauril 1926- 105
Alden, Douglas William 1912- 69-72
Alden, Henry Mills 1836-1919 .... DLB 79
Alden, Isabella (Macdonald) 1841(?)-1930 Brief entry 120
See also DLB 42
See also YABC 2
Alden, Jack
See Barrows, (Ruth) Marjorie
Alden, Joan 1944- 144
Alden, John D. 1921- 17-20R
Alden, John R(ichard) 1908-1991 .... CANR-11
Obituary 135
Earlier sketch in CA 61-64
Alden, Michele
See Avallone, Michael (Angelo, Jr.)
Alden, Robert L(eslie) 1937- 65-68
Alden, Sue
See Francis, Dorothy Brenner
Alder, Francis A(nthony) 1937- 61-64
Alder, Henry (Ludwig) 1922- 49-52
Alderfer, Clayton P. 1940- 37-40R
Alderfer, E. G.
See Alderfer, E. Gordon
Alderfer, E. Gordon 1915- 121
Alderfer, Harold F(reed) 1903- 9-12R
Alderman, Clifford Lindsey 1902- CANR-3
Earlier sketch in CA 1-4R
See also SATA 3
Alderman, Ellen 1957(?)- 162
Alderman, Geoffrey 1944- CANR-55
Earlier sketches in CA 93-96, CANR-29
Alderman, (Barbara) Joy 1931- 61-64
Aldersey-Williams, Hugh 1959- 138
Alderson, Jo(anne) Bartels 1930- 65-68
Alderson, Michael (Rowland) 1931-1988 Obituary 126
Alderson, (Arthur) Stanley 1927- 5-8R
Alderson, Sue Ann 1940- .... SATA 59
See also SATA-Brief 48
Alderson, William T(homas), Jr. 1926- 9-12R
Alding, Peter
See Jeffries, Roderic (Graeme)
Aldington, Richard 1892-1962 .... CANR-45
Earlier sketch in CA 85-88
See also CLC 49
See also DLB 20, 36, 100, 149
Aldis, Dorothy (Keeley) 1896-1966 .... CANR-34
Earlier sketch in CA 1-4R
See also DLB 22
See also SATA 2
Aldis, H. G. 1863-1919 .... DLB 184
Aldiss, Brian W(ilson) 1925- CANR-64
Earlier sketches in CA 5-8R, CANR-5, 28
See also CAAS 2
See also CLC 5, 14, 40
See also DAM NOV
See also DLB 14
See also MTCW 1
See also SATA 34

Aldon, Adair
See Meigs, Cornelia Lynde
Aldon, Howard
See Wilson, (Alan) Doric
Aldouby, Zwy H(erbert) 1931- ... 33-36R
Aldous, Allan (Charles) 1911- ... SATA 27
Aldous, Anthony Michael 1935- ... CANR-25
Earlier sketch in CA 69-72
Aldous, Tony
See Aldous, Anthony Michael
Aldred, Cyril 1914-1991 ... CANR-6
Obituary ... 134
Earlier sketch in CA 57-60
Aldrich, Ann
See Meaker, Marijane (Agnes)
Aldrich, C(larence) Knight 1914- ... 25-28R
Aldrich, Frederic DeLong 1899- ... CAP-1
Earlier sketch in CA 11-12
Aldrich, Jonathan 1936- Brief entry ... 112
Aldrich, Joseph C(offin) 1940- ... CANR-37
Earlier sketch in CA 114
Aldrich, Nelson W(ilmarth), Jr. 1935- ... 141
Aldrich, Nelson Wilmarth, Jr. 1935- Brief entry . 110
Aldrich, Richard (Stoddard)
1902-1986 Obituary ... 119
Aldrich, Ruth I(sabelle) ... 105
Aldrich, Sandra Picklesimer 1945- ... 111
Aldrich, Thomas Bailey 1836-1907 Brief entry .. 111
See also DLB 42, 71, 74, 79
See also SATA 17
Aldridge, A(lfred) Owen 1915- ... 17-20R
Aldridge, Adele 1934- ... CANR-28
Earlier sketch in CA 49-52
Aldridge, Alan 1943- ... 125
See also SATA-Brief 33
Aldridge, Delores P(atricia) ... 142
See also BW 2
Aldridge, (Harold Edward) James 1918- .. CANR-51
Earlier sketches in CA 61-64, CANR-13
See also SATA 87
Aldridge, Jeffrey 1938- ... 25-28R
Aldridge, John W(atson) 1922- ... CANR-3
Earlier sketch in CA 1-4R
Aldridge, Josephine Haskell ... 73-76
See also SATA 14
Aldridge, Richard Boughton 1930- ... CANR-3
Earlier sketch in CA 9-12R
Aldridge, Sarah
See Marchant, Anyda
Aldrin, Edwin E(ugene), Jr. 1930- ... 89-92
Aldwinckle, Russell (Foster) 1911- ... 69-72
Aldyne, Nathan
See McDowell, Michael
Al-E Ahmad, Jalal 1923-1969 ... 152
Alegria, Ciro 1909-1967 ... CANR-72
Earlier sketch in CA 131
See also DLB 113
Alegria, Claribel 1924- ... CANR-66
Earlier sketch in CA 131
See also CAAS 15
See also CLC 75
See also DAM MULT
See also DLB 145
See also HW
Alegria, Fernando 1918- ... CANR-72
Earlier sketches in CA 9-12R, CANR-5, 32
See also CLC 57
See also HW
Alegria, Ricardo E(nrique) 1921- ... CANR-72
Earlier sketches in CA 25-28R, CANR-15, 32
See also HW
See also SATA 6
Aleichem, Sholom
See Rabinovitch, Sholem
See also TCLC 1, 35
Aleixandre, Vicente 1898-1984 ... CANR-26
Obituary ... 114
Earlier sketch in CA 85-88
See also CLC 9, 36
See also DAM POET
See also DLB 108
See also HW
See also MTCW 1
See also PC 15
Alejandro, Carlos F(ederico) Diaz
See Diaz-Alejandro, Carlos F(ederico)
Aleksandrov, Aleksandr Andreevich
See Durova, Nadezhda Andreevna
Aleksandrov, Pavel S(ergeevich) 1896-1982 ... 159
Aleksin, Anatolii Georgievich 1924- ... CANR-29
Earlier sketch in CA 109
See also SATA 36
Aleman, Miguel 1903(?)-1983 Obituary ... 110
Alenov, Lydia 1948- ... SATA 61
Alent, Rose Marie Bachem
See Bachem Alent, Rose M(arie Baake)
Alepoudelis, Odysseus
See Elytis, Odysseus
Aleramo, Sibilla 1876-1960 ... DLB 114
Aleshkovsky, Joseph 1929- ... 128
Brief entry ... 121
See also Aleshkovsky, Yuz
Aleshkovsky, Yuz
See Aleshkovsky, Joseph
See also CLC 44
Alessandra, Anthony J(oseph) 1947- ... 103
Alessandra, Tony ... 160
Alessandrini, Federico 1906(?)-1983 Obituary .. 109
Alex, Ben (a pseudonym) 1946- ... 114
See also SATA 45
Alex, Marlee (a pseudonym) 1948- ... 114
See also SATA 45
Alexander, Adele Logan 1938- ... 142
Alexander, Albert 1914- ... 25-28R
Alexander, Alfred 1908-1983 Obituary ... 110
Alexander, Anna B(arbara Cooke) 1913- ... 57-60
See also SATA 1
Alexander, Anne
See Alexander, Anna B(arbara Cooke)
Alexander, Anthony Francis 1920- ... 1-4R
Alexander, Arthur (Wilson) 1927- ... 5-8R
Alexander, Bevin (Ray) 1928- ... CANR-48
Earlier sketch in CA 122
Alexander, Bill 1910- ... 130
Alexander, Boyd 1913-1980 ... 53-56
Obituary ... 97-100
Alexander, Bruce 1932- ... 166
Alexander, Caroline 1956- ... 132
Alexander, Cecil Frances 1818-1895 ... DLB 199
Alexander, Charles
See Hadfield, (Ellis) Charles (Raymond)
Alexander, Charles 1868-1923 ... DLB 91
Alexander, Charles C(omer) 1935- ... 13-16R
Alexander, Charles Stevenson 1916- ... CANR-2
Earlier sketch in CA 5-8R
Alexander, Christine 1893-1975 Obituary ... 61-64
Alexander, Christine (Anne) 1949- ... 117
Alexander, Colin James 1920- ... 13-16R
Alexander, Conel Hugh O'Donel 1909-1974 .. 73-76
Alexander, David 1907-1973 ... 1-4R
Obituary ... 41-44R
Alexander, David M(ichael) 1945- ... 81-84
Alexander, Denis 1945- ... 45-48
Alexander, Donna
See Vitek, Donna Kimel
Alexander, Doris (Muriel) 1922- ... 143
Alexander, Edward 1936- ... 13-16R
Alexander, Edward P(orter) 1907- ... 33-36R
Alexander, Edwin P. 1905- ... 29-32R
Alexander, Elizabeth 1962- ... 135
Alexander, Ellen 1938- ... SATA 91
Alexander, Eric 1910(?)-1982 Obituary ... 106
Alexander, Ernest R(obert) 1933- ... 103
Alexander, Estella Conwill 1949- ... 143
See also BW 2
Alexander, Faith
See Bentley, Margaret
Alexander, Floyce 1938- ... CANR-13
Earlier sketch in CA 33-36R
Alexander, Frances (Laura) 1888- ... CANR-35
Earlier sketch in CA 25-28R
See also SATA 4
Alexander, Frank 1943- ... 65-68
Alexander, Franklin Osborne 1897- ... CAP-2
Earlier sketch in CA 25-28
Alexander, Franz (Gabriel) 1891-1964 ... 5-8R
Alexander, Gary 1941- ... 135
Alexander, George Jonathan 1931- ... 73-76
Alexander, George M(oyer) 1914- ... 5-8R
Alexander, Gil
See Ralston, Gilbert A(lexander)
Alexander, H. G. ... 129
See also Alexander, Horace G(undry)
Alexander, Harold Lee 1934- ... 69-72
Alexander, Harriet Semmes 1949- ... 156
Alexander, Henry
See McAllister, Alister
Alexander, Herbert (Mortimer)
1910-1988 Obituary ... 127
Alexander, Herbert E(phraim) 1927- ... 41-44R
Alexander, Holmes (Moss) 1906-1985 ... CANR-36
Obituary ... 118
Earlier sketch in CA 61-64
Alexander, Horace G(undry)
1889-1989 Obituary ... 129
See also Alexander, H. G.
Alexander, Hubert G(riggs) 1909- ... 21-24R
Alexander, I. J. 1905(?)-1974 Obituary ... 53-56
Alexander, Ian W(elsh) 1911- ... 13-16R
Alexander, J(onathan) J(ames) G(raham) 1935- ...
CANR-13
Earlier sketch in CA 21-24R
Alexander, James 1691-1756 ... DLB 24
Alexander, James E(ckert) 1913- ... 73-76
Alexander, Jan
See Banis, Victor J(erome)
Alexander, Janet 1907- ... CANR-4
Earlier sketch in CA 9-12R
See also McNeill, Janet
Alexander, Jean 1926- ... CANR-27
Earlier sketch in CA 49-52
Alexander, Jeb 1899-1965 ... 146
Alexander, Joan
See Wetherell-Pepper, Joan Alexander
Alexander, Jocelyn Anne Arundel 1930- .. CANR-4
Earlier sketch in CA 1-4R
See also SATA 22
Alexander, John A(leck) 1912- ... 9-12R
Alexander, John Kurt 1941- ... 102
Alexander, John N. 1941- ... 69-72
Alexander, John T(horndike) 1940- ... 33-36R
Alexander, John W(esley) 1918- ... CANR-3
Earlier sketch in CA 5-8R
Alexander, Jon 1940- ... 33-36R
Alexander, Joseph H(ammond) 1938- ... 150
Alexander, Josephine 1909- ... 104
Alexander, (Charles) K(halil)
1923-1980 Obituary ... 103
Alexander, Karl 1944- ... 134
Alexander, Kate
See Armstrong, Tilly
Alexander, Kathryn
See Caldwell, Kathryn (Smoot)
Alexander, Ken
See Alexander, Kenneth John Wilson
Alexander, Kenneth John Wilson 1922- ... 61-64
Alexander, L(ouis) G(eorge) 1932- ... CANR-42
Earlier sketches in CA 102, CANR-19
Alexander, Lawrence 1939- Brief entry ... 122
Alexander, Leo 1905-1985 Obituary ... 116
Alexander, Lewis M(cElwain) 1921- ... 21-24R
Alexander, Linda 1935- ... 21-24R
See also SATA 2
Alexander, Liza
See Campbell, Louisa D.
Alexander, Lloyd (Chudley) 1924- ... CANR-55
Earlier sketches in CA 1-4R, CANR-1, 24, 38
See also AAYA 1, 27
See also CLC 35
See also CLR 1, 5, 48
See also DLB 52
See also JRDA
See also MAICYA
See also MTCW 1
See also SAAS 19
See also SATA 3, 49, 81
Alexander, Louis 1917- ... 121
Alexander, Marc 1929- ... CANR-34
Earlier sketches in CA 5-8R, CANR-14
Alexander, Marge
See Edwards, Roselyn
Alexander, Martha (G.) 1920- ... CANR-44
Earlier sketch in CA 85-88
See also MAICYA
See also SATA 11, 70
Alexander, Marthann 1907- ... 53-56
Alexander, Martin 1930- ... CANR-27
Earlier sketch in CA 49-52
Alexander, Mary Jean McCutcheon ... 9-12R
Alexander, Meena 1951- ... CANR-70
Earlier sketches in CA 115, CANR-38
Alexander, Michael (Joseph) 1941- ... CANR-45
Earlier sketches in CA 45-48, CANR-22
Alexander, Michael Van Cleave 1937- ... 102
Alexander, Milton 1917- ... 17-20R
Alexander, Pamela 1948- ... 122
Alexander, Pat(ricia June) 1937- ... 113
Alexander, Paul 1955- ... 149
Alexander, Peter F. 1949- ... 138
Alexander, R(obert) McNeill 1934- ... CANR-51
Earlier sketch in CA 124
Alexander, R(obert) P(ercival)
1905(?)-1985 Obituary ... 117
Alexander, Rae Pace
See Alexander, Raymond Pace
Alexander, Ralph (Holland) 1936- ... 115
Alexander, Raymond Pace 1898-1974 ... 97-100
See also SATA 22
Alexander, Ric
See Long, Richard A(lexander)
Alexander, Richard Dale 1929- ... 110
Alexander, Robert
See Gross, Michael (Robert)
Alexander, Robert
See Legat, Michael (Ronald)
Alexander, Robert J. 1918- ... CANR-39
Earlier sketches in CA 1-4R, CANR-3, 18
Alexander, Robert Lester 1920- ... 108
Alexander, Robert William
1906(?)-1980 Obituary ... 97-100
Alexander, Rod
See Pellowski, Michael (Joseph)
Alexander, (Eben) Roy 1899(?)-1978 ... 85-88
Obituary ... 81-84
Alexander, Roy 1928- ... CANR-42
Earlier sketch in CA 118
Alexander, Ruth M. 1954- ... 154
Alexander, Sally Hobart 1943- ... 150
See also SATA 84
Alexander, Samuel 1859-1938 ... TCLC 77
Alexander, Shana 1925- ... CANR-58
Earlier sketches in CA 61-64, CANR-26
Interview in ... CANR-26
Alexander, Sidney 1912- ... CANR-6
Earlier sketch in CA 9-12R
Alexander, Stanley Walter
1895-1980 Obituary ... 97-100
Alexander, Stella Tucker 1912- ... 105
Alexander, Sue 1933- ... CANR-57
Earlier sketches in CA 53-56, CANR-4, 19
See also SAAS 15
See also SATA 12, 89
Alexander, Taylor Richard 1915- ... 107
Alexander, Theron 1913- ... CANR-3
Earlier sketch in CA 5-8R
Alexander, Thomas G(len) 1935- ... 65-68
Alexander, Thomas W(illiamson), Jr. 1930- ... 9-12R
Alexander, Victoria N. 1965- ... 152
Alexander, Vincent Arthur 1925-1980 Obituary . 101
See also SATA-Obit 23
Alexander, W(illiam) M(ortimer) 1928- ... 69-72
Alexander, SirWilliam 1557(?)-1640 ... DLB 121
Alexander, William M(arvin) 1912- ... 33-36R
Alexander, Yonah 1931- ... 61-64
Alexander, Zane
See Alexander, Harold Lee
Alexanderson, Gerald L(ee) 1933- ... CANR-42
Earlier sketch in CA 118
Alexandersson, Gunnar V(ilhelm) 1922- ... 17-20R
Alexandre, Philippe 1932- ... 41-44R
Alexandrowicz, Charles Henry 1902-1975 . CANR-1
Earlier sketch in CA 1-4R
Alexeev, Wassilij 1906- ... 89-92
Alexeieff, Alexandre A. 1901- ... SATA 14
Alexeyev, Constantin (Sergeivich)
See Stanislavsky, Constantin (Sergeivich)
Alexeyeva, Ludmilla 1927- ... 144
Alexie, Sherman (Joseph, Jr.) 1966- ... CANR-65
Earlier sketch in CA 138
See also CLC 96
See also DAM MULT
See also DLB 175
See also NNAL
Alexiou, Margaret 1939- ... 69-72
Alexis, Katina
See Strauch, Katina (Parthemos)
Alexis, Willibald 1798-1871 ... DLB 133
Aley, Albert 1919-1986 Obituary ... 118
Alfandary-Alexander, Mark 1923- ... 5-8R
al-Farabi 870(?)-950 ... DLB 115
al-Faruqi, Isma'il Raji 1921- ... CANR-13
Earlier sketch in CA 69-72
Alfau, Felipe 1902- ... 137
See also CLC 66
Alford, Bernard William Ernest 1937- ... 101
Alford, C(harles) Fred(erick) 1947- ... 131
Alford, Edna 1947- ... 152
Alford, Kenneth D. 1939- ... 150
Alford, Norman (William) 1929- ... 37-40R
Alford, Robert R(oss) 1928- ... 41-44R
Alford, Terry (L.) 1945- Brief entry ... 110
Alfred 849-899 ... DLB 146
Alfred, Richard
See Haverstock, Nathan Alfred
Alfred, William 1922- ... CANR-67
Earlier sketch in CA 13-16R
Alfven, Hannes O(lof) G(oesta) 1908-1995 .. 29-32R
Obituary ... 148
Algarin, Miguel 1941- ... CANR-20
Earlier sketch in CA 69-72
Algeo, John (Thomas) 1930- ... CANR-7
Earlier sketch in CA 17-20R
Alger, Horatio, Jr.
See Stratemeyer, Edward L.
Alger, Horatio, Jr. 1832-1899 ... DLB 42
See also SATA 16
Alger, Leclaire (Gowans) 1898-1969 ... 73-76
See also MAICYA
See also SATA 15
Alger, Philip Langdon 1894-1979 Obituary ... 109
Algery, Andre
See Coulet du Gard, Rene
al-Ghazali 1058-1111 ... DLB 115
Algren, Nelson 1909-1981 ... CANR-61
Obituary ... 103
Earlier sketches in CA 13-16R, CANR-20
See also CDALB 1941-1968
See also CLC 4, 10, 33
See also DLB 9
See also DLBY 81, 82
See also MTCW 1
Alhadeff, Gini q 1951- ... 164
Alhaique, Claudio 1913- ... 29-32R
Ali, Agha Shahid 1949- ... 153
Ali, Ahmed 1910- ... CANR-34
Earlier sketches in CA 25-28R, CANR-15
See also CLC 69
Ali, Chaudhri Mohamad 1905-1980 Obituary ... 105
Ali, Muhammad 1942- Brief entry ... 116
Ali, Salim (A.) 1896-1987 ... 132
Obituary ... 123
Ali, Schavi M(ali) 1948- ... CANR-26
Earlier sketches in CA 61-64, CANR-11
Ali, Shahrazad 1947- ... 152
See also BW 2
Ali, Sheikh R(ustum) 1932-1994 ... 141
Obituary ... 161
Ali, Tariq 1943- ... CANR-10
Earlier sketch in CA 25-28R
Aliano, Richard Anthony 1946- ... CANR-10
Earlier sketch in CA 65-68
Aliav, Ruth
See Kluger, Ruth
Aliber, Robert Z. 1930- ... CANR-25
Earlier sketches in CA 21-24R, CANR-8
Alibrandi, Tom 1941- ... CANR-12
Earlier sketch in CA 65-68
Alice (Mary Victoria Augusta Pauline), Princess
1883-1981 Obituary ... 103
Alicea, Gil C. 1979- ... 152
Aliesan, Jody 1943- ... CANR-7
Earlier sketch in CA 57-60
Alighieri, Dante
See Dante
Alihan, Milla ... CAP-2
Earlier sketch in CA 29-32
Ali Khan, Shirley 1951- ... 118
Aliki
See Brandenberg, Aliki Liacouras
See also CLR 9
Alilunas, Leo John 1912- ... 17-20R
Alimayo, Chikuyo
See Franklin, Harold L(eroy)
Alinder, Martha Wheelock
See Wheelock, Martha E.
Alinder, Mary Street 1946- ... 141
Aline, Countess of Romanones
See Quintanilla, (Maria) Aline (Griffith y Dexter)
Alinsky, Saul (David) 1909-1972 ... 133
Obituary ... 37-40R
Alioto, Robert F(ranklyn) 1933- ... 45-48
Alisky, Marvin (Howard) 1923- ... CANR-42
Earlier sketches in CA 13-16R, CANR-5, 20
Alisov, Boris P. 1892-1972 Obituary ... 37-40R
Al-Issa, Ihsan 1931- ... 109
Alitto, Guy S(alvatore) 1942- ... 93-96
Alix, Ernest Kahlar 1939- Brief entry ... 112
Al-Jahiz
See Jahiz, Al-
Alkalay-Gut, Karen 1945- ... 129
Alkema, Chester Jay 1932- ... 53-56
See also SATA 12
Alker, Hayward R(ose), Jr. 1937- ... 17-20R
al-Khadim, Sa'd
See Elkhadem, Saad (Eldin Amin)
al-Khalil, Samir a pseudonym ... 140
al-Kharrat, Edwar 1926- ... 136
Alkire, Leland George, (Jr.) 1937- ... 101
Alkire, William Henry 1935- ... 107
Alkon, Paul K. ... 150
Allaback, Steven Lee 1939- ... 97-100
Allaby, (John) Michael 1933- ... CANR-42
Earlier sketches in CA 45-48, CANR-1, 20

Allahar, Anton L. 1949- 153
Allain, Marie-Francoise 1945- 142
Allaire, Joseph L(eo) 1929- 41-44R
Allamand, Pascale 1942- CANR-12
Earlier sketch in CA 69-72
See also SATA 12
Allan, Adrian R. 168
Allan, Alfred K. 1930- 17-20R
Allan, Andrew 1907-1974 ..... DLB 88
Allan, Andrew (Edward Fairbairn) 1907-1974 ... 145
Allan, D(avid) G(uy) C(harles) 1925- CANR-15
Earlier sketch in CA 25-28R
Allan, David 1964- 148
Allan, Elkan 1922- 101
Allan, Harry T. 1928- 25-28R
Allan, J(ohn) David 1945- 41-44R
Allan, John B.
See Westlake, Donald E(dwin)
Allan, Keith 1943- 141
Allan, Lewis
See Meeropol, Abel
Allan, Mabel Esther 1915-1998 ..... CANR-47
Obituary 167
Earlier sketches in CA 5-8R, CANR-2, 18
See also CLR 43
See also MAICYA
See also SAAS 11
See also SATA 5, 32, 75
Allan, Mea 1909-1982 ..... CANR-2
Obituary 107
Earlier sketch in CA 5-8R
Allan, Nicholas 1956- ..... SATA 79
Allan, Norman B. 1921- Brief entry 105
Allan, Robert Alexander 1914-1979 Obituary ... 106
Allan, Robin 1934- 107
Allan, Sidney
See Hartmann, Sadakichi
Allan, Sydney
See Hartmann, Sadakichi
Allan, Ted 1918(?)-1995 ..... CANR-67
Obituary 149
Earlier sketch in CA 77-80
See also DLB 68
Allana, Ghulam Ali 1906-1985 Obituary 115
Allana, Ghulamali
See Allana, Ghulam Ali
Allanbrook, Douglas 1921- 151
Allanbrook, Wye J(amison) 1943- 110
Alland, Alexander, Jr. 1931- 21-24R
Alland, Guy 1944- 69-72
Allan-Meyer, Kathleen 1918- CANR-50
Earlier sketch in CA 123
See also SATA 51
See also SATA-Brief 46
Allard, Bessie Butler Newsom
(?)-1987 Obituary 122
Allard, Dean C(onrad) 1933- CANR-1
Earlier sketch in CA 45-48
Allard, Harry
See Allard, Harry G(rover), Jr.
Allard, Harry G(rover), Jr. 1928- CANR-38
Earlier sketch in CA 113
Interview in 113
See also MAICYA
See also SATA 42, 102
Allard, Michel (Adrien) 1924-1976 Obituary .. 65-68
Allard, Sven 1896-1975 ..... CAP-2
Earlier sketch in CA 29-32
Allard, William Albert 1937- 115
Allardt, Erik 1925- CANR-56
Earlier sketches in CA 73-76, CANR-13, 30
Allardt, Linda 1926- 126
Brief entry 104
Allardyce, Gilbert Daniel 1932- 33-36R
Allardyce, Paula
See Torday, Ursula
Allason, Rupert (W. S.) 1951- 132
Allaun, Frank (Julian) 1913- 103
Allbeck, Willard Dow 1898- 21-24R
Allbery, Debra 1957- 141
Allbeury, Ted
See Allbeury, Theodore Edward le Bouthillier
See also DLB 87
Allbeury, Theodore Edward le Bouthillier 1917- ....
CANR-72
Earlier sketches in CA 53-56, CANR-5, 34
See also Allbeury, Ted
Allchin, A(rthur) M(acdonald) 1930- CANR-38
Earlier sketches in CA 25-28R, CANR-17
Allcorn, Seth 1946- 138
Alldridge, James Charles 1910- 29-32R
Alldritt, Keith 1935- CANR-42
Earlier sketch in CA 25-28R
See also DLB 14
Allee, John Gage, (Jr.) 1918-1987 Obituary 121
Allee, Marjorie Hill 1890-1945 ..... SATA 17
Alleger, Daniel E(ugene) 1903- 33-36R
Allegretto, Michael 1944- 167
Allegro, John Marco 1923-1988 ..... CANR-20
Obituary 124
Earlier sketches in CA 9-12R, CANR-4
Allen, A(rthur) B(ruce) 1903-1975 ..... CAP-2
Earlier sketch in CA 23-24
Allen, A(rvon) Dale, Jr. 1935- 21-24R
Allen, Adam
See Epstein, Beryl (M. Williams)
and Epstein, Samuel
Allen, Agnes Rogers 1893-1986 Obituary 121
Allen, Alex B.
See Heide, Florence Parry
Allen, Allyn
See Eberle, Irmengarde
Allen, Anita
See Schenck, Anita A(llen)
Allen, Arthur A(ugustus) 1885-1964 ..... CANR-19
Earlier sketch in CA 1-4R
Allen, Barbara
See Stuart, (Violet) Vivian (Finlay)
Allen, Barry 1957- 145
Allen, Betsy
See Harrison, Elizabeth Cavanna
Allen, Betty (Jeanne) 1929- 113
Allen, Bob 1948- 118
Allen, Bob 1961- 143
See also SATA 76
Allen, Brian 1952- 126
Allen, Captain Quincy CANR-26
Earlier sketches in CAP-2, CA 19-20
Allen, Carl 1961- 69-72
Allen, Catherine B(ryant) 1942- 129
Allen, Cecil J(ohn) 1886-1973 ..... CAP-2
Earlier sketch in CA 25-28
Allen, Charles L(ivingstone) 1913- CANR-56
Earlier sketches in CA 111, CANR-28
Allen, Charlotte Hale 1928- 130
Allen, Charlotte Vale 1941- CANR-54
Earlier sketches in CA 69-72, CANR-12, 30
Allen, Chester
See Holding, Vera Zumwalt
Allen, Chris 1929- 29-32R
Allen, Clabon Walter 1904-1987 Obituary 124
Allen, Clay
See Paine, Lauran (Bosworth)
Allen, Clifford Edward 1902- CAP-1
Earlier sketch in CA 9-10
Allen, Clifton Judson 1901- 108
Allen, Craig M(itchell) 1954- 145
Allen, Daniel 1947- 125
Allen, David 1925- 33-36R
Allen, David 1939- 115
Allen, David Elliston 1932- 25-28R
Allen, David F(ranklyn) 1943- 103
Allen, David Grayson 1943- 115
Allen, David Rayvern 1938- 129
Allen, David W. 1922- Brief entry 113
Allen, Derek Fortrose 1910-1975 Obituary 114
Allen, Dick 1939- 33-36R
See also CAAS 11
Allen, Diogenes 1932- CANR-25
Earlier sketches in CA 25-28R, CANR-10
Allen, Dizzy
See Allen, H(ubert) R(aymond)
Allen, Don Cameron 1903-1972 ..... CANR-4
Earlier sketch in CA 5-8R
Allen, Donald Emerson 1917- 45-48
Allen, Donald M(erriam) 1912- CANR-10
Earlier sketch in CA 17-20R
Allen, Donald R. 1930- 45-48
Allen, Douglas (Malcolm) 1941- 113
Allen, Durward L(eon) 1910- 41-44R
Allen, Dwight W(illiam) 1931- 13-16R
Allen, E. C.
See Ward, Elizabeth Campbell
Allen, E. John B. 1933- 146
Allen, Edith Beavers 1920- 9-12R
Allen, Edith Marion CAP-1
Earlier sketch in CA 13-16
Allen, Edward 1948- ..... CLC 59
Allen, Edward (Hathaway) 1948- 161
Allen, Edward D(avid) 1923- CANR-31
Earlier sketch in CA 49-52
Allen, Edward Heron
See Heron-Allen, Edward
Allen, Edward J(oseph) 1907- CAP-1
Earlier sketch in CA 17-18
Allen, Edward Lawrence 1913-1989 Obituary .. 130
Allen, Edward Switzer 1887-1985 Obituary 116
Allen, Elisabeth Offutt 1895- 57-60
Allen, Elizabeth
See Thompson, Elizabeth Allen
Allen, (Evelyn) Elizabeth 1918- 121
Allen, Elizabeth 1955- 122
Allen, Elizabeth Cooper
See Allen, Betty (Jeanne)
Allen, Eric 1916- 133
Brief entry 111
Allen, Esther 1962- 158
Allen, Ethan 1738-1789 ..... DLB 31
Allen, Everett S(locum) 1916-1990 147
Brief entry 110
Allen, Fergus 1921- 162
Allen, Francis A(lfred) 1919- 13-16R
Allen, Francis R(obbins) 1908- 77-80
Allen, Frank 1939- CANR-26
Earlier sketch in CA 109
Allen, Frederick G(arfield) 1936-1986 .... CANR-26
Obituary 121
Earlier sketch in CA 57-60
Allen, Frederick Lewis 1890-1954 ..... DLB 137
Allen, Frederick S(tetson) 1930- Brief entry 112
Allen, G(eorge) C(yril) 1900-1982 ..... CANR-32
Obituary 107
Earlier sketches in CA 1-4R, CANR-3
Allen, G(eorge) Francis 1907- CAP-1
Earlier sketch in CA 9-10
Allen, Garland E(dward) 1936- 53-56
Allen, Gary
See Allen, Frederick G(arfield)
Allen, Gay Wilson 1903-1995 ..... CANR-3
Obituary 149
Earlier sketch in CA 5-8R
See also DLB 103
See also DLBY 95
Allen, Geoffrey Francis 1902- CAP-1
Earlier sketch in CA 13-14
Allen, George 1808-1876 ..... DLB 59
Allen, George (Herbert) 1922- 111
Allen, Gerald 1942- CANR-16
Earlier sketch in CA 93-96
Allen, Gertrude E(lizabeth) 1888- 61-64
See also SATA 9
Allen, Gilbert (Bruce) 1951- 111
Allen, Gina 1918- CANR-43
Earlier sketch in CA 1-4R
Allen, Grace
See Hogarth, Grace (Weston Allen)
Allen, Grant 1848-1899 ..... DLB 70, 92, 178
Allen, Gwenfread Elaine 1904- 61-64
Allen, H. Fredericka
See Allen, H(elena) G(ronlund)
Allen, H(elena) G(ronlund) 29-32R
Allen, H(ubert) R(aymond) 1919-1987 Obituary . 122
Allen, Harold B(yron) 1902- CANR-10
Earlier sketch in CA 17-20R
Allen, Harold J(oseph) 1925- 45-48
Allen, Harry Cranbrook 1917- 5-8R
Allen, Hazel
See Hershberger, Hazel Kuhns
Allen, Henry
See Adams, Henry H(itch)
Allen, Henry Wilson 1912-1991 ..... CANR-64
Obituary 135
Earlier sketch in CA 89-92
See also DLBY 85
Allen, Herman R. 1913(?)-1979 Obituary 89-92
Allen, (William) Hervey, (Jr.) 1889-1949 Brief
entry 108
See also DLB 9, 45
Allen, Howard W. 1931- 33-36R
Allen, Ida (Cogswell) Bailey
1885-1973 Obituary 110
Allen, Ira R. 1948- 65-68
Allen, Irene 1903- CAP-1
Earlier sketch in CA 13-16
Allen, Irving L(ewis), Jr. 1931- 110
Allen, Ivan, Jr. 1911- 109
Allen, Jack 1899- ..... SATA-Brief 29
Allen, Jack 1914- CANR-4
Earlier sketch in CA 9-12R
Allen, James
See Ader, Paul (Fassett)
Allen, James 1739-1808 ..... DLB 31
Allen, James B(rown) 1927- 105
Allen, James B(eekman) 1931- 105
Allen, James Egert 1896-1980 Obituary 97-100
Allen, James L(ovic), Jr. 1929- CANR-17
Earlier sketch in CA 33-36R
Allen, James Lane 1849-1925 ..... DLB 71
Allen, James S. 1906(?)-1986 Obituary 120
Allen, James Smith 1949- 111
Allen, Jay Presson 1922- CANR-45
Earlier sketch in CA 73-76
See also DLB 26
Allen, Jeffner 1947- 155
Allen, Jeffrey (Yale) 1948- 112
See also SATA 42
Allen, Jeffrey G(rant) 1943- 116
Allen, Jerry 1911-1994 ..... 9-12R
Obituary 147
Allen, Jim
See Allen, James L(ovic), Jr.
Allen, Johannes 1916-1973 ..... CANR-14
Earlier sketch in CA 29-32R
Allen, John
See Perry, Ritchie (John Allen)
Allen, John Alexander 1922- 25-28R
Allen, John D(aniel) 1898-1972 ..... CAP-2
Earlier sketch in CA 33-36
Allen, John Jay 1932- CANR-18
Earlier sketch in CA 33-36R
Allen, John Logan 1941- 85-88
Allen, John Stuart 1907-1982 Obituary 109
Allen, Jon L(ewis) 1931- 57-60
Allen, Jordan
See Dumke, Glenn S.
Allen, Judson B(oyce) 1932- CANR-17
Earlier sketch in CA 81-84
Allen, Judy (Christina) 1941- ..... SATA 80
Allen, K. Eileen 1918- 113
Allen, Katharine Martin 1906(?)-1984 Obituary . 113
Allen, Kenneth (William) 1941- 69-72
Allen, Kenneth S. 1913-1981 ..... CANR-32
Earlier sketch in CA 77-80
See also SATA 56
Allen, L(ouis) David 1940- 130
Brief entry 117
Allen, Lafe Franklin 1914- Brief entry 111
Allen, Laura Jean 133
Brief entry 110
See also SATA-Brief 53
Allen, Lawrence A. 1926- 45-48
Allen, Layman E(dward) 1927- 5-8R
Allen, Lee 1915-1969 ..... CANR-1
Earlier sketch in CA 1-4R
Allen, Leonard 1915(?)-1981 Obituary 102
Allen, Leroy 1912- 65-68
See also SATA 11
Allen, Leslie Christopher 1935- CANR-13
Earlier sketch in CA 73-76
Allen, Leslie H. 1887(?)-1973 Obituary 49-52
Allen, Linda 1925- 102
See also SATA 33
Allen, Loring
See Allen, Robert Loring
Allen, Louis 1922-1991 ..... 41-44R
Obituary 136
Allen, Louis A. 1917- 5-8R
Allen, M(arion) C. 1914- 9-12R
Allen, M(alcolm) D(ennis) 1951- 138
Allen, Marcus
See Donicht, Mark Allen
Allen, Marjorie 1931- 69-72
See also SATA 22
Allen, Marjory (Gill) 1897- CAP-1
Earlier sketch in CA 9-10
Allen, Mark
See Donicht, Mark Allen
Allen, Martha Mitten 1937- 125
Allen, Mary
See Cleveland, Mary
Allen, Mary (Charlotte Chocqueel) 1909- 109
Allen, Maury 1932- CANR-11
Earlier sketch in CA 17-20R
See also SATA 26
Allen, Merrill J(ames) 1918- 69-72
Allen, Merritt Parmelee 1892-1954 ..... SATA 22
Allen, Michael (Derek) 1939- CANR-39
Earlier sketch in CA 77-80
Allen, Michael J(ohn) B(ridgman) 1941- 102
Allen, Michael Patrick 1945- 137
Allen, Minerva C(rantz) 1935- CANR-6
Earlier sketch in CA 57-60
Allen, Miriam Marx 1927- 138
Allen, Myron Sheppard 1901- CAP-1
Earlier sketch in CA 9-10
Allen, Nancy 1938- 165
Allen, Nina (Stroemgren) 1935- ..... SATA 22
Allen, Oliver E. 1922- CANR-53
Earlier sketch in CA 126
Allen, Pamela 1934- CANR-53
Earlier sketch in CA 126
See also CLR 44
See also SATA 50, 81
Allen, Pat 1938- 118
Allen, Paul 1948- 81-84
Allen, Paula Gunn 1939- CANR-63
Brief entry 112
Earlier sketch in CA 143
See also CLC 84
See also DAM MULT
See also DLB 175
See also NNAL
Allen, Peter Christopher 1905- 108
Allen, Philip M(ark) 1932- 150
Allen, Phyllis (Greig) 65-68
Allen, Phyllis S(loan) 1908- 65-68
Allen, Polly Reynolds 1940- 110
Allen, R. Earl 1922- CANR-6
Earlier sketch in CA 9-12R
Allen, R(onald) R(oyce) 1930- 17-20R
Allen, Reginald E. 1931- CANR-13
Earlier sketch in CA 33-36R
Allen, Richard (Hugh Sedley) 1903-1996 ... 25-28R
Obituary 151
Allen, (Alexander) Richard 1929- CANR-11
Earlier sketch in CA 65-68
Allen, Richard C.
See Taylor, John M(axwell)
Allen, Richard C. 1926- CANR-17
Earlier sketch in CA 25-28R
Allen, Richard Sanders 1917- 21-24R
Allen, Richard V(incent) 1936- 21-24R
Allen, Roach Van 1917- 9-12R
Allen, Robert
See Garfinkel, Bernard Max
Allen, Robert 1946- 97-100
Allen, Robert C(lyde) 1950- CANR-41
Earlier sketch in CA 117
Allen, Robert Day 1927-1986 107
Obituary 125
Allen, Robert F(rancis) 1928-1987 ..... CANR-36
Obituary 123
Earlier sketch in CA 33-36R
Allen, Robert J. 1930- 13-16R
Allen, Robert L(ee) 1942- 101
See also BW 1
Allen, Robert Livingston 1916- 17-20R
Allen, Robert Loring 1921- CANR-6
Earlier sketch in CA 1-4R
Allen, Robert M. 1909-1979 ..... CANR-2
Earlier sketch in CA 1-4R
Allen, Robert Porter 1905-1963 ..... 5-8R
Allen, Robert S(haron) 1900-1981 ..... CANR-6
Obituary 103
Earlier sketch in CA 57-60
Allen, Robert Thomas 1911- Brief entry 110
Allen, Roberta L. 1945- 144
Allen, Rodney F. 1938- 61-64
See also SATA 27
Allen, Roger M(ichael) A(shley) 1942- ... CANR-51
Earlier sketches in CA 111, CANR-28
Allen, Roger MacBride 1957- 162
Allen, Roland
See Ayckbourn, Alan
Allen, Ronald B(arclay) 1941- 114
Allen, Ronald Royce 1930- CANR-32
Earlier sketch in CA 113
Allen, Ross R(oundy) 1928- 33-36R
Allen, Roy (George Douglas)
1906-1983 Obituary 110
Allen, Rupert C(lyde) 1927- 65-68
Allen, Ruth
See Peterson, Esther (Allen)
Allen, Ruth Finney 1898-1979 93-96
Obituary 85-88
Allen, Sam
See Allen, M(arion) C.
Allen, Samuel W(ashington) 1917- CANR-26
Earlier sketch in CA 49-52
See also BW 1
See also DLB 41
See also SATA 9
Allen, Sarah A.
See Hopkins, Pauline Elizabeth
Allen, Sarah (Pearson) Sawyer 1920- 89-92
Allen, Sheila Rosalynd 1942- 135
Allen, Shirley Seifried 1921- 57-60
Allen, Shirley Walter 1883- CAP-2
Earlier sketch in CA 25-28
Allen, Sidney H.
See Hartmann, Sadakichi
Allen, Stephen (Valentine Patrick William) 1921- ...
CANR-46
Earlier sketches in CA 25-28R, CANR-18

Allen, Steve
See Allen, Stephen (Valentine Patrick William)
Allen, Sue P. 1913- ... 25-28R
Allen, Sydney (Earl), Jr. 1929- ... 29-32R
Allen, T. D.
See Allen, Terril Diener
Allen, Terril Diener 1908- ... CANR-61
Earlier sketches in CA 5-8R, CANR-2
See also SATA 35
Allen, Terry D.
See Allen, Terril Diener
Allen, Thomas B(enton) 1929- ... CANR-45
Earlier sketches in CA 13-16R, CANR-5, 20
See also SATA 45
Allen, Tim 1953- ... 158
See also AAYA 24
Allen, Tom
See Allen, Thomas B(enton)
Allen, Tony 1945- ... 77-80
Allen, Vernon L(esley) 1933- ... 29-32R
Allen, W(illiam) Sidney 1918- ... 49-52
Allen, Wallace (Wilbur) 1919- ... 118
Allen, Walter Ernest 1911-1994 ... CANR-25
Obituary ... 147
Earlier sketch in CA 61-64
See also CAAS 6
Allen, William 1940- ... 65-68
Allen, William A(ustin) 1916- ... CANR-13
Earlier sketch in CA 33-36R
Allen, William R(ichard) 1924- ... 17-20R
Allen, William Sheridan 1932- ... 13-16R
Allen, William Stannard 1913- ... 101
Allen, Woody 1935- ... CANR-63
Earlier sketches in CA 33-36R, CANR-27, 38
See also AAYA 10
See also CLC 16, 52
See also DAM POP
See also DLB 44
See also MTCW 1
Allende, Isabel 1942- ... CANR-51
Brief entry ... 125
Earlier sketch in CA 130
Interview in ... 130
See also AAYA 18
See also CLC 39, 57, 97
See also DAM MULT, NOV
See also DLB 145
See also HLC
See also HW
See also MTCW 1
See also WLCS
Allendoerfer, Carl B(arnett) 1911-1974 ... CANR-11
Earlier sketches in CAP-2, CA 17-18
Allen of Hurtwood, Lady
See Allen, Marjory (Gill)
Allentuch, Harriet Ray 1933- ... 13-16R
Allentuck, Andrew 1943- ... 111
Allentuck, Marcia Epstein 1928- ... 33-36R
Allerton, Mary
See Govan, Christine Noble
Alletzhauser, Albert J. 1960- ... 136
Alley, Brian 1933- ... 111
Alley, Henry Melton 1945- ... CANR-35
Earlier sketch in CA 112
Alley, Louis Edward 1914- ... 17-20R
Alley, Norman William 1895-1981 Obituary ... 115
Alley, Rewi 1897-1987 ... CANR-36
Obituary ... 124
Earlier sketches in CA 73-76, CANR-13
Alley, Robert S. 1932- ... 33-36R
Alley, Stephen L(ewis) 1915- Brief entry ... 110
Alleyn, Ellen
See Rossetti, Christina (Georgina)
Alleyne, Mervyn (C.) 1933- ... 130
Allfrey, Anthony 1930- ... 137
Allgire, Mildred J. 1910- ... CAP-2
Earlier sketch in CA 25-28
Allgood, Myralyn F(rizzelle) 1939- ... 137
Allibone, T(homas) E(dward) 1903- ... 131
Alliluyeva, Svetlana (Iosifovna Stalina) 1926- . 57-60
Allin, Clinton Harrop
See Harrop-Allin, Clinton
Allin, Craig Willard 1946- ... CANR-51
Earlier sketches in CA 108, CANR-25
Alline, Henry 1748-1784 ... DLB 99
Allingham, Margery (Louise) 1904-1966 ... CANR-58
Obituary ... 25-28R
Earlier sketches in CA 5-8R, CANR-4
See also CLC 19
See also DLB 77
See also MTCW 1
Allingham, Michael 1943- ... 97-100
Allingham, William 1824-1889 ... DLB 35
Allington, Maynard 1931- ... 148
Allington, Richard L(loyd) 1947- ... CANR-57
Earlier sketches in CA 112, CANR-30
See also SATA 39
See also SATA-Brief 35
Allinsmith, Wesley 1923- ... 85-88
Allinson, Beverley (Lynn Rouse) 1936- ... CANR-4
Earlier sketch in CA 49-52
Allinson, Gary D(ean) 1942- ... 77-80
Allis, Frederick Scouller, Jr. 1913- ... 115
Allis, Oswald T(hompson)
1880-1973 Obituary ... 37-40R
Allison, A(ntony) F(rancis) 1916- ... 106
Allison, Alexander Ward 1919- ... 5-8R
Allison, Anne Marie 1931- ... 114
Allison, Anthony C(lifford) 1928- ... CANR-25
Earlier sketch in CA 29-32R
Allison, Bob ... SATA 14
Allison, C(hristopher) FitzSimons 1927- ... CANR-4
Earlier sketch in CA 1-4R
Allison, Clay
See Keevill, Henry J(ohn)
Allison, Diane Worfolk ... SATA 78
Allison, Dorothy E. 1949- ... CANR-66
Earlier sketch in CA 140
See also CLC 78
Allison, E. M. A.
See Allison, Eric W(illiam)
and Allison, Mary Ann
Allison, Eric W(illiam) 1947- ... 122
Allison, Graham T(illett), Jr. 1940- ... CANR-35
Earlier sketches in CA 49-52, CANR-2
Allison, Harrison C(larke) 1917- ... CANR-35
Earlier sketch in CA 49-52
Allison, Henry E(dward) 1937- ... 133
Brief entry ... 110
Allison, John Murray 1889- ... 73-76
Allison, Joseph D(avid) 1950- ... 111
Allison, Linda 1948- ... 113
See also SATA 43
Allison, Marian
See Reid, Frances P(ugh)
Allison, Mary Ann 1949- ... 122
Allison, Michael Frederick Lister 1936- ... 57-60
Allison, Mike
See Allison, Michael Frederick Lister
Allison, Oliver Claude 1908-1989 ... 129
Allison, Penny
See Katz, Carol
Allison, R(ichard) Bruce 1949- ... CANR-19
Earlier sketches in CA 49-52, CANR-3
Allison, Ralph B(rewster) 1931- ... 101
Allison, Rand
See McCormick, Wilfred
Allison, Rosemary 1953- ... 93-96
Allison, Roy (Anthony) 1957- ... 119
Allison, Sam
See Loomis, Noel M(iller)
Allman, Eileen Jorge 1940- ... 128
Allman, James 1943- ... 112
Allman, John 1935- ... CANR-25
Earlier sketch in CA 85-88
See also CAAS 15
Allman, T. D. 1944- ... CANR-17
Earlier sketch in CA 93-96
Allmand, C. T. ... 154
Allmand, Christopher
See Allmand, C. T.
Allmendinger, David F(rederick), Jr. 1938- ... 61-64
See also SATA 35
Allnutt, Gillian (Marguerite) 1949- ... 128
Allon, Yigal 1918-1980 ... CANR-36
Obituary ... 97-100
Earlier sketch in CA 73-76
Allott, Kenneth 1912-1973 ... 129
Obituary ... 89-92
See also DLB 20
Allott, Miriam 1920- ... 112
Alloway, David N(elson) 1927- ... CANR-10
Earlier sketch in CA 21-24R
Alloway, Lawrence 1926- ... 41-44R
Allport, Gordon (Willard) 1897-1967 ... CANR-3
Obituary ... 25-28R
Earlier sketch in CA 1-4R
Allport, Susan 1950- ... CANR-72
Earlier sketches in CA 124, CANR-54
Allred, Dorald M(ervin) 1923- ... 65-68
Allred, G. Hugh 1932- ... CANR-8
Earlier sketch in CA 61-64
Allred, Gordon T(hatcher) 1930- ... CANR-10
Earlier sketch in CA 17-20R
See also SATA 10
Allred, Ruel A(cord) 1929- ... 106
Allsen, Philip E(dmond) 1932- ... CANR-4
Earlier sketch in CA 53-56
Allsobrook, David Ian 1940- ... 151
Allsop, Kenneth 1920-1973 ... CANR-6
Earlier sketch in CA 1-4R
See also SATA 17
Allsopp, (Harold) Bruce 1912- ... CANR-18
Earlier sketches in CA 5-8R, CANR-2
Allsopp, (Stanley Reginald) Richard 1923- ... 166
Allston, Washington 1779-1843 ... DLB 1
Allswang, John M(yers) 1937- ... 41-44R
Allum, Nancy (Patricia Eaton) 1920- ... CAP-1
Earlier sketch in CA 9-10
Allvine, Fred C. 1936- ... 61-64
Allvine, Glendon 1893(?)-1977 Obituary ... 73-76
Allward, Maurice (Frank) 1923- ... CANR-19
Earlier sketches in CA 5-8R, CANR-3
Allwood, Martin (Samuel) 1916- ... CANR-29
Earlier sketch in CA 110
Allworth, Edward (Alfred) 1920- ... CANR-43
Earlier sketch in CA 101
Allyn, Doug 1942- ... 148
Allyn, Jennifer
See Jones, Jeannette
Allyn, Paul
See Schosberg, Paul A.
Allyson, Kym
See Kimbro, John M.
Alma, Peter
See Nemeshegyi, Peter
Alman, David 1919- ... 9-12R
Al-Marayati, Abid A(min) 1931- ... 33-36R
Almaraz, Felix D(iaz), Jr. 1933- ... 33-36R
Almasi, Janice F. 1963- ... 165
Almaz, Michael 1921- ... 81-84
Almedingen, E. M.
See Almedingen, Martha Edith von
See also CLC 12
See also SATA 3
Almedingen, Martha Edith von 1898-1971 . CANR-1
Earlier sketch in CA 1-4R
See also Almedingen, E. M.
Almendros, Nestor 1930-1992 ... 142
Almodovar, Norma Jean 1951- ... 142
Almodovar, Pedro 1949(?)- ... CANR-72
Earlier sketch in CA 133
Almon, Bert 1943- ... 110
Almon, Clopper, Jr. 1934- ... 21-24R
Almon, Russell
See Clevenger, William R(ussell)
and Downing, David A(lmon)
Almond, Brenda 1937- ... 151
Almond, Gabriel Abraham 1911- ... CANR-18
Earlier sketch in CA 101
Almond, Linda Stevens 1881(?)-1987 Obituary . 121
See also SATA-Obit 50
Almond, Paul 1931- ... 73-76
Almond, Richard 1938- ... 53-56
Almonte, Rosa
See Paine, Lauran (Bosworth)
Almquist, Don 1929- ... SATA 11
Almquist, Gregg (Andrew) 1948- ... 126
Almquist, L. Arden 1921- ... 29-32R
Almy, Millie 1915- ... 85-88
Alnasrawi, Abbas ... 140
Aloff, Mindy 1947- ... 135
Alofsin, Anthony 1949- ... 146
Aloian, David 1928- ... 25-28R
Aloma, Rene R(amon) 1947- ... 113
Alonie de Lestres, Lionel Montal
See Groulx, Lionel (Adolphe)
Alonso, Damaso 1898-1990 ... CANR-72
Obituary ... 130
Brief entry ... 110
Earlier sketch in CA 131
See also CLC 14
See also DLB 108
See also HW
Alonso, J(uan) M(anuel) 1936- ... 102
Alonso, Maria Teresa Manjon
See Manjon De Read, Maria Teresa
Alonso, William 1933- ... CANR-6
Earlier sketch in CA 9-12R
Alotta, Robert I(gnatius) 1937- ... CANR-14
Earlier sketch in CA 65-68
Alov
See Gogol, Nikolai (Vasilyevich)
Aloysius, Sister Mary
See Schaldenbrand, Mary
Alpaugh, Craig 1945- ... 117
Alper, Benedict S(olomon) 1905- ... CANR-27
Earlier sketch in CA 49-52
Alper, M(ax) Victor 1944- ... 69-72
Alpern, Andrew 1938- ... CANR-52
Earlier sketches in CA 69-72, CANR-11, 27
Alpern, David M(ark) 1942- ... 73-76
Alpern, Gerald D(avid) 1932- ... 53-56
Alpern, Sara 1942- ... 128
Alperovitz, Gar 1936- ... CANR-29
Earlier sketch in CA 49-52
Alpers, Antony 1919- ... CANR-35
Earlier sketches in CA 1-4R, CANR-3
Alpers, Bernard J. 1900-1981 Obituary ... 105
Alpers, Edward Alter 1941- ... 109
Alpers, Paul (Joel) 1932- ... 85-88
Alpers, Svetlana (Leontief) 1936- ... 115
Alpert, Cathryn 1952- ... 151
Alpert, Hollis 1916- ... CANR-46
Earlier sketches in CA 1-4R, CANR-6, 23
Alpert, Jane (Lauren) 1947- ... 107
Alpert, Mark I(ra) 1942- ... 61-64
Alpert, Paul 1907- ... 41-44R
Alpert, Richard 1931- ... 89-92
Alpha and Omega
See Gogarty, Oliver St. John
Alphin, Elaine Marie 1955- ... SATA 80
Alphonso-Karkala, John B. 1923- ... CANR-14
Earlier sketch in CA 37-40R
Alplaus, N. Y.
See Rubin, Cynthia Elyce
Al-Qazzaz, Ayad (Sayyid Ali) 1941- ... 112
Alred, Gerald J(ames) 1943- ... 105
AlRoy, Gil Carl 1924-1985 ... CANR-17
Obituary ... 116
Earlier sketch in CA 41-44R
Als, Hilton ... 162
Alschuler, Rose Haas 1887-1979 ... CAP-2
Obituary ... 89-92
Earlier sketch in CA 25-28
Alsen, Eberhard 1939- ... 110
Al Sharouni, Youssef 1924- ... 131
Alshawi, Hiyan 1957- ... 143
al-Shaykh, Hanan 1945- ... 135
Alson, Peter (H.) 1955- ... 156
Alsop, George 1636-(?) ... DLB 24
Alsop, Gulielma Fell 1881-1978 Obituary ... 77-80
Alsop, Joseph (Wright) 1910-1989 ... 129
Obituary ... 122
Alsop, Mary O'Hara 1885-1980 ... CANR-65
Obituary ... 102
Earlier sketches in CA 9-12R, CANR-4
See also MAICYA
See also SATA 2, 34
See also SATA-Obit 24
Alsop, Richard 1761-1815 ... DLB 37
Alsop, Stewart (Johonnot Oliver) 1914-1974 ... 89-92
Obituary ... 49-52
Alstad, Diana ... 147
Alsterlund, Betty
See Pilkington, Betty
Alstern, Fred
See Stern, Alfred
Alston, J(ames) M(axwell)
1901(?)-1990 Obituary ... 131
Alston, Mary Niven 1918- ... 33-36R
Alston, Patrick L(ionel) 1926- ... 25-28R
Alston, Philip 1950- ... 140
Alston, Robin (Carfrae) 1933- ... 131
Alston, Walter Emmons 1911-1984 Obituary ... 113
Alston, William P(ayne) 1921- ... CANR-37
Earlier sketches in CA 5-8R, CANR-7
Alswang, Betty 1920(?)-1978 Obituary ... 77-80
Alt, Betty L. 1931- ... 162
Alt, Betty Sowers 1931- ... 133
Alt, David D. 1933- ... CANR-27
Earlier sketch in CA 49-52
Alt, Herschel 1897(?)-1981 Obituary ... 105
Alt, (Arthur) Tilo 1931- ... 41-44R
Alta 1942- ... 57-60
See also CLC 19
Altabe, Joan B. 1935- ... 53-56
Altbach, Edith Hoshino 1941- ... 57-60
Altbach, Philip G(eoffrey) 1941- ... CANR-10
Earlier sketch in CA 25-28R
Altemeyer, Bob 1940- ... 163
Alten, Steve 1959- ... 165
Altenberg, Peter 1859-1919 ... DLB 81
Altenbernd, (August) Lynn 1918- ... CANR-1
Earlier sketch in CA 45-48
Alter, J(ohn) Cecil 1879-1964 ... 5-8R
Alter, Jean V(ictor) 1925- ... 45-48
Alter, Jonathan Hammerman 1957- ... 129
Alter, Joseph Dinsmore 1923- ... 111
Alter, Judith (MacBain) 1938- ... CANR-31
Earlier sketches in CA 81-84, CANR-14
See also SATA 52, 101
Alter, Judy
See Alter, Judith (MacBain)
Alter, Nora M. ... 167
Alter, Robert B(ernard) 1935- ... CANR-47
Earlier sketches in CA 49-52, CANR-1
See also CLC 34
Alter, Robert Edmond 1925-1965 ... CANR-1
Earlier sketch in CA 1-4R
See also SATA 9
Alter, Stephen 1956- ... 109
Alteras, Isaac 1938- ... 144
Alterman, Eric (Ross) 1960- ... 151
Alterman, Nathan 1910-1970 Obituary ... 25-28R
Altfest, Karen Caplan ... 105
Alth, Max O(ctavious) 1927- ... CANR-17
Earlier sketch in CA 41-44R
Althauser, Robert P(ierce) 1939- ... 57-60
Althea
See Braithwaite, Althea
Alther, Lisa 1944- ... CANR-51
Earlier sketches in CA 65-68, CANR-12, 30
See also CAAS 30
See also CLC 7, 41
See also MTCW 1
Althoff, Phillip 1941- ... 33-36R
Altholz, Josef L(ewis) 1933- ... CANR-35
Earlier sketch in CA 9-12R
Althouse, Larry
See Althouse, Lawrence Wilson
Althouse, LaVonne 1932- ... 17-20R
Althouse, Lawrence Wilson 1930- ... 101
Althusser, L.
See Althusser, Louis
Althusser, Louis 1918-1990 ... 131
Obituary ... 132
See also CLC 106
Altick, Richard Daniel 1915- ... CANR-40
Earlier sketches in CA 1-4R, CANR-4, 19
Altieri, Charles F(rancis) 1942- ... 106
Altizer, Thomas J(onathan) J(ackson) 1927- ...
CANR-3
Earlier sketch in CA 1-4R
Altman, Dennis 1943- ... CANR-34
Earlier sketches in CA 33-36R, CANR-15
Altman, Edward I(ra) 1941- ... CANR-22
Earlier sketches in CA 57-60, CANR-7
Altman, Frances 1937- ... 65-68
Altman, Irwin 1928- ... 81-84
Altman, Irwin 1930- ... CANR-21
Earlier sketch in CA 69-72
Altman, Jack 1938- ... 21-24R
Altman, Janet Gurkin 1945- ... 128
Altman, Larry
See Altman, Irwin
Altman, Linda Jacobs 1943- ... CANR-30
Earlier sketch in CA 29-32R
See also SATA 21
Altman, Nathaniel 1948- ... CANR-44
Earlier sketches in CA 57-60, CANR-6, 21
Altman, Richard Charles 1932- ... 41-44R
Altman, Rick 1945- ... 128
Altman, Robert 1925- ... CANR-43
Earlier sketch in CA 73-76
See also CLC 16
Altman, Robert A. 1943- ... 29-32R
Altman, Suzanne
See Orgel, Doris
and Schecter, Ellen
Altman, Thomas
See Black, Campbell
Altman, Wilfred 1927- ... CAP-1
Earlier sketch in CA 9-10
Altmann, Alexander 1906-1987 ... CANR-35
Obituary ... 122
Earlier sketches in CA 61-64, CANR-8
Altmann, Berthold 1902(?)-1977 Obituary ... 69-72
Altmann, Simon L(eonardo) 1924- ... 143
Altolaguirre, Manuel 1905-1959 ... DLB 108
Altoma, Salih J(awad) 1929- ... 49-52
Alton, Thomas
See Bryant, T(homas) Alton
Altrocchi, Julia Cooley 1893-1972 ... CAP-1
Earlier sketch in CA 13-14
Altschul, Aaron Mayer 1914-1994 ... 105
Obituary ... 146
Altschul, b j 1948- ... 114
Altschul, Selig 1914- ... 108
Altschuler, Franz 1923- ... SATA 45
Altsheler, Joseph A(lexander) 1862-1919 ... 167
See also YABC 1
Altshuler, Alan Anthony 1936- ... 108
Altshuler, Edward A. 1919- ... 17-20R

Altshuler, Harry 1913(?)-1990 Obituary........131
Aluko, T(imothy) M(ofolorunso) 1918(?)-. CANR-62
Earlier sketches in CA 65-68, CANR-10
See also BW 1
See also DLB 117
Alurista
See Urista, Alberto H.
See also DLB 82
Al-Van-Gar
See Radwanski, Pierre A(rthur)
Alvarado (green), Manuel (Bernardo) 1948-.... 147
Alvarez, A(lfred) 1929-................. CANR-63
Earlier sketches in CA 1-4R, CANR-3, 33
See also CLC 5, 13
See also DLB 14, 40
Alvarez, Alejandro Rodriguez 1903-1965...... 131
Obituary................................ 93-96
See also Casona, Alejandro
See also HW
Alvarez, Eugene 1932-.................... 57-60
Alvarez, John
See del Rey, Lester
Alvarez, Joseph A. 1930-.............. CANR-17
Earlier sketch in CA 33-36R
See also SATA 18
Alvarez, Julia 1950-.................. CANR-69
Earlier sketch in CA 147
See also AAYA 25
See also CLC 93
Alvarez, Luis W(alter) 1911-1988 Obituary..... 126
Alvarez, Lynne..............................131
See also HW
Alvarez, Max Joseph 1960-.................. 112
Alvarez, Walter C(lement) 1884-1978.... CANR-10
Earlier sketch in CA 61-64
Alvarez-Altman, Grace (DeJesus) 1926-.... 33-36R
Alvarez del Vayo, Julio 1891-1975 Obituary.. 61-64
Alvarez Murena, Hector Alberto 1923-.........HW
Alvaro, Corrado 1896-1956................. 163
See also TCLC 60
Alverson, Charles (E.) 1935-.......... CANR-13
Earlier sketch in CA 25-28R
Alverson, Donna 1933-.................... 65-68
Alverson, Marianne 1942-.................. 126
Alves, Colin 1930-..................... CANR-2
Earlier sketch in CA 5-8R
Alves, Marcio Moreira 1936-............ CANR-2
Earlier sketch in CA 45-48
Alves, Michael (Joseph) 1956-.............. 118
Alvey, Edward, Jr. 1902-..................53-56
Alvey, R(ichard) Gerald 1935-................121
Alvi, Moniza 1954-........................153
Alvin, Juliette (Louise) (?)-1982............77-80
Obituary.................................108
Alvord, Burt
See Keevill, Henry J(ohn)
Alworth, E. P(aul) 1918-.................25-28R
Alwyn, William 1905-1985 Obituary.......... 117
Aly, Bower 1903-...................... CANR-5
Earlier sketch in CA 5-8R
Aly, Lucile Folse 1913-..................21-24R
Alyer, Philip A.
See Stratemeyer, Edward L.
Alyeshmerni, Mansoor 1943-..............29-32R
Alyn, Marc (a pseudonym) 1937-............. 101
Alzado, Lyle (Martin) 1949- Brief entry....... 110
Alzaga, Florinda 1930-.................... 73-76
Amabile, George 1936-.................... 33-36R
Amacher, Richard Earl 1917-............. CANR-3
Earlier sketch in CA 1-4R
Amacher, Ryan C(uster) 1945-.............. 105
Amadi, Elechi (Emmanuel) 1934-....... CANR-63
Earlier sketches in CA 29-32R, CANR-16, 38
See also BW 1
See also DLB 117
Amado, Jorge 1912-................. CANR-35
Earlier sketch in CA 77-80
See also CLC 13, 40, 106
See also DAM MULT, NOV
See also DLB 113
See also HLC
See also MTCW 1
Amadon, Dean 1912-..................... 61-64
Amalrik, Andrei Alekseyevich 1938-1980.......155
Obituary.................................102
Amamoo, Joseph Godson 1931-.......... 13-16R
Aman, Mohammed M(ohammed) 1940-.. CANR-16
Earlier sketches in CA 49-52, CANR-1
Amanda
See Wynne-Tyson, Esme
Amann, Janet 1951-...................... 147
See also SATA 79
Amann, Peter H. 1927-.................. 61-64
Amann, Richard 1945-.................... 106
Amann, Ronald 1943-......................112
Amann, Victor F(rancis) 1927-............ 41-44R
Amanuddin, Syed 1934-................ CANR-17
Earlier sketches in CA 49-52, CANR-1
Amar, Akhil Reed 1958-......................167
Amaral, Anthony 1930-1982............ CANR-11
Earlier sketch in CA 21-24R
Amaral, Jose Vazquez
See Vazquez Amaral, Jose
Amare, Rothayne
See Byrne, Stuart J(ames)
Amaron, Douglas 1914-1985 Obituary....... 117
Amary, Issam B(ahjat) 1942-........... CANR-8
Earlier sketch in CA 61-64
Amato, Carol A. 1942-.................... 156
See also SATA 92
Amato, Joseph Anthony 1938-.......... CANR-6
Earlier sketch in CA 57-60
Amatora, Sister Mary......................9-12R
Amaya, Ismael E(liseo) 1928-1986 Obituary... 120
Amaya, Mario (Anthony) 1933-1986..... CANR-36
Obituary................................119
Earlier sketches in CA 61-64, CANR-9
Amazing Randi, The
See Randi, James
Ambasz, Emilio 1943-.................... 73-76
Amberg, George H. 1901-1971 Obituary.......110
Amberg, (Martin) Hans 1913-..............77-80
Amberg, Richard H(iller), Jr. 1942-.......... 77-80
Amberg, Richard Hiller 1912-1967 Obituary....114
Ambert, Anne-Marie 1940-..................145
Ambhanwong, Suthilak 1924-.......... CANR-18
Earlier sketch in CA 73-76
Ambirajan, Srinivasa 1936-............. CANR-7
Earlier sketch in CA 17-20R
Ambler, C(hristopher) Gifford 1886-..SATA-Brief 29
Ambler, Effie 1936-...................... 77-80
Ambler, Eric 1909-................... CANR-38
Earlier sketches in CA 9-12R, CANR-7
See also CLC 4, 6, 9
See also DLB 77
See also MTCW 1
Ambler, John S(teward) 1932-.......... CANR-27
Earlier sketch in CA 49-52
Ambler, Marjane 1948-.....................135
Ambrose, Alice
See Lazerowitz, Alice Ambrose
Ambrose, David (Edwin) 1943-.............. 144
Brief entry.............................. 116
Ambrose, Eric (Samuel) 1908-............ CAP-1
Earlier sketch in CA 11-12
Ambrose, John W(illiam), Jr. 1931-.........57-60
Ambrose, Stephen E(dward) 1936-...... CANR-57
Earlier sketches in CA 1-4R, CANR-3, 43
See also SATA 40
Ambrose, W. Haydn 1922-................25-28R
Ambrosi, Hans Georg 1925-................ 103
Ambrosini, Maria Luisa.................... 33-36R
Ambrosini, Richard 1955-..................143
Ambroz, Oton 1905-......................41-44R
Ambrus, Gyozo Laszlo 1935-.......... CANR-53
Earlier sketches in CA 25-28R, CANR-11, 28
See also Ambrus, Victor G.
See also MAICYA
See also SATA 41
Ambrus, Victor G.
See Ambrus, Gyozo Laszlo
See also SAAS 4
See also SATA 1
Amburn, Ellis 1933-.......................138
Amdur, Neil 1939-........................ 106
Amdur, Nikki 1950-....................... 111
Amelio, Gianni 1945-......................156
Amelio, Ralph J. 1939-..................37-40R
Amen, Carol 1934(?)-1987 Obituary.......... 123
Amend, Victor E(arl) 1916-............... 33-36R
Ament, Pat 1946-........................85-88
Amerika, Mark...............................152
Amerine, Maynard A(ndrew) 1911-1998.... 41-44R
Obituary..................................166
Ameringer, Charles D. 1926-.............. 57-60
Amerman, Lockhart 1911-1969............ CAP-2
Earlier sketch in CA 29-32
See also SATA 3
Amery, Francis
See Stableford, Brian (Michael)
Amery, (Harold) Julian 1919-............ 61-64
Ames, Charles Edgar 1895-1972.......... CAP-2
Earlier sketch in CA 25-28
Ames, Christopher 1956-................... 164
Ames, Delano L. 1906-....................107
Ames, Elinor
See Ranzini, Addis Durning
Ames, Evelyn 1908-1990.................. 57-60
Obituary..................................130
See also SATA 13
See also SATA-Obit 64
Ames, Felicia
See Burden, Jean
Ames, Fisher 1758-1808................. DLB 37
Ames, Francis H. 1900-................. 17-20R
Ames, Gerald 1906-1993.................. 73-76
Obituary..................................140
See also SATA 11
See also SATA-Obit 74
Ames, Jennifer
See Greig, Maysie
Ames, Jocelyn Green........................5-8R
Ames, John 1944-..........................111
Ames, John Dawes 1904-1987 Obituary.......122
Ames, Kenneth L. 1942-....................143
Ames, Lee J(udah) 1921-............... CANR-18
Earlier sketches in CA 1-4R, CANR-3
See also SATA 3
Ames, Leslie
See Rigoni, Orlando (Joseph)
and Ross, W(illiam) E(dward) D(aniel)
Ames, Lois (Winslow Sisson) 1931-............101
Ames, Louise Bates 1908-1996.......... CANR-39
Obituary..................................154
Earlier sketches in CA 1-4R, CANR-3, 18
Ames, Mary Clemmer 1831-1884..........DLB 23
Ames, Mildred 1919-1994............... CANR-11
Obituary..................................146
Earlier sketch in CA 69-72
See also SATA 22, 81, 85
Ames, Noel
See Barrows, (Ruth) Marjorie
Ames, Norma 1920-.................... CANR-12
Earlier sketch in CA 29-32R
Ames, Rachel 1922-..................... 97-100
Ames, Ruth M(argaret) 1918-............. 29-32R
Ames, (Polly) Scribner 1908-............... 69-72
Ames, Van Meter 1898-1985.............. CAP-1
Obituary..................................117
Earlier sketch in CA 13-16
Ames, Walter Lansing 1946-.................106
Ames, Winslow 1907-.................... CAP-2
Earlier sketch in CA 25-28
Ames-Lewis, Francis 1943-..................108
Amey, Lloyd Ronald 1922-............. CANR-20
Earlier sketch in CA 45-48
Amfitheatrof, Erik 1931-.................. 89-92
Amft, M(arian) J(anet) 1920-1985 Obituary.... 117
Amherst, Wes
See Shaver, Richard S(harpe)
Ami, Ben
See Eliav, Arie L(ova)
Ami, Shlomo Ben
See Ben-Ami, Shlomo
Amichai, Yehuda 1924-................ CANR-60
Earlier sketches in CA 85-88, CANR-46
See also CLC 9, 22, 57
See also MTCW 1
Amichai, Yehudah
See Amichai, Yehuda
Amick, Robert Gene 1933-............... 33-36R
Amidon, Bill (Vincent) 1935-1979.......... 45-48
Obituary..................................103
Amidon, Stephen 1959-.................... 132
Amiel, Barbara 1940-...................... 101
Amiel, Joseph 1937-....................... 101
Amies, (Edwin) Hardy 1909-................ 129
Amin, Ali 1913(?)-1976 Obituary............65-68
Amin, Mohamed 1943-1996...................158
Amin, Samir 1931-.................... CANR-35
Earlier sketches in CA 89-92, CANR-15
Amini, Johari M.
See Kunjufu, Johari M. Amini
See also DLB 41
Amir, Menachem 1930-....................45-48
Amis, Breton
See Best, Rayleigh Breton Amis
Amis, Kingsley (William) 1922-1995..... CANR-54
Obituary..................................150
Earlier sketches in CA 9-12R, CANR-8, 28
Interview in CANR-8
See also AITN 2
See also CDBLB 1945-1960
See also CLC 1, 2, 3, 5, 8, 13, 40, 44
See also DA
See also DAB
See also DAC
See also DAM MST, NOV
See also DLB 15, 27, 100, 139
See also DLBY 96
See also MTCW 1
Amis, Martin (Louis) 1949-............. CANR-54
Earlier sketches in CA 65-68, CANR-8, 27
Interview in CANR-27
See also BEST 90:3
See also CLC 4, 9, 38, 62, 101
See also DLB 14, 194
Amishai-Maisels, Ziva
See Maisels, Maxine S.
Amling, Frederick 1926-.....................133
Brief entry............................... 112
Amlund, Curtis Arthur 1927-.............. 21-24R
Ammar, Abbas 1907(?)-1974 Obituary.......53-56
Amme, Carl H., Jr. 1913-................. 25-28R
Ammer, Christine (Parker) 1931-.............106
Ammer, Dean S. 1926-.................. CANR-7
Earlier sketch in CA 17-20R
Ammerman, David L(eon) 1938-.............57-60
Ammerman, Gale Richard 1923-..............107
Ammerman, Leila T(remaine) 1912-........33-36R
Ammerman, Nancy T(atom) 1950-............ 167
Ammerman, Robert R(ay) 1927-...........13-16R
Ammon, Harry 1917-......................73-76
Ammons, A(rchie) R(andolph) 1926-..... CANR-51
Earlier sketches in CA 9-12R, CANR-6, 36
See also AITN 1
See also CLC 2, 3, 5, 8, 9, 25, 57, 108
See also DAM POET
See also DLB 5, 165
See also MTCW 1
See also PC 16
Amo, Tauraatua i
See Adams, Henry (Brooks)
Amoaku, J. K. 1936-..................... 45-48
Amoia, Alba della Fazia 1928-..............144
Amon, Aline 1928-..................... CANR-8
Earlier sketch in CA 61-64
See also SATA 9
Amor, Amos
See Harrell, Irene B(urk)
Amor, Anne Clark 1933-............... CANR-59
Earlier sketches in CA 112, CANR-31
Amore, Roy Clayton 1942-..................105
Amorim, Enrique (Manuel) 1900-1960.......... HW
Amory, Anne Reinberg 1931-............. 17-20R
Amory, Cleveland 1917-............... CANR-29
Earlier sketch in CA 69-72
Interview in CANR-29
See also AITN 1
See also DAM POP
Amory, Mark 1941-................... CANR-36
Earlier sketch in CA 114
Amory, Robert, Jr. 1915-1989 Obituary........128
Amos, James H., Jr. 1946-..................132
Amos, William (David) 1933-............... 146
Amos, William E. 1926-.................. 17-20R
Amos, Winsom 1921-.................. CANR-27
Earlier sketch in CA 49-52
Amosov, N.
See Amosov, N(ikolai) M(ikhailovich)
Amosov, N(ikolai) M(ikhailovich) 1913- Brief entry...............................112
Amoss, Benjamin McRae, Jr. 1960-...........139
Amoss, Berthe 1925-.................. CANR-14
Earlier sketch in CA 21-24R
See also SATA 5
Amplegirth, Antony
See Dent, Anthony Austen
Amprimoz, Alexandre 1948-............ CANR-15
Earlier sketch in CA 37-40R
Amram, David (Werner III) 1930-........ CANR-28
Earlier sketch in CA 29-32R
Amram, Philip Werner 1900-1990 Obituary.... 131
Amrine, Michael 1919(?)-1974.............73-76
Obituary..................................49-52
Amsel, Abram 1922-................... CANR-35
Earlier sketch in CA 114
Amstead, B(illy) H(oward) 1921-...........21-24R
Amster, Linda 1938-.................. CANR-22
Earlier sketch in CA 45-48
Amsterdam, Morey 1914(?)-1996.............148
Obituary..................................154
Brief entry...............................111
Amstutz, Arnold E. 1936-.................21-24R
Amstutz, Mark R(obert) 1944-...............105
Amter, Joseph A. (?)-1982 Obituary...........109
Amundsen, Kirsten 1932-.................37-40R
Amundsen, Roald Engelbregt Gravning 1872-1928 Brief entry......................117
Amusin, Joseph 1910-1984 Obituary..........113
Amuzegar, Jahangir 1920-............. CANR-15
Earlier sketch in CA 41-44R
Analyticus
See Wise, James Waterman
Anand, Mulk Raj 1905-................ CANR-64
Earlier sketches in CA 65-68, CANR-32
See also CLC 23, 93
See also DAM NOV
See also MTCW 1
Anand, Valerie 1937-................. CANR-61
Earlier sketches in CA 73-76, CANR-13
Anania, Michael 1939-................... 25-28R
See also DLB 193
Anastaplo, George 1925-..................37-40R
Anastas, Lila L. 1940-......................122
Anastas, Peter 1937-................... CANR-1
Earlier sketch in CA 45-48
Anastasi, Anne 1908-................. CANR-17
Earlier sketches in CA 5-8R, CANR-2
Anastasio, Dina 1941-................ CANR-68
Earlier sketch in CA 107
See also SATA 37, 94
See also SATA-Brief 30
Anastasiou, Clifford (John) 1929-........ CANR-18
Earlier sketches in CA 49-52, CANR-3
Anastos, Andrea La Sonde (Melrose) 1951-.... 117
Anatol
See Schnitzler, Arthur
Anatol, A.
See Kuznetsov, Anatoli
Anaya, Rudolfo A(lfonso) 1937-......... CANR-51
Earlier sketches in CA 45-48, CANR-1, 32
See also CAAS 4
See also AAYA 20
See also CLC 23
See also DAM MULT, NOV
See also DLB 82
See also HLC
See also HW 1
See also MTCW 1
Anber, Paul
See Baker, Pauline H(alpern)
Anbinder, Tyler (Gregory) 1962-............. 141
Ancel, Marc 1902-................... CANR-12
Earlier sketch in CA 69-72
Ancelet, Barry Jean 1951-................. 131
Anchell, Melvin 1919-.................. 25-28R
Anchor, Robert 1937-...................... 69-72
Anckarsvard, Karin Inez Maria 1915-1969... 9-12R
Obituary..................................103
See also SATA 6
Ancona, George 1929-................ CANR-19
Earlier sketches in CA 53-56, CANR-4
See also SAAS 18
See also SATA 12, 85
Andelin, Helen B. 1920-................... 89-92
Andelman, Eddie 1936-....................57-60
Andelman, Samuel L(ouis) 1916- Brief entry... 114
Andelson, Robert V(ernon) 1931-..........33-36R
Andenaes, Johannes 1912-............ CANR-68
Earlier sketch in CA 129
Anderegg, Karen Klok 1940-.................137
Andereich, Justus
See Steiner, Gerolf
Anderman, Janusz 1949-.................... 142
Anders, Allison 1954-...................... 165
Anders, Donna Carolyn 1938-...............125
Anders, Edith (Mary) England 1899-....... CAP-1
Earlier sketch in CA 13-16
Anders, Evelyn 1916-................... 29-32R
Anders, Isabel 1946-......................161
See also SATA 101
Anders, Jeanne
See Anderson, Joan Wester
Anders, Leslie 1922-....................13-16R
Anders, Sarah Frances 1927-................ 105
Andersch, Alfred 1914-1980............ CANR-37
Obituary................................ 93-96
Earlier sketch in CA 33-36R
See also DLB 69
Andersch, Elizabeth Genevieve 1913-........5-8R
Andersdatter, Karla M(argaret) 1938-.... CANR-44
Earlier sketches in CA 104, CANR-21
See also SATA 34
Andersen, Arlow W. 1906-.............. CAP-1
Earlier sketch in CA 11-12
Andersen, Benny (Allan) 1929-.............. 101
Andersen, Christopher P(eter) 1949-.... CANR-31
Earlier sketches in CA 69-72, CANR-14
Andersen, D(ennis) R(ichard) 1947-...........108
Andersen, Doris 1909-................ CANR-11
Earlier sketch in CA 21-24R

Andersen, Francis Ian 1925- CANR-27
Earlier sketch in CA 108
Andersen, Georg 1941- 112
Andersen, Hans Christian 1805-1875 .... CLR 6
See also DA
See also DAB
See also DAC
See also DAM MST, POP
See also MAICYA
See also SATA 100
See also SSC 6
See also WLC
See also YABC 1
Andersen, Jefferson 1955(?)-1979 Obituary .. 85-88
Andersen, Juel 1923- CANR-22
Earlier sketch in CA 105
Andersen, Kenneth E(ldon) 1933- 37-40R
Andersen, Kurt 1954- CANR-23
Earlier sketch in CA 106
Andersen, Marianne S(inger) 1934- 65-68
Andersen, Marion Lineaweaver
1912(?)-1971 Obituary 29-32R
Andersen, R(udolph) Clifton 1933- 33-36R
Andersen, Richard 1931- CANR-24
Earlier sketches in CA 57-60, CANR-8
Andersen, Richard 1946- 102
Andersen, Ted
See Boyd, Waldo T.
Andersen, Uell Stanley 1917- 1-4R
Andersen, Wayne V. 1928- 9-12R
Andersen, Wilhelm 1911- 29-32R
Andersen, Yvonne 1932- 29-32R
See also SATA 27
Anderson, A(rthur) J(ames) 1933- 106
Anderson, Alan B(rauer) 1934- 133
Anderson, Alan H., Jr. 1943- 69-72
Anderson, Alan Ross 1925-1973 .... CAP-2
Obituary 45-48
Earlier sketch in CA 17-18
Anderson, Alexander 1775-1870 .... DLB 188
Anderson, Alison 1950- .... CAAS 30
Anderson, Allan 1915- 97-100
Anderson, Alpha E. 1914-1970 .... CAP-2
Earlier sketch in CA 23-24
Anderson, Ann Kiemel 1945- 121
Anderson, Arthur J(ames) O(utram) 1907- ....
CANR-15
Earlier sketch in CA 85-88
Anderson, B(asil) W(illiam) 1901-1984 Obituary 112
Anderson, Barbara 1948- 93-96
Anderson, Barbara Gallatin 1926- Brief entry .. 111
Anderson, Barry (Franklin) 1935- 17-20R
Anderson, Bern 1900-1963 .... 1-4R
Anderson, Bernard Eric 1936- CANR-5
Earlier sketch in CA 53-56
Anderson, Bernhard Word 1916- CANR-8
Earlier sketch in CA 57-60
Anderson, Bernice G(oudy) 1894- 101
See also SATA 33
Anderson, Bertha Moore 1892- 5-8R
Anderson, Beverly
See Nemiro, Beverly Anderson
Anderson, Beverly M.
See Nemiro, Beverly Anderson
Anderson, Bob 1947- 69-72
Anderson, Brad(ley Jay) 1924- 106
See also SATA 33
See also SATA-Brief 31
Anderson, Burton 1938- 149
Anderson, C. C.
See Anderson, Catherine Corley
Anderson, C. Farley
See Mencken, H(enry) L(ouis)
and Nathan, George Jean
Anderson, C(arl) L(eonard) 1901- 25-28R
Anderson, Camilla M(ay) 1904- 33-36R
Anderson, Carl Dicmann 1912- 33-36R
Anderson, Carl L(ennart) 1919- 41-44R
Anderson, Carolyn 1941- 73-76
Anderson, Catherine C.
See Anderson, Catherine Corley
Anderson, Catherine Corley 1909- 1-4R
See also SATA 72
Anderson, Charles 1933- CANR-27
Earlier sketch in CA 49-52
Anderson, Charles Burroughs 1905-1985 65-68
Obituary 115
Anderson, Charles C. 1931- 29-32R
Anderson, Charles Roberts 1902- CANR-3
Earlier sketch in CA 1-4R
Anderson, Charles W(illiam) 1934- 9-12R
Anderson, Charlotte Maria 1923- 81-84
Anderson, Chester 1932- 131
Brief entry 117
Anderson, Chester G(rant) 1923- 25-28R
Anderson, Chuck
See Anderson, Charles
Anderson, Clarence William 1891-1971 73-76
Obituary 29-32R
See also SATA 11
Anderson, Clifford
See Gardner, Richard (M.)
Anderson, Colena M(ichael) 1891- CANR-11
Earlier sketch in CA 21-24R
Anderson, Cortland 1935-1985 Obituary 118
Anderson, Courtney 1906- CAP-1
Earlier sketch in CA 19-20
Anderson, Daphne 1919- 130
Anderson, Daryl Shon 1963- .... SATA 93
Anderson, Dave
See Anderson, David Poole
See also AITN 2
Anderson, David 1952- 130
Anderson, David D(aniel) 1924- CANR-5
Earlier sketch in CA 13-16R
Anderson, David L(eonard) 1919- 5-8R
Anderson, David Poole 1929- 89-92
See also Anderson, Dave
See also SATA 60
Anderson, Dillon 1906-1974 .... 1-4R
Obituary 45-48
Anderson, Don 1939- 128
Anderson, Donald F(rancis) 1938- 53-56
Anderson, Donald K(ennedy), Jr. 1922- 37-40R
Anderson, Donna K. 1935- 142
Anderson, Doris (Hilda) 1925- 89-92
Anderson, Douglas A(llen) 1959- 147
Anderson, Dwight G(ale) 1938- 107
Anderson, E. Ruth 1907- 93-96
Anderson, E. W. 1901-1981 Obituary 104
Anderson, Earl Robert 1943- 111
Anderson, Edgar 1920- CANR-30
Earlier sketches in CA 33-36R, CANR-13
Anderson, Edward F. 1932- 146
Anderson, Einar 1909- 13-16R
Anderson, Elbridge Gerry 1907- 69-72
Anderson, Elijah 1943- 140
Anderson, Elizabeth (S.) 1959- 147
Anderson, Elliott 1944- 93-96
Anderson, Eloise Adell 1927- 53-56
See also SATA 9
Anderson, Emily 1891-1962 124
Anderson, Eric (Douglas) 1949- 106
Anderson, Erica 1914- 57-60
Anderson, Eugene N(ewton) 1900- 29-32R
Anderson, (William) Ferguson 1914- 107
Anderson, Frank J(ohn) 1919- CANR-4
Earlier sketch in CA 9-12R
Anderson, Fred 1949- 117
Anderson, Frederick Irving 1877-1947 Brief
entry 112
See also DLB 202
Anderson, Freeman B(urket) 1922- 41-44R
Anderson, Gary Clayton 1948- 117
Anderson, Gary L. 1948- 167
Anderson, Gary Lee 1939- Brief entry 115
Anderson, George
See Groom, Arthur William
Anderson, George
See Weissman, Jack
Anderson, George B. 1908(?)-1985 Obituary ... 114
Anderson, George Christian 1907-1976 ..... CAP-2
Obituary 69-72
Earlier sketch in CA 29-32
Anderson, George K(umler) 1901- CAP-2
Earlier sketch in CA 23-24
Anderson, George L(aVerne) 1905-1971 .. CANR-9
Earlier sketch in CA 13-16R
Anderson, George Lee 1934- Brief entry 111
Anderson, Gerald Dwight 1944- CANR-37
Earlier sketch in CA 115
Anderson, Gerald H(arry) 1930- CANR-7
Earlier sketch in CA 17-20R
Anderson, Godfrey Tryggve 1909- 41-44R
Anderson, Grace Fox 1932- 121
See also SATA 43
Anderson, Gregory 1946- 135
Anderson, H(ugh) Allen, (Jr.) 1950- 120
Anderson, H(obson) Dewey 1897-1975 65-68
Obituary 61-64
Anderson, Harold H(omer) 1897- CAP-2
Earlier sketch in CA 21-22
Anderson, Harry 1952- 152
Anderson, Harry V(ernon) 1903-1983 Obituary . 110
Anderson, Henry L(ee Norman) 1934- 142
See also BW 2
Anderson, Henry P. 1927- 33-36R
Anderson, Howard Jeremy
1915(?)-1983 Obituary 111
Anderson, Howard Peter 1932- 61-64
Anderson, Hugh 1920- 9-12R
Anderson, Ian Gibson 1933- 85-88
Anderson, Irvine H(enry) 1928- CANR-11
Earlier sketch in CA 69-72
Anderson, J(ohn) E(dward) 1903- 37-40R
Anderson, J(ohn) K(inloch) 1924- CANR-28
Earlier sketches in CA 17-20R, CANR-10
Anderson, J(ohn) Kerby 1951- 97-100
Anderson, J. N.
See Anderson, (James) Norman (Dalrymple)
Anderson, J(ohn) R(ichard) L(ane) 1911-1981 .....
CANR-18
Obituary 104
Earlier sketch in CA 25-28R
See also SATA 15
See also SATA-Obit 27
Anderson, Jack(son Northman) 1922- ... CANR-44
Earlier sketches in CA 57-60, CANR-6
See also AITN 1
Anderson, Jack 1935- CANR-24
Earlier sketch in CA 33-36R
Anderson, James C(letus) 1943- 111
Anderson, James D(esmond) 1933- CANR-27
Earlier sketch in CA 49-52
Anderson, James E(lliott) 1933- CANR-21
Earlier sketches in CA 9-12R, CANR-6
Anderson, James F(rancis) 1910- 41-44R
Anderson, James G(eorge) 1936- 25-28R
Anderson, James LaVerne 1940- Brief entry ... 111
Anderson, James M(axwell) 1933- 33-36R
Anderson, Janet A. 1934- 140
Anderson, (Helen) Jean 1931- CANR-57
Earlier sketches in CA 41-44R, CANR-14, 31
Anderson, Jeanne 1934(?)-1979 Obituary 85-88
Anderson, Jennifer 1942- 57-60
Anderson, Jerry M(aynard) 1933- 41-44R
Anderson, Jervis (B.) 1936- 141
See also BW 2
Anderson, Jessica (Margaret) Queale 1916- ....
CANR-62
Earlier sketches in CA 9-12R, CANR-4
See also CLC 37
Anderson, Jim 1937- 134
Anderson, Joan Wester 1938- CANR-24
Earlier sketches in CA 65-68, CANR-9
Anderson, John Bayard 1922- 33-36R
Anderson, John F(reeman) 1945- 53-56
Anderson, John K.
See Anderson, J(ohn) K(inloch)
Anderson, John L(onzo) 1905- CANR-35
Earlier sketch in CA 25-28R
See also Anderson, Lonzo
Anderson, John M(ueller) 1914- 17-20R
Anderson, John Q. 1916-1975 .... CANR-3
Earlier sketch in CA 1-4R
Anderson, Jon (Stephen) 1936- 133
Anderson, Jon (Victor) 1940- CANR-20
Earlier sketch in CA 25-28R
See also CLC 9
See also DAM POET
Anderson, Joy 1928- 25-28R
See also SATA 1
Anderson, Judith H(elena) 1940- CANR-50
Earlier sketch in CA 123
Anderson, Judith I(cke) 1939- 112
Anderson, Judy 1943- 149
Anderson, Kare 1950- 142
Anderson, Karen (Kruse) 1932- 136
Anderson, Kay 1958- 152
Anderson, Ken 1917- 25-28R
Anderson, Kenneth Norman 1921- CANR-18
Earlier sketch in CA 102
Anderson, Kevin J(ames) 1962- 161
See also SATA 74
Anderson, Kirk 1965- 140
Anderson, Kristin
See Du Breuil, (Elizabeth) L(or)inda
Anderson, Laurie 1947- 156
Anderson, Laurie Halse 1961- 160
See also SATA 95
Anderson, LaVere Francis Shoenfelt 1907- 101
See also SATA 27
Anderson, Lee 1896-1972 .... 1-4R
Obituary 37-40R
Anderson, Lee Stratton 1925- 101
Anderson, Leone Castell 1923- 126
See also SATA 53
See also SATA-Brief 49
Anderson, Lester William 1918-1973 .... 5-8R
Obituary 103
Anderson, Lindsay (Gordon) 1923-1994 128
Obituary 146
Brief entry 125
See also CLC 20
Anderson, Lonzo
See Anderson, John L(onzo)
See also SATA 2
Anderson, Louie 1953- 139
Anderson, Lucia (Lewis) 1922- 41-44R
See also SATA 10
Anderson, Luther A(dolph) 65-68
Anderson, M(ary) D(esiree) 1902- 9-12R
Anderson, M. T(obin) 1968- 163
See also SATA 97
Anderson, Madeleine Paltenghi 1899- CAP-1
Earlier sketch in CA 19-20
Anderson, Madelyn Klein CANR-28
Earlier sketches in CA 69-72, CANR-11
See also SATA 28
Anderson, Maggie
See Anderson, Margaret
Anderson, Malcolm 1934- 33-36R
Anderson, Margaret (Vance) 1917- 21-24R
Anderson, Margaret 1948- 101
Anderson, Margaret Bartlett 1922- 9-12R
Anderson, Margaret C(aroline) 1886-1973 108
Obituary 45-48
See also DLB 4, 91
Anderson, Margaret J(ohnson) 1909- CANR-3
Earlier sketch in CA 1-4R
Anderson, Margaret J(ean) 1931- CANR-26
Earlier sketches in CA 69-72, CANR-11
See also SAAS 8
See also SATA 27
Anderson, Mark M. 1955- 139
Anderson, Martin 1936- CANR-9
Earlier sketch in CA 13-16R
Anderson, Marvin Walter 1933- 41-44R
Anderson, Mary 1939- CANR-16
Earlier sketches in CA 49-52, CANR-1
See also SAAS 23
See also SATA 7, 82
Anderson, Mary M. 1919- 136
Anderson, Matthew Smith 1922- 13-16R
Anderson, Maxie (Leroy) 1934-1983 Obituary .. 115
Anderson, Maxwell 1888-1959 152
Brief entry 105
See also DAM DRAM
See also DLB 7
See also TCLC 2
Anderson, Michael Falconer 1947- 136
Anderson, Molly D(elCarmen) 1955- 147
Anderson, Mona 1910- CANR-6
Earlier sketch in CA 57-60
See also SATA 40
Anderson, Mrs. Melvin
See Anderson, Catherine Corley
Anderson, Nancy Fix 1941- 126
Anderson, Nancy Scott 1939- 137
Anderson, (James) Norman (Dalrymple) 1908- .....
CANR-4
Earlier sketch in CA 9-12R
Anderson, Norman Dean 1928- CANR-42
Earlier sketches in CA 33-36R, CANR-15
See also SATA 22
Anderson, Norman G(ulden) 1913- 133
Brief entry 114
Anderson, O(rvil) Roger 1937- 33-36R
Anderson, Odin W(aldemar) 1914- 25-28R
Anderson, Olive M(ary) 1915- CANR-42
Earlier sketches in CA 81-84, CANR-14
Anderson, Olive Ruth 1926- 107
Anderson, P(aul) Howard 1947- 61-64
Anderson, Patricia J. 1950- 152
Anderson, Patrick (John MacAllister)
1915-1979 93-96
Obituary 85-88
See also DLB 68
Anderson, Patrick 1936- 33-36R
Anderson, Paul E. 1925- 33-36R
Anderson, Paul Seward 1913-1975 .... CANR-6
Earlier sketch in CA 1-4R
Anderson, Paul Y. 1893-1938 .... DLB 29
Anderson, Peggy 1938- 93-96
Anderson, Peggy Perry 1953- .... SATA 84
Anderson, Perry 1938- 151
Anderson, Philip 1956- 158
Anderson, Philip Warren 1923- 159
Anderson, Poul (William) 1926- CANR-64
Earlier sketches in CA 1-4R, CANR-2, 15, 34
Interview in CANR-15
See also CAAS 2
See also AAYA 5
See also CLC 15
See also DLB 8
See also MTCW 1
See also SATA 90
See also SATA-Brief 39
Anderson, Quentin 1912- CANR-3
Earlier sketch in CA 1-4R
Anderson, R. C. 1883(?)-1976 Obituary 69-72
Anderson, R(oy) C(laude) 1931- 124
Anderson, Rachel 1943- CANR-50
Earlier sketches in CA 21-24R, CANR-9, 24
See also SAAS 18
See also SATA 34, 86
Anderson, Randall C. 1934- 41-44R
Anderson, Ray Sherman 1925- CANR-10
Earlier sketch in CA 65-68
Anderson, Raymond L(loyd) 1927- 106
Anderson, Richard
See Anderson, J(ohn) R(ichard) L(ane)
Anderson, Richard Chase 1934- Brief entry ... 112
Anderson, Richard Lloyd 1926- 37-40R
Anderson, Robert 1750-1830 .... DLB 142
Anderson, Robert (Woodruff) 1917- CANR-32
Earlier sketch in CA 21-24R
See also AITN 1
See also CLC 23
See also DAM DRAM
See also DLB 7
Anderson, Robert (David) 1927- 150
Anderson, Robert A(ndrew) 1944- 109
Anderson, Robert C(harles) 1930-1990 85-88
Obituary 130
Anderson, Robert David 1942- 73-76
Anderson, Robert H(enry) 1918- CANR-27
Earlier sketch in CA 49-52
Anderson, Robert Mapes 1929- 108
Anderson, Robert N(orris) 1944- 126
Anderson, Robert Newton 1929- 49-52
Anderson, Robert T(homas) 1926- 9-12R
Anderson, Robert W(illiam) 1926- 17-20R
Anderson, Roberta 1942- CANR-42
Brief entry 111
Earlier sketch in CA 115
Anderson, Rodney Dean 1938- 108
Anderson, Ronald Kinloch 1911-1984 Obituary . 111
Anderson, Roy
See Anderson, R(oy) C(laude)
Anderson, Roy 1936- 13-16R
Anderson, Roy Allan 1895- CANR-9
Earlier sketch in CA 13-16R
Anderson, Ruth I(rene) 1919- CANR-18
Earlier sketch in CA 1-4R
Anderson, Ruth Nathan 1934- 69-72
Anderson, Sarah 1947- 168
Anderson, Scarvia (Bateman) 1926- CANR-14
Earlier sketch in CA 41-44R
Anderson, Sherwood 1876-1941 .... CANR-61
Brief entry 104
Earlier sketch in CA 121
See also CDALB 1917-1929
See also DA
See also DAB
See also DAC
See also DAM MST, NOV
See also DLB 4, 9, 86
See also DLBD 1
See also MTCW 1
See also SSC 1
See also TCLC 1, 10, 24
See also WLC
Anderson, Sparky
See Anderson, George Lee
Anderson, Stanford 1934- 25-28R
Anderson, Stanley Edwin 1900-1977 ..... CANR-3
Earlier sketch in CA 1-4R
Anderson, Stanley V(ictor) 1928- 21-24R
Anderson, Susan 1952- .... SATA 90
Anderson, Sydney 1927- 106
Anderson, T(heodore) W(ilbur) 1918- CANR-29
Earlier sketch in CA 49-52
Anderson, Teresa 1944- 85-88
Anderson, Terry (A.) 1949- 147
Anderson, Terry H(oward) 1946- 128
Anderson, Theodore R(obert) 1927- 41-44R
Anderson, Thomas 1929- 1-4R
Anderson, Thomas D. 1929- 111
Anderson, Tom 1910- 69-72
Anderson, Tommy (Nolan) 1918- 45-48
Anderson, Totton J(ames) 1909-1992 .... 1-4R
Obituary 136
Anderson, Trevor A(ndrew) 1959- 154

Anderson, Verily (Bruce) 1915- CANR-3
Earlier sketch in CA 5-8R
Anderson, Vernon E(llsworth) 1908- CANR-5
Earlier sketch in CA 1-4R
Anderson, Virgil Antris 1899- CANR-16
Earlier sketch in CA 1-4R
Anderson, Virginia (R. Cronin) 1920- 21-24R
Anderson, Virginia DeJohn 1954- 150
Anderson, Vivienne 1916- 17-20R
Anderson, W. B.
See Schultz, James Willard
Anderson, Wallace Ludwig 1917- 17-20R
Anderson, Walt
See Anderson, Walter Truett
Anderson, Walter 1944- 101
Anderson, Walter Truett 1933- 105
Anderson, Warren DeWitt 1920- 17-20R
Anderson, Wayne 1946- 107
See also SATA 56
Anderson, Wayne Jeremy 1908- 49-52
Anderson, Wendell B(ernhard) 1920- 105
Anderson, Wilda (Christine) 1951- 139
Anderson, William A(verette) 1937- Brief entry . 114
Anderson, William Charles 1920- CANR-2
Earlier sketch in CA 5-8R
Anderson, William Davis 1938- 33-36R
Anderson, William Eugene 1926- Brief entry ... 111
Anderson, William G(ary) 1945- 115
Anderson, William H(arry) 1905-1972 49-52
Anderson, William L(ouis) 1941- 135
Anderson, William Robert 1921- 5-8R
Anderson, William Scovil 1927- 61-64
Anderson, Wilton T(homas) 1916- 17-20R
Anderson-Dargatz, Gail 1963- 158
Anderson Imbert, Enrique 1910- CANR-26
Earlier sketches in CA 17-20R, CANR-10
See also HW
Andersons, Edgars
See Anderson, Edgar
Anders-Richards, Donald 1928- 25-28R
Andersson, Ingvar 1899(?)-1974 Obituary 53-56
Andersson, Theodore 1903- CANR-29
Earlier sketch in CA 49-52
Andersson, Theodore M(urdock) 1934- 25-28R
Anderton, David A(lbin) 1919- CANR-9
Earlier sketch in CA 65-68
Anderton, Joanne (Marie) Gast 1930- 61-64
Anderton, Johana Gast
See Anderton, Joanne (Marie) Gast
Andervont, Howard Bancroft
1898-1981 Obituary 103
Andes, Karen 1956- 154
Andier, Pierre
See Desnos, Robert
Andonian, Jeanne (Beghian)
1891(?)-1976 Obituary 65-68
Andonov-Poljanski, Hristo 1927- CANR-9
Earlier sketch in CA 21-24R
Andouard
See Giraudoux, (Hippolyte) Jean
Andrade, Carlos Drummond de
See Drummond de Andrade, Carlos
See also CLC 18
Andrade, E(dward) N(eville) da C(osta) 1887-1971 .
CAP-1
Earlier sketch in CA 11-12
Andrade, Jorge Carrera
See Carrera Andrade, Jorge
Andrade, Mario de 1893-1945 .... TCLC 43
Andrade, Victor (Manuel) 1905- 69-72
Andrain, Charles F(ranklin) 1937- 69-72
Andre, Evelyn M(arie) 1924- CANR-11
Earlier sketch in CA 69-72
See also SATA 27
Andre, Judith 1941- 140
Andre, (Kenneth) Michael 1946- 114
See also CAAS 13
Andre, Rae 1946- 116
Andreach, Robert J. 1930- 33-36R
Andreae, Johann V(alentin) 1586-1654 ... DLB 164
Andreano, Ralph L(ouis) 1929- CANR-6
Earlier sketch in CA 5-8R
Andreas, Burton G(ould) 1921- 81-84
Andreas, Thomas
See Williams, Thomas (Andrew)
Andreasen, Alan R(obert) 1934- 65-68
Andreasen, Nancy C(oover) 1938- 108
Andreas-Salome, Lou 1861-1937 .... DLB 66
See also TCLC 56
Andreassen, Karl
See Boyd, Waldo T.
Andree, Louise
See Coury, Louise Andree
Andree, R(ichard) V(ernon) 1919- CANR-8
Earlier sketch in CA 57-60
Andree, Robert G(erald) 1912-1987 .... 29-32R
Obituary 124
Andreissen, David
See Poyer, David
Andreopoulos, George J. 1953- 168
Andreopoulos, Spyros (George) 1929- 77-80
Andres, Glenn M(erle) 1941- 73-76
Andres, Stefan 1906-1970 Obituary 29-32R
See also DLB 69
Andresen, Jack
See Andresen, John H(enry), Jr.
Andresen, John H(enry), Jr. 1917- 57-60
Andresen, Julie Tetel
See Tetel, Julie
Andreski, Iris
See Gillespie, I(ris) S(ylvia)
Andreski, Stanislav Leonard 1919- 61-64
Andress, Lesley
See Sanders, Lawrence
Andreu, Blanca 1959- .... DLB 134
Andrew, Christopher (Maurice) 1941- 136
Andrew, David S. 1943- 123
Andrew, J(ames) Dudley 1945- CANR-9
Earlier sketch in CA 65-68
Andrew, John (Alfred III) 1943- 165
Andrew, Joseph J(erald) 1960- 143
Andrew, Joseph Maree
See Occomy, Marita (Odette) Bonner
Andrew, Malcolm (Ross) 1945- 105
Andrew, Prudence (Hastings) 1924- CANR-52
Earlier sketches in CA 1-4R, CANR-1
See also SATA 87
Andrew, Sheila M. 1938- 165
Andrew, Warren 1910- 21-24R
Andrewes, Christopher Howard 1896- 17-20R
Andrewes, Lancelot 1555-1626 ...... DLB 151, 172
Andrewes, Patience
See Bradford, Patience Andrewes
Andrews, A. A.
See Paine, Lauran (Bosworth)
Andrews, Allen 1913- CANR-1
Earlier sketch in CA 49-52
Andrews, Arthur (Douglas, Jr.) 1923- 69-72
Andrews, Barry G(eoffrey) 1943- CANR-2
Earlier sketch in CA 49-52
Andrews, Bart 1945- CANR-24
Earlier sketches in CA 65-68, CANR-9
Andrews, Benny 1930- 106
See also SATA 31
Andrews, Bruce 1948- CANR-10
Earlier sketch in CA 49-52
Andrews, Burton (Allen) 1906- CAP-2
Earlier sketch in CA 33-36
Andrews, Charles M(cLean) 1863-1943 Brief
entry 119
See also DLB 17
Andrews, Cicily Fairfield
See West, Rebecca
Andrews, Claire 1940- 33-36R
Andrews, Clarence A(delbert) 1912- CANR-20
Earlier sketch in CA 33-36R
Andrews, Colin 1946- 133
Andrews, Donald H(atch) 1898-197(?) CAP-2
Earlier sketch in CA 23-24
Andrews, Dorothea Harris
1916-1976 Obituary 69-72
Andrews, E(ric) M(ontgomery) 1933- 93-96
Andrews, Eamonn 1922-1987 120
Obituary 124
Andrews, Edgar Harold 1932- 105
Andrews, Eleanor Lattimore
See Lattimore, Eleanor Frances
Andrews, Elmer 1948- 132
Andrews, Elton V.
See Pohl, Frederik
Andrews, Ernest E(ugene) 1932- 57-60
Andrews, F(rank) Emerson 1902-1978 .... CANR-1
Obituary 81-84
Earlier sketch in CA 1-4R
See also SATA 22
Andrews, (Earl) Frank 1937- 61-64
Andrews, Frank M(eredith) 1935- CANR-14
Earlier sketch in CA 41-44R
Andrews, George (Clinton) 1926- 21-24R
Andrews, George F(redrick) 1918- 65-68
Andrews, George Reid 1951- 141
Andrews, Henry N(athaniel), Jr. 1910- 93-96
Andrews, J. Cutler 1908-1972 Obituary 37-40R
Andrews, J(ames) S(ydney) 1934- 29-32R
See also SATA 4
Andrews, James David 1924- 53-56
Andrews, James Frederick
1936-1980 Obituary 107
Andrews, James J. C. 1943(?)-1985 Obituary .. 116
Andrews, James R(obertson) 1936- 129
Brief entry 117
Andrews, Jan 1942- 122
See also SATA 58, 98
See also SATA-Brief 49
Andrews, John F(rank) 1942- CANR-48
Earlier sketch in CA 119
Andrews, John Henry 1939- 107
Andrews, John Malcolm 1936- CANR-67
Earlier sketches in CA 117, CANR-41
Andrews, John Williams 1898-1975 Obituary . 57-60
Andrews, Julie 1935- 37-40R
See also SATA 7
Andrews, Keith 1930- 33-36R
Andrews, Kenneth R(ichmond) 1916- CANR-37
Earlier sketches in CA 1-4R, CANR-16
Andrews, Kevin 1924- 124
Andrews, Laura
See Coury, Louise Andree
Andrews, Lewis M. 1946- 65-68
Andrews, (William) Linton 1886-1972 .... 9-12R
Obituary 120
Andrews, Lucilla (Mathew) CANR-61
Brief entry 116
Earlier sketch in CA 128
Andrews, Lyman 1938- 49-52
Andrews, Lynn V. 129
Brief entry 125
Andrews, Margaret E(lizabeth) 33-36R
Andrews, Mark Edwin 1903- CAP-1
Earlier sketch in CA 19-20
Andrews, (Daniel) Marshall
1899(?)-1973 Obituary 45-48
Andrews, Mary Evans 5-8R
Andrews, Michael
See Andrews, Michael Alford
Andrews, Michael Alford 1939- 116
Andrews, Michael F(rank) 1916- CANR-27
Earlier sketch in CA 49-52
Andrews, Mike
See Andrews, Michael Alford
Andrews, Miles Peter (?)-1814 .... DLB 89
Andrews, Paul Revere 1906-1983 Obituary 110
Andrews, Peter 1931- CANR-11
Earlier sketch in CA 17-20R
Andrews, Ralph W(arren) 1897- 9-12R
Andrews, Raymond 1934-1991 .... CANR-42
Obituary 136
Earlier sketches in CA 81-84, CANR-15
See also BW 2
Andrews, Robert D.
See Andrews, (Charles) Robert Douglas (Hardy)
Andrews, (Charles) Robert Douglas (Hardy) 1908- .
CAP-1
Earlier sketch in CA 9-10
Andrews, Roy Chapman 1884-1960 ...... SATA 19
Andrews, Stanley 1894- CANR-22
Earlier sketch in CA 45-48
Andrews, Tom 1961- 147
Andrews, V(irginia) C(leo) (?)-1986 ...... CANR-21
Obituary 121
Earlier sketch in CA 97-100
See also AAYA 4
See also DAM POP
See also MTCW 1
See also SATA-Obit 50
Andrews, Wayne 1913-1987 .... CANR-70
Obituary 123
Earlier sketches in CA 9-12R, CANR-3
Andrews, William G(eorge) 1930- CANR-48
Earlier sketches in CA 5-8R, CANR-7
See also SATA 74
Andrews, William L(eake) 1946- 136
Andrews, William R(obert) 1937- 53-56
Andreyev, Leonid (Nikolaevich) 1871-1919 Brief
entry 104
See also TCLC 3
Andreyev, Nikolay Efremych
1908-1982 Obituary 106
Andrezel, Pierre
See Blixen, Karen (Christentze Dinesen)
Andrian, Gustave W(illiam) 1918- Brief entry ... 114
Andrian, Leopold von 1875-1951 .... DLB 81
Andriani, Renee
See Williams-Andriani, Renee
Andric, Ivo 1892-1975 .... CANR-60
Obituary 57-60
Earlier sketches in CA 81-84, CANR-43
See also CLC 8
See also DLB 147
See also MTCW 1
Andriekus, (Kazimieras) Leonardas 1914- ... 25-28R
Andrien, Kenneth James 1951- 120
Andriessen, Hendrik (Franciscus)
1892-1981 Obituary 108
Andriola, Alfred J. 1912-1983 Obituary 109
See also SATA-Obit 34
Andrist, Ralph K. 1914- CANR-20
Earlier sketches in CA 9-12R, CANR-5
See also SATA 45
Andropov, Yuri (Vladimirovich)
1914-1984 Obituary 111
Andros, Dee G(us) 1924- 69-72
Andros, Phil
See Steward, Samuel M(orris)
Androvar
See Prado (Calvo), Pedro
Andrus, (Vincent) Dyckman 1942- 102
Andrus, Hyrum L(eslie) 1924- 37-40R
Andrus, Jeff 1947- 155
Andrus, Paul 1931- 65-68
Andrus, Vera 1895- CAP-2
Earlier sketch in CA 21-22
Andryszewski, Tricia 1956- 152
See also SATA 88
Andrzejewski, Jerzy 1909-1983 .... CANR-29
Obituary 109
Earlier sketch in CA 25-28R
Andrzejewski, Julie 1945- 129
Andrzeyevski, George
See Andrzejewski, Jerzy
Anduze-Dufy, Raphael
See Coulet du Gard, Rene
Anees, Munawar Ahmad 1948- 123
An Elderly Spinster
See Wilson, Margaret (Wilhemina)
Anfinsen, Christian Boehmer 1916- 159
Anfousse, Ginette 1944- .... SATA-Brief 48
Ang, Ien 1954- 133
Angebert, Jean
See Bertrand, Michel
Angebert, Jean-Michel
See Bertrand, Michel
Angebert, Michel
See Bertrand, Michel
Angel, Daniel D. 1939- 33-36R
Angel, Heather 1941- CANR-25
Earlier sketch in CA 69-72
Angel, J(ohn) Lawrence 1915-1986 101
Obituary 120
Angel, Marc D(wight) 1945- 101
Angel, Marie 1923- CANR-15
Earlier sketch in CA 29-32R
See also SATA 47
Angela, Alberto 1962- 144
Angelella, Michael 1953- 97-100
Angeles, Jose 1930- 33-36R
Angeles, Peter A. 1931- 33-36R
See also SATA 40
Angeles, Philip 1909- 5-8R
Angeli, Marguerite (Lofft) de
See de Angeli, Marguerite (Lofft)
Angelilli, Frank Joseph
See Angell, Frank Joseph
Angelin, Patricia 119
Angelino, Marie
See Garbutt, Janice (D.) Lovoos
Angelique, Pierre
See Bataille, Georges
Angell, Ernest 1889-1973 Obituary 37-40R
Angell, Frank Joseph 1919- 17-20R
Angell, George 1945- 101
Angell, James Burrill 1829-1916 .... DLB 64
Angell, James W(aterhouse)
1898-1986 Obituary 119
Angell, Judie
See Gaberman, Judie Angell
Angell, Madeline 1919- CANR-10
Earlier sketch in CA 65-68
See also SATA 18
Angell, (Ralph) Norman 1872(?)-1967 ...... CAP-1
Earlier sketch in CA 13-14
Angell, Richard B(radshaw) 1918- 13-16R
Angell, Robert Cooley 1899- 101
Angell, Roger 1920- CANR-70
Earlier sketches in CA 57-60, CANR-13, 44
See also CLC 26
See also DLB 171, 185
Angell, Tony 1940- CANR-4
Earlier sketch in CA 53-56
Angelo, Bonnie Brief entry 113
Angelo, Frank 1914- CANR-4
Earlier sketch in CA 53-56
Angelo, Valenti 1897- CANR-68
Earlier sketch in CA 73-76
See also SATA 14
Angelocci, Angelo 1926- 21-24R
Angelou, Maya 1928- CANR-65
Earlier sketches in CA 65-68, CANR-19, 42
See also AAYA 7, 20
See also BLC 1
See also BW 2
See also CLC 12, 35, 64, 77
See also DA
See also DAB
See also DAC
See also DAM MST, MULT, POET, POP
See also DLB 38
See also MTCW 1
See also SATA 49
See also WLCS
Anger, Kenneth 1930- 106
Interview in 106
Angermann, Gerhard O(tto) 1904- 65-68
Angier, Bradford CANR-7
Earlier sketch in CA 5-8R
See also SATA 12
Angier, Carole 1943- 120
Angier, Roswell P. 1940- 101
Angiolillo, Paul F(rancis) 1917- 105
Anglade, Jean 1915- CANR-43
Earlier sketches in CA 103, CANR-20
Angle, Barbara 1947- 150
Angle, Jim 1946- 133
Angle, Paul M(cClelland) 1900-1975 .... CAP-2
Obituary 57-60
Earlier sketch in CA 21-22
See also SATA-Obit 20
Anglesey, Zoe (Rita) 1941- 147
Anglin, Douglas G(eorge) 1923- CANR-14
Earlier sketch in CA 37-40R
Anglo, Sydney 1934- 89-92
Anglund, Joan Walsh 1926- CANR-15
Earlier sketch in CA 5-8R
See also CLR 1
See also SATA 2
Ango, Fan D.
See Longyear, Barry Brookes
Angoff, Allan 1910- CANR-20
Earlier sketch in CA 45-48
Angoff, Charles 1902-1979 .... CANR-68
Obituary 85-88
Earlier sketches in CA 5-8R, CANR-4
Angremy, Jean-Pierre 1937- 106
Angress, R(uth) K(lueger) 1931- 37-40R
Angress, Werner T(homas) 1920- 13-16R
Angrist, Shirley S(arah) 1933- 25-28R
Angrist, Stanley W(olff) 1933- 25-28R
See also SATA 4
Anguizola, G. A.
See Anguizola, Gustave (A.)
Anguizola, Gustave (A.) 1927- Brief entry 116
Angus, Douglas Ross 1909- CANR-3
Earlier sketch in CA 1-4R
Angus, Fay 1929- CANR-33
Earlier sketches in CA 89-92, CANR-15
Angus, Ian
See Mackay, James (Alexander)
Angus, J(ohn) Colin 1907- 107
Angus, Margaret 1908- 21-24R
Angus, Sylvia 1921-1982 .... CANR-10
Earlier sketch in CA 61-64
Angus, Tom
See Powell, Geoffrey Stewart
Angus-Butterworth, Lionel Milner 1900- ... CANR-4
Earlier sketch in CA 53-56
Anhalt, Edward 1914- CANR-29
Earlier sketch in CA 85-88
See also DLB 26
Anholt, Catherine 1958- .... SATA 74
Anholt, Laurence 1959- .... SATA 74
Anicar, Tom
See Raucina, Thomas Frank
Aniebo, I(feanyichukwu) N(dubuisi) C(hikezie)
1939- CANR-62
Earlier sketch in CA 134
Anikouchine, William A(lexander) 1929- Brief
entry 117
Anita
See Daniel, Anita
Ankenbrand, Frank, Jr. 1905- CAP-2
Earlier sketch in CA 19-20
Anker, Charlotte 1934- 93-96
Ankerson, Dudley (Charles) 1948- CANR-53
Earlier sketch in CA 126

Anmar, Frank
  See Nolan, William F(rancis)
Anna, Timothy E. 1944- ... 101
Annan, Noel Gilroy 1916- ... CANR-63
  Earlier sketch in CA 61-64
Annand, J(ames) K(ing) 1908- ... CANR-18
  Earlier sketch in CA 101
Annandale, Barbara
  See Bowden, Jean
Annas, George J. 1945- ... 77-80
Anne (Elizabeth Alice Louise Windsor), Princess
  1950- ... 140
Anne-Mariel
  See Goud, Anne
Annensky, Innokenty (Fyodorovich) 1856-1909 . 155
  Brief entry ... 110
  See also TCLC 14
Annerino, John ... 144
Anness, Milford E(dwin) 1918- ... 17-20R
Annett, Cora
  See Scott, Cora Annett (Pipitone)
Annett, John 1930- ... 29-32R
Annigoni, Pietro 1910-1988 Obituary ... 127
Annikova, Galina
  See Dutkina, Galina (Borisovna)
Annis, Linda Ferrill 1943- ... 85-88
Annixter, Jane
  See Sturtzel, Jane Levington
Annixter, Paul
  See ENTER
Anno, Mitsumasa 1926- ... CANR-44
  Earlier sketches in CA 49-52, CANR-4
  See also CLR 2, 14
  See also MAICYA
  See also SATA 5, 38, 77
Annunzio, Gabriele d'
  See D'Annunzio, Gabriele
Anobile, Richard J(oseph) 1947- ... CANR-5
  Earlier sketch in CA 53-56
Anobile, Ulla (Kakonen) 1945- ... 111
Anodos
  See Coleridge, Mary E(lizabeth)
Anoff, I(sador) S(amuel) 1892- ... 45-48
Anon, Charles Robert
  See Pessoa, Fernando (Antonio Nogueira)
Anouilh, Jean (Marie Lucien Pierre) 1910-1987 ...
  CANR-32
  Obituary ... 123
  Earlier sketch in CA 17-20R
  See also CLC 1, 3, 8, 13, 40, 50
  See also DAM DRAM
  See also DC 8
  See also MTCW 1
Anozie, Sunday O(gbonna) 1942- ... 143
  See also BW 2
Anquillare, John 1942- ... 105
Ansa, Tina McElroy 1949- ... 142
  See also BW 2
Ansara, Michael
  See Crowther, Bruce (Ian)
Ansay, A. Manette 1964- ... 148
Ansbacher, Heinz L(udwig) 1904- ... CAP-1
  Earlier sketch in CA 9-10
Ansbacher, Max G. 1935- ... 89-92
Ansberry, William F. 1926- ... 33-36R
Anschel, Eugene 1907- ... 53-56
Anschel, Kurt R. 1936- ... 41-44R
Anscombe, Elizabeth
  See Anscombe, G(ertrude) E(lizabeth) M(argaret)
Anscombe, G(ertrude) E(lizabeth) M(argaret)
  1919- ... 129
  Brief entry ... 122
Anscombe, Isabelle (Mary) 1954- ... 108
Anscombe, Roderick 1947- ... 147
Ansel, Talvikki 1962- ... 164
Ansel, Walter (Charles) 1897-1977 ... 45-48
  Obituary ... 73-76
Ansell, Helen 1940- ... 25-28R
Ansell, Jack 1925-1976 ... 17-20R
  Obituary ... 69-72
Anselm, Felix
  See Pollak, Felix
Anselm of Canterbury 1033-1109 ... DLB 115
Ansen, Alan 1922- ... CANR-4
  Earlier sketch in CA 1-4R
Anshaw, Carol 1946- ... 164
Anshen, Melvin (Leon) 1912- ... 124
Ansky, S.
  See Rappoport, Shloyme Zanul
Ansley, Gladys Piatt 1906- ... 5-8R
Anslinger, Harry Jacob 1892-1975 ... CANR-70
  Obituary ... 61-64
  Earlier sketches in CAP-1, CA 11-12
Anson, Bill 1907-1983 Obituary ... 110
Anson, Cyril J(oseph) 1923- ... 49-52
Anson, Jay 1921-1980 ... CANR-29
  Obituary ... 97-100
  Earlier sketch in CA 81-84
Anson, John
  See Firth, (Frederick) Anson
Anson, Peter Frederick 1889- ... 9-12R
Anson, Robert Sam 1945- ... CANR-52
  Brief entry ... 115
  Earlier sketch in CA 125
  Interview in ... 125
Anspach, Donald F. 1942- ... 69-72
Anstey, Caroline 1958- ... SATA 81
Anstey, Edgar
  See Slusser, George Edgar
Anstey, Edgar 1917- ... CANR-3
  Earlier sketch in CA 5-8R
Anstey, F.
  See Guthrie, Thomas Anstey
  See also DLB 141, 178
Anstey, Roger T(homas) 1927- ... 13-16R
Anstey, Vera (Powell) 1889- ... CAP-1
  Earlier sketch in CA 17-18
Anstruther, Godfrey 1903-1988 Obituary ... 126
Anstruther, Ian 1922- ... CANR-59
  Earlier sketch in CA 128
Anstruther, James
  See Maxtone Graham, James Anstruther
An Tai-sung 1931- ... 133
  Brief entry ... 113
Antal, Dan 1954- ... 152
Antar, Johanna 1953- ... 140
Antell, Gerson 1926- ... 53-56
Antell, Will D. 1935- ... 104
  See also SATA 31
Anthes, Richard A(llen) 1944- ... 107
Anthony
  See Taber, Anthony Scott
Anthony, Barbara 1932- ... CANR-21
  Earlier sketch in CA 103
  See also SATA 29
Anthony, C. L.
  See Smith, Dorothy Gladys
Anthony, Carolyn (Taylor) 1928- ... 147
Anthony, Catherine
  See Adachi, Barbara (Curtis)
Anthony, David
  See Smith, William Dale
Anthony, Diana 1951- ... 114
Anthony, Edward 1895-1971 ... CANR-68
  Obituary ... 33-36R
  Earlier sketch in CA 73-76
  See also SATA 21
Anthony, Evelyn
  See Ward-Thomas, Evelyn Bridget Patricia
    Stephens
Anthony, Florence
  See Ai
Anthony, Geraldine (Cecilia) 1919- ... CANR-52
  Earlier sketches in CA 69-72, CANR-11, 28
Anthony, Gordon
  See Stannus, (James) Gordon (Dawson)
Anthony, Inid E. 1925- ... 104
Anthony, J(oseph) Garner 1899- ... 61-64
Anthony, James R(aymond) 1922- ... CANR-27
  Earlier sketch in CA 49-52
Anthony, John
  See Beckett, Ronald Brymer
  and Ciardi, John (Anthony)
  and Sabini, John Anthony
Anthony, Julie 1948- ... 106
Anthony, Katharine (Susan)
  1877-1965 Obituary ... 25-28R
Anthony, Michael 1932- ... CANR-43
  Earlier sketches in CA 17-20R, CANR-10, 27
  See also CAAS 18
  See also BW 2
  See also DLB 125
Anthony, Patricia 1947- ... 166
Anthony, Peter
  See Shaffer, Anthony (Joshua)
  and Shaffer, Peter (Levin)
Anthony, Piers 1934- ... CANR-56
  Earlier sketches in CA 21-24R, CANR-28
  See also AAYA 11
  See also CLC 35
  See also DAM POP
  See also DLB 8
  See also MTCW 1
  See also SAAS 22
  See also SATA 84
Anthony, Rebecca (Jespersen) 1950- ... 118
Anthony, Robert N(ewton) 1916- ... CANR-5
  Earlier sketch in CA 13-16R
Anthony, Susan B(rownell) 1916-1991 ... 89-92
  Obituary ... 134
  See also TCLC 84
Anthony, Susan C(arol) 1953- ... SATA 87
Anthony, Susanna 1726-1791 ... DLB 200
Anthony, Tony
  See Alessandra, Tony
Anthony, William G. 1934- ... 17-20R
Anthony, William P(hilip) 1943- ... CANR-29
  Earlier sketches in CA 77-80, CANR-13
Anthrop, Donald F. 1935- Brief entry ... 111
Anticaglia, Elizabeth 1939- ... CANR-1
  Earlier sketch in CA 45-48
  See also SATA 12
Antico, John 1924- ... 29-32R
Antill, James Macquarie 1912- ... CANR-13
  Earlier sketch in CA 33-36R
Antin, David 1932- ... 73-76
  See also DLB 169
Antin, Mary 1881-1949 Brief entry ... 118
  See also DLBY 84
Antle, Nancy 1955- ... SATA 102
Antoine, Marc
  See Proust, (Valentin-Louis-George-Eugene-)
    Marcel
Antoine-Dariaux, Genevieve 1914- ... 57-60
Antokoletz, Elliott (Maxim) 1942- ... 129
Antol, Marie Nadine 1930- ... 152
Antol, Nikki
  See Antol, Marie Nadine
Antolini, Margaret Fishback
  1904-1985 Obituary ... 117
  See also SATA-Obit 45
Anton, Frank Robert 1920- ... 41-44R
Anton, Hector R(oque) 1919- ... 73-76
Anton, John P(eter) 1920- ... CANR-9
  Earlier sketch in CA 21-24R
Anton, Michael J(ames) 1940- ... 57-60
  See also SATA 12
Anton, Rita (Kenter) 1920- ... 9-12R
Anton, Ted 1957- ... 153
Antonacci, Robert J(oseph) 1916- ... CANR-9
  Earlier sketch in CA 5-8R
  See also SATA 45
  See also SATA-Brief 37
Antoncich, Betty (Kennedy) 1913- ... 13-16R
Antone, Evan Haywood 1922- ... 126
Antoni
  See Iranek-Osmecki, Kazimierz
Antoni, Brian 1959- ... 147
Antoni, Robert (William) 1958- ... 139
Antoniak, Helen Elizabeth 1947- ... 105
Antonick, Robert J. 1939- ... 37-40R
Antoninus, Brother
  See Everson, William (Oliver)
Antonio, Robert J(ohn) 1945- ... 120
Antonioni, Michelangelo 1912- ... CANR-45
  Earlier sketch in CA 73-76
  See also CLC 20
Antoniutti, Ildebrando 1898-1974 Obituary ... 53-56
Antonovsky, Aaron 1923- ... CANR-12
  Earlier sketch in CA 29-32R
Antonucci, Francesco 1956- ... 149
Antony, Jonquil 1916(?)-1980 ... 13-16R
  Obituary ... 120
Antoun, Richard T(aft) 1932- ... 65-68
Antreasian, Garo Z(areh) 1922- ... 81-84
Antrim, Donald 1959(?)- ... 167
Antrim, Harry Thomas 1936- ... 33-36R
Antrim, William H. 1928- ... 69-72
Antrobus, John 1933- ... CANR-67
  Earlier sketches in CA 57-60, CANR-11
Antschel, Paul 1920-1970 ... CANR-61
  Earlier sketches in CA 85-88, CANR-33
  See also Celan, Paul
  See also MTCW 1
Anttila, Raimo (Aulis) 1935- ... 33-36R
Anunobi, Fredoline O. 1956- ... 146
Anvic, Frank
  See Sherman, Jory (Tecumseh)
Anvil, Christopher
  See Crosby, Harry C., Jr.
Anwar, Chairil 1922-1949 Brief entry ... 121
  See also TCLC 22
Anweiler, Oskar 1925- ... CANR-9
  Earlier sketch in CA 65-68
Anyon, G(eorge) Jay 1909- ... 5-8R
Anzaldua, Gloria 1942- ... DLB 122
Anzengruber, Ludwig 1839-1889 ... DLB 129
Anzovin, Steven 1954- ... 124
Aoki, Haruo 1930- ... CANR-52
  Earlier sketches in CA 49-52, CANR-27
Aoki, Hisako 1942- ... 115
  See also SATA 45
Aoki, Michiko Y(amaguchi) ... 107
Apel, Karl-Otto 1922- ... CANR-46
  Earlier sketches in CA 105, CANR-22
Apel, Willi 1893- ... CANR-2
  Earlier sketch in CA 1-4R
Apelian, Albert Solomon 1893-1986 Obituary .. 121
Apess, William 1798-1839(?) ... DAM MULT
  See also DLB 175
  See also NNAL
Apfel, Necia H(alpern) 1930- ... CANR-46
  Earlier sketches in CA 107, CANR-23
  See also SATA 51
  See also SATA-Brief 41
Apffel, Edmund R., Jr. 1948- ... 107
Apgar, Virginia 1909-1974 ... 73-76
  Obituary ... 53-56
Aphrodite, J.
  See Livingston, Carole
Aphrontis, Hippoclides
  See Humez, Nicholas (David)
Apikuni
  See Schultz, James Willard
Apilentz
  See Apelian, Albert Solomon
Apitz, Bruno 1900-1979 Obituary ... 85-88
Aplon, Roger 1937- ... 119
Apodaca, Rudy S(amuel) 1939- ... 131
  See also DLB 82
  See also HW
Apolinar, Danny 1934- ... 61-64
Apollinaire, Guillaume 1880-1918 ... 152
  See also Kostrowitzki, Wilhelm Apollinaris de
  See also DAM POET
  See also PC 7
  See also TCLC 3, 8, 51
Aponte, Barbara (Ann) Bockus 1936- Brief
  entry ... 111
Aponte, Harry J. 1935- ... 149
Apostle, Chris(tos) N(icholas) 1935- ... 21-24R
Apostolon, Billy (Michael) 1930- ... 97-100
Apostolos-Cappadona, Diane 1948- ... CANR-30
  Earlier sketch in CA 112
Apostolou, Christine Hale 1955- ... SATA 82
Apostolou, John L. 1930- ... 127
App, Austin Joseph 1902-1984 ... 101
  Obituary ... 112
Appachana, Anjana 1956- ... 148
Appadorai, A(ngadipuram) 1902- ... 102
Appel, Alfred, Jr. 1934- ... 133
  Brief entry ... 113
Appel, Allan 1946- ... 77-80
Appel, Allen (R.) 1945- ... 138
Appel, Benjamin 1907-1977 ... CANR-69
  Obituary ... 69-72
  Earlier sketches in CA 13-16R, CANR-6
  See also SATA 39
  See also SATA-Obit 21
Appel, Frederic C. 1935(?)-1984 Obituary ... 112
Appel, John J. 1921- ... 33-36R
Appel, Kenneth Ellmaker
  1896-1979 Obituary ... 89-92
Appel, Libby E(ve Sundel) 1937- ... 117
Appel, Martin E(liot) 1948- ... CANR-15
  Earlier sketch in CA 85-88
  See also SATA 45
Appel, Marty
  See Appel, Martin E(liot)
Appel, Willa 1946- ... 117
Appel, William 1939- ... 114
Appelbaum, Diana Karter 1953- ... 122
Appelbaum, Judith (Pilpel) 1939- ... CANR-14
  Earlier sketch in CA 77-80
  Interview in ... CANR-14
Appelbaum, Paul S(tuart) 1951- ... 108
Appelbaum, Stephen A(rthur) 1926- ... 101
Appelfeld, Aharon 1932- ... 133
  Brief entry ... 112
  See also CLC 23, 47
Appell, Don 1917(?)-1990 Obituary ... 131
Appelman, Hyman (Jedidiah) 1902- ... 5-8R
Appelt, Kathi 1954- ... 150
  See also SATA 83
Appere, Guy 1923- ... CANR-41
  Earlier sketch in CA 117
Appiah, (K.) Anthony 1954- ... 140
  See also BW 2
Appiah, Peggy 1921- ... CANR-53
  Earlier sketch in CA 41-44R
  See also SAAS 19
  See also SATA 15, 84
Appignanesi, Lisa 1946- ... CANR-50
  Earlier sketches in CA 49-52, CANR-27
Applbaum, Ronald L. 1943- ... CANR-7
  Earlier sketch in CA 57-60
Apple, Hope 1942- ... 152
Apple, Jacki 1941- ... 127
Apple, Margot ... SATA 64
  See also SATA-Brief 42
Apple, Max (Isaac) 1941- ... CANR-54
  Earlier sketches in CA 81-84, CANR-19
  See also CLC 9, 33
  See also DLB 130
Apple, Michael W(hitman) 1942- ... 109
Apple, R(aymond) W(alter), Jr. 1934- ... 89-92
Apple, Rima D. 1944- ... 147
Applebaum, Anne 1964- ... 149
Applebaum, Edmond L(ewis) 1924- ... 117
Applebaum, Samuel 1904- ... 65-68
Applebaum, Stan 1922- ... 85-88
  See also SATA 45
Applebaum, William 1906-1979(?) ... CANR-6
  Earlier sketch in CA 9-12R
Applebee, Arthur N(oble) 1946- ... CANR-57
  Earlier sketches in CA 81-84, CANR-14, 31
Appleby, Andrew Bell 1929-1980 ... 108
Appleby, David P. 1925- ... 110
Appleby, John T. 1909(?)-1974 Obituary ... 53-56
Appleby, Jon 1948- ... 33-36R
Appleby, Joyce Oldham 1929- ... CANR-11
  Earlier sketch in CA 69-72
Appleby, Louis 1955- ... 146
Applegarth, Margaret Tyson
  1886-1976 Obituary ... 69-72
Applegate, James (Earl) 1923- ... 33-36R
Applegate, Richard 1913(?)-1979 Obituary ... 85-88
Applegath, John 1935- ... 115
Appleman, John Alan 1912-1982 ... CANR-2
  Obituary ... 108
  Earlier sketch in CA 5-8R
Appleman, M(arjorie) H. 1928- ... CANR-43
  Earlier sketch in CA 118
Appleman, Margie
  See Appleman, M(arjorie) H.
Appleman, Mark J(erome) 1917- ... 29-32R
Appleman, Philip (Dean) 1926- ... CANR-56
  Earlier sketches in CA 13-16R, CANR-6, 29
  See also CAAS 18
  See also CLC 51
Appleman, Roy Edgar 1904- ... CAP-1
  Earlier sketch in CA 9-10
Appleton, Arthur 1913- ... 93-96
Appleton, George 1902- ... 126
Appleton, James Henry 1919- ... CANR-2
  Earlier sketch in CA 5-8R
Appleton, Jane (Frances) 1934- ... 102
Appleton, Jay
  See Appleton, James Henry
Appleton, Lawrence
  See Lovecraft, H(oward) P(hillips)
Appleton, Marion Brymner 1906- ... 105
Appleton, Sarah 1930- ... 37-40R
Appleton, Sheldon Lee 1933- ... 1-4R
Appleton, Victor ... CANR-27
  Earlier sketches in CAP-2, CA 19-20
  See also Macdonald, James D.
  and Vardeman, Robert E(dward)
  See also SATA 1, 67
Appleton, Victor II ... CANR-27
  Earlier sketch in CA 17-20R
  See also SATA 1, 67
Appleton, William S. 1934- ... 101
Appleton, William W(orthen) 1915- Brief entry ... 113
Applewhite, Cynthia ... 89-92
Applewhite, E(dgar) J(arratt, Jr.) 1919- ... 89-92
Applewhite, Harriet Branson 1940- ... 106
Applewhite, James W(illiam) 1935- ... CANR-50
  Earlier sketches in CA 85-88, CANR-25
  See also DLB 105
Applewhite, Philip B(oatman) 1938- ... 112
Appley, Lawrence A. 1904- ... 121
Appley, M(ortimer) H(erbert) 1921- ... 13-16R
Appleyard, Bryan (Edward) 1951- ... 141
Appleyard, Donald 1928- ... CANR-4
  Earlier sketch in CA 5-8R
Appleyard, Reginald Thomas 1927- ... 17-20R
Applezweig, M. H.
  See Appley, M(ortimer) H(erbert)

Apps, Jerold W(illard) 1934- ... CANR-37
Earlier sketches in CA 49-52, CANR-1, 16
Apps, Jerry
See Apps, Jerold W(illard)
apRoberts, Ruth ... 111
Apsler, Alfred 1907- ... CANR-3
Earlier sketch in CA 5-8R
See also SATA 10
Apstein, Theodore 1918- ... 131
Apt, (Jerome) Leon 1929- ... 53-56
Apte, Mahadev L(akshuman) 1931- ... 117
Apted, M(ichael) R. 1919- ... 25-28R
Aptekar, Jane 1935- ... 81-84
Apter, David Ernest 1924- ... CANR-3
Earlier sketch in CA 1-4R
Apter, Emily (S.) 1954- ... 137
Apter, Michael J(ohn) 1939- ... 29-32R
Apter, Samson 1910- ... 104
Apter, T(erri) E. 1949- ... 134
Apteryx
See Eliot, T(homas) S(tearns)
Aptheker, Bettina 1944- ... CANR-6
Earlier sketch in CA 29-32R
Aptheker, Herbert 1915- ... CANR-6
Earlier sketch in CA 5-8R
Interview in ... CANR-6
Aquarius, Qass
See Buskirk, Richard H(obart)
Aquilano, Nicholas Joseph 1930- ... 112
Aquin, Hubert 1929-1977 ... 105
See also CLC 15
See also DLB 53
Aquina, Sister Mary
See Weinrich, A(nna) K(atharina) H(ildegard)
Aquinas, Thomas 1224(?)-1274 ... DLB 115
Aquino, Benigno S(imeon), Jr.
1932-1983 Obituary ... 110
Aquino, Luis Hernandez
See Hernandez Aquino, Luis
Aquino, Ninoy
See Aquino, Benigno S(imeon), Jr.
Arad, Yitshak 1926- ... 134
Arafat, Ibtihaj Said 1934- ... 85-88
Aragbabalu, Omidiji
See Beier, Ulli
Aragon, Louis 1897-1982 ... CANR-71
Obituary ... 108
Earlier sketches in CA 69-72, CANR-28
See also CLC 3, 22
See also DAM NOV, POET
See also DLB 72
See also MTCW 1
Aragon, Luis Cardoza y
See Cardoza y Aragon, Luis
Aragones, Sergio 1937- ... 122
See also SATA 48
See also SATA-Brief 39
Arai, Masami 1953- ... 140
Arakawa, Yoichi 1962- ... 163
Araki, James T(omomasa) 1925- ... 13-16R
Aralica, Ivan 1930- ... DLB 181
Arango, Jorge Sanin 1916- ... 61-64
Aranha, Ray 1939- Brief entry ... 112
Aranow, Edward Ross 1909-1993 ... 41-44R
Obituary ... 143
Araoz, Daniel Leon 1930- ... 108
Arapoff, Nancy 1930- ... 29-32R
Arasteh, A(bdol) Reza 1927-1992 ... CANR-46
Obituary ... 139
Earlier sketch in CA 105
Arata, Esther S(pring) 1918- ... 89-92
Arata, Luis O(scar) 1950- ... 115
Aratus of Soli c. 315B.C.-c. 239B.C. ... DLB 176
Araujo, Frank P. 1937- ... 151
See also SATA 86
Arax, Mark 1956- ... 154
Arbasino, Alberto 1930- ... DLB 196
Arbatov, G. A.
See Arbatov, Georgi (Arkadevich)
Arbatov, Georgi (Arkadevich) 1923- ... 116
Arbatov, Yuri Arkadevich
See Arbatov, Georgi (Arkadevich)
Arbeiter, Jean S(onkin) 1937- ... 106
Arberry, A(rthur) J(ohn) 1905-1969 ... CANR-4
Earlier sketch in CA 1-4R
Arbib, Robert
See Arbib, Robert S(imeon), Jr.
Arbib, Robert S(imeon), Jr. 1915-1987 ... 33-36R
Obituary ... 123
Arbingast, Stanley A(lan) 1910- ... CANR-10
Earlier sketch in CA 17-20R
Arbogast, William F. 1908-1979 Obituary ... 89-92
Arbuckle, Dorothy Fry 1910-1982 Obituary ... 108
See also SATA-Obit 33
Arbuckle, Dugald S(inclair) 1912- ... 13-16R
Arbuckle, Robert D(ean) 1940- ... 61-64
Arbuckle, W(endell) S(herwood)
1911-1987 Obituary ... 122
Arbuckle, Wanda Rector 1910- ... 41-44R
Arbus, Amy 1954- ... 127
Arbus, Diane 1923-1971 ... 166
Arbuthnot, John 1667-1735 ... DLB 101
Arbuthnot, May Hill 1884-1969 ... 9-12R
See also SATA 2
Arbuthnott, Hugh (James) 1936- ... 125
Arbuzov, Alexei Nikolaevich 1908-1986 ... 69-72
Obituary ... 119
Arca, Julie Anne 1953- ... 111
Arcana, Judith 1943- ... 103
Arcand, Bernard ... 164
Arcand, Denys 1941- ... 133
Arce, Hector 1935-1980 ... 97-100
Arce, Julio G.
See Ulica, Jorge
Arceneaux, Jean
See Ancelet, Barry Jean
Arceneaux, Thelma Hoffmann Tyler ... AITN 1
Arch, E. L.
See Payes, Rachel C(osgrove)
ar C'halan, Reun
See Galand, Rene
Archambault, John ... 135
See also MAICYA
See also SATA 67
Archambault, Paul 1937- ... 81-84
Archbold, Rick 1950- ... 154
See also SATA 97
Archdeacon, Thomas J(ohn) 1942- ... 65-68
Archer, A. A.
See Joscelyn, Archie L.
Archer, Chalmers, Jr. 1938- ... 138
See also BW 2
Archer, Dennis
See Paine, Lauran (Bosworth)
Archer, Frank
See O'Connor, Richard
Archer, Fred 1915- ... CANR-7
Earlier sketch in CA 57-60
Archer, Fred C. 1916(?)-1974 Obituary ... 53-56
Archer, Gleason Leonard, Jr. 1916- ... 65-68
Archer, H(orace) Richard 1911-1978 ... CANR-6
Obituary ... 89-92
Earlier sketch in CA 13-16R
Archer, Herbert Winslow
See Mencken, H(enry) L(ouis)
Archer, Ian W. 1960- ... 135
Archer, Jane (a pseudonym) ... 113
Archer, Jeffrey (Howard) 1940- ... CANR-52
Earlier sketches in CA 77-80, CANR-22
Interview in ... CANR-22
See also AAYA 16
See also BEST 89:3
See also CLC 28
See also DAM POP
Archer, John H(all) 1914- ... 101
Archer, Jules 1915- ... CANR-69
Earlier sketches in CA 9-12R, CANR-6
See also CLC 12
See also SAAS 5
See also SATA 4, 85
Archer, Keith (Allan) 1955- ... 135
Archer, Lee
See Ellison, Harlan (Jay)
Archer, Leonie (Jane) 1955- ... 132
Archer, Marion Fuller 1917- ... 5-8R
See also SATA 11
Archer, Mildred 1911- ... 104
Archer, Myrtle (Lilly) 1926- ... 102
Archer, Nathan 1958- ... 154
Archer, Nuala 1955- ... CANR-59
Earlier sketch in CA 121
Archer, Peter Kingsley 1926- ... CANR-2
Earlier sketch in CA 5-8R
Archer, Ron
See White, Theodore Edwin
Archer, S. E.
See Soderberg, Percy Measday
Archer, Sellers G. 1908-1980 ... 17-20R
Obituary ... 134
Archer, Stanley (Louis) 1935- ... 145
Archer, Stephen H(unt) 1928- ... 17-20R
Archer, Stephen M(urphy) 1934- ... 105
Archer, W(illiam) G(eorge) 1907-1979 ... 57-60
Obituary ... 125
Archer, William 1856-1924 Brief entry ... 108
See also DLB 10
Archerd, Armand ... 115
Brief entry ... 110
Archerd, Army
See Archerd, Armand
Archer Houblon, Doreen (Lindsay) 1899-1977 .. 106
Archery, Helen
See Argers, Helen
Archibald, (Rupert) Douglas 1919- ... 101
Archibald, Douglas N(elson) 1933- ... 128
Brief entry ... 113
Archibald, James Montgomery
1920-1983 Obituary ... 110
Archibald, Joe
See Archibald, Joseph S(topford)
Archibald, John J. 1925- ... 5-8R
Archibald, Joseph S(topford) 1898-1986 .. CANR-5
Obituary ... 118
Earlier sketch in CA 9-12R
See also SATA 3
See also SATA-Obit 47
Archibald, Sandra O(rr) 1945- ... 113
Archibald, William 1924-1970 Obituary ... 29-32R
Archilochus c. 7th cent. B.C.- ... DLB 176
Archpoet, The c. 1130-(?) ... DLB 148
Arciniegas, German 1900- ... CANR-29
Earlier sketches in CA 61-64, CANR-10
See also HW
Arcone, Sonya 1925-1978 ... 21-24R
Obituary ... 77-80
Ard, Ben N(eal), Jr. 1922- ... CANR-12
Earlier sketch in CA 33-36R
Ard, William (Thomas) 1922-1960 ... CANR-72
Earlier sketch in CA 5-8R
Ardagh, John 1928- ... CANR-50
Earlier sketch in CA 25-28R
Ardai, Charles 1969- ... 136
See also SATA 85
Ardalan, Nader 1939- ... 69-72
Arden, Barbi
See Stoutenburg, Adrien (Pearl)
Arden, Gothard Everett 1905- ... CAP-1
Earlier sketch in CA 11-12
Arden, J. E. M.
See Conquest, (George) Robert (Acworth)
Arden, Jane ... 61-64
Arden, John 1930- ... CANR-67
Earlier sketches in CA 13-16R, CANR-31, 65
See also CAAS 4
See also CLC 6, 13, 15
See also DAM DRAM
See also DLB 13
See also MTCW 1
Arden, Leon 1932- ... 107
Arden, Noele
See Dambrauskas, Joan Arden
Arden, William
See Lynds, Dennis
Ardener, Edwin (William) 1927-1987 ... 5-8R
Obituary ... 123
Ardies, Tom 1931- ... CANR-59
Earlier sketch in CA 33-36R
Ardizzone, Edward (Jeffrey Irving) 1900-1979 ...
CANR-8
Obituary ... 89-92
Earlier sketch in CA 5-8R
See also CLR 3
See also DLB 160
See also MAICYA
See also SATA 1, 28
See also SATA-Obit 21
Ardizzone, Tony 1949- ... 85-88
Ardley, Gavin 1915- ... 129
Ardley, Neil (Richard) 1937- ... CANR-39
Earlier sketch in CA 115
See also SATA 43
Ardmore, Jane Kesner 1915- ... 5-8R
Ardoin, John (Louis) 1935- ... 57-60
Ardrey, Robert 1908-1980 ... 33-36R
Obituary ... 93-96
Arecco, Vera Lustig
See Lustig-Arecco, Vera
Areeda, Phillip E. 1930-1995 ... 21-24R
Obituary ... 150
Arehart-Treichel, Joan 1942- ... CANR-6
Earlier sketch in CA 57-60
See also SATA 22
Arellanes, Audrey Spencer 1920- ... 33-36R
Arellano, Diana Ramirez de
See Ramirez de Arellano, Diana (T. Clotilde)
Arellano, Juan Estevan 1947- ... DLB 122
Arellano, Rafael W(illiam) Ramirez de
See Ramirez de Arellano, Rafael W(illiam)
Arem, Joel E(dward) 1943- ... 89-92
Arena, Jay M(orris) 1909- ... 107
Arena, John I. 1929- ... CANR-20
Earlier sketch in CA 45-48
Arenas, Reinaldo 1943-1990 ... 128
Obituary ... 133
Brief entry ... 124
See also CLC 41
See also DAM MULT
See also DLB 145
See also HLC
See also HW
Arendt, Hannah 1906-1975 ... CANR-60
Obituary ... 61-64
Earlier sketches in CA 17-20R, CANR-26
See also CLC 66, 98
See also MTCW 1
Arenella, Roy 1939- ... SATA 14
Arens, Katherine (Marie) 1953- ... 164
Arens, Richard 1921-1984 ... 73-76
Obituary ... 112
Arens, William 1940- ... 89-92
Arensberg, Ann 1937- ... 114
Interview in ... 114
See also DLBY 82
Arensberg, Conrad Maynadier 1910-1997 ... 61-64
Obituary ... 156
Arenson, Gloria 1935- ... 118
Arent, Arthur 1904-1972 ... CAP-2
Obituary ... 33-36R
Earlier sketch in CA 23-24
Areskoug, Kaj 1933- ... 29-32R
Arestis, Philip 1941- ... 148
Aresty, Esther B(radford) ... 9-12R
Areta, Mavis
See Winder, Mavis Areta
Arevalo Martinez, Rafael 1884-1975 ... HW
Arey, James A(rthur) 1936-1988 ... 41-44R
Obituary ... 125
Arey, Leslie Brainerd 1891-1988 Obituary ... 125
Argan, Giulio Carlo 1909-1992 ... CANR-46
Obituary ... 139
Earlier sketch in CA 65-68
Argenti, John 1926- ... 115
Argenti, Philip 1891(?)-1974 Obituary ... 49-52
Argenzio, Victor 1902- ... 53-56
Argers, Helen ... 148
Argersinger, Peter H(ayes) 1944- Brief entry ... 112
Arghezi, Tudor 1880-1967 ... 167
See also Theodorescu, Ion N.
See also CLC 80
Argiri, Laura 1958- ... 163
Argiro, Larry 1909- ... 5-8R
Argo, Ellen
See Johnson, Ellen Argo
Argow, Waldemar 1916- ... 21-24R
Arguedas, Jose Maria 1911-1969 ... 89-92
See also CLC 10, 18
See also DLB 113
See also HW
Arguelles, Ivan (Wallace) 1939- ... 158
See also CAAS 24
Arguelles, Jose A(nthony) 1939- ... CANR-20
Earlier sketch in CA 45-48
Arguelles, Miriam Tarcov 1943- ... 45-48
Argueta, Manlio 1936- ... 131
See also CLC 31
See also DLB 145
See also HW
Argus
See Osusky, Stefan
and Phillips-Birt, Douglas Hextall Chedzey
Argyle, Aubrey William 1910- ... CAP-1
Earlier sketch in CA 17-18
Argyle, Michael 1925- ... CANR-50
Earlier sketches in CA 21-24R, CANR-9, 25
Argyris, Chris 1923- ... CANR-20
Earlier sketch in CA 1-4R, CANR-5
Arian, Alan (Asher) 1938- ... CANR-1
Earlier sketch in CA 49-52
Arian, Edward 1921- ... 33-36R
Arias, Ron(ald Francis) 1941- ... 131
See also DAM MULT
See also DLB 82
See also HLC
See also HW
Arias-Misson, Alain 1936- ... 77-80
Arias Sanchez, Oscar 1941- ... HW
Aricha, Amos 1933- ... 162
Arico, Santo L. 1938- ... 162
Aridas, Chris 1947- ... CANR-42
Earlier sketch in CA 112
Aridjis, Homero 1940- ... 131
See also HW
Ariel
See Moraes, Frank Robert
Aries, Philippe 1914-1984 ... 89-92
Obituary ... 112
Arieti, James Alexander 1948- ... 108
Arieti, Silvano 1914-1981 ... CANR-10
Obituary ... 104
Earlier sketch in CA 21-24R
Arimond, Carroll 1909-1979 Obituary ... 89-92
Aring, Charles D(air) 1904- ... 49-52
Arinze, Francis 1932- ... 138
Aris, Rutherford 1929- ... 117
Arishima Takeo 1878-1923 ... DLB 180
Arismendi, Rodney 1913-1989 Obituary ... 130
Aristide, Jean-Bertrand 1953- ... 147
Aristides
See Epstein, Joseph
Aristophanes 450B.C.-385B.C. ... DA
See also DAB
See also DAC
See also DAM DRAM, MST
See also DC 2
See also DLB 176
See also WLCS
Aristotle 384B.C.-322B.C. ... DA
See also DAB
See also DAC
See also DAM MST
See also DLB 176
See also WLCS
Ariyoshi, Sawako 1931-1984 ... 105
Obituary ... 113
See also DLB 182
Ariyoshi, Shoichiro 1939(?)-1979 Obituary ... 89-92
Arkadyev, N.
See Shevchenko, Arkady N(ikolaevich)
Arkell, Anthony John 1898-1980 ... 102
Obituary ... 97-100
Arkell, David 1913- ... 142
Arkhurst, Frederick S(iegfried) 1920- ... CANR-25
Earlier sketch in CA 29-32R
Arkhurst, Joyce Cooper 1921- ... 17-20R
Arkin, Alan (Wolf) 1934- ... 112
Brief entry ... 110
See also SATA 59
See also SATA-Brief 32
Arkin, David 1906- ... 21-24R
Arkin, Frieda 1917- ... CANR-11
Earlier sketch in CA 65-68
Arkin, Herbert 1906- ... 5-8R
Arkin, Joseph 1922- ... 5-8R
Arkin, Marcus 1926- ... 53-56
Arkley, Arthur J(ames) 1919- ... 112
Arkoun, Mohammed 1928- ... 156
Arkow, Phil 1947- ... 128
Arksey, Laura L(ee) 1936- ... 119
Arkush, Arthur Spencer 1925-1979 Obituary . 85-88
Arkush, Michael 1958- ... 148
Arland, Marcel 1899-1986 ... DLB 72
Arlandson, Leone 1917- ... 29-32R
Arlen, Leslie
See Nicole, Christopher (Robin)
Arlen, Michael 1895-1956 Brief entry ... 120
See also DLB 36, 77, 162
Arlen, Michael J. 1930- ... CANR-13
Earlier sketch in CA 61-64
Arleo, Joseph 1933- ... 29-32R
Arley, Catherine 1935- ... CANR-2
Earlier sketch in CA 45-48
Arley, Robert
See Jackson, Mike
Arlington, Taryn
See Palmer, Randy
Arliss, Leslie 1901-1987 Obituary ... 124
Arlott, (Leslie Thomas) John 1914-1991 ... 9-12R
Obituary ... 136
Arlotto, Anthony (Thomas) 1939- ... 33-36R
Arlow, Jacob A. 1912- ... 53-56
Arlt, Roberto (Godofredo Christophersen)
1900-1942 ... CANR-67
Brief entry ... 123
Earlier sketch in CA 131
See also DAM MULT
See also HLC
See also HW
See also TCLC 29
Arluke, Arnold 1947- ... 162
Armacost, Michael Hayden 1937- ... 101

Armah, Ayi Kwei 1939- ... CANR-64
  Earlier sketches in CA 61-64, CANR-21
  See also BLC 1
  See also BW 1
  See also CLC 5, 33
  See also DAM MULT, POET
  See also DLB 117
  See also MTCW 1
Armand, Louis 1905-1971 ... CAP-2
  Obituary ... 33-36R
  Earlier sketch in CA 29-32
Armand, Octavio Rafael 1946- ... 131
  See also HW
Armantrout, (Mary) Rae 1947- ... CANR-69
  Earlier sketch in CA 153
  See also CAAS 25
  See also DLB 193
Armatas, James P. 1931- ... 41-44R
Armatrading, Joan 1950- Brief entry ... 114
  See also CLC 17
Armbrister, Trevor 1933- ... 89-92
Armbruster, Carl J. 1929- ... 33-36R
Armbruster, F(ranz) O(wen) 1929- ... 49-52
Armbruster, Francis E(dward) 1923- ... 29-32R
Armbruster, Frank
  See Armbruster, Francis E(dward)
Armbruster, Maxim Ethan 1902- ... 1-4R
Armens, Sven 1921- ... 21-24R
Armentrout, Fred S(herman) 1946- ... 119
Armentrout, William W(infield) 1918- ... 33-36R
Armer, Alberta (Roller) 1904- ... 5-8R
  See also SATA 9
Armer, J(ohn) Michael 1937- ... 106
Armer, Laura (Adams) 1874-1963 ... 65-68
  See also MAICYA
  See also SATA 13
Armerding, Carl Edwin 1936- ... 104
Armerding, George D. 1899- ... 85-88
Armerding, Hudson Taylor 1918- ... CANR-11
  Earlier sketch in CA 21-24R
Armes, Roy (Philip) 1937- ... CANR-13
  Earlier sketch in CA 73-76
Armington, John Calvin 1923- ... 53-56
Armington, R(aymond) Q(uintin) 1907- ... 131
Armistead, John 1941- ... 150
Armistead, Samuel (Gordon) 1927- ... 53-56
Armitage, A(rthur) L(lewellyn)
  1916-1984 Obituary ... 112
Armitage, Angus 1902- ... CAP-1
  Earlier sketch in CA 13-14
Armitage, David 1943- ... 167
  See also SATA 99
  See also SATA-Brief 38
Armitage, E(dward) Liddall 1887- ... CAP-1
  Earlier sketch in CA 9-10
Armitage, Frank
  See Carpenter, John (Howard)
Armitage, G(ary) E(dric) 1956- ... 121
Armitage, Merle 1893-1975 Obituary ... 61-64
Armitage, Michael 1930- ... CANR-41
  Earlier sketch in CA 117
Armitage, Ronda (Jacqueline) 1943- ... CANR-47
  Earlier sketch in CA 121
  See also SATA 47, 99
  See also SATA-Brief 38
Armitage, Shelley S(ue) 1947- ... CANR-47
  Earlier sketch in CA 121
Armitage, Simon 1963- ... 134
Armory, Thomas 1691(?)-1788 ... DLB 39
Armour, John
  See Paine, Lauran (Bosworth)
Armour, Leslie 1931- ... 110
Armour, Lloyd R. 1922- ... 29-32R
Armour, Peter 1940- ... CANR-59
  Earlier sketch in CA 128
Armour, Richard (Willard) 1906-1989 ... CANR-32
  Obituary ... 128
  Earlier sketches in CA 1-4R, CANR-4
  See also SATA 14
  See also SATA-Obit 61
Armour, Rollin Stely 1929- ... 33-36R
Arms, George (Warren) 1912- ... 5-8R
Arms, Johnson
  See Halliwell, David (William)
Arms, Suzanne 1944- ... 57-60
Armstrong, (Walter) Alan 1936- ... 73-76
Armstrong, Alexandra 1939- ... 142
Armstrong, Ann Seidel 1917- ... 9-12R
Armstrong, Anne(tte) 1924- ... 13-16R
Armstrong, Anthony
  See Willis, (George) Anthony Armstrong
Armstrong, Anthony C.
  See Armstrong, Christopher J(ohn) R(ichard)
Armstrong, (Grace) April (Oursler) 1926- ... 89-92
Armstrong, Arthur Hilary 1909-1997 ... 69-72
  Obituary ... 162
Armstrong, Benjamin Leighton 1923- ... 93-96
Armstrong, Brian G(ary) 1936- ... 69-72
Armstrong, Charles B. 1923-1985 Obituary ... 115
Armstrong, Charlotte 1905-1969 ... CANR-71
  Obituary ... 25-28R
  Earlier sketches in CA 1-4R, CANR-3
Armstrong, Christopher J(ohn) R(ichard)
  1935- ... 69-72
Armstrong, Claude Blakely
  1889-1982 Obituary ... 108
Armstrong, D(avid) M(alet) 1926- ... CANR-31
  Earlier sketches in CA 25-28R, CANR-11
Armstrong, (James) David 1945- ... 107
Armstrong, David M(ichael) 1944- ... 57-60
Armstrong, Diana 1943- ... 107
Armstrong, Douglas Albert 1920- ... 9-12R
Armstrong, Edward Allworthy 1900-1978 ... CANR-4
  Earlier sketch in CA 5-8R
Armstrong, (Annette) Elizabeth 1917- ... 25-28R
Armstrong, F. W.
  See Wright, T. M.
Armstrong, Frederick H(enry) 1926- ... 33-36R
Armstrong, Garner Ted 1929(?)- Brief entry ... 113
Armstrong, George D. 1927- ... SATA 10
Armstrong, Gerry (Breen) 1929- ... 13-16R
  See also SATA 10
Armstrong, Gregory T(imon) 1933- ... 9-12R
Armstrong, Hamilton Fish 1893-1973 ... 93-96
  Obituary ... 41-44R
Armstrong, Henry
  See Jackson, Henry
Armstrong, Henry H.
  See Arvay, Harry
Armstrong, Herbert W. 1892-1986 ... 142
  Obituary ... 118
  Brief entry ... 116
Armstrong, J(on) Scott 1937- ... CANR-1
  Earlier sketch in CA 45-48
Armstrong, (A.) James 1924- ... 29-32R
Armstrong, Jeannette (C.) 1948- ... 149
  See also DAC
  See also NNAL
  See also SATA 102
Armstrong, Jennifer 1961- ... CANR-67
  Earlier sketch in CA 145
  See also SAAS 24
  See also SATA 77
Armstrong, Joe C. W.
  See Armstrong, Joseph Charles Woodland
Armstrong, John A(lexander, Jr.) 1922- ... CANR-3
  Earlier sketch in CA 1-4R
Armstrong, John Borden 1926- ... 33-36R
Armstrong, John Byron 1917-1976 ... 5-8R
  Obituary ... 65-68
Armstrong, Joseph Charles Woodland 1934- ...
  CANR-57
  Earlier sketch in CA 127
Armstrong, Joseph Gravitt 1943- ... 101
Armstrong, Judith Mary 1935- ... 102
Armstrong, Karen 1945(?)- ... 147
Armstrong, Keith F(rancis) W(hitfield) 1950- ... 29-32R
Armstrong, Leslie 1940- ... 124
Armstrong, (Daniel) Louis
  1900-1971 Obituary ... 29-32R
Armstrong, Louise ... 117
  Brief entry ... 111
  See also SATA 43
  See also SATA-Brief 33
Armstrong, Marjorie Moore 1912- ... 89-92
Armstrong, Martin (Donisthorpe)
  1882-1974 Obituary ... 49-52
  See also DLB 197
Armstrong, Mary (Elizabeth) Willems 1957- ... 134
Armstrong, Neil (Alden) 1930- ... 155
Armstrong, O(rland) K(ay) 1893-1987 ... 93-96
  Obituary ... 122
Armstrong, (Raymond) Paul 1912- ... 37-40R
Armstrong, Paul B(radford) 1949- ... 112
Armstrong, Richard 1903- ... CANR-70
  Earlier sketch in CA 77-80
  See also DLB 160
  See also SATA 11
Armstrong, Richard B(yron) 1956- ... 134
Armstrong, Richard G. 1932- ... 73-76
Armstrong, Robert H(oward) 1936- ... 108
Armstrong, Robert L(aurence) 1926- ... 29-32R
Armstrong, Robert Plant 1919-1984 ... 41-44R
  Obituary ... 113
Armstrong, Roger D. 1939- ... 17-20R
Armstrong, Ruth Gallup 1891- ... CAP-1
  Earlier sketch in CA 9-10
Armstrong, (Russell) Scott 1945- ... 108
  Interview in ... 108
Armstrong, Terence Ian Fytton 1912-1970 ... CAP-2
  Obituary ... 29-32R
  Earlier sketch in CA 17-18
Armstrong, Thomas 1899-1978 ... 5-8R
  Obituary ... 103
Armstrong, Tilly 1927- ... CANR-47
  Earlier sketches in CA 107, CANR-23
Armstrong, Wallace Edwin
  1896-1980 Obituary ... 97-100
Armstrong, William A(lexander) 1912- ... 13-16R
Armstrong, William A(rthur) 1915- ... 17-20R
Armstrong, William H(oward) 1914- ... CANR-69
  Earlier sketches in CA 17-20R, CANR-9
  See also AAYA 18
  See also AITN 1
  See also CLR 1
  See also JRDA
  See also MAICYA
  See also SAAS 7
  See also SATA 4
Armstrong, William M(artin) 1919- ... 49-52
Armstrong-Jones, Antony (Charles Robert) 1930- ...
  CANR-43
  Earlier sketch in CA 118
Armstrong Jones, Tony
  See Armstrong-Jones, Antony (Charles Robert)
Armytage, Walter Harry Green 1915- ... 9-12R
Arnade, Charles W(olfgang) 1927- ... 33-36R
Arnandez, Richard 1912- ... CANR-6
  Earlier sketch in CA 13-16R
Arnason, David 1940- ... 114
Arnason, Eleanor (Atwood) 1942- ... 156
Arnason, H(jorvardur) H(arvard) 1909-1986 ...
  CANR-13
  Obituary ... 119
  Earlier sketch in CA 61-64
Arnau, Frank
  See Schmitt, Heinrich
Arnaud, Claude 1955- ... 143
Arnaud, Georges
  See Girard, Henri Georges Charles Achille
Arnaz, Desi
  See Arnaz y de Acha, Desiderio Alberto III
Arnaz y de Acha, Desiderio Alberto III
  1917(?)-1986 Obituary ... 121
  Brief entry ... 114
Arncliffe, Andrew
  See Walker, Peter N.
Arndt, Elise 1943- ... 116
Arndt, Ernst H(einrich) D(aniel) 1899- ... CAP-2
  Earlier sketch in CA 23-24
Arndt, Ernst Moritz 1769-1860 ... DLB 90
Arndt, H(einz) W(olfgang) 1915- ... CANR-29
  Earlier sketches in CA 21-24R, CANR-10
Arndt, Karl John Richard 1903- ... CANR-23
  Earlier sketches in CA 17-20R, CANR-7
Arndt, Ursula (Martha H.) ... SATA 56
  See also SATA-Brief 39
Arndt, Walter W(erner) 1916- ... CANR-5
  Earlier sketch in CA 13-16R
Arnebeck, Bob 1947- ... 108
Arneson, D(on) J(on) 1935- ... 106
  See also SATA 37
Arnett, Caroline
  See Cole, Lois Dwight
Arnett, Carroll 1927- ... CANR-11
  Earlier sketch in CA 21-24R
Arnett, Harold E(dward) 1931- ... CANR-8
  Earlier sketch in CA 21-24R
Arnett, Peter (Gregg) 1934- ... 152
Arnett, Ronald C. 1952- ... 144
Arnett, Ross H(arold), Jr. 1919- ... CANR-17
  Earlier sketches in CA 49-52, CANR-2
Arnette, Robert
  See Silverberg, Robert
Arney, James
  See Russell, Martin
Arney, William Ray 1950- ... CANR-43
  Earlier sketch in CA 110
Arnez, Nancy Levi 1928- ... 29-32R
Arnheim, Daniel D(avid) 1930- ... CANR-5
  Earlier sketch in CA 9-12R
Arnheim, Rudolf 1904- ... CANR-69
  Earlier sketches in CA 1-4R, CANR-3
Arnim, Achim von (Ludwig Joachim von Arnim)
  1781-1831 ... DLB 90
  See also SSC 29
Arnim, Bettina von 1785-1859 ... DLB 90
Arno, Enrico 1913-1981 ... SATA 43
  See also SATA-Obit 28
Arno, Peter 1904-1968 ... 73-76
  Obituary ... 25-28R
Arnold, A(lbert) James, (Jr.) 1939- ... 132
Arnold, Adlai F(ranklin) 1914- ... 33-36R
Arnold, Alan 1922- ... 5-8R
Arnold, Alvin L(incoln) 1929- ... 93-96
Arnold, Anthony 1928- ... 111
Arnold, Armin H. 1931- ... CANR-18
  Earlier sketches in CA 9-12R, CANR-3
Arnold, Arnold (Ferdinand) 1921- ... CANR-44
  Earlier sketches in CA 17-20R, CANR-10, 27
Arnold, Benjamin 1943- ... 144
Arnold, Bob 1952- ... CANR-21
  Earlier sketch in CA 105
  See also CAAS 25
Arnold, Bruce 1936- ... 93-96
Arnold, Carl
  See Raknes, Ola
Arnold, Caroline 1944- ... CANR-24
  Earlier sketch in CA 107
  See also SAAS 23
  See also SATA 36, 85
  See also SATA-Brief 34
Arnold, Carroll C(lyde) 1912- Brief entry ... 116
Arnold, Catharine 1959- ... 125
Arnold, Charles Harvey 1920- ... 65-68
Arnold, Charlotte E(lizabeth) Cramer ... 57-60
Arnold, Corliss Richard 1926- ... 49-52
Arnold, Denis Midgley 1926-1986 ... CANR-2
  Obituary ... 119
  Earlier sketch in CA 5-8R
Arnold, Duane W(ade-) H(ampton) 1953- ... 127
Arnold, Edmund C(larence) 1913- ... CANR-3
  Earlier sketch in CA 1-4R
Arnold, Edwin 1832-1904 ... DLB 35
Arnold, Edwin L(ester Linden) 1857(?)-1935 ... 154
  Brief entry ... 109
  See also DLB 178
Arnold, Edwin T. 1947- ... 134
Arnold, Eleanor 1929- ... 143
Arnold, Elliott 1912-1980 ... CANR-65
  Obituary ... 97-100
  Earlier sketches in CA 17-20R, CANR-24
  See also SATA 5
  See also SATA-Obit 22
Arnold, Emily 1939- ... 109
  See also McCully, Emily Arnold
  See also MAICYA
  See also SATA 50, 76
Arnold, Emmy (von Hollander) 1884-1980 ... CANR-9
  Earlier sketch in CA 21-24R
Arnold, Eve 1913- ... CANR-52
  Earlier sketches in CA 112, CANR-31
Arnold, Francena H(arriet Long) 1888- ... CAP-1
  Earlier sketch in CA 17-18
Arnold, G. L.
  See Lichtheim, George
Arnold, Gary Howard 1942- Brief entry ... 117
Arnold, Gladys (M.) 1905- ... 128
Arnold, Guy 1932- ... CANR-53
  Earlier sketches in CA 25-28R, CANR-11, 28
Arnold, H(arry) J(ohn) P(hilip) 1932- ... CANR-2
  Earlier sketch in CA 5-8R
Arnold, Heini
  See Arnold, Johann Heinrich
Arnold, Herbert 1935- ... 37-40R
Arnold, Janet 1932- ... 93-96
Arnold, Janis ... 160
Arnold, Johann Heinrich 1913-1982 ... 122
  Obituary ... 111
Arnold, John D(avid) 1933- ... 111
Arnold, Joseph H.
  See Hayes, Joseph
Arnold, June (Davis) 1926-1982 ... CANR-58
  Obituary ... 133
  Earlier sketch in CA 21-24R
Arnold, Katya 1947- ... SATA 82
Arnold, Kenneth L. 1957- ... 148
Arnold, L. J.
  See Cameron, Lou
Arnold, Leslie
  See Lazarus, A(rnold) L(eslie)
Arnold, Lloyd R. 1906-1970 ... CAP-2
  Earlier sketch in CA 25-28
Arnold, Lois B(arber) ... 107
Arnold, Madelyn M. a pseudonym 1948- ... 129
Arnold, Magda B(londiau) 1903- ... 5-8R
Arnold, Margot
  See Cook, Petronelle Marguerite Mary
Arnold, Marilyn 1935- ... 122
Arnold, Marsha Diane 1948- ... 158
  See also SATA 93
Arnold, Mary Ann 1918- ... 65-68
Arnold, Matthew 1822-1888 ... CDBLB 1832-1890
  See also DA
  See also DAB
  See also DAC
  See also DAM MST, POET
  See also DLB 32, 57
  See also PC 5
  See also WLC
Arnold, Milo Lawrence 1903- ... 57-60
Arnold, Olga Moore 1900-1981 Obituary ... 102
Arnold, Oren 1900- ... CANR-2
  Earlier sketch in CA 5-8R
  See also SATA 4
Arnold, Pauline 1894-1974 ... CANR-2
  Earlier sketch in CA 1-4R
Arnold, Peter 1931- ... 123
Arnold, Peter 1943- ... CANR-1
  Earlier sketch in CA 49-52
Arnold, R. Douglas 1950- ... 101
Arnold, Ray Henry 1895- ... 5-8R
Arnold, Richard 1912- ... CANR-3
  Earlier sketch in CA 9-12R
Arnold, Richard E(ugene) 1908- ... CAP-2
  Earlier sketch in CA 33-36
Arnold, Richard K(lein) 1923- ... 69-72
Arnold, Robert E(vans) 1932- ... 49-52
Arnold, Rollo (Davis) 1926- ... 21-24R
Arnold, Ron 1937- ... CANR-25
  Earlier sketch in CA 108
Arnold, Roseanne 1952- ... 139
  See also BEST 90:1
Arnold, Stephen H. 1942- ... 117
Arnold, Susan (Riser) 1951- ... SATA 58
Arnold, Tedd 1949- ... 137
  See also SATA 69
Arnold, Terrell E. 1925- ... 130
Arnold, Thomas 1795-1842 ... DLB 55
Arnold, Thurman Wesley 1891-1969 ... CAP-1
  Earlier sketch in CA 13-16
Arnold, William Robert 1933- ... 29-32R
Arnold, William Van 1941- ... 110
Arnold-Baker, Charles 1918- ... 5-8R
Arnold-Forster, Mark 1920-1981 ... 65-68
  Obituary ... 105
Arnoldy, Julie
  See Bischoff, Julia Bristol
Arnosky, James Edward 1946- ... CANR-32
  Earlier sketches in CA 69-72, CANR-12
  See also Arnosky, Jim
  See also CLR 15
  See also SATA 22
Arnosky, Jim
  See Arnosky, James Edward
  See also MAICYA
  See also SATA 70
Arnothy, Christine 1930- ... CANR-10
  Earlier sketch in CA 65-68
Arnott, (Margaret) Anne 1916- ... CANR-13
  Earlier sketch in CA 73-76
Arnott, J(ames) F(ullarton) 1914-1982 Obituary ... 108
Arnott, Kathleen 1914- ... 57-60
  See also SATA 20
Arnott, Peter D(ouglas) 1931- ... CANR-3
  Earlier sketch in CA 1-4R
Arnoux, Alexandre (Paul)
  1884-1973 Obituary ... 37-40R
Arnov, Boris, Jr. 1926- ... CANR-3
  Earlier sketch in CA 1-4R
  See also SATA 12
Arnove, Robert Fred 1937- ... 111
Arnow, Harriette (Louisa) Simpson 1908-1986 ...
  CANR-14
  Obituary ... 118
  Earlier sketch in CA 9-12R
  See also CLC 2, 7, 18
  See also DLB 6
  See also MTCW 1
  See also SATA 42
  See also SATA-Obit 47
Arnow, L(eslie) Earle 1909- ... 69-72
Arnsteen, Katy Keck 1934- ... 136
  See also SATA 68
Arnstein, Flora Jacobi 1885- ... 5-8R
Arnstein, Helene S(olomon) 1915- ... 57-60
  See also SATA 12
Arnstein, Walter L(eonard) 1930- ... CANR-46
  Earlier sketches in CA 13-16R, CANR-5, 23
Arntson, Herbert E(dward) 1911- ... 17-20R
  See also SATA 12
Arny, Mary (Travis) 1909- ... 61-64

Arny, Thomas Travis 1940- . . . 85-88
Arom, Simha 1930- . . . 139
Aron, Jean-Paul 1925(?)-1988 Obituary . . . 126
Aron, Michael 1946- . . . 146
Aron, Raymond (Claude Ferdinand) 1905-1983 . . . CANR-2
Obituary . . . 111
Earlier sketch in CA 49-52
Aron, Robert 1898-1975 . . . 93-96
Obituary . . . 57-60
Arond, Miriam 1955- . . . 127
Aroner, Miriam . . . 149
See also SATA 82
Aronfreed, Justin 1930- . . . 25-28R
Aronin, Ben 1904-1980 Obituary . . . 102
See also SATA-Obit 25
Aronoff, Craig E(llis) 1951- . . . 145
Aronoff, Myron J(oel) 1940- . . . CANR-24
Earlier sketch in CA 107
Aronowitz, Stanley 1933- . . . 131
Arons, Arnold B. 1916- . . . 162
Aronson, Alex 1912- . . . 45-48
Aronson, Alvin 1928- . . . 25-28R
Aronson, David 1894-1988 Obituary . . . 126
Aronson, Elliot 1932- . . . CANR-12
Earlier sketch in CA 33-36R
Aronson, Harvey 1929- . . . 85-88
Aronson, I(rwin) Michael 1942- . . . 137
Aronson, J(ay) Richard 1937- . . . CANR-34
Earlier sketch in CA 81-84
Aronson, James (Allan) 1915-1988 . . . 29-32R
Obituary . . . 126
Aronson, Joseph 1898- . . . CAP-1
Earlier sketch in CA 19-20
Aronson, Marvin L. 1925- . . . 41-44R
Aronson, Ronald 1938- . . . 133
Aronson, Shlomo 1936- . . . 73-76
Aronson, Steven M. L. . . . 153
Aronson, Theo 1930- . . . CANR-25
Earlier sketches in CA 9-12R, CANR-4
Aronson, Virginia 1954- . . . CANR-25
Earlier sketch in CA 108
Arora, Shirley (Lease) 1930- . . . 1-4R
See also SATA 2
Aros, Andrew A(lexandre) 1944- . . . 97-100
Arout, Gabriel 1909-1982 Obituary . . . 106
Aroutunova, Bayara 1926- . . . 152
Arozarena, Marcelino 1912- . . . HW
Arp, Bill
See Smith, Charles Henry
Arp, Hans
See Arp, Jean
Arp, Jean 1887-1966 . . . CANR-42
Obituary . . . 25-28R
Earlier sketch in CA 81-84
See also CLC 5
Arpad, Joseph J(ohn) 1937- . . . 49-52
Arpel, Adrien
See Newman, Adrien Ann
Arpino, Giovanni 1927-1987 . . . DLB 177
Arps, Louisa Ward 1901-1986 Obituary . . . 118
Arquette, Cliff(ord) 1905-1974 Obituary . . . 53-56
Arrabal
See Arrabal, Fernando
Arrabal, Fernando 1932- . . . CANR-15
Earlier sketch in CA 9-12R
See also CLC 2, 9, 18, 58
Arre, Helen
See Ross, Zola Helen
Arre, John
See Holt, John (Robert)
Arreola, Juan Jose 1918- . . . 131
Brief entry . . . 113
See also DAM MULT
See also DLB 113
See also HLC
See also HW
Arrian c. 89-c. 155 . . . DLB 176
Arrick, Fran
See Gaberman, Judie Angell
See also CLC 30
Arriey, Richmond
See Delaney, Samuel R(ay, Jr.)
Arrighi, Mel 1933-1986 . . . CANR-18
Obituary . . . 120
Earlier sketches in CA 49-52, CANR-1
Arrington, Leonard J(ames) 1917- . . . CANR-30
Earlier sketches in CA 17-20R, CANR-9
Arrington, Stephen L(ee) 1948- . . . 163
See also SATA 97
Arriola, Gus 1917- . . . 129
Arrow, Kenneth J(oseph) 1921- . . . CANR-13
Earlier sketch in CA 13-16R
Arroway, Francis M.
See Rosmond, Babette
Arrowood, (McKendrick Lee) Clinton 1939- . . . SATA 19
Arrowsmith, Marvin Lawrence
1913-1995 Obituary . . . 150
Brief entry . . . 116
Arrowsmith, Pat 1930- . . . 101
See also Barton, Pat
Arrowsmith, William Ayres 1924-1992 . . . CANR-4
Obituary . . . 136
Earlier sketch in CA 9-12R
Arroyo, Antonio M. Stevens
See Stevens-Arroyo, Antonio M.
Arroyo, Stephen J(oseph) 1946- . . . 61-64
Arrufat, Anton B. 1935- . . . HW
Art, Robert (Jeffrey) 1942- . . . 65-68
Artaud, Antonin (Marie Joseph) 1896-1948 . . . 149
Brief entry . . . 104
See also DAM DRAM
See also TCLC 3, 36
Arteaga, Alfred 1950- . . . 163
Arteaga, Lucio 1924- . . . 49-52
Arteaga, William De
See De Arteaga, William
Artel, Jorge 1909- . . . HW
Artell, Mike 1948- . . . 155
See also SATA 89
Arterburn, Stephen (Forrest) 1953- . . . 147
Artes, Dorothy Beecher 1919- . . . 57-60
Arther, Richard O. 1928- . . . 17-20R
Arthos, John 1908- . . . 9-12R
Arthur, Alan
See Edmonds, Arthur Denis
Arthur, Anthony 1937- . . . 119
Arthur, Art(hur) 1911-1985 Obituary . . . 116
Arthur, Burt
See Shappiro, Herbert (Arthur)
Arthur, Don(ald) R(amsay) 1917-1984 . . . 29-32R
Obituary . . . 114
Arthur, Elizabeth 1953- . . . CANR-21
Earlier sketch in CA 105
Arthur, Eric (Ross) 1898-1982 Obituary . . . 112
Arthur, Frank
See Ebert, Arthur Frank
Arthur, George
See Phillips, Bluebell Stewart
Arthur, Gladys
See Osborne, Dorothy (Gladys) Yeo
Arthur, Herbert
See Shappiro, Herbert (Arthur)
Arthur, Hugh
See Christie-Murray, David (Hugh Arthur)
Arthur, Kay L(ee) 1933- . . . CANR-42
Earlier sketch in CA 118
Arthur, Lee . . . 122
Arthur, Martin (Forest) 1951- . . . 116
Arthur, Max 1939- . . . 121
Arthur, Percy E. 1910- . . . CAP-1
Earlier sketch in CA 9-10
Arthur, Robert
See Feder, Robert Arthur
Arthur, Ruth M(abel) 1905-1979 . . . CANR-4
Obituary . . . 85-88
Earlier sketch in CA 9-12R
See also CLC 12
See also SATA 7, 26
Arthur, Thomas H. 1937- . . . 122
Arthur, Tiffany
See Pelton, Robert W(ayne)
Arthur, Timothy Shay 1809-1885 . . . DLB 3, 42, 79
See also DLBD 13
Arthur, Tom
See Arthur, Thomas H.
Arthur, William
See Neubauer, William Arthur
Arthurs, Peter 1933- . . . 106
Artin, Thomas 1938- Brief entry . . . 116
Artin, Tom
See Artin, Thomas
Artis, Vicki Kimmel 1945- . . . 53-56
See also SATA 12
Artmann, H(ans) C(arl) 1921- . . . 101
Artobolevsky, Ivan I. 1905-1977 Obituary . . . 73-76
Artom, Guido 1906-1982 . . . CANR-12
Earlier sketch in CA 29-32R
Arts, Herwig (W. J.) 1935- . . . CANR-32
Earlier sketch in CA 113
Artsybashev, Mikhail (Petrovich) 1878-1927 . . TCLC 31
Artus, Nancy
See Dargel, Nancy
Artz, Frederick B(inkerd) 1894-1983 . . . CANR-18
Earlier sketch in CA 1-4R
Artzybasheff, Boris (Miklailovich) 1899-1965 . . SATA 14
Aruego, Ariane
See Dewey, Ariane
Aruego, Jose (Espiritu) 1932- . . . CANR-42
Earlier sketch in CA 37-40R
See also CLR 5
See also MAICYA
See also SATA 6, 68
Arundale, G. S.
See Arundale, George S(ydney)
Arundale, George S(ydney) 1878-1945 Brief entry . . . 119
Arundel, Honor (Morfydd) 1919-1973 . . . CAP-2
Obituary . . . 41-44R
Earlier sketch in CA 21-22
See also CLC 17
See also CLR 35
See also SATA 4
See also SATA-Obit 24
Arundel, Jocelyn
See Alexander, Jocelyn Anne Arundel
Arundel, Russell M. 1903-1978 Obituary . . . 77-80
Arundell, Dennis Drew 1898-1988 Obituary . . . 127
Aruri, Naseer H. . . . 161
Arvay, Harry 1925- . . . CANR-8
Earlier sketch in CA 57-60
Arvay, Stephen 1937- . . . 114
Arvensis, Alauda
See Furdyna, Anna M.
Arvey, Michael 1948- . . . 147
See also SATA 79
Arvey, Verna 1910- . . . 157
Arvill, Robert
See Boote, Robert Edward
Arvin, Kay K(rehbiel) 1922- . . . 65-68
Arvin, (Frederic) Newton, (Jr.)
1900-1963 Obituary . . . 116
See also DLB 103
Arvio, Raymond Paavo 1930-1986 . . . 77-80
Obituary . . . 120
Ary, Donald E(ugene) 1930- . . . 41-44R
Ary, Sheila M(ary Littleboy) 1929- . . . 13-16R
Arya, Usharbudh 1934- . . . 105
Arzhak, Nikolai
See Daniel, Yuli (Markovich)
Arzner, Dorothy 1897-1979 . . . CLC 98
Arzoomanian, Raffi
See Arzoomanian, Ralph Sarkis
Arzoomanian, Ralph Sarkis 1937- . . . 118
Arzt, Max 1897-1975 Obituary . . . 61-64
Asals, Frederick (John) 1935- . . . 124
Asamani, Joseph Owusu 1934- . . . 49-52
Asante, Molefi K(ete) 1942- . . . CANR-21
Earlier sketch in CA 33-36R
See also BW 2
Asare, Bediako
See Konadu, S(amuel) A(sare)
Asare, Meshack (Yaw) 1945- . . . CANR-52
Earlier sketches in CA 61-64, CANR-11
See also SATA 86
Asaro, Catherine (Ann) 1955- . . . 161
See also SATA 101
Asbell, Bernard 1923- . . . CANR-50
Earlier sketches in CA 45-48, CANR-1, 25
Asbjoernsen, Peter Christen 1812-1885 . . . MAICYA
See also SATA 15
Asbury, Herbert 1891-1963 Obituary . . . 116
Ascani, Sparky (Wilson) 1922- . . . 111
Ascanio, Pam 1950- . . . 142
Asch, Frank 1946- . . . 41-44R
See also SATA 5, 66, 102
Asch, Nathan 1902-1964 . . . 109
See also DLB 4, 28
Asch, Peter 1937-1990 . . . 133
Brief entry . . . 114
Asch, Sholem 1880-1957 Brief entry . . . 105
See also TCLC 3
Aschan, Ulf 1937- . . . 138
Ascheim, Skip 1943- . . . 53-56
Ascher, Abraham 1928- . . . 81-84
Ascher, Barbara Lazear 1946(?)- . . . 138
Brief entry . . . 130
Interview in . . . 138
Ascher, Carol 1941- . . . CANR-29
Earlier sketch in CA 105
Ascher, Kate (J.) 1958- . . . 128
Ascher, Maria Louise . . . 140
Ascher, Sheila . . . CANR-23
Earlier sketch in CA 105
Ascher/Straus
See Ascher, Sheila
and Straus, Dennis
Ascher, William (Louis) 1947- . . . 114
Ascherson, (Charles) Neal 1932- . . . CANR-57
Earlier sketch in CA 13-16R
Aschmann, Alberta 1921- . . . CANR-7
Earlier sketch in CA 13-16R
Aschmann, Helen Tann . . . 13-16R
Ascoli, Max 1898-1978 Obituary . . . 77-80
Ash, Anthony Lee 1931- . . . CANR-3
Earlier sketch in CA 49-52
Ash, Bernard 1910- . . . CAP-1
Earlier sketch in CA 19-20
Ash, Brian 1936- Brief entry . . . 114
Ash, Christopher (Edward) 1914- . . . 1-4R
Ash, Constance (Lee) 1950- . . . 154
Ash, David W(ilfred) 1923- . . . 9-12R
Ash, Douglas 1914- . . . CANR-2
Earlier sketch in CA 5-8R
Ash, Fenton
See Atkins, Francis Henry
Ash, Jennifer 1964- . . . 149
Ash, John 1948- . . . 127
Brief entry . . . 123
Interview in . . . 127
See also DLB 40
Ash, Jutta 1942- . . . SATA 38
Ash, Lee (Michael) 1917- . . . 110
Ash, Mary Kay (Wagner) . . . 112
Ash, Maurice Anthony 1917- . . . 101
Ash, Rene Lee 1939- . . . 57-60
Ash, Roberta
See Garner, Roberta
Ash, Sarah Leeds 1904- . . . CAP-1
Earlier sketch in CA 9-10
Ash, Shalom
See Asch, Sholem
Ash, Stephen V. 1948- . . . 153
Ash, Timothy Garton
See Garton Ash, Timothy
Ash, William Franklin 1917- . . . CANR-18
Earlier sketches in CA 5-8R, CANR-2
Ashabranner, Brent (Kenneth) 1921- . . . CANR-57
Earlier sketches in CA 5-8R, CANR-10, 27
See also AAYA 6
See also CLR 28
See also JRDA
See also MAICYA
See also SAAS 14
See also SATA 1, 67
Ashabranner, Melissa 1950- . . . 134
Ashall, Frank 1957- . . . 146
Ashbaugh, Nancy 1929- . . . 73-76
Ashbee, Paul 1918- . . . 93-96
Ashbery, John (Lawrence) 1927- . . . CANR-66
Earlier sketches in CA 5-8R, CANR-9, 37
Interview in . . . CANR-9
See also CLC 2, 3, 4, 6, 9, 13, 15, 25, 41, 77
See also DAM POET
See also DLB 5, 165
See also DLBY 81
See also MTCW 1
Ashbolt, Allan Campbell 1921- . . . 104
Ashbridge, Elizabeth 1713-1755 . . . DLB 200
Ashbrook, James B(arbour) 1925- . . . CANR-57
Earlier sketches in CA 37-40R, CANR-14, 31
Ashbrook, Joseph 1918-1980 . . . 122
Obituary . . . 117
Ashbrook, William (Sinclair) 1922- . . . 29-32R
Ashburne, Jim G. 1912- . . . 1-4R
Ashburnham, Bertram Lord 1797-1878 . . . DLB 184
Ashby, Carter
See Paine, Lauran (Bosworth)
Ashby, Cliff 1919- . . . 25-28R
See also CAAS 6
Ashby, Eric 1904-1992 . . . 61-64
Obituary . . . 139
Ashby, Gwynneth 1922- . . . 25-28R
See also SATA 44
Ashby, LaVerne 1922- . . . 21-24R
Ashby, (Darrel) LeRoy 1938- . . . 33-36R
Ashby, Lloyd W. 1905- . . . 89-92
Ashby, Lynn 1938- . . . 127
Ashby, Neal 1924- . . . 89-92
Ashby, Nora
See Africano, Lillian
Ashby, Philip Harrison 1916- . . . 17-20R
Ashcraft, Allan Coleman 1928- . . . 9-12R
Ashcraft, Laura 1945- . . . 107
Ashcraft, Laurie
See Ashcraft, Laura
Ashcraft, Morris 1922- . . . 45-48
Ashcroft, John (David) 1942- . . . 112
Ashdown, Clifford
See Freeman, R(ichard) Austin
Ashdown, Dulcie M(argaret) 1946- . . . 122
Brief entry . . . 112
Ashdown, Paul G(eorge) 1944- . . . 119
Ashe, Arthur (Robert, Jr.) 1943-1993 . . . CANR-42
Earlier sketches in CA 65-68, CANR-18, 35
See also BW 2
See also SATA 65
See also SATA-Obit 87
Ashe, Douglas
See Bardin, John Franklin
Ashe, Geoffrey (Thomas) 1923- . . . CANR-57
Earlier sketches in CA 5-8R, CANR-12, 31
See also SATA 17
Ashe, Gerald C. 1924(?)-1984 Obituary . . . 112
Ashe, Gordon
See Creasey, John
Ashe, Mary Ann
See Lewis, Mary (Christianna)
Ashe, Penelope
See Greene, Robert W.
and Karman, Mal
and Young, Billie
Ashe, Rebecca
See Meluch, R(ebecca) M.
Asheim, Lester E(ugene) 1914-1997 . . . 17-20R
Obituary . . . 159
Ashenfelter, David L. 1948- . . . 108
Ashenfelter, Orley C(lark) 1942- . . . CANR-8
Earlier sketch in CA 61-64
Asher, Don 1926- . . . 73-76
Asher, Harry (Maurice Felix) 1909- . . . CANR-2
Earlier sketch in CA 5-8R
Asher, Jane 1946- . . . 133
Asher, John A(lexander) 1921- . . . 21-24R
Asher, Maxine 1930- . . . 105
Asher, Michael 1953- . . . 151
Asher, Miriam
See Mundis, Hester
Asher, R. E. 1926- . . . 149
Asher, Ramona M. 1945- . . . 143
Asher, Robert 1944- . . . 111
Asher, Robert Eller 1910- . . . 61-64
Asher, Sandra Fenichel 1942- . . . CANR-53
Earlier sketches in CA 105, CANR-22
See also Asher, Sandy
See also JRDA
See also MAICYA
Asher, Sandy
See Asher, Sandra Fenichel
See also AAYA 17
See also DLBY 83
See also SAAS 13
See also SATA 36, 71
See also SATA-Brief 34
Asheron, Sara
See Moore, Lilian
Ashey, Bella
See Breinburg, Petronella
Ashfield, Helen
See Bennetts, Pamela
Ashford, Daisy
See Ashford, Margaret Mary
Ashford, Douglas E(lliott) 1928- . . . CANR-37
Earlier sketches in CA 73-76, CANR-16
Ashford, Gerald 1907- . . . 41-44R
Ashford, Janet Isaacs 1949- . . . 113
Ashford, Jeffrey
See Jeffries, Roderic (Graeme)
Ashford, Margaret Mary
1881-1972 Obituary . . . 33-36R
See also SATA 10
Ashford, Nicholas 1943(?)-1990 Obituary . . . 130
Ashford, Nigel (John Gladwell) 1952- . . . 137
Ashford, (H.) Ray 1926- . . . 65-68
Ashford, Theodore Askounes
1908-1987 Obituary . . . 122
Ashihara Yoshinobu 1918- . . . CANR-65
Earlier sketch in CA 129
Ashkenazy, Vladimir D(avidovich) 1937- . . . 137
Ashley, A.
See Aasheim, Ashley
Ashley, Bernard 1935- . . . CANR-44
Earlier sketches in CA 93-96, CANR-25
See also CLR 4
See also MAICYA
See also SATA 47, 79
See also SATA-Brief 39
Ashley, Douglas . . . 155
Ashley, Elizabeth
See Salmon, Annie Elizabeth

Ashley, Ellen
See Gasparotti, Elizabeth Seifert
Ashley, (Arthur) Ernest 1906-.... CAP-1
Earlier sketch in CA 13-16
Ashley, Franklin 1942-.... CANR-1
Earlier sketch in CA 45-48
Ashley, Fred
See Atkins, Francis Henry
Ashley, Graham
See Organ, John
Ashley, Jack 1922-.... 106
Ashley, Leonard R(aymond) N(elligan) 1928-....
CANR-24
Earlier sketches in CA 13-16R, CANR-9
Ashley, Maurice (Percy) 1907-.... 41-44R
Ashley, Michael (Raymond Donald) 1948-....
CANR-56
Earlier sketches in CA 69-72, CANR-13, 30
Ashley, Nova Trimble 1911-.... 65-68
Ashley, Paul P(ritchard) 1896-1979.... CANR-10
Obituary.... 85-88
Earlier sketch in CA 21-24R
Ashley, Perry J(onathan) 1928-.... 120
Ashley, Ray
See Abrashkin, Raymond
Ashley, Renee 1949-.... 148
Ashley, Robert P(aul), Jr. 1915-.... 17-20R
Ashley, Rosalind Minor 1923-.... 69-72
Ashley, Sally 1935-.... 109
Ashley, Steven
See McCaig, Donald
Ashley-Montagu, Montague Francis
See Montagu, Ashley
Ashlin, John
See Cutforth, John Ashlin
Ashlock, Patrick (Robert) 1937-.... 61-64
Ashlock, Robert B. 1930-.... CANR-28
Earlier sketches in CA 29-32R, CANR-12
Ashman, Howard (Elliott) 1950-1991.... 131
Obituary.... 133
Brief entry.... 122
Ashmead, John, Jr. 1917-1992.... CANR-28
Obituary.... 136
Earlier sketch in CA 1-4R
Ashmole, Bernard 1894-1988.... 106
Obituary.... 124
Ashmore, Harry S(cott) 1916-1998.... 13-16R
Obituary.... 163
Ashmore, Jerome 1901-.... CAP-2
Earlier sketch in CA 33-36
Ashmore, Lewis
See Raborg, Frederick A(shton), Jr.
Ashmore, Owen 1920-.... 106
Ashner, Sonie Shapiro 1938-.... 57-60
Ashrawi, Hanan (Mikhail) 1946-.... 162
Ashrawi-Mikhail, Hanan
See Ashrawi, Hanan (Mikhail)
Ashton, Ann
See Kimbro, John M.
Ashton, Dore 1928-.... CANR-57
Earlier sketches in CA 5-8R, CANR-2, 30
Ashton, (Arthur) Leigh (Bolland)
1897-1983 Obituary.... 114
Ashton, Lorayne
See Gottfried, Theodore Mark
Ashton, Robert 1924-.... CANR-3
Earlier sketch in CA 1-4R
Ashton, Rosemary 1947-.... 138
Ashton, Sharon
See Van Slyke, Helen (Lenore)
Ashton, (Margery) Violet 1908-.... 73-76
Ashton, Warren T.
See Adams, William Taylor
Ashton, Winifred 1888-1965 Obituary.... 93-96
See also Dane, Clemence
Ashton-Warner, Sylvia (Constance) 1908-1984....
CANR-29
Obituary.... 112
Earlier sketch in CA 69-72
See also CLC 19
See also MTCW 1
Ashworth, Kenneth H(ayden) 1932-.... 41-44R
Ashworth, Mary Wells Knight 1903-.... 5-8R
Ashworth, Wilfred 1912-.... 13-16R
Ashworth, William 1920-1991.... 5-8R
Obituary.... 134
Ashworth, (Lewis) William 1942-.... 133
Asimov, Isaac 1920-1992.... CANR-60
Obituary.... 137
Earlier sketches in CA 1-4R, CANR-2, 19, 36
Interview in.... CANR-19
See also AAYA 13
See also BEST 90:2
See also CLC 1, 3, 9, 19, 26, 76, 92
See also CLR 12
See also DAM POP
See also DLB 8
See also DLBY 92
See also JRDA
See also MAICYA
See also MTCW 1
See also SATA 1, 26, 74
Asimov, Janet (Jeppson) 1926-.... CANR-36
Asimow, Michael 1939-.... 154
Asin, Alfredo Quispez
See Moro, Cesar
Asin, Cesar Quispez
See Moro, Cesar
Asinof, Eliot 1919-.... CANR-7
Earlier sketch in CA 9-12R
See also SATA 6
Aska, Warabe
See Masuda, Takeshi
See also SATA 56
Askari, Hussaini Muhammad
See Pereira, Harold Bertram
Askenasy, Hans George 1930-.... 77-80
Askew, Jack
See Hivnor, Robert
Askew, Thomas A(delbert, Jr.) 1931-.... 130
Askew, William C(larence) 1910-.... 49-52
Askham, Francis
See Greenwood, Julia Eileen Courtney
Askin, A. Bradley 1943-.... 73-76
Askin, Alma 1911-.... 57-60
Askin, I(da) Jayne 1940-.... 109
Askwith, Betty Ellen 1909-1995.... CANR-13
Obituary.... 148
Earlier sketch in CA 61-64
Askwith, Herbert 1889-1985 Obituary.... 117
Brief entry.... 113
Aslanapa, Oktay 1914-.... 37-40R
Aslet, Clive (William) 1955-.... CANR-32
Earlier sketch in CA 113
Aslin, Elizabeth (Mary) 1923-1989 Obituary.... 128
Asman, David 1954-.... 127
Aspaturian, Vernon V. 1922-.... 105
Aspel, Michael (Terence) 1933- Brief entry.... 117
Aspell, Patrick J(oseph) 1930-.... 25-28R
Asper, Kathrin 1941-.... 146
Aspin, Les(lie, Jr.) 1938-1995.... 108
Obituary.... 148
Aspinall, (Honor) Ruth (Alastair) 1922-.... CANR-2
Earlier sketch in CA 5-8R
Aspinwall, Dorothy B(rown) 1910-.... 49-52
Aspiz, Harold 1921-.... 105
Aspler, Tony 1939-.... CANR-25
Earlier sketch in CA 105
Asprey, Robert B. 1923-.... CANR-6
Earlier sketch in CA 5-8R
Asprin, Robert L(ynn) 1946-.... CANR-57
Earlier sketch in CA 85-88
See also SATA 92
Aspy, David N(athanial) 1930-.... CANR-20
Earlier sketch in CA 45-48
Asquith, Cynthia Mary Evelyn (Charteris)
1887-1960.... 166
Obituary.... 110
Asquith, Glenn Hackney 1904-.... CANR-16
Earlier sketches in CA 1-4R, CANR-1
Asquith, Nan
See Pattinson, Nancy Evelyn
Asquith, Stewart 1948-.... 116
Assael, Henry 1935-.... 41-44R
Assagioli, Roberto 1893(?)-1974 Obituary.... 53-56
Asselbroke, Archibald Algernon 1923-.... 77-80
Asselin, E(dward) Donald 1903-1970.... CAP-1
Earlier sketch in CA 11-12
Asselin, Olivar 1874-1937.... DLB 92
Asselineau, Roger (Maurice) 1915-.... CANR-26
Earlier sketch in CA 97-100
Assensoh, A(kwasi) B(retuo) 1946(?)-.... 120
Assiac
See Fraenkel, Heinrich
Assis, Joaquim Maria Machado de
See Machado de Assis, Joaquim Maria
Assmann, Jan 1938-.... 168
Assouline, Pierre 1953-.... 162
Astaire, Fred 1899-1987 Obituary.... 122
Astarita, Tommaso 1961-.... 143
Aster, Sidney 1942-.... CANR-10
Earlier sketch in CA 65-68
Astier, Pierre A(rthur) G(eorges) 1927-.... CANR-20
Earlier sketch in CA 45-48
Astill, Kenneth N. 1923-.... 53-56
Astin, Alexander W(illiam) 1932-.... CANR-53
Earlier sketches in CA 17-20R, CANR-7, 28
Astin, Helen S(tavridou) 1932-.... CANR-28
Earlier sketch in CA 29-32R
Astin, Patty Duke
See Duke, Anna Marie
Astiz, Carlos A. 1933-.... 25-28R
Astley, Joan Bright 1910-.... 33-36R
Astley, Juliet
See Lofts, Norah (Robinson)
Astley, Neil 1953-.... 132
Astley, Thea (Beatrice May) 1925-.... CANR-43
Earlier sketches in CA 65-68, CANR-11
See also CLC 41
Aston, Athina (Leka) 1934-.... 117
Aston, James
See White, T(erence) H(anbury)
Aston, Margaret 1932-.... 73-76
Aston, Michael (Anthony) 1946-.... 61-64
Aston, Trevor Henry 1925-1985 Obituary.... 118
Astor, Brooke 1902-.... 148
Astor, (Francis) David (Langhorne) 1912- Brief
entry.... 113
Astor, Gavin 1918-1984 Obituary.... 113
Astor, Gerald (Morton) 1926-.... CANR-24
Earlier sketch in CA 107
Astor, Mary 1906-1987.... CANR-3
Obituary.... 123
Earlier sketch in CA 5-8R
Astor, Michael Langhorne 1916-1980.... 61-64
Obituary.... 97-100
Astor, Susan 1946-.... 105
Astrachan, Samuel 1934-.... 69-72
Astro, Richard 1941-.... CANR-27
Earlier sketch in CA 29-32R
Asturias, Miguel Angel 1899-1974.... CANR-32
Obituary.... 49-52
Earlier sketches in CAP-2, CA 25-28
See also CLC 3, 8, 13
See also DAM MULT, NOV
See also DLB 113
See also HLC
See also HW
See also MTCW 1
Aswad, Betsy (Becker) 1939-.... CANR-25
Earlier sketch in CA 104
Aswell, Mary Louise 1902-1984 Obituary.... 114
Aswin
See Nandakumar, Prema
Atamian, David 1892(?)-1978 Obituary.... 81-84
Atares, Carlos Saura
See Saura (Atares), Carlos
Atcheson, Richard 1934-.... 29-32R
Atchison, Sandra Dallas 1939-.... CANR-62
Earlier sketches in CA 17-20R, CANR-10
Atchity, Kenneth John 1944-.... CANR-16
Earlier sketches in CA 49-52, CANR-1
Atchley, Bob
See Atchley, Robert C.
Atchley, Dana W(inslow) 1941-.... 61-64
Atchley, Robert C. 1939-.... CANR-1
Earlier sketch in CA 45-48
Atene, Ann
See Atene, (Rita) Anna
Atene, (Rita) Anna 1922-.... SATA 12
Athanassiadis, Nikos 1904-.... CANR-17
Earlier sketch in CA 33-36R
Athans, George (Stanley), Jr. 1952-.... 104
Athar
See Afzal, Omar
Athas, Daphne 1923-.... CANR-3
Earlier sketch in CA 1-4R
Athay, R(obert) E. 1925-.... 33-36R
Athearn, Robert G(reenleaf) 1914-1983.. CANR-70
Earlier sketches in CA 1-4R, CANR-3
Atheling, William
See Pound, Ezra (Weston Loomis)
Atheling, William, Jr.
See Blish, James (Benjamin)
Atherden, Margaret Ann 1947-.... 147
Atherton, Alexine 1930-.... 37-40R
Atherton, Gertrude (Franklin Horn) 1857-1948.. 155
Brief entry.... 104
See also DLB 9, 78, 186
See also TCLC 2
Atherton, James C(hristian) 1915-.... 49-52
Atherton, James S(tephen) 1910-.... CAP-1
Earlier sketch in CA 13-16
Atherton, Lewis E. 1905-.... 1-4R
Atherton, Lucius
See Masters, Edgar Lee
Atherton, Maxine.... 5-8R
Atherton, Pauline
See Cochrane, Pauline A(therton)
Atherton, Sarah
See Bridgman, Sarah Atherton
Atherton, Wallace N(ewman) 1927-.... 49-52
Athey, Irene J(owett) 1919-.... 61-64
Athill, Diana 1917-.... CANR-2
Earlier sketch in CA 1-4R
Athlone, Countess of
See Alice (Mary Victoria Augusta Pauline),
Princess
Atholl, Desmond 1956-.... 134
Athos
See Walkerley, Rodney Lewis (de Burgh)
Athos, Anthony G(eorge) 1934-.... CANR-19
Earlier sketch in CA 25-28R
Athos, Jonathan
See Mallett, Daryl F(urumi)
Atil, Esin 1938-.... CANR-67
Earlier sketches in CA 113, CANR-32
Atiya, Aziz S. 1898-.... 5-8R
Atiya, Nayra 1943-.... 128
Atiyah, P(atrick) S(elim) 1931-.... 37-40R
Atiyeh, George N(icholas) 1923-.... 57-60
Atkeson, Roy A. 1907-1990.... CANR-11
Obituary.... 131
Earlier sketch in CA 69-72
Atkey, Philip 1908-1985.... 148
Obituary.... 118
Brief entry.... 112
Atkin, Flora B(lumenthal) 1919-.... CANR-37
Earlier sketches in CA 93-96, CANR-16
Atkin, J. Myron 1927-.... 45-48
Atkin, Mary Gage 1929-.... 81-84
Atkin, William Wilson 1912(?)-1976 Obituary. 65-68
Atkins, Burton M(ark) 1944- Brief entry.... 115
Atkins, Chester Burton 1924- Brief entry.... 113
Atkins, Chester G(reenough) 1948-.... 45-48
Atkins, Chet
See Atkins, Chester Burton
Atkins, E(dward) Wulstan 1904-.... 128
Atkins, Francis Henry 1840-1927.... 167
Atkins, Frank
See Atkins, Francis Henry
Atkins, G(eorge) Douglas 1943-.... 114
Atkins, G(eorge) Pope 1934-.... CANR-17
Earlier sketch in CA 33-36R
Atkins, Gary 1949-.... 126
Atkins, (Arthur) Harold 1910-.... 105
Atkins, Harry 1933-.... 25-28R
Atkins, Hedley (John Barnard)
1905-1983 Obituary.... 111
Atkins, Jack
See Harris, Mark
Atkins, James G. 1932-.... 17-20R
Atkins, Jim
See Atkins, James G.
Atkins, John (Alfred) 1916-.... CANR-19
Earlier sketches in CA 9-12R, CANR-3
Atkins, Josiah 1755(?)-1781.... DLB 31
Atkins, Kenneth R(obert) 1920-.... 73-76
Atkins, Mary
See Sternau, Cynthia
Atkins, Meg Elizabeth.... 102
Atkins, Oliver F. 1916-1977.... 73-76
Atkins, Ollie
See Atkins, Oliver F.
Atkins, P(eter) W(illiam) 1940-.... CANR-41
Earlier sketch in CA 117
Atkins, Paul Moody 1892-1977 Obituary.... 69-72
Atkins, Robert C(oleman) 1930-.... 128
Atkins, Russell 1926-.... CANR-53
Earlier sketches in CA 45-48, CANR-1, 25
See also CAAS 16
See also BW 1
See also DLB 41
Atkins, Stephen E. 1941-.... 144
Atkins, Stuart (Pratt) 1914-.... 25-28R
Atkins, Thomas R(adcliffe) 1939-.... CANR-8
Earlier sketch in CA 61-64
Atkinson, Allen G. 1953(?)-1987.... SATA 60
See also SATA-Brief 46
See also SATA-Obit 55
Atkinson, Anthony Barnes 1944-.... CANR-11
Earlier sketch in CA 69-72
Atkinson, Basil F(erris) C(ampbell) 1895-.... 5-8R
Atkinson, (Justin) Brooks 1894-1984.... CANR-14
Obituary.... 111
Earlier sketch in CA 61-64
Atkinson, Carroll (Holloway) 1896-.... CAP-1
Earlier sketch in CA 13-16
Atkinson, David J(ohn) 1943-.... 107
Atkinson, Frank 1922-.... 108
Atkinson, Geoffrey 1955-.... 118
Atkinson, Hugh C(raig) 1933-1986.... CANR-28
Obituary.... 120
Earlier sketch in CA 49-52
Atkinson, James 1914-.... 25-28R
Atkinson, James B(lakely) 1934-.... 119
Atkinson, Jennifer (Elizabeth) McCabe 1937- Brief
entry.... 116
Atkinson, John W(illiam) 1923-.... CANR-11
Earlier sketch in CA 21-24R
Atkinson, Kate.... 166
See also CLC 99
Atkinson, Linda 1941-.... 135
Atkinson, M. E.
See Frankau, Mary Evelyn Atkinson
Atkinson, Margaret Fleming.... 73-76
See also SATA 14
Atkinson, Mary
See Hardwick, Mollie
Atkinson, Michael (J.).... 167
Atkinson, Phillip S. 1921-.... 25-28R
Atkinson, R(ichard) C(hatham) 1929-.... 17-20R
Atkinson, Rick 1952-.... 133
See also BEST 90:2
Atkinson, Ron 1932-.... 57-60
Atkinson, Ronald Field 1928-.... 17-20R
Atkinson, W. W.
See Atkinson, William Walker
Atkinson, Walter S(ydney)
1891-1978 Obituary.... 73-76
Atkinson, William Christopher 1902-1992.... 109
Obituary.... 139
Atkinson, William Walker 1862-1932 Brief
entry.... 120
Atkisson, Arthur A(lbert, Jr.) 1930-.... 61-64
Atkyns, Glenn C(hadwick) 1921-.... 49-52
Atlas, Helen Vincent 1931-.... 101
Atlas, James (Robert) 1949-.... 138
Atlas, Martin 1914-.... 5-8R
Atlas, Samuel 1899-1977 Obituary.... 73-76
Atmore, Anthony 1932-.... 25-28R
Attanasio, A(lfred) A(ngelo) 1951-.... CANR-69
Earlier sketch in CA 137
Attanasio, Paul 1959-.... 160
Attaway, Robert J(oseph) 1942-.... 49-52
Attaway, William (Alexander) 1911-1986.... 143
See also BLC 1
See also BW 2
See also CLC 92
See also DAM MULT
See also DLB 76
Attea, Mary
See Spahn, Mary Attea
Atteberry, William L(ouis) 1939-.... 53-56
Attema, Martha 1949-.... 159
See also SATA 94
Attenborough, Bernard George.... CANR-2
Earlier sketch in CA 49-52
Attenborough, David (Frederick) 1926-.... CANR-30
Earlier sketches in CA 1-4R, CANR-6
Attenborough, John 1908-1994.... 101
Obituary.... 146
Attenborough, Richard (Samuel) 1923-.... 139
Brief entry.... 127
Atterton, Julian (Harold) 1956-.... 122
Attfield, Robin.... 137
Atthill, Robin 1912-.... 69-72
Atticus
See Davies, Hunter
and Fleming, Ian (Lancaster)
and Pawle, Gerald Strachan
and Wilson, (Thomas) Woodrow
Attiyeh, Richard E. 1937- Brief entry.... 113
Attlee, C. R.
See Attlee, Clement R(ichard)
Attlee, Clement R(ichard) 1883-1967 Obituary. 112
Attneave, Carolyn L(ewis) 1920-.... CANR-1
Earlier sketch in CA 45-48
Attridge, Derek 1945-.... 105
Attwell, Arthur A(lbert) 1917-.... 49-52
Attwood, William (Hollingsworth) 1919-1989 21-24R
Obituary.... 128
Atwater, C(onstance) Elizabeth (Sullivan)
1923-.... 13-16R
Atwater, Eastwood 1925-.... 110
Atwater, Florence (Hasseltine Carroll)
1896-1979.... 135
See also CLR 19
See also MAICYA
See also SATA 16, 66
Atwater, James David 1928-1996.... 101
Obituary.... 151
Atwater, Lynn 1935-.... 111

Atwater, Montgomery Meigs 1904-1976 .. CANR-70
Earlier sketch in CA 73-76
See also SATA 15
Atwater, P(hyllis) M. H. 1937- 133
Atwater, Richard (Tupper) 1892-1948 135
Brief entry 111
See also CLR 19
See also MAICYA
See also SATA 54, 66
See also SATA-Brief 27
Atwell, Debby 1953- .... SATA 87
Atwood, Ann (Margaret) 1913- 41-44R
See also SATA 7
Atwood, Drucy
See Morrison, Eula Atwood
Atwood, Margaret (Eleanor) 1939- CANR-59
Earlier sketches in CA 49-52, CANR-3, 24, 33
Interview in CANR-24
See also AAYA 12
See also BEST 89:2
See also CLC 2, 3, 4, 8, 13, 15, 25, 44, 84
See also DA
See also DAB
See also DAC
See also DAM MST, NOV, POET
See also DLB 53
See also MTCW 1
See also PC 8
See also SATA 50
See also SSC 2
See also WLC
Atwood, Nina 168
Atwood, Robert B. .... AITN 2
Atwood, William G(oodson) 1932- 142
Atxaga, Bernardo
See Garmendia, Joseba Irazu
Atyeo, Don 1950- 93-96
Atzeni, Sergio 1952-1995 168
Auberjonois, Fernand 1910- 77-80
Aubert, Alvin (Bernard) 1930- CANR-26
Earlier sketch in CA 81-84
See also CAAS 20
See also BW 1
See also DLB 41
Aubert, Jacques 1932- 147
Aubert, Rosemary 1946- 113
Aubert de Gaspe, Philippe-Ignace-Francois
1814-1841 .... DLB 99
Aubert de Gaspe, Philippe-Joseph 1786-1871 . DLB 99
Aubery, Pierre 1920- 37-40R
Aubey, Robert T(haddeus) 1930- 21-24R
Aubigny, Pierre d'
See Mencken, H(enry) L(ouis)
Aubin, Henry (Trocme) 1942- 77-80
Aubin, Napoleon 1812-1890 .... DLB 99
Aubin, Penelope 1685-1731(?) .... DLB 39
Aubrac, Lucie 1912- 151
Aubrey, Crispin 1946- 129
Aubrey, Frank
See Atkins, Francis Henry
Aubrey, Meg Kelleher 1963- .... SATA 83
Aubrey-Fletcher, Henry Lancelot
1887-1969 Obituary 111
See also Wade, Henry
Aubry, Claude B. 1914-1984 106
See also SATA 29
See also SATA-Obit 40
Auburn, Mark Stuart 1945- 89-92
Auchincloss, Louis (Stanton) 1917- CANR-55
Earlier sketches in CA 1-4R, CANR-6, 29
Interview in CANR-29
See also CLC 4, 6, 9, 18, 45
See also DAM NOV
See also DLB 2
See also DLBY 80
See also MTCW 1
See also SSC 22
Auchmuty, James Johnston 1909-1981 101
Obituary 109
Auchterlonie, Dorothy
See Green, Dorothy (Auchterlonie)
Auclair, Joan 1960- .... SATA 68
Audax
See Oaksey, John
Audemars, Pierre 1909- CANR-58
Earlier sketches in CA 17-20R, CANR-7
Auden, Renee
See West, Uta
Auden, W(ystan) H(ugh) 1907-1973 ..... CANR-61
Obituary 45-48
Earlier sketches in CA 9-12R, CANR-5
See also AAYA 18
See also CDBLB 1914-1945
See also CLC 1, 2, 3, 4, 6, 9, 11, 14, 43
See also DA
See also DAB
See also DAC
See also DAM DRAM, MST, POET
See also DLB 10, 20
See also MTCW 1
See also PC 1
See also WLC
Audi, Robert (N.) 1941- 123
Audiard, Michel 1920-1985 Obituary 116
Audiberti, Jacques 1900-1965 Obituary 25-28R
See also CLC 38
See also DAM DRAM
Audubon, John Woodhouse 1812-1862 ... DLB 183
Auel, Jean M(arie) 1936- CANR-64
Earlier sketches in CA 103, CANR-21
Interview in CANR-21
See also AAYA 7
See also BEST 90:4
See also CLC 31, 107
See also DAM POP
See also SATA 91
Auer, J(ohn) Jeffery 1913- CANR-6
Earlier sketch in CA 9-12R
Auer, James M(atthew) 1928- 133
Auer, Martin 1951- 145
See also SATA 77
Auerbach, Aline B.
See Auerbach, Aline Sophie (Buchman)
Auerbach, Aline Sophie (Buchman)
1899(?)-1985 Obituary 116
Auerbach, Arnold (Jacob) 1917- 131
Auerbach, Arnold M. 1912- 17-20R
Auerbach, Berthold 1812-1882 .... DLB 133
Auerbach, Erich 1892-1957 155
Brief entry 118
See also TCLC 43
Auerbach, Erna (?)-1975 Obituary 61-64
Auerbach, George 1905(?)-1973 Obituary 45-48
Auerbach, Jerold S(tephen) 1936- CANR-69
Earlier sketch in CA 21-24R
Auerbach, Jessica (Lynn) 1947- 114
Auerbach, Loyd 1956- 166
Auerbach, Marjorie (Hoffberg) 9-12R
Auerbach, Nina 1943- CANR-34
Earlier sketches in CA 85-88, CANR-15
Auerbach, Red
See Auerbach, Arnold (Jacob)
Auerbach, Stevanne 1938- CANR-24
Earlier sketches in CA 57-60, CANR-8
Auerbach, Stuart C(harles) 1935- 89-92
Auerbach, Sylvia CANR-4
Earlier sketch in CA 53-56
Auernheimer, Raoul 1876-1948 .... DLB 81
Auf der Maur, Nick 1942- 129
Aufricht, Hans 1902- 45-48
Augarde, Steve 1950- CANR-21
Earlier sketch in CA 104
See also SATA 25
Augarde, Tony 1936- 118
Augarten, Stan 1952- 115
Auge, Bud
See Auge, Henry J., Jr.
Auge, Henry J., Jr. 1930(?)-1983 Obituary 109
Augelli, John P(at) 1921- 17-20R
See also SATA 46
Augenbraum, Harold 1953- 142
Auger, C(harles) P(eter) 1931- 147
Aughtry, Charles Edward 1925- 5-8R
Augier, Emile 1820-1889 .... DLB 192
Augsburger, A(aron) Don(ald) 1925- 21-24R
Augsburger, David W. 1938- CANR-13
Earlier sketch in CA 33-36R
Augsburger, Myron S. 1929- CANR-6
Earlier sketch in CA 13-16R
Augspurger, Everett F. 1904(?)-1986 Obituary .. 118
Augstein, Rudolf (Karl) 1923- 110
Auguet, Roland (Jacques) 1935- 105
August, Bille 1948- 144
August, Eugene R(obert) 1935- CANR-27
Earlier sketch in CA 49-52
August, John
See De Voto, Bernard (Augustine)
Augustin, Ann Sutherland 1934- 57-60
Augustin, Pius 1934- 17-20R
Augustine 354-430 .... DA
See also DAC
See also DAM MST
See also DLB 115
See also WLCS
Augustine, Erich
See Stoil, Michael Jon
Augustine, Mildred
See Benson, Mildred (Augustine Wirt)
Augustine, Norman R(alph) 1935- 121
Augustine, St. 354-430 .... DAB
Augustinos, Gerasimos 1939- 145
Augustson, Ernest
See Ryden, Ernest Edwin
Augustus, Albert, Jr.
See Nuetzel, Charles (Alexander)
Aukerman, Dale 1930- 112
Aukerman, Robert C. 1910- 33-36R
Aukofer, Frank A(lexander) 1935- 65-68
Auld, Rhoda L(andsman) 105
Auleta, Michael S. 1909- CAP-2
Earlier sketch in CA 25-28
Auletta, Ken 1942- CANR-72
Earlier sketches in CA 69-72, CANR-12
See also DLBY 97
Auletta, Richard P(aul) 1942- 53-56
Auletta, Robert 1940- CANR-48
Brief entry 115
Earlier sketch in CA 119
Interview in 119
Aulich, James 1952- 132
Aulicino, Armand 1920(?)-1983 Obituary 109
Aulick, June L. 1906- 25-28R
Ault, Donald D(uane) 1942- 81-84
Ault, Phil
See Ault, Phillip H(alliday)
Ault, Phillip H(alliday) 1914- CANR-18
Earlier sketch in CA 101
See also SATA 23
Ault, Rosalie Sain 1942- 107
See also SATA 38
Ault, Roz
See Ault, Rosalie Sain
Aultman, Donald S. 1930- 17-20R
Aultman, Richard E(ugene) 1933- CANR-9
Earlier sketch in CA 65-68
Aumann, Francis R(obert) 1901- 41-44R
Aumbry, Alan
See Bayley, Barrington J(ohn)
Aumont, Jean-Pierre 1913- 29-32R
Aune, Bruce (Arthur) 1933- 73-76
Aung, (Maung) Htin 1909- CANR-3
Earlier sketch in CA 5-8R
See also SATA 21
Aunger, Edmund A(lexander) 1949- 112
Auntie Deb
See Coury, Louise Andree
Auntie Louise
See Coury, Louise Andree
Aurand, Harold Wilson 1940- 41-44R
Aurand, L(eonard) W(illiam) 1920- 53-56
Aurandt, Paul (Harvey II) 1948- 129
Aurandt, Paul Harvey 1918- 102
Aurelio, John R. 1937- CANR-28
Earlier sketch in CA 111
Aurelius
See Bourne, Randolph S(illiman)
Aurell, Tage 1895-1976 Obituary 113
Aurner, Robert R(ay) 1898- 5-8R
Aurobindo, Sri
See Ghose, Aurabinda
Aurthur, Robert Alan 1922-1978 .... CANR-34
Earlier sketch in CA 81-84
Ausland, John C(ampbell) 1920-1996 93-96
Obituary 152
Auslander, Audrey (May) Wurdemann
1911-1960 Obituary 116
Auslander, Joseph 1897-1965 Obituary 116
Ausmus, Harry Jack 1937- 115
Austen, Carrie
See Bennett, Cherie
Austen, Jane 1775-1817 .... AAYA 19
See also CDBLB 1789-1832
See also DA
See also DAB
See also DAC
See also DAM MST, NOV
See also DLB 116
See also WLC
Austen, Michael (Edward) 1951- 109
Austen, Ralph A. 1937- 25-28R
Auster, Nancy (Eileen) R(oss) 1926- 65-68
Auster, Paul 1947- CANR-52
Earlier sketches in CA 69-72, CANR-23
See also CLC 47
Austerlitz, Paul 1957- 165
Austerlitz, Robert Paul 1923-1994 111
Obituary 146
Austerman, Wayne R. 1948- 122
Austgen, Robert Joseph 1932- 21-24R
Austin, Alfred 1835-1913 .... DLB 35
Austin, Allan Edward 1929- 73-76
Austin, Allen 1922- 33-36R
Austin, Anthony 1919- 33-36R
Austin, (Mildred) Aurelia 53-56
Austin, Barbara Leslie
See Linton, Barbara Leslie
Austin, Brett
See Floren, Lee
Austin, Carrie
See Seuling, Barbara
Austin, Charles M(arshall) 1941- 69-72
Austin, David E(dwards) 1926- 29-32R
Austin, Elizabeth S. 1907- CAP-2
Earlier sketch in CA 25-28
See also SATA 5
Austin, Frank
See Faust, Frederick (Schiller)
Austin, Guy 1966- 163
Austin, Harry
See McInerny, Ralph
Austin, Henry Wilfred 1906- 101
Austin, James C(layton) 1923- 13-16R
Austin, James Henry 1925- 81-84
Austin, Jane Goodwin 1831-1894 .... DLB 202
Austin, John 1922- 61-64
Austin, John Langshaw 1911-1960 Obituary ... 112
Austin, K(enneth) A(shurst) 1911- 102
Austin, Lettie J(ane) 1925- 65-68
Austin, Lewis 1936- 73-76
Austin, Lloyd James 1915-1994 .... CAP-1
Obituary 147
Earlier sketch in CA 13-14
Austin, M(ichel) M(ervyn) 1943- CANR-19
Earlier sketch in CA 85-88
Austin, Margot 1909(?)-1990 .... CAP-1
Obituary 132
Earlier sketch in CA 9-10
See also SATA 11
See also SATA-Obit 66
Austin, Mary (Hunter) 1868-1934 Brief entry ... 109
See also DLB 9, 78
See also TCLC 25
Austin, Mary C(arrington) 1915- 5-8R
Austin, Michael 165
Austin, Neal F(uller) 1926- 25-28R
Austin, (John) Norman 1937- 89-92
Austin, Oliver L(uther), Jr. 1903-1988 49-52
Obituary 127
See also SATA 7
See also SATA-Obit 59
Austin, R. G.
See Gelman, Rita Golden
and Lamb, Nancy
Austin, (Stewart) Reid 1931- 89-92
Austin, Richard B(uckner), Jr. 1930- 73-76
Austin, Stephen
See Stevens, Austin N(eil)
Austin, Timothy R(obert) 1952- 117
Austin, Virginia .... SATA 80
Austin, William 1778-1841 .... DLB 74
Austin, William W(eaver) 1920- 21-24R
Austwick, John
See Lee, Austin
Ausubel, Herman 1920-1977 .... 1-4R
Obituary 69-72
Ausubel, Marynn H. 1913(?)-1980 Obituary . 97-100
Auten, James H(udson) 1938- 41-44R
Auteur, Hillary
See Gottfried, Theodore Mark
Auth, Tony
See Auth, William Anthony, Jr.
Auth, William Anthony, Jr. 1942- CANR-72
Brief entry 108
Earlier sketch in CA 111
Interview in 111
See also SATA 51
Autran Dourado, Waldomiro
See Dourado, (Waldomiro Freitas) Autran
Autrey, C. E. 1904- CANR-2
Earlier sketch in CA 1-4R
Autry, Ewart (Arthur) 1900- 13-16R
Autry, (Orvon) Gene 1907- Brief entry 112
Autry, Gloria Diener
See Allen, Terril Diener
Autry, James A(rthur) 1933- 135
Brief entry 115
Autton, Norman William James 1920- 101
Auty, Phyllis 1910- CANR-2
Earlier sketch in CA 5-8R
Auty, Robert 1914-1978 Obituary 111
Auvert, Elizabeth CANR-14
Earlier sketch in CA 37-40R
Auvil, Kenneth W(illiam) 1925- 17-20R
Avakian, Arlene Voski 1939- 139
Avakian, Arra S(teve) 1912- 85-88
Avakumovic, Ivan 1926- 41-44R
Avalle-Arce, Juan Bautista de 1927- CANR-32
Earlier sketches in CA 33-36R, CANR-13
See also HW
Avallone, Michael (Angelo, Jr.) 1924- CANR-39
Earlier sketches in CA 5-8R, CANR-4
Interview in CANR-4
Avalon, Arthur
See Woodroffe, John George
Avancini, Nicolaus 1611-1686 .... DLB 164
Avanzini, John F. 1936- CANR-49
Earlier sketch in CA 122
Avarius
See Stolk, Anthonie
Avedis, Hikmet 132
Avedis, Howard
See Avedis, Hikmet
Aveline, Claude 1901- CANR-6
Earlier sketch in CA 5-8R
Aveling, Hugh
See Aveling, J(ohn) C(edric) H(ugh)
Aveling, J(ohn) C(edric) H(ugh) 1917-1993 131
Obituary 140
Avella, Steven M. 1951- 145
Avellano, Albert
See Marlowe, Dan J(ames)
Avendano, Fausto 1941- 131
See also DLB 82
See also HW
Aveni, Anthony F(rancis) 1938- 81-84
Averbach, Albert 1902-1975 .... CAP-2
Earlier sketch in CA 21-22
Averill, E(dgar) W(aite) 1906-1980 53-56
Averill, Esther (Holden) 1902-1992 ...... CANR-12
Obituary 139
Earlier sketch in CA 29-32R
See also SATA 1, 28
See also SATA-Obit 72
Averill, Gage 1954- 166
Averill, James H(alsey) 1947- 129
Averill, John Hillier 1923-1984 Obituary 111
Averill, Lloyd J(ames) 1923- CANR-10
Earlier sketch in CA 21-24R
Averitt, Robert T(abor) 1931- 21-24R
Averroes 1126-1198 .... DLB 115
Avers, Charlotte J(o) 1926-1990 Obituary 131
Aversa, Elizabeth Smith 1946- 127
Avery, Al
See Montgomery, Rutherford George
Avery, Burniece 1908- 73-76
Avery, Catherine B(arber) 1909- 57-60
Avery, Edwina Austin 1896-1983 Obituary 110
Avery, George C(ostas) 1926- 25-28R
Avery, Gillian (Elise) 1926- CANR-69
Earlier sketches in CA 9-12R, CANR-4
See also DLB 161
See also MAICYA
See also SAAS 6
See also SATA 7, 75
Avery, Ira 1914- 81-84
Avery, James S. 1923- 126
Avery, Jeanne 1931- 111
Avery, June
See Rees, Joan
Avery, Kay 1908- 1-4R
See also SATA 5
Avery, Kevin J. 1950- 149
Avery, Laurence G(reen) 1934- 33-36R
Avery, Lynn
See Cole, Lois Dwight
Avery, Martin 1955- 113
Avery, Mary Ellen 1927- 118
Avery, Peter 1923- 13-16R
Avery, Richard
See Cooper, Edmund
Avery, Robert J., Jr. 1911(?)-1983 Obituary 110
Avery, Robert Sterling 1917- 13-16R
Avery, Valeen Tippetts 1936- 129
Avery, Valerie 1940- 111
Averyt, Anne C. 1946- 127

Avey, Albert E(dwin) 1886-1963 ... CAP-1
Earlier sketch in CA 17-18
Avey, Ruby 1927- ... CANR-39
Earlier sketches in CA 89-92, CANR-16
Avi
See Wortis, Avi
See also AAYA 10
See also CLR 24
See also SATA 71
Aviad, Janet 1942- ... 115
Avice, Claude (Pierre Marie) 1925- ... CANR-49
Earlier sketches in CA 61-64, CANR-8, 24
Avicenna 980-1037 ... DLB 115
Avigad, Nachman 1905-1992 ... 129
Obituary ... 136
Avila, Charles 1945- ... 129
Avila, Lilian Estelle ... 45-48
Avila (Penagos), Rafael 1941- ... 132
Avineri, Shlomo 1933- ... 25-28R
Avirgan, Anthony Lance 1944- ... CANR-31
Earlier sketch in CA 112
Avirgan, Tony
See Avirgan, Anthony Lance
Avis, Paul (David Loup) 1947- ... CANR-45
Earlier sketch in CA 120
Avishai, Susan 1949- ... SATA 82
Avison, Margaret 1918- ... 17-20R
See also CLC 2, 4, 97
See also DAC
See also DAM POET
See also DLB 53
See also MTCW 1
Avison, N(eville) Howard 1934- ... 29-32R
Avi-Yonah, M(ichael) 1904-1974 ... CANR-6
Earlier sketch in CA 5-8R
Avnery, Uri 1923- ... CANR-25
Earlier sketch in CA 105
Avni, Abraham Albert 1921- ... 33-36R
Avni, Haim 1930- ... 133
Avramides, Anita 1952- ... 133
Avramovic, Dragoslav 1919- ... CANR-17
Earlier sketch in CA 41-44R
Avrelin, M.
See Steinberg, Aaron Zacharovich
Avrett, Robert 1901- ... 1-4R
Avrett, Rosalind Case 1933- ... 110
Avrett, Roz
See Avrett, Rosalind Case
Avrich, Paul (Henry) 1931- ... CANR-5
Earlier sketch in CA 49-52
Avriel, Ehud 1917-1980 ... 69-72
Obituary ... 133
Avril, Pierre 1930- ... 29-32R
Avruch, Kevin Andrew 1950- ... CANR-50
Earlier sketch in CA 123
Avrutis, Raymond 1948- ... 69-72
Avvakum (Petrovich) 1620(?)-1682 ... DLB 150
AvZ
See Von Zelewsky, Alexander
Awa, Eme Onuoha 1921- ... 13-16R
Awad, Elias M. 1934- ... CANR-11
Earlier sketch in CA 17-20R
Awdry, Christopher Vere 1940- ... 136
See also SATA 67
Awdry, Wilbert Vere 1911-1997 ... 103
Obituary ... 157
See also CLR 23
See also DLB 160
See also SATA 94
Awe, Chulho 1927- ... 33-36R
Awe, Susan C. 1948- ... 166
Awiakta, Marilou 1936- ... 148
Awolowo, Obafemi Awo 1909-1987 ... CANR-14
Obituary ... 122
Earlier sketch in CA 65-68
See also BW 2
Awoonor, Kofi (Nyidevu) 1935- ... CANR-42
Earlier sketches in CA 29-32R, CANR-15
See also CAAS 13
See also BW 2
See also DLB 117
Awoonor-Williams, George
See Awoonor, Kofi (Nyidevu)
Awret, Irene 1921- ... 131
Awwad, Tawfiq Yusuf 1911-1988 ... 154
Axell, Herbert (Ernest) 1915- ... CANR-14
Earlier sketch in CA 81-84
Axelrad, Jacob 1899- ... 61-64
Axelrad, Sidney 1913-1976 ... 122
Obituary ... 110
Axelrad, Sylvia Brody 1914- ... 104
Axelrod, Alan 1952- ... 110
Axelrod, D(avid) B(ruce) 1943- ... CANR-1
Earlier sketch in CA 45-48
Axelrod, George 1922- ... 65-68
Axelrod, Herbert Richard 1927- ... 85-88
Axelrod, Joseph 1918- ... 33-36R
Axelrod, Mark (R.) 1946- ... 145
Axelrod, Paul (Douglas) 1949- ... 110
Axelrod, Robert 1943- ... 33-36R
Axelrod, Steven Gould 1944- ... 81-84
Axelson, Eric (Victor) 1913- ... CANR-25
Earlier sketches in CA 21-24R, CANR-9
Axford, H. William 1925- ... 37-40R
Axford, Joseph Mack 1879-1970 ... CAP-2
Earlier sketch in CA 25-28
Axford, Lavonne B(rady) 1928- ... 33-36R
Axford, Roger W(illiam) 1920- ... 33-36R
Axinn, Donald E(verett) 1929- ... CANR-53
Brief entry ... 115
Earlier sketch in CA 125
Axinn, June 1923- ... 89-92
Axler, Leo
See Lazuta, Gene
Axline, W. Andrew 1940- ... 25-28R
Axtell, James Lewis 1941- ... CANR-54
Earlier sketches in CA 108, CANR-25
Axthelm, Peter M(acrae) 1943- ... 107
Interview in ... 107
Axton, David
See Koontz, Dean R(ay)
Axton, W(illiam) F(itch) 1926- ... 21-24R
Ayal, Igal 1942- ... 37-40R
Ayala, Emilie Smith
See Smith-Ayala, Emilie
Ayala, Francisco 1934- ... 85-88
Ayala, Mitzi 1941- ... 110
Ayandele, E(mmanuel) A(yankanmi) 1936- ... CANR-13
Earlier sketch in CA 21-24R
Ayars, Albert L(ee) 1917- ... 29-32R
Ayars, James S(terling) 1898- ... CANR-2
Earlier sketch in CA 5-8R
See also SATA 4
Ayatey, Siegfried B. Y. 1934- ... 25-28R
Ayckbourn, Alan 1939- ... CANR-59
Earlier sketches in CA 21-24R, CANR-31
See also CLC 5, 8, 18, 33, 74
See also DAB
See also DAM DRAM
See also DLB 13
See also MTCW 1
Aycliffe, Jonathan
See MacEoin, Denis
Aycock, Don M(ilton) 1951- ... 106
Aydelotte, William Osgood 1910-1996 ... 57-60
Obituary ... 151
Aydy, Catherine
See Tennant, Emma (Christina)
Ayearst, Morley 1899-1983 ... CAP-2
Obituary ... 109
Earlier sketch in CA 29-32
Ayer, A(lfred) J(ules) 1910-1989 ... CANR-34
Obituary ... 129
Earlier sketches in CA 5-8R, 129, CANR-5
Ayer, Eleanor H. 1947- ... 146
See also SATA 78
Ayer, Frederick, Jr. 1917(?)-1974 ... CANR-70
Obituary ... 45-48
Earlier sketch in CA 73-76
Ayer, Jacqueline 1930- ... CANR-70
Earlier sketch in CA 69-72
See also SATA 13
Ayer, Margaret (?)-1981 ... CANR-13
Earlier sketch in CA 65-68
See also SATA 15
Ayers, Bradley Earl 1935- ... 69-72
Ayers, Donald Murray 1923- ... 17-20R
Ayers, Edward L(ynn) 1953- ... 115
Ayers, M(ichael) R(ichard) 1935- ... 25-28R
Ayers, Robert H(yman) 1918- ... 45-48
Ayers, Ronald 1948- ... 61-64
Ayers, Rose
See Greenwood, Lillian Bethel
Ayerst, David (George Ogilvy) 1904- Brief entry ... 113
Ayim, May 1960- ... 139
See also BW 2
Ayittey, George B. N. 1945- ... 167
Aykroyd, Dan(iel Edward) 1952- ... 123
Aykroyd, Wallace Ruddell 1899-1979 Obituary . 110
Aylen, Leo (William) 1935- ... CANR-19
Earlier sketch in CA 102
Aylesworth, Jim 1943- ... CANR-45
Earlier sketches in CA 106, CANR-22
See also SATA 38, 89
Aylesworth, Thomas G(ibbons) 1927-1995 ... CANR-26
Obituary ... 149
Earlier sketches in CA 25-28R, CANR-10
See also CLR 6
See also SAAS 17
See also SATA 4, 88
Ayling, (Harold) Keith (Oliver) 1898-1976 ... 73-76
Obituary ... 69-72
Ayling, Stanley (Edward) 1909- ... CANR-44
Earlier sketches in CA 45-48, CANR-21
Aylmer, Felix
See Jones, Felix Edward Aylmer
Aylmer, G(erald) E(dward) 1926- ... CANR-5
Earlier sketch in CA 13-16R
Aylward, Gladys 1902(?)-1970 Obituary ... 111
Aylward, Marcus
See Alexander, Marc
Aymar, Brandt 1911- ... CANR-37
Earlier sketches in CA 1-4R, CANR-16
See also SATA 22
Aymar, Gordon C(hristian) 1893- ... 5-8R
Ayme, Marcel (Andre) 1902-1967 ... CANR-67
Earlier sketch in CA 89-92
See also CLC 11
See also CLR 25
See also DLB 72
See also SATA 91
Aymes, Sister Maria de la Cruz ... 21-24R
Aynes, Edith A(nnette) 1909- ... 45-48
Aynes, Pat Edith
See Aynes, Edith A(nnette)
Aynesworth, Hugh (G.) 1931- ... 120
Brief entry ... 115
Interview in ... 120
Ayrault, Evelyn West 1922- ... 9-12R
Ayre, Jessica
See Appignanesi, Lisa
Ayre, Robert (Hugh) 1900- ... 1-4R
Ayres, Alison
See Carter, Robert A(yres)
Ayres, Carole Briggs
See Briggs, Carole S(uzanne)
Ayres, Gene
See Ayres, E. C.
Ayres, Ian 1959- ... 144
Ayres, James Eyvind 1939- ... 103
Ayres, Mary Jo 1953- ... 162
Ayres, Pam 1947- ... 155
See also SATA 90
Ayres, Patricia Miller 1923-1985 Obituary ... 117
See also SATA-Obit 46
Ayres, Paul
See Aarons, Edward S(idney)
Ayres, Philip 1944- ... 134
Ayres, Robert U(nderwood) 1932- ... CANR-16
Earlier sketch in CA 93-96
Ayres, Ruby M(ildred) 1883-1955 Brief entry ... 117
Ayrton, Elisabeth Walshe 1910(?)-1991 .. CANR-21
Obituary ... 136
Earlier sketches in CA 5-8R, CANR-3
Ayrton, Michael 1921-1975 ... CANR-21
Obituary ... 61-64
Earlier sketches in CA 5-8R, CANR-9
See also CLC 7
Aytoun, SirRobert 1570-1638 ... DLB 121
Aytoun, William Edmonstoune 1813-1865 .. DLB 32, 159
Ayub Khan, Mohammad 1907-1974 ... CAP-2
Earlier sketch in CA 23-24
Ayvazian, L. Fred 1919- ... 69-72
Azaid
See Zaidenberg, Arthur
Azar, Edward E(lias) 1938-1991 ... CANR-28
Obituary ... 134
Earlier sketch in CA 49-52
Azarian, Mary 1940- ... 118
Azarya, Victor 1946- ... 129
Azbel, Mark Ya. 1932- ... 105
Azcarate y Florez, Pablo de 1890-1971 Obituary ... 113
Azevedo, Carlos de 1918- ... 136
Azevedo, Ross E(ames) ... 105
Aziz, Sartaj 1929- ... 111
Aznavour, Charles
See Aznavourian, Varenagh
Aznavourian, Varenagh 1924- Brief entry ... 112
Azneer, J. Leonard 1921- ... 33-36R
Azorin
See Martinez Ruiz, Jose
See also CLC 11
Azoy, A(nastasio) C. M. 1891- ... CAP-1
Earlier sketch in CA 13-14
Azoy, G. Whitney 1940- ... 128
Azrael, Judith Anne 1938- ... CANR-10
Earlier sketch in CA 65-68
Azrin, Nathan H(arold) 1930- ... CANR-16
Earlier sketches in CA 45-48, CANR-1
Azuela, Arturo 1938- ... 131
See also HW
Azuela, Mariano 1873-1952 ... 131
Brief entry ... 104
See also DAM MULT
See also HLC
See also HW
See also MTCW 1
See also TCLC 3
Azumi, Atsushi 1907- ... 102
Azumi, Koya 1930- ... 29-32R

B

Ba, Mariama 1929-1981 ... 141
See also BLCS
See also BW 2
Baack, Lawrence James 1943- ... 109
Baade, (Wilhelm Heinrich) W(alter) 1893-1960 Obituary ... 112
Baali, Fuad (G.) 1930- Brief entry ... 117
Baal-Teshuva, Jacob 1929- ... 5-8R
Baantjer, Albert Cornelis 1923- ... 141
Baar, James A. 1929- ... 102
Baars, Conrad W(alterus) 1919-1981 ... CANR-8
Earlier sketch in CA 57-60
Baars, Donald Lee 1928- ... 121
Baarslag, Karl Herman William 1900-1984 Obituary ... 111
Baastad, Babbis Friis
See Friis-Baastad, Babbis Ellinor
Baatz, Charles A(lbert) 1916-1982 ... 104
Obituary ... 162
Baatz, Olga K. 1921- ... 104
Bab
See Gilbert, W(illiam) S(chwenck)
Baba, Meher 1894-1969 ... 109
Obituary ... 106
Babb, Howard S(elden) 1924-1978 ... 13-16R
Obituary ... 120
Babb, Hugh Webster 1887-197(?) ... CAP-1
Earlier sketch in CA 13-14
Babb, Janice Barbara
See Bentley, Janice Babb
Babb, Lawrence 1902-1979 ... CAP-2
Obituary ... 162
Earlier sketch in CA 33-36
Babb, Lawrence Alan 1941- Brief entry ... 105
Babb, Sanora 1907- ... 13-16R
Babb, Valerie (Melissa) 1955- ... 142
See also BW 2
Babbage, Stuart Barton 1916- ... CANR-8
Earlier sketch in CA 5-8R
Babbidge, Homer D(aniels), Jr. 1925-1984 ... CANR-13
Obituary ... 112
Earlier sketch in CA 61-64
Babbie, Earl (Robert) 1938- ... CANR-48
Earlier sketches in CA 61-64, CANR-8, 23
Babbis, Eleanor
See Friis-Baastad, Babbis Ellinor
Babbitt, Bruce E(dward) 1938- ... 97-100
Babbitt, Irving 1865-1933 ... DLB 63
Babbitt, Lucy Cullyford 1960- ... 151
See also SATA 85
Babbitt, Natalie (Zane Moore) 1932- ... CANR-38
Earlier sketches in CA 49-52, CANR-2, 19
See also CLR 2
See also DLB 52
See also JRDA
See also MAICYA
See also SAAS 5
See also SATA 6, 68
Babbitt, Robert
See Bangs, Robert B(abbitt)
Babbitt, Susan E. 1953- ... 159
Babbs, Ken 1936- ... 158
Babcock, C(larence) Merton 1908- ... CANR-5
Earlier sketch in CA 5-8R
Babcock, Chris 1963- ... 150
See also SATA 83
Babcock, Dennis Arthur 1948- ... 61-64
See also SATA 22
Babcock, Dorothy E(llen) 1931- ... 65-68
Babcock, Frederic 1896- ... 5-8R
Babcock, Frederick Morrison 1897(?)-1983 Obituary ... 110
Babcock, Havilah 1898-1964 ... 122
Obituary ... 110
Babcock, Leland S. 1922- Brief entry ... 106
Babcock, Nicolas
See Lewis, Tom
Babcock, Robert J(oseph) 1928- ... 13-16R
Babe, Thomas 1941- ... CANR-67
Earlier sketch in CA 101
Interview in ... 101
Babel, Isaac
See Babel, Isaak (Emmanuilovich)
Babel, Isaak (Emmanuilovich) 1894-1941(?) ... 155
Brief entry ... 104
See also SSC 16
See also TCLC 2, 13
Baber, Asa 1936- ... 140
Baber, Carolyn Stonnell 1936- ... 161
See also SATA 96
Baber, Walter F(rank) 1953- ... 120
Babich, Babette E. 1956- ... 149
Babiiha, Thaddeo K(itasimbwa) 1945- ... 110
Babin, David E. 1925- ... 21-24R
Babin, Maria Teresa 1910- Brief entry ... 107
See also HW
Babington, Anthony Patrick 1920- ... 61-64
Babington Smith, Constance 1912- ... 131
Babits, Mihaly 1883-1941 Brief entry ... 114
See also TCLC 14
Babitz, Eve 1943- ... CANR-28
Earlier sketch in CA 81-84
Babitz, Sol 1911-1982 ... CANR-28
Earlier sketch in CA 41-44R
Babladelis, Georgia 1931- ... CANR-8
Earlier sketch in CA 21-24R
Babris, Peter J. 1917- ... CANR-10
Earlier sketch in CA 21-24R
Babrius c. 150-c. 200 ... DLB 176
Babson, Marian ... CANR-66
Earlier sketch in CA 102
Babson, Roger W(ard) 1875-1967 Obituary .. 89-92
Babula, William 1943- ... CANR-45
Earlier sketches in CA 105, CANR-21
Babushka
See Malamud-Goti, Jaime
Baca, Jimmy Santiago 1952- ... 131
See also DAM MULT
See also DLB 122
See also HLC
See also HW
Baca, Jose Santiago
See Baca, Jimmy Santiago
Baca, Manuel Cabeza de 1853-1915 ... DLB 122
Baca, Murtha ... 154
Baca Gilbert, Fabiola Cabeza de 1898- ... DLB 122
Bacall, Lauren 1924- ... 93-96
Bacchelli, Riccardo 1891-1985 ... 29-32R
Obituary ... 117
See also CLC 19
Bacciocco, Edward J(oseph), Jr. 1935- ... 45-48
Bach, Alice (Hendricks) 1942- ... CANR-60
Earlier sketch in CA 101
See also SATA 30, 93
See also SATA-Brief 27
Bach, Bert C(oates) 1936- ... 21-24R
Bach, George Leland 1915- ... CANR-3
Earlier sketch in CA 1-4R
Bach, George Robert 1914- ... 104
Bach, Ira J(ohn) 1906-1985 ... 115
Bach, Jean
See Greif, Martin
Bach, Kent 1943- ... 85-88
Bach, Marcus (Louis) 1906- Brief entry ... 115
Bach, Orville E(uing), Jr. 1946- ... 115
Bach, P. D. Q.
See Schickele, Peter
Bach, Richard (David) 1936- ... CANR-18
Earlier sketch in CA 9-12R
See also AITN 1
See also BEST 89:2
See also CLC 14
See also DAM NOV, POP
See also MTCW 1
See also SATA 13
Bach, Steven 1940- ... 141
Bach, Wilfrid 1936- ... CANR-10
Earlier sketch in CA 61-64

Bacharach, Alfred L(ouis) 1891-1966 .... CAP-1
Earlier sketch in CA 11-12
Bacharach, Bert(ram Mark)
1898-1983 Obituary 110
Bache, Benjamin Franklin 1769-1798 ...... DLB 43
Bache, Ellyn 1942- CANR-65
Earlier sketch in CA 129
Bache, William B. 1922- 25-28R
Bachelard, Gaston 1884-1962 97-100
Obituary 89-92
Bachelder, Thomas 1958- 139
Bacheller, Irving 1859-1950 .... DLB 201
Bachem Alent, Rose M(arie Baake) 49-52
Bacher, June Masters 1918- 108
Bachkatov, Nina 1946- 134
Bachman, David C(hristian) 1934- 124
Bachman, Fred 1949- 53-56
See also SATA 12
Bachman, Jerald G(raybill) 1936- 41-44R
Bachman, John Walter 1916- 5-8R
Bachman, Richard
See King, Stephen (Edwin)
Bachman, W(illiam) Bryant, Jr. 1941- 145
Bachmann, Gideon 1927- 104
Bachmann, Ingeborg 1926-1973 .... CANR-69
Obituary 45-48
Earlier sketch in CA 93-96
See also CLC 69
See also DLB 85
Bachmura, Frank T(homas) 1922- 45-48
Bacho, Peter 1950- 167
Bachrach, Bernard S. 1939- 113
Bachrach, Deborah 147
See also SATA 80
Bachrach, Judy 1948- 114
Bacik, James Joseph 1936- 105
Back, Joe (W.) 1899-1986 .... CAP-2
Obituary 120
Earlier sketch in CA 17-18
Back, Kurt W(olfgang) 1919- 13-16R
Backer, Dorothy 1925- 85-88
Backer, John H. 1902-1985 ....33-36R
Obituary 116
Backer, Morton 1918- 17-20R
Backes, Clarus 1935-1988 Obituary 127
Backes, David James 1957- 166
Backgammon, Daisy
See Murray, John F(rancis)
Backhouse, Janet 1938- CANR-54
Earlier sketches in CA 109, CANR-26
Backhouse, Sally 1927- 21-24R
Backlund, Ralph T. 1918- 73-76
Backman, Carl W(ard) 1923- 17-20R
Backman, Jules 1910- CANR-3
Earlier sketch in CA 1-4R
Backman, Melvin (Abraham) 1919- 21-24R
Backman, Milton V., Jr. 1927- CANR-13
Earlier sketch in CA 33-36R
Backscheider, Paula R(ice) 1943- 138
Backstrom, Charles H(erbert) 1926- 13-16R
Backus, James Gilmore 1913-1989 Obituary ... 129
See also SATA-Obit 63
Backus, Jean L(ouise) 1914-1986 .... 33-36R
Obituary 119
Backus, Jim
See Backus, James Gilmore
Backus, Oswald P(rentiss) III 1921-1972 .... CAP-2
Obituary 37-40R
Earlier sketch in CA 33-36
Backus, (D.) William 1926- 135
Bacle, Claude
See Grignon, Claude-Henri
Bacmeister, Rhoda W(arner) 1893-1991 .... CAP-1
Obituary 133
Earlier sketch in CA 13-16
See also SATA 11
Bacon, Daisy Sarah 1899(?)-1986 Obituary 118
Bacon, Delia 1811-1859 .... DLB 1
Bacon, Donald C(onrad) 1935- 133
Bacon, Edmund N(orwood) 1910- 41-44R
Bacon, Edward 1906-1981 .... 29-32R
Obituary 102
Bacon, Elizabeth 1914- 29-32R
See also SATA 3
Bacon, Elizabeth E(maline) 1904- CAP-1
Earlier sketch in CA 19-20
Bacon, Ernst 1898-1990 Obituary 131
Bacon, Frances Atchinson 1903- 1-4R
Bacon, Francis 1561-1626 .... CDBLB Before 1660
See also DLB 151
Bacon, Joan Chase
See Bowden, Joan Chase
Bacon, John 1940- 53-56
Bacon, Josephine Dodge (Daskam)
1876-1961 97-100
See also SATA 48
Bacon, Lenice Ingram 1895- 45-48
Bacon, Margaret 106
Bacon, Margaret Frances
See Bacon, Peggy
See also SATA-Obit 50
Bacon, Margaret Hope 1921- 25-28R
See also SATA 6
Bacon, Marion 1901(?)-1975 Obituary 57-60
Bacon, Mark S. 1948- 151
Bacon, Martha Sherman 1917-1981 85-88
Obituary 104
See also CLR 3
See also SATA 18
See also SATA-Obit 27
Bacon, Melvin (L.) 1950- 159
See also SATA 93
Bacon, Nancy 1940- 93-96
Bacon, Nicholas c. 1510-1579 .... DLB 132
Bacon, Peggy 1895-1987 .... CAP-2
Obituary 121
Earlier sketch in CA 23-24
See also Bacon, Margaret Frances
See also SATA 2
Bacon, Phillip 1922- 41-44R
Bacon, R(onald) L(eonard) 1924- CANR-51
Earlier sketch in CA 104
See also SATA 26, 84
Bacon, Roger 1214(?)-1292 .... DLB 115
Bacon, Thomas 1700(?)-1768 ....DLB 31
Bacon, Wallace A(lger) 1914- 17-20R
Bacote, Clarence A(lbert) 1906- CAP-2
Earlier sketch in CA 33-36
Bacovia, G.
See Vasiliu, Gheorghe
Bacovia, George
See Vasiliu, Gheorghe
See also TCLC 24
Bacque, James 1929- 101
Bada, Constantina 1950- 145
Badanes, Jerome 1937- ....CLC 59
Badash, Lawrence 1934- CANR-14
Earlier sketch in CA 37-40R
Badawi, M(ohamed) M(ustafa) 1925- CANR-1
Earlier sketch in CA 49-52
Badawi, Muhammed Mustafa
See Badawi, M(ohamed) M(ustafa)
Badcock, Christopher Robert 1946- 101
Badcock, Gary D. 1961- 164
Baddeley, Alan D(avid) 1934- 69-72
Baddeley, Hermione 1906(?)-1986 133
Obituary 120
Baddeley, V. C. Clinton
See Clinton-Baddeley, V.C.
Baddock, James 1950- 137
Bade, Jane (Ruth) 1932- 89-92
Bade, Patrick 1951- 89-92
Baden, Robert 1936- 138
See also SATA 70
Baden-Powell, Dorothy 1920- 103
Baden-Powell, Robert (Stephenson Smyth)
1857-1941 Brief entry 114
See also SATA 16
Bader, Douglas (Robert Steuart) 1910-1982 101
Obituary 107
Bader, Julia 1944- 69-72
Bader, Robert S(mith) 1925- 120
Badger, John d'Arcy 1917- 45-48
Badger, Ralph E(astman) 1890-1978 .... CAP-2
Obituary 73-76
Earlier sketch in CA 21-22
Badger, Reid 1942- 97-100
Badgley, John 1930- 37-40R
Badgley, Robin F(rancis) 1931- 101
Badham, Leslie (Stephen Ronald)
1908-1975 Obituary 114
Badham, Roger A. 167
Badia, Leonard F(rancis) 1934- 113
Badian, Ernst 1925- 37-40R
Badillo, Herman 1929- 85-88
Badinter, Elisabeth 1944- 118
Badough, Rose Marie 1938- 117
Badt, Karin L(uisa) 1963- 155
See also SATA 91
Badura-Skoda, Eva 1929- CANR-14
Earlier sketch in CA 37-40R
Baechler, Jean 1937- CANR-56
Earlier sketches in CA 73-76, CANR-13, 30
Baeck, Leo 1873-1956 Brief entry 115
Baeder, John 1938- 111
Baehr, Consuelo 1938- 103
Baehr, Harry William 1907-1987 Obituary 123
Baehr, Kingsley M. 1937- 155
See also SATA 89
Baehr, Patricia (Goehner) 1952- CANR-35
Earlier sketch in CA 103
See also SATA 65
Baen, James P. 1943- Brief entry 112
Baensch, Willy E(dward)
1893-1972 Obituary 37-40R
Baenziger, Hans 1917- 49-52
Baer, Adela S(wenson) 1931- 101
Baer, Curtis O. 1898- 49-52
Baer, Daniel J(oseph) 1929- 33-36R
Baer, Donald Merle 1931- 81-84
Baer, Earl E. 1928- 57-60
Baer, Edith R(uth) 1920- CANR-21
Earlier sketch in CA 104
Baer, Eleanora A(gnes) 1907- 9-12R
Baer, Gabriel 1919- CANR-2
Earlier sketch in CA 5-8R
Baer, George Webster 1935- 21-24R
Baer, Hans A. 1944- CANR-44
Earlier sketch in CA 119
Baer, Jean L. CANR-9
Earlier sketch in CA 13-16R
Interview in CANR-9
Baer, Jill
See Gilbert, (Agnes) Joan (Sewell)
Baer, John 1886-1970 Obituary 29-32R
Baer, Judith A(bbott) 1945- 81-84
Baer, Judy 1951- .... SATA 71
Baer, Marc (Bradley) 1945- 138
Baer, Marianne 1932- 81-84
Baer, Martha 1961- 158
Baer, Max Frank 1912- 9-12R
Baer, Rosemary 1913- 41-44R
Baer, Walter S. III 1937- 65-68
Baer, Werner 1931- 9-12R
Baerg, Harry J(ohn) 1909- CANR-4
Earlier sketch in CA 9-12R
See also SATA 12
Baerwald, Hans H(erman) 1927- 33-36R
Baerwald, Sara 1948- 61-64
Baes, Katharine Lee 1859-1929 ....DLB 71
Baeten, Lieve 1954- ....SATA 83
Baetjer, Anna M(edora) 1899-1984 Obituary ... 112
Baetzhold, Howard G(eorge) 1923- 29-32R
Baeuml, Franz H(einrich) 1926- 49-52
Baez, Joan (Chandos) 1941- CANR-55
Earlier sketches in CA 21-24R, CANR-26
See also HW
Bagarag, Shibli
See Lawlor, Patrick Anthony
Bagby, George
See Stein, Aaron Marc
Bagby, Wesley M(arvin) 1922- CANR-37
Earlier sketches in CA 1-4R, CANR-16
Bagdikian, Ben Haig 1920- CANR-6
Earlier sketch in CA 9-12R
Bage, Robert 1728-1801 ....DLB 39
Bagehot, Walter 1826-1877 .... DLB 55
Bagert, Brod 1947- 147
See also SATA 80
Bagg, Graham (William) 1917- 57-60
Bagg, Robert Ely 1935- CANR-42
Earlier sketches in CA 65-68, CANR-15
Baggaley, Andrew R(obert) 1923- 13-16R
Baggett, Nancy 1943- 117
Baggley, John (Samuel) 1940- 124
Bagin, Don(ald Richard) 1938- 77-80
Baginski, Frank 1938- 93-96
Bagley, Christopher 1937- 119
Bagley, Desmond 1923-1983 .... CANR-29
Obituary 109
Earlier sketch in CA 17-20R
See also DLB 87
Bagley, Edward R(osecrans) 1926- CANR-5
Earlier sketch in CA 53-56
Bagley, J(ohn) J(oseph) 1908-1989 ...... CANR-2
Obituary 127
Earlier sketch in CA 5-8R
Bagley, Michael 1947- 129
Bagnall, Nigel (Thomas) 1927- 136
Bagnel, Joan 1933- 49-52
Bagni, Gwen
See Dubov, Gwen Bagni
Bagnold, Enid 1889-1981 .... CANR-40
Obituary 103
Earlier sketches in CA 5-8R, CANR-5
See also CLC 25
See also DAM DRAM
See also DLB 13, 160, 191
See also MAICYA
See also SATA 1, 25
Bagnold, Ralph Alger 1896-1990 Obituary 131
Bagramian, Ivan K(ristoforovich)
1897-1982 Obituary 107
Bagritsky, Eduard 1895-1934 .... TCLC 60
Bagrjana, Elisaveta
See Belcheva, Elisaveta
Bagryana, Elisaveta
See Belcheva, Elisaveta
See also CLC 10
See also DLB 147
Bagster, Hubert
See Trumper, Hubert Bagster
Bagwell, Philip S(idney) 1914- CANR-70
Earlier sketches in CA 33-36R, CANR-13, 29
Bagwell, William Francis, Jr. 1923- CANR-31
Earlier sketch in CA 33-36R
Bahadur, K(rishna) P(rakash) 1924- CANR-28
Earlier sketch in CA 57-60
Bahat, Dan 1938- 77-80
Bahl, Roy W., (Jr.) 1939- 21-24R
Bahlke, George W(ilbon) 1934- 29-32R
Bahlke, Valerie Worth 1933-1994 .... CANR-44
Obituary 146
Earlier sketches in CA 41-44R, CANR-15
See also Worth, Valerie
See also SATA 81
Bahlman, Dudley Ward Rhodes 1923- 85-88
Bahm, Archie J(ohn) 1907- CANR-3
Earlier sketch in CA 9-12R
Bahmueller, Charles F(erdinand) 1942- 112
Bahn, Eugene 1906- 21-24R
Bahn, Margaret (Elizabeth) Linton 1907-1969 ......
CAP-2
Earlier sketch in CA 25-28
Bahn, Paul (Gerard) 1953- 146
Bahous, Sally 1939- ....SATA 86
Bahr, Edith-Jane 1926- 65-68
Bahr, Erhard 1932- 33-36R
Bahr, Hermann 1863-1934 Brief entry 121
See also DLB 81, 118
Bahr, Howard M. 1938- CANR-12
Earlier sketch in CA 29-32R
Bahr, Jerome 1909- 33-36R
Bahr, Mary M(adelyn) 1946- CANR-65
Earlier sketch in CA 136
See also SATA 95
Bahr, Robert 1940- CANR-9
Earlier sketch in CA 65-68
See also SATA 38
Bahti, Tom 1926-1972 ....SATA 57
See also SATA-Brief 31
Baier, Kurt Erich 1917- 65-68
Baigell, Matthew 1933- 107
Bai Jieming
See Barme, Geremie
Bail, Murray 1941- CANR-62
Earlier sketch in CA 127
Bailes, Kendall E(ugene) 1940- Brief entry 112
Bailey, Abigail Abbot 1746-1815 .... DLB 200
Bailey, Alfred Goldsworthy 1905- 25-28R
See also DLB 68
Bailey, Alfred M(arshall) 1894-1978 ....41-44R
Bailey, Alice A(nne La Trobe-Bateman)
1880(?)-1949 Brief entry 116
Bailey, Alice Cooper 1890-1978 .... CANR-70
Earlier sketches in CAP-1, CA 13-16
See also SATA 12
Bailey, Anne 1958- ....SATA 71
Bailey, Anthony 1933- CANR-44
Earlier sketches in CA 1-4R, CANR-3
Bailey, Barry 1926- 107
Bailey, Bernadine (Freeman) 1901- CANR-7
Earlier sketch in CA 5-8R
See also SATA 14
Bailey, Beryl Loftman 1920(?)-1977 Obituary . 69-72
Bailey, Beth L. 1957- 142
Bailey, Carolyn Sherwin 1875-1961 73-76
See also MAICYA
See also SATA 14
Bailey, Charles W(aldo) II 1929- CANR-1
Earlier sketch in CA 1-4R
Bailey, Chris H(arvey) 1946- 65-68
Bailey, Conrad Charles Maitland 1922- 105
Bailey, D. F. 1950- 125
Bailey, D. R. Shackleton
See Shackleton Bailey, D(avid) R(oy)
Bailey, David (Royston) 1938- 120
Bailey, David C(harles) 1930- 45-48
Bailey, Derrick Sherwin 1910-1984 .... CANR-2
Obituary 112
Earlier sketch in CA 5-8R
Bailey, Don 1942- 93-96
Bailey, Donna (Veronica Anne) 1938- 136
See also SATA 68
Bailey, Dudley 1918- 17-20R
Bailey, Eric 1933- 33-36R
Bailey, F(rancis) Lee 1933- 89-92
Bailey, Fred Arthur 1947- CANR-72
Earlier sketch in CA 129
Bailey, (John) Frederick (II) 1946- 133
Bailey, Frederick George 1924- CANR-9
Earlier sketch in CA 13-16R
Bailey, Frederick Marshman 1882-1967 .... CAP-1
Earlier sketch in CA 13-14
Bailey, George 1919- CANR-38
Earlier sketches in CA 25-28R, CANR-17
Bailey, Gerald Earl 1929- CANR-10
Earlier sketch in CA 25-28R
Bailey, Gordon Keith 1936- 112
Bailey, H(enry) C(hristopher)
1878-1961 Obituary 108
See also DLB 77
Bailey, Harold (Walter) 1899-1996 109
Obituary 151
Bailey, Harry A(ugustine), Jr. 1932- 21-24R
Bailey, Helen Miller 1909- 13-16R
Bailey, Herbert S(mith), Jr. 1921- Brief entry ... 112
Bailey, Hilary 1936- 158
Bailey, Hillary G(oodsell) 1894- 57-60
Bailey, Hugh C(oleman) 1929- 9-12R
Bailey, J(ames) Martin 1929- 49-52
Bailey, J(ames) O(sler) 1903-1979 ....17-20R
Obituary 126
Bailey, Jackson Holbrook 1925-1996 .... CANR-21
Obituary 153
Earlier sketch in CA 45-48
Bailey, Jacob 1731-1808 ....DLB 99
Bailey, James H(enry) 1919- 106
Bailey, James R(ichard) A(be) 1919- 53-56
Bailey, (Corinne) Jane 1943- 77-80
Bailey, Jane H(orton) 1916- CANR-4
Earlier sketch in CA 53-56
See also SATA 12
Bailey, Joan H(auser) 1922- 21-24R
Bailey, Joe A(llen) 1929- 37-40R
Bailey, John (Robert) 1940- 121
See also SATA 52
Bailey, John A(medee) 1929- 37-40R
Bailey, K. C.
See Bailey, Kathleen C.
Bailey, Kathleen C. 1949- 149
Bailey, Kenneth K(yle) 1923- 21-24R
Bailey, Kenneth P. 1912- CANR-4
Earlier sketch in CA 53-56
Bailey, Lee 1930- 144
Bailey, Linda 1948- 166
Bailey, Lloyd Richard 1936- CANR-15
Earlier sketch in CA 85-88
Bailey, M(innie Elizabeth) Thomas 57-60
Bailey, Maralyn Collins (Harrison) 1941- 53-56
See also SATA 12
Bailey, Martha (J.) 1929- 151
Bailey, Martin 1947- 134
Bailey, Matilda
See Radford, Ruby L(orraine)
Bailey, Maurice Charles 1932- 53-56
See also SATA 12
Bailey, Norman A(lishan) 1931- CANR-13
Earlier sketch in CA 21-24R
Bailey, Patrick 1925- 57-60
Bailey, Paul 1937- CANR-62
Earlier sketches in CA 21-24R, CANR-16
See also CLC 45
See also DLB 14
Bailey, Paul Dayton 1906-1987 .... CANR-6
Obituary 124
Earlier sketch in CA 5-8R
Bailey, Pearl (Mae) 1918-1990 .... CANR-42
Obituary 132
Earlier sketches in CA 61-64, CANR-14
See also BW 2
See also SATA 81
Bailey, Philip James 1816-1902 .... DLB 32
Bailey, Ralph Edgar 1893-1982 .... CANR-70
Earlier sketches in CAP-1, CA 17-18
See also SATA 11
Bailey, Raymond H(amby) 1938- CANR-8
Earlier sketch in CA 61-64
Bailey, Richard W(eld) 1939- CANR-10
Earlier sketch in CA 25-28R

Bailey, Robert, Jr. 1945- 49-52
Bailey, Robert W(ilson) 1943- CANR-21
Earlier sketch in CA 69-72
Bailey, Robin W(ayne) 1952- 154
Bailey, Stephen Kemp 1916-1982 .... CANR-4
Obituary 106
Earlier sketch in CA 1-4R
Bailey, Sydney D(awson) 1916-1995 .... CANR-31
Obituary 150
Earlier sketches in CA 69-72, CANR-12
Bailey, Thomas A(ndrew) 1902-1983 .... CANR-18
Obituary 110
Earlier sketch in CA 17-20R
Bailey, Victor 1948- 125
Bailie, Victoria Worley 1894- CAP-1
Earlier sketch in CA 13-16
Bailkey, Nels M(artin) 1911- 33-36R
Baillargeon, Pierre 1916-1967 152
See also DLB 88
Baillen, Claude
See Delay(-Tubiana), Claude
Baillie, Allan (Stuart) 1943- CANR-42
Earlier sketch in CA 118
See also AAYA 25
See also CLR 49
See also SAAS 21
See also SATA 87
Baillie, Hugh 1890-1966 Obituary 89-92
See also DLB 29
Baillie, Isobel 1895-1983 Obituary 110
Baillie, Joanna 1762-1851 .... DLB 93
Baillie, Kate 1957- 124
Baillie-Hamilton, George 1894-1986 Obituary .. 121
Baily, Charles M(ichael) 1944- 117
Baily, Leslie 1906-1976 .... CAP-2
Earlier sketch in CA 25-28
Baily, Nathan A(riel) 1920- CANR-6
Earlier sketch in CA 9-12R
Baily, Samuel L(ongstreth) 1936- 29-32R
Bailyn, Bernard 1922- CANR-46
Earlier sketches in CA 61-64, CANR-8
See also DLB 17
Bailyn, Lotte 1930- 146
Bain, A(ndrew) D(avid) 1936- Brief entry 111
Bain, Carl E. 1930- 85-88
Bain, Chester A(rthur) 1912- 29-32R
Bain, Chester Ward 1919- 85-88
Bain, David Haward 1949- 141
Bain, George Sayers 1939- 132
Bain, Joe S. 1912- 33-36R
Bain, Kenneth (Ross) 1923- 130
Bain, Kenneth Bruce Findlater 1921-1985 93-96
Obituary 115
Bain, Kenneth Ray 1942- 104
Bain, Robert 1932- 77-80
Bain, Trevor 1931- 145
Bain, Willard S., Jr. 1938- 25-28R
Bainbridge, Beryl (Margaret) 1933- CANR-55
Earlier sketches in CA 21-24R, CANR-24
See also CLC 4, 5, 8, 10, 14, 18, 22, 62
See also DAM NOV
See also DLB 14
See also MTCW 1
Bainbridge, Cyril 1928- 129
Bainbridge, Geoffrey 1923- 5-8R
Bainbridge, John (Lakin) 1913-1992 ..... CANR-46
Obituary 139
Earlier sketch in CA 13-16R
Bainbridge, William Sims 1940- 120
Baine, Rodney M(ontgomery) 1913- 69-72
Baines, Anthony C(uthbert) 1912- 5-8R
Baines, Frank 1915-1987 Obituary 124
Baines, Jocelyn 1925-1973 106
Obituary 104
Baines, John (David) 1943- .... SATA 71
Baines, John M. 1935- 41-44R
Baines, John Robert 1946- 123
Bains, Larry
See Sabin, Louis
Bains, William (Arthur) 1955- 145
Bainton, Roland H(erbert) 1894-1984 ..... CANR-5
Obituary 113
Earlier sketch in CA 1-4R
Bair, Deirdre 1935- 81-84
See also BEST 90:4
Bair, Frank E. 1927- 102
Baird, A(lbert) Craig 1883- CAP-1
Earlier sketch in CA 13-14
Baird, Alexander (John) 1925- 9-12R
Baird, Bil
See Baird, William Britton
See also SATA 30
See also SATA-Obit 52
Baird, Duncan H. 1917- 65-68
Baird, Forrest J. 1905- CAP-1
Earlier sketch in CA 19-20
Baird, Irene 1901-1981 .... DLB 68
Baird, Irene (Todd) 1901-1981 145
Baird, J(oseph) Arthur 1922- CANR-3
Earlier sketch in CA 5-8R
Baird, J(oseph) L. 1933- 85-88
Baird, Jack
See Baird, John Charlton
Baird, Jay Warren 1936- 41-44R
Baird, Jesse Hays 1889- 13-16R
Baird, John Charlton 1938- 126
Baird, John D. 1941- 109
Baird, John Edward 1922- 17-20R
Baird, Joseph Armstrong, (Jr.) 1922-1992 ....
CANR-57
Obituary 142
Earlier sketches in CA 33-36R, CANR-12
Baird, Lorrayne Y. 1927- 112
Baird, Marie-Terese 1918- 57-60
Baird, Martha (Joanna) 1921-1981 .... CANR-9
Earlier sketch in CA 61-64

Baird, Nancy Disher 1935- CANR-32
Earlier sketches in CA 89-92, CANR-15
Baird, Patrick D(ouglas) 1912-1984 Obituary ... 112
Baird, Robert D(ahlen) 1933- 53-56
Baird, Robert M. 1937- 139
Baird, Ronald J(ames) 1929- 53-56
Baird, Russell N. 1922- 17-20R
Baird, Thomas (P.) 1923-1990 .... CANR-21
Obituary 131
Earlier sketches in CA 53-56, CANR-4
See also SATA 45
See also SATA-Brief 39
See also SATA-Obit 64
Baird, W(illiam) David 1939- 41-44R
Baird, Wilhelmina 1935- 163
Baird, William (Robb) 1924- 13-16R
Baird, William Britton 1904-1987 106
Obituary 122
See also Baird, Bil
See also SATA 30
Baird-Smith, Robin 1946- 123
Bairstow, Jeffrey N(oel) 1939- CANR-8
Earlier sketch in CA 61-64
Baity, Elizabeth Chesley 1907- 29-32R
See also SATA 1
Baitz, Jon Robin 1961- CANR-72
Earlier sketch in CA 134
Bajema, Carl Jay 1937- CANR-12
Earlier sketch in CA 33-36R
Bakal, Carl 1918- 21-24R
Bakalar, James B. 1943- 97-100
Bakalian, Anny 1951- 145
Bakalis, Michael J. 1938- 85-88
Bakan, David 1921- 25-28R
Bakan, Paul 1928- 21-24R
Bakaric, Vladimir 1912-1983 Obituary 114
Bake, William A(lbert) 1938- 110
Bakeless, John (Edwin) 1894-1978 .... CANR-5
Obituary 118
Earlier sketch in CA 5-8R
See also SATA 9
Bakeless, Katherine Little 1895- 5-8R
See also SATA 9
Bakely, Don(ald Carlisle) 1928- 65-68
Baker, A(rthur) D(avidson) III 1941- 161
Baker, Adelaide N(ichols) 1894-1974 45-48
Obituary 134
Baker, Adolph 1917- 53-56
Baker, Al .... AITN 1
Baker, Alan 1951- CANR-68
Earlier sketches in CA 97-100, CANR-16, 38
See also SATA 22, 93
Baker, (Allen) Albert 1910- 104
Baker, Alfred Thornton 1915(?)-1983 Obituary . 110
Baker, Alison 1953- 144
Baker, Allison
See Crumbaker, Alice
Baker, Alton Wesley 1912- 33-36R
Baker, Asa
See Dresser, Davis
Baker, Augusta 1911-1998 .... CANR-17
Obituary 164
Earlier sketch in CA 1-4R
See also BW 1
See also SATA 3
Baker, Augustine 1575-1641 .... DLB 151
Baker, Benjamin 1915- 1-4R
Baker, Betty D(oreen Flook) 1916- CANR-6
Earlier sketch in CA 9-12R
Baker, Betty Lou 1928-1987 .... CANR-38
Earlier sketches in CA 1-4R, CANR-2
See also JRDA
See also MAICYA
See also SATA 5, 73
See also SATA-Obit 54
Baker, Bill
See Baker, C(harles) William
Baker, Bill 1936- 77-80
Baker, Bill Russell 1933- 57-60
Baker, Bobby
See Baker, Alfred Thornton
and Baker, Robert G.
Baker, C. J.
See Baker, Christopher John
Baker, C(harles) William 1919- 57-60
Baker, Calvin 1972- 163
Baker, Carin Greenberg 1959- .... SATA 79
Baker, Carlos (Heard) 1909-1987 .... CANR-63
Obituary 122
Earlier sketches in CA 5-8R, CANR-3
See also DLB 103
Baker, Carroll 1931- 142
Baker, Charlotte 1910- 17-20R
See also SATA 2
Baker, Christina Looper 1939- 161
Baker, Christopher John 1948- 135
Brief entry 117
Baker, D(onald) Philip 1937- 102
Baker, David (Anthony) 1954- 118
See also DLB 120
Baker, Deborah 1959- 158
Baker, Dennis 1942- 107
Baker, Denys Val 1917-1984 .... CANR-72
Obituary 113
Earlier sketches in CA 9-12R, CANR-6
Baker, Donald G(ene) 1932- 33-36R
Baker, Donald N(oel) 1936- 21-24R
Baker, Donald W(hitelaw) 1923- CANR-12
Earlier sketch in CA 73-76
Baker, Dorothy 1907-1968 .... CANR-1
Obituary 25-28R
Earlier sketch in CA 1-4R
Baker, Eleanor Z(uckerman) 1932- CANR-8
Earlier sketch in CA 57-60

Baker, (Mary) Elizabeth (Gillette) 1923- .. CANR-70
Earlier sketches in CA 1-4R, CANR-3
See also SATA 7
Baker, Elizabeth Faulkner 1886(?)-1973 .... CAP-1
Obituary 41-44R
Earlier sketch in CA 13-16
Baker, Elliott 1922- CANR-63
Earlier sketches in CA 45-48, CANR-2
See also CLC 8
Baker, Elsie 1929- 65-68
Baker, Elsworth F. 1903- CAP-2
Earlier sketch in CA 25-28
Baker, Eric Wilfred 1899-1973 Obituary 45-48
Baker, Eugene H. .... SATA-Brief 50
Baker, F(rederick) Sherman
1902-1976 Obituary 65-68
Baker, Falcon (O., Jr.) 1916- 135
Baker, Frank 1910- 9-12R
Baker, Frank 1936- CANR-18
Earlier sketches in CA 49-52, CANR-2
Baker, Frank S. 1899(?)-1983 Obituary 109
Baker, Frank S(heaffer) 1910- 17-20R
Baker, G. P.
See Baker, Gordon (P.)
Baker, Gary G. 1939- 21-24R
Baker, Gayle Cunningham 1950- 105
See also SATA 39
Baker, George 1915-1975 93-96
Obituary 57-60
Baker, George W(alter) 1915- 21-24R
Baker, Gilbert
See Baker, John Gilbert Hindley
Baker, Gladys L(ucille) 1910- 41-44R
Baker, Gordon (P.) 1938- 130
Baker, Gordon Pratt 1910- 1-4R
Baker, Herbert G(eorge) 1920- 41-44R
Baker, Herschel Clay 1914- 61-64
See also DLB 111
Baker, Houston A., Jr. 1943- CANR-42
Earlier sketches in CA 41-44R, CANR-14
See also BW 2
See also DLB 67
Baker, Howard H(enry), Jr. 1925- 124
Brief entry 113
Baker, Howard Wilson 1905-1990 .... CAP-2
Obituary 132
Earlier sketch in CA 19-20
Baker, Hugh D. R. 1937- CANR-12
Earlier sketch in CA 25-28R
Baker, Ivon 1928- 73-76
Baker, J(ohn) A(lec) 1926- 25-28R
Baker, James C(alvin) 1935- CANR-55
Brief entry 117
Earlier sketch in CA 125
Baker, James Lawrence 1941- 53-56
Baker, James R(upert) 1925- 29-32R
Baker, James T. 1940- 85-88
Baker, James Volant 1903- 57-60
Baker, James W. 1924- 77-80
See also SATA 22, 65
Baker, James W. 1926- 133
Baker, Jameson
See Spencer, David
Baker, Jane Howard 1950- 110
Baker, Janice E(dla) 1941- 57-60
See also SATA 22
Baker, Jean H.
See Russell, George William
See also TCLC 3, 10
Baker, Jean H(ogarth Harvey) 1933- CANR-59
Earlier sketch in CA 41-44R
Baker, Jean-Claude 1944(?)- 150
Baker, Jeannie 1950- CANR-69
Earlier sketch in CA 97-100
See also CLR 28
See also SATA 23, 88
Baker, Jeffrey J(ohn) W(heeler) 1931- CANR-1
Earlier sketch in CA 49-52
See also SATA 5
Baker, Jerry 105
See also AITN 2
Baker, Jill 1951- 127
Baker, Jim
See Baker, James W.
Baker, John 1901(?)-1971 Obituary 104
Baker, John C(hester) 1909- 106
Baker, John F(leetwood) 1901-1985 Obituary .. 117
Baker, John F. 1931- 85-88
Baker, John Gilbert Hindley
1910-1986 Obituary 119
Baker, John H(enry) 1936- 33-36R
Baker, John R(andal) 1900-1984 .... CANR-27
Obituary 113
Earlier sketch in CA 49-52
Baker, John W(esley) 1920- 61-64
Baker, Joseph E(llis) 1905- 33-36R
Baker, Josephine 1906-1975 Obituary 105
Baker, Kage 1952- 164
Baker, Keith Michael 1938- 57-60
Baker, Kenneth F(rank) 1908- CANR-27
Earlier sketch in CA 49-52
Baker, Kevin (Breen) 1958- 143
Baker, Laura Nelson 1911- CANR-70
Earlier sketches in CA 5-8R, CANR-5
See also SATA 3
Baker, Lawrence M(anning) 1907- CAP-1
Earlier sketch in CA 13-14
Baker, Leonard S(tanley) 1931-1984 .... 21-24R
Obituary 114
Baker, Letha Elizabeth (Mitts) 1913- 33-36R
Baker, Lewis
See Baker, Lewis T(urner) III
Baker, Lewis T(urner) III 1953- 129
Baker, Liliane L.
See Baker, Lillian (L.)
Baker, Lillian (L.) 1921- 139

Baker, Liva 1930- 29-32R
Baker, Lori 1962- 156
Baker, Lucinda 1916- 65-68
Baker, Lynn S. 1948- 109
Baker, M(ary) E(llen) Penny 45-48
Baker, Margaret 1890- CANR-6
Earlier sketch in CA 13-16R
See also SATA 4
Baker, Margaret J(oyce) 1918- CANR-22
Earlier sketches in CA 13-16R, CANR-7
See also SAAS 8
See also SATA 12
Baker, Marilyn 1929- Brief entry 111
Baker, Mark 1950- 143
Baker, Mary Gladys Steel 1892-1974 .... CAP-1
Earlier sketch in CA 13-16
See also SATA 12
Baker, Maureen 1948- 162
Baker, (Robert) Michael (Graham) 1938- ... 25-28R
See also SATA 4
Baker, Michael H(enry) C(hadwick) 1937- ....
CANR-23
Earlier sketches in CA 57-60, CANR-8
Baker, Miriam Hawthorn
See Nye, Miriam (Maurine Hawthorn) Baker
Baker, Nancy C(arolyn Moll) 1944- 81-84
Baker, Nancy V. 1952- 144
Baker, Nelson B(laisdell) 1905- 17-20R
Baker, Nicholson 1957- CANR-63
Earlier sketch in CA 135
See also CLC 61
See also DAM POP
Baker, Nikki 1962- 137
See also BW 2
Baker, Nina (Brown) 1888-1957 .... SATA 15
Baker, Norma Jean 1926-1962 129
Obituary 113
Baker, Olaf 187(?)- 129
Baker, Oleda 1934- 69-72
Baker, Pamela J. 1947- 127
See also SATA 66
Baker, Paul R(aymond) 1927- CANR-41
Earlier sketches in CA 9-12R, CANR-4, 19
Baker, Paul T(hornell) 1927- 33-36R
Baker, Pauline H(alpern) 1941- 105
Baker, Pearl Biddlecome 1907- 17-20R
Baker, Peter (Gorton) 1926- CANR-10
Earlier sketch in CA 21-24R
Baker, Philip John Noel
See Noel-Baker, Philip John
Baker, R(onald) J(ames) 1924- 33-36R
Baker, R. R.
See Baker, R(eginald) Robin
Baker, R(eginald) Robin 1944- 110
Baker, Rachel 1904-1978 .... 5-8R
Obituary 103
See also SATA 2
See also SATA-Obit 26
Baker, Ray Stannard 1870-1946 Brief entry 118
See also TCLC 47
Baker, Richard A(llan) 1940- 140
Baker, Richard E. 1950- 148
Baker, Richard M(ason), Jr. 1924-1978 ..... 13-16R
Obituary 135
Baker, Richard St. Barbe 1889-1982 .... CAP-1
Obituary 110
Earlier sketch in CA 11-12
Baker, Richard Terrill 1913-1981 .... 1-4R
Obituary 104
Baker, Robert Allen, Jr. 1921- 108
Baker, Robert Andrew 1910- 109
Baker, Robert B(ernard) 1937- CANR-6
Earlier sketch in CA 53-56
Baker, Robert D(onald) 1927- 121
Baker, Robert G. 1928- 85-88
Baker, Robert J(unior) 1920- 116
Baker, Robert K(erry) 1948- 108
Baker, Robin
See Baker, R(eginald) Robin
Baker, Robin Campbell 1941- 17-20R
Baker, (John) Roger 1934-1993 .... 25-28R
Obituary 143
Baker, Rollin H(arold) 1916- 118
Baker, Ronald L(ee) 1937- 105
Baker, Ross K(enneth) 1938- 29-32R
Baker, Russell (Wayne) 1925- CANR-59
Earlier sketches in CA 57-60, CANR-11, 41
See also BEST 89:4
See also CLC 31
See also MTCW 1
Baker, Samm Sinclair 1909-1997 .... CANR-21
Obituary 157
Earlier sketches in CA 5-8R, CANR-3
See also SATA 12
See also SATA-Obit 96
Baker, Scott (MacMartin) 1947- CANR-72
Earlier sketch in CA 93-96
Baker, Sharlene 1954- 136
Baker, Sharon 1938- 117
Baker, Sheridan (Warner, Jr.) 1918- CANR-18
Earlier sketches in CA 5-8R, CANR-2
Baker, Sir Samuel White 1821-1893 ...... DLB 166
Baker, Stephen 1921- CANR-19
Earlier sketches in CA 1-4R, CANR-3
Baker, Susan (Catherine) 1942- 105
See also SATA 29
Baker, T(homas) F(rancis) Timothy 1935- ... 25-28R
Baker, T(homas) Lindsay 1947- CANR-47
Earlier sketch in CA 121
Baker, Thomas George Adames 1920- 108
Baker, Thomas Harrison 1933- 33-36R
Baker, Victor Richard 1945- 109
Baker, Wesley C. 21-24R
Baker, William 1944- 163
Baker, William Avery 1911- CANR-2
Earlier sketch in CA 5-8R

Baker, William D. 1924- 105
Baker, William E(dwin) 1935- 21-24R
Baker, William Howard
See McNeilly, Wilfred (Glassford)
Baker, William Joseph 1938- CANR-24
Earlier sketch in CA 97-100
Baker, William W(allace) 1921- 73-76
Baker-Carr, Janet 1934- 93-96
Baker White, John 1902- 101
Bakewell, K(enneth) G(raham) B(artlett) 1931- CANR-42
Earlier sketches in CA 102, CANR-19
Bakewell, Paul, Jr. 1889-1972 CAP-1
Earlier sketch in CA 11-12
Bakewell, Peter J(ohn) 1943- 119
Bakhtiar, Laleh Mehree 1938- 69-72
Bakhtin, M.
See Bakhtin, Mikhail Mikhailovich
Bakhtin, M. M.
See Bakhtin, Mikhail Mikhailovich
Bakhtin, Mikhail
See Bakhtin, Mikhail Mikhailovich
Bakhtin, Mikhail Mikhailovich 1895-1975 128
Obituary 113
See also CLC 83
Bakis, Kirsten 1968(?)- 159
Bakish, David (Joseph) 1937- 45-48
Bakjian, Andy 1915- 53-56
Bakke, E(dward) Wight 1903-1971 Obituary 110
Bakke, Mary S(terling) 1904-1987 37-40R
Obituary 121
Bakken, Dick 1941- CANR-25
Earlier sketch in CA 106
Bakken, Henry Harrison 1896- CANR-11
Earlier sketch in CA 65-68
Bakker, Cornelius B(ernardus) 1929- 57-60
Bakker, Elna S(undquist) 1921-1995 69-72
Obituary 149
Bakker, James Orson 1940- 128
Bakker, Jim
See Bakker, James Orson
Bakker, Robert T. 1946(?)- 152
Bakker, Tamara Faye 128
Bakker, Tammy Faye
See Bakker, Tamara Faye
Bakker-Rabdau, Marianne K(atherine) 1935- 73-76
Baklanoff, Eric N. 1925- CANR-13
Earlier sketch in CA 33-36R
Bakr, Abd Al-Wahhab 1933- 139
Bakr el Toure, Askia Muhammad Abu
See Toure, Askia Muhammad Abu Bakr el
Bakshi, Ralph 1938(?)- 138
Brief entry 112
See also CLC 26
Bakshian, Aram 1944- 102
Bakst, Harold 1953- 142
Bakula, William J(ohn), Jr. 1936- 49-52
Bakwin, Harry 1894-1973 CAP-2
Obituary 45-48
Earlier sketch in CA 19-20
Bakwin, Ruth Morris 1898- 17-20R
Bal, Mieke (Maria Gertrudis) 1946- 156
Balaam
See Lamb, G(eoffrey) F(rederick)
Balaam, David N(orman) 1950- 112
Balaban, John B. 1943- CANR-70
Earlier sketches in CA 65-68, CANR-12, 29
See also DLB 120
Balaban, Nancy 1928- 126
Balabkins, Nicholas (W.) 1926- 9-12R
Balachandran, M(adhavarao) 1938- CANR-40
Earlier sketch in CA 102
Balachandran, Sarojini 1934- CANR-40
Earlier sketches in CA 102, CANR-18
Balagura, Saul 1943- 81-84
Balaguru, P(erumalsamy) N(aidu) 1947- 144
Balakian, Anna (Elizabeth) 1916-1997 129
Obituary 160
Balakian, Nona 1919-1991 85-88
Obituary 134
Balakian, Peter 1951- CANR-69
Earlier sketch in CA 102
Balakrishnan, N. 1956- 157
Balanchine, George 1904-1983 111
Obituary 109
Balancy, Pierre Guy Girald 1924-1979 Obituary 89-92
Balandier, Georges (Leon) 1920- CANR-8
Earlier sketch in CA 61-64
Balas, David L(aszlo) 1929- 33-36R
Balaskas, Arthur 1940- 103
Balaskas, Janet (Marion) 1946- 117
Balassa, Bela 1928-1991 CANR-3
Obituary 134
Earlier sketch in CA 1-4R
Balawyder, Aloysius 1924- CANR-15
Earlier sketch in CA 41-44R
Balbontin, Jose Antonio 1893- CAP-1
Earlier sketch in CA 11-12
Balbus
See Huxley, Julian (Sorell)
Balcarce, Alberto G. 1946- 128
Balch, Glenn 1902-1989 CANR-3
Earlier sketch in CA 1-4R
See also SAAS 11
See also SATA 3
See also SATA-Obit 83
Balchen, Bernt 1899-1973 Obituary 45-48
Balchin, John Frederick 1937- 122
Balchin, Nigel (Marlin) 1908-1970 CANR-21
Obituary 29-32R
Earlier sketch in CA 97-100
Balchin, W(illiam) G(eorge) V(ictor) 1916- CANR-18
Earlier sketch in CA 101
Balcomb, Mary N. 1928- 149
Balcomb, Raymond E. 1923- 21-24R
Balcon, Michael 1896-1977 77-80
Obituary 73-76
Bald, F(rederick) Clever 1897-1970 CAP-1
Earlier sketch in CA 13-14
Bald, R(obert) C(ecil) 1901-1965 CANR-6
Earlier sketch in CA 5-8R
Bald, Wambly 1902- DLB 4
Baldanza, Frank 1924- 1-4R
Baldassarri, Mario 1946- 146
Balde, Jacob 1604-1668 DLB 164
Baldelli, Giovanni 1914- 45-48
Baldeosingh, Kevin 1963- 156
Balderose, Nancy Ward 1952- 158
See also SATA 93
Balderson, Margaret 25-28R
Balderston, Daniel 1952- 144
Balderston, Frederick E(mery) 1923- 133
Brief entry 112
Balderston, John L.
See Balderston, John Lloyd
Balderston, John Lloyd 1889-1954 Brief entry 121
See also DLB 26
Balderston, Katharine Canby 1895-1979 Obituary 93-96
Baldick, Chris(topher Giles) 1954- 128
Baldick, Robert 1927-1972 Obituary 89-92
Baldinger, Stanley 1932- 29-32R
Baldinger, Wallace S(pencer) 1905- 1-4R
Baldree, J(asper) Martin, Jr. 1927- 53-56
Baldrey, Keith (Donald) 1958- 133
Baldridge, Cyrus LeRoy 1889- SATA-Brief 29
Baldridge, Mary Humphrey 1937- 114
Baldrige, Letitia (Katherine) CANR-17
Earlier sketch in CA 25-28R
Baldry, Cherith 1947- SATA 72
Baldry, Harold (Caparne) 1907- 17-20R
Balducci, Carolyn (Feleppa) 1946- 33-36R
See also SATA 5
Balducci, Ernesto 1922- CANR-28
Earlier sketches in CA 29-32R, CANR-12
Baldwin, Alex
See Butterworth, W(illiam) E(dmund III)
Baldwin, Anna P. 1947- 128
Baldwin, Anne fl. 1680-1713 DLB 170
Baldwin, Anne Norris 1938- 29-32R
See also SATA 5
Baldwin, Arthur W. 1904(?)-1976 Obituary 69-72
Baldwin, Bates
See Jennings, John (Edward, Jr.)
Baldwin, Billy
See Baldwin, William, Jr.
Baldwin, Christina 1946- CANR-31
Earlier sketches in CA 77-80, CANR-13
Baldwin, Cinda K. 1954- 147
Baldwin, Clara 61-64
See also SATA 11
Baldwin, David A. 1936- 17-20R
Baldwin, Dick
See Raborg, Frederick A(shton), Jr.
Baldwin, Ed(ward A.) 1935- 118
Baldwin, Edward R(obinson) 1935- CANR-21
Earlier sketch in CA 45-48
Baldwin, Faith 1893-1978 CANR-59
Obituary 77-80
Earlier sketches in CA 5-8R, CANR-4
See also AITN 1
Baldwin, Gordo
See Baldwin, Gordon C.
Baldwin, Gordon C. 1908- CANR-62
Earlier sketches in CA 1-4R, CANR-3
See also SATA 12
Baldwin, Hanson W(eightman) 1903-1991 CANR-70
Obituary 136
Earlier sketch in CA 61-64
Baldwin, James 1841-1925 Brief entry 111
See also SATA 24
Baldwin, James (Arthur) 1924-1987 CANR-24
Obituary 124
Earlier sketches in CA 1-4R, CANR-3
See also CABS 1
See also AAYA 4
See also BLC 1
See also BW 1
See also CDALB 1941-1968
See also CLC 1, 2, 3, 4, 5, 8, 13, 15, 17, 42, 50, 67, 90
See also DA
See also DAB
See also DAC
See also DAM MST, MULT, NOV, POP
See also DC 1
See also DLB 2, 7, 33
See also DLBY 87
See also MTCW 1
See also SATA 9
See also SATA-Obit 54
See also SSC 10
See also WLC
Baldwin, John D. 1930- 101
Baldwin, John W(esley) 1929- 105
Baldwin, Joseph B(urkette) 1918-1994 111
Obituary 147
Baldwin, Joseph Glover 1815-1864 DLB 3, 11
Baldwin, Joyce G(ertrude) 1921- CANR-8
Earlier sketch in CA 61-64
Baldwin, Leland D(ewitt) 1897-1981 41-44R
Obituary 103
Baldwin, Lewis V. 1949- 135
Baldwin, Margaret
See Weis, Margaret (Edith)
Baldwin, Marshall W(hithed) 1903-1975 61-64
Obituary 57-60
Baldwin, Michael 1930- CANR-3
Earlier sketch in CA 9-12R
Baldwin, Monica 1896(?)-1975 Obituary 104
Baldwin, Ned
See Baldwin, Edward R(obinson)
Baldwin, Neil 1947- 130
Baldwin, Raymond Earl 1893-1986 Obituary 121
Baldwin, Rebecca
See Chappell, Helen
Baldwin, Richard fl. 1680-1713 DLB 170
Baldwin, Richard S(heridan) 1910- 105
Baldwin, Robert E(dward) 1924- 41-44R
Baldwin, Roger (Nash) 1884-1981 Obituary 105
Baldwin, Roger E(dwin) 1929- 49-52
Baldwin, Stan(ley C.) 1929- CANR-38
Earlier sketches in CA 49-52, CANR-2, 17
See also SATA 62
See also SATA-Brief 28
Baldwin, William, Jr. 1903-1983 129
Obituary 111
Baldwin, William c. 1515-1563 DLB 132
Baldwin, William 1944- 152
Baldwin, William Lee 1928- CANR-3
Earlier sketch in CA 1-4R
Bale, John 1495-1563 DLB 132
Bale, Robert Osborne 1912- 1-4R
Bales, Carol Ann 1940- 45-48
See also SATA 57
See also SATA-Brief 29
Bales, Jack
See Bales, James E(dward)
Bales, James D(avid) 1915- 5-8R
Bales, James E(dward) 1951- CANR-30
Earlier sketch in CA 107
Bales, Kevin 1952- 140
Bales, Robert F(reed) 1916- 93-96
Bales, William Alan 1917-1996 5-8R
Obituary 152
Balester, Valerie M. 1952- 147
Balestrini, Nanni 1935- DLB 128, 196
Balet, Jan (Bernard) 1913- 85-88
See also SATA 11
Baley, James A. 1918- CANR-5
Earlier sketch in CA 13-16R
Balfort, Neil
See Fanthorpe, R(obert) Lionel
Balfour, A. J.
See Balfour, Arthur James
Balfour, Arthur J.
See Balfour, Arthur James
Balfour, Arthur James 1848-1930 Brief entry 120
See also DLB 189
Balfour, Conrad George 1928- 53-56
Balfour, Henry H(allowell), Jr. 1940- 117
Balfour, James 1925- 25-28R
Balfour, John
See Moore, James
Balfour, Michael (Leonard) Graham 1908- CANR-6
Obituary 150
Earlier sketch in CA 9-12R
Balfour, (John) Patrick Douglas 1904-1976 CANR-6
Earlier sketch in CA 9-12R
Balfour, Victoria 1954- 129
Balfour-Kinnear, George Purvis Russell 1888- 5-8R
Balian, Lorna 1929- CANR-40
Earlier sketches in CA 53-56, CANR-4, 19
See also SATA 9, 91
Baligh, Helmy H. 1931- 21-24R
Balikci, Asen 1929- 29-32R
Balinky, Alexander 1919- 21-24R
Balint, Michael 1896-1970 CAP-1
Earlier sketch in CA 9-10
Balis, Andrea F. 1948- 108
Balit, Christina 1961- SATA 102
Balizet, Carol 1933- 114
Baljeu, Joost 1925- 97-100
Balk, Alfred (W.) 1930- 25-28R
Balk, H(oward) Wesley 1932- Brief entry 111
Balka, Marie
See Balkany, Marie (Romoka Zelinger) de
Balkany, Marie (Romoka Zelinger) de 1930- 104
Balke, Willem 1933- 107
Balken, Debra Bricker 1954- 168
Balkey, Rita 1922- CANR-30
Earlier sketch in CA 111
Balkin, Richard 1938- 77-80
Balkoff, Zuri
See Stavans, Ilan
Ball, Angela 1952- 135
Ball, Ann 1944- 148
Ball, Ann E. Bolton
See Ball, Ann
Ball, B. N.
See Ball, Brian N(eville)
Ball, Brian N(eville) 1932- 33-36R
Ball, (Frederick) Clive 1941- Brief entry 114
Ball, David 1937- 65-68
Ball, Desmond (John) 1947- CANR-24
Earlier sketch in CA 106
Ball, Donald W(inston) 1934-1976 122
Obituary 110
Ball, Donna 1951- 108
Ball, Doris Bell (Collier) 1897-1987 CANR-58
Obituary 122
Earlier sketches in CA 1-4R, CANR-2, 18
Ball, Duncan 1941- SATA 73
Ball, Edith L. 1905- 85-88
Ball, Edward 1959- 167
Ball, (Katherine) Eve(lyn) 1890-1984 122
Obituary 114
Ball, F(rederick) Carlton 1911- 17-20R
Ball, George W(ildman) 1909-1994 73-76
Obituary 145
Ball, Howard 1937- CANR-17
Earlier sketch in CA 33-36R
Ball, Jane Eklund 1921- 33-36R
Ball, Jennifer (M. V.) 1958- 136
Ball, John (Dudley, Jr.) 1911-1988 CANR-58
Obituary 126
Earlier sketches in CA 5-8R, CANR-3, 18
Ball, John C. 1924- CANR-8
Earlier sketch in CA 5-8R
Ball, John M(iller) 1923- 33-36R
Ball, Joseph H(urst) 1905-1993 CAP-2
Obituary 143
Earlier sketch in CA 23-24
Ball, Larry Durwood Sr. 1940- 123
Ball, Lucille (Desiree) 1911-1989 164
Ball, M(ary) Margaret 1909- 25-28R
Ball, Marion J(okl) 1940- CANR-15
Earlier sketch in CA 89-92
Ball, Nelson 1942- 134
Ball, Nicole (Janice) 1948- CANR-31
Earlier sketch in CA 112
Ball, Robert Edward 1911- 108
Ball, Robert Hamilton 1902-1988 9-12R
Obituary 127
Ball, Robert J(erome) 1941- 128
Ball, Robert M(yers) 1914- 97-100
Ball, Stuart 1956- 130
Ball, Sylvia Patricia 1936- 57-60
Ball, Terence 1944- 138
Ball, Zachary
See Janas, Frankie-Lee
and Masters, Kelly R.
Ballantine, Bill
See Ballantine, William (Oliver)
Ballantine, David 1926- 115
Ballantine, John
See da Cruz, Daniel, Jr.
Ballantine, John (Winthrop) 1920- 53-56
Ballantine, Joseph W. 1890(?)-1973 Obituary 41-44R
Ballantine, Lesley Frost
See Frost, Lesley
Ballantine, Richard 1940- CANR-1
Earlier sketch in CA 45-48
Ballantine, William (Oliver) 1911- 106
Ballantyne, David (Watt) 1924- CANR-10
Earlier sketch in CA 65-68
Ballantyne, Dorothy Joan (Smith) 1922- 5-8R
Ballantyne, R(obert) M(ichael) 1825-1894 DLB 163
See also JRDA
See also SATA 24
Ballantyne, Sheila 1936- CANR-25
Earlier sketch in CA 101
Ballard, Allen B(utler, Jr.) 1930- 61-64
Ballard, Charles E. 1914(?)-1987 Obituary 123
Ballard, Dean
See Wilkes-Hunter, R(ichard)
Ballard, Edward Goodwin 1910- CANR-30
Earlier sketches in CA 33-36R, CANR-13
Ballard, I. Edward 1909(?)-1985 Obituary 117
Ballard, J(ames) G(raham) 1930- CANR-65
Earlier sketches in CA 5-8R, CANR-15, 39
See also AAYA 3
See also CLC 3, 6, 14, 36
See also DAM NOV, POP
See also DLB 14
See also MTCW 1
See also SATA 93
See also SSC 1
Ballard, Joan Kadey 1928- 5-8R
Ballard, K. G.
See Roth, Holly
Ballard, Lowell C(lyne) 1904-1986 CAP-1
Obituary 120
Earlier sketch in CA 11-12
See also SATA 12
See also SATA-Obit 49
Ballard, Martha Moore 1735-1812 DLB 200
Ballard, (Charles) Martin 1929- 25-28R
See also SATA 1
Ballard, Michael B. 1946- 156
Ballard, Mignon Franklin 1934- 121
See also SATA 64
See also SATA-Brief 49
Ballard, P. D.
See Ballard, (Willis) Todhunter
Ballard, Robert D(uane) 1942- 112
See also SATA 85
Ballard, Terry 1946- 163
Ballard, (Willis) Todhunter 1903-1980 CANR-59
Earlier sketches in CA 13-16R, CANR-29
Ballard, W. T.
See Ballard, (Willis) Todhunter
Ballard, Willis T.
See Ballard, (Willis) Todhunter
Ballem, John 1925- 81-84
Ballen, Roger 1950- 103
Ballendorf, Dirk Anthony 1939- 165
Ballentine, Lee (Kenney) 1954- 162
Ballentine, Rudolph 1941- 114
Baller, Warren Robert 1900- 69-72
Ballerini, Luigi 1940- DLB 128
Ballet, Arthur H(arold) 1924- Brief entry 111
Balliett, Whitney 1926- CANR-57
Earlier sketches in CA 17-20R, CANR-13, 30
Ballin, Caroline 17-20R
Balling, Robert C., Jr. 1952- 138
Ballingall, James (Gordon Mackie) 1958- 117
Ballinger, Bill S.
See Ballinger, William Sanborn
Ballinger, Harry (Russell) 1892- CAP-2
Earlier sketch in CA 23-24
Ballinger, James Lawrence 1919- 17-20R
Ballinger, Louise Bowen 1909- 13-16R
Ballinger, (Violet) Margaret (Livingstone) 1894-1980 CANR-13
Obituary 105
Earlier sketch in CA 61-64
Ballinger, Raymond A. 1907- 5-8R

Ballinger, W. A.
See McNeilly, Wilfred (Glassford)
Ballinger, William Sanborn 1912-1980 ... CANR-58
Obituary ... 97-100
Earlier sketches in CA 1-4R, CANR-1
Ballon, Robert J(ean) 1919- ... CANR-44
Earlier sketches in CA 45-48, CANR-21
Ballonoff, Paul A(lan) 1943- ... 57-60
Ballou, Arthur W. 1915-1981 ... 25-28R
Obituary ... 134
Ballou, Ellen B(artlett) 1905- ... CAP-2
Earlier sketch in CA 29-32
Ballou, Maturin Murray 1820-1895 ... DLB 79, 189
Ballouhey, Pierre 1944- ... SATA 90
Ballowe, James 1933- ... CANR-12
Earlier sketch in CA 29-32R
Ballstadt, Carl A. 1931- ... CANR-54
Earlier sketch in CA 124
Balma, Michael J(ames) 1930- ... 17-20R
Balmain, Pierre (Alexandre)
1914-1982 Obituary ... 107
Balme, Maurice (George) 1925- ... 61-64
Balmer, Edwin 1883-1959 Brief entry ... 114
Balmont, Konstantin (Dmitriyevich) 1867-1943 .. 155
Brief entry ... 109
See also TCLC 11
Balmuth, Miriam S. ... 124
Balodis, Janis (Maris) 1950- ... CANR-67
Earlier sketch in CA 134
Balogh, Mary 1944- ... 161
Balogh, Penelope 1916-1975 ... CAP-2
Earlier sketch in CA 25-28
See also SATA 1
See also SATA-Obit 34
Balogh, Thomas 1905-1985 ... 57-60
Obituary ... 115
Balota, D(avid) A. 1954- ... 135
Balow, Tom 1931- ... 45-48
See also SATA 12
Baloyra, Enrique Antonio 1942- ... 111
Balsdon, (John Percy Vyvian) Dacre 1901-1977 ...
CANR-13
Obituary ... 73-76
Earlier sketch in CA 5-8R
Balsdon, J. P. V. D.
See Balsdon, (John Percy Vyvian) Dacre
Balseiro, Jose Agustin 1900- ... CANR-72
Earlier sketch in CA 81-84
See also AITN 1
See also HW
Balsiger, Dave
See Balsiger, David (Wayne)
Balsiger, David (Wayne) 1945- ... CANR-28
Earlier sketches in CA 61-64, CANR-11
Balsley, Howard L(loyd) 1913- ... CANR-4
Earlier sketch in CA 1-4R
Balsley, Irol Whitmore 1912- ... 13-16R
Balswick, Jack Orville ... 136
Balswick, Judith K. 1939- ... 136
Baltake, Joe 1945- ... 118
Baltazar, Eulalio R. 1925- ... 17-20R
Baltazzi, Evan S(erge) 1921- ... CANR-57
Earlier sketch in CA 65-68
See also SATA 90
Baltensperger, Peter 1938- ... 115
Balterman, Marcia Ridlon 1942- ... 25-28R
See also Ridlon, Marci
Baltes, Paul B. 1939- ... 89-92
Balthasar, Hans Urs von
See von Balthasar, Hans Urs
Balthazar, Earl E(dward) 1918- ... 53-56
Baltimore, J.
See Catherall, Arthur
Baltz, Howard B(url) 1930- ... 29-32R
Baltzell, E(dward) Digby 1915-1996 ... CANR-48
Obituary ... 153
Earlier sketch in CA 33-36R
Baltzer, Hans (Adolf) 1900- ... SATA 40
Balukas, Jean 1959- Brief entry ... 111
Balutansky, Kathleen M(arie) 1954- ... 145
Balwers, Renato
See La Barre, Weston
Baly, (Alfred) Denis 1913- ... 17-20R
Baly, Monica Eileen 1914- ... 102
Balzac, Honore de 1799-1850 ... DA
See also DAB
See also DAC
See also DAM MST, NOV
See also DLB 119
See also SSC 5
See also WLC
Balzano, Jeanne (Koppel) 1912- ... 5-8R
See also Bell, Gina
and Bell-Zano, Gina
and Iannone, Jeanne
Balzer, Richard J(ay) 1944- ... 45-48
Balzer, Robert Lawrence 1912- ... 103
Bambara, Toni Cade 1939-1995 ... CANR-49
Obituary ... 150
Earlier sketches in CA 29-32R, CANR-24
See also AAYA 5
See also BLC 1
See also BW 2
See also CLC 19, 88
See also DA
See also DAC
See also DAM MST, MULT
See also DLB 38
See also MTCW 1
See also WLCS
Bamber, Linda 1945- ... 109
Bamberger, Bernard J(acob) 1904-1980 .. CANR-6
Obituary ... 101
Earlier sketch in CA 13-16R
Bamberger, Carl 1902- ... CAP-2
Earlier sketch in CA 21-22
Bamberger, Fritz 1902-1984 Obituary ... 113
Bamberger, Michael (F.) 1960- ... 134
Bambrough, (John) Renford 1926- ... 61-64
Bamdad, A.
See Shamlu, Ahmad
Bamford, James 1946- ... 123
Bamford, Paul W(alden) 1921- ... 41-44R
Bamford, Samuel 1788-1872 ... DLB 190
Bamfylde, Walter
See Bevan, Tom
Bamm, Peter
See Emmrich, Curt
Bamman, Henry A. 1918- ... CANR-7
Earlier sketch in CA 5-8R
See also SATA 12
Ban, (Maria) Eva 1934- ... 73-76
Ban, Joseph D(aniel) 1926- ... CANR-23
Earlier sketches in CA 21-24R, CANR-8
Ban, Thomas A. 1929- ... CANR-10
Earlier sketch in CA 21-24R
Banani, Amin 1926- ... 33-36R
Banat, D. R.
See Bradbury, Ray (Douglas)
Banazek, Jeanne M. (Carpenter) 1943- ... 156
Banbury, Jen(nifer Marie) 1966- ... 167
Banbury, Philip 1914- ... 102
Bance, Alan F. 1939- ... 111
Banchs, Enrique J. 1888-1968 ... HW
Bancroft, Anne 1923- ... 57-60
Bancroft, Caroline 1900- ... CAP-2
Earlier sketch in CA 21-22
Bancroft, George 1800-1891 ... DLB 1, 30, 59
Bancroft, Griffing 1907- ... 29-32R
See also AITN 1
See also SATA 6
Bancroft, Hubert Howe 1832-1918 ... DLB 47, 140
Bancroft, Iris (May Nelson) 1922- ... CANR-19
Earlier sketch in CA 102
Interview in ... CANR-19
Bancroft, Laura
See Baum, L(yman) Frank
Bancroft, Mary 1903-1997 ... 118
Obituary ... 156
Bancroft, Peter 1916- ... 41-44R
Bancroft, Robert
See Kirsch, Robert R.
Bandarage, Asoka 1950- ... 167
Bandeira (Filho), Manuel (Carneiro de Sousa)
1886(?)-1968 Obituary ... 115
Bandel, Betty 1912- ... 106
See also SATA 47
Bandele, Biyi 1967- ... 167
Bandele-Thomas, Biyi
See Bandele, Biyi
Bandelier, Adolph F. 1840-1914 ... DLB 186
Bander, Edward J. 1923- ... CANR-5
Earlier sketch in CA 13-16R
Bandera, V(ladimir) N(icholas) 1932- ... 33-36R
Bandi, Hans-Georg 1920- ... 85-88
Bandinelli, Ranuccio Bianchi
1901(?)-1975 Obituary ... 53-56
Bandman, Bertram 1930- ... 21-24R
Bandoff, Hope
See Guthrie, Thomas Anstey
Bandow, Doug(las) 1957- ... 127
Bandrauk, Andre D. 1941- ... 149
Bandura, Albert 1925- ... 13-16R
Bandy, (Eugene) Franklin 1914-1987 ... CANR-24
Obituary ... 122
Earlier sketch in CA 33-36R
Bandy, Leland A. 1935- ... 77-80
Bandy, Melanie 1932- ... 114
Bandy, W(illiam) T(homas) 1903-1989 ... 37-40R
Obituary ... 129
Bandy, Way 1941(?)-1986 ... 123
Obituary ... 120
Bane, Mary Jo 1942- ... 126
Brief entry ... 112
Bane, Michael 1950- ... 108
Banel, Joseph 1943- ... 45-48
Baner, Skulda Vanadis 1897-1964 ... CAP-1
Earlier sketch in CA 13-14
See also SATA 10
Banerjee, Asit 1940- ... 146
Banerjee, H(emendra) N(ath) 1929- Brief entry . 114
Banerji, Ranan B(ihari) 1928- ... CANR-11
Earlier sketch in CA 29-32R
Banerji, S(riranjan) 1938- ... 147
Banerji, Sara 1932- ... 126
Banet, Doris Beatrice Robinson 1925- ... 5-8R
Banfield, A(lexander) W(illiam) F(rancis)
1918- ... 61-64
Banfield, Edward C(hristie) 1916- ... 57-60
See also AITN 1
Banfield, Stephen 1951- ... 149
Banfill, A. Scott 1956- ... SATA 98
Bang, Betsy 1912- ... 102
See also SATA 48
See also SATA-Brief 37
Bang, Garrett
See Bang, Molly Garrett
Bang, Molly Garrett 1943- ... 102
See also CLR 8
See also MAICYA
See also SATA 24, 69
Bangert, Ethel E(lizabeth) 1912- ... CANR-1
Earlier sketch in CA 45-48
Bangert, Sharon 1951- ... 146
Bangert, William V(alentine) 1911- ... 45-48
Bangerter, Lowell A(llen) 1941- ... CANR-26
Earlier sketches in CA 69-72, CANR-11
Bangham, Mary Dickerson 1896- ... CAP-2
Earlier sketch in CA 23-24
Banghart, Charles K(enneth)
1910(?)-1980 Obituary ... 97-100
Banghart, Kenneth
See Banghart, Charles K(enneth)
Bangley, Bernard K. 1935- ... CANR-51
Earlier sketches in CA 110, CANR-28
Bangs, Carl (Oliver) 1922- ... CANR-7
Earlier sketch in CA 17-20R
Bangs, Carol Jane 1949- ... 114
Bangs, John Kendrick 1862-1922 Brief entry ... 110
See also DLB 11, 79
Bangs, Lester 1949(?)-1982 Obituary ... 106
Bangs, Richard 1950- ... 122
Bangs, Robert B(abbitt) 1914- ... 37-40R
Banham, (Peter) Reyner 1922-1988 ... CANR-35
Obituary ... 125
Earlier sketch in CA 29-32R
Banim, John 1798-1842 ... DLB 116, 158, 159
Banim, Michael 1796-1874 ... DLB 158, 159
Banis, Victor J(erome) 1937- ... 81-84
Bani-Sadr, Abolhassan 1933- ... 143
Banister, Gary L. 1948- ... 57-60
Banister, Judith 1943- ... CANR-57
Earlier sketch in CA 127
Banister, Manly (Miles) 1914- ... 41-44R
Banister, Margaret 1894(?)-1977 Obituary ... 73-76
Banjo, The
See Paterson, A(ndrew) B(arton)
Bank, Dena Citron 1912- ... 123
Bank, Mirra 1945- ... 102
Bank, Stephen Paul 1941- ... 110
Bank, Ted
See Bank, Theodore P(aul) II
Bank, Theodore P(aul) II 1923- ... 41-44R
Banker, James R. 1938- ... 132
Banker, Mark T(ollie) 1951- ... 143
Bankier, David 1947- ... 145
Bank-Jensen, Thea
See Ottesen, Thea Tauber
Bankoff, George Alexis
See Milkomane, George Alexis Milkomanovich
Bankole, Timothy 1920(?)- ... BW 2
Bankowsky, Richard James 1928- ... 1-4R
Banks, A. L.
See Banks, Arthur Leslie
Banks, A. Leslie
See Banks, Arthur Leslie
Banks, Ann 1943- ... 105
Banks, Arthur Leslie 1904-1989 Obituary ... 129
Banks, Arthur S. 1926- ... CANR-27
Earlier sketch in CA 33-36R
Banks, Brian R. 1956- ... 138
Banks, Carolyn 1941- ... CANR-23
Earlier sketch in CA 105
Banks, Geraldine 1942- ... 147
Banks, Hal N(orman) 1921- ... 102
Banks, Harlan Parker 1913- ... 89-92
Banks, Iain
See Banks, Iain M(enzies)
Banks, Iain M(enzies) 1954- ... CANR-61
Brief entry ... 123
Earlier sketch in CA 128
Interview in ... 128
See also CLC 34
See also DLB 194
Banks, J(ohn) Houston 1911- ... 33-36R
Banks, James A(lbert) 1941- ... CANR-68
Earlier sketches in CA 33-36R, CANR-13, 32
Banks, James Houston 1925- ... 89-92
Banks, Jane 1913- ... 65-68
Banks, Jeri
See Banks, Geraldine
Banks, Jimmy
See Banks, James Houston
Banks, John 1653(?)-1706 ... DLB 80
Banks, Laura Stockton Voorhees
1908(?)-1980 Obituary ... 101
See also SATA-Obit 23
Banks, Leslie 1920- ... 145
Banks, Lynne Reid
See Reid Banks, Lynne
See also AAYA 6
See also CLC 23
Banks, Michael A. 1951- ... 161
See also SATA 101
Banks, Oliver 1941- ... 107
Banks, Richard L. 1920- ... 9-12R
Banks, Roger 1929- ... 107
Banks, Ronald F(illmore) 1934- ... 29-32R
Banks, Russell 1940- ... CANR-52
Earlier sketches in CA 65-68, CANR-19
See also CAAS 15
See also CLC 37, 72
See also DLB 130
Banks, Sara (Jeanne Gordon Harrell)
See Harrell, Sara (Jeanne) Gordon
See also SATA 26
Banks, Taylor
See Banks, Jane
Banks, William L(ove) 1928- ... 112
Bankson, Douglas (Henneck) 1920- ... CANR-31
Earlier sketch in CA 45-48
Bankwitz, Philip Charles Farwell 1924- ... 33-36R
Bann, Stephen 1942- ... 137
Bannatyne-Cugnet, (Elizabeth) Jo(-Anne) 1951- 160
See also SATA 101
Banner, Angela
See Maddison, Angela Mary
See also CLR 24
Banner, Charla Ann Leibenguth 1942- ... CANR-24
Earlier sketch in CA 106
Banner, Hubert Stewart 1891-1964 ... CAP-1
Earlier sketch in CA 11-12
Banner, James M(orrill), Jr. 1935- ... 49-52
Banner, Lois W(endland) 1939- ... CANR-1
Earlier sketch in CA 49-52
Banner, Melvin Edward 1914- ... 53-56
Banner, William Augustus 1915- ... 45-48
Banner-Haley, Charles T. 1948- ... 148
Bannerman, Helen (Brodie Cowan Watson)
1862(?)-1946 ... 136
Brief entry ... 111
See also CLR 21
See also DLB 141
See also MAICYA
See also SATA 19
Bannerman, Mark
See Lewing, Anthony Charles
Bannerman, Roland
See Hartston, W(illiam) R(oland)
Bannerman, W. Mary 1894-1984 Obituary ... 114
Bannet, Eve Tavor ... CANR-55
Earlier sketch in CA 127
Bannick, Nancy (Meredith) 1926- ... 41-44R
Banning, Evelyn I. 1903- ... 73-76
See also SATA 36
Banning, Lance (Gilbert) 1942- ... CANR-52
Earlier sketch in CA 89-92
Banning, Margaret Culkin 1891-1982 ... CANR-70
Obituary ... 105
Earlier sketches in CA 5-8R, CANR-4
Bannister, Don
See Bannister, Donald
Bannister, Donald 1928- ... CANR-9
Earlier sketch in CA 61-64
Bannister, Jo 1951- ... CANR-48
Earlier sketch in CA 119
Bannister, Pat
See Davis, Lou Ellen
Bannister, Patricia Valeria 1923- ... 150
Brief entry ... 115
Bannister, Robert C(orwin), Jr. 1935- ... 21-24R
Bannister, Sally
See Pratt, James Norwood
Bannock, Graham 1932- ... 33-36R
Bannon, Barbara Anne 1928- ... 101
Bannon, John Francis 1905-1986 ... CANR-4
Obituary ... 119
Earlier sketch in CA 1-4R
Bannon, Laura (?)-1963 ... 1-4R
See also SATA 6
Bannon, Peter
See Durst, Paul
Bansal, Vipul K. 1959- ... 142
Bansemer, Roger 1948- ... 137
Banta, Martha 1928- ... CANR-29
Earlier sketch in CA 81-84
Banta, R(ichard) E(lwell) 1904- ... CAP-2
Earlier sketch in CA 33-36
Banta, Trudy W. ... 148
Bantel, Linda 1943- ... 113
Banti, Anna 1895-1985 ... DLB 177
Banting, Keith G. 1947- ... 129
Banting, Peter M(yles) 1936- ... 112
Bantock, G(eoffrey) H(erman) 1914- ... CANR-11
Earlier sketch in CA 25-28R
Bantock, Gavin (Marcus August) 1939- ... 33-36R
Bantock, Nick 1950(?)- ... CANR-65
Earlier sketch in CA 142
See also DAM POP
See also SATA 95
Banton, Coy
See Norwood, Victor G(eorge) C(harles)
Banton, Michael (Parker) 1926- ... CANR-2
Earlier sketch in CA 5-8R
Banville, John 1945- ... 128
Brief entry ... 117
Interview in ... 128
See also CLC 46
See also DLB 14
Banville, Thomas G(eorge) 1924- ... 81-84
Bany, Mary A. 1913- ... 9-12R
Banz, George 1928- ... 29-32R
Banziger, Hans
See Baenziger, Hans
Bapu
See Khare, Narayan Bhaskar
Barabas, Gabor 1948- ... 134
Barabas, Steven 1904-1983 ... 5-8R
Obituary ... 109
Barabas, SuzAnne 1949- ... 134
Barabtarlo, Gene
See Barabtarlo, Gennady
Barabtarlo, Gennady 1949- ... 147
Barach, Alvan L(eroy) 1895-1977 Obituary ... 73-76
Barach, Arnold B(auer) 1913-1987 ... 97-100
Obituary ... 122
Barack, Nathan A. 1913- ... 13-16R
Barackman, Floyd Hays, Jr. 1923- ... 115
Barackman, Paul F(reeman) 1894- ... 1-4R
Baracks, Barbara 1951- ... 106
Barada, Bill
See Barada, William Richard
Barada, William Richard 1913- ... 45-48
Bar-Adon, Aaron 1923- Brief entry ... 114
Baraheni, Reza 1935- ... 69-72
Barak, Gregg 1948- ... CANR-35
Earlier sketch in CA 114
Barak, Michael
See Bar-Zohar, Michael

Baraka, Amiri 1934- CANR-61
Earlier sketches in CA 21-24R, CANR-27, 38
See also Jones, LeRoi
See also CABS 3
See also BLC 1
See also BW 2
See also CDALB 1941-1968
See also CLC 1, 2, 3, 5, 10, 14, 33
See also DA
See also DAC
See also DAM MST, MULT, POET, POP
See also DC 6
See also DLB 5, 7, 16, 38
See also DLBD 8
See also MTCW 1
See also PC 4
See also WLCS
Baral, Robert 1910- CAP-1
Earlier sketch in CA 9-10
Baram, Amatzia 1938- 146
Baram, Phillip J(ason) 1938- 85-88
Baram, Robert 1919- Brief entry 112
Baran, Annette 1927- Brief entry 114
Baranczak, Stanislaw 1946- 149
Baranet, Nancy Neiman 1933- 41-44R
Baranov, Alexander A. 1931(?)-1983 Obituary 109
Baranson, Jack 1924- 119
Barany, George 1922- 25-28R
Barasch, Frances K. 1928- 37-40R
Barasch, Lynne 1939- SATA 74
Barasch, Marc Ian 1949- 113
Barasch, Moshe 1920- 97-100
Barash, David P(hilip) 1946- 144
Barash, Meyer 1916- 1-4R
Barash, Samuel T(heodore) 1921- 107
Baratta, Joseph Preston 1943- 154
Barayon, Ramon Sender
See Sender Barayon, Ramon
Barazangi, Nimat Hafez 1943- 160
Barba, Harry 1922- CANR-1
Earlier sketch in CA 1-4R
Barbach, Lonnie (Villoldo) 1946- CANR-25
Earlier sketches in CA 61-64, CANR-9
Barbalet, Margaret 1949- 145
See also SATA 77
Barbanell, Maurice 1902-1981 Obituary 113
Barbara, Dominick A. 1914- 37-40R
Barbare, Rholf
See Volkoff, Vladimir
Barbarese, J. T. 1948- 135
Barbary, James
See Beeching, Jack
Barbash, Jack 1910-1994 CANR-16
Obituary 145
Earlier sketch in CA 1-4R
Barbash, Shepard 1957- 150
See also SATA 84
Barbato, Joseph 1944- 150
Barbauld, Anna Laetitia 1743-1825 .. DLB 107, 109, 142, 158
Barbe, Walter Burke 1926- 13-16R
See also SATA 45
Barbeau, Arthur E(dward) 1936- 49-52
Barbeau, Clayton C(harles) 1930- 73-76
Barbeau, Edward J(oseph) 1938- 159
Barbeau, (Frederic Charles Joseph) Marius 1883-1969 148
Obituary 25-28R
See also DLB 92
Barbee, David E(dwin) 1936- 57-60
Barbee, Phillips
See Sheckley, Robert
Barbellion, W. N. P.
See Cummings, Bruce F(rederick)
See also TCLC 24
Barber, Antonia
See Anthony, Barbara
Barber, Benjamin R. 1939- CANR-64
Earlier sketches in CA 29-32R, CANR-12, 32
Barber, Bernard 1918- CANR-14
Earlier sketch in CA 65-68
Barber, Charles (Laurence) 1915- CANR-22
Earlier sketches in CA 17-20R, CANR-7
Barber, Cyril J(ohn) 1934- CANR-9
Earlier sketch in CA 65-68
Barber, D(ulan) F(riar Whilberton) 1940-1988 ...... CANR-71
Earlier sketches in CA 61-64, CANR-21
Barber, E(lizabeth) J. W(ayland) 1940- 146
Barber, James David 1930- CANR-6
Earlier sketch in CA 13-16R
Barber, James G(eoffrey) 1952- 110
Barber, Jesse 1893-1979 Obituary 85-88
Barber, John 1944- 128
Barber, John Warner 1798-1885 DLB 30
Barber, Joseph 1909-1982 Obituary 107
Barber, Karin 138
Barber, Lucie W(elles) 1922- 108
Barber, Lucy L(ombardi) 1882(?)-1974 Obituary 49-52
Barber, Lynda
See Graham-Barber, Lynda
Barber, Lynda Graham
See Graham-Barber, Lynda
Barber, Lynn 1944- 97-100
Barber, Noel (John Lysberg) 1909-1988 Obituary 126
Brief entry 115
Barber, Patricia 1946- CANR-48
Barber, Paul (Thomas) 1941- 134
Barber, Philip W. 1903-1981 Obituary 103
Barber, Phyllis (Nelson) 1943- 139
Barber, Red
See Barber, Walter Lanier
Barber, Richard (William) 1941- CANR-72
Earlier sketches in CA 33-36R, CANR-13, 32
See also SATA 35
Barber, Richard J. 1932- 29-32R
Barber, Samuel 1910-1981 Obituary 103
Barber, Stephen Guy 1921-1980 69-72
Obituary 97-100
Barber, T(heodore) X(enophon) 1927- 41-44R
Barber, Walter Lanier 1908-1992 141
Brief entry 113
Barber, Willard F(oster) 1909- CAP-2
Earlier sketch in CA 21-22
Barber, William Henry 1918- 5-8R
Barber, William Joseph 1925- CANR-8
Earlier sketch in CA 61-64
Barbera, Henry 1929- 105
Barbera, Jack (Vincent) 1945- CANR-45
Earlier sketch in CA 110
See also CLC 44
Barbera, Joe
See Barbera, Joseph Roland
Barbera, Joseph Roland 1911- 150
See also SATA 51
Barberis
See Barberis, Franco
Barberis, Franco 1905- 25-28R
Barberis, Juan C(arlos) 1920- SATA 61
Barberi Squarotti, Giorgio 1929- DLB 128
Barbero, Yves Regis Francois 1943- 57-60
Barbet, Pierre
See Avice, Claude (Pierre Marie)
Barbette, Jay
See Spicer, Bart
Barbey d'Aurevilly, Jules Amedee 1808-1889 .. DLB 119
See also SSC 17
Barbier, Patrick 1956- 157
Barbieri, Elaine 1936- 138
Barbotin, Edmond 1920- 57-60
Barbour, Alan G. 1933- Brief entry 117
Barbour, Arthur Joseph 1926- 57-60
Barbour, Brian M(ichael) 1943- 49-52
Barbour, Douglas (Fleming) 1940- CANR-54
Earlier sketches in CA 69-72, CANR-11, 27
Barbour, Frances Martha 1895- 17-20R
Barbour, George 1890-1977 Obituary 73-76
Barbour, Hugh (Stewart) 1921- 21-24R
Barbour, Ian G(raeme) 1923- CANR-8
Earlier sketch in CA 21-24R
Barbour, J(ames) Murray 1897-1970 CAP-1
Earlier sketch in CA 11-12
Barbour, John c. 1316-1395 DLB 146
Barbour, John D. 1951- 150
Barbour, Julian B. 1937- 133
Barbour, Karen 1956- 127
See also SATA 63
Barbour, Kenneth Michael 1921- CANR-7
Earlier sketch in CA 5-8R
Barbour, Michael G(eorge) 1942- CANR-2
Earlier sketch in CA 49-52
Barbour, Nevill 1895-1972 5-8R
Obituary 103
Barbour, Philip L(emont) 1898- 9-12R
Barbour, Ralph Henry 1870-1944 DLB 22
See also SATA 16
Barbour, Roger W(illiam) 1919- 61-64
Barbour, Russell B. 1906- CAP-2
Earlier sketch in CA 23-24
Barbour, Ruth P(eeling) 1924- 89-92
Barbour, Thomas L.
See Lesure, Thomas B(arbour)
Barbrook, Alec
See Barbrook, Alexander Thomas
Barbrook, Alexander Thomas 1927- 45-48
Barbusse, Henri 1873-1935 154
Brief entry 105
See also DLB 65
See also TCLC 5
Barchek, James Robert 1935- 41-44R
Barchiesi, Robert 1955- 137
Barchilon, Jacques 1923- CANR-5
Earlier sketch in CA 13-16R
Barchus, Agnes J(osephine) 1893- 97-100
Barcia, Jose Rubia
See Rubia Barcia, Jose
Barck, Oscar Theodore, Jr. 1902- 21-24R
Barclay, Alexander c. 1475-1552 DLB 132
Barclay, Andrew M(ichael) 1941- 113
Barclay, Ann
See Greig, Maysie
Barclay, Barbara 1938- 29-32R
Barclay, Bill
See Moorcock, Michael (John)
Barclay, Cyril Nelson 1896- 5-8R
Barclay, Florence L(ouisa Charlesworth) 1862-1921 157
Barclay, Glen St. J(ohn) 1930- 77-80
Barclay, Harold B. 1924- 9-12R
Barclay, Hartley Wade 1903-1978 85-88
Obituary 81-84
Barclay, Isabel
See Dobell, I(sabel) M(arian) B(arclay)
Barclay, Oliver R(ainsford) 1919- CANR-8
Earlier sketch in CA 57-60
Barclay, Robert 1946- 143
Barclay, Virginia
See McDonnell, Virginia B(leecker)
Barclay, William 1907-1978 CANR-29
Obituary 73-76
Earlier sketch in CA 77-80
Barclay, William Ewert
See Moorcock, Michael (John)
Barcus, James E(dgar) 1938- 21-24R
Barcus, Nancy B(idwell) 1937- CANR-40
Earlier sketch in CA 117
Barcynski, Leon Roger 1949- CANR-10
Earlier sketch in CA 93-96
Barcynski, Vivian G(odfrey) 1917- CANR-10
Earlier sketch in CA 61-64
Bard, Bernard 1927- 25-28R
Bard, Harry 1906-1976 33-36R
Bard, James (Alan) 1925- 102
Bard, Mitchell G. 1959- 148
Bard, Morton 1924- 97-100
Obituary 163
Bard, Patti 1935- 21-24R
Bard, Rachel 1921- 117
Bardach, John E(ugene) 1915- 41-44R
Bardarson, Hjalmar R(oegnvaldur) 1918- 57-60
Barden, Leonard (William) 1929- CANR-2
Earlier sketch in CA 1-4R
Barden, Thomas E(arl) 1946- 136
Bardens, Amey E. 1894(?)-1974 Obituary 53-56
Bardens, Dennis (Conrad) 1911- 5-8R
Bardhan, Pranab 1939- 139
Bardi, Pietro Maria 1900- CANR-42
Earlier sketches in CA 85-88, CANR-19
Bardin, John Franklin 1916-1981 CANR-66
Obituary 104
Earlier sketch in CA 81-84
Bardis, Panos D(emetrios) 1924- CANR-46
Earlier sketches in CA 25-28R, CANR-10
Bard of Avondale
See Jacobs, Howard
Bardolph, Richard 1915- 61-64
Bardon, Edward J(ohn) 1933- 81-84
Bardon, Jack Irving 1925- 101
Bardos, Marie (Dupuis) 1935- 13-16R
Bardot, Louis 1896-1975 Obituary 61-64
Bardsley, Cuthbert K(illick) N(orman) 1907-1991 ... CAP-2
Obituary 133
Earlier sketch in CA 25-28
Bardwell, George E(ldred) 1924- 1-4R
Bardwick, Judith M(arcia) 1933- CANR-19
Earlier sketch in CA 103
Bare, Arnold Edwin 1920- SATA 16
Bare, Colleen Stanley 102
See also SATA 32
Barea, Arturo 1897-1957 Brief entry 111
See also TCLC 14
Bareham, Lindsey 1948- 140
Bareham, Terence 1937- 109
Barell, John 1938- 111
Barendrecht, Cor W(illiam) 1934- 114
Barenholtz, Bernard 1914-1989 SATA-Obit 64
Barer, Burl (Roger) 1947- 162
Baretski, Charles Allan 1918- 77-80
Barfield, (Arthur) Owen 1898-1997 CANR-2
Obituary 163
Earlier sketch in CA 5-8R
Barfield, Woodrow 1950- 168
Barfoot, Audrey Ilma 1918-1964 5-8R
Barfoot, Joan 1946- 105
See also CLC 18
Barford, Carol 1931- 89-92
Barford, Philip (Trevelyan) 1925- 93-96
Bargad, Warren 1940- CANR-49
Earlier sketch in CA 122
Bargar, B(radley) D(uffee) 1924- 17-20R
Bargar, Gary W. 1947-1985 SATA 63
Bargate, Verity 1941(?)-1981 Obituary 103
Bargebuhr, Frederick P(erez) 1904- CAP-2
Earlier sketch in CA 33-36
Bargellini, Piero 1897-1980(?) Obituary 97-100
Barger, Harold 1907- CAP-2
Earlier sketch in CA 19-20
Barger, James (David) 1947- 57-60
Barham, Patte B. 143
Barham, Richard Harris 1788-1845 DLB 159
Bar-Hillel, Yehoshua 1915-1975 Obituary 115
Bari, Nina Karlovna 1901-1961 161
Bari, Ruth Aaronson 1917- 161
Barich, Bill 1943- CANR-68
Earlier sketch in CA 149
See also DLB 185
Barille, Elisabeth 1960- 137
Baring, Arnulf Martin 1932- 41-44R
Baring, Maurice 1874-1945 168
Brief entry 105
See also DLB 34
See also TCLC 8
Baringer, William E(ldon) 1909- 1-4R
Baring-Gould, Sabine 1834-1924 DLB 156, 190
Baring-Gould, William Stuart 1913-1967 Obituary 25-28R
Barish, Evelyn 1935- 132
Barish, Jonas A. 1922-1998
Obituary 165
Earlier sketch in CA 21-24R
Barish, Matthew 1907- 57-60
See also SATA 12
Baritz, Loren 1928- 13-16R
Barjavel, Rene (Gustave Henri) 1911-1985 162
Brief entry 107
Bar-Joseph, Uri 1949- 155
Bark, Dennis L(aistner) 1942- CANR-41
Earlier sketch in CA 117
Bark, William (Carroll) 1908-1996 CAP-1
Obituary 154
Earlier sketch in CA 13-14
Barkalow, Frederick Schenck, Jr. 1914- 61-64
Barkan, Elliott Robert 1940- 21-24R
Barkan, Joanne 145
See also SATA 77
Barkan, Leonard 1944- 122
Brief entry 116
Barkas, J. L.
See Yager, Jan
Barkas, Janet
See Yager, Jan
Barkdoll, Robert S. 1913(?)-1984 Obituary 112
Barkee, Asouff
See Strung, Norman
Barker, A(rthur) J(ames) 1918-1981 CANR-70
Obituary 104
Earlier sketches in CA 13-16R, CANR-7
Barker, A(udrey) L(ilian) 1918- CANR-53
Earlier sketches in CA 9-12R, CANR-3, 27
See also DLB 14, 139
Barker, A(nthony) W(ilhelm) 1930- CANR-32
Earlier sketch in CA 113
Barker, Albert W. 1900- CANR-14
Earlier sketch in CA 73-76
See also SATA 8
Barker, Andrew (Dennison) 1943- 130
Barker, Bill
See Barker, William J(ohn)
Barker, Carol (Minturn) 1938- 107
See also SATA 31
Barker, Carol M. 1942- 45-48
Barker, Charles Albro 1904-1993 93-96
Obituary 142
Barker, Charles M., Jr. 1926- 13-16R
Barker, Cicely Mary 1895-1973 121
Obituary 117
See also SATA 49
See also SATA-Brief 39
Barker, Clive 1952- CANR-71
Brief entry 121
Earlier sketch in CA 129
Interview in 129
See also AAYA 10
See also BEST 90:3
See also CLC 52
See also DAM POP
See also MTCW 1
Barker, D(erek) R(oland) 1930- 5-8R
Barker, Dennis (Malcolm) 1929- CANR-32
Earlier sketches in CA 25-28R, CANR-14
Barker, Dudley 1910-1980(?) CANR-58
Obituary 102
Earlier sketches in CA 1-4R, CANR-1
Barker, E. M.
See Barker, Elsa (McCormick)
Barker, Elisabeth 1910-1986 136
Obituary 118
Barker, Elliott S(peer) 1886-1988 89-92
Obituary 125
Barker, Elsa (McCormick) 1906- CAP-2
Earlier sketch in CA 17-18
Barker, Elspeth 1940- 138
Barker, Elver A. 1920- 25-28R
Barker, Eric 1905-1973 CANR-27
Obituary 41-44R
Earlier sketch in CA 1-4R
Barker, Ernest 1874-1960 103
Obituary 93-96
Barker, Esther T(emperley) 1910- CANR-2
Earlier sketch in CA 49-52
Barker, Felix 1917- 130
Barker, Frank Granville 1923- CAP-1
Earlier sketch in CA 11-12
Barker, Garry 1943- 140
Barker, George Granville 1913-1991 CANR-38
Obituary 135
Earlier sketches in CA 9-12R, CANR-7
See also CLC 8, 48
See also DAM POET
See also DLB 20
See also MTCW 1
Barker, Gerard A(rthur) 1930- 69-72
Barker, Graham H(arold) 1949- 106
Barker, Harley Granville
See Granville-Barker, Harley
See also DLB 10
Barker, Howard 1946- 102
See also CLC 37
See also DLB 13
Barker, Jack M. 1924(?)-1985 Obituary 117
Barker, James Nelson 1784-1858 DLB 37
Barker, Jane Valentine 1930- CANR-11
Earlier sketch in CA 65-68
Barker, John W(alton, Jr.) 1933- 17-20R
Barker, Jonathan 1949- 139
Barker, Joseph 1929- 103
Barker, Keith 1947- 135
Barker, Kenneth S(tacey) 1932- 110
Barker, Lady Mary Anne 1831-1911 DLB 166
Barker, Larry L(ee) 1941- CANR-17
Earlier sketch in CA 81-84
Barker, M(uhammad) A(bd-Al-)R(ahman) 1929- 116
Barker, Margaret 1944- 138
Barker, Melvern 1907- CAP-1
Earlier sketch in CA 9-10
See also SATA 11
Barker, Myrtie Lillian 1910- 5-8R
Barker, Nancy Nichols 1925- Brief entry 114
Barker, Nicola 1966- 141
Barker, Nicolas (John) 1932- CANR-43
Earlier sketch in CA 102
Barker, Pat(ricia) 1943- CANR-50
Brief entry 117
Earlier sketch in CA 122
Interview in 122
See also CLC 32, 94
Barker, Philip 1929- 114
Barker, Raffaella 1964- 146
Barker, Ralph 1917- CANR-38
Earlier sketches in CA 1-4R, CANR-1, 16
Barker, Robert L(ee) 1937- 25-28R
Barker, Rocky
See Barker, Roland
Barker, Rodney (Steven) 1942- 45-48
Barker, Rodney 1946- 160
Barker, Roger Garlock 1903- CANR-11
Earlier sketches in CAP-1, CA 11-12

Barker, Roland 1953- 146
Barker, Ronald 1921(?)-1976 Obituary 65-68
Barker, S(quire) Omar 1894-1985 .... CANR-64
Earlier sketches in CAP-2, CA 17-18
See also SATA 10
Barker, Sally
See McMurry, Sarah L.
Barker, Sebastian 1945- CANR-54
Earlier sketch in CA 124
Barker, Shirley Frances 1911-1965 .... CANR-70
Earlier sketch in CA 5-8R
Barker, T(heodore Cardwell) 1923- CANR-5
Earlier sketch in CA 13-16R
Barker, T(erence) S(narr) 1941- CANR-21
Earlier sketch in CA 45-48
Barker, Thomas M. 1929- 21-24R
Barker, W(illiam) Alan 1923-1988(?) CANR-1
Obituary 125
Earlier sketch in CA 1-4R
Barker, Wendy B. 1942- CANR-52
Earlier sketch in CA 125
Barker, Will 1913-1983 .... 9-12R
Obituary 110
See also SATA 8
Barker, William c. 1520-1576(?) .... DLB 132
Barker, William J(ohn) 65-68
Barker, William P(ierson) 1927- 9-12R
Barker-Benfield, G(raham) J(ohn) 1941- Brief entry 113
Barkey, Karen 1958- 168
Barkhouse, Joyce 1913- 93-96
See also SATA-Brief 48
Barkin, Carol 1944- 135
Brief entry 118
See also SATA 42, 52
Barkin, David Peter 1942- 37-40R
Barkin, Kenneth D(avid) 1939- 41-44R
Barkin, Solomon 1907- 9-12R
Barkins, Evelyn (Warner) 1919- 29-32R
Barklem, Jill 1951- 161
See also CLR 31
See also SATA 96
Barkley, Deanne 1931- Brief entry 114
Barkley, James Edward 1941- .... SATA 6
Barkley, T(heodore) M(itchell) 1934- 120
Barkley, Vada Lee 1919- 57-60
Barkman, Alma 1939- CANR-35
Earlier sketch in CA 114
Barkman, Paul Friesen 1921- 17-20R
Barkov, Ivan Semenovich 1732-1768 .... DLB 150
Barkow, Al 1932- CANR-4
Earlier sketch in CA 53-56
Barks, Carl 1901- 115
See also SATA 37
Barks, Coleman (Bryan) 1937- CANR-12
Earlier sketch in CA 25-28R
See also DLB 5
Barksdale, E(thelbert) C(ourtland) 1944- 57-60
Barksdale, Hiram C(ollier) 1921- 9-12R
Barksdale, Richard (Kenneth) 1915- 49-52
Barkton, S. Rush
See Brav, Stanley R(osenbaum)
Barkun, Michael 1938- 135
Brief entry 114
Barkworth, Peter (Wynn) 1929- 107
Barlach, Ernst 1870-1938 .... DLB 56, 118
See also TCLC 84
Barlay, Bennett
See Crossen, Kendell Foster
Barlay, Stephen 1930- CANR-12
Earlier sketch in CA 25-28R
Barlett, Donald L(eon) 1936- CANR-68
Earlier sketch in CA 115
Interview in 115
Barlett, Peggy F. 1947- 144
Barley, Janet Crane 1934- 160
See also SATA 95
Barley, M. W.
See Barley, Maurice Willmore
Barley, Maurice Willmore 1909-1991 122
Obituary 134
Barlin, Anne L(ief) 1916- 97-100
Barling, Charles
See Barling, Muriel Vere Mant
Barling, Muriel Vere Mant 1904- 5-8R
Barlough, J(effrey) Ernest 1953- 49-52
Barlow, Claude W(illis) 1907-1976 .... CAP-2
Earlier sketch in CA 33-36
Barlow, Connie 1952- 154
Barlow, Frank 1911- CANR-30
Earlier sketches in CA 9-12R, CANR-3
Barlow, Genevieve 1910- 21-24R
Barlow, J(ames) Stanley, (Jr.) 1924- 41-44R
Barlow, James 1921-1973 .... CANR-69
Obituary 41-44R
Earlier sketches in CAP-1, CA 13-14
Barlow, Jane 1857-1917 Brief entry 115
Barlow, Joel 1754-1812 .... DLB 37
Barlow, John A(lfred) 1924- 21-24R
Barlow, John D(enison) 1934- 120
Barlow, Judith E(llen) 1946- 107
Barlow, Maude 1947- 135
Barlow, (Emma) Nora 1885- CAP-2
Earlier sketch in CA 25-28
Barlow, Robert O.
See Meyer, Heinrich
Barlow, Roger
See Leckie, Robert (Hugh)
Barlow, Ronald S. 1936- 142
Barlow, Samuel L(atham) M(itchell) 1892-1982 Obituary 107
Barlow, Sanna Morrison
See Rossi, Sanna Morrison Barlow
Barlow, T(homas) Edward 1931- CANR-3
Earlier sketch in CA 45-48
Barlow, Tani E. 1950- 130
Barlow, Wilfred 1915- 101
Barlow, William 1943- 139
Barlowe, Raleigh 1914- 17-20R
Barlowe, Wayne Douglas 1958- 134
Barltrop, Robert 1922- CANR-19
Earlier sketch in CA 73-76
Barman, Alicerose 1919- 65-68
Barman, Charles R(oy) 1945- 106
Barmann, Lawrence Francis 1932- 9-12R
Barmash, Isadore 1921- CANR-17
Earlier sketches in CA 45-48, CANR-1
Barme, Geremie 1954- 131
Barmine, Alexander (G.) 1899-1987 Obituary 125
Barna, George 1954- 114
Barna, Joel Warren 1951- 138
Barna, Yon 1927- 53-56
Barnabas
See Blandford, Brian E(rnest) and West, Charles Converse
Barnaby, (Charles) Frank 1927- CANR-56
Earlier sketches in CA 33-36R, CANR-13, 29
Barnaby, Ralph S(tanton) 1893- 61-64
See also SATA 9
Barnao, Jack
See Wood, Edward John
Barnard, A. M.
See Alcott, Louisa May
Barnard, (James) Alan 1928- 9-12R
Barnard, Charles N(elson III) 1924- CANR-1
Earlier sketch in CA 49-52
Barnard, Christiaan (Neethling) 1922- CANR-14
Earlier sketch in CA 61-64
Barnard, Ellsworth 1907- CANR-26
Earlier sketches in CA 21-24R, CANR-11
Barnard, F(rederick) M(echner) 1921- 25-28R
Barnard, Harry 1906-1982 .... CANR-3
Obituary 107
Earlier sketch in CA 5-8R
Barnard, Howard Clive 1884-1985 85-88
Obituary 117
Barnard, J(ohn) Darrell 1906- 5-8R
Barnard, J(ohn) Lawrence 1912-1977 77-80
Obituary 73-76
Barnard, John 1681-1770 .... DLB 24
Barnard, (Virgil) John 1932- CANR-45
Earlier sketch in CA 33-36R
Barnard, Judith 1934- 139
See also DAM POP
Barnard, Marjorie Faith 1897-1987 156
Barnard, Mary (Ethel) 1909- CAP-2
Earlier sketch in CA 21-22
See also CLC 48
Barnard, Nicholas 1958- 139
Barnard, Robert 1936- CANR-54
Earlier sketches in CA 77-80, CANR-20
Interview in CANR-20
Barnard, Tom
See Geldenhuys, Deon
Barnard, William Dean 1942- 69-72
Bar-Natan, Moshe
See Louvish, Misha
Barne, Kitty
See Barne, Marion Catherine
See also DLB 160
Barne, Marion Catherine 1883-1957 154
Brief entry 112
See also Barne, Kitty
See also SATA 97
Barner, Bob 1947- 93-96
See also SATA 29
Bar Ner, R.
See Brenner, Reeve R(obert)
Barnes, Adrienne Martine
See Martine-Barnes, Adrienne
Barnes, Annie S. 1932- 146
Barnes, Barnabe 1571-1609 .... DLB 132
Barnes, Barry 1943- 97-100
Barnes, Burton V(erne) 1930- 130
Barnes, Chesley Virginia
See Young, Chesley Virginia
Barnes, Christopher J(ohn) 1942- 132
Barnes, Clara Ernst 1895- 5-8R
Barnes, Clive (Alexander) 1927- CANR-26
Earlier sketch in CA 77-80
See also AITN 2
Barnes, Djuna 1892-1982 .... CANR-55
Obituary 107
Earlier sketches in CA 9-12R, CANR-16
See also CLC 3, 4, 8, 11, 29
See also DLB 4, 9, 45
See also MTCW 1
See also SSC 3
Barnes, Douglas 1927- CANR-41
Earlier sketches in CA 103, CANR-19
Barnes, Duncan 1935- 127
Barnes, Edward F.
See Marquis, Max
Barnes, Elmer Tracey CANR-26
Earlier sketches in CAP-2, CA 19-20
Barnes, (Frank) Eric Wollencott 1907-1962 .... SATA 22
Barnes, Gregory Allen 1934- CANR-25
Earlier sketches in CA 25-28R, CANR-10
Barnes, Harry Elmer 1889-1968 89-92
Obituary 25-28R
Barnes, Hazel E(stella) 1915- CANR-3
Earlier sketch in CA 5-8R
Barnes, Henry A. 1906-1968 .... CAP-1
Earlier sketch in CA 13-16
Barnes, Irston Roberts 1904-1988 Obituary 124
Barnes, J. 1944- 85-88
Barnes, J(ohn) A(rundel) 1918- 101
Barnes, Jack 1920- 89-92
Barnes, Jack 1940- CANR-9
Earlier sketch in CA 61-64
Barnes, James A(nderson) 1898- 9-12R
Barnes, James J(ohn) 1931- CANR-4
Earlier sketch in CA 9-12R
Barnes, James N(eil) 1944- 117
Barnes, Jane
See Casey, Jane Barnes
Barnes, Jay 1958- 154
Barnes, Jim 1933- 108
See also CAAS 28
See also DLB 175
See also NNAL
Barnes, Joanna 1934- 57-60
Barnes, John 1908- CANR-2
Earlier sketch in CA 45-48
Barnes, (Ernest) John (Ward) 1917- 108
Barnes, John (Allen) 1957- 137
Barnes, John B(ertram) 1924- 33-36R
Barnes, Joseph Fels 1907-1970 Obituary 104
Barnes, Joyce Annette 1958- 151
See also SATA 85
Barnes, Julian (Patrick) 1946- CANR-54
Earlier sketches in CA 102, CANR-19
See also CLC 42
See also DAB
See also DLB 194
See also DLBY 93
Barnes, Kenneth Charles 1903- 106
Barnes, Kim 163
Barnes, Leonard (John) 1895- CAP-2
Earlier sketch in CA 29-32
Barnes, Lilly I. 1935- 126
Barnes, Linda
See Barnes, Linda J(oyce)
Barnes, Linda J(oyce) 1949- CANR-62
Earlier sketch in CA 132
Barnes, Loutricia
See Barnes-Svarney, Patricia L(ou)
Barnes, Malcolm 1909(?)-1984 Obituary 114
See also SATA-Obit 41
Barnes, Margaret Ayer 1886-1967 Obituary 25-28R
See also DLB 9
Barnes, Mary 1923- 85-88
Barnes, Melvyn (Peter Keith) 1942- 122
Barnes, Michael 1934- .... SATA 55
Barnes, Michael (Anthony) 1947- 137
Barnes, Patience P(lummer) 1932- 108
Barnes, Peter 1931- CANR-64
Earlier sketches in CA 65-68, CANR-33, 34
See also CAAS 12
See also CLC 5, 56
See also DLB 13
See also MTCW 1
Barnes, Phoebe 1908- CAP-2
Earlier sketch in CA 23-24
Barnes, R(ichard) G(ordon) 1932- 33-36R
Barnes, Ralph M(osser) 1900-1984 .... CAP-2
Obituary 114
Earlier sketch in CA 17-18
Barnes, Robert J(ay) 1925- 21-24R
Barnes, Robert M(orson) 1940- CANR-25
Earlier sketch in CA 45-48
Barnes, Sam(uel) G(ill) 1913- 13-16R
Barnes, Samuel H(enry) 1931- 21-24R
Barnes, Simon 1951- 130
Barnes, Stephen Emory 1952- CANR-55
Earlier sketch in CA 105
Barnes, Steven
See Barnes, Stephen Emory
Barnes, Suzanne Falter
See Falter-Barns, Suzanne
Barnes, Thomas Garden 1930- CANR-1
Earlier sketch in CA 1-4R
Barnes, Timothy David 1942- 114
Barnes, Trevor 1955- 143
Barnes, Valerie 115
Barnes, Viola Florence 1885- 1-4R
Barnes, Walter 1880-1969 Obituary 116
Barnes, William 1801-1886 .... DLB 32
Barnes-Murphy, Frances 1951- .... SATA 88
Barnes-Murphy, Rowan 1952- .... SATA 88
Barness, Richard 1917- 65-68
Barnes-Svarney, Patricia L(ou) 1953- 135
See also SATA 67
Barnet, Miguel 1940- .... DLB 145
Barnet, Nancy 1954- .... SATA 84
Barnet, Richard J. 1929- CANR-49
Earlier sketch in CA 13-16R
Barnet, Sylvan 1926- CANR-4
Earlier sketch in CA 1-4R
Barnetson, William Denholm 1917-1981 Obituary 103
Barnett, A. Doak 1921- CANR-15
Earlier sketch in CA 5-8R
Barnett, Adam
See Fast, Julius
Barnett, Correlli (Douglas) 1927- CANR-46
Earlier sketches in CA 13-16R, CANR-15
Barnett, Franklin 1903- 69-72
Barnett, George L(eonard) 1915- 29-32R
Barnett, (Nicolas) Guy 1928- 17-20R
Barnett, H(omer) G(arner) 1906- 45-48
Barnett, Isobel (Morag) 1918-1980 Obituary 105
Barnett, Ivan 1947- .... SATA 70
Barnett, James Monroe 1925- 114
Barnett, Joe R(ichard) 1933- 106
Barnett, Joel 1923- 129
Barnett, L. David
See Laschever, Barnett D.
Barnett, Leo 1925- 29-32R
Barnett, Leonard (Palin) 1919- CANR-12
Earlier sketches in CAP-1, CA 13-14
Barnett, Lincoln (Kinnear) 1909-1979 102
Obituary 89-92
See also SATA 36
Barnett, Malcolm Joel 1941- 45-48
Barnett, Marva T(uttle) 1913- 57-60
Barnett, Maurice 1917-1980 Obituary 97-100
Barnett, Michael 1930- 57-60
Barnett, Moneta 1922-1976 .... SATA 33
Barnett, Naomi 1927- CANR-7
Earlier sketch in CA 5-8R
See also SATA 40
Barnett, Peter Herbert 1945- 124
Barnett, Richard B(aity) 1941- 105
Barnett, Richard C(hambers) 1932- 33-36R
Barnett, Robert W(arren) 1911-1997 126
Obituary 159
Barnett, Rosalind C(hait) 1937- 129
Barnett, S(amuel) A(nthony) 1915- CANR-6
Earlier sketch in CA 13-16R
Barnett, Sanford 1909(?)-1988 Obituary 125
Barnett, Suzanne Wilson 1940- 120
Barnett, Ursula A(nnemarie) 1924- 123
Barnett, Victoria (Joan) 1950- 147
Barnett, Vivian E(ndicott) 1944- 115
Barnette, Henlee H(ulix) 1911- CANR-31
Earlier sketch in CA 49-52
Barnette, Martha 1957- 136
Barnette, W(arren) Leslie, Jr. 1910- CAP-1
Earlier sketch in CA 11-12
Barnewall, Gordon G(ouverneur) 1924- 121
Barney, Harry
See Lottman, Eileen
Barney, Kenneth D. 1921- 69-72
Barney, Laura D(reyfus) 1880(?)-1974 Obituary 53-56
Barney, LeRoy 1930- 33-36R
Barney, Maginel Wright 1881(?)-1966 Obituary 111
See also SATA 39
See also SATA-Brief 32
Barney, Natalie (Clifford) 1878(?)-1972 Obituary 33-36R
See also DLB 4
Barney, Stephen A(llen) 1942- 102
Barney, William L(esko) 1943- 41-44R
Barnfield, Richard 1574-1627 .... DLB 172
Barnhardt, Deanna
See Kawatski, Deanna
Barnhardt, Wilton 1960- 148
Barnhart, Clarence L(ewis) 1900-1993 .... 13-16R
Obituary 143
See also SATA 48
See also SATA-Obit 78
Barnhart, Joe Edward 1931- 41-44R
Barnhart, Michael A(ndrew) 1951- 127
Barnhart, Robert K. 1933- 127
Barnhill, Myrtle Fait 1896-1986 .... CAP-1
Obituary 119
Earlier sketch in CA 13-16
Barnhouse, Donald 103
Barnhouse, Donald Grey 1895-1960 123
Obituary 113
Barnhouse, Ruth Tiffany 1923- CANR-15
Earlier sketch in CA 85-88
Barnie, John 1941- 57-60
Barnitt, Nedda Lemmon 9-12R
Barnitz, Harry W. 1920-1973 .... CAP-2
Earlier sketch in CA 25-28
Barnoon, Shlomo 1940- 41-44R
Barnouw, Adriaan Jacob 1877-1968 Obituary 104
See also SATA-Obit 27
Barnouw, Dagmar 1936- 139
Barnouw, Erik 1908- CANR-72
Earlier sketches in CA 13-16R, CANR-12
Barnouw, Victor 1915- 85-88
See also SATA 43
See also SATA-Brief 28
Barn Owl
See Howells, Roscoe
Barnright, Julia
See Bancroft, Iris (May Nelson)
Barns, John W(intour) B(aldwin) 1912-1974 Obituary 49-52
Barns, Suzanne Falter
See Falter-Barns, Suzanne
Barnsley, Alan Gabriel 1916-1986 .... 13-16R
Obituary 121
Barnstone, Aliki 1956- 105
Barnstone, Howard 1923-1987 Obituary 122
Barnstone, Willis 1927- CANR-68
Earlier sketches in CA 17-20R, CANR-45
See also CAAS 15
See also SATA 20
Barnum, Barbara (J.) Stevens 1937- 162
Barnum, Jay Hyde 1888(?)-1962 .... SATA 20
Barnum, P. T., Jr.
See Stratemeyer, Edward L.
Barnum, Richard CANR-26
Earlier sketches in CAP-2, CA 19-20
See also SATA 1, 67
Barnum, Theodore
See Stratemeyer, Edward L.
Barnum, Vance CANR-26
Earlier sketches in CAP-2, CA 19-20
Barnum, W(illiam) Paul 1933- 29-32R
Barnwell, D. Robinson 1915- 17-20R
Barnwell, John (Gibbes, Jr.) 1947- 113
Barnwell, William Curtis 1943- 103
Baro, Gene 1924-1982 Obituary 112
Baroff, George Stanley 1924- 101
Baroja (y Nessi), Pio 1872-1956 Brief entry 104
See also HLC
See also TCLC 8
Barolini, Antonio 1910-1971 .... CANR-1
Earlier sketch in CA 1-4R
Barolini, Helen 1925- CANR-45
Earlier sketches in CA 73-76, CANR-16, 39
Barolini, Teodolinda 1951- 124
Barolsky, Paul 1941- 81-84
Baron, (Joseph) Alexander 1917- CANR-14
Earlier sketch in CA 5-8R
Baron, Beth 1958- 138
Bar-On, Dan 1938- 139

Baron, David
See Pinter, Harold
Baron, Dennis E(mery) 1944- CANR-54
Earlier sketches in CA 110, CANR-27
Baron, Elizabeth Frank
See Frank-Baron, Elizabeth
Baron, Frank 1936- 119
Baron, Hans 1900- 17-20R
Baron, Herman 1941- 61-64
Baron, J. W.
See Krauzer, Steven M(ark)
Baron, Kathy 1954- .... SATA 90
Baron, Mary (Kelley) 1944- CANR-2
Earlier sketch in CA 49-52
Baron, Mikan
See Barba, Harry
Baron, Naomi S(usan) 1946- 140
Baron, Oscar 1908(?)-1976 Obituary 65-68
Baron, Othello
See Fanthorpe, R(obert) Lionel
Baron, Robert Alex 1920- 41-44R
Baron, Salo W(ittmayer) 1895-1989 69-72
Obituary 130
Baron, Samuel H(askell) 1921- CANR-3
Earlier sketch in CA 9-12R
Baron, Virginia Olsen 1931- 25-28R
See also SATA 46
See also SATA-Brief 28
Baron, (Ora) Wendy 1937- 41-44R
Baron Amulree
See Mackenzie, Basil William Sholto
Baron-Cohen, Simon 1958- 151
Baron Corvo
See Rolfe, Frederick (William Serafino Austin Lewis Mary)
Barondess, Sue K(aufman) 1926-1977 .... CANR-1
Obituary 69-72
Earlier sketch in CA 1-4R
See also Kaufman, Sue
See also CLC 8
Baron de Teive
See Pessoa, Fernando (Antonio Nogueira)
Barone, Michael 1944- 93-96
Barone, Mike
See Albert, Marvin H(ubert)
Baroness Von S.
See Zangwill, Israel
Baron Lloyd of Hampstead
See Lloyd, Dennis
Baron of Remenham
See Thomas, (William) Miles (Webster)
Baron Tebbit of Chingford
See Tebbit, Norman
Baron Visi
See Vian, Boris
Baroody, Jamil Murad 1905-1979 Obituary ... 85-88
Barooshian, (Dickran) Vahan 1932- 85-88
Barovsky, Sharon Daley 1939- 128
Barr, Alfred H(amilton), Jr. 1902-1981 ... CANR-29
Obituary 105
Earlier sketch in CA 49-52
Barr, (Chester) Alwyn, (Jr.) 1938- 33-36R
Barr, Amelia Edith Huddleston 1831-1919 . DLB 202
Barr, Andrew 1961- 130
Barr, Anthony 1921- 109
Barr, Betty 1932- 97-100
Barr, Beverly 61-64
Barr, Densil Neve
See Buttrey, Douglas N(orton)
Barr, Donald 1921- 9-12R
See also SATA 20
Barr, Donald Roy 1938- 69-72
Barr, Doris W(ilson) 1923- 33-36R
Barr, George 1907- CANR-1
Earlier sketch in CA 1-4R
See also SATA 2
Barr, Gladys Hutchison 1904-1976 .... CANR-6
Earlier sketch in CA 1-4R
Barr, James 1924- CANR-20
Earlier sketches in CA 1-4R, CANR-4
Barr, Jeff 1941- 69-72
Barr, Jene
See Cohen, Jene Barr
See also SATA 16
See also SATA-Obit 42
Barr, Jennifer 1945- 102
Barr, John J(ay) 1942- 61-64
Barr, Margaret Scolari 1901-1987 Obituary 124
Barr, Marleen Sandra 1953- 120
Barr, Murray L(lewellyn) 1908- 130
Barr, Nevada 1952(?)- 161
Barr, Nicholas 1943- 143
Barr, O(rlando) Sydney 1919- 13-16R
Barr, Pat(ricia Miriam) 1934- CANR-60
Earlier sketches in CA 21-24R, CANR-12, 30, 56
Barr, Robert 1850-1912 .... DLB 70, 92
Barr, Robert R(ussell) 1931- 110
Barr, Stephen 1904- CAP-1
Earlier sketch in CA 13-16
Barr, Stringfellow 1897-1982 .... CANR-1
Obituary 106
Earlier sketch in CA 1-4R
Barr, Tony
See Barr, Anthony
Barr, William G. 1920(?)-1987 Obituary 121
Barraclough, Geoffrey 1908-1984 101
Obituary 114
Barraclough, June (Mary) 1930- 132
Barraclough, Solon L(ovett) 1922- 41-44R
Barraga, Natalie Carter 1915- 41-44R
Barral, Carlos 1928(?)-1989 Obituary 130
See also DLB 134
Barral, Mary-Rose 1925- 33-36R
Barranger, M(illy) S(later) 1937- CANR-53
Earlier sketches in CA 29-32R, CANR-12, 28
Barratt, Barnaby B. 147
Barratt, G. R.
See Barratt, Glynn (Richard V.)
Barratt, G. R. V.
See Barratt, Glynn (Richard V.)
Barratt, Glynn (Richard V.) 1944- 127
Brief entry 110
Barratt-Brown, Michael 1918- CANR-38
Earlier sketches in CA 97-100, CANR-17
Barrault, Jean-Louis 1910-1994 105
Obituary 143
Barrax, Gerald William 1933- CANR-10
Earlier sketch in CA 65-68
See also BW 2
See also DLB 41, 120
Barre, Michael Lee 1943- 118
Barre, Richard 1943- CANR-72
Earlier sketch in CA 150
Barreca, Regina 1957- 145
Barreiro, Alvaro 1936- 131
Barrell, Geoffrey Richard 1917-1983 Obituary .. 111
Barrell, Rex A(rthur) 1921- CANR-65
Earlier sketch in CA 129
Barrell, Sarah Webb 1946(?)-1979 Obituary .. 89-92
Barren, Charles (MacKinnon) 1913- CANR-4
Earlier sketch in CA 9-12R
Barreno, Maria Isabel
See Martins, Maria Isabel Barreno de Faria
See also AITN 1
Barrer, Gertrude
See Barrer-Russell, Gertrude
Barrera, Mario 1939- 97-100
Barrer-Russell, Gertrude 1921- .... SATA 27
Barres, (Auguste-) Maurice 1862-1923 164
See also DLB 123
See also TCLC 47
Barres, Oliver 1921- 13-16R
Barreto, Afonso Henrique de Lima
See Lima Barreto, Afonso Henrique de
Barrett, Andrea 1965- 156
Barrett, Angela (Jane) 1955- .... SATA 75
Barrett, Anne Mainwaring (Gillett) 1911- CAP-2
Earlier sketch in CA 29-32
Barrett, Anthony A(rthur) 1941- 134
Barrett, Bob 1925- 73-76
Barrett, Buckley Barry 1948- 149
Barrett, C(harles) Kingsley 1917- CANR-50
Earlier sketches in CA 21-24R, CANR-10, 25
Barrett, C(lifton) Waller 1901- 41-44R
Barrett, Clifford L(eslie) 1894-1971 Obituary 33-36R
Barrett, David M(arshall) 1951- 154
Barrett, Dean 1942- 69-72
Barrett, Donald N(eil) 1920- 13-16R
Barrett, Eaton Stannard 1786-1820 ....DLB 116
Barrett, Edward L(ouis), Jr. 1917- 25-28R
Barrett, Edward W(are) 1910-1989 Obituary 130
Barrett, Ethel 134
See also SATA 87
See also SATA-Brief 44
Barrett, Eugene F(rancis) 1921- 57-60
Barrett, George W(est) 1908- 17-20R
Barrett, George W. 1913(?)-1984 Obituary 114
Barrett, Gerald Van 1936- 37-40R
Barrett, Harold 1925- 81-84
Barrett, Harry B(emister) 1922- 85-88
Barrett, Henry Charles 1923- 53-56
Barrett, Ivan J. 1910- 49-52
Barrett, J(ohn) Edward 1932- 37-40R
Barrett, James H(enry) 1906- 33-36R
Barrett, James Lee 1929- 81-84
Barrett, Jennifer
See Plecas, Jennifer
Barrett, John Gilchrist 1921- CANR-2
Earlier sketch in CA 5-8R
Barrett, John Henry 1913- 101
Barrett, Joyce Durham 1943- 138
Barrett, Judi
See Barrett, Judith
Barrett, Judith 1941- 103
See also SATA 26
Barrett, Julia
See Kessler, Julia Braun
Barrett, Julia
See Kessler, Julia Braun
Barrett, Laurence I(rwin) 1935- 69-72
Barrett, Leonard E(manuel) 1920- 65-68
Barrett, (Eseoghene) Lindsay 1941- 143
See also BW 2
Barrett, Linton Lomas 1904-1972 ....5-8R
Obituary 134
Barrett, Lois (Yvonne) 1947- CANR-53
Earlier sketch in CA 125
Barrett, Marvin 1920- CANR-11
Earlier sketch in CA 69-72
Barrett, Mary Ellin 1927- 17-20R
Barrett, Max 81-84
Barrett, Maye
See Barrett, Max
Barrett, Michael Dennis 1947- 85-88
Barrett, N. S.
See Barrett, Norman (S.)
Barrett, Nancy Smith 1942- 37-40R
Barrett, Nathan N(oble) 1933- 17-20R
Barrett, Norman (S.) 1935- CANR-24
Earlier sketch in CA 107
Barrett, Patricia 1914-1987 .... 5-8R
Obituary 121
Barrett, Paul F(rancis) 1943- 117
Barrett, Raina
See Kelly, Pauline Agnes
Barrett, Robert T(heodore) 1949- .... SATA 92
Barrett, Ron 1937- .... SATA 14
Barrett, Rona 1936- 103
Interview in 103
See also AITN 1
Barrett, Russel H(unter) 1919- 17-20R
Barrett, Stanley R. 1938- 128
Barrett, Susan (Mary) 1938- 138
Brief entry 109
Barrett, (Roger) Syd 1946- .... CLC 35
Barrett, Sylvia 1914- 25-28R
Barrett, Tracy 1955- 150
See also SATA 84
Barrett, Ward J. 1927- 29-32R
Barrett, William (Christopher) 1913-1992 . CANR-67
Obituary 139
Earlier sketches in CA 13-16R, CANR-11
Interview in CANR-11
See also CLC 27
Barrett, William E(dmund) 1900-1986 .... CANR-22
Obituary 120
Earlier sketch in CA 5-8R
See also SATA-Obit 49
Barrett, William R. 1922(?)-1977 Obituary 73-76
Barretto, Larry
See Barretto, Laurence Brevoort
Barretto, Laurence Brevoort 1890-1971 Obituary 33-36R
Barretton, Grandall
See Garrett, (Gordon) Randall (Phillip)
Barriault, Arthur 1915(?)-1976 Obituary 65-68
Barricelli, Jean-Pierre 1924- CANR-45
Earlier sketches in CA 105, CANR-21
Barrick, Mac E(ugene) 1933- 33-36R
Barrie, Alexander 1923- CANR-5
Earlier sketch in CA 1-4R
Barrie, Donald C(onway) 1905- 17-20R
Barrie, J(ames) M(atthew) 1860-1937 136
Brief entry 104
See also CDBLB 1890-1914
See also CLR 16
See also DAB
See also DAM DRAM
See also DLB 10, 141, 156
See also MAICYA
See also SATA 100
See also TCLC 2
See also YABC 1
Barrie, Jane
See Savage, Mildred (Spitz)
Barrie, Patricia
See Barber, Patricia
Barrie, Thomas (Matthew) 1955- 161
Barrier, (John) Michael 1940- 109
Barrier, Norman G(erald) 1940- CANR-4
Earlier sketch in CA 53-56
Barriger, John Walker 1899-1976 Obituary ... 69-72
Barrile, Jackie 1943- 117
Barrington, H. W.
See Brannon, William T.
Barrington, John
See Brownjohn, Alan
Barrington, Maurice
See Brogan, D(enis) W(illiam)
Barrington, Michael
See Moorcock, Michael (John)
Barrington, P. V.
See Barling, Muriel Vere Mant
Barrington, Pamela
See Barling, Muriel Vere Mant
Barrington, Thomas Joseph 1916- 104
Barrio, Raymond 1921- CANR-32
Earlier sketches in CA 25-28R, CANR-11
See also CAAS 15
See also DLB 82
See also HW
Barrio-Garay, Jose Luis 1932- 81-84
Barrios, Eduardo 1884-1963 .... HW
Barrios, Gregg 1945- .... DLB 122
Barrios, Pilar E. 1889- .... HW
Barris, Alex 1922- 61-64
Barris, Chuck 1929- Brief entry 109
Barris, George 1925- .... SATA 47
Barritt, Denis P(hillips) 1914- 21-24R
Barro, Robert Joseph 1944- 97-100
Barrol, Grady
See Bograd, Larry
Barroll, John Leeds III 1928- 101
Barron, Ann Forman 69-72
Barron, Bruce 1960- 123
Barron, Charlie Nelms 1922-1977 Obituary ...69-72
Barron, Ed
See Bernhardt, Clyde Edric Barron
Barron, Frank (Xavier) 1922- CANR-8
Earlier sketch in CA 5-8R
Barron, Fred CANR-41
Earlier sketch in CA 117
Barron, Gayle 1945- 109
Barron, Gloria Joan 1934- 81-84
Barron, Greg 1952- 110
Barron, Jerome A(ure) 1933- CANR-49
Earlier sketches in CA 45-48, CANR-24
Barron, Judy 1939- 137
Barron, Milton L. 1918- CANR-18
Earlier sketch in CA 1-4R
Barron, (Richard) Neil 1934- CANR-37
Earlier sketch in CA 102
Barron, Rex 1951- .... SATA 84
Barron, T(om) A. 1952- 150
See also SATA 83
Barrosse, Thomas 1926- 9-12R
Barrow, Andrew 1945- 97-100
Barrow, Geoffrey W(allis) S(teuart) 1924- . CANR-30
Earlier sketches in CA 17-20R, CANR-7
Barrow, Harold M(arion) 1909- 106
Barrow, Henry 1906(?)-1985 Obituary 117
Barrow, Jedediah
See Benson, Gerard
Barrow, John D(avid) 1952- 115
Barrow, Joseph Louis 1914-1981 Obituary 103
Barrow, Keith E. 1954-1983 Obituary 111
Barrow, Kenneth 1945-1993 119
Obituary 142
Barrow, Leo (Lebron) 1925- Brief entry 110
Barrow, Lloyd H. 1942- .... SATA 73
Barrow, Pamela
See Howarth, Pamela
Barrow, R. H. 1894(?)-1984 Obituary 114
Barrow, Rhoda
See Lederer, Rhoda Catharine (Kitto)
Barrow, Robin 1944- CANR-10
Earlier sketch in CA 65-68
Barrow, Terence 1923- 41-44R
Barrow, Thomas C(hurchill) 1929- 21-24R
Barrow, William
See Fuller, Hoyt (William)
Barrows, Anita 1947- CANR-31
Earlier sketch in CA 49-52
Barrows, Chester L. 1892(?)-1975 Obituary 104
Barrows, (Ruth) Marjorie 1892(?)-1983 ..... CAP-2
Obituary 109
Earlier sketch in CA 21-22
Barrows, R. M.
See Barrows, (Ruth) Marjorie
Barrows, Ruth
See Barrows, (Ruth) Marjorie
Barrows, Susanna Isabel 1944- 108
Barrows, Sydney (Biddle) 1952- 126
Barry, Ann 1942-1996 152
Barry, Anne 1940- 85-88
Barry, Colman J(ames) 1921-1994 ....13-16R
Obituary 143
Barry, Dave 1947- 134
Brief entry 129
Interview in 134
See also AAYA 14
See also BEST 90:4
Barry, Herbert III 1930- CANR-43
Earlier sketches in CA 37-40R, CANR-14
Barry, Iris 1895-1969 Obituary 104
Barry, Jack 1939- 69-72
Barry, Jackson G(ranville) 1926- 29-32R
Barry, James Donald 1926- 33-36R
Barry, James P(otvin) 1918- CANR-24
Earlier sketch in CA 37-40R
See also SATA 14
Barry, Jane (Powell) 1925- CANR-62
Earlier sketch in CA 5-8R
Barry, Jerome B(enedict) 1894-1975 .... CANR-68
Obituary 61-64
Earlier sketch in CA 1-4R
Barry, Jocelyn
See Bowden, Jean
Barry, John A(bbott) 1948- 139
Barry, John M. 1947- 165
Barry, John Vincent William 1903-1969 ....1-4R
Obituary 103
Barry, Joseph (Amber) 1917-1994 .... CANR-14
Obituary 144
Earlier sketch in CA 57-60
Barry, Katharina Watjen 1936- 9-12R
See also SATA 4
Barry, Kathleen (L.) 1941- 129
Barry, Kevin
See Laffan, Kevin (Barry)
Barry, Laurel D. 1922- 144
Barry, Lucy (Brown) 1934- 17-20R
Barry, Lynda (Jean) 1956- 138
See also AAYA 9
See also DAM POP
Barry, Margaret Stuart 1927- CANR-25
Earlier sketch in CA 106
Barry, Mary J(ane) 1928- 49-52
Barry, Mike
See Malzberg, Barry N(athaniel)
Barry, Norman P. 1944- 134
Barry, P(atricia) S(teepee) 1926- 140
Barry, Philip 1896-1949 Brief entry 109
See also DLB 7
See also TCLC 11
Barry, Raymond Walker 1894- CAP-1
Earlier sketch in CA 17-18
Barry, Robert (Everett) 1931- CANR-2
Earlier sketch in CA 5-8R
See also SATA 6
Barry, Roger Graham 1935- 102
Barry, Roxana
See Robinson, Roxana (Barry)
Barry, Scott 1952- 89-92
See also SATA 32
Barry, Sebastian 1955- 117
Barry, Sheila Anne CANR-57
Earlier sketch in CA 135
See also SATA 91
Barry, Spranger
See Kauffmann, Stanley
Barry, Stephen P. 1948(?)-1986 123
Obituary 120
Barry, Tom 1950- 139
Barry, William A(nthony) 1930- CANR-38
Earlier sketch in CA 115
Barry, William David 1946- 114
Barrymore, Drew 1975- 139
Barsacq, Andre 1909-1973 Obituary 41-44R
Barsacq, Leon 1906-1969 Obituary 113
Barsby, John A. 1935- 121
Barsh, Russel Lawrence 1950- 105
Barsis, Max 1894(?)-1973 Obituary 41-44R
Barsky, Arthur 1900(?)-1982(?) Obituary 106
Barsky, Robert F. 1961- 161
Barsness, John 1952- 139
Barson, John 1936- 85-88
Barson, Michael 1951- 129
Barsotti, C(harles) 1933- 65-68
Barstow, Anne Llewellyn 1929- 111
Barstow, Phyllida 1937- CANR-27
Earlier sketch in CA 121

Barstow, Stan(ley) 1928- ... CANR-62
Earlier sketches in CA 1-4R, CANR-1, 44
See also DLB 14, 139
Bart, Andre Schwarz
See Schwarz-Bart, Andre
Bart, Benjamin F(ranklin) 1917- ... 25-28R
Bart, Lionel 1930- ... 65-68
Bart, Pauline B(ernice) 1930- ... 53-56
Bart, Peter 1932- ... CANR-19
Earlier sketch in CA 93-96
Bartek, E(dward) J(ohn) 1921- ... 37-40R
Bartel, Pauline C(hristine) 1952- ... 81-84
Bartel, Roland 1919- ... 17-20R
Bartell, Ernest 1932- ... 33-36R
Bartell, Linda Lang 1948- ... 125
Bartels, Robert 1913- ... 13-16R
Bartels, Robert A. 1923- ... CANR-16
Earlier sketch in CA 1-4R
Bartels, Susan Ludvigson
See Ludvigson, Susan
Barten, Harvey H(arold) 1933- ... 33-36R
Bartenbach, Jean 1918- ... 115
See also SATA 40
Bartenieff, Irmgard 1900(?)-1981 Obituary ... 105
Barter, A(lice) K(nar) 1918- ... 57-60
Barth, Alan 1906-1979 ... CANR-5
Obituary ... 104
Earlier sketch in CA 1-4R
Barth, Charles P. 1895- ... CAP-2
Earlier sketch in CA 25-28
Barth, Christoph F. 1917- ... 29-32R
Barth, Edna 1914-1980 ... CANR-27
Obituary ... 102
Earlier sketch in CA 41-44R
See also SATA 7
See also SATA-Obit 24
Barth, Fredrik 1928- ... CANR-11
Earlier sketch in CA 65-68
Barth, Gunther 1925- ... 103
Barth, Ilene Joan 1944- ... 134
Barth, J(ohn) Robert 1931- ... 29-32R
Barth, John (Simmons) 1930- ... CANR-64
Earlier sketches in CA 1-4R, CANR-5, 23, 49
See also CABS 1
See also AITN 1, 2
See also CLC 1, 2, 3, 5, 7, 9, 10, 14, 27, 51, 89
See also DAM NOV
See also DLB 2
See also MTCW 1
See also SSC 10
Barth, Karl 1886-1968 ... 134
Obituary ... 25-28R
Barth, Lois
See Freihofer, Lois Diane
Barth, Markus Karl 1915- ... CANR-2
Earlier sketch in CA 5-8R
Barth, Peter S. 1937- ... CANR-25
Earlier sketch in CA 106
Barth, Richard 1943- ... 81-84
Barth, Roland S(awyer) 1937- ... CANR-1
Earlier sketch in CA 45-48
Barthel, Diane L(ee) 1949- ... 115
Barthel, Joan 1932- ... 114
Brief entry ... 111
Interview in ... 114
Barthelme, Donald 1931-1989 ... CANR-58
Obituary ... 129
Earlier sketches in CA 21-24R, CANR-20
See also CLC 1, 2, 3, 5, 6, 8, 13, 23, 46, 59
See also DAM NOV
See also DLB 2
See also DLBY 80, 89
See also MTCW 1
See also SATA 7
See also SATA-Obit 62
See also SSC 2
Barthelme, Frederick 1943- ... 122
Brief entry ... 114
Interview in ... 122
See also CLC 36
See also DLBY 85
Barthelme, Peter R. 1939- ... 127
Barthelme, Steve(n) 1947- ... 136
Barthelmes, (Albert) Wes(ley, Jr.) 1922-1976 . 69-72
Obituary ... 65-68
Barthes, Roland (Gerard) 1915-1980 ... CANR-66
Obituary ... 97-100
Earlier sketch in CA 130
See also CLC 24, 83
See also MTCW 1
Bartholet, Elizabeth 1940- ... 141
Bartholomay, Julia A. 1923- ... 45-48
Bartholomeusz, Dennis 1930- ... 130
Bartholomew, Barbara 1941- ... 135
Brief entry ... 118
See also SATA 86
See also SATA-Brief 42
Bartholomew, Bart
See Bartholomew, Frank H.
Bartholomew, Cecilia 1907- ... CAP-1
Earlier sketch in CA 13-14
Bartholomew, Ed(ward Ellsworth) 1914- ... 25-28R
Bartholomew, Frank H. 1898-1985 Obituary ... 115
See also DLB 127
Bartholomew, James 1950- ... 132
Bartholomew, Jean
See Beatty, Patricia (Robbins)
Bartholomew, John Eric
See Morecambe, Eric
Bartholomew, Paul C(harles) 1907-1975 . CANR-10
Earlier sketch in CA 17-20R
Bartier, Pierre 1945- ... 21-24R
Bartky, Sandra Lee 1935- ... 154
Bartlett, Amy 1949- ... 124
Bartlett, Basil Hardington 1905-1985 Obituary .. 115
Bartlett, Bruce R(eeves) 1951- ... CANR-19
Earlier sketch in CA 89-92
Bartlett, C(hristopher) J(ohn) 1931- ... 17-20R
Bartlett, Charles (Leffingwell) 1921- ... 29-32R
Bartlett, David
See Mason, Madeline
Bartlett, Donald L. Brief entry ... 110
Bartlett, Elizabeth (Winters) ... CANR-9
Earlier sketch in CA 17-20R
Bartlett, Elsa Jaffe 1935- ... CANR-15
Earlier sketch in CA 33-36R
Bartlett, Eric George 1920- ... CANR-41
Earlier sketches in CA 5-8R, CANR-2, 19
Bartlett, F. C.
See Bartlett, Frederic Charles
Bartlett, Frederic Charles 1886-1969 Obituary .. 115
Bartlett, Gene E(bert) 1910-1989 Obituary ... 130
Bartlett, Gerald (Robert) 1935- ... 21-24R
Bartlett, Harriett M(oulton) 1897-1987 Obituary . 121
Bartlett, Hubert Moyse
See Moyse-Bartlett, Hubert
Bartlett, Irving H(enry) 1923- ... CANR-9
Earlier sketch in CA 21-24R
Bartlett, Jean Anne 1927- ... 97-100
Bartlett, Jennifer Losch 1941- ... 136
Bartlett, John 1820-1905 ... DLB 1
Bartlett, Jonathan 1931- ... 93-96
Bartlett, Kathleen
See Paine, Lauran (Bosworth)
Bartlett, Kim 1941- ... 89-92
Bartlett, Lee Anthony 1950- ... 114
Bartlett, Margaret Farrington 1896- ... CANR-5
Earlier sketch in CA 5-8R
Bartlett, Marie (Swan) 1918- ... 21-24R
Bartlett, Merrill L(ewis) 1939- ... 117
Bartlett, Nancy W(hite) 1913-1972 ... CAP-2
Obituary ... 41-44R
Earlier sketch in CA 23-24
Bartlett, Paul 1909- ... CAP-2
Earlier sketch in CA 17-18
Bartlett, Philip A. ... CANR-26
Earlier sketches in CAP-2, CA 19-20
See also SATA 1
Bartlett, Phyllis 1908(?)-1973 Obituary ... 41-44R
Bartlett, Richard A(dams) 1920- ... CANR-2
Earlier sketch in CA 5-8R
Bartlett, Robert (John) 1950- ... 125
Bartlett, Robert Merrill 1899- ... CANR-68
Earlier sketches in CA 5-8R, CANR-2
See also SATA 12
Bartlett, Robert V(irgil) 1953- ... CANR-22
Earlier sketch in CA 104
Bartlett, Ruhl J. 1897- ... CAP-1
Earlier sketch in CA 11-12
Bartlett, Ruth ... 17-20R
Bartlett, Sarah 1955- ... 140
Bartlett, (Charles) Vernon (Oldfield) 1894-1983 ... CANR-68
Obituary ... 108
Earlier sketch in CA 61-64
Bartley, Diana E(sther) Pelaez-Rivera 1940- .. 69-72
Bartley, Leigh
See Riker, Leigh
Bartley, Numan V(ache) 1934- ... CANR-12
Earlier sketch in CA 69-72
Bartley, Robert L(eRoy) 1937- ... 97-100
Interview in ... 97-100
Bartley, William Warren III 1934- ... CANR-15
Earlier sketch in CA 37-40R
Bartocci, Gianni 1925- ... 21-24R
Bartol, Cyrus Augustus 1813-1900 ... DLB 1
Bartole, Genevieve 1927- ... 101
Bartoletti, Susan Campbell 1958- ... 152
See also SATA 88
Bartolome de Roxas, Juan
See Rubia Barcia, Jose
Bartolomeo, Joseph F(rancis) 1958- ... 151
Barton, Allen H(oisington) 1924- ... CANR-10
Earlier sketch in CA 25-28R
Barton, Anne 1933- ... 144
Barton, Bernard 1784-1849 ... DLB 96
Barton, Bruce Walter 1935- ... 89-92
Barton, Byron 1930- ... CANR-57
Earlier sketches in CA 57-60, CANR-13
See also SATA 9, 90
Barton, Charles (Albert) 1920- ... 139
Barton, Del 1925-1971 Obituary ... 103
Barton, Erle
See Fanthorpe, R(obert) Lionel
Barton, Eustace Robert 1854-1943 Brief entry . 114
Barton, Fredrick (Preston) 1948- ... CANR-43
Earlier sketch in CA 119
Barton, H. Arnold 1929- ... 77-80
Barton, Harriett ... SATA-Brief 43
Barton, Humphrey (Douglas Elliott) 1900- ... CAP-2
Earlier sketch in CA 19-20
Barton, Jill(ian) 1940- ... SATA 75
Barton, Jim Tom ... 123
Barton, John 1948- ... 137
Barton, John (Stuart) 1957- ... 114
Barton, John Bernard Adie 1928- ... 81-84
Barton, John H(ays) 1936- ... 111
Barton, John Mackintosh Tilney 1898- ... CAP-1
Earlier sketch in CA 17-18
Barton, Jon
See Harvey, John (Barton)
Barton, Lee
See Fanthorpe, R(obert) Lionel
Barton, Lew(is Randolph) 1918- ... 73-76
Barton, M. Xaveria 1910- Brief entry ... 105
Barton, Margaret D(over) 1902- ... CAP-1
Earlier sketch in CA 13-16
Barton, Mary Neill 1899- ... CAP-2
Earlier sketch in CA 19-20
Barton, May Hollis ... CANR-26
Earlier sketches in CAP-2, CA 19-20
See also SATA 1, 67
Barton, Michael (Lee) 1943- ... 110
Barton, Pat
See Arrowsmith, Pat
See also SATA 59
Barton, Pat 1928- ... SATA 59
Barton, Richard F(leming) 1924- ... 61-64
Barton, Roger A(very) 1903-1976 Obituary ... 65-68
Barton, S. W.
See Whaley, Barton Stewart
Barton, Tamsyn (S.) 1962- ... 151
Barton, Thomas Frank 1905- ... CANR-1
Earlier sketch in CA 45-48
Barton, Thomas Pennant 1803-1869 ... DLB 140
Barton, V(ernon) Wayne ... 1-4R
Barton, Walter Elbert 1886-1983 Obituary ... 111
Barton, Wayne 1944- ... CANR-64
Earlier sketch in CA 124
Barton, Weldon V. 1938- ... 21-24R
Barton, William (Renald III) 1950- ... CANR-1
Earlier sketch in CA 45-48
Bartos, Otomar J(an) 1927- ... 105
Bartos-Hoeppner, Barbara 1923- ... CANR-10
Earlier sketch in CA 25-28R
See also SATA 5
Bartoszewski, Wladyslaw T(eofil) 1955- ... 146
Bartov, Hanoch 1926- ... CANR-65
Brief entry ... 117
Earlier sketch in CA 129
Bartov, Omer 1954- ... 135
Bartram, George
See Cameron, Kenneth M.
Bartram, Graham 1946- ... 116
Bartram, John 1699-1777 ... DLB 31
Bartram, William 1739-1823 ... DLB 37
Bartran, Margaret 1913-1976 ... CAP-2
Earlier sketch in CA 29-32
Bartrum, Douglas A(lbert) 1907- ... CANR-6
Earlier sketch in CA 9-12R
Bartsch, Jochen 1906- ... SATA 39
Bartsch, William H. 1933- ... 138
Bartscht, Waltraud 1924- ... 41-44R
Bartusiak, Marcia 1950- ... 129
Bartusis, Mary Ann 1930- ... 101
Bart-Williams, Gaston 1938- ... BW 2
Bartz, Albert E(dward) 1933- ... 21-24R
Bartz, Patricia McBride 1921- ... 102
Bartz, Wayne R(onald) 1938- ... 111
Baruch, Dorothy W(alter) 1899-1962 ... SATA 21
Baruch, Grace K. 1936(?)-1988 Obituary ... 126
Baruch, Ruth-Marion 1922- ... 29-32R
Baruchello, Gianfranco 1924- ... 153
Baruk, Henri Marc 1897- ... 85-88
Barwick, Steven 1921- ... 13-16R
Barwood, Hal ... 129
Brief entry ... 125
Baryshnikov, Mikhail (Nikolayevich) 1948- ... CANR-72
Brief entry ... 113
Earlier sketch in CA 133
Barzanti, Sergio 1925- ... 17-20R
Barzilay, Isaac Eisenstein 1915- ... 113
Barzini, Luigi (Giorgio, Jr.) 1908-1984 ... CANR-23
Obituary ... 112
Earlier sketch in CA 13-16R
Barzman, Ben 1912- ... 132
Bar-Zohar, Michael 1938- ... CANR-35
Earlier sketches in CA 21-24R, CANR-12
Barzun, Jacques (Martin) 1907- ... CANR-22
Earlier sketch in CA 61-64
See also CLC 51
Bas, Joe 1932- ... 53-56
Bas, Rutger
See Rutgers van der Loeff-Basenau, An(na) Maria Margaretha
Basa, Eniko Molnar 1939- ... 77-80
Basart, Ann Phillips 1931- ... CANR-1
Earlier sketch in CA 1-4R
Basch, Michael Franz ... 130
Basch, Rachel 1959- ... 168
Basche, James 1926- ... 29-32R
Bascio, Patrick 1927- ... CANR-44
Earlier sketch in CA 119
Bascom, David 1912- ... 93-96
Bascom, Harold A(dolphus) 1951- ... 135
Bascom, Willard N. 1916- ... CANR-6
Earlier sketch in CA 1-4R
Bascom, William R(ussel) 1912-1981 ... 17-20R
Obituary ... 125
Basdekis, Demetrios 1930- ... 25-28R
Base, Graeme (Rowland) 1958- ... CANR-69
Earlier sketch in CA 134
See also CLR 22
See also MAICYA
See also SATA 67, 101
Baseley, Godfrey 1904-1997 ... 102
Obituary ... 156
Basgoz, M(ehmet) Ilhan 1921- ... 113
Bash, Deborah M. Blumenthal 1940- ... 109
Bash, Frank N(ess) 1937- ... 107
Bash, Harry H(arvey) 1926- ... 89-92
Basham, Don W(ilson) 1926- ... 65-68
Basham, Richard Dalton 1945- ... 111
Basham, William Randolph
1933(?)-1986 Obituary ... 118
Bashe, Patricia Ann Romanowski 1956- ... 127
Bashe, Philip (Scott) 1954- ... 134
Bashevis, Isaac
See Singer, Isaac Bashevis
Bashevkin, Sylvia B. 1954- ... 121
Bashira, Damali 1951- ... 57-60
Basho
See Matsuo Basho
Bashshur, Rashid L. 1933- ... 89-92
Basichis, Gordon (Allen) 1947- ... 85-88
Basie, Count
See Basie, William James
Basie, William James 1904(?)-1984 ... 134
Basil, Douglas C. 1923- ... 41-44R
Basil, Otto 1901-1983 ... 49-52
Obituary ... 113
Basile, Gloria Vitanza 1929- ... CANR-12
Earlier sketch in CA 69-72
Basile, Joseph 1912- ... CANR-11
Earlier sketch in CA 25-28R
Basile, Leon 1955- ... 113
Basile, Robert M(anlius) 1916- ... 53-56
Basil-Hart, James
See Hough, Harold
Basilius, Harold A. 1905-1977 ... CANR-2
Earlier sketch in CA 1-4R
Basinger, Jeanine (Deyling) 1936- ... CANR-18
Earlier sketch in CA 97-100
Basinski, Michael 1950- ... CAAS 29
Basiuk, Victor 1932- ... 93-96
Baskerville, Barnet 1916- ... 1-4R
Baskerville, Patricia 1951- ... 108
Baskett, John 1930- ... 97-100
Baskette, Floyd K(enneth) 1910-1979 ... CANR-29
Earlier sketch in CA 33-36R
Baskin, Barbara H(olland) 1929- ... CANR-22
Earlier sketch in CA 103
Baskin, Esther Tane 1926(?)-1973 Obituary 37-40R
Baskin, Judith R. 1950- ... 137
Baskin, Leonard 1922- ... 106
See also SATA 30
See also SATA-Brief 27
Baskin, Robert E(dward) 1917-1983 Obituary .. 110
Baskin, Samuel 1921- ... 17-20R
Baskin, Wade 1924-1974 ... CAP-2
Earlier sketch in CA 23-24
Basler, Roy P(rentice) 1906-1989 ... CANR-4
Obituary ... 130
Earlier sketch in CA 5-8R
Basler, Thomas G(ordon) 1940- ... 103
Bason, Fred
See Bason, Frederick (Thomas)
Bason, Frederick (Thomas) 1907-1973 ... 5-8R
Obituary ... 89-92
Bason, Lillian 1913- ... 69-72
See also SATA 20
Basra, Amarjit S(ingh) 1958- ... 151
Bass, Altha Leah (Bierbower) 1892-1988 ... CAP-2
Obituary ... 126
Earlier sketch in CA 23-24
Bass, Althea
See Bass, Altha Leah (Bierbower)
Bass, Bernard M(orris) 1925- ... CANR-19
Earlier sketches in CA 1-4R, CANR-4
Bass, Clarence B(eaty) 1922- ... 5-8R
Bass, Cynthia 1949- ... 160
Bass, Eben E(dward) 1924- ... 107
Bass, Ellen 1947- ... CANR-2
Earlier sketch in CA 49-52
Bass, George F(letcher) 1932- ... CANR-48
Earlier sketch in CA 122
Bass, Henry B(enjamin) 1897-1975 Obituary . 57-60
Bass, Herbert Jacob 1929- ... CANR-1
Earlier sketch in CA 1-4R
Bass, Howard 1923- ... CANR-2
Earlier sketch in CA 5-8R
Bass, Howard L(arry) 1942- ... 69-72
Bass, Jack 1934- ... CANR-19
Earlier sketch in CA 29-32R
Bass, Jack A(lexander) 1946- ... 97-100
Bass, Kingsley B., Jr.
See Bullins, Ed
Bass, Lawrence W(ade) 1898- ... 49-52
Bass, Madeline Tiger
See Tiger, Madeline
Bass, Milton R. 1923- ... 25-28R
Bass, Nelson Estupinan
See Estupinan Bass, Nelson
Bass, Rick 1958- ... CANR-53
Earlier sketch in CA 126
See also CLC 79
Bass, Robert D(uncan) 1904- ... 61-64
Bass, Ron
See Bass, Ronald
Bass, Ronald ... 165
Bass, T. J.
See Bassler, Thomas J(oseph)
See also DLBY 81
Bass, Thomas A. 1951- ... 124
Bass, Virginia W(auchope) 1905- ... 61-64
Bass, William M(arvin III) 1928- ... CANR-31
Earlier sketch in CA 41-44R
Bassan, Maurice 1929- ... 25-28R
Bassani, Giorgio 1916- ... CANR-33
Earlier sketch in CA 65-68
See also CLC 9
See also DLB 128, 177
See also MTCW 1
Basse, Eli 1904-1979 Obituary ... 93-96
Basse, William 1583(?)-1653 ... DLB 121
Basseches, Michael 1950- ... 114
Bassermann, Lujo
See Schreiber, Hermann (Otto Ludwig)
Basset, Bernard 1909-1988 ... CANR-6
Obituary ... 125
Earlier sketch in CA 9-12R
Bassett, Edward Eryl 1940- ... 33-36R
Bassett, Flora Marjorie
1890(?)-1980 Obituary ... 97-100
Bassett, George William 1910- ... 102
Bassett, Glenn Arthur 1930- ... 17-20R
Bassett, (Mary) Grace 1927- ... 73-76
Bassett, Jack
See Rowland, D(onald) S(ydney)

Bassett, James E(lias) 1912-1978 ... 61-64
Obituary ... 81-84
Bassett, Jan(ice Mary) 1953- ... 145
Bassett, Jeni 1959- ... SATA 64
See also SATA-Brief 43
Bassett, John Earl, Jr. 1942- ... 123
Bassett, John Keith
See Keating, Lawrence A.
Bassett, John Spencer 1867-1928 Brief entry .. 122
See also DLB 17
Bassett, Lisa 1958- ... CANR-53
Earlier sketch in CA 126
See also SATA 61
Bassett, Marnie
See Bassett, Flora Marjorie
Bassett, Richard 1900- ... CAP-2
Earlier sketch in CA 25-28
Bassett, Ronald 1924- ... 81-84
Bassett, T(homas) D(ay) Seymour 1913- .. CANR-8
Earlier sketch in CA 21-24R
Bassett, William B. K. 1908- ... CAP-1
Earlier sketch in CA 9-10
Bassett, William Travis 1923- ... 9-12R
Bassett, William W. 1932- ... CANR-34
Earlier sketch in CA 25-28R
Bassford, Christopher 1953- ... 152
Bassil, Andrea 1948- ... 161
See also SATA 96
Bassin, Donna 1950- ... 148
Bassiouni, M. Cherif 1937- ... CANR-34
Earlier sketch in CA 29-32R
Bassler, Thomas J(oseph) 1932- ... 115
See also Bass, T. J.
Bassnett, Susan (Edna) 1947- ... 128
Bassnett-McGuire, Susan
See Bassnett, Susan (Edna)
Basso, Aldo P(eter) 1922- ... 65-68
Basso, (Joseph) Hamilton 1904-1964 ... CANR-67
Earlier sketch in CA 89-92
Basso, Keith H(amilton) 1940- ... 131
Bassoff, Bruce 1941- ... 69-72
Bassoff, Evelyn S(ilten) 1944- ... 166
Basson, Helene Carol Weldt
See Weldt-Basson, Helene Carol
Basta, Lofty L. 1933- ... 156
Bastable, Bernard
See Barnard, Robert
Basten, Fred E(rnest) ... CANR-22
Earlier sketches in CA 57-60, CANR-7
Bastian, F(rank) 1913- ... 128
Bastias, Constantine
1901(?)-1972 Obituary ... 37-40R
Bastico, Ettore 1876-1972 Obituary ... 37-40R
Bastin, J(ohn) S(turgus) 1927- ... CANR-11
Earlier sketch in CA 21-24R
Bastlund, Knud 1925- ... 21-24R
Bastos, Augusto (Antonio) Roa
See Roa Bastos, Augusto (Antonio)
Basu, Arindam 1948- ... 61-64
Basu, Asoke (Kumar) 1940- ... 106
Basu, Dipak R. 1951- ... 112
Basu, Kaushik 1952- ... CANR-38
Earlier sketch in CA 115
Basu, Romen 1923- ... CANR-56
Earlier sketches in CA 77-80, CANR-13, 30
Baswell, Christopher 1952- ... 149
Bataille, Georges 1897-1962 ... 101
Obituary ... 89-92
See also CLC 29
Bataille, Gretchen M. 1944- ... 102
Bat-Ami, Miriam 1950- ... 150
See also SATA 82
Batbedat, Jean 1926- ... 37-40R
Batchelder, Alan Bruce 1931- ... 21-24R
Batchelder, Howard T(imothy) 1909- ... CAP-2
Earlier sketch in CA 19-20
Batcheller, John M. 1918- ... 45-48
Batchelor, C(larence) D(aniel)
1888-1977 Obituary ... 73-76
Batchelor, David 1943- ... CANR-18
Earlier sketch in CA 101
Batchelor, Edward, Jr. 1930- ... 110
Batchelor, John 1942- ... 93-96
Batchelor, John (Dennis) 1947- ... 109
Batchelor, John Calvin 1948- ... CANR-45
Earlier sketch in CA 105
Batchelor, Joy 1914- ... SATA-Brief 29
Batchelor, Julie F(rances) E(lizabeth) 1947- ... 109
Batchelor, R. E. 1934- ... 146
Batchelor, Reg
See Paine, Lauran (Bosworth)
Batcher, Elaine Kotler 1944- ... 109
Bate, Jonathan 1958- ... 134
Bate, Lucy 1939- ... 69-72
See also SATA 18
Bate, Norman (Arthur) 1916- ... 1-4R
See also SATA 5
Bate, Sam 1907- ... 102
Bate, W(alter) Jackson 1918- ... 5-8R
See also DLB 67, 103
Bateman, Barbara Dee 1933- ... 41-44R
Bateman, Christopher fl. 1684-1731 ... DLB 170
Bateman, Colin 1962- ... 153
Bateman, Robert (Moyes Carruthers) 1922-1973 ...
CANR-7
Earlier sketch in CA 5-8R
Bateman, Walter L(ewis) 1916- ... 29-32R
Bates, Alan Lawrence 1923- ... 17-20R
Bates, Arthenia J.
See Millican, Arthenia Jackson Bates
Bates, Barbara S(nedeker) 1919- ... 17-20R
See also SATA 12
Bates, Betty
See Bates, Elizabeth
See also SATA 19
Bates, Carol Neuls
See Neuls-Bates, Carol
Bates, Caroline (Philbrick) 1932- ... 103
Bates, Catherine 1964- ... 139
Bates, Charles C(arpenter) 1918- ... 121
Bates, Craig D. 1952- ... 140
Bates, Daisy Lee 1914- ... 127
Bates, (Julian) Darrell 1913-1989 ... CAP-1
Obituary ... 129
Earlier sketch in CA 9-10
Bates, David Vincent 1922- ... 110
Bates, Elizabeth 1921- ... CANR-32
Earlier sketches in CA 77-80, CANR-14
See also Bates, Betty
Bates, H(erbert) E(rnest) 1905-1974 ... CANR-34
Obituary ... 45-48
Earlier sketch in CA 93-96
See also CLC 46
See also DAB
See also DAM POP
See also DLB 162, 191
See also MTCW 1
See also SSC 10
Bates, Harry 1900-1981 ... 162
Bates, Helen L. Z.
See Yakobson, Helen B(ates)
Bates, J. Douglas 1946- ... 142
Bates, J(ames) Leonard 1919- ... 13-16R
Bates, Jefferson D(avis) 1920- ... CANR-34
Earlier sketches in CA 81-84, CANR-15
Bates, Jerome E. 1917- ... 17-20R
Bates, Kenneth Francis 1904- ... CAP-1
Earlier sketch in CA 13-14
Bates, Lucius Christopher
1901(?)-1980 Obituary ... 101
Bates, Margaret J(ane) 1918- ... 17-20R
Bates, Marston 1906-1974 ... CANR-7
Obituary ... 49-52
Earlier sketch in CA 5-8R
Bates, Milton J(ames) 1945- ... 128
Bates, Paul A(llen) 1920- ... 37-40R
Bates, Peter Watson 1920- ... 102
Bates, Ralph Samuel 1906- ... 1-4R
Bates, Robert H(inrichs) 1942- ... CANR-28
Earlier sketches in CA 69-72, CANR-11
Bates, Robert L(atimer) 1912-1994 ... CANR-46
Obituary ... 145
Brief entry ... 116
Earlier sketch in CA 121
Bates, Ronald (Gordon Nudell) 1924- ... 25-28R
Bates, Scott 1923- ... 49-52
Bates, Stephen 1958- ... 122
Bates, Steven Latimer 1940- ... 114
Bates, Su
See Bates, Susannah (Vacella)
Bates, Susannah (Vacella) 1941- ... 112
Bates, Timothy M(ason) 1946- ... 53-56
Bates, Tom 1944- ... 143
Bateson, Charles (Henry) 1903- ... 69-72
Bateson, F(rederick) W(ilse) 1901-1978 ... CANR-6
Earlier sketch in CA 5-8R
Bateson, Gregory 1904-1980 ... 41-44R
Obituary ... 101
Bateson, Mary Catherine 1939- ... 137
Batey, Mavis 1921- ... CANR-51
Earlier sketch in CA 125
Batey, Richard (Alexander) 1933- ... 33-36R
Batey, Tom 1946- ... 107
See also SATA 52
See also SATA-Brief 41
Bath, Philip Ernest 1898- ... CAP-1
Earlier sketch in CA 9-10
Batherman, Muriel
See Sheldon, Muriel
Bathke, Edwin A(lbert) 1936- ... 57-60
Bathke, Nancy E(dna) 1938- ... 57-60
Batho, Edith C(lara) 1895- ... CAP-1
Earlier sketch in CA 11-12
Bathurst, Sheila
See Sullivan, Sheila
Batista, Fulgencio
See Batista y Zaldivar, Fulgencio
Batista y Zaldivar, Fulgencio
1901-1973 Obituary ... 111
Batiuk, Thomas M(artin) 1947- ... 69-72
See also SATA-Brief 40
Batki, John 1942- ... 45-48
Batman, Richard (Dale) 1932- ... 124
Bator, Robert 1939- ... 115
Batra, Raveendra N(ath) 1943- ... CANR-31
Earlier sketch in CA 89-92
Interview in ... CANR-31
Batra, Ravi
See Batra, Raveendra N(ath)
Batson, C(harles) Daniel 1943- ... 129
Batson, George (Donald) 1918-1977 ... 33-36R
Obituary ... 73-76
Batson, Larry 1930- ... 57-60
See also SATA 35
Batson, Wade Thomas 1912- ... 125
Battaglia, Anthony 1939- ... 108
Battaglia, Aurelius 1910- ... SATA 50
See also SATA-Brief 33
Battaglia, Elio Lee 1928- ... CANR-1
Earlier sketch in CA 1-4R
Battalia, O. William 1928- ... 45-48
Battan, Louis J(oseph) 1923- ... 13-16R
Battcock, Gregory 1938-1980 ... CANR-11
Obituary ... 105
Earlier sketch in CA 21-24R
Battelle, Phyllis (Marie) 1922- ... 77-80
Batten, Charles Linwood, Jr. 1942- ... 85-88
Batten, H(arry) Mortimer 1888-1958 Brief entry . 112
See also SATA 25
Batten, Jack (Hubert, Jr.) 1932- ... CANR-44
Earlier sketch in CA 49-52
Batten, James Knox 1936-1995 ... 102
Obituary ... 148
Batten, James William 1919- ... 33-36R
Batten, Jean (Gardner) 1909-1982 ... 106
Obituary ... 123
Batten, Joyce Mortimer
See Mankowska, Joyce Kells Batten
Batten, Mary 1937- ... 41-44R
See also SATA 5, 102
Batten, (Richard) Peter 1916- ... 97-100
Batten, Thomas Reginald 1904- ... 13-16R
Battenhouse, Roy W(esley) 1912-1995 ... 13-16R
Obituary ... 148
Batterberry, Ariane Ruskin 1935- ... CANR-13
Earlier sketch in CA 69-72
See also SATA 13
Batterberry, Michael Carver 1932- ... 77-80
See also SATA 32
Battersby, Christine 1946- ... 132
Battersby, James L(yons) 1936- ... 41-44R
Battersby, Martin 1914(?)-1982 Obituary ... 106
Battersby, William J(ohn) 1904-1976 ... CANR-4
Earlier sketch in CA 5-8R
Battestin, Martin C(arey) 1930- ... 13-16R
Battie, David 1942- ... 135
Battin, B(rinton) W(arner) 1941- ... CANR-57
Earlier sketches in CA 112, CANR-30
Battin, R(osabell) Ray 1925- ... CANR-6
Earlier sketch in CA 9-12R
Battin, Wendy 1953- ... 121
Battis, Emery John 1915- ... 1-4R
Battiscombe, E(sther) Georgina (Harwood) 1905- ..
CANR-53
Earlier sketches in CAP-1, CA 9-10, CANR-14
See also DLB 155
Battison, Brian 1939- ... 147
Battista, Miriam 1912(?)-1980 Obituary ... 103
Battista, O(rlando) A(loysius) 1917- ... CANR-7
Earlier sketch in CA 13-16R
Battisti, Eugenio 1924- ... 37-40R
Battle, Allen Overton 1927- ... 41-44R
Battle, Gerald N(ichols) 1914- ... 57-60
Battle, Jean Allen 1914- ... 25-28R
Battle, Lois 1942- ... CANR-27
Earlier sketch in CA 106
Battle, Richard John Vulliamy
1907-1982 Obituary ... 106
Battle, Sol(omon Oden) 1934- ... 25-28R
Battle-Lavert, Gwendolyn 1951- ... 151
See also SATA 85
Battles, (Roxy) Edith 1921- ... 41-44R
See also SATA 7
Battles, Ford Lewis 1915- ... 13-16R
Batto, Bernard Frank 1941- ... 57-60
Batts, Michael S. 1929- ... 41-44R
Batty, C(harles) D(avid) 1932- ... 17-20R
Batty, Joyce D(orothea) 1919- ... 17-20R
Batty, Linda Schmidt 1940- ... 61-64
Battye, Gladys Starkey 1915- Brief entry ... 111
Battye, Louis Neville 1923- ... 5-8R
Baty, Gordon B(ruce) 1938- ... 57-60
Baty, Roger M(endenhall) 1937- ... 77-80
Baty, Wayne 1925- ... CANR-5
Earlier sketch in CA 13-16R
Bauby, Cathrina 1927- ... 49-52
Bauby, Jean-Dominique 1952(?)-1997 ... 163
Bauchart
See Camus, Albert
Bauchau, Henry 1913- ... 166
Baucom, Donald R. 1940- ... 145
Baudelaire, Charles 1821-1867 ... DA
See also DAB
See also DAC
See also DAM MST, POET
See also PC 1
See also SSC 18
See also WLC
Baudet, Henri 1919- ... 134
Baudhuin, John S. 1948- ... 112
Baudino, Gael 1955(?)- ... 154
Baudot, Georges 1935- ... 162
Baudouy, Michel-Aime 1909- ... CAP-2
Earlier sketch in CA 33-36
See also SATA 7
Baudrillard, Jean 1929- ... CLC 60
Baudry, Bernard
See Guindey, Guillaume Louis
Bauduc, R.
See Segre, Dan V(ittorio)
Baudy, Nicolas 1904(?)-1971 Obituary ... 33-36R
Bauer, Bruno 1809-1882 ... DLB 133
Bauer, Caroline Feller 1935- ... CANR-67
Earlier sketch in CA 77-80
See also SAAS 24
See also SATA 52, 98
See also SATA-Brief 46
Bauer, Douglas 1945- ... 166
Bauer, E. Charles 1916- ... 9-12R
Bauer, Erwin A. 1919- ... CANR-6
Earlier sketch in CA 9-12R
Bauer, Florence Marvyne ... CAP-2
Earlier sketch in CA 17-18
Bauer, Fred 1934- ... CANR-13
Earlier sketch in CA 29-32R
See also SATA 36
Bauer, George C. 1942- ... 73-76
Bauer, George Howard 1933-1996 ... CANR-15
Obituary ... 152
Earlier sketch in CA 29-32R
Bauer, (Jo) Hanna R(uth Goldsmith) 1918- ... 57-60
Bauer, Harry C(harles) 1902-1979 ... CAP-1
Obituary ... 85-88
Earlier sketch in CA 13-14
Bauer, Helen 1900- ... 5-8R
See also SATA 2
Bauer, Henry H. 1931- ... 149
Bauer, Josef Martin 1901- ... CANR-5
Earlier sketch in CA 5-8R
Bauer, K(arl) Jack 1926-1987 ... CANR-10
Obituary ... 123
Earlier sketch in CA 25-28R
Bauer, Malcolm Clair 1914- ... 102
Bauer, Maria 1919- ... 117
Bauer, Marion Dane 1938- ... CANR-50
Earlier sketches in CA 69-72, CANR-11, 26
See also AAYA 19
See also JRDA
See also MAICYA
See also SAAS 9
See also SATA 20, 69
Bauer, Nancy 1934- ... 113
Bauer, Peter Thomas 1915- ... 103
Bauer, Raymond A(ugustine) 1916-1977 . CANR-11
Obituary ... 73-76
Earlier sketch in CA 61-64
Bauer, Robert A(lbert) 1910- ... 69-72
Bauer, Roy A. 1945- ... 137
Bauer, Royal D(aniel) M(ichael) 1889- ... 33-36R
Bauer, Steven 1948- ... 128
Bauer, Tricia ... 153
Bauer, Walter 1904- ... 101
Bauer, William Waldo 1892-1967 ... CANR-7
Earlier sketch in CA 5-8R
Bauer, Wolfgang 1941- ... 151
See also DLB 124
Bauer, Wolfgang L(eander) 1930- ... 13-16R
Bauer, Yehuda 1926- ... CANR-12
Earlier sketch in CA 29-32R
Bauerle, Ruth (Ellen) H(awkins) 1924- ... 112
Bauerlein, Mark (Weightman) 1959- ... 141
Bauernfeind, Harry B. 1904- ... CAP-2
Earlier sketch in CA 19-20
Bauerschmidt, Marjorie 1926- ... SATA 15
Baugh, Albert C(roll) 1891-1981 ... 107
Obituary ... 103
Baugh, Daniel A(lbert) 1931- ... 69-72
Baughan, Peter E(dward) 1934- ... 107
Baughman, Dorothy 1940- ... 65-68
See also SATA 61
Baughman, Ernest W(arren) 1916- ... 33-36R
Baughman, James L(ewis) 1952- ... CANR-41
Earlier sketch in CA 118
Baughman, James P(orter) 1936- ... 25-28R
Baughman, John Lee 1913- ... 97-100
Baughman, M(illard) Dale 1919- ... 41-44R
Baughman, Michael 1937- ... 150
Baughman, Ray Edward 1925- ... CANR-22
Earlier sketches in CA 9-12R, CANR-4
Baughman, Ronald 1940- ... 122
Baughman, T. H. 1947- ... 145
Baughman, Urbanus E., Jr.
1905(?)-1978 Obituary ... 81-84
Baughn, William Hubert 1918- ... CANR-17
Earlier sketch in CA 1-4R
Baukhage, Hilmar Robert
1889-1976 Obituary ... 65-68
See also AITN 2
Baul, Lee Khepa
See Lozowick, Lee
Bauland, Peter 1932- ... 25-28R
Baulch, Jerry T. 1913- ... 77-80
Baulch, Lawrence 1926- ... 25-28R
Baum, Allyn Z(elton) 1924-1997 ... 17-20R
Obituary ... 158
See also SATA 20, 98
Baum, Bernard H(elmut) 1926- ... 37-40R
Baum, Dale 1943- ... 118
Baum, Daniel (Jay) 1934- ... CANR-6
Earlier sketch in CA 13-16R
Baum, David William 1940- ... 53-56
Baum, Gregory 1923- ... CANR-15
Earlier sketch in CA 25-28R
Baum, Joan 1937- ... 134
Baum, L. Frank
See Thompson, Ruth Plumly
Baum, L(yman) Frank 1856-1919 ... 133
Brief entry ... 108
See also CLR 15
See also DLB 22
See also JRDA
See also MAICYA
See also MTCW 1
See also SATA 18, 100
See also TCLC 7
Baum, Louis 1948- ... 124
See also SATA 64
See also SATA-Brief 52
Baum, Louis F.
See Baum, L(yman) Frank
Baum, Paull F(ranklin) 1886-1964 ... 5-8R
Obituary ... 103
Baum, Rainer C(arl) 1934- ... 107
Baum, Richard (Dennis) 1940- ... 57-60
Baum, Richard Fitzgerald 1913- ... 5-8R
Baum, Robert J(ames) 1941- ... CANR-17
Earlier sketch in CA 85-88
Baum, Thomas 1940- ... 65-68
Baum, Vicki 1888-1960 ... 93-96
Interview in ... 93-96
See also DLB 85
Baum, Willi 1931- ... 29-32R
See also SATA 4
Bauman, Clarence 1928- ... CANR-32
Earlier sketch in CA 45-48
Bauman, Edward Walter 1927- ... 106
Bauman, H(erman) Carl 1913- ... 9-12R
Bauman, Janina (G.) 1926- ... 134
Bauman, Karl R. 1902(?)-1989 Obituary ... 130
Bauman, Richard W. 1951- ... 163
Bauman, Zygmunt 1925- ... 127
Baumann, Amy (Brown) Beeching 1922- ... 21-24R
See also SATA 10

Baumann, Carol Edler 1932-....33-36R
Baumann, Charles Henry 1926-....73-76
Baumann, Charly 1928-....89-92
Baumann, Edward (Weston) 1925-....109
Baumann, Elwood D. Brief entry....111
See also SATA-Brief 33
Baumann, Gerd 1953-....125
Baumann, Hans 1914-....CANR-3
Earlier sketch in CA 5-8R
See also CLR 35
See also SATA 2
Baumann, Hans Felix S(iegismund)
1893-1985 Obituary....115
Baumann, Kurt 1935-....CANR-13
Earlier sketch in CA 77-80
See also SATA 21
Baumann, Walter 1935-....29-32R
Baumbach, Jonathan 1933-....CANR-66
Earlier sketches in CA 13-16R, CANR-12
Interview in....CANR-12
See also CAAS 5
See also CLC 6, 23
See also DLBY 80
See also MTCW 1
Baumback, Clifford M(ason) 1915-....CANR-6
Earlier sketch in CA 57-60
Baumber, Michael (Leslie) 1935-....133
Baume, Michael 1930-....25-28R
Baumel, Judith 1956-....125
Baumer, Franklin L(e Van) 1913- Brief entry....110
Baumer, William H(enry) 1909-1989....CANR-1
Obituary....127
Earlier sketch in CA 1-4R
Baumgaertel, (Max) Walter 1902-....69-72
Baumgard, Herbert Mark 1920-....13-16R
Baumgardt, David 1890-1963....CANR-15
Obituary....103
Earlier sketch in CA 1-4R
Baumgartel, Walter
See Baumgaertel, (Max) Walter
Baumgarten, Sylvia 1933-....112
Baumgartner, A. Marguerite 1909-....145
Baumgartner, Barbara 1939-....SATA 86
Baumgartner, Frederic J(oseph) 1945-....CANR-52
Earlier sketches in CA 110, CANR-27
Baumgartner, Frederick Milton 1910-....154
Baumgartner, John Stanley 1924-....9-12R
Bauml, Franz H.
See Baeuml, Franz H(einrich)
Baumol, William J(ack) 1922-....CANR-49
Earlier sketches in CA 13-16R, CANR-7, 24
Baumrin, Bernard H(erbert) 1934-....9-12R
Baumrin, Stefan
See Baumrin, Bernard H(erbert)
Baumslag, Naomi 1936-....167
Baur, Francis G. 1930-....111
Baur, John E(dward) 1922-....9-12R
Baur, John I(reland) H(owe)
1909-1987 Obituary....122
Baur, Susan 1940-....CANR-62
Earlier sketch in CANR-40
Baus, Herbert M(ichael) 1914-....CANR-11
Earlier sketch in CA 25-28R
Bausani, Alessandro 1921-....CANR-43
Earlier sketch in CA 45-48
Bausch, Richard (Carl) 1945-....CANR-61
Earlier sketches in CA 101, CANR-43
See also CAAS 14
See also CLC 51
See also DLB 130
Bausch, Robert (Charles) 1945-....109
See also CAAS 14
Bausch, William J. 1929-....CANR-11
Earlier sketch in CA 29-32R
Bausher, Mildred Jordan 1901-1982 Obituary....133
Bavarel, Michel (Joseph) 1940-....CANR-35
Earlier sketch in CA 114
Bavier, Robert Newton, (Jr.) 1918-....115
Bavin, Bill 1919-....73-76
Bavinck, J(ohan) H(erman)
1895-1965 Obituary....113
Bavly, Dan (Abraham) 1929-....130
Bawcutt, Priscilla (June) 1931-....141
Bawden, Nina (Mary Mabey) 1925-....CANR-54
Earlier sketches in CA 17-20R, CANR-8, 29
See also Kark, Nina Mary (Mabey)
See also CLR 2, 51
See also DAB
See also DLB 14, 161
See also JRDA
See also MAICYA
See also SAAS 16
See also SATA 72
Bawer, (Theodore) Bruce 1956-....144
Bawly, Dan
See Bavly, Dan (Abraham)
Bawn, Mary
See Wright, Mary Pamela Godwin
Bax
See Baxter, Gordon F(rancis), Jr.
Bax, Clifford 1886-1962 Obituary....113
See also DLB 10, 100
Bax, Martin C(harles) O(wen) 1933-....65-68
Bax, Roger
See Winterton, Paul
Baxandall, Rosalyn Fraad 1939-....81-84
Baxt, George 1923-....21-24R
Baxter, Angus 1912-....CANR-28
Earlier sketch in CA 111
Baxter, Anne 1923-1985....114
Obituary....118
Brief entry....111
Baxter, Annette Kar 1926-....CANR-4
Earlier sketch in CA 1-4R
Baxter, Batsell Barrett 1916-....33-36R
Baxter, Charles (Morley) 1947-....CANR-64
Earlier sketches in CA 57-60, CANR-40
See also CLC 45, 78
See also DAM POP
See also DLB 130
Baxter, Craig 1929-....CANR-52
Earlier sketches in CA 25-28R, CANR-11, 26
Baxter, Douglas Clark 1942-....85-88
Baxter, Edna May 1890-....CAP-1
Earlier sketch in CA 17-18
Baxter, Eric George 1918-....17-20R
Baxter, Eric P(eter) 1913-....9-12R
Baxter, George Owen
See Faust, Frederick (Schiller)
Baxter, Glen 1944-....CANR-56
Earlier sketches in CA 109, CANR-28
Baxter, Gordon F(rancis), Jr. 1923-....CANR-1
Earlier sketch in CA 45-48
Baxter, Hazel
See Rowland, D(onald) S(ydney)
Baxter, Ian F. G.....CANR-11
Earlier sketch in CA 21-24R
Baxter, James K(eir) 1926-1972....77-80
See also CLC 14
Baxter, James P(hinney) III 1893-1975....65-68
Obituary....57-60
Baxter, James Sidlow 1903-....73-76
Baxter, John
See Hunt, E(verette) Howard, (Jr.)
Baxter, John 1939-....CANR-25
Earlier sketch in CA 29-32R
Baxter(-Wright), Keith (Stanley) 1935-....135
Baxter, Mary Lynn 1943-....152
Baxter, Maurice Glen 1920-....13-16R
Baxter, Michael John 1944-....103
Interview in....103
Baxter, Mike
See Baxter, Michael John
Baxter, Patricia E. W.....107
Baxter, Phyllis
See Wallmann, Jeffrey M(iner)
Baxter, Shane V.
See Norwood, Victor G(eorge) C(harles)
Baxter, Stephen 1957-....161
Baxter, Stephen B(artow) 1929-....17-20R
Baxter, Valerie
See Meynell, Laurence Walter
Baxter, William F(rancis) 1929-....89-92
Baxter, William T(hreipland) 1906-....107
Bay, Austin 1951-....131
Bay, Christian 1921-1990....33-36R
Obituary....131
Bay, Howard 1912-1986....81-84
Obituary....121
Bay, Jeanette Graham 1928-....152
See also SATA 88
Bayard, Jean 1923-....114
Baybars, Taner 1936-....CANR-4
Earlier sketch in CA 53-56
Bayer, Eleanor
See Perry, Eleanor (Rosenfeld Bayer)
Bayer, Harold
See Gregg, Andrew K.
Bayer, Herbert 1900-1985 Obituary....117
Bayer, Jane E. (?)-1985 Obituary....116
See also SATA-Obit 44
Bayer, Konrad 1932-1964....DLB 85
Bayer, Linda 1948-....CANR-26
Earlier sketch in CA 107
Bayer, Oliver Weld
See Perry, Eleanor (Rosenfeld Bayer)
Bayer, Patricia 1952-....141
Bayer, Ronald 1943-....106
Bayer, Sandra Lee 1945-....127
Bayer, Sandy
See Bayer, Sandra Lee
Bayer, Sylvia
See Glassco, John
Bayer, Valerie Townsend 1924-....141
Bayer, William 1939-....CANR-48
Earlier sketch in CA 33-36R
Bayer-Berenbaum, Linda
See Bayer, Linda
Bayerle, Gustav 1931-....53-56
Bayes, Marjorie 1934-....115
Bayes, Ronald H(omer) 1932-....CANR-10
Earlier sketch in CA 25-28R
Bayh, Birch E(vans), Jr. 1928-....41-44R
Bayh, Marvella (Hern) 1933-1979....93-96
Obituary....85-88
Bay Laurel, Alicia
See Laurel, Alicia Bay
Baylen, Joseph O(scar) 1920-....CANR-10
Earlier sketch in CA 25-28R
Bayles, Ernest E(dward) 1897-....73-76
Bayles, Martha 1948-....134
Bayles, Michael D(ale) 1941-....CANR-18
Earlier sketches in CA 49-52, CANR-1
Bayless, John 1913(?)-1983 Obituary....109
Bayless, Kenneth 1913(?)-1972 Obituary....104
Bayless, Raymond 1920-....85-88
Bayley, Barrington J(ohn) 1937-....CANR-43
Earlier sketches in CA 37-40R, CANR-14
Bayley, Charles C(alvert) 1907-....33-36R
Bayley, David H(ume) 1933-....13-16R
Bayley, Edwin Richard 1918-....108
Bayley, John (Oliver) 1925-....85-88
Bayley, Monica Worsley 1919-....111
Bayley, Nicola 1949-....118
See also MAICYA
See also SATA 41, 69
Bayley, Peter Charles 1921-....101
Bayley, Stephen 1951-....106
Bayley, Viola (Powles) 1911-....CANR-5
Earlier sketch in CA 5-8R
Baylis, Janice H(inshaw) 1928-....161
Baylis, John 1946-....CANR-39
Earlier sketches in CA 101, CANR-18
Bayliss, John Clifford 1919-....13-16R
Bayliss, Timothy
See Baybars, Taner
Bayliss, William Maddock 1860-1924....159
Baylor, Byrd 1924-....81-84
See also CLR 3
See also MAICYA
See also SATA 16, 69
Baylor, Robert 1925-....13-16R
Bayly, Joseph T(ate) 1920-....17-20R
Baym, Max I. 1895-....41-44R
Baym, Nina 1936-....CANR-64
Earlier sketches in CA 112, CANR-32
Bayme, Steven 1950-....151
Bayne, David C(owan) 1918-....41-44R
Bayne, Nicholas (Peter) 1937-....130
Bayne, Stephen F(ielding), Jr.
1908-1974 Obituary....45-48
Bayne-Jardine, C(olin) C(harles) 1932-....25-28R
Baynes, Cary F. 1873(?)-1977 Obituary....104
Baynes, Dorothy Colston
See Colston-Baynes, Dorothy
Baynes, John (Christopher Malcolm) 1928-....21-24R
Baynes, Ken 1934- Brief entry....110
Baynes, Kenneth R(ichard) 1954-....141
Baynes, Pauline (Diana) 1922-....CANR-37
Earlier sketch in CA 120
See also DLB 160
See also MAICYA
See also SATA 19, 59
Baynham, Henry (W. F.) 1933-....29-32R
Baynton, Barbara 1857-1929....TCLC 57
Bayor, Ronald H(oward) 1944-....CANR-60
Earlier sketch in CA 128
Bayrd, Edwin 1944-....97-100
Bays, Gwendolyn McKee....13-16R
Bazelon, David T. 1923-....17-20R
Bazelon, Irwin 1922-....102
Bazin, Andre 1918-1958 Brief entry....113
Bazin, Germain (Rene Michel) 1901-1990....
CANR-12
Obituary....131
Earlier sketch in CA 5-8R
Bazin, Herve
See Herve-Bazin, Jean Pierre Marie
See also DLB 83
Bazin, Nancy Topping 1934-....41-44R
Bazley, Margaret C. 1938-....106
Bazzoni, Jana O'Keefe 1941-....154
BB
See Watkins-Pitchford, Denys James
Beach, Bert Beverly 1928-....57-60
Beach, Charles
See Reid, (Thomas) Mayne
Beach, Charles Amory....CANR-26
Earlier sketches in CAP-2, CA 19-20
See also SATA 1
Beach, Dale S. 1923-....13-16R
Beach, David (Williams) 1938-....115
Beach, Earl F(rancis) 1912-....13-16R
Beach, Edward L(atimer) 1918-....CANR-6
Earlier sketch in CA 5-8R
See also SATA 12
Beach, Eric 1947-....160
Beach, Frank Ambrose 1911-1988....110
Obituary....125
Beach, Hugh 1949-....143
Beach, Lynn
See Lance, Kathryn
Beach, Mark B. 1937-....69-72
Beach, Robert C. 1934-....139
Beach, Stewart T(aft) 1899-1979....93-96
Obituary....85-88
See also SATA 23
Beach, Sylvia (Woodbridge) 1887-1962....108
See also DLB 4
See also DLBD 15
Beach, Vincent W(oodrow) 1917-....33-36R
Beach, (William) Waldo 1916-....61-64
Beacham, Richard C. 1946-....141
Beachcomber
See Morton, John (Cameron Andrieu) Bingham
(Michael)
Beachcroft, Nina 1931-....CANR-19
Earlier sketch in CA 97-100
See also SATA 18
Beachcroft, T(homas) O(wen) 1902-....CAP-1
Earlier sketch in CA 9-10
Beachey, Duane 1948-....112
Beachum, Larry M(ahon) 1948-....113
Beachy, Lucille 1935-....77-80
Beadell, Len 1923-....102
Beadle, G. W.
See Beadle, George Wells
Beadle, George
See Beadle, George Wells
Beadle, George Wells 1903-1989....159
Obituary....128
Beadle, Leigh P(atric) 1941-....65-68
Beadle, Muriel (McClure Barnett)
1915-1994....21-24R
Obituary....144
Beadles, William T(homas) 1902-....17-20R
Beagle, Peter S(oyer) 1939-....CANR-51
Earlier sketches in CA 9-12R, CANR-4
Interview in....CANR-4
See also CLC 7, 104
See also DLBY 80
See also SATA 60
Beaglehole, J(ohn) C(awte) 1901-1971....CAP-2
Obituary....33-36R
Earlier sketch in CA 21-22
Beakley, George Carroll, Jr. 1922-....CANR-16
Earlier sketches in CA 45-48, CANR-1
Beal, Anthony (Ridley) 1925-....9-12R
Beal, Bob 1949-....130
Beal, George M(elvin) 1917-....CANR-13
Earlier sketch in CA 21-24R
Beal, Graham W(illiam) J(ohn) 1947-....118
Beal, Gwyneth 1943-....69-72
Beal, John Robinson 1906(?)-1985 Obituary....116
Beal, M. F. 1937-....73-76
See also DLBY 81
Beal, Merrill D. 1898-....CANR-5
Earlier sketch in CA 1-4R
Beal, Richard S(mith) 1945-1984....122
Obituary....114
Beal, Virginia
See Dabney, Virginia Bell
Beale, Betty....73-76
Beale, Calvin L(unsford) 1923-....1-4R
Beale, Christopher Griffin
See Griffin-Beale, Christopher
Beale, Howard 1898-....109
Beale, Howard K. 1899-1959....DLB 17
Beale, Paul (Christian) 1933-....130
Beale, Walter H(enry) 1945- Brief entry....118
Bealer, Alex W(inkler III) 1921-1980....CANR-2
Obituary....97-100
Earlier sketch in CA 45-48
See also SATA 8
See also SATA-Obit 22
Bealer, George Persson 1944-....CANR-32
Earlier sketch in CA 113
Beales, Derek (Edward Dawson) 1931-....CANR-16
Earlier sketch in CA 73-76
Beales, H(ugh) L(ancelot) 1889-1988 Obituary....125
Beales, Peter 1936-....CANR-48
Earlier sketch in CA 122
Beales, Valerie 1915-....SATA 74
Bealey, (Frank) William 1922-....CANR-2
Earlier sketch in CA 5-8R
Beall, Anne E. 1966-....147
Beall, James Lee 1924-....CANR-11
Earlier sketch in CA 65-68
Beall, Karen F(riedmann) 1938-....106
Beall, Otho T(hompson), Jr.
1908-1977 Obituary....113
Beals, Alan R(obin) 1928-....37-40R
Beals, Carleton 1893-1979....CANR-66
Earlier sketches in CA 1-4R, CANR-3
See also SATA 12
Beals, Frank Lee 1881-1972....5-8R
Obituary....103
See also SATA-Obit 26
Beals, Melba Patillo
See Beals, Melba Pattillo
Beals, Melba Pattillo 1941-....159
Beals, Ralph L(eon) 1901-....21-24R
Beam, Alex 1954-....135
Beam, Alvin Wesley 1912-1982 Obituary....107
Beam, C. Richard....45-48
Beam, George D(ahl) 1934-....69-72
Beam, Philip C(onway) 1910-....97-100
Beaman, Joyce Proctor 1931-....29-32R
Beame, Rona 1934-....45-48
See also SATA 12
Beamer, (George) Charles (Jr.) 1942-....121
See also SATA 43
Beamish, Annie O'Meara de Vic 1883-....13-16R
Beamish, Anthony Hamilton (?)-1983 Obituary....109
Beamish, Huldine V. 1904-....CAP-1
Earlier sketch in CA 13-14
Beamish, Noel de Vic
See Beamish, Annie O'Meara de Vic
Beamish, Tufton Victor Hamilton
See Chelwood, Tufton Victor Hamilton
Bean, Constance A(ustin)....41-44R
Bean, George E(wart) 1903-1977....25-28R
Obituary....133
Bean, Gregory (K.) 1952-....CANR-72
Earlier sketch in CA 152
Bean, Henry (Schorr) 1945-....109
Bean, Jonathan J. 1962-....164
Bean, Keith F(enwick) 1911-....CAP-1
Earlier sketch in CA 11-12
Bean, Lowell John 1931-....41-44R
Bean, Mabel Greene 1898(?)-1977 Obituary....73-76
Bean, Normal
See Burroughs, Edgar Rice
Bean, Orson 1928-....77-80
Bean, Walton (Elbert) 1914-....25-28R
Bean, William B(ennett) 1909-1989....111
Obituary....128
Beaney, Jan
See Udall, Jan Beaney
Beaney, Jane
See Udall, Jan Beaney
Bear, Bullen
See Donnelly, Austin Stanislaus
Bear, David 1949-....106
Bear, Greg(ory Dale) 1951-....CANR-35
Earlier sketch in CA 113
See also AAYA 24
See also SATA 65
Bear, James A(dam), Jr. 1919-....21-24R
Bear, Joan 1918-....57-60
Bear, John (Boris) 1938-....CANR-29
Earlier sketches in CA 73-76, CANR-13
Bear, O. L.
See Putnam, William L(owell)
Bear, Roberta Meyer 1942-....21-24R
Bearce, George D(onham) 1922-....9-12R
Bearchell, Charles 1925-....93-96
Beard, Belle Boone 1898-1984 Obituary....114
Beard, Charles A(ustin) 1874-1948 Brief entry....115
See also DLB 17
See also SATA 18
See also TCLC 15
Beard, Dan(iel Carter) 1859-1941....SATA 22

Beard, Darleen Bailey 1961- ... 161
See also SATA 96
Beard, Estle S. 1908-1983 ... 111
Beard, Geoffrey 1929- ... 130
Beard, Helen 1931- ... CANR-32
Earlier sketch in CA 113
Beard, James (Andrews) 1903-1985 ... CANR-15
Obituary ... 114
Earlier sketch in CA 81-84
Beard, James F(ranklin) 1919-1989 ... 1-4R
Obituary ... 130
Beard, Marna L(ouise) 1942- ... 112
Beard, Peter H. 1938- ... 13-16R
Beard, Robert Eric 1911-1983 Obituary ... 111
Bearden, James Hudson 1933- ... 21-24R
Bearden, Romare (Howard) 1914(?)-1988 ... 102
Obituary ... 125
See also SATA 22
See also SATA-Obit 56
Beardmore, Cedric
See Beardmore, George
Beardmore, George 1908-1979 ... 69-72
Obituary ... 126
See also SATA 20
Beardsell, Peter R. 1940- ... 143
Beardslee, John W(alter) III 1914- ... 37-40R
Beardsley, Charles Noel 1914- ... CANR-2
Earlier sketch in CA 1-4R
Beardsley, (John) Douglas 1941- ... 113
Beardsley, Elizabeth Lane ... 29-32R
Beardsley, John 1952- ... CANR-28
Earlier sketch in CA 109
Beardsley, (Betty) Lou 1925- ... 118
Beardsley, Monroe C(urtis) 1915-1985 ... 17-20R
Obituary ... 117
Beardsley, Richard K(ing) 1918-1978 ... CANR-11
Obituary ... 77-80
Earlier sketch in CA 17-20R
Beardsley, Theodore S(terling), Jr. 1930- ... 33-36R
Beardsworth, Millicent Monica 1915- ... 103
Beardwood, Roger 1932- ... 89-92
Beardwood, Valerie Fairfield ... 5-8R
Beare, Francis W(right) 1902- ... CANR-16
Earlier sketch in CA 1-4R
Beare, (M. A.) Nikki 1928- ... 37-40R
Bearman, Jane (Ruth) 1917- ... 105
See also SATA 29
Bearne, C(olin) G(erald) 1939- ... 97-100
Bearss, Edwin C(ole) 1923- ... CANR-10
Earlier sketch in CA 25-28R
Beaser, Herbert W. 1913(?)-1979 Obituary ... 85-88
Beasley, Bruce 1958- ... 159
Beasley, Faith E. 1958- ... 139
Beasley, Jerry C(arr) 1940- ... CANR-14
Earlier sketch in CA 37-40R
Beasley, M. Robert 1918- ... 9-12R
Beasley, Maurine 1936- ... CANR-42
Earlier sketches in CA 104, CANR-20
Beasley, Rex 1925- ... 9-12R
Beasley, Ruth 1942- ... 135
Beasley, W(illiam) Conger, Jr. 1940- ... CANR-4
Earlier sketch in CA 53-56
Beasley, W(illiam) G(erald) 1919- ... 53-56
Beasley-Murray, George Raymond 1916- ... 65-68
Beason, Doug 1953- ... 164
Beason, Robert G(ayle) 1927- ... 114
Beath, Paul Robert 1905- ... 5-8R
Beath, Warren Newton 1951- ... 136
Beaton, Alan A. 1947- ... 123
Beaton, Anne
See Washington, (Catherine) Marguerite Beauchamp
Beaton, Cecil (Walter Hardy) 1904-1980 ... CANR-68
Obituary ... 93-96
Earlier sketch in CA 81-84
Beaton, George
See Brenan, (Edward Fitz)Gerald
Beaton, (Donald) Leonard 1929-1971 ... CANR-4
Obituary ... 29-32R
Earlier sketch in CA 5-8R
Beaton, M. C.
See Chesney, Marion
Beaton-Jones, Cynon 1921- ... 5-8R
Beattie, Ann 1947- ... CANR-53
Earlier sketch in CA 81-84
See also BEST 90:2
See also CLC 8, 13, 18, 40, 63
See also DAM NOV, POP
See also DLBY 82
See also MTCW 1
See also SSC 11
Beattie, Carol 1918- ... 29-32R
Beattie, Edward J(ames), Jr. 1918- ... 106
Beattie, James 1735-1803 ... DLB 109
Beattie, Jessie Louise 1896- ... CANR-17
Earlier sketches in CA 5-8R, CANR-2
Beattie, John (Hugh Marshall) 1915-1990 ... 37-40R
Obituary ... 131
Beattie, Melody (Lynn) 1948- ... 141
See also BEST 90:4
Beattie, Sally 1941- ... 122
Beattie, Susan 1938- ... 123
Beatts, Anne Patricia 1947- ... 102
Beatty, Barbara (R.) 1946- ... 152
Beatty, Bernard 1938- ... 127
Beatty, Chester 1875-1968 ... DLB 201
Beatty, Elizabeth
See Holloway, Teresa (Bragunier)
Beatty, Hetty Burlingame 1907-1971 ... 1-4R
Obituary ... 103
See also SATA 5
Beatty, Jerome, Jr. 1918- ... CANR-3
Earlier sketch in CA 9-12R
See also SATA 5
Beatty, John (Louis) 1922-1975 ... CANR-4
Obituary ... 57-60
Earlier sketch in CA 5-8R
See also SATA 6
See also SATA-Obit 25
Beatty, Morgan 1902-1975 Obituary ... 61-64
Beatty, Patricia (Robbins) 1922-1991 ... CANR-55
Obituary ... 134
Earlier sketches in CA 1-4R, CANR-3
See also AAYA 16
See also JRDA
See also MAICYA
See also SAAS 4
See also SATA 1, 30, 73
See also SATA-Obit 68
Beatty, Paul ... 154
Beatty, Rita Gray 1930- ... 45-48
Beatty, Robert Owen 1924-1976 Obituary ... 69-72
Beatty, Warren
See Beaty, Warren
Beatty, William Alfred 1912-(?) ... CAP-1
Earlier sketch in CA 13-14
Beatty, William K(ave) 1926- ... 41-44R
Beaty, Betty ... CANR-18
Earlier sketch in CA 73-76
Beaty, (Arthur) David 1919- ... CANR-18
Earlier sketches in CA 1-4R, CANR-2
Beaty, Janice J(anowski) 1930- ... 13-16R
Beaty, Jerome 1924- ... 85-88
Beaty, Shirley MacLean
See MacLaine, Shirley
Beaty, Warren 1937(?)- ... 126
Brief entry ... 109
Beaubien, Anne K(athleen) 1947- ... 123
Beauchamp, Cari ... 167
Beauchamp, Edward R(obert) 1933- ... 61-64
Beauchamp, Gorman 1938- ... 121
Beauchamp, Kathleen Mansfield 1888-1923 ... 134
Brief entry ... 104
See also Mansfield, Katherine
See also DA
See also DAC
See also DAM MST
Beauchamp, Kenneth L(loyd) 1939- ... 29-32R
Beauchamp, Pat
See Washington, (Catherine) Marguerite Beauchamp
Beauchamp, Tom L. 1939- ... CANR-13
Earlier sketch in CA 73-76
Beauchemin, Neree 1850-1931 ... DLB 92
Beauchemin, Yves 1941- ... 129
See also DLB 60
Beauclerk, Helen De Vere 1892-1969 Obituary ... 114
Beauclerk, Jane
See Engh, M(ary) J(ane)
Beaud, Michel 1935- ... 146
Beaudoin, Kenneth Lawrence 1913- ... 29-32R
Beaudouin, John T(yrell) 1920- Brief entry ... 114
Beaufitz, William
See Critchley, Julian (Michael Gordon)
Beaufort, John (David) 1912- ... 104
Beaufre, Andre 1902-1975 ... 65-68
Obituary ... 57-60
Beaugrand, Honore 1848-1906 ... DLB 99
Beaulac, Willard L(eon) 1899-1990 ... 9-12R
Obituary ... 132
Beaulieu, Victor-Levy 1945- ... 146
See also DLB 53
Beauman, E(ric) Bentley 1891-1989 ... 9-12R
Obituary ... 129
Beauman, Katharine (Burgoyne) Bentley 1902- ... 102
Beauman, Nicola 1944- ... 152
Beauman, Sally 1944(?)- ... 134
Beaumarchais, Pierre-Augustin Caron de 1732-1799 ... DAM DRAM
See also DC 4
Beaumont, Beverly
See von Block, Sylvia
Beaumont, Charles 1929-1967 ... 5-8R
Obituary ... 103
Beaumont, Charles Allen 1926- ... 1-4R
Beaumont, Cyril William 1891-1976 ... CANR-68
Obituary ... 65-68
Earlier sketch in CA 13-16R
Beaumont, Francis 1584(?)-1616 ... CDBLB Before 1660
See also DC 6
See also DLB 58, 121
Beaumont, George Ernest 1888-1974 Obituary ... 49-52
Beaumont, SirJohn 1583(?)-1627 ... DLB 121
Beaumont, Joseph 1616-1699 ... DLB 126
Beaumont, Keith (Stanley) 1944- ... 118
Beaumont, Roger A(lban) 1935- ... 65-68
Beauregard, Erving E. 1920- ... CANR-43
Earlier sketch in CA 111
Beaurline, L(ester) A(lbert) 1927- ... 21-24R
Beausang, Michael F(rancis), Jr. 1936- ... 57-60
Beausay, Florence E(dith) 1911- ... 21-24R
Beausoleil, Beau 1941- ... CANR-14
Earlier sketch in CA 81-84
Beauvais, Robert 1911- ... 104
Beauvoir, Simone (Lucie Ernestine Marie Bertrand) 1908-1986 ... CANR-61
Obituary ... 118
Earlier sketches in CA 9-12R, CANR-28
See also CLC 1, 2, 4, 8, 14, 31, 44, 50, 71
See also DA
See also DAB
See also DAC
See also DAM MST, NOV
See also DLB 72
See also DLBY 86
See also MTCW 1
See also WLC
Beaver, Bruce (Victor) 1928- ... 97-100
Beaver, Frank E(ugene) 1938- ... 114
Beaver, Harold (Lothar) 1929- ... 21-24R
Beaver, (Jack) Patrick 1923- ... 33-36R
Beaver, Paul (Eli) 1953- ... CANR-40
Earlier sketch in CA 115
Beaver, R(obert) Pierce 1906- ... CANR-7
Earlier sketch in CA 5-8R
Beaver, Stanley H(enry) 1907-1984 Obituary ... 114
Beaverbrook, William Maxwell Aitken 1879-1964 ... 103
Obituary ... 89-92
Beazley, John Davidson 1885-1970 Obituary ... 115
Bebb, Russ(ell H.), Jr. 1930- ... 49-52
Bebbington, D(avid) W(illiam) 1949- ... 133
Bebell, Mildred Hoyt 1909- ... CAP-1
Earlier sketch in CA 13-16
Bebey, Francis 1929- ... CANR-25
Earlier sketch in CA 69-72
See also BW 1
Bebler, A(lex) Anton 1937- ... CANR-2
Earlier sketch in CA 49-52
Becerra, Rosina M. 1939- ... CANR-48
Earlier sketch in CA 122
Bechard, Margaret 1953- ... 151
See also SATA 85
Bechdel, Alison 1960- ... 138
Becher, Ulrich 1910- ... 101
See also DLB 69
Bechert, Heinz 1932- ... 136
Bechervaise, John Mayston 1910- ... CANR-5
Earlier sketch in CA 13-16R
Bechhoefer, Bernhard G. 1904- ... 1-4R
Bechko, P(eggy) A(nne) 1950- ... CANR-63
Earlier sketches in CA 49-52, CANR-2
Bechler, Curt 1958- ... 145
Bechmann, Roland 1919- ... 136
Becht, J. Edwin 1918- ... 29-32R
Bechtel, Louise Seaman 1894-1985 ... CAP-2
Obituary ... 116
Earlier sketch in CA 29-32
See also SATA 4
See also SATA-Obit 43
Bechtel, Paul M(oyer) 1909- ... 116
Bechtel, Stefan D. 1951- ... 163
Bechtol, William M(ilton) 1931- ... CANR-34
Earlier sketch in CA 49-52
Beck, Aaron T(emkin) 1921- ... CANR-11
Earlier sketch in CA 21-24R
Beck, Alan M(arshall) 1942- ... CANR-21
Earlier sketch in CA 45-48
Beck, Barbara L. 1927- ... 17-20R
See also SATA 12
Beck, Calvin Thomas 1937- ... 97-100
Beck, Carl 1930- ... CANR-1
Earlier sketch in CA 1-4R
Beck, Clive 1939- ... CANR-27
Earlier sketch in CA 49-52
Beck, Doc
See Beck, Earl Clifton
Beck, Earl Clifton 1891-1977 Obituary ... 110
Beck, Earl R(ay) 1916- ... 33-36R
Beck, Emily M(orison) 1915- ... 114
Beck, Evelyn Torton 1933- ... CANR-13
Earlier sketch in CA 33-36R
Beck, Harry
See Paine, Lauran (Bosworth)
Beck, Helen L(ouise) 1908- ... 73-76
Beck, Henry G(abriel) J(ustin) 1914- ... 9-12R
Beck, Horace P(almer) 1920- ... 77-80
Beck, Hubert (F.) 1931- ... CANR-12
Earlier sketch in CA 29-32R
Beck, James (H.) 1930- ... 85-88
Beck, James Murray 1914- ... 101
Beck, Joan (Wagner) 1923- Brief entry ... 118
Beck, John Jacob, Jr. 1941- ... 53-56
Beck, Julian 1925-1985 ... 102
Obituary ... 117
Beck, K(athrine) K(ristine) 1950- ... 142
Beck, Leslie 1907(?)-1978 Obituary ... 104
Beck, Lewis White 1913- ... CANR-2
Earlier sketch in CA 5-8R
Beck, M. Susan 1941- ... 113
Beck, Marilyn (Mohr) 1928- ... 65-68
Beck, Mary L. (Giraudo) 1924- ... 131
Beck, Pamela 1954- ... 120
Beck, Paul 1933(?)-1985 Obituary ... 116
Beck, Phineas
See Chamberlain, Samuel
Beck, Robert Edward 1941- ... 104
Beck, Robert H(olmes) 1918- ... 29-32R
Beck, Robert J. 1961- ... 149
Beck, Robert Nelson 1924-1980 ... CANR-4
Earlier sketch in CA 1-4R
Beck, Thomas D(avis) 1943- ... 57-60
Beck, Toni 1925- ... 57-60
Beck, Victor Emanuel 1894-1963 ... 5-8R
Beck, Warren 1896-1986 ... CANR-68
Obituary ... 119
Earlier sketches in CA 1-4R, CANR-3
Beck, Warren Albert 1918-1991 ... CANR-6
Obituary ... 135
Earlier sketch in CA 5-8R
Beckel, Graham 1913- ... 1-4R
Beckelhymer, (Paul) Hunter 1919- ... CANR-3
Earlier sketch in CA 1-4R
Becker, A(dolph) C(arl), Jr. 1920- ... 65-68
Becker, Abraham S(amuel) 1927- ... 33-36R
Becker, Albert B. 1903-1972 ... CAP-2
Earlier sketch in CA 29-32
Becker, Arthur P(eter) 1918- ... 29-32R
Becker, B. Jay 1904-1987 ... 65-68
Obituary ... 123
Becker, Beril 1901- ... CAP-1
Earlier sketch in CA 9-10
See also SATA 11
Becker, Bill
See Becker, William
Becker, Bruce ... 57-60
Becker, Carl (Lotus) 1873-1945 ... 157
See also DLB 17
See also TCLC 63
Becker, Carol 1947- ... 124
Becker, Charles M(axwell) 1954- ... 146
Becker, Elizabeth 1947- ... 141
Becker, Ernest 1925-1974 ... 97-100
Becker, Florence
See Lennon, Florence Becker (Tanenbaum)
Becker, Gary S(tanley) 1930- ... CANR-11
Earlier sketch in CA 61-64
Becker, George J(oseph) 1908-1989 ... CANR-7
Obituary ... 130
Earlier sketch in CA 5-8R
Becker, Harold K(auffman) 1933- ... CANR-13
Earlier sketch in CA 29-32R
Becker, Howard S(aul) 1928- ... 134
Brief entry ... 115
Becker, Irving 1945- ... 122
Becker, Jasper 1956- ... CANR-62
Earlier sketch in CA 139
Becker, Jillian (Ruth) 1932- ... CANR-25
Earlier sketch in CA 77-80
Becker, John (Leonard) 1901- ... CAP-1
Earlier sketch in CA 11-12
See also SATA 12
Becker, John E(dward) 1930- ... 49-52
Becker, Joseph M(aria) 1908- ... CANR-7
Earlier sketch in CA 17-20R
Becker, Joyce 1936- ... SATA 39
Becker, Juergen 1932- ... 154
See also DLB 75
Becker, Jurek 1937-1997 ... CANR-60
Obituary ... 157
Earlier sketch in CA 85-88
See also CLC 7, 19
See also DLB 75
Becker, Jurgen
See Becker, Juergen
Becker, Klaus
See Koch, Kurt E(mil)
Becker, Lawrence C(arlyle) 1939- ... 85-88
Becker, Lucille F(rackman) 1929- ... CANR-12
Earlier sketch in CA 29-32R
Becker, Manning H. 1922- ... 13-16R
Becker, Marion Rombauer 1903-1976 ... 37-40R
Obituary ... 69-72
Becker, Marvin Burton 1922- ... 107
Becker, May Lamberton 1873-1958 Brief entry ... 112
See also SATA 33
Becker, Murray 1909(?)-1986 Obituary ... 118
Becker, Olga
See Frank, Rudolf
Becker, Palmer (Joseph) 1936- ... 143
Becker, Paula Lee 1941- ... 17-20R
Becker, Peter 1921- ... 53-56
Becker, Robert O(tto) 1923- ... 123
Becker, Robin 1951- ... CANR-70
Earlier sketch in CA 110
Becker, Ruby Wirt 1915- ... 33-36R
Becker, Russell J(ames) 1923- ... 37-40R
Becker, Samuel L(eo) 1923- ... CANR-7
Earlier sketch in CA 13-16R
Becker, Seymour 1934- ... 25-28R
Becker, Stephen (David) 1927- ... CANR-62
Earlier sketches in CA 5-8R, CANR-3
See also CAAS 1
Becker, Ted
See Becker, Theodore L(ewis)
Becker, Theodore L(ewis) 1932- Brief entry ... 116
Becker, Thomas W(illiam) 1933- ... 5-8R
Becker, Walter 1950- ... CLC 26
Becker, Wesley C(lemence) 1928- ... 33-36R
Becker, William 1903(?)-1983 Obituary ... 110
Becker, William H(enry) 1943- ... 125
Beckerman, Bernard 1921-1985 ... CANR-19
Obituary ... 117
Earlier sketch in CA 1-4R
Beckerman, Ilene 1935- ... 151
Beckerman, Paul 1948- ... 141
Beckerman, Wilfred 1925- ... CANR-7
Earlier sketch in CA 17-20R
Becket, Henry S. A.
See Goulden, Joseph C. (Jr.)
Beckett, Ian F(rederick) W(illiam) 1950- ... CANR-45
Earlier sketch in CA 120
Beckett, J(ames) C(amlin) 1912-1996 Obituary ... 151
Brief entry ... 114
Beckett, John A(ngus) 1916- ... 33-36R
Beckett, Kenneth A(lbert) 1929- ... CANR-51
Earlier sketches in CA 65-68, CANR-10, 28
Beckett, Lucy 1942- ... 49-52
Beckett, Mary 1926- ... 127
Beckett, Ralph L(awrence) 1923- ... 5-8R
Beckett, Ronald Brymer 1891- ... 5-8R
Beckett, Samuel (Barclay) 1906-1989 ... CANR-61
Obituary ... 130
Earlier sketches in CA 5-8R, CANR-33
See also CDBLB 1945-1960
See also CLC 1, 2, 3, 4, 6, 9, 10, 11, 14, 18, 29, 57, 59, 83
See also DA
See also DAB
See also DAC
See also DAM DRAM, MST, NOV
See also DLB 13, 15
See also DLBY 90
See also MTCW 1
See also SSC 16
See also WLC
Beckett, Sheilah 1913- ... SATA 33
Beckey, Fred W(olfgang) 1923- ... 109
Beckford, George L(eslie Fitz-Gerald) 1934- ... 97-100

Beckford, William 1760-1844 .... DLB 39
Beckham, Barry (Earl) 1944- CANR-62
  Earlier sketches in CA 29-32R, CANR-26
  See also BLC 1
  See also BW 1
  See also DAM MULT
  See also DLB 33
Beckham, Stephen Dow 1941- CANR-51
  Earlier sketches in CA 61-64, CANR-12, 28
Beckhart, Benjamin Haggott
  1897-1975 Obituary 57-60
Beckingham, Charles Fraser 1914- 61-64
Beckinsale, Monica 1914- 69-72
Beckinsale, Robert Percy 1908- CANR-2
  Earlier sketch in CA 5-8R
Becklake, Sue 1943- 120
Beckler, Marion Floyd 1889- CAP-1
  Earlier sketch in CA 11-12
Beckles Willson, Robina (Elizabeth) 1930- ....
  CANR-43
  Earlier sketches in CA 13-16R, CANR-5, 20
  See also Willson, Robina Beckles
Beckley, Harlan R. 1943- 145
Beckman, Aldo Bruce 1934- 73-76
Beckman, Delores 1914- 121
  See also SATA 51
Beckman, Gail McKnight 1938- 53-56
Beckman, Gunnel 1910- CANR-15
  Earlier sketch in CA 33-36R
  See also CLC 26
  See also CLR 25
  See also MAICYA
  See also SAAS 9
  See also SATA 6
Beckman, Kaj
  See Beckman, Karin
Beckman, Karin 1913- .... SATA 45
Beckman, Patti
  See Boeckman, Patti
Beckman, Per (Frithiof) 1913- .... SATA 45
Beckman, Robert C(harles) 1934- 120
Beckmann, David M(ilton) 1948- CANR-8
  Earlier sketch in CA 61-64
Beckmann, George Michael 1926- 5-8R
Beckmann, Martin J(osef) 1924- 37-40R
Beckmann, Petr 1924- 69-72
Beckner, Weldon (Earnest) 1933- 33-36R
Beckovic, Matija 1939- 33-36R
  See also DLB 181
Beckson, Karl 1926- CANR-2
  Earlier sketch in CA 5-8R
Beckwith, B(rainerd) K(ellogg) 1902- 73-76
Beckwith, Burnham Putnam 1904- 33-36R
Beckwith, Charles E(milio) 1917- 37-40R
Beckwith, Harry 1949- 168
Beckwith, John Gordon 1918- 9-12R
Beckwith, Lillian
  See Comber, Lillian
Beckwith, Paul 1905-1975 Obituary 113
Beckwith, Yvonne 106
Becque, Henri 1837-1899 .... DLB 192
Becquer, Gustavo Adolfo 1836-1870 ... DAM MULT
Bedard, Michael 1949- 159
  See also AAYA 22
  See also CLR 35
  See also SATA 93
Bedard, Michelle
  See Finnigan, Joan
Bedard, Patrick Joseph 1941- 112
Bedau, Hugo Adam 1926- CANR-41
  Earlier sketches in CA 9-12R, CANR-4, 19
Beddall, Barbara G(ould) 1919- 33-36R
Beddall-Smith, Charles John 1916- 13-16R
Beddoe, Ellaruth
  See Elkins, Ella Ruth
Beddoes, Richard H(erbert) 1926- 37-40R
Beddoes, Thomas 1760-1808 .... DLB 158
Beddoes, Thomas Lovell 1803-1849 .... DLB 96
Beddows, Eric
  See Nutt, Ken
Bede c. 673-735 .... DLB 146
Bede, Andrew
  See Beha, Ernest
Bede, Jean-Albert 1903-1977 Obituary 69-72
Bedeian, Arthur G(eorge) 1946- 110
Bedell, George C(hester) 1928- 41-44R
Bedell, L. Frank 1888- CAP-1
  Earlier sketch in CA 13-16
Bedell, Madelon (Jane Berns) 1922(?)-1986 136
  Obituary 119
Bedells, Phyllis 1893-1985 Obituary 116
Bederman, Gail 1952- 151
Bedford, A. N.
  See Watson, Jane Werner
Bedford, Ann
  See Rees, Joan
Bedford, Annie North
  See Watson, Jane Werner
Bedford, Charles Harold 1929- 57-60
Bedford, Denton R. 1907-(?) .... NNAL
Bedford, Donald F.
  See Fearing, Kenneth (Flexner)
Bedford, Emmett G(runer) 1922- 45-48
Bedford, Henry F(rederick) 1931- 9-12R
Bedford, Kenneth
  See Paine, Lauran (Bosworth)
Bedford, Martyn 1959- 154
Bedford, Norton M(oore) 1916- 5-8R
Bedford, Sybille 1911- CANR-47
  Earlier sketch in CA 9-12R
Bedford-Jones, H(enry James O'Brien)
  1887-1949 157
Bediako, Kwabena Asare
  See Konadu, S(amuel) A(sare)
Bedikian, Antriganik A.
  1886(?)-1980 Obituary 93-96
Bedinger, Margery 1891- 57-60
Bedinger, Singleton B(erry) 1907- 49-52
Bedini, Silvio A. 1917- CANR-55
  Earlier sketches in CA 33-36R, CANR-13, 29
Bednarik, Charles (Philip) 1925- 77-80
Bednarik, Chuck
  See Bednarik, Charles (Philip)
Bedoukian, Kerop 1907-1981 93-96
  See also SATA 53
Bedoyere, Michael De La
  See De La Bedoyere, Michael
Bedrij, Orest (John) 1933- CANR-16
  Earlier sketch in CA 85-88
Bedsole, Adolph 1914- 13-16R
Bee, Clair (Francis) 1900-1983 .... 1-4R
  Obituary 109
Bee, (John) David (Ashford) 1931- 17-20R
Bee, Helen L. 1939- CANR-16
  Earlier sketch in CA 89-92
Bee, Jay
  See Brainerd, John W(hiting)
Bee, Robert L(awrence) 1938- 113
Bee, Ronald J. 1955- 140
Beebe, (Ida) Ann 1919- 41-44R
Beebe, B(urdetta) F(aye)
  See Johnson, B(urdetta) F(aye)
  See also SATA 1
Beebe, Frank L(yman) 1914- 89-92
Beebe, Frederick S(essions)
  1914-1973 Obituary 41-44R
Beebe, H. Keith 1921- 29-32R
Beebe, Lucius 1902-1966 Obituary 25-28R
Beebe, Maurice (Laverne) 1926- CANR-1
  Earlier sketch in CA 1-4R
Beebe, Ralph K(enneth) 1932- 33-36R
Beebe, (Charles) William 1877-1962 73-76
  See also SATA 19
Beeby, Betty 1923- .... SATA 25
Beeby, C(larence) E(dward) 1902- 109
Beeby, Dean 1954- 151
Beech, George T(homas) 1931- 9-12R
Beech, Harold Reginald 1925- 25-28R
Beech, Keyes 1913-1990 .... 33-36R
  Obituary 130
Beech, Robert (Paul) 1940- 33-36R
Beech, Webb
  See Butterworth, W(illiam) E(dmund III)
Beecham, Justin
  See Wintle, Justin (Beecham)
Beecham, Thomas 1879-1961 Obituary 112
Beechcroft, William
  See Hallstead, William F(inn III)
Beecher, Catharine Esther 1800-1878 ...... DLB 1
Beecher, Donald A(llen) 1942- 135
Beecher, Henry Ward 1813-1887 .... DLB 3, 43
Beecher, John 1904-1980 .... CANR-8
  Obituary 105
  Earlier sketch in CA 5-8R
  See also AITN 1
  See also CLC 6
Beecher, Jonathan French 1937- 128
Beecher, Maureen Ursenbach 1935- 137
Beecher, William (M.) 1933- 65-68
Beechert, Edward D. 1920- 124
Beechhold, Henry F(rank) 1928- 33-36R
Beechick, Ruth 1925- CANR-25
  Earlier sketch in CA 108
Beeching, Jack 1922- CANR-13
  Earlier sketch in CA 21-24R
  See also SATA 14
Beechy, Winifred
  See Beechy, Winifred Nelson
Beechy, Winifred Nelson 1915- 116
Beecroft, John William Richard 1902-1966 .... 5-8R
Beedell, Suzanne (Mollie) 1921- CANR-20
  Earlier sketch in CA 69-72
Beeding, Francis
  See Palmer, John (Leslie)
  and Saunders, Hilary Aidan St. George
Beegle, Charles William 1928- 106
Beegle, Dewey Maurice 1919- 5-8R
Beegle, J(oseph) Allan 1918- 119
Beehler, Bruce M(cPherson) 1951- CANR-55
  Earlier sketch in CA 127
Beek, Martin(us) A(drianus) 1909- 13-16R
Beekman, Allan 1913- 33-36R
Beekman, E(ric) M(ontague) 1939- CANR-14
  Earlier sketch in CA 33-36R
Beekman, John 1918-1980 61-64
  Obituary 135
Beekman, Ross
  See Dey, Frederic (Merrill) Van Rensselaer
Beeks, Graydon 1919- 65-68
Beeler, Cecil Freeman 1915- 139
Beeler, Janet
  See Shaw, Janet
Beeler, Nelson F(rederick) 1910- 69-72
  See also SATA 13
Beeman, Richard R(oy) 1942- 77-80
Beeman, Robin 1940- 151
Beer, Barrett L(ynn) 1936- 49-52
Beer, Edith Lynn 1930- CANR-28
  Earlier sketches in CA 61-64, CANR-11
Beer, Eloise C. S. 1903- 13-16R
Beer, Ethel S(ophia) 1897-1975 .... CAP-2
  Obituary 57-60
  Earlier sketch in CA 25-28
Beer, Francis Anthony 1939- CANR-10
  Earlier sketch in CA 25-28R
Beer, George L. 1872-1920 .... DLB 47
Beer, Gillian (Patricia Kempster) 1935- 142
Beer, Jeanette (Mary Ayres) CANR-51
  Earlier sketch in CA 124
Beer, Johann 1655-1700 .... DLB 168
Beer, John B(ernard) 1926- CANR-49
  Earlier sketches in CA 5-8R, CANR-7, 23
Beer, Kathleen Costello 1926- 25-28R
Beer, Lawrence W(ard) 1932- 37-40R
Beer, Lisl
  See Beer, Eloise C. S.
Beer, Patricia 1924- CANR-46
  Earlier sketches in CA 61-64, CANR-13
  See also CLC 58
  See also DLB 40
Beer, Ralph (Robert) 1947- CANR-64
  Earlier sketch in CA 120
Beer, Samuel Hutchison 1911- CANR-31
  Earlier sketch in CA 61-64
Beer, Vic
  See Bird, Vivian
Beer, William Reed 1943- CANR-31
  Earlier sketch in CA 112
Beerbohm, Max
  See Beerbohm, (Henry) Max(imilian)
Beerbohm, (Henry) Max(imilian) 1872-1956 154
  Brief entry 104
  See also DLB 34, 100
  See also TCLC 1, 24
Beere, Peter 1951- 151
  See also SATA 97
Beer-Hofmann, Richard 1866-1945 160
  See also DLB 81
  See also TCLC 60
Beers, Burton F(loyd) 1927- CANR-41
  Earlier sketches in CA 1-4R, CANR-19
Beers, Dorothy Sands 1917- 49-52
  See also SATA 9
Beers, Henry A. 1847-1926 .... DLB 71
Beers, Henry Putney 1907- 13-16R
Beers, Lorna 1897- 49-52
  See also SATA 14
Beers, Mark H. 1954- 140
Beers, Paul Benjamin 1931- 102
Beers, V(ictor) Gilbert 1928- CANR-36
  Earlier sketches in CA 49-52, CANR-1, 16
  See also SATA 9
Beers, William 1948- 137
Beery, Mary 1907- 5-8R
Beesly, Patrick 1913-1986 .... CANR-15
  Obituary 120
  Earlier sketch in CA 85-88
Beeson, Trevor Randall 1926- 93-96
Beeth, Howard 1942- 144
Beeton, Max
  See Redding, Robert Hull
Beeton, (Douglas) Ridley 1929- 93-96
Beevers, John (Leonard) 1911-1975 61-64
Beevor, Antony 1946- CANR-67
  Earlier sketch in CA 129
Beezley, P(aul) C. 1895- 5-8R
Beezley, William H(oward Taft) 1942- CANR-27
  Earlier sketch in CA 49-52
Befu, Harumi 1930- 53-56
Beg, Toran
  See McKillop, Norman
Begam, Robert G(eorge) 1928- 127
Begelman, Mitchell (Craig) 1953- 154
Begg, A(lexander) Charles 1912- 102
Begg, Howard Bolton 1896- 5-8R
Begg, Neil Colquhoun 1915- 102
Beggs, David W(hiteford) III 1931-1966 ..... CAP-1
  Earlier sketch in CA 13-16
Beggs, Donald L(ee) 1941- 33-36R
Beggs, Edward Larry 1933- CANR-56
  Earlier sketch in CA 89-92
Begiebing, Robert J(ohn) 1946- CANR-40
  Earlier sketch in CA 122
  See also CLC 70
Begin, Maryjane 1963- .... SATA 82
Begin, Menachem 1913- Brief entry 109
Begin, Menahem
  See Begin, Menachem
Begin-Callanan, Maryjane
  See Begin, Maryjane
Begleiter, Henri 1935- 119
Begley, James 1929- 25-28R
Begley, Kathleen A(nne) 1948- 77-80
  See also SATA 21
Begley, Louis 1933- 140
Begnal, Michael H(enry) 1939- 73-76
Begner, Edith 1918-1989 .... CANR-3
  Obituary 129
  Earlier sketch in CA 1-4R
Bego, Mark 1952- 145
Begon, Elisabeth 1696-1755 .... DLB 99
Beha, Ernest 1908- CAP-1
  Earlier sketch in CA 13-14
Beha, Sister Helen Marie 1926- 21-24R
Behan, Brendan 1923-1964 .... CANR-33
  Earlier sketch in CA 73-76
  See also CDBLB 1945-1960
  See also CLC 1, 8, 11, 15, 79
  See also DAM DRAM
  See also DLB 13
  See also MTCW 1
Behan, Dominic 1928(?)-1989 Obituary 129
Behan, Leslie
  See Gottfried, Theodore Mark
Behar, Ruth 1956- 159
Behara, Devendra Nath 1940- 41-44R
Behee, John 1933- 112
Behle, William H(arroun) 1909- 5-8R
Behler, Ernst 1928- 41-44R
Behlmer, George K(inkel) 1948- 123
Behlmer, Rudy 1926- CANR-8
  Earlier sketch in CA 57-60
Behm, Marc 1925- 101
Behm, William H(erman), Jr. 1922- 13-16R
Behme, Robert Lee 1924- 57-60
Behn, Aphra 1640(?)-1689 .... DA
  See also DAB
  See also DAC
  See also DAM DRAM, MST, NOV, POET
  See also DC 4
  See also DLB 39, 80, 131
  See also PC 13
  See also WLC
Behn, Harry 1898-1973 .... CANR-5
  Obituary 53-56
  Earlier sketch in CA 5-8R
  See also DLB 61
  See also SATA 2
  See also SATA-Obit 34
Behn, Noel 1928- 129
  Brief entry 116
Behn, Robert Dietrich 1941- 137
Behney, John Bruce 1905- 101
Behnke, Charles A(lbert) 1891- CAP-2
  Earlier sketch in CA 19-20
Behnke, Frances L. 33-36R
  See also SATA 8
Behnke, John 1945- 69-72
Behnke, Leo 1933- 111
Behr, Edward (Samuel) 1926- CANR-42
  Earlier sketches in CA 1-4R, CANR-3
Behr, Joyce 1929- .... SATA 15
Behr, Marion 1939- 105
Behr, Mark 152
Behrend, Jeanne 1911- 17-20R
Behrens, Earl (Charles) 1892-1985 Obituary ... 116
Behrens, Ellen 1957- 153
Behrens, Helen Kindler 1922-1995 61-64
  Obituary 148
Behrens, Herman D(aniel) 1901- 33-36R
Behrens, John C. 1933- CANR-14
  Earlier sketch in CA 37-40R
Behrens, June York 1925- CANR-24
  Earlier sketches in CA 17-20R, CANR-8
  See also SATA 19
Behrens, Roy R(ichard) 1946- 110
Behrman, Carol H(elen) 1925- CANR-46
  Earlier sketches in CA 61-64, CANR-7, 22
  See also SATA 14
Behrman, Cynthia F(ansler) 1931- 123
Behrman, Daniel 1923-1990 65-68
  Obituary 131
Behrman, Jack N(ewton) 1922- CANR-30
  Earlier sketch in CA 29-32R
Behrman, Lucy Creevey
  See Creevey, Lucy E.
Behrman, S(amuel) N(athaniel) 1893-1973 .. CAP-1
  Obituary 45-48
  Earlier sketch in CA 13-16
  See also CLC 40
  See also DLB 7, 44
Behrstock, Barry 1948- 106
Bei, Dao 1949- 139
  See also Zhenkai, Zhao
Beichman, Arnold 1913- CANR-31
  Earlier sketch in CA 49-52
Beichner, Paul E(dward) 1912- 33-36R
Beidelman, T(homas) O(wen) 1931- 129
Beiderwell, Bruce 1952- 137
Beier, Ernst G(unter) 1916- 21-24R
Beier, Ulli 1922- CANR-4
  Earlier sketch in CA 9-12R
Beifuss, John, (Jr.) 1959- 156
  See also SATA 92
Beigel, Allan 1940-1996 101
  Obituary 152
Beigel, Herbert 1944- 97-100
Beigel, Hugo George 1897- 37-40R
Beik, Paul H(arold) 1915- 13-16R
Beik, William (Humphrey) 1941- 123
Beilenson, Edna 1909-1981 .... CANR-29
  Obituary 103
  Earlier sketch in CA 85-88
Beilenson, Laurence W. 1899-1988 .... 29-32R
  Obituary 125
Beiler, Edna 1923- CANR-1
  Earlier sketch in CA 1-4R
  See also SATA 61
Beilharz, Edwin Alanson 1907-1986 ..... CANR-27
  Obituary 120
  Earlier sketch in CA 33-36R
Beilharz, Peter (Michael) 1953- CANR-55
  Earlier sketch in CA 127
Beim, Norman 1923- 85-88
Beine, George Holmes 1893- 93-96
Beineix, Jean-Jacques 1946- 124
Beiner, Ronald 1953- CANR-42
  Earlier sketch in CA 117
Beinhart, Larry 1947- 138
Beinicke, Steve 1956- .... SATA 69
Beining, Guy 1938- .... CAAS 30
Beirne, Barbara 1933- .... SATA 71
Beirne, Brother Kilian 1896-1976 .... 21-24R
  Obituary 134
Beirne, Gerald E(dward) 1936- 118
Beirne, Joseph Anthony 1911-1974 45-48
  Obituary 53-56
Beiser, Arthur 1931- 93-96
  See also SATA 22
Beiser, Frederick C. 1949- 128
Beiser, Germaine 1931- .... SATA 11
Beisner, Robert L(ee) 1936- 25-28R
Beissel, Henry Eric 1929- CANR-10
  Earlier sketch in CA 65-68
Beisser, Arnold R(ay) 1925- 25-28R
Beissinger, Steven R. 1953- 146
Beistle, Shirley
  See Climo, Shirley
Beit-Hallahmi, Benjamin 1943- 105
Beitler, Ethel Jane (Heinkel) 1906- CANR-2
  Earlier sketch in CA 5-8R

Beitler, Stanley (Samuel) 1924- ... 5-8R
Beitz, Charles R(ichard) 1949- ... CANR-1
Earlier sketch in CA 49-52
Beitzell, Edwin Warfield 1905(?)-1984 Obituary . 114
Beitzell, Robert (E.) 1930- Brief entry ... 115
Beitzinger, A(lfons) J(oseph) 1918- ... 45-48
Beizer, Boris 1934- ... 105
Beja, Morris 1935- ... 29-32R
Bejerot, Nils 1921- ... 29-32R
Bekessy, Jean
See Habe, Hans
Bekker, Hugo 1925- ... 41-44R
Bekker-Nielsen, Hans 1933- ... CANR-16
Earlier sketch in CA 25-28R
Belair, Felix, Jr. 1907-1978 Obituary ... 77-80
Belair, Richard L. 1934- ... 13-16R
See also SATA 45
Beland, Pierre 1947- ... 153
Belaney, Archibald Stansfeld 1888-1938 Brief entry ... 114
See also Grey Owl
See also DLBD 17
See also SATA 24
Belanger, Jerome D(avid) 1938- ... 69-72
Belasco, David 1853-1931 ... 168
Brief entry ... 104
See also DLB 7
See also TCLC 3
Belcastro, Joseph 1910- ... CAP-2
Earlier sketch in CA 19-20
Belch, Caroline Jean 1916- ... 45-48
Belchem, David
See Belchem, R(onald) F(rederick) K(ing)
Belchem, R(onald) F(rederick) K(ing) 1911-1981 ... 122
Obituary ... 108
Belcher, Jerry 1930-1987 Obituary ... 124
Belcher, Wendy (Laura) 1962- ... 130
Belcheva, Elisaveta 1893-
See Bagryana, Elisaveta
See also CLC 10
Belden, Gail
See Belden, Louise Conway
Belden, Jack 1910-1989 Obituary ... 128
Belden, Louise Conway 1910- ... 104
Belden, Wilanne Schneider 1925- ... CANR-23
Earlier sketch in CA 106
See also SATA 56
Belding, Robert E(dward) 1911- ... 33-36R
Beldone, Phil "Cheech"
See Ellison, Harlan (Jay)
Belehradek, Jan 1896-1980 Obituary ... 97-100
Belen
See Kaplan, Nelly
Beleno
See Azuela, Mariano
Belew, M. Wendell 1922- ... 33-36R
Belfer, Nancy 1930- ... 85-88
Belfield, Eversley (Michael Gallimore) 1918- ... CANR-11
Earlier sketch in CA 25-28R
Belfiglio, Valentine J(ohn) 1934- ... CANR-51
Earlier sketches in CA 49-52, CANR-11, 28
Belford, Barbara 1935- ... CANR-59
Earlier sketch in CA 136
Belford, Lee A(rcher) 1913- ... 17-20R
Belfrage, Cedric H. 1904-1990 ... CANR-3
Obituary ... 132
Earlier sketch in CA 9-12R
Belfrage, Sally 1936-1994 ... CANR-45
Obituary ... 144
Earlier sketch in CA 105
See also SATA 65
See also SATA-Obit 79
Bel Geddes, Joan
See Geddes, Joan Bel
Belgion, (Harold) Montgomery 1892-1973 ... CAP-1
Earlier sketch in CA 13-14
Belgum, David 1922- ... CANR-6
Earlier sketch in CA 13-16R
Belieu, Erin 1965- ... 160
Belin, David W. 1928- ... 85-88
Beling, Willard A(dolf) 1919- ... 53-56
Belinkov, Arkady Viktorovich 1922(?)-1970 Obituary ... 29-32R
Belinski, Vissarion Grigoryevich 1811-1848 ... DLB 198
Belisle, Louis-Alexandre 1902-1985 Obituary ... 117
Belitsky, A(braham) Harvey 1929- ... 33-36R
Belitt, Ben 1911- ... CANR-7
Earlier sketch in CA 13-16R
See also CAAS 4
See also CLC 22
See also DLB 5
Belk, Fred Richard 1937- ... 115
Belkaoui, Ahmed R.
See Riahi-Belkaoui, Ahmed
Belkin, Gary S(tuart) 1945- ... 114
Belkin, Lisa 1960- ... 141
Belkin, Samuel 1911-1976 ... CANR-6
Obituary ... 65-68
Earlier sketch in CA 1-4R
Belkind, Allen 1927- ... 29-32R
Belknap, B. H.
See Ellis, Edward S(ylvester)
Belknap, Boynton
See Ellis, Edward S(ylvester)
Belknap, Boynton M.D.
See Ellis, Edward S(ylvester)
Belknap, Ivan (Carl) 1916- ... 5-8R
Belknap, Jeremy 1744-1798 ... DLB 30, 37
Belknap, Robert H(arlan) 1917- ... 45-48
Belknap, Robert L(amont) 1929- ... 33-36R
Belknap, S(ally) Yancey 1895- ... CAP-1
Earlier sketch in CA 11-12
Bell, A(rthur) Donald 1920- ... 25-28R
Bell, Adrian (Hanbury) 1901-1980 ... CANR-69
Obituary ... 102
Earlier sketch in CA 97-100
See also DLB 191
Bell, Alan P(aul) 1932- ... CANR-13
Earlier sketch in CA 33-36R
Bell, Albert A., Jr. 1945- ... 142
Bell, Anne Olivier 1916- ... 112
Bell, Anthea 1936- ... 152
See also SATA 88
Bell, Arthur 1939-1984 ... CANR-72
Obituary ... 112
Earlier sketch in CA 85-88
Bell, Barbara Currier 1941- ... 115
Bell, Barbara Mosallai 1937- ... 150
Bell, Bernard W(illiam) 1936- Brief entry ... 117
Bell, Betty
See Bell, Lorna Beatrice
Bell, Betty Louise 1949- ... 145
Bell, Carol
See Flavell, Carol Willsey Bell
Bell, Carolyn
See Rigoni, Orlando (Joseph)
Bell, Carolyn Shaw 1920- ... 29-32R
Bell, Charles G. 1929- ... 37-40R
Bell, Charles Greenleaf 1916- ... CANR-2
Earlier sketch in CA 1-4R
See also CAAS 12
Bell, Chip R(ay) 1944- ... 121
Bell, Clare (Louise) 1952- ... 157
See also SATA 99
Bell, (Arthur) Clive (Howard) 1881-1964 ... CANR-72
Obituary ... 89-92
Earlier sketch in CA 97-100
See also DLBD 10
See also MTCW 1
Bell, Colin (John) 1938- ... CANR-32
Earlier sketch in CA 29-32R
Bell, Corydon Whitten 1894- ... 5-8R
See also SATA 3
Bell, Daniel 1919- ... CANR-4
Earlier sketch in CA 1-4R
Bell, David A(rnold) 1945- ... 156
Bell, David Owen 1949- ... 167
See also SATA 99
Bell, David R(obert) 1932- ... 93-96
Bell, David S(heffield) 1945- ... 61-64
Bell, David Victor John 1944- ... CANR-38
Earlier sketches in CA 45-48, CANR-1, 17
Bell, Derrick Albert, Jr. 1930- ... 104
See also BW 2
Bell, Earl Hoyt 1903-1963 ... 1-4R
Bell, Eileen 1907- ... 33-36R
Bell, Elizabeth Rose 1912- ... 106
Bell, Elizabeth S. 1946- ... 128
Bell, Elliot V(allance) 1902-1983 Obituary ... 108
Bell, Emerson
See Stratemeyer, Edward L.
Bell, Emily Mary
See Cason, Mabel Earp
Bell, Frank
See Benson, Mildred (Augustine Wirt)
Bell, Gail Winther 1936- ... 41-44R
Bell, Gawain (Westray) 1909- ... 131
Bell, Geoffrey (Lakin) 1939- Brief entry ... 114
Bell, Geoffrey Foxall 1896-1984 Obituary ... 111
Bell, Gerald D(ean) 1937- ... 49-52
Bell, Gertrude (Margaret Lowthian) 1868-1926 . 167
See also DLB 174
See also TCLC 67
Bell, Gertrude (Wood) 1911- ... 13-16R
See also SATA 12
Bell, Gina
See Balzano, Jeanne (Koppel)
See also SATA 7
Bell, Gordon Bennett 1934- ... 104
Bell, H(arold) Idris 1879-1967 ... CAP-1
Earlier sketch in CA 13-14
Bell, Harry McAra 1899- ... CAP-1
Earlier sketch in CA 13-14
Bell, Herbert C(lifford Francis) 1881-1966 Obituary ... 113
Bell, Herbert W. 1922- ... 123
Bell, Ian A.
See Bell, Ian F. A.
Bell, Ian F. A. 1932- ... 152
Bell, Irene Wood 1944- ... 89-92
Bell, J. Bowyer 1931- ... 17-20R
Bell, J. Freeman
See Zangwill, Israel
Bell, Jack L. 1904-1975 ... CANR-6
Obituary ... 61-64
Earlier sketch in CA 1-4R
Bell, James (Adrian) 1917- ... 73-76
Bell, James B. 1932- ... 101
Bell, James Edward 1941- ... 33-36R
Bell, James K(enton) 1937- ... 25-28R
Bell, James Madison 1826-1902 ... 124
Brief entry ... 122
See also BLC 1
See also BW 1
See also DAM MULT
See also DLB 50
See also TCLC 43
Bell, Janet
See Clymer, Eleanor
Bell, John
See Johnson, Victor Hugo
Bell, John (Donnelly) 1944- ... 97-100
Bell, John C. 1902(?)-1981 Obituary ... 103
Bell, John Elderkin 1913- ... 81-84
Bell, John Patrick 1935- ... 101
Bell, Joseph N. 1921- ... 5-8R
Bell, Josephine
See Ball, Doris Bell (Collier)
Bell, Joyce 1920- ... CANR-8
Earlier sketch in CA 57-60
Bell, Joyce Denebrink 1936- ... 17-20R
Bell, Julian (Heward) 1908-1937 ... 158
Bell, L. Nelson 1894-1973 ... CAP-1
Obituary ... 45-48
Earlier sketch in CA 19-20
Bell, Leland V(irgil) 1934- ... 49-52
Bell, Linda R. 1949- ... 117
Bell, Lorna Beatrice 1902- ... 117
Bell, Louise Price ... CAP-1
Earlier sketch in CA 9-10
Bell, Madison Smartt 1957- ... CANR-54
Earlier sketches in CA 111, CANR-28
See also CLC 41, 102
Bell, Malcolm (H.) 1931- ... 122
Bell, Margaret E(lizabeth) 1898- ... CANR-1
Earlier sketch in CA 1-4R
See also SATA 2
Bell, Marvin (Hartley) 1937- ... CANR-59
Earlier sketch in CA 21-24R
See also CAAS 14
See also CLC 8, 31
See also DAM POET
See also DLB 5
See also MTCW 1
Bell, Mary Hayley
See Hayley Bell, Mary
Bell, Mary Reeves 1946- ... 152
See also SATA 88
Bell, Michael Davitt 1941- ... CANR-15
Earlier sketch in CA 81-84
Bell, Millicent (L.) ... CANR-36
Earlier sketch in CA 114
See also DLB 111
Bell, Neill 1946- ... 118
See also SATA-Brief 50
Bell, Norman (Edward) 1899- ... 61-64
See also SATA 11
Bell, Norman W. 1928- ... CANR-1
Earlier sketch in CA 1-4R
Bell, Oliver (Sydney) 1913- ... 53-56
Bell, Philip W(ilkes) 1924- ... CANR-26
Earlier sketch in CA 29-32R
Bell, Quentin (Claudian Stephen) 1910-1996 ... CANR-51
Obituary ... 155
Earlier sketch in CA 57-60
See also DLB 155
Bell, R(obert) C(harles) 1917- ... CANR-24
Earlier sketches in CA 17-20R, CANR-7
Bell, Raymond Martin 1907- ... 29-32R
See also SATA 13
Bell, Richard H. 1938- ... 145
Bell, Robert (Ivan) 1942- ... 101
Bell, Robert E(ugene) 1914- ... 37-40R
Bell, Robert E(ugene) 1926- ... 138
Bell, Robert Roy 1924- ... CANR-1
Earlier sketch in CA 1-4R
Bell, Robert S(tanley) W(arren) 1871-1921 Brief entry ... 115
See also SATA-Brief 27
Bell, Robert Vaughn 1924- ... CANR-64
Earlier sketch in CA 110
Bell, Robin
See Jones, John F(inbar)
Bell, Roger 1947- ... CANR-48
Earlier sketch in CA 122
Bell, (Caroline) Rose (Buchanan) 1939- ... 29-32R
Bell, Roseann P. 1945- ... 120
See also BW 2
Bell, Rudolph M(ark) 1942- ... CANR-48
Earlier sketch in CA 45-48
Bell, Sallie Lee ... CANR-1
Earlier sketch in CA 1-4R
Bell, Sarah Fore 1920- ... 53-56
Bell, Sidney 1929- ... 41-44R
Bell, Stephen (Scott) 1935- ... 65-68
Bell, Terrel H(oward) 1921-1996 ... 144
Obituary ... 152
Bell, Thelma Harrington 1896- ... CANR-69
Earlier sketch in CA 1-4R
See also SATA 3
Bell, Thornton
See Fanthorpe, R(obert) Lionel
Bell, Vanessa 1879-1961 ... 145
See also DLBD 10
Bell, Vicars W(alker) 1904- ... CAP-1
Earlier sketch in CA 13-16
Bell, W. L. D.
See Mencken, H(enry) L(ouis)
Bell, Wendell 1924- ... CANR-4
Earlier sketch in CA 1-4R
Bell, Whitfield Jenks, Jr. 1914- ... 105
Bell, William 1945- ... 155
See also SATA 90
Bell, William J. ... AITN 1
Bell, William Stewart 1921- ... 1-4R
Bell, Winifred 1914- ... CANR-9
Earlier sketch in CA 17-20R
Bellah, James Warner 1899-1976 ... CANR-61
Obituary ... 69-72
Earlier sketch in CA 5-8R
Bellah, Robert N(eelly) 1927- ... 21-24R
Bellairs, George
See Blundell, Harold
Bellairs, John (A.) 1938-1991 ... CANR-24
Obituary ... 133
Earlier sketches in CA 21-24R, CANR-8
See also CLR 37
See also JRDA
See also MAICYA
See also SATA 2, 68
See also SATA-Obit 66
Bellak, Leopold 1916- ... CANR-40
Earlier sketches in CA 85-88, CANR-16
Bellamy, Atwood C.
See Mencken, H(enry) L(ouis)
Bellamy, Christopher (David) 1955- ... 157
Bellamy, David (James) 1933- Brief entry ... 114
Bellamy, Edward 1850-1898 ... DLB 12
Bellamy, Francis Rufus 1886-1972 Obituary ... 33-36R
Bellamy, Guy 1935- ... CANR-34
Earlier sketches in CA 65-68, CANR-9
Bellamy, Harmon
See Bloom, Herman Irving
Bellamy, James A(ndrew) 1925- ... 49-52
Bellamy, Joe David 1941- ... CANR-34
Earlier sketches in CA 41-44R, CANR-15
Bellamy, John fl. 1620-1651 ... DLB 170
Bellamy, Joseph 1719-1790 ... DLB 31
Bellamy, Peter 1914- Brief entry ... 117
Bellamy, Ralph (Rexford) 1904-1991 ... 101
Obituary ... 136
Bellamy, Richard (Paul) 1957- ... 141
Bellan, Ruben C. 1918- ... 13-16R
Belle, Pamela 1952- ... CANR-61
Earlier sketches in CA 115, CANR-38
Beller, Anne Scott ... 77-80
Beller, Elmer Adolph 1894-1980 Obituary ... 97-100
Beller, Jacob 1896- ... CAP-2
Earlier sketch in CA 25-28
Beller, Joel 1926- ... 113
Beller, Miles 1951- ... 134
Beller, Steven (Peter) 1958- ... 133
Beller, Susan Provost 1949- ... 151
See also SATA 84
Beller, Thomas
See Beller, Tom
Beller, Tom 1965- ... 150
Beller, William Stern 1919- ... 5-8R
Bellerby, (Mary Eireen) Frances Parker 1899-1975 ... 101
Bellezza, Dario 1944- ... DLB 128
Bellhouse, Alan Robert 1914-1980 Obituary ... 108
Belli, Angela 1935- ... 37-40R
Belli, Carlos German 1927- ... 131
See also HW
Belli, Gioconda 1949- ... 152
Belli, Melvin M(ouron) 1907-1996 ... CANR-34
Obituary ... 152
Earlier sketch in CA 104
Bellin, Edward J.
See Kuttner, Henry
Bellingham, Brenda 1931- ... CANR-54
Earlier sketch in CA 123
See also SATA 99
See also SATA-Brief 51
Bellingham, Helen Mary Dorothea
See Beauclerk, Helen De Vere
Bellini delle Stelle, Pier Luigi 1920(?)-1984 Obituary ... 111
Belliotti, Raymond A(ngelo) 1948- ... 143
Bellis, David James 1944- ... 108
Bellisario, Donald P. 1935- ... 151
Bellman, Richard (Ernest) 1920-1984 ... CANR-12
Obituary ... 112
Earlier sketch in CA 69-72
Bellman, Samuel Irving 1926- ... CANR-7
Earlier sketch in CA 17-20R
Bellman, Willard F. 1920- ... 113
Bell-Metereau, Rebecca 1949- ... 122
Bellmon, Patricia 1948- ... 140
Bello, Francis (Cesare) 1917-1987 Obituary ... 121
Belloc, (Joseph) Hilaire (Pierre Sebastien Rene Swanton) 1870-1953 ... 152
Brief entry ... 106
See also DAM POET
See also DLB 19, 100, 141, 174
See also TCLC 7, 18
See also YABC 1
Belloc, Joseph Peter Rene Hilaire
See Belloc, (Joseph) Hilaire (Pierre Sebastien Rene Swanton)
Belloc, Joseph Pierre Hilaire
See Belloc, (Joseph) Hilaire (Pierre Sebastien Rene Swanton)
Belloc, M. A.
See Lowndes, Marie Adelaide (Belloc)
Bellochio, Marco 1939- ... 110
Bellocq, Louise
See Boudat, Marie-Louise
Belloli, Andrea P. A. 1947- ... 151
See also SATA 86
Bellonci, Maria 1902-1986 Obituary ... 120
See also DLB 196
Bellone, Enrico 1938- ... 106
Bellony, Alice 1925- ... 118
Bellony-Rewald, Alice
See Bellony, Alice
Bellos, David 1945- ... 153
Bellot, Leland J(oseph) 1936- Brief entry ... 115
Bellotti, Laura Golden 1947- ... 137
Bellow, Saul 1915- ... CANR-53
Earlier sketches in CA 5-8R, CANR-29
See also CABS 1
See also AITN 2
See also BEST 89:3
See also CDALB 1941-1968
See also CLC 1, 2, 3, 6, 8, 10, 13, 15, 25, 33, 34, 63, 79
See also DA
See also DAB
See also DAC
See also DAM MST, NOV, POP
See also DLB 2, 28
See also DLBD 3
See also DLBY 82
See also MTCW 1
See also SSC 14
See also WLC

Bellows, Barbara L(awrence) 1950- ... 145
Bellows, James G(ilbert) 1922- ... 102
Interview in ... 102
Bellows, Roger Marion 1905- ... 1-4R
Bellows, Thomas J(ohn) 1935- ... CANR-31
Earlier sketch in CA 45-48
Bellush, Bernard 1917- ... 132
Brief entry ... 120
Bellush, Jewel (Lubin) 1959- ... 152
Bell-Villada, Gene Harold 1941- ... 105
Bellville, Cheryl Walsh 1944- ... CANR-71
Earlier sketch in CA 109
See also SATA 54
See also SATA-Brief 49
Bellville, Rod 1944- ... 117
Bell-Zano, Gina
See Balzano, Jeanne (Koppel)
See also SATA 7
Belmont, Eleanor Robson
1879-1979 Obituary ... 97-100
Belmont, Georges 1909- ... 29-32R
Belmont, Herman S. 1920- ... 41-44R
Belmonte, Thomas 1946-1995 ... 93-96
Obituary ... 148
Belnap, Nuel 1930- ... 144
Belo, Fernando 1933- ... 131
Beloff, John 1920- ... 147
Beloff, Max 1913- ... CANR-18
Earlier sketch in CA 5-8R
Beloff, Michael 1942- ... 21-24R
Beloff, Nora 1919-1997 ... 106
Obituary ... 156
Belok, Michael V(ictor) 1923- ... 33-36R
Beloof, Robert 1923- ... 21-24R
Belote, James H(ine) 1922- ... 33-36R
Belote, Julianne 1929- ... 61-64
Belote, William Milton 1922- ... 49-52
Belotserkovsky, Vladimir Naumovich Bill
See Bill-Belotserkovsky, Vladimir Naumovich
Belous, Russell E. 1925- ... 25-28R
Belozersky, Andrei (Nicolaevich)
1905-1972 Obituary ... 37-40R
Belpre, Pura 1899-1982 ... 73-76
Obituary ... 109
See also SATA 16
See also SATA-Obit 30
Belser, Lee 1925(?)-1988 ... 73-76
Obituary ... 127
Belser, Reimond Karel Maria de 1929- ... 152
See also Ruyslinck, Ward
Belsey, Catherine 1940- ... 142
Belshaw, Cyril S(hirley) 1921- ... 9-12R
Belshaw, Michael (Horace) 1928- ... 21-24R
Belshaw, Patrick (Edward Blakiston) 1936- ... 148
Belsky, Dick 1945- ... CANR-48
Earlier sketch in CA 122
Belsley, David A(lan) 1939- ... 29-32R
Belth, Joseph M(orton) 1929- ... 112
Belth, Nathan C. 1909(?)-1989 Obituary ... 128
Belting, Hans 1951- ... 155
Belting, Natalia Maree 1915-1997 ... CANR-70
Earlier sketches in CA 1-4R, CANR-3
See also SATA 6
Beltman, Brian W. 1945- ... 156
Belton, John Raynor 1931- ... 69-72
See also SATA 22
Belton, Sandra (Yvonne) 1939- ... 151
See also SATA 85
Beltrametti, Franco 1937- ... CAAS 13
Beltran, Alberto 1923- ... SATA 43
Beltran, Miriam 1914- ... 33-36R
Beltran, Pedro (Gerardo) 1897-1979 ... 93-96
Obituary ... 85-88
Beltran-Hernandez, Irene 1945- ... SATA 74
Belushi, John 1949-1982 Obituary ... 106
Belveal, L(orenzo) Dee 1918- ... 21-24R
Belvedere, Lee
See Grayland, Valerie (Merle Spanner)
Bely, Andrey
See Bugayev, Boris Nikolayevich
See also PC 11
See also TCLC 7
Bely, Jeanette L(obach) 1916- ... 33-36R
Belyaev, Aleksandr 1884-1942(?) ... 166
Belyi, Andrei
See Bugayev, Boris Nikolayevich
Belz, Carl 1937- ... CANR-26
Earlier sketches in CA 29-32R, CANR-11
Belz, Herman (Julius) 1937- ... 65-68
Bemelmans, Ludwig 1898-1962 ... 73-76
See also CLR 6
See also DLB 22
See also MAICYA
See also SATA 15, 100
Bemis, Samuel Flagg 1891-1973 ... 9-12R
Obituary ... 45-48
See also DLB 17
Bemis, Stephen Edward 1937-1985 Obituary ... 115
Bemister, Henry
See Barrett, Harry B(emister)
Bemporad, Jules (Richard) 1937- ... 122
Ben, Ilke
See Harper, Carol Ely
Benagh, Jim 1937- ... CANR-9
Earlier sketch in CA 57-60
Ben-Ami, Shlomo 1943- ... 116
Ben-Ami, Yitshaq 1913- ... 130
Ben-Amos, Dan 1934- ... CANR-11
Earlier sketch in CA 69-72
Ben-Amotz, Dan 1923(?)-1989 Obituary ... 130
Benamou, Michel J(ean) 1929-1978 ... CANR-3
Earlier sketch in CA 5-8R
Benander, Carl D. 1941- ... 141
See also SATA 74
Benante, Joseph P(hilip) 1936- ... 33-36R
Benarde, Melvin A(lbert) 1923- ... 25-28R
Benardete, Jane Johnson 1930- ... 45-48
Benario, Herbert W. 1929- ... 25-28R
Benarria, Allan
See Goldenthal, Allan Benarria
Benary, Margot
See Benary-Isbert, Margot
Benary-Isbert, Margot 1889-1979 ... CANR-72
Obituary ... 89-92
Earlier sketches in CA 5-8R, CANR-4
See also CLC 12
See also CLR 12
See also MAICYA
See also SATA 2
See also SATA-Obit 21
Benasutti, Marion 1908- ... 21-24R
See also SATA 6
Benatar, Stephen (Royce) 1937- ... 110
Benaud, Richard 1930- ... 131
Benaud, Richie
See Benaud, Richard
Benavente (y Martinez), Jacinto 1866-1954 ... 131
Brief entry ... 106
See also DAM DRAM, MULT
See also HW
See also MTCW 1
See also TCLC 3
Ben-Avraham, Chofetz Chaim
See Pickering, Stephen
Benbow, Charles (Clarence) 1929- ... 122
Bence, Evelyn ... 110
Bence-Jones, Mark 1930- ... CANR-48
Earlier sketches in CA 13-16R, CANR-5
Bench, Johnny (Lee) 1947- ... 133
Brief entry ... 113
Benchley, Nathaniel (Goddard) 1915-1981 ... CANR-12
Obituary ... 105
Earlier sketches in CA 1-4R, CANR-2
See also SATA 3, 25
See also SATA-Obit 28
Benchley, Peter (Bradford) 1940- ... CANR-66
Earlier sketches in CA 17-20R, CANR-12, 35
See also AAYA 14
See also AITN 2
See also CLC 4, 8
See also DAM NOV, POP
See also MTCW 1
See also SATA 3, 89
Benchley, Robert (Charles) 1889-1945 ... 153
Brief entry ... 105
See also DLB 11
See also TCLC 1, 55
Bencke, Matthew
See Von Bencke, Matthew Justin
Benda, Harry J(indrich) 1919-1971 ... 9-12R
Obituary ... 134
Benda, Julien 1867-1956 ... 154
Brief entry ... 120
See also TCLC 60
Bendavid, Avrom 1942- ... 41-44R
Ben-David, Joseph 1920-1986 ... 157
Obituary ... 118
Bendell, Frederick H.
See McCarty, Hanoch
Bender, Coleman C. 1921- ... 33-36R
Bender, David L(eo) 1936- ... 123
Bender, David R(ay) 1942- ... 102
Bender, Edna 1941- ... SATA 92
Bender, Esther 1942- ... 152
See also SATA 88
Bender, Frederic L(awrence) 1943- ... 69-72
Bender, Henry E(dwin), Jr. 1937- ... 33-36R
Bender, James F(rederick) 1905-1997 ... 17-20R
Obituary ... 162
Bender, Jay
See Deindorfer, Robert Greene
Bender, John B(ryant) 1940- ... 65-68
Bender, Louis W. 1927- ... CANR-32
Earlier sketches in CA 33-36R, CANR-14
Bender, Lucy Ellen 1942- ... 25-28R
See also SATA 22
Bender, Marylin 1925- ... CANR-12
Earlier sketch in CA 21-24R
Bender, Norman J(ohn) 1927- ... 118
Bender, Richard 1930- ... 45-48
Bender, Robert 1962- ... SATA 79
Bender, Robert M. 1936- ... 33-36R
Bender, Ross Thomas 1929- ... 61-64
Bender, Stephen (Joseph) 1942- ... 61-64
Bender, Thomas 1944- ... CANR-35
Earlier sketches in CA 73-76, CANR-12
Bender, Todd K. 1936- ... CANR-24
Earlier sketches in CA 21-24R, CANR-9
Benderly, Beryl Lieff 1943- ... CANR-30
Earlier sketch in CA 108
Bendersky, Margaret (Irene) 1949- ... 151
Bendick, Jeanne 1919- ... CANR-48
Earlier sketches in CA 5-8R, CANR-2
See also CLR 5
See also MAICYA
See also SAAS 4
See also SATA 2, 68
Bendick, Marc, Jr. 1946- ... 118
Bendick, Robert L(ouis) 1917- ... 61-64
See also SATA 11
Bendiner, Elmer 1916- ... CANR-7
Earlier sketch in CA 57-60
Bendiner, Kenneth Paul 1947- ... 119
Bendiner, Robert 1909- ... 9-12R
Bendit, Gladys Williams 1885- ... CAP-1
Earlier sketch in CA 13-14
Bendit, Laurence John 1898-1974 ... CAP-2
Earlier sketch in CA 25-28
Bendix, Deanna Marohn 1938- ... 152
Bendix, Reinhard 1916-1991 ... CANR-4
Obituary ... 133
Earlier sketch in CA 1-4R
Bendixen, Alfred 1952- ... 128
Bendixson, Terence 1934- ... 93-96
Ben-Dov, Meir
See Bernet, Michael M.
Bendroth, Margaret Lamberts 1954- ... 151
Benecke, Gerhard (?)-1985 Obituary ... 117
Benedek, Barbara ... 165
Benedek, Therese 1892-1977 ... 41-44R
Benedetti, Jean (Norman) 1930- ... 160
Benedetti, Mario 1920- ... 152
See also DAM MULT
See also DLB 113
See also HW
Benedetti, Robert L(awrence) 1939- ... 29-32R
Benedetto, Antonio di
See di Benedetto, Antonio
Benedetto, Arnold J(oseph) 1916-1966 ... 5-8R
Benedict, Barbara M. 1955- ... 151
Benedict, Bertram 1892(?)-1978 Obituary ... 77-80
Benedict, Burton 1923- ... 109
Benedict, Dianne 1941- ... 110
Benedict, Dorothy Potter 1889-1979 ... CAP-1
Obituary ... 93-96
Earlier sketch in CA 13-14
See also SATA 11
See also SATA-Obit 23
Benedict, Elizabeth 1954- ... CANR-69
Brief entry ... 126
Earlier sketch in CA 131
Interview in ... 131
Benedict, Helen 1952- ... 140
Benedict, Howard (S.) 1928- ... 147
Benedict, Lois Trimble 1902-1967 ... CAP-2
Earlier sketch in CA 19-20
See also SATA 12
Benedict, Marion 1923- ... 109
Benedict, Michael Les 1945- ... 45-48
Benedict, Philip (Joseph) 1949- ... 130
Benedict, Rex 1920- ... 17-20R
See also SATA 8
Benedict, Robert P(hilip) 1924-1986 ... 41-44R
Obituary ... 119
Benedict, Ruth (Fulton) 1887-1948 ... 158
See also TCLC 60
Benedict, Stewart H(urd) 1924- ... 13-16R
See also SATA 26
Benedictus, David (Henry) 1938- ... CANR-66
Earlier sketches in CA 73-76, CANR-24
See also DLB 14
Benedikt, Michael 1935- ... CANR-7
Earlier sketch in CA 13-16R
See also CLC 4, 14
See also DLB 5
Benefield, June 1921- ... 45-48
Beneke, Walter 1923- ... HW
Benell, Florence B(elle) 1912- ... 33-36R
Benell, Julie 1906(?)-1982 Obituary ... 105
Benello, C. George 1926- ... 33-36R
Ben-Ephraim, Gavriel 1946- ... 116
Beneria, Lourdes 1939- ... 161
Benes, Jan 1936- ... 29-32R
Benet, Edouard
See Edwards, William B(ennett)
Benet, James 1914- ... CANR-8
Earlier sketch in CA 61-64
Benet, Juan 1927- ... 143
See also CLC 28
Benet, Laura 1884-1979 ... CANR-70
Obituary ... 85-88
Earlier sketches in CA 9-12R, CANR-6
See also SATA 3
See also SATA-Obit 23
Benet, Mary Kathleen 1943- ... 57-60
Benet, Stephen Vincent 1898-1943 ... 152
Brief entry ... 104
See also DAM POET
See also DLB 4, 48, 102
See also DLBY 97
See also SSC 10
See also TCLC 7
See also YABC 1
Benet, Sula 1906-1982 ... 89-92
Obituary ... 108
See also SATA 21
See also SATA-Obit 33
Benet, William Rose 1886-1950 ... 152
Brief entry ... 118
See also DAM POET
See also DLB 45
See also TCLC 28
Benetar, Judith 1941- ... 53-56
Benevolo, Leonardo 1923- ... 89-92
Ben-Ezer, Ehud 1936- ... CANR-24
Earlier sketches in CA 61-64, CANR-8
Benezra, Barbara (Beardsley) 1921- ... CANR-72
Earlier sketch in CA 13-16R
See also SATA 10
Benezra, Neal 1953- ... 141
Benfield, Derek 1926- ... CANR-56
Earlier sketches in CA 21-24R, CANR-10, 30
Benfield, G(raham) J(ohn) Barker
See Barker-Benfield, G(raham) J(ohn)
Benfield, Richard E. 1940- ... 77-80
Benford, Gregory (Albert) 1941- ... CANR-49
Earlier sketches in CA 69-72, CANR-12, 24
See also CAAS 27
See also CLC 52
See also DLBY 82
Benford, Harry (Bell) 1917- ... 89-92
Benford, Timothy B(artholomew) 1941- ... CANR-11
Earlier sketch in CA 69-72
Benge, Eugene J(ackson) 1896- ... CANR-9
Earlier sketch in CA 57-60
Bengelsdorf, Irving S. 1922- ... 57-60
Bengtson, Vern L. 1941- ... CANR-4
Earlier sketch in CA 49-52
Bengtsson, Arvid 1916- ... 33-36R
Bengtsson, Frans (Gunnar) 1894-1954 ... TCLC 48
Ben-Gurion, David 1886-1973 ... 101
Obituary ... 45-48
Benham, Leslie 1922- ... 9-12R
See also SATA 48
Benham, Lois (Dakin) 1924- ... 9-12R
See also SATA 48
Benham, Mary Lile 1914- ... 102
See also SATA 55
Ben-Horav, Naphthali
See Kravitz, Nathaniel
Ben-Horin, Meir 1918- ... CANR-14
Earlier sketch in CA 29-32R
Benichou, Paul 1908- ... 57-60
Benig, Irving 1944- ... 152
Beniger, James R. 1946- ... 111
Benington, John (Elson) 1921-1969 ... 5-8R
Obituary ... 134
Benison, C. C.
See Whiteway, Doug(las) Alfred
Ben-Israel-Kidron, Hedva ... 33-36R
Benitez, Fernando 1911- ... 152
See also HW
Benitez, Sandra (Ables) 1941- ... 144
Benitez-Rojo, Antonio 1931- ... 137
Benjamin, Alice
See Brooke, Avery (Rogers)
Benjamin, Anna Shaw 1925- ... 41-44R
Benjamin, Annette Francis 1928- ... 17-20R
Benjamin, Bry 1924- ... 17-20R
Benjamin, Burton Richard 1917-1988 ... 101
Obituary ... 126
Benjamin, Claude (Max Edward Pohlman)
1911- ... 9-12R
Benjamin, Curtis G. 1901-1983 ... 122
Obituary ... 111
Benjamin, David
See Slavitt, David R(ytman)
Benjamin, Denis R(ichard) 1945- ... 154
Benjamin, Edward Bernard 1897-1980 ... 69-72
Obituary ... 133
Benjamin, Gerald 1945- ... CANR-46
Earlier sketch in CA 49-52
Benjamin, Harold H. 1924- ... 154
Benjamin, Harry 1885-1986 ... CAP-1
Obituary ... 120
Earlier sketch in CA 11-12
Benjamin, Herbert S(tanley) 1922- ... 5-8R
Benjamin, Joan 1956- ... 167
Benjamin, Joseph 1921- ... 57-60
Benjamin, Judy-Lynn
See del Rey, Judy-Lynn
Benjamin, Kathleen Kelly
See Kelly-Benjamin, Kathleen
Benjamin, Lois
See Gould, Lois
Benjamin, Nora
See Kubie, Nora Gottheil Benjamin
Benjamin, Park 1809-1864 ... DLB 3, 59, 73
Benjamin, Philip (Robert) 1922-1966 ... 5-8R
Obituary ... 25-28R
Benjamin, Robert (Irving) 1949- ... 109
Benjamin, Roger W. 1942- ... 37-40R
Benjamin, Ruth 1934- ... 125
Benjamin, S. G. W. 1837-1914 ... DLB 189
Benjamin, Saragail Katzman 1953- ... 151
See also SATA 86
Benjamin, Walter 1892-1940 ... 164
See also TCLC 39
Benjamin, William E(arl) 1942- ... 25-28R
Benjaminson, Peter 1945- ... CANR-12
Earlier sketch in CA 73-76
Ben Jelloun, Tahar 1944- ... 135
Benji, Thomas
See Robinson, Frank M(alcolm)
ben-Jochannan, Yosef 1918- ... CANR-12
Earlier sketch in CA 69-72
See also BW 2
Benko, Stephen 1924- ... 9-12R
Benkovitz, Miriam J(eanette) 1911-1986 ... CANR-4
Obituary ... 119
Earlier sketch in CA 9-12R
Benlowes, Edward 1602-1676 ... DLB 126
Benn, Anthony Neil Wedgwood 1925- ... 131
Benn, Gottfried 1886-1956 ... 153
Brief entry ... 106
See also DLB 56
See also TCLC 3
Benn, John Andrews 1904-1984 Obituary ... 115
Benn, June
See Barraclough, June (Mary)
Benn, June Wedgwood
See Barraclough, June (Mary)
Benn, Matthew
See Siegel, Benjamin
Benn, S. I.
See Benn, Stanley I(saac)
Benn, Stanley I(saac) 1920-1986 ... 129
Benn, Tony
See Benn, Anthony Neil Wedgwood
Bennahum, Judith Chazin 1937- ... 146
Bennani, B(en) M(ohammed) 1946- ... CANR-13
Earlier sketch in CA 61-64
Bennassar, Bartolome 1929- ... 158
Benne, Kenneth D(ean) 1908-1992 ... CANR-46
Obituary ... 139
Earlier sketch in CA 33-36R
Benner, Cheryl 1962- ... SATA 80
Benner, Judith Ann 1942- ... CANR-62
Earlier sketch in CA 122
See also SATA 94
Benner, Ralph Eugene (Jr.) 1932- ... 33-36R

Bennet, Glin 1927- 123
Bennet, Richard Bruce 1957- 150
Bennet, Rick
See Bennet, Richard Bruce
Bennet, Ruth
See Straubing, Harold (Elk)
Bennett, A(bram) E(lting Hasbrouck) 1898- 65-68
Bennett, Addison C(urtis) 1918- CANR-7
Earlier sketch in CA 5-8R
Bennett, Adrian A(rthur) 1941- 53-56
Bennett, Alan 1934- CANR-55
Earlier sketches in CA 103, CANR-35
See also CLC 45, 77
See also DAB
See also DAM MST
See also MTCW 1
Bennett, Alice
See Ziner, Florence
Bennett, Anna Elizabeth 1914- 17-20R
Bennett, Archibald F. 1896- CAP-1
Earlier sketch in CA 13-16
Bennett, (Enoch) Arnold 1867-1931 155
Brief entry 106
See also CDBLB 1890-1914
See also DLB 10, 34, 98, 135
See also TCLC 5, 20
Bennett, Betty T. 115
Bennett, Boyce McLean, Jr. 1928- 115
Bennett, Bruce (William) 1952- 110
Bennett, Bruce L(anyon) 1917- 25-28R
Bennett, Carl D(ouglas) 1917- 140
Bennett, Charles 1899-1995 146
Obituary 149
See also DLB 44
Bennett, Charles 1901- CAP-1
Earlier sketch in CA 13-16
Bennett, Charles 1932- 25-28R
Bennett, Charles E(dward) 1910- 9-12R
Bennett, Cherie 1960- 163
See also SATA 97
Bennett, Christine
See Neubauer, William Arthur
Bennett, Clinton 1955- 157
Bennett, Colin J. 1955- 138
Bennett, Daniel
See Gilmore, Joseph L(ee)
Bennett, Daphne Nicholson 41-44R
Bennett, David H. 1935- 25-28R
Bennett, Dennis J. 1917- CANR-20
Earlier sketch in CA 49-52
Bennett, Dorothea
See Young, Dorothea Bennett
Bennett, Dwight
See Newton, D(wight) B(ennett)
Bennett, E(thel) M. Granger 1891- CAP-1
Earlier sketch in CA 13-14
Bennett, E. N.
See Bennett, Ernest N(athaniel)
Bennett, Edward (Martin) 1924- 5-8R
Bennett, Edward M(oore) 1927- 33-36R
Bennett, Elizabeth
See Mitchell, Margaret (Munnerlyn)
Bennett, Elizabeth
See Harrod-Eagles, Cynthia
Bennett, Elizabeth Deare
See Merwin, Sam(uel Kimball), Jr.
Bennett, Emerson 1822-1905 DLB 202
Bennett, Ernest N(athaniel) 1868-1947 Brief entry 119
Bennett, Frances Grant 1899- CAP-2
Earlier sketch in CA 25-28
Bennett, Fredna W(illis) 1906- CAP-1
Earlier sketch in CA 9-10
Bennett, G. V.
See Bennett, Gareth Vaughan
Bennett, Gareth Vaughan 1929-1987 Obituary 124
Bennett, Gary L. 1940- 138
Bennett, Geoffrey (Martin) 1909-1983 13-16R
Obituary 110
Bennett, George 1920-1969 5-8R
Obituary 134
Bennett, George Harold 1930- 97-100
See also Bennett, Hal
See also BW 1
Bennett, Georgette 1946- 143
Bennett, Gertrude Ryder 53-56
Bennett, Gordon A(nderson) 1940- 29-32R
Bennett, Gordon C. 1935- CANR-31
Earlier sketches in CA 33-36R, CANR-14
Bennett, Gwendolyn B. 1902-1981 125
See also BW 1
See also DLB 51
Bennett, Hal
See Bennett, George Harold
See also CLC 5
See also DLB 33
Bennett, Hal 1930- CAAS 13
Bennett, Hal Zina 1936- CANR-40
Earlier sketch in CA 41-44R
Bennett, Hall
See Hall, Bennie Caroline (Humble)
Bennett, Harve
See Fischman, Harve
Bennett, Howard Franklin 1911-1974 1-4R
Bennett, Isadora 1900-1980 Obituary 93-96
Bennett, J(ohn) G(odolphin) 1897-1974 Obituary 111
Bennett, Jack Arthur Walter 1911-1981 CANR-6
Obituary 103
Earlier sketch in CA 9-12R
Bennett, James (W.) 1942- 158
See also AAYA 26
See also SATA 93
Bennett, James D(avid) 1926- 61-64
Bennett, James Gordon, Jr. 1841-1918 DLB 23
Bennett, James Gordon 1795-1872 DLB 43
Bennett, James R(ichard) 1932- 33-36R
Bennett, James Thomas 1942- CANR-23
Earlier sketch in CA 106
Bennett, Jay 1912- CANR-42
Earlier sketches in CA 69-72, CANR-11
See also AAYA 10
See also CLC 35
See also JRDA
See also SAAS 4
See also SATA 41, 87
See also SATA-Brief 27
Bennett, Jean Francis
See Dorcy, Sister Mary Jean
Bennett, Jeremy
See Bennett, John Jerome Nelson
Bennett, Jill (Crawford) 1934- SATA 41
Bennett, Jill 1947- 106
Bennett, Joan S. 1941- 132
Bennett, John 1865-1956 DLB 42
See also YABC 1
Bennett, John (Frederic) 1920- 29-32R
Bennett, John Jerome Nelson 1939- 21-24R
Bennett, John M(ichael) 1942- CANR-41
Earlier sketches in CA 49-52, CANR-2, 18
See also CAAS 25
Bennett, John W. 1918- 69-72
Bennett, John William 1915- CANR-4
Earlier sketch in CA 1-4R
Bennett, Jon 1955- 127
Bennett, Jonathan (Francis) 1930- CANR-1
Earlier sketch in CA 45-48
Bennett, Joseph D. 1922-1972 1-4R
Obituary 33-36R
Bennett, Josephine Waters 1899-1975 1-4R
Obituary 103
Bennett, Judith (?)-1979 Obituary 85-88
Bennett, Kathleen 1946- 138
Bennett, Kay Curley 1922-1997 17-20R
Obituary 162
Bennett, Kenneth A(lan) 1935- 131
Bennett, Lerone, Jr. 1928- CANR-25
Earlier sketches in CA 45-48, CANR-2
See also BW 2
Bennett, Linda L(eveque) 1946- 115
Bennett, Louise (Simone) 1919- 151
See also BLC 1
See also BW 2
See also CLC 28
See also DAM MULT
See also DLB 117
Bennett, M. J.
See Bennett, Marcia J(oanne)
Bennett, Marcia J(oanne) 1945- CANR-35
Earlier sketch in CA 114
Bennett, Margaret E(laine) 1893- 5-8R
Bennett, Margot 1912-1980 Obituary 105
Bennett, Marion T(insley) 1914- 9-12R
Bennett, Melba Berry 1901-1968 CAP-2
Earlier sketch in CA 19-20
Bennett, Meridan 1927- 25-28R
Bennett, Merit 1947- 160
Bennett, Michael 1943-1987 101
Obituary 122
Bennett, Mildred R. 1909-1989 CAP-2
Obituary 130
Earlier sketch in CA 25-28
Bennett, Neville 1937- CANR-41
Earlier sketches in CA 102, CANR-19
Bennett, Noel 1939- 45-48
Bennett, Norman Robert 1932- CANR-39
Earlier sketches in CA 9-12R, CANR-3, 18
Bennett, Patrick (H.) 1931- 122
Bennett, Paul Lewis 1921- CANR-4
Earlier sketch in CA 1-4R
Bennett, Penelope (Agnes) 1938- CANR-65
Earlier sketch in CA 13-16R
See also SATA 94
Bennett, Rachel
See Hill, Margaret (Ohler)
Bennett, Rainey 1907- SATA 15
Bennett, Richard 1899- SATA 21
Bennett, Rita (Marie) 1934- CANR-20
Earlier sketch in CA 69-72
Bennett, Robert A(ndrew) 1927- CANR-5
Earlier sketch in CA 13-16R
Bennett, Robert D(onald) 1947- 118
Bennett, Robert L. 1931- 41-44R
Bennett, Robert Russell 1894-1981 Obituary 105
Bennett, Ronan 1956- 142
Bennett, Russell H(oradley) 1896- SATA 25
Bennett, Saxon 1961- 163
Bennett, Scott (Boyce) 1939- 33-36R
Bennett, Shelley M. 1947- 131
Bennett, Thomas L(eroy) 1942- 85-88
Bennett, Victor 1919- CANR-7
Earlier sketch in CA 5-8R
Bennett, W(illiam) R(obert) 1921- 13-16R
Bennett, Wilhelmine 1933- 167
Bennett, William (Ira) 1941- 107
Bennett, William (John) 1943- 153
See also SATA 102
Bennett, William L. 1924- 17-20R
Bennett-England, Rodney Charles 1936- 61-64
Bennetts, Pamela 1922-1986 CANR-60
Earlier sketch in CA 37-40R
Benni, Stefano 1947- DLB 196
Bennie, William A(ndrew) 1921- 69-72
Bennigsen, Alexandre (A.) 1913-1988(?) Obituary 125
Benning, Elizabeth
See Rice, Bebe Faas
Benning, (Barbara) Lee Edwards 1934- 53-56
Bennion, Barbara Elisabeth 1930- 110
Bennion, Sherilyn Cox 1935- 137
Bennis, Warren G. 1925- CANR-5
Earlier sketch in CA 53-56
Benoff, Mac 1915(?)-1972 Obituary 37-40R
Benoist-Mechin, Jacques 1901-1983 105
Obituary 109
Benoit, Emile 1910-1978 CANR-3
Obituary 77-80
Earlier sketch in CA 5-8R
Benoit, Jacques 1941- DLB 60
Benoit, Leroy James 1913- 33-36R
Benoit, Pierre 1886-1962 Obituary 93-96
Benoit, Pierre Maurice 1906-1987 41-44R
Obituary 122
Benoit, Richard 1899(?)-1969 Obituary 104
Benoit, William L. 1953- 163
Benoliel, Jeanne Quint 1919- CANR-27
Earlier sketch in CA 49-52
Ben-Rafael, Eliezer 1938- 141
Bense, Walter F(rederick) 1932- CANR-1
Earlier sketch in CA 45-48
Bensel, Richard Franklin 1949- 141
Bensen, Alice R. 1911- 69-72
Bensen, Donald R. 1927- CANR-20
Earlier sketches in CA 9-12R, CANR-5
Bensko, John 1949- 105
Bensley, Connie 1929- 135
Bensman, David 1949- 144
Bensman, Joseph 1922- CANR-10
Earlier sketch in CA 21-24R
Bensol, Oscar
See Gilbert, Willie
Benson, A. C. 1862-1925 DLB 98
Benson, A. George 1924- 69-72
Benson, B. A.
See Beyea, Basil
Benson, Ben(jamin) 1915-1959 Brief entry 112
Benson, C(arl) David 1942- 123
Benson, C. Randolph 1923- 29-32R
Benson, Carmen 1921- 57-60
Benson, Charles S(cott) 1922-1994 CANR-8
Obituary 146
Earlier sketch in CA 17-20R
Benson, Constantine Walter 1909-1982 Obituary 108
Benson, D(avid) Frank 1928- 151
Benson, Daniel
See Cooper, Colin Symons
Benson, Dennis C(arroll) 1936- 37-40R
Benson, E(dward) F(rederic) 1867-1940 157
Brief entry 114
See also DLB 135, 153
See also TCLC 27
Benson, Elizabeth P(olk) 1924- CANR-35
Earlier sketch in CA 93-96
See also SATA 65
Benson, Eugene 1928- 89-92
Benson, Evelyn 1924- 167
Benson, Frederick R. 1934- 33-36R
Benson, Frederick William 1948- CANR-43
Earlier sketches in CA 101, CANR-19
Benson, Gerard 1931- 144
Benson, Gigi (Dian Daniels) 1941- 108
Benson, Ginny
See Benson, Virginia
Benson, Harry 1929- 108
Benson, Herbert 1935- 85-88
Benson, J(ack) L(eonard) 1920- 105
Benson, Jackson J. 1930- 25-28R
See also CLC 34
See also DLB 111
Benson, Jeffrey 1937- 120
Benson, John 1945- 131
Benson, Judi 1947- 147
Benson, Kathleen 1947- 85-88
See also SATA 62
Benson, Larry D(ean) 1929- 37-40R
Benson, Linda M(aria) 1959- SATA 84
Benson, Lyman (David) 1909- CANR-32
Earlier sketch in CA 49-52
Benson, Margaret H. Benson 1899- 5-8R
Benson, Mary 1919- CANR-17
Earlier sketches in CA 49-52, CANR-1
Benson, Maxine (Frances) 1939- 65-68
Benson, Mildred (Augustine Wirt) 1905- 134
See also MAICYA
See also SATA 65, 100
Benson, Mildred Wirt
See Benson, Mildred (Augustine Wirt)
Benson, Peter 1956- 137
Benson, R(obert) H(ugh) 1871-1914 167
See also DLB 153
Benson, Rachel
See Jowitt, Deborah
Benson, Raymond 1955- 118
Benson, Richard
See Cooper, Saul
Benson, Robert G(reen) 1930- 29-32R
Benson, Robert S(later) 1942- 33-36R
Benson, Rolf Eric 1951- 102
Benson, Ruth Crego 1937- 41-44R
Benson, Sally 1900-1972 CAP-1
Obituary 37-40R
Earlier sketch in CA 19-20
See also CLC 17
See also SATA 1, 35
See also SATA-Obit 27
Benson, Stella 1892-1933 155
Brief entry 117
See also DLB 36, 162
See also TCLC 17
Benson, Stephana Vere 1909- 13-16R
Benson, Ted
See Benson, Frederick William
Benson, Thomas Godfrey 1899- CAP-1
Earlier sketch in CA 11-12
Benson, Thomas W(alter) 1937- CANR-19
Earlier sketch in CA 29-32R
Benson, Virginia 1923- 57-60
Benson, Warren S(ten) 1929- 114
Benson, William Howard 1902- 1-4R
Benstead, Steven 1951- 113
Bensted-Smith, Richard (Brian) 1929- 13-16R
Benstock, Bernard 1930- CANR-29
Earlier sketches in CA 17-20R, CANR-7
Benstock, Shari 1944- CANR-29
Earlier sketch in CA 97-100
Bent, Alan Edward 1939- CANR-4
Earlier sketch in CA 49-52
Bent, Charles N. 1935- 21-24R
Bent, James Theodore 1852-1897 DLB 174
Bent, Mabel Virginia Anna (?)-(?) DLB 174
Bent, Rudyard K(ipling) 1901- CANR-18
Earlier sketch in CA 1-4R
Bent, Timothy (David) 1955- 157
Benteen, John
See Haas, Ben(jamin) L(eopold)
Bentel, Pearl B(ucklen) 1901- CAP-2
Earlier sketch in CA 21-22
Benthall, Jonathan 1941- 41-44R
Bentham, Frederick 1911- 105
Bentham, Jay
See Bensman, Joseph
Bentham, Jeremy 1748-1832 DLB 107, 158
Benthic, Arch E.
See Stewart, Harris B(ates), Jr.
Benthul, Herman F(orrest) 1911- 33-36R
Bentley, Beth (Rita) 1928- 101
Bentley, Bill
See Bentley, William (George)
Bentley, Colin 1936- 118
Bentley, E(dmund) C(lerihew) 1875-1956 Brief entry 108
See also DLB 70
See also TCLC 12
Bentley, Eric (Russell) 1916- CANR-67
Earlier sketches in CA 5-8R, CANR-6
Interview in CANR-6
See also CLC 24
Bentley, G(erald) E(ades), Jr. 1930- CANR-4
Earlier sketch in CA 1-4R
Bentley, Gerald Eades 1901-1994 41-44R
Obituary 146
Bentley, Howard Beebe 1925- 9-12R
Bentley, Janice Babb 1933- 13-16R
Bentley, Jayne
See Krentz, Jayne Ann
Bentley, Jeffery W(estwood) 1955- 143
Bentley, Jerry H(arrell) 1949- CANR-55
Earlier sketch in CA 127
Bentley, Joanne 1928- 130
Bentley, Joyce 1928- 144
Bentley, Judith (McBride) 1945- CANR-48
Earlier sketches in CA 107, CANR-23
See also SATA 40, 89
Bentley, Margaret 1926- CANR-25
Earlier sketch in CA 108
Bentley, Michael (John) 1948- 145
Bentley, Nancy 1946- 146
See also SATA 78
Bentley, Nicolas Clerihew 1907-1978 CANR-11
Obituary 81-84
Earlier sketch in CA 65-68
See also SATA-Obit 24
Bentley, Phyllis Eleanor 1894-1977 CANR-59
Earlier sketches in CA 1-4R, CANR-3
See also DLB 191
See also SATA 6
See also SATA-Obit 25
Bentley, Richard
See Browning, Alice C(rolley)
Bentley, Roy 1947- 127
See also SATA 46
Bentley, Sarah 1946- 29-32R
Bentley, Toni 1958- CANR-56
Earlier sketch in CA 123
Bentley, Ursula 1945- 125
Bentley, Virginia W(illiams) 1908- 57-60
Bentley, William (George) 1916- 150
See also SATA 84
Bentley-Taylor, David 1915- CANR-14
Earlier sketch in CA 77-80
Benton, D(ebra) A. 1953- 141
Benton, Dorothy Gilchrist 1919- 57-60
Benton, F(red) Warren 1948- 119
Benton, Helen Hemingway 1902(?)-1974 Obituary 104
Benton, John Frederic 1931-1988 69-72
Obituary 124
Benton, John W. 1933- CANR-12
Earlier sketch in CA 29-32R
Benton, Joseph Nelson, Jr. 1924-1988 Obituary 124
Benton, Josephine Moffett 1905- 5-8R
Benton, Karla
See Rowland, D(onald) S(ydney)
Benton, Kenneth (Carter) 1909- CANR-1
Earlier sketch in CA 49-52
Benton, Lewis R(obert) 1920- 17-20R
Benton, (Joseph) Nelson (Jr.) 1924- 112
Brief entry 110
Interview in 112
Benton, Patricia 1907- 5-8R
Benton, Peggie 1906- CANR-31
Earlier sketch in CA 49-52
Benton, Richard G(lasscock) 1938- 81-84
Benton, Robert
See Buse, Renee
Benton, Robert (Douglass) 1932- CANR-2
Earlier sketch in CA 1-4R
See also DLB 44
Benton, Thomas Hart 1889-1975 93-96
Obituary 53-56
Benton, Wilbourn Eugene 1917- 1-4R

Benton, Will
See Paine, Lauran (Bosworth)
Benton, William 1900-1973 .... CAP-1
Obituary 41-44R
Earlier sketch in CA 13-16
Bentov, Itzhak 1923(?)-1979 Obituary 85-88
Bentsen, Cheryl 1950- 138
Bentwich, Norman 1883-1971 Obituary 111
Bentz, Thomas 1943- 112
Bentz, William F(rederick) 1940- 53-56
ben Uzair, Salem
See Horne, Richard Henry
Benveniste, Asa 1925-1990 .... CANR-33
Obituary 131
Earlier sketch in CA 69-72
Benveniste, Emile 1902-1976 Obituary 115
Benveniste, Guy 1927- CANR-8
Earlier sketch in CA 61-64
Ben-Veniste, Richard 1943- Brief entry 114
Benvenisti, Meron (Shmuel) 1934- CANR-35
Earlier sketches in CA 65-68, CANR-12
Benward, Bruce (Charles) 1921- CANR-9
Earlier sketch in CA 9-12R
Beny, Roloff
See Beny, Wilfred Roy
Beny, Wilfred Roy 1924-1984 .... CANR-32
Obituary 112
Earlier sketch in CA 21-24R
Ben-Yehuda, Nachman 1948- 159
Ben-Yishai, Yonatan
See Wachsmann, Shelley
Benyo, Richard (Stephen) 1946- CANR-29
Earlier sketches in CA 77-80, CANR-13
Ben-Yosef, Avraham C(haim)
See Matsuba, Moshe
Benz, Ernst (Wilhelm) 1907-1978 .... CANR-13
Earlier sketch in CA 13-16R
Benz, Frank L(eonard) 1930- 41-44R
Benzie, William 1930- 37-40R
Benziger, Barbara Field 1918- Brief entry 115
Benziger, James 1914- 13-16R
Ben-Zion
See Weinman, Benzion
Benzoni, Juliette (Andree Marguerite) 1920- CANR-18
Earlier sketch in CA 101
Beorse, Bryn 1896- 45-48
Bequaert, Lucia H(umes) 65-68
Beranek, Leo L(eroy) 1914- 5-8R
Beranek, William 1922- 5-8R
Berard, J(ules) Aram 1933- 17-20R
Berardo, Felix M(ario) 1934- CANR-24
Earlier sketches in CA 57-60, CANR-8
Berberick, Nancy Varian 1951- 154
Berberova, Nina (Nikolaevna) 1901-1993 .... CANR-56
Obituary 142
Earlier sketches in CA 33-36R, CANR-14
Berbrich, Joan D. 1925- CANR-12
Earlier sketch in CA 29-32R
Berbusse, Edward J(oseph) 1912- 21-24R
Berch, Bettina 1950- 129
Berch, William O.
See Coyne, Joseph E.
Berchen, Ursula 1919- 65-68
Berchen, William 1920- 65-68
Berck, Judith 1960- 142
See also SATA 75
Berck, Martin G(ans) 1928- 65-68
Berckman, Evelyn Domenica 1900-1978 .... CANR-71
Earlier sketches in CA 1-4R, CANR-1
Bercovici, Rion 1903(?)-1976 Obituary 69-72
Bercovitch, Reuben 1923- 104
Bercovitch, Sacvan 1933- 41-44R
Berczeller, Richard 1902-1994 .... 9-12R
Obituary 143
Berdanier, Carolyn D. 1936- 150
Berdes, George R. 1931- 29-32R
Berdie, Douglas R(alph) 1946- 53-56
Berdie, Ralph F(reimuth) 1916-1974 .... CANR-11
Earlier sketch in CA 17-20R
Berding, Andrew H(enry) 1902- 5-8R
Berdyaev, Nicolas
See Berdyaev, Nikolai (Aleksandrovich)
Berdyaev, Nikolai (Aleksandrovich) 1874-1948 157
Brief entry 120
See also TCLC 67
Berdyayev, Nikolai (Aleksandrovich)
See Berdyaev, Nikolai (Aleksandrovich)
Bere, Rennie Montague 1907- 65-68
Bereday, George Z(ygmunt) F(ijalkowski) 1920-1983 .... CANR-4
Obituary 111
Earlier sketch in CA 1-4R
Bereiter, Carl 1930- Brief entry 113
Berelson, Bernard R(euben) 1912-1979 .... CANR-3
Obituary 89-92
Earlier sketch in CA 5-8R
Berelson, David 1943- 25-28R
Berelson, Howard 1940- .... SATA 5
Berenbaum, Linda Bayer
See Bayer, Linda
Berenbaum, Michael 1945- 146
Berends, Polly Berrien 1939- 108
See also SATA 50
See also SATA-Brief 38
Berendsohn, Walter A(rthur) 1884-1984(?) CANR-34
Earlier sketch in CA 33-36R
Berendt, Joachim Ernst 1922- CANR-30
Earlier sketches in CA 69-72, CANR-12
Berendt, John (Lawrence) 1939- 146
See also CLC 86
Berendzen, Richard (Earl) 1938- 85-88
Berenson, Conrad 1930- 9-12R
Berenson, F(rances) M(aria) 1929- CANR-64
Earlier sketch in CA 129
Berenstain, Jan(ice) 1923- CANR-36
Earlier sketches in CA 25-28R, CANR-14
See also CLR 19
See also MAICYA
See also SAAS 20
See also SATA 12, 64
Berenstain, Michael 1951- CANR-36
Earlier sketches in CA 97-100, CANR-14
See also SATA 45
Berenstain, Stan(ley) 1923- CANR-36
Earlier sketches in CA 25-28R, CANR-14
See also CLR 19
See also MAICYA
See also SAAS 20
See also SATA 12, 64
Bereny, Gail Rubin 1942- 85-88
Berenzy, Alix 1957- 133
See also SATA 65
Beresford, Anne 1929- CANR-70
Earlier sketch in CA 97-100
See also DLB 40
Beresford, Elisabeth CANR-53
Earlier sketch in CA 102
See also SAAS 20
See also SATA 25, 86
Beresford, J(ohn) D(avys) 1873-1947 155
Brief entry 112
See also DLB 162, 178, 197
See also TCLC 81
Beresford, Maurice Warwick 1920- CANR-72
Earlier sketch in CA 13-16R
Beresford-Howe, Constance 1922- 53-56
See also AITN 2
See also DLB 88
Beresiner, Yasha 1940- CANR-12
Earlier sketch in CA 69-72
Beretta, Lia 1934- 17-20R
Berg, A(ndrew) Scott 1949(?)- 81-84
See also BEST 89:3
Berg, Adriane G(ilda) 1948- 119
Berg, Alan (David) 1932- CANR-22
Earlier sketch in CA 45-48
Berg, Barbara J. 124
Berg, Bjoern 1923- .... SATA-Brief 47
Berg, Darrel E. 1920- 17-20R
Berg, Dave
See Berg, David
Berg, David 1920- CANR-10
Earlier sketch in CA 21-24R
See also SATA 27
Berg, Elizabeth 1948- 147
Berg, Fred Anderson 1948- 37-40R
Berg, Frederick S(ven) 1928- 53-56
Berg, Friedrich Kantor
See Kantor-Berg, Friedrich
Berg, Goesta 1903- 69-72
Berg, Irwin August 1913- 13-16R
Berg, Ivar E(lis), Jr. 1929- CANR-13
Earlier sketch in CA 21-24R
Berg, Jean Horton 1913- CANR-4
Earlier sketch in CA 53-56
See also SATA 6
Berg, Joan
See Victor, Joan Berg
Berg, John C. 1943- 150
Berg, Larry L(ee) 1939- 41-44R
Berg, Lasse 1943- CANR-12
Earlier sketch in CA 73-76
Berg, Leila Rita 1917- 101
Berg, Louis 1901-1972 Obituary 37-40R
Berg, Orley M. 1918- 17-20R
Berg, Paul Conrad 1921- 33-36R
Berg, Richard F(rederick) 1936- 115
Berg, Rick 1951- 93-96
Berg, Ron 1952- .... SATA 48
Berg, Stephen 1934- CANR-8
Earlier sketch in CA 13-16R
See also DLB 5
Berg, Thomas L(eRoy) 1930- 69-72
Berg, Viola Jacobson 1918- CANR-5
Earlier sketch in CA 53-56
Berg, William 1938- 97-100
Bergamini, David H(owland) 1928-1983 .... CANR-15
Obituary 110
Earlier sketch in CA 1-4R
Bergamini, John D. 1925(?)-1982 Obituary 108
Bergaust, Erik 1925-1978 .... CANR-32
Obituary 77-80
Earlier sketch in CA 73-76
See also SATA 20
Berge, Carol 1928- CANR-7
Earlier sketch in CA 13-16R
See also CAAS 10
Bergeijk, Peter A(drianus) G(errit) van 1959- 152
Bergel, Egon Ernst 1894-1969 .... CAP-2
Earlier sketch in CA 21-22
Bergelson, David 1884-1952 .... TCLC 81
Bergen, Candice 1946- 142
Bergen, David 1957- 161
Bergen, Joyce 1949- .... SATA 95
Bergen, Polly 1930- 57-60
Bergendoff, Conrad J(ohn) I(mmanuel) 1895- CANR-13
Earlier sketch in CA 33-36R
Bergengruen, Werner 1892-1964(?) Obituary 114
See also DLB 56
Berger, Andrew J(ohn) 1915- CANR-14
Earlier sketch in CA 41-44R
Berger, Anna Maria Busse 146
Berger, Arthur Asa 1933- CANR-51
Earlier sketches in CA 25-28R, CANR-10, 26
Berger, Barbara (Helen) 1945- 145
See also SATA 77
Berger, Bennett Maurice 1926- CANR-4
Earlier sketch in CA 1-4R
Berger, Brigitte (M. L.) 1928- 131
Berger, Bruce 1938- CANR-56
Earlier sketches in CA 112, CANR-30
Berger, Carl 1925- 9-12R
Berger, Charles R. 167
Berger, Colonel
See Malraux, (Georges-)Andre
Berger, David 1943- 115
Berger, David G. 1941- 129
Berger, Elmer 1908-1996 61-64
Obituary 154
Berger, Evelyn Miller 1896- CANR-14
Earlier sketch in CA 37-40R
Berger, Fredericka 1932- 131
Berger, Gilda 1935- 134
Brief entry 118
See also SATA 88
See also SATA-Brief 42
Berger, H. Jean 1924- 13-16R
Berger, Harry, Jr. 1924- 110
Berger, Hilbert J. 1920- 57-60
Berger, Ivan (Bennett) 1939- CANR-17
Earlier sketch in CA 97-100
Berger, John (Peter) 1926- CANR-51
Earlier sketch in CA 81-84
See also CLC 2, 19
See also DLB 14
Berger, John J(oseph) 1945- 69-72
Berger, Josef 1903-1971 .... 5-8R
Obituary 33-36R
See also SATA 36
Berger, Joseph 1924- 41-44R
Berger, Karen 1944- 122
Berger, Klaus 1901- CAP-1
Earlier sketch in CA 13-14
Berger, Marilyn 1935- 101
Berger, Marjorie Sue 1916- 13-16R
Berger, Mark L(ewis) 1942- Brief entry 109
Berger, Melvin H. 1927- CANR-4
Earlier sketch in CA 5-8R
See also CLC 12
See also CLR 32
See also SAAS 2
See also SATA 5, 88
Berger, Meyer 1898-1959(?) 154
Brief entry 120
See also DLB 29
Berger, Michael L(ouis) 1943- CANR-32
Earlier sketches in CA 77-80, CANR-14
Berger, Morroe 1917-1981 .... CANR-4
Obituary 103
Earlier sketch in CA 1-4R
Berger, Nan 1914- 113
Berger, Peter Ludwig 1929- CANR-1
Earlier sketch in CA 1-4R
Berger, Phil 1942- CANR-55
Earlier sketches in CA 61-64, CANR-12
See also SATA 62
Berger, Rainer 1930- 37-40R
Berger, Raoul 1901- CANR-44
Earlier sketch in CA 93-96
Berger, Raymond M(ark) 1950- 109
Berger, Robert W(illiam) 1936- 49-52
Berger, Stefan 1964- 154
Berger, Stuart 1953-1994 112
Obituary 144
Berger, Suzanne E(lizabeth) 1944- 105
Berger, Terry 1933- 37-40R
See also SATA 8
Berger, Thomas (Louis) 1924- CANR-51
Earlier sketches in CA 1-4R, CANR-5, 28
Interview in CANR-28
See also CLC 3, 5, 8, 11, 18, 38
See also DAM NOV
See also DLB 2
See also DLBY 80
See also MTCW 1
Berger, Thomas R(odney) 1933- 143
Berger, Yves 1934- 85-88
Bergeret, Ida Treat 1889(?)-1978 Obituary 77-80
Bergeron, Arthur W(illiam), Jr. 1946- 141
Bergeron, David M(oore) 1938- CANR-2
Earlier sketch in CA 45-48
Bergeron, Paul H. 1938- 101
Bergeron, Victor (Jules, Jr.) 1902-1984 89-92
Obituary 114
Bergerud, Eric M. 1948- 141
Berges, Emily Trafford 1937- 132
Berges, Marshall (William) 1921(?)-1988 Obituary 126
Bergeson, John B(rian) 1935- 69-72
Bergevin, Paul (Emile) 1906- CANR-2
Earlier sketch in CA 5-8R
Bergey, Alyce (Mae) 1934- CANR-7
Earlier sketch in CA 5-8R
See also SATA 45
Berggren, W(illiam) A(lfred) 1931- 123
Berghahn, Volker R(olf) 1938- CANR-20
Earlier sketch in CA 103
Bergier, Jacques 1912-1978 .... CANR-37
Obituary 81-84
Earlier sketch in CA 85-88
Bergin, Allen E. 1934- 45-48
Bergin, John 1966- 148
Bergin, Kenneth Glenny 1911-1981 Obituary 103
Bergin, Thomas Goddard 1904-1987 .... CANR-3
Obituary 124
Earlier sketch in CA 9-12R
Bergin, Thomas J. (Tim) 1940- 160
Bergland, Martha 1945- CANR-68
Earlier sketch in CA 130
Berglas, Steven 1949- 142
Bergman, Andrew 1945- 149
Bergman, Arlene Eisen 1942- 61-64
Bergman, Bernard A(aron) 1894-1980 102
Obituary 97-100
Bergman, Bo 1869-1967 Obituary 25-28R
Bergman, David (L.) 1950- CANR-51
Earlier sketches in CA 106, CANR-22
Bergman, Donna 1934- .... SATA 73
Bergman, Eugene 1930- 135
Bergman, Floyd L(awrence) 1927- CANR-17
Earlier sketches in CA 49-52, CANR-2
Bergman, Hannah E(stermann) 1925-1981 69-72
Obituary 135
Bergman, Hjalmar (Frederik Elgerus) 1883-1931 Brief entry 119
Bergman, (Shmuel) Hugo 1883-1975 Obituary 57-60
Bergman, (Ernst) Ingmar 1918- CANR-70
Earlier sketches in CA 81-84, CANR-33
See also CLC 16, 72
Bergman, Ingrid 1915-1982 132
Obituary 107
Bergman, Jay Asa 1948- 110
Bergman, Jules (Verne) 1929-1987 108
Obituary 121
Interview in 108
Bergman, Lewis 1918-1988 Obituary 127
Bergman, Tamar 1939- CANR-68
Earlier sketch in CA 138
See also SATA 95
Bergmann, Ernst W. 1896(?)-1977 Obituary 69-72
Bergmann, Fred L(ouis) 1916- 61-64
Bergmann, Frithjof H. 1930- 101
Bergmann, Peter G(abriel) 1915- 21-24R
Bergon, Frank 1943- 152
Bergonzi, Bernard 1929- CANR-8
Earlier sketch in CA 17-20R
Bergonzo, Jean Louis 1939-(?) CAP-2
Earlier sketch in CA 25-28
Bergquist, Laura (Cecelia) 1918-1982 Obituary 108
Bergquist, William Hastings 1940- 144
Bergreen, Laurence R. 1950- CANR-72
Earlier sketches in CA 104, CANR-42
See also BEST 90:4
Bergson, Abram 1914- 13-16R
Bergson, Henri(-Louis) 1859-1941 164
See also TCLC 32
Bergson, Leo
See Stebel, S(idney) L(eo)
Bergstein, Eleanor 1938- CANR-5
Earlier sketch in CA 53-56
See also CLC 4
Bergsten, C. Fred 1941- 111
Bergsten, Staffan 1932- CANR-6
Earlier sketch in CA 57-60
Bergstrom, Elaine 1946- 149
Bergstrom, Joan M(argosian) 1940- 144
Bergstrom, Louise 1914- 29-32R
Beringause, Arthur F. 1919- 33-36R
Beringer, Richard E. 1933- 81-84
Berio, Luciano 1925- 146
Berk, Fred 1911(?)-1980 Obituary 97-100
Berke, Joel S(ommers) 1936-1981 110
Obituary 105
Berke, Joseph H(erman) 1939- 57-60
Berke, Roberta 1943- CANR-43
Earlier sketch in CA 106
Berkebile, Don(ald) H(erbert) 1926- CANR-8
Earlier sketch in CA 61-64
Berkebile, Fred D(onovan) 1900-1978 .... 5-8R
Obituary 103
See also SATA-Obit 26
Berkeley, Anthony
See Cox, A(nthony) B(erkeley)
See also DLB 77
Berkeley, David S(helley) 1917- 41-44R
Berkeley, Edmund 1912- 133
Brief entry 112
Berkeley, Ellen Perry 1931- 110
Berkeley, George 1685-1753 .... DLB 101
Berkeley, Sara 1967- 152
Berkemeyer, William C. 1908- CAP-2
Earlier sketch in CA 25-28
Berkey, Barry Robert 1935- 69-72
See also SATA 24
Berkey, Helen 1898- CAP-2
Earlier sketch in CA 23-24
Berkey, Jonathan P. 1959- 140
Berkhofer, Robert Frederick, Jr. 1931- 13-16R
Berkin, Carol Ruth 1942- CANR-11
Earlier sketch in CA 69-72
Berkley, George E(ugene) 1928- 127
Brief entry 113
Berkman, Edward O(scar) 1914- CANR-9
Earlier sketch in CA 61-64
Berkman, Harold W(illiam) 1926- CANR-44
Earlier sketches in CA 53-56, CANR-5, 21
Berkman, Richard Lyle 1946- CANR-1
Earlier sketch in CA 45-48
Berkman, Sue 1936- 45-48
Berkman, Ted
See Berkman, Edward O(scar)
Berkoff, Steven 1937- CANR-72
Earlier sketch in CA 104
See also CLC 56
Berkove, Lawrence Ivan 1930- CANR-36
Earlier sketch in CA 106
Berkovits, Eliezer 1908- CANR-37
Earlier sketches in CA 1-4R, CANR-2
Berkovitz, Irving H(erbert) 1924- 57-60
Berkovitz, Jay R. 1951- 134
Berkow, Ira 1940- 97-100
Berkowitz, Bernard 1909- .... AITN 1
Berkowitz, David Sandler 1913- 33-36R
Berkowitz, Freda Pastor 1910- CAP-1
Earlier sketch in CA 9-10
See also SATA 12
Berkowitz, Gerald M(artin) 1942- 110
Berkowitz, Leonard 1926- 125
Berkowitz, Luci 1938- 33-36R

Berkowitz, Marvin 1938- CANR-30
Earlier sketch in CA 29-32R
Berkowitz, Monroe 1919- 130
Berkowitz, Morris Ira 1931- 53-56
Berkowitz, Pearl H(enriette) 1921- 21-24R
Berkowitz, Peter 1959- 151
Berkowitz, Sol 1922- CANR-1
Earlier sketch in CA 45-48
Berkowitz, William R(obby) 1939- CANR-43
Earlier sketch in CA 112
Berkson, Bill 1939- CANR-49
Earlier sketches in CA 21-24R, CANR-9, 24
Berkson, William Koller 1944- 102
Berkus, Clara Widess 1909- 146
See also SATA 78
Berlak, Harold 1932- 33-36R
Berlan, Kathryn Hook 1946- 146
See also SATA 78
Berland, Alwyn 1920- 125
Berland, Theodore 1929- CANR-18
Earlier sketches in CA 5-8R, CANR-2
Berlanstein, Lenard R(ussell) 1947- 69-72
Berlant, Anthony 1941- Brief entry 112
Berlant, Tony
See Berlant, Anthony
Berle, Adolf A(ugustus), Jr. 1895-1971 ..... CAP-2
Obituary 29-32R
Earlier sketch in CA 23-24
Berle, Beatrice Bishop 1902-1993 114
Obituary 141
Berle, Gustav 1920-1996 140
Obituary 153
Berle, Milton 1908- 77-80
See also AITN 1
Berleant, Arnold 1932- 29-32R
Berler, Beatrice (Adele) 1915- 139
Berlfein, Judy Reiss 1958- 147
See also SATA 79
Berlin, Ellin (Mackay) 1904(?)-1988 65-68
Obituary 126
Berlin, Ira 1941- CANR-56
Earlier sketch in CA 101
Berlin, Irving 1888-1989 108
Obituary 129
Berlin, Irving N. 1917- CANR-13
Earlier sketch in CA 21-24R
Berlin, Isaiah 1909-1997 85-88
Obituary 162
Berlin, Jean V. 1962- 150
Berlin, Lucia 1936- .... DLB 130
Berlin, Michael J(oseph) 1938- 69-72
Berlin, Normand 1931- 57-60
Berlin, Richard Emmett 1894(?)-1986 Obituary . 118
Berlin, Sven 1911- CANR-15
Earlier sketch in CA 85-88
Berlind, Bruce 1926- 33-36R
Berliner, Don 1930- CANR-45
Earlier sketches in CA 105, CANR-21
See also SATA 33
Berliner, Franz 1930- CANR-29
Earlier sketches in CA 29-32R, CANR-12
See also SATA 13
Berliner, Herman A(lbert) 1944- 77-80
Berliner, Janet 1939- 163
Berliner, Joseph S(cholom) 1921- 69-72
Berliner, Michael S. 1938- 153
Berlitz, Charles (L. Frambach) 1914- CANR-9
Earlier sketch in CA 5-8R
Interview in CANR-9
See also SATA 32
Berl-Lee, Maria
See Lee, Maria Berl
Berloni, William 1956- 77-80
Berlow, Alan 1950- 159
Berlye, Milton K. 1915- CANR-31
Earlier sketch in CA 49-52
Berlyne, D(aniel) E(llis) 1924- 13-16R
Berman, Arthur I(rwin) 1925- 97-100
Berman, Bennett H(erbert) 1927- 105
Berman, Bruce D(avid) 1944- 41-44R
Berman, Claire 1936- CANR-10
Earlier sketch in CA 25-28R
Berman, Connie 1949- 93-96
Berman, Daniel M(arvin) 1928-1967 ...... CANR-1
Earlier sketch in CA 1-4R
Berman, David 1942- 147
Earlier sketch in CA 135
Berman, Ed 1941- 106
Berman, Edgar F(rank) 1915(?)-1987 97-100
Obituary 124
Berman, Eleanor 1934- 85-88
Berman, Emile Zola 1902-1981 Obituary 104
Berman, Harold Joseph 1918- CANR-15
Earlier sketch in CA 89-92
Berman, Jeffrey 1945- 134
Berman, Larry 1951- CANR-48
Earlier sketch in CA 93-96
Berman, Linda 1948- 113
See also SATA 38
Berman, Louise M(arguerite) 1928- 21-24R
Berman, Marshall 1940- 29-32R
Berman, Milton 1924- 1-4R
Berman, Mitch 1956- 136
Berman, Morris 1944- 139
Berman, Morton 1924- CANR-2
Earlier sketch in CA 5-8R
Berman, Morton M(ayer) 1899-1986 Obituary .. 118
Berman, Paul (Lawrence) 1949- 110
See also SATA 66
Berman, Ronald 1930- 13-16R
Berman, Ruth 1958- 156
Berman, Sanford 1933- 37-40R
Berman, Simeon M(oses) 1935- 49-52
Berman, Susan 1945- CANR-17
Earlier sketch in CA 65-68
Berman, William C(arl) 1932- 41-44R
Bermange, Barry 1933- CANR-67
Earlier sketch in CA 57-60
Bermann, Sandra L/ 1947- 156
Bermant, Chaim (Icyk) 1929- CANR-57
Earlier sketches in CA 57-60, CANR-6, 31
See also CLC 40
Bermant, Gordon 1936- 120
Bermel, Albert (Cyril) 1927- CANR-11
Earlier sketch in CA 69-72
Bermeo, Nancy 1951- 131
Bermingham, Ann 1948- 128
Bermont, Hubert Ingram 1924- CANR-5
Earlier sketch in CA 9-12R
Bermosk, Loretta Sue 1918- CANR-3
Earlier sketch in CA 9-12R
Bern, Maria Rasputin Soloviev
1900(?)-1977 Obituary 73-76
Bern, Victoria
See Fisher, M(ary) F(rances) K(ennedy)
Berna, Paul 1910-1994 73-76
Obituary 143
See also CLR 19
See also SATA 15
See also SATA-Obit 78
Bernabei, Alfio 1941- CANR-14
Earlier sketch in CA 77-80
Bernadette
See Watts, (Anna) Bernadette
Bernal (y Garcia y Pimentel), Ignacio 1910-1992 ...
CANR-5
Obituary 136
Earlier sketch in CA 9-12R
Bernal, J(ohn) D(esmond) 1901-1971 97-100
Obituary 33-36R
Bernal, Judith F. 1939- 57-60
Bernal, Martin Gardiner 1937- 104
Bernal, Vicente J. 1888-1915 .... DLB 82
See also HW
Bernanos, (Paul Louis) Georges 1888-1948 130
Brief entry 104
See also DLB 72
See also TCLC 3
Bernanos, Michel 1924-1964 167
Bernard, Andre 1956- 132
Bernard, April 1956- 131
See also CLC 59
Bernard, Bruce 152
See also SATA 78
Bernard, George 1939- 73-76
Bernard, George I. 1949- .... SATA 39
Bernard, Guy
See Barber, Stephen Guy
Bernard, H(arvey) Russell 1940- 41-44R
Bernard, Harold W. 1908- CANR-4
Earlier sketch in CA 1-4R
Bernard, Harry 1898-1979 145
See also DLB 92
Bernard, Hugh Y(ancey), Jr. 1919- 21-24R
Bernard, Jack F. 1930- 21-24R
Bernard, Jacqueline (de Sieyes) 1921-1983 . 21-24R
Obituary 117
See also SATA 8
See also SATA-Obit 45
Bernard, Jami 1956- 152
Bernard, Jay
See Forbes, Colin
Bernard, Jean-Jacques
1888-1972 Obituary 37-40R
Bernard, Jessie (Shirley) 1903- 151
Bernard, John 1756-1828 .... DLB 37
Bernard, Kenneth 1930- CANR-67
Earlier sketch in CA 41-44R
Bernard, Kenneth A(nderson) 1906- 29-32R
Bernard, Laureat J(oseph) 1922- 25-28R
Bernard, Marley
See Graves, Susan B(ernard)
Bernard, Nelson T(ed), Jr. 1925- 123
Bernard, Oliver 1925- 13-16R
Bernard, Paul Peter 1929- 89-92
Bernard, Richard Marion 1948- 105
Bernard, Robert
See Martin, Robert Bernard
Bernard, Sidney 1918- 29-32R
Bernard, Stefan
See Baumrin, Bernard H(erbert)
Bernard, Thelma Rene 1940- 57-60
Bernard, Thomas J(oseph) 1945- 138
Bernard, Will 1915- 93-96
Bernard, William Spencer 1907-1986 Obituary . 118
Bernardin, Joseph (Louis Cardinal) 1928-1996 .. 160
Bernardini, Joe 1937- 136
Bernardo, Aldo S(isto) 1920- CANR-4
Earlier sketch in CA 1-4R
Bernardo, James V. 1913- 17-20R
Bernardo, Stephanie
See Johns, Stephanie Bernardo
Bernard of Chartres 1060(?)-1124(?) ...... DLB 115
Bernards, Neal 1963- .... SATA 71
Bernari, Carlo 1909-1992 .... DLB 177
Bernarn, Terrave
See Burnett, David (Benjamin Foley)
Bernau, George 1945- 127
Bernauer, George F. 1941- 29-32R
Bernays, Anne
See Kaplan, Anne Bernays
Bernays, Edward L. 1891-1995 .... 17-20R
Obituary 147
Bernazza, Ann Marie
See Haase, Ann Marie Bernazza
Bernbach, William 1911-1982 Obituary 108
Bernd, Joseph Laurence 1923- 17-20R
Berndt, Ronald Murray 1916- CANR-19
Earlier sketches in CA 5-8R, CANR-3
Berndt, Walter 1900(?)-1979 Obituary 89-92
Berndtson, Arthur 1913- 108
Berne, Eric (Lennard) 1910-1970 .... CANR-4
Obituary 25-28R
Earlier sketch in CA 5-8R
See also MTCW 1
Berne, Leo
See Davies, L(eslie) P(urnell)
Berne, Patricia H(iggins) 1934- 110
Berne, Stanley 1923- CANR-72
Earlier sketches in CA 45-48, CANR-1
Berne, Victoria
See Fisher, M(ary) F(rances) K(ennedy)
Berner, Carl Walter 1902- CANR-37
Earlier sketch in CA 49-52
Berner, Jeff 1940- 89-92
Berner, Robert A(rbuckle) 1935- 155
Berner, Robert B(arry) 1940- 41-44R
Bernert, Eleanor H.
See Sheldon, Eleanor Bernert
Bernet, Michael M. 1930- 25-28R
Bernhard, Durga T. 1961- .... SATA 80
Bernhard, Emery 1950- .... SATA 80
Bernhard, Sandra 1955(?)- 137
Bernhard, Thomas 1931-1989 .... CANR-57
Obituary 127
Earlier sketches in CA 85-88, CANR-32
See also CLC 3, 32, 61
See also DLB 85, 124
See also MTCW 1
Bernhard, Virginia Purington 1937- 112
Bernhardsen, Bris
See Bernhardsen, (Einar) Christian (Rosenvinge)
Bernhardsen, (Einar) Christian (Rosenvinge)
1923- 29-32R
Bernhardt, Clyde Edric Barron
1905-1986 Obituary 119
Bernhardt, Frances Simonsen 1932- 103
Bernhardt, Karl S. 1901-1967 .... CAP-1
Earlier sketch in CA 13-14
Bernhardt, Sarah (Henriette Rosine)
1844-1923 157
See also TCLC 75
Bernhardt, William 1960- 151
Bernheim, Emmanuelle 1955- 148
Bernheim, Evelyne 1935- 21-24R
Bernheim, Kayla F. 1946- 108
Bernheim, Marc 1924- 21-24R
Bernheimer, Charles 1942- 134
Bernheimer, Martin 1936- 69-72
Bernier, Alexis 1956- 130
Bernier, Olivier 1941- CANR-30
Earlier sketch in CA 105
Bernikow, Louise 1940- 132
Berninghausen, David K(nipe) 1916- 111
Berns, Julie 1899(?)-1983 Obituary 111
Berns, Walter (Fred) 1919- CANR-24
Earlier sketch in CA 101
Bernstam, Mikhail S. 1943- 130
Bernstein, Alvin H(owell) 1939- 89-92
Bernstein, Anne C(arolyn) 1944- 105
Bernstein, Arnold 1920- 29-32R
Bernstein, Barton J(annen) 1936- 37-40R
Bernstein, Basil (Bernard) 1924- Brief entry 119
Bernstein, Blanche 1912-1993 110
Obituary 140
Bernstein, Burton 1932- CANR-21
Earlier sketches in CA 1-4R, CANR-4
Bernstein, Carl 1944- 81-84
See also AITN 1
Bernstein, Charles 1950- 129
See also CAAS 24
See also DLB 169
Bernstein, Daryl (Evan) 1976- 149
See also SATA 81
Bernstein, David 1915(?)-1974 Obituary 53-56
Bernstein, Dorothy Lewis 1914-1988 161
Bernstein, Douglas A. 1942- 45-48
Bernstein, Gail Lee 1939- 115
Bernstein, Gerry 1927- 105
Bernstein, Harry 1909- CANR-1
Earlier sketch in CA 1-4R
Bernstein, Hilda 1915- 130
Bernstein, Hillel 1892(?)-1977 Obituary 69-72
Bernstein, Irving 1916- Brief entry 114
Bernstein, J(erome) S(traus) 1936- 25-28R
Bernstein, Jacob 1946- 104
Bernstein, Jane 1949- 104
Bernstein, Jared 1955- 145
Bernstein, Jeremy 1929- CANR-27
Earlier sketch in CA 13-16R
Bernstein, Jerry Marx 1908-1969 .... CAP-2
Earlier sketch in CA 25-28
Bernstein, Joanne E(ckstein) 1943- CANR-29
Earlier sketches in CA 77-80, CANR-13
See also SATA 15
Bernstein, John Andrew 1944- 124
Bernstein, Joseph M(ilton)
1908(?)-1975 Obituary 57-60
Bernstein, Leonard 1918-1990 .... CANR-21
Obituary 132
Earlier sketches in CA 1-4R, CANR-2
Bernstein, Lewis 1915- 33-36R
Bernstein, Margery 1933- 57-60
Bernstein, Marilyn 1929- 21-24R
Bernstein, Marver H(illel) 1919- CANR-2
Earlier sketch in CA 1-4R
Bernstein, Marvin David 1923- 45-48
Bernstein, Merton C(lay) 1923- 17-20R
Bernstein, Michael Andre 1947- CANR-51
Earlier sketch in CA 124
Bernstein, Mordechai 1893-1983 Obituary 109
Bernstein, Morey 1919- 21-24R
Bernstein, Norman R. 1927- CANR-13
Earlier sketch in CA 33-36R
Bernstein, Paula 1944- 125
Bernstein, Philip S(idney) 1901-1985 .... CANR-28
Earlier sketch in CA 49-52
Bernstein, Richard J(acob) 1932- Brief entry ... 113
Bernstein, Richard K. 1934- 105
Bernstein, Seymour CANR-26
Earlier sketch in CA 109
Bernstein, Theodore M(enline) 1904-1979 . CANR-3
Earlier sketch in CA 1-4R
See also SATA 12
See also SATA-Obit 27
Bernstein, Thomas P(aul) 1937- 113
Bernstein, Walter 1919- 106
Interview in 106
Bernzweig, Eli P. 1927- CANR-26
Earlier sketch in CA 29-32R
Berofsky, Bernard 1935- 89-92
Berque, Jacques Augustin 1910-1995 85-88
Obituary 149
Berquist, Goodwin F(auntleroy) 1930- 21-24R
Berrellez, Robert 1920(?)-1985 Obituary 116
Berrett, Delwyn G(reen) 1935- 128
Berrett, LaMar C(ecil) 1926- 53-56
Berri, Claude 1934- 152
Berrian, Albert H. 1925- 37-40R
Berriault, Gina 1926- CANR-66
Brief entry 116
Earlier sketch in CA 129
See also CLC 54, 109
See also DLB 130
See also SSC 30
Berridge, Celia 1943- CANR-28
Earlier sketch in CA 110
Berridge, Elizabeth 1921- CANR-6
Earlier sketch in CA 57-60
Berridge, G. R. 1947- 146
Berridge, P(ercy) S(tuart) A(ttwood) 1901- .. 29-32R
Berrien, Edith Heal
See Heal, Edith
Berrien, F. Kenneth 1909-1971 .... CANR-1
Obituary 29-32R
Earlier sketch in CA 1-4R
Berrigan, Daniel 1921- CANR-43
Earlier sketches in CA 33-36R, CANR-11
See also CAAS 1
See also CLC 4
See also DLB 5
Berrigan, Edmund Joseph Michael, Jr. 1934-1983 ..
CANR-14
Obituary 110
Earlier sketch in CA 61-64
See also Berrigan, Ted
Berrigan, Philip (Francis) 1923- CANR-11
Earlier sketch in CA 13-16R
Interview in CANR-11
Berrigan, Ted
See Berrigan, Edmund Joseph Michael, Jr.
See also CLC 37
See also DLB 5, 169
Berrill, Jacquelyn (Batsel) 1905- 17-20R
See also SATA 12
Berrill, N(orman) J(ohn) 1903- 17-20R
Berrington, Hugh B(ayard) 1928- 49-52
Berrington, John
See Brownjohn, Alan
Berrisford, Judith Mary
See Lewis, Judith Mary
Berry, Adrian M(ichael) 1937- CANR-25
Earlier sketches in CA 57-60, CANR-9
Berry, B. J.
See Berry, Barbara J.
Berry, Barbara J. 1937- 33-36R
See also SATA 7
Berry, Boyd M(cCulloch) 1939- 69-72
Berry, Brewton 1901- CANR-3
Earlier sketch in CA 1-4R
Berry, Brian J(oe) L(obley) 1934- CANR-5
Earlier sketch in CA 13-16R
Berry, Bryan 1930-1955 Brief entry 112
Berry, Burton Yost 1901- 85-88
Berry, Carole 167
Berry, Charles Edward Anderson 1931- 115
See also Berry, Chuck
Berry, Charles H. 1930- 69-72
Berry, Chuck
See Berry, Charles Edward Anderson
See also CLC 17
Berry, Cicely 1926- 93-96
Berry, D. C.
See Berry, David (Chapman)
Berry, David (Ronald) 1942- 29-32R
Berry, David (Chapman) 1942- CANR-27
Earlier sketch in CA 45-48
Berry, David (Adams) 1943- 108
Berry, Don (George) 1932- CANR-67
Earlier sketch in CA 106
Berry, Edmund G(rindlay) 1915- 1-4R
Berry, Edward I. 1940- 57-60
Berry, Eliot 1949- 139
Berry, (Julia) Elizabeth 1920- 21-24R
Berry, Erick
See Best, (Evangel) Allena Champlin
Berry, Faith 1939- 133
Berry, Francis 1915- CANR-5
Earlier sketch in CA 5-8R
Berry, Frederic Aroyce, Jr.
1906-1978 Obituary 77-80
Berry, Geoffrey 1912-1988 Obituary 124
Berry, Helen
See Rowland, D(onald) S(ydney)
Berry, Henry 1926- 85-88
Berry, Herbert 1922- CANR-29
Earlier sketch in CA 111
Berry, I. William 1934- CANR-25
Earlier sketch in CA 105
Berry, J. Bill 1945- 137
Berry, J. W. 1939- 149
Berry, Jack 1918- 37-40R
Berry, Jake 1959- .... CAAS 24

Berry, James 1925- ... 135
See also CLR 22
See also JRDA
See also SATA 67
Berry, James 1932- ... 21-24R
Berry, James Gomer 1883-1968 Obituary ... 89-92
Berry, Jane Cobb 1915(?)-1979 Obituary ... 85-88
See also SATA-Obit 22
Berry, Jason 1949- ... 45-48
Berry, Jim
See Berry, James
Berry, Jim 1946- ... 107
Berry, Jo(ycelyn) 1933- ... CANR-18
Earlier sketch in CA 102
Berry, John Nichols (III) 1933- Brief entry ... 113
Berry, John Stevens 1938- ... 132
Berry, Jonas
See Ashbery, John (Lawrence)
Berry, Joy
See Berry, Joy Wilt
Berry, Joy Wilt 1944- ... 134
See also SATA 58
See also SATA-Brief 46
Berry, Katherine F(iske) 1877-(?) ... CAP-2
Earlier sketch in CA 17-18
Berry, Leonidas Harris 1902-1995 ... 159
Berry, Lloyd E(ason) 1935-1977 ... 13-16R
Obituary ... 133
Berry, Lynn 1948- ... 61-64
Berry, Mary Frances 1938- ... CANR-14
Earlier sketch in CA 33-36R
See also BW 1
Berry, Nicholas O(rlando) 1936- ... 93-96
Berry, Paul 1919- ... 102
Berry, R(obert) J(ames) 1934- ... 121
Berry, R(alph) M(arion) 1947- ... 128
Berry, Roland (Brian) 1951- ... 93-96
Berry, Ron(ald Anthony) 1920-1997 ... 25-28R
Obituary ... 159
Berry, Rynn 1945- ... 164
Berry, Scyld 1954- ... 136
Berry, Sister Mary Virginia
1908(?)-1987 Obituary ... 122
Berry, Stephen Ames 1947- ... 118
Berry, Thomas 1914- ... 21-24R
Berry, Thomas Edwin 1930- ... 102
Berry, Thomas Elliott 1917- ... 33-36R
Berry, Wallace Taft 1928- ... CANR-8
Earlier sketch in CA 17-20R
Berry, Wendell (Erdman) 1934- ... CANR-50
Earlier sketch in CA 73-76
See also AITN 1
See also CLC 4, 6, 8, 27, 46
See also DAM POET
See also DLB 5, 6
Berry, William D(avid) 1926- ... 73-76
See also SATA 14
Berry, William Turner 1888- ... CAP-2
Earlier sketch in CA 23-24
Berryman, Charles (Beecher) 1939- ... 112
Berryman, Jack W. 1947- ... 143
Berryman, James Thomas
1902-1971 Obituary ... 93-96
Berryman, Jim
See Berryman, James Thomas
Berryman, John 1914-1972 ... CANR-35
Obituary ... 33-36R
Earlier sketches in CAP-1, CA 13-16
See also CABS 2
See also CDALB 1941-1968
See also CLC 1, 2, 3, 4, 6, 8, 10, 13, 25, 62
See also DAM POET
See also DLB 48
See also MTCW 1
Berryman, Phillip E. 1938- ... 158
Bers, Lipman 1914-1993 ... 159
Bersani, Leo 1931- ... CANR-5
Earlier sketch in CA 53-56
Berscheid, Ellen 1936- ... 25-28R
Bershadsky, Luba 1916-1986 ... 131
Obituary ... 162
Bershtel, Sara 1947- ... 139
Bersianik, Louky 1930- ... DLB 60
Berson, Harold 1926- ... 33-36R
See also SATA 4
Berson, Lenora E. 1926- ... 93-96
Berssenbrugge, Mei-mei 1947- ... 104
Berst, Charles A(shton) 1932- ... 41-44R
Berst, Jesse ... 116
Bert, Norman A(llen) 1942- ... 149
Bertcher, Harvey (Joseph) 1929- ... 85-88
Bertelson, David (Earl) 1934- ... 21-24R
Bertematti, Richard 1971- ... 160
Berthelet, Thomas fl. 1524(?)-1555 ... DLB 170
Berthelot, Helen Washburn 1904-1996 ... 159
Berthelot, Joseph A. 1927- ... 21-24R
Berthoff, Ann (Rhys) E(vans) 1924- ... CANR-65
Earlier sketch in CA 129
Berthoff, Rowland (Tappan) 1921- ... 33-36R
Berthoff, Warner (Bement) 1925- ... CANR-2
Earlier sketch in CA 5-8R
Berthold, Dennis (Alfred) 1942- ... 117
Berthold, Margot 1922- ... CANR-48
Earlier sketch in CA 73-76
Berthold, Mary Paddock 1909- ... 53-56
Berthold, Richard M(artin) 1946- ... 131
Bertholf, Diana 1946- ... 115
Berthoud, Jacques (Alexandre) 1935- ... CANR-10
Earlier sketch in CA 17-20R
Berthoud, Roger 1934- ... 128
Berthrong, Donald J(ohn) 1922- ... 81-84
Berthrong, Evelyn Nagai
See Nagai Berthrong, Evelyn
Bertin, Charles-Francois
See Berlitz, Charles (L. Frambach)
Bertin, Jack
See Bertin, John
Bertin, John 1904-1963 Obituary ... 116
Bertin, Leonard M. 1918- ... 13-16R
Bertling, Tom 1956- ... 167
Bertman, Stephen (Samuel) 1937- ... 45-48
Berto, Giuseppe 1914-1978 ... DLB 177
Bertocci, Peter A(nthony) 1910- ... 17-20R
Bertolet, Paul
See McLaughlin, Frank
Bertolino, James 1942- ... CANR-17
Earlier sketches in CA 45-48, CANR-1
Bertolucci, Attilio 1911- ... DLB 128
Bertolucci, Bernardo 1940- ... 106
See also CLC 16
Berton, Dick
See Roquebrune, Robert (Laroque) de
Berton, Peter (Alexander Menquez) 1922- ... 77-80
Berton, Pierre (Francis Demarigny) 1920- ...
CANR-56
Earlier sketches in CA 1-4R, CANR-2
See also CLC 104
See also DLB 68
See also SATA 99
Berton, Ralph 1910-1993 ... 49-52
Obituary ... 143
Bertonasco, Marc F(rancis) 1934- ... 89-92
Bertram, Anthony 1897-1978 Obituary ... 104
Bertram, (George) Colin (Lawder) 1911- ... 13-16R
Bertram, James Munro 1910- ... 65-68
Bertram, Jean De Sales ... CANR-12
Earlier sketch in CA 45-48
Bertram, Noel
See Fanthorpe, R(obert) Lionel
Bertram-Cox, Jean De Sales
See Bertram, Jean De Sales
Bertrand, Alvin L(ee) 1918- ... CANR-30
Earlier sketch in CA 45-48
Bertrand, Cecile 1953- ... 143
See also SATA 76
Bertrand, Charles
See Carter, David C(harles)
Bertrand, Lewis 1897(?)-1974 Obituary ... 53-56
Bertrand, Lynne 1963- ... 149
See also SATA 81
Bertrand, Marsha 1950- ... 162
Bertrand, Michel 1944- ... CANR-13
Earlier sketch in CA 73-76
Bertrand, Sandra 1943- ... 130
Berube, Maurice R. 1933- ... 139
Berwanger, Eugene H. ... 21-24R
Berwick, Jean Shepherd 1929- ... 9-12R
Berwick, Keith (Bennet) 1928- ... 33-36R
Besag, Frank P. 1935- ... 119
Besanceney, Paul H. 1924- ... 45-48
Besancon, Alain J. 1932- ... 130
Besant, Annie (Wood) 1847-1933 Brief entry ... 105
See also TCLC 9
Besant, SirWalter 1836-1901 ... DLB 135, 190
Besas, Peter 1933- ... 77-80
Beschloss, Michael R(ichard) 1955- ... CANR-42
Earlier sketch in CA 101
Besdine, Matthew 1905(?)-1986 Obituary ... 120
Beshers, James M(onahan) 1931- ... 1-4R
Beshoar, Barron B(enedict) 1907- ... 69-72
Beskow, Bo 1906- ... CANR-11
Earlier sketch in CA 61-64
Beskow, Elsa (Maartman) 1874-1953 ... 135
See also CLR 17
See also MAICYA
See also SATA 20
Besner, Hilda F. 1950- ... 157
Besner, Neil K. 1949- ... 137
Besoyan, Rick 1924(?)-1970 Obituary ... 25-28R
Bess, Clayton 1944-
See Locke, Robert
See also CLR 39
Bessborough, Tenth Earl of
See Ponsonby, Frederick Edward Neuflize
Bessel, Richard 1948- ... 145
Bessell, Peter (Joseph) 1921-1985 Obituary ... 117
Besser, Gretchen R(ous) 1928- ... CANR-14
Earlier sketch in CA 41-44R
Besser, Joe 1907-1988 Obituary ... 124
Besser, Milton 1911-1976 ... 69-72
Obituary ... 65-68
Bessette, Gerard 1920- ... CANR-14
Earlier sketch in CA 37-40R
See also DLB 53
bes-Shahar, Eluki 1956- ... 168
Bessie, Alvah 1904-1985 ... CANR-2
Obituary ... 116
Earlier sketch in CA 5-8R
See also CLC 23
See also DLB 26
Bessie, Constance Ernst
1918(?)-1985 Obituary ... 115
Bessinger, Jess B(alsor), Jr. 1921-1994 ... 13-16R
Obituary ... 146
Bessom, Malcolm E(ugene) 1940-1988 ... 57-60
Obituary ... 126
Besson, Luc 1959- ... 152
Bessy, Maurice 1910-1993 ... CANR-26
Obituary ... 143
Earlier sketches in CA 65-68, CANR-10
Best, Adam
See Carmichael, William Edward
Best, Alan C. G. 1939- ... 111
Best, (Evangel) Allena Champlin 1892-1974 ...
CANR-71
Earlier sketches in CAP-2, CA 25-28
See also SATA 2
See also SATA-Obit 25
Best, Charles H(erbert) 1899-1978 ... CANR-29
Obituary ... 103
Earlier sketch in CA 45-48
Best, D. Minor
See Best, Don(ald M.)
Best, Don(ald M.) 1949- ... 147
Best, Ernest 1917- ... CANR-35
Earlier sketch in CA 114
Best, Ernest E. 1919- ... 112
Best, G. F. A.
See Best, Geoffrey (Francis Andrew)
Best, Gary A(llen) 1939- ... 33-36R
Best, Gary Dean 1936- ... CANR-40
Earlier sketch in CA 117
Best, Geoffrey (Francis Andrew) 1928- ... 142
Brief entry ... 114
Best, (Oswald) Herbert 1894-1980 ... CANR-71
Earlier sketches in CAP-2, CA 25-28
See also SATA 2
Best, Hugh 1920- ... 115
Best, James J(oseph) 1938- ... 37-40R
Best, Joel 1946- ... 139
Best, John Wesley 1909- ... 17-20R
Best, Judith A. 1938- ... 69-72
Best, Marc
See Lemieux, Marc
Best, Marshall A. 1901(?)-1982 Obituary ... 106
Best, Michael R. ... 37-40R
Best, Nicholas 1948- ... 138
Best, Otto F(erdinand) 1929- ... CANR-25
Earlier sketch in CA 69-72
Best, Rayleigh Breton Amis 1905- ... CAP-1
Earlier sketch in CA 13-16
Best, Robin Hewitson (?)-1984 Obituary ... 113
Best, Thomas W(aring) 1939- ... 29-32R
Bestall, A(lfred) E(dmeades) 1892-1986 ... 155
Obituary ... 119
See also SATA 97
See also SATA-Obit 48
Beste, R(aymond) Vernon 1908- ... CANR-4
Earlier sketch in CA 1-4R
Bester, Alfred 1913-1987 ... CANR-36
Obituary ... 123
Earlier sketches in CA 13-16R, CANR-12
See also DLB 8
See also MTCW 1
Besterman, Theodore (Deocatus Nathaniel)
1904-1976 Obituary ... 105
See also DLB 201
Bestic, Alan Kent 1922- ... 13-16R
Beston, Henry 1888-1968 Obituary ... 25-28R
Bestor, Arthur (Eugene, Jr.) 1908- ... CANR-6
Earlier sketch in CA 1-4R
Bestor, Dorothy K(och) ... 118
Bestul, Thomas H(oward) 1942- ... 53-56
Bestuzhev, Aleksandr Aleksandrovich
1797-1837 ... DLB 198
Bestuzhev, Nikolai Aleksandrovich 1791-1855 . DLB 198
Betancourt, Jeanne 1941- ... CANR-67
Earlier sketches in CA 49-52, CANR-31
See also SATA 55, 96
See also SATA-Brief 43
Betancourt, John (Gregory) 1963- ... 149
Betancourt, Romulo 1908-1981 ... 104
Beteille, Andre 1934- ... 130
Betenson, Lula Parker 1884-1980 ... 61-64
Obituary ... 133
Beth
See Winship, Elizabeth
Beth, Loren Peter 1920- ... CANR-3
Earlier sketch in CA 1-4R
Beth, Mary
See Miller, Mary Beth
Betham-Edwards, Matilda Barbara 1836-1919 . DLB 174
Bethancourt, T. Ernesto
See Paisley, Tom
See also AAYA 20
See also CLR 3
See also SATA 11
Bethe, H. A.
See Bethe, Hans Albrecht
Bethe, Hans A.
See Bethe, Hans Albrecht
Bethe, Hans Albrecht 1906- Brief entry ... 115
Bethea, J. D.
See Bethea, James D.
Bethea, James D. 1933(?)-1990 Obituary ... 130
Bethel, Dell 1929- ... CANR-26
Earlier sketch in CA 29-32R
See also SATA 52
Bethel, Elizabeth Rauh 1942- ... 106
Bethel, Paul D(uane) 1919- ... 25-28R
Bethell, Jean (Frankenberry) 1922- ... CANR-3
Earlier sketch in CA 9-12R
See also SATA 8
Bethell, Nicholas William 1938- ... CANR-1
Earlier sketch in CA 45-48
Bethell, Tom 1940- ... 77-80
Bethers, Ray 1902- ... CAP-1
Earlier sketch in CA 11-12
See also SATA 6
Bethge, Eberhard 1909- ... 85-88
Bethlen, T. D.
See Silverberg, Robert
Bethmann, Erich Waldemar 1904-1993 ... CAP-2
Obituary ... 141
Earlier sketch in CA 23-24
Bethune, J. G.
See Ellis, Edward S(ylvester)
Bethune, J. H.
See Ellis, Edward S(ylvester)
Bethurum, F(rances) Dorothy 1897- ... CAP-2
Earlier sketch in CA 17-18
Beti, Mongo
See Biyidi, Alexandre
See also BLC 1
See also CLC 27
See also DAM MULT
Betjeman, John 1906-1984 ... CANR-56
Obituary ... 112
Earlier sketches in CA 9-12R, CANR-33
See also CDBLB 1945-1960
See also CLC 2, 6, 10, 34, 43
See also DAB
See also DAM MST, POET
See also DLB 20
See also DLBY 84
See also MTCW 1
Betjeman, Penelope Chetwode
See Chetwode, Penelope
Betocchi, Carlo 1899- ... CANR-4
Earlier sketch in CA 9-12R
See also DLB 128
Betsko, Kathleen
See Yale, Kathleen Betsko
Bett, Walter R(eginald) 1903- ... CAP-1
Earlier sketch in CA 13-14
Bettarini, Mariella 1942- ... 156
See also DLB 128
Bettelheim, Bruno 1903-1990 ... CANR-61
Obituary ... 131
Earlier sketches in CA 81-84, CANR-23
See also CLC 79
See also MTCW 1
Bettelheim, Charles 1913- ... CANR-13
Earlier sketch in CA 73-76
Bettelheim, Frederick A(braham) 1923- ... 49-52
Betten, Neil B. 1939- ... 105
Bettenbender, John (I.) 1921-1988 Obituary ... 125
Bettenson, Henry (Scowcroft) 1908- ... 13-16R
Betteridge, Anne
See Potter, Margaret (Newman)
Betteridge, Don
See Newman, Bernard (Charles)
Betteridge, H(arold) T(homas) 1910- ... 5-8R
Bettersworth, John K(nox) 1909- ... CANR-2
Earlier sketch in CA 5-8R
Bettey, J(oseph) H(arold) 1932- ... 130
Betti, Liliana 1939- ... 101
Betti, Ugo 1892-1953 ... 155
Brief entry ... 104
See also TCLC 5
Bettina
See Ehrlich, Bettina Bauer
Bettini, Maurizio 1947- ... 139
Bettis, Joseph Dabney 1936- ... 33-36R
Bettmann, Otto Ludwig 1903-1998 ... 17-20R
Obituary ... 167
See also SATA 46
Betts, Charles L(ancaster), Jr. 1908- ... 101
Betts, Clive 1943- ... 153
Betts, Donni 1948- ... CANR-5
Earlier sketch in CA 53-56
Betts, Doris (Waugh) 1932- ... CANR-66
Earlier sketches in CA 13-16R, CANR-9
Interview in ... CANR-9
See also CLC 3, 6, 28
See also DLBY 82
Betts, Emmett Albert 1903- ... 33-36R
Betts, George 1944- ... CANR-2
Earlier sketch in CA 45-48
Betts, Glynne Robinson 1934- ... 105
Betts, James
See Haynes, Betsy
Betts, John (Edward) 1939- ... 106
Betts, Raymond F. 1925- ... CANR-3
Earlier sketch in CA 1-4R
Betts, Richard K(evin) 1947- ... CANR-40
Earlier sketches in CA 85-88, CANR-16
Betts, William W(ilson), Jr. 1926- ... 33-36R
Betty, L(ewis) Stafford 1942- ... CANR-42
Earlier sketch in CA 118
Betz, Betty 1920- ... 1-4R
Betz, Eva Kelly 1897-1968 ... CAP-1
Earlier sketch in CA 11-12
See also SATA 10
Betz, Hans Dieter 1931- ... CANR-41
Earlier sketches in CA 53-56, CANR-4, 19
Beuf, Ann H(ill) 1939- ... 85-88
Beum, Robert (Lawrence) 1929- ... 9-12R
Beurdeley, Michel 1911- ... CANR-30
Earlier sketch in CA 49-52
Beutel, William Charles 1930- ... 101
Beuttler, Edward Ivan Oakley ... 73-76
Beuve-Mery, Hubert 1902-1989 Obituary ... 129
Bevan, Alistair
See Roberts, Keith (John Kingston)
Bevan, Aneurin 1897-1960 Obituary ... 106
Bevan, Bryan 1913- ... 13-16R
Bevan, E. Dean 1938- ... 33-36R
Bevan, Gloria (Isabel) ... CANR-59
Brief entry ... 117
Earlier sketch in CA 134
Bevan, Jack 1920- ... 13-16R
Bevan, James (Stuart) 1930- ... 106
Bevan, Tom 1868-193(?) ... YABC 2
Bevenot, Maurice 1897-1980 Obituary ... 105
Beveridge, Albert J. 1862-1927 ... DLB 17
Beveridge, Andrew A(lan) 1945- ... 93-96
Beveridge, George David, Jr. 1922-1987 ... 102
Obituary ... 121
Beveridge, Oscar Maltman 1913- ... 9-12R
Beveridge, William (Henry) 1879-1963 Obituary 112
Beveridge, William (Ian Beardmore) 1908- ... 106
Beverley, Jo 1947- ... 166
Beverley, Mary Frances 1925- ... 120
Beverley, Robert 1673(?)-1722 ... DLB 24, 30
BeVier, Michael J(udson) ... 97-100

Bevilacqua, Alberto 1934- CANR-26
Earlier sketch in CA 29-32R
See also DLB 196
Bevington, David M(artin) 1931- CANR-3
Earlier sketch in CA 1-4R
Bevington, Helen (Smith) 1906- CANR-69
Earlier sketch in CA 13-16R
Bevington, Louisa Sarah 1845-1895 ...... DLB 199
Bevis, Em Olivia 1932- CANR-1
Earlier sketch in CA 49-52
Bevis, H(erbert) U(rlin) 1902- CAP-2
Earlier sketch in CA 29-32
Bevis, James
See Cumberland, Marten
Bevis, William W. 1941- 153
Bevlin, Marjorie Elliott 1917- 9-12R
Bewes, Richard 1934- CANR-20
Earlier sketch in CA 102
Bewick, Thomas 1753-1828 .... SATA 16
Bewkes, Eugene Garrett 1895- 5-8R
Bewley, Charles Henry 1888- 5-8R
Bewley, Christina (Mary Erskine) 1924- 129
Bewley, Marius 1918-1973 .... CANR-3
Obituary 41-44R
Earlier sketch in CA 5-8R
Bey, Isabelle
See Bosticco, (Isabel Lucy) Mary
Bey, Pilaff
See Douglas, (George) Norman
Beye, Charles Rowan 1930- 93-96
Beyea, Basil 1910- 61-64
Beyer, (Richard) Andrew 1943- CANR-11
Earlier sketch in CA 69-72
Beyer, Audrey White 1916- CANR-72
Earlier sketch in CA 13-16R
See also SATA 9
Beyer, Edvard (Freydar) 1920- 121
Brief entry 116
Beyer, Evelyn M. 1907- CAP-2
Earlier sketch in CA 25-28
Beyer, Glenn H. 1913-1969 .... CANR-2
Earlier sketch in CA 1-4R
Beyer, Paul J. III 1950- .... SATA 74
Beyer, Robert 1913(?)-1978 Obituary 77-80
Beyer, Steven L(arsen) 1943- 123
Beyer, Werner William 1911- 9-12R
Beyerchen, Alan 1945- 81-84
Beyerhaus, Peter (Paul Johannes) 1929- . CANR-38
Earlier sketches in CA 93-96, CANR-16
Beyerlin, Walter W(ilhelm) 1929- 124
Beyers, Charlotte K(empner) 1931- 85-88
Beyfus, Drusilla 1927- 107
Beyle, Hank
See Buchanan, James David
Beyle, Thad L. 1934- 37-40R
Beynon, Huw 1942- 107
Beynon, John
See Harris, John (Wyndham Parkes Lucas) Beynon
Beytagh, Gonville (Aubie) ffrench
See ffrench-Beytagh, Gonville (Aubie)
Bezencon, Jacqueline (Buxcel) 1924- ..... SATA 48
Bezilla, Michael 1950- 111
Bezio, May Rowland (?)-1977 Obituary 69-72
Bezruchka, Stephen (Anthony) 1943- 107
Bhabra, H(argurchet) S(ingh) 1955- 145
Bhagat, G(oberdhan) 1928- 29-32R
Bhagavatula, Murty S. 1921- 29-32R
Bhagwati, Jagdish N. 1934- 17-20R
Bhajan, Yogi
See Yogiji, Harbhajan Singh Khalsa
Bhaktivedanta Swami, A. C.
See Prabhupada, A. C. Bhaktivedanta
Bhala, Raj K. 1962- 151
Bhana, Surendra 1939- 57-60
Bharath, Ramachandran 1935- 148
Bharati, Agehananda 1923-1991 .... CANR-4
Obituary 134
Earlier sketch in CA 1-4R
Bhardwaj, Surinder Mohan 1934- 45-48
Bharti, Ma Satya 1942- 102
Bhatia, Hans Raj 1904-1979 53-56
Obituary 133
Bhatia, Jamunadevi 1919- CANR-45
Earlier sketch in CA 101
See also Edwards, June
and Forrester, Helen
Bhatia, June
See Bhatia, Jamunadevi
Bhatia, Krishan 1926(?)-1974 Obituary 53-56
Bhatnagar, Joti 1935- 41-44R
Bhatt, Jagdish J(eyshanker) 1939- CANR-31
Earlier sketches in CA 77-80, CANR-14
Bhatt, Sujata 1956- 153
Bhattacharji, Sukumari 1921- 33-36R
Bhattacharya, Bhabani 1906- CANR-9
Earlier sketch in CA 5-8R
Bhattacharya, Nalinaksha 1949- 163
Bhave, Vinoba 1895-1982 Obituary 108
Bhide, Amar 1955- 130
Bhote, Keki R. 1925- 142
Bhutto, Benazir 1953- 131
Bhutto, Zulfikar Ali 1928-1979 .... CANR-11
Earlier sketch in CA 53-56
Biaggini, Adriana Ivancich
1930(?)-1983 Obituary 109
Biagi, Shirley 1944- CANR-32
Earlier sketches in CA 85-88, CANR-15
Bial, Morrison David 1917- 61-64
See also SATA 62
Bial, Raymond 1948- 143
See also SATA 76
Biale, Rachel 1952- 167
See also SATA 99
Bialik, Chaim Nachman 1873-1934 .... TCLC 25
Bialk, Elisa
See Krautter, Elisa (Bialk)
Bialostocki, Jan 1921- CANR-48
Earlier sketch in CA 104
Bialostosky, Don H(oward) 1947- 120
Bianchi, Engene C(arl) 1930- 25-28R
Bianchi, Hombert 1912(?)-1980 Obituary ... 97-100
Bianchi, John 1947- .... SATA 91
Bianchi, Robert S(teven) 1943- CANR-54
Earlier sketch in CA 109
See also SATA 92
Bianco, Anthony 1953- 134
Bianco, Lucien Andre 1930- CANR-15
Earlier sketch in CA 85-88
Bianco, Margery (Williams) 1881-1944 155
Brief entry 109
See also CLR 19
See also DLB 160
See also MAICYA
See also SATA 15
Bianco, Pamela 1906- 85-88
See also SATA 28
Biancolli, Louis Leopold 1907-1992 65-68
Obituary 139
Bianconi, Lorenzo (Gennaro) 1946- 134
Biasin, Gian-Paolo 1933- 25-28R
Bibaud, Adele 1854-1941 .... DLB 92
Bibaud, Michel 1782-1857 .... DLB 99
Bibb, (David) Porter III 1937- 65-68
Bibby, Cyril 1914- CANR-7
Earlier sketch in CA 13-16R
Bibby, John F(ranklin) 1934- CANR-35
Earlier sketch in CA 45-48
Bibby, T(homas) Geoffrey 1917- CANR-4
Earlier sketch in CA 1-4R
Bibby, Violet 1908- 102
See also SATA 24
Bibee, John 1954- 112
Biberman, Edward 1904-1986 49-52
Obituary 118
Biberman, Herbert 1900-1971 .... CAP-1
Obituary 33-36R
Earlier sketch in CA 13-16
Bibesco, Marthe Lucie 1887-1973 .... CANR-68
Obituary 49-52
Earlier sketch in CA 93-96
Bible, Charles 1937- 69-72
See also SATA 13
Bibo, Bobette
See Gugliotta, Bobette
Bicanic, Rudolf 1905-1968 85-88
Bicat, Tony 1945- 130
Bicchieri, Cristina 1950- 149
Bice, Clare 1909-1976 .... SATA 22
Bicerano, Jozef 1952- 145
Bichakjian, Bernard H. 1937- 136
Bichler, Joyce 1954- 107
Bichsel, Peter 1935- CANR-71
Earlier sketch in CA 81-84
See also DLB 75
Bick, Edgar Milton 1902-1978 Obituary 77-80
Bickel, Alexander M(ordecai) 1924-1974 .. CANR-1
Obituary 53-56
Earlier sketch in CA 1-4R
Bickelhaupt, David L(ynn) 1929- 69-72
Bickerman, Elias J(oseph) 1897-1981 ... CANR-20
Obituary 104
Earlier sketch in CA 25-28R
Bickers, Richard (Leslie) Townshend 1917- ....
CANR-42
Earlier sketches in CA 45-48, CANR-1
Bickerstaff, Isaac
See Swift, Jonathan
Bickersteth, Geoffrey Langdale
1884-1974 Obituary 49-52
Bickerton, Derek 1926- CANR-66
Earlier sketch in CA 61-64
Bicket, Zenas J(ohan) 1932- 37-40R
Bickford, David 1953- 133
Bickford, Elwood Dale 1927- 61-64
Bickford, Lawrence 1921- 147
Bickford-Smith, Vivian 1955- 150
Bickham, Jack M(iles) 1930-1997 .... CANR-23
Obituary 159
Earlier sketches in CA 5-8R, CANR-8
Bickle, Judith Brundrett (?)-(?) CANR-66
Earlier sketches in CAP-1, CA 13-14
Bickley, R(obert) Bruce, Jr. 1942- CANR-9
Earlier sketch in CA 65-68
Bickman, Martin 1945- 104
Bida, Constantine 1916- CANR-13
Earlier sketch in CA 61-64
Bidart, Frank 1939- 140
See also CLC 33
Bidault, Georges 1899-1983 Obituary 109
Biddiss, Michael Denis 1942- CANR-4
Earlier sketch in CA 53-56
Biddle, Arthur W(illiam) 1936- 45-48
Biddle, Bruce J(esse) 1928- CANR-7
Earlier sketch in CA 17-20R
Biddle, Francis (Beverley) 1886-1968 .... 5-8R
Obituary 103
Biddle, George 1885-1973 Obituary 45-48
Biddle, Katherine Garrison Chapin 1890-1977 .....
CANR-5
Obituary 73-76
Earlier sketch in CA 5-8R
Biddle, Marcia McKenna 1931- 112
Biddle, Perry H(arvey), Jr. 1932- 57-60
Biddle, Phillips R. 1933- 37-40R
Biddle, Wayne 1948- 106
Biddle, William W(ishart) 1900-(?) CAP-2
Earlier sketch in CA 17-18
Biderman, Albert D. 1923- CANR-47
Earlier sketches in CA 5-8R, CANR-8, 23
Biderman, Sol 1936- 25-28R
Bidermann, Jacob 1577-1639 .... DLB 164
Bidney, David 1908- 9-12R
Bidney, Martin 1943- 165
Bidwell, Dafne (Mary) 1929- 97-100
Bidwell, Marjory Elizabeth Sarah 77-80
Bidwell, Percy W(ells) 1888-(?) CAP-1
Earlier sketch in CA 9-10
Bidwell, Walter Hilliard 1798-1881 .... DLB 79
Biebel, David B. 1949- 125
Bieber, Konrad (F.) 1916- 141
Bieber, Margarete 1879-1978 .... CANR-11
Obituary 77-80
Earlier sketch in CA 17-20R
Biebuyck, Daniel P. 1925- CANR-30
Earlier sketches in CA 25-28R, CANR-11
Bieder, Robert E. 1938- 152
Biederman, Marcia (Squire) 1949- 127
Biegel, John E(dward) 1925- 49-52
Biegel, Paul 1925- CANR-32
Earlier sketches in CA 77-80, CANR-14
See also CLR 27
See also SAAS 18
See also SATA 16, 79
Biehler, Robert F(rederick) 1927- 37-40R
Biel, Steven 1960- 159
Bielby, Cliff 1919-1984 Obituary 111
Bielby, Denise D. 155
Bielenberg, Christabel 1909- 29-32R
Bieler, Ludwig 1906-1981 .... 5-8R
Obituary 103
Bielfield, Sidney 1904(?)-1984 Obituary 112
Bielski, Feliks
See Giergielewicz, Mieczyslaw F.
Bielyi, Sergei
See Hollo, Anselm
Bieman, Elizabeth 1923- 137
Biemiller, Carl L(udwig), Jr.) 1912-1979 121
Obituary 106
See also SATA 40
See also SATA-Obit 21
Biemiller, Ruth Cobbett 1914- 37-40R
Bien, David Duckworth 1930- 5-8R
Bien, Joseph Julius 1936- CANR-31
Earlier sketches in CA 53-56, CANR-5
Bien, Peter (Adolph) 1930- 9-12R
Bienek, Horst 1930- 73-76
See also CLC 7, 11
See also DLB 75
Bienen, Henry Samuel 1939- 81-84
Bienenfeld, Florence L(ucille) 1929- CANR-23
Earlier sketch in CA 106
See also SATA 39
Bienes, Nicholas Peter 1952- 136
Bienstock, Mike
See Bienstock, Myron Joseph
Bienstock, Myron Joseph 1922- 9-12R
Bienvenu, Bernard J(efferson) 1925- 53-56
Bienvenu, Marcelle 1945- 154
Bienvenu, Richard (Thomas) 1936- 61-64
Bier, Jesse 1925- CANR-3
Earlier sketch in CA 5-8R
Bier, William C(hristian) 1911-1980 .... 33-36R
Obituary 97-100
Bierbaum, Margaret 1916- 33-36R
Bierbaum, Otto Julius 1865-1910 .... DLB 66
Bierbrier, M(orris) L(eonard) 1947- CANR-60
Earlier sketch in CA 128
Bierce, Ambrose (Gwinett) 1842-1914(?) 139
Brief entry 104
See also CDALB 1865-1917
See also DA
See also DAC
See also DAM MST
See also DLB 11, 12, 23, 71, 74, 186
See also SSC 9
See also TCLC 1, 7, 44
See also WLC
Bierce, Jane 1940- 144
Bierds, Linda 1945- 147
Bierhorst, John (William) 1936- CANR-51
Earlier sketches in CA 33-36R, CANR-13, 28
See also SAAS 10
See also SATA 6, 91
Bieri, Arthur Peter 1931- 61-64
Bierley, Paul E(dmund) 1926- CANR-13
Earlier sketch in CA 77-80
Bierman, Arthur K(almer) 1923- 85-88
Bierman, Harold, Jr. 1924- CANR-9
Earlier sketch in CA 17-20R
Bierman, Judah 1917- 114
Bierman, Mildred Thornton 1912- 5-8R
Bierman, Stanley M(elvin) 1935- 106
Biermann, Lillian
See Wehmeyer, Lillian (Mabel) Biermann
Biermann, Pieke 1950- 153
Biermann, Wolf 1936- 81-84
Biernatzki, William E(ugene) 1931- CANR-6
Earlier sketch in CA 57-60
Biers, William Richard 1938- CANR-23
Earlier sketch in CA 106
Bierstedt, Robert 1913- CANR-2
Earlier sketch in CA 1-4R
Biery, William (Richard) 1933- 57-60
Biesanz, Mavis Hiltunen 1919- 33-36R
Biesanz, Richard 1944- 112
Biesel, David B. 1931- 140
Biesterveld, Betty Parsons 1923- CANR-1
Earlier sketch in CA 1-4R
Bietenholz, Peter G(erard) 1933- 101
Biezanek, Anne C(ampbell) 1927- 17-20R
Bigard, (Albany) Barney (Leon) 1906-1980 134
Bigart, Robert James 1947- 33-36R
Bigelow, Brian J(ohn) 1947- 164
Bigelow, Donald N(evius) 1918- 41-44R
Bigelow, Gordon Ellsworth 1919- 110
Bigelow, Karl Worth 1898-1980 Obituary ... 97-100
Bigelow, Kathryn 1952- 139
Bigelow, Marybelle S(chmidt) 1923- 25-28R
Bigelow, Robert P(ratt) 1927- Brief entry 118
Bigelow, Robert Sydney 1918- 102
Bigelow, William F. 1879-1966 .... DLB 91
Biger, Gideon 1945- 144
Bigg, Patricia Nina 1932- 102
Bigge, Morris L. 1908- 9-12R
Biggers, Earl Derr 1884-1933 153
Brief entry 108
See also TCLC 65
Biggers, John Thomas 1924- CANR-2
Earlier sketch in CA 1-4R
Biggle, Lloyd, Jr. 1923- CANR-35
Earlier sketches in CA 13-16R, CANR-5, 20
See also DLB 8
See also SATA 65
Biggs, Anselm G. 1914- 33-36R
Biggs, Bradley 1920- 124
Biggs, Cheryl 1947- 152
Biggs, Cheryln
See Biggs, Cheryl
Biggs, Chester M(axwell), Jr. 1921- 151
Biggs, John, Jr. 1895-1979 Obituary 85-88
Biggs, John B(urville) 1934- CANR-6
Earlier sketch in CA 57-60
Biggs, Margaret Key 1933- 114
Biggs, Mary 1944- 137
Biggs, (Marvin) Mouzon, Jr. 1941- 111
Biggs, Peter
See Rimel, Duane (Weldon)
Biggs-Davison, John (Alec) 1918- 13-16R
Bigiaretti, Libero 1906- CANR-12
Earlier sketch in CA 29-32R
See also DLB 177
Bigland, Eileen 1898-1970 .... DLB 195
Bigler, Vernon 1922- 21-24R
Bignell, Alan 1928- 103
Bigo, Pierre (Auguste) 1906- 136
Bigongiari, Piero 1914- .... DLB 128
Bigsby, C(hristopher) W(illiam) E(dgar) 1941- ......
CANR-55
Earlier sketches in CA 25-28R, CANR-11, 28
Bihalji-Merin, Oto 1904- CANR-34
Earlier sketches in CA 81-84, CANR-15
Bihler, Penny 1940- 77-80
Bijou, Sidney W(illiam) 1908- CANR-14
Earlier sketch in CA 37-40R
Bikel, Theodore 1924- CANR-1
Earlier sketch in CA 1-4R
Bikerstaff, Isaac John 1733-1808 .... DLB 89
Bikkie, James A(ndrew) 1929- 53-56
Biklen, Douglas Paul 1945- CANR-15
Earlier sketch in CA 85-88
Bilal, Abdel W(ahab) 1970- .... SATA 92
Bilas, Richard A(llen) 1935- 53-56
Bilbo, Queenie (?)-1972 Obituary 37-40R
Bilbow, Antony 1932- 25-28R
Bilby, Joanne Stroud 1927- 149
Bilderback, Dean Loy 1932- 97-100
Bilderback, Diane E(lizabeth) 1951- 110
Bileck, Marvin 1920- .... SATA 40
Bilek, Arthur J(ohn) 1929- 115
Bilgrami, Akeel 1950- 140
Bilibin, Ivan (Iakolevich) 1876-1942 .... SATA 61
Bilich, Marion Yellin 1949- 114
Bilinsky, Yaroslav 1932- 13-16R
Bilkey, Warren J(oseph) 1920- 29-32R
Bill, Alfred Hoyt 1879-1964 .... CANR-68
Earlier sketch in CA 107
See also SATA 44
Bill, J(ohn) Brent 1951- 117
Bill, James A(lban) 1939- Brief entry 114
Bill, Valentine T. 13-16R
Billam, Rosemary 1952- 123
See also SATA 61
Bill-Belotserkovsky, Vladimir Naumovich
1884-1970 Obituary 104
Billcliffe, Roger (George) 1946- 132
Biller, Henry B(urt) 1940- CANR-35
Earlier sketch in CA 114
Billetdoux, Francois (Paul) 1927- 21-24R
Billetdoux, Raphaele 1951- 159
Billett, Roy O(ren) 1891- 13-16R
Billias, George Athan 1919- CANR-6
Earlier sketch in CA 9-12R
Billig, Otto 1910- 129
Billing, Graham (John) 1936- 147
Billinger, Richard 1890-1965 .... DLB 124
Billings, Charlene W(interer) 1941- CANR-49
Earlier sketches in CA 107, CANR-24
See also SATA 41
Billings, Charles E(dward) 1938- 121
Billings, Evelyn L(ivingston) 1918- 112
Billings, Ezra
See Halla, (Robert) Chris(tian)
Billings, Hammatt 1818-1874 .... DLB 188
Billings, Harold (Wayne) 1931- 25-28R
Billings, John Shaw 1898-1975 Obituary 104
See also DLB 137
Billings, Josh
See Shaw, Henry Wheeler
Billings, Peggy 1928- 25-28R
Billings, Richard N. 1930- 103
Billings, Robert 1949- 113
Billings, Warren M(artin) 1940- 61-64
Billings, William Dwight 1910- 113
Billingsley, Andrew 1926- 57-60
See also BW 2
Billingsley, Edward Baxter 1910- CAP-2
Earlier sketch in CA 25-28
Billington, David P(erkins) 1927- 134
Billington, Dora May 1890-1968 .... CAP-1
Earlier sketch in CA 13-14

Billington, Elizabeth T(hain) 101
See also SATA 50
See also SATA-Brief 43
Billington, James H(adley) 1929- 132
Brief entry 117
Interview in 132
Billington, John
See Beaver, (Jack) Patrick
Billington, Joy 1931- 77-80
Billington, Michael 1939- 102
Billington, Monroe Lee 1928- 21-24R
Billington, (Lady) Rachel (Mary) 1942- CANR-44
Earlier sketch in CA 33-36R
See also AITN 2
See also CLC 43
Billington, Ray Allen 1903-1981 .... CANR-5
Obituary 103
Earlier sketch in CA 1-4R
Billington, Raymond John 1930- 110
Billmeyer, Fred Wallace, Jr. 1919- 85-88
Billout, Guy (Rene) 1941- CANR-26
Earlier sketch in CA 85-88
See also CLR 33
See also SATA 10
Bills, Robert E(dgar) 1916- 107
Bills, Scott L(aurence) 1948- CANR-38
Earlier sketch in CA 112
Billson, Anne 1954- CANR-72
Earlier sketch in CA 143
Billson, Janet Mancini 1941- 152
Billy, Andre 1882-1971 Obituary 29-32R
Bilow, Pat 1941- 106
Bilsland, Bilko
See Bilsland, E(rnest) C(harles)
Bilsland, E(rnest) C(harles) 1931- 69-72
Bilson, Geoffrey 1938-1987 160
See also SATA 99
Bimler, Richard William 1940- CANR-14
Earlier sketch in CA 41-44R
Bina, Cyrus 1946- 140
Binch, Caroline 1947- .... SATA 81
Binchy, Maeve 1940- CANR-50
Brief entry 127
Earlier sketch in CA 134
Interview in 134
See also BEST 90:1
See also DAM POP
Binder, Aaron 1927- 57-60
Binder, David 1931- 65-68
Binder, Eando
See Binder, Otto O(scar)
Binder, Frederick M(elvin) 1931- 29-32R
Binder, Frederick Moore 1920- 41-44R
Binder, Leonard 1927- 61-64
Binder, Otto O(scar) 1911-1974 .... CANR-3
Obituary 53-56
Earlier sketch in CA 1-4R
Binder, Pearl
See Elwyn-Jones, Pearl Binder
Binding, Rudolf G. 1867-1938 .... DLB 66
Bindman, Arthur J(oseph) 1925- 45-48
Bindoff, Stanley Thomas 1908-1980 73-76
Obituary 102
Bindra, Dalbir 1922-1980 122
Obituary 117
Binford, Chapman H(unter)
1900-1990 Obituary 130
Binford, Lewis R(oberts) 1930- 131
Bing, Elisabeth D. 1914- CANR-11
Earlier sketch in CA 69-72
Bing, Leon 1950- 140
Bing, Rudolf 1902-1997 89-92
Obituary 161
Bingaman, Ron 1936- 61-64
Binger, Carl A(lfred) L(anning) 1889-1976 73-76
Obituary 65-68
Binger, Norman H(enry) 1914- 33-36R
Binger, Walter 1888(?)-1979 Obituary 85-88
Bingham, (George) Barry, Jr. 1933- 106
Interview in 106
Bingham, (George) Barry 1906-1988 Obituary .. 126
See also DLB 127
Bingham, Caleb 1757-1817 .... DLB 42
Bingham, Caroline 1938- CANR-10
Earlier sketch in CA 57-60
Bingham, Carson
See Cassiday, Bruce (Bingham)
Bingham, Charlotte (Mary Therese) 1942- ....
CANR-11
Earlier sketch in CA 105
Bingham, David A(ndrew) 1926- 53-56
Bingham, Edwin R(alph) 1920- CANR-2
Earlier sketch in CA 5-8R
Bingham, Evangeline M(arguerite) L(adys) (Elliot)
1899- 65-68
Bingham, Jane Marie 1941- 104
Bingham, John (Michael Ward) 1908-1988 ....
CANR-58
Obituary 126
Earlier sketches in CA 21-24R, CANR-11
Bingham, Jonathan Brewster 1914-1986 .... 33-36R
Obituary 119
Bingham, June Rossbach 1919- 1-4R
Bingham, M(orley) P(aul) 1918- 49-52
Bingham, Madeleine (Mary Ebel) 1912-1988 ....
CANR-11
Obituary 124
Earlier sketch in CA 13-16R
Bingham, Melinda 1950- 119
Bingham, Mindy
See Bingham, Melinda
Bingham, Richard D. 1937- 112
Bingham, Robert C(harles) 1927- 21-24R
Bingham, Robert E. 1925- 29-32R
Bingham, Robert Kamerer
1925(?)-1982 Obituary 107
Bingham, Sallie 1937- CANR-55
Earlier sketches in CA 1-4R, CANR-18
Bingham, Sam(uel A.) 1944- 161
See also SATA 96
Bingham, Woodbridge 1901-1986 Obituary 119
Bingley, Clive (Hamilton) 1936- 17-20R
Bingley, D. E.
See Bingley, David Ernest
Bingley, David Ernest 1920-1985 .... CANR-42
Earlier sketches in CA 45-48, CANR-2, 18
Bingley, Margaret (Jane) 1947- .... SATA 72
Binham, Philip Frank 1924- 107
Binion, Rudolph 1927- CANR-4
Earlier sketch in CA 1-4R
bin Ishak, Yusof
See Ishak, Yusof bin
Binkley, Anne
See Rand, Ann (Binkley)
Binkley, Luther John 1925- 5-8R
Binkley, Olin T(rivette) 1908- 45-48
Binkley, Thomas (Eden) 1931- 135
Binkley, William Campbell 1889-1970 107
Obituary 104
Binnie, G(eoffrey) M(orse) 1908-1989 Obituary . 128
Binns, Archie (Fred) 1899-1971 .... CANR-71
Obituary 133
Earlier sketch in CA 73-76
Binns, Brigit (Legere) 161
Binns, J(ames) W(allace) 1940- 53-56
Binski, Paul 1956- 150
Binstock, R. C. 1958- CANR-63
Earlier sketch in CA 138
Binswanger, Ludwig 1881-1966 Obituary 107
Binyon, Claude 1905-1978 Obituary 77-80
Binyon, Helen 1904-1982(?) Obituary 111
Binyon, (Robert) Laurence 1869-1943 Brief
entry 115
See also DLB 19
Binyon, Michael (Roger) 1944- 142
Binyon, T(imothy) J(ohn) 1936- CANR-28
Earlier sketch in CA 111
See also CLC 34
Binzen, Bill
See Binzen, William
See also SATA 24
Binzen, Peter (Husted) 1922- 136
Binzen, William 89-92
See also Binzen, Bill
Biossat, Bruce 1910(?)-1974 Obituary 104
Biot, Francois 1923- 13-16R
Biow, Milton H. 1882(?)-1976 Obituary 65-68
Bioy Casares, Adolfo 1914-1984 .... CANR-66
Earlier sketches in CA 29-32R, CANR-19, 43
See also CLC 4, 8, 13, 88
See also DAM MULT
See also DLB 113
See also HLC
See also HW
See also MTCW 1
See also SSC 17
Biram, Brenda 1930(?)-1984 Obituary 112
Birch, Alison Wyrley 1922- 85-88
Birch, Anthony H(arold) 1924- CANR-5
Earlier sketch in CA 13-16R
Birch, Beryl Bender 1942- 147
Birch, Bruce C(harles) 1941- CANR-51
Earlier sketches in CA 65-68, CANR-10, 25
Birch, Carol 1951- 127
Birch, Charles
See Birch, L(ouis) C(harles)
Birch, Cyril 1925- 85-88
Birch, Daniel R(ichard) 1937- 101
Birch, David (W.) 1913- 155
See also SATA 89
Birch, David L. 1937- CANR-16
Earlier sketch in CA 25-28R
Birch, Herbert G. 1918-1973 Obituary 41-44R
Birch, L(ouis) C(harles) 1918- CANR-44
Earlier sketch in CA 120
Birch, Leo Bedrich 1902- 33-36R
Birch, Lionel (?)-1982(?) Obituary 106
Birch, (Evelyn) Nigel (Chetwode)
1906-1981 Obituary 108
Birch, Reginald B(athurst) 1856-1943 .... SATA 19
Birch, William G(arry) 1909- 53-56
Birchall, Ian H(arry) 1939- 97-100
Bircham, Deric Neale 1934- 89-92
Birchman, David 1949- .... SATA 72
Birchmore, Daniel A. 1951- 156
See also SATA 92
Birchmore, Fred (Agnew) 1911- 153
Bird, Al
See Mandel, Leon
Bird, Anthony (Cole) 1917-1974 .... 13-16R
Obituary 135
Bird, Brandon
See Evans, George Bird
and Evans, Kay Harris
Bird, Carmel 1940- 128
Bird, Caroline 1915- CANR-11
Earlier sketch in CA 17-20R
Bird, Cordwainer
See Ellison, Harlan (Jay)
Bird, David 1926(?)-1987 Obituary 121
Bird, Dennis L(eslie) 1930- 116
Bird, Dorothy Maywood 1899- CAP-1
Earlier sketch in CA 17-18
Bird, E(lzy) J(ay) 1911- .... SATA 58
Bird, Florence (Bayard) 1908- 97-100
Bird, George L(loyd) 1900- CANR-2
Earlier sketch in CA 5-8R
Bird, Harrison K. 1910- 85-88
Bird, Isabella L(ucy) 1831-1904
See Bishop, Isabella Lucy (Bird)
See also DLB 166
Bird, James Harold 1923- 102
Bird, John 1941- 130
Bird, Junius Bouton 1907-1982 Obituary 106
Bird, (Cyril) Kenneth 1887-1965 .... CAP-1
Earlier sketch in CA 13-14
Bird, Larry (Joe) 1956- 139
Bird, Lewis P(enhall) 1933- CANR-17
Earlier sketch in CA 97-100
Bird, Patricia Amy 1941- CANR-46
Earlier sketches in CA 61-64, CANR-7, 22
Bird, Richard (Miller) 1938- CANR-19
Earlier sketches in CA 9-12R, CANR-4
Bird, Robert Montgomery 1806-1854 .... DLB 202
Bird, Sarah McCabe 1949- CANR-44
Earlier sketch in CA 111
Bird, Veronica 1932- 112
Bird, Vivian 1910- 102
Bird, W(illiam) Ernest 1890- CAP-1
Earlier sketch in CA 19-20
Bird, Wendell R(aleigh) CANR-40
Earlier sketch in CA 116
Bird, Will R. 1891- 13-16R
Bird, William 1889-1963 Obituary 112
See also DLB 4
See also DLBD 15
Birdsall, Steve 1944- CANR-7
Earlier sketch in CA 53-56
Birdsell, Joseph B(enjamin) 1908- 119
Birdsell, Sandra 1942- 130
Birdseye, Clarence (Frank) 1886-1956 Brief
entry 122
Birdseye, Tom 1951- 133
See also SATA 66, 98
Birdwell, Russell (Juarez) 1903-1977 Obituary . 107
Birdwhistell, Ray L. 1918- 45-48
Birdzell, L(uther) E(arle), Jr. 1916- 154
Bireley, Robert 1933- 137
Birenbaum, Arnold 1939- 108
Birenbaum, Barbara 1941- 136
See also SATA 65
Birenbaum, Halina 1929- 45-48
Birenbaum, Harvey 1936- 109
Birenbaum, William M. 1923- 29-32R
Birimisa, George 1924- CANR-67
Earlier sketch in CA 89-92
Interview in 89-92
Birkenhead, Lord
See Smith, Frederick Winston Furneaux
Birkenmayer, Sigmund Stanley 1923- 21-24R
Birkerts, Sven 1951- 133
Brief entry 128
Interview in 133
See also CAAS 29
Birket-Smith, Kaj 1893- CAP-1
Earlier sketch in CA 13-14
Birkhoff, George David 1884-1944 155
Birkin, Andrew (Timothy) 1945- CANR-41
Earlier sketch in CA 97-100
Birkin, Charles (Lloyd) 1907-1986 .... CANR-72
Earlier sketch in CA 69-72
Birkley, Marilyn 1916- 41-44R
Birkner, Michael John 1950- 125
Birkos, Alexander S(ergei) 1936- 25-28R
Birks, Tony 1937- CANR-50
Earlier sketches in CA 69-72, CANR-12
Birksted-Breen, Dana 1946- 102
Birla, Ghanshyamdas 1894-1983 Obituary 110
Birla, Lakshminiwas N. 1909- CAP-1
Earlier sketch in CA 13-14
Birley, Anthony (Richard) 1937- 129
Birley, Anthony R.
See Birley, Anthony (Richard)
Birley, Julia (Davies) 1928- 13-16R
Birley, Robert 1903-1982 Obituary 110
Birmelin, Blair T. 1939- 117
Birmingham, David (Bevis) 1938- 17-20R
Birmingham, F(rederic) A(lexander) 1911-1982 ....
CANR-11
Obituary 107
Earlier sketch in CA 17-20R
Birmingham, Frances A(therton) 1920- 17-20R
Birmingham, John 1951- 45-48
Birmingham, Lloyd P(aul) 1924- .... SATA 12, 83
Birmingham, Maisie 1914- 101
Birmingham, Stephen 1932- CANR-20
Earlier sketches in CA 49-52, CANR-2
Interview in CANR-20
See also AITN 1
Birmingham, Walter (Barr) 1913- 17-20R
Birn, Donald S. 1937- 132
Birn, Randi (Marie) 1935- 73-76
Birn, Raymond Francis 1935- 102
Birnbach, Lisa 1957- 164
Birnbach, Martin 1929- 1-4R
Birnbaum, Eleazar 1929- 37-40R
Birnbaum, Louis 1909-1983 125
Birnbaum, Milton 1919- 33-36R
Birnbaum, Norman 1926- CANR-5
Earlier sketch in CA 53-56
Birnbaum, Philip 1904-1988 .... CANR-1
Obituary 125
Earlier sketch in CA 49-52
Birnbaum, Phyllis 1945- 102
Birnbaum, Solomon Asher 1891-1989 Obituary . 130
Birnbaum, Stephen (Norman) 1937-1991 129
Obituary 136
Brief entry 125
Birnbaum, Steve
See Birnbaum, Stephen (Norman)
Birnberg, Thomas B.
See Brooks, Thomas
Birne, Henry 1921- 17-20R
Birney, Alice L(otvin) 1938- 33-36R
Birney, Betty G. 1947- 165
See also SATA 98
Birney, (Alfred) Earle 1904-1995 .... CANR-20
Earlier sketches in CA 1-4R, CANR-5
See also CLC 1, 4, 6, 11
See also DAC
See also DAM MST, POET
See also DLB 88
See also MTCW 1
Birnie, Whittlesey 1945- 97-100
Birnkrant, Arthur 1906(?)-1983 Obituary 108
Biro, B.
See Biro, B(alint) S(tephen)
Biro, B(alint) S(tephen) 1921- CANR-39
Earlier sketches in CA 25-28R, CANR-11
See also Biro, Val
See also MAICYA
See also SATA 67
Biro, Charlotte Slovak 1904- 57-60
Biro, Val
See Biro, B(alint) S(tephen)
See also CLR 28
See also SAAS 13
See also SATA 1
Biro, Yvette 111
Birrell, Anne (Margaret) 130
Birrell, Augustine 1850-1933 .... DLB 98
Birren, Faber 1900- CANR-7
Earlier sketch in CA 13-16R
Birren, James E(mmett) 1918- 17-20R
Birringer, Johannes (H.) 1953- 158
Birse, A(rthur) H(erbert) 1889- CAP-2
Earlier sketch in CA 23-24
Birstein, Ann 1927- CANR-28
Earlier sketch in CA 17-20R
Birt, David 1936- CANR-35
Earlier sketches in CA 73-76, CANR-13
Birtha, Becky 1948- 142
See also BW 2
Biryukov, Nikolai (Ivanovich) 1949- 149
Bischof, Ledford Julius 1914- 9-12R
Bischoff, David F(redrick) 1951- 81-84
Bischoff, F(rederick) A(lexander) 1928- 89-92
Bischoff, Julia Bristol 1909-1970 .... CAP-2
Earlier sketch in CA 21-22
See also SATA 12
Bish, Robert L(ee) 1942- 53-56
Bishai, Wilson B. 1923- 33-36R
Bi Shang-guan
See Shen, Congwen
Bisher, Furman 1918- .... DLB 171
Bisher, James F(urman) 1918- CANR-2
Earlier sketch in CA 5-8R
Bishin, William R(obert) 1939- 61-64
Bishir, John (William) 1933- 41-44R
Bishop, Bonnie 1943- 103
See also SATA 37
Bishop, Claire Huchet 1899(?)-1993 .... CANR-36
Obituary 140
Earlier sketch in CA 73-76
See also MAICYA
See also SATA 14
See also SATA-Obit 74
Bishop, Claudia
See Stanton, Mary
Bishop, Courtney
See Ruemmler, John D(avid)
Bishop, Crawford M. 1885- CAP-2
Earlier sketch in CA 17-18
Bishop, Curtis (Kent) 1912-1967 .... CAP-1
Earlier sketch in CA 11-12
See also SATA 6
Bishop, Donald
See Steward, Samuel M(orris)
Bishop, Donald G. 1907- CANR-3
Earlier sketch in CA 1-4R
Bishop, Donald H(arold) 1920- 105
Bishop, E. Morchard
See Stonor, Oliver
Bishop, Elizabeth 1911-1979 .... CANR-61
Obituary 89-92
Earlier sketches in CA 5-8R, CANR-26
See also CABS 2
See also CDALB 1968-1988
See also CLC 1, 4, 9, 13, 15, 32
See also DA
See also DAC
See also DAM MST, POET
See also DLB 5, 169
See also MTCW 1
See also PC 3
See also SATA-Obit 24
Bishop, Eugene C. 1909-1983 Obituary 109
Bishop, Ferman 1922- 21-24R
Bishop, Gavin 1946- CANR-48
Earlier sketch in CA 121
See also SATA 97
Bishop, George (Victor) 1924- CANR-2
Earlier sketch in CA 49-52
Bishop, George W(esley), Jr. 1910- 13-16R
Bishop, Gordon (Bruce) 1938- 118
Bishop, Ian Benjamin 1927- 106
Bishop, Isabella Bird
See Bishop, Isabella Lucy (Bird)
Bishop, Isabella L.
See Bishop, Isabella Lucy (Bird)
Bishop, Isabella Lucy (Bird) 1831-1904 Brief
entry 123
See also Bird, Isabella L(ucy)
Bishop, James, Jr. 1936- 154
Bishop, James 1929- 97-100
Bishop, James Alonzo 1907-1987 .... CANR-71
Obituary 123
Earlier sketch in CA 17-20R
See also Bishop, Jim
Bishop, Jerry E. 1931- 142

Bishop, Jim
See Bishop, James Alonzo
See also AITN 1, 2
Bishop, John
See Willis, Edward Henry
Bishop, John 1908- ... 65-68
Bishop, John 1935- ... 105
See also CLC 10
Bishop, John L(yman) 1913-1974 ... CAP-2
Earlier sketch in CA 33-36
Bishop, John Melville 1946- ... CANR-13
Earlier sketch in CA 77-80
Bishop, John Peale 1892-1944 ... 155
Brief entry ... 107
See also DLB 4, 9, 45
Bishop, John Wesley 1927- ... 128
Bishop, Jonathan P(eale) 1927- ... 129
Bishop, Joseph W(arren), Jr. 1915-1985 ... 33-36R
Obituary ... 116
Bishop, Leonard 1922- ... CANR-70
Earlier sketch in CA 13-16R
Bishop, Lloyd (Ormond) 1933- ... 114
Bishop, Louis Faugeres 1901(?)-1986 ... 122
Obituary ... 119
Bishop, Martin
See Paine, Lauran (Bosworth)
Bishop, Maurice 1944-1983 ... 123
Obituary ... 111
See also BW 1
Bishop, Maxine H. 1919- ... 25-28R
Bishop, Michael 1945- ... CANR-49
Earlier sketches in CA 61-64, CANR-9
See also CAAS 26
See also AITN 2
Bishop, Morchard
See Stonor, Oliver
Bishop, Morris 1893-1973 ... CANR-6
Obituary ... 45-48
Earlier sketch in CA 1-4R
Bishop, Mrs. J. F.
See Bishop, Isabella Lucy (Bird)
Bishop, Patrick 1952- ... 132
Bishop, Pike
See Obstfeld, Raymond
Bishop, Robert 1938-1991 ... CANR-35
Obituary ... 135
Earlier sketches in CA 81-84, CANR-15
Bishop, Robert Lee 1931- ... 13-16R
Bishop, Ron 1922(?)-1988 Obituary ... 124
Bishop, Susan M. 1921(?)-1970 Obituary ... 104
Bishop, Tania Kroitor 1906- ... CAP-2
Earlier sketch in CA 29-32
Bishop, Thomas W(alter) 1929- ... CANR-18
Earlier sketches in CA 1-4R, CANR-1
Bishop, Tom
See Bishop, Thomas W(alter)
Bishop, W(illiam) Arthur 1923- ... 21-24R
Bishop, Wendy 1953- ... 137
Bishop, William W(arner), Jr. 1906- ... 17-20R
Bishop of Marsland
See Duncan, Ronald
Bishop of Truro
See Leonard, Graham Douglas
Bisignani, J(oseph) D(aniel) 1947- ... CANR-35
Earlier sketch in CA 112
Biskin, Miriam 1920- ... 21-24R
Bismarck, Otto von 1815-1898 ... DLB 129
Bisnow, Mark (C.) 1952- ... 130
Bisque, Anatole
See Bosquet, Alain
Bissell, Claude T(homas) 1916- ... 101
Bissell, Elaine ... 81-84
Bissell, LeClair 1928- ... 133
Bissell, Richard (Pike) 1913-1977 ... CANR-6
Obituary ... 69-72
Earlier sketch in CA 1-4R
Bisset, Donald 1910-1995 ... CANR-51
Earlier sketches in CA 33-36R, CANR-13
See also SATA 7, 86
Bisset, Robert c. 1759-1805 ... DLB 142
Bisset, Ronald 1950- ... 103
Bissett, Bill 1939- ... CANR-15
Earlier sketch in CA 69-72
See also CAAS 19
See also CLC 18
See also DLB 53
See also MTCW 1
See also PC 14
Bissett, Donald J(ohn) 1930- ... 97-100
Bissinger, H(arry) G(erard III) 1954- ... 140
Bisson, Terry (Ballantine) 1942- ... CANR-59
Earlier sketch in CA 127
See also SATA 99
Bisson, Thomas N(oel) 1931- ... 119
Bissoondath, Neil (Devindra) 1955- ... 136
See also DAC
Bissoondoyal, Basdeo 1906- ... CANR-11
Earlier sketch in CA 25-28R
Bisztray, George 1938- ... 106
Bita, Lili
See Zaller, Angelika Bita
Bite, Ben
See Schneck, Stephen
Bitker, Marjorie M(arks) 1901-1990 ... 77-80
Obituary ... 132
Bitov, Andrei (Georgievich) 1937- ... 142
See also CLC 57
Bitsios, Dimitri S. 1915-1984 Obituary ... 111
Bittel, Lester Robert 1918- ... CANR-45
Earlier sketches in CA 13-16R, CANR-6, 21
Bitter, Francis 1902-1967 Obituary ... 113
Bitter, Gary G(len) 1940- ... CANR-31
Earlier sketches in CA 69-72, CANR-14
See also SATA 22
Bittermann, Henry J(ohn) 1904- ... 33-36R
Bittinger, Desmond W(right) 1905- ... 37-40R
Bittinger, Emmert F(oster) 1925- ... 37-40R
Bittker, Boris I(rving) 1916- Brief entry ... 109
Bittle, William E(lmer) 1926- ... 53-56
Bittlinger, Arnold (Georg) 1928- ... CANR-31
Earlier sketch in CA 49-52
Bittner, Donald F(rancis) 1941- ... 122
Bittner, Rosanne 1945- ... 143
Bittner, Vernon (John) 1932- ... 69-72
Bittner, William (Robert) 1921- ... 5-8R
Bitton, Davis 1930- ... CANR-31
Earlier sketches in CA 33-36R, CANR-14
Bitton, Livia Elvira
See Bitton Jackson, Livia E(lvira)
Bitton-Jackson, Livia
See Bitton Jackson, Livia E(lvira)
Bitton Jackson, Livia E(lvira) 1931- ... 130
Biven, W(illiam) Carl 1925- ... 21-24R
Bivins, John 1940- ... 85-88
Bixby, Jay Lewis
See Bixby, Jerome Lewis
Bixby, Jerome Lewis 1923- ... 17-20R
Bixby, Ray Z.
See Tralins, S(andor) Robert
Bixby, William (Courtney) 1920-1986 ... CANR-71
Obituary ... 118
Earlier sketches in CA 1-4R, CANR-6
See also SATA 6
See also SATA-Obit 47
Bixler, Julius Seelye 1894-1985 Obituary ... 115
Bixler, Norma 1905- ... 49-52
Bixler, Paul (Howard) 1899- ... 69-72
Bixler, R(oy) Russell, Jr. 1927- ... 61-64
Biyidi, Alexandre 1932- ... 124
Brief entry ... 114
See also Beti, Mongo
See also BW 1
See also MTCW 1
Bizardel, Yvon 1891- ... 61-64
Bizzarro, Salvatore 1939- ... 53-56
Bizzarro, Tina Waldeier 1950- ... 144
Bizzell, Patricia (Lynn) 1948- ... 139
Bjarkman, Peter C(hristian) 1941- ... 130
Bjarme, Brynjolf
See Ibsen, Henrik (Johan)
Bjerke, Robert Alan 1939- ... 41-44R
Bjerke, Ward (Ollie) 1920- Brief entry ... 108
Bjerre, Jens 1921- ... 9-12R
Bjoerk, Christina 1938- ... 135
See also CLR 22
See also SATA 67, 99
Bjoerneboe, Jens 1920-1976 ... CANR-28
Obituary ... 65-68
Earlier sketch in CA 69-72
Bjoernson, Bjoernstjerne (Martinius)
1832-1910 Brief entry ... 104
See also TCLC 7, 37
Bjorge, Gary J(ohn) 1940- ... 130
Bjork, Christina
See Bjoerk, Christina
Bjork, Daniel W. 1940- ... 143
Bjorkelo, Anders 1947- ... 138
Bjorklund, Lorence F. 1913-1978 ... SATA 35
See also SATA-Brief 32
Bjorn, Thyra Ferre 1905-1975 ... CANR-69
Obituary ... 57-60
Earlier sketches in CA 5-8R, CANR-3
Bjornard, Reidar B(ernhard) 1917- ... 33-36R
Bjorneboe, Jens
See Bjoerneboe, Jens
Bjornson, Richard 1938- ... 77-80
Bjornson, (Kristjan) Val(dimar)
1906-1987 Obituary ... 121
Bjornstad, James 1940- ... 29-32R
Bjorset, Bryniolf
See Beorse, Bryn
Blaazer, David (Paul) 1957- ... 141
Blachford, George 1913- ... 9-12R
Blachly, Frederick (Frank)
1881(?)-1975 Obituary ... 57-60
Blachly, Lou 1889- ... CAP-1
Earlier sketch in CA 13-14
Black, Albert George 1928- ... 45-48
Black, Algernon David 1900-1993 ... CANR-2
Obituary ... 141
Earlier sketch in CA 1-4R
See also SATA 12
See also SATA-Obit 76
Black, Angus 1943- ... 29-32R
Black, Antony 1936- ... 121
Black, Arthur (Raymond) 1943- ... 138
Black, Baxter 1945- ... 147
Black, Betty
See Schwartz, Betty
Black, Bonnie Lee 1945- ... 107
Black, Brady Forrest 1908- ... 102
Black, Campbell 1944- ... CANR-72
Earlier sketch in CA 89-92
Black, Charles
See Black, Charles L(und), Jr.
Black, Charles 1928- ... 132
Black, Charles L(und), Jr. 1915- ... CANR-3
Earlier sketch in CA 1-4R
Black, Clinton V(ane De Brosse) 1918- ... CANR-30
Earlier sketch in CA 102
Black, Creed C(arter) 1925- ... 73-76
Black, Cyril Edwin 1915-1989 ... CANR-3
Obituary ... 129
Earlier sketch in CA 1-4R
Black, D. M.
See Black, David (Macleod)
Black, David
See Way, Robert E(dward)
Black, David (Macleod) 1941- ... 25-28R
See also DLB 40
Black, David 1945- ... 136
Black, Dianne (a pseudonym) 1940- ... 97-100
Black, Donald 1941- ... 146
Black, Dorothy 1899-1985 Obituary ... 115
Black, Dorothy 1914- ... CANR-30
Earlier sketch in CA 111
Black, Douglas M. 1896(?)-1977 Obituary ... 104
Black, Duncan 1908- ... CAP-2
Earlier sketch in CA 19-20
Black, E(dward) L(oring) 1915- ... 9-12R
Black, Earl 1942- ... 101
Black, Elizabeth 1908(?)-1987 Obituary ... 122
Black, Eugene C(harlton) 1927- ... 9-12R
Black, Eugene R(obert) 1898- ... CAP-2
Earlier sketch in CA 25-28
Black, Floyd H. 1888-1983 Obituary ... 111
Black, Gavin
See Wynd, Oswald Morris
Black, Hallie 1943- ... 108
Black, Harry George 1933- ... 61-64
Black, Hugh C(leon) 1920- ... 37-40R
Black, Hugo Lafayette 1886-1971 Obituary ... 33-36R
Black, Ian Stuart 1915- ... CANR-6
Earlier sketch in CA 9-12R
Black, Irma Simonton 1906-1972 ... CANR-68
Obituary ... 37-40R
Earlier sketches in CA 1-4R, CANR-6
See also SATA 2
See also SATA-Obit 25
Black, Ishi
See Gibson, Walter B(rown)
Black, Ivan 1904(?)-1979 Obituary ... 85-88
Black, James A(llen) 1937- ... 121
Black, James Menzies 1913- ... CANR-5
Earlier sketch in CA 5-8R
Black, Jeremy (Martin) 1955- ... 136
Black, John N(icholson) 1922- ... CANR-13
Earlier sketch in CA 33-36R
Black, John Wilson 1906- ... CAP-1
Earlier sketch in CA 17-18
Black, Jonathan
See von Block, Bela W(illiam)
Black, Joseph E. 1921- ... 9-12R
Black, Kenneth, Jr. 1925- ... CANR-7
Earlier sketch in CA 13-16R
Black, Kitty
See Black, Dorothy
Black, Lionel
See Barker, Dudley
Black, Maggie
See Black, Margaret K(atherine)
Black, Malcolm Charles Lamont 1928- ... 85-88
Black, Mansell
See Trevor, Elleston
Black, Margaret K(atherine) 1921- ... CANR-32
Earlier sketches in CA 29-32R, CANR-14
Black, Martha E(llen) 1901- ... 33-36R
Black, Mary (Childs) 1922-1992 ... CANR-13
Obituary ... 137
Earlier sketch in CA 21-24R
Black, MaryAnn
See Easley, MaryAnn
Black, Matthew W(ilson) 1895- ... CAP-2
Earlier sketch in CA 25-28
Black, Max 1909- ... 61-64
Black, Michael (Hugo) 1928- ... 131
Black, Michael L(awrence) 1940- ... 121
Black, Millard H. 1912- ... 25-28R
Black, Misha 1910-1977 ... CAP-1
Obituary ... 133
Earlier sketch in CA 11-12
Black, Nancy B(reMiller) 1941- Brief entry ... 107
Black, Percy 1922- ... 33-36R
Black, R(obert) D(enis) Collison 1922- ... 131
Black, Robert
See Holdstock, Robert P.
Black, Robert 1946- ... 121
Black, Robert B(ruce) 1920- ... 109
Black, Robert C(lifford) III 1914- ... 41-44R
Black, Roe C(oddington) 1926- ... 89-92
Black, Shane 1962(?)- ... 152
Black, Shirley Temple 1928- ... BEST 89:2
Black, Stanley Warren III 1939- ... CANR-31
Earlier sketch in CA 45-48
Black, Susan Adams 1953- ... 105
See also SATA 40
Black, Theodore Michael 1919-1994 ... 109
Obituary ... 144
Black, Veronica
See Peters, Maureen
Black, William Joseph 1934(?)-1977 Obituary 73-76
Black, Winifred 1863-1936 ... DLB 25
Blackall, Eric Albert 1914-1989 ... 65-68
Obituary ... 130
Blackamore, Arthur 1679-(?) ... DLB 24, 39
Blackbeard, Bill 1926- ... CANR-66
Earlier sketch in CA 97-100
Interview in ... 97-100
Blackbourn, David 1949- ... 132
Blackburn, Alexander (Lambert) 1929- ... 97-100
See also DLBY 85
Blackburn, Barbara
See Leader, (Evelyn) Barbara (Blackburn)
Blackburn, Claire
See Altman, Linda Jacobs
Blackburn, Fred M(onroe) 1950- ... 166
Blackburn, George M. III 1950- ... 123
Blackburn, Graham (John) 1940- ... CANR-22
Earlier sketch in CA 69-72
Blackburn, John (Fenwick) 1923- ... CANR-58
Earlier sketches in CA 1-4R, CANR-2, 22
Blackburn, John(ny) Brewton 1952- ... SATA 15
Blackburn, John O. 1929- ... 127
Blackburn, Joyce Knight 1920- ... 17-20R
See also SATA 29
Blackburn, Laurence Henry 1897- ... 57-60
Blackburn, Michael 1954- ... CANR-43
Earlier sketch in CA 118
Blackburn, Norma Davis 1914- ... 69-72
Blackburn, Norman 1904(?)-1990 Obituary ... 131
Blackburn, Paul 1926-1971 ... CANR-34
Obituary ... 33-36R
Earlier sketch in CA 81-84
See also CLC 9, 43
See also DLB 16
See also DLBY 81
Blackburn, R(obert) M(artin) 1934- ... 119
Blackburn, Robert T. 1923- ... 121
Blackburn, Robin 1940- ... CANR-63
Earlier sketch in CA 128
Blackburn, Simon 1944- ... CANR-40
Earlier sketch in CA 49-52
Blackburn, Thomas (Eliel Fenwick) 1916-1977 ...
CANR-69
Obituary ... 113
Earlier sketch in CA 73-76
See also DLB 27
Blackburn, Thomas C(arl) 1936- ... CANR-22
Earlier sketch in CA 69-72
Blackburne, Kenneth (William)
1907-1980 Obituary ... 105
Blackburne, Neville Alfred Edmund 1913- ... 53-56
Black Elk 1863-1950 ... 144
See also DAM MULT
See also NNAL
See also TCLC 33
Blacker, C(arlos) P(aton)
1895-1975 Obituary ... 57-60
Blacker, Carmen Elizabeth 1924- ... 9-12R
Blacker, Irwin R(obert) 1919-1985 ... CANR-3
Obituary ... 115
Earlier sketch in CA 1-4R
Blackett, Patrick (Maynard Stuart)
1897-1974 Obituary ... 49-52
Blackett, Veronica Heath 1927- ... 53-56
See also SATA 12
Blackey, Robert 1941- ... CANR-4
Earlier sketch in CA 53-56
Blackford, Charles Minor III 1898- ... 69-72
Blackford, Mansel G(riffiths) 1944- ... 142
Blackford, Staige D(avis) 1931- ... 103
Blackhall, David Scott 1910- ... 5-8R
Blackham, Garth J. 1926- ... 33-36R
Blackham, H(arold) J(ohn) 1903- ... 21-24R
Black Hawk 1767-1838 ... NNAL
Black Hobart
See Sanders, (James) Ed(ward)
Blackie, Bruce L(othian) 1936- ... 57-60
Blackie, Jean Cutler 1943- ... SATA 79
Blackie, John (Ernest Haldane) 1904-1985 ... 73-76
Obituary ... 116
Blackie, Pamela 1917- ... 103
Blacking, John (Anthony Randoll) 1928- ... CANR-3
Earlier sketch in CA 9-12R
Blackledge, Ethel H(ale) ... CANR-11
Earlier sketch in CA 21-24R
Blacklin, Malcolm
See Chambers, Aidan
Blackman, Audrey (Babette) 1907-1990(?) ... 109
Obituary ... 132
Blackman, Malorie 1962- ... 150
See also SATA 83
Blackman, Raymond V(ictor) B(ernard)
1910-1989 Obituary ... 128
Blackman, Sheldon 1935- ... 33-36R
Blackman, Sue Anne Batey 1948- ... 132
Blackman, Victor 1922- ... 103
Blackmer, Donald L. M. 1929- ... 33-36R
Black-Michaud, Jacob 1938- ... 61-64
Blackmon, C(harles) Robert 1925- ... 33-36R
Blackmon, Rosemary Barnsdall
1921(?)-1983 Obituary ... 111
Blackmore, Charles (David) 1957- ... 124
Blackmore, Dorothy S. 1914- ... 41-44R
Blackmore, John T(homas) 1931- ... CANR-15
Earlier sketch in CA 41-44R
Blackmore, Peter 1909-1984 ... 9-12R
Obituary ... 114
Blackmore, R(ichard) D(oddridge) 1825-1900 Brief
entry ... 120
See also DLB 18
See also TCLC 27
Blackmore, Richard 1654-1729 ... DLB 131
Blackmore, Robert Long 1919- ... 113
Blackmore, Susan (Jane) 1951- ... 146
Blackmur, R(ichard) P(almer) 1904-1965 ... CANR-71
Obituary ... 25-28R
Earlier sketches in CAP-1, CA 11-12
See also CLC 2, 24
See also DLB 63
Blackoff, Edward M. 1934- ... 9-12R
Blackshear, Helen F(riedman) 1911- ... CANR-10
Earlier sketch in CA 25-28R
Blacksnake, George
See Richardson, Gladwell
Blackstock, Charity
See Torday, Ursula
Blackstock, Lee
See Torday, Ursula
Blackstock, Nelson 1944- ... 97-100
Blackstock, Paul W(illiam) 1913- ... CANR-69
Earlier sketch in CA 13-16R
Blackstock, Terri 1957- ... 153
Blackstock, Walter 1917- ... CANR-9
Earlier sketch in CA 5-8R
Blackstone, Bernard 1911-1983 ... 69-72
Obituary ... 111
Blackstone, Geoffrey Vaughan 1910- ... CAP-1
Earlier sketch in CA 9-10
Blackstone, Harry
See Blackstone, Harry (Bouton), Jr.
Blackstone, Harry (Bouton), Jr. 1934-1997 ... 114
Obituary ... 158

Blackstone, James
See Brosnan, John
and Brosnan, John
Blackstone, Tessa Ann Vosper 1942- ... CANR-42
Earlier sketches in CA 102, CANR-19
Blackstone, William T(homas) 1931- ... CANR-11
Earlier sketch in CA 17-20R
Black Tarantula
See Acker, Kathy
Blackton, Peter
See Wilson, Lionel
Blackwelder, Bernice Fowler 1902- ... 1-4R
Blackwelder, Boyce W(atson) 1913-1976 ... 17-20R
Obituary ... 135
Blackwelder, Jerry 1950- ... 122
Blackwell, Basil (Henry) 1889-1984 Obituary ... 112
Blackwell, Betsy Talbot 1905(?)-1985 Obituary . 115
Blackwell, (Samuel) Earl (Jr.) 1913-1995 ... 81-84
Obituary ... 148
Blackwell, James
See Blackwell, James A., Jr.
Blackwell, James A., Jr. ... 140
Blackwell, James E(dward) 1926- ... 133
Brief entry ... 114
Blackwell, Leslie 1885- ... 9-12R
Blackwell, Lois S. 1943- ... 85-88
Blackwell, (Annie) Louise 1919-1977 ... 37-40R
Blackwell, Marilyn Johns 1948- ... 116
Blackwell, Muriel F(ontenot) 1929- ... 108
Blackwell, Richard Joseph 1929- ... 33-36R
Blackwell, Roger D(ale) 1940- ... 93-96
Blackwell, William L. 1929- ... 21-24R
Blackwood, Alan 1932- ... CANR-53
Earlier sketches in CA 110, CANR-28
See also SATA 70
Blackwood, Algernon (Henry) 1869-1951 ... 150
Brief entry ... 105
See also DLB 153, 156, 178
See also TCLC 5
Blackwood, Andrew W(atterson), Jr. 1915- ...
CANR-5
Earlier sketch in CA 1-4R
Blackwood, Andrew W(atterson) 1882-1966 ...
CANR-69
Obituary ... 103
Earlier sketch in CA 5-8R
Blackwood, Caroline 1931-1996 ... CANR-65
Obituary ... 151
Earlier sketches in CA 85-88, CANR-32, 61
See also CLC 6, 9, 100
See also DLB 14
See also MTCW 1
Blackwood, Cheryl Prewitt 1957- ... 108
Blackwood, Easley 1903- ... 115
Blackwood, Gary L. 1945- ... SATA 72
Blackwood, George D(ouglas) 1919- ... 13-16R
Blackwood, James R. 1918- ... 21-24R
Blackwood, Margaret 1959- ... 144
Blackwood, Paul Everett 1913- ... 102
Blade, Alexander
See Garrett, (Gordon) Randall (Phillip)
and Hamilton, Edmond
and Silverberg, Robert
Bladel, Roderick L(eRoy) ... 97-100
Bladen, Ashby 1929- ... 106
Bladen, V(incent) W(heeler) 1900- ... 61-64
Blades, Ann (Sager) 1947- ... CANR-48
Earlier sketches in CA 77-80, CANR-13
See also CLR 15
See also JRDA
See also MAICYA
See also SATA 16, 69
Blades, Brian Brewer 1906-1977 Obituary ... 73-76
Blades, James 1901- ... 65-68
Blades, John (D.) 1936- ... 140
Blades, Ruben 1948- ... 131
See also HW
Blades, William 1824-1890 ... DLB 184
Bladow, Suzanne Wilson 1937- ... 61-64
See also SATA 14
Blaffer, Sarah C.
See Hrdy, Sarah Blaffer
Blaga, Lucian 1895-1961 ... 157
See also CLC 75
Blagden, Cyprian 1906-1962 ... 1-4R
Blagden, David 1944- ... 53-56
Blagden, Isabella 1817(?)-1873 ... DLB 199
Blagowidow, George 1923- ... 77-80
Blaher, Damian J(oseph) 1913- ... 21-24R
Blaich, Theodore Paul 1902- ... CAP-1
Earlier sketch in CA 13-14
Blaike, Avona
See MacIntosh, Joan
Blaikie, Robert J. 1923- ... 33-36R
Blaiklock, Edward Musgrave 1903- ... CANR-7
Earlier sketch in CA 17-20R
Blain, W. Edward 1951- ... 139
Blaine, James
See Avallone, Michael (Angelo, Jr.)
Blaine, John
See Goodwin, Harold L(eland)
Blaine, Marge
See Blaine, Margery Kay
Blaine, Margery Kay 1937- ... 61-64
See also SATA 11
Blaine, Thomas R(obert) 1895- ... 106
Blaine, Tom R.
See Blaine, Thomas R(obert)
Blaine, William L(ee) 1931- ... 65-68
Blainey, Ann (Warriner) 1935- ... 25-28R
Blainey, Geoffrey (Norman) 1930- ... CANR-69
Earlier sketch in CA 25-28R
Blair
See Blair-Fish, Wallace Wilfrid
Blair, Anne Denton 1914- ... 110
See also SATA 46
Blair, Calvin Patton 1924- ... 13-16R
Blair, Carvel Hall 1924- ... 49-52
Blair, Charles E. 1920- ... 25-28R
Blair, Claude 1922- ... CANR-11
Earlier sketch in CA 5-8R
Blair, Clay Drewry, Jr. 1925- ... CANR-68
Earlier sketch in CA 77-80
See also AITN 2
Blair, Cynthia 1953- ... 118
Blair, David Nelson 1954- ... 147
See also SATA 80
Blair, (Robert) Dike 1919- ... 9-12R
Blair, Don 1933- ... 65-68
Blair, Dorothy L. 1890- ... 114
Blair, Dorothy S(ara Greene) 1913- Brief entry . 113
Blair, E(lizabeth) Anne 1946- ... 153
Blair, Edward H. 1938- ... CANR-7
Earlier sketch in CA 17-20R
Blair, Edward P(ayson) 1910- ... CANR-26
Earlier sketches in CAP-1, CA 13-14, CANR-11
Blair, Eric (Arthur) 1903-1950 ... 132
Brief entry ... 104
See also Orwell, George
See also DA
See also DAB
See also DAC
See also DAM MST, NOV
See also MTCW 1
See also SATA 29
Blair, Everetta Love 1907- ... CAP-2
Earlier sketch in CA 25-28
Blair, Francis Preston 1791-1876 ... DLB 43
Blair, Frank 1915-1995 ... 93-96
Obituary ... 148
Blair, George S(imms) 1924- ... 17-20R
Blair, Glenn Myers 1908- ... 5-8R
Blair, Gwenda (Linda) 1943- ... 125
Blair, Harry Wallace 1938- ... 109
Blair, Helen 1910- ... SATA-Brief 29
Blair, J(oseph) Allen 1913- ... 89-92
Blair, James 1655(?)-1743 ... DLB 24
Blair, Jane N(emec) 1911- ... 57-60
Blair, Jay 1953- ... SATA 45
Blair, Jessica
See Spence, William John Duncan
Blair, John Durburrow 1759-1823 ... DLB 37
Blair, John G(eorge) 1934- ... 13-16R
Blair, John M(alcolm) 1914-1976 ... 73-76
Obituary ... 69-72
Blair, Kay Reynolds 1942- ... 33-36R
Blair, Leon Borden 1917- ... 29-32R
Blair, Leona ... 165
Blair, Lorraine Louise 1899(?)-1984 Obituary ... 114
Blair, Lucile
See Yeakley, Marjory Hall
Blair, Pauline Hunter ... SATA 3
Blair, Paxton 1892-1974 Obituary ... 53-56
Blair, Peter Hunter
See Hunter Blair, Peter
Blair, Philip M(ark) 1928-1979 ... 41-44R
Obituary ... 133
Blair, Ruth Van Ness 1912- ... 21-24R
See also SATA 12
Blair, Sam 1932- ... 53-56
Blair, Shannon
See Kaye, Marilyn
Blair, Sheila ... 166
Blair, Thomas (Lucien Vincent) 1926- ... 106
Blair, Walter 1900-1992 ... CANR-18
Obituary ... 139
Earlier sketches in CA 5-8R, CANR-3
See also SATA 12
See also SATA-Obit 72
Blair, Wilfrid
See Blair-Fish, Wallace Wilfrid
Blair-Fish, Wallace Wilfrid 1889-1968 ... CAP-2
Earlier sketch in CA 29-32
Blais, Andre 1947- ... 167
Blais, Madeleine 1947- ... 104
Blais, Marie-Claire 1939- ... CANR-38
Earlier sketch in CA 21-24R
See also CAAS 4
See also CLC 2, 4, 6, 13, 22
See also DAC
See also DAM MST
See also DLB 53
See also MTCW 1
Blaisdell, Donald C(hristy) 1899-1988 ... 37-40R
Obituary ... 126
Blaisdell, Foster W(arren) 1927- ... 69-72
Blaisdell, Harold F. 1914- ... 65-68
Blaisdell, Paul H(enry) 1908- ... 61-64
Blaisdell, Thomas C(harles), Jr.
1895-1988 Obituary ... 127
Blaise, Clark 1940- ... CANR-66
Earlier sketches in CA 53-56, CANR-5
See also CAAS 3
See also AITN 2
See also CLC 29
See also DLB 53
Blake, Alfred
See Janifer, Laurence M(ark)
Blake, Andrew
See Janifer, Laurence M(ark)
Blake, Brian 1918- ... 109
Blake, Bud
See Blake, Julian Watson
Blake, Christina
See Chandler, Bryn
Blake, David H(aven) 1940- ... 41-44R
Blake, Eubie
See Blake, James Hubert
Blake, Eugene Carson 1906-1985 Obituary ... 116
Blake, Fairley
See De Voto, Bernard (Augustine)
Blake, Fay M(ontaug) 1920- ... 53-56
Blake, Gary 1944- ... CANR-15
Earlier sketch in CA 85-88
Blake, George 1893-1961 ... DLB 191
Blake, Gerald H(enry) 1936- ... CANR-51
Earlier sketch in CA 124
Blake, Harlan Morse 1923- ... 25-28R
Blake, I(srael) George 1902- ... 21-24R
Blake, J. W.
See Blake, John William
Blake, James 1922-1979 ... 93-96
Obituary ... 85-88
Blake, James C(arlos) 1950(?)- ... 158
Blake, James Hubert 1883-1983 Obituary ... 109
Blake, Jennifer
See Maxwell, Patricia
Blake, John W.
See Blake, John William
Blake, John William 1911-1987 Obituary ... 122
Blake, Jon 1954- ... 135
See also SATA 78
Blake, Judith (Kincade) 1926-1993 ... CANR-47
Obituary ... 141
Earlier sketch in CA 1-4R
Blake, Julian Watson 1918- ... 65-68
Blake, Justin
See Bowen, John (Griffith)
Blake, Katherine
See Walter, Dorothy Blake
Blake, Kathleen 1944- ... 57-60
Blake, Kay
See Walter, Dorothy Blake
Blake, Ken
See Bulmer, (Henry) Kenneth
Blake, L(eslie) J(ames) 1913- ... CANR-11
Earlier sketch in CA 25-28R
Blake, Laurel
See Palencia, Elaine Fowler
Blake, Lillie Devereux 1833-1913 ... DLB 202
Blake, Margaret
See Trimble, Barbara Margaret
Blake, Michael 1945- ... 140
Blake, Mike 1950- ... 148
Blake, Minden V(aughan) 1913- ... 69-72
Blake, Mindy
See Blake, Minden V(aughan)
Blake, Monica
See Muir, Marie
Blake, Nelson Manfred 1908-1996 ... CANR-71
Earlier sketches in CA 1-4R, CANR-3
Blake, Nicholas
See Day Lewis, C(ecil)
See also DLB 77
Blake, Norman (Francis) 1934- ... 93-96
Blake, Olive
See Supraner, Robyn
Blake, Patricia 1933- ... CANR-46
Earlier sketch in CA 49-52
Blake, Patrick
See Egleton, Clive (Frederick)
Blake, Paul C. 1916- ... 25-28R
Blake, Peter (Jost) 1920- ... CANR-14
Earlier sketch in CA 65-68
Blake, Quentin (Saxby) 1932- ... CANR-67
Earlier sketches in CA 25-28R, CANR-11, 37
See also CLR 31
See also MAICYA
See also SATA 9, 52, 96
Blake, Raymond B. 1958- ... 148
Blake, Reed H(arris) 1933- ... 57-60
Blake, Richard A(loysius) 1939- ... 93-96
Blake, Robert
See Davies, L(eslie) P(urnell)
Blake, Robert (Norman William) 1916- ... CANR-45
Earlier sketches in CA 9-12R, CANR-22
Blake, Robert 1949- ... SATA 42
Blake, Robert R(ogers) 1918- ... CANR-13
Earlier sketch in CA 21-24R
Blake, Robert W(illiam) 1930- ... CANR-31
Earlier sketch in CA 33-36R
Blake, Robin (James) 1948- ... 127
Blake, Sally
See Saunders, Jean
Blake, Sally Mirliss 1925-1986 ... 17-20R
Obituary ... 118
Blake, Stephanie
See Pearl, Jacques Bain
Blake, Stephen P. 1942- ... 139
Blake, Vanessa
See Brown, May
Blake, Walker E.
See Butterworth, W(illiam) E(dmund III)
Blake, Wendon
See Holden, Donald
Blake, William 1757-1827 ... CDBLB 1789-1832
See also CLR 52
See also DA
See also DAB
See also DAC
See also DAM MST, POET
See also DLB 93, 163
See also MAICYA
See also PC 12
See also SATA 30
See also WLC
Blake, William J(ames) 1894-1969 ... 5-8R
Obituary ... 25-28R
Blakeborough, Jack Fairfax
See Fairfax-Blakeborough, John Freeman
Blakeborough, John Freeman Fairfax
See Fairfax-Blakeborough, John Freeman
Blakeley, Phyllis (Ruth) 1922- ... 61-64
Blakeley, Thomas J(ohn) 1931- ... CANR-3
Earlier sketch in CA 9-12R
Blakely, Allison 1940- ... CANR-51
Earlier sketch in CA 125
Blakely, Mary Kay 1948- ... 131
Blakely, R(obert) J(ohn) 1915-1994 ... 37-40R
Obituary ... 147
Blakely, Roger K. 1922- ... 149
See also SATA 82
Blakemore, Colin (Brian) 1944- ... 85-88
Blakemore, Harold 1930-1991 ... 146
Blakeney, Jay D.
See Chester, Deborah
Blaker, Alfred A(rthur) 1928- ... 65-68
Blakeslee, Alton (Lauren) 1913-1997 ... 105
Obituary ... 158
Blakeslee, Sandra 1943- ... 131
Blakeslee, Thomas R(obert) 1937- ... 101
Blakesley, Christopher L. 1945- ... 146
Blakeston, Oswell 1907(?)-1985(?) Obituary ... 116
Blakey, George T., Jr. 1939- ... 120
Blakey, Nancy 1955- ... 159
See also SATA 94
Blakey, Scott 1936- ... 85-88
Blakey, Walker Jameson 1940- ... 69-72
Blakiston, Georgiana 1903-1995 ... 69-72
Obituary ... 150
Blakiston, Noel 1905-1984 Obituary ... 115
Blakney, Raymond D. 1897(?)-1970 Obituary .. 104
Blalock, Hubert M(orse), Jr. 1926-1991 ... CANR-5
Obituary ... 133
Earlier sketch in CA 13-16R
Blalock, Jane B. 1945- Brief entry ... 112
Blamires, Alcuin (Godfrey) 1946- ... 141
Blamires, David (Malcolm) 1936- ... CANR-14
Earlier sketch in CA 65-68
Blamires, Harry 1916- ... CANR-42
Earlier sketches in CA 9-12R, CANR-5, 20
Blanc, Esther S. 1913- ... 131
See also SATA 66
Blanc, Mel 1908-1989 ... SATA-Obit 64
Blanc, Michel H(enri) A(mbroise) 1929- ... 133
Blance, Ellen 1931- ... CANR-7
Earlier sketch in CA 57-60
Blanch, Lesley 1907- ... CANR-70
Earlier sketch in CA 102
Blanch, Robert J. 1938- ... 21-24R
Blanch, Stuart Yarworth 1918-1994 ... 106
Obituary ... 145
Blanchard, Alice 1959- ... 163
Blanchard, Allan E(dward) 1929- ... 69-72
Blanchard, B(irdsall) Everard 1909- ... 41-44R
Blanchard, Carroll Henry, Jr. 1928- ... 13-16R
Blanchard, Fessenden Seaver 1888-1963 ... 5-8R
Blanchard, Howard L(awrence) 1909- ... 5-8R
Blanchard, J. Richard 1912- ... 89-92
Blanchard, Kendall A(llan) 1942- ... CANR-11
Earlier sketch in CA 69-72
Blanchard, Kenneth H(artley) 1939- ... 111
Blanchard, Nina ... 101
Blanchard, Olivier Jean 1948- ... 141
Blanchard, Paula (Barber) 1936- ... 81-84
Blanchard, Peter 1946- ... 117
Blanchard, Ralph Harrub 1890-1973 ... CAP-1
Earlier sketch in CA 13-14
Blanchard, Stephen (Thomas) 1950- ... 161
Blanchard, William H(enry) 1922- ... CANR-8
Earlier sketch in CA 21-24R
Blanche, Pierre 1927- ... 25-28R
Blanchet, Eileen 1924- ... 57-60
Blanchet, M(uriel) Wylie 1891-1961 ... 168
Blanchette, Oliva 1929- ... 53-56
Blanchot, Maurice 1907- ... 144
Brief entry ... 117
See also DLB 72
Blanck, Gertrude 1914- ... 85-88
Blanck, Jacob Nathaniel 1906-1974 ... CANR-69
Obituary ... 53-56
Earlier sketches in CAP-1, CA 11-12
Blanck, Rubin 1914- ... 25-28R
Blanckenburg, Christian Friedrich von
1744-1796 ... DLB 94
Blanco, Luis Anado 1903(?)-1975 Obituary ... 104
Blanco, Richard L(idio) 1926- ... 57-60
See also SATA 63
Blanco Fombona, Rufino 1874-1944 ... HW
Blanco White, Amber 1887-1981 Obituary ... 105
Bland, Alexander
See Gosling, Nigel
Bland, E.
See Nesbit, E(dith)
Bland, Edith Nesbit
See Nesbit, E(dith)
Bland, Eleanor Taylor ... 166
Bland, Fabian
See Nesbit, E(dith)
Bland, Hester Beth 1906- ... 57-60
Bland, Jeffrey 1946- ... 106
Bland, Jennifer
See Bowden, Jean
Bland, Larry I(rvin) 1940- ... 109
Bland, Lucy ... 158
Bland, Peter 1934- ... 153
Bland, Randall Walton 1942- ... CANR-5
Earlier sketch in CA 53-56
Blanda, George (Frederick) 1927- Brief entry .. 114
Blandford, Brian E(rnest) 1937- ... 118
Blandford, Percy William 1912- ... 9-12R
Blandiana, Ana 1942- ... 152
Blanding, Forrest H(arvey) 1917- ... 111
Blandino, Giovanni 1923- ... 21-24R
Blandy, Doug(las E.) 1951- ... 138
Blane, Gertrude
See Blumenthal, Gertrude
Blane, Howard T(homas) 1926- ... CANR-51
Earlier sketches in CA 25-28R, CANR-10, 28
Blanford, James T. 1917- ... 33-36R
Blank, Blanche D(avis) ... 41-44R
Blank, Clarissa Mabel 1915-1965 ... SATA 62
Blank, G(regory) Kim 1952- ... 151
Blank, George (W. III) 1945- ... 110

Blank, Joseph P. 1919- 93-96
Blank, Leonard 1927- CANR-12
Earlier sketch in CA 33-36R
Blank, Les 1935- 131
Blank, Robert H(enry) 1943- 148
Blank, Sheldon H(aas) 1896- 1-4R
Blankenhorn, David (George III) 1955- 151
Blankenship, A(lbert) B. 1914- CANR-7
Earlier sketch in CA 13-16R
Blankenship, Edward Gary 1943- 45-48
Blankenship, Lela (McDowell) 1886- 5-8R
Blankenship, William D(ouglas) 1934- 33-36R
Blankfort, (Seymour) Michael 1907-1982 . CANR-70
Obituary 107
Earlier sketches in CA 1-4R, CANR-2
Blanksten, George I(rving) 1917- CANR-1
Earlier sketch in CA 1-4R
Blanpied, Pamela Wharton 1937- 102
Blanshard, Brand 1892-1987 CANR-16
Obituary 124
Earlier sketch in CA 1-4R
Blanshard, Paul (Beecher) 1892-1980 135
Obituary 93-96
Blanton, (Martha) Catherine 1907- CANR-70
Earlier sketch in CA 1-4R
Blantz, Thomas E(dward) 1934- 111
Blanzaco, Andre C. 1934- 29-32R
Blasco Ibanez, Vicente 1867-1928 131
Brief entry 110
See also DAM NOV
See also HW
See also MTCW 1
See also TCLC 12
Blase, Melvin G(eorge) 1933- 33-36R
Blaser, Robin (Francis) 1925- CANR-8
Earlier sketch in CA 57-60
See also DLB 165
Blaser, Werner 1924- 136
Blashford-Snell, John (Nicholas) 1936- CANR-42
Earlier sketches in CA 102, CANR-19
Blasi, Anthony J(oseph) 1946- 140
Blasier, (Stewart) Cole 1925- 21-24R
Blasing, Mutlu Konuk 1944- CANR-35
Earlier sketch in CA 89-92
Blasing, Randy 1943- CANR-50
Earlier sketches in CA 114, CANR-35
Blass, Birgit A(nnelise) 1940- 29-32R
Blass, Ron(ald J.) 1922-1984 Obituary 114
Blassingame, John W(esley) 1940- CANR-25
Earlier sketch in CA 49-52
See also BW 1
Blassingame, Wyatt Rainey 1909-1985 CANR-68
Obituary 114
Earlier sketches in CA 1-4R, CANR-3
See also SATA 1, 34
See also SATA-Obit 41
Blatchford, Christie 1951- 73-76
Blatchford, Claire H. 1944- 159
See also SATA 94
Blathwayt, Jean 1918- 106
Blatner, David 1966- 168
Blatt, Burton 1927- CANR-14
Earlier sketch in CA 41-44R
Blatt, Sidney J(ules) 1928- 37-40R
Blatter, Dorothy (Gertrude) 1901- CAP-1
Earlier sketch in CA 11-12
Blatty, William Peter 1928- CANR-9
Earlier sketch in CA 5-8R
See also CLC 2
See also DAM POP
Blau, Abram 1907-1979 Obituary 85-88
Blau, Eric 1921- 85-88
Blau, Francine D(ee) 1946- CANR-51
Earlier sketches in CA 106, CANR-25
Blau, Herbert 1926- CANR-36
Earlier sketch in CA 111
Blau, Joel 1945- 137
Blau, Joseph L(eon) 1909-1986 9-12R
Obituary 121
Blau, Joshua 1919- CANR-7
Earlier sketch in CA 13-16R
Blau, Judith R. 1942- CANR-48
Earlier sketch in CA 122
Blau, Milton
See Blau, Eric
Blau, Peter M(ichael) 1918- CANR-1
Earlier sketch in CA 1-4R
Blau, Sheldon Paul 1935- 57-60
Blau, Tom 1913(?)-1984 Obituary 113
Blau, Yehoshua
See Blau, Joshua
Blau, Zena Smith 1922- CANR-1
Earlier sketch in CA 45-48
Blauer, Ettagale 1940- CANR-24
Earlier sketch in CA 103
See also SATA 49
Blaufarb, Douglas S(amuel) 1918- 85-88
Blaug, Mark 1927- CANR-16
Earlier sketches in CA 1-4R, CANR-1
Blaukopf, Herta 1924- 131
Blaukopf, Kurt 1914- Brief entry 114
Blauner, Peter 1959- 136
Blauner, Robert 1929- 17-20R
Blaushild, Babette 1927- 29-32R
Blaustein, Albert Paul 1921- CANR-19
Earlier sketches in CA 1-4R, CANR-1
Blaustein, Arthur I. 1933- CANR-10
Earlier sketch in CA 25-28R
Blaustein, Elliott H(arold) 1915- 41-44R
Blaustein, Esther 1935- 45-48
Blauw, Johannes 1912- 9-12R
Blauw, Pieter Wilhelmus 1942- 137
Blauw, Wim
See Blauw, Pieter Wilhelmus
Blaxland, John 1917- 5-8R
Blaxland, W(illiam) Gregory 1918- CANR-3
Earlier sketch in CA 9-12R
Blaylock, James P(aul) 1950- CANR-53
Earlier sketches in CA 110, CANR-27
Blayn, Hugo
See Fearn, John Russell
Blayne, Diana
See Kyle, Susan (Spaeth)
Blayne, Sara
See Howl, Marcia (Yvonne Hurt)
Blayney, Margaret S(tatler) 1926- 53-56
Blayre, Christopher
See Heron-Allen, Edward
Blaze, Wayne 1951- 61-64
Blazek, Douglas 1941- 25-28R
Blazek, Ron(ald David) 1936- 111
Blazer, Dan G(erman) II 1944- 110
Blazer, J. S.
See Scott, Justin
Blazier, Kenneth D(ean) 1933- CANR-11
Earlier sketch in CA 69-72
Bleakley, David (Wylie) 1925- 102
Bleamer, Burton 1906(?)-1986 Obituary 118
Blechman, Barry M. 1943- 97-100
Blechman, Burt 1927- CANR-72
Earlier sketches in CA 21-24R, CANR-65
Blecker, Robert A. 1956- 145
Bledlow, John
See Vale, (Henry) Edmund (Theodoric)
Bledsoe, Albert Taylor 1809-1877 DLB 3, 79
Bledsoe, Jerry 1941- CANR-49
Earlier sketch in CA 85-88
Bledsoe, Joseph C(ullie) 1918- 33-36R
Bledsoe, Lucy Jane 1957- 152
See also SATA 97
Bledsoe, Thomas (Alexander) 1914- CANR-9
Earlier sketch in CA 13-16R
Bledsoe, Timothy 1953- 146
Bledsoe, William Ambrose 1906-1981 Obituary . 104
Bleeck, Oliver
See Thomas, Ross (Elmore)
Bleeker, Ann Eliza 1752-1783 DLB 200
Bleeker, Mordecia
See Morgan, Fred Troy
Bleeker, Sonia
See Zim, Sonia Bleeker
See also SATA 2
See also SATA-Obit 26
Blees, Robert A(rthur) 1922- 17-20R
Blegen, Carl (William) 1887-1971 Obituary 33-36R
Blegen, Daniel M. 1950- 156
See also SATA 92
Blegen, Theodore C(hristian) 1891-1969 . CANR-69
Earlier sketches in CA 5-8R, CANR-3
Blegvad, Erik 1923- 97-100
See also MAICYA
See also SATA 14, 66
Blegvad, Lenore 1926- CANR-31
Earlier sketches in CA 69-72, CANR-14
See also SATA 14, 66
Blehl, Vincent Ferrer 1921- 9-12R
Blei, Norbert 1935- 143
Bleiberg, Robert Marvin 1924-1997 103
Obituary 162
Bleich, Alan R. 1913- 13-16R
Bleich, Harold 1930(?)-1980 Obituary 93-96
Bleich, J(udah) David 1936- 116
Bleicher, Michael N(athaniel) 1935- 37-40R
Bleier, Robert Patrick 1946- 85-88
Bleier, Rocky
See Bleier, Robert Patrick
Bleiler, Everett F(ranklin) 1920- 164
Blench, J(ohn) W(heatley) 1926- 13-16R
Blend, Charles D(aniels) 1918-1971 21-24R
Obituary 134
Blenk, K. T.
See Blenk, Katie
Blenk, Katie 1954- 152
Blenkinsopp, Joseph 1927- 37-40R
Blennerhassett, Margaret Agnew 1773-1842 ... DLB 99
Bleser, Carol K. 1935- 107
Blesh, Rudi
See Blesh, Rudolph Pickett
Blesh, Rudolph Pickett 1899-1985 CANR-72
Obituary 117
Earlier sketch in CA 17-20R
Blessing, Lee 1949- CLC 54
Blessing, Richard Allen 1939- 53-56
Blessington, Francis C(harles) 1942- 130
Blethen, H(arold) Tyler 1945- 166
Bletter, Robert 1933(?)-1976 Obituary 61-64
Bletter, Rosemarie Haag 1939- 57-60
Blevins, James Lowell 1936- 106
Blevins, Leon W(ilford) 1937- 57-60
Blevins, William L. 1937- 33-36R
Blevins, Winfred (Ernest, Jr.) 1938- CANR-1
Earlier sketch in CA 45-48
Blewett, Daniel K(eith) 1957- 152
Bleything, Dennis H(ugh) 1946- 61-64
Bleznick, Donald W(illiam) 1924- 21-24R
Blezzard, Judith 1944- 134
Blicker, Seymour 1940- 77-80
Blickle, Peter 1938- 144
Blicq, Anthony 1926- 33-36R
Blier, Bertrand 1939- 143
Bligh, Norman
See Neubauer, William Arthur
Blight, David W. 1949- 147
Blight, John 1913- CANR-22
Earlier sketch in CA 69-72
Blight, Rose
See Greer, Germaine
Blind, Mathilde 1841-1896 DLB 199
Blinder, Alan S(tuart) 1945- CANR-32
Earlier sketch in CA 113
Blinder, Elliot 1949- 106
Blinderman, Abraham 1916- 61-64
Blinderman, Charles 1930- 135
Blinn, Johna
See Dorsey, Helen
Blinn, Keith Wayne 1917-1990 Obituary 131
Blinn, Walter Craig 1930- 61-64
Blish, James (Benjamin) 1921-1975 CANR-3
Obituary 57-60
Earlier sketch in CA 1-4R
See also CLC 14
See also DLB 8
See also MTCW 1
See also SATA 66
Blishen, Bernard Russell 1919- CANR-3
Earlier sketch in CA 1-4R
Blishen, Edward (William) 1920-1996 CANR-27
Obituary 155
Earlier sketches in CA 17-20R, CANR-11
See also SATA 8, 66
See also SATA-Obit 93
Bliss, A. J.
See Bliss, Alan (Joseph)
Bliss, Alan (Joseph) 1921-1985 134
Obituary 118
Bliss, Carey S(tillman) 1914-1994 41-44R
Obituary 145
Bliss, Carolyn (Jane) 1947- 128
Bliss, Corinne Demas 1947- CANR-28
Earlier sketch in CA 104
See also SATA 37
Bliss, Dorothy E(lizabeth) 1916-1987 118
Obituary 124
Bliss, Edward, Jr. 1912- 41-44R
Bliss, Edwin C(rosby) 1923- 131
Bliss, George William 1918-1978 85-88
Obituary 81-84
Bliss, Lee 1943- CANR-49
Earlier sketch in CA 122
Bliss, (John) Michael 1941- CANR-60
Earlier sketches in CA 103, CANR-31
Bliss, Michael (J.) 1947- 150
Bliss, Patricia Lounsbury 1929- CANR-55
Earlier sketch in CA 127
Bliss, Reginald
See Wells, H(erbert) G(eorge)
Bliss, Ronald G(ene) 1942- 53-56
See also SATA 12
Blissett, Luther
See Home, Stewart
Blissett, Marlan 1938- 41-44R
Blistein, Elmer M(ilton) 1920-1993 9-12R
Obituary 142
Blitch, Fleming Lee
See Lee, Fleming
Blitchington, Evelyn G(rant) 1947- 114
Blits, Jan H. 1943- 110
Blitzer, Wolf 1948- 136
Blitzstein, Marc 1905-1964 Obituary 110
Bliven, Bruce, Jr. 1916- CANR-7
Earlier sketch in CA 17-20R
See also SATA 2
Bliven, Bruce 1889-1977 CANR-70
Obituary 69-72
Earlier sketch in CA 37-40R
See also DLB 137
Bliven, Naomi 1925- 33-36R
Blix, Jacqueline 1949- 163
Blixen, Karen (Christentze Dinesen) 1885-1962 ... CANR-50
Earlier sketches in CAP-2, CA 25-28, CANR-22
See also Dinesen, Isak
See also MTCW 1
See also SATA 44
Blizzard, Gladys S. (?)-1992 SATA 79
Blizzard, S(amuel) W(ilson, Jr.) 1914(?)-1976 Obituary 65-68
Bloch, Ariel A(lfred Karl) 1933- 41-44R
Bloch, Arthur McBride 1938- 128
Bloch, Barbara 1925- CANR-49
Earlier sketches in CA 106, CANR-24
Bloch, Bertram 1892-1987 Obituary 122
Bloch, Blanche 1890-1980 Obituary 97-100
Bloch, Chana 1940- CANR-70
Earlier sketch in CA 105
Bloch, Dan 1943- 140
Bloch, Dorothy 1912- 93-96
Bloch, Douglas 1949- 138
Bloch, E. Maurice 25-28R
Bloch, Ernst 1885-1977 CANR-34
Obituary 73-76
Earlier sketch in CA 29-32R
Bloch, Herbert A(aron David) 1904-1965 1-4R
Obituary 134
Bloch, Herman D(avid) 1914- 29-32R
Bloch, Jeff(rey W.) 1959- 130
Bloch, Konrad E. 1912- 150
Bloch, Lucienne 1909- SATA 10
Bloch, Lucienne S(chupf) 1937- 93-96
Bloch, Marc 1886-1944 Brief entry 118
Bloch, Marie Halun 1910- CANR-19
Earlier sketches in CA 1-4R, CANR-4
See also SAAS 9
See also SATA 6
Bloch, Robert (Albert) 1917-1994 CANR-5
Obituary 146
Earlier sketch in CA 5-8R
Interview in CANR-5
See also CAAS 20
See also CLC 33
See also DLB 44
See also SATA 12
See also SATA-Obit 82
Blocher, Henri (Arthur) 1937- CANR-10
Earlier sketch in CA 65-68
Blochman, Lawrence G(oldtree) 1900-1975 CANR-58
Obituary 53-56
Earlier sketches in CAP-2, CA 19-20
See also SATA 22
Block, Allan (Forrest) 1923- CANR-31
Earlier sketch in CA 49-52
Block, Andrew 1892-1985 Obituary 118
Block, Arthur John 1916(?)-1981 Obituary 105
Block, Eugene B. 1890-1988 CANR-72
Earlier sketches in CA 5-8R, CANR-2
Block, Francesca (Lia) 1962- CANR-56
Earlier sketch in CA 131
See also AAYA 13
See also CLR 33
See also SAAS 21
See also SATA 80
Block, Geoffrey 1948- 162
Block, Hal 1914(?)-1981 Obituary 104
Block, Herbert (Lawrence) 1909- 111
Block, Irvin 1917- 17-20R
See also SATA 12
Block, Irving (Leonard) 1930- 118
Block, Jack 1921- 33-36R
Block, Jack 1931- 53-56
Block, Jean Libman 5-8R
Block, Joel D(avid) 1943- CANR-15
Earlier sketch in CA 89-92
Block, Joyce 1951- 145
Block, Julian 1934- 106
Block, Laurie S. 1951- 127
Block, Lawrence 1938- CANR-63
Earlier sketches in CA 1-4R, CANR-6, 45
See also CAAS 11
See also DAM POP
Block, Libbie 1910(?)-1972 Obituary 33-36R
Block, Marvin Avram 1903-1989 106
Obituary 128
Block, Michael 1942- 101
Block, Ned Joel 1942- 117
Block, Paul, Jr. 1911-1987 Obituary 122
Block, Ralph 1889-1974 Obituary 45-48
Block, Rudolph
See Lessing, Bruno
Block, Seymour Stanton 1918- 89-92
Block, Stanley Byron 1939- 85-88
Block, Thomas H(arris) 1945- CANR-18
Earlier sketch in CA 101
Block, Walter (Edward) 1941- CANR-22
Earlier sketches in CA 57-60, CANR-6
Block, Zenas 1916- 107
Blocker, Clyde (Edward) 1918- 33-36R
Blocker, H(arry) Gene 1937- 116
Blockinger, Betty
See Blocklinger, Peggy O'More
Blocklinger, Peggy O'More 1895- 5-8R
Blocksma, Mary 1942- 130
See also SATA-Brief 44
Blockson, Charles L(eRoy) 1933- 141
See also BW 2
Blodgett, Beverley 1926- 57-60
Blodgett, E(dward) D(ickinson) 1935- 112
Blodgett, Geoffrey Thomas 1931- 17-20R
Blodgett, Harold William 1900- 13-16R
Blodgett, Harriet Eleanor 1919- 33-36R
Blodgett, Richard 1940- CANR-1
Earlier sketch in CA 49-52
Bloem, Diane Brummel 1935- CANR-16
Earlier sketch in CA 85-88
Bloesch, Donald G. 1928- 13-16R
Bloesser, Robert 1930- 37-40R
Blofeld, John (Eaton Calthorpe) 1913-1987 CANR-19
Obituary 123
Earlier sketches in CA 53-56, CANR-4
Blois, Marsden S(cott, Jr.) 1919- 132
Blok, Alexander (Alexandrovich) 1880-1921 Brief entry 104
See also PC 21
See also TCLC 5
Blok, Anton 1935- 97-100
Blom, Gaston E(ugene) 1920- 25-28R
Blom, Jan
See Breytenbach, Breyten
Blom, Karl Arne 1946- CANR-51
Earlier sketches in CA 69-72, CANR-11, 28
Blom, Lynne Anne 1942- 120
Blom, Philipp
See Sievert, Philipp
Blom-Cooper, Louis Jacques 1926- 5-8R
Blond, Anthony 1928- 106
Blondal, Patricia 1926-1959 DLB 88
Blondel, Jean Fernand Pierre 1929- 101
Blondel, Nathalie 1960- 138
Blondell, (Rose) Joan 1906(?)-1979 115
Obituary 93-96
Blood, Bob
See Blood, Robert O(scar), Jr.
Blood, Charles Lewis 1929- 73-76
See also SATA 28
Blood, Jerome W. 1926- 9-12R
Blood, Marje 41-44R
Blood, Matthew
See Dresser, Davis
Blood, Robert O(scar), Jr. 1921- CANR-3
Earlier sketch in CA 1-4R
Bloodstein, Oliver 1920- 146
Bloodstone, John
See Byrne, Stuart J(ames)
Bloom, Alan (Herbert Vawser) 1906- CANR-3
Earlier sketch in CA 9-12R
Bloom, Alexander 1947- 114
Bloom, Allan (David) 1930-1992 131
Obituary 139
Brief entry 125
Interview in 131

Bloom, Amy 1953- CANR-61
Earlier sketch in CA 144
Bloom, Claire 1931- CANR-59
Earlier sketch in CA 114
Bloom, Clive 1953- 131
Bloom, Daniel Halevi 1949- 120
Bloom, Edward A(lan) 1914- CANR-2
Earlier sketch in CA 1-4R
Bloom, Erick Franklin 1944- 57-60
Bloom, Floyd E(lliott) 1936- 120
Bloom, Freddy 1914- 101
See also SATA 37
Bloom, Gordon F. 1918- 13-16R
Bloom, Harold 1930- CANR-39
Earlier sketch in CA 13-16R
See also CLC 24, 103
See also DLB 67
Bloom, Harry 1913(?)-1981 Obituary 104
Bloom, Herman Irving 1908- 102
Bloom, James D. 1951- 163
Bloom, John 1921- 5-8R
Bloom, John Porter 1924- 49-52
Bloom, Jonathan M(ax) 1950- 150
Bloom, Ken(neth) 1949- CANR-38
Earlier sketch in CA 115
Bloom, Lillian D. 1920- CANR-11
Earlier sketch in CA 17-20R
Bloom, Lisa E. 1958- 144
Bloom, Lloyd SATA-Brief 43
Bloom, Lynn (Marie) Z(immerman) 1934- CANR-49
Earlier sketches in CA 13-16R, CANR-6, 21
Bloom, Melvyn H(arold) 1938- 45-48
Bloom, Miriam 1934- 151
Bloom, Murray Teigh 1916- CANR-69
Earlier sketch in CA 17-20R
Bloom, Patrice 1936- 128
Bloom, Pauline 41-44R
Bloom, Robert 1930- 17-20R
Bloom, Samuel William 1921- CANR-3
Earlier sketch in CA 9-12R
Bloom, Steven 1942- 159
Bloom, Ursula (Harvey) 1893-1984 CANR-48
Obituary 114
Earlier sketch in CA 25-28R
Blooman, Percy A. 1906- CAP-1
Earlier sketch in CA 11-12
Bloomberg, Edward (Michael) 1937- 41-44R
Bloomberg, Marty
See Bloomberg, Max Arthur
Bloomberg, Max Arthur 1938- 101
Bloomberg, Michael (Rubens) 1942- 160
Bloomberg, Morton 1936- 53-56
Bloome, Enid P. 1925- 85-88
Bloomer, Amelia 1818-1894 DLB 79
Bloomer, Kent C(ress) 1935- 125
Bloomfield, Anthony (John Westgate) 1922- CANR-49
Earlier sketch in CA 1-4R
Bloomfield, Arthur (John) 1931- 65-68
Bloomfield, Arthur Irving 1914- 41-44R
Bloomfield, Aurelius
See Bourne, Randolph S(illiman)
Bloomfield, B(arry) C(ambray) 1931- CANR-5
Earlier sketch in CA 9-12R
Bloomfield, Harold H. 1944- CANR-9
Earlier sketch in CA 57-60
Bloomfield, Lincoln Palmer 1920- CANR-5
Earlier sketch in CA 1-4R
Bloomfield, Louis A(ub) 1956- 163
Bloomfield, Masse 1923- CANR-8
Earlier sketch in CA 61-64
Bloomfield, Maxwell H(erron III) 1931- 122
Brief entry 118
Bloomfield, Michaela 1966- SATA 70
Bloomfield, Morton W(ilfred) 1913-1987 CANR-2
Obituary 122
Earlier sketch in CA 5-8R
Bloomfield, Robert 1766-1823 DLB 93
Bloomingdale, Teresa 1930- CANR-21
Earlier sketch in CA 105
Bloomquist, Edward R. 1924- 29-32R
Bloomstein, Morris J. 1928- 25-28R
Bloor, Edward (William) 1950- 166
See also SATA 98
Blos, Joan W(insor) 1928- CANR-21
Earlier sketch in CA 101
See also CLR 18
See also JRDA
See also MAICYA
See also SAAS 11
See also SATA 33, 69
See also SATA-Brief 27
Blos, Peter 1904-1997 89-92
Obituary 158
Bloss, F(red) Donald 1920- 53-56
Bloss, Meredith 1908-1982 Obituary 107
Blossom, Frederick A.
1878(?)-1974 Obituary 49-52
Blossom, Thomas 1912- 21-24R
Blotner, Joseph (Leo) 1923- CANR-35
Earlier sketches in CA 17-20R, CANR-13
See also CAAS 25
See also AITN 1
See also DLB 111
Blotnick, Elihu 1939- 106
Blotnick, Srully (D.) 1941- 136
Brief entry 123
Blouet, Brian Walter 1936- CANR-15
Earlier sketches in CA 93-96, CANR-32
Blouet, Olwyn M(ary) 1948- 130
Blough, Glenn O(rlando) 1907- CANR-68
Earlier sketches in CAP-1, CA 11-12
See also SATA 1
Blough, Roger M(iles) 1904-1985 Obituary 117
Blount, Charles (Harold Clavell) 1913- 17-20R
Blount, Margaret 1924- 69-72
Blount, Roy (Alton), Jr. 1941- CANR-61
Earlier sketches in CA 53-56, CANR-10, 28
Interview in CANR-28
See also CLC 38
See also MTCW 1
Bloustein, Edward J. 1925- 41-44R
Blow, Michael 1930- 130
Blow, Suzanne (Katherine) 1932- 45-48
Blowsnake, Sam 1875-(?) NNAL
Bloy, Leon 1846-1917 Brief entry 121
See also DLB 123
See also TCLC 22
Blu, Karen I(sobell) 1941- 121
Blue, Betty (Anne) 1922- CANR-1
Earlier sketch in CA 45-48
Blue, Frederick Judd 1937- 53-56
Blue, Martha Ward 1942- 104
Blue, Rose 1931- CANR-60
Earlier sketches in CA 41-44R, CANR-14
See also SAAS 24
See also SATA 5, 91, 93
Blue, Vida (Rochelle) 1949- Brief entry 112
Blue, Wallace
See Kraenzel, Margaret (Powell)
Blue, Zachary
See Stine, R(obert) L(awrence)
Bluebond-Langner, Myra 1948- 81-84
Blue Cloud, Peter (Aroniawenrate) 1933- CANR-40
Earlier sketch in CA 117
See also DAM MULT
See also NNAL
Bluefarb, Samuel 1919- 37-40R
Bluemel, Kristin 1964- 166
Bluemle, Andrew (Waltz) 1929- 1-4R
Blues, Elwood
See Aykroyd, Dan(iel Edward)
Bluestein, Barry (M.) 1950- 154
Bluestein, Daniel Thomas 1943- 65-68
Bluestein, Gene 1928- 81-84
Bluestone, Barry A(lan) 1944- 115
Bluestone, George 1928- CANR-1
Earlier sketch in CA 1-4R
Bluestone, Irving 1917- 136
Bluestone, Max 1926- 13-16R
Bluh, Bonnie 1926- 97-100
Bluhm, Heinz 1907- CAP-1
Earlier sketch in CA 17-18
Bluhm, William T(heodore) 1923- 13-16R
Blum, Albert A(lexander) 1924- CANR-11
Earlier sketch in CA 5-8R
Blum, Bruce I(van) 1931- 144
Blum, Carol (Kathlyn) O'Brien 1934- CANR-17
Earlier sketch in CA 101
Blum, D. Steven 1951- 118
Blum, David 1935-1998 107
Obituary 166
Blum, Deborah (Leigh) 1954- 151
Blum, Eleanor 1914- 1-4R
Blum, Fred 1932- 13-16R
Blum, Harold P. 1929- 103
Blum, Henrik L(eo) 1915- CANR-6
Earlier sketch in CA 9-12R
Blum, Howard 1948- 146
Blum, Jerome 1913-1993 CANR-19
Obituary 141
Earlier sketch in CA 1-4R
Blum, John Morton 1921- CANR-72
Earlier sketches in CA 5-8R, CANR-2
Blum, Lawrence A. 1943- CANR-54
Earlier sketch in CA 124
Blum, Leon 1872-1950 Brief entry 119
Blum, Louise A(gnes) 1960- 151
Blum, Lucille Hollander 1904- 101
Blum, Mark E. 1937- 121
Blum, Ralph AITN 1
Blum, Richard H(osmer Adams) 1927- CANR-69
Earlier sketch in CA 13-16R
Blum, Rudolf 1909- 144
Blum, Shirley Neilsen 1932- 33-36R
Blum, Stella 1916-1985 97-100
Obituary 116
Blum, Virgil C(larence) 1913- 13-16R
Blum, William (Henry) 1933- CANR-51
Earlier sketch in CA 125
Blumberg, Arnold 1925- 33-36R
Blumberg, Dorothy Rose 1904- CAP-2
Earlier sketch in CA 25-28
Blumberg, Gary 1938- CANR-2
Earlier sketch in CA 45-48
Blumberg, Harry 1903- 73-76
Blumberg, Leda 1956- SATA 59
Blumberg, Leonard U. 1920- 101
Blumberg, Morris B. 1917- 123
Blumberg, Myrna 1932- 21-24R
Blumberg, Nathan(iel) Bernard 1922- 41-44R
Blumberg, Paul (Marvin) 1935- Brief entry 113
Blumberg, Phillip I(rvin) 1919- CANR-35
Earlier sketch in CA 101
Blumberg, Rena J(oy) 1934- 109
Blumberg, Rhoda 1917- CANR-26
Earlier sketches in CA 65-68, CANR-9
See also CLR 21
See also MAICYA
See also SATA 35, 70
Blumberg, Rhoda L(ois Goldstein) 1926- CANR-30
Earlier sketches in CA 57-60, CANR-6
Blumberg, Richard E(lliot) 1944- 113
Blumberg, Robert S(tephen) 1945- 57-60
Blumberg, Stanley A. 1912- 136
Blume, Friedrich 1893-1975 73-76
Blume, Harvey 1946- 141
Blume, Helmut 1920- 138
Blume, Judy (Sussman) 1938- CANR-66
Earlier sketches in CA 29-32R, CANR-13, 37
See also AAYA 3, 26
See also CLC 12, 30
See also CLR 2, 15
See also DAM NOV, POP
See also DLB 52
See also JRDA
See also MAICYA
See also MTCW 1
See also SATA 2, 31, 79
Blumenfeld, Gerry 1906- 21-24R
Blumenfeld, Hans 1892- CAP-2
Earlier sketch in CA 21-22
Blumenfeld, Harold 1905(?)-1991 97-100
Obituary 133
Blumenfeld, Meyer 1905-1980 Obituary 97-100
Blumenfeld, Samuel L(eon) 1926- 41-44R
Blumenfeld, (F.) Yorick 1932- 25-28R
Blumenson, Martin 1918- CANR-21
Earlier sketches in CA 1-4R, CANR-4
Blumenstock, David Irving 1913-1963 Obituary 116
Blumenthal, Arthur L. 1936- 29-32R
Blumenthal, David Reuben 1938- 112
Blumenthal, Eileen (Flinder) 1948- 120
Blumenthal, Fred(erick G.)
1919(?)-1986 Obituary 118
Blumenthal, Gerda Renee 1923- 1-4R
Blumenthal, Gertrude 1907-1971 Obituary 104
See also SATA-Obit 27
Blumenthal, Henry 1911-1987 29-32R
Obituary 121
Blumenthal, Howard J. 1952- 136
Blumenthal, John 1949- 129
Blumenthal, L. Roy 1908-1975 Obituary 61-64
Blumenthal, Lassor Agoos 1926- 25-28R
Blumenthal, Michael C. 1949- 110
Blumenthal, Monica David 1930-1981 73-76
Obituary 103
Blumenthal, Norm 97-100
Blumenthal, Shirley 1943- 108
See also SATA 46
Blumenthal, Sid
See Blumenthal, Sidney
Blumenthal, Sidney 1909- 106
Blumenthal, Sidney 1948- 142
Blumenthal, Susan
See Tribich, Susan
Blumenthal, Walter Hart 1883- CAP-1
Earlier sketch in CA 11-12
Blumin, Stuart M(ack) 1940- 65-68
Bluming, Mildred G. 1919- 106
Blumlein, Michael 1948- 156
Blumrich, Josef F(ranz) 1913- 93-96
Blumrosen, Alfred W(illiam) 1928- 53-56
Blunck, Hans Friedrich 1888-1961 DLB 66
Blundel, Anne
See Conley, Enid Mary
Blundell, (Walter) Derek (George) 1929- 135
Blundell, Derek (John) 1933- 144
Blundell, Harold 1902- 101
Blundell, Sue 1947- 151
Blunden, Caroline 1948- 132
Blunden, Edmund (Charles) 1896-1974 CANR-54
Obituary 45-48
Earlier sketches in CAP-2, CA 17-18
See also CLC 2, 56
See also DLB 20, 100, 155
See also MTCW 1
Blunden, Margaret (Anne) 1939- 21-24R
Blunk, Frank M. 1897(?)-1976 Obituary 69-72
Blunsden, John (Beresford) 1930- 57-60
Blunsdon, Norman (Victor Charles) 1915-1968 CAP-1
Earlier sketch in CA 13-14
Blunt, Anthony (Frederick) 1907-1983 113
Obituary 109
Blunt, Don
See Booth, Edwin
Blunt, Lady Anne Isabella Noel 1837-1917 DLB 174
Blunt, Wilfrid (Jasper Walter) 1901-1987 CANR-68
Obituary 121
Earlier sketches in CA 13-16R, CANR-5, 21
Blunt, Wilfrid Scawen 1840-1922 DLB 19, 174
Bluphocks, Lucien
See Seldes, Gilbert (Vivian)
Bluth, B(etty) J(ean) 1934- CANR-49
Earlier sketches in CA 106, CANR-24
Bluth, Don 1938- 156
Blutig, Eduard
See Gorey, Edward (St. John)
Bly, Amy Sprecher 1955- 126
Bly, Carol(yn) 1930- CANR-51
Earlier sketches in CA 108, CANR-26
Bly, Janet (Chester) 1945- CANR-40
Earlier sketch in CA 116
See also SATA 43
Bly, Mark J. 1949- 165
Bly, Nellie
See Cochrane, Elizabeth
Bly, Peter A(nthony) 1944- CANR-38
Earlier sketch in CA 116
Bly, Robert (Elwood) 1926- CANR-41
Earlier sketch in CA 5-8R
See also CLC 1, 2, 5, 10, 15, 38
See also DAM POET
See also DLB 5
See also MTCW 1
Bly, Robert W(ayne) 1957- CANR-40
Earlier sketch in CA 117
See also SATA-Brief 48
Bly, Stephen A(rthur) 1944- CANR-40
Earlier sketch in CA 121
See also SATA 43
Bly, Thomas J. 1918(?)-1979 Obituary 85-88
Blyler, Allison Lee 1966- SATA 74
Blyn, George 1919- CANR-14
Earlier sketch in CA 37-40R
Blyth, Alan 1929- CANR-1
Earlier sketch in CA 49-52
Blyth, Chay 1940- Brief entry 110
Blyth, Estelle 1882(?)-1983 Obituary 109
Blyth, Henry 1910-1983 CANR-69
Obituary 110
Earlier sketch in CA 21-24R
Blyth, Jeffrey 1926- 65-68
Blyth, John
See Hibbs, John
Blyth, Myrna 1939- CANR-10
Earlier sketch in CA 65-68
Blythe, (William) LeGette 1900- CANR-68
Earlier sketches in CA 1-4R, CANR-1
Blythe, Martin 1954- 149
Blythe, Ronald (George) 1922- CANR-48
Earlier sketch in CA 5-8R
Blyton, Carey 1932- 49-52
See also SATA 9
Blyton, Enid (Mary) 1897-1968 CANR-33
Obituary 25-28R
Earlier sketch in CA 77-80
See also CLR 31
See also DLB 160
See also MAICYA
See also SATA 25
Boa, Kenneth 1945- CANR-27
Earlier sketches in CA 61-64, CANR-8
Boadella, David 1931- 53-56
Boaden, James 1762-1839 DLB 89
Boadt, Lawrence 1942- 114
Boag, Peter G. 1961- 147
Boak, Arthur Edward Romilly 1888-1962 5-8R
Boak, (Charles) Denis 1932- 13-16R
Boal, Augusto 1931- 158
Boalch, Donald (Howard) 1914- 9-12R
Boalt, (Hans) Gunnar 1910- CANR-7
Earlier sketch in CA 57-60
Board, C(hester) Stephen 1942- 57-60
Board, Joseph B(reckinridge), Jr. 1931- 29-32R
Boardman, Arthur 1927- 61-64
Boardman, Barrington 1933- 130
Boardman, Brigid M. 1931- CANR-65
Earlier sketch in CA 129
Boardman, Charles C. 1932- 29-32R
Boardman, Eunice
See Meske, Eunice Boardman
Boardman, Fon Wyman, Jr. 1911- CANR-72
Earlier sketches in CA 1-4R, CANR-3
See also SATA 6
Boardman, Francis 1915-1976 Obituary 69-72
Boardman, Gwenn R.
See Petersen, Gwenn Boardman
See also SATA 12
Boardman, John 1927- CANR-72
Earlier sketch in CA 101
Boardman, Michael Moore 1945- 118
Boardman, Neil S(ervis) 1907- CAP-1
Earlier sketch in CA 13-14
Boardman, Peter (David) 1950-1982 97-100
Obituary 108
Boardman, Robert (B.) 1943- 138
Boardman, Thomas Leslie 1919-1990 Obituary 131
Brief entry 111
Boardwell, Robert Lee 1926- 103
Boaretto, Claire 1947- 134
Boarino, Gerald L(ouis) 1931- 21-24R
Boarman, Patrick M(adigan) 1922- CANR-28
Earlier sketches in CA 13-16R, CANR-9
Boas, Claudio Villas
See Villas Boas, Claudio
Boas, Franz 1858-1942 Brief entry 115
See also TCLC 56
Boas, Frederick S. 1862-1957 DLB 149
Boas, Guy (Herman Sidney) 1896-1966 CAP-1
Earlier sketch in CA 11-12
Boas, Jacob 1943- 120
Boas, Louise Schutz 1885-1973 CANR-70
Earlier sketch in CA 5-8R
Boas, Marie
See Hall, Marie Boas
Boas, Maurits Ignatius 1892- CANR-5
Earlier sketch in CA 1-4R
Boas, Orlando Villas
See Villas Boas, Orlando
Boase, Alan Martin 1902-1982 CANR-10
Obituary 108
Earlier sketch in CA 5-8R
Boase, Paul H(enshaw) 1915- 37-40R
Boase, Thomas Sherrer Ross 1898-1974 CANR-70
Earlier sketches in CAP-2, CA 23-24
Boase, Wendy 1944- 106
See also SATA 28
Boast, Philip 1952- 135
Boateng, E(rnest) A(mano) 1920- CANR-28
Earlier sketches in CA 21-24R, CANR-11
Boateng, Yaw Maurice
See Brunner, Maurice Yaw
Boatman, Don Earl 1913- 1-4R
Boatner, Mark Mayo III 1921- 21-24R
See also SATA 29
Boatright, Mody Coggin 1896-1970 CANR-72
Obituary 89-92
Earlier sketches in CA 5-8R, CANR-3
Boatwright, Howard (Leake, Jr.) 1918- 53-56
Boatwright, James III 1933-1988 119
Obituary 126
Boaz, David 1953- 144
Boaz, Martha (Tearosse) CANR-19
Earlier sketches in CA 9-12R, CANR-3
Boaz, Noel T(homas) 1952- CANR-72
Earlier sketch in CA 146

Boba, Imre 1919- 69-72
Bobb, Bernard E(arl) 1917- 5-8R
Bobbe, Dorothie de Bear 1905-1975 ..... CAP-2
  Obituary 57-60
  Earlier sketch in CA 25-28
  See also SATA 1
  See also SATA-Obit 25
Bobbitt, Philip 1948- 108
Bober, Harry 1915-1988 Obituary 125
Bober, Natalie S. 1930- 151
  See also SAAS 23
  See also SATA 87
Bober, P(hyllis) P(ray) 1920- CANR-55
  Earlier sketch in CA 127
Bober, Stanley 1932- CANR-11
  Earlier sketch in CA 21-24R
Bobette
  See Simenon, Georges (Jacques Christian)
Bobette, Bibo
  See Gugliotta, Bobette
Bobinski, George S(ylvan) 1929- 29-32R
Bobker, Lee R(obert) 1925- CANR-9
  Earlier sketch in CA 53-56
Bobo, Lawrence (Douglas) 1958- 124
Bobri, Vladimir V. 1898- 105
  See also Bobritsky, Vladimir
Bobritsky, Vladimir
  See Bobri, Vladimir V.
  See also SATA 47
  See also SATA-Brief 32
Bobroff, Edith
  See Marks, Edith Bobroff
Bobrov, Semen Sergeevich 1763(?)-1810 . DLB 150
Bobrow, Davis Bernard 1936- CANR-7
  Earlier sketch in CA 57-60
Bobrow, Edwin E. 1928- CANR-24
  Earlier sketches in CA 21-24R, CANR-8
Bobrowski, Johannes 1917-1965 ..... CANR-33
  Earlier sketch in CA 77-80
  See also DLB 75
Bobst, Elmer H(olmes) 1884-1978 122
  Obituary 113
Bocardo, Claire 1939- 141
Bocca, Al
  See Winter, Bevis (Peter)
Bocca, Geoffrey 1923-1983 Obituary 110
Boccaccio, Giovanni 1313-1375 ..... SSC 10
Bochak, Grayce 1956- ..... SATA 76
Bochco, Steven 1943- 138
  Brief entry 124
  See also AAYA 11
  See also CLC 35
Bochenski, Innocentius M.
  See Bochenski, Joseph M.
Bochenski, Joseph M. 1902- CANR-7
  Earlier sketch in CA 5-8R
Bochin, Hal W(illiam) 1942- 137
Bochner, Salomon 1899- 41-44R
Bochroch, Albert R(obert) 1909- CANR-39
  Earlier sketch in CA 111
Bock, Alan W(illiam) 1943- 41-44R
Bock, Carl H(einz) 1930-(?) CAP-2
  Earlier sketch in CA 19-20
Bock, Fred 1939- CANR-10
  Earlier sketch in CA 25-28R
Bock, Frederick 1916- 9-12R
Bock, Gisela 1942- 138
Bock, Hal
  See Bock, Harold I.
Bock, Harold I. 1939- 29-32R
  See also SATA 10
Bock, Joanne 1940- 57-60
Bock, Paul J(ohn) 1922- 53-56
Bock, Philip K. 1934- CANR-11
  Earlier sketch in CA 25-28R
Bock, William Sauts Netamux'we 1939- ... SATA 14
Bockelman, Wilfred 1920- 37-40R
Bockl, George 1909- 61-64
Bockle, Franz
  See Boeckle, Franz
Bockmon, Guy Alan 1926- 5-8R
Bockstoce, John R(oberts) 1944- 121
Bockus, H(erman) William 1915- 53-56
Bocock, Robert (James) 1940- CANR-28
  Earlier sketches in CA 69-72, CANR-12
Boczek, Boleslaw Adam 1922- CANR-4
  Earlier sketch in CA 1-4R
Bod, Peter
  See Vesenyi, Paul E.
Bodansky, Oscar 1901-1977 Obituary 73-76
Bodard, Lucien (Albert) 1914-1998 149
  Obituary 165
  Brief entry 116
Bodart, Joni
  See Bodart-Talbot, Joni
Bodart-Talbot, Joni 1947- CANR-23
  Earlier sketch in CA 106
Boddewyn, J(ean) J. 1929- CANR-39
  Earlier sketches in CA 25-28R, CANR-17
Boddie, Charles Emerson 1911- 65-68
Boddington, Craig Thornton 1952- CANR-28
  Earlier sketch in CA 111
Boddy, David 1940- 119
Boddy, Frederick A(rthur) 1914- 61-64
Boddy, Janice 1951- 134
Boddy, William Charles 1913- 101
Bode, Carl 1911-1993 ..... CANR-20
  Obituary 140
  Earlier sketches in CA 1-4R, CANR-3
Bode, Elroy 1931- CANR-10
  Earlier sketch in CA 25-28R
Bode, Janet 1943- CANR-67
  Earlier sketches in CA 69-72, CANR-12
  See also AAYA 21
  See also SATA 60, 96
Bode, Roy E. 1948- 77-80
Bodecker, N(iels) M(ogens) 1922-1988 .. CANR-40
  Obituary 124
  Earlier sketches in CA 49-52, CANR-4
  See also MAICYA
  See also SATA 8, 73
  See also SATA-Obit 54
Bodeen, DeWitt 1908-1988 ..... CANR-10
  Obituary 125
  Earlier sketch in CA 25-28R
Bodell, Mary
  See Pecsok, Mary Bodell
Bodelsen, Anders 1937- 128
Boden, Hilda
  See Bodenham, Hilda Morris
Boden, Margaret A. 1936- 93-96
Bodenham, Hilda Morris 1901- CANR-6
  Earlier sketch in CA 9-12R
  See also SATA 13
Bodenhamer, David J(ackson) 1947- 142
Bodenheim, Maxwell 1892-1954 Brief entry 110
  See also DLB 9, 45
  See also TCLC 44
Bodenheimer, Edgar 1908- CANR-20
  Earlier sketch in CA 33-36R
Bodenstedt, Friedrich von 1819-1892 ..... DLB 129
Bodet, Jaime Torres
  See Torres Bodet, Jaime
Bodett, Thomas Edward 1955- CANR-64
  Earlier sketches in CA 123, CANR-44
  See also Bodett, Tom
Bodett, Tom
  See Bodett, Thomas Edward
  See also SATA 70
Bodey, Donald 1946- 128
Bodey, Hugh (Arthur) 1939- CANR-12
  Earlier sketch in CA 61-64
Bodger, Joan
  See Mercer, Joan Bodger
Bodian, Nat G. 1921- CANR-44
  Earlier sketches in CA 103, CANR-20
Bodie, Idella F(allaw) 1925- CANR-55
  Earlier sketch in CA 41-44R
  See also SATA 12, 89
Bodin, Paul 1909- 65-68
Bodine, Eunice
  See Lapp, Eunice Willis Bodine
Bodington, Nancy H(ermione) 1912- CANR-67
  Earlier sketch in CA 53-56
Bodington, Stephen 1909- 123
Bodini, Vittorio 1914-1970 ..... DLB 128
Bodker, Cecil 1927- CANR-44
  Earlier sketches in CA 73-76, CANR-13
  See also CLC 21
  See also CLR 23
  See also MAICYA
  See also SATA 14
Bodkin, Cora 1944- 69-72
Bodkin, M(atthias) M'Donnell 1850-1933 Brief entry 114
  See also DLB 70
Bodkin, Maud 1875- CAP-1
  Earlier sketch in CA 11-12
Bodkin, Ronald G(eorge) 1936- 33-36R
Bodle, Yvonne Gallegos 1939- 33-36R
Bodley, Hal
  See Bodley, Harley Ryan, Jr.
Bodley, Harley Ryan, Jr. 1936- 126
Bodmer, Johann Jakob 1698-1783 ..... DLB 97
Bodmer, Walter Fred 1936- 102
Bodmershof, Imma von 1895-1982 ..... DLB 85
Bodnar, John Edward 1944- 110
Bodo, Murray 1937- CANR-46
  Earlier sketches in CA 57-60, CANR-7, 23
Bodo, Peter T. 1949- 85-88
Bodoh, John J(ames) 1931- 45-48
Bodsworth, (Charles) Fred(erick) 1918- .. CANR-66
  Earlier sketches in CA 1-4R, CANR-3
  See also DLB 68
  See also SATA 27
Bodwell, Richard
  See Spring, Gerald M(ax)
Boeckle, Franz 1921- 101
Boeckman, Charles 1920- 13-16R
  See also SATA 12
Boeckman, Patti CANR-28
  Earlier sketch in CA 109
Boege, Ulrich Gustav 1940- 97-100
Boegehold, Alan L(indley) 1927- 146
Boegehold, Betty (Doyle) 1913-1985 ..... CANR-12
  Obituary 115
  Earlier sketch in CA 69-72
  See also SATA-Obit 42
Boegner, Marc 1881-1970 Obituary 29-32R
Boehling, Rebecca L. 1955- 164
Boehlke, Frederick J(ohn), Jr. 1926- 21-24R
Boehlke, Robert R(ichard) 1925- 5-8R
Boehlow, Robert H(enry) 1925- 53-56
Boehm, Christopher 1937- 121
Boehm, Eric H. 1918- 13-16R
Boehm, Herb
  See Varley, John (Herbert)
Boehm, Karl 1894-1981 Obituary 105
Boehm, Sydney 1908-1990 147
  See also DLB 44
Boehm, William D(ryden) 1946- 61-64
Boehme, Gernot 1937- 145
Boehme, Jakob 1575-1624 ..... DLB 164
Boehme, Lillian R.
  See Rodberg, Lillian
Boehmer, Elleke 1961- 164
Boehning, W. R.
  See Bohning, W(olf) R(uediger)
Boehringer, Robert 1885(?)-1974 Obituary ... 53-56
Boelcke, Willi A(lfred) 1929- Brief entry 107
Boelen, Bernard J(acques) 1916- 41-44R
Boell, Heinrich (Theodor) 1917-1985 ..... CANR-24
  Obituary 116
  Earlier sketch in CA 21-24R
  See also CLC 2, 3, 6, 9, 11, 15, 27, 32, 72
  See also DA
  See also DAB
  See also DAC
  See also DAM MST, NOV
  See also DLB 69
  See also DLBY 85
  See also MTCW 1
  See also SSC 23
  See also WLC
Boelts, Maribeth 1964- 146
  See also SATA 78
Boeman, John (Sigler) 1923- 108
Boer, Charles 1939- 69-72
  See also DLB 5
Boer, Harry R(einier) 1913- CANR-4
  Earlier sketch in CA 1-4R
Boerne, Alfred
  See Doeblin, Alfred
Boerne, Ludwig 1786-1837 ..... DLB 90
Boers, Arthur Paul 1957- 138
Boesch, Hans Heinrich 1911-1978 Obituary ... 116
Boesch, Mark J(oseph) 1917- 21-24R
  See also SATA 12
Boesel, David 1938- 41-44R
Boesen, Victor 1908- 37-40R
  See also SATA 16
Boesiger, Willi 1904- 102
Boessenecker, John 1953- 138
Boeth, Richard 1933-1982 Obituary 107
Boethius 480(?)-524(?) ..... DLB 115
Boethius of Dacia 1240(?)-(?) ..... DLB 115
Boetie, Dugmore 1920(?)-1966 Obituary 109
Boettcher, Henry J. 1893- CAP-1
  Earlier sketch in CA 19-20
Boettcher, Robert B. 1941(?)-1984 Obituary ... 112
Boettcher, Thomas D. 1944- 129
Boetticher, Budd 1916- 157
Boettinger, Henry M(aurice) 1924- 73-76
Boeve, Edgar G. 1929- 21-24R
Boewe, Charles (Ernst) 1924- 9-12R
Boff, Leonardo (Genezio Darci) 1938- 150
  See also DAM MULT
  See also HLC
Boff, Vic 1915- 103
Boffa, Giuseppe 1923- 140
Boffey, David Barnes 1945- 110
Bogaduck
  See Lindsay, Harold Arthur
Bogaerts, Gert 1965- ..... SATA 80
Bogan, Christopher E(ric) 1954- 144
Bogan, James 1945- 103
Bogan, Louise 1897-1970 ..... CANR-33
  Obituary 25-28R
  Earlier sketch in CA 73-76
  See also CLC 4, 39, 46, 93
  See also DAM POET
  See also DLB 45, 169
  See also MTCW 1
  See also PC 12
Bogard, Travis (Miller) 1918-1997 69-72
  Obituary 157
Bogarde, Dirk
  See Van Den Bogarde, Derek Jules Gaspard Ulric Niven
  See also CLC 19
  See also DLB 14
Bogardus, Emory Stephen 1882-1973 Obituary . 116
Bogart, Carlotta 1929- 61-64
Bogart, E. A.
  See Bogart, Eleanor A(nne)
Bogart, Eleanor A(nne) 1928- 137
Bogart, Frank L. 1914-1993 161
Bogart, Jo Ellen 1945- 156
  See also SATA 92
Bogart, Leo 1921- CANR-14
  Earlier sketch in CA 41-44R
Bogart, Mary Hattan 1916- 161
Bogart, Stephen Humphrey 1949- CANR-72
  Earlier sketch in CA 150
Bogat, Shatan
  See Kacew, Romain
Bogatyryov, Konstantin
  1924(?)-1976 Obituary 65-68
Bogdan, Robert 1941- 128
Bogdanor, Vernon 1943- CANR-35
  Earlier sketches in CA 81-84, CANR-14
Bogdanov, Michael 1938- 129
Bogdanovich, Ippolit Fedorovich c. 1743-1803 . DLB 150
Bogdanovich, Peter 1939- CANR-71
  Earlier sketches in CA 5-8R, CANR-21
Bogen, Hyman 1924- 140
Bogen, James Benjamin 1935- 89-92
Bogen, Laurel Ann 1950- CANR-35
  Earlier sketch in CA 112
Bogen, Nancy R(uth) 1932- 97-100
Boger, Louise Ade 1909- Brief entry 115
Bogert, L(otta) Jean 1888-1970 ..... CAP-1
  Earlier sketch in CA 11-12
Boggan, E(lton) Carrington 1943- 101
Boggess, Louise Bradford 1912- CANR-53
  Earlier sketches in CA 13-16R, CANR-7, 28
Boggs, Bill
  See Boggs, William III
Boggs, James 1919- 77-80
Boggs, Jean Sutherland 1922- 108
Boggs, Marcus 1947- 108
Boggs, Ralph Steele 1901- CAP-1
  Earlier sketch in CA 11-12
  See also SATA 7
Boggs, W(ilmot) Arthur 1916- 17-20R
Boggs, Wade Hamilton, Jr. 1916- 13-16R
Boggs, William III 1942- 102
Bogin, George 1920- 104
Bogin, Magda 1950- 148
Bogin, Meg
  See Bogin, Magda
Bogin, Ruth 1920- 122
Bogle, Donald ..... AITN 1
Bogle, Warren
  See Bergman, Andrew
Bogner, Norman 1935- CANR-15
  Earlier sketch in CA 5-8R
  See also AITN 2
Bogomolny, Robert L(ee) 1938- 121
Bogosian, Eric 1953- 138
  See also CLC 45
Bogoslovsky, Christina Stael
  1888(?)-1974 Obituary 49-52
Bograd, Larry 1953- CANR-57
  Earlier sketch in CA 93-96
  See also CLC 35
  See also SAAS 21
  See also SATA 33, 89
Bogue, Allan G(eorge Britton) 1921- 107
Bogue, Jesse C. 1912(?)-1983 Obituary 111
Bogue, Lucile 1911- CANR-13
  Earlier sketch in CA 37-40R
Bogue, Merwyn (Alton) 1908-1994 131
  Obituary 145
Boguraev, Branimir Konstantinov 1950- 163
Bogus, SDiane (Adams) 1946- 141
  See also BW 2
Boguslaw, Robert 1919- 132
Boguslawski, Dorothy Beers
  1911(?)-1978 Obituary 77-80
Bohan, Peter 33-36R
Bohana, Aileen Stein 1951- 103
Bohannan, Paul (James) 1920- 9-12R
Bohdal, Susi 1951- 97-100
  See also SATA 22, 101
Bohem, Endre 1901(?)-1990 Obituary 131
Bohen, Halcyone H(arger) 1937- 108
Bohen, Sister Marian 1930- 5-8R
Bohi, Charles W(esley) 1940- 89-92
Bohi, M. Janette 1927- 25-28R
Bohjalian, Chris 1960- 139
Bohlander, Jill 1936- 37-40R
Bohle, Bruce 1918- CANR-9
  Earlier sketch in CA 21-24R
Bohle, Edgar (Henry) 1909- 1-4R
Bohlen, Charles Eustis 1904-1974 Obituary 111
Bohlen, Joe M(erl) 1919- 5-8R
Bohlen, Nina 1931- ..... SATA 58
Bohlke, L(andall) Brent 1942-1987 124
Bohlman, (Mary) Edna McCaull 1897- CAP-1
  Earlier sketch in CA 9-10
Bohlman, Herbert W(illiam) 1896- CAP-1
  Earlier sketch in CA 19-20
Bohlmeijer, Arno 1956- 156
  See also SATA 94
Bohme, Gernot
  See Boehme, Gernot
Bohn, Frank 1878-1975 Obituary 57-60
Bohn, Joyce Illig 1940(?)-1976 Obituary 69-72
Bohn, Martin J(ohn), Jr. 1938- 116
Bohn, Ralph C. 1930- CANR-11
  Earlier sketch in CA 17-20R
Bohner, Charles (Henry) 1927- 118
  See also SATA 62
Bohnet, Michael 1937- 102
Bohnhoff, Maya Kaathryn 1954- 152
  See also SATA 88
Bohning, W(olf) R(uediger) 1942- 111
Bohnstedt, John W(olfgang) 1927- 33-36R
Bohr, Niels (Henrik David) 1885-1962 155
  Obituary 112
Bohr, R(ussell) L(eRoi) 1916- 25-28R
Bohr, Theophilus
  See Thistle, Mel(ville William)
Bohren, Craig F. 1940- CANR-60
  Earlier sketch in CA 128
Bohrnstedt, George W(illiam) 1938- CANR-44
  Earlier sketches in CA 33-36R, CANR-20
Bohrod, Aaron 1907- 21-24R
Bohse, August 1661-1742 ..... DLB 168
Boice, James Montgomery 1938- CANR-51
  Earlier sketches in CA 29-32R, CANR-12, 28
Boie, Heinrich Christian 1744-1806 ..... DLB 94
Boiko, Claire Taylor 1925- 93-96
Boiles, Charles Lafayette (Jr.) 1932- 65-68
Boime, Albert 1933- 125
Bois, J(oseph) Samuel 1892- 33-36R
Boisgilbert, Edmund M.D.
  See Donnelly, Ignatius
Boissard, Janine 1932- ..... SATA 59
Boisset, Caroline 1955- 134
Boissevain, Jeremy 1928- CANR-21
  Earlier sketches in CA 57-60, CANR-6
Boissiere, Robert 1914- 119
Boissoneau, Robert 1937- 105
Boissonneau, Alice 101
Boitani, Piero 1947- 137
Bojaxhiu, Agnes Gonxha
  See Mother Teresa
Bojer, Johan 1872-1959 ..... TCLC 64
Bok, Bart J(an) 1906-1983 ..... CANR-30
  Obituary 110
  Earlier sketch in CA 49-52
Bok, Cary W(illiam) 1905-1970 Obituary 29-32R
Bok, Derek (Curtis) 1930- CANR-64
  Earlier sketch in CA 106
Bok, Edward W. 1863-1930 ..... DLB 91
  See also DLBD 16
Bok, Hannes (Vajn) 1914-1964 154
Bok, Priscilla F(airfield) 1896- 49-52
Bok, Sissela Ann 1934- CANR-32
  Earlier sketch in CA 112

Bokenkotter, Thomas 1924- CANR-17
Earlier sketch in CA 85-88
Bokina, John 1948- 148
Bokser, Ben Zion 1907-1984 .... CANR-69
Obituary 111
Earlier sketches in CA 65-68, CANR-11
Bokum, Fanny Butcher 1888-1987 .... 37-40R
Obituary 122
Bokun, Branko 1920- 45-48
Boland, Bridget 1913-1988 101
Obituary 124
Boland, Charles Michael 1917- 9-12R
Boland, Daniel 1891- CAP-1
Earlier sketch in CA 13-14
Boland, Eavan (Aisling) 1944- CANR-61
Earlier sketch in CA 143
See also CLC 40, 67, 113
See also DAM POET
See also DLB 40
Boland, Janice 165
See also SATA 98
Boland, (Bertram) John 1913-1976 .... CANR-10
Earlier sketch in CA 9-12R
Boland, Lillian C(anon) 1919- 29-32R
Bolch, Ben W(ilsman) 1938- 57-60
Bolcom, William E(lden) 1938- 93-96
Bold, Alan Norman 1943- CANR-30
Earlier sketch in CA 25-28R
Bolden, Tonya (Wilyce) 1959- 147
See also SATA 79
Bolding, Amy 1910- 73-76
Boldizsar, Ivan 1912-1988 Obituary 127
Boldt, Menno 1930- CANR-46
Earlier sketch in CA 120
Bolen, Jean Shinoda 1936- 110
Boles, Donald Edward 1926- CANR-18
Earlier sketch in CA 1-4R
Boles, Harold W(ilson) 1915- 17-20R
Boles, John B. 1943- CANR-48
Earlier sketches in CA 37-40R, CANR-14
Boles, Paul Darcy 1916-1984 .... CANR-4
Obituary 112
Earlier sketch in CA 9-12R
See also SATA 9
See also SATA-Obit 38
Boles, Robert (E.) 1943- .... BW 2
Bolgan, Anne C(atherine) 1923-1992(?) 41-44R
Obituary 136
Bolgar, (Caius Coriolanus) R(obert) R(alph)
1913-1985 Obituary 117
Bolger, Daniel P(atrick) 1957- 150
Bolger, Dermot 1959- 145
Bolger, Philip C(unningham) 1927- CANR-6
Earlier sketch in CA 57-60
Bolgiano, Chris(tina) 1948- 151
Bolian, Polly 1925- 33-36R
See also SATA 4
Bolin, Luis (A.) 1894-1969 .... CAP-2
Earlier sketch in CA 23-24
Boling, Katharine (Singleton) 1933- 57-60
Bolingbroke, Viscount
See St. John, Henry
Bolinger, Dwight (L.) 1907-1992 .... CANR-7
Obituary 137
Earlier sketch in CA 13-16R
Bolino, August C(onstantino) 1922- CANR-18
Earlier sketch in CA 1-4R
Bolitho, Archie A(rdella) 1886- CAP-1
Earlier sketch in CA 9-10
Bolitho, Harold 1939- 103
Bolitho, (Henry) Hector 1897-1974 .... CANR-68
Obituary 53-56
Earlier sketches in CAP-1, CA 9-10
Bolitho, Ray D.
See Blair, Dorothy S(ara Greene)
Bolkhovitinov, Nikolai Nikolaevich 1930- 97-100
Bolkosky, Sidney M(arvin) 1944- 65-68
Boll, Carl R. 1894- CAP-1
Earlier sketch in CA 17-18
Boll, David 1931- 21-24R
Boll, Ernest
See Boll, Theophilus E(rnest) M(artin)
Boll, Heinrich
See Boell, Heinrich (Theodor)
Boll, Theo
See Boll, Theophilus E(rnest) M(artin)
Boll, Theophilus E(rnest) M(artin) 1902- 37-40R
Bolland, O(rlando) Nigel 1943- 110
Bolle, Kees W. 1927- CANR-17
Earlier sketch in CA 25-28R
Bollen, Roger 1941(?)- .... AITN 1
See also SATA 83
See also SATA-Brief 29
Bollens, John C(onstantinus) 1920-1983 .... CANR-3
Obituary 111
Earlier sketch in CA 1-4R
Boller, Paul Franklin, Jr. 1916- CANR-41
Earlier sketches in CA 1-4R, CANR-3, 19
Bolles, (Edmund) Blair 1911-1990 .... 9-12R
Obituary 130
Bolles, Donald F. 1928-1976 73-76
Obituary 65-68
Bolles, Richard Nelson 1927- CANR-1
Earlier sketch in CA 45-48
Bolles, Robert C(harles) 1928- 21-24R
Bollettieri, Nick J(ames) 1931- 110
Bolliger, Max 1929- 25-28R
See also SATA 7
Bolling, Hal
See Schwalberg, Carol(yn Ernestine Stein)
Bolling, Richard (Walker) 1916-1991 .... 17-20R
Obituary 134
Bolling, Robert 1738-1775 .... DLB 31
Bollinger, Lee C. 1946- 138
Bolloten, Burnett 1909-1987 93-96
Obituary 123
Bolls, Imogene (Lamb) 1938- 149
Bolman, Frederick deWolfe, Jr.
1912-1985 Obituary 117
Bolman, Lee G. 1941- 149
Bolner, James (Jerome) 1936- 61-64
Bologna, Joseph 77-80
Bolognese, Don(ald Alan) 1934- CANR-45
Earlier sketch in CA 97-100
See also MAICYA
See also SATA 24, 71
Bolognese, Elaine (Raphael Chionchio)
1933- 97-100
See also Raphael, Elaine
Bolotin, Norman (Phillip) 1951- 159
See also SATA 93
Bolotov, Andrei Timofeevich 1738-1833 .... DLB 150
Bolotowsky, Ilya 1907-1981 Obituary 108
Bolshakoff, Serge 1901- 93-96
Bolster, John 1910-1984 89-92
Obituary 111
Bolster, W(illiam) Jeffrey 1954- 161
Bolsterli, Margaret Jones 1931- 111
Bolt, Bruce A(lan) 1930- CANR-10
Earlier sketch in CA 65-68
Bolt, Carol 1941- CANR-70
Earlier sketch in CA 101
See also DLB 60
Bolt, David (Michael) Langstone 1927- CANR-6
Earlier sketch in CA 1-4R
Bolt, Ernest C(ollier), Jr. 1936- 77-80
Bolt, Jonathan 1935- 145
Bolt, Lee
See Faust, Frederick (Schiller)
Bolt, Martin 1944- 118
Bolt, Robert (Oxton) 1924-1995 .... CANR-67
Obituary 147
Earlier sketches in CA 17-20R, CANR-35
See also CLC 14
See also DAM DRAM
See also DLB 13
See also MTCW 1
Bolten, Steven E. 1941- 37-40R
Boltho, Andrea 1939- CANR-42
Earlier sketch in CA 69-72
Bolton, Carole 1926- CANR-1
Earlier sketch in CA 49-52
See also SATA 6
Bolton, Edmund 1575(?)-1633(?) .... DLB 121
Bolton, Elizabeth
See St. John, Nicole
Bolton, Evelyn
See Bunting, Anne Evelyn
Bolton, Guy (Reginald) 1884-1979 .... 5-8R
Obituary 89-92
Bolton, H(arold) Philip 1944- 127
Bolton, Herbert E. 1870-1953 .... DLB 17
Bolton, Isabel
See Miller, Mary Britton
Bolton, James 1917(?)-1981 Obituary 103
Bolton, John Robert 1948- 115
Bolton, Kenneth (Ewart) 1914- 9-12R
Bolton, Maisie Sharman 1915- 9-12R
Bolton, Muriel Roy 1909(?)-1983 Obituary 109
Bolton, Ruthie 1961- 147
Bolton, Theodore 1889(?)-1973 Obituary 45-48
Bolton, W(hitney) F(rench) 1930- 17-20R
Bolton, Whitney 1900-1969 Obituary 25-28R
Bolus, James Michael 1943- 111
Bolus, Jim
See Bolus, James Michael
Bolz, Frank A., Jr. 1930- 127
Boman, Thorleif Gustav 1894- 21-24R
Bomans, Godfried J(an) A(rnold) 1913-1971 .... CAP-2
Earlier sketch in CA 29-32
Bomar, Cora Paul 1913- 41-44R
Bombal, Maria Luisa 1910-1980 .... CANR-72
Earlier sketch in CA 127
See also HW
Bombardieri, Merle 1949- 107
Bombeck, Erma (Louise) 1927-1996 .... CANR-39
Obituary 151
Earlier sketches in CA 21-24R, CANR-12
Interview in CANR-12
See also AITN 1
See also BEST 89:4
See also DAM POP
See also MTCW 1
Bombelles, Joseph T. 1930- 25-28R
Bombet, Louis-Alexandre-Cesar
See Stendhal
Bomeli, Edwin C(larence) 1920- 21-24R
Bomkauf
See Kaufman, Bob (Garnell)
Bommarito, James W. 1922- 121
Bona, Mercy
See Ziegler, Alan
Bonachea, E(nrique) Rolando 1943- 41-44R
Bonacich, Edna 1940- 45-48
Bonanno, Margaret Wander 1950- CANR-40
Earlier sketch in CA 85-88
Bonansea, Bernardino M(aria) 1908- CANR-14
Earlier sketch in CA 41-44R
Bonansinga, Jay R. 166
Bonaparte, Felicia 1937- CANR-11
Earlier sketch in CA 61-64
Bonar, Veronica
See Bailey, Donna (Veronica Anne)
Bonatti, Walter 1930- CANR-48
Earlier sketches in CA 106, CANR-23
Bonaventura .... DLB 90
Bonaventure 1217(?)-1274 .... DLB 115
Bonavia, David Michael 1940-1988 106
Obituary 126
Bonavia-Hunt, Noel Aubrey 1882-1965 .... CAP-1
Earlier sketch in CA 9-10
Bonaviri, Giuseppe 1924- .... DLB 177
Bonbright, James C(ummings) 1891-1985 .... 1-4R
Obituary 117
Bond, Alma H(albert) 1923- 130
Bond, B. J.
See Heneghan, James
Bond, Brian 1936- CANR-6
Earlier sketch in CA 57-60
Bond, Bruce 1939- .... SATA 61
Bond, Charles R(ankin), Jr. 1915- 124
Bond, Christopher Godfrey 1945- 101
Bond, Donald F(rederic) 1898-1987 .... 13-16R
Obituary 121
Bond, Douglas Danford 1911-1976 Obituary 69-72
Bond, E(dward) J(arvis) 1930- 114
Bond, Edward 1934- CANR-67
Earlier sketches in CA 25-28R, CANR-38
See also CLC 4, 6, 13, 23
See also DAM DRAM
See also DLB 13
See also MTCW 1
Bond, Elaine 1924-1984 Obituary 112
Bond, Evelyn
See Hershman, Morris
Bond, Felicia 1954- 127
See also SATA 49
Bond, Geoffrey 1924-1978 .... 29-32R
Obituary 134
Bond, George C(lement) 1936- 147
Bond, Gladys Baker 1912- CANR-2
Earlier sketch in CA 5-8R
See also SATA 14
Bond, Harold 1939- CANR-11
Earlier sketch in CA 65-68
Bond, Higgins 1951- .... SATA 83
Bond, Horace Mann 1904-1972 .... CANR-1
Obituary 37-40R
Earlier sketch in CA 1-4R
Bond, J. Harvey
See Winterbotham, R(ussell) R(obert)
Bond, James 1900-1989 Obituary 127
Bond, Jean Carey 106
Bond, Julian 1940- 49-52
See also BW 1
Bond, Lewis H.
See Paine, Lauran (Bosworth)
Bond, Marshall, Jr. 1908- CAP-2
Earlier sketch in CA 25-28
Bond, Mary Fanning Wickham 1898- 21-24R
Bond, Maurice Francis 1916-1983 Obituary 111
Bond, (Thomas) Michael 1926- CANR-49
Earlier sketches in CA 5-8R, CANR-4, 24
See also CLR 1
See also MAICYA
See also SAAS 3
See also SATA 6, 58
Bond, Michael 1926-
Interview in CANR-24
See also DLB 161
Bond, Mrs. James
See Bond, Mary Fanning Wickham
Bond, Nancy (Barbara) 1945- CANR-36
Earlier sketches in CA 65-68, CANR-9
See also CLR 11
See also JRDA
See also MAICYA
See also SAAS 13
See also SATA 22, 82
Bond, Nelson S(lade) 1908- CANR-58
Earlier sketches in CAP-1, CA 19-20
Bond, Otto F(erdinand) 1885- 1-4R
Bond, Ray
See Smith, Richard Rein
Bond, Raymond T. 1893(?)-1981 Obituary 104
Bond, Richmond Pugh 1899- CAP-2
Earlier sketch in CA 33-36
Bond, Ruskin 1934- CANR-52
Earlier sketches in CA 29-32R, CANR-14, 31
See also SATA 14, 87
Bond, Simon 1947- 104
Bond, Ted
See Bond, E(dward) J(arvis)
Bond, William Henry 1915- CANR-54
Earlier sketch in CA 124
Bond, William J(oseph) 1941- CANR-51
Earlier sketches in CA 108, CANR-26
Bondanella, Peter Eugene 1943- CANR-29
Earlier sketches in CA 65-68, CANR-10
Bonder, Nilton 1957- 164
Bonderoff, Jason (Dennis) 1946- 97-100
Bondi, Joseph C. 1936- CANR-28
Earlier sketches in CA 29-32R, CANR-11
Bondie, J. D.
See Cunningham, Chet
Bondurant, Joan V(alerie) 1918- 41-44R
Bondy, Sebastian Salazar
See Salazar Bondy, Sebastian
Bone, Edith 1889(?)-1975 Obituary 57-60
Bone, Hugh A(lvin) 1909- CANR-3
Earlier sketch in CA 1-4R
Bone, J. F.
See Bone, Jesse F(ranklin)
Bone, Jesse F(ranklin) 1916- CANR-55
Earlier sketch in CA 57-60
Bone, Quentin 1918- 85-88
Bone, Robert (Adamson) 1924- 69-72
Bone, Robert C(larke) 1917- 37-40R
Bonehill, Captain Ralph
See Stratemeyer, Edward L.
Bonelli, Robert Allen 1950- 112
Bonellie, Helen-Janet 1937- 41-44R
Bonello, Frank J. 1939- 154
Bones, James C., Jr. 1943- 125
Bones, Jim, Jr.
See Bones, James C., Jr.
Boness, A. James 1928- 37-40R
Bonestell, Chesley 1888-1986 Obituary 119
See also SATA-Obit 48
Bonett, Emery
See Coulson, Felicity Carter
Bonett, John
See Coulson, John H(ubert) A(rthur)
Bonetti, Edward 1928- 93-96
Bonewits, Isaac
See Bonewits, P(hilip) E(mmons) I(saac)
Bonewits, P(hilip) E(mmons) I(saac) 1949- 93-96
Boney, Elaine E(mesette) 1921- Brief entry 110
Boney, F(rancis) N(ash) 1929- CANR-46
Earlier sketches in CA 41-44R, CANR-15
Boney, Mary Lily
See Sheats, Mary Boney
Boney, William Jerry 1930- 21-24R
Bonfante, Giuliano 1904- 158
Bonfante, Larissa CANR-11
Earlier sketch in CA 69-72
Bongar, Emmet W(ald) 1919- 33-36R
Bongard, David L(awrence) 1959- 140
Bongartz, Heinz
See Thorwald, Juergen
Bongartz, Roy 1924-1989 .... 13-16R
Obituary 128
Bongie, Laurence L(ouis) 1929- 61-64
Bonham, Barbara Thomas 1926- CANR-7
Earlier sketch in CA 17-20R
See also SATA 7
Bonham, Frank 1914-1989 .... CANR-36
Earlier sketches in CA 9-12R, CANR-4
See also AAYA 1
See also CLC 12
See also JRDA
See also MAICYA
See also SAAS 3
See also SATA 1, 49
See also SATA-Obit 62
Bonham-Carter, Victor 1913- 9-12R
Bonham Carter, (Helen) Violet (Asquith)
1887-1969 .... CAP-2
Earlier sketch in CA 17-18
Bonheim, Helmut 1930- CANR-4
Earlier sketch in CA 1-4R
Bonhoeffer, Dietrich 1906-1945 148
Brief entry 122
Bonhomme, Denise 1926- 104
Boni, Albert 1892-1981 65-68
Obituary 104
Boni, Margaret Bradford
1893(?)-1974 Obituary 53-56
Boniface, William 1963- .... SATA 102
Bonifacio, Amelia Lapena
See Lapena-Bonifacio, Amelia
Bonime, Florence 1907- 49-52
Bonime, Walter 1909- CAP-2
Earlier sketch in CA 17-18
Bonine, Gladys Nichols 1907- CAP-1
Earlier sketch in CA 13-16
Bonington, Chris(tian John Storey) 1934- CANR-34
Earlier sketches in CA 45-48, CANR-1
Bonini, Charles P(ius) 1933- 13-16R
Bonino, Louise
See Williams, Louise Bonino
Bonjean, Charles M. 1935- 41-44R
Bonk, James 1932- 123
Bonk, Wallace J. 1923- 9-12R
Bonn, Pat
See Bonn, Patricia Carolyn
Bonn, Patricia Carolyn 1948- .... SATA 43
Bonn, Robert Lewis 1937- 125
Bonn, Thomas L. 1939- 109
Bonnamy, Francis
See Walz, Audrey Boyers
Bonnar, Alphonsus 1895-1968 .... CAP-1
Earlier sketch in CA 9-10
Bonnay, Charles (Louis) 1930-1986 Obituary 119
Bonnefoy, Yves 1923- CANR-33
Earlier sketch in CA 85-88
See also CLC 9, 15, 58
See also DAM MST, POET
See also MTCW 1
Bonnell, Dorothy Haworth 1914- CANR-3
Earlier sketch in CA 1-4R
Bonnell, F(raser) C(larence) 1908-1983 118
Bonnell, F(lorence Rhodes) W(inn) 1915- 118
Bonnell, John Sutherland 1893-1992 .... 5-8R
Obituary 136
Bonner, Arthur 1922- 135
Bonner, Brian 1917- CANR-21
Earlier sketch in CA 104
Bonner, Cindy 1953- 139
Bonner, Gerald 1926- CANR-5
Earlier sketch in CA 9-12R
Bonner, Jack
See Paine, Lauran (Bosworth)
Bonner, James Calvin 1904- CANR-9
Earlier sketch in CA 9-12R
Bonner, Joey 1948- 122
Bonner, John Tyler 1920- CANR-48
Earlier sketch in CA 49-52
Bonner, Marita
See Occomy, Marita (Odette) Bonner
Bonner, Mary Graham 1890-1974 .... CANR-68
Obituary 49-52
Earlier sketch in CA 73-76
See also SATA 19
Bonner, Michael
See Glasscock, Anne Bonner
Bonner, Parker
See Ballard, (Willis) Todhunter
Bonner, Paul Hyde 1893-1968 .... CANR-72
Obituary 103
Earlier sketch in CA 1-4R
See also DLBD 17
Bonner, Raymond T(homas) 1942- 117

Bonner, Sherwood 1849-1883 ... DLB 202
Bonner, Terry Nelsen
See Castoro, Laura A(nn)
and Krauzer, Steven M(ark)
and Raeschild, Sheila
and Yarbro, Chelsea Quinn
Bonner, Thomas, Jr. 1942- ... 110
Bonner, Thomas N(eville) 1923- ... 9-12R
Bonner, William H(omer) 1924- ... 53-56
Bonner, William Hallam 1899-1980 Obituary ... 115
Bonners, Susan 1947- ... SATA 85
See also SATA-Brief 48
Bonnette, Jeanne 1907- ... 41-44R
Bonnette, Victor
See Roy, Ewell Paul
Bonneville, Douglas A(lan) 1931- ... 21-24R
Bonney, Bill
See Keevill, Henry J(ohn)
Bonney, H(anning) Orrin 1903-1979 ... 9-12R
Obituary ... 103
Bonney, Lorraine G(agnon) 1922- ... CANR-1
Earlier sketch in CA 45-48
Bonney, Merl E(dwin) 1902- ... CAP-2
Earlier sketch in CA 33-36
Bonney, (Mabel) Therese
1897-1978 Obituary ... 73-76
Bonnice, Joseph G(regory) 1930- ... 49-52
Bonnie, Fred 1945- ... 127
Bonnie, Richard J(effrey) 1945- ... CANR-4
Earlier sketch in CA 53-56
Bonnifield, Paul 1937- ... 104
Bonnin, Gertrude 1876-1938 ... 150
See also DAM MULT
See also NNAL
Bonnor, William (Bowen) 1920- ... 9-12R
Bonny, Helen L(indquist) 1921- ... CANR-19
Earlier sketches in CA 49-52, CANR-2
Bono, Philip 1921- ... 101
Bonoma, T(homas) V(incent) 1946- ... CANR-33
Earlier sketches in CA 85-88, CANR-15
Bonomi, Patricia U(pdegraff) 1928- ... 85-88
Bononno, Robert 1949- ... 159
Bonosky, Phillip 1916- ... 128
Bonsal, Philip Wilson 1903- ... 85-88
Bonsall, Crosby Barbara (Newell) 1921-1995 ...
CANR-72
Obituary ... 147
Earlier sketch in CA 73-76
See also SATA 23
See also SATA-Obit 84
Bonsanti, Alessandro 1904-1984 ... DLB 177
Bonta, Marcia Myers 1940- ... 148
Bonta, Vanna ... 152
Bonte, Pierre 1942- ... 143
Bontebal, Henk
See Heertje, Arnold
Bontecou, Eleanor 1890(?)-1976 Obituary ... 65-68
Bontempo, Charles J(oseph) 1931- ... 61-64
Bontemps, Arna(ud Wendell) 1902-1973 . CANR-35
Obituary ... 41-44R
Earlier sketches in CA 1-4R, CANR-4
See also BLC 1
See also BW 1
See also CLC 1, 18
See also CLR 6
See also DAM MULT, NOV, POET
See also DLB 48, 51
See also JRDA
See also MAICYA
See also MTCW 1
See also SATA 2, 44
See also SATA-Obit 24
Bontly, Thomas (John) 1939- ... 57-60
Bontrager, G(erald) Edwin 1939- ... 114
Bontrager, John K(enneth) 1923- ... 65-68
Bonvie, Thomas L. 1940- ... 114
Bony, Jean (Victor) 1908- ... 101
Bonzon, Paul-Jacques 1908-1978 ... 93-96
See also SATA 22
Boodman, David M(orris) 1923- ... 21-24R
Boody, Shirley Bright 1919- ... 89-92
Boog Watson, Elspeth Janet 1900- ... CAP-1
Earlier sketch in CA 11-12
Booher, Dianna Daniels 1948- ... 103
See also SATA 33
Bookbinder, David J(oel) 1951- ... 101
Bookbinder, Robert 1950- ... 110
Bookchin, Murray 1921- ... CANR-48
Earlier sketches in CA 1-4R, CANR-1
Booker, Anton S.
See Randolph, Vance
Booker, Christopher (John Penrice) 1937- ... 136
Booker, Malcolm (Richard) 1915- ... 108
Booker, Simeon Saunders 1918- ... 9-12R
Bookman, Charlotte
See Zolotow, Charlotte S(hapiro)
Book-Senninger, Claude 1928- ... 45-48
Bookspan, Martin 1926- ... 41-44R
Bookstein, Abraham 1940- ... 53-56
Boom, Alfred B. 1928- ... CANR-14
Earlier sketch in CA 25-28R
Boom, Corrie ten
See ten Boom, Corrie
Boon, Emilie (Laetitia) 1958- ... 131
See also SATA 86
Boon, Francis
See Bacon, Edward
Boon, Louis-Paul 1912-1979 ... CANR-13
Earlier sketch in CA 73-76
Boone, Bruce 1940- ... 112
Boone, Buford 1909(?)-1983 Obituary ... 109
Boone, Catherine 1958- ... 144
Boone, Charles Eugene
See Boone, Pat
Boone, Daniel R. 1927- ... CANR-12
Earlier sketch in CA 33-36R
Boone, Debby
See Boone, Deborah Ann
Boone, Deborah Ann 1956- ... 110
Boone, Gene 1962- ... CANR-33
Earlier sketch in CA 113
Boone, Gray Davis 1938- ... 93-96
Boone, Louis E(ugene) 1941- ... CANR-15
Earlier sketch in CA 41-44R
Boone, Muriel 1893- ... 69-72
Boone, Pat 1934- ... CANR-2
Earlier sketch in CA 1-4R
See also SATA 7
Boontje
See Boon, Louis-Paul
Boore, W(alter) H(ugh) 1904- ... CANR-5
Earlier sketch in CA 5-8R
Boorer, Wendy 1931- ... CANR-6
Earlier sketch in CA 57-60
Boorman, Howard L(yon) 1920- ... 41-44R
Boorman, John 1933- ... 121
Brief entry ... 112
See also AAYA 3
Boorman, Linda (Kay) 1940- ... 121
See also SATA 46
Boorman, Scott A(rcher) 1949- ... 29-32R
Boorman, Stanley (Harold) 1939- ... 127
Boorstein, Edward 1915- ... 73-76
Boorstin, Daniel J(oseph) 1914- ... CANR-71
Earlier sketches in CA 1-4R, CANR-1, 28
Interview in ... CANR-28
See also AITN 2
See also DLB 17
See also SATA 52
Boorstin, Jon ... 134
Boorstin, Paul (Terry) 1944- ... 103
Boorstin, Ruth F.
See Boorstin, Ruth (Carolyn) Frankel
Boorstin, Ruth (Carolyn) Frankel 1917- ... 134
Boos, Frank Holgate 1893-1968 ... CAP-2
Earlier sketch in CA 33-36
Boostrom, Robert E(dward) 1949- ... 147
Boot, John C. G. 1936- ... 17-20R
Boote, Robert Edward 1920- ... 65-68
Booth, Alan R. 1934- Brief entry ... 107
Booth, Bradford A(llen) 1909-1968 Obituary ... 116
Booth, Brian 1936- ... 143
Booth, Catherine Bramwell
See Bramwell-Booth, Catherine
Booth, Charles Orrell 1918- ... 13-16R
Booth, Edward
See Booth, Geoffrey Thornton
Booth, Edwin ... CANR-63
Earlier sketches in CA 17-20R, CANR-7
Booth, Ernest Sheldon 1915-1984 ... 53-56
See also SATA 43
Booth, Franklin 1874-1948 ... DLB 188
Booth, Geoffrey
See Tann, Jennifer
Booth, Geoffrey Thornton 1928- ... 132
Booth, George C(live) 1901- ... CAP-1
Earlier sketch in CA 11-12
Booth, Graham (Charles) 1935- ... SATA 37
Booth, Helen Sutton 1890(?)-1985 Obituary ... 117
Booth, Irwin
See Hoch, Edward D(entinger)
Booth, James 1945- ... 119
Booth, John A(llan) 1946- ... CANR-28
Earlier sketch in CA 111
Booth, John E(rlanger) 1919- ... 9-12R
Booth, Ken 1943- ... 102
Booth, Mark Warren 1943- ... 107
Booth, Martin 1944- ... 93-96
See also CAAS 2
See also CLC 13
Booth, Mary L. 1831-1889 ... DLB 79
Booth, Nyla ... 121
Booth, Pat(rick John) 1929- ... CAP-1
Earlier sketch in CA 9-10
Booth, Pat 1945(?)- ... 130
See also BEST 90:1
See also DAM POP
Booth, Paul Henry Gore
See Gore-Booth, Paul Henry
Booth, Philip 1907-1981 ... 106
Booth, Philip 1925- ... CANR-5
Earlier sketch in CA 5-8R
See also CLC 23
See also DLBY 82
Booth, Rosemary Frances 1928- ... 53-56
Booth, Stanley 1942- ... 136
Booth, Stephen 1933- ... 69-72
Booth, Taylor L(ockwood) 1933- ... 53-56
Booth, Warren Scripps 1894-1987 Obituary ... 121
Booth, Wayne C(layson) 1921- ... CANR-43
Earlier sketches in CA 1-4R, CANR-3
See also CAAS 5
See also CLC 24
See also DLB 67
Booth, William 1829-1912 ... DLB 190
Booth, Windsor Peyton 1912-1989 Obituary ... 130
Boothby, Robert
See Boothby, Robert John Graham
Boothby, Robert John Graham 1900-1986 ... 117
Obituary ... 120
Boothroyd, (John) Basil 1910-1988 ... CANR-13
Obituary ... 124
Earlier sketch in CA 33-36R
Bootle, Stan Kelly
See Kelly-Bootle, Stan
Booton, (Catherine) Kage 1919- ... 61-64
Booty, John Everitt 1925- ... CANR-43
Earlier sketches in CA 85-88, CANR-17
Bopp, Karl Richard 1906-1979 Obituary ... 107
Bopp, Mary S.
See Strow, Mary R.
Bor, Jonathan (Steven) 1953- ... 133
Bor, Josef 1906-1979 Obituary ... 115
Bor, Norman 1893(?)-1973 Obituary ... 104
Boraas, Roger S(tuart) 1926- ... 33-36R
Borah, Woodrow (Wilson) 1912- ... CANR-3
Earlier sketch in CA 5-8R
Borch, Ted
See Lund, A. Morten
Borchard, Ruth (Berendsohn) 1910- ... 13-16R
Borchardt, D(ietrich) H(ans) 1916- ... CANR-49
Earlier sketches in CA 21-24R, CANR-9, 24
Borchardt, Frank L(ouis) 1938- ... 33-36R
Borchardt, Rudolf 1877-1945 ... DLB 66
Borchers, Gladys L. 1891- ... CAP-1
Earlier sketch in CA 17-18
Borchert, Gerald L(eo) 1932- ... CANR-36
Earlier sketches in CA 37-40R, CANR-14
Borchert, James 1941- ... 104
Borchert, Wolfgang 1921-1947 Brief entry ... 104
See also DLB 69, 124
See also TCLC 5
Borch-Jacobsen, Mikkel ... 163
Borden, Bob
See Rees, Clair (Francis)
Borden, Charles A. 1912-1968 ... 5-8R
Borden, Henry 1901- ... 41-44R
Borden, Lee
See Deal, Borden
Borden, Leigh
See Deal, Borden
Borden, Linda 1951(?)- ... 125
Borden, Lizzie
See Borden, Linda
Borden, Louise (Walker) 1949- ... 136
See also SATA 68
Borden, M.
See Saxon, Gladys Relyea
Borden, Mary 1886-1968 ... CANR-59
Obituary ... 25-28R
Earlier sketches in CAP-1, CA 13-16
Borden, Morton 1925- ... 9-12R
Borden, Neil Hopper 1895- ... CANR-6
Earlier sketch in CA 1-4R
Borden, Norman E(aston), Jr. 1907- ... 17-20R
Borden, Richard Carman 1900- ... CAP-1
Earlier sketch in CA 11-12
Borden, William (Vickers) 1938- ... CANR-25
Earlier sketches in CA 25-28R, CANR-10
Borden-Turner, Mary
See Borden, Mary
Borderieux, Carita 1874-1953 Brief entry ... 113
Borders, William Alexander 1939- ... 134
Bordes, Francois 1919-1981 Obituary ... 103
Bordier, Georgette 1924- ... SATA 16
Bordin, Edward S. 1913- ... 57-60
Bordin, Ruth B(irgitta) Anderson 1917-1994 ...
CANR-56
Earlier sketches in CA 21-24R, CANR-11, 27
Bordley, James III 1900-1979 ... 69-72
Obituary ... 133
Bordman, Gerald 1931- ... 107
Bordo, Susan (Rebecca) 1947- ... 159
Bordo, Susan R.
See Bordo, Susan (Rebecca)
Bordow, Joan (Wiener) 1944- ... 85-88
Borea, Phyllis Gilbert 1924- ... 29-32R
Boreham, Gordon F. 1928- ... 41-44R
Borek, Ernest 1911-1986 ... 106
Obituary ... 118
Borel, Jacques 1925- ... CANR-49
Earlier sketches in CA 33-36R, CANR-13
Borel, Raymond C. 1927- ... 73-76
Borell, Helene
See Hegeler, Sten
Boreman, Jean 1909- ... CAP-2
Earlier sketch in CA 21-22
Boren, Henry C(harles) 1921- ... 17-20R
Boren, James H(arlan) 1925- ... 41-44R
Borenstein, Audrey F(arrell) 1930- ... CANR-28
Earlier sketches in CA 77-80, CANR-13
Borenstein, Emily 1923- ... 104
Borer, Mary (Irene) Cathcart 1906- ... CANR-4
Earlier sketch in CA 9-12R
Boretz, Allen 1900-1986 Obituary ... 119
Boretz, Alvin 1919- ... CANR-48
Brief entry ... 118
Earlier sketch in CA 124
Interview in ... 124
Boretz, Benjamin (Aaron) 1934- ... CANR-43
Earlier sketch in CA 69-72
Borg, Bjoern (Rune) 1956- ... 134
Brief entry ... 114
Borg, Bjorn
See Borg, Bjoern (Rune)
Borg, Dorothy 1902-1993 ... 21-24R
Obituary ... 143
Borg, Susan 1947- ... 131
Borg, Walter R(aymond) 1921- ... CANR-13
Earlier sketch in CA 33-36R
Borgen, Robert 1945- ... 124
Borges, Jorge Luis 1899-1986 ... CANR-33
Earlier sketches in CA 21-24R, CANR-19
See also AAYA 26
See also CLC 1, 2, 3, 4, 6, 8, 9, 10, 13, 19, 44, 48, 83
See also DA
See also DAB
See also DAC
See also DAM MST, MULT
See also DLB 113
See also DLBY 86
See also HLC
See also HW
See also MTCW 1
See also PC 22
See also SSC 4
See also WLC
Borgese, Elisabeth Mann 1918- ... CANR-24
Earlier sketch in CA 73-76
Borghese, Junio Valerio
1906(?)-1974 Obituary ... 53-56
Borglum, (James) Lincoln (De La Mothe)
1912-1986 ... 122
Obituary ... 118
Borgman, James Mark 1954- ... 133
Borgman, Jim
See Borgman, James Mark
Borgmann, Albert 1937- ... 117
Borgmann, Dmitri A(lfred) 1927-1985 ... 17-20R
Obituary ... 118
Borgo, Ludovico 1930- ... 65-68
Borgos, Seth 1952- ... 119
Borgstrom, Georg A(rne) 1912-1990 ... 17-20R
Obituary ... 130
Borgzinner, Jon A. 1938-1980 ... 108
Obituary ... 97-100
Borhek, Mary V(irginia) 1922- ... 113
Borich, Michael 1949- ... 105
Boring, Edwin G(arrigues) 1886-1968 ... CANR-6
Earlier sketch in CA 1-4R
Boring, M(aynard) Eugene 1935- ... 107
Boring, Mel 1939- ... 106
See also SATA 35
Boring, Phyllis Zatlin
See Zatlin, Phyllis
Boris, Edna Z(wick) 1943- ... 113
Boris, Martin 1930- ... 89-92
Borish, Elaine ... 132
Boritt, Gabor S(zappanos) 1940- ... 147
Borja, Corinne 1929- ... 97-100
See also SATA 22
Borja, Robert 1923- ... 97-100
See also SATA 22
Bork, Alfred M. 1926- ... 17-20R
Bork, Robert H(eron) 1927- ... 130
Brief entry ... 111
See also BEST 90:2
Borkin, Joseph 1911-1979 ... 97-100
Obituary ... 89-92
Borklund, C(arl) W(ilbur) 1930- ... 21-24R
Borko, Harold 1922- ... 13-16R
Borkovec, Thomas D. 1944- ... 45-48
Borland, Barbara Dodge 1904(?)-1991 ... CAP-1
Obituary ... 133
Earlier sketch in CA 9-10
Borland, Hal
See Borland, Harold Glen
See also SATA 5
See also SATA-Obit 24
Borland, Harold Glen 1900-1978 ... CANR-63
Obituary ... 77-80
Earlier sketches in CA 1-4R, CANR-6
See also Borland, Hal
Borland, Kathryn Kilby 1916- ... CANR-4
Earlier sketch in CA 53-56
See also SATA 16
Borlenghi, Patricia 1951- ... SATA 79
Borman, Kathryn M. 1941- ... 117
Borman, William Alan 1948- ... 126
Bormann, Ernest G(ordon) 1925- ... 17-20R
Born, Adolf 1930- ... SATA 49
Born, Ernest Alexander 1898- ... 102
Born, Max 1882-1970 ... 5-8R
Obituary ... 25-28R
Borne, Dorothy
See Rice, Dorothy Mary
Borne, Lawrence Roger 1939- ... 121
Borneman, Ernest 1915- ... CANR-41
Earlier sketches in CA 9-12R, CANR-3, 19
Borneman, H.
See Gottshall, Franklin Henry
Borneman, John 1952- ... 140
Bornemann, Alfred H(enry) 1908-1991 ... 13-16R
Obituary ... 134
Bornet, Vaughn Davis 1917- ... CANR-42
Earlier sketches in CA 1-4R, CANR-5, 20
Bornheimer, Deane G(ordon) 1935- ... 89-92
Bornholdt, Jennifer Mary 1960- ... 153
Bornholdt, Jenny
See Bornholdt, Jennifer Mary
Borning, Bernard C(arl) 1913- ... CANR-3
Earlier sketch in CA 1-4R
Bornkamm, Guenther 1905- Brief entry ... 116
Bornstein, Diane (Dorothy) 1942-1984 ... CANR-8
Obituary ... 112
Earlier sketch in CA 57-60
Bornstein, George (Jay) 1941- ... 29-32R
Bornstein, Morris 1927- ... CANR-2
Earlier sketch in CA 5-8R
Bornstein, Sam 1913- Brief entry ... 112
Bornstein-Lercher, Ruth 1927- ... CANR-8
Earlier sketch in CA 61-64
See also SATA 14, 88
Bornstein-Somoza, Miriam 1950- ... HW
Borntrager, Karl A. 1892- ... 89-92
Borntrager, Mary Christner 1921- ... 144
Borodacz, William (?)-1986 Obituary ... 118
Borodin, George
See Milkomane, George Alexis Milkomanovich
Boroff, David 1917-1965 ... CAP-1
Obituary ... 29-32R
Earlier sketch in CA 11-12
Boroson, Warren 1935- ... 21-24R
Borovik, Artyom 1960- ... 141
Borovik, Genrikh (Aviezerovich) 1929- ... 151
Borovski, Conrad 1930- ... 37-40R
Borovsky, Natasha 1924- ... 121
Borowiec, Andrew 1928- ... 127
Borowitz, Albert (Ira) 1930- ... CANR-32
Earlier sketches in CA 85-88, CANR-15
Borowitz, Eugene B(ernard) 1924- ... CANR-1
Earlier sketch in CA 49-52

Borowski, Tadeusz 1922-1951 ... 154
Brief entry ... 106
See also TCLC 9
Borras, Frank Marshall (?)-1980 Obituary ... 102
Borrello, Alfred 1931- ... 29-32R
Borrie, John 1915- ... 103
Borrie, Wilfred David 1913- ... 109
Borroff, Edith 1925- ... 65-68
Borroff, Marie 1923- ... CANR-2
Earlier sketch in CA 5-8R
Borror, Donald J(oyce) 1907-1988 ... CANR-29
Earlier sketch in CA 1-4R
Borror, Gordon L(amar) 1936- ... 117
Borrow, George (Henry) 1803-1881 ... DLB 21, 55, 166
Borrus, Michael (Glen) 1956- ... 141
Borsch, Frederick Houk 1935- ... CANR-25
Earlier sketches in CA 25-28R, CANR-10
Borski, Lucia Merecka ... 73-76
See also SATA 18
Borsodi, Ralph 1888-1977 Obituary ... 73-76
Borson, Roo
See Borson, Ruth Elizabeth
Borson, Ruth Elizabeth 1952- ... CANR-46
Earlier sketch in CA 112
Borst, Raymond R(ichard) 1909- ... 107
Borstelmann, Thomas 1958- ... 142
Borsten, Orin 1912- ... 85-88
Borsten, Rick 1955- ... 140
Borten, Helen Jacobson 1930- ... CANR-3
Earlier sketch in CA 5-8R
See also SATA 5
Borth, Christian C. 1895(?)-1976 Obituary ... 65-68
Bortin, George ... 114
Bortin, V. G.
See Bortin, George
and Bortin, Virginia
Bortin, Virginia 1936- ... 114
Bortner, Doyle M(cClean) 1915- ... 33-36R
Bortner, Morton 1925- ... 33-36R
Bortnik, Aida (Beatriz) 1938- ... 163
Bortoli, Georges 1923- ... 65-68
Borton, D. B.
See Carpenter, Lynette
Borton, Elizabeth
See Trevino, Elizabeth B(orton) de
Borton, John C., Jr. 1938- ... CANR-27
Earlier sketch in CA 29-32R
Borton, Lady 1942- ... 147
See also SATA 98
Borton, Terry
See Borton, John C., Jr.
Bortstein, Larry 1942- ... 33-36R
See also SATA 16
Bortz, Edward L(eRoy) 1896-1970 ... CAP-1
Earlier sketch in CA 11-12
Bortz, Fred 1944- ... 141
See also SATA 74
Boruch, Robert F(rancis) 1942- ... 69-72
Borus, Michael E(liot) 1938-1987 ... 37-40R
Obituary ... 122
Borza, Eugene N(icholas) 1935- ... 25-28R
Bosanquet, N(icholas) F(rancis) G(ustavus) 1942- ... 131
Bosanquet, Nick
See Bosanquet, N(icholas) F(rancis) G(ustavus)
Bosanquet, Reggie
See Bosanquet, Reginald
Bosanquet, Reginald 1932-1984 Obituary ... 113
Bosch, David J(acobus) 1929- ... 118
Bosch, Henry G(erard) 1914- ... 135
Bosch (Gavino), Juan 1909- ... 151
See also DAM MST, MULT
See also DLB 145
See also HW
Bosch, William Joseph 1928- ... 29-32R
Bosco, Antoinette (Oppedisano) 1928- ... 13-16R
Bosco, Dominick 1948- ... 145
Bosco, (Fernand Joseph Marius) Henri 1888-1976 ... 69-72
Obituary ... 65-68
See also DLB 72
Bosco, Jack
See Holliday, Joseph
Bosco, Joseph (Augustus) 1948- ... 147
Bosco, Monique 1927- ... 160
See also DLB 53
Bose, Buddhadeva 1908- Brief entry ... 119
Bose, Irene Mott 1899(?)-1974 Obituary ... 53-56
Bose, N(irmal) K(umar) 1901-1972 ... CAP-2
Earlier sketch in CA 23-24
Bose, Tarun Chandra 1931- ... CANR-48
Earlier sketch in CA 45-48
Boserup, Ester 1910- ... 57-60
Boshell, Buris R(aye) 1923- ... 105
Boshell, Gordon 1908- ... 77-80
See also SATA 15
Boshinski, Blanche 1922- ... 21-24R
See also SATA 10
Boskin, Joseph 1929- ... 25-28R
Boskoff, Alvin 1924- ... 13-16R
Bosland, Chelcie Clayton 1901- ... 5-8R
Bosler, Raymond Thomas 1915- ... 112
Bosley, Harold A(ugustus) 1907-1975 ... 49-52
Obituary ... 53-56
Bosley, Keith 1937- ... CANR-6
Earlier sketch in CA 57-60
Boslooper, Thomas 1923- ... 81-84
Bosmajian, Haig Aram 1928- ... CANR-7
Earlier sketch in CA 17-20R
Bosmajian, Hamida 1936- ... 107
Bosman, Herman Charles 1905-1951 ... 160
See also Malan, Herman
See also TCLC 49
Bosoni, Anthony J. 1952- ... 151
Bosquet, Alain 1919-1998 ... 13-16R
Obituary ... 166
Boss, Judy 1935- ... 57-60
Boss, Richard W(oodruff) 1937- ... 103
Bosschere, Jean de 1878(?)-1953 Brief entry ... 115
See also TCLC 19
Bosse, Malcolm (Joseph, Jr.) 1933- ... CANR-49
Earlier sketch in CA 106
See also AAYA 16
See also SATA 35
Bosserman, (Charles) Phillip 1931- ... 102
See also SATA 84
Bossert, Steven T(homas) 1948- ... 104
Bossom, Naomi 1933- ... 102
See also SATA 35
Bossone, Richard M. 1924- ... 33-36R
Bostdorff, Denise M. 1959- ... 147
Bosticco, (Isabel Lucy) Mary ... 102
Bostick, William A(llison) 1913- ... 89-92
Boston, Anne 1945- ... 130
Boston, Bruce 1943- ... 146
See also CAAS 30
Boston, Charles K.
See Gruber, Frank
Boston, Jonathan 1957- ... 140
Boston, L(ucy) M(aria Wood) 1892-1990 ... CANR-58
Obituary ... 131
Earlier sketch in CA 73-76
See also CLR 3
See also DLB 161
See also JRDA
See also MAICYA
See also SATA 19
See also SATA-Obit 64
Boston, Noel 1910-1966 ... CAP-1
Earlier sketch in CA 13-16
Boston, Ray(mond J.) 1927- ... 128
Boston, Robert 1940- ... CANR-60
Earlier sketch in CA 65-68
Bostwick, Burdette Edwards 1908- ... 106
Boswell
See Gordon, Giles (Alexander Esme)
Boswell, Barbara (S.) 1946- ... 122
Boswell, Charles (Meigs, Jr.) 1909- ... 5-8R
Boswell, Jackson Campbell 1934- ... 61-64
Boswell, James 1740-1795 ... CDBLB 1660-1789
See also DA
See also DAB
See also DAC
See also DAM MST
See also DLB 104, 142
See also WLC
Boswell, Jeanetta 1922- ... CANR-22
Earlier sketch in CA 106
Boswell, John (Eastburn) 1947-1994 ... 121
Obituary ... 147
Boswell, Robert 1953- ... 136
Boswell, Thomas 1947- ... 118
Bosworth, Allan R(ucker) 1901-1986 ... CANR-64
Obituary ... 120
Earlier sketch in CA 1-4R
Bosworth, Clifford Edmund 1928- ... CANR-7
Earlier sketch in CA 13-16R
Bosworth, David 1947- ... 113
Bosworth, Frank
See Paine, Lauran (Bosworth)
Bosworth, J. Allan 1925- ... SATA 19
Bosworth, Patricia 1933- ... CANR-65
Earlier sketch in CA 77-80
Bosworth, R(ichard) J(ames) B(oon) 1943- ... CANR-46
Earlier sketches in CA 106, CANR-23
Bote, Hermann c. 1460-c. 1520 ... DLB 179
Botein, Bernard 1900-1974 Obituary ... 45-48
Botel, Morton 1925- ... 105
Botev, Khristo 1847-1876 ... DLB 147
Botham, Noel 1940- ... 104
Bothmer, Dietrich Felix von
See von Bothmer, Dietrich Felix
Bothwell, Jean (?)-1977 ... CANR-68
Earlier sketches in CA 1-4R, CANR-3
See also SATA 2
Bothwell, Robert (Selkirk) 1944- ... 143
Botjer, George (Francis) 1937- ... 97-100
Botkin, B(enjamin) A(lbert) 1901-1975 ... CAP-1
Obituary ... 57-60
Earlier sketch in CA 13-16
See also SATA 40
Botkin, Daniel B. 1937- ... 136
Botkin, James W. 1943- ... 112
Botman, Selma 1950- ... 135
Boto, Eza
See Biyidi, Alexandre
Botsch, Robert Emil 1947- ... 104
Botsford, Keith 1928- ... 9-12R
Botsford, Ward 1927- ... 110
See also SATA 66
Bott, Anita F. 1970- ... 151
Bott, George 1920- ... 104
Bott, Raoul 1923- ... 164
Botta, Anne Charlotte (Lynch) 1815-1891 ... DLB 3
Bottel, Helen 1914- ... 25-28R
Botterill, Cal(vin Bruce) 1947- ... 57-60
Botterill, Joyce 1939- ... 138
Bottigheimer, Ruth B. 1939- ... 125
Bottiglia, William F(ilbert) 1912- ... 21-24R
Botting, Douglas (Scott) 1934- ... CANR-37
Earlier sketches in CA 45-48, CANR-1, 16
See also SATA 43
Bottner, Barbara 1943- ... CANR-60
Earlier sketches in CA 61-64, CANR-8, 23
See also SAAS 26
See also SATA 14, 93
Bottom, Raymond 1927- ... 33-36R
Bottome, Edgar M. 1937- ... 33-36R
Bottome, Phyllis
See Forbes-Dennis, Phyllis
See also DLB 197
Bottomley, Gordon 1874-1948 Brief entry ... 120
See also DLB 10
Bottomly, Heath 1919- ... 105
Bottomore, T(homas) B(urton) 1920-1992 ... CANR-20
Obituary ... 140
Earlier sketches in CA 9-12R, CANR-4
Bottoms, A(nthony) E(dward) 1939- ... 73-76
Bottoms, David 1949- ... CANR-22
Earlier sketch in CA 105
See also CLC 53
See also DLB 120
See also DLBY 83
Bottoms, Lawrence W(endell) 1908- ... 89-92
Bottrall, Margaret Florence Saumarez 1909- ... 104
Bottrall, (Francis James) Ronald 1906-1989 ... 53-56
Obituary ... 129
See also DLB 20
Botvinnik, Mikhail Moiseyevich 1911-1995 ... 112
Obituary ... 148
Botwin, Carol 1929-1997 ... 159
Botwinick, Jack 1923- ... 41-44R
Bouce, Paul-Gabriel 1936- ... 73-76
Bouchard, Constance B(rittain) 1948- ... CANR-60
Earlier sketch in CA 128
Bouchard, Lois Kalb 1938- ... 25-28R
Bouchard, Robert H. 1923- ... 17-20R
Bouchardy, Joseph 1810-1870 ... DLB 192
Bouchelle, Joan Hoiness 1928- ... 146
Boucher, Alan (Estcourt) 1918-1996 ... CANR-54
Earlier sketches in CA 5-8R, CANR-9, 24
Boucher, Anthony
See White, William A(nthony) P(arker)
See also DLB 8
Boucher, Bruce (Ambler) 1948- ... 146
Boucher, David 1951- ... 135
Boucher, Frank 1901-1977 ... 122
Obituary ... 110
Boucher, John G(regory) 1930- ... 37-40R
Boucher, Jonathan 1738-1804 ... DLB 31
Boucher, Paul Edward 1893- ... CAP-1
Earlier sketch in CA 13-14
Boucher, Philip P. 1944- ... 146
Boucher, Sandy 1936- ... 110
Boucher, Wayne I(rving) 1934- ... 53-56
Boucherville, Georges Boucher de 1814-1894 ... DLB 99
Boucolon, Maryse 1937(?)- ... CANR-53
Earlier sketches in CA 110, CANR-30
See also Conde, Maryse
Boudat, Marie-Louise 1909- ... CAP-1
Earlier sketch in CA 11-12
Boudon, Raymond 1934- ... CANR-56
Earlier sketches in CA 49-52, CANR-30
Boudreau, Eugene H(oward) 1934- ... 45-48
Boudreaux, Patricia Duncan 1941- ... 33-36R
Bough, Lee
See Huser, (La)Verne (Carl)
Boughey, Arthur S(tanley) 1913- Brief entry ... 113
Boughner, Daniel C(liness) 1909-1974 ... CAP-2
Obituary ... 49-52
Earlier sketch in CA 23-24
Boughton, Doug(las Gordon) 1944- ... 163
Boughton, James M(urray) 1940- ... 41-44R
Boughton, Richard 1954- ... 142
See also SATA 75
Boughton, Willis A(rnold) 1885-1977 Obituary ... 73-76
Bouissac, Paul (Antoine Rene) 1934- ... 65-68
Boukreev, Anatoli 1958(?)-1997 ... 166
Boulanger, Nadia (Juliette) 1887-1979 ... 127
Boularan, Jacques 1890-1972 Obituary ... 37-40R
Boulby, Mark 1929- ... 37-40R
Boulding, Elise (Biorn-Hansen) 1920- ... CANR-51
Earlier sketches in CA 21-24R, CANR-8, 26
Boulding, Kenneth E(wart) 1910-1993 ... CANR-26
Obituary ... 140
Earlier sketches in CA 5-8R, CANR-7
Boulet, Susan Seddon 1941- ... SATA 50
Boulez, Pierre 1925- ... 148
Boulger, James Denis 1931-1979 ... 109
Boulle, Pierre (Francois Marie-Louis) 1912-1994 ... CANR-24
Obituary ... 143
Earlier sketch in CA 9-12R
See also SATA 22
See also SATA-Obit 78
Boulogne, Jean 1942- ... 93-96
Boult, Adrian (Cedric) 1889-1983 ... 114
Obituary ... 109
Boult, S. Kye
See Cochrane, William E.
Boulter, Eric Thomas 1917-1989 Obituary ... 129
Boulting, John (Edward) 1913-1985 Obituary ... 116
Boulton, David 1935- ... CANR-15
Earlier sketch in CA 25-28R
Boulton, James T(hompson) 1924- ... 29-32R
Boulton, Jane 1921- ... CANR-57
Earlier sketch in CA 65-68
See also SATA 91
Boulton, Laura Theresa Craytor 1899(?)-1980 Obituary ... 110
Boulton, Marjorie 1924- ... CANR-9
Earlier sketch in CA 65-68
Boulton, Wayne G(ranberry) 1941- ... 115
Boultwood, Alban 1911- ... 118
Boulware, Marcus H(anna) 1907- ... CANR-1
Earlier sketch in CA 45-48
Bouma, Donald H(erbert) 1918- ... 41-44R
Bouma, Mary La Grand ... 93-96
Bouman, Pieter M(arinus) 1938- ... CANR-12
Earlier sketch in CA 29-32R
Bouman, Walter Richard 1929- ... 29-32R
Boumelha, Penelope Ann 1950- ... 110
Boumelha, Penny
See Boumelha, Penelope Ann
Boumphrey, Robert Stavely 1916(?)-1987 Obituary ... 123
Bouquet, Mary (Rose) 1955- ... 146
Bour, Daniele 1939- ... SATA 62
Bouraoui, H(edi) A(ndre) 1932- ... CANR-25
Earlier sketches in CA 65-68, CANR-9
Bourassa, Napoleon 1827-1916 ... DLB 99
Bourbaki, Nicolas
See Cartan, Henri (Paul)
and Weil, Andre
Bourbon, Ken
See Bauer, Erwin A.
Bourdain, Anthony 1957(?)- ... 154
Bourdeaux, Michael 1934- ... CANR-14
Earlier sketch in CA 33-36R
Bourdier, James A(aron) 1929-1987 Obituary ... 124
Bourdieu, Pierre 1930- ... 130
Bourdon, David 1934- ... CANR-46
Earlier sketches in CA 37-40R, CANR-13
See also SATA 46
Bourdon, Sylvia Diane Eve 1949- ... 85-88
Bouregy, Thomas 1909(?)-1978 Obituary ... 104
Bouret, Jean 1914- ... 85-88
Bourgeois, Paulette 1951- ... 137
Bourget, Paul (Charles Joseph) 1852-1935 Brief entry ... 107
See also DLB 123
See also TCLC 12
Bourgholtzer, Frank 1919- ... 25-28R
Bourguignon, Erika (Eichhorn) 1924- ... 85-88
Bourinot, Arthur Stanley 1893-1969 ... 159
Bourinot, John George 1837-1902 ... DLB 99
Bourjaily, Monte Ferris 1894-1979 ... 97-100
Obituary ... 85-88
Bourjaily, Vance (Nye) 1922- ... CANR-72
Earlier sketches in CA 1-4R, CANR-2
See also CAAS 1
See also CLC 8, 62
See also DLB 2, 143
Bourke, Vernon J(oseph) 1907- ... CANR-3
Earlier sketch in CA 9-12R
Bourke-White, Margaret 1904-1971 ... CAP-1
Obituary ... 29-32R
Earlier sketch in CA 13-16
Bourliaguet, Leonce 1895-1965 ... 102
Bourliere, Francois (Marie Gabriel) 1913-1993 ... 159
Brief entry ... 113
Bourne, Aleck William 1885(?)-1974 Obituary 53-56
Bourne, Charles P. 1931- ... 9-12R
Bourne, Dorothy D(ulles) 1893-(?) ... CAP-2
Earlier sketch in CA 23-24
Bourne, Edward Gaylord 1860-1908 ... DLB 47
Bourne, Eulalia ... 97-100
Bourne, Frank Card 1914- ... 17-20R
Bourne, Geoffrey Howard 1909-1988 ... 33-36R
Obituary ... 126
Bourne, J(ohn) M. 1949- ... 124
Bourne, James R. 1897-(?) ... CAP-2
Earlier sketch in CA 21-22
Bourne, Joanna Watkins 1949- ... 112
Bourne, John
See John, Owen
Bourne, Kenneth 1930-1992 ... CANR-11
Obituary ... 140
Earlier sketch in CA 25-28R
Bourne, L(arry) S(tuart) 1939- ... CANR-56
Earlier sketches in CA 33-36R, CANR-12, 27
Bourne, Lesley
See Marshall, Evelyn
Bourne, Lyle E(ugene), Jr. 1932- ... 53-56
Bourne, Miriam Anne 1931-1989 ... CANR-10
Earlier sketch in CA 21-24R, 129
See also SATA 16
See also SATA-Obit 63
Bourne, Peter
See Jeffries, Graham Montague
Bourne, Peter Geoffrey 1939- ... CANR-64
Earlier sketches in CA 57-60, CANR-7
Bourne, Randolph S(illiman) 1886-1918 ... 155
Brief entry ... 117
See also DLB 63
See also TCLC 16
Bourne, Russell 1928- ... 133
Bourne, Ruth (May) 1897-1986 ... 33-36R
Obituary ... 120
Bourneuf, Alice E. 1912-1980 Obituary ... 102
Bourque, Antoine
See Brasseaux, Carl A(nthony)
Bourricaud, Francois 1922- ... CANR-26
Earlier sketch in CA 29-32R
Bouscaren, Anthony Trawick 1920- ... CANR-69
Earlier sketches in CA 1-4R, CANR-5
Bouscaren, T(imothy) Lincoln 1884- ... CAP-1
Earlier sketch in CA 11-12
Bouson, J. Brooks ... 151
Bousono, Carlos 1923- ... DLB 108
Bousquet, Joe 1897-1950 ... DLB 72
Bousquet, Marie-Louis Valentin 1887(?)-1975 Obituary ... 104
Boussard, Jacques Marie 1910- ... 29-32R
Boustani, Rafic 1942- ... 141
Boustead, John Edmund Hugh 1895-1980 Obituary ... 97-100
Boutell, Clarence Burley 1908-1981 Obituary ... 104
Boutell, Clip
See Boutell, Clarence Burley
Boutelle, Ann Edwards 1943- ... 131
Boutelle, Sara Holmes ... 130
Boutet de Monvel, (Louis) M(aurice) 1850(?)-1913 ... CLR 32
See also SATA 30
Boutilier, Mary A(nn) 1943- ... 105
Boutilier, Robert 1950- ... 145

Bouton, James Alan 1939- 89-92
Bouton, Jim
See Bouton, James Alan
Boutros-Ghali, Boutros 1922- 166
Bouvard, Marguerite Guzman 1937- 149
Bouvier, Emile 1906- 37-40R
Bouvier, Leon F(rancis) 1922- 105
Bouvier, Nicolas 1929- 153
Bova, Ben(jamin William) 1932- CANR-56
Earlier sketches in CA 5-8R, CANR-11
Interview in CANR-11
See also CAAS 18
See also AAYA 16
See also CLC 45
See also CLR 3
See also DLBY 81
See also MAICYA
See also MTCW 1
See also SATA 6, 68
Bovaird, Anne E(lizabeth) 1960- 155
See also SATA 90
Bovard, Oliver K. 1872-1945 .... DLB 25
Bovasso, Julie 1930- 25-28R
Bove, Emmanuel 1898-1945 .... DLB 72
Bove, Paul A(nthony) 1949- 125
Bovee, Courtland L(owell) 1944- CANR-27
Earlier sketch in CA 49-52
Bovee, Ruth
See Paine, Lauran (Bosworth)
Boven, William 1887(?)-1970 Obituary 104
Bovet, Eric D(avid) 1900- 118
Bovey, John (Alden, Jr.) 1913- 107
Bovis, H(enry) Eugene 1928- 29-32R
Bow, Russell 1925- 21-24R
Bowden, Betsy 1948- 107
Bowden, Charles 1945(?)- 156
Bowden, Edwin T(urner), Jr. 1924- CANR-8
Earlier sketch in CA 13-16R
Bowden, Elbert Victor 1924- CANR-48
Earlier sketches in CA 41-44R, CANR-15
Bowden, Gregory Houston 1948- 41-44R
Bowden, Henry Warner 1939- CANR-27
Earlier sketch in CA 49-52
Bowden, J(ocelyn) J(ean) 1927- 29-32R
Bowden, Jean 1925- CANR-7
Earlier sketch in CA 53-56
Bowden, Jim
See Spence, William John Duncan
Bowden, Joan Chase 1925- 89-92
See also SATA 51
See also SATA-Brief 38
Bowden, Leonard (Walter) 1933-1979 .... 17-20R
Obituary 134
Bowden, Mark 1951- 148
Bowden, Mary Weatherspoon 1941- 110
Bowden, Roland Heywood 1916- CANR-24
Earlier sketch in CA 106
Bowden, Susan White
See White-Bowden, Susan
Bowder, Diana (Ruth) 1942- 109
Bowditch, James L(owell) 1939- 89-92
Bowdle, Donald N(elson) 1935- 49-52
Bowdler, Roger 1934- 97-100
Bowdring, Paul (Edward) 1946- 135
Bowe, Frank 1947- 104
Bowe, Gabriel P(aul) 1923- 21-24R
Bowe, Kate
See Taylor, Mary Ann
Bowe, (Paul Thomas) Patrick 1945- 106
Bowen, Alexandria Russell 163
See also SATA 97
Bowen, Andy Russell
See Bowen, Alexandria Russell
Bowen, Barbara C(herry) 1937- 37-40R
Bowen, Betty Morgan
See West, Betty
Bowen, Catherine (Shober) Drinker 1897-1973 ....
CANR-68
Obituary 45-48
Earlier sketches in CA 5-8R, CANR-15
See also SATA 7
Bowen, Croswell 1905-1971 Obituary 33-36R
Bowen, David
See Bowen, Joshua David
Bowen, Desmond 1921- 33-36R
Bowen, Earl Kenneth 1918- 5-8R
Bowen, Edmund (John) 1898-1980 Obituary 105
Bowen, Elbert Russell 1918- 13-16R
Bowen, Elizabeth (Dorothea Cole) 1899-1973 .....
CANR-35
Obituary 41-44R
Earlier sketches in CAP-2, CA 17-18
See also CDBLB 1945-1960
See also CLC 1, 3, 6, 11, 15, 22
See also DAM NOV
See also DLB 15, 162
See also MTCW 1
See also SSC 3, 28
Bowen, Emrys George 1900-1983 Obituary 111
Bowen, Ezra 1927- 85-88
Bowen, Francis 1811-1890 .... DLB 1, 59
Bowen, Gail 1942- 138
Bowen, Haskell L. 1929- 41-44R
Bowen, Howard R(othmann) 1908-1989 .. CANR-8
Obituary 130
Earlier sketch in CA 21-24R
Bowen, (Ivor) Ian 1908-1984 105
Obituary 115
Bowen, J(ean) Donald 1922- CANR-8
Earlier sketch in CA 17-20R
Bowen, James Keith 1932- 37-40R
Bowen, John 1916- 103
Bowen, John (Griffith) 1924- CANR-67
Earlier sketches in CA 1-4R, CANR-2
See also DLB 13
Bowen, Joshua David 1930- 105
See also SATA 22
Bowen, Marjorie
See Campbell, (Gabrielle) Margaret (Vere)
See also DLB 153
Bowen, Mary
See Hall, Mary Bowen
Bowen, Michael 1951- 134
Bowen, Peter 1939- 57-60
Bowen, Ralph H(enry) 1919- 69-72
Bowen, Richard M. 1928- 21-24R
Bowen, Robert O. 1920- 9-12R
Bowen, Robert Sydney 1900-1977 .... CANR-28
Obituary 69-72
Earlier sketch in CA 73-76
See also SATA 52
See also SATA-Obit 21
Bowen, Roger W. 1947- 146
Bowen, Zack (Rhollie) 1934- 29-32R
Bowen-Judd, Sara (Hutton) 1922-1985 .. CANR-58
Obituary 117
Earlier sketches in CA 9-12R, CANR-5
Bower, Barbara
See Todd, Barbara Euphan
Bower, David A(llan) 1945- 37-40R
Bower, Donald E(dward) 1920- 77-80
Bower, Eli M(ichael) 1917- 89-92
Bower, Fay Louise 1929- 53-56
Bower, Gordon H(oward) 1932- 17-20R
Bower, John Morton 1942- 143
Bower, Joseph L(yon) 1938- 112
Bower, Julia Wells 1903- 41-44R
Bower, Keith
See Beckett, Kenneth A(lbert)
Bower, Louise 1900- CAP-2
Earlier sketch in CA 21-22
Bower, Muriel 1921- 49-52
Bower, Robert T(urrell) 1919-1990 .... CANR-27
Obituary 132
Earlier sketch in CA 49-52
Bower, Sharon Anthony 1932- 65-68
Bower, Tom 1946- CANR-72
Earlier sketch in CA 144
Bower, Ursula Violet Graham
1914-1988 Obituary 127
Bower, William Clayton 1878- 5-8R
Bowering, George 1935- CANR-10
Earlier sketch in CA 21-24R
See also CAAS 16
See also CLC 15, 47
See also DLB 53
Bowering, Marilyn R(uthe) 1949- CANR-49
Earlier sketch in CA 101
See also CLC 32
Bowermaster, Jon 1954- 127
See also SATA 77
Bowers, Bathsheba 1671-1718 .... DLB 200
Bowers, C. A. 1935- 29-32R
Bowers, Claude G. 1878-1958 .... DLB 17
Bowers, Edgar 1924- CANR-24
Earlier sketch in CA 5-8R
See also CLC 9
See also DLB 5
Bowers, Faubion 1917- 5-8R
Bowers, Fredson (Thayer) 1905-1991 ... CANR-48
Obituary 134
Earlier sketches in CA 5-8R, CANR-2
See also DLB 140
See also DLBY 91
Bowers, George K. 1916- CANR-2
Earlier sketch in CA 1-4R
Bowers, Jane Palatini 1945- 145
Bowers, Janice Emily 1950- 162
Bowers, John 1928- 33-36R
Bowers, John M. 1949- 126
Bowers, John Waite 1935- 41-44R
Bowers, Kenneth S. 1937- 97-100
Bowers, Margaretta K(eller) 1908- 5-8R
Bowers, Mary Beacom 1932- 105
Bowers, Neal 1948- CANR-55
Earlier sketches in CA 110, CANR-28
Bowers, Q(uentin) David 1938- CANR-37
Earlier sketches in CA 41-44R, CANR-16
Bowers, Ronald (Lee) 1941- 41-44R
Bowers, Terrell L. 1945- 168
See also SATA 101
Bowers, Terry
See Bowers, Terrell L.
Bowers, Warner Fremont 1906- 61-64
Bowers, William 1916-1987 102
Obituary 122
Interview in 102
Bowers, William J(oseph) 1935- 97-100
Bowers, William L(avalle) 1930- Brief entry 114
Bowersock, G(len) W(arren) 1936- 81-84
Bowes, Anne LaBastille
See LaBastille, Anne
Bowett, Derek William 1927- CANR-6
Earlier sketch in CA 9-12R
Bowick, Dorothy Mueller
See Mueller, Dorothy
Bowie, Andrew (S.) 1952- 134
Bowie, David
See Jones, David Robert
See also CLC 17
Bowie, Janetta (Hamilton) 1907- 102
Bowie, Jim
See Norwood, Victor G(eorge) C(harles)
and Stratemeyer, Edward L.
Bowie, Malcolm (McNaughtan) 1943- 128
Bowie, Norman E. 1942- CANR-29
Earlier sketches in CA 33-36R, CANR-13
Bowie, Robert R(ichardson) 1909- CAP-1
Earlier sketch in CA 11-12
Bowie, Sam
See Ballard, (Willis) Todhunter
Bowie, Walter Russell 1882-1969 .... CANR-3
Earlier sketch in CA 5-8R
Bowker, Francis E. 1917- 41-44R
Bowker, Gordon 1934- 155
Bowker, John (Westerdale) 1935- CANR-12
Earlier sketch in CA 25-28R
Bowker, Lee Harrington 1940- CANR-25
Earlier sketch in CA 108
Bowker, Margaret 1936- 25-28R
Bowker, R(obin) M(arsland) 1920- 65-68
Bowker, Richard (J.) 1950- 127
Bowkett, Stephen 1953- 134
See also SATA 67
Bowlby, (Edward) John (Mostyn) 1907-1990 ....
CANR-34
Obituary 132
Earlier sketch in CA 49-52
Bowlby, Rachel 1957- 130
Bowle, John (Edward) 1905-1985 .... CANR-1
Obituary 117
Earlier sketch in CA 1-4R
Bowler, Jan Brett
See Brett, Jan (Churchill)
Bowler, Peter J(ohn) 1944- CANR-65
Earlier sketch in CA 129
Bowler, R(eginald) Arthur 1930- 57-60
Bowles, Chester (Bliss) 1901-1986 69-72
Obituary 119
Bowles, D(elbert) Richard 1910- 33-36R
Bowles, Edmund A(ddison) 1925- CANR-32
Earlier sketch in CA 33-36R
Bowles, Ella Shannon 1886-1975 Obituary ... 57-60
Bowles, Frank H(amilton) 1907-1975 .... 13-16R
Obituary 57-60
Bowles, George A., Jr. 1924(?)-1986 Obituary .. 118
Bowles, Gordon Townsend 1904- CAP-1
Earlier sketch in CA 11-12
Bowles, Jane (Sydney) 1917-1973 .... CAP-2
Obituary 41-44R
Earlier sketch in CA 19-20
See also CLC 3, 68
Bowles, John 1938- 106
Bowles, Kerwin
See Abeles, Elvin
Bowles, Norma L(ouise) 77-80
Bowles, Paul (Frederick) 1910-1986 .... CANR-50
Earlier sketches in CA 1-4R, CANR-1, 19
See also CAAS 1
See also CLC 1, 2, 19, 53
See also DLB 5, 6
See also MTCW 1
See also SSC 3
Bowles, Samuel III 1826-1878 .... DLB 43
Bowles, William Lisle 1762-1850 .... DLB 93
Bowley, Rex Lyon 1925- 103
Bowling, Ann (Patricia) 1951- 113
Bowling, Jackson M(ichael) 1934- 5-8R
Bowlt, John E(llis) 1943- 130
Bowman, Albert Hall 1921- 41-44R
Bowman, Alfred C(onner) 1904-1982 117
Bowman, Bob
See Bowman, Robert T.
Bowman, Bruce 1938- 65-68
Bowman, Buck
See Bowman, J. Wilson
Bowman, Clell Edgar 1904- 105
Bowman, Crystal 1951- 165
Bowman, David 1957- 140
Bowman, David J. 1919-1993 .... 9-12R
Obituary 142
Bowman, Derek 1931- 102
Bowman, Frank Paul 1927- 33-36R
Bowman, Henry A(delbert) 1903- CAP-1
Earlier sketch in CA 13-14
Bowman, Herbert E(ugene) 1917- 65-68
Bowman, J. Wilson 151
Bowman, James Cloyd 1880-1961 97-100
See also SATA 23
Bowman, Jeanne
See Blocklinger, Peggy O'More
Bowman, John S(tewart) 1931- CANR-41
Earlier sketches in CA 9-12R, CANR-5, 19
See also SATA 16
Bowman, John Wick 1894- CANR-6
Earlier sketch in CA 1-4R
Bowman, Karl M. 1888-1973 Obituary 41-44R
Bowman, Kathleen (Gill) 1942- 69-72
See also SATA 52
See also SATA-Brief 40
Bowman, Larry G(ene) 1935- Brief entry 115
Bowman, LeRoy 1887-1971 Obituary 33-36R
Bowman, Locke E., Jr. 1927- CANR-2
Earlier sketch in CA 5-8R
Bowman, Louise Morey 1882-1944 .... DLB 68
Bowman, Marcelle 1914- 25-28R
Bowman, Mary D. 1924- 25-28R
Bowman, Mary Jean 1908- 33-36R
Bowman, Ned A(lan) 1932- 41-44R
Bowman, Paul Hoover 1914- 33-36R
Bowman, Peter 1917(?)-1985 Obituary 114
Bowman, Raymond Albert
1903-1979 Obituary 89-92
Bowman, Robert 1928- 25-28R
Bowman, Robert T. 1910- 73-76
Bowman, Sylvia E(dmonia) 1914- 1-4R
Bowman, Ward S(imon), Jr. 1911- 49-52
Bowmer, Angus L(ivingston)
1904-1979 Obituary 85-88
Bown, Deni 1944- 154
Bowne, (William) Alan 1945(?)-1989 Obituary .. 130
Bowne, Ford
See Brown, Forrest
Bowness, Alan 1928- 130
Bowood, Richard
See Daniell, Albert Scott
Bowra, (Cecil) Maurice 1898-1971 .... CANR-69
Obituary 29-32R
Earlier sketches in CA 1-4R, CANR-2
Bowring, Richard (John) 1947- 114
Bowron, Edgar Peters 1943- 130
Bowser, Benjamin P(aul) 1946- 146
Bowser, Eileen 1928- CANR-51
Earlier sketches in CA 69-72, CANR-11, 26
Bowser, Frederick P(ark) 1937- 49-52
Bowser, Hallowell 1922(?)-1990 Obituary 130
Bowser, Joan
See Bowser, Pearl
Bowser, Pearl 1931- CANR-13
Earlier sketch in CA 33-36R
Bowskill, Derek 1928- CANR-47
Earlier sketches in CA 77-80, CANR-13
Bowyer, (Raymond) Chaz 1926- CANR-72
Earlier sketches in CA 93-96, CANR-15, 33
Bowyer, John W(alter) 1921- 37-40R
Bowyer, Mathew J(ustice) 1926- CANR-13
Earlier sketch in CA 37-40R
Box, Edgar
See Vidal, Gore
Box, Sydney 1907-1983 Obituary 109
Boxer, Charles Ralph 1904- CANR-72
Earlier sketch in CA 102
Boxer, (Charles) Mark (Edward)
1931-1988 Obituary 126
Boxerman, David Samuel 1945- 61-64
Boxill, Roger 1928- 126
Boxman
See Chambliss, William J(oseph)
Boy, Angelo V(ictor) 1929- 69-72
Boyajian, Cecile
See Starr, Cecile
Boyarsky, Bill 1936- 25-28R
Boyce, (Joseph) Chris(topher) 1943- 73-76
Boyce, David George 1942- 103
Boyce, George A(rthur) 1898- 53-56
See also SATA 19
Boyce, Gray Cowan 1899- 5-8R
Boyce, Joseph Nelson 1937- 102
Boyce, Richard Fyfe 1896-1985 69-72
Obituary 116
Boyce, Ronald R(eed) 1931- CANR-18
Earlier sketches in CA 9-12R, CANR-3
Boycott, Desmond (Lionel) Morse
See Morse-Boycott, Desmond (Lionel)
Boycott, Geoff
See Boycott, Geoffrey
Boycott, Geoffrey 1940- 131
Boycott, Rosie 1951- 132
Boyd, Alamo
See Bosworth, Allan R(ucker)
Boyd, Andrew (Kirk Henry) 1920- CANR-48
Earlier sketch in CA 1-4R
Boyd, Ann S.
See Schoonmaker, Ann
Boyd, Anne Morris 1884-1974 Obituary 113
Boyd, Beverly M(ary) 1925- 69-72
Boyd, Blanche M.
See Boyd, Blanche McCrary
Boyd, Blanche McCrary 1945- 162
Boyd, Bob
See Boyd, Robert T(hompson)
Boyd, Brian (David) 1952- 139
Boyd, Candy Dawson 1946- 138
See also BW 2
See also CLR 50
See also JRDA
See also SATA 72
Boyd, Carl 1936- 141
Boyd, Carolyn Patricia 1944- 112
Boyd, Carse
See Stacton, David (Derek)
Boyd, Claude E. 1939- 151
Boyd, Dean (Wallace) 5-8R
Boyd, E(lizabeth) 1904(?)-1974 Obituary 53-56
Boyd, Edward M. 1927- 120
Boyd, Frank
See Kane, Frank
Boyd, Harper W(hite), Jr. 1917- 13-16R
Boyd, Herb 1938- 110
Boyd, J(ohn) Francis 1910- 5-8R
Boyd, Jack 1932- CANR-34
Earlier sketch in CA 49-52
Boyd, James 1888-1944 .... DLB 9
See also DLBD 16
Boyd, James M(oore) 1919- 33-36R
Boyd, James S(terling) 1917- 49-52
Boyd, John
See Upchurch, Boyd (Bradfield)
See also DLB 8
Boyd, John D. 1916- 25-28R
Boyd, Julian P(arks) 1903-1980 65-68
Obituary 97-100
Boyd, Malcolm 1923- CANR-51
Earlier sketches in CA 5-8R, CANR-4, 26
Interview in CANR-26
See also CAAS 11
Boyd, (Charles) Malcolm 1932- 126
Boyd, Marion M.
See Havighurst, Marion (M.)
Boyd, Martin a Beckett 1893- CAP-1
Earlier sketch in CA 13-14
Boyd, Maurice 1921- 9-12R
Boyd, Mildred Worthy 1921- 17-20R
Boyd, Myron F(enton) 1909-1978 .... 41-44R
Boyd, Nancy
See Millay, Edna St. Vincent
Boyd, Neil
See DeRosa, Peter (Clement)
Boyd, Neil 1951- 129
Boyd, Pauline
See Schock, Pauline
Boyd, R(obert) L(ewis) F(ullarton) 1922- 57-60

Boyd, Robert H. 1912- ... 53-56
Boyd, Robert S. 1928- ... 13-16R
Boyd, Robert T(hompson) 1914- ... 108
Boyd, Robin (Gerard Penleigh) 1919-1971 .. 17-20R
Obituary ... 133
Boyd, Selma
See Acuff, Selma Boyd
Boyd, Shylah 1945- ... 61-64
Boyd, Steven R(ay) 1946- ... 146
Boyd, Sue Abbott 1921- ... CANR-14
Earlier sketch in CA 65-68
Boyd, Thomas (Alexander) 1898-1935 Brief entry ... 111
See also DLB 9
See also DLBD 16
Boyd, Waldo T. 1918- ... CANR-12
Earlier sketch in CA 29-32R
See also SATA 18
Boyd, William 1885-1979 ... 41-44R
Obituary ... 135
Boyd, William 1952- ... CANR-71
Brief entry ... 114
Earlier sketches in CA 120, CANR-51
See also CLC 28, 53, 70
Boyd, William C(louser) 1903-1983 Obituary ... 109
Boyd, William Harland 1912- ... CANR-11
Earlier sketch in CA 69-72
Boyd-Carpenter, John (Archibald) 1908- ... 131
Boyden, David D(odge) 1910-1986 Obituary ... 120
Boyden, Donald P. 1957- ... 128
Boyden, Sarah B. (?)-1989 Obituary ... 128
Boydston, Jo Ann 1924- ... 29-32R
Boye, Karin Maria 1900-1941 ... 165
Boyer, Brian D. 1939- ... 45-48
Boyer, Bruce Hatton 1946- ... 101
Boyer, Carl B(enjamin) 1906-1976 Obituary .. 65-68
Boyer, Dwight 1912- ... 65-68
Boyer, Elizabeth (Mary) 1913- ... 81-84
Boyer, Ernest LeRoy 1928-1995 ... 110
Obituary ... 150
Boyer, G. G.
See Boyer, Glenn G.
Boyer, Glenn G. 1924- ... 130
Boyer, Harold W. 1908- ... 1-4R
Boyer, Jay 1947- ... 147
Boyer, John (William) 1946- ... 103
Boyer, Mildred (Vinson) 1926- ... 112
Boyer, Paul Samuel 1935- ... CANR-41
Earlier sketches in CA 49-52, CANR-1, 18
Boyer, Richard Edwin 1932- ... 21-24R
Boyer, Richard Lewis 1943- ... CANR-62
Earlier sketches in CA 69-72, CANR-11, 27
Boyer, Richard O. 1903-1973 Obituary ... 45-48
Boyer, Rick
See Boyer, Richard Lewis
Boyer, Robert
See Lake, Kenneth R(obert)
Boyer, Robert E(rnst) 1929- ... 41-44R
See also SATA 22
Boyer, Ruth Gasink 1913- ... 114
Boyer, Sophia Ames 1907(?)-1972 Obituary ... 37-40R
Boyer, William H(arrison) 1924- ... CANR-22
Earlier sketch in CA 106
Boyer, William W., (Jr.) 1923- ... 13-16R
Boyers, Margaret Anne ... 118
Boyers, Peggy
See Boyers, Margaret Anne
Boyers, Robert 1942- ... CANR-4
Earlier sketch in CA 53-56
Boyesen, Hjalmar Hjorth 1848-1895 ... DLB 12, 71
See also DLBD 13
Boyett, Jimmie T. 1948- ... 149
Boyett, Joseph H. 1945- ... 149
Boyett, Steven R. 1960- ... 154
Boyington, (Gregory) Pappy 1912-1988 Obituary ... 124
Boykin, James H(andy) 1914- ... CANR-2
Earlier sketch in CA 5-8R
Boykin, Keith 1965- ... 156
Boylan, Bernard R(obert) 1927- ... 127
Boylan, Boyd
See Whiton, James Nelson
Boylan, Brian Richard 1936- ... 81-84
Boylan, Clare 1948- ... 136
Boylan, Eleanor 1916- ... 132
Boylan, James (Richard) 1927- ... CANR-16
Earlier sketches in CA 1-4R, CANR-1
Boylan, Leona Davis 1910- ... 61-64
Boylan, Lucile 1906- ... CAP-1
Earlier sketch in CA 11-12
Boylan, Mary 1913(?)-1984 Obituary ... 112
Boyle, Alistair 1952- ... 157
Boyle, Andrew (Philip More) 1919-1991 ... 102
Obituary ... 134
Boyle, Ann (Peters) 1916- ... CANR-26
Earlier sketch in CA 29-32R
See also SATA 10
Boyle, Charles 1951- ... 113
Boyle, David (Courtney) 1958- ... 133
Boyle, Deirdre 1949- ... CANR-28
Earlier sketch in CA 110
Boyle, Edward Charles Gurney 1923-1981 Obituary ... 108
Boyle, Eleanor Vere (Gordon) 1825-1916 . SATA 28
Boyle, Freddie M. 1915(?)-1984 Obituary ... 113
Boyle, Gerry 1956- ... CANR-72
Earlier sketch in CA 144
Boyle, Hal
See Boyle, Harold V(incent)
Boyle, Harold V(incent) 1911-1974 ... 101
Obituary ... 89-92
Boyle, Harry Joseph 1915- ... CANR-7
Earlier sketch in CA 13-16R
Boyle, J(ohn) A(ndrew) 1916-1979 ... CANR-9
Obituary ... 85-88
Earlier sketch in CA 61-64
Boyle, Jimmy 1944- ... 130
Boyle, John Hunter 1930- ... 41-44R
Boyle, John P(hillips) 1931- Brief entry ... 114
Boyle, Josephine 1935- ... 148
Boyle, (Emily) Joyce 1901- ... CAP-1
Earlier sketch in CA 13-14
Boyle, Kay 1902-1992 ... CANR-61
Obituary ... 140
Earlier sketches in CA 13-16R, CANR-29
See also CAAS 1
See also CLC 1, 5, 19, 58
See also DLB 4, 9, 48, 86
See also DLBY 93
See also MTCW 1
See also SSC 5
Boyle, (C.) Kevin 1943- ... CANR-50
Earlier sketch in CA 123
Boyle, Leonard E(ugene) 1923- ... 127
Boyle, Mark
See Kienzle, William X(avier)
Boyle, Mary 1882(?)-1975 Obituary ... 53-56
Boyle, Nicholas 1946- ... 140
Boyle, Patrick 1905-1982 ... 127
See also CLC 19
Boyle, Richard J(ohn) 1932- ... 129
Boyle, Robert (Richard) 1915- ... 13-16R
Boyle, Robert H. 1928- ... CANR-12
Earlier sketch in CA 17-20R
See also SATA 65
Boyle, Roger 1621-1679 ... DLB 80
Boyle, Samuel J. III 1920-1985 Obituary ... 118
Boyle, Sarah Patton 1906-1994 ... CAP-1
Obituary ... 144
Earlier sketch in CA 13-16
Boyle, Stanley E(ugene) 1927- ... 41-44R
Boyle, T. C. 1948-
See Boyle, T(homas) Coraghessan
Boyle, T(homas) Coraghessan 1948- ... CANR-44
Earlier sketch in CA 120
See also BEST 90:4
See also CLC 36, 55, 90
See also DAM POP
See also DLBY 86
See also SSC 16
Boyle, Ted Eugene 1933- ... 21-24R
Boyle, Thomas 1939- ... CANR-44
Earlier sketch in CA 118
Boyle, Thomas A. 1922- ... 161
Boyle, Timm
See Boyle, Timothy R(obert)
Boyle, Timothy R(obert) 1953- ... 118
Boylen, Margaret Currier 1921-1967 ... 1-4R
Obituary ... 103
Boyles, C(larence) S(cott), Jr. 1905- ... CANR-64
Earlier sketch in CA 1-4R
Boyles, Denis 1946- ... 140
Boylston, Helen Dore 1895-1984 ... CANR-21
Obituary ... 113
Earlier sketch in CA 73-76
See also MAICYA
See also SATA 23
See also SATA-Obit 39
Boym, Svetlana 1959- ... 139
Boyne, Walter J(ames) 1929- ... 107
Boynton, Lewis Delano 1909- ... CANR-6
Earlier sketch in CA 5-8R
Boynton, Peter S. 1920(?)-1971 Obituary ... 104
Boynton, Robert W(hitney) 1921- Brief entry ... 117
Boynton, Sandra (Keith) 1953- ... CANR-53
Earlier sketch in CA 126
See also SATA 57
See also SATA-Brief 38
Boynton, Searles Roland 1926- ... 77-80
Boyum, Joy Gould 1934- ... 33-36R
Boyum, Keith O(rel) 1945- ... 102
Boz
See Dickens, Charles (John Huffam)
Bozarth-Campbell, Alla (Linda Renee) 1947- ... 105
Boze, Arthur Phillip 1945- ... 57-60
Bozeman, Adda B(ruemmer) 1908- ... CANR-3
Earlier sketch in CA 5-8R
Bozeman, Theodore Dwight 1942- ... 85-88
Bozic, Mirko 1919- ... DLB 181
Braasch, William Frederick 1878- ... CAP-2
Earlier sketch in CA 29-32
Brabazon, James
See Seth-Smith, Leslie James
Brabb, George J(acob) 1925- ... 41-44R
Brabec, Barbara 1937- ... CANR-65
Earlier sketches in CA 93-96, CANR-15, 32
Brabson, George Dana 1900- ... CAP-1
Earlier sketch in CA 19-20
Brace, Edward Roy 1936- ... CANR-19
Earlier sketch in CA 102
Brace, Geoffrey (Arthur) 1930- ... CANR-11
Earlier sketch in CA 69-72
Brace, Gerald Warner 1901-1978 ... CANR-71
Obituary ... 81-84
Earlier sketch in CA 13-16R
Brace, Paul (R.) 1954- ... 145
Brace, Richard Munthe 1915-1977 ... CANR-15
Obituary ... 69-72
Earlier sketch in CA 1-4R
Brace, Timothy
See Pratt, Theodore
Braceairdle, Cyril 1920- ... 45-48
Bracegirdle, Brian 1933- ... 101
Braceland, Francis J(ames) 1900-1985 Obituary ... 115
Bracewell, Michael 1958- ... 135
Bracewell, Ronald N(ewbold) 1921- ... 57-60
Bracewell-Milnes, (John) Barry 1931- ... CANR-37
Earlier sketches in CA 33-36R, CANR-13
Bracey, Howard E(dwin) 1905- ... 13-16R
Bracey, John H(enry, Jr.) 1941- ... 29-32R
Brach, Gerard 1927- ... 138
Bracher, Frederick (George) 1905- ... 111
Bracher, Karl Dietrich 1922- ... CANR-40
Earlier sketches in CA 45-48, CANR-1, 17
Bracher, Marjory (Louise) 1906- ... CAP-1
Earlier sketch in CA 13-16
Brack, Harold Arthur 1923- ... 17-20R
Brack, O M, Jr. 1938- ... 41-44R
Brack, Vektris
See Humphrys, Leslie George
Brack, William Dennis 1939- ... 136
Brackbill, Yvonne 1928- ... 21-24R
Brackeen, Steve
See Farris, John
Bracken, Charles
See Pellowski, Michael (Joseph)
Bracken, Dorothy K(endall) ... 21-24R
Bracken, James K. 1952- ... 142
Bracken, Joseph Andrew 1930- ... 37-40R
Bracken, Len 1961- ... 166
Bracken, Paul 1948- ... 115
Bracken, Peg 1920- ... CANR-6
Earlier sketch in CA 1-4R
Brackenbury, Alison 1953- ... 136
See also DLB 40
Brackenridge, Hugh Henry 1748-1816 .. DLB 11, 37
Brackenridge, R(obert) Douglas 1932- ... 101
Bracker, Jon 1936- ... 17-20R
Brackett, Charles 1892-1969 Obituary ... 113
See also DLB 26
Brackett, Leigh (Douglass) 1915-1978 ... CANR-1
Obituary ... 77-80
Earlier sketch in CA 1-4R
See also DLB 8, 26
Brackman, Arnold C(harles) 1923-1983 ... CANR-2
Obituary ... 111
Earlier sketch in CA 5-8R
See also AITN 1
Brackman, Barbara 1945- ... 146
Brackney, William (Henry) 1948- ... CANR-50
Earlier sketch in CA 123
Bracy, William 1915- ... 61-64
Bradbrook, M(uriel) C(lara) 1909-1993 ... CANR-23
Obituary ... 141
Earlier sketches in CA 13-16R, CANR-7
Bradburn, Norman M. 1933- ... CANR-13
Earlier sketch in CA 37-40R
Bradburne, E(lizabeth) S. 1915- ... 25-28R
Bradbury, Bianca (Ryley) 1908-1982 ... CANR-37
Earlier sketches in CA 13-16R, CANR-5
See also MAICYA
See also SATA 3, 56
Bradbury, Dorothy E(dith) 1902-1984 Obituary . 113
Bradbury, Edward P.
See Moorcock, Michael (John)
Bradbury, Jim 1937- ... 140
Bradbury, John M(ason) 1908-1969 ... CAP-1
Earlier sketch in CA 13-16
Bradbury, Katharine L(orraine) 1946- ... 111
Bradbury, Malcolm (Stanley) 1932- ... CANR-33
Earlier sketches in CA 1-4R, CANR-1
See also CLC 32, 61
See also DAM NOV
See also DLB 14
See also MTCW 1
Bradbury, Parnell 1904- ... 13-16R
Bradbury, Peggy 1930- ... 65-68
Bradbury, Ray (Douglas) 1920- ... CANR-30
Earlier sketches in CA 1-4R, CANR-2
See also AAYA 15
See also AITN 1, 2
See also CDALB 1968-1988
See also CLC 1, 3, 10, 15, 42, 98
See also DA
See also DAB
See also DAC
See also DAM MST, NOV, POP
See also DLB 2, 8
See also MTCW 1
See also SATA 11, 64
See also SSC 29
See also WLC
Braddock, Joseph (Edward) 1902- Brief entry ... 117
Braddock, Richard R(eed) 1920-1974 ... 1-4R
Obituary ... 103
Braddon, George
See Milkomane, George Alexis Milkomanovich
Braddon, Mary Elizabeth 1837(?)-1915 Brief entry ... 108
See also DLB 18, 70, 156
Braddon, Russell (Reading) 1921-1995 .. CANR-71
Obituary ... 148
Earlier sketches in CA 1-4R, CANR-2
Braddy, Haldeen 1908-1980 ... 17-20R
Obituary ... 101
Brade-Birks, S(tanley) Graham 1887- ... CAP-1
Earlier sketch in CA 13-16
Braden, Charles Samuel 1887- ... 5-8R
Braden, Donna R. 1953- ... 130
Braden, Irene A.
See Hoadley, Irene Braden
Braden, Spruille 1894-1978 Obituary ... 115
Braden, Thomas (Wardell) 1918- Brief entry ... 113
Braden, Tom
See Braden, Thomas (Wardell)
Braden, Waldo W(arder) 1911- ... CANR-5
Earlier sketch in CA 5-8R
Braden, William 1930- ... 21-24R
Bradfield, Carl 1942- ... SATA 91
Bradfield, James McComb 1917- ... 5-8R
Bradfield, Jolly Roger
See Bradfield, Roger
Bradfield, Nancy 1913- ... 29-32R
Bradfield, Richard 1896- ... CAP-2
Earlier sketch in CA 23-24
Bradfield, Roger 1924- ... 17-20R
Bradfield, Scott (Michael) 1955- ... 147
Bradford, Adam M.D.
See Wassersug, Joseph D.
Bradford, Alex 1927-1978 Obituary ... 112
Bradford, Andrew 1686-1742 ... DLB 43, 73
Bradford, Ann (Liddell) 1917- Brief entry ... 116
See also SATA 56
See also SATA-Brief 38
Bradford, Barbara Taylor 1933- ... CANR-56
Earlier sketches in CA 89-92, CANR-32
See also BEST 89:1
See also DAM POP
See also MTCW 1
See also SATA 66
Bradford, Benjamin 1925- ... CANR-47
Earlier sketch in CA 85-88
Bradford, David F(rantz) 1939- ... 124
Bradford, Dennis E(arle) 1946- ... 118
Bradford, Ernle (Dusgate Selby) 1922-1986 ... CANR-68
Obituary ... 119
Earlier sketch in CA 101
Bradford, Gamaliel 1863-1932 ... 160
See also DLB 17
See also TCLC 36
Bradford, James C(hapin) 1945- ... CANR-29
Earlier sketch in CA 111
Bradford, John 1749-1830 ... DLB 43
Bradford, Karleen 1936- ... CANR-67
Earlier sketch in CA 112
See also SATA 48, 96
Bradford, Leland P(owers) 1905- ... CANR-9
Earlier sketch in CA 13-16R
Bradford, Leroy 1922- ... 105
Bradford, Lois J(ean) 1936- ... 104
See also SATA 36
Bradford, M(elvin) E(ustace) 1934-1993 .. CANR-46
Obituary ... 140
Earlier sketches in CA 77-80, CANR-13
Bradford, Patience Andrewes 1918- ... 33-36R
Bradford, Peter Amory 1942- ... 61-64
Bradford, Reed H(oward) 1912- ... 49-52
Bradford, Richard (Roark) 1932- ... CANR-64
Earlier sketches in CA 49-52, CANR-2
See also SATA 59
Bradford, Richard H(eadlee) 1938- ... 89-92
Bradford, Roark (Whitney Wickliffe) 1896-1948 . 162
See also DLB 86
Bradford, Robert W(hitmore) 1918- ... 77-80
Bradford, Roy Hamilton 1920- ... 109
Bradford, S. W.
See Battin, B(rinton) W(arner)
Bradford, Sarah (Mary Malet) 1938- ... CANR-65
Earlier sketches in CA 128, CANR-60
Bradford, Sax(ton) 1907-1966 ... 1-4R
Bradford, Will
See Paine, Lauran (Bosworth)
Bradford, William III 1719-1791 ... DLB 43, 73
Bradford, William 1590-1657 ... DLB 24, 30
Bradford, William C(astle) 1910- ... 9-12R
Brading, D. A. 1936- ... 136
Bradlaugh, Charles 1833-1891 ... DLB 57
Bradlee, Benjamin C(rowninshield) 1921- ... 61-64
See also AITN 2
Bradlee, Frederic 1920- ... 21-24R
Bradley, Alfred 1925-1991 ... 105
Obituary ... 134
Bradley, Bert E(dward) 1926- ... 41-44R
Bradley, Bill
See Bradley, William Warren
Bradley, Brigitte L(ooke) 1924- ... 37-40R
Bradley, C. Paul 1918- ... 106
Bradley, Concho
See Paine, Lauran (Bosworth)
Bradley, David (Henry, Jr.) 1950- ... CANR-26
Earlier sketch in CA 104
See also BLC 1
See also BW 1
See also CLC 23
See also DAM MULT
See also DLB 33
Bradley, David G. 1916- ... 13-16R
Bradley, Duane
See Sanborn, Duane
Bradley, Ed 1911(?)-1983 Obituary ... 110
Bradley, Ed(ward R.) 1941- ... 113
Brief entry ... 108
Interview in ... 113
See also BW 1
Bradley, Edwin M(cKinley) 1958- ... 158
Bradley, Erwin S(tanley) 1906- ... CAP-2
Earlier sketch in CA 33-36
Bradley, George 1953- ... 134
Bradley, Harold Whitman 1903- ... 33-36R
Bradley, Hassell 1930- ... 65-68
Bradley, Helen G(enevieve) 1932- ... 112
Bradley, Ian Campbell 1950- ... 103
Bradley, James E. 1944- ... 136
Bradley, James V(andiver) 1924- ... 37-40R
Bradley, Jerry (Wayne) 1948- ... 137
Bradley, John (Francis Nejez) 1930- ... CANR-10
Earlier sketch in CA 25-28R
Bradley, John Ed(mund, Jr.) 1958- ... 139
See also CLC 55
Bradley, John Lewis 1917- ... 29-32R
Bradley, Joseph F(rancis) 1917- ... 21-24R
Bradley, Kenneth (Granville) 1904- ... CAP-1
Earlier sketch in CA 13-14

Bradley, Marion Zimmer 1930- CANR-51
Earlier sketches in CA 57-60, CANR-7, 31
See also CAAS 10
See also AAYA 9
See also CLC 30
See also DAM POP
See also DLB 8
See also MTCW 1
See also SATA 90
Bradley, Marjorie D. 1931- 25-28R
Bradley, Matt 1947- 105
Bradley, Melanie (Rose) Choukas
See Choukas-Bradley, Melanie (Rose)
Bradley, Michael
See Blumberg, Gary
Bradley, Michael 1944- 129
Bradley, Omar Nelson 1893-1981 Obituary 103
Bradley, Preston 1888-1983 Obituary 110
Bradley, R. C. 1929- CANR-14
Earlier sketch in CA 33-36R
Bradley, Ritamary 1916- 49-52
Bradley, Robert A(ustin) 1917- 21-24R
Bradley, Sam(uel McKee) 1917- 21-24R
Bradley, (Edward) Sculley 1897- 89-92
Bradley, Van Allen 1913-1984 .... 37-40R
Obituary 114
Bradley, Virginia 1912- CANR-8
Earlier sketch in CA 61-64
See also SATA 23
Bradley, Will
See Strickland, (William) Brad(ley)
Bradley, William 1934- 45-48
Bradley, William Aspenwall 1878-1939 Brief entry 107
See also DLB 4
Bradley, William L(ee) 1918- 21-24R
Bradley, William Warren 1943- CANR-55
Earlier sketch in CA 101
Bradlow, Edna Rom CAP-1
Earlier sketch in CA 9-10
Bradlow, Frank R(osslyn) 1913- CANR-13
Earlier sketches in CAP-1, CA 9-10
Bradman, Tony 1954- 149
See also SATA 81
Bradner, Enos 1892-1984 57-60
Obituary 111
Bradshaw, Brendan 1937- 73-76
Bradshaw, Buck
See Paine, Lauran (Bosworth)
Bradshaw, George 1909(?)-1973 Obituary ... 45-48
Bradshaw, Gillian (Marucha) 1956- CANR-58
Earlier sketch in CA 103
Bradshaw, Henry 1831-1886 .... DLB 184
Bradshaw, John 1933- CANR-61
Earlier sketch in CA 138
Bradshaw, Jon (Wayne) 1937-1986 145
Obituary 121
Bradshaw, Michael 1935- 143
Bradshaw, Terry (Paxton) 1948- 111
Bradshaw, Thornton F(rederick) 1917- 108
Bradsher, Henry S(t. Amant) 1931- 133
Bradstock, Andrew (William) 1955- 127
Bradstreet, Anne 1612(?)-1672 .. CDALB 1640-1865
See also DA
See also DAC
See also DAM MST, POET
See also DLB 24
See also PC 10
Bradstreet, Vallerie
See Roby, Mary Linn
Bradt, A(cken) Gordon 1896-1983 57-60
Obituary 110
Bradwardine, Thomas 1295(?)-1349 ...... DLB 115
Bradway, John S(aeger) 1890- CAP-2
Earlier sketch in CA 33-36
Bradwell, James
See Kent, Arthur William Charles
Brady, Alexander 1896-1985 Obituary 117
Brady, Ann 1947- 138
Brady, Charles Andrew 1912- 5-8R
Brady, Darlene A(nn) 1951- 102
Brady, Dave 1913(?)-1988 Obituary 125
Brady, David W(illiam) 1940- Brief entry 114
Brady, Esther Wood 1905-1987 93-96
Obituary 123
See also SATA 31
See also SATA-Obit 53
Brady, Frank 1924-1986 .... 13-16R
Obituary 120
See also DLB 111
Brady, Frank 1934- CANR-9
Earlier sketch in CA 61-64
Brady, Gene P(aul) 1927- 107
Brady, George Stuart 1887-1977 Obituary ... 73-76
Brady, Gerald Peter 1929- 5-8R
Brady, Ignatius Charles 1911- 113
Brady, Irene 1943- CANR-20
Earlier sketch in CA 33-36R
See also SATA 4
Brady, James B. 1939- 143
Brady, James Winston 1928- CANR-21
Earlier sketch in CA 101
Brady, Jane 1934- Brief entry 113
Brady, Joan 1939- 141
See also CLC 86
Brady, John 1942- CANR-10
Earlier sketch in CA 65-68
Brady, John (Mary) 1955- CANR-53
Earlier sketch in CA 130
Brady, John Paul 1928- CANR-5
Earlier sketch in CA 13-16R
Brady, Kathleen 1947- 129
Brady, Kimberley S(mith) 1953- 168
See also SATA 101
Brady, Kristin 1949- 109
Brady, Leo 1917-1984 69-72
Obituary 114
Brady, Lillian 1902- 105
See also SATA 28
Brady, Mary Lou 1937- 106
Brady, Maureen 1943- 112
Brady, Maxine L. 1941- 69-72
Brady, Michael 1928- 93-96
Brady, Nicholas
See Levinson, Leonard
Brady, Patricia 1943- 136
Brady, Peter
See Daniels, Norman
Brady, Sally Ryder 1939- 103
Brady, Terence 1939- 106
Brady, William S.
See Harvey, John (Barton)
Brady, William S.
See Wells, Angus
Braeker, Ulrich 1735-1798 .... DLB 94
Braenne, Berit 1918- 21-24R
Braestrup, Carl Bjorn 1897-1982 Obituary 107
Braestrup, Peter 1929-1997 97-100
Obituary 160
Braff, Allan James 1930- 108
Braganti, Nancy (Sue) 1941- CANR-40
Earlier sketch in CA 117
Bragdon, Clifford R(ichardson) 1940- 57-60
Bragdon, Elspeth MacDuffie 1897- CANR-5
Earlier sketch in CA 5-8R
See also SATA 6
Bragdon, Henry Wilkinson 1906-1980 ..... CANR-3
Obituary 97-100
Earlier sketch in CA 5-8R
Bragdon, Kathleen J. 163
Bragdon, Lillian Jacot 73-76
See also SATA 24
Bragg, Arthur N(orris) 1897- CAP-1
Earlier sketch in CA 17-18
Bragg, Bill
See Bragg, William Fredrick, Jr.
Bragg, Dobby
See Sykes, Roosevelt
Bragg, Mabel Caroline 1870-1945 .... SATA 24
Bragg, Melvyn 1939- CANR-48
Earlier sketches in CA 57-60, CANR-10
See also BEST 89:3
See also CLC 10
See also DLB 14
Bragg, Michael 1948- 128
See also SATA 46
Bragg, Richard Geoffrey 1909- 121
Bragg, Rick 1959- 165
Bragg, Ruth Gembicki 1943- .... SATA 77
Bragg, Sir W. H.
See Bragg, William Henry
Bragg, Sir William
See Bragg, William Henry
Bragg, Sir William Henry
See Bragg, William Henry
Bragg, Steven M. 1960- 162
Bragg, William Fredrick, Jr. 1922- 109
Bragg, William Henry 1862-1942 155
Brief entry 123
Bragg, William Lawrence 1890-1971 155
Obituary 115
Braggin, Mary Vetterling
See Vetterling-Braggin, Mary (Katherine)
Braginsky, Vladimir B. 1931- 145
Braham, Allan (John Witney) 1937- 105
Braham, (E.) Jeanne 1940- 150
Braham, Randolph L(ewis) 1922- CANR-41
Earlier sketches in CA 1-4R, CANR-5, 19
Brahm, Sumishta 1954- .... SATA 58
Brahms, Caryl
See Abrahams, Doris Caroline
Brahs, Stuart J(ohn) 1940- 57-60
Brahtz, John F(rederick) Peel 1918- 73-76
Braider, Donald 1923-1976 .... CAP-2
Obituary 65-68
Earlier sketch in CA 33-36
Braidwood, Robert John 1907- 108
Braiker, Harriet B. 1948- 141
Brailsford, Frances
See Wosmek, Frances
Braimah, Joseph Adam 1916- 61-64
Braiman, Susan 1943- 97-100
Brain, George B(ernard) 1920- 41-44R
Brain, J(oy) B(lundell) 1926- CANR-41
Earlier sketch in CA 118
Brain, James Lewton
See Lewton-Brain, James
Brain, Joseph J. 1920- 13-16R
Brain, Robert 1933- 73-76
Brainard, Cecilia Manguerra 1947- 146
Brainard, Harry Gray 1907- 1-4R
Brainard, Joe 1942-1994 .... CANR-12
Obituary 145
Earlier sketch in CA 65-68
Braine, David 1940- 155
Braine, John (Gerard) 1922-1986 .... CANR-33
Obituary 120
Earlier sketches in CA 1-4R, CANR-1
See also CDBLB 1945-1960
See also CLC 1, 3, 41
See also DLB 15
See also DLBY 86
See also MTCW 1
Brainerd, Barron 1928- 33-36R
Brainerd, Charles Jon 1944- 103
Brainerd, John W(hiting) 1918- 57-60
See also SATA 65
Braithwaite, Althea 1940- CANR-18
Earlier sketch in CA 97-100
See also SAAS 24
See also SATA 23
Braithwaite, (Eustace) E(dward) R(icardo) 1920- ... CANR-25
Earlier sketch in CA 106
See also BW 1
Braithwaite, Kenneth James
See Barrow, Kenneth
Braithwaite, Max 1911- 93-96
Braithwaite, Richard Bevan
1900-1990 Obituary 131
Braithwaite, William Stanley (Beaumont)
1878-1962 125
See also BLC 1
See also BW 1
See also DAM MULT
See also DLB 50, 54
Brake, Laurel 1941- 138
Brake, Mike 1936- 93-96
Brakel, Samuel J(ohannes) 1943- 33-36R
Brakhage, Stan 1933- CANR-15
Earlier sketch in CA 41-44R
Bralver, Eleanor 1913- 97-100
Braly, Malcolm 1925-1980 .... CANR-12
Obituary 97-100
Earlier sketch in CA 17-20R
Bram, Chris
See Bram, Christopher
Bram, Christopher 1952- 126
Bram, Elizabeth 1948- CANR-9
Earlier sketch in CA 65-68
See also SATA 30
Bram, Joseph 1904-1974 Obituary 110
Bramah, Ernest 1868-1942 156
See also DLB 70
See also TCLC 72
Bramall, Eric 1927- 9-12R
Braman, Sandra 1951- 114
Bramann, Jorn K(arl) 1938- CANR-43
Earlier sketch in CA 119
Brambell, Wilfrid 1912- 113
Brambeus, Baron
See Senkovsky, Osip Ivanovich
Bramble, Forbes 1939- 89-92
Brameld, Theodore (Burghard Hurt)
1904-1987 .... 17-20R
Obituary 123
Bramer, Jennie (Perkins) 1900- CAP-1
Earlier sketch in CA 13-14
Bramer, John C(onrad) Jr. 1924- 1-4R
Bramesco, Norton J. 1924- 106
Bramlett, John
See Pierce, John Leonard, Jr.
Bramly, Serge 1949- 142
Brammell, P(aris) Roy 1900- 65-68
Brammer, Lawrence M(artin) 1922- 13-16R
Brammer, William 1930(?)-1978 Obituary 77-80
See also CLC 31
Brams, Stanley Howard 1910- 9-12R
Brams, Steven J(ohn) 1940- CANR-52
Earlier sketches in CA 61-64, CANR-10, 26
Bramsch, Joan 1936- 122
Bramson, Leon 1930- CANR-4
Earlier sketch in CA 1-4R
Bramson, Robert M(ark) 1925- CANR-54
Earlier sketches in CA 108, CANR-25
Bramson, Susan (Jane) 1940- 128
Bramwell, Charlotte
See Kimbro, John M.
Bramwell, Dana G. 1948- 57-60
Bramwell, James Guy 1911- 9-12R
Bramwell-Booth, Catherine
1883-1987 Obituary 123
Branagan, Thomas 1774-1843 .... DLB 37
Branagh, Kenneth 1960- 156
See also AAYA 20
Brana-Shute, Gary 1945- 111
Branca, Albert A. 1916- 13-16R
Branca, Vittore (Felice Giovanni) 1913- 154
Brancaforte, Benito 1934- 37-40R
Brancati, Vitaliano 1907-1954 Brief entry 109
See also TCLC 12
Brancato, Gilda 1949- 107
Brancato, Robin F(idler) 1936- CANR-45
Earlier sketches in CA 69-72, CANR-11
See also AAYA 9
See also CLC 35
See also CLR 32
See also JRDA
See also SAAS 9
See also SATA 97
Branch, Alan E(dward) 1933- CANR-50
Earlier sketches in CA 105, CANR-25
Branch, Daniel Paulk 1931- 17-20R
Branch, Edgar Marquess 1913- 13-16R
Branch, Harold F(rancis) 1894-1966 .... 5-8R
Branch, Kip 1947- 108
Branch, Mary 1910- CANR-10
Earlier sketch in CA 25-28R
Branch, Melville C(ampbell) 1913- CANR-14
Earlier sketch in CA 41-44R
Branch, Muriel Miller 1943- 159
See also SATA 94
Branch, Taylor 1947- 131
Interview in 131
See also BEST 89:2
Branch, William (Blackwell) 1927- CANR-40
Earlier sketches in CA 81-84, CANR-16
See also BW 2
See also DLB 76
Brand, Alice Glarden 1938- 148
Brand, C(larence) E(ugene) 1895- CAP-2
Earlier sketch in CA 23-24
Brand, Carl F(remont) 1892-1981 .... 13-16R
Obituary 133
Brand, Charles M(acy) 1932- 21-24R
Brand, Charles Peter 1923- 13-16R
Brand, Christianna
See Lewis, Mary (Christianna)
Brand, Clay
See Norwood, Victor G(eorge) C(harles)
Brand, Dionne 1953- 143
See also BW 2
Brand, Eugene L(ouis) 1931- CANR-8
Earlier sketch in CA 61-64
Brand, Garrison
See Brandner, Gary (Phil)
Brand, Gerd 1921- Brief entry 113
Brand, Irene B. 1929- 124
Brand, Jeanne L(aurel) 1919- 13-16R
Brand, Max
See Faust, Frederick (Schiller)
Brand, Millen 1906-1980 .... CANR-72
Obituary 97-100
Earlier sketch in CA 21-24R
See also CLC 7
Brand, Myles 1942- 37-40R
Brand, Oscar 1920- CANR-4
Earlier sketch in CA 1-4R
Brand, Peter
See Larsen, Erling
Brand, Sandra 1918- 85-88
Brand, Stewart 1938- CANR-44
Earlier sketch in CA 81-84
See also AITN 1
Brand, Susan
See Roper, Susan Bonthron
Brandabur, Edward 1930- 41-44R
Brande, Ralph T. 1921- 25-28R
Brandeis, Irma 1906(?)-1990 Obituary 130
Brandeis, Irma 1906-1990 130
Brandeis, Louis Dembitz 1856-1941 166
Brief entry 118
Brandel, Arthur Meyer 1913(?)-1980 Obituary .. 102
Brandel, Marc 1919- CANR-25
Earlier sketch in CA 108
See also SATA 71
Brandell, (Erik) Gunnar 1916- CANR-42
Earlier sketches in CA 103, CANR-20
Branden, Barbara 148
See also CLC 44
Branden, Nathaniel 1930- CANR-27
Earlier sketch in CA 33-36R
Interview in CANR-27
Branden, Victoria (Fremlin) 101
Brandenberg, Alexa (Demetria) 1966- 163
See also SATA 97
Brandenberg, Aliki Liacouras 1929- CANR-30
Earlier sketches in CA 1-4R, CANR-4, 12
See also Aliki
See also MAICYA
See also SATA 2, 35, 75
Brandenberg, Franz 1932- CANR-30
Earlier sketches in CA 29-32R, CANR-12
See also MAICYA
See also SATA 8, 35, 75
Brandenburg, David J(ohn)
1920-1987 Obituary 123
Brandenburg, Frank R(alph) 1926- 13-16R
Brandenburg, Jim 1945- 151
See also SATA 87
Brander, Michael (William) 1924- CANR-7
Earlier sketch in CA 53-56
Brandes, Georg (Morris Cohen) 1842-1927 Brief entry 105
See also TCLC 10
Brandes, Joseph 1928- 5-8R
Brandes, Norman Scott 1923- 57-60
Brandes, Paul D(ickerson) 1920- CANR-2
Earlier sketch in CA 45-48
Brandes, Stuart D. 1940- 160
Brandewyne, (Mary) Rebecca (Wadsworth) 1955- .. CANR-60
Earlier sketches in CA 107, CANR-23
Brandhorst, Carl T(heodore) 1898- CAP-2
Earlier sketch in CA 25-28
See also SATA 23
Brandi, John 1943- CANR-47
Earlier sketches in CA 73-76, CANR-12
Brandis, Marianne 1938- CANR-67
Earlier sketch in CA 117
See also SATA 59, 96
Brandner, Gary (Phil) 1933- CANR-72
Earlier sketches in CA 45-48, CANR-1, 17, 38
Brando, Marlon, (Jr.) 1924- 148
Brandon, Beatrice
See Krepps, Robert W(ilson)
Brandon, Brumsic, Jr. 1927- 61-64
See also SATA 9
Brandon, Curt
See Bishop, Curtis (Kent)
Brandon, Dick H. 1934-1981 .... CANR-10
Earlier sketch in CA 17-20R
Brandon, Donald (Wayne) 1926- 69-72
Brandon, Dorothy 1899(?)-1977 Obituary 69-72
Brandon, Frances Sweeney 1916- 9-12R
Brandon, Frank
See Bulmer, (Henry) Kenneth
Brandon, (Oscar) Henry 1916-1993 ..... CANR-48
Obituary 141
Earlier sketch in CA 49-52
Brandon, James Rodger 1927- CANR-11
Earlier sketch in CA 69-72
Brandon, Jay (Robert) 1953- 119
Brandon, Joe
See Davis, Robert P.
Brandon, John G(ordon) 1879(?)-1941 Brief entry 112
Brandon, Johnny 192(?)- CANR-45
Earlier sketch in CA 105
Brandon, Joyce A(lmeta) 1938- CANR-42
Earlier sketch in CA 118
Brandon, Robert Joseph 1918- 105

Brandon, Robin
See Brandon, Robert Joseph
Brandon, S(amuel) G(eorge) F(rederick) 1907-1971 .... CANR-69
Earlier sketch in CA 102
Brandon, Sheila
See Rayner, Claire (Berenice)
Brandon, William 1914- 77-80
Brandon-Cox, Hugh 1917- 93-96
Brandreth, Gyles 1948- 65-68
See also SATA 28
Brandreth, Henry R(enaud) T(urner) 1914-1984 Obituary 114
Brands, H. W. 1953- CANR-69
Earlier sketch in CA 147
Brandstatter, A(rthur) F. 1914- 107
Brandt, Allan M(orris) 1953- 144
Brandt, Alvin G. 1922- 13-16R
Brandt, Anthony 1936- 69-72
Brandt, Bill 1904(?)-1983 Obituary 111
Brandt, Carol 1904-1984 Obituary 114
Brandt, Catharine 1905- 106
See also SATA 40
Brandt, Charles 1942- 128
Brandt, Clare 1934- 145
Brandt, Deborah 1951- 138
Brandt, Floyd S(tanley) 1930- 21-24R
Brandt, George W(illiam) 1920- 131
Brandt, Harvey
See Edwards, William B(ennett)
Brandt, Jane Lewis 1915- 97-100
Brandt, Keith
See Sabin, Louis
Brandt, Leslie F. 1919- CANR-46
Earlier sketches in CA 21-24R, CANR-8, 23
Brandt, Lucile (Long Strayer) 1900- CANR-13
Earlier sketch in CA 61-64
Brandt, Nat
See Brandt, Nathan Henry, Jr.
Brandt, Nathan Henry, Jr. 1929- CANR-18
Earlier sketch in CA 102
Brandt, Rex(ford Elson) 1914- CANR-5
Earlier sketch in CA 13-16R
Brandt, Richard B(ooker) 1910- Brief entry 114
Brandt, Richard M(artin) 1922- 33-36R
Brandt, Roger
See Crawford, William (Elbert)
Brandt, Sue R(eading) 1916- 25-28R
See also SATA 59
Brandt, Tom
See Dewey, Thomas B(lanchard)
Brandt, Vincent S. R. 1924- 37-40R
Brandt, William E(dward) 1920- 5-8R
Brandt, Willy 1913- 85-88
Brandt, Yanna Kroyt 1933- 104
Brandts, Robert (Percival) 1930- 69-72
Brandwein, Chaim N(aftali) 1920- 21-24R
Brandys, Kazimierz 1916- .... CLC 62
Brandys, Marian 1912- 57-60
Branegan, James Augustus III 1950- 124
Branfield, John (Charles) 1931- CANR-72
Earlier sketches in CA 41-44R, CANR-14, 33
See also SATA 11
Branfoot, Gwynneth
See Holder, Gwynneth
Branick, Vincent P(atrick) 1941- 113
Branigan, Keith 1940- CANR-51
Earlier sketch in CA 124
Branin, M(anlif) Lelyn 1901- 85-88
Branley, Franklyn M(ansfield) 1915- CANR-39
Earlier sketches in CA 33-36R, CANR-14
See also CLC 21
See also CLR 13
See also MAICYA
See also SAAS 16
See also SATA 4, 68
Brann, Eva T(oni) H(elene) 1929- 93-96
Brannan, Robert Louis 1927- 21-24R
Brannen, J. P. 1927- 156
Brannen, Julia (M.) 1944- 130
Brannen, Noah S(amuel) 1924- CANR-11
Earlier sketch in CA 25-28R
Brannen, Ted R. 1924- 17-20R
Branner, Hans Christian 1903-1966 97-100
Obituary 89-92
Branner, R(obert) 1927-1973 .... CANR-3
Obituary 45-48
Earlier sketch in CA 5-8R
Brannigan, Bill
See Brannigan, William
Brannigan, Gary G(eorge) 1947- 139
Brannigan, William 1936- 65-68
Brannon, William T. 1906- CAP-1
Earlier sketch in CA 13-16
Branon, Bill 1937- 149
Branover, Herman 1931- 130
Branscomb, (Bennett) Harvie 1894- 106
Branscum, Robbie (Tilley) 1937-1997 .... CANR-8
Obituary 158
Earlier sketch in CA 61-64
See also AAYA 19
See also JRDA
See also MAICYA
See also SAAS 17
See also SATA 23, 72
See also SATA-Obit 96
Bransford, Kent Jackson 1953- 97-100
Bransford, Stephen 1949- 134
Bransom, (John) Paul 1885-1979 .... SATA 43
Branson, David 1909- CANR-21
Earlier sketch in CA 41-44R
Branson, Margaret Stimmann 1922- CANR-1
Earlier sketch in CA 49-52
Branston, (Ronald Victor) Brian 1914- 53-56
Brant, Beth (E.) 1941- 144
See also NNAL
Brant, Charles S(tanford) 1919- 25-28R
Brant, Irving (Newton) 1885-1976 .... CANR-68
Obituary 69-72
Earlier sketch in CA 9-12R
Brant, Lewis
See Rowland, D(onald) S(ydney)
Brant, Marley 1950- 140
Brant, Sebastian 1457-1521 .... DLB 179
Brantenberg, Gerd 1941- 162
Brantley, Cynthia Louise 1943- 109
Brantlinger, Patrick (Morgan) 1941- 145
Branyan, Brenda
See Branyan-Broadbent, Brenda
Branyan, Robert L(ester) 1930- 104
Branyan-Broadbent, Brenda 1932- 128
Branzburg, Paul M(arshal) 1941- 73-76
Braque, Georges 1882-1963 Obituary 112
Brasch, Charles (Orwell) 1909-1973 114
Obituary 104
Brasch, Ila Wales 1945- 57-60
Brasch, James D(aniel) 1929- 116
Brasch, Rudolph 1912- CANR-51
Earlier sketches in CA 21-24R, CANR-8, 27
Brasch, Walter Milton 1945- CANR-49
Earlier sketches in CA 57-60, CANR-6, 23
Braschi, Giannina 1953- 146
Brasher, Christopher William 1928- 5-8R
Brasher, N(orman) H(enry) 1922- 25-28R
Brasher, Nell 1912- CANR-7
Earlier sketch in CA 61-64
Brasher, Thomas L(owber) 1912- 69-72
Brashers, H(oward) C(harles) 1930- CANR-8
Earlier sketch in CA 5-8R
Brashler, William 1947- CANR-2
Earlier sketch in CA 45-48
Brasier, Virginia 1910- 61-64
Brasier-Creagh, Patrick
See Creagh, Patrick
Brasil, Emanuel 1940- 130
Brasnett, Bertrand R(ippington) 1893-1988 Obituary 124
Brason, Gill 1942- 112
Brass, Paul Richard 1936- 17-20R
Brassai
See Halasz, Gyula
Brasseaux, Carl A(nthony) 1951- 143
Brasselle, Keefe 1923(?)-1981 Obituary 104
Brassens, Georges 1921-1981 Obituary 105
Brasseur, Pierre
See Espinasse, Albert
Brassey, Lady Annie (Allnutt) 1839-1887 .... DLB 166
Braswell, George Wilbur, Jr. 1936- 112
Brata, Sasthi 1939- 143
Brater, Enoch 1944- CANR-48
Earlier sketch in CA 122
Brathwait, Richard c. 1588-1673 .... DLB 151
Brathwaite, Edward Kamau 1930- CANR-47
Earlier sketches in CA 25-28R, CANR-11, 26
See also BLCS
See also BW 2
See also CLC 11
See also DAM POET
See also DLB 125
Brathwaite, Errol (Freeman) 1924- CANR-66
Earlier sketches in CA 57-60, CANR-7, 11
Brathwaite, Sheila R. 1914- 25-28R
Bratt, Elmer Clark 1901-1970 .... 1-4R
Obituary 103
Bratt, John H(arold) 1909- CANR-9
Earlier sketch in CA 17-20R
Bratter, Herbert Max 1900-1976 Obituary 65-68
Bratter, Thomas Edward 1939- 120
Brattgarg, Helge (Axel Kristian) 1920- 5-8R
Bratton, Fred Gladstone 1896-(?) CANR-69
Earlier sketches in CAP-1, CA 11-12
Bratton, Helen 1899- CAP-2
Earlier sketch in CA 23-24
See also SATA 4
Bratton, Susan Power 1948- 145
Brattstrom, Bayard H(olmes) 1929- 57-60
Bratun, Katy 1950- .... SATA 83
Braude, Ann (Deborah) 1955- 132
Braude, Benjamin 1945- 111
Braude, Jacob M(orton) 1896-1970 .... CANR-5
Earlier sketch in CA 5-8R
Braude, Michael 1909-1986 Obituary 121
Braude, Michael 1936- 17-20R
See also SATA 23
Braude, William Gordon 1907- 33-36R
Braudel, Fernand (Paul) 1902-1985 .... CANR-42
Obituary 117
Earlier sketches in CA 93-96, CANR-14
Braudy, Leo 1941- 37-40R
Braudy, Susan (Orr) 1941- CANR-10
Earlier sketch in CA 65-68
Brauer, Carl M(alcolm) 1946- 85-88
Brauer, George C(harles), Jr. 1925- Brief entry 113
Brauer, Jerald C(arl) 1921- CANR-13
Earlier sketch in CA 33-36R
Brauer, Kinley J(ules) 1935- 21-24R
Brault, Gerard Joseph 1929- CANR-3
Earlier sketch in CA 5-8R
Brault, Jacques 1933- 161
See also DLB 53
Braun, Armin C(harles John) 1911-1986 Obituary 120
Braun, Arthur E. 1876-1976 Obituary 69-72
Braun, Barbara 1939- 162
Braun, Edward 1936- 134
Brief entry 115
Braun, Eric 1921- 102
Braun, Henry 1930- 25-28R
Braun, Hugh 1902- CANR-70
Earlier sketch in CA 25-28R
Braun, J(oachim) Werner 1914-1972 Obituary 37-40R
Braun, John R(ichard) 1928- 33-36R
Braun, Lev 1913- 41-44R
Braun, Lilian Jackson 1916(?)- CANR-59
Earlier sketch in CA 140
See also DAM POP
Braun, Marta (A.) 1946- 141
Braun, Richard Emil 1934- 9-12R
Braun, Sidney D(avid) 1912- CANR-10
Earlier sketch in CA 65-68
Braun, Stephen R. 1957- 162
Braun, Theodore E. D. 1933- CANR-7
Earlier sketch in CA 13-16R
Braun, Thomas (Felix Rudry Gerhart) 1935- 115
Braun, Volker 1939- .... DLB 75, 124
Braunbehrens, Volkmar 1941- 134
Braunburg, Rudolf 1924- CANR-29
Earlier sketch in CA 109
Braund, Hal
See Braund, Harold
Braund, Harold 1913-1988 61-64
Obituary 124
Braund, Kathryn E. Holland 1955- 145
Braunmuller, A(lbert) R(ichard) 1945- 132
Braunrot, Bruno 1936- 114
Braunstein, Daniel N(orman) 1938- 111
Braunstein, Mark M(athew) 1951- CANR-50
Earlier sketch in CA 113
Braunthal, Alfred 1898(?)-1980 Obituary 93-96
Braunthal, Gerard 1923- 13-16R
Braunthal, Julius 1891-1972 .... CAP-2
Earlier sketch in CA 23-24
Brautigan, Richard (Gary) 1935-1984 .... CANR-34
Obituary 113
Earlier sketch in CA 53-56
See also CLC 1, 3, 5, 9, 12, 34, 42
See also DAM NOV
See also DLB 2, 5
See also DLBY 80, 84
See also MTCW 1
See also SATA 56
Brav, Stanley R(osenbaum) 1908- 25-28R
Brave Bird, Mary 1953-
See Crow Dog, Mary (Ellen)
See also NNAL
Braveboy-Wagner, Jacqueline Anne 1948- 168
Braverman, Harry 1920-1976 53-56
Obituary 69-72
Braverman, Kate 1950- 89-92
See also CLC 67
Braverman, Melanie 1960- 156
Braverman, Terry 1953- 156
Bravmann, Rene A. 1939- 85-88
Brawer, Florence B(lum) 1922- 37-40R
Brawley, Benjamin (Griffith) 1882-1939 125
See also BW 1
Brawley, Ernest 1937- 53-56
Brawley, Paul Holm
See Brawley, Paul L(eroy)
Brawley, Paul L(eroy) 1942-1988 73-76
Obituary 126
Brawley, Robert L. 1939- 156
Brawn, Dympna 1931- 25-28R
Brawne, Michael 1925- 73-76
Braxton, Joanne M(argaret) 1950- 140
See also BW 2
See also DLB 41
Braxton, Jodi
See Braxton, Joanne M(argaret)
Bray, Alison
See Rowland, D(onald) S(ydney)
Bray, Allen Farris III 1926- 9-12R
Bray, Anna Eliza 1790-1883 .... DLB 116
Bray, Douglas W. 1918- 13-16R
Bray, Howard 1929- 105
Bray, J(ohn) J(efferson) 1912- 102
Bray, Nicholas 1948- 135
Bray, Thomas 1656-1730 .... DLB 24
Bray, Virginia Elizabeth Nuckolls 1895(?)-1979 Obituary 93-96
Bray, Warwick 1936- CANR-15
Earlier sketch in CA 25-28R
Braybon, (Charmian) Gail 1952- 131
Braybrooke, David 1924- CANR-18
Earlier sketches in CA 9-12R, CANR-3
Braybrooke, Neville (Patrick Bellairs) 1925- 5-8R
Brayce, William
See Rowland, D(onald) S(ydney)
Brayfield, Celia 1945- 128
Brayman, Harold 1900-1988 73-76
Obituary 124
Braymer, Marguerite
See Dodd, Marguerite
Braymer, Marjorie Elizabeth 1911- 1-4R
See also SATA 6
Braynard, Frank O(sborn) 1916- CANR-45
Earlier sketches in CA 17-20R, CANR-8
Braza, Jacque
See McKeag, Ernest L(ionel)
Brazeau, Peter (Alden) 1942-1986 111
Obituary 119
Brazell, Karen 1938- CANR-31
Earlier sketch in CA 45-48
Brazelton, T(homas) Berry 1918- 97-100
Brazer, Harvey E(lliott) 1922-1991 111
Obituary 134
Brazil, Angela 1869(?)-1947 Brief entry 112
Brazill, William J., Jr. 1935- 53-56
Brazos, Waco
See Jennings, Michael Glenn
Breach, Robert Walter 1927- 13-16R
Breakwell, Glynis M(arie) 1952- 122
Brealey, Richard A. 1936- 53-56
Brean, Herbert (J.) 1907-1973 .... CANR-58
Obituary 41-44R
Earlier sketch in CA 93-96
Brearley, Denis 1940- 37-40R
Brears, Peter C(harles) D(avid) 1944- 102
Breasted, Charles 1898(?)-1980 Obituary 93-96
Breasted, James Henry, Jr. 1908-1983 Obituary 109
Breasted, James Henry 1865-1935 .... DLB 47
Breathed, (Guy) Berke(ley) 1957- CANR-27
Earlier sketch in CA 110
See also AAYA 5
See also SATA 86
Breathett, George 1925- 13-16R
Breatnac, Seamus
See Walsh, James P(atrick)
Breault, William 1926- CANR-6
Earlier sketch in CA 57-60
Brebner, Philip 1955- 139
Brecher, Charles Martin 1945- CANR-4
Earlier sketch in CA 53-56
Brecher, Edward M(oritz) 1911-1989 .... CANR-7
Obituary 128
Earlier sketch in CA 13-16R
Brecher, Jeremy 1946- CANR-12
Earlier sketch in CA 69-72
Brecher, Michael 1925- CANR-72
Earlier sketches in CA 1-4R, CANR-4
Brecher, Ruth E(rnestine) 1911-1966 .... CAP-1
Earlier sketch in CA 13-14
Brechner, Irv 1951- 110
Brecht, Arnold 1884-1977 .... CANR-72
Obituary 73-76
Earlier sketch in CA 77-80
Brecht, (Eugen) Bertolt (Friedrich) 1898-1956 .... CANR-62
Brief entry 104
Earlier sketch in CA 133
See also DA
See also DAB
See also DAC
See also DAM DRAM, MST
See also DC 3
See also DLB 56, 124
See also MTCW 1
See also TCLC 1, 6, 13, 35
See also WLC
Brecht, Edith 1895-1975 .... CAP-2
Earlier sketch in CA 25-28
See also SATA 6
See also SATA-Obit 25
Brecht, Eugen Berthold Friedrich
See Brecht, (Eugen) Bertolt (Friedrich)
Brecht, George 1924- 106
Breck, Allen duPont 1914- CANR-9
Earlier sketch in CA 13-16R
Breck, Vivian
See Breckenfeld, Vivian Gurney
Breckenfeld, Vivian Gurney 1895- CANR-69
Earlier sketch in CA 5-8R
See also SATA 1
Breckenridge, Adam Carlyle 1916- 29-32R
Breckinridge, Mary 1881-1965 Obituary 114
Breckler, Rosemary 1920- 101
Breda, Tjalmar
See DeJong, David C(ornel)
Bredel, Willi 1901-1964 .... DLB 56
Bredemeier, Harry Charles 1920- CANR-8
Earlier sketch in CA 5-8R
Bredemeier, Mary E(lizabeth) 1924- 81-84
Bredero, Adriaan H(endrick) 1921- 159
Bredes, Don(ald) 1947- 110
Bredeson, Carmen 1944- 166
See also SATA 98
Bredow, Miriam
See Wolf, Miriam Bredow
Bredsdorff, Elias Lunn 1912- CAP-1
Earlier sketch in CA 9-10
Bredsdorff, Jan 1942- CANR-13
Earlier sketch in CA 21-24R
Bredvold, Louis I(gnatius) 1888-1977 .... 1-4R
Obituary 103
Bree, Germaine 1907- CANR-4
Earlier sketch in CA 1-4R
See also CAAS 15
Breech, (Earl) James 1944- 114
Breecher, Maury M. 1944- 156
Breed, Paul F. 1916- 33-36R
Breeden, Joann Elizabeth 1934- 145
Breeden, Stanley 1938- 106
Breem, Wallace (Wilfred Swinburne) 1926- Brief entry 113
Breen, Dana
See Birksted-Breen, Dana
Breen, (Joseph) John 1942- 149
Breen, Jon L(inn) 1943- CANR-63
Earlier sketch in CA 119
Breen, Quirinus 1896-1975 .... CAP-2
Earlier sketch in CA 33-36
Breen, Richard 1935- 110
Breen, Richard L. 1919-1967 Obituary 111
Breen, T(imothy) H(all) 1942- 101
Breen, William J(ames) 1937- 118
Breese, Dave
See Breese, David W(illiam)
Breese, David W(illiam) 1926- 118
Breese, Gerald (William) 1912- 41-44R
Breeskin, Adelyn Dohme 1896-1986 .... 33-36R
Obituary 119
Breetveld, Jim Patrick 1925- CANR-69
Earlier sketches in CA 1-4R, CANR-2
Breeze, Katie 1929- 111
Breffort, Alexandre 1901-1971 Obituary 29-32R
Breger, Louis 1935- 69-72
Breggin, Peter R(oger) 1936- CANR-34
Earlier sketches in CA 81-84, CANR-15
Bregman, Jacob I(srael Jack) 1923- 41-44R
Bregman, Jay 1940- 109
Brehm, Sharon S(tephens) 1945- CANR-30
Earlier sketch in CA 112

Brehm, Shirley A(lice) 1926- 69-72
Breig, Joseph A(nthony) 1905- 5-8R
Breihan, Carl W(illiam) 1916- CANR-1
Earlier sketch in CA 1-4R
Breillat, Catherine 1950- 33-36R
Breimyer, Harold F(rederick) 1914- 17-20R
Breinburg, Petronella 1927- CANR-4
Earlier sketch in CA 53-56
See also CLR 31
See also SATA 11
Breines, Paul 1941- 61-64
Breines, Simon 1906- Brief entry 114
Breines, Winifred 1942- 113
Breisach, Ernst Adolf 1923- CANR-18
Earlier sketch in CA 1-4R
Breisky, William J(ohn) 1928- 53-56
See also SATA 22
Breit, Harvey 1909-1968 .... CANR-6
Obituary 25-28R
Earlier sketch in CA 5-8R
Breit, Marquita E(laine) 1942- 57-60
Breit, William (Leo) 1933- CANR-13
Earlier sketch in CA 33-36R
Breitbart, Vicki 1942- 93-96
Breitenkamp, Edward C(arlton) 1913- CANR-25
Earlier sketches in CA 25-28R, CANR-10
Breitinger, Johann Jakob 1701-1776 .... DLB 97
Breitman, George 1916-1986 .... CANR-7
Obituary 119
Earlier sketch in CA 61-64
Breitman, Richard D(avid) 1947- CANR-21
Earlier sketch in CA 105
Breitner, I. Emery 1929- 57-60
Breland, Osmond P(hilip) 1910- CANR-69
Earlier sketch in CA 9-12R
Brelis, Dean 1924- CANR-72
Earlier sketch in CA 9-12R
Brelis, Matthew 1957- 132
Brief entry 126
Interview in 132
Brelis, Nancy (Burns) 1929- 21-24R
Brelsford, W(illiam) V(ernon) 1907- CAP-1
Earlier sketch in CA 13-14
Breman, Paul 1931- 21-24R
Brembeck, Winston Lamont 1912- Brief entry 115
Bremer, Arthur H(erman) 1950- Brief entry 113
Bremer, Francis J(ohn) 1947- 93-96
Bremer, Lisa
See Janas, Frankie-Lee
Bremmer, Ian A. 1969- 143
Bremner, Geoffrey 1930- CANR-38
Earlier sketch in CA 115
Bremner, John B(urton) 1920-1987 Obituary 123
Bremner, Robert H(amlett) 1917- CANR-9
Earlier sketch in CA 21-24R
Brems, Hans 1915- CANR-10
Earlier sketch in CA 25-28R
Bremser, Bonnie 1939- 153
See also DLB 16
Bremser, Ray 1934- 17-20R
See also DLB 16
Bremyer, Jayne Dickey 1924- 61-64
Brenan, (Edward Fitz)Gerald 1894-1987 .... CANR-72
Obituary 121
Earlier sketches in CA 1-4R, CANR-3
Brend, Ruth M(argaret) 1927- 105
Brendel, Otto Johannes 1901-1973 97-100
Brendon, Piers (George Rundle) 1940- CANR-57
Earlier sketches in CA 101, CANR-31
Brendtro, Larry K. 1940- 29-32R
Brener, Milton E. 1930- 29-32R
Brengelman, Fred(erick Henry) 1928- 134
Brief entry 115
Brengelmann, Johannes Clemens 1920- 5-8R
Brenlove, Milovan S. 1948- 126
Brennan, Anne 1936- 109
Brennan, Bernard P(atrick) 1918- 5-8R
Brennan, Carol 1934- 142
Brennan, Christopher
See Kininmonth, Christopher
Brennan, Christopher John 1870-1932 Brief entry 117
See also TCLC 17
Brennan, Donald (George) 1926-1980 Obituary 97-100
Brennan, Gale (Patrick) 1927- 125
See also SATA 64
See also SATA-Brief 53
Brennan, (Harold) Geoffrey 1944- 128
Brennan, John N(eedham) H(uggard) 1914- CANR-64
Earlier sketches in CA 1-4R, CANR-4, 20
Brennan, Joseph Gerard 1910- CANR-69
Earlier sketches in CA 1-4R, CANR-3
Brennan, Joseph K(illorin) 1952- 121
Brennan, Joseph Lomas 1903- CANR-2
Earlier sketch in CA 5-8R
See also SATA 6
Brennan, Joseph Payne 1918-1990 .... CANR-72
Earlier sketches in CA 1-4R, CANR-4, 19
Brennan, Lawrence D(avid) 1915- 5-8R
Brennan, Louis A(rthur) 1911-1983 .... CANR-71
Obituary 109
Earlier sketch in CA 17-20R
Brennan, Maeve 1917-1993 .... CANR-72
Earlier sketch in CA 81-84
See also CLC 5
Brennan, Mary C. 1959- 152
Brennan, Matthew C. 1955- 165
Brennan, Matthew J. 1917- 106
Brennan, Maynard J. 1921- 13-16R
Brennan, Michael Joseph, Jr. 1928- 13-16R
Brennan, Neil F(rancis) 1923- 37-40R
Brennan, Niall 1918- 13-16R
Brennan, Nicholas (Stephen) 1948- 106
Brennan, Ray 1908(?)-1972 Obituary 37-40R
Brennan, Richard O(liver) 1916- 89-92
Brennan, Tim
See Conroy, John Wesley
Brennan, Will
See Paine, Lauran (Bosworth)
Brennan, William J(oseph), Jr. 1906-1997 163
Brennand, Frank
See Lambert, Eric
Brennecke, John H(enry) 1934- 37-40R
Brenneman, Helen Good 1925-1994 .... CANR-46
Obituary 146
Earlier sketch in CA 21-24R
Brenner, Anita 1905-1974 .... CANR-71
Obituary 53-56
Earlier sketch in CA 49-52
See also SATA 56
Brenner, Barbara (Johnes) 1925- CANR-57
Earlier sketches in CA 9-12R, CANR-12, 31
See also JRDA
See also MAICYA
See also SAAS 14
See also SATA 4, 42, 76
Brenner, David 1945- 133
Brenner, Elizabeth 1954- 123
Brenner, Erma 1911- 69-72
Brenner, Fred 1920- .... MAICYA
See also SATA 36
See also SATA-Brief 34
Brenner, Gerry 1937- 110
Brenner, Isabel
See Schuchman, Joan
Brenner, Lenni 1937- 117
Brenner, Marie 1949- CANR-71
Earlier sketch in CA 73-76
Brenner, Mayer Alan 1956- 154
Brenner, Rebecca Summer 1945- CANR-10
Earlier sketch in CA 61-64
Brenner, Reeve R(obert) 1936- Brief entry 116
Brenner, Reuven 1947- 142
Brenner, Robert 1945- 162
Brenner, Summer
See Brenner, Rebecca Summer
Brenner, Wendy 1966- 166
Brenner, Yehojachin Simon 1926- CANR-11
Earlier sketch in CA 21-24R
Brennert, Alan (Michael) 1954- CANR-72
Earlier sketch in CA 118
Brenni, Vito J(oseph) 1923- CANR-31
Earlier sketch in CA 49-52
Brent, Beryl
See Ince, Martin (Jeffrey)
Brent, Harold Patrick 1943- 33-36R
Brent, Harry
See Brent, Harold Patrick
Brent, Hope 1935(?)-1984 .... SATA-Obit 39
Brent, Iris
See Bancroft, Iris (May Nelson)
Brent, Jonathan 1949- 113
Brent, Linda
See Jacobs, Harriet A(nn)
Brent, Madeleine
See O'Donnell, Peter
Brent, Peter (Ludwig) 1931-1984 .... CANR-13
Obituary 114
Earlier sketch in CA 65-68
Brent, Stuart 73-76
Brentano, Bernard von 1901-1964 .... DLB 56
Brentano, Clemens (Maria) 1778-1842 .... DLB 90
Brentano, Robert 1926- 21-24R
Brent-Dyer, Elinor Mary 1895-1969 101
Brentlinger, John 1934- 152
Brent of Bin Bin
See Franklin, (Stella Maria Sarah) Miles (Lampe)
Brenton, Howard 1942- CANR-67
Earlier sketches in CA 69-72, CANR-33
See also CLC 31
See also DLB 13
See also MTCW 1
Breo, Dennis L. 1942- 124
Brereton, Geoffrey 1906-1979 .... CANR-20
Earlier sketch in CA 25-28R
Bresee, Clyde W. 1916- CANR-48
Earlier sketch in CA 122
Bresky, Dushan 53-56
Breslau, Alan Jeffry 1926- 69-72
Breslauer, George W. 1946- CANR-12
Earlier sketch in CA 29-32R
Breslauer, Samuel Daniel 1942- 102
Breslin, Catherine 1936- 93-96
Breslin, Herbert H. 1924- 53-56
Breslin, James 1930-1996 .... CANR-31
Earlier sketch in CA 73-76
See also Breslin, Jimmy
See also DAM NOV
See also MTCW 1
Breslin, James E. B. 1935-1996 .... 33-36R
Obituary 151
Breslin, Jimmy
See Breslin, James
See also AITN 1
See also CLC 4, 43
See also DLB 185
Breslin, John B. 1943- 132
Breslin, Mark 1952- 121
Breslin, Paul 1946- 111
Breslin, Rosemary 1957- 162
Breslin, Theresa 138
See also SATA 70
Breslove, David 1891- 9-12R
Breslow, Lester 1915- 115
Breslow, Lou 1900(?)-1987 Obituary 124
Breslow, Maurice (A.) 1935- 133
See also SATA 72
Breslow, Susan 1951- 137
See also SATA 69
Bressett, Kenneth E(dward) 1928- 93-96
Bressler, Leo A(lbert) 1911- 57-60
Bressler, Marion Ann 1921- 57-60
Bresson, Robert 1901- CANR-49
Earlier sketch in CA 110
See also CLC 16
Bressoud, David M(arius) 1950- 141
Brestin, Dee 1944- 114
Brestol, Betsey Ann
See Ritchie, (Harry) Ward
Bret, David 1952- 134
Bretall, Robert Walter 1913-1980 Obituary 110
Bretecher, Claire 1940- Brief entry 113
Bretnor, Reginald 1911- CANR-25
Earlier sketches in CA 65-68, CANR-10
Breton, Albert 1929- 61-64
Breton, Andre 1896-1966 .... CANR-60
Obituary 25-28R
Earlier sketches in CAP-2, CA 19-20, CANR-40
See also CLC 2, 9, 15, 54
See also DLB 65
See also MTCW 1
See also PC 15
Breton, Marcela
See Jenkins, Marcella
Bretscher, Paul G(erhardt) 1921- CANR-8
Earlier sketch in CA 17-20R
Brett, Bernard 1925- CANR-17
Earlier sketch in CA 97-100
See also SATA 22
Brett, Bill 1922- 122
Brett, Brian 1950- 139
Brett, David
See Campbell, Will D(avis)
Brett, Donna W(hitson) 1947- 134
Brett, Dorothy 1883-1977 Obituary 73-76
Brett, Edward T(racy) 1944- 134
Brett, George P(latt), Jr. 1893-1984 Obituary 112
Brett, Grace N(eff) 1900-1975 .... 9-12R
Obituary 120
See also SATA 23
Brett, Hawksley
See Bell, Robert S(tanley) W(arren)
Brett, Jan (Churchill) 1949- CANR-41
Earlier sketch in CA 116
See also CLR 27
See also MAICYA
See also SATA 42, 71
Brett, John Michael
See Tripp, Miles (Barton)
Brett, Leo
See Fanthorpe, R(obert) Lionel
Brett, Lionel (Gordon Baliol) 1913- 131
Brett, Mary Elizabeth 9-12R
Brett, Michael
See Tripp, Miles (Barton)
Brett, Molly
See Brett, Mary Elizabeth
Brett, Peter David 1943- 77-80
Brett, Philip 1937- 129
Brett, Raymond Laurence 1917- CANR-3
Earlier sketch in CA 1-4R
Brett, Simon (Anthony Lee) 1945- CANR-63
Earlier sketches in CA 69-72, CANR-29
Brettell, Caroline B. 1950- CANR-55
Earlier sketch in CA 127
Brettell, Richard (Robson) 1949- 124
Brett-James, (Eliot) Antony 1920-1984 .... CANR-7
Obituary 112
Earlier sketch in CA 5-8R
Bretton, Barbara 1950- 162
Bretton, Henry L. 1916- CANR-2
Earlier sketch in CA 5-8R
Brettschneider, Bertram D(onald) 1924-1986 .... 33-36R
Obituary 121
Brett-Smith, Richard 1923- 21-24R
Brett-Young, Jessica (Hankinson) 1883-1970 .... CAP-1
Earlier sketch in CA 9-10
Bretuo, Akwasi
See Assensoh, A(kwasi) B(retuo)
Breuer, Bessie 1893-1975 .... CANR-70
Obituary 61-64
Earlier sketches in CAP-2, CA 17-18
Breuer, Ernest Henry 1902-1972 .... CAP-2
Earlier sketch in CA 19-20
Breuer, Georg 1919- 105
Breuer, Gustav J. 1915-1985 Obituary 114
Breuer, Gustl
See Breuer, Gustav J.
Breuer, Lee 1937- CANR-68
Earlier sketch in CA 110
Breuer, Marcel 1902-1981 .... CANR-5
Obituary 104
Earlier sketch in CA 5-8R
Breuer, Miles J(ohn) 1888-1947 Brief entry 112
Breuer, Reinhard 1946- CANR-38
Earlier sketch in CA 115
Breuer, William B(entley) 1924- 118
Breugelmans, Rene 1925- 103
Breunig, Jerome Edward 1917- CANR-45
Earlier sketch in CA 13-16R
Breunig, LeRoy C(linton) 1915-1996 61-64
Obituary 151
Brew, Douglas James 1949(?)-1985 Obituary 117
Brew, J(ohn) O(tis) 1906- 61-64
Brew, (Osborne Henry) Kwesi 1928- 142
See also BW 2
Breward, Christopher 1965- 151
Brewer, Annie M. 1925- 107
Brewer, D(erek) S(tanley) 1923- CANR-4
Earlier sketch in CA 1-4R
Brewer, Edward S(amuel) 1933- CANR-13
Earlier sketch in CA 33-36R
Brewer, (Lucie) Elisabeth 1923- 115
Brewer, Frances Joan 1913-1965 .... CAP-1
Earlier sketch in CA 11-12
Brewer, Fredric (Aldwyn) 1921- 17-20R
Brewer, Garry Dwight 1941- CANR-14
Earlier sketch in CA 33-36R
Brewer, Gay 1965- 146
Brewer, J(ohn) Mason 1896-1975 .... CAP-2
Earlier sketch in CA 25-28
Brewer, Jack A. 1933- 21-24R
Brewer, James H. Fitzgerald 1916- 9-12R
Brewer, Jeannie A. 1960- 158
Brewer, Jeutonne P. 1939- CANR-14
Earlier sketch in CA 77-80
Brewer, John D(avid) 1951- 131
Brewer, Kenneth W(ayne) 1941- 110
Brewer, Luther A. 1858-1933 .... DLB 187
Brewer, Margaret L. 1929- 29-32R
Brewer, Priscilla J. 1956- 122
Brewer, Sally King 1947- .... SATA 33
Brewer, Sam Pope 1909(?)-1976 Obituary 65-68
Brewer, Thomas B. 1932- 21-24R
Brewer, William C. 1897(?)-1974 Obituary 53-56
Brewer, William D(ean) 1955- 151
Brewer, Wilmon 1895- 5-8R
Brewerton, Derrick (Arthur) 1924- 143
Brewi, Janice 1933- 110
Brewington, Marion Vernon 1902-1974 .... CANR-3
Obituary 53-56
Earlier sketch in CA 5-8R
Brewster, Benjamin
See Folsom, Franklin (Brewster)
Brewster, David (C.) 1939- 139
Brewster, Dorothy 1883-1979 .... CANR-70
Obituary 85-88
Earlier sketches in CA 1-4R, CANR-3
Brewster, Elizabeth (Winifred) 1922- CANR-68
Earlier sketches in CA 25-28R, CANR-10, 25
See also CAAS 15
See also DLB 60
Brewster, Eva 1922- 132
Brewster, Hugh 1950- 160
See also SATA 95
Brewster, Patience 1952- CANR-46
Earlier sketch in CA 121
See also SATA 97
Brewster, Townsend 1924- CANR-29
Earlier sketch in CA 105
Brewton, John E(dmund) 1898- CANR-3
Earlier sketch in CA 5-8R
See also SATA 5
Brewton, Sara Westbrook (?)-1976 122
Breyer, N(orman) L(ane) 1942- CANR-31
Earlier sketch in CA 49-52
Breyer, Stephen G(erald) 1938- CANR-64
Earlier sketch in CA 107
Breytenbach, Breyten 1939(?)- CANR-61
Brief entry 113
Earlier sketch in CA 129
See also CLC 23, 37
See also DAM POET
Breza, Tadeusz 1905(?)-1970 Obituary 29-32R
Brezhnev, L. I.
See Brezhnev, Leonid I(lyich)
Brezhnev, Leonid
See Brezhnev, Leonid I(lyich)
Brezhnev, Leonid I(lyich) 1906-1982 132
Obituary 108
Breznitz, Shlomo 1936- 140
Brian
See Powell, Brian S(harples)
Brian, Alan B.
See Parulski, George R(ichard), Jr.
Brian, Denis 1923- 25-28R
Briand, Paul L., Jr. 1920- CANR-4
Earlier sketch in CA 1-4R
Briand, Rena 1935- 29-32R
Brians, Paul 1942- CANR-55
Earlier sketch in CA 127
Briarton, Grendel
See Bretnor, Reginald
Brice, Douglas 1916- 21-24R
Brice, Marshall Moore 1898- 17-20R
Brice, Valerie Kack
See Kack-Brice, Valerie
Brichant, Colette Dubois 1926- 13-16R
Brichto, Herbert Chanan 1925- 147
Brick, Howard 1953- 126
Brick, John 1922-1973 .... CANR-70
Obituary 45-48
Earlier sketches in CAP-1, CA 13-14
See also SATA 10
Brick, Michael 1922-1974 .... CANR-9
Earlier sketch in CA 13-16R
Bricker, Victoria Reifler 1940- 53-56
Brickhill, Paul Chester Jerome 1916-1991 .... CANR-69
Obituary 134
Earlier sketch in CA 9-12R
Bricklin, Mark Harris 1939- 111
Brickman, Marshall 1941- 81-84
Brickman, William Wolfgang 1913-1986 .... CANR-17
Obituary 119
Earlier sketches in CA 1-4R, CANR-1
Brickner, Richard P(ilpel) 1933- CANR-2
Earlier sketch in CA 5-8R
Bricktop
See Smith, Ada Beatrice Queen Victoria Louisa Virginia
Bricuth, John
See Irwin, John T(homas)
Bride, Nadja
See Nobisso, Josephine
Bridenbaugh, Carl 1903-1992 .... CANR-69
Obituary 136
Earlier sketches in CA 9-12R, CANR-4

Bridge, Ann
See O'Malley, Lady Mary Dolling (Sanders)
Bridge, Don(ald) U(lysses) 1894-1984 Obituary . 112
Bridge, Horatio 1806-1893 . . . . DLB 183
Bridge, Raymond 1943- CANR-32
Earlier sketch in CA 69-72
Bridgecross, Peter
See Cardinal, Roger (Thomas)
Bridgeman, Harriet 1942- 85-88
Bridgeman, Richard
See Davies, L(eslie) P(urnell)
Bridgeman, William Barton 1916- 9-12R
Bridger, Adam
See Bingley, David Ernest
Bridger, Gordon (Frederick) 1932- 65-68
Bridgers, Sue Ellen 1942- CANR-36
Earlier sketches in CA 65-68, CANR-11
See also AAYA 8
See also CLC 26
See also CLR 18
See also DLB 52
See also JRDA
See also MAICYA
See also SAAS 1
See also SATA 22, 90
Bridges, Emily
See Bruggen, Carol (Holmes)
Bridges, Hal 1918- 1-4R
Bridges, Herb 1929- 110
Bridges, James 1936-1993 127
Obituary 141
Brief entry 116
Bridges, Laurie 147
See also Bruck, Lorraine
Bridges, Robert (Seymour) 1844-1930 152
Brief entry 104
See also CDBLB 1890-1914
See also DAM POET
See also DLB 19, 98
See also TCLC 1
Bridges, William (Andrew) 1901-1984 . . . . CANR-69
Earlier sketch in CA 33-36R
See also SATA 5
Bridges, William (Emery) 1933- CANR-13
Earlier sketch in CA 33-36R
Bridges-Adams, William 1889-1965 . . . . CAP-1
Earlier sketch in CA 13-14
Bridgman, Elizabeth 1921- 73-76
Bridgman, Richard 1927- 129
Bridgman, Sarah Atherton
1889(?)-1975 Obituary 57-60
Bridgwater, (William) Patrick 1931- 5-8R
Bridie, James
See Mavor, Osborne Henry
See also DLB 10
See also TCLC 3
Bridson, Gavin (Douglas Ruthven) 1936- 105
Bridwell, Norman (Ray) 1928- CANR-46
Earlier sketches in CA 13-16R, CANR-5, 20
See also MAICYA
See also SATA 4, 68
Briefs, Goetz Antony 1889-1974 . . . . CAP-2
Obituary 49-52
Earlier sketch in CA 21-22
Briegel, Ann C(arrick) 1915- 33-36R
Brien, Alan 1925- 147
Brien, Mimi 1929- 111
Brien, Raley
See McCulley, Johnston
Brier, Bob 1943- 102
Brier, Howard M(axwell) 1903-1969 . . . . . . CANR-69
Earlier sketches in CAP-1, CA 13-14
See also SATA 8
Brier, Peter A. 1935- 105
Brier, Royce 1894-1975 Obituary 93-96
Brier, Warren Judson 1931- 25-28R
Brierley, (Louise) 1958- . . . . SATA 59
Brierley, Barry 1937- 153
Brierley, David 1936- 107
Brierley, Susan S.
See Isaacs, Susan (Sutherland Fairhurst)
Brieux, Eugene 1858-1932 . . . . DLB 192
Briffault, Herma 1898-1981 Obituary 104
Briggs, Asa 1921- CANR-7
Earlier sketch in CA 5-8R
Briggs, Austin (Eugene), Jr. 1931- 29-32R
Briggs, B(arry B.) Bruce
See Bruce-Briggs, B(arry B.)
Briggs, Berta N. 1884(?)-1976 Obituary 69-72
Briggs, Carl 1925- 114
Briggs, Carole S(uzanne) 1950- 110
See also SATA-Brief 47
Briggs, Charles Frederick 1804-1877 . . . . DLB 3
Briggs, Charlie 1927- CANR-1
Earlier sketch in CA 49-52
Briggs, Clarence E. III 1960- 136
Briggs, Desmond Lawther 1931- CANR-25
Earlier sketch in CA 108
Briggs, Dorothy Corkille 1924- 29-32R
Briggs, Ellis O(rmsbee) 1899-1976 73-76
Obituary 65-68
Briggs, F(red) Allen 1916- 33-36R
Briggs, Fred 1932-1995 73-76
Obituary 147
Briggs, G. A. 1891(?)-1978 Obituary 104
Briggs, George M(cSpadden) 1919- 33-36R
Briggs, Jean 1925- 93-96
Briggs, Joe Bob 1959- 131
Briggs, John 1945- 132
Briggs, Julia 1943- 147
Briggs, Katharine Mary 1898-1980 . . . . CANR-58
Obituary 102
Earlier sketches in CA 9-12R, CANR-12
See also SATA 101
See also SATA-Obit 25
Briggs, Kenneth Arthur 1941- 101
Briggs, Kenneth R. 1934- 33-36R
Briggs, L(loyd) Cabot 1909-1975 . . . . CANR-3
Obituary 57-60
Earlier sketch in CA 5-8R
Briggs, Michael (David) 1951- 135
Briggs, Peter 1921-1975 . . . . CANR-70
Obituary 57-60
Earlier sketches in CAP-2, CA 25-28
See also SATA 39
See also SATA-Obit 31
Briggs, R(obert) C(ook) 1915- 37-40R
Briggs, Raymond Redvers 1934- CANR-70
Earlier sketch in CA 73-76
See also CLR 10
See also MAICYA
See also SATA 23, 66
Briggs, Shirley Ann 1918- 106
Briggs, Vernon M(ason), Jr. 1937- 73-76
Briggs, Walter Ladd 1919- 69-72
Briggs, Ward W(right, Jr.) 1945- 135
Brigham, Besmilr 1923- CANR-12
Earlier sketch in CA 29-32R
Brigham, John C(arl) 1942- 41-44R
Brighouse, Harold 1882-1958 Brief entry 110
See also DLB 10
Bright, Deborah (Sue Tomberg) 1949- 97-100
Bright, Freda 1929- 136
Bright, Greg 1951- 93-96
Bright, John M. 1908-1995 . . . . CANR-70
Obituary 129
Earlier sketch in CA 5-8R
Bright, Myron H. 1919- 134
Bright, Pamela Mia 1914- 109
Bright, Richard (Eugene) 1931- 69-72
Bright, Robert (Douglas Sr.) 1902-1988 . . CANR-70
Obituary 127
Earlier sketch in CA 73-76
See also SATA 24, 63
See also SATA-Obit 60
Bright, Sarah
See Shine, Deborah
Bright, William 1928- 33-36R
Brightbill, Charles K(estner) 1910-1966 . . . . 1-4R
Obituary 103
Brightfield, Richard 1927- CANR-35
Earlier sketch in CA 118
See also SATA 65
See also SATA-Brief 53
Brightfield, Rick
See Brightfield, Richard
Brightman, Carol 1939- 158
Brightman, Robert 1920- 105
Brighton, Catherine 1943- 130
See also SATA 65
Brighton, Howard 1925- 57-60
Brighton, Wesley, Jr.
See Lovin, Roger Robert
Brightwell, L(eonard) R(obert) 1889- . SATA-Brief 29
Brignano, Russell C(arl) 1935- 57-60
Brignetti, Raffaello 1922(?)-1978 Obituary 104
Brigola, Alfredo L(uigi) 1923- 41-44R
Brijbhushan, Jamila 1918- 130
Briles, Judith 1946- 106
Briley, John (Richard) 1925- CANR-44
Earlier sketch in CA 101
Brilhart, John K. 1929- 21-24R
Brill, Alida 1949- 142
Brill, Earl H(ubert) 1925- 17-20R
Brill, Leon 1915- 110
Brill, Marlene Targ 1945- 145
See also SATA 77
Brill, Steven 85-88
Brilliant, Ashleigh (Ellwood) 1933- CANR-45
Earlier sketches in CA 65-68, CANR-11
Brilliant, Eleanor L(uria) 1930- 112
Brilliant, Richard 1929- 33-36R
Briloff, Abraham J(acob) 1917- 61-64
Brim, Orville G(ilbert), Jr. 1923- CANR-2
Earlier sketch in CA 5-8R
Brimberg, Stanlee 1947- 49-52
See also SATA 9
Brimblecombe, Peter 1949- 128
Brimelow, Peter 1947- CANR-71
Earlier sketch in CA 133
Brimner, Larry Dane 1949- . . . . SATA 79
Brin, David 1950- CANR-70
Earlier sketches in CA 102, CANR-24
Interview in CANR-24
See also AAYA 21
See also CLC 34
See also SATA 65
Brin, Herb(ert Henry) 1915- CANR-27
Earlier sketch in CA 49-52
Brin, Ruth Firestone 1921- CANR-8
Earlier sketch in CA 17-20R
See also SATA 22
Brinckerhoff, Sidney B(urr) 1933- Brief entry . . . 117
Brinckloe, Julie (Lorraine) 1950- 65-68
See also SATA 13
Brindel, June (Rachuy) 1919- CANR-31
Earlier sketch in CA 49-52
See also SATA 7
Brindle, Reginald Smith
See Smith Brindle, Reginald
Brindze, Ruth 1903-1984 . . . . CANR-70
Earlier sketch in CA 73-76
See also SATA 23
Brinegar, David F(ranklin) 1910- 77-80
Briner, Bob 1935- 162
Brines, Francisco 1932- . . . . DLB 134
Brines, Russell (Dean) 1911- 69-72
Briney, Robert E(dward) 1933- CANR-19
Earlier sketches in CA 53-56, CANR-4
Bring, Mitchell 1951- 106
Bringhurst, Robert 1946- CANR-44
Earlier sketches in CA 57-60, CANR-6, 21
Bringuier, Jean-Claude 1925- 133
Brinitzer, Carl 1907-1974 . . . . CANR-3
Obituary 53-56
Earlier sketch in CA 5-8R
Brink, Andre (Philippus) 1935- CANR-62
Earlier sketches in CA 104, CANR-39
Interview in 103
See also CLC 18, 36, 106
See also MTCW 1
Brink, Carol Ryrie 1895-1981 . . . . CANR-65
Obituary 104
Earlier sketches in CA 1-4R, CANR-3
See also CLR 30
See also JRDA
See also MAICYA
See also SATA 1, 31, 100
See also SATA-Obit 27
Brink, Jean R. 1942- 137
Brink, T(erry) L(ee) 1949- CANR-34
Earlier sketches in CA 89-92, CANR-15
Brink, Wellington 1895-1979 Obituary 85-88
Brinker, Nancy (Goodman) 1946- 134
Brinker, Paul A. 1919- 25-28R
Brinker, Robert Durie 1901-1983 Obituary 111
Brinkerhoff, Dericksen Morgan 1921- 85-88
Brinkley, Alan 1949- CANR-45
Earlier sketch in CA 107
Brinkley, Christie 1953- 122
Brinkley, David (McClure) 1920- 97-100
Brinkley, George A. (Jr.) 1931- 17-20R
Brinkley, Joel (Graham) 1952- CANR-61
Earlier sketch in CA 102
Brinkley, Roberta Florence
1892(?)-1967 Obituary 112
Brinkley, William (Clark) 1917-1993 . . . . . . CANR-11
Obituary 143
Earlier sketch in CA 21-24R
Brinkman, George L(oris) 1942- 53-56
Brinkman, Grover 1903- 73-76
Brinks, Herbert J(ohn) 1935- CANR-44
Earlier sketches in CA 29-32R, CANR-12
Brinley, Bertrand R(ussell) 1917-1994 . . . . . . 29-32R
Obituary 147
Brinley, George, Jr. 1817-1875 . . . . DLB 140
Brinley, Maryann B(ucknum) 1949- 130
Brinner, William M(ichael) 1924- CANR-55
Earlier sketches in CA 111, CANR-29
Brinnin, John Malcolm 1916-1998 . . . . CANR-70
Earlier sketches in CA 1-4R, CANR-1
See also DLB 48
Brinsmead, H(esba) F(ay) 1922- CANR-10
Earlier sketch in CA 21-24R
See also CLC 21
See also CLR 47
See also MAICYA
See also SAAS 5
See also SATA 18, 78
Brint, Armand Ian 1952- 105
Brint, Michael (E.) 1955- 140
Brinton, Alexander
See Battin, B(rinton) W(arner)
Brinton, (Clarence) Crane 1898-1968 . . . . . CANR-69
Obituary 25-28R
Earlier sketch in CA 5-8R
Brinton, Henry 1901-1977 . . . . CANR-70
Earlier sketches in CA 1-4R, CANR-4
Brinton, Howard Haines 1884-1973 . . . . CANR-3
Earlier sketch in CA 5-8R
Brion, Guy
See Madsen, Axel
Brion, Irene 1919- 167
Brion, John M. 1922- 21-24R
Brion, Marcel 1895-1984 124
Obituary 114
Briquebec, John
See Rowland-Entwistle, (Arthur) Theodore (Henry)
Brisbane, Albert 1809-1890 . . . . DLB 3
Brisbane, Arthur 1864-1936 . . . . DLB 25
Brisbane, Henry R.
See Ellis, Edward S(ylvester)
Brisbane, Holly E. 1927- 33-36R
Brisbane, Katharine 1932- CANR-23
Earlier sketch in CA 107
Brisbane, Robert Hughes 1913-1998 77-80
Obituary 163
Brisco, P. A.
See Matthews, Patricia (Anne)
Brisco, Patty
See Matthews, Clayton (Hartley)
and Matthews, Patricia (Anne)
Briscoe, Connie 1952- 162
Briscoe, D(avid) Stuart 1930- CANR-50
Earlier sketches in CA 17-20R, CANR-9, 25
Briscoe, Jill (Pauline) 1935- CANR-8
Earlier sketch in CA 61-64
See also SATA 56
See also SATA-Brief 47
Briscoe, John 1938- 118
Briscoe, Mary Louise 1937- 109
Brisk, Melvin J. 1924-1981 Obituary 104
Briskin, Jacqueline 1927- CANR-60
Earlier sketches in CA 29-32R, CANR-13
See also BEST 89:4
See also DAM POP
Briskin, Mae 1924- 134
Brisley, Joyce Lankester 1896-1978 97-100
Obituary 147
See also SATA 22
See also SATA-Obit 84
Brisman, Leslie 1944- 61-64
Brissenden, Alan (Theo) 1932- 132
Brissenden, Paul F(rederick) 1885-1974 . . . . . CAP-2
Obituary 53-56
Earlier sketch in CA 17-18
Brissenden, R(obert) F(rancis) 1928- CANR-10
Earlier sketch in CA 21-24R
Brisson, Pat 1951- 134
See also SATA 67
Brister, C(ommodore) W(ebster), Jr. 1926- CANR-7
Earlier sketch in CA 13-16R
Brister, Richard 1915- 13-16R
Bristol, Goldie M(ae) 1918- 121
Bristol, Julius
See Abel, Alan (Irwin)
Bristol, Lee Hastings, Jr. 1923-1979 . . . . . . CANR-4
Obituary 89-92
Earlier sketch in CA 5-8R
Bristow, Allen P. 1929- CANR-57
Earlier sketches in CA 21-24R, CANR-8
Bristow, Gwen 1903-1980 . . . . CANR-59
Obituary 102
Earlier sketches in CA 17-20R, CANR-12
Bristow, Robert O'Neil 1926- 25-28R
Bristowe, Anthony (Lynn) 1921-(?) CAP-1
Earlier sketch in CA 11-12
Britain, Dan
See Pendleton, Don(ald Eugene)
Britain, Ian (Michael) 1948- 130
Britchky, Seymour 1930- 102
Brite, Poppy Z. 1967- 141
Britindian
See Solomon, Samuel
Britnell, R(ichard) H. 1944- 142
Brito, Aristeo 1942- . . . . DLB 122
See also HW
Britsch, Ralph A(dam) 1912- 101
Britsch, Todd A(dam) 1937- 101
Britt, Albert 1874-1969 . . . . CANR-70
Obituary 103
Earlier sketch in CA 5-8R
See also SATA-Obit 28
Britt, Dell 1934- 25-28R
See also SATA 1
Britt, George (William Hughes)
1895-1988 Obituary 124
Britt, Steuart Henderson 1907-1979 . . . . CANR-2
Obituary 85-88
Earlier sketch in CA 1-4R
Brittain, Bill
See Brittain, William (E.)
See also JRDA
See also SAAS 7
Brittain, C. Dale 1948- 149
See also SATA 82
Brittain, Frederick (?)-1969 . . . . CANR-3
Earlier sketch in CA 5-8R
Brittain, Joan Tucker 1928- 37-40R
Brittain, John A(shleigh) 1923- 73-76
Brittain, Vera (Mary) 1893(?)-1970 . . . . CANR-58
Obituary 25-28R
Earlier sketches in CAP-1, CA 13-16
See also CLC 23
See also DLB 191
See also MTCW 1
Brittain, William (E.) 1930- CANR-57
Earlier sketches in CA 77-80, CANR-13, 30
See also Brittain, Bill
See also MAICYA
See also SATA 36, 76
Brittan, Gordon G(oodhue), Jr. 1939- 89-92
Brittan, Samuel 1933- 29-32R
Britten, Milton R(eese) 1924-1985 125
Obituary 115
Britten Austin, Paul 1922- CANR-13
Earlier sketch in CA 21-24R
Britter, Eric V(alentine) B(lakeney)
1906-1977 Obituary 73-76
Brittin, Norman A(ylsworth) 1906- 17-20R
Brittin, Phil (Henry) 1953- 108
Brittingham, Geoffrey (Hugh) 1959- . . . . SATA 76
Britton, Bruce K. 1944- 145
Britton, Bryce 1943- 110
Britton, Christopher (Q.) 1943- Brief entry 118
Britton, Dorothea S(prague) 1926- CANR-16
Earlier sketches in CA 45-48, CANR-1
Britton, Dorothy (Guyver) 1922- 107
Britton, John A(ndrew) 1943- CANR-55
Earlier sketch in CA 126
Britton, Karl (William) 1909-1983 . . . . CANR-47
Obituary 110
Earlier sketch in CA 29-32R
Britton, Kate
See Stegeman, Janet Allais
See also SATA 49
Britton, Louisa
See McGuire, Leslie (Sarah)
Britton, Mattie Lula Cooper 1914- 5-8R
Britton, Peter Ewart 1936- CANR-40
Earlier sketches in CA 97-100, CANR-18
Britton, Rick 1952- . . . . SATA 82
Brivic, Sheldon Roy 1943- 122
Brkic, Jovan 1927- 41-44R
Bro, Bernard (Gerard Marie) 1925- CANR-39
Earlier sketches in CA 97-100, CANR-17
Bro, Harmon Hartzell 1919-1997 . . . . 25-28R
Obituary 161
Bro, Margueritte (Harmon) 1894-1977 . . . . . CANR-71
Earlier sketch in CA 77-80
See also SATA 19
See also SATA-Obit 27
Broad, C(harlie) D(unbar) 1887-1971 . . . . . . CANR-70
Obituary 89-92
Earlier sketch in CA 101
Broad, Charles Lewis 1900- 5-8R
Broad, Jay 1930- CANR-19
Earlier sketch in CA 97-100
Broad, Robin 1954- 143
Broadbent, Donald E(ric) 1926- 105
Broadbent, Edward 1936- 45-48
Broadbent, W. W. 1919- 69-72
Broaddus, J(ohn) Morgan, Jr. 1929- 21-24R
Broadfoot, Barry 1926- 89-92

Broadhead, Helen Cross 1913- 103
See also SATA 25
Broadhurst, Allan R. 1932- 5-8R
Broadhurst, Kent 1940- 137
Broadhurst, Ronald Joseph Callender 1906- CAP-1
Earlier sketch in CA 11-12
Broadley, Margaret E(ricson) 1904-1985 97-100
Obituary 117
Broadribb, Violet 41-44R
Broadus, Catherine 1929- 37-40R
Broadus, Loren, Jr. 1928- 37-40R
Broadus, Robert N(ewton) 1922- 73-76
Broadwater, Jeff 1955- 144
Broadwell, Martin M. 1927- CANR-28
Earlier sketches in CA 73-76, CANR-13
Broadwin, John 1944- 164
Broat, I(sidore) G(erald) 1927- 97-100
Brobeck, Florence 1895-1979 Obituary 85-88
Broby-Johansen, R(udolf) 1900- CANR-12
Earlier sketch in CA 25-28R
Broce, Thomas Edward 1935- 69-72
Broch, Harald Beyer 1944- 135
Broch, Hermann 1886-1951 Brief entry 117
See also DLB 85, 124
See also TCLC 20
Brochmann, Elizabeth 1938- 112
See also SATA 41
Brochu, Andre 1942- 162
See also DLB 53
Brock, Alice May 1941- 41-44R
Brock, Arthur Guy Clutton
See Clutton-Brock, Arthur Guy
Brock, Ben
See Howells, Roscoe
Brock, Betty 1923- 29-32R
See also SATA 4
Brock, C(harles) E(dmund) 1870-1938 .... SATA 42
See also SATA-Brief 32
Brock, D(ewey) Heyward 1941- 53-56
Brock, Delia
See Ephron, Delia
Brock, Dewey Clifton, Jr. 1930- 5-8R
Brock, Edwin 1927- 130
Brief entry 119
See also DLB 40
Brock, Eleanor (Hope) 1921- 130
Brock, Emma L(illian) 1886-1974 .... 5-8R
Obituary 103
See also SATA 8
Brock, Gavin
See Lindsay, (John) Maurice
Brock, Gerald Wayne 1948- 57-60
Brock, H(enry) M(atthew) 1875-1960 ..... SATA 42
Brock, Horace 1908(?)-1981 Obituary 105
Brock, Horace Rhea 1927- CANR-33
Earlier sketch in CA 113
Brock, James 1958- 160
Brock, Lou(is Clark) 1939- Brief entry 113
Brock, Lynn
See McAllister, Alister
Brock, Mary Duncan Howe
1909(?)-1984 Obituary 112
Brock, Michael George 1920- 93-96
Brock, P. W.
See Brock, Patrick Willet
Brock, Patrick Willet 1902- 112
Brock, Peter (de Beauvoir) 1920- CANR-5
Earlier sketch in CA 9-12R
Brock, Rose
See Hansen, Joseph
Brock, Russell Claude 1903-1980 Obituary 105
Brock, Stanley E(dmunde) 1936- 57-60
Brock, Stuart
See Trimble, Louis P(reston)
Brock, Van(dall) K(line) 1932- CANR-11
Earlier sketch in CA 61-64
Brock, W(illiam) H(odson) 1936- 21-24R
Brock, William R(anulf) 1916- CANR-20
Earlier sketches in CA 1-4R, CANR-4
Brockbank, (John) Philip 1922-1989 Obituary .. 129
Brockbank, Reed 1923- 21-24R
Brock-Broido, Lucie 1956- 153
Brockelman, Paul T(aylor) 1935- 110
Brockes, Barthold Heinrich 1680-1747 .... DLB 168
Brockett, Eleanor Hall 1913-1967 .... CAP-1
Earlier sketch in CA 9-10
See also SATA 10
Brockett, Oscar Gross 1923- CANR-22
Earlier sketches in CA 13-16R, CANR-7
Brockington, J(ohn) L(eonard) 1940- 146
Brockley, Fenton
See Rowland, D(onald) S(ydney)
Brockman, C(hristian) Frank 1902- 5-8R
See also SATA 26
Brockman, David Drake
See Drake-Brockman, David
Brockman, Harold 1902-1980 Obituary 101
Brockman, James R(aymond) 1926- CANR-53
Earlier sketches in CA 110, CANR-28
Brockman, Norbert 1934- 73-76
Brockriede, Wayne Elmer 1922- CANR-4
Earlier sketch in CA 1-4R
Brockway, Allan R(eitz) 1932- 21-24R
Brockway, Connie 1954- 162
Brockway, Edith E. 1914- 17-20R
Brockway, (Archibald) Fenner 1888-1988 ... CAP-1
Obituary 125
Earlier sketch in CA 11-12
Brockway, George P(ond) 1915- CANR-49
Earlier sketch in CA 123
Brockway, Thomas P(armelee) 1898- CAP-2
Earlier sketch in CA 17-18
Brockway, Wallace 1905-1972 Obituary 37-40R
Brod, Harry 1951- 143
Brod, Max 1884-1968 .... CANR-7
Obituary 25-28R
Earlier sketch in CA 5-8R
See also DLB 81
Brod, Ruth Hagy 1911-1980 166
Obituary 97-100
Brodatz, Philip 1915- 57-60
Brodbeck, L. Emma 1893(?)-1989 Obituary 130
Brodber, Erna (May) 1940- 143
See also BW 2
See also DLB 157
Brode, Douglas 1943- 57-60
Brode, Patrick 1950- 132
Brode, Wallace R. 1900(?)-1974 Obituary 53-56
Broder, David S(alzer) 1929- CANR-65
Earlier sketches in CA 97-100, CANR-58
Broder, Patricia Janis 1935- CANR-6
Earlier sketch in CA 57-60
Broderick, Carlfred B(artholomew) 1932- . CANR-10
Earlier sketch in CA 25-28R
Broderick, Damien (Francis) 1944- CANR-58
Earlier sketches in CA 111, CANR-28
Broderick, Dorothy M. 1929- 13-16R
See also SATA 5
Broderick, Francis L(yons) 1922-1992 ... CANR-46
Obituary 139
Earlier sketch in CA 101
Broderick, John 1927-1989 143
Broderick, John C(aruthers) 1926- 1-4R
Broderick, John F. 1909- CAP-2
Earlier sketch in CA 33-36
Broderick, Richard L(awrence) 1927- CANR-1
Earlier sketch in CA 45-48
Broderick, Robert C(arlton) 1913- CANR-8
Earlier sketch in CA 21-24R
Brodeur, Paul (Adrian, Jr.) 1931- CANR-65
Earlier sketches in CA 5-8R, CANR-25
Brodeur, Ruth Wallace
See Wallace-Brodeur, Ruth
Brodhead, John R. 1814-1873 .... DLB 30
Brodhead, Michael John 1935- 105
Brodie, Bernard 1910-1978 .... CANR-10
Obituary 81-84
Earlier sketch in CA 17-20R
Brodie, Fawn M(cKay) 1915-1981 .... CANR-71
Obituary 102
Earlier sketches in CA 17-20R, CANR-10
Brodie, H(arlowe) Keith H(ammond) 1939- 103
Brodie, John (Riley) 1935- Brief entry 115
Brodie, Sally
See Cavin, Ruth (Brodie)
Brodin, Pierre Eugene 1909-1997 85-88
Obituary 156
Brodine, Karen 1947- 123
Brodine, Virginia Warner 1915- 41-44R
Brodkey, Harold (Roy) 1930-1996 .... CANR-71
Obituary 151
Earlier sketch in CA 111
See also CLC 56
See also DLB 130
Brodribb, (Arthur) Gerald (Norcott) 1915- . CANR-72
Earlier sketches in CA 113, CANR-33
Brodsky, Archie 1945- CANR-7
Earlier sketch in CA 61-64
Brodsky, Beverly
See McDermott, Beverly Brodsky
Brodsky, Iosif Alexandrovich 1940-1996 . CANR-37
Obituary 151
Earlier sketch in CA 41-44R
See also Brodsky, Joseph
See also AITN 1
See also DAM POET
See also MTCW 1
Brodsky, Joseph 1940-1996
See Brodsky, Iosif Alexandrovich
See also CLC 4, 6, 13, 36, 100
See also PC 9
Brodsky, Louis Daniel 1941- 111
Brodsky, Michael (Mark) 1948- CANR-58
Earlier sketches in CA 102, CANR-18, 41
See also CLC 19
Brodsky, Stanley L. 1939- CANR-29
Earlier sketch in CA 29-32R
Brodsky, Vera
See Lawrence, Vera Brodsky
Brodwin, Leonora Leet 1929- 53-56
Brody, Baruch A(lter) 1943- CANR-14
Earlier sketch in CA 33-36R
Brody, David 1930- 33-36R
Brody, Elaine 1923-1987 .... 37-40R
Obituary 123
Brody, J(acob) J(erome) 1929- CANR-32
Earlier sketch in CA 113
Brody, Jane E(llen) 1941- CANR-23
Earlier sketch in CA 102
Interview in CANR-23
Brody, Jean 148
Brody, Jules 1928- CANR-9
Earlier sketch in CA 13-16R
Brody, Marc
See Wilkes-Hunter, R(ichard)
Brody, Miriam 1940- 147
Brody, Nathan 1935- 111
Brody, Polly 1919- 57-60
Brody, Saul Nathaniel 1938- 53-56
Brody, Sylvia
See Axelrad, Sylvia Brody
Broe, Mary Lynn 1946- 110
Broe, Ruth Hammond 1912(?)-1983 Obituary .. 110
Broeg, Bob
See Broeg, Robert M.
See also DLB 171
Broeg, Robert M. 1918- CANR-62
Earlier sketches in CA 13-16R, CANR-5
See also Broeg, Bob
Broeger, Achim 1944- CANR-48
Earlier sketch in CA 107
See also SATA 31
Broegger, Fredrik Chr(istian) 1945- 138
Broehl, Wayne G(ottlieb), Jr. 1922- 9-12R
Broek, J(an) O(tto) M(arius) 1904-1974 ..... CAP-2
Earlier sketch in CA 19-20
Broekel, Rainer Lothar 1923- CANR-45
Earlier sketches in CA 9-12R, CANR-3, 19
See also SATA 38
Broekel, Ray
See Broekel, Rainer Lothar
Broeker, Galen 1920-1978 .... 41-44R
Obituary 133
Broekman, Marcel 1922- 57-60
Broer, Lawrence R(ichard) 1938- 69-72
Broer, Marion Ruth 1910- 13-16R
Broerman, Bruce M(artin) 1945- 126
Broesamle, John J(oseph) 1941- 57-60
Broeze, Frank 1945- 148
Brof, Janet 1929- 37-40R
Brog, Molly (Jane) 1950- 113
Brogan, D(enis) W(illiam) 1900-1974 .... CANR-71
Obituary 45-48
Earlier sketch in CA 97-100
Brogan, Elise
See Urch, Elizabeth
Brogan, Frankie Fonde 1922- 109
Brogan, Gerald E(dward) 1924-1981 .... 29-32R
Obituary 104
Brogan, Hugh 1936- 144
Brogan, Jacque Vaught
See Brogan, Jacqueline Vaught
Brogan, Jacqueline Vaught 1952- CANR-57
Earlier sketch in CA 125
Brogan, James
See Hodder-Williams, (John) Christopher (Glazebrook)
Brogan, James E(dmund) 1941- 41-44R
Brogan, Phil(ip) F(rancis) 1896- 9-12R
Brogan, T(erry) V. F. 1951- 119
Broger, Achim
See Broeger, Achim
Brogger, Fredrik Chr.
See Broegger, Fredrik Chr(istian)
Broglie, Marguerite de 1897-1973 Obituary . 37-40R
Broh, C(harles) Anthony 1945- 61-64
Broh-Kahn, Eleanor 1924- 45-48
Broido, Ethel 1917- 143
Broido, Vera
See Cohn, Vera
Brokamp, Marilyn 1920- CANR-46
Earlier sketch in CA 49-52
See also SATA 10
Brokaw, Thomas John 1940- 108
Brokaw, Tom
See Brokaw, Thomas John
Brokensha, David W(arwick) 1923- 25-28R
Brokhin, Yuri 1934- 57-60
Brokhoff, John R(udolph) 1913- CANR-23
Earlier sketches in CA 61-64, CANR-8
Brolin, Brent C(ruse) 1940- 65-68
Bromage, Mary Cogan 1906- CAP-1
Earlier sketch in CA 13-16
Bromberg, Walter 1900- 65-68
Bromberger, Merry (Marie Louis)
1906-1979 Obituary 110
Bromberger, Serge Paul 1912- 29-32R
Brombert, Victor (Henri) 1923- CANR-45
Earlier sketches in CA 13-16R, CANR-7
Brome, Richard 1590(?)-1652 .... DLB 58
Brome, (Herbert) Vincent 1910- CANR-52
Earlier sketches in CA 77-80, CANR-14
See also DLB 155
Bromell, Henry 1947- CANR-9
Earlier sketch in CA 53-56
See also CLC 5
Bromfield, Louis (Brucker) 1896-1956 155
Brief entry 107
See also DLB 4, 9, 86
See also TCLC 11
Bromhall, Winifred .... SATA 26
Bromhead, Peter (Alexander) 1919- 61-64
Bromige, David (Mansfield) 1933- CANR-16
Earlier sketch in CA 25-28R
See also CAAS 26
See also DLB 193
Bromiley, Geoffrey W(illiam) 1915- CANR-19
Earlier sketches in CA 5-8R, CANR-4
Bromke, Adam 1928- 13-16R
Bromley, David G(rover) 1941- 41-44R
Bromley, Dorothy Dunbar 1896-1986 Obituary . 118
Bromley, Dudley 1948- 77-80
See also SATA-Brief 51
Bromley, Gordon 1910- 112
Bromley, John Carter 1937- 33-36R
Bromley, John Selwyn 1913-1985 Obituary 116
Bromley, Simon 1961- 147
Bromley, Yulian Vladimirovich
1921-1990 Obituary 131
Brommer, Gerald F(rederick) 1927- CANR-21
Earlier sketch in CA 105
See also SATA 28
Bromwich, David (Lee) 1951- 127
Brief entry 121
Interview in 127
Bron, Eleanor 1938- 156
Bronaugh, Robert Brett 1947- 106
Brondfield, Jerome 1913- 73-76
See also SATA 22
Brondfield, Jerry
See Brondfield, Jerome
Broneer, Oscar (Theodore) 1894-1992 168
Broner, E(sther) M(asserman) 1930- CANR-72
Earlier sketches in CA 17-20R, CANR-8, 25
See also CLC 19
See also DLB 28
Bronfeld, Stewart 1929- 109
Bronfenbrenner, Martin 1914- 13-16R
Bronfenbrenner, Urie 1917- CANR-16
Earlier sketch in CA 97-100
Bronin, Andrew 1947- 45-48
Bronk, William 1918- CANR-23
Earlier sketch in CA 89-92
See also CLC 10
See also DLB 165
Bronnen, Arnolt 1895-1959 .... DLB 124
Bronner, Edwin B(laine) 1920- CANR-22
Earlier sketches in CA 5-8R, CANR-7
Bronner, Ethan (Samuel) 1954- 140
Bronner, Leila Leah 1930- 155
Bronner, Simon J. 1954- CANR-46
Earlier sketch in CA 121
Bronner, Stephen Eric 1949- CANR-72
Earlier sketches in CA 113, CANR-32
See also SATA 101
Bronowski, Jacob 1908-1974 .... CANR-71
Obituary 53-56
Earlier sketches in CA 1-4R, CANR-3
See also SATA 55
Bronsen, David 1926- 37-40R
Bronson, Bertrand Harris 1902-1986 .... CANR-71
Obituary 118
Earlier sketch in CA 61-64
Bronson, Jill (Dorothy) Ireland
1936-1990 Obituary 131
Bronson, Lita
See Bell, Louise Price
Bronson, Lynn
See Lampman, Evelyn Sibley
Bronson, Oliver
See Rowland, D(onald) S(ydney)
Bronson, Po 1964- 153
Bronson, Wilfrid Swancourt 1894-1985 73-76
Obituary 116
See also SATA-Obit 43
Bronson, William (Knox) 1926-1976 .... 41-44R
Obituary 65-68
Bronson, Wolfe
See Raborg, Frederick A(shton), Jr.
Bronstein, Arthur J. 1914- 9-12R
Bronstein, Leo 1903(?)-1976 Obituary 65-68
Bronstein, Lev Davidovich
See Trotsky, Leon
Bronstein, Lynne 1950- 77-80
Bronstein, Yetta
See Abel, Jeanne
Bronte, Anne 1820-1849 .... DLB 21, 199
Bronte, Charlotte 1816-1855 .... AAYA 17
See also CDBLB 1832-1890
See also DA
See also DAB
See also DAC
See also DAM MST, NOV
See also DLB 21, 159, 199
See also WLC
Bronte, D(iana) Lydia 1938- 125
Bronte, Emily (Jane) 1818-1848 .... AAYA 17
See also CDBLB 1832-1890
See also DA
See also DAB
See also DAC
See also DAM MST, NOV, POET
See also DLB 21, 32, 199
See also PC 8
See also WLC
Bronte, Louisa
See Roberts, Janet Louise
Bronwell, Arthur B. 1909- 33-36R
Bronzino, Joseph D. 1937- 136
Brook, Barry S(helley) 1918-1997 .... CANR-16
Obituary 163
Earlier sketch in CA 25-28R
Brook, David 1932- 13-16R
Brook, Elaine (Isabel) 1949- 143
Brook, G. L.
See Brook, George Leslie
Brook, George Leslie 1910-1987 .... CANR-5
Obituary 123
Earlier sketch in CA 9-12R
Brook, Judith (Penelope) 1926- 122
See also SATA 59
See also SATA-Brief 51
Brook, Judy
See Brook, Judith (Penelope)
Brook, Peter (Stephen Paul) 1925- CANR-38
Earlier sketch in CA 105
See also MTCW 1
Brook, Stephen 1947- 147
Brook, Timothy (James) 1951- 140
Brook, Victor John Knight 1887-1974 .... 1-4R
Obituary 103
Brooke, A. B.
See Jennings, Leslie Nelson
Brooke, Avery (Rogers) 1923- CANR-21
Earlier sketches in CA 57-60, CANR-6
Brooke, Brian 1911- 85-88
Brooke, Bryan (Nicholas) 1915- CANR-1
Earlier sketch in CA 45-48
Brooke, Carol
See Ramskill, Valerie Patricia Roskams
Brooke, Christopher N(ugent) L(awrence) 1927- ... CANR-42
Earlier sketches in CA 5-8R, CANR-2, 18, 40
Brooke, Dinah 1936- CANR-4
Earlier sketch in CA 49-52
Brooke, Eleanor (Golden)
1905(?)-1987 Obituary 122
Brooke, Frances 1724-1789 .... DLB 39, 99

Brooke, George Mercer, Jr. 1914- 122
Brooke, Harold 1910- Brief entry 113
Brooke, Henry 1703(?)-1783 .... DLB 39
Brooke, James B. 1955- 135
Brooke, (Bernard) Jocelyn 1908- 5-8R
Brooke, John 1920-1985 Obituary 118
Brooke, John L. 1953- 140
Brooke, Joshua
See Miller, Victor (Brooke)
Brooke, L(eonard) Leslie 1862-1940 .... CLR 20
See also DLB 141
See also MAICYA
See also SATA 17
Brooke, Margaret 1849-1936 .... DLB 174
Brooke, Maxey 1913- 9-12R
Brooke, Nicholas Stanton 1924- 25-28R
Brooke, Rosalind B(eckford) 1925- 148
Brooke, Rupert (Chawner) 1887-1915 ... CANR-61
Brief entry 104
Earlier sketch in CA 132
See also CDBLB 1914-1945
See also DA
See also DAB
See also DAC
See also DAM MST, POET
See also DLB 19
See also MTCW 1
See also TCLC 2, 7
See also WLC
Brooke, (Robert) Tal(iaferro) 1945- 93-96
Brooke, William J. 1946- 134
Brooke-Haven, P.
See Wodehouse, P(elham) G(renville)
Brooke-Little, John 1927- CANR-10
Earlier sketch in CA 21-24R
Brooker, Barbara 1936- 127
Brooker, Bertram 1888-1955 .... DLB 88
Brooker, Clark
See Fowler, Kenneth A(brams)
Brooker, Jewel Spears 1940- CANR-69
Earlier sketch in CA 135
Brooke-Rose, Christine 1926(?)- CANR-58
Earlier sketch in CA 13-16R
See also CLC 40
See also DLB 14
Brookes, Edgar Harry 1897- CANR-70
Earlier sketches in CA 1-4R, CANR-3
Brookes, John A. 1933- 137
Brookes, Kenneth John 1909-1984 Obituary ... 111
Brookes, Owen
See Barber, D(ulan) F(riar Whilberton)
Brookes, Pamela 1922- 25-28R
Brookes, Reuben Solomon 1914- CAP-1
Earlier sketch in CA 9-10
Brookes, Tim 1953- 147
Brookhiser, Richard 1955- 139
Brookhouse, (John) Christopher 1938- ... CANR-52
Earlier sketch in CA 29-32R
Brookhouser, Frank 1912(?)-1975 .... 1-4R
Obituary 61-64
Brookins, Dana 1931- 69-72
See also SATA 28
Brookman, Denise Cass 1921- 1-4R
Brookman, Rosina Francesca 1932- 61-64
Brookner, Anita 1928- CANR-56
Brief entry 114
Earlier sketches in CA 120, CANR-37
See also CLC 32, 34, 51
See also DAB
See also DAM POP
See also DLB 194
See also DLBY 87
See also MTCW 1
Brookover, Wilbur B(one) 1911- 33-36R
Brooks, A(lfred) Russell 1906- CAP-2
Earlier sketch in CA 33-36
Brooks, Albert
See Einstein, Albert
Brooks, Andree (Nicole) Aelion 1937- 133
Brooks, Anita
See Abramovitz, Anita (Zeltner Brooks)
See also SATA 5
Brooks, Anne Tedlock 1905- CANR-1
Earlier sketch in CA 1-4R
Brooks, B. David 1938- 113
Brooks, Betty 1936- 162
Brooks, Bill 1939- .... SATA 59
Brooks, Bruce 1950- 137
See also AAYA 8
See also CLR 25
See also JRDA
See also MAICYA
See also SATA 72
See also SATA-Brief 53
Brooks, C(larence) Carlyle 1888- CAP-1
Earlier sketch in CA 13-14
Brooks, Caryl 1924- 150
See also SATA 84
Brooks, Charles (Gordon) 1920- 115
Brooks, Charles B(enton) 1921- 1-4R
Brooks, Charles E(dward) 1921- 53-56
Brooks, Charles Timothy 1813-1883 .... DLB 1
Brooks, Charles V. W. 1912- 77-80
Brooks, Charlotte K(endrick) 1918- CANR-45
Earlier sketch in CA 89-92
See also SATA 24
Brooks, Cleanth 1906-1994 .... CANR-35
Obituary 145
Earlier sketches in CA 17-20R, CANR-33
Interview in CANR-35
See also CLC 24, 86, 110
See also DLB 63
See also DLBY 94
See also MTCW 1
Brooks, D(avid) P. 1915- CANR-11
Earlier sketch in CA 25-28R
Brooks, David (Gordon) 1953- 140
Brooks, David H(opkinson) 1929- 61-64
Brooks, Deems M(arkham) 1934- 69-72
Brooks, Douglas
See Brooks-Davies, Douglas
Brooks, Douglas L(ee) 1916- CANR-35
Earlier sketch in CA 114
Brooks, Elston (Harwood) 1930- 125
Brooks, Emerson M. 1905(?)-1982 Obituary ... 108
Brooks, Gary D(onald) 1942- 41-44R
Brooks, George
See Baum, L(yman) Frank
Brooks, George E(dward), Jr. 1933- 33-36R
Brooks, Gladys Rice 1886(?)-1984 Obituary ... 111
Brooks, Glenn E(llis), Jr. 1931- 1-4R
Brooks, Gregory 1961- 102
Brooks, Gwendolyn 1917- CANR-52
Earlier sketches in CA 1-4R, CANR-1, 27
See also AAYA 20
See also AITN 1
See also BLC 1
See also BW 2
See also CDALB 1941-1968
See also CLC 1, 2, 4, 5, 15, 49
See also CLR 27
See also DA
See also DAC
See also DAM MST, MULT, POET
See also DLB 5, 76, 165
See also MTCW 1
See also PC 7
See also SATA 6
See also WLC
Brooks, H(arold) Allen 1925- CANR-31
Earlier sketches in CA 81-84, CANR-14, 31
Brooks, Harold F(letcher) 1907- 128
Brooks, Harvey 1915- 25-28R
Brooks, Hindi Brief entry 115
Brooks, Hugh C. 1922- 29-32R
Brooks, Hunter O(tis) 1929- 77-80
Brooks, James L. 1940- CANR-54
Earlier sketches in CA 73-76, CANR-32
See also AAYA 17
Brooks, Janice Young 1943- CANR-69
Earlier sketches in CA 65-68, CANR-9, 39
Brooks, Jeanne
See Brooks-Gunn, Jeanne
Brooks, Jeremy 1926-1994 .... CANR-7
Obituary 146
Earlier sketch in CA 5-8R
See also DLB 14
Brooks, Jerome 1931- CANR-2
Earlier sketch in CA 49-52
See also SATA 23
Brooks, Jerome E(dmund)
1895(?)-1983 Obituary 109
Brooks, John
See Sugar, Bert Randolph
Brooks, John (Nixon) 1920-1993 .... CANR-55
Obituary 142
Earlier sketches in CA 13-16R, CANR-6
Brooks, Juanita 1898- Brief entry 114
Brooks, Karen 1949- 57-60
Brooks, Keith 1923- 17-20R
Brooks, (Frank) Leonard 1911- 13-16R
Brooks, LeRoy D(avis) II 1943- Brief entry 113
Brooks, Lester 1924- CANR-42
Earlier sketches in CA 33-36R, CANR-13
See also SATA 7
Brooks, (Mary) Louise 1906-1985 134
Obituary 117
Brooks, Lyman Beecher 1910-1984 122
Obituary 112
Brooks, Maggie
See Brooks, Margaret Ann
Brooks, Margaret Ann 1951- 132
Brooks, Maria (Zagorska) 1933- 41-44R
Brooks, Martha 136
See also SATA 68
Brooks, Maurice (Graham) 1900- .... SATA 45
Brooks, Mel
See Kaminsky, Melvin
See also AAYA 13
See also CLC 12
See also DLB 26
Brooks, Nelson Herbert 1902-1978 Obituary . 77-80
Brooks, Noah 1830-1903 .... DLB 42
See also DLBD 13
Brooks, Pat 1931- CANR-7
Earlier sketch in CA 57-60
Brooks, Patricia 1926- CANR-11
Earlier sketch in CA 25-28R
Brooks, Paul 1909- CANR-70
Earlier sketches in CA 13-16R, CANR-7
Brooks, Peter 1938- CANR-1
Earlier sketch in CA 45-48
See also CLC 34
Brooks, Peter Newman 1931- 131
Brooks, Peter W(right) 1920- 9-12R
Brooks, Philip 1899(?)-1975 Obituary 104
Brooks, Polly Schoyer 1912- CANR-17
Earlier sketch in CA 1-4R
See also SATA 12
Brooks, Richard 1912-1992 73-76
Obituary 137
See also DLB 44
Brooks, Richard A. 1931- 153
Brooks, Richard Oliver 1934- 112
Brooks, Robert A(ngus) 1920-1976 Obituary . 65-68
Brooks, Robert Emanuel 1941- 57-60
Brooks, Romaine 1874-1970 163
Brooks, Ron(ald George) 1948- 159
Brief entry 111
See also SATA 94
See also SATA-Brief 33
Brooks, Roy L(avon) 1950- 166
Brooks, Seth Rogers 1901-1987 Obituary 123
Brooks, Stewart M. 1923- CANR-9
Earlier sketch in CA 17-20R
Brooks, Terry 1944- CANR-51
Earlier sketches in CA 77-80, CANR-14
See also AAYA 18
See also DAM POP
See also SATA 60
Brooks, Thomas 1941- 120
Brooks, Thomas R(eed) 1925- CANR-34
Earlier sketch in CA 73-76
Brooks, Tim(othy Haley) 1942- CANR-19
Earlier sketch in CA 102
Brooks, Van Wyck 1886-1963 .... CANR-6
Earlier sketch in CA 1-4R
See also CLC 29
See also DLB 45, 63, 103
Brooks, W. Hal 1933- 57-60
Brooks, Walter R(ollin) 1886-1958 Brief entry .. 111
See also SATA 17
Brooks, William D(ean) 1929- 33-36R
Brooks-Davies, Douglas 1942- CANR-12
Earlier sketch in CA 73-76
Brooks-Gunn, Jeanne 1946- 135
Brook-Shepherd, (Frederick) Gordon 1918- ....
CANR-70
Earlier sketches in CA 9-12R, CANR-3
Brookshier, Frank 93-96
Brooks-Hill, Helen (Mason) 1908- .... SATA 59
Brookter, Marie 1934(?)- .... AITN 1
Broom, Leonard 1911- CANR-5
Earlier sketch in CA 13-16R
Broomall, Robert W(alter) 1946- CANR-44
Earlier sketch in CA 119
Broome, Charles L(arue) 1925- 41-44R
Broome, Harvey 1902-1968 122
Obituary 110
Broomell, Myron H(enry) 1906-1970 .... CAP-1
Earlier sketch in CA 9-10
Broomfield, Gerald W(ebb) 1895-1976 .... 5-8R
Obituary 103
Broomfield, J(ohn) H(indle) 1935- 25-28R
Brophy, Ann 1931- 106
Brophy, Brigid (Antonia) 1929-1995 ..... CANR-53
Obituary 149
Earlier sketches in CA 5-8R, CANR-25
See also CAAS 4
See also CLC 6, 11, 29, 105
See also DLB 14
See also MTCW 1
Brophy, Donald F(rancis) 1934- CANR-10
Earlier sketch in CA 21-24R
Brophy, Elizabeth Bergen 1929- 61-64
Brophy, James David, Jr. 1926- CANR-3
Earlier sketch in CA 1-4R
Brophy, James J(oseph) 1912- 65-68
Brophy, Jere E(dward) 1940- CANR-2
Earlier sketch in CA 45-48
Brophy, Jim
See Brophy, James J(oseph)
Brophy, John 1899-1965 .... CANR-71
Earlier sketches in CAP-1, CA 11-12
See also DLB 191
Brophy, Liam 1910- 9-12R
Brophy, Nannette 1963- .... SATA 73
Brophy, Robert J(oseph) 1928- CANR-5
Earlier sketch in CA 53-56
Brose, Olive J(ohnson) 1919- 41-44R
Brosman, Catharine Savage 1934- CANR-46
Earlier sketches in CA 61-64, CANR-21
See also CLC 9
Brosnahan, Leonard Francis 1922- 102
Brosnahan, Tom 1945- 119
Brosnan, James Patrick 1929- CANR-3
Earlier sketch in CA 1-4R
See also SATA 14
Brosnan, Jim
See Brosnan, James Patrick
Brosnan, John 1947- 160
See also Blackstone, James
Bross, Donald G. 1932- 154
Bross, Irwin D(udley) J(ackson) 1921- 37-40R
Brossard, Chandler 1922-1993 .... CANR-56
Obituary 142
Earlier sketches in CA 61-64, CANR-8
See also CAAS 2
See also DLB 16
Brossard, Nicole 1943- 122
See also CAAS 16
See also DLB 53
Brossier, Margaret 1918(?)-1984 Obituary 113
Broster, Dorothy Kathleen 1877-1950 ..... DLB 160
Brostowin, Patrick Ronald 1931- 13-16R
Broszat, Martin 1926-1989 Obituary 130
Brother Antoninus
See Everson, William (Oliver)
Brother Bob
See Buell, Robert Kingery
Brother Choleric
See van Zeller, Claud
Brothers, (M.) Jay 1931- 103
Brothers, Joyce (Diane Bauer) 1929- CANR-13
Earlier sketch in CA 21-24R
See also AITN 1
Brothers Hildebrandt, The
See Hildebrandt, Tim(othy)BROTHERS
The Brothers Quay
See Quay, Stephen
and Quay, Timothy
Brotherston, James Gordon 1939- CANR-11
Earlier sketch in CA 25-28R
Brotherton 1856-1930 .... DLB 184
Brotherton, Manfred 1900(?)-1981 Obituary 102
Broude, Norma (Freedman) 1941- 113
Broudy, Harry S(amuel) 1905- CANR-3
Earlier sketch in CA 1-4R
Broue, Pierre 1926- CANR-12
Earlier sketch in CA 69-72
Brough, James 1918- 111
Brough, John 1917-1984 Obituary 111
Brough, R(obert) Clayton 1950- CANR-7
Earlier sketch in CA 57-60
Brougham, Henry Peter 1778-1868 .. DLB 110, 158
Brougham, John 1810-1880 .... DLB 11
Broughton, Bradford B. 1926- 21-24R
Broughton, Diane 1943- 81-84
Broughton, Geoffrey 1927- 102
Broughton, Jack(sel Markham) 1925- 73-76
Broughton, James (Richard) 1913- CANR-57
Earlier sketches in CA 49-52, CANR-2, 30
See also CAAS 12
See also DLB 5
Broughton, Panthea Reid 1940- CANR-7
Earlier sketch in CA 57-60
Broughton, R(obert) Peter 1940- 148
Broughton, Rhoda 1840-1920 .... DLB 18
Broughton, T(homas) Alan 1936- CANR-48
Earlier sketches in CA 45-48, CANR-2, 23
See also CLC 19
Brouillette, Jeanne S. 1-4R
Broumas, Olga 1949- CANR-69
Earlier sketches in CA 85-88, CANR-20
See also CLC 10, 73
Broun, Emily
See Sterne, Emma Gelders
Broun, Heywood 1888-1939 .... DLB 29, 171
Broun, Heywood Hale 1918- CANR-12
Earlier sketch in CA 17-20R
Broun, Heywood Oren 1950(?)-1987 144
Obituary 124
Broun, Hob
See Broun, Heywood Oren
Broussard, Louis 1922- 25-28R
Broussard, Vivian L.
See Martinetz, V(ivian) L.
Brouwer, Luitzen Egbertus Jan
1881-1966 Obituary 116
Brouwer, S. W.
See Brouwer, Sigmund
Brouwer, Sigmund 1959- 164
Brovka, Petr (Pyatrus Ustinovich)
1905-1980 Obituary 105
Brovkin, Vladimir N. 1951- 137
Brow, Robert 1924- CANR-10
Earlier sketch in CA 21-24R
Brow, Thea 1934- .... SATA 60
Broward, Donn
See Halleran, Eugene E(dward)
Broward, Robert C. 1926- 122
Browder, Earl Russell 1891(?)-1973 Obituary . 45-48
Browder, Lesley H(ughes), Jr. 1935- 45-48
Browder, Olin L(orraine), Jr. 1913- 41-44R
Browder, Robert P(aul) 1921- 122
Browder, Sue 1946- 77-80
Browder, Walter Everett 1939- 53-56
Brower, Brock (Hendrickson) 1931- 25-28R
Brower, Charles Hendrickson 1901-1984 102
Obituary 113
Brower, Charlie
See Brower, Charles Hendrickson
Brower, Daniel R(oberts) 1936- 41-44R
Brower, David R(oss) 1912- CANR-9
Earlier sketch in CA 61-64
Brower, Kenneth (David) 1944- CANR-10
Earlier sketch in CA 25-28R
Brower, Linda A. 1945- 33-36R
Brower, Millicent CANR-15
Earlier sketch in CA 41-44R
See also SATA 8
Brower, Pauline 1929- 77-80
See also SATA 22
Brower, Reuben Arthur 1908-1975 ...... CANR-69
Obituary 57-60
Earlier sketches in CA 1-4R, CANR-6
Browin, Frances Williams 1898- CANR-69
Earlier sketches in CAP-1, CA 19-20
See also SATA 5
Brown, A(lfred) R(eginald) Radcliffe
See Radcliffe-Brown, A(lfred) R(eginald)
Brown, Alan 163
Brown, Alan 1950- 156
See also CLC 99
Brown, Alan A. 1929- CANR-16
Earlier sketch in CA 25-28R
Brown, Alan R. 1938- 105
Brown, Alberta L(ouise) 1894- CAP-1
Earlier sketch in CA 11-12
Brown, Alexander (Crosby) 1905- CANR-3
Earlier sketch in CA 1-4R
Brown, Alexis
See Baumann, Amy (Brown) Beeching
Brown, Alice 1856-1948 .... DLB 78
Brown, Alice Very
See Very, Alice (N.)
Brown, Allen 1926- 13-16R
Brown, Andreas Le 1933- 108
Brown, Anne Ensign 1937- 101
See also SATA 61
Brown, Anne M. Wyatt
See Wyatt-Brown, Anne M(arbury)
Brown, Anne S(eddon) K(insolving)
1906-1985 .... 17-20R
Obituary 117
Brown, Annice Harris 1897- 45-48
Brown, Annora 1899-1987(?) Obituary 121
Brown, Anthony Cave 1930- 139
Brown, Anthony Eugene 1937- 89-92
Brown, Archibald Haworth 1938- CANR-44
Earlier sketches in CA 103, CANR-20
Brown, Arnold 1927- 117
Brown, Arthur A(llen) 1900- 73-76

Brown, Arthur Wayne 1917- CANR-8
Earlier sketch in CA 5-8R
Brown, Ashley 1923- CANR-20
Earlier sketches in CA 1-4R, CANR-3
Brown, B(artley) Frank 1917- CANR-4
Earlier sketch in CA 9-12R
Brown, B(essie) Katherine (Taylor) 1917- 13-16R
Brown, Barbara B(anker) 1917- 69-72
Brown, Barbara W(ood) 1928- 105
Brown, Beatrice C.
See Curtis Brown, Beatrice
Brown, Benjamin F. 1930- CANR-1
Earlier sketch in CA 45-48
Brown, Bernard E(dward) 1925- CANR-21
Earlier sketches in CA 1-4R, CANR-4
Brown, Bert R(obert) 1936- 41-44R
Brown, Beth CANR-69
Earlier sketches in CAP-2, CA 21-22
Brown, Betty
See Jones, Elizabeth B(rown)
Brown, Beverly Swerdlow SATA 97
Brown, Bill
See Brown, William L(ouis)
Brown, Billye Walker
See Cutchen, Billye Walker
Brown, Blanche R. (Levine) 1915- 13-16R
Brown, Bob
See Brown, Robert Carlton
and Brown, Robert Joseph
See also DLB 4, 45
Brown, Bob Burton 1925- 21-24R
Brown, Brian A. 1942- 161
Brown, Bryan T(urner) 1952- 139
Brown, Buck 1936- SATA 45
Brown, Calvin S(mith) 1909- 49-52
Brown, Camille 1917- 9-12R
Brown, Carl F(raser) 1910- 41-44R
Brown, Carol Williams 1941- 111
Brown, Carolyn S. 1950- 127
Brown, Carrie
See Brown, Carolyn S.
Brown, Carter
See Yates, A(lan) G(eoffrey)
Brown, Cassie 1919-1986 CANR-23
Earlier sketch in CA 45-48
See also SATA 55
Brown, Cecil 1907-1987 Obituary 123
Brown, Cecil H(ooper) 1944- 109
Brown, Cecil M(orris) 1943- CANR-27
Earlier sketch in CA 73-76
See also BW 1
See also DLB 33
Brown, Charles
See Cadet, John
Brown, Charles Brockden 1771-1810 CDALB 1640-1865
See also DLB 37, 59, 73
Brown, Charles H. 1910- 21-24R
Brown, Charles N(ikki) 1937- 93-96
Brown, Charles T(homas) 1912- 41-44R
Brown, Christopher P(aterson) 1939- CANR-10
Earlier sketch in CA 65-68
Brown, Christy 1932-1981 CANR-72
Obituary 104
Earlier sketch in CA 105
See also CLC 63
See also DLB 14
Brown, Clarence (Fleetwood, Jr.) 1929- Brief entry 112
Brown, Clark 1935- 25-28R
Brown, Claude 1937- 73-76
See also AAYA 7
See also BLC 1
See also BW 1
See also CLC 30
See also DAM MULT
Brown, Clifford Waters, Jr. 1942- 77-80
Brown, (John) Clive (Anthony) 1947- 121
Brown, Conrad 1922- SATA 31
Brown, Constantine 1889-1966 CAP-1
Earlier sketch in CA 11-12
Brown, Courtney C(onrades) 1904-1990 77-80
Obituary 131
Brown, Craig McFarland 1947- SATA 73
Brown, Croswell 1905(?)-1971 Obituary 104
Brown, Curtis F(ranklin) 1925- 61-64
Brown, Cynthia 1952- 121
Brown, Dale 1956(?)- CANR-60
Brief entry 129
Earlier sketch in CA 138
See also BEST 89:4
Brown, Dale W. 1926- 37-40R
Brown, Daniel G(ilbert) 1924- 45-48
Brown, Daniel Russell
See Curzon, Daniel
Brown, Daphne Faunce
See Faunce-Brown, Daphne (Bridget)
Brown, David
See Brown, David A(lan)
and Myller, Rolf
Brown, David 1916- 13-16R
Brown, David (Clifford) 1929- 57-60
Brown, David A(lan) 1922-1982 129
Obituary 110
Brown, David E(arl) 1938- CANR-64
Earlier sketches in CA 113, CANR-32
Brown, David Grant 1936- 13-16R
Brown, David S(pringer) 1915- 29-32R
Brown, Deaver David 1943- 102
Brown, Dee (Alexander) 1908- CANR-60
Earlier sketches in CA 13-16R, CANR-11, 45
See also CAAS 6
See also CLC 18, 47
See also DAM POP
See also DLBY 80
See also MTCW 1
See also SATA 5
Brown, Delwin (Wray) 1935- 135
Brief entry 117
Brown, Deming 1919- 147
Brown, Denise Scott 1931- 41-44R
Brown, Dennis A(lbert) 1926-1978 CANR-13
Earlier sketch in CA 61-64
Brown, Derek Ernest Denny
See Denny-Brown, Derek Ernest
Brown, Diana 1928- CANR-40
Earlier sketches in CA 101, CANR-18
Brown, Dona 1956- 151
Brown, Donald Eugene 1909-1996 CAP-1
Obituary 155
Earlier sketch in CA 13-16
Brown, Donald Fowler 1909- 41-44R
Brown, Donald Robert 1925- 41-44R
Brown, Doris E. 1910(?)-1975 Obituary 61-64
Brown, Dorothy
See Oxley, Dorothy (Anne)
Brown, Dorothy M. 1932- 125
Brown, Douglas
See Gibson, Walter B(rown)
Brown, Douglas (Frank Lambert) 1907- 25-28R
Brown, Drew T. III 1955- 150
See also SATA 83
Brown, Drollene P. 1939- CANR-48
Earlier sketch in CA 122
See also SATA 53
Brown, Duane 1937- 33-36R
Brown, E(dward) K(illoran) 1905-1951 Brief entry 107
Brown, E(ugene) Richard 1942- CANR-40
Earlier sketches in CA 97-100, CANR-18
Brown, Edgar S., Jr. 1922- 9-12R
Brown, Edmund G. (Pat)
See Brown, Edmund G(erald)
Brown, Edmund G(erald) 1905-1996 132
Obituary 151
Brown, Edward J(ames) 1909-1991 CANR-69
Earlier sketch in CA 25-28R
Brown, Elaine 1943- 142
See also BW 2
Brown, Eleanor Frances 1908- 29-32R
See also SATA 3
Brown, Eleanor Gertrude 1887-1968 Obituary 104
Brown, Elisabeth Potts 1939- 133
Brown, Elizabeth Louise 1924- 53-56
Brown, Elizabeth M(yers) 1915- 107
See also SATA 43
Brown, Emily Clara 1911- 53-56
Brown, Erik 1923- 114
Brown, Ernest Henry Phelps 1906- 108
Brown, Evelyn M. 1911- 21-24R
Brown, F(rancis) Andrew 1915- 41-44R
Brown, F. Keith 1913(?)-1976 Obituary 69-72
Brown, F(rancis Charles Claypon) Yeats
See Yeats-Brown, F(rancis Charles Claypon)
Brown, Felicia M. Jefferson 1971- 162
Brown, Fern G. 1918- CANR-40
Earlier sketches in CA 97-100, CANR-17
See also SATA 34
Brown, (Robert) Fletch 1923- 116
See also SATA 42
Brown, Fornan 1901-1996 SATA 71
See also SATA-Obit 88
Brown, Forrest 49-52
Brown, (Ernest) Francis 1903-1995 CANR-69
Obituary 150
Earlier sketch in CA 73-76
Brown, Francis R(obert) 1914- 41-44R
Brown, Frank A(rthur), Jr. 1908- 69-72
Brown, Frank E(dward) 1908- 101
Brown, Frank London 1927-1962 141
See also BW 2
See also DLB 76
Brown, Frederick 1934- CANR-66
Earlier sketch in CA 25-28R
Brown, Frederick G(ramm) 1932- CANR-12
Earlier sketch in CA 29-32R
Brown, Fredric (William) 1906-1972 CANR-59
Obituary 33-36R
Earlier sketch in CA 121
See also DLB 8
Brown, G(eorge) Neville 1932- 17-20R
Brown, Geoff 1932- 61-64
Brown, George
See Wertmueller, Lina
Brown, George Alfred George
See George-Brown, George Alfred
Brown, George Douglas 1869-1902 162
See also TCLC 28
Brown, George Earl 1883-1964 5-8R
See also SATA 11
Brown, George Isaac 1923- 73-76
Brown, George Mackay 1921-1996 CANR-67
Obituary 151
Earlier sketches in CA 21-24R, CANR-12, 37
See also CAAS 6
See also CLC 5, 48, 100
See also DLB 14, 27, 139
See also MTCW 1
See also SATA 35
Brown, George Thompson 1921- 111
Brown, Gerald Saxon 1911- 9-12R
Brown, Gerald W(illiam) 1916- 33-36R
Brown, Giles T(yler) 1916- 17-20R
Brown, Ginny
See Brown, Virginia Sharpe
Brown, Gwilym Slater 1928-1974 9-12R
Obituary 53-56
Brown, H. Jackson, Jr. 1940- 140
Brown, H. Rap
See Al-Amin, Jamil Abdullah
Brown, Hamish M. 1934- 129
Brown, Harcourt 1900-1990 CANR-20
Obituary 141
Earlier sketch in CA 101
Brown, Harold O(gden) J(oseph) 1933- CANR-10
Earlier sketch in CA 25-28R
Brown, Harriett M. 1897- 5-8R
Brown, Harrison Scott 1917-1986 69-72
Obituary 121
Brown, Harry (Peter McNab, Jr.) 1917-1986 CANR-72
Obituary 120
Earlier sketch in CA 69-72
See also DLB 26
Brown, Harry Clifford 1953- 168
Brown, Harry G(unnison) 1880-1975 Obituary 57-60
Brown, Harry M(atthew) 1921- CANR-10
Earlier sketch in CA 25-28R
Brown, Hazel E(lizabeth) 1893- 57-60
Brown, Helen Gurley 1922- CANR-5
Earlier sketch in CA 5-8R
Interview in CANR-5
Brown, Herbert Ross 1902- CAP-1
Earlier sketch in CA 13-16
Brown, Howard Mayer 1930-1993 CANR-49
Obituary 140
Earlier sketches in CA 1-4R, CANR-3
Brown, Hugh Auchincloss 1879-1975 Obituary 61-64
Brown, Huntington 1899- CAP-1
Earlier sketch in CA 19-20
Brown, Ian 1954(?)- 156
Brown, Ida Mae 1908- CAP-2
Earlier sketch in CA 29-32
Brown, Ina Corinne 5-8R
Brown, Ina Ladd 1905- CAP-1
Earlier sketch in CA 13-14
Brown, Ira Vernon 1922- 5-8R
Brown, Irene Bennett 1932- CANR-12
Earlier sketch in CA 29-32R
See also SATA 3
Brown, Irving
See Adams, William Taylor
Brown, Irwin
See Murray, David Stark
Brown, Ivor (John Carnegie) 1891-1974 CANR-69
Obituary 49-52
Earlier sketches in CA 9-12R, CANR-12
See also SATA 5
See also SATA-Obit 26
Brown, J(ames) Douglas 1898-1986 Obituary 118
Brown, J(oseph) P(aul) S(ummers) 1930- CANR-63
Earlier sketch in CA 61-64
Brown, James (Wiley) 1909-1983 77-80
Obituary 135
Brown, James (Montgomery) 1921- 1-4R
Brown, James (Joe, Jr.) 1928(?)- 146
Brown, James 1934- CANR-27
Earlier sketches in CA 65-68, 139, CANR-10
Brown, James 1957- 139
Brown, James Alan Calvert 1922-1984 Obituary 114
Brown, James Bush
See Bush-Brown, James
Brown, James Cooke 1921- 29-32R
Brown, James I(saac) 1908- CANR-7
Earlier sketch in CA 17-20R
Brown, James Patrick 1948- 29-32R
Brown, James S(eay), Jr. 1944- 120
Brown, James Wilson 1913- 41-44R
Brown, Jamie 1945- CANR-20
Earlier sketch in CA 101
Brown, Jane Clark 1930- SATA 81
Brown, Janet 1947- 69-72
Brown, Janet Mitsui 151
See also SATA 87
Brown, Jared Allen 1936- 142
Brown, Jay A(llen) 1935- 110
Brown, Jeff
See Brown, Sevellon III
Brown, Jennifer S. H. 1940- 130
Brown, Jerry Earl 1940- 105
Brown, Jerry Wayne 1936- 25-28R
Brown, Jim (M.) 1940- 69-72
Brown, Jo Giese 1947- 108
Brown, Joan Sayers 1925(?)-1983 Obituary 110
Brown, Joe David 1915-1976 CANR-70
Obituary 65-68
Earlier sketch in CA 13-16R
See also SATA 44
Brown, John 1887- CAP-1
Earlier sketch in CA 13-14
Brown, John 1920- 5-8R
Brown, John (E.) 1934- CANR-45
Earlier sketch in CA 25-28R
Brown, John A. 1898- 112
Brown, John Arthur 1914- CANR-11
Earlier sketch in CA 17-20R
Brown, John Buchanan
See Buchanan-Brown, John
Brown, John Gracen 1936- CANR-44
Earlier sketch in CA 104
Brown, John Gregory 160
Brown, John J. 1916- 13-16R
Brown, John L(ackey) 1914- CANR-46
Earlier sketch in CA 49-52
Brown, John Mason 1900-1969 CANR-70
Obituary 25-28R
Earlier sketch in CA 9-12R
Brown, John Pairman 1923- 33-36R
Brown, John Russell 1923- CANR-70
Earlier sketches in CA 21-24R, CANR-11
Brown, Jonathan (Mayer) 1939- 132
Brown, Jonathan (M.) 1939- Brief entry 112
Brown, Joseph E(dward) 1929- CANR-6
Earlier sketch in CA 53-56
See also SATA 59
See also SATA-Brief 51
Brown, Judith C(ora) 136
Brown, Judith Gwyn 1933- CANR-21
Earlier sketch in CA 93-96
See also SATA 20
Brown, Judith K. CANR-51
Earlier sketch in CA 124
Brown, Judith M(argaret) 1944- CANR-72
Earlier sketches in CA 41-44R, CANR-15, 32
Brown, Julia (Prewitt) 1948- 93-96
Brown, Karl 1895(?)-1970 Obituary 104
Brown, Karl 1897-1990 Obituary 131
Brown, Kathryn 1955- 166
See also SATA 98
Brown, Kenneth H. 1936- CANR-69
Earlier sketch in CA 13-16R
Brown, Kevin 1960- 148
See also SATA 101
Brown, Kevin V. 1922- 89-92
Brown, Kitt
See Vandergriff, (Lola) Aola
Brown, L(aurence) B(inet) 1927- 65-68
Brown, L. Carl
See Brown, Leon Carl
Brown, L. J.
See Du Breuil, (Elizabeth) L(or)inda
Brown, Larry
See Brown, Lawrence, Jr.
Brown, (William) Larry 1951- 134
Brief entry 130
Interview in 133
See also CLC 73
Brown, Laurene Krasny 1945- CANR-54
Earlier sketch in CA 117
See also SATA 54, 99
Brown, Laurie Krasny
See Brown, Laurene Krasny
Brown, Lawrence, Jr. 1947- Brief entry 114
Brown, Lawrence R. 1904(?)-1986 Obituary 119
Brown, Lee Dolph 1890-1971 Obituary 29-32R
Brown, Leigh 65-68
Brown, Leland 1914- 1-4R
Brown, Lennox (John) 1934- 93-96
Brown, Leon Carl 1928- Brief entry 117
Brown, LeRoy Chester 1908- CANR-13
Earlier sketches in CAP-1, CA 11-12
Brown, Les(ter Louis) 1928- CANR-13
Earlier sketch in CA 33-36R
Brown, Leslie H(ilton) 1917-1980 CANR-7
Earlier sketch in CA 9-12R
Brown, Leslie Wilfrid 1912- 17-20R
Brown, Lester
See Brown, Lester R(ussell)
Brown, Lester R(ussell) 1934- 132
Brown, Letitia Woods 1915-1976 73-76
Obituary 69-72
Brown, Linda Beatrice 1939- 148
Brown, Lloyd Arnold 1907-1966 CAP-1
Earlier sketch in CA 11-12
See also SATA 36
Brown, Lloyd L(ouis) 1913- 143
See also BW 2
Brown, Louis M(orris) 1909-1996 CANR-47
Obituary 154
Earlier sketch in CA 49-52
Brown, Lyle C(larence) 1926- CANR-15
Earlier sketch in CA 41-44R
Brown, Lyn Mikel 140
Brown, Lynne P. 1952- 138
Brown, M(ary) L(oretta) T(herese) 13-16R
Brown, Mac Alister 1924- 89-92
Brown, Mahlon A.
See Ellis, Edward S(ylvester)
Brown, Mandy
See Brown, May
Brown, Marc (Tolon) 1946- CANR-36
Earlier sketch in CA 69-72
See also CLR 29
See also MAICYA
See also SATA 10, 53, 80
Brown, Marcia 1918- CANR-46
Earlier sketch in CA 41-44R
See also CLR 12
See also DLB 61
See also MAICYA
See also SATA 7, 47
Brown, Marel 1899- 102
Brown, Margaret Wise 1910-1952 136
Brief entry 108
See also CLR 10
See also DLB 22
See also MAICYA
See also SATA 100
See also YABC 2
Brown, Margery (Wheeler) CANR-26
Earlier sketch in CA 25-28R
See also BW 2
See also SATA 5, 78
Brown, Marian A. 1911- 73-76
Brown, Marilyn McMeen Miller 1938- CANR-6
Earlier sketch in CA 57-60
Brown, Marion Marsh 1908- CANR-70
Earlier sketches in CA 1-4R, CANR-3
See also SATA 6
Brown, Mark 165
Brown, Mark H(erbert) 1900-1988 CANR-70
Earlier sketches in CAP-2, CA 21-22
Brown, Marshall 1945- CANR-48
Earlier sketch in CA 111

Brown, Marshall L. 1924- ... 21-24R
Brown, Marvin L(uther), Jr. 1920- ... CANR-70
Earlier sketch in CA 53-56
Brown, Mary Ellen 1939- ... CANR-41
Earlier sketch in CA 117
Brown, Mary Ward 1917- ... 133
Brown, Maurice F(red) 1928-1985 ... 41-44R
Obituary ... 116
Brown, May 1913- ... 118
Brown, Melissa Mather 1917- ... 121
Brown, Merle Elliott 1925-1978 ... 108
Brown, Michael 1931- ... CANR-55
Earlier sketch in CA 33-36R
Brown, Michael 1938- ... 127
Brown, Michael Barratt
See Barratt-Brown, Michael
Brown, Michael F(obes) 1950- ... 142
Brown, Michael H(arold) 1952- ... 121
Brown, Michael John 1932- ... 29-32R
Brown, Michael P. 1966- ... 168
Brown, Michelle P(atricia) 1959- ... 139
Brown, Milton Perry, Jr. 1928- ... 9-12R
Brown, Milton W(olf) 1911-1998 Obituary ... 164
Brief entry ... 113
Brown, Montague 1952- ... 162
Brown, Morna Doris 1907-1995 ... CANR-59
Obituary ... 148
Earlier sketches in CA 5-8R, CANR-5
See also Ferrars, Elizabeth
Brown, Morris Cecil 1943- ... 37-40R
Brown, Moses
See Barrett, William (Christopher)
Brown, Muriel 1938- ... 107
Brown, Muriel W(hitbeck) 1892- ... CAP-2
Earlier sketch in CA 23-24
Brown, Murray 1929- ... 37-40R
Brown, Myra Berry 1918- ... CANR-3
Earlier sketch in CA 1-4R
See also SATA 6
Brown, Nathaniel Hapgood 1929- ... 101
Brown, Ned 1882(?)-1976 Obituary ... 65-68
Brown, Neville (George) 1932- ... 9-12R
Brown, Newell 1917- ... 97-100
Brown, Norman D(onald) 1935- ... 53-56
Brown, Norman O(liver) 1913- ... CANR-70
Earlier sketch in CA 21-24R
Brown, Oliver Madox 1855-1874 ... DLB 21
Brown, Palmer 1919- ... CANR-69
Earlier sketch in CA 107
See also SATA 36
Brown, Pamela (Beatrice) 1924-1989 ... CANR-70
Obituary ... 127
Earlier sketch in CA 13-16R
See also SATA 5
See also SATA-Obit 61
Brown, Parker B(oyd) 1928- ... 53-56
Brown, Pat
See Brown, Edmund G(erald)
Brown, Patricia Fortini 1936- ... CANR-72
Earlier sketch in CA 131
Brown, Paul B. 1954- ... 138
Brown, Paula 1925- ... CANR-47
Earlier sketch in CA 110
Brown, Peter 1926(?)-1984(?) Obituary ... 112
Brown, Peter (Robert Lamont) 1935- ... CANR-13
Earlier sketch in CA 21-24R
Brown, Peter A. 1949- ... 138
Brown, Peter Carter
See Yates, A(lan) G(eoffrey)
Brown, Peter Douglas 1925- ... CANR-16
Earlier sketch in CA 25-28R
Brown, Peter G. 1940- ... 151
Brown, Peter Harry 1939- ... 143
Brown, Peter Lancaster
See Lancaster-Brown, Peter
Brown, R(eginald) Allen 1924-1989 ... CANR-11
Obituary ... 128
Earlier sketch in CA 5-8R
Brown, R(onald) G(ordon) S(clater) 1929-1978 ... CANR-48
Earlier sketch in CA 29-32R
Brown, Rae
See Brown, Forrest
Brown, Ralph Adams 1908- ... 33-36R
Brown, Raymond Bryan 1923-1977 ... 17-20R
Obituary ... 133
Brown, Raymond E(dward) 1928- ... CANR-17
Earlier sketch in CA 97-100
Brown, Raymond George 1924- ... 109
Brown, Raymond Kay 1936- ... 102
Brown, Raymond Lamont
See Lamont-Brown, Raymond
Brown, Re Mona 1917- ... 41-44R
Brown, Rebecca
See Ore, Rebecca
Brown, Rebecca 1956- ... 124
Brown, Rex V(andesteene) 1933- ... 53-56
Brown, Richard 1935- ... 114
Brown, Richard C(arl) 1917- ... CANR-17
Earlier sketches in CA 5-8R, CANR-2
Brown, Richard D(avid) 1939- ... 53-56
Brown, Richard E(ugene) 1937- ... 73-76
Brown, Richard E. 1946- ... 130
See also SATA 61
Brown, Richard E(arl) 1948- ... 149
Brown, Richard H(olbrook) 1927- ... 9-12R
Brown, Richard H(arvey) 1940- ... CANR-38
Earlier sketch in CA 109
Brown, Richard Howard 1929- ... 57-60
Brown, Richard Maxwell 1927- ... CANR-11
Earlier sketch in CA 17-20R

Brown, Rita Mae 1944- ... CANR-62
Earlier sketches in CA 45-48, CANR-2, 11, 35
Interview in ... CANR-11
See also CLC 18, 43, 79
See also DAM NOV, POP
See also MTCW 1
Brown, Robert Carlton 1886-1959 Brief entry ... 107
See also Brown, Bob
Brown, Robert Craig 1935- ... 101
Brown, Robert D. 1924- ... CANR-20
Earlier sketch in CA 104
Brown, Robert E(ldon) 1907- ... 5-8R
Brown, Robert Edward 1945- ... CANR-15
Earlier sketch in CA 65-68
Brown, Robert Fath 1941- ... 111
Brown, Robert Goodell 1923- ... 33-36R
Brown, Robert Hanbury 1916- ... 112
Brown, Robert Joseph 1907- ... CANR-13
Earlier sketches in CAP-1, CA 9-10
See also Brown, Bob
See also SATA 14
Brown, Robert L. 1921- ... 21-24R
Brown, Robert McAfee 1920- ... CANR-69
Earlier sketches in CA 13-16R, CANR-7
Brown, Robert T(homas) 1943- ... 113
Brown, Roberta Simpson 1939- ... 150
Brown, Robin 1937- ... 97-100
Brown, Roderick (Langmere) Haig-
See Haig-Brown, Roderick (Langmere)
Brown, Roger Glenn 1941- ... 77-80
Brown, Roger H(amilton) 1931- ... 9-12R
Brown, Roger William 1925-1997 ... 13-16R
Obituary ... 163
Brown, Ronald 1900- ... 81-84
Brown, Rosalie
See Moore, Rosalie (Gertrude)
See also SATA 9
Brown, Rosel George 1926-1967 Obituary ... 102
Brown, Rosellen 1939- ... CANR-44
Earlier sketches in CA 77-80, CANR-14
See also CAAS 10
See also CLC 32
Brown, Rosemary (Eleanor) 1938- Brief entry ... 115
Brown, Roswell
See Webb, Jean Francis
Brown, Roy (Frederick) 1921-1982 ... 65-68
Obituary ... 117
See also SATA 51
See also SATA-Obit 39
Brown, Rustie 1930(?)-1988 Obituary ... 125
Brown, Sanborn C(onner) 1913-1981 ... CANR-11
Obituary ... 106
Earlier sketch in CA 17-20R
Brown, Sandra 1948- ... CANR-63
Earlier sketch in CA 139
Brown, Sanford J(ay) 1946- ... 118
Brown, Sevellon III 1913-1983 Obituary ... 110
Brown, Seyom 1933- ... CANR-17
Earlier sketch in CA 65-68
Brown, Sheldon S. 1933- ... 122
Brown, Sheldon S. 1937- ... CANR-7
Earlier sketch in CA 53-56
Brown, Sidney DeVere 1925- ... 33-36R
Brown, Spencer 1909- ... 130
Brown, Stanley (Branson) 1914- ... 49-52
Brown, Stanley C(oleman) 1928- ... 77-80
Brown, Stanley H(arold) 1927- ... 45-48
Brown, Stephen W. 1940- ... CANR-13
Earlier sketch in CA 33-36R
Brown, Sterling Allen 1901-1989 ... CANR-26
Obituary ... 127
Earlier sketch in CA 85-88
See also BLC 1
See also BW 1
See also CLC 1, 23, 59
See also DAM MULT, POET
See also DLB 48, 51, 63
See also MTCW 1
Brown, Steven R(andall) 1939- ... 49-52
Brown, Stewart 1951- ... 135
Brown, Stuart C(ampbell) 1938- ... CANR-50
Earlier sketches in CA 29-32R, CANR-25
Brown, Stuart Gerry 1912-1991 ... CANR-70
Obituary ... 135
Earlier sketch in CA 21-24R
Brown, Sue Ellen 1954- ... SATA 81
Brown, Susan Jenkins 1896- ... 85-88
Brown, T. E. 1830-1897 ... DLB 35
Brown, T(illman) Merritt 1913- ... 41-44R
Brown, Terence 1944- ... CANR-41
Earlier sketches in CA 102, CANR-19
Brown, Theo W(atts) 1934- ... CANR-8
Earlier sketch in CA 61-64
Brown, Theodore L(awrence) 1928- ... 33-36R
Brown, Theodore M(orey) 1925- ... 33-36R
Brown, Thomas H., Jr. 1950- ... CANR-56
Earlier sketch in CA 127
Brown, Thomas H. 1930- ... 57-60
Brown, Thomas McPherson
1906-1989 Obituary ... 128
Brown, Tim W. 1961- ... 164
Brown, Tina 1953- ... 118
Brief entry ... 116
Brown, Tom, Jr.
See Brown, Thomas H., Jr.
Brown, Truesdell S(parhawk) 1906- ... 13-16R
Brown, Turner, Jr.
See Hample, Stuart
Brown, Velma Darbo 1921- ... 97-100
Brown, Vinson 1912- ... CANR-1
Earlier sketch in CA 1-4R
See also SATA 19
Brown, Virginia (Suggs) 1924- ... 69-72
Brown, Virginia Pounds 1916- ... 114
Brown, Virginia Sharpe 1916- ... 13-16R
Brown, W. Anthony 1933- Brief entry ... 110

Brown, W(illiam) Norman 1892-1975 ... 61-64
Obituary ... 57-60
Brown, Wallace 1933- ... 17-20R
Brown, Walter Lee 1924- ... 33-36R
Brown, Walter R(eed) 1929- ... CANR-2
Earlier sketch in CA 45-48
See also SATA 19
Brown, Warner
See Boroson, Warren
Brown, Warren (William) 1894-1978 ... 85-88
Obituary ... 81-84
Brown, Warren A. 1917(?)-1985 Obituary ... 117
Brown, Wayne 1944- ... 101
Brown, Weldon A(mzy) 1911- ... 65-68
Brown, Wenzell 1912-1981 ... CANR-70
Obituary ... 162
Earlier sketches in CA 1-4R, CANR-5
Brown, Wesley 1945- ... 125
See also BW 2
Brown, Wilfred (Banks Duncan) 1908-1985 ... 9-12R
Obituary ... 116
Brown, Wilfred A(rthur) Gavin
See Gavin-Brown, Wilfred A(rthur)
Brown, Will
See Ainsworth, William Harrison
Brown, Will C.
See Boyles, C(larence) S(cott), Jr.
Brown, William Anthony 1933- ... 125
Brief entry ... 110
See also BW 1
Brown, William Campbell 1928- ... 57-60
Brown, William E(nglish) 1907-1975 ... CAP-2
Earlier sketch in CA 29-32
Brown, William Edward 1904- ... 126
Brown, William F. 1906(?)-1990 Obituary ... 131
Brown, William F(rank) 1920- ... 33-36R
Brown, William F(erdinand) 1928- ... 33-36R
Brown, William Hill 1765-1793 ... DLB 37
Brown, William J. ... 97-100
Brown, William James 1889- ... 5-8R
Brown, William L(ouis) 1910-1964 ... CANR-70
Earlier sketch in CA 1-4R
See also SATA 5
Brown, William Wells 1813-1884 ... BLC 1
See also DAM MULT
See also DC 1
See also DLB 3, 50
Brown, Zenith Jones 1898-1983 ... 9-12R
Obituary ... 110
Brown-Azarowicz, Marjory F. 1922- ... 33-36R
Brownback, Paul 1940- ... 113
Browne, Anthony (Edward Tudor) 1946- ... CANR-36
Earlier sketch in CA 97-100
See also CLR 19
See also MAICYA
See also SATA 45, 61
See also SATA-Brief 44
Browne, Barum
See Saunders, Hilary Aidan St. George
Browne, Charles Farrar 1834-1867 ... DLB 11
Browne, Colette (Victoria) 1950- ... 121
Browne, Courtney 1915- ... 21-24R
Browne, Dik
See Browne, Richard Arthur Allen
See also AITN 1
See also SATA 38
Browne, E(lliott) Martin 1900-1980 ... CAP-2
Obituary ... 97-100
Earlier sketch in CA 25-28
Browne, Frances 1816-1879 ... DLB 199
Browne, Francis Fisher 1843-1913 ... DLB 79
Browne, G(erald) P(eter) 1930- ... 21-24R
Browne, Gary Lawson 1939- ... 101
Browne, George Stephenson 1890-1970 ... CAP-2
Earlier sketch in CA 29-32
Browne, Gerald A(ustin) 1928- ... 166
Browne, Hablot Knight 1815-1882 ... SATA 21
Browne, Harry
See Browne, Henry
Browne, Harry 1933- ... CANR-3
Earlier sketch in CA 49-52
Browne, Henry 1918- ... 102
Browne, Howard 1908- ... 73-76
Browne, J. Ross 1821-1875 ... DLB 202
Browne, (Clyde) Jackson 1948(?)- ... 120
See also CLC 21
Browne, Joseph William 1914- ... 105
Browne, Joy 1944- ... 97-100
Browne, Malcolm W(ilde) 1931- ... 17-20R
Browne, Mary T. 1955- ... 148
Browne, Matthew
See Rands, William Brighty
Browne, Michael Dennis 1940- ... CANR-15
Earlier sketch in CA 29-32R
See also CAAS 20
See also DLB 40
Browne, Ray B(roadus) 1922- ... CANR-49
Earlier sketches in CA 17-20R, CANR-11
Browne, Raymond 1897- ... 73-76
Browne, Richard Arthur Allen
1917-1989 Obituary ... 128
See also Browne, Dik
See also SATA 67
See also SATA-Brief 38
Browne, Robert
See Karlins, Marvin
Browne, Robert S(pan) 1924- ... CANR-14
Earlier sketch in CA 37-40R
Browne, Roland A. 1910- ... 65-68
Browne, Sam
See Smith, Ronald Gregor
Browne, Theodore R. 1911(?)-1979 Obituary ... 81-84
Browne, Thomas 1605-1682 ... DLB 151
Browne, Vee F(rances) 1956- ... SATA 90
Browne, Walter A(nderson) 1895- ... 37-40R

Browne, William P(aul) 1945- ... CANR-54
Earlier sketches in CA 109, CANR-25
Browne, Wynyard (Barry) 1911-1964 Obituary ... 113
See also DLB 13
Brownell, Blaine Allison 1942- ... 65-68
Brownell, Charles E(dward III) 1943- ... 139
Brownell, John Arnold 1924- ... 21-24R
Brownell, Susan 1960- ... 155
Brownell, W. C. 1851-1928 ... DLB 71
Browne Miller, Angela 1952- ... 135
Browne of Tavistock, William 1590-1645 ... DLB 121
Browning, Alice C(rolley) 1907-1985 Obituary ... 117
Browning, Christopher R(obert) 1944- ... 112
Browning, Columban
See Browning, William
Browning, David (George) 1938- ... 37-40R
Browning, Dixie Burrus 1930- ... CANR-66
Earlier sketches in CA 110, CANR-64
Browning, Don S(pencer) 1934- ... CANR-2
Earlier sketch in CA 49-52
Browning, (Grayson) Douglas 1929- ... 13-16R
Browning, Elizabeth 1924- ... 57-60
Browning, Elizabeth Barrett 1806-1861 ... CDBLB 1832-1890
See also DA
See also DAB
See also DAC
See also DAM MST, POET
See also DLB 32, 199
See also PC 6
See also WLC
Browning, Frank 1946- ... 107
Browning, Gordon 1938- ... 37-40R
Browning, Iben 1918- Brief entry ... 113
Browning, J(ohn) D. 1942- ... 125
Browning, John S.
See Williams, Robert Moore
Browning, L. J.
See Du Breuil, (Elizabeth) L(or)inda
Browning, Mary 1887- ... CAP-1
Earlier sketch in CA 11-12
Browning, Norma Lee 1914- ... CANR-8
Earlier sketch in CA 61-64
Browning, Peter 1928- ... 104
Browning, Preston M(ercer), Jr. 1929- ... 57-60
Browning, Reed 1938- ... 57-60
Browning, Robert 1812-1889 ... CDBLB 1832-1890
See also DA
See also DAB
See also DAC
See also DAM MST, POET
See also DLB 32, 163
See also PC 2
See also WLCS
See also YABC 1
Browning, Robert 1914-1997 ... CANR-13
Obituary ... 157
Earlier sketch in CA 33-36R
Browning, Robert L(ynn) 1924- ... CANR-16
Earlier sketch in CA 85-88
Browning, Rufus P(utnam) 1934- ... 124
Browning, (Zerilda) Sinclair 1946- ... CANR-49
Earlier sketch in CA 112
Browning, Sterry
See Gribble, Leonard (Reginald)
Browning, Tod 1882-1962 ... 141
Obituary ... 117
See also CLC 16
Browning, Wilfrid (Robert Francis) 1918- ... 5-8R
Browning, William 1921- ... 113
Brownjohn, Alan 1931- ... CANR-72
Earlier sketch in CA 25-28R
See also DLB 40
See also SATA 6
Brownjohn, J(ohn Nevil) Maxwell 1929- ... 129
Brownlee, David B(ruce) 1951- ... 132
Brownlee, O(swald) H(arvey) 1917- ... 65-68
Brownlee, W(ilson) Elliot, Jr. 1941- ... 69-72
Brownlee, W(illiam) H(ugh) 1917- ... 9-12R
Brownlee, Walter 1930- ... 57-60
See also SATA 62
Brownlie, Ian 1932- ... CANR-2
Earlier sketch in CA 5-8R
Brownlow, Cecil Alexander III
1926-1988 Obituary ... 124
Brownlow, Kevin 1938- ... CANR-12
Earlier sketch in CA 25-28R
See also SATA 65
Brownmiller, Susan 1935- ... CANR-35
Earlier sketch in CA 103
See also DAM NOV
See also MTCW 1
Brownridge, William R(oy) 1932- ... 159
See also SATA 94
Brownrigg, Walter Grant 1940- ... 110
Brownson, Orestes Augustus 1803-1876 ... DLB 1, 59, 73
Brownson, William C(larence), Jr. 1928- ... 69-72
Brownstein, Karen (Osney) 1944-1989 ... 124
Obituary ... 130
Brownstein, Michael 1943- ... 33-36R
Brownstein, Oscar Lee 1928- ... 113
Brownstein, Rachel M. 1937- ... 122
Brownstein, Ronald J. 1958- ... 106
Brownstein, Samuel C. 1909-1996 ... 5-8R
Obituary ... 155
Brownstone, David M. 1928- ... CANR-65
Earlier sketches in CA 104, CANR-21
Brox, Jane (Martha) 1956- ... 153
Broxholme, John Franklin 1930- ... CANR-31
Earlier sketches in CA 65-68, CANR-12
Broxon, Mildred Downey 1944- ... CANR-58
Earlier sketch in CA 107
Broy, Anthony 1916- ... 102

Broyard, Anatole 1920-1990 .... CANR-44
Obituary 132
Earlier sketch in CA 105
Broyles, J(ohn) Allen 1934- 9-12R
Broyles, Michael 1939- 146
Broyles, William Dodson, Jr. 1944- 73-76
Broz, J. Lawrence 1956- 167
Brozek, Josef (Maria) 1913- CANR-48
Earlier sketch in CA 45-48
Brozen, Yale 1917-1998 109
Obituary 166
Bru, Hedin
See Jacobsen, Hans Jacob
Brubach, Holly 1953- 110
Brubacher, John Seiler 1898-1988 .... CANR-1
Obituary 162
Earlier sketch in CA 1-4R
Brubaker, Carol
See Stolk, Anthonie
Brubaker, Dale L(ee) 1937- CANR-4
Earlier sketch in CA 53-56
Brubaker, Earl R(oy) 1932- 107
Brubaker, Sterling 1924- 21-24R
Bruccoli, Matthew J(oseph) 1931- CANR-7
Earlier sketch in CA 9-12R
See also CLC 34
See also DLB 103
Bruce, Ben F., Jr. 1920- 13-16R
Bruce, Charles (Tory) 1906-1971 152
See also DLB 68
Bruce, Colin John 1960- 150
Bruce, Curt 1946- 97-100
Bruce, David (Kirkpatrick Este)
1898-1977 Obituary 105
Bruce, Debra 1951- 118
Bruce, Dickson D., Jr. 1946- 53-56
Bruce, Donald (James) 1930- 17-20R
Bruce, Dorita Fairlie 1885-1970 Obituary 107
See also SATA-Obit 27
Bruce, Evangeline 153
Bruce, F(rederick) F(yvie) 1910-1990 .... CANR-41
Earlier sketches in CA 1-4R, CANR-3, 19
Bruce, George 1909- CANR-69
Earlier sketch in CA 65-68
Bruce, Harold (R., Jr.) 1934(?)-1987 Obituary 122
Bruce, (William) Harry 1934- 145
See also SATA 77
Bruce, Harry J. 1931- 21-24R
Bruce, Janet
See Campbell, Janet Bruce
Bruce, Jeannette M. 1922- 5-8R
Bruce, Lennart 1919- CANR-13
Earlier sketch in CA 33-36R
See also CAAS 27
Bruce, Lenny
See Schneider, Leonard Alfred
See also CLC 21
Bruce, Leo
See Croft-Cooke, Rupert
See also DLB 77
Bruce, Mary 1927- 25-28R
See also SATA 1
Bruce, Maurice 1913(?)-1988 Obituary 125
Bruce, Mildred Mary 1896(?)-1990 Obituary 131
Bruce, Monica
See Melaro, Constance L(oraine)
Bruce, Philip Alexander 1856-1933 .... DLB 47
Bruce, R(aymon) R(ene) 1934- 89-92
Bruce, Richard
See Nugent, Richard Bruce
Bruce, Robert 1927- CAP-1
Earlier sketch in CA 9-10
Bruce, Robert V(ance) 1923- 53-56
Bruce, Shelley
See Merklinghaus, Michele
Bruce, Sylvia (Valerie) 1936- 33-36R
Bruce, Violet R(ose) 29-32R
Bruce-Briggs, B(arry B.) 112
Bruce-Gardyne, Jock
See Bruce-Gardyne, John
Bruce-Gardyne, John 1930-1990 Obituary 131
Bruce Lockhart, Robin 1920- 25-28R
Bruce-Novoa
See Bruce-Novoa, Juan D.
Bruce-Novoa, John David
See Bruce-Novoa, Juan D.
Bruce-Novoa, Juan D. 1944- CANR-32
Brief entry 117
See also CAAS 18
See also DLB 82
See also HW
Bruch, Hilde 53-56
See also AITN 1
Bruchac, Joseph III 1942- CANR-47
Earlier sketches in CA 33-36R, CANR-13
See also AAYA 19
See also CLR 46
See also DAM MULT
See also JRDA
See also NNAL
See also SATA 42, 89
Bruchey, Stuart (Weems) 1917- 33-36R
Bruck, Connie 1946- 140
Bruck, Lilly 1918- 109
Bruck, Lorraine 1921- 147
See also Bridges, Laurie
See also SATA 55
See also SATA-Brief 46
Brucker, Clara (Hantel)
1892(?)-1980 Obituary 97-100
Brucker, Gene (Adam) 1924- Brief entry 114
Brucker, Herbert 1898-1977 .... CANR-4
Obituary 69-72
Earlier sketch in CA 5-8R
Brucker, Roger W(arren) 1929- CANR-11
Earlier sketch in CA 65-68
Bruckman, Clyde 1894-1955 .... DLB 26
Bruckner, D. J. R. 1933- 132
Bruckner, Ferdinand 1891-1958 .... DLB 118
Bruckner, Pascal 1948- 150
Bruder, Judith 97-100
Bruder, Mary Newton 1939- 127
Bruegel, Johann Wolfgang 1905-1986 77-80
Obituary 121
Bruegel, John Wolfgang
See Bruegel, Johann Wolfgang
Brueggemann, Walter (A.) 1933- Brief entry 117
Bruegmann, Robert 1948- 101
Bruehl, Anton 1900-1982 Obituary 110
Bruemmer, Fred 1929- CANR-69
Earlier sketch in CA 102
See also SATA 47
Bruening, William H(arry) 1943- 57-60
Bruess, Clint E. 1941- 33-36R
Bruff, Nancy
See Gardner, Nancy Bruff
Bruffee, Kenneth A. 1934- 37-40R
Bruford, Walter Horace 1894-1988 Obituary 126
Bruggen, Carol (Holmes) 1932- 117
Brugger, Bill
See Brugger, William (Christian)
Brugger, Robert J(ohn) 1943- CANR-38
Earlier sketches in CA 85-88, CANR-16
Brugger, William (Christian) 1941- CANR-44
Earlier sketches in CA 73-76, CANR-12
Bruggink, Donald J. 1929- CANR-7
Earlier sketch in CA 13-16R
Brugioni, Dino A. 1921- 137
Bruhn, Eric (Belton Evers) 1928-1986 Obituary 118
Bruhn, John Glyndon 1934- 89-92
Bruhns, Karen Olsen 1941- 154
Bruin, John
See Brutus, Dennis
Bruins, Elton J(ohn) 1927- 53-56
Bruland, Esther (Byle) 1956- 116
Brulard, Henri
See Stendhal
Brulard, Henri
See Baillargeon, Pierre
Bruller, Jean (Marcel) 1902-1991 .... CANR-47
Obituary 134
Earlier sketches in CA 65-68, CANR-12
Brulls, Christian
See Simenon, Georges (Jacques Christian)
Brulotte, Gaetan 1945- 150
Brumback, Carl V. 1917(?)-1987 Obituary 123
Brumbaugh, Robert Sherrick 1918-1992 .... CANR-70
Earlier sketches in CA 5-8R, CANR-3
Brumbaugh, Thomas B(rendle) 1921- 49-52
Brumble, H(erbert) David III 1943- 107
Brumfield, William C.
See Brumfield, William Craft
Brumfield, William Craft 1944- 144
Brumgardt, John R(aymond) 1946- 97-100
Brumm, Ursula 1919- 29-32R
Brummel, Mark Joseph 1933- 103
Brummet, R. Lee 1921- 21-24R
Brummitt, Wyatt B. 1897- 9-12R
Brun, Ellen 1933- 103
Brun, Henri 1939- 53-56
Bruna, Dick 1927- CANR-36
Earlier sketch in CA 112
See also CLR 7
See also MAICYA
See also SATA 43, 76
See also SATA-Brief 30
Brundage, Burr Cartwright 1912-1993 .... CANR-70
Earlier sketch in CA 41-44R
Brundage, Dorothy J(une) 1930- 104
Brundage, James A(rthur) 1929- CANR-7
Earlier sketch in CA 5-8R
Brundage, John Herbert 1926- 101
See also Herbert, John
Brundage, Percival F(lack) 1892-1979 101
Obituary 89-92
Brundage, W(illiam) Fitzhugh 1959- 142
Brune, Lester H(ugo) 1926- CANR-48
Earlier sketches in CA 33-36R, CANR-13
Bruneau, Jean
See Sylvestre, (Joseph Jean) Guy
Bruneau, Thomas C. 1939- 53-56
Brunelli, Jean 1934- 138
Bruner, Edward M. 1924- 121
Bruner, Herbert B. 1894(?)-1974 Obituary 53-56
Bruner, Jerome S(eymour) 1915- CANR-1
Earlier sketch in CA 45-48
Bruner, Margaret E. (Baggerly) 1886-197(?) CAP-1
Earlier sketch in CA 17-18
Bruner, Phillip L. 1944- 127
Bruner, Richard W(allace) 1926- 49-52
Bruner, Wally 1931-1997 49-52
Obituary 162
Brunet, Michel 1917-1985 .... CANR-18
Obituary 117
Earlier sketch in CA 102
Brunette, Peter (Clark), Jr. 1943- CANR-53
Earlier sketch in CA 126
Brunetti, Cledo 1910-1971 .... CAP-2
Earlier sketch in CA 29-32
Brunetti, Mendor Thomas
1894-1979 Obituary 89-92
Brunhoff, Jean de 1899-1937 137
Brief entry 118
See also CLR 4
See also MAICYA
See also SATA 24
Brunhoff, Laurent de 1925- CANR-45
Earlier sketch in CA 73-76
See also CLR 4
See also MAICYA
See also SATA 24, 71
Brunhouse, Robert Levere 1908-1996 .... CANR-2
Obituary 162
Earlier sketch in CA 49-52
Bruning, Nancy P(auline) 1948- CANR-46
Earlier sketches in CA 106, CANR-23
Brunn, Harry O(tis), Jr. 1919- 1-4R
Brunner, Edmund de S(chweinitz) 1889-1973 ....
CAP-1
Obituary 45-48
Earlier sketch in CA 13-16
Brunner, Edward J. 1946- 127
Brunner, Elizabeth 1920-1983 Obituary 111
Brunner, James A(lbertus) 1923- 37-40R
Brunner, John (Kilian Houston) 1934-1995 ....
CANR-37
Obituary 149
Earlier sketches in CA 1-4R, CANR-2
See also CAAS 8
See also CLC 8, 10
See also DAM POP
See also MTCW 1
Brunner, Karl 1916-1989 Obituary 128
Brunner, Maurice Yaw 1950- 103
Brunner, Theodore F(riederich) 1934- 33-36R
Brunnings, Florence E(mery) 1916- 112
Bruno, Carole A. 1942- 144
Bruno, Frank
See St. Bruno, Albert Francis
Bruno, Frank J(oe) 1930- 107
Bruno, Harold R., Jr. 1928- 77-80
Bruno, James Edward 1940- 41-44R
Bruno, Michael 1921- 33-36R
Bruno, Vincent J. 1926- 65-68
Bruns, Frederick R., Jr.
1913(?)-1979 Obituary 85-88
Bruns, George 1914(?)-1983 Obituary 109
Bruns, J(ames) Edgar 1923- CANR-2
Earlier sketch in CA 5-8R
Bruns, Joe
See Altshuler, Harry
Bruns, Roger A. 1941- 144
Bruns, William A(lan) 1942- 113
Bruns, William J(ohn), Jr. 1935- 37-40R
Brunskill, Elizabeth Ann Flatt 1966- .... SATA 88
Brunskill, Ronald (William) 1929- 85-88
Brunstein, Karl (Avrum) 1933- 97-100
Brunswick, Heinrich Julius of 1564-1613 .... DLB 164
Brunt, P(eter) A(stbury) 1917- 101
Bruntjen, Scott 1943- 111
Brunton, David W(alter) 1929- 41-44R
Brunton, Paul 1898-1981 Obituary 115
Bruntz, George G. 1901- 5-8R
Brunvand, Jan Harold 1933- CANR-51
Earlier sketches in CA 108, CANR-26
Brus, Wlodzimierz 1921- 73-76
Brusati, Franco 1927-1993 148
Brush, Craig B(alcombe) 1930- 21-24R
Brush, Douglas P(eirce) 1930- CANR-7
Earlier sketch in CA 57-60
Brush, John E(dwin) 1919- 33-36R
Brush, Judith M(arie) 1938- CANR-7
Earlier sketch in CA 57-60
Brush, Karen A(lexandra) 1960- 127
See also SATA 85
Brush, Stephanie 1954- 138
Brush, Stephen G(eorge) 73-76
Brushwood, John S(tubbs) 1920- CANR-9
Earlier sketch in CA 21-24R
Brusiloff, Phyllis 1935- 57-60
Bruss, Elizabeth W(issman) 1944-1981 108
Brussel, Jacob 1900(?)-1979 Obituary 104
Brussel, James Arnold 1905-1982 .... CANR-70
Earlier sketches in CA 1-4R, CANR-3
Brussel-Smith, Bernard 1914- .... SATA 58
Brust, Harold
See Cheyney, (Reginald Evelyn) Peter (Southouse)
Brust, Steven K. (Zoltan) 1955- CANR-37
Earlier sketch in CA 115
See also SATA 86
Brustein, Robert S(anford) 1927- CANR-71
Earlier sketches in CA 9-12R, CANR-7
Brustein, William I. 1947- 162
Bruster, Bill(y) G(lenn) 1940- 111
Brustlein, Daniel 1904- .... SATA 40
Brustlein, Janice Tworkov 9-12R
See also SATA 40
Bruteau, Beatrice 1930- 57-60
Bruton, Eric (Moore) 1915- CANR-23
Earlier sketches in CA 13-16R, CANR-5
Bruton, Henry J(ackson) 1921- 21-24R
Bruton, J(ack) G(ordon) 1914- 9-12R
Brutschy, Jennifer 1960- .... SATA 84
Brutten, Gene J. 1928- 37-40R
Brutten, Milton 1922- 45-48
Brutus
See Spooner, John D.
Brutus, Dennis 1924- CANR-42
Earlier sketches in CA 49-52, CANR-2, 27
See also CAAS 14
See also BLC 1
See also BW 2
See also CLC 43
See also DAM MULT, POET
See also DLB 117
Bruun, Bertel 1937- 45-48
Bruun, (Arthur) Geoffrey 1898-1988 .... CANR-70
Obituary 126
Earlier sketch in CA 1-4R
Bruun, Ruth Dowling 1937- 108
Bruyn, Kathleen 1903- CAP-2
Earlier sketch in CA 33-36
Bruzelius, Caroline 1949- 121
Bry, Adelaide 1920- 33-36R
Bry, Gerhard 1911- 41-44R
Bryan, Ashley F. 1923- CANR-43
Earlier sketches in CA 107, CANR-26
See also BW 2
See also CLR 18
See also MAICYA
See also SATA 31, 72
Bryan, C(ourtlandt) D(ixon) B(arnes) 1936- ....
CANR-68
Earlier sketches in CA 73-76, CANR-13
Interview in CANR-13
See also CLC 29
See also DLB 185
Bryan, Carter R(oyston) 1911-1986 .... 33-36R
Obituary 162
Bryan, Christopher 1935- CANR-43
Earlier sketches in CA 104, CANR-20
Bryan, Dorothy M. 1896(?)-1984 Obituary 114
See also SATA-Obit 39
Bryan, Ford R. 1912- 134
Bryan, G(eorge) McLeod 1920- 1-4R
Bryan, George B(arton) 1939- 117
Bryan, J(oseph) III 1904-1993 .... CANR-47
Obituary 141
Earlier sketches in CA 61-64, CANR-11
Bryan, J(ack) Y(eaman) 1907- 73-76
Bryan, John E. 1931- CANR-4
Earlier sketch in CA 53-56
Bryan, Julien (Hequembourg)
1899-1974 Obituary 53-56
Bryan, Lynne 1961- 149
Bryan, M(erwyn) Leonard 1937- 103
Bryan, Marian K(nighton)
1900(?)-1974 Obituary 53-56
Bryan, Martin 1908- 1-4R
Bryan, Mavis
See O'Brien, Marian P(lowman)
Bryan, Michael
See Moore, Brian
Bryan, Mina R(uese) 1908-1985 Obituary 115
Bryan, Sharon 1943- CANR-37
Earlier sketch in CA 115
Bryan, (William) Wright 1905-1991 77-80
Obituary 133
Bryans, Robert Harbinson 1928- CANR-11
Earlier sketch in CA 5-8R
Bryans, Robin
See Bryans, Robert Harbinson
Bryant, Al
See Bryant, T(homas) Alton
Bryant, Anita
See Green, Anita Jane
Bryant, Arthur (Wynne Morgan) 1899-1985 ....
CANR-72
Obituary 114
Earlier sketch in CA 105
See also DLB 149
Bryant, Bear
See Bryant, Paul W(illiam)
Bryant, Bernice (Morgan) 1908- CAP-1
Earlier sketch in CA 9-10
See also SATA 11
Bryant, Beth Elaine 1936- 13-16R
Bryant, Christopher G. A. 1944- 164
Bryant, Cyril E(ric, Jr.) 1917- 61-64
Bryant, Donald C(ross) 1905- 13-16R
Bryant, Dorothy 1930- CANR-41
Earlier sketches in CA 53-56, CANR-4, 19
See also CAAS 26
Bryant, Edward (Albert) 1928- CANR-11
Earlier sketch in CA 9-12R
Bryant, Edward (Winslow, Jr.) 1945- CANR-72
Earlier sketches in CA 45-48, CANR-1
Bryant, Edward (Arnot) 1948- 141
Bryant, Gay 1945- CANR-13
Earlier sketch in CA 73-76
Bryant, Henry A(llen), Jr. 1943- CANR-4
Earlier sketch in CA 53-56
Bryant, J(oseph) A(llen), Jr. 1919- 5-8R
Bryant, J. M.
See Bryant, Jonathan M.
Bryant, James C(ecil), Jr. 1931- CANR-48
Earlier sketch in CA 49-52
Bryant, Jennifer F(isher) 1960- 159
See also SATA 94
Bryant, Jerry H(olt) 1928- 33-36R
Bryant, Jon
See Bryant, Jonathan M.
Bryant, Jonathan M. 1957- 161
Bryant, Katherine Cliffton 1912- 13-16R
Bryant, Keith L(ynn), Jr. 1937- 49-52
Bryant, Lynwood 1908- 139
Bryant, Margaret M. 1900-1993 .... CANR-4
Obituary 141
Earlier sketch in CA 1-4R
Bryant, Michael
See Brennert, Alan (Michael)
Bryant, Paul W(illiam) 1913-1983 111
Obituary 108
Bryant, Ralph C(lement) 1938- 117
Bryant, Robert H(arry) 1925- 21-24R
Bryant, Shasta M(onroe) 1924- 41-44R
Bryant, T(homas) Alton 1926- CANR-29
Earlier sketches in CA 25-28R, CANR-10
Bryant, Traphes L(emon) 1914- 77-80
Bryant, Verda E. 1910- CAP-2
Earlier sketch in CA 21-22
Bryant, William Cullen 1794-1878 .... CDALB
1640-1865
See also DA
See also DAB
See also DAC
See also DAM MST, POET
See also DLB 3, 43, 59, 189
See also PC 20
Bryant, Willis Rooks 1892-1965 .... 5-8R
Obituary 103

Bryce, Gladysann 1934- 116
Bryce, James
See Mobley, James Bryce
Bryce, Murray D(avidson) 1917- 13-16R
Bryce, Viscount James 1838-1922 ... DLB 166, 189
Bryce Echenique, Alfredo 1939- .... DLB 145
Brychta, Alex 1956- CANR-20
Earlier sketch in CA 103
See also SATA 21
Bryde, John F(rancis) 1920- 33-36R
Bryden, Bill
See Bryden, William Campbell Rough
Bryden, John (Herbert) 1943- 134
Bryden, John Marshall 1941- CANR-1
Earlier sketch in CA 49-52
Bryden, John R(ennie) 1913- 33-36R
Bryden, William Campbell Rough 1942- 105
Brydges, Samuel Egerton 1762-1837 . DLB 107, 142
Bryer, Jackson R(obert) 1937- CANR-40
Earlier sketches in CA 9-12R, CANR-3, 18
Bryer, (Alastair) Robin (Mornington) 1944- 111
Bryers, Paul 1945- 73-76
Bryfonski, Dedria (Anne) 1947- 101
BRYHER
See ELLERMAN, Annie Winifred
Bryks, Rachmil 1912-1974 97-100
Brymer, Jack 1915- 110
Bryner, Gary C. 1951- 145
Brynildsen, Ken(neth) 1944- 110
Brynner, Yul
See Khan, Taidje
Bryskett, Lodowick 1546(?)-1612 .... DLB 167
Bryson, Bernarda 1905- CANR-70
Earlier sketch in CA 49-52
See also SATA 9
Bryson, Bill
See Bryson, William
Bryson, Conrey 1905- 93-96
Bryson, John 1923- 133
Bryson, John (Noel) 1935- 142
Bryson, Norman 1949- 147
Bryson, Phillip J(ames) 1939- 69-72
Bryson, Reid Allen 1920- 101
Bryson, W(illiam) Hamilton 1941- CANR-36
Earlier sketch in CA 114
Bryson, William 1951(?)- CANR-72
Earlier sketch in CA 142
Bryusov, Valery Yakovlevich 1873-1924 155
Brief entry 107
See also TCLC 10
Brzezinski, Zbigniew K(azimierz) 1928- .. CANR-41
Earlier sketches in CA 1-4R, CANR-5
See also BEST 89:3
Buarque De Holanda (Ferreira), Aurelio
1911(?)-1989 Obituary 128
Buba, Joy Flinsch 1904- .... SATA 44
Bubar, Margaret Weber
1920(?)-1978 Obituary 77-80
Bubb, Mel
See Whitcomb, Ian
Bube, Richard H. 1927- CANR-8
Earlier sketch in CA 21-24R
Bubeck, Mark I(rving) 1928- 61-64
Buber, Martin 1878-1965 125
Obituary 25-28R
See also MTCW 1
Bubner, Rudiger
See Bubner, Ruediger
Bubner, Ruediger 1941- 121
Bucaille, Maurice 1920- 137
Buccellati, Giorgio 1937- 41-44R
Bucchieri, Theresa F. 1908- 73-76
Buccini, Stefania 1959- 166
Bucco, Martin 1929- CANR-14
Earlier sketch in CA 29-32R
Buchan, Alastair (Francis) 1918-1976 73-76
Obituary 65-68
Buchan, Bryan 1945- 107
See also SATA 36
Buchan, David
See Womack, David A(lfred)
Buchan, James 1916- 130
Brief entry 119
Buchan, John 1875-1940 145
Brief entry 108
See also DAB
See also DAM POP
See also DLB 34, 70, 156
See also TCLC 41
See also YABC 2
Buchan, Kate
See Erskine, Barbara
Buchan, Norman Findlay 1922-1990 109
Obituary 132
Buchan, Perdita 1940- 21-24R
Buchan, Stuart 1942-1987 57-60
Obituary 123
See also SATA-Obit 54
Buchan, Thomas Buchanan 1931- CANR-16
Earlier sketch in CA 25-28R
Buchan, Tom
See Buchan, Thomas Buchanan
Buchan, Ursula 1953- 128
Buchan, William (James de l'Aigle) 1916- 161
Buchanan, A(lbert) Russell 1906- 13-16R
Buchanan, Annette 1933- 118
Buchanan, Betty (Joan) 1923- 101
Buchanan, Chuck
See Rowland, D(onald) S(ydney)
Buchanan, Colin O(gilvie) 1934- 25-28R
Buchanan, Cynthia 1942- CANR-1
Earlier sketch in CA 45-48
Buchanan, Cynthia D(ee) 1937- 5-8R
Buchanan, Daniel C(rump) 1892- 17-20R
Buchanan, (Eric) David 1933- 57-60
Buchanan, David A(lan) 1949- 118
Buchanan(-Berrigan), Dawna Lisa 1954- 137
Buchanan, Debby 1952- 149
See also SATA 82
Buchanan, Deborah Leevonne
See Buchanan, Debby
Buchanan, Donald W(illiam) 1908-(?) CAP-1
Earlier sketch in CA 11-12
Buchanan, Edna (Rydzik) 1939(?)- CANR-52
Brief entry 125
Earlier sketch in CA 132
Interview in 132
Buchanan, George 1506-1582 .... DLB 152
Buchanan, George (Henry Perrott) 1904-1989 .....
CANR-3
Obituary 129
Earlier sketch in CA 9-12R
Buchanan, George Wesley 1921- CANR-14
Earlier sketch in CA 37-40R
Buchanan, James David 1929- 130
Buchanan, James J(unkin) 1925- 33-36R
Buchanan, James McGill 1919- CANR-22
Earlier sketches in CA 5-8R, CANR-3
Buchanan, Keith 1919- CANR-10
Earlier sketch in CA 21-24R
Buchanan, Ken 1952- 149
Buchanan, Laura
See King, Florence
Buchanan, Marie 1922- CANR-72
Earlier sketches in CA 65-68, CANR-10, 25
Buchanan, Patrick
See Corley, Edwin (Raymond)
Buchanan, Paul G. 1954- 154
Buchanan, Pegasus 1920- 9-12R
Buchanan, R(obert) A(ngus) 1930- CANR-7
Earlier sketch in CA 17-20R
Buchanan, Robert 1841-1901 .... DLB 18, 35
Buchanan, Thomas G(ittings) 1919- 1-4R
Buchanan, Wiley T(homas), Jr.
1914-1986 Obituary 118
Buchanan, William
See Buck, William Ray
Buchanan, William J(esse) 1926- CANR-39
Earlier sketch in CA 73-76
Buchanan-Brown, John 1929- 102
Buchard, Robert 1931- 33-36R
Buchdahl, Gerd 1914- 57-60
Bucheister, Patt 1942- CANR-48
Earlier sketch in CA 122
Buchele, William Martin 1895- 57-60
Buchen, Irving H. 1930- 25-28R
Bucher, Bradley 1932- 37-40R
Bucher, Charles A(ugustus) 1912- CANR-3
Earlier sketch in CA 9-12R
Bucher, Francois 1927- CANR-3
Earlier sketch in CA 5-8R
Bucher, Glenn R(ichard) 1940- 57-60
Bucher, Magnus 1927- 41-44R
Buchheim, Lothar-Guenther 1918- 85-88
See also CLC 6
Buchheimer, Naomi Barnett
See Barnett, Naomi
Buchheit, Lee C(harles) 1950- 81-84
Buchholz, Todd G. 1961- 150
Buchignani, Walter 1965- 150
See also SATA 84
Buchler, Justus 1914-1991 .... 5-8R
Obituary 134
Buchman, Dian Dincin CANR-8
Earlier sketch in CA 61-64
Buchman, Frank N(athan) D(aniel)
1878-1961 Obituary 112
Buchman, Herman 1920- 41-44R
Buchman, Marion 121
Buchman, Randall L(oren) 1929- CANR-1
Earlier sketch in CA 45-48
Buchman, Sidney 1902-1975 93-96
Obituary 61-64
See also DLB 26
Buchmann, Stephen L. 162
Buchner, Augustus 1591-1661 .... DLB 164
Bucholtz, Andreas Heinrich 1607-1671 .... DLB 168
Bucholz, Arden 1936- 167
Buchsbaum, Tony 1961- 128
Buchwald, Ann 1920-1994 128
Obituary 146
Buchwald, Art(hur) 1925- CANR-67
Earlier sketches in CA 5-8R, CANR-21
See also AITN 1
See also CLC 33
See also MTCW 1
See also SATA 10
Buchwald, Emilie 1935- CANR-2
Earlier sketch in CA 49-52
See also SATA 7
Buchwalter, Andrew 1949- 145
Buck, Ashley (?)-1980 Obituary 97-100
Buck, Charles (Henry, Jr.) 1915- 33-36R
Buck, Craig 1952- 141
Buck, David 1934(?)-1989 Obituary 128
Buck, Doris P(itkin) 1898(?)-1980 Obituary 102
Buck, Edith V(irginia) 1919- 117
Buck, Frederick Silas 5-8R
Buck, George C(rawford) 1918- 69-72
Buck, Gisela 1941- 168
See also SATA 101
Buck, Harry M(erwyn, Jr.) 1921- CANR-13
Earlier sketch in CA 33-36R
Buck, James H. 1924- 104
Buck, Joan Juliet 1948- CANR-25
Earlier sketch in CA 108
Buck, John Lossing 1890-1975 .... CANR-2
Obituary 61-64
Earlier sketch in CA 45-48
Buck, John N(elson) 1906- CAP-2
Earlier sketch in CA 29-32
Buck, Lewis 1925- 73-76
See also SATA 18
Buck, Margaret Waring 1910- CANR-70
Earlier sketch in CA 5-8R
See also SATA 3
Buck, Marion A(shby) 1909- CAP-1
Earlier sketch in CA 13-14
Buck, Paul H(erman) 1899-1978 Obituary 81-84
Buck, Pearl S(ydenstricker) 1892-1973 .. CANR-34
Obituary 41-44R
Earlier sketches in CA 1-4R, CANR-1
See also AITN 1
See also CLC 7, 11, 18
See also DA
See also DAB
See also DAC
See also DAM MST, NOV
See also DLB 9, 102
See also MTCW 1
See also SATA 1, 25
Buck, Peggy S(ullivan) 1930- 65-68
Buck, Philip W(allenstein) 1900- 65-68
Buck, Rinker 1951(?)- 166
Buck, Robert N. 1914- 103
Buck, Ross (Workman) 1941- 128
Buck, Siegfried 1941- 168
See also SATA 101
Buck, Stratton 1906- CAP-2
Earlier sketch in CA 17-18
Buck, Susan J. 1947- 141
Buck, Vernon E(llis) 1934- 37-40R
Buck, William Ray 1930- 1-4R
Buckaway, C. M.
See Buckaway, Catherine M(argaret)
Buckaway, Catherine M(argaret) 1919- 130
Bucke, Charles 1781-1846 .... DLB 110
Bucke, Richard Maurice 1837-1902 .... DLB 99
Buckelew, Albert R., Jr. 1942- 150
Buckeridge, Anthony (Malcolm) 1912- ... CANR-52
Earlier sketches in CA 49-52, CANR-2
See also SATA 6, 85
Buckeye, Donald A(ndrew) 1930- CANR-47
Earlier sketch in CA 49-52
Buckholdt, David R. 1942- 101
Buckholtz, Eileen (Garber) 1949- 117
See also SATA 54
See also SATA-Brief 47
Buckhout, Robert 1935-1990 45-48
Obituary 133
Buckingham, Burdette H.
1907(?)-1977 Obituary 73-76
Buckingham, Clyde E(dwin) 1907- CAP-1
Earlier sketch in CA 13-16
Buckingham, Edwin 1810-1833 .... DLB 73
Buckingham, James (William) 1932-1992 CANR-47
Obituary 136
Earlier sketch in CA 29-32R
Buckingham, Jamie
See Buckingham, James (William)
Buckingham, Joseph Tinker 1779-1861 .... DLB 73
Buckingham, Robert W(illiam) III 113
Buckingham, Walter S(amuel), Jr. 1924-1967 .. 1-4R
Obituary 103
Buckingham, Willis J(ohn) 1938- 29-32R
Buckland, Michael K(eeble) 1941- 97-100
Buckland, Raymond 1934- 73-76
Buckle, (Christopher) Richard (Sandford) 1916- ....
CANR-70
Earlier sketch in CA 97-100
Buckler, Beatrice 1933- 127
Buckler, Ernest 1908-1984 .... CAP-1
Obituary 114
Earlier sketch in CA 11-12
See also CLC 13
See also DAC
See also DAM MST
See also DLB 68
See also SATA 47
Buckler, John 1945- 121
Buckler, William Earl 1924- CANR-20
Earlier sketches in CA 1-4R, CANR-5
Buckley, Anthony D. 1945- CANR-47
Earlier sketch in CA 120
Buckley, Christopher (Taylor) 1952- 139
Buckley, Cornelius M(ichael) 1925- 138
Buckley, Doris Heather
See Buckley Neville, Heather
Buckley, Fergus Reid 1930- 21-24R
Buckley, Fiona
See Anand, Valerie
Buckley, Francis J(oseph) 1928- CANR-13
Earlier sketch in CA 33-36R
Buckley, Gail Lumet 1937- 142
See also BW 2
Buckley, Helen 1923- 144
Buckley, Helen E(lizabeth) 1918- CANR-3
Earlier sketch in CA 5-8R
See also SATA 2, 90
Buckley, J(ames) Taylor, Jr. 1939- 127
Buckley, James Lane 1923- 61-64
Buckley, Jerome Hamilton 1917- CANR-70
Earlier sketches in CA 1-4R, CANR-3
Buckley, John (F.) 1961- 148
Buckley, Julian Gerard 1905- 41-44R
Buckley, Kevin 1941(?)- 140
Buckley, Mary L(orraine) 53-56
Buckley, Michael F. 1880(?)-1977 Obituary ... 69-72
Buckley, Michael J(oseph) 1931- 73-76
Buckley, Paul 1938- 162
Buckley, Peter 1938-1991 112
Obituary 134
Buckley, Priscilla 1921- 81-84
Buckley, Roger N(orman) 1937- 97-100
Buckley, Shawn 1943- 93-96
Buckley, Suzanne Shelton 1946- 108
Buckley, Thomas H(ugh) 1932- 29-32R
Buckley, Vincent (Thomas) 1925-1988 101
See also CLC 57
Buckley, Walter (Frederick) 1921- 121
Buckley, William F(rank), Jr. 1925- CANR-53
Earlier sketches in CA 1-4R, CANR-1, 24
Interview in CANR-24
See also AITN 1
See also CLC 7, 18, 37
See also DAM POP
See also DLB 137
See also DLBY 80
See also MTCW 1
Buckley Neville, Heather 1910- 103
Bucklin, Louis P(ierre) 1928- 97-100
Buckman, Peter 1941- CANR-11
Earlier sketch in CA 65-68
Buckman, Rob
See Buckman, Robert (Alexander Amiel)
Buckman, Robert (Alexander Amiel) 1948- 128
Buckmaster, Henrietta
See Stephens, Henrietta Henkle
See also SATA 6
Buckminster, Joseph Stevens 1784-1812 ... DLB 37
Bucknall, Barbara J(ane) 1933- CANR-14
Earlier sketch in CA 33-36R
Bucknell, Howard III 1924-1986 125
Buckner, Rheuben
See McCoy, Max
Buckner, Robert (Henry) 1906- 1-4R
See also DLB 26
Buckner, Sally Beaver 1931- 61-64
Buckser, Andrew (S.) 1964- 164
Buckstaff, Kathryn 1947- 147
Buckstead, Richard C(hris) 1929- 49-52
Buckvar, Felice (Spitz) 1938- 107
Bucuvalas, Tina 1951- 149
Buczkowski, Leopold 1905- 41-44R
Budapest, Zsuzsanna E(mese) 1940- 154
Buday, George
See Buday, Gyorgy
Buday, Gyorgy 1907-1990(?) 107
Obituary 132
Budberg, Moura 1892(?)-1974 Obituary 53-56
Budbill, David 1940- 73-76
Budd, Carol (Pellegrini) 1951- 128
Budd, Edward C(arhart) 1920- 21-24R
Budd, Elaine 1925- 101
Budd, Kenneth George 1904-1972 .... CAP-1
Earlier sketch in CA 13-14
Budd, Lillian (Peterson) 1897-1989 ...... CANR-72
Earlier sketches in CA 1-4R, CANR-4
See also SATA 7
Budd, Louis J(ohn) 1921- CANR-3
Earlier sketch in CA 1-4R
Budd, Mavis CANR-19
Earlier sketch in CA 102
Budd, Richard W. 1934- 21-24R
Budd, Thomas (?)-1698 .... DLB 24
Budd, William C(laude) 1923- 49-52
Budde, Michael L(eo) 1958- 168
Buddee, Paul Edgar 1913- 103
Budden, Julian (Medforth) 1924- 130
Budden, Laura M(adeline) 1894- 5-8R
Buddensieg, Tilmann 1928- 138
Bude, John
See Elmore, Ernest Carpenter
Budenz, Louis F(rancis) 1891-1972 Obituary . 89-92
Buderi, Robert 1954- 162
Budge, Ian 1936- CANR-12
Earlier sketch in CA 29-32R
Budgen, Frank Spencer Curtis
1882-1971 Obituary 29-32R
Budiansky, Stephen (Philip) 1957- 150
Budick, Sanford 1942- CANR-71
Earlier sketch in CA 33-36R
Budimir, (Simo) Velimir 1926- 65-68
Budinger, Peyton Bailey 1939- 114
Budoff, Penny Wise 1939- 110
Budrys, Algirdas Jonas 1931- CANR-20
Earlier sketches in CA 1-4R, CANR-4
See also Budrys, Algis
See also DLB 8
Budrys, Algis
See Budrys, Algirdas Jonas
See also CAAS 14
Budurowycz, Bohdan B(asil) 1921- CANR-3
Earlier sketch in CA 5-8R
Budzik, Janet K. Sims 1942- 37-40R
Budziszewski, J(ay Dalton) 1952- 125
Buechner, (Carl) Frederick 1926- CANR-64
Earlier sketches in CA 13-16R, CANR-11, 39
Interview in CANR-11
See also CLC 2, 4, 6, 9
See also DAM NOV
See also DLBY 80
See also MTCW 1
Buechner, Georg 1813-1837 .... DLB 133
Buechner, John C(harles) 1934- 21-24R
Buechner, Thomas S(charman) 1926- ... CANR-47
Earlier sketch in CA 49-52
Buehler, Curt F(erdinand) 1905-1985 .... 1-4R
Obituary 117
Buehler, Evelyn Judy 1953- 167
Buehler, Stephanie Jona 1956- 150
See also SATA 83
Buehlmann, Walbert 1916- CANR-38
Earlier sketch in CA 115
Buehnau, Ludwig
See Schreiber, Hermann (Otto Ludwig)
Buehner, Andrew J(ohn) 1905- 17-20R
Buehr, Walter Franklin 1897-1971 .... CANR-3
Obituary 33-36R
Earlier sketch in CA 5-8R
See also SATA 3
Buehrig, Edward H(enry) 1910- 37-40R
Buehrig, Gordon M. 1904- 101

Buel, Richard (Van Wyck), Jr. 1933- CANR-13
Earlier sketch in CA 73-76
Bueler, Lois E(aton) 1940- 57-60
Bueler, William Merwin 1934- 37-40R
Buell, Ellen Lewis
See Cash, Ellen Lewis Buell
Buell, Emmett H., Jr. 1941- 138
Buell, Frederick H(enderson) 1942- 33-36R
Buell, Janet 1945- 127
Buell, John (Edward) 1927- CANR-71
Earlier sketch in CA 1-4R
See also CLC 10
See also DLB 53
Buell, Jon A. 1939- 102
Buell, Lawrence 1939- CANR-47
Earlier sketch in CA 49-52
Buell, Robert Kingery 1908-1971 ..... CANR-71
Earlier sketches in CAP-2, CA 25-28
Buell, Victor P(aul) 1914- CANR-8
Earlier sketch in CA 21-24R
Buelow, George J. 1929- 21-24R
Buenaventura, Enrique 1925- 151
See also DAM MULT
See also HW
Buendia, Manuel
See Giron, Manuel Buendia Tellez
Buenker, John D(avid) 1937- CANR-16
Earlier sketches in CA 45-48, CANR-1
Bueno, Jose de la Torre
1905(?)-1980 Obituary 93-96
Bueno de Mesquita, Bruce James 1946- 108
Buergel, Paul-Hermann H. 1949- ..... SATA 83
Buergenthal, Thomas 1934- 37-40R
Buerger, Gottfried August 1747-1794 ..... DLB 94
Buerger, Peter 1936- 144
Buerkle, Jack Vincent 1923- 41-44R
Buero Vallejo, Antonio 1916- CANR-49
Earlier sketches in CA 106, CANR-24
See also CLC 15, 46
See also HW
See also MTCW 1
Bueschel, Richard M. 1926- CANR-26
Earlier sketches in CA 25-28R, CANR-11
Buetow, Harold A(ndrew) 1919- 53-56
Buettner, Dan 1960- 160
See also SATA 95
Buettner-Janusch, John 1924-1992 49-52
Obituary 138
Bufalari, Giuseppe 1927- CANR-16
Earlier sketch in CA 25-28R
Bufalino, Gesualdo 1920(?)- ..... CLC 74
See also DLB 196
Buferd, Norma Bradley 1937- 69-72
Buff, Conrad 1886-1975 135
See also MAICYA
See also SATA 19
Buff, Mary (E. Marsh) 1890-1970 135
Obituary 116
See also MAICYA
See also SATA 19
Buffa, Dudley W. 1940- 121
Buffalo Chuck
See Barth, Charles P.
Buffaloe, Neal D(ollison) 1924- 53-56
Buffett, Jimmy 1946- 141
See also BEST 90:2
See also SATA 76
Buffie, Margaret 1945- 160
See also AAYA 23
See also CLR 39
See also JRDA
See also SATA 71
Buffington, Albert F(ranklin) 1905-1980 ..... 33-36R
Obituary 162
Buffington, Robert (Ray) 1933- 21-24R
Bufkin, Ernest Claude, Jr. 1929- 101
Buford, Bill 1954- 143
Buford, Thomas O(liver) 1932- 29-32R
Buford, William Holmes
See Buford, Bill
Bugajski, Janusz 1954- 144
Bugayev, Boris Nikolayevich 1880-1934 165
Brief entry 104
See also Bely, Andrey
See also PC 11
See also TCLC 7
Bugbee, Emma 1888(?)-1981 Obituary 105
See also SATA-Obit 29
Bugbee, Ruth Carson 1903- CANR-1
Earlier sketch in CA 1-4R
Bugeja, Michael J. 1952- 138
See also CAAS 29
Bugental, James F(rederick) T(homas) 1915- .....
CANR-50
Earlier sketches in CA 21-24R, CANR-10, 25
Bugg, James L(uckin), Jr. 1920- 5-8R
Bugg, Ralph 1922- 73-76
Buggie, Frederick D(enman) 1929- 97-100
Buglass, Leslie J. 1917- 13-16R
Bugliarello, George 1927- 41-44R
Bugliosi, Vincent (T.) 1934- CANR-46
Earlier sketches in CA 73-76, CANR-13
Bugnet, Georges (-Charles-Jules) 1879-1981 ... 148
See also DLB 92
Bugos, Glenn E. 1961- 164
Bugul, Ken
See Mbaye, Marietou (Bileoma)
Buhagiar, Marion 1932- 141
Buhite, Russell D(evere) 1938- 101
Buhle, Mari Jo 1943- 108
Buhle, Paul 1944- CANR-63
Earlier sketch in CA 127
Buhler, Charlotte B(ertha) 1893-1974(?) . CANR-72
Earlier sketches in CAP-2, CA 17-18
Buhler, Charlotte Malachowski
See Buhler, Charlotte B(ertha)
Buhler, Curt F(erdinand)
See Buehler, Curt F(erdinand)
Buhlmann, Walbert
See Buehlmann, Walbert
Buies, Arthur 1840-1901 ..... DLB 99
Buisseret, David 1934- 124
Buist, Charlotte
See Patterson, Charlotte (Buist)
Buist, Vincent 1919(?)-1979 Obituary 89-92
Buitenhuis, Peter (Martinus) 1925- 25-28R
Buitrago, Ann Mari 1929- 105
Bujold, Lois McMaster 1949- 139
See also AAYA 19
Bukalski, Peter J(ulian) 1941- CANR-15
Earlier sketch in CA 41-44R
Bukatman, Scott 1957- 151
Buker, George E(dward) 1923- 53-56
Bukey, Evan Burr 1940- 131
Bukharin, Nikolai (Ivanovich) 1888-1938 Brief
entry 120
Bukiet, Melvin Jules 154
Bukowczyk, John J(oseph) 1950- 125
Bukowski, Charles 1920-1994 ..... CANR-62
Obituary 144
Earlier sketches in CA 17-20R, CANR-40
See also CLC 2, 5, 9, 41, 82, 108
See also DAM NOV, POET
See also DLB 5, 130, 169
See also MTCW 1
See also PC 18
Buktenica, Norman A(ugust) 1930- 33-36R
Bulatkin, Eleanor Webster 1913- 33-36R
Bulatovic, Miodrag 1930-1991 ..... CANR-72
Obituary 133
Earlier sketches in CA 5-8R, CANR-21
See also DLB 181
Bulbeck, Chilla 1951- 145
Buley, R(oscoe) Carlyle 1893-1968 ..... CAP-2
Obituary 25-28R
Earlier sketch in CA 21-22
Bulfinch, Thomas 1796-1867 ..... SATA 35
Bulgakov, Mikhail (Afanas'evich) 1891-1940 ... 152
Brief entry 105
See also DAM DRAM, NOV
See also SSC 18
See also TCLC 2, 16
Bulgarin, Faddei Venediktovich 1789-1859 .... DLB
198
Bulger, Bozeman 1877-1932 ..... DLB 171
Bulger, Margaret Anne
See Bulger, Peggy A.
Bulger, Peggy A. 1949- 149
Bulger, William M. 1934- 153
Bulger, William T(homas) 1927- 69-72
Bulgya, Alexander Alexandrovich 1901-1956 Brief
entry 117
See also Fadeyev, Alexander
See also TCLC 53
Bulka, Reuven P(inchas) 1944- CANR-49
Earlier sketch in CA 113
Bulkeley, Christy C. ..... AITN 2
Bulkeley, William M. 1950- 135
Bulkley, Dwight H(atfield) 1919- 105
Bull, Angela (Mary) 1936- CANR-24
Earlier sketches in CA 21-24R, CANR-9
See also SATA 45
Bull, Barry L. 1947- 146
Bull, Christopher Neil 1940- 145
Bull, Emma 1954- 127
See also SATA 99
Bull, Geoffrey Taylor 1921- CANR-3
Earlier sketch in CA 9-12R
Bull, George (Anthony) 1929- CANR-39
Earlier sketch in CA 115
Bull, Guyon B(oys) G(arrett) 1912- CANR-5
Earlier sketch in CA 5-8R
Bull, Hedley Norman 1932-1985 ..... 5-8R
Obituary 116
Bull, John 1914- 69-72
Bull, Norman John 1916- CANR-16
Earlier sketch in CA 93-96
See also SATA 41
Bull, Odd 1907- 81-84
Bull, Peter (Cecil) 1912-1984 ..... CANR-11
Obituary 112
Earlier sketch in CA 25-28R
See also SATA-Obit 39
Bull, Robert J(ehu) 1920- 97-100
Bull, Storm 1913- 9-12R
Bull, William E(merson) 1909-1972 ..... CAP-1
Earlier sketch in CA 13-16
Bulla, Clyde Robert 1914- CANR-40
Earlier sketches in CA 5-8R, CANR-3, 18
See also MAICYA
See also SAAS 6
See also SATA 2, 41, 91
Bullard, Beth 1939- 149
Bullard, E(dgar) John III 1942- 33-36R
Bullard, Fred Mason 1901- 25-28R
Bullard, Helen 1902- CANR-7
Earlier sketch in CA 17-20R
Bullard, Oral 1922- CANR-23
Earlier sketches in CA 61-64, CANR-8
Bullard, Pamela 1948- 106
Bullard, Roger A(ubrey) 1937- 33-36R
Bulle, Florence (Elizabeth) 1925- CANR-15
Earlier sketch in CA 93-96
Bulleid, H(enry) A(nthony) V(aughan) 1912- .....
CANR-13
Earlier sketches in CAP-1, CA 9-10
Bullein, William c. 1520-1576 ..... DLB 167
Bullen, Dana R(ipley) 1931- 73-76
Bullen, Keith Edward 1906-1976 Obituary 106
Bullen, Robert 1926(?)-1976 Obituary 69-72
Buller, Herman 1923- 61-64
Bullett, Gerald (William) 1893-1958 155
Bulliet, Richard W(illiams) 1940- CANR-7
Earlier sketch in CA 57-60
Bullingham, Rodney
See Sladen, Norman St. Barbe
Bullins, Ed 1935- CANR-46
Earlier sketches in CA 49-52, CANR-24
See also CAAS 16
See also BLC 1
See also BW 2
See also CLC 1, 5, 7
See also DAM DRAM, MULT
See also DC 6
See also DLB 7, 38
See also MTCW 1
Bullis, Harry Amos 1890-1963 ..... CAP-2
Earlier sketch in CA 17-18
Bullis, Jerald 1944- CANR-1
Earlier sketch in CA 49-52
Bullitt, John M(arshall) 1921-1985 Obituary 117
Bullitt, Orville H(orwitz) 1894-1979 ..... 33-36R
Obituary 89-92
Bullitt, Stimson 1919- 112
Bullitt, William C(hristian)
1891-1967 Obituary 89-92
Bulloch, John 1928- 134
Bullock, Alan (Louis Charles) 1914- CANR-41
Earlier sketch in CA 1-4R
Bullock, Alice 1904- 89-92
Bullock, Barbara
See Bullock-Wilson, Barbara
Bullock, C(larence) Hassell 1939- 89-92
Bullock, Charles S(pencer) III 1942- CANR-13
Earlier sketch in CA 33-36R
Bullock, Frederick W(illiam) B(agshawe) 1903-(?) ..
CANR-4
Earlier sketch in CA 5-8R
Bullock, Henry 1907(?)-1973 Obituary 41-44R
Bullock, Kathleen (Mary) 1946- ..... SATA 77
Bullock, Michael 1918- CANR-38
Earlier sketches in CA 17-20R, CANR-7
Bullock, Paul 1924-1986 ..... CANR-11
Obituary 118
Earlier sketch in CA 29-32R
Bullock, Robert (D.) 1947- ..... SATA 92
Bullock-Wilson, Barbara 1945- 65-68
Bullough, Bonnie 1927- CANR-49
Earlier sketches in CA 69-72, CANR-11
Bullough, D(onald) A(uberon) 1928- 107
Bullough, Geoffrey 1901-1982 ..... CANR-5
Obituary 106
Earlier sketch in CA 1-4R
Bullough, Robert V., Jr. 1949- 135
Bullough, Vern (LeRoy) 1928- CANR-52
Earlier sketches in CA 9-12R, CANR-4, 11, 26
Bullough, William A(lfred) 1933- 101
Bullrich (Palenque), Silvina 1915- ..... HW
Bulman, Joan (Carroll Boone) 1904- 103
Bulman, Oliver (Meredith Boone)
1902-1974 Obituary 49-52
Bulmer, (Henry) Kenneth 1921- CANR-9
Earlier sketch in CA 13-16R
Bulmer, Martin 1943- 113
Bulmer, Ralph N(eville) H(ermon)
1928-1988 Obituary 126
Bulmer-Thomas, Ivor 1905-1993 ..... CAP-1
Obituary 143
Earlier sketch in CA 11-12
Buloff, Joseph 1899-1985 141
Obituary 115
Bulpin, T(homas) V(ictor) 1918- CANR-4
Earlier sketch in CA 9-12R
Bulpin, (Barbara) Vicki 156
See also SATA 92
Bultmann, Rudolf Karl 1884-1976 ..... CANR-29
Obituary 65-68
Earlier sketch in CA 5-8R
See also MTCW 1
Bulwer-Lytton, Edward (George Earle Lytton)
1803-1873 ..... DLB 21
Bumagin, Victoria E. 1923- 89-92
Bumiller, Elisabeth 1956- 153
Bump, Jerome 1943- 109
Bumppo, Nathaniel John Balthazar 1940- ... 97-100
Bumppo, Natty
See Bumppo, Nathaniel John Balthazar
Bumpus, Jerry 1937- CANR-44
Earlier sketches in CA 65-68, CANR-10
See also DLBY 81
Bumstead, Kathleen Mary 1918-1987 121
See also SATA 53
Bumsted, J(ohn) M(ichael) 1938- 41-44R
Bunce, Alan 1939- 77-80
Bunce, Frank David 1907- CAP-1
Earlier sketch in CA 11-12
Bunce, Linda Susan (Staines) 1956- 107
Bunch, Charlotte (Anne) 1944- CANR-72
Earlier sketch in CA 126
Bunch, Chris(topher R.) 1943- 163
Bunch, Clarence 53-56
Bunch, David R(oosevelt) 29-32R
Bunche, Ralph J(ohnson) 1904-1971 125
Obituary 33-36R
See also BW 2
See also DAM MULT
Bunch-Weeks, Charlotte
See Bunch, Charlotte (Anne)
Bunck, Julie Marie 1960- 148
Bundles, A'Lelia Perry 1952- 144
See also SATA 76
Bundtzen, Lynda K(athryn) 1947- 127
Bundy, Clarence E(verett) 1906- 85-88
Bundy, McGeorge 1919-1996 160
Bundy, William P(utnam) 1917- 104
Bungay, Stephen 1954- 127
Bunge, Mario A(ugusto) 1919- 163
Bunge, Nancy L(iddell) 1942- 124
Bunge, Robert Pierce 1930- 124
Bunge, Walter R(ichard) 1911- 25-28R
Bungert, D. Edward 1957- 140
Bung Karno
See Sukarno, (Ahmed)
Buni, Andrew 1931- 21-24R
Bunim, Amos 1929- 132
Bunim, Irving M. 1901(?)-1980 Obituary 103
Bunin, Catherine 1967- 93-96
See also SATA 30
Bunin, Ivan Alexeyevich 1870-1953 Brief entry . 104
See also SSC 5
See also TCLC 6
Bunin, Sherry 1925- 93-96
See also SATA 30
Buning, Sietze
See Wiersma, Stanley M(arvin)
Bunke, H(arvey) Charles 1922- 9-12R
Bunker, Edward 1933- CANR-65
Earlier sketch in CA 41-44R
Bunker, Gerald Edward 1938- 37-40R
Bunker, Linda K. 1947- CANR-29
Earlier sketch in CA 111
Bunkers, Suzanne L. 1950- 160
Bunn, John T(homas) 1924- 37-40R
Bunn, John W. 1898- CAP-2
Earlier sketch in CA 23-24
Bunn, Ronald F(reeze) 1929- 21-24R
Bunn, Scott (Middelton) 1943- 111
Bunn, Thomas 1944- 69-72
Bunnell, Peter C(urtis) 1937- CANR-30
Earlier sketches in CA 33-36R, CANR-12
Bunnell, William S(tanley) 1925- CAP-1
Earlier sketch in CA 11-12
Bunner, H. C. 1855-1896 ..... DLB 78, 79
Bunt, Lucas N(icolaas) H(endrik) 1905- 69-72
Bunting, A. E.
See Bunting, Anne Evelyn
Bunting, Anne Evelyn 1928- CANR-59
Earlier sketches in CA 53-56, CANR-5, 19
See also Bunting, Eve
See also AAYA 5
See also SATA 18
Bunting, Bainbridge 1913-1981 ..... CANR-8
Earlier sketch in CA 61-64
Bunting, Basil 1900-1985 ..... CANR-7
Obituary 115
Earlier sketch in CA 53-56
See also CLC 10, 39, 47
See also DAM POET
See also DLB 20
Bunting, Eve
See Bunting, Anne Evelyn
See also CLR 28
See also JRDA
See also MAICYA
See also SATA 64
Bunting, Glenn (Davison) 1957- ..... SATA 22
Bunting, Josiah III 1939- CANR-71
Earlier sketch in CA 45-48
Buntline, Ned
See Judson, Edward Zane Carroll
Bunuan, Josefina S(antiago) 1935- 33-36R
Bunuel, Luis 1900-1983 ..... CANR-32
Obituary 110
Earlier sketch in CA 101
See also CLC 16, 80
See also DAM MULT
See also HLC
See also HW
Bunyan, John 1628-1688 ..... CDBLB 1660-1789
See also DA
See also DAB
See also DAC
See also DAM MST
See also DLB 39
See also WLC
Bunzel, John H(arvey) 1924- 17-20R
Bunzel, Ruth L(eah) 1898-1990 Obituary 130
Buol, S(tanley) W(alter) 1934- 49-52
Burack, Abraham Saul 1908-1978 ..... CANR-4
Obituary 77-80
Earlier sketch in CA 9-12R
Burack, Elmer H(oward) 1927- CANR-37
Earlier sketches in CA 37-40R, CANR-16
Burack, Sylvia K. 1916- CANR-9
Earlier sketch in CA 21-24R
See also SATA 35
Burak, Carl S. 1942- 147
Burak, Linda (Gallina) 116
Buranelli, Vincent 1919- CANR-43
Earlier sketches in CA 9-12R, CANR-5, 20
Burbank, Addison (Buswell) 1895-1961 ... SATA 37
Burbank, Garin 1940- 69-72
Burbank, Natt B(ryant) 1903- CAP-2
Earlier sketch in CA 25-28
Burbank, Nelson L(incoln) 1898- CAP-1
Earlier sketch in CA 11-12
Burbank, Rex James 1925- CANR-18
Earlier sketch in CA 1-4R
Burbidge, Peter George 1919-1985 Obituary ... 116
Burbridge, Branse 1921- 97-100
Burby, Raymond J(oseph) III 1942- CANR-11
Earlier sketch in CA 69-72
Burby, William E(dward) 1893- CAP-1
Earlier sketch in CA 11-12
Burch, Claire R. 1925- 101
Burch, Francis F(loyd) 1932- 29-32R
Burch, Geoff 1951- 156
Burch, George Bosworth 1902-1973 122
Obituary 109
Burch, Jennings Michael 1941- 118
Burch, Joann J(ohansen) 142
See also SATA 75
Burch, Mark H(etzel) 1953- 122
Burch, Mary Lou 1914- 104

Burch, Monte G. 1943- 103
Burch, Pat 1944- 57-60
Burch, Philip H. 1930- 106
Burch, Preston M. 1884-1978 Obituary 77-80
Burch, Robert J(oseph) 1925- CANR-71
Earlier sketches in CA 5-8R, CANR-2, 17
See also DLB 52
See also JRDA
See also MAICYA
See also SATA 1, 74
Burcham, Nancy A(nn) 1942- 89-92
Burchard, John Ely 1898-1975 .... CANR-6
Obituary 61-64
Earlier sketch in CA 1-4R
Burchard, Max N(orman) 1925- 21-24R
Burchard, Peter Duncan 1921- CANR-39
Earlier sketches in CA 5-8R, CANR-3, 18
See also MAICYA
See also SAAS 13
See also SATA 5, 74
Burchard, Rachael C(aroline) 1921- 33-36R
Burchard, S. H.
See Burchard, Sue
Burchard, Sue 1937- CANR-19
Earlier sketches in CA 53-56, CANR-4
See also SATA 22
Burchardt, Bill
See Burchardt, William Robert
Burchardt, Nellie 1921- 21-24R
See also SATA 7
Burchardt, William Robert 1917- CANR-16
Earlier sketch in CA 89-92
Burchell, Mary
See Cook, Ida
Burchell, R(obert) A(rthur) 1941- 106
Burchett, Randall E. (?)-1971 .... 1-4R
Obituary 103
Burchett, Wilfred (Graham) 1911-1983 .... CANR-72
Obituary 110
Earlier sketches in CA 49-52, CANR-2
Burchfield, Joe D(onald) 1937- 85-88
Burchfield, Robert William 1923- CANR-35
Earlier sketches in CA 41-44R, CANR-14
Burchill, Julie 1960- 135
Burchwood, Katharine T(yler) 57-60
Burciaga, Jose Antonio 1940-1996 131
Obituary 154
See also DLB 82
See also HW
Burck, Jacob 1907-1982 Obituary 106
Burckel, Nicholas C(lare) 1943- CANR-19
Earlier sketch in CA 103
Burckhardt, C(arl) J(akob) 1891-1974 93-96
Obituary 49-52
Burd, Laurence Hull 1915-1983 Obituary 109
Burd, Van Akin 1914- 41-44R
Burda, R(obert) W(arren) 1932- 73-76
Burdekin, Katharine (Penelope) 1896-1963 162
Burdekin, Kay
See Burdekin, Katharine (Penelope)
Burden, Jean 1914- CANR-3
Earlier sketch in CA 9-12R
Burden, Shirley C. 1909(?)-1989 Obituary 128
Burden, William Douglas 1898-1978 Obituary 81-84
Burder, John 1940- 110
Burdett, John 1951- 151
Burdett, Winston 1913- 29-32R
Burdette, Franklin L. 1911-1975 65-68
Obituary 61-64
Burdge, Rabel J(ames) 1937- 69-72
Burdick, Carol (Ruth) 1928- 132
Burdick, Donald W(alter) 1917- 53-56
Burdick, Eric 1934- 29-32R
Burdick, Eugene (Leonard) 1918-1965 .... CANR-71
Obituary 25-28R
Earlier sketch in CA 5-8R
See also SATA 22
Burdick, Loraine 1929- 57-60
Burdon, R(andal) M(athews) 1896- CAP-1
Earlier sketch in CA 13-14
Bureau, William H(obbs) 1913- 102
Buren, Martha Margareta Elisabet 1910- CAP-1
Earlier sketch in CA 13-14
Burenstam Linder, Staffan
See Linder, Staffan Burenstam
Burfield, Eva
See Ebbett, (Frances) Eva
Burford, Anne M(cGill) 1942- 127
Burford, E(phraim) J(ohn) 1905- CANR-52
Earlier sketch in CA 124
Burford, Eleanor
See Hibbert, Eleanor Alice Burford
Burford, Lolah 1931- CANR-58
Earlier sketch in CA 41-44R
Burford, Roger L(ewis) 1930- 41-44R
Burford, William (Skelly) 1927- CANR-71
Earlier sketches in CA 5-8R, CANR-7
Burg, B(arry) R(ichard) 1938- 129
Burg, Dale R(onda) 1942- CANR-47
Earlier sketches in CA 106, CANR-23
Burg, David
See Dolberg, Alexander
Burg, David F(rederick) 1936- 116
Burge, Doris 1909- 120
Burge, Ethel 1916- 65-68
Burgeon, G. A. L.
See Barfield, (Arthur) Owen
Burger, Albert E. 1941- 37-40R
Burger, Alfred 1905- 122
Burger, Angela Sutherland (Brown) 1936- 81-84
Burger, Carl 1888-1967 .... CAP-2
Earlier sketch in CA 19-20
See also SATA 9
Burger, Chester 1921- 9-12R
Burger, Edward J(ames), Jr. 1933- 110
Burger, George V(anderkarr) 1927- 57-60
Burger, Henry G. 1923- CANR-15
Earlier sketch in CA 41-44R
Burger, Hermann 1942-1989 Obituary 128
Burger, Jack
See Burger, John R(obert)
Burger, Joanna 1941- 136
Burger, John
See Marquard, Leo(pold)
Burger, John R(obert) 1942- 81-84
Burger, Nash K(err) 1908- CAP-2
Earlier sketch in CA 23-24
Burger, Peter
See Buerger, Peter
Burger, Robert E(ugene) 1931- 85-88
Burger, Robert S. 1913- 29-32R
Burger, Ronna Cheryl 1947- 117
Burger, Ruth (Pazen) 1917- 17-20R
Burger, Sarah Greene 1935- 69-72
Burgess, Ann Marie
See Gerson, Noel Bertram
Burgess, Anthony
See Wilson, John (Anthony) Burgess
See also AAYA 25
See also AITN 1
See also CDBLB 1960 to Present
See also CLC 1, 2, 4, 5, 8, 10, 13, 15, 22, 40, 62, 81, 94
See also DAB
See also DLB 14, 194
Burgess, Barbara Hood 1926- 138
See also SATA 69
Burgess, C(hester) F(rancis) 1922- 21-24R
Burgess, Charles (Orville) 1932- 33-36R
Burgess, Christopher Victor 1921- 9-12R
Burgess, Em
See Burgess, Mary Wyche
Burgess, Eric (Alexander) 1912- 101
Burgess, Eric 1920- CANR-42
Earlier sketches in CA 5-8R, CANR-3, 18
Burgess, (Frank) Gelett 1866-1951 Brief entry . 113
See also DLB 11
See also SATA 32
See also SATA-Brief 30
Burgess, Granville Wyche 1947- 137
Burgess, Helen S(teers) 1906-1987 Obituary 123
Burgess, Jackson (Visscher) 1927- 9-12R
Burgess, Jane K. 1928- CANR-42
Earlier sketches in CA 73-76R, CANR-13
Burgess, John H(enry) 1923- 33-36R
Burgess, John Lawie 1912-1987 Obituary 121
Burgess, John W. 1844-1931 .... DLB 47
Burgess, Linda Cannon 1911- 73-76
Burgess, Lorraine Marshall 1913- 106
Burgess, M(argaret) Elaine 13-16R
Burgess, M. R.
See Burgess, Michael (Roy)
Burgess, Mary Wyche 1916- 61-64
See also SATA 18
Burgess, Melvin 1954- 161
See also SATA 96
Burgess, Michael
See Gerson, Noel Bertram
Burgess, Michael (Roy) 1948- CANR-42
Earlier sketches in CA 57-60, CANR-6
Burgess, Mike
See Burgess, Michael (Roy)
Burgess, Norman 1923- 25-28R
Burgess, Patricia 1947- 151
Burgess, Philip M(ark) 1939- CANR-16
Earlier sketch in CA 25-28R
Burgess, Robert F(orrest) 1927- CANR-11
Earlier sketch in CA 25-28R
See also SATA 4
Burgess, Robert H(errmann) 1913- CANR-5
Earlier sketch in CA 9-12R
Burgess, Robert J(ohn) 1961- 143
Burgess, Robert L. 1938- 29-32R
Burgess, Thornton Waldo 1874-1965 .... CANR-41
Earlier sketch in CA 73-76
See also DLB 22
See also MAICYA
See also SATA 17
Burgess, Trevor
See Trevor, Elleston
Burgess, W(arren) Randolph 1889-1978 .... CAP-2
Obituary 81-84
Earlier sketch in CA 29-32
Burgess-Kohn, Jane
See Burgess, Jane K.
Burgett, Donald R(obert) 1925- 21-24R
Burggraaff, Winfield J. 1940- Brief entry 114
Burghard, August 1901- CANR-7
Earlier sketch in CA 17-20R
See also AITN 2
Burghardt, Andrew Frank 1924- 5-8R
Burghardt, Walter J(ohn) 1914- CANR-41
Earlier sketches in CA 1-4R, CANR-4, 19
Burgin, C(harles) David 1939- 73-76
Burgin, (Weston) Richard 1947- 25-28R
Burgos, Joseph A(gner), Jr. 1945- 106
Burgoyne, Bruce E. 1924- 135
Burgoyne, Elizabeth
See Pickles, M(abel) Elizabeth
Burgwyn, Diana 1937- 108
Burgwyn, Mebane Holoman 1914-1992 .... CANR-71
Earlier sketch in CA 49-52
See also SATA 7
Burhoe, Ralph Wendell 1911- 17-20R
Buri, Fritz 1907- CANR-8
Earlier sketch in CA 17-20R
Burian, Jarka M(arsano) 1927- 33-36R
Burian, Richard M(artin) 1941- CANR-47
Earlier sketch in CA 121
Burich, Nancy J(ane) 1943- 29-32R
Burick, Si(mon) 1909-1986 .... CANR-62
Obituary 121
Earlier sketch in CA 85-88
See also DLB 171
Burk, Bill E(ugene) 1932- 65-68
Burk, Bruce 1917- 61-64
Burk, John Daly 1772(?)-1808 .... DLB 37
Burk, Kathleen 1946- 130
Burk, Robert F(redrick) 1955- 134
Burkard, Michael 1947- 132
Burke, Alan Dennis 1949- 106
Burke, Anna Mae Walsh 1938- 111
Burke, Avid J. 1906- 21-24R
Burke, C(letus) J(oseph) 1917-1973 45-48
Burke, Carl F(rancis) 1917- 25-28R
Burke, Carol 1950- CANR-14
Earlier sketch in CA 65-68
Burke, Colin Bradley 1936- CANR-50
Earlier sketch in CA 113
Burke, David 1927- CANR-47
Earlier sketches in CA 105, CANR-23
See also SATA 46
Burke, Desmond William Lardner
See Lardner-Burke, Desmond William
Burke, Dianne O'Quinn 1940- .... SATA 89
Burke, Edmund 1729(?)-1797 .... DA
See also DAB
See also DAC
See also DAM MST
See also DLB 104
See also WLC
Burke, Edmund M. 1928- 9-12R
Burke, Fielding
See Dargan, Olive (Tilford)
Burke, Fred G(eorge) 1926- 13-16R
Burke, Gerald 1914- CANR-1
Earlier sketch in CA 45-48
Burke, J(ohn) Bruce 1933- 37-40R
Burke, J(ackson) F(rederick Augustine) 1915- CANR-12
Earlier sketch in CA 65-68
Burke, James 1936- CANR-28
Earlier sketch in CA 102
Burke, James Lee 1936- CANR-64
Earlier sketches in CA 13-16R, CANR-7, 22, 41
See also CAAS 19
Burke, James Wakefield 1916- CANR-1
Earlier sketch in CA 45-48
Burke, Jan 1953- 142
Burke, John
See O'Connor, Richard
Burke, John (Frederick) 1922- CANR-50
Earlier sketches in CA 5-8R, CANR-9, 25
Burke, John Emmett 1908- 37-40R
Burke, John Garrett 1917- 77-80
Burke, John J(oseph), Jr. 1942- 114
Burke, Jonathan
See Burke, John (Frederick)
Burke, Joseph (Terence Anthony) 1913- 103
Burke, Kenneth (Duva) 1897-1993 .... CANR-39
Obituary 143
Earlier sketch in CA 5-8R
See also CLC 2, 24
See also DLB 45, 63
See also MTCW 1
Burke, Leda
See Garnett, David
Burke, Maggie
See Snyder, Marilyn
Burke, Martyn 1947(?)- 144
Burke, (Omar) Michael 1927- 73-76
Burke, Owen
See Burke, John (Frederick)
Burke, (Ulick) Peter 1937- CANR-63
Earlier sketches in CA 25-28R, CANR-16
Burke, Phyllis 1951- 164
Burke, Ralph
See Garrett, (Gordon) Randall (Phillip) and Silverberg, Robert
Burke, Richard C(ullen) 1932- 53-56
Burke, Richard E. 1953- 143
Burke, Robert E(ugene) 1921- 21-24R
Burke, Russell 1946- 33-36R
Burke, S(amuel) M(artin) 1906- 49-52
Burke, Sean 1961- 151
Burke, Shifty
See Benton, Peggie
Burke, Stanley 1923- 101
Burke, T(homas) Patrick 1934- 121
Burke, Ted 1934(?)-1978 Obituary 77-80
Burke, Thomas 1886-1945 155
Brief entry 113
See also DLB 197
See also TCLC 63
Burke, Tom 73-76
Burke, Vee
See Burke, Velma Whitgrove
Burke, Velma Whitgrove 1921- CANR-4
Earlier sketch in CA 53-56
Burke, Vincent John 1919-1973 122
Obituary 111
Burke, Virginia M. 1916- 45-48
Burke, W. Warner 1935- CANR-14
Earlier sketch in CA 37-40R
Burkert, Nancy Ekholm 1933- .... MAICYA
See also SAAS 14
See also SATA 24
Burkert, Walter 1931- CANR-34
Earlier sketch in CA 103
Burket, Harriet 1908- 37-40R
Burkett, David (Young III) 1934- CANR-9
Earlier sketch in CA 65-68
Burkett, Eva M(ae) 1903- 33-36R
Burkett, Jack 1914- 101
Burkett, Larry 1939- 140
Burkett, Molly 1932- CANR-9
Earlier sketch in CA 53-56
Burke-Weiner, Kimberly 1962- 160
See also SATA 95
Burkey, Richard M(ichael) 1930- 93-96
Burkey, Stan 1938- 144
Burkhalter, Barton R. 1938- CANR-11
Earlier sketch in CA 25-28R
Burkhardt, Richard Wellington 1918- 1-4R
Burkhart, Charles 1924- 13-16R
Burkhart, James A(ustin) 1914-1979 .... 9-12R
Burkhart, John E(rnest) 1927- 116
Burkhart, Kathryn Watterson 1942- CANR-34
Earlier sketch in CA 45-48
Burkhart, Kitsi
See Burkhart, Kathryn Watterson
Burkhart, Robert E(dward) 1937- 29-32R
Burkhead, Jesse 1916- CANR-3
Earlier sketch in CA 1-4R
Burkholder, J(ames) Peter 1954- 119
Burkholder, John Richard 1928- CANR-37
Earlier sketch in CA 115
Burkholz, Herbert 1932- CANR-41
Earlier sketches in CA 25-28R, CANR-11
Burkill, T(om) A(lec) 1912- 33-36R
Burkitt, Denis (Parsons) 1911-1993 112
Obituary 141
Burkitt, Ian 1956- 144
Burkle, Howard R(ussell) 1925- Brief entry 107
Burkman, Katherine H. 1934- 29-32R
Burkowsky, Mitchell R(oy) 1931- 29-32R
Burks, Ardath Walter 1915- 107
Burks, Arthur W(alter) 1915- CANR-48
Earlier sketch in CA 49-52
Burks, Brian 1955- 160
See also SATA 95
Burks, David D. 1924- 33-36R
Burks, Edward C. 1921(?)-1983 Obituary 111
Burks, Gordon E(ngledow) 1904- 1-4R
Burks, Jean M. 1949- 151
Burks, Ned
See Burks, Edward C.
Burl, (Harry) Aubrey (Woodruff) 1926- 97-100
Burland, Brian (Berkeley) 1931- CANR-23
Earlier sketches in CA 13-16R, CANR-7
See also SATA 34
Burland, C. A.
See Burland, Cottie (Arthur)
Burland, Cottie (Arthur) 1905- CANR-72
Earlier sketches in CA 5-8R, CANR-5
See also SATA 5
Burleigh, Anne Husted 1941- 29-32R
Burleigh, David Robert 1907- 1-4R
Burleigh, John H. S. 1894-1985 Obituary 116
Burleigh, Michael 1955- 135
Burleigh, Robert 1936- 166
See also SATA 55, 98
Burlew, A(nn) Kathleen 145
Burley, George (Joseph) 1939- Brief entry 107
Burley, W(illiam) J(ohn) 1914- CANR-55
Earlier sketches in CA 33-36R, CANR-13, 29
Burling, Robbins 1926- 17-20R
Burling, William J. 1949- 145
Burlingame, Edward Livermore 1848-1922 .... DLB 79
Burlingame, (William) Roger 1889-1967 .... CANR-72
Earlier sketch in CA 5-8R
See also SATA 2
Burlingame, Virginia (Struble) 1900- CAP-2
Earlier sketch in CA 23-24
Burlingham, Dorothy (Tiffany) 1891-1979 109
Obituary 93-96
Burma, John H(armon) 1913- CANR-5
Earlier sketch in CA 1-4R
Burman, Alice Caddy 1896(?)-1977 .... SATA-Obit 24
Burman, Ben Lucien 1896-1984 .... CANR-32
Obituary 114
Earlier sketches in CA 5-8R, CANR-8
See also SATA 6
See also SATA-Obit 40
Burman, Edward 1947- 134
Burman, Jose Lionel 1917- CANR-53
Earlier sketches in CA 109, CANR-28
Burmeister, Edwin 1939- CANR-26
Earlier sketch in CA 29-32R
Burmeister, Eva (Elizabeth) 1899- CAP-1
Earlier sketch in CA 13-14
Burmeister, Jon 1933- 29-32R
Burmeister, Lou E(lla) 1928- CANR-26
Earlier sketch in CA 45-48
Burn, A(ndrew) R(obert) 1902- CANR-72
Earlier sketches in CA 1-4R, CANR-1, 17
Burn, Barbara 1940- CANR-17
Earlier sketch in CA 85-88
Burn, Doris 1923- 29-32R
See also SATA 1
Burn, Duncan (Lyall) 1902-1988 Obituary 124
Burn, Gordon 1948- 123
Burn, J(oshua) Harold 1892-1982 .... CAP-1
Obituary 108
Earlier sketch in CA 11-12
Burn, Mary (Wynn) 1910- 122
Burnaby, John 1891-1978 .... CAP-1
Obituary 104
Earlier sketch in CA 13-14
Burnam, Tom 1913- 61-64
Burne, Glen
See Green, Alan (Baer)
Burne, Glenn S. 1921- 21-24R
Burne, Kevin G. 1925- 13-16R
Burner, David (B.) 1937- CANR-48
Earlier sketches in CA 25-28R, CANR-10
Burnes, Caroline
See Haines, Carolyn
Burness, Tad
See Burness, Wallace B(inny)

Burness, Wallace B(inny) 1933- CANR-21
Earlier sketch in CA 69-72
Burnet, George Bain 1894- CAP-2
Earlier sketch in CA 23-24
Burnet, Gilbert 1643-1715 .... DLB 101
Burnet, Jean R. 1920- 130
Burnet, (Frank) Macfarlane 1899-1985 ... CANR-70
Obituary 117
Earlier sketch in CA 73-76
Burnet, Mary E(dith) 1911- 53-56
Burnett, Alan 1932- 146
Burnett, Alfred David 1937- CANR-41
Earlier sketches in CA 102, CANR-19
Burnett, Anne Pippin 1925- 113
Burnett, Avis 1937- 41-44R
Burnett, Ben G(eorge) 1924-1975 .... CANR-3
Earlier sketch in CA 1-4R
Burnett, Calvin 1921- 33-36R
Burnett, Carol 1933- 127
Burnett, Collins W. 1914- CANR-3
Earlier sketch in CA 9-12R
Burnett, Constance Buel 1893-1975 ..... CANR-72
Earlier sketch in CA 5-8R
See also SATA 36
Burnett, David (Benjamin Foley) 1931-1971 .. 9-12R
Obituary 33-36R
Burnett, David (Alan) 1946- 121
Burnett, Dorothy Kirk 1924- 5-8R
Burnett, Frances (Eliza) Hodgson 1849-1924 ... 136
Brief entry 108
See also CLR 24
See also DLB 42, 141
See also DLBD 13, 14
See also JRDA
See also MAICYA
See also SATA 100
See also YABC 2
Burnett, Gail Lemley 1953- 151
Burnett, Hallie Southgate (Zeisel) 1909(?)-1991 ....
CANR-37
Obituary 135
Earlier sketches in CA 13-16R, CANR-6
Burnett, Janet 1915- 49-52
Burnett, Joe Ray 1928- 17-20R
Burnett, John 1925- 57-60
Burnett, June 1936- 113
Burnett, Laurence 1907- 49-52
Burnett, Leo 1891-1971 Obituary 116
Burnett, Leon R. 1925(?)-1983 Obituary 109
Burnett, Ron 1947- 157
Burnett, Virgil 1928- 161
Burnett, W(illiam) R(iley) 1899-1982 ..... CANR-59
Obituary 106
Earlier sketches in CA 5-8R, CANR-22
See also DLB 9
Burnett, Whit(ney Ewing) 1899-1973 .... CAP-2
Obituary 41-44R
Earlier sketch in CA 13-14
See also DLB 137
Burnette, O(llen) Lawrence, Jr. 1927- 33-36R
Burney, Anton
See Hopkins, (Hector) Kenneth
Burney, Elizabeth (Mary) 1934- 21-24R
Burney, Eugenia 1913- 29-32R
Burney, Fanny 1752-1840 .... DLB 39
Burnford, S. D.
See Burnford, Sheila (Philip Cochrane Every)
Burnford, Sheila (Philip Cochrane Every)
1918-1984 .... CANR-49
Obituary 112
Earlier sketches in CA 1-4R, CANR-1
See also CLR 2
See also JRDA
See also MAICYA
See also SATA 3
See also SATA-Obit 38
Burnham, Alan 1913-1984 .... 13-16R
Obituary 112
Burnham, Charles
See Paine, Lauran (Bosworth)
Burnham, David (Bright) 1933- CANR-48
Earlier sketch in CA 122
Burnham, Dorothy E(dith) 1921- 65-68
Burnham, (Linden) Forbes (Sampson)
1923-1985 Obituary 117
Burnham, J. W.
See Burnham, Jack (Wesley)
Burnham, Jack (Wesley) 1931- 115
Burnham, James 1905-1987 Obituary 123
Burnham, John
See Beckwith, Burnham Putnam
Burnham, John C(hynoweth) 1929- 33-36R
Burnham, Linda Frye 1940- 125
Burnham, Richard 1940- 118
Burnham, Robert Ward, Jr. 1913- 17-20R
Burnham, Sophy 1936- CANR-38
Earlier sketch in CA 41-44R
See also AITN 1
See also SATA 65
Burnham, Walter Dean 1930- 101
Burnim, Kalman A(aron) 1928- 1-4R
Burningham, John (Mackintosh) 1936- CANR-36
Earlier sketch in CA 73-76
See also CLR 9
See also MAICYA
See also SATA 16, 59
Burnley, (John) David 1941- CANR-40
Earlier sketch in CA 117
Burnley, Judith CANR-16
Earlier sketch in CA 97-100
Interview in CANR-16
Burns, Aidan 1943- 121
Burns, Ailsa (Milligan) 1930- 148
Burns, Alan 1929- CANR-34
Earlier sketches in CA 9-12R, CANR-5
See also DLB 14, 194
Burns, Alan Cuthbert 1887-1980 Obituary 102
Burns, Allan P. 1935- 125
Burns, Alma 1919- 81-84
Burns, Arthur F(rank) 1904-1987 .... CANR-46
Obituary 122
Earlier sketch in CA 13-16R
Burns, Betty 1909- CAP-2
Earlier sketch in CA 19-20
Burns, Bobby
See Burns, Vincent Godfrey
Burns, Carol 1934- 29-32R
Burns, Chester R(ay) 1937- 103
Burns, David D. 1942- 114
Burns, Deborah E(dwards) 1951- 147
Burns, Diane L. 1950- CANR-55
Earlier sketch in CA 135
See also SAAS 24
See also SATA 81
Burns, E(dward) Bradford 1932- CANR-72
Earlier sketch in CA 17-20R
Burns, Edward McNall 1897-1972 .... 1-4R
Obituary 103
Burns, Eedson Louis Millard 1897-1985 ... CANR-5
Obituary 117
Earlier sketch in CA 5-8R
Burns, Eveline M(abel Richardson)
1900-1985 Obituary 117
Burns, Florence M. 1905-1988 .... SATA 61
Burns, Geoff 1954- 115
Burns, George 1896-1996 .... CANR-63
Obituary 151
Earlier sketch in CA 112
See also BEST 89:2
Burns, Gerald P(hillip) 1918- 17-20R
Burns, Grant (Francis) 1947- 146
Burns, Helen M(arie) 1922- 110
Burns, Hobert Warren 1925- CANR-47
Earlier sketch in CA 1-4R
Burns, James MacGregor 1918- CANR-43
Earlier sketches in CA 5-8R, CANR-19
Burns, James W(illiam) 1937- 33-36R
Burns, Jean (Ellen) 1934- 103
Burns, Jim 1936- 101
Burns, Jimmy 1953- 134
Burns, Joan Simpson 1927- 65-68
Burns, John Horne 1916-1953 Brief entry 115
See also DLBY 85
Burns, John McLauren 1932- Brief entry 109
Burns, John V. 1907- CAP-2
Earlier sketch in CA 33-36
Burns, Ken(neth Lauren) 1953- 141
Burns, Khephra 1950- 156
See also SATA 92
Burns, Marilyn 1941- 161
See also SATA 96
See also SATA-Brief 33
Burns, Michael 1947- 121
Burns, Norman T(homas) 1930- 69-72
Burns, Olive Ann 1924-1990 .... CANR-41
Obituary 132
Earlier sketch in CA 120
See also SATA 65
Burns, Paul C. CANR-4
Earlier sketch in CA 1-4R
See also SATA 5
Burns, Ralph 1949- 162
Burns, Ralph J. 1901- CAP-2
Earlier sketch in CA 25-28
Burns, Ray
See Burns, Raymond (Howard)
Burns, Raymond (Howard) 1924- .... SATA 9
Burns, Rex (Sehler) 1935- CANR-13
Earlier sketch in CA 77-80
Burns, Ric 1955(?)- 141
Burns, Richard (William) 1958-1992 ..... CANR-60
Obituary 139
Earlier sketch in CA 128
Burns, Richard Dean 1929- CANR-8
Earlier sketch in CA 17-20R
Burns, Richard Gordon 1925- 142
Burns, Richard W(ebster) 1920- 69-72
Burns, Rio
See Burns, Deborah E(dwards)
Burns, Robert 1759-1796 .... CDBLB 1789-1832
See also DA
See also DAB
See also DAC
See also DAM MST, POET
See also DLB 109
See also PC 6
See also WLC
Burns, Robert E(lliott) 1891(?)-1955 138
Burns, Robert Edward 1919- 111
Burns, Robert Grant 1938- CANR-16
Earlier sketch in CA 25-28R
Burns, Robert I(gnatius) 1921- CANR-52
Earlier sketches in CA 17-20R, CANR-7, 26
Burns, Robert M(ilton) C(lark), Jr. 1940- 102
Burns, Ruby V(ermillion) 1901- 106
Burns, Scott
See Burns, Robert M(ilton) C(lark), Jr.
Burns, Sheila
See Bloom, Ursula (Harvey)
Burns, Stanley B(enjamin) 1938- 147
Burns, Stuart L(eroy) 1932- 127
Burns, Tex
See L'Amour, Louis (Dearborn)
Burns, Theresa 1961- .... SATA 84
Burns, Thomas (Jr.) 1928- CANR-14
Earlier sketch in CA 41-44R
Burns, Thomas J. 1942- 127
Burns, Thomas Stephen 1927- CANR-45
Earlier sketch in CA 49-52
Burns, Tom 1913- CANR-22
Earlier sketches in CA 5-8R, CANR-5
Burns, Vincent Godfrey 1893-1979 .... 41-44R
Obituary 85-88
See also AITN 2
Burns, Wayne 1918- CANR-1
Earlier sketch in CA 1-4R
Burns, William A. 1909- CANR-11
Earlier sketches in CAP-1, CA 13-14
See also SATA 5
Burns, Zed H(ouston) 1903- 33-36R
Burns-Bisogno, Louisa 1936- 134
Burnshaw, Stanley 1906- 9-12R
See also CLC 3, 13, 44
See also DLB 48
See also DLBY 97
Burnside, John 1955- 153
Burnside, Wesley M(ason) 1918- 65-68
Buros, Oscar Krisen 1905-1978 Obituary 77-80
Burow, Daniel R(obert) 1931- CANR-11
Earlier sketch in CA 29-32R
Burr, Alfred Gray 1919- 25-28R
Burr, Anne 1937- 25-28R
See also CLC 6
Burr, C. Chauncey 1815(?)-1883 .... DLB 79
Burr, Charles 1922(?)-1976 Obituary 69-72
Burr, Dan 1951- .... SATA 65
Burr, Esther Edwards 1732-1758 .... DLB 200
Burr, Gray 1919- 69-72
Burr, John R(oy) 1933- CANR-45
Earlier sketch in CA 45-48
Burr, Keith 1946- 115
Burr, Lonnie 1943- 103
See also SATA 47
Burr, Samuel Engle, Jr. 1897-1987 Obituary ... 124
Burr, Wesley R(ay) 1936- 37-40R
Burrell, Berkeley G(raham) 1919-1979 ..... 33-36R
Obituary 89-92
Burrell, David B(akewell) 1933- 33-36R
Burrell, Evelyn Patterson 1920- CANR-7
Earlier sketch in CA 53-56
Burrell, Roy E(ric) C(harles) 1923- 33-36R
See also SATA 72
Burridge, Kenelm (Oswald Lancelot) 1922- ....
CANR-70
Earlier sketch in CA 93-96
Burridge, Trevor David 1932- 137
Burrin, Frank K. 1920- 25-28R
Burrington, David E. 1931- 73-76
Burris, B. C(ullen) 1924- 21-24R
Burris-Meyer, Harold 1902- 41-44R
Burros, Marian (Fox) CANR-30
Earlier sketch in CA 89-92
Burrough, Bryan 1961- 140
See also BEST 90:3
Burroughs, Ben(jamin F.) 1918-1980 65-68
Obituary 122
Burroughs, Edgar Rice 1875-1950 132
Brief entry 104
See also AAYA 11
See also DAM NOV
See also DLB 8
See also MTCW 1
See also SATA 41
See also TCLC 2, 32
Burroughs, Jean Mitchell 1908- 65-68
See also SATA 28
Burroughs, John 1837-1921 167
Brief entry 109
See also DLB 64
Burroughs, Margaret G.
See Burroughs, Margaret Taylor (Goss)
Burroughs, Margaret Taylor (Goss) 1917- ....
CANR-25
Earlier sketch in CA 21-24R
See also BW 1
See also DLB 41
Burroughs, Polly 1925- 25-28R
See also SATA 2
Burroughs, Raleigh (Simpson) 1901- 106
Burroughs, William (Seward), Jr. 1947-1981 .. 73-76
Obituary 112
See also DLB 16
Burroughs, William James 1942- 144
Burroughs, William S(eward) 1914-1997 . CANR-52
Obituary 160
Earlier sketches in CA 9-12R, CANR-20
See also AITN 2
See also CLC 1, 2, 5, 15, 22, 42, 75, 109
See also DA
See also DAB
See also DAC
See also DAM MST, NOV, POP
See also DLB 2, 8, 16, 152
See also DLBY 81, 97
See also MTCW 1
See also WLC
Burrow, James Gordon 1922- CANR-2
Earlier sketch in CA 5-8R
Burrow, John A(nthony) 1932- 97-100
Burrow, John W(yon) 1935- CANR-30
Earlier sketches in CA 21-24R, CANR-12
Burroway, Janet (Gay) 1936- CANR-44
Earlier sketches in CA 21-24R, CANR-12
See also CAAS 6
See also DLB 6
See also SATA 23
Burrowes, Michael Anthony Bernard 1937- 103
Burrowes, Mike
See Burrowes, Michael Anthony Bernard
Burrows, Abe
See Burrows, Abram Solman
Burrows, Abram Solman 1910-1985 110
Obituary 116
Burrows, David J(ames) 1936- 41-44R
Burrows, E(dwin) G(ladding) 1917- CANR-14
Earlier sketch in CA 77-80
Burrows, Fredrika Alexander 1908- CANR-6
Earlier sketch in CA 57-60
Burrows, James C. 1944- 29-32R
Burrows, John 1945- CANR-69
Earlier sketch in CA 101
Burrows, Miles 1936- 21-24R
Burrows, Millar 1889-1980 .... CANR-72
Obituary 97-100
Earlier sketch in CA 81-84
Burrows, William E. 1937- 65-68
Burrows, William R(ichard) 1942- 117
Burrup, Percy E. 1910- 1-4R
Bursk, Christopher 1943- CANR-24
Earlier sketch in CA 85-88
Bursk, Edward C(ollins) 1907-1990 .... CANR-5
Obituary 130
Earlier sketch in CA 1-4R
Burstall, Aubrey F(rederic) 1902-1984 Obituary . 113
Burstein, Alvin G(eorge) 1931- 85-88
Burstein, Chaya M(alamud) 1923- CANR-53
Earlier sketch in CA 126
See also SATA 64
Burstein, Fred 1950- 151
See also SATA 83
Burstein, John 1949- CANR-21
Earlier sketch in CA 69-72
See also SATA 54
See also SATA-Brief 40
Burstein, Patricia (Ann) 1945- 108
Burstein, Paul 1946- 123
Burstiner, Irving 1919- 104
Burston, Daniel 1954- 158
Burston, W. H. 1915-1981 Obituary 103
Burstow, Bonnie 1945- 145
Burstyn, Harold L(ewis) 1930- CANR-5
Earlier sketch in CA 9-12R
Burt, Al(vin Victor, Jr.) 1927- 25-28R
Burt, Alfred LeRoy 1888- CAP-1
Earlier sketch in CA 9-10
Burt, Cyril (Lodowic) 1883-1971 .... CAP-1
Obituary 33-36R
Earlier sketch in CA 13-14
Burt, Donald X(avier) 1929- CANR-39
Earlier sketch in CA 116
Burt, Frances R(iemer) 1917- 69-72
Burt, Jesse Clifton 1921-1976 .... CANR-4
Earlier sketch in CA 9-12R
See also SATA 46
See also SATA-Obit 20
Burt, John J. 1934- CANR-11
Earlier sketch in CA 29-32R
Burt, Larry W(ayne) 1950- 122
Burt, Leonard James 1892-1983 Obituary 114
Burt, Mala S(chuster) 1943- 112
Burt, Maxwell Struthers 1882-1954 .... DLB 86
See also DLBD 16
Burt, Nathaniel 1913- CANR-72
Earlier sketch in CA 17-20R
Burt, Olive Woolley 1894-1981 .... CANR-71
Earlier sketches in CA 5-8R, CANR-5
See also SATA 4
Burt, Robert Amsterdam 1939- 102
Burt, Roger B(ivens) 1939- 113
Burt, Samuel M(athew) 1915- 21-24R
Burt, Simon 1947- 123
Burt, William Henry 1903- 106
Burtch, Brian 1949- 148
Burtchaell, James Tunstead 1934- CANR-52
Earlier sketches in CA 25-28R, CANR-11, 27
Burtis, C(harles) Edward 1907- 41-44R
Burtle, James (L.) 1919- Brief entry 113
Burtless, Gary 1950- 144
Burtness, Paul Sidney 1923- 17-20R
Burton, Anne
See Bowen-Judd, Sara (Hutton)
Burton, Anthony 1933- 61-64
Burton, Anthony 1934- 97-100
Burton, Arthur 1914-1982 .... CANR-10
Earlier sketch in CA 21-24R
Burton, Carl D. 1913- 1-4R
Burton, David H(enry) 1925- CANR-3
Earlier sketch in CA 49-52
Burton, Dolores Marie 1932- 25-28R
Burton, Dwight L(owell) 1922- 61-64
Burton, Edward J. 1917- 21-24R
Burton, (Alice) Elizabeth 1908- CANR-72
Earlier sketches in CA 65-68, CANR-15
Burton, Gabrielle 1939- 45-48
Burton, Genevieve 1912- 33-36R
Burton, Gennett 1945- 160
See also SATA 95
Burton, H(arry) M(cGuire Philip)
1898(?)-1979 Obituary 93-96
Burton, Hal
See Burton, Harold Bernard
Burton, Harold Bernard 1908-1992 ...... CANR-70
Earlier sketch in CA 97-100
Burton, Hester (Wood-Hill) 1913- CANR-10
Earlier sketch in CA 9-12R
See also CLR 1
See also DLB 161
See also MAICYA
See also SAAS 8
See also SATA 7, 74
Burton, Ian 1935- 17-20R
Burton, Ivor Flower 1923- 109
Burton, Jane 1933- CANR-29
Earlier sketch in CA 105
Burton, Joe Wright 1907-1976 107
Burton, John A(ndrew) 1944- CANR-14
Earlier sketch in CA 65-68
Burton, John Wear 1915- 103
Burton, Katherine (Kurz) 1890-1969 ..... CANR-71
Earlier sketch in CA 77-80
Burton, L(awrence) DeVere 1943- 156
Burton, Lady Isabel Arundell 1831-1896 ... DLB 166

Burton, Leslie
See McGuire, Leslie (Sarah)
Burton, Levar 1957- ... 166
Burton, Lindy 1937- ... 25-28R
Burton, Lloyd E. 1922- ... 53-56
Burton, M. Garlinda 1958- ... 156
Burton, Marilee Robin 1950- ... CANR-46
Earlier sketch in CA 121
See also SATA 46, 82
Burton, Martin A. 1911-1984 Obituary ... 114
Burton, Mary E(lizabeth) 1900- ... 106
Burton, Maurice 1898-1992 ... CANR-29
Obituary ... 139
Earlier sketches in CA 65-68, CANR-9
See also SATA 23
Burton, Miles
See Rhode, John
Burton, Nelson, Jr. 1942- ... 57-60
Burton, Orville Vernon 1947- ... 126
Burton, Philip 1904-1995 ... 25-28R
Obituary ... 147
Burton, Richard 1925-1984 Obituary ... 113
Burton, Richard F. 1821-1890 ... DLB 55, 184
Burton, Robert 1577-1640 ... DLB 151
Burton, Robert (Wellesley) 1941- ... CANR-29
Earlier sketches in CA 45-48, CANR-1, 17
See also SATA 22
Burton, Robert E(dward) 1927- ... CANR-13
Earlier sketch in CA 61-64
Burton, Robert H(enderson) 1934- ... 37-40R
Burton, Roger V(ernon) 1928- ... 45-48
Burton, S(amuel) H(olroyd) 1919- ... 102
Burton, Sandra ... 132
Burton, Sir Richard Francis 1821-1890 ... DLB 166
Burton, Thomas
See Longstreet, Stephen
Burton, Thomas G(len) 1935- ... 145
Burton, Tim 1958- ... 148
See also AAYA 14
Burton, Virginia Lee 1909-1968 ... CAP-1
Obituary ... 25-28R
Earlier sketch in CA 13-14
See also CLR 11
See also DLB 22
See also MAICYA
See also SATA 2, 100
Burton, William Evans 1804-1860 ... DLB 73
Burton, William H(enry) 1890-1964 ... CANR-1
Earlier sketch in CA 1-4R
See also SATA 11
Burton, William L(ester) 1928- ... 21-24R
Burton-Bradley, Burton Gyrth 1914- ... 77-80
Burtschi, Mary 1911- ... CANR-19
Earlier sketches in CA 9-12R, CANR-5
Burtt, Edwin Arthur 1892-1989 ... 5-8R
Obituary ... 129
Burtt, Everett Johnson, Jr. 1914- ... 9-12R
Burtt, George 1914- ... CANR-11
Earlier sketch in CA 61-64
Burtt, Harold E(rnest) 1890- ... CAP-2
Earlier sketch in CA 17-18
Burtt, Shelley 1959- ... 139
Buruma, Ian 1951- ... CANR-65
Earlier sketch in CA 128
Burwash, Peter 1945- ... 119
Burwell, Adam Hood 1790-1849 ... DLB 99
Burwell, Jennifer 1962- ... 166
Bury, Frank
See Harris, Herbert
Bury, J(ohn) P(atrick) T(uer) 1908- ... 17-20R
Bury, Lady Charlotte 1775-1861 ... DLB 116
Buryn, Ed(ward Casimir) 1934- ... 85-88
Busbee, Shirlee (Elaine) 1941- ... CANR-60
Earlier sketch in CA 77-80
Busby, Edith (A. Lake) (?)-1964 Obituary ... 109
See also SATA-Obit 29
Busby, F. M. 1921- ... CANR-49
Earlier sketches in CA 65-68, CANR-9, 24
Busby, John 1928- ... CANR-39
Earlier sketch in CA 116
Busby, Mabel Janice
See Stanford, Sally
Busby, Mark 1945- ... 151
Busby, Roger (Charles) 1941- ... CANR-60
Earlier sketch in CA 105
Buscaglia, (Felice) Leo(nardo) 1924- ... CANR-30
Brief entry ... 110
Earlier sketch in CA 112
Interview in ... CANR-30
See also Buscaglia, Leo F.
See also DAM POP
See also SATA 65
Buscaglia, Leo F.
See Buscaglia, (Felice) Leo(nardo)
See also BEST 89:4
Busch, Briton Cooper 1936- ... CANR-36
Earlier sketches in CA 21-24R, CANR-8
Busch, Charles 1954- ... 145
Busch, Francis X(avier) 1879-1975 ... CAP-1
Obituary ... 61-64
Earlier sketch in CA 13-14
Busch, Frederick 1941- ... CANR-45
Earlier sketch in CA 33-36R
See also CAAS 1
See also CLC 7, 10, 18, 47
See also DLB 6
Busch, Hans (Peter) 1914-1996 ... 109
Obituary ... 153
Busch, Julia 1940- ... CANR-39
Earlier sketch in CA 57-60
Busch, Lawrence (Michael) 1945- ... 161
Busch, Niven 1903-1991 ... CANR-7
Obituary ... 135
Earlier sketch in CA 13-16R
See also DLB 44
Busch, Noel F(airchild) 1906-1985 ... 49-52
Obituary ... 117
Busch, Phyllis S. 1909- ... CANR-71
Earlier sketch in CA 107
See also SATA 30
Busch, Ronald 1928-1987 Obituary ... 123
Buschkuehl, Matthias 1953- ... CANR-47
Earlier sketch in CA 121
Buschkuhl, Matthias
See Buschkuehl, Matthias
Buse, D(ieter) K(urt) 1941- ... 137
Buse, R. F.
See Buse, Renee
Buse, Renee 1914(?)-1979 Obituary ... 85-88
Buse, Rueben C. 1932- ... 109
Buser, Pierre 1921- ... 146
Busey, James L. 1916- ... 5-8R
Bush, Alan (Dudley) 1900-1995 ... 110
Obituary ... 150
Bush, Anne Kelleher 1959- ... 151
See also SATA 97
Bush, Barbara (Pierce) 1925- ... 141
Bush, Barbara Holstein 1935- ... CANR-12
Earlier sketch in CA 69-72
Bush, Barney (Furman) 1946- ... 145
See also NNAL
Bush, Barry (Michael) 1938- ... 110
Bush, Catherine 1961- ... 151
Bush, Charlie Christmas 1885-1973 ... CANR-58
Obituary ... 104
Earlier sketch in CA 107
Bush, Christopher
See Bush, Charlie Christmas
Bush, Clifford L(ewis) 1915- ... 33-36R
Bush, Donald J(ohn) ... 114
Bush, (John Nash) Douglas 1896-1983 ... CANR-41
Obituary ... 109
Earlier sketch in CA 37-40R
Bush, Duncan 1946- ... 153
Bush, Eric Wheler 1899-1985 ... 65-68
Obituary ... 117
Bush, Frederic W(illiam) 1929- ... 125
Bush, George Edward, Jr. 1938- ... 109
Bush, George P(ollock) 1892- ... 17-20R
Bush, George S(idney) 1925- ... 110
Bush, Grace A(bhau) 1936- ... 104
Bush, Ian (Elcock) 1928-1986 ... 157
Bush, Jim 1926- ... 57-60
Bush, John W(illiam) 1917-1976 ... CAP-2
Earlier sketch in CA 33-36
Bush, L(uther) Russ(ell III) 1944- ... CANR-47
Earlier sketch in CA 121
Bush, Larry
See Bush, Lawrence Dana
Bush, Lawrence Dana 1951- ... 109
Bush, Lewis William 1907- ... 81-84
Bush, M(ichael) L(accohee) 1938- ... 132
Bush, Martin H(arry) 1930- ... CANR-71
Earlier sketches in CA 29-32R, CANR-12
Bush, Patricia (Jahns) 1932- ... CANR-24
Earlier sketch in CA 105
Bush, Richard C(larence) 1923- Brief entry ... 114
Bush, Robert (Burton) 1917- ... 116
Bush, Robert (Ray) 1920-1972 Obituary ... 33-36R
Bush, Ronald 1946- ... 136
See also CLC 34
Bush, Sargent, Jr. 1937- ... CANR-56
Earlier sketches in CA 65-68, CANR-29
Bush, Susan 1933- ... 127
Bush, Ted J. 1922- ... 17-20R
Bush, Vannevar 1890-1974 ... 97-100
Obituary ... 53-56
Bush, William (Shirley, Jr.) 1929- ... CANR-32
Earlier sketches in CA 37-40R, CANR-14
Busha, Charles Henry 1931- ... CANR-5
Earlier sketch in CA 53-56
Bush-Brown, Albert 1926- ... 128
Bush-Brown, James 1892-1985 ... 5-8R
Obituary ... 118
Bush-Brown, Louise 1896(?)-1973 Obituary ... 49-52
Bushell, Agnes 1949- ... 135
Bushell, Don(ald Gair), Jr. 1934- Brief entry ... 113
Bushell, Raymond 1910-1998 ... CANR-20
Obituary ... 164
Earlier sketches in CA 13-16R, CANR-5
Bushey, Jeanne 1944- ... 149
Bushey, Jerry 1941- ... CANR-25
Earlier sketch in CA 108
Bushinsky, Jay (Joseph Mason) 1932- ... 77-80
Bushman, Claudia L(auper) 1934- ... CANR-22
Earlier sketch in CA 106
Bushman, Richard L(yman) 1931- ... CANR-22
Earlier sketch in CA 21-24R
Bushmiller, Ernest Paul 1905-1982 ... 29-32R
Obituary ... 107
See also Bushmiller, Ernie
See also AITN 1
Bushmiller, Ernie
See Bushmiller, Ernest Paul
See also SATA-Obit 31
Bushnell, Candace 1959(?)- ... 163
Bushnell, David S(herman) 1927- ... 41-44R
Bushnell, Horace 1802-1876 ... DLBD 13
Bushnell, Jack 1952- ... 151
See also SATA 86
Bushong, Carolyn N(ordin) 1947- ... 164
Bushrui, S(uheil) B(adi) 1929- ... 17-20R
Bushyager, Linda E(yster) 1947- ... 154
Earlier sketch in CA 93-96
Busia, Akosua ... 161
Busia, Kofi Abrefa 1913-1978 ... CANR-46
Obituary ... 126
Earlier sketch in CA 69-72
See also BW 2
Buske, Morris Roger 1912- ... 13-16R
Buskin, Martin 1930-1976 Obituary ... 65-68
Buskin, Richard 1959- ... 164
Buskirk, Richard H(obart) 1927-1994 ... CANR-1
Obituary ... 145
Earlier sketch in CA 1-4R
Busoni, Rafaello 1900-1962 Obituary ... 117
See also SATA 16
Buss, Arnold H. 1924- ... CANR-4
Earlier sketch in CA 1-4R
Buss, Claude Albert 1903- ... 109
Buss, David M. 1953- ... 151
Buss, Gerald (Vere Austen) 1936- ... 127
Buss, Helen M.
See Clarke, Margaret
Buss, Leo W. 1953- ... 121
Buss, Martin J(ohn) 1930- ... 33-36R
Buss, Robin (Caron) 1939- ... 141
Bussard, Paul 1904-1983 Obituary ... 109
Bussche, Henri O(mer) A(ntoine) Van den 1920-1965 ... CANR-5
Earlier sketch in CA 5-8R
Busse, Thomas V(alentine) 1941-1986 ... 77-80
Obituary ... 119
Bussell, Harold L. 1941- ... 125
Busselle, Rebecca 1941- ... 135
See also SATA 80
Bussey, Ellen M(arion) 1926- ... CANR-2
Earlier sketch in CA 49-52
Bussieres, Arthur de 1877-1913 ... DLB 92
Bussieres, Simone 1918- ... 53-56
Bustad, Leo Kenneth 1920- ... 106
Bustamante, A(gustin) Jorge 1938- ... 33-36R
Bustanoby, Andre S(teven) 1930- ... 101
Bustard, Robert 1938- ... 65-68
Busteed, Marilyn 1937- ... 61-64
Bustos, F(rancisco)
See Borges, Jorge Luis
Bustos Domecq, H(onorio)
See Bioy Casares, Adolfo
and Borges, Jorge Luis
Buswell, J(ames) Oliver, Jr. 1895- ... 5-8R
Butcher, Fanny
See Bokum, Fanny Butcher
Butcher, Geoffrey (Arthur John) 1936- ... 111
Butcher, Grace 1934- ... 25-28R
Butcher, H(arold) J(ohn) 1920- ... 21-24R
Butcher, Harry Cecil 1901-1985 Obituary ... 115
Butcher, James Neal 1933- ... CANR-14
Earlier sketch in CA 33-36R
Butcher, (Anne) Judith 1927- ... 57-60
Butcher, (Charles) Philip 1918- ... CANR-4
Earlier sketch in CA 1-4R
Butcher, Russell Devereux 1938- ... CANR-8
Earlier sketch in CA 61-64
Butcher, Thomas Kennedy 1914- ... CAP-1
Earlier sketch in CA 11-12
Butcher, (Charles) William 1951- ... 131
Butchvarov, Panayot K. 1933- ... 33-36R
Butck, Zulie
See Jones, Thomas W(arren)
Butel, Jane
See de Calles, Jane F. Butel
Butenko, Bohdan 1931- ... SATA 90
Butera, Mary C. 1925- ... 21-24R
Buteux, Paul E. 1939- ... 121
Buth, Lenore 1932- ... 89-92
Buthelezi, Gatsha 1928- ... 102
Butland, Gilbert J(ames) 1910- ... 21-24R
Butler, Albert 1923- ... CANR-5
Earlier sketch in CA 13-16R
Butler, Annie L(ouise) 1920-1979 ... CANR-28
Earlier sketch in CA 33-36R
See also BW 2
Butler, Arthur D. 1923- ... 1-4R
Butler, B. C.
See Butler, Basil Christopher
Butler, Basil Christopher 1902-1986 ... CANR-2
Obituary ... 120
Earlier sketch in CA 1-4R
Butler, Beverly Kathleen 1932- ... CANR-72
Earlier sketches in CA 1-4R, CANR-4
See also SATA 7
Butler, Bill
See Butler, Ernest Alton
and Butler, William Huxford
and Butler, William (Arthur) Vivian
Butler, Bishop B. C.
See Butler, Basil Christopher
Butler, Charles Henry 1894-(?) ... CAP-2
Earlier sketch in CA 23-24
Butler, Christina Violet 1884-1982 Obituary ... 106
Butler, Christopher
See Butler, Basil Christopher
Butler, Colin Gasking 1913- ... 109
Butler, David Edgeworth 1924- ... CANR-13
Earlier sketch in CA 5-8R
Butler, David Francis 1928- ... 41-44R
Butler, David Jonathon 1946- ... 69-72
Butler, Dorothy 1925- ... 133
See also SATA 73
Butler, E(dward) H(arry) 1913- ... 13-16R
Butler, Edgar W(ilbur) 1929- ... 77-80
Butler, Erica Bracher 1905- ... CAP-2
Earlier sketch in CA 17-18
Butler, Ernest Alton 1926- ... 33-36R
Butler, Francelia McWilliams 1913- ... CANR-3
Earlier sketch in CA 9-12R
Butler, G(eorge) Paul 1900- ... CAP-2
Earlier sketch in CA 17-18
Butler, Geoff 1945- ... 159
See also SATA 94
Butler, George D. 1893- ... 17-20R
Butler, George Tyssen 1943- ... 103
Butler, Grace Kipp Pratt
See Pratt-Butler, Grace Kipp
Butler, Gregory S. 1961- ... 145
Butler, (Frederick) Guy 1918- ... CANR-41
Earlier sketches in CA 101, CANR-18
Butler, Gwendoline Williams 1922- ... CANR-63
Earlier sketches in CA 9-12R, CANR-6
Butler, Hal 1913- ... 57-60
Butler, Iris 1905- ... 21-24R
Butler, Ivan
See Beuttler, Edward Ivan Oakley
Butler, J. Donald 1908- ... 1-4R
Butler, Jack 1944- ... CANR-53
Earlier sketch in CA 114
Butler, James 1904- ... CAP-1
Earlier sketch in CA 11-12
Butler, James H(armon) 1908- ... 41-44R
Butler, James R(amsay) M(ontagu) 1889-1975 ... CAP-1
Earlier sketch in CA 13-14
Butler, Jean Campbell (MacLaurin) 1918- ... 9-12R
Butler, Jean Rouverol 1916- ... 97-100
Butler, Jeffrey (Ernest) 1922- ... 65-68
Butler, Jerry P. 1944- ... 65-68
Butler, Joan
See Alexander, Robert William
Butler, John Alfred Valentine 1899-1977 ... CANR-5
Obituary ... 106
Earlier sketch in CA 5-8R
Butler, Jon 1940- ... 134
Butler, Joseph Thomas 1932- ... 13-16R
Butler, Josephine Elizabeth 1828-1906 ... DLB 190
Butler, Joyce 1933- ... CANR-25
Earlier sketches in CA 65-68, CANR-9
Butler, Juan (Antonio) 1942-1981 ... 146
See also DLB 53
Butler, Judith P. ... 154
Butler, Lance St. John 1947- ... 144
Butler, Lionel Harry 1923-1981 ... 110
Obituary ... 105
Butler, Lucius (Albert, Jr.) 1928- ... 69-72
Butler, M. Christina 1934- ... SATA 72
Butler, Margaret Gwendoline ... 104
Butler, Marilyn (Speers) 1937- ... 102
Butler, Mildred Allen 1897- ... CAP-2
Earlier sketch in CA 29-32
Butler, Mollie 1907- ... 128
Butler, Natalie Sturges 1908- ... 53-56
Butler, Nathan
See Sohl, Jerry
Butler, Octavia E(stelle) 1947- ... CANR-38
Earlier sketches in CA 73-76, CANR-12, 24
See also AAYA 18
See also BLCS
See also BW 2
See also CLC 38
See also DAM MULT, POP
See also DLB 33
See also MTCW 1
See also SATA 84
Butler, Pat(rick) (Trevor) 1929- ... 5-8R
Butler, Pierce 1884-1953 ... DLB 187
Butler, Pierce A. 1952- ... 146
Butler, Rab
See Butler, Richard Austen
Butler, Richard
See Allbeury, Theodore Edward le Bouthillier
Butler, Richard 1925- ... CANR-8
Earlier sketch in CA 57-60
Butler, Richard Austen 1902-1982 Obituary ... 106
Butler, Rick 1946- ... 97-100
Butler, Robert Albert 1934- ... CANR-11
Earlier sketch in CA 61-64
Butler, Robert Lee 1918- ... 57-60
Butler, Robert M. 1928(?)-1989 Obituary ... 129
Butler, Robert N(eil) 1927- ... 41-44R
Butler, Robert Olen (Jr.) 1945- ... CANR-66
Earlier sketch in CA 112
Interview in ... 112
See also CLC 81
See also DAM POP
See also DLB 173
Butler, Rohan D'Olier 1917-1996 ... 109
Obituary ... 154
Butler, Ron(ald William) 1934- ... 69-72
Butler, Ronnie 1931- ... 130
Butler, Ruth (Ann) 1931- ... 151
Butler, Samuel 1612-1680 ... DLB 101, 126
Butler, Samuel 1835-1902 ... 143
See also CDBLB 1890-1914
See also DA
See also DAB
See also DAC
See also DAM MST, NOV
See also DLB 18, 57, 174
See also TCLC 1, 33
See also WLC
Butler, Sandra (Ada) 1938- ... 105
Butler, Stanley 1914- ... 57-60
Butler, Stefan Congrat
See Congrat-Butler, Stefan
Butler, Stuart Thomas 1926- ... 107
Butler, Suzanne
See Perreard, Suzanne Louise Butler
Butler, Ted
See Schweitzer, Darrell
Butler, Vivian
See Butler, William (Arthur) Vivian
Butler, Walter C.
See Faust, Frederick (Schiller)
Butler, Walter E(rnest) 1898- ... CANR-5
Earlier sketch in CA 5-8R
Butler, William
See Butler, William (Arthur) Vivian
Butler, William 1929- ... CANR-70
Earlier sketch in CA 107
Butler, William E(lliot II) 1939- ... CANR-38
Earlier sketches in CA 25-28R, CANR-11
Butler, William F(rank) 1917-1972 Obituary ... 113

Butler, William Francis 1838-1910 .... DLB 166
Butler, William Huxford 1934-1977 57-60
 Obituary 133
Butler, William (Arthur) Vivian 1927- 135
 See also SATA 79
Butlin, Martin (Richard Fletcher) 1929- ... CANR-19
 Earlier sketches in CA 5-8R, CANR-2
Butlin, Ron 1949- 136
Butman, John 1951- 142
Butor, Michel (Marie Francois) 1926- CANR-66
 Earlier sketches in CA 9-12R, CANR-33
 See also CLC 1, 3, 8, 11, 15
 See also DLB 83
 See also MTCW 1
Butow, Robert J. C. 1924- 13-16R
Butrym, Zofia Teresa 1927- 103
Butsch, Richard (J.) 1943- 135
Butscher, Edward 1943- 97-100
Butt, (Howard) Edward, Jr. 1927- 57-60
Butt, (Dorcas) Susan 1938- 89-92
Buttaci, Sal(vatore) St. John 1941- CANR-9
 Earlier sketch in CA 65-68
Buttel, Robert (William) 1923- 102
Buttenwieser, Ann L. 1935- 128
Buttenwieser, Paul (Arthur) 1938- CANR-35
 Earlier sketch in CA 104
Butter, Peter (Herbert) 1921- 5-8R
Butterfield, Fox 1939- CANR-55
 Earlier sketch in CA 119
 Interview in 119
Butterfield, Herbert 1900-1979 .... CANR-46
 Earlier sketch in CA 1-4R
Butterfield, Lyman H(enry) 1909-1982 Obituary . 106
Butterfield, Roger (Place) 1907-1981 .... CAP-1
 Obituary 103
 Earlier sketch in CA 9-10
Butterfield, Stephen T(homas) 1942- 57-60
Butterick, George F. 1942-1988 .... CANR-27
 Obituary 126
 Earlier sketches in CA 69-72, CANR-11
Butters, Dorothy Gilman
 See Gilman, Dorothy
Butterworth, Douglas Stanley 1930- 108
Butterworth, Emma Macalik 1928- 105
 See also SATA 43
Butterworth, F(rank) Edward (Jr.) 1917- 29-32R
Butterworth, Hezekiah 1839-1905 .... DLB 42
Butterworth, Lionel Milner Angus
 See Angus-Butterworth, Lionel Milner
Butterworth, Michael 1924-1986 .... CANR-10
 Obituary 121
 Earlier sketch in CA 25-28R
Butterworth, Neil 1934- CANR-56
 Earlier sketch in CA 125
Butterworth, Oliver 1915-1990 .... CANR-37
 Obituary 132
 Earlier sketch in CA 1-4R
 See also MAICYA
 See also SATA 1
 See also SATA-Obit 66
Butterworth, W(illiam) E(dmund III) 1929- CANR-64
 Earlier sketches in CA 1-4R, CANR-2, 18, 40
 See also SATA 5
Butti, Ken(neth Michael) 1950- 104
Buttigeig, Anton 1912-1983 Obituary 109
Buttimer, Anne 1938- 37-40R
Buttinger, Joseph 1906-1992 .... CANR-46
 Obituary 138
 Earlier sketch in CA 21-24R
Buttinger, Muriel Gardiner 1901-1985 .... CANR-39
 Obituary 115
 Earlier sketch in CA 77-80
Buttitta, Anthony 1907- 81-84
Buttitta, Ignazio 1899- .... DLB 114
Buttitta, Tony
 See Buttitta, Anthony
Buttlar, Lois J(acqueline) 1934- 112
Buttle, Myra
 See Purcell, Victor
Button, Daniel E(van) 1917- 89-92
Button, Dick 1929- 9-12R
Button, James W(ickham) 1942- 81-84
Button, Kenneth John 1948- CANR-20
 Earlier sketch in CA 103
Button, (Henry) Warren 1922- 97-100
Buttress, Frederick Arthur 1908- 33-36R
Buttrey, Douglas N(orton) CANR-40
 Earlier sketches in CA 101, CANR-18
Buttrick, George Arthur 1892-1980 61-64
 Obituary 93-96
Butts, Anthony 1969- 168
Butts, David P. 1932- 9-12R
Butts, Dennis 1932- 145
Butts, Edward 1951- 128
Butts, Ellen R(ubinstein) 1942- 158
 See also SATA 93
Butts, Jane Roberts 1929-1984 .... CANR-15
 Earlier sketch in CA 41-44R
Butts, Mary 1892(?)-1937 148
 See also TCLC 77
Butts, Porter (Freeman) 1903- 41-44R
Butts, R. Freeman 1910- 13-16R
Butwell, Richard 1929- CANR-1
 Earlier sketch in CA 45-48
Butzer, Karl W(ilhelm) 1934- CANR-8
 Earlier sketch in CA 21-24R
Buultjens, (Edward) Ralph 1936- CANR-4
 Earlier sketch in CA 53-56
Buxbaum, Edith 1902- CAP-2
 Earlier sketch in CA 25-28
Buxbaum, Martin (David) 1912-1991 ...... 17-20R
 Obituary 134
Buxbaum, Melvin H. 1934- 53-56
Buxbaum, Robert C(ourtney) 1930- 97-100
Buxton, Anne (Arundel) Brief entry 115
Buxton, Anthony 1892(?)-1970 Obituary 104
Buxton, (Evelyn June) Bonnie 1940- 69-72
Buxton, Charles R(oberts) 1913- 65-68
Buxton, Cindy 1950- 132
Buxton, Claude E(lmo) 1912- Brief entry 114
Buxton, David Roden 1910- 104
Buxton, Edward F(ulton) 1917-1990 ....41-44R
 Obituary 132
Buxton, Harold J(ocelyn) 1880-1976 Obituary .. 104
Buxton, (Edward) John (Mawby) 1912- ... CANR-31
 Earlier sketches in CA 9-12R, CANR-5
Buxton, Thomas H(amilton) 1940- 57-60
Buys, Donna 1944- 102
Buzan, Barry 1946- CANR-44
 Earlier sketch in CA 119
Buzard, James 1959- 141
Buzo, Alexander (John) 1944- CANR-69
 Earlier sketches in CA 97-100, CANR-17, 39
 See also CLC 61
Buzzard, John Huxley 1912-1984 Obituary 112
Buzzati, Dino 1906-1972 160
 Obituary 33-36R
 See also CLC 36
 See also DLB 177
Buzzell, Robert (Dow) 1933- 104
Buzzle, Buck
 See Rubin, Charles J.
Buzzotta, V. R(alph) 1931- 37-40R
Byalick, Marcia 1947- 154
 See also SATA 97
Byard, Carole (Marie) 1941- .... SATA 57
Byars, Betsy (Cromer) 1928- CANR-57
 Earlier sketches in CA 33-36R, CANR-18, 36
 Interview in CANR-18
 See also AAYA 19
 See also CLC 35
 See also CLR 1, 16
 See also DLB 52
 See also JRDA
 See also MAICYA
 See also MTCW 1
 See also SAAS 1
 See also SATA 4, 46, 80
Byatt, A(ntonia) S(usan Drabble) 1936- .. CANR-50
 Earlier sketches in CA 13-16R, CANR-13, 33
 See also CLC 19, 65
 See also DAM NOV, POP
 See also DLB 14, 194
 See also MTCW 1
Bychowski, Gustav 1895-1972 Obituary 33-36R
Byck, Robert 1933- 109
Bye, Beryl (Joyce Rayment) 1926- CANR-11
 Earlier sketch in CA 61-64
Bye, Ranulph (deBayeux) 1916- 53-56
Bye, Raymond T(aylor) 1892- 5-8R
Byer, Kathryn Stripling 1944- 142
Byerly, Greg (W.) 1949- 130
Byerly, Henry Clement 1935- 53-56
Byerly, Kenneth R(hodes) 1908- 1-4R
Byerly, Victoria 1949- 127
Byers, David (Milner) 1941- 53-56
Byers, Edward A(dams) 1939-1989 119
 Obituary 129
Byers, Edward E. 1921- CANR-3
 Earlier sketch in CA 1-4R
Byers, (Amy) Irene 1906- CANR-3
 Earlier sketch in CA 9-12R
Byers, R(ichard) McCulloch 1913- 69-72
Byfield, Barbara Ninde 1930- CANR-4
 Earlier sketch in CA 1-4R
 See also SATA 8
Byham, William C(larence) 1936- CANR-17
 Earlier sketch in CA 25-28R
Bykau, Vasilii Uladzimiravich
 See Bykov, Vasily Vladimirovich
Bykov, Vasily Vladimirovich 1924- 102
Byles, Mather 1707-1788 ....DLB 24
Bylinsky, Gene Michae 1930- 77-80
Bynagle, Hans E(dward) 1946- 120
Byng, Douglas 1893-1987 Obituary 123
Bynneman, Henry fl. 1566-1583 ....DLB 170
Bynner, Witter 1881-1968 .... CANR-4
 Obituary 25-28R
 Earlier sketch in CA 1-4R
 See also DLB 54
Bynum, David E(liab) 1936- CANR-20
 Earlier sketch in CA 37-40R
Bynum, Terrell Ward 1941- CANR-18
 Earlier sketch in CA 101
Bynum, Victoria E. 1947- 146
Byock, Jesse L(ewis) 1945- 110
Byrd, Bobby
 See Byrd, Robert James
Byrd, C. L.
 See Rosenkrantz, Linda
Byrd, Cecil Kash 1913- 17-20R
Byrd, Eldon A(rthur) 1939- 45-48
Byrd, Elizabeth 1912- CANR-5
 Earlier sketch in CA 5-8R
 See also SATA 34
Byrd, Emmett
 See Hinden, Michael C(harles)
Byrd, John Crowe
 See Hinden, Michael C(harles)
Byrd, Martha 1930- 29-32R
Byrd, Max (W.) 1942- CANR-72
 Earlier sketch in CA 142
Byrd, Richard E(dward) 1931- CANR-7
 Earlier sketch in CA 57-60
Byrd, Robert (John) 1942- .... SATA 33
Byrd, Robert James 1942- 65-68
Byrd, William II 1674-1744 .... DLB 24, 139
Byrd, William c. 1543-1623 .... DLB 172
Byrne, Charles Raymond 1916-1983 Obituary .. 111
Byrne, David 1952- 127
 See also CLC 26
Byrne, Donald E(dward), Jr. 1942- 73-76
Byrne, Donn (Erwin) 1931- CANR-20
 Earlier sketches in CA 9-12R, CANR-5
Byrne, Edmund F(rancis) 1933- 29-32R
Byrne, Edward M. 1935- 29-32R
Byrne, Frank L(oyola) 1928- 21-24R
Byrne, Gary C. 1942- 49-52
Byrne, Herbert Winston 1917- 1-4R
Byrne, James E. 1945- 81-84
Byrne, John 1940- CANR-69
 Earlier sketch in CA 104
Byrne, John Keyes 1926- 102
 Interview in 102
 See also Leonard, Hugh
Byrne, Malcolm 1955- 127
Byrne, Muriel St. Clare 1895-1983 .... CAP-1
 Obituary 111
 Earlier sketch in CA 17-18
Byrne, Peter 1925- 65-68
Byrne, Ralph
 See Burns, Ralph J.
Byrne, Richard Hill 1915- 21-24R
Byrne, Robert (Eugene) 1928- Brief entry 110
Byrne, Robert 1930- CANR-35
 Earlier sketches in CA 73-76, CANR-13
Byrne, Stuart J(ames) 1913- 102
Byrnes, Edward T(homas) 1929- 53-56
Byrnes, Eugene F. 1890(?)-1974 Obituary ... 49-52
Byrnes, Garrett D(avis) 1904(?)-1985 Obituary . 118
Byrnes, James Francis 1879-1972 Obituary 112
Byrnes, Joseph Francis 1939- 114
Byrnes, Robert F(rancis) 1917-1997 ...... CANR-10
 Obituary 158
 Earlier sketch in CA 25-28R
Byrnes, Thomas Edmund 1911- 13-16R
Byrom, James
 See Bramwell, James Guy
Byrom, (Robert) Michael 1925- 5-8R
Byron, Carl R(oscoe) 1948- 97-100
Byron, Christopher M. 1944- 77-80
Byron, George Gordon (Noel) 1788-1824 ... CDBLB 1789-1832
 See also DA
 See also DAB
 See also DAC
 See also DAM MST, POET
 See also DLB 96, 110
 See also PC 16
 See also WLC
Byron, Gilbert (Valliant) 1903-1991 .... 17-20R
 Obituary 134
Byron, John
 See Armstrong, John Byron
Byron, Robert 1905-1941 160
 See also DLB 195
 See also TCLC 67
Byron, William J(ames) 1927- 81-84
Bytwerk, Randall Lee 1950- 109
Bywater, William G(len), Jr. 1940- 61-64

C

C. 3. 3.
 See Wilde, Oscar (Fingal O'Flahertie Wills)
C. E. M.
 See Mastrangelo, Charles E.
Caballero, Ann Mallory 1928- 17-20R
Caballero, Manuel 1931- 132
 See also HW
Caballero Bonald, Jose Manuel 1926- .... DLB 108
Caballero Calderon, E.
 See Caballero Calderon, Eduardo
Caballero Calderon, Eduardo 1910- .... HW
Cabanero, Eladio 1930- ....DLB 134
Cabanis, Jose 1922- Brief entry 111
Cabaniss, J(ames) Allen 1911- 1-4R
 See also SATA 5
Cabarga, Leslie 1954- CANR-13
 Earlier sketch in CA 77-80
Cabassa, Victoria 1912- 49-52
Cabat, Erni 1914- .... SATA 74
Cabbell, Edward J. 1946- 121
Cabbell, Paul 1942- 53-56
Cabeen, David Clark 1886-(?) CAP-1
 Earlier sketch in CA 13-14
Cabell, Branch
 See Cabell, James Branch
Cabell, James Branch 1879-1958 152
 Brief entry 105
 See also DLB 9, 78
 See also TCLC 6
Cabezas (Lacayo), Omar 1951(?)- 131
 See also HW
Cabibi, John F(rank) J(oseph) 1912- 53-56
Cable, George Washington 1844-1925 155
 Brief entry 104
 See also DLB 12, 74
 See also DLBD 13
 See also SSC 4
 See also TCLC 4
Cable, James (Eric) 1920- CANR-33
 Earlier sketches in CA 85-88, CANR-15
Cable, John L(aurence) 1934- CANR-21
 Earlier sketch in CA 69-72
Cable, Mary 1920- CANR-28
 Earlier sketches in CA 25-28R, CANR-11
 See also SATA 9
Cable, Mildred 1878-1952 .... DLB 195
Cable, Thomas Monroe 1942- Brief entry 106
Cabot, Blake 1905(?)-1974 Obituary 53-56
Cabot, John Moors 1901-1981 Obituary 103
Cabot, Robert (Moors) 1924- 29-32R
Cabot, Thomas Dudley 1897- 93-96
Cabot, Tracy 1941- 81-84
Cabral, Alberto
 See White, Richard Alan
Cabral, Amilcar 1921-1973 Obituary 111
Cabral, Joao de Pina
 See Pina-Cabral, Joao de
Cabral, O. M.
 See Cabral, Olga
Cabral, Olga 1909- CANR-10
 Earlier sketch in CA 25-28R
 See also SATA 46
Cabral de Melo Neto, Joao 1920- 151
 See also CLC 76
 See also DAM MULT
Cabrera, James C. 1935-1997 109
 Obituary 161
Cabrera, Lydia 1900- .... DLB 145
 See also HW
Cabrera, Marcela 1966- ....SATA 90
Cabrera Infante, G(uillermo) 1929- CANR-65
 Earlier sketches in CA 85-88, CANR-29
 See also CLC 5, 25, 45
 See also DAM MULT
 See also DLB 113
 See also HLC
 See also HW
 See also MTCW 1
Caccia-Dominioni, Paolo 1896- 21-24R
Cacciatore, Vera (Signorelli) 1911- CANR-5
 Earlier sketch in CA 5-8R
Cachia, Pierre J. E. 1921- CANR-11
 Earlier sketch in CA 25-28R
Cacoyannis, Michael 1922- 101
Cadbury, Henry J(oel) 1883-1974 .... CAP-1
 Obituary 53-56
 Earlier sketch in CA 13-16
Cadbury, Paul Strangman 1895-1984 Obituary . 114
Caddel, Richard (Ivo) 1949- 137
Cadden, Joseph E. 1911(?)-1980 Obituary 101
Cadden, Thomas Scott 1923- 131
Cadden, Tom Scott
 See Cadden, Thomas Scott
Caddick, Arthur 1911-1987 Obituary 122
Caddy, Alice
 See Burman, Alice Caddy
Caddy, Caroline 1944- 153
Caddy, (Michael) Douglas 1938- 136
Cade, Alexander
 See Methold, Kenneth (Walter)
Cade, Robin
 See Nicole, Christopher (Robin)
Cade, Toni
 See Bambara, Toni Cade
Cadell, (Violet) Elizabeth 1903-1989 ..... CANR-72
 Earlier sketches in CA 57-60, CANR-11
Cadenhead, Ivie E(dward), Jr. 1923- 41-44R
Cader, Michael 1961- 147
Cadet, John 1935- 77-80
Cadieux, Charles L. 1919- 57-60
Cadieux, (Joseph Arthur) Lorenzo 1903-1976 .49-52
 Obituary 103
Cadieux, (Joseph David Romeo) Marcel 1915-1981 Obituary 108
Cadigan, Pat(ricia Kearney) 1953- 165
Cadle, Dean 1920- 25-28R
Cadle, Farris W(illiam) 1952- 135
Cadmus and Harmonia
 See Buchan, John
Cadnum, Michael 1949- 151
 See also AAYA 23
 See also SATA 87
Cadogan, Alexander (George Montagu) 1884-1968 Obituary 106
Cadogan, Mary (Rose) 1928- 106
Caduto, Michael J. 1955- 153
Cadwallader, Clyde T(homas) 5-8R
Cadwallader, Sharon 1936- CANR-17
 Earlier sketches in CA 49-52, CANR-1
 See also SATA 7
Cady, Arthur 1920-1983 Obituary 109
Cady, Edwin Harrison 1917- CANR-70
 Earlier sketches in CA 1-4R, CANR-4
 See also DLB 103
Cady, Ernest (Albert) 1899-1985 Obituary 117
Cady, (Walter) Harrison 1877(?)-1970 Obituary . 116
 See also SATA 19
Cady, Howard Stevenson 1914-1990 Obituary . 132
Cady, Jack A(ndrew) 1932- CANR-72
 Earlier sketches in CA 65-68, CANR-9
Cady, John Frank 1901-1996 .... CANR-72
 Earlier sketches in CA 1-4R, CANR-4
Cady, Steve (Noel) 1927-1995 45-48
 Obituary 149
Caedmon fl. 658-680 .... DLB 146
Caedmon, Father
 See Wahl, Thomas (Peter)
Caefer, Raymond J(ohn) 1926- 17-20R
Caeiro, Alberto
 See Pessoa, Fernando (Antonio Nogueira)
Caemmerer, Richard R(udolph) 1904- CANR-5
 Earlier sketch in CA 1-4R
Caen, Herb (Eugene) 1916-1997 .... CANR-1
 Obituary 156
 Earlier sketch in CA 1-4R
 See also AITN 1
Caesar, (Eu)Gene (Lee) 1927- CANR-72
 Earlier sketches in CA 1-4R, CANR-1
Caesar, Judith 1946- 167
Caesar, (Isaac) Sid(ney) 1922- 143
Cafferty, Bernard 1934- 41-44R
Cafferty, Pastora San Juan 1940- 114
Caffey, David L(uther) 1947- 45-48
Caffrey, John G(ordon) 1922- 17-20R
Caffrey, Kate CANR-1
 Earlier sketch in CA 49-52

Caffrey, Margaret M. 1947- 135
Cagan, Phillip D(avid) 1927- 17-20R
Cagan, Stephen M(ichael) 1943- 139
Cage, John (Milton, Jr.) 1912- CANR-9
Earlier sketch in CA 13-16R
Interview in CANR-9
See also CLC 41
See also DLB 193
Caggiano, Philip 1949- 114
Cagle, Malcolm W(infield) 1918- 108
See also SATA 32
Cagle, William R(ea) 1933- 65-68
Cagney, James (Francis, Jr.) 1899(?)-1986 144
Obituary 118
Brief entry 115
Cagney, Peter
See Winter, Bevis (Peter)
Cahalan, (John) Don(ald) 1912- 102
Cahalan, James Michael 1953- 145
Cahalane, Victor H(arrison) 1901- CAP-2
Earlier sketch in CA 23-24
Cahan, Abraham 1860-1951 154
Brief entry 108
See also DLB 9, 25, 28
See also TCLC 71
Cahan, William G. 1914- 139
Cahen, Alfred B. 1932- 17-20R
Cahill, Audrey Fawcett 1929- 21-24R
Cahill, Daniel J(oseph) 1929- 69-72
Cahill, Fred V(irgil), Jr. 1916-1984 Obituary 112
Cahill, Gilbert A. 1912- Brief entry 107
Cahill, Jack
See Cahill, John Denis
Cahill, James F(rancis) 1926- CANR-6
Earlier sketch in CA 1-4R
Cahill, Jane (Miller) 1901- CAP-2
Earlier sketch in CA 23-24
Cahill, John Denis 1926- 131
Cahill, Kevin Michael 1936- CANR-63
Earlier sketches in CA 102, CANR-18, 40
Cahill, Rick 1950- 126
Cahill, Robert S. 1933- 13-16R
Cahill, Susan Neunzig 1940- 37-40R
Cahill, Thomas (Quinn) 1940- CANR-53
Earlier sketch in CA 49-52
Cahill, Tim 1944- 164
See also AAYA 25
Cahill, Tom
See Cahill, Thomas (Quinn)
Cahn, Edgar S. 1935- 29-32R
Cahn, Rhoda 1922- 81-84
See also SATA 37
Cahn, Robert 1917-1997 108
Obituary 162
Cahn, Sammy 1913-1993 85-88
Obituary 140
Cahn, Steven M. 1942- CANR-53
Earlier sketches in CA 21-24R, CANR-13, 29
Cahn, Walter 1933- 129
Cahn, William 1912-1976 CANR-71
Obituary 69-72
Earlier sketch in CA 21-24R
See also SATA 37
Cahn, Zvi 1896- CAP-2
Earlier sketch in CA 23-24
Cahnman, Werner J(acob) 1902- 49-52
Caiden, Gerald E(lliot) 1936- CANR-14
Earlier sketch in CA 29-32R
Caidin, Martin 1927-1997 CANR-58
Obituary 157
Earlier sketches in CA 1-4R, CANR-2
See also AITN 2
Caiger-Smith, Alan 1930- 13-16R
Cail, Carol 1937- CANR-71
Earlier sketch in CA 140
Caillois, Roger 1913-1978 CANR-13
Obituary 85-88
Earlier sketch in CA 25-28R
Caillou, Alan
See Lyle-Smythe, Alan
Cain, Arthur H(omer) 1913- CANR-4
Earlier sketch in CA 1-4R
See also SATA 3
Cain, Bob
See Cain, Robert Owen
Cain, Bruce E. 1948- 122
Cain, G.
See Cabrera Infante, G(uillermo)
Cain, George (M.) 1943- 142
See also BW 2
See also DLB 33
Cain, Glen G. 1933- 21-24R
Cain, Guillermo
See Cabrera Infante, G(uillermo)
Cain, Jackson
See Gleason, Robert
Cain, James M(allahan) 1892-1977 CANR-61
Obituary 73-76
Earlier sketches in CA 17-20R, CANR-8, 34
See also AITN 1
See also CLC 3, 11, 28
See also MTCW 1
Cain, Mary (Dawson) 1904-1984 Obituary 112
Cain, Maureen 1938- 73-76
Cain, Michael Peter 1941- 93-96
Cain, Robert Owen 1934- 65-68
Cain, T. G. S. 1944- 124
Cain, Thomas H(enry) 1931- 93-96
Caine, Barbara 1948- 143
Caine, Geoffrey
See Walker, Robert W(ayne)
Caine, (Thomas Henry) Hall 1853(?)-1931 Brief entry 122
Caine, Jeffrey (Andrew) 1944- 85-88
Caine, Lynn 1924(?)-1987 Obituary 124
Caine, Mark
See Raphael, Frederic (Michael)
Caine, Michael 1933- 146
Caine, Mitchell
See Sparkia, Roy (Bernard)
Caine, Peter
See Hornig, Doug
Caine, Stanley P(aul) 1940- 41-44R
Caine, Sydney 1902- CAP-2
Earlier sketch in CA 25-28
Caines, Jeannette (Franklin) 1938- 152
See also BW 2
See also CLR 24
See also SATA 78
See also SATA-Brief 43
Caird, George Bradford 1917-1984 61-64
Obituary 112
Caird, Janet 1913- CANR-2
Earlier sketch in CA 49-52
Caird, John (Newport) 1948- 156
Caird, Mona 1854-1932 DLB 197
Cairncross, Alec
See Cairncross, Alexander Kirkland
Cairncross, Alexander Kirkland 1911- CANR-57
Earlier sketches in CA 61-64, CANR-8
Cairncross, Frances (Anne) 1944- 57-60
Cairney, John 1930- 105
Cairns, David 1904-1992 CANR-11
Obituary 140
Earlier sketch in CA 61-64
Cairns, (Thomas) Dorian 1901-1972 Obituary 37-40R
Cairns, Earle E(dwin) 1910- CANR-18
Earlier sketch in CA 1-4R
Cairns, (Samuel) Ed(mund) 1945- CANR-66
Earlier sketch in CA 128
Cairns, Grace Edith 1907- CANR-18
Earlier sketch in CA 1-4R
Cairns, Huntington 1904-1985 CANR-5
Obituary 114
Earlier sketch in CA 53-56
Cairns, J(ames) F(ord) 1914- 105
Cairns, John C(ampbell) 1924- CANR-5
Earlier sketch in CA 13-16R
Cairns, Scott 1954- 146
Cairns, Thomas W(illiam) 1931- 21-24R
Cairns, Trevor 1922- 33-36R
See also SATA 14
Cairns-Smith, A(lexander) G(raham) 1931- 123
Cairo, Jon
See Romano, Deane Louis
Caitlin, Elise 1953- 111
Cake, Patrick
See Welch, Timothy L.
Calabrese, Alphonse F. X. 1923- 69-72
Calabrese, Anthony 1938- 89-92
Calabresi, Guido 1932- CANR-20
Earlier sketch in CA 41-44R
Calabro, Marian 1954- 147
See also SATA 79
Calaferte, Louis 1928- CANR-17
Earlier sketches in CA 45-48, CANR-1
Calais, Jean
See Rodefer, Stephen
Calamandrei, Mauro 1925- 69-72
Calamari, John D(aniel) 1921- 37-40R
Calas, Nicholas 1907-1988 Obituary 127
Calasibetta, Charlotte M(ankey) 1917- 103
Calasso, Roberto 1941- 143
See also CLC 81
Calbom, Cherie 1947- 138
Calde, Mark A(ugustine) 1945- 69-72
Caldecott, Moyra 1927- CANR-30
Earlier sketches in CA 77-80, CANR-13
See also SATA 22
Caldecott, Randolph (J.) 1846-1886 CLR 14
See also DLB 163
See also MAICYA
See also SATA 17, 100
Calder, Alexander 1898-1976 167
Obituary 111
See also AAYA 25
Calder, Angus 1942- CANR-38
Earlier sketch in CA 29-32R
Calder, Bruce J. 1940- 132
Calder, C(larence) R(oy), Jr. 1928- 81-84
Calder, Daniel Gillmore 1939- 103
Calder, Jason
See Dunmore, John
Calder, Jenni 1941- CANR-38
Earlier sketches in CA 45-48, CANR-1
Calder, John (Mackenzie) 1927- 133
Calder, Kent E(yring) 1948- 107
Calder, Lyn
See Calmenson, Stephanie
Calder, Marie D(onais) 1948- 161
See also SATA 96
Calder, Nigel (David Ritchie) 1931- CANR-38
Earlier sketches in CA 21-24R, CANR-11
See also MTCW 1
Calder, Ritchie
See Ritchie-Calder, Peter Ritchie
Calder, Robert
See Mundis, Jerrold
Calder, Robert Lorin 1941- 65-68
Calder-Marshall, Arthur 1908-1992 CANR-72
Obituary 137
Earlier sketch in CA 61-64
Calderon, Eduardo Caballero
See Caballero Calderon, Eduardo
Calderon, Jose Vasconcelos
See Vasconcelos (Calderon), Jose
Calderon de la Barca, Pedro 1600-1681 DC 3
Calderone, Mary S(teichen) 1904- 104
See also AITN 1
Calderwood, Ivan E. 1899- 57-60
Calderwood, James D(ixon) 1917- CANR-3
Earlier sketch in CA 5-8R
Calderwood, James L(ee) 1930- 21-24R
Caldicott, Helen (Mary) 1938- CANR-66
Brief entry 114
Earlier sketch in CA 124
Interview in 124
See also MTCW 1
Caldwell, Ben(jamin) 1937- 124
Brief entry 117
See also BW 1
See also DLB 38
Caldwell, Bettye (McDonald) 1924- 104
Caldwell, C(harles) Edson 1906-1974 CAP-2
Earlier sketch in CA 29-32
Caldwell, Dan (Edward) 1948- 112
Caldwell, David H(epburn) 1951- 132
Caldwell, Doreen (Mary) 1942- SATA 71
Caldwell, Edward S(abiston) 1928- 65-68
Caldwell, Erskine (Preston) 1903-1987 CANR-33
Obituary 121
Earlier sketches in CA 1-4R, CANR-2
See also CAAS 1
See also AITN 1
See also CLC 1, 8, 14, 50, 60
See also DAM NOV
See also DLB 9, 86
See also MTCW 1
See also SSC 19
Caldwell, Gaylon L(oray) 1920- 33-36R
Caldwell, Grant 1947- 159
Caldwell, Harry B(oynton) 1935- 37-40R
Caldwell, Helen F. 1904- 77-80
Caldwell, Inga Gilson 1897- 61-64
Caldwell, Irene Catherine (Smith) 1908-1979 9-12R
Obituary 103
Caldwell, James
See Lowry, Robert (James Collas)
Caldwell, John 1928- CANR-12
Earlier sketch in CA 73-76
Caldwell, John C(ope) 1913- CANR-13
Earlier sketch in CA 21-24R
See also SATA 7
Caldwell, Joseph H(erman) 1934- 21-24R
Caldwell, Kathryn (Smoot) 1942- 69-72
Caldwell, Louis O(liver) 1935- 69-72
Caldwell, Lynton (Keith) 1913- CANR-12
Earlier sketch in CA 29-32R
Caldwell, (James Alexander) Malcolm 1931-1978 CANR-17
Earlier sketch in CA 25-28R
Caldwell, Marge 1914- 97-100
Caldwell, Nat(han Green) 1912-1985 Obituary 115
Caldwell, Oliver Johnson 1904- 37-40R
Caldwell, Robert G(ranville) 1882-1976 Obituary 65-68
Caldwell, Robert Graham 1904- 17-20R
Caldwell, Stratton F(ranklin) 1926- 136
Caldwell, (Janet Miriam) Taylor (Holland) 1900-1985 CANR-5
Obituary 116
Earlier sketch in CA 5-8R
See also CLC 2, 28, 39
See also DAM NOV, POP
See also DLBD 17
Caldwell, William A(nthony) 1906-1986 Obituary 119
Calef, George (Waller) 1944- 132
Calef, Wesley (Carr) 1914- 13-16R
Caley, Rod
See Rowland, D(onald) S(ydney)
Calhoon, Richard P(ercival) 1909- 57-60
Calhoon, Robert M(cCluer) 1935- CANR-4
Earlier sketch in CA 53-56
Calhoun, B. B. 1961- 165
See also SATA 98
Calhoun, Calfrey C. 1928- 37-40R
Calhoun, Chad
See Cunningham, Chet
and Goulart, Ron(ald Joseph)
Calhoun, Charles W(illiam) 1948- 125
Calhoun, Conyus 1946- 111
Calhoun, Craig (Jackson) 1952- 130
Calhoun, Daniel F(airchild) 1929- 65-68
Calhoun, Don Gilmore 1914- 85-88
Calhoun, Donald W(allace) 1917- 104
Calhoun, Eric
See Turner, Robert (Harry)
Calhoun, Jackie 1936- 138
Calhoun, James Frank 1941- 109
Calhoun, John Caldwell 1782-1850 DLB 3
Calhoun, Mary
See Wilkins, Mary Huiskamp
See also CLR 42
See also SATA 2
Calhoun, Richard James 1926- 33-36R
Calhoun, Robert L(owery) 1896-1983 Obituary 110
Calhoun, T. B.
See Bisson, Terry (Ballantine)
Calhoun, Thomas 1940- 89-92
Calia, Vincent F(rank) 1926- 53-56
Calian, Carnegie Samuel 1933- 25-28R
Caliban
See Reid, J(ohn) C(owie)
Calif, Ruth 1922- 134
See also SATA 67
Califano, Joseph A(nthony), Jr. 1931- CANR-2
Earlier sketch in CA 45-48
Califia, Pat 1954- 133
Calimani, Riccardo 1946- 137
Calin, William (Compaine) 1936- CANR-27
Earlier sketches in CA 21-24R, CANR-11
Calinescu, Matei (Alexe) 1934- 131
Calisch, Edith Lindeman 1898-1984 Obituary 114
Calisher, Hortense 1911- CANR-67
Earlier sketches in CA 1-4R, CANR-1, 22
Interview in CANR-22
See also CLC 2, 4, 8, 38
See also DAM NOV
See also DLB 2
See also MTCW 1
See also SSC 15
Calistro, Paddy
See Calistro McAuley, Patricia Ann
Calistro McAuley, Patricia Ann 1948- CANR-41
Earlier sketch in CA 118
Calitri, Charles J(oseph) 1916-1984 CANR-70
Earlier sketch in CA 5-8R
Calitri, Princine 33-36R
Calkin, Homer Leonard 1912- 41-44R
Calkin, Ruth Harms 1918- 102
Calkins, Fay
See Alailima, Fay C.
Calkins, Franklin
See Stratemeyer, Edward L.
Calkins, Lucy McCormick CANR-72
Earlier sketch in CA 125
Calkins, Robert G. 1932- 130
Calkins, Rodello 1920- Brief entry 105
Call, Alice E(lizabeth) LaPlant 1914- 13-16R
Call, Hughie Florence 1890-1969 CANR-70
Earlier sketch in CA 5-8R
See also SATA 1
Calladine, Andrew G(arfield) 1941- 102
Calladine, Carole E(lizabeth) 1942- 102
Callaghan, Barry 1937- 101
Interview in 101
Callaghan, Catherine A. 1931- 33-36R
Callaghan, Mary Rose 1944- CANR-43
Earlier sketch in CA 118
Callaghan, Morley Edward 1903-1990 CANR-33
Obituary 132
Earlier sketch in CA 9-12R
See also CLC 3, 14, 41, 65
See also DAC
See also DAM MST
See also DLB 68
See also MTCW 1
Callaghan, Thomas 1924- 114
Callahan, Bob 1942- 138
Callahan, Charles C(lifford) 1910- CAP-2
Earlier sketch in CA 17-18
Callahan, Claire Wallis 1890- 5-8R
Callahan, Daniel 1930- 21-24R
Callahan, David 1965(?)- 140
Callahan, Dorothy M(onahan) 1934- 114
See also SATA 39
See also SATA-Brief 35
Callahan, John
See Gallun, Raymond Z(inke)
Callahan, John F(rancis) 1912- 33-36R
Callahan, Mary
See Randazzo, Mary Callahan
Callahan, Nelson J. 1927- 33-36R
Callahan, North 1908- CANR-72
Earlier sketches in CA 1-4R, CANR-2
Callahan, Philip Serna 1923- 102
See also SATA 25
Callahan, Raymond (Aloysius) 1938- 69-72
Callahan, S. Alice 1868-1894 DLB 175
Callahan, Sidney Cornelia 1933- 17-20R
Callahan, Sterling G. 1916- 21-24R
Callahan, Steven (Patrick) 1952- 120
Callan, Edward T. 1917- 17-20R
Callan, Jamie 1954- 109
See also SATA 59
Callan, John P(atrick) 1939- 111
Callan, Richard J(erome) 1932- 53-56
Callanan, Frank 1956- 144
Callander, Don 1930- 146
Callard, D(avid) A(rthur) 1950- 144
Callard, Maurice (Frederick Thomas) 1912- CANR-3
Earlier sketch in CA 1-4R
Callard, Thomas Henry 1912- 9-12R
Callas, Theo
See McCarthy, Shaun (Lloyd)
Callaway, Ben (Anderson) 1927- 131
Callaway, Bernice (Anne) 1923- 121
See also SATA 48
Callaway, C. Wayne 1941- 138
Callaway, Joseph A(tlee) 1920- 65-68
Callaway, Kathy 1943- 107
See also SATA 36
Callcott, George H(ardy) 1929- 29-32R
Callcott, Margaret Law 1929- 61-64
Callcott, Wilfrid H(ardy) 1895-1969 Obituary 112
Calle, Francisco Rosillo
See Rosillo-Calle, Francisco
Callen, Larry
See Callen, Lawrence Willard, Jr.
Callen, Lawrence Willard, Jr. 1927- CANR-12
Earlier sketch in CA 73-76
See also SATA 19
Callen, Michael (Lane) 1955-1993 139
Obituary 143
Callen, William B. 1930- 21-24R
Callenbach, Ernest 1929- CANR-21
Earlier sketches in CA 57-60, CANR-6
Callender, Charles 1928- 41-44R
Callender, George 1916- 136
Callender, Julian
See Lee, Austin
Callender, Red
See Callender, George
Callender, Wesley P(ayne), Jr. 1923- 17-20R
Calleo, David P(atrick) 1934- CANR-57
Earlier sketches in CA 17-20R, CANR-10, 31
Calley, Karin 1965- SATA 92
Callicott, J(ohn) Baird 1941- 135

Callihan, E(lmer) L(ee) 1903- CAP-2
Earlier sketch in CA 25-28
Callimachus c. 305B.C.-c. 240B.C. .... DLB 176
Callinan, Bernard James 1913- 110
Callis, Helmut G(unther) 1906- CANR-5
Earlier sketch in CA 53-56
Callis, Robert 1920- 37-40R
Callison, Brian (Richard) 1934- CANR-60
Earlier sketches in CA 29-32R, CANR-31
Callister, Frank 1916- 13-16R
Callmann, Rudolf 1892-1976 69-72
Obituary 65-68
Callow, Alexander B., Jr. 1925- 21-24R
Callow, James T(homas) 1928- 41-44R
Callow, Philip (Kenneth) 1924- CANR-21
Earlier sketches in CA 13-16R, CANR-6
Callow, Simon 1949- 138
Calloway, Cab(ell III) 1907- Brief entry 113
Calloway, Colin G(ordon) 1953- 135
Calloway, Doris Howes 1923- 21-24R
Callum, Myles 1934- 9-12R
Callwood, June 1924- CANR-49
Earlier sketches in CA 101, CANR-24
Calman, Alvin R(ose) 1895-1983 Obituary 110
Calman, Mel 1931-1994 126
Obituary 144
Calmann, John 1935-1980 .... 21-24R
Obituary 97-100
Calmann-Levy, Robert 1899-1982 Obituary 108
Calmenson, Stephanie 1952- CANR-24
Earlier sketch in CA 107
See also SATA 51, 84
See also SATA-Brief 37
Calmer, Edgar 1907-1986 .... CANR-20
Obituary 118
Earlier sketch in CA 69-72
See also DLB 4
Calmer, Ned
See Calmer, Edgar
Calmus, Lawrence 1943- 111
Calnan, T(homas) D(aniel) 1915- 29-32R
Calne, Roy Yorke 1930- 61-64
Calonne, David Stephen 1953- 114
Calta, Louis 1913(?)-1990 Obituary 132
Caltagirone, Carmen L(illian) 1950- 114
Calter, Paul (Arthur) 1934- CANR-57
Earlier sketches in CA 41-44R, CANR-14, 31
Calverley, C. S. 1831-1884 .... DLB 35
Calvert, Elinor H.
See Lasell, Elinor H.
Calvert, Gene 1943- 144
Calvert, George Henry 1803-1889 .... DLB 1, 64
Calvert, John
See Leaf, (Wilbur) Munro
Calvert, Laura D. 1922- 37-40R
Calvert, Monte A(lan) 1938- 21-24R
Calvert, Patricia 1931- CANR-21
Earlier sketch in CA 105
See also AAYA 18
See also JRDA
See also MAICYA
See also SAAS 17
See also SATA 45, 69
Calvert, Peter (Anthony Richard) 1936- .. CANR-71
Earlier sketches in CA 25-28R, CANR-11
Calvert, Robert, Jr. 1922- 25-28R
Calvert, Theodora 1898-1988 Obituary 128
Calvez, Jean-Yves 1927- 57-60
Calvin, Henry
See Hanley, Clifford
Calvin, Melvin 1911- 155
Calvin, Ross 1890(?)-1970 Obituary 104
Calvin, William H(oward) 1939- 123
Calvino, Italo 1923-1985 .... CANR-61
Obituary 116
Earlier sketches in CA 85-88, CANR-23
See also CLC 5, 8, 11, 22, 33, 39, 73
See also DAM NOV
See also DLB 196
See also MTCW 1
See also SSC 3
Calvo, Lino Novas
See Novas Calvo, Lino
Calvocoressi, Peter (John Ambrose) 1912- ... 65-68
Cam, Helen Maud 1885-1968 .... CAP-1
Earlier sketch in CA 13-14
Camara, Helder Pessoa 1909- 61-64
Camarillo, Albert (M.) 1948- 132
Camarillo, Alberto
See Camarillo, Albert (M.)
Camazine, S(cott) 1952- 129
Camber, Andrew
See Bingley, David Ernest
Cambie, R(ichard) C(onrad) 1931- 143
Cambon, Glauco (Gianlorenzo) 1921-1988 ....
CANR-7
Obituary 125
Earlier sketch in CA 17-20R
Camden, Archie 1888-1979 114
Camden, William 1551-1623 .... DLB 172
Cameja, Pedro
See Camejo, Peter (Miguel)
Camejo, Pedro
See Camejo, Peter (Miguel)
Camejo, Pedro M.
See Camejo, Peter (Miguel)
Camejo, Peter (Miguel) 1939- 125
Brief entry 105
Camerini, Mario 1895-1981 Obituary 103
Cameron, A(rchibald) J(ames) 1920- 73-76
Cameron, Alan (Douglas Edward) 1938- .. CANR-8
Earlier sketch in CA 61-64
Cameron, Alexander
See Gibson, Alexander Cameron
Cameron, Allan Gillies 1930- 102
Cameron, Allan W(illiams) 1938- 33-36R
Cameron, Angus de Mille 1913- 102
Cameron, Angus Fraser 1941-1983 122
Obituary 109
Cameron, Ann 1943- CANR-57
Earlier sketch in CA 101
See also SAAS 20
See also SATA 27, 89
Cameron, (Barbara) Anne 1938- 136
Cameron, Betsy 1949- 101
Cameron, (Jack) Bruce 1913-1979 .... 1-4R
Obituary 133
Cameron, Carey 1952- 135
See also CLC 59
Cameron, Caryn
See Harper, Karen
Cameron, Charla
See Skinner, Gloria Dale
Cameron, Constance Carpenter 1937- 49-52
Cameron, D. A.
See Cameron, Donald (Allan)
Cameron, D. Y.
See Cook, Dorothy Mary
Cameron, David R(obertson) 1941- 73-76
Cameron, Deborah 1958- CANR-53
Earlier sketch in CA 126
Cameron, Donald
See Bryans, Robert Harbinson
Cameron, Donald (Allan) 1937- CANR-8
Earlier sketch in CA 21-24R
Cameron, Edna M. 1905- CAP-1
Earlier sketch in CA 9-10
See also SATA 3
Cameron, Eleanor (Frances) 1912-1996 . CANR-22
Obituary 154
Earlier sketches in CA 1-4R, CANR-2
See also CLR 1
See also DLB 52
See also JRDA
See also MAICYA
See also MTCW 1
See also SAAS 10
See also SATA 1, 25
See also SATA-Obit 93
Cameron, Eleanor Cranston 118
Cameron, Eleanor Elford 1910- 77-80
Cameron, Elizabeth
See Nowell, Elizabeth Cameron
Cameron, Elizabeth Jane 1910-1976 ..... CANR-1
Obituary 69-72
Earlier sketch in CA 1-4R
See also SATA 32
See also SATA-Obit 30
Cameron, Elspeth 1943- 113
Cameron, Frank T. 1909- CAP-1
Earlier sketch in CA 19-20
Cameron, George Frederick 1854-1885 .... DLB 99
Cameron, George Glenn
1905-1979 Obituary 89-92
Cameron, Harold W. 1905- 81-84
Cameron, Hope
See Morritt, Hope
Cameron, Ian
See Payne, Donald Gordon
Cameron, J(ames) M(unro) 1910- CANR-2
Earlier sketch in CA 5-8R
Cameron, (Mark) James (Walter)
1911-1985 .... 21-24R
Obituary 114
Cameron, James 1954- CANR-71
Earlier sketch in CA 137
See also AAYA 9, 27
Cameron, James R(eese) 1929- 33-36R
Cameron, James Sorel
See Sorel-Cameron, James (Robert)
Cameron, John 1914- 29-32R
Cameron, Joy 1912- 132
Cameron, Julie
See Cameron, Lou
Cameron, Kate
See Du Breuil, (Elizabeth) L(or)inda
and McGlamry, Beverly
Cameron, Kenneth 1922- 103
Cameron, Kenneth M. 1931- 129
Cameron, Kenneth Neill 1908-1994 ...... CANR-3
Obituary 144
Earlier sketch in CA 9-12R
Cameron, Kenneth Walter 1908- CANR-49
Earlier sketches in CA 21-24R, CANR-8, 24
Cameron, Kim S(terling) 1946- 109
Cameron, Lorna
See Fraser, Anthea
Cameron, Lou 1924- CANR-21
Earlier sketches in CA 1-4R, CANR-4
Cameron, Lucy Lyttelton 1781-1858 ...... DLB 163
Cameron, M(alcolm) G(ordon) Graham
See Graham-Cameron, M(alcolm) G(ordon)
Cameron, M. Graham
See Graham-Cameron, M(alcolm) G(ordon)
Cameron, M(alcolm) L(aurence) 1918- 146
Cameron, Mary Owen 1915- 13-16R
Cameron, Maxwell A. 1961- 151
Cameron, Meribeth E(lliott) 1905-1997 .... 1-4R
Obituary 159
Cameron, Mike Graham
See Graham-Cameron, M(alcolm) G(ordon)
Cameron, Neil 1920-1985 Obituary 115
Cameron, Peter 1959- CANR-50
Earlier sketch in CA 125
See also CLC 44
Cameron, Polly 1928- 17-20R
See also SATA 2
Cameron, Roderick (William) 1913-1985 . CANR-72
Obituary 117
Brief entry 113
Cameron, Rondo (Emmett) 1925- CANR-5
Earlier sketch in CA 1-4R
Cameron, Scott 1962- .... SATA 84
Cameron, Sharon 1947- 123
Cameron, Silver Donald
See Cameron, Donald (Allan)
Cameron, William Bleasdell 1862-1951 ..... DLB 99
Cameron, William Bruce 1920- 37-40R
Cameron, William J(ames) 1926- Brief entry ... 116
Cameron Watt, Donald 1928- CANR-14
Earlier sketch in CA 77-80
Camille, Michael 1958- 137
Camilleri, Joseph A. 1944- CANR-41
Earlier sketch in CA 117
Caminada, Jerome (Charles)
1911-1985 Obituary 117
Caminals-Heath, Roser 1956- 137
Camm, John 1718-1778 .... DLB 31
Cammack, Floyd M(cKee) 1933- CANR-6
Earlier sketch in CA 9-12R
Cammann, Schuyler (van Rensselaer) 1912- . 9-12R
Cammarata, Jerry F(rank) 1947- 81-84
Cammer, Leonard 1913- 65-68
Cammermeyer, Margarethe 1942- 152
Camner, James 1950- 108
Camnitzer, Luis 1937- 152
Camoin, Francois Andre 1939- 61-64
Camon, Ferdinando 1935- .... DLB 196
Camp, Candace (Pauline) 1949- CANR-42
Earlier sketch in CA 102
Camp, Charles L. 1893-1975 Obituary 61-64
See also SATA-Obit 31
Camp, Dalton Kingsley 1920- 61-64
Camp, Fred V(alterma) 1911- 49-52
Camp, Helen C(ollier) 1939- 152
Camp, James 1923- 33-36R
Camp, Joe
See Camp, Joseph Shelton, Jr.
Camp, John (Michael Francis) 1915- 93-96
Camp, John 1944- 138
Camp, Joseph Shelton, Jr. 1939- 129
Camp, Robert C. 1935- 150
Camp, Roderic (Ai) 1945- CANR-41
Earlier sketches in CA 102, CANR-18
Camp, T(homas) Edward 1929- 13-16R
Camp, Walter (Chauncey) 1859-1925 .... YABC 1
Camp, Wesley D(ouglass) 1915- 17-20R
Camp, William (Newton Alexander) 1926- ... 61-64
Campa, Arthur L(eon) 1905- CANR-40
Earlier sketch in CA 73-76
See also HW
Campaigne, Jameson Gilbert 1914-1985 ...... 1-4R
Obituary 114
Campana, Dino 1885-1932 Brief entry 117
See also DLB 114
See also TCLC 20
Campanella, Francis B. 1936- 53-56
Campanile, Archille 1900(?)-1977 Obituary ... 69-72
Campanile, Pasquale Festa
See Festa Campanile, Pasquale
Campbell, A. C.
See Campbell, Andrew C.
Campbell, Alan K(eith) 1923-1998 .... CANR-3
Obituary 164
Earlier sketch in CA 5-8R
Campbell, Alasdair Iain
See Hamilton, Iain (Betram)
Campbell, Albert A.
See Campbell, (Albert) Angus
Campbell, Alexander 1912-1977 61-64
Obituary 69-72
Campbell, Alistair 1907-1974 .... CAP-1
Earlier sketch in CA 17-18
Campbell, Alla (Linda Renee) Bozarth
See Bozarth-Campbell, Alla (Linda Renee)
Campbell, (Elizabeth) Andrea 1963- ...... SATA 50
Campbell, Andrew C. 1923- Brief entry 114
Campbell, Angus
See Chetwynd-Hayes, R(onald Henry Glynn)
Campbell, (Albert) Angus 1910-1980 129
Obituary 105
Campbell, Ann R. 1925- 21-24R
See also SATA 11
Campbell, Archibald Bruce 1881- CAP-1
Earlier sketch in CA 13-16
Campbell, Arnold Everitt 1906-1980 Obituary .. 108
Campbell, Arthur A(ndrews) 1924- CANR-43
Earlier sketch in CA 1-4R
Campbell, Ballard Crooker, Jr. 1940- 104
Campbell, Beatrice Murphy
See Murphy, Beatrice M.
Campbell, Beatrix 1947- 138
Campbell, Bebe Moore 1950- 139
See also AAYA 26
See also BW 2
Campbell, Bernard G(rant) 1930- 21-24R
Campbell, Bill 1960- .... SATA 89
Campbell, Blanche 1902- 5-8R
Campbell, Bruce
See Epstein, Samuel
Campbell, Camilla 1905-1992 .... CANR-72
Earlier sketches in CAP-2, CA 25-28
See also SATA 26
Campbell, Carlos Cardozo 1937- 102
Campbell, Charles Arthur
1897-1974 Obituary 49-52
Campbell, Charles S(outter) 1911- 69-72
Campbell, Clarice (Marjorie T(hompson) 1907- . 166
Campbell, Clive
See MacRae, Donald G.
Campbell, Clyde Crane
See Gold, H(orace) L(eonard)
Campbell, Colin Dearborn 1917- 33-36R
Campbell, Cy(ril Calvin) 1925- 97-100
Campbell, D(onald)
See Gilford, C(harles) B(ernard)
Campbell, D(onald) Ross 1939- 117
Campbell, Dan H(ampton) 1907-1974 Obituary . 112
Campbell, David (Watt Ian) 1915-1979 97-100
Campbell, David 1961- 146
Campbell, David A(itken) 1927- CANR-11
Earlier sketch in CA 25-28R
Campbell, David (John) Graham
See Graham-Campbell, David (John)
Campbell, David P. 1934- 21-24R
Campbell, Dennis M(arion) 1945- 73-76
Campbell, Don(ald Guy) 1922-1991 .... 17-20R
Obituary 135
Campbell, Donald 1940- CANR-56
Earlier sketches in CA 69-72, CANR-30
Campbell, Donald E. 1943- 138
Campbell, Duane E(ugene) 1941- 116
Campbell, E(lwood) G(ordon) 1923- 107
Campbell, E. Simms 1906-1971 Obituary 93-96
Campbell, Edward D(unscomb) C(hristian), Jr.
1946- CANR-26
Earlier sketch in CA 106
Campbell, Edward F(ay), Jr. 1932- 13-16R
Campbell, Elizabeth McClure 1891- 37-40R
Campbell, Enid (Mona) 1932- 109
Campbell, Ernest Q(ueener) 1926- 37-40R
Campbell, Eugene Edward 1915- 21-24R
Campbell, Ewing 1940- CANR-53
Earlier sketches in CA 73-76, CANR-13, 29
Campbell, F(enton) Gregory, Jr. 1939- 69-72
Campbell, Francis Stuart
See Kuehnelt-Leddihn, Erik (Maria) Ritter von
Campbell, G(aylon) S(anford) 1940- 107
Campbell, George F(rederick) 1915- CANR-14
Earlier sketch in CA 65-68
Campbell, Georgia Arianna Ziadie 1949- 140
Campbell, Graeme 1931- 77-80
Campbell, Hannah 9-12R
Campbell, Herbert James 1925- 97-100
Campbell, Hope 1925- CANR-10
Earlier sketch in CA 61-64
See also SATA 20
Campbell, Howard E(rnest) 1925- CANR-7
Earlier sketch in CA 57-60
Campbell, Hugh 1930- .... SATA 90
Campbell, Ian 1899-1978 53-56
Obituary 103
Campbell, Ian 1942- CANR-25
Earlier sketches in CA 65-68, CANR-9
Campbell, J(ames) Arthur 1916- 53-56
Campbell, Jack K(enagy) 1927- 21-24R
Campbell, James 1920- 57-60
Campbell, James B. 1944- 165
Campbell, James Dykes 1838-1895 .... DLB 144
Campbell, James E(dward) 1945- 107
Campbell, James Edwin 1867-1896 .... DLB 50
Campbell, James Howard 1928- 113
Campbell, James Marshall 1895-1977 73-76
Obituary 69-72
Campbell, Jane
See Edwards, Jane Campbell
Campbell, Jane 1934- 41-44R
Campbell, Janet Bruce 1955- 121
Campbell, (Mary) Jean 1943- 115
Campbell, Jeff(erson) H(olland) 1931- 41-44R
Campbell, Jeffrey
See Black, Campbell
Campbell, Jeremy 1931- CANR-29
Earlier sketch in CA 109
Interview in CANR-29
Campbell, Jim
See Campbell, James Howard
Campbell, Jo Ann (L.) 1958- 157
Campbell, Joan 1929- 109
Campbell, Joanna
See Bly, Carol(yn)
Campbell, John 1653-1728 .... DLB 43
Campbell, John 1947- CANR-35
Earlier sketch in CA 114
Campbell, John 1956- 149
Campbell, John Coert 1911- CANR-3
Earlier sketch in CA 1-4R
Campbell, John Creighton 1941- 111
Campbell, John Franklin
1940(?)-1971 Obituary 33-36R
Campbell, John Lorne 1906- 29-32R
Campbell, John R(oy) 1933- 53-56
Campbell, John W(ood, Jr.) 1910-1971 .. CANR-34
Obituary 29-32R
Earlier sketches in CAP-2, CA 21-22
See also CLC 32
See also DLB 8
See also MTCW 1
Campbell, Joseph 1904-1987 .... CANR-61
Obituary 124
Earlier sketches in CA 1-4R, CANR-3, 28
See also AAYA 3
See also BEST 89:2
See also CLC 69
See also MTCW 1
Campbell, Judith
See Pares, Marion (Stapylton)
Campbell, Julie
See Tatham, Julie Campbell
Campbell, Karen
See Beaty, Betty
Campbell, Karlyn Kohrs 1937- CANR-39
Earlier sketches in CA 53-56, CANR-4, 18
Campbell, Katie 1957- 136
Campbell, Keith 1938- 106
Campbell, Keith Oliver 1920- 110
Campbell, Ken 1941- 77-80
Campbell, Kenneth 1901(?)-1979 Obituary ... 85-88
Campbell, Lady Colin
See Campbell, Georgia Arianna Ziadie
Campbell, Laurence R(andolph) 1903-1987 126
Campbell, Lawrence James 1931- 106
Campbell, Litta Belle 1886-1980 .... CANR-5
Earlier sketch in CA 5-8R

Campbell, Louisa D. 1958- 121
Campbell, Louisa Dresser 1907-1989 Obituary . 129
Campbell, Luke
See Madison, Thomas A(lvin)
Campbell, Malcolm J(ames) 1930- CANR-21
Earlier sketches in CA 57-60, CANR-6
Campbell, Margaret 69-72
Campbell, (Gabrielle) Margaret (Vere) 1886-1952 Brief entry 116
See also Bowen, Marjorie and Shearing, Joseph
Campbell, Margaret 1916- 106
Campbell, Maria 1940- CANR-54
Earlier sketch in CA 102
See also CLC 85
See also DAC
See also NNAL
Campbell, Marion 1919- 162
Campbell, Marjorie Wilkins 97-100
Campbell, Mary B(aine) 1954- 136
Campbell, Mavis C. 148
Campbell, Michael Mussen 1924-1984 102
Obituary 113
Campbell, Oscar James, Jr. 1879-1970 Obituary 29-32R
Campbell, Patricia J(ean) 1930- CANR-35
Earlier sketch in CA 103
See also SATA 45
Campbell, Patricia Piatt 1901- 25-28R
Campbell, Patrick Gordon 1913-1980 Obituary . 102
Campbell, Patty
See Campbell, Patricia J(ean)
Campbell, Paul N. 1923- 21-24R
Campbell, Penelope 1935- 33-36R
Campbell, Peter (Walter) 1926- CANR-11
Earlier sketches in CAP-1, CA 13-14
Campbell, Peter A. 1948- 167
See also SATA 99
Campbell, Peter Anthony 1935- 21-24R
Campbell, R. T.
See Todd, Ruthven
Campbell, R. W.
See Campbell, Rosemae Wells
Campbell, R(obert) Wayne 1941- 167
Campbell, R(obert) Wright 1927- CANR-60
Earlier sketches in CA 57-60, CANR-6, 21, 24
Campbell, (John) Ramsey 1946- CANR-7
Earlier sketch in CA 57-60
Interview in CANR-7
See also CLC 42
See also SSC 19
Campbell, Randolph B(luford) 1940- 41-44R
Campbell, Rex R. 1931- 41-44R
Campbell, Rhonda 1962- 167
Campbell, Rita Ricardo
See Ricardo-Campbell, Rita
Campbell, Robert
See Campbell, R(obert) Wright
Campbell, Robert 1922-1977 .... CANR-8
Obituary 73-76
Earlier sketch in CA 53-56
Campbell, Robert B(lair) 1923- 69-72
Campbell, Robert C(harles) 1924- 49-52
Campbell, Robert Dale 1914- 9-12R
Campbell, Robert Wellington 1926- CANR-3
Earlier sketch in CA 1-4R
Campbell, Robin
See Strachan, Ian
Campbell, Rod 1945- 155
See also SATA 51, 98
See also SATA-Brief 44
Campbell, Rosemae Wells 1909- 13-16R
See also SATA 1
Campbell, (Ignatius) Roy (Dunnachie) 1901-1957 155
Brief entry 104
See also DLB 20
See also TCLC 5
Campbell, Sheldon 1919- 41-44R
Campbell, Sid 1944- CANR-48
Earlier sketch in CA 118
Campbell, Stanley W(allace) 1926- 49-52
Campbell, Stephen K(ent) 1935- 49-52
Campbell, Thomas 1777-1844 .... DLB 93; 144
Campbell, Thomas E.
See Campbell, Tom
Campbell, Thomas F. 1924- 21-24R
Campbell, Thomas M(oody) 1936-1993 .... CANR-53
Obituary 142
Earlier sketch in CA 49-52
Campbell, Tom 1938- 150
Campbell, Tom D. 1938- CANR-54
Earlier sketch in CA 126
Campbell, Tracy (A.) 1962- 146
Campbell, Wallace Justin 1910-1998 135
Obituary 163
Campbell, Wilfred
See Campbell, William
See also TCLC 9
Campbell, Will D(avis) 1924- CANR-45
Earlier sketches in CA 5-8R, CANR-7, 22
Campbell, William 1858(?)-1918 Brief entry 106
See also Campbell, Wilfred
See also DLB 92
Campbell, William Edward March 1893-1954 Brief entry 108
See also March, William
Campbell-Johnson, Alan 1913- 65-68
Campbell-Purdie, Wendy 1925- 21-24R
Campen, Richard N(ewman) 1912- 69-72
Camper, Carol 1954- 149
Camper, Shirley
See Soman, Shirley Camper
Campion, Dan(iel Ray) 1949- 157
Campion, Donald Richard 1921-1988 Obituary . 128
Campion, Edmund 1539-1581 .... DLB 167
Campion, Jane 138
See also CLC 95
Campion, Joan 1940- 124
Campion, Nardi Reeder 1917- CANR-6
Earlier sketch in CA 1-4R
See also SATA 22
Campion, Nicholas 1953- 162
Campion, Rosamond
See Rosmond, Babette
Campion, Sidney R(onald) 1891- CAP-1
Earlier sketch in CA 9-10
Campion, Thomas 1567-1620 . CDBLB Before 1660
See also DAM POET
See also DLB 58, 172
Camplin, Jamie (Robert) 1947- 97-100
Campling, Christopher R(ussell) 1925- 113
Campling, Elizabeth 1948- 123
See also SATA 53
Campobello, Nellie (Francisca Ernestina) 1912- 131
See also HW
Campolo, Anthony, Jr. 1935- CANR-26
Earlier sketches in CA 69-72, CANR-11
Campos, Alvaro de
See Pessoa, Fernando (Antonio Nogueira)
Camps, Arnulf (P. H. J. M.) 1925- 131
Camps, Francis Edward 1905-1972 .... 37-40R
Camps, Luis 1928- .... SATA 66
Campton, David 1924- CANR-47
Earlier sketches in CA 5-8R, CANR-5, 20
Camus, Albert 1913-1960 89-92
See also CLC 1, 2, 4, 9, 11, 14, 32, 63, 69
See also DA
See also DAB
See also DAC
See also DAM DRAM, MST, NOV
See also DC 2
See also DLB 72
See also MTCW 1
See also SSC 9
See also WLC
Camus, Raoul Francois 1930- 65-68
Camus, (Jean) Renaud (Gabriel) 1946- 108
Camuti, Louis J(oseph) 1893-1981 101
Obituary 103
Canada, Geoffrey 1954- 165
Canada, Lena 1942- 93-96
Canaday, John E(dwin) 1907-1985 .... CANR-7
Obituary 116
Earlier sketch in CA 13-16R
Canan, James William 1929- 61-64
Canary
See Conn, Canary Denise
Canary, Robert H(ughes) 1939- CANR-11
Earlier sketch in CA 29-32R
Canavaggio, Jean (Francois) 1936- 167
Canavan, Francis 1917- 118
Canaway, W(illiam) H(amilton) 1925- 93-96
Canby, Courtlandt 1914- 118
Canby, Henry Seidel 1878-1961 Obituary 89-92
See also DLB 91
Canby, Vincent 1924- 81-84
See also CLC 13
Cancale
See Desnos, Robert
Cancellare, Frank 1910-1985 Obituary 116
Cancian, Francesca M(icaela) 1937- 57-60
Cancian, Francis Alexander 1934- CANR-7
Earlier sketch in CA 53-56
Cancian, Frank
See Cancian, Francis Alexander
Candelaria, Cordelia (Chavez) 1943- 131
See also DLB 82
See also HW
Candelaria, Frederick (Henry) 1929- 17-20R
Candelaria, Nash 1928- CANR-72
Earlier sketches in CA 69-72, CANR-11, 32
See also DLB 82
See also HW
Candell, Victor 1903-1977 .... SATA-Obit 24
Candida
See Hoffman, Lisa
Candilis, Wray O. 1927- CANR-10
Earlier sketch in CA 25-28R
Candisky, Catherine A. 1961- 144
Candland, Douglas Keith 1934- CANR-2
Earlier sketch in CA 5-8R
Candler, Julie 1919- 65-68
Candlin, Enid Saunders 1909- CANR-1
Earlier sketch in CA 45-48
Candy, Edward
See Neville, B(arbara) Alison (Boodson)
Candy, John (Franklin) 1950-1994 155
Candy, Philip C(arne) 1950- 140
Cane, Melville (Henry) 1879-1980 .... CANR-72
Obituary 97-100
Earlier sketches in CA 1-4R, CANR-6, 8
Canellopoulos, Panayiotis 1902-1986 Obituary . 120
Canemaker, John 1943- 81-84
Caner, Mary Paul 1893- CAP-2
Earlier sketch in CA 21-22
Canetti, Elias 1905-1994 .... CANR-61
Obituary 146
Earlier sketches in CA 21-24R, CANR-23
See also CLC 3, 14, 25, 75, 86
See also DLB 85, 124
See also MTCW 1
Caney, Steven 1941- 104
Canfield, Cass 1897-1986 .... 41-44R
Obituary 118
Canfield, (Fayette) Curtis 1903-1986 Obituary .. 120
Canfield, D(elos) Lincoln 1903- 25-28R
Canfield, Dorothea F.
See Fisher, Dorothy (Frances) Canfield
Canfield, Dorothea Frances
See Fisher, Dorothy (Frances) Canfield
Canfield, Dorothy
See Fisher, Dorothy (Frances) Canfield
Canfield, Gae Whitney 1931- 113
Canfield, Jack 1944- 159
Canfield, James D(avid) 1937- 117
Canfield, James K(eith) 1925- 25-28R
Canfield, James Lewis 1942- 121
Canfield, Jane White 1897-1984 109
Obituary 112
See also SATA 32
See also SATA-Obit 38
Canfield, John A(lan) 1941- 37-40R
Canfield, Kenneth French 1909- CAP-1
Earlier sketch in CA 13-16
Canfield, Leon Hardy 1886- 1-4R
Canfield, Muriel
See Kanoza, Muriel Canfield
Canfield, Muriel 1935- 115
Canfield, Sandra (Kay Patterson) 1944- 146
Cang, Joel 1899-1974 .... CAP-2
Earlier sketch in CA 29-32
Cangemi, Sister Marie Lucita 1920- 21-24R
Canham, Erwin D(ain) 1904-1982 .... CAP-1
Obituary 105
Earlier sketch in CA 13-14
See also DLB 127
Canham, Kingsley 1945- 57-60
Caniff, Milton (Arthur) 1907-1988 .... CANR-47
Obituary 125
Earlier sketch in CA 85-88
See also AITN 1
See also SATA-Obit 58
Canin, Ethan 1960- 135
Brief entry 131
See also CLC 55
Canitz, Friedrich Rudolph Ludwig von 1654-1699 .... DLB 168
Cankar, Ivan 1876-1918 .... DLB 147
Cann, Marjorie Mitchell 1924- 89-92
Cannadine, David 1950- 151
Cannam, Peggie 1925- 13-16R
Cannan, Denis 1919- CANR-68
Earlier sketches in CA 57-60, CANR-7
Cannan, Gilbert E. 1884-1955 Brief entry 111
See also DLB 10, 197
Cannan, Joanna 1896-1961
See Pullein-Thompson, Joanna Maxwell
See also DLB 191
See also SATA 82
Cannell, Charles (Henry) 1882-1947 155
Cannell, Dorothy 165
Cannell, Kathleen Biggar (Eaton) 1891-1974 ... 106
See also DLB 4
Cannell, Skipwith 1887-1957 .... DLB 45
Cannell, Stephen J(oseph) 1941- 138
Canney, Donald L. 1947- 147
Canning, George 1770-1827 .... DLB 158
Canning, Jeff(rey Michael) 1947- 73-76
Canning, John 1920- 89-92
Canning, Paul 1947- 126
Canning, Peter 1937- 159
Canning, Ray R(ussell) 1920- 41-44R
Canning, Victor 1911-1986 .... CANR-63
Obituary 118
Earlier sketches in CA 13-16R, CANR-6
Cannistraro, Philip V(incent) 1942- 141
Cannon, A(nn) E(dwards) .... SATA 93
Cannon, Alexander 1896-1963(?) Obituary 111
Cannon, Beth 1951- 69-72
Cannon, Bettie (Waddell) 1922- 126
See also SATA 59
Cannon, Bill
See Cannon, William S.
Cannon, Cornelia (James) 1876-1969 Obituary . 109
See also SATA-Brief 28
Cannon, Curt
See Hunter, Evan
Cannon, David Wadsworth, Jr. 1911-1938 155
See also BW 2
Cannon, Dolores Eilene 1931- 166
Cannon, Dyan 1937- 167
Cannon, Eileen E(mily) 1948- 165
Cannon, Frank
See Mayhar, Ardath
Cannon, Garland (Hampton) 1924- CANR-57
Earlier sketches in CA 33-36R, CANR-13, 30
Cannon, Grant Groesbeck 1911-1969 Obituary . 117
Cannon, Harold C(harles) 1930- 45-48
Cannon, Helen 1921- 101
Cannon, James Monroe III 1918- 1-4R
Cannon, James P. 1890(?)-1974 Obituary 53-56
Cannon, Janell 1957- .... SATA 78
Cannon, Jimmy 1909-1973 Obituary 104
See also DLB 171
Cannon, John
See Newton, Michael
Cannon, John (Darcy) 1918- 154
Cannon, Le Grand, Jr. 1899-1979 Obituary .. 93-96
Cannon, Lou(is S.) 1933- CANR-43
Earlier sketch in CA 29-32R
Cannon, Marian G. 1923- 151
See also SATA 85
Cannon, Mark W(ilcox) 1928- 13-16R
Cannon, Michael 1929- 150
Cannon, Poppy
See White, Poppy Cannon
Cannon, Sarah Ophelia Colley 1912-1996 129
Obituary 151
Cannon, Taffy
See Cannon, Eileen E(mily)
Cannon, William Ragsdale 1916-1997 ... CANR-18
Obituary 158
Earlier sketches in CA 1-4R, CANR-4
Cannon, William S. 1918- 29-32R
Canny, Nicholas P(atrick) 1944- 69-72
Cano, Daniel 1947- 155
Cano-Ballesta, Juan 1932- CANR-1
Earlier sketch in CA 49-52
Canon, Lance Kirkpatrick 1939- 45-48
Canovan, Margaret 1939- 81-84
Cansdale, George (Soper) 1909-1993 .... 9-12R
Obituary 142
Cant, Gilbert 1909-1982 Obituary 107
Cant, Reginald (Edward) 1914-1987 Obituary .. 122
Cantacuzene, Julia 1876-1975 Obituary 61-64
Cantacuzino, Sherban 1928- 118
Cantalupo, Charles 1951- 126
Cantelon, John E(dward) 1924- 9-12R
Cantelon, Philip L(ouis) 1940- 124
Canter, Mark 1952- 152
Canterbery, E(stes) Ray 1935- 41-44R
Cantin, Eileen 1931- 53-56
Cantin, Eugene Thorpe 1944- 45-48
Cantinat, Jean 1902- 29-32R
Cantlupe, Joe 1951- 140
Canton, Katia 1962- 152
Cantone, Vic 1933- 138
Cantor, Arthur 1920- 29-32R
Cantor, Eli 1913- CANR-14
Earlier sketch in CA 77-80
Cantor, Geoffrey 1943- 135
Cantor, George (Nathan) 1941- 138
Cantor, Gilbert M. 1929(?)-1987 Obituary 122
Cantor, Harold 1926- 136
Cantor, Leonard M(artin) 1927- 69-72
Cantor, Louis 1934- 29-32R
Cantor, Milton 1925- Brief entry 112
Cantor, Muriel G. 1923- CANR-12
Earlier sketch in CA 33-36R
Cantor, Norman F(rank) 1929- 102
Cantor, Paul A(rthur) 1945- 89-92
Cantor, Paul David 1916-1979 Obituary 89-92
Cantori, Louis J. 1934- 29-32R
Cantrell, J(ohn) A(nthony) 1952- 123
Cantrell, Lisa W. 1945- 166
Cantril, Albert H(adley) 1940- 111
Cantsin, Monty
See Home, Stewart
Cantu, Norma Elia 152
Cantu, Robert Clark 1938- 108
Cantwell, Aston
See Platt, Charles
Cantwell, Dennis P(atrick) 1940-1997 57-60
Obituary 157
Cantwell, Lois 1951- 121
Cantwell, Mary 140
Cantwell, Robert Emmett 1908-1978 .... CANR-4
Obituary 81-84
Earlier sketch in CA 5-8R
See also DLB 9
Canty, Kevin 1954(?)- 151
Cantzlaar, George La Fond 1906-1967 .... CAP-1
Earlier sketch in CA 13-16
Canuck, Abe
See Bingley, David Ernest
Canusi, Jose
See Barker, S(quire) Omar
Canutt, Enos Edward 1895(?)-1986 155
Obituary 119
Brief entry 114
Canutt, Yakima
See Canutt, Enos Edward
Can Xue
See Deng, Xiao Hua
Canzoneri, Robert (Wilburn) 1925- 17-20R
Cao, Guanlong 163
Cao, Lan 1961- 165
See also CLC 109
Capaldi, Nicholas 1939- 21-24R
Cape, Judith
See Page, P(atricia) K(athleen)
Cape, Peter (Irwin) 1929- 108
Cape, William H(enry) 1920- 9-12R
Capeci, Dominic Joseph, Jr. 1940- 77-80
Capek, Karel 1890-1938 140
Brief entry 104
See also DA
See also DAB
See also DAC
See also DAM DRAM, MST, NOV
See also DC 1
See also TCLC 6, 37
See also WLC
Capek, Michael 1947- 150
See also SATA 96
Capek, Milic 1909- CANR-4
Earlier sketch in CA 1-4R
Capel, Roger
See Sheppard, Lancelot C(apel)
Capelle, Russell B(eckett) 1917- 5-8R
Capen, Joseph 1658-1725 .... DLB 24
Capers, Gerald Mortimer, Jr. 1909- CANR-70
Earlier sketch in CA 5-8R
Capes, Bernard 1854-1918 .... DLB 156
Capie, Forrest H(unter) 1940- 146
Capitan, William H(arry) 1933- 29-32R
Capitanchik, Maurice 1929(?)-1985 Obituary .. 118
Capitman, Barbara Baer 1920-1990 Obituary .. 131
Capitman, William G(ardiner) 1921-1975 122
Obituary 111
Capizzi, Michael 1941- 41-44R
Caplan, Arthur L(eonard) 1950- CANR-22
Earlier sketch in CA 106
Caplan, David 1947- 105
Caplan, Edwin H(arvey) 1926- 41-44R
Caplan, Frank 1911(?)-1988 110
Obituary 126
Caplan, Gerald 1917- CANR-40
Earlier sketches in CA 25-28R, CANR-18
Caplan, Harry 1896- CAP-2
Earlier sketch in CA 23-24
Caplan, Lincoln 1950- 138

Caplan, Lionel 33-36R
Caplan, Mariana 1969- 167
Caplan, Paula J(oan) 1947- 129
Caplan, Ralph 1925- 13-16R
Caplan, Ronald Mervyn 1937- 107
Caplan, Theresa 110
Caplan, Thomas (Mark) 1946- 107
Caples, John 1900-1990 .... 21-24R
Obituary 131
Caplin, Alfred Gerald 1909-1979 57-60
Obituary 89-92
See also Capp, Al
See also SATA 61
See also SATA-Obit 21
Caplovitz, David 1928-1992 .... 41-44R
Obituary 139
Caplow, Theodore 1920- CANR-20
Earlier sketches in CA 1-4R, CANR-4
Capon, Edmund (George) 1940- 107
Capon, (Harry) Paul 1912-1969 .... CANR-55
Obituary 103
Earlier sketch in CA 5-8R
Capon, Peter
See Oakley, Eric Gilbert
Capon, Robert Farrar 1925- 136
Brief entry 106
Caponigri, A(loysius) Robert 1915-1983 .. CANR-43
Earlier sketch in CA 37-40R
Caponigro, John Paul 1965- .... SATA 84
Caporale, Rocco 1927- 37-40R
Capote, Truman 1924-1984 .... CANR-62
Obituary 113
Earlier sketches in CA 5-8R, CANR-18
See also CDALB 1941-1968
See also CLC 1, 3, 8, 13, 19, 34, 38, 58
See also DA
See also DAB
See also DAC
See also DAM MST, NOV, POP
See also DLB 2, 185
See also DLBY 80, 84
See also MTCW 1
See also SATA 91
See also SSC 2
See also WLC
Capouya, Emile 122
Brief entry 118
Capp, Al
See Caplin, Alfred Gerald
See also SATA 61
Capp, B. S.
See Capp, Bernard (Stuart)
Capp, Bernard (Stuart) 1943- 130
Capp, Glenn Richard 1910- CANR-3
Earlier sketch in CA 1-4R
Capp, Richard 1935- 81-84
Cappadona, Diane Apostolos
See Apostolos-Cappadona, Diane
Cappel, Constance 1936- CANR-10
Earlier sketch in CA 21-24R
See also SATA 22
Cappelluti, Frank Joseph 1935-1972 .... 37-40R
Capper, Douglas Parode 1898(?)-1979 ...... 9-12R
Obituary 103
Cappo, Joseph 1936- 77-80
Cappon, Daniel 1921- 17-20R
Cappon, Lester J(esse) 1900-1981 106
Obituary 104
Capps, Benjamin (Franklin) 1922- CANR-61
Earlier sketches in CA 5-8R, CANR-7
See also SATA 9
Capps, Carroll M. 1917(?)-1971 Obituary 112
Capps, Clifford Lucille Sheats 1902-1976 ... 37-40R
Capps, Donald E(ric) 1939- CANR-12
Earlier sketch in CA 29-32R
Capps, Jack Lee 1926- 21-24R
Capps, Walter H(olden) 1934-1997 ...... CANR-12
Obituary 162
Earlier sketch in CA 29-32R
Cappy Dick
See Cleveland, George
Capra, Frank 1897-1991 61-64
Obituary 135
See also CLC 16
Capra, Fritjof 1939- 107
Capretta, Patrick J(ohn) 1929-1982 .... 21-24R
Obituary 135
Caprio, Betsy
See Caprio, Elizabeth (Blair) Whitworth
Caprio, Elizabeth (Blair) Whitworth 1933- . CANR-44
Earlier sketches in CA 110, CANR-30
Caprio, Frank S(amuel) 1906- 101
Capron, Alexander Morgan 1944- 115
Capron, Jean F. 1924- 21-24R
Capron, Louis (Bishop) 1891-1971 ...... CANR-71
Earlier sketches in CAP-1, CA 9-10
Capron, Walter Clark 1904-1979 .... CAP-1
Obituary 89-92
Earlier sketch in CA 17-18
Capron, William M(osher) 1920- 29-32R
Caproni, Giorgio 1912-1990 .... DLB 128
Capstick, Peter Hathaway 1940- 102
Captain Kangaroo
See Keeshan, Robert J.
Captain Wheeler
See Ellis, Edward S(ylvester)
Captain X
See Power-Waters, Brian
Captain Young of Yale
See Stratemeyer, Edward L.
Capucine
See Mazille, Capucine
Caputi, Anthony (Francis) 1924- CANR-3
Earlier sketch in CA 1-4R
Caputi, Jane 1953- 129
Caputo, David A(rmand) 1943- 65-68
Caputo, Philip 1941- CANR-40
Earlier sketch in CA 73-76
See also CLC 32
Caputo, Richard K. 1948- 139
Caputo, Robert 1949- 101
Carabelli, Giancarlo 1939- 154
Caradon, Lord
See Foot, Hugh Mackintosh
Caragiale, Ion Luca 1852-1912 157
See also TCLC 76
Caraker, Mary 1929- .... SATA 74
Caraley, Demetrios 1932- 103
Caraman, Philip (George) 1911-1998 .... CANR-70
Obituary 167
Earlier sketches in CA 9-12R, CANR-6, 21
Caramello, Charles 1948- 112
Carano, Paul 1919- 17-20R
Caras, Roger A(ndrew) 1928- CANR-47
Earlier sketches in CA 1-4R, CANR-5
See also SATA 12
Caras, Tracy 1953- 113
Carawan, Candie
See Carawan, Carolanne M.
Carawan, Carolanne M. 1939- 17-20R
Carawan, Guy H., Jr. 1927- 17-20R
Caraway, Caren 1939- .... SATA 57
Caraway, Charless 1888-1977 125
Carbajal, Xavier Joseph 1958- 163
Carballido, Emilio 1925- CANR-54
Earlier sketch in CA 33-36R
See also HW
Carbaugh, Robert J(ohn) 1946- 65-68
Carbery, Thomas F. 29-32R
Carbine, Patricia (Theresa) 1931- 107
Carbone, Elisa Lynn 1954- 149
See also SATA 81
Carbonell, Reyes 1917- 9-12R
Carbonnier, Jeanne 1894-1974 .... CANR-71
Earlier sketches in CAP-2, CA 33-36
See also SATA 3
See also SATA-Obit 34
Carbury, A. B.
See Carr, Albert H. Z(olotkoff)
Carby, Hazel V. 1948- 154
Carcaterra, Lorenzo 1954- 140
Carcopino, Jerome 1881(?)-1970 Obituary 104
Card, Orson Scott 1951- CANR-47
Earlier sketches in CA 102, CANR-27
Interview in CANR-27
See also AAYA 11
See also CLC 44, 47, 50
See also DAM POP
See also MTCW 1
See also SATA 83
Card, T. S. B. 1931- 147
Card, Tim
See Card, T. S. B.
Cardan, Paul
See Castoriadis, Cornelius
Cardarelli, Joseph 1944- 77-80
Cardarelli, Vincenzo 1887-1959 .... DLB 114
Carden, Karen W(ilson) 1946- CANR-1
Earlier sketch in CA 49-52
Carden, Maren Lockwood 53-56
Carden, Patricia J. 1935- 41-44R
Cardenal, Ernesto 1925- CANR-66
Earlier sketches in CA 49-52, CANR-2, 32
See also CLC 31
See also DAM MULT, POET
See also HLC
See also HW
See also MTCW 1
See also PC 22
Cardenas, Daniel N(egrete) 1917- CANR-26
Earlier sketch in CA 45-48
Cardenas, Gilbert 1947- 97-100
Cardenas, Reyes 1948- 152
See also DLB 122
See also HW
Cardew, Cornelius 1936-1981 130
Obituary 108
Cardew, Michael (Ambrose) 1901-1983 .. CANR-30
Obituary 109
Earlier sketch in CA 49-52
Cardiff, Gray Emerson 1949- 89-92
Cardinal, Marie 1929- .... DLB 83
Cardinal, Ora 1913- 111
Cardinal, Roger (Thomas) 1940- CANR-40
Earlier sketches in CA 45-48, CANR-1, 18
Cardinal, Sister Mary Ora
See Cardinal, Ora
Cardona, George 1936- 119
Cardona, Manuel 1934- 156
Cardona-Hine, Alvaro 1926- CANR-5
Earlier sketch in CA 9-12R
Cardone, Samuel S(teve) 1938- 17-20R
Cardoso, Onelio Jorge 1914-1986 .... HW
Cardoza y Aragon, Luis 1904- .... HW
Cardozo, Arlene Rossen 1938- CANR-19
Earlier sketch in CA 102
Cardozo, Benjamin N(athan) 1870-1938 164
Brief entry 117
See also TCLC 65
Cardozo, Michael H(art IV) 1910-1996 ..... 33-36R
Obituary 154
Cardozo, Nancy 103
Cardozo, Peter 1916- 61-64
Cardozo-Freeman, Inez 1928- 131
See also HW
Carducci, Giosue (Alessandro Giuseppe)
1835-1907 163
See also TCLC 32
Cardui, Van
See Wayman, Tony Russell
Cardui, Vanessa
See Wayman, Tony Russell
Cardus, Neville 1889-1975 .... CANR-70
Obituary 57-60
Earlier sketches in CA 61-64, CANR-11
Cardwell, D(onald) S(tephen) L(owell) 1919- ... 101
Cardwell, Guy A(dams) 1905- 13-16R
Care, Felicity
See Coury, Louise Andree
Care, Norman S. 1937- 25-28R
Careless, J(ames) M(aurice) S(tockford) 1919- . 102
Carens, James Francis 1927- CANR-12
Earlier sketch in CA 61-64
Carerra, Kathleen
See Carr, Jess(e Crowe, Jr.)
Cares, Paul B. 1911- 9-12R
Caress, James M. 1947- 122
Caress, Jay
See Caress, James M.
Carette, Louis 1913- 85-88
Carew, Dorothy 1910(?)-1973 Obituary 41-44R
Carew, Dudley Charles 1903-1981 Obituary 103
Carew, Jan (Rynveld) 1925- 77-80
See also BW 2
See also DLB 157
See also SATA 51
See also SATA-Brief 40
Carew, Jocelyn
See Aeby, Jacquelyn
Carew, John Mohun 1921-1980 .... CANR-7
Earlier sketch in CA 13-16R
Carew, Rod(ney Cline) 1945- 104
Carew, Thomas 1595(?)-1640 .... DLB 126
Carew, Tim
See Carew, John Mohun
Carewe, S. C.
See Du Breuil, (Elizabeth) L(or)inda
Carey, Anne
See Nevill, Barry St-John
Carey, Bonnie 1941- .... SATA 18
Carey, Diane 1954- 122
Carey, Drew 1958- 166
Carey, Eileen
See O'Casey, Eileen (Kathleen Reynolds)
Carey, Ernestine Gilbreth 1908- CANR-71
Earlier sketch in CA 5-8R
See also CLC 17
See also SATA 2
Carey, Gary 1938- CANR-34
Earlier sketches in CA 57-60, CANR-15
Carey, Henry 1687(?)-1743 .... DLB 84
Carey, Jacqueline 1954- 162
Carey, James Charles 1915- 13-16R
Carey, Jane Perry (Clark) 1898-1981 73-76
Obituary 105
Carey, John 1934- CANR-35
Earlier sketches in CA 57-60, CANR-6
Carey, John A(ndrew) 1949- 109
Carey, Joseph Kuhn 1957- 135
Carey, Kenneth Moir 1908-1979 Obituary 108
Carey, M. V.
See Carey, Mary V(irginia)
Carey, Mary V(irginia) 1925- CANR-38
Earlier sketches in CA 81-84, CANR-17
See also SATA 44
See also SATA-Brief 39
Carey, Mathew 1760-1839 .... DLB 37, 73
Carey, Michael
See Burton, Edward J.
Carey, Michael (Sausmarez)
1913-1985 Obituary 118
Carey, Michael L(awrence) 1948- 65-68
Carey, Mother Marme Aimee 1931- 13-16R
Carey, Omer L. 1929- CANR-23
Earlier sketches in CA 21-24R, CANR-8
Carey, Patrick W. 1940- 145
Carey, Peter 1943- CANR-53
Brief entry 123
Earlier sketch in CA 127
Interview in 127
See also CLC 40, 55, 96
See also MTCW 1
See also SATA 94
Carey, Richard John 1925- 53-56
Carey, Robert George 1926- Brief entry 108
Carey, Steven Harry 1946(?)-1989 Obituary 129
Carey, Valerie Scho 1949- 128
See also SATA 60
Carey Evans, Olwen (Elizabeth) 1892- 126
Carey-Jones, N(orman) S(tewart) 1911- 21-24R
Carfagne, Cyril
See Jennings, Leslie Nelson
Carfagno, Vincent R. 1935- 41-44R
Carfax, Catherine
See Fairburn, Eleanor
Cargas, Harry J(ames) 1932- CANR-21
Earlier sketches in CA 13-16R, CANR-6
Cargill, Jennifer S(ue) 1944- 109
Cargill, Oscar 1898-1972 .... CANR-15
Obituary 33-36R
Earlier sketch in CA 1-4R
Cargill, Robert L. 1929- 25-28R
Cargo, David N(iels) 1932- 57-60
Cargo, Robert T. 1933- 85-88
Cargoe, Richard
See Payne, (Pierre Stephen) Robert
Carhart, Arthur Hawthorne 1892-1978 ... CANR-71
Earlier sketches in CAP-1, CA 9-10
Caridi, Ronald J. 1941- 25-28R
Carigiet, Alois 1902-1985 73-76
Obituary 119
See also CLR 38
See also SATA 24
See also SATA-Obit 47
Carim, Enver 1938- 136
Carin, Arthur A. 1928- 29-32R
Carin, Michael 1951- 132
Carini, Edward 1923- 61-64
See also SATA 9
Carisella, P(asquale) J. 1922- 134
Caristi, Dom(inic) 1956- 143
Carkeet, David 1946- CANR-38
Earlier sketch in CA 102
See also SATA 75
Carl, Beverly May 1932- CANR-4
Earlier sketch in CA 53-56
Carl, Lillian Stewart 1949- CANR-42
Earlier sketch in CA 118
Carle, Eric 1929- CANR-25
Earlier sketches in CA 25-28R, CANR-10
See also CLR 10
See also MAICYA
See also SAAS 6
See also SATA 4, 65
Carlebach, Michael L(loyd) 1945- 143
Carlell, Lodowick 1602-1675 .... DLB 58
Carlen, Claudia 1906- 106
Carles, Emilie 1900-1979 141
Carless, Jennifer 1960- 146
Carleton, Barbee Oliver 1917- CANR-71
Earlier sketch in CA 21-24R
Carleton, Captain L. C.
See Ellis, Edward S(ylvester)
Carleton, Captain Latham C.
See Ellis, Edward S(ylvester)
Carleton, Latham C.
See Ellis, Edward S(ylvester)
Carleton, Mark T. 1935- CANR-12
Earlier sketch in CA 33-36R
Carleton, R(eginal) Milton 1899-1986 69-72
Obituary 120
Carleton, Will(iam McKendree) 1845-1912 Brief
entry 115
Carleton, William 1794-1869 .... DLB 159
Carleton, William G(raves) 1903- CAP-2
Earlier sketch in CA 25-28
Carley, Larry W. 1950- 139
Carley, Lionel (Kenneth) 1936- 132
Carley, V(an Ness) Royal 1906-1976 .... CAP-2
Earlier sketch in CA 29-32
See also SATA-Obit 20
Carli, Angelo 1937- 49-52
Carlile, Clancy 1930- 128
Carlile, Clark S(tites) 1912- 41-44R
Carlile, Henry 1934- 33-36R
Carlile, Richard 1790-1843 .... DLB 110, 158
Carlin, Gabriel S. 1921- 1-4R
Carlin, George (Denis) 1937- 158
Carlin, Martha 159
Carlin, Thomas W(illard) 1918- 25-28R
Carlin, Vivian F. 1919- 131
Carline, Richard (Cotton) 1896-1980 Obituary .. 105
Carling, Alan H(ugh) 1949- 143
Carling, Francis 1945- 25-28R
Carling, Paul J. 1945- 151
Carlino, Lewis John 1932- CANR-67
Earlier sketch in CA 77-80
Carlinsky, Dan 1944- CANR-47
Earlier sketches in CA 21-24R, CANR-8, 23
Carlip, Hillary 1956- 150
Carlise, Carris
See Pemberton, Margaret
Carlisle, Carol Jones 1919- 29-32R
Carlisle, Clark
See Holding, James (Clark Carlisle, Jr.)
Carlisle, D. M.
See Cook, Dorothy Mary
Carlisle, Douglas H(ilton) 1921- 45-48
Carlisle, E(rvin) Fred 1935- 53-56
Carlisle, Fred 1915- 73-76
Carlisle, Henry (Coffin) 1926- CANR-15
Earlier sketch in CA 13-16R
See also CLC 33
Carlisle, Howard M(yron) 1928- 69-72
Carlisle, Lilian (Matarose) Baker 1912- 53-56
Carlisle, Olga Andreyev 1930- CANR-7
Earlier sketch in CA 13-16R
See also SATA 35
Carlisle, Rodney P. 1936- CANR-49
Earlier sketch in CA 45-48
Carlisle, Thomas (Fiske) 1944- 53-56
Carlisle, Thomas John 1913-1992 .... CANR-40
Earlier sketches in CA 101, CANR-18
Carlock, John R(obert) 1921- 33-36R
Carlock, Lynn
See Cunningham, Marilyn
Carlon, Patricia Bernardette 1927- CANR-56
Earlier sketch in CA 13-16R
Carlquist, Sherwin 1930- 13-16R
Carls, (John) Norman 1907- CAP-2
Earlier sketch in CA 17-18
Carls, Stephen D(ouglas) 1944- 148
Carlsen, Chris
See Holdstock, Robert P.
Carlsen, G(eorge) Robert 1917- CANR-24
Earlier sketches in CA 17-20R, CANR-8
See also SATA 30
Carlsen, James C(aldwell) 1927- 25-28R
Carlsen, Ruth C(hristoffer) 1918- CANR-24
Earlier sketches in CA 17-20R, CANR-8
See also SATA 2
Carlson, Andrew R(aymond) 1934- CANR-71
Earlier sketch in CA 29-32R
Carlson, Arthur E(ugene) 1923- 37-40R
Carlson, Avis D(ungan) 1896-1987 73-76
Obituary 121
Carlson, Bernice Wells 1910- CANR-2
Earlier sketch in CA 5-8R
See also SATA 8
Carlson, Betty 1919- CANR-2
Earlier sketch in CA 1-4R
Carlson, C. C.
See Carlson, Carole C.

Carlson, Carl Walter 1907- 49-52
Carlson, Carole C. 1925- 113
Carlson, Dale (Bick) 1935- CANR-49
Earlier sketches in CA 9-12R, CANR-3
See also SATA 1
Carlson, Daniel (Bick) 1960- 105
See also SATA 27
Carlson, Edgar M(agnus) 1908- 105
Carlson, Ellsworth C. 1917- Brief entry 105
Carlson, Elof Axel 1931- CANR-44
Earlier sketch in CA 45-48
Carlson, Eric W(alter) 1910- 25-28R
Carlson, Esther Elisabeth 1920- 5-8R
Carlson, Harry Gilbert 1930- CANR-29
Earlier sketch in CA 109
Carlson, John A(llyn) 1933- 29-32R
Carlson, Judith Lee 1952- 104
Carlson, Laurie (Winn) 1952- 140
See also SATA 101
Carlson, Leland H(enry) 1908- 17-20R
Carlson, Lewis H(erbert) 1934- 41-44R
Carlson, Loraine 1923- CANR-14
Earlier sketch in CA 37-40R
Carlson, Marvin 1935- CANR-71
Earlier sketches in CA 21-24R, CANR-8
Carlson, Maureen 1947- 163
Carlson, Nancy L(ee) 1953- CANR-57
Earlier sketch in CA 110
See also SATA 56, 90
See also SATA-Brief 45
Carlson, Natalie Savage 1906- CANR-57
Earlier sketches in CA 1-4R, CANR-3
See also JRDA
See also MAICYA
See also SAAS 4
See also SATA 2, 68
Carlson, P. M.
See Carlson, Patricia M(cElroy)
Carlson, Patricia M(cElroy) 1940- CANR-36
Earlier sketch in CA 114
Carlson, Paul Robins 1928- 101
Carlson, Raymond 1906-1983 Obituary 109
Carlson, Reynold Edgar 1901- CANR-4
Earlier sketch in CA 1-4R
Carlson, Richard 1912(?)-1977 Obituary 73-76
Carlson, Richard C. 1942- 149
Carlson, Richard Stocks 1942- 57-60
Carlson, Rick J. 1940- 65-68
Carlson, Robert E(ugene) 1922- 41-44R
Carlson, Ron(ald F.) 1947- CANR-27
Earlier sketch in CA 105
See also CLC 54
Carlson, Ronald L. 1934- CANR-35
Earlier sketches in CA 33-36R, CANR-13
Carlson, Roy L(incoln) 1930- 41-44R
Carlson, Ruth (Elizabeth) Kearney 1911- 29-32R
Carlson, Susan Johnston 1953- SATA 88
Carlson, Theodore L(eonard) 1905- 45-48
Carlson, Vada F. 1897- CANR-28
Earlier sketches in CA 21-24R, CANR-10
See also SATA 16
Carlson, William H(ugh) 1898- CAP-2
Earlier sketch in CA 23-24
Carlson, William S(amuel) 1905-1994 1-4R
Obituary 145
Carlston, Kenneth S. 1904- 5-8R
Carlstrom, Nancy White 1948- CANR-57
Earlier sketch in CA 121
See also SATA 53, 92
See also SATA-Brief 48
Carlton, Alva
See Delk, Robert Carlton
Carlton, Charles 1941- 53-56
Carlton, Charles Merritt 1928- CANR-43
Earlier sketch in CA 45-48
Carlton, David 1938- 103
Carlton, Henry F(isk)
1893(?)-1973 Obituary 41-44R
Carlton, Jay
See Obrecht, Jas
Carlton, Jim 1955- 167
Carlton, Lessie 1903- 49-52
Carlton, Robert G(oodrich) 1927- 17-20R
Carlton, Roger
See Rowland, D(onald) S(ydney)
Carlton, Wendy 1949- 101
Carlut, Charles E. 1911- 153
Brief entry 107
Carlyle, Jane Welsh 1801-1866 DLB 55
Carlyle, Thomas 1795-1881 CDBLB 1789-1832
See also DA
See also DAB
See also DAC
See also DAM MST
See also DLB 55; 144
Carlyon, Richard SATA 55
Carm, Mac
See Armstrong, Keith F(rancis) W(hitfield)
Carmack, Robert M. 1934- 45-48
Carman, Barry (Francis) 1922- 118
Carman, (William) Bliss 1861-1929 152
Brief entry 104
See also DAC
See also DLB 92
See also TCLC 7
Carman, Dulce
See Drummond, Edith Marie Dulce Carman
Carman, J(ustice) Neale 1897-1972 CAP-1
Earlier sketch in CA 9-10
Carman, Robert A(rchibald) 1931- CANR-7
Earlier sketch in CA 57-60
Carman, William Y(oung) 1909- 13-16R
Carmel, Catherine 1939- CANR-46
Earlier sketch in CA 69-72
Carmel, Hesi 1937- 103
Carmell, Aryeh 1917- 118
Carmen, Arlene 1936- 69-72
Carmen, Ira H. 1934- 128
Carmen, Leon 1950- 164
Carmen, Sister (M.) Joann 1941- 21-24R
Carmen Sylva
See Elisabeth (Ottilie Luise), Queen (Pauline)
Carmer, Carl (Lamson) 1893-1976 CANR-70
Obituary 69-72
Earlier sketches in CA 5-8R, CANR-4
See also SATA 37
See also SATA-Obit 30
Carmer, Elizabeth Black 1904- SATA 24
Carmi, Giora 1944- SATA 79
Carmi, T.
See Charny, Carmi
Carmichael, Ann
See MacAlpine, Margaret H(esketh Murray)
Carmichael, Ann G(ayton) 1947- 125
Carmichael, Calum M. 1938- 53-56
Carmichael, Carrie
See Carmichael, Harriet
See also SATA 40
Carmichael, D(ouglas) R(oy) 1941- 33-36R
Carmichael, Fred 1924- CANR-51
Earlier sketches in CA 17-20R, CANR-10, 25
Carmichael, Harriet 115
See also Carmichael, Carrie
Carmichael, Harry
See Ognall, Leopold Horace
Carmichael, Hoagland Howard
1899-1981 Obituary 108
Carmichael, Hoagy
See Carmichael, Hoagland Howard
Carmichael, Ian (Gillett) 1920- 129
Carmichael, Joel 1915- CANR-71
Earlier sketches in CA 1-4R, CANR-2
Carmichael, John P(eerless)
1902-1986 Obituary 119
Carmichael, Leonard 1898-1973 41-44R
Obituary 45-48
Carmichael, Marie
See Stonov, Natasha
Carmichael, Oliver C(romwell) 1891-1966 CAP-1
Earlier sketch in CA 9-10
Carmichael, Peter A(rchibald) 1897- CAP-2
Earlier sketch in CA 17-18
Carmichael, Peter S. 1966- 152
Carmichael, Stokely 1941- CANR-25
Earlier sketch in CA 57-60
See also BW 1
Carmichael, Thomas N(ichols) 1919-1972 CAP-2
Earlier sketch in CA 29-32
Carmichael, William Edward 1922- 37-40R
Carmilly, Moshe 1908- 41-44R
Carmines, Al(vin Allison, Jr.) 1936- 103
Carmody, Denise Lardner 1935- 93-96
Carmody, Jay 1900(?)-1973 Obituary 41-44R
Carmoy, Guy de 1907- 89-92
Carnac, Carol
See Rivett, Edith Caroline
Carnac, Levin
See Griffith-Jones, George Chetwynd
Carnahan, Walter H(ervey) 1891- CAP-1
Earlier sketch in CA 9-10
Carnall, Geoffrey 1927- 13-16R
Carnap, Rudolf P. 1891-1970 CAP-1
Obituary 29-32R
Earlier sketch in CA 9-10
Carnarvon, The Earl of
See Herbert, Henry George Alfred Marius Victor Francis
Carne, Judy
See Botterill, Joyce
Carnegie, Dale 1888-1955 TCLC 53
Carnegie, Dorothy Vanderpool AITN 1
Carnegie, Raymond Alexander 1920- CANR-11
Earlier sketch in CA 21-24R
Carnegie, Sacha
See Carnegie, Raymond Alexander
Carnegy, Patrick 1940- 81-84
Carneiro, Maurina Pereira
See Pereira Carneiro, Maurina
Carnell, Corbin Scott 1929- CANR-10
Earlier sketch in CA 65-68
Carnell, E. J.
See Carnell, (Edward) John
Carnell, Edward John 1919-1967 CAP-1
Earlier sketch in CA 13-14
Carnell, (Edward) John 1912-1972 25-28R
Obituary 104
Carner, Gary 1955- 140
Carner, Mosco 1904-1985 CANR-38
Obituary 116
Earlier sketches in CAP-1, CA 11-12, CANR-12
Carnero, Guillermo 1947- DLB 108
Carnes, Conrad D(ew) 1936- 85-88
Carnes, Mark C(hristopher) 1950- CANR-56
Earlier sketches in CA 112, CANR-30
Carnes, Paul N(athaniel) 1921-1979 Obituary 85-88
Carnes, Ralph L(ee) 1931- 33-36R
Carnes, Valerie Folts-Bohanan 1945- 33-36R
Carnesale, Albert 1936- 142
Carnevale, Anthony P(atrick) 1946- 135
Carnevali, Doris L(orrain) CANR-44
Earlier sketches in CA 69-72, CANR-21
Carney, Daniel 1944- 119
Carney, Dora Sanders 1903-1986 Obituary 120
Carney, Edward John 1913-1989 Obituary 128
Carney, James (Patrick) 1914- 21-24R
Carney, John J(oseph), Jr. 1932- 69-72
Carney, John Otis 1922- CANR-3
Earlier sketch in CA 1-4R
Carney, Matthew 1922- CANR-25
Earlier sketch in CA 108
Carney, Raymond 1950- 137
Carney, Richard Edward 1929- 37-40R
Carney, T(homas) F(rancis) 1931- CANR-39
Earlier sketches in CA 49-52, CANR-1, 17
Carney, W(illiam) Alderman 1922- 25-28R
Carnicelli, D(omenick) D. 1931- 61-64
Carnochan, W(alter) B(liss) 1930- 33-36R
Carnot, Joseph B(arry) 1941- 45-48
Carnoy, Martin 1938- CANR-10
Earlier sketch in CA 65-68
Caro, Francis G(eorge) 1936- CANR-54
Earlier sketches in CA 69-72, CANR-11, 28
Caro, Robert A. 1935- CANR-40
Earlier sketch in CA 101
See also BEST 90:2
Caroe, Olaf Kirkpatrick 1892-1981 113
Carol, Bill J.
See Knott, William C(ecil, Jr.)
Carol, Jacqueline
See Cooper, Jacqueline
Caroli, Betty Boyd 1938- CANR-43
Earlier sketch in CA 118
Caroll, Nonie 1926- 103
Caron, Leslie (Claire Margaret) 1931- 152
Caron, Roger 1938- 89-92
Caron, Romi
See Caron-Kyselkova', Romana
Carona, Philip B(en) 1925- CANR-4
Earlier sketch in CA 1-4R
Caronia, Guiseppe 1884(?)-1977 Obituary 69-72
Caron-Kyselkova', Romana 1967- SATA 94
Caroselli, Remus F(rancis) 1916- 97-100
See also SATA 36
Carossa, Hans 1878-1956 DLB 66
See also TCLC 48
Carosso, Vincent P(hillip) 1922-1993 CANR-48
Obituary 141
Earlier sketches in CA 9-12R, CANR-3
Carothers, J. Edward 1907- 41-44R
Carothers, Robert Lee 1942- CANR-45
Earlier sketch in CA 45-48
Carousso, Georges 1909- 89-92
Carozzi, Albert V(ictor) 1925- 53-56
Carp, Frances Merchant 1918- 21-24R
Carpelan, Bo (Gustaf Bertelsson) 1926- CANR-52
Earlier sketches in CA 49-52, CANR-2, 27
See also SATA 8
Carpenter
See Arnold, June (Davis)
Carpenter, (John) Allan 1917- CANR-42
Earlier sketches in CA 9-12R, CANR-3
See also SATA 3, 81
Carpenter, Andrew 1943- 93-96
Carpenter, Angelica Shirley 1945- SATA 71
Carpenter, Bogdana 1941- 135
Carpenter, Cal
See Carpenter, Clarence A(lfred)
Carpenter, Charles A. (Jr.) 1929- 33-36R
Carpenter, Charles H(ope), Jr. 1916- 111
Carpenter, Clarence A(lfred) 1921- 116
Carpenter, Clarence Ray
1905-1975 Obituary 57-60
Carpenter, D(avid) A(rscott) 1946- 134
Carpenter, David A(llen) 1949- 111
Carpenter, David C. 1941- 121
Carpenter, Delores Bird 1942- CANR-53
Earlier sketch in CA 126
Carpenter, Don(ald Richard) 1931-1995 CANR-71
Obituary 149
Earlier sketches in CA 45-48, CANR-1
See also CLC 41
Carpenter, Duffy
See Hurley, John J(erome)
Carpenter, Edward 1844-1929 163
Carpenter, Elizabeth Sutherland 1920- 41-44R
Carpenter, Frances 1890-1972 CANR-71
Obituary 37-40R
Earlier sketches in CA 5-8R, CANR-4
See also SATA 3
See also SATA-Obit 27
Carpenter, Francis Ross 1925- 101
Carpenter, Fred
See Hand, (Andrus) Jackson
Carpenter, Frederic I.
See Carpenter, Frederic Ives (Jr.)
Carpenter, Frederic Ives (Jr.) 1903-1991 CANR-38
Obituary 134
Earlier sketch in CA 5-8R
Carpenter, Humphrey (William Bouverie) 1946- CANR-53
Earlier sketches in CA 89-92, CANR-13
Interview in CANR-13
See also DLB 155
Carpenter, J(ohn) D(avid) 1948- 115
Carpenter, James A. 1928- 37-40R
Carpenter, John (Randell) 1936- CANR-38
Earlier sketches in CA 65-68, CANR-9
Carpenter, John (Howard) 1948- 134
See also AAYA 2
See also SATA 58
Carpenter, John A(lcott) 1921-1978 9-12R
Obituary 77-80
Carpenter, John Jo
See Reese, John (Henry)
Carpenter, Joyce Frances 33-36R
Carpenter, Kenneth E(dward) 1936- 137
Carpenter, Kenneth J(ohn) 1923- CANR-50
Earlier sketch in CA 124
Carpenter, Liz
See Carpenter, Elizabeth Sutherland
Carpenter, Lucas 1947- CANR-53
Earlier sketch in CA 126
Carpenter, Lynette 1951- 138
Carpenter, Margaret Haley (?)-1985 5-8R
Obituary 116
Carpenter, Marjorie 1896- 45-48
Carpenter, Michael (Anthony) 1940- 119
Carpenter, Mimi Gregoire 1947- CANR-30
Earlier sketch in CA 111
Carpenter, Nan Cooke 1912- 25-28R
Carpenter, Patricia (Healy Evans) 1920- 29-32R
See also SATA 11
Carpenter, Peter 1922- 13-16R
Carpenter, Rhys 1889-1980 CANR-71
Obituary 93-96
Earlier sketch in CA 57-60
Carpenter, Richard C(oles) 1916- 13-16R
Carpenter, Stephen Cullen (?)-1820(?) DLB 73
Carpenter, Teresa (Suzanne) 1948- 162
Carpenter, William 1940- 106
Carpenter, Willow
See Browning, (Zerilda) Sinclair
Carpentier (y Valmont), Alejo 1904-1980 CANR-70
Obituary 97-100
Earlier sketches in CA 65-68, CANR-11
See also CLC 8, 11, 38, 110
See also DAM MULT
See also DLB 113
See also HLC
See also HW
Carper, Jean Elinor 1932- CANR-7
Earlier sketch in CA 17-20R
Carper, L. Dean 1931- 49-52
Carpi, Daniel (V.) 1926- 149
Carpozi, George, Jr. 1920- CANR-71
Earlier sketches in CA 13-16R, CANR-11
Carr, A. H. Z.
See Carr, Albert H. Z(olotkoff)
Carr, Albert H. Z(olotkoff) 1902-1971 CANR-71
Obituary 33-36R
Earlier sketches in CA 1-4R, CANR-1
Carr, Annemarie Weyl 1941- 144
Carr, Annie Roe CANR-26
Earlier sketches in CAP-2, CA 19-20
Carr, Archie (Fairly, Jr.) 1909-1987 CANR-71
Obituary 122
Earlier sketch in CA 13-16R
Carr, Arthur C(harles) 1918- 37-40R
Carr, Arthur Japheth 1914- 57-60
Carr, Blair 166
Carr, Bruce (A.) 1938- 114
Carr, C(harles) T(elford) 1905-1976 Obituary 65-68
Carr, Caleb 1955(?)- 147
See also CLC 86
Carr, Catharine
See Wade, Rosalind Herschel
Carr, David William 1911- 37-40R
Carr, Donald Eaton 1903- CANR-71
Earlier sketch in CA 13-16R
Carr, Dorothy Stevenson Laird 1912- 9-12R
Carr, Duane 1934- 166
Carr, Edward Hallet 1892-1982 CANR-14
Obituary 108
Earlier sketch in CA 61-64
Carr, Edwin George 1937- 61-64
Carr, Emily 1871-1945 159
See also DLB 68
See also TCLC 32
Carr, Gerald F(rancis) 1930- 118
Carr, Glyn
See Styles, (Frank) Showell
Carr, Gwen B. 1924- 41-44R
Carr, Harriett H(elen) 1899-1977 CANR-71
Earlier sketches in CAP-1, CA 9-10
See also SATA 3
Carr, Herbert R(eginald) C(ulling)
1896-1986 Obituary 119
Carr, Ian (Henry Randell) 1933- CANR-46
Earlier sketch in CA 110
Carr, J(ames Joseph) L(loyd) 1912-1994 CANR-37
Obituary 144
Earlier sketch in CA 102
Carr, Jan 1953- 155
See also SATA 89
Carr, Janet Baker
See Baker-Carr, Janet
Carr, Jay Phillip 1936- 89-92
Carr, Jayge 1940- 158
See also Krueger, Marj
Carr, Jess(e Crowe, Jr.) 1930-1990 CANR-29
Obituary 130
Earlier sketches in CA 29-32R, CANR-12
Carr, (Bettye) Jo (Crisler) 1926- 21-24R
Carr, John C(harles) 1929- 53-56
Carr, John Dickson 1906-1977 CANR-60
Obituary 69-72
Earlier sketches in CA 49-52, CANR-3, 33
See also Fairbairn, Roger
See also CLC 3
See also MTCW 1
Carr, John Laurence 1916- 49-52
Carr, Josephine 1952- 111
Carr, Karen L. 1960- 142
Carr, Lois Green 1922- 61-64
Carr, M. J.
See Carr, Jan
Carr, Margaret 1935- 105
Carr, Marvin (N.) 1927- 148
Carr, Mary Jane 1899-1988 CAP-1
Obituary 124
Earlier sketch in CA 9-10
See also SATA 2
See also SATA-Obit 55
Carr, Michael Harold 1935- 109
Carr, Pat 1932- CANR-57
Earlier sketches in CA 65-68, CANR-14, 31
Carr, Philippa
See Hibbert, Eleanor Alice Burford
Carr, Raymond 1919- CANR-8
Earlier sketch in CA 17-20R
Carr, Robert K(enneth) 1908-1979 93-96
Obituary 85-88

Carr, Roberta
See Roberts, Irene
Carr, Robyn 1951- ... CANR-38
Earlier sketch in CA 115
Carr, Roger Vaughan 1937- ... 160
See also SATA 95
Carr, Roland T. 1908(?)-1983 ... 122
Obituary ... 111
Carr, Stephen L(amoni) ... 57-60
Carr, Terry (Gene) 1937- ... 81-84
Carr, Virginia Mason
See Vaughan, Virginia M(ason)
Carr, Virginia Spencer 1929- ... 61-64
See also CLC 34
See also DLB 111
Carr, Warren Tyree 1917- ... 5-8R
Carr, William 1921- ... 73-76
Carr, William G(eorge) 1901-1996 ... 53-56
Obituary ... 151
Carr, William H(enry) A(lexander) 1924- ... CANR-7
Earlier sketch in CA 13-16R
Carraco, Carol Crowe
See Crowe-Carraco, Carol
Carradice, Ian A. 1953- ... 163
Carraher, Charles E. (Jr.) 1941- ... 135
Carranco, Lynwood 1921- ... CANR-21
Earlier sketches in CA 57-60, CANR-6
Carras, Mary C(alliope) ... 85-88
Carrasco, David ... 112
Carrel, Alexis (Marie Joseph Auguste Billiard) 1873-1944 ... 157
Brief entry ... 120
Carrel, Annette Felder 1929- ... 155
See also SATA 90
Carrel, Mark
See Paine, Lauran (Bosworth)
Carrell, Norman (Gerald) 1905- ... CAP-2
Earlier sketch in CA 25-28
Carrera Andrade, Jorge 1903-1978 ... 155
Obituary ... 85-88
See also HW
Carreras, Jose 1946- ... 141
Carrere, Emmanuel 1957- ... CLC 89
Carretta, Vincent (Albert) 1945- ... 131
Carr-Hill, Roy A. 1943- ... 141
Carrick, A. B.
See Lindsay, Harold Arthur
Carrick, Burt
See Cassiday, Bruce (Bingham)
Carrick, Carol (Hatfield) 1935- ... CANR-70
Earlier sketches in CA 45-48, CANR-1, 17, 37
See also MAICYA
See also SAAS 18
See also SATA 7, 63
Carrick, Donald (F.) 1929-1989 ... CANR-37
Earlier sketches in CA 53-56, CANR-5, 20
See also MAICYA
See also SATA 7, 63
Carrick, Edward
See Craig, Edward Anthony
Carrick, John
See Crosbie, (Hugh) Provan
Carrick, Malcolm 1945- ... CANR-14
Earlier sketch in CA 77-80
See also SATA 28
Carrier, Constance 1908- ... 33-36R
Carrier, Esther Jane 1925- ... 17-20R
Carrier, James G(olden) 1947- ... 149
Carrier, Jean-Guy 1945- ... 101
Carrier, Lark 1947- ... SATA 71
See also SATA-Brief 50
Carrier, Roch 1937- ... CANR-61
Earlier sketch in CA 130
See also CLC 13, 78
See also DAC
See also DAM MST
See also DLB 53
Carrier, Warren (Pendleton) 1918- ... CANR-71
Earlier sketches in CA 9-12R, CANR-3, 18
Carriere, Jean-Claude 1931- ... 140
Carrigan, Andrew G(ardner) 1935- ... CANR-1
Earlier sketch in CA 45-48
Carrigan, D(avid) Owen 1933- ... 25-28R
Carrigan, Richard A(lfred), Jr. 1932- ... CANR-30
Earlier sketch in CA 112
Carrighar, Sally 1898-1985 ... CANR-70
Earlier sketch in CA 93-96
See also SATA 24
Carriker, Robert C(harles) 1940- ... 69-72
Carrillo, Adolfo 1855-1926 ... DLB 122
Carrillo, Lawrence W(ilbert) 1920- ... 13-16R
Carringer, Robert L. 1941- ... CANR-17
Earlier sketch in CA 97-100
Carrington, Charles Edmund 1897-1990 ... CANR-71
Obituary ... 132
Earlier sketch in CA 5-8R
Carrington, Frank G(amble, Jr.) 1936- ... 57-60
Carrington, G. A.
See Cunningham, Chet
Carrington, George C(abell), Jr. 1928-1990 ... 122
Obituary ... 132
Brief entry ... 118
Carrington, Grant 1938- ... 104
Carrington, Leonora 1917- ... 124
Brief entry ... 114
Carrington, Molly
See Matthews, C(onstance) M(ary)
Carrington, Paul D(eWitt) 1931- ... 29-32R
Carrington, Richard (Temple Murray) 1921- ... 9-12R
Carrington, William Langley 1900-1970 ... CAP-1
Earlier sketch in CA 13-14
Carrion, Arturo Morales
See Morales Carrion, Arturo
Carris, Joan Davenport 1938- ... CANR-27
Earlier sketch in CA 106
See also SATA 44
See also SATA-Brief 42
Carrison, Daniel J. 1917- ... 37-40R
Carrison, Muriel Paskin 1928- ... 127
Carrithers, David W. 1943- ... 110
Carrithers, Gale H(emphill), Jr. 1932- ... 41-44R
Carrithers, Wallace M(axwell) 1911- ... 25-28R
Carrol, Shana
See Newcomb, Kerry
and Schaefer, Frank
Carroll, Anne Kristin
See Gales, Barbara J.
Carroll, Archie B(enjamin III) 1943- ... 109
Carroll, B(illy) D(an) 1940- ... 53-56
Carroll, Berenice A(nita) 1932- ... 41-44R
Carroll, Bob 1936- ... CANR-65
Earlier sketch in CA 129
Carroll, Brendan G. 1952- ... 164
Carroll, C(armal) Edward 1923- ... 29-32R
Carroll, Carroll 1902-1991 ... 101
Obituary ... 133
Carroll, Charles Francis 1936- ... 53-56
Carroll, Christina
See Henderson, M(arilyn) R(uth)
Carroll, Curt
See Bishop, Curtis (Kent)
Carroll, Daniel B(ernard) 1928-1977 ... 41-44R
Carroll, David
See Carroll, David L.
Carroll, David L. 1942- ... 129
Carroll, Dennis 1940- ... 114
Carroll, Donald K(ingery) 1909- ... CAP-2
Earlier sketch in CA 17-18
Carroll, Elizabeth
See Barkin, Carol
and James, Elizabeth
Carroll, Faye 1937- ... 21-24R
Carroll, Gerry 1947-1993 ... 151
Carroll, Ginny 1948- ... 130
Carroll, Gladys Hasty 1904- ... CANR-5
Earlier sketch in CA 1-4R
See also DLB 9
Carroll, Herbert A(llen) 1897- ... CAP-1
Earlier sketch in CA 11-12
Carroll, J. Larry 1946- ... 129
Carroll, Jackson W(alker) 1932- ... CANR-16
Earlier sketch in CA 85-88
Carroll, James P. 1943(?)- ... 81-84
See also CLC 38
Carroll, Jeffrey 1950- ... 85-88
Carroll, Jim 1951- ... CANR-42
Earlier sketch in CA 45-48
See also AAYA 17
See also CLC 35
Carroll, John 1735-1815 ... DLB 37
Carroll, John 1809-1884 ... DLB 99
Carroll, John 1944- ... CANR-7
Earlier sketch in CA 57-60
Carroll, John B(issell) 1916- ... CANR-3
Earlier sketch in CA 1-4R
Carroll, John J(oseph) 1924- ... 13-16R
Carroll, John M(elvin) 1928- ... 37-40R
Carroll, John Millar 1925- ... CANR-23
Earlier sketches in CA 5-8R, CANR-8
Carroll, Jonathan 1949- ... CANR-21
Earlier sketch in CA 105
Carroll, Joseph 1912(?)-1989 Obituary ... 128
Carroll, Joseph T(homas) 1935- ... 102
Carroll, Joy 1924- ... 102
Carroll, Kenneth Lane 1924- ... 37-40R
Carroll, L(awrence) Patrick 1936- ... 111
Carroll, (Archer) Latrobe 1894- ... CANR-3
Earlier sketch in CA 1-4R
See also SATA 7
Carroll, Laura
See Parr, Lucy
Carroll, Lewis
See Dodgson, Charles Lutwidge
See also CDBLB 1832-1890
See also CLR 2, 18
See also DLB 18, 163, 178
See also JRDA
See also PC 18
See also WLC
Carroll, Loren 1904-1978 ... 85-88
Obituary ... 81-84
Carroll, Martin
See Carr, Margaret
Carroll, Mary
See Sanford, Annette
Carroll, Matthew S. 1955- ... 152
Carroll, Paul 1927- ... 25-28R
See also DLB 16
Carroll, Paul Vincent 1900-1968 ... 9-12R
Obituary ... 25-28R
See also CLC 10
See also DLB 10
Carroll, Peter N(eil) 1943- ... 102
Carroll, Phil 1895-1971 ... CAP-1
Earlier sketch in CA 13-14
Carroll, Raymond 1924- ... 126
See also SATA 86
See also SATA-Brief 47
Carroll, Rebecca 1969- ... 147
Carroll, Robert
See Alpert, Hollis
Carroll, Robert P(eter) 1941- ... CANR-43
Earlier sketch in CA 105
Carroll, Rosalynn
See Katz, Carol
Carroll, Ruth (Robinson) 1899- ... CANR-1
Earlier sketch in CA 1-4R
Carroll, St. Thomas Marion
See Carroll, Tom M.
Carroll, Sheila Baker 1918(?)-1984 Obituary ... 113
Carroll, Sister Mary Gerald 1913- ... 21-24R
Carroll, Stephen J(ohn), Jr. 1930- ... 41-44R
Carroll, Ted
See Carroll, Thomas Theodore, Jr.
Carroll, Theodus (Catherine) 1928- ... CANR-49
Earlier sketch in CA 69-72
Carroll, Thomas J. 1909-1971 ... 1-4R
Obituary ... 103
Carroll, Thomas Theodore, Jr. 1925- ... 9-12R
Carroll, Tom M. 1950- ... 53-56
Carroll, Vern 1933- ... 57-60
Carroll, Vinnette (Justine) ... 123
Brief entry ... 114
Interview in ... 123
See also BW 1
Carron, Malcolm 1917- Brief entry ... 105
Carrott, Richard G. 1924- ... 85-88
Carrouges, Michel
See Couturier, Louis (Joseph)
Carrow, Milton M(ichael) 1912- ... CANR-16
Earlier sketch in CA 25-28R
Carr-Saunders, Alexander (Morris) 1886-1966 ... CANR-20
Obituary ... 103
Earlier sketch in CA 1-4R
Carruth, Estelle 1910- ... 9-12R
Carruth, Gorton Veeder 1925- ... CANR-6
Earlier sketch in CA 57-60
Carruth, Hayden 1921- ... CANR-59
Earlier sketches in CA 9-12R, CANR-4, 38
Interview in ... CANR-4
See also CLC 4, 7, 10, 18, 84
See also DLB 5, 165
See also MTCW 1
See also PC 10
See also SATA 47
Carruthers, Ben F(rederick) 1911- ... 114
Carruthers, Malcolm Euan 1938- ... 102
Carruthers, Peter 1952- ... 126
Carry, (Benjamin) Peter 1942- ... 105
Carryaway, Nick
See Murray, John F(rancis)
Carryl, Charles E. 1841-1920 ... DLB 42
Carsac, Francis
See Bordes, Francois
Carsberg, Bryan Victor 1939- ... CANR-29
Earlier sketches in CA 29-32R, CANR-12
Carse, James P(earce) 1932- ... 21-24R
Carse, Robert 1902-1971 ... CANR-1
Obituary ... 29-32R
Earlier sketch in CA 1-4R
See also SATA 5
Carskadon, Thomas R. 1901(?)-1983(?) Obituary ... 108
Carson, Ada Lou 1932- ... 110
Carson, Alan 1951- ... 115
Carson, Anne (Regina) 1950- ... CANR-53
Earlier sketch in CA 132
See also DLB 193
Carson, Barbara Harrell 1943- ... 143
Carson, Benjamin S(olomon) 1951- ... 157
Carson, Captain James ... CANR-26
Earlier sketches in CAP-2, CA 19-20
Carson, Ciaran 1948- ... 153
Brief entry ... 112
Carson, Clarence B. 1925- ... 130
Carson, Clayborne 1944- ... CANR-62
Earlier sketch in CA 105
Carson, D(onald) A(rthur) 1946- ... 142
Carson, F(ranklin) John 1920- ... 9-12R
Carson, Gerald (Hewes) 1899-1989 ... CANR-16
Obituary ... 130
Earlier sketches in CA 1-4R, CANR-1
Carson, Hampton L(awrence) 1914- ... 5-8R
Carson, Hank
See Fearn, John Russell
Carson, Herbert L(ee) 1929- ... 29-32R
Carson, J(ohn) Franklin 1920- ... 13-16R
See also SATA 1
Carson, Jane Dennison (?)-1984 Obituary ... 114
Carson, Josephine 1919- ... CAAS 28
Carson, Kit
See Carson, Xanthus
Carson, Mary 1934- ... 41-44R
Carson, Michael (Charles) 1946- ... 130
Carson, Rachel Louise 1907-1964 ... CANR-35
Earlier sketch in CA 77-80
See also CLC 71
See also DAM POP
See also MTCW 1
See also SATA 23
Carson, Ray F(ritziof) 1939- ... 61-64
Carson, Robert 1909-1983 ... 21-24R
Obituary ... 108
Carson, Robert B. 1934- ... CANR-6
Earlier sketch in CA 57-60
Carson, Robert C(harles) 1930- ... 29-32R
Carson, Ronald A(lan) 1940- ... 119
Carson, Rosalind
See Chittenden, Margaret
Carson, Ruth
See Bugbee, Ruth Carson
Carson, S. M.
See Gorsline, (Sally) Marie
Carson, William Glasgow Bruce 1891- ... 5-8R
Carson, Xanthus 1910- ... 57-60
Carstairs, George Morrison 1916- ... 69-72
Carstairs, Kathleen
See Pendower, Jacques
Carsten, Francis Ludwig 1911- ... 13-16R
Carstens, Catherine Mansell
See Mayo, C(atherine) M(ansell)
Carstens, Grace Pearce ... 1-4R
Carstensen, Roger Norwood 1920- ... CANR-2
Earlier sketch in CA 5-8R
Carswell, Catherine 1879-1946 ... DLB 36
Carswell, Evelyn M(edicus) 1919- ... 57-60
Carswell, John (Patrick) 1918-1997 ... CANR-21
Obituary ... 162
Earlier sketch in CA 9-12R
Carswell, Leslie
See Stephens, Rosemary
Cartan, Henri (Paul) 1904- ... 164
Cartano, Tony 1944- ... 129
Carte, Gene E(dward) 1938- ... 61-64
Carter, Alan 1936- ... 33-36R
Carter, Albert Howard 1913-1970 ... CAP-2
Earlier sketch in CA 25-28
Carter, Alden R(ichardson) 1947- ... CANR-58
Earlier sketch in CA 135
See also AAYA 17
See also CLR 22
See also SAAS 18
See also SATA 67
Carter, Alfred Edward 1914- ... 33-36R
Carter, Amon Giles, Jr. 1919-1982 Obituary ... 111
Carter, Angela (Olive) 1940-1992 ... CANR-61
Obituary ... 136
Earlier sketches in CA 53-56, CANR-12, 36
See also CLC 5, 41, 76
See also DLB 14
See also MTCW 1
See also SATA 66
See also SATA-Obit 70
See also SSC 13
Carter, Ann
See Brooks, Anne Tedlock
Carter, Anne
See Brooks, Anne Tedlock
Carter, Anne Pitts 1925- Brief entry ... 106
Carter, Arthur M. 1911-1988 Obituary ... 125
Carter, Ashley
See Whittington, Harry (Benjamin)
Carter, Ashton B. 1954- ... 137
Carter, Avis Murton
See Allen, Kenneth S.
Carter, Barbara (Ellen) 1925-1988 ... CANR-10
Obituary ... 126
Earlier sketch in CA 53-56
Carter, Boyd (George) 1908-1980 ... CANR-7
Earlier sketch in CA 13-16R
Carter, Bruce
See Hough, Richard (Alexander)
Carter, Burnham 1901(?)-1979 Obituary ... 89-92
Carter, Byron L. 1924- ... 21-24R
Carter, C(edric) O(swald) 1917-1984 Obituary ... 112
Carter, Carmen 1954- ... 128
Carter, Carolle J(ean) 1934- ... 81-84
Carter, Charles Frederick 1919- ... CANR-20
Earlier sketches in CA 1-4R, CANR-4
Carter, Charles H(oward) 1927- ... 9-12R
Carter, Charles W(ebb) 1905- ... 21-24R
Carter, Chris 1956- ... 160
See also AAYA 23
Carter, Dan T. 1940- ... CANR-52
Earlier sketch in CA 65-68
Carter, David C(harles) 1946- ... 45-48
Carter, Don E(arl) 1917- ... 73-76
Carter, Dorothy Sharp 1921- ... 49-52
See also SATA 8
Carter, E. Lawrence 1910-1997 ... 25-28R
Obituary ... 158
Carter, Edward Julian 1902-1982 ... 5-8R
Obituary ... 107
Carter, Elizabeth 1717-1806 ... DLB 109
Carter, Elizabeth Eliot
See Holland, Cecelia (Anastasia)
Carter, Elliott Cook 1908- ... 89-92
Carter, Ernestine (Marie) (?)-1983 ... 130
Obituary ... 110
Carter, Everett 1919- ... 13-16R
Carter, Forrest 1927(?)-1979 ... 107
See also DAM POP
See also SATA 32
Carter, Frances Monet 1923- ... 37-40R
Carter, Frances Tunnell ... 37-40R
Carter, George F(rancis) 1912- ... CANR-4
Earlier sketch in CA 5-8R
Carter, Gwendolen M(argaret) 1906-1991 ... CANR-19
Obituary ... 133
Earlier sketches in CA 1-4R, CANR-4
Carter, Harold 1925- ... 33-36R
Carter, Harry Graham 1901-1982 Obituary ... 106
Carter, Harvey L(ewis) 1904- ... 21-24R
Carter, Helene 1887-1960 ... SATA 15
Carter, Henry
See Leslie, Frank
Carter, Henry Hare 1905- ... 41-44R
Carter, Hodding, Jr. 1907-1972 ... DLB 127
Carter, (William) Hodding 1907-1972 ... CAP-1
Obituary ... 33-36R
Earlier sketch in CA 13-14
See also SATA 2
See also SATA-Obit 27
Carter, Hugh 1895- ... 37-40R
Carter, Hurricane
See Carter, Rubin
Carter, J(ohn) Anthony 1943- ... 61-64
Carter, James E(dward) 1935- ... CANR-22
Earlier sketches in CA 57-60, CANR-7
Carter, James Earl, Jr. 1924- ... CANR-32
Earlier sketch in CA 69-72
See also MTCW 1
See also SATA 79
Carter, James Puckette 1933- ... 33-36R
Carter, James Richard 1940- ... 33-36R
Carter, Jane Robbins
See Robbins, Jane (Borsch)
Carter, Janet 1938- ... 104
Carter, Jared 1939- ... 145

Carter, Jimmy
See Carter, James Earl, Jr.
Carter, John (Waynflete) 1905-1975 .... 5-8R
Obituary 57-60
See also DLB 201
Carter, John E. 1950- 141
Carter, John Franklin 1897-1967 Obituary .. 25-28R
Carter, John Mack 1928- 103
Carter, John Marshall 1949- 143
Carter, John Stewart 1912-1965 .... CAP-1
Earlier sketch in CA 11-12
Carter, John T(homas) 1921- 33-36R
Carter, Joseph 1912-1984 49-52
Obituary 112
Carter, Joseph H(enry Sr.) 1932- 139
Carter, K(ay) Codell 1939- 110
Carter, Katharine J(ones) 1905- 5-8R
See also SATA 2
Carter, Landon 1710-1778 .... DLB 31
Carter, Lief Hastings 1940- CANR-6
Earlier sketch in CA 57-60
Carter, (Bessie) Lillian (Gordy) 1898-1983 118
Obituary 111
Brief entry 105
Carter, Lin(wood Vrooman) 1930-1988 ... CANR-30
Earlier sketch in CA 41-44R
See also DLBY 81
See also SATA 91
Carter, Lonnie 1942- CANR-67
Earlier sketches in CA 65-68, CANR-9
Carter, Luther J(ordan) 1927- 57-60
Carter, M(argaret) L(ouise) 1948- 33-36R
Carter, Margaret (Mary) 1923- 107
Carter, Marilyn
See Ross, W(illiam) E(dward) D(aniel)
Carter, Martin (Wylde) 1927- CANR-42
Earlier sketch in CA 102
See also BW 2
See also DLB 117
Carter, Martin R(oger) 1946- 147
Carter, Mary CANR-5
Earlier sketch in CA 9-12R
Carter, Mary Ellen 1923- 25-28R
Carter, Mary Kennedy 65-68
Carter, Neil 1913- 17-20R
Carter, Nevada
See Paine, Lauran (Bosworth)
Carter, Nicholas
See Dey, Frederic (Merrill) Van Rensselaer
Carter, Nick
See Avallone, Michael (Angelo, Jr.)
and Ballard, (Willis) Todhunter
and Cassiday, Bruce (Bingham)
and Crider, (Allen) Bill(y)
and Dey, Frederic (Merrill) Van Rensselaer
and Garside, (Clifford) Jack
and Hayes, Ralph E(ugene)
and Henderson, M(arilyn) R(uth)
and Lynds, Dennis
and Lynds, Gayle (Hallenbeck)
and Rasof, Henry
and Smith, Martin Cruz
and Stratemeyer, Edward L.
and Swain, Dwight V(reeland)
and Vardeman, Robert E(dward)
and Wallmann, Jeffrey M(iner)
and White, Lionel
Carter, Paul (Hugh) 1951- 129
Carter, Paul A(llen) 1926- CANR-13
Earlier sketch in CA 33-36R
Carter, Paul J(efferson), Jr. 1912-1975 ..... CAP-2
Earlier sketch in CA 21-22
Carter, Peter 1929- CANR-44
Earlier sketch in CA 69-72
See also SATA 57
Carter, Phyllis Ann
See Eberle, Irmengarde
Carter, Ralph
See Neubauer, William Arthur
Carter, Randolph 1914- 101
Carter, Raphael 164
Carter, Richard 1918- CANR-8
Earlier sketch in CA 61-64
Carter, Richard D(uane) 1929- 111
Carter, Robert 1945- 128
Carter, Robert A(yres) 1923- 33-36R
Carter, Robert M(ack) 1925- 33-36R
Carter, Roger 1939- CANR-43
Earlier sketch in CA 119
Carter, (Eleanor) Rosalynn (Smith) 1927- 113
Carter, Rubin 1937- Brief entry 113
Carter, Samuel (Thomson) III 1904-1988 57-60
Obituary 127
See also SATA 37
See also SATA-Obit 60
Carter, Sebastian 1941- 126
Carter, Stephen L(isle) 1954- 147
Carter, Steven 1956- 137
Carter, Steven R(ay) 1942- 141
Carter, (Elizabeth) Susanne 1950- 141
Carter, Thomas Earl 1947- 133
Carter, Tom
See Carter, Thomas Earl
Carter, Victor A(lbert) 1902- CAP-1
Earlier sketch in CA 9-10
Carter, Walter 1950- 149
Carter, William 1934- 33-36R
Carter, William Ambrose 1899- CAP-1
Earlier sketch in CA 17-18
Carter, William Beverly, Jr. 1921-1982 Obituary 110
Carter, William E. 1926-1983 .... 17-20R
Obituary 110
See also SATA 1
See also SATA-Obit 35
Carter, William Lee 1925- 1-4R
Carter, Worrall Reed 1885(?)-1975 Obituary .. 57-60
Carter-Brown, Peter
See Yates, A(lan) G(eoffrey)
Carterette, Edward C(alvin) 1921- 41-44R
Carter-Harrison, Paul
See Harrison, Paul Carter
Carter-Ruck, Peter F(rederick) 1914- 97-100
Cartey, Wilfred (George Onslow) 1931-1992 ....
CANR-25
Obituary 137
Earlier sketch in CA 73-76
See also BW 2
Carthy, Mother Mary Peter 1911- 13-16R
Cartier, Xam Wilson 1949(?)- 125
See also BW 2
Cartland, Barbara (Hamilton) 1901- CANR-34
Earlier sketches in CA 9-12R, CANR-6
Interview in CANR-6
See also CAAS 8
See also DAM POP
See also MTCW 1
Cartledge, Paul 1947- CANR-51
Earlier sketch in CA 124
Cartledge, Samuel Antoine 1903- 1-4R
Cartlidge, Barbara 1922- 121
Cartlidge, Michelle 1950- CANR-68
Earlier sketch in CA 93-96
See also SATA 49, 96
See also SATA-Brief 37
Cartmill, Cleve 1908-1964 161
Cartmill, Matt 1943- 146
Cartnal, Alan 1950- 105
Cartner, William Carruthers 1910- 73-76
See also SATA 11
Carto, Willis A(llison) 1926- 114
Cartter, Allan Murray 1922-1976 .... CANR-8
Earlier sketch in CA 5-8R
Cartwright, Ann 1940- .... SATA 78
Cartwright, Desmond S(pencer) 1924- 89-92
Cartwright, Gary 1934- 89-92
Cartwright, James McGregor
See Jennings, Leslie Nelson
Cartwright, John 1740-1824 .... DLB 158
Cartwright, Joseph H. 1939- 73-76
Cartwright, Justin 1933- 144
Cartwright, N.
See Scofield, Norma Margaret Cartwright
Cartwright, Reg(inald Ainsley) 1938- ...... SATA 64
Cartwright, Rosalind Dymond 1922- 81-84
Cartwright, Sally 1923- CANR-2
Earlier sketch in CA 49-52
See also SATA 9
Cartwright, Vanessa
See Preston, Harry
Cartwright, William 1611(?)-1643 .... DLB 126
Cartwright, William H(olman) 1915- 9-12R
Carty, David 1955- 139
Carty, James William, Jr. 1925- 53-56
Caruba, Alan 1937- 65-68
Caruso, Enrico 1873-1921 Brief entry 115
Caruso, John Anthony 1907- 33-36R
Carusone, Al 1949- 155
See also SATA 89
Carus-Wilson, Eleanora M(ary) 1897- 5-8R
Caruth, Donald L(ewis) 1935- 29-32R
Caruthers, Osgood 1915-1985 Obituary 117
Caruthers, William Alexander 1802-1846 .... DLB 3
Carvajal, Ricardo
See Meneses, Enrique
Carvalho-Neto, Paulo de 1923- CANR-4
Earlier sketch in CA 53-56
Carvell, Fred J. 1934- 29-32R
Carver, Dave
See Bingley, David Ernest
Carver, Frank G(ould) 1928- CANR-45
Earlier sketch in CA 49-52
Carver, Fred D(onald) 1936- 29-32R
Carver, Jeffrey A(llan) 1949- CANR-18
Earlier sketch in CA 101
Carver, John
See Gardner, Richard (M.)
Carver, Jonathan 1710-1780 .... DLB 31
Carver, M. O. H.
See Carver, Martin
Carver, Martin 1941- 145
Carver, (Richard) Michael (Power) 1915- . CANR-14
Earlier sketch in CA 69-72
Carver, Norman F., Jr. 1928- 41-44R
Carver, Raymond 1938-1988 .... CANR-61
Obituary 126
Earlier sketches in CA 33-36R, CANR-17, 34
See also CLC 22, 36, 53, 55
See also DAM NOV
See also DLB 130
See also DLBY 84, 88
See also MTCW 1
See also SSC 8
Carver, Saxon Rowe 1905- CAP-1
Earlier sketch in CA 13-14
Carver, Terrell 1946- 133
Carvic, Heron (?)-1980 .... CANR-72
Obituary 103
Earlier sketch in CA 53-56
Carville, (Chester) James, (Jr.) 1944- 147
Carwardine, Richard J(ohn) 1947- 146
Carwell, L'Ann
See McKissack, Patricia (L'Ann) C(arwell)
Cary
See Cary, Louis F(avreau)
Cary, Alice 1820-1871 .... DLB 202
Cary, Arthur
See Cary, (Arthur) Joyce (Lunel)
Cary, Barbara Knapp 1912(?)-1975 Obituary . 61-64
See also SATA-Obit 31
Cary, Bob 1921- 105
Cary, Diana Serra
See Cary, Peggy-Jean Montgomery
Cary, Falkland L. 1897-1989 Obituary 128
Cary, Harold Whiting 1903- CAP-1
Earlier sketch in CA 9-10
Cary, James Donald 1919- 5-8R
Cary, John H. 1926- 9-12R
Cary, (Arthur) Joyce (Lunel) 1888-1957 164
Brief entry 104
See also CDBLB 1914-1945
See also DLB 15, 100
See also TCLC 1, 29
Cary, Jud
See Tubb, E(dwin) C(harles)
Cary, Lee J(ames) 1925- 29-32R
Cary, Lorene 1956- 135
See also BW 2
Cary, Louis F(avreau) 1915- .... SATA 9
Cary, Lucian 1886-1971 .... 33-36R
Cary, Otis 1921- 61-64
Cary, Patrick 1623(?)-1657 .... DLB 131
Cary, Peggy-Jean Montgomery 1918- 57-60
Cary, Richard 1909- 21-24R
Cary, William L(ucius) 1910-1983 Obituary 109
Cary, Zenja Saft 1932(?)-1983 Obituary 110
Caryl, Jean
See Kaplan, Jean Caryl Korn
Caryl, Warren 1920- 21-24R
Casaccia, Gabriel
See Casaccia Bibolini, G(abriel)
Casaccia Bibolini, G(abriel) 1907- .... HW
Casada, James A(llen) 1942- CANR-43
Earlier sketch in CA 109
Casado, Pablo Gil 1931- CANR-47
Earlier sketch in CA 49-52
Casady, Cort (Boon) 1947- CANR-22
Earlier sketch in CA 105
Casady, Donald Rex 1926- 13-16R
Casalandra, Estelle
See Estelle, Sister Mary
Casale, Anne L. 1930- 146
Casale, Joan T(herese) 1935- 61-64
Casale, Ottavio M(ark) 1934- 104
Casals, Pablo
See Casals, Pau Carlos Salvador Defillo de
Casals, Pau Carlos Salvador Defillo de
1876-1973 93-96
Obituary 45-48
Casanova, Mary 1957- 159
See also SATA 94
Casares, Adolfo Bioy
See Bioy Casares, Adolfo
Casart, Jonathan
See St. Martin, Hardie
Casart, Julian
See St. Martin, Hardie
Casas, Penelope 1943- 114
Casati, Roberto 1961- 148
Casberg, Melvin Augustus 1909- 104
Cascardi, Anthony J(oseph) 1953- 132
Cascio, Chuck 1946- 93-96
Casdorph, Herman Richard 1928- 101
Casdorph, Paul D(ouglas) 1932- 106
Case, Bill
See Case, Theodore Willard
Case, Brian (David) 1937- 25-28R
Case, (Brian) David (Francis) 1937- CANR-72
Earlier sketch in CA 107
Case, Elinor Rutt 1914- 1-4R
Case, Fred E. 1918- CANR-31
Earlier sketches in CA 5-8R, CANR-4
Case, Geoffrey 77-80
Case, George (Andrew Thomas) 1967- 164
Case, Jack Gaylord 1918(?)-1970 Obituary 104
Case, John 1944- 114
Case, Josephine Young 1907-1990 .... CAP-2
Obituary 130
Earlier sketch in CA 25-28
Case, Justin
See Gleadow, Rupert Seeley
Case, L. L.
See Lewin, Leonard C(ase)
Case, Leland D(avidson) 1900- 17-20R
Case, Lynn M(arshall) 1903- 13-16R
Case, Marshal T(aylor) 1941- 57-60
See also SATA 9
Case, Maurice 1910-1968 .... CAP-2
Earlier sketch in CA 19-20
Case, Michael
See Howard, Robert West
Case, Patricia J(une) 1952- CANR-53
Earlier sketches in CA 110, CANR-27
Case, Theodore Willard 1920- 133
Case, Victoria 1897- 5-8R
Case, Walter 1909(?)-1983 Obituary 110
Casebier, Allan (Frank) 1934- 65-68
Casebier, Marjorie
See McCoy, Marjorie Casebier
Casebier, Virginia (Eleanor) 1918- 41-44R
Caseley, Judith 1951- CANR-48
Earlier sketch in CA 121
See also SATA 87
See also SATA-Brief 53
Caseleyr, Cam(ille Auguste Marie) 1909- CAP-1
Earlier sketch in CA 9-10
Casely-Hayford, Gladys May 1904-1950 152
See also BW 2
Casely-Hayford, J(oseph) E(phraim) 1866-1930 . 152
Brief entry 123
See also BLC 1
See also BW 2
See also DAM MULT
See also TCLC 24
Casement, Richard 1942-1982 Obituary 108
Casemore, Robert 1915- CANR-35
Earlier sketch in CA 73-76
Casewit, Curtis W(erner) 1922- CANR-21
Earlier sketches in CA 13-16R, CANR-6
See also SATA 4
Casey, Barbara 1944- .... SATA 79
Casey, Beatrice Vivian 1898(?)-1986 Obituary .. 120
Casey, Bernard Terry 1939- 152
See also BW 2
Casey, Bernie
See Casey, Bernard Terry
Casey, Bill Harris 1930- 1-4R
Casey, Brigid 1950- CANR-28
Earlier sketch in CA 49-52
See also SATA 9
Casey, Daniel J(oseph) 1937- CANR-22
Earlier sketches in CA 57-60, CANR-6
Casey, Douglas R(obert) 1946- Brief entry 118
Casey, Edward Scott 1939- 102
Casey, Genevieve M(ary) 1916- CANR-39
Earlier sketch in CA 116
Casey, Gladys
See Grier, Barbara G(ene Damon)
Casey, Jack
See Casey, John
Casey, Jane Barnes 1942- 104
Casey, John (Dudley) 1939- CANR-23
Earlier sketch in CA 69-72
See also BEST 90:2
See also CLC 59
Casey, John 1950- 120
Casey, Juanita 1925- CANR-45
Earlier sketch in CA 49-52
See also DLB 14
Casey, Kevin 1940- 25-28R
Casey, Lawrence B. 1905-1977 73-76
Obituary 69-72
Casey, Linda M. 136
Casey, Mart
See Casey, Michael T.
Casey, Michael 1947- 65-68
See also CLC 2
See also DLB 5
Casey, Michael T. 1922- 21-24R
Casey, Patrick
See Thurman, Wallace (Henry)
Casey, Richard Gardiner 1890-1976 61-64
Obituary 65-68
Casey, Robert J(oseph) 1890-1962 Obituary . 89-92
Casey, Rosemary 1904-1976 Obituary 65-68
Casey, Rosemary Alice (Christmann) 1922- ... 5-8R
Casey, Thomas Francis 1923- 13-16R
Casey, W. Wilson 1954- 107
Casey, Warren (Peter) 1935-1988 101
Obituary 127
Interview in 101
See also CLC 12
Casey, William J(oseph) 1913-1987 Obituary ... 122
Casey, William Van Etten 1914-1990 57-60
Obituary 131
Casgrain, Therese F. 1896(?)-1981 110
Obituary 108
Cash, Anthony 1933- 102
Cash, Arthur H(ill) 1922- Brief entry 110
Cash, Catherine 1939- 141
Cash, Ellen Lewis Buell 1905-1989 Obituary ... 130
See also SATA-Obit 64
Cash, Grace (Savannah) 1915- 21-24R
Cash, Grady
See Cash, Grace (Savannah)
Cash, J(ames) Allan 1901- CANR-4
Earlier sketch in CA 5-8R
Cash, John R.
See Cash, Johnny
Cash, Johnny 1932- 142
Brief entry 110
Cash, Joseph H(arper) 1927- 41-44R
Cash, Kevin (Richard) 1926-1985 77-80
Obituary 115
Cash, Philip 1931- 106
Cash, Sebastian
See Smithells, Roger (William)
Cashdan, Linda 1942- 132
Cashen, Richard A(nthony) 1938- 112
Cashin, Edward J(oseph, Jr.) 1927- CANR-9
Earlier sketch in CA 21-24R
Cashin, Edward L(awrence)
See Cashin, Edward J(oseph, Jr.)
Cashin, James A. 1911-1982 .... CANR-10
Earlier sketch in CA 17-20R
Cashman, John
See Davis, Timothy Francis Tothill
Cashman, Paul Harrison 1924- 13-16R
Cashman, Sean Dennis 1943- 107
Cashmore, E. Ellis 1949- 116
Cashmore, Ernest
See Cashmore, E. Ellis
Casilla, Robert 1959- .... SATA 75
Casimir, H(endrik) B(rugt) G(erhard) 1909- 129
Casimir, Hendrik
See Casimir, H(endrik) B(rugt) G(erhard)
Caskey, John L. 1908- 13-16R
Casler, Lawrence (Ray) 1932- 49-52
Casmier, Adam A(nthony) 1934- 33-36R
Casmir, Fred L. 1928- 37-40R
Casner, A(ndrew) James 1907-1990 ...... CANR-4
Obituary 132
Earlier sketch in CA 5-8R
Caso, Adolph 1934- CANR-7
Earlier sketch in CA 57-60
Casolaro, Daniel 1949- 114
Cason, Mabel Earp 1892-1965 .... CAP-1
Earlier sketch in CA 13-14
See also SATA 10
Casona, Alejandro
See Alvarez, Alejandro Rodriguez
See also CLC 49
Casotti, Fred 1923- 93-96

Caspari, Ernest W(olfgang) 1909- 41-44R
Caspary, Vera 1899-1987 CANR-59
Obituary 122
Earlier sketches in CA 13-16R, CANR-9
Casper, Barry M(ichael) 1939- 69-72
Casper, Bill, Jr.
See Casper, William Earl, Jr.
Casper, Billy
See Casper, William Earl, Jr.
Casper, Henry W. 1909- 37-40R
Casper, Jonathan D(avid) 1942- 53-56
Casper, Joseph Andrew 1941- 65-68
Casper, Leonard Ralph 1923- 1-4R
Casper, Linda Ty
See Ty-Casper, Linda
Casper, William Earl, Jr. 1931- 121
Casque, Sammy
See Davis, Sydney Charles Houghton
Casriel, H(arold) Daniel 1924-1983 13-16R
Obituary 110
Cass, Carl Bartholomew 1901- CAP-1
Earlier sketch in CA 9-10
Cass, James (Michael) 1915-1992 101
Obituary 140
Cass, Joan E(velyn) CANR-20
Earlier sketches in CA 1-4R, CANR-5
See also SATA 1
Cass, Ronald A(ndrew) 1949- 106
Cass, Zoe
See Low, Lois Dorothea
Cassady, Carolyn (Elizabeth Robinson) 1923- 133
See also DLB 16
Cassady, Claude
See Paine, Lauran (Bosworth)
Cassady, Marsh 1936- 167
Cassady, Neal 1926-1968 141
See also DLB 16
Cassady, Ralph, Jr. 1900-1978 CANR-4
Obituary 77-80
Earlier sketch in CA 1-4R
Cassandra
See Connor, William (Neil)
Cassara, Ernest 1925- 41-44R
Cassata, Mary B. 1930- 121
Cassatt, Mary AAYA 22
Cassavant, Sharron Greer 1939- 125
Cassavetes, John 1929-1989 85-88
Obituary 127
See also CLC 20
Cass-Beggs, Barbara 1904- SATA 62
Cassedy, James H(iggins) 1919- CANR-46
Earlier sketch in CA 1-4R
Cassedy, Sylvia 1930-1989 CANR-22
Earlier sketch in CA 105
See also CLR 26
See also JRDA
See also SATA 27, 77
See also SATA-Obit 61
Cassel, Don 1942- CANR-28
Earlier sketch in CA 110
Cassel, Lili
See Wronker, Lili Cassel
Cassel, Mana-Zucca 1891-1981 Obituary 103
Cassel, Russell N. 1911- 37-40R
Cassel, Virginia Cunningham 105
Cassell, Anthony K. 1941- CANR-48
Earlier sketch in CA 120
Cassell, Eric J. 1928- 137
Cassell, Frank A(llan) 1941- 33-36R
Cassell, Frank Hyde 1916- 37-40R
Cassell, Joan 1929- 135
Cassell, Richard A(llan) 1921- 21-24R
Cassell, Sylvia 1924- 5-8R
Cassells, Cyrus (Curtis III) 1957- CANR-49
Earlier sketch in CA 112
Cassells, John
See Duncan, W(illiam) Murdoch
Casselman, Karen Leigh 1942- 107
Cassels, Alan 1929- CANR-13
Earlier sketch in CA 33-36R
Cassels, J(ohn) W(illiam) S(cott) 1922- 142
Cassels, Louis 1922-1974 CANR-4
Obituary 45-48
Earlier sketch in CA 9-12R
Casserley, H(enry) C(yril) 1903- CANR-9
Earlier sketch in CA 65-68
Casserley, Julian Victor Langmead 1909-1978 9-12R
Obituary 133
Casserly, Jack
See Casserly, John J(oseph)
Casserly, John J(oseph) 1927- CANR-44
Earlier sketch in CA 120
Cassian, Nina 1924- PC 17
Cassiday, Bruce (Bingham) 1920- CANR-47
Earlier sketches in CA 1-4R, CANR-4, 19
Cassidy, Daniel J(ames) 1956- 119
Cassidy, David (Bruce) 1950- 153
Cassidy, David C(harles) 1945- 140
Cassidy, Frederic Gomes 1907- 1-4R
Cassidy, George
See Vance, William E.
Cassidy, Harold G(omes) 1906- 25-28R
Cassidy, John 1928- CANR-35
Earlier sketch in CA 114
Cassidy, John A(lbert) 1908- 33-36R
Cassidy, John R(ufus) 1922- 89-92
Cassidy, Jude (Anne) 1955- 121
Cassidy, Michael 1936- 97-100
Cassidy, Richard J(oseph) 1942- 114
Cassidy, Vincent H. 1923- 21-24R
Cassidy, William L(awrence Robert) 103
Cassilis, Robert
See Edwardes, Michael (F. H.)
Cassill, Kay 89-92
Cassill, R(onald) V(erlin) 1919- CANR-45
Earlier sketches in CA 9-12R, CANR-7
See also CAAS 1
See also CLC 4, 23
See also DLB 6
Cassils, Peter
See Keele, Kenneth D(avid)
Cassin, Rene Samuel 1887-1976 Obituary 65-68
Cassinelli, C(harles) W(illiam, Jr.) 1925- 1-4R
Cassini, Igor (Loiewski) 1915- 129
Cassirer, Ernst 1874-1945 157
See also TCLC 61
Cassity, (Allen) Turner 1929- CANR-11
Earlier sketch in CA 17-20R
See also CAAS 8
See also CLC 6, 42
See also DLB 105
Cassius Dio c. 155-c. 229 DLB 176
Casso, Evans J(oseph) 1914- 57-60
Cassola, Albert M(aria) 1915- CAP-1
Earlier sketch in CA 9-10
Cassola, Carlo 1917-1987 CANR-71
Obituary 121
Earlier sketch in CA 01
See also DLB 177
Casson, Hugh Maxwell 1910- CANR-36
Earlier sketches in CA 103, CANR-20
See also SATA 65
Casson, Lionel 1914- CANR-3
Earlier sketch in CA 9-12R
Casson, Mark (Christopher) 1945- 143
Casstevens, Thomas W(illiam) 1937- 17-20R
Cassuto, David N(athan) 1963- 145
Cassutt, Michael (Joseph) 1954- 146
Cast, David (Jesse Dale) 1942- 109
Castagna, Edwin 1909-1983 CAP-2
Obituary 111
Earlier sketch in CA 17-18
Castagnola, Lawrence A. 1933- CANR-12
Earlier sketch in CA 29-32R
Castaldo, Nancy Fusco 1962- Obituary 152
See also SATA 93
Castaneda, Carlos 1931(?)- CANR-66
Earlier sketches in CA 25-28R, CANR-32
See also CLC 12
See also HW
See also MTCW 1
Castaneda, Christopher James 1959- 145
Castaneda, Hector-Neri 1924- CANR-19
Earlier sketches in CA 5-8R, CANR-3
Castaneda, James A(gustin) 1933- 41-44R
Castaneda, Jorge G. 1953- 144
Castaneda, Omar S. 1954- 135
See also SATA 71
Castedo, Elena 1937- 132
See also CLC 65
Castedo-Ellerman, Elena
See Castedo, Elena
Castel, Albert 1928- CANR-5
Earlier sketch in CA 1-4R
Castel, J(ean) G(abriel) 1928- CANR-50
Earlier sketches in CA 21-24R, CANR-9, 25
Castel, Robert 1933- CANR-68
Earlier sketch in CA 129
Casteleyn, Mary (Teresa) 1941- 131
Castell, Megan
See Williams, Jeanne
Castellan, N(orman) John, Jr. 1939- 37-40R
Castellaneta, Carlo 1930- CANR-11
Earlier sketch in CA 13-16R
Castellano, Giuseppe 1893-1977 Obituary 73-76
Castellano, Olivia 1944- DLB 122
Castellanos, Jane Mollie Robinson 1913- 9-12R
See also SATA 9
Castellanos, Rosario 1925-1974 CANR-58
Obituary 53-56
Earlier sketch in CA 131
See also CLC 66
See also DAM MULT
See also DLB 113
See also HLC
See also HW
Castellon, Federico 1914-1971 SATA 48
Castells, Manuel 1942- CANR-37
Earlier sketch in CA 115
Castells, Matilde O(livella) 1929- 69-72
Castelnuovo-Tedesco, P(ietro) 1925- 21-24R
Caster, Andrew I. 1954- 165
Castetter, William Benjamin 1914- CANR-4
Earlier sketch in CA 1-4R
Casti, J.
See Casti, John L(ouis)
Casti, J. L.
See Casti, John L(ouis)
Casti, John
See Casti, John L(ouis)
Casti, John L(ouis) 1943- 141
Castile, Rand 1938- 138
Castillo, Ana (Hernandez Del) 1953- CANR-51
Earlier sketch in CA 131
See also DLB 122
See also HW
Castillo, Debra A(nn Garsow) 1953- 136
Castillo, Edmund L. 1924- 29-32R
See also SATA 1
Castillo, Richard Griswold del
See Griswold del Castillo, Richard
Castillo Puche, Jose Luis 1919- Brief entry 110
Castle, Alfred L. 1948- 139
Castle, Anthony (Percy) 1938- CANR-32
Earlier sketch in CA 113
Castle, Barbara (Anne) 1910- 130
Castle, Charles 1939- 33-36R
Castle, Coralie 1924- 57-60
Castle, Damon
See Smith, Richard Rein
Castle, Edgar Bradshaw 1897-1973 Obituary 104
Castle, Emery N(eal) 1923- 1-4R
Castle, Frances
See Leader, (Evelyn) Barbara (Blackburn)
Castle, Frederick Ted 1938- 137
Castle, Jayne
See Krentz, Jayne Ann
Castle, Kate 123
Castle, Kathryn 164
Castle, Keith 1927(?)-1985 Obituary 118
Castle, Lee
See Ogan, George F.
and Ogan, Margaret E. (Nettles)
Castle, Leonard L. 1912(?)-1989 129
Castle, Linda
See Crockett, Linda Lea
Castle, Marian (Johnson) CAP-2
Earlier sketch in CA 17-18
Castle, Mort 1946- CANR-14
Earlier sketch in CA 81-84
Castle, Nick 1947- 156
Castle, Paul
See Howard, Vernon (Linwood)
Castle, Robert
See Hamilton, Edmond
Castle, Robert W., Jr. 1929- 25-28R
Castle, Sue G(aronzik) 1942- 105
Castle, Terry (Jacqueline) 1953- 112
Castle, Tony
See Castle, Anthony (Percy)
Castle, William 1914-1977 77-80
Obituary 69-72
Castleden, Rodney 1945- 138
Castle-Kanerova, Mita 1948- 142
Castleman, Harry 1953- 109
Castleman, Michael 1950- 108
Castleman, (Esther) Riva 1930- CANR-40
Brief entry 117
Earlier sketch in CA 128
Castlemon, Harry
See Fosdick, Charles Austin
Castles, Francis G(eoffrey) 1943- CANR-17
Earlier sketch in CA 25-28R
Castles, Lance 1937- 25-28R
Castleton, Virginia 1925- 49-52
Castor, Grahame (Douglas) 1932- CANR-7
Earlier sketch in CA 13-16R
Castor, Henry 1909- 17-20R
Castoriadis, Cornelius 1922- 138
Castoro, Laura A(nn) 1948- 124
Castro (y Quesada), Americo 1885-1972 HW
Castro, Americo 1885-1972 37-40R
Castro, Antonio 1946- 53-56
Castro, Brian (Albert) 1950- 167
Castro (Ruz), Fidel 1926(?)- 129
Brief entry 110
See also DAM MULT
See also HLC
Castro, Jan Garden 1945- 120
Castro, Michael 1945- 132
Castro, Rosalia de 1837-1885 DAM MULT
Castro, Tony
See Castro, Antonio
Castro-Klaren, Sara 1942- 61-64
Castronovo, David 1945- CANR-55
Earlier sketches in CA 114, CANR-35
Casty, Alan Howard 1929- CANR-4
Earlier sketch in CA 1-4R
Casule, Kole 1921- DLB 181
Caswall, Edward 1814-1878 DLB 32
Caswell, Brian 1954- 163
See also SATA 97
Caswell, Helen (Rayburn) 1923- 33-36R
See also SATA 12
Caswell, Margaret (Betsy) R(oss) 1903(?)-1982 Obituary 107
Catacalos, Rosemary 1944- DLB 122
Catala, Rafael 1942- CANR-32
Earlier sketches in CA 73-76, CANR-13
See also HW
Catalano, Dominic 1956- SATA 76
Catalano, Donald B(ernard) 1920- 57-60
Catalano, Grace (A.) 1961- 141
See also SATA 99
Catalano, Joseph S(tellario) 1928- 102
Catalano, Stephen 1952- 135
Catalanotto, Peter 1959- CANR-68
Earlier sketch in CA 138
See also SATA 70
Cataldo, Michael F. 1947- 122
Catanese, Anthony James (Jr.) 1942- CANR-32
Earlier sketches in CA 29-32R, CANR-14
Catania, A(nthony) Charles 1936- 37-40R
Catanzariti, John 1942- CANR-51
Earlier sketch in CA 124
Cate, Benjamin W(ilson) 1931- 73-76
Cate, Curtis 1924- CANR-9
Earlier sketch in CA 53-56
Cate, Curtis Wolsey 1884-1976 Obituary 61-64
Cate, Dick
See Cate, Richard Edward Nelson
Cate, Richard Edward Nelson 1932- 73-76
See also SATA 28
Cate, Robert L(ouis) 1932- CANR-28
Earlier sketch in CA 111
Cate, William Burke 1924- 13-16R
Cateora, Philip Rene 1932- 5-8R
Cater, (Silas) Douglass, (Jr.) 1923-1995 CANR-1
Obituary 149
Earlier sketch in CA 1-4R
Cates, Jo A. 1958- 134
Cates, Ray A., Jr. 1940- 29-32R
Cates, Tory
See Bird, Sarah McCabe
Cateura, Linda Brandi 1924- 135
Cathcart, Helen CANR-2
Earlier sketch in CA 5-8R
See also Albert, Harold A.
Cathcart, Noble Aydelotte 1898-1988 Obituary 126
Cathcart, Robert S(tephen) 1923- 101
Cather, Willa
See Cather, Willa Sibert
Cather, Willa Sibert 1873-1947 128
Brief entry 104
See also AAYA 24
See also CDALB 1865-1917
See also DA
See also DAB
See also DAC
See also DAM MST, NOV
See also DLB 9, 54, 78
See also DLBD 1
See also MTCW 1
See also SATA 30
See also SSC 2
See also TCLC 1, 11, 31
See also WLC
Catherall, Arthur 1906-1980 CANR-38
Earlier sketch in CA 5-8R
See also MAICYA
See also SATA 3, 74
Catherine II 1729-1796 DLB 150
Cathers, David M. 1941- 111
Cathers, Ken 1951- 112
Catherwood, (Henry) Frederick (Ross) 1925- 106
Catherwood, Mary Hartwell 1847-1902 DLB 78
Cathey, Cornelius Oliver 1908- 1-4R
Cathon, Laura E(lizabeth) 1908- 5-8R
See also SATA 27
Catledge, Turner 1901-1983 57-60
Obituary 109
See also AITN 1
See also DLB 127
Catlett, Elizabeth 1919(?)- SATA 82
Catlin, George 1796-1872 DLB 186, 189
Catlin, George E(dward) G(ordon) 1896-1979 13-16R
Obituary 85-88
Catlin, Warren Benjamin 1881-1968 1-4R
Obituary 103
Catlin, Wynelle 1930- 65-68
See also SATA 13
Catling, Darrel (Charles) 1909- 5-8R
Catling, Patrick Skene 1925- Brief entry 115
Catlow, Joanna
See Lowry, Joan (Catlow)
Cato
See Howard, Peter D(unsmore)
Cato, Nancy (Fotheringham) 1917- CAP-1
Earlier sketch in CA 49-52
Catoir, John T. 1931- CANR-11
Earlier sketch in CA 25-28R
Caton, Charles E(dwin) 1928- 9-12R
Caton, Hiram P. 1936- CANR-4
Earlier sketch in CA 53-56
Caton-Thompson, Gertrude 1888-1985 122
Obituary 116
Catran, Jack 1933- 128
Catron, Louis E. 1932- 45-48
Cattafi, Bartolo 1922-1979 DLB 128
Cattan, Henry 1906- 29-32R
Cattaui, Georges 1896-1974 CAP-2
Earlier sketch in CA 25-28
Cattell, Everett L(ewis) 1905- 1-4R
Cattell, Psyche 1893- 41-44R
Cattell, Raymond Bernard 1905- CANR-2
Earlier sketch in CA 5-8R
Catterall, Lee 1944- 141
Catterall, Peter 1961- 134
Catto, Max(well Jeffrey) 1909(?)-1992 105
Obituary 137
Catton, (Charles) Bruce 1899-1978 CANR-7
Obituary 81-84
Earlier sketch in CA 5-8R
See also AITN 1
See also CLC 35
See also DLB 17
See also SATA 2
See also SATA-Obit 24
Catton, William Bruce 1926- CANR-1
Earlier sketch in CA 1-4R
Catton, William R(obert), Jr. 1926- 109
Catudal, Honore M(arc, Jr.) 1944- CANR-12
Earlier sketch in CA 69-72
Catz, Max
See Glaser, Milton
Caudell, Marian 1930- 121
See also SATA 52
Caudill, Harry M(onroe) 1922-1990 CANR-71
Obituary 133
Earlier sketches in CA 33-36R, CANR-14
Caudill, Rebecca 1899-1985 CANR-44
Obituary 117
Earlier sketches in CA 5-8R, CANR-2
See also MAICYA
See also SATA 1
See also SATA-Obit 44
Caudill, William W(ayne) 1914-1983 Obituary 110
Caudle, Neil 1952- 132
Caudwell, Christopher
See Sprigg, C(hristopher) St. John
Cauffiel, Lowell 1951- 132
Caufield, Catherine 161
Caughey, John L(yon) 1941- 115
Caughey, John Walton 1902-1995 Obituary 150
Brief entry 106
Caulder, Colline 1945- 113
Cauldwell, Frank
See King, Francis (Henry)
Cauley, John R(owan) 1908-1976 Obituary 65-68

Cauley, Lorinda Bryan 1951- 101
See also SATA 46
See also SATA-Brief 43
Cauley, Terry
See Cauley, Troy Jesse
Cauley, Troy Jesse 1902- CANR-1
Earlier sketch in CA 1-4R
Caulfield, Carlota 1953- .... CAAS 25
Caulfield, Malachy Francis 1915- CANR-14
Earlier sketch in CA 77-80
Caulfield, Max
See Caulfield, Malachy Francis
Caulfield, Peggy F. 1926-1987 .... 5-8R
Obituary 123
See also SATA-Obit 53
Caulfield, Sean 1925- 108
Cauliflower, Sebastian
See Seldes, Gilbert (Vivian)
Cauman, Samuel 1910-1971 .... CAP-2
Earlier sketch in CA 23-24
See also SATA 48
Caunitz, William J. 1933-1996 130
Obituary 152
Brief entry 125
Interview in 130
See also BEST 89:3
See also CLC 34
Causley, Charles (Stanley) 1917- CANR-35
Earlier sketches in CA 9-12R, CANR-5
See also CLC 7
See also CLR 30
See also DLB 27
See also MTCW 1
See also SATA 3, 66
Caute, (John) David 1936- CANR-64
Earlier sketches in CA 1-4R, CANR-1, 33
See also CAAS 4
See also CLC 29
See also DAM NOV
See also DLB 14
Cautela, Joseph R(ichard) 1927- 106
Cauthen, Baker James 1909-1985 Obituary 115
Cauthen, Irby Bruce, Jr. 1919- 111
Cauthen, W(ilfred) Kenneth 1930- CANR-7
Earlier sketch in CA 5-8R
Cauvin, Jean-Pierre (Bernard) 1936- 116
Cauwels, Janice M(arie) 1949- 110
Cava, Esther Laden 1916- 37-40R
Cavafy, C(onstantine) P(eter) 1863-1933 148
See also Kavafis, Konstantinos Petrou
See also DAM POET
See also TCLC 2, 7
Cavaiani, Mabel 1919- CANR-45
Earlier sketches in CA 57-60, CANR-6, 21
Cavalcanti, Alberto (de Almeida)
1897-1982 Obituary 107
Cavalier, Julian 1931- CANR-2
Earlier sketch in CA 49-52
Cavaliero, Glen 1927- CANR-53
Earlier sketches in CA 73-76, CANR-13, 29
Cavallari, Alberto 1927- CANR-10
Earlier sketch in CA 21-24R
Cavallaro, Ann (Abelson) 1918- 5-8R
See also SATA 62
Cavalletti, Sofia 1917- 130
Cavallo, Diana 1931- CANR-2
Earlier sketch in CA 1-4R
See also SATA 7
Cavallo, Evelyn
See Spark, Muriel (Sarah)
Cavallo, Robert M. 1932- CANR-10
Earlier sketch in CA 65-68
Cavan, Romilly 1914(?)-1975 Obituary 61-64
Cavan, Sherri 1938- 17-20R
Cavanagh, Gerald F(rancis) 1931- 41-44R
Cavanagh, Helen (Carol) 1939- 104
See also SATA 48, 98
See also SATA-Brief 37
Cavanagh, John B. 1908-1983 Obituary 110
Cavanagh, John Richard 1904- CAP-2
Earlier sketch in CA 19-20
Cavanagh, Richard E(dward) 1946- 121
Cavanah, Frances 1899-1982 .... 13-16R
Obituary 133
See also SATA 1, 31
Cavanaugh, Arthur 1926- 17-20R
Cavani, Liliana 1936- 110
Cavanna, Betty
See Harrison, Elizabeth Cavanna
See also CLC 12
See also JRDA
See also MAICYA
See also SAAS 4
See also SATA 1, 30
Cavanna, Elizabeth Allen
See Harrison, Elizabeth Cavanna
Cavazos-Gaither, Alma E(lisa) 1955- 165
Cave, Alfred A. 1935- 37-40R
Cave, (John) David 1957- 138
Cave, Hugh B(arnett) 1910- CANR-72
Earlier sketches in CA 5-8R, CANR-2
Cave, Kathryn 1948- 143
See also SATA 76
Cave, Roderick (George James Munro) 1935- ....
CANR-2
Earlier sketch in CA 5-8R
Cave, Terence (Christopher) 1938- 142
Cave, Thomas
See Steward, Samuel M(orris)
Cave Brown, Anthony
See Brown, Anthony Cave
Cavell, Marcia 1931- 147
Cavell, Stanley (Louis) 1926- CANR-11
Earlier sketch in CA 61-64
Cavelti, Peter C(hristian) 1948- 116
Cavendish, J(ean) M(avis) 1932- 118
Cavendish, Margaret Lucas 1623-1673 .... DLB 131
Cavendish, Peter
See Horler, Sydney
Cavendish, Richard 1930- CANR-20
Earlier sketches in CA 9-12R, CANR-5
Cavendish, (Michael) William (Patrick) 1964- 143
Caveney, Philip (Richard) 1951- CANR-19
Earlier sketch in CA 102
Caverhill, Nicholas
See Kirk-Greene, Anthony (Hamilton Millard)
Caverhill, William Melville 1910-1983 Obituary . 111
Cavers, David F(arquhar) 1902-1988 .... 17-20R
Obituary 125
Cavert, Samuel McCrea 1888-1976 .... 37-40R
Cavert, Walter Dudley 1891- 1-4R
Caves, Richard E(arl) 1931- CANR-41
Earlier sketches in CA 1-4R, CANR-4, 19
Cavett, Dick
See Cavett, Richard A.
Cavett, Richard A. 1936- 108
Cavin, Ruth (Brodie) 1918- CANR-8
Earlier sketch in CA 61-64
See also SATA 38
Cavitch, David 1933- 29-32R
Cavnes, Max P(arvin) 1922- 9-12R
Cavoukian, Raffi 1948- 136
See also SATA 68
Cavrell, Jean 1927- 107
Cawein, Madison 1865-1914 .... DLB 54
Cawelti, John G(eorge) 1929- 21-24R
Cawley, Linda 1949- 113
Cawley, Robert Ralston 1893-1973 .... CAP-2
Obituary 41-44R
Earlier sketch in CA 21-22
Cawley, Winifred 1915- 69-72
See also SATA 13
Cawood, John W. 1931- 33-36R
Caws, Ian 1945- 118
Caws, Mary Ann 1933- CANR-55
Earlier sketches in CA 25-28R, CANR-10, 31
Caws, Peter (James) 1931- CANR-8
Earlier sketch in CA 17-20R
Cawthorne, Graham 1906(?)-1980 Obituary . 97-100
Cawthorne, Nigel 1951- 136
Caxton, Pisistratus
See Lytton, Edward G(eorge) E(arle) L(ytton)
Bulwer-Lytton Baron
Caxton, William 1421(?)-1491(?) .... DLB 170
Cayce, Edgar E(vans) 1918- 21-24R
Cayce, Hugh Lynn 1907-1982 .... CANR-34
Obituary 107
Earlier sketch in CA 25-28R
Cayer, D. M.
See Duffy, Maureen
Cayleff, Susan E. 1954- 147
Cayley, Michael (Forde) 1950- 53-56
Cayrol, Jean 1911- 89-92
See also CLC 11
See also DLB 83
Cayton, Andrew R(obert) L(ee) 1954- 126
Cayton, Horace R(oscoe) 1903-1970 .... CAP-1
Obituary 29-32R
Earlier sketch in CA 13-14
Cayton, Mary Kupiec 1954- 137
Cazalet-Keir, Thelma 1900(?)-1989 .... 25-28R
Obituary 127
Cazamian, Louis Francois
1877-1965 Obituary 93-96
Cazden, Courtney B(orden) 1925- 146
Cazden, Elizabeth 1950- 65-68
Cazden, Norman 1914- 37-40R
Cazden, Robert E. 1930- 33-36R
Cazeau, Charles J(ay) 1931- 104
See also SATA 65
Cazeaux, Isabelle 1926- 53-56
Cazel, Fred A(ugustus), Jr. 1921- 9-12R
Cazelles, Brigitte Jacqueline 1944- 102
Cazemajou, Jean 1924- 73-76
Cazet, Denys 1938- 108
See also SATA 52, 99
See also SATA-Brief 41
Cazzola, Gus 1934- CANR-46
Earlier sketch in CA 108
See also SATA 73
Ceadel, Martin (Eric) 1948- 128
Cebula, Richard J(ohn) 1944- 111
Cebulash, Mel 1937- CANR-57
Earlier sketches in CA 29-32R, CANR-12, 30
See also SATA 10, 91
Cecchetti, Giovanni 1922- Brief entry 107
Cecelski, Elizabeth 1953- 119
Cech, John O(tto) 1944- CANR-46
Earlier sketch in CA 120
Cecil, (Edward Christian) David (Gascoyne)
1902-1986 .... CANR-34
Obituary 118
Earlier sketches in CA 61-64, CANR-13
See also DLB 155
Cecil, Henry
See Keller, David H(enry)
and Leon, Henry Cecil
Cecil, Hugh Mortimer
See Roberts, William
Cecil, Lamar (John Ryan, Jr.) 1932- 21-24R
Cecil, Lord David
See Cecil, (Edward Christian) David (Gascoyne)
Cecil, R. H.
See Hewitt, Cecil Rolph
Cecil, Robert 1913-1994 .... CANR-72
Obituary 144
Earlier sketch in CA 53-56
Cecil-Fronsman, Bill 1953- 143
Ceder, Georgiana Dorcas 1-4R
See also SATA 10
Cefkin, J. Leo 1916- 25-28R
Cegielka, Francis A(nthony) 1908- 37-40R
Ceitho, Dewi
See Jones, Evan David
Cejka, Jaroslav 1943- 132
Cela, Camilo Jose 1916- CANR-32
Earlier sketches in CA 21-24R, CANR-21
See also CAAS 10
See also BEST 90:2
See also CLC 4, 13, 59
See also DAM MULT
See also DLBY 89
See also HLC
See also HW
See also MTCW 1
Celaeno
See Harper, George W(illiam)
Celan, Paul
See Antschel, Paul
See also CLC 10, 19, 53, 82
See also DLB 69
See also PC 10
Celati, Gianni 1937- .... DLB 196
Celaya, Gabriel 1911-1991 .... DLB 108
Celeste, Sister Marie CANR-30
Earlier sketch in CA 49-52
Celestino, Martha Laing 1951- 107
See also SATA 39
Celine, Louis-Ferdinand
See Destouches, Louis-Ferdinand
See also CLC 1, 3, 4, 7, 9, 15, 47
See also DLB 72
Celizic, Mike 1948- 135
Cell, Edward (Charles) 1928- 21-24R
Cell, John W(hitson) 1935- 41-44R
Cellario, Alberto R. 1910(?)-1984 Obituary 112
Celler, Emanuel 1888-1981 Obituary 108
Celnik, Max 1933- 17-20R
Celoria, Francis (S. C.) 1926- 102
Celtis, Conrad 1459-1508 .... DLB 179
Cemach, Harry P(aul) 1917- 57-60
Cenci, Louis 1918- 17-20R
Cendrars, Blaise 1887-1961
See Sauser-Hall, Frederic
See also CLC 18, 106
Censer, Jane T(urner) 1951- 123
Cente, H. F.
See Rocklin, Ross Louis
Center, Allen Harry 1912- CANR-4
Earlier sketch in CA 5-8R
Centlivre, Susanna 1669(?)-1723 .... DLB 84
Cento
See Cobbing, Bob
Centolella, Thomas Carmen 1952- 140
Centore, F. F. 1938- 25-28R
Ceram, C. W.
See Marek, Kurt W(illi)
Ceravolo, Joseph 1934-1988 102
Obituary 126
Cerf, Bennett (Alfred) 1898-1971 .... CAP-2
Obituary 29-32R
Earlier sketch in CA 19-20
See also SATA 7
Cerf, Christopher (Bennett) 1941- CANR-48
Earlier sketch in CA 25-28R
See also SATA 2
Cerf, Jay H(enry) 1923-1974 .... CAP-2
Obituary 53-56
Earlier sketch in CA 19-20
Cerling, Charles (Edward), Jr. 1943- 111
Cermak, Laird S(cott) 1942- CANR-4
Earlier sketch in CA 53-56
Cermak, Martin
See Duchacek, Ivo D(uka)
Cerminara, Gina 17-20R
Cernada, George P. 166
Cerney, James Vincent 1914- 21-24R
Cernuda (y Bidon), Luis 1902-1963 131
Obituary 89-92
See also CLC 54
See also DAM POET
See also DLB 134
See also HW
Cerra, Frances 1946- 97-100
Cerri, Lawrence J. 1923- CANR-17
Earlier sketch in CA 89-92
Cerruti, James Smith 1918-1997 103
Obituary 158
Certner, Simon 1909(?)-1979 Obituary 89-92
Cerullo, Mary M. 1949- 151
See also SATA 86
Cerutti, Maria Antonietta 1932- 25-28R
Cerutti, Toni
See Cerutti, Maria Antonietta
Cerutty, Percy Wells 1895-1975 .... CAP-2
Obituary 61-64
Earlier sketch in CA 25-28
Cervantes, Alfonso J(uan) 1920-1983 Obituary . 110
Cervantes, Lorna Dee 1954- 131
See also DLB 82
See also HW
Cervantes, Lucius F. 1914- 13-16R
Cervantes (Saavedra), Miguel de 1547-1616 .... DA
See also DAB
See also DAC
See also DAM MST, NOV
See also SSC 12
See also WLC
Cervenka, Jarda 1933- 152
Cerveri, Doris 1914- 101
Cervon, Jacqueline
See Moussard, Jacqueline
Cerwinske, Laura 1948- 111
Cerych, Ladislav 1925- CANR-7
Earlier sketch in CA 13-16R
Cesaire, Aime (Fernand) 1913- CANR-43
Earlier sketches in CA 65-68, CANR-24
See also BLC 1
See also BW 2
See also CLC 19, 32, 112
See also DAM MULT, POET
See also MTCW 1
Cesara, Manda
See Poewe, Karla
Cespedes, Frank V. 1950- 154
Cessac, Catherine 1952- 153
Cetin, Frank Stanley 1921- 1-4R
See also SATA 2
Cetron, Marvin Jerome 1930- 107
Cetta, Lewis T(homas) 1933- 53-56
Cevasco, George A(nthony) 1924- CANR-2
Earlier sketch in CA 5-8R
Chabe, Alexander M(ichael) 1923- 53-56
Chaber, M. E.
See Crossen, Kendell Foster
Chabod, Federico 1901-1960 Obituary 116
Chabon, Michael 1963- CANR-57
Earlier sketch in CA 139
See also CLC 55
Chabrol, Claude 1930- 110
See also CLC 16
Chace, Isobel
See de Guise, Elizabeth (Mary Teresa)
Chace, James (Clarke) 1931- CANR-30
Earlier sketches in CA 1-4R, CANR-1
Chace, Rebecca 1960- 144
Chace, William M(urdough) 1938- 69-72
Chacel, Rosa 1898- .... DLB 134
Chacholiades, Miltiades 1937- CANR-1
Earlier sketch in CA 45-48
Chacko, David 1942- CANR-31
Earlier sketch in CA 49-52
Chacko, George K(uttickal) 1930- CANR-13
Earlier sketch in CA 73-76
Chacon, Eusebio 1869-1948 131
See also DLB 82
See also HW
Chacon, Felipe Maximiliano 1873-(?) .... DLB 82
Chaconas, D(oris) J. 1938- 21-24R
Chadbourne, Richard M(cClain) 1922- 21-24R
Chadeayne, Lee 1933- 53-56
Chadourne, Marc 1896(?)-1975 Obituary 53-56
Chadwick, Alex
See Zoss, Joel
Chadwick, Bruce A(lbert) 1940- 97-100
Chadwick, Cydney 1959- 164
Chadwick, Henry 1920- CANR-50
Earlier sketches in CA 21-24R, CANR-9, 25
Chadwick, James 1891-1974 157
Obituary 49-52
Chadwick, Janet (Bachand) 1933- 97-100
Chadwick, (Gerald William St.) John 1915- .. 25-28R
Chadwick, John 1920- 1-4R
Chadwick, Lee 1909- 69-72
Chadwick, Lester CANR-27
Earlier sketches in CAP-2, CA 19-20
See also SATA 1, 67
Chadwick, Margaret Lee (Gill)
1893-1984 Obituary 112
Chadwick, Nora Kershaw 1891-1972 .... CAP-1
Earlier sketch in CA 13-16
Chadwick, (William) Owen 1916- CANR-41
Earlier sketches in CA 1-4R, CANR-1, 19
Chadwick, Ronald P(aul) 1935- 116
Chadwick, Whitney 1943- 132
Chadwin, Mark Lincoln 1939- CANR-17
Earlier sketch in CA 25-28R
Chae, Man-Sik 1902-1950 166
Chaet, Bernard 1924- 69-72
Chafe, Wallace L. 1927- 29-32R
Chafe, William H(enry) 1942- CANR-12
Earlier sketch in CA 49-52
Chafel, Judith A. 1945- 149
Chafets, Ze'ev 1947(?)- 137
Chafets, Zev
See Chafets, Ze'ev
Chafetz, Gary S. 1947- 145
Chafetz, Henry 1916-1978 .... CANR-3
Obituary 73-76
Earlier sketch in CA 1-4R
Chafetz, Janet Saltzman 1942- 69-72
Chafetz, Morris E(dward) 1924- CANR-5
Earlier sketch in CA 13-16R
Chaffee, Allen CAP-1
Earlier sketch in CA 9-10
See also SATA 3
Chaffee, John 1946- 85-88
Chaffee, Steven Henry 1935- 106
Chaffin, Lillie D(orton) 1925- CANR-13
Earlier sketch in CA 33-36R
See also SATA 4
Chaffin, Yule M. 1914- 21-24R
Chafin, Andrew 1937- 53-56
Chagall, David 1930- CANR-3
Earlier sketch in CA 9-12R
Chagall, Marc 1887-1985 122
Obituary 114
See also AAYA 24
Chagla, M(ohamedali) C(urrim)
1900-1981 Obituary 108
Chagnon, Napoleon A. 1938- 130
Chai, Arlene J. 1955- 155
Chai, Chen kang 1916- 21-24R
Chai, Ch'u 1906- 9-12R
Chai, Hon-chan 1931- 21-24R
Chai, Winberg 1932- CANR-9
Earlier sketch in CA 5-8R
Chaij, Fernando 1909- CANR-8
Earlier sketch in CA 21-24R

Chaikin, Miriam 1928- CANR-14
Earlier sketch in CA 81-84
See also SATA 24, 102
Chais, Pamela (Herbert) 1930- 73-76
Chaisson, Eric (Joseph) 1946- CANR-25
Earlier sketch in CA 108
Chajkowsky, William E(ugene) 1938- 116
Chakerian, Charles (Garabed) 1904- 45-48
Chakour, Charles M. 1929- 33-36R
Chakovsky, Sergei 1949- 144
Chakravarty, Amiya (Chandra) 1901- CANR-1
Earlier sketch in CA 1-4R
Chakravarty, Birendra Narayan 1904-1980(?) 102
Chakravarty, Sumita S(inha) 1951- 148
Chaleff, Ira 1945- 150
Chalfant, Edward Allan 1921- 111
Chalfant, William Y. 1928- 149
Chalfont, Alun
See Jones, (Alun) Arthur Gwynne
Chalhoub, Michael 1932- 89-92
Chalidze, Valery Nikolaevich 1938- 103
Chalk, John Allen 1937- 57-60
Chalk, Ocania 1927- CANR-1
Earlier sketch in CA 45-48
Chalker, Jack L(aurence) 1944- CANR-47
Earlier sketch in CA 73-76
Chalker, Sylvia 146
Chall, Jeanne S(ternlicht) 1921- CANR-10
Earlier sketch in CA 25-28R
Challand, Helen J(ean) 1921- 121
Brief entry 118
See also SATA 64
Challans, Mary 1905-1983 81-84
Obituary 111
See also Renault, Mary
See also SATA 23
See also SATA-Obit 36
Challice, Kenneth
See Hutchin, Kenneth Charles
Challinor, John 1894- 73-76
Challis, Chris 131
Challis, George
See Faust, Frederick (Schiller)
Challis, Mary
See Bowen-Judd, Sara (Hutton)
Challis, Simon
See Phillips, D(ennis) J(ohn Andrew)
Challoner, H. K.
See Mills, J(anet) M(elanie) A(ilsa)
Challoner, Robert
See Butterworth, Michael
Chalmers, Alan D(ouglas) 1957- 152
Chalmers, David Mark 1927- 25-28R
Chalmers, Eric Brownlie 1929- 102
Chalmers, Floyd S(herman) 1898- CAP-2
Earlier sketch in CA 25-28
Chalmers, George 1742-1825 DLB 30
Chalmers, Harvey II 1890-1971 Obituary 33-36R
Chalmers, John W. 1910- 93-96
Chalmers, Malcolm 1956- 120
Chalmers, Mary (Eileen) 1927- 5-8R
See also SAAS 14
See also SATA 6
Chalmers, Penny
See Kemp, Penny
Chalon, Jean 1935- CANR-40
Earlier sketches in CA 97-100, CANR-16
Chalon, Jon
See Chaloner, John Seymour
Chaloner, John Seymour 1924- 93-96
Chaloner, Sir Thomas 1520-1565 DLB 167
Chaloner, W. H.
See Chaloner, William Henry
Chaloner, William Henry 1914-1987 Obituary 122
Chamberlain, Anne 1917- 77-80
Chamberlain, Betty 1908-1983 33-36R
Obituary 109
Chamberlain, Elinor 1901- CAP-1
Earlier sketch in CA 13-16
Chamberlain, Elwyn M. 1928- 131
Chamberlain, Ena
See Cooper, Penny
Chamberlain, Houston Stewart 1855-1927(?) Brief entry 120
Chamberlain, John (Rensselaer) 1903-1995 57-60
Obituary 148
Chamberlain, Jonathan Mack 1928- 101
Chamberlain, Joseph Miles 1923- 107
Chamberlain, Lesley 1951- 137
Chamberlain, Lorna M(arie) 1945- 146
Chamberlain, Margaret 1954- SATA 46
Chamberlain, Mary (Christina) 1947- CANR-44
Earlier sketch in CA 115
Chamberlain, Muriel Evelyn 1932- CANR-16
Earlier sketch in CA 93-96
Chamberlain, Narcisse 1924- 13-16R
Chamberlain, Neil Wolverton 1915- CANR-6
Earlier sketch in CA 13-16R
Chamberlain, (Arthur) Neville 1869-1940 Brief entry 113
Chamberlain, Robert Lyall 1923- 13-16R
Chamberlain, Samuel 1895-1975 CAP-2
Obituary 53-56
Earlier sketch in CA 23-24
Chamberlain, Samuel S. 1851-1916 DLB 25
Chamberlain, Wilson
See Crandall, Norma
Chamberlain, Wilt(on Norman) 1936- 103
Chamberland, Paul 1939- DLB 60
Chamberlin, Ann 1954- 159
Chamberlin, E(ric) R(ussell) 1926- CANR-19
Earlier sketch in CA 97-100
Chamberlin, Enid C. S.
1900(?)-1982(?) Obituary 106
Chamberlin, J. E(ward) 1943- 85-88
Chamberlin, J(ohn) Gordon 1914- CANR-4
Earlier sketch in CA 1-4R
Chamberlin, Judi 1944- 81-84
Chamberlin, Lee
See La Pallo, A. Elise
Chamberlin, Leslie J(oseph) 1926- 53-56
Chamberlin, M. Hope 1920-1974 45-48
Obituary 49-52
Chamberlin, Mary 1914- 45-48
Chamberlin, Thomas Chrowder 1843-1928 158
Chamberlin, Waldo 1905- 65-68
Chamberlin, William Henry 1897-1969 5-8R
See also DLB 29
Chambers, Aidan 1934- CANR-58
Earlier sketches in CA 25-28R, CANR-12, 31
See also AAYA 27
See also CLC 35
See also JRDA
See also MAICYA
See also SAAS 12
See also SATA 1, 69
Chambers, Anne 1949- CANR-53
Earlier sketch in CA 126
Chambers, Anthony H(ood) 1943- 108
Chambers, Bradford 1922-1984 Obituary 113
See also SATA-Obit 39
Chambers, Catherine E.
See St. John, Nicole
Chambers, Charles Haddon 1860-1921 Brief entry 110
See also DLB 10
Chambers, Clarke A(lexander) 1921- 41-44R
Chambers, Colin 1950- 134
Chambers, Dewey W. 1929- CANR-12
Earlier sketch in CA 29-32R
Chambers, Edward J(ames) 1925- 17-20R
Chambers, Frances 1940- CANR-29
Earlier sketch in CA 111
Chambers, Frank P(entland) 1900- CAP-1
Earlier sketch in CA 9-10
Chambers, Howard V.
See Lowenkopf, Shelly A(lan)
Chambers, Iain 1949- 126
Chambers, James 1948- Brief entry 124
See also Cliff, Jimmy
Chambers, Jane 1937-1983 85-88
Obituary 109
Chambers, Jessie
See Lawrence, D(avid) H(erbert Richards)
Chambers, John W. 1933- 124
See also SATA 57
See also SATA-Brief 46
Chambers, John Whiteclay II 1936- 137
Chambers, Jonathan David 1898-1970 CANR-3
Earlier sketch in CA 1-4R
Chambers, Kate
See St. John, Nicole
Chambers, Leland H. 1928- 140
Chambers, Lenoir 1891-1970 111
Obituary 104
Chambers, Lucille Arcola
1909(?)-1988 Obituary 125
Chambers, M(erritt) M(adison) 1899- CANR-5
Earlier sketch in CA 9-12R
Chambers, Margaret Ada Eastwood 1911- 9-12R
See also SATA 2
Chambers, Mortimer Hardin, Jr. 1927- CANR-6
Earlier sketch in CA 9-12R
Chambers, Peggy
See Chambers, Margaret Ada Eastwood
Chambers, Peter
See Phillips, D(ennis) J(ohn Andrew)
Chambers, R(aymond) J(ohn) 1917- 17-20R
Chambers, Robert W(illiam) 1865-1933 165
See also DLB 202
See also TCLC 41
Chambers, Robin Bernard 1942- 103
Chambers, Veronica 1970(?)- 167
Chambers, W(illiam) Walker 1913- 29-32R
Chambers, (David) Whittaker
1901-1961 Obituary 89-92
Chambers, William E. 1943- 73-76
Chambers, William Nisbet 1916- CANR-8
Earlier sketch in CA 5-8R
Chambers, William Trout 1896- CAP-1
Earlier sketch in CA 13-14
Chambers-Schiller, Lee Virginia 1948- 120
Chambertin, Ilya
See von Block, Bela W(illiam)
and von Block, Sylvia
Chambliss, Bill
See Chambliss, William J(oseph)
Chambliss, William C. 1908(?)-1975 Obituary 57-60
Chambliss, William J(ones) 1923- 13-16R
Chambliss, William J(oseph) 1933- CANR-14
Earlier sketch in CA 77-80
Chamelin, Neil Charles 1942- 69-72
Chametzky, Jules 1928- 33-36R
Chamisso, Adelbert von 1781-1838 DLB 90
Chamlee, Ruth Miller 1893(?)-1983 Obituary 110
Chamoiseau, Patrick 1953- 162
Champagne, Marian 1915- 5-8R
Champe, Flavia Waters 1902- 115
Champernowne, David (Gawen) 1912- 104
Champigny, Robert J(ean) 1922- 33-36R
Champion, Dick
See Champion, Richard Gordon
Champion, J(ustin) A. I. 1960- 141
Champion, John C(arr) 1923- CANR-8
Earlier sketch in CA 17-20R
Champion, John E(lmer) 1922- 13-16R
Champion, Larry S(tephen) 1932- CANR-9
Earlier sketch in CA 21-24R
Champion, R(ichard) A(nnells) 1925- 29-32R
Champion, Richard Gordon 1931- 77-80
Champkin, Peter 1918- 5-8R
Champlin, Charles (Davenport) 1926- 69-72
Champlin, James R(aymond) 1928- 21-24R
Champlin, John Michael 1937- CANR-52
Earlier sketches in CA 110, CANR-27
Champlin, Joseph M(asson) 1930- CANR-20
Earlier sketches in CA 49-52, CANR-1
Champlin, Margaret Derby 1925- 148
Champlin, Peggy
See Champlin, Margaret Derby
Champlin, Tim
See Champlin, John Michael
Champney, Freeman 1911- 25-28R
Chamson, Andre J(ules) L(ouis) 1900-1983 CANR-2
Obituary 111
Earlier sketch in CA 5-8R
Ch'an, Chu
See Blofeld, John (Eaton Calthorpe)
Ch'An, Chu
See Blofeld, John (Eaton Calthorpe)
Chan, Gillian 1954- 160
See also SATA 102
Chan, Loren Briggs 1943- CANR-8
Earlier sketch in CA 57-60
Chanaidh, Fear
See Campbell, John Lorne
Chanakya
See Panikkar, K(avalam) Madhava
Chanan, Ben
See Yaffe, Richard
Chanan, Gabriel 1942- CANR-7
Earlier sketch in CA 57-60
Chanan, Michael 1946- 106
Chance, Britton 1913- 157
Chance, John Newton 1911-1983 CANR-59
Obituary 110
Earlier sketch in CA 102
Chance, John T.
See Carpenter, John (Howard)
Chance, Jonathan
See Chance, John Newton
Chance, Megan 1959- 167
Chance, Michael R(obin) A(lexander) 1915- 85-88
Chance, Roger (James Ferguson)
1893-1987 Obituary 122
Chance, Stephen
See Turner, Philip (William)
Chancellor, John 1900-1971 CAP-2
Earlier sketch in CA 23-24
Chancellor, John (William) 1927-1996 109
Obituary 152
Interview in 109
See also AITN 1
See also BEST 90:4
Chancellor, Paul 1900-1975 Obituary 57-60
Chancer, Lynn S. 1955- 144
Chand, Meira (Angela) 1942- 106
Chand, Munshi Prem
See Srivastava, Dhanpat Rai
Chand, Prem
See Srivastava, Dhanpat Rai
Chanda, Asok Kumar 1902- 17-20R
Chandler, A(rthur) Bertram 1912-1984 CANR-13
Earlier sketch in CA 21-24R
Chandler, Alfred D(upont), Jr. 1918- CANR-4
Earlier sketch in CA 9-12R
Chandler, Alice 1931- 53-56
Chandler, Allison 1906- CAP-1
Earlier sketch in CA 9-10
Chandler, B. J. 1921- 1-4R
Chandler, Billy Jaynes 1932- 122
Chandler, Bryn 1945- 118
Chandler, Caroline A(ugusta) 1906-1979 17-20R
Obituary 93-96
See also SATA 22
See also SATA-Obit 24
Chandler, David (Geoffrey) 1934- CANR-52
Earlier sketches in CA 25-28R, CANR-11, 28
Chandler, David Leon 1937(?)-1994 CANR-38
Obituary 143
Earlier sketches in CA 49-52, CANR-1, 16
Chandler, David Porter 1933- CANR-54
Earlier sketches in CA 45-48, CANR-29
See also SATA 28
Chandler, E(dwin) Russell, Jr. 1932- 77-80
Chandler, Edna Walker 1908-1982 CANR-4
Obituary 108
Earlier sketch in CA 1-4R
See also SATA 11
See also SATA-Obit 31
Chandler, Frank
See Harknett, Terry
Chandler, George 1915- CANR-5
Earlier sketch in CA 9-12R
Chandler, Harry 1864-1944 DLB 29
Chandler, Howard 1915(?)-1981 Obituary 104
Chandler, James 1948- 168
Chandler, Jennifer
See Westwood, Jennifer
Chandler, Laurel
See Holder, Nancy L.
Chandler, Lester Vernon 1905-1988 Obituary 126
Chandler, Linda S(mith) 1929- CANR-23
Earlier sketch in CA 106
See also SATA 39
Chandler, Margaret Kueffner 1922- 17-20R
Chandler, Marilyn R(uth) 1949- 140
Chandler, Norman 1899-1973 Obituary 89-92
See also DLB 127
Chandler, Otis 1927- 111
See also DLB 127
Chandler, Raymond (Thornton) 1888-1959 CANR-60
Brief entry 104
Earlier sketch in CA 129
See also AAYA 25
See also CDALB 1929-1941
See also DLBD 6
See also MTCW 1
See also SSC 23
See also TCLC 1, 7
Chandler, Richard Eugene 1916- 5-8R
Chandler, Robert 1953- 112
See also SATA 40
Chandler, Robert Wilbur 1921- 102
Chandler, Ruth Forbes 1894-1978 1-4R
Obituary 103
See also SATA 2
See also SATA-Obit 26
Chandler, S(tanley) Bernard 1921- 21-24R
Chandler, T(ony) J(ohn) 1928- 107
Chandler, Tertius 1915- CANR-19
Earlier sketch in CA 102
Chandola, Anoop C. 1937- CANR-14
Earlier sketch in CA 37-40R
Chandonnet, Ann F. 1943- CANR-47
Earlier sketches in CA 61-64, CANR-8, 23
See also SATA 92
Chandor, (Peter John) Anthony 1932- CANR-26
Earlier sketch in CA 29-32R
Chandos, Fay
See Swatridge, Irene Maude (Mossop)
Chandos, John
See McConnell, John Lithgow Chandos
Chandra, Pramod 1930- 77-80
Chandra, Smita 1960- 138
Chandra, Vikram 1961- 149
Chandrasekhar, Sripati 1918- 89-92
Chandrasekhar, Subrahmanyan 1910- 157
Chaneles, Sol 1926- 41-44R
Chaney, Edward (Paul de Gruyter) 1951- 131
Chaney, Jill 1932- CANR-52
Earlier sketches in CA 25-28R, CANR-11
See also SATA 87
Chaney, Norman 1935- 110
Chaney, Otto Preston, Jr. 1931- 33-36R
Chaney, William A(lbert) 1922- 33-36R
Chang, Chen-chi 1920- 153
Brief entry 115
Chang, Ch'eng-chi
See Chang, Chen-chi
Chang, Chung-yuan 1900- 117
Chang, Cindy 1968- SATA 90
Chang, Constance D(an) 1917- 61-64
Chang, Dae H(ong) 1928- CANR-6
Earlier sketch in CA 57-60
Chang, David Wen-wei 1929- 130
Chang, Eileen 1920-1995 166
See also SSC 28
Chang, Garma C. C.
See Chang, Chen-chi
Chang, Hsin-hai 1898(?)-1972 5-8R
Chang, Isabelle C(hin) 1924- 21-24R
Chang, Jen-chi 1903- CAP-1
Earlier sketch in CA 11-12
Chang, Jung 1952- 142
See also CLC 71
Chang, Kevin O'Brien 1958- 168
Chang, Kia-Ngau 1889- 5-8R
Chang, Kwang-chih 1931- CANR-15
Earlier sketch in CA 41-44R
Chang, Lee
See Levinson, Leonard
Chang, Leonard 1968- 168
Chang, Margaret (Scrogin) 1941- SATA 71
Chang, Pang-Mei Natasha 1965- 156
Chang, Parris (Hsu-Cheng) 1936- CANR-6
Earlier sketch in CA 57-60
Chang, Raymond 1939- CANR-47
Earlier sketch in CA 121
See also SATA 71
Chang, Richard T(aiwon) 1933- 61-64
Chang Ai-Ling
See Chang, Eileen
Chang Chieh
See Zhang, Jie
Chang Chien
See Zhang, Jie
Changeux, Jean-Pierre 1936- 134
Chang-Rodriguez, Eugenio 1926- CANR-21
Earlier sketches in CA 9-12R, CANR-6
Chanin, Abraham (Solomon) 1921- 89-92
Chanin, Michael 1952- SATA 84
Chankin, Donald O(liver) 1934- 57-60
Channel, A. R.
See Catherall, Arthur
Channels, Vera G(race) 1915- 69-72
Channing, Edward (Perkins) 1856-1931 Brief entry 122
See also DLB 17
Channing, Edward Tyrrell 1790-1856 DLB 1, 59
Channing, Steven A. 1940- CANR-29
Earlier sketches in CA 33-36R, CANR-13
Channing, William Ellery II 1817-1901 DLB 1
Channing, William Ellery 1780-1842 DLB 1, 59
Channing, William Henry 1810-1884 DLB 1, 59
Channon, Henry 1897-1958 Brief entry 121
Chanoff, David 1943- 138
Chanover, E(dmond) Pierre 1932- 29-32R
Chanover, Hyman 1920- CANR-2
Earlier sketch in CA 49-52
Chansky, Norman M(orton) 1929- 21-24R
Chant, Barry (Mostyn) 1938- CANR-29
Earlier sketches in CA 65-68, CANR-11
Chant, Donald (Alfred) 1928- CANR-18
Earlier sketch in CA 101

Chant, Joy
See Rutter, Eileen Joyce
Chant, Ken(neth David) 1933- ... 89-92
Chantiles, Vilma Liacouras 1925- ... CANR-6
Earlier sketch in CA 57-60
Chantler, David T(homas) 1925- ... 93-96
Chao, Buwei Yang 1889-1981 ... 61-64
Obituary ... 120
Chao, Evelina 1949- ... 120
Chao, Kang 1929- ... 33-36R
Chao, Patricia 1955- ... 163
Chao, Paul 1919- ... 114
Chao, Yuen Ren 1892-1982 ... CAP-2
Obituary ... 106
Earlier sketch in CA 21-22
Chapel, Paul 1926- ... 25-28R
Chapelle, Howard I(rving) 1901-1975 ... CAP-2
Obituary ... 57-60
Earlier sketch in CA 25-28
Chapian, Marie 1938- ... CANR-22
Earlier sketch in CA 106
See also SATA 29
Chapin, Alene Olsen Dalton
1915(?)-1986 Obituary ... 119
See also SATA-Obit 47
Chapin, Dwight Allan 1938- ... 41-44R
Chapin, F(rancis) Stuart, Jr. 1916- ... CANR-2
Earlier sketch in CA 5-8R
Chapin, Harry (Forster) 1942-1981 ... 105
Obituary ... 104
Chapin, Henry 1893-1983 ... 93-96
Obituary ... 110
Chapin, June Roediger 1931- ... CANR-13
Earlier sketch in CA 37-40R
Chapin, Katherine Garrison
See Biddle, Katherine Garrison Chapin
Chapin, Kim 1942- ... CANR-9
Earlier sketch in CA 53-56
Chapin, Louis Le Bourgeois, Jr. 1918-1981 ... 103
Chapin, Miles 1954- ... 147
Chapin, Ned 1927- ... 13-16R
Chapin, Sarah 1931- ... 148
Chapin, Schuyler G(arrison) 1923- ... 77-80
Chapin, Tom 1945- ... SATA 83
Chapin, Victor 1919(?)-1983 Obituary ... 109
Chapin, William 1918- ... 37-40R
Chaplin, Bill
See Chaplin, W. W.
Chaplin, Charles Spencer 1889-1977 ... 81-84
Obituary ... 73-76
See also Chaplin, Charlie
See also CLC 16
Chaplin, Charlie
See Chaplin, Charles Spencer
See also DLB 44
Chaplin, Dora P. 1906(?)-1990 Obituary ... 132
Chaplin, George 1914- ... 69-72
See also AITN 2
Chaplin, James P(atrick) 1919- ... CANR-1
Earlier sketch in CA 1-4R
Chaplin, L(inda) Tarin 1941- ... CANR-40
Earlier sketch in CA 116
Chaplin, Sid(ney) 1916-1986 ... CANR-39
Obituary ... 118
Earlier sketches in CAP-1, CA 9-10, CANR-16
Chaplin, W. W. 1895(?)-1978 Obituary ... 81-84
Chapman, A(rthur) H(arry) 1924- ... CANR-19
Earlier sketch in CA 25-28R
Chapman, Abraham 1915- ... 45-48
Chapman, Allen ... CANR-27
Earlier sketches in CAP-2, CA 19-20
See also SATA 1, 67
Chapman, Alvah H., Jr. ... AITN 2
Chapman, Brian 1923- ... 9-12R
Chapman, Carl H(aley) 1915-1987 ... 133
Chapman, Carleton B(urke) 1915- ... 69-72
Chapman, Charles F(rederic)
1881-1976 Obituary ... 65-68
Chapman, Cheryl O(rth) 1948- ... SATA 80
Chapman, Christine 1933- ... CANR-12
Earlier sketch in CA 73-76
Chapman, Clark Russell 1945- ... CANR-28
Earlier sketch in CA 110
Chapman, Colin 1937- ... CANR-26
Earlier sketch in CA 29-32R
Chapman, David L. 1948- ... 148
Chapman, (William) Donald 1923- ... 109
Chapman, Dorothy Hilton 1934- ... 57-60
Chapman, Edmund H(aupt) 1906- ... CAP-1
Earlier sketch in CA 13-16
Chapman, (Constance) Elizabeth (Mann) 1919- ...
CAP-1
Earlier sketch in CA 9-10
See also SATA 10
Chapman, Elwood N. 1916- ... 37-40R
Chapman, Frances
See Chapman, Frank M(onroe)
Chapman, Frank
See Chapman, Frank M(onroe)
Chapman, Frank M(onroe) 1930- ... 113
Chapman, G(eorge) W(arren) Vernon 1925- ...
CANR-26
Earlier sketch in CA 29-32R
Chapman, Gaynor 1935- ... SATA 32
Chapman, George 1559(?)-1634 ... DAM DRAM
See also DLB 62, 121
Chapman, Graham 1941-1989 ... CANR-35
Obituary ... 129
Earlier sketch in CA 116
See also Monty Python
See also CLC 21
Chapman, Guy (Patterson) 1889-1972 ... 101
Obituary ... 89-92
Chapman, Hester W(olferstan) 1899-1976 . CANR-9
Obituary ... 65-68
Earlier sketch in CA 9-12R
Chapman, J. Dudley 1928- ... CANR-8
Earlier sketch in CA 21-24R
Chapman, James (Keith) 1919- ... CANR-33
Earlier sketches in CA 41-44R, CANR-15
Chapman, Jean ... 97-100
See also SATA 34
Chapman, Jennifer 1950- ... CANR-42
Earlier sketch in CA 118
Chapman, John 1900-1972 Obituary ... 33-36R
Chapman, John Jay 1862-1933 Brief entry ... 104
See also TCLC 7
Chapman, John L(eslie) 1920- ... 1-4R
Chapman, John Roy 1927- ... CANR-15
Earlier sketch in CA 77-80
Chapman, John Stanton Higham
1891-1972 Obituary ... 107
See also SATA-Obit 27
Chapman, Joseph Irvine 1912- ... 61-64
Chapman, June R(amey) 1918- ... 5-8R
Chapman, Karen C. 1942- ... 65-68
Chapman, Kenneth F(rancis) 1910- ... CAP-1
Earlier sketch in CA 13-16
Chapman, Kenneth G. 1927- ... 13-16R
Chapman, Laura 1935- ... 105
Chapman, Lee
See Bradley, Marion Zimmer
Chapman, Loren J(ames) 1927- ... 53-56
Chapman, Lynne F(erguson) 1963- ... 159
See also SATA 94
Chapman, M(ary) Winslow 1903- ... 93-96
Chapman, Marie M(anire) 1917- ... CANR-11
Earlier sketch in CA 61-64
Chapman, Maristan
See Chapman, John Stanton Higham
Chapman, Nancy W(hisnant) Collins
See Collins-Chapman, Nancy W(hisnant)
Chapman, Olive Murray 1892-1977 ... DLB 195
Chapman, Paul K. 1931- ... 139
Chapman, Phil 1944- ... 121
Chapman, R. W. 1881-1960 ... DLB 201
Chapman, Raymond 1924- ... CANR-42
Earlier sketches in CA 5-8R, CANR-2
Chapman, Richard A(rnold) 1937- ... 133
Brief entry ... 105
Chapman, Rick M. 1943- ... 49-52
Chapman, Robert (DeWitt) 1937- ... 107
Chapman, Robert L(undquist) 1920- ... 122
Chapman, Roger E(ddington) 1916- ... 21-24R
Chapman, Ronald (George) 1917-1994 ... 5-8R
Obituary ... 147
Chapman, Ruth 1912(?)-1979 Obituary ... 104
Chapman, Samuel Greeley 1929- ... CANR-9
Earlier sketch in CA 17-20R
Chapman, Stanley D(avid) 1935- ... CANR-9
Earlier sketch in CA 21-24R
Chapman, Stepan ... 41-44R
Chapman, Steven
See Chapman, Stepan
Chapman, Sydney 1888-1970 ... 106
Chapman, Vera (Ivy May) 1898- ... CANR-58
Earlier sketch in CA 81-84
See also SATA 33
Chapman, Victoria L(ynn) 1944- ... 57-60
Chapman, Walker
See Silverberg, Robert
Chapman, William 1850-1917 ... DLB 99
Chapman-Mortimer, William Charles 1907- ... 13-16R
Chapnick, Howard 1922-1996 ... 65-68
Obituary ... 152
Chappel, Bernice M(arie) 1910- ... CANR-37
Earlier sketches in CA 89-92, CANR-16
Chappell, Audrey 1954- ... 140
See also SATA 72
Chappell, Clovis G(illham) 1882-1972 ... 65-68
Chappell, Fred (Davis) 1936- ... CANR-67
Earlier sketches in CA 5-8R, CANR-8, 33
See also CAAS 4
See also CLC 40, 78
See also DLB 6, 105
Chappell, Gordon (Stelling) 1939- ... 57-60
Chappell, Helen 1947- ... 104
Chappell, Jeannette
See Kalt, Jeannette Chappell
Chappell, Mollie ... 102
Chappell, Vere Claiborne 1930- ... 5-8R
Chappell, Warren 1904-1991 ... CANR-47
Obituary ... 134
Earlier sketches in CA 17-20R, CANR-8
See also MAICYA
See also SAAS 10
See also SATA 6, 68
See also SATA-Obit 67
Chappell, William (Evelyn) 1908-1994 ... 106
Obituary ... 143
Chapple, Christopher Key 1954- ... CANR-52
Earlier sketch in CA 126
Chapple, Eliot D(ismore) 1909- ... 41-44R
Chapple, (Clement) Gerald 1937- ... 111
Chapple, J(ohn) A(lfred) V(ictor) 1928- ... 21-24R
Chapple, Richard L(ynn) 1944- ... 112
Chapple, Steve 1949- ... 77-80
Chaput, Donald (Charles) 1933- ... 122
Brief entry ... 117
Chaqueri, Cosroe
See Shakeri, Khosrow
Char, K. T. Narasimha
See Narasimha Char, K. T.
Char, Rene(-Emile) 1907-1988 ... CANR-32
Obituary ... 124
Earlier sketch in CA 13-16R
See also CLC 9, 11, 14, 55
See also DAM POET
See also MTCW 1
Char, Tin-Yuke 1905- ... 57-60
Char, Wai Jane Chun 1912- ... 118
Char, Yum
See Barrett, Dean
Charanis, Peter 1908-1985 ... 37-40R
Obituary ... 115
Charbonneau, Eileen 1951- ... 150
See also SATA 84
Charbonneau, Jean 1875-1960 ... DLB 92
Charbonneau, Louis (Henry) 1924- ... CANR-55
Earlier sketch in CA 85-88
Charbonneau, Robert 1911-1967 ... DLB 68
Charbonnet, Gabrielle 1961- ... 149
See also SATA 81
Charby, Jay
See Ellison, Harlan (Jay)
Charchat, Isaac 1904(?)-1985 Obituary ... 116
Chard, (Maire) Brigid 1934- ... 105
Chard, Judy 1916- ... CANR-31
Earlier sketches in CA 77-80, CANR-14
Chard, Leslie F. II 1934- ... 33-36R
Chardiet, Bernice (Kroll) 1927(?)- ... 103
See also SATA 27
Chardin, Pierre Teilhard de
See Teilhard de Chardin, (Marie Joseph) Pierre
Chargaff, Erwin 1905- ... CANR-39
Earlier sketches in CA 101, CANR-18
Charhadi, Driss ben Hamed ... 13-16R
Chari, V. Krishna 1924- ... 17-20R
Charland, William (Alfred), Jr. 1937- ... 97-100
Charles, Amy M(arie) 1922- ... 116
Charles, C(arol) M(organ) 1931- ... CANR-1
Earlier sketch in CA 49-52
Charles, David
See Mondey, David (Charles)
and Taylor, Charles D(oonan)
Charles, Don C(laude) 1918- ... 9-12R
Charles, Donald
See Meighan, Donald Charles
Charles, Franklin
See Adams, Cleve F(ranklin)
Charles, Gerda 1914- ... CANR-68
Earlier sketches in CA 1-4R, CANR-1
See also DLB 14
Charles, Gordon H(ull) 1920- ... 104
Charles, Henry
See Harris, Marion Rose (Young)
Charles, Kate 1950- ... CANR-72
Earlier sketch in CA 141
Charles, Louis
See Stratemeyer, Edward L.
Charles, Maggi
See Koehler, Margaret (Hudson)
Charles, Mark
See Bickers, Richard (Leslie) Townshend
Charles, Nathanael
See Franklin, Benjamin V
Charles, Nicholas J.
See Kuskin, Karla (Seidman)
Charles, Ray
See Robinson, Ray Charles
Charles, Robert
See Smith, Robert Charles
Charles, Sara C(onnor) 1934- ... 132
Charles, Sascha 1896(?)-1972 Obituary ... 37-40R
Charles, Searle F(ranklin) 1923- ... 9-12R
Charles, Theresa
See Swatridge, Charles (John)
Charles, Will
See Willeford, Charles (Ray III)
Charles-Roux, Edmonde 1920- ... 85-88
Charles the Clown
See Kraus, Charles E.
Charleston, Robert E.
See Robinson, Charles M. III
Charleston, Robert Jesse 1916- ... 102
Charlesworth, Arthur Riggs 1911- ... 53-56
Charlesworth, Edward A(llison) 1949- ... 125
Charlesworth, James Clyde 1900-1974 ... 9-12R
Obituary ... 45-48
Charlesworth, James H(amilton) 1940- ... 130
Charlesworth, John Kaye 1889- ... CAP-1
Earlier sketch in CA 9-10
Charlesworth, Maxwell John 1925- ... CANR-40
Earlier sketches in CA 1-4R, CANR-2, 18
Charlier, Patricia (Mary) Simonet 1923- ... 37-40R
Charlier, Roger H(enri) 1921- ... CANR-60
Earlier sketches in CA 37-40R, CANR-13, 31
Charlip, Remy 1929- ... CANR-44
Earlier sketch in CA 33-36R
See also CLR 8
See also MAICYA
See also SATA 4, 68
Charlot, Jean 1898-1979 ... CANR-4
Earlier sketch in CA 5-8R
See also SATA 8
See also SATA-Obit 31
Charlot, John (Pierre) 1941- ... 120
Charlot, Martin (Day) 1944- ... CANR-35
Earlier sketch in CA 114
See also SATA 64
Charlotte, Susan 1954- ... 109
Charlson, David
See Holmes, David Charles
Charlton, David 1946- ... 127
Charlton, Donald Geoffrey 1925- ... CANR-17
Earlier sketches in CA 1-4R, CANR-1
Charlton, Evan 1912-1983 Obituary ... 110
Charlton, Jack
See Charlton, John
Charlton, James (Mervyn) 1939- ... 81-84
Charlton, John
See Woodhouse, Martin (Charlton)
Charlton, John 1935- ... 109
Charlton, Linda
See Murray, Linda Charlton
Charlton, Michael (Alan) 1923- ... SATA 34
Charlwood, D(onald) E(rnest) 1915- ... CANR-9
Earlier sketch in CA 21-24R
Charlwood, Don
See Charlwood, D(onald) E(rnest)
Charmatz, Bill 1925- ... 29-32R
See also SATA 7
Charme, Stuart Zane 1951- ... 137
Charmley, John 1955- ... 143
Charnance, L. P.
See Hannaway, Patricia H(inman)
Charnas, Suzy McKee 1939- ... CANR-39
Earlier sketches in CA 93-96, CANR-18
See also SATA 61
Charney, Ann ... 102
Charney, David H. 1923- ... CANR-15
Earlier sketch in CA 81-84
Charney, George 1905(?)-1975 Obituary ... 61-64
Charney, Hanna (Kurz) 1931- ... CANR-29
Earlier sketch in CA 49-52
Charney, Mark J. 1956- ... 141
Charney, Maurice (Myron) 1929- ... CANR-40
Earlier sketches in CA 9-12R, CANR-3, 18
Charnin, Martin (Jay) 1934- ... 103
Charnley, John 1911-1982 Obituary ... 107
Charnley, Mitchell V(aughn) 1898- ... 69-72
Charnock, Joan 1903- ... CAP-2
Earlier sketch in CA 33-36
Charnon-Deutsch, Lou 1946- ... 162
Charny, Carmi 1925- ... CANR-45
Earlier sketches in CA 13-16R, CANR-7
Charny, Israel W(olf) 1931- ... 57-60
Charosh, Mannis 1906- ... 29-32R
See also SATA 5
Charpak, Georges 1924- ... 157
Charques, Dorothy (Taylor) 1899-1976 ... 73-76
Obituary ... 65-68
Charren, Peggy 1928- ... 129
Charrette, Robert N. 1953- ... 160
Charriere, Henri 1906-1973 ... 101
Charron, Shirley 1935- ... 69-72
Charry, Elias 1906- ... 69-72
Charter, S(teve) P. R. 1915(?)-1984 Obituary ... 114
Charteris, Hugo (Francis Guy) 1922-1970 ... 105
Obituary ... 89-92
Charteris, James Donald 1948- ... 117
Charteris, Leslie 1907-1993 ... CANR-58
Obituary ... 141
Earlier sketches in CA 5-8R, CANR-10
See also DLB 77
Charters, Alexander N(athaniel) 1916- ... 120
Charters, Ann (Danberg) 1936- ... CANR-34
Earlier sketches in CA 17-20R, CANR-9
Charters, Lowell
See Maxwell, Ann (Elizabeth)
Charters, Samuel (Barclay) 1929- ... CANR-34
Earlier sketches in CA 9-12R, CANR-9
Chartham, Robert
See Seth, Ronald (Sydney)
Chartier, Emile-Auguste
See Alain
Chartier, Emilio
See Estenssoro, Hugo
Chartier, Normand L. 1945- ... SATA 66
Chartier, Roger 1945- ... 137
Chartkoff, Joseph L(ouis) 1942- ... 119
Chartkoff, Kerry K(ona) 1943- ... 119
Charvat, Frank John 1918- ... 1-4R
Charvet, John 1938- ... CANR-15
Earlier sketch in CA 85-88
Chary, Frederick B(arry) 1939- ... 49-52
Charyn, Jerome 1937- ... CANR-61
Earlier sketches in CA 5-8R, CANR-7
See also CAAS 1
See also CLC 5, 8, 18
See also DLBY 83
See also MTCW 1
Chasan, Daniel Jack 1943- ... 29-32R
Chase, A(lice) Elizabeth 1906- ... CAP-1
Earlier sketch in CA 11-12
Chase, Adam
See Fairman, Paul W.
and Marlowe, Stephen
and Thomson, James C(utting)
Chase, Alan (Louis) 1929- ... 1-4R
Chase, Alice
See McHargue, Georgess
Chase, Alston Hurd 1906- ... 5-8R
Chase, Alyssa 1965- ... 156
See also SATA 92
Chase, Andra 1942- ... SATA 91
Chase, Borden
See Fowler, Frank
See also DLB 26
Chase, Caroline
See DuBay, Sandra
Chase, Chevy 1943- ... 164
Chase, Chris ... AITN 1
Chase, Cleveland B(ruce)
1904(?)-1975 Obituary ... 53-56
Chase, Clinton I(rvin) 1927- ... 106
Chase, Cora G(ingrich) 1898- ... CANR-7
Earlier sketch in CA 61-64
Chase, Donald 1943- ... 53-56
Chase, Edna Woolman 1877-1957 ... DLB 91
Chase, Elaine R(aco) 1949- ... CANR-36
Earlier sketch in CA 114
Chase, Emily
See Aks, Patricia
and Sachs, Judith
and White, Carol
Chase, Gilbert 1906-1992 ... 17-20R
Obituary ... 137
Chase, Glen
See Fox, G(ardner) F(rancis)
and Levinson, Leonard

Chase, Harold W(illiam) 1922- CANR-4
Earlier sketch in CA 9-12R
Chase, Ilka 1905-1978 .... CANR-9
Obituary 77-80
Earlier sketch in CA 61-64
Chase, James Hadley
See Raymond, Rene (Brabazon)
Chase, James S(taton) 1932- 85-88
Chase, Joan 134
Brief entry 129
Interview in 134
Chase, Judith Wragg 1907- 41-44R
Chase, Larry
See Chase, Lawrence
Chase, Lawrence 1943- 97-100
Chase, Loriene Eck 102
Chase, Loring D. 1916- 25-28R
Chase, Lyndon
See Chard, Judy
Chase, Mary (Coyle) 1907-1981 77-80
Obituary 105
See also DC 1
See also SATA 17
See also SATA-Obit 29
Chase, Mary Ellen 1887-1973 .... CAP-1
Obituary 41-44R
Earlier sketch in CA 13-16
See also CLC 2
See also SATA 10
Chase, Mildred Portney 1921- 106
Chase, Naomi Feigelson 1932- 104
Chase, Nicholas
See Hyde, Anthony
Chase, Otta Louise 1909-1987 .... CANR-32
Earlier sketch in CA 49-52
Chase, Philander D(ean) 1943- CANR-51
Earlier sketch in CA 124
Chase, Richard 1904-1988 61-64
Obituary 125
See also SATA 64
See also SATA-Obit 56
Chase, Samuel B(rown), Jr. 1932- 5-8R
Chase, Stuart 1888-1985 65-68
Obituary 117
Chase, Sylvia (Belle) 1938- 115
Brief entry 110
Interview in 115
Chase, Truddi 1937(?)- 142
Chase, Virginia Lowell
See Perkins, Virginia Chase
Chase, W. Linwood 1897(?)-1983 Obituary 110
Chasen, Nancy H. 1945- 130
Chase-Riboud, Barbara (Dewayne Tosi) 1939- . 113
See also BW 2
See also DAM MULT
See also DLB 33
Chasin, Barbara 1940- 69-72
Chasins, Abram 1903-1987 .... CANR-14
Obituary 122
Earlier sketch in CA 37-40R
Chasman, Herbert 1938- 121
Chast, Roz 1954- 149
See also SATA 97
Chastain, Madye Lee 1908- 5-8R
See also SATA 4
Chasteen, Edgar R(ay) 1935- 33-36R
Chastel, Andre (Adrien) 1912-1990 Obituary ... 132
Chastenet de Castaing, Jacques
1893-1978 Obituary 77-80
Chaston, Gloria Duncan 1929- 69-72
Chatalbash, Ron 1959- 111
Chateaubriand, Francois Rene de 1768-1848 .. DLB 119
Chatelain, Nicolas 1913-1976 Obituary 65-68
Chatelet, Albert 1928- CANR-6
Earlier sketch in CA 13-16R
Chatellier, Louis 1935- 161
Chater, Elizabeth (Eileen) 1910- 111
Chatfield, (Earl) Charles (Jr.) 1934- 37-40R
Chatfield, Hale 1936- CANR-13
Earlier sketch in CA 33-36R
Chatfield, Michael 1934- CANR-10
Earlier sketch in CA 25-28R
Chatham, Doug(las) M. 1938- CANR-8
Earlier sketch in CA 61-64
Chatham, James R(ay) 1931- 33-36R
Chatham, Josiah G(eorge) 1914- 49-52
Chatham, Larry
See Bingley, David Ernest
Chatham, Russell 1939- 69-72
Chatman, Seymour B(enjamin) 1928- 37-40R
Chatov, Robert 1927- 105
Chatt, Orville K(eith) 1924- 53-56
Chatterje, Sarat Chandra 1876-1936(?) Brief entry 109
See also Chatterji, Saratchandra
Chatterjee, Debjani 1952- 150
See also SATA 83
Chatterjee, Margaret (Gantzer) 1925- CANR-20
Earlier sketches in CA 5-8R, CANR-3
Chatterjee, Upamanyu 1959- 160
Chatterji, Joya 1964- 149
Chatterji, Saratchandra
See Chatterje, Sarat Chandra
See also TCLC 13
Chatterji, Suniti Kumar 1890-1977 .... CANR-46
Earlier sketch in CA 81-84
Chatterton, Thomas 1752-1770 .... DAM POET
See also DLB 109
Chatterton, Wayne 1921- 37-40R
Chatwin, (Charles) Bruce 1940-1989 85-88
Obituary 127
See also AAYA 4
See also BEST 90:1
See also CLC 28, 57, 59
See also DAM POP
See also DLB 194
Chaucer, Daniel
See Ford, Ford Madox
Chaucer, Geoffrey 1340(?)-1400 .... CDBLB Before 1660
See also DA
See also DAB
See also DAC
See also DAM MST, POET
See also DLB 146
See also PC 19
See also WLCS
Chaudhuri, Amit 1962- 146
Chaudhuri, Haridas 1913- CANR-4
Earlier sketch in CA 5-8R
Chaudhuri, Nirad C(handra) 1897- 128
Chaudhuri, Pranay 1957- 143
Chaudhuri, Sukanta 1950- 57-60
Chauffard, Rene-Jacques
1920(?)-1972 Obituary 37-40R
Chaulieu, Pierre
See Castoriadis, Cornelius
Chauncey, George 152
Chauncy, Charles 1705-1787 .... DLB 24
Chauncy, Nan(cen Beryl Masterman) 1900-1970 ... CANR-4
Earlier sketch in CA 1-4R
See also CLR 6
See also MAICYA
See also SATA 6
Chaundler, Christine 1887-1972 .... CAP-2
Earlier sketch in CA 29-32
See also SATA 1
See also SATA-Obit 25
Chaurette, Normand 1954- 165
Chauveau, Pierre-Joseph-Olivier 1820-1890 DLB 99
Chauvin, Remy 1913- 108
Chavasse, Michael Louis Maude
1923-1983 Obituary 110
Chavchavadze, Paul 1899-1971 .... CAP-2
Obituary 29-32R
Earlier sketch in CA 25-28
Chave, Anna C. 155
Chavel, Charles Ber 1906- CANR-4
Earlier sketch in CA 49-52
Chaves, Jonathan 1943- CANR-9
Earlier sketch in CA 65-68
Chavez, Angelico
See Chavez, Manuel
Chavez, Denise (Elia) 1948- CANR-56
Earlier sketch in CA 131
See also DAM MULT
See also DLB 122
See also HLC
See also HW
Chavez, Fray Angelico
See Chavez, Manuel
Chavez, Fray Angelico 1910- .... DLB 82
Chavez, Jeffrey A. 1971- 164
Chavez, John R(ichard) 1949- 118
See also HW
Chavez, Manuel 1910-1996 .... CANR-32
Obituary 151
Earlier sketch in CA 93-96
See also HW
Chavez, Patricia 1934- 103
Chaviaras, Strates 1935- 105
See also Haviaras, Stratis
Chayefsky, Paddy
See Chayefsky, Sidney
See also CLC 23
See also DLB 7, 44
See also DLBY 81
Chayefsky, Sidney 1923-1981 .... CANR-18
Obituary 104
Earlier sketch in CA 9-12R
See also Chayefsky, Paddy
See also DAM DRAM
Chayes, Abram 1922- CANR-14
Earlier sketch in CA 65-68
Chaytor, Lee
See Chater, Elizabeth (Eileen)
Chazanof, William 1915- 33-36R
Chaze, (Lewis) Elliott 1915- 113
Cheape, Charles Windsor 1945- CANR-28
Earlier sketch in CA 105
Cheatham, K(aryn) Follis 1943- 81-84
Cheavens, (Sam) Frank 1905- 33-36R
Cheavens, Martha Louise (Schuck)
1898-1975 Obituary 57-60
Check, Otto Premier
See Berman, Ed
Check, William A. 1943- 118
Checkland, Olive 152
Checkland, S(ydney) G(eorge) 1916-1986 .. 17-20R
Obituary 118
Checkoway, Julie 1963- 160
Chedid, Andree 1920- 145
See also CLC 47
Chee, Cheng-Khee 1934- .... SATA 79
Cheech
See Marin, Richard Anthony
Cheek, Frances Edith 1923- 41-44R
Cheek, Mavis 1948- 128
Cheeks, James E. 1930- 124
Cheesman, Evelyn 1881-1969 .... DLB 195
Cheesman, Paul R. 1921- CANR-1
Earlier sketch in CA 49-52
Cheetham, Erika (McMahon-Turner) 1939-1998 .... CANR-30
Obituary 167
Earlier sketch in CA 109
Cheetham, Hal
See Cheetham, J(ames) H(arold)
Cheetham, J(ames) H(arold) 1921- 108
Cheetham, Nicholas (John Alexander) 1910- CANR-15
Earlier sketch in CA 81-84
Cheever, Ezekiel 1615-1708 .... DLB 24
Cheever, George Barrell 1807-1890 .... DLB 59
Cheever, John 1912-1982 .... CANR-27
Obituary 106
Earlier sketches in CA 5-8R, CANR-5
Interview in CANR-5
See also CABS 1
See also CDALB 1941-1968
See also CLC 3, 7, 8, 11, 15, 25, 64
See also DA
See also DAB
See also DAC
See also DAM MST, NOV, POP
See also DLB 2, 102
See also DLBY 80, 82
See also MTCW 1
See also SSC 1
See also WLC
Cheever, Susan 1943- CANR-51
Earlier sketches in CA 103, CANR-27
Interview in CANR-27
See also CLC 18, 48
See also DLBY 82
Cheffins, Ronald I. 1930- 45-48
Chehak, Susan Taylor 1951- CANR-52
Earlier sketch in CA 130
Cheifetz, Dan 1926- 69-72
Cheifetz, Philip M(orris) 1944- 53-56
Cheim, John 1953- 138
Chein, Isidor 1912- Brief entry 105
Chejne, Anwar G(eorge) 1923-1983 ..... CANR-18
Earlier sketch in CA 25-28R
Cheke, John 1514-1557 .... DLB 132
Chekenian, Aram Haigaz 1900-1986 Obituary .. 119
Chekenian, Jane
See Gerard, Jane
Chekhonte, Antosha
See Chekhov, Anton (Pavlovich)
Chekhov, Anton (Pavlovich) 1860-1904 124
Brief entry 104
See also DA
See also DAB
See also DAC
See also DAM DRAM, MST
See also DC 9
See also SATA 90
See also SSC 2, 28
See also TCLC 3, 10, 31, 55
See also WLC
Chekhova, Olga 1897-1980 Obituary 97-100
Chekki, Dan(esh) A(yyappa) 1935- CANR-47
Earlier sketches in CA 61-64, CANR-7, 23
Cheldelin, Larry V(ernon) 1945- 116
Cheles, Luciano 1948- CANR-55
Earlier sketch in CA 127
Chelf, Carl P. 1937- 37-40R
Chelius, James R(obert) 1943- 115
Chellis, Marcia 1940- 121
Chelminski, Rudolph 1934- 93-96
Chelsea, David 1959- 148
Chelton, John
See Durst, Paul
Chelwood, Tufton Victor Hamilton 1917-1989 .65-68
Obituary 128
Chen, Anthony 1929- CANR-14
Earlier sketch in CA 37-40R
See also SATA 6
Chen, Ching-chih 1937- CANR-45
Earlier sketches in CA 106, CANR-22
Ch'En, Chi-yun 1933- 108
Chen, Chung-Hwan 1906- 45-48
Chen, Edwin (Hung-teh) 1934- Brief entry 116
Chen, Edwin 1948- 159
Chen, Jack 1908- CANR-15
Earlier sketch in CA 41-44R
Chen, Janey 1922- 73-76
Ch'en, Jerome 1921- CANR-9
Earlier sketch in CA 13-16R
Chen, Joseph Tao 1925- 37-40R
Chen, Ju-Hong 1941- .... SATA 78
Chen, Kan 1928- CANR-45
Earlier sketch in CA 49-52
Chen, Kenneth K(uan-) S(heng) 1907- 17-20R
Chen, King C(hing) 1926- CANR-4
Earlier sketch in CA 53-56
Chen, Kuan I. 1926- 41-44R
Chen, Lincoln C(hih-ho) 1942- CANR-47
Earlier sketch in CA 49-52
Chen, Nai-Ruenn 1927- CANR-9
Earlier sketch in CA 21-24R
Chen, Philip S(tanley) 1903-1978 .... CANR-5
Earlier sketch in CA 9-12R
Chen, Samuel Shih-Tsai 1915- 41-44R
Chen, Theodore Hsi-En 1902- CANR-17
Earlier sketches in CA 1-4R, CANR-1
Chen, Tony
See Chen, Anthony
Chen, Vincent 1917- 37-40R
Chen, Yuan-tsung 1932- 106
See also SATA 65
Chenault, Lawrence R(oyce) 1897- CAP-2
Earlier sketch in CA 17-18
Chenault, Nell
See Smith, Linell Nash
Chenery, Hollis Burnley 1918- 111
Chenery, Janet (Dai) 1923- 103
See also SATA 25
Chenery, William Ludlow 1884-1974 97-100
Obituary 53-56
Chenetier, Marc 1946- 143
Cheney, Anne 1944- 61-64
Cheney, Brainard (Bartwell) 1900-1990 ..... CAP-2
Obituary 130
Earlier sketch in CA 25-28
Cheney, C. R.
See Cheney, Christopher Robert
Cheney, Christopher Robert
1906-1987 Obituary 123
Cheney, Cora 1916- CANR-4
Earlier sketch in CA 1-4R
See also SATA 3
Cheney, Ednah Dow (Littlehale) 1824-1904 .. DLB 1
Cheney, Frances Neel 1906- 33-36R
Cheney, Glenn Alan 1951- CANR-70
Earlier sketch in CA 109
See also SATA 99
Cheney, Harriet Vaughan 1796-1889 .... DLB 99
Cheney, Jean E. 1921- 118
Cheney, Lois A. 1931- 29-32R
Cheney, Lynne V. 1941- CANR-58
Earlier sketch in CA 89-92
Cheney, Margaret 1921- 101
Cheney, Richard B(ruce) 1941- 113
Cheney, Robert S(impson) 1922- 118
Cheney, Roberta Carkeek 1912- 73-76
Cheney, Ruth G(ordon) 1908- 113
Cheney, Sheldon Warren 1886-1980 Obituary .. 102
Cheney, Ted
See Cheney, Theodore Albert
Cheney, Theodore A. Rees
See Cheney, Theodore Albert
Cheney, Theodore Albert 1928- CANR-23
Earlier sketches in CA 61-64, CANR-8
See also SATA 11
Cheney, Thomas E. 1901- 41-44R
Cheney-Coker, Syl 1945- 101
Cheng, Chu-yuan 1927- CANR-42
Earlier sketches in CA 13-16R, CANR-5, 20
Cheng, F.T.
See Cheng, Tien-hsi
Cheng, Hang-Sheng 1927- 69-72
Cheng, Hou-Tien 1944- 69-72
Cheng, J(ames) Chester 1926- 9-12R
Cheng, James K(uo) C(hiang) 1936- 25-28R
Cheng, Judith 1955- .... SATA 36
Cheng, Naishan 167
Cheng, Ronald Ye-lin 1933- 41-44R
Cheng, Tien-hsi 1884-1970 Obituary 104
Cheng, Yi
See Cheng, James K(uo) C(hiang)
Cheng, Ying-wan 41-44R
Chenier, Marie-Joseph 1764-1811 .... DLB 192
Chen Jia
See Shen, Congwen
Chen Jo-hsi
See Tuann, Lucy H(siu-mei) C(hen)
Chennault, Anna (Chan) 1925- 61-64
Chennells, Roy D. 1912(?)-1981 Obituary 105
Chenneviere, Daniel
See Rudhyar, Dane
Chenoweth, Vida S. 1928- CANR-11
Earlier sketch in CA 25-28R
Cher, Ming 1947- 149
Cheraskin, Emanuel 1916- 53-56
Cherim, Stanley M(arshall) 1929- 53-56
Cherington, Paul Whiton 1918-1974 ...... CANR-6
Obituary 53-56
Earlier sketch in CA 1-4R
Cheripko, Jan 1951- 150
See also SATA 83
Cherkovski, Neeli 1945- 158
See also CAAS 24
Chermayeff, Ivan 1932- 97-100
See also SATA 47
Chermayeff, Serge (Ivan) 1900-1996 .... 21-24R
Obituary 152
Chernaik, Judith 1934- CANR-39
Earlier sketches in CA 61-64, CANR-11
Chernaik, Warren L(ewis) 1931- 151
Chernenko, K. U.
See Chernenko, Konstantin U(stinovich)
Chernenko, Konstantin U(stinovich) 1911-1985 . 132
Obituary 115
Cherner, Anne 1954- 109
Chernev, Irving 1900-1981 Obituary 105
Cherniavsky, Michael
1923(?)-1973 Obituary 41-44R
Chernik, Barbara E(ileen) 1938- 117
Chernin, Kim 1940- CANR-63
Earlier sketch in CA 107
Cherniss, Harold
See Cherniss, Harold Fredrik
Cherniss, Harold Fredrik 1904-1987 93-96
Obituary 123
Cherniss, Michael D(avid) 1940- 37-40R
Cherniss, Norman A(rnold) 1926-1984 122
Obituary 114
Chernoff, Dorothy A.
See Ernst, (Lyman) John
Chernoff, Goldie Taub 1909- 33-36R
See also SATA 10
Chernoff, John Miller 1947- 105
Chernoff, Maxine 1952- 136
Chernofsky, Barbara J. 1949- 152
Chernofsky, Jacob L. 1928- 73-76
Chernow, Barbara A. 1948- 144
Chernow, Burt 1933-1997 110
Obituary 158
Chernow, Carol 1934- 57-60
Chernow, Fred B. 1932- 57-60
Chernow, Ron 1949- 142

Chernowitz, Maurice E. 1909-1977 Obituary . . 73-76
Cherns, Albert
See Cherns, Albert B(ernard)
Cherns, Albert B(ernard) 1921-1987 Obituary . . 122
Cherny, Robert W(allace) 1943- 131
Chernykh, E(vgenij) N(ikolaevich) 1935- 147
Cherrington, Ernest H(urst), Jr. 1909- 33-36R
Cherrington, John 1909- 116
Cherrington, Leon G. 1926- 33-36R
Cherry, C. Conrad 1937- CANR-11
Earlier sketch in CA 21-24R
Cherry, Caroline L(ockett) 1942- 57-60
Cherry, Carolyn Janice 1942- CANR-10
Earlier sketch in CA 65-68
See also Cherryh, C. J.
Cherry, Charles L(ester) 1942- 57-60
Cherry, (Edward) Colin 1914-1979 . . . . . CANR-12
Obituary 93-96
Earlier sketch in CA 69-72
Cherry, George Loy 1905- 5-8R
Cherry, Gordon E(manuel) 1931- CANR-57
Earlier sketch in CA 125
Cherry, Kelly CANR-68
Earlier sketches in CA 49-52, CANR-3, 47
See also AITN 1
See also DLBY 83
Cherry, Lynne 1952- 167
See also SATA 34, 99
Cherry, Neeli
See Cherkovski, Neeli
Cherry, Sheldon H(arold) 1934- CANR-27
Earlier sketch in CA 49-52
Cherryh, C. J.
See Cherry, Carolyn Janice
See also AAYA 24
See also CLC 35
See also DLBY 80
See also SATA 93
Cherryholmes, Anne
See Price, Olive
Chertok, Haim
See Chertok, Harvey
Chertok, Harvey 1938- CANR-55
Earlier sketch in CA 127
Chervin, Ronda 1937- CANR-21
Earlier sketches in CA 57-60, CANR-6
Chervokas, John V(incent) 1936- 129
Cherwinski, Joseph 1915- CANR-5
Earlier sketch in CA 13-16R
Chesbro, George C(lark) 1940- CANR-58
Earlier sketch in CA 77-80
Chesebro', Caroline 1825-1873 . . . . . DLB 202
Chesebro, James William 1944- 108
Chesebrough, David B. 1932- 164
Chesen, Eli S. 1944- 37-40R
Chesham, Henry
See Bingley, David Ernest
Chesham, Sallie CANR-26
Earlier sketch in CA 29-32R
Chesher, Kim 1955- CANR-19
Earlier sketch in CA 102
Chesher, Richard (Harvey) 1940- 106
Cheshire, David 1944- 97-100
Cheshire, Geoffrey Leonard 1917- CAP-1
Earlier sketch in CA 13-14
Cheshire, Herbert 1925(?)-1985 Obituary 118
Cheshire, Maxine 1930- 108
Cheskin, Louis 1909-1981 . . . . . CANR-5
Obituary 105
Earlier sketch in CA 5-8R
Chesler, Bernice 1932- CANR-16
Earlier sketch in CA 25-28R
See also SATA 59
Chesler, Ellen 1947- 140
Chesler, Phyllis 1940- CANR-59
Earlier sketches in CA 49-52, CANR-4
Cheslock, Louis 1898- CAP-1
Earlier sketch in CA 11-12
Chesman, Andrea 1952- 135
Chesney, Ann
See Dummett, (Agnes Margaret) Ann
Chesney, Elizabeth Anne
See Zegura, Elizabeth Chesney
Chesney, SirGeorge Tomkyns 1830-1895 . DLB 190
Chesney, Inga L. 1928- 45-48
Chesney, Kellow (Robert) 1914- 29-32R
Chesney, Marion 1936- CANR-53
Brief entry 111
Earlier sketch in CA 115
Interview in 115
Chesney, Weatherby
See Hyne, C(harles) J(ohn) Cutcliffe (Wright)
Chesnoff, Richard Z(eltner) 1937- CANR-10
Earlier sketch in CA 25-28R
Chesnut, J(ames) Stanley 1926- 21-24R
Chesnutt, Charles W(addell) 1858-1932 125
Brief entry 106
See also BLC 1
See also BW 1
See also DAM MULT
See also DLB 12, 50, 78
See also MTCW 1
See also SSC 7
See also TCLC 5, 39
Chesnutt, David R(ogers) 1940- 122
Chess, Richard 1953- 150
Chess, Stella 1914- 85-88
Chess, Victoria 1939- 107
See also SATA 33
Chess, Victoria (Dickerson) 1939- . . . . . SATA 92
Chessare, Michele . . . . . SATA-Brief 42
Chesser, Eustace 1902-1973 . . . . . CANR-4
Obituary 45-48
Earlier sketch in CA 9-12R
Chessex, Jacques 1934- 65-68
Chesshyre, Robert (Coxhead) 1941- 128
Chessman, Caryl (Whittier) 1921-1960 73-76
Chessman, G(eorge) Wallace 1919- 13-16R
Chessman, Ruth (Green) 1910- CAP-2
Earlier sketch in CA 17-18
Chester, Alfred 1929(?)-1971 Obituary 33-36R
See also CLC 49
See also DLB 130
Chester, Allan Griffith 1900-1976 Obituary 111
Chester, Deborah 1957- CANR-72
Earlier sketches in CA 102, CANR-18, 41
See also SATA 85
Chester, Edward W(illiam) 1935- CANR-13
Earlier sketch in CA 21-24R
Chester, Eric Thomas 1943- 152
Chester, George Randolph 1869-1924 . . . . . DLB 78
Chester, Laura 1949- CANR-50
Earlier sketches in CA 65-68, CANR-9
Chester, Mark (S.) 1945- 144
Chester, Michael (Arthur) 1928- CANR-1
Earlier sketch in CA 1-4R
Chester, (Daniel) Norman 1907-1986 109
Obituary 120
Chester, Peter
See Phillips, D(ennis) J(ohn Andrew)
Chester, Tessa Rose 1950- 130
Chesterman, Charles W(esley) 1913- 107
Chesterman, Clement (Clapton)
1894-1983 Obituary 110
Chesterson, Denise
See Robins, Denise (Naomi)
Chesterton, A(rthur) K(enneth) 1899- CAP-1
Earlier sketch in CA 11-12
Chesterton, G(ilbert) K(eith) 1874-1936 132
Brief entry 104
See also CDBLB 1914-1945
See also DAM NOV, POET
See also DLB 10, 19, 34, 70, 98, 149, 178
See also MTCW 1
See also SATA 27
See also SSC 1
See also TCLC 1, 6, 64
Chestnut, Harold 1917- 157
Chestor, Rui
See Courtier, S(idney) H(obson)
Chetham-Strode, Warren 1896- CAP-1
Earlier sketch in CA 13-14
Chethimattam, John B(ritto) 1922- 25-28R
Chetin, Helen 1922- CANR-12
Earlier sketch in CA 29-32R
See also SATA 6
Chetkovich, Carol A. 1948- 164
Chetwin, Grace CANR-52
Earlier sketch in CA 123
See also SATA 86
See also SATA-Brief 50
Chetwode, Penelope 1910-1986 102
Obituary 119
Chetwynd, Berry
See Rayner, Claire (Berenice)
Chetwynd, Lionel 1940- 137
Chetwynd, Tom 1938- 45-48
Chetwynd-Hayes, R(onald Henry Glynn) 1919- . . . . .
CANR-58
Earlier sketches in CA 61-64, CANR-12, 30
Chetwynd-Talbot, Edward Hugh Frederick
1909- 116
Cheung, Steven N(g-) S(heong) 1935- 25-28R
Cheuse, Alan 1940- CANR-52
Earlier sketches in CA 49-52, CANR-27
Chevalier, Christa 1937- CANR-24
Earlier sketch in CA 107
See also SATA 35
Chevalier, Elizabeth (Pickett)
1896-1984 Obituary 111
Chevalier, Haakon (Maurice) 1901-1985 61-64
Obituary 116
Chevalier, Louis 1911- CANR-35
Earlier sketch in CA 85-88
Chevalier, Maurice 1888-1972 Obituary 33-36R
Chevalier, Paul Eugene George 1925- 106
Chevallier, Gabriel 1895-1969 Obituary 113
Chevallier, Raymond 1929- 103
Chevigny, Bell Gale 1936- 57-60
Chevigny, Paul G. 1935- 97-100
Cheville, Roy A(rthur) 1897- 97-100
Chevremont, Evaristo Ribera
See Ribera Chevremont, Evaristo
Chew, Ada Nield 1870-1945 . . . . . DLB 135
Chew, Allen F. 1924- 33-36R
Chew, Geoffrey Foucar 1924- 157
Chew, Peter 1924- 57-60
Chew, Ruth 1920- CANR-14
Earlier sketches in CA 41-44R, CANR-31
See also SATA 7
Cheyette, Bryan (Henry) 1959- 146
Cheyette, Irving 1904- CANR-22
Earlier sketch in CA 69-72
Cheyney, Arnold B. 1926- CANR-23
Earlier sketches in CA 21-24R, CANR-8
Cheyney, Edward P. 1861-1947 . . . . . DLB 47
Cheyney, (Reginald Evelyn) Peter (Southouse)
1896-1951 Brief entry 113
Cheyney-Coker, Syl 1945- 153
Chi, Madeleine 1930- CANR-11
Earlier sketch in CA 69-72
Chi, Richard Hu See-Yee 1918- 37-40R
Chi, Wen-shun 1910- 13-16R
Chiang, Kai-shek 1886(?)-1975 Obituary 112
Chiang, Pin-chin 1904-1986 Obituary 118
See also Ding Ling
Chiang Yee 1903-1977 . . . . . CANR-15
Obituary 73-76
Earlier sketch in CA 65-68
Ch'iao, Sung
See Chou, Eric
Chiappelli, Fredi 1921-1990 Obituary 131
Chiara, Piero 1913-1986 . . . . . CANR-8
Obituary 121
Earlier sketch in CA 53-56
See also DLB 177
Chiarella, Tom 1961- 161
Chiarello, Michael 1962- 149
Chiarenza, Carl 1935- CANR-29
Earlier sketch in CA 109
Chiari, Joseph 1911- CANR-29
Earlier sketches in CA 5-8R, CANR-4
Chiaromonte, Nicola (?)-1972 Obituary 104
Chiba, Atsuko 1941(?)-1987 Obituary 123
Chibnall, Marjorie (McCallum) 1915- 29-32R
Chicago, Judy 1939- CANR-64
Earlier sketches in CA 85-88, CANR-21
Chichester, Francis (Charles) 1901-1972 . . . CAP-1
Obituary 37-40R
Earlier sketch in CA 13-14
Chichester, Jane
See Longrigg, Jane Chichester
Chichester Clark, Emma 1955- 132
See also Clark, Emma Chichester
Chick, Edson M(arland) 1924- 21-24R
Chick, Jean M.
See Snook, Jean M(cGregor)
Chickering, Arthur W. 1927- 29-32R
Chickering, Roger (Philip) 1942- 73-76
Chickos, James Speros 1941- 49-52
Chicorel, Marietta 85-88
Chideya, Farai 1969- 156
Chidsey, Donald Barr 1902-1981 . . . . . CANR-2
Obituary 103
Earlier sketch in CA 5-8R
See also SATA 3
See also SATA-Obit 27
Chidzero, Bernard Thomas Gibson 1927- 1-4R
Chiefari, Janet D. 1942- . . . . . SATA 58
Chief Eagle, Dallas 1925-1978 144
Chief Joseph 1840-1904 152
See also DAM MULT
See also NNAL
Chief Seattle 1786(?)-1866 . . . . . DAM MULT
See also NNAL
Chief Standing Bear
See Standing Bear, Luther
Chieger, Bob 1945- 114
Chielens, Edward E(rnest) 1943- 53-56
Ch'ien, Ts'un-hsun
See Tsien, Tsuen-hsuin
Ch'ien Chung-shu 1910- 130
See also CLC 22
See also MTCW 1
Chiesa, Francesco 1871(?)-1973 Obituary 104
Chignon, Niles
See Lingeman, Richard R(oberts)
Chigounis, Evans 1931- 45-48
Chilcote, Ronald H. 1935- CANR-49
Earlier sketches in CA 21-24R, CANR-8, 24
Chilcott, John H(enry) 1924- 41-44R
Child, Alan
See Langner, Lawrence
Child, Charles Manning 1869-1954 157
Child, Francis James 1825-1896 . . . . . DLB 1, 64
Child, Heather 1912- 9-12R
Child, Irvin L(ong) 1915- 41-44R
Child, John 1922- 93-96
Child, Julia 1912- CANR-19
Earlier sketch in CA 41-44R
Child, Kenneth 1916-1983 Obituary 111
Child, L. Maria
See Child, Lydia Maria
Child, Lydia Maria 1802-1880 . . . . . DLB 1, 74
See also SATA 67
Child, Mrs.
See Child, Lydia Maria
Child, Philip 1898-1978 . . . . . CAP-1
Earlier sketch in CA 13-14
See also CLC 19, 68
See also SATA 47
Child, Roderick 1949- 25-28R
Childer, Simon Ian
See Brosnan, John
Childers, (Robert) Erskine 1870-1922 153
Brief entry 113
See also DLB 70
See also TCLC 65
Childers, Thomas (Allen) 1940- 37-40R
Children's Shepherd, The
See Westphal, Arnold Carl
Childress, Alice 1920-1994 . . . . . CANR-50
Obituary 146
Earlier sketches in CA 45-48, CANR-3, 27
See also AAYA 8
See also BLC 1
See also BW 2
See also CLC 12, 15, 86, 96
See also CLR 14
See also DAM DRAM, MULT, NOV
See also DC 4
See also DLB 7, 38
See also JRDA
See also MAICYA
See also MTCW 1
See also SATA 7, 48, 81
Childress, James Franklin 1940- CANR-11
Earlier sketch in CA 65-68
Childress, Mark 1957- 134
Childress, William 1933- CANR-34
Earlier sketch in CA 41-44R
Childs, Barney 1926- 21-24R
Childs, Brevard S(prings) 1923- 128
Brief entry 117
Childs, C. Sand
See Childs, Maryanna
Childs, Craig 1967- 163
Childs, David (Haslam) 1933- CANR-58
Earlier sketches in CA 37-40R, CANR-14, 31
Childs, Elizabeth C(atharine) 1954- 138
Childs, George W. 1829-1894 . . . . . DLB 23
Childs, H(alla) Fay (Cochrane) 1890-1971 . . CAP-1
Earlier sketch in CA 13-16
See also SATA 1
See also SATA-Obit 25
Childs, Harwood Lawrence 1898-1972 . . . . . CAP-2
Obituary 37-40R
Earlier sketch in CA 25-28
Childs, J(ames) Rives 1893-1987 Obituary 123
Childs, James Bennett 1896-1977 Obituary . . 73-76
Childs, John Steven 1947- 128
Childs, Marilyn Grace Carlson 1923- 9-12R
Childs, Marquis W(illiam) 1903-1990 . . . . . CANR-12
Obituary 132
Earlier sketch in CA 61-64
Childs, Maryanna 1910- 9-12R
Childs, Michael J. 1956- 146
Childs, Timothy 1941- 97-100
Childs, W(illiam) H(arold) J(oseph)
1905(?)-1983 Obituary 109
Chiles, Robert E(ugene) 1923- 17-20R
Chiles, Webb 1941- 108
Chill, Dan S(amuel) 1945- 69-72
Chilman, Catherine (Earles) S(treet) 1914- 121
Chilson, Richard William 1943- CANR-6
Earlier sketch in CA 57-60
Chilson, Rob(ert Dean) 1945- CANR-58
Earlier sketch in CA 69-72
Chilson, Robert
See Chilson, Rob(ert Dean)
Chilton, Bruce 1949- 158
Chilton, Charles (Frederick William) 1917- 163
See also SATA 102
Chilton, Irma 1930- CANR-19
Earlier sketch in CA 103
Chilton, John (James) 1932- CANR-8
Earlier sketch in CA 61-64
Chilton, Lance 1944- 123
Chilton, Shirley R(ay) 1923- 77-80
Chilver, Guy (Edward Farquhar) 1910-1982 109
Obituary 107
Chilver, Peter 1933- CANR-38
Earlier sketches in CA 25-28R, CANR-17
Chimaera
See Farjeon, Eleanor
Chin, Chuan
See Chi, Richard Hu See-Yee
Chin, Frank (Chew, Jr.) 1940- CANR-71
Earlier sketch in CA 33-36R
See also DAM MULT
See also DC 7
Chin, Marilyn (Mei Ling) 1955- CANR-70
Earlier sketch in CA 129
Chin, Richard (M.) 1946- 121
See also SATA 52
Chin, Robert 1918- 61-64
Chin, Yin-lien C. 1930- 141
Chinard, Gilbert 1882(?)-1972 Obituary 104
Chinas, Beverly N(ewbold) 1924- 89-92
Chinery, Michael 1938- CANR-20
Earlier sketch in CA 103
See also SATA 26
Ching, Frank 1940- 129
Ching, James C(hristopher) 1926- 37-40R
Ching, Julia (Chia-yi) 1934- CANR-37
Earlier sketch in CA 101
Chinitz, Benjamin 1924- 9-12R
Chin-Lee, Cynthia D. 1958- . . . . . SATA 102
Chinmoy, Sri 1931- CANR-2
Earlier sketch in CA 49-52
Chinn, Carl 1956- 150
Chinn, Laurene Chambers 1902-1978 . . . . . 1-4R
Obituary 103
Chinn, Robert (Edward) 1928- 69-72
Chinn, William G. 1919- 33-36R
Chinodya, Shimmer 1957- 139
Chinoy, Ely 1921-1975 . . . . . CANR-1
Obituary 57-60
Earlier sketch in CA 1-4R
Chinoy, Helen Krich 1922- 17-20R
Chinweizu 1943- 103
See also DLB 157
Chioino, Joan D. Koss
See Koss-Chioino, Joan D.
Chipasula, Frank (Mkalawile) 1949- 121
Chipman, Bruce L(ewis) 1946- 37-40R
Chipman, Donald E(ugene) 1928- 29-32R
Chipman, John S(omerset) 1926- 104
Chipp, D(onald) L(eslie) 1925- 108
Chipp, Herschel B(rowning) 1913- 25-28R
Chipperfield, Joseph Eugene 1912-1980(?) . . . . .
CANR-6
Earlier sketch in CA 9-12R
See also SATA 2, 87
Chipperfield, Richard 1904-1988 Obituary 125
Chiras, Daniel D. 1950- 143
Chiraska, B. S.
See Chinodya, Shimmer
Chirenje, J. Mutero 1935- 65-68
Chironis, Nicholas P. 1921- 140
Chirot, Daniel 1942- 132
Chirovsky, Nicholas L. 1919- CANR-4
Earlier sketch in CA 53-56
Chisholm, A(rthur) M(urray) 1872-1960 . . CANR-64
Obituary 114
Chisholm, A(lan) R(owland) 1888- 5-8R
Chisholm, Anne 109
Chisholm, Dianne 1953- 137
Chisholm, Hugh J., Jr. 1913-1972 Obituary . 37-40R
Chisholm, K. Lomneth 1919- 61-64
Chisholm, Mary K(athleen) 1924- 37-40R
Chisholm, Matt
See Watts, Peter Christopher

Chisholm, Michael (Donald Inglis) 1931- ... 37-40R
Chisholm, R(obert) F(erguson) 1904- ... CAP-2
Earlier sketch in CA 29-32
Chisholm, Roderick Milton 1916- ... 102
Chisholm, Roger K. 1937- ... 33-36R
Chisholm, Sam(uel) Whitten 1919- ... 5-8R
Chisholm, Shirley (Anita St. Hill) 1924- ... CANR-27
Earlier sketch in CA 29-32R
See also BW 1
Chisholm, William S(herman), Jr. 1931- ... CANR-27
Earlier sketch in CA 49-52
Chishti, Hakim M.
See Thomson, Robert
Chislett, (Margaret) Anne 1943- ... 151
See also CLC 34
Chislett, Gail (Elaine) 1948- ... SATA 58
Chisolm, Lawrence W(ashington) 1929- ... 9-12R
Chissell, Joan Olive ... 61-64
Chitham, Edward (Harry Gordon) 1932- ... CANR-41
Earlier sketches in CA 103, CANR-19
See also DLB 155
Chitnis, Anand C. 1942- ... 123
Chitrabhanu, Gurudev Shree 1922- ... 89-92
Chittenden, Elizabeth F. 1903- ... 61-64
See also SATA 9
Chittenden, Hiram Martin 1858-1917 ... DLB 47
Chittenden, Margaret 1935- ... CANR-59
Earlier sketches in CA 53-56, CANR-4, 19
See also SATA 28
Chittick, Donald Ernest 1932- ... 115
Chittick, William O(liver) 1937- ... 41-44R
Chittum, Ida 1918- ... CANR-14
Earlier sketch in CA 37-40R
See also SATA 7
Chitty, Arthur Benjamin 1914- ... CANR-20
Earlier sketches in CA 53-56, CANR-4
Chitty, Letitia 1897-1982 Obituary ... 108
Chitty, Susan Elspeth 1929- ... CAP-1
Earlier sketch in CA 9-10
Chitty, Thomas Willes 1926- ... 5-8R
See also Hinde, Thomas
See also CLC 11
Chitwood, B(illy) J(ames) 1931- ... 97-100
Chitwood, Marie Downs 1918- ... 9-12R
Chitwood, Oliver Perry 1874-1971 ... CAP-1
Earlier sketch in CA 13-14
Chiu, Hong-Yee 1932- ... 53-56
Chiu, Hungdah 1936- ... CANR-60
Earlier sketches in CA 37-40R, CANR-14, 31
Chiu, Tony ... 143
Chivers, Thomas Holley 1809-1858 ... DLB 3
Chivian, Eric 1942- ... 147
Chi-wei
See Shu, Austin Chi-wei
Chlamyda, Jehudil
See Peshkov, Alexei Maximovich
Chloros, A(lexander) G(eorge)
1926-1982 Obituary ... 108
Chloros, Aleck George
See Chloros, A(lexander) G(eorge)
Chmaj, Betty E. 1930- ... 97-100
Chmielarz, Sharon 1940- ... 121
See also SATA 72
Chmielewski, Edward 1928- ... 13-16R
Chmielewski, Wendy E. 1955- ... 139
Ch'o, Chou
See Shu-Jen, Chou
Cho, Yong Hyo 1934- Brief entry ... 105
Cho, Yong Sam 1925- ... 5-8R
Choate, Ernest A(lfred) 1900- ... 49-52
Choate, Gwen Peterson 1922- ... 1-4R
Choate, J(ulian) E(rnest, Jr.) 1916- ... 33-36R
Choate, Judith (Newkirk) 1940- ... 105
See also SATA 30
Choate, Pat 1941(?)- ... 146
Choate, R. G.
See Choate, Gwen Peterson
Chobanian, Aram V(an) 1929- ... 108
Chocano, Jose Santos 1875-1934 ... 131
See also HW
Chochlik
See Radwanski, Pierre A(rthur)
Chociolko, Christina 1958- ... 149
Chocolate, Debbi 1954- ... 161
See also SATA 96
Chocolate, Deborah M. Newton
See Chocolate, Debbi
Chodes, John 1939- ... CANR-25
Earlier sketches in CA 61-64, CANR-9
Chodorov, Edward 1904-1988 ... 102
Obituary ... 126
Chodorov, Jerome 1911- ... CANR-15
Earlier sketch in CA 65-68
Chodorov, Stephan 1934- ... 17-20R
Chodorow, Nancy (Julia) 1944- ... CANR-59
Earlier sketch in CA 105
Chodos, Robert 1947- ... 142
Chodron, Pema 1936- ... 162
Chogyam Trungpa 1939-1987 ... CANR-42
Obituary ... 122
Earlier sketches in CA 25-28R, CANR-12
Choi, Frederick D. S. 1942- ... 167
Choi, Hyaeweol 1962- ... 147
Choi, Sook Nyul ... SATA 73
Choi, Sunu 1916-1984 Obituary ... 115
Choldin, Marianna Tax 1942- ... CANR-26
Earlier sketch in CA 109
Choleric, Brother
See van Zeller, Claud
Cholmondeley, Alice
See Russell, CountessMary Annette Beauchamp
Cholmondeley, Mary 1859-1925 ... DLB 197
Chomette, Rene Lucien 1898-1981 Obituary ... 103
See also Clair, Rene
Chommie, John C(ampbell) 1914-1974 ... CAP-2
Earlier sketch in CA 29-32
Chomsky, Aviva 1957- ... 167
Chomsky, (Avram) Noam 1928- ... CANR-62
Earlier sketches in CA 17-20R, CANR-28
See also MTCW 1
Chomsky, William 1896-1977 ... 77-80
Obituary ... 73-76
Chona, Maria 1845(?)-1936 ... 144
See also NNAL
Chong
See Chong, Tommy
Chong, Denise ... 159
Chong, Kyong-Jo
See Chung, Kyung Cho
Chong, Peng-Khuan ... 25-28R
Chong, Tommy 1938- ... 164
Brief entry ... 112
Choper, Jesse H(erbert) 1935- ... CANR-5
Earlier sketch in CA 13-16R
Chopey, Nicholas P. ... 147
Chopin, Kate
See Chopin, Katherine
See also CDALB 1865-1917
See also DA
See also DAB
See also DLB 12, 78
See also SSC 8
See also TCLC 5, 14
See also WLCS
Chopin, Katherine 1851-1904 ... 122
Brief entry ... 104
See also Chopin, Kate
See also DAC
See also DAM MST, NOV
Chopin, Rene 1885-1953 ... DLB 92
Chopra, Deepak (K.) 1946- ... 153
Choquette, Adrienne 1915-1973 ... DLB 68
Choquette, Robert 1905- ... DLB 68
Chorafas, Dimitris N. 1926- ... CANR-48
Earlier sketches in CA 5-8R, CANR-4, 20
Chorao, (Ann Mc)Kay (Sproat) 1936- ... CANR-19
Earlier sketches in CA 49-52, CANR-1
See also MAICYA
See also SATA 8, 69
Chorbajian, Levon 1942- ... 154
Chorell, Walentin 1912-1984(?) Obituary ... 111
Chorley, Katharine Campbell (Hopkinson)
1897-1986 Obituary ... 120
Chorley, R. J.
See Chorley, Richard J(ohn)
Chorley, Richard J(ohn) 1927- ... 121
Brief entry ... 116
Chorlton, David 1948- ... 144
Chorny, Merron 1922- ... 41-44R
Choron, Jacques 1904-1972 ... CAP-1
Obituary ... 33-36R
Earlier sketch in CA 9-10
Chorpenning, Charlotte (Lee Barrows)
1872-1955 Brief entry ... 114
See also SATA-Brief 37
Chothia, Jean 1944- ... 105
Chotjewitz, Peter O(tto) 1934- ... 129
Chotzinoff, Samuel 1889-1964 Obituary ... 93-96
Chou, En-lai 1898-1976 Obituary ... 112
Chou, Eric 1915- ... 132
Chou, Mark 1910-1988 Obituary ... 128
Chou, Tsu-Wei 1940- ... 144
Chou, Ya-luu 1924- ... 41-44R
Chou, Yu-jui
See Chou, Eric
Choucri, Nazli 1943- ... CANR-14
Earlier sketch in CA 81-84
Choudhury, Ashok 1957- ... 145
Choudhury, G(olam) W(ahed) 1926- ... CANR-17
Earlier sketch in CA 25-28R
Choudhury, Malay Roy 1939- ... CAAS 14
Choudhury, Masudul Alam 1948- ... 146
Choueiri, Youssef M. 1948- ... 136
Choukas, Michael (Eugene) 1901-1989 ... CAP-2
Obituary ... 129
Earlier sketch in CA 17-18
Choukas-Bradley, Melanie (Rose) 1952- ... 124
Choukri, Mohamed 1935- ... 136
Chouraqui, Andre (Nathanael) 1917- ... CANR-10
Earlier sketch in CA 65-68
Chow, Claire S. 1952- ... 166
Chow, Gregory C. 1929- ... 13-16R
Chow, Yung-Teh 1916- ... 37-40R
Chowder, Ken 1950- ... CANR-48
Earlier sketch in CA 102
Chowdhary, Savitri Devi (Dumra) 1907- ... CAP-1
Earlier sketch in CA 11-12
Chowning, Larry S(hepherd) 1949- ... 111
Choy, Bong-youn 1914- ... 69-72
Choyce, Lesley 1951- ... CANR-68
Earlier sketch in CA 130
See also SATA 94
Chraibi, Driss 1926- ... 151
Chrimes, Stanley Bertram 1907-1984 ... 5-8R
Obituary ... 113
Chrislock, Carl H(endrick) 1917- ... 45-48
Chrisman, Arthur Bowie 1889-1953 ... YABC 1
Chrisman, Harry E. 1906-1993 ... CANR-45
Earlier sketch in CA 1-4R
Chrisman, Katherine (G.)
1940(?)-1987 Obituary ... 122
Chrisman, Miriam Usher 1920- ... 131
Chriss, Nicholas C. 1928(?)-1990 Obituary ... 131
Christ, Carl F(inley) 1923- ... 21-24R
Christ, Carol P(atrice) 1945- ... 154
Christ, Carol T(ecla) 1944- ... 93-96
Christ, Henry I(rvine) 1915- ... CANR-2
Earlier sketch in CA 5-8R
Christ, John M(ichael) 1934- ... 106
Christ, Karl 1923- ... CANR-45
Earlier sketch in CA 120
Christ, Ronald 1936- ... CANR-10
Earlier sketch in CA 25-28R
Christain, David 1938-
See Gaulden, Albert Clayton
Christaller, Walter 1893-1969 Obituary ... 115
Christelow, Eileen 1943- ... CANR-57
Earlier sketch in CA 111
See also SATA 38, 90
See also SATA-Brief 35
Christen, Robert J. 1928-1981 Obituary ... 108
Brief entry ... 107
Christen, William L. 1942- ... 149
Christensen, Ann 1946- ... 108
Christensen, Anna
See Mayer, Deborah Anne
Christensen, Clyde M. 1905- ... 53-56
Christensen, David E(mun) 1921- ... 13-16R
Christensen, Edward L. 1913- ... 25-28R
Christensen, Eleanor Ingalls 1913- ... 53-56
Christensen, Erwin O(ttomar) 1890- ... CAP-1
Earlier sketch in CA 13-14
Christensen, Francis 1902-(?) ... CAP-2
Earlier sketch in CA 23-24
Christensen, Gardell Dano 1907- ... 9-12R
See also SATA 1
Christensen, Harold T(aylor) 1909- ... 45-48
Christensen, J(ack) A(rden) 1927- ... 53-56
Christensen, James L(ee) 1922- ... 97-100
Christensen, Jerome 1948- ... 110
Christensen, Jo Ippolito
See Christensen, Yolanda Maria Ippolito
Christensen, Otto H(enry) 1898- ... 33-36R
Christensen, Paul 1943- ... CANR-15
Earlier sketch in CA 77-80
Christensen, Sandra 1944- ... 110
Christensen, Terry 1944- ... 127
Christensen, Yolanda Maria Ippolito 1943- CANR-7
Earlier sketch in CA 57-60
Christenson, Cornelia V(os) 1903- ... CAP-2
Earlier sketch in CA 33-36
Christenson, Evelyn (Carol) 1922- ... 117
Christenson, James A. 1944- ... 143
Christenson, Larry 1928- ... CANR-8
Earlier sketch in CA 57-60
Christenson, Nordis 1929- ... 108
Christenson, Reo M. 1918- ... 37-40R
Christesen, Barbara 1940- ... 107
See also SATA 40
Christesen, Clement Byrne 1911- ... 102
Christgau, Alice Erickson 1902- ... CAP-2
Earlier sketch in CA 17-18
See also SATA 13
Christgau, John (Frederick) 1934- ... 103
Christgau, Robert (Thomas) 1942- ... 65-68
Christian, A. B.
See Yabes, Leopoldo Y(abes)
Christian, Barbara T. 1943- ... CANR-57
Earlier sketch in CA 110
See also BW 1
Christian, C(urtis) W(allace) 1927- ... 21-24R
Christian, Carol (Cathay) 1923- ... 53-56
Christian, Frederick
See Gehman, Richard (Boyd)
Christian, Frederick H.
See Nolan, Frederick William
Christian, Garna L. 1935- ... 151
Christian, Garth Hood 1921-1967 ... CAP-1
Earlier sketch in CA 9-10
Christian, George (Eastland) 1927- ... 65-68
Christian, Glynn 1942- ... 115
Christian, Henry A(rthur) 1931- ... CANR-14
Earlier sketch in CA 33-36R
Christian, James L(ee) 1927- ... 57-60
Christian, Jill
See Dilcock, Noreen
Christian, John
See Dixon, Roger
Christian, Louise
See Grill, Nannette L.
Christian, Marcus Bruce 1900- ... 73-76
Christian, Mary Blount 1933- ... CANR-17
Earlier sketches in CA 45-48, CANR-1
See also SATA 9
Christian, Nick
See Pollitz, Edward A(lan), Jr.
Christian, Peter
See Steinbrunner, (Peter) Chris(tian)
Christian, Portia 1908- ... 103
Christian, Rebecca 1952- ... 107
Christian, Reginald Frank 1924- ... CANR-3
Earlier sketch in CA 5-8R
Christian, Roy Cloberry 1914- ... 93-96
Christian, Shirley (Ann) 1938- ... 125
Brief entry ... 119
Interview in ... 125
Christian, William 1945- ... 150
Christian, William A(rmistead), Jr. 1944- ... 107
Christiani, Dounia Bunis 1913- ... 13-16R
Christians, Clifford Glenn 1939- ... 104
Christiansen, Arthur 1904-1963 ... 1-4R
Christiansen, Eugene Martin 1944- ... 121
Christiansen, Harley Duane 1930- ... CANR-4
Earlier sketch in CA 53-56
Christiansen, Keith 1947- ... 112
Christiansen, Michael Robin
1927-1984 Obituary ... 113
Christiansen, Richard (Dean) 1931- ... 121
Christiansen, Rupert 1954- ... 135
Christianson, Elin B(allantyne) 1936- ... 111
Christianson, Gale E. 1942- ... 81-84
Christianson, John Robert 1934- ... 21-24R
Christianson, Sven-Ake 1954- ... 161
Christie
See Ichikawa, Kon
Christie, Agatha (Mary Clarissa) 1890-1976 ...
CANR-37
Obituary ... 61-64
Earlier sketches in CA 17-20R, CANR-10
See also AAYA 9
See also AITN 1, 2
See also CDBLB 1914-1945
See also CLC 1, 6, 8, 12, 39, 48, 110
See also DAB
See also DAC
See also DAM NOV
See also DLB 13, 77
See also MTCW 1
See also SATA 36
Christie, George C(ustis) 1934- ... 37-40R
Christie, Hugh
See Christie-Murray, David (Hugh Arthur)
Christie, Ian 1956- ... 145
Christie, Ian R(alph) 1919- ... CANR-51
Earlier sketches in CA 5-8R, CANR-2, 20, 42
Christie, James R(ichard) 1952- ... 129
Christie, Jean 1912- ... 101
Christie, John Aldrich 1920- ... 65-68
Christie, Keith
See Haynes, Alfred H(enry)
Christie, Lindsay H. 1906(?)-1976 Obituary ... 61-64
Christie, Milton 1921- ... 17-20R
Christie, (Ann) Philippa ... CANR-4
Earlier sketch in CA 5-8R
See also Pearce, Philippa
Christie, Trevor L. 1905-1969 ... CAP-2
Earlier sketch in CA 21-22
Christie, William 1960- ... 140
Christie-Murray, David (Hugh Arthur) 1913- ...
CANR-4
Earlier sketch in CA 53-56
Christina, Teresa
See Taylor, Delores
Christine, Charles T(hornton) 1936- ... 33-36R
Christine, Dorothy Weaver 1934- ... 33-36R
Christ-Janer, Albert W. 1910-1973 ... CANR-4
Obituary ... 45-48
Earlier sketch in CA 1-4R
Christman, Al(bert B.) 1923- ... 168
Christman, Don(ald) R. 1919- ... 17-20R
Christman, Elizabeth 1914- ... 89-92
Christman, Henry 1906-1980 Obituary ... 103
Christman, Henry Max 1932- ... 65-68
Christman, Luther (Parmalee) 1915- ... 124
Christman, Paul J. 1952- ... 132
Christman, R(aymond) J(ohn) 1919- ... 89-92
Christmas, Joyce 1939- ... CANR-72
Earlier sketches in CA 123, CANR-50
Christmas, Linda (Irene) 1943- ... 149
Christodoulou, Anastasios 1932- ... 120
Christodoulou, Demetrios 1919- ... 136
Christoff, Peter K. 1911- ... 121
Christol, Carl Quimby 1914- ... CANR-4
Earlier sketch in CA 5-8R
Christoph, Florence A(nna) 1937- ... 137
Christoph, James B(ernard) 1928- ... CANR-4
Earlier sketch in CA 5-8R
Christoph, Peter R(ichard) 1938- ... 137
Christopher, Beth
See Steinke, Ann E(lizabeth)
Christopher, Georgia B. 1932- ... 111
Christopher, Joe R(andell) 1935- ... CANR-4
Earlier sketch in CA 53-56
Christopher, John
See Youd, (Christopher) Samuel
See also AAYA 22
See also CLR 2
Christopher, John B. 1914- ... 13-16R
Christopher, Kenneth
See Brophy, Donald F(rancis)
Christopher, Louise
See Hale, Arlene
Christopher, Matt(hew Frederick) 1917-1997 ...
CANR-36
Obituary ... 161
Earlier sketches in CA 1-4R, CANR-5
See also CLR 33
See also JRDA
See also MAICYA
See also SAAS 9
See also SATA 2, 47, 80
See also SATA-Obit 99
Christopher, Maurine (Brooks) ... 65-68
Christopher, Milbourne 1914(?)-1984 ... 105
Obituary ... 113
See also SATA 46
Christopher, Nicholas 1951- ... CANR-43
Earlier sketch in CA 108
Christopher, Renny (Teresa) 1957- ... 159
Christopher, Robert Collins 1924-1992 ... CANR-46
Obituary ... 138
Earlier sketch in CA 102
Christophersen, Paul (Hans) 1911- ... 57-60
Christowe, Stoyan 1898- ... 65-68
Christy, Betty 1924- ... 57-60
Christy, George ... 9-12R
Christy, Howard Chandler 1873-1952 ... DLB 188
See also SATA 21
Christy, Jim 1945- ... 138
Christy, Joe
See Christy, Joseph M.
Christy, Joseph M. 1919- ... CANR-14
Earlier sketch in CA 29-32R
Christy, Marian 1932- ... 65-68
Christy, Teresa E(lizabeth) 1927- ... 73-76
Chroman, Eleanor 1937- ... 45-48
Chroman, Nathan 1929- ... 77-80
Chronic, Halka (Pattison) 1923- ... 118
Chroust, Anton-Hermann 1907- ... CAP-1
Earlier sketch in CA 9-10
Chruden, Herbert J(efferson) 1918- ... 5-8R

Chryssides, Helen 167
Chrystie, Frances N(icholson) 1904-1986 . SATA 60
Chu, Arthur (T. S.) 1916-1979 81-84
Obituary 133
Chu, Daniel 1933- 13-16R
See also SATA 11
Chu, Godwin C(hien) 1927- 114
Chu, Grace (Goodyear) 1916- 81-84
Chu, Grace Zia 1899- CANR-4
Earlier sketch in CA 5-8R
Chu, Kong 1926- 49-52
Chu, Louis H. 1915- 13-16R
Chu, Petra ten-Doesschate 1942- 138
Chu, Samuel C. 1929- 69-72
Ch'u, Tung-tsu 1910- CANR-2
Earlier sketch in CA 1-4R
Chu, Valentin (Yuan-ling) 1919- 9-12R
Chu, W. R.
See Chu, Arthur (T. S.)
Chuan-Hsiang
See Shih, Chih-yu
Chubb, Elmer
See Masters, Edgar Lee
Chubb, Judith (Ann) 1947- 113
Chubb, Thomas Caldecot 1899-1972 ..... CANR-6
Obituary 33-36R
Earlier sketch in CA 1-4R
Chubin, Barry 1943- 124
Chudacoff, Howard P(eter) 1943- 45-48
Chudley, Ron(ald Alexander) 1937- 110
Chughtai, Ismat 1915-1991 166
Chuikov, Vasili Ivanovich 1900-1982 Obituary .. 106
Chukovskaya, Lydia (Korneeva) 1907-1996 128
Obituary 151
Brief entry 117
Chukovsky, Kornei (Ivanovich) 1882-1969 ....
CANR-42
Obituary 25-28R
Earlier sketches in CA 5-8R, CANR-4
See also MAICYA
See also SATA 5, 34
Chulak, Armando (?)-1975 Obituary 109
Chulkov, Mikhail Dmitrievich 1743-1792 ... DLB 150
Chumacero, Ali 1918- ..... HW
Chuman, Frank Fujio 1917- 69-72
Chun, Jinsie K(yung) S(hien) 1902- 49-52
Chun, Richard 1935- 65-68
Chung, Connie
See Chung, Constance Yu-Hwa
Chung, Constance Yu-Hwa 1946- 132
Brief entry 119
Chung, Edward K(oo-Young) 1931- 107
Chung, Hyung C(han) 1931- 57-60
Chung, Joseph Sang-hoon 1929- 49-52
Chung, Kyung Cho 1921- 33-36R
Chung-yu, Chu
See Hsu, Benedict (Pei-Hsiung)
Chunn, Jay Carrington II 1938- 116
Chupack, Henry 1915- 49-52
Church, Albert M(arion) 1940- 111
Church, Alonzo 1903- 157
Church, Benjamin 1734-1778 ..... DLB 31
Church, F(rank) Forrester (IV) 1948- 133
Church, Francis Pharcellus 1839-1906 ..... DLB 79
Church, Jeffrey
See Kirk, Richard (Edmund)
Church, Joseph 1918- 1-4R
Church, Kristine
See Jensen, Kristine Mary
Church, Margaret 1920- 13-16R
Church, Peter
See Nuttall, Jeff
Church, Ralph (Bruce) 1927- 37-40R
Church, Richard 1893-1972 ..... CANR-3
Obituary 33-36R
Earlier sketch in CA 1-4R
See also DLB 191
See also SATA 3
Church, Robert L(eValley) 1938- 61-64
Church, Ronald James Harrison
See Harrison Church, Ronald James
Church, Roy A. 1935- 124
Church, Ruth Ellen (Lovrien) 1910(?)-1991 ....
CANR-7
Obituary 135
Earlier sketch in CA 5-8R
Church, Suzanne
See Bates, Susannah (Vacella)
Church, William Conant 1836-1917 ..... DLB 79
Church, William Farr 1912- Brief entry 105
Churchett, Stephen 1947- 163
Churchill, Allen 1911-1988 97-100
Obituary 124
Churchill, Bill
See Churchill, Gail Winston
Churchill, Caryl 1938- CANR-46
Earlier sketches in CA 102, CANR-22
See also CLC 31, 55
See also DC 5
See also DLB 13
See also MTCW 1
Churchill, Charles 1731-1764 ..... DLB 109
Churchill, Creighton 1912-1984 69-72
Obituary 114
Churchill, David 1935- 106
Churchill, E(lmer) Richard 1937- CANR-56
Earlier sketches in CA 17-20R, CANR-11, 30
See also SATA 11
Churchill, Edward Delos
1895-1972 Obituary 37-40R
Churchill, Elizabeth
See Hough, Richard (Alexander)
Churchill, Gail Winston 1903(?)-1984 Obituary . 112
Churchill, Guy E. 1926- 29-32R
Churchill, J(ohn) H(oward) 1920-1990 Obituary . 131
Churchill, Jill
See Brooks, Janice Young
Churchill, Joyce
See Harrison, M(ichael) John
Churchill, Linda R. 1938- CANR-11
Earlier sketch in CA 21-24R
Churchill, R(eginald) C(harles) 1916- 9-12R
Churchill, Randolph (Frederick Edward Spencer)
1911-1968 Obituary 89-92
Churchill, Reba 1932(?)-1985 Obituary 116
Churchill, Rhona Adelaide 1913- 5-8R
Churchill, Rogers Platt 1902-1989 Obituary 129
Churchill, Samuel 1911- 17-20R
Churchill, Sarah (Millicent Hermione)
1914-1982 129
Obituary 107
Churchill, Thomas Bell Lindsay
1907-1990 Obituary 131
Churchill, Ward 1947- 135
Churchill, Winston 1871-1947 ..... DLB 202
Churchill, Winston (Leonard Spencer)
1874-1965 97-100
See also CDBLB 1890-1914
See also DLB 100
See also DLBD 16
See also MTCW 1
Churchill, Winston S(pencer) 1940- 131
Churchland, Patricia Smith 1943- CANR-50
Earlier sketch in CA 123
Churchland, Paul M. 1942- 152
Churchman, C(harles) West 1913- CANR-9
Earlier sketch in CA 21-24R
Churchman, Michael 1929- 37-40R
Churchyard, Thomas 1520(?)-1604 ..... DLB 132
Chute, B(eatrice) J(oy) 1913-1987 ..... 1-4R
Obituary 123
See also SATA 2
See also SATA-Obit 53
Chute, Carolyn 1947- 123
See also CLC 39
Chute, Marchette (Gaylord) 1909-1994 ... CANR-5
Obituary 145
Earlier sketch in CA 1-4R
See also DLB 103
See also SATA 1
Chute, Robert M. 1926- 109
Chute, Rupert
See Cleveland, Philip Jerome
Chute, William J(oseph) 1914- 9-12R
Chvidkovski, Dmitri
See Shvidkovsky, Dimitri
Chwalek, Henryka C. 1918- 17-20R
Chwast, Jacqueline 1932- CANR-5
Earlier sketch in CA 49-52
See also SATA 6
Chwast, Seymour 1931- 161
See also SATA 18, 96
Chyet, Stanley F. 1931- 33-36R
Cialente, Fausta
See Terni-Cialente, Fausta
Cianciolo, Patricia Jean 1929- CANR-13
Earlier sketch in CA 37-40R
Ciaramitaro, Andrew James 1955- 110
Ciaramitaro, Barbara 1946- 107
Ciarcia, Steve 1947- 110
Ciardi, John (Anthony) 1916-1986 ..... CANR-33
Obituary 118
Earlier sketches in CA 5-8R, CANR-5
Interview in CANR-5
See also CAAS 2
See also CLC 10, 40, 44
See also CLR 19
See also DAM POET
See also DLB 5
See also DLBY 86
See also MAICYA
See also MTCW 1
See also SAAS 26
See also SATA 1, 65
See also SATA-Obit 46
Ciavolella, Massimo 1942- 135
Cibber, Colley 1671-1757 ..... DLB 84
Ciccone, Madonna Louise Veronica
See Madonna
Ciccorella, Aubra Dair 65-68
Cicellis, Kay 1926- CANR-3
Earlier sketch in CA 1-4R
Cicognani, Amleto Giovanni Cardinal
1883-1973 Obituary 45-48
Cicourel, Aaron V. 1928- 53-56
Cid Perez, Jose (Diego) 1906- CANR-4
Earlier sketch in CA 53-56
Ciechanowski, Jan 1888(?)-1973 Obituary .. 41-44R
Ciee, Grace 1961- 140
See also BW 2
Cienciala, Anna M(aria) 1929- 89-92
Cieplak, Tadeusz N(owak) 1918- CANR-11
Earlier sketch in CA 69-72
Cigler, Allan J(ames) 1943- CANR-29
Earlier sketch in CA 111
Cikovsky, Nicolai, Jr. 1933- 113
Cilffriw, Gwynfor
See Griffith, Thomas Gwynfor
Cima, Annalisa 1941- ..... DLB 128
Cimbala, Stephen J. 1943- 142
Cimbollek, Robert (Carl) 1937- 57-60
Ciment, Jill 1953- 154
Ciment, Michel 1938- CANR-44
Earlier sketch in CA 97-100
Cimino, Michael 1943- 105
See also CLC 16
Cinberg, Bernard L. 1905-1979 Obituary 85-88
Cincinnatus
See Currey, Cecil B(arr)
Cinel, Dino 1941- 111
Cingo, Zivko 1935-1987 ..... DLB 181
Cinquin, Emmanuelle 1908- 131
Cinquin, Sister Emmanuelle
See Cinquin, Emmanuelle
Ciochon, Russell L. 1948- 145
Cioffari, Vincenzo 1905- 17-20R
Cioffi, Lou(is James) 1926-1998 120
Obituary 167
Brief entry 109
Interview in 120
Cioran, E(mil) M. 1911-1995 ..... 25-28R
Obituary 149
See also CLC 64
Cipes, Robert M. 1930- 21-24R
Ciplijauskaite, Birute 1929- CANR-14
Earlier sketches in CA 37-40R, CANR-31
Cipolla, Carlo M(anlio) 1922- CANR-39
Earlier sketches in CA 5-8R, CANR-2, 18
Cipolla, Joan Bagnel
See Bagnel, Joan
Cipriano, Anthony (John) 1941- 102
Circus, Anthony
See Hoch, Edward D(entinger)
Circus, Jim
See Roseyear, John
Cire
See Hayden, Eric W(illiam)
Cirese, Eugenio 1884-1955 ..... DLB 114
Ciresi, Rita 1960- 149
Ciria, Alberto 1934- 73-76
Cirino, Linda D(avis) 1941- 65-68
Cirino, Robert 1937- 61-64
Cismaru, Alfred 1933- 61-64
Cisneros, Antonio 1942-1989 ..... CANR-72
Earlier sketch in CA 131
See also HW
Cisneros, Sandra 1954- CANR-64
Earlier sketch in CA 131
See also AAYA 9
See also CLC 69
See also DAM MULT
See also DLB 122, 152
See also HLC
See also HW
Ciszek, Walter 1904- CAP-1
Earlier sketch in CA 13-14
Citati, Pietro 1930- CANR-43
Earlier sketches in CA 53-56, CANR-4
Citino, David 1947- 104
Citrine, Walter McLennan 1887-1983 Obituary . 109
Cittafino, Ricardo
See Bickers, Richard (Leslie) Townshend
Ciuba, Edward J(oseph) 1935- 61-64
Civille, John R(aphael) 1940- CANR-11
Earlier sketch in CA 69-72
Cixous, Helene 1937- CANR-55
Earlier sketch in CA 126
See also CLC 92
See also DLB 83
See also MTCW 1
Cizmar, Paula 1949- 122
Claassen, Harold 1905- CAP-2
Earlier sketch in CA 19-20
Clabaugh, Gary K(enneth) 1940- 69-72
Clabby, John 1911- 104
Clack, Robert Wood 1886-1964 122
Obituary 110
Claerbaut, David 1946- CANR-1
Earlier sketch in CA 45-48
Claeyssens, Astere E(varist)
1924-1990 Obituary 132
Claffey, William J. 1925- 21-24R
Claflin, Edward 1949- 97-100
Clagett, John (Henry) 1916- CANR-6
Earlier sketch in CA 5-8R
Clagett, Marshall 1916- CANR-5
Earlier sketch in CA 1-4R
Claghorn, Charles E.
See Claghorn, Charles Eugene
Claghorn, Charles Eugene 1911- CANR-44
Earlier sketch in CA 57-60
Claghorn, Gene
See Claghorn, Charles Eugene
Clague, Christopher K. 1938- 141
Clague, Ewan 1896-1987 ..... 29-32R
Obituary 122
Clague, Maryhelen 1930- 81-84
Claiborne, Craig 1920- CANR-5
Earlier sketch in CA 1-4R
Claiborne, Robert (Watson, Jr.) 1919-1990 ....
CANR-31
Obituary 130
Earlier sketches in CA 29-32R, CANR-12
Claiborne, Sybil 1923-1992 128
Obituary 140
Clain-Stefanelli, Vladimir 1914-1982 111
Obituary 108
Clair, Andree 29-32R
See also SATA 19
Clair, Bernard (Eddy) 1951- 102
Clair, Rene
See Chomette, Rene Lucien
See also CLC 20
Claire, Keith
See Andrews, Claire
and Andrews, Keith
Claire, William Francis 1935- CANR-7
Earlier sketch in CA 57-60
Clairmont, Elva 1937- 117
Clammer, David 1943- 69-72
Clampett, Bob 1914(?)-1984 Obituary 112
See also Clampett, Robert
See also AITN 1
See also SATA-Obit 38
Clampett, Robert
See Clampett, Bob
See also SATA 44
Clampitt, Amy 1920-1994 ..... CANR-29
Obituary 146
Earlier sketch in CA 110
See also CLC 32
See also DLB 105
See also PC 19
Clance, Pauline Rose 1938- 126
Clancy, Francis Michael 1903-1986 Obituary ... 121
Clancy, John Gregory 1922- 13-16R
Clancy, Joseph P(atrick) 1928- CANR-18
Earlier sketch in CA 101
Clancy, King
See Clancy, Francis Michael
Clancy, Laurence James 1942- 108
Clancy, Laurie
See Clancy, Laurence James
Clancy, Thomas H(anley) 1923- CANR-7
Earlier sketch in CA 13-16R
Clancy, Thomas L., Jr. 1947- CANR-62
Brief entry 125
Earlier sketch in CA 131
Interview in 131
See also Clancy, Tom
See also MTCW 1
Clancy, Tom
See Clancy, Thomas L., Jr.
See also AAYA 9
See also BEST 89:1, 90:1
See also CLC 45, 112
See also DAM NOV, POP
Clancy, William 1922-1982 Obituary 106
Clanton, (Orval) Gene 1934- 41-44R
Clanton, Gordon 1942- 57-60
Clapham, Arthur Roy 1904-1990 109
Obituary 133
Clapham, Christopher (S.) 1941- CANR-60
Earlier sketch in CA 128
Clapham, John 1908- CANR-10
Earlier sketch in CA 25-28R
Clapp, James Gordon 1909-1970 ..... CAP-1
Earlier sketch in CA 9-10
Clapp, Margaret (Antoinette)
1910-1974 Obituary 49-52
Clapp, Patricia 1912- CANR-37
Earlier sketches in CA 25-28R, CANR-10
See also JRDA
See also MAICYA
See also SAAS 4
See also SATA 4, 74
Clapp, Verner W(arren)
1901-1972 Obituary 37-40R
Clapper, Gregory S(cott) 1951- 166
Clapper, Raymond 1892-1944 ..... DLB 29
Clapperton, Richard 1934- 25-28R
Clar, C(harles) Raymond 1903- 37-40R
Clardy, Andrea Fleck 1943- CANR-17
Earlier sketch in CA 97-100
Clardy, J(esse) V. 1929- 33-36R
Clare, Elizabeth
See Cook, Dorothy Mary
Clare, Ellen
See Sinclair, Olga
Clare, Francis D.
See Aschmann, Alberta
Clare, George P. 1920- 111
Clare, Helen CANR-45
Clare, John 1793-1864 ..... DAB
See also DAM POET
See also DLB 55, 96
See also PC 23
Clare, Josephine 1933- 73-76
Clare, Margaret
See Maison, Margaret M(ary Bowles)
Clare, Samantha
See Dawson, Janis
Claremont, Chris(topher Simon) 1950- 151
See also SATA 87
Clarens, Carlos (Figueredo y) 1936(?)-1987 . 21-24R
Obituary 121
Clareson, Thomas D(ean) 1926-1993 .... CANR-39
Obituary 141
Earlier sketches in CA 1-4R, CANR-2, 18
Clarfield, Gerard Howard 1936- 103
Claridge, Gordon S. 1932- 21-24R
Clarie, Thomas C(ashin) 1943- 93-96
Clarin
See Alas (y Urena), Leopoldo (Enrique Garcia)
Clarizio, Harvey F(rank) 1934- 33-36R
Clark, A(ilsa) M. 1926- 144
Clark, Admont Gulick 1919- 53-56
Clark, Al C.
See Goines, Donald
Clark, Alan 1928- 13-16R
Clark, Alfred Alexander Gordon 1900-1958 Brief
entry 112
See also Hare, Cyril
Clark, Alice S(andell) 1922- 41-44R
Clark, Andrew Hill 1911-1975 ..... CAP-2
Earlier sketch in CA 25-28
Clark, Andy 1957- 163
Clark, Ann L(ivezey) 1913- CANR-7
Earlier sketch in CA 17-20R
Clark, Ann Nolan 1896-1995 ..... CANR-48
Obituary 150
Earlier sketches in CA 5-8R, CANR-2
See also CLR 16
See also DLB 52
See also MAICYA
See also SAAS 16
See also SATA 4, 82
See also SATA-Obit 87
Clark, Anne
See Amor, Anne Clark
Clark, Anne 1909- 29-32R
Clark (of Herriotshall), Arthur Melville 1895- .. 9-12R

Clark, Badger
See Paine, Lauran (Bosworth)
Clark, Ben T. 1928- 53-56
Clark, Bill
See Clark, William A(rthur)
Clark, Billy C(urtis) 1928- CANR-22
Earlier sketch in CA 1-4R
Clark, Blue
See Clark, C(arter) Blue
Clark, (Robert) Brian 1932- CANR-67
Earlier sketch in CA 41-44R
See also CLC 29
Clark, Bruce B(udge) 1918- 69-72
Clark, Burton R(obert) 1921- CANR-52
Earlier sketches in CA 110, CANR-28
Clark, C(arter) Blue 1946- 150
Clark, C. E. Frazer, Jr. 1925- 33-36R
See also DLB 187
Clark, C. H. Douglas 1890- CAP-2
Earlier sketch in CA 23-24
Clark, C(harles) M(anning) H(ope) 1915- 97-100
Clark, Carol (Lois) 1948- 57-60
Clark, Carol Higgins 1956(?)- 152
Clark, Catherine Anthony (Smith) 1892-1977 CAP-1
Earlier sketch in CA 11-12
See also DLB 68
See also JRDA
Clark, Champ 1923- 108
See also SATA 47
Clark, Charles E(dwin) 1929- 29-32R
Clark, Charles Heber 1841-1915 Brief entry 111
See also DLB 11
Clark, Charles Michael Andres 1960- 144
Clark, Charles Tallifero 1917- 13-16R
Clark, China (Debra) 1950- 45-48
Clark, Christopher (Anthony) Stuart
See Stuart-Clark, Christopher (Anthony)
Clark, Clara Gillow 1951- 150
See also SATA 84
Clark, Clifford E(dward), Jr. 1941- 81-84
Clark, Colin (Grant) 1905-1989 CANR-8
Obituary 129
Earlier sketch in CA 61-64
Clark, Curt
See Westlake, Donald E(dwin)
Clark, D. M. J.
See Clark, Douglas (Malcolm Jackson)
Clark, David
See Hardcastle, Michael
Clark, David (George) 1939- 130
Clark, David Allen
See Ernst, (Lyman) John
Clark, David Gillis 1933- 53-56
Clark, David Ridgley 1920- CANR-9
Earlier sketch in CA 17-20R
Clark, Davis Wasgatt 1812-1871 DLB 79
Clark, Dennis E. 1916- 29-32R
Clark, Dennis J. 1927-1993 CANR-53
Obituary 142
Earlier sketches in CA 1-4R, CANR-1
Clark, Diana Cooper
See Cooper-Clark, Diana
Clark, Dick
See Clark, Richard Wagstaff
Clark, Don(ald Rowlee) 1925- 57-60
Clark, Don(ald Henry) 1930- 29-32R
Clark, Donald E. 1933- CANR-8
Earlier sketch in CA 21-24R
Clark, Dora Mae 1893- 41-44R
Clark, Dorothy Park 1899- 5-8R
Clark, Douglas (Malcolm Jackson) 1919-1993 CANR-71
Earlier sketch in CA 114
Clark, E. Ritchie 1912- 122
Clark, Edward W(illiam) 1943- 123
Clark, Eleanor 1913-1996 CANR-41
Obituary 151
Earlier sketch in CA 9-12R
See also CLC 5, 19
See also DLB 6
Clark, Electa 1910- 69-72
Clark, Eliot (Candee) 1883-1980 Obituary 97-100
Clark, Ella E(lizabeth) 1896- 105
Clark, Ellery Harding, Jr. 1909-1997 CANR-10
Obituary 160
Earlier sketch in CA 65-68
Clark, Elmer Talmage 1886-1966 5-8R
Clark, Emma Chichester
See Chichester Clark, Emma
See also SATA 69
Clark, Eric 1911- CANR-9
Earlier sketch in CA 13-16R
Clark, Eric 1937- 102
Clark, Eugenie 1922- 49-52
Clark, Evans 1888-1970 Obituary 104
Clark, Evert 1926(?)-1988 Obituary 126
Clark, F(rederick) Stephen 1908-1977 CANR-14
Earlier sketch in CA 21-24R
Clark, Francis 1919- 17-20R
Clark, Frank J(ames) 1922- CANR-17
Earlier sketch in CA 13-16R
See also SATA 18
Clark, Fred George 1890-1972 Obituary 37-40R
Clark, Gail 1944- CANR-16
Earlier sketch in CA 97-100
Clark, Garel
See Garelick, May
Clark, Garth (Reginald) 1947- 115
Clark, Geoffrey (D.) 1940- 144
Clark, George 1932- 136
Clark, George Norman 1890-1979 65-68
Obituary 85-88
Clark, George Sidney Roberts Kitson
See Kitson Clark, George Sydney Roberts
Clark, Gerald 1918- 13-16R
Clark, Gordon H(addon) 1902-1985 CANR-17
Earlier sketches in CA 1-4R, CANR-1
Clark, Gordon L. 1950- 148
Clark, (John) Grahame (Douglas) 1907-1995 CANR-10
Obituary 149
Earlier sketch in CA 65-68
Clark, Gregory 1892-1977 Obituary 89-92
Clark, Harry 1917- 61-64
Clark, Harry Hayden 1901-1971 CAP-2
Earlier sketch in CA 29-32
Clark, Henry B(alsley) II 1930- CANR-8
Earlier sketch in CA 5-8R
Clark, Howard
See Haskin, Dorothy C(lark)
Clark, Hunter R. 1955- 141
Clark, Ira G(ranville, Jr.) 1909- 127
Clark, J(onathan) C(harles) D(ouglas) 1951- CANR-47
Earlier sketch in CA 121
Clark, J(ohn) H(oward) 1929- 106
Clark, J(ustus) Kent 1917- 128
Clark, J. P.
See Clark, John Pepper
See also DLB 117
Clark, J. R.
See Clark, John R(ussell)
Clark, J(eff) R(ay) 1947- CANR-22
Earlier sketch in CA 106
Clark, James Anthony 1907- 65-68
Clark, James C. 1947- CANR-48
Earlier sketch in CA 122
Clark, James M(ilford) 1930- 21-24R
Clark, James V(aughan) 1927- 13-16R
Clark, Janie 1956- 138
Clark, Jean C(ashman) 1920- 93-96
Clark, Jere Walton 1922- 21-24R
Clark, Jerome 1946- 143
Clark, Jerome L. 1928- 37-40R
Clark, Jerry E(ugene) 1942- 73-76
Clark, Joan
See Benson, Mildred (Augustine Wirt)
Clark, Joan 1934- CANR-67
Earlier sketch in CA 93-96
See also SATA 59, 96
Clark, John Desmond 1916- 61-64
Clark, John Drury 1907- 37-40R
Clark, John G(arretson) 1932- 17-20R
Clark, John Maurice 1884-1963 5-8R
Clark, John Pepper 1935- CANR-72
Earlier sketches in CA 65-68, CANR-16
See also Clark, J. P.
See also BLC 1
See also BW 1
See also CLC 38
See also DAM DRAM, MULT
See also DC 5
Clark, John R(ussell) 1927- 120
Clark, John R(ichard) 1930- 37-40R
Clark, John R(alph) K(ukeakalani) 1946- 101
Clark, John W(illiams) 1907- 13-16R
Clark, Joseph D(eadrick) 1893- CAP-2
Earlier sketch in CA 33-36
Clark, Joseph James 1893-1971 CAP-2
Obituary 29-32R
Earlier sketch in CA 19-20
Clark, Joseph L(ynn) 1881- CAP-2
Earlier sketch in CA 17-18
Clark, Joseph S(ill, Jr.) 1901-1990 Obituary 130
Clark, Joshua Reuben, Jr. 1871-1961 165
Clark, Katerina 1941- CANR-58
Earlier sketch in CA 110
Clark, Katharine (Jarman) 1911(?)-1986 Obituary 118
Clark, Keith 1939- 124
Clark, Kenneth (Mackenzie) 1903-1983 CANR-36
Obituary 109
Earlier sketch in CA 93-96
See also MTCW 1
Clark, Kenneth B(ancroft) 1914- 33-36R
See also BW 1
Clark, L. D. 1922- CANR-1
Earlier sketch in CA 1-4R
Clark, Laurence (Walter) 1914- 13-16R
Clark, LaVerne Harrell 1929- CANR-46
Earlier sketches in CA 13-16R, CANR-11
Clark, Leonard 1905-1981 CANR-7
Obituary 105
Earlier sketch in CA 13-16R
See also SATA 30
See also SATA-Obit 29
Clark, Leonard H(ill) 1915- CANR-4
Earlier sketch in CA 53-56
Clark, Leroy D. CANR-11
Earlier sketch in CA 61-64
Clark, Lewis Gaylord 1808-1873 DLB 3, 64, 73
Clark, Lindley H(oag), Jr. 1920- 65-68
Clark, Lydia Benson
See Meaker, Eloise
Clark, M. R.
See Clark, Mavis Thorpe
Clark, Mabel Margaret (Cowie) 1903-1975 101
Clark, Malcolm (Hamilton), Jr. 1917- 106
Clark, (Charles) Manning (Hope) 1915-1991 9-12R
Obituary 134
Clark, Marcia (Rachel) 1953- 161
Clark, Marden J. 1916- 61-64
Clark, Margaret Goff 1913- CANR-43
Earlier sketches in CA 1-4R, CANR-5, 20
See also SATA 8, 82
Clark, Marguerite Sheridan 1892(?)-1982 Obituary 107
Clark, Maria Louisa Guidish 1926- 5-8R
Clark, Marion L. 1943-1977 77-80
Obituary 73-76
Clark, Marjorie A. 1911- 33-36R
Clark, Mark (Wayne) 1896-1984 Obituary 112
Clark, (Bennett) Marsh 1928-1985 122
Obituary 117
Clark, Marv T. 37-40R
Clark, Mary Higgins 1929- CANR-51
Earlier sketches in CA 81-84, CANR-16, 36
See also AAYA 10
See also BEST 89:4
See also DAM POP
See also JRDA
See also MTCW 1
See also SATA 46
Clark, Mary Jane 1915- 57-60
Clark, Mary Lou
See Clark, Maria Louisa Guidish
Clark, Mary Margaret 1929- 113
Clark, Mary T(wibill) 102
Clark, Mavis Thorpe 1909- CANR-37
Earlier sketches in CA 57-60, CANR-8
See also CLC 12
See also CLR 30
See also MAICYA
See also SAAS 5
See also SATA 8, 74
Clark, Melissa 1949- CANR-22
Earlier sketch in CA 104
Clark, Merle
See Gessner, Lynne
Clark, Michael D(orsey) 1937- 111
Clark, Miles (Morton) 1920- 21-24R
Clark, Naomi 1932- 77-80
Clark, Neal 1950- 113
Clark, Neil M(cCullough) 1890- 5-8R
Clark, Nicholas (Alexander) 1959-1984 132
Clark, Norman H(arold) 1925- 69-72
Clark, Parlin
See Trigg, Harry Davis
Clark, Patricia Finrow 1929- 17-20R
See also SATA 11
Clark, Paul F. 1954- 138
Clark, R. Milton
See Clark, Reginald M.
Clark, (William) Ramsey 1927- 29-32R
Clark, Randall 1957- 120
Clark, Reginald M. 1949- 128
Clark, Richard Charles 1935- 133
Brief entry 114
Clark, Richard Wagstaff 1929- 130
Brief entry 113
Clark, Robert Alfred 1908- 101
Clark, Robert E(ugene) 1912- 41-44R
Clark, Robert E(dward) D(avid) 1906- CANR-21
Earlier sketch in CA 5-8R
Clark, Robert L(loyd), Jr. 1945- 103
Clark, Robert P(hillips) 1921- 126
Clark, Rolf 1937- 114
Clark, Romane Lewis 1925- 17-20R
Clark, Ronald Harry 1904- 110
Clark, Ronald William 1916-1987 CANR-47
Obituary 122
Earlier sketch in CA 25-28R
See also SATA 2
See also SATA-Obit 52
Clark, Ruth C(ampbell) 1920- 69-72
Clark, Samuel 1945- 89-92
Clark, Samuel Delbert 1910- CANR-11
Earlier sketches in CAP-1, CA 13-14
Clark, Septima Poinsette 1898-1987 5-8R
Obituary 124
Clark, Stephen R(ichard) L(yster) 1945- CANR-72
Earlier sketches in CA 77-80, CANR-13, 32
Clark, Sue C(assidy) 1935- 41-44R
Clark, Sydney A(ylmer) 1890-1975 CANR-4
Obituary 57-60
Earlier sketch in CA 5-8R
Clark, Terry N(ichols) 1940- 25-28R
Clark, Thomas D(ionysious) 1903- CANR-4
Earlier sketch in CA 5-8R
Clark, Thomas Willard 1941- CANR-43
Earlier sketch in CA 81-84
See also CAAS 22
Clark, Tom
See Clark, Thomas Willard
Clark, Truman R(oss) 1935- 61-64
Clark, Van D(eusen) 1909- CAP-1
Earlier sketch in CA 13-14
See also SATA 2
Clark, Virginia
See Gray, Patricia (Clark)
Clark, Walter Houston 1902- 37-40R
Clark, Walter Van Tilburg 1909-1971 CANR-63
Obituary 33-36R
Earlier sketch in CA 9-12R
See also CLC 28
See also DLB 9
See also SATA 8
Clark, Wesley James 1950- CANR-31
Earlier sketch in CA 112
Clark, Will 1939- 166
Clark, William 1770-1838 DLB 186
Clark, William (Donaldson) 1916-1985 29-32R
Obituary 116
Clark, William A(rthur) 1931- 33-36R
Clark, William Andrews, Jr. 1877-1934 DLB 187
Clark, William Bedford 1947- CANR-51
Earlier sketches in CA 109, CANR-27
Clark, William R. 1938- 152
Clark, William Smith II 1900-1969 CAP-2
Earlier sketch in CA 25-28
Clark Bekederemo, J(ohnson) P(epper)
See Clark, John Pepper
Clarke, A. F. N. 1948- 128
Clarke, Anna 1919- CANR-39
Earlier sketches in CA 102, CANR-18
Clarke, Arthur C(harles) 1917- CANR-55
Earlier sketches in CA 1-4R, CANR-2, 28
See also AAYA 4
See also CLC 1, 4, 13, 18, 35
See also DAM POP
See also JRDA
See also MAICYA
See also MTCW 1
See also SATA 13, 70
See also SSC 3
Clarke, Arthur G(ladstone) 1887- CAP-2
Earlier sketch in CA 17-18
Clarke, Austin 1896-1974 CAP-2
Obituary 49-52
Earlier sketch in CA 29-32
See also CLC 6, 9
See also DAM POET
See also DLB 10, 20
Clarke, Austin C(hesterfield) 1934- CANR-68
Earlier sketches in CA 25-28R, CANR-14, 32
See also CAAS 16
See also BLC 1
See also BW 1
See also CLC 8, 53
See also DAC
See also DAM MULT
See also DLB 53, 125
Clarke, Basil F(ulford) L(owther) 1908-1978 CANR-4
Obituary 89-92
Earlier sketch in CA 5-8R
Clarke, Boden
See Burgess, Michael (Roy)
Clarke, Brenda (Margaret Lilian) 1926- CANR-49
Earlier sketches in CA 65-68, CANR-9, 24
Clarke, Captain Jafar
See Nesmith, Robert I.
Clarke, Charles (Richard Astley) 1944- 118
Clarke, Charles Galloway 1899-1983 Obituary 110
Clarke, Cheryl 1947- 143
See also BW 2
Clarke, Clorinda 1917- 25-28R
See also SATA 7
Clarke, D(erek) A(shdown) 1921- 125
Clarke, D(avid) Waldo 1907- 9-12R
Clarke, David E(gerton) 1920- 17-20R
Clarke, David Leonard 1937-1976 Obituary 111
Clarke, Derrick Harry 1919- 103
Clarke, Dorothy Clotelle
See Shadi, Dorothy Clotelle Clarke
Clarke, Dudley (Wrangel) 1899-1974 CAP-1
Earlier sketch in CA 13-16
Clarke, Duncan L(ynn) 1941- CANR-16
Earlier sketch in CA 97-100
Clarke, Dwight Lancelot 1885-1971 1-4R
Obituary 103
Clarke, Edith 1883-1959 157
Clarke, Ernest George 1927- 102
Clarke, Garry E(vans) 1943- 77-80
Clarke, George Timothy CANR-1
Earlier sketch in CA 1-4R
Clarke, George Wallace
See Wallace-Clarke, George
Clarke, Gillian 1937- 106
See also CLC 61
See also DLB 40
Clarke, H. Harrison 1902- CANR-5
Earlier sketch in CA 1-4R
Clarke, Hans Thacher 1887-1972 Obituary 37-40R
Clarke, Harry Eugene, Jr. 1921- 5-8R
Clarke, Henry Charles 1899- 102
Clarke, Hockley
See Clarke, Henry Charles
Clarke, Howard William 1929- 37-40R
Clarke, Hugh Vincent 1919- CANR-41
Earlier sketches in CA 102, CANR-19
Clarke, I. F.
See Clarke, Ignatius (Ian) Frederick
Clarke, Ian
See Clarke, Ignatius (Ian) Frederick
Clarke, Ignatius (Ian) Frederick 1918- 116
Clarke, J.
See Clarke, Judith
Clarke, J(ohn) F(rederick) Gates 1905-1990 CAP-1
Obituary 132
Earlier sketch in CA 13-14
Clarke, Jack Alden 1924- 29-32R
Clarke, James 1934- 127
Clarke, James F(ranklin) 1906- 69-72
Clarke, James Freeman 1810-1888 DLB 1, 59
Clarke, James Hall
See Rowland-Entwistle, (Arthur) Theodore (Henry)
Clarke, James W(eston) 1937- CANR-42
Earlier sketch in CA 110
Clarke, Joan (Lorraine) 1920- 104
Clarke, Joan B. 1921- SATA 42
See also SATA-Brief 27
Clarke, Joan Dorn 1924- 9-12R
Clarke, John
See Laklan, Carli
and Sontup, Dan(iel)
Clarke, John (Campbell) 1913-(?) CAP-1
Earlier sketch in CA 13-16
Clarke, John Henrik 1915- CANR-43
Earlier sketches in CA 53-56, CANR-24
See also AITN 1
See also BW 2
Clarke, John Joseph 1879- CANR-5
Earlier sketch in CA 5-8R
Clarke, John R. 1945- 141
Clarke, Judith 1943- 142
See also SATA 75
Clarke, Kenneth W(endell) 1917- 17-20R
Clarke, Lea
See Rowland-Entwistle, (Arthur) Theodore (Henry)
Clarke, Lige 1942- 41-44R

Clarke, (Victor) Lindsay 1939- 127
Clarke, Margaret 1941- 130
Clarke, Martin Lowther 1909- CANR-2
Earlier sketch in CA 5-8R
Clarke, Mary 1923- 104
Clarke, Mary Stetson 1911- CANR-8
Earlier sketch in CA 21-24R
See also SATA 5
Clarke, Mary Washington 1913- CANR-11
Earlier sketch in CA 25-28R
Clarke, Mary Whatley 1899- CANR-2
Earlier sketch in CA 5-8R
Clarke, Michael
See Newlon, (Frank) Clarke
Clarke, Nicholas Goodrick
See Goodrick-Clarke, Nicholas
Clarke, P(eter) F(rederick) 1942- 73-76
Clarke, Patricia 1926- 143
Clarke, Pauline 1921- CANR-45
See also CLR 28
See also DLB 161
See also MAICYA
Clarke, Peter 1936- 104
Clarke, Rebecca Sophia 1833-1906 Brief entry . 119
See also DLB 42
Clarke, Richard
See Paine, Lauran (Bosworth)
Clarke, Richard (William Barnes)
1910-1975 Obituary 115
Clarke, Robert
See Paine, Lauran (Bosworth)
and Platt, Charles
Clarke, Robin Harwood 1937- CANR-9
Earlier sketch in CA 13-16R
Clarke, Ron 1937- 107
Clarke, Ronald Francis 1933- 21-24R
Clarke, Shirley 1925- . . . . CLC 16
Clarke, Simon 1946- 122
Clarke, Stephan P(aul) 1945- 69-72
Clarke, Terence 1943- . . . . CAAS 28
Clarke, Thomas E(mmet) 1918- 53-56
Clarke, Thomas Ernest Bennett 1907-1989 . . . .
CANR-19
Obituary 127
Earlier sketch in CA 103
Clarke, Thurston 1946- CANR-63
Earlier sketches in CA 77-80, CANR-13
Clarke, Tom E(ugene) 1915- 5-8R
Clarke, William Dixon 1927- 5-8R
Clarke, William Kendall 1911(?)-1981 Obituary . 104
Clarke, William M(alpas) 1922- CANR-34
Earlier sketches in CA 41-44R, CANR-15
Clarke, William Thomas 1932- 57-60
Clarke-Stewart, K(athleen) Alison 1943- . CANR-32
Earlier sketch in CA 113
Clark-Kennedy, A. E.
See Clark-Kennedy, Archibald Edmund
Clark-Kennedy, Archibald Edmund 1893-1985 . . 134
Obituary 117
Clark-Pendarvis, China 1950- 129
Clarkson, Adrienne 1939- 49-52
Clarkson, E(dith) Margaret 1915- CANR-20
Earlier sketches in CA 1-4R, CANR-5
See also SATA 37
Clarkson, Ewan 1929- CANR-17
Earlier sketch in CA 25-28R
See also SATA 9
Clarkson, Geoffrey P. E. 1934- CANR-2
Earlier sketch in CA 5-8R
Clarkson, Helen
See McCloy, Helen (Worrell Clarkson)
Clarkson, J. F.
See Tubb, E(dwin) C(harles)
Clarkson, Jan Nagel 1943- 93-96
Clarkson, Jesse Dunsmore 1897-1973 . . . . 5-8R
Obituary 45-48
Clarkson, L(eslie) A(lbert) 1933- 73-76
Clarkson, Orman
See Richardson, Gladwell
Clarkson, Paul S(tephen) 1905- 29-32R
Clarkson, Stephen 1937- 41-44R
Clarkson, Thomas 1760-1846 . . . . DLB 158
Clarkson, Tom 1913- 103
Clarkson, Wensley 1956- 156
Clary, Jack 1932- 57-60
Clary, Killarney 1953- 148
Clary, Margie Willis 1931- 164
Clasen, Claus-Peter 1931- 41-44R
Clash, The
See Headon, (Nicky) Topper
and Jones, Mick
and Simonon, Paul
and Strummer, Joe
Clasper, Paul D(udley) 1923- 1-4R
Claspy, Everett M. 1907(?)-1973 Obituary . . 41-44R
Claster, Daniel S(tuart) 1932- 21-24R
Clatworthy, Nancy M(oore) K. 1924- 124
Claude, Richard (P.) 1934- 29-32R
Claudel, Alice Moser CANR-2
Earlier sketch in CA 49-52
Claudel, Paul (Louis Charles Marie) 1868-1955 . 165
Brief entry 104
See also DLB 192
See also TCLC 2, 10
Claudia, Sister Mary 1906- CAP-1
Earlier sketch in CA 9-10
Claudia, Susan
See Johnston, William
Claudius, Matthias 1740-1815 . . . . DLB 97
Claus, Hugo (Maurice Julius) 1929- 168
Brief entry 116
Claus, Marshall R. 1936-1970 . . . . CAP-2
Earlier sketch in CA 29-32
Clausen, Aage R. 1932- 49-52
Clausen, Andy 1943- Brief entry 117
See also DLB 16
Clausen, Christopher (John) 1942- 130
Clausen, Connie 1923-1997 . . . . 1-4R
Obituary 161
Clausen, Dennis M(onroe) 1943- 106
Clausen, Meredith L(eslie) 1942- 151
Clausen, W. V.
See Clausen, Wendell (Vernon)
Clausen, Wendell (Vernon) 1923- 121
Clauser, Suzanne (P.) 1929- 37-40R
Clavel, Bernard (Charles Henri) 1923- CANR-2
Earlier sketch in CA 45-48
Clavel, Maurice 1920-1979 Obituary 85-88
Clavel, Pierre 143
Clavell, James (duMaresq) 1925-1994 . . . CANR-48
Obituary 146
Earlier sketches in CA 25-28R, CANR-26
See also CLC 6, 25, 87
See also DAM NOV, POP
See also MTCW 1
Claverie, Jean 1946- . . . . SATA 38
Clawson, Calvin C. 1941- 148
Clawson, James G. 1947- 145
Clawson, John L. 1865-1933 . . . . DLB 187
Clawson, Marion 1905-1998 . . . . CANR-10
Obituary 165
Earlier sketch in CA 65-68
Clawson, Robert W(ayne) 1939- CANR-25
Earlier sketch in CA 108
Clay, Alison
See Keevill, Henry J(ohn)
Clay, Bertha M.
See Dey, Frederic (Merrill) Van Rensselaer
Clay, Cassius
See Ali, Muhammad
Clay, Cassius Marcellus 1810-1903 Brief entry . 120
See also DLB 43
Clay, Charles Travis 1885-1978 Obituary 77-80
Clay, Christopher (G. A.) 1940- 128
Clay, Comer 1910- 45-48
Clay, Diskin 1938- 115
Clay, Edith 1910- 125
Clay, Floyd M(artin) 1927- 45-48
Clay, G. A.
See Trotter, Michael H(amilton)
Clay, Grady E. 1916- 93-96
Clay, James 1924- 17-20R
Clay, Jenny Strauss 125
Clay, Jim
See Clay, James
Clay, Lucius D(uBignon) 1897-1978 81-84
Obituary 77-80
Clay, Marie M(ildred) 1926- CANR-22
Earlier sketches in CA 61-64, CANR-8
Clay, Patrice 1947- 106
See also SATA 47
Clay, Rita
See Estrada, Rita Clay
Clay, Roberta 1900- CAP-2
Earlier sketch in CA 29-32
Claybaugh, Amos L(incoln) 1917- 69-72
Claybourne, Casey 167
Claydon, Leslie Francis 1923- 53-56
Clayes, Stanley A(rnold) 1922- 29-32R
Claypool, Jane
See Miner, Jane Claypool
Clayre, Alasdair 1935-1984 102
Obituary 111
Clayson, Alan 1951- 145
Clayson, (S.) Hollis 1946- 140
Clayton, Aileen Bowen 1918-1981 113
Clayton, Barbara
See Pluff, Barbara Littlefield
Clayton, Bruce 1939- 69-72
Clayton, C. Guy 1936- 122
Clayton, Charles C(urtis) 1902- 73-76
Clayton, Donald D(elbert) 1935- 65-68
Clayton, Elaine 1961- 159
See also SATA 94
Clayton, (Francis) Howard 1918- CANR-12
Earlier sketch in CA 29-32R
Clayton, Howard 1929- 65-68
Clayton, James E(dwin) 1929- 9-12R
Clayton, James L. 1931- CANR-12
Earlier sketch in CA 29-32R
Clayton, Jo 1939-1997 81-84
Obituary 164
Clayton, John
See Beevers, John (Leonard)
Clayton, John 1892-1979 . . . . 33-36R
Obituary 89-92
Clayton, John J(acob) 1935- CANR-11
Earlier sketch in CA 25-28R
Clayton, Keith (M.) 1928- CANR-11
Earlier sketch in CA 21-24R
Clayton, Lawrence (Ray) 1938- 137
Clayton, Lawrence (Otto, Jr.) 1945- 142
See also SATA 75
Clayton, Martin 1967- 152
Clayton, Mary 1954- 136
Clayton, Michael 1934- 144
Clayton, Paul C(lark) 1932- 61-64
Clayton, Peter A(rthur) 1937- 130
Clayton, Richard Henry Michael 1907-1993 . . . . . .
CANR-62
Obituary 143
Earlier sketches in CA 5-8R, CANR-4, 29
See also Haggard, William
Clayton, Susan
See Bailey, Alfred Goldsworthy
Clayton, Sylvia 103
Clayton, Thomas (Swoverland) 1932- 41-44R
Clayton, Thompson B(owker) 1904- 57-60
Claytor, Gertrude Boatwright
1890(?)-1973 Obituary 45-48
Cleage, Albert B., Jr. 1911- 65-68
Cleage, Pearl (Michelle) 1948- CANR-27
Earlier sketch in CA 41-44R
See also BW 2
Cleall, Charles 1927- 5-8R
Clear, Todd R. 1949- 117
Cleare, John 1936- 65-68
Clearman, Brian (Patrick Joseph) 1941- . . CANR-38
Earlier sketch in CA 115
Cleary, Beverly (Atlee Bunn) 1916- CANR-66
Earlier sketches in CA 1-4R, CANR-2, 19, 36
Interview in CANR-19
See also AAYA 6
See also CLR 2, 8
See also DLB 52
See also JRDA
See also MAICYA
See also MTCW 1
See also SAAS 20
See also SATA 2, 43, 79
Cleary, Brian P. 1959- 159
See also SATA 93
Cleary, David Powers 1915- 106
Cleary, Edward L. 1929- 140
Cleary, Florence Damon 1896-1982 81-84
Obituary 133
Cleary, James W(illiam) 1927- 17-20R
Cleary, Johanna L. 1961- 122
Cleary, Jon 1917- CANR-52
Earlier sketches in CA 1-4R, CANR-3, 26
Cleary, Robert E(dward) 1932- 41-44R
Cleator, P(hilip) E(llaby) 1908- 102
Cleaver, Anastasia N. CANR-18
Earlier sketch in CA 97-100
Cleaver, Bill . . . . CLR 6
See also DLB 52
See also SATA 22
See also SATA-Obit 27
Cleaver, Carole 1934- 49-52
See also SATA 6
Cleaver, Dale G. 1928- 17-20R
Cleaver, (Leroy) Eldridge 1935-1998 . . . . CANR-16
Obituary 167
Earlier sketch in CA 21-24R
See also BLC 1
See also BW 1
See also CLC 30
See also DAM MULT
Cleaver, Elizabeth (Mrazik) 1939-1985 97-100
Obituary 117
See also CLR 13
See also SATA 23
See also SATA-Obit 43
Cleaver, Hylton Reginald 1891-1961 73-76
See also SATA 49
Cleaver, Nancy
See Mathews, Evelyn Craw
Cleaver, Vera (Allen) 1919-1992 . . . . CANR-38
Obituary 161
Earlier sketch in CA 73-76
See also AAYA 12
See also CLR 6
See also DLB 52
See also JRDA
See also MAICYA
See also SATA 22, 76
Cleaver, William J(oseph) 1920-1981 . . . . CANR-38
Obituary 104
See also JRDA
See also MAICYA
Cleaves, Emery N(udd) 1902- 33-36R
Cleaves, Freeman 1904- 1-4R
Cleaves, Peter S(hurtleff) 1943- 69-72
Clebsch, William Anthony 1923-1984 . . . . . . 13-16R
Obituary 113
Clecak, Peter (E.) 1938- 41-44R
Cleckley, Hervey Milton 1903-1984 122
Obituary 111
Cleek, Richard K. 1945- 151
Cleese, John (Marwood) 1939- CANR-35
Brief entry 112
Earlier sketch in CA 116
See also Monty Python
See also CLC 21
See also MTCW 1
Cleeve, Brian (Talbot) 1921- CANR-16
Earlier sketches in CA 49-52, CANR-1
Clegg, Alec
See Clegg, Alexander Bradshaw
Clegg, Alexander Bradshaw 1909- 85-88
Clegg, Charles (Myron, Jr.) 1916- CANR-17
Earlier sketch in CA 25-28R
Clegg, Holly Berkowitz 1955- 154
Clegg, Jerry S(tephen) 1933- 77-80
Clegg, John 1909- 118
Clegg, Reed K. 1907- CAP-1
Earlier sketch in CA 13-14
Clegg, Stewart (Roger) 1947- CANR-27
Earlier sketches in CA 69-72, CANR-11
Cleghorn, Reese 1930- 25-28R
Cleishbotham, Jebediah
See Scott, Walter
Cleland, Charles C(arr) 1924- CANR-14
Earlier sketch in CA 41-44R
Cleland, Charles E(dward) 1936- 111
Cleland, David I. 1926- CANR-10
Earlier sketch in CA 25-28R
Cleland, Hugh
See Clarke, John (Campbell)
Cleland, John 1710-1789 . . . . DLB 39
Cleland, Mabel
See Widdemer, Mabel Cleland
Cleland, (Joseph) Max(well) 1942- 129
Brief entry 113
Cleland, Morton
See Rennie, James Alan
Cleland, W(illiam) Wendell
1888-1972 Obituary 37-40R
Clelland, Catherine
See Townsend, Doris McFerran
Clelland, Richard C(ook) 1921- 17-20R
Clem, Alan L(eland) 1929- CANR-3
Earlier sketch in CA 9-12R
Clem, Margaret H(ollingsworth) 1923- 155
See also SATA 90
Clemeau, Carol
See Esler, Carol Clemeau
Clemen, Wolfgang Hermann 1909- CANR-2
Earlier sketch in CA 1-4R
Clemence, Richard V(ernon) 1910- 1-4R
Clemenceau, Georges (Eugene Benjamin)
1841-1929 Brief entry 114
Clemenko, Harold B. 1905-1984 Obituary 113
Clemens, Alphonse H. 1905-1977 Obituary . . 73-76
Clemens, Brian (Horace) 1931- 167
Clemens, Bryan T. 1934- 97-100
Clemens, Cyril . . . . AITN 2
Clemens, Diane S(haver) 1936- 29-32R
Clemens, Rodgers
See Lovin, Roger Robert
Clemens, Samuel Langhorne 1835-1910 135
Brief entry 104
See also Twain, Mark
See also CDALB 1865-1917
See also DA
See also DAB
See also DAC
See also DAM MST, NOV
See also DLB 11, 12, 23, 64, 74, 186, 189
See also JRDA
See also MAICYA
See also SATA 100
See also YABC 2
Clemens, Virginia Phelps 1941- CANR-15
Earlier sketch in CA 85-88
See also SATA 35
Clemens, Walter C., Jr. 1933- CANR-7
Earlier sketch in CA 17-20R
Clement, A(lfred) J(ohn) 1915- 25-28R
Clement, Aeron 1936(?)-1989 Obituary 127
Clement, Charles Baxter 1940- 105
Clement, Evelyn Geer 1926- 53-56
Clement, George H. 1909- 29-32R
Clement, Hal
See Stubbs, Harry C(lement)
See also CAAS 16
See also DLB 8
Clement, Herbert F(lint) 1927- 81-84
Clement, Jane Tyson 1917- 25-28R
Clement, Rod 163
See also SATA 97
Clement, Roland C(harles) 1912- 49-52
Clement, Wallace 1949- CANR-28
Earlier sketch in CA 111
Clemente, Vince(nt L.) 1932- CANR-55
Earlier sketch in CA 127
Clements, A(rthur) L(eo) 1932- 29-32R
Clements, Barbara Evans 1945- 89-92
Clements, Bruce 1931- CANR-68
Earlier sketches in CA 53-56, CANR-5
See also SATA 27, 94
Clements, Colleen D(ianne) 1936- 110
Clements, E(llen) Catherine (Scott) 1920- . . . 13-16R
Clements, E(ileen) H(elen) 1905- CAP-1
Earlier sketch in CA 9-10
Clements, Frank A. 1942- 93-96
Clements, Harold M. Sr. 1907- 69-72
Clements, John 1916- CANR-11
Earlier sketch in CA 69-72
Clements, Jonathan 1963- 164
Clements, Julia 1906- CAP-1
Earlier sketch in CA 13-14
Clements, Kendrick Alling 1939- 110
Clements, Marcelle 1948- 121
Clements, Mark A. 1955- 136
Clements, Robert John 1912-1993 . . . . CANR-47
Obituary 142
Earlier sketches in CA 1-4R, CANR-5
Clements, Robert W(illiam) 1939- 110
Clements, Ronald Ernest 1929- 13-16R
Clements, Tad S. 1922- 25-28R
Clements, Traverse 1900(?)-1977 Obituary . . . 69-72
Clements, William 1933(?)-1983 Obituary 110
Clements, William M(orris) 1943- 106
Clemhout, Simone 1934- 73-76
Cleminshaw, Clarence Higbee 1902-1985 134
Obituary 116
Brief entry 106
Clemmer, Richard O. 1945- 158
Clemmons, Francois 1945- 41-44R
Clemmons, Larry 1906(?)-1988 Obituary 127
Clemmons, Robert S(tarr) 1910- CAP-2
Earlier sketch in CA 21-22
Clemmons, William (Preston) 1932- 57-60
Clemo, Jack
See Clemo, Reginald John
See also DLB 27
Clemo, Reginald John 1916-1994 . . . . CANR-6
Obituary 146
Earlier sketch in CA 13-16R
See also Clemo, Jack
Clemo, Richard F(rederick)
1920-1976 Obituary 65-68
Clemoes, Peter Alan Martin 1920-1996 102
Obituary 151
Clemons, Elizabeth
See Nowell, Elizabeth Cameron
Clemons, Harry 1879-(?) CAP-1
Earlier sketch in CA 13-14
Clemons, Lulamae 1917- 73-76

Clemons, Walter, Jr. 1929-1994 ... CANR-6
Obituary ... 146
Earlier sketch in CA 1-4R
Clendenen, Clarence Clemens 1899- ... 1-4R
Clendenin, John C(ameron) 1903- ... 17-20R
Clendenin, William R(itchie) 1917-1979 ... 13-16R
Obituary ... 120
Clendenning, John 1934- ... 123
Clendenning, Sheila T. 1939- ... 25-28R
Clendinnen, Inga 1934- ... 138
Cleobury, Frank Harold 1892- ... CAP-1
Earlier sketch in CA 13-14
Cleophil
See Congreve, William
Clephane, Elizabeth Cecilia 1830-1869 ... 166
Clephane, Irene (Amy) ... 13-16R
Clepper, Henry (Edward) 1901-1987 ... CANR-1
Obituary ... 122
Earlier sketch in CA 45-48
Clepper, Irene E(lizabeth) ... 53-56
Clerc, Charles 1926- ... CANR-14
Earlier sketch in CA 37-40R
Clergue, Lucien (Georges) 1934- ... 163
Clerici, Gianni 1930- ... 65-68
Clerihew, E.
See Bentley, E(dmund) C(lerihew)
Clerk, N. W.
See Lewis, C(live) S(taples)
Clery, (Reginald) Val(entine) 1924- ... CANR-3
Earlier sketch in CA 49-52
Cleugh, Mary F(rances) 1913- ... CANR-4
Earlier sketch in CA 1-4R
Cleve, Janita
See Rowland, D(onald) S(ydney)
Cleve, John
See Green, Roland (James)
and Haldeman, Jack C(arroll II)
and Offutt, Andrew J(efferson V)
and Swain, Dwight V(reeland)
Cleveland, Bob
See Cleveland, George
Cleveland, Carles 1952- ... 85-88
Cleveland, Clifford S.
See Goldsmith, David H(irsh)
Cleveland, George 1903(?)-1985 Obituary ... 116
See also SATA-Obit 43
Cleveland, (James) Harlan 1918- ... CANR-4
Earlier sketch in CA 1-4R
Cleveland, Harold van B(uren) 1916-1993 ... CANR-13
Obituary ... 140
Earlier sketch in CA 21-24R
Cleveland, John
See McElfresh, (Elizabeth) Adeline
Cleveland, John 1613-1658 ... DLB 126
Cleveland, Leslie 1921- ... 102
Cleveland, Mary 1917- ... 104
Cleveland, Philip Jerome 1903- ... 9-12R
Cleveland, Ray L(eRoy) 1929- ... 21-24R
Cleveland, Sidney E(arl) 1919- ... 9-12R
Cleveland-Peck, Patricia ... 147
See also SATA 80
Cleven, Cathrine
See Cleven, Kathryn Seward
Cleven, Kathryn Seward ... 1-4R
See also SATA 2
Clevenger, Ernest Allen, Jr. 1929- ... CANR-8
Earlier sketch in CA 57-60
Clevenger, Theodore, Jr. 1929- ... 41-44R
Clevenger, William R(ussell) 1954- ... 150
See also SATA 84
Clever, (Warren) Glenn 1918- ... 57-60
Cleverdon, (Thomas) Douglas (James) 1903-1987 ... 29-32R
Obituary ... 123
Cleverley Ford, D(ouglas) W(illiam) 1914- ... CANR-52
Earlier sketches in CA 25-28R, CANR-11, 28
Cleves, Bernard
See Moore, Bernard
Clevin, Joergen 1920- ... 29-32R
See also SATA 7
Clevin, Jorgen
See Clevin, Joergen
Clew, Jeffrey Robert 1928- ... CANR-44
Earlier sketches in CA 57-60, CANR-6, 21
Clew, William J(oseph) 1904- ... 77-80
Clewell, David 1955- ... 147
Clewes, Dorothy (Mary) 1907- ... CANR-52
Earlier sketches in CA 5-8R, CANR-3
See also SATA 1, 86
Clewes, Howard (Charles Vivian) 1912(?)-1988 Obituary ... 125
Clews, Roy 1937- ... 65-68
Click, J(ohn) W(illiam) 1936- ... 57-60
Cliff, Jimmy
See Chambers, James
See also CLC 21
Cliff, Michelle 1946- ... CANR-72
Earlier sketches in CA 116, CANR-39
See also BLCS
See also BW 2
See also DLB 157
Clifford, Alexandra
See Smith-Brown, Fern
Clifford, Anne 1590-1676 ... DLB 151
Clifford, Christine 1954- ... 164
Clifford, Clark (McAdams) 1906- ... 140
Clifford, Craig Edward 1951- ... 125
Clifford, David
See Rosenberg, Ethel (Clifford)
Clifford, Deborah Pickman 1933- ... 138
Clifford, Derek Plint 1915- ... CANR-4
Earlier sketch in CA 5-8R
Clifford, Eth
See Rosenberg, Ethel (Clifford)
See also SAAS 22
See also SATA 92
Clifford, Francis
See Thompson, A(rthur) L(eonard) B(ell)
Clifford, George 1934(?)-1985 Obituary ... 118
Clifford, Geraldine Joncich 1931- ... 25-28R
Clifford, H(enry) Dalton 1911- ... 9-12R
Clifford, Harold B(urton) 1893- ... CAP-1
Earlier sketch in CA 11-12
See also SATA 10
Clifford, J(ohn) Garry 1942- ... CANR-40
Earlier sketch in CA 53-56
Clifford, James L(owry) 1901-1978 ... CANR-6
Obituary ... 77-80
Earlier sketch in CA 1-4R
See also DLB 103
Clifford, John
See Bayliss, John Clifford
Clifford, John E(dward) 1935- ... 37-40R
Clifford, John McLean 1904-1979 ... 85-88
Clifford, John W(illiam) 1918- ... 17-20R
Clifford, Laurie B(erry) 1948- ... 112
Clifford, Lucy Lane 1853-1929 .. DLB 135, 141, 197
Clifford, Margaret Cort 1929- ... CANR-23
Earlier sketch in CA 25-28R
See also SATA 1
Clifford, Martin
See Hamilton, Charles (Harold St. John)
Clifford, Martin 1910- ... CANR-11
Earlier sketch in CA 25-28R
Clifford, Mary Louise Beneway 1926- ... CANR-3
Earlier sketch in CA 5-8R
See also SATA 23
Clifford, Nicholas R(owland) 1930- ... 21-24R
Clifford, Peggy
See Clifford, Margaret Cort
Clifford, Rachel Mark
See Lewis, Brenda Ralph
Clifford, Richard J(ohn) 1934- ... 112
Clifford, Sarah 1916-1976 ... CANR-11
Earlier sketch in CA 25-28R
Clifford, Theodore
See von Block, Sylvia
Clifford, Tony
See Slide, Anthony
Cliffton, Katherine Potter
See Bryant, Katherine Cliffton
Clift, Virgil Alfred 1912- ... 9-12R
Clift, Wallace Bruce 1926- ... 110
Clifton, Bernice Marie 1901(?)-1985 ... 5-8R
Obituary ... 116
Clifton, Bud
See Stacton, David (Derek)
Clifton, Chas S. 1951- ... 144
Clifton, Fred J. 1935(?)-1984 Obituary ... 114
Clifton, Harry
See Hamilton, Charles (Harold St. John)
Clifton, Jack (Whitney) 1912- ... 106
Clifton, James A(lfonso) 1927- ... CANR-25
Earlier sketches in CA 25-28R, CANR-10
Clifton, James M(alcolm) 1930- ... 112
Clifton, Lewis
See Linedecker, Clifford L.
Clifton, (Thelma) Lucille 1936- ... CANR-42
Earlier sketches in CA 49-52, CANR-2, 24
See also BLC 1
See also BW 2
See also CLC 19, 66
See also CLR 5
See also DAM MULT, POET
See also DLB 5, 41
See also MAICYA
See also MTCW 1
See also PC 17
See also SATA 20, 69
Clifton, Marguerite Ann 1925- ... 13-16R
Clifton, Mark (Irvin) 1906-1963 ... 136
Obituary ... 117
Clifton-Taylor, Alec 1907-1985 ... 125
Clignet, Remi Pierre 1931- ... 104
Climo, Shirley 1928- ... CANR-49
Earlier sketches in CA 107, CANR-24
See also SATA 39, 77
See also SATA-Brief 35
Clinard, Dorothy Long 1909- ... 5-8R
Clinard, Helen Hall 1931- ... 124
Clinard, Marshall B(arron) 1911- ... CANR-4
Earlier sketch in CA 5-8R
Clinard, Turner N(orman) 1917-1981 ... 37-40R
Obituary ... 135
Clinch, Nicholas (Bayard) 1930- ... 111
Clinchy, Everett R(oss) 1896-1986 Obituary ... 118
Cline, Bev
See Fink Cline, Beverly
Cline, Beverly
See Fink Cline, Beverly
Cline, Beverly Fink
See Fink Cline, Beverly
Cline, C(harles) Terry, Jr. 1935- ... CANR-50
Earlier sketches in CA 61-64, CANR-8, 25
Cline, Catherine Ann 1927- ... 17-20R
Cline, Charles (William) 1937- ... CANR-7
Earlier sketch in CA 61-64
Cline, Denzel C(ecil) 1903- ... CAP-2
Earlier sketch in CA 21-22
Cline, Edward 1946- ... CANR-40
Earlier sketch in CA 101
Cline, Foster W. 1940- ... 145
Cline, Gloria Griffen 1929-1973 ... 5-8R
Obituary ... 125
Cline, Joan
See Hamilton, Joan Lesley
Cline, Linda 1941- ... 65-68
Cline, Lynn Hunter 1961- ... 167
Cline, Ray S(teiner) 1918- ... 133
Brief entry ... 106
Cline, Rodney 1903- ... 61-64
Cline, S(arah) L(ouise) 1948- ... 129
Cline, Victor (Bailey) 1925- ... 65-68
Cline, William R. 1941- ... 145
Clinebell, Howard J., Jr. 1922- ... CANR-13
Earlier sketch in CA 33-36R
Clines, Francis X. 1938- ... DLB 185
Clinton, Bill
See Clinton, William Jefferson
Clinton, Catherine 1952- ... 130
Clinton, (Lloyd) D(eWitt) 1946- ... CANR-38
Earlier sketch in CA 116
Clinton, Dirk
See Silverberg, Robert
Clinton, F. G.
See Campbell, R(obert) Wright
Clinton, Hillary Rodham 1947- ... 153
Clinton, Iris A. (Corbin) 1901- ... CAP-1
Earlier sketch in CA 11-12
Clinton, James H(armon) 1946- ... 166
Clinton, James W(illiam) 1929- ... 163
Clinton, Jeff
See Bickham, Jack M(iles)
Clinton, Jon
See Prince, J(ack) H(arvey)
Clinton, Richard Lee 1938- ... CANR-23
Earlier sketches in CA 61-64, CANR-8
Clinton, Rupert
See Bulmer, (Henry) Kenneth
Clinton, William Jefferson 1946- ... 165
Clinton-Baddeley, V.C. 1911(?)-1970 Obituary .. 104
Clipman, William 1954- ... CANR-46
Earlier sketch in CA 106
Clipper, Lawrence Jon 1930- ... 49-52
Clish, (Lee) Marian 1946- ... SATA 43
Clissmann, Anne
See Clune, Anne
Clissold, (John) Stephen (Hallet) 1913-1982 ... 110
Obituary ... 107
Clistier, Adeline
See Denny, Alma
Clithero, Myrtle E(ly) 1906- ... CAP-2
Earlier sketch in CA 25-28
Clithero, Sally
See Clithero, Myrtle E(ly)
Clive, Caroline (V) 1801-1873 ... DLB 199
Clive, Clifford
See Hamilton, Charles (Harold St. John)
Clive, Dennis
See Fearn, John Russell
Clive, Geoffrey 1927-1976 ... 33-36R
Clive, John
See Clive, John Leonard
Clive, John 1933- ... 103
Clive, John Leonard 1924-1990 ... CANR-43
Obituary ... 130
Earlier sketch in CA 85-88
Clive, Mary 1907- ... 21-24R
Clive, William
See Bassett, Ronald
Cloake, John (Cecil) 1924- ... 133
Clodfelter, (William) Frank(lin) 1911- ... 103
Clodfelter, Micheal D. 1946- ... CANR-31
Earlier sketch in CA 69-72
Cloeren, Hermann J(osef) 1934- ... 41-44R
Cloete, Stuart 1897-1976 ... CANR-3
Obituary ... 65-68
Earlier sketch in CA 1-4R
Clogan, Paul M(aurice) 1934- ... 33-36R
Clogg, Clifford C(ollier) 1949-1995 ... 112
Obituary ... 148
Cloke, Richard 1916- ... CANR-11
Earlier sketch in CA 69-72
Clokey, Art 1921- ... SATA 59
Clokey, Richard M(ontgomery) 1936- ... 127
Brief entry ... 107
Clones, N(icholas) J. ... 97-100
Clopton, Beverly Virginia B(eck) ... 106
Clor, Harry M(ortimer) 1929- ... 53-56
Clore, Gerald L(ewis, Jr.) 1939- ... 37-40R
Close, A. Kathryn 1908(?)-1973 Obituary ... 41-44R
Close, Frank (E.) 1945- ... 126
Close, Henry T(hompson) 1928- ... 1-4R
Close, Reginald Arthur 1909-1996 ... 17-20R
Obituary ... 154
Close, Upton
See Hall, Josef Washington
Closen, Michael L. 1949- ... 121
Closs, August 1898-1990 ... CANR-2
Obituary ... 132
Earlier sketch in CA 5-8R
Closs, Elizabeth
See Traugott, Elizabeth Closs
Clot, Andre 1909- ... 156
Clotfelter, Beryl E(dward) 1926- ... 53-56
Clotfelter, Cecil F. 1929- ... 53-56
Clotfelter, Charles T. 1947- ... 131
Clotfelter, Mary (Eunice) L(ong) ... 103
Clothier, Peter (Dean) 1936- ... 65-68
Cloud, (Joseph) Fred (Jr.) 1925- ... 13-16R
Cloud, Patricia
See Strother, Pat Wallace
Cloud, Preston (Ercelle) 1912-1991 ... 93-96
Obituary ... 133
Cloud, Yvonne
See Kapp, Yvonne (Mayer)
Cloudsley-Thompson, J(ohn) L(eonard) 1921- ... CANR-23
Earlier sketches in CA 17-20R, CANR-8
See also SATA 19
Clough, Arthur Hugh 1819-1861 ... DLB 32
Clough, B(renda) W(ang) 1955- ... CANR-65
Earlier sketch in CA 116
Clough, Brenda
See Clough, B(renda) W(ang)
Clough, Francis F(rederick) 1912- ... CAP-1
Earlier sketch in CA 9-10
Clough, Neil 1950- ... 112
Clough, Ralph Nelson 1916- Brief entry ... 105
Clough, Rosa Trillo 1906- ... 13-16R
Clough, Shepard B(ancroft) 1901-1990 ... CANR-4
Obituary ... 131
Earlier sketch in CA 1-4R
Clough, William 1911(?)-1976 Obituary ... 69-72
Clough, William A. 1899- ... CAP-2
Earlier sketch in CA 21-22
Clough, Wilson O(ber) 1894-1990 ... 17-20R
Obituary ... 161
Clouse, Nancy L. 1938- ... SATA 78
Clouse, Robert Gordon 1931- ... CANR-12
Earlier sketch in CA 29-32R
Clouser, John William 1932- ... 61-64
Clouser, Roy A. 1937- ... 146
Clout, Hugh Donald 1944- ... CANR-34
Earlier sketches in CA 41-44R, CANR-15
Cloutier, Cecile
See Cloutier-Wojciechowska, Cecile
See also DLB 60
Cloutier, David 1951- ... CANR-49
Earlier sketches in CA 57-60, CANR-7
Cloutier-Wojciechowska, Cecile 1930- ... CANR-12
Earlier sketch in CA 65-68
See also Cloutier, Cecile
Clover, Frank Metlar III 1940- ... 101
Clovis, Allen M. 1953- ... 143
Clow, Barbara Hand 1943- ... 133
Clow, Martha de Mev 1932- ... 29-32R
Cloward, Richard Andrew 1926- ... 41-44R
Clower, Robert W(ayne) 1926- ... 89-92
Clowney, Edmund P(rosper) 1917- ... CANR-8
Earlier sketch in CA 5-8R
Clowse, Converse Dilworth 1929- ... 127
Brief entry ... 108
Clubb, Louise George 1930- ... 69-72
Clubb, O(liver) Edmund 1901-1989 ... 37-40R
Obituary ... 128
Clubb, Oliver E., Jr. 1929- ... 5-8R
Clubbe, John 1938- ... CANR-11
Earlier sketch in CA 25-28R
Clube, (Stace) Victor (Murray) 1934- ... 130
Cluff, Charles E. 1937- ... 65-68
Cluff, Russell M. 1946- ... 154
Clugston, Richard 1938- ... 41-44R
Clum, John M(acKenzie) 1941- ... 69-72
Clun, Arthur
See Polsby, Nelson W(oolf)
Clune, Anne 1945- ... 103
Clune, Francis Patrick 1893-1971 ... CAP-2
Obituary ... 29-32R
Earlier sketch in CA 23-24
Clune, Frank
See Clune, Francis Patrick
Clune, Henry W. 1890-1995 ... CANR-5
Obituary ... 161
Earlier sketch in CA 1-4R
Clunies Ross, Anthony (Ian) 1932- ... 53-56
Clunis, D. Merilee ... 166
Clurman, Harold 1901-1980 ... CANR-2
Obituary ... 101
Earlier sketch in CA 1-4R
Cluster, Dick 1947- ... 97-100
Clute, Morrel J. 1912- ... 13-16R
Clute, Robert E(ugene) 1924- ... 41-44R
Clutha, Janet Paterson Frame 1924- ... CANR-36
Earlier sketches in CA 1-4R, CANR-2
See also Frame, Janet
See also MTCW 1
Clutterbuck, David Ashley 1947- ... 113
Clutterbuck, Richard 1917-1998 ... CANR-50
Obituary ... 163
Earlier sketches in CA 21-24R, CANR-9, 25
Clutton-Brock, Arthur 1868-1924 ... DLB 98
Clutton-Brock, Arthur Guy 1906-1995 ... 110
Obituary ... 147
Cluver, Eustace Henry 1894- ... CAP-1
Earlier sketch in CA 9-10
Cluysenaar, Anne (Alice Andree Jackson) 1936- ... 102
Clyde, Leslie
See Kipps, Harriet C(lyde)
Clyde, Norman Asa 1885-1972 ... 41-44R
Clyde Cool
See Frazier, Walt(er)
Clymer, Eleanor 1906- ... CANR-51
Earlier sketches in CA 61-64, CANR-9
See also SAAS 17
See also SATA 9, 85
Clymer, (Joseph) Floyd 1895-1970 Obituary ... 104
Clymer, Kenton James 1943- ... 127
Brief entry ... 109
Clymer, Reuben Swinburne 1878- ... CAP-1
Earlier sketch in CA 11-12
Clynder, Monica
See Muir, Marie
Clyne, James F. 1898(?)-1977 Obituary ... 69-72
Clyne, Patricia (Edwards) ... 101
See also SATA 31
Clyne, Terence
See Blatty, William Peter
Clytus, John 1929- ... 29-32R
Cnudde, Charles F(rancis) 1938- ... CANR-26
Earlier sketch in CA 29-32R
Coad, F(rederick) Roy 1925- ... 103
Coad, Oral Sumner 1887- ... 45-48
Coade, Jessie 1911- ... 120
Coakley, Lakme 1912- ... 69-72
Coakley, Mary Lewis ... CAP-1
Earlier sketch in CA 13-16
Coakley, Michael 1947(?)-1988 Obituary ... 126

Coale, Samuel Chase 1943- CANR-52
Earlier sketches in CA 65-68, CANR-11, 27
Coalson, Glo 1946- CANR-68
Earlier sketch in CA 103
See also SATA 26, 94
Coan, Eugene V(ictor) 1943- 110
Coan, Otis W(elton) 1895- CAP-2
Earlier sketch in CA 33-36
Coan, Richard Welton 1928- CANR-12
Earlier sketch in CA 69-72
Coates, Anna 1958- .... SATA 73
Coates, Austin 1922- 102
Coates, Belle 1896-1986 .... 5-8R
Obituary 161
See also SATA 2
Coates, Charles (K.) 1929- 146
Coates, Charles R(obert) 1915- 106
Coates, David 1946- CANR-57
Earlier sketch in CA 125
Coates, Donald R(obert) 1922- CANR-2
Earlier sketch in CA 49-52
Coates, Doreen (Frances) 1912- 107
Coates, Gary J(oseph) 1947- 110
Coates, Geoffrey Edward 1917- 37-40R
Coates, J(ohn) F(rancis) 1922- CANR-49
Earlier sketch in CA 123
Coates, K. S.
See Coates, Kenneth (Stephen)
Coates, Ken
See Coates, Kenneth (Stephen)
Coates, Ken 1930- CANR-50
Earlier sketch in CA 123
Coates, Ken S.
See Coates, Kenneth (Stephen)
Coates, Kenneth (Stephen) 1956- 130
Coates, Robert C(rawford) 1937- 134
Coates, Robert M(yron) 1897-1973 .... 5-8R
Obituary 41-44R
See also DLB 4, 9, 102
Coates, Ruth Allison 1915- 57-60
See also SATA 11
Coates, W. Paul 1945- 136
Coates, William Ames 1916-1973 .... 37-40R
Coates, Willson H(avelock) 1899-1976 ... CANR-33
Obituary 69-72
Earlier sketch in CA 37-40R
Coats, Alice M(argaret) 1905- 53-56
See also SATA 11
Coats, George W. 1936- 21-24R
Coats, Peter 1910-1990 .... CANR-1
Obituary 132
Earlier sketch in CA 49-52
Coatsworth, Elizabeth (Jane) 1893-1986 .. CANR-4
Obituary 120
Earlier sketch in CA 5-8R
See also CLR 2
See also DLB 22
See also MAICYA
See also SATA 2, 56, 100
See also SATA-Obit 49
Coatsworth, John H(enry) 1940- 148
Cobalt, Martin
See Mayne, William (James Carter)
Cobb, Alice 1909- 5-8R
Cobb, Carl W(esley) 1926- 21-24R
Cobb, Charles E(arl), Jr. 1943- 142
See also BW 2
See also DLB 41
Cobb, Clifford (William) 1951- 162
Cobb, David 1934- 112
Cobb, Faye Davis 1932- 9-12R
Cobb, Frank I. 1869-1923 .... DLB 25
Cobb, Geoffrey Belton 1892(?)-1971 Obituary .. 104
Cobb, Irvin S. 1876-1944 .... DLB 11, 25, 86
See also TCLC 77
Cobb, James Charles 1947- CANR-31
Earlier sketch in CA 112
Cobb, James H(arvey) 1953- 154
Cobb, Jane
See Berry, Jane Cobb
Cobb, John B(oswell), Jr. 1925- CANR-2
Earlier sketch in CA 1-4R
Cobb, Jonathan 1946- 93-96
Cobb, Mary 1931- .... SATA 88
Cobb, Nancy (Howard) 1949- 137
Cobb, Nathan 1943- 105
Cobb, R. C.
See Cobb, Richard (Charles)
Cobb, Richard (Charles) 1917-1996 128
Obituary 151
Brief entry 116
Cobb, Robert A. 1941- 69-72
Cobb, Roger W(illiam) 1941- 104
Cobb, Thomas 1947- 136
Cobb, Vicki 1938- CANR-14
Earlier sketch in CA 33-36R
See also CLR 2
See also JRDA
See also MAICYA
See also SAAS 6
See also SATA 8, 69
Cobban, Alfred 1901-1968 Obituary 111
Cobbe, Frances Power 1822-1904 .... DLB 190
Cobbett
See Ludovici, Anthony M(ario)
Cobbett, Richard
See Pluckrose, Henry (Arthur)
Cobbett, William 1763-1835 ..... DLB 43, 107, 158
Cobbing, Bob 1920- 101
Cobbledick, Gordon 1898-1969 .... DLB 171
Cobbledick, James R. 1935- 97-100
Cobbs, Elizabeth Anne 1956- 144
Cobbs, John L(ewis) 1917- Brief entry 115
Cobbs, Lisa
See Cobbs, Elizabeth Anne
Cobbs, Price M(ashaw) 1928- 21-24R
Coben, Harlan 1962- 164
Coben, Lawrence A(llan) 1926- 111
Coben, Stanley 1929- 122
Cober, Alan E(dwin) 1935-1998 .... SATA 7
See also SATA-Obit 101
Cobham, Sir Alan
See Hamilton, Charles (Harold St. John)
Coble, John (Lawrence) 1924- 9-12R
Cobleigh, Ira U(nderwood) 1903- 81-84
Coblentz, Stanton A(rthur) 1896-1982 ... CANR-21
Obituary 161
Earlier sketch in CA 5-8R
Cobley, John 1914- 13-16R
Cobos, Ruben 1911- 135
Cobrin, Harry Aaron 1902- CAP-2
Earlier sketch in CA 29-32
Coburn, Andrew 1932- CANR-36
Earlier sketches in CA 53-56, CANR-4
Coburn, Broughton 1951- 111
Coburn, D(onald) L(ee) 1938- 89-92
See also CLC 10
Coburn, John Bowen 1914- CANR-2
Earlier sketch in CA 1-4R
Coburn, Karen Levin 1941- 65-68
Coburn, Kathleen 1905-1991 93-96
Obituary 135
Coburn, L. J.
See Harvey, John (Barton)
Coburn, Louis 1915- 104
Coburn, Thomas B(owen) 1944- 110
Coburn, Walt(er John) 1889-1971 .... CANR-61
Obituary 161
Earlier sketches in CAP-1, CA 9-10
Cocagnac, Augustin Maurice(-Jean) 1924- ....
CANR-17
Earlier sketch in CA 25-28R
See also SATA 7
Cocca-Leffler, Maryann 1958- .... SATA 80
Coccioli, Carlo 1920- CANR-9
Earlier sketches in CA 13-16R, CANR-31
Cochard, Thomas S(ylvester) 1893- 57-60
Cochet, Gabriel 1888-1973 Obituary 45-48
Cochran, Bert 1917-1984 45-48
Obituary 113
Cochran, Bobbye A. 1949- .... SATA 11
Cochran, Charles L(eo) 1940- 57-60
Cochran, Clarke E(dward) 1945- 107
Cochran, Elizabeth
See Cochrane, Elizabeth
Cochran, Hamilton 1898-1977 .... CANR-6
Obituary 73-76
Earlier sketch in CA 1-4R
Cochran, Jacqueline 1910(?)-1980 Obituary ... 101
Cochran, Jeff
See Durst, Paul
Cochran, John A(rthur) 1921- 122
Cochran, John R(obert) 1937- 41-44R
Cochran, Leslie H(ershel) 1939- CANR-2
Earlier sketch in CA 49-52
Cochran, Molly 156
Cochran, Rice E.
See Monroe, Keith
Cochran, Robert B(rady) 1943- 141
Cochran, Thomas C(hilds) 1902- CANR-8
Earlier sketch in CA 61-64
See also DLB 17
Cochrane, A(rchibald) L(eman)
1909(?)-1988 Obituary 125
Cochrane, Arthur C(aspersz) 1909- CANR-4
Earlier sketch in CA 5-8R
Cochrane, Elizabeth 1864-1922 Brief entry 118
See also DLB 25, 189
Cochrane, Eric W. 1928-1985 .... CANR-28
Obituary 118
Earlier sketch in CA 49-52
Cochrane, Glynn 1940- 53-56
Cochrane, Hugh (Ferrier) 1923- 103
Cochrane, James D(avid) 1938- 29-32R
Cochrane, James L. 1941- CANR-13
Earlier sketch in CA 33-36R
Cochrane, Jennifer (Ann Frances) 1936- 102
Cochrane, Louise Morley 1918- 9-12R
Cochrane, Pauline A(therton) 1929- 110
Cochrane, Willard W(esley) 1914- CANR-11
Earlier sketch in CA 21-24R
Cochrane, William E. 1926- 97-100
Cochrane de Alencar, Gertrude E. L. 1906- 5-8R
Cochran-Smith, Marilyn 1951- 115
Coch-y-Bonddhu
See Arnold, Richard
Cockburn, Alexander 1941- 144
Brief entry 123
Cockburn, (Francis) Claud 1904-1981 102
Obituary 105
Cockburn, Patricia (Evangeline Anne)
1914-1989 144
Cockburn, Thomas Aiden 1912- 9-12R
Cockcroft, George Powers 1932- 116
Cockcroft, James D(onald) 1935- CANR-65
Earlier sketches in CA 25-28R, CANR-10, 25
Cockcroft, John (Douglas) 1897-1967 .... CAP-2
Earlier sketch in CA 21-22
Cockerell, H(ugh) A(nthony) L(ewis) 1909- .. CAP-1
Earlier sketch in CA 13-14
Cockerell, SirSydney 1867-1962 .... DLB 201
Cockerell, Sydney M(orris) 1906-1987 Obituary 124
Cockerill, A(rthur) W(illiam) 1929- 131
Cockerill, John A. 1845-1896 .... DLB 23
Cockett, Mary CANR-19
Earlier sketches in CA 9-12R, CANR-4
See also SATA 3
Cockfield, Jamie (Hartwell) 1945- 115
Cocking, Clive 1938- 105
Cocking, J(ohn) M(artin) 1914- 53-56
Cockrell, Amanda
See Crowe, Amanda Cockrell
Cockrell, Marian (Brown) 1909- CAP-2
Earlier sketch in CA 17-18
Cockrell, Thomas D(errell) 1949- 154
Cocks, Geoffrey (Campbell) 1948- CANR-47
Earlier sketch in CA 121
Cockshut, A(nthony) O(liver) J(ohn) 1927- ....
CANR-10
Earlier sketch in CA 17-20R
Coco, James (Emil) 1930(?)-1987 Obituary 121
Cocozzella, Peter 1937- 37-40R
Cocozzoli, Gary R(ichard) 1951- 119
Cocquyt, Kathryn Marie 1960- 147
Cocteau, Jean (Maurice Eugene Clement)
1889-1963 .... CANR-40
Earlier sketches in CAP-2, CA 25-28
See also CLC 1, 8, 15, 16, 43
See also DA
See also DAB
See also DAC
See also DAM DRAM, MST, NOV
See also DLB 65
See also MTCW 1
See also WLC
Codd, Carson
See Sommers, Robert (Thomas)
Codding, George A(rthur), Jr. 1923- CANR-13
Earlier sketch in CA 33-36R
Code, Grant Hyde 1896-1974 49-52
Codel, Martin 1903(?)-1973 Obituary 41-44R
Codel, Michael R(ichard) 1939- 73-76
Coder, S(amuel) Maxwell 1902-1997 .... CANR-14
Obituary 159
Earlier sketch in CA 37-40R
Codere, Helen (Frances) 1917- 69-72
Coderre, Emile 1893-1970 148
See also Narrache, Jean
Codevilla, (Maria) Angelo 1943- 61-64
Codrescu, Andrei 1946- CANR-53
Earlier sketches in CA 33-36R, CANR-13, 34
See also CAAS 19
See also CLC 46
See also DAM POET
Codrington, Kenneth de Burgh
1899-1986 Obituary 118
Cody, Al
See Joscelyn, Archie L.
Cody, C. S.
See Waller, Leslie
Cody, D(ouglas) Thane R(omney) 1932- 57-60
Cody, Fred 1916- 107
Cody, James P.
See Rohrbach, Peter Thomas
Cody, Jess
See Cunningham, Chet
Cody, John 1925- 101
Cody, John J. 1930- 29-32R
Cody, Liza 1944- CANR-71
Brief entry 125
Earlier sketch in CA 129
Cody, Martin L(eonard) 1941- 53-56
Cody, Morrill 1901-1987 125
Obituary 161
Cody, Paul 1953- 153
Cody, Robin 1943- 153
Cody, Walt
See Norwood, Victor G(eorge) C(harles)
Coe, Anne (E.) 1949- .... SATA 95
Coe, Charles Norton 1915- 1-4R
Coe, Christine Sadler
See Sadler, Christine
Coe, Douglas
See Epstein, Beryl (M. Williams)
and Epstein, Samuel
Coe, Fred(erick) 1914-1979 Obituary 85-88
Coe, Jonathan 1961- 133
Coe, Lewis 1911- 154
Coe, Lloyd 1899(?)-1976 Obituary 69-72
See also SATA-Obit 30
Coe, Malcolm (James) 1930- 123
Coe, Max
See Bourne, Randolph S(illiman)
Coe, Michael Douglas 1929- CANR-41
Earlier sketches in CA 1-4R, CANR-4, 19
Coe, Michelle E(ileen) 1917- 106
Coe, Peter 1929-1987 Obituary 122
Coe, Ralph T(racy) 1929- CANR-1
Earlier sketch in CA 1-4R
Coe, Richard L(ivingston) 1916- 65-68
Coe, Richard N(elson) 1923- CANR-12
Earlier sketch in CA 25-28R
Coe, Rodney Michael 1933- 41-44R
Coe, Sue 1951- 151
Coe, Tucker
See Westlake, Donald E(dwin)
Coe, William C(harles) 1930- 37-40R
Coel, Margaret 1937- CANR-72
Earlier sketches in CA 106, CANR-39
Coelho, George Victor 1918- CANR-1
Earlier sketch in CA 45-48
Coelho, Paulo 152
Coello, Dennis (L.) 129
Coen, Ethan 1958- 126
See also CLC 108
Coen, Joel 1955- 126
See also CLC 108
Coen, Rena Neumann 1925- 13-16R
See also SATA 20COEN
The Coen Brothers
See Coen, Ethan
and Coen, Joel
Coens, Sister Mary Xavier 1918- 21-24R
Coerr, Eleanor (Beatrice) 1922- CANR-11
Earlier sketch in CA 25-28R
See also MAICYA
See also SATA 1, 67
Coers, Donald V. 1941- 139
Coetzee, J(ohn) M(ichael) 1940- CANR-54
Earlier sketches in CA 77-80, CANR-41
See also CLC 23, 33, 66
See also DAM NOV
See also MTCW 1
Cofacci, Gino P. 1914(?)-1989 Obituary 128
Cofer, Charles N(orval) 1916- 37-40R
Cofer, Judith Ortiz 1952- CANR-72
Earlier sketches in CA 115, CANR-32
See also HW
Coffe, M.
See Gourmont, Remy (-Marie-Charles) de
Coffee, Lenore J. 1897(?)-1984 Obituary 113
See also DLB 44
Coffey, Alan R. 1931- 33-36R
Coffey, Brian
See Koontz, Dean R(ay)
Coffey, (Helen) Dairine 1933- 21-24R
Coffey, Daniel 1950- 131
Coffey, Frank 136
Coffey, J(oseph) I(rving) 1916- 41-44R
Coffey, John W(ill), Jr. 1925- 45-48
Coffey, Marilyn 1937- CANR-2
Earlier sketch in CA 45-48
Coffey, Michael 1926- 139
Coffey, Rebecca 166
Coffey, Robert E(dward) 1931- 65-68
Coffey, Thomas Patrick 1928- 120
Coffin, Arthur B. 1929- 29-32R
Coffin, Berton 1910- CANR-5
Earlier sketch in CA 9-12R
Coffin, David R(obbins) 1918- 5-8R
Coffin, Dean (Fiske) 1911-1992 .... 33-36R
Obituary 139
Coffin, Frank M(orey) 1919- 9-12R
Coffin, Geoffrey
See Mason, F(rancis) van Wyck
Coffin, George S(turgis) 1903- 5-8R
Coffin, Harold 1905(?)-1981 Obituary 104
Coffin, Harold Glen 1926- 115
Coffin, Joseph (John) 1899- 57-60
Coffin, Lewis A(ugustus) III 1932- 61-64
Coffin, Lyn 1943- 110
Coffin, Patricia 1912-1974 .... CAP-2
Obituary 49-52
Earlier sketch in CA 33-36
Coffin, Robert P(eter) Tristram 1892-1955 Brief
entry 123
See also DLB 45
Coffin, Tristram 1912-1997 .... 21-24R
Obituary 158
Coffin, Tristram Potter 1922- CANR-2
Earlier sketch in CA 5-8R
Coffin, William Sloane, Jr. 1924- 103
Coffinet, Julien 1907- 61-64
Coffman, Barbara Frances 1907- CAP-1
Earlier sketch in CA 13-16
Coffman, Charles DeWitt 1909- 102
Coffman, Edward M. 1929- 33-36R
Coffman, Paul B(rown) 1900- CAP-2
Earlier sketch in CA 21-22
Coffman, Ramon Peyton 1896-1989 .... CAP-2
Obituary 161
Earlier sketch in CA 17-18
See also SATA 4
Coffman, Virginia (Edith) 1914- CANR-2
Earlier sketch in CA 49-52
Cofyn, Cornelius
See Saunders, Hilary Aidan St. George
Cogan, Mike
See Lottman, Eileen
Cogane, Gerald
See Fonarow, Jerry
Coger, Leslie Irene 1912- 21-24R
Coggan, (Frederick) Donald 1909- 17-20R
Coggin, Philip A(nnett) 1917- 117
Coggins, Jack (Banham) 1914- CANR-2
Earlier sketch in CA 5-8R
See also SATA 2
Coggins, Paul E. 1951- 126
Coggins, Ross 1927- 13-16R
Coghill, Nevill (Henry Kendall Aylmer) 1899-1980 ..
CANR-11
Obituary 102
Earlier sketch in CA 13-16R
Coghlan, Brian (Laurence Dillon) 1926- 17-20R
Coghlan, Margaret M. 1920- 106
Cogley, John 1916-1976 .... CANR-2
Obituary 65-68
Earlier sketch in CA 45-48
Cogswell, Coralie (Norris) 1930- 13-16R
Cogswell, Fred(erick William) 1917- CANR-43
Earlier sketches in CA 5-8R, CANR-3, 18
See also DLB 60
Cogswell, James A(rthur) 1922- 33-36R
Cogswell, Mason Fitch 1761-1830 .... DLB 37
Cogswell, Theodore R(ose) 1918-1987 ... CANR-4
Obituary 161
Earlier sketch in CA 1-4R
Cohan, Avery B(erlow) 1914-1977 61-64
Obituary 69-72
Cohan, George M(ichael) 1878-1942 157
See also TCLC 60
Cohan, Tony 1939- 108
Cohane, John Philip 1911- 101
Cohane, Tim(othy Sylvester) 1912-1989 ..... 9-12R
Obituary 161
Cohart, Mary 1911- 57-60
Cohen, Aaron (Samuel) 1935- 110
Cohen, Aharon 1910- 69-72
Cohen, Albert 1895(?)-1981 Obituary 105
Cohen, Albert J. 1903(?)-1984 Obituary 114
Cohen, Albert Kircidel 1918- 13-16R
Cohen, Allan R(ay) 1938- 148
Cohen, Allan Y. 1939- 33-36R
Cohen, Allen 1940- 139

Cohen, Alvin 1931- ... 145
Cohen, Amnon 1936- ... 85-88
Cohen, Andrew (Z.) 1955- ... 135
Cohen, Anne Billings 1937- ... 57-60
Cohen, Anthea 1913- ... CANR-40
Earlier sketches in CA 97-100, CANR-18
Cohen, Arthur A(llen) 1928-1986 ... CANR-42
Obituary ... 120
Earlier sketches in CA 1-4R, CANR-1, 17
See also CLC 7, 31
See also DLB 28
Cohen, Arthur M. 1927- ... 33-36R
Cohen, B(enjamin) Bernard 1922- ... 9-12R
Cohen, Barbara 1932-1992 ... CANR-19
Obituary ... 140
Earlier sketches in CA 53-56, CANR-4
See also AAYA 24
See also JRDA
See also SAAS 7
See also SATA 10, 77
See also SATA-Obit 74
Cohen, Bella
See Spewack, Bella
Cohen, Benjamin J(erry) 1937- ... CANR-18
Earlier sketch in CA 101
Cohen, Benjamin Victor 1894-1983 ... CAP-1
Obituary ... 110
Earlier sketch in CA 11-12
Cohen, Bernard 1937- ... 103
Cohen, Bernard 1956- ... 166
Cohen, Bernard 1963- ... 167
Cohen, Bernard Lande 1902- ... 29-32R
Cohen, Bernard P. 1930- ... 45-48
Cohen, Brenda
See Almond, Brenda
Cohen, Bruce J. 1938- ... 89-92
Cohen, Carl 1931- ... CANR-5
Earlier sketch in CA 1-4R
Cohen, Charles 1943- ... 111
Cohen, Daniel (E.) 1936- ... CANR-44
Earlier sketches in CA 45-48, CANR-1, 20
See also AAYA 7
See also CLR 3, 43
See also JRDA
See also MAICYA
See also SAAS 4
See also SATA 8, 70
Cohen, Daniel A. 1957- ... 144
Cohen, David 1946- ... 129
Cohen, David 1952- ... 108
Cohen, David Steven 1943- ... 53-56
Cohen, Donald J. 1940- ... 145
Cohen, Donna 1947- ... 122
Cohen, Dorothy H. 1915- Brief entry ... 105
Cohen, Edgar H. 1913- ... 29-32R
Cohen, Edmund D(avid) 1943- ... 57-60
Cohen, Edward H. 1941- Brief entry ... 115
Cohen, Edward M(artin) 1936- ... 21-24R
Cohen, Elaine (Marsha Perlman) 1938- ... 110
Cohen, Elie Aron 1909- ... 53-56
Cohen, Eliot A(sher) 1956- ... 113
Cohen, Elliot D. 1951- ... 138
Cohen, Florence Chanock 1927- ... 5-8R
Cohen, Gary B(ennett) 1948- ... 107
Cohen, Gary G. 1934- ... CANR-7
Earlier sketch in CA 57-60
Cohen, George Michael 1931- ... 81-84
Cohen, Harry 1936- ... 106
Cohen, (Henry) Hennig 1919- ... CANR-5
Earlier sketch in CA 1-4R
Cohen, Henry 1933- ... 33-36R
Cohen, Hiyaguha (Rachelle) 1951- ... 152
Cohen, Howard Martin 1926- Brief entry ... 107
Cohen, hubert I. 1930- ... 155
Cohen, I. Bernard 1914- ... CANR-56
Earlier sketch in CA 69-72
Cohen, Ira Sheldon 1924- ... CANR-10
Earlier sketch in CA 5-8R
Cohen, J. M.
See Cohen, John Michael
Cohen, Jack S(idney) 1938- ... 130
Cohen, Jacob 1918- ... 123
Cohen, James (E.) 1956- ... 137
Cohen, Jane R(abb) 1938- ... 130
Cohen, Janet 1940- ... CANR-55
Earlier sketch in CA 126
Cohen, Jason 1967- ... 152
Cohen, Jean Louise 1946- ... 111
Cohen, Jeffrey A. 1952- ... 141
Cohen, Jene Barr 1900-1985 ... CANR-42
Obituary ... 115
See also Barr, Jene
Cohen, Jeremy 1953- ... 130
Cohen, Jerome Alan 1930- ... CANR-30
Earlier sketches in CA 49-52, CANR-13
Cohen, Jerome B(ernard) 1915-1986 ... 9-12R
Obituary ... 121
Cohen, Joan Lebold 1932- ... CANR-30
Earlier sketches in CA 25-28R, CANR-13
See also SATA 4
Cohen, John 1911- ... CANR-6
Earlier sketch in CA 13-16R
Cohen, John Michael 1903-1989 ... CANR-4
Obituary ... 129
Earlier sketch in CA 5-8R
Cohen, Joseph 1926- ... CANR-10
Earlier sketch in CA 65-68
Cohen, Jozef (B.) 1921-1995 ... 29-32R
Obituary ... 161
Cohen, Judith Beth 1943- ... 118
Cohen, Judith Love 1933- ... 146
See also SATA 78
Cohen, Kalman J(oseph) 1931- ... 13-16R
Cohen, Karl F. 1940- ... 167
Cohen, Kathleen Rogers 1933- ... 53-56
Cohen, Keith 1945- ... 101
Cohen, Larry 1945- ... 142
Cohen, Lawrence Jonathan 1923- ... 65-68
Cohen, Leonard (Norman) 1934- ... CANR-69
Earlier sketches in CA 21-24R, CANR-14
See also CLC 3, 38
See also DAC
See also DAM MST
See also DLB 53
See also MTCW 1
Cohen, Marcel 1937- ... 153
Cohen, Margie K(anter) 1912- ... 109
Cohen, Mark Nathan 1943- ... 135
Cohen, (Stephen) Marshall 1929- ... CANR-23
Earlier sketches in CA 45-48, CANR-2
Cohen, Martin A(aron) 1928- Brief entry ... 113
Cohen, Marvin 1931- ... CANR-17
Earlier sketch in CA 25-28R
Cohen, Matt 1942- ... CANR-40
Earlier sketch in CA 61-64
See also CAAS 18
See also CLC 19
See also DAC
See also DLB 53
Cohen, Michael J. 1940- ... CANR-65
Earlier sketch in CA 129
Cohen, Michael P. 1944- ... CANR-47
Earlier sketch in CA 121
Cohen, Mike
See Cohen, Morris
Cohen, Miriam 1926- ... 106
See also SAAS 11
See also SATA 29
Cohen, Morris 1912- ... 17-20R
Cohen, Morris L(eo) 1927- ... CANR-53
Earlier sketches in CA 49-52, CANR-29
Cohen, Mortimer J. 1894-1972 Obituary ... 104
Cohen, Morton N(orton) 1921- ... CANR-56
Earlier sketches in CA 1-4R, CANR-5, 28
Cohen, Myron 1903(?)-1986 Obituary ... 118
Cohen, Nancy Wainer 1947- ... 111
Cohen, Naomi W(iener) 1927- Brief entry ... 114
Cohen, Nora ... SATA 75
Cohen, Norm(an) 1936- ... 109
Cohen, Octavus Roy 1891-1959 Brief entry ... 112
Cohen, Paul Andrew 1934- ... 115
Cohen, Paul S. 1945- ... 123
See also SATA 58
Cohen, Peter Zachary 1931- ... CANR-12
Earlier sketch in CA 33-36R
See also SATA 4
Cohen, Philip G(ary) 1954- ... 136
Cohen, Ralph 1917- ... 138
Cohen, Richard 1952- ... 140
Cohen, Richard M(artin) 1941- ... 146
Cohen, Richard Murry 1938- ... CANR-19
Earlier sketch in CA 103
Cohen, Robert 1938- ... CANR-34
Earlier sketches in CA 29-32R, CANR-12
Cohen, Robert 1957- ... 158
Cohen, Robert Carl 1930- ... 57-60
See also SATA 8
Cohen, Roberta G. 1937- ... 49-52
Cohen, Robin 1944- ... 134
Cohen, Ronald 1930- ... CANR-29
Earlier sketches in CA 33-36R, CANR-13
Cohen, Ronald Dennis 1940- ... 105
Cohen, Ronald Jay 1949- ... 97-100
Cohen, Rosalyn
See Higgins, Rosalyn (Cohen)
Cohen, S. Alan 1933- ... 29-32R
Cohen, S. Ralph 1917-1983 Obituary ... 110
Cohen, Sanford 1920- ... 1-4R
Cohen, Sara Kay Sherman 1943- ... 102
Cohen, Sarah Blacher 1936- ... 81-84
Cohen, Saul Bernard 1925- ... 130
Cohen, Scott 1946- ... 116
Cohen, Selma Jeanne 1920- ... 25-28R
Cohen, Seymour Jay 1922- ... 25-28R
Cohen, Sharleen Cooper ... CANR-41
Earlier sketches in CA 97-100, CANR-19
Cohen, Sheldon S. 1931- ... 25-28R
Cohen, Sherry Suib 1934- ... 102
Cohen, Sholom 1951- ... 159
See also SATA 94
Cohen, Sidney 1910-1987 ... 13-16R
Obituary ... 122
Cohen, Stanley 1928- ... CANR-34
Earlier sketches in CA 29-32R, CANR-15
Cohen, Stephen 1941- ... 118
Cohen, Stephen D(avid) 1942- ... 111
Cohen, Stephen F(rand) 1938- ... CANR-35
Earlier sketch in CA 49-52
Cohen, Stephen S. 1941- ... 33-36R
Cohen, Stephen Z(olman) 1931- ... 121
Cohen, Steve (Michael) 1951- ... 114
Cohen, Steven (A.) 1953- ... 142
Cohen, Stewart 1940- ... 65-68
Cohen, Susan (Lois) 1938- ... CANR-44
Earlier sketches in CA 53-56, CANR-5, 20
Cohen, Warren I. 1934- ... CANR-9
Earlier sketch in CA 21-24R
Cohen, Wilbur J(oseph) 1913-1987 ... CANR-17
Obituary ... 122
Earlier sketch in CA 25-28R
Cohen, William A(lan) 1937- ... CANR-42
Earlier sketches in CA 103, CANR-19
Cohen, William B(enjamin) 1941- ... 37-40R
Cohen, William Howard 1927- ... 17-20R
Cohen, William S(ebastian) 1940- ... CANR-27
Earlier sketch in CA 108
Cohen, Yehudi A(ryeh) 1928- ... 13-16R
Cohen, Youssef 1947- ... 151
Cohen-Solal, Annie 19(?)- ... CLC 50
Cohen-Stratyner, Barbara Naomi 1951- ... 113
Cohler, Anne M(eyers) 1940(?)-1989 Obituary ... 130
Cohler, Bertram J(oseph) 1938- ... 109
Cohler, David Keith 1940- ... 104
Cohn, Adrian A. 1922- ... 25-28R
Cohn, Alan M(artin) 1926-1989 ... 110
Obituary ... 129
Cohn, Angelo 1914- ... CANR-4
Earlier sketch in CA 5-8R
See also SATA 19
Cohn, Arthur 1910-1998 ... 110
Obituary ... 164
Cohn, Dorrit 1924- ... 93-96
Cohn, Elchanan 1941- ... 73-76
Cohn, Haim H(erman) 1911- ... 45-48
Cohn, Helen Desfosses
See Desfosses, Helen
Cohn, Henry S. 1945- ... 141
Cohn, Jan Kadetsky 1933- ... 102
Cohn, Jules 1930- ... 33-36R
Cohn, Keith E(van) 1935- ... 107
Cohn, Lester
See Cole, Lester
Cohn, Marguerite A. 1898(?)-1984 Obituary ... 113
Cohn, Marvin L(ester) 1924-1990 ... 105
Obituary ... 131
Cohn, Nik 1946- ... 102
Cohn, Norman 1915- ... 57-60
Cohn, Robert Greer 1921- ... 9-12R
Cohn, Roy M(arcus) 1927-1986 ... CANR-29
Obituary ... 119
Earlier sketch in CA 108
Cohn, Rubin (Goodman) 1911-1986 ... 57-60
Obituary ... 119
Cohn, Ruby 1922- ... CANR-32
Earlier sketch in CA 93-96
Cohn, Samuel Kline, Jr. 1949- ... CANR-52
Earlier sketch in CA 125
Cohn, Stanley H(arold) 1922- ... 29-32R
Cohn, Theodore 1923- ... 89-92
Cohn, Vera 1907- ... 97-100
Cohn, Victor (Edward) 1919- ... 65-68
Cohn-Sherbok, Dan 1945- ... 137
Cohon, Barry
See Cohon, Baruch J(oseph)
Cohon, Baruch J(oseph) 1926- ... 29-32R
Cohon, Beryl David 1898- ... CANR-6
Earlier sketch in CA 1-4R
Coigney, Virginia 1917- ... 103
Coit, John Hamilton 1947(?)-1986 Obituary ... 118
Coit, Lew Garrison 1897(?)-1985 Obituary ... 116
Coit, Margaret Louise 1919- ... CANR-5
Earlier sketch in CA 1-4R
See also SATA 2
Cojeen, Robert H. 1920- ... 37-40R
Coke, Tom S(tephen) 1943- ... 115
Coke, Van Deren 1921- ... CANR-22
Earlier sketches in CA 13-16R, CANR-7
Coker, C(harles) F(rederick) W(illiams) 1932-1983 Obituary ... 110
Coker, Carolyn ... 125
Coker, Christopher ... 158
Coker, Elizabeth Boatwright 1909-1993 ... 45-48
Obituary ... 142
Coker, Gylbert 1944- ... 93-96
Coker, Jerry 1932- ... CANR-6
Earlier sketch in CA 9-12R
Coker, Syl Cheney
See Cheney-Coker, Syl
Colacci, Mario 1910-1968 ... 5-8R
Obituary ... 135
Colacello, Bob 1947- ... 138
Coladarci, Arthur Paul 1917-1991 ... 5-8R
Obituary ... 161
Colaiaco, James A(lfred) 1945- ... 115
Colander, Pat(ricia) 1952- ... 110
Colaneri, John Nunzio 1930- ... 103
Colaw, Emerson S. 1921- ... 13-16R
Colbach, Edward M(ichael) 1939- ... 69-72
Colbeck, Maurice 1925- ... CANR-34
Earlier sketches in CA 13-16R, CANR-5
Colbeck, Norman 1903-1987 ... DLB 201
Colberg, Marshall R(udolph) 1913- ... CANR-1
Earlier sketch in CA 1-4R
Colbert, Anthony 1934- ... 89-92
See also SATA 15
Colbert, Douglas A(lbert) 1933- ... 57-60
Colbert, Edwin Harris 1905- ... CANR-8
Earlier sketch in CA 61-64
Colbert, Evelyn S(peyer) 1918- ... 102
Colbert, James 1951- ... CANR-54
Earlier sketch in CA 122
Colbert, Roman 1921- ... 53-56
Colborn, Nigel 1944- ... 128
Colbourn, H(arold) Trevor 1927- ... 33-36R
Colburn, C(lyde) William 1939- ... 37-40R
Colburn, David Richard 1942- ... 110
Colburn, George A(bbott) 1938- ... 41-44R
Colby, Averil 1900-1983(?) Obituary ... 108
Colby, Benjamin N(ick) 1931- ... 61-64
Colby, C(arroll) B(urleigh) 1904-1977 ... CANR-6
Earlier sketch in CA 1-4R
See also SATA 3, 35
Colby, Douglas (Steven) 1954- ... 116
Colby, Elbridge 1891-1982 ... CAP-1
Obituary ... 108
Earlier sketch in CA 13-16
Colby, Jean Poindexter 1909- ... CANR-5
Earlier sketch in CA 1-4R
See also SATA 23
Colby, Joan 1939- ... CANR-13
Earlier sketch in CA 77-80
Colby, Robert A(lan) 1920- ... 53-56
Colby, Roy (Edward) 1910- ... 25-28R
Colby, Vineta (Blumoff) 1922- ... 9-12R
Colby, William Egan 1920-1996 ... 81-84
Obituary ... 151
Colchie, Elizabeth Schneider
See Schneider, Elizabeth (Susan)
Colden, Cadwallader 1688-1776 ... DLB 24, 30
Colden, Jane 1724-1766 ... DLB 200
Coldham, James D(esmond Bowden) 1924-1987 ... 113
Obituary ... 121
Coldrey, Jennifer (M.) 1940- ... 121
Coldsmith, Don(ald Charles) 1926- ... CANR-50
Earlier sketches in CA 105, CANR-21
Coldwell, David F(rederick) C(larke) 1923-1973 ... 17-20R
Obituary ... 134
Coldwell, Joan 1936- ... 106
Coldwell, M(ichael) J. 1888-1974 Obituary ... 53-56
Cole, Adrian 1949- ... CANR-59
Earlier sketch in CA 121
Cole, Allan 1943- ... 150
Cole, Allison
See Coker, Carolyn
Cole, Andrew Thomas, Jr. 1933- ... 102
Cole, Ann 1937- ... 65-68
Cole, Ann Kilborn
See Callahan, Claire Wallis
Cole, Annette
See Steiner, Barbara A(nnette)
Cole, Arthur C(harles) 1886-1976 Obituary ... 65-68
Cole, Babette 1949- ... 161
See also SATA 61, 96
Cole, Barry 1936- ... CANR-68
Earlier sketches in CA 25-28R, CANR-16
See also DLB 14
Cole, Betsy 1940- ... 150
See also SATA 83
Cole, Bill
See Cole, William Shadrack
Cole, Brock 1938- ... 136
See also AAYA 15
See also CLR 18
See also JRDA
See also MAICYA
See also SATA 72
Cole, Bruce 1938- ... CANR-15
Earlier sketch in CA 65-68
Cole, Burt 1930- ... 73-76
Cole, C. Donald 1923- ... 125
Cole, C(harles) Robert 1939- ... 65-68
Cole, Cannon
See Cook, Arlene Ethel
Cole, Charles C(hester), Jr. 1922- ... 118
Cole, Charles L(eland) 1927- ... 69-72
Cole, Charles Woolsey 1906-1978 ... CANR-22
Obituary ... 77-80
Earlier sketch in CA 69-72
Cole, Clifford A. 1915- ... 13-16R
Cole, Cozy
See Cole, William R.
Cole, Dandridge MacFarlan 1921- ... 13-16R
Cole, David C(hamberlin) 1928- ... 127
Brief entry ... 106
Cole, Davis
See Elting, Mary
Cole, Davis
See Elting, Mary
Cole, Diane 1952- ... 138
Cole, Donald Barnard 1922- ... 5-8R
Cole, Doris 1938- ... 89-92
Cole, Douglas 1934- ... CANR-2
Earlier sketch in CA 5-8R
Cole, E(ugene) R(oger) 1930- ... CANR-31
Earlier sketches in CA 53-56, CANR-4, 19
Cole, Eddie-Lou 1909- ... 65-68
Cole, Edward B(ender) 1923- ... 107
Cole, Edward C(yrus) 1904- ... 13-16R
Cole, Frank R(aymond) 1892- ... 69-72
Cole, G(eorge) D(ouglas) H(oward) 1889-1959 Brief entry ... 108
Cole, George F(raser) 1935- ... 65-68
Cole, George Watson 1850-1939 ... DLB 140
Cole, Gordon
See Cole, Gordon H(enry)
Cole, Gordon H(enry) 1912-1988 Obituary ... 125
Cole, H. S. D.
See Cole, (Hugh) Sam(uel David)
Cole, Hank
See Fearn, John Russell
Cole, Hannah 1954- ... SATA 74
Cole, (Roger) Henri 1956- ... 121
Cole, Howard C(handler) 1934- ... 49-52
Cole, Hubert (Archibald Noel) 1908- ... CANR-5
Earlier sketch in CA 5-8R
Cole, J(ohn) A(lfred) 1905- ... CAP-1
Earlier sketch in CA 13-16
Cole, J. P.
See Cole, John P(eter)
Cole, Jack
See Stewart, John (William)
Cole, Jackson
See Germano, Peter B.
and Schisgall, Oscar
Cole, Janet
See Hunter, Kim
Cole, Jean Hascall 1922- ... 139
Cole, Jennifer
See Zach, Cheryl (Byrd)
Cole, Joan 1957- ... 113
Cole, Joanna 1944- ... CANR-70
Earlier sketches in CA 115, CANR-36, 55
See also CLR 5, 40
See also MAICYA
See also SATA 49, 81
See also SATA-Brief 37
Cole, John N(elson) 1923- ... 93-96
Cole, John P(eter) 1928- ... CANR-41
Earlier sketches in CA 5-8R, CANR-3, 19
Cole, John Y(oung), Jr. 1940- ... CANR-41
Earlier sketches in CA 103, CANR-19
Cole, Johnnetta B(etsch) 1936- ... 157

Cole, Jonathan R(ichard) 1942- 53-56
Cole, Juan R(icardo) I(rfan) 1952- 121
Cole, K. C. 1946- 105
Cole, Kay
See Colominas, Kathleen Adele
Cole, (Edmund) Keith 1919- CANR-19
Earlier sketch in CA 102
Cole, Larry 1936- 45-48
Cole, Leonard A(aron) 1933- 81-84
Cole, Leonard Leslie 1909-1980 103
Cole, Lester 1904(?)-1985 Obituary 117
Cole, Lewis 1946- 109
Cole, Lois Dwight 1903-1979 .... CANR-4
Obituary 104
Earlier sketch in CA 1-4R
See also SATA 10
See also SATA-Obit 26
Cole, Luella (Winifred) 1893-(?) CAP-1
Earlier sketch in CA 19-20
Cole, Margaret Alice CANR-6
Earlier sketch in CA 9-12R
Cole, Margaret Isabel 1893-1980 .... CANR-4
Obituary 97-100
Earlier sketch in CA 5-8R
Cole, Martha 1916(?)-1986 Obituary 118
Cole, Mary
See Hanna, Mary T.
Cole, Michael 1938- 97-100
Cole, Michael 1947- .... SATA 59
Cole, Michelle 1940- 29-32R
Cole, Monica M(ary) 1922-1994 .... 1-4R
Obituary 144
Cole, Richard Cargill 1926- CANR-51
Earlier sketch in CA 124
Cole, Robert 1939- 146
Cole, Robert E(van) 1937- 69-72
Cole, Robert H. 1918- 33-36R
Cole, Robert J(ason) 1925- 133
Cole, Roger L. 1933- 25-28R
Cole, (Hugh) Sam(uel David) 1943- 130
Cole, Sandi Gelles
See Gelles-Cole, Sandi
Cole, Sheila R(otenberg) 1939- CANR-68
Earlier sketches in CA 53-56, CANR-4
See also SATA 24, 95
Cole, Sonia (Mary) 1918-1982 93-96
Obituary 106
Cole, Stephen
See Webbe, Gale D(udley)
Cole, Stephen 1941- 29-32R
Cole, Susan Letzler 1940- 168
Cole, Sylvan, Jr. 1918- 69-72
Cole, Terrence (Michael) 1953- 135
Cole, (Andrew) Thomas (Jr.) 1933- 33-36R
Cole, Thomas R(ichard) 1949- 141
Cole, Toby 1916- 153
Cole, Tom
See Cole, Thomas R(ichard)
Cole, W(illiam) Owen 1931- CANR-43
Earlier sketch in CA 118
Cole, Wayne S. 1922- 21-24R
Cole, Wendell 1914- 21-24R
Cole, William (Rossa) 1919- CANR-47
Earlier sketches in CA 9-12R, CANR-7
See also MAICYA
See also SAAS 9
See also SATA 9, 71
Cole, William Earle 1904-1979 .... 17-20R
Obituary 126
Cole, William Graham 1917- 17-20R
Cole, William R. 1909-1981 Obituary 108
Cole, William Shadrack 1937- 101
Colean, Miles Lanier 1898-1980 .... CAP-2
Obituary 161
Earlier sketch in CA 21-22
Coleburt, J(ames) Russell 1920- 13-16R
Colecchia, Francesca Maria 89-92
Colegate, Isabel 1931- CANR-22
Earlier sketches in CA 17-20R, CANR-8
Interview in CANR-22
See also CLC 36
See also DLB 14
See also MTCW 1
Colegrove, Kenneth 1886-1975 .... CANR-4
Obituary 53-56
Earlier sketch in CA 5-8R
Coleman, A(llan) D(ouglass) 1943- CANR-15
Earlier sketch in CA 73-76
Coleman, Almand R(ouse) 1905-1996 ...... CAP-2
Obituary 161
Earlier sketch in CA 29-32
Coleman, Andrew
See Pine, Nicholas
Coleman, Arthur 1924- 81-84
Coleman, Bernard D(avid) 1919- 25-28R
Coleman, Bill
See Coleman, William V(incent)
Coleman, Bob
See Coleman, Robert David
Coleman, Bruce P(umphrey) 1931- 37-40R
Coleman, Buck
See Richardson, Gladwell
Coleman, Clare
See Bell, Clare (Louise)
Coleman, Clayton W(ebster) 1901- 29-32R
Coleman, D(onald) C(uthbert) 1920- 13-16R
Coleman, David (Firth) 1945- 153
Coleman, Dorothy Gabe 1935-1992 ..... CANR-46
Obituary 139
Earlier sketch in CA 93-96
Coleman, Elliott 1906-1980 .... 17-20R
Obituary 97-100
Coleman, Emily Holmes 1899-1974 105
See also DLB 4
Coleman, Emily R. 1947- 135
Coleman, Emmett
See Reed, Ishmael
Coleman, Evelyn Scherabon
See Firchow, Evelyn Scherabon
Coleman, Felicia Slatkin
1916(?)-1981 Obituary 102
Coleman, Francis Xavier Jerome 1939- 108
Coleman, J(ohn) Winston, Jr. 1898-1983 . CANR-27
Earlier sketch in CA 49-52
Coleman, James A(ndrew) 1921- 5-8R
Coleman, James C(ovington) 1914- CANR-1
Earlier sketch in CA 1-4R
Coleman, James S(amuel) 1926- 13-16R
Coleman, James Smoot 1919- 1-4R
Coleman, Jane Candia 1939- 136
Coleman, John R(oyston) 1921- CANR-1
Earlier sketch in CA 1-4R
See also AITN 1
Coleman, Jonathan 1951(?)- Brief entry 129
Coleman, Jonathan (Mark) 1951- CANR-70
Earlier sketch in CA 138
Interview in 138
Coleman, Kenneth 1916- CANR-33
Earlier sketches in CA 21-24R, CANR-8
Coleman, Lee
See Lapidus, Elaine
Coleman, Lonnie
See Coleman, William Laurence
Coleman, Loren (Elwood, Jr.) 1947- 133
Coleman, Lucile 73-76
Coleman, Marion (Reeves) Moore 1900- . CANR-11
Earlier sketch in CA 17-20R
Coleman, Mary Ann 1928- 150
See also SATA 83
Coleman, Mary DeLorse 1954- 143
Coleman, Michael C(hristopher) 1946- ... CANR-43
Earlier sketch in CA 119
Coleman, Patricia R(egister) 1936- CANR-51
Earlier sketches in CA 109, CANR-25
Coleman, Patty R.
See Coleman, Patricia R(egister)
Coleman, Peter J(arrett) 1926- 5-8R
Coleman, Ray 1937-1996 137
Obituary 153
Coleman, Raymond James 1923- CANR-36
Earlier sketch in CA 49-52
Coleman, Richard J(ames) 1941- 41-44R
Coleman, Richard M(ark) 1951- 121
Coleman, Richard Patrick 1927- 33-36R
Coleman, Robert David 1951- 121
Coleman, Robert E(merson) 1928- CANR-35
Earlier sketches in CA 13-16R, CANR-7
Coleman, Robert William Alfred 1916- 9-12R
Coleman, Roy V. 1885-1971 Obituary 104
Coleman, Terry 1931- CANR-58
Earlier sketches in CA 13-16R, CANR-10, 27
Coleman, Thomas R. 1942- 57-60
Coleman, Verna (Scott) 134
Coleman, Vernon 1946- 81-84
Coleman, Victor (Art) 1944- 153
Coleman, Wanda 1946- CANR-43
Earlier sketch in CA 119
See also CAAS 29
See also BW 2
See also DLB 130
Coleman, William L(eRoy) 1938- CANR-21
Earlier sketch in CA 69-72
See also SATA 49
See also SATA-Brief 34
Coleman, William Laurence 1920-1982 .. CANR-39
Coleman, William Oliver 154
Coleman, William V(incent) 1932- CANR-51
Earlier sketches in CA 57-60, CANR-9, 25
Coleman-Norton, P(aul) R(obinson)
1898-1971 Obituary 29-32R
Colen, B. D. 1946- CANR-23
Earlier sketch in CA 65-68
Colenbrander, Joanna 1908- 121
Coleridge, Hartley 1796-1849 .... DLB 96
Coleridge, John
See Binder, Otto O(scar)
Coleridge, M. E.
See Coleridge, Mary E(lizabeth)
Coleridge, Mary E(lizabeth) 1861-1907 166
Brief entry 116
See also DLB 19, 98
See also TCLC 73
Coleridge, Nicholas (David) 1957- 144
Coleridge, Samuel Taylor 1772-1834 .... CDBLB
1789-1832
See also DA
See also DAB
See also DAC
See also DAM MST, POET
See also DLB 93, 107
See also PC 11
See also WLC
Coleridge, Sara 1802-1852 .... DLB 199
Coles, Alan 1927- 124
Coles, Cyril Henry 1899-1965 .... CANR-62
Earlier sketches in CAP-1, CA 9-10
Coles, Don 1928- CANR-38
Earlier sketch in CA 115
See also CLC 46
Coles, Flournoy (Arthur), Jr. 1915- 57-60
Coles, Harry L(ewis) 1920- 9-12R
Coles, Janis
See Dawson, Janis
Coles, Joan M(yers) 1947- 133
Coles, John M(orton) 1930- CANR-34
Earlier sketches in CA 29-32R, CANR-12
Coles, Kaines Adlard 1901-1985 .... CAP-1
Obituary 117
Earlier sketch in CA 13-14
Coles, Manning
See Coles, Cyril Henry
Coles, Robert (Martin) 1929- CANR-70
Earlier sketches in CA 45-48, CANR-3, 32, 66
Interview in CANR-32
See also CLC 108
See also SATA 23
Coles, Robert R(eed) 1908(?)-1985 Obituary ... 116
Coles, S(ydney) F(rederick) Arthur 1896- 5-8R
Coles, Susan Vaughan Ebershoff
See Ebershoff-Coles, Susan Vaughan
Coles, William Allan 1930- 33-36R
Coles, William E., Jr. 1932- CANR-10
Earlier sketch in CA 61-64
Colet, John 1467-1519 .... DLB 132
Coletta, Paolo Enrico 1916- CANR-56
Earlier sketches in CA 41-44R, CANR-14, 31
Colette, (Sidonie-Gabrielle) 1873-1954 131
Brief entry 104
See also DAM NOV
See also DLB 65
See also MTCW 1
See also SSC 10
See also TCLC 1, 5, 16
Colette, Jacques 1929- 89-92
Colfax, David (John) 1936- 140
Colfax, J. David
See Colfax, David (John)
Colford, Paul D(ennis) 1953- 110
Colford, William E(dward) 1908-1971 .... 5-8R
Obituary 33-36R
Colgin, Russell W(eymount) 1925- 121
Colgrave, Bertram 1888-1968 .... CAP-2
Earlier sketch in CA 25-28
Colie, Rosalie L(ittell) 1924-1972 Obituary 106
Colimore, Vincent J(erome) 1914- 37-40R
Colin, Ann
See Ure, Jean
Colin, Jean
See Bell, Joyce
Colina, Tessa Patterson 1915- CANR-7
Earlier sketch in CA 17-20R
Colinas, Antonio 1946- .... DLB 134
Colinvaux, Paul (Alfred) 1930- CANR-14
Earlier sketch in CA 41-44R
Colish, Marcia L. 1937- CANR-10
Earlier sketch in CA 25-28R
Coll, Alberto R(aoul) 1955- 145
Coll, Joseph Clement 1881-1921 .... DLB 188
Coll, Regina A(udrey) 1929- 112
Coll, Steve 1958- 137
Collard, Cyril 1957-1993 152
Collard, Edgar Andrew 1911- 102
Collard, Sneeed B. III 1959- 150
See also SATA 84
Collas, J. P. 1911-1984 Obituary 114
Collector, Stephen 1951- 139
Colledge, Malcolm A(ndrew) R(ichard) 1939- ......
CANR-10
Earlier sketch in CA 25-28R
Collee, John (Gerald) 1955- 145
Collen, Neil
See Lee, Lincoln
Coller, Richard Walter 1925- 119
Collery, Arnold (Peter) 1927-1989 Obituary 128
Collett, Barry 1934- CANR-64
Earlier sketch in CA 128
Collett, Rosemary K(ing) 1931- 69-72
Colletta, Nat J(oseph) 1944- 104
Collette, Christine 1947- 132
Colley, Ann C(heetham) 1940- CANR-30
Earlier sketch in CA 112
Colley, Iain 1940- 97-100
Colley, Linda 1949- 130
Collias, Joe G. 1928- CANR-14
Earlier sketch in CA 41-44R
Collias, Nicholas E(lias) 1914- 131
Collicott, Sharleen 1937- 165
See also SATA 98
Collie, Michael (John) 1929- CANR-39
Earlier sketches in CA 49-52, CANR-3, 18
Collier, (John) Basil 1908- CANR-2
Earlier sketch in CA 5-8R
Collier, Boyd D(ean) 1938- 57-60
Collier, Calhoun C(rofford) 1916- 25-28R
Collier, Christopher 1930- CANR-33
Earlier sketches in CA 33-36R, CANR-13
See also AAYA 13
See also CLC 30
See also JRDA
See also MAICYA
See also SATA 16, 70
Collier, David 1942- 69-72
Collier, David S(wanson) 1923-1983 .... 21-24R
Obituary 111
Collier, Douglas
See Fellowes-Gordon, Ian (Douglas)
Collier, Ethel 1903- 65-68
See also SATA 22
Collier, Eugenia W(illiams) 1928- 49-52
See also BW 2
Collier, Gary 1947- 138
Collier, Gaydell M(aier) 1935- CANR-70
Earlier sketch in CA 93-96
Collier, Gaylan Jane 1924- 37-40R
Collier, (Alan) Graham 1923- 17-20R
Collier, (James) Graham 1937- 105
Collier, Herbert L(eon) 1933- 103
Collier, James L(incoln) 1928- CANR-60
Earlier sketches in CA 9-12R, CANR-4, 33
See also AAYA 13
See also CLC 30
See also CLR 3
See also DAM POP
See also JRDA
See also MAICYA
See also SAAS 21
See also SATA 8, 70
Collier, Jane
See Collier, Zena
Collier, John 1901-1980 .... CANR-10
Obituary 97-100
Earlier sketch in CA 65-68
See also DLB 77
See also SSC 19
Collier, John Payne 1789-1883 .... DLB 184
Collier, Johnnie Lucille
See Collier, Lucille Ann
Collier, Joy
See Millar, (Minna Henrietta) Joy
Collier, Kenneth Gerald 1910- CANR-18
Earlier sketch in CA 85-88
Collier, Leo(nard) D(awson) 1908- 5-8R
Collier, Louise Wilbourn 1925- 109
Collier, Lucille Ann 1919(?)- Brief entry 109
Collier, Lucy Ann
See Collier, Lucille Ann
Collier, Margaret
See Taylor, Margaret Stewart
Collier, Mary 1690-(?) .... DLB 95
Collier, Michael 1953- 137
Collier, Peter 1939- CANR-44
Earlier sketch in CA 65-68
Collier, Phyllis K(ay) 1939- 110
Collier, Richard 1924- CANR-25
Earlier sketches in CA 1-4R, CANR-5
Collier, Robert J. 1876-1918 .... DLB 91
Collier, Simon 1938- 21-24R
Collier, Steven 1942- .... SATA 61
Collier, Zena 1926- CANR-43
See also SATA 23
Colligan, Francis J(ames) 1908-(?) CAP-2
Earlier sketch in CA 19-20
Collignon, Jean Henri 1918- 1-4R
Collignon, Jeff 1953- 137
Collignon, Joseph 1930- 89-92
Collignon, Rick 1948- 167
Collin, Marion (Cripps) 1928- CANR-5
Earlier sketch in CA 9-12R
Collin, Richard H(arvey) 1932- 122
Collin, Richard Oliver 1940- 105
Collinge, William B. 1949- 162
Collings, Ellsworth 1887- 73-76
Collings, Gillian 1939- .... SATA 102
Collings, I. J(illie) 1950- CANR-38
Earlier sketch in CA 115
Collings, Michael R(obert) 1947- CANR-56
Earlier sketches in CA 111, CANR-30
Collington, Peter 1948- 127
See also SATA 59, 99
Collingwood, Charles (Cummings)
1917-1985 .... 29-32R
Obituary 117
Collingwood, Donna K. 145
Collingwood, R(obin) G(eorge) 1889(?)-1943 ... 155
Brief entry 117
See also TCLC 67
Collingwood, W. G. 1854-1932 .... DLB 149
Collins, Ace 1953- 149
See also SATA 82
Collins, Alan 1928- 132
Collins, Alice H(esslein) 1907- 65-68
Collins, An fl. c. 1653- .... DLB 131
Collins, Andrew J.
See Collins, Ace
Collins, Arnold Quint 1935- 73-76
Collins, Arthur Worth, Jr. 1929- 131
Collins, Barbara J(ane) 1929- CANR-6
Earlier sketch in CA 57-60
Collins, Barry 1941- 102
Collins, Barry E(merson) 1937- CANR-7
Earlier sketch in CA 13-16R
Collins, Beulah Stowe 1923-1983 122
Obituary 110
Collins, Billy 1941- 151
Collins, Bud
See Collins, Arthur Worth, Jr.
Collins, Carvel 1912-1990 .... CANR-8
Obituary 131
Earlier sketch in CA 17-20R
Collins, Catherine Fisher 165
Collins, Cecil (James Henry)
1908-1989 Obituary 128
Collins, Charles C. 1919- 25-28R
Collins, Charles William 1880-1964 Obituary . 89-92
Collins, Christopher 1936- 49-52
Collins, Cindy
See Smith, Richard Rein
Collins, Clark
See Reynolds, Dallas McCord
Collins, Colette
See Knaack, Twila
Collins, D.
See Bulleid, H(enry) A(nthony) V(aughan)
Collins, David A(lmon) 1931- 21-24R
Collins, David R(aymond) 1940- CANR-51
Earlier sketches in CA 29-32R, CANR-11, 26
See also SATA 7
Collins, Desmond 1940- CANR-14
Earlier sketch in CA 73-76
Collins, Donald E(dward) 1934- 122
Collins, Douglas 1912-1972 Obituary 33-36R
Collins, Eliza G. C. 1938- 129
Collins, F(rederick) Herbert 1890- CAP-1
Earlier sketch in CA 11-12
Collins, Fletcher, Jr. 1906- 53-56
Collins, Freda
See Collins, Frederica Joan Hale
Collins, Frederica Joan Hale 1904- CAP-1
Earlier sketch in CA 13-14
Collins, Gary (Ross) 1934- CANR-45
Earlier sketches in CA 57-60, CANR-7, 22

Collins, George R(oseborough) 1917-1993 .... CANR-1
Obituary 140
Earlier sketch in CA 1-4R
Collins, Harold R(eeves) 1915- 25-28R
Collins, Heather 1946- .... SATA 81
Collins, Helen (Francis) 141
Collins, Henry 1917- 17-20R
Collins, Henry B(ascom), Jr. 1899-1987 Obituary 123
Collins, Herbert Ridgeway 1932- 118
Collins, Hugh 1953- 158
Collins, Hunt
See Hunter, Evan
Collins, Irene 1925- 151
Collins, Jackie 1941- CANR-64
Earlier sketches in CA 102, CANR-22
See also BEST 90:4
See also DAM POP
Collins, James Daniel 1917- CANR-5
Earlier sketch in CA 1-4R
Collins, Jean E(lizabeth) 1948- 110
Collins, Joan 1933- 116
Collins, Jodie 1941- 121
Collins, John H. 1893- 1-4R
Collins, John J(oseph) 1946- 112
Collins, John Lawrence, Jr. 1929- CANR-19
Earlier sketch in CA 65-68
Interview in CANR-19
Collins, John M(artin) 1921- CANR-56
Earlier sketches in CA 49-52, CANR-31
Collins, Joseph B. 1898(?)-1975 Obituary 53-56
Collins, Joseph T. 1939- CANR-45
Earlier sketch in CA 120
Collins, Josie
See Bentley, Joyce
Collins, Judith Graham 1942- 115
Collins, Judy (Marjorie) 1939- 103
Collins, Julie (Hubbard) 1959- 131
Collins, June Irene 1935- 37-40R
Collins, Kathleen 1931-1988 119
Collins, L(ewis) John 1905-1982 .... CAP-1
Obituary 108
Earlier sketch in CA 13-14
Collins, Larry
See Collins, John Lawrence, Jr.
Collins, Lawrence D. 1907- 149
Collins, Linda 1931- 125
See also CLC 44
Collins, Lorraine (Hill) 1931- 57-60
Collins, Mabel
See Cook, Mabel Collins
Collins, Margaret (Brandon James) 1909- 89-92
Collins, Marie (Margaret) 1935- 53-56
Collins, Marjorie A(nn) 1930- CANR-11
Earlier sketch in CA 65-68
Collins, Marva (Deloise Nettles) 1936- 111
Collins, Max
See Collins, Max Allan, (Jr.)
Collins, Max Allan, (Jr.) 1948- CANR-58
Earlier sketches in CA 103, CANR-27
Collins, Meghan 1926- 101
Collins, Merle 1950- .... DLB 157
Collins, Michael
See Lynds, Dennis
Collins, Michael 1930- CANR-5
Earlier sketch in CA 53-56
See also SATA 58
Collins, Miki (Dickey) 1959- 131
Collins, Mortimer 1827-1876 .... DLB 21, 35
Collins, Myron D(ean) 1901- CAP-1
Earlier sketch in CA 13-16
Collins, Myrtle T(elleen) 1915- 101
Collins, Nancy A. 1959- 148
Collins, Nancy W.
See Collins-Chapman, Nancy W(hisnant)
Collins, Norman Richard 1907-1982 105
Obituary 107
Collins, Orvis F(loyd) 1918- 69-72
Collins, Pat(ricia) Lowery 1932- CANR-49
Earlier sketches in CA 107, CANR-24
See also SATA 31
Collins, Patricia Hill 1948- 154
Collins, Paul 1936- 153
Collins, Peter (Sheridan) 1942- 77-80
Collins, Philip (Arthur William) 1923- CANR-22
Earlier sketches in CA 5-8R, CANR-8
Collins, R(obert) G(eorge) 1926- 112
Collins, Raymond F(rancis) 1935- 112
Collins, Robert 1924- CANR-15
Earlier sketch in CA 89-92
Collins, Robert E(mmet) 1927- 69-72
Collins, Robert M. 1943- 110
Collins, Robert O(akley) 1933- CANR-48
Earlier sketches in CA 1-4R, CANR-4, 22
Collins, Ronald K. L. 1949- 154
Collins, Rowland Lee 1934-1985 .... 9-12R
Obituary 116
Collins, Ruth Philpott 1890-1975 .... CANR-4
Obituary 53-56
Earlier sketch in CA 1-4R
See also SATA-Obit 30
Collins, Stephen L. 1949- 140
Collins, Thomas Hightower 1910- 102
Collins, Tom
See Furphy, Joseph
Collins, Trish 1927- 106
Collins, (William) Wilkie 1824-1889 .... CDBLB 1832-1890
See also DLB 18, 70, 159
Collins, Will
See Corley, Edwin (Raymond)
Collins, William 1721-1759 .... DAM POET
See also DLB 109
Collins, William Alexander Roy 1900-1976 Obituary 69-72
Collins, William Bernard 1913- 5-8R
Collins-Chapman, Nancy W(hisnant) 1933- 112
Collinson, A. S.
See Collinson, Alan S.
Collinson, Alan S. 1934- 147
See also SATA 80
Collinson, Laurence (Henry) 1925- 103
Collinson, Roger (Alfred) 1936- 110
Collinson, Sarah 1965- 147
Collis, John Stewart 1900-1984 61-64
Obituary 112
Collis, Kevin F(rancis) 1930- 107
Collis, Louise 1925- 21-24R
Collis, Maurice 1889-1973 .... CANR-4
Obituary 89-92
Earlier sketch in CA 5-8R
See also DLB 195
Collis, William Robert Fitzgerald 1900- CAP-1
Earlier sketch in CA 9-10
Collison, David (John) 1937- 105
Collison, Gary 1947- 158
Collison, Koder M(acklin) 1910- 53-56
Collison, Robert Lewis Wright 1914- CANR-2
Earlier sketch in CA 5-8R
Colliss, Gertrude Florence Mary (Jones) 1908- 5-8R
Collodi, Carlo 1826-1890
See Lorenzini, Carlo
See also CLR 5
Collom, Jack 1931- 77-80
Colloms, Brenda 1919- CANR-7
Earlier sketch in CA 61-64
See also SATA 40
Collura, Mary-Ellen Lang 1949- 165
Collver, Michael 1953- 165
Collyer, Mary 1716(?)-1763(?) .... DLB 39
Collyns, Robin 1940- 69-72
Colm, Gerhard 1897-1968 .... 5-8R
Obituary 103
Colman, Arthur D. 1937- 33-36R
Colman, Benjamin 1673-1747 .... DLB 24
Colman, E(rnest) A(drian) M(ackenzie) 1930- . 57-60
Colman, George 1732-1794
See Glassco, John
Colman, Hila CANR-7
Earlier sketch in CA 13-16R
See also AAYA 1
See also JRDA
See also MAICYA
See also SAAS 14
See also SATA 1, 53
Colman, John E. 1923- 21-24R
Colman, Juliet Benita 1944- 61-64
Colman, Libby Lee 1940- 33-36R
Colman, Morris 1899(?)-1981 .... SATA-Obit 25
Colman, Penny (Morgan) 1944- 145
See also SATA 77
Colman, Warren (David) 1944- 136
See also SATA 67
Colmer, John (Anthony) 1921- CANR-34
Earlier sketches in CA 85-88, CANR-15
Colmer, Michael (J.) 1942- CANR-21
Earlier sketch in CA 69-72
Colodny, Len 1938- 162
Colodny, Robert G. 1915- CANR-14
Earlier sketch in CA 37-40R
Cologne-Brookes, Gavin (John) 1961- 152
Colombo, Dale
See Monroe, Keith
Colombo, Furio 1931- CANR-30
Earlier sketch in CA 111
Colombo, John Robert 1936- CANR-48
Earlier sketches in CA 25-28R, CANR-11
See also CAAS 22
See also DLB 53
See also SATA 50
Colominas, Kathleen Adele 1948- 134
Colon, Jesus 1901-1974 .... CANR-72
Earlier sketch in CA 131
See also HW
Colonel Sanders
See Sanders, Harland
Colonius, Lillian 1911- 21-24R
See also SATA 3
Colony, Horatio 1900-1977 .... 37-40R
Colorado, Antonio J.
See Colorado (Capella), Antonio J(ulio)
Colorado (Capella), Antonio J(ulio) 1903-1994 ..... CANR-32
Obituary 144
Earlier sketch in CA 17-20R
See also HW
See also SATA 23
See also SATA-Obit 79
Colp, Ralph, Jr. 1924- 126
Colquhoun, Archibald 1912-1964 129
Obituary 89-92
Colquhoun, Frank 1909-1997 106
Obituary 157
Colquhoun, Ithell 1906-1988 .... 13-16R
Obituary 125
Colquhoun, Keith 1927- 102
Colquhoun, Patrick 1745-1820 .... DLB 158
Colquitt, Betsy Feagan 1926- 53-56
Colson, Charles W(endell) 1931- CANR-54
Earlier sketches in CA 102, CANR-29
Colson, Elizabeth 1917- 53-56
Colson, Frederick
See Geis, Richard E(rwin)
Colson, Greta (Scotchmur) 1913- CAP-1
Earlier sketch in CA 9-10
Colson, Howard P(aul) 1910- 29-32R
Colson, Laramie
See Richardson, Gladwell
Colston, Lowell G(wen) 1919-1985 53-56
Obituary 118
Colston-Baynes, Dorothy 1881(?)-1973 Obituary 104
Colt, Clem
See Nye, Nelson C(oral)
Colt, John W. 1900(?)-1983 Obituary 111
Colt, Martin
See Epstein, Beryl (M. Williams) and Epstein, Samuel
Colt, Winchester Remington
See Hubbard, L(afayette) Ron(ald)
Colt, Zandra
See Stevenson, Florence
Coltart, James M(ilne) 1903-1986 Obituary 120
Coltart, Nina 1927-1997 144
Obituary 159
Colter, Cyrus 1910- CANR-66
Earlier sketches in CA 65-68, CANR-10
See also BW 1
See also CLC 58
See also DLB 33
Colter, Dale
See Broomall, Robert W(alter)
Colter, Shayne
See Norwood, Victor G(eorge) C(harles)
Coltharp, Lurline H(ughes) 1913- 17-20R
Coltman, Ernest Vivian
See Dudley, Ernest
Coltman, Will
See Bingley, David Ernest
Colton, C(larence) E(ugene) 1914- CANR-2
Earlier sketch in CA 5-8R
Colton, Harold S(ellers) 1881-1970 .... CANR-3
Earlier sketch in CA 1-4R
Colton, Helen 1918- 57-60
Colton, James
See Hansen, Joseph
Colton, James B(yers) II 1908- 37-40R
Colton, Joel 1918- CANR-2
Earlier sketch in CA 1-4R
Colton, Timothy J. 1947- CANR-63
Earlier sketch in CA 124
Coltrane, James
See Wohl, James P(aul)
Colum, Padraic 1881-1972 .... CANR-35
Obituary 33-36R
Earlier sketch in CA 73-76
See also CLC 28
See also CLR 36
See also MAICYA
See also MTCW 1
See also SATA 15
Columbu, Franco 1941- 125
Columbus, Chris(topher) 1959- 154
See also SATA 97
Columella
See Moore, Clement Clarke
Colver, A(nthony) Wayne 1923- 93-96
Colver, Alice Mary (Ross) 1892-1988 69-72
Obituary 161
Colver, Anne 1908- CANR-2
Earlier sketch in CA 45-48
See also SATA 7
Colvert, James B(rumley) 1921- 116
Colvett, Latayne
See Scott, Latayne Colvett
Colville, Derek Kent 1923- Brief entry 105
Colville, John Rupert 1915-1987 .... CANR-10
Obituary 124
Earlier sketch in CA 61-64
Colvin, Brenda 1897-1981 Obituary 108
Colvin, Clare 1943- 123
Colvin, Elaine Wright 1942- 106
Colvin, Howard Montagu 1919- 61-64
Colvin, Ian G(oodhope) 1912-1975 .... CAP-2
Obituary 57-60
Earlier sketch in CA 19-20
Colvin, James
See Moorcock, Michael (John)
Colvin, Ralph W(hitmore) 1920-1981 107
Obituary 104
Colvin, Sidney 1845-1927 .... DLB 149
Colwell, C(harles) Carter 1932- 41-44R
Colwell, Eileen (Hilda) 1904- CANR-12
Earlier sketch in CA 29-32R
See also SATA 2
Colwell, Ernest Cadman 1901-1974 .... CANR-4
Obituary 53-56
Earlier sketch in CA 5-8R
Colwell, Richard J(ames) 1930- 69-72
Colwell, Rita R. 1934- 157
Colwell, Robert 1931- 33-36R
Colwin, Laurie (E.) 1944-1992 .... CANR-46
Obituary 139
Earlier sketches in CA 89-92, CANR-20
See also CLC 5, 13, 23, 84
See also DLBY 80
See also MTCW 1
Colwyn, Stewart
See Pepper, Frank S.
Colyer, Penrose 1940- CANR-20
Earlier sketches in CA 65-68, CANR-14
Colyer, Richard Moore
See Moore-Colyer, Richard
Coman, Dale Rex 1906- 81-84
Coman, Edwin Truman, Jr. 1903-1995 .... 9-12R
Obituary 161
Comaroff, Jean 1946- 139
Comaroff, John L(ionel) 1945- CANR-57
Earlier sketch in CA 125
Comaromi, John P(hillip) 1937- 111
Comarow, Avery 1945- 127
Comay, Joan 103
Comber, Lillian 1916- CANR-3
Earlier sketch in CA 9-12R
Combs, A(rthur) W(right) 1912- CANR-10
Earlier sketch in CA 17-20R
Combs, Ann 1935- 117
Combs, David 1934- 108
Combs, Eugene 1934- 118
Combs, Harry (Benjamin) 1913- 129
Combs, James E(verett) 1941- CANR-19
Earlier sketch in CA 101
Combs, Jerald A(rthur) 1937- 110
Combs, Richard Earl 1934- 33-36R
Combs, Robert
See Murray, John
Combs, (Elisha) Tram(mell, Jr.) 1924- 13-16R
Combuchen, Sigrid
See Combuechen, Sigrid
Combuechen, Sigrid 1942- 136
Comden, Betty 1919- CANR-40
Earlier sketches in CA 49-52, CANR-2
See also DLB 44
Comeau, Arthur M. 1938- 61-64
Comencini, Luigi 1916- 149
Comer, James P(ierpont) 1934- CANR-43
Earlier sketch in CA 61-64
See also BW 2
Comey, Dennis J. 1896-1987 Obituary 123
Comey, James Hugh 1947- 65-68
Comfort, Alex(ander) 1920- CANR-45
Earlier sketches in CA 1-4R, CANR-1
See also CLC 7
See also DAM POP
Comfort, B(arbara) 1916- CANR-72
Earlier sketch in CA 150
Comfort, Howard 1904-1993 .... 37-40R
Obituary 161
Comfort, Iris Tracy CANR-6
Earlier sketch in CA 13-16R
Comfort, Jane Levington
See Sturtzel, Jane Levington
Comfort, Mildred Houghton 1886- 9-12R
See also SATA 3
Comfort, Montgomery
See Campbell, (John) Ramsey
Comfort, Ray 1949- 150
Comfort, Richard A(llen) 1933- 21-24R
Comi, Girolamo 1890-1968 .... DLB 114
Comidas, Chinas
See Genser, Cynthia
Comini, Alessandra 1934- 93-96
Comins, Ethel M(ae) CANR-8
Earlier sketch in CA 61-64
See also SATA 11
Comins, Jeremy 1933- CANR-14
Earlier sketch in CA 65-68
See also SATA 28
Comitas, Lambros 1927- Brief entry 113
Comito, Terry (Allen) 1935- CANR-29
Earlier sketch in CA 109
Commager, Henry Steele 1902-1998 ..... CANR-68
Obituary 165
Earlier sketches in CA 21-24R, CANR-26
See also DLB 17
See also MTCW 1
See also SATA 23
See also SATA-Obit 102
Commager, (Henry) Steele (Jr.) 1932-1984 Obituary 112
Commins, William Dollard Sr. 1899-1983 Obituary 109
Commire, Anne CANR-44
Earlier sketches in CA 69-72, CANR-21
Committe, Thomas C. 1922- 65-68
Commoner, Barry 1917- CANR-33
Earlier sketch in CA 65-68
See also MTCW 1
Commons, Dorman L(eland) 1918- 129
Comnena, Anna
See Sonnenberg, Ben
Como, (Michael) William 1925-1989 69-72
Obituary 127
Comparetti, Alice (Pattee) 1907-1996 ...... 37-40R
Obituary 161
Compere, Mickie
See Davidson, Margaret
Compitello, Malcolm Alan 1946- 136
Compio, Sister Jannita Marie 1935- 57-60
Compo, Susan 1955- 134
Comprone, Joseph J(ohn) 1943- CANR-35
Earlier sketches in CA 53-56, CANR-5
Compton, Ann
See Prebble, Marjorie Mary Curtis
Compton, Arthur Holly 1892-1962 158
Obituary 116
Compton, D(avid) G(uy) 1930- CANR-17
Earlier sketch in CA 25-28R
Compton, Guy
See Compton, D(avid) G(uy)
Compton, Henry (Pasfield) 1909- 9-12R
Compton, James V(incent) 1928- 29-32R
Compton, Patricia A. 1936- 142
See also SATA 75
Compton, Piers 1903- 122
Compton-Burnett, I(vy) 1884(?)-1969 ...... CANR-4
Obituary 25-28R
Earlier sketch in CA 1-4R
See also CLC 1, 3, 10, 15, 34
See also DAM NOV
See also DLB 36
See also MTCW 1
Compton-Hall, (Patrick) Richard 1929- ... CANR-49
Earlier sketches in CA 107, CANR-24
Comrey, Andrew Laurence 1923- Brief entry ... 106
Comroe, Julius H(iram), Jr. 1911-1984 122
Obituary 113
Comstock, Anthony 1844-1915 Brief entry 110
See also TCLC 13
Comstock, Christine 1942- CANR-20
Earlier sketch in CA 104
Comstock, Gary 1954- 127

Comstock, Gary D(avid) 1945- 162
Comstock, George Adolphe 1932- 124
Comstock, Helen 1893-1970 CANR-4
Obituary 89-92
Earlier sketch in CA 5-8R
Comstock, Henry B. 1908- CAP-2
Earlier sketch in CA 33-36
Comstock, Mary Bryce 1934- 105
Comstock, W(illiam) Richard 1928- 73-76
Comte, P. D. Q.
See Hilbert, Richard A.
Comte, The Great
See Hawkesworth, Eric
Comus
See Ballantyne, R(obert) M(ichael)
Comyns, Barbara
See Comyns-Carr, Barbara Irene Veronica
Comyns, Nance
See Comyns-Toohey, Nantz
Comyns-Carr, Barbara Irene Veronica 1912- 5-8R
Comyns-Toohey, Nantz 1956- SATA 86
Conacher, D(esmond) J(ohn) 1918- 25-28R
Conacher, J(ames) B(lennerhasset) 1916- 25-28R
Conan, Laure 1845-1924 DLB 99
Conan Doyle, Adrian Malcolm 1910-1970 5-8R
Obituary 29-32R
Conan Doyle, Arthur
See Doyle, Arthur Conan
Conant, Eaton H. 1930- 53-56
Conant, Howard (Somers) 1921- CANR-8
Earlier sketch in CA 17-20R
Conant, James Bryant 1893-1978 13-16R
Obituary 77-80
Conant, Kenneth John 1894-1984 1-4R
Obituary 161
Conant, Michael 1924- 138
Conant, Ralph W(endell) 1926- CANR-31
Earlier sketches in CA 29-32R, CANR-14
Conant, Roger 1909- Brief entry 107
Conant, Susan CANR-72
Earlier sketch in CA 139
Conard, Alfred Fletcher 1911- 13-16R
Conard, Joseph W. 1911- 13-16R
Conard, Rebecca 1946- 162
Conard, Robert C. 1933- CANR-53
Earlier sketch in CA 126
Conarroe, Joel (Osborne) 1934- 29-32R
Conarroe, Richard R(iley) 1928- 69-72
Conati, Marcello 1928- 154
Conaway, James (Alley) 1941- 33-36R
Conchon, Georges 1925-1990 Obituary 132
Conconi, Charles N. 1938- 77-80
Conde, Carmen 1901- DLB 108
Conde, Jesse C(lay) 1912- 57-60
Conde, Maryse 1937-
See Boucolon, Maryse
See also BLCS
See also BW 2
See also CLC 52, 92
See also DAM MULT
Condee, Ralph Waterbury 1916- 17-20R
Condit, Carl Wilbur 1914- CANR-4
Earlier sketch in CA 1-4R
Condit, Martha Olson 1913- 73-76
See also SATA 28
Condliffe, John B(ell) 1891-1981 CAP-1
Obituary 106
Earlier sketch in CA 13-16
Condon, David Rensing 1924-1994 114
Obituary 147
Condon, E(dward) U(hler) 1902-1974 Obituary 112
Condon, Eddie 1905-1973 Obituary 45-48
Condon, George Edward 1916- CANR-1
Earlier sketch in CA 45-48
Condon, Jack
See Condon, John C(arl), Jr.
Condon, Jane 1951- 128
Condon, John C(arl), Jr. 1938- CANR-10
Earlier sketch in CA 21-24R
Condon, Judith 150
See also SATA 83
Condon, Richard (Thomas) 1915-1996 CANR-23
Obituary 151
Earlier sketches in CA 1-4R, CANR-2
Interview in CANR-23
See also CAAS 1
See also BEST 90:3
See also CLC 4, 6, 8, 10, 45, 100
See also DAM NOV
See also MTCW 1
Condon, Robert 1921(?)-1972 Obituary 37-40R
Condor, Gladyn
See Davison, Gladys Patton
Condray, Bruno
See Humphrys, Leslie George
Condry, William Moreton 1918- 103
Condy, Roy 1942- SATA 96
Cone, Carl B(ruce) 1916-1995 9-12R
Obituary 161
Cone, Edward Toner 1917- 110
Cone, Fairfax Mastick 1903-1977 73-76
Obituary 69-72
Cone, Ferne Geller 1921- 107
See also SATA 39
Cone, James H. 1938- 33-36R
Cone, John F(rederick) 1926- 17-20R
Cone, Molly Lamken 1918- CANR-37
Earlier sketches in CA 1-4R, CANR-1, 16
See also SAAS 11
See also SATA 1, 28
Cone, Patrick 1954- SATA 89
Cone, William F. 1919- 57-60
Conerly, Perian Collier 1926- 5-8R
Coney, Michael G(reatrex) 1932- CANR-56
Earlier sketch in CA 97-100
See also SATA 61
Coney, Michael Greatrex
See Coney, Michael G(reatrex)
Coney, Mike
See Coney, Michael G(reatrex)
Coney, Sandra 1944- 150
Confer, Dennis W. 1941- 157
Confer, Vincent 1913- 21-24R
Conford, Ellen 1942- CANR-54
Earlier sketches in CA 33-36R, CANR-13, 29
See also AAYA 10
See also CLR 10
See also JRDA
See also MAICYA
See also SATA 6, 68
Confucius
See Lund, Philip R(eginald)
Confucius 551B.C.-479B.C. DA
See also DAB
See also DAC
See also DAM MST
See also WLCS
Congar, Marie Joseph
See Congar, (Georges) Yves Marie-Joseph
Congar, Y. M.
See Congar, (Georges) Yves Marie-Joseph
Congar, Yves
See Congar, (Georges) Yves Marie-Joseph
Congar, Yves M.-J.
See Congar, (Georges) Yves Marie-Joseph
Congar, Yves M. J.
See Congar, (Georges) Yves Marie-Joseph
Congar, (Georges) Yves Marie-Joseph
1904-1995 130
Obituary 149
Congdon, Constance S. 1944- CANR-67
Earlier sketch in CA 123
Congdon, Herbert Wheaton 1876-1965 5-8R
Congdon, Kirby 1924- CANR-7
Earlier sketch in CA 13-16R
Congdon, Kristin G. 1948- 138
Congdon, Lee (Walter) 1939- 130
Congdon, William Grosvenor 1912- CANR-24
Earlier sketches in CA 17-20R, CANR-7
Conger, (Seymour) Beach III
1912-1969 Obituary 115
Conger, Jay A. 1952- 132
Conger, John (Janeway) 1921- CANR-6
Earlier sketch in CA 13-16R
Conger, Lesley
See Suttles, Shirley (Smith)
Conger, Marion (C.) 1915-1990 Obituary 130
Conger, Syndy McMillen 1942- 152
Congrat-Butler, Stefan 1914(?)-1979 103
Obituary 89-92
Congreve, Willard J(ohn) 1921-1979 57-60
Obituary 134
Congreve, William 1670-1729 CDBLB 1660-1789
See also DA
See also DAB
See also DAC
See also DAM DRAM, MST, POET
See also DC 2
See also DLB 39, 84
See also WLC
Conigliaro, Vincenzo 1928- 165
Conil, Jean 1917- CANR-53
Earlier sketches in CA 13-16R, CANR-13, 29
Conine, (Odie) Ernest 1925- 69-72
Coniston, Ed
See Bingley, David Ernest
Conkin, Paul K(eith) 1929- 33-36R
Conkle, E(llsworth) P(routy) 1899-1994 65-68
Obituary 144
Conklin, Barbara P. 1927- 109
Conklin, Gladys Plemon 1903- CANR-4
Earlier sketch in CA 1-4R
See also SATA 2
Conklin, Groff 1904-1968 CANR-3
Earlier sketch in CA 1-4R
Conklin, Harold C(olyer) 1926- 118
Conklin, John E(van) 1943- CANR-14
Earlier sketch in CA 37-40R
Conklin, Mike 1944- 120
Conklin, Paul 115
Brief entry 111
See also SATA 43
See also SATA-Brief 33
Conkling, Hilda 1910- SATA 23
Conlay, Iris 1910- CAP-1
Earlier sketch in CA 11-12
Conley, Carolyn A. 145
Conley, Ellen Alexander 1938- CANR-20
Earlier sketch in CA 103
Conley, Enid Mary 1917- CANR-10
Earlier sketch in CA 65-68
Conley, John (Allan) 1912- 61-64
Conley, Phillip Mallory 1887- 69-72
Conley, Robert J(ackson) 1940- CANR-45
Earlier sketches in CA 41-44R, CANR-15, 34
See also DAM MULT
See also NNAL
Conley, Tom (Clark) 1943- 155
Conley, Verena Andermatt 1943- 117
Conlin, David A. 1897- 17-20R
Conlin, Joseph Robert 1940- CANR-40
Earlier sketch in CA 49-52
Conlon, Denis J. 1932- 37-40R
Conlon, Kathleen (Annie) 1943- 130
Brief entry 114
Conlon-McKenna, Marita 1956- SATA 71
Conly, Jane Leslie 1948- SATA 80
Conly, Robert Leslie 1918(?)-1973 73-76
Obituary 41-44R
See also O'Brien, Robert C.
See also MAICYA
See also SATA 23
Conn, Canary Denise 1949- 57-60
Conn, Charles Paul 1945- CANR-6
Earlier sketch in CA 57-60
Conn, Charles William 1920- CANR-10
Earlier sketch in CA 21-24R
Conn, Frances G. 1925- 33-36R
Conn, Jan E(velyn) 1952- CANR-31
Earlier sketch in CA 110
Conn, Martha Orr 1935- 93-96
Conn, Nicole 1959- 144
Conn, Peter J. 1942- 33-36R
Conn, Stetson 1908- CAP-1
Earlier sketch in CA 9-10
Conn, Stewart 1936- 153
Brief entry 117
Conn, Walter E(ugene) 1940- 110
Connable, Alfred 1931- 81-84
Connally, Eugenia (Maye) Horstman 1931- 103
Connally, John (Bowden, Jr.) 1917-1993 145
Connell, Brian (Reginald) 1916- CANR-4
Earlier sketch in CA 1-4R
Connell, Evan S(helby), Jr. 1924- CANR-39
Earlier sketches in CA 1-4R, CANR-2
See also CAAS 2
See also AAYA 7
See also CLC 4, 6, 45
See also DAM NOV
See also DLB 2
See also DLBY 81
See also MTCW 1
Connell, Francis J. 1888- CAP-1
Earlier sketch in CA 13-14
Connell, George B(oyce II) 1957- 141
Connell, Jan
See Connell, Janice T(imchak)
Connell, Janice T(imchak) 1939- 140
Connell, Jon 1952- 97-100
Connell, K(enneth) H(ugh) 1917-1973 CAP-2
Earlier sketch in CA 25-28
Connell, Kirk
See Chapman, John Stanton Higham
Connell, Maureen 1931- 104
Connell, William Fraser 1916- 104
Connellan, Leo 1928- 81-84
Connelly, Bridget 1941- 127
Connelly, Douglas 1949- 121
Connelly, Frances S(usan) 151
Connelly, Karen 1969- 149
Connelly, Marc(us Cook) 1890-1980 CANR-30
Obituary 102
Earlier sketch in CA 85-88
See also CLC 7
See also DLB 7
See also DLBY 80
See also SATA-Obit 25
Connelly, Michael 1956- 158
Connelly, Owen (Sergeson, Jr.) 1924- 17-20R
Connelly, Philip M(arshal)
1904(?)-1981 Obituary 104
Connelly, Thomas L(awrence) 1938- CANR-11
Earlier sketch in CA 17-20R
Connelly, Willard 1888-1967 CAP-2
Earlier sketch in CA 17-18
Conner, Berenice Gillete 1908- 65-68
Conner, Daryl R(iles) 1946- 142
Conner, Floyd D(avis) 1951- 119
Conner, K. Patrick 1952- CANR-54
Earlier sketch in CA 127
Conner, Patrick (Roy Mountifort) 1947- 106
Conner, Patrick Reardon 1907- 5-8R
Conner, Paul Willard 1937-1984 17-20R
Obituary 114
Conner, Rearden
See Conner, Patrick Reardon
Conner, Valerie Jean 1945- 114
Conners, Bernard F. 1926- 41-44R
Conners, Kenneth Wray 1909- 29-32R
Connery, Donald S(tuart) 1926- Brief entry 114
Connery, George Edward
1907(?)-1985 Obituary 116
Connery, John (R.) 1913-1987 Obituary 124
Connery, Robert H(owe) 1907- 41-44R
Connett, Eugene Virginius III 1891-1969 CAP-1
Earlier sketch in CA 13-14
Connette, Earle 1910- CAP-1
Earlier sketch in CA 13-16
Connick, C(harles) Milo 1917- 1-4R
Conniff, Frank 1914-1971 Obituary 93-96
Conniff, James C(lifford) G(regory) 21-24R
Conniff, Michael L(ee) 1942- 118
Conniff, Richard 1951- 124
Connolly, Cyril (Vernon) 1903-1974 CANR-61
Obituary 53-56
Earlier sketches in CAP-2, CA 21-22
See also DLB 98
See also MTCW 1
Connolly, Francis X(avier) 1909-1965 CAP-1
Earlier sketch in CA 13-14
Connolly, James B. 1868-1957 DLB 78
Connolly, Jerome P(atrick) 1931- SATA 8
Connolly, Joseph 1950- 130
Connolly, Pat 1943- SATA 74
Connolly, Paul
See Wicker, Thomas Grey
Connolly, Peter 1935- 103
See also SATA 47
Connolly, Ray 1940- 101
Connolly, Robert D(uggan, Jr.) 1917- 69-72
Connolly, S(ean) J. 1951- 138
Connolly, Thomas Edmund 1918- CANR-4
Earlier sketch in CA 1-4R
Connolly, Vivian 1925- CANR-1
Earlier sketch in CA 49-52
Connon, Bryan (James Milne) 1927- 137
Connor, Anthony J(oseph) 1946- 144
Connor, J. Robert 1927- 123
Connor, Jim 1935- 107
Connor, Joan 1954- 168
Connor, John Anthony 1930- 13-16R
See also Connor, Tony
Connor, Joyce Mary 1929- CANR-10
Earlier sketch in CA 65-68
Connor, Kevin
See O'Rourke, Frank
Connor, Lawrence S(tanton) 1925- 89-92
Connor, Patricia 1943- 25-28R
Connor, Ralph
See Gordon, Charles William
See also DLB 92
See also TCLC 31
Connor, Seymour V(aughan) 1923- 53-56
Connor, Steven 1955- 141
Connor, Susanna Pflaum
See Pflaum, Susanna Whitney
Connor, Tony
See Connor, John Anthony
See also DLB 40
Connor, W(alter) Robert 1934- 41-44R
Connor, Walter Downing 1942- 106
Connor, William (Neil)
1909(?)-1967 Obituary 25-28R
Connors, Bruton
See Rohen, Edward
Connors, Dorsey 45-48
Connors, John Stanley 1925-1984 Obituary 112
Connors, Joseph 1945- 106
Conolly, L(eonard) W(illiam) 1941- 106
Conolly, Violet 1901(?)-1988(?) Obituary 124
Conor, Glen
See Cooney, Michael
Conot, Robert E. 1929- CANR-2
Earlier sketch in CA 45-48
Conover, C(harles) Eugene 1903- 5-8R
Conover, Carole 1941- 89-92
Conover, Chris 1950- 128
See also SATA 31
Conover, David (Beals) 1919-1983 115
Conover, Hobart H. 1914- 13-16R
Conover, Jessica Arline Wilcox
See Jones, Candy
Conover, Roger L(loyd) 1950- 130
Conover, Ted 1958- 129
Conquest, Edwin Parker, Jr. 1931- 29-32R
Conquest, John 1943- 144
Conquest, Ned
See Conquest, Edwin Parker, Jr.
Conquest, Owen
See Hamilton, Charles (Harold St. John)
Conquest, (George) Robert (Acworth) 1917-
CANR-50
Earlier sketches in CA 13-16R, CANR-9, 25
See also DLB 27
Conrad, Alfred Borys 1899(?)-1979 Obituary 104
Conrad, Andree 1945- 29-32R
Conrad, Barnaby (Jr.) 1922- CANR-6
Earlier sketch in CA 9-12R
Conrad, Brenda
See Brown, Zenith Jones
Conrad, David Eugene 1928- 17-20R
Conrad, Earl 1912-1986 CANR-10
Obituary 118
Earlier sketch in CA 1-4R
Conrad, Edna (G.) 1893- CAP-2
Earlier sketch in CA 33-36
Conrad, Hal
See Conrad, Harold
Conrad, Harold 1911-1991 112
Obituary 134
Conrad, Jack (Randolph) 1923- 9-12R
Conrad, Jean
See Martinez, Nancy C.
Conrad, John W(ilfred) 1935- CANR-4
Earlier sketch in CA 53-56
Conrad, Jon(athan) J(ames) 1920- 114
Conrad, Joseph 1857-1924 CANR-60
Brief entry 104
Earlier sketch in CA 131
See also AAYA 26
See also CDBLB 1890-1914
See also DA
See also DAB
See also DAC
See also DAM MST, NOV
See also DLB 10, 34, 98, 156
See also MTCW 1
See also SATA 27
See also SSC 9
See also TCLC 1, 6, 13, 25, 43, 57
See also WLC
Conrad, Kenneth
See Lottich, Kenneth V(erne)
Conrad, L. K.
See Conrad, Andree
Conrad, Mark J. 1957- 164
Conrad, Pam 1947-1996 CANR-36
Obituary 151
Earlier sketch in CA 121
See also AAYA 18
See also CLR 18
See also JRDA
See also MAICYA
See also SAAS 19
See also SATA 52, 80
See also SATA-Brief 49
See also SATA-Obit 90
Conrad, Paul (Francis) 1924- CANR-38
Earlier sketch in CA 113
Interview in 113
Conrad, Peter 1945- 139
Conrad, Robert 1928- 41-44R
Conrad, Robert Arnold
See Hart, Moss

Conrad, Susan P(hinney) 1941- Brief entry 113
Conrad, Sybil 1921- 21-24R
Conrad, Tex
See Yates, A(lan) G(eoffrey)
Conrad, Tod
See Wilkes-Hunter, R(ichard)
Conrad, Will C. 1882- CAP-1
Earlier sketch in CA 13-14
Conradi, Peter J(ohn) 1945- 133
Conradis, Heinz 1907- CAP-1
Earlier sketch in CA 13-14
Conrads, Ulrich 1923- 9-12R
Conran, Anthony 1931- CANR-14
Earlier sketch in CA 65-68
Conran, Shirley (Ida) 1932- CANR-22
Earlier sketch in CA 103
See also MTCW 1
Conran, Terence Orby 1931- 85-88
Conron, (Alfred) Brandon 1919- 17-20R
Conrow, Robert 1942- 57-60
Conroy, Al
See Albert, Marvin H(ubert)
Conroy, Albert
See Albert, Marvin H(ubert)
Conroy, Barbara 1934- 111
Conroy, Charles W. 1922- 13-16R
Conroy, Donald Pat(rick) 1945- CANR-53
Earlier sketches in CA 85-88, CANR-24
See also AAYA 8
See also AITN 1
See also CLC 30, 74
See also DAM NOV, POP
See also DLB 6
See also MTCW 1
Conroy, Frank 1936- 77-80
Conroy, (Francis) Hilary 1919- CANR-39
Earlier sketch in CA 115
Conroy, Jack
See Conroy, John Wesley
See also DLBY 81
See also SATA 19
Conroy, John 1951- 136
Conroy, John Wesley 1899-1990 .... CANR-3
Obituary 131
Earlier sketch in CA 5-8R
See also Conroy, Jack
See also SATA-Obit 65
Conroy, Mary 1941- 110
Conroy, Michael R(alph) 1945- CANR-9
Earlier sketch in CA 53-56
Conroy, Pat
See Conroy, Donald Pat(rick)
Conroy, Patricia 1941- 93-96
Conroy, Peter V(incent), Jr. 1944- 53-56
Conroy, Robert
See Goldston, Robert (Conroy)
Conroy, Thomas F(rancis) 1935- 143
Considine, Bob
See Considine, Robert (Bernard)
See also AITN 2
Considine, Douglas M(axwell) 1915- CANR-11
Earlier sketch in CA 69-72
Considine, John J(oseph) 1897- 1-4R
Considine, Robert (Bernard) 1906-1975 93-96
Obituary 61-64
See also Considine, Bob
Considine, Shaun 1940- 137
Consilvio, Thomas 1947- 57-60
Consolo, Dominick P(eter) 1923- 33-36R
Consolo, Vincenzo 1933- .... DLB 196
Constable, George 1941(?)- 160
Constable, Giles 1929- 159
Constable, John W. 1922- 81-84
Constable, Trevor James 1925- 89-92
Constable, W(illiam) G(eorge) 1887-1976 .... 5-8R
Obituary 65-68
Constant, Alberta Wilson 1908-1981 .... CANR-4
Obituary 109
Earlier sketch in CA 1-4R
See also SATA 22
See also SATA-Obit 28
Constant (de Rebecque), (Henri) Benjamin
1767-1830 .... DLB 119
Constant, Jan
See Dawson, Janis
Constante, Lena 1909- 156
Constantelos, Demetrios J. 1927- CANR-49
Earlier sketches in CA 21-24R, CANR-8, 24
Constantin, James A. 1922- 13-16R
Constantin, Maurice
See Constantin-Weyer, Maurice
Constantin, Robert W(ilfrid) 1937- 25-28R
Constantine, David (John) 1944- 142
See also DLB 40
Constantine, Greg(ory John) 1938- 117
Constantine, J. Robert 1924- 154
Constantine, K. C. 1934- CANR-71
Earlier sketch in CA 138
Constantine, K. C. (a pseudonym) 1935(?)- Brief
entry 114
Constantine, Larry L(eRoy) 1943- CANR-14
Earlier sketch in CA 81-84
Constantine, Mildred 1914- 112
Brief entry 105
Constantine, Murray
See Burdekin, Katharine (Penelope)
Constantine, Stephen 1947- CANR-45
Earlier sketch in CA 120
Constantine, Storm 1956- 156
Constantino, Renato 1919- CANR-42
Earlier sketch in CA 118
Constantin-Weyer, Maurice 1881-1964 148
See also DLB 92
Conte, Gian Biagio 1941- 136
Contini, Gianfranco 1912-1990 Obituary 130
Conton, William (Farquhar) 1925- 1-4R
Contoski, Victor 1936- CANR-17
Earlier sketch in CA 25-28R
Contosta, David R(ichard) 1945- 104
Contreras, Heles 1933- CANR-14
Earlier sketch in CA 37-40R
Converse, John Marquis 1909-1980 Obituary .. 102
Converse, Paul D(ulaney) 1889-1968 .... CAP-2
Earlier sketch in CA 17-18
Converse, Philip E. 1928- CANR-6
Earlier sketch in CA 13-16R
Convict Writer, The
See Torok, Lou
Conway, Alan (Arthur) 1920- CANR-2
Earlier sketch in CA 1-4R
Conway, Arlington B.
See Burns, Eedson Louis Millard
Conway, D. J. 1939- 154
Conway, David 1939- 106
Conway, Denise
See Prebble, Marjorie Mary Curtis
Conway, Diana C(ohen) 1943- 155
See also SATA 91
Conway, Freda 1911- 25-28R
Conway, Gordon
See Hamilton, Charles (Harold St. John)
Conway, Harry 1927- 154
Conway, J(ohn) D(onald) 1905-1967 .... CANR-2
Earlier sketch in CA 1-4R
Conway, J(ack) North 1949- 145
Conway, Jill K(er) 1934- 130
Conway, Jim 1932- CANR-39
Earlier sketch in CA 116
Conway, Joan Ditzel 1933- 97-100
Conway, John Seymour 1929- 25-28R
Conway, Lynn Ann 1938- 157
Conway, (Mary) Margaret 1935- 37-40R
Conway, Moncure Daniel 1832-1907 .... DLB 1
Conway, Peter
See Milkomane, George Alexis Milkomanovich
Conway, Sally 1934- CANR-39
Earlier sketch in CA 116
Conway, Theresa (Ann) 1951- CANR-19
Earlier sketch in CA 103
Conway, Thomas D(aniel) 1934- 21-24R
Conway, Thomas Daniel 1933- 112
Conway, Tim
See Conway, Thomas Daniel
Conway, Tom
See Yates, A(lan) G(eoffrey)
Conway, Troy
See Avallone, Michael (Angelo, Jr.)
Conway, Ward
See Westmoreland, Reg(inald Conway)
Conway, William J. 1904-1983 Obituary 110
Conybeare, Charles Augustus
See Eliot, T(homas) S(tearns)
Conyers, James E(rnest) 1932- 41-44R
Conyngham, William Joseph 1924- 53-56
Conyus
See Calhoun, Conyus
Conze, Edward J. D. 1904- 13-16R
Conzelman, James Gleason
1898-1970 Obituary 104
Conzelman, Jimmy
See Conzelman, James Gleason
Coogan, Daniel (Francis, Jr.) 1915-1980 .... 21-24R
Obituary 134
Coogan, John W(illiam) 1947- 107
Coogan, Joseph Patrick 1925- CANR-4
Earlier sketch in CA 1-4R
Coogan, Michael David 1942- Brief entry 112
Coogan, Tim(othy) Pat(rick) 1935- CANR-62
Earlier sketch in CA 145
Cook, Adrian 1940- 49-52
Cook, Alan Hugh 1922- 106
Cook, Albert S(paulding) 1925- CANR-37
Earlier sketches in CA 1-4R, CANR-1, 16
See also CAAS 27
Cook, Alice H(anson) 1903-1998 115
Obituary 164
Cook, Alice Rice 1899-1973 Obituary 41-44R
Cook, Ann Jennalie 1934- 105
Cook, Arlene Ethel 1936- 65-68
Cook, Bernadine 1924- .... SATA 11
Cook, Beverly Blair 1926- 37-40R
Cook, Blanche Wiesen 1941- CANR-4
Earlier sketch in CA 53-56
Cook, Bob 1961- 134
Cook, Bruce 1932- 33-36R
See also CAAS 28
Cook, Chris(topher) 1945- CANR-23
Earlier sketches in CA 57-60, CANR-6
Cook, Daniel 1914- 33-36R
Cook, Daniel J(oseph) 1938- 53-56
Cook, David (John) 1929- 107
Cook, David 1940- CANR-48
Earlier sketches in CA 103, CANR-22
Cook, David A. 1945- 107
Cook, David C(harles) III 1912- 57-60
Cook, David T. 1946- 65-68
Cook, Deanna F. 156
Cook, Don(ald Paul) 1920-1995 .... CANR-14
Obituary 148
Earlier sketch in CA 13-16R
Cook, Don Lewis 1928- 69-72
Cook, Dorothy Mary 1907- CANR-20
Earlier sketch in CA 103
Cook, Ebenezer 1667(?)-1732(?) .... DLB 24
Cook, Edward M(arks), Jr. 1944- 123
Brief entry 118
Cook, Edward Tyas 1857-1919 .... DLB 149
Cook, Eliza 1818-1889 .... DLB 199
Cook, Elsa E(stelle) 1932- 125
Cook, Eugene 1917(?)-1986 Obituary 120
Cook, F(rederick) P. 1937- 93-96
Cook, Ferris 1950- 145
Cook, Fred J(ames) 1911- CANR-23
Earlier sketches in CA 9-12R, CANR-3
Interview in CANR-23
See also SATA 2
Cook, Geoffrey 1946- 77-80
Cook, George Allan 1916- 21-24R
Cook, George S. 1920- 49-52
Cook, Gervis Frere
See Frere-Cook, Gervis
Cook, Gladys Emerson 5-8R
Cook, Gladys Moon 1907- 33-36R
Cook, Glen (Charles) 1944- CANR-58
Earlier sketch in CA 122
Cook, Glenn J. 1913- 25-28R
Cook, Gregory M(orton) 1942- 117
Cook, Harold Reed 1902- 13-16R
Cook, Hugh (Walter Gilbert) 1956- 132
See also SATA 85
Cook, Hugh C(hristopher) B(ult) 1910- 57-60
Cook, Ida (?)-1987(?) 153
Obituary 121
Cook, (Harold) J. 1952- 120
Cook, J(ames) Gordon 1916- 9-12R
Cook, J(ohn) M(anuel) 1910- 130
Cook, Jack
See Cook, John Augustine
Cook, (Harold) James 1926- 73-76
Cook, James Graham 1925-1966 .... 1-4R
Obituary 103
Cook, James L(ister) 1932- 142
Cook, James W(yatt) 1932- 69-72
Cook, Jean Thor 1930- 159
See also SATA 94
Cook, Jeffrey 1934- 97-100
Cook, Joan Marble 1920- 57-60
Cook, Joel 1934- .... SATA 79
Cook, John Augustine 1940- 45-48
Cook, John Lennox 1923- 106
Cook, Joseph Jay 1924- CANR-2
Earlier sketch in CA 1-4R
See also SATA 8
Cook, Judith (Anne) 1933- 132
Cook, Kenneth (Bernard) 1929- 130
Cook, Lennox
See Cook, John Lennox
Cook, Lila
See Africano, Lillian
Cook, Louise (Celia) 1942-1984 Obituary 112
Cook, Luther T(ownsend) 1901- 89-92
Cook, Lyn
See Waddell, Evelyn Margaret
Cook, Mabel Collins 1851-1927(?) Brief entry .. 121
Cook, Margaret G(erry) 1903- 5-8R
Cook, Marjorie 1920- 81-84
Cook, Mark 1942- CANR-14
Earlier sketch in CA 37-40R
Cook, Mary Jane 1929- 93-96
Cook, Melva Janice 1919- CANR-9
Earlier sketch in CA 21-24R
Cook, Melvin A(lonzo) 1911- CANR-2
Earlier sketch in CA 49-52
Cook, (Will) Mercer 1903-1987 .... CANR-25
Obituary 124
Earlier sketch in CA 77-80
See also BW 1
Cook, Michael 1931- CANR-50
Earlier sketch in CA 123
Cook, Michael 1933- CANR-68
Earlier sketch in CA 93-96
See also CLC 58
See also DLB 53
Cook, Michael Lewis 1929- 112
Cook, Myra B. 1933- 21-24R
Cook, Nicholas (John) 1950- 128
Cook, Nilla Cram 1908-1982 Obituary 108
Cook, Olive 1916- CANR-19
Earlier sketches in CA 5-8R, CANR-3
Cook, Olive Rambo 1892- 13-16R
Cook, P(auline) Lesley 1922- 13-16R
Cook, Paul H(arlin) 1950- 163
Cook, Peter D(onald) 1939- 112
Cook, Petronelle Marguerite Mary 1925- . CANR-15
Earlier sketch in CA 81-84
Cook, Philip J. 1946- 133
Cook, Ramona Graham 5-8R
Cook, Ramsay 1931- CANR-50
Earlier sketches in CA 102, CANR-25
Cook, Raymond Allen 1919- 45-48
Cook, Rebecca J. 1946- 168
Cook, Reginald L. 1903- 65-68
Cook, Richard I(rving) 1927- 21-24R
Cook, Robert 1958- 149
Cook, Robert Andrew 1912-1991 117
Obituary 133
Cook, Robert I. 1920- 33-36R
Cook, Robert William Arthur 1931-1994 .... 25-28R
Obituary 146
Cook, Robin
See Cook, Robert William Arthur
Cook, Robin 1940- CANR-41
Brief entry 108
Earlier sketch in CA 111
Interview in 111
See also BEST 90:2
See also CLC 14
See also DAM POP
Cook, Roderick 1932- 9-12R
Cook, Roy
See Silverberg, Robert
Cook, Stanley 1922- 93-96
Cook, Stephani 1944- CANR-23
Earlier sketch in CA 106
Cook, Stephen 1949- 118
Cook, Stephen L(loyd) 1962- 161
Cook, Stuart W(ellford) 1913-1993 .... CANR-1
Obituary 141
Earlier sketch in CA 1-4R
Cook, Sylvia (Carol) 1938- 49-52
Cook, T(homas) S(tephen) 1947- 128
Cook, Terry 1942- CANR-12
Earlier sketch in CA 73-76
Cook, Thomas H. 1947- CANR-57
Earlier sketches in CA 111, CANR-32
Cook, Thomas Ira 1907-1976 Obituary 111
Cook, W(illiam) Robert 1928- 115
Cook, Warren L. 1925- 37-40R
Cook, Wesley
See Abu-Jamal, Mumia
Cook, (George) Whitfield 1909- 107
Cook, William H(arleston) 1931- 104
Cook, William J(esse), Jr. 1938- 29-32R
Cook, William Wallace 1867-1933 Brief entry .. 116
Cooke, (Alfred) Alistair 1908- CANR-34
Earlier sketches in CA 57-60, CANR-9
See also AITN 1
Cooke, Ann
See Cole, Joanna
Cooke, Arthur
See Lowndes, Robert A(ugustine) W(ard)
Cooke, Barbara
See Alexander, Anna B(arbara Cooke)
Cooke, Barclay 1912-1981 97-100
Obituary 105
Cooke, Bernard J. 1922- CANR-34
Earlier sketches in CA 13-16R, CANR-9
Cooke, Charles Harris
1904(?)-1977 Obituary 73-76
Cooke, David Coxe 1917- CANR-2
Earlier sketch in CA 1-4R
See also SATA 2
Cooke, Deryck (Victor) 1919-1976 Obituary 115
Cooke, Donald Ewin 1916-1985 .... CANR-4
Obituary 117
Earlier sketch in CA 1-4R
See also SATA 2
See also SATA-Obit 45
Cooke, Edward F(rancis) 1923- 41-44R
Cooke, Elizabeth 1948- 129
See also CLC 55
Cooke, Frank E. 1920- .... SATA 87
Cooke, George Willis 1848-1923 .... DLB 71
Cooke, Gerald 1925- 13-16R
Cooke, Gilbert William 1899- CAP-1
Earlier sketch in CA 11-12
Cooke, Greville (Vaughan Turner) 1894- 13-16R
Cooke, Hereward Lester 1916-1973 .... CANR-1
Obituary 45-48
Earlier sketch in CA 1-4R
Cooke, Hope 1940- 108
Cooke, Jacob E(rnest) 1924- CANR-34
Earlier sketch in CA 1-4R
Cooke, James Francis 1875-1960 Obituary 115
Cooke, Jean (Isobel Esther) 1929- .... SATA 74
Cooke, John Byrne 1940- CANR-43
Earlier sketch in CA 119
Cooke, John D(aniel) 1892-1972 Obituary 106
Cooke, John Esten 1830-1886 .... DLB 3
Cooke, John Estes
See Baum, L(yman) Frank
Cooke, John Fletcher
See Fletcher-Cooke, John
Cooke, John Peyton 1967- 158
Cooke, Joseph R(obinson) 1926- 65-68
Cooke, M. E.
See Creasey, John
Cooke, Margaret
See Creasey, John
Cooke, Michael F.R.C.
See Cook, Michael Lewis
Cooke, Michael G(eorge) 1934-1990 110
Obituary 132
Cooke, Nancy
See de Herrera, Nancy Cooke
Cooke, Philip Pendleton 1816-1850 .... DLB 3, 59
Cooke, Robert (Gordon) 1930-1987 101
Obituary 121
Cooke, Robert William 1935- 123
Cooke, Rose Terry 1827-1892 .... DLB 12, 74
Cooke, Terence James 1921-1983 Obituary 110
Cooke, Thomas D(arlington) 1933- 115
Cooke, William 1942- CANR-14
Earlier sketch in CA 33-36R
Cook-Lynn, Elizabeth 1930- 133
See also CLC 93
See also DAM MULT
See also DLB 175
See also NNAL
Cookridge, E. H.
See Spiro, Edward
Cookson, Catherine (McMullen) 1906- CANR-68
Earlier sketches in CA 13-16R, CANR-9, 28
See also MTCW 1
See also SATA 9
Cookson, Frank Barton 1912-1977 Obituary . 69-72
Cookson, Peter (W.) 1913-1990 49-52
Obituary 130
Cookson, Peter W., Jr. 1942- 121
Cookson, William 1939- CANR-30
Earlier sketch in CA 49-52
Cool, Joyce 1938- 111
Cool, Ola C. 1890(?)-1977 Obituary 69-72
Coolbrith, Ina 1841-1928 .... DLB 54, 71, 186
Coole, W. W.
See Kulski, Wladyslaw W(szebor)
Cooley, Denton A(rthur) 1920- CANR-53
Earlier sketch in CA 126
Cooley, John Kent 1927- 13-16R
Cooley, Lee Morrison 1919- CANR-3
Earlier sketch in CA 9-12R

Cooley, Leland Frederick 1909- ... CANR-4
Earlier sketch in CA 5-8R
Cooley, Margaret L. 1906(?)-1985 Obituary ... 117
Cooley, Nicole (Ruth) 1966- ... 154
Cooley, Peter (John) 1940- ... CANR-47
Earlier sketches in CA 69-72, CANR-21
See also DLB 105
Cooley, Richard A(llen) 1925- ... 21-24R
Coolidge, Archibald C(ary), Jr. 1928- ... 37-40R
Coolidge, Clark 1939- ... 33-36R
See also DLB 193
Coolidge, Harold Jefferson
1904-1985 Obituary ... 115
Coolidge, John 1913- ... 144
Coolidge, Olivia E(nsor) 1908- ... CANR-2
Earlier sketch in CA 5-8R
See also MAICYA
See also SATA 1, 26
Coolidge, Susan
See Woolsey, Sarah Chauncy
Cooling, Benjamin Franklin 1938- ... 53-56
Coolwater, John
See Conniff, James C(lifford) G(regory)
Coomaraswamy, A. K.
See Coomaraswamy, Ananda K(entish)
Coomaraswamy, Ananda K(entish) 1877-1947 ... 154
Brief entry ... 115
Coombes, B. L. 1894(?)-1974 Obituary ... 53-56
Coombs, Ann
See Pykare, Nina
Coombs, Charles Anthony 1918-1981 ... 109
Obituary ... 105
Coombs, Charles I(ra) 1914- ... CANR-36
Earlier sketches in CA 5-8R, CANR-4, 19
See also MAICYA
See also SAAS 15
See also SATA 3, 43
Coombs, Chick
See Coombs, Charles I(ra)
Coombs, Douglas (Stafford) 1924- ... 13-16R
Coombs, H. Samm 1928- ... 93-96
Coombs, Herbert Cole 1906-1997 ... 93-96
Obituary ... 162
Coombs, Murdo
See Davis, Frederick C(lyde)
Coombs, Nina
See Pykare, Nina
Coombs, Orde M. 1939(?)-1984 ... CANR-25
Obituary ... 113
Earlier sketch in CA 73-76
See also BW 1
Coombs, Patricia 1926- ... CANR-1
Earlier sketch in CA 1-4R
See also MAICYA
See also SAAS 22
See also SATA 3, 51
Coombs, (Robert) Peter 1913- ... 116
Coombs, Philip H(all) 1915- ... CANR-23
Earlier sketches in CA 17-20R, CANR-8
Coombs, Robert H(olman) 1934- ... CANR-41
Earlier sketch in CA 41-44R
Coomer, Joe 1958- ... 125
Coon, Carleton Stevens 1904-1981 ... CANR-2
Obituary ... 104
Earlier sketch in CA 5-8R
Coon, Gene L(ee) 1924-1973 ... CANR-15
Obituary ... 103
Earlier sketch in CA 1-4R
Coon, Martha Sutherland 1884- ... CAP-2
Earlier sketch in CA 25-28
Coon, Nelson 1895- ... 69-72
Coon, Stephen 1948- ... 57-60
Cooney, Barbara 1917- ... CANR-67
Earlier sketches in CA 5-8R, CANR-3, 37
See also CLR 23
See also MAICYA
See also SATA 6, 59, 96
Cooney, Blanche 1917- ... 142
Cooney, Caroline B. 1947- ... CANR-37
Earlier sketch in CA 97-100
See also AAYA 5
See also JRDA
See also MAICYA
See also SATA 48, 80
See also SATA-Brief 41
Cooney, David M(artin) 1930- ... 17-20R
Cooney, Eugene J(erome) 1931- ... 45-48
Cooney, John 1942- ... 115
Cooney, Michael 1921- ... 25-28R
Cooney, Nancy Evans 1932- ... 105
See also SATA 42
Cooney, Ray ... CLC 62
Cooney, Ray(mond George Alfred) 1932- ... 148
Cooney, Seamus (Anthony) 1933- ... 53-56
Cooney, Timothy J. 1929- ... 107
Coons, Frederica Bertha (Safley) 1910- ... 17-20R
Coons, William R(ichard) 1934- ... 41-44R
Coonts, Stephen (Paul) 1946- ... CANR-59
Brief entry ... 127
Earlier sketch in CA 133
Interview in ... 133
See also BEST 89:2
See also DAM POP
Coontz, Otto 1946- ... 105
See also SATA 33
Coontz, Stephanie ... CANR-72
Earlier sketch in CA 132
Coop, Howard 1928- ... 25-28R
Coope, Rosalys 1921- ... 45-48
Cooper, Alfred Morton 1890- ... CAP-1
Earlier sketch in CA 11-12
Cooper, Alice 1948- ... 106
Cooper, Allan 1954- ... 118
Cooper, Allan D. 1952- ... 121
Cooper, Anthony Ashley 1671-1713 ... DLB 101
Cooper, Arnold Cook 1933- ... 17-20R
Cooper, Artemis 1953- ... CANR-54
Earlier sketch in CA 127
Cooper, B(rian) Lee 1942- ... CANR-40
Earlier sketch in CA 117
Cooper, Barbara (Ann) 1929- ... 9-12R
Cooper, (Fraser) Barry 1943- ... 126
Cooper, Barry (Anthony Raymond) 1949- ... 150
Cooper, Bernard 1951- ... 134
Cooper, Bernarr 1912- ... 41-44R
Cooper, Bev 1936- ... 119
Cooper, Brian (Newman) 1919- ... CANR-45
Earlier sketches in CA 1-4R, CANR-22
Cooper, Bruce M(ichael) 1925- ... CANR-9
Earlier sketch in CA 13-16R
Cooper, Bryan (Robert Wright) 1932- ... 25-28R
Cooper, C(hristopher) D(onald) H(untington)
1942- ... 29-32R
Cooper, C. Everett
See Burgess, Michael (Roy)
Cooper, Carl
See Cooper, Kenneth C(arlton)
Cooper, Carolyn (Joy) 1950- ... 152
Cooper, Charles 1936- ... 151
Cooper, Charles M(uhlenberg) 1909- ... 41-44R
Cooper, Charles W(illiam) 1904- ... CAP-2
Earlier sketch in CA 21-22
Cooper, Chester L. 1917- ... 29-32R
Cooper, Christopher (John) 1941- ... 107
Cooper, (Brenda) Clare 1935- ... CANR-41
Earlier sketch in CA 118
Cooper, Clarence L(avaugn), Jr. 1942- ... 152
See also BW 2
Cooper, Colin Symons 1926- ... 102
Cooper, Darien B(rown) 1934- ... 116
Cooper, Darien B(irla) 1937- ... CANR-16
Earlier sketches in CA 49-52, CANR-1
Cooper, David (Graham) 1931-1986 ... 97-100
Obituary ... 119
Cooper, David A. 1939- ... 168
Cooper, David D. 1948- ... 137
Cooper, David E(dward) 1942- ... CANR-31
Earlier sketch in CA 49-52
Cooper, Dennis 1953- ... CANR-72
Earlier sketch in CA 133
Cooper, Derek Macdonald 1925- ... 102
Cooper, Diana (Olivia Winifred Maud Manners)
1892(?)-1986 Obituary ... 119
Cooper, Dominic (Xavier) 1944- ... 65-68
Cooper, Douglas 1911-1984 ... 130
Obituary ... 112
Cooper, Douglas 1960- ... CLC 86
Cooper, Duff 1890-1954 ... 158
Cooper, Edmund 1926-1982 ... CANR-31
Earlier sketch in CA 33-36R
Cooper, Elisha 1971- ... 167
See also SATA 99
Cooper, Elizabeth Ann 1927- ... 1-4R
Cooper, Elizabeth Keyser ... CANR-1
Earlier sketch in CA 1-4R
See also SATA 47
Cooper, Emmanuel 1938- ... CANR-3
Earlier sketch in CA 49-52
Cooper, Esther
See Kellner, Esther
Cooper, Floyd ... 161
See also SATA 96
Cooper, Frank E(dward) 1910-1968 ... CAP-2
Earlier sketch in CA 21-22
Cooper, George 1937- ... 144
Cooper, Giles (Stannus) 1918-1966 Obituary ... 113
See also DLB 13
Cooper, Gladys 1888-1971 Obituary ... 33-36R
Cooper, Gordon 1932- ... 61-64
See also SATA 23
Cooper, Grace Rogers 1924- ... 41-44R
Cooper, Hannah
See Spence, William John Duncan
Cooper, Harold E(ugene) 1928- ... 45-48
Cooper, Harold H. 1911(?)-1976 Obituary ... 69-72
Cooper, Harold R. 1911(?)-1978 Obituary ... 77-80
Cooper, Helen 1947- ... 129
Cooper, Helen 1963- ... SATA 102
Cooper, Henry S(potswood) F(enimore), Jr. 1933- ..
CANR-13
Earlier sketch in CA 69-72
See also SATA 65
Cooper, Henry St. John
See Creasey, John
Cooper, I(rving) S(pencer) 1922-1985 ... CANR-26
Obituary ... 117
Earlier sketch in CA 69-72
Cooper, Ilene ... 163
See also SATA 66, 97
Cooper, J(ean) C. 1905- ... CANR-54
Earlier sketch in CA 127
Cooper, J(oan) California ... CANR-55
Earlier sketch in CA 125
See also AAYA 12
See also BW 1
See also CLC 56
See also DAM MULT
Cooper, Jackie 1922- ... 133
Cooper, Jacqueline 1924- ... 107
Cooper, James A. ... CANR-26
Earlier sketches in CAP-2, CA 19-20
Cooper, James Fenimore 1789-1851 ... AAYA 22
See also CDALB 1640-1865
See also DLB 3
See also SATA 19
Cooper, James L(ouis) 1934- ... 53-56
Cooper, James M. 1939- ... 45-48
Cooper, Jamie Lee ... 9-12R
Cooper, Jane (Marvel) 1924- ... CANR-69
Earlier sketches in CA 25-28R, CANR-17
Cooper, Jeff 1920- ... 41-44R
Cooper, Jefferson
See Fox, G(ardner) F(rancis)
Cooper, Jennifer Gough
See Gough-Cooper, Jennifer
Cooper, Jeremy (Francis Peter) 1946- ... 93-96
Cooper, Jilly 1937- ... CANR-30
Earlier sketch in CA 105
Cooper, John 1934-1984 Obituary ... 113
Cooper, John C(harles) 1933- ... CANR-56
Earlier sketches in CA 21-24R, CANR-9, 30
Cooper, John Cobb 1887- ... 5-8R
Cooper, John Dean
See Cooper, Jeff
Cooper, John E(llsworth) 1922- ... 25-28R
Cooper, John Irwin 1905- ... 41-44R
Cooper, John L. 1936- ... CANR-13
Earlier sketch in CA 21-24R
Cooper, John M(iller) 1912- ... 21-24R
Cooper, John Milton, Jr. 1940- ... 128
Brief entry ... 105
Cooper, John O(wen) 1938- ... 89-92
Cooper, John R. ... CANR-27
Earlier sketches in CAP-2, CA 19-20
See also SATA 1
Cooper, Joseph Bonar 1912- ... 17-20R
Cooper, Joseph D(avid) 1917-1975 ... CANR-4
Obituary ... 57-60
Earlier sketch in CA 5-8R
Cooper, Julian M. 1945- ... 130
Cooper, Kay 1941- ... CANR-37
Earlier sketches in CA 45-48, CANR-1, 16
See also SATA 11
Cooper, Kenneth C(arlton) 1948- ... 110
Cooper, Kenneth H(ardy) 1931- ... 134
Brief entry ... 126
Interview in ... 134
Cooper, Kenneth Schaaf 1918- ... 9-12R
Cooper, Kent 1880-1965 Obituary ... 89-92
See also DLB 29
Cooper, Lee Pelham 1926- ... CANR-4
Earlier sketch in CA 5-8R
See also SATA 5
Cooper, Leon N. 1930- ... 157
Cooper, Leslie M(uir) 1930- ... 41-44R
Cooper, Lester (Irving) 1919-1985 ... 108
Obituary ... 116
See also SATA 32
See also SATA-Obit 43
Cooper, Lettice (Ulpha) 1897-1994 ... CANR-68
Obituary ... 146
Earlier sketches in CA 9-12R, CANR-5
See also SATA 35
See also SATA-Obit 82
Cooper, Louise 1952- ... CANR-53
Earlier sketch in CA 107
Cooper, Louise Field 1905-1992 ... CANR-4
Obituary ... 139
Earlier sketch in CA 1-4R
Cooper, Lynna
See Fox, G(ardner) F(rancis)
Cooper, Mae (Klein) ... 17-20R
Cooper, Mario (Ruben) 1905-1995 ... 21-24R
Obituary ... 161
Cooper, Martin Du Pre 1910-1986 ... 103
Obituary ... 118
Cooper, Matthew (Heald) 1952- ... 85-88
Cooper, Mattie Lula
See Britton, Mattie Lula Cooper
Cooper, Melrose
See Kroll, Virginia L(ouise)
Cooper, Michael (John) 1930- ... 13-16R
Cooper, Michael L. 1950- ... SATA 79
Cooper, Michele F(reda) 1941- ... 85-88
Cooper, Morley
See Cooper, Alfred Morton
Cooper, Neil (Louis) 1930- ... CANR-44
Earlier sketch in CA 119
Cooper, Parley J(oseph) 1937- ... CANR-26
Earlier sketches in CA 65-68, CANR-10
Cooper, Patricia J(ean) 1936- ... 97-100
Cooper, Paul 1926- ... CANR-34
Earlier sketch in CA 49-52
Cooper, Paul F(enimore)
1900(?)-1970 Obituary ... 104
Cooper, Paulette 1942- ... 149
Earlier sketch in CA 37-40R
Cooper, Penny 1918- ... 137
Cooper, Peter Lee 1949- ... 111
Cooper, Philip (Jr.) 1926- ... 33-36R
Cooper, Phyllis 1939- ... 53-56
Cooper, R(obert) C(ecil) 1917- ... 143
Cooper, Richard N(ewell) 1934- ... CANR-10
Earlier sketch in CA 25-28R
Cooper, Robert G(ravlin) 1943- ... 110
Cooper, Robert St. John
1905(?)-1984 Obituary ... 111
Cooper, Ron L. 1960- ... 147
Cooper, Rosaleen 1894-1989 Obituary ... 129
Cooper, Sandi E. 1936- ... CANR-29
Earlier sketch in CA 49-52
Cooper, Saul 1934- ... 1-4R
Cooper, Signe Skott 1921- ... CANR-4
Earlier sketch in CA 53-56
Cooper, Sister Mary Ursula 1925- ... 5-8R
Cooper, Sophie
See Amory, Mark
Cooper, Susan (Mary) 1935- ... CANR-63
Earlier sketches in CA 29-32R, CANR-15, 37
See also AAYA 13
See also CLR 4
See also DLB 161
See also JRDA
See also MAICYA
See also SAAS 6
See also SATA 4, 64
Cooper, Susan Rogers 1947- ... CANR-71
Earlier sketch in CA 136
Cooper, Sylvia 1903- ... CAP-2
Earlier sketch in CA 17-18
Cooper, Terry L. 1938- ... 142
Cooper, Thomas W. 1950- ... 163
Cooper, Wayne 1938- ... 93-96
Cooper, Wendy (Lowe) 1919- ... CANR-6
Earlier sketch in CA 13-16R
Cooper, Wilhelmina (Behmenburg)
1939(?)-1980 Obituary ... 97-100
Cooper, Will 1929- ... 69-72
Cooper, William fl. 1669-1689 ... DLB 170
Cooper, William 1910- ... CANR-42
Earlier sketches in CA 1-4R, CANR-2, 20
Cooper, William F(razier) 1932- ... 69-72
Cooper, William Hurlbert 1924- ... 49-52
Cooper, William J(ames), Jr. 1940- ... 69-72
Cooper, William W(ager) 1914- ... 13-16R
Cooper, Wyatt (Emory) 1927-1978 ... 73-76
Obituary ... 77-80
See also AITN 2
Cooper-Clark, Diana 1945- ... 109
Cooper-Klein, Nina
See Cooper, Mae (Klein)
Cooperman, Hasye 1909- ... 37-40R
Cooperman, Stanley 1929-1976 ... CAP-2
Earlier sketch in CA 33-36
Cooperrider, Allen Y(ale) 1944- ... 148
Coopersmith, Harry 1903- ... CAP-2
Earlier sketch in CA 21-22
Coopersmith, Jerome 1925- ... 73-76
Coopersmith, Stanley 1926-1979 ... 21-24R
Obituary ... 133
Cooperstein, Claire (Louise) 1923- ... 158
Cooter, Roger James 1948- ... 123
Cootner, Paul H(arold) 1930- ... 9-12R
Coover, James B(urrell) 1925- ... CANR-23
Earlier sketches in CA 57-60, CANR-6
Coover, Robert (Lowell) 1932- ... CANR-58
Earlier sketches in CA 45-48, CANR-3, 37
See also CLC 3, 7, 15, 32, 46, 87
See also DAM NOV
See also DLB 2
See also DLBY 81
See also MTCW 1
See also SSC 15
Coox, Alvin D(avid) 1924- ... 29-32R
Copani, Peter 1942- ... 89-92
Cope, David 1941- ... 33-36R
Cope, Edward A(llen) 1948- ... 121
Cope, Jack
See Cope, Robert Knox
Cope, Jackson I(rving) 1925- ... CANR-34
Earlier sketch in CA 103
Cope, Lewis 1934- ... 125
Cope, Myron 1929- ... 57-60
Cope, Oliver 1902- Brief entry ... 109
Cope, Robert Knox 1913- ... 9-12R
Cope, Wendy 1945- ... 140
Cope, (Vincent) Zachary 1881-1974 ... CAP-1
Earlier sketch in CA 9-10
Copel, Sidney L(eroy) 1930- ... 21-24R
Copelan, Rachel 1934- ... 114
Copeland, Ann
See Furtwangler, Virginia W(alsh)
Copeland, Bill
See Copeland, Paul William
Copeland, Bonnie Chapman 1919- ... 101
Copeland, Carolyn Faunce 1930- ... 65-68
Copeland, E(dwin) Luther 1916- ... CANR-3
Earlier sketch in CA 9-12R
Copeland, Gary A. 1952- ... 138
Copeland, Helen 1920- ... 25-28R
See also SATA 4
Copeland, James E(verett) 1937- ... 125
Copeland, James Isaac 1910- ... 106
Copeland, Lennie 1946- ... 120
Copeland, Lori 1941- ... 142
Copeland, Melvin T. 1884-1975 ... CAP-2
Obituary ... 57-60
Earlier sketch in CA 21-22
Copeland, Miles 1916(?)-1991 ... 29-32R
Obituary ... 133
Copeland, Morris A(lbert) 1895-1989 ... CAP-1
Obituary ... 128
Earlier sketch in CA 17-18
Copeland, Pat
See Bellmon, Patricia
Copeland, Paul W. ... 105
See also SATA 23
Copeland, Paul William 1917- ... 25-28R
Copeland, Peter 1957- ... 139
Copeland, Ray (M.) 1926-1984 Obituary ... 112
Copeland, Rebecca L. 1956- ... 163
Copeland, Ross H(ugh) 1930-1980 ... 25-28R
Obituary ... 133
Copeland, Stewart (Armstrong) 1952- ... CLC 26
Copeland, Thomas Wellsted 1907-1979 ... 5-8R
Copeman, George H(enry) 1922- ... CANR-8
Earlier sketch in CA 5-8R
Copenhaver, Charles L(eonard)
1915-1982 Obituary ... 107
Copenhaver, John D., Jr. 1949- ... 146
Coper, Rudolf 1904- ... CAP-1
Earlier sketch in CA 13-14
Copetas, A. Craig 1951- ... 121
Copi, Irving M(armer) 1917- ... CANR-5
Earlier sketch in CA 1-4R
Copic, Branko 1915-1984 ... DLB 181
Coplan, David B. 1948- ... 151
Coplan, Kate M(ildred) 1901- ... 5-8R
Copland, Aaron 1900-1990 ... 5-8R
Obituary ... 133
Coplans, John (Rivers) 1920- Brief entry ... 112
Coplans, Peta 1951- ... SATA 84

Copleston, Frederick Charles (John Paul) 1907- ... CANR-7
Earlier sketch in CA 13-16R
Copley, Frederick S.
See Greif, Martin
Copley, Gerald L. C.
See Cole, Lester
Copley (Diana) Heather Pickering 1918- .. SATA 45
Coplin, William D(avid) 1939- CANR-32
Earlier sketches in CA 21-24R, CANR-12
Copman, Louis 1934- 57-60
Copp, Andrew James (III) 1916- 25-28R
Copp, E. Anthony 1945- 102
Copp, Jim
See Copp, Andrew James (III)
Copp, (John) Terry 1938- 134
Coppa, Frank John 1937- CANR-55
Earlier sketches in CA 33-36R, CANR-13, 29
Coppard, A(lfred) E(dgar) 1878-1957 167
Brief entry 114
See also DLB 162
See also SSC 21
See also TCLC 5
See also YABC 1
Coppard, Audrey 1931- CANR-27
Earlier sketch in CA 29-32R
Coppe, Abiezer
See Taylor, John (Alfred)
Coppee, Francois 1842-1908 .... TCLC 25
Coppel, Alec 1909(?)-1972 Obituary 33-36R
Coppel, Alfred 1921- CANR-10
Earlier sketch in CA 17-20R
See also CAAS 9
See also DLBY 83
Copper, (Robert) Arnold (de Vignier) 1934- .. 97-100
Copper, Basil 1924- CANR-72
Earlier sketch in CA 133
Copper, John Franklin 1940- CANR-11
Earlier sketch in CA 69-72
Copper, Marcia S(nyder) 1934- 53-56
Copperman, Paul 1947- 101
Copperud, Roy H(erman) 1915-1991 .... 9-12R
Obituary 136
Coppock, John (Oates) 1914- 13-16R
Coppock, John Terence 1921- 102
Coppock, Joseph D(avid) 1909- 49-52
Coppola, Francis Ford 1939- CANR-40
Earlier sketch in CA 77-80
See also CLC 16
See also DLB 44
Coppola, Raymond T(homas) 1947- 102
Copus, Julia 1969- 151
Copway, George 1818-1869 .... DAM MULT
See also DLB 175
See also NNAL
Coquery-Vidrovitch, Catherine 1935- 168
Coralie
See Anderson, Catherine Corley
Coram, Christopher
See Walker, Peter N.
Corazzini, Sergio 1886-1907 .... DLB 114
Corbalis, Judy 1941- 125
Corballis, Michael C(harles) 1936- 115
Corbally, John Edward, Jr. 1924- 5-8R
Corbett, Chan
See Schachner, Nathan(iel)
Corbett, Christopher 1951- 123
Corbett, Edward P(atrick) J(oseph) 1919- . CANR-9
Earlier sketch in CA 17-20R
Corbett, Elizabeth (Frances) 1887-1981 ... CANR-2
Obituary 102
Earlier sketch in CA 5-8R
Corbett, Grahame 116
See also SATA 43
See also SATA-Brief 36
Corbett, J(ack) Elliott 1920- 29-32R
Corbett, James A(rthur) 1908- 65-68
Corbett, Janice M. 1935- 37-40R
Corbett, (John) Patrick 1916- 17-20R
Corbett, Pearson H(arris) 1900- CAP-1
Earlier sketch in CA 9-10
Corbett, Richard 1582-1635 .... DLB 121
Corbett, Richard (Graham) 1955- 143
Corbett, Richmond McLain 1902- CAP-1
Earlier sketch in CA 13-16
Corbett, Ruth 1912- 29-32R
Corbett, Scott 1913- CANR-23
Earlier sketches in CA 1-4R, CANR-1
See also CLR 1
See also JRDA
See also MAICYA
See also SAAS 2
See also SATA 2, 42
Corbett, Thomas H(enry) 1938- 77-80
Corbett, W(illiam) J(esse) 1938- 137
See also CLR 19
See also MAICYA
See also SATA 50, 102
See also SATA-Brief 44
Corbin, Alain 1936- 146
Corbin, Arnold 1911- 9-12R
Corbin, Charles B. 1940- CANR-14
Earlier sketches in CA 29-32R, CANR-31
Corbin, Claire 1913- 41-44R
Corbin, Donald A(lvin) 1920- 33-36R
Corbin, H(ayman) Dan 1912- 41-44R
Corbin, Iris
See Clinton, Iris A. (Corbin)
Corbin, Jane 1954- 146
Corbin, John B(oyd) 1935- CANR-22
Earlier sketch in CA 105
Corbin, Michael
See Cartmill, Cleve
Corbin, Richard 1911-1988 .... CANR-3
Obituary 125
Earlier sketch in CA 5-8R
Corbin, Sabra Lee
See Malvern, Gladys
Corbin, Steven 1953- 131
See also BW 2
Corbin, William
See McGraw, William Corbin
Corbishley, Thomas 1903-1976 .... CANR-7
Obituary 65-68
Earlier sketch in CA 13-16R
Corbitt, Helen Lucy 1906-1978 .... CANR-4
Obituary 89-92
Earlier sketch in CA 5-8R
Corby, Dan
See Catherall, Arthur
Corcoran, Barbara 1911- CANR-48
Earlier sketches in CA 21-24R, CANR-11, 28
See also CAAS 2
See also AAYA 14
See also CLC 17
See also CLR 50
See also DLB 52
See also JRDA
See also SAAS 20
See also SATA 3, 77
Corcoran, Gertrude B(eatty) 1922- 29-32R
Corcoran, Jean (Kennedy) 1926- 1-4R
Corcoran, Neil (Cornelius) 1948- 135
Corcos, Lucille 1908-1973 .... 21-24R
Obituary 134
See also SATA 10
Cord, Barry
See Germano, Peter B.
Cord, Robert L. 1935- 33-36R
Cord, Steven Benson 1928- 21-24R
Cord, William O. 1921- 37-40R
Cordasco, Francesco 1920- CANR-46
Earlier sketches in CA 13-16R, CANR-6, 21
Cordeiro, Patricia (A.) 1944- 145
Cordelier, Maurice
See Giraudoux, (Hippolyte) Jean
Cordell, Alexander
See Graber, Alexander
Cordell, Alexander
See Graber, (George) Alexander
Cordell, Richard Albert 1896- 1-4R
Cordelli, Franco 1943- .... DLB 196
Corden, W(arner) M(ax) 1927- 33-36R
Corder, Brice W(ood) 1936- 53-56
Corder, Eric
See Mundis, Jerrold
Corder, George Edward 1904- 110
Corder, Jim(my Wayne) 1929- 17-20R
Cordier, Andrew W(ellington)
1901-1975 Obituary 106
Cordier, Gilbert
See Scherer, Jean-Marie Maurice
Cordier, Ralph Waldo 1902-1990 .... 37-40R
Obituary 161
Cordingley, Patrick 1944- 114
Cordingly, David 1938- 93-96
Cordis, Lonny
See Donson, Cyril
Cordle, Thomas 1918- 144
Cords, Nicholas J. 1929- 105
Cordtz, Dan 1927- 73-76
Cordwell, Miriam 1908-1986 89-92
Obituary 120
Corea, Gena
See Corea, Genoveffa
Corea, Genoveffa 1946- 81-84
Corelli, Marie 1855-1924
See Mackay, Mary
See also DLB 34, 156
See also TCLC 51
Coren, Alan 1938- CANR-54
Earlier sketches in CA 69-72, CANR-29
See also SATA 32
Coren, Michael 1959- 153
Coren, Stanley 1942- 137
Coren, Victoria 1972- 131
Corey, Deborah Joy 1958- 168
Corey, Dorothy CANR-26
Earlier sketches in CA 69-72, CANR-11
See also SATA 23
Corey, Gerald F(rancis) 1937- 114
Corey, Melinda (Ann) 1957- 144
Corey, Paul (Frederick) 1903- CANR-2
Earlier sketch in CA 5-8R
Corey, Stephen 1948- CANR-52
Earlier sketch in CA 124
Corfe, Thomas Howell 1928- 103
See also SATA 27
Corfe, Tom
See Corfe, Thomas Howell
Corfield, Conrad Laurence 1893-1980 Obituary . 105
Corfield, Robin Bell 1952- .... SATA 74
Corfman, Eunice (Luccock)
1928-1980 Obituary 97-100
Corina, Maurice 1936- 57-60
Cork, Patrick
See Cockburn, (Francis) Claud
Cork, Richard (Graham) 1947- CANR-50
Earlier sketches in CA 107, CANR-24
Corke, Helen 1882- CAP-1
Earlier sketch in CA 9-10
Corke, Hilary 1921- 97-100
Corkey, R(obert) 1881-1966 .... CAP-1
Earlier sketch in CA 13-16
Corkran, David Hudson, Jr. 1902- 5-8R
Corkran, Herbert, Jr. 1924- 29-32R
Corle, Edwin 1906-1956 .... DLBY 85
Corless, Roger (Jonathan) 1938- 108
Corlett, Mary Lee 1957- 139
Corlett, William 1938- 103
See also SATA 46
See also SATA-Brief 39
Corlew, Robert Ewing 1922- 110
Corley, (Thomas) Anthony (Buchanan) 1923- ......
CANR-34
Earlier sketch in CA 1-4R
Corley, Edwin (Raymond) 1931-1981 .... CANR-12
Obituary 105
Earlier sketch in CA 25-28R
Corley, Ernest
See Bulmer, (Henry) Kenneth
Corley, Nora T(eresa) 118
Corley, Ray
See Corley, Edwin (Raymond)
Corley, Robert N(eil) 1930- CANR-19
Earlier sketches in CA 9-12R, CANR-3
Corliss, Charlotte N(uzum) 1932- 53-56
Corliss, Richard (Nelson) 1944- 157
Corliss, William R(oger) 1926- CANR-37
Earlier sketches in CA 45-48, CANR-1, 16
Cormack, Alexander James Ross 1942- 65-68
Cormack, James Maxwell Ross 1909-1975 . CAP-1
Earlier sketch in CA 9-10
Cormack, M(argaret) Grant 1913- 1-4R
See also SATA 11
Cormack, Margaret Lawson 1912- CANR-35
Earlier sketch in CA 1-4R
Cormack, Maribelle B. 1902-1984 .... SATA 39
Cormack, Robert J. 1946- 139
Cormack, Sandy
See Cormack, Alexander James Ross
Corman, Avery 1935- 85-88
Corman, Cid 1924-
See Corman, Sidney
See also CAAS 2
See also CLC 9
See also DLB 5, 193
Corman, Roger (William) 1926- 158
Corman, Sidney 1924- CANR-44
Earlier sketch in CA 85-88
See also Corman, Cid
See also DAM POET
Cormany, Michael 1951- 135
Cormier, Bruno M. 1919- Brief entry 114
Cormier, Frank 1927-1994 .... 21-24R
Obituary 144
Cormier, Ramona 1923- 49-52
Cormier, Raymond J(oseph) 1938- CANR-19
Earlier sketches in CA 53-56, CANR-4
Cormier, Robert (Edmund) 1925- CANR-23
Earlier sketches in CA 1-4R, CANR-5
Interview in CANR-23
See also AAYA 3, 19
See also CDALB 1968-1988
See also CLC 12, 30
See also CLR 12
See also DA
See also DAB
See also DAC
See also DAM MST, NOV
See also DLB 52
See also JRDA
See also MAICYA
See also MTCW 1
See also SATA 10, 45, 83
Cormillot, Albert E. J. 1938- 69-72
Corn, Alfred (DeWitt III) 1943- CANR-44
Earlier sketch in CA 104
See also CAAS 25
See also CLC 33
See also DLB 120
See also DLBY 80
Corn, Charles 1936- 168
Corn, David 1959- 149
Corn, Ira George, Jr. 1921-1982 .... CANR-35
Obituary 106
Earlier sketch in CA 85-88
Corn, Joseph J. 1938- 166
Cornea, Carol
See Koch, Kurt E(mil)
Cornebise, Alfred E(mile) 1929- CANR-38
Earlier sketch in CA 115
Cornehls, James V(ernon) 1936- 93-96
Corneille, Pierre 1606-1684 .... DAB
See also DAM MST
Cornelisen, Ann 1926- CANR-17
Earlier sketch in CA 25-28R
corneliszavandenheuvel
See van den Heuvel, Cornelisz A.
Cornelius, Carol 1942- 115
See also SATA 40
Cornelius, Temple H. 1891-1964 .... CAP-1
Earlier sketch in CA 11-12
Cornelius, Wanda Pyle 1936- 105
Cornell, Douglas B. 1906(?)-1982 Obituary 106
Cornell, Felix M. 1896(?)-1970 Obituary 104
Cornell, Francis Griffith 1906-1979 Obituary .. 89-92
Cornell, George W. 1920-1994 .... 9-12R
Obituary 146
Cornell, J.
See Cornell, Jeffrey
Cornell, James (Clayton, Jr.) 1938- CANR-11
Earlier sketch in CA 69-72
See also SATA 27
Cornell, Jean Gay 1920- CANR-1
Earlier sketch in CA 45-48
See also SATA 23
Cornell, Jeffrey 1945- .... SATA 11
Cornell, Jennifer C 1967- 158
Cornell, Katherine 1898(?)-1974 Obituary 49-52
Cornell, Tim 1946- 115
Corner, E. J. H.
See Corner, Edred John Henry
Corner, Edred John Henry 1906- Brief entry ... 116
Corner, George W(ashington) 1889-1981 102
Obituary 104
Corner, James 1961- 163
Corner, Philip 1933- 21-24R
Cornett, Joe D(elayne) 1935- 53-56
Corney, Estelle 1911- 115
Cornfeld, Betty S. 1944(?)-1988 Obituary 128
Cornfeld, Gaalyah 1902- CANR-12
Earlier sketch in CA 73-76
Cornford, A(ndrew) J(ohn) 1942- 112
Cornford, Adam 1950- .... CAAS 28
Cornforth, Maurice 1909-1980 .... CANR-4
Obituary 102
Earlier sketch in CA 5-8R
Corngold, Stanley Alan 1934- CANR-32
Earlier sketches in CA 37-40R, CANR-14
Cornillon, John Raymond Koppleman 1941- 17-20R
Cornish, Dudley T(aylor) 1915- 17-20R
Cornish, Edward (Seymour) 1927- CANR-25
Earlier sketch in CA 108
Cornish, Geoffrey (St. John) 1914- 125
Cornish, John (Buckley) 1914- 25-28R
Cornish, Sam(uel James) 1935- CANR-24
Earlier sketch in CA 41-44R
See also BW 1
See also DLB 41
See also SATA 23
Cornish, W(illiam) R(odolph) 1937- 29-32R
Cornish, William c. 1465-c. 1524 .... DLB 132
Cornman, James W(elton) 1929-1978 ... CANR-11
Earlier sketch in CA 69-72
Cornock, (John) Stroud 1938- 25-28R
Cornthwaite, Robert 1917- 152
Cornuelle, Richard C. 1927- 17-20R
Cornum, Rhonda (Leah Scott) 1954- 139
Cornwall, E(spie) Judson 1924- CANR-6
Earlier sketch in CA 57-60
Cornwall, I(an) W(olfran) 1909- 9-12R
Cornwall, J. Spencer 1888(?)-1983 Obituary ... 109
Cornwall, James (Handyside) Marshall
See Marshall-Cornwall, James (Handyside)
Cornwall, Jim
See Rikhoff, James C.
Cornwall, John 1928- CANR-37
Earlier sketch in CA 115
Cornwall, Martin
See Cavendish, Richard
Cornwall, Nellie
See Sloggett, Nellie
Cornwallis the Younger, William c. 1579-1614 . DLB 151
Cornwell, Anita (R.) 1923- CANR-71
Earlier sketch in CA 142
See also BW 2
Cornwell, Bernard 1944- 104
Cornwell, David (John Moore) 1931- CANR-59
Earlier sketches in CA 5-8R, CANR-13, 33
See also le Carre, John
See also CLC 9, 15
See also DAM POP
See also MTCW 1
Cornwell, Elmer E(ckert), Jr. 1924- Brief entry .. 118
Cornwell, John 157
Cornwell, Patricia Daniels 1956- CANR-53
Earlier sketch in CA 134
See also AAYA 16
See also DAM POP
Cornwell, Smith
See Smith, David (Jeddie)
Coronel, Jorge Icaza
See Icaza (Coronel), Jorge
Corp, Edward 1948- 156
Corpi, Lucha 1945- 131
See also DLB 82
See also HW
Corporal Trim
See Bolger, Philip C(unningham)
Corradi, Gemma 1939- 21-24R
Corradi, Juan E. 1943- 113
Corrado, Anthony 1957- 143
Corrall, Alice Enid 1916- 5-8R
Corran, Mary 1953- 154
Corre, Alan D. 1931- 37-40R
Correa
See Galbraith, Jean
Correa, Gustavo 1914- 49-52
Correia-Afonso, John 1924- CANR-13
Earlier sketch in CA 33-36R
Corren, Grace
See Hoskins, Robert
Correnti, Mario
See Togliatti, Palmiro
Correu, Larry M. 1931- 114
Correy, Lee
See Stine, G(eorge) Harry
Corrick, James A. 1945- 143
See also SATA 76
Corrie, Elva
See Clairmont, Elva
Corrigan, (Helen) Adeline 1909- 69-72
See also SATA 23
Corrigan, Barbara 1922- 57-60
See also SATA 8
Corrigan, Francis Joseph 1919- 5-8R
Corrigan, John D(avitt) 1900- 41-44R
Corrigan, John Thomas 1936- CANR-10
Earlier sketch in CA 65-68
Corrigan, Ralph L(awrence), Jr. 1937- 33-36R
Corrigan, Robert A(nthony) 1935- 9-12R
Corrigan, Robert W(illoughby) 1927-1993 . CANR-6
Obituary 142
Earlier sketch in CA 5-8R
Corrigan, Simon 1964- 143
Corrigan, Timothy (J.) 1951- 129
Corrin, Jay P(atrick) 1943- 125
Corrin, Sara 1918- 120
See also SATA 86
See also SATA-Brief 48

Corrin, Stephen 121
See also SATA 86
See also SATA-Brief 48
Corrington, John William 1932-1988 .... CANR-8
Obituary 127
Earlier sketch in CA 13-16R
Interview in CANR-8
See also DLB 6
Corris, Peter 1942- 135
Corriveau, Monique (Chouinard) 1927-1976 ....
CANR-12
Obituary 122
Earlier sketch in CA 61-64
Corrothers, James D(avid) 1869-1917 141
See also BW 2
See also DLB 50
Corry, Emmett 1934- 111
Corry, J(ames) A(lexander)
1899-1985 Obituary 120
Corsa, Helen Storm 1915- 17-20R
Corsaro, Francesco Andrea 1924- 85-88
Corsaro, Frank
See Corsaro, Francesco Andrea
Corsaro, Maria C(ecelia) 1949- 107
Corsel, Ralph 1920- 25-28R
Corsi, Jerome R(obert) 1946- 89-92
Corsini, Raymond J. 1914- CANR-45
Earlier sketches in CA 1-4R, CANR-3, 21
Corso, (Nunzio) Gregory 1930- CANR-41
Earlier sketch in CA 5-8R
See also CLC 1, 11
See also DLB 5, 16
See also MTCW 1
Corson, Fred Pierce 1896-1985 .... CAP-2
Obituary 115
Earlier sketch in CA 23-24
Corson, Hazel W. 1906- CANR-2
Earlier sketch in CA 1-4R
Corson, John J(ay III) 1905-1990 .... CANR-5
Obituary 132
Earlier sketch in CA 1-4R
Corson, Richard 41-44R
Corson-Finnerty, Adam Daniel 1944- CANR-14
Earlier sketch in CA 81-84
Corstanje, Auspicius van
See van Corstanje, Charles
Corstanje, Charles van
See van Corstanje, Charles
Cort, David 1904-1983 .... 9-12R
Obituary 111
Cort, M. C.
See Clifford, Margaret Cort
Cort, Margaret
See Clifford, Margaret Cort
Cort, Ned
See Jagninski, Tom
Cortada, James W(illiam) 1946- 133
Brief entry 114
Cortazar, Julio 1914-1984 .... CANR-32
Earlier sketches in CA 21-24R, CANR-12
See also CLC 2, 3, 5, 10, 13, 15, 33, 34, 92
See also DAM MULT, NOV
See also DLB 113
See also HLC
See also HW
See also MTCW 1
See also SSC 7
Cortazzi, (Henry Arthur) Hugh 1924- CANR-39
Earlier sketch in CA 115
Cortazzo, Carman 1936- 109
Corteen, Wes
See Norwood, Victor G(eorge) C(harles)
Corten, Irina H. 1941- 137
Cortes, Carlos E(liseo) 1934- CANR-8
Earlier sketch in CA 61-64
Cortes, Juan B(autista) 1925- 37-40R
Cortese, A(nthony) James 1917- 65-68
Cortese, Peter A. 1928- 149
Cortesi, Lawrence
See Cerri, Lawrence J.
Cortez, Jayne 1936- CANR-68
Earlier sketches in CA 73-76, CANR-13, 31
See also BW 2
See also DLB 41
Cortez-Villon, Juan
See Herzinger, Kim A(llen)
Corti, Eugenio 1921- 163
Cortinez, Carlos 1934- 123
Cortner, Richard C(arroll) 1935- 104
Cortright, Barbara 1927- 112
Cortright, David 1946- 57-60
Corty, Floyd L(ouis) 1916- 13-16R
Corum, James S(terling) 1953- 139
Corvinus, Gottlieb Siegmund 1677-1746 .. DLB 168
Corvinus, Jakob
See Raabe, Wilhelm (Karl)
Corwen, Leonard 1921- CANR-15
Earlier sketch in CA 93-96
Corwin, Adele Beatrice Lewis 1922-1990 123
Obituary 131
Corwin, Cecil
See Kornbluth, C(yril) M.
Corwin, Edward S(amuel) 1878-1963 122
Obituary 113
Corwin, Judith H(offman) 1946- CANR-32
Earlier sketch in CA 113
See also SATA 10
Corwin, Norman 1910- CANR-24
Earlier sketches in CA 1-4R, CANR-1
See also AITN 2
Corwin, Ronald G(ary) 1932- CANR-23
Earlier sketches in CA 17-20R, CANR-8
Cory, Annie Sophie
See Cross, Victoria
Cory, Caroline
See Freeman, Kathleen
Cory, Charlotte 1956- 137
Cory, Corrine
See Cory, Irene E.
Cory, Daniel 1904-1972 Obituary 37-40R
Cory, David 1872-1966 Obituary 25-28R
Cory, Desmond
See McCarthy, Shaun (Lloyd)
Cory, Howard L.
See Jardine, Jack
Cory, Irene E. 1910- 49-52
Cory, Jean-Jacques 1947- 57-60
Cory, Ray
See Marshall, Mel(vin D.)
Cory, Rowena
See Lindquist, Rowena Cory
Cory, William Johnson 1823-1892 .... DLB 35
Corya, I. E.
See Cory, Irene E.
Coryate, Thomas 1577(?)-1617 .... DLB 151, 172
Coryell, Janet L(ee) 1955- 135
Cosby, Bill
See Cosby, William Henry, Jr.
See also BEST 89:4
Cosby, Camille (Olivia Hanks) 1945- 156
Cosby, William Henry, Jr. 1937- CANR-42
Earlier sketches in CA 81-84, CANR-27
See also Cosby, Bill
See also BW 2
See also SATA 66
Cosby, Yvonne Shepard
1886(?)-1980 Obituary 97-100
Coscarelli, Kate 1927- 142
Cose, Ellis Jonathan 1951- 119
See also BW 2
Cosell, Howard 1918-1995 108
Obituary 148
Cosentino, Andrew J(oseph) 1931- 120
Cosentino, Donald J(ohn) 1941- 108
Cosentino, Frank 1937- 132
Coser, Lewis A. 1913- CANR-4
Earlier sketch in CA 1-4R
Coser, Rose Laub 1916- 13-16R
Cosgrave, John O'Hara II 1908-1968 .... CANR-1
Earlier sketch in CA 1-4R
See also SATA-Obit 21
Cosgrave, Patrick 1941- 33-36R
Cosgrove, Carol Ann
See Twitchett, Carol Cosgrove
Cosgrove, Denis (Edmund) 1948- 146
Cosgrove, Margaret (Leota) 1926- CANR-6
Earlier sketch in CA 9-12R
See also SATA 47
Cosgrove, Mark P. 1947- 85-88
Cosgrove, Maynard G(iles) 1895- 57-60
Cosgrove, Rachel
See Payes, Rachel C(osgrove)
Cosgrove, Richard A(lfred) 1941- 104
Cosgrove, Stephen E(dward) 1945- CANR-22
Earlier sketch in CA 69-72
See also AITN 1
See also SATA 53
See also SATA-Brief 40
Cosh, (Ethel Eleanor) Mary 5-8R
Cosic, Dobrica 1921- 138
Brief entry 122
See also CLC 14
See also DLB 181
Cosin, John 1595-1672 .... DLB 151
Coskey, Evelyn 1932- 41-44R
See also SATA 7
Coskran, Kathleen 1943- 139
Coslow, Sam(son) 1905-1982 .... CANR-29
Obituary 106
Earlier sketch in CA 77-80
Cosman, Carol 104
Cosman, Madeleine Pelner 1937- 127
Brief entry 105
Cosman, Mark 1945- 152
Cosneck, Bernard Joseph 1912- 49-52
Cosner, Shaaron 1940- CANR-38
Earlier sketch in CA 116
See also SATA 43
Coss, Thurman L. 1926- 13-16R
Cossart, Theophilus
See Glass, Montague (Marsden)
Cosseboom, Kathy Groehn
See El-Messidi, Kathy Groehn
Cossi, Olga 1921- 81-84
See also SATA 67, 102
Cosslett, Tess 1947- 115
Cossman, E(li) Joseph 1918- 17-20R
Cossolotto, Matthew 1953- 153
Cost, March
See Morrison, Margaret Mackie
Costa, Albert Bernard 1929- 13-16R
Costa, (Elena) Alexandra 1944- 145
Costa, Gustavo 1930- 37-40R
Costa, Horacio (L.) de la 1916-1977 Obituary .. 112
Costa, Manuel J(oseph) 1933- 161
Costa, Richard Hauer 1921- 21-24R
Costabel, Eva Deutsch 1924- 125
See also SATA 45
Costabel-Deutsch, Eva
See Costabel, Eva Deutsch
Costain, Thomas B(ertram) 1885-1965 .... 5-8R
Obituary 25-28R
See also CLC 30
See also DLB 9
Costantin, M(ary) M(cCaffrey) 1935- 45-48
Costantini, Humberto 1924(?)-1987 131
Obituary 122
See also CLC 49
See also HW
Costanza, Mary S(carpone) 1927- 158
Costas, Orlando E(nrique) 1942-1987 101
Obituary 124
Costas, Procope 1900(?)-1974 Obituary 53-56
Coste, Donat 1912-1957 .... DLB 88
Costello, Anne 1937- 102
Costello, Bonnie 1950- 129
Costello, Chris 1947- 107
Costello, David F(rancis) 1904- 33-36R
See also SATA 23
Costello, Donald P(aul) 1931- 17-20R
Costello, Elvis 1955- .... CLC 21
Costello, Gerald M. 1931- 127
Costello, Grace Seymour 1883-1983 Obituary .. 110
Costello, John E(dward) 1943- 85-88
Costello, Joseph P(atrick) 1924- 115
Costello, Louisa Stuart 1799-1870 .... DLB 166
Costello, Michael
See Detzer, Karl
Costello, Peter 1946- 93-96
Costello, William Aloysious 1904-1969 .... 1-4R
Obituary 103
Costelloe, M(artin) Joseph 1914- 41-44R
Coster, Robert
See Barltrop, Robert
Costigan, Daniel M. 1929- CANR-56
Earlier sketches in CA 33-36R, CANR-14, 31
Costigan, Giovanni 1905- CAP-1
Earlier sketch in CA 13-16
Costigan, James 1928- 73-76
Costikyan, Edward N. 1924- 17-20R
Costikyan, Greg 1959- 142
Costinescu, Tristan
See Gross, Terence
Costis, Harry George 1928- 45-48
Costley, Bill
See Costley, William K(irkwood), Jr.
Costley, William K(irkwood), Jr. 1942- CANR-56
Earlier sketches in CA 81-84, CANR-35
Costonis, John J(oseph) 1937- CANR-4
Earlier sketch in CA 49-52
Cota-Cardenas, Margarita 1941- .... DLB 122
Cote, Richard G(eorge) 1934- 69-72
Cote, Richard N. 1945- 147
Cotes, Cecil V.
See Duncan, Sara Jeannette
Cotes, Peter 1912- CANR-26
Earlier sketches in CA 5-8R, CANR-4
Cothem, Fayly H(ardcastle) 1926- 1-4R
Cothen, Joe H(erbert) 1926- 113
Cothran, J(oseph) Guy 1897- CAP-2
Earlier sketch in CA 29-32
Cothran, James R(obert) 1940- 150
Cothran, Jean 1910- 93-96
Cotich, Felicia 1926- 115
Cotler, Gordon 1923- 1-4R
Cotler, Sherwin B(arry) 1941- 65-68
Cotlow, Lewis N(athaniel) 1898-1987 65-68
Obituary 122
Cotman, John Walton 1954- 146
Cotner, Robert Crawford 1906- 37-40R
Cotner, Thomas E. 1916- 37-40R
Cott, Hugh B(amford) 1900-1987 Obituary 122
Cott, Jonathan 1942- 53-56
See also SATA 23
Cott, Nancy F(alik) 1945- CANR-59
Earlier sketch in CA 81-84
Cottam, Clarence 1899-1974 97-100
See also SATA 25
Cottam, Keith M. 1941- 81-84
Cottam, Walter P(ace) 1894- CAP-1
Earlier sketch in CA 13-16
Cotten, Bruce 1873-1954 .... DLB 187
Cotten, Lee 1942- CANR-56
Earlier sketch in CA 127
Cotten, Nell(ie) Wyllie 1908- 1-4R
Cotter, Charles H(enry) 1919- 13-16R
Cotter, Cornelius Philip 1924- CANR-1
Earlier sketch in CA 1-4R
Cotter, Edward F(rancis) 1917- CANR-6
Earlier sketch in CA 5-8R
Cotter, James Finn 1929- 33-36R
Cotter, Janet M(errill) 1914- 61-64
Cotter, Joseph Seamon Sr. 1861-1949 124
See also BLC 1
See also BW 1
See also DAM MULT
See also DLB 50
See also TCLC 28
Cotter, Joseph Seamon, Jr. 1895-1919 .... DLB 50
Cotter, Richard V(ern) 1930- CANR-47
Earlier sketches in CA 41-44R, CANR-14
Cotterell, Geoffrey 1919- 5-8R
Cotterell, (Francis) Peter 1930- CANR-1
Earlier sketch in CA 49-52
Cotterill, Rodney M(ichael) J(ohn) 1933- . CANR-42
Earlier sketch in CA 118
Cotterrell, Roger (B. M.) 1946- 142
Cottingham, John (Graham) 1943- CANR-49
Earlier sketch in CA 133
Cottle, Charles
See Anderson, Robert C(harles)
Cottle, Thomas J. 1937- CANR-17
Earlier sketch in CA 33-36R
Cottle, William C(ullen) 1913- 41-44R
Cottler, Joseph 1899- CAP-2
Earlier sketch in CA 25-28
See also SATA 22
Cotton, Charles 1630-1687 .... DLB 131
Cotton, (Thomas) Henry 1907-1987 Obituary 124
Cotton, John 1584-1652 .... DLB 24
Cotton, John 1925- CANR-52
Earlier sketches in CA 65-68, CANR-11, 27
Cotton, John W(healdon) 1925- 33-36R
Cotton, Norris 1900- 103
Cottonwood, Joe 1947- 156
See also SATA 92
Cottrell, Alan (Howard) 1919- CANR-10
Earlier sketch in CA 65-68
Cottrell, Alan P. 1935-1984 120
Cottrell, Alvin J. 1925(?)-1984 Obituary 112
Cottrell, (William) Fred(erick) 1903- 1-4R
Cottrell, Jack (Warren) 1938- CANR-23
Earlier sketch in CA 107
Cottrell, Leonard 1913-1974 .... CANR-4
Earlier sketch in CA 5-8R
See also SATA 24
Cottrell, Leonard S(later), Jr. 1899-1985 107
Obituary 115
Cottrell, Richard 1936- 130
Cottrell, Robert C. 1950- 142
Cottrell, Robert D(uane) 1930- 53-56
Cottret, Bernard 1951- 143
Cottringer, Anne 1952- 163
See also SATA 97
Couch, Arthur Thomas Quiller
See Quiller-Couch, SirArthur (Thomas)
Couch, Helen F(ox) 1907- CAP-2
Earlier sketch in CA 17-18
Couch, Osma Palmer
See Tod, Osma Gallinger
Couch, William, Jr. 152
See also BW 2
Couch, William T(erry) 1901-1988 Obituary 127
Coudenhove-Kalergi, Richard N(icolas)
1894-1972 Obituary 37-40R
Coudert, Allison P(ierce) 1941- 110
Coudert, Jo 1923- 17-20R
Coudray, Jean-Marc
See Castoriadis, Cornelius
Couffer, Jack 1924- CANR-1
Earlier sketch in CA 1-4R
Couger, J(ames) Daniel 1929- CANR-8
Earlier sketch in CA 53-56
Coughlan, John W. 1927- 21-24R
Coughlan, Margaret N(ourse) 1925- 107
Coughlan, (John) Robert 1914- 65-68
Coughlan, William C(arlisle), Jr. 1946- 115
Coughlin, Bernard J. 1922- 13-16R
Coughlin, Charles E(dward)
1891-1979 Obituary 97-100
Coughlin, George G(ordon) 1900- 107
Coughlin, Joseph Welter 1919- 1-4R
Coughlin, T(homas) Glen 1958- 136
Coughlin, Violet L(ouise) 73-76
Coughlin, William J(eremiah) 1929-1992 139
Coughran, Larry C. 1925- 21-24R
Coughtry, Jay 1945- 111
Couldery, Fred(erick) A(lan) J(ames) 1928- .. 9-12R
Coulet du Gard, Rene 1919- CANR-4
Earlier sketch in CA 53-56
Coulette, Henri Anthony 1927-1988 .... CANR-14
Obituary 125
Earlier sketch in CA 65-68
Coulling, Mary (Price) 1928- 142
Coulling, Sidney Baxter 1924- 102
Coulmas, Florian 1949- 132
Couloumbis, Theodore A. 1935- CANR-7
Earlier sketch in CA 17-20R
Coulson, C(harles) A(lfred) 1910-1974 .... CANR-4
Earlier sketch in CA 5-8R
Coulson, Felicity Carter 1906- 9-12R
Coulson, John H(ubert) A(rthur) 1906- 9-12R
Coulson, Juanita (Ruth) 1933- CANR-52
Earlier sketches in CA 25-28R, CANR-9, 26
Coulson, N. J.
See Coulson, Noel J(ames)
Coulson, Noel J(ames) 1928-1986 124
Obituary 120
Coulson, Robert 1924- CANR-36
Earlier sketch in CA 49-52
Coulson, Robert S(tratton) 1928- CANR-24
Earlier sketches in CA 21-24R, CANR-9
Coulson, William D(onald) E(dward) 1942- 89-92
Coulter, Catherine CANR-71
Earlier sketch in CA 139
Coulter, E(llis) Merton 1890-1981 .... CANR-3
Obituary 104
Earlier sketch in CA 9-12R
Coulter, Edwin M(artin) 1937- 104
Coulter, Harris L. 1932- 136
Coulter, Hope Norman 1961- 129
Coulter, John (William) 1888-1980 .... CANR-3
Earlier sketch in CA 5-8R
See also DLB 68
Coulter, N(orman) Arthur, Jr. 1920- 65-68
Coulter, Olivia W. 1915(?)-1989 Obituary 129
Coulter, Stephen 1914- Brief entry 109
Coulton, James
See Hansen, Joseph
Coultrap-McQuin, Susan (M.) 1947- 137
Council, Norman Briggs 1936- 102
Cound, John J(ames) 1928- 37-40R
Counsel, June 1926- 138
See also SATA 70
Counsell, John William 1905-1987 57-60
Obituary 121
Counselman, Mary Elizabeth 1911-1994 . CANR-72
Earlier sketch in CA 106
Counsilman, James E(dward) 1920- 126
Count, Earl W(endel) 1899-1996 .... 37-40R
Obituary 155
Counter, Kenneth (Norman Samuel) 1930- .. 25-28R
Countess of Blessington, Marguerite
1789-1849 .... DLB 166
Countess of Longford
See Longford, Elizabeth (Harmon Pakenham)
Countess of Pembroke
See Sidney Herbert, Mary
Countryman, The
See Whitlock, Ralph
Countryman, Vern 1917- 13-16R
Counts, Charles Richard 1934- 49-52
Counts, George S(ylvester) 1889-1974 .... 5-8R
Obituary 53-56

Couper, Heather 1949- 124
Couper, J(ohn) M(ill) 1914- 45-48
Couper, Stephen
See Gallagher, Stephen
Couperus, Louis (Marie Anne) 1863-1923 Brief entry 115
See also TCLC 15
Coupey, Philippe 1937- 104
Coupland, Douglas 1961- CANR-57
Earlier sketch in CA 142
See also CLC 85
See also DAC
See also DAM POP
Coupling, J. J.
See Pierce, John Robinson
Courage, James Francis 1903-1963 77-80
Courant, Richard 1888-1972 157
Obituary 33-36R
Couratin, Arthur Hubert 1902-1988 Obituary 126
Courlander, Harold 1908-1996 CANR-40
Obituary 151
Earlier sketches in CA 9-12R, CANR-3, 18
See also SATA 6
See also SATA-Obit 88
Cournand, Andre (Frederic) 1895-1988 157
Cournos, John 1881-1966 CAP-2
Earlier sketch in CA 13-14
See also DLB 54
Courouсli, Jennifer 1922- 29-32R
Course, Alfred George 1895- 9-12R
Course, Edwin 1922- 77-80
Coursen, Herbert R(andolph), Jr. 1932- CANR-41
Earlier sketches in CA 53-56, CANR-4, 19
Coursen, Valerie 1965(?)- SATA 102
Court, Harold
See Swycaffer, Jefferson P(utnam)
Court, Margaret Smith 1942- Brief entry 106
Court, Sharon
See Rowland, D(onald) S(ydney)
Court, W(illiam) H(enry) B(assano) 1905(?)-1971 Obituary 104
Court, Wesli
See Turco, Lewis (Putnam)
Court, Wesli 1940- CANR-11
Earlier sketch in CA 69-72
Courtauld, George 1938- 129
Courteline, Georges 1858-1929 DLB 192
Courtenay, Ashley (Reginald) 1888-1986 Obituary 121
Courtenay, Bryce 1933- 138
See also CLC 59
Courtenay, William J(ames) 1935- 9-12R
Courter, Gay 1944- CANR-26
Earlier sketches in CA 57-60, CANR-7
Courthion, Pierre (Barthelemy) 1902- CANR-14
Earlier sketch in CA 81-84
Courtice, Katie 1942- 121
Courtier, S(idney) H(obson) 1904-197(?) CAP-2
Earlier sketch in CA 25-28
Courtine, Robert 1910- CANR-14
Earlier sketch in CA 81-84
Courtis, Stuart Appleton 1874-1969 Obituary 105
See also SATA-Obit 29
Courtland, Roberta
See Dern, Erolie Pearl Gaddis
Courtneidge, Cicely 1893-1980 Obituary 105
Courtney, Dayle
See Goldsmith, Howard
Courtney, E(dward) 1932- 129
Courtney, Gwendoline CAP-1
Earlier sketch in CA 9-10
Courtney, John
See Judd, Frederick Charles
Courtney, Nicholas (Piers) 1944- CANR-32
Earlier sketch in CA 113
Courtney, Ragan 1941- 97-100
Courtney, (John) Richard 1927- CANR-48
Earlier sketches in CA 105, CANR-23
Courtney, Robert
See Ellison, Harlan (Jay)
Courtney, William J(ohn) 1921- 102
Courtney, Winifred F(isk) 1918- 109
Courtwright, David T(odd) 1952- CANR-28
Earlier sketch in CA 110
Courville, Donovan A(mos) 1901- 45-48
Coury, Louise Andree 1895(?)-1983 Obituary 109
See also SATA-Obit 34
Couse, Harold C. 1925- 17-20R
Cousens, Frances Reissman 1913-1985 Obituary 115
Couser, G(riffith) Thomas 1946- 89-92
Cousineau, Phil 1952- 146
Cousins, Albert Newton 1919- 41-44R
Cousins, Geoffrey (Esmond) 1900- 25-28R
Cousins, Linda 1946- 155
See also SATA 90
Cousins, Margaret 1905-1996 CANR-1
Obituary 152
Earlier sketch in CA 1-4R
See also DLB 137
See also SATA 2
See also SATA-Obit 92
Cousins, Norman 1915-1990 CANR-61
Earlier sketches in CA 17-20R, CANR-13, 33
See also BEST 90:2
See also DLB 137
See also MTCW 1
Cousins, Peter Edward 1928- 104
Cousse, Raymond 1942- 101
Cousteau, Jacques-Yves 1910-1997 CANR-67
Obituary 159
Earlier sketches in CA 65-68, CANR-15
See also CLC 30
See also MTCW 1
See also SATA 38, 98
Cousteau, Philippe Pierre 1940-1979 33-36R
Obituary 89-92
Coustillas, Pierre 1930- 73-76
Coutard, Wanda Lundy Hale 1902(?)-1982 Obituary 106
Coutinho, Joaquim 1886(?)-1978 Obituary 77-80
Couto, Nancy Vieira 1942- 136
Couto, Richard A. 1941- CANR-15
Earlier sketch in CA 89-92
Coutts, Frederick Lee 1899-1986 CANR-36
Earlier sketch in CA 109
Couture, Andrea 1943- 85-88
Couture, Christin 1951- SATA 73
Couturier, Louis (Joseph) 1910- 101
Couzyn, Jeni 1942- 85-88
Covarrubias, Barbara Faith 1932- 113
Covatta, Anthony Gallo 1944- 53-56
Covell, Alan C(arter) 1952- 118
Covell, Jon Carter 1910- CANR-17
Earlier sketch in CA 97-100
Coven, Brenda 110
Coveney, James 1920- 41-44R
Coveney, Peter (Vivian) 1958- 140
Coventry, Francis 1725-1754 DLB 39
Coventry, John (Joseph Seton) 1915-1998 93-96
Obituary 165
Cover, Arthur Byron 1950- CANR-57
Earlier sketch in CA 107
Cover, Robert M. 1943-1986 57-60
Obituary 119
Coverdale, John F(oy) 1940- 73-76
Coverdale, Miles c. 1487-1569 DLB 167
Coverley, Louise Bennett
See Bennett-Coverley, Louise
Covert, James Thayne 1932- 37-40R
Covert, Paul 1941- CANR-20
Earlier sketch in CA 103
Covey, Cyclone 1922- 21-24R
Covey, Stephen R. 1932- CANR-41
Earlier sketches in CA 33-36R, CANR-12
Covici, Pascal, Jr. 1930- 1-4R
Coville, Bruce 1950- CANR-22
Earlier sketch in CA 97-100
See also JRDA
See also SATA 32, 77
Coville, Walter J(oseph) 1914- CANR-5
Earlier sketch in CA 5-8R
Covin, David L(eroy) 1940- 143
See also BW 2
Covin, Theron Michael 1947- 57-60
Covina, Gina 1952- 101
Covington, James W. 1917- 33-36R
Covington, Martin Vaden 1936- 37-40R
Covington, Vicki 1952- CANR-59
Earlier sketch in CA 133
Covino, Frank 1931- 57-60
Covino, Joseph, Jr. 1954- 113
Covino, Michael 1950- 132
Covvey, H(arry) Dominic J(oseph) 1944- CANR-28
Earlier sketch in CA 110
Cowan, Alan
See Gilchrist, Alan W.
Cowan, Charles Donald 1923- 102
Cowan, Edward James 1944- 103
Cowan, G(ordon) 1933- 25-28R
Cowan, G(eorge) H(amilton) 1917- 17-20R
Cowan, Geoffrey 1942- 97-100
Cowan, George McKillop 1916- 102
Cowan, Gregory M(ac) 1935-1979 CANR-9
Earlier sketch in CA 65-68
Cowan, Henry J(acob) 1919- CANR-19
Earlier sketches in CA 53-56, CANR-4
Cowan, Ian Borthwick 1932-1990 CANR-24
Obituary 133
Earlier sketches in CA 61-64, CANR-8
Cowan, J(oseph) L(loyd) 1929- 25-28R
Cowan, James (Granville) 1942- 139
Cowan, James C(ostello) 1927- CANR-29
Earlier sketch in CA 29-32R
Cowan, Janice 1941- 97-100
Cowan, Louise (Shillingburg) 1916- CANR-47
Earlier sketch in CA 1-4R
Cowan, Lyn 1942- 116
Cowan, Michael H(eath) 1937- 21-24R
Cowan, Paul 1940-1988 Obituary 126
Cowan, Peter (Walkinshaw) 1914- CANR-50
Earlier sketches in CA 21-24R, CANR-9, 25
See also SSC 28
Cowan, Richard O(lsen) 1934- 53-56
Cowan, Robert Granniss 1895- CAP-1
Earlier sketch in CA 11-12
Cowan, Ruth Schwartz 1941- 115
Cowan, Stuart DuBois 1917- 104
Cowan, Walter G(reaves) 1912- 120
Cowan, Wood (Messick) 1896-1977 69-72
Coward, Barry 1941- 131
Coward, Noel (Peirce) 1899-1973 CANR-35
Obituary 41-44R
Earlier sketches in CAP-2, CA 17-18
See also AITN 1
See also CDBLB 1914-1945
See also CLC 1, 9, 29, 51
See also DAM DRAM
See also DLB 10
See also MTCW 1
Cowart, David (Guyland) 1947- CANR-30
Earlier sketch in CA 104
Cowasjee, Saros 1931- CANR-43
Earlier sketches in CA 9-12R, CANR-5, 20
Cowden, Dudley J(ohnstone) 1899- 41-44R
Cowden, Jeanne 1918- 85-88
Cowden, Joanna Dunlap 1933- 53-56
Cowden, Robert H. 1934- 143
Cowdrey, A(lbert) E(dward) 1933- 17-20R
Cowdrey, (Herbert) Colin 1932- 105
Cowdrey, H(erbert) E(dward) J(ohn) 1926- 129
Cowell, (John) Adrian 1934- 103
Cowell, Cyril 1888- CAP-2
Earlier sketch in CA 21-22
Cowell, Frank A. 135
Cowell, Frank Richard 1897- CANR-8
Earlier sketch in CA 53-56
Cowell, Henry Dixon 1897-1965 Obituary 116
Cowell, Stephanie 1943- 144
Cowen, David L(aurence) 1909- CANR-47
Earlier sketch in CA 13-16R
Cowen, Emory L(eland) 1926- CANR-51
Earlier sketch in CA 69-72
Cowen, Eve
See Werner, Herma
Cowen, Frances
See Munthe, Frances
Cowen, Ida 1898- 45-48
See also SATA 64
Cowen, Robert Churchill 1927- 13-16R
Cowen, Ron(ald) 1944- CANR-67
Earlier sketch in CA 85-88
Cowen, Roy C(hadwell) 1930- CANR-12
Earlier sketch in CA 33-36R
Cowen, Zelman 1919- CANR-1
Earlier sketch in CA 1-4R
Cowgill, Donald O(len) 1911- 37-40R
Cowherd, Raymond Gibson 1909- 124
Cowie, Alexander 1896- 33-36R
Cowie, Donald 1911- 116
Cowie, Evelyn E(lizabeth) 1924- CANR-9
Earlier sketch in CA 13-16R
Cowie, Hamilton Russell 1931- 102
Cowie, Leonard W(allace) 1919- CANR-9
Earlier sketch in CA 13-16R
See also SATA 4
Cowie, Mervyn (Hugh) 1909-1996 CAP-1
Obituary 152
Earlier sketch in CA 9-10
Cowie, Peter 1939- CANR-18
Earlier sketches in CA 49-52, CANR-1
Cowle, Jerome Milton 1917- 93-96
Cowle, Jerry
See Cowle, Jerome Milton
Cowler, Rosemary (Elizabeth) 1925- 25-28R
Cowles, Fleur CANR-24
Earlier sketches in CA 9-12R, CANR-4
See also AITN 1
Cowles, Frank, Jr. 1918- 57-60
Cowles, Gardner 1861-1946 DLB 29
Cowles, Gardner A., Jr. 1903-1985 Obituary 116
See also DLB 127, 137
Cowles, Ginny 1924- 57-60
Cowles, John Sr. 1898-1983 Obituary 109
Cowles, Kathleen
See Krull, Kathleen
Cowles, Lois Thornburg 1909-1980 Obituary 101
Cowles, Mike
See Cowles, Gardner A., Jr.
Cowles, Raymond B(ridgeman) 1896-1975 Obituary 61-64
Cowles, S(amuel) Macon, Jr. 1916- 21-24R
Cowles, Virginia (Spencer) 1912-1983 CANR-12
Obituary 110
Earlier sketch in CA 65-68
Cowley, Abraham 1618-1667 DLB 131, 151
Cowley, Hannah 1743-1809 DLB 89
Cowley, Joseph (Gilbert) 1923- 106
Cowley, (Cassia) Joy 1936- CANR-57
Earlier sketches in CA 25-28R, CANR-11
See also SATA 4, 90
Cowley, Joy 1936- SAAS 26
Cowley, Malcolm 1898-1989 CANR-55
Obituary 128
Earlier sketches in CA 5-8R, CANR-3
See also CLC 39
See also DLB 4, 48
See also DLBY 81, 89
See also MTCW 1
Cowley, Marjorie 1925- 148
Cowlin, Dorothy
See Whalley, Dorothy
Cowling, Elizabeth 1910- Brief entry 110
Cowling, Ellis 1905- CAP-1
Earlier sketch in CA 13-16
Cowling, Maurice John 1926- CANR-3
Earlier sketch in CA 5-8R
Cowlishaw, Ranson 1894- 5-8R
Cowper, Richard
See Middleton-Murry, John (Jr.)
Cowper, William 1731-1800 DAM POET
See also DLB 104, 109
Cox, A(nthony) B(erkeley) 1893-1971 CANR-58
Earlier sketch in CA 97-100
See also Berkeley, Anthony
Cox, Albert W(esley) 1921- 53-56
Cox, Allan 1937- 93-96
Cox, Alva Irwin, Jr. 1925- 17-20R
Cox, Archibald 1912- 73-76
Cox, (Christopher) Barry 1931- 103
See also SATA 62
Cox, Bertha Mae (Hill) 1901- 17-20R
Cox, Bill 1910- 9-12R
Cox, Brad J. 1944- 160
Cox, C. Benjamin 1925- 97-100
Cox, Carol 1946- 117
Cox, Charles B(rian) 1928- 25-28R
Cox, Claire 1919- CANR-2
Earlier sketch in CA 5-8R
Cox, Clinton SATA 74
Cox, Constance 1915- CANR-24
Earlier sketches in CA 21-24R, CANR-9
Cox, David (Dundas) 1933- 119
See also SATA 56
Cox, Donald William 1921- CANR-4
Earlier sketch in CA 1-4R
See also SATA 23
Cox, Edith Muriel 102
Cox, Edward Finch 1946- 29-32R
Cox, Edward Franklin 1925- 33-36R
Cox, Edward Locksley 1943- 121
Cox, Edwin B(urk) 1930- 37-40R
Cox, Elizabeth 1942- 130
Cox, Elizabeth 1953- 136
Cox, Erle (Harold) 1873-1950 Brief entry 112
Cox, Eugene L. 1931- 21-24R
Cox, Frank D. 1933- 29-32R
Cox, Fred(erick) M(oreland) 1928- CANR-1
Earlier sketch in CA 45-48
Cox, G. William 1949(?)-1988 Obituary 125
Cox, Gary D(uane) 1947- 113
Cox, Gary W(alter) 1955- 139
Cox, Geoffrey Sandford 1910- 103
Cox, George W(yatt) 1935- 115
Cox, Geraldine Vang 1944- 157
Cox, Gordon 1942- 146
Cox, Harvey (Gallagher, Jr.) 1929- 77-80
See also AITN 1
Cox, (William) Harvey 1939- 45-48
Cox, Hebe 1909- CAP-1
Earlier sketch in CA 13-14
Cox, Hugh Brandon
See Brandon-Cox, Hugh
Cox, Hugh S(towell) 1874-1969 CAP-2
Earlier sketch in CA 21-22
Cox, J(ohn) Gray 1952- 123
Cox, J. Halley 1910-1974 Obituary 112
Cox, Jack
See Cox, John Roberts
Cox, James Anthony 1926- 104
Cox, James M(elville) 1925- 13-16R
Cox, James McMahon 1903-1974 DLB 127
Cox, James Middleton, Jr. 1903-1974 Obituary 89-92
Cox, James Middleton 1870-1957 DLB 127
Cox, James W(illiam) 1923- 33-36R
Cox, Jennifer Lloyd 1947- 158
Cox, Jeri
See Kimes, Beverly Rae
Cox, Joan (Irene) 1942- 101
Cox, John H(enry) 1907-1975 Obituary 115
Cox, John Roberts 1915-1981 CANR-14
Earlier sketch in CA 29-32R
See also SATA 9
Cox, John Stuart 1931- 117
Cox, Joseph A. 1896(?)-1980 Obituary 97-100
Cox, Joseph Mason Andrew 1930- CANR-2
Earlier sketch in CA 49-52
See also BW 1
Cox, Joseph W(illiam) 1937- 81-84
Cox, Keith (Kohn) 1931- CANR-12
Earlier sketch in CA 69-72
Cox, Kevin R. 1939- 37-40R
Cox, LaWanda Fenlason 1909- 9-12R
Cox, Lee Sheridan 1916- 25-28R
Cox, Madison 1958- 144
Cox, Marie-Therese Henriette 1925-1991 105
Obituary 136
Cox, Marion Monroe 1898-1983 Obituary 110
See also Monroe, Marion
Cox, Mark 1956- 128
Cox, Martha Heasley 1919- 13-16R
Cox, Mary Elizabeth
See Headapohl, Betty R.
Cox, Maxwell E(varts) 1922-1996 25-28R
Obituary 153
Cox, Miriam Stewart 9-12R
Cox, Molly
See Cox, Marie-Therese Henriette
Cox, Oliver Cromwell 1901-1974 1-4R
Obituary 103
Cox, P(atrick) Brian 45-48
See also Stuart, Kenneth
Cox, Palmer 1840-1924 Brief entry 111
See also CLR 24
See also DLB 42
See also SATA 24
Cox, Paul(us) 1940- 143
Cox, R(obert) David 1937- CANR-13
Earlier sketch in CA 29-32R
Cox, R(alph) Merritt 1939- 33-36R
Cox, Rachel Dunaway 1904- 33-36R
Cox, Reavis 1900-1992 CAP-1
Obituary 139
Earlier sketch in CA 13-16
Cox, Richard 1931- CANR-30
Earlier sketches in CA 21-24R, CANR-11
Cox, Richard Howard 1925- CANR-8
Earlier sketch in CA 13-16R
Cox, Robert H(enry) 1961- 147
Cox, Roger L. 1931- 135
Cox, Stephen (LeRoy) 1966- 130
Cox, Steve 1962- 156
Cox, Thomas R(ichard) 1933- 53-56
Cox, Vic 1942- 152
See also SATA 88
Cox, Victoria
See Garretson, Victoria Diane
Cox, Wallace (Maynard) 1924-1973 97-100
Obituary 41-44R
See also Cox, Wally
Cox, Wally
See Cox, Wallace (Maynard)
See also SATA 25
Cox, Warren E(arle) 1895-1977 CAP-2
Obituary 69-72
Earlier sketch in CA 33-36
Cox, William E(dwin), Jr. 1930- 106

Cox, William R(obert) 1901-1988 ... CANR-59
Obituary ... 126
Earlier sketches in CA 9-12R, CANR-6, 24
See also SATA 46
See also SATA-Brief 31
See also SATA-Obit 57
Cox, William Trevor 1928- ... CANR-55
Earlier sketches in CA 9-12R, CANR-4, 37
Interview in ... CANR-37
See also Trevor, William
See also CLC 9, 14, 71
See also DAM NOV
See also DLB 14
See also MTCW 1
Coxe, Antony D(acres) Hippisley
See Hippisley Coxe, Antony D(acres)
Coxe, George Harmon 1901-1984 ... CANR-59
Earlier sketch in CA 57-60
Coxe, Louis (Osborne) 1918- ... 13-16R
See also DLB 5
Coxe, Molly 1959- ... 137
See also SATA 69, 101
Coxe, Tench 1755-1824 ... DLB 37
Cox-George, Noah Arthur William 1915- ... CANR-6
Earlier sketch in CA 13-16R
Coxhead, Elizabeth 1909(?)-1979 Obituary ... 89-92
Cox-Johnson, Ann
See Saunders, Ann Loreille
Coxon, Michele 1950- ... SATA 76
Coy, Fred E. 1923- ... 164
Coy, Harold 1902- ... CANR-4
Earlier sketch in CA 5-8R
See also SATA 3
Coyle, Beverly (Jones) 1946- ... 133
Coyle, David Cushman 1887-1969 ... CANR-15
Obituary ... 103
Earlier sketch in CA 1-4R
Coyle, Harold (W.) 1952- ... 140
Coyle, J(ohn) J(ames) 1928- ... 129
Coyle, L(eslie) Patrick 1934- ... 110
Coyle, Lee
See Coyle, Leo (Perry)
Coyle, Leo (Perry) 1925- ... 41-44R
Coyle, Neva 1943- ... 138
Coyle, William 1917- ... CANR-2
Earlier sketch in CA 1-4R
Coyne, James K(itchenman) 1946- ... 141
Coyne, John (P.) 1940- ... CANR-12
Earlier sketch in CA 93-96
Interview in ... CANR-12
Coyne, John R(ichard), Jr. 1935- ... 37-40R
Coyne, Joseph E. 1918-1978 ... 13-16R
Obituary ... 134
Coyne, Michael ... 167
Coyne, P. J.
See Masters, Hilary
Coysh, A(rthur) W(ilfred) 1905- ... CANR-13
Earlier sketch in CA 73-76
Coysh, Victor 1906- ... CANR-8
Earlier sketch in CA 61-64
Coze, Paul 1903(?)-1974 Obituary ... 53-56
Cozzens, Frederic S. 1818-1869 ... DLB 202
Cozzens, James Gould 1903-1978 ... CANR-19
Obituary ... 81-84
Earlier sketch in CA 9-12R
See also CDALB 1941-1968
See also CLC 1, 4, 11, 92
See also DLB 9
See also DLBD 2
See also DLBY 84, 97
See also MTCW 1
Cozzens, Peter 1957- ... 140
Crabb, Alfred Leland 1884- ... CAP-1
Earlier sketch in CA 13-14
Crabb, Cecil V., Jr. 1924- ... 13-16R
Crabb, E(dmund) W(illiam) 1912- ... CAP-1
Earlier sketch in CA 11-12
Crabb, Lawrence J(ames), Jr. 1944- ... CANR-14
Earlier sketches in CA 65-68, CANR-31
Crabb, Richard 1914- ... 21-24R
Crabbe, Buster
See Crabbe, Clarence Linden
Crabbe, Clarence Linden 1908-1983 ... CANR-11
Obituary ... 109
Earlier sketch in CA 69-72
Crabbe, George 1754-1832 ... DLB 93
Crabbe, Katharyn W. 1945- ... 130
Crabtree, Adam 1938- ... 146
Crabtree, Arthur B(amford) 1910- ... CAP-2
Earlier sketch in CA 17-18
Crabtree, John 1950- ... 145
Crabtree, Judith 1928- ... CANR-42
Earlier sketch in CA 118
See also SATA 63, 98
Crabtree, Lou V. P. 1913- ... 167
Crabtree, T(homas) T(avron) 1924- ... 21-24R
Crace, Jim 1946- ... CANR-70
Brief entry ... 128
Earlier sketches in CA 135, CANR-55
Interview in ... 135
Crackanthorpe, Hubert 1870-1896 ... DLB 135
Crackel, Theodore J(oseph) 1938- ... 33-36R
Crackers, Fritz
See Frank, Philip Norman
Cracknell, Basil Edward 1925- ... 103
Cracraft, James (Edward) 1939- ... 53-56
Cracroft, Richard Holton 1936- ... 53-56
Craddock, Charles Egbert
See Murfree, Mary Noailles
Craddock, Fred B(renning) 1928- ... 132
Craddock, Patricia (Bland) 1938- ... CANR-4
Earlier sketch in CA 53-56
Craddock, William J(ames) 1946- ... 85-88
Cradock, Thomas 1718-1770 ... DLB 31
Craft, K. Y.
See Craft, Kinuko Y(amabe)
Craft, Kinuko
See Craft, Kinuko Y(amabe)
Craft, Kinuko Y(amabe) 1940- ... SATA 65
Craft, Maurice 1932- ... CANR-28
Earlier sketches in CA 65-68, CANR-11
Craft, Michael 1928- ... 25-28R
Craft, Robert 1923- ... CANR-7
Earlier sketch in CA 9-12R
Craft, Ruth 1935- ... 133
Brief entry ... 110
See also SATA 87
See also SATA-Brief 31
Crafton, Donald (Clayton) 1947- ... 138
Crafts, Glenn Alty 1918- ... 9-12R
Crafts, Kathy 1952- ... 109
Crafts, Roger Conant 1911- ... 106
Cragg, D. J.
See Cragg, Dan
Cragg, Dan 1939- ... CANR-45
Earlier sketch in CA 115
Cragg, Gerald R(obertson) 1906- ... 61-64
Cragg, (Albert) Kenneth 1913- ... CANR-46
Earlier sketches in CA 17-20R, CANR-7, 22
Craggs, Stewart R. 1943- ... 164
Craghan, John Francis 1936- ... 53-56
Crago, Hugh 1946- ... 116
Crago, Maureen 1939- ... 116
Crago, T(homas) Howard 1907- ... CAP-1
Earlier sketch in CA 13-16
Crahan, Margaret E(llen) 1939- ... 114
Craib, Ian 1945- ... 69-72
Craib, Ralph G(rant) 1925- ... 136
Craig, A. A.
See Anderson, Poul (William)
Craig, Albert M(orton) 1927- ... 37-40R
Craig, Alec
See Craig, Alexander George
Craig, Alexander George 1897- ... CAP-1
Earlier sketch in CA 9-10
Craig, Alisa
See MacLeod, Charlotte (Matilda)
Craig, Amanda 1959- ... 137
Craig, Archibald Campbell 1888-1985 Obituary ... 117
Craig, Barbara Hinkson 1942- ... 135
Craig, Barbara M(ary St. George) 1914- ... 37-40R
Craig, Bill 1930- ... 33-36R
Craig, Brian
See Stableford, Brian (Michael)
Craig, (Robert) Cairns 1949- ... 131
Craig, Charlotte M(arie) 1929- ... 73-76
Craig, Christine (Angela) 1943- ... 120
Craig, Daniel H. 1811-1895 ... DLB 43
Craig, David
See Tucker, James
Craig, David 1932- ... CANR-37
Earlier sketches in CA 41-44R, CANR-14
Craig, Denys
See Stoll, Dennis G(ray)
Craig, Don(ald) Laurence 1946- ... 73-76
Craig, E(velyn) Quita 1917- ... 103
Craig, Edward Anthony 1905- ... 13-16R
Craig, Edward (Henry) Gordon
1872-1966 Obituary ... 25-28R
Craig, Eleanor 1929- ... 93-96
Craig, Elizabeth (Josephine) 1883-1980 ... CANR-11
Obituary ... 101
Earlier sketch in CA 9-12R
Craig, G(illian) M(ary) 1949- ... 139
Craig, Georgia
See Dern, Erolie Pearl Gaddis
Craig, Gerald M(arquis) 1916- ... 9-12R
Craig, Gordon A(lexander) 1913- ... CANR-17
Earlier sketch in CA 25-28R
Craig, H(enry) A(rmitage) L(lewellyn)
1921-1978 ... 85-88
Obituary ... 81-84
Craig, Hazel Thompson 1904- ... 1-4R
Craig, Helen 1934- ... CANR-68
Earlier sketch in CA 117
See also SATA 46, 49, 94
Craig, James 1930- ... 73-76
Craig, Jasmine
See Cresswell, Jasmine (Rosemary)
Craig, Jean T. 1936- ... 5-8R
Craig, John David 1903- ... CAP-2
Earlier sketch in CA 17-18
Craig, John Eland
See Chipperfield, Joseph Eugene
Craig, John Ernest 1921- ... 101
See also SATA 23
Craig, John H(erbert) 1885- ... CAP-1
Earlier sketch in CA 9-10
Craig, Jonathan
See Smith, Frank E.
Craig, Kenneth M., Jr. 1960- ... 147
Craig, Larry
See Coughran, Larry C.
Craig, Lee A(llen) ... 159
See also Sands, Leo G(eorge)
Craig, M. F.
See Craig, Mary (Francis) Shura
Craig, M. Jean ... 73-76
See also SATA 17
Craig, M. S.
See Craig, Mary (Francis) Shura
Craig, Margaret (Maze) 1911-1964 ... 1-4R
See also SATA 9
Craig, Mary
See Craig, Mary (Francis) Shura
Craig, Mary S.
See Craig, Mary (Francis) Shura
Craig, Mary (Francis) Shura 1923-1991 ... CANR-26
Obituary ... 133
Earlier sketches in CA 1-4R, CANR-4
See also SAAS 7
See also SATA 6, 86
See also SATA-Obit 65
Craig, (Elizabeth) May 1889(?)-1975 ... 101
Obituary ... 89-92
Craig, Nancy
See Maslin, Alice
Craig, Pamela Tudor
See Tudor-Craig, Pamela
Craig, Patricia 1949- ... 128
Craig, Peggy
See Kreig, Margaret B. (Baltzell)
Craig, Philip R. 1933- ... CANR-72
Earlier sketch in CA 25-28R
Craig, Randolph
See Page, Norvell W(ooten)
Craig, Raymond C. 1928- ... 124
Craig, Richard B(lythe) 1935- ... 53-56
Craig, Robert B(ruce) 1944- ... 49-52
Craig, Robert C(harles) 1921- ... 17-20R
Craig, Robert D(ean) 1934- ... CANR-14
Earlier sketch in CA 81-84
Craig, Robert H. 1942- ... 140
Craig, Ruth 1922- ... 160
See also SATA 95
Craig, Stephen C. 1948- ... 147
Craig, Vera
See Rowland, D(onald) S(ydney)
Craig, Webster
See Russell, Eric Frank
Craig, William Lane 1949- ... 116
Craige, Betty Jean 1946- ... CANR-40
Earlier sketch in CA 117
Craighead, Frank C(ooper), Jr. 1916- ... 97-100
Craighead, W(ade) Edward 1942- Brief entry ... 118
Craigie, E(dward) Horne 1894- ... CAP-2
Earlier sketch in CA 25-28
Craik, Arthur
See Craig, Alexander George
Craik, Dinah Maria (Mulock) 1826-1887 ... DLB 35, 163
See also MAICYA
See also SATA 34
Craik, Elizabeth M(ary) 1939- ... 131
Craik, Kenneth H(enry) 1936- ... CANR-1
Earlier sketch in CA 45-48
Craik, Thomas Wallace 1927- ... 106
Craik, W(endy) A(nn) 1934- ... 25-28R
Craille, Wesley
See Rowland, D(onald) S(ydney)
Crain, Jeff
See Meneses, Enrique
Crain, John 1926(?)-1979 Obituary ... 89-92
Crain, Robert L(ee) 1934- ... CANR-13
Earlier sketch in CA 21-24R
Crain, Sharie 1942- ... 77-80
Craine, Eugene R(ichard) 1917-1977 ... 33-36R
Crais, Clifton C(harles) 1960- ... 143
Craker, Lyle E(ugene) 1941- ... 116
Cram, Donald J(ames) 1919- ... 157
Cram, Mildred 1889- ... 49-52
Cram, Ralph Adams 1863-1942 ... 160
See also TCLC 45
Cramer, Clarence H(enley) 1905-1982 ... CANR-9
Earlier sketch in CA 13-16R
Cramer, Eugene H. 1930- ... 150
Cramer, George H. 1913- ... 21-24R
Cramer, Harold 1927- ... 29-32R
Cramer, J(an) S(olomon) 1928- ... 29-32R
Cramer, James 1915- ... 21-24R
Cramer, John F. 1913(?)-1989 Obituary ... 128
Cramer, John Francis 1899-1967 ... CAP-1
Earlier sketch in CA 17-18
Cramer, Kathryn 1943- ... 25-28R
Cramer, Richard Ben 1950- ... CANR-68
Earlier sketch in CA 140
See also DLB 185
Cramer, Richard L(ouis) 1947- ... 102
Cramer, Richard S(eldon) 1928- ... 29-32R
Cramer, Stanley H. 1933- ... 29-32R
Cramp, H(arold) St. G(eorge) 1912- ... 130
Cramp, Rosemary (Jean) 1929- ... 121
Crampton, C(harles) Gregory 1911- ... 21-24R
Crampton, Georgia Ronan 1925- ... 57-60
Crampton, Helen
See Chesney, Marion
Crampton, Luke 1959- ... 139
Crampton, Roger C. 1929- ... 33-36R
Cranbrook, James L.
See Edwards, William B(ennett)
Cranch, Christopher Pearse 1813-1892 ... DLB 1, 42
Crandall, James E(dward) 1930- ... 41-44R
Crandall, Joy
See Martin, Joy
Crandall, Norma 1907- ... 69-72
Crandall, Robert Warren 1940- ... 124
Crandell, Anne (Elizabeth) Shaver
See Shaver-Crandell, Anne (Elizabeth)
Crandell, Richard F. 1901-1974 Obituary ... 53-56
Crane, Alex
See Wilkes-Hunter, R(ichard)
Crane, Barbara (Joyce) 1934- ... CANR-29
Earlier sketch in CA 107
See also SATA 31
Crane, Bill
See Crane, William B.
Crane, Caroline 1930- ... CANR-41
Earlier sketches in CA 9-12R, CANR-3, 19
See also SATA 11
Crane, Catherine C(owle) 1940- ... 101
Crane, Conrad C(harles) 1952- ... 147
Crane, Diana 1933- ... 89-92
Crane, Donald P(aul) 1933- ... 61-64
Crane, (Lauren) Edgar 1917- ... 17-20R
Crane, Edna Temple
See Eicher, (Ethel) Elizabeth
Crane, Elaine Forman 1939- ... CANR-48
Earlier sketch in CA 122
Crane, Frank H. 1912- ... 89-92
Crane, Hamilton
See Mason, Sarah J.
Crane, (Harold) Hart 1899-1932 ... 127
Brief entry ... 104
See also CDALB 1917-1929
See also DA
See also DAB
See also DAC
See also DAM MST, POET
See also DLB 4, 48
See also MTCW 1
See also PC 3
See also TCLC 2, 5, 80
See also WLC
Crane, Hewitt D(avid) 1927- ... 116
Crane, Jacob L(eslie) 1892-1988 Obituary ... 125
Crane, James G(ordon) 1927- ... 13-16R
Crane, Jim
See Crane, James G(ordon)
Crane, Joan St. C(lair) 1927- ... 73-76
Crane, Julia G(orham) 1925- ... 41-44R
Crane, M. A.
See Wartski, Maureen (Ann Crane)
Crane, Milton 1917-1985 Obituary ... 117
Crane, Morley Benjamin 1890-1983 Obituary ... 110
Crane, Peter R(obert) 1954- ... 167
Crane, Philip Miller 1930- ... 9-12R
Crane, R(onald) S(almon) 1886-1967 ... 85-88
See also CLC 27
See also DLB 63
Crane, Richard (Arthur) 1944- ... CANR-67
Earlier sketch in CA 77-80
Crane, Robert
See Glemser, Bernard
and Robertson, Frank C(hester)
and Sellers, Con(nie Leslie, Jr.)
Crane, Robert Dickson 1929- ... 81-84
Crane, Royston Campbell
1901-1977 Obituary ... 89-92
See also SATA-Obit 22
Crane, Stephen (Townley) 1871-1900 ... 140
Brief entry ... 109
See also AAYA 21
See also CDALB 1865-1917
See also DA
See also DAB
See also DAC
See also DAM MST, NOV, POET
See also DLB 12, 54, 78
See also SSC 7
See also TCLC 11, 17, 32
See also WLC
See also YABC 2
Crane, Sylvia E(ngel) 1918- ... 33-36R
Crane, Theodore Rawson 1929- ... 97-100
Crane, Verner W(inslow) 1889-1974 Obituary ... 113
Crane, Walter 1845-1915 ... 168
See also DLB 163
See also MAICYA
See also SATA 18, 100
Crane, Wilder (Willard) 1928- ... 45-48
Crane, William B. 1904-1981 ... 107
Crane, William D(wight) 1892- ... 5-8R
See also SATA 1
Crane, William Earl 1899- ... 103
Cranefield, Paul F. 1925- ... 141
Cranfield, Charles E(rnest) B(urland) 1915- ... CANR-18
Earlier sketches in CA 5-8R, CANR-2
Cranfield, Geoffrey Alan 1920- ... 5-8R
Cranfield, Ingrid 1945- ... 141
See also SATA 74
Cranford, Clarence William 1906- ... 1-4R
Cranford, Robert J(oshua) 1908- ... CAP-2
Earlier sketch in CA 17-18
Cranin, A(braham) Norman 1927- ... 73-76
Cranko, John 1927-1973 Obituary ... 45-48
Crankshaw, Edward 1909-1984 ... CANR-23
Obituary ... 114
Earlier sketch in CA 25-28R
Cranmer, Thomas 1489-1556 ... DLB 132
Cranny, Titus (Francis) 1921-1981 ... CANR-27
Earlier sketch in CA 25-28R
Cranor, Phoebe 1923- ... 112
Cranshaw, Stanley
See Fisher, Dorothy (Frances) Canfield
Cranston, Edward
See Fairchild, William
Cranston, Maurice (William) 1920-1993 ... CANR-3
Obituary ... 143
Earlier sketch in CA 5-8R
Cranston, Mechthild ... 53-56
Cranstone, B(ryan) A(llan) L(efevre)
1918-1989 Obituary ... 129
Cranton, Elmer M(itchell) 1932- ... 118
Cranwell, John Philips 1904- ... 61-64
Crapanzano, Vincent 1939- ... CANR-5
Earlier sketch in CA 53-56
Crapol, Edward P(aul) 1936- ... 45-48
Crapps, Robert W. 1925- ... 53-56
Crapsey, Adelaide 1878-1914 ... DLB 54
Crary, Catherine S. 1909- ... CAP-1
Earlier sketch in CA 13-16
Crary, Elizabeth (Ann) 1942- ... 158
See also SATA 99
See also SATA-Brief 43
Crary, Margaret (Coleman) 1906- ... 5-8R
See also SATA 9
Crary, Ryland W(esley) 1913-1984 Obituary ... 113

Crase, Douglas 1944- 106
See also CLC 58
Crashaw, Richard 1612(?)-1649 DLB 126
Crassweller, Robert D. 1915- 21-24R
Craster, John Montagu 1901-1975 Obituary 108
Crathern, Alice Tarbell 1894-1973 Obituary 110
Craton, Michael (John) 1931- 41-44R
Cratty, Bryant J. 1929- CANR-11
Earlier sketch in CA 25-28R
Cravath, Lynne W. 1951- SATA 98
Craven, Avery (Odelle) 1885(?)-1980 143
Obituary 113
See also DLB 17
Craven, George M(ilton) 1929- 61-64
Craven, Margaret 1901-1980 103
See also CLC 17
See also DAC
Craven, Roy C., Jr. 1924- 69-72
Craven, Thomas 1889-1969 97-100
See also SATA 22
Craven, Wayne 1930- 127
Craven, Wes(ley Earl) 1939- CANR-70
Earlier sketch in CA 137
See also AAYA 6, 25
Craven, Wesley Frank (Jr.) 1905-1981 61-64
Obituary 103
Cravens, Gwyneth 85-88
Cravens, Hamilton 1938- 162
Craveri, Marcello 1914- 21-24R
Crawells, Carl
See Herm, Gerhard
Crawford, Alan 1953- 101
Crawford, Ann Fears 1932- CANR-9
Earlier sketch in CA 21-24R
Crawford, Bill
See Crawford, William Hulfish
Crawford, C(harles) Merle 1924- 45-48
Crawford, Char 1935- 57-60
Crawford, Charles 1752-1815(?) DLB 31
Crawford, Charles F. (?)-1983 Obituary 109
Crawford, Charles O(len) 1934- 37-40R
Crawford, Charles P. 1945- CANR-24
Earlier sketch in CA 45-48
See also SATA 28
Crawford, Charles W(ann) 1931- CANR-8
Earlier sketch in CA 61-64
Crawford, Cheryl 1902-1986 Obituary 120
Brief entry 112
Crawford, Christina 1939- 85-88
Crawford, Clan, Jr. 1927- 57-60
Crawford, Daniel J. 1942- 136
Crawford, David
See Kettelhack, Guy
Crawford, David L. 1890(?)-1974 Obituary 45-48
Crawford, Dean (Adams) 1949- 127
Crawford, Deborah 1922- 49-52
See also SATA 6
Crawford, Donald W(esley) 1938- 45-48
Crawford, F(rancis) Marion 1854-1909 168
Brief entry 107
See also DLB 71
See also TCLC 10
Crawford, Fred D. 1947- 117
Crawford, Fred Roberts 1924- CANR-2
Earlier sketch in CA 45-48
Crawford, Hank
See Rummel, (Louis) Jack(son)
Crawford, Iain (Padruig) 1922- CANR-23
Earlier sketch in CA 1-4R
Crawford, Isabella Valancy 1850-1887 DLB 92
Crawford, James M. 1925- 89-92
Crawford, Jean 1907(?)-1976 Obituary 104
Crawford, Jerry L(eroy) 1934- 106
Crawford, Joan
See Le Sueur, Lucille
Crawford, Joanna 1941- 9-12R
Crawford, John E(dmund) 1904-1971 CAP-2
Earlier sketch in CA 17-18
See also SATA 3
Crawford, John R. 1915(?)-1976 Obituary 65-68
Crawford, John Richard 1932- 106
Crawford, John S(herman) 1928- 106
Crawford, John W(illiam) 1914- CANR-30
Earlier sketch in CA 1-4R
Crawford, John W(illiam) 1936- CANR-4
Earlier sketch in CA 53-56
Crawford, Joyce 1931- 25-28R
Crawford, Kenneth G(ale) 1902-1983 81-84
Obituary 108
Crawford, Linda 1938- CANR-23
Earlier sketch in CA 65-68
Crawford, Marion (Kirk) 1910(?)-1988 Obituary 124
Crawford, Mary 1942- 144
Crawford, Matsu W(offord) 1902- CAP-2
Earlier sketch in CA 17-18
Crawford, Max 1938- 77-80
Crawford, Mel 1925- SATA 44
See also SATA-Brief 33
Crawford, Oliver 1917- 85-88
Crawford, Patricia 103
Crawford, Phyllis 1899- SATA 3
Crawford, Richard (Arthur) 1935- CANR-9
Earlier sketch in CA 57-60
Crawford, Robert
See Rae, Hugh C(rauford)
Crawford, Robert Platt 1893- CAP-2
Earlier sketch in CA 17-18
Crawford, Stanley (Gottlieb) 1937- 69-72
Crawford, T. Hugh 1956- 146
Crawford, T(erence Gordon) S(harman)
1945- 29-32R
Crawford, Tad 1946- 133
Brief entry 114
Crawford, Terrence Michael 1945- 129
Crawford, Terry
See Crawford, Terrence Michael
Crawford, Thelmar Wyche 1905- 1-4R
Crawford, Theresa 1956- 110
Crawford, Thomas 1920- CANR-62
Earlier sketch in CA 128
Crawford, Vaughn Emerson
1917(?)-1981 Obituary 104
Crawford, Vernon (E.) 1946- 136
Crawford, Walter B(yron) 1919- 116
Crawford, William (Elbert) 1929- CANR-4
Earlier sketch in CA 1-4R
Crawford, William H. 1907(?)-1973 Obituary 104
Crawford, William Hulfish 1913-1982 Obituary 105
Crawford, William P(atrick) 1922- 106
Crawley, Aidan Merivale 1908-1993 61-64
Obituary 143
Crawley, Alan 1887-1975 146
See also DLB 68
Crawley, C(harles) W(illiam) 1899- 109
Crawley, Gerard M(arcus) 1938- 106
Crawley, Harriet 1948- 134
Crawley, Thomas Edward 1920- 111
Crawley, Tony 1938- 129
Cray, Ed(ward) 1933- CANR-37
Earlier sketches in CA 81-84, CANR-16
Crayder, Dorothy 33-36R
See also SATA 7
Crayder, Teresa
See Colman, Hila
Crayon, Geoffrey
See Irving, Washington
Crayon, Porte
See Strother, David Hunter
Craz, Albert G. 1926- CANR-8
Earlier sketch in CA 17-20R
See also SATA 24
Creager, Alfred L(eon) 1910- 17-20R
Creagh, Patrick 1930- CANR-18
Earlier sketch in CA 25-28R
Creagh-Osborne, Richard 1928- CANR-7
Earlier sketch in CA 9-12R
Creamer, J. Shane 1929- Brief entry 116
Creamer, Robert W. 1922- CANR-63
Earlier sketch in CA 21-24R
See also DLB 171
Crean, John Edward, Jr. 1939- 41-44R
Crean, Patrick (G.) 1949- 123
Crean, Susan M. 1945- 158
Creasey, John 1908-1973 CANR-59
Obituary 41-44R
Earlier sketches in CA 5-8R, CANR-8
See also CLC 11
See also DLB 77
See also MTCW 1
Creasy, Robert K(enwood) 1934- 118
Creasy, Rosalind R. CANR-28
Earlier sketch in CA 110
Creaturo, Barbara 1943-1990 129
Obituary 132
Crebbin, June 1938- SATA 80
Crecelius, Daniel 1937- 139
Crechales, Anthony George 1926- 29-32R
Crechales, Tony
See Crechales, Anthony George
Crecine, John Patrick 1939- CANR-7
Earlier sketch in CA 57-60
Crecy, Jeanne
See Williams, Jeanne
Credland, Peter (Francis) 1946- 69-72
Credle, Ellis 1902- CANR-9
Earlier sketch in CA 13-16R
See also SATA 1
Credo
See Creasey, John
Credo, Alvaro J. de
See Prado (Calvo), Pedro
Creech, Sharon 1945- 159
See also AAYA 21
See also CLR 42
See also SATA 94
Creed, David
See Guthrie, James Shields
Creede, Thomas fl. 1593-1619(?) DLB 170
Creeden, Sharon 1938- 155
See also SATA 91
Creekmore, Betsey B(eeler) 1915- 69-72
Creekmore, Mildred C. 1905(?)-1987 Obituary 123
Creel, George 1876-1953 Brief entry 115
See also DLB 25
Creel, Herrlee G(lessner) 1905-1994 85-88
Obituary 145
Creel, Stephen Melville 1938- 69-72
Creeley, Robert (White) 1926- CANR-43
Earlier sketches in CA 1-4R, CANR-23
See also CAAS 10
See also CLC 1, 2, 4, 8, 11, 15, 36, 78
See also DAM POET
See also DLB 5, 16, 169
See also DLBD 17
See also MTCW 1
Creelman, James 1859-1915 DLB 23
Creelman, Marjorie B(roer) 1908- CAP-2
Earlier sketch in CA 21-22
Creer, Thomas L(aselle) 1934- CANR-22
Earlier sketch in CA 69-72
Creese, Bethea CANR-5
Earlier sketch in CA 9-12R
Creese, Walter L(ittlefield) 1919- 125
Creeth, Edmund Homer 1928- 102
Creevey, Lucy E. 1940- 29-32R
Creevy, Patrick Joseph 1947- 141
Crefeld, Donna Carolyn Anders
See Anders, Donna Carolyn
Cregan, David (Appleton Quartus) 1931- CANR-67
Earlier sketches in CA 45-48, CANR-1
See also DLB 13
Creger, Ralph (Clinton) 1914- 13-16R
Cregier, Don M(esick) 1930- 69-72
Crehan, Stewart 1942- 118
Crehan, Thomas 1919- CANR-2
Earlier sketch in CA 5-8R
Creigh, Dorothy (Weyer) 1921- 105
Creighton, Basil 1885-1989 Obituary 128
Creighton, Don
See Drury, Maxine Cole
Creighton, Donald Grant 1902-1979 101
Obituary 93-96
See also DLB 88
Creighton, (Mary) Helen 1899-1989 41-44R
Obituary 130
See also SATA-Obit 64
Creighton, Helen (Evelyn) 1914- 33-36R
Creighton, Jill 1949- 161
See also SATA 96
Creighton, Joanne V(anish) 1942- 69-72
Creighton, Linn 1917- 143
Creighton, Luella Bruce 1901- CAP-1
Earlier sketch in CA 17-18
Creighton, Thomas 1915(?)-1987 Obituary 123
Creighton, Thomas H(awk) 1904-1984 CANR-6
Obituary 114
Earlier sketch in CA 5-8R
Crellin, John 1916- 69-72
Cremazie, Octave 1827-1879 DLB 99
Cremeans, Charles D(avis) 1915- 5-8R
Cremer, Jan 1940- 13-16R
Cremer, Robert Roger 1947- 61-64
Cremer, Robert Wyndham Ketton
See Ketton-Cremer, Robert Wyndham
Cremer, Victoriano 1909(?)- DLB 108
Cremin, Lawrence A(rthur) 1925-1990 CANR-29
Obituary 132
Earlier sketch in CA 33-36R
Cremo, Michael (A.) 1948- 143
Crena de Iongh, Mary (Dows Herter Norton)
1894(?)-1985 Obituary 116
Crena de Iongh, Daniel 1888-1970 CAP-2
Obituary 29-32R
Earlier sketch in CA 25-28
Crenna, C. David 1944- 128
Crennen, Robert Earl 1929-1984 Obituary 112
Crenner, James 1938- 13-16R
Crenshaw, Charles A(ndrew) 1933- 140
Crenshaw, James L. 1934- CANR-34
Earlier sketches in CA 37-40R, CANR-14
Crenshaw, Marshall (H.) 1953- 149
Crenshaw, Mary Ann CANR-8
Earlier sketch in CA 57-60
Crenson, Victoria 1952- 152
See also SATA 88
Crepeau, Richard C(harles) 1941- 105
Crerar, Duff (Willis) 1955- 156
Crescas, Hasdai 1340(?)-1412(?) DLB 115
Crespo, Angel 1926- DLB 134
Crespo, George 1962- SATA 82
Cressey, Donald R(ay) 1919-1987 CANR-6
Obituary 123
Earlier sketch in CA 13-16R
Cressey, William W. 1939- 33-36R
Cresson, Bruce Collins 1930- 45-48
Cresswell, Helen 1934- CANR-37
Earlier sketches in CA 17-20R, CANR-8
See also AAYA 25
See also CLR 18
See also DLB 161
See also JRDA
See also MAICYA
See also SAAS 20
See also SATA 1, 48, 79
Cresswell, Jasmine (Rosemary) 1941- CANR-29
Earlier sketch in CA 110
Cresswell, Stephen 1956- 152
Cressy, David 1946- 130
Creston, Dormer
See Colston-Baynes, Dorothy
Creswell, K(eppel) A(rchibald) C(ameron) 1879- CAP-1
Earlier sketch in CA 9-10
Cretan, Gladys (Yessayan) 1921- 29-32R
See also SATA 2
Cretcher, Dorothy 1934- 112
Cretzmeyer, F(rancis) X(avier), Jr. 1913- 13-16R
Crevecoeur, Michel Guillaume Jean de
1735-1813 DLB 37
Crevier, Daniel 1947- 142
Crew, Francis Albert Eley 1888-1973 CAP-2
Earlier sketch in CA 17-18
Crew, Gary 1947- 142
See also AAYA 17
See also CLR 42
See also SATA 75
Crew, Helen (Cecilia) Coale 1866-1941 Brief entry 121
See also YABC 2
Crew, Linda 1951- CANR-56
Earlier sketch in CA 130
See also AAYA 21
See also SATA 71
Crew, Louie 1936- 81-84
Crewdson, John (Mark) 1945- 132
Brief entry 128
Crewe, Candida 1964- 135
Crewe, Jonathan V(ere) 1941- 116
Crewe, Quentin (Hugh) 1926- 144
Crews, Clyde F. 1944- CANR-38
Earlier sketch in CA 116
Crews, Donald 108
See also CLR 7
See also MAICYA
See also SATA 32, 76
See also SATA-Brief 30
Crews, Frederick C(ampbell) 1933- CANR-44
Earlier sketches in CA 1-4R, CANR-1
Crews, Harry (Eugene) 1935- CANR-57
Earlier sketches in CA 25-28R, CANR-20
See also AITN 1
See also CLC 6, 23, 49
See also DLB 6, 143, 185
See also MTCW 1
Crews, Judson (Campbell) 1917- CANR-24
Earlier sketches in CA 13-16R, CANR-7
See also CAAS 14
Crews, Nina 1963- 163
See also SATA 97
Crews, William J. 1931- 25-28R
Cribb, Larry 1934- 109
Cribb, Robert (Bridson) 1957- 137
Cribbet, John E(dward) 1918- 17-20R
Cribbin, James J(oseph) 1915- 121
Crichton, James Dunlop 1907- CANR-5
Earlier sketch in CA 13-16R
Crichton, Jennifer 1957- 123
Crichton, John 1916- 17-20R
Crichton, Kyle Samuel 1896-1960 Obituary 89-92
Crichton, (John) Michael 1942- CANR-54
Earlier sketches in CA 25-28R, CANR-13, 40
Interview in CANR-13
See also AAYA 10
See also AITN 2
See also CLC 2, 6, 54, 90
See also DAM NOV, POP
See also DLBY 81
See also JRDA
See also MTCW 1
See also SATA 9, 88
Crichton, Robert 1925-1993 CANR-46
Obituary 140
Earlier sketch in CA 17-20R
See also AITN 1
Crichton, Robin 1940- 139
Crichton, Ronald 1913- 128
Crick, Bernard (Rowland) 1929- CANR-5
Earlier sketch in CA 1-4R
Crick, Donald Herbert 1916- 102
Crick, Francis (Harry Compton) 1916- 121
Brief entry 113
Crick, Michael (Lawrence) 1958- CANR-42
Earlier sketch in CA 118
Criddle, Byron 1942- 149
Criddle, Joan D(ewey) 1935- 126
Criden, Joseph 1916- 77-80
Criden, Yosef
See Criden, Joseph
Crider, (Allen) Bill(y) 1941- CANR-56
Earlier sketches in CA 112, CANR-30
See also SATA 99
Cridland, Nancy C. 1932- 111
Crighton, John C(lark) 1903- 33-36R
Crighton, Richard E. 1921- 109
Crile, Barney
See Crile, George, Jr.
Crile, George, Jr. 1907- 89-92
Crim, Keith R(enn) 1924- CANR-43
Earlier sketch in CA 29-32R
Crim, Mort 1935- 41-44R
Crimmins, James Custis 1935- CANR-11
Earlier sketch in CA 5-8R
Crinkley, Richmond (Dillard) 1940-1989 29-32R
Obituary 127
Cripe, Helen 1932- CANR-8
Earlier sketch in CA 61-64
Cripps, (Matthew) Anthony (Leonard) 1913- 13-16R
Cripps, L(ouise) L(ilian) 1914- 97-100
Cripps, Thomas (Robert) 1932- 97-100
Crisler, Fritz
See Crisler, Herbert Orin
Crisler, Herbert Orin 1899-1982 Obituary 107
Crisler, Lois (Brown) (?)-1971 Obituary 104
Crisman, Ruth 1914- SATA 73
Crisp, Anthony Thomas 1937- 101
Crisp, C(olin) G(odfrey) 1936- 37-40R
Crisp, Frank R(obson) 1915- 9-12R
Crisp, Norman James 1923- 93-96
Crisp, Quentin 1908- CANR-59
Brief entry 109
Earlier sketch in CA 116
Interview in 116
Crisp, Robert (James) 1-4R
Crisp, Tony
See Crisp, Anthony Thomas
Crispin, A(nn) C(arol) 1950- CANR-32
Earlier sketch in CA 113
See also SATA 86
Crispin, Edmund
See Montgomery, (Robert) Bruce
See also CLC 22
See also DLB 87
Crispin, John 1936- 53-56
Crispin, Ruth Helen Katz 1940- 93-96
Crispin, Suzy
See Cartwright, Justin
Crispo, John 1933- 37-40R
Crissey, Elwell 1899- CAP-2
Earlier sketch in CA 23-24
Crist, Judith (Klein) 1922- CANR-17
Earlier sketch in CA 81-84
See also AITN 1
Crist, Lyle M(artin) 1924- 53-56
Crist, Raymond E. 1904- 73-76
Crist, Steven G(ordon) 1956- 101
Cristabel
See Abrahamsen, Christine Elizabeth
Cristall, Barbara 147
See also SATA 79
Cristina, Frank
See Laughlin, Tom
Cristina, Teresa
See Laughlin, Tom

Cristofer, Michael 1945(?)- ... 152
Brief entry ... 110
See also CLC 28
See also DAM DRAM
See also DLB 7
Cristol, Vivian ... 17-20R
Cristy, Ann
See Mittermeyer, Helen (Hayton Monteith)
Cristy, R. J.
See De Cristoforo, R(omeo) J(ohn)
Criswell, Cloyd M. 1908- ... CAP-1
Earlier sketch in CA 17-18
Criswell, W(allie) A(mos) 1909- ... 17-20R
Critchfield, Howard J(ohn) 1920- ... 53-56
Critchfield, Richard (Patrick) 1931-1994 .. CANR-40
Obituary ... 147
Earlier sketches in CA 41-44R, CANR-16
Critchley, Edmund M(ichael) R(hys) 1931- .. 21-24R
Critchley, Julian (Michael Gordon) 1930- ... 85-88
Critchley, Lynne
See Radford, Richard F(rancis), Jr.
Critchley, T(homas) A(lan) 1919-1991 ... 29-32R
Obituary ... 134
Critchlow, Donald T. 1948- ... 156
Crites, Ronald W(ayne) 1945- ... CANR-18
Earlier sketch in CA 102
Crites, Stephen D(ecatur) 1931- ... 41-44R
Critic
See Martin, (Basil) Kingsley
Criticus
See Harcourt, Melville
and Roe, F(rederic) Gordon
Criton
See Alain
Crittenden, Mabel (Buss) 1917- ... 103
Crnjanski, Milos 1893- ... CANR-50
Earlier sketches in CAP-1, CA 9-10
See also DLB 147
Crnobrnja (Tsernobernya), Mihailo 1946- ... 150
Croall, Jonathan 1941- ... 130
Crobaugh, Emma ... AITN 2
Croce, Arlene 1934- ... 104
Interview in ... 104
Croce, Benedetto 1866-1952 ... 155
Brief entry ... 120
See also TCLC 37
Croce, Paul Jerome 1957- ... 154
Crocetti, Guido M. 1920-1979 ... 85-88
Crock, Stan 1950- ... 134
Crocker, Hannah Mather 1752-1829 ... DLB 200
Crocker, Helen Bartter 1929- ... 69-72
Crocker, Lester G(ilbert) 1912- ... CANR-5
Earlier sketch in CA 5-8R
Crocker, Lionel (George) 1897- ... CAP-2
Earlier sketch in CA 25-28
Crocker, Mary Wallace 1941- ... 93-96
Crocker, Thomas Dunstan 1936- Brief entry ... 108
Crocker, Walter Russell 1902- ... 17-20R
Crockett, Albert Stevens 1873-1969 Obituary 89-92
Crockett, Christina
See Crockett, Linda
and Gray, Linda Crockett
Crockett, David 1786-1836 ... DLB 3, 11
Crockett, Davy
See Crockett, David
Crockett, G(eorge) Ronald 1906- ... CAP-1
Earlier sketch in CA 11-12
Crockett, H(arold) Dale 1933- ... 111
Crockett, James Underwood 1915-1979 . CANR-13
Obituary ... 89-92
Earlier sketch in CA 33-36R
Crockett, Linda 1943- ... 144
See also Crockett, Christina
and Gray, Linda Crockett
Crockett, Linda Lea 1962- ... 155
Crockett, S(amuel) R(utherford) 1860-1914 Brief entry ... 116
Crocombe, Ronald G(ordon) 1929- ... 13-16R
Crofford, Emily (Ardell) 1927- ... 107
See also SATA 61
Crofford, Lena H(enrichson) 1908- ... CAP-1
Earlier sketch in CA 9-10
Croft, Julian (Charles Basset) 1941- ... CANR-55
Earlier sketch in CA 124
Croft, Michael (John) 1922-1986 Obituary ... 121
Croft, Peter John 1929-1984 ... 122
Obituary ... 114
Croft, Sutton
See Lunn, Arnold
Croft-Cooke, Rupert 1903-1979 ... CANR-60
Obituary ... 89-92
Earlier sketches in CA 9-12R, CANR-4
See also Bruce, Leo
Croft-Murray, Edward 1907-1980 Obituary ... 102
Crofton, Denis Hayes 1908- ... 109
Crofts, Freeman Wills 1879-1957 Brief entry ... 115
See also DLB 77
See also TCLC 55
Crofts, John E(rnest) V(ictor) 1887-1972 ... CAP-2
Earlier sketch in CA 25-28
Crofts, William ... 137
Crofut, William E. III 1934- ... 25-28R
See also SATA 23
Crohn, Burrill B(ernard) 1884-1983 Obituary ... 110
Croise, Jacques
See Schakovskoy, Zinaida
Croizat, Victor J. 1919- ... 163
Croizier, Ralph 1935- ... 61-64
Croker, John Wilson 1780-1857 ... DLB 110
Croll, Carolyn 1945- ... CANR-49
Earlier sketch in CA 123
See also SATA 56, 102
See also SATA-Brief 52
Croll, (Joan) Elisabeth 1944- ... 158
Croly, George 1780-1860 ... DLB 159
Croly, Herbert 1869-1930 ... DLB 91
Croly, Jane Cunningham 1829(?)-1901 Brief entry ... 118
See also DLB 23
Croman, Dorothy Young
See Rosenberg, Dorothy
Crombie, A(listair) C(ameron) 1915- ... 151
Cromer, Alan (Herbert) 1935- ... 146
Cromie, Alice Hamilton 1914- ... CANR-3
Earlier sketch in CA 9-12R
See also SATA 24
Cromie, Robert (Allen) 1909- ... CANR-16
Earlier sketches in CA 1-4R, CANR-1
Cromie, William J(oseph) 1930- ... 13-16R
See also SATA 4
Crommelynck, Fernand 1885-1970 Obituary . 89-92
See also CLC 75
Crompton, Anne Eliot 1930- ... CANR-46
Earlier sketches in CA 33-36R, CANR-13
See also SATA 23, 73
Crompton, John
See Lamburn, John Battersby Crompton
Crompton, Louis (William) 1925- ... 33-36R
Crompton, Margaret (Norah Mair) 1901- ... CAP-1
Earlier sketch in CA 13-14
Crompton, Richmal
See Lamburn, Richmal Crompton
See also DLB 160
Cromwell, Chester R. 1925- ... 89-92
Cromwell, Elsie
See Lee, Elsie
Cromwell, Harvey 1907-1977 ... 17-20R
Obituary ... 134
Cromwell, James H(enry) R(oberts) 1897(?)-1990 Obituary ... 131
Cromwell, John 1887-1979 Obituary ... 89-92
Cromwell, John 1914(?)-1979 Obituary ... 89-92
Cromwell, Link
See Kaye, Lenny
Cromwell, Richard Sidney 1925- ... 53-56
Cromwell, Rue L(eVelle) 1928- ... 149
Cronbach, Abraham 1882-1965 ... 1-4R
See also SATA 11
Crone, Alla 1923- ... 113
Crone, G(erald) R(oe) 1899-1982 ... 121
Crone, Moira 1952- ... CANR-59
Earlier sketch in CA 125
Crone, (Hans-) Rainer 1942- ... CANR-14
Earlier sketch in CA 33-36R
Crone, Ruth 1919- ... 9-12R
See also SATA 4
Cronenberg, David 1943- ... 138
Croner, Helga 1914- ... 107
Croner, John A(lton) 1916- ... 121
Cronin, A(rchibald) J(oseph) 1896-1981 ... CANR-5
Obituary ... 102
Earlier sketch in CA 1-4R
See also CLC 32
See also DLB 191
See also SATA 47
See also SATA-Obit 25
Cronin, Anthony 1926- ... 137
Cronin, Audrey Kurth 1958- ... 125
Cronin, George 1933- ... 101
Cronin, James E(mmet) 1908- ... CANR-24
Earlier sketch in CA 45-48
Cronin, John F(rancis) 1908-1994 ... 37-40R
Obituary ... 143
Cronin, Joseph M(arr) 1935- ... CANR-31
Earlier sketch in CA 49-52
Cronin, Mary J. 1947- ... 148
Cronin, Sylvia 1929- ... 89-92
Cronin, Thomas E(dward) 1940- ... CANR-42
Earlier sketches in CA 85-88, CANR-20
Cronin, Vincent (Archibald Patrick) 1924- .. CANR-5
Earlier sketch in CA 9-12R
Cronkhite, Bernice Brown 1893-1983 Obituary . 110
Cronkite, Walter (Leland, Jr.) 1916- ... CANR-62
Earlier sketches in CA 69-72, CANR-37
See also AITN 1, 2
Cronley, Jay 1943- ... 81-84
Cronne, H(enry) A(lfred) 1904- ... 65-68
Cronon, E(dmund) David 1924- ... CANR-1
Earlier sketch in CA 1-4R
Cronon, William (John) 1954- ... 111
Cronus, Diodorus
See Taylor, Richard
Cronyn, Hume 1911- ... CANR-50
Earlier sketch in CA 123
Crook, Bette (Jean) 1921- ... 73-76
Crook, Beverly Courtney ... 115
See also SATA 38
See also SATA-Brief 35
Crook, Compton Newby 1908- ... 121
Crook, Connie Brummel
See Crook, Constance
Crook, Constance ... 166
See also SATA 98
Crook, D(avid) P(aul) 1937- ... 128
Crook, David 1910- ... 97-100
Crook, Howard (Hawthorne) 1937- ... 107
Crook, Isabel 1915- ... 97-100
Crook, J(ohn) A(nthony) 1921- ... 21-24R
Crook, J(oseph) Mordaunt 1937- ... 41-44R
Crook, Margaret Brackenbury 1886- ... CAP-1
Earlier sketch in CA 13-16
Crook, Marion 1941- ... 163
Crook, Roger H(awley) 1921- ... CANR-4
Earlier sketch in CA 1-4R
Crook, W. Melvin 1912(?)-1984 Obituary ... 112
Crook, William 1933- ... 102
Crook, William G. 1917- ... 129
Crookall, Robert 1890-1981 ... CANR-30
Earlier sketch in CA 33-36R
Crookenden, Napier 1915- ... CANR-11
Earlier sketch in CA 69-72
Crooks, James B(enedict) 1933- ... 25-28R
Cropp, Ben(jamin) 1936- ... 33-36R
Cropper, Margaret 1886-1980 Obituary ... 102
Crosbie, John S(haver) 1920- ... CANR-12
Earlier sketch in CA 73-76
Crosbie, Lynn 1963- ... 146
Crosbie, (Hugh) Provan 1912- ... 9-12R
Crosbie, Sylvia Kowitt 1938- ... 73-76
Crosby, Alexander L. 1906-1980 ... 29-32R
Obituary ... 93-96
See also SATA 2
See also SATA-Obit 23
Crosby, Alfred W., Jr. 1931- ... CANR-68
Earlier sketch in CA 17-20R
Crosby, Bing
See Crosby, Harry Lillis
Crosby, (Mary Jacob) Caresse 1892-1970 Obituary ... 25-28R
See also DLB 4, 48
Crosby, Donald A(llen) 1932- ... 53-56
Crosby, Donald F(rancis) 1933- ... 77-80
Crosby, Elizabeth Caroline 1888-1983 ... 157
Crosby, Faye J. 1947- ... CANR-36
Earlier sketch in CA 114
Crosby, Harry 1898-1929 Brief entry ... 107
See also DLB 4, 48
See also DLBD 15
Crosby, Harry C., Jr. ... 161
See also SATA 102
Crosby, Harry H(erbert) 1919- ... CANR-5
Earlier sketch in CA 13-16R
Crosby, Harry Lillis 1904-1977 Obituary ... 73-76
Crosby, Harry W(illiams) 1926- ... 149
Crosby, Henry Grew
See Crosby, Harry
Crosby, Henry Sturgis
See Crosby, Harry
Crosby, Jackie
See Crosby, Jacqueline Garton
Crosby, Jacqueline Garton 1961- ... 133
Crosby, James O('Hea) 1924- ... 89-92
Crosby, Jeremiah
See Crosby, Michael (Hugh)
Crosby, John (Campbell) 1912-1991 ... CANR-4
Obituary ... 135
Earlier sketch in CA 1-4R
Crosby, John F. 1931- ... CANR-7
Earlier sketch in CA 17-20R
Crosby, Michael (Hugh) 1940- ... CANR-11
Earlier sketch in CA 17-20R
Crosby, Muriel (Estelle) 1908- ... 17-20R
Crosby, Philip B(ayard) 1926- ... 73-76
Crosby, Ruth 1897- ... 49-52
Crosby, Sumner McK(night) 1909-1982 ... 13-16R
Obituary ... 108
Crosby, Theo 1925- ... 133
Crosher, G. R. ... 69-72
See also SATA 14
Crosland, Andrew T(ate) 1944- ... 53-56
Crosland, (Charles) Anthony (Raven) 1918-1977 ... 73-76
Obituary ... 69-72
Crosland, Margaret 1920- ... CANR-45
Earlier sketches in CA 49-52, CANR-1, 21
Cross, Ian (Robert) 1925- ... 161
Cross, Aleene (Ann) 1922- ... CANR-26
Earlier sketch in CA 29-32R
Cross, Amanda
See Heilbrun, Carolyn G(old)
Cross, Anthony (Glenn) 1936- ... CANR-17
Earlier sketch in CA 37-40R
Cross, (Alan) Beverley 1931-1998 ... CANR-67
Obituary ... 166
Earlier sketch in CA 102
Cross, Claire 1932- ... 21-24R
Cross, Colin (John) 1928-1985 ... CANR-7
Obituary ... 118
Earlier sketch in CA 9-12R
Cross, David
See Chesbro, George C(lark)
Cross, Donna Woolfolk 1947- ... 97-100
Cross, Frank Moore, Jr. 1921- ... 65-68
Cross, Gary Scott 1946- ... 115
Cross, George Lynn 1905- ... 125
Cross, Gilbert B. 1939- ... CANR-47
Earlier sketches in CA 105, CANR-23
See also SATA 60
See also SATA-Brief 51
Cross, Gillian (Clare) 1945- ... CANR-38
Earlier sketch in CA 111
See also AAYA 24
See also CLR 28
See also DLB 161
See also JRDA
See also MAICYA
See also SATA 38, 71
Cross, Helen Reeder
See Broadhead, Helen Cross
Cross, Herbert James 1934- ... 45-48
Cross, Ira Brown 1880-1977 Obituary ... 106
Cross, James
See Parry, Hugh J(ones)
Cross, Jennifer 1932- ... 29-32R
Cross, John Keir 1914-1967 ... CANR-72
Earlier sketch in CA 73-76
Cross, John R(ay) 1939- ... 120
Cross, K(enneth) G(ustav) W(alter) 1927-1967 ... CAP-1
Earlier sketch in CA 13-16
Cross, K(athryn) Patricia 1926- ... CANR-49
Earlier sketches in CA 33-36R, CANR-13
Cross, Leslie (Frank) 1909-1977 ... 65-68
Obituary ... 89-92
Cross, M. Claire
See Cross, Claire
Cross, Milton (John) 1897-1975 Obituary ... 53-56
Cross, Nigel 1942- ... CANR-38
Earlier sketch in CA 116
Cross, Peter 1951- ... 141
See also SATA 95
Cross, Polton
See Fearn, John Russell
Cross, Ralph D(onald) 1931- ... CANR-17
Earlier sketch in CA 93-96
Cross, Richard 1950(?)-1983 Obituary ... 110
Cross, Richard K(eith) 1940- ... CANR-12
Earlier sketch in CA 33-36R
Cross, Robert Brandt 1914- ... 37-40R
Cross, Robert Dougherty 1924- ... 1-4R
Cross, Robert Singlehurst 1925- ... 5-8R
Cross, (Alfred) Rupert (Neal) 1912-1980 Obituary ... 102
Cross, (Alfred) Rupert (Neale) 1912-1980 ... 105
Cross, Samuel S(tephen) 1919- ... 45-48
Cross, Sister Mary Francilda 1902(?)-1984 Obituary ... 114
Cross, Stewart
See Drago, Harry Sinclair
Cross, T. T.
See da Cruz, Daniel, Jr.
Cross, Theodore L(amont) 1924- ... CANR-27
Earlier sketch in CA 45-48
Cross, Thomas B. 1949- ... 123
Cross, Verda 1914- ... 142
See also SATA 75
Cross, Victor
See Coffman, Virginia (Edith)
Cross, Victoria 1868-1952 ... DLB 135, 197
Cross, Wilbur Lucius III 1918- ... CANR-2
Earlier sketch in CA 1-4R
See also SATA 2
Crossan, Darryl
See Smith, Richard Rein
Crosscountry
See Campbell, Thomas F.
Crossen, Ken
See Crossen, Kendell Foster
Crossen, Kendell Foster 1910-1981 ... CANR-60
Earlier sketches in CA 1-4R, CANR-4
See also Foster, Richard
Crosser, Paul K. 1902-1976 ... CANR-3
Earlier sketch in CA 1-4R
Crossette, George 1910-1984 Obituary ... 114
Crosskill, W. E. 1904- ... 129
Crossland, Caroline 1964- ... SATA 83
Crossley, Archibald M(addock) 1896-1985 Obituary ... 116
Crossley, Pamela Kyle 1955- ... 154
Crossley, Robert 1945- ... 127
Crossley-Holland, Kevin 1941- ... CANR-47
Earlier sketch in CA 41-44R
See also CLR 47
See also DLB 40, 161
See also MAICYA
See also SAAS 20
See also SATA 5, 74
Crossman, Richard (Howard Stafford) 1907-1974 .. CANR-43
Obituary ... 49-52
Earlier sketch in CA 61-64
Croteau, John T(ougas) 1910- ... 9-12R
Crothers, George D. 1909- ... CAP-1
Earlier sketch in CA 13-16
Crothers, J(essie) Frances 1913- ... 33-36R
Crothers, Jessie F.
See Crothers, J(essie) Frances
Crothers, Rachel 1878(?)-1958 Brief entry ... 113
See also DLB 7
See also TCLC 19
Crotty, William J(oseph) 1936- ... CANR-13
Earlier sketch in CA 21-24R
Crouch, Bill, Jr.
See Crouch, William Maxwell, Jr.
Crouch, David 1948- ... 129
Crouch, Harold (Arthur) 1940- ... CANR-15
Earlier sketch in CA 89-92
Crouch, Marcus 1913- ... CANR-23
Earlier sketches in CA 9-12R, CANR-5
See also SATA 4
Crouch, Stanley 1945- ... 141
Crouch, Steve 1915-1983 ... CANR-9
Obituary ... 109
Earlier sketch in CA 53-56
Crouch, Thomas W(illiam) 1932- ... 73-76
Crouch, Tom D. 1944- ... 106
Crouch, W(illiam) George (Alfred) 1903-1970 .. 5-8R
Obituary ... 89-92
Crouch, William Maxwell, Jr. 1945- ... 126
Crouch, Winston Winford 1907- Brief entry ... 106
Croucher, Michael 1930- ... 128
Croudace, Glynn 1917- ... 29-32R
Crouse, Russell M. 1893-1966 ... 77-80
Obituary ... 25-28R
Crouse, Timothy 1947- ... 77-80
Crouse, William H(arry) 1907- ... CANR-6
Earlier sketch in CA 5-8R
Crout, George C(lement) 1917- ... CANR-11
Earlier sketch in CA 29-32R
See also SATA 11
Crout, Robert Rhodes 1946- ... 116
Croutier, Alev Lytle 1944- ... 142
Crouzet, Francois Marie-Joseph 1922- ... CANR-42
Earlier sketches in CA 9-12R, CANR-3, 19
Croves, Hal
See Traven, B.
Crovitz, Herbert F(loyd) 1932- ... 29-32R
Crow, Alice (von Bauer) 1894-1966 ... CAP-1
Earlier sketch in CA 13-16
Crow, Bill 1927- ... 140
Crow, C(harles) P(atrick) 1938- ... 102
Crow, Charles L(loyd) 1940- ... 112

Crow, Donna Fletcher 1941- CANR-50
Earlier sketches in CA 108, CANR-25
See also SATA 40
Crow, Duncan 1920- 85-88
Crow, Elizabeth Smith 1946- 103
Crow, Francis Luther
See Luther, Frank
Crow, Jeffrey J(ay) 1947- CANR-19
Earlier sketch in CA 85-88
Crow, John A(rmstrong) 1906- 13-16R
Crow, Lester D(onald) 1897-1983 CAP-1
Obituary 110
Earlier sketch in CA 13-16
Crow, Mark (Alan) 1948- 57-60
Crow, Martin M(ichael) 1901- CAP-2
Earlier sketch in CA 19-20
Crow, Mary 1933- 138
Crow, William Bernard 1895-1976 CAP-1
Obituary 65-68
Earlier sketch in CA 13-14
Crowbate, Ophelia Mae
See Smith, C. U.
Crowcroft, Andrew 1923- 21-24R
Crowcroft, Jane
See Crowcroft, Peter
Crowcroft, Peter 1923- 101
Crowder, Ashby Bland (Jr.) 1941- 151
Crowder, Christopher M. D. 1922- 103
Crowder, George 1956- 146
Crowder, Herbert 1925- 127
Crowder, Michael 1934-1988 CANR-1
Obituary 126
Earlier sketch in CA 1-4R
Crowder, Richard (Henry) 1909- CAP-1
Earlier sketch in CA 17-18
Crowder, Robert G. 1939- 138
Crow Dog, Mary (Ellen) (?)- 154
See also Brave Bird, Mary
See also CLC 93
Crowe, Amanda Cockrell 1948- 101
Crowe, Bettina Lum 1911- 9-12R
See also SATA 6
Crowe, C. B.
See Gibson, Walter B(rown)
Crowe, Cameron 1957- 153
See also AAYA 23
Crowe, Cecily (Teague) Brief entry 115
Crowe, Charles 1928- 17-20R
Crowe, Charles Monroe 1902-1978 1-4R
Obituary 103
Crowe, E. Odell 1925(?)-1983 Obituary 110
Crowe, F. J.
See Johnston, Jill
Crowe, Frederick Ernest 1915- CANR-29
Earlier sketch in CA 111
Crowe, Gregory D(ennis) 1963- 116
Crowe, John
See Lynds, Dennis
Crowe, Kenneth C(harles) 1934- 103
Crowe, Norman 1938- 151
Crowe, Philip Kingsland 1908-1976 65-68
Obituary 69-72
Crowe, Robert L(ee) 1937- 69-72
Crowe, Sylvia 1901- CAP-1
Earlier sketch in CA 9-10
Crowe, Thomas Rain 1949- 166
Crowe, William J., Jr. 1925- 142
Crowe-Carraco, Carol 1943- 93-96
Crowell, George H. 1931- 25-28R
Crowell, Grace Noll 1877-1969 107
See also SATA 34
Crowell, Jenn(ifer) 1978- 159
Crowell, Joan 1921- 57-60
Crowell, Muriel Beyea 1916- 57-60
Crowell, Norton B. 1914- 9-12R
Crowell, Pers 1910- 29-32R
See also SATA 2
Crowell, Robert Leland 1909- 109
See also SATA 63
Crowfield, Christopher
See Stowe, Harriet (Elizabeth) Beecher
Crowl, Philip A(xtell) 1914-1991 110
Obituary 134
Crowl, Samuel 1940- 142
Crowley, Aleister
See Crowley, Edward Alexander
See also TCLC 7
Crowley, Arthur McBlair 1945- 107
See also SATA 38
Crowley, Daniel J(ohn) 1921-1998 CANR-9
Obituary 166
Earlier sketch in CA 21-24R
Crowley, David 1966- 146
Crowley, Diane 1939- 135
Crowley, Edward Alexander 1875-1947 Brief entry 104
See also Crowley, Aleister
Crowley, Ellen T(eresa) 1943- CANR-17
Earlier sketch in CA 97-100
Crowley, Frances G(eyer) 1921- 105
Crowley, George (David) 1913-1987 Obituary 123
Crowley, J(oseph) Donald 1932- 122
Crowley, James B. 1929- 21-24R
Crowley, John 1942- CANR-43
Earlier sketch in CA 61-64
See also CLC 57
See also DLBY 82
See also SATA 65
Crowley, John Edward 1943- 53-56
Crowley, John W(illiam) 1945- 69-72
Crowley, Mart 1935- 73-76
See also DLB 7
Crowley, Mary C. 1915- 97-100
Crowley, Raymond 1895-1982 Obituary 106
Crowley, Robert T(inkham) 1913- 161
Crowley, William R. 1946- 162
Crowley-Milling, Michael C. 1917- 146
Crown, Alan D(avid) 1932- 141
Crown, David A. 1928- CANR-10
Earlier sketch in CA 25-28R
Crown, Paul 1928- 17-20R
Crowne, John 1641-1712 DLB 80
Crownfield, Gertrude 1867-1945 YABC 1
Crowninshield, Edward Augustus 1817-1859 DLB 140
Crowninshield, Frank 1872-1947 DLB 91
Crowson, P(aul) S(piller) 1913- 53-56
Crowther, Betty 1939- 61-64
Crowther, (Francis) Bosley 1905-1981 CANR-38
Obituary 103
Earlier sketch in CA 65-68
Crowther, Brian
See Grierson, Edward
Crowther, Bruce (Ian) 1933- 128
Crowther, Duane S(wofford) 1934- CANR-17
Earlier sketch in CA 25-28R
Crowther, Geoffrey 1907-1972 Obituary 33-36R
Crowther, James Gerald 1899- 73-76
See also SATA 14
Crowther, Jean D(ecker) 1937- 120
Crowther, Peter 1949- CANR-72
Earlier sketch in CA 148
Crowther, Wilma (Beryl) 1918-1989 5-8R
Obituary 128
Crowther-Hunt, Norman Crowther 1920-1987 133
Obituary 121
Croxford, Leslie 1944- 81-84
Croxton, Anthony H(ugh) 1902- 61-64
Croxton, Frederick E(mory) 1899-1991 CAP-2
Obituary 133
Earlier sketch in CA 23-24
Croy, Homer 1883-1965 110
Obituary 89-92
See also DLB 4
Croydon, Michael (Benet) 1931- 158
Crozet, Charlotte 1926- 25-28R
Crozetti, R(uth G.) Warner
See Warner-Crozetti, R(uth G.)
Crozier, Andrew 1943- 153
Crozier, Brian (Rossiter) 1918- CANR-3
Earlier sketch in CA 9-12R
Crozier, Lorna 1948- CANR-68
Earlier sketches in CA 113, CANR-32
Crozier, Michael (Paul) 1956- 161
Crozier, Michel J. 1922- 130
Crud
See Crumb, R(obert)
Cruden, Robert 1910- 33-36R
Cruger, Melvin J. 1925(?)-1983 Obituary 111
Cruickshank, Allan D(udley) 1907-1974 Obituary 53-56
Cruickshank, C. G.
See Cruickshank, Charles (Greig)
Cruickshank, Charles (Greig) 1914-1989 CANR-25
Obituary 128
Earlier sketches in CA 21-24R, CANR-9
Cruickshank, Helen Gere 1907- CAP-1
Earlier sketch in CA 13-14
Cruickshank, John 1924- CANR-20
Earlier sketches in CA 1-4R, CANR-4
Cruickshank, Marjorie 1920-1983 122
Obituary 111
Cruickshank, William M(ellon) 1915-1992 89-92
Obituary 139
Cruikshank, George 1792-1878 SATA 22
Cruise, David 1950- 128
Crumarums
See Crumb, R(obert)
Crumb, R(obert) 1943- 106
See also CLC 17
Crumbaker, Alice 1911- 81-84
Crumbaugh, James C(harles) 1912- 37-40R
Crumbley, D(onald) Larry 1941- CANR-46
Earlier sketches in CA 29-32R, CANR-12
Crumbley, Paul 1952- 168
Crumbum
See Crumb, R(obert)
Crumley, James 1939- CANR-65
Earlier sketches in CA 69-72, CANR-21
See also DLBY 84
Crummey, Robert O(wen) 1936- CANR-17
Earlier sketch in CA 25-28R
Crump, Barry (John) 1935- CANR-8
Earlier sketch in CA 13-16R
Crump, Fred H., Jr. 1931- CANR-41
Earlier sketches in CA 9-12R, CANR-3, 19
See also SATA 11, 76
Crump, Galbraith Miller 1929- 57-60
Crump, Geoffrey (Herbert) 1891- CAP-1
Earlier sketch in CA 13-14
Crump, J(ames) Irving 1887-1979 73-76
Obituary 89-92
See also SATA 57
See also SATA-Obit 21
Crump, Kenneth G(ordon), Jr. 1931- 21-24R
Crump, Paul (Orville) 1930(?)- BW 2
Crump, Spencer (M., Jr.) 1933- CANR-9
Earlier sketch in CA 21-24R
Crump, (Stephen) Thomas 1929- CANR-47
Earlier sketch in CA 49-52
Crumpacker, Laurie 1941- 118
Crumpet, Peter
See Buckley, Fergus Reid
Crumpler, Frank H(unter) 1935- 77-80
Crumpler, Gus H(unt) 1911- 69-72
Crumrine, N(orman) Ross II 1934- CANR-8
Earlier sketch in CA 13-16R
Crumski
See Crumb, R(obert)
Crum the Bum
See Crumb, R(obert)
Crunden, Reginald
See Cleaver, Hylton Reginald
Crunden, Robert M. 1940- CANR-15
Earlier sketch in CA 29-32R
Crunk
See Crumb, R(obert)
Cruse, Harold 77-80
Crush, Jonathan 1953- 141
Cruso, Thalassa 1909-1997 65-68
Obituary 158
Crussi, F(rank) Gonzalez
See Gonzalez-Crussi, F(rank)
Crustt
See Crumb, R(obert)
Crutcher, Anne Neilson 1919-1983 Obituary 111
Crutcher, Chris(topher C.) 1946- CANR-36
Earlier sketch in CA 113
See also AAYA 9
See also CLR 28
See also JRDA
See also MAICYA
See also SATA 52, 99
Cruz, Arturo, Jr. 1954(?)- 131
See also HW
Cruz, Gilbert R(alph) 1929- 131
See also HW
Cruz, Gilberto Rafael
See Cruz, Gilbert R(alph)
Cruz, Joan Carroll 1931- 73-76
Cruz, Nicomedes Santa
See Santa Cruz (Gamarra), Nicomedes
Cruz, Ray(mond) 1933- SATA 6
Cruz, Ricardo Cortez 1964- 139
See also BW 2
Cruz, Victor Hernandez 1949- CANR-32
Earlier sketches in CA 65-68, CANR-14
See also CAAS 17
See also BW 2
See also DAM MULT, POET
See also DLB 41
See also HLC
See also HW
Cruz Martinez, Alejandro (?)-1987 SATA 74
Cruz Monclova, Lidio 1899- HW
Cryer, Gretchen (Kiger) 1935- 123
Brief entry 114
See also CLC 21
Cryer, Jon 1965- 155
Crying Wind
See Stafford, Linda (Crying Wind)
Crystal, David 1941- CANR-47
Earlier sketches in CA 17-20R, CANR-7, 23
Crystal, John C(urry) 1920- 102
Csaba, Laszlo 1954- 154
Csath, Geza 1887-1919 Brief entry 111
See also TCLC 13
Csepeli, Gyorgy 1946- 145
Csicsery-Ronay, Istvan 1917- 21-24R
Csikos-Nagy, Bela 1915- 73-76
Csikszentmihalyi, Mihaly 1934- 125
Csokor, Franz Theodor 1885-1969 DLB 81
Csoori, Sandor 1930- 154
Ctvrtek, Vaclav 1911-1976 Obituary 107
See also SATA-Obit 27
Cua, Antonio S. 1932- CANR-7
Earlier sketch in CA 17-20R
Cuadra, Pablo Antonio 1912- 131
See also HW
Cuadrado, Carlos Mellizo
See Mellizo (Cuadrado), Carlos
Cuban, Larry 1934- CANR-12
Earlier sketch in CA 29-32R
Cubas, Braz
See Dawes, Robyn M(ason)
Cuber, John F(rank) 1911- 9-12R
Cubeta, Paul Marsden 1925- 5-8R
Cuciti, Peggy L. 1949- 123
Cudahy, Brian J(ames) 1936- 41-44R
Cudahy, Sheila 1920- 159
Cuddihy, John Murray 1922- 85-88
Cuddon, John Anthony 1928-1996 CANR-19
Obituary 151
Earlier sketches in CA 5-8R, CANR-3
Cuddy, Don 1925- 69-72
Cudjoe, Selwyn Reginald 1943- 118
Cudlip, David 1933- CLC 34
Cudlipp, Lord
See Cudlipp, Hugh
Cudlipp, Edythe 1929- CANR-12
Earlier sketch in CA 33-36R
Cudlipp, Hugh 1913-1998 Obituary 167
Brief entry 116
Cudmore, Dana (D.) 1954- 134
Cuelho, Art 1943- 61-64
Cuevas, Clara 1933- 57-60
Cuevas, Judy
See Cuevas, Judy
Cuff, Barry
See Koste, Robert Francis
Cuff, Robert Dennis 1941- Brief entry 109
Cuffari, Richard 1925-1978 MAICYA
See also SATA 6, 66
See also SATA-Obit 25
Cugat, Xavier 1900-1990 Obituary 132
Cuisenaire, Emile-Georges 1891(?)-1976 Obituary 61-64
Cuisenier, Jean 1927- CANR-20
Earlier sketch in CA 73-76
Culbert, David H(olbrook) 1943- CANR-31
Earlier sketch in CA 112
Culbert, Samuel Alan 1938- 69-72
Culbert, Steven (Tye) 1950- 144
Culbert, T(homas) Patrick 1930- Brief entry 107
Culbertson, Don S(tuart) 1927- 9-12R
Culbertson, Hugh M. 77-80
Culbertson, J(ohn) M(athew) 1921- 9-12R
Culbertson, James T(homas) 1911- 118
Culbertson, Judi 1941- CANR-60
Earlier sketches in CA 85-88, CANR-31
Culbertson, Manie 1927- 49-52
Culbertson, Paul T(homas) 1905- 37-40R
Culex
See Stanier, Maida Euphemia Kerr
Culhane, Claire 1918- 118
Culhane, John (William) 1934- 144
Culhane, Shamus 1908-1996 121
Obituary 151
Culican, William 1929(?)-1984 Obituary 113
Culkin, Ann Marie 1918- 9-12R
Cull, John G(uinn, Jr.) 1934- 41-44R
Cullen, Charles T(homas) 1940- 53-56
Cullen, Countee 1903-1946 124
Brief entry 108
See also BLC 1
See also BW 1
See also CDALB 1917-1929
See also DA
See also DAC
See also DAM MST, MULT, POET
See also DLB 4, 48, 51
See also MTCW 1
See also PC 20
See also SATA 18
See also TCLC 4, 37
See also WLCS
Cullen, George Francis 1901-1980 Obituary 102
Cullen, Jim 1962- 151
Cullen, Joseph P(atrick) 1920- 49-52
Cullen, Lee Stowell 1922- 103
Cullen, Mark 1956- 141
Cullen, Maurice R(aymond), Jr. 1927- 73-76
Cullen, Patrick (Colborn) 1940- 29-32R
Cullen, Peta
See Pyle, Hilary
Cullen, Robert (B.) 1949- 134
Cullen Brown, Joanna 1930- 128
Culler, A(rthur) Dwight 1917- 17-20R
Culler, Annette Lorena
See Penney, Annette Culler
Culler, Jonathan 1944- 104
See also DLB 67
Cullerne Bown, Matthew 1956- 132
Culleton, Beatrice 1949- 120
See also DAC
See also NNAL
Culley, Thomas R(obert) 1931- 33-36R
Culliford, Pierre 1928-1992 124
Obituary 140
See also SATA 40
See also SATA-Obit 74
Culliford, Stanley George 1920- 65-68
Culligan, Joe
See Culligan, Matthew J(oseph)
Culligan, Matthew J(oseph) 1918- CANR-20
Earlier sketch in CA 81-84
Cullinan, Bernice Ellinger 1926- 104
Cullinan, Elizabeth 1933- CANR-11
Earlier sketch in CA 25-28R
Cullinan, Gerald 1916- 21-24R
Cullinan, Patrick 1932- 153
Cullinane, Leo Patrick 1907(?)-1978 Obituary 77-80
Culliney, John L. 1942- 65-68
Cullingford, Cecil H(oward) D(unstan) 1904-1990 CANR-7
Obituary 132
Earlier sketch in CA 5-8R
Cullingford, Guy
See Taylor, Constance Lindsay
Cullingworth, J(ohn) Barry 1929- CANR-1
Earlier sketch in CA 1-4R
Cullman, Marguerite Wagner 1908- 1-4R
Cullman, W. Arthur 1914- Brief entry 111
Cullman, W(illiam) Arthur 1914- 113
Cullmann, Oscar 1902- 106
Cullop, Charles P. 1927- 25-28R
Cully, Iris V(irginia Arnold) 1914- CANR-17
Earlier sketches in CA 1-4R, CANR-1
Cully, Kendig Brubaker 1913- CANR-17
Earlier sketches in CA 1-4R, CANR-1
Culme, John 1946- 128
Culotta, Nino
See O'Grady, John (Patrick)
Culp, Delos Poe 1911- 17-20R
Culp, John H(ewett, Jr.) 1907- CANR-61
Earlier sketch in CA 29-32R
Culp, Louanna McNary 1901-1965 CAP-1
Earlier sketch in CA 13-16
See also SATA 2
Culp, Paula 1941- 57-60
Culp, Stephanie (Anne) 1947- 136
Culpepper, R(ichard) Alan 1946- 115
Culpepper, Robert H(arrell) 1924- 77-80
Culross, Michael (Gerard) 1942- 33-36R
Culshaw, John (Royds) 1924-1980 CANR-11
Obituary 97-100
Earlier sketch in CA 21-24R
Culver, Dwight W(endell) 1921- 9-12R
Culver, Elsie Thomas 1898- CAP-2
Earlier sketch in CA 21-22
Culver, Kathryn
See Dresser, Davis
Culver, Kenneth Leon 1903- 103
Culver, Robert Duncan 1916- 120
Culver, Roger B(ruce) 1940- 104
Cum, R.
See Crumb, R(obert)
Cumbaa, Stephen 1947- SATA 72
Cumberland, Charles C(urtis) 1914-1970 CANR-2
Earlier sketch in CA 1-4R
Cumberland, John H(ammett) 1924- 127
Brief entry 106
Cumberland, Kenneth Brailey 1913- 53-56

Cumberland, Marten 1892-1972 .... CAP-1
Earlier sketch in CA 11-12
Cumberland, Richard 1732-1811 .... DLB 89
Cumberland, William Henry 1929- 17-20R
Cumberlege, Marcus (Crossley) 1938- ... CANR-17
Earlier sketch in CA 97-100
Cumberlege, Vera 1908- 81-84
Cumbler, John T(aylor) 1946- 89-92
Cumes, J(ames) W(illiam) C(rawford) 1922- .. 73-76
Cuming, Geoffrey John 1917-1988 ...... CANR-18
Obituary 125
Earlier sketches in CA 5-8R, CANR-3
Cuming, Pamela 1944- 107
Cumings, Bruce Glenn 1943- 107
Cumming, Constance Gordon 1837-1924 . DLB 174
Cumming, Elizabeth (Skeoch) 1948- 137
Cumming, Patricia (Arens) 1932- CANR-11
Earlier sketch in CA 61-64
Cumming, Peter 1951- 129
Cumming, Primrose Amy 1915- 33-36R
See also SATA 24
Cumming, Robert 1945- CANR-44
Earlier sketch in CA 106
See also SATA 65
Cumming, Robert Denoon 1916- Brief entry ... 107
Cumming, William P(atterson) 1900- 33-36R
Cummings, Ann
See Rudolph, Lee (Norman)
Cummings, Arthur J. 1920(?)-1979 Obituary .. 89-92
Cummings, Betty Sue 1918- CANR-14
Earlier sketch in CA 73-76
See also SAAS 9
See also SATA 15
Cummings, Bruce F(rederick) 1889-1919 Brief entry 123
See also Barbellion, W. N. P.
Cummings, Charles 1940- 107
Cummings, D(onald) W(ayne) 1935- 101
Cummings, E(dward) E(stlin) 1894-1962 . CANR-31
Earlier sketch in CA 73-76
See also CDALB 1929-1941
See also CLC 1, 3, 8, 12, 15, 68
See also DA
See also DAB
See also DAC
See also DAM MST, POET
See also DLB 4, 48
See also MTCW 1
See also PC 5
See also WLC 2
Cummings, Florence
See Bonime, Florence
Cummings, Gary 1941(?)-1987 Obituary 125
Cummings, Jack
See Cummings, John W(illiam), Jr.
Cummings, Jean 1930- 33-36R
Cummings, Joe 1952- 137
Cummings, John W(illiam), Jr. 1940- CANR-41
Earlier sketch in CA 117
Cummings, Larry L(ee) 1937- 53-56
Cummings, Milton C(urtis), Jr. 1933- 13-16R
Cummings, Monette 1914- CANR-40
Earlier sketch in CA 116
Cummings, Parke 1902-1987 .... CAP-1
Obituary 123
Earlier sketch in CA 13-14
See also SATA 2
See also SATA-Obit 53
Cummings, Pat (Marie) 1950- CANR-44
Earlier sketch in CA 122
See also BW 2
See also CLR 48
See also MAICYA
See also SAAS 13
See also SATA 42, 71
Cummings, Paul 1933-1997 .... CANR-8
Obituary 156
Earlier sketch in CA 21-24R
Cummings, Phil 1957- .... SATA 74
Cummings, Ray(mond King) 1887-1957 .. CANR-31
Brief entry 113
See also DLB 8
Cummings, Richard
See Gardner, Richard (M.)
Cummings, Richard (Marshall) 1938- 113
Cummings, Richard LeRoy 1933- 45-48
Cummings, Scott 112
Cummings, Thomas G(erald) 1944- CANR-16
Earlier sketch in CA 97-100
Cummings, Violet M(ay) 1905- 57-60
Cummings, W(alter) T(hies) 1933- 1-4R
Cummins, C. Lyle, Jr. 1930- 149
Cummins, D. Duane 1935- CANR-14
Earlier sketch in CA 37-40R
Cummins, Geraldine Dorothy 1890-1969 .... CAP-1
Earlier sketch in CA 9-10
Cummins, James 1948- 122
Cummins, Light Townsend 1946- 141
Cummins, Maria Susanna 1827-1866 ...... DLB 42
See also YABC 1
Cummins, Paul F. 1937- 33-36R
Cummins, Walter (Merrill) 1936- CANR-15
Earlier sketch in CA 41-44R
Cundieff, Rusty 1965(?)- 156
Cundiff, Edward William 1919- CANR-4
Earlier sketch in CA 1-4R
Cundiff, Margaret Joan 1932- CANR-56
Earlier sketches in CA 112, CANR-30
Cundy, Henry Martyn 1913- 5-8R
Cuneo, Ernest (L.) 1905-1988 Obituary 125
Cuneo, Gilbert Anthony 1913-1978 Obituary . 77-80
Cuneo, John R(obert) 1911- 53-56
Cuneo, Mary Louise .... SATA 85
Cuney, Waring
See Cuney, William Waring
Cuney, William Waring 1906-1976 125
See also BW 1
See also DLB 51
Cunha, Euclides (Rodrigues Pimenta) da 1866-1909 Brief entry 123
See also TCLC 24
Cunha, George Martin 1911- 25-28R
Cuninggim, Merrimon 1911- 41-44R
Cunliffe, Barrington Windsor 1939- CANR-49
Earlier sketches in CA 53-56, CANR-9, 24
Cunliffe, Barry
See Cunliffe, Barrington Windsor
Cunliffe, Elaine 33-36R
Cunliffe, John Arthur 1933- CANR-52
Earlier sketches in CA 61-64, CANR-11
See also SATA 11, 86
Cunliffe, Marcus (Falkner) 1922-1990 .... CANR-10
Obituary 132
Earlier sketch in CA 21-24R
See also SATA 37
See also SATA-Obit 66
Cunliffe, William Gordon 1929- 25-28R
Cunningham, Aline CANR-9
Earlier sketch in CA 57-60
Cunningham, Allan 1784-1842 .... DLB 116; 144
Cunningham, Barry 1940- 73-76
Cunningham, Bob
See May, Julian
Cunningham, Captain Frank
See Glick, Carl (Cannon)
Cunningham, Cathy
See Cunningham, Chet
Cunningham, Chet 1928- CANR-62
Earlier sketches in CA 49-52, CANR-4, 19
See also Dalton, Kit
See also SATA 23
Cunningham, Dale S(peers) 1932- CANR-8
Earlier sketch in CA 13-16R
See also SATA 11
Cunningham, Donald H(ayward) 1935- ... CANR-20
Earlier sketch in CA 103
Cunningham, Dru 155
See also SATA 91
Cunningham, E. V.
See Fast, Howard (Melvin)
Cunningham, Elaine 1957- 160
Cunningham, Eldon L. 1956- 144
Cunningham, Floyd F(ranklin) 1899- CAP-1
Earlier sketch in CA 13-16
Cunningham, Frank R. 1937- 137
Cunningham, H(orace) H(erndon) 1913-1969 ...... CAP-1
Earlier sketch in CA 11-12
Cunningham, Hugh 1942- 151
Cunningham, Imogen 1883-1976 Obituary ... 65-68
Cunningham, J(ames) V(incent) 1911-1985 .... CANR-72
Obituary 115
Earlier sketches in CA 1-4R, CANR-1
See also CLC 3, 31
See also DLB 5
Cunningham, James F. 1901- CAP-2
Earlier sketch in CA 19-20
Cunningham, James V. 1923- 135
Cunningham, Jim
See Cunningham, James V.
Cunningham, John D(onovan) 1933- 111
Cunningham, Joseph F. X. 1925- 69-72
Cunningham, Joseph Sandy 1928- 61-64
Cunningham, Julia (Woolfolk) 1916- CANR-36
Earlier sketches in CA 9-12R, CANR-4, 19
See also CLC 12
See also JRDA
See also MAICYA
See also SAAS 2
See also SATA 1, 26
Cunningham, Keith 1939- 139
Cunningham, Laura 1947- CANR-47
Earlier sketches in CA 85-88, CANR-23
Cunningham, Lawrence 1935- CANR-15
Earlier sketch in CA 85-88
Cunningham, Lyda Sue Martin 1938- 17-20R
Cunningham, Marilyn 1927- 125
Cunningham, Mary (Elizabeth) 1951- 114
Cunningham, Michael 1952- 136
See also CLC 34
Cunningham, Michael A(lan) 1945- 41-44R
Cunningham, Noble E., Jr. 1926- 81-84
Cunningham, Patricia (A.) 1937- 151
Cunningham, Paul James, Jr. 1917- 73-76
Cunningham, R(onnie) Walter 1932- 103
Cunningham, Richard 1939- 101
Cunningham, Robert Louis 1926- 41-44R
Cunningham, Robert M(aris), Jr. 1909-1992 .... CANR-1
Obituary 137
Earlier sketch in CA 49-52
Cunningham, Robert Stanley 1907- 53-56
Cunningham, Rosemary 1916- 9-12R
Cunningham, Virginia
See Holmgren, Virginia C(unningham)
Cunningham, W(infield) Scott 1899(?)-1986 Obituary 118
Cunninghame Graham, R(obert) B(ontine) 1852-1936 Brief entry 119
See also Graham, R(obert) B(ontine) Cunninghame
See also DLB 98
See also TCLC 19
Cunnington, Phillis 1887-1974 Obituary 53-56
Cuno, Kenneth M. 1950- 147
Cunquerio, Alvaro 1911-1981 .... DLB 134
Cunz, Dieter 1910-1969 .... CAP-2
Earlier sketch in CA 19-20
Cuomo, George (Michael) 1929- CANR-50
Earlier sketches in CA 5-8R, CANR-7
See also DLBY 80
Cuomo, Mario Matthew 1932- CANR-40
Earlier sketch in CA 103
Cupitt, Don 1934- CANR-48
Earlier sketches in CA 41-44R, CANR-14
Cuppleditch, David 1946- CANR-56
Earlier sketches in CA 116, CANR-38
Cuppy, Will(iam Jacob) 1884-1949 Brief entry .. 108
See also DLB 11
Cure, Karen 1949- CANR-9
Earlier sketch in CA 65-68
Curiae, Amicus
See Fuller, Edmund (Maybank)
Curie, Eve 1904- CAP-1
Earlier sketch in CA 9-10
See also SATA 1
Curie, Marie (Sklodowska) 1867-1934 166
Brief entry 118
Curl, David H. 1932- 93-96
Curl, Donald Walter 1935- 33-36R
Curl, James Stevens 1937- CANR-14
Earlier sketch in CA 37-40R
Curle, Adam
See Curle, Charles T. W.
Curle, Charles T. W. 1916- 33-36R
Curlee, Lynn 1947- 165
See also SATA 98
Curler, (Mary) Bernice 1915- 85-88
Curley, Arthur 1938- CANR-9
Earlier sketch in CA 21-24R
Curley, Charles 1949- 57-60
Curley, Daniel 1918-1988 .... CANR-18
Obituary 127
Earlier sketches in CA 9-12R, CANR-3
See also SATA 23
See also SATA-Obit 61
Curley, Dorothy Nyren
See Nyren, Dorothy Elizabeth
Curley, Michael J. 1900-1972 Obituary 37-40R
Curley, Walter J(oseph) P(atrick) 1922- 53-56
Curling, Audrey 61-64
Curling, Bill
See Curling, Bryan William Richard
Curling, Bryan William Richard 1911- 102
Curnow, (Thomas) Allen (Monro) 1911- .. CANR-48
Earlier sketch in CA 69-72
Curnow, Frank
See Atkinson, Frank
Curnow, Ray(mond) 1928- 117
Curran, Bob
See Curran, Robert
Curran, Charles (John) 1921-1980 130
Obituary 105
Curran, Charles A(rthur) 1913-1978 ..... CANR-29
Earlier sketch in CA 33-36R
Curran, Charles E. 1934- CANR-48
Earlier sketches in CA 21-24R, CANR-14
Curran, Daniel J. 1950- 139
Curran, Dolores 1932- CANR-6
Earlier sketch in CA 57-60
Curran, Donald J. 1926- 45-48
Curran, Francis X. 1914- 17-20R
Curran, Jan Goldberg 1937- 101
Curran, Joseph M(aroney) 1932- 103
Curran, Mona (Elisa) 5-8R
Curran, Peter Malcolm 1922- 103
Curran, Phil(ip) R(ead) 1911- 73-76
Curran, Robert 1923- 89-92
Curran, Samuel (Crowe) 1912- 109
Curran, Stuart (Alan) 1940- 29-32R
Curran, Susan 1952- 113
Curran, Terrie 1942- 127
Curran, Thomas J(oseph) 1929- 45-48
Curran, Ward S(chenk) 1935- 41-44R
Curran, William John 1925- 108
Curren, Polly 1917- CANR-4
Earlier sketch in CA 1-4R
Current, Richard N(elson) 1912- CANR-5
Earlier sketch in CA 1-4R
Current-Garcia, Eugene 1908- 17-20R
Currer-Briggs, Noel 1919- CANR-13
Earlier sketch in CA 73-76
Currey, Cecil B(arr) 1932- CANR-51
Earlier sketches in CA 25-28R, CANR-25
Currey, Dave 1953- 140
Currey, R(onald) F(airbridge) 1894-1983 .... CAP-1
Obituary 109
Earlier sketch in CA 9-10
Currey, R(alph) N(ixon) 1907- 93-96
Currey, Richard 1949- 163
Earlier sketch in CA 117
Currie, Ann (Brooke Peterson) 1922(?)-1980 Obituary 102
Currie, Barton Wood 1878-1962 Obituary 116
Currie, David
See Allen, Sydney (Earl), Jr.
Currie, David P(ark) 1936- 134
Brief entry 106
Currie, Donald Glenne 1926-1984 Obituary 111
Currie, Edwina 1946- 152
Currie, Ellen 19(?)- .... CLC 44
Currie, Elliott (?)-1993(?) 155
Currie, James 1756-1805 .... DLB 142
Currie, Katy
See Kyle, Susan (Spaeth)
Currie, Lauchlin (Bernard) 1902-1993 .... CANR-15
Obituary 143
Earlier sketch in CA 73-76
Currie, Mary Montgomerie Lamb Singleton
See Fane, Violet
Currie, Philip J(ohn) 1949- 168
Currie, Robert 1937- 112
Currie, Stephen 1960- 149
See also SATA 82
Currier, Alvin C. 1932- 21-24R
Currier, Chester S. 1945- 129
Currier, Frederick P(lumer) 1923- 85-88
Currier, Richard L(eon) 1940- 57-60
Curro, Evelyn Malone 1907- 5-8R
Curry, Andrew 1931- 57-60
Curry, Ann (Gabrielle) 1934- .... SATA 72
Curry, Avon
See Bowden, Jean
Curry, Constance (Winifred) 1933- 151
Curry, David 1942- 69-72
Curry, Dean C(onrad) 1952- 118
Curry, Estell H. 1907- CAP-2
Earlier sketch in CA 23-24
Curry, F. Hayden 1940- 108
Curry, G(len) David 1948- 136
Curry, George E(dward) 1947- 69-72
Curry, Gladys J.
See Washington, Gladys J(oseph)
Curry, Jane L(ouise) 1932- CANR-44
Earlier sketches in CA 17-20R, CANR-7, 24
See also CLR 31
See also MAICYA
See also SAAS 6
See also SATA 1, 52, 90
Curry, Jennifer 1934- 77-80
Curry, Kenneth 1910- CANR-8
Earlier sketch in CA 17-20R
Curry, Leonard Preston 1929- 29-32R
Curry, Lerond (Loving) 1938- 33-36R
Curry, Martha Mulroy 1926- 61-64
Curry, Neil 1937- 149
Curry, Paul (J.) 1917-1986 49-52
Obituary 118
Curry, Peggy Simson 1911-1987 .... CANR-61
Obituary 121
Earlier sketches in CA 33-36R, CANR-12
See also SATA 8
See also SATA-Obit 50
Curry, Richard Orr 1931- 13-16R
Curry, Thomas A. 1901(?)-1976 Obituary 69-72
Curry, Windell
See Sujata, Anagarika
Curry-Lindahl, Kai 1917- CANR-19
Earlier sketches in CA 49-52, CANR-2
Curtayne, Alice 1898- 53-56
Curteis, Ian Bayley 1935- CANR-36
Earlier sketch in CA 103
Curti, Merle Eugene 1897-1996 .... CANR-4
Obituary 151
Earlier sketch in CA 5-8R
See also DLB 17
Curtin, Dave 1955- 132
Curtin, Deane 1951- 138
Curtin, James R(udd) 1922- 17-20R
Curtin, Mary Ellen 1922- 57-60
Curtin, Patricia Romero
See Romero, Patricia W.
Curtin, Philip
See Lowndes, Marie Adelaide (Belloc)
Curtin, Phillip D. 1922- CANR-7
Earlier sketch in CA 13-16R
Curtin, Valerie 130
Curtin, William M(artin) 1927- 53-56
Curtis, Alan R(obert) 1936- 105
Curtis, Anthony 1926- CANR-40
Earlier sketches in CA 101, CANR-18
See also DLB 155
Curtis, (Hubert) Arnold 1917- CANR-29
Earlier sketches in CA 29-32R, CANR-12
Curtis, Bruce (Richard) 1944- .... SATA 30
Curtis, C(hristopher) Michael 1934- 136
Curtis, Carol Edwards 1943- 77-80
Curtis, Chara M(ahar) 1950- .... SATA 78
Curtis, Charles J(ohn) 1921- 21-24R
Curtis, Charles Ralph 1899- 5-8R
Curtis, Charlotte (Murray) 1928-1987 .... 9-12R
Obituary 122
See also AITN 2
Curtis, Christopher Paul 1954(?)- 159
See also SATA 93
Curtis, Cyrus H. K. 1850-1933 .... DLB 91
Curtis, Dan(iel Meyer) 1928- 145
Curtis, David Paul 1942- CANR-13
Earlier sketch in CA 21-24R
Curtis, Donald 1915- CANR-44
Earlier sketches in CA 103, CANR-20
Curtis, Edith Roelker 1893-1977 .... 1-4R
Obituary 103
Curtis, George William 1824-1892 .... DLB 1, 43
Curtis, Gerald 1904-1983 Obituary 109
Curtis, Howard J(ames) 1906-1972 Obituary 37-40R
Curtis, J(ulie) A. E. 1955- 141
Curtis, J(osiah) Montgomery 1905-1982 Obituary 108
Curtis, Jack 1922- 103
Curtis, Jackie
See Holder, John, Jr.
Curtis, James (Richard) 1953- 108
Curtis, James C. 1938- Brief entry 105
Curtis, James Malcolm 1940- 119
Curtis, Jamie Lee 1958- 160
See also SATA 95
Curtis, Jared Ralph 1936- 101
Curtis, John
See Prebble, John Edward Curtis
Curtis, Lewis Perry 1900-1976 .... CAP-2
Obituary 65-68
Earlier sketch in CA 23-24
Curtis, Lindsay R(aine) 1916- 41-44R
Curtis, Lynn A(lan) 1943- 61-64
Curtis, Margaret James 1897- 1-4R
Curtis, Marjorie
See Prebble, Marjorie Mary Curtis
Curtis, Mark H(ubert) 1920- 5-8R
Curtis, Michael K. 1942- 128
Curtis, Michael Raymond 1923- CANR-22
Earlier sketch in CA 103

Curtis, Nancy 1947- 159
Curtis, Norman 1914- 45-48
Curtis, Patricia 1921- CANR-18
Earlier sketch in CA 69-72
See also SATA 23, 101
Curtis, Paul
See Czura, R(oman) P(eter)
Curtis, Peter
See Lofts, Norah (Robinson)
Curtis, Philip (Delacourt) 1920- 109
See also SATA 62
Curtis, Price
See Ellison, Harlan (Jay)
Curtis, Richard (Alan) 1937- CANR-25
Earlier sketch in CA 106
See also SATA 29
Curtis, Richard 1956- 157
Curtis, Richard Hale
See Levinson, Leonard
and Rothweiler, Paul Roger
Curtis, Richard Kenneth 1924- CANR-47
Earlier sketch in CA 1-4R
Curtis, Rosemary Ann (Stevens) 1935- 9-12R
Curtis, Sharon 1951- CANR-68
Brief entry 116
Earlier sketch in CA 126
Curtis, Susan 1956- 145
Curtis, Thomas Bradford 1911-1993 61-64
Obituary 140
Curtis, Thomas Dale 1952- 126
Brief entry 116
Curtis, Tom
See Curtis, Thomas Dale
and Pendower, Jacques
Curtis, Tony 1925- CANR-45
Earlier sketch in CA 73-76
Curtis, Tony 1946- CANR-22
Earlier sketch in CA 106
Curtis, Wade
See Pournelle, Jerry (Eugene)
Curtis, Will
See Nunn, William Curtis
Curtis, William J(oseph) R. 1948- 110
Curtis Brown, Beatrice 1901-1974 .... CANR-69
Earlier sketches in CAP-2, CA 25-28
Curtiss, A(rlene) B. 1934- 155
See also SATA 90
Curtiss, John S(helton) 1899- CAP-2
Earlier sketch in CA 19-20
Curtiss, Mina (Stein Kirstein) 1896-1985 133
Obituary 118
Curtiss, Ursula Reilly 1923-1984 .... CANR-60
Obituary 114
Earlier sketches in CA 1-4R, CANR-5
Curtius, Ernst Robert 1886-1956 154
Curtler, Hugh Mercer 1937- CANR-15
Earlier sketch in CA 89-92
Curto, Josephine J. 1927- 17-20R
Curwin, Richard L(eonard) 1944- 77-80
Curzon, Clare
See Buchanan, Marie
Curzon, Daniel 73-76
Curzon, David 1941- 137
Curzon, Lucia
See Stevenson, Florence
Curzon, Robert 1810-1873 .... DLB 166
Curzon, Sam
See Krasney, Samuel A.
Curzon, Sarah Anne 1833-1898 .... DLB 99
Curzon, Virginia
See Hawton, Hector
Cusac, Marian H(ollingsworth) 1932- 33-36R
Cusack, (Ellen) Dymphna 1902-198(?) CANR-11
Earlier sketch in CA 9-12R
Cusack, Lawrence X(avier) 1919- 5-8R
Cusack, Margaret 1945- .... SATA 58
Cusack, Michael J(oseph) 1928- 69-72
Cush, Carol Gregor
See Gregor, Carol
Cushing, Barry E(dwin) 1945- CANR-4
Earlier sketch in CA 53-56
Cushing, Eliza Lanesford 1794-1886 ....DLB 99
Cushing, Harvey 1869-1939 .... DLB 187
Cushing, Jane 1922- 29-32R
Cushing, Mary W(atkins)
189(?)-1974 Obituary 53-56
Cushing, Peter (Wilton) 1913-1994 133
Obituary 146
Cushing, Richard Cardinal
See Cushing, Richard James
Cushing, Richard James 1895-1970 Obituary .. 112
Cushing, Winifred 1907-1990 Obituary 132
Cushion, John P(atrick) 1915- 93-96
Cushman, Clarissa Fairchild
1889-1980 Obituary 93-96
Cushman, Dan 1909- CANR-64
Earlier sketches in CA 5-8R, CANR-3, 18
Cushman, Doug 1953- CANR-54
Earlier sketch in CA 117
See also SATA 65, 101
Cushman, Jerome 1-4R
See also SATA 2
Cushman, Joseph David, Jr. 1925- 111
Cushman, Karen 1941- 155
See also AAYA 22
See also SATA 89
Cushman, Keith (Maxwell) 1942- 124
Cushman, Robert F(airchild) 1918- 77-80
Cushman, Stephen B. 1956- CANR-50
Earlier sketch in CA 123
Cusic, Don 1948- 145
Cusick, Heidi Haughy 1946- 150
Cusick, Philip A. 1937- 69-72
Cusick, Richie Tankersley 1952- 134
See also AAYA 14
See also JRDA
See also SATA 67
Cuskelly, Eugene James 1924- 5-8R
Cuskey, (Raymond) Walter 1934- 41-44R
Cuss, (Theodore Patrick) Camerer
1909(?)-1970 Obituary 104
Cussen, Antonio 1952- 144
Cussler, Clive (Eric) 1931- CANR-50
Earlier sketches in CA 45-48, CANR-1, 21
Interview in CANR-21
See also AAYA 19
See also BEST 90:4
See also DAM POP
Custer, Chester Eugene 1920- 41-44R
Custer, Clint
See Paine, Lauran (Bosworth)
Custer, Robert (Laverne) 1927-1990 Obituary .. 132
Cusumano, Michael A. 1954- 125
Cutchen, Billye Walker 1930- CANR-13
Earlier sketch in CA 77-80
See also SATA 15
Cutchins, Judy 1947- 127
See also SATA 59
Cutcliffe, Stephen H(osmer) 1947- CANR-48
Earlier sketch in CA 116
Cutforth, John Ashlin 1911- 9-12R
Cutforth, Rene 1909(?)-1984 123
Obituary 112
Cuthbert, Diana Daphne Holman-Hunt 1913- ....
CANR-54
Earlier sketch in CA 1-4R
Cuthbert, Eleonora Isabel (McKenzie) 1902- CAP-1
Earlier sketch in CA 11-12
Cuthbert, John A. 167
Cuthbert, Mary
See Hellwig, Monika Konrad
Cuthbert, Neil 1951- 146
Cuthbertson, Gilbert Morris 1937- 57-60
Cuthbertson, Tom 1945- CANR-1
Earlier sketch in CA 45-48
Cutler, Bruce 1930- CANR-41
Earlier sketches in CA 1-4R, CANR-2, 18
Cutler, Carl C(uster) 1878-1966 ....1-4R
Obituary 103
Cutler, Carol 1926- CANR-19
Earlier sketch in CA 103
Cutler, Charles L(ocke, Jr.) 1930- 65-68
Cutler, Daniel S(olomon) 1951- 120
See also SATA 78
Cutler, David 1956- 137
Cutler, Donald R. 1930- 21-24R
Cutler, (May) Ebbitt 1923- CANR-4
Earlier sketch in CA 49-52
See also SATA 9
Cutler, Irving H. 1923- CANR-9
Earlier sketch in CA 21-24R
Cutler, Ivor 1923- CANR-9
Earlier sketch in CA 5-8R
See also SATA 24
Cutler, Jane 1936- 142
See also SATA 75
Cutler, Judith 1946- 149
Cutler, Katherine Noble 1905- CANR-4
Earlier sketch in CA 5-8R
Cutler, Roland 1938- CANR-50
Earlier sketches in CA 102, CANR-25
Cutler, Samuel
See Folsom, Franklin (Brewster)
Cutler, Stan 1925- 137
Cutler, William Worcester III 1941- 103
Cutler, Winnifred B(erg) 1944- CANR-40
Earlier sketch in CA 117
Cutlip, Scott M. 1915- 5-8R
Cutrate, Joe
See Spiegelman, Art
Cutrer, Thomas W(illiam) 1947- 123
Cutright, Paul Russell 1897- 65-68
Cutright, Phillips 1930- 5-8R
Cutshall, Alden (D.) 1911-1997 .... CANR-3
Obituary 162
Earlier sketch in CA 9-12R
Cutsumbis, Michael N(icholas) 1935- 45-48
Cutt, W(illiam) Towrie 1898-1981 81-84
Obituary 115
See also SATA 16
See also SATA-Obit 85
Cutten, M. J.
See Cutten, Mervyn (James)
Cutten, Mervyn (James) 1916- CANR-46
Earlier sketch in CA 120
Cutter, Charles 1936- 148
Cutter, Charles R. 1950- 127
Cutter, Donald C(olgett) 1922- CANR-13
Earlier sketch in CA 33-36R
Cutter, Fred 1924- 57-60
Cutter, Robert Arthur 1930- CANR-8
Earlier sketch in CA 57-60
Cutter, Tom
See Randisi, Robert J(oseph)
and Wallmann, Jeffrey M(iner)
Cutting, Edith E(lsie) 1918- 106
Cutting, Linda Katherine 1954(?)- 168
Cutting, Pauline 1952- 128
Cuttino, G(eorge) P(eddy) 1914- 21-24R
Cuttle, Evelyn Roeding 57-60
Cuttler, Charles D(avid) 1913- 29-32R
Cutts, John P. 1927-1986 45-48
Obituary 121
Cutts, Richard 1923- 33-36R
Cutul, Ann-Marie 1945- 103
Cuyler, Louise E. 1908- 21-24R
Cuyler, Margery S(tuyvesant) 1948- 117
See also SATA 39, 99
Cuyler, Stephen
See Bates, Barbara S(nedeker)
Cuyler, Susanna (Stevens) 1946- 61-64
Cuza Male, Belkis 1942- 131
See also HW
Cykler, Edmund A(lbert) 1903- 9-12R
Cylwicki, Albert 1932- CANR-38
Earlier sketch in CA 116
Cynan
See Evans-Jones, Albert
Cynthia
See King, Florence
Cyprys, Ruth Altbeker 19(?)-1979 166
Cyr, Arthur 1945- 125
Cyr, Don(ald Joseph) 1935- 103
Cyr, Gilles 1940- 168
Cyr, John Edwin 1915- 103
Cyr, Mary 1946- 145
Cytowic, Richard E(dmund) 1952- 144
Czaczkes, Shmuel Yosef
See Agnon, S(hmuel) Y(osef Halevi)
Czaja, Michael 1911- 57-60
Czaplinski, Suzanne 1943- 61-64
Czekanowska, Anna 1929- 140
Czepko, Daniel 1605-1660 .... DLB 164
Czerneda, Julie E(lizabeth) 1955- 164
Czerniawski, Adam 1934- CANR-48
Earlier sketches in CA 37-40R, CANR-14
Czerny, Peter G(erd) 1941- 65-68
Czestochowski, Joseph S(tephen) 1950- 113
Czigany, Lorant (Gyorgy) 1935- 130
Czobor, Agnes 1920- 37-40R
Czura, R(oman) P(eter) 1913- 89-92

D

Daalder, Hans 1928- 133
Daane, Calvin J(ohn) 1925- 41-44R
Daane, James 1914- 21-24R
Dabberdt, Walter F. 1942- CANR-23
Earlier sketch in CA 107
Dabbs, Jack Autrey 1914- 17-20R
Dabbs, James McBride 1896-1970 .... CAP-1
Earlier sketch in CA 13-16
Dabcovich, Lydia 124
See also SATA 58, 99
See also SATA-Brief 47
Dabit, Eugene 1898-1936 .... DLB 65
Dabkin, Edwin Franden
1898(?)-1976 Obituary 65-68
Dabney, Dick 1933-1981 69-72
Obituary 105
Dabney, Joseph Earl 1929- 49-52
Dabney, Ross H. 1934- 21-24R
Dabney, Virginia Bell 1919- 139
Dabney, Virginius 1901-1995 .... CANR-29
Obituary 150
Earlier sketches in CA 45-48, CANR-1
Dabney, William M(inor) 1919- 9-12R
Daborne, Robert 1580(?)-1628 ....DLB 58
D'Abreu, Gerald Joseph 1916-(?) CAP-2
Earlier sketch in CA 19-20
Dabringhaus, Erhard 1917- 115
Dabrowska, Maria (Szumska) 1889-1965 106
See also CLC 15
Dabydeen, Cyril 1945- CANR-48
Brief entry 122
Earlier sketch in CA 133
Dabydeen, David 1955- CANR-56
Earlier sketch in CA 125
See also BW 1
See also CLC 34
DaCal, Ernesto Guerra 1911-1994 .... CANR-19
Obituary 162
Earlier sketches in CA 5-8R, CANR-4
Dace, Dolores B(oelens) 1929- 155
See also SATA 89
Dace, Letitia (Skinner) 1941- 106
Dace, Tish
See Dace, Letitia (Skinner)
Dace, (Edwin) Wallace 1920- CANR-34
Earlier sketch in CA 61-64
Dacey, Norman F(ranklyn) 1908-1994 .... CANR-2
Obituary 144
Earlier sketch in CA 5-8R
Dacey, Philip 1939- CANR-64
Earlier sketches in CA 37-40R, CANR-14, 32
See also CAAS 17
See also CLC 51
See also DLB 105
Dach, Simon 1605-1659 .... DLB 164
Dachman, Ken 1958- 110
Dachs, David 1922-1980 .... CANR-11
Earlier sketch in CA 69-72
Dack, Gail Monroe 1901-1976 Obituary 111
da Cruz, Daniel, Jr. 1921- CANR-19
Earlier sketches in CA 5-8R, CANR-3
Dacy, Douglas Calvin 1927- Brief entry 104
Dacyczyn, Amy 1955- 143
Dadamo, Amadeo F(iliberto), Jr. 1929- 168
Dadey, Debbie 1959- ....SATA 73
Dadie, Bernard B(inlin) 1916- CANR-17
Earlier sketch in CA 25-28R
See also BW 1
Dadlez, E(va) M(aria) 1956- 167
Daedalus
See Bramesco, Norton J.
Daehlin, Reidar A. 1910-1978 .... CAP-1
Obituary 162
Earlier sketch in CA 17-18
Daem, Thelma (Mary) Bannerman 1914- 5-8R
Daemer, Will
See Miller, (H.) Bill(y)
and Wade, Robert (Allison)
Daemmrich, Horst S. 1930- CANR-1
Earlier sketch in CA 45-48
Daenzer, Bernard John 1916- 53-56
da Fonseca, Eduardo Giannetti 1957- 141
Daftary, Farhad 1938- 136
Dagan, Avigdor 1912- CANR-30
Earlier sketches in CA 33-36R, CANR-13
Dagenais, James J(oseph) 1928- 41-44R
Dager, Edward Z(icca) 1921- 61-64
Dagerman, Stig (Halvard) 1923-1954 155
Brief entry 117
See also TCLC 17
Dagg, Anne Innis 1933- CANR-28
Earlier sketches in CA 69-72, CANR-11
Daggett, Rollin M. 1831-1901 .... DLB 79
Daglish, Eric Fitch 1892-1966 102
D'Agostino, Angelo 1926- 17-20R
D'Agostino, Anthony 1937- 128
D'Agostino, Dennis John 1957- 106
D'Agostino, Giovanna P. 1914- 57-60
D'Agostino, Joseph David 1929- 69-72
Dagover, Lil 1897-1980 Obituary 105
D'Aguiar, Fred 1960- 148
See also DLB 157
Daheim, Mary 1937- 110
Dahinden, Justus 1925- 81-84
Dahl, Arlene (Carol) 1928- 140
Brief entry 105
Dahl, Borghild (Margarethe) 1890-1984 .... CANR-2
Obituary 112
Earlier sketch in CA 1-4R
See also SATA 7
See also SATA-Obit 37
Dahl, Curtis 1920- CANR-2
Earlier sketch in CA 1-4R
Dahl, Georg 1905- 85-88
Dahl, Gordon J. 1932- 49-52
Dahl, John 1956- 164
Dahl, Linda 1949- 122
Dahl, Murdoch Edgcumbe 1914- CAP-1
Earlier sketch in CA 9-10
Dahl, Nils A(lstrup) 1911- 65-68
Dahl, Roald 1916-1990 .... CANR-62
Obituary 133
Earlier sketches in CA 1-4R, CANR-6, 32, 37
See also AAYA 15
See also CLC 1, 6, 18, 79
See also CLR 1, 7, 41
See also DAB
See also DAC
See also DAM MST, NOV, POP
See also DLB 139
See also JRDA
See also MAICYA
See also MTCW 1
See also SATA 1, 26, 73
See also SATA-Obit 65
Dahl, Robert A(lan) 1915- CANR-56
Earlier sketches in CA 65-68, CANR-30
Dahlberg, Arthur O. 1898(?)-1989 124
Obituary 129
Dahlberg, Edward 1900-1977 .... CANR-62
Obituary 69-72
Earlier sketches in CA 9-12R, CANR-31
See also CLC 1, 7, 14
See also DLB 48
See also MTCW 1
Dahlberg, Edwin T(heodore) 1892-1986 .... CAP-2
Obituary 120
Earlier sketch in CA 17-18
Dahlberg, Jane S. 1923- 21-24R
Dahlen, Beverly (Jean) 1934- 163
Dahlhaus, Carl 1928-1989 Obituary 128
Dahlie, Hallvard 1925- 128
Dahlinger, John Cote 1923-1984 Obituary 114
Dahlstedt, Marden (Stewart) 1921-1983 .... CANR-1
Obituary 163
Earlier sketch in CA 45-48
See also SATA 8
Dahlsten, Donald L. 1933- 132
Dahlstrand, Frederick Charles 1945- 111
Dahlstrom, Earl C(arl) 1914-1992 .... 17-20R
Obituary 139
Dahl-Wolfe, Louise (Emma Augusta)
1895-1989 Obituary 130
Dahm, Charles W(illiam) 1937- 107
Dahmer, Lionel (Herbert) 1936- 152
Dahms, Alan M(artin) 1937- 49-52
Dahmus, Joseph Henry 1909- 21-24R
Dahn, Felix 1834-1912 ....DLB 129
Dahood, Mitchell (Joseph) 1922-1982 .... CANR-20
Obituary 106
Earlier sketch in CA 25-28R
Dahrendorf, Ralf 1929- CANR-28
Earlier sketches in CA 1-4R, CANR-3
Daiches, David 1912- CANR-54
Earlier sketches in CA 5-8R, CANR-7, 29
Daigh, Ralph (Foster) 1907-1986 Obituary 121
Daigon, Arthur 1928- 33-36R
Daigon, Ruth 1923- 159
See also CAAS 25
Daiken, Leslie Herbert 1912- 1-4R
Dailey, Charles A(lvin) 1923- 89-92
Dailey, Janet (Ann) 1944- CANR-63
Earlier sketches in CA 89-92, CANR-17, 39
Interview in CANR-17
See also BEST 89:3
See also DAM POP
See also MTCW 1
Daily, Ann 1926- CANR-45
Daily, Jay E(lwood) 1923- 33-36R
Daims, Diva 1925- 113

Dain, Catherine
See Garwood, Judith
Dain, Martin J. 1924- ... 13-16R
See also SATA 35
Dain, Norman 1925- ... 9-12R
Dain, Phyllis 1929- ... 69-72
Dainton, (William) Courtney 1920- ... 9-12R
Daintrey, Adrian (Maurice) 1902-1988 Obituary . 127
Daitch, Susan 1954- ... 161
See also CLC 103
Daiute, Robert James 1926- ... 13-16R
Dajani, M(unther) S(uleiman) 1951- ... 132
Dakers, Elaine Kidner 1905-1978 ... CANR-30
Earlier sketch in CA 85-88
Dakin, Arthur Hazard 1905- Brief entry ... 106
Dakin, D(avid) Martin 1908- ... 73-76
Dakin, Edwin Franden 1898-1976 Obituary ... 104
Dakin, (David) Julian 1939-1971 ... CAP-2
Earlier sketch in CA 25-28
Dakin, Shaun 1966- ... 162
Dakos, Kalli 1950- ... SATA 80
Dal', Vladimir Ivanovich 1801-1872 ... DLB 198
Dalai Lama XIV
See Gyatso, Tenzin
Dalal, Nergis 1920- Brief entry ... 116
Daland, Robert T(heodore) 1919- ... 21-24R
Dalbor, John B(ronislaw) 1929- ... 17-20R
Dal Co, Francesco 1945- ... 133
Dalcourt, Gerard J. 1927- ... 33-36R
Dale, (Mary) Alzina Stone 1931- ... CANR-38
Earlier sketch in CA 114
Dale, Antony 1912- ... 107
Dale, Arbie Myron, Jr. 1924- ... 122
Dale, Celia (Marjorie) ... CANR-3
Earlier sketch in CA 5-8R
Dale, Colin
See Lawrence, T(homas) E(dward)
See also TCLC 18
Dale, D(ion) M(urray) C(rosbie) 1930- ... 21-24R
Dale, DeArmond 1914- ... SATA 70
Dale, Doris Cruger 1927- ... 116
Dale, Edgar 1900-1985 Obituary ... 117
Dale, Edward Everett 1879-1972 ... CANR-4
Earlier sketch in CA 5-8R
Dale, Edwin L., Jr. 1923- ... 69-72
Dale, Ernest 1917-1996 ... 13-16R
Obituary ... 153
Dale, George E.
See Asimov, Isaac
Dale, Henry Hallett 1875-1968 ... 157
Dale, Jack
See Holliday, Joseph
Dale, James 1886-1985 ... CAP-2
Obituary ... 116
Earlier sketch in CA 33-36
Dale, John B. 1905- ... 13-16R
Dale, Kathleen 1895-1984 Obituary ... 112
Dale, Laura A(bbott) 1919-1983 Obituary ... 113
Dale, Magdalene L(arsen) 1904- ... 13-16R
Dale, Margaret J(essy) Miller 1911- ... CANR-19
Earlier sketches in CA 5-8R, CANR-3
See also SATA 39
Dale, Norman
See Denny, Norman (George)
Dale, Paul W(orthen) 1923- ... 25-28R
Dale, Penny 1954- ... 138
See also SATA 70
Dale, Peter (John) 1938- ... CANR-39
Earlier sketches in CA 45-48, CANR-1, 16
See also DLB 40
Dale, Peter N(icholas) 1950- ... 126
Dale, Reginald R. 1907- ... 21-24R
Dale, Richard 1932- ... 33-36R
Dale, Robert D(ennis) 1940- ... CANR-33
Earlier sketch in CA 113
Dale, Roman
See Czura, R(oman) P(eter)
d'Alelio, Ellen F. 1938- ... 17-20R
Dales, Douglas S. 1907(?)-1985 Obituary ... 114
Dales, Richard C(lark) 1926- ... CANR-49
Earlier sketches in CA 45-48, CANR-24
Daleski, H(illel) M(atthew) 1926- ... 33-36R
D'Alessandro, Robert (Philip) 1942- ... 61-64
Dalet, Roger (Charles) 1927- ... 107
Daley, Adeline 1922(?)-1984 Obituary ... 112
Daley, Arthur (John) 1904-1974 ... CANR-62
Obituary ... 45-48
Earlier sketches in CAP-2, CA 23-24
See also DLB 171
Daley, Bill
See Appleman, John Alan
Daley, Brian 1947-1996 ... CANR-54
Earlier sketch in CA 126
Daley, Eliot A. 1936- ... 97-100
Daley, Harry 1901-1971 ... 134
Daley, Janet 1944- ... 125
Daley, Joseph A(ndrew) 1927- ... 53-56
Daley, Robert 1930- ... CANR-24
Earlier sketches in CA 1-4R, CANR-2
Interview in ... CANR-24
Daley, Sharon
See Barovsky, Sharon Daley
Daley, Stephen Dennis 1948- ... 133
Dalfiume, Richard Myron 1936- ... 25-28R
D'Alfonso, Antonio 1953- ... 129
D'Alfonso, John 1918- ... 29-32R
Dalgleish, Oakley Hedley 1910-1963 Obituary ... 115
Dalgliesh, Alice 1893-1979 ... 73-76
Obituary ... 89-92
See also MAICYA
See also SATA 17
See also SATA-Obit 21
Dalglish, Edward R(ussell) 1913- ... 37-40R
Dali, Salvador (Domenech Felipe Jacinto)
1904-1989 ... 104
Obituary ... 127
See also AAYA 23
Dalkey, Kara (Mia) 1953- ... 154
Dall, Caroline Wells (Healey) 1822-1912 ... DLB 1
D'Allard, Hunter
See Ballard, (Willis) Todhunter
Dallas, Athena Gianakas
See Dallas-Damis, Athena G(ianakas)
Dallas, E. S. 1828-1879 ... DLB 55
Dallas, John
See Duncan, W(illiam) Murdoch
Dallas, Philip 1921- ... 61-64
Dallas, Ruth
See Mumford, Ruth
Dallas, Sandra
See Atchison, Sandra Dallas
Dallas-Damis, Athena G(ianakas) 1925- ... 81-84
Dallek, Robert 1934- ... CANR-17
Earlier sketch in CA 25-28R
D'Allenger, Hugh
See Kershaw, John (Hugh D'Allenger)
Dallimore, Arnold A(rthur) 1911- ... 112
Dallin, Alexander 1924- ... CANR-19
Earlier sketches in CA 1-4R, CANR-5
Dallin, Leon 1918- ... CANR-1
Earlier sketch in CA 1-4R
Dallmann, Martha (Elsie) 1904- ... 1-4R
Dallmayr, Fred R(einhard) 1928- ... CANR-1
Earlier sketch in CA 49-52
Dally, Ann 1926- ... CANR-21
Earlier sketches in CA 5-8R, CANR-3
Dalmas, John
See Jones, John R(obert)
D'Alonzo, C(onstance) Anthony
1912-1972 Obituary ... 37-40R
Daloz, Laurent A. Parks 1940- ... 158
Dalpadado, J(ames) Kingsley (Evold) 1922- ... 112
Dalphin, John R(obert) 1942- ... 118
Dal Poggetto, Newton Francis 1922- ... 61-64
d'Alpuget, Blanche 1944- ... CANR-68
Earlier sketch in CA 114
Dalrymple, Byron W(illiam) 1910-1994 ... CANR-6
Obituary ... 163
Earlier sketch in CA 57-60
Dalrymple, Douglas J(esse) 1934- ... 73-76
Dalrymple, G. Brent 1937- ... 157
Dalrymple, Gertrude Bradley
1901(?)-1984 Obituary ... 113
Dalrymple, Ian (Murray) 1903-1989 ... 115
Obituary ... 128
Dalrymple, Jean 1910- ... CANR-5
Earlier sketch in CA 5-8R
Dalrymple, Willard 1921- ... 21-24R
Dalsass, Diana 1947- ... 106
Dalton, Alene
See Chapin, Alene Olsen Dalton
Dalton, Annie 1948- ... 156
See also SATA 40
Dalton, Claire
See Burns, Alma
Dalton, Clive
See Clark, F(rederick) Stephen
Dalton, (John) David 1944- ... CANR-72
Earlier sketch in CA 97-100
Dalton, Dennis (Gilmore) 1938- ... 115
Dalton, Dorothy 1915- ... 21-24R
Dalton, Elizabeth 1936- ... 85-88
Dalton, Gene W(ray) 1928- ... 25-28R
Dalton, George 1926-1991 ... 127
Obituary ... 135
Brief entry ... 106
Dalton, (Edward) Hugh (John Neale)
1887-1962 ... 144
Dalton, Kit
See Cunningham, Chet
Dalton, Lord
See Dalton, (Edward) Hugh (John Neale)
D'Alton, Louis (Lynch) 1900-1951 Brief entry ... 110
See also DLB 10
Dalton, Priscilla
See Avallone, Michael (Angelo, Jr.)
Dalton, Richard 1930- ... 57-60
Dalton, Sean
See Chester, Deborah
Dalton, Stephen 1937- ... 85-88
Dalven, Rae 1904-1992 ... 33-36R
Obituary ... 139
Daly, Anne 1896- ... CAP-2
Earlier sketch in CA 29-32
Daly, Brenda 1941- ... 162
Daly, Cahal Brendan 1917- ... CANR-52
Earlier sketches in CA 104, CANR-28
Daly, Carroll John 1889-1958 Brief entry ... 112
Daly, Christopher B. 1954- ... 126
Daly, Donald F(remont) ... 69-72
Daly, Edith Iglauer ... CANR-14
Earlier sketch in CA 77-80
Daly, Elizabeth 1878-1967 ... CANR-60
Obituary ... 25-28R
Earlier sketches in CAP-2, CA 23-24
See also CLC 52
Daly, Emily Joseph 1913- ... 9-12R
Daly, Faye Kennedy 1936- ... 97-100
Daly, Gay 1951- ... 131
Daly, Herman E. 1938- ... 89-92
Daly, Ita 1945- ... 136
Daly, Jim
See Stratemeyer, Edward L.
Daly, John Jay 1888(?)-1976 Obituary ... 69-72
Daly, Kathleen N(orah) Brief entry ... 115
See also SATA-Brief 37
Daly, (Arthur) Leo 1920- ... CANR-50
Earlier sketches in CA 105, CANR-25
Daly, Lowrie John 1914- ... 13-16R
Daly, Mary 1928- ... CANR-62
Earlier sketches in CA 25-28R, CANR-30
See also MTCW 1
Daly, Mary Tinley 1904(?)-1979 ... 85-88
Daly, Maureen 1921- ... CANR-37
See also AAYA 5
See also CLC 17
See also JRDA
See also MAICYA
See also SAAS 1
See also SATA 2
Daly, Nicholas 1946- ... CANR-36
Earlier sketch in CA 111
See also Daly, Niki
See also CLR 41
See also MAICYA
See also SATA 37, 76
Daly, Niki
See Daly, Nicholas
See also SAAS 21
Daly, Reginald Aldworth 1871-1957 ... 158
Daly, Robert 1943- ... 104
Daly, Robert Welter 1916-1975 ... CANR-71
Obituary ... 103
Earlier sketch in CA 9-12R
Daly, Saralyn R(uth) 1924- ... 57-60
Daly, Sister Mary Virginia 1925- ... 17-20R
Daly, T(homas) A(ugustine) 1871-1948 Brief
entry ... 111
See also DLB 11
Dalyell, Tam 1932- ... 142
Dalzel, Peter
See Dalzel Job, P(atrick)
Dalzel Job, P(atrick) 1913- ... 13-16R
Dalzell, Alexander 1925- ... 165
Dalzell, Robert (Fenton), Jr. 1937- ... 81-84
Dam, Hari N(arayan) 1921- ... 57-60
Dam, Kenneth W. 1932- ... CANR-12
Earlier sketch in CA 69-72
Damachi, (Godwin) Ukandi 1942- ... CANR-2
Earlier sketch in CA 45-48
Damas, David (John) 1926- ... 132
Damas, Leon-Gontran 1912-1978 ... 125
Obituary ... 73-76
See also BW 1
See also CLC 84
Damasio, Antonio R. 1944- ... 151
Damata, Ted 1909(?)-1988 Obituary ... 125
D'Amato, Alex 1919- ... CANR-18
Earlier sketch in CA 81-84
See also SATA 20
D'Amato, Alfonse 1937- ... 152
D'Amato, Anthony A. 1937- ... 29-32R
D'Amato, Barbara 1938- ... 69-72
D'Amato, Brian ... 141
D'Amato, Janet (Potter) 1925- ... CANR-18
Earlier sketches in CA 49-52, CANR-1
See also SATA 9
Damaz, Paul F. 1917- ... 5-8R
d'Amboise, Christopher 1960- ... 115
d'Amboise, Jacques Joseph 1934- ... 143
Dambrauskas, Joan Arden 1933- ... 104
D'Ambrosio, Charles ... 153
D'Ambrosio, Charles A. 1932- ... 21-24R
D'Ambrosio, Richard A(nthony) 1927- ... 102
D'Ambrosio, Vinnie-Marie 1928- ... 45-48
Dame, Lawrence 1898-1981 ... CAP-1
Obituary ... 163
Earlier sketch in CA 11-12
D'Amelio, Dan 1927- ... 33-36R
Dameron, J(ohn) Lasley 1925- ... 53-56
Damerow, Gail (Jane) 1944- ... 150
See also SATA 83
Damerst, William A. 1923- ... 17-20R
Dames, Rob(ert L.) 1944- ... 133
Damiani, Bruno Mario 1942- ... 57-60
D'Amico, John Francis 1947(?)-1987 Obituary . 124
Damis, John 1940- ... 118
Damm, John S. 1926- ... 37-40R
Damocles
See Benedetti, Mario
Damon, Gene
See Grier, Barbara G(ene Damon)
Damon, Matt(hew Paige) 1970- ... 168
Damon, S(amuel) Foster 1893-1971 ... 101
See also DLB 45
Damon, Virgil Green 1895-1972 ... CAP-1
Obituary ... 37-40R
Earlier sketch in CA 9-10
Damon, William 1944- ... 147
Damor, Hakji
See Lesser, R(oger) H(arold)
D'Amore, Arcangelo R. T. 1920-1986 Obituary . 118
Damore, Leo J. 1929-1995 ... CANR-35
Obituary ... 149
Earlier sketch in CA 81-84
See also BEST 89:2
Damrell, Liz 1956- ... SATA 77
Damrosch, Helen
See Tee-Van, Helen Damrosch
Damrosch, Leopold, Jr. 1941- ... 45-48
Dams, Jeanne M(artin) 1941- ... 155
Damsker, Matt(hew Harry) 1951- ... 108
Damtoft, Walter A(tkinson) 1922- ... 57-60
Dan, John 1926- ... 147
Dana, Amber
See Paine, Lauran (Bosworth)
Dana, Barbara 1940- ... CANR-8
Earlier sketch in CA 17-20R
See also SATA 22
Dana, Charles Anderson 1819-1897 ... DLB 3, 23
Dana, E. H.
See Hamel Peifer, Kathleen
Dana, Richard
See Paine, Lauran (Bosworth)
Dana, Richard H(enry) 1927- ... CANR-15
Earlier sketch in CA 85-88
Dana, Richard Henry, Jr. 1815-1882 ... DLB 1
See also SATA 26
Dana, Robert (Patrick) 1929- ... 33-36R
Dana, Rose
See Ross, W(illiam) E(dward) D(aniel)
Danachair, Caoimhin O
See Danaher, Kevin
Danagher, Edward F. 1919- ... 9-12R
Danaher, Kevin 1913- ... 33-36R
See also SATA 22
Danakas, John 1963- ... 159
See also SATA 94
Danan, Alexis 1889(?)-1979 Obituary ... 89-92
Danby, Hope (Smedley) 1899- ... CAP-1
Earlier sketch in CA 13-14
Danby, John B(lench) 1905-1983 Obituary ... 109
Danby, Mary (Heather) 1941- ... CANR-39
Danby, Miles William 1925- ... 13-16R
Dance, Daryl Cumber 1938- ... 131
See also BW 2
Dance, E(dward) H(erbert) 1894- ... 37-40R
Dance, F(rancis) E(sburn) X(avier) 1929- . CANR-16
Earlier sketches in CA 1-4R, CANR-1
Dance, Frank E. X.
See Dance, F(rancis) E(sburn) X(avier)
Dance, Helen Oakley 1913- ... 140
Dance, Jim 1924(?)-1983 Obituary ... 110
Dance, S(tanley) Peter 1932- ... CANR-13
Earlier sketch in CA 69-72
Dance, Stanley (Frank) 1910- ... CANR-8
Earlier sketch in CA 17-20R
Dancer, J. B.
See Harvey, John (Barton)
Dancer, J. B.
See Wells, Angus
Danco, Katharine L(eck) 1929- ... 112
Danco, Katy
See Danco, Katharine L(eck)
Danco, Leon A(ntoine) 1923- ... 112
Dancocks, Daniel G. 1950- ... 120
D'Ancona, Matthew 1968- ... 154
D'Ancona, Mirella Levi 1919- ... CANR-6
Earlier sketch in CA 53-56
Dancy, John Christopher 1920- ... 107
Dandrea, Don(ald E.) 1936- ... 120
D'Andrea, Kate
See Steiner, Barbara A(nnette)
D'Andrea, Paul 1939- ... 120
Dandridge, Ray G.
See Dandridge, Raymond Garfield
Dandridge, Raymond Garfield 1882-1930 ... 125
See also BW 1
See also DLB 51
Dandridge, Rita B(ernice) 1940- ... 141
See also BW 2
Dandy, James Edgar 1903-1976 Obituary ... 104
Dane, Carl
See Adams, F(rank) Ramsay
Dane, Clemence
See Ashton, Winifred
See also DLB 10, 197
Dane, Les(lie A.) 1925- ... 89-92
Dane, Mark
See Avallone, Michael (Angelo, Jr.)
Dane, Mary
See Morland, Nigel
Dane, Nathan II 1916-1980 ... 108
Obituary ... 97-100
Dane, Zel
See Timms, E(dward) V(ivian)
Daneff, Stephen Constantine 1931- ... 106
Daneke, Gregory A(llen) 1950- ... 112
Danelski, David J. 1930- ... 13-16R
Danenberg, Leigh 1893-1976 Obituary ... 69-72
Danesh, Abol Hassan 1952- ... 140
Danford, Howard G(orby) 1904- ... CAP-1
Earlier sketch in CA 11-12
Danforth, Art(hur Louis) 1913(?)-1987 Obituary . 122
Danforth, John 1660-1730 ... DLB 24
Danforth, John C(laggett) 1936- ... 148
Danforth, Loring M(andell) 1949- ... 111
Danforth, Samuel I 1626-1674 ... DLB 24
Danforth, Samuel II 1666-1727 ... DLB 24
Dangaard, Colin (Edward) 1942- ... 85-88
Dangarembga, Tsitsi 1959- ... 163
D'angelo, Edward 1932- ... 37-40R
D'Angelo, Frank J(oseph) 1928- ... 120
D'Angelo, Lou
See D'Angelo, Luciano
D'Angelo, Luciano 1932- ... 33-36R
Dangerfield, Balfour
See McCloskey, (John) Robert
Dangerfield, Clint
See Norwood, Victor G(eorge) C(harles)
Dangerfield, George (Bubb) 1904-1986 ... 9-12R
Obituary ... 121
Dangerfield, Harlan
See Padgett, Ron
Dangerfield, Rodney 1922(?)- ... 102
Danhof, Clarence H(enry) 1911- ... 37-40R
Dani, Ahmad Hasan 1920- ... 13-16R
Daniel, Alan 1939- ... SATA 76
See also SATA-Brief 53
Daniel, Anita 1893(?)-1978 Obituary ... 77-80
See also SATA 23
See also SATA-Obit 24
Daniel, Anne
See Steiner, Barbara A(nnette)
Daniel, Becky 1947- ... SATA 56
Daniel, Charles 1933- ... 114
Daniel, Cletus E(dward) 1943- ... 107
Daniel, (Elbert) Clifton, (Jr.) 1912- ... 142
Brief entry ... 113

Daniel, Colin
See Windsor, Patricia
Daniel, Daniel 1890(?)-1981 Obituary ... 104
Daniel, Elna Worrell
See Stone, Elna
Daniel, Emmett Randolph 1935- ... 102
Daniel, Errol Valentine ... 111
Daniel, George Bernard, Jr. 1927- ... 13-16R
Daniel, Glenda 1943- ... 111
Daniel, Glyn (Edmund) 1914-1986 ... CANR-30
Obituary ... 121
Earlier sketches in CA 57-60, CANR-13
Daniel, Hawthorne 1890- ... 5-8R
See also SATA 8
Daniel, James 1916- ... 69-72
Daniel, Jerry C(layton) 1937- ... 33-36R
Daniel, John M. 1825-1865 ... DLB 43
Daniel, Julie Goldsmith 1949- ... CANR-14
Earlier sketch in CA 77-80
Daniel, Lee
See Reid, Daniel P. (Jr.)
Daniel, (Donna) Lee 1944- ... SATA 76
Daniel, Lorne (MacLeod Lyons) 1953- ... 118
Daniel, Malcolm R. 1956- ... 150
Daniel, Mark 1954- ... 133
Daniel, Norman (Alexander) 1919- ... CANR-6
Earlier sketch in CA 57-60
Daniel, Pete 1938- ... CANR-14
Earlier sketch in CA 37-40R
Daniel, Price, Jr. 1941-1981 Obituary ... 103
Daniel, Ralph T(homas) 1921- ... 53-56
Daniel, Rebecca
See Daniel, Becky
Daniel, Robert L(eslie) 1923- ... 33-36R
Daniel, Robert W(oodham) 1915- ... 25-28R
Daniel, Samuel 1562(?)-1619 ... DLB 62
Daniel, Stephen H(artley) 1950- ... 119
Daniel, Tony 1963- ... 141
Daniel, Urcel 1908(?)-1984 Obituary ... 113
Daniel, Walter C(larence) 1922- ... 110
Daniel, Wayne W. 1929- ... 135
Daniel, Yuli (Markovich) 1925-1988 ... 116
Obituary ... 127
Daniele, Joseph William 1927- ... 89-92
Daniell, Albert Scott 1906-1965 ... CANR-3
Earlier sketch in CA 5-8R
Daniell, David Scott
See Daniell, Albert Scott
Daniell, Jere Rogers 1932- ... CANR-11
Earlier sketch in CA 29-32R
Daniell, Rosemary 1935- ... CANR-44
Earlier sketch in CA 118
Danielle, Maria 1945- ... 114
Danielli, James Frederic 1911-1984 Obituary ... 113
Daniells, Lorna M(cLean) 1918- ... CANR-18
Earlier sketch in CA 89-92
Daniells, Roy 1902-1979 ... 57-60
See also DLB 68
Danielou, Alain 1907-1994 ... CANR-57
Earlier sketches in CA 73-76, CANR-14, 31
Danielou, Jean 1905-1974 ... CAP-2
Obituary ... 49-52
Earlier sketch in CA 23-24
Daniel-Rops, Henri
See Petiot, Henri Jules Charles
Daniels, Anna Kleegman
1893-1970 Obituary ... 29-32R
Daniels, Arlene Kaplan 1930- ... CANR-27
Earlier sketches in CA 29-32R, CANR-12
Daniels, Brett
See Adler, Renata
Daniels, Bruce C(olin) 1943- ... CANR-48
Earlier sketch in CA 122
Daniels, Charlie 1936- ... 138
Daniels, David 1933- ... 53-56
Daniels, Derick January 1926- Brief entry ... 112
Daniels, Dewey
See McKimmey, James
Daniels, Doris Groshen 1931- ... 131
Daniels, Dorothy 1915- ... CANR-15
Earlier sketch in CA 89-92
See also Somers, Suzanne
Daniels, Douglas Henry 1943- ... 125
Daniels, Draper 1913-1983 ... 53-56
Obituary ... 109
Daniels, Elizabeth Adams 1920- ... 37-40R
Daniels, Farrington 1889-1972 ... 5-8R
Obituary ... 37-40R
Daniels, Frank Arthur 1904-1986 Obituary ... 121
Daniels, Frank James 1900(?)-1983 Obituary ... 110
Daniels, George H. 1935- ... CANR-10
Earlier sketch in CA 25-28R
Daniels, George M(orris) 1927- ... 29-32R
Daniels, Guy 1919-1989 ... 21-24R
Obituary ... 128
See also SATA 11
See also SATA-Obit 62
Daniels, Harold R(obert) 1919- ... 17-20R
Daniels, James R(aymond) 1956- ... CANR-47
Earlier sketch in CA 121
See also Daniels, Jim
Daniels, Jim
See Daniels, James R(aymond)
See also DLB 120
Daniels, John Clifford 1915- ... 13-16R
Daniels, John S.
See Overholser, Wayne D.
Daniels, Jonathan (Worth) 1902-1981 ... CANR-29
Obituary ... 105
Earlier sketch in CA 49-52
See also DLB 127
Daniels, Josephus 1862-1948 Brief entry ... 122
See also DLB 29
Daniels, Kate 1953- ... 124
Daniels, Les(lie Noel III) 1943- ... CANR-49
Earlier sketches in CA 65-68, CANR-9, 24
Daniels, Mark R. 1952- ... 167
Daniels, Mary 1937- ... 93-96
Daniels, Max
See Gellis, Roberta L(eah Jacobs)
Daniels, Norman ... CANR-15
Earlier sketch in CA 89-92
Daniels, Norman 1942- ... CANR-22
Earlier sketch in CA 106
Daniels, Olga
See Sinclair, Olga
Daniels, Pamela 1937- ... 101
Daniels, Patricia 1955- ... SATA 93
Daniels, Philip
See Phillips, D(ennis) J(ohn Andrew)
Daniels, R(obertson) Balfour 1900- ... 49-52
Daniels, Randy (Allan) 1949- ... 81-84
Daniels, Rebecca 1949- ... 164
Daniels, Robert V(incent) 1926- ... CANR-70
Earlier sketches in CA 1-4R, CANR-2
Daniels, Roger 1927- ... CANR-47
Earlier sketches in CA 5-8R, CANR-8, 23
Daniels, Sally 1931- ... 1-4R
Daniels, Sarah 1956- ... 133
Daniels, Shouri
See Ramanujan, Molly
Daniels, Steven Lloyd 1945-1973 ... 33-36R
Daniels, Velma Seawell 1931- ... 108
Daniels, Zoe
See Laux, Constance
Danielson, Elena S(chafer) 1947- ... 116
Danielson, J. D.
See James, M. R.
Danielson, Michael N(ils) 1934- ... 33-36R
Danielson, Wayne Allen 1929- ... 77-80
Danielsson, Bengt (Emmerik) 1921- ... CANR-23
Earlier sketch in CA 107
Daniere, Andre L(ucien) 1926- ... 9-12R
Daniloff, Nicholas 1934- ... 85-88
Danilov, Victor J(oseph) 1924- ... CANR-45
Earlier sketches in CA 13-16R, CANR-6, 21
Daninos, Pierre 1913- ... CANR-15
Earlier sketch in CA 77-80
Danish, Barbara 1948- ... 57-60
Dank, Gloria Rand 1955- ... 114
See also SATA 56
See also SATA-Brief 46
Dank, Leonard D(ewey) 1929- ... SATA 44
Dank, Milton 1920- ... CANR-28
Earlier sketches in CA 69-72, CANR-11
See also SATA 31
Danker, Frederick William 1920- ... CANR-5
Earlier sketch in CA 13-16R
Danker, W(illiam) John 1914- ... 13-16R
Dankleff, Richard E(lden) 1925- ... 114
Dankner, Laura ... 142
Danko, William D(avid) 1952- ... 162
Danky, James Philip 1947- ... CANR-12
Earlier sketch in CA 69-72
Danley, John R(obert) 1948- ... 152
Danly, Robert Lyons 1947- ... 108
Dann, Colin (Michael) 1943- ... 108
Dann, Jack 1945- ... CANR-30
Earlier sketches in CA 49-52, CANR-2
See also CAAS 20
Dann, John C(hristie) 1944- ... 126
Dann, Max 1955- ... 118
See also SATA 62
Dann, Uriel 1922- ... 25-28R
Dannay, Frederic 1905-1982 ... CANR-39
Obituary ... 107
Earlier sketches in CA 1-4R, CANR-1
See also Queen, Ellery
See also CLC 11
See also DAM POP
See also DLB 137
See also MTCW 1
Dannelley, Paul (Edward, Jr.) 1919- ... 122
Dannemiller, Lawrence 1925- ... 1-4R
Dannen, Fredric 1955- ... 140
Dannenfeldt, Karl H(enry) 1916- ... 25-28R
Danner, Margaret (Essie) 1915- ... 29-32R
See also BW 1
See also DLB 41
Danner, Mark (David) 1958- ... 146
Dannett, Sylvia G. L. 1909- ... CANR-4
Earlier sketch in CA 1-4R
D'Annunzio, Gabriele 1863-1938 ... 155
Brief entry ... 104
See also TCLC 6, 40
Dano, Linda 1943- ... 167
Danoff, I. Michael 1940- ... 97-100
Danois, N. le
See Gourmont, Remy (-Marie-Charles) de
Danow, David K. 1944- ... 154
Danowski, T(haddeus) S(tanley) 1914-1987 .. 9-12R
Obituary ... 123
Danska, Herbert 1928- ... 29-32R
Danson, Lawrence Neil 1942- ... 85-88
Dante 1265-1321 ... DA
See also DAB
See also DAC
See also DAM MST, POET
See also PC 21
See also WLCS
Danter, John fl. 1586-1599 ... DLB 170
d'Antibes, Germain
See Simenon, Georges (Jacques Christian)
Danticat, Edwidge 1969- ... 152
See also CLC 94
Dantin, Louis 1865-1945 ... DLB 92
Danto, Arthur C(oleman) 1924- ... CANR-56
Earlier sketch in CA 17-20R
Danto, Bruce L. 1927- ... CANR-7
Earlier sketch in CA 53-56
Danton, J(oseph) Periam 1908- ... CANR-71
Earlier sketch in CA 9-12R
Danton, Rebecca
See Roberts, Janet Louise
D'Antonio, Michael 1955- ... 140
Dantzer, Robert 1944- ... 149
Dantzic, Cynthia Maris 1933- ... 101
Dantzig, George Bernard 1914- ... 155
Brief entry ... 106
Danvers, Dennis 1947- ... CLC 70
Danvers, Jack
See Caseleyr, Cam(ille Auguste Marie)
Danzell, George
See Bond, Nelson S(lade)
Danzig, Allan (Peter) 1931- ... 45-48
Danzig, Allison 1898-1987 ... CANR-62
Obituary ... 121
Earlier sketch in CA 37-40R
See also DLB 171
Danzig, Fred P(aul) 1925- ... 65-68
Danziger, Charles 1962- ... 145
Danziger, Edmund J(efferson), Jr. 1938- ... 102
Danziger, Kurt 1926- ... 41-44R
Danziger, Marlies K(allmann) 1926- ... CANR-16
Earlier sketch in CA 25-28R
Danziger, Nick 1958- ... 129
Danziger, Paula 1944- ... CANR-37
Brief entry ... 112
Earlier sketch in CA 115
See also AAYA 4
See also CLC 21
See also CLR 20
See also JRDA
See also MAICYA
See also SATA 36, 63, 102
See also SATA-Brief 30
Danziger, Sheldon H. 1948- ... CANR-43
Earlier sketch in CA 119
Daoud, Hazim S. 1930-1976 ... 122
Daoudi, M(ohammed) S(uleiman) 1946- ... 132
Daoust, Jean-Paul 1946- ... 164
Dapper, Gloria 1922- ... 17-20R
Dapping, William Osborne 1880-1969 Obituary . 115
D'Aprix, Roger M. 1932- ... 33-36R
Darack, Arthur J. 1918- ... CANR-37
Earlier sketch in CA 115
Darbelnet, Jean (Louis) 1904- ... CANR-10
Earlier sketch in CA 25-28R
Darby, Catherine
See Peters, Maureen
Darby, Edwin Wheeler 1922- ... 125
Darby, Gene Kegley
See Darby, Jean (Kegley)
Darby, Henry Clifford 1909- ... 5-8R
Darby, J. N.
See Govan, Christine Noble
Darby, Jean (Kegley) 1921- ... CANR-39
See also SATA 68
Darby, John 1940- ... 105
Darby, Michael 1944- ... CANR-38
Earlier sketch in CA 116
Darby, Patricia (Paulsen) ... 73-76
See also SATA 14
Darby, Ray(mond) 1912- ... 17-20R
See also SATA 7
Darby, William D(uane) 1942- ... 141
d'Arch Smith, Timothy 1936- ... 13-16R
Darcy, Clare ... 102
D'Arcy, Ella c. 1857-1937 ... DLB 135
D'Arcy, G(eorge) Minot 1930- ... 9-12R
Darcy, Jean
See Lepley, Jean Elizabeth
D'Arcy, Jean (Marie) 1913-1983 Obituary ... 109
D'Arcy, Margaretta (Ruth) 1934- ... CANR-58
Earlier sketches in CA 104, CANR-31
D'Arcy, Martin C(yril) 1888-1976 ... CANR-3
Obituary ... 69-72
Earlier sketch in CA 5-8R
D'Arcy, Pamela
See Roby, Mary Linn
D'Arcy, Paul F(rancis) 1921- ... 17-20R
d'Arcy, Willard
See Cox, William R(obert)
Darden, Christopher 1957(?)- ... 155
Darden, Lloyd (Nestor) 1931- Brief entry ... 113
Darden, Norma Jean ... 114
Darden, Robert 1954- ... 152
Darden, William R(aymond) 1936- ... 77-80
Dardess, John W(olfe) 1937- ... 45-48
Dardig, Jill C(arolyn) 1948- ... 69-72
Dardis, Tom 1926- ... CANR-53
Earlier sketches in CA 65-68, CANR-9
Dare, Evelyn
See Everett-Green, Evelyn
Dareff, Hal 1920- ... 65-68
Darga, Bert 1931- ... 110
Dargan, Olive (Tilford) 1869-1968 Obituary ... 111
Dargel, Nancy ... 152
Dargo, George 1935- ... 115
d'Argyre, Gilles
See Klein, Gerard
Darian, Shea 1959- ... 163
See also SATA 97
Dariaux, Genevieve Antoine
See Antoine-Dariaux, Genevieve
Darien, Peter
See Bassett, William B. K.
Daringer, Helen Fern 1892- ... CAP-2
Earlier sketch in CA 17-18
See also SATA 1
Dario, Ruben 1867-1916 ... 131
See also DAM MULT
See also HLC
See also HW
See also MTCW 1
See also PC 15
See also TCLC 4
Darion, Joe
See Darion, Joseph
Darion, Joseph 1917- Brief entry ... 113
Dark, Alvin Ralph 1922- ... 105
Dark, Harris Edward 1922- ... 57-60
Dark, Johnny
See Norwood, Victor G(eorge) C(harles)
Dark, Larry 1959- ... 136
Dark, Philip J(ohn) C(rosskey) 1918- ... CANR-18
Earlier sketches in CA 49-52, CANR-2
Darke, Marjorie 1929- ... CANR-34
Earlier sketches in CA 81-84, CANR-15
See also SATA 16, 87
Darley, F(elix) O(ctavius) C(arr) 1822-1888 ... DLB 188
See also SATA 35
Darley, George 1795-1846 ... DLB 96
Darley, John M(cConnon) 1938- ... 93-96
Darling, Arthur Burr 1892-1971 ... 5-8R
Obituary ... 33-36R
Darling, David J. 1953- ... 138
See also SATA 60
See also SATA-Brief 44
Darling, Diana 1947- ... 142
Darling, Edward 1907-1974 ... CANR-3
Obituary ... 53-56
Earlier sketch in CA 49-52
Darling, Frank Clayton 1925- ... 17-20R
Darling, Frank Fraser
See Fraser Darling, Frank
Darling, Jay Norwood 1876-1962 Obituary ... 93-96
Darling, John R(othburn) 1937- ... 93-96
Darling, Kathy
See Darling, Mary Kathleen
Darling, Lois MacIntyre 1917-1989 ... CANR-38
Obituary ... 130
Earlier sketches in CA 5-8R, CANR-3
See also MAICYA
See also SATA 3
See also SATA-Obit 64
Darling, Louis, Jr. 1916-1970 ... CANR-38
Obituary ... 89-92
Earlier sketches in CA 5-8R, CANR-3
See also MAICYA
See also SATA 3
See also SATA-Obit 23
Darling, Mary Kathleen 1943- ... CANR-4
Earlier sketch in CA 53-56
See also SATA 9, 79
Darling, Richard L(ewis) 1925- ... 21-24R
Darling, Sandra
See Day, Alexandra
Darling, Sharon (Sandling) 1943- ... 128
Darling, T. H.
See Harris, Thomas Walter
Darlington, Alice B(enning) 1906-1973 ... CAP-2
Obituary ... 41-44R
Earlier sketch in CA 25-28
Darlington, C(yril) D(ean) 1903-1981 ... CANR-10
Obituary ... 108
Earlier sketch in CA 9-12R
Darlington, Charles F. 1904-1986 ... CAP-2
Obituary ... 119
Earlier sketch in CA 25-28
Darlington, David 1951- ... CANR-61
Earlier sketch in CA 127
Darlington, Joy 1947- ... 89-92
Darlington, William Aubrey (Cecil) 1890-1979 ... CANR-58
Earlier sketches in CAP-1, CA 13-16
Darlow, Michael (George) 1934- ... 104
Darlton, Clark
See Ernsting, Walter
Darmstadter, Joel 1928- ... 121
Darnay, Arsen (Julius) 1936- ... 111
Darnley, John
See Drinkwater, John
Darnton, John (Townsend) 1941- ... CANR-53
Brief entry ... 119
Earlier sketch in CA 126
Interview in ... 126
Darnton, Robert (Choate) 1939- ... 116
Brief entry ... 113
Interview in ... 116
Darr, Ann 1920- ... CANR-7
Earlier sketch in CA 57-60
Darracott, Joseph C(orbould) 1934- ... 106
Darrah, William C(ulp) 1909- ... 57-60
Darrell, R(obert) D(onaldson)
1903-1988 Obituary ... 125
Darroch, James L. 1951- ... 148
Darroch, Maurice A. 1903-(?) ... CAP-2
Earlier sketch in CA 19-20
Darroch, Sandra Jobson 1942- ... 89-92
Darroll, Sally
See Odgers, Sally Farrell
Darroll, Sally
See Odgers, Sally Farrell
Darrow, Clarence (Seward) 1857-1938 ... 164
See also TCLC 81
Darrow, Ralph C(arroll) 1918- ... 61-64
Darrow, Richard W(illiam) 1915-1976 ... 21-24R
Obituary ... 120
Darrow, Whitney, (Jr.) 1909- ... CANR-71
Earlier sketches in CA 61-64, CANR-14
See also SATA 13
Dart, Iris Rainer ... 149
Dart, John 1936- ... 65-68
Dart, Raymond A(rthur) 1893-1988 ... CAP-1
Obituary ... 127
Earlier sketch in CA 13-14
Darton, Eric 1950- ... 160
Darton, G(erald) C(hristopher)
1913(?)-1987 Obituary ... 122
Daruwalla, Keki N(asserwanji) 1937- ... 153
Darvas, Nicolas 1920- ... 61-64

Darveaux, Terry A(lan) 1943- ... 65-68
Darvi, Andrea
See Plate, Andrea
Darvill, Fred T(homas), Jr. 1927- ... CANR-6
Earlier sketch in CA 57-60
Darvill, Timothy (C.) 1957- ... 127
Darville, Helen (Fiona) 1971- ... 168
Darwall, Stephen L(eicester) 1946- ... 113
Darweesh, Mahmoud
See Darwish, Mahmoud
Darwin, Charles 1809-1882 ... DLB 57, 166
Darwin, Erasmus 1731-1802 ... DLB 93
Darwin, Len
See Darwin, Leonard
Darwin, Leonard 1916- ... SATA 24
Darwin, M. B.
See McDavid, Raven I(oor), Jr.
Darwish, Adel 1945- ... 135
Darwish, Mahmoud 1942- ... 164
Darwish, Mahmud
See Darwish, Mahmoud
Dary, David A. 1934- ... CANR-54
Earlier sketches in CA 29-32R, CANR-13, 29
Daryush, Elizabeth 1887-1977 ... CANR-3
Earlier sketch in CA 49-52
See also CLC 6, 19
See also DLB 20
Das, Deb Kumar 1935- ... 102
Das, Durga 1900-1974 ... CAP-2
Obituary ... 49-52
Earlier sketch in CA 29-32
Das, G. K. 1934- ... 128
Das, Gurcharan 1943- ... 33-36R
Das, Jagannath Prasad 1931- ... CANR-6
Earlier sketch in CA 57-60
Das, Kamala 1934- ... CANR-59
Earlier sketches in CA 101, CANR-27
Das, Lama Surya 1950- ... 168
Das, Manmath Nath 1926- ... CANR-8
Earlier sketch in CA 13-16R
Das, Suranjan 1954- ... 139
Dasa, Drutakarma
See Cremo, Michael (A.)
Dascal, Marcelo 1940- ... 140
Dasenbrock, Reed Way 1953- ... CANR-56
Earlier sketch in CA 125
Dasent, Sir George Webbe 1817-1896 ... SATA 62
See also SATA-Brief 29
Das Gupta, Jyotirindra 1933- ... 53-56
Dasgupta, Subrata 1944- ... 150
Dasgupta, Surendranath 1887-1952 ... 157
See also TCLC 81
Dash, Irene G(olden) ... 125
Dash, Jack Brien 1907-1989 Obituary ... 128
Dash, Joan 1925- ... CANR-57
Earlier sketches in CA 49-52, CANR-31
Dash, Julie ... 168
Dash, Samuel 1925- Brief entry ... 105
Dash, Tony 1945- ... 33-36R
Dashiell, Alfred Sheppard
1901-1970 Obituary ... 89-92
Dashkova, Ekaterina Romanovna 1743-1810 .. DLB 150
Dashti, Ali 1894- ... 85-88
Dashwood, Edmee Elizabeth Monica de la Pasture
1890-1943 ... 154
Brief entry ... 119
See also Delafield, E. M.
Dashwood, Robert Julian 1899- ... CAP-1
Earlier sketch in CA 13-14
da Silva, Howard 1909-1986 Obituary ... 118
DaSilva, Leon
See Wallmann, Jeffrey M(iner)
DaSilva, Zenia Sacks 1925- ... 121
Daskam, Josephine Dodge
See Bacon, Josephine Dodge (Daskam)
Dasmann, Raymond (Fredric) 1919- ... CANR-71
Earlier sketch in CA 5-8R
Dass, Ram
See Alpert, Richard
Dassanowsky, Robert 1960- ... 150
Dassault, Marcel (Bloch) 1892-1986 Obituary .. 119
Brief entry ... 115
Dassin, Jules 1911- ... 132
Dassonville, Michel A(uguste) 1927- ... 73-76
Daston, Lorraine 1951- ... 128
Dater, Henry M. 1909(?)-1974 Obituary ... 49-52
Dates, Jannette L. ... 140
See also BW 2
Datesh, John Nicholas 1950- ... 97-100
Dathorne, O(scar) R(onald) 1934- ... CANR-67
Earlier sketches in CA 57-60, CANR-26
See also BW 1
Dattel, Eugene R. 1944- ... 146
Daube, David 1909- ... CANR-72
Earlier sketches in CA 1-4R, CANR-1
Daubeny, Peter (Lauderdale) 1921-1975 ... 61-64
Dauber, Kenneth Marc 1945- ... CANR-37
Earlier sketch in CA 114
Dauber, Philip M. 1942- ... 162
Daudet, (Louis Marie) Alphonse 1840-1897 ... DLB 123
Daudet, Leon 1867-1942 Brief entry ... 121
Dauenhauer, Richard L(eonard) 1942- ... CANR-11
Earlier sketch in CA 61-64
Dauer, Dorothea W. 1917- ... 37-40R
Dauer, Lesley 1965- ... 165
Dauer, Manning J(ulian) 1909- ... 89-92
Dauer, Rosamond 1934- ... CANR-10
Earlier sketch in CA 65-68
See also SATA 23
Dauer, Victor Paul 1909- ... 17-20R
Daugert, Stanley M(atthew) 1918- ... 17-20R
Daugharty, Janice 1944- ... 156
Daughdrill, James H(arold), Jr. 1934- ... 41-44R
Daughen, Joseph R(obert) 1935- ... 33-36R
Daugherty, Carroll R(oop) 1900-1988 Obituary . 125
Daugherty, Charles Michael 1914- ... 73-76
See also SATA 16
Daugherty, Greg(ory Ash) 1953- ... 145
Daugherty, James (Henry) 1889-1974 ... 73-76
Obituary ... 49-52
See also MAICYA
See also SATA 13
Daugherty, Richard D(eo) 1922- ... 108
See also SATA 35
Daugherty, Sarah Bowyer 1949- ... 106
Daugherty, Sonia Medwedeff (?)-1971 Obituary 104
See also SATA-Obit 27
Daugherty, Tracy 1955- ... CANR-54
Earlier sketch in CA 127
Daughtrey, Anne Scott 1920- ... 17-20R
d'Aulaire, Edgar Parin 1898-1986 ... CANR-29
Obituary ... 119
Earlier sketch in CA 49-52
See also CLR 21
See also DLB 22
See also MAICYA
See also SATA 5, 66
See also SATA-Obit 47
d'Aulaire, Ingri (Mortenson Parin) 1904-1980 ... CANR-29
Obituary ... 102
Earlier sketch in CA 49-52
See also CLR 21
See also DLB 22
See also MAICYA
See also SATA 5, 66
See also SATA-Obit 24
Daumal, Rene 1908-1944 Brief entry ... 114
See also TCLC 14
Daunton, M(artin) J(ames) 1949- ... CANR-52
Earlier sketch in CA 125
Dausset, Jean 1916- ... 155
Dauster, Frank (Nicholas) 1925- ... 53-56
Dauten, Carl Anton 1913-1976 ... CANR-3
Earlier sketch in CA 5-8R
Dauw, Dean C(harles) 1933- ... CANR-6
Earlier sketch in CA 53-56
D'Avanzo, Mario Louis 1931- ... 41-44R
Davar, Ashok ... 69-72
Dave, Shyam
See Gantzer, Hugh
Daveluy, Paule Cloutier 1919- ... 9-12R
See also SATA 11
Davenant, William 1606-1668 ... DLB 58, 126
Davenport, Doris 1915-1980 ... 152
See also BW 2
Davenport, Elaine 1946- ... 102
Davenport, Francine
See Tate, Velma
Davenport, Francis Garvin 1905-1975 Obituary . 111
Davenport, Gene L(ooney) 1935- ... 33-36R
Davenport, Guy (Mattison, Jr.) 1927- ... CANR-23
Earlier sketch in CA 33-36R
See also CLC 6, 14, 38
See also DLB 130
See also SSC 16
Davenport, Gwen 1910- ... 9-12R
Davenport, John 1905-1987 Obituary ... 122
Davenport, Marcia 1903-1996 ... 9-12R
Obituary ... 151
See also DLBD 17
Davenport, Paul 1946- ... 132
Davenport, Robert ... DLB 58
Davenport, Roger (Hamilton) 1946- ... 131
Davenport, Spencer ... CANR-26
Earlier sketches in CAP-2, CA 19-20
Davenport, T(homas) R(odney) H(ope) 1926- . 77-80
Davenport, Walter 1889-1971 Obituary ... 104
Davenport, William H. 1908- ... CANR-4
Earlier sketch in CA 1-4R
Davenport-Hines, Richard (Peter Treadwell)
1953- ... 134
Daventry, Leonard John 1915- ... 17-20R
Daves, Delmer Lawrence
1904(?)-1977 Obituary ... 73-76
See also DLB 26
Daves, Francis Marion 1903- ... 45-48
Daves, Jessica 1898(?)-1974 Obituary ... 53-56
Daves, Michael 1938- ... 9-12R
See also SATA 40
Davey, Cyril J(ames) 1911- ... CANR-41
Earlier sketches in CA 5-8R, CANR-2, 18
Davey, Frank 1907(?)-1983 Obituary ... 109
Davey, Frank(land Wilmot) 1940- ... CANR-65
Earlier sketches in CA 65-68, CANR-13, 32
See also CAAS 27
Davey, Gilbert (Walter) 1913- ... CANR-12
Earlier sketches in CAP-1, CA 9-10
Davey, Harold W(illiam) 1915-1986 ... 120
Davey, Jocelyn
See Raphael, Chaim
Davey, John
See Richey, David
Davey, Peter (John) 1940- ... 135
Davey, Thomas A. 1954- ... 126
Daviau, Donald G(eorge) 1927- ... CANR-66
Earlier sketches in CA 81-84, CANR-14, 32
David, A. R.
See David, A(nn) Rosalie
David, A(nn) Rosalie 1946- ... CANR-37
Earlier sketch in CA 114
David, Alfred 1929- ... 85-88
David, Andrew
See Whittingham, Richard
David, Anne 1924-1987 ... CANR-12
Obituary ... 122
Earlier sketch in CA 29-32R
David, Carl 1949- ... 108
David, Catherine 1949(?)- ... 168
David, Catherine 1954- ... 161
David, Ed
See Wohlmuth, Ed
David, Emily
See Alman, David
David, Gerald 1941- ... 114
David, Heather M(acKinnon) 1937- ... 37-40R
David, Henry 1907-1984 Obituary ... 111
David, Henry P. 1923- ... CANR-6
Earlier sketch in CA 13-16R
David, Hugh (Housdon) 1954- ... 129
David, Irene 1921- ... 110
David, Jack 1946- ... CANR-30
Earlier sketch in CA 110
David, Jay
See Adler, William
David, Jonathan
See Ames, Lee J(udah)
David, Joseph Ben
See Ben-David, Joseph
David, Lawrence 1963- ... 144
David, Lester 1914-1997 ... CANR-14
Obituary ... 162
Earlier sketch in CA 37-40R
David, Marjorie 1950- ... 112
David, Martin H(eidenhain) 1935- ... 37-40R
David, Michael Robert 1932- ... 53-56
David, Nicholas
See Morgan, Thomas Bruce
David, Paul A(llan) 1935- ... 97-100
David, Paul T(heodore) 1906-1994 ... CANR-2
Obituary ... 146
Earlier sketch in CA 5-8R
David, R. W.
See David, Richard (W.)
David, Richard (W.) 1912- ... 129
David, Rosalie
See David, A(nn) Rosalie
David, Saul 1921- ... 124
Brief entry ... 114
David, Stephen M(ark) 1934-1985 ... 33-36R
Obituary ... 115
David, William
See Sandman, Peter M(ark)
David-Neel, Alexandra 1868-1969 Obituary . 25-28R
Davidoff, Leonore 1932- ... 167
Davidow, Michael
See Davidow, Mike
Davidow, Mike 1913-1996 ... 57-60
Obituary ... 153
Davidow-Goodman, Ann
See Goodman, Ann (Davidow)
Davids, Anthony 1923- ... 41-44R
Davids, Bob
See Davids, L(eonard) Robert
Davids, L(eonard) Robert 1926- ... 115
Davids, Lewis Edmund 1917- ... 37-40R
Davids, Richard Carlyle 1913- ... 97-100
Davidson, Abraham A. 1935- ... 53-56
Davidson, Alan Eaton 1924- ... 103
Davidson, Alastair 1939- ... 29-32R
Davidson, Alice Joyce 1932- ... 115
See also SATA 54
See also SATA-Brief 45
Davidson, Angus (Henry Gordon) 1898-1980 ... CANR-71
Obituary ... 97-100
Earlier sketch in CA 25-28R
Davidson, Arnold E(dward) 1936- ... 111
Davidson, Avram 1923- ... CANR-26
Earlier sketch in CA 101
See also Queen, Ellery
See also DLB 8
Davidson, Basil 1914- ... CANR-17
Earlier sketches in CA 1-4R, CANR-1
See also SATA 13
Davidson, Bill
See Davidson, William
Davidson, Bill R.
See Davidson, William R.
Davidson, Caroline 1953- ... 122
Davidson, Cathy Notari 1949- ... CANR-23
Earlier sketch in CA 106
Davidson, Chalmers Gaston 1907-1994 .. CANR-72
Earlier sketch in CA 29-32R
Davidson, Chandler 1936- ... 45-48
Davidson, Clarissa Start
See Lippert, Clarissa Start
Davidson, Clifford 1932- ... 45-48
Davidson, Dana H. 1949- ... 143
Davidson, David 1908-1985 ... 49-52
Obituary ... 117
Davidson, (Marie) Diane 1924- ... CANR-57
Earlier sketch in CA 29-32R
See also SATA 91
Davidson, Donald (Grady) 1893-1968 ... CANR-4
Obituary ... 25-28R
Earlier sketch in CA 5-8R
See also CLC 2, 13, 19
See also DLB 45
Davidson, Donald 1917- ... CANR-2
Earlier sketch in CA 45-48
Davidson, E(phraim) E(dward) 1923- ... 33-36R
Davidson, Ellen Prescott ... 49-52
Davidson, Eugene (Arthur) 1902- ... CANR-72
Earlier sketches in CA 1-4R, CANR-3
Davidson, Eva Rucker
1894(?)-1974 Obituary ... 53-56
Davidson, F(rank) G(eoffrey) 1920- ... 29-32R
Davidson, Frank P(aul) 1918- ... CANR-40
Earlier sketch in CA 116
Davidson, Glen W(illiam) 1936- ... CANR-9
Earlier sketch in CA 61-64
Davidson, Greg (Stuart) 1961- ... 129
Davidson, Gustav 1895-1971 Obituary ... 29-32R
Davidson, H(ilda) R(oderick) Ellis 1914- .. CANR-11
Earlier sketch in CA 17-20R
Davidson, Harold G(ordon) 1912- ... 65-68
Davidson, Henry A(lexander)
1905-1973 Obituary ... 45-48
Davidson, Herbert A(lan) 1932- ... 17-20R
Davidson, Hugh
See Hamilton, Edmond
Davidson, Hugh M(acCullough) 1918- ... 102
Davidson, Irwin Delmore 1906-1981 Obituary .. 105
Davidson, James Dale 1947- ... 107
Davidson, James West 1946- ... CANR-15
Earlier sketch in CA 85-88
Davidson, Jeffrey P(hilip) 1951- ... CANR-48
Earlier sketches in CA 122, CANR-41
Davidson, Jessica 1915- ... CANR-14
Earlier sketch in CA 41-44R
See also SATA 5
Davidson, John
See Reid, Charles (Stuart)
Davidson, John 1857-1909 Brief entry ... 118
See also DLB 19
See also TCLC 24
Davidson, John 1941- ... 156
Davidson, John Wells 1903-1986 Obituary ... 120
Davidson, Judith 1953- ... 116
See also SATA 40
Davidson, Julian M. 1931- ... 102
Davidson, Lionel 1922- ... CANR-43
Earlier sketches in CA 1-4R, CANR-1
See also DLB 14
See also SATA 87
Davidson, Margaret 1936- ... CANR-17
Earlier sketch in CA 25-28R
See also SATA 5
Davidson, Marion
See Garis, Howard R(oger)
Davidson, Mark 1940- ... 138
Davidson, Marshall B(owman) 1907-1989 ... CANR-42
Obituary ... 129
Earlier sketch in CA 33-36R
Davidson, Mary R. 1885-1973 ... 5-8R
See also SATA 9
Davidson, Mary S. 1940- ... 107
See also SATA 61
Davidson, Max 1955- ... 139
Davidson, Max D. 1899(?)-1977 Obituary ... 73-76
Davidson, Melanie
See Arnold, Madelyn M. a pseudonym
Davidson, Michael
See Rorvik, David M(ichael)
Davidson, Michael 1944- ... 106
Davidson, Michael Childers 1897- ... 29-32R
Davidson, Mickie
See Davidson, Margaret
Davidson, Mildred 1935- ... 93-96
Davidson, Miriam 1960- ... 128
Davidson, Morris 1898-1979 ... CANR-72
Earlier sketch in CA 85-88
Davidson, Muriel 1924(?)-1983 Obituary ... 110
Davidson, Nicole
See Jensen, Kathryn
Davidson, Norman 1933- ... 119
Davidson, Osha Gray 1954- ... 145
Davidson, Pamela 1954- ... 133
Davidson, Paul 1930- ... CANR-52
Earlier sketches in CA 13-16R, CANR-6, 28
Davidson, Philip (Grant) 1902- ... 73-76
Davidson, Phillip B. 1915- ... 130
Davidson, R.
See Davidson, Raymond
Davidson, Raymond 1926- ... SATA 32
Davidson, Robert F(ranklin) 1902- ... 49-52
Davidson, Robyn 1950- ... 142
Davidson, Roger H(arry) 1936- ... CANR-49
Earlier sketches in CA 21-24R, CANR-9, 24
Davidson, Rosalie 1921- ... 69-72
See also SATA 23
Davidson, Sandra Calder 1935- ... 41-44R
Davidson, Sara 1943- ... CANR-68
Earlier sketches in CA 81-84, CANR-44
See also CLC 9
See also DLB 185
Davidson, Sol M. 1924- ... 17-20R
Davidson, William 1918- ... 93-96
Davidson, William H. 1951- ... 128
Davidson, William R. 1929(?)-1987 Obituary ... 122
Davidson, William Robert 1919- ... 17-20R
Davidson-Houston, J(ames) Vivian 1901-1965 . 5-8R
Davie, Donald (Alfred) 1922-1995 ... CANR-44
Obituary ... 149
Earlier sketches in CA 1-4R, CANR-1
See also CAAS 3
See also CLC 5, 8, 10, 31
See also DLB 27
See also MTCW 1
Davie, Elspeth 1919-1995 ... 126
Obituary ... 150
Brief entry ... 120
See also DLB 139
Davie, Helen K(ay) 1952- ... SATA 77
Davie, Ian 1924- ... 102
Davie, Maurice R(ea) 1893-1964 ... 5-8R
Davie, Michael 1924- ... 57-60
Davie, Peter (Edward Sidney) 1936- ... 114
Davied, Camille
See Rose, Camille Davied
Davie-Martin, Hugh
See McCutcheon, Hugh Davie-Martin
Davies, A(lfred) Mervyn 1899-1976 ... 17-20R
Obituary ... 69-72
Davies, Ada Hilton 1893- ... CAP-2
Earlier sketch in CA 17-18
Davies, Alan T(rewartha) 1933- ... 33-36R
Davies, Alfred T(homas) 1930- ... 13-16R
Davies, Andrew (Wynford) 1936- ... 105
See also SATA 27

Davies, Bettilu D(onna) 1942- CANR-18
Earlier sketch in CA 101
See also SATA 33
Davies, Charles (Michael) 1946- 128
Davies, Christie 1941- CANR-48
Davies, Colin
See Elliot, Ian
Davies, (George) Colliss (Boardman) 1912- . CAP-1
Earlier sketch in CA 11-12
Davies, D(avid) Jacob 1916-1974 .... 5-8R
Obituary 103
Davies, Daniel R. 1911- 37-40R
Davies, David Margerison 1923- 5-8R
Davies, David Michael 1929- Brief entry 109
Davies, David W(illiam) 1908- CANR-3
Earlier sketch in CA 9-12R
Davies, Duncan (Sheppey) 1921-1987 124
Obituary 122
Davies, Ebenezer Thomas 1903- CAP-1
Earlier sketch in CA 13-14
Davies, Eileen Winifred 1910- CAP-1
Earlier sketch in CA 13-14
Davies, Evelyn 1924- CANR-8
Earlier sketch in CA 61-64
Davies, Evelyn A(dele) 1915- 61-64
Davies, Glyn 1919- 158
Davies, Harriet Vaughn
1879(?)-1978 Obituary 77-80
Davies, Horton (Marlais) 1916- CANR-7
Earlier sketch in CA 5-8R
Davies, Hugh Sykes 1909-1984(?) Obituary 113
Davies, Hunter 1936- CANR-12
Earlier sketch in CA 57-60
See also SATA 55
See also SATA-Brief 45
Davies, (David) Ioan 1936- 21-24R
Davies, Ivor K(evin) 1930- 53-56
Davies, J. Clarence III 1937- CANR-71
Earlier sketch in CA 29-32R
Davies, J(ohn) D(avid) 1957- 139
Davies, J. Kenneth 1925- 57-60
Davies, James A. 1939- 129
Davies, James Chowning 1918- 45-48
Davies, Jennifer (Eileen) 1950- 139
Davies, Joan 1934- 124
See also SATA 50
See also SATA-Brief 47
Davies, John Evan Weston 1914- 113
Brief entry 111
Interview in 113
Davies, John Gordon 1919- 69-72
Davies, John K(enyon) 1937- 120
Davies, John Paton, Jr. 1908- CANR-72
Earlier sketch in CA 9-12R
Davies, L(eslie) P(urnell) 1914- CANR-59
Earlier sketches in CA 21-24R, CANR-9
Davies, Laurence 1926- CANR-72
Earlier sketch in CA 57-60
Davies, Linda 1963- 149
Davies, Loma G. 1934- 137
Davies, Mansel Morris 1913- 9-12R
Davies, Margaret C(onstance Brown) 1923- .. 9-12R
Davies, Margaret Lloyd 1935- 106
Davies, Marion
See Douras, Marion Cecilia
Davies, Martin Brett 1936- 102
Davies, Martin L. 1948- 155
Davies, Merton E(dward) 1917- 85-88
Davies, Morton Rees 1939- 37-40R
Davies, Nick 1953- 136
Davies, Nicola 1958- 167
See also SATA 99
Davies, (Claude) Nigel (Byam) 1920- CANR-19
Earlier sketch in CA 102
Davies, Norman 1939- 41-44R
Davies, Oliver 1905- CAP-2
Earlier sketch in CA 25-28
Davies, P. C. W.
See Davies, Paul (Charles William)
Davies, Paul (Charles William) 1946- CANR-31
Earlier sketch in CA 106
Davies, (William Thomas) Pennar
1911-1996 .... 13-16R
Obituary 155
Davies, Peter J. 1937- 135
See also SATA 52
Davies, Philip John 1948- 152
Davies, Piers (Anthony David) 1941- 103
Davies, R(onald) E. G. 1921- 17-20R
Davies, R(obert) R(ees) 1938- 135
Davies, R(eginald) T(horne) 1923- 9-12R
Davies, R(obert) W(illiam) 1925- CANR-54
Earlier sketches in CA 33-36R, CANR-13, 29
Davies, Ray(mond Douglas) 1944- 146
Brief entry 116
See also CLC 21
Davies, Rhys 1901-1978 .... CANR-4
Obituary 81-84
Earlier sketch in CA 9-12R
See also CLC 23
See also DLB 139, 191
Davies, Richard Llewelyn
See Llewelyn-Davies, Richard
Davies, Richard O. 1937- 17-20R
Davies, (William) Robertson 1913-1995 .. CANR-42
Obituary 150
Earlier sketches in CA 33-36R, CANR-17
Interview in CANR-17
See also BEST 89:2
See also CLC 2, 7, 13, 25, 42, 75, 91
See also DA
See also DAB
See also DAC
See also DAM MST, NOV, POP
See also DLB 68
See also MTCW 1
See also WLC
Davies, Rod 1941- 61-64
Davies, Rosemary Reeves 1925- 49-52
Davies, Rupert Eric 1909- CANR-39
Earlier sketches in CA 5-8R, CANR-3, 18
Davies, Ruth A(nn) 1915- CANR-26
Earlier sketch in CA 29-32R
Davies, Sally Kevill
See Kevill-Davies, Sally
Davies, Samuel 1723-1761 .... DLB 31
Davies, Sir John 1569-1626 .... DLB 172
Davies, Stan Gebler 1943-1994 65-68
Obituary 146
Davies, Stanley Powell 1892-1985 Obituary 115
Davies, Stephanie 1946- 147
Davies, Stevan L(awrence) 1948- 107
Davies, Stevie
See Davies, Stephanie
Davies, Sumiko 1942- 126
See also SATA 46
Davies, T(refor) Rendall 1913- CAP-1
Earlier sketch in CA 9-10
Davies, Terence 1945- 156
Davies, Terry
See Davies, J. Clarence III
Davies, Thomas 1712(?)-1785 .... DLB 142
Davies, Thomas 1941- 115
Davies, Thomas M(ockett), Jr. 1940- CANR-6
Earlier sketch in CA 57-60
Davies, Tom
See Davies, Thomas
Davies, W(illiam) H(enry) 1871-1940 Brief
entry 104
See also DLB 19, 174
See also TCLC 5
Davies, Walter C.
See Kornbluth, C(yril) M.
Davies, William David 1911- CANR-1
Earlier sketch in CA 1-4R
Davies, Wyndham (Roy) 1926- 25-28R
Davies of Hereford, John 1565(?)-1618 ... DLB 121
Davila, Virgilio 1869-1943 131
See also HW
Davin, D(aniel) M(arcus) 1913- CANR-30
Earlier sketches in CA 9-12R, CANR-3
Davin, Dan
See Davin, D(aniel) M(arcus)
Davin, Nicholas Flood 1840(?)-1901 .... DLB 99
Davinson, Donald E(dward) 1932- CANR-3
Earlier sketch in CA 5-8R
Daviot, Gordon
See Mackintosh, Elizabeth
See also DLB 10
Davis, Ada Romaine
See Romaine-Davis, Ada
Davis, Adelle 1904-1974 .... CANR-30
Obituary 49-52
Earlier sketch in CA 37-40R
Davis, Alan (R.) 1950- 156
Davis, Albert Belisle 1947- 138
Davis, Alice Taylor 1903-1989 Obituary 129
Davis, Allen III 1929- 108
Davis, Allen F(reeman) 1931- CANR-50
Earlier sketches in CA 21-24R, CANR-10, 25
Davis, (William) Allison 1902-1983 125
Obituary 111
Brief entry 106
See also BW 1
Davis, Andrew Jackson 1826-1910 Brief entry . 120
Davis, Angela (Yvonne) 1944- CANR-10
Earlier sketch in CA 57-60
See also BW 2
See also CLC 77
See also DAM MULT
Davis, Ann 1946- 137
Davis, Ann E(lizabeth) 1932- 69-72
Davis, Archie K. 1911- 124
Davis, Arthur G. 1915- 13-16R
Davis, Arthur Hoey 1868-1935 Brief entry 121
Davis, Arthur Kennard 1910- CAP-1
Earlier sketch in CA 13-14
Davis, Arthur Kyle, Jr. 1897-(?) CAP-2
Earlier sketch in CA 17-18
Davis, Arthur P(aul) 1904-1996 61-64
Obituary 151
See also BW 2
Davis, Audrey
See Paine, Lauran (Bosworth)
Davis, B. Lynch
See Bioy Casares, Adolfo
and Borges, Jorge Luis
Davis, Barbara Kerr 1946- 104
Davis, Bart 1950- 153
Davis, Ben Reeves 1927- 77-80
Davis, Benjamin O(liver), Jr. 1912- 134
See also BW 2
Davis, (Mary) Bernice
See Curler, (Mary) Bernice
Davis, Berrie 1922- 101
Davis, Bertram H(ylton) 1918- CANR-1
Earlier sketch in CA 1-4R
Davis, Bette
See Davis, Ruth Elizabeth
Davis, Bette J. 1923- 93-96
See also SATA 15
Davis, Bill C. 1951- 110
Davis, Brian 1925-1988 Obituary 126
Davis, Burke 1913- CANR-50
Earlier sketches in CA 1-4R, CANR-4, 25
See also SATA 4
Davis, Calvin DeArmond 1927- 5-8R
Davis, Charles 1923- CANR-21
Earlier sketch in CA 5-8R
Davis, Charles A. 1795-1867 .... DLB 11
Davis, Charles T(witchell) 1918-1981 125
See also BW 1
Davis, Charles T(ill) 1929- 37-40R
Davis, Christopher 1928- CANR-3
Earlier sketch in CA 9-12R
See also CAAS 20
See also SATA 6
Davis, (Elvis) Clark (III) 1964- 151
Davis, Cliff
See Smith, Richard Rein
Davis, Clive E(dward) 1914- CANR-72
Earlier sketch in CA 17-20R
Davis, Clyde Brion 1894-1962 .... 5-8R
See also DLB 9
Davis, Creath 1939-1987 .... CANR-21
Obituary 145
Earlier sketches in CA 57-60, CANR-6
Davis, Curtis Carroll 1916-1997 .... CANR-72
Earlier sketches in CA 9-12R, CANR-6
Davis, Curtis Wheeler 1928-1986 136
Obituary 119
Davis, D(elbert) Dwight 1908-1965 Obituary ... 111
See also SATA 33
Davis, D(onald) Evan 1923-1979 .... 17-20R
Obituary 122
Davis, Daniel S(heldon) 1936- 45-48
See also SATA 12
Davis, Daphne 65-68
Davis, David Brion 1927- CANR-51
Earlier sketches in CA 17-20R, CANR-9, 26
Davis, David C(harles) L. 1928- 33-36R
Davis, David Howard 1941- 53-56
Davis, Deane C(handler) 1900- 108
Davis, Deborah 1949- 129
Davis, Dick 1945- 155
See also DLB 40
Davis, Don
See Dresser, Davis
Davis, Donald (D) 1944- CANR-68
Earlier sketch in CA 146
See also SATA 93
Davis, Donald Gordon, Jr. 1939- CANR-6
Earlier sketch in CA 53-56
Davis, Dorothy Salisbury 1916- CANR-32
Earlier sketches in CA 37-40R, CANR-14
Davis, Douglas (Matthew) 1933- 111
Davis, Douglas F(redell) 1935- 105
Davis, E. Adams
See Davis, Edwin Adams
Davis, Earl C(linton) 1938- CANR-46
Earlier sketch in CA 111
Davis, Earle (Rosco) 1905-1991 .... CANR-72
Earlier sketch in CA 65-68
Davis, Edwin Adams 1904- CAP-2
Earlier sketch in CA 25-28
Davis, Eleanor Harmon 1909- 106
Davis, Elise Miller 1915- 69-72
Davis, Elizabeth
See Davis, Lou Ellen
Davis, Elizabeth G. 1910(?)-1974 Obituary ... 53-56
Davis, Elwood Craig 1896- CANR-3
Earlier sketch in CA 1-4R
Davis, F(loyd) James 1920- CANR-4
Earlier sketch in CA 1-4R
Davis, Fitzroy 1912-1980 .... CANR-31
Obituary 102
Earlier sketch in CA 49-52
Davis, Flora 1934- CANR-10
Earlier sketch in CA 65-68
Davis, Forest K(endall) 1918- 41-44R
Davis, Francis 1946- CANR-50
Earlier sketch in CA 123
Davis, Frank (Cecil) 1892-1990 Obituary 131
Davis, Frank G(reene) 1915- 85-88
Davis, Frank Marshall 1905-1987 .... CANR-42
Obituary 123
Earlier sketch in CA 125
See also BLC 1
See also BW 2
See also DAM MULT
See also DLB 51
Davis, Franklin M(ilton), Jr. 1918-1981 .... CANR-4
Earlier sketch in CA 1-4R
Davis, Fred 1925- 13-16R
Davis, Frederick Barton 1909-1975 ...... CANR-17
Obituary 116
Earlier sketch in CA 1-4R
Davis, Frederick C(lyde) 1902-1977 Obituary ... 115
Davis, Gail Barbara 1956- 164
Davis, Garold N(eil) 1932- 41-44R
Davis, Gary A(lan) 1938- 106
Davis, Genevieve 1928- 65-68
Davis, Genny Wright 1948- 105
Davis, George 1939- CANR-9
Earlier sketch in CA 65-68
See also BW 1
Davis, George L(ittleton) Sr. 1921- 57-60
Davis, Gerry 1930- Brief entry 117
Davis, Gibbs 1953- 111
See also SATA 46, 102
See also SATA-Brief 41
Davis, Gil
See Gilmore, Don
Davis, Gilbert 1899-1983 Obituary 109
Davis, Gordon
See Levinson, Leonard
Davis, Gordon B(itter) 1930- CANR-4
Earlier sketch in CA 53-56
Davis, Grania 1943- CANR-39
Earlier sketches in CA 85-88, CANR-16
See also SATA 88
See also SATA-Brief 50
Davis, Grant Miller 1937- CANR-11
Earlier sketch in CA 29-32R
Davis, Gwen 1936- CANR-2
Earlier sketch in CA 1-4R
See also AITN 1
Davis, H(enry) Grady 1890- CAP-2
Earlier sketch in CA 21-22
Davis, Harley
See Green, Kay
Davis, Harold Eugene 1902-1988 .... CANR-1
Obituary 126
Earlier sketch in CA 1-4R
Davis, Harold Lenoir 1896-1960 Obituary 89-92
See also CLC 49
See also DLB 9
Davis, Harold S(eaton) 1919- 57-60
Davis, Harriet Eager 1892(?)-1974 Obituary .. 49-52
Davis, Harry Rex 1921- 1-4R
Davis, Helen Dick 1899-1992 143
Davis, Henry P. 1894(?)-1970 Obituary 104
Davis, Herbert (John) 1893-1967 .... CANR-1
Earlier sketch in CA 1-4R
Davis, Hope Hale 25-28R
Davis, Hope Harding 1915(?)-1976 Obituary . 69-72
Davis, Horace B(ancroft) 1898- 21-24R
Davis, Horance G(ibbs), Jr. 1924- 65-68
Davis, Howard V(aughn) 1915- 25-28R
Davis, Hubert J(ackson) 1904- 107
See also SATA 31
Davis, I(rene) M(ary) 1926- 61-64
Davis, J(ames) C(olin) 1940- 127
Davis, J(ohn) Cary 1905- 41-44R
Davis, J(ames) Madison (Jr.) 1951- 134
Davis, J. Morton 1929- 124
Davis, J(ames) William 1908- 102
Davis, Jack Leonard 1917- 106
Davis, James Allan 1929- CANR-1
Earlier sketch in CA 1-4R
Davis, James C(urran) 1895-1981 Obituary 108
Davis, James C(ushman) 1931- Brief entry 117
Davis, James H. 1932- 89-92
Davis, James Kirkpatrick 1939- 127
Davis, James Kotsilibas
See Kotsilibas-Davis, James
Davis, James Richard 1936- 65-68
Davis, James Robert 1945- CANR-41
Earlier sketches in CA 85-88, CANR-16
See also Davis, Jim
See also SATA 32
Davis, James W(arren, Jr.) 1935- CANR-72
Earlier sketch in CA 29-32R
Davis, Jan Haddle 1950- 93-96
Davis, Jean Reynolds 1927- 61-64
Davis, Jean Walton 1909- 1-4R
Davis, Jed H(orace, Jr.) 1921- 17-20R
Davis, Jenny 1953- CANR-66
Earlier sketch in CA 128
See also AAYA 21
See also SATA 74
Davis, Jerome 1891-1979 .... CANR-3
Obituary 89-92
Earlier sketch in CA 5-8R
Davis, Jim
Interview in CANR-16
See also Davis, James Robert
and Smith, Richard Rein
See also AAYA 8
Davis, Jimmie Dan 1940- 127
Davis, Jinnie Y(eh) 1945- 107
Davis, Jodie 1959- 139
Davis, Joe 1901-1978 Obituary 112
Davis, Joe Lee 1906-1974 .... 5-8R
Obituary 103
Davis, Joel 1948- 146
Davis, Johanna 1937-1974 .... 41-44R
Obituary 53-56
Davis, John 1774-1854 .... DLB 37
Davis, John D(avid) 1937- 29-32R
Davis, John H(erbert) 1904- 29-32R
Davis, John H. 1929- CANR-40
Earlier sketches in CA 25-28R, CANR-18
Davis, John J(ames) 1936- 33-36R
Davis, John King 1884-1967 .... CAP-1
Earlier sketch in CA 9-10
Davis, Jon 1952- 151
Davis, Joseph C(ole) 1908- 97-100
Davis, Joseph S(tancliffe) 1885-1975 101
Obituary 57-60
Davis, Judith 1925- 106
Davis, Julia
See Marsh, John
Davis, Julia 1900(?)-1993 .... CANR-1
Obituary 140
Earlier sketch in CA 1-4R
See also SATA 6
See also SATA-Obit 75
Davis, Julian 1902(?)-1974 Obituary 53-56
Davis, K(eith) 1918- CANR-20
Earlier sketches in CA 1-4R, CANR-5
Davis, Karen Padgett 1942- 112
Davis, Kathryn 1946- 149
Davis, Keith F. 1952- CANR-50
Earlier sketch in CA 123
Davis, Ken(neth Pickett) 1906-1982 49-52
Obituary 135
Davis, Kenneth C. 139
Davis, Kenneth Culp 1908- Brief entry 115
Davis, Kenneth R(exton) 1921- 17-20R

Davis, Kenneth S(idney) 1912- CANR-30
Earlier sketch in CA 13-16R
Davis, Kingsley 1908-1997 .... CANR-8
Obituary 156
Earlier sketch in CA 13-16R
Davis, L(awrence) J(ames) 1940- CANR-72
Earlier sketches in CA 25-28R, CANR-11
Davis, Lance E(dwin) 1928- 53-56
Davis, Lanny J(esse) 1945- 57-60
Davis, Lawrence B(ennion) 1939- 45-48
Davis, Lennard J. 1949- CANR-39
Earlier sketch in CA 116
Davis, Lenwood G. 1939- CANR-35
Earlier sketch in CA 25-28R
Davis, Leslie
See Guccione, Leslie Davis
Davis, Leslie
See Guccione, Leslie Davis
Davis, Lew A(rter) 1930- 21-24R
Davis, Linda H(onor) 1953- 127
Davis, Linda W. 1945- 146
Davis, Lindsey 1949- 164
Davis, Lloyd (Moore) 1931- 69-72
Davis, Lou Ellen 1936- 81-84
Davis, Louis E(lkin) 1918- 53-56
Davis, Louise Littleton 1921- 103
See also SATA 25
Davis, Loyal Edward 1896-1982 Obituary 107
Davis, Luther 1921- 105
Davis, Lydia 1947- 139
See also DLB 130
Davis, M(orris) Edward 1899- 5-8R
Davis, Maggie (Hill) CANR-9
Earlier sketch in CA 13-16R
Davis, Maggie S. 1943- .... SATA 57
Davis, Maralee G.
See Gibson, Maralee G.
Davis, Marc 1934- 29-32R
Davis, Margaret Banfield 1903- CAP-1
Earlier sketch in CA 11-12
Davis, Margaret Thomson 1926- 102
See also DLB 14
Davis, Marguerite 1889- .... SATA 34
Davis, Marilyn (Illaine) 1930- 153
Davis, Marilyn K(ornreich) 1928- 5-8R
Davis, Mark H. 1953- 158
Davis, Martha 1942- CANR-4
Earlier sketch in CA 49-52
Davis, Martin 1928- 148
Davis, Mary Byrd 1936- 158
Davis, Mary Dymond
See Davis, Mary Byrd
Davis, Mary L(ee) 1935- CANR-4
Earlier sketch in CA 49-52
See also SATA 9
Davis, Mary Octavia 1901- CAP-2
Earlier sketch in CA 25-28
See also SATA 6
Davis, Maxine
See McHugh, Maxine Davis
Davis, Mel
See Arnold, Madelyn M. a pseudonym
Davis, Melodie M(iller) 1951- CANR-71
Earlier sketches in CA 113, CANR-33
Davis, Melton S(amillow) 1910- 41-44R
Davis, (John) Michael 1940- 33-36R
Davis, Michael D. 1939- 141
See also BW 2
Davis, Michael Justin 1925- 102
Davis, Michele Weiner
See Weiner-Davis, Michele
Davis, Mildred 77-80
Davis, Mildred Ann (Campbell) 1916- 5-8R
Davis, Millard C. 1930- 69-72
Davis, Monte 1949- 103
Davis, Morris 1933- CANR-11
Earlier sketch in CA 61-64
Davis, Morton D(avid) 1930- 65-68
Davis, Moshe 1916- CANR-20
Earlier sketches in CA 9-12R, CANR-4
Davis, Murray S(tuart) 1940- 53-56
Davis, Myrna (Mushkin) 1936- 69-72
Davis, Natalie Zemon 1928- CANR-58
Earlier sketch in CA 53-56
Davis, Nathaniel 1925- 128
Davis, Neil
See Davis, T(homas) Neil
Davis, Neil 1934(?)-1985 Obituary 117
Davis, Nelle 1958- .... SATA 73
Davis, Nicholas 1965- 136
Davis, Nick
See Davis, Nicholas
Davis, Nolan 1942- CANR-25
Earlier sketch in CA 49-52
See also BW 1
Davis, Norah Deakin 1941- 111
Davis, Norman 1913- Brief entry 106
Davis, Norman Maurice 1936- 69-72
Davis, Nuel Pharr 1915- 29-32R
Davis, Olivia 1922- 81-84
Davis, Ossie 1917- CANR-53
Earlier sketches in CA 112, CANR-26
See also AAYA 17
See also BW 2
See also DAM DRAM, MULT
See also DLB 7, 38
See also SATA 81
Davis, Patrick (David Channer) 1925- 93-96
Davis, Patti 1952- 134
Davis, Paul (Benjamin) 1934- 135
Davis, Paxton 1925-1994 .... CANR-3
Obituary 145
Earlier sketch in CA 9-12R
See also DLBY 94
See also SATA 16
Davis, Peter (Frank) 1937- CANR-54
Earlier sketches in CA 107, CANR-29
Davis, Peter G(raffam) 1936- 165
Davis, Philip E(dward) 1927- 49-52
Davis, Philip J. 1923- CANR-51
Earlier sketch in CA 124
Davis, Polly Ann 1931- 102
Davis, R. G. 1933- 57-60
Davis, R(alph) H(enry) C(arless) 1918-1991 ....
CANR-6
Obituary 134
Earlier sketch in CA 5-8R
Davis, Ralph C(urrier) 1894- 33-36R
Davis, Rebecca (Blaine) Harding 1831-1910 Brief
entry 104
See also DLB 74
See also TCLC 6
Davis, Reuben
See Ship, Reuben
Davis, Reuben G. 1889-1966 143
Davis, Rex D. 1924- 9-12R
Davis, Richard CANR-26
Earlier sketches in CA 53-56, CANR-7
Davis, Richard A., (Jr.) 1937- 146
Davis, Richard Beale 1907- CANR-2
Earlier sketch in CA 5-8R
Davis, Richard Harding 1864-1916 Brief entry .. 114
See also DLB 12, 23, 78, 79, 189
See also DLBD 13
See also TCLC 24
Davis, Richard W. 1935- 33-36R
Davis, Robert 1881-1949 .... YABC 1
Davis, Robert Con 1948- CANR-23
Earlier sketch in CA 104
Davis, Robert Murray 1934- CANR-52
Earlier sketches in CA 33-36R, CANR-12, 28
Davis, Robert P. 1929- CANR-3
Earlier sketch in CA 5-8R
Davis, Robert Ralph, Jr. 1941- 37-40R
Davis, Robin W(orks) 1962- 151
See also SATA 87
Davis, Rocky 1927- 61-64
Davis, Ronald L(eroy) 1936- CANR-50
Earlier sketch in CA 37-40R
Davis, Rosemary 5-8R
Davis, Rosemary L.
See Davis, Rosemary
Davis, Roy Eugene 1931- CANR-6
Earlier sketch in CA 9-12R
Davis, Rupert (Charles) Hart
See Hart-Davis, Rupert (Charles)
Davis, Russell Gerard 1922- 5-8R
See also SATA 3
Davis, Ruth Elizabeth 1908-1989 .... CANR-21
Obituary 129
Earlier sketch in CA 61-64
Davis, Sammy, Jr. 1925-1990 108
Obituary 131
Interview in 108
Davis, Samuel 1930- 29-32R
Davis, Samuel Cole 1764-1809 .... DLB 37
Davis, Samuel Post 1850-1918 .... DLB 202
Davis, Sandra T. W. 1937- 124
Davis, Sara deSaussure 1943- 125
Davis, Shelley L(orraine) 1956- 161
Davis, Simon J. M. 1950- 128
Davis, Stanley Nelson 1924- 108
Davis, Stephen 1947- 128
Davis, Stephen M. 1955- 127
Davis, Stephen R(andy) 1956- 159
Davis, Steven Andrew 1947- 112
Davis, Steven J(oseph) 1957- 161
Davis, Stratford
See Bolton, Maisie Sharman
Davis, Suzanne
See Sugar, Bert Randolph
Davis, Sydney Charles Houghton 1887- 5-8R
Davis, Sylvan 1927(?)-1984 Obituary 112
Davis, T. N.
See Davis, T(homas) Neil
Davis, T(homas) Neil 1932- CANR-49
Earlier sketch in CA 123
Davis, Terence 1924- 21-24R
Davis, Thomas J(oseph) 1946- CANR-4
Earlier sketch in CA 53-56
Davis, Thulani .... BW 2
Davis, Tim(othy N.) 1957- 159
See also SATA 94
Davis, Timothy Francis Tothill 1941- 81-84
Davis, Tom Edward 1929- 85-88
Davis, Verne Theodore 1889-1973 .... 1-4R
See also SATA 6
Davis, (Benton) Vincent (Jr.) 1930- CANR-23
Earlier sketches in CA 17-20R, CANR-7
Davis, W(illiam) Jackson 1942- 107
Davis, W(arren) Jefferson 1885-1973 .... CAP-2
Earlier sketch in CA 29-32
Davis, W(illiam) N(ewell), Jr. 1915- 81-84
Davis, (Edmund) Wade 1953- 131
Davis, Walter A(lbert III) 1942- 114
Davis, Walter Richardson 1928- 102
Davis, Wayne H(arry) 1930- 33-36R
Davis, Wendi
See Holder, Nancy L.
Davis, Wiley H. 1913- 25-28R
Davis, William 1933- CANR-28
Earlier sketches in CA 65-68, CANR-10
Davis, William C(harles) 1946- CANR-23
Earlier sketches in CA 61-64, CANR-8
Davis, William H(atcher) 1939- 33-36R
Davis, William S(terling) 1943- CANR-53
Earlier sketches in CA 111, CANR-28
Davis, William Virgil 1940- CANR-47
Earlier sketches in CA 106, CANR-23
Davis, Winston (Bradley) 1939- 104
Davis-Friedmann, Deborah 1945- CANR-41
Earlier sketch in CA 118
Davis-Gardner, Angela 1942- 110
Davis-Goff, Annabel 1942- 85-88
Davison, Edward 1898-1970 Obituary 29-32R
Davison, Frank Dalby 1893-1970 Obituary 116
See also CLC 15
Davison, Geoffrey 1927- 110
Davison, Gladys Patton 1905- CAP-1
Earlier sketch in CA 13-16
Davison, Jane 1932(?)-1981 Obituary 104
Davison, Jean 1937- CANR-10
Earlier sketch in CA 65-68
Davison, Kenneth E(dwin) 1924- 9-12R
Davison, Lawrence H.
See Lawrence, D(avid) H(erbert Richards)
Davison, Liam 1957- 161
Davison, Ned J. 1926- 45-48
Davison, Peter (Hobley) 1926- 160
Davison, Peter (Hubert) 1928- CANR-43
Earlier sketches in CA 9-12R, CANR-3
See also CAAS 4
See also CLC 28
See also DLB 5
Davison, Roderic H(ollett) 1916- 37-40R
Davison, Verne E(lbert) 1904- 69-72
Davisson, Charles Nelson 1917- 25-28R
Davisson, William I. 1929- CANR-11
Earlier sketch in CA 17-20R
Davis-Weyer, Caecilia 1929- 41-44R
Davitt, Thomas E(dward) 1904-1980 .... 25-28R
Obituary 117
Davitz, J. R.
See Davitz, Joel R(obert)
Davitz, Joel R(obert) 1926- 134
Brief entry 114
Davol, Marguerite W. 1928- .... SATA 82
DaVolls, Andy (P.) 1967- .... SATA 85
DaVolls, Linda 1966- 151
See also SATA 85
d'Avray, David L. 129
Davy, Francis X(avier) 1916- 29-32R
Davy, George Mark Oswald
1898-1983 Obituary 110
Davy, John Charles 1927-1984 Obituary 114
Davys, Mary 1674-1732 .... DLB 39
Davys, Sarah
See Manning, Rosemary (Joy)
Dawdy, Doris Ostrander 53-56
Dawe, (Donald) Bruce 1930- CANR-52
Earlier sketches in CA 69-72, CANR-11, 27
Dawe, Donald G. 1926- 33-36R
Dawe, Frederick
See Gettings, Fred
Dawe, (Chartres) Gerald 1952- CANR-36
Earlier sketch in CA 114
Dawe, Margaret 1957- 148
Dawe, R(oger) D(avid) 1934- CANR-3
Earlier sketch in CA 146
Dawes, Dorothy
See Cooper, Parley J(oseph)
Dawes, Frank 1933- 69-72
Dawes, Nathaniel Thomas, Jr. 1937- 49-52
Dawes, Neville 1926- 13-16R
Dawes, Robyn M(ason) 1936- 37-40R
Dawick, John 1934- 148
Dawid, Annie 1960- 141
Dawidowicz, Lucy S(childkret) 1915-1990 ....
CANR-18
Obituary 133
Earlier sketch in CA 25-28R
Dawis, Rene V(illaneuva) 1928- 45-48
Dawisha, Adeed Isam 1944- CANR-18
Earlier sketch in CA 102
Dawisha, Karen (Lea) 1949- 120
Dawkins, Cecil 1927- CANR-36
Earlier sketch in CA 5-8R
Dawkins, Louisa a pseudonym 1940- 128
Dawkins, Richard 1941- CANR-51
Earlier sketches in CA 69-72, CANR-26
Dawley, Alan 1943- 140
Dawley, David 1941- 45-48
Dawley, Powel Mills 1907- 57-60
Dawlish, Peter
See Kerr, James Lennox
Dawn, C(larence) Ernest 1918- 61-64
Dawn, Marva J. 1948- 139
Dawood, N(essim) J(oseph) 1927- CANR-28
Earlier sketch in CA 49-52
Dawson, Alan David 1942- 77-80
Dawson, Carl 1938- CANR-1
Earlier sketch in CA 45-48
Dawson, Carol 1951- 141
Dawson, Christopher (Henry) 1889-1970 .. CANR-6
Obituary 29-32R
Earlier sketch in CA 1-4R
Dawson, Clay
See Levinson, Leonard
Dawson, Elizabeth
See Geach, Christine
Dawson, Elmer A. CANR-27
Earlier sketches in CAP-2, CA 19-20
See also SATA 1, 67
Dawson, Ernest 1882-1947 .... DLB 140
Dawson, Fielding 1930- 85-88
See also CLC 6
See also DLB 130
Dawson, Frank G(ates, Jr.) 1925- 69-72
Dawson, George G(lenn) 1925- 37-40R
Dawson, Giles E(dwin) 1903-1994 .... CAP-2
Obituary 146
Earlier sketch in CA 19-20
Dawson, Grace S(trickler) 1891- 17-20R
Dawson, Howard A. 1895(?)-1979 Obituary .. 89-92
Dawson, Imogen (Zoe) 1948- 155
See also SATA 90
Dawson, James Lee 1949- 127
Dawson, Jan 1939(?)-1980 Obituary 101
Dawson, Janet 1949- 162
Dawson, Janis 1936- 135
Dawson, Jennifer CANR-68
Earlier sketches in CA 57-60, CANR-10
Dawson, Jerry F. 1933- 33-36R
Dawson, Jim
See Dawson, James Lee
Dawson, Joseph G(reen) III 1945- 110
Dawson, Mary 1919- 21-24R
See also SATA 11
Dawson, Mildred A(gnes) 1897- CANR-12
Earlier sketch in CA 17-20R
Dawson, Minnie E. 1906-1978 85-88
Dawson, Peter
See Faust, Frederick (Schiller)
Dawson, (John) Philip 1928- 21-24R
Dawson, Richard E(vans) 1939- 73-76
Dawson, Robert (Merril) 1941- 21-24R
Dawson, Robert L(ewis) 1943- 105
Dawson, Robert MacGregor 1895-1958 159
Dawson, Roger 1940- 142
Dawson, William 1704-1752 .... DLB 31
Dawson-Scott, C(atharine) A(my) 1865-1934 Brief
entry 113
Day, A(rthur) Colin 1935- 145
Day, A(rthur) Grove 1904- CANR-23
Earlier sketches in CA 21-24R, CANR-8
See also SATA 59
Day, Aidan 1952- 132
Day, Alan 1932- 147
Day, Alan Charles Lynn 1924- 1-4R
Day, Alan J(ohn) 1942- 105
Day, Albert Edward 1884-1973 .... CAP-2
Obituary 45-48
Earlier sketch in CA 23-24
Day, Albert M. 1897-1979 93-96
Obituary 85-88
Day, Alexandra 136
See also CLR 22
See also SAAS 19
See also SATA 67, 97
Day, Alice Taylor 1928- 17-20R
Day, Angel fl. 1586- .... DLB 167
Day, Benjamin Henry 1810-1889 .... DLB 43
Day, Beth (Feagles) 1924- CANR-40
Earlier sketches in CA 9-12R, CANR-3, 18, 40
See also SATA 33
Day, Bradford M(arshall) 1916- 104
Day, Clarence (Shepard, Jr.) 1874-1935 Brief
entry 108
See also DLB 11
See also TCLC 25
Day, Clarence Burton 1889-1987 Obituary 121
Day, David 1944- 93-96
Day, (Stephen) Deforest 1941- 134
Day, Dianne 1938- 127
Day, Donald
See Harding, Donald Edward
Day, Dorothy 1897-1980 65-68
Obituary 102
See also DLB 29
Day, Douglas (Turner III) 1932- CANR-8
Earlier sketch in CA 9-12R
Day, Edward C. 1932- 133
See also SATA 72
Day, Frank Parker 1881-1950 .... DLB 92
Day, Gardiner Mumford 1900-1981 Obituary ... 104
Day, George 1950- 117
Day, George Harold 1900- CAP-1
Earlier sketch in CA 13-14
Day, Gwynn McLendon 1908- CAP-1
Earlier sketch in CA 11-12
Day, Holliday T. 1936- 137
Day, Houston
See Day, Sam Houston
Day, J(ames) Edward 1914-1996 .... 17-20R
Obituary 154
Day, J(ohn) Laurence 1934- 65-68
Day, James F(rancis) 1917- 33-36R
Day, James Wentworth 1899-1983(?) CANR-10
Obituary 108
Earlier sketch in CA 13-16R
Day, John 1574(?)-1640(?) .... DLB 62, 170
Day, John A(rthur) 1913- 17-20R
Day, John Patrick 1919- 5-8R
Day, John R(obert) 1917- CANR-9
Earlier sketch in CA 5-8R
Day, Jon 1936(?)- .... SATA 79
Day, Kathleen (Mary) 1944- 144
Day, Kenneth 1912- 9-12R
Day, Laura (Globus) 1959- 160
Day, LeRoy Judson 1917- 21-24R
Day, Lincoln H(ubert) 1928- 17-20R
Day, Lucille 1947- 110
Day, M(ichael) H(erbert) 1927- 102
Day, Martin Steele 1917- CANR-7
Earlier sketch in CA 5-8R
Day, Maurice 1892- .... SATA-Brief 30
Day, Max
See Cassiday, Bruce (Bingham)
Day, Melvin Norman 1923- 109
Day, Michael
See Dempewolff, Richard F(rederic)
Day, Nancy Raines 1951- CANR-60
Earlier sketch in CA 111
See also SATA 93
Day, Neil (Atherton) 1945- 140
Day, (Truman) Owen 1890-1983 69-72
Obituary 163
Day, Paul Woodford 1916- 25-28R
Day, Peter (Morton) 1914- 1-4R
Day, Price 1907-1978 85-88
Obituary 81-84
Day, R(oss) H(enry) 1927- 29-32R

Day, Ralph L(ewis) 1926- CANR-7
Earlier sketch in CA 5-8R
Day, Richard B(ruce) 1942- CANR-27
Earlier sketch in CA 49-52
Day, Richard E. 1929- 33-36R
Day, Richard Hollis 1933- 114
Day, Robert Adams 1924- 53-56
Day, Robin 1923- 144
Day, Sam Houston 1896-1984 Obituary 113
Day, Shirley 1962- 159
See also SATA 94
Day, Sir Robin
See Day, Robin
Day, Stacey B(iswas) 1927- CANR-57
Earlier sketches in CA 33-36R, CANR-29
Day, Thomas 1748-1789 DLB 39
See also YABC 1
Dayal, Rajeshwar 1909- 130
Dayan, Moshe 1915-1981 CANR-22
Obituary 105
Earlier sketch in CA 21-24R
Dayan, Yael 1939- 89-92
See also AITN 1
Dayananda, James Yesupriya 1934- 81-84
Daydi-Tolson, Santiago 1943- 127
Day Lewis, C(ecil) 1904-1972 CANR-34
Obituary 33-36R
Earlier sketches in CAP-1, CA 13-16
See also Blake, Nicholas
See also CLC 1, 6, 10
See also DAM POET
See also DLB 15, 20
See also MTCW 1
See also PC 11
Day-Lewis, Sean (Francis) 1931- 132
Daynes, Byron W(ilford) 1937- 110
Daysh, G(eorge) H(enry) J(ohn)
1901-1987 Obituary 122
Dayton, Charles (W.) 1943- 145
Dayton, Donald W(ilber) 1942- CANR-24
Earlier sketch in CA 69-72
Dayton, Edward R(isedorph) 1924- CANR-16
Earlier sketch in CA 85-88
Dayton, Eldorous L. 1906-1987 Obituary 122
Dayton, Irene 1922- CANR-6
Earlier sketch in CA 57-60
Dazai Osamu 1909-1948 164
See also Tsushima, Shuji
See also DLB 182
See also TCLC 11
d'Azevedo, Warren L. 1920- 93-96
Dazey, Agnes J(ohnston) CAP-2
Earlier sketch in CA 23-24
See also SATA 2
Dazey, Frank M. CAP-2
Earlier sketch in CA 23-24
See also SATA 2
Deacon, Eileen
See Geipel, Eileen
Deacon, George Edward Raven
1906-1984 Obituary 114
Deacon, Joseph John 1920- 69-72
Deacon, Richard
See McCormick, (George) Donald (King)
Deacon, Richard 1922-1984 Obituary 113
Deacon, Ruth E. 1923- 102
Deadman, Ronald 1919-1988(?) Obituary 125
See also SATA-Obit 56
Deagon, Ann (Fleming) 1930- 57-60
Deak, Edward Joseph, Jr. 1943- 53-56
Deak, Francis 1899-1972 Obituary 33-36R
Deak, Istvan 1926- CANR-52
Earlier sketches in CA 25-28R, CANR-11, 28
Deakin, Frederick William 1913- CANR-5
Earlier sketch in CA 5-8R
Deakin, James 1929- CANR-24
Earlier sketches in CA 21-24R, CANR-8
Deakin, Motley F. 1920- 120
Deakin, Rose 1937- 109
Deakins, Roger Lee 1933- 61-64
Deal, Babs H(odges) 1929- CANR-1
Earlier sketch in CA 1-4R
Deal, Borden 1922-1985 CANR-43
Obituary 114
Earlier sketches in CA 1-4R, CANR-2
See also BW 2
See also DLB 6
Deal, Ernest L(afayette, Jr.) 1918-1984 132
Deal, Terrance E. 1939- 130
Deal, William S(anford) 1910- CANR-3
Earlier sketch in CA 5-8R
Deale, Kenneth Edwin Lee 1907-(?) CANR-4
Earlier sketch in CA 5-8R
Dealey, E(dward) M(usgrove) 1892-1969 CAP-2
Earlier sketch in CA 23-24
Dealey, Ted
See Dealey, E(dward) M(usgrove)
deAlmeida, Hermione (Beatrice) 1950- 118
Dean, Abner 1910-1982 Obituary 107
Dean, Amber 1902-1985 CANR-2
Obituary 116
Earlier sketch in CA 5-8R
Dean, Anabel 1915- CANR-14
Earlier sketch in CA 37-40R
See also SATA 12
Dean, Barbara 1946- 113
Dean, Basil (Herbert) 1888-1978 69-72
Obituary 134
Dean, Beryl 1911- 9-12R
Dean, Bradley P. 1954- 141
Dean, Burton V(ictor) 1924- CANR-20
Earlier sketches in CA 45-48, CANR-1
Dean, Christopher G(eorge) 1940- 111
Dean, Dennis R(ichard) 1938- 137
Dean, Dorothy 1932(?)-1987 Obituary 121
Dean, Dwight G(antz) 1918- 17-20R
Dean, E. Douglas 1916- 97-100
Dean, Edith M(ae) 1915- 111
Dean, Edwin R(obinson) 1933- 17-20R
Dean, Elinor
See McCann, Helen
Dean, Frances Mary 1905(?)-1983 Obituary 110
Dean, Herbert Morris 1938- 105
Dean, Howard E(dward) 1916- 41-44R
Dean, Ida
See Grae, Ida
Dean, Jeffrey S. 1939- 37-40R
Dean, (Alfreda) Joan 1925- 101
Dean, Joan FitzPatrick 1949- 118
Dean, Joel 1906- 33-36R
Dean, John
See Bumppo, Nathaniel John Balthazar
Dean, John A(urie) 1921- 53-56
Dean, John Wesley III 1938- 105
Dean, Karen Strickler 1923- CANR-26
Earlier sketch in CA 109
See also SATA 49
Dean, Leonard Fellows 1909- Brief entry 105
Dean, Luella Jo 1908(?)-1977 Obituary 69-72
Dean, Malcolm 1948- CANR-31
Earlier sketch in CA 105
Dean, Morton 1935- 69-72
Dean, Nancy 1930- 65-68
Dean, Nell Marr 1910- 21-24R
Dean (Dyer-Bennett), Pamela (Collins) 1953- 154
Dean, Robert George 1904(?)-1989 Obituary 130
Dean, Roger 1944- Brief entry 114
Dean, Roy 1925- CANR-6
Earlier sketch in CA 57-60
Dean, Stanley (Rochelle) 1908- 73-76
Dean, Vera Micheles 1903-1972 Obituary 37-40R
Dean, Warren 1932-1994 29-32R
Obituary 145
Dean, William D(enard) 1937- 37-40R
Dean, William F(rishe) 1899-1981 Obituary 105
Dean, Winton Basil 1916- CANR-10
Earlier sketch in CA 65-68
Dean, Yetive H(ornor) 1909- CAP-1
Earlier sketch in CA 9-10
de Andrade, Carlos Drummond
See Drummond de Andrade, Carlos
DeAndrea, William L(ouis) 1952-1996 CANR-59
Earlier sketches in CA 81-84, CANR-20
Interview in CANR-20
Deane, Dee Shirley 1928- 81-84
Deane, Elisabeth
See Beilenson, Edna
Deane, Herbert Andrew 1921- 1-4R
Deane, James G(arner) 1923- 89-92
Deane, Lorna
See Wilkinson, Lorna Hilda Kathleen
Deane, Nancy H(ilts) 1939- 29-32R
Deane, Norman
See Creasey, John
Deane, Seamus (Francis) 1940- CANR-42
Earlier sketch in CA 118
Deane, Shirley Joan 1920- CANR-2
Earlier sketch in CA 1-4R
de Angeli, Marguerite (Lofft) 1889-1987 CANR-3
Obituary 122
Earlier sketch in CA 5-8R
See also AITN 2
See also CLR 1
See also DLB 22
See also MAICYA
See also SATA 1, 27, 100
See also SATA-Obit 51
De Angelis, Barbara (Ann) 1951- 139
See also BEST 90:3
De Angelis, Milo 1951- DLB 128
DeAngelis, William 1943- 113
Deans, Sis Boulos 1955- 146
See also SATA 78
de Antonio, Emile 1922-1989 117
Obituary 130
Brief entry 113
Interview in 117
Dear, William (C.) 1937- 125
de Aragon, Ray John 1946- 115
De Araugo, Tess (S.) 1930- 135
De Araugo-O'Mullane, Tess
See De Araugo, Tess (S.)
Dearborn, Mary V. 1955- 142
Dearden, Harold 1882(?)-1962 Obituary 116
Dearden, James 1949- 136
Dearden, James A(rthur) 1924-1976 33-36R
Dearden, James S(hackley) 1931- CANR-12
Earlier sketch in CA 25-28R
Dearden, John 1919- 33-36R
Deardorff, Robert 1912- 61-64
Deardorff, Tom 1940- 89-92
Dearing, James (William) 1959- 114
Dearing, Vinton Adams 1920- 110
Dearlove, John 1944- 97-100
DeArmand, Frances Ullmann 1904(?)-1984 5-8R
Obituary 112
See also SATA 10
See also SATA-Obit 38
de Armas, Frederick A(lfred) 1945- 37-40R
de Armas, Jose R(afael) 1924- 113
DeArment, Robert K(endall) 1925- 93-96
Dearmer, Geoffrey 1893-1996 CAP-2
Obituary 153
Earlier sketch in CA 23-24
Dearmin, Jeannie Tarascou 1924- 5-8R
DeArmond, Dale 1914- 138
DeArmond, Dale Burlison
See Dale, DeArmond
and DeArmond, Dale
Dearstyne, Howard (Best) 1903-1979 121
Obituary 85-88
De Arteaga, William 1943- 111
Deary, Terry 1946- 110
See also SATA 51, 101
See also SATA-Brief 41
Deason, Hilary J(ohn) 1903- 73-76
d'Easum, Cedric (Godfrey) 1907-1990 CANR-12
Obituary 163
Earlier sketch in CA 73-76
d'Easum, Dick
See d'Easum, Cedric (Godfrey)
Deasy, C(ornelius) M(ichael) 1918- 93-96
Deasy, Mary (Margaret) 1914- 5-8R
Deathridge, John (William) 1944- 133
Deaton, Charles W. 1942- 93-96
Deaton, John (Graydon) 1939- CANR-11
Earlier sketch in CA 61-64
Deats, Paul (Kindred), Jr. 1918- 13-16R
Deats, Randy 1954- 93-96
Deats, Richard L(ouis) 1932- 21-24R
D'Eau, Jean
See Gould, Allan (Mendel)
Deaux, George 1931- 5-8R
Deaux, Kay 1941- 114
Deaver, Jeff
See Deaver, Jeffery Wilds
Deaver, Jeffery
See Deaver, Jeffery Wilds
Deaver, Jeffery Wilds 1950- 163
Deaver, Julie Reece 1953- CANR-37
Earlier sketch in CA 129
See also SATA 68
DeBakey, Michael E(llis) 1908- 73-76
de Banke, Cecile 1889-1965 CAP-1
Earlier sketch in CA 13-14
See also SATA 11
de Bary, Brett
See Nee, Brett de Bary
deBary, William Theodore 1919- CANR-37
Earlier sketch in CA 57-60
DeBeaubien, Philip Francis
1913-1979 Obituary 85-88
de Beausobre, Iulia
See Namier, Julia
de Beauvoir, Simone (Lucie Ernestine Marie Bertrand)
See Beauvoir, Simone (Lucie Ernestine Marie Bertrand) de
de Becker, Gavin 166
de Bedts, Ralph F(ortes) 1914- 9-12R
De Beer, E(smond) S(amuel) 1895-1990 CAP-1
Obituary 132
Earlier sketch in CA 13-14
de Beer, Gavin R(ylands) 1899-1972 CAP-1
Earlier sketch in CA 13-16
de Beer, P.
See Bosman, Herman Charles
De Bello, Rosario 1923- SATA 89
DeBenedetti, Charles Louis 1943-1987 102
Obituary 121
DeBerard, Ella 1900- 73-76
Deberdt-Malaquais, Elisabeth 1937- 57-60
de Bernieres, Louis 1954- CANR-72
Earlier sketch in CA 133
de Betancourt, Cressy
See Dobkin De Rios, Marlene
DeBetz, Barbara Holstein 123
de Beus, Jacobus Gysbertus 1909- 102
Debevec Henning, Sylvie Marie 1948- 109
Debicki, Andrew P(eter) 1934- CANR-37
Earlier sketch in CA 37-40R
Debicki, Roman 1896-1980 1-4R
Obituary 163
Debin, David 1942- 150
de Blank, Joost 1908-1968 CAP-1
Earlier sketch in CA 13-14
De Blasis, Celeste (N.) 1946- CANR-63
Earlier sketches in CA 53-56, CANR-4
Deblieu, Jan 1955- 146
de Blij, Harm J(an) 1935- CANR-23
Earlier sketches in CA 13-16R, CANR-8
Debo, Angie 1890-1988 CANR-40
Obituary 124
Earlier sketch in CA 69-72
De Boe, David C. 1942- 127
DeBoer, John C(harles) 1923- CANR-26
Earlier sketch in CA 29-32R
DeBoer, John James 1903-1969 CANR-3
Earlier sketch in CA 1-4R
de Bois, Helma
See de Bois, Wilhelmina J. E.
de Bois, Wilhelmina J. E. 1923- 17-20R
de Boissiere, Ralph (Anthony) 1907- CANR-67
Earlier sketch in CA 106
DeBold, Richard C. 1927- 21-24R
DeBolt, Margaret Wayt 1930- 115
De Bona, Maurice, Jr. 1926- 65-68
DeBonis, Steven 1949- 150
de Bono, Edward 1933- CANR-43
Earlier sketches in CA 21-24R, CANR-10
See also MTCW 1
See also SATA 66
De Bonville, Bob 1926- 69-72
De Borchgrave, Arnaud 1926- 73-76
de Borchgrave, Baroness Sheri 1952- 145
De Borhegyi, Suzanne Sims 1926- 5-8R
de Born, Edith 25-28R
De Botton, Alain 1969- 159
De Bow, James Dunwoody Brownson
1820-1867 DLB 3, 79
DeBoy, James J(oseph), Jr. 1942- 113
Debray, (Jules) Regis 1942- CANR-43
Earlier sketch in CA 21-24R
Debreczeny, Paul 1932- CANR-12
Earlier sketch in CA 33-36R
De Breffny, Brian (O'Rorke) 1931(?)-1989 77-80
Obituary 127
Debrett, Hal
See Dresser, Davis
Debreu, Gerard 1921- CANR-23
Earlier sketch in CA 37-40R
de Brissac, Malcolm
See Dickinson, Peter (Malcolm)
de Broca, Philippe (Claude Alex) 1933- 126
de Broglie, L.
See de Broglie, Louis (Victor Pierre Raymond)
de Broglie, Louis (Victor Pierre Raymond)
1892-1987 155
Obituary 122
de Brunhoff, Jean
See Brunhoff, Jean de
De Brunhoff, Laurent
See Brunhoff, Laurent de
de Bruyn, Guenter 1926- DLB 75
de Bruyn, Monica (Jean) G(rembowicz)
1952- 65-68
See also SATA 13
DeBry, Roger K. 1942- 155
See also SATA 91
Debs, Victor, Jr. 1949- 164
de Burgos, Julia 1914-1953 164
Debus, Allen G(eorge) 1926- CANR-57
Earlier sketches in CA 37-40R, CANR-14, 31
Debussy, (Achille) Claude 1862-1918 Brief entry 118
deBuys, William (Eno, Jr.) 1949- 136
de Calles, Jane F. Butel 1938- 126
Decalo, Samuel 1937- 121
de Camp, Catherine Crook 1907- CANR-20
Earlier sketches in CA 21-24R, CANR-9
See also SATA 12, 83
DeCamp, Graydon 1934- 97-100
de Camp, L(yon) Sprague 1907- CANR-20
Earlier sketches in CA 1-4R, CANR-1, 9
See also DLB 8
See also SATA 9, 83
de Campi, John Webb 1939- 69-72
De Campos, L.
See Dahl, Linda
De Canio, Stephen J(ohn) 1942- 57-60
De Capite, Raymond Anthony 1924- 1-4R
Decarie, Therese Gouin 1923- 41-44R
DeCarl, Lennard 1940- 81-84
De Carlo, Andrea 1952- 132
See also DLB 196
de Carvalho, Fernando Jose Cardim 1953- 143
de Carvalho, Mario 1944- 164
de Castro, Fernando J(ose) 1937- 53-56
De Castro, Josue 1908-1973 33-36R
De Caux, Len
See De Caux, Leonard Howard
De Caux, Leonard Howard 1899- 29-32R
Decaux, Lucile
See Bibesco, Marthe Lucie
DeCecco, John Paul 1925- 17-20R
de Cervera, Alejo 1919- 21-24R
de Chair, Somerset (Struben) 1911-1995 CANR-1
Obituary 147
Earlier sketch in CA 45-48
DeChancie, John 1946- CANR-41
Earlier sketch in CA 118
Dechant, Emerald V(ictor) 1926- 9-12R
DeChant, John A(loysius) 1917-1974 CAP-2
Obituary 53-56
Earlier sketch in CA 23-24
de Chardin, Pierre Teilhard
See Teilhard de Chardin, (Marie Joseph) Pierre
deCharms, Richard IV 1927- 41-44R
de Chasca, Edmund V(illela) 1903- Brief entry 117
de Chatellerault, Victor
See Beaudoin, Kenneth Lawrence
Dechausay, Sonia E. 159
See also SATA 94
Dechert, Charles R(ichard) 1927- CANR-10
Earlier sketch in CA 21-24R
Dechert, Robert 1895-1975 DLB 187
de Chirico, Giorgio 1888-1978 89-92
Obituary 81-84
De Christoforo, Ron(ald) 1951- 81-84
Deci, Edward L(ewis) 1942- CANR-39
Earlier sketch in CA 53-56
Deck, Allen F.
See Deck, Allen Figueroa
Deck, Allen Figueroa 1945- 150
Decker, Albert 1895-1988 Obituary 127
Decker, Beatrice 1919- 61-64
Decker, Donald M(ilton) 1923- 37-40R
Decker, Duane 1910-1964 5-8R
See also SATA 5
Decker, Hannah S(hulman) 1937- 85-88
Decker, Leslie E(dward) 1930- 9-12R
Decker, Robert Owen 1927- 65-68
Decker, William 1926- Brief entry 115
Deckers, Jeanine 1933(?)-1985 Obituary 115
Deckert, Alice Mae 13-16R
DeClements, Barthe 1920- CANR-45
Earlier sketches in CA 105, CANR-22
See also CLR 23
See also JRDA
See also SATA 35, 71
De Cock, Liliane 1939- CANR-2
Earlier sketch in CA 45-48
Decolta, Ramon
See Whitfield, Raoul
DeConde, Alexander 1920- CANR-6
Earlier sketch in CA 5-8R
de Conte, Sieur Louis
See Clemens, Samuel Langhorne
De Costa, Elena M. 1949- 144
de Costa, (George) Rene 1939- 102
DeCosta-Willis, Miriam 1934- 142
See also BW 2

deCoste, Fredrik 1910- CAP-2
Earlier sketch in CA 21-22
DeCoster, Cyrus C(ole) 1914- CANR-29
Earlier sketch in CA 49-52
deCourcy Hinds, Michael 1947- 114
DeCoursey, Virginia 1924- 114
deCoy, Robert H(arold), Jr. 1920- 25-28R
DeCredico, Mary A. 1959- 135
De Crescenzo, Luciano 1928- 133
de Crespigny, (Richard) Rafe (Champion) 1936- 57-60
De Cristoforo, R(omeo) J(ohn) 1917- CANR-3
Earlier sketch in CA 9-12R
DeCrow, Karen 1937- CANR-37
Earlier sketch in CA 33-36R
Decter, Midge (Rosenthal) 1927- CANR-2
Earlier sketch in CA 45-48
Dedek, John F. 1929- 33-36R
Dederer, John Morgan 1951- 136
Dederick, Robert 1919- Brief entry 116
de Dienes, Andre 1913- 41-44R
Dedijer, Vladimir 1914-1990 CANR-4
Obituary 133
Earlier sketch in CA 1-4R
Dedina, Michel 1933- 33-36R
Dedini, Eldon 1921- 65-68
Dedman, Stephen 166
Dedmon, Emmett 1918-1983 CANR-5
Obituary 110
Earlier sketch in CA 9-12R
De Duve, Christian (Rene) 1917- 157
Dee, Ed(ward J., Jr.) 1940- CANR-72
Earlier sketch in CA 146
Dee, Henry
See Torbett, Harvey Douglas Louis
Dee, Johnny
See Krauzer, Steven M(ark)
Dee, Ruby
See Wallace, Ruby Ann
See also SATA 77
Deeb, Gary (James) 1945- 138
Deedy, John 1923- 33-36R
See also SATA 24
Deegan, Paul Joseph 1937- 102
See also SATA 48
See also SATA-Brief 38
Deeken, Alfons 1932- 77-80
Deeley, Roger 1944- 53-56
Deelman, Christian Felling 1937-1964 CAP-1
Earlier sketch in CA 11-12
Deem, James M(organ) 1950- 142
See also SATA 75
Deemer, Bill 1945- 17-20R
Deemer, Charles (Robert, Jr.) 1939- 73-76
Deen, Edith Alderman 1905- CANR-2
Earlier sketch in CA 5-8R
Deener, David R(ussell) 1920-1976 17-20R
Obituary 134
Deep Chin
See Gould, Allan (Mendel)
Deeping, (George) Warwick 1877-1950 Brief entry 114
See also DLB 153
Deeps, Frederick
See Speed, F(rederick) Maurice
Deer, Irving 1924- 17-20R
Deer, Sandra 1940- CLC 45
Deese, Helen 1925- 126
Deese, James (Earle) 1921- CANR-5
Earlier sketch in CA 1-4R
Deeter, Allen C. 1931- 45-48
de Extramuros, Quixote
See Espino, Federico (Licsi, Jr.)
DeFalco, Joseph Michael 1931- 13-16R
DeFanti, Charles 1942- 89-92
DeFelice, Cynthia 1951- SATA 79
DeFelice, James (V.) 1940- 128
DeFelice, Jim 1956- 142
DeFelice, Louise P(aula) 1945- 61-64
De Felitta, Frank (Paul) 1921- CANR-28
Earlier sketch in CA 61-64
De Ferrari, Gabriella 1941- 146
See also CLC 65
Deferrari, Roy J(oseph) 1890-1969 CAP-1
Earlier sketch in CA 13-14
DeFerrari, Sister Teresa Mary 1930- 9-12R
Deffaa, Chip 1951- 153
Deffner, Donald L(ouis) 1924- CANR-11
Earlier sketch in CA 17-20R
de Filippo, Eduardo 1900-1984 132
Obituary 114
See also MTCW 1
de Fletin, P.
See Fielden, T(homas) P(erceval)
Defoe, Daniel 1660(?)-1731 AAYA 27
See also CDBLB 1660-1789
See also DA
See also DAB
See also DAC
See also DAM MST, NOV
See also DLB 39, 95, 101
See also JRDA
See also MAICYA
See also SATA 22
See also WLC
de Fontaine, Felix Gregory 1834-1896 DLB 43
deFontaine, Wade Hampton 1893-1969 5-8R
Obituary 103
De Forbes
See Forbes, DeLoris (Florine) Stanton
Deford, Frank 1938- CANR-45
Earlier sketch in CA 33-36R
See also AAYA 14
deFord, Miriam Allen 1888-1975 CANR-4
Earlier sketch in CA 1-4R
deFord, Sara (Whitcraft) 1916- 25-28R
DeForest, Charlotte B. 1879-1971 CAP-2
Earlier sketch in CA 25-28
De Forest, John William 1826-1906 Brief entry 119
See also DLB 12, 189
De Forest, Lee 1873-1961 157
Obituary 112
DeForest, Orrin L. 1923- 134
de Forrest, Julie
See DeWitt, Edith Openshaw
de Fossard, R(onald) A(lfred) 1929- 41-44R
de Fox, Lucia Ungaro
See Lockert, Lucia (Alicia Ungaro Fox)
deFrance, Anthony
See DiFranco, Anthony (Mario)
DeFrancis, John 1911- Brief entry 106
DeFrank, Thomas M. 1945- 152
See also DeFrank, Tom
DeFrank, Tom
See DeFrank, Thomas M.
DeFrees, Madeline 1919- CANR-4
Earlier sketch in CA 9-12R
See also DLB 105
de Funiak, William Q(uinby) 1901- 33-36R
de Gamez, Cielo Cayetana Alba
See Alba de Gamez, Cielo Cayetana
de Gamez, Tana
See Alba de Gamez, Cielo Cayetana
Degani, Meir H(ershtenkorn) 1909- 102
DeGarmo, Kenneth Scott 1943- 81-84
de Gaulle, Charles (Andre Joseph Marie) 1890-1970 130
Obituary 111
de Gaury, Gerald 1897-1984 13-16R
Obituary 112
Degen, Bruce 1945- 124
See also SATA 57, 97
See also SATA-Brief 47
Degeneres, Ellen 1958- 165
Degenhardt, Henry W(illiam) 1910- CANR-23
Earlier sketch in CA 106
De Gennaro, Angelo Anthony 1919- 13-16R
De Gennes, Pierre-Gilles 1932- 157
Degenshein, George A. 1918(?)-1979 Obituary 93-96
De George, Richard T(homas) 1933- CANR-39
Earlier sketches in CA 5-8R, CANR-2, 17
DeGering, Etta Fowler 1898- CAP-1
Earlier sketch in CA 9-10
See also SATA 7
Degh, Linda 1920- 85-88
Deghy, Guy (Stephen) 1912-1992 CAP-1
Obituary 137
Earlier sketch in CA 9-10
DeGidio, Sandra 1943- 112
Degler, Carl N(eumann) 1921- CANR-3
Earlier sketch in CA 5-8R
Degler, Stanley E. 1929- 25-28R
Degnan, James Philip 1933- 41-44R
DeGolyer, Everette Lee 1886-1956 DLB 187
Degonwadonti
See Brant, Beth (E.)
de Gourmont, Remy(-Marie-Charles)
See Gourmont, Remy (-Marie-Charles) de
DeGraaff, Robert M(ark) 1942- 141
De Graeff, Allen
See Blaustein, Albert Paul
de Graff, Robert F(air) 1895-1981 Obituary 105
See also DLBY 81
de Graffe, Richard
See St. Clair, Leonard
de Graft, Joe (Coleman) 1924-1978 CANR-43
Earlier sketch in CA 73-76
See also DLB 117
de Graft, John Coleman 1919- 21-24R
See also BW 2
de Gramont, Sanche
See Morgan, Ted
De Grave, Kathleen 1950- 152
DeGrave, Philip
See DeAndrea, William L(ouis)
de Grazia, Alfred 1919- CANR-5
Earlier sketch in CA 13-16R
de Grazia, Edward 1927- 129
DeGrazia, Emilio 1941- 140
De Grazia, Ettore 1909-1982 CANR-13
Earlier sketch in CA 61-64
See also De Grazia, Ted
De Grazia, Sebastian 1917- CANR-43
Earlier sketch in CA 65-68
De Grazia, Ted
See De Grazia, Ettore
See also SATA 39
DeGre, Muriel (Harris) 1914-1971 CAP-1
Earlier sketch in CA 17-18
De Greene, Kenyon B(renton) CANR-14
Earlier sketch in CA 37-40R
De Gregori, Thomas R(oger) 1935- CANR-12
Earlier sketch in CA 29-32R
DeGregorio, William A(lfred) 1946- 117
DeGregory, Jerry L(ouis) 1945- 119
de Groat, Diane 1947- CANR-57
Earlier sketch in CA 107
See also SATA 31, 90
DeGrood, David H. 1937- 33-36R
DeGroot, Alfred Thomas 1903- CANR-5
Earlier sketch in CA 5-8R
de Groot, Roy Andries 1910-1983 Obituary 110
deGros, J. H.
See Villiard, Paul
de Gruchy, John W(esley) 1939- 131
de Grummond, Lena Young CANR-1
Earlier sketch in CA 1-4R
See also SATA 6, 62
de Grunwald, Constantine 9-12R
de Guadaloupe, Brother Jose
See Mojica, Jose
Deguine, Jean-Claude 1943- 81-84
de Guingand, Francis Wilfred 1900-1979 Obituary 89-92
de Guise, Elizabeth (Mary Teresa) 1934- 126
de Gunzburg, Nicholas
See Gunzburg, Nicholas de
deGuzman, Daniel 1911- 93-96
De Haan, Margaret
See Freed, Margaret De Haan
De Haan, Richard W. 1923- 21-24R
De Haas, Elsa 1901-1984 45-48
Obituary 163
de Hamel, Christopher 1950- CANR-45
Earlier sketch in CA 120
de Hamel, Joan Littledale 1924- CANR-51
Earlier sketch in CA 103
See also SATA 86
de Hart, Allen 1926- 119
de Hartmann, Olga 1883(?)-1979 Obituary 89-92
de Hartog, Jan 1914- CANR-1
Earlier sketch in CA 1-4R
See also CLC 19
De Haven, Tom 1949- 133
See also SATA 72
Dehejia, Vidya 1942- 136
de Herrera, Nancy Cooke 142
de Hevesy, Paul 1883-1988 Obituary 125
Dehn, Olive 1914- 117
Dehn, Paul (Edward) 1912-1976 89-92
Dehoney, W(illiam) Wayne 1918- 17-20R
de Hostos, E. M.
See Hostos (y Bonilla), Eugenio Maria de
de Hostos, Eugenio M.
See Hostos (y Bonilla), Eugenio Maria de
de Hoyos, Angela
See Hoyos, Angela de
Dehqani-Tafti, H. B. 1920- 106
Dehr, Dorothy 1915- 29-32R
Dei-Anang, Michael 1909- 53-56
Deibler, William E. 1932- 89-92
Deichmann, Ute 1951- 164
Deighton, Lee C(ecil) 1906-1987 124
Obituary 122
Deighton, Len
See Deighton, Leonard Cyril
See also AAYA 6
See also BEST 89:2
See also CDBLB 1960 to Present
See also CLC 4, 7, 22, 46
See also DLB 87
Deighton, Leonard Cyril 1929- CANR-68
Earlier sketches in CA 9-12R, CANR-19, 33
See also Deighton, Len
See also DAM NOV, POP
See also MTCW 1
Deikman, Arthur J(oseph) 1929- 65-68
Deindorfer, Robert Greene 1922-1983 CANR-3
Obituary 109
Earlier sketch in CA 9-12R
Deindorfer, Scott 1967- 81-84
Deinzer, Harvey T. 1908- 17-20R
de longh, Mary (Dows Herter Norton) Crena
See Crena de longh, Mary (Dows Herter Norton)
Deisenhofer, Johann 1943- 157
Deiss, Joseph Jay 1915- CANR-14
Earlier sketch in CA 33-36R
See also SATA 12
Deist, Wilhelm 1931- 136
Deitrick, Frances I. 1962- 137
Deitsch, Jeremy Stafford
See Stafford-Deitsch, Jeremy
Deitz, Susan 1934- 110
Deitz, Tom 1952- 154
De Jaegher, Raymond-Joseph 1905-1980 CAP-2
Obituary 93-96
Earlier sketch in CA 21-22
DeJean, Joan (Elizabeth) 1948- 134
De Jenkins, Lyll Becerra 1925-1997 SATA 102
De Jong, Arthur J(ay) 1934- 69-72
DeJong, David C(ornel) 1905-1967 5-8R
See also SATA 10
deJong, Dola 5-8R
See also SATA 7
de Jong, Eveline D(orothea) 1948- 130
De Jong, Gerald Francis 1921- 61-64
de Jong, Gerrit, Jr. 1892- 37-40R
De Jong, Gordon F(rederick) 1935- 25-28R
DeJong, Meindert 1906-1991 CANR-36
Obituary 134
Earlier sketch in CA 13-16R
See also CLR 1
See also DLB 52
See also MAICYA
See also SATA 2
See also SATA-Obit 68
De Jong, Peter 1945- 69-72
De Jong, Russell N(elson) 1907-1990 Obituary 132
de Jonge, Alex 1938- CANR-42
Earlier sketches in CA 53-56, CANR-5
DeJonge, Joanne E. 1943- SATA 56
De Jonge, Marinus 1925- CANR-50
Earlier sketch in CA 123
de Jongh, James 1942- 85-88
de Journlet, Marie
See Little, Paul H(ugo)
de Jouvenel, Bertrand
See de Jouvenel des Ursins, Edouard Bertrand
de Jouvenel, Hugues Alain 1946- 130
de Jouvenel des Ursins, Edouard Bertrand 1903-1987 Obituary 121
De Jovine, F(elix) Anthony 1927-1976 CAP-2
Earlier sketch in CA 29-32
Deju, Raul A(ntonio) 1946- 53-56
Deka, Connie
See Laux, Constance
DeKalb, Lorimer
See Knorr, Marian L(ockwood)
de Kay, James T(ertius) 1930- CANR-10
Earlier sketch in CA 25-28R
de Kay, Ormonde (Jr.) 1923- 49-52
See also SATA 7
de Kerpely, Theresa 1898- 119
deKieffer, Donald (Eulette) 1945- 112
de Kiewiet, Cornelis W(illem) 1902-1986 Obituary 118
de Kiewiet, Cornelius W(illiam)
See de Kiewiet, Cornelis W(illem)
de Kiewit, Cornelis W(illem)
See de Kiewiet, Cornelis W(illem)
de Kiriline, Louise
See Lawrence, Louise de Kiriline
Dekker, Carl
See Laffin, John (Alfred Charles)
and Lynds, Dennis
Dekker, George 1934- 104
Dekker, Rudolf M(ichel) 1951- 132
Dekker, Thomas 1572(?)-1632 CDBLB Before 1660
See also DAM DRAM
See also DLB 62, 172
Dekkers, Midas 1946- 153
Dekle, Bernard 1905- 17-20R
Dekmejian, Richard Hrair 1933- 37-40R
Deknatel, F(rederick) B(rockway) 1905-1973 Obituary 45-48
Dekobra, Maurice
See Tessier, (Ernst) M(aurice)
De Koenigswerther, Edwin Raymond 1930- 49-52
DeKok, David (Paul) 1953- 124
de Kooning, Elaine (Marie Catherine) 1920-1989 148
DeKosky, Robert K. 1945- 93-96
DeKoster, Lester Ronald 1915- 13-16R
De Koven, Bernard 1941- 85-88
De Koven, Bernie
See De Koven, Bernard
Dekovic, Gene 1922- CANR-26
Earlier sketch in CA 108
deKruif, Paul (Henry) 1890-1971 9-12R
Obituary 29-32R
See also SATA 5, 50
de Kun, Nicolas 1923- 17-20R
de la Barca, Fanny Calderon 1804-1882 DLB 183
De La Bedoyere, Michael 1900-1973 Obituary 104
de la Billiere, Peter (Edgar de la Cour) 1934- 143
Delacato, Carl H(enry) 1923- 41-44R
Delacorta
See Odier, Daniel
Delacorte, George T., Jr. 1894- DLB 91
Delacorte, Peter 1943- 105
de la Costa, Horacio (L.)
See Costa, Horacio (L.) de la
Delacour, Jean
See Delacour, Jean Theodore
Delacour, Jean Theodore 1890-1985 Obituary 117
Delacre, Lulu 1957- SATA 36
DeLaCroix, Alice 1940- 142
See also SATA 75
DeLacy, Margaret (Eisenstein) 1951- 122
DeLaet, Sigfried J(an) 1914- CANR-18
Earlier sketches in CA 5-8R, CANR-3
Delafield, E. M. 1890-1943
See Dashwood, Edmee Elizabeth Monica de la Pasture
See also DLB 34
See also TCLC 61
de la Garza, Rodolfo O(ropea) 1942- 77-80
Delage, Denys 1942- 149
De Lage, Ida 1918- CANR-14
Earlier sketch in CA 41-44R
See also SATA 11
de La Glannege, Roger-Maxe
See Legman, G(ershon)
De La Grange, Henry Louis 1924- 69-72
de la Guardia, Ernesto, Jr. 1904-1983 Obituary 109
de Laguna, Frederica (Annis) 1906- 37-40R
de Laguna, Grace Mead A(ndrus) 1878-1978 CAP-1
Obituary 77-80
Earlier sketch in CA 11-12
Delahanty, Randolph
See Delehanty, Randolph
Delahay, E(ileen) A(vril) 1915-1982 25-28R
Obituary 117
Delahaye, Guy 1888-1969 DLB 92
De La Iglesia, Maria Elena 1936- 29-32R
Delamaide, Darrell (George) 1949- 146
de la Mare, Albinia Catherine 1932- 33-36R
de la Mare, Richard (Herbert Ingpen) 1901-1986 Obituary 118
de la Mare, Walter (John) 1873-1956 163
See also CDBLB 1914-1945
See also CLR 23
See also DAB
See also DAC
See also DAM MST, POET
See also DLB 162
See also SATA 16
See also SSC 14
See also TCLC 4, 53
See also WLC
DeLamarter, Jeanne
See Bonnette, Jeanne
DeLamotte, Roy Carroll 1917- CANR-15
Earlier sketch in CA 41-44R
DeLancey, Mark W(akeman) 1939- 93-96
Deland, Margaret(ta Wade Campbell) 1857-1945 Brief entry 122
See also DLB 78
Delaney, Bud
See Delaney, Francis, Jr.

Delaney, C(ornelius) F. 1938- CANR-16
Earlier sketch in CA 25-28R
Delaney, Daniel J(oseph) 1938- 41-44R
Delaney, Denis
See Green, Peter (Morris)
Delaney, Edmund T. 1914- 13-16R
Delaney, Francis, Jr. 1931- 57-60
Delaney, Franey
See O'Hara, John (Henry)
Delaney, Frank 1942- 126
Delaney, Gayle (M. V.) 1949- 142
Delaney, Harry 1932- 25-28R
See also SATA 3
Delaney, Jack J(ames) 1921- 21-24R
Delaney, John
See Rowland, D(onald) S(ydney)
Delaney, John Joseph 1910-1985 CANR-5
Obituary 115
Earlier sketch in CA 1-4R
Delaney, Joseph H(enry) 1932- 156
DeLaney, Joseph Lawrence 1917- 102
Delaney, Lolo M(ae) 1937- 57-60
Delaney, Marshall
See Fulford, Robert
Delaney, Mary Murray 1913- 53-56
Delaney, Michael 1955- 161
See also SATA 96
Delaney, Ned
See Delaney, Thomas Nicholas III
See also SATA 28
Delaney, Norman Conrad 1932- 37-40R
Delaney, Robert Finley 1925- CANR-6
Earlier sketch in CA 1-4R
Delaney, Samuel R(ay, Jr.) 1942- SATA 92
Delaney, Shelagh 1939- CANR-67
Earlier sketches in CA 17-20R, CANR-30
See also CDBLB 1960 to Present
See also CLC 29
See also DAM DRAM
See also DLB 13
See also MTCW 1
Delaney, Steve 1938- 121
Brief entry 110
Interview in 121
Delaney, Thomas Nicholas III 1951- CANR-10
Earlier sketch in CA 65-68
See also Delaney, Ned
Delaney, William A(nthony) 1926- 106
de Lange, Nicholas (Robert Michael) 1944- CANR-15
Earlier sketch in CA 89-92
Delano, Amasa 1763-1823 DLB 183
Delano, Anthony 1930- 102
Delano, Hugh 1933- 65-68
See also SATA 20
Delano, Isaac O. 1904- 25-28R
Delano, Kenneth J(oseph) 1934- 57-60
De-la-NOY, Michael 1934- 153
de Lantagne, Cecile
See Cloutier-Wojciechowska, Cecile
Delany, George (Battle) 1946- 114
Delany, Kevin F(rancis) X(avier) 1927- 73-76
Delany, Martin Robinson 1812-1885 DLB 50
Delany, Paul 1937- CANR-41
Earlier sketches in CA 29-32R, CANR-19
Delany, Samuel R(ay, Jr.) 1942- CANR-43
Earlier sketches in CA 81-84, CANR-27
See also AAYA 24
See also BLC 1
See also BW 2
See also CLC 8, 14, 38
See also DAM MULT
See also DLB 8, 33
See also MTCW 1
Delany, Sheila 1940- 112
De La Pedraja, Rene 1951- 145
de la Pena, Augustin (Mateo) 1942- 115
Delaplane, Stanton Hill 1907-1988 25-28R
Obituary 125
Delaporte, Ernest P(ierre) 1924- 97-100
Delaporte, Francois Louis 1941- 137
Delaporte, Theophile
See Green, Julian (Hartridge)
de la Portilla, Marta (Rosa) 1927- 61-64
De Lapp, Ardyce Lucile 1903- 97-100
DeLapp, George Leslie 1895- 102
De La Ramee, (Marie) Louise 1839-1908
See Ouida
See also SATA 20
de la Renta, Francoise de Langiade 1921(?)-1983 Obituary 110
de la Roche, Mazo 1879-1961 CANR-30
Earlier sketch in CA 85-88
See also CLC 14
See also DLB 68
See also SATA 64
De La Roche Saint Andre, Anne 1950- SATA 75
Delarue, Jean
See Dreze, Jean
De La Salle, Innocent
See Hartmann, Sadakichi
Delasanta, Rodney 1932- 33-36R
de las Cuevas, Raymon
See Harrington, Mark Raymond
de las Lunas, Carmencita
See Trocchi, Alexander
de la Torre, Jose 1943- 112
De La Torre, Lillian
See McCue, Lillian Bueno
de la Torre, Victor Raul Haya
See Haya de la Torre, Victor Raul
de la Torre-Bueno, Lillian
See McCue, Lillian Bueno
DeLatte, Carolyn E(lizabeth) 1943- 112
Delattre, Pierre 1930- 105
Delatush, Edith G. 1921- 124
de Laubenfels, David J(ohn) 1925- 53-56
Delaunay, Charles 1911-1988 Obituary 125
de Launay, Jacques F(orment) 1924- CANR-3
Earlier sketch in CA 9-12R
Delaunay(-Terk), Sonia 1885-1979 128
Delaune, (Jewel) Lynn (de Grummond) CANR-21
Earlier sketch in CA 1-4R
See also SATA 7
DeLaura, David J(oseph) 1930- 21-24R
DeLaurentis, Louise Budde 1920- 5-8R
See also SATA 12
Delavigne, Jean-Francois Casimir 1793-1843 DLB 192
de la Warr, George Walter 1904-1969 CAP-1
Earlier sketch in CA 13-16
Delay(-Tubiana), Claude 1944- CANR-33
Earlier sketches in CA 53-56, CANR-4
Delbanco, Nicholas (Franklin) 1942- CANR-55
Earlier sketches in CA 17-20R, CANR-29
See also CAAS 2
See also CLC 6, 13
See also DLB 6
del Barco, Lucy Salamanca 1900(?)-1989 17-20R
Obituary 130
See also SATA-Obit 64
Delblanc, Sven (Axel Herman) 1931- 149
Del Boca, Angelo 1925- 25-28R
Delbridge, Rosemary 1949(?)-1981 Obituary 105
Del Caro, Adrian 1952- 137
del Castillo, Michel 1933- 109
See also CLC 38
del Castillo, Richard Griswold
See Griswold del Castillo, Richard
Delcroix, Carlo 1896-1977 Obituary 73-76
Delderfield, Eric R(aymond) 1909- CANR-4
Earlier sketch in CA 53-56
See also SATA 14
Delderfield, Ronald Frederick 1912-1972 CANR-47
Obituary 37-40R
Earlier sketch in CA 73-76
See also DAM POP
See also SATA 20
Delear, Frank J. 1914- CANR-9
Earlier sketch in CA 21-24R
Deledda, Grazia (Cosima) 1875(?)-1936 Brief entry 123
See also TCLC 23
DeLeeuw, Adele (Louise) 1899-1988 CANR-1
Obituary 125
Earlier sketch in CA 1-4R
See also SATA 1, 30
See also SATA-Obit 56
DeLeeuw, Cateau 1903-1975 CANR-3
Earlier sketch in CA 1-4R
de Leeuw, Hendrik 1891-1977 Obituary 73-76
Delehanty, Randolph 1944- 123
de Leiris, Alain 1922- 73-76
DeLeon, David (Henry) 1947- Brief entry 114
De Leon, Nephtali 1945- 152
See also DLB 82
See also HW
See also SATA 97
deLeon, Peter 1943- 146
DeLeon, Richard Edward 1942- 140
de Lerma, Dominique-Rene 1928- CANR-1
Earlier sketch in CA 45-48
Delessert, Etienne 1941- CANR-37
Earlier sketches in CA 21-24R, CANR-13
See also MAICYA
See also SATA 46
See also SATA-Brief 27
Delessert, Jacquine
See Reiter, Victoria (Kelrich)
DeLey, Herbert (Clemone, Jr.) 1936- 21-24R
Delfano, M. M.
See Flammonde, Paris
DelFattore, Joan 142
Delfgaauw, Bernard(us Maria Ignatius) 1912- 21-24R
Delgado, Abelardo B(arrientos) 1931- 131
See also CAAS 15
See also DAM MST, MULT
See also DLB 82
See also HLC
See also HW
Delgado, Alan (George) 1909- CANR-5
Earlier sketch in CA 9-12R
Delgado, Hector L. 1949- 146
Delgado, James P. 1958- 136
Delgado, Jose Manuel R(odriguez) 1915- 29-32R
Delgado, Ramon (Louis) 1937- CANR-15
Earlier sketch in CA 85-88
Del Giudice, Daniele 1949- DLB 196
D'Elia, Donald John 1933- 57-60
D'Elia, Maria
See Goudiss, Maria Agnes D'Elia
De Libero, Libero 1906-1981 DLB 114
Delibes, Miguel
See Delibes Setien, Miguel
See also CLC 8, 18
Delibes Setien, Miguel 1920- CANR-32
Earlier sketches in CA 45-48, CANR-1
See also Delibes, Miguel
See also HW
See also MTCW 1
Delicado, Pepe
See Raskin, Jonah (Seth)
Deligiorgis, Stavros (George) 1933- 61-64
Deligne, Pierre (R.) 1944- 155
DeLillo, Don 1936- CANR-21
Earlier sketch in CA 81-84
See also BEST 89:1
See also CLC 8, 10, 13, 27, 39, 54, 76
See also DAM NOV, POP
See also DLB 6, 173
See also MTCW 1
de Lima, Agnes 1887(?)-1974 Obituary 53-56
De Lima, Clara Rosa 1922- CANR-6
Earlier sketch in CA 57-60
de Lima, Sigrid 1921- 25-28R
Delinsky, Barbara (Ruth Greenberg) 1945- CANR-30
Earlier sketch in CA 111
de Lint, Charles (Henri Diederick Hoefsmit) 1951- 126
Delisle, Francoise 1886(?)-1974 Obituary 53-56
De Lisle, Harold F. 1933- 158
de Lisser, H. G.
See De Lisser, H(erbert) G(eorge)
See also DLB 117
De Lisser, H(erbert) G(eorge) 1878-1944 152
Brief entry 109
See also de Lisser, H. G.
See also BW 2
See also TCLC 12
Delius, Anthony (Ronald St. Martin) 1916- CANR-12
Earlier sketch in CA 17-20R
Delk, Robert Carlton 1920- 45-48
Dell, Belinda
See Bowden, Jean
Dell, Christopher 1927- 65-68
Dell, E(dward) T(homas), Jr. 1923- 13-16R
Dell, Edmund 1921- 103
Dell, Floyd 1887-1969 Obituary 89-92
See also DLB 9
Dell, Jeffrey 1899-1985(?) Obituary 116
Dell, Roberta E(lizabeth) 1946- 81-84
Dell, Sidney 1918- CANR-17
Earlier sketches in CA 5-8R, CANR-2
Della Femina, Jerry 1936- Brief entry 111
Della-Piana, Gabriel M. 1926- 73-76
delle Grazie, Marie Eugenie 1864-1931 DLB 81
Deller, John J. 1931- 134
delle Stelle, Pier Luigi Bellini
See Bellini delle Stelle, Pier Luigi
Dellheim, Charles (Jay) 1952- 128
Dellin, Lubomir A. D. 1920- 45-48
Dellinger, David (T.) 1915- 65-68
Delloff, Irving Arthur 1920- 13-16R
Delman, David 1924- Brief entry 115
Delmar, Ken 1941- 121
Del Mar, Marcia 1950- 105
Del Mar, Norman (Rene) 1919- 149
Delmar, Roy
See Wexler, Jerome (LeRoy)
Delmar, Vina (Croter) 1905-1990 65-68
Obituary 130
Del Martia, Astron
See Fearn, John Russell
Delmer, Denis Sefton 1904- 5-8R
Delmonico, Andrea
See Morrison, Eula Atwood
Delo, David Michael 1938- 146
De Loach, Allen (Wayne) 1939- CANR-16
Earlier sketch in CA 85-88
DeLoach, Charles F. 1927- 37-40R
DeLoach, Clarence, Jr. 1936- 57-60
de Lomellini, C. A.
See Kelley, (Kathleen) Alita
Delon, Floyd G(urney) 1929- CANR-21
Earlier sketch in CA 69-72
de Lone, Richard H. 1940- 101
DeLone, Ruth
See Rankin, Ruth (DeLone) I(rvine)
Deloney, Thomas (?)-1600 DLB 167
De Long, David G. 1939- 139
De Long, Julie
See Hay, Millicent V.
DeLong, Lea Rosson 1947- CANR-48
Earlier sketch in CA 119
DeLong, Thomas A(nderton) 1935- CANR-25
Earlier sketch in CA 106
de Longchamps, Joanne (Cutten) 1923- CANR-3
Earlier sketch in CA 9-12R
De Lora, Joann S.
See Sandlin, Joann S(chepers) De Lora
DeLorean, John Z(achary) 1925- 122
DeLorenzo, Lorisa Mernette 1951- 117
DeLorenzo, Robert John 1947- 117
Deloria, Ella (Cara) 1889-1971(?) 152
See also DAM MULT
See also DLB 175
See also NNAL
Deloria, Vine (Victor), Jr. 1933- CANR-48
Earlier sketches in CA 53-56, CANR-5, 20
See also CLC 21
See also DAM MULT
See also DLB 175
See also MTCW 1
See also NNAL
See also SATA 21
Delorme, Andre
See Julien, Charles-Andre
Delorme, Michele
See Cranston, Mechthild
Delort, Robert 1932- 102
de los Reyes, Gabriel 45-48
de los Rios, Francisco Giner
See Giner de los Rios, Francisco
Deloughery, Grace L. 1933- 33-36R
de Loune, Henry
See Popham, Peter (Nicholas Home)
Delp, Michael W(illiam) 1948- 77-80
Delpar, Helen 1936- 53-56
Delphos, Omar
See Ald, Roy A(llison)
del Rey, Judy-Lynn 1943-1986 124
Obituary 118
del Rey, Lester 1915-1993 CANR-17
Obituary 141
Earlier sketch in CA 65-68
See also DLB 8
See also MTCW 1
See also SATA 22
See also SATA-Obit 76
Del Rio, Rikki
See Gordon, Lewis Ricardo
Delta
See Dennett, Herbert Victor
Delton, Jina 1961- 106
Delton, Judy 1931- CANR-25
Earlier sketches in CA 57-60, CANR-8
See also AAYA 6
See also JRDA
See also SAAS 9
See also SATA 14, 77
Delton, Julie 1959- 108
DeLuca, A(ngelo) Michael 1912-1976 21-24R
Obituary 120
De Luca, Charles J. 1927- 73-76
De Lucca, John 1920- 41-44R
Delulio, John 1938- SATA 15
Delumeau, Jean 1923- 97-100
De Luna, Frederick Adolph 1928- 65-68
Delupis, Ingrid 1939- 103
del Valle, Teresa 1937- 149
Del Vecchio, Deborah 1950- 146
Del Vecchio, John M(ichael) 1947- 110
See also CLC 29
See also DLBD 9
Delves, Peter J(ohn) 1951- 144
Delving, Michael
See Williams, Jay
DeLynn, Jane 1946- CANR-72
Earlier sketch in CA 77-80
DeLyser, Femmy 1935- 110
Delzell, Charles F(loyd) 1920- CANR-2
Earlier sketch in CA 1-4R
Demac, Donna A. 1952- 121
de Madariaga, Isabel 1919- 107
Demaine, Don
See Drinkall, Gordon (Don)
de Man, Paul (Adolph Michel) 1919-1983 CANR-61
Obituary 111
Earlier sketch in CA 128
See also CLC 55
See also DLB 67
See also MTCW 1
de Mandiargues, Andre Pieyre
See Pieyre de Mandiargues, Andre
de Manio, Jack 1914-1988 61-64
Obituary 127
Demant, Vigo Auguste 1893-1983 Obituary 109
de Mar, Esmeralda
See Mellen, Ida M(ay)
Demaray, Donald E(ugene) 1926- CANR-37
Earlier sketches in CA 1-4R, CANR-1, 16
De Marco, Angelus A. 1916- 9-12R
De Marco, Arlene AITN 1
DeMarco, Donald 1937- CANR-49
Earlier sketches in CA 61-64, CANR-7, 24
de Mare, Eric S. 1910- CANR-6
Earlier sketch in CA 9-12R
deMare, George 1912- 21-24R
Demarest, Bruce A(lvin) 1935- 118
Demarest, Chris(topher) L(ynn) 1951- 109
See also SATA 45, 82
See also SATA-Brief 44
Demarest, Doug
See Barker, Will
Demarest, Michael 1924(?)-1984 Obituary 112
Demarest, Phyllis Gordon 1911-1969 Obituary 104
Demarest, Rosemary Regina 1914- 116
Demarest, Victoria Booth(-Clibborn) 1890-1982 124
Obituary 112
Demaret, James Newton 1910-1983 Obituary 111
Demaret, Jimmy
See Demaret, James Newton
Demaret, Pierre 1943- CANR-12
Earlier sketch in CA 61-64
De Maria, Robert 1928- CANR-5
Earlier sketch in CA 1-4R
De Marinis, Marco 1949- 156
De Marinis, Rick 1934- CANR-50
Earlier sketches in CA 57-60, CANR-9, 25
See also CAAS 24
See also CLC 54
Demaris, Ovid
See Desmarais, Ovid E.
De Marly, Diana 1939- 125
DeMarr, Mary Jean 1932- 151
DeMartini, Rodney J(ames) 1947- 113
De Martino, Manfred F(rank) 1924- Brief entry 117
Demas, Vida 1927- 49-52
See also SATA 9
deMatteo, Donna 1941- 25-28R
de Mauny, Erik 1920- CANR-13
Earlier sketch in CA 33-36R
deMause, Lloyd 1931- 65-68
Demb, Ada 1948- 138
Dembart, Lee 1946- 133
Dembner, Red
See Dembner, S. Arthur
Dembner, S. Arthur 1920-1990 Obituary 131
Dembo, L(awrence) S(anford) 1929- CANR-2
Earlier sketch in CA 1-4R
Dembry, R. Emmet
See Murfree, Mary Noailles
Dembski, Stephen (Michael) 1949- 128

Demby, William 1922- 81-84
See also BLC 1
See also BW 1
See also CLC 53
See also DAM MULT
See also DLB 33
de Medici, Lorenza 1926- 141
de Medici, Marino 1933- 89-92
De Mejo, Oscar 1911- 111
See also SATA 40
Dement, William Charles 1928- Brief entry 105
De Mente, Boye 1928- CANR-8
Earlier sketch in CA 21-24R
de Menton, Francisco
See Chin, Frank (Chew, Jr.)
Demeny, Janos 1915- 118
Demers, David (Pearce) 1953- 162
Demers, James 1942- 97-100
de Mesne, Eugene (Frederick Peter Cheshire)
CANR-25
Earlier sketch in CA 41-44R
de Mesquita, Bruce James Bueno
See Bueno de Mesquita, Bruce James
de Messieres, Nicole 1930- 107
See also SATA 39
Demetillo, Ricaredo 1920- 102
Demetrakopoulos, Stephanie Anne 1937- 111
Demetrius, James Kleon 1924- CANR-13
Earlier sketch in CA 21-24R
Demetz, Peter 1922- CANR-14
Earlier sketch in CA 65-68
de Meung, Jean
See de Meun, Jean
Demi
See Hitz, Demi
De Michael, Don(ald Anthony)
1928-1982 Obituary 106
Demidenko, Helen
See Darville, Helen (Fiona)
Demijohn, Thom
See Disch, Thomas M(ichael)
and Sladek, John
de Milan, Sister Jean
See Jean, Gabrielle (Lucille)
D'Emilio, A. Edward 1919(?)-1987 Obituary 122
D'Emilio, John 1948- 135
de Mille, Agnes
See Prude, Agnes George de Mille
DeMille, Alexandria
See Du Breuil, (Elizabeth) L(or)inda
De Mille, Cecil B(lount) 1881-1959 149
Brief entry 115
De Mille, James 1833-1880 DLB 99
De Mille, Nelson
See Levinson, Leonard
DeMille, Nelson (Richard) 1943- CANR-62
Earlier sketches in CA 57-60, CANR-6, 25, 46
See also BEST 90:3
See also DAM POP
de Mille, Richard 1922- CANR-13
Earlier sketch in CA 21-24R
Deming, Alison Hawthorne 1946- 148
Deming, Barbara 1917-1984 CANR-71
Earlier sketches in CA 85-88, CANR-15
Deming, Kirk
See Drago, Harry Sinclair
Deming, Louise Macpherson
1916-1976 Obituary 61-64
Deming, Philander 1829-1915 DLB 74
Deming, Richard 1915- CANR-3
Earlier sketch in CA 9-12R
See also SATA 24
Deming, Robert H. 1937- 21-24R
DeMirjian, Arto, Jr. 1931- 57-60
De Molen, Richard Lee 1938- 45-48
Demone, Harold W(ellington), Jr. 1924- CANR-9
Earlier sketch in CA 5-8R
De Monfried, Henri 1879(?)-1974 Obituary 53-56
Demong, Phyllis 1920- 106
de Montalvo, Luis Galvez
See Avalle-Arce, Juan Bautista de
DeMonte, Claudia 1947- 114
de Montebello, Guy-Philippe Lannes 1936- 45-48
de Montfort, Guy
See Johnson, Donald Mcl(ntosh)
de Montherlant, Henry (Milon)
See Montherlant, Henry (Milon) de
De MONTREVILLE POLAK, Doris
1904(?)-1974 Obituary 49-52
De Mordaunt, Walter J(ulius) 1925- 33-36R
Demorest, Jean-Jacques 1920- 5-8R
Demorest, Stephen 1949- CANR-20
Earlier sketch in CA 101
Demorest, William Jennings 1822-1895 DLB 79
De Morgan, William 1839-1917 DLB 153
De Morny, Peter
See Wynne-Tyson, Esme
Demos, John Putnam 1937- 137
Demos, Paul 1888-1983 Obituary 109
Demosthenes 384B.C.-322B.C. DLB 176
Demotes, Michael
See Burgess, Michael (Roy)
DeMott, Benjamin (Hailer) 1924- CANR-49
Earlier sketch in CA 5-8R
De Mott, Donald W(arren) 1928- 61-64
DeMott, Robert (James) 1943- 141
DeMott, Wes 1952- 164
de Mourgues, Odette (Marie Helene Louise)
1914-1988 5-8R
Obituary 126
Dempewolff, Richard F(rederic) 1914- CANR-1
Earlier sketch in CA 1-4R
Dempsey, David Knapp 1914- CANR-2
Earlier sketch in CA 5-8R
Dempsey, Hugh Aylmer 1929- CANR-51
Earlier sketches in CA 69-72, CANR-11, 26
Dempsey, Jack
See Dempsey, William Harrison
Dempsey, Lotta 101
Dempsey, Paul K(enneth) 1935- CANR-19
Earlier sketch in CA 25-28R
Dempsey, Richard A(llen) 1932- 61-64
Dempsey, William Harrison 1895-1983 89-92
Obituary 109
Dempster, Barry 1952- CANR-32
Earlier sketch in CA 113
Dempster, Chris 1943- 106
Dempster, Derek David 1924- 13-16R
Dempster, Stuart 1936- 104
Demske, James Michael 1922-1994 29-32R
Obituary 145
Demski, Eva 1944- 135
Demski, Joel S. 1940- 148
de Munck, Victor C. 1948- 168
Demura, Fumio 1940- CANR-12
Earlier sketch in CA 61-64
Demus, Otto 1902-1990 144
Demuth, Norman (Frank) 1898-1968 CAP-1
Earlier sketch in CA 13-14
Demuth, Patricia Brennan 1948- 118
See also SATA 84
See also SATA-Brief 51
Demy, Jacques 1931-1990 148
Den, Petr
See Radimsky, Ladislaw
Denali, Peter
See Holm, Don(ald Raymond)
de Natale, Francine
See Malzberg, Barry N(athaniel)
Denbeaux, Fred J. 1914- 5-8R
Denbie, Roger
See Green, Alan (Baer)
Denbigh, Kenneth George 1911- 106
Den Boer, James (Drew) 1937- CANR-10
Earlier sketch in CA 21-24R
Denby, David 1943(?)- 158
Denby, Edwin (Orr) 1903-1983 138
Obituary 110
See also CLC 48
Dendel, Esther (Sietmann Warner) 1910- 102
Dender, Jay
See Deindorfer, Robert Greene
Dendle, Brian J(ohn) 1936- CANR-42
Earlier sketch in CA 116
Dendy, Marshall C(oleman) 1902- CAP-2
Earlier sketch in CA 17-18
DeNeef, Arthur Leigh 1942- 102
Deneen, James R. 1928- 45-48
Denenberg, Herbert S(idney) 1929- 37-40R
Denes, Magda 1934-1996 158
de Neufville, Richard 1939- 53-56
Denevan, William M(axfield) 1931- 41-44R
de Nevers, Noel (Howard) 1932- 37-40R
DeNevi, Donald P. 1937- 37-40R
Denevi, Marco 1922- HW
Denfeld, Duane (Henry) 1939- 41-44R
Deng, Francis Mading 1938- 157
Deng, William 1929- 13-16R
Deng, Xiao Hua 1953- 139
Dengler, Dieter 1938- 102
Dengler, Marianna (Herron) 1935- 102
Dengler, Sandy 1939- CANR-30
Earlier sketch in CA 112
See also SATA 54
See also SATA-Brief 40
Denham, Alice 1933- 21-24R
Denham, Avery Strakosch (?)-1970 Obituary 104
Denham, Bertie 1927- 93-96
Denham, H(enry) M(angles) 1897-1993 61-64
Obituary 142
Denham, Henry fl. 1559-1590(?) DLB 170
Denham, John 1615-1669 DLB 58, 126
Denham, Mary Orr 1918- CANR-2
Earlier sketch in CA 1-4R
Denham, Reginald 1894-1983 CAP-1
Obituary 109
Earlier sketch in CA 13-16
Denham, Robert D(ayton) 1938- 53-56
Denham, Sully
See Budd, Mavis
Denhardt, Robert Moorman 1912- 101
den Hollander, A(rie) Nicolaas Jan 1906-1976
CAP-2
Earlier sketch in CA 29-32
Denholm, Therese Mary Zita White 1933- 9-12R
Denholtz, Elaine (Grudin) CANR-13
Earlier sketch in CA 73-76
Dening, Greg 1931- 107
Denis, Armand 1896(?)-1971 Obituary 104
Denis, Charlotte
See Plimmer, Charlotte
and Plimmer, Denis
Denis, Julio
See Cortazar, Julio
Denis, Manuel Maldonado
See Maldonado-Denis, Manuel
Denis, Michaela Holdsworth 13-16R
Denis, Paul 1909- 21-24R
Denisoff, R. Serge 1939- 33-36R
Denison, Barbara 1926- 13-16R
Denison, Corrie
See Partridge, Eric (Honeywood)
Denison, Edward F(ulton) 1915-1992 21-24R
Obituary 140
Denison, Merrill 1893-1975 DLB 92
Denison, (John) Michael (Terence Wellesley)
1915- 109
Denison, Norman 1925- 65-68
Denker, Henry 1912- CANR-57
Earlier sketches in CA 33-36R, CANR-31
See also AITN 1
Denkler, Horst 1935- CANR-19
Earlier sketches in CA 53-56, CANR-4
Denkstein, Vladimir 1906- 103
Denlinger, A(nna) Martha 1931- 113
Denman, D(onald) R(obert) 1911- CANR-8
Earlier sketch in CA 61-64
Denmark, Florence L. 1932- 85-88
Denmark, Harrison
See Zelazny, Roger (Joseph)
Dennard, Deborah 1953- 146
See also SATA 78
Dennehy, Raymond L(eo) 1934- 109
Dennery, Adolphe Philippe 1811-1899 DLB 192
Dennes, William Ray 1898- 73-76
Dennett, Daniel C(lement) 1942- CANR-53
Earlier sketches in CA 97-100, CANR-35
Dennett, Herbert Victor 1893- CANR-5
Earlier sketch in CA 5-8R
Dennett, Nolan A. 1950- 147
Denney, Diana 1910- 104
See also SATA 25
Denney, Myron Keith 1930- 102
Denney, Reuel (Nicholas) 1913-1995 CANR-2
Obituary 148
Earlier sketch in CA 1-4R
Denney, Robert (Eugene) 1929- 140
Dennie, Joseph 1768-1812 DLB 37, 43, 59, 73
Denning, A. T.
See Denning, Alfred Thompson
Denning, Alfred Thompson 1899- 143
Brief entry 115
Denning, Basil W. 1928- 33-36R
Denning, Candace 1946- 125
Denning, Melita
See Barcynski, Vivian G(odfrey)
Denning, Patricia
See Willis, Corinne Denneny
Dennis, Arthur
See Edmonds, Arthur Denis
Dennis, Benjamin G. 1929- 45-48
Dennis, Carl 1939- 77-80
Dennis, Charles 1946- CANR-17
Earlier sketch in CA 65-68
Dennis, Deborah Ellis 1950- 116
Dennis, Everette E. 1942- 41-44R
Dennis, Henry C(harles) 1918- 41-44R
Dennis, Ian 1952- 125
Dennis, Jack B(onnell) 1931- 155
Dennis, James M(unn) 1932- 102
Dennis, John 1658-1734 DLB 101
Dennis, John V(alue) 1916- 107
Dennis, Landt 1937- 65-68
Dennis, Lane T(imothy) 1943- 93-96
Dennis, Lawrence 1893-1977 Obituary 73-76
Dennis, Morgan 1891(?)-1960 SATA 18
Dennis, Nigel (Forbes) 1912-1989 25-28R
Obituary 129
See also CLC 8
See also DLB 13, 15
See also MTCW 1
Dennis, Patrick
See Tanner, Edward Everett III
Dennis, Peggy 1909-1993 77-80
Obituary 143
Dennis, Peter (John) 1945- 41-44R
Dennis, Ralph AITN 1
Dennis, Richard (John) 1949- 118
Dennis, Robert C. 1920-1983 101
Obituary 110
Dennis, Rutledge M(elvin) 1939- 115
Dennis, Suzanne Easton 1922- 25-28R
Dennis, Wayne 1905-1976 17-20R
Obituary 69-72
Dennis, Wesley 1903-1966 135
See also MAICYA
See also SATA 18
Dennis-Jones, H(arold) 1915- CANR-8
Earlier sketch in CA 57-60
Dennison, A(lfred) Dudley, Jr. 1914- CANR-9
Earlier sketch in CA 57-60
Dennison, George (Harris) 1925-1987 CANR-44
Obituary 123
Earlier sketch in CA 101
See also CAAS 6
Dennison, George M(arshel) 1935- 53-56
Dennison, Milo
See Cantwell, Lois
Dennison, Peter (John) 1942- 124
Dennison, Sam 1926- CANR-28
Earlier sketch in CA 109
Dennison, Shane 1933- 73-76
Denniston, Denise 1946- 69-72
Denniston, Elinore 1900-1978 Obituary 81-84
See also SATA-Obit 24
Denniston, Lyle (William) 1931- 65-68
Denny, Alma 1912- 89-92
Denny, Brian
See Doughty, Bradford
Denny, Carol
See Brandt, Carol
Denny, John Howard 1920- CAP-1
Earlier sketch in CA 9-10
Denny, Ludwell 1894-1970 Obituary 29-32R
Denny, M(aurice) Ray 1918- CANR-14
Earlier sketch in CA 41-44R
Denny, Norman (George) 1901-1982 107
See also SATA 43
Denny, Robert 1920- 135
Denny-Brown, Derek Ernest
1901-1981 Obituary 103
Dennys, Joyce (a pseudonym) 1895- 121
Dennys, Rodney Onslow 1911-1993 85-88
Obituary 142
Denoeu, Francois 1898-1975 53-56
Denomme, Robert T. 1930- 25-28R
Denoon, Donald (John Noble) 1940- CANR-14
Earlier sketch in CA 73-76
DeNovo, John A(ugust) 1916- 9-12R
Densen-Gerber, Judianne 1934- 37-40R
Denslow, Sharon Phillips 1947- 136
See also SATA 68
Denslow, W(illiam) W(allace) 1856-1915 CLR 15
See also DLB 188
See also SATA 16
Densmore, John 1944- 136
Denson, John Lee 1903-1982 Obituary 108
Dent, Alan (Holmes) 1905-1978 CANR-5
Earlier sketch in CA 9-12R
Dent, Anthony Austen 1915- CANR-15
Earlier sketch in CA 25-28R
Dent, Colin 1921- 13-16R
Dent, Harold (Collett) 1894-1995 CANR-5
Obituary 147
Earlier sketch in CA 5-8R
Dent, Harry (Shuler) 1930- 81-84
Dent, Lester 1904(?)-1959 161
Brief entry 112
See also TCLC 72
Dent, Richard J. 1951- 153
Dent, Robert William 1917- 105
Dent, Thomas C(ovington) 1932- 125
Brief entry 122
See also Dent, Tom
See also BW 1
Dent, Tom
See Dent, Thomas C(ovington)
See also DLB 38
Dentan, Robert C(laude) 1907- CANR-2
Earlier sketch in CA 1-4R
Dentinger, Jane 1951- CANR-56
Earlier sketch in CA 123
Dentinger, Stephen
See Hoch, Edward D(entinger)
Dentler, Robert A(rnold) 1928- CANR-17
Earlier sketches in CA 1-4R, CANR-1
Denton, Bradley (Clayton) 1958- 158
Denton, Charles F(rederick) 1942- 37-40R
Denton, D. Keith 1948- 112
Denton, Daniel 1626(?)-1703 DLB 24
Denton, H(arry) M. 1882- CAP-1
Earlier sketch in CA 11-12
Denton, Herbert H(oward), Jr.
1943-1989 Obituary 128
Denton, J(effrey) H(oward) 1939- CANR-15
Earlier sketch in CA 41-44R
Denton, Jeremiah A(ndrew), Jr. 1924- CANR-31
Earlier sketch in CA 69-72
Denton, Kady MacDonald 134
See also SATA 66
Denton, Wallace 1928- 1-4R
d'Entreves, Alexander (Passerin)
1902-1985 Obituary 118
Dentry, Robert
See White, Osmar (Egmont Dorkin)
Denues, Celia 1915- 41-44R
Den Uyl, Douglas J(ohn) 1950- 117
Denver, Boone
See Rennie, James Alan
Denver, Drake C.
See Nye, Nelson C(oral)
Denver, John 1943-1997 159
Denver, Lee
See Gribble, Leonard (Reginald)
Denver, Rod
See Edson, J(ohn) T(homas)
Denver, Walt
See Redding, Robert Hull
and Sherman, Jory (Tecumseh)
Denvir, Bernard 1917- 115
Denyer, Nicholas (Charles) 1955- 136
Denys, Teresa (a pseudonym) 1947- 105
Denzel, Justin F(rancis) 1917- CANR-42
Earlier sketches in CA 53-56, CANR-4
See also SATA 46
See also SATA-Brief 38
Denzer, Ann Wiseman
See Wiseman, Ann (Sayre)
Denzer, Peter W(orthington) 1921- 5-8R
Denzin, Norman K(ent) 1941- CANR-57
Earlier sketches in CA 29-32R, CANR-12, 30
de Obaldia, Rene
See Obaldia, Rene de
de Oca, Marco Antonio Montes
See Montes de Oca, Marco Antonio
de Oliveira, Paulo C(arlos) 1953- 114
Deon, Michel 1919- CANR-37
Earlier sketches in CA 37-40R, CANR-16
de Palchi, Alfredo 1926- 163
De Palma, Brian (Russell) 1940- 109
See also CLC 20
dePaola, Thomas Anthony 1934- CANR-37
Earlier sketches in CA 49-52, CANR-2
See also dePaola, Tomie
See also MAICYA
See also SATA 11, 59
dePaola, Tomie
See dePaola, Thomas Anthony
See also CLR 4, 24
See also DLB 61
See also SAAS 15
de Paor, Risteard
See Power, Richard
Depardieu, Gerard 1948- 156
deParrie, Paul 1949- SATA 74
Depas, Spencer 1925- 69-72
DePaul, Edith
See Delatush, Edith G.
DePauw, Linda Grant 1940- CANR-9
Earlier sketch in CA 21-24R
See also SATA 24
Depel, Jim 1936- 73-76

de Pereda, Prudencio 1912- ... CANR-4
Earlier sketch in CA 1-4R
Depestre, Rene 1926- Brief entry ... 113
DePew, Alfred (Mansfield) 1952- ... 141
Depew, Arthur M(c Kinley) 1896-1976 ... 41-44R
Depew, Wally
See Depew, Walter Westerfield
Depew, Walter Westerfield 1924- ... 5-8R
De Pietro, Albert 1913- ... 69-72
de Polman, Willem
See Nichols, Dale (William)
De Polnay, Peter 1906-1984 ... 73-76
Obituary ... 114
DePorte, Anton W. 1928- ... 124
DePorte, Michael V(ital) 1939- ... 49-52
Depp, Roberta J. 1947- ... 101
de Pre, Jean-Anne
See Avallone, Michael (Angelo, Jr.)
DePree, Gladis (Lenore) 1933- ... 101
DePree, Gordon 1930- ... 101
Depta, Victor M(arshall) 1939- ... 49-52
De Puy, Norman R(obert) 1929- ... 97-100
Dequasie, Andrew 1929- ... CANR-35
Earlier sketch in CA 114
De Quille, Dan
See Wright, William
De Quincey, Thomas 1785-1859 ... CDBLB 1789-1832
See also DLB 110; 144
DeRan, David 1946- ... SATA 76
Der arme Hartmann (?)-c. 1150(?) ... DLB 148
D'Erasmo, Martha 1939- ... 81-84
Derber, Milton 1915- Brief entry ... 106
Derby, George Horatio 1823-1861 ... DLB 11
Derby, Pat 1942- ... 69-72
Derby, Sally 1934- ... 155
See also SATA 89
Der Derian, James (Arthur) 1955- ... 152
Derderian, Yeghishe 1910(?)-1990 Obituary ... 130
de Regniers, Beatrice Schenk (Freedman) 1914- ... CANR-26
Earlier sketches in CA 13-16R, CANR-6
See also MAICYA
See also SAAS 6
See also SATA 2, 68
Dereksen, David
See Stacton, David (Derek)
Deren, Eleanora 1908(?)-1961 Obituary ... 111
See also Deren, Maya
Deren, Maya 1917-1961
See Deren, Eleanora
See also CLC 16, 102
Derenberg, Walter J(ulius) 1903-1975 Obituary ... 61-64
De Reneville, Mary Margaret Motley Sheridan 1912- ... 5-8R
Dereske, Jo 1947- Obituary ... 163
See also SATA 72
de Reyna, Rudy 1914- ... CANR-10
Earlier sketch in CA 57-60
Derfler, (Arnold) Leslie 1933- ... CANR-9
Earlier sketch in CA 5-8R
deRham, Edith 1933- ... 13-16R
Derham, (Arthur) Morgan 1915- ... 13-16R
Der Hovanessian, Diana ... 124
Deriabin, Peter 1921- ... 134
Deric, Arthur J. 1926- ... 21-24R
de Ricci, Seymour 1881-1942 ... DLB 201
Dering, Joan (Rosalind Cordelia) 1917- ... 9-12R
De Risi, William J(oseph) 1938- ... 53-56
de Rivera, Joseph H(osmer) 1932- ... 41-44R
Derksen, Jeff 1958- ... 153
Derleth, August (William) 1909-1971 ... CANR-4
Obituary ... 29-32R
Earlier sketch in CA 1-4R
See also CLC 31
See also DLB 9
See also DLBD 17
See also SATA 5
Derman, Lou 1914(?)-1976 Obituary ... 65-68
Derman, Martha (Winn) ... SATA 74
Derman, Sarah Audrey 1915- ... CANR-17
Earlier sketch in CA 1-4R
See also SATA 11
Dermid, Jack 1923- ... 49-52
Dermout, Maria
See Dermout-Ingermann, Helena Antonia Maria Elisabeth
Dermout-Ingermann, Helena Antonia Maria 1888-1962 Obituary ... 114
Dern, Erolie Pearl Gaddis 1895-1966 ... CANR-6
Obituary ... 25-28R
Earlier sketch in CA 1-4R
Dern, Karl L(udwig) 1894- ... 57-60
Dern, Peggy
See Dern, Erolie Pearl Gaddis
Dernburg, Thomas F(rederick) 1930- ... CANR-2
Earlier sketch in CA 1-4R
Der Nersessian, Sirarpie 1896- ... 102
Der Nister 1884-1950 ... TCLC 56
de Robeck, Nesta 1886- ... CAP-2
Earlier sketch in CA 25-28
De Rochemont, Richard (Guertis) 1903-1982 Obituary ... 108
de Rocher, Gregory (David) 1943- ... 114
DeRoin, Nancy 1934- ... 65-68
de Romaszkan, Gregor 1894- ... 13-16R
de Romilly, Jacqueline (David) 1913- ... 144
de Roo, Anne Louise 1931- ... CANR-51
Earlier sketch in CA 103
See also SATA 25, 84
de Roos, Robert (William) 1912- ... 9-12R
de Ropp, Robert S(ylvester) 1913- ... 17-20R
Deror, Yehezkel
See Dror, Yehezkel
deRosa, Dee ... SATA 70
DeRosa, Peter (Clement) 1932- ... CANR-9
Earlier sketch in CA 21-24R
DeRose, David J(oseph) 1957- ... 144
DeRosier, Arthur H(enry), Jr. 1931- ... 29-32R
De Rosis, Helen A. 1918- ... 122
Brief entry ... 107
De Rossi, Claude J(oseph) 1942- ... 53-56
Derossi, Flavia 1926- ... 112
de Rothschild, Guy (Edouard Alphonse Paul) 1909- ... 129
de Rothschild, Pauline (Fairfax-Potter) 1908(?)-1976 Obituary ... 65-68
de Rougemont, Denis (Louis) 1906-1985 ... 154
Obituary ... 118
de Roussan, Jacques 1929- ... 123
Brief entry ... 110
See also SATA-Brief 31
de Routisie, Albert
See Aragon, Louis
de Roxas, Juan Bartolome
See Rubia Barcia, Jose
Derr, Mark (Burgess) 1950- ... 135
Derr, Richard L(uther) 1930- ... 53-56
Derr, Thomas Sieger 1931- ... 53-56
Derrett, J(ohn) Duncan M(artin) 1922- ... CANR-44
Earlier sketches in CA 13-16R, CANR-6, 21
Derrick, Graham
See Raby, Derek Graham
Derrick, Lionel
See Cunningham, Chet
Derrick, Paul 1916- ... CAP-1
Earlier sketch in CA 9-10
Derricotte, Toi 1941- ... CANR-32
Earlier sketch in CA 113
See also BW 2
Derrida, Jacques 1930- ... 127
Brief entry ... 124
See also CLC 24, 87
Derriman, James Parkyns 1922- ... 106
Derry, John W(esley) 1933- ... CANR-3
Earlier sketch in CA 5-8R
Derry, (Thomas) Ramsay 1939- ... 110
Derry, Thomas Kingston 1905- ... CANR-4
Earlier sketch in CA 1-4R
Derry Down Derry
See Lear, Edward
Dershowitz, Alan M(orton) 1938- ... CANR-44
Earlier sketches in CA 25-28R, CANR-11
Dersonnes, Jacques
See Simenon, Georges (Jacques Christian)
Dertouzos, Michael L. 1936- ... 21-24R
Derum, James Patrick 1893- ... CAP-1
Earlier sketch in CA 13-14
De Ruth, Jan 1922- ... 33-36R
Dervaes, Claudine 1954- ... 167
Dervin, Brenda 1938- ... 29-32R
Dervin, Daniel A(rthur) 1935- ... 57-60
Derwent, Lavinia ... CANR-27
Earlier sketch in CA 69-72
See also SATA 14
Derwin, Jordan 1931- ... 13-16R
Dery, Mark 1959- ... 153
Dery, Tibor 1894-1977 Obituary ... 73-76
de Rycke, Laurence Joseph 1907-1989 Obituary ... 129
Derzhavin, Gavriil Romanovich 1743-1816 ... DLB 150
Desai, Anita 1937- ... CANR-53
Earlier sketches in CA 81-84, CANR-33
See also CLC 19, 37, 97
See also DAB
See also DAM NOV
See also MTCW 1
See also SATA 63
Desai, Boman 1950- ... CANR-71
Earlier sketch in CA 134
Desai, Meghnad 1940- ... 126
Desai, P(rasannavadan) B(hagwanji) 1924- ... 29-32R
Desai, Ram 1926- ... 5-8R
Desai, Rashmi H(arilal) 1928- ... 13-16R
Desai, Rupin W(alter) 1934- ... 45-48
de Ste. Croix, G(eoffrey) E(rnest) M(aurice) 1910- ... 73-76
de Saint-Gall, Auguste Amedee
See Strich, Christian
de St. Jorre, John 1936- ... 102
de Saint-Luc, Jean
See Glassco, John
de Saint Phalle, Therese 1930- ... CANR-21
Earlier sketch in CA 29-32R
de Saint Phalle, Thibaut 1918- ... 108
de Saint Roman, Arnaud
See Aragon, Louis
De Salamanca, Cristina Enriquez
See Enriquez de Salamanca, Cristina
DeSalvo, Joseph S(alvatore) 1938- ... 45-48
DeSalvo, Louise A(nita) 1942- ... CANR-62
Earlier sketches in CA 102, CANR-23
Desan, Wilfrid 1908- ... 61-64
Desani, G(ovindas) V(ishnoodas) 1909- ... CANR-70
Earlier sketch in CA 45-48
de Santa Ana, Julio 1934- ... 132
de Santillana, Giorgio Diaz 1902- ... CAP-1
Earlier sketch in CA 13-14
DeSantis, Mary Allen (Carpe) 1930- ... 9-12R
De Santis, Vincent P. 1916- ... CANR-4
Earlier sketch in CA 9-12R
De Santo, Charles P(asquale) 1923- ... 116
De Satge, John (Cosmo) 1928-1984 ... 124
Obituary ... 113
Desatnick, Robert L(awrence) 1931- ... 41-44R
Desaulniers, Gonzalve 1863-1934 ... DLB 92
de Sausmarez, (Lionel) Maurice 1915-1969 ... CAP-1
Earlier sketch in CA 11-12
de Saussure, Eric 1925- ... 105
de Saussure, Ferdinand 1857-1913 ... 168
Desbarats, Peter 1933- ... CANR-10
Earlier sketch in CA 17-20R
See also SATA 39
Des Barres, Pamela (Ann) 1948- ... CANR-57
Earlier sketch in CA 128
Desbiens, Jean-Paul 1927- ... DLB 53
Desborough, Vincent Robin d'Arba 1914-1978 Obituary ... 111
Descargues, Pierre 1925- ... CANR-14
Earlier sketch in CA 37-40R
Deschampsneufs, Henry Pierre Bernard 1911- ... CANR-6
Earlier sketch in CA 5-8R
de Schanschieff, Juliet Dymoke 1919- ... 106
Descharnes, Robert (Pierre) 1926- ... 69-72
De Schauensee, Rodolphe Meyer 1901-1984 ... 155
Deschenaux, Jacques 1945- ... 61-64
Deschin, Celia Spalter 1903- ... 104
Deschin, Jacob 1900(?)-1983 Obituary ... 110
Deschler, Lewis 1905-1976 Obituary ... 65-68
Deschner, Donald (Anthony) 1933- ... 21-24R
Deschner, (Hans) Guenther 1941- ... 41-44R
Deschner, Gunther
See Deschner, (Hans) Guenther
Deschner, John 1923- ... 81-84
de Schweinitz, Karl 1887-1975 ... 61-64
Descola, Philippe 1949- ... 151
Descombes, Vincent 1943- ... 136
de Selincourt, Aubrey 1894-1962 ... 73-76
See also SATA 14
DeSena, Carmine 1957- ... 151
de Sena, Jorge 1919-1978 Obituary ... 77-80
De Seversky, Alexander P(rocofieff) 1894-1974 Obituary ... 53-56
DeSeyn, Donna E. 1933- ... 21-24R
des Forets, Louis-Rene 1918- ... DLB 83
Desfosses, Helen 1945- ... 41-44R
Des Gagniers, Jean 1929- ... CANR-9
Earlier sketch in CA 65-68
Desguin, Guillard
See Humez, Nicholas (David)
DeShazo, Edith K(ind) 1920- ... 61-64
DeShazo, Elmer Anthony 1924- ... 37-40R
Deshen, Shlomo 1935- ... 57-60
Deshler, G(eorge) Byron 1903- ... 53-56
Deshpande, Chris 1950- ... 137
See also SATA 69
Deshpande, Shashi 1938- ... CANR-60
Earlier sketch in CA 128
DeSiano, Francis P(atrick) 1945- ... CANR-31
Earlier sketch in CA 112
Desiato, Luca 1941- ... DLB 196
De Sica, Vittorio 1901(?)-1974 Obituary ... 117
See also CLC 20
Desiderato, Otello 1926- ... 37-40R
de Silva, Alvaro 1949- ... 138
De Silva, Cara ... 165
Desimini, Lisa 1964- ... SATA 86
De Simone, Daniel V. 1930- ... 25-28R
Desjarlais, John 1953- ... 135
See also SATA 71
Desmangles, Leslie G. 1941- ... 144
Desmarais, Barbara G.
See Taylor, Barbara G.
Des Marais, Louise M(ercier) 1923- ... 110
Desmarais, Ovid E. 1919- ... CANR-23
Earlier sketches in CA 1-4R, CANR-4
Desmond, Adrian J(ohn) 1947- ... CANR-8
Earlier sketch in CA 61-64
See also SATA 51
Desmond, Alice Curtis 1897- ... CANR-2
Earlier sketch in CA 1-4R
See also SATA 8
Desmond, (Clarice) J(oanne) Patrick (Scholes) 1910- ... 9-12R
Desmond, John 1909(?)-1977 Obituary ... 73-76
Desmond, John F(rancis) 1939- ... 112
Desmond, Ray 1925- ... 120
Desmond, Robert W(illiam) 1900- ... CANR-12
Earlier sketch in CA 73-76
Desmond, Shaw 1877-1960 Obituary ... 89-92
Desmonde, William H(erbert) 1921- ... 1-4R
Desnica, Vladan 1905-1967 ... DLB 181
Desnos, Robert 1900-1945 ... 151
Brief entry ... 121
See also TCLC 22
De Sola, John
See Morland, Nigel
De Sola, Ralph 1908- ... 53-56
de Sousa, Ronald 1940- ... 127
de Souza, Eunice 1940- ... 153
Desowitz, Robert S. 1926- ... 126
DeSpain, Pleasant 1943- ... 151
See also SATA 87
Despalatovic, Elinor Murray 1933- ... 105
Despert, J(uliette) Louise 1892- ... 69-72
Desplaines, Baroness Julie
See Jennings, Leslie Nelson
Despland, Michel 1936- ... CANR-29
Earlier sketch in CA 49-52
Despres, Leo A(rthur) 1932- ... 25-28R
Des Pres, Terrence 1939-1987 ... 73-76
Obituary ... 124
Desputeaux, Helene 1959- ... 160
See also SATA 95
des Rivieres, Jim 1953- ... 141
DesRochers, Alfred 1901-1978 ... DLB 68
DesRochers, Diane 1937- ... 150
Desrosiers, Leo-Paul 1892-1967 ... 148
See also DLB 68
Dess, G. D. ... 135
Dessaix, Robert 1944- ... 161
Dessau, Joanna 1921- ... CANR-24
Earlier sketch in CA 106
Dessauer, John H(ans) 1905-1993 ... 104
Obituary ... 142
Dessauer, John P(aul) 1924- ... 53-56
Dessaulles, Louis-Antoine 1819-1895 ... DLB 99
Dessel, Norman F(rank) 1932- ... 61-64
Dessen, Alan C(harles) 1935- ... 69-72
Dessent, Michael H(arold) 1942- ... 110
Desser, David 1953- ... 145
Dessi, Giuseppe 1909-1977 ... 65-68
Obituary ... 126
See also DLB 177
d'Estaing, Valery Giscard
See Giscard d'Estaing, Valery
Deste, Carlo 1936- ... 153
De Steuch, Harriet Henry 1897(?)-1974 Obituary ... 49-52
Destler, Chester McArthur 1904-1984 ... CANR-16
Obituary ... 114
Earlier sketch in CA 5-8R
Destler, I. M. 1939- ... CANR-15
Earlier sketch in CA 89-92
Destouches, Louis-Ferdinand 1894-1961 ... CANR-28
Earlier sketch in CA 85-88
See also Celine, Louis-Ferdinand
See also CLC 9, 15
See also MTCW 1
Destry, Vince
See Norwood, Victor G(eorge) C(harles)
De Sua, William Joseph 1930- ... 13-16R
de Swaan, Abram 1942- ... CANR-13
Earlier sketch in CA 69-72
de Sylva, Donald Perrin 1928- ... 53-56
De Tabley, Lord 1835-1895 ... DLB 35
De Tarr, Francis 1926- ... 17-20R
Deter, Dean (Allen) 1945- ... 53-56
de Teran, Lisa St. Aubin
See St. Aubin de Teran, Lisa
Deterline, William A(lexander) 1927- ... CANR-8
Earlier sketch in CA 5-8R
de Terra, Helmut 1900-1981 Obituary ... 104
de Terra, Rhoda Hoff 1901- ... 1-4R
Detherage, May 1908- ... CAP-2
Earlier sketch in CA 23-24
Dethier, Vincent Gaston 1915-1993 ... CANR-9
Obituary ... 142
Earlier sketch in CA 65-68
Dethlefsen, Merle 1934- ... 119
Dethloff, Henry C(lay) 1934- ... 21-24R
De Thomasis, Louis 1940- ... CANR-49
Earlier sketch in CA 123
de Thulstrup, Thure 1848-1930 ... DLB 188
Detine, Padre
See Olsen, Ib Spang
de Tirtoff, Romain 1892-1990 ... 69-72
Obituary ... 131
Detjen, Ervin W(infred) 1909- ... CAP-2
Earlier sketch in CA 19-20
Detjen, Mary (Elizabeth) Ford 1904- ... CAP-1
Earlier sketch in CA 13-14
de Todany, James
See Beaudoin, Kenneth Lawrence
de Toledano, Ralph
See Toledano, Ralph de
de Tolignac, Gaston
See Griffith, D(avid Lewelyn) W(ark)
De Tolnay, Charles Erich 1899- ... 73-76
de Tonquedec, Jospeh
See Tonquedec, Joseph de
de Toth, Andre 1913- ... 154
de Trevino, Elizabeth B.
See Trevino, Elizabeth B(orton) de
Detrez, Conrad (Jean) 1937-1985 ... 132
Detro, Gene 1935- ... CANR-12
Earlier sketch in CA 61-64
Detter, Ingrid
See Delupis, Ingrid
Dettmar, Kevin J(ohn) H(offmann) 1958- ... 145
Detweiler, Robert 1932- ... 33-36R
Detwiler, Donald S(caife) 1933- ... 37-40R
Detwiler, Susan Dill 1956- ... SATA 58
Detz, Joan (Marie) 1951- ... 118
Detz, Phyllis 1911- ... CAP-2
Earlier sketch in CA 33-36
Detzer, David William 1937- ... 93-96
Detzer, Karl 1891- ... CAP-1
Earlier sketch in CA 9-10
Detzler, Jack J. 1922- ... 33-36R
Detzler, Wayne Alan 1936- ... 105
Deuchar, Margaret 1952- ... 113
Deuel, Thorne 1890-1984 Obituary ... 112
Deuker, Carl 1950- ... 149
See also AAYA 26
See also SATA 82
Deutermann, P(eter) T(homas) 1941- ... 142
Deutrich, Mabel E. 1915- ... 5-8R
Deutsch, Alfred H(enry) 1914- ... 116
Deutsch, Arnold R. 1919- ... 101
Deutsch, Babette 1895-1982 ... CANR-4
Obituary ... 108
Earlier sketch in CA 1-4R
See also CLC 18
See also DLB 45
See also SATA 1
See also SATA-Obit 33
Deutsch, Bernard Francis 1925- ... 13-16R
Deutsch, Eberhard Paul 1897-1980 Obituary ... 93-96
Deutsch, Eliot (Sandler) 1931- ... CANR-10
Earlier sketch in CA 65-68
Deutsch, Eva Costabel
See Costabel, Eva Deutsch
Deutsch, Harold C(harles) 1904- ... 21-24R
Deutsch, Helen 1906-1992 ... 112
Obituary ... 137
Brief entry ... 108
Interview in ... 112
See also SATA 76
Deutsch, Helene (Rosenbach) 1884-1982 ... 128
Obituary ... 106

Deutsch, Herbert A(rnold) 1932- ... 89-92
Deutsch, Hermann Bacher
1889-1970 Obituary ... 93-96
Deutsch, John James 1911-1976 Obituary ... 111
Deutsch, Karl W(olfgang) 1912-1992 ... CANR-46
Obituary ... 139
Earlier sketch in CA 41-44R
Deutsch, Marilyn Weisberg 1950- ... 102
Deutsch, Morton 1920- ... 1-4R
Deutsch, Patrizia Giampieri
See Giampieri-Deutsch, Patrizia
Deutsch, Ronald M(artin) 1928- ... CANR-4
Earlier sketch in CA 1-4R
Deutscher, Irwin 1923- ... 25-28R
Deutscher, Isaac 1907-1967 ... CANR-4
Obituary ... 25-28R
Earlier sketch in CA 5-8R
Deutscher, Max 1916(?)-1979 Obituary ... 93-96
Deutscher, Tamara (Lebenhaft)
1913(?)-1990 Obituary ... 132
Deutscher, Thomas (Brian) 1949- ... 124
Deutschkron, Inge 1922- ... 29-32R
Deutschman, Alan (Barry) 1965- ... 116
Devadutt, Vinjamuri E(verett) 1908- ... CAP-2
Earlier sketch in CA 23-24
De Vaere, Ulric Josef 1932- ... 1-4R
Devahuti, D. 1929- ... 45-48
Devajee, Ved
See Gool, Reshard
Deval, Gord 1930- ... 124
Deval, Jacques
See Boularan, Jacques
De Valera, Eamon 1882-1975 Obituary ... 89-92
De Valera, Sinead 1879(?)-1975 Obituary ... 53-56
See also SATA-Obit 30
de Vallbona, Rima
See Vallbona, Rima-Gretel Rothe
Devalle, Susana B(eatriz) C(ristina) 1945- ... 147
de Valois, Ninette 1898- Brief entry ... 115
Devaney, John 1926-1994 ... CANR-23
Obituary ... 145
Earlier sketches in CA 17-20R, CANR-7
See also SATA 12
Devaraja, N(and) K(ishore) 1917- ... 104
de Varona, Frank J. 1943- ... 150
See also SATA 83
Devas, Nicolette (Macnamara)
1911-1987(?) ... 13-16R
Obituary ... 122
Devashish, Donald Acosta 1956- ... 162
DeVault, M(arion) Vere 1922- ... CANR-20
Earlier sketches in CA 1-4R, CANR-4
De Vaux, Roland 1903-1971 Obituary ... 33-36R
De Veaux, Alexis 1948- ... CANR-71
Earlier sketches in CA 65-68, CANR-26
See also BW 1
See also DLB 38
De Vecchi, Nicolo 1943- ... 151
D'Evelyn, Katherine E(dith) 1899- ... 17-20R
Dever, Joseph 1919-1970 ... CAP-2
Obituary ... 29-32R
Earlier sketch in CA 19-20
Dever, William Gwinn 1933- Brief entry ... 109
Deveraux, Jude
See White, Jude Gilliam
See also BEST 90:1
de Vere, Aubrey 1814-1902 ... DLB 35
de Vere, Edward 1550-1604 ... DLB 172
de Vere, Jane
See Watson, Julia
Deverell, Rex (Johnson) 1941- ... 132
Deverell, William H(erbert) 1937- ... CANR-43
Earlier sketch in CA 115
Devereux, Frederick L(eonard), Jr. 1914- ... CANR-1
Earlier sketch in CA 49-52
See also SATA 9
Devereux, George 1908- ... 69-72
Devereux, Hilary 1919- ... 13-16R
Devereux, Robert (Essex) 1922- ... 5-8R
Deverson, Harry 1909(?)-1972 Obituary ... 104
De Vet, Charles V(incent) 1911-1997 ... 102
Obituary ... 163
Devi, Gayatri 1919- ... 159
Devi, Indra 1899- ... CAP-1
Earlier sketch in CA 13-14
Devi, Nila
See Woody, Regina Jones
Devi, Ragini 1894(?)-1982 Obituary ... 110
Deview, Lucille 1920- ... 73-76
De Vilbiss, Philip
See Mebane, John (Harrison)
Deville, Rene
See Kacew, Romain
de Villiers, Gerard 1929- ... 61-64
De Villiers, Marq 1940- ... 166
de Vilmorin, Louise Leveque
See Vilmorin, Louise Leveque de
DeVincentes-Hayes, Nan ... 142
de Vinck, Antoine 1924- ... 53-56
de Vinck, Catherine 1922- ... CANR-6
Earlier sketch in CA 57-60
deVinck, Christopher 1951- ... 151
See also SATA 85
de Vinck, (Baron) Jose M. G. A. 1912- ... 17-20R
Devine, Betsy 1946- ... 142
Devine, D(avid) M(cDonald) 1920- ... CANR-1
Earlier sketch in CA 1-4R
Devine, Dominic
See Devine, D(avid) M(cDonald)
Devine, Donald J. 1937- ... 81-84
Devine, (Mary) Elizabeth 1938- ... CANR-38
Earlier sketch in CA 116
Devine, George 1941- ... CANR-1
Earlier sketch in CA 45-48
Devine, Janice 1909(?)-1973 Obituary ... 41-44R
Devine, (Joseph) Lawrence 1935- ... 73-76
Devine, T(homas) M(artin) 1945- ... 136
Devine, Thomas G. 1928- ... 17-20R
De Vinne, Theodore Low 1828-1914 ... DLB 187
DeVinney, Richard 1936- ... 45-48
Devins, Joseph H(erbert), Jr. 1930- ... 21-24R
Devious, B. K.
See Herring, Peggy J.
DeVitis, Angelo A(nthony) 1925- ... 107
DeVito, Cara 1956- ... 147
See also SATA 80
De Vito, Joseph Anthony 1938- ... 37-40R
Devkota, Laxmiprasad 1909-1959 Brief entry ... 123
See also TCLC 23
Devletoglou, Nicos E. 1936- ... 41-44R
Devlin, Bernadette (Josephine) 1947- ... 105
Devlin, Diana (Mary) 1941- ... CANR-37
Earlier sketch in CA 114
Devlin, Gerard M(ichael) 1933- ... 105
Devlin, Harry 1918- ... CANR-37
Earlier sketches in CA 65-68, CANR-8
See also MAICYA
See also SATA 11, 74
Devlin, John C. 1911(?)-1984 Obituary ... 113
Devlin, John J(oseph), Jr. 1920- ... 37-40R
Devlin, Keith 1947- ... 141
Devlin, L. Patrick 1939- ... 61-64
Devlin, Patrick (Arthur) 1905-1992 ... CANR-46
Obituary ... 138
Earlier sketch in CA 69-72
Devlin, (Dorothy) Wende 1918- ... CANR-37
Earlier sketches in CA 61-64, CANR-8
See also MAICYA
See also SATA 11, 74
Devney, Darcy C(ampion) 1960- ... 138
DeVoe, Shirley Spaulding 1899-1991 ... 77-80
Obituary ... 163
Devol, Kenneth S(towe) 1929-1997 ... 49-52
Obituary ... 163
Devon, D. G.
See Demorest, Stephen
and Gross, Michael (Robert)
Devon, John Anthony
See Payne, (Pierre Stephen) Robert
Devon, Paddie 1953- ... 156
See also SATA 92
Devons, Sonia 1974- ... SATA 72
Devor, John W(esley) 1901- ... CAP-1
Earlier sketch in CA 11-12
DeVore, Gary 1941-1997 ... 166
Devore, Irven 1934- ... 21-24R
DeVorkin, David H(yam) 1944- ... CANR-26
Earlier sketch in CA 108
De Vorsey, Louis, Jr. 1929- ... 21-24R
DeVos, George A(lphonse) 1922- ... CANR-11
Earlier sketch in CA 21-24R
De Vos, Karen Helder 1939- ... 102
De Vos, Susan 1953- ... 153
de Vosjoli, Philippe L. Thyraud 1920- ... 29-32R
De Voto, Bernard (Augustine) 1897-1955 ... 160
Brief entry ... 113
See also DLB 9
See also TCLC 29
de Vries, Anne 1904-1964 Obituary ... 116
De Vries, Carrow 1906- ... 53-56
deVries, Egbert 1901- ... 61-64
de Vries, Herbert A. 1917- ... CANR-13
Earlier sketch in CA 33-36R
de Vries, Jan 1943- ... CANR-26
Earlier sketch in CA 69-72
DeVries, Kelly 1956- ... 168
de Vries, Leonard
See Vries, Leonard de
de Vries, Manfred F. R. Kets
See Kets de Vries, Manfred F. R.
De Vries, Peter 1910-1993 ... CANR-41
Obituary ... 142
Earlier sketch in CA 17-20R
See also CLC 1, 2, 3, 7, 10, 28, 46
See also DAM NOV
See also DLB 6
See also DLBY 82
See also MTCW 1
de Vries, Rachel (Guido) 1947- ... 123
De Vries, Simon J(ohn) 1921- ... 57-60
De Vries, Walter (Dale) 1929- ... 69-72
Dew, Charles B(urgess) 1937- ... CANR-29
Earlier sketch in CA 21-24R
Dew, Donald 1928- ... 106
Dew, Edward MacMillan 1935- ... 81-84
Dew, Joan King 1932- ... 104
Dew, Robb (Reavill) Forman 1946- ... CANR-29
Earlier sketch in CA 104
de Waal, Frans 1948- ... 110
De Waal, Ronald Burt 1932- ... CANR-14
Earlier sketch in CA 37-40R
de Waal, Victor (Alexander) 1929- ... 29-32R
de Waal Malefijt, Annemarie 1914-1982 ... 61-64
Obituary ... 109
De Waard, E(lliott) John 1935- ... CANR-2
Earlier sketch in CA 49-52
See also SATA 7
Dewald, Paul A. 1920- ... 17-20R
Dewar, David R(oss) 1913-1990 Obituary ... 131
Dewar, Deborah 1946(?)-1986 Obituary ... 118
Dewar, Diana Ill 1928(?)-1984 Obituary ... 112
Dewar, Margaret E(lizabeth) 1948- ... 114
Dewar, Mary (Williamson) 1921- ... 13-16R
Dewart, Edward Hartley 1828-1903 ... DLB 99
Dewart, Gilbert 1932- ... 135
Dewart, Leslie 1922- ... 9-12R
de Water, Frederic F(ranklyn) Van
See Van de Water, Frederic F(ranklyn)
Dewberry, Elizabeth 1962- ... 150
Dewdney, A(lexander) K(eewatin) 1941- ... 142
Dewdney, Christopher 1951- ... CANR-53
Earlier sketch in CA 125
See also DLB 60
Dewdney, John Christopher 1928- ... 103
Dewdney, Selwyn (Hanington) 1909-1979 ...
CANR-27
Earlier sketch in CA 69-72
See also DLB 68
See also SATA 64
DeWeerd, Harvey A. 1902- ... 73-76
DeWeese, Gene
See DeWeese, Thomas Eugene
DeWeese, Jean
See DeWeese, Thomas Eugene
DeWeese, Thomas Eugene 1934- ... CANR-24
Earlier sketches in CA 65-68, CANR-9
See also SATA 46
See also SATA-Brief 45
De Welt, Don Finch 1919- ... CANR-1
Earlier sketch in CA 1-4R
de Wet, Hugh Oloff 1912(?)-1976(?) Obituary ... 104
Dewey, Ariane 1937- ... CANR-3
Earlier sketch in CA 49-52
See also SATA 7
Dewey, Bradley R. 1934- ... 29-32R
Dewey, Donald O(dell) 1930- ... 37-40R
Dewey, Edward R(ussell) 1895-1978 ... 41-44R
Dewey, Frank L. 1906- ... 122
Dewey, Godfrey 1887-1977 ... CAP-2
Obituary ... 73-76
Earlier sketch in CA 29-32
Dewey, Irene Sargent 1896- ... CAP-2
Earlier sketch in CA 17-18
Dewey, Jennifer (Owings) 1941- ... 126
See also SATA 58
See also SATA-Brief 48
Dewey, John 1859-1952 Brief entry ... 114
Dewey, Kenneth Francis 1940- ... 112
See also SATA 39
Dewey, Melvil 1851-1931 Brief entry ... 118
Dewey, Melville Louis Kossuth
See Dewey, Melvil
Dewey, Robert D(yckman) 1923- ... 9-12R
Dewey, Robert E(ugene) 1923- ... 13-16R
Dewey, Thomas B(lanchard) 1915-1981 ... CANR-59
Earlier sketches in CA 1-4R, CANR-1
Dewhirst, Ian 1936- ... 102
Dewhurst, Colleen 1924-1991 ... 158
Dewhurst, Eileen (Mary) 1929- ... CANR-27
Earlier sketch in CA 109
Dewhurst, J(ames) Frederic 1895-1967 ... CAP-2
Earlier sketch in CA 17-18
Dewhurst, Keith 1931- ... CANR-68
Earlier sketches in CA 61-64, CANR-18
Dewhurst, Kenneth 1919- ... CANR-2
Earlier sketch in CA 5-8R
deWit, Dorothy (May Knowles) 1916-1980 ... 113
Obituary ... 109
See also SATA 39
See also SATA-Obit 28
de Wit, Wim 1948- ... 128
DeWitt, Addison
See Newman, Kim (James)
DeWitt, Calvin B. 1935- ... 136
DeWitt, Edith Openshaw 1920- ... 111
DeWitt, James
See Lewis, Mildred D.
DeWitt, John 1910(?)-1984 Obituary ... 113
Dewitt, Katherine, Jr. 1943- ... 153
Dewlen, Al 1921- ... CANR-63
Earlier sketches in CA 1-4R, CANR-2
de Wohl, Louis 1903-1961 Obituary ... 111
De Wolf, L. Harold 1905- ... CANR-2
Earlier sketch in CA 1-4R
DeWolf, Rose (Doris) 1934- ... CANR-11
Earlier sketch in CA 29-32R
de Wolfe, Ivor
See Hastings, Hubert de Cronin
de Wolfe, Ivy
See Hastings, Hubert de Cronin
de Worde, Wynkyn 1491-1535 ... DLB 170
Dewsbury, Donald A(llen) 1939- ... CANR-15
Earlier sketch in CA 89-92
Dexter, Al
See Poindexter, Clarence Albert
Dexter, Beverly L(iebherr) 1943- ... 114
Dexter, Byron (Vinson) 1900-1973 Obituary ... 113
Dexter, (Norman) Colin 1930- ... CANR-53
Earlier sketches in CA 65-68, CANR-10, 25
See also DAM POP
See also DLB 87
Dexter, John
See Zachary, Hugh
Dexter, John
See Bradley, Marion Zimmer
Dexter, Lewis Anthony 1915-1995 ... CANR-4
Obituary ... 148
Earlier sketch in CA 9-12R
Dexter, Martin
See Faust, Frederick (Schiller)
Dexter, N. C.
See Dexter, (Norman) Colin
Dexter, (Ellen) Pat(ricia) Egan ... 81-84
Dexter, Pete 1943- ... 131
Brief entry ... 127
Interview in ... 131
See also BEST 89:2
See also CLC 34, 55
See also DAM POP
See also MTCW 1
Dexter, Peter
See Shaver, Richard S(harpe)
Dexter, Susan (Elizabeth) 1955- ... CANR-50
Earlier sketches in CA 108, CANR-25
Dey, Frederic (Merrill) Van Rensselaer
1865-1922 Brief entry ... 113
Dey, Joseph C(harles), Jr. 1907-1991 ... CAP-1
Obituary ... 133
Earlier sketch in CA 11-12
Dey, Marmaduke
See Dey, Frederic (Merrill) Van Rensselaer
Deyermond, Alan D(avid) 1932- ... CANR-6
Earlier sketch in CA 13-16R
Deyneka, Anita 1943- ... CANR-26
Earlier sketches in CA 61-64, CANR-11
See also SATA 24
Deyneka, Peter (N. Sr.) 1898-1987 Obituary ... 123
de Young, M. H. 1849-1925 ... DLB 25
DeYoung, Mary 1949- ... 112
Deyrup, Astrith Johnson 1923- ... 65-68
See also SATA 24
Deza, Ernest C. 1923- ... 53-56
de Zegher, M. Catherine 1955- ... 162
Dhalla, Nariman K. 1925- ... 25-28R
Dharker, Imtiaz ... 168
Dharmi, Santana 1914- ... CANR-20
Earlier sketch in CA 101
d'Harnoncourt, Anne (Julie) 1943- ... 120
Dhavamony, Mariasusai 1925- ... 33-36R
Dhiegh, Khigh (Alx) ... 93-96
Dhlomo, H. I. E. 1903-1956 ... DLB 157
Dhokalia, (Ramaa) Prasad 1925- ... 41-44R
Dhondy, Farrukh 1944- ... 132
See also AAYA 24
See also CLR 41
See also MAICYA
See also SATA 65
Dhrymes, Phoebus J(ames) 1932- ... CANR-12
Earlier sketch in CA 29-32R
Dhuoda c. 803-c. 843 ... DLB 148
Diack, Hunter 1908-1974 ... CAP-2
Earlier sketch in CA 21-22
Dial, Joan 1937- ... CANR-24
Earlier sketch in CA 81-84
Diallo, Nafissatou (Niang) 1941-(?) ... 116
Diamano, Silmang
See Senghor, Leopold Sedar
Diamant, Anita 1951- ... 145
Diamant, Lincoln 1923- ... 33-36R
Diamond, Ann
See McLean, Anne (Julia)
Diamond, Arthur 1957- ... 144
See also SATA 76
Diamond, Arthur Sigismund 1897- ... CAP-1
Earlier sketch in CA 9-10
Diamond, Cora A(nn) 1937- ... 121
Diamond, Donna 1950- ... 115
See also MAICYA
See also SATA 35, 69
See also SATA-Brief 30
Diamond, Edwin 1925-1997 ... CANR-9
Obituary ... 159
Earlier sketch in CA 13-16R
Diamond, Ellen 1938- ... 133
Diamond, Graham 1945- ... CANR-60
Earlier sketch in CA 85-88
Diamond, Harold J(ames) 1934- ... 110
Diamond, I(sidore) A. L. 1920-1988 ... 81-84
Obituary ... 125
See also DLB 26
Diamond, Jacqueline
See Hyman, Jackie (Diamond)
Diamond, Jared (Mason) 1937- ... 158
Diamond, Jay 1934- ... CANR-33
Earlier sketches in CA 65-68, CANR-14
Diamond, John 1907- ... 109
Diamond, John 1934- ... 85-88
Diamond, Malcolm L(uria) 1924- ... 25-28R
Diamond, Marc 1944- ... CANR-44
Earlier sketch in CA 119
Diamond, Martin 1919-1977 ... 77-80
Obituary ... 73-76
Diamond, Milton 1934- ... 89-92
Diamond, Neil 1941- ... 108
See also CLC 30
Diamond, Norma Joyce 1933- Brief entry ... 108
Diamond, Petra
See Sachs, Judith
Diamond, Rebecca
See Sachs, Judith
Diamond, Rickey Gard 1946- ... 164
Diamond, Robert Mach 1930- ... CANR-7
Earlier sketch in CA 9-12R
Diamond, Sander A. 1942- ... CANR-57
Earlier sketch in CA 49-52
Diamond, Sara 1958- ... 153
Diamond, Selma 1920-1985 Obituary ... 116
Diamond, Sigmund 1920- ... 1-4R
Diamond, Solomon 1906- ... 102
Diamond, Stanley 1922-1991 ... 102
Obituary ... 134
Diamond, Stephen A(rthur) 1946- ... 89-92
Diamond, William 1917- ... 65-68
Diamonstein, Barbaralee D. ... CANR-35
Earlier sketches in CA 85-88, CANR-15
Diar, Prakash 1956- ... 137
Diara, Agadem Lumumba 1947- ... 65-68
Diara, Schavi M.
See Ali, Schavi M(ali)
Dias, Earl Joseph 1916- ... 21-24R
See also SATA 41
Dias, Ron 1937- ... SATA 71
Diaz, David 1958- ... SATA 96
Diaz, Henry Frank 1948- ... 157
Diaz, Janet W(inecoff) 1935- ... 53-56
Diaz, Jorge 1930- ... HW
Diaz, Junot 1968- ... 161
Diaz-Alejandro, Carlos F(ederico) 1937-1985 ... 131
Obituary ... 116
See also HW
Diaz-Guerrero, Rogelio 1918- ... 101
Diaz Miron, Salvador 1858-1928 ... HW

Diaz Plaja, Guillermo 1909-1984 ... 131
Obituary ... 113
See also HW
Diaz-Stevens, Ana Maria 1942- ... 144
Diaz Valcarcel, Emilio 1929- ... 135
See also HW
DiBartolomeo, Albert 1952- ... 141
di Bassetto, Corno
See Shaw, George Bernard
DiBattista, Maria 1947- ... 113
Dibb, Paul 1939- ... CANR-1
Earlier sketch in CA 45-48
Dibba, Ebou 1943- ... 124
Dibble, J(ames) Birney 1925- ... 17-20R
Dibble, Nancy Ann 1942- ... 103
Dibble, Vadna Davis 1902(?)-1983 Obituary ... 110
Dibdin, Michael 1947- ... CANR-66
Earlier sketches in CA 77-80, CANR-45
Dibdin, Thomas Frognall 1776-1847 ... DLB 184
Dibelius, Otto (Friedrich Karl)
1880-1967 Obituary ... 114
Dibell, Ansen
See Dibble, Nancy Ann
Di Bella, Anna 1933- Brief entry ... 110
di Benedetto, Antonio 1922- ... HW
Di Berardino, Angelo 1936- ... 135
Di Blasi, Debra 1957- ... 157
Dible, Donald M(eredith) 1936- ... 110
Dibner, Andrew Sherman 1926- Brief entry ... 110
Dibner, Bern 1897- ... 107
Dibner, Martin 1911-1992 ... CANR-4
Obituary ... 136
Earlier sketch in CA 1-4R
DiBona, Joseph E. 1927- Brief entry ... 109
Di Cavalcanti, Emiliano
1898(?)-1976 Obituary ... 69-72
Dice, Lee R. 1889(?)-1976 Obituary ... 69-72
Di Certo, J(oseph) J(ohn) 1933- ... CANR-42
Earlier sketches in CA 21-24R, CANR-13
See also SATA 60
Di Cesare, Mario A(nthony) 1928- ... CANR-3
Earlier sketch in CA 5-8R
Dichter, Ernest 1907-1991 ... CANR-44
Earlier sketch in CA 17-20R
Dichter, Harry 1900(?)-1978(?) Obituary ... 104
Di Cicco, Pier Giorgio 1949- ... CANR-17
Earlier sketch in CA 97-100
See also DLB 60
Dick, Bernard F(rancis) 1935- ... CANR-9
Earlier sketch in CA 21-24R
Dick, Daniel T. 1946- ... 61-64
Dick, Everett 1898- ... 25-28R
Dick, Ignace 1926- ... CANR-12
Earlier sketch in CA 25-28R
Dick, Kay 1915- ... CANR-57
Earlier sketches in CA 13-16R, CANR-15
Dick, Philip K(indred) 1928-1982 ... CANR-16
Obituary ... 106
Earlier sketches in CA 49-52, CANR-2
See also AAYA 24
See also CLC 10, 30, 72
See also DAM NOV, POP
See also DLB 8
See also MTCW 1
Dick, R. A.
See Leslie, Josephine Aimee Campbell
Dick, Robert C. 1938- ... 37-40R
Dick, Susan 1940- ... CANR-44
Earlier sketch in CA 120
Dick, Trella Lamson 1889-1974 ... 5-8R
See also SATA 9
Dick, Trevor J. O. 1934- Brief entry ... 106
Dick, William M(ilner) 1933- ... 41-44R
Dickason, David Howard 1907-1974 ... CAP-2
Earlier sketch in CA 33-36
Dickason, Olive Patricia 1920- ... 132
Dick B.
See Burns, Richard Gordon
Dicke, Robert H(enry) 1916-1997 ... 53-56
Obituary ... 157
Dicke, Thomas S(cott) 1955- ... 143
Dicken, E(ric) W(illiam) Trueman 1919- ... 9-12R
Dickens, A(rthus) G(eoffrey) 1910- ... 53-56
Dickens, Charles (John Huffam) 1812-1870 .. AAYA 23
See also CDBLB 1832-1890
See also DA
See also DAB
See also DAC
See also DAM MST, NOV
See also DLB 21, 55, 70, 159, 166
See also JRDA
See also MAICYA
See also SATA 15
See also SSC 17
See also WLC
Dickens, Floyd, Jr. 1940- ... 111
Dickens, Frank
See Huline-Dickens, Frank William
Dickens, Jacqueline B(ass) 1941- ... 112
Dickens, Milton 1908- ... 1-4R
Dickens, Monica (Enid) 1915-1992 ... CANR-46
Obituary ... 140
Earlier sketches in CA 5-8R, CANR-2
See also SATA 4
See also SATA-Obit 74
Dickens, Norman
See Eisenberg, Lawrence B(enjamin)
Dickens, Peter (Gerald Charles) 1917-1987 ... 124
Obituary ... 122
Dickens, Roy S(elman), Jr. 1938- ... CANR-9
Earlier sketch in CA 65-68
Dickenson, Fred 1909-1986 Obituary ... 119
Dickenson, James R. 1931- ... CANR-50
Earlier sketch in CA 65-68
Dickenson, Mollie 1935- ... 129
Dickenson, Reginald 1912- ... 155
Dicker, Davie
See Ritchie, (Harry) Ward
Dicker, Eva Barash 1936- ... 107
Dicker, Ralph Leslie 1914- ... 65-68
Dickerman, Edmund H. 1935- Brief entry ... 110
Dickerson, Dennis C. 1949- ... 168
Dickerson, F(rederick) Reed 1909- ... 17-20R
Dickerson, Grace Leslie 1911- ... 5-8R
Dickerson, John 1939- ... 57-60
Dickerson, Martha Ufford 1922- ... 81-84
Dickerson, Nancy H(anschman) 1930-1997 .. 69-72
Obituary ... 162
Dickerson, Oliver M(orton) 1875-1966 Obituary . 106
Dickerson, Robert B(radford), Jr. 1955- ... 106
Dickerson, Roy Ernest 1886-1965 ... 5-8R
Obituary ... 103
See also SATA-Obit 26
Dickerson, William E(ugene) 1897-1971 ... CAP-2
Earlier sketch in CA 21-22
Dickey, Charley 1920- ... 69-72
Dickey, Christopher 1951- ... 146
Dickey, Franklin M(iller) 1921- ... 21-24R
Dickey, Glenn (Ernest, Jr.) 1936- ... CANR-4
Earlier sketch in CA 53-56
Dickey, James (Lafayette) 1923-1997 ... CANR-61
Obituary ... 156
Earlier sketches in CA 9-12R, CANR-10, 48
Interview in ... CANR-10
See also CABS 2
See also AITN 1, 2
See also CDALB 1968-1988
See also CLC 1, 2, 4, 7, 10, 15, 47, 109
See also DAM NOV, POET, POP
See also DLB 5, 193
See also DLBD 7
See also DLBY 82, 93, 96, 97
See also MTCW 1
Dickey, Lee
See Bremyer, Jayne Dickey
Dickey, Page 1940- ... 139
Dickey, R(obert) P(reston) 1936- ... CANR-44
Earlier sketches in CA 29-32R, CANR-25
Dickey, William 1928-1994 ... CANR-24
Obituary ... 145
Earlier sketch in CA 9-12R
See also CLC 3, 28
See also DLB 5
Dickie, Edgar P(rimrose) 1897- ... CAP-1
Earlier sketch in CA 11-12
Dickie, George (Thomas) 1926- ... 33-36R
Dickie, James 1934- ... 97-100
Dickie, John 1923- ... 13-16R
Dickie, Margaret (McKenzie) 1935- ... 162
Dickie-Clark, H(amish) F(indlay) 1922- ... 21-24R
Dickins, A. S. M.
See Dickins, Anthony (Stewart Mackay)
Dickins, Anthony (Stewart Mackay)
1914-1987 Obituary ... 124
Dickinson, A(lan) E(dgar) F(rederic) 1899- ... 73-76
Dickinson, A(rthur) T(aylor), Jr. 1925- ... 5-8R
Dickinson, Charles 1951- ... 128
See also CLC 49
Dickinson, Don(ald Percy) 1947- ... 137
Dickinson, Donald C. 1927- ... 21-24R
Dickinson, Edward C(live) 1938- ... 61-64
Dickinson, Eleanor 1931- ... 65-68
Dickinson, Emily (Elizabeth) 1830-1886 ... AAYA 22
See also CDALB 1865-1917
See also DA
See also DAB
See also DAC
See also DAM MST, POET
See also DLB 1
See also PC 1
See also SATA 29
See also WLC
Dickinson, H(arry) T(homas) 1939- ... 33-36R
Dickinson, John 1732-1808 ... DLB 31
Dickinson, John K(ellogg) 1918- ... 25-28R
Dickinson, Jonathan 1688-1747 ... DLB 24
Dickinson, Leon T. 1912- ... 13-16R
Dickinson, Lois Stice 1898(?)-1970 Obituary ... 104
Dickinson, Margaret
See Muggeson, Margaret Elizabeth
Dickinson, Mary 1949- ... 110
See also SATA 48
See also SATA-Brief 41
Dickinson, Patric Thomas 1914-1994 ... CANR-43
Obituary ... 144
Earlier sketches in CA 9-12R, CANR-3
See also DLB 27
Dickinson, Peter (Malcolm) 1927- ... CANR-58
Earlier sketches in CA 41-44R, CANR-31
See also AAYA 9
See also CLC 12, 35
See also CLR 29
See also DLB 87, 161
See also JRDA
See also MAICYA
See also SATA 5, 62, 95
Dickinson, Peter A(llen) 1926- ... 102
Dickinson, Richard D(onald) N(ye, Jr.) 1929- Brief entry ... 109
Dickinson, Robert Eric 1905- ... CANR-3
Earlier sketch in CA 5-8R
Dickinson, Ruth F(rankenstein) 1933- ... 37-40R
Dickinson, (William) Stirling 1909- ... CAP-2
Earlier sketch in CA 33-36
Dickinson, Susan 1931- ... 57-60
See also SATA 8
Dickinson, Terence 1943- ... 160
See also SATA 102
Dickinson, Thorold (Barron) 1903-1984 ... 45-48
Obituary ... 112
Dickinson, W(illiam) Croft 1897-1963 ... CANR-6
Earlier sketch in CA 1-4R
See also SATA 13
Dickinson, William Boyd 1908-1978 ... 85-88
Obituary ... 81-84
Dick-Lauder, George (Andrew) 1917- ... 102
Dickler, Gerald 1912- ... 9-12R
Dickman, James B(ruce) 1949- ... 138
Dickman, Thomas 1955- ... 146
Dickmeyer, Lowell A. 1939- ... 109
See also SATA-Brief 51
Dicks, Henry V(ictor) 1900- ... 102
Dicks, Russell Leslie 1906-1965 ... CAP-1
Earlier sketch in CA 13-16
Dicks, Shirley 1940- ... 138
Dickson, Athol 1955- ... 166
Dickson, Carr
See Carr, John Dickson
Dickson, Carter
See Carr, John Dickson
Dickson, Charles W., Jr. 1926- ... 25-28R
Dickson, Donald R(ichard) 1951- ... 126
Dickson, Franklyn 1941- ... 53-56
Dickson, George E(dmond) 1918- ... 49-52
Dickson, Gordon R(upert) 1923- ... CANR-6
Earlier sketch in CA 9-12R
See also DLB 8
See also SATA 77
Dickson, Helen
See Reynolds, Helen Mary Greenwood Campbell
Dickson, K. A.
See Dickson, Kwesi A(botsia)
Dickson, Kwesi A(botsia) 1929- ... 134
Brief entry ... 109
Dickson, (Horatio Henry) Lovat 1902-1987 ... CANR-46
Obituary ... 121
Earlier sketch in CA 13-16R
Dickson, Margaret (Smith) 1947- ... 114
Dickson, Mora (Hope-Robertson) 1918- ... CANR-5
Earlier sketch in CA 13-16R
Dickson, Naida 1916- ... 37-40R
See also SATA 8
Dickson, Paul (Andrew) 1939- ... CANR-52
Earlier sketches in CA 33-36R, CANR-27
Dickson, Peter George Muir 1929- ... 13-16R
Dickson, Robert J(ames) 1919- ... 21-24R
Dickson, Stanley 1927- ... 53-56
Dickstein, Morris 1940- ... 85-88
Di Cyan, Erwin 1918- ... 37-40R
Didato, Salvatore V. 1926- ... 122
Brief entry ... 107
Didinger, Ray 1946- ... 93-96
Didion, Joan 1934- ... CANR-52
Earlier sketches in CA 5-8R, CANR-14
See also AITN 1
See also CDALB 1968-1988
See also CLC 1, 3, 8, 14, 32
See also DAM NOV
See also DLB 2, 173, 185
See also DLBY 81, 86
See also MTCW 1
di Donato, Georgia 1932- ... 103
di Donato, Pietro 1911-1992 ... 101
Obituary ... 136
See also DLB 9
Didsbury, Howard F(rancis), Jr. 1924- ... 111
Didsbury, Peter 1946- ... 112
Diebold, Janet
See Sylvester, Janet Hart
Diebold, Janet Oline
See Sylvester, Janet Hart
Diebold, John (Theurer) 1926- ... 53-56
Diebold, William, Jr. 1918- ... CANR-6
Earlier sketch in CA 13-16R
Dieckmann, Ed(ward Adolph), Jr. 1920- .. CANR-21
Earlier sketch in CA 102
Dieckmann, Liselotte 1902- ... 97-100
Diederich, Bernard 1926- ... 77-80
Diefendorf, Barbara B(oonstoppel) 1946- ... 124
Diefendorf, Jeffry M(indlin) 1945- ... 104
Diefenthaler, Jon 1943- ... 124
Diego, Gerardo
See Diego Cendoya, Gerardo
See also DLB 134
Diego Cendoya, Gerardo 1896-1987 Obituary .. 123
See also Diego, Gerardo
See also HW
Diehl, (Robert) Digby 1940- ... CANR-7
Earlier sketch in CA 53-56
Diehl, Jackson 1956- ... 135
Diehl, James M(ichael) 1938- ... 85-88
Diehl, Katharine Smith 1906- ... CAP-1
Earlier sketch in CA 11-12
Diehl, Kemper 1918- ... 118
Diehl, Lorraine B(uscaglia) 1940- ... 119
Diehl, W(illiam) W(ells) 1916-1974 ... 17-20R
Obituary ... 134
Diehl, William (Francis, Jr.) 1924- ... CANR-13
Earlier sketch in CA 101
Interview in ... CANR-13
Diehm, Floyd L(ee) 1925- Brief entry ... 110
Diehn, Gwen 1943- ... 147
See also SATA 80
Diekhoff, John S(iemon) 1905-1976 ... CAP-2
Obituary ... 69-72
Earlier sketch in CA 29-32
Diekman, John R(aymond) 1946- ... 110
Diekmann, Godfrey 1908- ... CANR-2
Earlier sketch in CA 1-4R
Diel, Paul 1893- ... 103
Diem, Max 1947- ... 151
Diener, Royce 1918- Brief entry ... 110
Diener, Theodor Otto 1921- ... 157
Dienes, C(harles) Thomas 1940- ... CANR-11
Earlier sketch in CA 69-72
Dienstag, Eleanor 1938- ... 65-68
Dienstein, William 1909- ... CAP-1
Earlier sketch in CA 17-18
Dierenfield, Bruce J(onathan) 1951- ... 145
Dierenfield, Richard B(ruce) 1922- ... 17-20R
Dierickx, C(harles) W(allace) 1921- ... 61-64
Dierks, Jack Cameron 1930- ... 29-32R
Diers, Carol Jean 1933- ... 33-36R
Diescho, Joseph 1955- ... 135
Diesing, Paul R. 1922- ... CANR-2
Earlier sketch in CA 1-4R
Dieska, L. Joseph 1913- ... 37-40R
Dieskau, Dietrich Fischer
See Fischer-Dieskau, Dietrich
Dieter, William 1929- ... 114
Dieterich, Michele M. 1962- ... 146
See also SATA 78
Dietl, (Kirsten) Ulla 1940- ... 33-36R
Dietrich, John E(rb) 1913- ... 17-20R
Dietrich, Noah 1889-1982 ... 45-48
Obituary ... 106
Dietrich, R(ichard) F(arr) 1936- ... 21-24R
Dietrich, Richard V(incent) 1924- ... CANR-44
Earlier sketches in CA 53-56, CANR-4, 19
Dietrich, Robert
See Hunt, E(verette) Howard, (Jr.)
Dietrich, William S. 1951- ... 150
Dietrich, Wilson G. 1916- ... 25-28R
Dietz, Betty Warner
See Dietz, Elisabeth H.
Dietz, David H(enry) 1897-1984 ... CANR-2
Obituary ... 114
Earlier sketch in CA 1-4R
See also SATA 10
See also SATA-Obit 41
Dietz, Elisabeth H. 1908- ... 29-32R
Dietz, Howard 1896-1983 ... 53-56
Obituary ... 110
Dietz, Lew 1907-1997 ... CANR-3
Obituary ... 157
Earlier sketch in CA 5-8R
See also SATA 11
See also SATA-Obit 95
Dietz, Marjorie (Priscilla) J(ohnson) 1918- ... CANR-14
Earlier sketch in CA 65-68
Dietz, Norman D. 1930- ... CANR-10
Earlier sketch in CA 21-24R
Dietz, Peter (John) 1924- ... 135
Dietz, Peter O(wen) 1935- ... 33-36R
Dietze, Charles Edgar 1919- ... 69-72
Dietze, Gottfried 1922- ... 21-24R
Dietzel, Paul F(ranklin) 1924- ... 21-24R
Diez Del Corral, Luis 1911- ... 13-16R
Diez de Medina, Raul 1909(?)-1985 Obituary ... 117
DiFederico, Frank R. 1933(?)-1987 Obituary ... 125
Di Filippo, Paul 1954- ... 157
See also CAAS 29
DiFranco, Anthony (Mario) 1945- ... 118
See also SATA 42
Di Franco, Fiorenza 1932- ... CANR-17
Earlier sketches in CA 45-48, CANR-1
Difusa, Pati
See Almodovar, Pedro
DiGaetani, John Louis 1943- ... CANR-35
Earlier sketch in CA 114
Digby, Anne 1935- ... SATA 72
Digby, George (Frederick) Wingfield
See Wingfield Digby, George (Frederick)
Digby, Joan (Hildreth) 1942- ... 126
Digby, John (Michael) 1938- ... 126
Digennaro, Joseph 1939- ... 53-56
Digges, Deborah 1950- ... 155
Digges, Jeremiah
See Berger, Josef
Digges, Sister Mary Laurentia 1910- ... CAP-2
Earlier sketch in CA 21-22
Diggett, Charles (P.) 1927- ... 128
Diggins, John P(atrick) 1935- ... 37-40R
Diggle, James 1944- ... CANR-13
Earlier sketch in CA 61-64
Diggory, James C(lark) 1920- ... CANR-9
Earlier sketch in CA 21-24R
Diggory, Terence (Elliott) 1951- ... 112
Diggs, Bernard James 1916- Brief entry ... 106
Diggs, Elizabeth 1939- ... 109
Diggs, Ellen Irene ... 114
Diggs, Irene
See Diggs, Ellen Irene
DiGiacomo, James J(oseph) 1924- ... CANR-57
Earlier sketches in CA 112, CANR-30
Di Girolamo, Vittorio 1928- ... 45-48
D'Ignazio, Fred(erick) 1949- ... 110
See also SATA 39
See also SATA-Brief 35
Di Grazia, Thomas (?)-1983 ... SATA 32
Di Gregorio, Mario A(urelio Umberto) 1950- ... 131
DiGregorio, Mario J. ... 168
di Guisa, Giano
See Praz, Mario
Dihoff, Gretchen 1942- ... 41-44R
Dijkstra, Bram (Abraham Jan) 1938- ... 37-40R
Dijkstra, Edsger W(ybe) 1930- ... 157
Dike, Kenneth Onwuka 1917-1983 Obituary ... 111
Dikshit, R(amesh) D(utta) 1939- ... CANR-10
Earlier sketch in CA 65-68
Dikty, Julian May
See May, Julian
Dil, Zakhmi
See Hilton, Richard
DiLauro, Stephen 1950- ... 112
Dilcock, Noreen 1907- ... 103
Di Lella, Alexander A. 1929- ... 21-24R
DiLello, Richard 1945- ... 41-44R
Di Leo, Joseph H. 1902- ... 33-36R

Diles, Dave 1931- ... CANR-8
Earlier sketch in CA 57-60
Diliberto, Gioia 1950- ... 128
Dilke, Annabel (Mary) 1942- ... CAP-1
Earlier sketch in CA 11-12
Dilke, Caroline (Sophia) 1940- ... 102
Dilke, Christopher Wentworth
1913(?)-1987 Obituary ... 125
Dilke, O(swald) A(shton) W(entworth)
1915-1993 ... 69-72
Obituary ... 142
Dilks, David (Neville) 1938- ... CANR-35
Earlier sketches in CA 61-64, CANR-8
Dill, Alonzo T(homas, Jr.) 1914- ... 37-40R
Dill, Clarence C(leveland) 1884-1978 Obituary . 115
Dill, (George) Marshall, Jr. 1916- ... 1-4R
Dill, W. S.
See Macbeth, Madge (Hamilton)
Dillard, Annie 1945- ... CANR-62
Earlier sketches in CA 49-52, CANR-3, 43
See also AAYA 6
See also CLC 9, 60
See also DAM NOV
See also DLBY 80
See also MTCW 1
See also SATA 10
Dillard, Dudley 1913-1991 ... 25-28R
Obituary ... 135
Dillard, Emil L(ee) 1921- ... 57-60
Dillard, Heath (Portmann) 1933- ... 119
Dillard, J(oey) L(ee) 1924- ... CANR-56
Earlier sketches in CA 41-44R, CANR-14, 31
Dillard, J. M. 1954- ... 128
Dillard, Polly Hargis 1916- ... CANR-5
Earlier sketch in CA 9-12R
See also SATA 24
Dillard, R(ichard) H(enry) W(ilde) 1937- .. CANR-10
Earlier sketch in CA 21-24R
See also CAAS 7
See also CLC 5
See also DLB 5
Dille, John M. 1921(?)-1971 Obituary ... 33-36R
Dille, Robert Crabtree 1924(?)-1983 Obituary .. 109
Dillehay, Ronald C(lifford) 1935- ... 21-24R
Dillenbeck, Marsden V. ... CAP-2
Earlier sketch in CA 25-28
Dillenberger, Jane 1916- ... CANR-23
Earlier sketches in CA 17-20R, CANR-7
Dillenberger, John 1918- ... CANR-38
Earlier sketches in CA 1-4R, CANR-2, 17
Diller, Edward 1925- ... 85-88
Diller, Harriett 1953- ... 146
See also SATA 78
Diller, Phyllis (Ada) 1917- ... CANR-22
Earlier sketch in CA 81-84
Dilles, James 1923- ... 1-4R
Dilley, Clyde H(obson) 1939- ... 113
Dilley, Frank B(rown) 1931- ... 13-16R
Dilliard, Irving (Lee) 1904- ... 21-24R
Dilligan, Robert J(ames) 1940- ... 127
Brief entry ... 108
Dilling, Judith
See Rhoades, Judith G(rubman)
Dilling, Yvonne 1955- ... 118
Dillingham, Beth 1927- ... 53-56
Dillingham, William B(yron) 1930- ... 13-16R
Dillistone, Frederick W(illiam) 1903- ... CANR-5
Earlier sketch in CA 1-4R
Dillman, Audrey 1922(?)-1984 Obituary ... 113
Dillman, David D. 1900(?)-1983 Obituary ... 110
Dillon, Barbara 1927- ... CANR-28
Earlier sketch in CA 110
See also SATA 44
See also SATA-Brief 39
Dillon, Bert 1937- ... 77-80
Dillon, Conley Hall 1906-1987 ... CANR-17
Obituary ... 123
Earlier sketch in CA 1-4R
Dillon, David 1941- ... 69-72
Dillon, Diane 1933- ... CLR 44
See also MAICYA
See also SATA 15, 51
Dillon, Eilis 1920-1994 ... CANR-38
Obituary ... 147
Earlier sketches in CA 9-12R, CANR-4
See also CAAS 3
See also CLC 17
See also CLR 26
See also MAICYA
See also SATA 2, 74
See also SATA-Obit 83
Dillon, George 1906-1968 Obituary ... 89-92
Dillon, George Lewis 1944- ... 102
Dillon, J(ames) T(homas) 1940- ... 33-36R
Dillon, John M(yles) 1939- ... 77-80
Dillon, Katherine V. 1916- ... 145
Dillon, Kathleen M. (Hynek) 1947- ... 146
Dillon, Lawrence S(amuel) 1910- ... CANR-25
Earlier sketch in CA 45-48
Dillon, Leo 1933- ... CLR 44
See also MAICYA
See also SATA 15, 51
Dillon, M(artin) C. 1938- ... 140
Dillon, Martin 1949- ... 61-64
Dillon, Merton L. 1924- ... 13-16R
Dillon, Millicent (Gerson) 1925- ... CANR-12
Earlier sketch in CA 65-68
Dillon, Richard H(ugh) 1924- ... CANR-8
Earlier sketch in CA 17-20R
Dillon, Sharon Saseen
See Saseen, Sharon (Dillon)
Dillon, Stuart
See Schwarcz, Vera
Dillon, Wallace Neil 1922- ... 1-4R
Dillon, Wilton S(terling) 1923- ... 37-40R
Dillow, Harry C. 1922- ... 123
Dilorenzo, Ronald Eugene 1931- Brief entry ... 110
Dils, Tracey E. 1958- ... 150
See also SATA 83
Dilson, Jesse 1914- ... 25-28R
See also SATA 24
Dilthey, Wilhelm 1833-1911 ... DLB 129
Diltz, Bert Case 1894- ... CANR-9
Earlier sketch in CA 65-68
Dilworth, David A. 1934- ... 136
Dilworth, Sharon 1958- ... 135
Dimancescu, Dan 1943- ... 113
di Marco, Gino
See Weiss, Irving J.
Di Marco, Luis Eugenio 1937- ... CANR-2
Earlier sketch in CA 45-48
Dimberg, Ronald G(ilbert) 1938- ... 61-64
Dimbleby, Jonathan 1944- ... 119
Brief entry ... 108
Di Meglio, Clara 1933- ... 97-100
DiMeglio, John E(dward) 1934- ... 77-80
Dimen, Muriel 1942- ... 127
Dimen-Schein, Muriel
See Dimen, Muriel
DiMento, Joseph F(rank) 1947- ... 69-72
DiMercurio, Michael 1958- ... 140
di Michele, Mary 1949- ... CANR-67
Earlier sketches in CA 97-100, CANR-17
Dimick, John M. 1898(?)-1983 Obituary ... 111
Dimick, Kenneth M. 1937- ... 29-32R
Dimitroff, Pashanko 1924- ... 129
Dimitrova, Blaga 1922- ... DLB 181
Dimmette, Celia (Puhr) 1896- ... CAP-2
Earlier sketch in CA 29-32
Dimmitt, Richard Bertrand 1925- ... 17-20R
Dimock, Edward Cameron, Jr. 1929- ... 102
Dimock, George E(dward) 1917- ... 133
Dimock, Gladys Ogden 1908- ... 5-8R
Dimock, Hedley G(ardiner) 1928- ... 5-8R
Dimock, Marshall E(dward) 1903-1991 ... CANR-2
Obituary ... 136
Earlier sketch in CA 1-4R
DiMona, Joseph ... 104
Dimond, E(dmunds) Grey 1918- ... 85-88
Dimond, Mary Clark ... 93-96
Dimond, Stanley E(llwood) 1905-1989 ... 13-16R
Obituary ... 128
Dimond, Stuart J. 1938-1981 ... CANR-27
Earlier sketch in CA 33-36R
Dimondstein, Geraldine 1926- ... 33-36R
Dimont, Madelon 1938- ... 41-44R
Dimont, Max I. 1912- ... 17-20R
Dimont, Penelope
See Mortimer, Penelope (Ruth)
Dimov, Dimitur 1909-1966 ... DLB 181
Dimrecken, B. Grayer
See de Mille, Richard
Dimsdale, Thomas J. 1831(?)-1866 ... DLB 186
Dimson, Wendy
See Baron, (Ora) Wendy
Din, Gilbert C. 1932- ... 118
Dinan, Carolyn ... 126
See also SATA 59
See also SATA-Brief 47
Dineley, David Lawrence 1927- ... 101
Diner, Hasia R(ena) 1946- ... CANR-9
Earlier sketch in CA 61-64
Diner, Steven J(ay) 1944- ... CANR-29
Earlier sketch in CA 110
Dinerman, Beatrice 1933- ... 13-16R
Dinerman, Helen Schneider
1921(?)-1974 Obituary ... 53-56
Dinerstein, Herbert S(amuel) 1919- Brief entry . 108
Dines, (Harry) Glen 1925- ... 9-12R
See also SATA 7
Dines, Michael 1916- ... 103
Dinesen, Isak
See Blixen, Karen (Christentze Dinesen)
See also CLC 10, 29, 95
See also SSC 7
Ding, J. N.
See Darling, Jay Norwood
Dingelstedt, Franz von 1814-1881 ... DLB 133
Dinges, John (Charles) 1941- ... 101
Dingle, Graeme 1945- ... 123
Dingle, Herbert 1890-1978 ... 13-16R
Obituary ... 122
Ding Ling
See Chiang, Pin-chin
See also CLC 68
Dingman, Roger 1938- ... 93-96
Dings, John (Garetson) 1939- ... 41-44R
Dingwall, E(ric) J(ohn) 1890-1986 ... 89-92
Obituary ... 120
Dingwall, W(illiam) Orr 1934- ... CANR-13
Earlier sketch in CA 21-24R
Dinhofer, A(lfred) 1929- ... 25-28R
Dinitz, Simon 1926- ... CANR-14
Earlier sketch in CA 37-40R
Dinkin, Robert J. 1940- Brief entry ... 107
Dinkmeyer, Don C. 1924- ... CANR-15
Earlier sketch in CA 41-44R
Dinman, Bertram David 1925- Brief entry ... 109
Dinnan, James A. 1929- ... 69-72
Dinneen, Betty 1929- ... CANR-8
Earlier sketch in CA 57-60
See also SATA 61
Dinnerstein, Harvey 1928- ... 112
See also SATA 42
Dinnerstein, Leonard 1934- ... CANR-24
Earlier sketches in CA 21-24R, CANR-9
Dino
See Dinhofer, A(lfred)
Dinsdale, Tim(othy Kay) 1924-1987 ... CANR-2
Obituary ... 124
Earlier sketch in CA 1-4R
See also SATA 11
Dinsky, Lazar 1891(?)-1976 Obituary ... 69-72
Dinsmore, Charles E(arle) 1947- ... 142
Dinsmore, Herman H.
1900(?)-1980 Obituary ... 97-100
Dintenfass, Mark 1941- ... CANR-11
Earlier sketch in CA 25-28R
Interview in ... CANR-11
See also DLBY 84
Dintiman, George B(lough) 1936- ... CANR-42
Earlier sketches in CA 53-56, CANR-5, 20
Dintrone, Charles V. 1942- ... 162
Dinwiddie, Elza Teresa ... 110
Dinwiddy, J(ohn) R(owland)
1939-1990 Obituary ... 131
Dinwiddy, John
See Dinwiddy, J(ohn) R(owland)
Diogenes Laertius c. 200- ... DLB 176
DioGuardi, Joseph J. 1940- ... 140
Diole, Philippe V. 1908- ... 53-56
Diomede, John K.
See Effinger, George Alec
Dion, Gerard 1912- ... 41-44R
Dion, Peter
See Chetwynd, Lionel
Dion, Sister Anita 1918- ... CANR-2
Earlier sketch in CA 5-8R
Dione, Robert L(ester) 1922- ... 57-60
Dionisopoulos, P(anagiotes) Allan
1921-1993 ... 29-32R
Obituary ... 141
Dionne, E(ugene) J., Jr. 1952- ... 140
Diop, Birago (Ismael) 1906-1989 ... 125
Obituary ... 130
See also BW 2
See also MTCW 1
See also SATA-Obit 64
Diop, Cheikh Anta 1923-1986 ... 125
Obituary ... 118
Brief entry ... 110
See also BW 2
Diop, David Mandessi 1927-1960 ... 143
See also BW 2
Dior, Christian 1905-1957 Brief entry ... 115
DiOrio, Al(bert John) 1950- ... CANR-9
Earlier sketch in CA 57-60
Diotima
See Wynne-Tyson, Esme
DiPalma, Ray(mond) 1943- ... CANR-49
Earlier sketches in CA 29-32R, CANR-24
DiPasquale, Dominic 1932- ... 57-60
DiPego, Gerald F(rancis) 1941- ... CANR-63
Earlier sketch in CA 85-88
DiPerna, Paula 1949- ... 112
DiPersio, Michael S(alvatore) 1934- ... 110
Di Peso, Charles C(orradino) 1920- ... 57-60
Diphusa, Patty
See Almodovar, Pedro
Di Piero, W(illiam) S. 1945- ... 138
Di Pietro, Robert Joseph 1932-1991 ... CANR-7
Obituary ... 136
Earlier sketch in CA 17-20R
Diplomaticus
See Guerra y Sanchez, Ramiro
Dipoko, Mbella Sonne 1936- ... 152
See also BW 2
Dippel, John V(an) H(outen) 1946- ... 154
Dipper, Alan 1922- ... 49-52
Dippie, Brian William 1943- ... CANR-50
Earlier sketches in CA 108, CANR-25
Dipple, Elizabeth (Dorothea) 1937-1996 ... 33-36R
Obituary ... 154
di Prima, Diane 1934- ... CANR-13
Earlier sketch in CA 17-20R
See also DLB 5, 16
Dirac, P. A. M.
See Dirac, Paul A(drien) M(aurice)
Dirac, Paul A(drien) M(aurice) 1902-1984 ... 133
Obituary ... 113
DiRenzo, Anthony 1960- ... 148
DiRenzo, Gordon J(ames) 1934- ... CANR-4
Earlier sketch in CA 53-56
Diringer, David 1900-1975 ... CANR-6
Obituary ... 57-60
Earlier sketch in CA 1-4R
Dirk
See Gringhuis, Richard H.
Dirk, R.
See Dietrich, Richard V(incent)
Dirks, Raymond L(ouis) 1934- ... 106
Dirks, Rudolph 1877-1968 Obituary ... 106
See also SATA-Brief 31
Dirks, Wilhelmina 1916- ... SATA 59
Dirks, Willy
See Dirks, Wilhelmina
Dirksen, Alvin Joseph 1915- ... 110
Dirksen, Charles J(oseph) 1912- ... 5-8R
Dirksen, Louella Carver 1899-1979 ... 103
Obituary ... 89-92
Dirlik, Arif 1940- ... 97-100
di Roccaferrera Ferrero, Giuseppe M. 1912- ...
CANR-7
Earlier sketch in CA 13-16R
Dirrim, Allen Wendell 1929- ... 21-24R
Dirscherl, Denis 1934- ... 21-24R
Dirvin, Joseph I. 1917-1993 ... CANR-2
Obituary ... 141
Earlier sketch in CA 5-8R
di Salerno, Masuccio
See dei Guardati, Tommaso
DiSalvo, Jacqueline 1943- ... 139
DiSalvo-Ryan, DyAnne 1954- ... SATA 59
Di Scala, Spencer M(ichael) 1941- ... 102
Disch, Thomas M(ichael) 1940- ... CANR-54
Earlier sketches in CA 21-24R, CANR-17, 36
See also CAAS 4
See also AAYA 17
See also CLC 7, 36
See also CLR 18
See also DLB 8
See also MAICYA
See also MTCW 1
See also SAAS 15
See also SATA 92
Disch, Tom
See Disch, Thomas M(ichael)
Dischell, Judy
See Lalli, Judy
Disher, Garry 1949- ... CANR-55
Earlier sketch in CA 127
See also SATA 81
Disher, Maurice Willson 1893-1969 ... CAP-1
Earlier sketch in CA 9-10
Dishman, Pat(ricia L.) 1939- ... 17-20R
Diski, Jenny 1947- ... 138
d'Isly, Georges
See Simenon, Georges (Jacques Christian)
Dismukes, Gwynelle
See Gwynelle (Dismukes)
Disney, Doris Miles 1907-1976 ... CANR-60
Obituary ... 65-68
Earlier sketches in CA 5-8R, CANR-3
Disney, Walt(er Elias) 1901-1966 ... 159
Obituary ... 107
See also AAYA 22
See also DLB 22
See also SATA 28
See also SATA-Brief 27
Dison, Norma 1928- ... 53-56
Dispenza, Joseph Ernest 1942- ... 81-84
Disraeli, Benjamin 1804-1881 ... DLB 21, 55
D'Israeli, Isaac 1766-1848 ... DLB 107
Disraeli, Robert 1903- ... CAP-1
Earlier sketch in CA 11-12
Disston, Harry 1899- ... 41-44R
Distel, Peter
See Koch, Kurt E(mil)
Distler, Ann G.
See Goethe, Ann
Distler, Paul Francis 1911- ... 5-8R
di Suvero, Victor 1927- ... CAAS 26
Ditchburn, R(obert) W(illiam) 1903-1987 ... 69-72
Obituary ... 122
Ditchoff, Pamela J. 1950- ... 150
Ditcum, Steve
See Crumb, R(obert)
Dito Und Idem
See Elisabeth (Ottilie Luise), Queen (Pauline)
Ditsky, John (Michael) 1938- ... CANR-9
Earlier sketch in CA 65-68
Dittes, James E(dward) 1926- ... 61-64
Dittmer, Lowell 1941- ... 89-92
Ditton, James
See Clark, Douglas (Malcolm Jackson)
Dittrich, John E(dward) 1931- ... 112
Ditzel, Paul C(alvin) 1926- ... 41-44R
Ditzen, Lowell Russell 1913-1987 ... 17-20R
Obituary ... 122
Ditzen, Rudolf 1893-1947 Brief entry ... 123
See also Fallada, Hans
Ditzion, Sidney 1908-1975 ... 41-44R
Obituary ... 57-60
Ditzler, James (R.) 1933- ... 135
Divale, William T(ulio) 1942- ... 33-36R
Di Valentin, Maria Messuri 1911- ... CANR-5
Earlier sketch in CA 5-8R
See also SATA 7
Divendal, Joost 1955- ... 132
Diverres, Armel Hugh 1914- ... 9-12R
Divine, Arthur Durham 1904-1987 ... 103
Obituary ... 122
See also SATA-Obit 52
Divine, David
See Divine, Arthur Durham
Divine, Floy (Sherman) 1881-1986 ... 113
Obituary ... 118
Divine, Robert A(lexander) 1929- ... CANR-42
Earlier sketches in CA 5-8R, CANR-3, 20
Divine, Thomas F(rancis) 1900- ... 37-40R
Divinsky, N. J.
See Divinsky, Nathan (Joseph)
Divinsky, Nathan (Joseph) 1925- ... 132
DiVitto, Barbara A(nn) 1947- ... 118
Divoky, Diane 1939- ... 33-36R
Dix, Albert V. 1901(?)-1983 Obituary ... 109
Dix, Dorothea Lynde 1802-1887 ... DLB 1
Dix, Dorothy
See Gilmer, Elizabeth Meriwether
Dix, Gertrude 1874(?)-(?) ... DLB 197
Dix, Robert H. 1930- ... 21-24R
Dix, William (Shepherd) 1910-1978 Obituary . 77-80
Dixie, Florence Douglas 1857-1905 ... DLB 174
Dixon, Ann R. 1954- ... 145
See also SATA 77
Dixon, Bernard 1938- ... CANR-51
Earlier sketches in CA 65-68, CANR-10, 26
Dixon, Christa Klingbeil 1935- ... 102
Dixon, Colin J. 1933- ... 105
Dixon, Dougal 1947- ... CANR-50
Earlier sketches in CA 107, CANR-25
See also SATA 45
Dixon, Ella Hepworth 1855(?)-1932 ... DLB 197
Dixon, Franklin W. ... CANR-27
Earlier sketch in CA 17-20R
See also MAICYA
See also SATA 1, 67, 100
Dixon, George
See Willis, Edward Henry
Dixon, Graham (Peter) 1956- ... 121

Dixon, H(arry) Vernor 1908- CAP-1
Earlier sketch in CA 9-10
Dixon, Janice T(horne) 1932- 107
Dixon, Jeane (L.) 1918-1997 CANR-21
Obituary 156
Earlier sketch in CA 65-68
Dixon, Jeanne 1936- 105
See also SATA 31
Dixon, Joan DeVee 1963- 142
Dixon, John W(esley), Jr. 1919- CANR-3
Earlier sketch in CA 9-12R
Dixon, Joseph L(awrence) 1896- 61-64
Dixon, Kenneth L. 1915(?)-1986 Obituary 119
Dixon, Laurinda S. 1948- 126
Dixon, Marjorie (Mack) 1887- CAP-2
Earlier sketch in CA 23-24
Dixon, Melvin (W.) 1950-1992 132
Obituary 139
See also BW 2
Dixon, Norman F(rank) 1922- 130
Dixon, Paige
See Corcoran, Barbara
Dixon, Penelope A(nn) 1948- 113
Dixon, Peter L(ee) 1931- CANR-2
Earlier sketch in CA 45-48
See also SATA 6
Dixon, Pierson (John) 1904-1965 CAP-1
Earlier sketch in CA 13-16
Dixon, Rachel 1952- SATA 74
Dixon, Richard Watson 1833-1900 Brief entry 122
See also DLB 19
Dixon, Robert G(alloway)
1920-1980 Obituary 97-100
Dixon, Roger 1930- 53-56
Dixon, Roger Edmund 1935-1983 Obituary 109
Dixon, Rosie
See Wood, Christopher (Hovelle)
Dixon, Ruth
See Barrows, (Ruth) Marjorie
Dixon, S(ydney) L(awrence) 1930- 69-72
Dixon, Stephen 1936- CANR-54
Earlier sketches in CA 89-92, CANR-17, 40
See also CLC 52
See also DLB 130
See also SSC 16
Dixon, Wheeler Winston 1950- 121
Dizard, Wilson P(aul) 1922- 17-20R
Dizdarevic, Zlatko 1948- 146
Dizenzo, Charles (John) 1938- CANR-67
Earlier sketch in CA 25-28R
Dizikes, John 1932- 156
Dizney, Henry (Franklin) 1926- 33-36R
Djassi, Abel
See Cabral, Amilcar
Djeddah, Eli 1911- 37-40R
Djerassi, Carl 1923- 131
Brief entry 111
See also CAAS 26
Djilas, Aleksa 1953- 139
Djilas, Milovan 1911-1995 127
Obituary 148
Djoleto, (Solomon Alexander) Amu 1929- 141
See also BW 2
See also SATA 80
Djonovich, Dusan J. 1920- 69-72
Djwa, Sandra (Ann) 1939- 131
Dluhosch, Eric 1927- 25-28R
Dluznowsky, Moshe 1906-1977 Obituary 73-76
Dmitriev, Ivan Ivanovich 1760-1837 DLB 150
Dmytryshyn, Basil 1925- CANR-26
Earlier sketches in CA 21-24R, CANR-11
Doak, Annie
See Dillard, Annie
Doak, (Dearle) Donn(ell) 1930- 65-68
Doak, Wade Thomas 1940- CANR-6
Earlier sketch in CA 57-60
Doan, Daniel 1914- 103
Doan, Eleanor Lloyd CANR-1
Earlier sketch in CA 1-4R
Doan, Richard K. 1911(?)-1989 Obituary 128
Doane, Donald P(aul) 1911- 77-80
Doane, Gilbert H(arry) 1897- CAP-1
Earlier sketch in CA 11-12
Doane, Janice (L.) 1950- 146
Doane, Marion S.
See Woodward, Grace Steele
Doane, (R.) Michael 1952- CANR-50
Earlier sketch in CA 135
Doane, Pelagie 1906-1966 CANR-6
Earlier sketch in CA 1-4R
See also SATA 7
Doan Van Toai 1946- 145
Dobb, Maurice (Herbert) 1900-1976 CANR-4
Obituary 69-72
Earlier sketch in CA 9-12R
Dobbie, Elliott Van Kirk 1907-1970 Obituary 111
Dobbin, John E. 1914-1979 9-12R
Obituary 103
Dobbin, Muriel 1935- 118
Dobbin, Murray 1945- 139
Dobbins, Austin C(harles) 1919- 57-60
Dobbins, Charles G(ordon) 1908-1988 CAP-1
Obituary 127
Earlier sketch in CA 13-16
Dobbins, Dorothy Wyeth 1929- 69-72
Dobbins, Gaines Stanley 1886-1978 CANR-2
Earlier sketch in CA 1-4R
Dobbins, Marybelle King 1900- 41-44R
Dobbs, Betty Jo Teeter 1930- 69-72
Dobbs, David 1958- 150
Dobbs, Farrell 1907-1983 CANR-14
Obituary 111
Earlier sketch in CA 49-52
Dobbs, Greg 1946- 65-68
Dobbs, Kildare (Robert Eric) 1923- CANR-19
Earlier sketch in CA 102
Dobbs, Michael 1948- 147
Dobbyn, John F(rancis) 1937- 53-56
Dobelis, M(iervaldis) C(hristian) 1929- 116
Dobell, Bertram 1842-1914 DLB 184
Dobell, Byron (Maxwell) 1927- Brief entry 112
Dobell, I(sabel) M(arian) B(arclay) 1909- CAP-1
Earlier sketch in CA 17-18
See also SATA 11
Dobell, Sydney Thompson 1824-1874 DLB 32
Dober, Richard P. 9-12R
Dobie, Ann B(rewster) 1935- 106
Dobie, Bertha McKee 1890(?)-1974 Obituary 53-56
Dobie, Edith 1894-1975 CAP-2
Obituary 57-60
Earlier sketch in CA 23-24
Dobie, J(ames) Frank 1888-1964 CANR-6
Earlier sketch in CA 1-4R
See also SATA 43
Dobin, Abraham 1907- 53-56
Dobinson, Charles Henry 1903-1980 Obituary 102
Dobkin, Alexander 1908-1975 Obituary 57-60
See also SATA-Obit 30
Dobkin, Bruce H. 1947- 122
Dobkin, Kathy
See Hamel Peifer, Kathleen
Dobkin, Kaye
See Hamel Peifer, Kathleen
Dobkin, Marjorie Housepian 1923- CANR-48
Earlier sketches in CA 33-36R, CANR-13
Dobkin De Rios, Marlene 1939- CANR-12
Earlier sketch in CA 61-64
Dobkins, J(ames) Dwight 1943- 49-52
Dobler, Bruce 1939- CANR-7
Earlier sketch in CA 53-56
Dobler, Lavinia G. 1910- CANR-2
Earlier sketch in CA 1-4R
See also SATA 6
Dobles, Fabian 1918- HW
Doblin, Alfred
See Doeblin, Alfred
See also TCLC 13
Dobner, Maeva Park 1918- 29-32R
Dobney, Frederick J(ohn) 1943- 53-56
Dobraczynski, Jan 1910- CAP-1
Earlier sketch in CA 11-12
Dobree, Bonamy 1891-1974 CANR-4
Obituary 53-56
Earlier sketch in CA 5-8R
Dobriansky, Lev E. 1918- CANR-2
Earlier sketch in CA 1-4R
Dobrin, Arnold 1928- CANR-11
Earlier sketch in CA 25-28R
See also SATA 4
Dobrin, Arthur 1943- CANR-8
Earlier sketch in CA 61-64
Dobrin, Lyn 1942- 135
Dobrin, Ronald L. 1938- 120
Dobriner, William M(ann) 1922- 65-68
Dobrovolsky, Sergei P(avlovich) 1908- CAP-2
Earlier sketch in CA 33-36
Dobrow, Larry 1925- 123
Dobrowolski, Tomasz B.
1914(?)-1976 Obituary 65-68
Dobrynin, Anatoly Fedorovich 1919- 151
Dobschiner, Johanna-Ruth 1925- 97-100
Dobson, Alan P. 1951- 139
Dobson, Andrew (Nicholas Howard) 1957- 132
Dobson, Austin 1840-1921 DLB 35; 144
See also TCLC 79
Dobson, (Richard) Barrie 1931- 33-36R
Dobson, Christopher (Joseph Edward) 1927- CANR-31
Earlier sketch in CA 97-100
Dobson, Dennis 1919(?)-1979(?) Obituary 104
Dobson, E. Philip 1910- CAP-1
Earlier sketch in CA 13-14
Dobson, Elinore (Lucille) 1934- 114
Dobson, Eric John 1913-1984 CANR-5
Obituary 112
Earlier sketch in CA 13-16R
Dobson, Eugene 1936- Brief entry 113
Dobson, James (Clayton, Jr.) 1936- CANR-68
Earlier sketches in CA 29-32R, CANR-27
Dobson, Jessie (?)-1984 Obituary 113
Dobson, Joanne 1942- 164
Dobson, John M(cCullough) 1940- 37-40R
Dobson, Julia 1941- 106
See also SATA 48
Dobson, Julia M(argaret) 1937- 73-76
Dobson, Margaret J(une) 1931- 53-56
Dobson, Michael 1960- 142
Dobson, Rosemary 1920- 77-80
Dobson, Terry 1937- 81-84
Dobson, Theodore E(lliott) 1946- CANR-28
Earlier sketch in CA 109
Dobson, William A(rthur) C(harles) H(arvey)
1913- 13-16R
Doby, John T(homas) 1920- Brief entry 114
Doby, Tibor 1914- 5-8R
Dobyns, Henry F(armer) 1925- CANR-32
Earlier sketches in CA 37-40R, CANR-15
Dobyns, Lloyd (Allen, Jr.) 1936- 119
Brief entry 110
Interview in 119
Dobyns, Stephen 1941- CANR-18
Earlier sketches in CA 45-48, CANR-2
See also CLC 37
Dobzhansky, Theodosius 1900-1975 CAP-1
Obituary 61-64
Earlier sketch in CA 13-14
Doc Abraham
See Abraham, George
Docherty, James C(airns) 1949- 144
Docherty, James L.
See Raymond, Rene (Brabazon)
Docherty, Thomas 1955- 120
Dockeray, J(ames) C(arlton) 1907-1984 45-48
Obituary 114
Dockery, Wallene T. 1941- CANR-22
Earlier sketch in CA 105
See also SATA 27
Dockrell, William Bryan 1929- CANR-32
Earlier sketches in CA 37-40R, CANR-14
Dockstader, Frederick J. 1919- 13-16R
Doc Lochard
See Lochard, Metz T(ullus) P(aul)
Doctor, Bernard
See Doctor, Bernard Aquina
Doctor, Bernard Aquina 1950- SATA 81
Doctor Baseball
See Bjarkman, Peter C(hristian)
Doctor Hispaniae
See Isidore of Seville
Doctorow, E(dgar) L(aurence) 1931- CANR-51
Earlier sketches in CA 45-48, CANR-2, 33
See also AAYA 22
See also AITN 2
See also BEST 89:3
See also CDALB 1968-1988
See also CLC 6, 11, 15, 18, 37, 44, 65, 113
See also DAM NOV, POP
See also DLB 2, 28, 173
See also DLBY 80
See also MTCW 1
Doctors, Samuel I(saac) 1936- CANR-5
Earlier sketch in CA 53-56
Doctor X
See Nourse, Alan E(dward)
Doczi, George Frederic 1909- 113
Dodd, A(rthur) E(dward) 1913- 9-12R
Dodd, Anne W(escott) 1940- 93-96
Dodd, Arthur Herbert 1893(?)-1975 Obituary 57-60
Dodd, Bella V.
See Dodd, Maria Assunta Isabella Visono
Dodd, Charles (Harold) 1884-1973 Obituary 45-48
Dodd, David L(e Fevre) 1895-1988 Obituary 126
Dodd, Donald B(radford) 1940- CANR-6
Earlier sketch in CA 57-60
Dodd, Ed(ward Benton) 1902-1991 73-76
Obituary 134
See also SATA 4
See also SATA-Obit 68
Dodd, Edward
See Dodd, Edward Howard, Jr.
Dodd, Edward Howard, Jr. 1905-1988 CANR-31
Obituary 127
Earlier sketch in CA 49-52
Dodd, James Harvey 1892-1969 1-4R
Obituary 103
Dodd, Lynley (Stuart) 1941- CANR-51
Earlier sketches in CA 107, CANR-25
See also SATA 35, 86
Dodd, Marguerite 1911- 5-8R
Dodd, Maria Assunta Isabella Visono
1904-1969 Obituary 111
Dodd, Martha
See Stern, Martha Eccles Dodd
Dodd, Philip W. 1904(?)-1983 Obituary 110
Dodd, Stuart C(arter) 1900-1975 41-44R
Dodd, Susan M. 1946- 116
Dodd, Thomas J. 1907-1971 Obituary 29-32R
Dodd, Valerie A. 1944- 134
Dodd, Wayne (Donald) 1930- 33-36R
Dodd, William E. 1869-1940 DLB 17
Dodderidge, Esme 1916- 97-100
Dodds, Bill 1952- 146
See also SATA 78
Dodds, Dayle Ann 1952- 142
See also SATA 75
Dodds, E(ric) R(obertson) 1893-1979 101
Dodds, Edward Charles 1899-1973 Obituary 115
Dodds, Gordon Barlow 1932- 5-8R
Dodds, John W(endell) 1902- 5-8R
Dodds, Robert Clyde 1918- 5-8R
Dodds, Robert H(ungerford) 1914-1976 CAP-2
Earlier sketch in CA 29-32
Dodds, Tracy 1952- 85-88
Dodek, Miriam (Joyce) Selker
1909-1986 Obituary 118
Doder, Dusko 1937- CANR-44
Earlier sketch in CA 102
Doderer, Heimito von
See von Doderer, Heimito
See also DLB 85
Dodge, Bayard 1888-1972 Obituary 111
Dodge, Bertha S(anford) 1902- CANR-2
Earlier sketch in CA 5-8R
See also SATA 8
Dodge, Calvert R(enaul) 1931- 61-64
Dodge, Daniel
See Du Breuil, (Elizabeth) L(or)inda
Dodge, David (Francis) 1910- 65-68
Dodge, David L(aurence) 1931- Brief entry 112
Dodge, Dick 1918(?)-1974 Obituary 49-52
Dodge, Dorothy R(ae) 1927- 45-48
Dodge, Ernest Stanley 1913-1980 CANR-2
Obituary 97-100
Earlier sketch in CA 1-4R
Dodge, Fremont
See Grimes, Lee
Dodge, Gil
See Hano, Arnold
Dodge, H(arry) Robert 1929- CANR-27
Earlier sketch in CA 29-32R
Dodge, Jim 1945- 141
Dodge, Langdon
See Wolfson, Victor
Dodge, Lowell 1940- 33-36R
Dodge, Marshall 1935- 89-92
Dodge, Mary (Elizabeth) Mapes 1831(?)-1905 137
Brief entry 109
See also DLB 42, 79
See also DLBD 13
See also MAICYA
See also SATA 21, 100
Dodge, Nicholas A. 1933- 65-68
Dodge, Norton T(ownshend) 1927- CANR-16
Earlier sketch in CA 25-28R
Dodge, Peter 1926- 37-40R
Dodge, Richard Holmes 1926- CANR-8
Earlier sketch in CA 13-16R
Dodge, Steve
See Becker, Stephen (David)
Dodge, Tom 1939- 154
Dodge, Wendell P(hillips)
1883-1976 Obituary 65-68
Dodgshon, Robert A(ndrew) 1941- 125
Dodgson, Charles Lutwidge 1832-1898
See Carroll, Lewis
See also CLR 2
See also DA
See also DAB
See also DAC
See also DAM MST, NOV, POET
See also MAICYA
See also SATA 100
See also YABC 2
Dodsley, Robert 1703-1764 DLB 95
Dodson, Daniel B(oone) 1918-1991 CANR-3
Obituary 133
Earlier sketch in CA 9-12R
Dodson, Fitzhugh (James) 1923-1993 CANR-24
Obituary 141
Earlier sketch in CA 29-32R
Dodson, James L. 1910- 53-56
Dodson, James Yarnell 1978- 164
Dodson, Jim
See Dodson, James Yarnell
Dodson, Kenneth MacKenzie 1907- 1-4R
See also SATA 11
Dodson, Leonidas 1900-1977 Obituary 111
Dodson, Oscar H(enry) 1905- 5-8R
Dodson, Owen (Vincent) 1914-1983 CANR-24
Obituary 110
Earlier sketch in CA 65-68
See also BLC 1
See also BW 1
See also CLC 79
See also DAM MULT
See also DLB 76
Dodson, Richard S(licer), Jr. 1896- CAP-1
Earlier sketch in CA 11-12
Dodson, Steve(n Yarnell) 1981- 164
Dodson, Susan 1941- 97-100
See also SATA 50
See also SATA-Brief 40
Dodson, Tom 1914- 29-32R
Dodwell, C(harles) R(eginald) 1922- 129
Dodwell, Peter C(arpenter) 1930- 29-32R
Dody, Sandford 1918- 129
Doebler, Bettie Anne 150
Doebler, Charles H. 1925- 21-24R
Doebler, John (Willard) 1932- 89-92
Doeblin, Alfred 1878-1957 141
Brief entry 110
See also Doblin, Alfred
See also DLB 66
See also TCLC 13
Doehring, Donald G(ene) 1927- 29-32R
Doell, Charles E(dward) 1894- CAP-1
Earlier sketch in CA 13-16
Doely, Sarah Bentley
See Bentley, Sarah
Doenecke, Justus Drew 1938- CANR-43
Earlier sketches in CA 104, CANR-20
Doenim, Susan
See Effinger, George Alec
Doenitz, Karl 1891-1980 Obituary 103
Doerffler, Alfred 1884- 1-4R
Doering, Jeanne
See Zornes, Jeanne Doering
Doeringer, Peter B(rantley) 1941- CANR-12
Earlier sketch in CA 61-64
Doerksen, Nan 1934- CANR-49
Earlier sketch in CA 123
See also SATA-Brief 50
Doerkson, Margaret 1921- 105
Doermann, Humphrey 1930- 25-28R
Doernberg, Myrna 1939- 120
Doerr, Arthur H(arry) 1924- 41-44R
Doerr, Harriet 1910- CANR-47
Brief entry 117
Earlier sketch in CA 122
Interview in 122
See also CLC 34
Doerrie, Doris 1955- 130
Doerschuk, Anna Beatrice
1880(?)-1974 Obituary 49-52
Doeser, Linda (Ann) 1950- 81-84
Doesticks, Q. K. Philander P. B.
See Thomson, Mortimer
Doezema, Linda Pegman 1948- 102
Dogan, Mattei 1920- CANR-56
Earlier sketches in CA 25-28R, CANR-12, 30
Dogg, Professor R. L.
See Berman, Ed
Doggett, Frank 1906- CANR-12
Earlier sketches in CAP-2, CA 21-22
Doggett, Rachel H. 1943- 124
Dogniez, Cecile 1953- 158
Dogyear, Drew
See Gorey, Edward (St. John)
Dohan, Mary Helen 1914- 85-88
Dohaney, Jean 129

Dohaney, M. T.
See Dohaney, Jean
Dohen, Dorothy M. 1923-1984 Obituary ... 111
Doheny, Carrie Estelle 1875-1958 ... DLB 140
Doherty, Barbara 1931- ... 116
Doherty, Berlie 1943- ... 131
See also AAYA 18
See also CLR 21
See also JRDA
See also MAICYA
See also SAAS 16
See also SATA 72
Doherty, Catherine de Hueck 1900- ... CANR-12
Earlier sketch in CA 65-68
Doherty, Charles Hugh 1913- ... 9-12R
See also SATA 6
Doherty, Craig A. 1951- ... 150
See also SATA 83
Doherty, Dennis J. 1932- ... 102
Doherty, Eddie
See Doherty, Edward J(oseph)
Doherty, Edward J(oseph) 1890-1975 ... 65-68
Obituary ... 57-60
Doherty, Herbert J(oseph), Jr. 1926- ... 1-4R
Doherty, Ivy Duffy
See Doherty, Ivy R. Duffy
Doherty, Ivy R. Duffy 1922- ... CANR-5
Earlier sketch in CA 9-12R
Doherty, John 1798(?)-1854 ... DLB 190
Doherty, Justin (Francis) 1960- ... 156
Doherty, Katherine M(ann) 1951- ... 150
See also SATA 83
Doherty, Robert W. 1935- ... 21-24R
Doherty, William 1911(?)-1984 Obituary ... 113
Doherty, William Thomas, Jr. 1923- ... 53-56
Dohme, Alvin R(obert) L(ouis) 1910- ... 110
Dohrenwend, Barbara Snell 1927-1982 ... CANR-11
Earlier sketch in CA 25-28R
Doig, Desmond 1921-1983 ... 69-72
Obituary ... 111
Doig, Ivan 1939- ... CANR-49
Earlier sketches in CA 81-84, CANR-24
Doig, Jameson W. 1933- ... CANR-32
Earlier sketches in CA 37-40R, CANR-15
Doimi di Delupis, Ingrid
See Delupis, Ingrid
Dokey, Cameron 1956- ... 152
See also SATA 97
Dolan, Anthony R(ossi) 1948- ... 73-76
Dolan, Edward F(rancis), Jr. 1924- ... CANR-68
Earlier sketch in CA 33-36R
See also SATA 45, 94
See also SATA-Brief 31
Dolan, Edwin G(eorge) 1943- ... 123
Dolan, Ellen M(eara) 1929- ... 152
See also SATA 88
Dolan, Frederick Michael 1955- ... 154
Dolan, Jay P(atrick) 1936- ... 81-84
Dolan, John Patrick 1923-1982(?) ... CANR-2
Obituary ... 106
Earlier sketch in CA 5-8R
Dolan, John Richard 1893- ... 9-12R
Dolan, Josephine A(loyse) 1913- ... 49-52
Dolan, Paul 1910- ... 9-12R
Dolan, Sean J. 1958- ... 141
See also SATA 74
Dolan, Winthrop W(iggin) 1909- ... 57-60
Dolbeare, Kenneth M(arsh) 1930- Brief entry ... 113
Dolberg, Alexander 1933- ... 33-36R
Dolbier, Maurice (Wyman) 1912-1993 ... 65-68
Obituary ... 143
Dolby, James L(ouis) 1926- ... 45-48
Dolce, J. Ellen 1948- ... SATA 75
Dolce, Philip C(harles) 1941- ... 57-60
Dolch, Edward William 1889-1961 ... SATA 50
Dolch, Marguerite Pierce 1891-1978 ... SATA 50
Dolci, Danilo (Bruno Pietro) 1924-1997 ... 127
Obituary ... 163
Brief entry ... 116
Dold, Gaylord 1947- ... 139
Dolden, A(lfred) Stuart 1893- ... 105
Dole, Gertrude E(velyn) 1915- ... 41-44R
Dole, Jeremy H(askell) 1932- ... 17-20R
Dolenz, Micky 1945- ... 152
Dolezel, Lubomir 1922- ... 45-48
Dolgoff, Ralph L. 1932- ... 33-36R
Dolgoff, Sam 1902-1990 ... 102
Obituary ... 132
Dolgun, Alexander (Michael) 1926-1986 ... 104
Obituary ... 120
Doliber, Earl L(awrence) 1947- ... 49-52
Dolim, Mary N(uzum) 1925- ... 17-20R
Dolin, Anton
See Healey-Kay, (Sydney Francis) Patrick (Chippendall)
Dolin, Edwin 1928- ... 45-48
Dolinar, Stephen J. 1926- ... 146
Doliner, Roy 1932- ... CANR-16
Earlier sketches in CA 1-4R, CANR-1
Dolinger, Jane ... AITN 2
Dolinsky, Meyer 1923- ... 57-60
Dolinsky, Mike
See Dolinsky, Meyer
Dolit, Alan 1934- ... 61-64
Doll, Mary A(swell) 1940- ... 130
Doll, (William) Richard (Shaboe) 1912- ... 108
Doll, Ronald C. 1913- ... CANR-8
Earlier sketch in CA 13-16R
Doll, Susan Marie 1954- ... 118
Dollar, Diane (Hills) 1933- ... SATA 57
Dollar, Jim
See Shaginyan, Marietta (Sergeyevna)
Dollar, Truman E. 1937- ... 97-100
Dollard, John 1900(?)-1980 Obituary ... 102
Dollar Investor
See D'Ambrosio, Charles A.
Dolle, Raymond F. 1952- ... 136
Dollen, Charles Joseph 1926- ... CANR-45
Earlier sketches in CA 5-8R, CANR-6, 21
Dolley, Michael 1925-1983 ... 123
Obituary ... 109
Dollimore, Jonathan 1948- ... 132
Dolliver, Barbara Babcock 1927- ... 5-8R
Dolloff, Eugene Dinsmore 1890-1972 ... 1-4R
Obituary ... 103
Dolmatch, Theodore B(ieley) 1924- ... 41-44R
Dolmetsch, Carl R(ichard, Jr.) 1924- ... 21-24R
Dolmetsch, Christopher L(ee) 1950- ... 111
Dolphin, Harry A. 1924- ... 128
Dolphin, Robert, Jr. 1935- ... 29-32R
Dols, Michael W(alters) 1942- ... 69-72
Dolson, Frank(lin Robert) 1933- ... 112
Dolson, Hildegarde
See Lockridge, Hildegarde (Dolson)
See also SATA 5
Doman, Glenn J(oseph) 1919- ... 61-64
Doman, June 1930- ... CANR-50
Domanska, Janina 1913(?)-1995 ... CANR-45
Obituary ... 147
Earlier sketches in CA 17-20R, CANR-11
See also AITN 1
See also CLR 40
See also MAICYA
See also SAAS 18
See also SATA 6, 68
See also SATA-Obit 84
Domaradzki, Theodore F(elix) 1910- ... CANR-1
Earlier sketch in CA 45-48
Domb, Cyril 1920- ... 109
Dombrowski, Daniel A. 1953- ... 142
Dombrowski, James A. 1897-1983 Obituary ... 109
Domecq, H(onorio) Bustos
See Bioy Casares, Adolfo and Borges, Jorge Luis
Domencich, Thomas A. ... 29-32R
Domergue, Maurice 1907- ... 25-28R
Domes, Juergen (Otto) 1932- ... 129
Dom Helder
See Camara, Helder Pessoa
Domhoff, G(eorge) William 1936- ... 45-48
Dominguez, Angel 1953- ... SATA 76
Dominguez, Jorge Ignacio 1945- ... CANR-70
Earlier sketch in CA 102
Dominguez, Richard H(enry) 1941- ... 102
Dominguez, Sergio D(anilo) Elizondo
See Elizondo (Dominguez), Sergio D(anilo)
Dominguez, Sylvia Maida 1935- ... DLB 122
Domini, Jon
See LaRusso, Dominic A(nthony)
Domini, Rey
See Lorde, Audre (Geraldine)
Dominian, Jack 1929- ... 104
Dominic, R. B.
See Hennissart, Martha and Latsis, Mary J(ane)
Dominic, Sister Mary
See Gallagher, Sister Mary Dominic
Dominick, Raymond Hunter III 1945- ... 110
Dominique
See Proust, (Valentin-Louis-George-Eugene-) Marcel
Dominique, Meg
See Sanford, Annette
Domino, John
See Averill, Esther (Holden)
Dominowski, Roger L. 1939- ... CANR-1
Earlier sketch in CA 45-48
Dominy, Eric (Norman) 1918- ... 9-12R
Domjan, Joseph (Spiri) 1907- ... CANR-24
Earlier sketches in CA 9-12R, CANR-3
See also SATA 25
Domke, Helmut Georg 1914-1974 ... CAP-1
Earlier sketch in CA 13-14
Domke, Martin 1892- ... CAP-1
Earlier sketch in CA 13-16
Domm, Jeffrey C. 1958- ... SATA 84
Dommen, Arthur J(ohn) 1934- ... 9-12R
Dommermuth, William P. 1925- ... 17-20R
Dommeyer, Frederick Charles 1909- ... 37-40R
Domotor, Tekla 1914- ... 132
Domville, Eric 1929- ... 41-44R
Don, A
See Stephen, SirLeslie
Donabedian, Avedis 1919- ... CANR-12
Earlier sketch in CA 73-76
Donagan, Alan (Harry) 1925- ... 5-8R
Donagan, Barbara (Galley) 1927- ... 17-20R
Donaghy, Henry J. 1930- ... 53-56
Donaghy, Michael 1954- ... 140
Donaghy, William A. 1910(?)-1975 Obituary ... 53-56
Donahoe, Bernard (Frances) 1932- ... 17-20R
Donahue, Don 1942- ... 69-72
Donahue, Francis J. 1917- ... 17-20R
Donahue, George T. 1911- ... 17-20R
Donahue, Jack (Clifford) 1917-1991 ... CANR-17
Obituary ... 135
Earlier sketch in CA 97-100
Donahue, June (Geserick) 1918(?)-1984 Obituary ... 111
Donahue, Kenneth 1915- ... 102
Donahue, Phil(lip John) 1935- ... 107
Donahue, Roy L(uther) 1908- ... CANR-34
Earlier sketches in CA 89-92, CANR-15
Donahue, Thomas John 1943- ... 112
Donald, Aida DiPace 1930- ... 21-24R
Donald, Anabel 1944- ... 122
Donald, Bruce H(arry) 1935- ... 111
Donald, David Herbert 1920- ... CANR-54
Earlier sketches in CA 9-12R, CANR-4
See also DLB 17
Donald, Diana 1938- ... 157
Donald, Larry W(atson) 1945- ... 93-96
Donald, Maxwell 1897-1978 Obituary ... 89-92
Donald, Merlin 1939- ... 137
Donald, Peter (Harry) 1962- ... 137
Donald, R. V.
See Floren, Lee
Donald, Vivian
See Mackinnon, Charles Roy
Donalds, Gordon
See Shirreffs, Gordon D(onald)
Donaldson, Betty 1923- ... 103
Donaldson, Bryna
See Stevens, Bryna
Donaldson, E(thelbert) Talbot 1910-1987 ... CANR-2
Obituary ... 122
Earlier sketch in CA 49-52
Donaldson, Elvin F. 1903-1972 ... 1-4R
Obituary ... 103
Donaldson, Frances (Annesley) 1907-1994 ... CANR-12
Obituary ... 144
Earlier sketch in CA 61-64
Donaldson, Frances (Gertrude) F(laacke) 1892(?)-1987 Obituary ... 122
Donaldson, Gordon 1913-1993 ... CANR-47
Obituary ... 141
Earlier sketches in CA 13-16R, CANR-5, 22
See also SATA 64
See also SATA-Obit 76
Donaldson, (Charles) Ian (Edward) 1935- ... CANR-35
Earlier sketches in CA 69-72, CANR-12
Donaldson, Islay (Eila) Murray 1921- ... 135
Donaldson, Joan 1953- ... 146
See also SATA 78
Donaldson, John W. 1893(?)-1979 Obituary ... 85-88
Donaldson, Julia 1948- ... 149
See also SATA 82
Donaldson, Kenneth 1908- ... 73-76
Donaldson, Loraine ... 140
Donaldson, Malcolm 1884-1973 ... CAP-1
Earlier sketch in CA 9-10
Donaldson, Margaret 1926- ... CANR-20
Earlier sketch in CA 103
Donaldson, Molla S(loane) 1944- ... 168
Donaldson, Norman 1922- ... 33-36R
Donaldson, Robert Herschel 1943- ... CANR-15
Earlier sketch in CA 85-88
Donaldson, S(imon) K. 1957- ... 163
Donaldson, Sam(uel Andrew) 1934- ... 111
Brief entry ... 109
Interview in ... 111
Donaldson, Scott 1928- ... CANR-27
Earlier sketches in CA 25-28R, CANR-11
See also DLB 111
Donaldson, Stephen R. 1947- ... CANR-55
Earlier sketches in CA 89-92, CANR-13
Interview in ... CANR-13
See also CLC 46
See also DAM POP
Donaldson, Thomas 1945- ... 139
Donaldson, (Charles) William 1935- ... 77-80
Donart, Arthur C(harles) 1936- ... 37-40R
Donat, Anton
See Donart, Arthur C(harles)
Donat, John (Annesley) 1933- ... 13-16R
Donato, Anthony 1909- ... CAP-1
Earlier sketch in CA 13-16
Donavan, John
See Morland, Nigel
Donawerth, Jane (Lynn) 1947- ... 118
Donceel, Joseph F. 1906- ... CANR-1
Earlier sketch in CA 1-4R
Donchess, Barbara (Briggs) 1922- ... 57-60
Donders, Jozef G(erardus) 1929- ... CANR-68
Earlier sketch in CA 129
Dondis, Donis A(snin) 1924- ... 85-88
Donelson, Irene W(itmer) 1913- ... 17-20R
Donelson, Kenneth L(avern) 1927- ... 69-72
Donelson, Kenneth W(ilber) 1910- ... 17-20R
Donem, Sue
See Ross, Stanley Ralph
Doner, Kim 1955- ... SATA 91
Doner, Mary Frances 1893- ... 13-16R
Donetta
See Chester, Tessa Rose
Doney, Willis (Frederick, Jr.) 1925- ... 21-24R
Donfried, Karl Paul 1940- ... 108
Donheiser, Alan D. 1936- ... 37-40R
Donhoff, Marion (Countess) 1909- ... 168
Doni, Rodolfo 1919- ... DLB 177
Donia, Robert J(ay) 1945- ... 155
Donicht, Mark Allen 1946- ... 93-96
Donigan, Robert L. 1903(?)-1989 Obituary ... 128
Doniger, Lester (Laurence) 1909-1971 Obituary ... 104
Donin, Hayim Halevy 1928- ... 77-80
Donington, Robert 1907-1990(?) ... 33-36R
Obituary ... 130
Donis, Miles 1937-1979 ... 29-32R
Obituary ... 93-96
Donker, Marjorie 1926- ... 145
Donkin, Nance (Clare) 1915- ... CANR-68
Earlier sketches in CA 103, CANR-20, 42
See also SATA 95
Donleavy, J(ames) P(atrick) 1926- ... CANR-62
Earlier sketches in CA 9-12R, CANR-24, 49
Interview in ... CANR-24
See also AITN 2
See also CLC 1, 4, 6, 10, 45
See also DLB 6, 173
See also MTCW 1
Donley, Carol C(ram) 1937- ... CANR-48
Earlier sketch in CA 122
Donley, Marshall O(wen), Jr. 1932- ... CANR-14
Earlier sketch in CA 65-68
Donna, Natalie 1934-1979 ... CANR-6
Earlier sketch in CA 9-12R
See also SATA 9
Donnachie, Ian Lowe 1944- ... 105
Donnan, Marcia Jeanne 1932- ... 104
Donne, John 1572-1631 ... CDBLB Before 1660
See also DA
See also DAB
See also DAC
See also DAM MST, POET
See also DLB 121, 151
See also PC 1
Donne, Maxim
See Duke, Madelaine (Elizabeth)
Donnell, David 1939(?)- ... CLC 34
Donnell, John C(orwin) 1919- ... 41-44R
Donnell, John D(ouglas) 1920- ... CANR-5
Earlier sketch in CA 53-56
Donnell, Susan ... 137
Donnellan, Michael T(homas) 1931- ... 37-40R
Donnelley, Dixon 1915-1982 Obituary ... 105
Donnell-Kotrozo, Carol 1947- ... 113
Donnelly, Alton S(tewart) 1920- ... 21-24R
Donnelly, Austin Stanislaus 1923- ... 112
Donnelly, Desmond L(ouis) 1920- ... 13-16R
Donnelly, Doris (Krimper) 1940- ... 123
Donnelly, Dorothy (Boillotat) 1903- ... CANR-3
Earlier sketch in CA 5-8R
Donnelly, Esmond
See Oberdorf, Charles (Donnell)
Donnelly, Gabrielle (Mary Teresa) 1952- ... 127
Donnelly, Ignatius 1831-1901 ... 162
Brief entry ... 110
See also DLB 12
Donnelly, James A. III 1929(?)-1984 Obituary ... 112
Donnelly, James H(oward), Jr. 1941- ... 29-32R
Donnelly, James S(tephen), Jr. 1943- ... 102
Donnelly, Joe 1950- ... 139
Donnelly, John 1941- ... 93-96
Donnelly, John Patrick 1934- ... 81-84
Donnelly, Joseph P(eter) 1905-1982 ... 81-84
Obituary ... 108
Donnelly, Sister Gertrude Joseph 1920- ... 13-16R
Donner, Fred McGraw 1945- ... 106
Donner, Joern 1933- ... CANR-9
Earlier sketch in CA 13-16R
Donner, Stanley T(emple) 1910- ... 61-64
Donnison, David Vernon 1926- ... 106
Donnison, F(rank) S(iegfried) V(ernon) 1898- ... 1-4R
Donnison, Jean 1925- ... 77-80
Donnithorne, Audrey 1922- ... 17-20R
Donnithorne, Larry 1944- ... 144
Donno, Elizabeth Story 1921- ... CANR-5
Earlier sketch in CA 1-4R
Donoghue, Denis 1928- ... CANR-16
Earlier sketch in CA 17-20R
Donoghue, Emma 1969- ... 155
See also SATA 101
Donoghue, Mildred R(ansdorf) ... CANR-10
Earlier sketch in CA 25-28R
Donoghue, P. S.
See Hunt, E(verette) Howard, (Jr.)
Donoghue, Quentin 1937- ... 122
Donoghue, William E(lliott) 1941- ... CANR-39
Earlier sketch in CA 116
Donohoe, Thomas 1917- ... 53-56
Donohoe, Tom 1957- ... 123
Donohue, Agnes McNeill 1917- ... 127
Donohue, Gail
See Storey, Gail Donohue
Donohue, James F(itzgerald) 1934- ... 73-76
Donohue, John J. 1926- ... CANR-48
Earlier sketch in CA 122
Donohue, John K. 1909- ... CAP-1
Earlier sketch in CA 11-12
Donohue, John W(aldron) 1917- ... CANR-3
Earlier sketch in CA 5-8R
Donohue, Joseph (Walter, Jr.) 1935- ... 69-72
Donohue, Mark 1937-1975 ... 57-60
Obituary ... 89-92
Donohue, Martin
See Gibson, Walter B(rown)
Donohue, William A. 1947- ... 144
Donoso (Yanez), Jose 1924-1996 ... CANR-32
Obituary ... 155
Earlier sketch in CA 81-84
See also CLC 4, 8, 11, 32, 99
See also DAM MULT
See also DLB 113
See also HLC
See also HW
See also MTCW 1
Donoughue, Bernard 1934- ... 17-20R
Donovan, Bonita R. 1947- ... 73-76
Donovan, Bonnie
See Donovan, Bonita R.
Donovan, Edward J(oseph) 1904- ... 5-8R
Donovan, Frank (Robert) 1906-1975 ... CANR-6
Obituary ... 61-64
Earlier sketch in CA 1-4R
See also SATA-Obit 30
Donovan, Hedley (Williams) 1914-1990 ... 115
Obituary ... 132
Brief entry ... 110
Interview in ... 115
Donovan, James A., Jr. 1917- ... 21-24R
Donovan, James Britt 1916-1970 ... 9-12R
Obituary ... 89-92
Donovan, John 1919- ... CANR-2
Earlier sketch in CA 1-4R

Donovan, John 1928-1992 97-100
Obituary 137
See also AAYA 20
See also CLC 35
See also CLR 3
See also MAICYA
See also SATA 72
See also SATA-Brief 29
Donovan, John C(hauncey) 1920-1984 .....37-40R
Obituary 114
Donovan, Josephine (Campbell) 1941- ... CANR-49
Earlier sketches in CA 106, CANR-24
Donovan, Katie 1962- 152
Donovan, Mary Lee 1961- 151
See also SATA 86
Donovan, Robert Alan 1921- 17-20R
Donovan, Robert J(ohn) 1912- CANR-41
Earlier sketches in CA 1-4R, CANR-2, 18
Donovan, Timothy Paul 1927- 53-56
Donovan, William
See Berkebile, Fred D(onovan)
Donow, Herbert S(tanton) 1936- 112
Don Roberto
See Cunninghame Graham, R(obert) B(ontine)
Donskoi, Mark Semyonovich
1901-1981 Obituary 103
Donson, Cyril 1919-1986 .... CANR-28
Earlier sketches in CA 21-24R, CANR-11
Don-Yehiya, Eliezer 1938- 111
Donze, Mary Terese 1911- CANR-50
Earlier sketches in CA 108, CANR-25
See also SATA 89
Doob, Anthony N(ewcomb) 1943- 33-36R
Doob, Leonard W(illiam) 1909- CANR-2
Earlier sketch in CA 5-8R
See also SATA 8
Doob, Penelope Billings Reed 1943- 53-56
Doody, Francis Stephen 1917- 13-16R
Doody, Margaret (Anne) 1939- CANR-27
Earlier sketches in CA 69-72, CANR-11
Doog, K. Caj
See Good, I(rving) John
Doohan, Leonard 1941- 118
Dooley, Allan C(harles) 1943- 138
Dooley, Arch R(ichard) 1925- 13-16R
Dooley, D(avid) J(oseph) 1921- CANR-16
Earlier sketch in CA 25-28R
Dooley, Ebon
See Ebon
Dooley, Howard J(ohn) 1944- 53-56
Dooley, John 1929(?)-1985 Obituary 119
Dooley, Maura 1957- 139
Dooley, Norah 1953- .... SATA 74
Dooley, Patrick K(iaran) 1942- 53-56
Dooley, Paul 1928- 133
Dooley, Peter C(hamberlain) 1937- 49-52
Dooley, Roger B(urke) 1920-1993 .... CANR-22
Obituary 143
Earlier sketch in CA 1-4R
Dooley, Thomas A(nthony)
1927-1961 Obituary 93-96
Dooley, William G(ermain)
1905(?)-1975 Obituary 57-60
Doolin, Dennis James 1933- 13-16R
Dooling, Dave
See Dooling, David, Jr.
Dooling, David, Jr. 1950- 125
Dooling, Richard (Patrick) 1954- 139
Doolittle, Hilda 1886-1961 .... CANR-35
Earlier sketch in CA 97-100
See also H. D.
See also CLC 3, 8, 14, 31, 34, 73
See also DA
See also DAC
See also DAM MST, POET
See also DLB 4, 45
See also MTCW 1
See also PC 5
See also WLC
Doolittle, James H(arold) 1896-1993 143
Doolittle, Jerome (Hill) 1933- CANR-71
Earlier sketch in CA 53-56
Doolittle, Jimmy
See Doolittle, James H(arold)
Doone, Jice
See Marshall, James Vance
Dooren, Ingrid van
See van Dooren, Ingrid
Doorly, Ruth K. 1919- 25-28R
Doornkamp, John Charles 1938- CANR-7
Earlier sketch in CA 57-60
Doplicher, Fabio 1938- ....DLB 128
Dopuch, Nicholas 1929- 61-64
Dor, Ana
See Ceder, Georgiana Dorcas
Dor, Milo 1923- ....DLB 85
Doran, Adelaide L(eMert) 1908- 116
Doran, Charles F(rancis) 1943- 73-76
Doran, David K. 1929- 143
Doran, Madeleine 1905- 121
Doran, Robert 1940- 150
Dorant, Gene
See Lent, D(ora) Geneva
Dorati, Antal 1906-1988 Obituary 127
Doray, Maya 1922- 45-48
Dorcy, Sister Mary Jean 1914- 9-12R
Dordick, Herbert S(halom) 1925- 116
Dore, Anita Wilkes 1914- 29-32R
Dore, Claire (Morin) 1934- 9-12R
Dore, (Louis Christophe Paul) Gustave
1832-1883 .... SATA 19
Dore, Ronald Philip 1925- CANR-34
Earlier sketches in CA 89-92, CANR-15
Doreian, Patrick 1942- 45-48
Doremus, Robert 1913- ....SATA 30
Doremus, Thomas Edmund 1922-1962 .... 1-4R
Doren, Marion (Walker) 1928- 125
See also SATA 57
Dorenkamp, Michelle 1957- .... SATA 89
Doreski, William 1946- CANR-17
Earlier sketches in CA 45-48, CANR-1
Dorey, T(homas) A(lan) 1921- 17-20R
Dorf, Fran 1953- 138
Dorf, Michael C. 1964- 135
Dorf, Richard C. 1933- CANR-52
Earlier sketches in CA 110, CANR-28
Dorfer, Ingemar (Nils Hans) 1939- 130
Dorff, Elliot N. 1943- CANR-51
Earlier sketch in CA 124
Dorflinger, Carolyn 1953- 155
See also SATA 91
Dorfman, Ariel 1942- CANR-70
Brief entry 124
Earlier sketches in CA 130, CANR-67
Interview in 130
See also CLC 48, 77
See also DAM MULT
See also HLC
See also HW
Dorfman, Dan 1932- 116
Brief entry 110
Interview in 116
Dorfman, Eugene 1917- 29-32R
Dorfman, Gerald Allen 1939- 118
Dorfman, John 1947- CANR-12
Earlier sketch in CA 69-72
Dorfman, Joseph 1904-1991 45-48
Obituary 135
Dorfman, Nancy S(chelling) 1922- 53-56
Dorfman, Nat N. 1895-1977 Obituary 73-76
Dorfman, Robert 1916- 17-20R
Dorgan, Charity Anne 1959- 134
Dorge, Jeanne Emilie Marie
See Marie-Andre du Sacre-Coeur, Sister
Dorgeles, Roland 1886-1973 .... DLB 65
Doria, Charles 1938- 73-76
Doria, Vincent Mark 1947- 138
Dorian, Edith M(cEwen) 1900- CAP-1
Earlier sketch in CA 9-10
See also SATA 5
Dorian, Frederick 1902- CAP-1
Earlier sketch in CA 11-12
Dorian, Harry
See Hamilton, Charles (Harold St. John)
Dorian, Marguerite 17-20R
See also SATA 7
Dorian, Nancy C(urrier) 1936- 104
Doriani, Beth Maclay 1961- 152
Dorin, Patrick C(arberry) 1939- CANR-34
Earlier sketches in CA 93-96, CANR-15
See also SATA 59
See also SATA-Brief 52
Doris, John Lawrence 1923- 102
Doris, Lillian 1899- 5-8R
Dorland, Henry
See Ash, Brian
Dorland, Michael 1948- 102
Dorliae, Peter Gondro 1935- 29-32R
Dorliae, Saint
See Dorliae, Peter Gondro
Dorman, Luke
See Bingley, David Ernest
Dorman, Michael 1932- CANR-5
Earlier sketch in CA 13-16R
See also SATA 7
Dorman, N. B. 1927- 106
See also SATA 39
Dorman, Sonya 1924- 73-76
Dormandy, Clara 1905- CAP-1
Earlier sketch in CA 9-10
Dorment, Richard 1946- 147
d'Ormesson, Jean (Bruno Waldemar
Francois-de-Paule Lefevre) 1925- Brief
entry 111
Dormon, James H(unter), Jr. 1936- 21-24R
Dorn, Edward (Merton) 1929- CANR-42
Earlier sketch in CA 93-96
Interview in 93-96
See also CLC 10, 18
See also DLB 5
Dorn, Frank 1901-1981 .... CANR-24
Obituary 104
Earlier sketch in CA 29-32R
Dorn, Jacob H(enry) 1939- 21-24R
Dorn, Phyllis Moore 1910(?)-1978 Obituary .. 77-80
Dorn, Sylvia O'Neill 1918- 69-72
Dorn, William S. 1928- 65-68
Dornan, James E., Jr. 1938(?)-1979 Obituary .85-88
Dornberg, John Robert 1931- CANR-1
Earlier sketch in CA 1-4R
Dornbusch, C(harles) E(mil) 1907- CAP-1
Earlier sketch in CA 9-10
Dorner, Marjorie 1942- 133
Dorner, Peter Paul 1925- CANR-14
Earlier sketch in CA 37-40R
Doro, Edward 1910- 21-24R
Doro, Marion Elizabeth 1928- 89-92
Doroch, Efim Yakovlevitch
1908(?)-1972 Obituary 37-40R
Doronzo, Emmanuel 1903- 21-24R
Doroshkin, Milton 1914- 33-36R
Dorothy, R. D.
See Charques, Dorothy (Taylor)
Dorpalen, Andreas 1911-1982 .... 17-20R
Obituary 109
Dorr, Donal 1935- CANR-44
Earlier sketch in CA 118
Dorr, Lawrence 168
Dorr, Rheta (Louise) Childe 1866-1948 Brief
entry 116
See also DLB 25
Dorrie, Doris
See Doerrie, Doris
Dorrien, Gary J. 1952- 135
Dorries, William (Lyle) 1923- 37-40R
Dorris, Michael (Anthony) 1945-1997 .... CANR-46
Obituary 157
Earlier sketches in CA 102, CANR-19
See also AAYA 20
See also BEST 90:1
See also CLC 109
See also DAM MULT, NOV
See also DLB 175
See also NNAL
See also SATA 75
See also SATA-Obit 94
Dorris, Michael A.
See Dorris, Michael (Anthony)
Dorris, R(obert) T. 1913- 29-32R
Dorritt, Susan
See Schlein, Miriam
Dorros, Arthur (M.) 1950- 146
See also CLR 42
See also SAAS 20
See also SATA 78
Dors, Diana
See Fluck, Diana
Dorsan, Luc
See Simenon, Georges (Jacques Christian)
Dorsange, Jean
See Simenon, Georges (Jacques Christian)
Dorsen, Norman 1930- 37-40R
Dorset, Gerald (Harris) 1920- 112
Dorset, Phyllis (Flanders) 1924- 25-28R
Dorset, Richard
See Shaver, Richard S(harpe)
Dorset, Ruth
See Ross, W(illiam) E(dward) D(aniel)
Dorsett, Danielle
See Daniels, Dorothy
Dorsett, Lyle W(esley) 1938- CANR-9
Earlier sketch in CA 21-24R
Dorsey, Candas Jane 1952- 156
Dorsey, David Frederick, Jr. 1934- 115
Dorsey, Hebe 1925-1987 Obituary 124
Dorsey, Helen 1928- 110
Dorsey, John M(orris) 1900- CANR-4
Earlier sketch in CA 5-8R
Dorsey, John R(ussell) 1938- 118
Dorsey, John Thornton, Jr. 1924- 111
D'Orso, Michael 1953- 154
D'Orso, Mike
See D'Orso, Michael
Dorson, Richard M(ercer) 1916-1981 106
Obituary 105
See also SATA 30
Dorsonville, Max 1943- 65-68
Dorst, Jean (Pierre) 1924- CANR-19
Earlier sketches in CA 5-8R, CANR-3
Dorst, Tankred 1925- CANR-30
Earlier sketch in CA 41-44R
See also DLB 75, 124
Dorwart, J(effrey) M(ichael) 1944- 97-100
Dorwart, Reinhold August 1911- 65-68
Dorworth, Alice Grey 1907- 5-8R
Dosa, Marta Leszlei 45-48
Doskocilova, Hana 1936- CANR-47
Earlier sketches in CA 61-64, CANR-8, 23
Doskow, Minna 1937- 118
Dos Passos, John (Roderigo) 1896-1970 .. CANR-3
Obituary 29-32R
Earlier sketch in CA 1-4R
See also CDALB 1929-1941
See also CLC 1, 4, 8, 11, 15, 25, 34, 82
See also DA
See also DAB
See also DAC
See also DAM MST, NOV
See also DLB 4, 9
See also DLBD 1, 15
See also DLBY 96
See also MTCW 1
See also WLC
Doss, Erika 159
Doss, Helen (Grigsby) 1918- CANR-6
Earlier sketch in CA 9-12R
See also SATA 20
Doss, James D(aniel) 1939- 163
Doss, Margot Patterson CANR-12
Earlier sketch in CA 29-32R
See also SATA 6
Doss, Richard W(eller) 1933- Brief entry 112
Dossage, Jean
See Simenon, Georges (Jacques Christian)
dos Santos, Joyce Audy 1949- 136
Brief entry 118
See also Zarins, Joyce Audy
See also SATA 57
See also SATA-Brief 42
Dossick, Philip 1941- 81-84
Doster, William C(lark) 1921- 13-16R
Dostoevsky, Fedor Mikhailovich 1821-1881 .....DA
See also DAB
See also DAC
See also DAM MST, NOV
See also SSC 2
See also WLC
Dothard, Robert Loos 1909(?)-1979 Obituary .85-88
Dothers, Anne
See Chess, Victoria (Dickerson)
Doti, Lynne Pierson 1948- 137
Dotsenko, Paul 1894-1988 117
Obituary 140
Dotson, Bob
See Dotson, Robert Charles
Dotson, Floyd 1917- 25-28R
Dotson, John L(ouis), Jr. 1937- 105
Dotson, Lillian O. 1921- 25-28R
Dotson, Robert Charles 1946- 134
Brief entry 119
Dott, R(obert) H(enry), Jr. 1929- 53-56
Dottig
See Grider, Dorothy
Dotto, Lydia 1949- 125
Dotts, M. Franklin 1929- 57-60
Dotts, Maryann J. 1933- CANR-30
Earlier sketches in CA 33-36R, CANR-12
See also SATA 35
Doty, Brant Lee 1921- 17-20R
Doty, C(harles) Stewart 1928- 65-68
Doty, Carolyn 1941- CANR-47
Earlier sketches in CA 105, CANR-23
Doty, Gladys 1908- 53-56
Doty, Gresdna Ann 1931- 41-44R
Doty, James Edward 1922- 37-40R
Doty, Jean Slaughter 1929- CANR-2
Earlier sketch in CA 45-48
See also SATA 28
Doty, Mark (A.) 1953(?)- 161
Doty, Richard (George) 1942- 109
Doty, Robert McIntyre 1933- 102
Doty, Roy 1922- CANR-8
Earlier sketch in CA 53-56
See also SATA 28
Doty, William G(uy) 1939- CANR-20
Earlier sketches in CA 53-56, CANR-5
Doty, William Lodewick 1919-1979 .... CANR-1
Earlier sketch in CA 1-4R
Doubiago, Sharon 1946- 112
Doubleday, Neal Frank 1905-1976 ....41-44R
Doubleday, Veronica 1948- 129
Doubrovsky, Serge 1928- 136
Brief entry 110
Doubtfire, Dianne (Abrams) 1918- CANR-39
Earlier sketches in CA 1-4R, CANR-1, 17
See also SATA 29
Doucet, Clive 1946- CANR-42
Earlier sketch in CA 118
Doucette, Leonard E(ugene) 1936- 33-36R
Douds, Charles Tucker 1898-1982 Obituary ... 106
Dougall, Herbert E(dward) 1902- CAP-1
Earlier sketch in CA 19-20
Dougall, Lily 1858-1923 ....DLB 92
Dougan, Michael B(ruce) 1944- 69-72
Dougherty, Betty 1922- 61-64
Dougherty, Charles 1922- ....SATA 18
Dougherty, Ching-yi (Hsu) 1915- 5-8R
Dougherty, David Mitchell 1903- 113
Dougherty, Flavian 1913(?)-1990 Obituary 130
Dougherty, James (Patrick) 1937- 106
Dougherty, James E(dward) 1923- 134
Brief entry 111
Dougherty, Joanna Foster
See Foster, Joanna
Dougherty, John J(oseph) 1907-1986 Obituary . 118
Dougherty, Jude P(atrick) 1930- 45-48
Dougherty, Philip H(ugh) 1923-1988 Obituary .. 126
Dougherty, Richard 1921-1986 .... CANR-2
Obituary 121
Earlier sketch in CA 1-4R
Dougherty, Richard M. 1935- 33-36R
Doughtie, Edward (Orth) 1935- 45-48
Doughty, Bradford 1921- 65-68
Doughty, Charles M(ontagu) 1843-1926 Brief
entry 115
See also DLB 19, 57, 174
See also TCLC 27
Doughty, Nina Beckett 1911- 53-56
Doughty, Oswald 1889- CAP-1
Earlier sketch in CA 9-10
Doughty, Paul L(arrabee) 1930- 85-88
Doughty, Robin W. 1941- 122
Douglas, Albert
See Armstrong, Douglas Albert
Douglas, Althea (Cleveland McCoy) 1926- 124
Douglas, Ann 1942- 149
Douglas, Ann C.
See Welch, Ann Courtenay (Edmonds)
Douglas, Arthur
See Hammond, Gerald (Arthur Douglas)
Douglas, Barbara
See Ovstedal, Barbara
Douglas, Blaise 1960- 168
See also SATA 101
Douglas, Carole Nelson 1944- CANR-53
Earlier sketches in CA 107, CANR-26
See also AAYA 17
See also SATA 73
Douglas, Charles H(erbert) 1926- Brief entry ... 109
Douglas, Christopher
See Neill, Christopher Harry Douglas
Douglas, Claire 1936- 144
Douglas, David C(harles) 1898-1982 .... CANR-28
Obituary 107
Earlier sketch in CA 73-76
Douglas, Ellen
See Haxton, Josephine Ayres
and Williamson, Ellen Douglas
See also CLC 73
Douglas, Emily (Taft) 1899-1994 107
Obituary 143
Douglas, Garry
See Kilworth, Garry (D.)
Douglas, Gavin 1475(?)-1522 .... DLB 132
Douglas, George
See Brown, George Douglas
Douglas, George H(alsey) 1934- CANR-14
Earlier sketch in CA 81-84
Douglas, Glenn
See Duckett, Alfred A.
Douglas, Gregory A.
See Cantor, Eli

Douglas, Helen Bee
See Bee, Helen L.
Douglas, Helen Gahagan 1900-1980 161
Obituary 101
Douglas, J(ames) D(ixon) 1922- CANR-44
Earlier sketches in CA 13-16R, CANR-6, 21
Douglas, Jack 1909(?)-1989 Obituary 128
Douglas, James McM.
See Butterworth, W(illiam) E(dmund III)
Douglas, Jeff
See Offutt, Andrew J(efferson V)
Douglas, John 162
Douglas, John (Frederick James) 1929- 116
Douglas, Kate
See Douglas, Kathleen
Douglas, Kathleen 1949- 117
Douglas, Kathryn
See Ewing, Kathryn
Douglas, Keith (Castellain) 1920-1944 160
See also DLB 27
See also TCLC 40
Douglas, Kirk 1916- 138
See also BEST 90:4
Douglas, Lauren Wright 1947- 129
Douglas, Leonard
See Bradbury, Ray (Douglas)
Douglas, Leonard M(arvin) 1910-(?) CAP-2
Earlier sketch in CA 23-24
Douglas, Lloyd C.
See Douglas, Lloyd Cassel
Douglas, Lloyd Cassel 1877-1951 Brief entry .. 120
Douglas, Louis H(artwell) 1907-1979 .... 21-24R
Obituary 133
Douglas, Mack R. 1922- 21-24R
Douglas, Marjory Stoneman 1890-1998 .. CANR-72
Obituary 167
Earlier sketches in CA 1-4R, CANR-2
See also AITN 2
See also SATA 10
Douglas, Mary (Tew) 1921- 97-100
Douglas, Melvyn 1901-1981 135
Douglas, Michael
See Bright, Robert (Douglas Sr.)
Douglas, Michael
See Crichton, (John) Michael
Douglas, Mike 1925- 89-92
Douglas, (George) Norman 1868-1952 157
Brief entry 119
See also DLB 34, 195
See also TCLC 68
Douglas, Paul Howard 1892-1976 69-72
Douglas, R. M.
See Mason, Douglas R(ankine)
Douglas, Robert
See Andrews, (Charles) Robert Douglas (Hardy)
Douglas, Roy (Ian) 1924- CANR-56
Earlier sketches in CA 73-76, CANR-13, 30
Douglas, Scott
See Smith, William Scott
Douglas, Shane
See Wilkes-Hunter, R(ichard)
Douglas, Susan J(eanne) 1950- 153
Douglas, Thorne
See Haas, Ben(jamin) L(eopold)
Douglas, William
See Brown, George Douglas
Douglas, William A(llison) 1934- 45-48
Douglas, William O(rville) 1898-1980 .... CANR-21
Obituary 93-96
Earlier sketch in CA 9-12R
Douglas-Hamilton, James 1942- CANR-13
Earlier sketch in CA 33-36R
Douglas-Home, Alec
See Home, Alexander Frederick (Douglas-)
Douglas-Home, Charles (Cospatrick)
1937-1985 Obituary 117
Douglas-Home, Henry 1907-1980 103
Obituary 101
Douglas-Home, Robin 1932-1968 .... CAP-2
Earlier sketch in CA 25-28
Douglas Home, William
See Home, William Douglas
Douglass, Amanda Hart
See Wallmann, Jeffrey M(iner)
Douglass, Barbara 1930- 114
See also SATA 40
Douglass, Billie
See Delinsky, Barbara (Ruth Greenberg)
Douglass, Donald McNutt 1899-1975 .... 1-4R
Obituary 103
Douglass, Elisha Peairs 1915- 81-84
Douglass, Frederick 1817(?)-1895 .... BLC 1
See also CDALB 1640-1865
See also DA
See also DAC
See also DAM MST, MULT
See also DLB 1, 43, 50, 79
See also SATA 29
See also WLC
Douglass, Harl R(oy) 1892- 5-8R
Douglass, Herbert Edgar 1927- CANR-13
Earlier sketch in CA 73-76
Douglass, James W. 1937- CANR-10
Earlier sketch in CA 25-28R
Douglass, Malcolm P(aul) 1923- CANR-13
Earlier sketch in CA 73-76
Douglass, Marcia Kent
See Doty, Gladys
Douglass, Paul F(ranklin) 1904- CANR-3
Earlier sketch in CA 5-8R
Douglass, Robert W. 1934- 57-60
Douglass, William 1691(?)-1752 .... DLB 24
Douglass, William A(nthony) 1939- 69-72
Douglas-Scott-Montagu, Edward
See Montagu of Beaulieu, Edward John Barrington

Douglas Wood, Ann
See Douglas, Ann
Doulis, Thomas 1931- CANR-11
Earlier sketch in CA 5-8R
Doulos, Jay
See Joyce, Jon L(oyd)
Doumato, Lamia 1947- 103
Dourado, (Waldomiro Freitas) Autran 1926- ....
CANR-34
Earlier sketch in CA 25-28R
See also CLC 23, 60
Dourado, Autran 1926- .... DLB 145
Dourado, Waldomiro Autran
See Dourado, (Waldomiro Freitas) Autran
Douras, Marion Cecilia 1897-1961 Obituary 111
Douskey, Franz 1941- 129
Doutremont, Henri
See Bugnet, Georges (-Charles-Jules)
Douty, Esther M(orris) 1909-1978 .... CANR-3
Obituary 85-88
Earlier sketch in CA 5-8R
See also SATA 8
See also SATA-Obit 23
Douty, Norman F(ranklin) 1899- CANR-31
Earlier sketch in CA 49-52
Douvan, Elizabeth (Ann Malcolm) 1926- 106
Dove, Arthur G. 1880-1946 .... DLB 188
Dove, Rita (Frances) 1952- CANR-68
Earlier sketches in CA 109, CANR-27, 42
See also CAAS 19
See also BLCS
See also BW 2
See also CLC 50, 81
See also DAM MULT, POET
See also DLB 120
See also PC 6
Doveglion
See Villa, Jose Garcia
Dover, C(larence) J(oseph) 1919- 13-16R
Dover, K(enneth) J(ames) 1920- CANR-56
Earlier sketches in CA 25-28R, CANR-12, 29
Dover Wilson, John 1881-1969 Obituary 25-28R
Dovey, Ken 1947- 120
Dovlatov, Sergei 1941-1990 .... CANR-45
Obituary 132
Earlier sketch in CA 115
Dow, Blanche H(innan)
1893-1973 Obituary 41-44R
Dow, Dorothy
See Fitzgerald, Dorothy (Minerva) Dow
Dow, Emily R. 1904- CAP-1
Earlier sketch in CA 11-12
See also SATA 10
Dow, George Francis 1868-1936 Brief entry ... 122
Dow, J(ose) Kamal 1936- 29-32R
Dow, Marguerite R(uth) 1926- 116
Dow, Neal 1906- 17-20R
Dow, Sterling 1903-1995 .... CAP-2
Obituary 147
Earlier sketch in CA 21-22
Dow, Vicki
See McVey, Vicki
Dowd, Douglas F(itzgerald) 1919- 5-8R
Dowd, John David 1945- 146
See also SATA 78
Dowd, Laurence P(hillips) 1914-1980 .... 17-20R
Obituary 133
Dowd, Maxine
See Jensen, Maxine Dowd
Dowd, Merle E(dward) 1918- 85-88
Dowdell, Dorothy (Florence) Karns 1910- ....
CANR-44
Earlier sketches in CA 9-12R, CANR-5, 20
See also SATA 12
Dowden, Anne Ophelia 1907- CANR-18
Earlier sketches in CA 9-12R, CANR-3
See also SAAS 10
See also SATA 7
Dowden, Edward 1843-1913 .... DLB 35, 149
Dowden, George 1932- CANR-22
Earlier sketches in CA 53-56, CANR-4
Dowden, Wilfred S(ellers) 1917- 125
Dowdey, Clifford (Shirley, Jr.) 1904- 9-12R
Dowdey, Landon Gerald 1923- 89-92
See also SATA 11
Dowding, Hugh Caswell Tremenheere
1882-1970 Obituary 112
Dowdy, Andrew 1936- 49-52
Dowdy, Homer E(arl) 1922- 5-8R
Dowdy, Mrs. Regera
See Gorey, Edward (St. John)
Dowell, Coleman 1925-1985 .... CANR-10
Obituary 117
Earlier sketch in CA 25-28R
See also CLC 60
See also DLB 130
Dowell, Jack (Larder) 1908- 57-60
Dowell, Richard W(alker) 1931- 116
Dower, J. W.
See Dower, John W(illiam)
Dower, John W(illiam) 1938- 137
Brief entry 128
Interview in 137
Dower, Penn
See Pendower, Jacques
Dowie, James Iverne 1911- 41-44R
Dowie, Mark 1939- 85-88
Dowland, John 1563-1626 .... DLB 172
Dowler, James R(oss) 1925- CANR-64
Earlier sketch in CA 29-32R
Dowley, D. M.
See Marrison, L(eslie) W(illiam)
Dowley, Timothy Edward 1946- CANR-18
Earlier sketch in CA 101
Dowling, Allan D. 1903-1983 Obituary 117
Dowling, Allen 1900- 29-32R

Dowling, Basil (Cairns) 1910- 97-100
Dowling, David (Hurst) 1950- 118
Dowling, Eddie 1894-1976 Obituary 65-68
Dowling, Harry Filmore 1904- 102
Dowling, Joseph A(lbert) 1926- 37-40R
Dowling, Maria 1955- 123
Dowling, Terry 1947- 161
See also SATA 101
Dowling, Thomas, Jr. 1921- 85-88
Dowling, Tom
See Dowling, Thomas, Jr.
Down, Goldie (Malvern) 1918- CANR-51
Earlier sketches in CA 25-28R, CANR-11, 26
Down, Michael (Graham) 1951- CANR-42
Earlier sketch in CA 118
Downard, William L. 1940- 49-52
Downer, Alan S(eymour) 1912-1970 .... CAP-1
Obituary 33-36R
Earlier sketch in CA 11-12
Downer, Lesley 1949- 131
Downer, Marion 1892(?)-1971 Obituary 33-36R
See also SATA 25
Downes, Bryan Trevor 1939- 33-36R
Downes, David A(nthony) 1927- 33-36R
Downes, Edward (Olin Davenport) 1911- 105
Downes, G. V.
See Downes, Gwladys (Violet)
Downes, Gwladys (Violet) 1915- 147
See also DLB 88
Downes, Kerry 1930- 119
Downes, Mollie Patricia Panter
See Panter-Downes, Mollie Patricia
Downes, Quentin
See Harrison, Michael
Downes, Randolph C(handler) 1901-1975 49-52
Obituary 61-64
Downey, Bill
See Downey, William L(eslie)
Downey, Fairfax D(avis) 1893-1990 .... CANR-1
Obituary 131
Earlier sketch in CA 1-4R
See also SATA 3
See also SATA-Obit 66
Downey, Glanville 1908- CANR-1
Earlier sketch in CA 1-4R
Downey, Harris 13-16R
Downey, James 1939- 101
Downey, Lawrence William (Lorne) 1921- ... 17-20R
Downey, Murray William 1910- CANR-1
Earlier sketch in CA 1-4R
Downey, William L(eslie) 1922- 110
Downie, Freda (Christina) 1929- 106
Downie, Jill 1938- CANR-25
Earlier sketch in CA 108
Downie, John 1931- CANR-26
Earlier sketch in CA 108
See also SATA 87
Downie, Leonard, Jr. 1942- CANR-1
Earlier sketch in CA 49-52
Downie, Mary Alice (Dawe) 1934- CANR-52
Earlier sketches in CA 25-28R, CANR-10, 26
See also SATA 13, 87
Downie, N(orville) M(organ) 1910- 17-20R
Downing, A(rthur) B(enjamin) 1915- 29-32R
Downing, Chris(tine) 1931- 57-60
Downing, David A(lmon) 1958- 150
See also SATA 84
Downing, David C(laude) 1951- 146
Downing, Douglas 1957- 114
Downing, Graham 1954- 136
Downing, J. Major
See Davis, Charles A.
Downing, John (Allen) 1922- CANR-20
Earlier sketches in CA 53-56, CANR-5
Downing, Julie 1956- .... SATA 81
Downing, Lester N. 1914- CANR-25
Earlier sketches in CA 25-28R, CANR-10
Downing, Major Jack
See Smith, Seba
Downing, Michael (Bernard) 1958- 166
Downing, Noel
See Shreffler, Philip A.
Downing, Paul B(utler) 1938- 104
Downing, Paula E. 1951- 136
See also SATA 80
Downing, Warwick 1931- 53-56
Downs, Anthony 1930- CANR-28
Earlier sketch in CA 49-52
Downs, Brian W(esterdale)
1893-1984 Obituary 112
Downs, Cal W. 1936- 103
Downs, Donald (Alexander) 1948- 119
Downs, Dorothy 1937- 151
Downs, Hugh (Malcolm) 1921- CANR-2
Earlier sketch in CA 45-48
Downs, Hunton (Leache) 1918- 1-4R
Downs, Jacques M. 1926- 37-40R
Downs, James Francis 1926- 81-84
Downs, Lenthiel H(owell) 1915- 25-28R
Downs, Norton 1918-1985 .... 1-4R
Obituary 114
Downs, Robert B.
See Downs, Robert Bingham
Downs, Robert Bingham 1903-1991 .... CANR-17
Obituary 133
Earlier sketches in CA 1-4R, CANR-2
Downs, Robert C. S. 1937- CANR-1
Earlier sketch in CA 45-48
Downs, William Randall, Jr. 1914-1978 81-84
Obituary 77-80
Dowpreeth, Hughbridge
See Kay, Jeremy
Dowriche, Anne 1560-1613(?) .... DLB 172
Dowse, Robert E. 1933- 21-24R
Dowse, (Dale) Sara 1938- 119
Dowsey-Magog, Paul 1950- 105

Dowson, Ernest (Christopher) 1867-1900 150
Brief entry 105
See also DLB 19, 135
See also TCLC 4
Dowst, Somerby R(ohrer) 1926-1990 .... 33-36R
Obituary 133
Dowty, Alan K. 1940- 122
Doxey, Roy W(atkins) 1908- 41-44R
Doxey, William S(anford, Jr.) 1935- CANR-25
Earlier sketches in CA 65-68, CANR-9
Doxiadis, Constantinos Apostolos
1913-1975 .... 41-44R
Obituary 57-60
Doyle, A. Conan
See Doyle, Arthur Conan
Doyle, Adrian M. C.
See Conan Doyle, Adrian Malcolm
Doyle, Arthur Conan 1859-1930 122
Brief entry 104
See also AAYA 14
See also CDBLB 1890-1914
See also DA
See also DAB
See also DAC
See also DAM MST, NOV
See also DLB 18, 70, 156, 178
See also MTCW 1
See also SATA 24
See also SSC 12
See also TCLC 7
See also WLC
Doyle, Brian 1930- 53-56
Doyle, Brian 1935- CANR-55
Earlier sketch in CA 135
See also AAYA 16
See also CLR 22
See also JRDA
See also MAICYA
See also SAAS 16
See also SATA 67
Doyle, Charles (Desmond) 1928- CANR-51
Earlier sketches in CA 25-28R, CANR-11, 26
Doyle, Charlotte (Lackner) 1937- CANR-65
Earlier sketch in CA 81-84
See also SATA 94
Doyle, Conan
See Doyle, Arthur Conan
Doyle, David
See Carter, David C(harles)
Doyle, Debra 1952- 165
Doyle, Denis P. 1940- CANR-26
Earlier sketch in CA 109
Doyle, Don H(arrison) 1946- CANR-14
Earlier sketch in CA 81-84
Doyle, Donovan
See Boegehold, Betty (Doyle)
Doyle, Edward (Gerard) 1949- 118
Doyle, Edward Park 1907-1985 Obituary 115
Doyle, Esther M. 1910- 45-48
Doyle, Frank D. 1909(?)-1983 Obituary 109
Doyle, Gerald A. 1898(?)-1986 Obituary 119
Doyle, Harold Edmund
See Stearns, Harold Edmund
Doyle, James (Stephen) 1935- 73-76
Doyle, Jerry
See Doyle, Gerald A.
Doyle, John
See Graves, Robert (von Ranke)
Doyle, John Robert, Jr. 1910- 25-28R
Doyle, Kirby 1932- .... DLB 16
Doyle, Mary Ellen 1932- 114
Doyle, Michael W. 1948- 120
Doyle, Mike
See Doyle, Charles (Desmond)
Doyle, Paul A. 1925- CANR-22
Earlier sketches in CA 13-16R, CANR-7
Doyle, Paul I(gnatius) 1959- 143
Doyle, Richard 1824-1883 .... SATA 21
Doyle, Richard 1948- 85-88
Doyle, Richard Edward 1929- 113
Doyle, Richard J(ames) 1923- 65-68
Doyle, Robert C. 1946- 145
Doyle, Robert J. 1931- 143
Doyle, Robert V(aughn) 1916- CANR-9
Earlier sketch in CA 65-68
Doyle, Roddy 1958(?)- 143
See also AAYA 14
See also CLC 81
See also DLB 194
Doyle, Sir A. Conan
See Doyle, Arthur Conan
Doyle, Sir Arthur Conan
See Doyle, Arthur Conan
Doyle, William 1942- 130
Doyno, Victor A(nthony) 1937- 37-40R
Dozer, Donald Marquand 1905- CANR-1
Earlier sketch in CA 1-4R
Dozier, Craig Lanier 1920- 41-44R
Dozier, Edward P. 1916-1971 Obituary 29-32R
Dozier, Robert R. 1932- 120
Dozier, Zoe
See Browning, Dixie Burrus
Dozois, Gardner R(aymond) 1947- CANR-27
Earlier sketch in CA 108
Dr. A
See Asimov, Isaac
and Silverstein, Alvin
Dr. Alphabet
See Morice, Dave
Dr. Guano
See Gootenberg, Paul
Dr. Hip
See Schoenfeld, Eugene
Dr. Hippocrates
See Schoenfeld, Eugene

Dr. Judy
See Kuriansky, Judith (Anne Brodsky)
Dr. Loon
See Martien, Jerry
Dr. NO
See Many, Seth E(dward)
Dr. Science
See Coffey, Daniel
Dr. Seuss
See Geisel, Theodor Seuss
See also CLR 1, 9
Dr. Spektor
See Glut, Donald F(rank)
Dr. Zed
See Penrose, Gordon
Drabble, Margaret 1939- ... CANR-63
Earlier sketches in CA 13-16R, CANR-18, 35
See also CDBLB 1960 to Present
See also CLC 2, 3, 5, 8, 10, 22, 53
See also DAB
See also DAC
See also DAM MST, NOV, POP
See also DLB 14, 155
See also MTCW 1
See also SATA 48
Drabble, Phil 1914- ... 102
Drabeck, Bernard A. 1932- ... 129
Drabek, Jan 1935- ... 93-96
Drabek, Thomas E(dward) 1940- ... CANR-37
Earlier sketches in CA 45-48, CANR-1, 16
Drach, Albert 1902- ... DLB 85
Drache, Sharon (Abron) 1943- ... CANR-47
Earlier sketch in CA 118
Drachkovitch, Milorad M. 1921- ... 17-20R
Drachler, Jacob 1909- ... 61-64
Drachler, Rose 1911- ... CANR-4
Earlier sketch in CA 53-56
Drachman, Edward Ralph 1940- ... 29-32R
Drachman, Julian M(oses) 1894- ... 61-64
Drachman, Theodore S(olomon) 1904- ... 81-84
Drackett, Phil(ip Arthur) 1922- ... CANR-3
Earlier sketch in CA 9-12R
See also SATA 53
Draco, F.
See Davis, Julia
Dracup, Angela 1943- ... 141
See also SATA 74
Drage, Charles H(ardinge) 1897- ... CANR-2
Earlier sketch in CA 5-8R
Drager, Marvin 1920- ... 81-84
Dragland, Stan L(ouis) 1942- ... CANR-52
Earlier sketch in CA 125
Dragnich, Alex N. 1912- ... CANR-15
Earlier sketch in CA 89-92
Drago, Edmund Leon 1942- ... 109
Drago, Harry Sinclair 1888-1979 ... CANR-63
Obituary ... 89-92
Earlier sketch in CA 113
Drago, Sinclair
See Drago, Harry Sinclair
Dragojevic, Danijel 1934- ... DLB 181
Dragon, Caroline
See Du Breuil, (Elizabeth) L(or)inda
Dragonette, Jessica (?)-1980 Obituary ... 97-100
Dragonwagon, Crescent 1952- ... CANR-36
Earlier sketches in CA 65-68, CANR-12
See also JRDA
See also MAICYA
See also SAAS 14
See also SATA 11, 41, 75
Dragun, Osvaldo 1929- ... HW
Drahos, Mary 1927- ... 116
Drainie, Bronwyn 1945- ... 129
Draitser, Emil 1937- ... CANR-18
Earlier sketch in CA 89-92
Drakakis, John 1944- ... 120
Drake, Albert (Dee) 1935- ... CANR-43
Earlier sketches in CA 33-36R, CANR-13
Drake, Alice Hutchins 1889(?)-1975 Obituary ... 61-64
Drake, Asa (a pseudonym) ... 113
Drake, Barbara (Ann) 1939- ... CANR-13
Earlier sketch in CA 33-36R
Drake, Bonnie
See Delinsky, Barbara (Ruth Greenberg)
Drake, Charles D(ominic) 1924- ... 116
Drake, David (Allen) 1945- ... CANR-38
Earlier sketches in CA 93-96, CANR-17
See also SATA 85
Drake, Donald C(harles) 1935- ... 85-88
Drake, Elizabeth 1948- ... 109
Drake, Francis Vivian 1894-1971 Obituary ... 104
Drake, Frank
See Hamilton, Charles (Harold St. John)
Drake, Frank D(onald) 1930- ... 17-20R
Drake, Frederick Charles 1937- ... 119
Drake, George Randolph 1938- ... CANR-11
Earlier sketch in CA 69-72
Drake, Harold Allen 1942- ... 97-100
Drake, James A. 1944- ... 130
Drake, Jane 1954- ... 149
See also SATA 82
Drake, Joan H(oward) ... CANR-24
Earlier sketch in CA 13-16R
Drake, Kimbal
See Gallagher, Rachel
Drake, Lisl
See Beer, Eloise C. S.
Drake, Michael 1935- ... CANR-16
Earlier sketch in CA 25-28R
Drake, Paul Winter 1944- ... 106
Drake, Richard Bryant 1925- ... 37-40R
Drake, Robert (Young, Jr.) 1930- ... 17-20R
Drake, (John Gibbs) St. Clair (Jr.) 1911-1990 ... 65-68
Obituary ... 131
Drake, Samuel Gardner 1798-1875 ... DLB 187
Drake, Shannon
See Pozzessere, Heather Graham
Drake, (Bryant) Stillman 1910- ... CANR-40
Earlier sketches in CA 41-44R, CANR-18
Drake, W. Anders
See Eshbach, Lloyd Arthur
Drake, W(inbourne) Magruder 1914- ... 41-44R
Drake, W(alter) Raymond 1913- ... CANR-5
Earlier sketch in CA 53-56
Drake, William D(onovan) 1922- ... 21-24R
Drake, William Daniel 1941- ... 69-72
Drake, William E(arle) 1903- ... CAP-1
Earlier sketch in CA 17-18
Drake-Brockman, David 1933- ... 114
Drakeford, John W. 1914- ... CANR-5
Earlier sketch in CA 1-4R
Drakulic, Slavenka 1949- ... 144
Drakulic-Ilic, Slavenka
See Drakulic, Slavenka
Dralle, Elizabeth (Mary) 1910- ... 1-4R
Drane, James F. 1930- ... CANR-7
Earlier sketch in CA 13-16R
Drane, John (William) 1946- ... CANR-15
Earlier sketch in CA 93-96
Drange, Theodore M. 1934- ... 37-40R
Dranoff, Linda Silver ... CANR-64
Earlier sketch in CA 129
Dranow, John (Theodore) 1948- ... 140
Dransfield, Michael (John Pender) 1948-1973 ... CANR-30
Earlier sketch in CA 37-40R
Drant, Thomas 1540(?)-1578(?) ... DLB 167
Draper, Alfred 1924- ... CANR-53
Earlier sketches in CA 33-36R, CANR-13, 29
Draper, Cena C(hristopher) 1907- ... CANR-10
Earlier sketch in CA 17-20R
Draper, Charles Stark 1901-1987 ... 157
Draper, Edgar 1926- ... 13-16R
Draper, (Ellinor) Elizabeth (Nancy) 1915- ... 17-20R
Draper, Hal 1914-1990 ... CANR-24
Obituary ... 130
Earlier sketches in CA 17-20R, CANR-7
Draper, Hastings
See Jeffries, Roderic (Graeme)
Draper, James P(atrick) 1959- ... 143
Draper, James T(homas), Jr. 1935- ... 89-92
Draper, Jo 1949- ... CANR-43
Earlier sketch in CA 119
Draper, John W. 1811-1882 ... DLB 30
Draper, John William 1893-1976 ... CANR-16
Obituary ... 69-72
Earlier sketches in CAP-1, CA 9-10
Draper, Lyman C. 1815-1891 ... DLB 30
Draper, Norman R(ichard) 1931- ... 53-56
Draper, Ronald Philip 1928- ... 69-72
Draper, Sharon M(ills) ... SATA 98
Draper, Theodore 1912- ... 13-16R
Draper, Thomas 1928- ... 108
Drapier, M. B.
See Swift, Jonathan
Drapkin, Herbert 1916- ... 33-36R
Drapkin, Israel 1906- ... 57-60
Draskovich, Slobodan M. 1910-1982 ... 93-96
Obituary ... 108
Drath, Viola Herms 1926- ... CANR-14
Earlier sketch in CA 65-68
Drawbell, James Wedgwood 1899- ... 65-68
Drawe, D. Lynn 1942- ... 146
Drawson, Blair 1943- ... 85-88
See also SATA 17
Dray, William H(erbert) 1921- ... CANR-13
Earlier sketch in CA 33-36R
Drayer, Adam Matthew 1913- ... 9-12R
Drayham, James
See Mencken, H(enry) L(ouis)
Drayne, George
See McCulley, Johnston
Drayton, Michael 1563-1631 ... DAM POET
See also DLB 121
Drazan, Joseph Gerald 1943- ... 110
Drazin, Israel 1935- ... 151
Dre, Dr. 1965(?)- ... 156
Dreadstone, Carl
See Campbell, (John) Ramsey
Drebinger, John 1891(?)-1979 Obituary ... 89-92
Drefus, Jean-Paul Etienne 1909-1985 Obituary ... 117
Dreger, Georgia 1918- ... 115
Dreger, Ralph Mason 1913- ... 73-76
Dreher, Carl 1896-1976 ... 73-76
Dreher, Diane Elizabeth 1946- ... 119
Dreher, Henry 1955- ... 149
Dreher, Melanie (Creagan) 1943- ... 114
Dreifort, John E. 1943- ... 45-48
Dreifus, Claudia 1944- ... CANR-1
Earlier sketch in CA 45-48
Dreifuss, Kurt 1897- ... CANR-16
Earlier sketches in CA 1-4R, CANR-1
Dreikurs, Rudolf 1897-1972 ... CANR-6
Obituary ... 33-36R
Earlier sketch in CA 1-4R
Dreiser, Theodore (Herman Albert) 1871-1945 ... 132
Brief entry ... 106
See also CDALB 1865-1917
See also DA
See also DAC
See also DAM MST, NOV
See also DLB 9, 12, 102, 137
See also DLBD 1
See also MTCW 1
See also SSC 30
See also TCLC 10, 18, 35, 83
See also WLC
Dreiser, Vera ... 69-72
Dreiss, Joseph G. 1949- ... 125
Dreiss-Tarasovic, Marcia M(argaret) 1943- ... 65-68
Dreitzel, Hans Peter 1935- ... 41-44R
Drekmeier, Charles 1927- ... 1-4R
Drennen, D(onald) A(rthur) 1925- ... CANR-17
Earlier sketches in CA 1-4R, CANR-2
Dresang, Eliza (Carolyn Timberlake) 1941- ... 69-72
See also SATA 19
Dresbach, Glen Ward 1889-1968 ... 5-8R
Drescher, Fran 1957- ... 155
Drescher, Henrik 1955- ... 135
See also CLR 20
See also MAICYA
See also SATA 67
Drescher, Joan E(lizabeth) 1939- ... 106
See also SATA 30
Drescher, John M(ummau) 1928- ... CANR-16
Earlier sketches in CA 49-52, CANR-1
Drescher, Sandra 1957- ... CANR-16
Earlier sketch in CA 85-88
Drescher, Seymour 1934- ... CANR-4
Earlier sketch in CA 9-12R
Drescher-Lehman, Sandra
See Drescher, Sandra
Dresner, Hal 1937- ... 13-16R
Dresner, Samuel H(ayim) 1923- ... CANR-9
Earlier sketch in CA 5-8R
Dressel, Paul L(eroy) 1910- ... CANR-3
Earlier sketch in CA 9-12R
Dresselhaus, Mildred S. 1930- ... 157
Dresser, Davis 1904-1977 ... CANR-49
Obituary ... 69-72
Earlier sketch in CA 77-80
Dresser, Helen
See McCloy, Helen (Worrell Clarkson)
Dresser, Norine 1931- ... 132
Dressler, Alan (Michael) 1948- ... 147
Dressman, Dennis L(ee) 1945- ... 106
Dressman, Denny
See Dressman, Dennis L(ee)
Dressman, John 1947- ... 122
Dretske, Frederick I(rwin) 1932- ... CANR-10
Earlier sketch in CA 25-28R
Dreux, William B(ehan) 1911- ... 89-92
Dreves, Veronica R. 1927-1986 Obituary ... 121
See also SATA-Obit 50
Drew, Bernard 1926(?)-1984 Obituary ... 111
Drew, Bettina 1956- ... 151
Drew, Donald J. 1920- ... 57-60
Drew, Eileen 1957- ... 143
Drew, Elizabeth 1887-1965 ... 5-8R
Drew, Elizabeth 1935- ... 104
Interview in ... 104
Drew, Fraser Bragg Robert 1913- ... 13-16R
Drew, George A(lexander) 1894-1973 Obituary ... 113
Drew, Katherine Fischer 1923- ... 9-12R
Drew, Kenneth
See Cockburn, (Francis) Claud
Drew, Mary Anne
See Cassiday, Bruce (Bingham)
Drew, Morgan
See Price, Robert
Drew, Patricia (Mary) 1938- ... 77-80
See also SATA 15
Drew, Philip 1943- ... 107
Drew, Wayland 1932- ... 154
Drew-Bear, Robert 1901- ... CAP-2
Earlier sketch in CA 33-36
Drewe, Robert (Duncan) 1943- ... 138
Drewery, Mary 1918- ... 25-28R
See also SATA 6
Drewes, Athena A. 1948- ... 146
Drewitz, Ingeborg 1923-1986 ... DLB 75
Drewnowski, Jan 1908- ... CANR-68
Earlier sketch in CA 129
Drewry, Guy Carleton 1901-1991 ... 5-8R
Obituary ... 135
Drewry, Henry N. 1924- ... 97-100
Drewry, John E(ldridge) 1902-1983 Obituary ... 109
Drexel, Jay B.
See Bixby, Jerome Lewis
Drexelius, J.
See Gourmont, Remy (-Marie-Charles) de
Drexler, Arthur 1925-1987 ... 97-100
Obituary ... 121
Drexler, J. F.
See Paine, Lauran (Bosworth)
Drexler, K(im) Eric 1955- ... CANR-48
Earlier sketch in CA 121
Drexler, Rosalyn 1926- ... CANR-68
Earlier sketch in CA 81-84
See also CLC 2, 6
Dreyer, Carl Theodor 1889-1968 Obituary ... 116
See also CLC 16
Dreyer, Edward C. 1937- ... 21-24R
Dreyer, Frederick 1932- ... 111
Dreyer, Peter (Richard) 1939- ... 81-84
Dreyfack, Raymond ... CANR-24
Earlier sketches in CA 65-68, CANR-9
Dreyfus, Edward A(lbert) 1937- ... 37-40R
Dreyfus, Fred
See Rosenblatt, Fred
Dreyfus, Hubert L(ederer) 1929- ... CANR-28
Earlier sketch in CA 33-36R
Dreyfus, Kay 1942- ... 124
Dreyfuss, Henry 1904-1972 ... 45-48
Obituary ... 37-40R
Dreyfuss, Joel 1945- ... 97-100
Dreyfuss, Larry 1928- ... 65-68
Dreyfuss, Randolph (Lowell) 1956- ... 97-100
Drez, Ronald J(oseph) 1940- ... 146
Dreze, Jean 1959- ... 133
Drial, J. E.
See Laird, Jean E(louise)
Dribben, Judith Strick 1923- ... 37-40R
Driberg, Thomas Edward Neil 1905-1976 ... 65-68
Obituary ... 104
Driberg, Tom
See Driberg, Thomas Edward Neil
Driedger, Leo ... 146
Drieu la Rochelle, Pierre(-Eugene) 1893-1945 Brief entry ... 117
See also DLB 72
See also TCLC 21
Driftwood, Penelope
See De Lima, Clara Rosa
Drimmer, Frederick 1916- ... CANR-23
Earlier sketches in CA 61-64, CANR-7
See also SATA 60
Drinan, Adam
See Macleod, Joseph (Todd Gordon)
Drinan, Robert F(rederick) 1920- ... CANR-3
Earlier sketch in CA 9-12R
Dring, Nathaniel
See McBroom, R. Curtis
Drinkall, Gordon (Don) 1927- ... 9-12R
Drinker, Elizabeth 1735-1807 ... DLB 200
Drinkle, Ruth Wolfley 1903- ... 93-96
Drinkrow, John
See Hardwick, (John) Michael (Drinkrow)
Drinkwater, Francis Harold 1886- ... CANR-1
Earlier sketch in CA 1-4R
Drinkwater, John 1882-1937 ... 149
Brief entry ... 109
See also DLB 10, 19, 149
See also TCLC 57
Drinkwater, Terry 1936-1989 ... 69-72
Obituary ... 128
Drinnon, Richard 1925- ... CANR-6
Earlier sketch in CA 13-16R
Driscoll, Gertrude 1898(?)-1975 Obituary ... 61-64
Driscoll, James P. 1946- ... 146
Driscoll, Peter (John) 1942- ... CANR-2
Earlier sketch in CA 49-52
Driscoll, R(obert) E(ugene) 1949- ... 85-88
Driskell, David Clyde 1931- ... 102
Driskill, Frank A. 1912- ... 130
Driskill, J. Lawrence 1920- ... 155
See also SATA 90
Driskill, Larry
See Driskill, J. Lawrence
Driver, C(harles) J(onathan) 1939- ... CANR-57
Earlier sketches in CA 29-32R, CANR-30
Driver, Christopher (Prout) 1932-1997 ... 57-60
Obituary ... 156
Driver, Cynthia C.
See Lovin, Roger Robert
Driver, David E. 1955- ... 155
Driver, Donald 1922-1988 Obituary ... 125
Driver, Edwin D(ouglas) 1925- ... 114
Driver, Godfrey Rolles 1892-1975 ... CAP-2
Obituary ... 57-60
Earlier sketch in CA 21-22
Driver, Harold Edson 1907- ... CANR-6
Earlier sketch in CA 1-4R
Driver, Tom F(aw) 1925- ... CANR-1
Earlier sketch in CA 1-4R
Driving Hawk, Virginia
See Sneve, Virginia Driving Hawk
Drlica, Karl 1943- ... 151
Drobot, Eve 1951- ... 131
Droege, Thomas Arthur 1931- ... 113
Droescher, Vitus B(ernward) 1925- ... 33-36R
Drogheda, Earl of
See Moore, Charles Garrett Ponsonby
Droit, Michel (Arnould Arthur) 1923- ... CANR-32
Earlier sketches in CA 5-8R, CANR-11
Droppers, Carl Hyink 1918- ... 5-8R
Drop Shot
See Cable, George Washington
Dror, Yehezkel 1928- ... CANR-13
Earlier sketch in CA 21-24R
Drosnin, Michael 1946- ... 163
Drossaart Lulofs, H(endrik) J(oan) 1906- ... 13-16R
Droste-Hulshoff, Annette Freiin von 1797-1848 DLB 133
Drotar, David Lee 1952- ... 112
Drotning, Phillip T(homas) 1920- ... CANR-10
Earlier sketch in CA 25-28R
Drought, James (William) 1931-1983 ... CANR-20
Obituary ... 110
Earlier sketch in CA 5-8R
Drouin, Francis M. 1901- ... 37-40R
Drouin, Marie-Josee 1949- ... 116
Drowatzky, John N(elson) 1936- ... 89-92
Drower, E(thel) S(tefana May) 1879-1972 ... CAP-1
Earlier sketch in CA 11-12
Drower, G(eorge) M(atthew) F(rederick) 1954- ... 131
Drown, Harold J(ames) 1904- ... 49-52
Drown, Merle 1943- ... 109
Drowne, Tatiana B(alkoff) 1913- ... 17-20R
Droz, Eugenie 1893(?)-1976 Obituary ... 104
Droze, Wilmon H(enry) 1924- ... CANR-10
Earlier sketch in CA 17-20R
Drubert, John H. 1925- ... 45-48
Druce, Christopher
See Pulling, Christopher Robert Druce
Drucker, Daniel Charles 1918- ... 157
Drucker, H. M.
See Drucker, Henry M(atthew)
Drucker, Henry M(atthew) 1942- ... CANR-29
Earlier sketch in CA 106
Drucker, Johanna 1952- ... 151
Drucker, Malka 1945- ... CANR-31
Earlier sketches in CA 81-84, CANR-14
See also SATA 39
See also SATA-Brief 29
Drucker, Mark L(ewis) 1947- ... 107
Drucker, Mort 1929- ... 133
Drucker, Olga Levy 1927- ... 147
See also SATA 79
Drucker, Peter 1958- ... 147
Drucker, Peter F(erdinand) 1909- ... CANR-46
Earlier sketch in CA 61-64
Druett, Joan 1939- ... 140

Drukker, J.
See Presser, (Gerrit) Jacob
Druks, Herbert 1937- CANR-9
Earlier sketch in CA 21-24R
Drum, Alice 1935- 154
Drum, Bob
See Drum, Robert F.
Drum, Robert F. 1918- 5-8R
Drumheller, Sidney J(ohn) 1923- 53-56
Drumm, D. B.
See Naha, Ed
Drummond, Alison 1903- 112
Drummond, Donald F(rasier) 1914- CANR-4
Earlier sketch in CA 1-4R
Drummond, Dorothy W(eitz) 1928- 41-44R
Drummond, Edith Marie Dulce Carman 1883-1970 . CAP-1
Earlier sketch in CA 9-10
Drummond, Ellen Lane 1897- 1-4R
Drummond, Harold D. 1916- CANR-12
Earlier sketch in CA 33-36R
Drummond, Ian (Macdonald) 1933- 37-40R
Drummond, Jack 1923(?)-1978 Obituary 81-84
Drummond, John
See Chance, John Newton
Drummond, John 1900-1982 Obituary 106
Drummond, John Dodds 1944- 102
Drummond, June 1923- CANR-72
Earlier sketches in CA 13-16R, CANR-7
Drummond, Kenneth H(erbert) 1922- 17-20R
Drummond, Maldwin Andrew Cyril 1932- . CANR-14
Earlier sketch in CA 73-76
Drummond, Richard H(enry) 1916- 41-44R
Drummond, (James) Roscoe 1902-1983 104
Obituary 110
Drummond, V(iolet) H(ilda) 1911- 13-16R
See also SATA 6
Drummond, Walter
See Silverberg, Robert
Drummond, William
See Calder-Marshall, Arthur
Drummond, William Henry 1854-1907 160
See also DLB 92
See also TCLC 25
Drummond, William Joe 1944- 77-80
See also BW 1
Drummond de Andrade, Carlos 1902-1987 132
Obituary 123
See also Andrade, Carlos Drummond de
See also CLC 18
Drummond of Hawthornden, William 1585-1649 .... DLB 121
Druon, Maurice (Samuel Roger Charles) 1918- CANR-12
Earlier sketch in CA 13-16R
Drury, Alan 1949- 106
Drury, Allen (Stuart) 1918- CANR-52
Earlier sketches in CA 57-60, CANR-18
Interview in CANR-18
See also CLC 37
Drury, Clare Marie
See Hoskyns-Abrahall, Clare (Constance Drury)
Drury, Clifford Merrill 1897- CANR-3
Earlier sketch in CA 9-12R
Drury, George H(erbert) 1940- CANR-47
Earlier sketch in CA 121
Drury, James Westbrook 1919- 5-8R
Drury, John 1898-1972 .... 5-8R
Obituary 33-36R
Drury, John 1936- 133
Drury, Margaret Josephine 1937- 53-56
Drury, Maxine Cole 1914- 5-8R
Drury, Michael CANR-27
Earlier sketch in CA 49-52
Drury, Roger W(olcott) 1914- 65-68
See also SATA 15
Drury, S(hadia) B(asilious) 1950- 116
Drury, Sally 1960- 139
Drury, Treesa Way 1937- 53-56
Drury, William 1918- 125
Drutman, Irving 1910-1978 85-88
Obituary 81-84
Druxman, Michael Barnett 1941- CANR-37
Earlier sketches in CA 49-52, CANR-1, 16
Drvota, Mojmir 1923- 57-60
Dryansky, G. Y. 49-52
Dryden, Cecil P(earl) 1887- 25-28R
Dryden, Charles 1860(?)-1931 .... DLB 171
Dryden, Edgar A. 1937- 89-92
Dryden, John
See Rowland, D(onald) S(ydney)
Dryden, John 1631-1700 .... CDBLB 1660-1789
See also DA
See also DAB
See also DAC
See also DAM DRAM, MST, POET
See also DC 3
See also DLB 80, 101, 131
See also WLC
Dryden, Ken(neth Wayne) 1947- 105
Dryden, Lennox
See Steen, Marguerite
Dryden, Pamela
See St. John, Nicole
Dryhurst, Edward
See Roberts, Edward Dryhurst
Drysdale, Frank R(eiff) 1943- 89-92
Drysdale, George Russell 1912-1981 Obituary . 108
Drysdale, Helena 1960- 125
Drysdale, Vera Louise 1923- 115
Drzazga, John 1907- CAP-1
Earlier sketch in CA 11-12
Drzemczewski, Andrew (Zbigniew) 1951- 116
Drzic, Marin c. 1508-1567 .... DLB 147
D'Souza, Dinesh 1961- CANR-54
Earlier sketch in CA 118

Dua, R(am) P(arkash) 1930- 25-28R
Duan, Le
See Le, Duan
Duane, Daniel 1967- 159
Duane, Daniel King
See Duane, Daniel
Duane, Diane (Elizabeth) 1952- CANR-66
Earlier sketch in CA 139
See also SATA 58, 95
See also SATA-Brief 46
Duane, Jim
See Hurley, Vic
Duane, William 1760-1835 .... DLB 43
Duarte (Fuentes), Jose Napoleon 1925-1990 ... 137
Obituary 131
Duarte, Joseph S(imon) 1913- 57-60
Dubal, David 1944- 118
Duball, Michael
See Ald, Roy A(llison)
Duban, James 1951- 125
Dubanevich, Arlene 1950- CANR-40
Earlier sketch in CA 116
See also SATA 56
Dubay, Robert W. 1943- 65-68
DuBay, Sandra 1954- CANR-47
Earlier sketches in CA 107, CANR-23
Dubay, Thomas Edward 1921- CANR-6
Earlier sketch in CA 1-4R
DuBay, William H. 1934- 17-20R
Dube, Marcel 1930- 129
Brief entry 117
See also DLB 53
Dube, Pierre Herbert 1943- CANR-10
Earlier sketch in CA 65-68
Dube, Rodolphe
See Hertel, Francois
Dubelaar, Thea 1947- .... SATA 60
Duberman, Lucile 1926- 69-72
Duberman, Martin (Bauml) 1930- CANR-63
Earlier sketches in CA 1-4R, CANR-2
See also CLC 8
Duberstein, Helen 1926- CANR-44
Earlier sketches in CA 45-48, CANR-1
Duberstein, Larry 1944- 135
Dubh, Cathal O
See Duff, Charles (St. Lawrence)
Dubie, Norman (Evans) 1945- CANR-12
Earlier sketch in CA 69-72
See also CLC 36
See also DLB 120
Dubin, Michael J. 1938- 137
Dubin, Robert 1916- CANR-1
Earlier sketch in CA 45-48
Dubin, Samuel Sanford 1914- 37-40R
Dubinsky, David 1892-1982 Obituary 107
Dubinsky, Rostislav (D.) 1923- 133
Dubitsky, Cora Marie 1933- 124
Dubkin, Lois Knudson 1911- 5-8R
du Blane, Daphne
See Groom, Arthur William
Dublin, Jack 1915- 21-24R
Dublin, Thomas Louis 1946- 101
Dubnick, Mel(vin Jay) 1946- CANR-30
Earlier sketch in CA 112
Dubnick, Randa Kay 1948- 112
Dubofsky, Melvyn 1934- CANR-37
Earlier sketches in CA 49-52, CANR-1, 16
Dubois, Charles
See Counselman, Mary Elizabeth
Du Bois, David G(raham) 1925- 65-68
See also BW 1
Dubois, Elfrieda T(heresia Pichler) 1916- 9-12R
DuBois, Ellen Carol 1947- 136
Brief entry 113
DuBois, Josiah Ellis, Jr. 1912-1983 Obituary ... 114
Dubois, M.
See Kent, Arthur William Charles
DuBois, Paul M(artin) 1945- 102
DuBois, Paul Z(inkhan) 1936- 111
DuBois, Rochelle (Lynn) Holt 1946- CANR-7
Earlier sketch in CA 57-60
See also Holt, Rochelle L.
DuBois, Rosemary
See Durrant, Rita D(elores)
Du Bois, Shirley Graham 1907(?)-1977 77-80
Obituary 69-72
See also Graham, Shirley
See also BW 1
See also SATA 24
Du Bois, W(illiam) E(dward) B(urghardt) 1868-1963 . CANR-34
Earlier sketch in CA 85-88
See also BLC 1
See also BW 1
See also CDALB 1865-1917
See also CLC 1, 2, 13, 64, 96
See also DA
See also DAC
See also DAM MST, MULT, NOV
See also DLB 47, 50, 91
See also MTCW 1
See also SATA 42
See also WLC
du Bois, William (Sherman) Pene 1916-1993 Obituary 140
See also SATA-Obit 74
Duboise, Novella 1911- 152
See also SATA 88
Dubos, Jean (Porter) 1918(?)-1988 Obituary ... 126
Dubos, Rene (Jules) 1901-1982 .... CANR-48
Obituary 106
Earlier sketch in CA 5-8R
DuBose, Fred 1945- 118
DuBose, LaRocque (Russ) 1926- 21-24R
See also SATA 2

DuBose, Louise Jones 1901- CAP-1
Earlier sketch in CA 13-14
Dubost, Thierry 1958- 164
Du Boulay, F(rancis) R(obin) H(oussemayne) 1920- 131
du Boulay, Shirley 1933- CANR-65
Earlier sketch in CA 129
Dubout, C(harles) A(lbert) 1905-1976 Obituary 65-68
Dubov, Gwen Bagni 97-100
Dubov, Paul (?)-1979 97-100
Obituary 89-92
DuBow, Fredric L(ee) 1944- 25-28R
Du Breuil, (Elizabeth) L(or)inda 1924-1980 104
Interview in 104
DuBrin, Andrew J(ohn) 1935- CANR-33
Earlier sketches in CA 41-44R, CANR-15
Dubro, Alec 1944- 133
Dubro, James (Richard) 1946- 129
Du Broff, Nedra 1931- 110
Du Broff, Sidney 1929- CANR-9
Earlier sketch in CA 21-24R
Dubrovin, Vivian 1931- CANR-71
Earlier sketches in CA 57-60, CANR-9, 40
See also SATA 65
DuBruck, Alfred J(oseph) 1922- 37-40R
DuBruck, Edelgard (Conradt) 1925- 17-20R
Du Brul, Paul 1938(?)-1987 Obituary 125
Dubs, Homer H(asenpflug) 1892-1969 ...... CAP-1
Earlier sketch in CA 13-16
Dubus, Andre III 1959- 132
Dubus, Andre 1936- CANR-17
Earlier sketch in CA 21-24R
Interview in CANR-17
See also CLC 13, 36, 97
See also DLB 130
See also SSC 15
Dubus, Elizabeth Nell 1933- 110
Duby, Georges (Michel Claude) 1919-1996 .... CANR-48
Obituary 154
Earlier sketches in CA 104, CANR-22
Duca Minimo
See D'Annunzio, Gabriele
Du Cane, Peter 1901-1984 Obituary 114
Ducange, Victor 1783-1833 .... DLB 192
du Cann, Charles Garfield Lott 1889(?)-1983 Obituary 109
Ducas, Dorothy 1905-1987 .... CANR-27
Earlier sketch in CA 5-8R
Ducasse, C(urt) J(ohn) 1881-1969 .... CANR-6
Earlier sketch in CA 1-4R
Duce, Robert 1908- 5-8R
Ducey, Jean Sparks 1915- 158
See also SATA 93
Duchac, Joseph 1932- 144
Duchacek, Ivo D(uka) 1913-1988 .... CANR-1
Obituary 124
Earlier sketch in CA 1-4R
See also SATA-Obit 55
Du Chaillu, Paul (Belloni) 1835(?)-1903 Brief entry 112
See also DLB 189
See also SATA 26
Duchamp, (Henri-Robert) Marcel 1887-1968 ... 116
Obituary 110
Ducharme, Rejean 1941- Obituary 165
See also CLC 74
See also DLB 60
Duche, Jean 1915- CANR-9
Earlier sketch in CA 9-12R
Duchein, Michel 1926- 135
Duchene, Louis-Francois 1927- 105
Duchesne, Antoinette
See Paine, Lauran (Bosworth)
Duchesne, Jacques
See Saint-Denis, Michel Jacques
Duchesne, Janet 1930- Brief entry 111
See also SATA-Brief 32
Duchess of Marlborough
See Spencer-Churchill, Laura
Duchess of Windsor
See Windsor, (Bessie) Wallis Warfield (Spencer) Simpson
Duchin, Faye 1944- 125
Ducic, Jovan 1871-1943 .... DLB 147
Duck, Stephen 1705(?)-1756 .... DLB 95
Duckat, Walter Benjamin 1911- 29-32R
Ducker, Bruce 1938- 65-68
Ducker, James H. 1950- 130
Duckert, Mary 1929- 53-56
Duckett, Alfred A. 1917(?)-1984 45-48
Obituary 114
Duckett, Eleanor Shipley 1880(?)-1976 Obituary 69-72
Duckham, A(lec) N(arraway) 1903-1988 73-76
Obituary 126
Duckham, Baron Frederick 1933- 103
Duckworth, Alistair M(cKay) 1936- 41-44R
Duckworth, Eleanor 1935- 142
Duckworth, F(rancis) R(obinson) G(ladstone) 1881-1964 Obituary 113
Duckworth, George E(ckel) 1903-1972 .... CANR-1
Obituary 33-36R
Earlier sketch in CA 1-4R
Duckworth, Leslie Blakey 1904- 105
Duckworth, Marilyn 1935- 163
Duckworth, William (Ervin) 1943- 151
Ducornet, Erica 1943- CANR-54
Earlier sketches in CA 37-40R, CANR-14, 34
See also SATA 7
Ducornet, Rikki
See Ducornet, Erica
Duda, Margaret B(arbalich) 1941- 65-68
Dudarew-Ossetynski, Leonidas 1911(?)-1989 Obituary 128

Dudden, Arthur P(ower) 1921- CANR-3
Earlier sketch in CA 5-8R
Dudek, Louis 1918- CANR-1
Earlier sketch in CA 45-48
See also CAAS 14
See also CLC 11, 19
See also DLB 88
Duder, Tessa 1940- 147
See also CLR 43
See also SAAS 23
See also SATA 80
Dudley, B(illy) J(oseph) 1931- 25-28R
Dudley, Barbara Hudson 1921- 65-68
Dudley, Carl Safford 1932- CANR-44
Earlier sketch in CA 116
Dudley, Donald Reynolds 1910-1972 ..... CANR-4
Earlier sketch in CA 5-8R
Dudley, Edward 1926- 45-48
Dudley, Ernest 1908- 13-16R
Dudley, Geoffrey A(rthur) 1917- CANR-6
Earlier sketch in CA 13-16R
Dudley, Guilford, Jr. 1907- CAP-2
Earlier sketch in CA 19-20
Dudley, Guilford A(llerton) 1921-1972 ...... 41-44R
Dudley, Helen
See Hope Simpson, Jacynth
Dudley, James F. 1942- 130
Dudley, Jay
See Chapman, J. Dudley
Dudley, Lavinia P(ratt) 1891(?)-1984 Obituary .. 113
Dudley, Louise 1884- 73-76
Dudley, Martha Ward 1909(?)-1985 Obituary ... 117
See also SATA-Obit 45
Dudley, Nancy
See Cole, Lois Dwight
Dudley, Robert
See Baldwin, James
Dudley, Ruth H(ubbell) 1905- 61-64
See also SATA 11
Dudley Edwards, Ruth 1944- 107
Dudley-Gordon, Tom
See Barker, Dudley
Dudley-Smith, T.
See Trevor, Elleston
Dudley-Smith, Timothy 1926- 103
Dudman, Richard (Beebe) 1918- 45-48
Due, Linnea A. 1948- 105
See also SATA 64
Dueck, Adele 1955- 163
See also SATA 97
Dueker, Christopher W(ayne) 1939- 57-60
Dueker, Joyce S(utherlin) 1942- 57-60
Dueland, Joy V(ivian) 106
See also SATA 27
Duell, Charles Halliwell 1905-1970 Obituary ... 104
Duerig, Alfred W. 1926- 129
Duerr, Edwin 1904- 73-76
Duerr, Gisela 1968- .... SATA 89
Duerrenmatt, Friedrich 1921-1990 .... CANR-33
Earlier sketch in CA 17-20R
See also CLC 1, 4, 8, 11, 15, 43, 102
See also DAM DRAM
See also DLB 69, 124
See also MTCW 1
Duettmann, Martina (Friederike) 1938- 142
Dufallo, Richard 1933- 133
Dufault, Peter Kane 1923- 33-36R
Dufault, Roseanna Lewis 1954- 138
Duff, Alan 1950- 147
Duff, Annis (James) 1904(?)-1986 Obituary 120
See also SATA-Obit 49
Duff, Charles (St. Lawrence) 1894-1966 ... CANR-2
Earlier sketch in CA 1-4R
Duff, David Skene 1912- 128
Brief entry 118
Duff, Ernest A(rthur) 1929- 25-28R
Duff, Gerald 1938- 45-48
Duff, John B. 1931- CANR-1
Earlier sketch in CA 45-48
Duff, Maggie
See Duff, Margaret K.
Duff, Margaret K. CANR-14
Earlier sketch in CA 37-40R
See also SATA 37
Duff, Raymond S(tanley) 1923- 21-24R
Duffee, David E(ugene) 1946- 104
Dufferin, Countess of GiffordHelen Lady 1807-1867 .... DLB 199
Duffey, Bernard I. 1917- 114
Duffey, Betsy (Byars) 1953- .... SATA 80
Duffey, Margery 1926- 73-76
Duff Gordon, Lady Lucie 1821-1869 ...... DLB 166
Duffield, Anne (Tate) 1893- CAP-1
Earlier sketch in CA 13-16
Duffin, Henry Charles 1884- CAP-1
Earlier sketch in CA 9-10
Duffus, R(obert) L(uther) 1888-1972 101
Obituary 37-40R
Duffy, Ben
See Duffy, Bernard C.
Duffy, Bernard C. 1902-1972 Obituary 37-40R
Duffy, Brian 1954- 143
Duffy, Bruce (?)- .... CLC 50
Duffy, Carol Ann 1955- CANR-70
Earlier sketch in CA 119
See also SATA 95
Duffy, Charles 1940- 104
Duffy, Clinton T(ruman) 1898-1982 Obituary ... 108
Duffy, Dennis 1938- 113
Duffy, Eamon 166
Duffy, Edmund 1899-1962 Obituary 93-96
Duffy, Elizabeth 1904(?)- CAP-2
Earlier sketch in CA 19-20
Duffy, Francis R(amon) 1915- CANR-30
Earlier sketch in CA 49-52
Duffy, Helene (Krainovich) 1926- 17-20R

Duffy, James (Edward) 1923- 129
Duffy, James H(enry) 1934- 131
Duffy, John 1915- CANR-8
Earlier sketch in CA 17-20R
Duffy, John J(oseph) 1934- 57-60
Duffy, Kevin 1929- 147
Duffy, Margaret 1942- 139
Duffy, Maureen 1933- CANR-68
Earlier sketches in CA 25-28R, CANR-33
See also CLC 37
See also DLB 14
See also MTCW 1
Duffy, Regis Anthony 1934- 110
Dufief, Nicholas Gouin 1776-1834 DLB 187
Dufner, Max 1920- 145
Dufrechou, Carole
See Monroe, Carole
Dufresne, Isabelle 1935- 136
DuFresne, Jim 1955- 154
Dufresne, John 1948- CANR-61
Earlier sketch in CA 139
Dufty, William 1916- 65-68
Dugan, Alan 1923- 81-84
See also CLC 2, 6
See also DLB 5
Dugan, George 1909-1982 Obituary 107
Dugan, J(ohn) Raymond 1935- 121
Dugan, Jack
See Butterworth, W(illiam) E(dmund III)
Dugan, James (Thomas) 1912-1967 CANR-4
Earlier sketch in CA 5-8R
Dugan, Michael (Gray) 1947- CANR-64
Earlier sketches in CA 77-80, CANR-14, 32
See also SATA 15
Dugard, C. J(ohn) R. 1936- 85-88
du Gard, Roger Martin
See Martin du Gard, Roger
Dugard, William fl. 1648-1662 DLB 170
Dugas, Marcel 1883-1947 DLB 92
Dugdale, Robert
See Hardy, Henry
Duggan, Alfred Leo 1903-1964 73-76
See also SATA 25
Duggan, Christopher 1957- 155
Duggan, George Henry 1912- 17-20R
Duggan, Joseph J(ohn) 1938- 29-32R
Duggan, Laurence James 1949- 153
Duggan, Laurie
See Duggan, Laurence James
Duggan, Mary M. 1921- 25-28R
Duggan, Maurice (Noel) 1922-1974 CANR-17
Obituary 53-56
Earlier sketch in CA 73-76
See also SATA 40
See also SATA-Obit 30
Duggan, William 1952- 122
Duggan, William Redman 1915- 69-72
Duggans, Pat
See Connolly, Robert D(uggan, Jr.)
Dugger, Ronnie 1930- CANR-12
Earlier sketch in CA 21-24R
Duggins, James (Harry), Jr. 1933- 37-40R
Duggleby, John 1952- 159
See also SATA 94
Dughi, Nancy 1-4R
Dugin, Andrej 1955- SATA 77
Dugina, Olga 1964- SATA 77
Dugmore, Clifford W(illiam) 1909-1990 13-16R
Obituary 132
Duguid, Charles 1884- 109
Duguid, John Bright 1895-1980 Obituary 102
Duguid, Robert
See Pring-Mill, Robert D(uguid) F(orrest)
Duhamel, Georges 1884-1966 CANR-35
Obituary 25-28R
Earlier sketch in CA 81-84
See also CLC 8
See also DLB 65
See also MTCW 1
Duhamel, Marcel 1900(?)-1977 Obituary 104
Duhamel, P(ierre) Albert 1920- 5-8R
du Hault, Jean
See Grindel, Eugene
Duhl, Leonard J. 1926- 13-16R
Duigan, John 1949- 164
Duignan, Peter 1926- CANR-11
Earlier sketch in CA 13-16R
Duiker, William J(ohn) 1932- CANR-16
Earlier sketch in CA 85-88
Duis, Perry R. 1943- 124
Dujardin, Edouard (Emile Louis) 1861-1949 Brief entry 109
See also DLB 123
See also TCLC 13
du Jardin, Rosamond Neal 1902-1963 1-4R
Obituary 103
See also SATA 2
Duka, Ivo
See Duchacek, Ivo D(uka)
Duka, John 1949-1989 Obituary 127
Dukakis, Katharine 1937(?)- 135
Dukakis, Kitty
See Dukakis, Katharine
Duke, Alvah (Carter) 1908- 45-48
Duke, Anna Marie 1946- 130
Duke, Benjamin 1931- 49-52
Duke, Charles (Richard) 1940- CANR-28
Earlier sketches in CA 69-72, CANR-11
Duke, David C. 1940- 112
Duke, Donald Norman 1929- CANR-7
Earlier sketch in CA 17-20R
Duke, Forrest R(eagan) 1918- 77-80
Duke, James A. 1929- 135
Duke, James T(aylor) 1933- 65-68
Duke, Jim
See Duke, James A.
Duke, John
See Chalmers, Floyd S(herman)
Duke, Judith S(ilverman) 1934- 118
Duke, Kate 1956- CLR 51
See also SATA 90
Duke, Madelaine (Elizabeth) 1925- CANR-9
Earlier sketch in CA 57-60
Duke, Martin 1930- 138
Duke, Maurice 1934- 112
Duke, Michael Geoffrey Hare
See Hare Duke, Michael Geoffrey
Duke, Michael S. 1940- 136
Duke, Patty
See Duke, Anna Marie
Duke, Richard DeLaBarre 1930- 57-60
Duke, Robin (Antony Hare)
1916-1984 Obituary 115
Duke, Simon (William) 1959- 127
Duke, Steven B. 1934- 144
Duke, Vernon 1903-1969 CAP-2
Earlier sketch in CA 29-32
Duke, Will
See Gault, William Campbell
Duke-Elder, Stewart 1896-1978 Obituary 77-80
Dukelsky, Vladimir
See Duke, Vernon
Duke of Beaufort
See Somerset, Henry Hugh Arthur FitzRoy
Duke of Brunswick-Luneburg
See Ulrich, Anton
Duker, Abraham G(ordon) 1907-1987 53-56
Obituary 164
Duker, Sam 1905-1978 13-16R
Obituary 77-80
Dukert, Joseph M(ichael) 1929- CANR-3
Earlier sketch in CA 5-8R
Dukes, Ashley 1885-1959 Brief entry 110
See also DLB 10
Dukes, Paul 1889-1967 Obituary 112
Dukes, Paul 1934- CANR-9
Earlier sketch in CA 21-24R
Dukes, Philip
See Bickers, Richard (Leslie) Townshend
Dukes, Tyrone 1946(?)-1983 Obituary 110
Dukore, Bernard F. 1931- CANR-53
Earlier sketches in CA 25-28R, CANR-12, 29
Dukore, Margaret Mitchell 1950- CANR-23
Earlier sketch in CA 106
Dulac, Edmund 1882-1953 SATA 19
Dulack, Thomas 1935- 25-28R
Dulaney, W. Marvin 1950- 156
Dulany, Don E., Jr. 1928- 69-72
Dulany, Harris 1940- 33-36R
Dulbecco, Renato 1914- 157
Dulieu, Jean
See van Oort, Jan
Dull, Jonathan R(omer) 1942- 69-72
Dulles, Allen W(elsh) 1893-1969 CAP-2
Earlier sketch in CA 23-24
Dulles, Avery (Robert) 1918- CANR-21
Earlier sketches in CA 9-12R, CANR-3
Dulles, Eleanor Lansing 1895-1996 9-12R
Obituary 154
Dulles, Foster Rhea 1900-1970 CAP-1
Obituary 29-32R
Earlier sketch in CA 13-14
Dulles, John Foster 1888-1959 149
Brief entry 115
See also TCLC 72
Dulles, John W(atson) F(oster) 1913- CANR-1
Earlier sketch in CA 1-4R
Duloup, Victor
See Volkoff, Vladimir
Dulsey, Bernard M. 1914- 9-12R
Duman, Daniel 1948- 129
Dumarchais, Pierre 1882-1970 Obituary 29-32R
Dumarchey, Pierre
See Dumarchais, Pierre
Dumas, Alexandre (Davy de la Pailleterie)
1802-1870 DA
See also DAB
See also DAC
See also DAM MST, NOV
See also DLB 119, 192
See also SATA 18
See also WLC
Dumas (fils), Alexandre 1824-1895 AAYA 22
See also DC 1
See also DLB 192
Dumas, Andre 1918- CANR-29
Earlier sketches in CA 73-76, CANR-13
Dumas, Claire
See Van Weddingen, Marthe
Dumas, Claudine
See Malzberg, Barry N(athaniel)
du Mas, Frank (Maurice) 1918- 106
Dumas, Frederic 1913- 69-72
Dumas, Gerald J. 1930- 25-28R
Dumas, Henry L. 1934-1968 85-88
See also BW 1
See also CLC 6, 62
See also DLB 41
Dumas, Jacqueline 1946- 123
See also SATA 55
Dumas, Philippe 1940- 107
See also SATA 52
du Maurier, Daphne 1907-1989 CANR-55
Obituary 128
Earlier sketches in CA 5-8R, CANR-6
See also CLC 6, 11, 59
See also DAB
See also DAC
See also DAM MST, POP
See also DLB 191
See also MTCW 1
See also SATA 27
See also SATA-Obit 60
See also SSC 18
Du Maurier, George 1834-1896 DLB 153, 178
Dumbauld, Edward 1905- 129
Dumbleton, Mike 1948- SATA 73
Dumbleton, William A(lbert) 1927- 37-40R
Dumbrell, John 1950- 151
Dumenil, Lynn 1950- 125
Dumery, Henry 1920- 101
Dumezil, Georges (Edmond Raoul) 1898-1986 165
Obituary 120
Dumitriu, Petru 1924- 155
Brief entry 116
Dumke, Edward J. 1946- 124
Dumke, Glenn S. 1917-1989 CANR-31
Obituary 129
Earlier sketch in CA 112
Dummett, (Agnes Margaret) Ann 1930- 135
Dummett, Michael Anthony Eardley 1925- 102
Dumond, Dwight Lowell 1895-1976 69-72
Obituary 65-68
Dumont, Jean-Paul 1940- CANR-12
Earlier sketch in CA 73-76
Dumoulin, Heinrich 1905- CANR-4
Earlier sketch in CA 5-8R
Dumpleton, John Le F(evre) 1924- 13-16R
Dumpty, Humpty S.
See Denenberg, Herbert S(idney)
Dun, Angus 1892-1971 Obituary 33-36R
Dun, Mao
See Yen-Ping, Shen
Dunant, Sarah 1950- 131
Dunas, Joseph C. 1900- 17-20R
Dunathan, Arni T(homas) 1936- 53-56
Dunaway, David King 1948- 107
Dunaway, Faye 1941- 155
Dunaway, John M(arson) 1945- 89-92
Dunayevskaya, Raya 1910-1987 130
Obituary 122
Dunbabin, J(ohn) P(aul) D(elacour) 1938- 69-72
Dunbabin, Jean 1939- 119
Dunbar, Alice
See Nelson, Alice Ruth Moore Dunbar
Dunbar, Alice Moore
See Nelson, Alice Ruth Moore Dunbar
Dunbar, Anthony P. 1949- CANR-71
Earlier sketch in CA 33-36R
Dunbar, Charles Stuart 1900- 107
Dunbar, David
See Baxter, Craig
Dunbar, Dorothy 1923- 9-12R
Dunbar, Edward
See Smith, David MacLeod
Dunbar, Ernest 1927- 25-28R
Dunbar, Gary S(eamans) 1931- 144
Dunbar, Janet 1901-1989(?) CANR-6
Obituary 129
Earlier sketch in CA 9-12R
Dunbar, John Greenwell 1930- 21-24R
Dunbar, Joyce 1944- 144
See also SATA 76
Dunbar, Leslie W(allace) 1921- CANR-52
Earlier sketch in CA 125
Dunbar, Maxwell John 1914- 103
Dunbar, Paul Laurence 1872-1906 124
Brief entry 104
See also BLC 1
See also BW 1
See also CDALB 1865-1917
See also DA
See also DAC
See also DAM MST, MULT, POET
See also DLB 50, 54, 78
See also PC 5
See also SATA 34
See also SSC 8
See also TCLC 2, 12
See also WLC
Dunbar, Robert E(verett) 1926- CANR-34
Earlier sketches in CA 85-88, CANR-15
See also SATA 32
Dunbar, Robert George 1907- 114
Dunbar, Tony
See Dunbar, Anthony P.
Dunbar, William 1460(?)-1530(?) DLB 132, 146
Dunbar, Willis F(rederick) 1902-1970 CANR-4
Earlier sketch in CA 5-8R
Dunbar-Nelson, Alice
See Nelson, Alice Ruth Moore Dunbar
Dunbar-Nelson, Alice Moore
See Nelson, Alice Ruth Moore Dunbar
Dunbaugh, Frank Montgomery 1895- 45-48
Duncan, A(nthony) D(ouglas) 1930- 33-36R
Duncan, Alastair 1942- CANR-40
Earlier sketch in CA 117
Duncan, Alex
See Duke, Madelaine (Elizabeth)
Duncan, Alice Faye 1967- 160
See also SATA 95
Duncan, Alistair (Charteris) 1927- 61-64
Duncan, Archibald A(lexander) M(cBeth)
1926- 81-84
Duncan, Ardinelle Bean 1913- 1-4R
Duncan, (Reid) Bingham 1911- 85-88
Duncan, Bowie 1941- 33-36R
Duncan, C(yril) J(ohn) 1916- 25-28R
Duncan, Carl P(orter) 1921- Brief entry 115
Duncan, Carol Greene 1936- 145
Duncan, Charles T(homas) 1914- 17-20R
Duncan, Chester 1913- 93-96
Duncan, Clyde H. 1903- 17-20R
Duncan, Colin A(drien) M(acKinley) 1954- 162
Duncan, Dave 1933- 143
Duncan, David 1913- 5-8R
Duncan, David Douglas 1916- 145
Brief entry 112
See also AITN 1
Duncan, Dayton 1949- 127
Duncan, Delbert J(ames) 1895- 41-44R
Duncan, Denis (Macdonald) 1920- CANR-23
Earlier sketch in CA 107
Duncan, Dora Angela
See Duncan, Isadora
Duncan, Dougal 1921- 102
Duncan, Elmer H(ubert) 1933- 69-72
Duncan, Florence Belle
1917(?)-1980 Obituary 97-100
Duncan, (Sandy) Frances (Mary) 1942- CANR-37
Earlier sketches in CA 97-100, CANR-17
See also SATA-Brief 48
Duncan, George
See Davison, Geoffrey
Duncan, Gregory
See McClintock, Marshall
Duncan, Harry (Alvin) 1916-1997 162
Duncan, Helen (Harger Bodwell) 1902- 125
Duncan, Hugh Dalziel 1909-1970 CAP-2
Earlier sketch in CA 23-24
Duncan, Irma 1897-1977 49-52
Obituary 73-76
Duncan, Isadora 1877(?)-1927 149
Brief entry 118
See also TCLC 68
Duncan, Jane
See Cameron, Elizabeth Jane
Duncan, Jennifer Ann 1940-1989 Obituary 128
Duncan, Joseph E(llis) 1921- 5-8R
Duncan, Julia Coley
See Sather, Julia Coley Duncan
Duncan, Julia K. CANR-27
Earlier sketches in CAP-2, CA 19-20
See also Benson, Mildred (Augustine Wirt)
See also SATA 1
Duncan, Kenneth S(andilands) 1912- 9-12R
Duncan, Kunigunde 1886- 5-8R
Duncan, Lois 1934- CANR-36
Earlier sketches in CA 1-4R, CANR-2, 23
See also AAYA 4
See also CLC 26
See also CLR 29
See also JRDA
See also MAICYA
See also SAAS 2
See also SATA 1, 36, 75
Duncan, Marion Moncure
1913-1978 Obituary 77-80
Duncan, Mark (Winchester) 1952- 130
Duncan, Norman 1871-1916 Brief entry 117
See also DLB 92
See also YABC 1
Duncan, Otis Dudley 1921- CANR-22
Earlier sketches in CA 13-16R, CANR-6
Duncan, Pam 1938- 37-40R
Duncan, Philip D. 1957- 158
Duncan, Pope A(lexander) 1920- 13-16R
Duncan, Quince 1940- DLB 145
See also HW
Duncan, Robert (Edward) 1919-1988 CANR-62
Obituary 124
Earlier sketches in CA 9-12R, CANR-28
See also CLC 1, 2, 4, 7, 15, 41, 55
See also DAM POET
See also DLB 5, 16, 193
See also MTCW 1
See also PC 2
Duncan, Robert F. 1890(?)-1974 Obituary 53-56
Duncan, Robert L(ipscomb) 1927- 106
See also CAAS 2
Duncan, Ronald 1914-1982 CANR-4
Obituary 107
Earlier sketch in CA 5-8R
See also DLB 13
Duncan, Sara Jeannette 1861-1922 157
See also DLB 92
See also TCLC 60
Duncan, T. Bentley 1929- 77-80
Duncan, Terence
See Nolan, William F(rancis)
Duncan, Theodore G(arfield) 1928- 128
Duncan, Thomas (William) 1905- CANR-1
Earlier sketch in CA 1-4R
Duncan, W(illiam) Murdoch 1909-1976 CANR-6
Earlier sketch in CA 13-16R
Duncan, W. R.
See Duncan, Robert L(ipscomb)
Duncan, W. Raymond 1936- 41-44R
Duncan, Wilbur H(oward) 1910- 116
Duncan, William (Robert) 1944- 115
Duncanson, Michael E(dward) 1948- 57-60
Duncker, Patricia 1951- 163
Duncombe, David C(ameron) 1928- 29-32R
Duncombe, Frances (Riker) 1900-1994 25-28R
Obituary 146
See also SATA 25
See also SATA-Obit 82
Dundee, Robert
See Kirsch, Robert R.
Dundes, Alan 1934- CANR-52
Earlier sketches in CA 21-24R, CANR-9, 26
Dundy, Elaine 1927- CANR-67
Earlier sketch in CA 97-100
Duneier, Mitchell 1961(?)- 144

Dunford, Judith 1933- 107
Dung, Van Tien 1917- 144
Dungan, David L(aird) 1936- 123
Dunham, Arthur 1893- 33-36R
Dunham, Barrows 1905- 5-8R
Dunham, Bob
  See Dunham, Robert
Dunham, Donald Carl 1908- CANR-17
  Earlier sketch in CA 1-4R
Dunham, H(enry) Warren 1906-1985 ..... CANR-8
  Obituary 118
  Earlier sketch in CA 13-16R
Dunham, John L. 1939- 29-32R
Dunham, Katherine 1910- CANR-17
  Earlier sketch in CA 65-68
  See also BW 1
Dunham, Lowell 1910- 37-40R
Dunham, (Bertha) Mabel 1881-1957 Brief
  entry 114
Dunham, Mikel 1948- 138
Dunham, Montrew Goetz 1919- 17-20R
Dunham, Robert 1931- 69-72
Dunham, William 1947- 133
Dunham, William Huse, Jr. 1901- 49-52
Dunhill, Alfred H(enry) 1896(?)-1971 Obituary .. 104
Dunhill, Mary 1907(?)-1988 Obituary 124
Dunk, Thomas W. 1955- 139
Dunkel, Elizabeth 1951- 142
Dunkel, Harold Baker 1912- 5-8R
Dunkel, Richard H(adley) 1933- 73-76
Dunkell, Samuel (V.) 1919- Brief entry 115
Dunkelman, Ben(jamin) 1913- Brief entry 111
Dunkerley, Elsie Jeanette (?)-1960 Obituary ... 116
Dunkerley, James 1953- 131
Dunkerley, Roderic 1884- CAP-1
  Earlier sketch in CA 13-14
Dunkin, Paul S(haner) 1905-1975 .... CAP-2
  Earlier sketch in CA 33-36
Dunkle, William F(rederick), Jr. 1911- 53-56
Dunkley, Christopher 1944- 121
Dunkling, Leslie Alan 1935- CANR-14
  Earlier sketch in CA 81-84
Dunkman, William E(dward) 1903- CAP-2
  Earlier sketch in CA 25-28
Dunlap, Anna
  See Higgins, Anna Dunlap
Dunlap, Aurie N(ichols) 1907-1977 .... 37-40R
Dunlap, David W. 157
Dunlap, G(eorge) D(ale) 1923- 49-52
Dunlap, Jan 65-68
Dunlap, Jane
  See Davis, Adelle
Dunlap, John 1747-1812 .... DLB 43
Dunlap, Joseph R(iggs) 1913- 85-88
Dunlap, Julie 1958- 150
  See also SATA 84
Dunlap, Leslie W(hittaker) 1911- 37-40R
Dunlap, Lon
  See McCormick, Wilfred
Dunlap, Orrin E(lmer), Jr. 1896-1970 .... CAP-1
  Earlier sketch in CA 11-12
Dunlap, Pat
  See Dunlap, Patricia Riley
Dunlap, Patricia Riley 1943- 162
Dunlap, Susan 1943- 165
Dunlap, Thomas R(ichard) 1943- 126
Dunlap, William 1766-1839 .... DLB 30, 37, 59
Dunlay, Thomas W. 1944- 112
Dunleavy, Gareth W(inthrop) 1923- 33-36R
Dunleavy, Janet Egleson 1928- CANR-21
  Earlier sketches in CA 57-60, CANR-6
Dunleavy, Patrick 1952- 123
Dunlop, Agnes M. R. (?)-1982 .... CANR-9
  Earlier sketch in CA 13-16R
  See also SATA 87
Dunlop, Derrick Melville 1902-1980 Obituary ... 101
Dunlop, Douglas Morton 1909-1987 Obituary .. 123
Dunlop, Eileen (Rhona) 1938- CANR-32
  Earlier sketches in CA 73-76, CANR-14
  See also JRDA
  See also MAICYA
  See also SAAS 12
  See also SATA 24, 76
Dunlop, Ian G(eoffrey) D(avid) 1925- CANR-24
  Earlier sketches in CA 9-12R, CANR-5
Dunlop, John B. 1942- 57-60
Dunlop, John Thomas 1914- CANR-5
  Earlier sketch in CA 13-16R
Dunlop, Richard (B.) 1921- CANR-25
  Earlier sketches in CA 17-20R, CANR-7
Dunlop, Robert 1953- 116
Dunlop, William Tiger 1792-1848 .... DLB 99
Dunmore, Helen 1952- 153
Dunmore, John 1923- CANR-47
  Earlier sketches in CA 106, CANR-23
Dunmore, Spencer (Sambrook) 1928- ... CANR-13
  Earlier sketch in CA 33-36R
Dunmore, Timothy 1948- 129
Dunn, Alan (Cantwell) 1900-1974 .... CAP-2
  Obituary 49-52
  Earlier sketch in CA 33-36
Dunn, Carola 1946- 118
Dunn, Catherine M(ary) 1930- 37-40R
Dunn, Charles W(illiam) 1915- 49-52
Dunn, Delmer D(elano) 1941- 25-28R
Dunn, Dennis J(ohn) 1942- 129
Dunn, Donald H(arley) 1929- 33-36R
Dunn, Douglas (Eaglesham) 1942- CANR-33
  Earlier sketches in CA 45-48, CANR-2
  See also CLC 6, 40
  See also DLB 40
  See also MTCW 1
Dunn, Durwood 1943- 166
Dunn, Edgar S(treeter), Jr. 1921- 9-12R
Dunn, Edward D. 1883(?)-1978 Obituary 77-80
Dunn, Esther Cloudman 1891-1977 Obituary . 73-76
Dunn, Ethel (Deikman) 1932- 21-24R
Dunn, Frederick Sherwood
  1893-1962 Obituary 113
Dunn, Halbert Louis 1896-1975 Obituary 61-64
Dunn, (Henry) Hampton 1916- 57-60
Dunn, Harold 1929- 9-12R
Dunn, Harris
  See Doerffler, Alfred
Dunn, Harvey T(homas) 1884-1952 .... DLB 188
  See also SATA 34
Dunn, Hugh Patrick 1916- CANR-48
  Earlier sketch in CA 122
Dunn, James
  See Wilkes-Hunter, R(ichard)
Dunn, James D(ouglas Grant) 1939- 73-76
Dunn, James Taylor 1912- CANR-43
  Earlier sketches in CA 5-8R, CANR-4, 20
Dunn, Jean 1921- 109
Dunn, Jerry G. 1916- CANR-11
  Earlier sketch in CA 21-24R
Dunn, John (Montfort) 1940- CANR-11
  Earlier sketch in CA 69-72
Dunn, John M. (III) 1949- 159
  See also SATA 93
Dunn, Joseph (Willcox, Jr.) 1937- 122
Dunn, Judith F.
  See Bernal, Judith F.
Dunn, Judy
  See Spangenberg, Judith Dunn
Dunn, Katherine (Karen) 1945- CANR-72
  Earlier sketch in CA 33-36R
  See also CLC 71
Dunn, Kaye
  See Dunham, Katherine
Dunn, Lloyd W. 1906-1991 57-60
  Obituary 134
Dunn, Marion Herndon 1920- 29-32R
Dunn, Mary Lois 1930- CANR-12
  Earlier sketch in CA 61-64
  See also SATA 6
Dunn, Mary Maples 1931- 114
Dunn, Nell (Mary) 1936- CANR-66
  See also Sandford, Nell Mary
Dunn, Patience (Louise Ralli) 1922- 5-8R
Dunn, Peter N(orman) 1926- 122
Dunn, Richard S(lator) 1928- 134
  Brief entry 112
Dunn, Ronald (Louis) 1936- Brief entry 120
Dunn, S. P.
  See Dunn, Stephen P(orter)
Dunn, Samuel Watson 1918- CANR-5
  Earlier sketch in CA 1-4R
Dunn, Si 1944- 77-80
Dunn, Stephen 1939- CANR-53
  Earlier sketches in CA 33-36R, CANR-12, 48
  See also CLC 36
  See also DLB 105
Dunn, Stephen P(orter) 1928- 124
Dunn, Stuart (James) 1900-1980 57-60
Dunn, Thomas G(eorge) 1950- CANR-44
  Earlier sketch in CA 119
Dunn, Thomas Tinsley 1901- 107
Dunn, Waldo H(ilary) 1882-1969 .... CAP-2
  Earlier sketch in CA 21-22
Dunn, Walter Scott, Jr. 1928- 101
Dunn, William J. 1906-1992 .... 33-36R
  Obituary 139
Dunn, William L(awrence, Jr.) 1924- 37-40R
Dunn, William Robert 1916- 113
Dunnahoo, Terry Janson 1927- CANR-57
  Earlier sketches in CA 41-44R, CANR-14, 31
  See also SATA 7
Dunnam, Maxie D(enton) 1934- 73-76
Dunnan, Nancy 1941- 112
Dunne, Colin 1937- 123
Dunne, Dominick 1925- CANR-46
  Earlier sketch in CA 121
  See also BEST 89:1, 90:4
  See also DAM POP
Dunne, Finley Peter 1867-1936 Brief entry 108
  See also DLB 11, 23
  See also TCLC 28
Dunne, George H(arold) 1905- CANR-5
  Earlier sketch in CA 1-4R
Dunne, Gerald T. 1919- CANR-1
  Earlier sketch in CA 45-48
Dunne, Gillian A(nne) 1956- 168
Dunne, Jeanette 1952- .... SATA 72
Dunne, John Gregory 1932- CANR-50
  Earlier sketches in CA 25-28R, CANR-14
  See also CLC 28
  See also DLBY 80
Dunne, John S(cribner) 1929- 13-16R
Dunne, (Christopher) Lee 1934- 120
Dunne, Marie
  See Clark, Ann Nolan
Dunne, Mary Collins 1914- CANR-14
  Earlier sketch in CA 41-44R
  See also SATA 11
Dunne, Mary Jo
  See Dunne, Mary Collins
Dunne, Philip 1908- CANR-11
  Earlier sketches in CAP-1, CA 9-10
  See also DLB 26
Dunne, Phillip 1908-1992 Obituary 137
Dunne, Robert Williams 1895-1977 Obituary . 69-72
Dunnell, Robert C(hester) 1942- 89-92
Dunner, Joseph 1908-1978 .... CANR-14
  Earlier sketch in CA 21-24R
Dunnett, Alastair M(acTavish) 1908- 65-68
Dunnett, Dorothy 1923- CANR-65
  Earlier sketches in CA 1-4R, CANR-3, 43
Dunnett, Margaret (Rosalind) 1909-1977 108
  See also SATA 42
Dunnigan, Alice Allison 1906-1983 125
  Obituary 109
  See also BW 1
Dunnigan, James F(rancis) 1943- 145
Dunning, Brad 1957- 102
Dunning, Bruce 1940- 77-80
Dunning, Chester S(idney) L(arson) 1949- 116
Dunning, Edward
  See Gilbert, R(obert) A(ndrew)
Dunning, Eric (Geoffrey) 1936- 116
Dunning, John 1942- CANR-16
  Earlier sketch in CA 93-96
Dunning, John H(arry) 1927- CANR-49
  Earlier sketches in CA 104, CANR-21
Dunning, Lawrence 1931- 77-80
Dunning, Ralph Cheever 1878-1930 Brief entry 107
  See also DLB 4
Dunning, Robert William 1938- CANR-42
  Earlier sketches in CA 53-56, CANR-5, 20
Dunning, (Arthur) Stephen (Jr.) 1924- CANR-12
  Earlier sketch in CA 25-28R
Dunning, William A. 1857-1922 .... DLB 17
Dunnington, Hazel Brain 1912- 21-24R
du Nouey, Pierre (-Andre-Leon) Lecomte
  See Lecomte du Nouey, Pierre (-Andre-Leon)
Dunoyer, Maurice
  See Domergue, Maurice
Dunoyer De Segonzac, Andre
  1884-1974 Obituary 53-56
Dunphy, Jack 1914-1992 .... 25-28R
  Obituary 137
Dunrea, Olivier Jean-Paul Dominique 1953- 124
  See also SATA 59
  See also SATA-Brief 46
Dunsany, Edward John Moreton Drax Plunkett
  1878-1957 148
  Brief entry 104
  See also Dunsany, Lord
  See also DLB 10
Dunsany, Lord
  See Dunsany, Edward John Moreton Drax Plunkett
  See also DLB 77, 153, 156
  See also TCLC 2, 59
Dunsheath, Joyce (Houchen) 1902- 5-8R
Dunsheath, Percy 1886- 107
Dunsmore, Roger 1938- 110
Dunson, Josh 1941- 25-28R
Duns Scotus, John 1266(?)-1308 .... DLB 115
Dunstan, Andrew
  See Chandler, A(rthur) Bertram
Dunstan, Don(ald Allan) 1926- 110
Dunstan, G(ordon) R(eginald) 1917- 130
Dunstan, Reginald (Ernest) 1914- 21-24R
Dunster, Julian A. 1954- 160
Dunster, Mark 1927- 85-88
Dunsterville, G(alfrid) C. K. 1905-1988 ...... CAP-1
  Obituary 127
  Earlier sketch in CA 9-10
Dunston, Arthur John 1922- 109
Dunton, (Arnold) Davidson 1912-1987 Obituary 121
Dunton, Dorothy 1912- 156
  See also SATA 92
Dunton, John fl. 1681-1711 .... DLB 170
Dunton, Samuel Cady 1910(?)-1975 Obituary 61-64
Dunton, W. Herbert 1878-1936 .... DLB 188
Duong, Thu Huong 1947- 152
Dupasquier, Philippe 1955- 130
  See also SATA 86
Dupea, Bobby
  See Crawley, Tony
Dupee, F(rederick) W(ilcox) 1904-1979 ..... CAP-1
  Obituary 85-88
  Earlier sketch in CA 13-14
du Perry, Jean
  See Simenon, Georges (Jacques Christian)
Dupin, August Dupont
  See Taylor, John (Alfred)
Dupin, Jacques 1927- Brief entry 119
Duplechan, Larry 1956- 141
  See also BW 2
  See also DAM MULT
DuPlessis, Rachel Blau 1941- 139
Duplessis, Yves
  See Duplessis, Yvonne
Duplessis, Yvonne 1912- CANR-3
  Earlier sketch in CA 9-12R
Dupont, Jacques 1915- 130
Dupont, Judith (Eva Maria) 1925- 136
Dupont, Paul
  See Frewin, Leslie Ronald
DuPont, Robert L(ouis) 1936- CANR-52
  Earlier sketch in CA 125
Dupre, Catherine CANR-16
  Earlier sketch in CA 25-28R
Dupre, J(osef) Stefan 1936- 102
Dupre, Louis CANR-39
  Earlier sketches in CA 9-12R, CANR-3, 18
Dupree, A(nderson) Hunter 1921- 9-12R
Dupree, Louis 1925- CANR-28
  Earlier sketch in CA 41-44R
Dupree, Nathalie 1939- 154
Dupree, Robert S(cott) 1940- 125
DuPree, Sherry Sherrod 1946- 153
Dupres, Henri
  See Fawcett, F(rank) Dubrez
Duprey, Richard A(llen) 1929- CANR-6
  Earlier sketch in CA 5-8R
Dupuis, Adrian M(aurice) 1919- 9-12R
Dupuis, Robert 1926- 141
Dupuy, Arnold C. 1962- 135
Dupuy, R(ichard) Ernest 1887-1975 ...... CANR-6
  Obituary 57-60
  Earlier sketch in CA 1-4R
Dupuy, T(revor) N(evitt) 1916-1995 ...... CANR-40
  Obituary 149
  Earlier sketches in CA 1-4R, CANR-2, 18
  See also SATA 4
  See also SATA-Obit 86
DuQuette, Keith 1960- .... SATA 90
Durac, Jack
  See Rachman, Stanley Jack
Durack, Mary 1913- CANR-17
  Earlier sketch in CA 97-100
Duram, James C(arl) 1939- CANR-4
  Earlier sketch in CA 53-56
Duran, Gloria Diana Bradley 1924- 107
Duran, Manuel E. 1925- CANR-11
  Earlier sketch in CA 25-28R
Duran, Richard (Paul) 1943- 114
Duran, Roberto (Tinoco) 1953- 131
  See also HW
Durand, G. Forbes
  See Burgess, Michael (Roy)
Durand, John Dana 1913-1981 .... CANR-9
  Earlier sketch in CA 61-64
Durand, Loup 1933- 124
Durand, Loyal, Jr. 1902-1970 .... CAP-2
  Earlier sketch in CA 21-22
Durand, Lucile
  See Bersianik, Louky
Durand, Robert 1944- 57-60
Durand, William F. 1859-1958 157
Durandeaux, Jacques 1926- 25-28R
Durang, Christopher (Ferdinand) 1949- .. CANR-50
  Earlier sketch in CA 105
  See also CLC 27, 38
Durant, Ariel K(aufman) 1898-1981 .... CANR-4
  Obituary 105
  Earlier sketch in CA 9-12R
Durant, David N(orton) 1925- 77-80
Durant, Frederick C(lark) III 1916- 113
Durant, Henry 1902-1982 Obituary 107
Durant, John 1902- CANR-5
  Earlier sketch in CA 9-12R
  See also SATA 27
Durant, Stuart 1932- 104
Durant, Will(iam James) 1885-1981 ..... CANR-61
  Obituary 105
  Earlier sketches in CA 9-12R, CANR-4
  See also MTCW 1
Durante, James Francis 1893-1980 Obituary . 93-96
Durante, Jimmy
  See Durante, James Francis
Duranti (Rossi), (Maria) Francesca 1935- 133
  See also DLB 196
Duranty, Walter 1884-1957 .... DLB 29
Duras, Marguerite 1914-1996 .... CANR-50
  Obituary 151
  Earlier sketch in CA 25-28R
  See also CLC 3, 6, 11, 20, 34, 40, 68, 100
  See also DLB 83
  See also MTCW 1
Duratschek, (Mary) Claudia 1894- 37-40R
Duratschek, Sister Mary Claudia
  See Duratschek, (Mary) Claudia
Durbahn, Walter E. 1895(?)-1981 Obituary 102
Durban, (Rosa) Pam 1947- 123
  See also CLC 39
Durband, Alan 1927- CANR-20
  Earlier sketches in CA 5-8R, CANR-2
Durbin, Brice 1899(?)-1983 Obituary 111
Durbin, Mary Lou 1927- 21-24R
Durbin, Richard Louis 1928- CANR-7
  Earlier sketch in CA 53-56
Durbridge, Francis (Henry) 1912-1998 ... CANR-24
  Obituary 166
  Earlier sketches in CA 77-80, CANR-6
Durcan, Paul 1944- 134
  See also CLC 43, 70
  See also DAM POET
Durden, Robert Franklin 1925- 9-12R
Durell, Ann 1930- 136
  See also SATA 66
Durey, Michael (John) 1947- 107
Durfee, David A(rthur) 1929- 29-32R
Durfee, Mary 1951- 154
Durfey, Thomas 1653-1723 .... DLB 80
Durgnat, Raymond (Eric) 1932- 17-20R
Durham, David
  See Vickers, Roy
Durham, Frank (Edington) 1935- 114
Durham, Jerry D. 1946- 146
Durham, John
  See Paine, Lauran (Bosworth)
Durham, John I 1933- CANR-13
  Earlier sketch in CA 29-32R
Durham, John 1925- 107
Durham, Mae
  See Roger, Mae Durham
Durham, Marilyn 1930- CANR-63
  Earlier sketch in CA 49-52
Durham, Philip 1912-1977 .... CANR-7
  Earlier sketch in CA 9-12R
Durham, Walter T. 1924- 168
Durka, Gloria 1939- CANR-45
  Earlier sketches in CA 65-68, CANR-14
Durkee, Mary C. 1921- 13-16R
Durkheim, Emile 1858-1917 .... TCLC 55
Durkin, Barbara W(ernecke) 1944- CANR-49
  Earlier sketch in CA 123
Durkin, Henry P(aul) 1940- 53-56
Durkin, Joseph Thomas 1903- CAP-1
  Earlier sketch in CA 11-12
Durland, Frances Caldwell 1892- 113
Durland, William R(eginald) 1931- CANR-7
  Earlier sketch in CA 57-60
Durnbaugh, Donald F. 1927- CANR-8
  Earlier sketch in CA 21-24R
Durnin, Richard G(erry) 1920- 110

Durning, Addis
See Ranzini, Addis Durning
Duro, Paul 1953- 143
Duroche, Leonard L(eRoy) 1933- 37-40R
DuRocher, Richard J(ames) 1955- 118
Duroselle, Jean-Baptiste (Marie Lucien Charles) 1917- CANR-45
Earlier sketches in CA 9-12R, CANR-3, 18
Durova, Nadezhda Andreevna 1783-1866 . DLB 198
Durr, Fred
See Durr, Frederick R(oland) E(ugene)
Durr, Frederick R(oland) E(ugene) 1921-1978 37-40R
Durr, William Kirtley 1924- 13-16R
Durrani, Mahmood Khan 1914- CAP-1
Earlier sketch in CA 13-14
Durrant, Digby 1926- CANR-13
Earlier sketch in CA 21-24R
Durrant, Lynda 1954- 161
See also SATA 96
Durrant, Rita D(elores) 108
Durrant, Theo
See Offord, Lenore Glen
and White, William A(nthony) P(arker)
Durrell, Donald D(e Witt) 1903- CANR-8
Earlier sketch in CA 17-20R
Durrell, Gerald (Malcolm) 1925-1995 CANR-59
Obituary 147
Earlier sketches in CA 5-8R, CANR-4, 25
See also MTCW 1
See also SATA 8
See also SATA-Obit 84
Durrell, Jacqueline Sonia Rasen 1929- 21-24R
Durrell, Jacquie
See Durrell, Jacqueline Sonia Rasen
Durrell, Julie 1955- 150
See also SATA 94
Durrell, Lawrence (George) 1912-1990 CANR-40
Obituary 132
Earlier sketch in CA 9-12R
See also CDBLB 1945-1960
See also CLC 1, 4, 6, 8, 13, 27, 41
See also DAM NOV
See also DLB 15, 27
See also DLBY 90
See also MTCW 1
Durrell, Zoe C(ompton) 1910- 89-92
Durrenberger, E. Paul 1943- 152
Durrenberger, Robert Warren 1918- CANR-10
Earlier sketch in CA 21-24R
Durrenmatt, Friedrich
See Duerrenmatt, Friedrich
Durrett, Deanne 1940- 156
See also SATA 92
Durschmied, Erik 1930- 140
Durslag, Melvin 1921- 101
Durst, Paul 1921- CANR-63
Earlier sketch in CA 21-24R
d'Urstelle, Pierre
See Dorst, Jean (Pierre)
Durville, Hector 1849-1923 Brief entry 117
Dury, George H(arry) 1916- 113
Duryee, Mary Ballard 1896-1988 Obituary 125
Durzak, Manfred 1938- CANR-1
Earlier sketch in CA 49-52
du Sautoy, Peter (Francis De Courcy) 1921- 5-8R
Dusay, Katherine M(ulholland) 1943- 118
Duscha, Julius (Carl) 1924- 73-76
Dusenberry, William Howard 1908- CAP-1
Earlier sketch in CA 19-20
Dusenbury, Winifred L.
See Frazer, Winifred L(oesch)
Dushkin, Alexander M(ordecai) 1890-1976 Obituary 65-68
Dushnitzky-Shner, Sara 1913- 29-32R
Duska, Ronald 1937- 97-100
Duskin, Ruthie
See Feldman, Ruth Duskin
Dusky, Lorraine 1942- 85-88
Du Soe, Robert C. 1892-1958 YABC 2
d'Usseau, Arnaud 1916-1990 Obituary 130
Dussel, Enrique D. 1934- 89-92
Dussere, Carol
See Dussere, Carolyn T(homas)
Dussere, Carolyn T(homas) 1942- 103
Dussinger, John A(ndrew) 1935- CANR-44
Earlier sketch in CA 113
Dussling, Jennifer 1970- 161
See also SATA 96
Duster, Alfreda Barnett 1904-1983 Obituary 109
Duster, Troy 1936- 29-32R
Dustin, Charles
See Giesy, J(ohn) U(lrich)
Duston, Hannah 1657-1737 DLB 200
Duthie, Charles S. 1911- CAP-2
Earlier sketch in CA 29-32
Dutile, Fernand N(eville) 1940- 107
Dutkina, Galina (Borisovna) 1952- 154
See also Annikova, Galina
Dutourd, Jean (Hubert) 1920- CANR-31
Earlier sketch in CA 65-68
Dutt, R(ajani) Palme 1896-1974 CAP-1
Obituary 53-56
Earlier sketch in CA 11-12
Dutta, Reginald 1914- 61-64
Dutta, Rex
See Dutta, Reginald
Duttman, Martina
See Duettmann, Martina (Friederike)
Dutton, Bertha P(auline) 1903- 122
Brief entry 117
Dutton, Diana B. 1943- 129
Dutton, Frederick G(ary) 1923- Brief entry 111
Dutton, Geoffrey (Piers Henry) 1922- CANR-68
Earlier sketches in CA 45-48, CANR-1, 17
Dutton, H(arold) I. (?)-1984 Obituary 116
Dutton, Joan Parry 1908- 9-12R
Dutton, John M(ason) 1926- 41-44R
Dutton, Mary 1922- 33-36R
Dutton, Michael R. 1967- 145
Dutton, Paul 1943- CANR-31
Earlier sketch in CA 112
Dutton, Paul Edward 1952- 148
Dutton, Ralph (Stawell) 1898-1985 13-16R
Obituary 116
Dutton, Richard Edward 1929- Brief entry 106
Dutz
See Davis, Mary Octavia
Duun, Olav 1876-1939 Brief entry 121
Duus, Masayo 1938- 89-92
Duus, Peter 1933- 25-28R
DuVal, F(rancis) Alan 1916- 33-36R
Duval, Jean-Jacques 1930- 69-72
DuVal, John 1940- 120
Duval, Katherine
See James, Elizabeth
Duval, Margaret
See Robinson, Patricia Colbert
DuVal, Miles P(ercy), Jr. 1896-1989 Obituary 130
Duvall, Evelyn Millis 1906- CANR-1
Earlier sketch in CA 1-4R
See also SATA 9
Duvall, Jill D(onovan) 1932- SATA 102
Duvall, Richard M. 1934- 45-48
Duvall, Robert (Selden) 1931- 146
Brief entry 116
Duvall, W(illiam) Clyde (Jr.) 1917- 17-20R
DuVaul, Virginia C.
See Coffman, Virginia (Edith)
Duveen, Geoffrey 1883-1975 Obituary 61-64
Duveneck, Josephine Whitney 1891-1978 114
Duverger, Maurice 1917- CANR-27
Earlier sketch in CA 65-68
Duvoisin, Roger Antoine 1904-1980 CANR-11
Obituary 101
Earlier sketch in CA 13-16R
See also CLR 23
See also DLB 61
See also MAICYA
See also SATA 2, 30
See also SATA-Obit 23
Duvoisin, Roger C(lair) 1927- 132
DuWors, Richard E(dward) 1914- 45-48
Duy, Pham 1927- 61-64
Duyckinck, Evert Augustus 1816-1878 DLB 3, 64
Duyckinck, George Long 1823-1863 DLB 3
Duyfhuizen, Bernard 1953- 145
Dvaipayan, Krishna
See Vyasa
Dvoretsky, Edward 1930- CANR-31
Earlier sketches in CA 37-40R, CANR-14
Dvorkin, David 1943- 118
Dvornik, Francis 1893-1975 CANR-6
Obituary 61-64
Earlier sketch in CA 1-4R
Dwaraki, Leela 1942- 106
Dweck, Susan 1943- 33-36R
Dwiggins, Don(ald J.) 1913-1988 CANR-23
Obituary 127
Earlier sketches in CA 17-20R, CANR-8
See also SATA 4
See also SATA-Obit 60
Dwight, Allan
See Cole, Lois Dwight
Dwight, John Sullivan 1813-1893 DLB 1
Dwight, Olivia
See Hazzard, Mary
Dwight, Timothy 1752-1817 DLB 37
Dworkin, Andrea 1946- CANR-39
Earlier sketches in CA 77-80, CANR-16
Interview in CANR-16
See also CAAS 21
See also CLC 43
See also MTCW 1
Dworkin, Gerald 1937- 53-56
Dworkin, James B(arnet) 1948- 112
Dworkin, R. M.
See Dworkin, Ronald M(yles)
Dworkin, Rita 1928- 21-24R
Dworkin, Ronald
See Dworkin, Ronald M(yles)
Dworkin, Ronald M(yles) 1931- 127
Brief entry 123
Interview in 127
Dwoskin, Charles 1922(?)-1980 Obituary 102
Dwoskin, Stephen 1939- 89-92
Dwyer, Augusta (Maria) 1956- 133
Dwyer, Deanna
See Koontz, Dean R(ay)
Dwyer, James Francis 1874-1952 154
Dwyer, Jim 1949- 159
Dwyer, John C. 1930- CANR-32
Earlier sketch in CA 113
Dwyer, Judith A(nne) 1948- 117
Dwyer, K. R.
See Koontz, Dean R(ay)
Dwyer, Richard A. 1934- 135
Dwyer, T. Ryle 1944- 105
Dwyer, Thomas A. 1923- 115
Dwyer, Vincent Michael 1912-1987 Obituary 123
Dwyer-Joyce, Alice 1913- CANR-4
Earlier sketch in CA 53-56
Dyal, Donald H(enriques) 1947- 156
Dyal, James A. 1928- CANR-10
Earlier sketch in CA 5-8R
Dyal, William M., Jr. 1928- 21-24R
Dyall, Valentine 1908-1985 Obituary 117
Dybek, Stuart 1942- CANR-39
Earlier sketch in CA 97-100
See also DLB 130
Dyck, Anni 1931- 25-28R
Dyck, Cornelius J(ohn) 1921- 89-92
Dyck, Harvey L(eonard) 1934- 69-72
Dyck, Ian 1954- 143
Dyck, J. William 1918- 57-60
Dyck, Martin 1927- 41-44R
Dyck, Peter J. 1914- 142
See also SATA 75
Dyckman, John William 1922-1987 CANR-2
Obituary 123
Earlier sketch in CA 1-4R
Dyckman, Thomas Richard 1932- CANR-13
Earlier sketch in CA 33-36R
Dye, Anne G.
See Phillips, Anne G(arvey)
Dye, Charles
See MacLean, Katherine
Dye, David L. 1925- 21-24R
Dye, Dwight L(atimer) 1931- 118
Dye, Frank Charles 1930- 103
Dye, H(ershel) Allan 1931- 93-96
Dye, Harold E(ldon) 1907- CANR-24
Earlier sketch in CA 29-32R
Dye, James W(ayne) 1934- 21-24R
Dye, Margaret 1932- 81-84
Dye, Richard
See De Voto, Bernard (Augustine)
Dye, Thomas R(oy) 1935- CANR-52
Earlier sketches in CA 33-36R, CANR-12, 28
Dyen, Isidore 1913- 53-56
Dyer, Beverly 1921- 61-64
Dyer, Braven 1900(?)-1983 Obituary 110
Dyer, Brian
See Petrocelli, Orlando R(alph)
and Rothery, Brian
Dyer, C. Raymond
See Dyer, Charles (Raymond)
Dyer, Charles (Raymond) 1928- CANR-44
Earlier sketch in CA 21-24R
See also DLB 13
Dyer, Donald R(ay) 1918- 140
Dyer, Elinor Mary Brent
See Brent-Dyer, Elinor Mary
Dyer, Esther R(uth) 1950- 102
Dyer, Frederick C. 1918- 17-20R
Dyer, Geoff 1958- 125
Dyer, George 1755-1841 DLB 93
Dyer, George Bell 1903-1978 85-88
Obituary 81-84
Dyer, George E(dward) 1928-1974 37-40R
Dyer, George J(ohn) 1927- 13-16R
Dyer, James (Frederick) 1934- 102
See also SATA 37
Dyer, Joel 1958- 164
Dyer, John 1699-1757 DLB 95
Dyer, John M. 1920- 13-16R
Dyer, John Percy 1902-1975 1-4R
Obituary 103
Dyer, Joyce 1947- 146
Dyer, Judith Clements 1947- 112
Dyer, K(enneth) F(rank) 1939- 114
Dyer, Lucinda 1947- 105
Dyer, T(homas) A(llan) 1947- 101
Dyer, Thomas G(eorge) 1943- CANR-25
Earlier sketch in CA 107
Dyer, Wayne W(alter) 1940- CANR-25
Earlier sketch in CA 69-72
Dyer, William G(ibb) 1925- CANR-14
Earlier sketch in CA 41-44R
Dyess, John (Foster) 1939- SATA 76
Dygard, Thomas J. 1931-1996 CANR-15
Obituary 153
Earlier sketch in CA 85-88
See also AAYA 7
See also JRDA
See also SAAS 15
See also SATA 24, 97
See also SATA-Obit 92
Dygat, Stanislaw 1914-1978 Obituary 111
Dygert, James H(erbert) 1934- CANR-10
Earlier sketch in CA 65-68
Dyja, Thomas 1962- 162
Dyja, Tom
See Dyja, Thomas
Dyk, Walter 1899-1972 Obituary 37-40R
Dyke, John 1935- CANR-12
Earlier sketch in CA 25-28R
See also SATA 35
Dykema, Karl W(ashburn) 1906-1970 CAP-2
Earlier sketch in CA 25-28
Dykeman, Richard M(ills) 1943- 93-96
Dykeman, Therese B(oos) 1936- 149
Dykeman, Wilma CANR-1
Earlier sketch in CA 1-4R
Dykes, Archie R(eece) 1931- CANR-7
Earlier sketch in CA 17-20R
Dykes, Jack
See Owen, Jack
Dykes, Jeff(erson) C(henowth) 1900- CANR-17
Earlier sketches in CA 5-8R, CANR-2
Dykhuizen, George 1899- 49-52
Dykstra, Craig Richard 1947- 112
Dykstra, Gerald 1922- 45-48
Dykstra, Robert R. 1930- 25-28R
Dylan, Bob 1941- 41-44R
See also CLC 3, 4, 6, 12, 77
See also DLB 16
Dymally, Mervyn M(alcolm) 1926- 41-44R
Dyment, Clifford (Henry) 1914-1971 CAP-1
Obituary 33-36R
Earlier sketch in CA 9-10
Dymoke, Juliet
See de Schanschieff, Juliet Dymoke
Dymond, Dorothy 1891-1985 Obituary 117
Dymond, Rosalind
See Cartwright, Rosalind Dymond
Dymsza, William A(lexander) 1920- CANR-2
Earlier sketch in CA 49-52
Dyne, Michael Bradley 1918-1989 Obituary 128
Dynes, Russell R(owe) 1923- CANR-23
Earlier sketches in CA 9-12R, CANR-6
Dyott, George (Miller) 1883-1972 Obituary 37-40R
Dyrness, William A(rthur) 1943- CANR-35
Earlier sketches in CA 33-36R, CANR-13
Dyroff, Jan Michael 1942- 61-64
Dyson, A(nthony) E(dward) 1928- 57-60
Dyson, Anne Jane 1912- 21-24R
Dyson, Freeman J(ohn) 1923- CANR-17
Earlier sketch in CA 89-92
Dyson, Geoffrey Harry George 1914-1981 Obituary 114
Dyson, George (Bernard) 1953- 126
Dyson, John 1943- 144
Dyson, Lowell Keith 1929- 107
Dyson, Michael Eric 1958- 154
Dyson, R(obert) W(illiam) 1949- CANR-49
Earlier sketch in CA 123
Dywasuk, Colette Taube 1941- 45-48
Dziech, Billie Wright 1941- CANR-43
Earlier sketch in CA 113
Dzielska, Maria 1942- 152
Dziewanowski, M(arian) Kamil 1913- 29-32R
Dzuback, Mary Ann 1950- 138
Dzung Wong, Baoswan 1949- 146
Dzwonkoski, Peter 1940- 123

E

Eade, Alfred Thompson 1891-1988 Obituary 125
Eadie, Donald 1919- 33-36R
Eadie, John W(illiam) 1935- 104
Eagan, Andrea Boroff 1943-1993 CANR-46
Obituary 140
Earlier sketch in CA 73-76
Eagan, Barbara Tiritilli 1935(?)-1986 Obituary 118
Eagar, Frances (Elisabeth Stuart) 1940-1978 61-64
Obituary 120
See also SATA 11
See also SATA-Obit 55
Eager, Edward McMaken 1911-1964 73-76
See also CLR 43
See also DLB 22
See also MAICYA
See also SATA 17
Eager, George B. 1921- SATA 56
Eager, Mary Ann 1905(?)-1984 Obituary 111
Eager, Molly
See Eager, Mary Ann
Eagle, Chester (Arthur) 1933- 57-60
Eagle, Dorothy 1912- CANR-9
Earlier sketch in CA 21-24R
Eagle, Ellen 1953- SATA 61
Eagle, Joanna 1934- 25-28R
Eagle, Kin
See Adlerman, Daniel
and Adlerman, Kimberly M.
Eagle, Mike 1942- SATA 11
Eagle, Robert H(arold) 1921-1969 CAP-2
Earlier sketch in CA 21-22
Eagles, Charles W. 1946- 138
Eagles, Douglas Alan 1943- 110
Eaglesfield, Francis
See Guirdham, Arthur
Eagleson, John 1941- 53-56
Eagleton, Terence (Francis) 1943- CANR-68
Earlier sketches in CA 57-60, CANR-7, 23
See also Eagleton, Terry
See also MTCW 1
Eagleton, Terry
See Eagleton, Terence (Francis)
See also CLC 63
Eagleton, Thomas Francis 1929- Brief entry 105
Eagly, Robert V(ictor) 1933- 49-52
Eaker, Ira
See Eaker, Ira C(larence)
Eaker, Ira C(larence) 1896-1987 Obituary 123
Eakin, Frank Edwin, Jr. 1936- 53-56
Eakin, Mary K(atherine) 1917- CANR-1
Earlier sketch in CA 1-4R
Eakin, Mary Mulford 1914-1980 126
Brief entry 106
Eakin, Paul John 1938- CANR-45
Earlier sketch in CA 120
Eakin, Richard M(arshall) 1910- 61-64
Eakin, Sue 1918- 69-72
Eakins, David W(alter) 1923- 49-52
Eakins, Pamela 1953- 117
Eales, John R(ay) 1910- 9-12R
Ealy, Lawrence O(rr) 1915- 33-36R
Eames, Alexandra 1942- 105
Eames, Andrew (John) 1958- 124
Eames, David 1934- 77-80
Eames, Edwin 1930- CANR-14
Earlier sketch in CA 41-44R
Eames, Elizabeth Ramsden 1921- 125
Eames, Hugh 1917- 45-48
Eames, John Douglas 1915- 69-72
Eames, Ray (Kaiser) 1915(?)-1988 162
Eames, S(amuel) Morris 1916- 57-60
Eames, Wilberforce 1855-1937 DLB 140
Ear, The
See McLellan, Diana
Eardley, George C(harles) 1926- 57-60
Earhart, H(arry) Byron 1935- CANR-14
Earlier sketch in CA 37-40R
Earl, David M(agarey) 1911- 13-16R
Earl, Donald (Charles) 1931-1996 57-60
Obituary 153
Earl, Johnrae 1919(?)-1978 Obituary 77-80

Earl, Lawrence 1915- ... 9-12R
Earl, Maureen 1944- ... 137
Earl, Paul Hunter 1945- ... CANR-2
Earlier sketch in CA 49-52
Earle, (Mary) Alice Morse 1853(?)-1911 Brief entry ... 117
Earle, Jean
See Burge, Doris
Earle, John 1600(?)-1665 ... DLB 151
Earle, Marilee
See Zdenek, Marilee
Earle, (Karl Mc)Neil 1947- ... 147
Earle, Olive L(ydia) 1888- ... 21-24R
See also SATA 7
Earle, Peter G. 1923- ... 17-20R
Earle, Ralph 1907- ... CANR-4
Earlier sketch in CA 1-4R
Earle, Sylvia A. 1935- ... 157
Earle, Timothy K. 1946- ... 125
Earle, William
See Johns, W(illiam) E(arle)
Earle, William (Alexander) 1919-1988 ... 85-88
Obituary ... 127
Earley, Charity (Edna) Adams 1918- ... 132
Earley, Martha
See Westwater, Sister Agnes Martha
Earley, Pete ... 163
Earley, Tom 1911- ... CAP-2
Earlier sketch in CA 33-36
Earley, Tony 1961- ... 156
Earll, Tony
See Buckland, Raymond
Earl Mountbatten of Burma
See Mountbatten, Louis (Francis Albert Victor Nicholas)
Earl of Arran
See Gore, Arthur Kattendyke S(trange) D(avid) A(rchibald)
Earl of Carnarvon
See Herbert, Henry George Alfred Marius Victor Francis
Earl of Longford
See Pakenham, Edward Arthur Henry and Pakenham, Francis Aungier
Earl of Orrey
See Boyle, Roger
Earls, Nick 1963- ... 160
See also SATA 95
Earlson, Ian Malcolm
See Dorn, William S.
Early, Gerald 1952- ... 133
Early, Jack
See Scoppettone, Sandra
Early, James 1923- ... 45-48
Early, Jon
See Johns, W(illiam) E(arle)
Early, Margaret 1951- ... SATA 72
Early, Richard E(lliott) 1908- ... 102
Early, Robert 1940- ... 49-52
Earnest, Ernest (Penney) 1901-1981 ... 33-36R
Obituary ... 164
Earney, Fillmore C(hristy) F(idelis) 1931- ... 57-60
Earnshaw, Anthony 1924- ... 53-56
Earnshaw, Brian 1929- ... CANR-27
Earlier sketches in CA 25-28R, CANR-11
See also SATA 17
Earnshaw, Micky
See Earnshaw, Spencer Wright
Earnshaw, Spencer Wright 1939- ... 152
See also SATA 88
Earp, Virgil
See Keevill, Henry J(ohn)
Easley, MaryAnn ... 159
See also SATA 94
Eason, Ruth P. 1898(?)-1978 Obituary ... 81-84
Easson, James 1895-1979 ... 5-8R
Obituary ... 103
Easson, Roger R(alph) 1945- ... 112
Easson, William M(cAlpine) 1931- ... 65-68
East, Ben 1898- ... CANR-27
Earlier sketch in CA 33-36R
East, Bob 1920(?)-1985 Obituary ... 115
East, Charles 1924- ... 17-20R
East, Churchill
See Harner, Stephen M.
East, John Marlborough 1936- ... 21-24R
East, John Porter 1931-1986 ... 17-20R
Obituary ... 119
East, Michael
See West, Morris L(anglo)
East, P. D. 1921-1971 ... 1-4R
Obituary ... 103
East, W(illiam) Gordon 1902- ... 69-72
Eastaugh, Kenneth 1929- ... 106
Eastaway, Edward
See Thomas, (Philip) Edward
Eastaway, Robert 1962- ... 139
Easter, Junior
See Easter, Willie, Jr.
Easter, Willie, Jr. 1963- ... 166
Easterbrook, Frank H. 1948- ... 138
Easterbrook, Gregg 1953- ... 140
Easterlin, Richard A(inley) 1926- ... 109
Easterling, Keller 1959- ... 142
Easterman, Alexander Levvey 1890-1983 Obituary ... 110
Easterman, Daniel
See MacEoin, Denis
Eastham, Thomas 1923- ... 77-80
Easthope, Antony 1939- ... 130
Easthope, Gary 1945- ... 69-72
Eastin, Roy B(randon) 1917- ... 41-44R
Eastlake, William (Derry) 1917-1997 ... CANR-63
Obituary ... 158
Earlier sketches in CA 5-8R, CANR-5
Interview in ... CANR-5
See also CAAS 1
See also CLC 8
See also DLB 6
Eastland, Terry 1950- ... 97-100
Eastlick, John Taylor 1912- ... 106
Eastman, Addison J. 1918- ... 85-88
Eastman, Ann Heidbreder 1933- ... CANR-14
Earlier sketch in CA 37-40R
Eastman, Arthur M(orse) 1918- ... 21-24R
Eastman, Carol ... 116
See also DLB 44
Eastman, Charles ... 116
Eastman, Charles A(lexander) 1858-1939 ... DAM MULT
See also DLB 175
See also NNAL
See also TCLC 55
See also YABC 1
Eastman, Edward Roe 1885- ... CAP-1
Earlier sketch in CA 13-14
Eastman, Frances W(hittier) 1915- ... CANR-28
Earlier sketch in CA 1-4R
Eastman, G. Don
See Oosterman, Gordon
Eastman, Harry Claude MacColl 1923- Brief entry ... 105
Eastman, Joel Webb 1939- ... 13-16R
Eastman, John 1935- ... CANR-41
Earlier sketch in CA 117
Eastman, Lloyd E. 1929- ... 126
Brief entry ... 112
Eastman, Max (Forrester) 1883-1969 ... 9-12R
Obituary ... 25-28R
See also DLB 91
Eastman, P(hilip) D(ey) 1909-1986 ... 107
Obituary ... 118
See also SATA 33
See also SATA-Obit 46
Eastman, Richard M(orse) 1916- ... 17-20R
Eastman, Robert E. 1913- ... 93-96
Eastman, Roger (Herbert) 1931- ... 53-56
Easton, Allan 1916- ... CANR-20
Earlier sketches in CA 49-52, CANR-2
Easton, Anthony Terrence 1947- ... 127
Easton, Carol 1932- ... CANR-39
Earlier sketch in CA 65-68
Easton, David 1917- ... 33-36R
Easton, Edward
See Malerich, Edward P.
Easton, Elizabeth Wynne 1956- ... 134
Easton, Jane 1918- ... 138
Easton, Loyd D(avid) 1915- ... 21-24R
Easton, Robert (Olney) 1915- ... CANR-27
Earlier sketches in CA 13-16R, CANR-7
See also CAAS 14
Easton, Stewart Copinger 1907- ... CANR-18
Earlier sketches in CA 1-4R, CANR-2
Easton, Thomas A(twood) 1944- ... CANR-45
Earlier sketch in CA 114
Eastwick, Ivy (Ethel) O(live) ... CANR-2
Earlier sketch in CA 5-8R
See also SATA 3
Eastwood, C(harles) Cyril 1916- ... 5-8R
Eastwood, Clint 1930- ... AAYA 18
Eastwood, Cyril
See Eastwood, C(harles) Cyril
Easum, Bill
See Easum, William M.
Easum, William M. 1939- ... 167
Eatock, Marjorie 1927- ... 89-92
Eaton, Anne T(haxter) 1881-1971 Obituary ... 111
See also SATA 32
Eaton, Charles Edward 1916- ... CANR-44
Earlier sketches in CA 5-8R, CANR-2, 20
See also CAAS 20
Eaton, Clement 1898-1980 ... CANR-4
Obituary ... 118
Earlier sketch in CA 1-4R
Eaton, Daniel Isaac 1753-1814 ... DLB 158
Eaton, Edith Maude 1865-1914 ... 154
Eaton, Evelyn (Sybil Mary) 1902- ... 53-56
Eaton, Faith (Sybil) 1927- ... 103
Eaton, George L.
See Verral, Charles Spain
Eaton, J(ohn) H(erbert) 1927- ... CANR-19
Earlier sketches in CA 1-4R, CANR-4
Eaton, Janet
See Givens, Janet E(aton)
Eaton, Jeanette 1886-1968 ... 73-76
See also MAICYA
See also SATA 24
Eaton, John
See Bodington, Stephen
Eaton, John P. ... 126
Eaton, Joseph W. 1919- ... CANR-4
Earlier sketch in CA 1-4R
Eaton, Leonard K. 1922- ... 21-24R
Eaton, Marcia M(uelder) 1938- ... 113
Eaton, Richard M. 1940- ... 148
Eaton, Theodore H(ildreth), Jr. 1907- ... 53-56
Eaton, Tom 1940- ... CANR-15
Earlier sketch in CA 41-44R
See also SATA 22
Eaton, Trevor 1934- ... 21-24R
Eaton, William Edward 1943- ... 69-72
Eatwell, Roger 1949- ... 152
Eauclaire, Sally 1950- ... 118
Eaves, James Clifton 1912- ... 13-16R
Eaves, Morris (Emery) 1944- ... CANR-45
Earlier sketch in CA 120
Eaves, T(homas) C(ary) Duncan 1918- ... 77-80
Eavey, Charles B(enton) 1889-1974 ... 5-8R
Obituary ... 164
Eavey, Louise Bone 1900-1971 ... 5-8R
Obituary ... 164
Eayrs, James George 1926- Brief entry ... 106
Eban, Abba (Solomon) 1915- ... CANR-26
Earlier sketch in CA 57-60
Eban, Aubrey
See Eban, Abba (Solomon)
Ebb, Fred 1935- ... CANR-24
Earlier sketch in CA 69-72
Ebbesen, Ebbe B(ruce) 1944- ... CANR-2
Earlier sketch in CA 49-52
Ebbett, (Frances) Eva 1925- ... 103
Ebbett, Eve
See Ebbett, (Frances) Eva
Ebejer, Francis 1925- ... CANR-40
Earlier sketches in CA 29-32R, CANR-16
Ebel, Alex 1927- ... SATA 11
Ebel, Henry 1938- ... 53-56
Ebel, Robert L(ouis) 1910- ... 89-92
Ebel, Roland H. 1928- ... 140
Ebel, Suzanne
See Goodwin, Suzanne
Ebeling, Gerhard 1912- ... CANR-5
Earlier sketch in CA 9-12R
Ebeling, Walter 1907- ... 119
Ebenstein, Ronnie Sue 1946- ... 103
Ebenstein, William 1910-1976 ... CANR-6
Obituary ... 65-68
Earlier sketch in CA 1-4R
Eber, Dorothy (Margaret) Harley 1930- ... 41-44R
See also SATA 27
Eber, Irene 1929- ... 102
Eberhard, Wolfram 1909- ... CANR-2
Earlier sketch in CA 49-52
Eberhardt, Newman Charles 1912- ... 1-4R
Eberhardt, Peter
See Adams, (Franklin) Robert
Eberhart, Dikkon 1946- ... 93-96
Eberhart, George M(artin) 1950- ... 105
Eberhart, Mignon G(ood) 1899-1996 ... CANR-60
Obituary ... 154
Earlier sketch in CA 73-76
See also AITN 2
Eberhart, (Wilfred) Perry 1924- ... 17-20R
Eberhart, Richard (Ghormley) 1904- ... CANR-2
Earlier sketch in CA 1-4R
See also CDALB 1941-1968
See also CLC 3, 11, 19, 56
See also DAM POET
See also DLB 48
See also MTCW 1
Eberle, Gary 1951- ... CANR-72
Earlier sketch in CA 150
Eberle, Irmengarde 1898-1979 ... CANR-2
Obituary ... 85-88
Earlier sketch in CA 1-4R
See also SATA 2
See also SATA-Obit 23
Eberle, Nancy (Oates) 1935(?)-1988 Obituary ... 125
Eberle, Paul 1928- ... 101
Eberle, Shirley 1929- ... 142
Eberman, (Gilbert) Willis 1917- ... 9-12R
Ebershoff-Coles, Susan Vaughan 1941- ... 102
Ebersohn, Wessel (Schalk) 1940- ... 97-100
Ebersole, A(lva) V(ernon), Jr. 1919- ... CANR-31
Earlier sketches in CA 37-40R, CANR-14
Ebersole, Lucinda 1956- ... 142
Eberstadt, Charles F. 1914(?)-1974 Obituary ... 53-56
Eberstadt, Fernanda 1960- ... CANR-69
Earlier sketch in CA 136
See also CLC 39
Eberstadt, Isabel 1933- ... 126
Eberstadt, Lindley E. 1910(?)-1985 Obituary ... 115
Eberstadt, Nicholas (Nash) 1955- ... 150
Ebert, Alan 1935- ... CANR-16
Earlier sketch in CA 85-88
Ebert, Arthur Frank 1902-1984 ... 5-8R
Obituary ... 114
Ebert, James I(an) 1948- ... 145
Ebert, John E(dward) 1922- ... 106
Ebert, Katherine 1921- ... 107
Ebert, Roger (Joseph) 1942- ... CANR-45
Earlier sketches in CA 69-72, CANR-22
Eberwein, Jane Donahue 1943- ... 111
Eberwein, Robert Thomas 1940- ... 111
Eblana, Sister 1907- ... CAP-1
Earlier sketch in CA 11-12
Eble, Connie 1942- ... 161
Eble, Diane 1956- ... SATA 74
Eble, Kenneth Eugene 1923- ... CANR-19
Earlier sketches in CA 1-4R, CANR-4
Eblen, Jack Ericson 1936- ... 33-36R
Eblis, J. Philip
See Phillips, James W.
Ebner, Jeannie 1918- ... DLB 85
Ebner-Eschenbach, Marie von 1830-1916 ... DLB 81
Ebon 1942- ... DLB 41
Ebon, Martin 1917- ... CANR-29
Earlier sketches in CA 21-24R, CANR-10
Ebsen, Buddy
See Ebsen, Christian
Ebsen, Christian 1908- ... 103
Ebsworth, (George Arthur) Raymond 1911- ... 1-4R
Eby, Cecil D(eGrotte) 1927- ... CANR-43
Earlier sketches in CA 1-4R, CANR-4
Eby, Richard E(ngle) 1912- ... 112
Eccles, David (McAdam) 1904- ... 53-56
Eccles, Frank 1923- ... 103
Eccles, Henry E. 1898- ... CAP-1
Earlier sketch in CA 13-16
Eccles, John Carew 1903-1997 ... CANR-9
Obituary ... 158
Earlier sketch in CA 65-68
Eccles, W(illiam) J(ohn) 1917- ... 9-12R
Ecclestone, Giles 1936-1990 Obituary ... 132
Eccles Williams, Ferelith 1920- ... CANR-21
Earlier sketch in CA 105
See also Williams, Ferelith Eccles
Eccli, Sandra Fulton 1936- ... 102
Echegaray (y Eizaguirre), Jose (Maria Waldo) 1832-1916 ... CANR-32
Brief entry ... 104
See also HW
See also MTCW 1
See also TCLC 4
Echenoz, Jean 1947- ... 147
Echeruo, Michael J(oseph) C(hukwudalu) 1937- ... CANR-8
Earlier sketch in CA 57-60
See also BW 2
Echevarria, Roberto Gonzalez
See Gonzalez-Echevarria, Roberto
Echeverria, Durand 1913- ... 9-12R
Echewa, T(homas) Obinkaram 1940- ... 73-76
Echikson, William 1959- ... 134
Echlin, Edward P. 1930- ... 21-24R
Echo
See Proust, (Valentin-Louis-George-Eugene-) Marcel
Echols, Barbara E(llen) 1934- ... 106
Echols, John M(inor) 1913-1982 ... CANR-2
Obituary ... 107
Earlier sketch in CA 5-8R
Echols, Margit 1944- ... 97-100
Eck, Diana L. 1945- ... 107
Eckardt, A(rthur) Roy 1918-1998 ... CANR-42
Obituary ... 167
Earlier sketches in CA 37-40R, CANR-14, 31
Eckardt, Alice L(yons) 1923- ... CANR-42
Earlier sketches in CA 37-40R, CANR-14
Eckardt, Arthur Roy
See Eckardt, A(rthur) Roy
Eckart, Gabriele 1954- ... 142
Eckaus, Richard S(amuel) 1926- ... 45-48
Eckblad, Edith Berven 1923- ... 17-20R
See also SATA 23
Eckbo, Garrett 1910- ... 25-28R
Ecke, Betty Tseng Yu-ho 1924- ... CANR-6
Earlier sketch in CA 5-8R
Ecke, Wolfgang 1927-1983 Obituary ... 111
See also SATA-Obit 37
Eckel, Malcolm W(illiam) 1912- ... 61-64
Eckel, Paul E(dward) 1908-1986 Obituary ... 119
Eckelberry, Grace Kathryn 1902- ... CAP-2
Earlier sketch in CA 33-36
Eckels, Jon ... CANR-3
Earlier sketch in CA 49-52
Ecker, Beverly A. 1938- ... 116
Ecker, H(erman) Paul 1922-1976 ... CAP-2
Earlier sketch in CA 29-32
Ecker-Racz, L. Laszlo 1906- ... 49-52
Eckerson, Olive Taylor 1901- ... 1-4R
Eckert, Allan W. 1931- ... CANR-45
Earlier sketches in CA 13-16R, CANR-14
Interview in ... CANR-14
See also AAYA 18
See also CLC 17
See also SAAS 21
See also SATA 29, 91
See also SATA-Brief 27
Eckert, Edward K(yle) 1943- ... 77-80
Eckert, Horst 1931- ... CANR-38
Earlier sketch in CA 37-40R
See also Janosch
See also MAICYA
See also SATA 8, 72
Eckert, Kathryn Bishop 1935- ... 147
Eckert, Martina 1960- ... 145
Eckert, Ruth E(lizabeth) 1905- ... 13-16R
Eckes, Alfred Edward, Jr. 1942- ... CANR-9
Earlier sketch in CA 61-64
Eckhardt, Bob
See Eckhardt, Robert Christian
Eckhardt, Celia Morris
See Morris, Celia
Eckhardt, Robert Christian 1913- ... 85-88
Eckhardt, Tibor 1888-1972 Obituary ... 37-40R
Eckhart, Meister 1260(?)-1328(?) ... DLB 115
Eckholm, Erik P(eter) 1949- ... CANR-6
Earlier sketch in CA 57-60
Eckley, Grace 1932- ... CANR-28
Earlier sketch in CA 45-48
Eckley, Mary M. ... 102
Eckley, Wilton Earl, Jr. 1929- ... CANR-28
Earlier sketch in CA 49-52
Eckman, Frederick (Willis) 1924- ... 33-36R
Eckman, Lester S(amuel) 1937- ... CANR-2
Earlier sketch in CA 49-52
Eckmar, F. R.
See de Hartog, Jan
Eckstein, Alexander 1915-1976 ... CANR-6
Obituary ... 69-72
Earlier sketch in CA 1-4R
Eckstein, Gustav 1890-1981 ... 57-60
Obituary ... 104
Eckstein, Harry 1924- ... CANR-1
Earlier sketch in CA 1-4R
Eckstein, Jerome 1925- ... CANR-36
Earlier sketch in CA 114
Eckstein, Otto 1927-1984 ... CANR-14
Obituary ... 112
Earlier sketch in CA 13-16R
Eckstein, Rick 1960- ... 165
Eclov, Shirley
See Pfoutz, Shirley Eclov

Eco, Umberto 1932- ... CANR-55
Earlier sketches in CA 77-80, CANR-12, 33
See also BEST 90:1
See also CLC 28, 60
See also DAM NOV, POP
See also DLB 196
See also MTCW 1
Economou, George 1934- ... CANR-38
Earlier sketch in CA 25-28R
Ecroyd, Donald H(owarth) 1923- ... CANR-4
Earlier sketch in CA 1-4R
Edari, Ronald S(amuel) 1943- ... 65-68
Edberg, Rolf 1912- ... CANR-54
Earlier sketches in CA 69-72, CANR-11, 26
Eddenden, A(rthur) E(dward) 1928- ... CANR-54
Earlier sketch in CA 127
Eddings, David (Carroll) 1931- ... CANR-53
Earlier sketches in CA 110, CANR-35
See also AAYA 17
See also BEST 90:2
See also DAM POP
See also SATA 91
Eddings, Leigh 1937- ... 164
Eddington, Arthur Stanley 1882-1944 ... 157
Eddins, Dwight L. 1939- ... 33-36R
Eddison, E(ric) R(ucker) 1882-1945 ... 156
Brief entry ... 109
See also TCLC 15
Eddison, John 1916- ... CANR-48
Earlier sketches in CA 61-64, CANR-8, 23
Eddison, Roger (Tatham) 1916- ... CAP-1
Earlier sketch in CA 11-12
Eddleman, H(enry) Leo 1911- ... CANR-9
Earlier sketch in CA 13-16R
Eddy, C. M., Jr.
See Eddy, Clifford Martin, Jr.
Eddy, Clifford Martin, Jr. 1896-1967 Obituary ... 113
Eddy, Edward D(anforth, Jr.) 1921- ... 73-76
Eddy, Elizabeth M. 1926- ... 21-24R
Eddy, John J(ude) 1933- ... 73-76
Eddy, John P(aul) 1932- ... CANR-9
Earlier sketch in CA 61-64
Eddy, John Percy 1881-1975 Obituary ... 61-64
Eddy, Mary (Morse) Baker 1821-1910 Brief entry ... 113
See also TCLC 71
Eddy, Paul 1944- ... CANR-15
Earlier sketch in CA 73-76
Eddy, Roger (Whittlesey) 1920- ... 17-20R
Eddy, Samuel K(ennedy) 1926- ... CANR-17
Earlier sketch in CA 1-4R
Ede, H(arold) S(tanley) 1895-1990 ... 131
Ede, Janina 1937- ... SATA 33
Ede, Jim
See Ede, H(arold) S(tanley)
Ede, Lisa S. 1947- ... 123
Edeiken, Louise 1956- ... 140
Edel, Abraham 1908- ... 1-4R
Edel, (Joseph) Leon 1907-1997 ... CANR-22
Obituary ... 161
Earlier sketches in CA 1-4R, CANR-1
Interview in ... CANR-22
See also CLC 29, 34
See also DLB 103
Edel, Marjorie
See Sinclair, Marjorie (Jane)
Edel, Matthew (David) 1941-1990 ... 29-32R
Obituary ... 133
Edel, Wilbur 1915- ... 138
Edelberg, Cynthia Dubin 1940- ... 89-92
Edelen, Georges 1924- ... 93-96
Edelhart, Michael 1951- ... 129
Edelhart, Mike
See Edelhart, Michael
Edelheit, Abraham J. 1958- ... 134
Edelheit, Hershel 1926- ... 134
Edell, Celeste ... 1-4R
See also SATA 12
Edelman, Alice Fisher 1940- ... 112
Edelman, Bernard 1946- ... 126
Edelman, Elaine ... 113
See also SATA-Brief 50
Edelman, Gerald Maurice 1929- ... 112
Edelman, John W(alter) 1893-1971 Obituary ... 113
Edelman, Lily (Judith) 1915-1981 ... 61-64
Obituary ... 102
See also SATA 22
Edelman, Marian Wright 1939- ... CANR-61
Earlier sketch in CA 124
See also BW 2
Edelman, Maurice 1911-1975 ... 65-68
Obituary ... 61-64
Edelman, Murray 1919- ... 33-36R
Edelman, Nathan 1911-1971 Obituary ... 113
Edelman, Paul S. 1926- ... 9-12R
Edelsberg, Herman 1909-1986 Obituary ... 120
Edelson, Edward 1932- ... CANR-13
Earlier sketch in CA 17-20R
See also SATA 51
Edelson, Julie 1949- ... CANR-48
Earlier sketch in CA 122
Edelson, Marshall 1928- ... 153
Brief entry ... 111
Edelstein, Alex S. 1920(?)- ... 133
Edelstein, Arthur ... CANR-9
Earlier sketch in CA 65-68
Edelstein, David S(imeon) 1913- ... 61-64
Edelstein, J(erome) M(elvin) 1924-1996 ... 53-56
Obituary ... 152
Edelstein, Morton A. 1925- ... 69-72
Edelstein, Scott 1954- ... CANR-49
Earlier sketch in CA 122
Edelstein, Stuart J. 1941- ... 122
Edelstein, Terese 1950- ... 135
Eden, Alvin N(oam) 1926- ... CANR-9
Earlier sketch in CA 61-64
Eden, (Robert) Anthony 1897-1977 ... 77-80
Obituary ... 69-72
Eden, Dorothy (Enid) 1912-1982 ... CANR-46
Obituary ... 106
Earlier sketch in CA 81-84
Eden, Laura
See Harrison, Claire (E.)
Eden, Marc
See Eden, Marcus
Eden, Marcus 1935- ... 147
Eden, Mark
See Eden, Marcus
Eden, Robert 1942- ... 113
Edens, Cooper 1945- ... SATA 49
Edens, (Bishop) David 1926- ... 108
See also SATA 39
Eder, George Jackson 1900- ... 85-88
Eder, Richard (Gray) 1932- ... 130
Brief entry ... 123
Interview in ... 130
Edes, Benjamin 1732-1803 ... DLB 43
Edey, Maitland A(rmstrong) 1910-1992 ... CANR-6
Obituary ... 137
Earlier sketch in CA 57-60
See also SATA 25
See also SATA-Obit 71
Edgar, David 1948- ... CANR-61
Earlier sketches in CA 57-60, CANR-12
See also CLC 42
See also DAM DRAM
See also DLB 13
See also MTCW 1
Edgar, Donald 1916- ... 121
Edgar, Frank Terrell Rhoades 1932- ... 69-72
Edgar, Josephine
See Mussi, Mary
Edgar, Ken(neth Frank) 1925- ... CANR-27
Earlier sketch in CA 49-52
Edgar, Neal Lowndes 1927-1983 ... CANR-27
Obituary ... 110
Earlier sketch in CA 69-72
Edgar, Stacey L. 1940- ... 147
Edge, David O(wen) 1932- ... 73-76
Edge, Findley B(artow) 1916- ... 5-8R
Edgell, Zee 1940- ... 135
Edgerton, Clyde (Carlyle) 1944- ... CANR-64
Brief entry ... 118
Earlier sketch in CA 134
Interview in ... 134
See also AAYA 17
See also CLC 39
Edgerton, David 1959- ... 138
Edgerton, Franklin 1885-1963 Obituary ... 110
Edgerton, Gary Richard 1952- ... 111
Edgerton, Harold E(ugene) 1903-1990 ... CANR-5
Obituary ... 130
Earlier sketch in CA 53-56
Edgerton, Joseph S. 1900(?)-1983 Obituary ... 109
Edgerton, Leslie H. 1943- ... 153
Edgerton, Lucile Selk 1896-1987 Obituary ... 122
Edgerton, Robert B(reckenridge) 1931- ... 53-56
Edgerton, Teresa (Ann) 1949- ... 154
Edgerton, William B(enbow) 1914- ... 29-32R
Edgeworth, Maria 1768-1849 ... DLB 116, 159, 163
See also SATA 21
Edghill, Rosemary
See bes-Shahar, Eluki
Edgington, Eugene S(inclair) 1924- ... 25-28R
Edgley, Charles K(enneth) 1943- ... 57-60
Edgley, Roy 1925- ... 29-32R
Edgren, Harry D(aniel) 1899- ... CAP-2
Earlier sketch in CA 33-36
Edgy, Wardore
See Gorey, Edward (St. John)
Edholm, O(tto) G(ustav) 1909-1985 Obituary ... 115
Edie, James M. 1927- ... 9-12R
Ediger, Peter J. 1926- ... 33-36R
Edinborough, Arnold 1922- ... 73-76
Edinger, Edward F(erdinand) 1922- ... 162
Edington, Andrew 1914- ... 73-76
Edison, Judith
See Paul, Judith Edison
Edison, Michael (G.) 1937- Brief entry ... 110
Edison, Theodore
See Stratemeyer, Edward L.
Edkardt, Roy
See Eckardt, A(rthur) Roy
Edkins, Anthony 1927- ... 97-100
Edkins, Diana M(aria) 1947- ... 41-44R
Edler, Peter 1934- ... 107
Edler, Tim(othy) 1948- ... SATA 56
Edlin, Herbert Leeson 1913-1976 ... CANR-9
Obituary ... 69-72
Earlier sketch in CA 61-64
Edlin, Rosabelle Alpern 1914- ... 9-12R
Edman, David 1930- ... 37-40R
Edman, Marion (Louise) 1901- ... CAP-1
Earlier sketch in CA 17-18
Edman, Victor Raymond 1900-1967 ... CANR-6
Earlier sketch in CA 1-4R
Edmands, Allan 1942- ... 117
Edmands, Dodie 1947- ... 116
Edmisten, Patricia Taylor 1939- ... 132
Edmiston, (Helen) Jean (Mary) 1913- ... 13-16R
Edmiston, Jim 1948- ... SATA 80
Edmiston, Susan 1940- ... 65-68
Edmond, Jay
See Jones, Jack
Edmond, Lauris (Dorothy) 1924- ... 153
Edmond, Mary 1916- ... 121
Edmond, Murray (Donald) 1949- ... 153
Edmonds, Alan
See Edmonds, Arthur Denis
Edmonds, Ann C.
See Welch, Ann Courtenay (Edmonds)
Edmonds, Arthur Denis 1932- ... 73-76
Edmonds, C(ecil) J(ohn) 1889- ... CAP-1
Earlier sketch in CA 13-14
Edmonds, Charles
See Carrington, Charles Edmund
Edmonds, Helen G(rey) 1911- ... 65-68
Edmonds, I(vy) G(ordon) 1917- ... CANR-30
Earlier sketches in CA 33-36R, CANR-13
See also SATA 8
Edmonds, Jae
See Edmonds, James A.
Edmonds, James A. 1947- ... 118
Edmonds, Margaret Hammett ... 101
Edmonds, Margot
See Edmonds, Margaret Hammett
Edmonds, Paul
See Kuttner, Henry
Edmonds, R(obert) H(umphrey) G(ordon) 1920- ... 69-72
Edmonds, (Sheppard) Randolph 1900-1983 ... 125
See also BW 1
See also DLB 51
Edmonds, Robert 1913-1990 ... 112
Obituary ... 132
Edmonds, Robin
See Edmonds, R(obert) H(umphrey) G(ordon)
Edmonds, Ronald R. 1935-1983 Obituary ... 110
Edmonds, Vernon H. 1927- ... 37-40R
Edmonds, Walter D(umaux) 1903-1998 ... CANR-2
Earlier sketch in CA 5-8R
See also CLC 35
See also DLB 9
See also MAICYA
See also SAAS 4
See also SATA 1, 27
See also SATA-Obit 99
Edmondson, Clifton Earl 1937- ... 102
Edmondson, G. C. 1922- ... CANR-26
Earlier sketches in CA 57-60, CANR-11
Edmondson, Garry C.
See Edmondson, G. C.
Edmondson, Wallace
See Ellison, Harlan (Jay)
Edmonson, Harold A(rthur) 1937- ... 41-44R
Edmonson, Munro Sterling 1924- ... CANR-28
Earlier sketch in CA 33-36R
Edmund, Sean
See Pringle, Laurence (Patrick)
Edmunds, H(enry) Tudor 1897- ... 106
Edmunds, Malcolm 1938- ... 73-76
Edmunds, (Thomas) Murrell 1898- ... CANR-4
Earlier sketch in CA 1-4R
Edmunds, R(ussell) David 1939- ... 149
Edmunds, Simeon 1917- ... 17-20R
Edmunds, Stahrl W(illiam) 1917- ... 69-72
Edmundson, Bruce 1952- ... 126
Edney, Matthew H(enry) 1962- ... 162
Edom, Clifton C. 1907- ... 105
Edric, Robert
See Armitage, G(ary) E(dric)
Edrich, William J(ohn) 1916-1986 Obituary ... 120
Edsall, Florence S(mall) 1898(?)-1986 Obituary 119
Edsall, Marian (Stickney) 1920- ... CANR-27
Earlier sketch in CA 49-52
See also SATA 8
Edsall, Mary D(eutsch) 1943- ... 142
Edsall, Thomas Byrne 1941- ... 126
Edschmid, Kasimir
See Schmid, Eduard
See also DLB 56
Edson, Harold
See Hall, Asa Zadel
Edson, J(ohn) T(homas) 1928- ... CANR-55
Earlier sketches in CA 29-32R, CANR-12, 30
Edson, Peter 1896-1977 Obituary ... 73-76
Edson, Russell ... 33-36R
See also CLC 13
Eduardi, Guillermo
See Edwards, William B(ennett)
Edwa
See Edwards, Bill
Edwardes, Allen
See Kinsley, D(aniel) A(llan)
Edwardes, Michael (F. H.) 1923- ... CANR-10
Earlier sketch in CA 57-60
Edwards, A. W. F. 1935- ... 73-76
Edwards, Al
See Nourse, Alan E(dward)
Edwards, Alexander
See Fleischer, Leonore
Edwards, Allen J(ack) 1926- ... 33-36R
Edwards, Allen L. 1914- ... CANR-10
Earlier sketch in CA 25-28R
Edwards, Amelia Anne Blandford 1831-1892 .. DLB 174
Edwards, Anne 1927- ... CANR-33
Earlier sketches in CA 61-64, CANR-13
Interview in ... CANR-33
See also SATA 35
Edwards, Anne-Marie 1932- ... CANR-38
Earlier sketches in CA 85-88, CANR-16
Edwards, Anthony David 1936- ... 13-16R
Edwards, Audrey 1947- ... 81-84
See also SATA 52
See also SATA-Brief 31
Edwards, Bertram
See Edwards, Herbert Charles
Edwards, Betty 1926- ... 105
Edwards, Bill 1929(?)-1987 Obituary ... 121
Edwards, Blake 1922- ... CANR-32
Earlier sketch in CA 81-84
Edwards, Bob
See Edwards, Robert Alan
Edwards, Bronwen Elizabeth
See Rose, Wendy
Edwards, Carl N(ormand) 1943- ... 57-60
Edwards, Cecile Pepin 1916- ... 5-8R
See also SATA 25
Edwards, Charles Edward 1930- ... 17-20R
Edwards, Charles Mundy, Jr. 1903-1985 ... 45-48
Obituary ... 117
Edwards, Charlotte 1907-1987 ... CANR-35
Earlier sketch in CA 29-32R
Edwards, Christine 1902- ... CAP-1
Earlier sketch in CA 19-20
Edwards, Claudia J(ane) 1943- ... 154
Edwards, Clifford D(uane) 1934- ... 61-64
Edwards, Clive D. 1947- ... 164
Edwards, Corwin D. 1901-1979 ... CANR-10
Obituary ... 85-88
Earlier sketch in CA 17-20R
Edwards, David C(harles) 1937- ... 41-44R
Edwards, David L(awrence) 1929- ... CANR-54
Earlier sketches in CA 5-8R, CANR-12, 29
Edwards, David V(andeusen) 1941- ... 126
Brief entry ... 105
Edwards, Deborah R. 1945- ... 166
Edwards, Donald (Isaac) 1904- ... 65-68
Edwards, Donald Earl
See Harding, Donald Edward
Edwards, Dorothy 1903(?)-1934 Brief entry ... 122
Edwards, Dorothy 1914-1982 ... CANR-12
Obituary ... 107
Earlier sketch in CA 25-28R
See also SATA 4, 88
See also SATA-Obit 31
Edwards, Douglas 1917-1990 ... 118
Obituary ... 132
Brief entry ... 110
Interview in ... 118
Edwards, Edgar O(wen) 1919- ... CANR-6
Earlier sketch in CA 1-4R
Edwards, Edward 1812-1886 ... DLB 184
Edwards, Eli
See McKay, Festus Claudius
Edwards, Elizabeth
See Inderlied, Mary Elizabeth
Edwards, Elwyn Hartley 1927- ... CANR-8
Earlier sketch in CA 61-64
Edwards, F. E.
See Nolan, William F(rancis)
Edwards, Francis
See Brandon, Johnny
Edwards, Frank Allyn 1908-1967 ... CANR-1
Earlier sketch in CA 1-4R
Edwards, Frank B. 1952- ... 158
See also SATA 93
Edwards, G(erald) B(asil) 1899-1976 Obituary .. 110
See also CLC 25
Edwards, Gawain
See Pendray, George Edward
Edwards, George 1914- ... 53-56
Edwards, George Charles III 1947- ... CANR-49
Earlier sketches in CA 107, CANR-24
Edwards, Gerald (Kenneth Savery) Hamilton
See Hamilton-Edwards, Gerald (Kenneth Savery)
Edwards, Gillian (Mary) 1918- ... 25-28R
Edwards, Graham 1965- ... 154
Edwards, Gunvor ... 107
See also SATA 32
Edwards, Gus 1939- ... 108
Interview in ... 108
See also CLC 43
Edwards, Hank
See Broomall, Robert W(alter)
Edwards, Harry
See Edwards, Henry James
Edwards, Harry (Jr.) 1942- ... 111
Brief entry ... 109
Interview in ... 111
Edwards, Harvey 1929- ... 25-28R
See also SATA 5
Edwards, Hazel (Eileen) 1945- ... 124
Edwards, Henry James 1893-1976 ... 13-16R
Obituary ... 122
Edwards, Herbert Charles 1912- ... 9-12R
See also SATA 12
Edwards, Hilton 1903- ... 65-68
Edwards, I(orwerth) E(iddon) S(tephen) 1909-1996 . CANR-7
Obituary ... 153
Earlier sketch in CA 13-16R
Edwards, India 1896(?)-1990 Obituary ... 130
Edwards, James Don(ald) 1926- ... CANR-4
Earlier sketch in CA 9-12R
Edwards, James Keith O'Neill 1920-1988 Obituary ... 126
Edwards, Jane Campbell 1932- ... 13-16R
See also SATA 10
Edwards, Jaroldeen 1932- ... 102
Edwards, Jerome E(arl) 1937- ... 37-40R
Edwards, Jimmy
See Edwards, James Keith O'Neill
Edwards, John 1943- ... 118
Edwards, John Milton
See Cook, William Wallace
Edwards, Jonathan, Jr. 1745-1801 ... DLB 37
Edwards, Jonathan 1703-1758 ... DA
See also DAC
See also DAM MST
See also DLB 24
Edwards, Josephine Cunnington 1904- ... 13-16R
Edwards, Josh
See Levinson, Leonard
Edwards, Julia
See Stratemeyer, Edward L.
Edwards, Julia Spalding 1920- ... 37-40R
Edwards, Julie
See Andrews, Julie
Edwards, June ... CANR-45
See also Bhatia, Jamunadevi

Edwards, Junius 1929- 142
See also BW 2
See also DLB 33
Edwards, K(enneth) Morgan 1912- 5-8R
Edwards, Kate F(lournoy) 1877-1980 107
Edwards, Larry 1957- 160
Edwards, Lee 1932- CANR-10
Earlier sketch in CA 25-28R
Edwards, Lee R. 1942- 124
Edwards, Leo
See Lee, Edward Edson
Edwards, Linda Strauss 1948- 126
See also SATA 49
See also SATA-Brief 42
Edwards, Louis 1962- 168
Edwards, Lyford Paterson 1882-1984 Obituary 113
Edwards, Lynne 1943- 73-76
Edwards, Margaret (Alexander) 1902-1988 .... CAP-2
Obituary 125
Earlier sketch in CA 29-32
See also SATA-Obit 56
Edwards, Marie Babare 57-60
Edwards, Mark U(lin), Jr. 1946- CANR-10
Earlier sketch in CA 65-68
Edwards, (Kenneth) Martin 1955- 137
Edwards, Marvin L(ouis) 1915- 13-16R
Edwards, Max
See Benjamin, Claude (Max Edward Pohlman)
Edwards, Michael 1932- 85-88
Edwards, Michael 1938- CANR-22
Earlier sketch in CA 106
Edwards, Michelle 1955- 138
See also SATA 70
Edwards, Monica le Doux Newton
1912-1998 .... 9-12R
Obituary 164
See also SATA 12
Edwards, Nicky 1958- 122
Edwards, Norman
See Carr, Terry (Gene)
and White, Theodore Edwin
Edwards, O(tis) C(arl), Jr. 1928- 53-56
Edwards, Oliver
See Haley, William (John)
Edwards, Olwen
See Gater, Dilys
Edwards, Owen Dudley 1938- CANR-7
Earlier sketch in CA 57-60
Edwards, P(rior) Max(imilian) H(emsley)
1914- 37-40R
Edwards, Page (Lawrence, Jr.) 1941- CANR-27
Earlier sketches in CA 45-48, CANR-1
See also SATA 59
Edwards, Paul 1923- 85-88
Edwards, Paul 1940- 123
Edwards, Paul Geoffrey 1926-1992 57-60
Obituary 137
Edwards, Paul M(adison) 1933- 41-44R
Edwards, Peter (William) 1934- 109
Edwards, Philip 1923- CANR-55
Earlier sketches in CA 25-28R, CANR-12, 29
Edwards, Phoebe
See Bloch, Barbara
Edwards, Phyllis Irene 1916-1984 Obituary 114
Edwards, R. M.
See Edwards, Roselyn
Edwards, (H. C.) Ralph 1894- CAP-1
Earlier sketch in CA 13-16
Edwards, Raoul D(urant) 1928-1987 Obituary 125
Edwards, Rem B(lanchard, Jr.) 1934- 37-40R
Edwards, Richard 1524-1566 .... DLB 62
Edwards, Richard Alan 1934- 69-72
Edwards, Richard C. 1944- CANR-2
Earlier sketch in CA 45-48
Edwards, Robert (John) 1925- 129
Edwards, Robert Alan 1947- 121
Interview in 121
Edwards, Ron(ald George) 1930- 105
Edwards, Roselyn 1929- 25-28R
Edwards, Ruth Dudley
See Dudley Edwards, Ruth
Edwards, S. W.
See Sublette, Walter (Edwards)
Edwards, Sally (Cary) 1929- 25-28R
See also SATA 7
Edwards, Samuel
See Gerson, Noel Bertram
Edwards, Sarah Pierpont 1710-1758 .... DLB 200
Edwards, Stephen
See Palestrant, Simon S.
Edwards, Susan 151
Edwards, T(homas) Bentley 1906- CAP-2
Earlier sketch in CA 23-24
Edwards, Thomas R(obert) Jr. 1928- 5-8R
Edwards, Tilden Hampton, Jr. 1935- CANR-18
Earlier sketch in CA 102
Edwards, Verne E(rvie), Jr. 1924- 33-36R
Edwards, Vince 1928-1996 159
Edwards, Ward 1927- 21-24R
Edwards, William 1896- CAP-1
Earlier sketch in CA 13-14
Edwards, William B(ennett) 1927- 5-8R
Edward VIII 1894-1972 Obituary 33-36R
Edwin, Brother B.
See Arnandez, Richard
Edzard, Christine 1945- 164
Eekelaar, John M(ichael) 1942- 116
Eekman, Thomas 1923- 81-84
Eells, George 1922- CANR-14
Earlier sketch in CA 21-24R
Eells, Richard S(edric) F(ox) 1917- 132
Eells, Robert J(ames) 1944- 102
Efemey, Raymond (Frederick) 1928- 21-24R
Effinger, George Alec 1947- CANR-23
Earlier sketch in CA 37-40R
See also DLB 8
Efimova, Alla 1961- 163
Efird, James M(ichael) 1932- CANR-31
Earlier sketches in CA 37-40R, CANR-14
Efremov, Ivan (Antonovich)
See Yefremov, Ivan (Antonovich)
Efron, Alexander 1897- CAP-2
Earlier sketch in CA 29-32
Efron, Arthur 1931- CANR-21
Earlier sketch in CA 69-72
Efron, Benjamin 1908- CANR-5
Earlier sketch in CA 5-8R
Efron, Edith Carol 1922- 102
Efron, Marina Ivanovna Tsvetaeva
See Tsvetaeva (Efron), Marina (Ivanovna)
Efron, Marshall 1938(?)- 126
Brief entry 112
Efros, Israel (Isaac) 1891-1981 .... 21-24R
Obituary 102
Efros, Susan Elyse 1947- 104
Efrot
See Efros, Israel (Isaac)
Egami, Tomi 1899- 61-64
Egan, Beresford Patrick 1905-1984 Obituary 111
Egan, Catherine 1943- 146
Egan, David R(onald) 1943- 102
Egan, Desmond 1936- 149
Egan, E(dward) W(elstead) 1922- CANR-9
Earlier sketch in CA 21-24R
See also SATA 35
Egan, Ferol 1923- 29-32R
Egan, Fred(erick Julian) 1905(?)-1986 Obituary 118
Egan, Gerard 1930- CANR-52
Earlier sketches in CA 29-32R, CANR-12, 28
Egan, Greg 1961- 165
Egan, Harvey Daniel 1937- 113
Egan, Jennifer 1962- 154
Egan, John P. 1934- 110
Egan, Kieran 1942- 161
Egan, Lesley
See Linington, (Barbara) Elizabeth
Egan, Lorraine Hopping 1960- 155
See also SATA 91
Egan, Melinda A(nne) 1950- 102
Egan, Michael 1941- 45-48
Egan, Philip S(idney) 1920- 1-4R
Egan, Robert 1945- 77-80
Egan, Tim 1957- 149
See also SATA 89
Egan, Timothy 1954- 141
Egbert, Donald Drew 1902-1973 .... CAP-2
Obituary 37-40R
Earlier sketch in CA 23-24
Egbert, Kathlyn Whitsitt 1950- 150
Egbert, Virginia Wylie
See Kilborne, Virginia Wylie
Egbuna, Obi B(enue Joseph) 1938- 102
Ege, Arvia MacKaye 1903(?)-1989 Obituary 128
Egejuru, Phanuel Akubueze 106
Egelhof, Joseph (Baird)
1919(?)-1980 Obituary 97-100
Eger, Jeffrey 1946- 125
Egermeier, Elsie E(milie) 1890-1986 .... 5-8R
See also SATA 65
Egerton, Frank N(icholas) III 1936- 110
Egerton, George 1859-1945 .... DLB 135
Egerton, George W(illiam) 1942- 85-88
Egerton, John (Walden) 1935- CANR-47
Earlier sketch in CA 85-88
Egerton, Lucy
See Malleson, Lucy Beatrice
Egg, Maria 1910- 29-32R
Egg-Benes, Maria
See Egg, Maria
Eggeling, Hans Friedrich 1878-1977 .... 1-4R
Obituary 73-76
Eggenberger, David 1918- 9-12R
See also SATA 6
Eggenschwiler, David 1936- 37-40R
Egger, M(aurice) David 1936- 57-60
Egger, Rowland (Andrews) 1908-1979 .... CANR-4
Earlier sketch in CA 5-8R
Eggers, J(ohn) Philip 1940- 33-36R
Eggers, Kerry 1953- 137
Eggers, William T. 1912- 29-32R
Eggert, Gerald G(ordon) 1926- 21-24R
Eggert, James (Edward) 1943- CANR-47
Earlier sketches in CA 107, CANR-23
Eggert, Jim
See Eggert, James (Edward)
Egginton, Joyce 142
Eggleston, Edward 1837-1902 Brief entry 111
See also DLB 12
See also SATA 27
Eggleston, George T(eeple)
1906-1990 Obituary 132
Eggleston, Wilfrid 1901-1986 .... CANR-8
Obituary 119
Earlier sketch in CA 21-24R
See also DLB 92
Eggum, Arne 1936- 134
Egharevba, Jacob U(wadiae) 1920(?)- 152
See also BW 2
Egielski, Richard 1952- .... MAICYA
See also SATA 11, 49
Egler, Claudio A(ntonio) G(oncalves) 1951- 144
Egler, Frank E(dwin) 1911-1996 .... 29-32R
Obituary 155
Egleson, Janet F.
See Dunleavy, Janet Egleson
Egleton, Clive (Frederick) 1927- CANR-22
Earlier sketch in CA 103
Egli, Ida Rae 1946- 137
Egoff, Sheila A. 1918- 132
Brief entry 116
Egoyan, Atom 1960- 157
Egremont, Max 1948- CANR-35
Earlier sketch in CA 93-96
Eguchi, Shinichi 1914-1979 Obituary 85-88
Egudu, R. N.
See Egudu, Romanus N(nagbo)
Egudu, Romanus N(nagbo) 1940- 143
See also BW 2
Egypt, Ophelia Settle 1903-1984 81-84
Obituary 112
See also SATA 16
See also SATA-Obit 38
Ehle, John (Marsden, Jr.) 1925- 9-12R
See also CLC 27
Ehler, R(ichard) L. 1930- 137
Ehlers, Henry James 1907- 13-16R
Ehlert, Lois (Jane) 1934- 137
See also CLR 28
See also MAICYA
See also SATA 35, 69
Ehling, Katalin Olah 1941- .... SATA 93
Ehmann, James 1948- 109
Ehninger, Douglas W(agner) 1913-1979 .... CANR-4
Earlier sketch in CA 5-8R
Ehre, Edward 1905- 9-12R
Ehre, Milton 1933- 53-56
Ehrenberg, John 1944- 159
Ehrenberg, Miriam 124
Ehrenberg, Otto 1926- 124
Ehrenberg, Victor (Leopold) 1891-1976 .... CANR-4
Obituary 65-68
Earlier sketch in CA 5-8R
Ehrenbourg, Ilya (Grigoryevich)
See Ehrenburg, Ilya (Grigoryevich)
Ehrenburg, Ilya (Grigoryevich) 1891-1967 102
Obituary 25-28R
See also CLC 18, 34, 62
Ehrenburg, Ilyo (Grigoryevich)
See Ehrenburg, Ilya (Grigoryevich)
Ehrenfeld, David W(illiam) 1938- 81-84
Ehrenfest, Paul 1880-1933 157
Ehrenfreund, Norbert 1921- 151
See also SATA 86
Ehrenhalt, Alan 1947- 112
Ehrenpreis, Anne Henry 1927- 53-56
Ehrenpreis, Irvin 1920-1985 121
Obituary 116
Brief entry 110
Ehrenreich, Barbara 1941- CANR-62
Earlier sketches in CA 73-76, CANR-16, 37
See also BEST 90:4
See also CLC 110
See also MTCW 1
Ehrenreich, Herman 1900(?)-1970 Obituary 104
Ehrenreich, John H. 1943- 125
Ehrenstein, Albert 1886-1950 .... DLB 81
Ehrensvaerd, Goesta (Carl Henrik) 1910- CANR-2
Earlier sketch in CA 49-52
Ehrenwald, Jan 1900-1988 .... CANR-2
Obituary 125
Earlier sketch in CA 49-52
Ehrenzweig, Albert A(rmin) 1906-1974 .... CAP-2
Earlier sketch in CA 29-32
Ehresmann, Donald L(ouis) 1937- 69-72
Ehresmann, Julia M. 1939- 33-36R
Ehret, Christopher 1941- 37-40R
Ehret, Terry 1955- 143
Ehrhardt, Reinhold 1900- 29-32R
Ehrhart, W(illiam) D(aniel) 1948- CANR-52
Earlier sketches in CA 61-64, CANR-7
See also DLBD 9
Ehricke, Krafft A(rnold) 1917-1984 Obituary 114
Ehrlich, Amy 1942- CANR-67
Earlier sketches in CA 37-40R, CANR-14, 32
See also SATA 25, 65, 96
Ehrlich, Anne (Fitzhugh) Howland 1933- CANR-8
Earlier sketch in CA 61-64
Ehrlich, Arnold 1923-1989 .... 33-36R
Obituary 129
Ehrlich, Bettina Bauer 1903- CAP-1
Earlier sketch in CA 13-14
See also SATA 1
Ehrlich, Carol H. 1927- 165
Ehrlich, Cyril 1925- 103
Ehrlich, David 1941- CANR-55
Earlier sketch in CA 127
Ehrlich, Eugene H. 1922- CANR-5
Earlier sketch in CA 1-4R
Ehrlich, Everett M. 1950- 112
Ehrlich, Gretel 1946- 140
Ehrlich, Howard J. 1932- 17-20R
Ehrlich, Isaac 1938- 118
Ehrlich, Jack
See Ehrlich, John Gunther
Ehrlich, Jacob Wilburn 1900-1971 Obituary 33-36R
Ehrlich, Jake
See Ehrlich, Jacob Wilburn
Ehrlich, John Gunther 1930- CANR-63
Earlier sketches in CA 1-4R, CANR-4
Ehrlich, Leonard Harry 1924- 102
Ehrlich, Max 1909-1983 .... CANR-72
Obituary 115
Earlier sketches in CA 1-4R, CANR-1
Ehrlich, Nathaniel J(oseph) 1940- 53-56
Ehrlich, Otto Hild 1892-1979 Obituary 85-88
Ehrlich, Paul R(alph) 1932- CANR-28
Earlier sketches in CA 65-68, CANR-8
Ehrlich, Robert S. 1935- 21-24R
Ehrlich, Thomas 1934- 113
Ehrlich, Walter 1921- 53-56
Ehrlichman, John Daniel 1925- CANR-45
Earlier sketch in CA 65-68
Ehrman, John (Patrick William) 1920- CANR-26
Earlier sketches in CA 5-8R, CANR-4
Ehrman, John 1959- 149
Ehrman, Lee 1935- 69-72
Ehrmann, Herbert B(rutus) 1891-1970 .... CAP-2
Earlier sketch in CA 25-28
Ehrsam, Theodore George 1909- 45-48
Eibel, Deborah 1940- 151
Eibl-Eibesfeldt, Irenaeus 1928- CANR-3
Earlier sketch in CA 9-12R
Eibling, Harold Henry 1905-1976 .... CANR-29
Earlier sketch in CA 37-40R
Eiby, George 1918- 53-56
Eich, Guenter 1907-1972 111
Obituary 93-96
See also CLC 15
See also DLB 69, 124
Eichelbaum, Stanley 1926- 73-76
Eichelberger, Clark M(ell)
1896-1980 Obituary 93-96
Eichelberger, Clayton L. 1925- 41-44R
Eichelberger, Ethyl 1945-1990 Obituary 132
Eichelberger, Rosa Kohler 1896- 102
Eichenbaum, Luise 1952- 126
Eichenberg, Fritz 1901-1990 .... CANR-57
Obituary 133
Earlier sketches in CA 57-60, CANR-6
See also MAICYA
See also SATA 9, 50
Eichendorff, Joseph Freiherr von 1788-1857 .... DLB 90
Eichenlaub, John Ellis 1922- CANR-4
Earlier sketch in CA 1-4R
Eicher, David J(ohn) 1961- 113
Eicher, (Ethel) Elizabeth 17-20R
Eicher, Joanne B(ubolz) 1930- CANR-28
Earlier sketch in CA 49-52
Eichhorn, David Max 1906- CAP-1
Earlier sketch in CA 11-12
Eichhorn, Werner 1899- 29-32R
Eichler, Margrit 1942- 107
See also SATA 35
Eichler, Ned 1930- 132
Eichman, Mark 1949- 109
Eichner, Alfred S. 1937-1988 .... CANR-5
Obituary 124
Earlier sketch in CA 13-16R
Eichner, Hans 1921- CANR-41
Earlier sketches in CA 5-8R, CANR-4, 19
Eichner, James A. 1927- 13-16R
See also SATA 4
Eichner, Maura 1915- CANR-14
Earlier sketch in CA 37-40R
Eichorn, Dorothy H(ansen) 1924- CANR-27
Earlier sketch in CA 49-52
Eickhoff, Andrew R(obert) 1924- 21-24R
Eicoff, Alvin Maurey 1921- 112
Eid, Leif 1908(?)-1976 Obituary 65-68
Eidelberg, Ludwig 1898-1970 .... CAP-1
Obituary 29-32R
Earlier sketch in CA 19-20
Eidelberg, Paul 1928- CANR-27
Earlier sketch in CA 21-24R
Eidenberg, Eugene 1939- 81-84
Eidesheim, Julie 1884-1972 Obituary 104
Eidsmoe, John 1945- CANR-40
Earlier sketch in CA 114
Eidsvik, Charles Vernon 1943- 101
Eidt, Robert C. 1923- 33-36R
Eiduson, Bernice T(abackman) 1921-1985 ....
CANR-27
Earlier sketch in CA 1-4R
Eifert, Virginia (Louise) S(nider) 1911-1966 ....
CANR-15
Earlier sketch in CA 1-4R
See also SATA 2
Eige, (Elizabeth) Lillian 1915- 136
See also SATA 65
Eigen, Manfred 1927- 108
Eigen, Michael 1936- CANR-39
Earlier sketch in CA 115
Eighner, Lars 1948- 143
Eigner, Edwin M(oss) 1931- 21-24R
Eigner, Larry
See Eigner, Laurence (Joel)
See also CAAS 23
See also CLC 9
See also DLB 5
Eigner, Laurence (Joel) 1927-1996 .... CANR-6
Obituary 151
Earlier sketch in CA 9-12R
See also Eigner, Larry
See also DLB 193
Eiland, Howard 1948- 111
Eiland, Murray L(ee) 1936- 85-88
Eilberg-Schwartz, Howard 1956- 147
Eilert, Richard E. 1947- 129
Eilert, Rick
See Eilert, Richard E.
Eilhart von Oberge c. 1140-c. 1195 .... DLB 148
Eilon, Samuel 1923- CANR-4
Earlier sketch in CA 5-8R
Eimer, D(ean) Robert 1927- 13-16R
Eimerl, Sarel (Henry) 1925- 21-24R
Einbond, Bernard Lionel 1937- 37-40R
Einhard c. 770-840 .... DLB 148
Einhorn, Barbara 1942- 156
Einhorn, Virginia Hilu
See Hilu, Virginia
Einsel, Mary E. 1929- 29-32R
Einsel, Naiad .... SATA 10
Einsel, Walter 1926- .... SATA 10
Einstein, Albert 1879-1955 133
Brief entry 121
See also MTCW 1
See also TCLC 65
Einstein, Albert 1947- CANR-37
Brief entry 109
Earlier sketch in CA 113

Einstein, Charles 1926- CANR-29
Earlier sketch in CA 65-68
Einstein, Elizabeth (Ann) 1939- CANR-27
Earlier sketch in CA 109
Einstein, Stanley 1934- CANR-4
Earlier sketch in CA 53-56
Einstoss, Ron 1930(?)-1977 Obituary 69-72
Einzig, Paul 1897-1973 .... CANR-5
Obituary 89-92
Earlier sketch in CA 9-12R
Einzig, Susan 1922- .... SATA 43
Eire, Carlos M(ario) N(ieto) 1950- 127
Eirelin, Glenn
See Evans, Glen
Eisdorfer, Carl 1930- 41-44R
Eisele, Albert A(lois) 1936- 41-44R
Eisele, Robert H. 1948- CANR-25
Earlier sketch in CA 108
Eiseley, Loren Corey 1907-1977 .... CANR-6
Obituary 73-76
Earlier sketch in CA 1-4R
See also AAYA 5
See also CLC 7
See also DLBD 17
Eiseman, Alberta 1925- 77-80
See also SATA 15
Eiseman, Alvord L. 1916- 112
Eisen, Carol G.
See Rinzler, Carol Eisen (Gene)
Eisen, Jack 1925- 73-76
Eisen, Sydney 1929- 135
Eisenach, Eldon J(ohn) 1938- 106
Eisenberg, Arlene 139
Eisenberg, Azriel (Louis) 1903-1985 ..... CANR-10
Obituary 164
Earlier sketch in CA 49-52
See also SATA 12
Eisenberg, Benjamin 1916-1984 Obituary 112
Eisenberg, Daniel Bruce 1946- CANR-6
Earlier sketch in CA 57-60
Eisenberg, Deborah 1945- 158
Eisenberg, Dennis (Harold) 1929- CANR-28
Earlier sketch in CA 25-28R
Eisenberg, Ellen M. 1962- 154
Eisenberg, Gerson G. 1909- 81-84
Eisenberg, Hershey H. 1927- 104
Eisenberg, Howard 1946- 101
Eisenberg, Larry 1919- 33-36R
Eisenberg, Lawrence B(enjamin) 77-80
Eisenberg, Lee 1946- CANR-9
Earlier sketch in CA 61-64
Eisenberg, Lisa 1949- 110
See also SATA 57
See also SATA-Brief 50
Eisenberg, Maurice 1902-1972 Obituary 37-40R
Eisenberg, Phyllis Rose 1924- 111
See also SATA 41
Eisenberg, Ralph 1930-1973 .... CANR-3
Obituary 45-48
Earlier sketch in CA 5-8R
Eisenberg, Robert 1956- 161
Eisenberg, Ronald L(ee) 1945- CANR-53
Earlier sketches in CA 73-76, CANR-13, 28
Eisenberger, Kenneth 1948- 81-84
Eisenbud, Jule 1908- CANR-27
Earlier sketch in CA 49-52
Eisendrath, Craig R. 1936- 49-52
Eisendrath, Polly Young
See Young-Eisendrath, Polly
Eisenhower, Dwight D(avid) 1890-1969 .. CANR-24
Earlier sketch in CA 65-68
Eisenhower, John S(heldon) D(oud) 1922- ....
CANR-32
Earlier sketches in CA 33-36R, CANR-14
Eisenhower, Julie Nixon 1948- 114
Eisenhower, Milton S(tover) 1899-1985 73-76
Obituary 116
Eisenhower, Susan (Elaine) 1951- 162
Eisenman, Peter D(avid) 1932- 108
Eisenman, Stephen F. 1956- CANR-71
Earlier sketch in CA 140
Eisenmenger, Robert Waltz 1926- 37-40R
Eisenreich, Herbert 1925-1986 .... DLB 85
Eisenschiml, Otto 1880-1963 .... 1-4R
Eisenson, Jon 1907- 17-20R
Eisenstadt, A(braham) S(eldin) 1920- CANR-4
Earlier sketch in CA 9-12R
Eisenstadt, Jill 1963- 140
See also CLC 50
Eisenstadt, Shmuel N(oah) 1923- 25-28R
Eisenstaedt, Alfred 1898-1995 108
Obituary 149
Eisenstat, Jane Sperry 1920- 1-4R
Eisenstein, Elizabeth L(ewisohn) 1923- 89-92
Eisenstein, Hester 1940- 137
Eisenstein, Ira 1906- 21-24R
Eisenstein, James 1940- Brief entry 111
Eisenstein, Phyllis 1946- CANR-36
Earlier sketches in CA 85-88, CANR-16
Eisenstein, Sam(uel Abraham) 1932- CANR-16
Earlier sketch in CA 61-64
Eisenstein, Sergei (Mikhailovich) 1898-1948 149
Brief entry 114
See also TCLC 57
Eiserer, Leonard Arnold 1948- 73-76
Eisiminger, Sterling (Jr.) 1941- 141
Eisinger, Chester E(manuel) 1915- 21-24R
Eisinger, Josef 1924- 167
Eisinger, Peter K(endall) 1942- 69-72
Eisler, Benita 1937- 136
Eisler, Colin (Tobias) 1931- 85-88
Eisler, Frieda Goldman
See Goldman-Eisler, Frieda
Eisler, Georg 1928- Brief entry 106
Eisler, George B. 1892(?)-1983 Obituary 111
Eisler, Hanns 1898-1962 Obituary 116
Eisler, Lawrence 1920- 122
Eisler, Paul (Erich) 1922-1978 61-64
Obituary 125
Eisler, Riane Tennenhaus 1931- 73-76
Eisman, Hy 1927- 65-68
Eisman, Mark 1948- 108
Eismann, Bernard N(orman) 1933- 1-4R
Eisner, Betty Grover 1915- 29-32R
Eisner, Elliot W(ayne) 1933- 123
Brief entry 118
Eisner, Gisela (Spanglet) 1925- CAP-1
Earlier sketch in CA 9-10
Eisner, Kurt 1867-1919 .... DLB 66
Eisner, Lotte (Henriette) 1896-1983 ..... CANR-14
Obituary 111
Earlier sketch in CA 45-48
Eisner, Robert 1922- 107
Eisner, Sigmund 1920- 124
Eisner, Simon
See Kornbluth, C(yril) M.
Eisner, Thomas 1929- 157
Eisner, Victor 1921- 53-56
Eisner, Vivienne
See Margolis, Vivienne
Eisner, Will(iam Erwin) 1917- 108
See also SATA 31
Eiss, Harry Edwin 1950- CANR-52
Earlier sketch in CA 124
Eissenstat, Bernard W. 1927- 45-48
Eister, Allan W(ardell) 1915-1979 .... CANR-2
Earlier sketch in CA 45-48
Eiteman, David (Kurt) 1930- 45-48
Eiteman, Wilford J(ohn) 1902- CANR-4
Earlier sketch in CA 1-4R
Eitinger, Leo S(hua) 1912- CANR-16
Earlier sketch in CA 89-92
Eitington, Julius E. 1918- 120
Eitner, Lorenz E. A. 1919- CANR-5
Earlier sketch in CA 1-4R
Eitzen, Allan 1928- .... SATA 9
Eitzen, D(avid) Stanley 1934- CANR-41
Earlier sketches in CA 53-56, CANR-4, 19
Eitzen, Ruth (Carper) 1924- 41-44R
See also SATA 9
Ekblaw, Sidney E(verette) 1903-1990 ...... 37-40R
Obituary 164
Ekdahl, Janis (Kay) 1946- Brief entry 112
Ekeblad, Frederick A(lfred) 1917- 5-8R
Ekeh, Peter P(almer) 1937- 102
Ekeloef, (Bengt) Gunnar 1907-1968 123
Obituary 25-28R
See also CLC 27
See also DAM POET
See also PC 23
Ekelof, (Bengt) Gunnar
See Ekeloef, (Bengt) Gunnar
Ekelund, Vilhelm 1880-1949 .... TCLC 75
Ekert-Rotholz, Alice Maria (Augusta) 1900- 129
Ekins, Paul (Whitfield) 1950- CANR-50
Earlier sketch in CA 123
Ekirch, A(rthur) Roger 1950- 109
Ekirch, Arthur A., Jr. 1915- CANR-2
Earlier sketch in CA 5-8R
Ekker, Charles 1930- 37-40R
Eklund, Gordon (Stewart) 1945- CANR-24
Earlier sketch in CA 33-36R
See also DLBY 83
Eklund, Jane Mary
See Ball, Jane Eklund
Ekman, Kerstin 1933- 154
Ekman, Paul 1934- CANR-14
Earlier sketch in CA 37-40R
Ekman, Rosalind 1933- 33-36R
Ekola, Giles C(hester) 1927- 17-20R
Ekstein, Rudolf 1912- CANR-4
Earlier sketch in CA 5-8R
Eksteins, Modris 1943- CANR-34
Earlier sketch in CA 77-80
Ekstroem, (Sigrid) Margareta 1930- 135
Ekstrom, Margareta
See Ekstroem, (Sigrid) Margareta
Ekstrom, Parmenia Migel 1908-1989 Obituary .. 130
Ekvall, Robert B(rainerd) 1898-1983 ...... CANR-5
Obituary 164
Earlier sketch in CA 1-4R
Ekwall, Eldon E(dward) 1933- CANR-12
Earlier sketch in CA 29-32R
Ekwensi, C. O. D.
See Ekwensi, Cyprian (Odiatu Duaka)
Ekwensi, Cyprian (Odiatu Duaka) 1921- .. CANR-42
Earlier sketches in CA 29-32R, CANR-18
See also BLC 1
See also BW 2
See also CLC 4
See also DAM MULT
See also DLB 117
See also MTCW 1
See also SATA 66
Ela, Jonathan P(ell) 1945- 81-84
Elad, Amikam 1946- 152
Elaine
See Leverson, Ada
See also TCLC 18
Elam, Richard M(ace, Jr.) 1920- 61-64
See also SATA 9
El-Aref, Aref (?)-1973 Obituary 41-44R
Elashoff, Janet Dixon 1942- 61-64
Elath, Eliahu 1903-1990 .... 13-16R
Obituary 132
El-Ayouty, Yassin 1928- CANR-14
Earlier sketch in CA 29-32R
Elazar, Daniel J(udah) 1934- CANR-13
Earlier sketch in CA 21-24R
El-Baz, Farouk 1938- CANR-51
Earlier sketches in CA 25-28R, CANR-10, 26
Elbert, Edmund J(oseph) 1923- 37-40R
Elbert, George A. 1911-1995 .... CANR-35
Obituary 149
Earlier sketch in CA 61-64
Elbert, Samuel H(oyt) 1907- CANR-5
Earlier sketch in CA 1-4R
Elbert, Sarah 1937- 135
Elbert, Virginie Fowler 1912- CANR-35
Earlier sketches in CA 61-64, CANR-8
Elbin, Paul Nowell 1905- CANR-35
Earlier sketch in CA 69-72
Elbing, Alvar O(liver), Jr. 1928- 21-24R
Elbing, Carol J(eppson) 1930- 21-24R
Elbogen, Paul 1894-1987 .... 5-8R
Obituary 164
Elborn, Geoffrey 1950- 109
Elbow, Peter (Henry) 1935- CANR-28
Earlier sketches in CA 65-68, CANR-12
Elbrecht, Paul G. 1921- 17-20R
El Bundukhari
See Dent, Anthony Austen
Elchamo, Jason
See Caballero, Manuel
Elchamo, Sebastian
See Caballero, Manuel
Elcock, Howard J(ames) 1942- CANR-56
Earlier sketches in CA 29-32R, CANR-12, 29
El Crummo
See Crumb, R(obert)
Eld, George fl. 1603-1624 .... DLB 170
Eldefonso, Edward 1933- CANR-14
Earlier sketch in CA 21-24R
Elder, Betty Doak 1938- 112
Elder, Ellen Rozanne 1940- 111
Elder, Gary 1939- 73-76
Elder, George Colman the 1732-1794 ...... DLB 89
Elder, Glen(nard) H(oll), Jr. 1934- CANR-3
Earlier sketch in CA 49-52
Elder, John 1947- 133
Elder, John William 1933- 111
Elder, Karl 1948- 77-80
Elder, Leon
See Young, Noel
Elder, Lonne III 1931-1996 .... CANR-25
Obituary 152
Earlier sketch in CA 81-84
See also BLC 1
See also BW 1
See also DAM MULT
See also DC 8
See also DLB 7, 38, 44
Elder, Mark 1935- CANR-2
Earlier sketch in CA 49-52
Elder, Michael (Aiken) 1931- 33-36R
Elder, Rob(ert Laurie) 1938- 125
Elder, Robert E(llsworth) 1915- 1-4R
Elder, Shirley (A.) 1931- 132
Brief entry 118
Elderfield, John 1943- 132
Elders, (Minnie) Joycelyn 1933- 156
Eldershaw, Flora Sydney Patricia 1897-1956 ... 156
Eldershaw, M. Barnard
See Eldershaw, Flora Sydney Patricia
Eldersveld, Samuel James 1917- 111
Eldin, Raymond
See Morton, James (Severs)
Eldjarn, Kristjan (Thorarinsson)
1916-1982 Obituary 110
Eldred, Vince 1924- 69-72
Eldredge, H(anford) Wentworth 1909-1991 . 41-44R
Obituary 133
Eldredge, Laurence H(oward) 1902- CAP-2
Earlier sketch in CA 25-28
Eldredge, Niles 1943- 157
Eldred-Grigg, Stevan (Treleaven) 1952- 162
Eldridge, Colin Clifford 1942- 107
Eldridge, Frank R. 1889(?)-1976 Obituary 69-72
Eldridge, J(ohn) E. T. 1936- CANR-11
Earlier sketch in CA 25-28R
Eldridge, Marian (Favel Clair) 1936- CANR-42
Earlier sketch in CA 118
Eldridge, Paul 1888- 9-12R
Eldridge, Retha Hazel (Giles) 1910- CAP-1
Earlier sketch in CA 13-14
Eleanor, Sister Joseph 25-28R
Elegant, Robert (Sampson) 1928- CANR-30
Earlier sketches in CA 1-4R, CANR-1
Elek, Paul 1906(?)-1976 Obituary 69-72
el-Erian, Abdullah Ali 1920-1981 Obituary 108
Elethea, Abba
See Thompson, James W.
Elevitch, M(orton) D. 1925- CANR-2
Earlier sketch in CA 49-52
Eley, Beverley 167
Eley, Geoff(rey Howard) 1949- 129
Eley, Lynn W. 1925- CANR-16
Earlier sketch in CA 25-28R
Elfenbein, Julien 1897-1983 .... CANR-5
Obituary 109
Earlier sketch in CA 1-4R
Elfman, Blossom 1925- CANR-39
Earlier sketches in CA 45-48, CANR-2, 17
See also SATA 8
Elfman, Danny 1953- CANR-71
Earlier sketch in CA 148
See also AAYA 14
Elford, Homer J. R. 1912- CANR-9
Earlier sketch in CA 21-24R
Elfstrom, Gerard 1945- 145
Elgar, Edward (William) 1857-1934 Brief entry . 116
Elgar, Frank 1899- 102
Elgin, Kathleen 1923- 25-28R
See also SATA 39
Elgin, Mary
See Stewart, Dorothy Mary
Elgin, (Patricia Anne) Suzette Haden 1936- ....
CANR-8
Earlier sketch in CA 61-64
Elgood, Robert (Francis Willard) 1948- 125
el Hajjam, Mohammed ben Chaib 1940- . CANR-38
Earlier sketches in CA 97-100, CANR-17
El Huitlacoche
See Keller, Gary D.
Elia
See Lamb, Charles
Eliach, Yaffa 1935- 110
Eliade, Mircea 1907-1986 .... CANR-62
Obituary 119
Earlier sketches in CA 65-68, CANR-30
See also CLC 19
See also MTCW 1
Elias, Albert J. 1920- 81-84
Elias, C(laude) E(dward), Jr. 1924- 13-16R
Elias, Christopher 1925- 33-36R
Elias, Eileen
See Davies, Eileen Winifred
Elias, Horace J(ay) 1910- CANR-16
Earlier sketch in CA 89-92
Elias, Jason 1947- 150
Elias, John L(awrence) 1933- CANR-51
Earlier sketches in CA 69-72, CANR-25
Elias, Norbert 1897-1990 Obituary 132
Elias, Robert H(enry) 1914- 61-64
Elias, Scott A. 1953- 148
Elias, Taslim Olawale 1914-1991 .... CANR-21
Obituary 145
Earlier sketches in CA 13-16R, CANR-6
Elias, Thomas S. 1942- CANR-35
Earlier sketch in CA 114
Elias, Victor J. 1937- 146
Eliason, Joyce 1934- 77-80
Eliav, Arie L(ova) 1921- CANR-28
Earlier sketches in CA 69-72, CANR-11
Elicker, Charles W. 1951-1978 Obituary 115
Elie, Lolis Eric 1963- 159
Elie, Robert 1915-1973 148
See also DLB 88
Elieff, Deanne D(esmond) 1926- 113
Elin Pelin 1877-1949 .... DLB 147
Elinson, Jack 1917- CANR-20
Earlier sketches in CA 45-48, CANR-2
Elioseff, Lee Andrew 1933- 17-20R
Eliot, A. D.
See Jewett, (Theodora) Sarah Orne
Eliot, Alexander 1919- CANR-1
Earlier sketch in CA 49-52
Eliot, Alice
See Jewett, (Theodora) Sarah Orne
Eliot, Anne
See Cole, Lois Dwight
Eliot, Dan
See Silverberg, Robert
Eliot, George 1819-1880 .... CDBLB 1832-1890
See also DA
See also DAB
See also DAC
See also DAM MST, NOV
See also DLB 21, 35, 55
See also PC 20
See also WLC
Eliot, George Fielding 1894-1971 Obituary . 29-32R
Eliot, John 1604-1690 .... DLB 24
Eliot, Karen
See Home, Stewart
Eliot, Nathan
See Kramer, Edward (E.)
Eliot, Sonny 1926- 81-84
Eliot, T(homas) S(tearns) 1888-1965 .... CANR-41
Obituary 25-28R
Earlier sketch in CA 5-8R
See also CDALB 1929-1941
See also CLC 1, 2, 3, 6, 9, 10, 13, 15, 24, 34, 41, 55, 57, 113
See also DA
See also DAB
See also DAC
See also DAM DRAM, MST, POET
See also DLB 7, 10, 45, 63
See also DLBY 88
See also MTCW 1
See also PC 5
See also WLC
Eliot, Thomas H(opkinson) 1907-1991 89-92
Obituary 135
Eliot Hurst, M(ichael) E(liot) 1938- 57-60
Eliovson, Sima (Benveniste) 1919- CANR-20
Earlier sketches in CA 13-16R, CANR-5
Elis, Islwyn Ffowc 1924- 93-96
Elisabeth (Ottilie Luise), Queen (Pauline)
1843-1916 Brief entry 123
Eliscu, Frank 1912-1996 57-60
Obituary 152
Elish, Dan 1960- 136
See also SATA 68
Elisofon, Eliot 1911-1973 Obituary 41-44R
See also SATA-Obit 21
Elison, George 1937- 53-56
Elium, Don 1954- 139
Elium, Jeanne (Ann) 1947- 138
Elizabeth
See Russell, CountessMary Annette Beauchamp
Elizabeth 1866-1941 .... TCLC 41
Elizabeth Marie, Sister 1914- 9-12R
Elizondo, Salvador 1932- .... DLB 145
Elizondo, Sergio
See Elizondo (Dominguez), Sergio D(anilo)
Elizondo (Dominguez), Sergio D(anilo) 1930- ... 131
See also DLB 82
See also HW
Elizur, Joel 1952- 135
Elkann, Alain 1950- 127

Elkhadem, Saad (Eldin Amin) 1932- 131
Elkholy, Abdo A. 1925- 21-24R
Elkin, Benjamin 1911- CANR-4
Earlier sketch in CA 1-4R
See also SATA 3
Elkin, Frederick 1918- 41-44R
Elkin, H. V.
See Hinkle, Vernon
Elkin, Judith Laikin 1928- CANR-41
Earlier sketches in CA 53-56, CANR-4, 19
Elkin, Stanley L(awrence) 1930-1995 .... CANR-46
Obituary 148
Earlier sketches in CA 9-12R, CANR-8
Interview in CANR-8
See also CLC 4, 6, 9, 14, 27, 51, 91
See also DAM NOV, POP
See also DLB 2, 28
See also DLBY 80
See also MTCW 1
See also SSC 12
Elkin, Stephen L(loyd) 1941- 93-96
Elkind, David 1931- CANR-1
Earlier sketch in CA 45-48
Elkins, Aaron J. 1935- 126
See also CAAS 18
See also BEST 89:1
Elkins, Charlotte 1948- 167
Elkins, Dov Peretz 1937- CANR-30
Earlier sketches in CA 29-32R, CANR-12
See also SATA 5
Elkins, Ella Ruth 1929- 25-28R
Elkins, James P. 1955- 162
Elkins, Stanley Maurice 1925- 102
Elkins, T(homas) H(enry) 1926- Brief entry 111
Elkins, William R. 1926- 33-36R
Elkon, Jon 1949- 134
Elkon, Juliette
See Elkon-Hamelecourt, Juliette
Elkon-Hamelecourt, Juliette 1912- 57-60
Elkouri, Frank 1921- 69-72
Elkus, Jonathan Britton 1931- 111
Ellacott, S(amuel) E(rnest) 1911- CANR-3
Earlier sketch in CA 5-8R
See also SATA 19
Elledge, Jim 1950- CANR-39
Earlier sketches in CA 102, CANR-19
Elledge, Scott .... CLC 34
Elledge, Scott (Bowen) 1914- 145
Elledge, W(aymon) Paul 1938- 25-28R
Ellen, Barbara 1938- 5-8R
Ellen, Jaye
See Nixon, Joan Lowery
Ellenberger, Henri F(rederic) 1905- CAP-2
Earlier sketch in CA 29-32
Ellenbogen, Eileen 1917- 104
Ellender, Raphael 1906-1972 Obituary 37-40R
Ellens, J(ay) Harold 1932- CANR-58
Earlier sketches in CA 57-60, CANR-7, 31
Ellenson, Gene 1921- 57-60
Eller, John 1935- 105
Eller, Ronald D 1948- 110
Eller, Scott
See Holinger, William (Jacques)
and Shepard, Jim
Eller, Vernard (Marion) 1927- CANR-24
Earlier sketches in CA 21-24R, CANR-9
Eller, William 1921- 77-80
Ellerbeck, Rosemary (Anne L'Estrange) CANR-24
Earlier sketch in CA 106
Ellerbee, Linda (Jane) 1944- CANR-54
Brief entry 110
Earlier sketch in CA 115
Interview in 115
See also AAYA 16
ELLERMAN, Annie Winifred 1894-1983 .. CANR-60
Obituary 108
Earlier sketch in CA 104
Ellery, John Blaise 1920- 9-12R
Elles, Dora Amy
See Wentworth, Patricia
Ellet, Elizabeth F. 1818(?)-1877 .... DLB 30
Ellett, Marcella H. 1931- 21-24R
Ellfeldt, Lois 1910- 33-36R
Ellicott, V. L.
See Ellicott, Valcoulon MeMoyne
Ellicott, Valcoulon MeMoyne
1893-1983 Obituary 109
Ellin, E(lizabeth) M(uriel) 1905- CAP-2
Earlier sketch in CA 29-32
Ellin, Stanley (Bernard) 1916-1986 .... CANR-28
Obituary 119
Earlier sketches in CA 1-4R, CANR-4
See also DAM POP
See also MTCW 1
Elling, Karl A(lwin) 1935- 25-28R
Elling, Ray H. 1929- 33-36R
Ellingham, Lewis 1933- 167
Ellingsworth, Huber W. 1928- CANR-10
Earlier sketch in CA 21-24R
Ellington, Duke
See Ellington, Edward Kennedy
Ellington, Edward Kennedy 1899-1974 97-100
Obituary 49-52
Ellington, James W(esley) 1927- 37-40R
Ellington, Mercer (Kennedy)
1919-1996 Obituary 151
Brief entry 113
Ellington, Richard 1915(?)-1980 Obituary 102
Ellinwood, Leonard Webster 1905- 1-4R
Elliot, Alistair 1932- CANR-64
Earlier sketch in CA 129
Elliot, Asa
See Blinder, Elliot
Elliot, Daniel
See Feldman, Leonard
Elliot, Don
See Silverberg, Robert
Elliot, Edith M(arie Farmer) 1912- 21-24R
Elliot, Elisabeth (Howard) 1926- CANR-6
Earlier sketch in CA 5-8R
Elliot, Frances Minto (Dickinson) 1820-1898 ... DLB 166
Elliot, Geraldine
See Bingham, Evangeline M(arguerite) L(adys) (Elliot)
Elliot, Ian 1925- 69-72
Elliot, Jeffrey M. 1947- CANR-24
Earlier sketch in CA 106
Elliot, John 1898-1988 Obituary 126
Elliott, Alan C(urtis) 1952- CANR-18
Earlier sketch in CA 102
Elliott, Allan
See Elliott, K(enneth) A(llan) C(aldwell)
Elliott, Aubrey (George) 1917- 93-96
Elliott, Ben
See Haas, Ben(jamin) L(eopold)
Elliott, Bob
See Elliott, Robert B.
Elliott, Brian (Robinson) 1910- 25-28R
Elliott, Bruce (Walter Gardner Lively Stacy)
1915(?)-1973 Obituary 41-44R
Elliott, C(larence) Orville 1913- 33-36R
Elliott, Charles 1951- 138
Elliott, Charlotte 1789-1871 .... DLB 199
Elliott, Chip
See Elliott, E(scalus) E(mmert) III
Elliott, Chris 1960- 147
Elliott, Clark A. 1941- 137
Elliott, David W. 1939- 45-48
Elliott, Don
See Silverberg, Robert
Elliott, Donald 1928- 69-72
Elliott, Douglas B(yron) 1947- 113
Elliott, E(scalus) E(mmert) III 1945- 29-32R
Elliott, Ebenezer 1781-1849 .... DLB 96, 190
Elliott, Elaine M. 1931- 166
Elliott, Emory 1942- CANR-23
Earlier sketch in CA 69-72
Elliott, Errol T(homas) 1894-1992 69-72
Obituary 164
Elliott, Gary E(ugene) 1941- 151
Elliott, George 1923- .... DLB 68
Elliott, George P(aul) 1918-1980 .... CANR-2
Obituary 97-100
Earlier sketch in CA 1-4R
See also CLC 2
Elliott, Harley 1940- CANR-4
Earlier sketch in CA 49-52
Elliott, Hugh (Francis Ivo) 1913- Brief entry 112
Elliott, Inger McCabe 1933- 127
Elliott, James Francis 1914-1981 Obituary 110
Elliott, Jan Walter 1939- 37-40R
Elliott, Janice 1931- CANR-29
Earlier sketches in CA 13-16R, CANR-8
See also CLC 47
See also DLB 14
Elliott, Joey
See Houk, Randy
Elliott, John 1938- 25-28R
Elliott, John E(d) 1931- CANR-5
Earlier sketch in CA 1-4R
Elliott, John H(uxtable) 1930- CANR-3
Earlier sketch in CA 5-8R
Elliott, John H(all) 1935- 126
Brief entry 113
Elliott, John R., Jr. 1937- 25-28R
Elliott, Jumbo
See Elliott, James Francis
Elliott, K(enneth) A(llan) C(aldwell) 1903-1986 .. 108
Obituary 119
Elliott, Kate
See Rasmussen, Alis A.
Elliott, Kit 1936- 29-32R
Elliott, Lawrence 1924- CANR-21
Earlier sketches in CA 5-8R, CANR-3
Elliott, Leonard M. 1902- CAP-1
Earlier sketch in CA 13-14
Elliott, Lesley 1905- CANR-14
Earlier sketch in CA 77-80
Elliott, Malissa Childs 1929(?)-1979 101
Obituary 85-88
Elliott, Marianne 1948- 132
Elliott, Mark Rowe 1947- CANR-24
Earlier sketch in CA 107
Elliott, Melinda 1947- 157
Elliott, Neil 1939- 25-28R
Elliott, Odette 1939- 142
See also SATA 75
Elliott, Osborn 1924- CANR-12
Earlier sketch in CA 69-72
Elliott, P(hilip) R(oss) C(ourtney)
1943(?)-1983 Obituary 110
Elliott, Ralph H. 1925- CANR-2
Earlier sketch in CA 1-4R
Elliott, Ralph W(arren) V(ictor) 1921- 127
Elliott, Raymond Pruitt 1904- 17-20R
Elliott, Richard V. 1934- 33-36R
Elliott, Robert
See Garfinkel, Bernard Max
Elliott, Robert B. 1923- 134
Brief entry 109
Elliott, Robert C(arl) 1914-1981 .... CANR-21
Earlier sketch in CA 1-4R
Elliott, Roberta 97-100
Elliott, Russell Richard 1912- 69-72
Elliott, Sarah M(cCarn) 1930- 41-44R
See also SATA 14
Elliott, Sheldon D(ouglass)
1906-1972 Obituary 33-36R
Elliott, Spencer H(ayward) 1883-1967 .... CAP-1
Earlier sketch in CA 11-12
Elliott, Sumner Locke 1917-1991 .... CANR-21
Obituary 134
Earlier sketches in CA 5-8R, CANR-2
See also CLC 38
Elliott, Susan (Anthony) 1947- 104
Elliott, Thomas Joseph 1941- 49-52
Elliott, Ward E(dward) Y(andell) 1937- 85-88
Elliott, William
See Bradbury, Ray (Douglas)
Elliott, William III 1788-1863 .... DLB 3
Elliott, William Douglas 1938- CANR-9
Earlier sketch in CA 65-68
Elliott, William M(arion), Jr. 1903- CAP-1
Earlier sketch in CA 9-10
Elliott, William Yandell 1896-1979 Obituary .. 85-88
Ellis, A. E. .... CLC 7
Ellis, Albert 1913- CANR-40
Earlier sketches in CA 1-4R, CANR-2, 17
Ellis, Alec (Charles Owen) 1932- CANR-1
Earlier sketch in CA 45-48
Ellis, Alice Thomas
See Haycraft, Anna
See also CLC 40
See also DLB 194
Ellis, (Mary) Amabel (Nassau Strachey) Williams
See Williams-Ellis, (Mary) Amabel (Nassau Strachey)
Ellis, Amanda M. 1898-1969 .... CAP-2
Earlier sketch in CA 23-24
Ellis, Anyon
See Rowland-Entwistle, (Arthur) Theodore (Henry)
Ellis, Audrey CANR-10
Earlier sketch in CA 65-68
Ellis, B(yron) Robert 1940- 53-56
Ellis, Barbara W. 1953- 139
Ellis, Bret Easton 1964- CANR-51
Brief entry 118
Earlier sketch in CA 123
Interview in 123
See also AAYA 2
See also CLC 39, 71
See also DAM POP
Ellis, Brooks (Fleming) 1897-1976 Obituary .. 65-68
Ellis, C(uthbert) Hamilton 1909- 13-16R
Ellis, Carl F., Jr. 1946- 121
Ellis, Carolyn Sue 1950- CANR-48
Earlier sketch in CA 122
Ellis, Charles D(aniel) 1937- Brief entry 115
Ellis, Charles Drummond 1895-1980 Obituary .. 105
Ellis, Charles Howard 1895- CAP-1
Earlier sketch in CA 13-14
Ellis, Clyde 1958- 162
Ellis, Clyde T(aylor) 1908- CAP-2
Earlier sketch in CA 23-24
Ellis, Dan C. 1949- 125
Ellis, David Maldwyn 1914- 9-12R
Ellis, Dock (Phillip, Jr.) 1945- Brief entry 111
Ellis, E. S.
See Ellis, Edward S(ylvester)
Ellis, Edward Robb 1911- CANR-53
Earlier sketch in CA 25-28R
Ellis, Edward S(ylvester) 1840-1916 Brief entry .122
See also DLB 42
See also YABC 1
Ellis, Ella Thorp 1928- CANR-2
Earlier sketch in CA 49-52
See also SAAS 9
See also SATA 7
Ellis, Elma I(srael) 1918- 33-36R
Ellis, Evelyn 1948- 138
Ellis, Florence Hawley 1906- 61-64
Ellis, (J.) Frank(lyn) 1904(?)-1976 Obituary 65-68
Ellis, Frank Hale 1916- 73-76
Ellis, Frank K. 1933- 25-28R
Ellis, Harry Bearse 1921- CANR-2
Earlier sketch in CA 1-4R
See also SATA 9
Ellis, (Henry) Havelock 1859-1939 Brief entry .. 109
See also DLB 190
See also TCLC 14
Ellis, Helen E. (Oickle) 1926- CANR-45
Earlier sketch in CA 120
Ellis, Henry C(arlton) 1927- CANR-17
Earlier sketch in CA 97-100
Ellis, Herbert
See Wilson, Lionel
Ellis, Hilda Roderick
See Davidson, H(ilda) R(oderick) Ellis
Ellis, Howard S(ylvester) 1898-1992 .... CANR-28
Obituary 137
Earlier sketch in CA 49-52
Ellis, Howard W(oodrow) 1914- CANR-38
Earlier sketches in CA 1-4R, CANR-17
Ellis, Humphry F(rancis) 1907- 5-8R
Ellis, J(ames) H(ervey) S(tewart) 1893- CAP-2
Earlier sketch in CA 23-24
Ellis, J(ohn) R(ichard) 1938- 85-88
Ellis, Jack C(lare) 1922- 89-92
Ellis, Jack D. 1941- 121
Ellis, James 1935- 37-40R
Ellis, Jerry 1947- 153
Ellis, Jody 1925- 57-60
Ellis, John H. 1931- CANR-52
Earlier sketch in CA 125
Ellis, John M(artin) 1936- CANR-66
Earlier sketches in CA 49-52, CANR-3
Ellis, John Marion 1917- 49-52
Ellis, John O(liver) 1917- 85-88
Ellis, John Tracy 1905-1992 .... CANR-46
Obituary 139
Earlier sketches in CA 1-4R, CANR-5
Ellis, Joseph J(ohn) 1943- 53-56
Ellis, Joyce K. (Eileen) 1950- 116
Ellis, Julie 1933- 142
Brief entry 111
Ellis, Kail C. 1940- 127
Ellis, Kathy
See Bentley, Margaret
Ellis, Keith Stanley 1927- 102
Ellis, L(ewis) Ethan 1898-1977 .... CANR-4
Earlier sketch in CA 5-8R
Ellis, Landon
See Ellison, Harlan (Jay)
Ellis, Leigh 1959- 105
Ellis, Leo R(oy) 1909- 9-12R
Ellis, M(adeleine) B(lanche) 1915- 69-72
Ellis, M(arion) LeRoy 1928- 37-40R
Ellis, Marc H. 1952- CANR-24
Earlier sketch in CA 107
Ellis, Mark Karl 1945- 103
Ellis, Mary Jackson 1916- CANR-17
Earlier sketch in CA 1-4R
Ellis, Mary Leith 1921- 21-24R
Ellis, Mel(vin Richard) 1912-1984 .... 13-16R
Obituary 113
See also SATA 7
See also SATA-Obit 39
Ellis, Norman R. 1924- 13-16R
Ellis, Olivia
See Wintle, Anne
Ellis, Peter Berresford 1943- CANR-56
Earlier sketches in CA 81-84, CANR-21
Ellis, Peter F(rancis) 1921- 115
Ellis, Ray C. 1898- CAP-2
Earlier sketch in CA 21-22
Ellis, Richard 1938- 104
Ellis, Richard (J.) 1960- 135
Ellis, Richard E(manuel) 1937- 61-64
Ellis, Richard N(athaniel) 1939- 33-36R
Ellis, Richard White Bernard 1902- CAP-1
Earlier sketch in CA 13-16
Ellis, Roger (Melville) 1943- 126
Ellis, Ron(ald Walter) 1941- 77-80
Ellis, (Christopher) Royston (George) 1941- 5-8R
Ellis, Sarah 1952- CANR-50
Earlier sketch in CA 123
See also CLR 42
See also JRDA
See also SATA 68
Ellis, Scott
See Schorr, Mark
Ellis, Steven G. 1950- 158
Ellis, Trey 1962- 146
See also CLC 55
Ellis, Ulrich Ruegg 1904-1981 Obituary 108
Ellis, Walter M. 1943- 137
Ellis, Wesley
See Wallmann, Jeffrey M(iner)
Ellis, William Donahue 1918- CANR-29
Earlier sketch in CA 49-52
Ellis, William E. 1940- 163
Ellisen, Stanley A(rthur) 1922- 133
Ellison, Alfred 1916- 1-4R
Ellison, Craig W(illiam) 1944- CANR-6
Earlier sketch in CA 57-60
Ellison, Fred P(ittman) 1922- Brief entry 113
Ellison, George R. 1907(?)-1983 Obituary 110
Ellison, Gerald Alexander 1910-1992 .... CAP-1
Obituary 139
Earlier sketch in CA 13-14
Ellison, Glenn 1911- 89-92
Ellison, Glenn "Tiger"
See Ellison, Glenn
Ellison, H(enry) L(eopold) 1903- CANR-6
Earlier sketch in CA 5-8R
Ellison, Harlan (Jay) 1934- CANR-46
Earlier sketches in CA 5-8R, CANR-5
Interview in CANR-5
See also CLC 1, 13, 42
See also DAM POP
See also DLB 8
See also MTCW 1
See also SSC 14
Ellison, Henry 1931-1965 .... 5-8R
Ellison, Herbert J(ay) 1929- 13-16R
Ellison, James E. 1927- 13-16R
Ellison, James Whitfield 1929- CANR-1
Earlier sketch in CA 1-4R
Ellison, Jerome 1907-1981 .... 29-32R
Obituary 104
Ellison, Joan Jarvis 1948- 158
Ellison, John Malcus 1889-1979 .... CANR-25
Earlier sketch in CA 1-4R
Ellison, Katherine (White) 1941- 101
Ellison, Katherine 1957- 127
Ellison, Lucile Watkins 1907(?)-1979 109
Obituary 93-96
See also SATA 50
See also SATA-Obit 22
Ellison, Max 1914-1985 57-60
Obituary 116
See also AITN 1
Ellison, Ralph (Waldo) 1914-1994 .... CANR-53
Obituary 145
Earlier sketches in CA 9-12R, CANR-24
See also AAYA 19
See also BLC 1
See also BW 1
See also CDALB 1941-1968
See also CLC 1, 3, 11, 54, 86
See also DA
See also DAB
See also DAC
See also DAM MST, MULT, NOV
See also DLB 2, 76
See also DLBY 94
See also MTCW 1
See also SSC 26
See also WLC
Ellison, Randall Erskine 1904-1984 Obituary ... 113
Ellison, Reuben Young 1907- 13-16R

Ellison, Virginia H(owell) 1910- ... 33-36R
See also SATA 4
Ellison, William McLaren 1919(?)-1978 Obituary ... 81-84
Elliston, Frederick Allen 1944- ... 105
Elliston, Thomas R(alph) 1919-1977 Obituary ... 73-76
Elliston, Valerie Mae (Watkinson) 1929- ... 9-12R
Ellithorpe, Harold (Earle) 1925- ... 77-80
Ellman, Michael 1942- ... 45-48
Ellmann, Lucy (Elizabeth) 1956- ... 128
See also CLC 61
Ellmann, Richard (David) 1918-1987 ... CANR-61
Obituary ... 122
Earlier sketches in CA 1-4R, CANR-2, 28
See also BEST 89:2
See also CLC 50
See also DLB 103
See also DLBY 87
See also MTCW 1
Ellroy, James 1948- ... 138
See also BEST 90:4
Ellsberg, Daniel 1931- ... 69-72
Ellsberg, Edward 1891- ... 5-8R
See also SATA 7
Ellsworth, L(ida) E(lizabeth) 1948- ... 118
Ellsworth, P(aul) T(heodore) 1897- ... 17-20R
Ellsworth, Ralph Eugene 1907- ... CANR-2
Earlier sketch in CA 1-4R
Ellsworth, S(amuel) George 1916- ... 45-48
Ellsworth, Scott 1954- ... 109
Ellul, Jacques 1912-1994 ... 81-84
Obituary ... 145
Ellvinger, Barbara Anne Price
See Price, Barbara Anne Ellvinger
Ellwood, Edith E(lizabeth)
See Muesing-Ellwood, Edith E(lizabeth)
Ellwood, Gracia-Fay 1938- ... 29-32R
Ellwood, Robert S(cott), Jr. 1933- ... CANR-14
Earlier sketch in CA 41-44R
Ellwood, Sheelagh (Margaret) 1949- ... 146
Ellyard, David ... 147
El Mallakh, Ragaei (William) 1925- ... 112
Elman, Richard (Martin) 1934-1997 ... CANR-47
Obituary ... 163
Earlier sketch in CA 17-20R
See also CAAS 3
See also CLC 19
Elman, Robert 1930- ... CANR-3
Earlier sketch in CA 45-48
Elmandjra, Mahdi 1933- ... 89-92
Elmblad, Mary (B.) 1927- ... 108
El-Meligi, A(bdel) Moneim 1923- ... 17-20R
Elmen, Paul H. 1913- ... 89-92
Elmendorf, Mary Lindsay 1917- ... 57-60
Elmer, Carlos Hall 1920- ... 102
Elmer, Gary W. 1941- ... 122
Elmer, Irene (Elizabeth) 1937- ... 1-4R
Elmer, Robert 1958- ... 167
See also SATA 99
El-Messidi, Kathy Groehn 1946- ... 57-60
Elmhirst, Leonard Knight 1893-1974 Obituary ... 115
Elmore, Ernest Carpenter 1901-1957 Brief entry ... 114
Elmore, (Carolyn) Patricia 1933- ... 114
See also SATA 38
See also SATA-Brief 35
El-Moslimany, Ann P(axton) 1937- ... 155
See also SATA 90
Elms, Alan C(linton) 1938- ... 69-72
Elmslie, Kenward 1929- ... CANR-50
Earlier sketches in CA 21-24R, CANR-9, 25
Elmslie, William Alexander Leslie 1885-1965 ... CAP-1
Earlier sketch in CA 13-14
Elmstrom, George P. 1925- ... 5-8R
El Muhajir 1944- ... CANR-26
Earlier sketch in CA 49-52
See also Marvin X
See also BW 1
Elon, Amos 1926- ... 128
Brief entry ... 121
Interview in ... 128
Elovitz, Mark H(arvey) 1938- ... 69-72
Elphick, Richard Hall 1943- ... CANR-48
Earlier sketch in CA 112
Elphinstone, Francis
See Powell-Smith, Vincent (Walter Francis)
Elphinstone, Murgatroyd
See Kahler, Hugh (Torbert) MacNair
Elrick, George S(eefurth) 1921-1997 ... 112
Obituary ... 163
Elron
See Hubbard, L(afayette) Ron(ald)
el Ropo, Smokestack
See Perry, Charles
El Saadawi, Nawal 1931- ... CANR-44
Earlier sketch in CA 118
See also CAAS 11
El Saffar, Ruth (Ann) 1941- ... 69-72
Elsasser, Albert B(ertrand) 1918- ... CANR-22
Earlier sketch in CA 69-72
Elsasser, Glen Robert 1935- ... 65-68
Elsberry, Terence 1943- ... 45-48
Elsbree, Langdon 1929- ... 33-36R
Else, Gerald Frank 1908-1982 ... 61-64
Obituary ... 107
Elsea, Janet G(ayle) 1942- ... 119
Elsen, Albert E(dward) 1927-1995 ... CANR-26
Obituary ... 147
Earlier sketches in CA 5-8R, CANR-11
El-Shabazz, El-Hajj Malik
See Little, Malcolm
Elshtain, Jean Bethke 1941- ... 106
Elsmere, Jane Shaffer 1932- ... 37-40R
Elsner, Gisela 1937- ... 9-12R
Elsner, Henry, Jr. 1930- ... 21-24R
Elsom, John Edward 1934- ... 65-68
Elson, Edward L(ee) R(oy) 1906-1993 ... CANR-3
Obituary ... 142
Earlier sketch in CA 5-8R
Elson, Lawrence M(cClellan) 1935- ... 53-56
Elson, R. N.
See Nelson, R(adell) Faraday
Elson, Robert T(ruscott) 1906-1987 ... 77-80
Obituary ... 121
Elson, Ruth Miller 1917- ... 13-16R
Elspeth
See Bragdon, Elspeth MacDuffie
Elstar, Dow
See Gallun, Raymond Z(inke)
Elstob, Peter 1915- ... CANR-1
Earlier sketch in CA 1-4R
Elston, Allan Vaughan 1887-1976 ... CANR-63
Earlier sketches in CA 1-4R, CANR-3
Elston, Gene 1922- ... 33-36R
Elston, Robert 1934-1987 Obituary ... 124
Elston, Wilbur E(vans) 1913- Brief entry ... 112
Elstun, Esther N(ies) 1935- ... 117
Elsy, (Winifred) Mary ... 93-96
Elting, John R(obert) 1911- ... CANR-57
Earlier sketches in CA 112, CANR-31
Elting, Mary 1906- ... CANR-19
Earlier sketches in CA 9-12R, CANR-4
See also SAAS 20
See also SATA 2, 88
Eltis, David 1940- ... 127
Eltis, Walter (Alfred) 1933- ... 131
Elton, Edwin J(oel) 1939- ... 53-56
Elton, G(eoffrey) R(udolph) 1921- ... CANR-30
Earlier sketches in CA 9-12R, CANR-3
Elton, Hugh 1964- ... 153
Elton, John
See Marsh, John
Elton, W(illiam) R. 1921- Brief entry ... 111
el-Toure, Askia Muhammad Abu Bakr
See Toure, Askia Muhammad Abu Bakr el
Eltringham, S(tewart) K(eith) 1929- ... 110
Eluard, Paul
See Grindel, Eugene
See also TCLC 7, 41
El Uqsor
See Borgmann, Dmitri A(lfred)
Elvenstar, Diane C.
See Medved, Diane
Elvin, Drake
See Beha, Ernest
Elvin, Harold 1909-1985 ... CANR-4
Obituary ... 115
Earlier sketch in CA 5-8R
Elvin, (Herbert) Lionel 1905- ... CAP-1
Earlier sketch in CA 13-14
Elvin, Mark 1938- ... 73-76
Elward, James (Joseph) 1928-1996 ... CANR-12
Obituary ... 153
Earlier sketch in CA 29-32R
Elwart, Joan Potter 1927- ... 25-28R
See also SATA 2
Elwell, Fayette Herbert 1885- ... 5-8R
Elwell, Jerry MacElroy 1922- ... 57-60
Elwell, Stillman J. 1894-1977 Obituary ... 110
Elwell, Walter A(lexander) 1937- ... 119
Elwell-Sutton, L(aurence) P(aul) 1912-1984 ... 5-8R
Obituary ... 114
Elwin, Malcolm 1903-1973 Obituary ... 89-92
Elwin, William
See Ebenstein, William
Elwood, Ann 1931- ... 125
See also SATA 55
See also SATA-Brief 52
Elwood, Catharyn 1903(?)-1975 Obituary ... 61-64
Elwood, Douglas J(ames) 1924- ... 116
Elwood, Muriel 1902- ... CAP-1
Earlier sketch in CA 9-10
Elwood, Roger 1943- ... CANR-10
Earlier sketch in CA 57-60
See also SATA 58
Elwyn-Jones, Pearl Binder 1904- ... 107
Ely, David 1927- ... 53-56
Ely, Donald P(aul) 1930- ... 29-32R
Ely, James W(allace), Jr. 1938- ... 73-76
Ely, John Hart 1938- ... 103
Ely, John Wilton
See Wilton-Ely, John
Ely, Melvin Patrick 1952- ... 140
Ely, Paul (Henri) 1897-1975 Obituary ... 53-56
Ely, Scott 1944- ... 127
Ely, Virginia (Shackelford) 1899- ... CANR-24
Earlier sketch in CA 1-4R
Elytis, Odysseus 1911-1996 ... 102
Obituary ... 151
See also CLC 15, 49, 100
See also DAM POET
See also MTCW 1
See also PC 21
Elzbieta ... SATA 88
Elzinga, Kenneth G(erald) 1941- ... CANR-13
Earlier sketches in CA 49-52, CANR-1
Emans, Robert 1934- ... 53-56
Emanuel, Ezekiel J(onathan) 1957- ... 139
Emanuel, James A. 1921- ... CANR-12
Earlier sketch in CA 29-32R
See also CAAS 18
See also BW 1
See also DLB 41
Emanuel, James A(ndrew, Sr.) 1921- ... 153
Ember, Carol R(uchlis) 1943- ... 77-80
Emberley, Barbara A(nne) 1932- ... CANR-5
Earlier sketch in CA 5-8R
See also CLR 5
See also MAICYA
See also SATA 8, 70
Emberley, Ed(ward Randolph) 1931- ... CANR-36
Earlier sketches in CA 5-8R, CANR-5
See also CLR 5
See also MAICYA
See also SATA 8, 70
Emberley, Michael 1960- ... 104
See also SATA 34, 80
Emberley, Peter C. 1956- ... 151
Embey, Philip
See Philipp, Elliot Elias
Emblen, D(onald) L(ewis) 1918- ... 33-36R
Embling, John 1952- ... 111
Emboden, William A(llen), Jr. 1935- ... CANR-34
Earlier sketches in CA 41-44R, CANR-14
Embree, Ainslie Thomas 1921- ... CANR-2
Earlier sketch in CA 1-4R
Embry, Margaret Jacob 1919-1975 ... CANR-3
Earlier sketch in CA 1-4R
See also SATA 5
Emecheta, (Florence Onye) Buchi 1944- ... CANR-27
Earlier sketch in CA 81-84
See also BLC 2
See also BW 2
See also CLC 14, 48
See also DAM MULT
See also DLB 117
See also MTCW 1
See also SATA 66
Emeneau, Murray Barnson 1904- ... CANR-5
Earlier sketch in CA 1-4R
Emenegger, Bob
See Emenegger, Robert
Emenegger, Robert 1933- ... 102
Emenhiser, JeDon A(llen) 1933- ... 37-40R
Emerick, Kenneth F(red) 1925- ... 53-56
Emerson, Alice B. ... CANR-27
Earlier sketches in CAP-2, CA 19-20
See also Benson, Mildred (Augustine Wirt)
See also SATA 1, 67
Emerson, Caroline D. 1891-1973 ... CAP-1
Obituary ... 45-48
Earlier sketch in CA 17-18
Emerson, Caryl (Geppert) 1944- ... 123
Emerson, Connie 1930- ... 109
Emerson, (Alan) David 1900- ... CANR-2
Earlier sketch in CA 5-8R
Emerson, Donald (Conger) 1913- ... 21-24R
Emerson, Earl W. 1948- ... CANR-66
Earlier sketches in CA 123, CANR-51
Emerson, Everett Harvey 1925- ... CANR-22
Earlier sketches in CA 13-16R, CANR-5
Emerson, Frank C(reighton) 1936- ... 53-56
Emerson, H(enry) O(liver) 1893- ... CAP-2
Earlier sketch in CA 23-24
Emerson, James G(ordon), Jr. 1926- ... 17-20R
Emerson, Kathy Lynn 1947- ... CANR-54
Earlier sketch in CA 127
See also SATA 63
Emerson, Laura S(alome) 1907- ... CAP-1
Earlier sketch in CA 13-16
Emerson, Mary Lee
See Kennedy, Mary
Emerson, O. B. 1922- ... CANR-16
Earlier sketch in CA 25-28R
Emerson, Ralph Waldo 1803-1882 ... CDALB 1640-1865
See also DA
See also DAB
See also DAC
See also DAM MST, POET
See also DLB 1, 59, 73
See also PC 18
See also WLC
Emerson, Ronald
See Scotland, James
Emerson, Ru 1944- ... CANR-44
Earlier sketch in CA 121
See also SATA 70
Emerson, Rupert 1899-1979 ... CANR-2
Obituary ... 85-88
Earlier sketch in CA 1-4R
Emerson, Steven A. 1954- ... 140
Emerson, Thomas E. 1945- ... 165
Emerson, Thomas I(rwin) 1907-1991 ... 21-24R
Obituary ... 134
Emerson, William 1769-1811 ... DLB 37
Emerson, William K(eith) 1925- ... 41-44R
See also SATA 25
Emerson, William R. 1923-1997 ... DLBY 97
Emert, Phyllis R(aybin) 1947- ... 159
See also SATA 93
Emery, Alan E(glin) H(eathcote) 1928- ... 69-72
Emery, Allan C(omstock), Jr. 1919- ... 104
Emery, Anne (McGuigan) 1907- ... CANR-2
Earlier sketch in CA 1-4R
See also SATA 1, 33
Emery, Clayton 1953- ... 156
Emery, David A(mos) 1920- ... 29-32R
Emery, Edwin 1914-1993 ... CANR-11
Obituary ... 142
Earlier sketch in CA 69-72
Emery, Fred 1933- ... 65-68
Emery, Gary 1942- ... CANR-29
Earlier sketch in CA 110
Emery, Glenn D. 1954- ... 135
Emery, Kenneth Orris 1914-1998 ... 107
Obituary ... 165
Emery, Marc 1932- ... 132
Emery, Michael 1940-1995 ... 73-76
Obituary ... 150
Emery, Pierre-Yves 1929- ... 101
Emery, Ralph 1932(?)- ... 142
Emery, Robert F(irestone) 1927- ... 37-40R
Emery, Tom 1971- ... 164
Emery, Walter Byron 1907-1973 ... CANR-22
Earlier sketch in CA 1-4R
Emett, Rowland 1906-1990 ... 102
Obituary ... 133
Emig, Janet Ann ... 73-76
Emiliani, Cesare 1922- ... 144
Emin, Fedor Aleksandrovich c. 1735-1770 ... DLB 150
Emlen, Robert P. 1946- ... 135
Emma, Ronald David 1920- ... 25-28R
Emmanuel, Philip D. 1909- ... CAP-1
Earlier sketch in CA 13-16
Emmanuel, Pierre
See Mathieu, Noel Jean
Emme, Eugene M(orlock) 1919-1985 ... CANR-8
Obituary ... 116
Earlier sketch in CA 13-16R
Emmel, Thomas C. 1941- Brief entry ... 111
Emmens, Carol Ann 1944- ... 106
See also SATA 39
Emmerich, Andre 1924- ... 9-12R
Emmerick, R(onald) E(ric) 1937- ... CANR-11
Earlier sketch in CA 25-28R
Emmerson, Donald K(enneth) 1940- ... CANR-32
Earlier sketches in CA 65-68, CANR-14
Emmerson, Henry Russell 1899- ... 5-8R
Emmerson, John K(enneth) 1908-1984 ... CANR-14
Obituary ... 112
Earlier sketch in CA 57-60
Emmerson, Richard Kenneth 1948- ... 106
Emmet, Alan 1927- ... 158
Emmet, Dorothy Mary 1904- ... 9-12R
Emmet, E(ric) R(evell) 1909- ... 107
Emmet, Herman LeRoy 1943- ... 141
Emmet, Olivia (Lily) 1933- ... 146
Emmett, Ayala 1935- ... 163
Emmett, Bruce 1949- ... 57-60
Emmitt, Robert (P.) 1925- ... 29-32R
Emmons, Charles F(rank) 1942- ... 110
Emmons, Della (Florence) Gould 1890-1983 Obituary ... 111
See also SATA-Obit 39
Emmons, Michael 1938- ... 107
Emmons, Nuel 1927- ... 125
Emmons, Phillip
See Little, Bentley
Emmons, Shirlee 1923- ... 147
Emmott, Bill
See Emmott, William John
Emmott, William John 1956- ... 136
Emmrich, Curt 1897-1975 ... CAP-2
Earlier sketch in CA 29-32
Emmrich, Kurt
See Emmrich, Curt
Emorey, N.
See Ellison, Jerome
Emory, Alan (Steuer) 1922- ... CANR-12
Earlier sketch in CA 69-72
Emory, Jerry 1957- ... 161
See also SATA 96
Empedocles c. 5th cent. B.C.- ... DLB 176
Empey, Arthur Guy 1883-1963 Obituary ... 107
Empey, LaMar T(aylor) 1923- ... CANR-30
Earlier sketch in CA 29-32R
Employee X
See Fautsko, Timothy F(rank)
Empringham, Antoinette F(leur) 1939- ... 124
Empringham, Toni
See Empringham, Antoinette F(leur)
Empson, William 1906-1984 ... CANR-61
Obituary ... 112
Earlier sketches in CA 17-20R, CANR-31
See also CLC 3, 8, 19, 33, 34
See also DLB 20
See also MTCW 1
Emrich, Duncan (Black Macdonald) 1908-197(?) ... CANR-9
Earlier sketch in CA 61-64
See also SATA 11
Emshwiller, Carol 1921- ... CANR-52
Earlier sketch in CA 53-56
Emsley, Clare
See Plummer, Clare (Emsley)
Emsley, John 1938- ... 142
Emsley, Michael Gordon 1930- ... 97-100
Emslie, M. L.
See Simpson, Myrtle L(illias)
Emswiler, Sharon Neufer 1944- ... 119
Emy, Hugh (Vincent) 1944- ... 77-80
Enamurado Cuesta, Jose 1892- ... HW
Encausse, Gerard (Anaclet Vincent) 1865-1916 Brief entry ... 113
Encel, Sol
See Encel, Solomon
Encel, Solomon 1925- ... CANR-37
Earlier sketch in CA 115
Enchi, Fumiko (Ueda) 1905-1986 ... 129
Obituary ... 121
See also CLC 31
Enchi, Fumiko 1905-1986 ... DLB 182
Encinias, Miguel 1923- ... 144
Endacott, G(eorge) B(eer) 1901- ... 5-8R
Endacott, M(arie) Violet 1915- ... 9-12R
Ende, Jean 1947- ... 53-56
Ende, Michael (Andreas Helmuth) 1929-1995 ... CANR-36
Obituary ... 149
Brief entry ... 118
Earlier sketch in CA 124
See also CLC 31
See also CLR 14
See also DLB 75
See also MAICYA
See also SATA 61
See also SATA-Brief 42
See also SATA-Obit 86
Ende, Richard Chaffey von
See von Ende, Richard Chaffey
Endelman, Todd M(ichael) 1946- ... 125

Enderle, Judith (Ann) Ross 1941- CANR-49
Earlier sketches in CA 106, CANR-22
See also SAAS 26
See also SATA 38, 89
Enders, Richard
See Fenster, Robert
Endersby, Clive 1944- 133
Endfield, Mercedes
See von Block, Bela W(illiam)
Endicott, Frank S(impson) 1904-1990 Obituary . 131
Endicott, Ruth Belmore CANR-26
Earlier sketches in CAP-2, CA 19-20
Endicott, Stephen Lyon 1928- 107
Endleman, Robert 152
Endler, Norman S(olomon) 1931- CANR-9
Earlier sketch in CA 21-24R
Endo, Mitsuko 1942- 65-68
Endo, Shusaku 1923-1996 .... CANR-54
Obituary 153
Earlier sketches in CA 29-32R, CANR-21
See also CLC 7, 14, 19, 54, 99
See also DAM NOV
See also DLB 182
See also MTCW 1
Endore, (Samuel) Guy 1900-1970 .... CANR-72
Obituary 25-28R
Earlier sketches in CA 1-4R, CANR-6
Endres, Clifford 1941- 108
Endy, Melvin B(ecker), Jr. 1938- 81-84
Enell, Trinka (Gochenour) 1951- .... SATA 79
Enelow, Allen J(ay) 1922- CANR-7
Earlier sketch in CA 17-20R
Ener, Guener 1935- 146
Ener, Guner
See Ener, Guener
Enfield, Carrie
See Smith, Susan Vernon
Eng--, Tom
See Engelhardt, Thomas Alexander
Engberg, Edward 1928- 21-24R
Engberg, Holger L(aessoe) 1930- 37-40R
Engberg, (Johanna) Susan 1940- CANR-41
Earlier sketch in CA 117
Engdahl, Sylvia Louise 1933- CANR-14
Earlier sketch in CA 29-32R
See also CLR 2
See also JRDA
See also MAICYA
See also SAAS 5
See also SATA 4
Engebrecht, P(atricia) A(nn) 1935- 57-60
Engel, A. J.
See Engel, Arthur (Jason)
Engel, Alan
See Engelberg, Alan (D.)
Engel, Alan S(tuart) 1932- 37-40R
Engel, Arthur (Jason) 1944- 129
Engel, Bernard F. 1921- 13-16R
Engel, Diana 1947- 138
See also SATA 70
Engel, Herbert M. 1918- CANR-43
Earlier sketch in CA 120
Engel, Howard 1931- CANR-66
Earlier sketches in CA 112, CANR-44
Engel, J. Ronald 1936- CANR-51
Earlier sketch in CA 124
Engel, James F. 1934- CANR-13
Earlier sketch in CA 21-24R
Engel, (Aaron) Lehman 1910-1982 .... CANR-31
Obituary 107
Earlier sketch in CA 41-44R
Engel, Louis (Henry, Jr.) 1909-1982 .... 21-24R
Obituary 108
Engel, Lyle Kenyon 1915-1986 85-88
Obituary 120
Engel, Madeline H(elena) 1941- 85-88
Engel, Margorie L(ouise) 1943- 147
Engel, Marian 1933-1985 .... CANR-12
Earlier sketch in CA 25-28R
Interview in CANR-12
See also CLC 36
See also DLB 53
Engel, Mary June Montgomery
1920(?)-1985 Obituary 117
Engel, Matthew (Lewis) 1951- 146
Engel, Monroe 1921- 5-8R
Engel, Pauline Newton 1918- 17-20R
Engel, Peter H. 1935- CANR-15
Earlier sketch in CA 81-84
Engel, S(rul) Morris (von) 1931- CANR-14
Earlier sketch in CA 37-40R
Engel, Salo 1908-1972 .... CAP-2
Earlier sketch in CA 33-36
Engel, Samuel G. 1904-1984 Obituary 112
Engelbach, David (Charles) 1946- 133
Engelberg, Alan (D.) 1941- 132
Engelberg, Edward 1929- 37-40R
Engelhard, Jack 1940- 132
Engelhardt, Frederick
See Hubbard, L(afayette) Ron(ald)
Engelhardt, H(ugo) Tristram, Jr. 1941- 139
Engelhardt, Thomas Alexander 1930- 133
Engelhardt, Tom
See Engelhardt, Thomas Alexander
Engelhart, Margaret S. 1924- 122
See also SATA 59
Engelking, L. L. 1903(?)-1980 Obituary 102
Engell, James 1951- 135
Engelman, Rose C. 1919(?)-1979 Obituary ... 89-92
Engelmann, Hugo O(tto) 1917- 41-44R
Engelmann, Kim (V.) 1959- 151
See also SATA 87
Engelmann, Larry 1941- 101
Engelmann, Ruth 1919- 106
Engelmann, Siegfried E. 1931- CANR-13
Earlier sketch in CA 21-24R
Engelmayer, Sheldon David 1945- 114
Engels, Donald (W.) 1946- 102
Engels, Friedrich 1820-1895 .... DLB 129
Engels, John David 1931- CANR-6
Earlier sketch in CA 13-16R
Engels, Norbert (Anthony) 1903- CAP-2
Earlier sketch in CA 17-18
Engeman, Thomas S(ledge) 1944- 109
Engen, Rodney K(ent) 1948- CANR-15
Earlier sketch in CA 65-68
Enger, Norman L. 1937- CANR-10
Earlier sketch in CA 25-28R
Engerman, Stanley L(ewis) 1936- 53-56
Enggass, Robert 1921- CANR-9
Earlier sketch in CA 13-16R
Engh, M(ary) J(ane) 1933- CANR-58
Earlier sketch in CA 69-72
Engh, Rohn 1938- 69-72
Engholm, Eva 1909- 93-96
Engl, Lieselotte 1918- 49-52
Engl, Theodor 1925- 49-52
Englade, Ken(neth Francis) 1938- 157
England, Anthony Bertram 1939- 85-88
England, Barry 1932- 25-28R
England, Colin
See Jeans, Michael
England, E. M.
See Anders, Edith (Mary) England
England, E Squires
See Ball, Sylvia Patricia
England, George Allan 1877-1936 161
Brief entry 112
See also SATA 102
England, George W(illiam) 1927- 104
England, John C(arol) 1930- 116
England, Martha Winburn 1909- CAP-1
Earlier sketch in CA 11-12
England, Maurice Derrick 1908-1980 104
England, Rodney Charles Bennett
See Bennett-England, Rodney Charles
England, Wilbur Birch 1903- 1-4R
Engle, Eloise
See Paananen, Eloise (Katherine)
See also SATA 9
Engle, Jeff(rey) 1947- 103
Engle, John D(avid), Jr. 1922- CANR-25
Earlier sketches in CA 57-60, CANR-7
Engle, Louise Boardman Proctor
1897(?)-1987 Obituary 121
Engle, Margarita 1951- 152
Engle, Parke F. 1900(?)-1984 Obituary 111
Engle, Paul (Hamilton) 1908-1991 .... CANR-5
Obituary 134
Earlier sketch in CA 1-4R
See also DLB 48
Engle, T(helburn) L(aRoy) 1901- 13-16R
Englebert, Victor 1933- 57-60
See also SATA 8
Englefield, Ronald 1891-1975 Obituary 105
Englehart, Bob
See Englehart, Robert (Wayne), Jr.
Englehart, Robert (Wayne), Jr. 1945- 133
Englekirk, John E(ugene) 1905-1983 Obituary .. 112
Engleman, Finis E(wing) 1895-1978 .... 9-12R
Obituary 134
Engleman, Paul 1953- 131
Engler, Larry 1949- 53-56
Engler, Richard E(mil), Jr. 1925- 37-40R
Engler, Robert 1922- CANR-2
Earlier sketch in CA 1-4R
Englert, Clement Cyril 1910- CANR-5
Earlier sketch in CA 1-4R
English, Adrian J(oseph) 1939- 118
English, Arnold
See Hershman, Morris
English, Barbara (Anne) 1933- CANR-13
Earlier sketch in CA 33-36R
English, Charles
See Nuetzel, Charles (Alexander)
English, David 1931- 69-72
English, Deirdre (Elena) 1948- 85-88
English, E(ugene) Schuyler 1899-1981 107
Obituary 103
English, Earl (Franklin) 1905- 37-40R
English, Edward (H.) 19(?)-1973 Obituary ... 41-44R
English, Fenwick Walter 1939- CANR-1
Earlier sketch in CA 45-48
English, Isobel 1925(?)-1994 53-56
Obituary 145
English, James W(ilson) 1915- 21-24R
See also SATA 37
English, (Emma) Jean M(artin) 1937- 29-32R
English, John W(esley) 1940- 69-72
English, Lyn D. 1953- 154
English, Maurice 1909-1983 .... CANR-12
Obituary 111
Earlier sketch in CA 9-12R
English, O(liver) Spurgeon 1901-1993 .... CAP-2
Obituary 143
Earlier sketch in CA 33-36
English, Richard
See Shaver, Richard S(harpe)
English, Ronald (Frederick) 1913- CAP-1
Earlier sketch in CA 9-10
English, Thomas Dunn 1819-1902 .... DLB 202
English, Thomas H(opkins) 1895- CANR-2
Earlier sketch in CA 5-8R
English, Thomas Saunders 1928- Brief entry ... 105
Englizian, H. Crosby 1923- 21-24R
Engquist, Richard 1933- 29-32R
Engren, Edith
See McCaig, Robert Jesse
Engs, Robert Francis 1943- 101
Engs, Ruth C(lifford) 1939- 160
Engstrand, Iris (H.) Wilson 1935- 107
Engstrom, Ted W.
See Engstrom, Theodore W(ilhelm)
Engstrom, Theodore W(ilhelm) 1916- CANR-25
Earlier sketches in CA 65-68, CANR-9
Engstrom, W(infred) A(ndrew) 1925- 57-60
Enis, Ben M(elvin) 1942- CANR-22
Earlier sketches in CA 57-60, CANR-7
Enke, Stephen 1916-1974 65-68
Obituary 53-56
Enloe, Cynthia H(olden) 1938- CANR-39
Earlier sketches in CA 37-40R, CANR-17
Enlow, David R(oland) 1916- CANR-10
Earlier sketch in CA 5-8R
Ennes, James M(arquis), Jr. 1933- CANR-34
Earlier sketch in CA 102
Ennis, Bruce J. 1940- Brief entry 110
Ennis, Robert H(ugh) 1927- CANR-10
Earlier sketch in CA 25-28R
Ennulat, Egbert M. 1929- 142
Eno, Susan 101
Enoch, Kurt 1895-1982 Obituary 106
Enockson, Paul G(eorge) 1938- 110
Enomiya-Lassalle, Hugo M(akibi) 1898- ... 21-24R
Enquist, Per Olov 1934- Brief entry 109
Enrick, Norbert Lloyd 1920- CANR-43
Earlier sketches in CA 13-16R, CANR-6
Enright, D(ennis) J(oseph) 1920- CANR-42
Earlier sketches in CA 1-4R, CANR-1
See also CLC 4, 8, 31
See also DLB 27
See also SATA 25
Enright, Elizabeth 1909-1968 61-64
Obituary 25-28R
See also CLR 4
See also DLB 22
See also MAICYA
See also SATA 9
Enright, Maureen Patricia Ford
1908(?)-1983 Obituary 111
Enright, Michael J(ohn) 1958- 139
Enriquez de Salamanca, Cristina 1952- 158
Enroth, Clyde A(dolph) 1926- 37-40R
Enscoe, Gerald (Eugene) 1926- CANR-10
Earlier sketch in CA 5-8R
Ense, Wolfgang
See Frank, Rudolf
Ensign, Thomas 1940- 101
Ensign, Tod
See Ensign, Thomas
Ensley, Evangeline 1907- 122
Brief entry 114
Interview in 122
Ensley, Francis Gerald 1907- CAP-1
Earlier sketch in CA 13-16
Enslin, Morton S(cott) 1897-1980 .... 17-20R
Obituary 134
Enslin, Theodore (Vernon) 1925- CANR-41
Earlier sketches in CA 53-56, CANR-4, 19
See also CAAS 3
Enslow, Sam 1946- 136
Ensminger, Audrey H(elen) 1919- 149
Ensminger, Marion Eugene 1908- CANR-16
Earlier sketches in CA 49-52, CANR-1
Ensor, Allison (Rash) 1935- 25-28R
Ensor, (Alick Charles) David(son)
1906-1987 Obituary 121
Ensor, Robert 1922- 158
See also SATA 93
Enstice, Wayne 1943- 139
Enstrom, Robert (William) 1946- 104
Enteman, Willard F(inley) 1936- 33-36R
Entenza, John Dymock
1905-1984 Obituary 112ENTER
ENTER CANR-70
Earlier sketches in CA 1-4R, CANR-6
See also SATA 1
Enterline, James Robert 1932- 41-44R
Enters, Angna 1907-1989 Obituary 128
Enthoven, Alain C(harles) 1930- CANR-27
Earlier sketch in CA 49-52
Entine, Alan D(avid) 1936- 21-24R
Entman, Robert M. 1949- 130
Entwisle, Doris R(oberts) 1924- 5-8R
Entwistle, Florence Vivienne
1889(?)-1982 Obituary 105
Entwistle, Harold 1923- 29-32R
Entwistle, Noel (James) 1936- CANR-39
Earlier sketches in CA 93-96, CANR-16
Entwistle, (Arthur) Theodore (Henry) Rowland
See Rowland-Entwistle, (Arthur) Theodore (Henry)
Enyeart, James L(yle) 1943- 113
Enys, Sarah L.
See Sloggett, Nellie
Enz, Jacob J(ohn) 1919- 41-44R
Enzensberger, Hans Magnus 1929- 119
Brief entry 116
See also CLC 43
Enzler, Clarence J. 1910(?)-1976 Obituary ... 69-72
Enzweiler, Joseph A. 1950- 151
Eoyang, Eugene Chen 1939- 140
Epafrodito
See Wagner, C(harles) Peter
Epand, Len 1950- 85-88
Epanya, Christian A(rthur Kingue) 1956- .. SATA 91
Epernay, Mark
See Galbraith, John Kenneth
Ephraim, Gavriel Ben
See Ben-Ephraim, Gavriel
Ephraim, Shelly S(chonebaum) 1952- .... SATA 97
Ephron, Amy 1955- 138
Ephron, Delia 1944- CANR-52
Earlier sketches in CA 97-100, CANR-12
See also SATA 65
See also SATA-Brief 50
Ephron, Henry 1911(?)-1992 73-76
Obituary 139
Ephron, Nora 1941- CANR-39
Earlier sketches in CA 65-68, CANR-12
See also AITN 2
See also CLC 17, 31
Ephron, Phoebe (Wolkind)
1916-1971 Obituary 33-36R
Epictetus c. 55-c. 125 .... DLB 176
Epicurus 341B.C.-270B.C. .... DLB 176
Epler, Doris M. 1928- .... SATA 73
Epler, Percy H. 1872-1975 Obituary 57-60
Epp, Eldon Jay 1930- CANR-7
Earlier sketch in CA 17-20R
Epp, Frank H(enry) 1929-1986 .... CANR-29
Earlier sketch in CA 29-32R
Epp, Margaret A(gnes) 1913- CANR-3
Earlier sketch in CA 9-12R
See also SATA 20
Eppard, Philip B(lair) 1945- 112
Eppenbach, Sarah 1947- 114
Eppenstein, Louise (Kohn) 1892-1987 Obituary 123
See also SATA-Obit 54
Epperly, Elizabeth Rollins 1951- 106
Epperson, Gordon 1921- 25-28R
Eppie
See Naismith, Helen
Eppinga, Jacob D. 1917- 33-36R
Eppinger, Josh 1940- 89-92
Eppink, Norman R(oland) 1906- 53-56
Epple, Anne Orth 1927- 33-36R
See also SATA 20
Epps, Bernard 1936- .... DLB 53
Epps, Bradley S. 1958- 166
Epps, Edgar G(ustavas) 1929- 49-52
Epps, Garrett 1950- 69-72
Epps, Jack, Jr. 1949- 133
Epps, Preston H(erschel) 1888-1982 .... 37-40R
Obituary 133
Epps, Robert L(ee) 1932- 17-20R
Eppstein, John 1895-1988 Obituary 125
Epsilon
See Betjeman, John
Epstein, Ann Wharton
See Wharton, Annabel (Jane)
Epstein, Anne Merrick 1931- 69-72
See also SATA 20
Epstein, Barbara 1928- Brief entry 110
Epstein, Benjamin Robert 1912-1983 45-48
Obituary 109
Epstein, Beryl (M. Williams) 1910- CANR-39
Earlier sketches in CA 5-8R, CANR-2, 18
See also CLR 26
See also SAAS 17
See also SATA 1, 31
Epstein, Charlotte 1921- CANR-8
Earlier sketch in CA 61-64
Epstein, Cy(ril Robert) 1942- Brief entry 108
Epstein, Cynthia Fuchs 1933- CANR-14
Earlier sketch in CA 29-32R
Epstein, Daniel Mark 1948- CANR-53
Earlier sketches in CA 49-52, CANR-2
See also CLC 7
Epstein, David G(eorge) 1943- 69-72
Epstein, Dena J. 1916- 41-44R
Epstein, Edmund L(loyd) 1931- 118
Epstein, Edward Jay 1935- CANR-71
Earlier sketches in CA 17-20R, CANR-13
Epstein, Edwin M(ichael) 1937- 25-28R
Epstein, Ellen Robinson 1947- 115
Epstein, Erwin H(oward) 1939- 29-32R
Epstein, Eugene 1944- 69-72
Epstein, Fritz T(heodor) 1898-1979 .... CANR-22
Earlier sketch in CA 69-72
Epstein, Helen 1947- 89-92
Epstein, Howard M(ichael) 1927- 21-24R
Epstein, Jacob 1880-1959 163
Brief entry 120
Epstein, Jacob 1956- 114
See also CLC 19
Epstein, Jason 1928- 57-60
Epstein, Joseph 1937- CANR-65
Brief entry 112
Earlier sketches in CA 119, CANR-50
See also CLC 39
Epstein, Judith Sue 1947- 69-72
Epstein, Julius 1901-1975 Obituary 57-60
Epstein, Julius J. 1909- 124
Brief entry 113
See also DLB 26
Epstein, June CANR-57
Earlier sketches in CA 73-76, CANR-13, 30
Epstein, Lawrence J(effrey) 1946- 132
Epstein, Lee 1958- 119
Epstein, Leon D. 1919- 13-16R
Epstein, Leslie 1938- CANR-69
Earlier sketches in CA 73-76, CANR-23
See also CAAS 12
See also CLC 27
Epstein, Melech (Michael)
1889(?)-1979 Obituary 89-92
Eps(h)tein, Mikhail N. 1950- 156
Epstein, Morris 1921-1973 .... CAP-1
Obituary 45-48
Earlier sketch in CA 13-16
Epstein, Perle S(herry) 1938- CANR-9
Earlier sketch in CA 65-68
See also SATA 27
Epstein, Philip G. 1909-1952 Brief entry 117
See also DLB 26
Epstein, Rachel S. 1941- .... SATA 102
Epstein, Richard A(llen) 1943- 158
Epstein, Robert M(orris) 1948- 149
Epstein, Samuel 1909- CANR-39
Earlier sketches in CA 9-12R, CANR-4, 18
See also CLR 26
See also SAAS 17
See also SATA 1, 31

Epstein, Samuel S(tanley) 1926- 115
Epstein, Seymour 1917- CANR-25
Earlier sketches in CA 1-4R, CANR-5
Epstein, Stephan R. 1960- 144
Epstein, William 1912- CANR-11
Earlier sketch in CA 69-72
Epstein, William H(enry) 1944- 61-64
Epton, Nina C(onsuelo) CANR-11
Earlier sketch in CA 5-8R
Equiano, Olaudah 1745(?)-1797 .... BLC 2
See also DAM MULT
See also DLB 37, 50ER
ER 160
See also DLB 85
See also TCLC 33
Eramus, M. Nott
See Stuber, Stanley I(rving)
Erasmus, Charles J(ohn) 1921- 1-4R
Erasmus, M. Nott
See Stuber, Stanley I(rving)
Erazmus, Edward T. 1920- Brief entry 106
Erb, Alta Mae 1891- CAP-1
Earlier sketch in CA 9-10
Erb, Paul 1894- 9-12R
Erb, Peter C. 1943- CANR-32
Earlier sketch in CA 113
Erba, Luciano 1922- .... DLB 128
Erbsen, Claude E. 1938- 89-92
Ercoli, Ercole
See Togliatti, Palmiro
Erdahl, Carol Syvertsen 1932- 108
Erdahl, Lowell O. 1931- 109
Erdman, David V(orse) 1911- CANR-17
Earlier sketches in CA 1-4R, CANR-1
Erdman, Harley 1962- 162
Erdman, Howard Loyd 1935- 21-24R
Erdman, Loula Grace 1905(?)-1976 ..... CANR-63
Earlier sketches in CA 5-8R, CANR-10
See also SATA 1
Erdman, Nikolai R. 1902(?)-1970 Obituary .. 29-32R
Erdman, Paul E(mil) 1932- CANR-43
Earlier sketches in CA 61-64, CANR-13
See also AITN 1
See also CLC 25
Erdoes, Richard 1912- 77-80
See also SATA 33
See also SATA-Brief 28
Erdos, Paul L(ouis) 1914- 29-32R
Erdrich, Louise 1954- CANR-62
Earlier sketches in CA 114, CANR-41
See also AAYA 10
See also BEST 89:1
See also CLC 39, 54
See also DAM MULT, NOV, POP
See also DLB 152, 175
See also MTCW 1
See also NNAL
See also SATA 94
Erdt, Terrence 1942- 106
Ereira, Alan 1943- 137
Erenberg, Arthur 1909(?)-1980 Obituary 114
Erenberg, Lewis A. 1944- 125
Erenburg, Ilya (Grigoryevich)
See Ehrenburg, Ilya (Grigoryevich)
Erens, Patricia 1938- 93-96
E-Rex
See Hilbert, Richard A.
Erhard, Ludwig 1897-1977 Obituary 112
Erhard, Thomas A. 1923- CANR-29
Earlier sketches in CA 33-36R, CANR-13
Erhard, Walter 1920- .... SATA-Brief 30
Erhart, Margaret 1953- 127
Eribon, Didier 1953- 138
Eric, Kenneth
See Henley, Arthur
Erichsen, Heino R(ichard) 1924- 110
Erichsen-Brown, Gwethalyn Graham
See Graham, Gwethalyn
Erichsen-Nelson, Jean 1934- 109
Ericksen, Ephraim Gordon 1917- 5-8R
Ericksen, Gerald L(awrence) 1931- 29-32R
Ericksen, Kenneth J(errold) 1939- 37-40R
Ericksen, Stanford Clark 1911- Brief entry 108
Erickson, Ann 1943- .... CAAS 29
Erickson, Arthur (Charles) 1924- 89-92
Erickson, Arvel Benjamin 1905-1974 .... CAP-2
Earlier sketch in CA 21-22
Erickson, Betty J(ean) ' 1923- 163
See also SATA 97
Erickson, Bonnie H(eather) 1944- 112
Erickson, Carolly 1943- CANR-11
Earlier sketch in CA 69-72
Erickson, Darlene (E.) Williams 1941- 143
Erickson, Don 1932- 110
Erickson, Donald A(rthur) 1925- 29-32R
Erickson, E(rnst) Walfred 1911- CANR-5
Earlier sketch in CA 5-8R
Erickson, Edsel L(ee) 1928- 53-56
Erickson, Erling Arthur 1934- 33-36R
Erickson, Hal 1950- 142
Erickson, John 1929- 101
Erickson, John R. 1943- 138
See also SATA 70
Erickson, Keith V. 1943- 29-32R
Erickson, M(elvin) E(ddy) 1918-(?) 9-12R
Erickson, Marilyn T. 1936- 73-76
Erickson, Marion J. 1913- 17-20R
Erickson, Millard J. 1932- 93-96
Erickson, Milton H(yland) 1901-1980 106
Obituary 97-100
Erickson, Peter (Brown) 1945- 126
Erickson, Phoebe CANR-3
Earlier sketch in CA 1-4R
See also SATA 59
Erickson, Robert 1917-1997 Obituary 157
Brief entry 109
Erickson, Russell E(verett) 1932- 93-96
See also SATA 27
Erickson, Sabra Rollins 1912- CANR-5
Earlier sketch in CA 5-8R
See also SATA 35
Erickson, Stephen A(nthony) 1940- 85-88
Erickson, Stephen Michael 1950- 129
See also Erickson, Steve
Erickson, Steve 1950- CANR-68
Earlier sketch in CANR-60
See also Erickson, Stephen Michael
See also CLC 64
Erickson, W(alter) Bruce 1938- 49-52
Erickson, Winston P(ercy) 1943- 151
Ericson, David F. 1950- 142
Ericson, Edward E(inar) 1939- 69-72
Ericson, Joe Ellis 1925- 41-44R
Ericson, Julia
See Leisy, James (Franklin)
Ericson, Richard V(ictor) 1948- 168
Ericson, Walter
See Fast, Howard (Melvin)
Ericsson, Emily (Alice) 1904-1976 Obituary .. 65-68
Ericsson, Mary Kentra 1910- CANR-20
Earlier sketches in CA 1-4R, CANR-5
Ericsson, Ronald James 1935- 110
Erikson, Erik H(omburger) 1902-1994 .... CANR-33
Obituary 145
Earlier sketch in CA 25-28R
See also MTCW 1
Erikson, Kai T(heodor) 1931- 142
Brief entry 107
Erikson, Mel 1937- ....SATA 31
Erikson, Robert 1938- 161
Erikson, Roy L. 1939(?)-1985 Obituary 116
Erikson, Stanley 1906- 37-40R
Eriksson, Buntel
See Bergman, (Ernst) Ingmar
Eriksson, Edward 1941- 77-80
Eriksson, Marguerite A. 1911- 13-16R
Erim, Kenan Tevfik 1929-1990 Obituary 132
Eringer, Robert 1954- 114
Erisman, Fred (Raymond) 1937- CANR-29
Earlier sketch in CA 110
Eriugena, John Scottus 810(?)-877(?) ..... DLB 115
Erkkila, Betsy 1944- 140
Erlander, Tage Fritiof 1901-1985 Obituary 116
Erlanger, Baba
See Trahey, Jane
Erlanger, Ellen (Louise) 1950- CANR-32
Earlier sketches in CA 85-88, CANR-15
See also SATA-Brief 52
Erlanger, Joseph 1874-1965 157
Erlanger, Philippe 1903- CANR-20
Earlier sketches in CA 5-8R, CANR-5
Erlanger, Steven Jay 1952- 133
Erlbach, Arlene 1948- 146
See also SATA 78
Erlewine, Michael 1941- 145
Erlich, Alexander 1912-1985 Obituary 114
Erlich, Gloria C. 125
Erlich, Lillian (Feldman) 1910- CANR-5
Earlier sketch in CA 1-4R
See also SATA 10
Erlich, Victor 1914- CANR-3
Earlier sketch in CA 9-12R
Erline, N. T.
See Ragen, Naomi
Erlmann, Veit 1951- 139
Ermarth, Elizabeth 1939- 117
Ermine, Will
See Drago, Harry Sinclair
Ermolaev, Herman Sergei 1924- 107
Ernaux, Annie 1940- 147
See also CLC 88
Ernest, Victor (Hugo) 1911- CAP-2
Earlier sketch in CA 33-36
Ernest, William
See Berkebile, Fred D(onovan)
Ernharth, Ronald Louis 1936- 45-48
Erno, Richard B. 1923- 13-16R
Ernotte, Andre (Gilbert) 1943- 164
Ernst, Barbara 1945- 65-68
Ernst, Carl Henry 1938- 45-48
Ernst, Carl W. 1950- 163
Ernst, Clara
See Barnes, Clara Ernst
Ernst, Earle 1911- 5-8R
Ernst, Eldon G(ilbert) 1939- 85-88
Ernst, Jimmy 1920-1984 Obituary 112
Ernst, (Lyman) John 1940- 45-48
See also SATA 39
Ernst, Joseph Albert 1931- Brief entry 109
Ernst, Kathryn (Fitzgerald) 1942- CANR-12
Earlier sketch in CA 61-64
See also SATA 25
Ernst, Lisa Campbell 1957- CANR-67
Earlier sketch in CA 114
See also SATA 55, 95
See also SATA-Brief 44
Ernst, Margaret Samuels 1894- CAP-1
Earlier sketch in CA 13-14
Ernst, Margot Klebe 1939- 21-24R
Ernst, Max(imillian) 1891-1976 152
Obituary 65-68
Ernst, Morris L(eopold) 1888-1976 .... CANR-7
Obituary 65-68
Earlier sketch in CA 5-8R
Interview in CANR-7
Ernst, Paul 1866-1933 ....DLB 66, 118
Ernst, Richard R(obert) 1933- 158
Ernst, Robert 1915- 21-24R
Ernst, Sheila 1941- 109
Ernsting, Walter 1920- 37-40R
Erny, Pierre Jean Paul 1933- CANR-13
Earlier sketch in CA 73-76
Erofeyev, Victor 1947- 140
Eron, Carol (Lehman) 1945- 112
Eron, Leonard D(avid) 1920- Brief entry 110
Errington, Frederick (Karl) 1940- 104
Errington, (Elizabeth) Jane 1951- CANR-60
Earlier sketch in CA 128
Erskine, Albert 1911-1993 .... DLBY 93
Erskine, Barbara 1944- CANR-50
Earlier sketch in CA 123
Erskine, Chester 1904(?)-1986 Obituary 121
Erskine, Jim 1956- 107
Erskine, John 1879-1951 159
Brief entry 112
See also DLB 9, 102
See also TCLC 84
Erskine, Laurie York 1894(?)-1976 Obituary .. 69-72
Erskine, Margaret
See Williams, (Margaret) Wetherby
Erskine, Mrs. Steuart (?)-1948 .... DLB 195
Erskine, Noel Leo 116
Erskine, Rosalind
See Longrigg, Roger (Erskine)
Erskine, Thomas L(eonard) 1939- 65-68
Erskine, Wilson Fiske 1911-1972(?) 1-4R
Obituary 134
Erskine-Lindop, Audrey (Beatrice Noel)
1920-1986 69-72
Obituary 121
Erspamer, Peter R(oy) 1959- 165
Erte
See de Tirtoff, Romain
Ertel, (Richard) James 1922-1985 .... 9-12R
Obituary 117
Ertz, Susan 1894-1985 .... CANR-63
Obituary 116
Earlier sketch in CA 5-8R
Ervin, Janet Halliday 1923- 29-32R
See also SATA 4
Ervin, Sam(uel) J(ames), Jr. 1896-1985 119
Obituary 115
Brief entry 113
Ervin, Susan
See Ervin-Tripp, Susan Moore
Ervin, Theodore Robert 1928- 13-16R
Ervine, St. John Greer 1883-1971 Obituary . 29-32R
See also DLB 10
Ervin-Tripp, Susan Moore 1927- 53-56
Erwin, Annabel
See Barron, Ann Forman
Erwin, Douglas H. 1958- 165
Erwin, Edward (James) 1937- 29-32R
Erwin, John D(raper) 1883-1983 Obituary 109
Erwin, John Seymour 1911- 105
Erwin, Will
See Eisner, Will(iam Erwin)
Esau, Helmut 1941- 57-60
Esau, Katherine 1898- 158
Esbensen, Barbara Juster 1925- 134
See also SATA 62, 97
See also SATA-Brief 53
Escandon, Ralph 1928- CANR-33
Earlier sketches in CA 37-40R, CANR-14
Escarpenter, Claudio 1922-1977 ....17-20R
Obituary 120
Escarraz, Donald Ray 1932- 21-24R
Eschelbach, Claire John 1929- 1-4R
Eschenbach, Wolfram von
See Wolfram von Eschenbach
Eschenburg, Johann Joachim 1743-1820 ... DLB 97
Escher, Franklin (Jr.) 1915- 9-12R
Escher, M(aurits) C(ornelis) 1898-1972 164
See also AAYA 16
Escherich, Elsa Falk 1888- 5-8R
Eschholz, Paul A(nderson) 1942- CANR-14
Earlier sketch in CA 37-40R
Eschmeyer, R(einhart) E(rnst) 1898- 105
See also Eshmeyer, R. E.
Eschmeyer, William N(eil) 1939- 112
Escoto, Julio 1944- ....DLB 145
Escott, Colin 1949- 107
Escott, Jonathan 1922- CANR-20
Earlier sketch in CA 65-68
Escott, Paul David 1947- 93-96
Escriva, Josemaria
See Escriva de Balaguer, Josemaria
Escriva de Balaguer, Josemaria
1902-1975 Obituary 57-60
Esdaile, Arundell 1880-1956 ....DLB 201
Eseki, Bruno
See Mphahlele, Ezekiel
Esenin, Sergei (Alexandrovich) 1895-1925 Brief
entry 104
See also TCLC 4
Eseoghene
See Barrett, (Eseoghene) Lindsay
Esfandiary, F M
See Fm-2030
Eshbach, Lloyd Arthur 1910- CANR-42
Earlier sketch in CA 118
Eshelman, Byron E(lias) 1915- 1-4R
Esherick, Joseph W(harton) 1942- 65-68
Eshleman, Clayton 1935- 33-36R
See also CAAS 6
See also CLC 7
See also DLB 5
Eshleman, Edwin D(uing) 1920-1985 Obituary .. 114
Eshleman, J. Ross 1936- 101
Eshmeyer, R. E.
See Eschmeyer, R(einhart) E(rnst)
See also SATA 29
Eskelin, Neil J(oyner) 1938- 33-36R
Eskelund, Karl 1918-1972 .... CAP-2
Earlier sketch in CA 23-24
Eskenazi, Gerald 1936- CANR-7
Earlier sketch in CA 61-64
Eskew, Glenn T. 1962- 166
Eskey, Kenneth 1930- 77-80
Eskin, Frada 1936- 37-40R
Eskow, John 1949- 105
Eskow, Seymour 1924- 9-12R
Eskridge, Ann E. 1949- 150
See also SATA 84
Esler, Anthony (James) 1934- CANR-26
Earlier sketches in CA 21-24R, CANR-8
Esler, Carol Clemeau 1935- 108
Esler, William K. 1930- CANR-5
Earlier sketch in CA 53-56
Esman, Aaron H(irsh) 1924- CANR-11
Earlier sketch in CA 61-64
Esman, Milton J. 1918- 81-84
Esmein, Jean 1923- CANR-57
Earlier sketches in CA 49-52, CANR-31
Esmond, Harriet
See Burke, John (Frederick)
Esohg, Lama
See Ghose, Amal
Eson, Morris E. 1921- 13-16R
Espada, Martin 1957- 159
Espeland, Pamela (Lee) 1951- 107
See also SATA 52
See also SATA-Brief 38
Espenshade, Edward B(owman), Jr. 1910- 1-4R
Esper, Erwin A(llen) 1895-(?) CAP-1
Earlier sketch in CA 13-16
Espey, John (Jenkins) 1913- CANR-50
Earlier sketches in CA 5-8R, CANR-4, 25
Espinasse, Albert 1905-1972 Obituary 37-40R
'Espinasse, Margaret 1903(?)-1980 Obituary ... 114
Espino, Federico (Licsi, Jr.) 1939- 93-96
Espinosa, Aurelio M(acedonio), Jr. 1907- 131
See also HW
Espinosa, Aurelio M(acedonio) 1880-1958 131
See also HW
Espinosa, Jose E(dmundo) 1900-1967 ..... CAP-2
Earlier sketch in CA 25-28
Espinosa, Maria 1939- .... CAAS 30
Espinosa, Rudy
See Espinoza, Rudolph Louis
Espinoza, Guillermo
See Robinson, William I.
Espinoza, Rudolph Louis 1933- 73-76
Esposito, John C(abrino) 1940- 33-36R
Esposito, John L(ouis) 1940- 116
Esposito, Joseph L(ouis) 1941- CANR-35
Earlier sketch in CA 114
Esposito, Mary Ann 1942- 153
Esposito, Phil(ip Anthony) 1942- Brief entry 108
Espriella, Don Manuel Alvarez
See Southey, Robert
Espriu, Salvador 1913-1985 154
Obituary 115
See also CLC 9
See also DLB 134
Espy, Richard 1952- 105
Espy, Willard R(ichardson) 1910- CANR-2
Earlier sketch in CA 49-52
See also SATA 38
Esquenazi-Mayo, Roberto 1920- 45-48
Esquivel, Laura 1951(?)- CANR-68
Earlier sketch in CA 143
Essame, Hubert 1896-1976 .... CANR-28
Obituary 65-68
Earlier sketch in CA 49-52
Esse, James
See Stephens, James
Esser, Robin 1933- 29-32R
Esses, Michael (Isaiah) 1923- Brief entry 110
Essex, Harry J. 1910(?)-1997 .... 33-36R
Obituary 156
Essex, Mary
See Bloom, Ursula (Harvey)
Essex, Rosamund (Sibyl) 1900-1985 107
Obituary 116
Essick, Robert N(ewman) 1942- CANR-41
Earlier sketches in CA 53-56, CANR-5, 19
Esslin, Martin (Julius) 1918- CANR-27
Earlier sketch in CA 85-88
See also MTCW 1
Esslinger, Dean R(obert) 1942- 61-64
Esslinger, Pat M.
See Carr, Pat
Essoe, Gabe (Attila) 1944- 25-28R
Essop, Ahmed 1931- CANR-50
Earlier sketch in CA 123
Essrig, Harry 1912- 108
See also SATA 66
Estabrook, Robert Harley 1918- 69-72
Estabrooks, George H.
1896(?)-1973 Obituary 45-48
Estang, Luc 1911-1992 61-64
Obituary 139
Estarellas, Juan 1918- CANR-2
Earlier sketch in CA 45-48
Estaver, Marguerite M. 1893- 97-100
Estelle, Sister Mary 1907- CAP-1
Earlier sketch in CA 11-12
Estenssoro, Hugo 1946- 69-72
Estep, Irene Compton 1-4R
See also SATA 5
Estep, Maggie 1962(?)- 159
Estep, W(illiam) R(oscoe), Jr. 1920- CANR-51
Earlier sketches in CA 13-16R, CANR-9, 25
Esterbrook, Tom
See Hubbard, L(afayette) Ron(ald)
Estergreen, M. Morgan
See Estergreen, Marian Morgan
Estergreen, Marian Morgan 1910- 17-20R
Esterhammer, Angela 1961- 146
Esterhazy, Peter 1950- 140
Esterl, Arnica 1933- .... SATA 77
Esterly, Glenn 1942- 33-36R
Estermann, Carlos (?)-1976 Obituary 105

Esterow, Milton 1928- 17-20R
Estes, Bill 1941- 107
Estes, Clarissa Pinkola 1943- CANR-67
Earlier sketch in CA 143
Estes, Eleanor 1906-1988 CANR-20
Obituary 126
Earlier sketches in CA 1-4R, CANR-5
See also CLR 2
See also DLB 22
See also JRDA
See also MAICYA
See also SATA 7, 91
See also SATA-Obit 56
Estes, J(oseph) Worth 1934- 104
Estes, John E(dward) 1939- 57-60
Estes, Rice 1907- CAP-1
Earlier sketch in CA 11-12
Estes, Richard J. 1942- CANR-41
Earlier sketch in CA 118
Estes, Steve(n Douglas) 1952- 97-100
Estes, Winston M(arvin) 1917-1982 29-32R
Obituary 126
Estess, Sybil P. 1942- 129
Estess, Ted L(ynn) 1942- 114
Esteven, John
See Shellabarger, Samuel
Estevez, Emilio 1962- 159
Estey, George F. 1924- 33-36R
Estey, Ralph H(oward) 1916- 148
Esthus, Raymond Arthur 1925- 13-16R
Estleman, Loren D. 1952- CANR-27
Earlier sketch in CA 85-88
Interview in CANR-27
See also AAYA 27
See also CLC 48
See also DAM NOV, POP
See also MTCW 1
Estner, Lois J(ane) 1947- 114
Estock, Anne (Martin) 1923- 1-4R
Estoril, Jean
See Allan, Mabel Esther
Estow, Clara 1945- 154
Estrada, Doris (Perkins) 1923- 17-20R
Estrada, Jacquelyn (Ann) 1946- 29-32R
Estrada, Pau 1961- SATA 74
Estrada, Rita Clay 164
Estragon, Vladimir
See Stokes, Geoffrey
Estrin, Herman A. 1915- CANR-7
Earlier sketch in CA 17-20R
Estroff, Sue E. 1950- 105
Estupinan Bass, Nelson 1915- HW
Esty, John Cushing, Jr. 1928- Brief entry 106
Eszterhas, Joe
See Eszterhas, Joseph A.
Eszterhas, Joseph A. 1944- CANR-68
Brief entry 124
Earlier sketch in CA 130
See also DLB 185
Etchebaster, Pierre 1894-1980 102
Obituary 97-100
Etchemendy, Nancy 1952- 106
See also SATA 38
Etcheson, Craig Carlyle 1955- 117
Etcheson, Warren W(ade) 1920- 41-44R
Etchison, Birdie L(ee) 1937- 106
See also SATA 38
Etchison, Dennis (William) 1943- 118
Brief entry 115
Interview in 118
Eterovich, Adam S(lav) 1930- CANR-27
Earlier sketch in CA 49-52
Eterovich, Francis Hyacinth 1913-1980 CANR-28
Earlier sketch in CA 37-40R
Ethell, Jeffrey L(ance) 1947-1997 CANR-39
Obituary 158
Earlier sketches in CA 101, CANR-18
Etherege, George 1636-1692 DAM DRAM
See also DLB 80
Etheridge, Eugene Wesley 1925- 5-8R
Etherington, Charles Leslie 1903- 5-8R
Etherington, Frank 1945- SATA 58
Etherton, Michael (James) 1939- 121
Ethridge, James M(erritt) 1921- 114
Ethridge, Mark Foster, Jr. 1924-1985 Obituary 115
Ethridge, Mark Foster 1896-1981 Obituary 103
See also DLB 127
Ethridge, Willie Snow 1900-1983(?) 17-20R
Obituary 108
See also AITN 1
Etienne
See King-Hall, (William) Stephen (Richard)
Etkin, Anne (Dunwody Little) 1923- 73-76
Etlin, Richard A. 1947- 155
Etmekjian, James 1915- CANR-3
Earlier sketch in CA 5-8R
Eton, Robert
See Meynell, Laurence Walter
Etra, Jonathan 1952-1991 102
Obituary 133
Ets, Marie Hall 1893-1984 CANR-4
Earlier sketch in CA 1-4R
See also CLR 33
See also DLB 22
See also MAICYA
See also SATA 2
Ets-Hokin, Judith Diane 1938- 61-64
Etteldorf, Raymond P. 1911- 9-12R
Etter, Dave 1928- CANR-49
Earlier sketches in CA 17-20R, CANR-8, 24
See also DLB 105
Etter, Les(ter Frederick) 1904- 25-28R
Etter, Patricia A. 1932- CANR-56
Earlier sketch in CA 120
Ettin, Andrew V(ogel) 1943- 124
Ettinger, Elzbieta 1925- CANR-52
Earlier sketch in CA 29-32R
Ettinger, Richard Prentice
1893-1971 Obituary 29-32R
Ettinger, Robert C(hester) W(ilson) 1918- 13-16R
Ettinghausen, Maurice Leon
1883-1974 Obituary 116
Ettinghausen, Richard 1906-1979 CANR-9
Obituary 85-88
Earlier sketch in CA 65-68
Ettleson, Abraham 1897- CAP-2
Earlier sketch in CA 23-24
Ettling, John 1944- 125
Ettlinger, Gerard H(erman) 1935- 61-64
Ettlinger, L. D.
See Ettlinger, Leopold David
Ettlinger, Leopold D.
See Ettlinger, Leopold David
Ettlinger, Leopold David 1913-1989 Obituary 129
Brief entry 111
Ettner, Johann Christoph 1654-1724 DLB 168
Etulain, Richard W(ayne) 1938- CANR-16
Earlier sketches in CA 45-48, CANR-1
Etzioni, Amitai (Werner) 1929- CANR-22
Earlier sketches in CA 1-4R, CANR-5
Etzioni, Minerva M(orales)
1938(?)-1985 Obituary 118
Etzioni-Halevy, Eva 1934- CANR-58
Earlier sketch in CA 127
Etzkorn, K(laus) Peter 1932- 49-52
Etzkowitz, Henry 1940- 25-28R
Etzold, Thomas H(erman) 1945- CANR-14
Earlier sketch in CA 81-84
Euba, Femi 1941- 141
See also BW 2
Eubank, (Weaver) Keith (Jr.) 1920- CANR-2
Earlier sketch in CA 5-8R
Eubank, Nancy 1934- 41-44R
Eubanks, Ralph T(ravis) 1920- 17-20R
Euchner, Charles C. 1960- 164
Eucken, Rudolf (Christof) 1846-1926 Brief entry 119
Eugenides, Jeffrey 1960(?)- 144
See also CLC 81
Eula, Michael J(ames) 1957- 150
Eulau, Heinz 1915- Brief entry 107
Eulenspiegel, Alexander
See Shea, Robert (Joseph)
Eulert, Don(ald Dean) 1935- CANR-40
Earlier sketches in CA 49-52, CANR-2, 18
Euller, John E(lmer) 1926- 9-12R
Eulo, Ken 1939- CANR-72
Brief entry 109
Earlier sketch in CA 126
Eunson, (John) Dale 1904- 41-44R
See also SATA 5
Eunson, Robert C(harles) 1912-1975 13-16R
Obituary 61-64
Euphan
See Todd, Barbara Euphan
Euphemides, Aristos
See von Koerber, Hans Nordewin
Eupolemius fl. c. 1095- DLB 148
Eurich, Alvin C(hristian) 1902-1987 17-20R
Obituary 123
Eurich, Nell 1919- CANR-12
Earlier sketch in CA 73-76
Euripides c. 485B.C.-406B.C. DA
See also DAB
See also DAC
See also DAM DRAM, MST
See also DC 4
See also DLB 176
See also WLCS
European
See Mosley, Oswald (Ernald)
Eurui, Yoshikichi 1937- DLB 182
Eusden, John (Dykstra) 1922- 45-48
Eustace, Cecil John 1903- 49-52
Eustace, May (Corcoran) 1904- 5-8R
Eustace, Robert
See Barton, Eustace Robert
Eustis, Alvin Allen, Jr. 1917- 102
Eustis, Laurette
See Murdock, Laurette P.
Eustis, O. B.
See Eustis, Orville B.
Eustis, Orville B. 1913-1986 124
Euwe, Machgielis 1901-1981 Obituary 105
Euwe, Max
See Euwe, Machgielis
Evain, Elaine 1931- 57-60
Evan, Carol
See Goldsmith, Carol Evan
Evan, Evin
See Faust, Frederick (Schiller)
Evan, William (Martin) 1922- CANR-2
Earlier sketch in CA 1-4R
Evang, Karl 1902- 65-68
Evanier, David Brief entry 108
Evanoff, Vlad 1916- CANR-6
Earlier sketch in CA 5-8R
See also SATA 59
Evanovich, Janet 167
Evans, A(lfred) Alexander 1905- CAP-1
Earlier sketch in CA 9-10
Evans, Abbie Huston 1881- 57-60
Evans, Alan
See Stoker, Alan
Evans, Albert 1917- 85-88
Evans, Alice Frazer 1939- CANR-58
Earlier sketches in CA 112, CANR-30
Evans, Arthur Bruce 1948- 61-64
Evans, Barbara Lloyd
See Lloyd Evans, Barbara
Evans, Benjamin Ifor 1899-1982 Obituary 107
Evans, Bennett
See Berger, Ivan (Bennett)
Evans, Bergen (Baldwin) 1904-1978 CANR-4
Obituary 77-80
Earlier sketch in CA 5-8R
Evans, Brendan 1944- 158
Evans, Bruce A. 1946- 134
Evans, C(harles) Stephen 1948- CANR-29
Earlier sketches in CA 33-36R, CANR-13
Evans, C. Stephen 1948- 162
Evans, Calvin (Donald) 1931- 146
Evans, Chad (Arthur) 1951- 131
Evans, Charles 1850-1935 DLB 187
Evans, (Jean) Cherry (Drummond) 1928- CAP-1
Earlier sketch in CA 9-10
Evans, Christopher (Riche) 1931-1979 102
Evans, Clifford 1916(?)-1983 Obituary 110
Evans, Constance May 1890- 9-12R
Evans, Craig A. 1952- CANR-66
Earlier sketch in CA 129
Evans, D(avid) Ellis 1930- CANR-16
Earlier sketch in CA 25-28R
Evans, Dale
See Rogers, Dale Evans
Evans, David Allan 1940- CANR-57
Earlier sketches in CA 49-52, CANR-31
Evans, David Beecher 1928- Brief entry 105
Evans, David Huhn, Jr. 1944- 110
Evans, David R(ussell) 1937- CANR-17
Earlier sketch in CA 33-36R
Evans, David R(ichard) 1940- CANR-39
Earlier sketch in CA 116
Evans, David S(tanley) 1916- 41-44R
Evans, Debra 1953- 122
Evans, Don 1938- 111
Evans, Donald 1884-1921 Brief entry 123
See also DLB 54
Evans, Donald (Dwight) 1927- 41-44R
Evans, Donald P(aul) 1930-1992 CANR-46
Obituary 140
Earlier sketches in CA 57-60, CANR-7
Evans, Dorinda 1944- 121
Evans, Douglas 1953- 159
See also SATA 93
Evans, E(myr) Estyn 1905-1989 CANR-5
Obituary 129
Earlier sketch in CA 5-8R
Evans, E(dward) Everett 1893-1958 160
Brief entry 113
Evans, Edward G(ordon), Jr. 1916- 45-48
Evans, Eli N. 1936- 45-48
See also AITN 1
Evans, Elizabeth 1932- 53-56
Evans, Ellen
See Du Breuil, (Elizabeth) L(or)inda
Evans, Emerald
See Du Breuil, (Elizabeth) L(or)inda
Evans, Eric J(ohn) 1945- 108
Evans, Eva (Knox) 1905- 73-76
See also SATA 27
Evans, Evan
See Faust, Frederick (Schiller)
Evans, (Francis) Fallon 1925- 1-4R
Evans, Fanny-Maude 1914- 117
Evans, F.M.G.
See Higham, Florence May Grier
Evans, Frances Monet Carter
See Carter, Frances Monet
Evans, Frank Bernard 1927- CANR-36
Earlier sketch in CA 114
Evans, G. B.
See Evans, Gwynne Blakemore
Evans, G. Blakemore
See Evans, Gwynne Blakemore
Evans, G(ayle) Edward 1937- 33-36R
Evans, G(eraint) N(antglyn) D(avies) 1935-1971 CAP-2
Earlier sketch in CA 33-36
Evans, G. R.
See Evans, Gillian (Rosemary)
Evans, Gareth Lloyd
See Lloyd Evans, Gareth
Evans, Gavin 1960- 167
Evans, Geoffrey (Charles) 1901-1987 17-20R
Obituary 121
Evans, George Bird 1906- CANR-2
Earlier sketch in CA 1-4R
Evans, George Ewart 1909-1988(?) 61-64
Obituary 124
Evans, George Henry 1805-1856 DLB 43
Evans, George W(illiam) II 1920- 21-24R
Evans, Giles (Edwin) 1949-1988 141
Evans, Gillian (Rosemary) 1944- CANR-53
Earlier sketch in CA 126
Evans, Glen 1921- 85-88
Evans, Gordon H(eyd) 1930- 13-16R
Evans, Greg 1947- 160
See also AAYA 23
See also SATA 73
Evans, Gwynfor 1912- 61-64
Evans, Gwynne B.
See Evans, Gwynne Blakemore
Evans, Gwynne Blakemore 1912- 125
Evans, Harold 1911-1983 129
Obituary 109
Evans, Harold Matthew 1928- 41-44R
Evans, Harris
See Evans, George Bird
and Evans, Kay Harris
Evans, Harry 1896(?)-1988 Obituary 126
Evans, Herndon J. 1895-1976 69-72
Evans, Hilary 1929- CANR-42
Earlier sketches in CA 1-4R, CANR-5, 20
Evans, Howard Ensign 1919- CANR-52
Earlier sketch in CA 5-8R
Evans, Hubert John Filmer
1904-1989 Obituary 129
Evans, Hubert Reginald 1892-1986 103
Obituary 119
See also DLB 92
See also SATA-Obit 48
Evans, Humphrey (Marshall, Jr.) 1914- 29-32R
Evans, I(drisyn) O(liver) 1894-1977 CANR-15
Earlier sketch in CA 13-16R
Evans, Ian
See Wells, Angus
Evans, Idella M(arie Crowe) 1924- 29-32R
Evans, Ilona 1918(?)-1980 Obituary 102
Evans, J(ames) A(llan) S(tewart) 1931- 37-40R
Evans, J(ohn) D(avid) G(emmill) 1942- 127
Evans, J. Martin 1935- 85-88
Evans, J(ack) N(aunton) 1920- 25-28R
Evans, J(ohn) Robert 1942- CANR-7
Earlier sketch in CA 57-60
Evans, Jacob A. 1920- 25-28R
Evans, James Allen 1926(?)-1983 Obituary 110
Evans, James H., Jr. 145
Evans, James R(ichard) 1908- 141
Evans, Jay 1925- 61-64
Evans, Jean 1939- 102
Evans, Jessica
See Lottman, Eileen
Evans, Joan 1893-1977 13-16R
Obituary 73-76
Evans, John
See Browne, Howard
Evans, John Davies 1925- 127
Evans, John Lewis 1930- 85-88
Evans, John W(alker) 1904- 33-36R
Evans, John X(avier) 1933- 37-40R
Evans, Jonathan
See Freemantle, Brian (Harry)
Evans, Joseph S., Jr. 1909(?)-1978 85-88
Obituary 81-84
Evans, Joseph W(illiam) 1921- 21-24R
Evans, Julia (Rendel) 1913- 13-16R
Evans, K(athleen) M(arianne) 1911- 9-12R
Evans, Katherine (Floyd) 1901-1964 5-8R
See also SATA 5
Evans, Kay Harris 1906- CANR-2
Earlier sketch in CA 1-4R
Evans, (Cyril) Kenneth 1917- 53-56
Evans, Kenneth R. 1938- 134
Brief entry 110
Evans, Larry
See Evans, Laurence Chubb
Evans, Larry (Melvyn) 1932- 129
Evans, Laura 1949(?)- 158
Evans, Laurence 1923- 37-40R
Evans, Laurence Chubb 1939- 152
See also SATA 88
Evans, Lawrence Watt 1954- CANR-32
Earlier sketch in CA 102
See also Watt-Evans, Lawrence
Evans, Lee
See Forrest, Richard (Stockton)
Evans, Lloyd (Lloyd Thomas) 1927- 69-72
Evans, Louis Hadley Sr. 1897-1981 116
Evans, Luther Harris 1902-1981 CANR-9
Obituary 106
Earlier sketch in CA 17-20R
Evans, M(edford) Stanton 1934- 65-68
Evans, Mari 1923- CANR-27
Earlier sketches in CA 49-52, CANR-2
See also BW 1
See also DLB 41
See also SATA 10
Evans, Marian
See Eliot, George
Evans, Mark 65-68
See also SATA 19
Evans, Marvin R(ussell) 1915- 49-52
Evans, Mary 1946- CANR-48
Earlier sketch in CA 122
Evans, Mary Ann
See Eliot, George
Evans, Mary Lowe
See Lowe-Evans, Mary
Evans, Max 1925(?)- CANR-64
Earlier sketches in CA 1-4R, CANR-1
Evans, Medford (Bryon) 1907- 25-28R
Evans, Mel 1912(?)-1984 Obituary 112
Evans, Melbourne G(riffith) 1912- CAP-2
Earlier sketch in CA 33-36
Evans, Michael K(aye) 1938- 132
Evans, Morgan
See Davies, L(eslie) P(urnell)
Evans, N(orman) Dean 1925- CANR-13
Earlier sketch in CA 21-24R
Evans, Nancy 1950- CANR-34
Earlier sketch in CA 77-80
See also SATA 65
Evans, Nathaniel 1742-1767 DLB 31
Evans, Oliver 1915- 17-20R
Evans, Olwen (Elizabeth) Carey
See Carey Evans, Olwen (Elizabeth)
Evans, Patricia Healy
See Carpenter, Patricia (Healy Evans)
Evans, Paul Richer 1925- Brief entry 106
Evans, (Alice) Pearl 1927- SATA 83
Evans, Peter (Andrew) 131
Evans, Philip 1944- Brief entry 110
Evans, Rand B(oyd) 1942- Brief entry 107
Evans, Richard 1939- 106
Evans, Richard Evan 1898-1983 Obituary 109
Evans, Richard I(sadore) 1922- 131
Brief entry 108
Evans, Richard J. 1947- 138
Evans, Richard L(ouis) 1906-1971 9-12R
Obituary 29-32R
Evans, Robert, Jr. 1932- 17-20R

Evans, Robert 1930- 147
Evans, Robert Allen 1937- 112
Evans, Robert C. 1955- 148
Evans, Robert F(ranklin) 1930-1974 CAP-2
Earlier sketch in CA 23-24
Evans, Robert Henry 1937- 21-24R
Evans, Robert L(eonard) 1917- CANR-32
Earlier sketch in CA 49-52
Evans, Robert Owen 1919- 13-16R
Evans, Robert P. 1918- 13-16R
Evans, Rodney E(arl) 1939- 49-52
Evans, Rowland, Jr. 1921- CANR-15
Earlier sketch in CA 21-24R
Evans, Rupert N. 1921- 37-40R
Evans, Sara 1943- 93-96
Evans, Sebastian 1830-1909 DLB 35
Evans, Shirlee 1931- 61-64
See also SATA 58
Evans, Stanley G(eorge) 1912-1965 CAP-1
Earlier sketch in CA 9-10
Evans, Stephen S(tewart) 1954- 168
Evans, (Edwin) Stuart (Gomer) 1934-1994 124
Obituary 147
Brief entry 118
Interview in 124
Evans, Susan H(ope) 1951- 115
Evans, Tabor
See Cameron, Lou
and Knott, William C(ecil, Jr.)
and Wallmann, Jeffrey M(iner)
Evans, Thomas W(illiam) 1930- 45-48
Evans, Travers Moncure 1938- 57-60
Evans, Virginia Moran 1909- CANR-5
Earlier sketch in CA 5-8R
Evans, W(illiam) Glyn 1918- 89-92
Evans, W(illiam) McKee 1923- 21-24R
Evans, Walker 1903-1975 Obituary 89-92
Evans, (William Edis) Webster 1908-1982 41-44R
Obituary 133
Evans, Wilbur 1913- 97-100
Evans, William 1895-1988 81-84
Obituary 126
Evans, William David 1912-1985 Obituary 117
Evans, William Howard 1924- 21-24R
Evans, William R. 1938- 105
Evans Davies, Gloria 1932- 5-8R
Evansen, Virginia Besaw 1921- 13-16R
Evans-Jones, Albert 1895- 5-8R
Evans-Pritchard, Edward Evan 1902-1973 65-68
Evanzz, Karl 1953- 140
See also BW 2
Evarts, Esther
See Benson, Sally
Evarts, Hal G(eorge) 1887-1934 Brief entry 121
Evarts, Hal G. (Jr.) 1915-1989 CANR-63
Earlier sketches in CA 49-52, CANR-2
See also SATA 6
Eve, Barbara
See Reiss, Barbara Eve
Eveland, Bill
See Eveland, Wilbur Crane
Eveland, Wilbur Crane 1918- 101
Eveling, (Harry) Stanley 1925- 61-64
Evely, Louis 1910- 85-88
Evelyn, Anthony
See Ward-Thomas, Evelyn Bridget Patricia Stephens
Evelyn, (John) Michael 1916-1992(?) CANR-69
Obituary 140
Earlier sketches in CA 5-8R, CANR-6, 22, 46
Evenhuis, Gertie 1932- 107
Evenson, Brian 1966- 148
Everage, Dame Edna
See Humphries, Barry
Everdell, William R(omeyn) 1941- 164
Evered, James F(letcher) 1928- 107
Everest, Allan S(eymour) 1913- CANR-51
Earlier sketches in CA 29-32R, CANR-11, 26
Everett, Alexander Hill 1790-1847 DLB 59
Everett, Arthur (W., Jr.) 1914- 103
Everett, Donald E(dward) 1920- 9-12R
Everett, Edward 1794-1865 DLB 1, 59
Everett, Gail
See Hale, Arlene
Everett, Glenn D. 1921- 69-72
Everett, Percival L. 1956- 129
See also BW 2
See also CLC 57
Everett, Peter 1931- CANR-31
Earlier sketch in CA 69-72
Everett, Peter W(illiam) 1924- 13-16R
Everett, Rupert 1960(?)- 142
Everett, T(homas) H(enry) 1903(?)-1986 133
Obituary 120
Everett, Walter 1936- 93-96
Everett-Green, Evelyn 1856-1932 Brief entry 114
Evergood, Philip 1901-1973 Obituary 41-44R
Everhart, James W(illiam), Jr. 1924- 89-92
Everhart, Jim
See Everhart, James W(illiam), Jr.
Everitt, Alan (Milner) 1926- CANR-11
Earlier sketch in CA 21-24R
Everitt, Arva Graham Johnson 1916(?)-1982 Obituary 107
Everitt, Bridget Mary 1924- 45-48
Everitt, C(harles) W(illiam) F(rancis) 1934- 65-68
Everitt, David Samuel 1952- 110
Everman, Welch D(uane) 1946- 57-60
Evernden, Margery 1916- 5-8R
See also SATA 5
Evers, (James) Charles 1923(?)- Brief entry 111
Evers, Christopher 1940- 122
Evers, Larry 1946- 135
Eversley, D(avid) E(dward) C(harles) 1921- CANR-1
Earlier sketch in CA 1-4R
Eversole, Finley T. 1933- 9-12R
Eversole, Robyn Harbert 1971- SATA 74
Everson, Dale Millar 1928- 17-20R
Everson, David H. 1941- 124
Everson, Ida Gertrude 1898- 37-40R
Everson, R(onald) G(ilmour) 1903- 17-20R
See also CLC 27
See also DLB 88
Everson, William (Oliver) 1912-1994 CANR-20
Obituary 145
Earlier sketch in CA 9-12R
See also CLC 1, 5, 14
See also DLB 5, 16
See also MTCW 1
Everson, William Keith 1929-1996 CANR-2
Obituary 151
Earlier sketch in CA 1-4R
Eversz, Robert McLeod 1954- 127
Everton, Macduff 1947- 104
Evertts, Eldonna L(ouise) 1917- 21-24R
Everwine, Peter Paul 1930- 73-76
Every, George 1909- CANR-6
Earlier sketch in CA 13-16R
Eves, Douglas 1922- 119
Evetts, Julia 1944- 69-72
Evinger, William R. 1943- 150
Evins, Joseph Landon 1910- 61-64
Eviota, Elizabeth Uy 1946- 146
Evitts, William J(oseph) 1942- 121
Brief entry 112
EVOE
See Knox, Edmund George Valpy
Evold, Bent 1936- 129
Evoy, John J(oseph) 1911- 5-8R
Evslin, Bernard 1922-1993 CANR-48
Obituary 142
Earlier sketches in CA 21-24R, CANR-9
See also SATA 45, 83
See also SATA-Brief 28
See also SATA-Obit 77
Evslin, Dorothy 1923- 57-60
Evtushenko, Evgenii Aleksandrovich
See Yevtushenko, Yevgeny (Alexandrovich)
Ewald, Wendy Taylor 1951- 120
Ewald, William Bragg, Jr. 1925- CANR-27
Earlier sketch in CA 107
Ewans, Michael (Christopher) 1946- 129
Ewart, Andrew 1911- 17-20R
Ewart, Charles
See Lyte, Charles
Ewart, Claire 1958- 144
See also SATA 76
Ewart, Gavin (Buchanan) 1916-1995 CANR-46
Obituary 150
Earlier sketches in CA 89-92, CANR-17
See also CLC 13, 46
See also DLB 40
See also MTCW 1
Ewart, Simon
See Herd, Michael
Ewbank, Henry L(ee), Jr. 1924- 73-76
Ewbank, Walter F(rederick) 1918- CANR-38
Earlier sketches in CA 25-28R, CANR-17
Ewell, Barbara C(laire) 1947- CANR-35
Earlier sketch in CA 114
Ewell, Judith 1943- 107
Ewen, David 1907-1985 CANR-2
Obituary 118
Earlier sketch in CA 1-4R
See also SATA 4
See also SATA-Obit 47
Ewen, Elizabeth 1943- 124
Ewen, Frederic 1899-1988 73-76
Obituary 126
Ewen, Robert B. 1940- CANR-15
Earlier sketch in CA 37-40R
Ewen, Stuart 1945- CANR-12
Earlier sketch in CA 69-72
Ewens, James 1939- 116
Ewers, Hanns Heinz 1871-1943 149
Brief entry 109
See also TCLC 12
Ewers, John C(anfield) 1909-1997 CANR-22
Obituary 158
Earlier sketches in CA 17-20R, CANR-7
Ewert, David 1922- 105
Ewing, Alfred Cyril 1899-1973 CANR-4
Earlier sketch in CA 5-8R
Ewing, David Walkley 1923- CANR-5
Earlier sketch in CA 1-4R
Ewing, Donald M. 1895(?)-1978 Obituary 81-84
Ewing, Elizabeth 1904- 41-44R
Ewing, Frederick R.
See Sturgeon, Theodore (Hamilton)
Ewing, George W(ilmeth) 1923- 45-48
Ewing, John A(lexander) 1923- 125
Brief entry 105
Ewing, John Melvin 1925- 53-56
Ewing, John S(inclair) 1916- 13-16R
Ewing, Juliana (Horatia Gatty) 1841-1885 DLB 21, 163
See also SATA 16
Ewing, Kathryn 1921- CANR-7
Earlier sketch in CA 61-64
See also SATA 20
Ewing, Sherman 1901-1975 Obituary 57-60
Ewing, Steve 1941- 160
Ewton, Ralph W(aldo), Jr. 1938- 81-84
Ewy, Donna 1934- CANR-14
Earlier sketch in CA 33-36R
Ewy, Rodger 1931- CANR-14
Earlier sketch in CA 33-36R
Exall, Barry
See Nugent, John Peer
Excellent, Matilda
See Farson, Daniel (Negley)
Exell, Frank Kingsley 1902- 5-8R
Exetastes
See Harakas, Stanley Samuel
Exley, Frederick (Earl) 1929-1992 81-84
Obituary 138
See also AITN 2
See also CLC 6, 11
See also DLB 143
See also DLBY 81
Exley, Jo Ella Powell 1940- 122
Exman, Eugene 1900-1975 CAP-1
Obituary 61-64
Earlier sketch in CA 17-18
Ex-R. S. M.
See Lindsay, Harold Arthur
Exton, Clive (Jack Montague) 1930- 61-64
Exton, William, Jr. 1907-1988 45-48
Obituary 127
Eyck, Frank 1921- CANR-11
Earlier sketch in CA 25-28R
Eye, Glen G(ordon) 1904- CANR-2
Earlier sketch in CA 49-52
Eyen, Jerome
See Eyen, Tom
Eyen, Tom 1941-1991 CANR-22
Obituary 134
Earlier sketch in CA 25-28R
Eyer, Diane E(lizabeth) 1944- 143
Eyerly, Jeannette (Hyde) 1908- CANR-51
Earlier sketches in CA 1-4R, CANR-4, 19
See also SAAS 10
See also SATA 4, 86
Eyestone, Robert 1942- 41-44R
Eykman, Christoph 1937- 41-44R
Eyles, Wilfred Charles 1891- CAP-2
Earlier sketch in CA 17-18
Eynhardt, Guillermo
See Quiroga, Horacio (Sylvestre)
Eyre, Annette
See Worboys, Anne(tte Isobel) Eyre
Eyre, Dorothy
See McGuire, Leslie (Sarah)
Eyre, Frank 1910-1988 SATA-Obit 62
Eyre, Katherine Wigmore 1901-1970 Obituary 104
See also SATA 26
Eyre, Peter 1942- 140
Eyre, Richard M(elvin) 1944- CANR-13
Earlier sketch in CA 61-64
Eyre, Ronald 1929- 104
Eyre, S(amuel) R(obert) 1922- 21-24R
Eysenck, Hans J(urgen) 1916-1997 CANR-50
Obituary 161
Earlier sketches in CA 9-12R, CANR-4, 25
Eysenck, Michael (William) 1944- 131
Eysman, Harvey (Allen) 1939- 104
Eyster, C(harles) William 1917- 29-32R
Eyvindson, Peter (Knowles) 1946- 124
See also SATA-Brief 52
Ezekiel, Mordecai J(oseph) B(rill) 1899-1974 65-68
Obituary 53-56
Ezekiel, Nissim 1924- 61-64
See also CLC 61
Ezekiel, Raphael S. 1931- 53-56
Ezekiel, Tish O'Dowd 1943- 129
See also CLC 34
Ezell, Edward C(linton) 1939-1993 128
Obituary 143
Ezell, Harry E(ugene) 1918-1974 1-4R
Obituary 103
Ezell, John Samuel 1917- 1-4R
Ezell, Macel D. 1934- 77-80
Ezell, Margaret J. M. 1955- 146
Ezera, Kalu 1925- 13-16R
Ezergailis, Andrew 1930- 89-92
Ezorsky, Gertrude 89-92
Ezzell, Marilyn 1937- 109
See also SATA 42
See also SATA-Brief 38
Ezzo (?)-c. 1065 DLB 148

F

F. P. A.
See Adams, Franklin P(ierce)
Faas, (K.) Ekbert 1938- 130
Faas, Larry A(ndrew) 1936- 29-32R
Fabbri, Diego 1911-1980 Obituary 105
Fabe, Maxene 1943- 77-80
See also SATA 15
Faber, Adele 1928- CANR-37
Earlier sketch in CA 77-80
Faber, Charles F(ranklin) 1926- CANR-12
Earlier sketch in CA 29-32R
Faber, Doris (Greenberg) 1924- CANR-56
Earlier sketches in CA 17-20R, CANR-8, 30
See also SATA 3, 78
Faber, Frederick William 1814-1863 DLB 32
Faber, Harold 1919- CANR-55
Earlier sketches in CA 13-16R, CANR-8, 29
See also SATA 5
Faber, Heije 1907- 139
Faber, John Henry 1918- 13-16R
Faber, Nancy W(eingarten) 1909-1976 5-8R
Obituary 65-68
Faber, Richard Stanley 1924- 61-64
Faber-Kaiser, Andreas 1944- 73-76
Fabian, Donald L(eroy) 1919- 21-24R
Fabian, Josephine C(unningham) 1903-1984 CAP-1
Obituary 114
Earlier sketch in CA 9-10
Fabian, Robert (Honey) 1901-1978 81-84
Obituary 77-80
Fabian, Ruth
See Quigley, Aileen
Fabilli, Mary 1914- CAAS 29
Fabinyi, Andrew 1908-1978 Obituary 108
Fabio, Sarah Webster 1928-1979 CANR-22
Earlier sketch in CA 69-72
See also BW 1
Fabisch, Judith Patricia 1938- CANR-19
Earlier sketch in CA 103
Fabos, Julius Gy(ula) 1932- 97-100
Fabre, Genevieve E. 1936- 109
Fabre, Jean Henri (Casimir) 1823-1915 SATA 22
Fabre, Michel J(acques) 1933- CANR-37
Earlier sketches in CA 45-48, CANR-1, 16
Fabrega, Horacio, Jr. 1934- 73-76
Fabri, Ralph 1894-1975 CAP-2
Obituary 57-60
Earlier sketch in CA 19-20
Fabricand, Burton Paul 1923- 93-96
Fabricant, Carole 1944- 113
Fabricant, Michael B. 1948- 143
Fabricant, Solomon 1906-1989 Obituary 129
Fabricius, Johan (Johannes) 1899- CANR-5
Earlier sketch in CA 53-56
Fabrizio, Ray 1930- 33-36R
Fabrizio, Timothy C(harles) 1948- 165
Fabrizius, Peter
See Fabry, Joseph B(enedikt)
and Knight, Max
Fabry, Joseph B(enedikt) 1909- 25-28R
Fabrycky, Wolter Joseph 1932- 21-24R
Fabun, Don 1920- 45-48
Fackenheim, Emil L(udwig) 1916- 21-24R
Facklam, Margery (Metz) 1927- CANR-48
Earlier sketches in CA 5-8R, CANR-6, 21
See also SATA 20, 85
Fackler, Eli
See Fackler, Elizabeth
Fackler, Elizabeth 1947- 118
Fackre, Gabriel Joseph 1926- CANR-7
Earlier sketch in CA 17-20R
Facos, James F(rancis) 1924- 41-44R
Factor, Regis A(nthony) 1937- 118
Fader, Daniel 1930- 33-36R
Fader, Shirley Sloan 1931- CANR-14
Earlier sketch in CA 77-80
Faderman, Lillian 1940- CANR-37
Earlier sketches in CA 33-36R, CANR-16
Fadeyev, A.
See Bulgya, Alexander Alexandrovich
Fadeyev, Alexander
See Bulgya, Alexander Alexandrovich
See also TCLC 53
Fadiman, Clifton (Paul) 1904- CANR-44
Earlier sketches in CA 61-64, CANR-9
See also SATA 11
Fadiman, Edwin, Jr. 1925- 29-32R
Fadiman, James 1939- 33-36R
Fadiman, Jeffrey A(ndrew) 1936- 116
Fadner, Frank (Leslie) 1910-1987 9-12R
Obituary 123
Faegre, Torvald 1941- 89-92
Faelten, Sharon 1950- CANR-23
Earlier sketch in CA 106
Faessler, Shirley 1921(?)- 106
Fagan, Brian M(urray) 1936- CANR-56
Earlier sketches in CA 41-44R, CANR-14, 31
Fagan, Cary 1957- 136
Fagan, Edward R(ichard) 1924- CANR-20
Earlier sketches in CA 9-12R, CANR-5
Fage, John Donnelly 1921- CANR-7
Earlier sketch in CA 5-8R
Fagen, Donald 1948- CLC 26
Fagen, Richard R. 1933- CANR-22
Earlier sketches in CA 17-20R, CANR-7
Fagen, Stanley Alan 1936- 102
Fager, Charles E(ugene) 1942- 21-24R
Fagerstrom, Stan 1923- 57-60
Fagg, Elizabeth
See Olds, Elizabeth Fagg
Fagg, John (Edwin) 1916- 81-84
Fagg, William Buller 1914- 102
Fagles, Robert 1933- 165
Brief entry 104
Fagley, Richard M(artin) 1910- 1-4R
Fagon, Alfred 1937-1986 Obituary 120
Fagothey, Austin 1901- CAP-1
Earlier sketch in CA 11-12
Fague, William Robert 1927- 109
Fagundo, Ana Maria 1938- 37-40R
See also DLB 134
Fagunwa, D(aniel) O(lorunfemi) 1910(?)-1963 Obituary 116
Fagyas, Maria 33-36R
Faherty, William B(arnaby) 1914- CANR-5
Earlier sketch in CA 5-8R
Fahey, David (Allen) 1948- 131
Fahey, Frank M(ichael) 1917- 101
Fahey, James C(harles) 1903-1974 Obituary 53-56
Fahlman, Clyde 1931- 161
Fahlstrom, Oyvind (Axel Christian) 1928-1976 Obituary 69-72
Fahmy, Ismail 1922-1997 133
Obituary 162
Fahnestock, Beatrice Beck 1899(?)-1980 Obituary 97-100
Fahs, Ivan J. 1932- 45-48
Fahs, Sophia Blanche Lyon 1876-1978 164
Obituary 77-80
See also SATA 102
Fahy, Christopher 1937- CANR-55
Earlier sketches in CA 69-72, CANR-11, 29
Faig, Kenneth W(alter), Jr. 1948- 154
Faigley, Lester 1947- 146

Failing, Patricia 1944- ... 151
Fain, Haskell 1926- ... 33-36R
Fain, Michael 1937- ... 139
Fain, Tyrus Gerard 1933- ... 104
Fainlight, Ruth (Esther) 1931- ... CANR-51
Earlier sketches in CA 17-20R, CANR-8, 26
Fainsod, Merle 1907-1972 ... CAP-1
Obituary ... 33-36R
Earlier sketch in CA 13-16
Fainstein, Norman Ira 1944- ... 102
Fainstein, Susan S. 1938- ... 93-96
Fainzilberg, Ilya Arnoldovich 1897-1937 ... 165
Brief entry ... 120
See also Ilf, Ilya
Fair, A. A.
See Gardner, Erle Stanley
Fair, Charles M. 1916- ... CANR-10
Earlier sketch in CA 13-16R
Fair, David 1952- ... 161
See also SATA 96
Fair, Harold L(loyd) 1924- ... 89-92
Fair, James 1898(?)-1984 Obituary ... 112
Fair, James R(utherford), Jr. 1920- ... CANR-34
Earlier sketch in CA 29-32R
Fair, Marvin L(uke) 1897(?)-1983 Obituary ... 110
Fair, Ray C(larence) 1942- ... 29-32R
Fair, Ronald L. 1932- ... CANR-25
Earlier sketch in CA 69-72
See also BW 1
See also CLC 18
See also DLB 33
Fair, Sylvia 1933- ... 69-72
See also SATA 13
Fairbairn, Ann
See Tait, Dorothy
Fairbairn, Douglas 1926- ... 33-36R
Fairbairn, Garry L. 1947- ... 77-80
Fairbairn, Helen
See Southard, Helen Fairbairn
Fairbairn, Ian J(ohn) 1933- ... 53-56
Fairbairn, Roger
See Carr, John Dickson
Fairbairns, Zoe (Ann) 1948- ... CANR-21
Earlier sketch in CA 103
See also CLC 32
Fairbank, Alfred John 1895-1982 ... CANR-6
Obituary ... 106
Earlier sketch in CA 5-8R
Fairbank, John K(ing) 1907-1991 ... CANR-3
Obituary ... 135
Earlier sketch in CA 1-4R
Fairbanks, Carol 1935- ... 69-72
Fairbanks, Henry G(eorge) 1914- Brief entry ... 112
Fairbrother, Nan 1913-1971 ... CANR-3
Obituary ... 33-36R
Earlier sketch in CA 5-8R
Fairburn, Eleanor 1928- ... CANR-8
Earlier sketch in CA 61-64
Fairchild, Hoxie Neale 1894-1973 ... 5-8R
Obituary ... 45-48
Fairchild, John B(urr) 1927- Brief entry ... 117
Fairchild, Louis W. 1901-1981 Obituary ... 105
Fairchild, William ... 73-76
Fairclough, Adam 1952- ... CANR-54
Earlier sketch in CA 127
Fairclough, Chris 1951- ... 112
Faire, Zabrina
See Stevenson, Florence
Fairfax, Ann
See Chesney, Marion
Fairfax, Beatrice
See Scarberry, Alma Sioux
Fairfax, Beatrice
See Manning, Marie
and McCarroll, Marion C(lyde)
Fairfax, Felix
See Gibson, Walter B(rown)
Fairfax, John 1930- ... 97-100
Fairfax, John 1937- ... 49-52
Fairfax, Warwick (Oswald) 1901-1987 Obituary ... 121
Fairfax-Blakeborough, Jack
See Fairfax-Blakeborough, John Freeman
Fairfax-Blakeborough, John Freeman
1883-1978(?) ... 102
Fairfax-Lucy, Brian (Fulke Cameron-Ramsay)
1898-1974 ... CAP-2
Earlier sketch in CA 29-32
See also SATA 6
See also SATA-Obit 26
Fairfield, Darrell
See Larkin, Rochelle
Fairfield, James G(lencairn) T(homson) 1926- ... 126
Fairfield, John
See Livingstone, Harrison Edward
Fairfield, John D. 1955- ... 148
Fairfield, Lesley 1949- ... 130
Fairfield, Leslie P(arke) 1941- Brief entry ... 107
Fairfield, Richard 1937- ... 41-44R
Fairfield, Roy P(hillip) 1918- ... 33-36R
Fairhall, David Keir 1934- ... 103
Fairholme, Elizabeth 1910- ... 97-100
Fairless, Caroline S. 1947- ... 105
Fairley, Barker 1887-1986 ... 1-4R
Obituary ... 121
Fairley, Irene R. 1940- ... 73-76
Fairley, James Stewart 1940- ... 102
Fairley, John (Alexander) 1939- ... 131
Fairley, M(ichael) C(harles) 1937- ... CANR-14
Earlier sketch in CA 37-40R
Fairley, Peter 1930- ... CANR-24
Earlier sketch in CA 29-32R
Fairlie, Gerard 1899-1983 Obituary ... 109
See also DLB 77
See also SATA-Obit 34
Fairlie, Henry (Jones) 1924-1990 ... 104
Obituary ... 131
Fairman, Charles 1897- ... 45-48
Fairman, Herbert Walter 1907-1982 ... 111
Obituary ... 108
Fairman, Honora C. 1927(?)-1978 Obituary ... 81-84
Fairman, Joan A(lexandra) 1935- ... 33-36R
See also SATA 10
Fairman, Paul W. 1916-1977 Obituary ... 114
Fairn, (Richard) Duncan 1906-1986 Obituary ... 119
Fairstein, Linda A. 1947(?)- ... 154
Fairweather, Digby 1946- ... CANR-58
Earlier sketch in CA 127
Fairweather, Eileen 1954- ... 125
Fairweather, Eugene Rathbone 1920- Brief entry ... 108
Fairweather, George W. 1921- ... 13-16R
Fairweather, Janet (Anne) 1945- ... 124
Fairweather, Sally (Hallberg) 1917- ... 112
Fairweather, Virginia 1922- ... 29-32R
Faison, S(amson) Lane, Jr. 1907- ... 89-92
Faissler, Margareta 1902- ... 5-8R
Fait, Hollis F. 1918- ... CANR-5
Earlier sketch in CA 1-4R
Faith, Barbara
See Covarrubias, Barbara Faith
Faith, (Richard) Mack 1944- ... 125
Faith, William Robert
See Fague, William Robert
Faithfull, Gail 1936- ... 57-60
See also SATA 8
Faithfull, Marianne 1946- ... 148
Faiz, Faiz Ahmad 1912(?)-1984 Obituary ... 115
Fakhry, Majid 1923- ... 29-32R
Fakinos, Aris 1935- ... 81-84
Falassi, Alessandro 1945- ... 105
Falb, Lewis W(illiam) 1935- ... 102
Falck, (Adrian) Colin 1934- ... 65-68
Falco, Edward 1948- ... 134
Falco, Gian
See Papini, Giovanni
Falco, Maria J(osephine) 1932- ... CANR-12
Earlier sketch in CA 61-64
Falcoff, Mark 1941- ... 65-68
Falcon
See Nestle, John Francis
Falcon, Richard
See Shapiro, Samuel
Falcon, Walter P(hillip) 1936- ... 126
Brief entry ... 109
Falcon, William D(yche) 1932- ... 17-20R
Falcon-Barker, Ted 1923- ... 25-28R
Falconer, A. F.
See Falconer, Alexander Frederick
Falconer, Alexander Frederick
1908-1987 Obituary ... 122
Falconer, Alun (?)-1973 Obituary ... 104
Falconer, James
See Kirkup, James
Falconer, Kenneth
See Kornbluth, C(yril) M.
Falconer, Lee N.
See May, Julian
Falconieri, John V(incent) 1920- ... 130
Falero, Frank, Jr. 1937- ... 37-40R
Fales, Dean Abner, Jr. 1925- Brief entry ... 110
Fales, Edward (Daniel, Jr.) 1906- ... 97-100
Falk, Avner 1943- ... 163
Falk, Candace 1947- ... 136
Falk, Charles J(ohn) 1899-1971 ... CAP-2
Earlier sketch in CA 23-24
Falk, Doris Virginia 1919- Brief entry ... 111
Falk, Elsa
See Escherich, Elsa Falk
Falk, Eugene H(annes) 1913- ... 116
Falk, Gerhard 1931- ... CANR-55
Earlier sketches in CA 117, CANR-39, 40
Falk, Harvey 1932- ... 127
Brief entry ... 112
Falk, I(sidore) S(ydney) 1899-1984 Obituary ... 114
Falk, Irving A. 1921- ... 21-24R
Falk, Kathryn 1940- ... CANR-20
Earlier sketch in CA 97-100
Interview in ... CANR-20
Falk, Lee
See Copper, Basil
Falk, Lee Harrison 1915- ... 97-100
Falk, Leslie A. 1915- ... 9-12R
Falk, Louis A. 1896(?)-1979 Obituary ... 85-88
Falk, Marvin W. 1943- ... 122
Falk, Minna Regina 1900-1983 Obituary ... 109
Falk, Pamela S. 1953- ... 122
Falk, Peter H(astings) 1950- ... 139
Falk, Quentin 1948- ... CANR-48
Earlier sketch in CA 122
Falk, Richard A(nderson) 1930- ... CANR-12
Earlier sketch in CA 5-8R
Falk, Robert 1914- ... 89-92
Falk, Roger (Salis) 1910- ... 65-68
Falk, S(tephen) J(ohn) 1942-1997 ... 124
Obituary ... 156
Falk, Signi Lenea 1906- ... 5-8R
Falk, Stanley L(awrence) 1927- ... CANR-2
Earlier sketch in CA 1-4R
Falk, Susan Meyers 1942- ... 117
Falk, Thomas H(einrich) 1935- ... 145
Falk, Toby
See Falk, S(tephen) J(ohn)
Falk, Ursula Adler ... 114
Falk, Ze'ev W(ilhelm) 1923- ... CANR-42
Earlier sketches in CA 21-24R, CANR-15
Falkender, Baroness Marcia
See Williams, Marcia
Falkingham, Jane (Cecelia) 1963- ... 144
Falkirk, Richard
See Lambert, Derek
Falkland, Samuel
See Heijermans, Herman
Falkner, Leonard 1900- ... 21-24R
See also SATA 12
Falkner, Murry (Charles) 1899- ... CAP-2
Earlier sketch in CA 23-24
Falk-Roenne, Arne 1920- ... CANR-14
Earlier sketch in CA 21-24R
Falkus, Hugh Edward Lance 1917-1996 ... 111
Obituary ... 151
Fall, Bernard B. 1926-1967 ... CANR-6
Obituary ... 25-28R
Earlier sketch in CA 1-4R
Fall, Frieda Kay 1913- ... 41-44R
Fall, Thomas
See Snow, Donald Clifford
Fallaci, Oriana 1930- ... CANR-58
Earlier sketches in CA 77-80, CANR-15
See also CLC 11, 110
See also MTCW 1
Fallada, Hans
See Ditzen, Rudolf
See also DLB 56
Fallaw, Wesner 1907- ... 1-4R
Faller, Kevin 1920- ... CANR-4
Earlier sketch in CA 53-56
Fallers, Lloyd A(shton, Jr.) 1925-1974 ... CANR-4
Obituary ... 49-52
Earlier sketch in CA 9-12R
Falley, Margaret Dickson 1898-1983 Obituary ... 110
Fallon, Carlos 1909- ... 41-44R
Fallon, Eileen Brydon 1954- ... 118
Fallon, Frederic (Michael) 1944-1970 ... 41-44R
Fallon, George
See Bingley, David Ernest
Fallon, Ivan (Gregory) 1944- ... 137
Fallon, Jack
See Fallon, John W(illiam)
Fallon, John W(illiam) 1924- ... 77-80
Fallon, Martin
See Patterson, Harry
Fallon, Padraic 1905-1974 ... 103
Obituary ... 89-92
Fallon, Peter 1951- ... 133
Brief entry ... 106
Fallon, Robert T(homas) 1927- ... 121
Fallowell, Duncan (Richard) 1948- ... 137
Fallows, James M(ackenzie) 1949- ... CANR-43
Earlier sketches in CA 45-48, CANR-2
Falls, C(harles) B(uckles) 1874-1960 Obituary ... 116
See also SATA 38
See also SATA-Brief 27
Falls, Cyril Bentham 1888- ... CAP-1
Earlier sketch in CA 13-14
Falls, Joe 1928- ... 77-80
Fallwell, Marshall Leigh, Jr. 1943- ... 69-72
Falola, Toyin 1953- ... 151
Falorp, Nelson P.
See Jones, Stephen (Phillip)
Falstein, Louis 1909- ... 97-100
See also SATA 37
Faltas Youssef, Edwar Kolta
See al-Kharrat, Edwar
Falter-Barns, Suzanne 1958- ... 141
Faludi, Susan 1959- ... 138
Faludy, George 1913- ... 21-24R
See also CLC 42
Faludy, Gyoergy
See Faludy, George
Falvey, Jack 1938- ... 122
Falwell, Jerry 1933- ... 102
Falzeder, Ernst 1955- ... 146
Fama, Eugene F. 1939- Brief entry ... 113
Famiglietti, Eugene Paul
1931(?)-1980 Obituary ... 97-100
Famularo, Joseph John 1922- ... CANR-4
Earlier sketch in CA 1-4R
Fan, Kuang Huan 1932- ... 21-24R
Fanburg, Walter H. 1936- Brief entry ... 114
Fancher, Betsy 1928- ... 143
See also DLBY 83
Fancher, Ewilda 1928- ... 61-64
Fancher, Raymond E(lwood), Jr. 1940- ... 69-72
Fancher, Robert T. 1954- ... 135
Fanchon, Lisa
See Floren, Lee
Fancutt, Walter 1911- ... CANR-12
Earlier sketches in CAP-1, CA 9-10
Fandel, John 1925- ... CANR-23
Earlier sketch in CA 69-72
Fane, Bron
See Fanthorpe, R(obert) Lionel
Fane, Julian Charles 1927- ... CANR-6
Earlier sketch in CA 13-16R
Fane, Violet 1843-1905 ... DLB 35
Fanelli, Sara 1969- ... SATA 89
Fang, Chaoying 1908(?)-1985 Obituary ... 116
Fang, Irving E. 1929- ... CANR-31
Earlier sketch in CA 49-52
Fang, Josephine (Maria) Riss 1922- ... 69-72
Fang, L. Z.
See Fang, Lizhi
Fang, Lizhi 1936- ... 135
Fanger, Donald (Lee) 1929- ... 13-16R
Fann, K(uang) T(ih) 1937- ... 61-64
Fann, William E(dwin) 1930- ... CANR-2
Earlier sketch in CA 49-52
Fannin, Allen 1939- ... 69-72
Fanning, Buckner 1926- ... 69-72
Fanning, Charles (Frederick, Jr.) 1942- ... 81-84
Fanning, Katherine 1927- ... DLB 127
Fanning, Leonard M(ulliken) 1888-1967 ... 5-8R
See also SATA 5
Fanning, Louis A(lbert) 1927- ... 69-72
Fanning, Michael 1942- ... 89-92
Fanning, Odom 1920- ... 53-56
Fanning, Richard (Ward) 1953- ... 152
Fanning, Robbie 1947- ... CANR-31
Earlier sketches in CA 77-80, CANR-14
Fanon, Frantz 1925-1961 ... 116
Obituary ... 89-92
See also BLC 2
See also BW 1
See also CLC 74
See also DAM MULT
Fanshawe, David 1942- ... 97-100
Fanshawe, Richard 1608-1666 ... DLB 126
Fant, Joseph Lewis III 1928- ... 13-16R
Fant, Louis J(udson), Jr. 1931- ... 37-40R
Fanta, J. Julius 1907- ... 33-36R
Fante, John (Thomas) 1911-1983 ... CANR-23
Obituary ... 109
Earlier sketch in CA 69-72
See also CLC 60
See also DLB 130
See also DLBY 83
Fantel, Hans 1922- ... CANR-31
Earlier sketch in CA 49-52
Fanthorpe, Patricia Alice 1938- ... CANR-14
Earlier sketch in CA 89-92
Fanthorpe, R(obert) Lionel 1935- ... CANR-32
Earlier sketches in CA 73-76, CANR-14
Fanthorpe, U(rsula) A(skham) 1929- ... 156
Fantini, Mario D. 1927(?)-1989 ... 77-80
Obituary ... 129
Fantoni, Barry (Ernest) 1940- ... 129
Faqih, Ahmed 1942- ... 154
Farabee, Barbara 1944- ... 57-60
Farace, Joe 1941- ... 162
Faraday, Ann 1935- ... 77-80
Faraday, M. M.
See Rorvik, David M(ichael)
Faraday, Robert
See Cassiday, Bruce (Bingham)
Faragher, John Mack 1945- ... 147
Brief entry ... 111
Farago, Ladislas 1906-1980 ... CANR-10
Obituary ... 102
Earlier sketch in CA 65-68
Farah, Caesar Elie 1929- ... 41-44R
Farah, Madelain 1934- ... 73-76
Farah, Nuruddin 1945- ... 106
See also BLC 2
See also BW 2
See also CLC 53
See also DAM MULT
See also DLB 125
Faralla, Dana 1909- ... 49-52
See also SATA 9
Faralla, Dorothy W.
See Faralla, Dana
Faramelli, Norman Joseph 1932- Brief entry ... 109
Farau, Alfred 1904-1972 Obituary ... 37-40R
Farb, Peter 1929-1980 ... CANR-12
Obituary ... 97-100
Earlier sketch in CA 13-16R
See also SATA 12
See also SATA-Obit 22
Farber, Bernard 1922- ... 21-24R
Farber, Daniel A. 1950- ... 128
Farber, Donald C. ... CANR-30
Earlier sketches in CA 29-32R, CANR-13
Farber, Edward (Rolke) 1914-1982 Obituary ... 110
Farber, Joseph C. 1903- ... 33-36R
Farber, Leslie Hillel 1912-1981 ... 110
Obituary ... 103
Farber, Marvin 1901-1980 ... CANR-42
Earlier sketch in CA 49-52
Farber, Norma 1909-1984 ... 102
Obituary ... 112
See also DLB 61
See also MAICYA
See also SATA 25, 75
See also SATA-Obit 38
Farber, Paul Lawrence 1944- ... 112
Farber, Seymour M(organ) 1912-1995 ... 57-60
Obituary ... 150
Farber, Stephen E. 1943- ... CANR-19
Earlier sketch in CA 103
Farber, Susan L. 1945- ... 106
Farber, Thomas (David) 1944- ... 103
Farberman, Harvey A(lan) 1939- ... CANR-35
Earlier sketch in CA 45-48
Farberow, Norman L(ouis) 1918- ... CANR-7
Earlier sketch in CA 17-20R
Farbman, Albert I. 1934- ... 145
Farca, Marie C. 1935- ... 37-40R
Farcau, Bruce 1951- ... 138
Farel, Conrad
See Bardens, Dennis (Conrad)
Farely, Alison
See Poland, Dorothy (Elizabeth Hayward)
Farer, Tom J. 1935- ... CANR-8
Earlier sketch in CA 17-20R
Farewell, Nina
See Cooper, Mae (Klein)
Fargis, Paul (McKenna) 1939- ... CANR-13
Earlier sketch in CA 21-24R
Fargo, Doone
See Norwood, Victor G(eorge) C(harles)
Fargo, Joe
See Rikhoff, James C.
Fargue, Leon-Paul 1876(?)-1947 Brief entry ... 109
See also TCLC 11
Farhi, Moris 1935- ... CANR-13
Earlier sketch in CA 77-80
Faria, A(nthony) J(ohn) 1944- ... CANR-40
Earlier sketches in CA 102, CANR-19
Farias, Victor 1940- ... 135
Faricy, Robert L(eo) 1926- ... CANR-34
Earlier sketches in CA 37-40R, CANR-15
Faridi, S. N.
See Faridi, Shah Nasiruddin Mohammad

Faridi, Shah Nasiruddin Mohammad 1929- . . 29-32R
Faries, Clyde J. 1928- 37-40R
Faries, David A(llan) 1938- 112
Farigoule, Louis
See Romains, Jules
Farina, John 1950- 114
Farina, Richard 1936(?)-1966 81-84
Obituary 25-28R
See also CLC 9
Faris, (Earl) Barry 1889-1966 Obituary 114
Faris, Robert E. L(ee) 1907- 17-20R
Faris, Wendy B(ush) 1945- 115
Farisani, Tshenuwani Simon 1947- 134
See also BW 2
Farish, Donald J(ames) 1942- 106
Farish, Margaret Kennedy 1918- 5-8R
Farish, Terry 1947- 137
See also SATA 82
Farjeon, (Eve) Annabel 1919- 53-56
See also SATA 11
Farjeon, Eleanor 1881-1965 . . . . . CAP-1
Earlier sketch in CA 11-12
See also CLR 34
See also DLB 160
See also MAICYA
See also SATA 2
Farkas, Emil 1946- CANR-32
Earlier sketch in CA 69-72
Farkas, George 1946- 163
Farkas, Philip (Francis) 1914-1992 . . . . . CANR-31
Earlier sketch in CA 49-52
Farley, Carol 1936- CANR-50
Earlier sketches in CA 21-24R, CANR-10, 25
See also SATA 4
Farley, (William) Edward 1929- 61-64
Farley, Eugene J. 1916- CANR-12
Earlier sketch in CA 33-36R
Farley, James A(loysius) 1888-1976 Obituary 65-68
Farley, Jean 1928- 21-24R
Farley, Jennie (Tiffany Towle) 1932- 132
Farley, Miriam Southwell
1907(?)-1975 Obituary 57-60
Farley, Rawle 1922- 45-48
Farley, Walter (Lorimer) 1915-1989 . . . . . CANR-29
Earlier sketches in CA 17-20R, CANR-8
See also CLC 17
See also DLB 22
See also JRDA
See also MAICYA
See also SATA 2, 43
Farley-Hills, David 1931- 73-76
Farlie, Barbara L(eitzow) 1936- 65-68
Farlow, James O(rville, Jr.) 1951- 142
See also SATA 75
Farlow, John King
See King-Farlow, John
Farmacevten
See Holm, Sven (Aage)
Farman Farmaian, Sattareh 1921- 142
Farmer, Hugh William 1908-1987 Obituary 123
Farmer, Albert J(ohn) 1894-1976 . . . . . 21-24R
Obituary 120
Farmer, Bernard James 1902- 5-8R
Farmer, Bertram Hughes 1916- 104
Farmer, Charles J(oseph) 1943- CANR-10
Earlier sketch in CA 57-60
Farmer, David Hugh 1923- CANR-54
Earlier sketch in CA 125
Farmer, Don 1938- 65-68
Farmer, Gary R(ay) 1923- 57-60
Farmer, Gene 1919-1972 Obituary 37-40R
Farmer, Herbert Henry 1892-1981(?) Obituary . . 102
Farmer, Kathleen 1946- CANR-10
Earlier sketch in CA 65-68
Farmer, Laurence 1895(?)-1976 Obituary 65-68
Farmer, Martha L(ouise) 1912- 21-24R
Farmer, Nancy 1941- 167
See also AAYA 26
See also SATA 79
Farmer, Norman K(ittrell, Jr.) 1934- 123
Farmer, Patti 1948- . . . . . SATA 79
Farmer, Penelope (Jane) 1939- CANR-37
Earlier sketches in CA 13-16R, CANR-9
See also CLR 8
See also DLB 161
See also JRDA
See also MAICYA
See also SAAS 22
See also SATA 40
See also SATA-Brief 39
Farmer, Peter 1950- . . . . . SATA 38
Farmer, Philip Jose 1918- CANR-35
Earlier sketches in CA 1-4R, CANR-4
See also CLC 1, 19
See also DLB 8
See also MTCW 1
See also SATA 93
Farmer, R. L.
See Lamont, Rosette C(lementine)
Farmer, Richard Neil 1928- CANR-8
Earlier sketch in CA 17-20R
Farmer, Robert Allen 1938- 21-24R
Farmer, William R(euben) 1921- CANR-49
Brief entry 109
Earlier sketch in CA 123
Farmer Jones
See Jones, Bryan L.
Farmiloe, Dorothy Alicia 1920- CANR-8
Earlier sketch in CA 61-64
Farnan, D(orothy) J(eanne-Therese) 1919- 130
Farnash, Hugh
See Luff, S(tanley) G(eorge) A(nthony)
Farndale, W(illiam) A(rthur) J(ames) 1916- . . . . .
CANR-11
Earlier sketch in CA 25-28R
Farner, Donald S(ankey) 1915- 53-56
Farnham, Burt
See Clifford, Harold B(urton)
Farnham, Emily 1912- 69-72
Farnham, Marynia F. 1900(?)-1979 Obituary . 85-88
Farnham, Thomas J(avery) 1938- CANR-4
Earlier sketch in CA 53-56
Farnie, D(ouglas) A(ntony) 1926- CANR-12
Earlier sketch in CA 73-76
Farnsworth, Bill 1958- . . . . . SATA 84
Farnsworth, Clyde A. 1908(?)-1984 Obituary . . . 112
Farnsworth, Dana (Lyda) 1905-1986 61-64
Obituary 119
Farnsworth, E(dward) Allan 1928- 13-16R
Farnsworth, James
See Pohle, Robert W(arren), Jr.
Farnsworth, Jerry 1895- CAP-1
Earlier sketch in CA 13-16
Farnsworth, Lee W(infield) 1932- 33-36R
Farnsworth, Paul Randolph 1899- CAP-2
Earlier sketch in CA 29-32
Farnsworth, Robert M. 1929- 53-56
Farnum, K. T.
See Rips, Ervine M(ilton)
Farnworth, Warren 1935- 93-96
Farny, Michael H(olt) 1934- 65-68
Faron, Fay 1949- 157
Faron, Louis C. 1923- 9-12R
Farquhar, Francis P(eloubet) 1887-1975 . . . . . CAP-1
Obituary 57-60
Earlier sketch in CA 19-20
Farquhar, George 1677-1707 . . . . . DAM DRAM
See also DLB 84
Farquhar, Margaret C(utting) 1905- 69-72
See also SATA 13
Farquharson, Alexander 1944- . . . . . SATA 46
Farquharson, Charlie
See Harron, Don(ald)
Farquharson, Martha
See Finley, Martha
Farr, Bill
See Farr, William T.
Farr, David M. L. 1922- 37-40R
Farr, Diana (Pullein-Thompson) CANR-20
Earlier sketches in CA 13-16R, CANR-7
See also Pullein-Thompson, Diana
See also SATA 82
Farr, Dorothy M(ary) 1905- 77-80
Farr, Douglas
See Gilford, C(harles) B(ernard)
Farr, Finis (King) 1904-1982 . . . . . CANR-1
Obituary 105
Earlier sketch in CA 1-4R
See also SATA 10
Farr, Hilary
See Foster, Jeannette Howard
Farr, John
See Webb, Jack (Randolph)
Farr, Jory 1952- 146
Farr, Judith 1937- CANR-12
Earlier sketch in CA 29-32R
Farr, Kenneth R(aymond) 1942- 73-76
Farr, Michael 1924- 29-32R
Farr, Roger C. 33-36R
Farr, Sidney Saylor 1932- 114
Farr, Walter Greene, Jr. 1925- Brief entry 106
Farr, William T. 1934-1987 Obituary 121
Farra, Madame E.
See Fawcett, F(rank) Dubrez
Farrand, Phil 1958- 148
Farrant, Leda 1927- 21-24R
Farrar, Frederic William 1831-1903 . . . . . DLB 163
Farrar, John C(hipman) 1896-1974 65-68
Obituary 53-56
Farrar, Lancelot Leighton, Jr. 1932- CANR-4
Earlier sketch in CA 53-56
Farrar, Larston Dawn 1915-1970 . . . . . 1-4R
Obituary 29-32R
Farrar, Margaret Petherbridge
1897-1984 Obituary 113
Farrar, Richard B(artlett), Jr. 1939- 65-68
Farrar, Ronald T(ruman) 1935- 33-36R
Farrar, Rowena Rutherford 1903- 108
Farrar, Susan Clement 1917- 101
See also SATA 33
Farrar-Hockley, Anthony Heritage 1924- 69-72
Farrell, Alan 1920- 13-16R
Farrell, Anne A. 1916- 25-28R
Farrell, B. A.
See Farrell, Brian Anthony
Farrell, Barry 1935(?)-1984 Obituary 114
Farrell, Ben
See Cebulash, Mel
Farrell, Brian
See Farrell, Brian Anthony
Farrell, Brian 1929- 135
Farrell, Brian Anthony 1912- 130
Farrell, Bryan (Henry) 1923- CANR-2
Earlier sketch in CA 49-52
Farrell, C(larence) Frederick, Jr. 1934- . . . CANR-48
Earlier sketch in CA 122
Farrell, Catharine
See O'Connor, Sister Mary Catharine
Farrell, Cliff 1899-1977 . . . . . CANR-64
Obituary 125
Earlier sketch in CA 65-68
Farrell, David
See Smith, Frederick E(screet)
Farrell, Desmond
See Organ, John
Farrell, Edith R(odgers) 1933- CANR-48
Earlier sketch in CA 122
Farrell, Edmund J(ames) 1927- 120
Farrell, Francis (Thomas) 1912-1983 Obituary . . 109
Farrell, Frank
See Farrell, Francis (Thomas)
Farrell, Gillian B. 140
Farrell, Harry (Guy) 1924- 139
Farrell, J(ames) G(ordon) 1935-1979 . . . . CANR-36
Obituary 89-92
Earlier sketch in CA 73-76
See also CLC 6
See also DLB 14
See also MTCW 1
Farrell, James T(homas) 1904-1979 . . . . . CANR-61
Obituary 89-92
Earlier sketches in CA 5-8R, CANR-9
See also CLC 1, 4, 8, 11, 66
See also DLB 4, 9, 86
See also DLBD 2
See also MTCW 1
See also SSC 28
Farrell, John J(oseph) 1934- Brief entry 110
Farrell, John Philip 1939- 102
Farrell, Kathleen (Amy) 1912- 5-8R
Farrell, Kirby 1942- 33-36R
Farrell, M. J.
See Keane, Mary Nesta (Skrine)
Farrell, Matthew Charles 1921- 49-52
Farrell, Melvin L(loyd) 1930- CANR-5
Earlier sketch in CA 13-16R
Farrell, Michael 1944- CANR-23
Earlier sketch in CA 69-72
Farrell, Patricia
See Zelver, Patricia (Farrell)
Farrell, Robert T(homas) 1938- 93-96
Farrell, Sally
See Odgers, Sally Farrell
Farrell, Sally
See Odgers, Sally Farrell
Farrell, Susan Caust 1944- 112
Farrell, Suzanne 1945(?)- 141
Farrell, Warren (Thomas) 1943- 146
Farrell, William E. 1936(?)-1985 Obituary 115
Farrelly, M(ark) John 1927- 13-16R
Farrelly, Peter (John) 1956- 127
Farren, David
See McFerran, Douglass David
Farren, Mick 1943- 156
Farren, Richard J.
See Betjeman, John
Farren, Richard M.
See Betjeman, John
Farrer, Claire R(afferty) 1936- CANR-51
Earlier sketches in CA 65-68, CANR-10, 26
Farrer, (Bryan) David 1906-1983 . . . . . 25-28R
Obituary 109
Farrer, Katharine Dorothy (Newton) 1911- 5-8R
Farrer, Keith Thomas Henry 1916- 110
Farrimond, John 1913- 102
Farrington, Benjamin 1891-1974 65-68
Obituary 53-56
See also SATA-Obit 20
Farrington, D. P.
See Farrington, David P.
Farrington, David P. 1944- 130
Farrington, (Mary) Elizabeth Pruett
1898-1984 Obituary 113
Farrington, (Roland) Gene 1931- 130
Farrington, S(elwyn) Kip, Jr. 1904-1983 73-76
Obituary 109
See also SATA 20
Farris, Jack 1921- 129
Farris, John 1936- CANR-72
Earlier sketch in CA 101
Farris, Martin T(heodore) 1925- CANR-11
Earlier sketch in CA 21-24R
Farris, Paul L(eonard) 1919- 9-12R
Farris, William Wayne 1951- 150
Farrison, William Edward 1902- 29-32R
Farriss, N(ancy) M(arguerite) 1938- 25-28R
Farrow, J.
See Fonarow, Jerry
Farrow, James S.
See Tubb, E(dwin) C(harles)
Farrow, Mia 1946- 166
Farson, Daniel (Negley) 1927-1997 . . . . . CANR-37
Obituary 162
Earlier sketches in CA 93-96, CANR-16
Farson, (James Scott) Negley
1890-1960 Obituary 93-96
Farstad, Arthur L(eonard) 1935- 109
Farthing, Alison 1936- 117
See also SATA 45
See also SATA-Brief 36
Farthing-Knight, Catherine 1933- 156
See also SATA 92
Farwell, Byron E. 1921- CANR-47
Earlier sketches in CA 13-16R, CANR-9
Farwell, George Michell 1911-1976 . . . . . 21-24R
Obituary 69-72
Farwell, Loring C(hapman) 1915- Brief entry . . . 111
Farzan, Massud 1936- 53-56
Fasana, Paul James 1933- CANR-14
Earlier sketch in CA 37-40R
Fasching, Darrell J. 1944- 145
Faschinger, Lilian 1950- 166
Fasel, George W(illiam) 1938- 21-24R
Fasick, Adele M(ongan) 1930- CANR-54
Earlier sketch in CA 125
Fasold, Ralph W(illiam August) 1940- 29-32R
Fasolt, Constantin 1951- 139
Fass, Paula S. 1947- CANR-66
Brief entry 112
Earlier sketch in CA 129
Fassbinder, Rainer Werner 1946-1982 . . . CANR-31
Obituary 106
Earlier sketch in CA 93-96
See also CLC 20
Fassett, James 1904-1986 49-52
Obituary 121
Fassett, John D. 1926- 157
Fassler, Joan (Grace) 1931- 61-64
See also SATA 11
Fassmann, Heinz 1955- 151
Fast, Barbara 1924- 104
Fast, Howard (Melvin) 1914- CANR-54
Earlier sketches in CA 1-4R, CANR-1, 33
Interview in CANR-33
See also CAAS 18
See also AAYA 16
See also CLC 23
See also DAM NOV
See also DLB 9
See also SATA 7
Fast, Jonathan (David) 1948- CANR-34
Earlier sketch in CA 77-80
Fast, Julius 1919- CANR-27
Earlier sketches in CA 25-28R, CANR-11
Fastlife
See Grogan, Emmett
Fasulo, Michael 1963- 150
See also SATA 83
Fatchen, Max 1920- CANR-53
Earlier sketches in CA 25-28R, CANR-11, 28
See also SAAS 20
See also SATA 20, 84
Fate, Terry 1949- 116
Fatemi, Nasrollah S(aifpour) 1910-1990 77-80
Obituary 131
Father Xavier
See Hurwood, Bernhardt J.
Fathy, Hassan 1900-1989 Obituary 130
Fatigati, (Frances) Evelyn 1948- 77-80
See also SATA 24
Fatio, Louise 1904- 37-40R
See also SATA 6
Fatjo, Thomas Joseph, Jr. 1940- 107
Fatouros, A(rghyrios) A. 1932- 13-16R
Fatout, Paul 1897- 21-24R
Fatt, Amelia 1943- 118
Faucher, Real 1940- 101
Faucher, W. Thomas 1945- 57-60
Faulcon, Robert
See Holdstock, Robert P.
Faulhaber, Charles Bailey 1941- 53-56
Faulhaber, Martha 1926- 33-36R
See also SATA 7
Faulk, Charles Johnson, Jr.
1916(?)-1990 Obituary 131
Faulk, John Henry 1913-1990 102
Obituary 131
Faulk, Odie B. 1933- CANR-14
Earlier sketch in CA 25-28R
Faulkes, Anthony 1937- 138
Faulkner, Alex 1905(?)-1983 Obituary 109
Faulkner, Anne Irvin 1906- CANR-2
Earlier sketch in CA 1-4R
See also SATA 23
Faulkner, Charles H. 1937- 25-28R
Faulkner, Christopher G(raham) 1942- 125
Faulkner, Edwin J. 1900(?)-1987 Obituary 121
Faulkner, Elsie 1905- 65-68
Faulkner, Frank
See Ellis, Edward S(ylvester)
Faulkner, Harold Underwood 1890-1968 . . . . . 1-4R
Obituary 103
Faulkner, Howard J. 1945- 135
Faulkner, John 1901-1963 . . . . . CANR-1
Earlier sketch in CA 1-4R
Faulkner, Joseph E. 1928- 45-48
Faulkner, Nancy
See Faulkner, Anne Irvin
Faulkner, Peter 1933- CANR-20
Earlier sketches in CA 5-8R, CANR-3
Faulkner, Ray (Nelson) 1906- 5-8R
Faulkner, Trader 1930- 102
Faulkner, Virginia (Louise) 1913-1980 . . . CANR-11
Earlier sketch in CA 65-68
Faulkner, (Herbert Winthrop) Waldron
1898-1979 93-96
Obituary 85-88
Faulkner, William (Cuthbert) 1897-1962 . . CANR-33
Earlier sketch in CA 81-84
See also AAYA 7
See also CDALB 1929-1941
See also CLC 1, 3, 6, 8, 9, 11, 14, 18, 28, 52, 68
See also DA
See also DAB
See also DAC
See also DAM MST, NOV
See also DLB 9, 11, 44, 102
See also DLBD 2
See also DLBY 86, 97
See also MTCW 1
See also SSC 1
See also WLC
Faulknor, Cliff(ord Vernon) 1913- CANR-51
Earlier sketches in CA 17-20R, CANR-8
See also SATA 86
Faulks, Neville 1908-1985 Obituary 118
Faulks, Sebastian 1953- CANR-58
Earlier sketch in CA 131
Faunce, Roland Cleo 1905- 1-4R
Faunce, William A(lden) 1928- 25-28R
Faunce-Brown, Daphne (Bridget) 1938- 115
Faupel, John F(rancis) 1906- 5-8R
Faure, Lucie 1908-1977 Obituary 73-76
Faure, William C(aldwell), Jr. 1949- 109
Faurot, Albert 1914- 77-80
Faurot, Jean H(iatt) 1911- 29-32R
Faurot, Jeannette 1943- 106
Faurot, Ruth Marie 1916- 85-88
Fauset, Arthur Huff 25-28R

Fauset, Jessie Redmon 1884(?)-1961 109
See also BLC 2
See also BW 1
See also CLC 19, 54
See also DAM MULT
See also DLB 51
Fausett, David 1950- 158
Fausold, Martin L. 1921- 21-24R
Fausset, Hugh I'Anson 1895-1965 Obituary .. 93-96
Faust, Clarence H(enry) 1901-1975 Obituary . 57-60
Faust, Drew Gilpin 1947- 110
Faust, Frederick (Schiller) 1892-1944(?) 152
Brief entry 108
See also DAM POP
See also TCLC 49
Faust, Irvin 1924- CANR-67
Earlier sketches in CA 33-36R, CANR-28
See also CLC 8
See also DLB 2, 28
See also DLBY 80
Faust, Jeff 1966- 167
Faust, John R. 1930- 151
Faust, Naomi F(lowe) 61-64
Fausti, Remo P(hilip) 1917- 41-44R
Fausto-Sterling, Anne 1944- 137
Fauth, Robert T. 1916- 1-4R
Fautsko, Timothy F(rank) 1945- 85-88
Faux, Marian 1945- CANR-14
Earlier sketch in CA 81-84
Fava, Sylvia Fleis 1927- 115
Faverty, Frederic Everett 1902-1981 45-48
Obituary 104
Favilla, Candice Lynn 1949- 139
Faville, David Ernest 1899-1970 .... 1-4R
Obituary 103
Favret, Andrew G. 1925- 17-20R
Favretti, Rudy J(ohn) 1932- CANR-4
Earlier sketch in CA 53-56
Fawcett, Brian 1906- 102
Fawcett, Chris 1950- 107
Fawcett, Clara Hallard 1887- CAP-1
Earlier sketch in CA 13-16
Fawcett, Claude W(eldon) 1911- 49-52
Fawcett, Edgar 1847-1904 .... DLB 202
Fawcett, F(rank) Dubrez 1891-1968 .... CAP-1
Earlier sketch in CA 9-10
Fawcett, J(ames) E(dmund) S(anford) 1913- 97-100
Fawcett, Ken(neth Richard) 1944- 104
Fawcett, Marion
See Sanderson, Sabina W(arren)
Fawcett, Millicent Garrett 1847-1929 .... DLB 190
Fawcett, Robin P(owell) 1937- 119
Fawcett, Roger Knowlton
1909-1979 Obituary 89-92
Fawcett, Ron
See Harrison, M(ichael) John
Fawcett, Webster
See Albert, Harold A.
Fawdry, Marguerite 1912- 135
Fawkes, Guy
See Benchley, Robert (Charles)
Fawkes, Richard (Brian) 1944- CANR-20
Earlier sketch in CA 103
Fax, Elton Clay 1909- CANR-43
Earlier sketches in CA 13-16R, CANR-15
See also BW 2
See also SATA 25
Faxon, Alicia Craig 1931- CANR-53
Earlier sketches in CA 69-72, CANR-29
Faxon, Arba D. 1895(?)-1975 Obituary 61-64
Faxon, Lavinia
See Russ, Lavinia (Faxon)
Fay, Allen 1934- 123
Brief entry 118
Fay, Erica
See Stopes, Marie (Charlotte) Carmichael
Fay, Erica
See Stonov, Natasha
Fay, Frederic L(eighton) 1890- CAP-2
Earlier sketch in CA 21-22
Fay, Gerard (Francis Arthur) 1913-1968 .... CAP-1
Earlier sketch in CA 13-16
Fay, Gordon S(haw) 1912- 53-56
Fay, Jim 1934- 145
Fay, John 1921- 57-60
Fay, Leo (Charles) 1920- 13-16R
Fay, Mary Helen
See Fagyas, Maria
Fay, Peter Ward 1924- 57-60
Fay, S(amuel) P(rescott), Jr. 1926- 89-92
Fay, Stanley
See Shulman, Fay Grissom Stanley
Fay, Stephen (Francis John) 1938- CANR-61
Earlier sketches in CA 25-28R, CANR-31
Fay, Theodore Sedgwick 1807-1898 .... DLB 202
Fay, Thomas A(rthur) 1927- 102
Faye, Jean Pierre 1925- 102
Fayer, Mischa Harry 1902-1977 .... CANR-6
Earlier sketch in CA 1-4R
Fayer, Steve 1935- 132
Fayerweather, John 1922- CANR-1
Earlier sketch in CA 1-4R
Fazakas, Ray 1932- 101
Fazakerley, George Raymond 1921- 13-16R
Fazal, M(uhammad) A(bul) 1939- 29-32R
Fazzano, Joseph E. 1929- 5-8R
Feagans, Lynne 1945- 117
Feagans, Raymond (John) 1953- 57-60
Feagin, Joe R(ichard) 1938- CANR-55
Earlier sketches in CA 37-40R, CANR-13, 46
Feagles, Anita M(acRae) 1927- CANR-4
Earlier sketch in CA 1-4R
See also SATA 9
Feagles, Elizabeth
See Day, Beth (Feagles)
Feague, Mildred H. 1915- 29-32R
See also SATA 14
Feal-Deibe, Carlos 1935- 37-40R
Fear, David E. 1941- 53-56
Fear, Richard Arthur 1909- 125
Fear Chanaidh
See Campbell, John Lorne
Fearing, Kenneth (Flexner) 1902-1961 ... CANR-59
Earlier sketch in CA 93-96
See also CLC 51
See also DLB 9
Fearn, John Russell 1908-1960 162
Fearnley-Whittingstall, Jane 1939- 139
Fearon, George Edward 1901- CAP-1
Earlier sketch in CA 9-10
Fearon, John D(aniel) 1920- 37-40R
Fearon, Peter (Shaun) 1942- 29-32R
Fears, Gerald 81-84
Feather, John 1947- CANR-48
Earlier sketch in CA 122
Feather, Leonard G(eoffrey) 1914-1994 61-64
Obituary 146
Feather, Norman 1904-1978 Obituary 111
Feather, Norman T(homas) 1930- 73-76
Featherstone, D.
See Warren, David
Featherstone, Helen 1944- 102
Featherstone, Joseph (Luke) 1940- 33-36R
Featherstonehaugh, Francis
See MacGregor, Alasdair Alpin (Douglas)
Feaver, George (Arthur) 1937- 29-32R
Feaver, J(ohn) Clayton 1911- CAP-2
Earlier sketch in CA 25-28
Feaver, Vicki 1943- 129
Feaver, William Andrew 1942- 103
February, Vernie A.
See February, Vernon Alexander
February, Vernon Alexander 1938- 129
Fecamps, Elise
See Creasey, John
Fecher, Charles A(dam) 1917- 81-84
Fecher, Constance
See Heaven, Constance
Fechter, Alyce Shinn 1909- CAP-1
Earlier sketch in CA 13-16
Fecit
See Barclay, Robert
Feck, Luke 1935- 69-72
Fedde, Norman A(ndreas) 1914- 5-8R
Fedden, Henry (Romilly) 1908- 9-12R
Fedden, Robin
See Fedden, Henry (Romilly)
Fedder, Edwin H(ersh) 1929- 37-40R
Fedder, Norman J(oseph) 1934- CANR-50
Earlier sketches in CA 21-24R, CANR-9, 25
Fedder, Ruth 1907- CANR-2
Earlier sketch in CA 5-8R
Feder, Bernard 1924- CANR-15
Earlier sketch in CA 33-36R
Feder, Chris Welles 1938- 149
See also SATA 81
Feder, Ernest 1913- 37-40R
Feder, Harriet K. 1928- .... SATA 73
Feder, Jane 1940- 93-96
Feder, Jose 1917- 105
Feder, Karah (Tal) 1920- 17-20R
Feder, Lillian 41-44R
Feder, Martin E(lliott) 1951- 145
Feder, Paula (Kurzband) 1935- 105
See also SATA 26
Feder, Robert Arthur 1909-1969 Obituary 110
See also SATA-Brief 35
Federbusch, Simon
See Federbush, Simon
Federbush, Arnold 1935- 104
Federbush, Simon 1892(?)-1969 Obituary 115
Federico, Ronald Charles 1941- 89-92
Federman, Raymond 1928- CANR-43
Earlier sketches in CA 17-20R, CANR-10
See also CAAS 8
See also CLC 6, 47
See also DLBY 80
Federoff, Alexander 1927(?)-1979 Obituary .. 89-92
Federspiel, J(uerg) F. 1931- 146
See also CLC 42
Fedin, Konstantin A(lexandrovich) 1892-1977 ......
CANR-28
Obituary 73-76
Earlier sketch in CA 81-84
Fedler, Fred 1940- 97-100
Fedoroff, Alexander 1927-1979 .... CANR-5
Earlier sketch in CA 1-4R
Fedoroff, Nina (V.) 1942- 143
Fedorov, Yevgeny Konstantinovich
1910-1981 Obituary 106
Fedorowicz, J(an) K(rzysztof) 1949- 130
Feduccia, (John) Alan 1943- 124
Fedyshyn, Oleh S(ylvester) 1928- 49-52
Fee, Elizabeth 1946- 126
Fee, Gordon D(onald) 1934- 117
Feegel, John R(ichard) 1932- CANR-9
Earlier sketch in CA 57-60
Feeley, Gregory 1955- 135
Feeley, Kathleen 1929- 33-36R
Feeley, Malcolm M(cCollum) 1942- 142
Brief entry 105
Feeley, Pat(ricia Falk) 1941- 81-84
Feelings, Muriel (Grey) 1938- 93-96
See also BW 1
See also CLR 5
See also MAICYA
See also SAAS 8
See also SATA 16
Feelings, Thomas 1933- CANR-25
Earlier sketch in CA 49-52
See also Feelings, Tom
See also BW 1
See also MAICYA
See also SATA 8
Feelings, Tom
See Feelings, Thomas
See also AAYA 25
See also CLR 5
See also SAAS 19
See also SATA 69
Feely, Terence John 1928- CANR-25
Earlier sketch in CA 106
Feenberg, Eugene 1906-1977 Obituary 73-76
Feeney, Leonard 1897-1978 81-84
Obituary 77-80
Feeney, Stephanie S(inger) 1939- 118
Feenstra, Henry John 1936- 37-40R
Feerick, John D(avid) 1936- 69-72
Fegan, Camilla 1939- 21-24R
Fegan, Patrick W. 1947- 111
Fegely, Thomas D(avid) 1941- 97-100
Fehl, Philipp P(inhas) 1920- 33-36R
Fehler, Gene 1940- .... SATA 74
Fehr, Howard Franklin 1901-1982 Obituary 106
Fehr, Richard 1920- 147
Fehren, Henry 1920- CANR-9
Earlier sketch in CA 21-24R
Fehrenbach, T(heodore) R(eed, Jr.) 1925- CANR-1
Earlier sketch in CA 1-4R
See also SATA 33
Fehrenbacher, Don E. 1920-1997 .... CANR-2
Obituary 163
Earlier sketch in CA 1-4R
Fehrman, Carl (Abraham Daniel) 1915- 133
Brief entry 113
Feibes, Walter 1928- 53-56
Feibleman, James K(ern) 1904- CANR-22
Earlier sketches in CA 5-8R, CANR-7
See also AITN 2
Feibleman, Peter S(teinam) 1930- 110
Brief entry 108
Interview in 110
Feiden, Karyn L. 1954- 140
Feider, Paul 1951- CANR-35
Earlier sketch in CA 114
Feied, Frederick (James) 1925- 13-16R
Feierman, Steven 1940- 53-56
Feifel, Herman 1915- 101
Feifer, George 1934- 148
Feiffer, Jules (Ralph) 1929- CANR-59
Earlier sketches in CA 17-20R, CANR-30
Interview in CANR-30
See also AAYA 3
See also CLC 2, 8, 64
See also DAM DRAM
See also DLB 7, 44
See also MTCW 1
See also SATA 8, 61
Feig, Barbara Krane 1937- 104
See also SATA 34
Feig, Barry 1948- 162
Feig, Douglas 1946- 114
Feige, Hermann Albert Otto Maximilian
See Traven, B.
Feigelson, Naomi
See Chase, Naomi Feigelson
Feigenbaum, Edward A(lbert) 1936- 134
Feigenbaum, Lawrence H. 1918- 25-28R
Feigert, Frank B(rook) 1937- CANR-19
Earlier sketches in CA 53-56, CANR-4
Feigl, Herbert 1902- CAP-1
Earlier sketch in CA 13-14
Feigon, Lee (Nathan) 1945- 117
Fei-Kan, Li
See Li Fei-kan
Feikema, Feike
See Manfred, Frederick (Feikema)
Feil, Hila 1942- 37-40R
See also SATA 12
Feild, Reshad 1934- CANR-25
Earlier sketch in CA 69-72
Feilding, Charles (Rudolph) 1902- CAP-2
Earlier sketch in CA 25-28
Feilen, John
See May, Julian
Feiler, Bruce 1964- 145
Feiler, Seymour 1919- 41-44R
Fein, Albert 1930-1989 115
Obituary 128
Fein, Ellen 159
Fein, Helen 1934- 110
Fein, Irving A(shley) 1911- 69-72
Fein, John M(orton) 1922- 120
Fein, Judith 1941- 107
Fein, Leah Gold 49-52
Fein, Leonard J. 1934- 13-16R
Fein, Rashi 1926- 122
Fein, Richard J(acob) 1929- 45-48
Feinberg, Abraham L. 1899-1986 .... 9-12R
Obituary 120
Feinberg, Barbara Jane 1938- CANR-45
Earlier sketches in CA 106, CANR-22
See also SATA 58
Feinberg, Barry (Vincent) 1938- 29-32R
Feinberg, Beatrice Cynthia Freeman 1915(?)-1988 .
CANR-29
Obituary 126
Earlier sketch in CA 81-84
Feinberg, Charles E. 1899-1988 .... DLB 187
See also DLBY 88
Feinberg, David B. 1956-1994 135
Obituary 147
See also CLC 59
Feinberg, Gerald 1933- CANR-12
Earlier sketch in CA 25-28R
Feinberg, Gloria (Granditer) 1923- Brief entry .. 109
Feinberg, Hilda 49-52
Feinberg, Joel 1926- CANR-45
Earlier sketches in CA 17-20R, CANR-22
Feinberg, Lawrence B(ernard) 1940- 73-76
Feinberg, Leonard 1914- CANR-2
Earlier sketch in CA 5-8R
Feinberg, Leslie 1949- 159
Feinberg, Mortimer R(obert) 1922- 102
Feinberg, Renee 1940- CANR-42
Earlier sketch in CA 112
Feinberg, Richard E. 1947- 158
Feinberg, Walter 1937- 57-60
Feinbloom, Deborah Heller 1940- 65-68
Feinbloom, Richard I. 1935- 135
Feind, Barthold 1678-1721 .... DLB 168
Feingold, Ben(jamin) F(ranklin) 1900-1982 .. 97-100
Obituary 106
Feingold, Eugene (Neil) 1931- CANR-22
Earlier sketch in CA 17-20R
Feingold, Henry L(eo) 1931- CANR-56
Earlier sketches in CA 29-32R, CANR-31
Feingold, Jessica 1910- CAP-2
Earlier sketch in CA 25-28
Feingold, Michael 1945- 89-92
Feingold, S. Norman 1914- CANR-56
Earlier sketches in CA 13-16R, CANR-13, 30
Feininger, Andreas (Bernhard Lyonel) 1906- ......
CANR-20
Earlier sketch in CA 85-88
Feininger, Lyonel 1871-1956 149
Feinman, Jeffrey 1943- CANR-10
Earlier sketch in CA 65-68
Feinsilver, Alexander 1910- 13-16R
Feinsilver, Lillian Mermin 1917- 29-32R
Feinsinger, Nathan Paul 1902-1983 Obituary ... 111
Feinstein, Alan (Shawn) 1931- 25-28R
Feinstein, David 1946- 135
Feinstein, Elaine 1930- CANR-68
Earlier sketches in CA 69-72, CANR-31
See also CAAS 1
See also CLC 36
See also DLB 14, 40
See also MTCW 1
Feinstein, George W(illiamson) 1913- 73-76
Feinstein, John 1956- 133
Feinstein, Lloyd L(eonard) 1941- 113
Feinstein, Moshe 1895-1986 Obituary 118
Feinstein, Otto 1930- 104
Feinstein, Roni 1954- 134
Feinstein, Sascha 1963- 165
Feinstein, Sherman C. 1923- CANR-7
Earlier sketch in CA 57-60
Feintuch, Burt H. 1949- 124
Feirstein, Bruce 1953- 108
Feirstein, Frederick 1940- CANR-1
Earlier sketch in CA 45-48
See also CAAS 11
Feis, Herbert 1893-1972 .... CAP-1
Obituary 33-36R
Earlier sketch in CA 9-10
Feis, Ruth (Stanley-Brown) 1892- CAP-2
Earlier sketch in CA 19-20
Feise, Ernst 1884-1966 .... CAP-2
Earlier sketch in CA 17-18
Feiss, Paul Louis 1875-1952 .... DLB 187
Feist, Aubrey (Noel Lydston) 1903- 41-44R
Feist, Gene 1930- 129
Feist, Raymond E(lias) 1945- 154
Feit, E(wald) Edward 1924- CANR-10
Earlier sketch in CA 5-8R
Feitel, Donald G. 1925(?)-1976 Obituary 65-68
Feith, Herbert 1930- CANR-47
Earlier sketch in CA 1-4R
Feiwel, George R(ichard) 1929- CANR-23
Earlier sketches in CA 17-20R, CANR-8
Feiwel, Raphael Joseph 1907-1985 129
Obituary 117
Fejes, Claire 1920- CANR-13
Earlier sketch in CA 21-24R
Fejes, Endre 1923- 25-28R
Fejto, Francois (Philippe) 1909- 29-32R
Fekete, John 1946- CANR-72
Earlier sketch in CA 129
Fekrat, M. Ali 1937- 45-48
Felber, Stanley B. 1932- 77-80
Feld, Bernard (David III) 1947- 125
Feld, Bernard T(aub) 1919- 104
Feld, Michael 1938- 33-36R
Feld, Rose Caroline 1895-1981 Obituary 105
Feld, Ross 1947- CANR-16
Earlier sketch in CA 33-36R
Feld, Werner (Joachim) 1910- CANR-24
Earlier sketches in CA 21-24R, CANR-8
Feldbaum, Eleanor G. 1935- 117
Feldberg, Michael 1943- 113
Feldenkrais, Moshe (Pinchas) 1904- 73-76
Felder, David W. 1945- 136
Felder, Paul
See Wellen, Edward (Paul)
Felder, Raoul Lionel 1934- 33-36R
Felderman, Eric 1944- CANR-46
Earlier sketch in CA 69-72
Feldhusen, John F. 1926- 141
Feldkamp, Fred 1915(?)-1981 Obituary 105
Feldkamp, Phyllis 102
Feldman, Abraham J(ehiel) 1893-1977 81-84
Obituary 73-76
Feldman, Alan 1945- CANR-13
Earlier sketch in CA 73-76
Feldman, Anne (Rodgers) 1939- 73-76
See also SATA 19
Feldman, Annette (Gerber) 1913-198(?) . CANR-34
Earlier sketch in CA 69-72

Feldman, Burton 1926- 33-36R
Feldman, Daniel L(ee) 1949- 131
Feldman, David Lewis 1951- 140
Feldman, Edmund Burke 1924- 33-36R
Feldman, Edwin B(arry) 1925- CANR-2
Earlier sketch in CA 5-8R
Feldman, Egal 1925- 125
Feldman, Elane 147
See also SATA 79
Feldman, Ellen (Bette) 1941- CANR-39
Earlier sketches in CA 97-100, CANR-18
Feldman, Gayle 1951- 146
Feldman, George J(ay) 1904- CAP-1
Earlier sketch in CA 13-14
Feldman, Gerald D(onald) 1937- CANR-52
Earlier sketches in CA 21-24R, CANR-9, 27
Feldman, Herbert (H. S.) 1910- 29-32R
Feldman, Irving (Mordecai) 1928- CANR-1
Earlier sketch in CA 1-4R
See also CLC 7
See also DLB 169
Feldman, Kenneth A. 1937- 29-32R
Feldman, Leon A(ryeh) 1921- CANR-16
Earlier sketch in CA 97-100
Feldman, Leonard 1927- 69-72
Feldman, Leslie AITN 1
Feldman, Louis H(arry) 1926- 53-56
Feldman, Lynne B. 1956- 138
Feldman, M(aurice) P(hilip) 1933- 41-44R
Feldman, Marty 1934(?)-1982 110
Obituary 108
Feldman, Paula R. 1948- 128
Feldman, Richard 1949- 128
Feldman, Robert A.
See Feldman, Robert Alan
Feldman, Robert Alan 1953- 123
Feldman, Ruth 1911- CANR-57
Earlier sketches in CA 106, CANR-31
Feldman, Ruth Duskin 1934- CANR-43
Earlier sketch in CA 119
Feldman, Samuel Nathan 1931- 25-28R
Feldman, Sandor S. 1891(?)-1973 Obituary 41-44R
Feldman, Saul D(aniel) 1943- 41-44R
Feldman, Sidney 1902(?)-1986 Obituary 121
Feldman, Silvia (Dash) 1928- 97-100
Feldman, Sol(omon) E. 1933- 25-28R
Feldman, Sophie 1930-1978 Obituary 108
Feldman, Stephen L. 1946-1990 Obituary 132
Feldmann, Susan Judith 1928-1969 Obituary 104
Feldmeir, Daryle M(atthew) 1923-1987 73-76
Obituary 122
Feldon, Leah 1944- 97-100
Feldstein, Martin S(tuart) 1939- 73-76
Feldstein, Paul J(oseph) 1933- 89-92
Feldstein, Stuart A(lan) 1948- 113
Feldt, Allan Gunnar 1932- 41-44R
Feldzamen, A(lvin) N(orman) 1931- 25-28R
Felheim, Marvin 1914- 1-4R
Felice, Cynthia 1942- CANR-56
Earlier sketch in CA 107
Felinto (Barbosa de Lima), Marilene 1957- 146
Felipe, Leon 1884-1968 DLB 108
Felix
See Vincent, Felix
Felix, Christopher
See McCargar, James (Goodrich)
Felix, David 1921- 45-48
Felix-Tchicaya, Gerald
See Tchicaya, Gerald Felix
Felkenes, George T(heodore) 1930- CANR-8
Earlier sketch in CA 57-60
Felker, Clay S(chuette) 1925- 73-76
Felker, Evelyn H. 1933- 57-60
Felker, Jere L. 1934- 21-24R
Felknor, Bruce L(ester) 1921- 21-24R
Fell, Alison 1944- 156
Fell, Barry
See Fell, H(oward) Barraclough
Fell, Derek (John) 1939- CANR-50
Earlier sketches in CA 108, CANR-25
Fell, H(oward) Barraclough 1917-1994 33-36R
Obituary 164
Fell, H. Barry
See Fell, H(oward) Barraclough
Fell, James E(dward), Jr. 1944- 107
Fell, John L(ouis) 1927- 53-56
Fell, Joseph P(hineas) III 1931- CANR-6
Earlier sketch in CA 13-16R
Fellig, Arthur H.
See Weegee
Fellig, Usher H.
See Weegee
Fellini, Federico 1920-1993 CANR-33
Obituary 143
Earlier sketch in CA 65-68
See also CLC 16, 85
Fellman, Gordon 1934- 53-56
Fellman, Michael (Dinion) 1943- 45-48
Fellmeth, Robert C(harles) 1945- CANR-2
Earlier sketch in CA 49-52
Fellner, William John 1905-1983 CANR-2
Obituary 110
Earlier sketch in CA 1-4R
Fellowes, Anne
See Mantle, Winifred (Langford)
Fellowes-Gordon, Ian (Douglas) 1921- CANR-10
Earlier sketch in CA 5-8R
Fellows, Brian John 1936- 25-28R
Fellows, Donald Keith 1920- 41-44R
Fellows, Hugh P. 1915- 37-40R
Fellows, Jay 1940- CANR-11
Earlier sketch in CA 61-64
Fellows, Lawrence (Perry) 1924- 49-52
Fellows, Malcolm Stuart 1924- 9-12R
Fellows, Muriel H. 53-56
See also SATA 10
Fellows, Otis (Edward) 1908-1993 CANR-1
Obituary 141
Earlier sketch in CA 1-4R
Fellows, Richard A(stley) 1947- CANR-47
Earlier sketch in CA 121
Felltham, Owen 1602(?)-1668 DLB 126, 151
Felman, Shoshana 162
Felmly, Lloyd McPherson 1894-1984 Obituary 112
Felperin, Howard (Michael) 1941- 136
Fels, Ludwig 1946- DLB 75
Fels, Rendigs 1917- 37-40R
Felsen, Henry Gregor 1916- CANR-1
Earlier sketch in CA 1-4R
See also CLC 17
See also SAAS 2
See also SATA 1
Felsenstein, Walter 1901-1975 Obituary 111
Felsenthal, Carol 1949- 108
Felsher, Howard D. 1927- 17-20R
Felske, Coerte V. W. 1960- 166
Felstein, Ivor 1933- 41-44R
Felstiner, L. John, Jr. 1936- 45-48
Felstiner, Mary Lowenthal 1941- 159
Felt, Jeremy P(ollard) 1930- 21-24R
Felt, Margaret Elley 1917- 9-12R
Felter, Emma K. (Schroeder) 1896- CAP-1
Earlier sketch in CA 13-16
Felton, Bruce 1946- 65-68
Felton, Cornelius Conway 1807-1862 DLB 1
Felton, Harold William 1902- CANR-1
Earlier sketch in CA 1-4R
See also SATA 1
Felton, John Richard 1917- 89-92
Felton, Ronald Oliver 1909- CANR-3
Earlier sketch in CA 9-12R
See also SATA 3
Felton, Sandra 1935- CANR-45
Earlier sketch in CA 120
Felts, Shirley 1934- SATA 33
Feltskog, E(lmer) N. 1935- 37-40R
Feltwell, John 1948- 142
Felver, Charles S(tanley) 1916- 33-36R
Felver, Chris 1946- 164
Femiano, Samuel D. 1932- 21-24R
Femina, Jerry Della
See Della Femina, Jerry
Fen, Elisaveta
See Jackson, Lydia
Fenady, Andrew J. 1928- CANR-13
Earlier sketch in CA 77-80
Fenander, Elliot W(atkins) 1938- 21-24R
Fenberg, Matilda 1888(?)-1977 Obituary 73-76
Fenby, Eric (William) 1906- 25-28R
Fendell, Bob 1925- 57-60
Fendelman, Helaine Woll 1942- 69-72
Fenderson, Lewis H., Jr. 1907-1983 106
Obituary 111
See also SATA 47
See also SATA-Obit 37
Fendrich, James Max 1938- 155
Fenelon, Fania 1918-1983 77-80
Obituary 111
Fenelon, Kevin G(erard) 1898-1983 73-76
Obituary 109
Feng, Chin
See Liu, Sydney (Chieh)
Feng, Jicai 1942- 146
Fenger, Henning Johannes Hauch 1921- 73-76
Fenical, Marlin Edward 1907-1983 Obituary 110
Fenichel, Carol Hansen 1935- 119
Fenichell, Stephen 1956- 108
Fenick, Barbara 1951- 118
Fenik, Bernard Carl 1934- 122
Fenin, George N(icolaievich) 1916- 9-12R
Fenlon, Dick 1930- 89-92
Fenlon, Paul Edward 1921- 13-16R
Fenn, Charles (Henry) 1907- 9-12R
Fenn, Dan H(untington), Jr. 1923- CANR-1
Earlier sketch in CA 1-4R
Fenn, Elizabeth A. 1959- 115
Fenn, Harry 1837-1911 DLB 188
Fenn, Henry Courtenay 1894-1978 Obituary 81-84
Fennario, David 1947- DLB 60
Fennell, Francis L(e Roy), Jr. 1942- CANR-39
Earlier sketch in CA 116
Fennell, John (Lister Illingworth) 1918-1992 CANR-19
Obituary 139
Earlier sketches in CA 1-4R, CANR-1
Fennell, William Oscar 1916- 101
Fennelly, Catherine 1918- 37-40R
Fennelly, John F(auntleroy) 1899-1974 Obituary 53-56
Fennelly, Parker W. 1891-1988 Obituary 125
Fennelly, Tony 1945- CANR-43
Earlier sketch in CA 119
Fennema, Owen Richard 1929- CANR-3
Earlier sketch in CA 49-52
Fenner, Carol (Elizabeth) 1929- CANR-57
Earlier sketches in CA 5-8R, CANR-3
See also SAAS 24
See also SATA 7, 89
Fenner, H(arry) Wolcott 1911-1972 CAP-2
Obituary 37-40R
Earlier sketch in CA 33-36
Fenner, James 1923- 37-40R
Fenner, James R.
See Tubb, E(dwin) C(harles)
Fenner, Kay Toy CAP-1
Earlier sketch in CA 9-10
Fenner, Mildred Sandison 1910- 33-36R
Fenner, Phyllis R(eid) 1899-1982 CANR-2
Obituary 106
Earlier sketch in CA 5-8R
See also SATA 1
See also SATA-Obit 29
Fenner, Theodore (Lincoln) 1919- 37-40R
Fennimore, Keith John 1917- 57-60
Fenno, Jack
See Calisher, Hortense
Fenno, Jenny 1765(?)-1803(?) DLB 200
Fenno, John 1751-1798 DLB 43
Fenno, R(ichard) Francis, Jr. 1926- 5-8R
Fenoglio, Beppe 1922-1963 DLB 177
Fensch, Edwin A. 1903- CAP-1
Earlier sketch in CA 13-16
Fensch, Thomas 1943- CANR-29
Earlier sketches in CA 25-28R, CANR-11
Fenster, Robert 1946- CANR-32
Earlier sketch in CA 113
Fenster, Valmai (Ruth) Kirkham 1939-1984 110
Obituary 114
Fensterheim, Herbert 1921- 112
Fenstermaker, J(oseph) Van 1933- 29-32R
Fenten, Barbara D(oris) 1935- CANR-5
Earlier sketch in CA 53-56
See also SATA 26
Fenten, D(onald) X. 1932- CANR-5
Earlier sketch in CA 33-36R
See also SATA 4
Fenton, Alexander 1929- 131
Fenton, Carroll Lane 1900-1969 CANR-6
Obituary 29-32R
Earlier sketch in CA 1-4R
See also SATA 5
Fenton, Clyde 1901-1982 Obituary 106
Fenton, Edward 1917-1995 CANR-34
Obituary 151
Earlier sketches in CA 9-12R, CANR-13
See also SATA 7
See also SATA-Obit 89
Fenton, Frank 1903-1971 Obituary 33-36R
Fenton, Freda
See Rowland, D(onald) S(ydney)
Fenton, James Martin 1949- 102
See also CLC 32
See also DLB 40
Fenton, John C(harles) 1921- CAP-1
Earlier sketch in CA 9-10
Fenton, John H(arold) 1921- 37-40R
Fenton, John Y(oung) 1933- 53-56
Fenton, Joseph Clifford 1906- 5-8R
Fenton, Julia
See Fenton, Robert L.
Fenton, Kate 1954- 141
Fenton, M(elville) Brockett 1943- 144
Fenton, Mildred Adams 1899- 77-80
See also SATA 21
Fenton, Robert L. 1929- 135
Fenton, Shane
See Stardust, Alvin
Fenton, Sophia Harvati 1914- 33-36R
Fenton, Thomas Patrick 1943- 89-92
Fenton, Thomas Trail 1930- 102
Fenton, William N(elson) 1908- 93-96
Fentress, John Simmons 1925(?)-1981 Obituary 104
Fenvessy, Stanley J(ohn) 1918- 106
Fenwick, Charles G(hequiere) 1880-1973 Obituary 41-44R
Fenwick, Kay
See Bean, Keith F(enwick)
Fenwick, (Ian Graham) Keith 1941- 102
Fenwick, Millicent Hammond 1910-1992 112
Obituary 139
Fenwick, Patti
See Grider, Dorothy
Fenwick, Sheridan 1942- 69-72
Fenwick-Owen, Roderic (Franklin Rawnsley) 1921- 129
Brief entry 111
Fenyvesi, Charles 1937- 102
Feola, Jose (Maria) 1926- 69-72
Feravolo, Rocco Vincent 1922- CANR-1
Earlier sketch in CA 1-4R
See also SATA 10
Ferazani, Larry 1938- 61-64
Ferber, Andrew 1935- 53-56
Ferber, Edna 1887-1968 CANR-68
Obituary 25-28R
Earlier sketch in CA 5-8R
See also AITN 1
See also CLC 18, 93
See also DLB 9, 28, 86
See also MTCW 1
See also SATA 7
Ferber, Ellen 1939- 102
Ferber, Robert 1922- 37-40R
Ferdinand, Theodore N(ichols) 1929- 21-24R
Ferdinand, Vallery III
See Salaam, Kalamu ya
Ferdon, Edwin N(elson), Jr. 1913- 21-24R
Ferejohn, John A(rthur) 1944- 53-56
Ferencz, Benjamin B(erell) 1920- CANR-19
Earlier sketch in CA 97-100
Fergus, Jan 1943- 125
Fergus, Patricia M(arguerita) 1918- 53-56
Ferguson, Alane 1957- 151
See also SATA 85
Ferguson, Alfred R(iggs) 1915-1974 CANR-6
Obituary 49-52
Earlier sketch in CA 1-4R
Ferguson, Annabelle Evelyn 1923- 102
Ferguson, Arthur B(owles) 1913- 5-8R
Ferguson, Bird
See Engh, M(ary) J(ane)
Ferguson, Bob
See Ferguson, Robert Bruce
Ferguson, Brad 1953- 166
Ferguson, C(harles) E(lmo) 1928-1972 17-20R
Obituary 134
Ferguson, Cecil 1931- SATA 45
Ferguson, Charles Albert 1921- CANR-46
Earlier sketch in CA 69-72
Ferguson, Charles Austin 1937- 121
Ferguson, Charles W. 1901-1987 13-16R
Obituary 124
Ferguson, Chris(topher Wilson) 1944- 57-60
Ferguson, Clarence Clyde, Jr. 1924-1983 CANR-6
Obituary 111
Earlier sketch in CA 5-8R
Ferguson, David L. 1930- 73-76
Ferguson, Donald N(ivison) 1882-1985 5-8R
Obituary 116
Ferguson, E(lmer) James 1917- 61-64
Ferguson, Everett 1933- 33-36R
Ferguson, Franklin C(ole) 1934- 69-72
Ferguson, Harry 1903-1980 Obituary 97-100
Ferguson, Helen
See Kavan, Anna
Ferguson, Howard 1908- CAP-1
Earlier sketch in CA 11-12
Ferguson, J(ohn) Halcro 1920-1968 1-4R
Obituary 103
Ferguson, James M(ilton) 1936- 21-24R
Ferguson, John 1921- CANR-25
Earlier sketches in CA 5-8R, CANR-8
Ferguson, John Henry 1907- 13-16R
Ferguson, Kathy E. 1950- 143
Ferguson, M(ilton) Carr, Jr. 1931- CANR-30
Earlier sketch in CA 49-52
Ferguson, M. J.
See Engh, M(ary) J(ane)
Ferguson, Margaret W(illiams) 1948- 112
Ferguson, Marilyn 1938- 114
Brief entry 110
Interview in 114
Ferguson, Mark W. J. 1955- 144
Ferguson, Mary Anne 1918- 77-80
Ferguson, Oliver W(atkins) 1924- 5-8R
Ferguson, Pamela 1943- 101
Ferguson, Peter R(oderick) I(nnes) 1933- CANR-3
Earlier sketch in CA 5-8R
Ferguson, R. Brian 1951- 155
Ferguson, Robert (Thomas) 1948- 135
Ferguson, Robert A. 1942- 131
Ferguson, Robert Bruce 1927- 69-72
See also SATA 13
Ferguson, Robert D(ouglas) 1921- 17-20R
Ferguson, Robert W(illiam) 1940- CANR-12
Earlier sketch in CA 61-64
Ferguson, Ronald 1939- 134
Ferguson, Rowena 1904- 85-88
Ferguson, Samuel 1810-1886 DLB 32
Ferguson, Sarah (Margaret) 1959- 135
See also SATA 66
Ferguson, Suzanne 1939- 57-60
Ferguson, Sybil (Rae) 1934- 129
Ferguson, Ted 1936- 65-68
Ferguson, Tom 1943- 107
Ferguson, Trevor 1947- CANR-40
Earlier sketch in CA 116
Ferguson, Walter (W.) 1930- 107
See also SATA 34
Ferguson, William (Rotch) 1943- CANR-33
Earlier sketch in CA 49-52
Ferguson, William M(cDonald) 1917- CANR-41
Earlier sketch in CA 117
Ferguson, William Scott 1875-1954 DLB 47
Fergusson, Adam 1932- Brief entry 112
Fergusson, Bernard Edward 1911-1980 CANR-7
Obituary 102
Earlier sketch in CA 9-12R
Fergusson, Bruce (Chandler) 1951- 154
Fergusson, Erna 1888-1964 CAP-1
Earlier sketch in CA 13-14
See also SATA 5
Fergusson, Francis (De Liesseline) 1904-1986 CANR-3
Obituary 121
Earlier sketch in CA 9-12R
Fergusson, Harvey 1890-1971 Obituary 33-36R
Fergusson, James 1904-1973 Obituary 104
Fergusson, Robert 1750-1774 DLB 109
Fergusson, Rosalind (Joyce) 1953- 117
Fergusson Hannay, Doris 1902(?)-1982 CANR-6
Obituary 107
Earlier sketch in CA 9-12R
See also DLB 191
Fericano, Paul 1951- CANR-29
Earlier sketches in CA 69-72, CANR-12
Ferkiss, Victor C(hristopher) 1925- 21-24R
Ferland, Albert 1872-1943 DLB 92
Ferland, Carol 1936- 102
Ferling, John E. 1940- 143
Ferling, Lawrence
See Ferlinghetti, Lawrence (Monsanto)
Ferlinghetti, Lawrence (Monsanto) 1919(?)- CANR-41
Earlier sketches in CA 5-8R, CANR-3
See also CDALB 1941-1968
See also CLC 2, 6, 10, 27, 111
See also DAM POET
See also DLB 5, 16
See also MTCW 1
See also PC 1
Ferlita, Ernest (Charles) 1927- CANR-54
Earlier sketches in CA 29-32R, CANR-11, 26
Ferm, Betty 1926- 21-24R
Ferm, Deane William 1927- CANR-13
Earlier sketch in CA 33-36R
Ferm, Max A(rnold) 1929- 116
Ferm, Robert Livingston 1931- 13-16R
Ferm, Vergilius (Ture Anselm) 1896-1974 9-12R
Obituary 49-52
Ferman, Edward L(ewis) 1937- 106
Ferman, Joseph W(olfe) 1906-1975 Obituary 104

Fermi, Enrico 1901-1954 157
Brief entry 115
Fermi, Laura 1907-1977 .... CANR-6
Earlier sketch in CA 1-4R
See also SATA 6
See also SATA-Obit 28
Fermi, Rachel 1964- 151
Fermor, Patrick Leigh
See Leigh Fermor, Patrick (Michael)
Fern, Alan M(axwell) 1930- CANR-12
Earlier sketch in CA 33-36R
Fern, Eugene A. 1919-1987 .... CANR-16
Obituary 123
Earlier sketch in CA 1-4R
See also SATA 10
See also SATA-Obit 54
Fern, Fanny
See Parton, Sara Payson Willis
Fernald, John (Bailey) 1905-1985 .... CAP-2
Obituary 115
Earlier sketch in CA 23-24
Fernandes, Eugenie 1943- .... SATA 77
Fernandez, Benedict J. (III) 1936- 85-88
Fernandez, Gladys Craven 1939- 106
Fernandez, Happy Craven
See Fernandez, Gladys Craven
Fernandez, James D. 1961- 139
Fernandez, James William 1930- CANR-23
Earlier sketch in CA 107
Fernandez, John P(eter) 1941- CANR-10
Earlier sketch in CA 65-68
Fernandez, Jose S(alvador)
1893-1967 Obituary 113
Fernandez, Joseph A. 1921- 37-40R
Fernandez, Julio A. 1936- 33-36R
Fernandez, Roberto G. 1951- CANR-68
Earlier sketch in CA 131
See also DAM MULT
See also HW
Fernandez, Vicente Garcia Huidobro
See Huidobro Fernandez, Vicente Garcia
Fernandez-Armesto, Felipe (Fermin Ricardo)
1950- 142
Fernandez de la Reguera, Ricardo 1914- . CANR-3
Earlier sketch in CA 5-8R
Fernandez-Marina, R(amon) 1909- 41-44R
Fernandez Mendez, E.
See Fernandez Mendez, Eugenio
Fernandez Mendez, Eugenio 1924- .... HW
Fernandez Moreno, Baldomero 1886-1950 .... HW
Fernandez Moreno, Cesar 1919- 131
See also HW
Fernandez Retamar, Roberto 1930- 131
See also HW
Fernandez-Shaw, Carlos M(anuel) 1924- 140
Fernando, Ajith 1948- 122
Fernando, Lloyd 1926- 77-80
Fernea, Elizabeth Warnock 1927- CANR-29
Earlier sketches in CA 13-16R, CANR-12
Fernea, Robert Alan 1932- CANR-29
Earlier sketch in CA 33-36R
Fernett, Gene 1924- 49-52
Fernie, Eric (Campbell) 1939- 119
Ferns, H(enry) S(tanley) 1913-1992 .... CANR-19
Obituary 137
Earlier sketches in CA 5-8R, CANR-4
Fernsworth, Lawrence
1893(?)-1977(?) Obituary 89-92
Ferracuti, Franco 1927- CANR-30
Earlier sketches in CA 25-28R, CANR-11
Ferrante, Don
See Gerbi, Antonello
Ferrante, Joan M(arguerite Aida) 1936- 85-88
Ferrar, Harold 1935- Brief entry 116
Ferrara, V(ernon) Peter 1912-1988 Obituary 127
Ferrari, Enzo 1898-1988 Obituary 126
Ferrari, R(onald) L(eslie) 1930- 135
Ferrarini, Elizabeth M. 1948- 124
Ferraro, Barbara 1943- 143
Ferraro, Gary P(aul) 1940- 89-92
Ferraro, Susan (Lyons) 1946- 148
Ferrars, E. X.
See Brown, Morna Doris
Ferrars, Elizabeth
See Brown, Morna Doris
See also DLB 87
Ferrat, Jacques Jean
See Merwin, Sam(uel Kimball), Jr.
Ferrater-Mora, Jose 1912- CANR-29
Earlier sketch in CA 1-4R
See also HW
Ferrato, Donna 1949- 147
Ferre, Frederick 1933- 13-16R
Ferre, Gustave A. 1918- 1-4R
Ferre, John P. 1956- 139
Ferre, Nels F(redrik) S(olomon) 1908-1971 . CAP-2
Earlier sketch in CA 29-32
Ferre, Rosario 1942- CANR-55
Earlier sketch in CA 131
See also DLB 145
See also HW
Ferree, Myra Marx 1949- 154
Ferreira de Castro, Jose Maria 1898-1974 102
Obituary 49-52
Ferrell, Frank 1940- 136
Ferrell, Mallory Hope 1935- CANR-56
Earlier sketches in CA 33-36R, CANR-13, 30
Ferrell, Nancy Warren 1932- 138
See also SATA 70
Ferrell, Robert H(ugh) 1921- CANR-22
Earlier sketches in CA 5-8R, CANR-6
Ferrell, Robert W(illingham) 1913- 13-16R
Ferreol, Marcel Auguste 1899-1974 97-100
Obituary 53-56
Ferrer, Aldo 1927- CANR-28
Earlier sketches in CA 25-28R, CANR-11
Ferrer, Gabriel (Francisco Victor) Miro
See Miro (Ferrer), Gabriel (Francisco Victor)
Ferrer, Gloria M. Pagan
See Pagan Ferrer, Gloria M.
Ferrer, Sister Vincent
See Doherty, Barbara
Ferreri, Marco 1928-1997 126
Obituary 158
Ferres, John H(oward) 1932- 41-44R
Ferridge, Philippa 1933- CANR-59
Earlier sketches in CA 102, CANR-18
Ferrier, Janet Mackay 1919- 9-12R
Ferrier, Lucy
See Penzler, Otto
Ferrier, Susan (Edmonstone) 1782-1854 .. DLB 116
Ferrigno, Robert 1948(?)- 140
See also CLC 65
Ferril, Thomas Hornsby 1896-1988 65-68
Obituary 127
Ferrill, Arther 1938- 129
Ferrini, Vincent 1913- 158
See also CAAS 24
See also DLB 48
Ferris, Helen Josephine 1890-1969 77-80
See also SATA 21
Ferris, James Cody CANR-27
Earlier sketches in CAP-2, CA 19-20
See also SATA 1
Ferris, Jean 1939- CANR-38
Earlier sketch in CA 116
See also SATA 56
See also SATA-Brief 50
Ferris, Jeri Chase 1937- 150
See also SATA 84
Ferris, John (Stephen) 1937- 146
Ferris, Norman (Bernard) 1931- 81-84
Ferris, Paul (Frederick) 1929- CANR-22
Earlier sketches in CA 5-8R, CANR-3
Ferris, Theodore P(arker)
1908-1972 Obituary 37-40R
Ferris, Timothy 1944- CANR-30
Earlier sketches in CA 69-72, CANR-11
Interview in CANR-30
Ferris, Tom
See Walker, Peter N.
Ferris, William (R.) 1942- 136
Ferriss, Abbott Lamoyne 1915- 29-32R
Ferritor, Daniel Edward 1939- CANR-35
Earlier sketch in CA 49-52
Ferro, Marc 1924- 77-80
Ferro, Robert (Michael) 1941-1988 .... 29-32R
Obituary 126
Ferron, Jacques 1921-1985 129
Brief entry 117
See also CLC 94
See also DAC
See also DLB 60
Ferron, Madeleine 1922- .... DLB 53
Ferrous, Vincent
See Ferrini, Vincent
Ferrucci, Franco 1936- .... DLB 196
Ferruolo, Stephen C(arl) 1949- 120
Ferry, Anne Davidson 1930- 17-20R
Ferry, Charles 1927- CANR-57
Earlier sketches in CA 97-100, CANR-16
See also CLR 34
See also SAAS 20
See also SATA 43, 92
Ferry, David (Russell) 1924- 13-16R
Ferry, W(illiam) Hawkins 1914(?)-1988 61-64
Obituary 124
Fersh, Seymour H. 1926- CANR-14
Earlier sketch in CA 37-40R
Ferster, C(harles) B(ohris) 1922-1981 97-100
Obituary 102
Ferster, Dorothy C(oben) 1922- 111
Ferster, Marilyn B(ender)
See Gilbert, Marilyn B(ender)
Ferullo, Dan 1948- 106
Feshbach, Murray 1929- 140
Feshbach, Norma Deitch 1926- CANR-8
Earlier sketch in CA 61-64
Feshbach, Seymour 1925- CANR-8
Earlier sketch in CA 37-40R
Fesler, James W(illiam) 1911- 21-24R
Fesperman, John (Thomas, Jr.) 1925- CANR-2
Earlier sketch in CA 5-8R
Fess, Philip E. 1931- 33-36R
Fessel, Murray 1927- 21-24R
Fessenden, Katherine 1896(?)-1974 Obituary 53-56
Fessenden, Seth A(rthur) 1903-1976 .... CANR-10
Earlier sketch in CA 17-20R
Fessenko, Tatiana (Sviatenko) 1915- 13-16R
Fessier, Michael 1905(?)-1988 Obituary 126
Fessler, Loren W. 1923- 9-12R
Fest, Joachim C. 1926- CANR-47
Earlier sketch in CA 49-52
Fest, Thorrel B(rooks) 1910- CAP-1
Earlier sketch in CA 13-16
Festa Campanile, Pasquale 1927-1986 162
Obituary 118
Festa-McCormick, Diana 117
Festinger, Leon 1919-1989 .... CANR-31
Obituary 127
Earlier sketch in CA 1-4R
Fetherling, Dale 1941- 77-80
Fetler, Andrew 1925- 13-16R
Fetridge, William Harrison 1906-1989 73-76
Obituary 129
Fetros, John G. 1932- 57-60
Fetscher, Iring 1922- CANR-12
Earlier sketch in CA 69-72
Fettamen, Ann
See Hoffman, Anita
Fetter, Elizabeth Head 1904-1973 .... 5-8R
Obituary 41-44R
Fetter, Frank Whitson 1899-1991 106
Obituary 135
Fetter, Richard (Leland) 1943- CANR-15
Earlier sketch in CA 89-92
Fetterley, Judith 1938- Brief entry 113
Fetterman, Elsie 1927- 97-100
Fetterman, John (Davis) 1920-1975 93-96
Obituary 61-64
Fettig, Art(hur John) 1929- CANR-53
Earlier sketches in CA 73-76, CANR-13, 29
Fetz, Ingrid 1915- .... SATA 30
Fetzer, John F(rancis) 1931- 61-64
Feucht, Oscar E(mil) 1895- 103
Feuchtersleben, Ernst Freiherr von 1797-1848 . DLB 133
Feuchtwanger, E(dgar) J(oseph) 1924- .. CANR-11
Earlier sketch in CA 69-72
Feuchtwanger, Lion 1884-1958 Brief entry 104
See also DLB 66
See also TCLC 3
Feuer, Avrohom Chaim 1946- CANR-32
Earlier sketch in CA 113
Feuer, Kathryn Beliveau 1926-1992 102
Obituary 137
Feuer, Lewis S(amuel) 1912- CANR-3
Earlier sketch in CA 5-8R
Feuerbach, Ludwig 1804-1872 .... DLB 133
Feuerlicht, Ignace CAP-2
Earlier sketch in CA 33-36
Feuerlicht, Roberta Strauss 1931-1991 .... 17-20R
Obituary 135
Feuerstein, Georg 1947- CANR-49
Earlier sketch in CA 123
Feuerstein, Phyllis A. 1930- 105
Feuerwerger, Marvin C(harles) 1950- 104
Feuerwerker, Albert 1927- CANR-8
Earlier sketch in CA 21-24R
Feuillet, Octave 1821-1890 .... DLB 192
Feulner, Edwin J(ohn), Jr. 1941- 115
Feulner, Patricia N(ancy) 1946- 105
Feur, D. C.
See Stahl, Fred Alan
Feurey, Benita S. 1940(?)-1989 Obituary 129
Fewster, Kevin (John) 1953- 125
Fey, Harold E(dward) 1898-1990 .... 17-20R
Obituary 130
Feydeau, Georges (Leon Jules Marie)
1862-1921 152
Brief entry 113
See also DAM DRAM
See also DLB 192
See also TCLC 22
Feydy, Anne Lindbergh
See Sapieyevski, Anne Lindbergh
See also SATA-Brief 32
Feyerabend, Paul K(arl) 1924-1994 150
Feynman, R. P.
See Feynman, Richard Phillips
Feynman, Richard
See Feynman, Richard Phillips
Feynman, Richard P.
See Feynman, Richard Phillips
See also BEST 89:3
Feynman, Richard Phillips 1918-1988 129
Obituary 125
Brief entry 119
See also Feynman, Richard P.
See also MTCW 1
Fezler, William 1945- CANR-48
Earlier sketch in CA 122
Ffinch, Michael 1934- 137
ffolkes
See Davis, Brian
Ffolkes, Michael
See Davis, Brian
ffolliott, Rosemary 1934- 97-100
ffrench-Beytagh, Gonville (Aubie) 1912- 103
ffrench Blake, Neil (St. John) 1940- 69-72
ffrench Blake, Robert L(ifford) V(alentine)
1913- 61-64
Fiacc, Padraic
See O'Connor, Patrick Joseph
Fialka, John J. 1938- CANR-60
Earlier sketch in CA 139
Fialkowski, Barbara 1946- 77-80
Fiammenghi, Gioia 1929- .... SATA 9, 66
Fiandt, Mary K. 1914- 89-92
Fiarotta, Noel
See Ficarotta, Noel
See also SATA 15
Fiarotta, Phyllis
See Ficarotta, Phyllis
See also SATA 15
Fiber, Alan 102
Ficarotta, Noel 1944- CANR-11
Earlier sketch in CA 69-72
See also Fiarotta, Noel
Ficarotta, Phyllis 1942- CANR-11
Earlier sketch in CA 69-72
See also Fiarotta, Phyllis
Fichte, Johann Gottlieb 1762-1814 .... DLB 90
Fichtelius, Karl-Erik 1924- 53-56
Fichter, Andrew J(ohn) 1945- 117
Fichter, George S. 1922- CANR-23
Earlier sketches in CA 17-20R, CANR-7
See also SATA 7
Fichter, Joseph (H.) 1908-1994 .... CANR-41
Obituary 144
Earlier sketches in CA 1-4R, CANR-4, 19
Fick, Carl 1918- 167
Ficke, Arthur Davison 1883-1945 .... DLB 54
Ficken, Frederick A(rthur)
1910-1978 Obituary 81-84
Ficker, Victor B. 1937- CANR-13
Earlier sketch in CA 33-36R
Fickert, Kurt J(on) 1920- CANR-57
Earlier sketches in CA 37-40R, CANR-14, 31
Fickett, Harold L., Jr. 1918- 13-16R
Fickett, Lewis P., Jr. 1926- 21-24R
Fickle, James Edward 1939- 106
Fickling, Forrest E. 1925-1998 .... 5-8R
Obituary 166
Fickling, G. G.
See Fickling, Forrest E.
Ficowski, Jerzy 1924- 154
Fidelio
See Hunt, Edgar H(ubert)
Fidler, James M. 1900-1988 Obituary 126
Fidler, Jimmie
See Fidler, James M.
Fidler, Kathleen (Annie) 1899-1980 .... CANR-20
Obituary 117
Earlier sketch in CA 25-28R
See also SATA 3, 87
See also SATA-Obit 45
Fido, Martin (Austin) 1939- 159
Fidrych, Mark 1954- Brief entry 112
Fie, Jacquelyn Joyce 1937- 57-60
Fiedel, Stuart J(ay) 1952- 128
Fiedeler, Hans
See Doeblin, Alfred
Fiedler, Fred E(dward) 1922- 21-24R
Fiedler, Jean(nette Feldman) CANR-11
Earlier sketch in CA 29-32R
See also SATA 4
Fiedler, Johanna 1946- 153
Fiedler, Leslie A(aron) 1917- CANR-63
Earlier sketches in CA 9-12R, CANR-7
See also CLC 4, 13, 24
See also DLB 28, 67
See also MTCW 1
Fiedler, Lois (Wagner) 1928- 17-20R
Fieg, Victor P. 1924- 106
Field, Adelaide (Anderson) 1916- 106
Field, Andrew 1938- CANR-25
Earlier sketch in CA 97-100
See also CLC 44
Field, Arthur J(ordan) 1927-1975 .... 33-36R
Field, Barbara 1935- 110
Field, Carol 1940- 113
Field, Charles
See Rowland, D(onald) S(ydney)
Field, Daniel 1938- 65-68
Field, David (McLucas) 1944- 133
Field, David D(udley) 1918- 73-76
Field, Dawn Stewart 1940- 57-60
Field, Dick 1912- 57-60
Field, Dorothy 1944- 163
See also SATA 97
Field, Edward 1924- CANR-10
Earlier sketch in CA 13-16R
See also CAAS 27
See also DLB 105
See also SATA 8
Field, Eleanor S. 1932- 122
Field, Elinor Whitney 1889-1980 Obituary 109
See also SATA-Obit 28
Field, Ernest R. 1925- 5-8R
Field, Eugene 1850-1895 .... DLB 23, 42, 140
See also DLBD 13
See also MAICYA
See also SATA 16
Field, Frances Fox 1913(?)-1977 Obituary 69-72
Field, Frank 1936- 21-24R
Field, Frank Chester
See Robertson, Frank C(hester)
Field, Frank McCoy 1887-1978 45-48
Obituary 103
Field, Frederick V.
See Field, Frederick Vanderbilt
Field, Frederick Vanderbilt 1905- 130
Field, G(eorge) W(allis) 1914- 37-40R
Field, Gans T.
See Wellman, Manly Wade
Field, George B(rooks) 1929- 101
Field, Gordon Lawrence 1939- 17-20R
Field, Harry
See Field, Henry
Field, Hartry H(amlin) 1946- CANR-52
Earlier sketch in CA 124
Field, Hazel E(lizabeth) 1891-(?) CAP-1
Earlier sketch in CA 19-20
Field, Henry 1902-1986 69-72
Obituary 118
Field, Hermann Haviland 1910- 135
Field, Irving M(edcraft) 1934- 25-28R
Field, James A(lfred), Jr. 1916-1996 .... 25-28R
Obituary 152
Field, Joanna
See Milner, Marion (Blackett)
Field, John 1545(?)-1588 .... DLB 167
Field, John (Leslie) 1910- 33-36R
Field, John P(aul) 1936- 37-40R
Field, Joyce W(olf) 1932- 29-32R
Field, Leslie A. 1926- 29-32R
Field, Mark G(eorge) 1923- 37-40R
Field, Marshall III 1893-1956 .... DLB 127
Field, Marshall IV 1916-1965 .... DLB 127
Field, Marshall V 1941- .... DLB 127
Field, Michael 1915-1971 Obituary 29-32R
See also TCLC 43
Field, Minna (Kagan) 25-28R
Field, Nathan 1587-1620(?) .... DLB 58
Field, Penelope
See Giberson, Dorothy (Dodds)
Field, Peter
See Drago, Harry Sinclair
and Hobson, Laura Z(ametkin)
Field, Phyllis Frances 1946- 107

Field, Rachel (Lyman) 1894-1942 137
Brief entry 109
See also CLR 21
See also DLB 9, 22
See also MAICYA
See also SATA 15
Field, Stanley 1911- CANR-9
Earlier sketch in CA 21-24R
Field, Thomas P(arry) 1914- 9-12R
Field, Walter S(herman) 1899- 49-52
Fielden, Charlotte 93-96
Fielden, T(homas) P(erceval) 1882- 5-8R
Fielder, Mildred (Craig) 1913- CANR-10
Earlier sketch in CA 13-16R
Fielding, A. W.
See Wallace, Alexander Fielding
Fielding, Daphne Winifred Louise 1904-1997 . 9-12R
Obituary 163
Fielding, G(ordon) J. 1934- 97-100
Fielding, Gabriel
See Barnsley, Alan Gabriel
Fielding, Henry 1707-1754 ......CDBLB 1660-1789
See also DA
See also DAB
See also DAC
See also DAM DRAM, MST, NOV
See also DLB 39, 84, 101
See also WLC
Fielding, Hubert
See Schonfield, Hugh J(oseph)
Fielding, Joy 1945- CANR-43
Earlier sketches in CA 49-52, CANR-2
Fielding, Nancy (Parker) 1913-1983 Obituary ...111
Brief entry 108
Fielding, Nigel G(oodwin) 1950- 131
Fielding, Raymond E. 1931- CANR-8
Earlier sketch in CA 17-20R
Fielding, Sarah 1710-1768 ....DLB 39
Fielding, Temple (Hornaday) 1913-1983 . CANR-14
Obituary 109
Earlier sketch in CA 21-24R
Fielding, Waldo L. 1921- 45-48
Fielding, William J(ohn) 1886-1973 ....13-16R
Obituary 134
Fielding, Xan
See Wallace, Alexander Fielding
Fields, Alan
See Duprey, Richard A(llen)
Fields, Arthur C. 1926(?)-1974 Obituary 49-52
Fields, Beverly 1917- 49-52
Fields, Debbi
See Fields, Debra J.
Fields, Debra J. 1956- 140
Fields, Dorothy 1905-1974 93-96
Obituary 49-52
Fields, Gracie 1898-1979 Obituary 112
Fields, Howard K(enneth) 1938- 81-84
Fields, James Thomas 1817-1881 ....DLB 1
Fields, Jeff ....AITN 2
Fields, Jennie 1953- 147
Fields, Joseph 1895-1966 Obituary 25-28R
Fields, Julia 1938- CANR-26
Earlier sketch in CA 73-76
See also BW 1
See also DLB 41
Fields, Kenneth (Wayne) 1939- Brief entry 110
Fields, L. Marc 1955- 146
Fields, Morgan
See Morgan, J(ill) M(eredith)
Fields, Nora 49-52
Fields, Rick 1942- CANR-27
Earlier sketches in CA 65-68, CANR-9
Fields, Rona M(arcia) 1934- 69-72
Fields, Scott (Gary) 1956- 134
Fields, Suzanne 1936- 129
Fields, Totie
See Feldman, Sophie
Fields, Victor A(lexander) 1901- 5-8R
Fields, W. C. 1880-1946 ....DLB 44
See also TCLC 80
Fields, Wayne 1942- 134
Fields, Wilbert J. 1917- 13-16R
Fields, Wilmer Clemont 1922- Brief entry 106
Fieler, Frank B(ernard) 1933- 41-44R
Fiene, Donald M(ark) 1930- 69-72
Fiene, Ernest 1894-1965 ....CAP-1
Earlier sketch in CA 13-14
Fiennes, Jini
See Lash, Jennifer
Fiennes, Ranulph (Twisleton-Wykeham) 1944- .....
CANR-48
Earlier sketches in CA 45-48, CANR-3, 20
Fiennes, Richard
See Twisleton-Wykeham-Fiennes, Richard Nathaniel
Fienup-Riordan, Ann 1948- 148
Fiering, Norman Sanford 1935- 105
Fierro, Robert Daniel 1945- 109
Fierstein, Harvey (Forbes) 1954- 129
Brief entry 123
See also CLC 33
See also DAM DRAM, POP
Fieser, Louis F(rederick) 1899-1977 157
Obituary 73-76
Fieser, Max E(ugene) 1930- 13-16R
Fiester, Mark (Lafayette) 1907- 65-68
Fieve, Ronald R(obert) 1930- Brief entry 107
Fife, Austin E(dwin) 1909- 53-56
Fife, Dale (Odile Hollerbach) 1901- CANR-19
Earlier sketch in CA 85-88
See also SATA 18
Fife, Robert Oldham 1918- 37-40R
Fifer, Elizabeth 1944- 139
Fifer, Ken 1947- 104
Fifield, Christopher G(eorge) 1945- 130
Fifield, William 1916-1987 ....CANR-9
Obituary 124
Earlier sketch in CA 13-16R
Fifo, Ray
See Glazar, Bob
Fifoot, Cecil Herbert Stuart
1899-1975 Obituary 107
Figes, Eva 1932- CANR-44
Earlier sketches in CA 53-56, CANR-4
See also CLC 31
See also DLB 14
Figes, Orlando (G.) 1959- 163
Figgie, Harry E., Jr. 1923- 143
Figgins, Ross 1936- CANR-11
Earlier sketch in CA 69-72
Figh, Margaret Gillis 1896- CAP-2
Earlier sketch in CA 29-32
Fighter Pilot, A
See Johnston, H(ugh) A(nthony) S(tephen)
Figler, Howard Elliot 1939- 127
Brief entry 109
Figler, Stephen K(enneth) 1942- 117
Figley, Marty Rhodes 1948- 152
See also SATA 88
Figueira, Thomas J. 1948- 142
Figuera, Angela 1902-1984 ....DLB 108
Figueroa, John
See Figueroa, John J(oseph Maria)
Figueroa, John J(oseph Maria) 1920- 125
Brief entry 108
See also BW 2
Figueroa, John L(ewis) 1936- 65-68
Figueroa (Mercado), Loida
See Figueroa-Mercado, Loida
See also HW
Figueroa, Pablo 1938- 61-64
See also HW
See also SATA 9
Figueroa-Chapel, Ramon 1935- 45-48
Figueroa-Mercado, Loida 1917- CANR-9
Earlier sketches in CAP-28, CA 57-60
See also Figueroa (Mercado), Loida
Figurito, Joseph 1922- 29-32R
Fijan, Carol 1918- 53-56
See also SATA 12
Fikes, Jay C(ourtney) 1951- 152
Fikso, Eunice Cleland 1927- 5-8R
Filas, Francis L(ad) 1915-1985 ....CANR-2
Obituary 115
Earlier sketch in CA 5-8R
Filby, P(ercy) William 1911- CANR-27
Earlier sketches in CA 9-12R, CANR-3
Filderman, Diane E(lizabeth) 1959- 151
See also SATA 87
Filene, Peter G. 1940- 21-24R
Filep, Robert Thomas 1931- CANR-19
Earlier sketches in CA 45-48, CANR-1
Filey, Mike 166
Filicchia, Ralph 1935- 103
Filip, Raymond 1950- 113
Filipacchi, Amanda 1967- 150
Filipovic, Zlata 1980- 148
Filipovitch, Anthony J(oseph) 1947- 102
Filippo, Eduardo de
See de Filippo, Eduardo
Fill, Joseph Herbert 1924- Brief entry 112
Filler, Louis 1912- CANR-2
Earlier sketch in CA 1-4R
Fillmer, Henry Thompson 1932- 21-24R
Fillmore, Lowell 1882- CAP-1
Earlier sketch in CA 9-10
Fillmore, Parker H(oysted) 1878-1944 ....YABC 1
Fillmore, Roscoe Alfred 1887- 5-8R
Filmer, Henry
See Childs, J(ames) Rives
Filmer, Robert c. 1586-1653 ....DLB 151
Filosa, Gary Fairmont Randolph de Marco II 1931- .
CANR-54
Earlier sketch in CA 65-68
Filreis, Alan 1956- 125
Filson, Floyd V(ivian) 1896- 61-64
Filson, John 1753(?)-1788 ....DLB 37
Filstrup, Chris
See Filstrup, E(dward) Christian
Filstrup, E(dward) Christian 1942- 113
See also SATA 43
Filstrup, Jane (Merrill) 1946- 110
Filstrup, Janie
See Filstrup, Jane (Merrill)
Filtzer, Donald (Arthur) 1948- CANR-53
Earlier sketch in CA 126
Finan, John J(oseph) 1925- 117
Finberg, H(erbert) P(atrick) R(eginald) 1900-1974 ..
CAP-1
Obituary 53-56
Earlier sketch in CA 13-16
Finch, A. R. C.
See Finch, Annie (Ridley Crane)
Finch, Anne 1661-1720 ....DLB 95
See also PC 21
Finch, Annie (Ridley Crane) 1956- 146
Finch, Caleb E(llicott) 1939- 139
Finch, Christopher 1939- 138
Brief entry 112
Finch, Donald George 1937- 53-56
Finch, Henry LeRoy 1918- 41-44R
Finch, Matthew
See Fink, Merton
Finch, Robert (Duer Claydon) 1900- CANR-49
Earlier sketches in CA 57-60, CANR-9, 24
See also CLC 18
See also DLB 88
Finch, Robert (Charles) 1943- 137
Finch, Roger 1937- 140
Finch, Sheila 1935- CANR-46
Earlier sketch in CA 121
Fincham, A(nthony) A(rthur) 1943- 117
Fincham, Francis D. 1954- 140
Fincham, Frank D.
See Fincham, Francis D.
Fincher, Cameron Lane 1926- 41-44R
Fincher, Ernest B(arksdale) 1910-1985 ....CANR-9
Obituary 115
Earlier sketch in CA 53-56
Finchler, Judy 1943- 158
See also SATA 93
Finck, Furman J(oseph) 1900- CAP-2
Earlier sketch in CA 33-36
Fincke, Gary (William) 1945- CANR-50
Earlier sketch in CA 57-60
Finckenauer, James O(liver) 1939- 108
Finder, Joseph 1958- CANR-62
Earlier sketch in CA 113
Finder, Martin
See Salzmann, Siegmund
Findlater, Richard
See Bain, Kenneth Bruce Findlater
Findlay, Bruce Allyn 1895-1972 ....CAP-1
Earlier sketch in CA 13-14
Findlay, David K. 1901- CAP-1
Earlier sketch in CA 13-14
Findlay, James Arthur 1883-1964 Obituary 111
Findlay, James F(ranklin), Jr. 1930- 49-52
Findlay, John N(iemeyer) 1903-1987 ....CANR-5
Obituary 123
Earlier sketch in CA 5-8R
Findlay, Robert R. 1932- 45-48
Findley, Carter Vaughn 1941- 102
Findley, Paul 1921- 29-32R
Findley, Timothy 1930- CANR-69
Earlier sketches in CA 25-28R, CANR-12, 42
See also CLC 27, 102
See also DAC
See also DAM MST
See also DLB 53
Findling, John Ellis 1941- 102
Fine, Anne 1947- CANR-38
Earlier sketch in CA 105
See also AAYA 20
See also CLR 25
See also JRDA
See also MAICYA
See also SAAS 15
See also SATA 29, 72
Fine, Benjamin 1905-1975 ....CANR-4
Obituary 57-60
Earlier sketch in CA 5-8R
Fine, Carla 1946- 112
Fine, Doris Landau 1949- 153
Fine, Elsa Honig 1930- CANR-28
Earlier sketch in CA 49-52
Fine, Estelle
See Jelinek, Estelle C.
Fine, Gary Alan 1950- CANR-46
Earlier sketch in CA 111
Fine, I(sadore) V. 1918- 17-20R
Fine, John (Van Antwerp), Jr. 1939- 117
Fine, John Van Antwerp (Sr.) 1903-1987 160
Fine, Jonathan 1949- 149
Fine, Judylaine 1948- 117
Fine, Marshall 1950- 137
Fine, Nathan 1893(?)-1979 Obituary 89-92
Fine, Ralph Adam 1941- 29-32R
Fine, Reuben 1914- CANR-12
Earlier sketch in CA 17-20R
Fine, Richard 1951- 146
Fine, S(eymour) Morton 1930- 104
Fine, Seymour H(oward) 1925- CANR-30
Earlier sketch in CA 111
Fine, Sidney 1920- CANR-1
Earlier sketch in CA 1-4R
Fine, Warren 1943- 21-24R
Fine, William Michael 1924- 13-16R
Fineberg, Robert Gene 1940- 107
Finegan, Jack 1908- CANR-1
Earlier sketch in CA 1-4R
Finegan, T(homas) Aldrich 1929- Brief entry 108
Finello, Dominick 1944- 149
Fineman, Howard (David) 1948- 133
Fineman, Irving 1893- 5-8R
Fineman, Joel 1947-1989 127
Obituary 128
Finer, Leslie 1921- 13-16R
Finer, S(amuel) E(dward) 1915-1993 ....CANR-48
Obituary 141
Earlier sketch in CA 41-44R
Finestone, Harold 1920- Brief entry 110
Finestone, Harry 1920- 45-48
Fingarette, Herbert 1921- 77-80
Finger, Charles J(oseph) 1869(?)-1941 Brief entry 119
See also SATA 42
Finger, Seymour Maxwell 1915- 104
Finger, William R(atliff) 1947- 111
Fingerhut, Eugene R. 1932- 111
Fingesten, Peter 1916-1987 ....13-16R
Obituary 123
Finifter, Ada W(eintraub) 1938- CANR-21
Earlier sketch in CA 104
Fink, Arthur Emil 1903- 1-4R
Fink, Augusta 1916- CANR-13
Earlier sketch in CA 33-36R
Fink, Carole 1940- 135
Fink, Deborah 1944- 144
Fink, Edith 1918- 61-64
Fink, Eli E. 1908(?)-1979 Obituary 85-88
Fink, Gary M. 1936- 53-56
Fink, Ida 1921- CANR-71
Earlier sketch in CA 136
Fink, Joanne 1954- 123
Fink, John (Philip) 1926- CANR-71
Earlier sketch in CA 139
Fink, Joseph 1915- 57-60
Fink, Karl J. 1942- 138
Fink, Lawrence Alfred 1930- 97-100
Fink, Leon 1948- 135
Fink, Merton 1921- 9-12R
Fink, Paul Jay 1933- 53-56
Fink, Stevanne Auerbach
See Auerbach, Stevanne
Fink, Steven (B.) 1948- 147
Fink, William
See Mencken, H(enry) L(ouis)
Fink, William B(ertrand) 1916- 41-44R
See also SATA 22
Fink, Z(era) S(ilver) 1902- CAP-1
Earlier sketch in CA 9-10
Fink Cline, Beverly 1951- 113
Finke, Blythe Foote 1922- 65-68
See also SATA 26
Finke, Jack A. 1918(?)-1979 Obituary 89-92
Finke, Ronald A. 1950- 143
Finkel, Alvin 1949- 131
Finkel, Donald 1929- CANR-59
Earlier sketches in CA 21-24R, CANR-9, 29
Finkel, George (Irvine) 1909-1975 ....CAP-2
Earlier sketch in CA 17-18
See also SATA 8
Finkel, Lawrence S. 1925- 13-16R
Finkel, LeRoy 1939- 105
Finkelhor, David 1947- 118
Finkelhor, Dorothy Cimberg 1902- 110
Finkell, Max
See Catto, Max(well Jeffrey)
Finkelman, Paul 1949- CANR-22
Earlier sketch in CA 105
Finkelstein, Bonnie B(lumenthal) 1946- 85-88
Finkelstein, Jacob Joel 1922-1974 Obituary ..53-56
Finkelstein, Leonid Vladimirovitch 1924- 21-24R
Finkelstein, Louis 1895-1991 ....13-16R
Obituary 136
Finkelstein, Marina S.
1921(?)-1972 Obituary 33-36R
Finkelstein, Milton 1920- 89-92
Finkelstein, Miriam 1928- 108
Finkelstein, Norman G. 1953- 162
Finkelstein, Norman H. 1941- ....SATA 73
Finkelstein, Sidney 1910(?)-1974 Obituary ... 45-48
Finkenstaedt, Rose L. H. 1927- 147
Finkle, Jason L(eonard) 1926- 21-24R
Finklehoffe, Fred F. 1910-1977 Obituary 73-76
Finkler, Kaja 1935- 114
Finlator, John Haywood 1911- 102
Finlay, Alice Sullivan 1946- ....SATA 82
Finlay, Campbell K(irkman) 1909- 5-8R
Finlay, David J(ames) 1934- CANR-16
Earlier sketch in CA 25-28R
Finlay, Fiona
See Stuart, (Violet) Vivian (Finlay)
Finlay, Ian Hamilton 1925- 81-84
See also DLB 40
Finlay, Matthew Henderson 1916- 13-16R
Finlay, Richard J(ason) 1962- 146
Finlay, Roger (Anthony Peter) 1952- 132
Finlay, William
See Mackay, James (Alexander)
Finlay, Winifred Lindsay Crawford (McKissack)
1910- 9-12R
See also SATA 23
Finlayson, Ann 1925- 29-32R
See also SATA 8
Finlayson, Geoffrey B(eauchamp) A(listair)
1934- 131
Finlayson, Iain (Thorburn) 1945- 144
Finlayson, Michael G(eorge) 1938- 128
Finlayson, Roderick (David) 1904- 81-84
Finler, Joel W(aldo) 1938- CANR-32
Earlier sketch in CA 77-80
Finletter, Thomas K(night) 1893-1980 Obituary . 101
Finley, Gerald Eric 1931- 105
Finley, Glenna
See Witte, Glenna Finley
Finley, Harold M(arshall) 1916- 17-20R
Finley, James 1943- 97-100
Finley, Joseph E(dwin) 1919-1997 69-72
Obituary 159
Finley, Karen 1956- 154
Finley, Lewis M(erren) 1929- 61-64
Finley, M(oses) I. 1912-1986 ....CANR-10
Obituary 119
Earlier sketch in CA 5-8R
Finley, Martha 1828-1909 Brief entry 118
See also DLB 42
See also SATA 43
Finley, Mary Peace 1942- ....SATA 83
Finley, Michael 1950- 166
Finley, Mitch 1945- 142
Finley, Randy 1954- 158
Finman, Ted 1931- Brief entry 110
Finn, David 1921- 73-76
Finn, Doug(las Arthur) 1946- 118
Finn, Edward E(rnest) 1908- 115
Finn, Elizabeth Anne (McCaul) 1825-1921 . DLB 166
Finn, Geraldine 1947- 118
Finn, James 1924- Brief entry 108
Finn, Jonathan 1884(?)-1971 Obituary 29-32R
Finn, Margot C. 1960- 146
Finn, R. Welldon
See Finn, Reginald Patrick Arthur Welldon
Finn, Ralph L(eslie) 1912- CANR-9
Earlier sketch in CA 5-8R
Finn, Reginald Patrick Arthur Welldon 1900-1971 ..
CANR-10
Earlier sketch in CA 13-16R
Finn, Rex Welldon
See Finn, Reginald Patrick Arthur Welldon
Finn, Susan C(alvert) 140
Finn, (Patrick) Timothy 1938- 129

Finnegan, Mary Jeremy 1907-...135
Finnegan, Robert
See Ryan, Paul William
Finnegan, Ruth H(ilary) 1933-... CANR-12
Earlier sketch in CA 25-28R
Finnegan, William (Patrick) 1952-...136
Finneran, Richard J(ohn) 1943-... CANR-29
Earlier sketches in CA 29-32R, CANR-12
Finnerty, Adam Daniel
See Corson-Finnerty, Adam Daniel
Finnerty, Daniel John
See Corson-Finnerty, Adam Daniel
Finney, Ben R(udolph) 1933-... CANR-1
Earlier sketch in CA 45-48
Finney, Charles G(randison) 1905-1984.. CANR-58
Obituary...112
Earlier sketches in CAP-2, CA 29-32
Finney, Ernest J....134
Finney, Gertrude Elva (Bridgeman) 1892-... CAP-1
Earlier sketch in CA 13-16
Finney, Gretchen Ludke 1901-... 9-12R
Finney, Humphrey S. 1902-... 97-100
Finney, Jack
See Finney, Walter Braden
See also DLB 8
Finney, Nathaniel Solon 1903-1982 Obituary...108
Finney, Patricia 1958-... 97-100
Finney, Paul B(urnham) 1929-...73-76
Finney, Shan 1944-...111
See also SATA 65
Finney, Theodore M(itchell) 1902-...61-64
Finney, Walter Braden 1911-1995... 133
Obituary...150
Brief entry...110
See also Finney, Jack
Finnigan, Joan 1925-... CANR-53
Earlier sketches in CA 17-20R, CANR-13, 29
Finnin, (Olive) Mary... 106
Finnis, John M(itchell) 1940-... 136
Finocchiaro, Mary (Bonomo) 1913-... CANR-27
Earlier sketch in CA 29-32R
Fins, Alice 1944-... 110
Finson, Jon W(illiam) 1950-... 125
Finstad, Suzanne 1955-... 131
Finucane, Ronald C(harles)... 135
Fiore, Edith 1930-...85-88
Fiore, Michael V. 1934-...45-48
Fiore, Peter Amadeus 1927-...33-36R
Fiore, Robert Louis 1935-...73-76
Fiore, Silvestro 1921-...17-20R
Fiorenza, Elisabeth Schuessler 1938-... CANR-39
Earlier sketch in CA 106
Fiorenza, Francis S(chuessler) 1941-... CANR-39
Earlier sketch in CA 115
Fiori, Pamela A. 1944-...89-92
Fiorina, Morris Paul, Jr. 1946-... 85-88
Fiorino, A(ngelo) John 1926-...29-32R
Fiorio, Franco Emilio 1912-1975 Obituary...61-64
Firbank, Louis 1942- Brief entry...117
See also Reed, Lou
Firbank, (Arthur Annesley) Ronald 1886-1926 Brief entry...104
See also DLB 36
See also TCLC 1
Firchow, Evelyn Scherabon 1932-... CANR-11
Earlier sketch in CA 21-24R
Firchow, Peter (Edgerly) 1937-...37-40R
Firda, Richard Arthur 1931-... 144
Firebrace, Aylmer (Newton George) 1886-... 5-8R
Firer, Ben Zion
See Firer, Benzion
Firer, Benzion 1914-... 131
See also SATA 64
Fires, Alicia
See Oglesby, Joseph
Fireside, Bryna J. 1932-... SATA 73
Fireside, Harvey 1929-...29-32R
Firestone, Harvey S(amuel), Jr. 1898-1973 Obituary... 41-44R
Firestone, O(tto) J(ohn) 1913-...41-44R
Firestone, Robert W. 1930-... 130
Firestone, Shulamith 1945-... 154
Firestone, Tom
See Newcomb, Duane G(raham)
Firey, Walter Irving (Jr.) 1916-...1-4R
Firkatian, Mari A. 1959-... 155
Firkins, Peter (Charles) 1926-... 107
Firmage, George J(ames) 1928-...9-12R
Firmat, Gustavo (Francisco) Perez
See Perez-Firmat, Gustavo (Francisco)
Firmin, Charlotte 1954-... CANR-47
Earlier sketches in CA 106, CANR-23
See also SATA 29
Firmin, Giles 1615-1697...DLB 24
Firmin, Peter 1928-... CANR-40
Earlier sketches in CA 81-84, CANR-17
See also SATA 15, 58
Firor, John (W.) 1927-...136
Firsching, F. Henry 1923-...163
Firsoff, V(aldemar) Axel 1910-... 93-96
First, Philip
See Williamson, Philip G.
First, Ruth 1925-1982... CANR-10
Obituary...107
Earlier sketch in CA 53-56
Firth, (Frederick) Anson 1902-...117
Firth, Grace (Ushler) 1922-...73-76
Firth, J. R.
See Firth, John Rupert
Firth, John Rupert 1890-1960 Obituary...116
Firth, Raymond (William) 1901-... 65-68
Firth, Robert E. 1921-... 77-80
Firth, Tony 1937(?)-1980 Obituary... 97-100
Fisch, Edith L. 1923-... 77-80
Fisch, Gerald G(rant) 1922-...13-16R
Fisch, Harold 1923-...37-40R
Fisch, Martin L. 1924-...109
Fisch, Max H(arold) 1900-...33-36R
Fisch, Richard 1926- Brief entry...106
Fischart, Johann c. 1546-c. 1590...DLB 179
Fischbach, Julius 1894-... CANR-2
Earlier sketch in CA 5-8R
See also SATA 10
Fischel, Walter J(oseph) 1902-1973... CAP-2
Obituary...41-44R
Earlier sketch in CA 23-24
Fischel, William A. 1945-... 156
Fischer, Alfred (George) 1920-... 73-76
Fischer, Ann 1919-1971... CAP-2
Earlier sketch in CA 25-28
Fischer, Arlene 1934-... 111
Fischer, Bobby
See Fischer, Robert James
Fischer, Bruno 1908-... CANR-59
Earlier sketch in CA 77-80
Fischer, Carl H(ahn) 1903-...17-20R
Fischer, Claude S(erge) 1948-...107
Fischer, David Hackett 1935-... 17-20R
Fischer, Dennis 1960-...140
Fischer, Dietrich 1941-...117
Fischer, Donald E(dward) 1935-...41-44R
Fischer, Edward (Adam) 1914-... CANR-37
Earlier sketches in CA 1-4R, CANR-1, 16
Fischer, Ernst 1899-1972 Obituary... 37-40R
Fischer, Ernst Otto 1918-...157
Fischer, Fritz 1908-... CANR-9
Earlier sketch in CA 65-68
Fischer, George 1923-... CANR-9
Earlier sketch in CA 53-56
Fischer, George 1932-... 25-28R
Fischer, Gerald C(harles) 1928-... CANR-9
Earlier sketch in CA 21-24R
Fischer, J(ohn) L(yle) 1923-...17-20R
Fischer, Joel 1939-... CANR-40
Earlier sketches in CA 53-56, CANR-4, 19
Fischer, John 1910-1978... CANR-4
Obituary... 81-84
Earlier sketch in CA 9-12R
Fischer, John Irwin 1940-...129
Fischer, John Martin 1952-... CANR-51
Earlier sketch in CA 124
Fischer, Karoline Auguste Fernandine 1764-1842... DLB 94
Fischer, Klaus P. 1942-... 150
Fischer, LeRoy H(enry) 1917-... CANR-8
Earlier sketch in CA 17-20R
Fischer, Louis 1896-1970... CAP-1
Obituary...25-28R
Earlier sketch in CA 11-12
Fischer, Lucy Rose 1944-... 138
Fischer, Lynn 1943-...150
Fischer, Michael R(obert) 1949-... 118
Fischer, Robert H. 1918-... 37-40R
Fischer, Robert James 1943-... 103
Fischer, Roger Adrian 1939- Brief entry... 109
Fischer, Tibor 1959-... 157
Fischer, Vera Kistiakowsky
See Kistiakowsky, Vera
Fischer, Victor 1924- Brief entry...110
Fischer, William F(rank) 1934- Brief entry...111
Fischer, Wolfgang Georg 1933-... 33-36R
Fischer-Dieskau, Dietrich 1925-...97-100
Fischer-Fabian, Siegfried 1922-... 130
Fischer-Galati, Stephen A(lexander) 1924-... 127
Brief entry... 117
Fischer-Nagel, Andreas 1951-...123
See also SATA 56
Fischer-Nagel, Heiderose 1956-... 123
See also SATA 56
Fischetti, John 1916-1980 Obituary...102
Fischl, Viktor
See Dagan, Avigdor
Fischler, Alan 1952-... 137
Fischler, Shirley (Walton)... 136
See also SATA 66
Fischler, Stan(ley I.)... 128
Brief entry... 116
See also SATA 66
See also SATA-Brief 36
Fischman, Dennis 1958-...140
Fischman, Harve 1930- Brief entry... 113
Fischman, Leonard L(ipman) 1919-... CANR-10
Earlier sketch in CA 13-16R
Fischtrom, Harvey 1933-1974... CAP-2
Obituary... 53-56
Earlier sketch in CA 25-28
See also Zemach, Harve
Fisdel, Steven A....163
Fish, Byron 1908-...45-48
Fish, Charles (K.) 1936-... 149
Fish, Joe
See Williamson, Philip G.
Fish, Julian
See Campbell, Blanche
Fish, Kenneth L(loyd) 1926-... 29-32R
Fish, Margery (Townshend) 1892-1969... CANR-4
Earlier sketch in CA 5-8R
Fish, Peter Graham 1937-... 69-72
Fish, Robert L(loyd) 1912-1981... CANR-61
Obituary... 103
Earlier sketches in CA 13-16R, CANR-13
Fish, Roy J(ason) 1930-... 123
Brief entry... 118
Fish, Stanley
See Fish, Stanley Eugene
Fish, Stanley E.
See Fish, Stanley Eugene
Fish, Stanley Eugene 1938-...132
Brief entry... 112
See also DLB 67
Fishacre, Richard 1205(?)-1248...DLB 115
Fishback, Margaret
See Antolini, Margaret Fishback
Fishback, Price V(anmeter) 1955-...138
Fishbane, Michael A(lton) 1943-...113
Fishbein, Harold D(ennis) 1938-... CANR-53
Brief entry... 105
Earlier sketch in CA 126
Fishbein, Meyer H(arry) 1916-...41-44R
Fishbein, Morris 1889-1976... CANR-4
Obituary... 69-72
Earlier sketch in CA 5-8R
Fishburn, Hummel 1901-... CAP-1
Earlier sketch in CA 19-20
Fishburn, Janet Forsythe 1937-... 108
Fishburn, Peter C(lingerman) 1936-... 45-48
Fishel, Edwin C. 1914-... 162
Fishel, Elizabeth 1950-... 103
Fishel, Leslie H(enry), Jr. 1921-... 21-24R
Fishel, Wesley R(obert) 1919-1977...73-76
Obituary... 69-72
Fisher, A(rnold) Garth 1933-... 104
Fisher, A(rthur) Stanley T(heodore) 1906-... 93-96
Fisher, Aileen (Lucia) 1906-... CANR-37
Earlier sketches in CA 5-8R, CANR-2, 17
See also CLR 49
See also MAICYA
See also SATA 1, 25, 73
Fisher, Alan (E.) 1929-... CANR-48
Earlier sketch in CA 121
Fisher, Alan W(ashburn) 1939-... 53-56
Fisher, Alden L(owell) 1928-1970... CAP-2
Earlier sketch in CA 25-28
Fisher, Allan C(arroll), Jr. 1919-... 112
Fisher, Allan G(eorge) B(arnard) 1895-1976 .33-36R
Fisher, Allen J. 1907(?)-1980 Obituary... 102
Fisher, Ameel J(oseph) 1909-... 104
Fisher, Angela 1947-...145
Fisher, Anne B. 1957-... 135
Fisher, Arthur 1931-... 110
Fisher, Barbara 1940-... CANR-56
Earlier sketches in CA 104, CANR-30
See also SATA 44
See also SATA-Brief 34
Fisher, Bart (Steven) 1943-... 45-48
Fisher, Benjamin Franklin IV 1940-... CANR-58
Earlier sketches in CA 112, CANR-30
Fisher, Bob
See Fisher, Robert Percival
Fisher, Bruce 1931-...118
Fisher, C(harles) William 1916-... CANR-6
Earlier sketch in CA 5-8R
Fisher, Carrie (Frances) 1956-...135
See also BEST 90:4
See also DAM POP
Fisher, Charles Alfred 1916-1982(?) Obituary.. 105
Fisher, Chris 1958-...SATA 80
Fisher, Clavin C(argill) 1912-... 65-68
See also SATA 24
Fisher, Clay
See Allen, Henry Wilson
Fisher, David 1946-...143
Fisher, David E(limelech) 1932-... CANR-45
Earlier sketches in CA 53-56, CANR-4, 22
Fisher, Dominic (Mayne Maitland) 1953-... 124
Fisher, Don 1933(?)-1983 Obituary... 111
Fisher, Dorothy (Frances) Canfield 1879-1958.. 136
Brief entry... 114
See also DLB 9, 102
See also MAICYA
See also YABC 1
Fisher, Douglas 1934-...102
Fisher, Douglas 1954-...118
Fisher, Douglas Mason 1919-... 89-92
Fisher, Edward 1902-...1-4R
Fisher, Elizabeth 1941-...117
Fisher, Ernest Arthur 1887-...13-16R
Fisher, Ernest F., Jr. 1918-... 150
Fisher, Esther Oshiver 1910-... 85-88
Fisher, Eugene J(oseph) 1943-... CANR-22
Earlier sketch in CA 105
Fisher, Florence (Anna) 1928- Brief entry...112
Fisher, Franklin M(arvin) 1934-...17-20R
Fisher, Fred L(ewis) 1911-... CANR-5
Earlier sketch in CA 1-4R
Fisher, (Donald) Gary 1938-... 103
Fisher, Gary L. 1949-... 151
See also SATA 86
Fisher, Gene H. 1922-... 41-44R
Fisher, Gene L(ouis) 1947-...81-84
Fisher, George E(dward) 1923-...127
Fisher, George W. 1910(?)-1987 Obituary... 124
Fisher, Glen H(arry) 1922- Brief entry... 111
Fisher, Glenn W(illiam) 1924-...53-56
Fisher, Gordon N(eil) 1928-1985 Obituary... 117
Fisher, Harold H. 1890-1975 Obituary... 61-64
Fisher, Harvey Irvin 1916-...69-72
Fisher, Helen E(lizabeth) 1945-...108
Fisher, Humphrey J(ohn) 1933-... 33-36R
Fisher, J(ohn) R(obert) 1943-... CANR-1
Earlier sketch in CA 45-48
Fisher, J(oseph) Thomas 1936-... 33-36R
Fisher, James (Maxwell McConnell) 1912-1970 .126
Obituary... 89-92
Fisher, James R(aymond), Jr. 1937-... 81-84
Fisher, Joe 1947-...103
Fisher, Johanna 1922-... 93-96
Fisher, John (Oswald Hamilton) 1909-... 81-84
See also SATA 15
Fisher, John C(harles) 1927-...41-44R
Fisher, John H(urt) 1919-... CANR-11
Earlier sketch in CA 21-24R
Fisher, John J(acob) III 1951(?)-1990 Obituary . 131
Fisher, Kenneth L(awrence) 1950-... 118
Fisher, Kim N. 1948-...121
Fisher, Laine
See Howard, James A(rch)
Fisher, Laura Harrison 1934-...13-16R
See also SATA 5
Fisher, Lawrence V. 1923-...17-20R
Fisher, Lee 1908-... 33-36R
Fisher, Leonard Everett 1924-... CANR-37
Earlier sketches in CA 1-4R, CANR-2
See also CLR 18
See also DLB 61
See also MAICYA
See also SAAS 1
See also SATA 4, 34, 73
Fisher, Lillian Estelle 1891-... CAP-1
Earlier sketch in CA 13-16
Fisher, Lois H(amilton) 1936-... 113
Fisher, Lois I. 1948-... 113
See also SATA 38
See also SATA-Brief 35
Fisher, Lois Jeannette 1909-...5-8R
Fisher, Louis 1934-...37-40R
Fisher, M(ary) F(rances) K(ennedy) 1908-1992... CANR-44
Obituary... 138
Earlier sketch in CA 77-80
See also CLC 76, 87
Fisher, Malcolm R(obertson) 1923- Brief entry . 110
Fisher, Margaret B(arrow) 1918-...17-20R
Fisher, Margery (Turner) 1913-1992... CANR-46
Obituary... 140
Earlier sketch in CA 73-76
See also SATA 20
See also SATA-Obit 74
Fisher, Margot
See Paine, Lauran (Bosworth)
Fisher, Marvin 1927-...21-24R
Fisher, Mary 1948-... 148
Fisher, Mary L. 1928-... 33-36R
Fisher, Michael John 1933-... CANR-3
Earlier sketch in CA 1-4R
Fisher, Miles Mark 1899-1970... CAP-1
Earlier sketch in CA 13-16
Fisher, Miriam Louise (Scharfe) 1939-...13-16R
Fisher, Morris 1922-... 21-24R
Fisher, Neal F(loyd) 1936-... 106
Fisher, Nigel 1913-... 102
Fisher, Nikki
See Strachan, Ian
Fisher, Norman George 1910-1972 Obituary... 107
Fisher, Peter Jack 1930-...69-72
Fisher, Philip 1941-... CANR-72
Earlier sketches in CA 113, CANR-33
Fisher, Philip A(rthur) 1907-... 61-64
Fisher, R. A.
See Fisher, Ronald A(ylmer)
Fisher, Ralph Talcott, Jr. 1920-...41-44R
Fisher, Rhoda Lee 1924-... 65-68
Fisher, Richard 1936-...17-20R
Fisher, Richard B(ernard) 1919-... 77-80
Fisher, Robert (Tempest) 1943-... CANR-52
Earlier sketches in CA 109, CANR-26
See also SATA 47
Fisher, Robert C(harles) 1930-... CANR-49
Earlier sketch in CA 53-56
Fisher, Robert J(ay) 1924-... 61-64
Fisher, Robert Percival 1935-...93-96
Fisher, Roger (Dummer) 1922-...37-40R
Fisher, Ronald A(ylmer) 1890-1962... 157
Obituary...112
Fisher, Roy 1930-... CANR-16
Earlier sketch in CA 81-84
See also CAAS 10
See also CLC 25
See also DLB 40
Fisher, Rudolph 1897-1934... 124
Brief entry... 107
See also BLC 2
See also BW 1
See also DAM MULT
See also DLB 51, 102
See also SSC 25
See also TCLC 11
Fisher, Seymour 1922-1996... CANR-12
Obituary... 155
Earlier sketch in CA 33-36R
Fisher, Shelton 1911-1985 Obituary... 115
Fisher, Sidney Thomson 1908-... 124
Fisher, Stephen L(ynn) 1944-... 139
Fisher, Sterling Wesley 1899(?)-1978...85-88
Obituary... 81-84
Fisher, Susan M(ichal) 1937-...119
Fisher, Suzanne
See Staples, Suzanne Fisher
Fisher, Sydney G.
See Fisher, Sydney George
Fisher, Sydney George 1856-1927 Brief entry.. 122
See also DLB 47
Fisher, Vardis (Alvero) 1895-1968... CANR-68
Obituary...25-28R
Earlier sketch in CA 5-8R
See also CLC 7
See also DLB 9
Fisher, Wade
See Norwood, Victor G(eorge) C(harles)
Fisher, Wallace E. 1918-... CANR-10
Earlier sketch in CA 21-24R
Fisher, Walter R. 1931-... 13-16R
Fisher, Welthy Honsinger 1879-1980... CANR-2
Obituary... 102
Earlier sketch in CA 1-4R
Fisher, Wesley Andrew 1944-... 104
Fisher, William Bayne 1916-1984... 65-68
Obituary...113
Fishkin, Shelley Fisher 1950-...145
Fishler, Mary Shiverick 1920-... 5-8R
Fishlock, David (Jocelyn) 1932-... 130
Fishlock, Trevor 1941-... 161
Fishman, Aryei 1922-... 142

Fishman, Betty G(oldstein) 1918- 5-8R
Fishman, Burton J(ohn) 1942- 45-48
Fishman, Charles 1942- CANR-7
Earlier sketch in CA 57-60
Fishman, George Samuel 1937- 25-28R
Fishman, Jack 1920- CANR-7
Earlier sketch in CA 9-12R
Fishman, Joshua A(aron) 1926- CANR-34
Earlier sketches in CA 41-44R, CANR-15
Fishman, Katherine Davis 1937- 130
Fishman, Ken 1950- 105
Fishman, Leo 1914-1975 17-20R
Obituary 120
Fishman, Lew 1939- CANR-11
Earlier sketch in CA 61-64
Fishman, Lisa 1966- 166
Fishman, Robert (Lawrence) 1946- 112
Fishman, Sterling 1932- 45-48
Fishof, David 1956- 115
Fishwick, Marshall William 1923- CANR-6
Earlier sketch in CA 5-8R
Fisk, E(rnest) K(elvin) 1917- 17-20R
Fisk, Erma J(onnie) 1905(?)-1990 Obituary 130
Fisk, McKee 1900- CAP-2
Earlier sketch in CA 21-22
Fisk, Nicholas CANR-28
Earlier sketches in CA 65-68, CANR-11
See also Higginbottom, David
See also SATA 25
Fisk, Pauline 1948- 136
See also SATA 66
Fisk, Robert 1946(?)- 140
Fisk, Samuel 1907- 57-60
Fiske, Edward B(ogardus) 1937- CANR-41
Earlier sketches in CA 85-88, CANR-16
Fiske, John 1608-1677 DLB 24
Fiske, John 1842-1901 DLB 47, 64
Fiske, Marjorie CANR-1
Earlier sketch in CA 45-48
Fiske, Robert H(artwell) 1948- 163
Fiske, Roger E(lwyn) 1910- 13-16R
Fiske, Sharon
See Hill, Pamela
Fiske, Tarleton
See Bloch, Robert (Albert)
Fisketjon, Gary 1954- 129
Brief entry 123
Interview in 129
Fiskin, A(bram) M. I. 1916-1975 CAP-2
Earlier sketch in CA 23-24
Fison, Joseph Edward 1906-1972 Obituary 114
Fiss, Owen M(itchell) 1938- 112
Fiszel, Henryk 1910- 29-32R
Fiszman, Joseph R. 1921- 41-44R
Fitch, Alger Morton, Jr. 1919- 53-56
Fitch, Bob
See Fitch, Robert Beck
Fitch, Clarke
See Sinclair, Upton (Beall)
Fitch, (William) Clyde 1865-1909 Brief entry 110
See also DLB 7
Fitch, Donald S(heldon) 1949- 106
Fitch, Edwin M(edbery) 1902- CAP-2
Earlier sketch in CA 25-28
Fitch, George Ashmore 1883-1979 Obituary 85-88
Fitch, Geraldine T(ownsend)
1892(?)-1976 Obituary 69-72
Fitch, James Marston 1909- 89-92
Fitch, John IV
See Cormier, Robert (Edmund)
Fitch, Kenneth (Leonard) 1929- 49-52
Fitch, Lyle C(raig) 1913-1996 13-16R
Obituary 155
Fitch, Noel Riley 1937- 144
Fitch, Raymond E(dward) 1930- 110
Fitch, Robert Beck 1938- 21-24R
Fitch, Stanley K. 1920- 29-32R
Fitch, Thomas 1700(?)-1774 DLB 31
Fitch, Willis Stetson 1896(?)-1978 Obituary 81-84
Fite, Gilbert C(ourtland) 1918- 33-36R
Fite, James David 1933- 107
Fite, Mack
See Schneck, Stephen
Fites, Philip 1946- 141
Fitler, Mary Biddle 1878(?)-1966 Obituary 25-28R
Fitschen, Dale 1937- 77-80
See also SATA 20
Fitt, Mary
See Freeman, Kathleen
Fitter, Chris 1955- 150
Fitter, Richard Sidney Richmond 1913- CANR-49
Earlier sketches in CA 65-68, CANR-11
Fitting, Greer A. 1943- 81-84
Fitting, James E. 1939- 45-48
Fitting, Melvin (Chris) 1942- CANR-11
Earlier sketch in CA 29-32R
Fitton, James 1899-1982 Obituary 106
Fitts, Dudley 1903-1968 93-96
Obituary 25-28R
Fitts, Henry (King) 1914- 113
Fitts, William Howard 1918- 21-24R
Fitz, Jean DeWitt 1912- 29-32R
Fitzalan, Roger
See Trevor, Elleston
Fitzell, John 1922- 13-16R
Fitzgeffrey, Charles 1575(?)-1638 DLB 121
Fitzgerald, Arlene J. CANR-8
Earlier sketch in CA 21-24R
Fitzgerald, Astrid 1938- 154
Fitzgerald, Barbara
See Newman, Mona Alice Jean
and Value, Barbara Ann
Fitzgerald, Barry Charles 1939- 37-40R
FitzGerald, Brian Seymour Vesey
See Vesey-FitzGerald, Brian Seymour
FitzGerald, C(harles) P(atrick) 1902-1992
CANR-11
Obituary 137
Earlier sketch in CA 17-20R
Fitzgerald, Captain Hugh
See Baum, L(yman) Frank
Fitz-Gerald, Carolyn 1932- 41-44R
FitzGerald, Cathleen 1932-1987 33-36R
Obituary 121
See also SATA-Obit 50
Fitzgerald, Dorothy (Minerva) Dow
1903(?)-1989 Obituary 128
Fitzgerald, E(dmund) V(alpy) K(nox) 1947- 73-76
FitzGerald, Edward 1809-1883 DLB 32
Fitzgerald, Edward 1898(?)-1982 Obituary 108
Fitzgerald, Edward Earl 1919- 73-76
See also SATA 20
Fitzgerald, Ellen
See Stevenson, Florence
Fitzgerald, Ernest A. 1925- CANR-12
Earlier sketch in CA 29-32R
Fitzgerald, F(rancis) A(nthony) 1940- SATA 15
Fitzgerald, F(rancis) Scott (Key) 1896-1940 123
Brief entry 110
See also AAYA 24
See also AITN 1
See also CDALB 1917-1929
See also DA
See also DAB
See also DAC
See also DAM MST, NOV
See also DLB 4, 9, 86
See also DLBD 1, 15, 16
See also DLBY 81, 96
See also MTCW 1
See also SSC 6, 31
See also TCLC 1, 6, 14, 28, 55
See also WLC
FitzGerald, Frances 1940- CANR-32
Earlier sketch in CA 41-44R
Interview in CANR-32
FitzGerald, Garret 1926- 109
Fitzgerald, George R. 1932- CANR-17
Earlier sketch in CA 97-100
Fitzgerald, Gerald (Pierce) 1930- 37-40R
Fitzgerald, Gerald (Norman)
1932-1990 Obituary 131
Fitzgerald, Gerald E(dward) 1920- 25-28R
Fitz Gerald, Gregory 1923- CANR-1
Earlier sketch in CA 49-52
Fitzgerald, Hal
See Johnson, Joseph E(arl)
Fitzgerald, Harold Alvin 1896-1984 Obituary 114
Fitzgerald, Hiram E(arl) 1940- CANR-16
Earlier sketch in CA 77-80
Fitzgerald, Jack
See Shea, John Gerald
Fitzgerald, James A(ugustine) 1892- CANR-1
Earlier sketch in CA 1-4R
Fitzgerald, James V. 1889(?)-1976 Obituary 69-72
Fitzgerald, John
See Fazzano, Joseph E.
Fitzgerald, John D(ennis) 1907(?)-1988 93-96
Obituary 126
See also CLR 1
See also MAICYA
See also SATA 20
See also SATA-Obit 56
Fitzgerald, John Joseph 1928- 37-40R
Fitzgerald, Judith 1952- CANR-62
Earlier sketches in CA 113, CANR-32
Fitzgerald, Julia
See Watson, Julia
FitzGerald, Kathleen Whalen 1938- 109
Fitzgerald, Kitty 1946- 129
Fitzgerald, Laurine Elisabeth 1930- 37-40R
Fitzgerald, Lawrence P(ennybaker) 1906-1976
CANR-2
Earlier sketch in CA 1-4R
Fitzgerald, Maury 1906(?)-1986 Obituary 121
Fitzgerald, Merni Ingrassia 1955- 124
See also SATA 53
Fitzgerald, Michael G(arrett) 1950- 77-80
Fitzgerald, Nancy 1951- 85-88
Fitzgerald, Patrick (John) 1928- 9-12R
Fitzgerald, Penelope 1916- CANR-56
Earlier sketch in CA 85-88
See also CAAS 10
See also CLC 19, 51, 61
See also DLB 14, 194
Fitzgerald, Randall 1950- 118
Fitzgerald, Richard (Ambrose) 1938- 45-48
Fitzgerald, Robert (Stuart) 1910-1985 CANR-1
Obituary 114
Earlier sketch in CA 1-4R
See also CLC 39
See also DLBY 80
FitzGerald, Robert D(avid) 1902-1987 17-20R
See also CLC 19
FitzGerald, Stephen (Arthur) 1938- 97-100
Fitzgerald, Tamsin 1950- 97-100
Fitzgerald, Thomas 1819-1891 DLB 23
Fitzgerald, Valerie 1927- 165
Fitzgerald, Zelda (Sayre) 1900-1948 126
Brief entry 117
See also DLBY 84
See also TCLC 52
FitzGibbon, (Robert Louis) Constantine (Lee-Dillon)
1919-1983 CANR-2
Obituary 109
Earlier sketch in CA 1-4R
Fitzgibbon, Russell H(umke) 1902-1979 CANR-14
Earlier sketch in CA 65-68
FitzGibbon, Theodora (Joanne Eileen Winifred)
1916- CANR-3
Earlier sketch in CA 5-8R
Fitzgibbons, James P. 1912(?)-1983 Obituary 110
Fitzhardinge, Joan Margaret 1912- CANR-36
Earlier sketches in CA 13-16R, CANR-6, 23
See also Phipson, Joan
See also MAICYA
See also SATA 2, 73
Fitzhenry, Robert Irvine 1918- 110
FitzHerbert, Margaret 1942-1986 130
Fitzhugh, Louise 1928-1974 CANR-34
Obituary 53-56
Earlier sketches in CAP-2, CA 29-32
See also AAYA 18
See also CLR 1
See also DLB 52
See also JRDA
See also MAICYA
See also SATA 1, 45
See also SATA-Obit 24
Fitzhugh, Percy Keese 1876-1950 133
See also SATA 65
Fitzhugh, Robert Tyson 1906-1981 Obituary 104
Fitzhugh, William 1651(?)-1701 DLB 24
Fitzlyon, (Cecily) April (Mead) 1920- 5-8R
Fitzlyon, Kyril 1910- 93-96
Fitzmaurice, Gabriel 1952- 137
Fitzmaurice, George 1877-1963 Obituary 93-96
Fitzmyer, Joseph A(ugustine) 1920- CANR-5
Earlier sketch in CA 9-12R
Fitzpatrick, Daniel Robert
1891-1969 Obituary 89-92
Fitzpatrick, David 1948- 156
Fitzpatrick, James K(evin) 1942- 65-68
Fitzpatrick, Joseph P(atrick) 1913- 17-20R
Fitzpatrick, Kathryn 1934- 113
Fitzpatrick, Mary Anne 1949- 145
FitzPatrick, Paul Joseph 1894-1984 Obituary 111
Fitzpatrick, Tom 1927- Brief entry 111
Fitzpatrick, Tony 1949- 140
Fitzpatrick, Vincent (dePaul III) 1950- 131
FitzRalph, Matthew
See McInerny, Ralph
Fitz-Randolph, Jane (Currens) 1915- 103
See also SATA 51
FitzRoy, Charles (Patrick Hugh) 1957- 136
Fitzroy, Rosamond
See Briggs, Desmond Lawther
Fitzsimmons, Cleo 1900- 1-4R
Fitzsimmons, Michael P. 1949- 129
Fitzsimmons, Thomas 1926- CANR-15
Earlier sketch in CA 33-36R
Fitz-Simon, Christopher 1934- CANR-48
Earlier sketch in CA 113
Fitzsimons, Cecilia (A. L.) 1952- 163
See also SATA 97
Fitzsimons, Louise 1932- 61-64
Fitzsimons, M(athew) A(nthony) 1912- 13-16R
Fitzsimons, Neal 1928- 33-36R
FitzSimons, Raymund CANR-15
Earlier sketch in CA 33-36R
FitzSimons, Ruth M(arie Mangan) 53-56
Fitzwilliam, Michael
See Lyons, J. B.
Five, Billy
See Obrecht, Jas
Fivelson, Scott 1954- 117
Fix, Michael 1950- 147
Fix, Paul
See Morrison, Paul Fix
Fix, William R. 1941- CANR-15
Earlier sketch in CA 85-88
Fixel, Lawrence 1917- 137
See also CAAS 28
Fixler, Michael 1927- 13-16R
Fixx, James F(uller) 1932-1984 CANR-13
Earlier sketch in CA 73-76
Fixx, Jim
See Fixx, James F(uller)
Fizer, John 1925- 53-56
Fjelde, Rolf (Gerhard) 1926- 17-20R
Flach, Frederic F(rancis) 1927- 81-84
Flachmann, Michael 1942- CANR-40
Earlier sketch in CA 117
Flack, Audrey L. 1931- CANR-26
Earlier sketch in CA 106
Flack, Dora D(utson) 1919- CANR-45
Earlier sketches in CA 57-60, CANR-6, 21
Flack, Elmer Ellsworth 1894- 17-20R
Flack, Harley E. 1943- 145
Flack, Jerry D(avid) 1943- 131
Flack, Marjorie 1897-1958 136
Brief entry 112
See also CLR 28
See also MAICYA
See also SATA 100
See also YABC 2
Flack, Naomi John White CANR-1
Earlier sketch in CA 1-4R
See also SATA 40
See also SATA-Brief 35
Flacks, Niki 1943- 110
Flacks, Richard 1938- 49-52
Fladeland, Betty 1919- 45-48
Flader, Susan L. 1941- 81-84
Fladmark, Knut R. 1946- 162
Flage, Daniel E(rvin) 1951- 127
Flagg, Fannie 1941- CANR-40
Earlier sketch in CA 111
See also DAM POP
Flagg, James Montgomery 1877-1960 DLB 188
Flagg, Kenneth
See Ayvazian, L. Fred
Flagstad, Kirsten 1895-1962 Obituary 112
Flaherty, Daniel Leo 1929- 89-92
Flaherty, David H(arris) 1940- 25-28R
Flaherty, Doug(las Ernest) 1939- 33-36R
Flaherty, Gloria 1938- 85-88
Flaherty, Joe 1936(?)-1983 141
Obituary 111
Flaherty, Mary Pat 1955- 132
Brief entry 127
Interview in 132
Flaherty, Michael G. 1952- 145
Flaherty, Robert J(oseph) 1884-1951 Brief
entry 115
Flaherty, Robert Joseph 1933- 73-76
Flaherty, Vincent X. 1908(?)-1977 Obituary 73-76
Flaiano, Ennio 1910-1972 Obituary 37-40R
Flake, Chad J(ohn) 1929- 29-32R
Flam, Jack D(onald) 1940- 144
Flambeau, Blossom
See Stocking, Kathleen
Flamhaft, Ziva 1944- 162
Flamholtz, Eric 1943- 57-60
Flamm, Dudley 1931- 25-28R
Flamm, Gerald R(obert) 1916- 77-80
Flamm, Jerry
See Flamm, Gerald R(obert)
Flammarion, (Nicolas) Camille 1842-1925 Brief
entry 120
Flammarion, Henri (Claude)
1910-1985 Obituary 117
Flammer, Philip M(eynard) 1928- 45-48
Flammonde, Paris 17-20R
Flanagan, Brenda A. 1948- 158
Flanagan, Cynthia
See Goss, Cynthia Flanagan
Flanagan, David 168
Flanagan, Dennis 1919- 128
Flanagan, Dorothy Belle
See Hughes, Dorothy B(elle)
Flanagan, John C(lemans) 1906- CANR-1
Earlier sketch in CA 1-4R
Flanagan, John T(heodore) 1906- 17-20R
Flanagan, Joseph David Stanislaus 1903- 13-16R
Flanagan, Mary 1943- CANR-54
Earlier sketch in CA 125
Flanagan, Michael 1943- 148
Flanagan, Mike 1950- 133
Flanagan, Neal M. 1920-1985 17-20R
Obituary 117
Flanagan, Owen J. 1949- 125
Flanagan, Robert (James) 1941- 33-36R
See also CAAS 17
Flanagan, Thomas (James Bonner) 1923-
CANR-55
Earlier sketch in CA 108
Interview in 108
See also CLC 25, 52
See also DLBY 80
See also MTCW 1
Flanagan, William G(eorge) 1940- CANR-15
Earlier sketch in CA 93-96
Flanagan, William G(eorge) 1942- 119
Flanagan, William I. 1916(?)-1986 Obituary 118
Flanders, Helen Hartness 1890-1972 CAP-1
Obituary 33-36R
Earlier sketch in CA 13-16
Flanders, Henry Jackson, Jr. 1921- 33-36R
Flanders, James P(rescott) 1942- 69-72
Flanders, Jane (Hess) 1940- 110
Flanders, Michael (Henry) 1922-1975 CANR-4
Obituary 57-60
Earlier sketch in CA 5-8R
Flanders, Ned A. 1918- 37-40R
Flanders, Ralph Edward 1880-1970 CAP-1
Earlier sketch in CA 11-12
Flanders, Rebecca
See Ball, Donna
Flanders, Robert Bruce 1930- 17-20R
Flanery, E(dward) B(oyd) 1932- 61-64
Flanigan, James 1936- 134
Flanigan, Lloyd A(llen) 1933- 33-36R
Flanner, Hildegarde 1899-1987 147
See also Monhoff, June Hildegarde Flanner
See also DLB 48
Flanner, Janet 1892-1978 CANR-13
Obituary 81-84
Earlier sketch in CA 65-68
See also DLB 4
Flannery, Edward H(ugh) 1912- 13-16R
Flannery, Harry W. 1900-1975 CAP-1
Obituary 57-60
Earlier sketch in CA 9-10
Flannery, James W(illiam) 1936- Brief entry 110
Flannery, Peter 1951- 104
Flannery, Sean
See Hagberg, David J(ames)
Flannery, Tim(othy Fridtjof) 1956- 154
Flasch, Joy 1932- 37-40R
Flaste, Richard (Alfred) 1942- 158
Flaster, Donald J(ohn) 1932- 115
Flath, Arnold W(illiam) J. 1929- 65-68
Flath, Carol Apollonio 1955- 146
Flato, Charles 1908(?)-1984 Obituary 111
Flatt, Lizann
See Brunskill, Elizabeth Ann Flatt
Flattau, Edward 1937- 65-68
Flaubert, Gustave 1821-1880 DA
See also DAB
See also DAC
See also DAM MST, NOV
See also DLB 119
See also SSC 11
See also WLC
Flavell, Carol Willsey Bell 1939- 73-76
Flavell, John H(urley) 1928- CANR-11
Earlier sketch in CA 17-20R
Flavin, Martin 1883-1967 5-8R
Obituary 25-28R
See also DLB 9
Flavius, Brother
See Ellison, James E.

Flavius Josephus 37-100 .... DLB 176
Flaxman, Traudl 1942- 25-28R
Flayderman, Phillip C(harles) 1930-1969 .... CAP-2
  Earlier sketch in CA 23-24
Flayhart, William Henry (III) 1944- 146
Fleck, Betty
  See Paine, Lauran (Bosworth)
Fleck, Henrietta 1903- 77-80
Fleck, Konrad fl. c. 1220- .... DLB 138
Fleck, Richard Francis 1937- CANR-40
  Earlier sketches in CA 102, CANR-18
Flecker, Herman Elroy
  See Flecker, (Herman) James Elroy
Flecker, (Herman) James Elroy 1884-1915 150
  Brief entry 109
  See also DLB 10, 19
  See also TCLC 43
Fleece, Jeffrey (Atkinson) 1920- 17-20R
Fleege, Urban H(erman) 1908- CANR-1
  Earlier sketch in CA 45-48
Fleer, Jack D(avid) 1937- 25-28R
Fleeson, Doris 1901-1970 Obituary 93-96
  See also DLB 29
Fleet, Michael 1941- 131
Fleetwood, Frances 1902- CANR-17
  Earlier sketches in CA 45-48, CANR-1
Fleetwood, Frank
  See Fleetwood, Frances
Fleetwood, Hugh (Nigel) 1944- 144
  Brief entry 112
Fleetwood, Jenni 1947- .... SATA 80
Fleetwood, Mick 1947- 143
Fleetwood-Hesketh, (Charles) Peter (Fleetwood)
  1905-1985 Obituary 115
Flegg, (Henry) Graham 1924- 114
Fleischbein, Sister M. Catherine Frederic
  1902- 5-8R
Fleischer, Cornell H(ugh) 1950- 128
Fleischer, Jane
  See Oppenheim, Joanne
Fleischer, Leonore Brief entry 109
  See also SATA-Brief 47
Fleischer, Manfred P(aul) 1928- 29-32R
Fleischer, Max 1889-1972 Obituary 109
  See also SATA-Brief 30
Fleischer, Nathaniel S.
  1888(?)-1972 Obituary 37-40R
Fleischhauer-Hardt, Helga 1936- 102
  See also SATA 30
Fleischman, Harry 1914- CANR-3
  Earlier sketch in CA 5-8R
Fleischman, Paul 1952- CANR-37
  Earlier sketch in CA 113
  See also AAYA 11
  See also CLR 20
  See also JRDA
  See also MAICYA
  See also SAAS 20
  See also SATA 39, 72
  See also SATA-Brief 32
Fleischman, Paul R. 1945- 160
Fleischman, (Albert) Sid(ney) 1920- CANR-67
  Earlier sketches in CA 1-4R, CANR-5, 37
  See also CLR 1, 15
  See also JRDA
  See also MAICYA
  See also SATA 8, 59, 96
Fleischmann, Glen H(arvey) 1909- 33-36R
Fleischmann, Harriet 1904- CAP-2
  Earlier sketch in CA 21-22
Fleischmann, Raoul H(erbert)
  1885-1969 Obituary 115
Fleischmann, Wolfgang Bernard 1928- 116
Fleischner, Jennifer 1956- 158
  See also SATA 93
Fleisher, Belton Mendel 1935- 69-72
Fleisher, Frederic 1933- 21-24R
Fleisher, Martin 1925- 45-48
Fleisher, Michael (Lawrence) 1942- 25-28R
Fleisher, Paul 1948- CANR-55
  Earlier sketch in CA 137
  See also SATA 81
Fleisher, Robbin 1951-1977 .... SATA 52
  See also SATA-Brief 49
Fleisher, Wilfried 1897(?)-1976 Obituary 65-68
Fleishman, Avrom (Hirsch) 1933- 21-24R
Fleishman, Edwin A(lan) 1927- CANR-11
  Earlier sketch in CA 21-24R
Fleishman, Lazar 1944- 133
Fleishman, Seymour 1918- 133
  Brief entry 111
  See also SATA 66
  See also SATA-Brief 32
Fleisser, Marieluise 1901-1974
  See Haindl, Marieluise
  See also DLB 56, 124
Fleissner, Robert F. 1932- 168
Flemer, William III 1922- 61-64
Fleming, Alice Mulcahey 1928- CANR-2
  Earlier sketch in CA 1-4R
  See also SATA 9
Fleming, Amalia 1912-1986 Obituary 118
Fleming, Anne 1928- 151
Fleming, Berry 1899-1989 .... CANR-18
  Obituary 129
  Earlier sketches in CA 1-4R, CANR-2
Fleming, C(harlotte) M(ary) 1894- 5-8R
Fleming, Candace 1962- 159
  See also SATA 94
Fleming, D(enna) F(rank) 1893- CANR-1
  Earlier sketch in CA 1-4R
Fleming, David A(rnold) 1939- 93-96
Fleming, Deborah (Diane) 1950- 145
Fleming, Denise 1950- .... SATA 81
Fleming, Donald M(ethuen) 1905-1986 130
  Obituary 121
Fleming, Elizabeth P. 1888-1985 Obituary 119
  See also SATA-Obit 48
Fleming, George J(oseph) 1917- 37-40R
Fleming, George James 1904(?)-1990 Obituary 132
Fleming, Gerald 1921- 53-56
Fleming, Guy
  See Masur, Harold Q.
Fleming, H(orace) K(ingston) 1901- 33-36R
Fleming, Harold (Lee) 1927- 17-20R
Fleming, Harold M(anchester) 1900-(?) CAP-2
  Earlier sketch in CA 21-22
Fleming, Ian (Lancaster) 1908-1964 ..... CANR-59
  Earlier sketch in CA 5-8R
  See also AAYA 26
  See also CDBLB 1945-1960
  See also CLC 3, 30
  See also DAM POP
  See also DLB 87, 201
  See also MTCW 1
  See also SATA 9
Fleming, Irene 1923(?)-1979 Obituary 89-92
Fleming, Jacky 1955- 142
Fleming, James Rodger 1949- 150
Fleming, Jennifer Baker 1943- 77-80
Fleming, Joan Margaret 1908-1980 ..... CANR-60
  Obituary 102
  Earlier sketch in CA 81-84
Fleming, John 1919- 129
Fleming, John V(incent) 1936- 139
Fleming, June 1935- 110
Fleming, Kate 1946- 137
Fleming, Lady Amalia
  See Fleming, Amalia
Fleming, Laurence (William Howie) 1929- 107
Fleming, Macklin 1911- 77-80
Fleming, May Agnes 1840-1880 .... DLB 99
Fleming, Miles 1919-1978 .... 29-32R
  Obituary 134
Fleming, Oliver
  See MacDonald, Philip
Fleming, Paul 1609-1640 .... DLB 164
Fleming, (Robert) Peter
  1907-1971 Obituary 33-36R
  See also DLB 195
Fleming, Ray(mond) 1945- 115
  See also BW 1
Fleming, Reid
  See Obrecht, Jas
Fleming, Robert E. 1936- 146
Fleming, Robert H(enry) 1912-1984 Obituary ... 114
Fleming, Ronald Lee 1941- 108
  See also SATA 56
Fleming, Sandford 1888- CAP-1
  Earlier sketch in CA 9-10
Fleming, Stuart
  See Knight, Damon (Francis)
Fleming, Susan 1932- CANR-14
  Earlier sketch in CA 81-84
  See also SATA 32
Fleming, Theodore B(owman), Jr. 1917- 45-48
Fleming, Thomas (James) 1927- CANR-10
  Earlier sketch in CA 5-8R
  Interview in CANR-10
  See also CLC 37
  See also SATA 8
Fleming, Virginia (Edwards) 1923- 150
  See also SATA 84
Fleming, William (Coleman) 1909- 17-20R
Flemming, Nicholas Coit 1936- 97-100
Flemmons, Jerry 1936- 124
Flender, Harold 1924-1975 49-52
  Obituary 135
Flesch, Janos Laszlo 1933(?)-1983 Obituary ... 111
Flesch, Rudolf (Franz) 1911-1986 .... CANR-3
  Obituary 120
  Earlier sketch in CA 9-12R
Flesch, Y.
  See Flesch, Yolande (Catarina)
Flesch, Yolande (Catarina) 1950- 122
  See also SATA 55
Flescher, Irwin 1926- 37-40R
Flescher, Joachim 1906(?)-1976 Obituary 65-68
Fletcher, Adele (Whitely) 1898- CAP-1
  Earlier sketch in CA 17-18
Fletcher, Alan Mark 1928- 73-76
Fletcher, Angus (John Stewart) 1930- 104
Fletcher, Anthony John 1941- 73-76
Fletcher, Arnold Charles 1917- 17-20R
Fletcher, Banister F.
  See Fletcher, Banister Flight
Fletcher, Banister Flight 1866-1953 Brief entry . 123
Fletcher, Barbara (Helen) 1935- 110
Fletcher, Basil Alais 1900-1983 65-68
  Obituary 109
Fletcher, Bramwell 1904(?)-1988 Obituary 125
Fletcher, Charlie May Hogue 1897- 9-12R
  See also SATA 3
Fletcher, Colin 1922- CANR-11
  Earlier sketch in CA 13-16R
  See also AITN 1
  See also SATA 28
Fletcher, David
  See Barber, D(ulan) F(riar Whilberton)
Fletcher, Dirk
  See Cunningham, Chet
Fletcher, Geoffrey Scowcroft 1923- 103
Fletcher, George U.
  See Pratt, (Murray) Fletcher
Fletcher, Gordon A(lan) 1942- 127
Fletcher, Grace Nies 1895- 5-8R
Fletcher, H(arry) L(utf) V(erne) 1902-197(?) ....
  CANR-4
  Earlier sketch in CA 9-12R
Fletcher, Harold Roy 1907-1978 Obituary 111
Fletcher, Harris Francis 1892-1979 .... 1-4R
  Obituary 103
Fletcher, Harvey 1884-1981 Obituary 108
Fletcher, Helen Jill 1911- 9-12R
  See also SATA 13
Fletcher, Henry Lancelot Aubrey
  See Aubrey-Fletcher, Henry Lancelot
Fletcher, Ian 1920-1988 Obituary 127
  Brief entry 124
Fletcher, (Minna) Inglis 5-8R
  See also AITN 1
Fletcher, J(oseph) S(mith) 1863-1935 Brief
  entry 109
  See also DLB 70
Fletcher, Jesse C. 1931- CANR-4
  Earlier sketch in CA 9-12R
Fletcher, John 1579-1625 ..... CDBLB Before 1660
  See also DC 6
  See also DLB 58
Fletcher, John (Walter James) 1937- CANR-15
  Earlier sketch in CA 81-84
Fletcher, John C(aldwell) 1931- 124
Fletcher, John Gould 1886-1950 167
  Brief entry 107
  See also DLB 4, 45
  See also TCLC 35
Fletcher, Joseph (Francis III) 1905-1991 . CANR-11
  Obituary 135
  Earlier sketch in CA 21-24R
Fletcher, Leon 1921- CANR-33
  Earlier sketch in CA 49-52
Fletcher, Lucille
  See Wallop, Lucille Fletcher
Fletcher, Marilyn P(endleton) 1940- 106
Fletcher, Marjorie 1941- Brief entry 113
Fletcher, Mary .... AITN 1
Fletcher, (William) Miles (III) 1946- 114
Fletcher, Phineas 1582-1650 .... DLB 121
Fletcher, Richard E. 1917(?)-1983 Obituary 109
  See also SATA-Obit 34
Fletcher, Rick
  See Fletcher, Richard E.
Fletcher, Robert H. 1885(?)-1972 Obituary . 37-40R
Fletcher, Roger A(nthony) 1942- 121
Fletcher, Ronald 1921-1992 .... CANR-42
  Earlier sketches in CA 33-36R, CANR-13
Fletcher, Sir Banister
  See Fletcher, Banister Flight
Fletcher, Susan (Clemens) 1951- CANR-71
  Earlier sketch in CA 138
  See also SATA 70
Fletcher, William C(atherwood) 1932- 21-24R
Fletcher, William W(higham) 1918- CANR-15
  Earlier sketch in CA 81-84
Fletcher, Winston 1937- CANR-42
  Earlier sketch in CA 118
Fletcher-Cooke, John 1911- 102
Fletcher the Younger, Giles 1585(?)-1623 . DLB 121
Flett, Una (Leonie) 1932- 137
Fleur, Anne 1901- .... SATA-Brief 31
Fleur, Paul
  See Pohl, Frederik
Fleure, H. J.
  See Fleure, Herbert John
Fleure, Herbert John 1877-1969 Obituary 115
Fleuridas, Ellie Rae
  See Sherman, Eleanor Rae
Fleury, Delphine
  See Amatora, Sister Mary
Flew, Antony G(arrard) N(ewton) 1923- .. CANR-40
  Earlier sketches in CA 5-8R, CANR-3, 18
Flexner, Eleanor 1908- 45-48
Flexner, James Thomas 1908- CANR-37
  Earlier sketches in CA 1-4R, CANR-2
  See also SATA 9
Flexner, Simon 1863-1946 156
Flexner, Stuart Berg 1928-1990 .... CANR-11
  Obituary 133
  Earlier sketch in CA 13-16R
Flick, Carlos Thomas 1927- 89-92
Fliegel, Frederick C(hristian) 1925- 49-52
Flieger, Verlyn 1933- 168
Flieger, Wilhelm 1931- 25-28R
Flier, Michael S(tephen) 1941- CANR-32
  Earlier sketches in CA 37-40R, CANR-14
Fliess, Peter J(oachim) 1915- 21-24R
Fligstein, Neil 1951- 135
Flinders, Neil J. 1934- 21-24R
Flink, James J(ohn) 1932- Brief entry 112
Flink, Salomon J. 1906-1983 .... CANR-17
  Earlier sketch in CA 1-4R
Flinn, M(ichael) W(alter) 1917-1983 ..... CANR-13
  Obituary 110
  Earlier sketch in CA 17-20R
Flint, Betty M. 1920- 21-24R
Flint, Cort R(ay) 1915- CANR-47
  Earlier sketch in CA 49-52
Flint, E. de P.
  See Fielden, T(homas) P(erceval)
Flint, F(rank) S(tuart) 1885-1960 Obituary 113
  See also DLB 19
Flint, Helen 1952- 128
  See also SATA 102
Flint, Homer Eon 1892-1924 160
  Brief entry 114
Flint, Jeremy 1928(?)-1989 Obituary 130
Flint, Jerry 1931- 127
Flint, John E(dgar) 1930- 37-40R
Flint, Kenneth C(ovey), Jr. 1947- 140
Flint, Lucy
  See Flint-Gohlke, Lucy
Flint, Roland (Henry) 1934- 153
Flint, Russ 1944- .... SATA 74
Flint, Timothy 1780-1840 .... DLB 73, 186
Flint-Gohlke, Lucy 1954- CANR-37
Flippo, Chet 1943- 89-92
Flippo, Edwin B(ly) 1925- CANR-13
  Earlier sketch in CA 33-36R
Flitner, David P(erkins), Jr. 1949- CANR-1
  Earlier sketch in CA 45-48
  See also SATA 7
Floan, Howard R(ussell) 1918- 17-20R
Floegstad, Kjartan 1944- 166
Floethe, Louise Lee 1913- CANR-2
  Earlier sketch in CA 1-4R
  See also SATA 4
Floethe, Richard 1901- 33-36R
  See also SATA 4
Floherty, John Joseph 1882-1964 .... SATA 25
Flood, Charles Bracelen 1929- 41-44R
Flood, Curt(is Charles) 1938-1997 Obituary 156
  Brief entry 115
Flood, E(dward) Thadeus 1932-1977 49-52
  Obituary 133
Flood, John A(nthony) 1949- 129
Flood, John M(ichael) 1947- 115
Flood, Kenneth Urban 1925- 9-12R
Flood, Norman 1935- 134
Flood, Robert G. 1935- CANR-22
  Earlier sketch in CA 106
Flooglebuckle, Al
  See Spiegelman, Art
Flook, Maria 1952- CANR-61
  Earlier sketch in CA 110
Flora, Fletcher 1914-1969 .... CANR-3
  Earlier sketch in CA 1-4R
Flora, James (Royer) 1914- CANR-3
  Earlier sketch in CA 5-8R
  See also SAAS 6
  See also SATA 1, 30
Flora, Joseph M(artin) 1934- CANR-44
  Earlier sketches in CA 13-16R, CANR-5, 21
Flora, Paul 1922- Brief entry 113
Floren, Lee 1910- CANR-64
  Earlier sketches in CA 5-8R, CANR-3, 18
Floren, Myron (Howard) 1919- 129
Florence, Philip Sargant 1890-1982 Obituary ... 106
Florence, Ronald 1942- CANR-15
  Earlier sketch in CA 33-36R
Florentin, Eddy 1923- 49-52
Flores, Angel 1900-1992 .... CANR-40
  Earlier sketches in CA 103, CANR-19, 32
  See also HW
Flores, Dan Louie 1948- CANR-47
  Earlier sketch in CA 121
Flores, Ivan 1923- CANR-22
  Earlier sketches in CA 17-20R, CANR-7
Flores, Janis 1946- CANR-51
  Earlier sketches in CA 65-68, CANR-10, 26
Flores, John 1943- 77-80
Florescu, Radu R. 1925- 41-44R
Florey, Howard Walter 1898-1968 158
Florey, Kitty B.
  See Florey, Kitty Burns
Florey, Kitty Burns 1943- 149
Florez, Pablo de Azcarate y
  See Azcarate y Florez, Pablo de
Florian, Douglas 1950- CANR-49
  Earlier sketch in CA 123
  See also SATA 19, 83
Florian, Tibor 1908- 73-76
Florida, Richard (L.) 1957- 139
Florin, Lambert F. 1905- CANR-7
  Earlier sketch in CA 17-20R
Florinsky, Michael T(imothy) 1894-1981 .. CANR-15
  Obituary 105
  Earlier sketch in CA 1-4R
Florio, John 1553(?)-1625 .... DLB 172
Floriot, Rene 1902-1975 Obituary 61-64
Florit (y Sanchez de Fuentes), Eugenio 1903- .....
  CANR-32
  Earlier sketch in CA 104
  See also HW
Florman, Samuel C(harles) 1925- 102
Florovsky, Georges (Vasilievich)
  1893-1979 Obituary 111
Flory, Charles D(avid) 1902- 41-44R
Flory, Harry R. 1899-1976 Obituary 69-72
Flory, Jane Trescott 1917- CANR-3
  Earlier sketch in CA 9-12R
  See also SATA 22
Flory, Julia McCune 1882-1971 .... CAP-2
  Obituary 29-32R
  Earlier sketch in CA 21-22
Flory, Paul (John) 1910-1985 156
  Obituary 117
Flory, Wendy Stallard 1943- 132
Floud, Roderick 1942- CANR-1
  Earlier sketch in CA 45-48
Flournoy, Don Michael 1937- 126
Flournoy, Valerie (Rose) 1952- 142
  See also BW 2
  See also SATA 95
Flower, Dean S. 1938- 21-24R
Flower, Desmond (John Newman)
  1907-1997 .... 9-12R
  Obituary 156
Flower, Elizabeth Farquhar 1914-1995 103
  Obituary 149
Flower, Harry A(lfred) 1901- CAP-1
  Earlier sketch in CA 11-12
Flower, Joe
  See Flower, Joseph Edward
Flower, (Harry) John 1936- 37-40R
Flower, Joseph Edward 1950- 130
Flower, Margaret Cameron Coss 61-64
Flower, Milton E(mbick) 1910- 129
Flower, (Walter) Newman 1879-1964 Obituary . 109
Flower, Raymond (Charles) 1921- 108
Flowerdew, Phyllis 103
  See also SATA 33
Flowers, Ann Moore 1923- 9-12R
Flowers, Betty S(ue) 1947- 65-68
Flowers, Charles 1942- 29-32R

Flowers, Charles E(ly, Jr.) 1920- ... 93-96
Flowers, Charles V., Jr. 1926(?)-1990 Obituary . 130
Flowers, John V(ictor) 1938- ... 106
Flowers, Paul Abbott 1905-1984 Obituary ... 112
Flowers, Ronald B(ruce) 1935- ... 151
Flowers, Sarah 1952- ... 166
See also SATA 98
Floyd, Barry Neil 1925- ... 33-36R
Floyd, Gareth 1940- ... SATA 62
See also SATA-Brief 31
Floyd, Harriet 1925- ... 69-72
Floyd, John E(arl) 1937- ... 145
Floyd, Lois Gray 1910(?)-1978 ... 85-88
Obituary ... 81-84
Floyd, Samuel A(lexander), Jr. 1937- ... CANR-39
Earlier sketch in CA 115
See also BW 2
Floyd, Troy S(mith) 1920- ... 37-40R
Floyd, W(illiam) E(dward) G(regory) 1939- .. 33-36R
Floyd, William Anderson 1928- ... 29-32R
Fluchere, Henri (Auguste) 1898-1987 Obituary . 123
Fluchere, Henri 1914- ... 77-80
See also SATA 40
Fluck, Diana 1931-1984 Obituary ... 113
Fluck, Reginald Alan Paul 1928- ... 9-12R
Fluehr-Lobban, Carolyn 1945- ... 144
Flugge-Lotz, Irmgard 1903-1974 ... 164
Fluke, Joanne
See Gibson, Jo
Flume, Violet S(igoloff) ... 116
Flumiani, Carlo M(aria) 1911- ... CANR-9
Earlier sketch in CA 13-16R
Fluno, Robert Y(ounger) 1916- ... 33-36R
Flusberg, Helen Tager
See Tager-Flusberg, Helen
Flusser, Martin 1947- ... 73-76
Flute, Molly
See Lottman, Eileen
Fly, Claude L(ee) 1905- ... 97-100
Flyat, Sten G(unnar) 1911- ... 9-12R
Flying Officer X
See Bates, H(erbert) E(rnest)
Flynn, Barbara 1928- ... SATA 9
Flynn, Bernice (Lydia Carlson) 1922- ... 114
Flynn, Carol Houlihan 1945- ... 112
Flynn, Casey
See Flint, Kenneth C(ovey), Jr.
Flynn, Charles F(rederick) 1949- ... 57-60
Flynn, David H(oughton) 1953- ... 115
Flynn, Don
See Flynn, Donald R(obert)
Flynn, Donald R(obert) 1928- ... CANR-30
Earlier sketches in CA 29-32R, CANR-12
Flynn, Elizabeth Gurley 1890-1964 Obituary ... 111
Flynn, Fahey 1916-1983 Obituary ... 110
Flynn, George
See Paine, Lauran (Bosworth)
Flynn, George L. 1931- ... CANR-24
Earlier sketches in CA 65-68, CANR-9
Flynn, George Q(uitman) 1937- ... 25-28R
Flynn, Gerard (Cox) 1924- ... 41-44R
Flynn, Jackson
See Bensen, Donald R.
and Shirreffs, Gordon D(onald)
Flynn, James Joseph 1911- ... 21-24R
Flynn, James R. 1934- ... 21-24R
Flynn, John Joseph 1936- ... 17-20R
Flynn, John Thomas 1882-1964 Obituary ... 89-92
Flynn, Leslie Bruce 1918- ... CANR-37
Earlier sketches in CA 1-4R, CANR-2, 17
Flynn, Paul P(atrick) 1942- ... 37-40R
Flynn, Robert (Lopez) 1932- ... CANR-55
Earlier sketch in CA 29-32R
Flynn, T(homas) T(heodore, Jr.) 1907-(?) ... 162
Flynt, Candace 1947- ... 102
Flynt, Larry ... AITN 2
Flynt, Wayne 1940- ... CANR-48
Earlier sketches in CA 37-40R, CANR-13
Flythe, Starkey S(harp), Jr. 1935- ... 69-72
Fm-2030 ... CANR-31
Fo, Dario 1926- ... CANR-68
Brief entry ... 116
Earlier sketch in CA 128
See also CLC 32, 109
See also DAM DRAM
See also DLBY 97
See also MTCW 1
Foat Tugay, Emine 1897- ... CAP-1
Earlier sketch in CA 13-14
Fobel, James M. 1946- ... 129
Fobel, Jim
See Fobel, James M.
Foda, Aun
See Foxe, Arthur N(orman)
Fodaski-Black, Martha 1929- ... 73-76
Fodden, Simon R. 1944- ... 131
Fodor, Eugene 1905-1991 ... CANR-14
Obituary ... 133
Earlier sketch in CA 21-24R
Fodor, M. W. 1890(?)-1977 Obituary ... 69-72
Fodor, Nandor 1895-1964 Obituary ... 112
Fodor, R(onald) V(ictor) 1944- ... CANR-15
Earlier sketch in CA 65-68
See also SATA 25
Foell, Earl W(illiam) 1929- ... 69-72
Foelsing, Albrecht 1940- ... 168
Foerstel, Lenora 1929- ... 144
Foerster, Eberhard
See Weisenborn, Guenther
Foerster, Leona M(itchell) 1930- ... 89-92
Foerster, Lotte B(rand) 1910-1986 ... 77-80
Obituary ... 119
Foerster, Norman 1887- ... 5-8R
Foff, Arthur R(aymond) 1925-1973 ... CAP-2
Earlier sketch in CA 33-36
Fogarty, John J. 1931- ... 128
Fogarty, Jonathan Titulescu Esq.
See Farrell, James T(homas)
Fogarty, Michael P(atrick) 1916- ... CANR-9
Earlier sketch in CA 21-24R
Fogarty, Robert S(tephen) 1938- ... CANR-9
Earlier sketch in CA 65-68
Fogel, Daniel
See Kahn-Fogel, Daniel (Mark)
Fogel, Daniel (Mark) Kahn
See Kahn-Fogel, Daniel (Mark)
Fogel, Ephim G(regory) 1920-1992 ... 120
Obituary ... 139
Fogel, Robert W(illiam) 1926- ... CANR-48
Earlier sketches in CA 77-80, CANR-13
Fogel, Ruby ... 17-20R
Fogelmark, Staffan 1939- ... 139
Fogelquist, Donald Frederick 1906- ... 69-72
Fogelson, Robert M(ichael) 1937- ... 81-84
Fogg, Sam R. 1917(?)-1987 Obituary ... 123
Fogle, Bruce 1944- ... 106
Fogle, French R(owe) 1912- ... 37-40R
Fogle, James 1936- ... 134
Fogle, Jeanne 1949- ... 145
Fogle, Richard Harter 1911- ... CANR-5
Earlier sketch in CA 5-8R
Foglio, Frank 1921- ... 57-60
Foiles, Keith Andrew 1926-1983 Obituary ... 109
Foin, Theodore C(hin) 1940- ... 93-96
Foisie, Jack 1919- ... 104
Foix, J. V. 1893-1987 ... DLB 134
Fokkema, D(ouwe) W(essel) 1931- ... CANR-23
Earlier sketches in CA 17-20R, CANR-7
Fol, Alexander 1933- Brief entry ... 111
Foladare, Joseph 1909- ... 102
Folb, Edith A(rlene) 1938- ... 102
Folch-Ribas, Jacques 1928- ... 69-72
Folda, Jaroslav (Thayer III) 1940- ... 127
Foldessy, Edward P(atrick) 1941- ... 126
Folds, Thomas M. ... 93-96
Foldvary, Fred E. 1946- ... 147
Folejewski, Zbigniew 1910- ... CANR-7
Earlier sketch in CA 17-20R
Foley, Allen Richard 1898-1978 ... 45-48
Obituary ... 77-80
Foley, (Anna) Bernice Williams 1902- ... CANR-12
Earlier sketch in CA 29-32R
See also SATA 28
Foley, Charles 1908- ... CAP-1
Obituary ... 148
Earlier sketch in CA 13-16
Foley, Daniel J(oseph) 1913- ... CANR-5
Earlier sketch in CA 5-8R
Foley, Denise (M.) 1950- ... 146
Foley, Doug 1942- ... 57-60
Foley, Duncan K(arl) 1942- ... 93-96
Foley, Gerald (Patrick) 1936- ... CANR-11
Earlier sketch in CA 69-72
Foley, Helen
See Fowler, Helen Rosa Huxley
Foley, Jack 1940- ... 160
See also CAAS 24
Foley, (Cedric) John 1917-1974 ... CANR-4
Obituary ... 53-56
Earlier sketch in CA 9-12R
Foley, John Miles 1947- ... CANR-45
Earlier sketch in CA 111
Foley, John Wayne Harold
See Foley, Jack
Foley, June 1944- ... 109
See also SATA 44
Foley, Leonard 1913- ... 89-92
Foley, (Mary) Louise Munro 1933- ... 37-40R
See also SATA 54
See also SATA-Brief 40
Foley, Martha 1897(?)-1977 ... 117
Obituary ... 73-76
See also DLB 137
Foley, Mary Mix 1918- ... 102
Foley, Michael F(rancis) 1940-1984 Obituary ... 113
Foley, Paul 1914-1983 Obituary ... 111
Foley, Rae
See Denniston, Elinore
Foley, Richard 1947- ... 126
Foley, Richard N. 1910(?)-1980 Obituary ... 102
Foley, Scott
See Dareff, Hal
Foley, Vincent D. 1933- ... 57-60
Foley, William E. 1938- ... 33-36R
Foley, Winifred 1914- ... 102
Folger, Henry Clay 1857-1930 ... DLB 140
Folk, Jerry ... 114
Folk, Thomas C. 1955- ... 168
Folkard, Charles James 1878-1963 Obituary ... 109
See also SATA-Brief 28
Folke, Will
See Bloch, Robert (Albert)
Folkenflik, Robert 1939- ... 162
Brief entry ... 111
Folkers, George Fulton 1929- ... 49-52
Folkerts, George W(illiam) 1938- ... 53-56
Folkman, Jerome (Daniel) 1907- ... CAP-2
Earlier sketch in CA 29-32
Folks, Jeffrey Jay 1948- ... 145
Follain, Jean (Rene) 1903-1971 ... 130
Folland, H(arold) F(reeze) 1906- ... 49-52
Follen, Eliza Lee (Cabot) 1787-1860 ... DLB 1
Follett, Helen Thomas 1884(?)-1970 Obituary ... 107
See also SATA-Obit 27
Follett, James 1939- ... 134
Brief entry ... 112
Follett, Ken(neth Martin) 1949- ... CANR-54
Earlier sketches in CA 81-84, CANR-13, 33
Interview in ... CANR-33
See also AAYA 6
See also BEST 89:4
See also CLC 18
See also DAM NOV, POP
See also DLB 87
See also DLBY 81
See also MTCW 1
Follett, Robert J(ohn) R(ichard) 1928- ... CANR-47
Earlier sketches in CA 21-24R, CANR-8, 23
Folley, Terence T. 1931- ... 21-24R
Folley, Vern L(eRoy) 1936- ... 49-52
Folliard, Edward T(homas)
1899-1976 Obituary ... 69-72
Follis, Anne Bowen 1947- ... 106
Follmann, J(oseph) F(rancis), Jr. 1908-1989 ...
CANR-7
Obituary ... 128
Earlier sketch in CA 17-20R
Folmar, J. Kent
See Folmar, John Kent
Folmar, John Kent 1932- ... 116
Folmsbee, Stanley J(ohn) 1899-1974 ... CAP-2
Earlier sketch in CA 29-32
Folsom, Allan (R.) 1941- ... 148
Folsom, Anne (Ferril) 1922- Brief entry ... 114
Folsom, Burton W(hitmore), Jr. 1947- ... 118
Folsom, Franklin (Brewster) 1907-1995 ... CANR-2
Obituary ... 150
Earlier sketch in CA 1-4R
See also SATA 5
See also SATA-Obit 88
Folsom, Jack
See Folsom, John B(entley)
Folsom, John B(entley) 1931- ... 45-48
Folsom, Kenneth E(verett) 1921- ... 21-24R
Folsom, Marion Bayard 1893- ... CAP-2
Earlier sketch in CA 17-18
Folsom, Marvin Hugh 1929- ... 57-60
Folsom, Michael (Brewster) 1938-1990 ... 112
Obituary ... 150
See also SATA 40
See also SATA-Obit 88
Folsom, Robert S(lade) 1915- ... 77-80
Folster, David 1937- ... 134
Folta, Jeannette R. 1934- ... 25-28R
Foltin, Lore Barbara 1913-(?) ... CAP-2
Earlier sketch in CA 25-28
Foltz, William J(ay) 1936- ... 9-12R
Folz, Hans c. 1435-1513 ... DLB 179
Fombona, Rufino Blanco
See Blanco Fombona, Rufino
Fombrun, Charles J. 1954- ... 144
Fomin
See Golomstock, Igor (Naumovitch)
Fomon, Samuel J(oseph) 1923- ... 53-56
Fonagy, Peter 1952- ... 146
Fonarow, Jerry 1935- ... CANR-4
Earlier sketch in CA 53-56
Fonda, Henry (Jaynes) 1905-1982 Obituary ... 107
Fonda, Jane (Seymour) 1937- ... 138
Fonda, Peter 1939(?)- Brief entry ... 112
Fon Eisen, Anthony T. 1917- ... 13-16R
Foner, Eric 1943- ... CANR-49
Earlier sketches in CA 29-32R, CANR-12
Foner, Jack D(onald) 1910- ... 77-80
Foner, Nancy 1945- ... 53-56
Foner, Naomi ... 166
Foner, Philip (Sheldon) 1910- ... CANR-47
Earlier sketches in CA 9-12R, CANR-3
Fong, C. K.
See Cassiday, Bruce (Bingham)
Fong, Leo 1928- ... 127
Fong, Wen Chih 1930- ... 103
Fong-Torres, Ben 1945- ... 93-96
Fonseca, Aloysius Joseph 1915- ... CANR-9
Earlier sketch in CA 13-16R
Fonseca, James W(illiam) 1947- ... 146
Fonseca, John R. 1925- ... CANR-8
Earlier sketch in CA 17-20R
Fonstad, Karen Wynn 1945- ... 104
Fontaine, Andre 1910- ... 65-68
Fontaine, Andre (Lucien Georges) 1921- . CANR-12
Earlier sketch in CA 25-28R
Fontaine, Joan 1917- ... 81-84
Fontana, Bernard L(ee) 1931- ... CANR-7
Earlier sketch in CA 17-20R
Fontana, Biancamaria 1952- ... CANR-51
Earlier sketch in CA 124
Fontana, Thomas M(ichael) 1951- ... 130
Brief entry ... 113
Fontana, Vincent James 1923- ... 13-16R
Fontane, Theodor 1819-1898 ... DLB 129
Fontanel, Beatrice 1957- ... 168
Fontanet, Joseph 1921-1980 Obituary ... 105
Fontcreuse, Marquis de
See Jaeger, Cyril Karel Stuart
Fontenay, Charles L(ouis) 1917- ... 25-28R
Fontenelle, Don H(arris) 1946- ... 106
Fontenot, Chester J. 1950- ... CANR-43
Earlier sketch in CA 112
Fontenot, Mary Alice 1910- ... CANR-57
Earlier sketches in CA 37-40R, CANR-14, 31
See also SATA 34, 91
Fontenrose, Joseph 1903- ... 5-8R
Fontes, Montserrat 1940- ... 136
Fonteyn, Margot
See Fonteyn de Arias, Margot
Fonteyn de Arias, Margot 1919-1991 ... 117
Obituary ... 133
Brief entry ... 110
Fonvizin, Denis Ivanovich 1744(?)-1792 ... DLB 150
Fonzi, Bruno 1913(?)-1976 Obituary ... 65-68
Foon, Dennis 1951- ... CANR-28
Earlier sketch in CA 111
Fooner, Michael ... 81-84
See also SATA 22
Foord, Archibald Smith 1914-1969 ... CAP-1
Earlier sketch in CA 11-12
Foos, Laurie 1966- ... 150
Foosaner, Samuel J. 1907(?)-1988 Obituary ... 125
Foot, David 1929- ... 136
Foot, Hugh Mackintosh 1907- ... 9-12R
Foot, M(ichael) R(ichard) D(aniell) 1919- . CANR-48
Earlier sketches in CA 5-8R, CANR-3
Foot, Michael 1913- ... 108
Foot, Mirjam M(ichaela) 1941- ... 139
Foot, Paul Mackintosh 1937- ... 17-20R
Foot, Philippa Ruth 1920- ... 101
Foote, A(von) Edward 1937- ... CANR-13
Earlier sketch in CA 73-76
Foote, Arthur 1911- ... 114
Foote, Darby Mozelle 1942- ... 61-64
Foote, Dorothy Norris (McBride) 1908- ... CAP-2
Earlier sketch in CA 21-22
Foote, Geoffrey 1950- ... 123
Foote, Horton 1916- ... CANR-51
Earlier sketches in CA 73-76, CANR-34
Interview in ... CANR-34
See also CLC 51, 91
See also DAM DRAM
See also DLB 26
Foote, Mary Hallock 1847-1938 . DLB 186, 188, 202
Foote, Patricia ... 165
Foote, Samuel 1721-1777 ... DLB 89
Foote, Shelby 1916- ... CANR-45
Earlier sketches in CA 5-8R, CANR-3
See also CLC 75
See also DAM NOV, POP
See also DLB 2, 17
Foote, Timothy (Gilson) 1926- ... 93-96
See also SATA 52
Foote, Victoria 1954- ... 118
Foote, Wilder 1905-1975 Obituary ... 57-60
Foote-Smith, Elizabeth 1913- ... 69-72
Footitt, Hilary 1948- ... 132
Footman, David (John) 1895-1983 ... 97-100
Obituary ... 111
Footman, Robert 1916- ... 126
Footner, (William) Hulbert 1879-1944 Brief
entry ... 114
Foran, Donald J. 1943- ... 33-36R
Forberg, Ati
See Forberg, Beate Gropius
See also SATA 22
Forberg, Beate Gropius 1925- ... 105
See also Forberg, Ati
Forbes, Anna 1954- ... 168
See also SATA 101
Forbes, Bryan 1926- ... CANR-44
Earlier sketch in CA 69-72
See also SATA 37
Forbes, Cabot L.
See Hoyt, Edwin P(almer), Jr.
Forbes, Calvin 1945- ... CANR-26
Earlier sketch in CA 49-52
See also CAAS 16
See also BW 1
See also DLB 41
Forbes, Clarence A(llen) 1901- ... 77-80
Forbes, Colin 1923- ... CANR-62
Earlier sketch in CA 103
See also Sawkins, Raymond H(arold)
Forbes, Daniel
See Kenyon, Michael
Forbes, DeLoris (Florine) Stanton 1923- .. CANR-5
Earlier sketch in CA 9-12R
Forbes, Donald (Galen) 1918-1987 Obituary ... 122
Forbes, Edith 1954- ... 159
Forbes, Elliot 1917- ... 9-12R
Forbes, Eric Gray 1933-1984 ... CANR-10
Obituary ... 114
Earlier sketch in CA 65-68
Forbes, Esther 1891-1967 ... CAP-1
Obituary ... 25-28R
Earlier sketch in CA 13-14
See also AAYA 17
See also CLC 12
See also CLR 27
See also DLB 22
See also JRDA
See also MAICYA
See also SATA 2, 100
Forbes, Graham B. ... CANR-27
Earlier sketches in CAP-2, CA 19-20
See also SATA 1
Forbes, Henry W(illiam) 1918- ... 1-4R
Forbes, J(ohn) V(an) G(elder) 1916- ... 9-12R
Forbes, Jack D. 1934- ... CANR-4
Earlier sketch in CA 1-4R
Forbes, Joanne R. (Triebel) 1930- ... 37-40R
Forbes, John Douglas 1910- ... 53-56
Forbes, Kathryn
See McLean, Kathryn (Anderson)
Forbes, Malcolm S(tevenson) 1919-1990 CANR-28
Obituary ... 131
Earlier sketch in CA 69-72
Forbes, Murray (M.) 1906-1987 Obituary ... 121
Forbes, (Christopher) Patrick 1925- ... 25-28R
Forbes, Rosita
See McGrath, Joan Rosita (Torr)
See also DLB 195
Forbes, Stanton
See Forbes, DeLoris (Florine) Stanton
Forbes, Thomas Rogers 1911- ... 41-44R
Forbes-Boyd, Eric 1897-1979 ... 13-16R
Obituary ... 125
Forbes-Dennis, Phyllis 1884-1963 Obituary .. 93-96
See also Bottome, Phyllis

Forbes-Robertson, Diana
See Sheean, Diana
Forbis, Judith 1934- ... 101
Forbis, William H. 1918- ... CANR-15
Earlier sketch in CA 37-40R
Forbus, Ina B(ell) ... 1-4R
Forcade, Robert J. 1935- ... 125
Force, Peter 1790-1868 ... DLB 30
Force, Roland W(ynfield) 1924-1996 ... 41-44R
Obituary ... 152
Force, William M. 1916- ... 21-24R
Forcey, Charles B(udd) 1925- ... CANR-1
Earlier sketch in CA 1-4R
Forche, Carolyn (Louise) 1950- ... CANR-50
Brief entry ... 109
Earlier sketch in CA 117
Interview in ... 117
See also CLC 25, 83, 86
See also DAM POET
See also DLB 5, 193
See also PC 10
Forchheimer, Paul 1913- ... 53-56
Forcione, Alban Keith 1938- ... CANR-13
Earlier sketch in CA 33-36R
Ford, A(lec) G(eorge) 1926- ... 5-8R
Ford, Adam 1940- ... 111
Ford, Agnes Gibbs 1902- ... CAP-2
Earlier sketch in CA 21-22
Ford, Albert Lee
See Stratemeyer, Edward L.
Ford, Alice 1906- ... CAP-1
Earlier sketch in CA 19-20
Ford, Amasa B. 1922- ... 21-24R
Ford, Arthur A. 1897-1971 Obituary ... 112
Ford, Arthur L(ewis) 1937- ... 57-60
Ford, Barbara ... 134
Brief entry ... 112
See also SATA 56
See also SATA-Brief 34
Ford, Betty
See Ford, Elizabeth Anne Bloomer
Ford, Boris 1917-1998 ... CANR-46
Obituary ... 167
Earlier sketch in CA 112
Ford, Brian J(ohn) 1939- ... CANR-34
Earlier sketches in CA 41-44R, CANR-15
See also SATA 49
Ford, Carolyn (Mott) 1938- ... 165
See also SATA 98
Ford, Cathy Diane 1952- ... 105
Ford, Charles Henri 1913- ... CANR-13
Earlier sketch in CA 25-28R
See also DLB 4, 48
Ford, Colin John 1934- ... 85-88
Ford, Collier
See Ford, James L(awrence) C(ollier)
Ford, Corey 1902-1969 Obituary ... 25-28R
See also DLB 11
Ford, D(ouglas) W(illiam) Cleverley
See Cleverley Ford, D(ouglas) W(illiam)
Ford, Daniel (Francis) 1931- ... CANR-11
Earlier sketch in CA 17-20R
Ford, David
See Harknett, Terry
Ford, Donald (Frank William) 1924- ... 5-8R
Ford, Donald H(erbert) 1926- ... 41-44R
Ford, Edmund Brisco 1901-1988 ... CANR-47
Obituary ... 124
Earlier sketch in CA 85-88
Ford, Edsel 1928-1970 ... CAP-1
Obituary ... 29-32R
Earlier sketch in CA 13-16
Ford, Edward (Charles) 1928- ... 89-92
Ford, Eileen (Otte) 1922- ... 120
Ford, Elaine 1938- ... CANR-19
Earlier sketch in CA 102
Ford, Elbur
See Hibbert, Eleanor Alice Burford
Ford, Elizabeth
See Bidwell, Marjory Elizabeth Sarah
Ford, Elizabeth Anne Bloomer 1918- ... CANR-23
Earlier sketch in CA 105
Ford, Ellen 1949- ... SATA 89
Ford, Florence
See Novelli, Florence
Ford, Ford Madox 1873-1939 ... 132
Brief entry ... 104
See also CDBLB 1914-1945
See also DAM NOV
See also DLB 162
See also MTCW 1
See also TCLC 1, 15, 39, 57
Ford, Frank B(ernard) 1932- ... 85-88
Ford, Franklin L(ewis) 1920- ... 17-20R
Ford, Fred
See Doerffler, Alfred
Ford, G. M. 1945- ... CANR-72
Earlier sketch in CA 154
Ford, George (Jr.) ... 107
See also SATA 31
Ford, George Barry 1885-1978 Obituary ... 81-84
Ford, George D. 1880(?)-1974 Obituary ... 53-56
Ford, George H(arry) 1914-1994 ... CANR-2
Obituary ... 147
Earlier sketch in CA 1-4R
Ford, George L(onnie) 1914- ... 5-8R
Ford, Gerald R(udolph, Jr.) 1913- ... 114
Brief entry ... 110
Ford, Glenn 1916- ... 167
Ford, Gordon B(uell), Jr. 1937- ... CANR-13
Earlier sketch in CA 21-24R
Ford, Guy B(arrett) 1922- ... 5-8R
Ford, Harvey Seabury 1905(?)-1978 Obituary 73-76
Ford, Henry II 1917-1987 ... 148
Obituary ... 123
Brief entry ... 111
Ford, Henry 1863-1947 ... 148
Brief entry ... 115
See also TCLC 73
Ford, Herbert Paul 1927- ... 17-20R
Ford, Hildegarde
See Morrison, Velma Ford
Ford, Hugh D. 1925- Brief entry ... 114
Ford, J. Massingberd
See Ford, Josephine Massyngbaerde
Ford, James Allan 1920- ... CAP-1
Earlier sketch in CA 9-10
Ford, James L(awrence) C(ollier) 1907- ... 29-32R
Ford, Jerome W. 1949- ... 146
See also SATA 78
Ford, Jerry
See Ford, Jerome W.
Ford, Jesse Hill (Jr.) 1928-1996 ... CANR-67
Obituary ... 152
Earlier sketches in CA 1-4R, CANR-1
See also CAAS 21
See also DLB 6
Ford, John 1586-(?) ... CDBLB Before 1660
See also DAM DRAM
See also DC 8
See also DLB 58
Ford, John 1895-1973 Obituary ... 45-48
See also CLC 16
Ford, Josephine Massyngbaerde ... 41-44R
Ford, Juwanda G(ertrude) 1967- ... SATA 102
Ford, Kathleen 1932- ... 25-28R
Ford, Kirk
See Spence, William John Duncan
Ford, Lee 1936- ... 25-28R
Ford, Leighton F. S. 1931- ... 17-20R
Ford, LeRoy 1922- ... 9-12R
Ford, Leslie
See Brown, Zenith Jones
Ford, Lewis
See Patten, Lewis B(yford)
Ford, Lewis S. 1933- ... 137
Ford, Marcia
See Radford, Ruby L(orraine)
Ford, Marcus Peter 1950- ... 108
Ford, Margaret Patricia 1925- ... 9-12R
Ford, Mary Forker 1905- ... 9-12R
Ford, Murray J(ohn) S(tanley) 1923- ... 93-96
Ford, Nancy K(effer) 1906-1961 Obituary ... 109
See also SATA-Obit 29
Ford, Nick Aaron 1904-1982 ... CANR-11
Earlier sketch in CA 25-28R
See also BW 1
Ford, Norman D(ennis) 1921- ... CANR-10
Earlier sketch in CA 21-24R
Ford, Norrey
See Dilcock, Noreen
Ford, Patrick 1914- ... 21-24R
Ford, Paul F(rancis X.) 1947- ... CANR-22
Earlier sketch in CA 105
Ford, Percy 1894-1983 Obituary ... 110
Ford, Peter 1936- ... 126
See also SATA 59
Ford, Philip J(ohn) 1949- ... 115
Ford, Phyllis M(arjorie) 1928- ... CANR-30
Earlier sketches in CA 33-36R, CANR-13
Ford, R(obert) A(rthur) D(ouglass) 1915- ... CANR-41
Earlier sketches in CA 97-100, CANR-19
See also DLB 88
Ford, R(ichard) Clyde 1870-1951 Brief entry ... 121
Ford, Richard 1944- ... CANR-47
Earlier sketches in CA 69-72, CANR-11
See also CLC 46, 99
Ford, Richard Brice 1935- ... 37-40R
Ford, Robert A. D.
See Ford, R(obert) A(rthur) D(ouglass)
Ford, Robert E. 1913-1975 ... CAP-2
Earlier sketch in CA 29-32
Ford, Robert N(icholas) 1909- ... 33-36R
Ford, Ronnie E. 1961- ... 151
Ford, Stephen 1949- ... 77-80
Ford, Thomas R(obert) 1923- ... CANR-47
Earlier sketch in CA 49-52
Ford, Thomas W(ellborn) 1924- ... 21-24R
Ford, W(illiam) Clay(ton, Jr.) 1946- ... 93-96
Ford, W(illiam) Herschel 1900- ... CANR-5
Earlier sketch in CA 9-12R
Ford, Webster
See Masters, Edgar Lee
Ford, Whitey
See Ford, Edward (Charles)
Ford, Worthington C. 1858-1941 ... DLB 47
Forde, Gerhard O(laf) 1927- ... 89-92
Forde-Johnston, James (Leo) 1927- ... CANR-3
Earlier sketch in CA 9-12R
Fordham, Frieda 1903-1988 Obituary ... 124
Fordham, Peta 1905- ... 106
Fordin, Hugh 1935- ... 57-60
Fordyce, Rachel (Poole) 1942- ... 121
Brief entry ... 118
Fore, William Frank 1928- ... 5-8R
Forell, George W(olfgang) 1919- ... CANR-16
Earlier sketches in CA 1-4R, CANR-1
Foreman, Carl 1914-1984 ... 41-44R
Obituary ... 113
See also DLB 26
Foreman, Clark H(owell) 1902-1977 Obituary .69-72
Foreman, Dave 1946- ... 139
Foreman, Gene 1934- ... 77-80
Foreman, Harry 1915- ... 33-36R
Foreman, Kenneth Joseph 1891- ... CAP-2
Earlier sketch in CA 33-36
Foreman, L(eonard) L(ondon) 1901-(?) ... CANR-63
Earlier sketches in CA 5-8R, CANR-5
Foreman, Lawton Durant 1913- ... 9-12R
Foreman, Lelia M. 1952- ... 150
Foreman, Lelia Rose
See Foreman, Lelia M.
Foreman, Michael 1938- ... CANR-68
Earlier sketches in CA 21-24R, CANR-10, 38
See also CLR 32
See also MAICYA
See also SAAS 21
See also SATA 2, 73
Foreman, Richard 1937- ... CANR-63
Earlier sketches in CA 65-68, CANR-32
See also CLC 50
Foreman, Russell 1921- ... 77-80
Forer, Lois G(oldstein) 1914-1994 ... 29-32R
Obituary ... 145
Forer, Lucille K(remith) ... 37-40R
Forer, Mort 1922- ... 97-100
Fores, John 1914- ... 25-28R
Forest, Antonia ... 103
See also SATA 29
Forest, Dial
See Gault, William Campbell
Forest, Ilse 1896- ... CAP-2
Earlier sketch in CA 19-20
Forest, James H. 1941- ... 136
Forest, Jim
See Forest, James H.
Forest, Lee
See Woods, Clee
Forester, Bruce (Michael) 1939- ... CANR-25
Earlier sketch in CA 107
Forester, C(ecil) S(cott) 1899-1966 ... 73-76
Obituary ... 25-28R
See also CLC 35
See also DLB 191
See also SATA 13
Forester, Frank
See Herbert, Henry William
Forester, Tom 1949- ... 127
Foreyt, John P(aul) 1943- ... CANR-41
Earlier sketch in CA 118
Forez
See Mauriac, Francois (Charles)
Forgie, George B(arnard) 1941- ... 89-92
Forgus, Ronald (Henry) 1928- ... 41-44R
Forio, Robert
See Weiss, Irving J.
Forisha, Barbara L.
See Forisha-Kovach, Barbara L(usk)
Forisha-Kovach, Barbara L(usk) 1941- ... 107
Forker, Charles R(ush) 1927- ... 136
Forkosch, Morris D(avid) 1908- ... 41-44R
Form, William H. 1917- ... 65-68
Forma, Warren 1923- ... 45-48
Forman, Brenda 1936- ... CANR-6
Earlier sketch in CA 9-12R
See also SATA 4
Forman, Celia Adler 1890(?)-1979 Obituary ... 85-88
Forman, Charles William 1916- ... 13-16R
Forman, Harrison 1904-1978 ... 5-8R
Obituary ... 77-80
Forman, Harry Buxton 1842-1917 ... DLB 184
Forman, Henry James 1879-1966 ... 5-8R
Forman, James Douglas 1932- ... CANR-42
Earlier sketches in CA 9-12R, CANR-4, 19
See also AAYA 17
See also CLC 21
See also JRDA
See also MAICYA
See also SATA 8, 70
Forman, Joan ... 102
Forman, Jonathan 1887-1974 ... CAP-2
Earlier sketch in CA 23-24
Forman, Leona S. 1940- ... 25-28R
Forman, Marc A(llan) 1935- ... 57-60
Forman, Max Leon 1909- ... 112
Forman, Milos 1932- ... 109
Forman, Robert E(dgar) 1924- ... 9-12R
Forman, Robert K. C. 1947- ... 145
Forman, Shepard (Lewis) 1938- Brief entry ... 112
Forman, (James Adam) Sholto 1915- ... 25-28R
Formby, William A(rthur) 1943- ... 109
Formento, Dan 1954- ... 112
Formhals, Robert W(illard) Y(ates) S(arguszko)
1919- ... 53-56
Formisano, Ronald P. 1939- ... 154
Brief entry ... 115
Formwalt, Lee W(illiam) 1949- ... 119
Fornara, Charles William 1935- ... 130
Fornari, Franco 1921- ... CANR-12
Earlier sketch in CA 29-32R
Fornari, Harry D(avid) 1919- ... 69-72
Fornell, Earl Wesley 1915-1969 ... 1-4R
Obituary ... 103
Fornes, Maria Irene 1930- ... CANR-28
Earlier sketch in CA 25-28R
Interview in ... CANR-28
See also CLC 39, 61
See also DLB 7
See also HW
See also MTCW 1
Forni, P(ier) M(assimo) 1951- ... 167
Forno, Lawrence J(oseph) 1943- ... 37-40R
Forrest, A(lfred) C(linton) 1916-1978 ... CANR-27
Obituary ... 103
Earlier sketch in CA 49-52
Forrest, Anthony
See MacKenzie, Norman (Ian)
Forrest, Caleb
See Telfer, Dariel (Doris)
Forrest, David
See Forrest-Webb, Robert
Forrest, Derek W(illiam) 1926- ... 77-80
Forrest, Earle Robert 1883-1969 ... 1-4R
Obituary ... 103
Forrest, Felix C.
See Linebarger, Paul M(yron) A(nthony)
Forrest, Gary Gran 1943- ... CANR-32
Earlier sketch in CA 113
Forrest, James Taylor 1921- ... 115
Forrest, John Galbraith 1898-1982 Obituary ... 107
Forrest, Julian
See Wagenknecht, Edward (Charles)
Forrest, Julie de
See DeWitt, Edith Openshaw
Forrest, Katherine V(irginia) 1939- ... 131
Forrest, Leon (Richard) 1937-1997 ... CANR-52
Obituary ... 162
Earlier sketches in CA 89-92, CANR-25
See also CAAS 7
See also BLCS
See also BW 2
See also CLC 4
See also DLB 33
Forrest, Norman
See Morland, Nigel
Forrest, Richard (Stockton) 1932- ... CANR-50
Earlier sketches in CA 57-60, CANR-9, 25
Forrest, Sybil
See Markun, Patricia Maloney
Forrest, W(illiam) G(eorge) 1925- ... 25-28R
Forrest, Wilbur S. 1887-1977 Obituary ... 69-72
Forrestal, Dan J(oseph), Jr. 1912- ... 77-80
Forrester, Duncan B(aillie) 1933- ... 131
Forrester, Frank H. 1919(?)-1986 Obituary ... 119
See also SATA-Obit 52
Forrester, Helen
See Bhatia, Jamunadevi
See also SATA 48
Forrester, Jay W(right) 1918- ... CANR-1
Earlier sketch in CA 45-48
Forrester, John 1949- ... 141
Forrester, Larry 1924- ... 25-28R
Forrester, Leland S. 1905(?)-1978 Obituary ... 81-84
Forrester, Leo
See Lee, Edward Edson
Forrester, Marian
See Schachtel, Roger (Bernard)
Forrester, Martyn (John) 1952- ... 129
Forrester, Mary
See Humphries, Mary
Forrester, Michael A. 1953- ... 146
Forrester, (William) Ray 1911- ... 21-24R
Forrester, Rex Desmond 1928- ... 103
Forrester, Sandra 1949- ... 155
See also SATA 90
Forrester, Sibelan 1961- ... 161
Forrester, Victoria 1940- ... CANR-25
Earlier sketch in CA 108
See also SATA 40
See also SATA-Brief 35
Forrest-Webb, Robert 1929- ... CANR-4
Earlier sketch in CA 49-52
Forsberg, (Charles) Gerald 1912- ... 102
Forsberg, Malcolm I. 1908- ... 21-24R
Forsberg, Roberta Jean 1914- Brief entry ... 105
Forsee, (Frances) Aylesa ... CANR-1
Earlier sketch in CA 1-4R
See also SATA 1
Forsey, Chris 1950- ... SATA 59
Forshay-Lunsford, Cin 1965- ... 119
See also SATA 60
Forssmann, Werner Theodor Otto
1904-1979 Obituary ... 111
Forstchen, William R. 1950- ... 165
Forstenzer, Thomas R. 1944- ... 154
Forstenzer, Tom
See Forstenzer, Thomas R.
Forster, Arnold 1912- ... 13-16R
Forster, E(dward) M(organ) 1879-1970 ... CANR-45
Obituary ... 25-28R
Earlier sketches in CAP-1, CA 13-14
See also AAYA 2
See also CDBLB 1914-1945
See also CLC 1, 2, 3, 4, 9, 10, 13, 15, 22, 45, 77
See also DA
See also DAB
See also DAC
See also DAM MST, NOV
See also DLB 34, 98, 162, 178, 195
See also DLBD 10
See also MTCW 1
See also SATA 57
See also SSC 27
See also WLC
Forster, Georg 1754-1794 ... DLB 94
Forster, John 1812-1876 ... DLB 144, 184
Forster, Kent 1916-1981 ... 21-24R
Obituary ... 125
Forster, Klaus 1945- ... 131
Forster, Marc R. 1959- ... 138
Forster, Margaret 1938- ... CANR-62
Earlier sketch in CA 133
See also DLB 155
Forster, Mark Arnold
See Arnold-Forster, Mark
Forster, Merlin H(enry) 1928- ... 41-44R
Forster, Peter 1926(?)-1982 Obituary ... 107
Forster, Robert 1926- ... 41-44R
Forstman, H(enry) Jackson 1929- ... 13-16R
Forsyth (Outram), Anne 1933- ... CANR-29
Earlier sketches in CA 29-32R, CANR-12
Forsyth, Bill 1948- ... 122
Forsyth, David J(ames) C(ameron) 1940- ... 41-44R
Forsyth, David P(ond) 1930- ... 9-12R
Forsyth, Frederick 1938- ... CANR-62
Earlier sketches in CA 85-88, CANR-38
See also BEST 89:4
See also CLC 2, 5, 36
See also DAM NOV, POP
See also DLB 87
See also MTCW 1
Forsyth, George H(oward), Jr. 1901-1991 ... 37-40R
Obituary ... 133
Forsyth, Ilene (Haering) 1928- ... 37-40R

Forsyth, James (Law) 1913- 73-76
Forsyth, Michael (de Jong) 1951- 133
Forsyth, Richard S(andes) 1948- 116
Forsythe, Elizabeth 1927- 93-96
Forsythe, Irene
See Hanson, Irene (Forsythe)
Forsythe, Robert
See Crichton, Kyle Samuel
Forsythe, Sidney A. 1920- 41-44R
Fort, Ilene Susan 1949- 140
Fort, John 1942- 77-80
Fort, Paul
See Stockton, Francis Richard
Fort, Paul 1872-1960 Obituary 114
Fort, Williams Edwards, Jr. 1905- 37-40R
Fortas, Abe 1910-1982 Obituary 106
Forte, Allen 1926- 41-44R
Forte, Dan 1935- 65-68
Forte, David F. 1941- 53-56
Fortebraccia, Donato
See Forte, Dan
Forten, Charlotte
See Grimke, Charlotte L(ottie) Forten
Forten, Charlotte L.
See Grimke, Charlotte L(ottie) Forten
See also BLC 2
See also DLB 50
See also TCLC 16
Fortes (De Leff), Jacqueline 1952- 148
Fortes, Meyer 1906-1983 129
Obituary 109
Fortescue, William (Archer Irvine) 1945- . CANR-48
Earlier sketch in CA 122
Forth, Melissa D(eal) 161
See also SATA 96
Fortin, Noonie 1947- 152
Fortini, Franco 1917- ....DLB 128
Fortman, Edmund J. 1901-1990 ....CANR-28
Obituary 130
Earlier sketches in CA 21-24R, CANR-11
Fortnum, Peggy
See Nuttall-Smith, Margaret Emily Noel
See also SATA 26
Fortune, T(imothy) Thomas 1856-1928 Brief entry 112
See also DLB 23
Forty, Adrian 1948- 123
Forty, George 1927- CANR-34
Earlier sketches in CA 89-92, CANR-15
Forward, Luke
See Patrick, Johnstone G(illespie)
Forward, Robert L(ull) 1932- CANR-20
Earlier sketch in CA 103
See also SATA 82
Forward, Susan 130
See also BEST 90:1
Forzano, Giovacchino 1884-1970 Obituary 104
Fosburgh, Hugh (Whitney) 1916-1976 Obituary 69-72
Fosburgh, Lacey 1942-1993 ....CANR-22
Obituary 140
Earlier sketch in CA 85-88
Fosburgh, Liza 1930- CANR-30
Earlier sketch in CA 112
Fosburgh, Pieter Whitney 1914(?)-1978 Obituary 77-80
Foscue, Edwin Jay 1899-1972 ....1-4R
Obituary 103
Fosdick, Charles Austin 1842-1915 Brief entry . 119
See also DLB 42
Fosdick, Harry Emerson 1878-1969 Obituary 25-28R
Fosdick, Raymond B(laine) 1883-1972 Obituary 37-40R
Foshay, Toby (Avard) 1950- 119
Foshee, John (Hugh) 1931- 69-72
Foskett, D(ouglas) J(ohn) 1918- CANR-5
Earlier sketch in CA 1-4R
Foskett, Daphne 1911- 102
Foskett, Reginald 1909-1973 ....CAP-2
Earlier sketch in CA 21-22
Foss, Christopher F(rank) 1946- 93-96
Foss, Clive (Frank Wilson) 1939- 132
Foss, Dennis C(arleton) 1947- 104
Foss, Phillip Oliver 13-16R
Foss, William O(tto) 1918- 17-20R
Fosse, Alfred
See Jelly, George Oliver
Fosse, Bob
See Fosse, Robert Louis
See also CLC 20
Fosse, Robert Louis 1927-1987 Obituary 123
Brief entry 110
See also Fosse, Bob
Fossedal, Gregory
See Fossedal, Gregory A.
Fossedal, Gregory A. 1959- 125
Fossey, Dian 1932-1985 ....CANR-34
Obituary 118
Earlier sketch in CA 113
See also MTCW 1
Fossum, Robert H. 1923- 25-28R
Foster, Alan Dean 1946- CANR-56
Earlier sketches in CA 53-56, CANR-5, 22
See also AAYA 16
See also DAM POP
See also SATA 70
Foster, Brad W. 1955- ....SATA 34
Foster, Brian 1920- Brief entry 112
Foster, Carno A(ugustus) 1916- 41-44R
Foster, Catharine Osgood 1907- 65-68
Foster, Cecil (A.) 1954- 154
Foster, Cedric 1900-1975 Obituary 89-92
Foster, Charles Howell 1913- 17-20R
Foster, Charles I(rving) 1898-197(?) 1-4R
Obituary 134
Foster, Charles R(obert) 1927- 110
Foster, Charles William 1939- 57-60
Foster, Chris(topher Joseph) 1932- 139
Foster, Daniel W(illet) 1930- 108
Foster, David 1908- 97-100
Foster, David Manning 1944- CANR-39
Earlier sketches in CA 97-100, CANR-18
Foster, David William (Anthony) 1940- ... CANR-50
Earlier sketches in CA 21-24R, CANR-8, 22
Foster, Don(ald) 1948- 33-36R
Foster, Donald (LeRoy) 1928- 53-56
Foster, Donald W. 1950- 132
Foster, Doris Van Liew 1899- 102
See also SATA 10
Foster, Dorothy 1936- 93-96
Foster, E(lizabeth) C(onnell) 1902- 53-56
See also SATA 9
Foster, Earl M(asters) 1940- 57-60
Foster, Edward Halsey 1942- CANR-40
Earlier sketches in CA 49-52, CANR-2, 18
See also CAAS 26
Foster, Elizabeth 1902- 85-88
See also SATA 12
Foster, Elizabeth 1905-1963 ....1-4R
See also SATA 10
Foster, Elizabeth Read 1912- 106
Foster, F. Blanche 1919- 61-64
See also SATA 11
Foster, Frances Smith 1944- 135
Foster, (Reginald) Francis 1896-1975 109
Obituary 107
Foster, Frederick
See Godwin, John (Frederick)
Foster, G(eorge) Allen 1907-1969 ....9-12R
See also SATA 26
Foster, Genevieve Stump 1893-1979 ....CANR-4
Obituary 89-92
Earlier sketch in CA 5-8R
See also CLR 7
See also DLB 61
See also MAICYA
See also SATA 2
See also SATA-Obit 23
Foster, Genevieve W(akeman) 1902- 69-72
Foster, George
See Haswell, Chetwynd John Drake
Foster, George M(cClelland, Jr.) 1913- Brief entry 113
Foster, H. Lincoln 1906-1989 ....CAP-1
Obituary 128
Earlier sketch in CA 19-20
Foster, Hal
See Foster, Harold (Rudolf)
See also AITN 2
Foster, Hannah Webster 1758-1840 ... DLB 37, 200
Foster, Harold (Rudolf) 1892-1982 Obituary ... 107
See also Foster, Hal
See also SATA 31
Foster, Harold D(ouglas) 1943- 111
Foster, Harry
See Paine, Lauran (Bosworth)
Foster, Henry H(ubbard), Jr. 1911-1988 ... CANR-2
Obituary 125
Earlier sketch in CA 1-4R
Foster, Herbert L(awrence) 1928- 57-60
Foster, Herbert W. 1920(?)-1979 Obituary ... 89-92
Foster, Idris Llywelyn 1911-1984 Obituary 113
Foster, Iris
See Posner, Richard
Foster, J(ames) A(nthony) 1932- 130
Foster, Jack Donald 1930- 29-32R
Foster, James C(aldwell) 1943- CANR-7
Earlier sketch in CA 57-60
Foster, Jeanne
See Williams, Jeanne
Foster, Jeanne Robert (Ollivier) 1884-1970 Obituary 104
Foster, Jeannette Howard 1895-1981 148
Foster, Joanna 1928- CANR-8
Earlier sketch in CA 5-8R
Foster, Jodie 1962- ....AAYA 24
Foster, John
See Foster, John L(ouis)
and Furcolo, Foster
Foster, John 1648-1681 ....DLB 24
Foster, John 1915- 5-8R
Foster, John (Thomas) 1925- 33-36R
See also SATA 8
Foster, John (Andrew) 1941- 126
Foster, John Bellamy 1953- 148
Foster, John Burt, Jr. 1945- 106
Foster, John L(awrence) 1930- 53-56
Foster, John L(ouis) 1941- 161
See also SATA 102
Foster, Joseph O'Kane 1898- 49-52
Foster, Julian F(rancis) S(herwood) 1926- . 29-32R
Foster, K(enneth) Neill 1935- CANR-4
Earlier sketch in CA 53-56
Foster, Laura Louise (James) 1918- 17-20R
See also SATA 6
Foster, (William) Lawrence 1947- 131
Foster, Lee 1923(?)-1977 Obituary 69-72
Foster, Lee Edwin 1943- 33-36R
Foster, Leila Merrell 1929- ....SATA 73
Foster, Lynn 1952- CANR-32
Earlier sketch in CA 113
Foster, Lynne 1937- ....SATA 74
Foster, M(ichael) A(nthony) 1939- CANR-25
Earlier sketches in CA 57-60, CANR-9
Foster, Malcolm (Burton) 1931- 109
Foster, Margaret Lesser 1899(?)-1979 Obituary 89-92
See also SATA-Obit 21
Foster, Margery S(omers) 1914- 5-8R
Foster, Marguerite H. 1909- CAP-2
Earlier sketch in CA 21-22
Foster, Marian Curtis 1909-1978 73-76
Obituary 85-88
See also SATA 23
Foster, Marion
See Shea, Shirley
Foster, Mark Stewart 1939- 106
Foster, Martha S(tanding) 5-8R
Foster, Michael 1904-1956 Brief entry 110
See also DLB 9
Foster, Michael S(immler) 1942- 117
Foster, Myles Birket 1825-1899 ....DLB 184
Foster, Nancy Haston 122
Foster, Nora R(akestraw) 1947- 140
Foster, O'Kane
See Foster, Joseph O'Kane
Foster, Paul 1931- CANR-26
Earlier sketches in CA 21-24R, CANR-9
Foster, Peter 1947- CANR-25
Earlier sketch in CA 108
Foster, Philip (John) 1927- 69-72
Foster, Richard 1946- 137
See also Crossen, Kendell Foster
Foster, Richard J(ames) 1942- CANR-34
Earlier sketches in CA 85-88, CANR-15
Foster, Robert A(lfred) 1949- 81-84
Foster, Ruel Elton 1916- 33-36R
Foster, Sally ....SATA 58
Foster, Shirley 1943- 122
Foster, Steven 1957- 135
Foster, Suzy
See Foster-Fritts, Suzy
Foster, Timothy R(ichard) V(ernon) 1938- 112
Foster, Tony
See Foster, J(ames) A(nthony)
Foster, Virginia Ramos 29-32R
Foster, Walter Roland 1925- Brief entry 116
Foster-Fritts, Suzy 1967- 164
Foster-Harris, William 1903(?)-1978 Obituary ... 104
Fothergill, (Arthur) Brian 1921-1990 ....17-20R
Obituary 132
Fothergill, Philip G(ilbert) 1908- 5-8R
Fotheringham, Nick 1943- 121
Foti, Veronique M. 1938- 141
Fottler, Myron David 1941- CANR-14
Earlier sketch in CA 37-40R
Foucault, Michel 1926-1984 ....CANR-34
Obituary 113
Earlier sketch in CA 105
See also CLC 31, 34, 69
See also MTCW 1
Fougasse
See Bird, (Cyril) Kenneth
Fought, John G(uy) 1938- Brief entry 113
Fouhy, Ed(ward Michael) 1934- 69-72
Foulds, Elfrida Vipont 1902- CANR-38
Earlier sketches in CA 53-56, CANR-4
See also Vipont, Elfrida
See also MAICYA
See also SATA 52
Foulke, Adrienne 1915- 65-68
Foulke, Robert (Dana) 1930- 45-48
Foulke, Roy Anderson 1896- CANR-1
Earlier sketch in CA 1-4R
Foulkes, A(lbert) Peter 1936- 37-40R
Foulkes, (William) David 1935- Brief entry 107
Foulkes, Fred K. 1941- CANR-12
Earlier sketch in CA 33-36R
Foulkes, Paul 1923- 153
Foulkes, Richard (George) 1944- 141
Fountain, Charles (Francis) 1950- 118
Fountain, Leatrice 1924- 21-24R
Fountain, Richard
See Sproat, Iain (MacDonald)
Fouque, Caroline de la Motte 1774-1831 ... DLB 90
Fouque, Friedrich (Heinrich Karl) de la Motte 1777-1843 ....DLB 90
Fouraker, Lawrence Edward 1923- 1-4R
Fourastie, Jean Joseph Hubert 1907-1990 Obituary 132
Fourcade, Marie-Madeleine 1909-1989 Obituary 129
Four Corners, George
See Viereck, George Sylvester
Fourest, Henry-Pierre 1911- 136
Brief entry 109
Fourest, Michel
See Wynne-Tyson, (Timothy) Jon (Lyden)
Fourie, Corlia 1944- 155
See also SATA 91
Fournet, Jean-Claude 1932- 124
Fournier, Frank
See Chapman, Frank M(onroe)
Fournier, Henri Alban 1886-1914 Brief entry ... 104
See also Alain-Fournier
Fournier, Pierre 1916- CANR-40
Earlier sketches in CA 89-92, CANR-16
See also Gascar, Pierre
See also CLC 11
Fourth, Clifton
See Morse, H(enry) Clifton IV
Fourth Brother, The
See Aung, (Maung) Htin
Fourth Earl of Chesterfield
See Stanhope, Philip Dormer
Foust, Paul J(ohn) 1920- 49-52
Fouste, E(thel) Bonita Rutledge 1926- 13-16R
Fout, John C(alvin) 1937- 57-60
Foveaux, Jessie Lee Brown 1899- 163
Fowke, Edith (Margaret) 1913- 37-40R
See also SATA 14
Fowkes, Robert Allen 1913- Brief entry 106
Fowle, Eleanor Cranston
See Cameron, Eleanor Cranston
Fowler, Alastair (David Shaw) 1930- CANR-39
Earlier sketch in CA 13-16R
Fowler, Austin 1928- 21-24R
Fowler, Carolyn 117
Fowler, Charles B(runer) 1931- CANR-49
Earlier sketches in CA 57-60, CANR-8, 24
Fowler, Christopher 1953- 137
Fowler, Connie May 1959(?)- 156
Fowler, David Covington 1921- CANR-58
Earlier sketches in CA 1-4R, CANR-28
Fowler, David Henry 1924- Brief entry 112
Fowler, Don D. 1936- CANR-45
Earlier sketches in CA 33-36R, CANR-15
Fowler, Doreen (Angela) 1948- 119
Fowler, Douglas 1940- 57-60
Fowler, Earlene 1954- 146
Fowler, Elaine W(otten) 1914- 93-96
Fowler, Elizabeth Millspaugh 1921- 102
Fowler, Eugene Devlan 1890-1960 97-100
Obituary 89-92
Fowler, Frank 1900-1971 ....CANR-64
Obituary 113
See also Chase, Borden
Fowler, Gene
See Fowler, Eugene Devlan
Fowler, Gene 1931- CANR-20
Earlier sketches in CA 53-56, CANR-5
Fowler, George P(almer) 1909- 41-44R
Fowler, Guy 1893(?)-1966 Obituary 25-28R
Fowler, Harry (Jr.) 1934- CANR-1
Earlier sketch in CA 45-48
Fowler, Heather T.
See Remoff, Heather T(rexler)
Fowler, Helen Rosa Huxley 1917- CAP-1
Earlier sketch in CA 9-10
Fowler, James W(iley) III 1940- 104
Fowler, Jim
See Fowler, James W(iley) III
Fowler, John M(ajor) 1926- 103
Fowler, Karen Joy 1950- 143
Fowler, Kenneth A(brams) 1900-1987 ... CANR-63
Obituary 122
Earlier sketch in CA 5-8R
Fowler, Marian (Elizabeth) 1929- CANR-48
Earlier sketch in CA 114
Fowler, Mark 1949- 65-68
Fowler, Mary Elizabeth 1911- CAP-2
Earlier sketch in CA 29-32
Fowler, Mary Jane
See Wheeler, Mary Jane
Fowler, (Edward) Michael (Coulson) 1929- 109
Fowler, Raymond Dalton, Jr. 1930- Brief entry . 110
Fowler, Raymond E(veleth) 1933- 85-88
Fowler, Richard A(lan) 1948- CANR-36
Earlier sketch in CA 113
Fowler, Richard Hindle 1910- 130
Fowler, Robert H(oward) 1926- 73-76
Fowler, Roger 1938- 65-68
Fowler, Sandra (Lynn) 1937- 106
Fowler, Sydney
See Wright, S(ydney) Fowler
Fowler, Virginia C. 1948- 145
Fowler, Virginie
See Elbert, Virginie Fowler
Fowler, Wilfred 1907- CAP-1
Earlier sketch in CA 13-14
Fowler, Will 1922- 5-8R
Fowler, William A. 1911- 156
Fowler, William Morgan, Jr. 1944- CANR-57
Earlier sketches in CA 45-48, CANR-1, 31
Fowler, Wilton B(onham) 1936- 53-56
Fowles, Jib 1940- 69-72
Fowles, John (Philip) 1926- CANR-71
Earlier sketches in CA 5-8R, CANR-25
See also CDBLB 1960 to Present
See also CLC 1, 2, 3, 4, 6, 9, 10, 15, 33, 87
See also DAB
See also DAC
See also DAM MST
See also DLB 14, 139
See also MTCW 1
See also SATA 22
Fowlie, Wallace 1908- CANR-5
Earlier sketch in CA 5-8R
Fowlkes, Diane L(owe) 1939- 143
Fox, Adam 1883-1977 ....CANR-10
Earlier sketches in CAP-1, CA 13-14
Fox, Aileen 1907- CANR-5
Earlier sketch in CA 5-8R
See also SATA 58
Fox, Alan John 13-16R
Fox, Alistair 1948- CANR-39
Earlier sketch in CA 116
Fox, Allan M(ark) 1948- 41-44R
Fox, Annette Baker 1912- Brief entry 109
Fox, Anthony
See Fullerton, Alexander (Fergus)
Fox, Bill
See Fox, William
Fox, Brian
See Ballard, (Willis) Todhunter
Fox, C(arol) Lynn 1948- CANR-29
Earlier sketch in CA 110
Fox, Charles Elliot 1878- CAP-1
Earlier sketch in CA 9-10
Fox, Charles Philip 1913- CANR-1
Earlier sketch in CA 1-4R
See also SATA 12
Fox, Col. Victor J.
See Winston, R(obert) A(lexander)
Fox, Connie
See Fox, Hugh (Bernard, Jr.)
Fox, Daniel Michael 1938- 112
Fox, David J(oseph) 1927- 13-16R
Fox, Dorothea Warren 1914- 61-64
Fox, Douglas A(llan) 1927- CANR-17
Earlier sketch in CA 41-44R
Fox, Douglas McMurray 1940- CANR-15
Earlier sketch in CA 33-36R

Fox, E(dward) Inman 1933- ... 17-20R
Fox, Edward J(ackson) 1913- ... 1-4R
Fox, Edward L. 1938-1983 ... 134
Brief entry ... 110
Fox, Edward Whiting 1911- Brief entry ... 106
Fox, Eleanor
See St. John, Wylly Folk
Fox, Fontaine Talbot, Jr. 1884-1964 Obituary 89-92
See also SATA-Obit 23
Fox, Frances Margaret
See Field, Frances Fox
Fox, Frank 1923- ... 159
Fox, Frank W(ayne) 1940- ... 109
Fox, Fred 1903(?)-1981 Obituary ... 104
See also SATA-Obit 27
Fox, Frederic Ewing 1917-1981 ... 1-4R
Obituary ... 103
Fox, Freeman
See Hamilton, Charles (Harold St. John)
Fox, G(ardner) F(rancis) 1911-1986 ... CANR-58
Earlier sketches in CA 5-8R, CANR-5
Fox, G(eoffrey) P. 1938- ... CANR-11
Earlier sketch in CA 21-24R
Fox, Gail 1942- ... CANR-19
Earlier sketch in CA 103
Fox, Geoffrey 1941- ... SATA 73
Fox, George (Richard) 1934- ... 37-40R
Fox, Gilbert T(heodore) 1915- ... 69-72
Fox, Gill
See Fox, Gilbert T(heodore)
Fox, Grace
See Anderson, Grace Fox
Fox, Grace (Estelle) 1899-1984 ... 37-40R
Obituary ... 111
Fox, Grace Imogene 1907- ... 1-4R
Fox, H(enry) B(enjamin) 1910- ... 57-60
Fox, Harrison W(illiam), Jr. 1944- ... 126
Fox, Helen Morgenthau
1885(?)-1974 Obituary ... 45-48
Fox, Hugh (Bernard, Jr.) 1932- ... CANR-54
Earlier sketches in CA 25-28R, CANR-11, 29
Fox, J. N.
See Janeczko, Paul B(ryan)
Fox, Jack C(urtis) 1925-1987 ... 21-24R
Obituary ... 122
Fox, Jack Vernon 1918-1982 Obituary ... 106
Fox, James (Lyttleton) 1945- ... 120
Fox, James M. 1908(?)-1989 ... 102
Obituary ... 128
Fox, John
See Todd, John M(urray)
Fox, John (William), Jr. 1862(?)-1919 Brief
entry ... 108
See also DLB 9
See also DLBD 13
Fox, John 1906-1984 Obituary ... 114
Fox, John 1952-1990 Obituary ... 132
Fox, John H(oward) 1925- ... CANR-8
Earlier sketch in CA 5-8R
Fox, John Roger 1896-1987 Obituary ... 125
Fox, Joseph M(ichael) 1934- ... 106
Fox, Karl A(ugust) 1917- ... CANR-7
Earlier sketch in CA 17-20R
Fox, Kenneth 1944- ... 125
Fox, Larry ... 106
See also SATA 30
Fox, Levi 1914- ... CANR-57
Earlier sketches in CA 77-80, CANR-14, 31
Fox, Logan J(ordan) 1922- ... 53-56
Fox, Lorraine 1922-1976 ... SATA 11, 27
Fox, Lucia
See Lockert, Lucia (Alicia Ungaro Fox)
Fox, Marcia R(ose) 1942- ... 105
Fox, Mary Virginia 1919- ... CANR-44
Earlier sketches in CA 29-32R, CANR-12
See also SATA 44, 88
See also SATA-Brief 39
Fox, Matthew (Timothy) 1940- ... 126
Brief entry ... 109
Fox, Mem
See Fox, Merrion Frances
See also CLR 23
See also MAICYA
Fox, Merrion Frances 1946- ... 127
See also Fox, Mem
See also SATA 51
Fox, Michael A(llen) 1940- ... CANR-19
Earlier sketch in CA 103
Fox, Michael W(ilson) 1937- ... CANR-14
Earlier sketch in CA 73-76
See also SATA 15
Fox, Milton S. 1904-1971 Obituary ... 33-36R
Fox, Nancy L. 1917- ... 122
Fox, Norman A(rnold) 1911-1960 Obituary ... 114
Fox, Owen
See Farmer, Bernard James
Fox, Paula 1923- ... CANR-62
Earlier sketches in CA 73-76, CANR-20, 36
See also AAYA 3
See also CLC 2, 8
See also CLR 1, 44
See also DLB 52
See also JRDA
See also MAICYA
See also MTCW 1
See also SATA 17, 60
Fox, Ralph H(artzler) 1913-1973 Obituary ... 49-52
Fox, Ray Errol 1941- ... 85-88
Fox, Renee C(laire) 1928- ... CANR-65
Earlier sketches in CA 49-52, CANR-47
Fox, Richard Allan, Jr. 1943- ... 147
Fox, Richard G(abriel) 1939- ... 41-44R
Fox, Richard Kyle 1846-1922 ... DLB 79
Fox, Richard Wightman 1945- ... CANR-27
Earlier sketch in CA 93-96
Fox, Robert 1943- ... 77-80
Fox, Robert Barlow 1930- ... 13-16R
Fox, Robert J. 1927- ... CANR-40
Earlier sketches in CA 45-48, CANR-1, 17
See also SATA 33
Fox, Robin 1934- ... 135
Fox, Ruth 1895-1989 ... 73-76
Obituary ... 128
Fox, Samuel 1905-1993 ... CAP-2
Obituary ... 143
Earlier sketch in CA 21-22
Fox, Samuel J. 1919- ... 53-56
Fox, Sharon E(lizabeth) 1938- ... 45-48
Fox, Sidney W(alter) 1912- ... 156
Fox, Siv Cedering 1939- ... 41-44R
Fox, Sonny 1925- ... 41-44R
Fox, Stephen
See Furthmann, Julius Grinnell
Fox, Stephen R. 1945- ... CANR-12
Earlier sketch in CA 29-32R
Fox, Ted
See Fox, Gilbert T(heodore)
and Fox, Theodore J.
Fox, Terry Curtis 1948- ... 117
Fox, Theodore J. 1954- ... 123
Fox, Uffa 1898-1972 Obituary ... 37-40R
Fox, V. Helen
See Couch, Helen F(ox)
Fox, Vernon (Brittain) 1916- ... CANR-35
Earlier sketch in CA 37-40R
Fox, Willard 1919- ... 21-24R
Fox, William 1919(?)-1985 Obituary ... 116
Fox, William L. 1953- ... 167
Fox, William Lloyd 1921- ... 17-20R
Fox, William McNair 1924- ... 5-8R
Fox, William Price (Jr.) 1926- ... CANR-11
Earlier sketch in CA 17-20R
See also CAAS 19
See also CLC 22
See also DLB 2
See also DLBY 81
Fox, William Thornton Rickert 1912- Brief
entry ... 108
Fox, William W(ellington) 1909- ... 1-4R
Foxall, Raymond (Jehoiada Campbell) 1916- ...
CANR-5
Earlier sketch in CA 9-12R
Foxe, Arthur N(orman) 1902-1982 ... CANR-4
Obituary ... 108
Earlier sketch in CA 9-12R
Foxe, John 1516(?)-1587 ... DLB 132
Foxell, Nigel 1931- ... 97-100
Fox-Genovese, Elizabeth 1941- ... CANR-55
Earlier sketches in CA 65-68, CANR-10, 26
Foxley, William M(cLachlan) 1926-1978 ... 77-80
Foxley-Norris, Christopher Neil 1917- ... 109
Fox-Lockert, Lucia
See Lockert, Lucia (Alicia Ungaro Fox)
Foxman, Sherri 1950- ... 112
Fox-Martin, Milton 1914(?)-1977 Obituary ... 69-72
Foxon, A(ndrew David) 1956- ... 121
Foxon, David Fairweather 1923- ... 102
Fox-Sheinwold, Patricia ... 102
Foxworth, Thomas G(ordon) 1937-1994 ... 114
Obituary ... 146
Foxworthy, Jeff 1958- ... 155
Foxx, Jack
See Pronzini, Bill
Foxx, Redd 1922-1991 ... 89-92
Obituary ... 135
Foxx, Richard M(ichael) 1944- ... CANR-17
Earlier sketches in CA 45-48, CANR-1
Foxx, Rosalind
See Haydon, June
and Simpson, Judith H(olroyd)
Foxx, Teralene S. 1939- ... 122
Foy, George 1952- ... 116
Foy, Kenneth R(ussell) 1922- ... 25-28R
Foy, Nancy 1934- ... CANR-2
Earlier sketch in CA 45-48
Fozdar, Jamshed K(hodadad) 1926- ... 49-52
Fraber, Daniel A. 1950- ... 128
Fracchia, Charles A(nthony) 1937- ... 89-92
Frackenpohl, Arthur R(oland) 1924- ... 17-20R
Frackman, Nathaline 1903(?)-1977 Obituary . 69-72
Fraddle, Farragut
See Mearns, David Chambers
Fradenburg, Louise Olga 1953- ... 142
Fradin, Dennis Brindell 1945- ... CANR-50
Earlier sketch in CA 69-72
See also SATA 29, 90
Fradin, Judith (Bernette) Bloom 1945- ... SATA 90
Fradkin, Elvira (Thekla) Kush
1890(?)-1972 Obituary ... 37-40R
Fradkin, Philip L(awrence) 1935- ... 107
Frady, Marshall (Bolton) 1940- ... 147
Fraelich, Richard O(ddly) 1924- ... 5-8R
Fraenkel, Abraham Adolf 1891-1965 ... 159
Fraenkel, Gerd 1919-1970 ... CAP-1
Earlier sketch in CA 11-12
Fraenkel, Gottfried S(amuel)
1901-1984 Obituary ... 114
Fraenkel, Heinrich 1897- ... 13-16R
Fraenkel, Jack R(unnels) 1932- ... 29-32R
Fraenkel, Michael 1896-1957 Brief entry ... 107
See also DLB 4
Fraenkel, Osmond K. 1888-1983 ... CAP-2
Obituary ... 109
Earlier sketch in CA 23-24
Fraenkel-Conrat, Heinz (Ludwig) 1910- ... 156
Frager, Robert 1940- ... 81-84
Frahm, Anne B. Schwerdt 1927- ... 9-12R
Fraiberg, Louis Benjamin 1913- ... 1-4R
Fraiberg, Selma 1918-1981 ... 97-100
Obituary ... 105
Frailey, Paige (Menefee) 1965- ... SATA 82
Fraine, Harold G(eorge) 1900- ... 1-4R
Frair, Wayne Franklin 1926- ... 113
Fraistat, Neil (Richard) 1952- ... 122
Fraistat, Rose Ann C. 1952- ... 123
Frake, Warner
See Musciano, Walter A.
Frakes, George Edward 1932- ... 29-32R
Frakes, William B. 1952- ... 141
Fraley, Oscar (B.) 1914- Brief entry ... 109
Fram, Eugene Harry 1929- ... 17-20R
Frame, Donald M(urdoch) 1911-1991 ... 17-20R
Obituary ... 133
Frame, Janet 1924-
See Clutha, Janet Paterson Frame
See also CLC 2, 3, 6, 22, 66, 96
See also SSC 29
Frame, Paul 1913-1994 Obituary ... 147
Brief entry ... 111
See also SATA 60
See also SATA-Brief 33
See also SATA-Obit 83
Frame, Ronald (William Sutherland) 1953- ... 143
Framo, James L(awrence) 1922- ... CANR-15
Earlier sketch in CA 41-44R
Frampton, Hollis 1936-1984 ... 141
Obituary ... 112
Frampton, Kenneth Brian 1930- ... 105
Frampton, Merle E(lbert) 1903- ... CAP-2
Earlier sketch in CA 25-28
Frampton, Peter (Kenneth) 1950- Brief entry ... 117
Franc, Helen M. 1908- ... 103
Franca, Celia 1921- ... 89-92
Franca, Jose-Augusto 1922- ... CANR-19
Earlier sketch in CA 102
France, Anatole
See Thibault, Jacques Anatole Francois
See also DLB 123
See also TCLC 9
France, Anna Kay 1940- ... 103
France, Beulah Sanford
1891-1971 Obituary ... 33-36R
France, Claire
See Dore, Claire (Morin)
France, David 1959- ... 140
France, Evangeline
See France-Hayhurst, Evangeline
(Chaworth-Musters)
France, Harold L(eroy) 1930- ... 49-52
France, Linda 1958- ... 141
France, Malcolm 1928- ... 21-24R
France, Miranda 1966- ... 168
France, Pierre Mendes
See Mendes France, Pierre
France, R(ichard) T(homas) 1938- ... 162
See also DLB 7
France-Hayhurst, Evangeline (Chaworth-Musters)
1904- ... CAP-1
Earlier sketch in CA 9-10
Francesca, Rosina
See Brookman, Rosina Francesca
Franceschini, Remo 1932- ... 144
Franchere, Ruth ... 73-76
See also SATA 18
Franchi, Eda
See Vickers, Antoinette L.
Francis, Anne
See Bird, Florence (Bayard)
and Wintle, Anne
Francis, Arlene 1912- ... 89-92
Francis, Arthur
See Gershwin, Ira
Francis, Basil (Hoskins) 1906- ... CAP-1
Earlier sketch in CA 13-14
Francis, C. D. E.
See Howarth, Patrick (John Fielding)
Francis, Cat
See Francis, Emile (Percy)
Francis, Charles
See Holme, Bryan
Francis, Clare 1946- ... CANR-34
Earlier sketches in CA 77-80, CANR-15
Francis, Claude 19(?)- ... CLC 50
Francis, Convers 1795-1863 ... DLB 1
Francis, Daniel
See Cranny, Titus (Francis)
Francis, Daniel 1947- ... 111
Francis, (Alan) David 1900- ... 21-24R
Francis, David Noel 1904- ... 5-8R
Francis, David R(ichard) 1933- ... 133
Francis, Dee
See Haas, Dorothy F.
Francis, Dennis S. 1943(?)-1980 Obituary ... 102
Francis, Devon (Earl) 1901-1986 ... 61-64
Obituary ... 118
Francis, Dick 1920- ... CANR-68
Earlier sketches in CA 5-8R, CANR-9, 42
Interview in ... CANR-9
See also AAYA 5, 21
See also BEST 89:3
See also CDBLB 1960 to Present
See also CLC 2, 22, 42, 102
See also DAM POP
See also DLB 87
See also MTCW 1
Francis, Dorothy Brenner 1926- ... CANR-49
Earlier sketches in CA 21-24R, CANR-9, 24
See also SATA 10
Francis, Emile (Percy) 1926- Brief entry ... 112
Francis, SirFrank Chalton 1901-1988 ... 65-68
Obituary ... 126
See also DLB 201
Francis, Gloria A(ileen) 1930-1988 Obituary ... 125
Brief entry ... 113
Francis, H(erbert) E(dward, Jr.) 1924- ... CANR-10
Earlier sketch in CA 25-28R
Francis, Helen Dannefer 1915- ... 13-16R
Francis, J. Alcuin
See Francis, James A.
Francis, James A. 1954- ... 151
See also Francis, James A.
Francis, John M(ichael) 1939- ... 118
Francis, Lesley Lee 1931- ... 151
Francis, Marilyn 1920- ... CANR-3
Earlier sketch in CA 5-8R
Francis, Matthew (Charles) 1956- ... 132
Francis, Michael J(ackson) 1938- ... 89-92
Francis, Michel
See Cattaui, Georges
Francis, Mother Mary
See Aschmann, Alberta
Francis, Nelle (Trew) 1914- ... 37-40R
Francis, Pamela (Mary) 1926- ... 29-32R
See also SATA 11
Francis, Paul
See Engleman, Paul
Francis, Philip
See Lockyer, Roger
Francis, Philip S(heridan) 1918- ... 17-20R
Francis, R. Mabel 1880-(?) ... CAP-2
Earlier sketch in CA 25-28
Francis, Richard (H.) 1945- ... CANR-49
Earlier sketches in CA 102, CANR-24
Francis, Robert (Churchill) 1901-1987 ... CANR-1
Obituary ... 123
Earlier sketch in CA 1-4R
See also CLC 15
Francis, Roy G. 1919- ... CANR-47
Earlier sketch in CA 1-4R
Francis, Samuel 1947- ... 144
Francis, Wayne L(ouis) 1935- ... 41-44R
Francisco, Charles 1930- ... 109
Francisco, Clyde Taylor 1916- Brief entry ... 106
Francisco, Nia 1952- ... 145
Francis-Williams, Lord
See Williams, Edward Francis
Franck, Dan 1952- ... 163
Franck, Eddie
See Cooke, Frank E.
Franck, Frederick 1909- ... CANR-5
Earlier sketch in CA 1-4R
Franck, Harry Alverson 1881-1962 Obituary ... 110
Franck, Irene M(ary) 1941- ... CANR-21
Earlier sketch in CA 104
Franck, Phyllis 1928- ... 53-56
Franck, Sebastian
See Jacoby, Henry
Franck, Sebastian 1499-1542 ... DLB 179
Franck, Thomas M. 1931- ... 33-36R
Franck, Violet M. 1949- ... 140
Francke, Donald Eugene
1910-1978 Obituary ... 81-84
Francke, Herbert W(erner) 1927- ... 156
Francke, Kuno 1855-1930 ... DLB 71
Francke, Linda Bird 1939- ... CANR-15
Earlier sketch in CA 85-88
Franco, Eloise (Bauder) 1910- ... SATA 62
Franco, Jean 1914-1971 ... CAP-2
Earlier sketch in CA 25-28
Franco, Jean 1924- ... CANR-9
Earlier sketch in CA 21-24R
Franco, Johan (Henri Gustave) 1908- ... 97-100
See also SATA 62
Franco, Marjorie ... 114
See also SATA 38
Francoeur, Anna K(otlarchyk) 1940- ... 53-56
Francoeur, Robert T(homas) 1931- ... CANR-57
Earlier sketches in CA 37-40R, CANR-14, 31
Francois, Andre 1915- ... 93-96
See also SATA 25
Francois, Louise von 1817-1893 ... DLB 129
Francois, Pierre 1932- ... 17-20R
Francois, William E. 1924- ... CANR-5
Earlier sketch in CA 13-16R
Francoise
See Seignobosc, Francoise
Francoise 1863-1910 ... DLB 92
Francois-Poncet, Andre 1887-1978 Obituary . 73-76
Franda, Marcus F. 1937- ... CANR-9
Earlier sketch in CA 21-24R
Frandsen, Arden N. 1902- ... 1-4R
Frandsen, Julius 1907-1976 Obituary ... 69-72
Franey, Pierre 1921-1996 ... CANR-15
Obituary ... 154
Earlier sketch in CA 89-92
Frangsmyr, Tore (Lennart) 1938- ... 129
Frank, Adolph F(rederick) 1918- ... 106
Frank, Andre Gunder 1929- ... CANR-28
Earlier sketch in CA 21-24R
Frank, Anne(lies Marie) 1929-1945 ... CANR-68
Brief entry ... 113
Earlier sketch in CA 133
See also AAYA 12
See also DA
See also DAB
See also DAC
See also DAM MST
See also MTCW 1
See also SATA 87
See also SATA-Brief 42
See also TCLC 17
See also WLC
Frank, Benis M. 1925- ... 37-40R
Frank, Benjamin 1902-1984 Obituary ... 113
Frank, Bernhard 1931- ... 105
Frank, Bruno 1887-1945 ... DLB 118
See also TCLC 81
Frank, Charles E(dward) 1911- ... 21-24R
Frank, Charles Paul 1935- Brief entry ... 112
Frank, Charles Raphael (Jr.) 1937- ... 37-40R
Frank, Daniel B. 1956- ... 117
See also SATA 55

Frank, Elizabeth 1945- 126
Brief entry 121
Interview in 126
See also CLC 39
Frank, Florence Kiper 1885(?)-1976 Obituary 65-68
Frank, Frederick S. 1935- 138
Frank, Gerold 1907- Brief entry 109
Frank, Goldalie 1908- CAP-1
Earlier sketch in CA 17-18
Frank, H(ans) Eric 1921- 49-52
Frank, Harry Thomas 1933-1980 53-56
Obituary 103
Frank, Helene
See Vautier, Ghislaine
Frank, Helmut J(ack) 1922- CANR-7
Earlier sketch in CA 17-20R
Frank, Irving 1910- CAP-2
Earlier sketch in CA 21-22
Frank, Isaiah 1917- CANR-1
Earlier sketch in CA 1-4R
Frank, Jacqueline (?)-1982 Obituary 114
Frank, Janet
See Dunleavy, Janet Egleson
Frank, Jeffrey 1942- 21-24R
Frank, Jerome (New) 1889-1957 Brief entry 121
Frank, Jerome D(avid) 1909- CANR-3
Earlier sketch in CA 5-8R
Frank, John G. 1896(?)-1978 Obituary 81-84
Frank, Joseph 1916- CANR-1
Earlier sketch in CA 1-4R
Interview in CANR-32
Frank, Joseph (Nathaniel) 1918- CANR-32
Earlier sketch in CA 77-80
Frank, Josette 1893-1989 .... CAP-1
Obituary 129
Earlier sketch in CA 19-20
See also SATA 10
See also SATA-Obit 63
Frank, Judith M. 127
Frank, Katherine CANR-49
Earlier sketch in CA 124
Frank, Lawrence K(elso) 1890-1968 .... 1-4R
Obituary 103
Frank, Lee
See Griffin, Arthur J.
Frank, Leonard
See King, Roger (Frank Graham)
Frank, Leonhard 1882-1961 Obituary 116
See also DLB 56, 118
Frank, Lucy 1947- 159
See also SATA 94
Frank, Mary 1933- .... SATA 34
Frank, Melvin 1913(?)-1988 Obituary 126
See also DLB 26
Frank, Morton 1912- 102
Frank, Murray 1908-1977 .... 37-40R
Obituary 73-76
Frank, Nathalie D. 1918- 9-12R
Frank, Pat (Harry Hart) 1907-1964 .... 5-8R
Frank, Peter (Solomon) 1950- CANR-15
Earlier sketch in CA 81-84
Frank, Philip Norman 1943- 113
Frank, Philipp (G.) 1884-1966 Obituary 25-28R
Frank, R., Jr.
See Ross, Frank (Xavier), Jr.
Frank, Reuven 1920- 81-84
Frank, Robert G(regg), Jr. 1943- 134
Brief entry 113
Frank, Robert J(oseph) 1939- 65-68
Frank, Robert Worth, Jr. 1914- 13-16R
Frank, Roberta 1941- 115
Frank, Ronald E(dward) 1933- CANR-18
Earlier sketches in CA 5-8R, CANR-3
Frank, Rudolf 1886-1979 121
Frank, Sheldon 1943- 77-80
Frank, Stanley B. 1908-1979 .... 5-8R
Obituary 85-88
Frank, T. C.
See Laughlin, Tom
Frank, Thaisa 1943- 117
Frank, Waldo (David) 1889-1967 93-96
Obituary 25-28R
See also DLB 9, 63
Frank, William G.
See Frank, Rudolf
Frank, William L(uke) 1929- 106
Frankau, Mary Evelyn Atkinson 1899- CAP-1
Earlier sketch in CA 9-10
See also SATA 4
Frankau, Pamela 1908-1967 Obituary 25-28R
Frank-Baron, Elizabeth 1911(?)-1982 Obituary 108
Franke, C(arl) W(ilfred) 1928- 21-24R
Franke, Christopher 1941- 77-80
Franke, David 1938- 49-52
Franke, Herbert W. 1927- 156
Brief entry 110
Franke, Holly L(ambro) 1943- 49-52
Franke, William 1956- 155
Frankel, A(rthur) Steven 1942- 53-56
Frankel, Alona 1937- 135
See also SATA 66
Frankel, Bernice 61-64
See also SATA 9
Frankel, Charles 1917-1979 .... CANR-4
Obituary 89-92
Earlier sketch in CA 5-8R
Frankel, Edward 1910- 85-88
See also SATA 44
Frankel, Eliot 1922-1990 77-80
Obituary 130
Frankel, Ellen 1951- 135
See also SATA 78
Frankel, Flo 1923- 105
Frankel, Glenn 1949- 150
Frankel, Hans H(ermann) 1916- 61-64
Frankel, Haskel 1926- 89-92
Frankel, Hermann F. 1899(?)-1977 Obituary 69-72
Frankel, J(oseph) 1913- CANR-3
Earlier sketch in CA 5-8R
Frankel, Julie 1947- CANR-36
Earlier sketch in CA 113
See also SATA 40
See also SATA-Brief 34
Frankel, Marvin E(arl) 1920- 154
Frankel, Max 1930- 65-68
Frankel, Otto (Herzberg) 1900- 108
Frankel, Sandor 1943- 33-36R
Frankel, Tobia (Brown) 1935(?)-1987 Obituary 122
Frankel, Valerie 1965- 138
Frankel, William 1917- 106
Frankel, Zygmunt 1929- 41-44R
Franken, Rose (Dorothy) 1895(?)-1988 Obituary 125
See also DLBY 84
Frankena, William K(laas) 1908-1994 .... CANR-10
Obituary 147
Earlier sketch in CA 17-20R
Frankenberg, Celestine Gilligan 9-12R
Frankenberg, Dirk 1937- 160
Frankenberg, Lloyd 1907-1975 .... CANR-6
Obituary 57-60
Earlier sketch in CA 1-4R
Frankenberg, Robert 1911- .... SATA 22
Frankenstein, Alfred Victor 1906-1981 .... CANR-2
Obituary 104
Earlier sketch in CA 1-4R
Frankenstein, Carl 1905- 9-12R
Frankenthal, Kate 1889-1976 Obituary 65-68
Frankfort, Ellen 1936-1987 .... CANR-44
Obituary 122
Earlier sketch in CA 29-32R
Frankforter, A(lbertus) Daniel (III) 1939- 81-84
Frankfurt, Harry Gordon 1929- 41-44R
Frankfurter, Felix 1882-1965 168
Brief entry 124
Frankl, Razelle 1932- 133
Frankl, Viktor E(mil) 1905-1997 65-68
Obituary 161
See also CLC 93
Frankland, Mark 1934- CANR-43
Earlier sketch in CA 69-72
Frankland, (Anthony) Noble 1922- CANR-49
Earlier sketches in CA 65-68, CANR-14
Franklet, Duane 1963- 162
Franklin, A.
See Arnold, Adlai F(ranklin)
Franklin, Ada C(rogman) (?)-1983 Obituary 111
Franklin, Adele 1887(?)-1977 Obituary 69-72
Franklin, Alexander (John) 1921- 13-16R
Franklin, Alfred White 1905- CANR-7
Earlier sketch in CA 57-60
Franklin, Ben(jamin) A. 1927- 89-92
Franklin, Benjamin
See Hasek, Jaroslav (Matej Frantisek)
Franklin, Benjamin V 1939- CANR-39
Earlier sketch in CA 115
Franklin, Benjamin 1706-1790 .. CDALB 1640-1865
See also DA
See also DAB
See also DAC
See also DAM MST
See also DLB 24, 43, 73
See also WLCS
Franklin, Billy J(oe) 1940- 33-36R
Franklin, Bob 1949- 124
Franklin, Burt 1903-1972 .... CAP-1
Earlier sketch in CA 13-16
Franklin, Carl (Mikal) 1930- 157
Franklin, Caroline 1949- 145
Franklin, Charles
See Usher, Frank (Hugh)
Franklin, Cheryl J. 1955- 138
See also SATA 70
Franklin, Colin 1923- 77-80
Franklin, Daniel P. 1954- 144
Franklin, David B. 1951- 151
Franklin, Denson Nauls 1914- 1-4R
Franklin, Edward Herbert 1930- 13-16R
Franklin, Elizabeth
See Campbell, Hannah
Franklin, Eugene
See Bandy, (Eugene) Franklin
Franklin, George E. 1890-1971 .... CAP-1
Earlier sketch in CA 19-20
Franklin, H. Bruce 1934- CANR-9
Earlier sketch in CA 5-8R
Franklin, Harold 1926- 29-32R
See also SATA 13
Franklin, Harold L(eroy) 1934- 57-60
Franklin, Harry 1906- CANR-12
Earlier sketches in CAP-1, CA 13-14
Franklin, J(ennie) E(lizabeth) 1937- 61-64
See also BW 1
Franklin, James 1697-1735 .... DLB 43
Franklin, Jane (Morgan) 1934- 161
Franklin, Jay
See Carter, John Franklin
Franklin, Jeffrey P. 1951- 168
Franklin, Jerome L(ee) 1943- 102
Franklin, Jill (Leslie) 1928-1988 Obituary 125
Franklin, Jimmie Lewis 1939- 126
Brief entry 106
Franklin, Joe 1926- 134
Brief entry 108
Franklin, John 1786-1847 .... DLB 99
Franklin, John Hope 1915- CANR-26
Earlier sketches in CA 5-8R, CANR-3
See also BW 2
Franklin, Jon (Daniel) 1942- CANR-27
Earlier sketch in CA 104
Franklin, Kay 1933-1996 118
Obituary 154
Franklin, Keith
See Foy, Kenneth R(ussell)
Franklin, Kerry
See Caldwell, Stratton F(ranklin)
Franklin, Kristine L. 1958- .... SATA 80
Franklin, Linda Campbell 1941- CANR-26
Earlier sketch in CA 105
Franklin, Marc A. 1932- 29-32R
Franklin, Marshall 1929- 53-56
Franklin, Max
See Deming, Richard
Franklin, Michael J(ohn) 1949- 159
Franklin, (Stella Maria Sarah) Miles (Lampe) 1879-1954 164
Brief entry 104
See also TCLC 7
Franklin, Nat
See Bauer, Erwin A.
Franklin, Olga 1912-1985 102
Obituary 115
Franklin, Pat
See Cady, Jack A(ndrew)
Franklin, Penelope (Florence) 1948- 125
Franklin, R(alph) W(illiam) 1937- CANR-9
Earlier sketch in CA 21-24R
Franklin, Richard 1918- 21-24R
Franklin, Robert M(ichael) 1954- 135
Franklin, S(amuel) Harvey 1928- CANR-26
Earlier sketch in CA 105
Franklin, Sidney 1903-1976 Obituary 65-68
Franklin, Steve
See Stevens, Franklin
Franklin, Ursula 1929- 112
Franklin, Wayne S(teven) 1945- 125
Franklyn, Charles Aubrey Hamilton 1896- 9-12R
Franklyn, Julian 1899-1970 Obituary 112
Franklyn, Robert Alan 1918- 89-92
Franklyn, Ross
See Hardy, Francis Joseph
Franko, Lawrence G. 1942- 37-40R
Frankowski, Leo 1943- 120
Franks, C(harles) E(dward) S(elwyn) 1936- 77-80
Franks, Claudia Stillman 1947- 117
Franks, Cyril Maurice 1923- 13-16R
Franks, Don(ald Richard) 1945- 160
Franks, Ed
See Brandon, Johnny
Franks, Felix 1926- 125
Franks, Helen 1934- 133
Franks, Kenny Arthur 1945- CANR-50
Earlier sketch in CA 123
Franks, Lucinda 1946- 53-56
Franks, Marlene Strong 1955- 125
Franks, Maurice R(udolph) 1942- 112
Franks, Robert S(leightholme) 1871-1963 .... 5-8R
Fransella, Fay CANR-13
Earlier sketch in CA 25-28R
Frantz, Charles 1925- CANR-3
Earlier sketch in CA 5-8R
Frantz, Douglas 1949- 126
Frantz, Harry Warner 1891-1982 Obituary 106
Frantz, Joe B. 1917-1993 .... CANR-1
Obituary 143
Earlier sketch in CA 1-4R
Frantz, Ralph Jules 1902-1979 77-80
Obituary 89-92
See also DLB 4
Frantzen, Allen J. 1947- 121
Frantzich, Stephen E. 1944- 164
Franz, Barbara E(van) 1946- 110
Franz, Carl 1944- 107
Franz, William S(trasser) 1945- 110
Franzblau, Abraham N(orman) 1901-1982 .. 29-32R
Obituary 108
Franzblau, Rose N(adler) 1905-1979 .... 29-32R
Obituary 89-92
Franzen, Gosta Knut 1906- 41-44R
Franzen, Jonathan 1959- 129
Franzen, Lavern G(erhardt) 1926- CANR-7
Earlier sketch in CA 61-64
Franzen, Nils-Olof 1916- CANR-25
Earlier sketch in CA 29-32R
See also SATA 10
Franzen, William Edward 1952- 129
Franzero, Carlo Maria 1892-1986 .... CANR-5
Obituary 120
Earlier sketch in CA 1-4R
Franzero, Charles Marie
See Franzero, Carlo Maria
Franzius, Enno 1901- 25-28R
Franzke, Andreas 1938- CANR-68
Earlier sketch in CA 129
Franzmann, Martin H. 1907-1976 .... CANR-3
Earlier sketch in CA 1-4R
Franzos, Karl Emil 1848-1904 .... DLB 129
Franzwa, Gregory M. 1926- CANR-9
Earlier sketch in CA 21-24R
Frappier-Mazur, Lucienne 1932- 158
Frary, Michael 1918- 77-80
Frasca, John (Anthony) 1916-1979 .... CANR-3
Obituary 93-96
Earlier sketch in CA 49-52
Frascatoro, Gerald
See Hornback, Bert G(erald)
Frascino, Edward CANR-37
Brief entry 111
Earlier sketch in CA 114
See also MAICYA
See also SAAS 9
See also SATA 48
See also SATA-Brief 33
Frascona, Joseph Lohengrin 1910- 17-20R
Frasconi, Antonio 1919- CANR-48
Earlier sketches in CA 1-4R, CANR-1
See also MAICYA
See also SAAS 11
See also SATA 6, 53
Frase, Larry E. 1945- 41-44R
Frase, Robert W(illiam) 1912- 33-36R
Fraser, Alex
See Brinton, Henry
Fraser, Allan 1900- 57-60
Fraser, Amy Stewart 1892- CANR-9
Earlier sketch in CA 49-52
Fraser, Anthea CANR-66
Earlier sketches in CA 65-68, CANR-10, 25, 50
Fraser, (Lady) Antonia (Pakenham) 1932- CANR-65
Earlier sketches in CA 85-88, CANR-44
See also CLC 32, 107
See also MTCW 1
See also SATA-Brief 32
Fraser, Arthur Ronald 1888-1974 Obituary 53-56
Fraser, Arvonne S. 1925- 33-36R
Fraser, B. Kay 1941- 69-72
Fraser, Betty
See Fraser, Elizabeth Marr
Fraser, Blair 1909-1968 .... CAP-2
Earlier sketch in CA 23-24
Fraser, Bruce (Donald) 1910-1993 109
Obituary 142
Fraser, Colin 1935- 21-24R
Fraser, Conon 1930- CAP-1
Earlier sketch in CA 9-10
Fraser, D(onald) M(urray) 1946-1985 117
Fraser, David (William) 1920- CANR-65
Earlier sketch in CA 129
Fraser, (William) Dean 1916- 45-48
Fraser, Diane Lynch
See Lynch-Fraser, Diane
Fraser, Dorothy May 1903(?)-1980 Obituary 102
Fraser, Douglas 1910- 102
Fraser, Douglas Ferrar 1929- CANR-4
Earlier sketch in CA 1-4R
Fraser, Edith Emily Rose Oram 1903- CAP-1
Earlier sketch in CA 11-12
Fraser, Elise Parker 1903- 1-4R
Fraser, Elizabeth Marr 1928- .... SATA 31
Fraser, Eric (George) 1902-1983 .... SATA 38
Fraser, Flora 1958- 124
Fraser, G(eorge) S(utherland) 1915-1980 .... CANR-45
Obituary 105
Earlier sketch in CA 85-88
See also DLB 27
Fraser, George (C.) 1945- 146
Fraser, George MacDonald 1925- CANR-48
Earlier sketches in CA 45-48, CANR-2
See also CLC 7
Fraser, Gordon 1943- 168
Fraser, Gordon Holmes 1898- CAP-1
Earlier sketch in CA 13-16
Fraser, Hamish 1913-1986 Obituary 120
Fraser, (William Jocelyn) Ian 1897-1974 Obituary 53-56
Fraser, J(ulius) T(homas) 1923- CANR-53
Earlier sketches in CA 61-64, CANR-8, 27
Fraser, James
See White, Alan
Fraser, Jane
See Pilcher, Rosamunde
Fraser, Janet Hobhouse
See Hobhouse, Janet
Fraser, John 1931- 29-32R
Fraser, Kathleen 1937- 106
See also DLB 169
Fraser, Keath 1944- 125
Fraser, Kennedy 163
Fraser, Margot 1936- 135
Fraser, Mary Ann 1959- 144
See also SAAS 23
See also SATA 76
Fraser, Maxwell
See Fraser, Dorothy May
Fraser, Morris 1941- 102
Fraser, Neil McCormick 1902- 5-8R
Fraser, Nicholas C(ampbell) 1958- 151
Fraser, Peter (Malcolm) 1928-1987 107
Obituary 121
Fraser, Peter (Shaw) 1932- 33-36R
Fraser, Ray
See Fraser, Raymond (Joseph)
Fraser, Raymond (Joseph) 1941- 130
Brief entry 107
Fraser, Robert (H.) 1947- 134
Fraser, Ronald
See Tiltman, Ronald Frank
Fraser, Ronald
See Fraser, Arthur Ronald
Fraser, Ronald (Angus) 1930- 131
Fraser, Russell A(lfred) 1927- 37-40R
Fraser, Stewart Erskine 1929- CANR-32
Earlier sketches in CA 13-16R, CANR-10
Fraser, Stuart
See Wood, James (Alexander Fraser)
Fraser, Sylvia 1935- CANR-60
Earlier sketches in CA 45-48, CANR-1, 16
See also CLC 64
Fraser, W(aller) B(rown) 1905- CAP-2
Earlier sketch in CA 25-28
Fraser, W(illiam) Hamish 1941- 103
Fraser, W(illiam) Lionel 18(?)-1965 .... CAP-1
Earlier sketch in CA 9-10
Fraser, Wynnette (McFaddin) 1925- 155
See also SATA 90
Fraser Darling, Frank 1903-1979 61-64
Obituary 89-92

Fraser Harrison, Brian 1918- ... CAP-1
Earlier sketch in CA 9-10
Fraser Roberts, J(ohn) A(lexander)
See Roberts, J(ohn) A(lexander) Fraser
Frasier, Debra 1953- ... 137
See also SATA 69
Frasier, James E(dwin) 1923- ... 17-20R
Frassanito, William A(llen) 1946- ... CANR-9
Earlier sketch in CA 57-60
Frasure, David W(illiam) 1942- ... 113
Fratcher, William F(ranklin) 1913- ... CANR-3
Earlier sketch in CA 5-8R
Frater, Alexander 1937- ... 140
Frater Perdurabo
See Crowley, Edward Alexander
Fratianni, Michele 1941- ... 144
Fraticelli, Marco 1945- ... 118
Fratkin, Elliot 1948- ... 144
Fratti, Mario 1927- ... 77-80
Frattini, Alberto 1922- ... DLB 128
Frau Ava (?)-1127 ... DLB 148
Fraustino, Lisa Rowe 1961- ... 150
See also SATA 84
Frautschi, R(ichard) L(ane) 1926- ... 17-20R
Frawley, Ernest D(avid) 1920-1984 Obituary ... 114
Frawley, William John 1953- ... 114
Fraydas, Stan 1918- ... 57-60
Frayling, Christopher 1946- ... 110
Frayn, Michael 1933- ... CANR-69
Earlier sketches in CA 5-8R, CANR-30
See also CLC 3, 7, 31, 47
See also DAM DRAM, NOV
See also DLB 13, 14, 194
See also MTCW 1
Frayser, Suzanne G. 1943- ... 127
Fraze, Candida (Merrill) 1945- ... 126
See also CLC 50
Frazee, Charles A(aron) 1929- ... 37-40R
Frazee, Steve (Charles) 1909-1992 ... CANR-70
Earlier sketches in CA 5-8R, CANR-5
Frazen, Bill
See Franzen, William Edward
Frazer, Andrew
See Marlowe, Stephen
Frazer, Fred
See Avallone, Michael (Angelo, Jr.)
Frazer, J(ames) G(eorge) 1854-1941 Brief entry ... 118
See also TCLC 32
Frazer, Mark Petrovich
See Maclean, Donald Duart
Frazer, Robert Caine
See Creasey, John
Frazer, Robert W(alter) 1911- ... 17-20R
Frazer, Sir James George
See Frazer, J(ames) G(eorge)
Frazer, Timothy C. 1941- ... 147
Frazer, William J(ohnson), Jr. 1924- ... 17-20R
Frazer, Winifred Dusenbury
See Frazer, Winifred L(oesch)
Frazer, Winifred L(oesch) ... 25-28R
Frazer-Hurst, Douglas 1883- ... CAP-1
Earlier sketch in CA 9-10
Frazetta, Frank 1928- ... CANR-46
Earlier sketch in CA 104
See also AAYA 14
See also SATA 58
Frazier, Allie M. 1932- Brief entry ... 110
Frazier, Anitra 1937- ... 113
Frazier, Arthur
See Bulmer, (Henry) Kenneth
Frazier, Charles 1950- ... 161
See also CLC 109
Frazier, Claude A(lbee) 1920- ... CANR-32
Earlier sketch in CA 29-32R
Frazier, Cliff(ord) 1934- Brief entry ... 109
Frazier, Donald S(haw) 1965- ... 151
Frazier, Edward Franklin 1894-1962 Obituary ... 108
Frazier, George 1911-1974 ... CAP-2
Obituary ... 49-52
Earlier sketch in CA 25-28
Frazier, Ian 1951- ... CANR-54
Earlier sketch in CA 130
See also CLC 46
Frazier, Kendrick (Crosby) 1942- ... CANR-39
Earlier sketches in CA 101, CANR-17
Frazier, Mansfield B. 1943- ... 150
Frazier, Neta (Osborn) Lohnes 1890-1990 . CANR-1
Obituary ... 131
Earlier sketch in CA 1-4R
See also SATA 7
Frazier, Sarah
See Wirt, Winola Wells
Frazier, Shervert Hughes 1921- ... 85-88
Frazier, Shirley George 1957- ... 164
Frazier, Thomas R(ichard) 1931- ... 33-36R
Frazier, Walt(er) 1945- ... 103
Frears, J(ohn) R(ussell) 1936- ... 107
Freas, Frank Kelly 1922- ... CANR-21
Earlier sketch in CA 102
Freburger, William J. 1940- ... 115
Frech, Frances 1923- ... 97-100
Frechet, (Rene) Maurice 1878-1973 ... 156
Frechette, Louis-Honore 1839-1908 ... DLB 99
Freda, Joseph 1951- ... 152
Freddi, Cris 1955- ... 106
Frede, Richard 1934- ... CANR-32
Earlier sketch in CA 69-72
Fredeman, William E(van) 1928- ... 33-36R
Fredenburgh, Franz A(lvah) 1906- ... 33-36R
Frederic, Harold 1856-1898 ... DLB 12, 23
See also DLBD 13
Frederic, Mike
See Cox, William R(obert)
Frederic, Sister M. Catherine
See Fleischbein, Sister M. Catherine Frederic
Frederick, Carl Louis 1942- ... 65-68
Frederick, David C. 1961- ... 156
Frederick, Dick
See Dempewolff, Richard F(rederic)
Frederick, John
See Faust, Frederick (Schiller)
Frederick, John H(utchinson) 1896- ... 1-4R
Frederick, John Towner 1893-1975 Obituary ... 111
Frederick, Lee
See Nussbaum, Al(bert F.)
Frederick, Oswald
See Snelling, O(swald) F(rederick)
Frederick, Pauline 1908-1990 ... 102
Obituary ... 131
See also SATA 27
Frederick, Robert Allen 1928- ... CANR-3
Earlier sketch in CA 45-48
Fredericks, Carlton 1910-1987 ... CANR-7
Obituary ... 123
Earlier sketch in CA 53-56
See also AITN 1
Fredericks, Frank
See Franck, Frederick
Fredericks, Frohm
See Kerner, Fred
Fredericks, Pierce Griffin 1920-1985 ... 13-16R
Obituary ... 117
Fredericks, Vic
See Majeski, William
Frederics, Jocko
See Frede, Richard
Frederics, Macdowell
See Frede, Richard
Frederika (Louise), Queen 1917-1981 Obituary . 108
Frederiksen, Alan Ryle 1935- ... 113
Frederiksen, Martin W. 1930-1980 Obituary ... 101
Frederikson, Edna 1904- ... 49-52
Fredge, Frederique 1906- ... CAP-2
Earlier sketch in CA 21-22
Fredman, Alice G(reen) 1924-1993 ... 102
Obituary ... 141
Fredman, Henry John 1927- ... 29-32R
Fredman, John
See Fredman, Henry John
Fredman, Ruth Gruber 1934- ... 106
Fredricks, Edgar J(ohn) 1942- ... 25-28R
Fredrickson, George M(arsh) 1934- ... CANR-49
Earlier sketches in CA 17-20R, CANR-8, 24
Fredrickson, Olive A(lta) 1901- ... 49-52
Fredriksson, Don 1926- ... 110
Fredriksson, Kristine 1940- ... 122
Free
See Hoffman, Abbie
Free, Ann Cottrell ... 9-12R
Free, James S(tillman) 1908-1996 ... 77-80
Obituary ... 151
Free, Lloyd A. 1908-1996 ... 13-16R
Obituary ... 154
Free, William Joseph 1933- ... 9-12R
Free, William Norris 1933- ... 25-28R
Freeborn, Brian (James) 1939- ... 65-68
Freeborn, Richard H. 1926- ... CANR-1
Earlier sketch in CA 1-4R
Freed, Alvyn M. 1913- ... CANR-8
Earlier sketch in CA 61-64
See also SATA 22
Freed, Anne O. 1917- ... 145
Freed, Arthur 1894-1973 Obituary ... 41-44R
Freed, Barry
See Hoffman, Abbie
Freed, Donald 1932- ... 85-88
Freed, Louis Franklin 1903- ... 5-8R
Freed, Lynn (R.) 1945- ... CANR-56
Earlier sketches in CA 108, CANR-27
Freed, Margaret De Haan 1917- ... 73-76
Freed, Ray 1939- ... CANR-40
Earlier sketch in CA 117
Freedberg, S(ydney) J(oseph) 1914-1997 ... CANR-17
Obituary ... 158
Earlier sketches in CA 1-4R, CANR-1
Freedeman, Charles E(ldon) 1926- ... 102
Freeden, Michael S(tephen) 1944- ... 127
Freedgood, Lillian (Fischel) 1911- ... 13-16R
Freedgood, Morton 1912- ... 128
Brief entry ... 108
See also AITN 1
Freedland, Michael 1934- ... CANR-29
Earlier sketches in CA 65-68, CANR-11
Freedland, Nat(haniel) 1936- ... 65-68
Freedley, George (Reynolds) 1904-1967 .. CANR-4
Earlier sketch in CA 5-8R
Freedman, Alfred M(ordecai) 1917- ... CANR-4
Earlier sketch in CA 49-52
Freedman, Anne (E.) 1938- ... 150
Freedman, Arthur M(erton) 1916- ... 41-44R
Freedman, Benedict 1919- ... 69-72
See also SATA 27
Freedman, Dan 1952- ... 126
Freedman, Daniel X. 1921-1993 ... 41-44R
Obituary ... 141
Freedman, David A(sa) 1918- ... 167
Freedman, David M(ichael) 1949- ... 112
Freedman, David Noel 1922- ... CANR-1
Earlier sketch in CA 1-4R
Freedman, Eric 1949- ... 144
Freedman, Hy 1914- ... 85-88
Freedman, J. F. ... 161
Freedman, James O. 1935- ... 152
Freedman, Jeff 1953- ... 155
See also SATA 90
Freedman, Jonathan (Borwick) 1950- ... 157
Freedman, Leonard 1924- ... CANR-1
Earlier sketch in CA 1-4R
Freedman, Luba 1953- ... 152
Freedman, M(orris) David 1938- ... CANR-16
Earlier sketch in CA 41-44R
Freedman, Marcia K(ohl) 1922- ... CANR-10
Earlier sketch in CA 25-28R
Freedman, Maurice 1920-1975 ... CAP-2
Obituary ... 61-64
Earlier sketch in CA 25-28
Freedman, Mervin B. 1920- ... 29-32R
Freedman, Michael H(artley) 1951- ... 161
Freedman, Monroe H(enry) 1928- Brief entry .. 107
Freedman, Morris 1920- ... CANR-3
Earlier sketch in CA 5-8R
Freedman, Nancy 1920- ... CANR-19
Earlier sketches in CA 45-48, CANR-1
Interview in ... CANR-19
See also SATA 27
Freedman, Paul H(arris) 1949- ... 122
Freedman, Ralph (William Bernard) 1920- ... 128
Brief entry ... 117
Freedman, Richard 1932-1991 ... 77-80
Obituary ... 134
Freedman, Robert Owen 1941- ... CANR-13
Earlier sketch in CA 33-36R
Freedman, Ronald 1917- ... CANR-6
Earlier sketch in CA 9-12R
Freedman, Russell (Bruce) 1929- ... CANR-46
Earlier sketches in CA 17-20R, CANR-7, 23
See also AAYA 4, 24
See also CLR 20
See also JRDA
See also MAICYA
See also SATA 16, 71
Freedman, Samuel Sumner 1927- ... 112
Freedman, Sarah Warshauer 1946- ... 160
Freedman, Warren 1921- ... 17-20R
Freehill, Maurice F(rancis) 1915- ... 5-8R
Freehling, Alison Goodyear 1941- ... 112
Freehof, Solomon B(ennett) 1892-1990 ... 93-96
Obituary ... 131
Freeland, Jay
See McLeod, John F(reeland)
Freeland, John Maxwell 1920- ... 13-16R
Freeland, Richard M. 1941- ... 81-84
Freeland, Stephen L. 1911(?)-1977 Obituary . 69-72
Freeley, Austin J. 1922- ... 5-8R
Freeling, Nicolas 1927- ... CANR-50
Earlier sketches in CA 49-52, CANR-1, 17
See also CAAS 12
See also CLC 38
See also DLB 87
Freely, Maureen 1952- ... 97-100
Freeman, A. Myrick III 1936- ... 85-88
Freeman, Anne Frances 1936- ... 1-4R
Freeman, Anne Hobson 1934- ... 154
Freeman, Arthur 1938- ... CANR-1
Earlier sketch in CA 1-4R
Freeman, Barbara C(onstance) 1906- ... 73-76
See also SATA 28
Freeman, Barbara M. 1947- ... 132
Freeman, Bill
See Freeman, William Bradford
Freeman, Bjorn
See Pratney, William Alfred
Freeman, C(lifford) Wade 1906- ... 5-8R
Freeman, Castle (William), Jr. 1944- ... 153
Freeman, Charles K. 1900-1980 Obituary ... 97-100
Freeman, Charles Wellman, Jr. 1943- ... 150
Freeman, Chas W.
See Freeman, Charles Wellman, Jr.
Freeman, Cynthia
See Feinberg, Beatrice Cynthia Freeman
Freeman, Daniel E(van) 1959- ... 144
Freeman, Darlene 1934- ... 29-32R
Freeman, Dave
See Freeman, David
Freeman, David 1922- ... 102
Freeman, David E(dgar) 1945- ... 131
Brief entry ... 108
Freeman, David Hugh 1924- ... CANR-17
Earlier sketch in CA 1-4R
Freeman, Davis
See Friedman, David F.
Freeman, Don 1908-1978 ... CANR-44
Earlier sketch in CA 77-80
See also CLR 30
See also MAICYA
See also SATA 17
Freeman, Donald Cary 1938- ... 53-56
Freeman, Donald McKinley 1931- ... CANR-15
Earlier sketch in CA 37-40R
Freeman, Douglas Southall 1886-1953 Brief entry ... 109
See also DLB 17
See also DLBD 17
See also TCLC 11
Freeman, Eugene 1906- ... CANR-26
Earlier sketch in CA 41-44R
Freeman, G(raydon) L(a Verne) 1904- ... CANR-13
Earlier sketch in CA 13-16R
Freeman, Gary 1945- ... 93-96
Freeman, Gillian 1929- ... CANR-43
Earlier sketches in CA 5-8R, CANR-3
Freeman, Harrop A(rthur) 1907- ... 13-16R
Freeman, Harry 1906-1978 ... 77-80
Freeman, Harry M. 1943- ... 154
Freeman, Howard E(dgar) 1929-1992 ... CANR-23
Obituary ... 139
Earlier sketches in CA 5-8R, CANR-6
Freeman, Ira Henry 1906-1997 ... CAP-1
Obituary ... 156
Earlier sketch in CA 13-16
Freeman, Ira Maximilian 1905- ... 73-76
See also SATA 21
Freeman, James Dillet 1912- ... 17-20R
Freeman, James Montague 1936- ... 102
Freeman, Jean Kenny 1929- ... 115
Freeman, Jean Todd 1929- ... 25-28R
Freeman, Jo 1945- ... CANR-45
Earlier sketches in CA 61-64, CANR-8
Freeman, John Crosby 1941- ... 13-16R
Freeman, Joseph 1897-1965 Obituary ... 89-92
Freeman, Joshua B. 1949- ... 139
Freeman, Judith 1946- ... 148
See also CLC 55
Freeman, Kathleen 1897-1959 Brief entry ... 112
Freeman, Larry
See Freeman, G(raydon) L(a Verne)
Freeman, Lea David 1887(?)-1976 Obituary .. 69-72
Freeman, Legh Richmond 1842-1915 ... DLB 23
Freeman, Leslie J(ane) 1944- ... 106
Freeman, Linton C(larke) 1927- ... 69-72
Freeman, Lucy (Greenbaum) 1916- ... CANR-3
Earlier sketch in CA 5-8R
See also SATA 24
Freeman, Mae (Blacker) 1907- ... 73-76
See also SATA 25
Freeman, Marcia S. 1937- ... SATA 102
Freeman, Margaret B. 1899-1980 ... 109
Obituary ... 97-100
Freeman, Margaret C(ooper) 1913- ... 57-60
Freeman, Margaret N(adgwick) 1915- ... 9-12R
Freeman, Martha 1956- ... 168
See also SATA 101
Freeman, Mary Eleanor Wilkins 1852-1930 Brief entry ... 106
See also DLB 12, 78
See also SSC 1
See also TCLC 9
Freeman, Max Herbert 1907- Brief entry ... 109
Freeman, Morton S(igmund) 1912- ... 118
Freeman, Nancy 1932- ... SATA 61
Freeman, Paul 1929(?)-1980 Obituary ... 101
Freeman, Peter J.
See Calvert, Patricia
Freeman, R(ichard) Austin 1862-1943 Brief entry ... 113
See also DLB 70
See also TCLC 21
Freeman, R(ichard) B(roke) 1915-1986 ... 133
Obituary ... 120
Freeman, Richard B(arry) 1944- ... CANR-15
Earlier sketch in CA 85-88
Freeman, Richard Borden 1908- ... CANR-17
Earlier sketch in CA 1-4R
Freeman, Roger A(dolph) 1904-1991 ... 25-28R
Obituary ... 136
Freeman, Roger A(nthony Wilson) 1928- . CANR-51
Earlier sketches in CA 65-68, CANR-10, 26
Freeman, Roger Anthony
See Freeman, Roger A(nthony Wilson)
Freeman, Roger K. 1935- ... 127
Freeman, Roger L(ouis) 1928- ... CANR-12
Earlier sketch in CA 69-72
Freeman, Ruth B(enson) 1906- ... 41-44R
Freeman, Ruth (Lazear) S(underlin) 1907- ... CANR-13
Earlier sketches in CAP-1, CA 13-16
Freeman, Sarah (Caroline) 1940- ... 133
See also SATA 66
Freeman, Simon (David) 1952- ... 133
Freeman, Susan Tax 1938- ... 85-88
Freeman, T(homas) W(alter) 1908-1988 ... 5-8R
Obituary ... 125
Freeman, Thomas 1919- ... 93-96
Freeman, Tony ... 134
See also SATA-Brief 44
Freeman, Walter (Jackson, Jr.) 1895-1972 .. CAP-1
Obituary ... 33-36R
Earlier sketch in CA 17-18
Freeman, Warren S(amuel) 1911- ... 5-8R
Freeman, William Bradford 1938- ... SATA 58
See also SATA-Brief 48
Freeman, William M. 1913-1990 Obituary ... 130
Freeman-Grenville, Greville Stewart Parker 1918- .. CANR-3
Earlier sketch in CA 5-8R
Freeman-Ishill, Rose 1895- ... CAP-1
Earlier sketch in CA 9-10
Freemantle, Brian (Harry) 1936- ... CANR-66
Earlier sketches in CA 65-68, CANR-16, 43
Freemon, Frank R(eed) 1938- ... 45-48
Freer, Coburn 1939- ... 125
Brief entry ... 105
Freer, Harold Wiley 1906- ... CAP-2
Earlier sketch in CA 21-22
Freese, Arthur S. 1917- ... 77-80
Freese, Mathias B(alogh) 1940- ... 164
Freestrom, Hubert J. 1928- ... 37-40R
Freeth, Zahra 1925- ... 121
Freeze, Gregory L. 1945- ... 168
Fregault, Guy 1918-1977 ... 101
Frege, (Friedrich Ludwig) Gottlob 1848-1925 Brief entry ... 120
Fregly, Bert 1922- ... CANR-8
Earlier sketch in CA 57-60
Fregosi, Claudia (Anne Marie) 1946- ... 69-72
See also SATA 24
Frei, Eduardo
See Frei Montalva, Eduardo
Frei, Hans W(ilhelm) 1922-1988 Obituary ... 126
Brief entry ... 111
Freiberg, Stanley K(enneth) 1923- ... CANR-31
Earlier sketch in CA 112
Freiberger, Steven Z. 1950- ... 138
Freid, Jacob L. 1913- ... CANR-17
Earlier sketch in CA 1-4R
Freidank c. 1170-c. 1233 ... DLB 138
Freidel, Frank (Burt, Jr.) 1916-1993 ... CANR-46
Obituary ... 140
Earlier sketches in CA 1-4R, CANR-5
Freidenreich, Harriet Pass 1947- ... 114
Freides, Thelma K(atz) 1930- ... 49-52

Freidin, Seymour K(enneth) 1917-1991 ... CANR-2
Obituary ... 134
Earlier sketch in CA 1-4R
Freidson, Eliot 1923- ... CANR-8
Earlier sketch in CA 5-8R
Freihofer, Lois Diane 1933- ... 13-16R
Freilich, Joan S(herman) 1941- ... 57-60
Freilich, Morris 1928- ... 37-40R
Freiligrath, Ferdinand 1810-1876 ... DLB 133
Frei Montalva, Eduardo 1911-1982 Obituary ... 110
Freire, P.
See Freire, Paulo
Freire, P.
See Freire, Paulo
Freire, Paulo 1921-1997 ... 132
Obituary ... 158
Brief entry ... 116
Freireich, Valerie J. 1952- ... 156
Freire-Maia, Newton 1918- ... 29-32R
Freitas, Margarete Elisabeth 1927- ... 45-48
Freivalds, John 1944- ... 69-72
Freixedo, Salvador 1923- ... CANR-46
Earlier sketch in CA 29-32R
Frelinghuysen, Joseph S. 1912- ... 134
Fremantle, Anne 1910- ... 13-16R
Fremgen, James Morgan 1933- ... 17-20R
Fremlin, Celia
See Goller, Celia (Fremlin)
Fremont, Jessie Benton 1834-1902 ... DLB 183
Fremont, John Charles 1813-1890 ... DLB 186
Fremont, W. B.
See Bowers, Warner Fremont
Fremont-Smith, Eliot 1929- ... 105
Frenay, Henri 1905-1988 Obituary ... 126
French, Albert 1943- ... 167
See also CLC 86
French, Alfred 1916- ... 102
French, Alice 1850-1934 ... DLB 74
See also DLBD 13
French, Allen 1870-1946 Brief entry ... 122
See also YABC 1
French, Anne 1956- ... 153
French, Ashley
See Robins, Denise (Naomi)
French, Bevan M(eredith) 1937- ... 97-100
French, Brandon 1944- ... 89-92
French, Calvin L(eonard) 1934- ... 53-56
French, Charles E(zra) 1923- ... CANR-1
Earlier sketch in CA 45-48
French, Christopher W. 1940(?)-1989 Obituary . 129
French, David 1939- ... 101
See also DAC
See also DLB 53
French, Doris
See Shackleton, Doris (Cavell)
French, Dorothy Kayser 1926- ... CANR-3
Earlier sketch in CA 9-12R
See also SATA 5
French, Edward L(ivingstone) 1916-1969 ... CAP-2
Earlier sketch in CA 21-22
French, Evangeline 1871-1960 ... DLB 195
French, Fiona 1944- ... CANR-40
Earlier sketch in CA 29-32R
See also CLR 37
See also MAICYA
See also SAAS 21
See also SATA 6, 75
French, Francesca 1874-1960 ... DLB 195
French, Herbert E(liot) 1912- ... 45-48
French, Kathryn
See Mosesson, Gloria R(ubin)
French, Marilyn 1929- ... CANR-31
Earlier sketches in CA 69-72, CANR-3
Interview in ... CANR-31
See also CLC 10, 18, 60
See also DAM DRAM, NOV, POP
See also MTCW 1
French, Michael 1944- ... 89-92
Interview in ... 89-92
See also SATA 49
See also SATA-Brief 38
French, Nicci
See French, Sean
French, Paul
See Asimov, Isaac
French, Peter 1918- ... 1-4R
French, Peter A(ndrew) 1942- ... CANR-38
Earlier sketches in CA 45-48, CANR-1, 17
French, Philip (Neville) 1933- ... 103
French, R(obert) B(utler) D(igby) 1904-1981 . CAP-2
Obituary ... 104
Earlier sketch in CA 25-28
French, R(oger) K(enneth) 1938- ... CANR-42
Earlier sketch in CA 118
French, Richard (De Land) 1947- ... CANR-11
Earlier sketch in CA 69-72
French, Ruth M. 1921(?)-1987 Obituary ... 122
French, Scott Robert 1948- ... 57-60
French, Sean 1959- ... 160
French, Simon 1957- ... CANR-49
Earlier sketches in CA 105, CANR-22
See also SATA 86
French, Warren G(raham) 1922- ... CANR-46
Earlier sketches in CA 1-4R, CANR-1, 16
French, Wendell L(owell) 1923- ... 116
French, Will 1890(?)-1979 Obituary ... 89-92
French, William (Harold) 1926- ... 69-72
French, William Marshall 1907- ... CAP-1
Earlier sketch in CA 13-16
Frend, A.
See Cleveland, Philip Jerome
Frend, W(illiam) H(ugh) C(lifford) 1916- ... CANR-9
Earlier sketch in CA 21-24R
Freneau, Philip Morin 1752-1832 ... DLB 37, 43
Freni, Melo 1934- ... DLB 128
Frenkel, Jacob A(haron) 1943- ... 89-92
Frenkel, Richard E(ugene) 1924- ... 21-24R
Frentzen, Jeffrey 1956- ... 109
Frenz, Horst 1912- ... 29-32R
Frenzel, Louis (Earl), Jr. 1938- ... 112
Frere, A. S.
See Frere-Reeves, Alexander Stuart
Frere, Emile (George) 1917-1974 ... 41-44R
Frere, James Arnold 1920- ... 5-8R
Frere, Paul 1917- ... CANR-14
Earlier sketch in CA 5-8R
Frere, Sheppard (Sunderland) 1916- ... 21-24R
Frere-Cook, Gervis 1928- Brief entry ... 111
Frere-Reeves, Alexander Stuart
1892-1984 Obituary ... 114
Frerichs, A(lbert) C(hristian) 1910- ... CAP-2
Earlier sketch in CA 25-28
Freschet, Berniece (Louise Speck) 1927- ...
CANR-11
Earlier sketch in CA 17-20R
Frese, Dolores Warwick 1936- ... CANR-9
Earlier sketch in CA 5-8R
Freshfield, Douglas W. 1845-1934 ... DLB 174
Fretheim, Terence E(rling) 1936- ... CANR-11
Earlier sketch in CA 25-28R
Fretter, T. W.
See Andre, (Kenneth) Michael
Fretter, William Bache 1916- ... 113
Fretwell, Stephen DeWitt 1942- ... 53-56
Freuchen, (Lorence) Peter (Elfred) 1886-1957 Brief entry ... 114
Freud, Anna 1895-1982 ... CANR-34
Obituary ... 108
Earlier sketch in CA 112
See also MTCW 1
Freud, Clement (Raphael) 1924- ... 102
Freud, Ernst L. 1892-1970 ... 160
Freud, Esther 1963- ... 144
Freud, Sigmund 1856-1939 ... CANR-69
Brief entry ... 115
Earlier sketch in CA 133
See also MTCW 1
See also TCLC 52
Freud, Sophie 1924- ... 134
Freudberg, Frank 1953- ... 118
Freudenberger, C(arlton) Dean 1930- ... 135
Freudenberger, Herman 1922- ... 13-16R
Freudenheim, Leslie Ann Mandelson 1941- .. 69-72
Freudenheim, Yehoshua (Oskar) 1894-1975 CAP-2
Earlier sketch in CA 21-22
Freudenthal, Gad 1944- ... 153
Freudenthal, Hans 1905- ... CANR-27
Earlier sketches in CA 25-28R, CANR-11
Freund, E(rnest) Hans 1905- ... 1-4R
Freund, Edith 1931- ... 118
Freund, Gerald 1930-1997 ... CANR-1
Obituary ... 158
Earlier sketch in CA 1-4R
Freund, Gisele 1912- ... 49-52
Freund, John E(rnst) 1921- ... 13-16R
Freund, Otto Kahn
See Kahn-Freund, Otto
Freund, Paul A(braham) 1908-1992 ... CANR-47
Obituary ... 136
Earlier sketch in CA 1-4R
Freund, Philip (Herbert) 1909- ... CANR-12
Earlier sketch in CA 13-16R
Freund, Rudolf 1915-1969 ... SATA-Brief 28
Freund, Thatcher 1955- ... 146
Freundlich, August L(udwig) 1924- ... CANR-49
Earlier sketch in CA 49-52
Frevert, Peter 1938- ... 81-84
Frew, David R(ichard) 1943- ... 77-80
Frewer, Glyn (M.) 1931- ... CANR-10
Earlier sketch in CA 13-16R
See also SATA 11
Frewin, Leslie Ronald 1917-1997 ... CANR-48
Obituary ... 160
Earlier sketches in CA 5-8R, CANR-11
Frey, Andrew 1905(?)-1983 Obituary ... 109
Frey, Bruno S. 1941- ... 166
Frey, Darcy ... 157
See also SATA 98
Frey, Erich A. 1931- ... 45-48
Frey, Frederick Ward 1929- ... 53-56
Frey, Henry A. 1923- ... 33-36R
Frey, John Andrew 1929- ... 89-92
Frey, Julia (Bloch) 1943- ... 149
Frey, Leonard H(amilton) 1927- ... 29-32R
Frey, Marlys
See Mayfield, Marlys
Frey, Richard L(incoln) 1905-1988 ... 89-92
Obituary ... 126
Frey, Robert Seitz 1955- ... 128
Frey, Stephen W. ... 157
Freyberg, Paul (Richard) 1923-1993 ... 135
Obituary ... 141
Freyd, Jennifer J. 1957- ... 158
Freyer, Frederic
See Ballinger, William Sanborn
Freyer, Tony (Allan) 1947- ... 143
Freyre, Gilberto (de Mello) 1900-1987 ... 126
Brief entry ... 116
Freyre, Ricardo Jaimes
See Jaimes Freyre, Ricardo
Freytag, Gustav 1816-1895 ... DLB 129
Freytag, Joseph
See Cooper, Parley J(oseph)
Freytag, Josephine
See Cooper, Parley J(oseph)
Frezza, Robert (A.) 1956- ... 154
Friar, Kimon 1911-1993 ... 85-88
Obituary ... 141
Friar Tuck
See Tucker, Irwin St. John
Fribourg, Marjorie G. 1920- ... CANR-4
Earlier sketch in CA 1-4R
Frick, C. H.
See Irwin, Constance Frick
Frick, Constance
See Irwin, Constance Frick
Frick, Ford Christopher 1894-1978 Obituary .. 89-92
Frick, George F(rederick) 1925- ... 13-16R
Fricke, Aaron 1962- ... 155
See also SATA 89
Fricke, Cedric V. 1928- ... 13-16R
Fricker, E(dward) G(eorge) 1910- ... 125
Fricker, Mary 1940- ... 134
Friday, Nancy 1937- ... CANR-70
Earlier sketches in CA 77-80, CANR-28
See also MTCW 1
Friday, Peter
See Harris, Herbert
Fridenson, Patrick 1944- ... 129
Frideres, James S(tephen) 1943- ... 113
Fridy, (William) Wallace 1910- ... CANR-17
Earlier sketch in CA 1-4R
Friebert, Stuart (Alyn) 1931- ... 65-68
Fried, Barbara 1924- ... 45-48
Fried, Charles 1935- ... CANR-12
Earlier sketch in CA 29-32R
Fried, Eleanor L.
See Furman, Eleanor L.
Fried, Emanuel 1913- ... 73-76
Fried, Erich 1921-1988 ... 126
Obituary ... 127
Brief entry ... 114
See also DLB 85
Fried, Eunice ... 124
Fried, Frederick 1908- ... 77-80
Fried, John J(ames) 1940- ... CANR-12
Earlier sketch in CA 33-36R
Fried, Jonathan L(ester) 1955- ... 113
Fried, Joseph P. 1939- ... 37-40R
Fried, Lawrence 1926-1983 Obituary ... 110
Fried, Marc (Allen) 1922- ... 77-80
Fried, Marc B(ernard) 1944- ... 77-80
Fried, Mary McKenzie Hill 1914- ... 93-96
Fried, Morton H(erbert) 1923-1986 ... 21-24R
Obituary ... 121
Fried, Peter A(lexander) 1943- ... 108
Fried, Richard M(ayer) 1941- ... 73-76
Fried, Stephen (Marc) 1958- ... 144
Fried, William 1945- ... 57-60
Friedan, Betty (Naomi) 1921- ... CANR-45
Earlier sketches in CA 65-68, CANR-18
See also CLC 74
See also MTCW 1
Friedberg, Ardy 1935- ... 108
Friedberg, Gertrude (Tonkonogy)
1908(?)-1989 ... 21-24R
Obituary ... 129
Friedberg, Joan Brest 1927- ... 124
Friedberg, Maurice 1929- ... CANR-5
Earlier sketch in CA 1-4R
Friede, Eleanor Kask 1920- ... 101
Friedeberg-Seeley, Frank (J. B.) 1912- ... 138
Friedelbaum, Stanley H(erman) 1927- ... 37-40R
Friedell, Aaron 1890(?)-1985 Obituary ... 116
Frieden, Bernard J. 1930- ... CANR-10
Earlier sketch in CA 13-16R
Frieden, Ken(neth) 1955- ... CANR-42
Earlier sketch in CA 118
Friedenberg, Edgar Zodiag 1921- ... CANR-29
Earlier sketch in CA 65-68
Friedenberg, Walter Drew 1928- ... 89-92
Friedenreich, Harriet Pass
See Freidenreich, Harriet Pass
Friedenthal, Richard 1896-1979 ... 103
Obituary ... 89-92
Frieder, Emma 1891- ... CAP-2
Earlier sketch in CA 33-36
Friederich, Werner P(aul) 1905- ... 13-16R
Friederichsen, Kathleen (Hockman) 1910- .. 17-20R
Friedgut, Theodore H. 1931- ... 89-92
Friedheim, Robert L(yle) 1934- ... CANR-12
Earlier sketch in CA 21-24R
Friedkin, William 1939- ... 107
Friedl, Erika (Loeffler) 1940- ... 147
Friedl, Ernestine 1920- ... 37-40R
Friedl, John 1945- ... CANR-4
Earlier sketch in CA 53-56
Friedlaender, Walter (Ferdinand)
1873-1966 Obituary ... 115
Friedland, Martin L(awrence) 1932- ... 146
Friedland, Ronald Lloyd 1937-1975 ... CAP-2
Obituary ... 57-60
Earlier sketch in CA 33-36
Friedland, Ronnie 1945- ... 106
Friedland, Seymour 1928- ... CANR-17
Earlier sketch in CA 25-28R
Friedland, William H. 1923- ... 13-16R
Friedlander, Albert H(oschander) 1927- .. CANR-51
Earlier sketches in CA 21-24R, CANR-9, 25
Friedlander, Henry (Egon) 1930- ... 153
Friedlander, Howard 1941- ... 105
Friedlander, Joanne K(ohn) 1930- ... 61-64
See also SATA 9
Friedlander, Michael W. 1929- ... 150
Friedlander, Saul 1932- ... CANR-72
Brief entry ... 117
Earlier sketch in CA 130
See also CLC 90
Friedlander, Stanley Lawrence 1938- ... 17-20R
Friedlander, Walter A(ndreas) 1891- ... 37-40R
Friedman, Alan ... 144
See also Horowitz, Shel Alan
Friedman, Alan J(acob) 1942- ... 125
Friedman, Alan Warren 1939- ... 25-28R
Friedman, Albert B(arron) 1920- ... CANR-17
Earlier sketch in CA 1-4R
Friedman, Alice R. 1900- ... 41-44R
Friedman, Amy 1952- ... 133
Friedman, Arnold D'Arcy 1900-1981 Obituary .. 109
Friedman, Arnold P(hineas) 1909- ... CANR-1
Earlier sketch in CA 45-48
Friedman, Avner 1932- ... 53-56
Friedman, B(ernard) H(arper) 1926- ... CANR-48
Earlier sketches in CA 1-4R, CANR-3
See also CLC 7
Friedman, Benjamin M. 1944- ... 139
Friedman, Bernard 1896-1983 Obituary ... 110
Friedman, Bruce Jay 1930- ... CANR-52
Earlier sketches in CA 9-12R, CANR-25
Interview in ... CANR-25
See also CLC 3, 5, 56
See also DLB 2, 28
Friedman, Charles 1902-1984 Obituary ... 113
Friedman, David 1945- ... 89-92
Friedman, David F. 1923- ... 134
Friedman, Edward H. 1948- ... 127
Friedman, Edward Ludwig 1903- ... 1-4R
Friedman, Elizabeth 1893(?)-1980 Obituary ... 102
Friedman, Estelle (Ehrenwald) 1920- ... 5-8R
See also SATA 7
Friedman, Francine 1948- ... 153
Friedman, Frieda 1905- ... SATA 43
Friedman, Hal
See Friedman, Harold
Friedman, Harold 1942- ... 89-92
Friedman, Herbert 1916- Brief entry ... 112
Friedman, Ina R(osen) 1926- ... 53-56
See also SATA 49
See also SATA-Brief 41
Friedman, Irving S(igmund) 1915-1989 ... CANR-3
Obituary ... 130
Earlier sketch in CA 45-48
Friedman, Isaiah 1921- ... 53-56
Friedman, Jerrold David
See Gerrold, David
Friedman, John Block 1934- ... 125
Friedman, John S(aul) 1942- ... 118
Friedman, Josephine Troth 1928- ... 77-80
Friedman, Josh(ua M.) 1941- ... 140
Brief entry ... 126
Friedman, Josh Alan 1956- ... 122
Friedman, Joy Troth
See Friedman, Josephine Troth
Friedman, Judi 1935- ... 65-68
See also AITN 2
See also SATA 59
Friedman, Julian R. 1920(?)-1983 Obituary ... 111
Friedman, Kathy V(allone) 1943- ... CANR-38
Earlier sketch in CA 114
Friedman, Ken(neth Scott) ... 65-68
Friedman, Ken(neth) 1939- ... CANR-48
Earlier sketch in CA 25-28R
Friedman, Kinky 1944- ... 147
Friedman, Lawrence J. 1940- ... 53-56
Friedman, Lawrence Meir 1930- ... CANR-43
Earlier sketches in CA 13-16R, CANR-5
Friedman, Lawrence S(amuel) 1936- ... 160
Friedman, Lenemaja 1924- ... 61-64
Friedman, Leon 1933- ... 81-84
Friedman, Lester David 1945- ... 108
Friedman, Marcia 1925- ... 57-60
Friedman, Marvin 1930- ... SATA 42
See also SATA-Brief 33
Friedman, Maurice S(tanley) 1921- ... 13-16R
Friedman, Max Motel 1899(?)-1988 Obituary ... 125
Friedman, Melvin J(ack) 1928- ... 21-24R
Friedman, Meyer 1910- ... 127
Brief entry ... 113
Friedman, Michael H(enry) 1945- ... 101
Friedman, Michael J(an) 1955- ... 119
Friedman, Michaele Thompson 1944- ... CANR-44
Earlier sketch in CA 111
Friedman, Mickey
See Friedman, Michaele Thompson
Friedman, Milton 1912- ... CANR-69
Earlier sketches in CA 1-4R, CANR-1, 22
See also MTCW 1
Friedman, Murray 1926- ... 57-60
Friedman, Myles I(van) 1924- ... CANR-6
Earlier sketch in CA 57-60
Friedman, Nancy 1950- ... 107
Friedman, Norman 1925- ... CANR-1
Earlier sketch in CA 1-4R
Friedman, Paul 1899-1972 Obituary ... 37-40R
Friedman, Paul 1937- ... 122
Friedman, Paul Belais 1953- ... 110
Friedman, Philip (J.) ... 141
Friedman, Ralph 1916- ... 69-72
Friedman, Rochelle (Rame) 1942- ... 112
Friedman, Ron 1943- ... 151
Friedman, Rose D(irector) ... CANR-22
Earlier sketch in CA 101
Friedman, (Eve) Rosemary (Tibber) 1929- ...
CANR-44
Earlier sketches in CA 5-8R, CANR-3, 21
Friedman, Roslyn Berger 1924- ... 17-20R
Friedman, Roy 1934- ... 25-28R
Friedman, Sanford 1928- ... 73-76
Friedman, Sara Ann 1935- ... 77-80
Friedman, Saul S. 1937- ... 57-60
Friedman, Stuart 1913- ... 1-4R
Friedman, Susan Stanford 1943- ... 109
Friedman, Thomas L(oren) 1953- ... CANR-38
Earlier sketch in CA 109
See also BEST 90:1
Friedman, Warner G(eorge) 1934- ... 97-100
Friedman, Winifred 1923(?)-1975 Obituary ... 61-64
Friedman, Yona 1923- ... 130
Friedmann, Arnold 1925- ... 41-44R
Friedmann, Deborah Davis
See Davis-Friedmann, Deborah
Friedmann, Elizabeth 1941- ... 142
Friedmann, Georges 1902(?)-1977 Obituary ... 104

Friedmann, Herbert 1900-1987 106
Obituary 122
Friedmann, John 1926- CANR-41
Earlier sketches in CA 85-88, CANR-15
Friedmann, Stan 1953- .... SATA 80
Friedmann, Thomas 1947- 118
Friedmann, Wolfgang (Gaston) 1907-1972 ....
CANR-6
Earlier sketch in CA 1-4R
Friedmann, Yohanan 1936- 33-36R
Friedrich, Anton
See Strich, Christian
Friedrich, Carl Joachim 1901-1984 .... CANR-30
Obituary 113
Earlier sketch in CA 69-72
Friedrich, Dick
See Friedrich, Richard
Friedrich, Gustav W(illiam) 1941- Brief entry 111
Friedrich, Otto (Alva) 1929-1995 .... CANR-3
Obituary 148
Earlier sketch in CA 5-8R
See also SATA 33
Friedrich, Paul 1927- CANR-12
Earlier sketch in CA 29-32R
Friedrich, Priscilla 1927- 113
See also SATA 39
Friedrich, Richard 1936- 103
Friedrichs, Christopher R(ichard) 1947- 89-92
Friedrichs, Robert W(inslow) 1923- 49-52
Friedrich von Hausen c. 1171-1190 .... DLB 138
Friedson, Anthony M(artin) 1924- 108
Friel, Brian 1929- CANR-69
Earlier sketches in CA 21-24R, CANR-33
See also CLC 5, 42, 59
See also DC 8
See also DLB 13
See also MTCW 1
Friel, James 1958- 139
Frielink, A(braham) Barend 1917- 21-24R
Frieman, Jerome 1942- 148
Friend, Dorie
See Friend, Theodore (Wood III)
Friend, Joseph H(arold) 1909-1972 .... CAP-2
Earlier sketch in CA 25-28
Friend, Krebs 1895(?)-1967(?) .... DLB 4
Friend, Robert 1913-1998 .... CANR-7
Obituary 163
Earlier sketch in CA 13-16R
Friend, Theodore (Wood III) 1931- 138
Friendlich, Dick
See Friendlich, Richard J.
Friendlich, Richard J. 1909- CAP-1
Earlier sketch in CA 13-16
See also SATA 11
Friendly, Alfred, Jr. 1938- 152
Friendly, Alfred 1911-1983 101
Obituary 111
Friendly, Fred W. 1915-1998 .... CANR-14
Obituary 165
Earlier sketch in CA 21-24R
Friendly, Henry Jacob 1903-1986 103
Obituary 118
Frier, Bruce W(oodward) 1943- 125
Friermood, Elisabeth Hamilton 1903- CANR-1
Earlier sketch in CA 1-4R
See also SATA 5
Fries, Albert Charles 1908- CANR-4
Earlier sketch in CA 1-4R
Fries, Fritz Rudolf 1935- CANR-11
Earlier sketch in CA 25-28R
See also DLB 75
Fries, James Franklin 1938- 89-92
Fries, Robert Francis 1911- 106
Friesel, Evyatar 1930- 135
Friesen, Bernice (Sarah Anne) 1966- 166
Friesen, Garry 1947- 114
Friesen, Gerald 1943- 120
Friesen, Patrick 1945- CANR-32
Earlier sketch in CA 113
Friesner, Esther M. 1951- CANR-41
See also AAYA 10
See also SATA 71
Friess, Horace L(eland) 1900-1975 65-68
Obituary 61-64
Friggens, Arthur (Henry) 1920- 103
Frigstad, David B. 1954- 150
Friis, Erik J(ohan) 1913- 69-72
Friis, Harald T(rap) 1893-1976 Obituary 65-68
Friis-Baastad, Babbis Ellinor 1921-1970 .... 17-20R
Obituary 134
See also CLC 12
See also SATA 7
Frijling-Schreuder, E(lisabeth) C. M. 1908- 61-64
Frillmann, Paul W. 1911-1972 .... CAP-2
Obituary 37-40R
Earlier sketch in CA 25-28
Friman, Alice 1933- CANR-65
Earlier sketch in CA 129
Frimbo, E. M.
See Whitaker, Rogers E(rnest) M(alcolm)
Friml, Rudolf 1879-1972 Obituary 37-40R
Frimmer, Steven 1928- 33-36R
See also SATA 31
Frimoth, Lenore B(eck) 1927- 5-8R
Frindall, Bill
See Frindall, William Howard
Frindall, William Howard 1939- 135
Frings, Ketti 1915-1981 101
Obituary 103
Frings, Manfred S. 1925- CANR-51
Earlier sketches in CA 17-20R, CANR-8, 26
Frink, Maurice 1895-1972 .... CAP-2
Earlier sketch in CA 25-28
Frinta, Mojmir S(vatopluk) 1922- 25-28R
Fripp, Patricia 1945- 93-96
Frisbie, Louise K(elley) 1913- 61-64
Frisbie, Margery (Rowbottom) 1923- 5-8R
Frisbie, Richard P(atrick) 1926- CANR-38
Earlier sketches in CA 5-8R, CANR-2, 17
Frisby, Terence (Peter Michael) 1932- 65-68
Frisch, Karl (Ritter) von 1886-1982 .... CANR-42
Obituary 115
Earlier sketch in CA 85-88
Frisch, Max (Rudolf) 1911-1991 .... CANR-32
Obituary 134
Earlier sketch in CA 85-88
See also CLC 3, 9, 14, 18, 32, 44
See also DAM DRAM, NOV
See also DLB 69, 124
See also MTCW 1
Frisch, Michael H(erbert) 1942- 126
Frisch, Morton J. 1923- 33-36R
Frisch, O(tto) R(obert) 1904- 9-12R
Frisch, Paul Z. 1926(?)-1977 Obituary 73-76
Frisch, Ragnar Anton Kittil 1895-1973 Obituary .115
Frischauer, Willi 1906- CANR-7
Earlier sketch in CA 5-8R
Frischer, Bernard D(avid) 1949- 113
Frischlin, Nicodemus 1547-1590 .... DLB 179
Frischmuth, Barbara 1941- .... DLB 85
Frischwasser-Ra'Anan, H. F.
See Ra'Anan, Uri
Friskey, Margaret (Richards) 1901-1995 . CANR-55
Earlier sketches in CA 5-8R, CANR-2
See also SATA 5
Frison, George C(arr) 1924- 93-96
Frist, William H. 1952- 136
Fritchman, Stephen Hole 1902- Brief entry 105
Frith, David (Edward John) 1937- 138
Frith, H(arold) J(ames) 1921- 102
Frith, Nigel (Andrew Silver) 1941- CANR-64
Earlier sketch in CA 69-72
Fritsch, Albert Joseph 1933- 102
Fritsch, Bruno 1926- CANR-41
Earlier sketches in CA 69-72, CANR-11
Fritsch, Charles Theodore 1912- 112
Fritschler, A. Lee 1937- 33-36R
Fritts, Mary Bahr
See Bahr, Mary M(adelyn)
Fritz
See Whitehall, Harold
Fritz, Henry E(ugene) 1927- 17-20R
Fritz, Jean (Guttery) 1915- CANR-37
Earlier sketches in CA 1-4R, CANR-5, 16
Interview in CANR-16
See also CLR 2, 14
See also DLB 52
See also JRDA
See also MAICYA
See also SAAS 2
See also SATA 1, 29, 72
Fritz, Leah 1931- 93-96
Fritze, Julius Arnold 1918- 103
Fritzell, Peter A(lgren) 1940- 133
Fritzsch, Harald 1943- 113
Fritzsche, Peter 1959- 139
Frobish, Nestle J(ohn) 1930- 101
Froboess, Harry (August) 1899- CAP-2
Earlier sketch in CA 17-18
Froehlich, Gustav 1902-1987 Obituary 124
Froehlich, Margaret W(alden) 1930- 115
See also SATA 56
Froelich, Robert E. 1929- CANR-3
Earlier sketch in CA 45-48
Frohlich, Gustav
See Froehlich, Gustav
Frohlich, Norman 1941- 77-80
Frohman, Charles E(ugene) 1901-1976 .... CAP-2
Earlier sketch in CA 29-32
Frohnen, Bruce (P.) 1962- 139
Frohnmayer, John 1942- 143
Frohock, Fred M(anuel) 1937- 163
Frohock, W(ilbur) M(errill) 1908-1984 73-76
Obituary 113
Frois, Jeanne 1953- .... SATA 73
Froissard, Lily Powell CANR-25
Earlier sketch in CA 45-48
Froissart, Jean 1338(?)-1410(?) .... SATA 28
Froman, Elizabeth Hull 1920-1975 .... CAP-1
Obituary 53-56
Earlier sketch in CA 13-16
See also SATA 10
Froman, Lewis A(crelius), Jr. 1935- 5-8R
Froman, Robert (Winslow) 1917- CANR-1
Earlier sketch in CA 1-4R
See also SATA 8
Frome, David
See Brown, Zenith Jones
Frome, Frieda
See Krieger, Frieda Frome
Frome, Michael 1920- CANR-16
Earlier sketches in CA 1-4R, CANR-1
Fromentin, Eugene (Samuel Auguste)
1820-1876 .... DLB 123
Fromer, Margot J(oan) 1939- 110
Fromkin, David 1932- 109
Fromkin, Howard L(arry) 1939- 121
Brief entry 118
Fromkin, Victoria A(lexandria) 1923- 89-92
Fromm, Erich 1900-1980 .... CANR-29
Obituary 97-100
Earlier sketch in CA 73-76
See also MTCW 1
Fromm, Erika 1910- 9-12R
Fromm, Gary 1933- CANR-7
Earlier sketch in CA 17-20R
Fromm, Gloria G(likin) 1931- Brief entry 112
Fromm, Harold 1933- 21-24R
Fromm, Herbert 1905- CANR-1
Earlier sketch in CA 49-52
Fromm, Lilo 1928- 81-84
See also SATA 29
Fromm, Pete 1958- 139
Fromme, Babbette Brandt 1925- 106
Frommel, Christoph Lvitpold 1933- 158
Frommer, Harvey 1937- CANR-51
Earlier sketches in CA 103, CANR-26
See also SATA 41
Frommer, Myrna 1941- 111
Froncek, Thomas (Walter) 1942- 81-84
Frondizi, Risieri 1910- 41-44R
Frontier, Tex
See Miller, J(ames) P(inckney)
Frooks, Dorothy 1899-1997 57-60
Obituary 157
Froomkin, Joseph 1927- CANR-13
Earlier sketch in CA 21-24R
Frosch, Thomas Richard 1943- 69-72
Froscher, Wingate 1918- 1-4R
Frost, A(rthur) B(urdett) 1851-1928 136
See also DLB 188
See also DLBD 13
See also MAICYA
See also SATA 19
Frost, Carol 1948- CANR-11
Earlier sketch in CA 69-72
Frost, David (Paradine) 1939- CANR-31
Earlier sketch in CA 69-72
Frost, Elizabeth
See Frost-Knappman, Elizabeth
Frost, Erica
See Supraner, Robyn
Frost, Ernest 1918- 9-12R
Frost, Everett L(loyd) 1942- 65-68
Frost, Frank (Jasper) 1929- 89-92
Frost, Frederick
See Faust, Frederick (Schiller)
Frost, Gavin 1930- CANR-1
Earlier sketch in CA 45-48
Frost, Gerhard Emanuel 1909- CAP-1
Earlier sketch in CA 9-10
Frost, Gregory 1951- 118
Frost, Helen 1898- CAP-1
Earlier sketch in CA 13-14
Frost, James A(rthur) 1918- 37-40R
Frost, Jason
See Obstfeld, Raymond
Frost, Joe L. 1933- 25-28R
Frost, Joni
See Paine, Lauran (Bosworth)
Frost, Lawrence A(ugust) 1907-1990 .... CANR-26
Obituary 132
Earlier sketches in CA 69-72, CANR-11
Frost, Lesley 1899-1983 .... 21-24R
Obituary 110
See also SATA 14
See also SATA-Obit 34
Frost, Leslie Miscampbell
1895-1973 Obituary 41-44R
Frost, M(ax) Gilbert 1908- CAP-1
Earlier sketch in CA 13-14
Frost, Marjorie 1914- 25-28R
Frost, Mark 1953- 168
Frost, O(rcutt) W(illiam) 1926- 136
Frost, Paul
See Castle, Anthony (Percy)
Frost, Peter Kip 1936- 33-36R
Frost, Richard 1929- 33-36R
Frost, Richard H(indman) 1930- 25-28R
Frost, Richard T. 1926-1972 .... CAP-1
Obituary 37-40R
Earlier sketch in CA 13-16
Frost, Robert (Lee) 1874-1963 .... CANR-33
Earlier sketch in CA 89-92
See also AAYA 21
See also CDALB 1917-1929
See also CLC 1, 3, 4, 9, 10, 13, 15, 26, 34, 44
See also DA
See also DAB
See also DAC
See also DAM MST, POET
See also DLB 54
See also DLBD 7
See also MTCW 1
See also PC 1
See also SATA 14
See also WLC
Frost, Robert Carlton 1926- 53-56
Frost, Roon 1943- 126
Frost, S. E., Jr. 1899- CAP-2
Earlier sketch in CA 19-20
Frost, Stanley Brice 1913- 61-64
Frost, William 1917- 41-44R
Frostic, Gwen 1906- 17-20R
Frostick, Michael 1917- 9-12R
Frost-Knappman, Elizabeth 1943- 149
Frothingham, Octavius Brooks 1822-1895 .... DLB 1
Froude, James Anthony 1818-1894 .... DLB 18, 57, 144
Frow, John 1948- 120
Froy, Herald
See Deghy, Guy (Stephen)
and Waterhouse, Keith (Spencer)
Frucht, Abby 1957- 127
Frucht, Phyllis 1936- 57-60
Fruchtenbaum, Arnold G(enekovich) 1943- ....
CANR-11
Earlier sketch in CA 61-64
Fruchter, Benjamin 1914- 1-4R
Fruchter, Norman D. 81-84
Frude, Neil 1946- 114
Fruehling, Rosemary T(herese) 1933- CANR-35
Earlier sketches in CA 33-36R, CANR-13
Frugoni, Cesare 1881-1978 Obituary 73-76
Fruhan, William E(dward), Jr. 1943- 41-44R
Fruin, W. Mark 1943- 140
Frum, Barbara 1937-1992 101
Obituary 137
Interview in 101
Frum, David 1960- 148
Fruman, Norman 1923- 37-40R
Frumkes, Lewis Burke 1939- CANR-36
Earlier sketch in CA 114
Frumkin, Gene 1928- CANR-4
Earlier sketch in CA 9-12R
Frumkin, Robert M. 1928- CANR-9
Earlier sketch in CA 21-24R
Fruton, Joseph S(tewart) 1912- CANR-34
Earlier sketch in CA 49-52
Fruzzetti, Lina M(aria) 1942- 113
Fry, Alan 1931- CANR-1
Earlier sketch in CA 45-48
Fry, Annette R(iley) .... SATA 89
Fry, Barbara 1932- 25-28R
Fry, C(harles) George 1936- CANR-57
Earlier sketches in CA 37-40R, CANR-14, 31
Fry, Christine 1943- 107
Fry, Christopher 1907- CANR-30
Earlier sketches in CA 17-20R, CANR-9
See also CAAS 23
See also CLC 2, 10, 14
See also DAM DRAM
See also DLB 13
See also MTCW 1
See also SATA 66
Fry, David
See Roper, William L(eon)
Fry, Dennis Butler 1907-1983 109
Obituary 110
Fry, Donald K(lein, Jr.) 1937- 25-28R
Fry, E(dwin) Maxwell 1899-1987 65-68
Obituary 123
Fry, Earl H(oward) 1947- 102
Fry, Edward Bernard 1925- CANR-5
Earlier sketch in CA 9-12R
See also SATA 35
Fry, Hilary G. 1922- 17-20R
Fry, Howard T(yrrell) 1919- 37-40R
Fry, John 1930- 93-96
Fry, Maggie Culver 1900- .... AITN 1
Fry, Maxwell
See Fry, E(dwin) Maxwell
Fry, Michael G(raham) 1934- CANR-48
Earlier sketches in CA 69-72, CANR-23
Fry, P(atricia) Eileen 1947- 104
Fry, Paul H. 1944- 129
Fry, Plantagenet Somerset
See Somerset Fry, (Peter George Robin) Plantagenet
Fry, Roger (Eliot) 1866-1934 Brief entry 115
See also DLBD 10
Fry, Ronald W(illiam) 1949- 57-60
Fry, Rosalie Kingsmill 1911- 9-12R
See also SAAS 11
See also SATA 3
Fry, Thomas Frederick 1919- 118
Fry, Tom
See Fry, Thomas Frederick
Fry, Virginia Lynn 1952- 160
See also SATA 95
Fry, William F(inley, Jr.) 1924- 5-8R
Fryatt, Norma R. 57-60
Fryburger, Vernon R(ay), Jr. 1918- 1-4R
Fryd, Norbert 1913-1976 Obituary 65-68
Fryd, Vivien Green 1952- 144
Frydman, Szajko 1911- CANR-48
Earlier sketch in CA 25-28R
Frye, (Charles) Alton 1936- 21-24R
Frye, Charles A(nthony) 1946- 153
See also BW 2
Frye, Ellen 1940- 49-52
Frye, John 1910- CANR-28
Earlier sketch in CA 49-52
Frye, Keith 1935- 53-56
Frye, Marilyn 1941- 154
Frye, (Herman) Northrop 1912-1991 .... CANR-37
Obituary 133
Earlier sketches in CA 5-8R, CANR-8
See also CLC 24, 70
See also DLB 67, 68
See also MTCW 1
Frye, Richard N(elson) 1920- CANR-3
Earlier sketch in CA 5-8R
Frye, Roland Mushat 1921- 9-12R
Frye, Sally
See Moore, Elaine
Frye, William R(uggles) 1918- 73-76
Fryer, Donald S.
See Sidney-Fryer, Donald
Fryer, Holly C(laire) 1908- CAP-1
Earlier sketch in CA 19-20
Fryer, Jonathan 1950- 85-88
Fryer, Judith 1939- 69-72
Fryer, Mary Beacock 1929- 97-100
Fryer, William T. 1900(?)-1980 Obituary 93-96
Frykenberg, Robert Eric 1930- 25-28R
Fryklund, Verne C(harles) 1896-1980 .... 13-16R
Obituary 126
Frykman, John H(arvey) 1932- CANR-43
Earlier sketch in CA 33-36R
Frym, Gloria 1947- 105
Frymier, Jack R(immel) 1925- 17-20R
Fryscak, Milan 1932- 53-56
Fu, Limin
See Freeman, Charles Wellman, Jr.
Fuchida, Mitsuo 1902(?)-1976 Obituary 65-68
Fuchs, Bernie 1932- .... SATA 95

Fuchs, Daniel 1909-1993 .... CANR-40
Obituary 142
Earlier sketch in CA 81-84
See also CAAS 5
See also CLC 8, 22
See also DLB 9, 26, 28
See also DLBY 93
Fuchs, Daniel 1934- CANR-48
Earlier sketches in CA 37-40R, CANR-14
See also CLC 34
Fuchs, Elinor 1933- 105
Fuchs, Erich 1916- 29-32R
See also SATA 6
Fuchs, Estelle 57-60
Fuchs, Guenter Bruno 1928-1977 Obituary 114
Fuchs, Jacob 1939- 21-24R
Fuchs, Jerome H(erbert) 1922- 69-72
Fuchs, Josef 1912- 21-24R
Fuchs, Lawrence H. 1927- CANR-5
Earlier sketch in CA 1-4R
Fuchs, Lucy 1935- CANR-30
Earlier sketches in CA 73-76, CANR-12
See also SATA-Brief 52
Fuchs, Miriam 1949- 147
Fuchs, Rachel G(innis) 1939- 144
Fuchs, Roland J(ohn) 1933- CANR-14
Earlier sketch in CA 81-84
Fuchs, Victor R(obert) 1924- CANR-41
Earlier sketches in CA 1-4R, CANR-2, 18
Fuchs, Vivian (Ernest) 1908- CANR-21
Earlier sketch in CA 104
Fuchshuber, Annegert 1940- 112
See also SATA 43
Fuchssteiner, Benno 1941- 149
Fucilla, Joseph G(uerin) 1897- 89-92
Fucini, Joseph J(ames) 1951- 120
Fucini, Suzy 1951- 120
Fudge, William Kingston 1904-1985 Obituary .. 116
Fuegi, John 1936- 37-40R
Fueloep-Miller, Rene 1891-1963 Obituary 110
Fuentes, Carlos 1928- CANR-68
Earlier sketches in CA 69-72, CANR-10, 32
See also AAYA 4
See also AITN 2
See also CLC 3, 8, 10, 13, 22, 41, 60, 113
See also DA
See also DAB
See also DAC
See also DAM MST, MULT, NOV
See also DLB 113
See also HLC
See also HW
See also MTCW 1
See also SSC 24
See also WLC
Fuentes, Gregorio Lopez y
See Lopez y Fuentes, Gregorio
Fuentes, Martha Ayers 1923- 73-76
Fuentes, Roberto 1934- 57-60
Fuentes Mohr, Alberto
1928(?)-1979 Obituary 85-88
Fuerer-Haimendorf, Christoph von 1909- . CANR-13
Earlier sketch in CA 13-16R
Fuermann, George Melvin 1918- 103
Fuertes, Gloria 1918- .... DLB 108
Fufuka, Karama
See Morgan, Sharon A(ntonia)
Fugard, (Harold) Athol 1932- CANR-54
Earlier sketches in CA 85-88, CANR-32
See also AAYA 17
See also CLC 5, 9, 14, 25, 40, 80
See also DAM DRAM
See also DC 3
See also MTCW 1
Fugard, Sheila 1932- 125
See also CLC 48
Fugate, Bryan I(rven) 1943- 120
Fugate, Francis L(yle) 1915- 25-28R
Fugate, Joe K. 1931- 21-24R
Fugate, Roberta B(auslin) 1917- 111
Fugate, Terence (McCuddy) 1930- 5-8R
Fuge, Charles 1966- .... SATA 74
Fugitt, Eva D(raper) 1929- 110
Fuhrman, Chris 1960-1991 151
Fuhrman, Ellsworth R(aymond) 1946- 112
Fuhrman, Lee 1903(?)-1977 Obituary 73-76
Fuhrman, Mark 1952(?)- 161
Fuhrmann, Joseph T(heodore) 1940- 73-76
Fuhro, Wilbur J. 1914- 9-12R
Fujikawa, Gyo 1908- CANR-46
Earlier sketch in CA 113
See also CLR 25
See also MAICYA
See also SAAS 16
See also SATA 39, 76
See also SATA-Brief 30
Fujimura, Joan H. 168
Fujita, Tamao 1905- 37-40R
See also SATA 7
Fujiwara, Iwaichi 1908- 132
Fujiwara, Kim 1957- .... SATA 81
Fujiwara, Michiko 1946- 77-80
See also SATA 15
Fujiwara, Yoichi 1909- CANR-22
Earlier sketch in CA 105
Fuka, Vladimir 1926-1977 Obituary 104
See also SATA-Obit 27
Fukei, Gladys Arlene (Harper) 1920- 13-16R
Fuks, Ladislav 1923- 118
Fukuda, Haruko 1946- 109
Fukuda, Tsutomu 1905- 103
Fukui, Haruhiro 1935- 29-32R
Fukui, Kenichi 1918-1998 156
Obituary 163
Fukutake, Tadashi 1917- CANR-5
Earlier sketch in CA 13-16R
Fukuyama, Francis 1952- CANR-72
Earlier sketch in CA 140
Fukuyama, Yoshio 1921- 41-44R
Fulani, Lenora (Branch) 1950- 155
Fulbecke, William 1560-1603(?) .... DLB 172
Fulbright, J(ames) William 1905-1995 .... 9-12R
Obituary 147
Fulbrook, Mary (Jean Alexandra) 1951- .. CANR-47
Earlier sketch in CA 121
Fulcher, James 1942- 139
Fulco, William J(ames) 1936- 49-52
Fuld, James J. 1916- 21-24R
Fuld, Leonard M. 1953- 120
Fulda, Carl H. 1909-1975 .... CAP-2
Earlier sketch in CA 33-36
Fuldauer, Ivan 1927- 69-72
Fuldheim, Dorothy (Violet Snell) 1893-1989 ....
CANR-29
Obituary 130
Earlier sketch in CA 49-52
Fulford, Robert 1932- 89-92
Fulford, Roger (Thomas Baldwin) 1902-1983 . 65-68
Obituary 109
Fulghum, Robert (L.) 1937- CANR-62
Earlier sketch in CA 139
See also BEST 89:2
See also DAM POP
Fulks, Bryan 1897- 97-100
Full, Harold 1919- 17-20R
Fullbrook, Kate 1950- 148
Fuller, Alfred C(arl) 1885-1973 Obituary 45-48
Fuller, Beverley 1927- 69-72
Fuller, Blair 1927- 9-12R
Fuller, Buckminster
See Fuller, R(ichard) Buckminster (Jr.)
Fuller, Catherine Leuthold 1916- 29-32R
See also SATA 9
Fuller, Charles (H., Jr.) 1939- 112
Brief entry 108
Interview in 112
See also BLC 2
See also BW 2
See also CLC 25
See also DAM DRAM, MULT
See also DC 1
See also DLB 38
See also MTCW 1
Fuller, Curtis G. 1912- Brief entry 120
Fuller, Daniel P(ayton) 1925- 127
Brief entry 112
Fuller, David O(tis) 1903- 53-56
Fuller, Dorothy Mason 1898- 101
Fuller, Edgar 1904-1973 Obituary 45-48
Fuller, Edmund (Maybank) 1914- 77-80
See also SATA 21
Fuller, Edward C. 1907- 53-56
Fuller, Elizabeth 1946- CANR-33
Earlier sketch in CA 113
Fuller, Harold 1940- 65-68
Fuller, Helen 1914(?)-1972 Obituary 37-40R
Fuller, Henry Blake 1857-1929 Brief entry 108
See also DLB 12
Fuller, Hoyt (William) 1927-1981 53-56
Obituary 103
See also BW 1
Fuller, Iola
See McCoy, Iola Fuller
Fuller, Jack (William) 1946- 130
Brief entry 125
Interview in 130
Fuller, Jean (Violet) Overton 1915- CANR-42
Earlier sketches in CA 5-8R, CANR-4, 19
Fuller, John (Harold) CAP-1
Earlier sketch in CA 9-10
Fuller, John (Leopold) 1937- CANR-44
Earlier sketches in CA 21-24R, CANR-9
See also CLC 62
See also DLB 40
Fuller, John Frederick Charles 1878-1966 .. CAP-1
Earlier sketch in CA 13-16
Fuller, John G(rant, Jr.) 1913-1990 .... CANR-2
Obituary 133
Earlier sketch in CA 1-4R
See also SATA 65
Fuller, Kathleen
See Gottfried, Theodore Mark
Fuller, Ken 1946- 125
Fuller, Lois Hamilton 1915- CANR-29
Earlier sketch in CA 1-4R
See also SATA 11
Fuller, Lon (Luvois) 1902-1978 .... CAP-2
Obituary 77-80
Earlier sketch in CA 33-36
Fuller, Margaret
See Ossoli, Sarah Margaret (Fuller marchesa d')
Fuller, Margaret 1810-1850 .... DLB 183
Fuller, Mary Lou 1929- 164
Fuller, Maud
See Petersham, Maud (Sylvia Fuller)
Fuller, Miriam Morris 1933- 37-40R
Fuller, Paul E(ugene) 1932- 73-76
Fuller, Peter (Michael) 1947- 97-100
Fuller, R(ichard) Buckminster (Jr.) 1895-1983 ......
CANR-12
Obituary 109
Earlier sketch in CA 9-12R
See also MTCW 1
Fuller, Reginald H(orace) 1915- CANR-39
Earlier sketches in CA 5-8R, CANR-3, 18
Fuller, Robert C(harles) 1952- CANR-38
Earlier sketch in CA 116
Fuller, Roger
See Tracy, Don(ald Fiske)
Fuller, Roy (Broadbent) 1912-1991 ...... CANR-53
Obituary 135
Earlier sketch in CA 5-8R
See also CAAS 10
See also CLC 4, 28
See also DLB 15, 20
See also SATA 87
Fuller, Ruth
See Perry, Ruth (Fuller)
Fuller, Sam
See Fuller, Samuel (Michael)
Fuller, Samuel (Michael) 1912- 129
Brief entry 112
See also DLB 26
Fuller, Sarah Margaret 1810-1850 .... CDALB
1640-1865
See also DLB 1, 59, 73
Fuller, Steve William 1959- 137
Fuller, Thomas 1608-1661 .... DLB 151
Fuller, Thomas C(harles) 1918- 126
Fuller, Wayne E(dison) 1919- 13-16R
Fuller, William A(lbert) 1924- 41-44R
Fullerton, Alexander (Fergus) 1924- CANR-48
Earlier sketches in CA 17-20R, CANR-7, 23
Fullerton, Gail Jackson 1927- 37-40R
Fullerton, Gail Putney
See Fullerton, Gail Jackson
Fullerton, Hugh 1873-1945 .... DLB 171
Fullinwider, Robert King 1942- 108
Fullinwider, S. P(endleton) 1933- 127
Brief entry 109
Fullmer, Daniel W(arren) 1922- CANR-29
Earlier sketches in CA 33-36R, CANR-13
Fullmer, June Z(immerman) 1920- 25-28R
Fulmer, Robert M(arion) 1939- CANR-10
Earlier sketch in CA 57-60
Fulop-Miller, Rene
See Fueloep-Miller, Rene
Fulton, A(lbert) R(ondthaler) 1902- 1-4R
Fulton, Alice 1952- CANR-57
Earlier sketch in CA 116
See also CLC 52
See also DLB 193
Fulton, Gere (Burke) 1939- 53-56
Fulton, Len 1934- 57-60
See also DLBY 86
Fulton, Norman 1927- 37-40R
Fulton, Paul C(edric) 1901-1985 .... CAP-1
Obituary 118
Earlier sketch in CA 13-16
Fulton, Robert Lester 1926- Brief entry 105
Fulton, Robin 1937- CANR-38
Earlier sketches in CA 33-36R, CANR-16
See also DLB 40
Fults, John Lee 1932- 53-56
See also SATA 33
Fultz, Walter J. 1924(?)-1971 Obituary 104
Fulweiler, Howard Wells 1932- 77-80
Fumento, Michael (Aaron) 1960- 139
Fumento, Rocco 1923- 1-4R
Fumerton, Patricia 140
Funabashi, Seiichi 1904(?)-1976 Obituary 65-68
Funai, Mamoru (Rolland) 1932- ..... SATA-Brief 46
Fundaburk, Emma Lila 1922- 41-44R
Funderburk, Guy B(ernard) 1902- 45-48
Funderburk, Thomas R(ay) 1928- 17-20R
Fung, Gong
See Goon, Fook Mun
Fung, Raymond (Wai Man) 1940- 123
Funiciello, Theresa 1947- 143
Funigiello, Philip J. 1939- 65-68
Funk, Arthur Layton 1914- 21-24R
Funk, Charles Earle, Jr. 1913- 122
Funk, Peter V(an) K(euren) 1921- CANR-13
Earlier sketch in CA 21-24R
Funk, Rainer 1943- 109
Funk, Robert W(alter) 1926- 33-36R
Funk, Thompson 1911- CANR-2
Earlier sketch in CA 49-52
See also SATA 7
Funk, Tom
See Funk, Thompson
Funk, Wilfred (John) 1883-1965 Obituary 89-92
Funke, Lewis 1912- 49-52
See also SATA 11
Funkhouser, Erica 1949- 135
Funston, Richard Y(ork) 1943- 123
Brief entry 118
Funt, Allen 1914- 146
Funt, Julian 1907(?)-1980 Obituary 97-100
Funt, Marilyn 1937- 102
Fuoss, Robert Martin 1912-1980 Obituary ... 93-96
Furbank, P(hilip) N(icholas) 1920- CANR-63
Earlier sketches in CA 21-24R, CANR-18, 40
See also DLB 155
Furbee, Leonard J. 1896(?)-1975 Obituary ... 61-64
Furchgott, Terry 1948- 105
See also SATA 29
Furcolo, Foster 1911(?)-1995 117
Obituary 149
Furdyna, Anna M. 1938- 143
Furer, Howard B(ernard) 1934- 33-36R
Furer-Haimendorf, Christoph von
See Fuerer-Haimendorf, Christoph von
Furey, Maggie 165
Furey, Michael
See Ward, Arthur Henry Sarsfield
Furfey, Paul Hanly 1896- CAP-2
Earlier sketch in CA 23-24
Furgurson, Ernest B(aker, Jr.) 1929- 73-76
Furgurson, Pat
See Furgurson, Ernest B(aker, Jr.)
Furia, Philip (G.) 1943- 136
Furino, Antonio 1931- 144
Furley, David John 1922- 108
Furlong, Monica (Mavis) 1930- 151
Brief entry 117
See also SATA 86
Furlonge, Geoffrey (Warren)
1903-1984 Obituary 114
Furman, Bess 1894-1969 Obituary 115
Furman, Eleanor L. 1913- CANR-12
Earlier sketch in CA 29-32R
Furman, Gertrude Lerner Kerman 1909- . CANR-31
Furman, Laura (J.) 1945- CANR-30
Earlier sketch in CA 104
See also CAAS 18
See also DLBY 86
Furman, Roger 1924(?)-1983 Obituary 111
Furnas, J(oseph) C(hamberlain) 1905- 77-80
Furneaux, Robin
See Smith, Frederick William Robin
Furneaux, Rupert 1908- CANR-1
Earlier sketch in CA 1-4R
Furness, Edna L(ue) 1906- 37-40R
Furness, Horace Howard 1833-1912 .... DLB 64
Furness, William Henry 1802-1896 .... DLB 1
Furnier, Vincent Damon
See Cooper, Alice
Furnish, Dorothy Jean 1921- 106
Furnish, Victor Paul 1931- CANR-25
Earlier sketches in CA 21-24R, CANR-10
Furniss, Edgar S(tephenson)
1890-1972 Obituary 37-40R
Furniss, Graham (Lytton) 1949- 156
Furniss, Norman Francis 1922- 1-4R
Furniss, Tim 1948- CANR-29
Earlier sketch in CA 109
See also SATA 49
Furniss, W(arren) Todd 1921- 57-60
Furnivall, Frederick James 1825-1910 .... DLB 184
Furphy, Joseph 1843-1912 163
See also TCLC 25
Furrer, Juerg 1939- 69-72
Furry, Elda 1890-1966 113
Furse, John 1932- 109
Fursenko, Aleksandr (A.) 165
Furst, Alan 1941- CANR-59
Earlier sketches in CA 69-72, CANR-12, 34
Furst, Lilian Renee 1931- CANR-40
Earlier sketches in CA 102, CANR-18
Furtado, Celso 1920- CANR-50
Earlier sketches in CA 17-20R, CANR-9, 25
Furth, Alex
See Sasuly, Richard
Furth, George 1932- 73-76
Furth, Hans G. 1920- 45-48
Furthman, Jules
See Furthmann, Julius Grinnell
See also DLB 26
Furthmann, Julius Grinnell 1888-1966 Obituary . 113
See also Furthman, Jules
Furtwangler, Albert (J.) 1942- CANR-41
Earlier sketch in CA 118
Furtwangler, Virginia W(alsh) 1932- CANR-41
Earlier sketch in CA 118
Furubotn, Eirik G. 1923- 137
Furukawa, Toshi 1924- CANR-2
Earlier sketch in CA 45-48
See also SATA 24
Furutani, Dale 1946- 164
Fusco, Margie 1949- 85-88
Fusero, Clemente 1913-1975 81-84
Fusfeld, Daniel R(oland) 1922- 45-48
Fusi (Aizpurua), Juan Pablo 1945- 131
See also HW
Fuson, Benjamin Willis 1911- 37-40R
Fuson, Robert H(enderson) 1927- 89-92
Fuss, Peter 1932- CANR-9
Earlier sketch in CA 21-24R
Fussell, Betty
See Fussell, Betty Harper
Fussell, Betty Harper 1927- 121
Fussell, Edwin 1922- 53-56
Fussell, G(eorge) E(dwin) 1889- CANR-3
Earlier sketch in CA 5-8R
Fussell, Paul 1924- CANR-69
Earlier sketches in CA 17-20R, CANR-8, 21, 35
Interview in CANR-21
See also BEST 90:1
See also CLC 74
See also MTCW 1
Fussner, F(rank) Smith 1920- CANR-5
Earlier sketch in CA 1-4R
Futabatei, Shimei 1864-1909 162
See also DLB 180
See also TCLC 44
Futcher, Jane P. 1947- 144
See also SATA 76
Futrell, Allan W. 1952- 123
Futrell, Gene Allen 1928- 107
Futrelle, Jacques 1875-1912 155
Brief entry 113
See also TCLC 19
Futuyma, Douglas Joel 1942- 108
Fye, W(allace) Bruce (III) 1946- 126
Fyffe, Don(ald Lewis) 1925- 25-28R
Fyfield, Frances
See Hegarty, Frances
Fyleman, Rose (Amy) 1877-1957 Brief entry ... 111
See also DLB 160
See also SATA 21
Fyler, John (Morgan) 1943- 89-92
Fyodorov, Yevgeny Konstantinovich
See Fedorov, Yevgeny Konstantinovich
Fysh, Wilmot Hudson 1895-1974 .... 17-20R
Obituary 134
Fyson, J(enny) G(race) 1904- CAP-2
Earlier sketch in CA 21-22
See also SATA 42

Fyvel, T. R.
See Feiwel, Raphael Joseph
Fyvel, Tosco Raphael
See Feiwel, Raphael Joseph

G

Gaa, Charles J(ohn) 1911- ... 17-20R
Gaan, Margaret 1914- ... 81-84
See also SATA 65
Gaar, Gillian G. 1959- ... 142
Gaard, David 1945- ... 25-28R
Gaard, Greta 1960- ... 140
Gaarder, Jostein 1952- ... 153
Gaastra, F(emme) S(imon) 1945- ... 132
Gaathon, A(ryeh) L(udwig) 1898- ... 49-52
GAB
See Russell, George William
Gabaldon, Diana 1950(?)- ... CANR-72
Earlier sketch in CA 149
Gabbard, Glen O(wens) 1949- ... CANR-53
Earlier sketch in CA 126
Gabbard, Krin 1948- ... 126
Gabbard, Lucina P(aquet) 1922- ... 110
Gabbett, Harry 1910(?)-1985 Obituary ... 116
Gabel, (W.) Creighton 1931- Brief entry ... 106
Gabel, Joseph 1912- ... 101
Gabel, Margaret 1938- ... 33-36R
Gabel, Medard 1946- ... CANR-11
Earlier sketch in CA 65-68
Gaberman, Judie Angell 1937- ... CANR-49
Earlier sketch in CA 77-80
See also AAYA 11
See also CLR 33
See also JRDA
See also SATA 22, 78
Gabhart, Ann 1947- ... 142
See also SATA 75
Gabin, Sanford B(yron) 1936- ... 114
Gable, Tom 1944- ... 93-96
Gablehouse, Charles 1928- ... 21-24R
Gabler, Mirko 1951- ... SATA 77
Gabler, Neal 1950(?)- ... 153
Gabler-Hover, Janet A. 1953- ... 135
Gablik, Suzi 1934- ... 33-36R
Gabo, Naum 1890-1977 ... CAP-2
Obituary ... 73-76
Earlier sketch in CA 33-36
Gabor, Dennis 1900-1979 ... 17-20R
Obituary ... 120
Gabor, Georgia M. 1930- ... 108
Gabor, Mark 1939- ... 81-84
Gabor, Thomas 1952- ... 149
Gaboury, Antonio 1919- ... CANR-2
Earlier sketch in CA 45-48
Gabre-Medhin, Tsegaye (Kawessa) 1936- ... 101
See also BW 2
Gabre-Tsadick, Marta 1932- ... 115
Gabriel, A(strik) L. 1907- ... CANR-6
Earlier sketch in CA 5-8R
Gabriel, Adriana
See Rojany, Lisa
Gabriel, H(enry) 1922- ... 77-80
Gabriel, Joyce 1949- ... 97-100
Gabriel, Jueri (Evald) 1940- ... 93-96
Gabriel, Kathryn (Ann) 1955- ... 140
Gabriel, Mabel McAfee
1884(?)-1976 Obituary ... 65-68
Gabriel, Philip L(ouis) 1918-1993 ... 93-96
Obituary ... 141
Gabriel, Ralph Henry 1890-1987 ... 13-16R
Obituary ... 122
Gabriel, Richard A(lan) 1942- ... 147
Gabriel, Richard Alan 1942- Brief entry ... 104
Gabriel, Roman 1940- Brief entry ... 107
Gabriel-Robinet, Louis 1909-1975 Obituary ... 61-64
Gabrielson, Frank 1911(?)-1980 Obituary ... 93-96
Gabrielson, Ira N(oel) 1889-1977 ... CAP-1
Obituary ... 73-76
Earlier sketch in CA 9-10
Gabrielson, James B. 1917- ... 29-32R
Gabrys, Ingrid Schubert
See Schubert-Gabrys, Ingrid
Gach, Gary 1947- ... 77-80
Gach, Michael Reed 1952- ... CANR-29
Earlier sketch in CA 110
Gackenbach, Dick 1927- ... CANR-38
Earlier sketch in CA 115
See also MAICYA
See also SATA 48, 79
See also SATA-Brief 30
Gadamer, Hans-Georg 1900- ... 85-88
Gadd, David 1912- ... 57-60
Gadd, Maxine 1940- ... 116
Gadda, Carlo Emilio 1893-1973 ... 89-92
See also CLC 11
See also DLB 177
Gaddes, Peter
See Sheldon, Peter
Gaddis, J. Wilson 1910(?)-1975 Obituary ... 57-60
Gaddis, John Lewis 1941- ... CANR-56
Earlier sketches in CA 45-48, CANR-30
Gaddis, Peggy
See Dern, Erolie Pearl Gaddis
Gaddis, Sarah 1955(?)- ... 142
Gaddis, Thomas E(ugene) 1908-1984 ... CANR-16
Obituary ... 114
Earlier sketch in CA 29-32R
Gaddis, Vincent H. 1913- ... 13-16R
See also SATA 35
Gaddis, William 1922- ... CANR-48
Earlier sketches in CA 17-20R, CANR-21
See also CLC 1, 3, 6, 8, 10, 19, 43, 86
See also DLB 2
See also MTCW 1
Gaddy, C(urtis) Welton 1941- ... 61-64
Gaddy, David Winfred 1932- ... 129
Gadler, Steve J. 1905- ... 97-100
See also SATA 36
Gadney, Reg 1941- ... CANR-50
Earlier sketches in CA 49-52, CANR-3, 18
Gado, Frank 1936- ... CANR-31
Earlier sketch in CA 49-52
Gadol, Peter 1964- ... 134
Gadpaille, Warren J(oseph) 1924- ... 61-64
Gaebelein, Frank Ely 1899- ... CANR-2
Earlier sketch in CA 13-16R
Gaeddert, Lou Ann (Bigge) 1931- ... CANR-29
Earlier sketches in CA 73-76, CANR-13
See also SATA 20
Gaedeke, Ralph M(ortimer) 1941- ... CANR-24
Earlier sketches in CA 65-68, CANR-9
Gaeng, Paul A. 1924- ... 37-40R
Gaenzl, Kurt (Friedrich) 1946- ... 134
Gaer, Joseph 1897-1969 ... 9-12R
Obituary ... 122
Gaer, Yossef
See Gaer, Joseph
Gaess, Roger 1943- ... 104
Gaff, Jerry G(ene) 1936- ... 85-88
Gaffen, Fred 1944- ... 127
Gaffney, Edward McGlynn, Jr. 1941- ... 114
Gaffney, James 1931- ... CANR-6
Earlier sketch in CA 57-60
Gaffney, (Merrill) Mason 1923- ... CANR-3
Earlier sketch in CA 49-52
Gaffney, Timothy R. 1951- ... 137
See also SATA 69
Gaffron, Norma (Bondeson) 1931- ... 163
See also SATA 97
Gag, Flavia 1907-1979 ... 5-8R
Obituary ... 104
See also SATA-Obit 24
Gag, Wanda (Hazel) 1893-1946 ... 137
Brief entry ... 113
See also CLR 4
See also DLB 22
See also MAICYA
See also SATA 100
See also YABC 1
Gagan, Bernard 1915-1984 Obituary ... 112
Gagarin, Ivan Sergeevich 1814-1882 ... DLB 198
Gagarin, Michael 1942- ... 89-92
Gagarin, Yuri A(lekseevich) 1934-1968 ... 157
Obituary ... 112
Gage, Diane 1954- ... 116
Gage, Edwin 1943- ... 85-88
Gage, Joy P. 1930- ... CANR-35
Earlier sketch in CA 114
Gage, Nathaniel Lees 1917- ... 69-72
Gage, Nicholas
See Ngagoyeanes, Nicholas
Gage, S. R. 1945- ... 134
Gage, Walter
See Inge, William (Motter)
Gage, William 1915-1973 ... CAP-2
Earlier sketch in CA 25-28
Gage, William W(hitney) 1925- ... 13-16R
Gage, Wilson
See Steele, Mary Q(uintard Govan)
Gager, John Goodrich, Jr. 1937- Brief entry ... 104
Gager, Nancy Land 1932(?)-1980 Obituary ... 93-96
Gagliano, Frank 1931- ... CANR-1
Earlier sketch in CA 45-48
Gagliardo, John G(arver) 1933- ... 21-24R
Gagliardo, Ruth Garver 1895(?)-1980 Obituary . 104
See also SATA-Obit 22
Gagne, Cole 1954- ... 112
Gagne, Robert M(ills) 1916- ... 121
Brief entry ... 116
Gagnier, Ed 1936- ... 65-68
Gagnier, Regenia (A.) 1953- ... CANR-53
Earlier sketch in CA 126
Gagnon, Cecile 1936- ... SATA 58
Gagnon, Jean-Louis 1913- ... 21-24R
Gagnon, John H(enry) 1931- ... 33-36R
Gagnon, Madeleine 1938- ... 160
See also DLB 60
Gagnon, Paul Adelard 1925- Brief entry ... 104
Gahagan, Helen
See Douglas, Helen Gahagan
Gahagan, Jayne D. 1929(?)-1983 Obituary ... 110
Gaherty, Sherry 1951- ... 57-60
Gaiduk, Ilya V(alerievich) 1961- ... 154
Gail, Marzieh ... CANR-11
Earlier sketch in CA 69-72
Gail, Otto 1896-1956 ... 160
Gailey, Harry A(lfred) 1926- ... CANR-16
Earlier sketches in CA 45-48, CANR-1
Gailey, James H(erbert), Jr. 1916- ... 5-8R
Gaillard, Frye 1946- ... 144
Gailmor, William S. 1910(?)-1970 Obituary ... 104
Gaiman, Neil (Richard) 1960- ... 133
See also AAYA 19
See also SATA 85
Gaine, Hugh 1726-1807 ... DLB 43
Gainer, Bernard 1944- Brief entry ... 109
Gainer, Cindy 1962- ... SATA 74
Gaines, Ann-Janine Morey
See Morey, Ann-Janine
Gaines, Bill
See Gaines, William Maxwell
Gaines, Charles (Latham, Jr.) 1942- ... 119
Gaines, Diana 1912- ... 1-4R
Gaines, Donna 1951- ... 136
Gaines, Ernest J(ames) 1933- ... CANR-42
Earlier sketches in CA 9-12R, CANR-6, 24
See also AAYA 18
See also AITN 1
See also BLC 2
See also BW 2
See also CDALB 1968-1988
See also CLC 3, 11, 18, 86
See also DAM MULT
See also DLB 2, 33, 152
See also DLBY 80
See also MTCW 1
See also SATA 86
Gaines, Jack
See Gaines, Jacob
Gaines, Jacob 1918- ... 101
Gaines, Patrice ... 162
Gaines, Pierce Welch 1905- ... 13-16R
Gaines, Richard L. 1925- ... 49-52
Gaines, Thomas A. 1923- ... 139
Gaines, William Maxwell 1922- Brief entry ... 108
Gainham, Sarah
See Ames, Rachel
Gains, Larry 1900-1983 Obituary ... 110
Gainsbrugh, Glen M. 1949- ... 25-28R
Gainsburgh, Martin R(euben)
1907-1977 Obituary ... 69-72
Gainsburg, Joseph (Charles) 1894- ... 5-8R
Gainza Paz, Alberto 1899-1977 ... 77-80
Obituary ... 73-76
Gaiser, Gerd 1908-1976 ... DLB 69
Gaitano, Nick
See Izzi, Eugene
Gaite, Francis
See Coles, Cyril Henry
Gaither, Carl C. 1944- ... 165
Gaither, Gant 1917- ... 9-12R
Gaither, Norman 1937- ... 112
Gaitskell, Charles D(udley) 1908- ... 29-32R
Gaitskell, H. T. N.
See Gaitskell, Hugh (Todd Naylor)
Gaitskell, Hugh (Todd Naylor)
1906-1963 Obituary ... 112
Gaitskill, Mary 1954- ... CANR-61
Earlier sketch in CA 128
See also CLC 69
Gajdusek, Robert Elemer 1925- ... 102
Gajdusek, Robin
See Gajdusek, Robert Elemer
Gakwandi, Shatto Arthur 1943- ... 131
Gal, Allon 1934- ... CANR-1
Earlier sketch in CA 45-48
Gal, Hans 1890- ... 5-8R
Gal, Istvan 1912-1982 Obituary ... 107
Gal, Laszlo 1933- ... 161
See also SATA 52, 96
See also SATA-Brief 32
Galai, Shmuel 1933- ... 107
Galambos, Louis (Paul) 1931- ... 81-84
Galamian, Ivan (Alexandrovitch)
1903-1981 Obituary ... 108
Galand, Rene 1923- ... CANR-49
Earlier sketches in CA 45-48, CANR-24
Galang, M. Evelina 1961- ... 155
Galanoy, Terry 1927- ... CANR-4
Earlier sketch in CA 45-48
Galanskov, Yuri 1939(?)-1972 Obituary ... 37-40R
Galantay, Ervin Yvan 1930- ... 101
Galante, Jane Hohfeld 1924- ... 132
Galante, Pierre 1909- ... 13-16R
Galanter, Eugene 1924- ... 1-4R
Galanter, Marc 1931- ... 122
Galantin, I(gnatius) J(oseph) 1910- ... 154
Galarza, Ernest
See Galarza, Ernesto
Galarza, Ernesto 1905-1984 ... 131
Obituary ... 113
See also DLB 122
See also HW
Galassi, Jonathan (White) 1949- ... 101
Galati, Stephen A(lexander) Fischer
See Fischer-Galati, Stephen A(lexander)
Galatopoulos, Stelios 1932- Brief entry ... 110
Galay, Ted 1941- ... 122
Galbraith, Clare K(earney) 1919- ... 33-36R
Galbraith, Georgie Starbuck 1909-1980 ... CAP-1
Obituary ... 97-100
Earlier sketch in CA 9-10
Galbraith, James K. 1952- ... 130
Galbraith, Jean 1906- ... 37-40R
Galbraith, John Kenneth 1908- ... CANR-68
Earlier sketches in CA 21-24R, CANR-34
Interview in ... CANR-34
See also MTCW 1
Galbraith, John S. 1916- ... CANR-6
Earlier sketch in CA 5-8R
Galbraith, Kathryn O(sebold) 1945- ... 151
See also SATA 85
Galbraith, Madelyn 1897-1976 ... CAP-2
Earlier sketch in CA 33-36
Galbraith, Stuart IV 1965- ... 159
Galbraith, Vivian Hunter 1889-1976 ... CANR-29
Obituary ... 69-72
Earlier sketch in CA 73-76
Galbreath, Robert (Carroll) 1938- ... 41-44R
Galdikas, Birute M. F. 1946- ... 152
Galdone, Paul 1907(?)-1986 ... CANR-13
Obituary ... 121
Earlier sketch in CA 73-76
See also CLR 16
See also MAICYA
See also SATA 17, 66
See also SATA-Obit 49
Galdos, Benito Perez
See Perez Galdos, Benito
Gale, Barry 1935- ... 110
Gale, Bill
See Gale, William
Gale, Bob
See Gale, Michael Robert
Gale, Elliot N(yman) 1938- Brief entry ... 110
Gale, Fredric G. 1933- ... 150
Gale, Herbert M(orrison) 1907- ... CAP-1
Earlier sketch in CA 13-16
Gale, John
See Gaze, Richard
Gale, Linda A(nn) 1939- ... 112
Gale, Michael Robert 1951- ... 133
Gale, Monica R(achel) 1966- ... 151
Gale, Patrick (Evelyn Hugh Sadler) 1962- ... 124
Gale, Raymond F(loyd) 1918- ... 25-28R
Gale, Richard M. 1932- ... 25-28R
Gale, Richard Nelson 1896-1982 Obituary ... 107
Gale, Robert L(ee) 1919- ... CANR-40
Earlier sketches in CA 9-12R, CANR-3, 18
Gale, Vi ... 33-36R
Gale, William 1925- ... 97-100
Gale, William C.
See Giles, Carl H(oward)
Gale, William Daniel 1906- ... 107
Gale, Zona 1874-1938 ... 153
Brief entry ... 105
See also DAM DRAM
See also DLB 9, 78
See also TCLC 7
Galeano, Eduardo (Hughes) 1940- ... CANR-32
Earlier sketches in CA 29-32R, CANR-13
See also CLC 72
See also HW
Galef, David 1959- ... 145
Galella, Ron 1931- ... CANR-14
Earlier sketch in CA 53-56
Interview in ... CANR-14
See also AITN 1
Galen of Pergamon c. 129-c. 210 ... DLB 176
Galenson, Walter 1914- ... CANR-51
Earlier sketches in CA 25-28R, CANR-11, 27
Galeotti, Mark 1965- ... 151
Gales, Barbara J. 1940- ... CANR-14
Earlier sketch in CA 81-84
Gales, Winifred Marshall 1761-1839 ... DLB 200
Galewitz, Herb 1928- ... CANR-14
Earlier sketch in CA 41-44R
Galfo, Armand J. 1924- ... 17-20R
Galford, Ellen 1947- ... 163
Galiano, Juan Valera y Alcala
See Valera y Alcala-Galiano, Juan
Galich, Alexander 1918(?)-1977 Obituary ... 73-76
Galilea, Segundo 1928- ... 105
Galindo, P.
See Hinojosa(-Smith), Rolando (R.)
Galinsky, Ellen 1942- ... CANR-9
Earlier sketch in CA 65-68
See also SATA 23
Galinsky, G(otthard) Karl 1942- ... 33-36R
Galkin, Elliott W(ashington)
1921-1990 Obituary ... 131
Gall, Auguste Amedee de Saint
See Strich, Christian
Gall, Lothar 1936- ... 157
Gall, Louise von 1815-1855 ... DLB 133
Gall, Meredith D(amien) 1942- ... CANR-44
Earlier sketches in CA 53-56, CANR-6, 21
Gall, Morris 1907- ... 45-48
Gall, Sally M(oore) 1941- ... 110
Gall, Sandy 1927- ... 130
Gallager, Gale
See Oursler, Will(iam Charles)
Gallagher, Buell Gordon 1904-1978 ... 65-68
Obituary ... 133
Gallagher, Carole 1950- ... 142
Gallagher, Charles A(ugustus) 1927- ... CANR-9
Earlier sketch in CA 61-64
Gallagher, David P. 1944- ... 45-48
Gallagher, Dorothy 1935- ... 65-68
Gallagher, Edward J. 1892(?)-1978 Obituary ... 81-84
Gallagher, Gary W(illiam) 1950- ... 136
Gallagher, Idella J(ane Smith) 1917- Brief entry ... 108
Gallagher, J(ames) Roswell 1903- ... 57-60
Gallagher, James J(ohn) 1926- ... 114
Gallagher, Jock 1938- ... 129
Gallagher, John (Andrew) 1919-1980 ... 133
Gallagher, John F(redrick) 1936- ... 17-20R
Gallagher, (John) Joseph 1929- ... 122
Gallagher, Kent G(rey) 1933- ... 33-36R
Gallagher, Louis J(oseph)
1885-1972 Obituary ... 37-40R
Gallagher, Lurlene Nora
See McDaniel, Lurlene
Gallagher, (Joseph) Mark 1953- ... 123
Gallagher, Marsha V. 1943- ... 117
Gallagher, Mary 1947- ... 97-100
Gallagher, Matthew P(hilip) 1919- ... 5-8R
Gallagher, Maureen 1938- ... 118
Gallagher, Neil 1941- ... 114
Gallagher, Patricia ... CANR-27
Earlier sketches in CA 65-68, CANR-11
Gallagher, Patricia C. 1957- ... 138
Gallagher, Patrick (Francis) 1930- ... 45-48
Gallagher, Rachel ... 89-92
Gallagher, Richard
See Levinson, Leonard
Gallagher, Richard (Farrington) 1926- ... CANR-6
Earlier sketch in CA 1-4R
Gallagher, Robert E(mmett) 1922- ... 13-16R
Gallagher, Sister Mary Dominic 1917- ... 17-20R
Gallagher, Stephen 1954- ... 138
Gallagher, Susan VanZanten 1955- ... 137

Gallagher, Tess 1943- 106
See also CLC 18, 63
See also DAM POET
See also DLB 120
See also PC 9
Gallagher, Thomas (Michael) 1918-1992 CANR-5
Obituary 140
Earlier sketch in CA 1-4R
Gallagher, Vera 1917- CANR-38
Earlier sketch in CA 115
Gallagher, (James) Wes(ley) 1911-1997 147
Obituary 162
See also DLB 127
Gallagher, William Davis 1808-1894 DLB 73
Gallagher, William M. 1923-1975 Obituary 89-92
Gallaher, Art, Jr. 1925- CANR-3
Earlier sketch in CA 1-4R
Gallaher, John G(erard) 1928- 126
Brief entry 112
Gallaher, (William) Rhea, Jr. 1945- 136
Gallahue, David L(ee) 1943- CANR-57
Earlier sketches in CA 77-80, CANR-13, 30
Gallahue, John (Jeremiah) 1930- Brief entry 110
Gallant, Christine C. 1940- Brief entry 106
Gallant, Felicia
See Dano, Linda
Gallant, Jennie
See Smith, Joan Gerarda
Gallant, Mavis 1922- CANR-69
Earlier sketches in CA 69-72, CANR-29
See also CLC 7, 18, 38
See also DAC
See also DAM MST
See also DLB 53
See also MTCW 1
See also SSC 5
Gallant, Roy A(rthur) 1924- CANR-54
Earlier sketches in CA 5-8R, CANR-4, 29
See also CLC 17
See also CLR 30
See also MAICYA
See also SATA 4, 68
Gallant, Stephen I. 1946- 145
Gallant, T(homas) Grady 1920- 5-8R
Gallardo, Edward 131
See also HW
Gallardo, Evelyn 1948- 146
See also SATA 78
Gallas, John (Edward) 1950- 143
Gallas, Karen 1949- 149
Gallati, Mary Ernestine 5-8R
Gallati, Robert R. J. 1913- CANR-1
Earlier sketch in CA 1-4R
Galle, F(rederick) C(harles) 1919- 61-64
Galle, William 1938- 93-96
Gallegly, J(oseph) S(tephen) 1898- 5-8R
Gallego, Laura (Matilde) 1924- HW
Gallegos (Freire), Romulo 1884-1969 131
See also HW
See also MTCW 1
Gallen, John (J.) 1932- Brief entry 113
Gallenkamp, Charles (Benton) 1930- 131
Galler, David 1929- 25-28R
Galler, Meyer 1914- 89-92
Gallerite, The
See Bason, Frederick (Thomas)
Gallery, Dan
See Gallery, Daniel V.
Gallery, Daniel V. 1901-1977 13-16R
Obituary 69-72
Gallico, Paul (William) 1897-1976 CANR-23
Obituary 69-72
Earlier sketch in CA 5-8R
See also AITN 1
See also CLC 2
See also DLB 9, 171
See also MAICYA
See also SATA 13
Gallie, Duncan (Ian Dunbar) 1946- 123
Gallie, Menna (Patricia Humphreys) 1920- CANR-1
Earlier sketch in CA 1-4R
Gallie, W(alter) B(ryce) 1912- 85-88
Galligan, Edward L(awrence) 1926- 126
Gallimard, Gaston 1881-1975 Obituary 61-64
Gallimore, Ronald 1938- 65-68
Gallin, Sister Mary Alice 1921- 13-16R
Gallinger, Osma Couch
See Tod, Osma Gallinger
Gallison, Kate
See Gallison, Kathleen
Gallison, Kathleen 1939- 120
Gallistel, C(harles) R(ansom) 1941- 119
Gallix, Francois 1939- CANR-26
Earlier sketch in CA 109
Gallman, Waldemar J(ohn) 1899-1980 CAP-1
Obituary 101
Earlier sketch in CA 11-12
Gallmann, Kuki 145
Gallner, Sheldon M(ark) 1949- 53-56
Gallo, Max Louis 1932- 85-88
See also CLC 95
Gallo, Patrick J. 1937- 139
Gallo, Robert C(harles) 1937- 143
Gallo, Rose Adrienne 1938- Brief entry 107
Gallois, Claire 1938- CANR-18
Earlier sketch in CA 85-88
Gallois, Lucien
See Desnos, Robert
Gallon, Arthur J(ames) 1915- 57-60
Gallop, David 1928- 65-68
Gallop, Jane 1952- 107
Galloping Gourmet
See Kerr, Graham
Galloway, A(llan) D(ouglas) 1920- 25-28R
Galloway, David D(arryl) 1937- CANR-37
Earlier sketches in CA 21-24R, CANR-16
Galloway, George Barnes 1898-1967 1-4R
Obituary 103
Galloway, Grace Growden 1727-1782 DLB 200
Galloway, Janice 1956- CANR-67
Earlier sketch in CA 137
Galloway, John C. 1915-1970 CAP-2
Earlier sketch in CA 25-28
Galloway, Jonathan F(uller) 1939- 77-80
Galloway, Joseph L(ee) 1941- CANR-12
Earlier sketch in CA 73-76
Galloway, Kara
See Cail, Carol
Galloway, Margaret C(ecilia) 1915- 13-16R
Galloway, Patricia Kay 1945- CANR-30
Earlier sketch in CA 112
Galloway, Priscilla 1930- 112
See also SATA 66
Gallu, Samuel 85-88
See also AITN 2
Gallucci, Robert L(ovis) 1946- 61-64
Gallun, Raymond Z(inke) 1911-1994 CANR-57
Earlier sketches in CA 65-68, CANR-9
Gallup, Dick 1941- 33-36R
Gallup, Donald (Clifford) 1913- CANR-58
Earlier sketches in CA 25-28R, CANR-11, 27
See also DLB 187
Gallup, George (Horace) 1901-1984 CANR-13
Earlier sketch in CA 13-16R
Gallup, Ralph
See Whitemore, Hugh (John)
Gallwey, W. Timothy 1938- CANR-4
Earlier sketch in CA 53-56
Gallwitz, Klaus 1930- 131
Brief entry 109
Galouchko, Annouchka Gravel 1960- 160
See also SATA 95
Galouye, Daniel Francis 1920-1976 9-12R
Obituary 134
Galper, Harvey 1937- 119
Galster, George C(harles) 1948- 126
Galston, Arthur William 1920- 102
Galsworthy, John 1867-1933 141
Brief entry 104
See also CDBLB 1890-1914
See also DA
See also DAB
See also DAC
See also DAM DRAM, MST, NOV
See also DLB 10, 34, 98, 162
See also DLBD 16
See also SSC 22
See also TCLC 1, 45
See also WLC 2
Galt, Alfreda Sill 114
Galt, Anthony H(oward) 1944- 137
Galt, John 1779-1839 DLB 99, 116, 159
Galt, Serena
See Donald, Anabel
Galt, Thomas Franklin, Jr. 1908- 5-8R
See also SATA 5
Galt, Tom
See Galt, Thomas Franklin, Jr.
Galt, Walter
See Mundy, Talbot
Galton, (Sir) Francis 1822-1911 Brief entry 121
See also DLB 166
Galton, Lawrence 1913- CANR-6
Earlier sketch in CA 57-60
Galub, Jack 1915- 85-88
Galus, Henry S(tanley) 1923- 5-8R
Galvez (Baluzera), Manuel 1882-1962 HW
Galvez de Montalvo, Luis
See Avalle-Arce, Juan Bautista de
Galvin, Brendan 1938- CANR-49
Earlier sketches in CA 45-48, CANR-1, 24
See also CAAS 13
See also DLB 5
Galvin, James 1951- CANR-26
Earlier sketch in CA 108
See also CLC 38
Galvin, John R(ogers) 1929- CANR-13
Earlier sketch in CA 21-24R
Galvin, Matthew R(eppert) 1950- 159
See also SATA 93
Galvin, Patrick Joseph 1927- CANR-18
Earlier sketch in CA 102
Galvin, Thomas J(ohn) 1932- CANR-10
Earlier sketch in CA 13-16R
Galway, James 1939- Brief entry 105
Gam, Rita (Elenore) 1927- 45-48
Gamarra, Eduardo (A.) 1957- 131
See also HW
Gambaccini, Peter 1950- 105
Gambaro, Griselda 1928- 131
See also HW
Gamba-Stonehouse, Virginia (Silvia Isabel)
1954- 134
Gambetta, Diego 1952- 144
Gambill, Edward Lee 1936- 112
Gambino, Richard 1939(?)- 160
Gambino, Thomas D(ominic) 1942- 101
Gamble, Andrew (Michael) 1947- CANR-12
Earlier sketch in CA 69-72
Gamble, Ed 1943- 133
Gamble, Frederick (John) 1904- CAP-1
Earlier sketch in CA 9-10
Gamble, Kim 1952- SATA 81
Gamble, Mary
See Murry, Mary Middleton
Gamble, Michael (Wesley) 1943- 110
Gamble, Sidney David 1890-1968 CAP-1
Earlier sketch in CA 11-12
Gamble, Teri (Susan) Kwal 1947- 110
Gamboa, Federico 1864-1939 167
See also TCLC 36
Gamboa, Harry, Jr. HW
Gamboa, Reymundo 1948- DLB 122
Gambrell, Herbert (Pickens) 1898- 1-4R
Gambrell, Jamey 149
See also SATA 82
Gambrill, Eileen 1934- CANR-34
Earlier sketches in CA 89-92, CANR-15
Gambs, John S(ake) 1899- 13-16R
Gamer, Robert E(manuel) 1938- 65-68
Gamerman, Martha 1941- 77-80
See also SATA 15
Gamm, David B(ernard) 1948- 69-72
Gammage, Allen Z. 1917- CANR-11
Earlier sketch in CA 5-8R
Gammage, Bill
See Gammage, William Leonard
Gammage, William Leonard 1942- CANR-10
Earlier sketch in CA 57-60
Gammell, Stephen 1943- CANR-55
Earlier sketch in CA 135
See also MAICYA
See also SATA 53, 81
Gammell, Susanna Valentine Mitchell
1897(?)-1979 Obituary 85-88
Gammer, Moshe 1950- 146
Gammie, John G(lenn) 1929- 121
Gammon, Roland I. 1920-1981 49-52
Obituary 103
Gammon, Samuel Rhea (III) 1924- Brief entry 112
Gammond, Peter 1925- CANR-31
Earlier sketches in CA 81-84, CANR-14
Gamoran, Mamie (Goldsmith) 1900- CANR-3
Earlier sketch in CA 5-8R
Gamow, George 1904-1968 102
Obituary 93-96
Gamson, Joshua (Paul) 1962- 150
Gamson, William A. 1934- CANR-13
Earlier sketch in CA 33-36R
Gamst, Frederick C(harles) 1936- CANR-11
Earlier sketch in CA 29-32R
Gan, Elena Andreevna 1814-1842 DLB 198
Gance, Abel 1889-1981 Obituary 108
Ganci, Dave 1937- 115
Gandalac, Lennard
See Berne, Eric (Lennard)
Gandee, Lee R(auss) 1917- 33-36R
Gander, Forrest 1956- 145
Gandevia, Bryan Harle 1925- CANR-45
Earlier sketches in CA 106, CANR-22
Gandhi, Indira (Priyadarshini Nehru) 1917-1984 128
Obituary 113
Gandhi, M. K.
See Gandhi, Mohandas Karamchand
Gandhi, Mahatma
See Gandhi, Mohandas Karamchand
Gandhi, Mohandas Karamchand 1869-1948 132
Brief entry 121
See also DAM MULT
See also MTCW 1
See also TCLC 59
Gandley, Kenneth Royce 1920- CANR-64
Earlier sketches in CA 69-72, CANR-12
Gandolfo, Joe M. 1936- 105
Gandossy, Robert P. 1951- 120
Ganey, Terry 1948- 144
Gangel, Kenneth O(tto) 1935- CANR-39
Earlier sketches in CA 25-28R, CANR-17
Gangemi, Kenneth 1937- CANR-67
Earlier sketch in CA 29-32R
Gangewere, Robert J(ay) 1936- 89-92
Gangloff, Deborah 1952- 130
Ganley, Albert Charles 1918- 13-16R
Ganley, Gladys Dickens 1929- CANR-41
Earlier sketch in CA 113
Ganley, Oswald Harold 1929- CANR-41
Earlier sketch in CA 112
Ganly, Helen (Mary) 1940- 125
See also SATA 56
Gann, Ernest Kellogg 1910-1991 CANR-1
Obituary 136
Earlier sketch in CA 1-4R
See also AITN 1
See also CLC 23
Gann, L(ewis) H(enry) 1924-1997 CANR-31
Obituary 156
Earlier sketches in CA 5-8R, CANR-3
Gannett, Frank E(rnest) 1876-1957 Brief entry 117
See also DLB 29
Gannett, Lewis Stiles 1891-1966 Obituary 89-92
Gannett, Ruth Chrisman (Arens) 1896-1979 SATA 33
Gannett, Ruth Stiles 1923- 21-24R
See also SATA 3
Gannon, Frank 1952- CANR-53
Earlier sketch in CA 126
Gannon, Martin John 1934- 145
Gannon, Robert Haines 1931- CANR-4
Earlier sketch in CA 9-12R
See also SATA 8
Gannon, Robert I(gnatius) 1893-1978 CAP-1
Obituary 77-80
Earlier sketch in CA 13-16
Gannon, Steve 1944- 162
Gannon, Thomas M(ichael) 1936- CANR-26
Earlier sketch in CA 109
Gano, Lila 1949- 144
See also SATA 76
Gans, Bruce Michael 1951- 81-84
Gans, Chaim 1948- 145
Gans, Eric L. 1941- 33-36R
Gans, Herbert J. 1927- CANR-63
Earlier sketches in CA 1-4R, CANR-6
Gans, Roma 1894-1996 CANR-32
Obituary 154
Earlier sketch in CA 77-80
See also SATA 45
See also SATA-Obit 93
Gansberg, Judith M. 1947- 85-88
Ganshof, Francois-Louis 1895- CAP-2
Earlier sketch in CA 19-20
Gansler, Jacques Singleton 1934- 135
Gans-Ruedin, E(rwin) 1915- 65-68
Ganss, George Edward 1905- CANR-31
Earlier sketch in CA 49-52
Gant, Chuck
See Galub, Jack
Gant, Jonathan
See Adams, Clifton
Gant, Matthew
See Hano, Arnold
Gant, Phyllis 1922- 57-60
Gant, Richard
See Freemantle, Brian (Harry)
Gantner, Neilma 1922- 104
Gantner, Susan (Verble) 1939- SATA 63
Gantos, Jack
See Gantos, John (Bryan), Jr.
See also CLR 18
Gantos, John (Bryan), Jr. 1951- CANR-56
Earlier sketches in CA 65-68, CANR-15
See also Gantos, Jack
See also SATA 20, 81
Gantry, Susan Nadler 1947- 61-64
Gantschev, Ivan 1925- 159
Gantt, Fred, Jr. 1922-197(?) CANR-3
Earlier sketch in CA 9-12R
Gantt, William Andrew Horsley 1893-1980 102
Obituary 97-100
Gantz, Charlotte Orr 1909- 49-52
Gantz, Joe
See Gantz, Joseph S.
Gantz, Joseph S. 1954- 168
Gantzer, Hugh 1931- 61-64
Ganz, Arthur (Frederick) 1928- CANR-46
Earlier sketch in CA 49-52
Ganz, David L(awrence) 1951- 105
Ganz, Lowell 1948- 154
Ganz, Margaret 1927- 45-48
Ganz, Yaffa 1938- 115
See also SATA 61
See also SATA-Brief 52
Ganzalass, Martin Richard 1941- 33-36R
Ganzel, Dewey Alvin, Jr. 1927- 25-28R
Ganzl, Kurt
See Gaenzl, Kurt (Friedrich)
Gaos, Vicente 1919-1980 DLB 134
Gao Xiaosheng 1928- 168
Gapanov, Boris 1934(?)-1972 Obituary 37-40R
Gapper, Patience 1928- 139
Gar, The
See Garfinkel, Charles H.
Gara, Larry 1922- 53-56
Garab, Arra M. 1930- 81-84
Garafano, Marie 1942- SATA 84
Garafola, Lynn 1946- 135
Garagiola, Joe
See Garagiola, Joseph Henry
Garagiola, Joseph Henry 1926- 126
Garard, Ira D(ufresne) 1888- 73-76
Garaudy, Roger 1913- 149
Garavaglia, Louis A(ubrey) 1940- 119
Garb, Solomon 1920- CANR-9
Earlier sketch in CA 13-16R
Garb, Tamar 1956- 153
Garbarino, Joseph W. 1919- 53-56
Garbarino, Merwyn S(tephens) 77-80
Garbe, Ruth Moore
See Moore, Ruth (Ellen)
Garber, Anne (Theresa) 1946- 138
Garber, Emil 1901(?)-1985 Obituary 115
Garber, Eugene K. 1932- CANR-6
Earlier sketch in CA 57-60
Garber, Frederick 1929- 53-56
Garber, Joseph R(ene) 1943- 132
Garber, Lawrence (Arnold) 1937- 122
Garber, Lee O(rville) 1900- 37-40R
Garber, Steven D(aniel) 1954- 128
Garber, Zev 1941- 154
Garbett, Colin (Campbell) 1881- CAP-1
Earlier sketch in CA 9-10
Garbini, Giovanni 1931- CANR-51
Earlier sketches in CA 21-24R, CANR-9, 25
Garbo, Norman 1919- CANR-9
Earlier sketch in CA 17-20R
Garbus, Martin 1934- 133
Garbutt, Bernard 1900- Brief entry 110
See also SATA-Brief 31
Garbutt, Janice (D.) Lovoos 124
Garceau, Oliver 1911- CAP-2
Earlier sketch in CA 29-32
Garchik, Leah (Lieberman) 1945- 133
Garchik, Morton (Lloyd) 1929- 119
Garcia, Alfredo 1952- 143
Garcia, Ann O'Neal 1939- 108
Garcia, C(elso-) R(amon) 1921- 118
Garcia, Cristina 1958- 141
See also CLC 76
Garcia, F(laviano) Chris 1940- CANR-4
Earlier sketch in CA 53-56
Garcia, George Haddad
See Haddad-Garcia, George
Garcia, Lionel G. 1935- 131
See also DLB 82
See also HW
Garcia, Mario R(amon) 1947- 77-80
Garcia, Nasario 1936- 134
Garcia, Richard A. 1941- HW
Garcia, Sam 1957- HW
Garcia Castaneda, Salvador 1932- 61-64

Garcia Lorca, Federico 1898-1936 ... 131
Brief entry ... 104
See also DA
See also DAB
See also DAC
See also DAM DRAM, MST, MULT, POET
See also DC 2
See also DLB 108
See also HLC
See also HW
See also MTCW 1
See also PC 3
See also TCLC 1, 7, 49
See also WLC
Garcia Marquez, Gabriel (Jose) 1928- ... CANR-50
Earlier sketches in CA 33-36R, CANR-10, 28
See also AAYA 3
See also BEST 89:1, 90:4
See also CLC 2, 3, 8, 10, 15, 27, 47, 55, 68
See also DA
See also DAB
See also DAC
See also DAM MST, MULT, NOV, POP
See also DLB 113
See also HLC
See also HW
See also MTCW 1
See also SSC 8
See also WLC
Garcia-Marquez, Vicente 1953- ... 134
Garcia Ponce, Juan 1932- ... 131
See also HW
Garcia Rocha, Rina 1954- ... 153
See also HW
Garcia Sanchez, Javier 1955- ... 136
Garcia Y Robertson, R(odrigo) 1949- ... 165
Gard, Janice
See Latham, Jean Lee
Gard, Joyce
See Reeves, Joyce
Gard, Richard A(bbott) 1914- ... CANR-1
Earlier sketch in CA 1-4R
Gard, Robert Edward 1910-1992 ... 85-88
Obituary ... 140
See also SATA 18
See also SATA-Obit 74
Gard, Roger Martin du
See Martin du Gard, Roger
Gard, (Sanford) Wayne 1899-1986 ... CANR-43
Obituary ... 120
Earlier sketch in CA 1-4R
See also SATA-Obit 49
Gardam, Jane 1928- ... CANR-54
Earlier sketches in CA 49-52, CANR-2, 18, 33
See also CLC 43
See also CLR 12
See also DLB 14, 161
See also MAICYA
See also MTCW 1
See also SAAS 9
See also SATA 39, 76
See also SATA-Brief 28
Gardaphe, Fred L(ouis) 1952- ... 136
Gardella, Robert (P.) 1943- ... 150
Gardella, Tricia 1944- ... 161
See also SATA 96
Garden, Alexander 1685(?)-1756 ... DLB 31
Garden, Bruce
See Mackay, James (Alexander)
Garden, Edward J(ames) C(larke) 1930- ... 25-28R
Garden, Graeme 1943- ... 107
Garden, John
See Fletcher, H(arry) L(utf) V(erne)
Garden, Nancy 1938- ... CANR-30
Earlier sketches in CA 33-36R, CANR-13
See also AAYA 18
See also CLR 51
See also JRDA
See also SAAS 8
See also SATA 12, 77
Garden, Robert Hal 1937- ... 69-72
Gardiner, C(linton) Harvey 1913- ... CANR-16
Earlier sketches in CA 1-4R, CANR-1
Gardiner, Charles Wrey 1901-1981 Obituary ... 103
Gardiner, Dorothy 1894-1979 Obituary ... 93-96
Gardiner, Glenn Lion 1896-1962 ... 1-4R
Gardiner, Jeremy 1957- ... 145
Gardiner, John Reynolds 1944- ... 127
See also SATA 64
Gardiner, Judith Kegan 1941- ... 138
Gardiner, Judy 1922- ... CANR-9
Earlier sketch in CA 21-24R
Gardiner, Margaret Power Farmer
See Countess of Blessington, Marguerite
Gardiner, Mary Summerfield
1896-1982 Obituary ... 106
Gardiner, Muriel
See Buttinger, Muriel Gardiner
Gardiner, Patrick (Lancaster) 1922-1997 ... CANR-5
Obituary ... 158
Earlier sketch in CA 1-4R
Gardiner, Robert K. A. 1914- ... 21-24R
Gardiner, Robert W(orthington) 1932- ... 53-56
Gardiner, Stephen 1925- ... 97-100
Gardinier, David E(lmer) 1932- ... 112
Gardiol, Rita M(azzetti) ... 81-84
Gardner, Alan (Harold) 1925- ... 21-24R
Gardner, Angela Davis
See Davis-Gardner, Angela
Gardner, Anne
See Shultz, Gladys Denny
Gardner, Ava (Lavinia) 1922-1990 ... 139
Gardner, Beau ... SATA-Brief 50
Gardner, (Robert) Brian 1931- ... 13-16R
Gardner, Carl 1931- ... 107
Gardner, Craig Shaw 1949- ... 157
See also SATA 99
Gardner, D(avid) Bruce 1924- ... 49-52
Gardner, David P(ierpont) 1933- ... 21-24R
Gardner, Dic
See Gardner, Richard (M.)
Gardner, Dorothy E. M. 1900-1972 ... CAP-2
Earlier sketch in CA 23-24
Gardner, E(dward) Clinton 1920- ... 13-16R
Gardner, Eldon J(ohn) 1909- ... 41-44R
Gardner, Frank Matthias 1908-1980 Obituary ... 109
Gardner, G(erald) B(rosseau)
1884-1964 Obituary ... 112
Gardner, Gerald 1929- ... CANR-5
Earlier sketch in CA 1-4R
Gardner, Helen (Louise) 1908- ... 97-100
Gardner, Herb(ert) 1934- ... 149
See also CLC 44
Gardner, Howard 1943- ... CANR-48
Earlier sketches in CA 65-68, CANR-9
Gardner, Hugh 1910-1986 Obituary ... 120
See also SATA-Obit 49
Gardner, Hy 1908-1989 ... 101
Obituary ... 128
Gardner, Isabella (Stewart) 1915-1981 ... 97-100
Obituary ... 104
Gardner, Jack Irving 1934- ... 102
Gardner, Jane Mylum 1946- ... 150
See also SATA 83
Gardner, Jani 1943- ... 25-28R
Gardner, Jeanne LeMonnier 1925- ... 17-20R
See also SATA 5
Gardner, Jeffrey
See Fox, G(ardner) F(rancis)
Gardner, John (Champlin), Jr. 1933-1982 ...
CANR-33
Obituary ... 107
Earlier sketch in CA 65-68
See also AITN 1
See also CLC 2, 3, 5, 7, 8, 10, 18, 28, 34
See also DAM NOV, POP
See also DLB 2
See also DLBY 82
See also MTCW 1
See also SATA 40
See also SATA-Obit 31
See also SSC 7
Gardner, John (Edmund) 1926- ... CANR-69
Earlier sketches in CA 103, CANR-15
See also CLC 30
See also DAM POP
See also MTCW 1
Gardner, John E(dward) 1917- ... 17-20R
Gardner, John W(illiam) 1912- ... CANR-4
Earlier sketch in CA 1-4R
Gardner, Joseph L(awrence) 1933- ... CANR-30
Earlier sketch in CA 29-32R
Gardner, Lawrence
See Brannon, William T.
Gardner, Leonard 1934- Brief entry ... 111
Gardner, Lewis 1943- ... 65-68
Gardner, Lloyd C(alvin) 1934- ... CANR-3
Earlier sketch in CA 9-12R
Gardner, (Alice) Lucille 1913- ... 69-72
Gardner, Marilyn ... 101
Gardner, Mark L(ee) 1960- ... 149
Gardner, Martin 1914- ... CANR-46
Earlier sketch in CA 73-76
See also SATA 16
Gardner, Mary 1936- ... 124
Gardner, Mary A(delaide) 1920- ... 21-24R
Gardner, Miriam
See Bradley, Marion Zimmer
Gardner, Nancy Bruff 1915- ... CANR-70
Earlier sketch in CA 13-16R
Gardner, Noel
See Kuttner, Henry
Gardner, Paul ... 69-72
Gardner, R(ufus) H(allette III) 1918- ... 33-36R
Gardner, Ralph D(avid) 1923- ... CANR-6
Earlier sketch in CA 13-16R
Gardner, Richard (M.) 1931- ... CANR-10
Earlier sketch in CA 21-24R
See also SATA 24
Gardner, Richard A. 1931- ... CANR-56
Earlier sketches in CA 33-36R, CANR-34
See also SATA 13
Gardner, Richard Kent 1928- ... CANR-27
Earlier sketch in CA 69-72
Gardner, Richard N(ewton) 1927- ... 89-92
Gardner, Riley W(etherell) 1921- ... 13-16R
Gardner, Robert 1911- ... 61-64
Gardner, Robert 1929- ... 147
See also SATA-Brief 43
Gardner, Robert W(ayne) 1940- ... 144
Gardner, Sandra 1940- ... 138
See also SATA 70
Gardner, Sheldon 1934- ... 104
See also SATA 33
Gardner, Theodore Roosevelt II 1934- ... 150
See also SATA 84
Gardner, Virginia (Marberry) 1904-1992 ... 112
Obituary ... 136
Gardner, Wanda Kirby 1914- ... 73-76
Gardner, Wayland Downing 1928- ... 73-76
Gardner, William Earl 1928- ... CANR-18
Earlier sketches in CA 5-8R, CANR-3
Gardner, William Henry 1902-1969 ... CAP-1
Earlier sketch in CA 13-16
Gardner, Wynelle B. 1918- ... 65-68
Gardner-Smith, Percival 1888-1985 ... CAP-2
Obituary ... 116
Earlier sketch in CA 17-18
Gardons, S. S.
See Snodgrass, W(illiam) D(e Witt)
Garduk, Harry David 1910(?)-1985 Obituary ... 116
Gare, Fran
See Mandell, Fran Gare
Gareau, Etienne 1915-1988 ... CANR-54
Earlier sketch in CA 45-48
Gareau, Frederick H(enry) 1923- ... 5-8R
Garebian, Keith 1943- ... 129
Gareffa, Peter M(ichael) 1952- ... CANR-43
Earlier sketch in CA 118
Garelick, May 1910-1989 ... 73-76
Obituary ... 130
See also SATA 19
Garetz, Mark 1953- ... 112
Garfield, Brian (Wynne) 1939- ... CANR-63
Earlier sketches in CA 1-4R, CANR-6
Garfield, Eugene 1925- ... 114
Garfield, Evelyn Picon 1940- ... CANR-25
Earlier sketches in CA 57-60, CANR-9
Garfield, James B. 1881-1984 Obituary ... 112
See also SATA 6
See also SATA-Obit 38
Garfield, Leon 1921-1996 ... CANR-41
Obituary ... 152
Earlier sketches in CA 17-20R, CANR-38
See also AAYA 8
See also CLC 12
See also CLR 21
See also DLB 161
See also JRDA
See also MAICYA
See also SATA 1, 32, 76
See also SATA-Obit 90
Garfield, Patricia L(ee) 1934- ... 85-88
Garfield, Sol L(ouis) 1918- ... CANR-12
Earlier sketch in CA 29-32R
Garfield, Sydney 1916(?)-1988 Obituary ... 124
Garfinkel, Alan 1941- ... CANR-21
Earlier sketch in CA 105
Garfinkel, Bernard Max 1929- ... CANR-17
Earlier sketch in CA 25-28R
Garfinkel, Charles H. 1939- ... 112
Garfinkel, Charlie
See Garfinkel, Charles H.
Garfinkel, Herbert 1920- ... 1-4R
Garfinkel, Perry 1948- ... 121
Garfinkle, Adam M. 1951- ... CANR-58
Earlier sketch in CA 112
Garfinkle, Louis (Alan) 1928- Brief entry ... 112
Garfitt, Roger 1944- ... CANR-13
Earlier sketch in CA 33-36R
Garforth, Francis William 1917- ... 9-12R
Garfunkel, Louis X. 1897(?)-1972 Obituary ... 37-40R
Garfunkel, Trudy 1944- ... 154
Gargan, Edward T(homas) 1922- Brief entry ... 111
Gargan, William (Michael) 1950- ... 111
Gargan, William Dennis 1905-1979 Obituary ... 106
Garibaldi, Gerald 1951- ... 108
Gariepy, Henry 1930- ... CANR-2
Earlier sketch in CA 49-52
Garioch, Robert Sutherland 1909-1981 ... 103
Garis, Howard R(oger) 1873-1962 ... CANR-27
Earlier sketch in CA 73-76
See also DLB 22
See also SATA 13
Garis, Robert (Erwin) 1925- ... 17-20R
Garitano, Rita 1939- ... 118
Garlan, Patricia Wallace 1926- ... 120
Garland, Alex 1970- ... 167
Garland, Bennett
See Garfield, Brian (Wynne)
Garland, Charles T(albot)
1910(?)-1976 Obituary ... 69-72
Garland, George
See Roark, Garland
Garland, (Hannibal) Hamlin 1860-1940 Brief
entry ... 104
See also DLB 12, 71, 78, 186
See also SSC 18
See also TCLC 3
Garland, Hazel (Barbara) 1913-1988 Obituary ... 125
Garland, Madge 1900(?)-1990 ... 25-28R
Obituary ... 132
Garland, Mark (A.) 1953- ... 147
See also SATA 79
Garland, Mary 1922- ... 89-92
Garland, Max 1950- ... 150
Garland, Phyl(lis T.) 1935- ... 69-72
Garland, Robert (Sandford John) 1947- ... 120
Garland, Sarah 1944- ... SATA 62
Garland, Sherry 1948- ... SATA 73
Garlick, Peter C(yril) 1923- ... 41-44R
Garlick, Raymond 1926- ... CANR-4
Earlier sketch in CA 53-56
Garlington, Phil 1943- ... 81-84
Garlington, Warren K(ing) 1923- ... 9-12R
Garlinski, Jozef 1914- ... 108
Garlock, Dorothy ... 160
Garmaise, Freda 1928- ... 134
Garmendia, Joseba Irazu 1951- ... 164
Garment, Grace R. 1927(?)-1976 Obituary ... 104
Garment, Leonard ... 158
Garment, Suzanne 1946- ... 142
Garmey, Jane 1942- ... 114
Garmon, William S. 1926- ... 21-24R
Garms, Walter I(rving, Jr.) 1925- ... 120
Garn, Edwin Jacob 1932- ... 107
Garn, Jake
See Garn, Edwin Jacob
Garneau, Francois-Xavier 1809-1866 ... DLB 99
Garneau, Michel 1939- ... 165
See also DLB 53
Garneau, (Hector de) Saint-Denys 1912-1943 Brief
entry ... 111
See also DLB 88
See also TCLC 13
Garner, Alan 1934- ... CANR-64
Earlier sketches in CA 73-76, CANR-15
See also AAYA 18
See also CLC 17
See also CLR 20
See also DAB
See also DAM POP
See also DLB 161
See also MAICYA
See also MTCW 1
See also SATA 18, 69
Garner, Alan (Francis) 1950- ... 132
Garner, Claud Wilton 1891- ... 9-12R
Garner, David 1958- ... SATA 78
Garner, Dwight L. 1913- ... 25-28R
Garner, Graham
See Rowland, D(onald) S(ydney)
Garner, H(essle) F(ilmore) 1926- ... 73-76
Garner, Harry Hyman 1910-1973 ... 17-20R
Obituary ... 134
Garner, Helen 1942- ... CANR-71
Brief entry ... 124
Earlier sketch in CA 127
Garner, Hugh 1913-1979 ... CANR-31
Earlier sketch in CA 69-72
See also CLC 13
See also DLB 68
Garner, James Finn 1960(?)- ... 153
See also SATA 92
Garner, John S. 1945- ... 146
Garner, Joseph John Saville
1908-1983 Obituary ... 111
Garner, (Samuel) Paul 1910- ... 37-40R
Garner, Roberta 1943- ... 85-88
Garner, Rolf
See Berry, Bryan
Garner, (Lafayette) Ross 1914- ... 33-36R
Garner, Wendell R(ichard) 1921- ... CANR-11
Earlier sketch in CA 5-8R
Garner, William 1920- ... CANR-12
Earlier sketch in CA 29-32R
Garner, William R(obin) 1936- ... 21-24R
Garnet, A. H.
See Slote, Alfred
Garnet, Eldon 1946- ... CANR-9
Earlier sketch in CA 61-64
Garnett, A(rthur) Campbell 1894-1970 ... CANR-2
Earlier sketch in CA 1-4R
Garnett, Angelica 1918- ... 136
Garnett, Bill
See Garnett, William John
Garnett, Christopher Browne
1906-1975 Obituary ... 61-64
Garnett, David 1892-1981 ... CANR-17
Obituary ... 103
Earlier sketch in CA 5-8R
See also CLC 3
See also DLB 34
Garnett, Eve C. R. 1900-1991 ... CANR-2
Obituary ... 134
Earlier sketch in CA 1-4R
See also DLB 160
See also SATA 3
See also SATA-Obit 70
Garnett, Henrietta (Catherine Vanessa) 1945- ... 125
Garnett, Isobel
See Waddington, Patrick (Haynes)
Garnett, Lynne 1942- ... 138
Garnett, Richard 1835-1906 ... DLB 184
Garnett, Richard (Duncan Carey) 1923- ... 5-8R
Garnett, Roger
See Morland, Nigel
Garnett, Tay 1894(?)-1977 Obituary ... 73-76
Garnett, William John 1941- ... 102
Garnham, Nicholas 1937- ... 33-36R
Garnham, Trevor 1947- ... 162
Garofalo, Reebee
See Garofalo, Robert L.
Garofalo, Robert L. 1944- ... 77-80
Garoogian, Andrew 1928- Brief entry ... 113
Garoogian, Rhoda 1933- ... CANR-19
Earlier sketch in CA 102
Garos, Stephanie
See Katz, Steve
and Krentz, Jayne Ann
Garou, Louis P.
See Bowkett, Stephen
Garoyan, Leon 1925- ... CANR-5
Earlier sketch in CA 1-4R
Garrad, Larch S(ylvia) 1936- ... 61-64
Garrard, Gene
See Garrard, Jeanne Sue
Garrard, J. G.
See Garrard, John (Gordon)
Garrard, Jeanne Sue ... 81-84
Garrard, John (Gordon) 1934- ... 151
Brief entry ... 114
Garrard, Lancelot Austin 1904-1993 ... CANR-46
Obituary ... 140
Earlier sketches in CAP-1, CA 9-10
Garrard, Lewis H. 1829-1887 ... DLB 186
Garrard, Mary D(ubose) 1937- ... 125
Garrard, Timothy F(rancis) 1943- ... 131
Garraty, John A(rthur) 1920- ... CANR-36
Earlier sketches in CA 1-4R, CANR-2
See also DLB 17
See also SATA 23
Garreau, Joel 1948- ... 101
Garret, Maxwell R. 1917- ... 106
See also SATA 39
Garretson, Lucy Reed 1936- ... 97-100
Garretson, Robert L. 1920- ... 17-20R
Garretson, Victoria Diane 1945- ... 108
See also SATA 44
Garrett, Albert Charles 1915-1983 Obituary ... 109
Garrett, Alfred B. 1906- ... 5-8R

Garrett, Charles 1925-1977 Obituary ... 73-76
Garrett, Charles C.
See Wells, Angus
Garrett, Clarke 1935- ... 73-76
Garrett, Eileen J(eanette) 1893-1970 ... CAP-2
Earlier sketch in CA 25-28
Garrett, Franklin M(iller) 1906- ... 57-60
Garrett, Garet 1878-1954 Brief entry ... 122
Garrett, George (Palmer) 1929- ... CANR-67
Earlier sketches in CA 1-4R, CANR-1, 42
See also CAAS 5
See also CLC 3, 11, 51
See also DLB 2, 5, 130, 152
See also DLBY 83
See also SSC 30
Garrett, Gerald R. 1940- ... CANR-53
Earlier sketches in CA 73-76, CANR-12, 28
Garrett, Gerard 1928- ... 73-76
Garrett, Gordon
See Garrett, (Gordon) Randall (Phillip)
Garrett, Helen 1895- ... SATA 21
Garrett, Howard 1931- ... 61-64
Garrett, James Leo, Jr. 1925- ... CANR-13
Earlier sketch in CA 33-36R
Garrett, (Ruth) Jane 1914- ... 105
Garrett, Jennifer 1960- ... 122
Garrett, John (Allen) 1920- ... CANR-16
Earlier sketch in CA 33-36R
Garrett, John Work 1872-1942 ... DLB 187
Garrett, Laurie 1951- ... 148
Garrett, Leonard J(oseph) 1926- ... 17-20R
Garrett, Leslie 1931- ... 17-20R
Garrett, Lillian ... 29-32R
Garrett, Peter K. 1940- ... 25-28R
Garrett, (Gordon) Randall (Phillip) 1927-1987 ... 130
Garrett, Richard 1920- ... CANR-37
Earlier sketches in CA 81-84, CANR-16
See also SATA 82
Garrett, Romeo Benjamin 1910- ... 37-40R
Garrett, Stephen A(rmour) 1939- ... 111
Garrett, Susan 1931- ... 146
Garrett, Thomas M(ichael) 1924- ... CANR-5
Earlier sketch in CA 1-4R
Garrett, Thomas S(amuel) 1913-1980 ... CANR-3
Earlier sketch in CA 1-4R
Garrett, Tom
See Garrett, Thomas S(amuel)
Garrett, Truman
See Judd, Margaret Haddican
Garrett, Wendell D(ouglas) 1929- ... 9-12R
Garrett, William 1890-1967 ... CAP-1
Earlier sketch in CA 11-12
Garrettson, Charles Lloyd (III) 1953- ... 144
Garrick, David 1717-1779 ... DAM DRAM
See also DLB 84
Garrigan, Owen (Walter) 1928- ... 21-24R
Garrigue, Jean 1914-1972 ... CANR-20
Obituary ... 37-40R
Earlier sketch in CA 5-8R
See also CLC 2, 8
Garrigue, Sheila 1931- ... 69-72
See also SATA 21
Garrigus, Charles B(yford) 1914- ... 136
Garris, Mick ... 165
Garrison, Barbara 1931- ... SATA 19
Garrison, Bruce 1950- ... 141
Garrison, Christian (Bascom) 1942- ... 65-68
Garrison, Daniel H. 1937- ... 136
Garrison, Dee 1934- ... 125
Garrison, Frederick
See Sinclair, Upton (Beall)
Garrison, J. Ritchie 1951- ... 137
Garrison, James (Dale) 1943- ... 61-64
Garrison, Jim (C.) 1921-1992 ... 132
Obituary ... 139
Brief entry ... 111
Garrison, Joan
See Neubauer, William Arthur
Garrison, Karl C(laudius) 1900-1980 ... CANR-31
Earlier sketch in CA 37-40R
Garrison, Omar V. 1913- ... 33-36R
Garrison, Paul 1918- ... CANR-48
Earlier sketch in CA 122
Garrison, Phil
See Brandner, Gary (Phil)
Garrison, R. Benjamin 1926- ... CANR-5
Earlier sketch in CA 13-16R
Garrison, Webb B(lack) 1919- ... CANR-18
Earlier sketches in CA 1-4R, CANR-2
See also SATA 25
Garrison, William Lloyd 1805-1879 ... CDALB 1640-1865
See also DLB 1, 43
Garrison, Winfred Ernest 1874-1969 ... CANR-6
Earlier sketch in CA 1-4R
Garrity
See Gerrity, David James
Garrity, Dave
See Gerrity, David James
Garrity, Devin Adair 1905-1981 ... 107
Obituary ... 103
Garrity, Joan Terry 1940- ... 69-72
See also AITN 1
Garrity, Richard (George) 1903- ... 77-80
Garrity, Terry
See Garrity, Joan Terry
Garro, Elena 1920(?)- ... 131
See also DLB 145
See also HW
Garrod, Rene J(eanette) 1954- ... CANR-49
Earlier sketch in CA 120
Garrow, David J(effries) 1953- ... 93-96
Garroway, Dave
See Garroway, David Cunningham
Garroway, David Cunningham 1913-1982 Obituary ... 107
Garry, Charles R. 1909- ... 73-76
Garside, Charles, Jr. 1927-1987 Obituary ... 122
Garside, (Clifford) Jack 1924- ... 127
Garside, Roger R(amsay) 1938- ... 107
Garskof, Michele Hoffnung
See Hoffnung, Michele
Garson, Barbara ... 33-36R
Garson, Clee
See Fairman, Paul W.
Garson, G(eorge) David 1943- ... CANR-4
Earlier sketch in CA 53-56
Garson, Helen Sylvia 1925- ... 107
Garson, Noel George 1931- ... 29-32R
Garson, Paul 1946- ... 49-52
Garst, Doris Shannon 1894- ... 1-4R
See also SATA 1
Garst, John Fredric 1932- ... 45-48
Garst, Robert E(dward) 1900-1980 ... 108
Obituary ... 97-100
Garst, Shannon
See Garst, Doris Shannon
Garstang, Jack
See Garstang, James Gordon
Garstang, James Gordon 1927- ... 13-16R
Garstein, Oskar Bernhard 1924- ... 13-16R
Gart, Murray Joseph 1924- ... 103
Garten, Hugh F(rederick) 1904-1975 ... CANR-3
Earlier sketch in CA 5-8R
Garten, Jeffrey E. 1946- ... 166
Gartenberg, Egon 1911- ... 57-60
Gartenberg, Leo 1906- ... 9-12R
Garth, Samuel 1661-1719 ... DLB 95
Garth, Will
See Hamilton, Edmond and Kuttner, Henry
Garthoff, Raymond L(eonard) 1929- ... 5-8R
Garthwaite, Malaby
See Dent, Anthony Austen
Garthwaite, Marion H(ook) 1893- ... 5-8R
See also SATA 7
Gartland, Robert Aldrich 1927- ... 17-20R
Gartman, Louise 1920- ... 17-20R
Gartner, Alan 1935- ... CANR-34
Earlier sketches in CA 33-36R, CANR-15
Gartner, Carol B(licker) 1935- ... 114
Gartner, Chloe (Maria) 1916- ... CANR-20
Earlier sketches in CA 1-4R, CANR-5
Gartner, Lloyd P. 1927- ... CANR-2
Earlier sketch in CA 1-4R
Gartner, Michael G(ay) 1938- ... 77-80
Garton, Charles 1926- ... CANR-45
Earlier sketches in CA 45-48, CANR-21
Garton, Janet 1944- ... CANR-36
Earlier sketch in CA 114
Garton, Jean Staker 1929- ... 114
Garton, Malinda D(ean) (?)-1976 ... 1-4R
Obituary ... 103
See also SATA-Obit 26
Garton, Nancy Wells 1908- ... 5-8R
Garton, Nina R. 1905- ... CAP-2
Earlier sketch in CA 21-22
Garton Ash, Timothy 1955- ... 166
Garton Ash, Timothy 1955- ... 166
Garve, Andrew
See Winterton, Paul
See also DLB 87
Garver, Newton 1928- ... 142
Garver, Richard B(ennett) 1934- ... 33-36R
Garverick, Linda M. 1959- ... 152
Garvey, Amy Jacques 1896(?)-1973 Obituary 45-48
Garvey, Edward B. 1914- ... 41-44R
Garvey, Gerald (Thomas) 1935- Brief entry ... 112
Garvey, John 1944- ... CANR-14
Earlier sketch in CA 65-68
Garvey, John H. 1948- ... 168
Garvey, Marcus (Moziah, Jr.) 1887-1940 ... 124
Brief entry ... 120
See also BLC 2
See also BW 1
See also DAM MULT
See also TCLC 41
Garvey, Mark 1959- ... 147
Garvey, Mona C. 1934- ... CANR-34
Earlier sketch in CA 29-32R
Garvey, Robert 1908-1983 ... 107
Obituary ... 109
Garvey, Steve(n Patrick) 1948- ... 133
Garvey, Terence Willcocks 1915- ... 103
Garvie, A(lexander) F(ermister) 1934- ... 73-76
Garvin, Charles D. 1929- ... CANR-6
Earlier sketch in CA 57-60
Garvin, Glenn 1954- ... 136
Garvin, (Hilda) Katharine 1904- ... 5-8R
Garvin, Lawrence 1945- ... 53-56
Garvin, Paul L(ucian) 1919- ... CANR-5
Earlier sketch in CA 13-16R
Garvin, Philip 1947- ... 73-76
Garvin, Richard M. 1934- ... 49-52
Garvin, Thomas Christopher 1943- ... 113
Garvin, Tom
See Garvin, Thomas Christopher
Garvin, William 1922- ... 25-28R
Garwood, Darrell (Nelson) 1909- ... 29-32R
Garwood, Judith 1941- ... 144
Garwood, Julie 1946- ... 138
Gary, Dorothy
See Page, Myra
Gary, Dorothy Page
See Page, Myra
Gary, Romain
See Kacew, Romain
See also CLC 25
See also DLB 83
Garza, Roberto J(esus) 1934- ... 104
See also HW
Garzilli, Enrico 1937- ... 41-44R
Gasca, Philip D. Ortego
See Ortego y Gasca, Philip D.
Gascar, Pierre
See Fournier, Pierre
See also CLC 11
Gasche, Rodolphe 1938- ... 135
Gaschnitz, Michael K. ... 168
Gascoigne, Bamber 1935- ... CANR-28
Earlier sketches in CA 25-28R, CANR-10
See also SATA 62
Gascoigne, John 1951- ... 133
Gascoigne, Marguerite
See Lazarus, Marguerite
Gascon, The
See Miller, F(rederick) W(alter) G(ascoyne)
Gascoyne, David (Emery) 1916- ... CANR-54
Earlier sketches in CA 65-68, CANR-10, 28
See also CLC 45
See also DLB 20
See also MTCW 1
Gash, Joe
See Granger, Bill
Gash, Jonathan
See Grant, John
Gash, Norman 1912- ... CANR-1
Earlier sketch in CA 1-4R
Gaskell, Elizabeth Cleghorn 1810-1865 ... CDBLB 1832-1890
See also DAB
See also DAM MST
See also DLB 21, 144, 159
See also SSC 25
Gaskell, Ivan 1955- ... 143
Gaskell, Jane 1941- ... CANR-58
Earlier sketches in CA 5-8R, CANR-11
Gaskell, (John) Philip (Wellesley) 1926- ... CANR-3
Earlier sketch in CA 5-8R
Gaskell, Thomas F. 1916- ... 17-20R
Gaskill, Harold V. 1905-1975 Obituary ... 57-60
Gaskin, Catherine 1929- ... CANR-10
Earlier sketch in CA 65-68
Gaskin, David Edward 1939- ... 69-72
Gaskin, Ina May 1940- ... 129
Gaskin, J(ohn) C(harles) A(ddison) 1936- ... 131
Gaskin, Stephen (F.) 1935- ... 129
Gaskins, Richard H. 1946- ... 145
Gasnick, Roy M(ichael) 1933- ... 117
Gasparini, Graziano 1926- ... 41-44R
Gasparotti, Elizabeth Seifert 1897-1983 ... CANR-68
Obituary ... 110
Earlier sketches in CA 1-4R, CANR-2
Gasper, Louis 1911- ... 13-16R
Gasperini, Jim 1952- ... 122
See also SATA 54
See also SATA-Brief 49
Gaspey, Thomas 1788-1871 ... DLB 116
Gasque, W(oodrow) Ward 1939- ... CANR-15
Earlier sketch in CA 65-68
Gass, William H(oward) 1924- ... CANR-71
Earlier sketches in CA 17-20R, CANR-30
See also CLC 1, 2, 8, 11, 15, 39
See also DLB 2
See also MTCW 1
See also SSC 12
Gassan, Arnold 1930- ... 73-76
Gassenheimer, Linda 1942- ... 137
Gassert, Robert G(eorge) 1921- ... 17-20R
Gasset, Jose Ortega y
See Ortega y Gasset, Jose
Gassier, Pierre 1915- ... CANR-34
Earlier sketch in CA 49-52
Gassner, John Waldhorn 1903-1967 ... CANR-3
Obituary ... 25-28R
Earlier sketch in CA 1-4R
Gassner, Julius S(tephen) 1915- ... 37-40R
Gast, Kelly P.
See Edmondson, G. C.
Gaster, T(heodor) Herzl 1906-1992 ... 73-76
Obituary ... 136
Gastil, John (Webster) 1967- ... 147
Gastil, Raymond D(uncan) 1931- ... 29-32R
Gastmann, Albert (Lodewijk) 1921- ... 97-100
Gaston, Edwin W(illmer), Jr. 1925- ... CANR-2
Earlier sketch in CA 1-4R
Gaston, Georg M(eri-) A(kri) 1938- ... 109
Gaston, Jerry (Collins) 1940- ... CANR-1
Earlier sketch in CA 45-48
Gaston, Patricia S. 1946- ... 144
Gaston, Wilber
See Gibson, Walter B(rown)
Gat, Azar 1959- ... 143
Gat, Dimitri V(sevolod) 1936- ... CANR-31
Earlier sketch in CA 29-32R
Gatch, Jean 1924- ... 127
Gatch, Milton McC(ormick, Jr.) 1932- ... CANR-27
Earlier sketch in CA 29-32R
Gatell, Frank Otto 1931- ... 9-12R
Gatenby, Greg 1950- ... 97-100
Gatenby, Rosemary 1918- ... CANR-9
Earlier sketch in CA 21-24R
Gater, Dilys 1944- ... 112
See also SATA 41
Gater, Hubert 1913(?)-1980 Obituary ... 101
Gates, Albert
See Glotzer, Albert
Gates, Arthur Irving 1890-1972 Obituary ... 37-40R
Gates, Bill 1955- ... 154
See also Gates, William Henry III
Gates, David 1947(?)- ... 140
Gates, David Murray 1921- ... 81-84
Gates, Doris 1901-1987 ... CANR-46
Obituary ... 124
Earlier sketches in CA 1-4R, CANR-1
See also DLB 22
See also MAICYA
See also SAAS 1
See also SATA 1, 34
See also SATA-Obit 54
Gates, Frieda 1933- ... 93-96
See also SATA 26
Gates, Henry Louis, Jr. 1950- ... CANR-53
Earlier sketches in CA 109, CANR-25
See also BLCS
See also BW 2
See also CLC 65
See also DAM MULT
See also DLB 67
Gates, J(eannette) M(cPherson) 1924- ... CANR-7
Earlier sketch in CA 57-60
Gates, Jean Key 1911- ... 33-36R
Gates, John A(lexander) 1898- ... 5-8R
Gates, John D. 1939- ... 89-92
Gates, John Floyd 1915- ... 1-4R
Gates, Lewis E. 1860-1924 ... DLB 71
Gates, Lillian Francis 1901- ... CAP-2
Earlier sketch in CA 25-28
Gates, Marilyn 1944- ... 145
Gates, Natalie ... 21-24R
Gates, Norman T(immins) 1914- ... 77-80
Gates, Paul W(allace) 1901- ... CANR-2
Earlier sketch in CA 1-4R
Gates, Philomene (A.) 1918- ... 134
Gates, Robbins L(adew) 1922- ... 13-16R
Gates, Ronda 1940- ... 161
Gates, Viola R. 1931- ... 168
See also SATA 101
Gates, William Byram 1917-1975 Obituary ... 61-64
Gates, William Henry III 1955-
See Gates, Bill
Gatewood, Willard B., Jr. 1931- ... 17-20R
Gathercole, Adrienne Lois
See Kaeppler, Adrienne Lois
Gatheridge, R. Edward
See Wilson, Robert (Edward)
Gathorne-Hardy, Jonathan G. 1933- ... CANR-39
Earlier sketch in CA 104
See also SATA 26
Gati, Charles 1934- ... 146
Gatley, Jimmy 1931(?)-1985 Obituary ... 115
Gatley, Richard Harry 1936- ... 101
Gatlin, Douglas S. 1928- ... 21-24R
Gatlin, Lila L(ee) 1928- ... 101
Gatner, Elliott S(herman) M(ozian) 1914- ... CANR-3
Earlier sketch in CA 9-12R
Gato, J. A.
See Keller, John E(sten)
Gattegno, Caleb 1911-1988 Obituary ... 126
Gattey, Charles Neilson 1921- ... CANR-20
Earlier sketches in CA 13-16R, CANR-5
Gatti, Arthur Gerard 1942- ... 65-68
Gatti, Daniel Jon 1946- ... 45-48
Gatti, Enzo
See Gatti, Vincenzo
Gatti, Richard DeY 1947- ... 45-48
Gatti, Vincenzo 1942- ... CANR-8
Earlier sketch in CA 61-64
Gattmann, Eric 1925- ... 49-52
Gatto, Alfonso 1909-1976 ... DLB 114
Gatty, Juliana Horatia
See Ewing, Juliana (Horatia Gatty)
Gatty, Margaret Scott 1809-1873 ... SATA-Brief 27
Gatty, Ronald 1929- ... 85-88
Gatzke, Hans W(ilhelm) 1915-1987 ... CANR-5
Obituary ... 123
Earlier sketch in CA 1-4R
Gaubatz, Kathlyn Taylor 1957- ... 154
Gauch, Patricia Lee 1934- ... CANR-9
Earlier sketch in CA 57-60
See also SAAS 21
See also SATA 26, 80
Gauchat, Dorothy 1921- ... 97-100
Gaudet, Frederick J(oseph) 1902-1977 ... 5-8R
Obituary ... 73-76
Gaudiose, Dorothy M(arie) 1920- ... 89-92
Gauer, Harold 1914- ... 13-16R
Gaugh, Harry F. ... 116
Gaul, Randy 1959- ... SATA 63
Gauld, Alan (Ogilvie) 1932- ... 144
Gauld, Charles A(nderson) 1911- ... 13-16R
Gauld, Joseph W(arren) 1927- ... 144
Gaulden, Albert Clayton 1938- ... 160
Gaulden, Ray 1914-(?) ... CANR-64
Earlier sketches in CA 17-20R, CANR-8
Gauldie, Enid 1928- ... CANR-14
Earlier sketch in CA 77-80
Gauldie, (William) Sinclair 1918- ... 33-36R
Gaulle, Charles (Andre Joseph Marie) de
See de Gaulle, Charles (Andre Joseph Marie)
Gault, Clare 1925- ... 97-100
See also SATA 36
Gault, Frank 1926-1982 ... CANR-11
Earlier sketch in CA 69-72
See also SATA 36
See also SATA-Brief 30
Gault, Henri (Andre Paul Victor) 1929- ... 130
Gault, Mark
See Cournos, John
Gault, Peter 1958- ... 138
Gault, William Campbell 1910- ... CANR-37
Earlier sketches in CA 49-52, CANR-1, 16
See also SATA 8
Gaumnitz, Jack E(rwin) 1935- ... 120
Gaumnitz, Walter Herbert 1891-1979 Obituary ... 89-92
Gaunt, Leonard 1921- ... CANR-3
Earlier sketch in CA 5-8R

Gaunt, Mary 1861-1942 ... DLB 174
Gaunt, Michael
See Robertshaw, (James) Denis
Gaunt, Peter
See Eshbach, Lloyd Arthur
Gaunt, William 1900-1980 ... CANR-6
Obituary ... 97-100
Earlier sketch in CA 9-12R
Gauquelin, Michel (Roland) 1928- ... CANR-31
Earlier sketch in CA 57-60
Gaur, Albertine 1932- ... CANR-47
Earlier sketch in CA 121
Gaus, Gerald F. 1952- ... 112
Gaustad, Edwin Scott 1923- ... CANR-1
Earlier sketch in CA 1-4R
Gautier, Theophile 1811-1872 ... DAM POET
See also DLB 119
See also PC 18
See also SSC 20
Gauvreau, Claude 1925-1971 ... 148
See also DLB 88
Gavaskar, Sunil 1949- ... 131
Gaver, Becky
See Gaver, Rebecca
Gaver, Jack 1906-1974 ... 97-100
Obituary ... 53-56
Gaver, Jessyca (Russell) 1915- ... CANR-9
Earlier sketch in CA 53-56
Gaver, Mary Virginia 1906-1991 ... CANR-34
Obituary ... 136
Earlier sketch in CA 1-4R
Gaver, Rebecca 1952- ... SATA 20
Gaverick, Linda M. 1959- ... 152
Gavett, J(oseph) William 1921- ... 25-28R
Gavett, Thomas W(illiam) 1932- ... 13-16R
Gavin
See Frost, Gavin
Gavin, Amanda
See Gibson-Jarvie, Clodagh
Gavin, Bill
See Gavin, William S.
Gavin, Catherine ... CANR-1
Earlier sketch in CA 1-4R
Gavin, Claire (E.) 1944- ... 150
Gavin, Eileen A. 1931- ... 45-48
Gavin, James M(aurice) 1907-1990 ... CAP-1
Obituary ... 131
Earlier sketch in CA 13-16
Gavin, Jamila 1941- ... CANR-68
Earlier sketch in CA 110
See also SATA 96
Gavin, Lettie 1922- ... 166
Gavin, Thomas 1941- ... 85-88
Gavin, Thomas F. 1910- ... 108
Gavin, William
See Houston, Douglas (Norman)
Gavin, William S. 1907(?)-1985 Obituary ... 114
Gavin-Brown, Wilfred A(rthur) 1904- ... CAP-1
Earlier sketch in CA 9-10
Gavron, Daniel 1935- ... CANR-12
Earlier sketch in CA 29-32R
Gavron, Susan J. 1947- ... 152
Gavronsky, Serge 1932- ... CANR-9
Earlier sketch in CA 65-68
Gavshon, Arthur L(eslie) 1916- ... 5-8R
Gaw, Walter A. 1904- ... 1-4R
Gawain, Shakti 1948- ... 93-96
Gawaine, John
See Hamilton-Hill, Donald
Gawron, Jean Mark 1953- ... 103
Gawsworth, John
See Armstrong, Terence Ian Fytton
and Bates, H(erbert) E(rnest)
Gawthrop, Louis C. 1930- ... 81-84
Gaxotte, Pierre 1895-1982 ... 111
Obituary ... 108
Gay, A. Nolder
See Koelsch, William Alvin
Gay, Amelia
See Hogarth, Grace (Weston Allen)
Gay, Carlo T(eofilo) E(berhard) 1913- ... CANR-51
Earlier sketches in CA 49-52, CANR-27
Gay, Ebenezer 1696-1787 ... DLB 24
Gay, Francis
See Gee, H(erbert) L(eslie)
Gay, John 1685-1732 ... DAM DRAM
See also DLB 84, 95
Gay, John E(dward) 1942- ... 81-84
Gay, John H. 1928- ... 143
See also BW 2
Gay, Kathlyn 1930- ... CANR-50
Earlier sketches in CA 21-24R, CANR-8, 25
See also SATA 9
Gay, Marie-Louise 1952- ... 135
See also CLR 27
See also SAAS 21
See also SATA 68
Gay, Oliver
See Gogarty, Oliver St. John
Gay, Peter (Jack) 1923- ... CANR-41
Earlier sketches in CA 13-16R, CANR-18
Interview in ... CANR-18
Gay, Ruth 1922- ... 139
Gay, Volney P(atrick) 1948- ... CANR-40
Earlier sketch in CA 117
Gay, Zhenya 1906-1978 ... 73-76
See also SATA 19
Gaya-Nuno, Juan Antonio 1913-1975 ... CANR-31
Earlier sketch in CA 81-84
Gayarre, Charles E. A. 1805-1895 ... DLB 30
Gay-Crosier, Raymond 1937- ... CANR-15
Earlier sketch in CA 41-44R
Gaydos, Michael J. 1940- ... 53-56
Gaye, Carol
See Shann, Renee
Gaye, Marvin (Penze) 1939-1984 Obituary ... 112
See also CLC 26
Gay-Kelly, Doreen 1952- ... 61-64
Gayle, Addison, Jr. 1932-1991 ... CANR-13
Obituary ... 135
Earlier sketch in CA 25-28R
See also BW 1
Gayle, Emma
See Fairburn, Eleanor
Gayle, Marilyn
See Hoff, Marilyn
Gayle, Stephen H. 1948(?)-1982 Obituary ... 107
Gayles, Anne Richardson 1923- ... 53-56
Gaylin, Willard (M.) 1925- ... CANR-44
Earlier sketches in CA 21-24R, CANR-13
Gaylord, Billy
See Gaylord, William (Gilbert)
Gaylord, Edward King 1873-1974 Obituary ... 89-92
See also DLB 127
Gaylord, Edward Lewis 1919- ... DLB 127
Gaylord, Sherwood Boyd 1914- Brief entry ... 105
Gaylord, William (Gilbert) 1945-1985 ... 69-72
Obituary ... 118
Gayn, Mark J. 1909-1981 Obituary ... 105
Gaynor, Gloria 1949(?)- ... 168
Gaynor, Harry J. ... 134
Gayre, G(eorge) R(obert) 1907- ... CANR-4
Earlier sketch in CA 5-8R
Gayre of Gayre, R.
See Gayre, G(eorge) R(obert)
Gayre of Gayre and Nigg, Robert
See Gayre, G(eorge) R(obert)
Gazaway, Rena 1910- ... CAP-2
Earlier sketch in CA 29-32
Gazda, George M(ichael) 1931- ... CANR-29
Earlier sketches in CA 61-64, CANR-13
Gazdanov, Gaito 1903-1971 Obituary ... 104
Gazdanov, Georgii
See Gazdanov, Gaito
Gaze, Gillian
See Barklem, Jill
Gaze, Richard 1917- ... 1-4R
Gazell, James A(lbert) 1942- ... 49-52
Gazi, Stephen 1914-1978 ... 45-48
Obituary ... 103
Gazis, Denos C(onstantinos) 1930- ... 57-60
Gazley, John G(erow) 1895- ... 61-64
Gazzaniga, Michael S(aunders) 1939- ... 121
Gdanski, Marek
See Thee, Marek
Geach, Christine 1930- ... CANR-10
Earlier sketch in CA 25-28R
Geach, Patricia Sullivan 1916- ... 29-32R
Geach, Peter Thomas 1916- ... 103
Gealt, Adelheid (Medicus) 1946- ... CANR-36
Earlier sketch in CA 114
Geanakoplos, Deno John 1916- ... CANR-2
Earlier sketch in CA 1-4R
Geaney, Dennis J(oseph) 1914-1992 ... CANR-20
Obituary ... 140
Earlier sketches in CA 5-8R, CANR-5
Gear, C. William 1935- ... 53-56
Gear, Kathleen M. O'Neal
See Gear, Kathleen O'Neal
Gear, Kathleen O'Neal 1954- ... SATA 71
Gear, Sheila 1942- ... 114
Gear, W. Michael 1955- ... SATA 71
Geare, Michael 1919- ... 117
Geare, Mildred Mahler
1888(?)-1977 Obituary ... 73-76
Gearey, John 1926- ... CANR-23
Earlier sketch in CA 45-48
Gearhart, Sally Miller 1931- ... CANR-59
Earlier sketch in CA 57-60
Gearheart, B(ill) R. 1928- ... CANR-9
Earlier sketch in CA 21-24R
Gearing, Catherine 1916- ... 103
Gearing, Fred(erick) O(smond) 1922- ... 29-32R
Gearing-Thomas, G.
See Norwood, Victor G(eorge) C(harles)
Geary, Douglas 1931- ... 13-16R
Geary, Frederick Charles
1886(?)-1975(?) Obituary ... 104
Geary, Herbert Valentine (Rupert) 1894-1965 ...
CAP-1
Earlier sketch in CA 9-10
Geary, Patricia (Carol) 1951- ... 134
Geary, Patrick J(oseph) 1948- ... 104
Geary, Roger 1950- ... CANR-49
Earlier sketch in CA 123
Geasland, Jack
See Geasland, John Buchanan, Jr.
Geasland, John Buchanan, Jr. 1944- ... 81-84
Gebhard, Anna Laura Munro 1914- ... 5-8R
Gebhard, Bruno (Frederic) 1901- ... 73-76
Gebhard, Paul H(enry) 1917- ... CANR-70
Earlier sketch in CA 5-8R
Gebhardt, James F(rederick) 1948- ... 147
Gebhart, Benjamin 1923- ... 53-56
Gebler, Carlo (Ernest) 1954- ... 133
Brief entry ... 119
See also CLC 39
Gebler, Ernest 1915-1998 ... CANR-3
Obituary ... 164
Earlier sketch in CA 5-8R
Geck, Francis J(oseph) 1900- ... 73-76
Geckle, George L. 1939- ... 77-80
Gecys, Casimir C. 1904- ... CAP-2
Earlier sketch in CA 19-20
Gedda, George 1941- ... 77-80
Geddes, Charles L(ynn) 1928- ... CANR-2
Earlier sketch in CA 49-52
Geddes, Gary 1940- ... 140
See also DLB 60
Geddes, Joan Bel 1916- ... 57-60
Geddes, Paul 1922- ... 136
Geddes, Virgil 1897-1989(?) ... 148
See also DLB 4
Geddie, John 1937- ... 69-72
Gedeon c. 1730-1763 ... DLB 150
Gedge, Pauline (Alice) 1945- ... 161
See also SATA 101
Gediman, Helen K. 1931- ... 150
Gedmin, Jeffrey (N.) 1958- ... 143
Gedo, John E. 1927- ... CANR-47
Earlier sketch in CA 121
Gedo, Mary M(athews) 1925- ... 104
Geduld, Harry M(aurice) 1931- ... CANR-42
Earlier sketches in CA 9-12R, CANR-5, 20
See also CAAS 21
Gedye, George Eric Rowe
1890-1970 Obituary ... 93-96
Gee, H(erbert) L(eslie) 1901-1977 ... 9-12R
Obituary ... 103
See also SATA-Obit 26
Gee, Maggie (Mary) 1948- ... 130
See also CLC 57
Gee, Maurice (Gough) 1931- ... CANR-67
Earlier sketch in CA 97-100
See also CLC 29
See also SATA 46, 101
Gee, Shirley 1932- ... 156
Geehr, Richard S. 1938- ... 136
Geemis, Joseph (Stephen) 1935- ... 69-72
Geen, Russell Glenn 1932- ... CANR-22
Earlier sketch in CA 104
Geer, Charles 1922- ... 108
See also SATA 42
See also SATA-Brief 32
Geer, Emily A(pt) 1912- ... 127
Geer, Stephen (DuBois) 1930- ... 69-72
Geer, William D. 1906(?)-1976 Obituary ... 104
Geering, R(onald) G(eorge) 1918- ... 133
Geertz, Clifford (James) 1926- ... CANR-36
Earlier sketch in CA 33-36R
Interview in ... CANR-36
Geertz, Hildred 1927- ... 77-80
Geeslin, Campbell 1925- ... 102
Geffen, Maxwell Myles 1896-1980 Obituary ... 102
Geffen, Roger 1919- ... 17-20R
Gefvert, Constance J(oanna) 1941- ... 53-56
Gega, Peter C(hristopher) 1924- ... 73-76
Geggus, David Patrick 1949- ... CANR-37
Earlier sketch in CA 114
Geha, Joseph (A.) 1944- ... 134
Geherin, David J(ohn) 1943- ... CANR-39
Earlier sketches in CA 101, CANR-17
Gehlbach, Frederick Renner 1935- ... 106
Gehlen, Reinhard 1902-1979 Obituary ... 89-92
Gehman, Betsy Holland 1932- ... 17-20R
Gehman, Christian 1948- ... 119
Gehman, Henry Snyder 1888- ... 13-16R
Gehman, Mary W. 1923- ... 151
See also SATA 86
Gehman, Richard (Boyd) 1921-1972 ... CANR-16
Obituary ... 33-36R
Earlier sketch in CA 1-4R
Gehr, Mary 1910(?)-1997 ... SATA 32
See also SATA-Obit 99
Gehrels, Franz 1922- ... 101
Gehri, Alfred 1896(?)-1972 Obituary ... 33-36R
Gehrig, Klaus 1946- ... 137
Gehring, Wes D(avid) 1950- ... 137
Gehris, Paul 1934- ... 45-48
Geibel, Emanuel 1815-1884 ... DLB 129
Geier, Arnold 1926- ... 1-4R
Geier, Woodrow A. 1914- ... 21-24R
Geigel Polanco, Vicente 1904-1979 Obituary ... 85-88
See also HW
Geiger, Don(ald) Jesse 1923- ... 5-8R
Geiger, H(omer) Kent 1922- ... CANR-5
Earlier sketch in CA 1-4R
Geiger, John (Grigsby) 1960- ... 129
Geiger, Louis G. 1913- ... 13-16R
Geiger, Ray(mond Aloysius) 1910-1994 ... 118
Obituary ... 145
See also AITN 1
Geiger, Theodore 1915- Brief entry ... 114
Geiogamah, Hanay 1945- ... 153
See also DAM MULT
See also DLB 175
See also NNAL
Geipel, Eileen 1932- ... 107
See also SATA 30
Geipel, John 1937- ... CANR-13
Earlier sketch in CA 73-76
Geiringer, Irene (Steckel) 1899-1983 Obituary ... 111
Geiringer, Karl (Johannes) 1899-1989 ... 13-16R
Obituary ... 127
Geis, Darlene Stern ... CANR-5
Earlier sketch in CA 1-4R
See also SATA 7
Geis, Florence L(indauer) 1933- ... CANR-8
Earlier sketch in CA 57-60
Geis, Gilbert 1925- ... CANR-6
Earlier sketch in CA 9-12R
Geis, Richard E(rwin) 1927- ... 101
Interview in ... 101
Geisel, Helen 1898-1967 Obituary ... 107
See also SATA 26
Geisel, Theodor Seuss 1904-1991 ... CANR-32
Obituary ... 135
Earlier sketches in CA 13-16R, CANR-13
See also Dr. Seuss
See also DLB 61
See also DLBY 91
See also MAICYA
See also MTCW 1
See also SATA 1, 28, 75, 100
See also SATA-Obit 67
Geiser, Robert L(ee) 1931- ... 97-100
Geisert, Arthur 1941- ... CANR-57
Earlier sketches in CA 120, CANR-44
See also SAAS 23
See also SATA 56, 92
See also SATA-Brief 52
Geisert, Bonnie 1942- ... SATA 92
Geisinger, David L. 1938- ... 110
Geisler, Norman L(eo) 1932- ... CANR-51
Earlier sketches in CA 25-28R, CANR-10, 27
Geismar, Ludwig L(eo) 1921- ... CANR-53
Earlier sketches in CA 25-28R, CANR-11, 29
Geismar, Maxwell (David) 1909-1979 ... CANR-33
Obituary ... 104
Earlier sketch in CA 1-4R
Geissman, Erwin William 1920-1980 Obituary ... 101
Geist, Bill
See Geist, William E.
Geist, Harold 1916- ... CANR-22
Earlier sketches in CA 17-20R, CANR-7
Geist, Kenneth L(ee) 1936- ... 81-84
Geist, Robert John 1912- ... 41-44R
Geist, Roland C. 1896- ... 89-92
Geist, Sidney 1914- Brief entry ... 112
Geist, Valerius 1938- ... CANR-8
Earlier sketch in CA 61-64
Geist, William E. 1945(?)- ... 140
Geitgey, Doris A. 1920- ... 53-56
Geiwitz, P(eter) James 1938- ... CANR-11
Earlier sketch in CA 29-32R
Gelatt, Roland 1920-1986 ... 13-16R
Obituary ... 121
Gelb, Alan
See Gelb, Alan Lloyd
Gelb, Alan Lloyd 1950- ... 126
Gelb, Arthur 1924- ... CANR-21
Earlier sketch in CA 1-4R
See also DLB 103
Gelb, Barbara (Stone) 1926- ... CANR-21
Earlier sketch in CA 1-4R
See also DLB 103
Gelb, Ignace J(ay) 1907-1985 ... 9-12R
Obituary ... 118
Gelb, Joyce 1940- ... 61-64
Gelb, Leslie H(oward) 1937- ... CANR-19
Earlier sketch in CA 103
Gelb, Michael J. 1952- ... 147
Gelb, Norman 1929- ... CANR-30
Earlier sketch in CA 108
Gelbart, Larry (Simon) 1923- ... CANR-45
Earlier sketch in CA 73-76
See also CLC 21, 61
Gelber, Harry G. 1926- ... 25-28R
Gelber, Jack 1932- ... CANR-2
Earlier sketch in CA 1-4R
See also CLC 1, 6, 14, 79
See also DLB 7
Gelber, Lionel (Morris) 1907-1989 ... 13-16R
Obituary ... 129
Gelber, Steven M(ichael) 1943- ... 53-56
Geld, Ellen Bromfield 1932- ... 37-40R
Geldard, Frank A(rthur) 1904-1984 ... 41-44R
Obituary ... 114
Geldart, William 1936- ... SATA 15
Geldenhuys, Deon 1950- ... 139
Gelderman, Carol Wettlaufer 1935- ... 105
Gelernt, Jules 1928- ... 21-24R
Gelernter, David (Hillel) 1955(?)- ... CANR-65
Earlier sketch in CA 149
Gelfand, Elissa D(eborah) 1949- ... 114
Gelfand, Lawrence Emerson 1926- ... CANR-3
Earlier sketch in CA 5-8R
Gelfand, Morris Arthur 1908- ... 49-52
Gelfman, Dick 1947- ... 122
Gelfman, Judith S(chlein) 1937- ... 65-68
Gelfond, Rhoda 1946- ... CANR-12
Earlier sketch in CA 49-52
Gelinas, Gratien 1909- ... DLB 88
Gelinas, Paul J. 1911- ... 41-44R
See also SATA 10
Gell, Frank
See Kowet, Don
Gell, Paul (Frederick William) 1928- ... 116
Gellatly, Peter 1923- Brief entry ... 111
Geller, Allen 1941- ... 25-28R
Geller, Bruce 1930-1978 Obituary ... 77-80
Geller, Evelyn
See Gottesfeld, Evelyn
Geller, Uri 1946- ... 69-72
Gellerman, Saul W(illiam) 1929- ... CANR-8
Earlier sketch in CA 5-8R
Gellert, Christian Furchtegott 1715-1769 ... DLB 97
Gellert, Judith 1925- ... 33-36R
Gellert, Lew
See Wellen, Edward (Paul)
Gelles, Richard J(ames) 1946- ... CANR-72
Earlier sketches in CA 61-64, CANR-8, 22, 45
Gelles, Sandi
See Gelles-Cole, Sandi
Gelles-Cole, Sandi 1949- ... 121
Gelley, Alexander 1933- ... 127
Brief entry ... 108
Gellhorn, Ernst 1893-1973 ... CAP-2
Earlier sketch in CA 21-22
Gellhorn, Martha (Ellis) 1908-1998 ... CANR-44
Obituary ... 164
Earlier sketch in CA 77-80
See also CLC 14, 60
See also DLBY 82
Gellhorn, Walter 1906-1995 ... 13-16R
Obituary ... 150
Gellinek, Christian 1930- ... CANR-9
Earlier sketch in CA 21-24R
Gellinek, Janis Little
See Solomon, Janis Little
Gellis, Roberta L(eah Jacobs) 1927- ... CANR-70
Earlier sketches in CA 5-8R, CANR-3, 22, 45

Gellman, Estelle Sheila 1941- 53-56
Gellman, Irwin F(rederick) 1942- CANR-1
Earlier sketch in CA 45-48
Gell-Mann, Murray 1929- 156
Gellner, Ernest (Andre) 1925-1995 .... CANR-22
Obituary 150
Earlier sketches in CA 5-8R, CANR-4
Gellner, John 1907- 29-32R
Gellrich, Jesse M. 1942- 118
Gelman, Amy 1961- .... SATA 72
Gelman, David Graham 1926- 103
Gelman, Jan 1963- .... SATA 58
Gelman, Juan 1930- .... HW
Gelman, Milton S. 1920(?)-1990 Obituary 131
Gelman, Mitch(ell Barry) 1962- CANR-51
Earlier sketch in CA 124
Gelman, Rita Golden 1937- CANR-16
Earlier sketch in CA 81-84
See also SATA 84
See also SATA-Brief 51
Gelman, Steve 1934- CANR-16
Earlier sketch in CA 25-28R
See also SATA 3
Gelman, Woodrow 1915(?)-1978 Obituary 104
Gelman, Woody
See Gelman, Woodrow
Gelmis, Joseph S(tephan) 1935- 45-48
Gelperin, L.
See Halpern, Leivick
Gelpi, Albert 1931- 33-36R
Gelpi, Barbara Charlesworth 1933- 112
Gelpi, Donald L. 1934- CANR-7
Earlier sketch in CA 17-20R
Geltman, Max 1906(?)-1984 Obituary 112
Gelula, Abner Joseph 1906-1985 Obituary 116
Gelven, (Charles) Michael 1937- 29-32R
Gelzer, Matthias 1886-1974 .... CAP-2
Earlier sketch in CA 25-28
Gemme, Francis Robert 1934- 21-24R
Gemme, Leila Boyle 1942- 81-84
Gemmell, Alan Robertson 1913- 114
Gemmell, David A(ndrew) 1948- 154
Gemmett, Robert J(ames) 1936- 33-36R
Gemmill, Jane Brown 1898- 1-4R
Gemmill, Paul F. 1890(?)-1976 Obituary 69-72
Gemming, Elizabeth 1932- CANR-9
Earlier sketch in CA 65-68
See also SATA 11
Gems, (Iris) Pam(ela) 1925- CANR-58
Earlier sketch in CA 107
See also DLB 13
Gemuenden, Gerd
See Gemunden, Gerd
Gemunden, Gerd 1959- 166
Genauer, Emily 1911- 106
Interview in 106
Gendel, Evelyn W. 1916(?)-1977 Obituary 104
See also SATA-Obit 27
Gendell, Murray 1924- CANR-5
Earlier sketch in CA 9-12R
Gendlin, Eugene T. 1926- 1-4R
Gendron, George M. 1949- 93-96
Gendzier, Irene Lefel 1936- 21-24R
Gendzier, Stephen J(ules) 1930- 33-36R
General, Lloyd 1924(?)-1986 Obituary 119
Genet
See Flanner, Janet
Genet, Jean 1910-1986 .... CANR-18
Earlier sketch in CA 13-16R
See also CLC 1, 2, 5, 10, 14, 44, 46
See also DAM DRAM
See also DLB 72
See also DLBY 86
See also MTCW 1
Genevoix, Maurice Charles Louis
1890-1980 Obituary 102
See also DLB 65
Geng, Veronica 1941-1997 .... CANR-51
Obituary 163
Brief entry 119
Earlier sketch in CA 124
Genini, Ronald 1946- 162
Genn, Calder
See Gillie, Christopher
Gennaro, Joseph F(rancis), Jr. 1924- 101
See also SATA 53
Genne, Elizabeth Steel 1911- Brief entry 108
Genne, William H. 1910-1997 .... 17-20R
Obituary 156
Genovese, Eugene D(ominick) 1930- CANR-10
Earlier sketch in CA 69-72
See also DLB 17
Genoves Tarazaga, Santiago 1923- 127
Brief entry 107
Gensemer, Robert Eugene 1936- Brief entry 110
Genser, Cynthia 1950- 69-72
Gensler, Kinereth 1922- 116
Genszler, G(eorge) William II 1915- CANR-9
Earlier sketch in CA 65-68
Gent, Peter 1942- 89-92
See also AITN 1
See also CLC 29
See also DLBY 82
Genthe, Charles V(incent) 1937- 29-32R
Gentil, Richard 1917- 102
Gentile, Gennaro L. 1946- 115
Gentile, Giovanni 1875-1944 Brief entry 119
Gentile, John S(amuel) 1956- 132
Gentile, Petrina 1969- .... SATA 91
Gentle, Mary 1956- CANR-56
Earlier sketch in CA 106
See also SATA 48
Gentleman, David (William) 1930- CANR-15
Earlier sketch in CA 25-28R
See also SATA 7
Gentles, Frederick (Ray) 1912- 29-32R
Gentlewoman in New England, A
See Bradstreet, Anne
Gentlewoman in Those Parts, A
See Bradstreet, Anne
Gentry, Byron B. 1913- 13-16R
Gentry, Curt 1931- CANR-5
Earlier sketch in CA 9-12R
Gentry, Diane Koos 1943- 128
Gentry, Dwight L. 1919- 1-4R
Gentry, Marshall Bruce 1953- CANR-47
Earlier sketch in CA 121
Gentry, Peter
See Newcomb, Kerry
and Schaefer, Frank
Gentz, William Howard 1918- 107
Gentzler, J(ennings) Mason 1930- 93-96
Genya, Monica 168
Geoff
See Dyson, Geoffrey Harry George
Geoffrey, Iqbal
See Jafree, Mohammed Jawaid Iqbal
Geoffrey, Theodate
See Wayman, Dorothy G.
Geoffrey of Monmouth c. 1100-1155 .... DLB 146
Geoghegan, Sister Barbara 1902- CAP-1
Earlier sketch in CA 11-12
Geoghegan, Thomas Dolan
1917(?)-1987 Obituary 121
Georgakas, Dan 1938- CANR-45
Earlier sketches in CA 45-48, CANR-1, 22
George, Alexander Lawrence 1920- 13-16R
George, Alfred Raymond 1912- 108
George, Barbara
See Katz, Bobbi
George, Charles H(illes) 1922- 9-12R
George, Chief Dan 1899-1981 110
Obituary 108
George, Claude Swanson, Jr. 1920- 13-16R
George, Collins Crusor 1909-1980 77-80
Obituary 133
George, Dan
See George, Chief Dan
George, David
See Vogenitz, David George
George, David (John) 1948- 146
George, E(dgar) Madison 1907-1975 .... 1-4R
Obituary 103
George, Edward
See Vardeman, Robert E(dward)
George, Eliot
See Freeman, Gillian
George, Elizabeth 1949- CANR-62
Earlier sketch in CA 137
George, Emery E(dward) 1933- CANR-36
Earlier sketches in CA 41-44R, CANR-16
George, Emily
See Katz, Bobbi
George, Eugene
See Chevalier, Paul Eugene George
George, Gail
See Katz, Bobbi
George, Henry 1839-1897 .... DLB 23
George, Hermon, Jr. 1945- 126
George, Jay
See Strachan, J(ohn) George
George, Jean Craighead 1919- CANR-25
Earlier sketch in CA 5-8R
See also AAYA 8
See also CLC 35
See also CLR 1
See also DLB 52
See also JRDA
See also MAICYA
See also SATA 2, 68
George, John 1936- 132
George, John E(dwin) 1936- 53-56
George, John L(othar) 1916- 5-8R
See also SATA 2
George, Jonathan
See Burke, John (Frederick)
and Theiner, George (Fredric)
George, Judith W(ordsworth) 1940- 143
George, Lindsay Barrett 1952- 160
See also SATA 95
George, M(ary) Dorothy CAP-1
Earlier sketch in CA 13-16
George, Malcom F(arris) 1930- 57-60
George, Margaret 1943- 143
George, Marion
See Benjamin, Claude (Max Edward Pohlman)
George, Mary Carolyn Hollers Jutson 1930- ....
CANR-12
Earlier sketch in CA 73-76
George, Mary Yanaga 1940- 29-32R
George, N(orvil) L(ester) 1902- CAP-2
Earlier sketch in CA 29-32
George, Nelson 1957- 119
George, Peter 1924-1966 Obituary 25-28R
George, Richard R(obert) 1943- 104
George, Robert Esmonde Gordon 1890-1969 ....
CAP-1
Earlier sketch in CA 11-12
George, Rolf 1930- 110
George, Roy E(dwin) 1923- CANR-14
Earlier sketch in CA 37-40R
George, S(idney) C(harles) 1898- 53-56
See also SATA 11
George, Sally
See Orr, Wendy
George, Sally 1945- 105
George, Sara 1947- 65-68
George, Stefan (Anton) 1868-1933 Brief entry . 104
See also TCLC 2, 14
George, Stephen (Alan) 1949- 139
George, Susan Akers 1934- 77-80
George, Susanne K. 1947- 141
George, W. L. 1882-1926 .... DLB 197
George, W(illiam) Lloyd
1900(?)-1975 Obituary 53-56
See also SATA-Obit 30
George, W(illiam) R(ichard) P(hilip) 1912- 69-72
George, Wilfred R(aymond) 1928- 111
George, Wilma
See Crowther, Wilma (Beryl)
George-Brown, George Alfred
1914-1985 Obituary 116
Brief entry 110
Georges, Georges Martin
See Simenon, Georges (Jacques Christian)
Georges, Robert A(ugustus) 1933- 111
Georgescu, Vlad 1937(?)-1988 Obituary 127
Georgescu-Roegen, Nicholas 1906-1994 .. CANR-9
Obituary 147
Earlier sketch in CA 21-24R
Georges-Michel, Michel 1883-1985 Obituary 116
Georgi, Charlotte CANR-17
Earlier sketches in CA 1-4R, CANR-2
Georgiana, Sister
See Terstegge, Mabel Alice
Georgi-Findlay, Brigitte 1956- 157
Georgiou, Constantine 1927- 13-16R
See also SATA 7
Georgiou, Steven Demetre 1948- 101
Georgopoulos, Basil S(pyros) 1926- 73-76
Gephart, William J(ay) 1928- 69-72
Geraci, Philip C. 1929- 77-80
Gerald, J(ames) Edward 1906- 5-8R
Gerald, John Bart 1940- CANR-45
Earlier sketches in CA 5-8R, CANR-7, 22
Gerald, Ziggy
See Zeigerman, Gerald
Gerard, Albert S(tanislas) 1920- CANR-13
Earlier sketch in CA 29-32R
Gerard, Andrew
See Gatti, Arthur Gerard
Gerard, Charles (Franklin) 1914- 29-32R
Gerard, Dave 1909- 53-56
Gerard, David 1923- 77-80
Gerard, Elaine
See Ryder, Eileen
Gerard, H(arold) B(enjamin) 1923- Brief entry .. 110
Gerard, Jane 1930- 1-4R
Gerard, Jean Ignace Isidore 1803-1847 .... SATA 45
Gerard, Jules B(ernard) 1929- 110
Gerard, Karen (Nina) 1932- 120
Gerard, Louise 1878(?)-1970 Obituary 104
Gerard, Philip 1955- 148
Gerard, Ralph W(aldo) 1900-1974 Obituary .. 49-52
Gerard-Libois, Jules C. 1923- 33-36R
Geras, Adele (Daphne) 1944- CANR-52
Earlier sketches in CA 97-100, CANR-19
Interview in CANR-19
See also SAAS 21
See also SATA 23, 87
Geras, Norman (Myron) 1943- CANR-19
Earlier sketch in CA 102
Gerasimov, Gennadi (Ivanovitch) 1930- .. CANR-32
Earlier sketch in CA 69-72
Gerasimov, Innokentii Petrovich
1905-1985 Obituary 115
Gerasimov, Mikhail Mikhaylovich
1907-1970 Obituary 107
Gerassi, John 1931- CANR-8
Earlier sketch in CA 5-8R
Geraud, (Charles Joseph) Andre 1882-1974 .. 69-72
Obituary 53-56
Gerber, Albert B(enjamin) 1913- 17-20R
Gerber, Barbara (Lin) 1942- 117
Gerber, Bobbie
See Gerber, Barbara (Lin)
Gerber, Dan(iel Frank) 1940- CANR-41
Earlier sketch in CA 33-36R
Gerber, David A(llison) 1944- 77-80
Gerber, Douglas E(arl) 1933- CANR-15
Earlier sketch in CA 29-32R
Gerber, Ellen W. 1936- Brief entry 107
Gerber, Helmut E. 1920-1981 .... CANR-10
Earlier sketch in CA 21-24R
Gerber, Israel J(oshua) 1918- 77-80
Gerber, John 1907(?)-1981 Obituary 103
Gerber, John C(hristian) 1908- 102
Gerber, Merrill Joan 1938- CANR-51
Earlier sketches in CA 13-16R, CANR-10, 26
See also CAAS 20
See also SATA 64
Gerber, Philip Leslie 1923- Brief entry 108
Gerber, Rudolph Joseph 1938- 105
Gerber, Sanford E(dwin) 1933- CANR-1
Earlier sketch in CA 49-52
Gerber, William 1908- 37-40R
Gerberding, Richard A. 1945- 128
Gerberg, Mort 1931- .... SATA 64
Gerbers, Teresa 1933- 53-56
Gerbi, Antonello 1904-1976 77-80
Gerbner, George 1919- CANR-1
Earlier sketch in CA 45-48
Gerboth, Walter W(illiam) 1925-1984 .... 13-16R
Obituary 112
Gerchunoff, Alberto 1883-1950 .... HW
Gerdes, Eckhard 1959- 147
Gerdes, Florence Marie 1919- 25-28R
Gerdts, William H. 1929- CANR-10
Earlier sketch in CA 13-16R
Gergely, Tibor 1900-1978 107
Obituary 106
See also SATA 54
See also SATA-Obit 20
Gergen, Kenneth J(ay) 1934- 33-36R
Gerhard, Happy 1920- 57-60
Gerhardi, William Alexander
See Gerhardie, William Alexander
Gerhardie, William Alexander 1895-1977 . CANR-18
Obituary 73-76
Earlier sketch in CA 25-28R
See also CLC 5
See also DLB 36
Gerhardt, Lydia A(nn) 1934- CANR-10
Earlier sketch in CA 61-64
Gerhardt, Paul 1607-1676 .... DLB 164
Gerhart, Gail M. 1943- 85-88
Gerhart, Genevra 1930- 57-60
Gerig, Reginald R(oth) 1919- 57-60
Gerin, Winifred 1901(?)-1981 .... CANR-20
Obituary 104
Earlier sketch in CA 25-28R
See also DLB 155
Geringer, Laura 1948- CANR-68
Earlier sketch in CA 107
See also SATA 29, 94
Gerlach, Barbara A(nn) 1946- 114
Gerlach, Don R(alph) 1932- 9-12R
Gerlach, John 1941- 101
Gerlach, Larry R(euben) 1941- 133
Brief entry 109
Gerlach, Luther P(aul) 1930- 41-44R
Gerlach, Russel L(ee) 1939- 89-92
Gerlach, Vernon S(amuel) 1922- 61-64
Gerler, William R(obert) 1917- 65-68
See also SATA 47
Germain, Edward B. 1937- 89-92
Germain, Walter 1889-1962 Obituary 112
German, Donald R(obert) 1931-1986 .... CANR-22
Obituary 119
Earlier sketches in CA 57-60, CANR-7
German, Gene Arlin 1933- 45-48
German, Joan
See German-Grapes, Joan
German, Tony 1924- 97-100
Germane, Gayton E. 1920- CANR-18
Earlier sketches in CA 1-4R, CANR-2
German-Grapes, Joan 1933- CANR-45
Germani, Gino 1911-1979 .... CANR-7
Earlier sketch in CA 53-56
Germanicus
See Dunner, Joseph
Germann, A(lbert) C(arl) 1921- 1-4R
Germann, Richard Wolf 1930- 104
Germano, Peter B. 1913- Brief entry 116
Germany, (Vera) Jo(sephine) CANR-9
Earlier sketch in CA 65-68
Germar, Herb
See Germar, William H(erbert)
Germar, William H(erbert) 1911- 21-24R
Germeshausen, Anna Louise
1906-1968 Obituary 108
Germino, Dante (Lee) 1931- 53-56
Germond, Jack W. 1928- 112
Brief entry 108
Interview in 112
Gernert, Eleanor Towles 1928- 37-40R
Gernes, Sonia 1942- 107
Gernet, Jacques 1921- 163
Gernsback, Hugo 1884-1967 Obituary 93-96
See also DLB 8, 137
Gernsheim, Helmut (Erich Robert) 1913-1995 ....
CANR-45
Obituary 149
Earlier sketches in CA 5-8R, CANR-5, 22
Gernstein, Mordicai Brief entry 117
See also SATA 36
Geroely, Kalman
See Gabel, Joseph
Gerold, Karl 1906-1973 Obituary 41-44R
Gerold, William 1932- 17-20R
Geroly, Kalman
See Gabel, Joseph
Gerome
See Thibault, Jacques Anatole Francois
Gerosa, Guido 1933- 73-76
Gerould, Daniel C. 1928- 29-32R
Gerould, Daniel C(harles) 1928- CANR-33
Gerould, Katharine Fullerton 1879-1944 .... DLB 78
Gerow, Edwin 1931- 53-56
Gerow, Josh(ua R.) 1941- 103
Gerrard, A. J.
See Gerrard, John
Gerrard, Jean 1933- 115
See also SATA 51
Gerrard, John 1944- 135
Gerrard, Michael B. 1951- 147
Gerrard, Roy 1935-1997 .... CANR-57
Obituary 160
Earlier sketch in CA 110
See also CLR 23
See also SATA 47, 90
See also SATA-Brief 45
See also SATA-Obit 99
Gerrietts, John 1912-1992 77-80
Obituary 136
Gerrig, Richard J. 1959- 147
Gerring, Ray H. 1926- 13-16R
Gerrish, B(rian) A(lbert) 1931- CANR-4
Earlier sketch in CA 5-8R
Gerritsen, Terry
See Gerritsen, Tess
Gerritsen, Tess 1953- 159
Gerrity, David James 1923- CANR-4
Earlier sketch in CA 1-4R
Gerrold, David 1944- 93-96
Interview in 93-96
See also DLB 8
See also SATA 66
Gerschenkron, Alexander (Pavlovich) 1904-1978 ...
CANR-1
Earlier sketch in CA 45-48
Gersh, Harry 1912- CANR-1
Earlier sketch in CA 1-4R

Gershator, David 1937- ... 115
Gershator, Phillis 1942- ... CANR-57
Earlier sketch in CA 102
See also SATA 90
Gershen, Martin 1924-1985 ... 33-36R
Obituary ... 114
Gershenson, Daniel E(noch) 1935- ... 5-8R
Gershman, Herbert S. 1926-1971 ... CAP-2
Obituary ... 33-36R
Earlier sketch in CA 25-28
Gershon, Karen
See Tripp, Karen
Gershoni, Israel 1946- ... 150
Gershoy, Leo 1897-1975 ... CAP-1
Obituary ... 57-60
Earlier sketch in CA 13-14
Gershuny, Grace 1950- ... 144
Gershwin, Ira 1896-1983 ... 164
Obituary ... 110
Brief entry ... 108
See also DLBY 96
Gerson, Corinne 1927- ... CANR-25
Earlier sketch in CA 93-96
See also SATA 37
Gerson, Kathleen 1947- ... 147
Gerson, Louis Leib 1921- ... 17-20R
Gerson, Mary-Joan ... SATA 79
Gerson, Noel Bertram 1914-1988 ... 81-84
Obituary ... 127
See also SATA 22
See also SATA-Obit 60
Gerson, Walter (Max) 1935- ... 41-44R
Gerson, Wolfgang 1916- ... 33-36R
Gersoni, Diane 1947- ... 53-56
Gersonides 1288-1344 ... DLB 115
Gersoni-Stavn, Diane
See Gersoni, Diane
Gerstad, John (Leif) 1924-1981 ... 103
Obituary ... 105
Gerstaecker, Friedrich 1816-1872 ... DLB 129
Gerstein, Arnold A. 1940- ... 124
Gerstein, Linda (Groves) 1938- Brief entry ... 110
Gerstein, Mordicai 1935- ... CANR-56
Earlier sketches in CA 127, CANR-36
See also MAICYA
See also SATA 47, 81
See also SATA-Brief 36
Gerstenberg, Heinrich Wilhelm von 1737-1823 . DLB 97
Gerstenberger, Donna Lorine 1929- ... CANR-4
Earlier sketch in CA 5-8R
Gerstenberger, Erhard S. 1932- ... 164
Gerster, Georg (Anton) 1928- ... 37-40R
Gerster, Patrick G(eorge) 1942- ... 57-60
Gerstine, Jack
See Gerstine, John
Gerstine, John 1915- ... 5-8R
Gerstl, Joel E. 1932- ... 21-24R
Gerstle, Kurt H(erman) 1923- ... 53-56
Gerstler, Amy 1956- ... 146
See also CLC 70
Gerstner, Edna Suckau 1914- ... 1-4R
Gerstner, John H(enry) 1914- ... CANR-2
Earlier sketch in CA 1-4R
Gert, Bernard 1934- ... 29-32R
Gerteiny, Alfred G(eorges) 1930- ... 21-24R
Gerteis, Louis S(axton) 1942- ... 45-48
Gerth, Donald Rogers 1928- ... 45-48
Gerth, Hans Heinrich 1908-1978 Obituary ... 81-84
Gertler, Menard M. 1919- ... 9-12R
Gertler, T. ... 121
Brief entry ... 116
Interview in ... 121
See also CLC 34
Gertman, Samuel 1915- ... 1-4R
Gertz, Elmer 1906- ... CANR-42
Earlier sketches in CA 13-16R, CANR-11
Gertz, Theodore G(erson) 1936- ... 115
Gertzog, Irwin N(orman) 1933- ... 29-32R
Gerulaitis, Leonardas Vytautas 1928- ... 77-80
Geruson, Richard J. 1957- ... 140
Gervais, Bernadette 1959- ... SATA 80
Gervais, C(harles) H(enry) 1946- ... 97-100
Gervais, Marty
See Gervais, C(harles) H(enry)
Gervais, (George) Paul 1946- ... 145
Gervasi, Eugene Michael 1937-1989 Obituary ... 127
Gervasi, Frank H(enry) 1908-1990 ... CAP-1
Obituary ... 130
Earlier sketch in CA 13-16
Gervasi, Tom
See Gervasi, Eugene Michael
Gervinus, Georg Gottfried 1805-1871 ... DLB 133
Gerwig, Anna Mary (Gerwig) 1907- ... CAP-2
Earlier sketch in CA 17-18
Gerwin, Donald 1937- ... 25-28R
Gery, John (Roy Octavius) 1953- ... 151
Gerzina, Gretchen (Aletha) Holbrook 1950- ... 140
Gerzon, Mark ... 81-84
Gerzon, Robert 1946- ... 164
Gesch, Dorothy K(atherine) 1923- ... 29-32R
Gesch, Roy G(eorge) 1920- ... 21-24R
Geschickter, Charles F(reeborn) 1901-1987 Obituary ... 123
Geschwender, James A(rthur) 1933- ... 41-44R
Gesell, Arnold Lucius 1880-1961 Obituary ... 116
Geserick, June
See Donahue, June (Geserick)
Gesler, Wilbert M. 1941- ... 138
Gesner, Carol 1922- ... 29-32R
Gesner, Clark 1938- ... 109
See also SATA 40
Gesner, Elsie Miller 1919- ... 17-20R
Gess, Denise 1952- ... 135
Gessel, Van C. 1950- ... 145
Gessert, Kate Rogers 1948- ... 113
Gessner, Lynne 1919- ... CANR-10
Earlier sketch in CA 25-28R
See also SATA 16
Gessner, Salomon 1730-1788 ... DLB 97
Geston, Mark S(ymington) 1946- ... CANR-58
Earlier sketch in CA 102
See also DLB 8
Gethers, Peter 1953- ... CANR-57
Earlier sketches in CA 103, CANR-31
Gethers, Steven 1922(?)-1989 Obituary ... 130
Gething, Thomas W(ilson) 1939- ... 41-44R
Gethner, Perry (J.) 1947- ... 151
Getlein, Dorothy Woolen 1921- ... 9-12R
Getlein, Frank 1921- ... CANR-6
Earlier sketch in CA 9-12R
Getman, Gerald Nathan 1914(?)-1990 Obituary 131
Getman, Julius (G.) 1931- ... 140
Gettel, Ronald 1931- ... 112
Gettens, Rutherford John 1900(?)-1974 Obituary ... 49-52
Gettings, Eunice J. 1901(?)-1978 Obituary ... 81-84
Gettings, Fred 1937- ... 123
Gettleman, Marvin E. 1933- ... 37-40R
Gettleman, Susan
See Braiman, Susan
Gettlin, Robert ... 160
Getty, Gerald W(inkler) 1913- ... 57-60
Getty, Hilda F. 1938- ... 61-64
Getty, J(ean) Paul 1892-1976 ... 69-72
Obituary ... 65-68
Getty, Mary Ann 1943- ... 114
Getz, David 1957- ... 155
See also SATA 91
Getz, Gene A(rnold) 1932- ... CANR-54
Earlier sketches in CA 29-32R, CANR-12, 29
Getz, Malcolm 1945- ... CANR-18
Earlier sketch in CA 101
Getz, Oscar 1897-1983 Obituary ... 110
Getzels, Jacob Warren 1912- ... CANR-30
Earlier sketch in CA 45-48
Getzoff, Carole 1943- ... 61-64
Geubtner, Virginia Reidel
See Reidel-Geubtner, Virginia
Geve, Thomas 1929- ... 127
Gevirtz, Don L(ee) 1928- ... 121
Gevirtz, Eliezer 1950- ... 121
See also SATA 49
Gevirtz, Stanley 1929-1988 Obituary ... 126
Brief entry ... 109
Gewe, Raddory
See Gorey, Edward (St. John)
Gewecke, Clifford George, Jr. 1932- ... 21-24R
Gewehr, Wolf M(ax) 1939- ... CANR-1
Earlier sketch in CA 45-48
Gewertz, Deborah B. 1948- ... 143
Gewirth, Alan 1912- Brief entry ... 107
Gewirtz, Jacob L(eon) 1924- ... 45-48
Gewirtz, Leonard Benjamin 1918- ... 1-4R
Geyer, Alan (Francis) 1931- ... 9-12R
Geyer, Georgie Anne 1935- ... CANR-17
Earlier sketch in CA 29-32R
Interview in ... CANR-17
Geyl, Pieter (Catharinus Arie) 1887-1966 ... 103
Obituary ... 89-92
Geyman, John P. 1931- ... CANR-14
Earlier sketch in CA 37-40R
Gezi, Kal
See Gezi, Kalil I(smail)
Gezi, Kalil I(smail) 1930- ... CANR-17
Earlier sketch in CA 25-28R
Ghadimi, Hossein 1922- ... 61-64
Ghai, Dharam P. 1936- ... CANR-34
Earlier sketches in CA 21-24R, CANR-15
Ghalib
See Ghalib, Hsadullah Khan
Ghalib, Hsadullah Khan 1797-1869
See Ghalib
See also DAM POET
Ghan, Linda (R.) 1947- ... 145
See also SATA 77
Gheddo, Piero 1929- ... CANR-15
Earlier sketch in CA 73-76
Ghelardi, Robert (Anthony) 1939- ... 69-72
Ghelderode, Michel de 1898-1962 ... CANR-40
Earlier sketch in CA 85-88
See also CLC 6, 11
See also DAM DRAM
Gheorghiu, (Constantin) Virgil 1916-1992 CANR-30
Obituary ... 138
Earlier sketch in CA 33-36R
Gherity, James Arthur 1929- ... 17-20R
Gherman, Beverly 1934- ... 136
See also SATA 68
Ghezzi, Bert (Bentil W.) 1941- ... 133
Ghigna, Charles 1946- ... 77-80
Ghilarducci, Teresa 1957- ... 144
Ghine, Wunnakyawhtin U Ohn
See Maurice, David (John Kerr)
Ghiotto, Renato 1923- ... 49-52
Ghiradella, Robert 1934- ... 114
Ghiselin, Brewster 1903- ... CANR-13
Earlier sketch in CA 13-16R
See also CAAS 10
See also CLC 23
Ghiselin, Michael T(enant) 1939- ... 49-52
Ghiselli, Edwin E(rnest) 1907- ... 37-40R
Ghnassia, Maurice (Jean-Henri) 1920- ... CANR-34
Earlier sketch in CA 49-52
Ghose, Amal 1929- ... CANR-28
Earlier sketch in CA 106
Ghose, Aurabinda 1872-1950 ... 163
See also TCLC 63
Ghose, Sri Chinmoy Kumar
See Chinmoy, Sri
Ghose, Sudhin(dra) N(ath) 1899- ... 5-8R
Ghose, Zulfikar 1935- ... CANR-67
Earlier sketch in CA 65-68
See also CLC 42
Ghosh, Amitav 1956- ... 147
See also CLC 44
Ghosh, Arun Kumar 1930- ... CANR-26
Earlier sketches in CA 21-24R, CANR-10
Ghosh, Dipali 1945- ... CANR-51
Earlier sketch in CA 124
Ghosh, Jyotis Chandra 1904(?)-1975 Obituary ... 57-60
Ghosh, Tapan 1928- ... 53-56
Ghougassian, Joseph P(eter) 1944- ... 49-52
Ghurye, G(ovind) S(adashiv) 1893- ... CANR-3
Earlier sketch in CA 5-8R
Giacconi, Riccardo 1931- ... 156
Giacosa, Giuseppe 1847-1906 Brief entry ... 104
See also TCLC 7
Giacumakis, George, Jr. 1937- ... 41-44R
Giallombardo, Rose (Mary) 1925- ... 61-64
Giamatti, A(ngelo) Bartlett 1938-1989 ... 97-100
Obituary ... 129
Giamatti, Valentine 1911-1982 Obituary ... 106
Giampieri-Deutsch, Patrizia ... 148
Gianakaris, C(onstantine) J(ohn) 1934- ... 25-28R
Giannaris, George (B.) 1936- ... CANR-45
Earlier sketches in CA 45-48, CANR-2, 22
Giannestras, Nicholas James 1909-1978 Obituary ... 105
Giannetti, Louis D. 1937- ... 33-36R
Giannini, Enzo 1946- ... SATA 68
Giannone, Richard 1934- ... 21-24R
Giannoni, Carlo Borromeo 1939- ... 41-44R
Giap Vo Nguyen
See Vo Nguyen, Giap
Giardina, Anthony 1950- ... 118
Giardina, Denise 1951- ... CANR-72
Earlier sketch in CA 119
Giauque, William Francis 1895-1982 Obituary ... 106
Gibaldi, Joseph 1942- ... CANR-15
Earlier sketch in CA 89-92
Gibans, Nina Freedlander 1932- ... 116
Gibb, Hamilton (Alexander Rosskeen) 1895-1971 ... CANR-6
Obituary ... 33-36R
Earlier sketch in CA 1-4R
Gibb, Jack (Rex) 1914- ... 17-20R
Gibb, Lee
See Deghy, Guy (Stephen) and Waterhouse, Keith (Spencer)
Gibbard, Allan (Fletcher) 1942- ... 136
Gibbard, Graham S(tewart) 1942- ... 53-56
Gibbens, T(revor) C(harles) N(oel) 1912-1983 Obituary ... 111
Gibberd, Frederick 1908-1984 Obituary ... 111
Gibbings, Robert 1889-1958 ... DLB 195
Gibbins, Peter 1947- ... 127
Gibble, Kenneth L(ee) 1941- ... 130
Gibbon, Edward 1737-1794 ... DLB 104
Gibbon, John Murray 1875-1952 ... 163
See also DLB 92
Gibbon, Lewis Grassic
See Mitchell, James Leslie
See also TCLC 4
Gibbon, (William) Monk 1896-1987 ... 69-72
Obituary ... 124
Gibbon, Vivian 1917- ... 103
Gibbons, Anne R(obert) 1947- ... 168
Gibbons, Barbara (Halloran) 1934- ... CANR-10
Earlier sketch in CA 61-64
Gibbons, Bob
See Gibbons, Robert
Gibbons, Brian 1938- ... CANR-11
Earlier sketch in CA 25-28R
Gibbons, Don C(ary) 1926- Brief entry ... 110
Gibbons, Euell (Theophilus) 1911-1975 ... CAP-2
Obituary ... 61-64
Earlier sketch in CA 23-24
See also AITN 1
Gibbons, Faye 1938- ... 109
See also SATA 65
Gibbons, Felton L(ewis) 1929-1990 ... 124
Obituary ... 131
Gibbons, (Raphael) Floyd (Phillips) 1887-1939 Brief entry ... 113
See also DLB 25
Gibbons, Gail 1944- ... CANR-12
Earlier sketch in CA 69-72
See also CLR 8
See also MAICYA
See also SAAS 12
See also SATA 23, 72
Gibbons, Helen Bay 1921- ... 17-20R
Gibbons, J. Whitfield 1939- ... CANR-35
Earlier sketch in CA 114
Gibbons, John H(oward) 1929- ... 127
Gibbons, John William 1907-1983 Obituary ... 109
Gibbons, Kaye 1960- ... 151
See also CLC 50, 88
See also DAM POP
Gibbons, Maurice 1931- ... 89-92
Gibbons, Reginald 1947- ... CANR-18
Earlier sketch in CA 97-100
See also CAAS 24
See also DLB 120
Gibbons, Robert 1949- ... CANR-39
Earlier sketch in CA 116
Gibbons, Stella (Dorothea) 1902-1989 ... 13-16R
Obituary ... 130
Gibbons, Whit
See Gibbons, J. Whitfield
Gibbons, William ... DLB 73
Gibbs, A(twood) James 1922- ... 17-20R
Gibbs, A(nthony) M(atthews) 1933- ... 33-36R
Gibbs, Alonzo (Lawrence) 1915- ... CANR-5
Earlier sketch in CA 5-8R
See also SATA 5
Gibbs, Anthony 1902-1975 ... CAP-2
Earlier sketch in CA 29-32
Gibbs, Barbara 1912- ... 25-28R
Gibbs, C. Earl 1935- ... 69-72
Gibbs, David N. 1958- ... 139
Gibbs, Esther 1904- ... 57-60
Gibbs, George 1870-1942 Brief entry ... 120
Gibbs, Henry
See Rumbold-Gibbs, Henry St. John Clair
Gibbs, Jack P(orter) 1927- ... 122
Brief entry ... 118
Gibbs, James A.
See Gibbs, James Atwood
Gibbs, James Atwood 1922- ... CANR-29
Earlier sketches in CA 69-72, CANR-11
Gibbs, Jim
See Gibbs, James Atwood
Gibbs, Joanifer 1947- ... 57-60
Gibbs, John G(amble) 1930- ... 41-44R
Gibbs, Mark 1920- ... 5-8R
Gibbs, Mary Ann
See Bidwell, Marjory Elizabeth Sarah
Gibbs, (Cecilia) May 1877-1969 Obituary ... 104
See also SATA-Obit 27
Gibbs, Norman Henry 1910-1990 Obituary ... 131
Gibbs, Paul T(homas) 1897- ... 9-12R
Gibbs, Peter Bawtree 1903- ... 1-4R
Gibbs, Philip (Hamilton) 1877-1962 Obituary . 89-92
Gibbs, Rafe
See Gibbs, Raphael Sanford
Gibbs, Raphael Sanford 1912- ... 5-8R
Gibbs, Tony
See Gibbs, Wolcott, Jr.
Gibbs, William E. 1936-(?) ... CAP-2
Earlier sketch in CA 21-22
Gibbs, Wolcott, Jr. 1935- ... CANR-72
Earlier sketch in CA 85-88
See also SATA 40
Gibbs-Smith, Charles Harvard 1909-1981 . CANR-4
Obituary ... 108
Earlier sketch in CA 9-12R
Gibbs-Wilson, Kathryn (Beatrice) 1930- ... CANR-10
Earlier sketch in CA 65-68
Gibby, Robert Gwyn 1916- ... 13-16R
Giberson, Dorothy (Dodds) ... CANR-2
Earlier sketch in CA 1-4R
Gibian, George 1924- ... CANR-19
Earlier sketches in CA 1-4R, CANR-5
Gibilisco, Stan 1953- ... 147
Giblin, Charles Homer 1928- ... 41-44R
Giblin, James Cross 1933- ... CANR-24
Earlier sketch in CA 106
See also CLR 29
See also MAICYA
See also SAAS 12
See also SATA 33, 75
Giblon, Shirley T(enhouse) 1935- ... 131
Gibney, Frank (Bray) 1924- ... CANR-11
Earlier sketch in CA 69-72
Gibney, Harriet
See Harvey, Harriet
Gibney, Sheridan 1904(?)-1988 Obituary ... 125
Giboire, Clive (John) 1945- ... 118
Gibran, Jean 1933- ... 69-72
Gibran, Kahlil 1883-1931 ... 150
Brief entry ... 104
See also DAM POET, POP
See also PC 9
See also TCLC 1, 9
Gibran, Khalil
See Gibran, Kahlil
Gibson, A(lex) J. S. 1958- ... 150
Gibson, Alexander Cameron 1926- ... 134
Gibson, Alexander Dunnett 1901-1978 Obituary ... 77-80
Gibson, Andrew (William) 1949- ... SATA 72
Gibson, Anne (E.) 1954- ... 125
Gibson, Arrell Morgan 1921- ... 41-44R
Gibson, Arthur 1943- ... 130
Gibson, Betty 1911- ... SATA 75
Gibson, Charles (Edmund) 1916- ... 5-8R
Gibson, Charles 1920- ... 21-24R
Gibson, Charles Dana 1867-1944 ... DLB 188
See also DLBD 13
Gibson, Charline 1937- ... 69-72
Gibson, D. Parke 1930-1979 ... 93-96
Obituary ... 85-88
Gibson, Derlyne 1936- ... 21-24R
Gibson, Donald B. 1933- ... 25-28R
See also BW 1
Gibson, E(rnest) Dana 1906- ... 29-32R
Gibson, E(dward) Lawrence 1935- ... 93-96
Gibson, Elizabeth 1949- ... 118
Gibson, Elsie (Edith) 1907- ... 61-64
Gibson, Eva 1939- ... CANR-35
Earlier sketch in CA 114
Gibson, Evan K(eith) 1909- ... 105
Gibson, Frank K. 1924- ... 37-40R
Gibson, George H(orner) 1932- Brief entry ... 114
Gibson, Gerald Don 1938- ... 104
Gibson, Gertrude Hevener 1906- ... 5-8R
Gibson, Gifford Guy 1943- ... 77-80
Gibson, Graeme 1934- ... CANR-69
Earlier sketch in CA 130
See also DLB 53
Gibson, H(amilton) B(ertie) 1914- ... 102
Gibson, Harry Clark
See Hubler, Richard Gibson
Gibson, Ian 1939- ... 145
Gibson, James (Charles) 1919- ... CANR-41
Earlier sketch in CA 117
Gibson, James C.
See Gibson, James (Charles)

Gibson, James J(erome) 1904- 85-88
Gibson, James L(awrence) 1935- CANR-8
Earlier sketch in CA 5-8R
Gibson, James W(illiam) 1932- 41-44R
Gibson, Janice T(horne) 1934- 41-44R
Gibson, Jo 152
See also SATA 88
Gibson, John 1907- 33-36R
Gibson, John M(endinghall) 1899-(?) 1-4R
Obituary 134
Gibson, John Michael 168
Gibson, Josephine
See Hine, Al(fred Blakelee)
and Hine, Sesyle Joslin
Gibson, Karon Rose (White) 1946- 105
Gibson, Maralee G. 1924- 17-20R
Gibson, Margaret 1944- 77-80
See also DLB 120
Gibson, Margaret 1948- 103
Gibson, Margaret Dunlop 1843-1920 .... DLB 174
Gibson, Mary Ellis 1952- 167
Gibson, Miles 1947- CANR-18
Earlier sketch in CA 102
Gibson, Morgan 1929- CANR-14
Earlier sketch in CA 25-28R
Gibson, (William) Morris(on) 1916- 117
Gibson, Nevin H(erman) 1915- 49-52
Gibson, P(atricia) J(oann) 142
See also BW 2
Gibson, Paul 1936- 144
Gibson, Raymond E(ugene) 1924- 21-24R
Gibson, Reginald Walter 1901- CAP-1
Earlier sketch in CA 13-14
Gibson, Richard (Thomas) 1931- 41-44R
See also BW 2
Gibson, Richard G. 1953- 159
Gibson, Robert (Donald Davidson) 1927- 65-68
Gibson, Robert L(eone) 1927- 121
Gibson, Robert William, Jr. 1923- 107
Gibson, Ronald George 1909- 109
Gibson, Rosemary
See Newell, Rosemary
Gibson, Shirley 1927- 103
Gibson, (William) Walker 1919- CANR-1
Earlier sketch in CA 1-4R
Gibson, Walter B(rown) 1897-1985 .... CANR-63
Obituary 118
Brief entry 108
Earlier sketch in CA 110
Interview in 110
Gibson, Walter Samuel 1932- 102
Gibson, Wilfrid Wilson 1878-1962 Obituary 113
See also DLB 19
Gibson, William 1914- CANR-42
Earlier sketches in CA 9-12R, CANR-9
See also CLC 23
See also DA
See also DAB
See also DAC
See also DAM DRAM, MST
See also DLB 7
See also SATA 66
Gibson, William (Ford) 1948- CANR-52
Brief entry 126
Earlier sketch in CA 133
See also AAYA 12
See also CLC 39, 63
See also DAM POP
Gibson, William Carleton 1913- 17-20R
Gibson, William E(dward) 1944- 33-36R
Gibson, William M(erriam) 1912-1987 121
Obituary 146
Gibson-Jarvie, Clodagh 1923- 105
Gichon, Mordechai 1922- 89-92
Gicovate, Bernard 1922- 37-40R
Gidal, Nachum
See Gidal, Tim Nachum
Gidal, Peter 1946- 103
Gidal, Sonia (Epstein) 1922- CANR-14
Earlier sketch in CA 5-8R
See also SATA 2
Gidal, Tim Nachum 1909-1996 .... CANR-44
Obituary 154
Earlier sketches in CA 5-8R, CANR-14, 20
See also SATA 2
Gidalewitsch, Nachum
See Gidal, Tim Nachum
Gidding, Nelson 1919- 142
Giddings, James Louis 1909-1964 .... CAP-1
Earlier sketch in CA 11-12
Giddings, John Calvin 1930- 109
Giddings, Paula 1948- 125
See also BW 1
Giddings, Robert (Lindsay) 1935- CANR-9
Earlier sketch in CA 21-24R
Giddins, Gary 1948- CANR-66
Earlier sketches in CA 77-80, CANR-13, 32
Giddy, Ian H. 1948- 114
Gide, Andre (Paul Guillaume) 1869-1951 124
Brief entry 104
See also DA
See also DAB
See also DAC
See also DAM MST, NOV
See also DLB 65
See also MTCW 1
See also SSC 13
See also TCLC 5, 12, 36
See also WLC
Gideonse, Harry David 1901-1985 Obituary 115
Gidley, Charles
See Wheeler, (Charles) Gidley
Gidley, (Gustavus) M(ick) 1941- 102
Gidlow, Elsa 1898-1986 77-80
Obituary 119
Gidney, James B. 1914- 45-48
Giedion, Sigfried 1888(?)-1968 Obituary 116
Giegling, John A(llan) 1935- 29-32R
See also SATA 17
Giele, Janet Z(ollinger) 1934- CANR-36
Earlier sketch in CA 114
Gielgud, Gwen Bagni
See Dubov, Gwen Bagni
Gielgud, (Arthur) John 1904- 147
Brief entry 111
Gielgud, Val (Henry) 1900- CANR-5
Earlier sketch in CA 9-12R
Gier, Scott G. 167
Giere, Ronald N(elson) 1938- CANR-4
Earlier sketch in CA 49-52
Giergielewicz, Mieczyslaw F. 1901-1983 .... CAP-2
Obituary 113
Earlier sketch in CA 25-28
Gierow, Karl Ragnar (Knut)
1904-1982 Obituary 108
Giersch, Herbert 1921- 147
Giersch, Julius
See Arnade, Charles W(olfgang)
Giertz, Bo H(arald) 1905- CANR-9
Earlier sketch in CA 21-24R
Gies, David T(hatcher) 1945- 151
Gies, Frances 1915- CANR-9
Earlier sketch in CA 25-28R
Gies, Joseph (Cornelius) 1916- CANR-9
Earlier sketch in CA 5-8R
Gies, Thomas G(eorge) 1921- 33-36R
Giesbrecht, Martin Gerhard 1933- CANR-4
Earlier sketch in CA 53-56
Gieseking, Hal E. 1932- 131
Giesey, Ralph E(dwin) 1923- 25-28R
Giessler, Phillip Bruce 1938- CANR-8
Earlier sketch in CA 61-64
Giesy, J(ohn) U(lrich) 1877-1947 Brief entry 112
Gifaldi, David 1950- 143
See also SATA 76
Giff, Patricia Reilly 1935- CANR-41
Earlier sketches in CA 101, CANR-18
See also JRDA
See also MAICYA
See also SATA 33, 70
Giffard, Hannah 1962- .... SATA 83
Giffen, Daniel H. 1938- 107
Giffin, Frederick Charles 1938- 41-44R
Giffin, James Manning 1935- 105
Giffin, Mary (Elizabeth) 1919- 130
Giffin, Sidney F. 1907-1977 Obituary 73-76
Gifford, Barry (Colby) 1946- CANR-40
Earlier sketches in CA 65-68, CANR-9, 30
See also CLC 34
Gifford, Denis 1927- CANR-18
Earlier sketch in CA 101
Gifford, Don (Creighton) 1919- 53-56
Gifford, Edward S(tewart), Jr. 1907- CAP-2
Earlier sketch in CA 19-20
Gifford, Francis Newton
See Gifford, Frank
Gifford, Frank 1930- Brief entry 109
Gifford, Griselda 1931- CANR-24
Earlier sketch in CA 107
See also SATA 42
Gifford, (Charles) Henry 1913- 17-20R
Gifford, James Fergus, Jr. 1940- 57-60
Gifford, James J. 1946- 160
Gifford, Kathie Lee 1953- 142
Gifford, Kerri 1961- .... SATA 91
Gifford, Prosser 1929- CANR-39
Earlier sketches in CA 101, CANR-18
Gifford, Terry 1946- CANR-24
Earlier sketch in CA 106
Gifford, Thomas (Eugene) 1937- 77-80
Gifford-Jones, W.
See Walker, Kenneth Francis
Gigerenzer, Gerd 1947- 135
Giggal, Kenneth 1927- CANR-44
Earlier sketches in CA 104, CANR-20
Giggans, Patricia O(cchiuzzo) 168
Giglio, Ernest D(avid) 1931- 33-36R
Giglio, James N. 1939- 138
Giguere, Diane 1937- 25-28R
See also DLB 53
Giguere, Roland 1929- .... DLB 60
Gih, Andrew 1901- 21-24R
Gil, David G(eorg) 1924- CANR-12
Earlier sketch in CA 29-32R
Gil, Federico Guillermo 1915- CANR-2
Earlier sketch in CA 1-4R
Gil, Moshe 1921- 143
Gil-Albert, Juan 1906- .... DLB 134
Gilb, Corinne Lathrop 1925- 17-20R
Gilb, Dagoberto 1950- 159
Gilbar, Steven 1941- 106
Gilberg, Gail H(osking) 1950- 162
Gilbert, Alan Graham 1944- 112
Gilbert, Allan H. 1888- 9-12R
Gilbert, Amy M(argaret) 1895-1980 49-52
Obituary 133
Gilbert, Ann
See Taylor, Ann
Gilbert, Anna
See Lazarus, Marguerite
Gilbert, Anne 1927- CANR-7
Earlier sketch in CA 57-60
Gilbert, Anthony
See Malleson, Lucy Beatrice
See also DLB 77
Gilbert, Arlene E(lsie) 1934- 49-52
Gilbert, Arthur 1926-1976 .... CANR-9
Earlier sketch in CA 17-20R
Gilbert, Barbara Snow 1954- 163
See also SATA 97
Gilbert, Ben W(illiam) 1918- 45-48
Gilbert, Benjamin Franklin 1918- CANR-22
Earlier sketches in CA 17-20R, CANR-7
Gilbert, Bentley B(rinkerhoff) 1924- 25-28R
Gilbert, Bil 1927- 134
Brief entry 129
Interview in 134
Gilbert, Bill 1931- 105
Gilbert, Celia 1932- 115
Gilbert, Charles 1913- 41-44R
Gilbert, Christine B(ell) 1909- 103
Gilbert, Christopher 1949- 120
See also BW 2
Gilbert, Creighton (Eddy) 1924- CANR-15
Earlier sketch in CA 33-36R
Gilbert, David 1913- 137
Gilbert, David T(hompson) 1953- 106
Gilbert, Doris Wilcox 17-20R
Gilbert, Doug 1938-1979 Obituary 104
Gilbert, Douglas 1942- 53-56
Gilbert, Douglas L. 1925- 13-16R
Gilbert, Edmund W(illiam) 1900-1973 65-68
Gilbert, Edwin 1907-1976 77-80
Obituary 69-72
Gilbert, Elliot L(ewis) 1930-1991 147
Gilbert, Felix 1905- 132
Brief entry 106
Gilbert, Frances
See Collings, Gillian
Gilbert, Frank
See De Voto, Bernard (Augustine)
Gilbert, George 1922- 69-72
Gilbert, Glenn Gordon 1936- CANR-13
Earlier sketch in CA 33-36R
Gilbert, Gordon Allan 1942- 103
Gilbert, Gorman 1943- 114
Gilbert, Gustave M. 1911-1977 Obituary 69-72
Gilbert, Harriett 1948- CANR-9
Earlier sketch in CA 57-60
See also SATA 30
Gilbert, Harry 1946- 106
Gilbert, Herman Cromwell 1923- CANR-12
Earlier sketch in CA 29-32R
See also BW 2
Gilbert, Jack 1925- 123
Brief entry 116
Gilbert, Jack G(lenn) 1934- 25-28R
Gilbert, James 1935- 29-32R
Gilbert, James B(urkhart) 1939- CANR-65
Earlier sketch in CA 129
Gilbert, Jarvey 1917- 33-36R
Gilbert, (Agnes) Joan (Sewell) 1931- 21-24R
See also SATA 10
Gilbert, John (Raphael) 1926- 107
See also SATA 36
Gilbert, Julie Goldsmith
See Daniel, Julie Goldsmith
Gilbert, Manu
See West, Joyce (Tarlton)
Gilbert, Marilyn B(ender) 1926- CANR-1
Earlier sketch in CA 1-4R
Gilbert, Martin (John) 1936- CANR-31
Earlier sketch in CA 9-12R
Gilbert, Michael (Francis) 1912- CANR-54
Earlier sketches in CA 1-4R, CANR-1, 28
See also CAAS 15
See also DLB 87
Gilbert, Milton 1909(?)-1979 Obituary 93-96
Gilbert, Miriam
See Presberg, Miriam Goldstein
Gilbert, Nan
See Gilbertson, Mildred Geiger
Gilbert, Neil 1940- 77-80
Gilbert, R(obert) A(ndrew) 1942- 124
Gilbert, Robert E(mile) 1939- 53-56
Gilbert, Roby Goodale 1966- .... SATA 90
Gilbert, Rod(rigue Gabriel) 1941- Brief entry 109
Gilbert, Russell Wieder 1905-1985 .... CANR-27
Obituary 115
Earlier sketch in CA 45-48
Gilbert, Ruth Gallard Ainsworth
See Ainsworth, Ruth (Gallard)
Gilbert, S(tuart) R(eid) 1948- 101
Gilbert, Sandra M(ortola) 1936- CANR-69
Earlier sketches in CA 41-44R, CANR-14, 33
See also DLB 120
See also MTCW 1
Gilbert, Sara (Dulaney) 1943- CANR-6
Earlier sketch in CA 57-60
See also SATA 11, 82
Gilbert, Sarah 1959- 139
Gilbert, Stephen 1912- 25-28R
Gilbert, Steven E(dward) 1943- 164
Gilbert, Suzie 1956- 164
See also SATA 97
Gilbert, Tom 1955- 142
Gilbert, W(illiam) S(chwenck) 1836-1911 Brief
entry 104
See also DAM DRAM, POET
See also SATA 36
See also TCLC 3
Gilbert, W(illiam) Stephen 1947- 155
Gilbert, Willie 1916-1980 .... CANR-37
Earlier sketch in CA 45-48
Gilbert, (Lerman) Zack 1925- 65-68
Gilberts, Helen 1909- 29-32R
Gilbertson, Merrill Thomas 1911- 9-12R
Gilbertson, Mildred Geiger 1908- CANR-2
Earlier sketch in CA 5-8R
See also SATA 2
Gilbo, Patrick F(rancis) 1937- 107
Gilboa, Amir 1917-1984 Obituary 114
Gilboa, Yehoshua A. 1918-1981 .... CANR-35
Earlier sketch in CA 29-32R
Gilborn, Alice 1936- 69-72
Gilbreath, Alice 1921- CANR-25
Earlier sketches in CA 25-28R, CANR-10
See also SATA 12
Gilbreath, (Larry) Kent 1945- 45-48
Gilbreth, Frank B., Jr. 1911- 9-12R
See also CLC 17
See also SATA 2
Gilbreth, Lillian (Evelyn) Moller 1878-1972 158
Obituary 33-36R
Gilcher, Edwin L. 1909- 29-32R
Gilchrist, Agnes A(ddison)
1907-1976 Obituary 65-68
Gilchrist, Alan W. 1913- 21-24R
Gilchrist, Alexander 1828-1861 .... DLB 144
Gilchrist, Andrew (Graham) 1910-1993 .... CANR-46
Obituary 140
Earlier sketches in CA 109, CANR-26
Gilchrist, Ellen 1935- CANR-61
Brief entry 113
Earlier sketches in CA 116, CANR-41
See also CLC 34, 48
See also DAM POP
See also DLB 130
See also MTCW 1
See also SSC 14
Gilchrist, J(ohn Thomas) 1927- 25-28R
Gilchrist, Jan Spivey 1949- .... SATA 72
Gilday, Robert M. 1925(?)-1980 Obituary 101
Gildea, Robert 1952- 154
Gildea, William 1939- 164
Gil de Biedma, Jaime 1929-1990 .... DLB 108
Gilden, Bert 1915(?)-1971 .... CAP-1
Obituary 29-32R
Earlier sketch in CA 11-12
Gilden, K. B.
See Gilden, Bert
and Gilden, Katya Alpert
Gilden, Katya Alpert 1919(?)-1991 .... 9-12R
Obituary 134
Gilden, Mel 1947- 153
See also SATA 97
Gilder, Eric 1911- CANR-46
Earlier sketches in CA 89-92, CANR-15
Gilder, George F. 1939- CANR-26
Earlier sketches in CA 17-20R, CANR-9
See also AITN 1
Gilder, Jeannette L. 1849-1916 .... DLB 79
Gilder, Richard Watson 1844-1909 .... DLB 64, 79
Gilder, Rosamond de Kay 1891-1986 .... 1-4R
Obituary 120
Gildersleeve, Basil 1831-1924 .... DLB 71
Gildersleeve, Thomas R(obert) 1927- 29-32R
Gildner, Gary 1938- CANR-12
Earlier sketch in CA 33-36R
Gildner, Judith 1943- 89-92
Gildrie, Richard P(eter) 1945- 73-76
Gildzen, Alex 1943- 41-44R
Gilead, Zerubavel 1912- 123
Giles, C(harles) W(ilfred) Scott
See Scott-Giles, C(harles) W(ilfred)
Giles, Carl H(oward) 1935- CANR-39
Earlier sketch in CA 29-32R
Giles, Elizabeth
See Holt, John (Robert)
Giles, Frank (Thomas Robertson) 1919- 133
Giles, Frederick John 1928- 93-96
Giles, Geoffrey J(ohn) 1947- 122
Giles, Gordon A.
See Binder, Otto O(scar)
Giles, Henry 1809-1882 .... DLB 64
Giles, James R(ichard) 1937- 73-76
Giles, Janice Holt 1909-1979 .... CANR-3
Earlier sketch in CA 1-4R
Giles, Jeff 1965- 137
Giles, John 1921- 104
Giles, Kris
See Nielsen, Helen Berniece
Giles, Mary E(lizabeth) 1934- 108
Giles, Molly 1942- 126
See also CLC 39
Giles, Paul 1957- 145
Giles, Raymond
See Holt, John (Robert)
Giles, Robert Hartmann 1933- 141
Giles of Rome 1243(?)-1316 .... DLB 115
Gilfillan, Edward S(mith), Jr. 1906- 57-60
Gilfillan, George 1813-1878 .... DLB 144
Gilfillan, Merrill (C.) 1910(?)-1996 138
Obituary 152
Gilfond, Henry CANR-24
Earlier sketches in CA 21-24R, CANR-9
See also SATA 2
Gilford, C(harles) B(ernard) 1920- 17-20R
Gilford, Madeline Lee 1923- 85-88
Gilge, Jeanette 1924- 61-64
See also SATA 22
Gilgen, Albert R(udolph) 1930- 37-40R
Gilgoff, Alice 1946- 85-88
Gilgun, John F(rancis) 1935- CANR-41
Earlier sketch in CA 117
Gilhooley, Jack
See Gilhooley, John
Gilhooley, John 1940- CANR-31
Earlier sketch in CA 85-88
Gilhooley, Leonard 1921- 37-40R
Gili, Phillida 1944- .... SATA 70
Gilien, Sasha 1925(?)-1971 Obituary 33-36R
Giliomee, Hermann (Buhr) 1938- 102
Gilison, Jerome Martin 1935- 103
Gilkerson, William 1936- 127
Gilkes, A(ntony) N(ewcombe) 1900- 5-8R
Gilkey, Langdon (Brown) 1919- CANR-7
Earlier sketch in CA 17-20R
Gilkyson, Bernice Kenyon
1898(?)-1982 Obituary 106

Gill, Alan
See Gillespie, Alfred
Gill, Anton 1948- 130
Gill, B. M.
See Trimble, Barbara Margaret
Gill, Bartholomew
See McGarrity, Mark
Gill, Bob 1931- CANR-48
Earlier sketch in CA 1-4R
Gill, Brendan 1914-1997 .... CANR-37
Obituary 163
Earlier sketch in CA 73-76
See also MTCW 1
Gill, (Ronald) Crispin 1916- CANR-12
Earlier sketch in CA 21-24R
Gill, David (Lawrence William) 1934- CANR-12
Earlier sketch in CA 29-32R
Gill, Derek (Lewis Theodore) 1919- CANR-19
Earlier sketches in CA 49-52, CANR-4
See also SATA 9
Gill, Dominic 1941- 106
Gill, Elizabeth
See Hankin, Elizabeth Rosemary
Gill, (Arthur) Eric (Rowton Peter Joseph) 1882-1940 Brief entry 120
See also DLB 98
Gill, Evan Robertson 1892- 9-12R
Gill, Frederick (Cyril) 1898- 5-8R
Gill, Gillian
See Gill, Gillian C(atherine)
Gill, Gillian C(atherine) 1942- 134
Gill, Graeme 1947- 144
Gill, I(nayat) K(hera) 1924- 61-64
Gill, Jerry H. 1933- CANR-28
Earlier sketches in CA 33-36R, CANR-12
Gill, John Edward 1938- 106
Gill, Joseph 1901- CANR-3
Earlier sketch in CA 9-12R
Gill, Kay 1944- 111
Gill, LaVerne McCain 1947- 164
Gill, Margery Jean 1925- .... SATA 22
Gill, Merton M(ax) 1914-1994 122
Obituary 147
Gill, Patrick
See Creasey, John
Gill, Peter 1939- CANR-22
Earlier sketch in CA 103
Gill, Richard 1922-1989 .... 41-44R
Obituary 128
Gill, Richard T(homas) 1927- CANR-13
Earlier sketch in CA 21-24R
Gill, Sam D. 1943- 130
Gill, Sarah Prince 1728-1771 .... DLB 200
Gill, Stephen 1932- .... SATA 63
Gill, Suzanne L(utz) 1941- 136
Gill, Traviss 1891- CAP-1
Earlier sketch in CA 13-14
Gill, Walter 1937- 146
Gillan, Garth J. 1939- 102
Gillan, Patricia Wagstaff 1936- 102
Gillchrest, Muriel Noyes 1905- 25-28R
Gillelan, G(eorge) Howard 1917-1998 .... CANR-6
Obituary 164
Earlier sketch in CA 1-4R, 164
Gillen, Lucy
See Stratton, Rebecca
Gillen, Mollie 1908- 41-44R
Gillen, Robert L(eonard) 1946- 114
Gillenson, Lewis William 1918-1992 .... 5-8R
Obituary 139
Giller, Robert M(aynard) 1942-1996 124
Obituary 154
Gilles, Albert S(imeon) Sr. 1888- 57-60
Gilles, Anthony E(ugene) 1945- 114
Gilles, Daniel 1917- 103
Gillese, John Patrick 1920- 13-16R
Gillespie, A(braham) Lincoln, Jr. 1895-1950 Brief entry 115
See also DLB 4
Gillespie, Alfred 1924- 77-80
Gillespie, Angus Kress 1942- 132
Gillespie, Cynthia K. 1941-1993 133
Obituary 140
Gillespie, Diane Filby 1943- 130
Gillespie, Dizzy
See Gillespie, John Birks
Gillespie, Gerald 1933- CANR-10
Earlier sketch in CA 25-28R
Gillespie, I(ris) S(ylvia) 1923- 65-68
Gillespie, J(ohn) David 1944- 144
Gillespie, James E(rnest), Jr. 1940- 53-56
Gillespie, Janet Wicks 1913- 5-8R
Gillespie, John Birks 1917- 104
Gillespie, John E. 1921- 17-20R
Gillespie, John T(homas) 1928- CANR-57
Earlier sketches in CA 73-76, CANR-13, 31
Gillespie, Kingsley 1895-1984 Obituary 112
Gillespie, Link
See Gillespie, A(braham) Lincoln, Jr.
Gillespie, Marcia Ann 1944- 134
See also AITN 2
Gillespie, Michael Patrick 1946- 127
Gillespie, Neal C(ephas) 1933- 33-36R
Gillespie, Robert B(yrne) 1917- CANR-29
Earlier sketch in CA 110
Gillespie, Robert W. 1922(?)-1983 Obituary 110
Gillespie, Susan
See Turton-Jones, Edith Constance (Bradshaw)
Gillet, Lev 1892(?)-1980 Obituary 97-100
Gillett, Charlie 1942- 33-36R
Gillett, Edward 1915- 131
Gillett, Eric (Walkey) 1893-1978 .... CANR-3
Earlier sketch in CA 5-8R
Gillett, Grant (Randall) 1950- 143
Gillett, J(ohn) D(avid) 1913- 49-52
Gillett, Margaret 1930- CANR-39
Earlier sketches in CA 1-4R, CANR-2, 17
Gillett, Mary (Bledsoe) CAP-2
Earlier sketch in CA 25-28
See also SATA 7
Gillette, Arnold S(impson) 1904- CANR-2
Earlier sketch in CA 1-4R
Gillette, Henry Sampson 1915- 5-8R
See also SATA 14
Gillette, J(ay) Michael 1939- 113
Gillette, Michael
See Gillette, J(ay) Michael
Gillette, Paul 1938-1996 53-56
Obituary 151
Gillette, Virginia M(ary) 1920- 57-60
Gillette, William 1933- 108
Gilley, Sheridan (Wayne) 1945- 133
Gillham, Bill
See Gillham, W(illiam) E(dwin) C(harles)
Gillham, D. G. 1921- 21-24R
Gillham, W(illiam) E(dwin) C(harles) 1936- 113
See also SATA 42
Gilliam, Dorothy B(utler) 1936- 97-100
Gilliam, Florence .... DLB 4
Gilliam, Stan 1946- .... SATA 39
See also SATA-Brief 35
Gilliam, Terry (Vance) 1940- CANR-35
Brief entry 108
Earlier sketch in CA 113
Interview in 113
See also Monty Python
See also AAYA 19
See also CLC 21
Gillian, Jerry
See Gilliam, Terry (Vance)
Gillian, Kay
See Smith, Kay Nolte
Gilliatt, Penelope (Ann Douglass) 1932-1993 .... CANR-49
Obituary 141
Earlier sketch in CA 13-16R
See also AITN 2
See also CLC 2, 10, 13, 53
See also DLB 14
Gillie, Christopher 1914- 102
Gillie, Oliver (John) 1937- CANR-12
Earlier sketch in CA 65-68
Gillies, Archibald L. 127
Gillies, David 1952- 164
Gillies, John 1925- CANR-28
Earlier sketches in CA 73-76, CANR-12
Gillies, Malcolm 1954- 137
Gillies, Mary Davis 1900- CAP-2
Earlier sketch in CA 25-28
Gilligan, Carol 1936- 142
Gilligan, Edmund 1898-1973 Obituary 45-48
Gilligan, James F. 1935- 164
Gilligan, Sonja Carl 1936- 57-60
Gilliland, Alexis A(rnaldus) 1931- CANR-50
Earlier sketches in CA 108, CANR-25
See also SATA 72
Gilliland, Charles
See Muller, Charles G(eorge Geoffrey)
Gilliland, Charles Edward, Jr. 1916-1975 Obituary 110
Gilliland, (Cleburne) Hap 1918- CANR-57
Earlier sketches in CA 53-56, CANR-5
See also SATA 92
Gillin, Caroline J(ulia) 1932- 45-48
Gillin, Donald George 1930- 33-36R
Gillin, John P(hilip) 1907-1973 .... 41-44R
Obituary 45-48
Gillingham, John (Bennett) 1940- CANR-18
Earlier sketch in CA 97-100
Gillings, Richard John 1902- 77-80
Gillion, Kenneth Lowell (Oliver) 1929- 93-96
Gillis, Chester 1951- 136
Gillis, Daniel 1935- 106
Gillis, Everett A(lden) 1914- CANR-47
Earlier sketches in CA 41-44R, CANR-15
Gillis, John R. 1939- 33-36R
Gillis, Patricia Ingle 1932- Brief entry 108
Gillis, Phyllis 1945- 116
Gillispie, Charles C(oulston) 1918- 13-16R
Gillman, Olga Marjorie 1894- 5-8R
Gillman, Peter (Charles) 1942- 131
Gillman, Richard 1929- 17-20R
Gillmer, Thomas C(harles) 1911- CANR-45
Earlier sketches in CA 57-60, CANR-6
Gillmer, Tom
See Gillmer, Thomas C(harles)
Gillmor, C(harles) Stewart 1938- 45-48
Gillmor, Daniel S. 1917(?)-1975 Obituary 61-64
Gillmor, Donald M(iles) 1926- 41-44R
Gillmor, Frances 1903- CAP-2
Earlier sketch in CA 17-18
Gillmore, David 1934- 21-24R
Gillmore, Margalo 1897-1986 Obituary 119
Gillon, Adam 1921- CANR-8
Earlier sketch in CA 5-8R
Gillon, Diana (Pleasance Case) 1915- 13-16R
Gillon, Meir Selig 1907- 13-16R
Gillon, Werner 1905- 126
Gillott, Jacky 1939-1980 102
See also DLB 14
Gillquist, Peter E. 1938- CANR-12
Earlier sketch in CA 29-32R
Gilluly, James 1896-1980 Obituary 102
Gillum, Helen L(ouise) 1909- 69-72
Gilman, Andrew D. 1951- 137
Gilman, C(harles) Malcolm B(rookfield) 1898-1981 107
Gilman, Caroline (Howard) 1794-1888 .... DLB 3, 73
Gilman, Charlotte (Anna) Perkins (Stetson) 1860-1935 150
Brief entry 106
See also SSC 13
See also TCLC 9, 37
Gilman, Dorothy 1923- CANR-30
Interview in CANR-30
Gilman, Esther 1925- .... SATA 15
Gilman, George G.
See Harknett, Terry
Gilman, J. D.
See Fishman, Jack
and Orgill, Douglas
Gilman, James
See Gilmore, Joseph L(ee)
Gilman, Owen W(inslow), Jr. 1947- 144
Gilman, Phoebe 1940- .... SATA 58
Gilman, Richard (Joan Thomas) 1925- CANR-5
Earlier sketch in CA 53-56
Gilman, Robert Cham
See Coppel, Alfred
Gilman, Sander L(awrence) 1944- CANR-5
Earlier sketch in CA 53-56
Gilman, Stephen 1917- 107
Gilman, William 1909-1978 .... 1-4R
Gilman, William H(enry) 1911-1976 .... 17-20R
Obituary 65-68
Gilmer, Ann
See Ross, W(illiam) E(dward) D(aniel)
Gilmer, B(everley) von Haller 1909- CANR-5
Earlier sketch in CA 5-8R
Gilmer, Elizabeth Meriwether 1861(?)-1951 Brief entry 114
See also DLB 29
Gilmer, Francis Walker 1790-1826 .... DLB 37
Gilmer, (Frank) Walker 1935- 33-36R
Gilmer, Wesley, Jr. 1928- 115
Gil-Montero, Martha 1940- 153
See also HW
Gilmore, Alec 1928- 93-96
Gilmore, Al-Tony 1946- CANR-7
Earlier sketch in CA 57-60
Gilmore, Anthony
See Bates, Harry
Gilmore, Cecile
See MacMillan, Cecile
Gilmore, Charles L(ee) 33-36R
Gilmore, Christopher Cook 1940- CANR-17
Earlier sketch in CA 101
Gilmore, Daniel F(rancis) 1922-1988 65-68
Obituary 126
Gilmore, David D. 1943- 133
Gilmore, Don 1930- 29-32R
Gilmore, Eddy (Lanier King) 1907- 5-8R
Gilmore, Edith Spacil 1920- 1-4R
Gilmore, Gene 1920- 33-36R
Gilmore, Grant 1910-1982 Obituary 111
Gilmore, Harold L(awrence) 1931- 53-56
Gilmore, Haydn 1928- 85-88
Gilmore, Iris 1900- 97-100
See also SATA 22
Gilmore, J. Herbert, Jr. 1925- 33-36R
Gilmore, Jene Carlton 1933- 33-36R
Gilmore, John 1935- 25-28R
Gilmore, John (Norman) 1951- 133
Gilmore, Joseph L(ee) 1929- 81-84
Gilmore, Kate 1931- 151
See also SATA 87
Gilmore, Maeve (?)-1983 102
Obituary 110
Gilmore, Mary (Jean Cameron) 1865-1962 114
See also SATA 49
Gilmore, Mikal (George) 1951- 149
Gilmore, Richard 1943- 107
Gilmore, Susan 1954- .... SATA 59
Gilmore, Thomas B(arry, Jr.) 1932- 73-76
Gilmore, William J(ames) 1945- 120
Gilmour, Barbara
See Trimble, Barbara Margaret
Gilmour, David 1949- 147
Earlier sketch in CA 138
See also CLC 35
Gilmour, Garth (Hamilton) 1925- CAP-1
Earlier sketch in CA 9-10
Gilmour, H. B. 1939- 81-84
Gilmour, John C. 1939- 136
Gilmour, Robert S(cott) 1940- 69-72
Gilmour, Robin 1943- 124
Gilner, Elias 1888(?)-1976 Obituary 65-68
Gilot, Francoise 1921- 108
Gilpatrick, Eleanor G(ottesfocht) 1930- CANR-9
Earlier sketch in CA 21-24R
Gilpin, Alan 1924- CANR-28
Earlier sketches in CA 25-28R, CANR-11
Gilpin, Alec Richard 1920- 45-48
Gilpin, John 1930-1983 Obituary 114
Gilpin, Laura 1891-1979 Obituary 111
Gilpin, Robert G., Jr. 1930- 5-8R
Gilray, J. D.
See Mencken, H(enry) L(ouis)
Gilray, James
See Madsen, (Mark) Hunter
Gilroy, Beryl 1924- 135
See also BW 2
See also SATA 80
Gilroy, Frank D(aniel) 1925- CANR-64
Earlier sketches in CA 81-84, CANR-32
See also CLC 2
See also DLB 7
Gilroy, Harry 1908(?)-1981 Obituary 104
Gilroy, Thomas Laurence 1951- 103
Gilroy, Tom
See Gilroy, Thomas Laurence
Gilson, Barbara
See Gilson, Charles James Louis
Gilson, Charles James Louis 1878-1943 .... YABC 2
Gilson, Estelle 1926- 148
Gilson, Etienne Henry 1884-1978 102
Obituary 81-84
Gilson, Goodwin Woodrow 1918- 17-20R
Gilson, Jamie 1933- CANR-57
Earlier sketch in CA 111
See also SATA 37, 91
See also SATA-Brief 34
Gilson, Thomas Q(uinleven) 1916- 5-8R
Gilstrap, John 1957(?)- 160
See also CLC 99
Gilstrap, Robert L(awrence) 1933- 9-12R
Gilzean, Elizabeth Houghton Blanchet 1913- 9-12R
Gimbel, John 1922- CANR-2
Earlier sketch in CA 1-4R
Gimbutas, Marija (Alseika) 1921-1994 .... 13-16R
Obituary 144
Gimferrer, Pere (Pedro) 1945- .... DLB 134
Gimmestad, Victor E(dward) 1912-1982 57-60
Obituary 109
Gimpel, Herbert J. 1915- 17-20R
Gimpel, Jean (Victor) 1918-1996 69-72
Obituary 152
Gimson, Alfred Charles 1917-1985 .... 5-8R
Obituary 116
Ginandes, Shepard 1928- 41-44R
Ginder, Richard 1914- 65-68
Gindin, James 1926- CANR-2
Earlier sketch in CA 5-8R
Giner de los Rios, Francisco 1839-1915 Brief entry 105
Gingell, Benjamin Broughton 1924- 104
Ginger, Ann Fagan 1925- CANR-44
Earlier sketches in CA 53-56, CANR-4, 19
Ginger, Helen 1916- 17-20R
Ginger, John 1933- 25-28R
Gingerich, Martin E(llsworth) 1933- 118
Gingerich, Melvin 1902-1975 .... CAP-2
Earlier sketch in CA 25-28
Gingerich, Owen (Jay) 1930- CANR-48
Earlier sketches in CA 53-56, CANR-5, 22
Gingher, Marianne 1947- 138
Gingher, Robert (S.) 1945- 141
Gingland, David R. 1913- 17-20R
Gingold, Hermione (Ferdinanda) 1897-1987 .... 5-8R
Obituary 122
Gingrich, Arnold 1903-1976 .... 13-16R
Obituary 69-72
See also DLB 137
Gingrich, F(elix) Wilbur 1901- CAP-2
Earlier sketch in CA 17-18
Gingrich, Newt(on Leroy) 1943- CANR-62
Earlier sketch in CA 131
Giniger, Carol Virginia Wilkins 1929(?)-1985 Obituary 117
Giniger, Kenneth Seeman 1919- CANR-3
Earlier sketch in CA 5-8R
Ginn, Robert Jay, Jr. 1946- 107
Ginnings, Harriett W.
See Harriett
Ginns, Patsy (Lee) M(oore) 1937- 69-72
Ginns, Ronald 1896- CAP-1
Earlier sketch in CA 11-12
Ginori Lisci, Leonardo 1908-1987 Obituary 122
Ginott, Haim G. 1922-1973 Obituary 45-48
Ginsberg, Allen 1926-1997 .... CANR-63
Obituary 157
Earlier sketches in CA 1-4R, CANR-2, 41
See also AITN 1
See also CDALB 1941-1968
See also CLC 1, 2, 3, 4, 6, 13, 36, 69, 109
See also DA
See also DAB
See also DAC
See also DAM MST, POET
See also DLB 5, 16, 169
See also MTCW 1
See also PC 4
See also WLC 3
Ginsberg, Benjamin 1947- CANR-48
Earlier sketch in CA 121
Ginsberg, Harold Louis 1903-1990 Obituary 132
Ginsberg, Joanne
See Summerfield, Joanne
Ginsberg, Leon H(erman) 1936- 105
Ginsberg, Louis 1895-1976 .... 13-16R
Obituary 65-68
Ginsberg, Morris 1889-1970 Obituary 116
Ginsberg, Robert 1937- 25-28R
Ginsberg, Ruta
See Colombo, John Robert
Ginsburg, Faye D(iana) 1952- 133
Ginsburg, Herbert (Paul) 1939- CANR-12
Earlier sketch in CA 73-76
Ginsburg, Mark B. 1949- 147
Ginsburg, Mirra CANR-54
Earlier sketches in CA 17-20R, CANR-11, 28
See also CLR 45
See also SATA 6, 92
Ginsburg, Ruth Bader 1933- 53-56
Ginsburg, Seymour 1927- CANR-13
Earlier sketch in CA 21-24R
Ginsburgh, Robert N(eville) 1923- 13-16R
Ginsburgs, George 1932- CANR-4
Earlier sketch in CA 53-56
Ginsbury, Norman 1902- 5-8R
Ginter, Maria 1922- 105
Ginther, John R(obert) 1922- Brief entry 107
Gintis, Herbert 1940- 57-60
Ginzberg, Eli 1911- CANR-52
Earlier sketches in CA 5-8R, CANR-8, 27
Ginzberg, Yevgeniya 1906(?)-1977 Obituary 69-72
Ginzburg, Carlo 1939- 147

Ginzburg, Natalia 1916-1991 .... CANR-33
Obituary 135
Earlier sketch in CA 85-88
See also CLC 5, 11, 54, 70
See also DLB 177
See also MTCW 1
Ginzburg, Ralph 1929- 21-24R
Ginzkey, Franz Karl 1871-1963 .... DLB 81
Gioia, (Michael) Dana 1950- CANR-70
Earlier sketch in CA 130
See also DLB 120
Gioia, Ted 1957- 127
Giono, Jean 1895-1970 .... CANR-35
Obituary 29-32R
Earlier sketches in CA 45-48, CANR-2
See also CLC 4, 11
See also DLB 72
See also MTCW 1
Giordan, Alma Roberts 1917- 57-60
Giordan, Marion (?)-1983 Obituary 110
Giordanetti, Elmo 1925-1984 Obituary 113
Giorno, John 1936- 33-36R
Gioseffi, Daniela 1941- CANR-3
Earlier sketch in CA 45-48
Giotti, Virgilio 1885-1957 .... DLB 114
Giovacchini, Peter L(ouis) 1922- 101
Giovannetti, Alberto 1913- 9-12R
Giovanni, Nikki 1943- CANR-60
Earlier sketches in CA 29-32R, CANR-18, 41
Interview in CANR-18
See also CAAS 6
See also AAYA 22
See also AITN 1
See also BLC 2
See also BW 2
See also CLC 2, 4, 19, 64
See also CLR 6
See also DA
See also DAB
See also DAC
See also DAM MST, MULT, POET
See also DLB 5, 41
See also MAICYA
See also MTCW 1
See also PC 19
See also SATA 24
See also WLCS
Giovannitti, Len 1920-1992 .... 13-16R
Obituary 137
Giovanopoulos, Paul (Arthur) 1939- .... SATA 7
Giovene, Andrea 1904- 85-88
See also CLC 7
Gipe, George 1933-1986 77-80
Obituary 120
Gippius, Zinaida (Nikolayevna) 1869-1945 Brief entry 106
See also Hippius, Zinaida
Gipson, Carolyn R. 1944- 147
Gipson, Fred(erick Benjamin) 1908-1973 . CANR-63
Obituary 45-48
Earlier sketches in CA 1-4R, CANR-3
See also JRDA
See also MAICYA
See also SATA 2
See also SATA-Obit 24
Gipson, John (Durwood) 1932- 61-64
Gipson, Lawrence Henry 1880-1971 .... CANR-3
Obituary 33-36R
Earlier sketch in CA 5-8R
See also DLB 17
Giragosian, Newman H. 1922- 93-96
Girard, Hazel Batten 1901-1989 .... CANR-48
Earlier sketch in CA 112
Girard, Henri Georges Charles Achille 1917-1987 Obituary 121
Girard, James P(reston) 1944- 69-72
Girard, Joe 1928- CANR-9
Earlier sketch in CA 77-80
Girard, John
See Messerly, John G.
Girard, Linda (Walvoord) 1942- 114
See also SATA 41
Girard, Marvin Eugene 1924- 112
Girard, Mustang Marve
See Girard, Marvin Eugene
Girard, Rene N(oel) 1923- CANR-28
Earlier sketches in CA 9-12R, CANR-4
Girard, Robert C(olby) 1932- 101
Girard, Rodolphe 1879-1956 .... DLB 92
Girardi, Joe
See Girard, Joe
Girardot, Norman J(ohn) 1943- 110
Giraud, Marcel 1900- 77-80
Giraudoux, (Hippolyte) Jean 1882-1944 Brief entry 104
See also DAM DRAM
See also DLB 65
See also TCLC 2, 7
Girdlestone, Cuthbert Morton 1895-1975 .. CANR-3
Obituary 65-68
Earlier sketch in CA 5-8R
Girgus, Sam B. 1941- 127
Girion, Barbara 1937- CANR-15
Earlier sketch in CA 85-88
See also SAAS 14
See also SATA 26, 78
Girling, John L(awrence) S(cott) 1926- 106
Girling, Richard 1945- 108
Girod, Gerald R(alph) 1939- 53-56
Girod, Gordon H. 1920- 1-4R
Girodias, Maurice 1919-1990 .... CANR-72
Obituary 132
Brief entry 112
Earlier sketch in CA 129
Girodo, Michel 1945- 81-84
Giron, Manuel Buendia Tellez 1926(?)-1984 Obituary 112
See also HW
Girondo, Oliverio 1891-1967 .... HW
Gironella, Jose Maria 1917- 101
See also CLC 11
Girouard, Mark 1931- 147
Giroud, Francoise 1916- CANR-39
Earlier sketches in CA 81-84, CANR-17
See also AITN 1
Giroux, Andre 1916-1977 166
Giroux, E. X.
See Shannon, Doris
Giroux, Henry A(rmand) 1943- CANR-30
Earlier sketch in CA 112
Giroux, Joan 1922- 93-96
Giroux, Robert 1914- CANR-52
Earlier sketches in CA 107, CANR-28
Girri, A.
See Girri, Alberto
Girri, Alberto 1919- .... HW
Girsh, Myers L. 1906- 166
Girson, Rochelle 21-24R
Girtin, Thomas 1913-1994 .... 9-12R
Obituary 145
Girtin, Tom
See Girtin, Thomas
Girvan, Helen (Masterman) 1891- 73-76
Girvetz, Harry K(enneth) 1910-1974 Obituary .. 111
Girzaitis, Loretta 1920- CANR-2
Earlier sketch in CA 49-52
Girzone, Joseph F(rancis) 1930- CANR-69
Earlier sketch in CA 130
See also BEST 90:1
See also DAM POP
See also SATA 76
Giscard, Valery
See Giscard d'Estaing, Valery
Giscard d'Estaing, Valery 1926- Brief entry 111
Giscombe, C. S. 1950- 127
Gish, Arthur G. 1939- 29-32R
Gish, Lillian (Diana) 1896(?)-1993 128
Obituary 140
Gish, Nancy K. 1942- 132
Gish, Robert F(ranklin) 1940- CANR-50
Earlier sketch in CA 133
Gishford, Anthony (Joseph) 1908-1975 Obituary 53-56
Gisolfi, Anthony M. 1909- CAP-2
Earlier sketch in CA 17-18
Gisselquist, David 1947- 112
Gissen, Max 1909(?)-1984 Obituary 114
Gissing, George (Robert) 1857-1903 167
Brief entry 105
See also DLB 18, 135, 184
See also TCLC 3, 24, 47
Gissler, Sig(vard Gunnar, Jr.) 1935- 134
Gist, Noel P(itts) 1899- CANR-1
Earlier sketch in CA 1-4R
Gist, Ronald R. 1932- 21-24R
Gitchoff, G(eorge) Thomas 1938- 53-56
Gitchoff, Tom
See Gitchoff, G(eorge) Thomas
Gitelman, Zvi Y(echiel) 1940- 128
Brief entry 112
Gitin, David (Daniel) 1941- CANR-2
Earlier sketch in CA 49-52
Gitin, Maria (Brians) 1946- CANR-8
Earlier sketch in CA 61-64
Gitisetan, Dariush 118
Gitisetan, Darrin Dariush
See Gitisetan, Dariush
Gitlin, Murray 1903- 1-4R
Gitlin, Todd 1943- CANR-50
Earlier sketches in CA 29-32R, CANR-25
Gitlow, A(braham) Leo 1918- 1-4R
Gitlow, Benjamin 1891-1965 Obituary 89-92
Gittell, Marilyn 1931- CANR-55
Earlier sketches in CA 21-24R, CANR-9, 29
Gittelsohn, Roland B(ertram) 1910- CANR-2
Earlier sketch in CA 5-8R
Gittelson, Celia 105
Gitter, A. George 1926- 102
Gittinger, J(ames) Price 41-44R
Gittings, Clare (St. Quentin) 1954- 130
Gittings, Jo (Grenville) Manton 1919- CANR-3
Earlier sketch in CA 5-8R
See also SATA 3
Gittings, John 1938- CANR-9
Earlier sketch in CA 21-24R
Gittings, Robert (William Victor) 1911-1992 .... CANR-43
Obituary 136
Earlier sketch in CA 25-28R
See also SATA 6
See also SATA-Obit 70
Gittins, Diana 1946- 113
Gittleman, Edwin 1929- 21-24R
Gittleman, Sol 1934- 65-68
Gittler, Joseph B(ertram) 1912- 37-40R
Giudici, Ann Couper 1929- 73-76
Giudici, Giovanni 1924- .... DLB 128
Giuliani, Alfredo 1924- .... DLB 128
Giuliani, George A. 1938- 120
Giunti, Renato 1905-1983 Obituary 109
Giurlani, Aldo
See Palazzeschi, Aldo
Giuseppi, John (Anthony) 1900- CAP-2
Earlier sketch in CA 23-24
Giuttari, Theodore Richard 1931- 29-32R
Given, David R(oger) 1943- 157
Givens, Charles J. 1942(?)- 140
See also BEST 90:3
Givens, David B(radley) 1944- 119
Givens, Douglas R. 1944- 145
Givens, Janet E(aton) 1932- 111
See also SATA 60
Givens, John 1943- 77-80
Givner, Abraham 1944- 89-92
Givner, Joan Mary 1936- CANR-50
Earlier sketches in CA 108, CANR-25
Gizycka, Eleanor M.
See Patterson, Eleanor Medill
Gizzi, Michael 1949- 117
Gjertsen, Derek 1933- 125
Glaab, Charles N(elson) 1927- CANR-8
Earlier sketch in CA 5-8R
Glackens, William J. 1870-1938 .... DLB 188
Glad, Betty 1929- 21-24R
Glad, Donald 1915- 13-16R
Glad, John 1941- 133
Glad, Paul W(ilbur) 1926- 73-76
Gladden, E(dgar) Norman 1897- 21-24R
Gladden, Vivianne Cervantes 1927- 102
Glade, William P(atton), Jr. 1929- 41-44R
Gladilin, Anatoly (Tikhonovich) 1935- CANR-44
Earlier sketches in CA 101, CANR-18
Gladish, David F(rancis) 1928- 41-44R
Gladkov, Fyodor (Vasilyevich) 1883-1958 . TCLC 27
Gladney, Heather 1957- 127
Gladney, Margaret Rose 1945- 156
Gladney Glasserow, Marion 1925- 118
Gladstone, Arthur M. 1921- 97-100
Gladstone, Eve
See Werner, Herma
Gladstone, Gary 1935- 29-32R
See also SATA 12
Gladstone, Josephine 1938- 21-24R
Gladstone, M(yron) J. 1923- 53-56
See also SATA 37
Gladstone, Maggie
See Gladstone, Arthur M.
Gladstone, Meredith 1939- 69-72
Gladstone, William Ewart 1809-1898 .. DLB 57, 184
Gladwin, William Zachary
See Zollinger, Gulielma
Gladych, B. Michael 1910- 5-8R
Glaeser, Ernst 1902-1963 .... DLB 69
Glaettli, Walter E(ric) 1920- 21-24R
Glahe, Fred R(ufus) 1934- CANR-14
Earlier sketch in CA 37-40R
Glaister, John 1892-1971 Obituary 104
Glaister, Lesley (G.) 1956- 134
Glamis, Walter
See Schachner, Nathan(iel)
Glancy, Diane 1941- 136
See also CAAS 24
See also DLB 175
See also NNAL
Glancy, Ruth F(ergusson) 1948- 141
Glantz, David M. 1942- 135
Glantz, Kalman 1937- 132
Glanville, Brian (Lester) 1931- CANR-70
Earlier sketches in CA 5-8R, CANR-3
See also CAAS 9
See also CLC 6
See also DLB 15, 139
See also SATA 42
Glanville, Maxwell 1918- 85-88
Glanville, Ranulph 1946- 114
Glanz, Edward C(oleman) 1924- 1-4R
Glanz, Karen 1953- 135
Glanz, Rudolf 1892-1978 .... CANR-3
Earlier sketch in CA 49-52
Glanzman, Louis S. 1922- .... SATA 36
Glapthorne, Henry 1610-1643(?) .... DLB 58
Glasberg, Davita Silfen 1951- 165
Glasco, Michael 1945- 153
Glaser, Daniel 1918- 61-64
Glaser, Dianne E(lizabeth) 1937- 77-80
See also SATA 50
See also SATA-Brief 31
Glaser, E(ric) M(ichael) 1913- 21-24R
Glaser, Edward 1918-1972 Obituary 37-40R
Glaser, Eleanor Dorothy
See Zonik, Eleanor Dorothy
Glaser, Elizabeth 1947-1994 138
Obituary 147
Glaser, Elton 1945- 111
Glaser, Eva Schocken 1918-1982 Obituary 105
Glaser, Isabel Joshlin 1929- CANR-65
Earlier sketch in CA 77-80
See also SATA 94
Glaser, James M. 1960- 163
Glaser, Kurt 1914- CANR-5
Earlier sketch in CA 1-4R
Glaser, Lynn 1943- 21-24R
Glaser, Milton 1929- CANR-11
Earlier sketch in CA 17-20R
See also SATA 11
Glaser, Robert 1921- CANR-7
Earlier sketch in CA 17-20R
Glaser, Rollin Oliver 1932- CANR-10
Earlier sketch in CA 25-28R
Glaser, William A(rnold) 1925- CANR-45
Earlier sketch in CA 1-4R
Glasgow, Douglas G. 108
Glasgow, Ellen (Anderson Gholson) 1873-1945 164
Brief entry 104
See also DLB 9, 12
See also TCLC 2, 7
Glasgow, Eric 1924- 69-72
Glasgow, Gordon H(enry) H(arper) 1926- 29-32R
Glasgow, Jack
See Larson, Doran
Glasgow, Mary Cecilia 1905-1983 Obituary 111
Glasheen, Adaline 1920- 101
Glasheen, Patrick 1897- CAP-1
Earlier sketch in CA 13-14
Glasier, Katharine Bruce 1867-1950 .... DLB 190
Glaskin, G(erald) M(arcus) 1923- CANR-46
Earlier sketches in CA 53-56, CANR-5
Glaskowsky, Nicholas A(lexander), Jr. 1928- CANR-3
Earlier sketch in CA 5-8R
Glaspell, Susan 1882(?)-1948 154
Brief entry 110
See also DLB 7, 9, 78
See also TCLC 55
See also YABC 2
Glasrud, Bruce (Alden) 1940- 41-44R
Glass, Albert J(ulius) 1908-1983 Obituary 109
Glass, Amanda
See Krentz, Jayne Ann
Glass, Andrew 1949- CANR-57
Earlier sketch in CA 134
See also SATA 90
See also SATA-Brief 46
Glass, Andrew J(ames) 1935- 65-68
Glass, Bill 1935- CANR-13
Earlier sketch in CA 73-76
Glass, Charles 1951- 139
Glass, David Victor 1911-1978 85-88
Obituary 81-84
Glass, Dee Dee 1948- 149
Glass, Ian Cameron 1926- 77-80
Glass, Joanna (McClelland) 1936- CANR-43
Earlier sketch in CA 81-84
Glass, John F(ranklin) 1936- 53-56
Glass, Justine C.
See Corrall, Alice Enid
Glass, Leslie 168
Glass, Malcolm (Sanford) 1936- CANR-20
Earlier sketch in CA 104
Glass, Montague (Marsden) 1877-1934 Brief entry 117
See also DLB 11
Glass, Ruth 1912-1990 Obituary 131
Glass, Sandra
See Shea, Robert (Joseph)
Glass, Stanley T(homas) 1932- 21-24R
Glassberg, B(ertrand) Y(ounker) 1902-(?) ... CAP-1
Earlier sketch in CA 13-16
Glassburner, Bruce 1920- 33-36R
Glassco, John 1909-1981 .... CANR-15
Obituary 102
Earlier sketch in CA 13-16R
See also CLC 9
See also DLB 68
Glasscock, Amnesia
See Steinbeck, John (Ernst)
Glasscock, Anne Bonner 1924- 1-4R
Glasscock, Sarah (Jean) 1952- 130
Glasse, Robert Marshall 1929-1993 .... 29-32R
Obituary 140
Glasser, Allen 1918- 9-12R
Glasser, Ira 1938- 137
Glasser, Paul H(arold) 1929- CANR-15
Earlier sketch in CA 29-32R
Glasser, Perry 1948- 127
Glasser, Ronald J. 1940(?)- .... CLC 37
Glasser, Selma 110
Glasser, Stephen A(ndrew) 1943- 53-56
Glasser, William 1925- 73-76
Glasserow, Mario N.
See Gladney Glasserow, Marion
Glasserow, Marion Gladney
See Gladney Glasserow, Marion
Glassford, Wilfred
See McNeilly, Wilfred (Glassford)
Glassgold, Peter 1939- 103
Glassie, Henry 1941- 148
Glassie, Henry H(aywood) 1914-1987 Obituary . 124
Glassman, Bernard Tetsugen 1939- 112
Glassman, Bruce 1961- 143
See also SATA 76
Glassman, James K(enneth) 1947- 127
Glassman, Jon David 1944- 69-72
Glassman, Jonathon P. 1956- 151
Glassman, Joyce
See Johnson, Joyce
Glassman, Michael 1899- 13-16R
Glassman, Peter Joel 1945- 113
Glassman, Ronald M. 1937- 134
Brief entry 111
Glassner, Barry 1952- 135
Glassner, Lester 1939- 107
Glassner, Martin Ira 1932- CANR-34
Earlier sketches in CA 41-44R, CANR-15
Glasson, Thomas Francis 1906- CAP-1
Earlier sketch in CA 9-10
Glassop, (Jack) Lawson 1913-1966 .... CAP-1
Earlier sketch in CA 9-10
Glasstone, Victor 1924- CANR-10
Earlier sketch in CA 65-68
Glatstein, Jacob 1896-1971 Obituary 33-36R
Glatt, John 1952- 155
Glatthaar, Joseph T(homas) 1957- 142
Glatthorn, Allan A. 1924- 13-16R
Glattstein, Judy 1942- 137
Glatzer, Hal 1946- 57-60
Glatzer, Nahum Norbert 1903-1990 .... CANR-7
Obituary 131
Earlier sketch in CA 13-16R
Glauber, Uta (Heil) 1936- 29-32R
See also SATA 17
Glaus, Marlene 1933- 21-24R
Glauser, Friedrich 1896-1938 .... DLB 56
Glavin, John P(atrick) 1933- 57-60
Glazar, Bob 1954- 115
Glaze, Andrew (Louis III) 1920- CANR-24
Earlier sketches in CA 17-20R, CANR-8
Glaze, Eleanor 1930- 49-52
Glaze, Thomas E(dward) 1914- 1-4R
Glazebrook, G(eorge) P(arkin) de T(wenebrokes) 1899- 102

Glazebrook, Philip 1937- ... 29-32R
Glazener, Mary U(nderwood) 1921- ... 17-20R
Glazer, Daphne (Fae) 1938- ... CANR-45
 Earlier sketch in CA 119
Glazer, Ellen Sarasohn 1947- ... 148
Glazer, Nathan 1923- ... CANR-64
 Earlier sketch in CA 5-8R
Glazer, Nona Y.
 See Glazer-Malbin, Nona
Glazer, Sidney 1905-1983 ... 1-4R
 Obituary ... 111
Glazer, Tom 1914- ... CANR-8
 Earlier sketch in CA 61-64
 See also SATA 9
Glazer-Malbin, Nona 1932- ... 33-36R
Glazier, Kenneth MacLean 1912- ... 9-12R
Glazier, Lyle (Edward) 1911- ... 37-40R
 See also CAAS 24
Glazier, Stephen 1947- ... 108
Glazner, Greg(ory Allen) 1958- ... 142
Glazner, Joseph Mark 1945- ... 104
Gleadow, Rupert Seeley 1909-1974 ... 9-12R
 Obituary ... 103
Gleasner, Diana (Cottle) 1936- ... CANR-33
 Earlier sketches in CA 65-68, CANR-15
 See also SATA 29
Gleason, Abbott 1938- ... CANR-21
 Earlier sketch in CA 104
Gleason, Eugene Franklin 1914- ... 1-4R
Gleason, Gene
 See Gleason, Eugene Franklin
Gleason, Harold 1892- ... CAP-1
 Earlier sketch in CA 9-10
Gleason, John (Marquis) 1942- ... 107
Gleason, John J(ames), Jr. 1934- ... 120
Gleason, Judith 1929- ... CANR-9
 Earlier sketch in CA 61-64
 See also SATA 24
Gleason, Ralph J(oseph) 1917-1975 ... 65-68
 Obituary ... 61-64
Gleason, Robert 1945- ... 118
Gleason, Robert J(ames) 1906- ... 73-76
Gleason, Robert Walter 1917- ... CANR-4
 Earlier sketch in CA 1-4R
Gleason, S(arel) Everett 1905-1974 Obituary . 53-56
Gleave, T(homas) P(ercy) 1908-1993 ... 127
 Obituary ... 141
Gleaves, Robert M(ilnor) 1938- ... 53-56
Gleaves, Suzanne 1904- ... 9-12R
Gleckner, Robert Francis 1925- ... CANR-17
 Earlier sketches in CA 1-4R, CANR-2
Gledhill, Alan 1895-1983 ... CAP-1
 Obituary ... 110
 Earlier sketch in CA 9-10
Gledhill, John 1949- ... 151
Glees, Anthony 1948- ... 134
Gleeson, Libby 1950- ... 149
 See also SATA 82
Gleeson, Ruth (Ryall) 1925- ... 9-12R
Gleick, James (W.) 1954- ... 137
 Brief entry ... 131
 Interview in ... 137
Gleim, Johann Wilhelm Ludwig 1719-1803 . DLB 97
Gleiman, Lubomir 1923- ... 41-44R
Gleisser, Marcus D(avid) 1923- ... 17-20R
Gleitman, Lila R. 1929- ... 114
Gleitzman, Morris 1953- ... 131
 See also SATA 88
Glemser, Bernard 1908-1990 Obituary ... 131
Glen, Duncan (Munro) 1933- ... CANR-12
 Earlier sketch in CA 21-24R
Glen, Eugene
 See Fawcett, F(rank) Dubrez
Glen, Frank Grenfell 1933- ... 106
Glen, J(ohn) Stanley 1907-1986 ... CAP-1
 Obituary ... 118
 Earlier sketch in CA 9-10
Glen, Maggie 1944- ... SATA 88
Glen, Robert S. 1925- ... 29-32R
Glenday, Alice 1920- ... 57-60
Glendenning, Donn
 See Paine, Lauran (Bosworth)
Glendenning, Raymond Carl
 1907-1974 Obituary ... 114
Glendinning, Miles
 See Horsey, Miles G.
Glendinning, Richard 1917- ... 21-24R
 See also SATA 24
Glendinning, Sally
 See Glendinning, Sara W(ilson)
Glendinning, Sara W(ilson) 1913- ... CANR-2
 Earlier sketch in CA 49-52
 See also SATA 24
Glendinning, Victoria 1937- ... CANR-59
 Brief entry ... 120
 Earlier sketch in CA 127
 See also CLC 50
 See also DLB 155
Glendon, Mary Ann 1938- ... 41-44R
Glenn, Armon 1912- ... 107
Glenn, Cheryl ... 162
Glenn, Christine Genevieve 1947- ... 115
Glenn, Constance W(hite) 1933- ... 128
Glenn, Dorothy
 See Garlock, Dorothy
Glenn, Edmund S(tanislas) 1915- ... 113
Glenn, Frank 1901-1982 Obituary ... 106
Glenn, Harold T(heodore) 1910- ... CANR-5
 Earlier sketch in CA 5-8R
Glenn, Jacob B. 1905-1974 ... CANR-4
 Obituary ... 49-52
 Earlier sketch in CA 9-12R
Glenn, James
 See Paine, Lauran (Bosworth)
Glenn, Jerry (Hesmer, Jr.) 1938- ... 45-48
Glenn, John H(erschel), Jr. 1921- ... 156
Glenn, Lois (Ruth) 1941- ... 61-64
Glenn, Mel 1943- ... CANR-68
 Earlier sketches in CA 123, CANR-49
 See also AAYA 25
 See also CLR 51
 See also SATA 51, 93
 See also SATA-Brief 45
Glenn, Morton B(ernard) 1922- ... 61-64
Glenn, Norval Dwight 1933- ... 17-20R
Glenn, Patricia Brown 1953- ... 151
 See also SATA 86
Glennon, James 1900- ... 25-28R
Glennon, Karen M. 1946- ... 151
 See also SATA 85
Glennon, Maurade 1926- ... 25-28R
Glenny, Lyman A. 1918- ... CANR-7
 Earlier sketch in CA 17-20R
Glenny, Michael Valentine 1927-1990 ... 102
 Obituary ... 132
Gles, Margaret Breitmaier 1940- ... 57-60
 See also SATA 22
Gleser, Goldine C(ohnberg) 1915- ... 17-20R
Gless, Darryl James 1945- ... 102
Glessing, Robert J(ohn) 1930- ... 29-32R
Gliauda, Jurgis 1906- ... CANR-3
 Earlier sketch in CA 5-8R
Glick, Bernard R. 1945- ... 150
Glick, Carl (Cannon) 1890-1971 ... 5-8R
 Obituary ... 103
 See also SATA 14
Glick, Edward Bernard 1929- ... CANR-8
 Earlier sketch in CA 21-24R
Glick, G(arland) Wayne 1921- ... 25-28R
Glick, Paul C(harles) 1910- ... 5-8R
Glick, Paula Brown
 See Brown, Paula
Glick, Ruth (Burtnick) 1942- ... CANR-16
 Earlier sketch in CA 89-92
Glick, Thomas F(rederick) 1939- ... CANR-34
 Earlier sketches in CA 29-32R, CANR-15
Glick, Virginia Kirkus 1893-1980 ... CAP-2
 Obituary ... 101
 Earlier sketch in CA 21-22
 See also SATA-Obit 23
Glick, Wendell 1916- ... 111
Glick, William H. 1952- ... 146
Glickman, Albert S(eymour) 1923- ... 53-56
Glickman, Arthur P. 1940- ... 61-64
Glickman, Beatrice Marden 1919- ... 102
Glickman, Gary 1959- ... 128
Glickman, James (A.) 1948- ... 157
Glickman, Norman J. 1942- ... 135
Glickman, S(teven) Craig 1947- ... 116
Glickman, Susan 1953- ... CANR-38
 Earlier sketch in CA 116
Glicksberg, Charles Irving 1900- ... CANR-2
 Earlier sketch in CA 1-4R
Glicksman, Abraham M(orton) 1911- ... 5-8R
Glidden, F. D.
 See Glidden, Frederick D(illey)
Glidden, Frederick D(illey) 1908-1975 ... CANR-71
 Obituary ... 61-64
 Earlier sketches in CAP-2, CA 21-22
Glidden, Horace Knight 1901- ... CAP-1
 Earlier sketch in CA 13-16
Gliddend, Fred
 See Glidden, Frederick D(illey)
Glidewell, John Calvin 1919- ... CANR-48
 Earlier sketches in CA 13-16R, CANR-7, 23
Glieberman, Herbert A(llen) 1930- ... 112
Gliewe, Unada (Grace) 1927- ... CANR-12
 Earlier sketch in CA 29-32R
 See also SATA 3
Glikes, Erwin (Arno) 1937-1994 ... 13-16R
 Obituary ... 145
Glimcher, Arnold B. 1938- ... 81-84
Glimm, James Y(ork) 1942- ... 132
Glimmerveen, Ulco 1958- ... 132
 See also SATA 85
Glines, Carroll V(ane), Jr. 1920- ... CANR-2
 Earlier sketch in CA 1-4R
 See also SATA 19
Gliori, Debi 1959- ... SATA 72
Gliozzo, Charles 1932- ... 45-48
Gliserman, Martin 1945- ... 157
Glissant, Edouard 1928- ... 153
 See also CLC 10, 68
 See also DAM MULT
Glisson, J(ake) T. 1927- ... 143
Glisson, Jerry (Lee) 1923- ... 113
Gloag, John (Edwards) 1896-1981 ... CANR-10
 Obituary ... 104
 Earlier sketch in CA 65-68
Gloag, Julian 1930- ... CANR-70
 Earlier sketches in CA 65-68, CANR-10
 See also AITN 1
 See also CLC 40
Glob, Peter Vilhelm 1911-1985 ... 97-100
 Obituary ... 117
Globe, Leah Ain 1900- ... 107
 See also SATA 41
Glock, Charles Y(oung) 1919- ... CANR-5
 Earlier sketch in CA 53-56
Glock, Marvin D(avid) 1912- ... 21-24R
Gloer, (William) Hulitt 1950- ... CANR-53
 Earlier sketch in CA 126
Glogau, Art(hur H.) 1922- ... 53-56
Glogau, Lillian Flatow Fleischer 1925- ... 85-88
Glogowski, Maryruth F(rancine) P(helps) 1950- . 120
Glorfeld, Louis E(arl) 1916- ... 53-56
Glos, Raymond E(ugene) 1903- ... 21-24R
Gloss, Molly 1944- ... 132
Glossop, Ronald J. 1933- ... 144
Glotzer, Albert 1908- ... 133
Glovach, Linda 1947- ... CANR-31
 Earlier sketches in CA 37-40R, CANR-14
 See also SATA 7
Glover, Albert Gould 1942- ... 89-92
Glover, Bob
 See Glover, Robert H.
Glover, Denis (James Matthews) 1912-1980 ...
 CANR-30
 Obituary ... 101
 Earlier sketch in CA 77-80
 See also SATA 7
Glover, Donald E(llsworth) 1933- ... 116
Glover, Douglas 1948- ... 137
 See also CAAS 23
Glover, Harry 1912- ... 77-80
Glover, Janice 1919- ... 17-20R
Glover, John D(esmond) 1915- ... CANR-2
 Earlier sketch in CA 5-8R
Glover, Jon 1943- ... 133
Glover, Judith 1943- ... CANR-22
 Earlier sketch in CA 106
Glover, Leland E(llis) 1917- ... 9-12R
Glover, Michael 1922- ... CANR-23
 Earlier sketches in CA 17-20R, CANR-8
Glover, Richard 1712-1785 ... DLB 95
Glover, Robert H. 1946- ... 116
Glover, Stephen (Charles Morton) 1952- ... 164
Glover, (David) Tony "Harp Dog" 1939- ... 13-16R
Gloversmith, Frank 1936- ... 127
Glowacki, Aleksander
 See Prus, Boleslaw
Glowacki, Janusz 1938- ... 116
Glubb, John Bagot 1897-1986 ... CANR-5
 Obituary ... 118
 Earlier sketch in CA 9-12R
Glubb Pasha
 See Glubb, John Bagot
Glubok, Shirley (Astor) ... CANR-43
 Earlier sketches in CA 5-8R, CANR-4
 See also CLR 1
 See also MAICYA
 See also SAAS 7
 See also SATA 6, 68
Gluck, Carol 1941- ... CANR-53
 Earlier sketch in CA 126
Gluck, Felix 1923-1981 Obituary ... 103
 See also SATA-Obit 25
Gluck, Herb 1925- ... CANR-31
 Earlier sketches in CA 45-48, CANR-2
Gluck, Jay 1927- ... CANR-12
 Earlier sketch in CA 21-24R
Gluck, Louise (Elisabeth) 1943- ... CANR-69
 Earlier sketches in CA 33-36R, CANR-40
 See also CLC 7, 22, 44, 81
 See also DAM POET
 See also DLB 5
 See also PC 16
Gluck, Mary 1947- ... 127
Gluck, Robert 1947- ... CANR-68
 Earlier sketches in CA 113, CANR-32
Gluckin, Doreen Sandra 1949- ... 108
Gluckman, Janet
 See Berliner, Janet
Gluckman, Max 1911-1975 ... 9-12R
 Obituary ... 57-60
Glucksberg, Harold 1939- ... 105
Glueck, Eleanor T(ouroff) 1898-1972 ... CANR-9
 Obituary ... 37-40R
 Earlier sketches in CAP-2, CA 17-18
Glueck, Nelson 1900-1971 ... CAP-2
 Earlier sketch in CA 17-18
Glueck, Sheldon 1896-1980 ... CANR-9
 Obituary ... 97-100
 Earlier sketch in CA 5-8R
Glueck, William F(rank) 1934-1980 ... CANR-27
 Earlier sketch in CA 33-36R
Glueckauf, Eugen 1906-1981 Obituary ... 108
Gluss, Brian 1930- ... 104
Glustrom, Simon W. 1924- ... 21-24R
Glut, Donald F(rank) 1944- ... CANR-13
 Earlier sketch in CA 33-36R
Gluyas, Constance 1920- ... 136
 Brief entry ... 115
Gluzman, Brian
 See Gluss, Brian
Glyn, Anthony 1922-1998 ... 53-56
 Obituary ... 164
Glyn, Caroline 1947- ... CANR-5
 Earlier sketch in CA 9-12R
Glyn, Elinor 1864-1943 ... DLB 153
 See also TCLC 72
Glyn, Richard Hamilton 1907-1980 ... 105
 Obituary ... 102
Glynn, James A. 1941- ... 57-60
Glynn, Jeanne Davis 1932- ... 29-32R
Glynn, Jenifer 1929- ... 128
Glynn, Leonard M. 1948- ... 130
Glynn, Prudence (Loveday) 1935-1986 ... 129
 Obituary ... 120
Glynn, Thomas P(eter) 1935- ... 93-96
Glynne-Jones, M(arjorie) L(ilian) 1936- Brief
 entry ... 111
Glynne-Jones, William 1907- ... 5-8R
 See also SATA 11
Gmelch, George 1944- ... 103
Gmelch, Sharon Bohn 1947- ... 103
Gmelch, Walter H(oward) 1947- ... 112
Gnaegy, Charles 1938- ... 89-92
Gnagey, Thomas D(avid) 1938- ... CANR-46
 Earlier sketch in CA 49-52
Gnagy, Jon
 See Gnagy, Michael Jacques
Gnagy, Michael Jacques
 1907(?)-1981 Obituary ... 103
Gnarowski, Michael 1934- ... 41-44R
Gneuss, Helmut (Walter Georg) 1927- ... 141
Gniffke, Rudolf
 See Hartmann, Rudolf A.
Gnosticus
 See Weschcke, Carl L(ouis)
Gnuse, Robert K(arl) 1947- ... 121
Go, Janet G. 1930- ... 166
Go, Puan Seng 1904- ... CAP-2
 Earlier sketch in CA 29-32
Goacher, Denis 1925- ... 104
Goaman, Muriel
 See Cox, Edith Muriel
Gobar, Ash 1930- ... 41-44R
Gobbato, Imero 1923- ... SATA 39
Gobbell, John J. 1937- ... 154
Gobbi, Tito 1915-1984 ... 129
 Obituary ... 112
 Brief entry ... 105
Gobineau, Joseph Arthur (Comte) de
 1816-1882 ... DLB 123
Goble, Alan 1938- ... 143
Goble, Danney 1946- ... 136
Goble, Dorothy ... 93-96
 See also SATA 26
Goble, Frank G. 1917- ... 112
Goble, (Lloyd) Neil 1933- ... 29-32R
Goble, Paul 1933- ... CANR-16
 Earlier sketch in CA 93-96
 See also CLR 21
 See also MAICYA
 See also SATA 25, 69
Goble, Warwick (?)-1943 ... SATA 46
Gocek, Matilda A(rkenbout) 1923- ... CANR-1
 Earlier sketch in CA 49-52
Gochfeld, Michael 1940- ... 137
Gockel, Herman W. 1906- ... CANR-1
 Earlier sketch in CA 1-4R
Godard, Jean-Luc 1930- ... 93-96
 See also CLC 20
Godbold, E(dward) Stanly, Jr. 1942- ... 37-40R
Godbolt, Jim 1922- ... 129
Godbout, Jacques 1933- ... 142
 Brief entry ... 125
 See also DLB 53
Goddard, Alfred
 See Harper, Carol Ely
Goddard, Beatrice Romaine
 See Brooks, Romaine
Goddard, Burton L(eslie) 1910- ... 21-24R
Goddard, Donald 1934- ... CANR-28
 Earlier sketches in CA 17-20R, CANR-11
Goddard, Gladys Benjamin
 1881(?)-1976 Obituary ... 61-64
Goddard, J(ack) R. 1930- ... 29-32R
Goddard, Kenneth (William) 1946- ... CANR-72
 Earlier sketch in CA 110
Goddard, Morrill 1865-1937 ... DLB 25
Goddard, Robert (William) 1954- ... CANR-72
 Earlier sketch in CA 134
Goddard, Robert H(utchings) 1882-1945 ... 156
 Brief entry ... 118
Goddard, William 1740-1817 ... DLB 43
Godden, Geoffrey 1929- ... 102
Godden, Jon 1906-1984 ... CANR-27
 Obituary ... 112
 Earlier sketch in CA 77-80
Godden, (Margaret) Rumer 1907- ... CANR-55
 Earlier sketches in CA 5-8R, CANR-4, 27, 36
 See also AAYA 6
 See also CLC 53
 See also CLR 20
 See also DLB 161
 See also MAICYA
 See also SAAS 12
 See also SATA 3, 36
Gode, Alexander
 See Gode von Aesch, Alexander (Gottfried
 Friedrich)
Godechot, Jacques Leon 1907- ... CANR-25
 Earlier sketches in CA 65-68, CANR-9
Godefroy, Vincent 1912- ... 69-72
Godel, Kurt
 See Goedel, Kurt
Godel, Kurt Friedrich 1906-1978 ... 157
Gode von Aesch, Alexander (Gottfried Friedrich)
 1906-1970 ... CAP-1
 Earlier sketch in CA 9-10
 See also SATA 14
Godey, John
 See Freedgood, Morton
Godey, Louis A. 1804-1878 ... DLB 73
Godfrey, Cuthbert John ... 5-8R
Godfrey, (William) Dave 1938- ... CANR-70
 Earlier sketches in CA 69-72, CANR-11
 See also DLB 60
Godfrey, Donald G. ... 140
Godfrey, Eleanor S(mith) 1914- ... 69-72
Godfrey, Ellen 1942- ... 113
Godfrey, Frederick M. 1901-1974 ... CAP-1
 Earlier sketch in CA 13-14
Godfrey, Henry F. 1906-1975 ... CAP-2
 Earlier sketch in CA 25-28
Godfrey, Jane
 See Bowden, Joan Chase
Godfrey, Laurie R(ohde) 1945- ... 113
Godfrey, Lionel (Robert Holcombe) 1932- ... 81-84
Godfrey, Martyn N. 1949- ... CANR-68
 Earlier sketch in CA 126
 See also SATA 95
Godfrey, Michael A. 1940- ... CANR-14
 Earlier sketch in CA 81-84
Godfrey, Neale S. 1951- ... 149
Godfrey, Peter 1917- ... 124
Godfrey, Thomas 1736-1763 ... DLB 31
Godfrey, Vincent H. 1895(?)-1975 Obituary .. 57-60
Godfrey, William
 See Youd, (Christopher) Samuel

Godin, Gabriel 1929- ... 73-76
Godine, David R(ichard) 1944- ... 101
Godkin, Celia (Marilyn) 1948- ... 133
See also SATA 66
Godkin, E. L. 1831-1902 ... DLB 79
Godley, John
See Kilbracken, John (Raymond Godley)
Godly, J. P.
See Plawin, Paul
Godman, Arthur 1916- ... CANR-24
Earlier sketch in CA 106
Godolphin, Francis R(ichard) B(orroum)
1903-1974 ... 65-68
Obituary ... 53-56
Godolphin, Sidney 1610-1643 ... DLB 126
Godown, Marian Bailey ... 103
Godoy Alcayaga, Lucila 1889-1957 ... 131
Brief entry ... 104
See also Mistral, Gabriela
See also BW 2
See also DAM MULT
See also HW
See also MTCW 1
Godsey, John Drew 1922- ... 13-16R
Godshalk, William Leigh 1937- ... 41-44R
Godson, John 1937- ... 77-80
Godson, Joseph 1913-1986 ... 142
Obituary ... 120
Godson, Roy (S.) 1942- ... 155
Brief entry ... 111
Godwin, Anthony Richard James Wylie
1920(?)-1976 Obituary ... 104
Godwin, Gail (Kathleen) 1937- ... CANR-69
Earlier sketches in CA 29-32R, CANR-15, 43
Interview in ... CANR-15
See also CLC 5, 8, 22, 31, 69
See also DAM POP
See also DLB 6
See also MTCW 1
Godwin, Gaylord 1906(?)-1979 Obituary ... 85-88
Godwin, George (Stanley) 1889- ... 5-8R
Godwin, Harry 1901-1985 ... 109
Obituary ... 117
Godwin, John (Frederick) 1922- ... CANR-41
Earlier sketches in CA 102, CANR-19
Godwin, John 1929- ... CANR-16
Earlier sketches in CA 1-4R, CANR-1
Godwin, Joscelyn 1945- ... CANR-55
Earlier sketches in CA 69-72, CANR-12, 29
Godwin, Mary Jane 1766-1841 ... DLB 163
Godwin, Parke 1816-1904 Brief entry ... 119
See also DLB 3, 64
Godwin, Parke 1929- ... 157
Godwin, Peter (Christopher) 1957- ... 143
Godwin, Phillip E(arl) 1954-1989 Obituary ... 130
Godwin, Rebecca T. 1950- ... 139
Godwin, Tom 1915-1980 ... 156
Godwin, Tony
See Godwin, Anthony Richard James Wylie
Godwin, William 1756-1836 ... CDBLB 1789-1832
See also DLB 39, 104, 142, 158, 163
Godwin-Jones, Robert 1949- ... 137
Goebbels, Josef
See Goebbels, (Paul) Joseph
Goebbels, (Paul) Joseph 1897-1945 ... 148
Brief entry ... 115
See also TCLC 68
Goebbels, Joseph Paul
See Goebbels, (Paul) Joseph
Goebel, Dorothy (Burne) 1898-1976 ... 69-72
Obituary ... 65-68
Goebel, Julius, Jr. 1893(?)-1973 Obituary ... 45-48
Goedecke, Christopher (John) 1951- ... 149
See also SATA 81
Goedecke, W(alter) Robert 1928- ... 29-32R
Goedel, Kurt 1906-1978 Obituary ... 108
Goedertier, Joseph M. 1907- ... CAP-2
Earlier sketch in CA 25-28
Goedicke, Hans 1926- ... CANR-19
Earlier sketches in CA 45-48, CANR-1
Goedicke, Patricia (McKenna) 1931- ... CANR-53
Earlier sketches in CA 25-28R, CANR-11, 27
Goedicke, Victor (Alfred) 1912- ... 17-20R
Goehlert, Robert 1948- ... 157
Goel, M(adan) Lal 1936- ... 53-56
Goeldner, Charles R. 1932- ... CANR-62
Earlier sketch in CA 128
Goeller, Carl 1930- ... 21-24R
Goelz, Paul Cornelius 1914- ... 109
Goen, Clarence C(urtis), Jr. 1924-1990 ... 1-4R
Obituary ... 133
Goen, Rayburne Wyndham, Jr. 1942- ... 107
Goen, Tex, Jr.
See Goen, Rayburne Wyndham, Jr.
Goeney, William M(orton) 1914- ... 5-8R
Goeppert-Mayer, Maria 1906-1972 ... 156
Goerdt, Arthur L(inus) 1912- ... 41-44R
Goergen, Donald 1943- ... 61-64
Goering, Helga
See Wallmann, Jeffrey M(iner)
Goering, Reinhard 1887-1936 ... DLB 118
Goerlach, Manfred 1937- ... 140
Goerler, Raimund E. 1948- ... 167
Goerling, Lars 1931-1966 ... CAP-2
Earlier sketch in CA 21-22
Goerner, E(dward) A(lfred) 1929- ... 49-52
Goerner, S. J.
See Goerner, Sally J.
Goerner, Sally J. 1952- ... 148
Goerres, Joseph 1776-1848 ... DLB 90
Goertz, Donald C(harles) 1939- ... 53-56
Goertzel, Ted George 1942- ... 69-72
Goes, Albrecht 1908- ... DLB 69
Goetchius, Eugene Van Ness 1921- ... 118
Goethals, George W. 1920- ... 13-16R
Goethe, Ann 1945- ... 143
Goethe, Johann Wolfgang von 1749-1832 ... DA
See also DAB
See also DAC
See also DAM DRAM, MST, POET
See also DLB 94
See also PC 5
See also WLC 3
Goetsch-Trevelyan, Katherine
See Trevelyan, Katharine
Goette, Ann
See Goethe, Ann
Goettel, Elinor 1930- ... 29-32R
See also SATA 12
Goetz, Billy E. 1904- ... CAP-1
Earlier sketch in CA 13-14
Goetz, Curt 1888-1960 ... DLB 124
Goetz, Delia 1898-1996 ... 73-76
Obituary ... 152
See also SATA 22
See also SATA-Obit 91
Goetz, Ignacio L. 1933- ... 37-40R
Goetz, Johann Nikolaus 1721-1781 ... DLB 97
Goetz, Joseph (William) 1933- ... 118
Goetz, Lee Garrett 1932- ... 25-28R
Goetze, Albrecht E. R. 1897-1971 Obituary ... 33-36R
Goetzmann, William H. 1930- ... 21-24R
Goetz-Stankiewicz, Marketa ... 122
Goff, Charles Ray 1889-1984 Obituary ... 114
Goff, Frederick Richmond 1916-1982 ... CANR-7
Obituary ... 108
Earlier sketch in CA 17-20R
Goff, James R., Jr. 1957- ... 126
Goff, Martyn 1923- ... CANR-2
Earlier sketch in CA 5-8R
Goffart, Walter (Andre) 1934- ... CANR-38
Earlier sketches in CA 37-40R, CANR-16
Goffe, Thomas 1592(?)-1629 ... DLB 58
Goffe, Toni 1936- ... SATA 61
Goffen, Rona 1944- ... 121
Goffin, Raymond C. 1890(?)-1976 Obituary ... 65-68
Goffman, Erving 1922-1982 ... CANR-9
Obituary ... 108
Earlier sketch in CA 21-24R
Goffstein, (Marilyn) Brooke 1940- ... CANR-28
Earlier sketches in CA 21-24R, CANR-9
See also CLR 3
See also DLB 61
See also MAICYA
See also SATA 8, 70
Gofman, John W(illiam) 1918- ... 65-68
Goforth, Ellen
See Francis, Dorothy Brenner
Gogarty, Oliver St. John 1878-1957 ... 150
Brief entry ... 109
See also DLB 15, 19
See also TCLC 15
Goggin, Dan 1943- ... 126
Goggin, Terrence P(atrick) 1941- ... 103
Gogisgi
See Arnett, Carroll
Gogol, Nikolai (Vasilyevich) 1809-1852 ... DA
See also DAB
See also DAC
See also DAM DRAM, MST
See also DC 1
See also DLB 198
See also SSC 4, 29
See also WLC
Gogol, Sara 1948- ... 147
See also SATA 80
Goh, Cheng-Teik 1943- ... 41-44R
Gohdes, Clarence Louis Frank 1901- ... 13-16R
Gohman, Fred Joseph 1918- ... 5-8R
Goines, David Lance 1945- ... 147
Goines, Donald 1937(?)-1974 ... 124
Obituary ... 114
See also AITN 1
See also BLC 2
See also BW 1
See also CLC 80
See also DAM MULT, POP
See also DLB 33
Goingback, Owl 1959- ... 154
Goins, Ellen H(aynes) 1927-1979 ... CANR-26
Earlier sketch in CA 33-36R
Goist, Park Dixon 1936- ... 37-40R
Goitein, S(helomo) D(ov) 1900-1985 ... CANR-8
Obituary ... 115
Earlier sketch in CA 61-64
Goitein, Solomon Dob Fritz
See Goitein, S(helomo) D(ov)
Gokak, Vinayak Krishna 1909- ... 69-72
Gokhale, Balkrishna Govind 1919- ... CANR-4
Earlier sketch in CA 1-4R
Gokhale, Namita 1956- ... 123
Golan, Aviezer 1922- ... 104
Golan, Matti 1936- ... 101
Golann, Cecil Paige 1921- ... 33-36R
See also SATA 11
Golann, Stuart E(ugene) 1936- ... 57-60
Golant, Stephen M(yles) 1945- ... 145
Golant, William 1937- ... 65-68
Golany, Gideon S. 1928- ... 143
Golay, Frank H(indman) 1915- ... CANR-1
Earlier sketch in CA 1-4R
Golay, Michael 1951- ... 147
Golbin, Andree 1923- ... SATA 15
Golburgh, Stephen J. 1935- ... 21-24R
Golby, J(ohn) M(ichael) 1935- ... 127
Gold, Aaron 1937-1983 ... 101
Obituary ... 109
Gold, Alan R(obert) 1948- ... 45-48
Gold, Alison Leslie 1945- ... 136
Gold, Arthur 1917- ... 132
Gold, Artie 1947- ... 114
Gold, Barbara K(irk) 1945- ... CANR-29
Earlier sketch in CA 110
Gold, Don 1931- ... CANR-9
Earlier sketch in CA 61-64
Gold, Doris B. 1919- ... CANR-9
Earlier sketch in CA 21-24R
Gold, Douglas 1894- ... CAP-1
Earlier sketch in CA 11-12
Gold, H(orace) L(eonard) 1914-1996 ... 167
Gold, Hazel 1953- ... 145
Gold, Herbert 1924- ... CANR-45
Earlier sketches in CA 9-12R, CANR-17
See also CLC 4, 7, 14, 42
See also DLB 2
See also DLBY 81
Gold, Ivan 1932- ... CANR-3
Earlier sketch in CA 5-8R
Gold, Janet N(owakowski) 1948- ... 149
Gold, Jerome 1943- ... 154
Gold, Joseph 1933- ... 21-24R
Gold, Lee 1919(?)-1985 Obituary ... 116
Gold, Martin 1931- ... 29-32R
Gold, Michael 1950- ... 139
See also Granich, Irving
See also DLB 9, 28
Gold, Michael Evan 1943- ... 138
Gold, Milton J. 1917- ... 17-20R
Gold, Phyllis
See Goldberg, Phyllis
See also SATA 21
Gold, Robert S(tanley) 1924- ... 53-56
See also SATA 63
Gold, Seymour M(urray) 1933- ... CANR-21
Earlier sketch in CA 41-44R
Gold, Sharlya ... CANR-8
Earlier sketch in CA 61-64
See also SATA 9
Gold, Steven J(ames) 1955- ... 141
Gold, Susan Dudley 1949- ... CANR-48
Gold, Thomas 1920- ... 156
Gold, Todd 1958- ... 136
Gold, Victor Roland 1924- ... 53-56
Gold, William E. 1912-1997 ... 69-72
Obituary ... 156
Goldbarth, Albert 1948- ... CANR-40
Earlier sketches in CA 53-56, CANR-6
See also CLC 5, 38
See also DLB 120
Goldbeck, David M. 1942- ... CANR-30
Earlier sketch in CA 49-52
Goldbeck, Frederick E(rnest) 1902- ... 102
Goldbeck, Nikki 1947- ... CANR-30
Earlier sketch in CA 49-52
Goldbeck, Willis 1899(?)-1979 Obituary ... 89-92
Goldberg, Adele (E.) 1945- ... 156
Goldberg, Albert (Levi) 1898-1990 Obituary ... 130
Goldberg, Alvin Arnold 1931- ... 41-44R
Goldberg, Anatol 1910-1982 ... 131
Obituary ... 117
See also CLC 34
Goldberg, Arnold I(rving) 1929- ... CANR-19
Earlier sketch in CA 103
Goldberg, Arthur J(oseph) 1908-1990 ... 65-68
Obituary ... 130
Goldberg, Barney 1918- ... 21-24R
Goldberg, Benjamin 1915- ... 120
Goldberg, Bruce (Edward) 1948- ... 163
Goldberg, Carl 1938- ... CANR-18
Earlier sketches in CA 49-52, CANR-3
Goldberg, David J. 1939- ... CANR-55
Earlier sketch in CA 127
Goldberg, Dick 1947- ... 97-100
Interview in ... 97-100
See also DLB 7
Goldberg, Dorothy K(urgans) 1909(?)-1988 ... 103
Obituary ... 124
Goldberg, E(lliott) Marshall 1930- ... CANR-26
Earlier sketches in CA 69-72, CANR-11
Goldberg, Edward M(orris) 1931- ... 53-56
Goldberg, Fats
See Goldberg, Larry
Goldberg, George 1935- ... 69-72
Goldberg, Gerald Jay 1929- ... 49-52
Goldberg, Grace 1956- ... SATA 78
Goldberg, Harvey E(llis) 1939- ... CANR-25
Earlier sketch in CA 45-48
Goldberg, Herb 1937- ... CANR-9
Earlier sketch in CA 61-64
Goldberg, Herbert S. 1926- ... 5-8R
See also SATA 25
Goldberg, Herman Raphael 1915- ... CANR-5
Earlier sketch in CA 9-12R
Goldberg, Hillel 1946- ... 116
Goldberg, Hyman 1908(?)-1970 Obituary ... 104
Goldberg, Jacob 1943- ... CANR-65
Earlier sketch in CA 159
See also SATA 94
Goldberg, Jacob 1948- ... 120
Goldberg, Jake
See Goldberg, Jacob
Goldberg, Jan
See Curran, Jan Goldberg
Goldberg, Jane G. 1946- ... 138
Goldberg, Joan Rachel 1955- ... 110
Goldberg, Jonathan 1943- ... 122
Goldberg, Joseph P(hilip) 1918- ... 37-40R
Goldberg, Kenneth P(hilip) 1945- ... 116
Goldberg, Larry 1934- ... 113
Goldberg, Leah 1911-1970 Obituary ... 25-28R
Goldberg, Lee 1962- ... CANR-72
Earlier sketch in CA 156
Goldberg, Leonard S. 1936- ... CANR-71
Earlier sketch in CA 153
Goldberg, Lester 1924- ... 126
Goldberg, Louis
See Grant, Louis T(heodore)
Goldberg, Louis 1908- ... 13-16R
Goldberg, Lucianne Cummings 1935- ... 85-88
Goldberg, M(ilton) A(llan) 1919-1970 ... CAP-2
Earlier sketch in CA 25-28
Goldberg, M(elvyn) Hirsh 1942- ... 73-76
Goldberg, Marie Waife
See Waife-Goldberg, Marie
Goldberg, Maxwell Henry 1907- ... CANR-24
Earlier sketch in CA 103
Goldberg, Miriam Levin 1914(?)-1996 ... 41-44R
Obituary ... 154
Goldberg, Moses H(aym) 1940- ... CANR-15
Earlier sketch in CA 93-96
Goldberg, Natalie ... 154
Goldberg, Nathan 1903(?)-1979 Obituary ... 85-88
Goldberg, Norman L(ewis) 1906-1982 ... 81-84
Obituary ... 133
Goldberg, P(ercy) Selvin 1917- ... 5-8R
Goldberg, Paul (Boris) 1959- ... 135
Goldberg, Philip 1944- ... CANR-15
Earlier sketch in CA 85-88
Goldberg, Phyllis 1941- ... 57-60
See also Gold, Phyllis
Goldberg, Ray A(llan) 1926- ... CANR-48
Earlier sketch in CA 49-52
Goldberg, Reuben L(ucius) 1883-1970 ... CANR-9
Earlier sketch in CA 5-8R
Goldberg, Robert Alan 1949- ... CANR-55
Earlier sketch in CA 105
Goldberg, RoseLee 1947- ... 120
Goldberg, Rube
See Goldberg, Reuben L(ucius)
Goldberg, Samuel Louis 1926- ... 112
Goldberg, Sidney 1931- ... 77-80
Goldberg, Stan J. 1939- ... 49-52
See also SATA 26
Goldberg, Steven 1941- ... 53-56
Goldberg, Susan 1948- ... SATA 71
Goldberg, Whoopi 1955- ... 165
Goldberger, Arthur Stanley 1930- ... 9-12R
Goldberger, Avriel H. 1928- ... 140
Goldberger, Judith M. 1948- ... 112
See also Mathews, Judith
Goldberger, Leo 1930- ... 127
Goldberger, Nancy Rule 1937- ... 124
Goldberger, Paul (Jesse) 1950- ... 129
Brief entry ... 122
Golde, Peggy 1930- ... 37-40R
Golde, Roger A(lan) 1934- ... 69-72
Goldemberg, Isaac 1945- ... CANR-32
Earlier sketches in CA 69-72, CANR-11
See also CAAS 12
See also CLC 52
See also HW
Goldemberg, Rose Leiman ... CANR-2
Earlier sketch in CA 49-52
Golden, Arthur 1924- ... CANR-72
Earlier sketch in CA 33-36R
Golden, Christopher 1967- ... 150
Golden, Eve 1957- ... 136
Golden, Harry, Jr. 1928(?)-1988 Obituary ... 125
Golden, Harry (Lewis) 1902-1981 ... CANR-2
Obituary ... 104
Earlier sketch in CA 1-4R
Golden, James L. 1919- Brief entry ... 109
Golden, Jeffrey S. 1950- ... 33-36R
Golden, L(ouis) L(awrence) L(ionel)
1909(?)-1983 ... 21-24R
Obituary ... 111
Golden, Leon 1930- ... 17-20R
Golden, Marita 1950- ... CANR-42
Earlier sketch in CA 111
See also BW 2
Golden, Mark 1948- ... 135
Golden, Morris 1926- ... 1-4R
Golden, Renny 1937- ... 142
Golden, Richard M(artin) 1947- ... 138
Golden, Robert Edward 1945- ... 65-68
Golden, Ruth I(sbell) 1910- ... CAP-2
Earlier sketch in CA 17-18
Golden, Samuel A(dler) 1909- Brief entry ... 110
Golden, Sean V(alentine) 1948- ... 107
Golden, Sherry (Lazar) 1945- ... 123
Goldenbaum, Sally 1941- ... 124
Goldenberg, Edie N. 1945- ... 69-72
Goldenberg, Herbert 1926- ... 41-44R
Goldenberg, I(sidore) Ira 1936- ... 113
Goldenberg, Robert 1942- ... 109
Goldenberg, Susan 1944- ... 134
Goldensohn, Barry 1937- ... 77-80
Goldenson, Daniel R. 1944- ... 25-28R
Goldenson, Robert M(yar) 1908- ... 29-32R
Goldenthal, Allan Benarria 1920- ... 17-20R
Goldentyer, Debra 1960- ... 150
See also SATA 84
Goldfader, Edward H. 1930- ... 29-32R
Goldfarb, Clare R(osett) 1934- ... 113
Goldfarb, Nathan 1913- ... 13-16R
Goldfarb, Ronald L. 1933- ... CANR-40
Earlier sketches in CA 21-24R, CANR-9
Goldfarb, Russell M. 1934- ... 37-40R
Goldfarb, Sally F(ay) 1957- ... 104
Goldfeder, Cheryl
See Pahz, (Anne) Cheryl Suzanne
Goldfeder, James
See Pahz, James Alon
Goldfeder, Jim
See Pahz, James Alon
Goldfein, Donna 1933- ... 116
Goldfrank, David M. ... 118
Goldfrank, Esther S(chiff) 1896-1997 ... 61-64
Obituary ... 157
Goldfrank, Helen Colodny 1912- ... CANR-3
Earlier sketch in CA 1-4R
See also SATA 6
Goldfrank, Lewis 1941- ... 127

Goldfried, Marvin R(obert) 1936- ... 37-40R
Goldgar, Bertrand A(lvin) 1927- ... 65-68
Goldhaber, Gerald Martin 1944- ... CANR-9
Earlier sketch in CA 57-60
Goldhamer, Herbert 1907-1977 ... CANR-2
Earlier sketch in CA 45-48
Goldhammer, Arthur 1946- ... 139
Goldhurst, Richard 1927- ... 57-60
Goldhurst, William 1929- ... 5-8R
Goldie, Frederick 1914-1980 Obituary ... 105
Goldie, Terrence William 1950- ... CANR-32
Earlier sketch in CA 113
Goldie, Terry
See Goldie, Terrence William
Goldin, Augusta 1906- ... CANR-7
Earlier sketch in CA 17-20R
See also SATA 13
Goldin, Barbara Diamond 1946- ... CANR-57
Earlier sketch in CA 132
See also SAAS 26
See also SATA 92
Goldin, Claudia 1946- ... 142
Goldin, David 1963- ... SATA 101
Goldin, Grace 1916- ... 115
Goldin, Judah 1914- ... 33-36R
Goldin, Kathleen Mckinney 1943- ... 133
Brief entry ... 118
Goldin, Milton 1927- ... 61-64
Goldin, Owen 1957- ... 158
Goldin, Stephen 1947- ... 77-80
Golding, Alan 1952- ... 154
Golding, Lawrence A(rthur) 1926- ... 61-64
Golding, Louis 1885-1958 ... DLB 195
Golding, Louis 1907- ... CAP-1
Earlier sketch in CA 9-10
Golding, Martin Philip 1930- ... 101
Golding, Morton J(ay) 1925- ... 21-24R
Golding, Peter 1947- ... 103
Golding, William (Gerald) 1911-1993 ... CANR-54
Obituary ... 141
Earlier sketches in CA 5-8R, CANR-13, 33
See also AAYA 5
See also CDBLB 1945-1960
See also CLC 1, 2, 3, 8, 10, 17, 27, 58, 81
See also DA
See also DAB
See also DAC
See also DAM MST, NOV
See also DLB 15, 100
See also MTCW 1
See also WLC
Goldknopf, David 1918- ... 53-56
Goldman, A(ndrew) E. O. 1947- ... 57-60
Goldman, Alan H(arris) 1945- ... 93-96
Goldman, Albert 1927-1994 ... CANR-48
Obituary ... 144
Earlier sketches in CA 17-20R, CANR-9
See also BEST 89:2
Goldman, Alex J. 1917- ... 49-52
See also SATA 65
Goldman, Alvin I(ra) 1938- ... 77-80
Goldman, Alvin L. 1938- ... CANR-1
Earlier sketch in CA 45-48
Goldman, Ari L. 1949- ... 140
Goldman, Arnold (Melvyn) 1936- ... 17-20R
Goldman, Bernard 1922- ... 53-56
Goldman, Bo 1932- ... 112
Brief entry ... 109
Interview in ... 112
Goldman, Bruce (Eliot) 1942- ... 61-64
Goldman, Carl A(lexander) 1942- ... 101
Goldman, Charles R(emington) 1930- ... 53-56
Goldman, Dave 1927- ... 107
Goldman, E. S. 1913- ... CANR-66
Earlier sketch in CA 128
Goldman, Elizabeth 1949- ... 155
See also SATA 90
Goldman, Emma 1869-1940 ... 150
Brief entry ... 110
See also TCLC 13
Goldman, Eric (Frederick) 1915-1989 ... 5-8R
Obituary ... 127
Goldman, Francisco 1954- ... 162
See also CLC 76
Goldman, Frederick 1921- ... 81-84
Goldman, George D(avid) 1923- ... 107
Goldman, Howard H(irsch) 1949- ... 112
Goldman, Irving 1911- ... 29-32R
Goldman, Ivan G. 1942- ... 143
Goldman, Jacquelin (Roberta) 1934- ... 69-72
Goldman, James A. 1927- ... CANR-1
Earlier sketch in CA 45-48
Goldman, Katherine (Wyse) 1951- ... 143
Goldman, Lee A. 1946- ... 25-28R
Goldman, Leo 1920- ... 85-88
Goldman, Lorraine 1940- ... 111
Goldman, Louis 1925- ... 125
Goldman, Marcus Selden 1894- ... 41-44R
Goldman, Marshall I(rwin) 1930- ... 9-12R
Goldman, Martin (Raymond Rubin) 1920- ... 69-72
Goldman, Martin 1950(?)-1984 Obituary ... 113
Goldman, Merle 1931- ... 33-36R
Goldman, Michael (Paul) 1936- ... CANR-8
Earlier sketch in CA 17-20R
Goldman, Norma Wynick 1922- ... CANR-56
Earlier sketch in CA 110
Goldman, Paul (Henry Joseph) 1950- ... CANR-65
Earlier sketch in CA 129
Goldman, Peter (Louis) 1933- ... CANR-49
Earlier sketches in CA 21-24R, CANR-8, 24
Goldman, Phyllis W. 1927- ... 29-32R
Goldman, Ralph M(orris) 1920- ... 89-92
Goldman, Richard Franko 1910-1980 ... CANR-5
Obituary ... 93-96
Earlier sketch in CA 9-12R
Goldman, Roger L. 1941- ... 142
Goldman, Ronald ... 21-24R
Goldman, Sheldon 1939- ... 21-24R
Goldman, Sherli E(vens) 1930- ... 25-28R
Goldman, Shifra M(eyerowitz) 1926- ... CANR-25
Earlier sketch in CA 106
Goldman, Susan 1939- ... 65-68
Goldman, William (W.) 1931- ... CANR-69
Earlier sketches in CA 9-12R, CANR-29
See also CLC 1, 48
See also DLB 44
Goldman-Eisler, Frieda 1909(?)-1982 Obituary ... 105
Goldmann, Lucien 1913-1970 ... CAP-2
Earlier sketch in CA 25-28
See also CLC 24
Goldmann, Nahum 1895-1982 Obituary ... 107
Goldmark, Peter C(arl) 1906-1977 ... 77-80
Obituary ... 73-76
Goldner, Bernard (Burton) 1919- ... 5-8R
Goldner, Jack 1900- ... CAP-2
Earlier sketch in CA 25-28
Goldner, Nancy 1943- ... 57-60
Goldner, Orville (Charles) 1906- ... 53-56
Goldoni, Carlo 1707-1793 ... DAM DRAM
Goldovsky, Boris 1908- ... CANR-16
Earlier sketch in CA 81-84
Goldring, Douglas 1887-1960 Obituary ... 93-96
See also DLB 197
Goldring, Patrick (Thomas Zachary) 1921- ... 29-32R
Goldsberry, Steven 1949- ... 131
See also CLC 34
Goldsborough, James Oliver 1936- ... 142
Goldsborough, June 1923- ... SATA 19
Goldsborough, Robert (Gerald) 1937- ... 138
Goldscheider, Calvin 1941- ... 122
Brief entry ... 108
Goldscheider, Ludwig 1896- ... 5-8R
Goldschmidt, Arthur (Eduard), Jr. 1938- ... 162
Goldschmidt, Clara Malraux
See Malraux, Clara (Goldschmidt)
Goldschmidt, Tijs ... 168
Goldschmidt, Victor (Moritz) 1888-1947 ... 156
Goldschmidt, Walter Rochs 1913- ... 9-12R
Goldschmidt, Yaagov 1927- ... 29-32R
Goldsen, Rose Kohn 1918- ... CANR-33
Earlier sketch in CA 1-4R
Goldsman, Akiva ... 167
Goldsmith
See Miller, Lynne (Ellen)
Goldsmith, Arnold L(ouis) 1928- ... 41-44R
Goldsmith, Arthur (A., Jr.) 1926- ... CANR-5
Earlier sketch in CA 13-16R
Goldsmith, Barbara 1931- ... CANR-5
Earlier sketch in CA 53-56
Goldsmith, Carol Evan 1930- ... 29-32R
Goldsmith, David H(irsh) 1933- ... 117
Goldsmith, Donald 1943- ... 77-80
Goldsmith, Edward ... 104
Goldsmith, Emanuel S(idney) 1935- Brief entry ... 109
Goldsmith, Howard 1943- ... CANR-40
Earlier sketches in CA 101, CANR-21
See also SATA 24
Goldsmith, Ilse Sondra (Weinberg) 1933- ... 37-40R
Goldsmith, Jack 1931- ... 57-60
Goldsmith, Joel S. 1892(?)-1964 Obituary ... 109
Goldsmith, John 1947- ... 125
Goldsmith, John Herman Thorburn
1903-1987 Obituary ... 122
See also SATA-Obit 52
Goldsmith, Lynn 1948- ... 142
Goldsmith, Oliver 1728-1774 ... CDBLB 1660-1789
See also DA
See also DAB
See also DAC
See also DAM DRAM, MST, NOV, POET
See also DC 8
See also DLB 39, 89, 104, 109, 142
See also SATA 26
See also WLC
Goldsmith, Oliver 1794-1861 ... DLB 99
Goldsmith, Olivia 1954(?)- ... 155
Goldsmith, Peter
See Priestley, J(ohn) B(oynton)
Goldsmith, Raymond W(illiam) 1904-1988 ... 115
Obituary ... 126
Goldsmith, Robert Hillis 1911- ... 49-52
Goldsmith, Ruth M. 1919- ... SATA 62
Goldsmith, Sharon S(weeney) 1948- ... 57-60
Goldsmith, Walter (Kenneth) 1938- ... 120
Goldson, Rae L(illian) Segalowitz 1893- ... 5-8R
Goldstein, Abraham 1903(?)-1982 Obituary ... 106
Goldstein, Abraham S(amuel) 1925- ... CANR-29
Earlier sketch in CA 33-36R
Goldstein, Alvin H. Sr. 1902-1972 Obituary ... 33-36R
Goldstein, Arthur D(avid) 1937- ... 73-76
Goldstein, Avram 1919- ... 156
Goldstein, Bernard R. 1938- ... 57-60
Goldstein, Carl 1938- ... 130
Goldstein, David 1933- ... CANR-11
Earlier sketch in CA 17-20R
Goldstein, David I. 1924-1987(?) ... 130
Goldstein, Donald M(aurice) 1932- ... CANR-26
Earlier sketch in CA 108
Goldstein, E. Ernest 1918- ... 9-12R
Goldstein, Edward 1923- ... 9-12R
Goldstein, Ernest A. 1933- ... 110
See also SATA-Brief 52
Goldstein, Gersham 1938- Brief entry ... 108
Goldstein, Howard 1922- ... 93-96
Goldstein, Imre 1938- ... 140
Goldstein, Irwin L. 1937- ... 41-44R
Goldstein, Israel 1896-1986 ... 53-56
Obituary ... 119
Goldstein, Jack 1930- ... 73-76
Goldstein, Jeffrey H(askell) 1942- ... CANR-32
Earlier sketches in CA 81-84, CANR-14
Goldstein, Jerome 1931- ... 101
Goldstein, Joan 1932- ... CANR-35
Earlier sketch in CA 114
Goldstein, Jonathan A(mos) 1929- ... 25-28R
Goldstein, Joseph 1923- ... 17-20R
Goldstein, Kenneth M(ichael) 1940- ... 33-36R
Goldstein, Kenneth S. 1927-1995 Obituary ... 150
Brief entry ... 107
Goldstein, Larry Joel 1944- ... 139
Goldstein, Laurence 1937(?)-1972 Obituary ... 33-36R
Goldstein, Laurence 1943- ... 93-96
Goldstein, Leo S. 1924- ... 13-16R
Goldstein, Leon J. 1927- ... 69-72
Goldstein, Lisa 1953- ... CANR-25
Earlier sketch in CA 108
Goldstein, Malcolm 1925- ... CANR-32
Earlier sketch in CA 49-52
Goldstein, Marc 1948- ... 109
Goldstein, Martin E(ugene) 1939- ... 41-44R
Goldstein, Melvyn C. 1938- ... CANR-47
Earlier sketch in CA 121
Goldstein, Michael J(oseph) 1930- ... 103
Goldstein, Michael S. 1944- ... 143
Goldstein, Milton 1915- ... CANR-24
Earlier sketch in CA 45-48
Goldstein, Nathan 1927- ... CANR-16
Earlier sketches in CA 45-48, CANR-1
See also SATA 47
Goldstein, Philip 1910- ... 53-56
See also SATA 23
Goldstein, Rebecca 1950- ... 144
Goldstein, Rhoda L.
See Blumberg, Rhoda L(ois Goldstein)
Goldstein, Richard 1944- ... CANR-68
Earlier sketch in CA 25-28R
See also DLB 185
Goldstein, Robert Justin 1947- ... 131
Goldstein, Roberta Butterfield 1917- ... 9-12R
Goldstein, Robin 1952- ... 133
Goldstein, Robin 1955(?)-1989 Obituary ... 129
Goldstein, Ruth M(artha) 1913- ... 113
Goldstein, Ruth Tessler 1924- ... 69-72
Goldstein, Sidney 1927- ... CANR-25
Earlier sketches in CA 21-24R, CANR-9
Goldstein, Stanley 1922- ... 103
Goldstein, Stephen R(obert) 1938- ... CANR-30
Earlier sketches in CA 61-64, CANR-13
Goldstein, Stewart 1941- ... 65-68
Goldstein, Thomas Eugene 1913- Brief entry ... 108
Goldstein, William Isaac 1932- ... 13-16R
Goldstein-Jackson, Kevin 1946- ... 106
Goldstine, Herman Heine 1913- ... 110
Goldston, Robert (Conroy) 1927- ... CANR-13
Earlier sketch in CA 17-20R
See also SATA 6
Goldstone, Aline L(ewis)
1878(?)-1976 Obituary ... 65-68
Goldstone, Harmon H(endricks) 1911- ... 77-80
Goldstone, Herbert 1921- ... 77-80
Goldstone, Lawrence A.
See Treat, Lawrence
Goldstone, Nancy Bazelon 1957(?)- ... 158
Goldstone, Richard H. 1921- ... 33-36R
Goldsworthy, David 1938- ... 33-36R
Goldsworthy, Graeme 1934- ... CANR-35
Earlier sketch in CA 114
Goldsworthy, Peter 1951- ... 118
Goldszmit, Henryk 1878-1942 ... 133
See also Korczak, Janusz
Goldthorpe, J(ohn) E(rnest) 1921- ... CANR-33
Earlier sketch in CA 49-52
Goldthorpe, Rhiannon 1934- ... 126
Goldthwait, Bob 1962- ... 164
Goldthwait, Bobcat
See Goldthwait, Bob
Goldthwaite, Eaton K. 1907- ... 25-28R
Goldthwaite, Richard A(llen) 1933- ... 136
Brief entry ... 108
Goldwasser, Thomas 1939- ... 135
Goldwater, Barry (Morris) 1909-1998 ... 41-44R
Obituary ... 167
Goldwater, Eleanor Lowenstein
1909(?)-1980 Obituary ... 102
Goldwater, John L. 1916- ... 131
See also AITN 1
Goldwater, Robert 1907-1973 Obituary ... 41-44R
Goldwater, Walter Delmar 1907-1985 Obituary ... 116
Goldwin, Robert Allen 1922- ... 102
Goldwyn, Robert M(alcolm) 1930- ... 122
Gole, Victor Leslie 1903- ... CANR-23
Earlier sketch in CA 107
Goleman, Daniel 1946- ... 111
Golembe, Carla 1951- ... SATA 79
Golembiewski, Robert T(homas) 1932- ... CANR-45
Earlier sketches in CA 5-8R, CANR-6, 21
Golenbock, Peter 1946- ... CANR-8
Earlier sketch in CA 57-60
See also SATA 99
Golenpaul, Ann 1907(?)-1986 Obituary ... 119
Golf, Loyal E.
See Golv, Loyal E(ugene)
Golffing, Francis (Charles) 1910- ... CANR-5
Earlier sketch in CA 5-8R
Goliard, Roy
See Shipley, Joseph T(wadell)
Golightly, Bonnie H(elen) 1919- ... 1-4R
Golinski, Jan 1957- ... 139
Goll, Reinhold W(eimar) 1897- ... 5-8R
See also SATA 26
Gollaher, David L. 1949- ... 149
Gollan, Robin 1917- ... 13-16R
Gollancz, SirIsrael 1864-1930 ... DLB 201
Gollancz, Victor 1893-1967 Obituary ... 116
Golledge, Reginald G(eorge) 1937- ... 41-44R
Goller, Celia (Fremlin) 1914- ... CANR-5
Earlier sketch in CA 13-16R
Golley, Frank Benjamin 1930- Brief entry ... 106
Gollin, Gillian Lindt
See Lindt, Gillian
Gollin, Rita K. 1928- ... 140
Gollings, Franklin O. A. 1919- ... 21-24R
Gollmar, Robert H. 1903(?)-1987 Obituary ... 123
Gollub, Matthew 1960- ... 150
See also SATA 83
Gollwitzer, Heinz 1917- ... 25-28R
Gologor, Ethan 1940- ... 101
Golomb, Claire 1928- ... 103
Golomb, Louis 1943- ... CANR-16
Earlier sketch in CA 85-88
Golombek, Harry 1911- ... 103
Golomstock, Igor (Naumovitch) 1929- ... 134
Golon, Serge(anne) 1903-1972 Obituary ... 37-40R
Golovine, Michael N(icholas) 1903-1965 ... 5-8R
Golson, G(eorge) Barry 1944- ... CANR-33
Earlier sketch in CA 69-72
Golubitsky, Martin 1945- ... 140
Golv, Loyal E(ugene) 1926- ... CANR-1
Earlier sketch in CA 1-4R
Golz, R(einhardt) Lud 1936- ... CANR-5
Earlier sketch in CA 13-16R
Gom, Leona 1946- ... 116
Gombault, Charles Henri 1907-1983 Obituary ... 110
Gomberg, Adeline Wishengrad 1915- ... 17-20R
Gomberg, William 1911-1985 ... 17-20R
Obituary ... 118
Gombossy, Zoltan
See Gabel, Joseph
Gombrich, E(rnst) H(ans Josef) 1909- ... CANR-71
Earlier sketches in CA 53-56, CANR-5, 32
Gombrich, Richard Francis 1937- ... 138
Gombrowicz, Witold 1904-1969 ... CAP-2
Obituary ... 25-28R
Earlier sketch in CA 19-20
See also CLC 4, 7, 11, 49
See also DAM DRAM
Gomery, Douglas 1945- ... CANR-29
Earlier sketch in CA 110
Gomes, Peter J(ohn) 1942- ... 162
Gomez, Alberto Perez
See Perez-Gomez, Alberto
Gomez, Carlos F. 1958- ... 129
Gomez, David F(ederico) 1940- ... 49-52
Gomez, Jewelle 1948- ... 142
See also BW 2
Gomez, Joseph A(nthony) 1942- ... 104
Gomez, Rudolph 1930- ... 53-56
Gomez de la Serna, Ramon 1888-1963 ... 153
Obituary ... 116
See also CLC 9
See also HW
Gomez-Gil, Alfredo 1936- ... CANR-49
Earlier sketch in CA 41-44R
See also AITN 1
Gomez-Pena, Guillermo 1955- ... 147
Gomez-Quinones, Juan (H.) 1942- ... 131
See also DLB 122
See also HW
Gomez Rosa, Alexis 1950- ... 153
See also Rosa, Alexis Gomez
See also HW
Gomi, Taro 1945- ... 162
See also SATA 64
Gommans, Jos J. L. 1963- ... 151
Gomori, George 1934- ... CANR-9
Earlier sketch in CA 21-24R
Gompertz, Rolf 1927- ... CANR-11
Earlier sketch in CA 69-72
Goncourt, Edmond (Louis Antoine Huot) de
1822-1896 ... DLB 123
Goncourt, Jules (Alfred Huot) de 1830-1870 ... DLB 123
Gondosch, Linda 1944- ... 127
See also SATA 58
Gongora, Maria Eugenia 1948- ... 104
Gonick, Jean 1950- ... 121
Gonick, Larry 1946- ... 127
Gontarski, S(tanley) E. 1942- ... 114
Gontier, Fernande 19(?)- ... CLC 50
Gonzales, (Elizabeth) Anne H. 1944- ... 138
Gonzales, John
See Terrall, Robert
Gonzales, Manuel G(arcia) 1943- ... 111
Gonzales, Pancho
See Gonzales, Richard Alonzo
Gonzales, Richard Alonzo 1928- Brief entry ... 105
Gonzales, Rodolfo "Corky" 1928- ... DLB 122
Gonzales, Sylvia Alicia 1943- ... 77-80
See also HW
Gonzalez, Alfonso 1927- ... 41-44R
Gonzalez, Angel 1925- ... CANR-15
Earlier sketch in CA 85-88
See also DLB 108
Gonzalez, Anibal 1956- ... 148
Gonzalez, Arturo 1928- ... 77-80
Gonzalez, Catherine Gunsalus 1934- ... 136
Gonzalez, Catherine Troxell 1917- ... 151
See also SATA 87
Gonzalez, Cesar A.
See Gonzalez T(rujillo), Cesar A.
Gonzalez, Edward 1933- Brief entry ... 109
Gonzalez (Mandri), Flora 1948- ... 151
Gonzalez, Genaro 1949- ... 148
See also AAYA 15
See also DLB 122
Gonzalez, Gloria 1940- ... CANR-49
Earlier sketches in CA 65-68, CANR-24
See also SATA 23
Gonzalez, Jaime Jose 1925- ... 103
Gonzalez, Jose Luis 1926- ... 131
See also HW
Gonzalez, Justo L(uis) 1937- ... CANR-54
Earlier sketches in CA 29-32R, CANR-16

Gonzalez, N(estor) V(icente) M(adali) 1915-.......
CANR-2
Earlier sketch in CA 1-4R
Gonzalez, Nancie L(oudon) 1929-............ 103
Gonzalez, Ray 1952-................... DLB 122
Gonzalez, Richard F(lorentz) 1927-........... 114
Gonzalez, Sergio A(ntonio) Torres
See Torres Gonzalez, Sergio A(ntonio)
Gonzalez-Aller, Faustino 1922-............. 81-84
Gonzalez-Balado, Jose Luis 1933-............162
Gonzalez-Crussi, F(rank) 1936-......... CANR-54
Brief entry 121
Earlier sketch in CA 126
Interview in 126
See also HW
Gonzalez de Mireles, Jovita 1899-1983 ... DLB 122
Gonzalez-Echevarria, Roberto 1943-.......... 106
Gonzalez-Gerth, Miguel 1926-..............69-72
Gonzalez Lopez, Emilio 1903-........... CANR-2
Earlier sketch in CA 49-52
Gonzalez Martinez, Enrique 1871-1952........166
See also HW
See also TCLC 72
Gonzalez-Mena, Janet 1937-.................111
Gonzalez-Paz, Elsie E. 1913-...............45-48
Gonzalez Prada, Manuel 1844-1918.......... HW
Gonzalez T(rujillo), Cesar A. 1931-............153
See also HW
Gonzalez-T., Cesar A. 1931-..............DLB 82
Gonzalez-Wippler, Migene 1936-............ 109
Gooby, Peter Taylor
See Taylor-Gooby, Peter
Gooch, Bob
See Gooch, Robert M(iletus)
Gooch, Brad 1952-......................... 132
Gooch, Brison D(owling) 1925-............13-16R
Gooch, Bryan Niel Shirley 1937-............93-96
Gooch, George Peabody 1873-1968......... 5-8R
Gooch, John 1945-..........................126
Gooch, Robert M(iletus) 1919-.......... CANR-55
Earlier sketches in CA 77-80, CANR-13, 29
Gooch, Stan(ley Alfred) 1932-.......... CANR-46
Earlier sketches in CA 77-80, CANR-14
Gooch, Steve 1945-..................... CANR-43
Earlier sketches in CA 101, CANR-20
Gooche, Terry, Jr. 1927-................... 145
Good, Alice 1950-..................... SATA 73
Good, Carter V(ictor) 1897-................. 5-8R
Good, David F(ranklin) 1943-................125
Good, Edwin M(arshall) 1928-.......... CANR-11
Earlier sketch in CA 17-20R
Good, H(arry) G(ehman) 1880-1971 ....1-4R
Obituary 103
Good, Howard 1951-..........................147
Good, I(rving) John 1916-............... CANR-3
Earlier sketch in CA 5-8R
Good, Kenneth 1942-........................ 134
Good, Lawrence R. 1924-................13-16R
Good, Mary L(owe) 1931-................... 156
Good, Paul 1929-..........................85-88
Good, Robert Crocker 1924-................ 73-76
Good, Thomas L(indall) 1943-........... CANR-22
Earlier sketches in CA 57-60, CANR-8
Goodacre, Elizabeth Jane 1929-.............102
Goodall, Daphne Machin
See Machin Goodall, Daphne (Edith)
Goodall, H(arold) L(loyd), Jr. 1952-.......... 132
Goodall, Jane 1934-.................... CANR-69
Earlier sketches in CA 45-48, CANR-2, 43
See also MTCW 1
Goodall, John Strickland 1908-1996....... 33-36R
Obituary 152
See also CLR 25
See also MAICYA
See also SATA 4, 66
See also SATA-Obit 91
Goodall, Leonard E. 1937-.................85-88
Goodall, Marcus C(ampbell) 1914-.........33-36R
Goodall, Melanie
See Drachman, Julian M(oses)
Goodall, Norman 1896-1985 Obituary.........115
Goodall, Vanne Morris
See Morris-Goodall, Vanne
Goodavage, Joseph F. 1925-............. 25-28R
Goodbody, Slim
See Burstein, John
Goodchild, Peter 1939-......................106
Goode, Barry 1938-..........................118
Goode, Diane (Capuozzo) 1949-......SATA 15, 84
Goode, Erica 166
Goode, Erich 1938-..................... CANR-37
Earlier sketches in CA 49-52, CANR-1, 16
Goode, Gerald 1899(?)-1983 Obituary........ 111
Goode, James (Arthur) 1924-1992 123
Obituary 140
Goode, James M. 1939-.................... 93-96
Goode, John 1927-..........................103
Goode, Kenneth G. 1932-.................. 49-52
Goode, Richard (Benjamin) 1916-......... 17-20R
Goode, Ruth 1905-1997 77-80
Obituary 162
Goode, Stephen H(ogue) 1924-.......... CANR-2
Earlier sketch in CA 45-48
Goode, Stephen Ray 1943-............ CANR-18
Earlier sketch in CA 57-60
See also SATA 55
See also SATA-Brief 40
Goode, William Josiah 1917-.................102
Goodell, Charles E(llsworth) 1926-1987 81-84
Obituary 121
Goodell, Donald (James) 1938-.............45-48
Goodell, Jeff 160
Goodell, John S. 1939-....................73-76
Goodell, Rae 1944-........................77-80
Goodenough, Erwin R(amsdell) 1893-1965 ....5-8R
Goodenough, Evelyn
See Pitcher, Evelyn G(oodenough)
Goodenough, Ward Hunt 1919-.......... CANR-2
Earlier sketch in CA 1-4R
Goodenow, Earle 1913-................. SATA 40
Gooders, John 1937-................... CANR-6
Earlier sketch in CA 57-60
Goodfellow, Peter 1935-.....................115
Goodfield, (Gwyneth) June 1927-...........9-12R
Goodfriend, Arthur 1907-...................5-8R
Goodgold, Edwin 1944-................ CANR-23
Earlier sketch in CA 21-24R
Goodhart, A. L.
See Goodhart, Arthur Lehman
Goodhart, Arthur Lehman 1891-1978 .... CANR-31
Obituary 81-84
Earlier sketch in CA 85-88
Goodhart, Robert S(tanley) 1909-...........89-92
Goodheart, Barbara 1934-................33-36R
Goodheart, Eugene 1931-............. CANR-39
Earlier sketches in CA 5-8R, CANR-3, 18
Goodheart, Lawrence B. 1944-.............. 135
Goodhue, Thomas W. 1949-................. 142
Goodin, Gayle 1938-....................33-36R
Goodin, Robert Edward 1950-.......... CANR-45
Earlier sketches in CA 105, CANR-22
Goodin, Sallie (Brown) 1953-............ SATA 74
Gooding, Cynthia 1924-.................. 33-36R
Gooding, John (Ervine) 1940-............ 21-24R
Gooding, Judson 1926-...................73-76
Gooding, Kathleen (Tinney) 116
Goodis, David 1917-1967 .... CANR-60
Earlier sketch in CA 1-4R
Goodison, Lorna 1947-......................142
See also DLB 157
Goodkin, Richard E. 1953-..................141
Goodkin, Sanford R(onald) 1929-........... 104
Goodkind, Henry M. 1904(?)-1970 Obituary 104
Goodkind, Terry 1948-..................... 165
See also AAYA 27
Goodlad, John I. 1920-................ CANR-43
Earlier sketches in CA 5-8R, CANR-3, 19
Goodman, A(lvin) Harold 1924-..............103
Goodman, A(dolph) W(inkler) 1915-......... 57-60
Goodman, Ann (Davidow) 1932-..............107
Goodman, Arnold Abraham 1913-1995........ 109
Obituary 148
Goodman, Benjamin David
1909(?)-1986 Obituary 119
Goodman, Benny
See Goodman, Benjamin David
Goodman, Celia (Mary) 1916-................123
Goodman, Charles S(chaffner) 1916-....... 33-36R
Goodman, Charlotte Margolis 1934-..........134
Goodman, David (Allen) 1941-............... 119
Goodman, David Michael 1936-............17-20R
Goodman, David S. 1917-..................29-32R
Goodman, Deborah Lerme 1956-.............121
See also SATA 50
See also SATA-Brief 49
Goodman, Edward J(ulius) 1916-............ 111
Goodman, Elaine 1930-...................37-40R
See also SATA 9
Goodman, Elizabeth B. 1912-............. 25-28R
Goodman, Ellen (Holtz) 1941-...............104
Interview in 104
Goodman, Elliot R(aymond) 1923-............ 1-4R
Goodman, Emily Jane 1940-................65-68
Goodman, Eric 1953-........................ 141
Goodman, Eugene B(enedict) 1922-.......... 113
Goodman, Felicitas D(aniels) 1914-...... CANR-46
Earlier sketches in CA 53-56, CANR-4, 23
Goodman, Fred 1950(?)-..................... 160
Goodman, George J(erome) W(aldo) 1930-.......
CANR-68
Earlier sketches in CA 21-24R, CANR-31
Interview in CANR-31
See also DLB 185
Goodman, Grant K(ohn) 1924-.......... CANR-15
Earlier sketch in CA 41-44R
Goodman, Hannah Grad
See Sverdlin, Hannah Grad
Goodman, Harriet Wilinsky 111
Goodman, Herman 1894-1971 Obituary....... 105
Goodman, James 1956-.......................146
Goodman, James M(arion) 1929-.............117
Goodman, Jay S. 1940-...................37-40R
Goodman, Joan Elizabeth 1950-......... CANR-67
Earlier sketch in CA 126
See also SATA 50, 94
Goodman, John 1952-....................... 146
Goodman, Jonathan 1931-.............. CANR-13
Earlier sketch in CA 33-36R
Goodman, Jordan E. 1954-.................. 147
Goodman, Joseph Irving 1908-.............. 102
Goodman, Kenneth S. 1927-...............25-28R
Goodman, Lenn Evan 1944-................ 53-56
Goodman, Leonard H(enry) 1941-........... 103
Goodman, Linda 1925-1995 .... CANR-52
Obituary 150
Earlier sketch in CA 89-92
Goodman, Lizbeth (L.) 1964-.................163
Goodman, Louis Wolf 1942-...............25-28R
Goodman, Mark 1939-....................... 126
Goodman, Melvin A. 1938-.................. 138
Goodman, Michael B(arry) 1949-............ 107
Goodman, Mitchell 1923-1997 .... CANR-4
Obituary 156
Earlier sketch in CA 1-4R
Goodman, (Henry) Nelson 1906-............45-48
Goodman, Norman 1934-............... CANR-17
Earlier sketches in CA 49-52, CANR-1
Goodman, Paul 1911-1972............. CANR-34
Obituary 37-40R
Earlier sketches in CAP-2, CA 19-20
See also CLC 1, 2, 4, 7
See also DLB 130
See also MTCW 1
Goodman, Percival 1904-1989............. 1-4R
Obituary 129
Goodman, Philip 1911-...................33-36R
Goodman, Randolph 1908-............. CANR-2
Earlier sketch in CA 5-8R
Goodman, Rebecca Gruver 1931-.......... 77-80
Goodman, Richard 1945-.....................136
Goodman, Richard Merle 1932-1989 .... CANR-40
Earlier sketches in CA 102, CANR-18
Goodman, Roger B. 1919-.............. CANR-9
Earlier sketch in CA 21-24R
Goodman, Ronald A. 1938-................ 73-76
Goodman, Rubin Robert 1913-1978 Obituary 81-84
Goodman, Saul 1919-........................103
Goodman, Seymour S. 1931-........... CANR-22
Earlier sketch in CA 45-48
Goodman, Sonya
See Arcone, Sonya
Goodman, Stanley J(oshua) 1910-............110
Goodman, Steve 1948-1984 Obituary.........113
Goodman, Steven M(ichael) 1957-............126
Goodman, Susan 1951-...................... 146
Goodman, Walter 1927-................ CANR-7
Earlier sketch in CA 9-12R
See also SATA 9
Goodnough, David L. 1930-................93-96
Goodnow, Henry F(rank) 1917-........... 13-16R
Goodnow, Jacqueline (Jarrett) 1924-..... CANR-5
Earlier sketch in CA 13-16R
Goodovitch, I(srael) M(eir) 1934-......... 25-28R
Goodpaster, Andrew J(ackson) 1915-......... 109
Goodpaster, Kenneth E(dwin) 1944-..... CANR-17
Earlier sketch in CA 97-100
Goodpasture, H(enry) McKennie 1929-........ 134
Goodreau, William Joseph, Jr. 1931-......... 1-4R
Goodrich, Chris 1956-.......................134
Goodrich, David L(loyd) 1930-..............85-88
Goodrich, Donna Clark 1938-................ 117
Goodrich, Foster E(dward)
1908-1972 Obituary 37-40R
Goodrich, Frances 1890(?)-1984 Obituary..... 111
See also DLB 26
Goodrich, Frances C. 1933-............. 21-24R
Goodrich, L(uther) Carrington 1894-1986 .. CANR-2
Obituary 120
Earlier sketch in CA 5-8R
Goodrich, Leland Matthew 1899-........... 81-84
Goodrich, Lloyd 1897-1987 .... CANR-31
Obituary 122
Earlier sketch in CA 69-72
Goodrich, Norma Lorre 1917-............. 53-56
Goodrich, Robert E(dward), Jr. 1909-...... 33-36R
Goodrich, Samuel Griswold 1793-1860 .. DLB 1, 42, 73
See also SATA 23
Goodrich, William Lloyd
1910(?)-1975 Obituary 61-64
Goodrick, Edward W(illiam) 1913-....... CANR-29
Earlier sketch in CA 111
Goodrick-Clarke, Nicholas 1953-........... 123
Goodrum, Charles A(lvin) 1923-......... CANR-57
Earlier sketches in CA 25-28R, CANR-12, 27
Goodsall, Robert Harold 1891-(?) CANR-4
Earlier sketch in CA 5-8R
Goodsell, Charles T(rue) 1932-.......... CANR-8
Earlier sketch in CA 61-64
Goodsell, Fred Field 1880-1976 .... 1-4R
Obituary 69-72
Goodsell, Jane Neuberger
1921(?)-1988 Obituary 126
See also SATA-Obit 56
Goodson, Felix E(mmett) 1922-.............49-52
Goodspeed, Donald J(ames) 1919-.......... 5-8R
Goodspeed, Edgar Johnson
1871-1962 Obituary 93-96
Goodspeed, Peter 1944-.................... 110
Goodstein, David B. 1932(?)-1985 Obituary 116
Goodstein, Leonard D(avid) 1927-...... CANR-13
Earlier sketch in CA 33-36R
Goodstein, Marvin (Elias) 1927-............ 125
Goodstein, R(euben) L(ouis) 1912-1985..... 53-56
Obituary 116
Goodwin, Albert 1906-..................... 5-8R
Goodwin, Bennie Eugene II 1933-........... 112
Goodwin, Craufurd D(avid) W(ycliffe) 1934-........
CANR-14
Earlier sketch in CA 37-40R
Goodwin, Dave 1926-........................113
Goodwin, Derek 1920-..................... 93-96
Goodwin, Donald W(illiam) 1931-........... 65-68
Goodwin, Doris (Helen) Kearns 1943-... CANR-53
Earlier sketch in CANR-23
Goodwin, Eugene D.
See Kaye, Marvin (Nathan)
Goodwin, Frederick K(ing) 1936-............ 148
Goodwin, Geoffrey (Lawrence) 1916-1995...... 106
Obituary 148
Goodwin, H(arry) Eugene 1922-.............126
Goodwin, Hal
See Goodwin, Harold L(eland)
Goodwin, Harold 1919-....................57-60
Goodwin, Harold L(eland) 1914-1990 .... CANR-29
Obituary 131
Earlier sketches in CA 1-4R, CANR-2
See also SATA 13, 51
See also SATA-Obit 65
Goodwin, Jan 1944-........................ 154
Goodwin, Joanne L. 1949-...................167
Goodwin, John Lonnen 1921-................ 108
Goodwin, John R(obert) 1929-..............77-80
Goodwin, Ken(neth Leslie) 1934-............. 131
Goodwin, Leonard 1929-..................41-44R
Goodwin, Mark
See Matthews, Stanley G(oodwin)
Goodwin, Michael 1949-.......................141
Goodwin, (Trevor) Noel 1927-.................124
Goodwin, R(ichard) M(urphey) 1913-1996 ....
CANR-29
Obituary 153
Earlier sketches in CA 29-32R, CANR-12
Goodwin, Richard N(aradhof) 1931-...........146
Brief entry 111
Goodwin, Robert L. 1928(?)-1983 Obituary.... 109
Goodwin, Ruby Berkley 1903-................153
See also BW 2
Goodwin, Stephen 1943-................ CANR-8
Earlier sketch in CA 57-60
See also DLBY 82
Goodwin, Suzanne CANR-31
Earlier sketches in CA 77-80, CANR-14
Goodwyn, Floyd L(owell) 1940-..............113
Goodwyn, Lawrence 1928-............... 21-24R
Goody, Joan Edelman 1935-..............17-20R
Goodyear, Frank H., Jr. 1944-................122
Goodyear, John H(enry) III 1941-....... CANR-41
Earlier sketch in CA 111
Goody-Jones
See Janko, (Kathleen) Susan
Googe, Barnabe 1540-1594 .... DLB 132
Gookin, Daniel 1612-1687 ....DLB 24
Gool, Reshard 1931-.....................97-100
Goolagong, Evonne 1951-................. 89-92
Goold-Adams, Richard (John Moreton)
1916-1995 ....13-16R
Obituary 148
Goon, Fook Mun 1917(?)-1984 Obituary.......113
Gooneratne, (Malini) Yasmine 1935-..... CANR-41
Earlier sketches in CA 29-32R, CANR-18
Goonetilleke, D(evapriya) C(hitra) R(anjan) A(lwis)
1938-.......................................130
Goor, Nancy (Ruth Miller) 1944-........ CANR-32
Earlier sketch in CA 113
See also SATA 39
See also SATA-Brief 34
Goor, Ron(ald Stephen) 1940-........... CANR-32
Earlier sketch in CA 113
See also SATA 39
See also SATA-Brief 34
Goossen, Agnes
See Epp, Margaret A(gnes)
Goossen, Irvy W. 37-40R
Goossen, Rachel Waltner 1960-..............167
Goot, Mary Vander
See Vander Goot, Mary
Gootenberg, Paul 1954-..................... 149
Gopal, Sarvepalli 1923-..................... 104
Gopalakrishnan, Chennat 1936-........ CANR-30
Earlier sketch in CA 112
Gopen, George D(avid) 1945-................113
Gopiah
See Keys, Kerry Shawn
Gopnik, Adam 1956-........................165
Gorak, Jan 1952-...................... CANR-58
Earlier sketch in CA 126
Goralski, Robert 1928-1988 105
Obituary 125
Goran, Lester 1928-................... CANR-48
Earlier sketch in CA 45-48
Goran, Morris 1918-................... CANR-2
Earlier sketch in CA 1-4R
Gorbachev, Mikhail (Sergeyevich) 1931-. CANR-69
Earlier sketch in CA 132
See also MTCW 1
Gorbachev, Raisa (Maksimovna) 1934(?)-..... 141
Gorbachev, Valeri 1944-.....................166
See also SATA 98
Gorbanevskaya, Natalya 1936-..............111
Gorbatov, Alexander V.
1891(?)-1973 Obituary 45-48
Gordeeva, Ekaterina 1971-................. 158
Gorden, Raymond L(owell) 1919-.......... 53-56
Gordenker, Leon 1923-................... 21-24R
Gordett, Marea (Beth) 1949-.................117
Gordh, George (Rudolph) 1912-..........13-16R
Gordievsky, Oleg 1938-..................... 140
Gordimer, Nadine 1923-................ CANR-56
Earlier sketches in CA 5-8R, CANR-3, 28
Interview in CANR-28
See also CLC 3, 5, 7, 10, 18, 33, 51, 70
See also DA
See also DAB
See also DAC
See also DAM MST, NOV
See also MTCW 1
See also SSC 17
See also WLCS
Gordin, Richard Davis 1928-.............. 53-56
Gordis, Robert 1908-.................. CANR-9
Earlier sketch in CA 13-16R
Gordon, Ad
See Hano, Arnold
Gordon, Alan F. 1947-..................... 102
Gordon, Albert I(saac) 1903-1968 .... CAP-1
Earlier sketch in CA 11-12
Gordon, Alex
See Cotler, Gordon
Gordon, Alison (Ruth) 1943-................ 121
Gordon, Alvin J. 1912-1989 ....33-36R
Obituary 130
Gordon, Ambrose, Jr. 1920-1987 ....33-36R
Obituary 122
Gordon, Andrew (Mark) 1945-................115
Gordon, Angela
See Paine, Lauran (Bosworth)
Gordon, Anne Wolrige
See Wolrige Gordon, Anne

Gordon, Antoinette K. 1892(?)-1975 Obituary 57-60
Gordon, April A. 1947- 162
Gordon, Archibald Victor Dudley
1913-1984 Obituary 114
Gordon, Archie
See Gordon, Archibald Victor Dudley
Gordon, Arthur 1912- 5-8R
Gordon, Barbara 1935- CANR-17
Earlier sketch in CA 89-92
Interview in CANR-17
Gordon, Barry (Lewis John) 1934- 102
Gordon, Bernard K. 1932- 85-88
Gordon, Bernard Ludwig 1931- 29-32R
See also SATA 27
Gordon, Bertram M(artin) 1943- 101
Gordon, Beverly 1948- 93-96
Gordon, Burton L(e Roy) 1920- 114
Gordon, Caroline 1895-1981 CANR-36
Obituary 103
Earlier sketches in CAP-1, CA 11-12
See also CLC 6, 13, 29, 83
See also DLB 4, 9, 102
See also DLBD 17
See also DLBY 81
See also MTCW 1
See also SSC 15
Gordon, Charles William 1860-1937 Brief entry 109
See also Connor, Ralph
Gordon, Colin 1962- 150
Gordon, Colonel H. R.
See Ellis, Edward S(ylvester)
Gordon, Cyrus H(erzl) 1908- CANR-5
Earlier sketch in CA 1-4R
Gordon, Dane R. 1925- 33-36R
Gordon, David
See Garrett, (Gordon) Randall (Phillip)
Gordon, David Cole 1922- 25-28R
Gordon, David J. 1929- Brief entry 105
Gordon, David M(ichael) 1944-1996 128
Obituary 151
Gordon, Deborah Hannes 1946- 130
Gordon, Diana
See Andrews, Lucilla (Mathew)
Gordon, Diana R(ussell) 1938- CANR-28
Earlier sketch in CA 49-52
Gordon, Donald
See Payne, Donald Gordon
Gordon, Donald Craigie 1911- 17-20R
Gordon, Donald E(dward) 1931-1984 Obituary 112
Gordon, Donald Ramsay 1929- CANR-31
Earlier sketches in CA 37-40R, CANR-14
Gordon, Doreen
See Chard, Judy
Gordon, Dorothy 1893-1970 73-76
See also SATA 20
Gordon, Edmund Wyatt 1921- 37-40R
Gordon, Edwin 1927- CANR-10
Earlier sketch in CA 17-20R
Gordon, Eric A(rthur) 1945- 132
Gordon, Ernest 1916- CANR-2
Earlier sketch in CA 1-4R
Gordon, (Alexander) Esme 1910- 108
Gordon, Esther S(aranga) 1935- CANR-7
Earlier sketch in CA 53-56
See also SATA 10
Gordon, Ethel Edison 1915- 53-56
Gordon, Felice 1939- 97-100
Gordon, Frances
See Wood, Bridget
Gordon, Frederick CANR-26
Earlier sketches in CAP-2, CA 19-20
See also SATA 1
Gordon, Fritz
See Jarvis, Fred(erick) G(ordon, Jr.)
Gordon, Gary
See Edmonds, I(vy) G(ordon)
Gordon, George
See Hasford, (Jerry) Gustav
Gordon, George Byron 1911- 33-36R
Gordon, George J(acob) 1943- 111
Gordon, George N(ewton) 1926- CANR-5
Earlier sketch in CA 1-4R
Gordon, Gerald 1909- CAP-1
Earlier sketch in CA 13-14
Gordon, Giles (Alexander Esme) 1940- CANR-69
Earlier sketches in CA 41-44R, CANR-43
See also DLB 14, 139
Gordon, Gordon 1912- CANR-7
Earlier sketch in CA 5-8R
Gordon, Graeme 1966- 151
Gordon, Guanetta Stewart 37-40R
Gordon, Hal
See Goodwin, Harold L(eland)
Gordon, Harold J(ackson), Jr. 1919- 33-36R
Gordon, Harry 1925- 137
See also Gordon, Henry Alfred
Gordon, (Charles) Harry (Clinton) Pirie
See Pirie-Gordon, (Charles) Harry (Clinton)
Gordon, Helen Cameron 1867-1949 DLB 195
Gordon, Henry Alfred 1925- CANR-5
Earlier sketch in CA 53-56
See also Gordon, Harry
Gordon, I(an) R(obert) F(raser) 1939- 69-72
Gordon, Ian
See Fellowes-Gordon, Ian (Douglas)
Gordon, Ian A(listair) 1908- CANR-11
Earlier sketch in CA 25-28R
Gordon, Ida L. 1907- CAP-2
Earlier sketch in CA 33-36
Gordon, Ira J(ay) 1923-1978 CANR-26
Earlier sketch in CA 69-72
Gordon, Jacob U. 1939- 147
Gordon, Jaimy 1944- 140
Gordon, (Gilbert) James 1918- 61-64
Gordon, James S(amuel) 1941- 158
Gordon, Jane
See Lee, Elsie
Gordon, Jeffie Ross
See Enderle, Judith (Ann) Ross
and Tessler, Stephanie Gordon
Gordon, Joanne J(oy) 1956- 108
Gordon, John
See Gesner, Clark
Gordon, John (Rutherford) 1890-1974 Obituary 104
Gordon, John (William) 1925- CANR-60
Earlier sketches in CA 103, CANR-11, 27, 51
See also SATA 84
Gordon, John Fraser 1916- CANR-45
Earlier sketches in CA 105, CANR-22
Gordon, John Steele 1944- 57-60
Gordon, Kermit 1916-1976 Obituary 65-68
Gordon, Kurtz
See Kurtz, C(larence) Gordon
Gordon, Leland J(ames) 1897-1982 41-44R
Obituary 133
Gordon, Leonard 1935- 53-56
Gordon, Leonard A. 1938- 37-40R
Gordon, Leonard H. D. 1928- 29-32R
Gordon, Lesley
See Elliott, Lesley
Gordon, Lew
See Baldwin, Gordon C.
Gordon, Lewis Ricardo 1962- 158
Gordon, Lillian L. 1925-1977 29-32R
Gordon, Lincoln 1913- 117
Gordon, (Irene) Linda 1940- CANR-50
Earlier sketches in CA 65-68, CANR-10, 25
Gordon, Lois G. 1938- CANR-55
Earlier sketches in CA 33-36R, CANR-13, 29
Gordon, Lou 1917(?)-1977 Obituary 69-72
Gordon, Lyndall (Felicity) 1941- 141
See also DLB 155
Gordon, Margaret (Anna) 1939- SATA 9
Gordon, Margaret T(aber) 1939- 81-84
Gordon, Mark 1942- 118
Gordon, Mary (Catherine) 1949- CANR-44
Earlier sketch in CA 102
Interview in 102
See also CLC 13, 22
See also DLB 6
See also DLBY 81
See also MTCW 1
Gordon, Mary Ebbitt
See Winters, Catherine (Mary)
Gordon, Mary McDougall 1929- 130
Gordon, Michael 1940- 41-44R
Gordon, Michael (David) 1952- 123
Gordon, Mike 1948- 168
See also SATA 101
Gordon, Mildred 1912-1979 CANR-7
Obituary 85-88
Earlier sketch in CA 5-8R
See also SATA-Obit 24
Gordon, Mitchell 1925- 5-8R
Gordon, Myron J(ules) 1920- CANR-6
Earlier sketch in CA 5-8R
Gordon, N. J.
See Bosman, Herman Charles
Gordon, Nancy
See Heinl, Nancy G(ordon)
Gordon, Noah 1926- CANR-62
Earlier sketch in CA 17-20R
Gordon, Oliver
See Emerson, H(enry) O(liver)
Gordon, Patricia 1909- 21-24R
Gordon, Percival Hector 1884-1975 41-44R
Gordon, Peter
See Wilkes-Hunter, R(ichard)
Gordon, Peter H. 1948- 130
Gordon, R(ichard) L(aurence) 1920- Brief entry 114
Gordon, Ray
See Wainwright, Gordon Ray
Gordon, Rex
See Hough, S(tanley) B(ennett)
Gordon, Richard
See Ostlere, Gordon (Stanley)
Gordon, Richard 1947- 160
Gordon, Richard L(ewis) 1934- 29-32R
Gordon, Robert A(aron) 1908-1978 CANR-4
Obituary 77-80
Earlier sketch in CA 5-8R
Gordon, Robert C(oningsby) 1921- 5-8R
Gordon, Robert Ellis 1954- 146
Gordon, Robert J. 1947- 121
Gordon, Ruth 1896-1985 CANR-31
Obituary 117
Earlier sketch in CA 81-84
Gordon, Samuel 1907(?)-1984 Obituary 114
Gordon, Sanford D(aniel) 1924- 33-36R
Gordon, Sarah (Ann) 1944- 132
Gordon, Selma
See Lanes, Selma Gordon
Gordon, Sheila 1927- 132
See also CLR 27
See also SATA 88
Gordon, Shirley 1921- 97-100
See also SATA 48
See also SATA-Brief 41
Gordon, Sol 1923- CANR-4
Earlier sketch in CA 53-56
See also CLC 26
See also SATA 11
Gordon, Spike
See Fearn, John Russell
Gordon, Steve 1938(?)-1982 Obituary 108
Gordon, Stewart
See Shirreffs, Gordon D(onald)
Gordon, Strathearn 1902-1983 Obituary 109
Gordon, Suzanne 1945- CANR-70
Earlier sketches in CA 49-52, CANR-4
Gordon, Sydney 1914- 29-32R
Gordon, Theodore J. 1930- 17-20R
Gordon, Thomas 1918- 29-32R
Gordon, Vivian V(erdell) 1934-1995 143
Obituary 147
See also BW 2
Gordon, W. Terrence 1942- 162
Gordon, Walter Kelly 1930- 33-36R
Gordon, Walter L(ockhart) 1906-1987 97-100
Obituary 122
Gordon, Wendell (Chaffee) 1916- 17-20R
Gordon, William A. 1950- 135
Gordone, Charles 1925-1995 CANR-55
Obituary 150
Earlier sketch in CA 93-96
Interview in 93-96
See also BW 1
See also CLC 1, 4
See also DAM DRAM
See also DC 8
See also DLB 7
See also MTCW 1
Gordons, The
See Gordon, Gordon
and Gordon, Mildred
Gordon Walker, Patrick (Chrestien) 1907- 29-32R
Gordon-Watson, Mary 1948- CANR-37
Earlier sketch in CA 112
Gordy, Berry Sr. 1888-1978 102
Gordy, Berry, Jr. 1929- 148
Gore, Al(bert, Jr.) 1948- 142
Gore, Albert (Arnold) 1907- Brief entry 112
Gore, Ariel 1971- 167
Gore, Arthur Kattendyke S(trange) D(avid)
1910-1983 Obituary 109
Gore, Catherine 1800-1861 DLB 116
Gore, Christopher 1946(?)-1988 Obituary 125
Gore, John Francis 1885-1983 Obituary 110
Gore, Mary Elizabeth 1948- 142
Gore, Robert Hayes 1886-1972 Obituary 89-92
Gore, Tipper
See Gore, Mary Elizabeth
Gore, William Jay 1924- 9-12R
Goreau, Angeline 1951- 102
Gore-Booth, Paul Henry 1909-1984 Obituary 113
Gorecki, Jan 1926- 57-60
Gorelick, Bryna Siegel
See Siegel-Gorelick, Bryna
Gorelick, Molly C. 1920- 21-24R
See also SATA 9
Gorelik, Mordecai 1899-1990 CAP-2
Obituary 131
Earlier sketch in CA 23-24
Goren, Arthur A(ryeh) 1926- 127
Brief entry 111
Goren, Charles H(enry) 1901-1991 CANR-48
Obituary 134
Earlier sketch in CA 69-72
Goren, Judith 1933- 61-64
Goren, Roberta C. 1943-1983 135
Gorenko, Anna Andreevna
See Akhmatova, Anna
Gorenstein, Paul 1934- 114
Gorenstein, Shirley 1928- 73-76
Gorer, Geoffrey (Edgar) 1905-1985 69-72
Obituary 116
Gores, Joe
See Gores, Joseph N(icholas)
Gores, Joseph N(icholas) 1931- CANR-54
Earlier sketches in CA 25-28R, CANR-10, 28
Gorey, Edward (St. John) 1925- CANR-30
Earlier sketches in CA 5-8R, CANR-9
Interview in CANR-30
See also CLR 36
See also DLB 61
See also MAICYA
See also SATA 29, 70
See also SATA-Brief 27
Gorey, Hays 57-60
Gorgias of Leontini c. 485B.C.-376B.C. DLB 176
Gorham, Charles Orson 1911-1975 CANR-6
Obituary 61-64
Earlier sketch in CA 1-4R
See also SATA 36
Gorham, J(eanne) U(rich) 1920- 53-56
Gorham, Maurice Anthony Coneys 1902- 9-12R
Gorham, Michael
See Folsom, Franklin (Brewster)
Gorkin, Jess 1913-1985 Obituary 115
Gorky, Maxim 1868-1936
See Peshkov, Alexei Maximovich
See also DAB
See also SSC 28
See also TCLC 8
See also WLC
Gorlach, Manfred
See Goerlach, Manfred
Gorling, Lars
See Goerling, Lars
Gorman, Beth
See Paine, Lauran (Bosworth)
Gorman, Burton W(illiam) 1907- 29-32R
Gorman, Ed
See Gorman, Edward
Gorman, Edward 1941- 138
Gorman, George H. 1916-1982 Obituary 106
Gorman, Ginny
See Zachary, Hugh
Gorman, James 1949- 152
Gorman, John Andrew 1938- 41-44R
Gorman, Katherine (?)-1972 CAP-2
Earlier sketch in CA 29-32
Gorman, Martha 1953- 147
Gorman, Michael E. 1952- 139
Gorman, Ralph 1897-1972 Obituary 37-40R
Gorman, T. Walter 1916(?)-1972 Obituary 37-40R
Gorman, Thomas David 1919-1986 123
Obituary 120
Gorman, Tom
See Gorman, Thomas David
Gormley, Beatrice 1942- 113
See also SATA 39
See also SATA-Brief 35
Gormley, Gerard (Joseph) 1931- CANR-14
Earlier sketch in CA 81-84
Gormley, Mike 1945- 69-72
Gorn, Janice L(eonora) 1915- 53-56
Gorn, Michael H. 1950- 139
Gorn, Mordechai Martin 1890-1986 Obituary 119
Gorney, Roderic 1924- 73-76
Gorney, Sondra 1918- 45-48
Gorni, Yosef
See Gorny, Yosef
Gornick, Vivian 1935- 101
Gorny, Joseph
See Gorny, Yosef
Gorny, Yosef 1933- 130
Goro, Fritz 1901-1986 Obituary 121
Gorodetsky, Gabriel 1945- 69-72
Gorog, Judith (Katharine Allen) 1938- CANR-45
Earlier sketch in CA 114
See also SATA 39, 75
Gorostiza, Celestino HW
Gorostiza, Jose 1901-1973 131
See also HW
Gorovitz, Samuel 1938- 140
Gorrell, Lorraine 146
Gorrell, Robert Mark 1914- CANR-5
Earlier sketch in CA 1-4R
Gorse, Brendan
See Benson, Gerard
Gorsky, Susan Rubinow 1944- 144
Gorsline, Douglas (Warner) 1913-1985 CANR-9
Obituary 116
Earlier sketch in CA 61-64
See also SATA 11
See also SATA-Obit 43
Gorsline, (Sally) Marie 1928- 106
See also SATA 28
Gorsline, S. M.
See Gorsline, (Sally) Marie
Gorst, Elliot Marcet 1885-1973 Obituary 104
Gortner, Ross A(iken), Jr. 1912- 5-8R
Gortner, Willis Alway 1913- 108
Gorton, Kaitlyn
See Emerson, Kathy Lynn
Gorton, Richard A. 1932- CANR-7
Earlier sketch in CA 57-60
Goryan, Sirak
See Saroyan, William
Goscilo, Helena 1945- 118
Goscinny, Rene 1926-1977 117
Obituary 113
See also CLR 37
See also SATA 47
See also SATA-Brief 39
Gosden, Freeman F(isher) 1899-1982 Obituary 108
Gosden, Peter Henry John Heather 1927- 93-96
Gosden, Roger 1948- 165
Gosdin, Rex 1938(?)-1983 Obituary 109
Gose, Elliott B(ickley), Jr. 1926- 33-36R
Gose, Peter 1955- 150
Goshay, Robert C. 1931- 13-16R
Goshen, Charles E(rnest) 1916- CANR-13
Earlier sketch in CA 21-24R
Goshen-Gottstein, Esther 1928- 137
Goshgarian, Gary 1942- 112
Goshorn, Elizabeth 1953- 61-64
Goslin, David A. 1936- 9-12R
Gosling, J(ustin) C(yril) B(ertrand) 1930- 77-80
Gosling, John Neville 1905- 5-8R
Gosling, Nigel 1909-1982 129
Obituary 106
Gosling, Paula 1939- CANR-57
Earlier sketches in CA 111, CANR-30
Gosling, William Flower 1901- 5-8R
Goslovich, Marianne
See Brown, Morris Cecil
Gosnell, Betty
See Gosnell, Elizabeth Duke Tucker
Gosnell, Elizabeth Duke Tucker 1921- 29-32R
Gosnell, Harold F(oote) 1896-1997 41-44R
Obituary 156
Gosoon, Stephen 1554-1624 DLB 172
Goss, Clay(ton E.) 1946- CANR-42
Earlier sketch in CA 57-60
See also BW 2
See also SATA 82
Goss, Cynthia Flanagan 1957- 149
Goss, Glenda Dawn 1947- 151
Gosse, Edmund (William) 1849-1928 Brief
entry 117
See also DLB 57, 144, 184
See also TCLC 28
Gosselin, Chris(topher C.) 1929- 110
Gosselin, Peter G. 1951- 133
Gosset, W(illiam) P(atrick) 1946- 126
Gossett, Philip 1941- CANR-15
Earlier sketch in CA 89-92
Gossett, Thomas F. 1916- 13-16R
Gossman, Lionel 1929- CANR-7
Earlier sketch in CA 17-20R
Gossop, Michael 1948- 127
Gostelow, Mary 1943- CANR-8
Earlier sketch in CA 61-64
Goswami, Amit 1936- 129
Goswami, Maggie 1937- 117
Gotanda, Philip Kan 1949(?)- 163
Gotchi, Iris 1933- 132
Gotesky, Rubin 1906- 45-48
Gotfryd, Bernard 1924- 133
Gotfurt, Frederick 1902(?)-1973 Obituary 104

Gotlieb, Phyllis Fay (Bloom) 1926- CANR-7
Earlier sketch in CA 13-16R
See also CLC 18
See also DLB 88
Gotlieb, Sondra 1936- 144
Brief entry 111
Goto, Hiromi 1966- 165
Goto, Junichi 1951- 141
Gotoff, Harold C(harles) 1936- Brief entry 112
Gots, Ronald E(ric) 1943- 65-68
Gotschalk, Felix C. 1929- 161
Gotshalk, D(ilman) W(alter) 1901-1973 .... CANR-6
Earlier sketch in CA 1-4R
Gott, K(enneth) D(avidson) 1923- 81-84
Gott, Richard (Willoughby) 1938- 81-84
Gottehrer, Barry H. 1935- 13-16R
Gotterer, Malcolm H(arold) 1924- 37-40R
Gottesfeld, Evelyn 1948- 104
Gottesfeld, Mary L. 1926(?)-1984 Obituary 113
Gottesman, Irving I(sadore) 1930- 37-40R
Gottesman, Ronald 1933- CANR-13
Earlier sketch in CA 33-36R
Gottesman, S. D.
See Kornbluth, C(yril) M.
and Lowndes, Robert A(ugustine) W(ard)
and Pohl, Frederik
Gottfried, Alex 1919- 1-4R
Gottfried, Manfred 1900-1985 Obituary 117
Gottfried, Martin 1933- CANR-63
Earlier sketches in CA 21-24R, CANR-14
Gottfried, Robert R(ichard) 1948- 154
Gottfried, Robert Steven 1949- 111
Gottfried, Ted
See Gottfried, Theodore Mark
Gottfried, Theodore Mark 1928- CANR-18
Earlier sketch in CA 33-36R
See also SATA 85
Gottfried von Strassburg fl. c. 1210- ...... DLB 138
Gotthelf, Jeremias 1797-1854 .... DLB 133
Gottlieb, Adolph 1903-1974 Obituary 49-52
Gottlieb, Alan M(erril) 1947- CANR-57
Earlier sketch in CA 125
Gottlieb, Alex 1906-1988 Obituary 126
Gottlieb, Alma 1954- 138
Gottlieb, Annie 1946- 135
Gottlieb, Arthur 1929- 137
Gottlieb, Beatrice 1925- 144
Gottlieb, Beatrice M. 1889(?)-1979 Obituary .. 89-92
Gottlieb, Bernhardt Stanley 1898- 1-4R
Gottlieb, Carl 143
Gottlieb, Carla 1912- 119
Gottlieb, Darcy 1922- 77-80
Gottlieb, Elaine 61-64
Gottlieb, Erika (Simon) 1938- 148
Gottlieb, Freema (Peninah) 1946- 137
Gottlieb, Gerald 1923- 5-8R
See also SATA 7
Gottlieb, Gilbert 1929- 138
Gottlieb, Lois Davidson 1926- 17-20R
Gottlieb, Moshe R(aphael) 1931- 113
Gottlieb, Naomi R(uth) 1925- 57-60
Gottlieb, Paul 1936- 93-96
Gottlieb, Robert A(dams) 1931- 129
Brief entry 125
Gottlieb, Robin (Grossman) 1928- CANR-2
Earlier sketch in CA 1-4R
Gottlieb, Stephen E. 1941- 138
Gottlieb, (Anne Ruth) Vera 1945- CANR-49
Earlier sketch in CA 117
Gottlieb, William P(aul) 1917- 101
See also SATA 24
Gottman, John M(ordechai) 1942- CANR-12
Earlier sketch in CA 69-72
Gottschalk c. 804-c. 866 .... DLB 148
Gottschalk, Elin Toona
See Toona, Elin(-Kai)
Gottschalk, Laura Riding
See Jackson, Laura (Riding)
Gottschalk, Louis (Reichenthal) 1899-1975 ....
CANR-9
Obituary 57-60
Earlier sketch in CA 13-16R
Gottschalk, Louis A(ugust) 1916- CANR-41
Earlier sketches in CA 53-56, CANR-5, 19
Gottschalk, Paul A. 1939- 61-64
Gottschalk, Shimon S. 1929- 89-92
Gottschalk, Stephen 1940- 77-80
Gottschalk, Edward M(aurice) 1915- 133
Gottsched, Johann Christoph 1700-1766 ... DLB 97
Gottsegen, Abby J. 1956- 105
Gottsegen, Gloria Behar 1930- 77-80
Gottshall, Franklin Henry 1902- CANR-2
Earlier sketch in CA 5-8R
Gottstein, Esther Goshen
See Goshen-Gottstein, Esther
Gottwald, Norman Karol 1926- 108
Gotwals, Vernon (Detwiler, Jr.) 1924- 5-8R
Gotz, Ignacio L.
See Goetz, Ignacio L.
Gotzsche, Anne-Lise 1939- 97-100
Goubert, Pierre 1915- 136
Goud, Anne 1917- 61-64
Goudeket, Maurice 1889-1977 Obituary 69-72
Goudey, Alice E. 1898- 73-76
See also SATA 20
Goudge, Eileen 1950- 126
See also AAYA 6
See also SATA 88
Goudge, Elizabeth (de Beauchamp) 1900-1984 ....
CANR-5
Obituary 112
Earlier sketch in CA 5-8R
See also DAM POP
See also DLB 191
See also MAICYA
See also SATA 2
See also SATA-Obit 38
Goudie, Andrew Shaw 1945- CANR-38
Earlier sketches in CA 49-52, CANR-1, 17
Goudinoff, Peter Alexis 1941- 112
Goudiss, Maria Agnes D'Elia 1941- 114
Goudsmit, Samuel A(braham) 1902-1978 157
Obituary 81-84
Gouge, Orson
See Larner, Jeremy
Gougeon, Len (G.) 1947- 135
Gough, Barry Morton 1938- CANR-58
Earlier sketches in CA 61-64, CANR-11, 30
Gough, Bill
See Gough, William (John)
Gough, Catherine
See Mulgan, Catherine
See also SATA 24
Gough, John W(iedhofft) 1900- 13-16R
Gough, Kathleen
See Aberle, Kathleen Gough
Gough, Lawrence 168
Gough, Michael 1939- 147
Gough, Philip 1908- .... SATA 45
Gough, Vera 25-28R
Gough, William (John) 1945- 131
Gough-Cooper, Jennifer 1942- 146
Gougov, Nikola Delchev 1914- CANR-37
Earlier sketch in CA 45-48
Goulart, Frances Sheridan 1938- CANR-25
Earlier sketches in CA 57-60, CANR-7
Goulart, Ron(ald Joseph) 1933- CANR-7
Earlier sketch in CA 25-28R
See also SATA 6
Goulbourne, Harry 1948- 137
Gould, Alan
See Canning, Victor
Gould, Alberta 1945- 161
See also SATA 96
Gould, Alfred Ernest 1909- 5-8R
Gould, Allan (Mendel) 1944- 132
Gould, Beatrice Blackmar 1898-1989 .... CAP-2
Obituary 127
Earlier sketch in CA 25-28
Gould, (Charles) Bruce 1898-1989 Obituary 129
Gould, Bruce Grant 1942- CANR-22
Earlier sketch in CA 45-48
Gould, Bryan 1939- 136
Gould, Carol C. 1946- 103
Gould, Cecil (Hilton Monk) 1918-1994 .... CANR-9
Obituary 145
Earlier sketch in CA 21-24R
Gould, Chester 1900-1985 .... CANR-30
Obituary 116
Earlier sketch in CA 77-80
See also AAYA 7
See also SATA 49
See also SATA-Obit 43
Gould, Douglas Parsons 1919- 1-4R
Gould, Ed(win Orrin) 1936- CANR-16
Earlier sketch in CA 93-96
Gould, Felix CAP-1
Earlier sketch in CA 11-12
Gould, James A(dams) 1922- 33-36R
Gould, James L. 1945- 130
Gould, James Warren 1924- CANR-2
Earlier sketch in CA 5-8R
Gould, Janice 1949- 147
Gould, Jay R(eid) 1906- CANR-24
Earlier sketch in CA 45-48
Gould, Jean R(osalind) 1909-1993 .... CANR-21
Obituary 142
Earlier sketches in CA 5-8R, CANR-3
See also SATA 11
See also SATA-Obit 77
Gould, Joan 1927- 107
Gould, John (Thomas) 1908- 65-68
Gould, John A(llen) 1944- 57-60
Gould, Joseph E(dmund) 1912- 9-12R
Gould, Josiah B(ancroft) 1928- 45-48
Gould, Joy
See Boyum, Joy Gould
Gould, Judith
See Bienes, Nicholas Peter
Gould, Leroy C. 1937- 93-96
Gould, Leslie 1902-1977 Obituary 73-76
Gould, Lettie
See Paxson, Ethel
Gould, Lewis L(udlow) 1939- 41-44R
Gould, Lilian CANR-2
Earlier sketch in CA 49-52
See also SATA 6
Gould, Lois CANR-29
Earlier sketch in CA 77-80
See also CLC 4, 10
See also MTCW 1
Gould, Marilyn 1928- .... SATA 15, 76
Gould, Mary Earle 1885- 5-8R
Gould, Maurice M. 1909- CANR-5
Earlier sketch in CA 5-8R
Gould, Michael
See Girsh, Myers L.
Gould, Milton Samuel 1909- 93-96
Gould, Peter R(obin) 1932- CANR-51
Earlier sketches in CA 1-4R, CANR-27
Gould, Philip 1925- 124
Gould, Randall 1898(?)-1979 Obituary 89-92
Gould, Richard A(llan) 1939- CANR-7
Earlier sketch in CA 53-56
Gould, Roger L(ouis) 1935- Brief entry 110
Gould, Ronald 1904- 102
Gould, Shirley (Goldman) 81-84
Gould, Stephen Jay 1941- CANR-56
Earlier sketches in CA 77-80, CANR-10, 27
Interview in CANR-27
See also AAYA 26
See also BEST 90:2
See also MTCW 1
Gould, Steven (Charles) 1955- 140
See also SATA 95
Gould, Wallace 1882-1940 .... DLB 54
Gould, Warwick 1947- 110
Gould, Wesley Larson 1917- CANR-2
Earlier sketch in CA 1-4R
Gould, William B(enjamin IV) 1936- 132
Brief entry 118
Goulden, Joseph C. (Jr.) 1934- CANR-31
Earlier sketches in CA 17-20R, CANR-8
Goulden, Mark 1896(?)-1980 Obituary 101
Goulder, Grace
See Izant, Grace Goulder
Goulding, Brian 1933- 103
Goulding, Dorothy Jane 1923- 65-68
Goulding, Edwin (John) 1938- 163
Goulding, Peter Geoffrey 1920- 106
Goulding, Ray(mond Walter) 1922-1990 . CANR-36
Obituary 131
Earlier sketch in CA 85-88
Gouldner, Alvin W(ard) 1920-1980 ...... CANR-17
Obituary 102
Earlier sketch in CA 13-16R
See also MTCW 1
Gouled, Vivian G(loria) 1911- 41-44R
Goulet, Denis A. 1931- CANR-15
Earlier sketch in CA 41-44R
Goulet, John 1942- 85-88
Goulet, Robert (Joseph) 1924- 1-4R
Goulet, Rosalina Morales 1930- 119
Goulett, Harlan M(ador) 1927-1969 .... CAP-2
Earlier sketch in CA 21-22
Goulianos, Joan Rodman 1939- 49-52
Gouliashki, (Stoianov) Andrei 1914- CANR-19
Earlier sketch in CA 101
Goullart, Peter 1902- CAP-1
Earlier sketch in CA 13-14
Goulson, Carlyn Floyd 1922- 113
Goulson, Cary F.
See Goulson, Carlyn Floyd
Goulter, Barbara 141
Gouma-Peterson, Thalia 1933- 140
Gourdie, Thomas 1913- CANR-1
Earlier sketch in CA 1-4R
Gourevitch, Doris-Jeanne 17-20R
Gourevitch, Peter A(lexis) 1943- 112
Gourhan, Andrè (Georges Leandre) Leroi
See Leroi-Gourhan, Andre (Georges Leandre)
Gouri, Haim 1923- 103
Gourlay, Elizabeth 1917- CANR-30
Earlier sketch in CA 112
Gourley, Catherine 1950- 160
See also SATA 95
Gourley, G(erald) Douglas 1911- 1-4R
Gourley, Jay 1947- 73-76
Gourlie, Norah Dundas CAP-1
Earlier sketch in CA 9-10
Gourmont, Remy (-Marie-Charles) de
1858-1915 150
Brief entry 109
See also TCLC 17
Gourse, Leslie 1939- CANR-57
Earlier sketch in CA 1-4R
See also SATA 89
Gourvish, T(erry) R. 1943- 125
Gouzenko, Igor 1919-1982 Obituary 107
Govan, Christine Noble 1898- CANR-2
Earlier sketch in CA 1-4R
See also SATA 9
Govan, Thomas P(ayne) 1907-1979 .... CANR-2
Earlier sketch in CA 45-48
Gove, Doris 1944- .... SATA 72
Gove, Philip Babcock 1902-1972 .... CAP-1
Obituary 37-40R
Earlier sketch in CA 13-14
Gove, Samuel K(imball) 1923- 33-36R
Gove, Walter R(oberts) 1938- 118
Goveia, Elsa V(esta) 1925- 21-24R
Govenar, Alan B(ruce) 1952- 109
Gover, (John) Robert 1929- CANR-70
Earlier sketch in CA 9-12R
Govern, Elaine 1939- 53-56
See also SATA 26
Govi, O.
See Gover, (John) Robert
Govier, Katherine 1948- CANR-40
Earlier sketches in CA 101, CANR-18
See also CLC 51
Govinda, Anagarika Brahmacari 1898- ... CANR-14
Earlier sketch in CA 21-24R
Govinda, Lama Anagarika Brahmacari
See Govinda, Anagarika Brahmacari
Govoni, Albert P(eter) 1914-1982 53-56
Obituary 108
Govoni, Corrado 1884-1965 .... DLB 114
Govoni, Laura E. 1914- 33-36R
Govorchin, Gerald Gilbert 1912- 13-16R
Gow, Andrew Colin 1962- 154
Gow, Donald 1920- 41-44R
Gow, Ronald 1897-1993 .... CANR-13
Obituary 141
Earlier sketches in CAP-2, CA 25-28
Gowan, Donald E(lmer) 1929- 69-72
Gowan, John Curtis 1912-1986 .... CANR-5
Obituary 121
Earlier sketch in CA 13-16R
Gowans, Alan 1923- CANR-40
Earlier sketches in CA 1-4R, CANR-2, 18
Gowar, Antonia
See Dunford, Judith
and Margolis, Susanna
Gowar, Michael Robert 1951- 127
Gowar, Mick
See Gowar, Michael Robert
Gowen, (Samuel) Emmett 1902- CAP-1
Earlier sketch in CA 11-12
Gowen, James A(nthony) 1928-1981 .... 17-20R
Obituary 134
Gowen, Kenneth K. 1924- 166
Gower, Herschel 1919- 5-8R
Gower, John c. 1330-1408 .... DLB 146
Gowers, Ernest (Arthur) 1880-1966 Obituary . 89-92
Gowin, D(ixie) Bob 1925- CANR-26
Earlier sketch in CA 108
Gowing, Lawrence (Burnett) 1918-1991 ..... 9-12R
Obituary 133
Gowing, Margaret (Margaret Mary) 1921- 81-84
Gowing, Peter Gordon 1930- 53-56
Gowland, Mariano E(zequiel) 1933- 5-8R
Goy, Richard J(ohn) 1947- 118
Goyder, George Armin 1908-1997 105
Obituary 156
Goyen, (Charles) William 1915-1983 ..... CANR-71
Obituary 110
Earlier sketches in CA 5-8R, CANR-6
Interview in CANR-6
See also AITN 2
See also CLC 5, 8, 14, 40
See also DLB 2
See also DLBY 83
Goyeneche, Gabriel
See Avalle-Arce, Juan Bautista de
Goyer, Robert S(tanton) 1923- CANR-16
Earlier sketch in CA 41-44R
Goytisolo, Jose Agustin 1928- .... DLB 134
Goytisolo, Juan 1931- CANR-61
Earlier sketches in CA 85-88, CANR-32
See also CLC 5, 10, 23
See also DAM MULT
See also HLC
See also HW
See also MTCW 1
Gozzano, Guido 1883-1916 154
See also DLB 114
See also PC 10
Gozzi, Raymond D(ante) 1920- 116
Graaf, Peter
See Youd, (Christopher) Samuel
Grabar, Andre 1896- 111
Grabar, Oleg 1929- CANR-51
Earlier sketch in CA 124
Grabbe, Christian Dietrich 1801-1836 ..... DLB 133
Grabbe, Crockett L(ane) 1951- 138
Grabbe, Paul 1902- 93-96
Graber, Alexander 1914- CANR-1
Obituary 159
Earlier sketch in CA 1-4R
See also SATA 7, 98
Graber, (George) Alexander 1914-1997 159
See also SATA 98
Graber, Doris A. 1923- CANR-13
Earlier sketch in CA 33-36R
Graber, Gerry S(amuel) 1928- 81-84
Graber, Julia A. 1961- 161
Graber, Richard (Fredrick) 1927- 85-88
See also SATA 26
Graber Miller, Keith Allen 1959- 164
Grabes, Herbert 1936- 130
Grabianski, Janusz 1928-1976 .... CANR-2
Earlier sketch in CA 45-48
See also SATA 39
See also SATA-Obit 30
Grabill, Joseph L. 1931- 29-32R
Grabner-Haider, Anton 1940- 73-76
Grabo, Norman Stanley 1930- CANR-49
Earlier sketch in CA 1-4R
Graboff, Abner 1919- 107
See also SATA 35
Grabois, Aryeh 1930- 105
Grabosky, Peter Nils 1945- 85-88
Grabow, Stephen (Harris) 1943- 121
Grabowski, Z(bigniew) Anthony 1903- 5-8R
Graburn, Nelson H(ayes) H(enry) 1936- ... CANR-1
Earlier sketch in CA 45-48
Grace, Alexander M.
See Farcau, Bruce
Grace, Carol
See Matthau, Carol
Grace, Deborah
See Winer, Deborah Grace
Grace, Edward
See de Grazia, Edward
Grace, F(rances Jane) 111
See also SATA 45
Grace, Gerald R(upert) 1936- CANR-22
Earlier sketch in CA 45-48
Grace, Helen K(ennedy) 1935- 53-56
Grace, J. Peter 1913-1995 126
Obituary 148
Grace, Joan C(arroll) 1921- 61-64
Grace, John Patrick 1942- CANR-31
Earlier sketch in CA 112
Grace, Joseph
See Hornby, John (Wilkinson)
Grace, Nancy McCampbell 1952- 151
Grace, Patricia 1937- .... CLC 56
Grace, Sherrill E(lizabeth) 1944- 110
Grace, William J(oseph), Jr. 1948- CANR-38
Earlier sketch in CA 111
Grace, William Joseph 1910- CAP-1
Earlier sketch in CA 13-14
Gracey, Harry L(ewis) 1933- 41-44R

Gracia, Jorge J(esus) E(miliano) 1942- ... CANR-56
  Earlier sketches in CA 109, CANR-30
  See also HW
Gracie, Archibald 1859-1912 Brief entry 122
Gracq, Julien
  See Poirier, Louis
  See also CLC 11, 48
  See also DLB 83
Gracy, David B(ergen) II 1941- CANR-16
  Earlier sketch in CA 25-28R
Gracza, Margaret Young 1928- 13-16R
  See also SATA 56
Grad, Bonnie L(ee) 1949- 117
Grad, Eli 1928- 115
Grad, Frank P. 1924- 33-36R
Grad, Laurie Burrows 1944- 168
Grade, Arnold (Edward) 1928- 29-32R
Grade, Chaim 1910-1982 93-96
  Obituary 107
  See also CLC 10
Gradidge, (John) Roderick (Warlow) 1929- ....
  CANR-41
  Earlier sketch in CA 117
Gradon, Pamela O(live) E(lizabeth) 1915- ... 97-100
Graduate of Oxford, A
  See Ruskin, John
Gradwohl, David M(ayer) 1934- CANR-51
  Earlier sketch in CA 125
Grady, Don(ald Wyndham) 1929- 115
Grady, Henry W. 1850-1889 .... DLB 23
Grady, James (Thomas) 1949- CANR-22
  Earlier sketch in CA 104
Grady, Ronan Calistus, Jr. 1921- 49-52
Grady, Tex
  See Webb, Jack (Randolph)
Grae, Ida 1918- 97-100
Graeber, Charlotte Towner 134
  See also SATA 56
  See also SATA-Brief 44
Graebner, Alan 1938- 61-64
Graebner, Norman A. 1915- CANR-49
  Earlier sketches in CA 13-16R, CANR-7, 24
Graebner, Walter 1909- CAP-1
  Earlier sketch in CA 13-16
Graebner, William Sievers 1943- 104
Graedon, Joe (David) 1945- 77-80
Graedon, Teresa 1947- 127
Graef, Hilda C(harlotte) 1907- 5-8R
Graeff, Grace M. 1918- 21-24R
Graeme, Bruce
  See Jeffries, Graham Montague
Graeme, David
  See Jeffries, Graham Montague
Graeme, Roderic
  See Jeffries, Roderic (Graeme)
Graeme, Sheila 1944- 25-28R
Graeub, Ralph 1921- 144
Graf, Le Roy Philip 1915- 41-44R
Graf, Oskar Maria 1894-1967 Obituary 115
  See also DLB 56
Graf, Rudolf F. 1926- 9-12R
Graf, William L. 1947- 156
Graff, Dale E(dward) 1934- 168
Graff, George 1886-1973 Obituary 41-44R
Graff, Gerald (Edward) 1937- CANR-31
  Earlier sketch in CA 29-32R
Graff, Harvey J. 1949- CANR-55
  Earlier sketch in CA 127
Graff, Henry F(ranklin) 1921- CANR-17
  Earlier sketches in CA 1-4R, CANR-1
Graff, Polly Anne Colver
  See Colver, Anne
Graff, (S.) Stewart 1908- CANR-29
  Earlier sketch in CA 49-52
  See also SATA 9
Grafftey, Heward 1928- 127
Grafftey-Smith, Laurence Barton
  1892-1989 Obituary 128
Grafton, Ann
  See Owens, Thelma
Grafton, Anthony T(homas) 1950- 166
Grafton, Carl 1942- 53-56
Grafton, David 1930- 126
Grafton, Garth
  See Duncan, Sara Jeannette
Grafton, Richard fl. 1534-1573 .... DLB 170
Grafton, Sue 1940- CANR-55
  Earlier sketches in CA 108, CANR-31
  See also AAYA 11
  See also BEST 90:3
  See also DAM POP
Gragg, Rod 1950- 134
Graglia, Lino A(nthony) 1930- 69-72
Graham, A(lexander) John 1930- CANR-8
  Earlier sketch in CA 13-16R
Graham, A(lexander) S(teel) 1917- 104
Graham, Ada 1931- CANR-4
  Earlier sketch in CA 29-32R
  See also SATA 11
Graham, Aelred 1907-1984 .... CANR-5
  Obituary 114
  Earlier sketch in CA 5-8R
Graham, Alastair 1945- 141
  See also SATA 74
Graham, Alice Walworth 1905- CANR-5
  Earlier sketch in CA 1-4R
Graham, Alistair (Dundas) 1938- CANR-46
  Earlier sketch in CA 49-52
Graham, Andrew Guillemard
  1913-1981 Obituary 103
Graham, Angus (Charles) 1919-1991 ...... 17-20R
  Obituary 134
Graham, Arthur Kennon
  See Harrison, David L(ee)
Graham, Billy
  See Graham, William Franklin

Graham, Bob 1942- 165
  See also CLR 31
  See also SATA 63, 101
Graham, Brenda Knight 1942- 103
  See also SATA 32
Graham, Carlotta
  See Wallmann, Jeffrey M(iner)
Graham, Caroline 1931- 119
Graham, Charles S.
  See Tubb, E(dwin) C(harles)
Graham, Charlotte
  See Bowden, Joan Chase
Graham, Clarence H. 1906-1971 Obituary .. 33-36R
Graham, Cosmo 1956- 138
Graham, Daniel O., Jr. 1952- 151
Graham, Daniel O(rrin) 1925- 132
Graham, David (Duane) 1927- 69-72
Graham, Desmond 1940- 73-76
Graham, Don(ald R.) 1947- 133
Graham, Don B. 1940- CANR-39
  Earlier sketches in CA 102, CANR-18
Graham, Donald W(ilkinson) 1903- CAP-2
  Earlier sketch in CA 29-32
Graham, Edward M(ontgomery) 1944- 141
Graham, Eleanor 1896-1984 73-76
  Obituary 112
  See also SATA 18
  See also SATA-Obit 38
Graham, Elizabeth
  See Edmonds, Arthur Denis
Graham, Ennis
  See Molesworth, Mary Louisa
Graham, Frank, Jr. 1925- CANR-4
  Earlier sketch in CA 9-12R
  See also SATA 11
Graham, Fred P(atterson) 1931- 37-40R
Graham, Gene S(wann) 1924- 41-44R
Graham, George J(ackson), Jr. 1938- CANR-48
  Earlier sketch in CA 45-48
Graham, George Rex 1813-1894 .... DLB 73
Graham, Gerald (Sandford) 1903-1988 102
  Obituary 126
Graham, Grace 1910- CAP-1
  Earlier sketch in CA 13-14
Graham, Gwethalyn 1913-1965 148
  See also DLB 88
Graham, Harriet 1935- 127
Graham, Harry Edward 1940- 29-32R
Graham, Heather
  See Pozzessere, Heather Graham
Graham, Henry 1930- 103
Graham, Howard Jay 1905- CAP-2
  Earlier sketch in CA 33-36
Graham, Hugh
  See Barrows, (Ruth) Marjorie
Graham, Hugh Davis 1936- CANR-13
  Earlier sketch in CA 21-24R
Graham, Ian (James Alastair) 1923- CANR-2
  Earlier sketch in CA 45-48
Graham, Ilse 1914-1988 .... CANR-8
  Obituary 127
  Earlier sketch in CA 57-60
Graham, J. W. 1925- 93-96
Graham, J(ames) Walter 1906- 1-4R
Graham, James
  See Patterson, Harry
Graham, Jefferson 1956- 145
Graham, John
  See Phillips, David Graham
Graham, John 1926- 33-36R
  See also SATA 11
Graham, John Alexander 1941- 25-28R
Graham, John D. 1956- 168
Graham, John Remington 1940- 33-36R
Graham, John Thomas 1928- 53-56
Graham, Jorie 1951- CANR-63
  Earlier sketch in CA 111
  See also CLC 48
  See also DLB 120
Graham, Jory 1925-1983 .... CANR-13
  Obituary 109
  Earlier sketch in CA 29-32R
Graham, Joseph M. 1911(?)-1971 Obituary 104
Graham, Katharine (Meyer) 1917- CANR-71
  Earlier sketch in CA 105
  See also AITN 1
  See also DLB 127
Graham, (George) Kenneth 1936- 77-80
Graham, Kennon
  See Harrison, David L(ee)
Graham, Larry
  See Graham, Lawrence (Otis)
Graham, Lawrence (Otis) 1962- 116
  See also SATA 63
Graham, Lawrence S(herman) 1936- CANR-47
  Earlier sketch in CA 45-48
Graham, Lee E. 1913(?)-1977 Obituary 73-76
Graham, Lloyd M. 1889- 97-100
Graham, Loren R. 1933- CANR-13
  Earlier sketch in CA 21-24R
Graham, Lorenz (Bell) 1902-1989 .... CANR-25
  Obituary 129
  Earlier sketch in CA 9-12R
  See also BW 1
  See also CLR 10
  See also DLB 76
  See also MAICYA
  See also SAAS 5
  See also SATA 2, 74
  See also SATA-Obit 63
Graham, Malcolm 1923- 53-56
Graham, Margaret Althea 1924- 9-12R
Graham, Margaret Bloy 1920- 77-80
  See also SATA 11
Graham, Martha 1894-1991 129
  Obituary 134

Graham, Matthew
  See Arnold, Peter
Graham, Michael 1898-1972 Obituary 104
Graham, Michael Angelo 1921-1985 Obituary .. 117
Graham, Milton D(uke) 1916- 45-48
Graham, Neile 1958- 113
Graham, Neill
  See Duncan, W(illiam) Murdoch
Graham, (Roger) Neill 1941- CANR-26
  Earlier sketch in CA 109
Graham, Otis L., Jr. 1935- CANR-11
  Earlier sketch in CA 21-24R
Graham, Patricia Albjerg 1935- 25-28R
Graham, Peter W(illiam) 1951- CANR-47
  Earlier sketch in CA 121
Graham, Philip Leslie 1915-1963 Obituary .. 89-92
  See also DLB 127
Graham, R(obert) B(ontine) Cunninghame
  See Cunninghame Graham, R(obert) B(ontine)
  See also DLB 98, 135, 174
Graham, Rachel (Metcalf) 1895- CAP-1
  Earlier sketch in CA 13-16
Graham, Ramona
  See Cook, Ramona Graham
Graham, Richard 1934- CANR-34
  Earlier sketches in CA 29-32R, CANR-15
Graham, Robert
  See Haldeman, Joe (William)
Graham, Robert G. 1925- CANR-12
  Earlier sketch in CA 25-28R
Graham, Robin Lee 1949- 49-52
  See also SATA 7
Graham, Ron 1948- 133
Graham, Ruth
  See Evans, Jean
Graham, Sean 1920- 21-24R
Graham, Sheilah 1904(?)-1988 108
  Obituary 127
  See also AITN 1
Graham, Shirley
  See Du Bois, Shirley Graham
  See also DLB 76
Graham, Sonia
  See Sinclair, Sonia
Graham, Stephen 1884-1975 Obituary 93-96
  See also DLB 195
Graham, (Maude Fitzgerald) Susan 1912- .. 17-20R
Graham, Thomas F(rancis) 1923- 21-24R
Graham, Tom
  See Lewis, (Harry) Sinclair
Graham, Vanessa
  See Fraser, Anthea
Graham, Victor E(rnest) 1920- 93-96
Graham, Virginia
  See Guttenberg, Virginia
Graham, W(illiam) Fred 1930- 33-36R
Graham, W(illiam) S(ydney) 1918-1986 73-76
  Obituary 118
  See also CLC 29
  See also DLB 20
Graham, William Franklin 1918- CANR-71
  Earlier sketches in CA 9-12R, CANR-20, 42
Graham, Winston (Mawdsley) 1910- CANR-66
  Earlier sketches in CA 49-52, CANR-2, 22, 45
  See also CLC 23
  See also DLB 77
Graham-Barber, Lynda 1944- 113
  See also SATA 42
Graham-Cameron, M.
  See Graham-Cameron, M(alcolm) G(ordon)
Graham-Cameron, M(alcolm) G(ordon) 1931- .. 123
  See also SATA 53
  See also SATA-Brief 45
Graham-Cameron, Mike
  See Graham-Cameron, M(alcolm) G(ordon)
Graham-Campbell, David (John) 1912- 113
Grahame, Kenneth 1859-1932 136
  Brief entry 108
  See also CLR 5
  See also DAB
  See also DLB 34, 141, 178
  See also MAICYA
  See also SATA 100
  See also TCLC 64
  See also YABC 1
Graham Scott, Peter 1923- 108
Graham-White, Anthony 1940- 61-64
Graham-Yooll, Andrew M(ichael) 1944- .. CANR-28
  Earlier sketch in CA 108
Grahn, Judith L. 1940- 122
  Brief entry 116
  Interview in 122
  See also CAAS 29
Grahn, Judy
  See Grahn, Judith L.
Grainger, A(nthony) J(ohn) 1929- 33-36R
Grainger, J(ohn) H(erbert) 1917- 77-80
Grainger, John D(ownie) 1939- 144
Grainger, Margaret 1936- 116
Grainger, Martin Allerdale 1874-1941 .... DLB 92
Gralapp, Leland Wilson 1921- 13-16R
Gram, Harold A(lbert) 1927- 25-28R
Gram, Moltke (Stefanus) 1938- CANR-13
  Earlier sketch in CA 69-72
Gramatky, Hardie 1907-1979 .... CANR-3
  Obituary 85-88
  Earlier sketch in CA 1-4R
  See also AITN 1
  See also CLR 22
  See also DLB 22
  See also MAICYA
  See also SATA 1, 30
  See also SATA-Obit 23
Grambling, Lois G. 1927- .... SATA 71
Grambs, David (Lawrence) 1938- 146

Grambs, Jean D(resden) 1919-1989 ...... CANR-7
  Obituary 129
  Earlier sketch in CA 17-20R
Gramer, Rod 1953- 147
Gramet, Charles 1-4R
Gramick, Jeannine 1942- 113
Grammaticus
  See Blaiklock, Edward Musgrave
Grammer, June Amos 1927- .... SATA 58
Grampp, William D(yer) 1914- 33-36R
Grams, Armin 1924- 45-48
Gran, Peter 1941- 156
Granados, Paul
  See Kent, Arthur William Charles
Granat, Robert 1925- CANR-2
  Earlier sketch in CA 1-4R
Granatstein, J(ack) L(awrence) 1939- ... CANR-10
  Earlier sketch in CA 25-28R
Granbeck, Marilyn
  See Henderson, M(arilyn) R(uth)
Granberg, W(ilbur) J(ohn) 1906- 5-8R
Granberry, Edwin 1897- CAP-2
  Earlier sketch in CA 21-22
Granby, Milton
  See Wallmann, Jeffrey M(iner)
Grand, Samuel 1912- 107
  See also SATA 42
Grand, Sarah 1854-1943 .... DLB 135, 197
Granda, Chabuca
  See Larco, Isabel Granda
Grandbois, Alain 1900-1975 148
  See also DLB 92
Grande, Luke M. 1922- CANR-2
  Earlier sketch in CA 5-8R
Grande Vitesse
  See Walkerley, Rodney Lewis (de Burgh)
Grandfield, Raymond J(oseph) 1931- 53-56
Grandin, Temple 1947- 154
Grandinetti, Fred M. 1961- 148
Grandower, Elissa
  See Waugh, Hillary Baldwin
Grandville, J. J.
  See Gerard, Jean Ignace Isidore
Grandville, Jean Ignace Isidore Gerard
  See Gerard, Jean Ignace Isidore
Grandy, Richard (Edward) 1942- 77-80
Granelli, Roger 1950- 151
Granfield, Linda 1950- CANR-60
  Earlier sketch in CA 128
  See also SATA 96
Grange, Chris
  See Gnaegy, Charles
Grange, Cyril 1900- CAP-1
  Earlier sketch in CA 13-16
Grange, Peter
  See Nicole, Christopher (Robin)
Granger, (Patricia) Ann 1939- 143
Granger, Bill 1941- 131
  Brief entry 127
Granger, Bruce Ingham 1920- CANR-47
  Earlier sketch in CA 1-4R
Granger, Byrd Howell 1912- 107
Granger, Clive W(illiam) J(ohn) 1934- CANR-8
  Earlier sketch in CA 9-12R
Granger, Darius John
  See Marlowe, Stephen
Granger, Guy
  See Green, Kay
Granger, Margaret Jane 1925(?)-1977 Obituary 104
  See also SATA-Obit 27
Granger, Michele 1949- 152
  See also SATA 88
Granger, Peggy
  See Granger, Margaret Jane
Granger, Percy 1945-1997 136
  Obituary 157
Granich, Irving 1894-1967 97-100
  Obituary 45-48
  See also Gold, Michael
Granick, David 1926- 1-4R
Granick, Harry 1898- CANR-48
  Earlier sketch in CA 85-88
Granik, (S.) Theodore 1906-1970 Obituary .. 89-92
Granit, Arthur 1917- 120
Granite, Harvey R. 1927- CANR-15
  Earlier sketch in CA 33-36R
Granite, Tony
  See Politella, Dario
Grannis, Chandler B(rinkerhoff) 1912- Brief
  entry 111
Granovetter, Mark S. 1943- 85-88
Granovsky, Anatoli 1922-1974 Obituary 53-56
Granovsky, Timofei Nikolaevich 1813-1855 .. DLB
  198
Granowsky, Alvin 1936- 21-24R
  See also SATA 101
Gransden, Antonia 1928- CANR-30
  Earlier sketch in CA 77-80
Granstaff, Bill 1925- .... SATA 10
Grant, Alan
  See Kennington, (Gilbert) Alan
Grant, Alexander T(homas) K(ingdom) 1906- . 53-56
Grant, Ambrose
  See Raymond, Rene (Brabazon)
Grant, Anne MacVicar 1755-1838 .... DLB 200
Grant, Anne Underwood 1946- 168
Grant, Anthony
  See Pares, Marion (Stapylton)
Grant, Barbara L.
  See Lachman, Barbara
Grant, Barbara M(oll) 1932- 53-56
Grant, Barry Keith 1947- 138
Grant, Ben
  See Henderson, M(arilyn) R(uth)
Grant, Brian W. 1939- CANR-7
  Earlier sketch in CA 57-60

Grant, Bruce 1893-1977 .... CANR-6
Obituary 69-72
Earlier sketch in CA 1-4R
See also SATA 5
See also SATA-Obit 25
Grant, Bruce Alexander 1925- 107
Grant, C. B. S.
See Haga, Enoch J.
Grant, Charles L. 1942- 85-88
Grant, Cynthia D. 1950- CANR-42
Earlier sketches in CA 104, CANR-20
See also AAYA 23
See also SATA 33, 77
Grant, Daniel 1954- 150
Grant, David
See Thomas, Craig (David)
Grant, Don
See Glut, Donald F(rank)
Grant, Donald J. 1939-1984 Obituary 113
Grant, Dorothy 1927- 114
Grant, Dorothy Fremont 1900- CAP-2
Earlier sketch in CA 23-24
Grant, Duncan (James Corrowr) 1885-1978 148
See also DLBD 10
Grant, Elliott Mansfield 1895-1969 .... CANR-5
Earlier sketch in CA 5-8R
Grant, Ellsworth Strong 1917- 57-60
Grant, Eva 1907- CANR-49
Earlier sketch in CA 49-52
See also SATA 7
Grant, Evva H. 1913-1977 Obituary 104
See also SATA-Obit 27
Grant, Frederick C(lifton) 1891-1974 ..... CANR-47
Obituary 49-52
Earlier sketch in CA 1-4R
Grant, George (Parkin) 1918-1988 Obituary 126
See also DLB 88
Grant, George Monro 1835-1902 ....DLB 99
Grant, Gerald 1938- 81-84
Grant, Gordon 1875-1962 102
See also SATA 25
Grant, Graeme 1961- 151
Grant, Gwen(doline Ellen) 1940- CANR-22
Earlier sketch in CA 106
See also SATA 47
Grant, H. Roger 1943- 89-92
Grant, Harry J(ohnston) 1881-1963 Obituary ... 114
See also DLB 29
Grant, Hilda Kay 1910- 1-4R
Grant, Isabel F(rances) 1887-1983 Obituary ... 110
Grant, J(ohn) B(arnard) 1940- CANR-28
Earlier sketches in CA 57-60, CANR-6
Grant, Jack
See Grant, J(ohn) B(arnard)
Grant, James
See Crowther, Bruce (Ian)
Grant, James Edward 1905-1966 Obituary 113
See also DLB 26
Grant, James G. 1926(?)-1979 Obituary 89-92
Grant, James Russell 1924- CANR-17
Earlier sketch in CA 101
Grant, Jane
See Leader, (Evelyn) Barbara (Blackburn)
Grant, Jane (Cole) 1895-1972 .... CAP-2
Obituary 33-36R
Earlier sketch in CA 25-28
Grant, Jill 1951- 148
Grant, Joan
See Kelsey, Joan Marshall
Grant, Joanne B(enzel) 1940- 106
Grant, John 1933- CANR-45
Earlier sketch in CA 77-80
Grant, John E(rnest) 1925- CANR-47
Earlier sketch in CA 41-44R
Grant, John J. 1932- 53-56
Grant, John Webster 1919- CANR-6
Earlier sketch in CA 5-8R
Grant, Judith 1929- 21-24R
Grant, Kay 21-24R
Grant, Kerry S. 1945- 121
Grant, Landon
See Gribble, Leonard (Reginald)
Grant, (Alice) Leigh 1947- ....SATA 10
Grant, Louis T(heodore) 1943- 53-56
Grant, Madeleine Parker 1895- 73-76
Grant, Margaret
See Franken, Rose (Dorothy)
Grant, Mary A(melia) 1890- CAP-2
Earlier sketch in CA 25-28
Grant, Mary Kathryn 1941- 81-84
Grant, Matthew G.
See May, Julian
Grant, Maxwell
See Gibson, Walter B(rown)
and Lynds, Dennis
Grant, Michael 1914- CANR-50
Earlier sketches in CA 1-4R, CANR-4, 25
Grant, Myrna (Lois) 1934- CANR-4
Earlier sketch in CA 53-56
See also SATA 21
Grant, Neil 1938- CANR-34
Earlier sketches in CA 33-36R, CANR-15
See also SATA 14
Grant, Nicholas
See Nicole, Christopher (Robin)
Grant, Nigel (Duncan Cameron) 1932- CANR-7
Earlier sketch in CA 17-20R
Grant, Ozro F. 1908- CAP-2
Earlier sketch in CA 21-22
Grant, Patrick 1941- 132
Grant, Richard 1948- 147
See also SATA 80
Grant, Richard B(abson) 1925- CANR-4
Earlier sketch in CA 1-4R
Grant, Robert B(ruce) 1933- 45-48
Grant, Robert M(cQueen) 1917- 65-68
Grant, Roderick 1941- Brief entry 112
Grant, Skeeter
See Spiegelman, Art
Grant, Stephanie 160
Grant, Ulysses S. III 1881-1968 Obituary 111
Grant, Verne E(dwin) 1917- 53-56
Grant, Vernon W(esley) 1904- 17-20R
Grant, W(illiam) Leonard 1914- 17-20R
Grant, Wilson Wayne 1941- 97-100
Grant, Wyn(ford) 1947- CANR-35
Earlier sketch in CA 114
Grant, Zalin (Belton) 1941- 73-76
Grant-Adamson, Lesley 1942- CANR-66
Earlier sketches in CA 121, CANR-47
Grant Duff, Shiela 1913- 159
Grantham, Alexander (William George Herder)
1899- CAP-2
Earlier sketch in CA 19-20
Grantham, Dewey Wesley 1921- CANR-1
Earlier sketch in CA 1-4R
Grantland, Keith
See Beaumont, Charles
Granton, Ester Fannie 1914(?)-1980 Obituary .. 101
Grant Wallace, Lewis
See Wallace, Lewis Grant
Granville, Evelyn Boyd 1924- 161
Granville, Joseph E(nsign) 1923- 65-68
Granville, W. Wilfred 1905- CAP-1
Earlier sketch in CA 9-10
Granville-Barker, Harley 1877-1946 Brief entry . 104
See also Barker, Harley Granville
See also DAM DRAM
See also TCLC 2
Granzotto, Gianni
See Granzotto, Giovanni Battista
Granzotto, Giovanni Battista 1914-1985 166
Grape, Oliver
See Wood, Christopher (Hovelle)
Grapho
See Oakley, Eric Gilbert
Grass, Guenter (Wilhelm) 1927- CANR-20
Earlier sketch in CA 13-16R
See also CLC 1, 2, 4, 6, 11, 15, 22, 32, 49, 88
See also DA
See also DAB
See also DAC
See also DAM MST, NOV
See also DLB 75, 124
See also MTCW 1
See also WLC
Grassi, Joseph A(ugustus) 1922- CANR-41
Earlier sketches in CA 103, CANR-19
Grassi, Maggi Lidchi
See Lidchi Grassi, Maggi
Grasso, Domenico 1917- 73-76
Grasty, Charles H. 1863-1924 .... DLB 25
Grater, Michael 1923- .... SATA 57
Grathwohl, Larry D(avid) 1947- 65-68
Grattan, C(linton) Hartley 1902-1980 ..... CANR-1
Obituary 101
Earlier sketch in CA 1-4R
Grattan, Virginia L(ee) 1932- 115
Grattan-Guinness, I. 1941- 73-76
Gratton, Thomas
See Hulme, T(homas) E(rnest)
Gratus, Jack 1935- CANR-48
Earlier sketch in CA 93-96
Grau, Joseph A(ugust) 1921- 65-68
Grau, Shirley Ann 1929- CANR-69
Earlier sketches in CA 89-92, CANR-22
Interview in CANR-22
See also CLC 4, 9
See also DLB 2
See also MTCW 1
See also SSC 15
Graubard, Mark A. 1904- CANR-5
Earlier sketch in CA 1-4R
Graubard, Paul S. 1932- 103
Graubard, S. R.
See Graubard, Stephen R(ichards)
Graubard, Stephen R(ichards) 1924- 161
Brief entry 113
Graubart, David 1907(?)-1984 Obituary 112
Grauer, Ben(jamin Franklin)
1908-1977 Obituary 69-72
Grauer, Neil A(lbert) 1947- 122
Graulich, Melody 1951- 128
Grauman, Lawrence, Jr. 1935- 33-36R
Graupe, Daniel 1934- 41-44R
Graupera, Carlos M(anuel) 1915- 49-52
Grava, Sigurd 1934- 77-80
Gravagnuolo, Benedetto 1949- 112
Grave, S(elwyn) A(lfred) 1916- 5-8R
Gravel, Fern
See Hall, James Norman
Gravel, Mike 1930- 41-44R
Gravelle, Jane G(ibson) 1947- 150
Gravelle, Karen 1942- 135
See also SATA 78
Gravely, William B(ernard) 1939- 49-52
Graver, Elizabeth 1964- CANR-71
Earlier sketch in CA 135
See also CLC 70
Graver, Jane (Ann) 1931- 117
Graver, Lawrence 1931- 25-28R
Graver, Suzanne 1936- 117
Graversen, Pat 1935- 109
Graves, Allen W(illis) 1915- 17-20R
Graves, Barbara Farris 1938- 41-44R
Graves, Charles Parlin 1911-1972 .... CANR-4
Obituary 37-40R
Earlier sketch in CA 5-8R
See also SATA 4
Graves, Edgar B(aldwin) 1898-1983 Obituary .. 109
Graves, Eleanor MacKenzie 1926- 102
Graves, John (Alexander III) 1920- CANR-68
Earlier sketches in CA 13-16R, CANR-9
See also DLBY 83
Graves, Keller
See Rogers, Evelyn
Graves, Leon B(erneil) 1946- 29-32R
Graves, Michael A(rthur) R(oy) 1933- 131
Graves, Nora Calhoun 1914- 73-76
Graves, Phillip E(arl) 1945- 115
Graves, Ralph (Augustus) 1924- 138
Graves, Richard 1715-1804 .... DLB 39
Graves, Richard L(atshaw) 1928- 57-60
Graves, Richard L(ayton) 1931- 53-56
Graves, Richard Perceval 1945- CANR-51
Earlier sketches in CA 65-68, CANR-9, 26
See also CLC 44
Graves, Robert (von Ranke) 1895-1985 . CANR-36
Obituary 117
Earlier sketches in CA 5-8R, CANR-5
See also CDBLB 1914-1945
See also CLC 1, 2, 6, 11, 39, 44, 45
See also DAB
See also DAC
See also DAM MST, POET
See also DLB 20, 100, 191
See also DLBD 18
See also DLBY 85
See also MTCW 1
See also PC 6
See also SATA 45
Graves, Susan B(ernard) 1933- 41-44R
Graves, Tricia
See Graversen, Pat
Graves, Valerie
See Bradley, Marion Zimmer
Graves, W(illiam) Brooke 1899- CAP-1
Earlier sketch in CA 9-10
Graves, Wallace 1922- 33-36R
Graves, Warren 1933- 128
Graveson, R(onald) H(arry) 1911- 122
Grawbarger, Josephine (Clara) 1908- 121
Grawoig, Sheila
See Raeschild, Sheila
Gray, A(lbert) W(illiam) 1940- CANR-71
Earlier sketch in CA 127
Gray, Alasdair (James) 1934- CANR-69
Earlier sketches in CA 126, CANR-47
Interview in 126
See also CLC 41
See also DLB 194
See also MTCW 1
Gray, Alexander 1882-1968 .... 5-8R
Gray, Alfred 1939- 146
Gray, Alfred O(rren) 1914- CANR-7
Earlier sketch in CA 17-20R
Gray, Amlin 1946- 138
See also CLC 29
Gray, Angela
See Daniels, Dorothy
Gray, Anne 1931- CANR-9
Earlier sketch in CA 65-68
Gray, Asa 1810-1888 .... DLB 1
Gray, Barry 1916-1996 155
Gray, Basil 1904-1989 .... CAP-1
Obituary 128
Earlier sketch in CA 9-10
Gray, Betsy
See Poole, Gray Johnson
Gray, Bettyanne 1934- 81-84
Gray, Bradford H(itch) 1942- 57-60
Gray, Captain Bill
See Gray, William Bittle
Gray, Caroline
See Nicole, Christopher (Robin)
Gray, Charles A(ugustus) 1938- 17-20R
Gray, Chris Hables 1953- 164
Gray, Clifford F. 1930- 25-28R
Gray, Darrell 1945- 65-68
Gray, David 1838-1861 .... DLB 32
Gray, David 1927-1983 Obituary 110
Gray, Dorothea Helen Forbes
(?)-1983 Obituary 110
Gray, Dorothy (Kamer) 1936- 69-72
Gray, Dorothy Kate 1918- 102
Gray, Douglas 1930- 117
Gray, Dulcie CANR-24
Earlier sketches in CA 5-8R, CANR-3
Gray, Dwight E(lder) 1903- CAP-2
Earlier sketch in CA 23-24
Gray, Eden 1907- 93-96
Gray, Edna Redmond 1905(?)-1983 Obituary .. 110
Gray, Edwyn 1927- 41-44R
Gray, Elizabeth Janet
See Vining, Elizabeth Gray
Gray, Ellington
See Jacob, Naomi Ellington
Gray, Ernest
See Gray, Ernest Alfred
Gray, Ernest A.
See Gray, Ernest Alfred
Gray, Ernest Alfred 1908- 118
Gray, Farnum 1940- 49-52
Gray, Floyd (Francis) 1926- CANR-10
Earlier sketch in CA 25-28R
Gray, Francine du Plessix 1930- CANR-33
Earlier sketches in CA 61-64, CANR-11
Interview in CANR-11
See also CAAS 2
See also BEST 90:3
See also CLC 22
See also DAM NOV
See also MTCW 1
Gray, Genevieve S(tuck) 1920- 33-36R
See also SATA 4
Gray, George Hugh 1922- CANR-7
Earlier sketch in CA 17-20R
Gray, Gibson 1922- 33-36R
Gray, Giles Wilkeson 1889- 5-8R
Gray, Gordon 1909-1982 Obituary 109
Gray, H(enry) Peter 1924- Brief entry 111
Gray, Harold (Lincoln) 1894-1968 107
See also SATA 33
See also SATA-Brief 32
Gray, Harold James 1907- 107
Gray, Harriet
See Robins, Denise (Naomi)
Gray, Ian 1951- 142
Gray, J(esse) Glenn 1913-1977 .... 37-40R
Obituary 73-76
Gray, J(ames) M(artin) 1930- 53-56
Gray, J(ohn) Richard 1929- CANR-5
Earlier sketch in CA 1-4R
Gray, J(ohn) Stanley 1894- CAP-2
Earlier sketch in CA 17-18
Gray, Jack 1927- 103
Gray, James 1899- 13-16R
Gray, James H(enry) 1906- 97-100
Gray, James R(obert) 1921- 33-36R
Gray, Jane
See Evans, Constance May
Gray, Jeffrey A(lan) 1934- 104
Gray, Jenny
See Gray, Genevieve S(tuck)
Gray, John (Henry) 1866-1934 162
Brief entry 119
See also TCLC 19
Gray, John 1951- CANR-66
Earlier sketch in CA 145
Gray, John E(dmund) 1922- 65-68
Gray, John Milner 1889-1970 Obituary 29-32R
Gray, John Morgan 1907- 103
Gray, John Rodger 1913-1984 Obituary 113
Gray, John S(tephens) 1910- 73-76
Gray, John W(ylie) 1935- 17-20R
Gray, Juanita R(uth) 1918- 61-64
Gray, Judith A(nne) 1949- 158
See also SATA 93
Gray, Lee Learner 1924- 73-76
Gray, Les 1929- .... SATA 82
Gray, Libba Moore 1937- .... SATA 83
Gray, Linda Crockett 1943- 109
See also Crockett, Linda
Gray, Luli 1945- 151
See also SATA 90
Gray, Malcolm
See Stuart, Ian
Gray, Margaret E(lla) 1956- 141
Gray, Margaret K. 1949- 123
Gray, Marian
See Pierce, Edith Gray
Gray, Marianne 1947- 110
Gray, Martin 1926- CANR-14
Earlier sketch in CA 77-80
See also AITN 1
Gray, Mayo Loiseau 1938- 104
Gray, Michael H(aslam) 1946- 103
Gray, Muriel 153
Gray, Nicholas Stuart 1922-1981 .... CANR-11
Obituary 103
Earlier sketch in CA 21-24R
See also SATA 4
See also SATA-Obit 27
Gray, Nicolete (Mary) 1911- 103
Gray, Nigel 1941- 85-88
See also SATA 33
Gray, (Lucy) Noel (Clervaux) 1898-1983 65-68
See also SATA 47
Gray, Oscar S(halom) 1926- 29-32R
Gray, Parke H. 1936(?)-1987 Obituary 121
Gray, Patience 1917- 142
Gray, Patricia (Clark) 29-32R
See also SATA 7
Gray, Patsey
See Gray, Patricia (Clark)
Gray, Peter 1908- 41-44R
Gray, Philip
See Perlman, Jess
Gray, Ralph D(ale) 1933- CANR-49
Earlier sketches in CA 21-24R, CANR-8, 24
Gray, Richard
See Gray, J(ohn) Richard
Gray, Richard A. 1927- 154
Gray, Richard B(utler) 1922- CANR-2
Earlier sketch in CA 1-4R
Gray, Richard G(eorge) 1932-1984 Obituary ... 114
Gray, Robert (Archibald Speir) 1942- 134
Gray, Robert F(red) 1912- 17-20R
Gray, Robert Keith 1923- 1-4R
Gray, Robert Mack 1922- 13-16R
Gray, Rod
See Fox, G(ardner) F(rancis)
Gray, Ronald (Douglas) 1919- CANR-22
Earlier sketches in CA 17-20R, CANR-7
Gray, Ronald Francis 1918- 5-8R
Gray, Russell
See Fischer, Bruno
Gray, Seymour 1911- 130
Gray, Simon (James Holliday) 1936- CANR-69
Earlier sketches in CA 21-24R, CANR-32
See also CAAS 3
See also AITN 1
See also CLC 9, 14, 36
See also DLB 13
See also MTCW 1
Gray, Spalding 1941- 128
See also CLC 49, 112
See also DAM POP
See also DC 7
Gray, Stephen E. 1925- 73-76

Gray, Thomas 1716-1771 ... CDBLB 1660-1789
See also DA
See also DAB
See also DAC
See also DAM MST
See also DLB 109
See also PC 2
See also WLC
Gray, Tony
See Gray, George Hugh
Gray, Vanessa
See Aeby, Jacquelyn
Gray, Wellington Burbank 1919-1977 ... 1-4R
Obituary ... 103
Gray, William Bittle 1891-1974 ... CANR-11
Earlier sketch in CA 13-16R
Gray, William R(alph) 1946- ... 97-100
Gray, Wood 1905(?)-1977 Obituary ... 69-72
Graybar, Lloyd J(oseph) 1938- ... 57-60
Graybeal, David M(cConnell) 1921- ... 17-20R
Graybill, Florence Curtis 1898- ... 97-100
Graybill, Ron(ald D.) 1944- ... 33-36R
Grayeff, Felix 1906- ... 77-80
Grayland, Eugene C(harles) 1916-1976 .. CANR-11
Earlier sketches in CAP-1, CA 9-10
Grayland, V. Merle
See Grayland, Valerie (Merle Spanner)
Grayland, Valerie (Merle Spanner) ... CANR-11
Earlier sketch in CA 9-12R
See also SATA 7
Graymont, Barbara ... 81-84
Graysmith, Robert 1942- ... CANR-41
Earlier sketch in CA 117
Grayson, A(lbert) K(irk) 1935- ... 41-44R
Grayson, Alice Barr
See Grossman, Jean Schick
Grayson, Benson Lee 1932- ... 93-96
Grayson, C(harles) Jackson, Jr. 1923- ... 106
Grayson, Cary Travers, Jr. 1919- ... CANR-10
Earlier sketch in CA 17-20R
Grayson, Cecil 1920-1998 ... 13-16R
Obituary ... 166
Grayson, Charles 1905-1973 Obituary ... 41-44R
Grayson, David
See Baker, Ray Stannard
Grayson, Donald K. 1945- ... 146
Grayson, Henry (Wesley) 1910- ... 41-44R
Grayson, Janet 1934- ... 53-56
Grayson, L(inda) M(ary) 1947- ... 89-92
Grayson, Marion F. 1906-1976 ... CANR-4
Obituary ... 69-72
Earlier sketch in CA 5-8R
Grayson, Melvin J(ay) 1924- ... 45-48
Grayson, Paul 1946- ... 147
See also SATA 79
Grayson, Richard
See Grindal, Richard
Grayson, Richard (A.) 1951- ... CANR-57
Earlier sketches in CA 85-88, CANR-14, 31
See also CLC 38
Grayson, Robert A. 1927- ... 33-36R
Grayson, Ruth (King) 1926- ... 73-76
Grayson, William John 1788-1863 ... DLB 3, 64
Graystone, Lynn
See Brennan, Joseph Lomas
Grayzel, Solomon 1896-1980 ... CANR-4
Earlier sketch in CA 1-4R
Grazhdanin, Misha
See Burgess, Michael (Roy)
Graziano, Anthony M(ichael) 1932- ... 93-96
Grealey, Thomas Louis 1916- ... 81-84
Grealis, Walt(er) 1929- ... 77-80
Grealy, Desmond 1923(?)-1979 Obituary ... 85-88
Grealy, Lucy 1963- ... 147
Grean, Stanley 1920- ... 29-32R
Greanias, George C. 1948- ... 126
Great Comte, The
See Hawkesworth, Eric
Great Merlini, The
See Rawson, Clayton
Greatorex, Wilfred 1921- ... 103
Greaves, Bettina Herbert Bien 1917- ... 144
Greaves, H(arold) R(ichard) G(oring) 1907- ... 5-8R
Greaves, (Brian) John 1898- ... 103
Greaves, Margaret 1914-1995 ... CANR-53
Earlier sketches in CA 25-28R, CANR-18
See also SATA 7, 87
Greaves, Nick 1955- ... 145
See also SATA 77
Greaves, Percy L(aurie), Jr. 1906- ... CANR-48
Earlier sketch in CA 49-52
Greaves, Richard L(ee) 1938- ... CANR-39
Earlier sketches in CA 33-36R, CANR-16
Greaves, William 1926- ... 125
See also BW 1
Grebanier, Bernard (David N.) 1903-1977 ...
CANR-10
Earlier sketch in CA 21-24R
Grebe, Maria Ester 1928- ... 25-28R
Greben, Stanley E(dward) 1927- ... CANR-45
Earlier sketch in CA 120
Greber, Judith 1939- ... 116
Grebstein, Lawrence C(harles) 1937- ... 29-32R
Grebstein, Sheldon Norman 1928- ... CANR-5
Earlier sketch in CA 1-4R
Grech, Nikolai Ivanovich 1787-1867 ... DLB 198
Greco, Jose 1918- ... 85-88
Greco, Margaret
See Fry, Barbara
Gree, Alain 1936- ... 89-92
See also SATA 28
Greeley, Andrew M(oran) 1928- ... CANR-69
Earlier sketches in CA 5-8R, CANR-7, 43
See also CAAS 7
See also CLC 28
See also DAM POP
See also MTCW 1
Greeley, Dana McLean 1908-1986 Obituary ... 119
Greeley, Horace 1811-1872 ... DLB 3, 43, 189
Greeley, Valerie 1953- ... CANR-43
Earlier sketch in CA 118
Green, A(dwin) Wigfall 1900-1971(?) ... CAP-1
Earlier sketch in CA 9-10
Green, Abel 1900-1973 Obituary ... 41-44R
Green, Adam
See Weisgard, Leonard (Joseph)
Green, Adolph 1915- ... 130
Brief entry ... 110
See also DLB 44
Green, Alan (Baer) 1906-1975 ... 53-56
Obituary ... 57-60
Green, Alan Singer 1907- ... 85-88
Green, Andrew (Malcolm) 1927- ... CANR-12
Earlier sketch in CA 73-76
Green, Anita Jane 1940- ... 85-88
Green, Anna Katharine 1846-1935 ... 159
Brief entry ... 112
See also DLB 202
See also TCLC 63
Green, Anne (Mitchell) 1947- ... 120
Green, Anne Canevari 1943- ... SATA 62
Green, Anne M. 1922- ... 1-4R
Green, Arnold W(ilfred) 1914- ... 5-8R
Green, Arthur 1941- ... 145
Green, Arthur S(amuel) 1927- ... 5-8R
Green, Ben K. 1911(?)-1974 Obituary ... 115
See also AITN 1
Green, Benny
See Green, Bernard
Green, Bernard 1927- ... 25-28R
Green, Betty Radley 1926-1978 Obituary ... 111
Green, Brian
See Card, Orson Scott
Green, Bryan S(tuart) W(estmacott) 1901-1993 ...
CAP-1
Obituary ... 140
Earlier sketch in CA 13-14
Green, Celia (Elizabeth) 1935- ... 65-68
Green, Cliff(ord) 1934- ... 131
Green, Connie Jordan 1938- ... 147
See also SATA 80
Green, Constance McLaughlin 1897-1975 ... 9-12R
Obituary ... 61-64
Green, D.
See Casewit, Curtis W(erner)
Green, Daniel W(illiam) E(dward) 1958- ... 121
Green, David 1942- ... 77-80
Green, David Bronte 1910- ... 13-16R
Green, David M(arvin) 1932- ... 41-44R
Green, Deborah 1948- ... 104
Green, December 1961- ... 144
Green, Dennis Howard 1922- ... 110
Green, Donald E(dward) 1936- ... CANR-1
Earlier sketch in CA 45-48
Green, Donald Ross 1924- ... 37-40R
Green, Dorothy (Auchterlonie) 1915- ... 112
Green, Duff 1791-1875 ... DLB 43
Green, Duncan 1958- ... 154
Green, Edith Pinero 1929- ... CANR-15
Earlier sketch in CA 77-80
Green, Edward 1920- ... 13-16R
Green, Edwin 1948- ... CANR-38
Earlier sketch in CA 116
Green, Elisabeth Sara 1940- ... CANR-42
Green, Elizabeth A(dine) H(erkimer) 1906- ... 21-24R
Green, Elizabeth Shippen 1871-1954 ... DLB 188
Green, Elmer Ellsworth 1917- ... 103
Green, Elna C. 1959- ... 166
Green, Ernestene L(everne) 1939- ... 57-60
Green, Evelyn Everett
See Everett-Green, Evelyn
Green, F(rederick) C(harles)
1891-1964 Obituary ... 89-92
Green, Fitzhugh 1917-1990 ... 77-80
Obituary ... 132
Green, Fletcher Melvin 1895-1978 ... CANR-6
Earlier sketch in CA 1-4R
Green, Frederick Pratt 1903- ... 102
Green, Galen 1949- ... 57-60
Green, George D(avid) 1938- Brief entry ... 114
Green, George MacEwan 1931- ... 81-84
Green, George S(herman) 1930- ... 97-100
Green, Georgia M. 1944- ... 93-96
Green, Gerald 1922- ... CANR-8
Earlier sketch in CA 13-16R
See also DLB 28
Green, Gil(bert) 1906-1997 ... 73-76
Obituary ... 158
Green, H(enry) Gordon 1912- ... 110
Green, Hannah
See Greenberg, Joanne (Goldenberg)
Green, Hannah 1927(?)-1996 ... CANR-59
Earlier sketch in CA 73-76
See also CLC 3
Green, Harold P(aul) 1922- ... 13-16R
Green, Harvey 1946- ... CANR-37
Earlier sketch in CA 115
Green, Henry 1905-1973
See Yorke, Henry Vincent
See also CLC 2, 13, 97
See also DLB 15
Green, Hollis Lynn 1933- ... 103
Green, J(ames) C. R. 1949- ... 104
Green, J. Paul 1929- ... 141
Green, James L(eroy) 1919- ... 17-20R
Green, James R(obert) 1944- ... 130
Green, Jane 1937- ... 61-64
See also SATA 9
Green, Jane Nugent 1918- ... 61-64
Green, Janet 1939- ... CANR-30
Earlier sketch in CA 112
Green, Jeffrey M. 1944- ... 140
Green, Jeffrey P(hillip) 1944- ... 111
Green, Jerome Frederic 1928- ... 125
Green, Jerry
See Green, Jerome Frederic
Green, Jesse 1958- ... 139
Green, Jim 1941- ... 114
Green, Joann 1938- ... 115
Green, John Alden 1925- ... CANR-3
Earlier sketch in CA 5-8R
Green, John F. 1943- ... 126
Green, John L(afayette), Jr. 1929- ... CANR-22
Earlier sketch in CA 45-48
Green, Jonas 1712-1767 ... DLB 31
Green, Jonathan (William) 1939- ... CANR-9
Earlier sketch in CA 61-64
Green, Jonathon 1948- ... 134
Green, Joseph 1706-1780 ... DLB 31
Green, Joseph 1931- ... 29-32R
Green, Joseph F(ranklin), Jr. 1924- ... 13-16R
Green, Judith
See Galbraith, Jean
and Rodriguez, Judith Green
Green, Julian (Hartridge) 1900- ... CANR-33
Earlier sketch in CA 21-24R
See also Green, Julien
See also DLB 4, 72
See also MTCW 1
Green, Julien
See Green, Julian (Hartridge)
See also CLC 3, 11, 77
Green, Kay 1927- ... CANR-41
Earlier sketch in CA 117
See also CAAS 11
Green, Kenneth Hart 1953- ... 162
Green, Landis K(night) 1940- ... 57-60
Green, Lawrence W(inter) 1940- ... CANR-42
Earlier sketches in CA 69-72, CANR-12
Green, Leslie Claude 1920- ... 13-16R
Green, Lewis 1946- ... 125
Green, Lewis W(allace) 1932- ... 119
Green, Louis 1929- ... 45-48
Green, Marc Edward 1943- ... CANR-42
Earlier sketch in CA 117
Green, Margaret (Murphy) 1926- ... CANR-1
Earlier sketch in CA 1-4R
Green, Maria A. 1922- ... 144
Green, Maria del Rosario
See Rosario Green (de Heller), Maria del
Green, Mark J(oseph) 1945- ... 41-44R
Green, Martin (Burgess) 1927- ... CANR-56
Earlier sketches in CA 17-20R, CANR-9, 29
Green, Martyn 1899-1975 Obituary ... 57-60
Green, Mary McBurney 1896- ... CAP-2
Earlier sketch in CA 29-32
Green, Mary Moore 1906- ... CAP-1
Earlier sketch in CA 13-14
See also SATA 11
Green, Maureen Patricia 1933- ... 101
Green, (James) Maurice (Spurgeon)
1906-1987 Obituary ... 123
Green, Maurice B(erkeley) 1920- ... 77-80
Green, Maurice R(ichard) 1922- ... 13-16R
Green, Maury 1916-1996 ... 155
Green, Michael Frederick 1927- ... CANR-41
Earlier sketches in CA 102, CANR-19
Green, Michelle 1953- ... 140
Green, Milton D(ouglas) 1903- ... 41-44R
Green, Miranda J(ane Aldhouse) 1947- ... 139
Green, Morton 1937- ... 57-60
See also SATA 8
Green, Norma B(erger) 1925- ... 41-44R
See also SATA 11
Green, O. O.
See Durgnat, Raymond (Eric)
Green, Otis H(oward) 1898- ... 9-12R
Green, Paul (Eliot) 1894-1981 ... CANR-3
Obituary ... 103
Earlier sketch in CA 5-8R
See also AITN 1
See also CLC 25
See also DAM DRAM
See also DLB 7, 9
See also DLBY 81
Green, Paul E(dgar) 1927- ... CANR-51
Earlier sketches in CA 69-72, CANR-11, 27
Green, Peter
See Bulmer, (Henry) Kenneth
Green, Peter (Morris) 1924- ... CANR-4
Earlier sketch in CA 5-8R
Green, Phyllis 1932- ... CANR-17
Earlier sketches in CA 45-48, CANR-1
See also SATA 20
Green, R. P. H. 1943- ... 138
Green, Rayna (Diane) 1942- ... 114
Green, Reginald Herbold 1935- ... CANR-17
Earlier sketch in CA 25-28R
Green, Richard 1936- ... 159
Brief entry ... 111
See also AITN 1
Green, Richard Lancelyn (Gordon) 1953- ... 160
Green, River
See Joyner, Stephen Christopher
Green, Robert
See Smith, Richard Rein
Green, Robert D(avid) 1942- ... 77-80
Green, Robert L(ee) 1933- ... CANR-15
Earlier sketch in CA 65-68
Green, Roger C(urtis) 1932- ... CANR-49
Earlier sketches in CA 45-48, CANR-24
Green, Roger James 1944- ... 123
See also SATA-Brief 52
Green, Roger (Gilbert) Lancelyn 1918-1987 ...
CANR-2
Obituary ... 123
Earlier sketch in CA 1-4R
See also SATA 2
See also SATA-Obit 53
Green, Roland (James) 1944- ... CANR-58
Earlier sketch in CA 77-80
Green, Ronald Michael 1942- ... 85-88
Green, Rosalie B(eth) 1917- ... 1-4R
Green, Rose Basile 1914- ... CANR-39
Earlier sketches in CA 41-44R, CANR-15
Green, (James Le)Roy 1948- ... SATA 89
Green, Samuel 1921(?)-1983 Obituary ... 111
Green, Samuel 1948- ... 77-80
Green, Scott E. 1951- ... 132
Green, Sharon 1942- ... CANR-45
Earlier sketch in CA 120
Green, Sharony Andrews 1967(?)- ... 168
Green, Sheila Ellen 1934- ... CANR-53
Earlier sketches in CA 1-4R, CANR-2, 17, 39
See also SATA 8, 87
Green, Simon
See Green, Simon R(ichard)
Green, Simon R(ichard) 1955- ... 164
Green, Smith Wendell 1917(?)-1987 Obituary ... 124
Green, Stanley 1923-1990 ... CANR-17
Obituary ... 133
Earlier sketches in CA 1-4R, CANR-1
Green, Stephen J(ohn) 1940- ... 131
Green, Susan 1941- ... 81-84
Green, Terence M(ichael) 1947- ... 157
Green, Thomas Andrew 1940- ... 125
Green, Thomas F. 1927- ... 57-60
Green, Thomas Hill 1836-1882 ... DLB 190
Green, Thomas J(ohn) 1946- ... 113
Green, Timothy (Seton) 1936- ... CANR-22
Earlier sketches in CA 49-52, CANR-5
Green, Timothy 1953- ... 155
See also SATA 91
Green, Vincent S(cott) 1953- ... 140
Green, Vivian Hubert Howard 1915- ... 9-12R
Green, William 1926- ... 53-56
Green, William A., Jr. 1935- ... 85-88
Green, William Baillie 1927- ... 118
Green, William M(ark) 1929- ... CANR-35
Earlier sketch in CA 45-48
Greenacre, Phyllis 1894- ... 5-8R
Greenall, Jack 1905-1983 Obituary ... 110
Greenawalt, R(obert) Kent 1936- ... 33-36R
Greenaway, George W(illiam) 1903- ... 118
Greenaway, Gladys 1901- ... 93-96
Greenaway, Kate 1846-1901 ... 137
See also CLR 6
See also DLB 141
See also MAICYA
See also SATA 100
See also YABC 2
Greenaway, Peter 1942- ... 127
Greenbank, Anthony Hunt 1933- ... CANR-19
Earlier sketches in CA 49-52, CANR-4
See also SATA 39
Greenbaum, Fred 1930- ... 37-40R
Greenbaum, Leonard 1930- ... 21-24R
Greenbaum, Sidney 1929-1996 ... CANR-33
Obituary ... 152
Earlier sketches in CA 33-36R, CANR-15
Greenberg, Alfred Henry 1924-1990 Obituary ... 131
Greenberg, Alvin (David) 1932- ... 33-36R
Greenberg, Arthur
See Granit, Arthur
Greenberg, Barbara L(evenson) 1932- ... 53-56
Greenberg, Bernard 1922- ... 69-72
Greenberg, Bernard L(ouis) 1917- ... 41-44R
Greenberg, Bradley S(ander) 1934- ... 104
Greenberg, Carl 1908-1984 Obituary ... 114
Greenberg, Cheryl Lynn 1958- ... 140
Greenberg, Clement 1909-1994 ... CANR-2
Obituary ... 145
Earlier sketch in CA 1-4R
Greenberg, Daniel A. 1934- ... 5-8R
Greenberg, Daniel S. 1931- ... 29-32R
Greenberg, Dolores 1934- ... 112
Greenberg, Douglas 1947- ... 117
Greenberg, Edward (Seymour) 1942- ... 53-56
Greenberg, Eliezer 1897(?)-1977 Obituary ... 69-72
Greenberg, Elinor Miller 1932- ... 143
Greenberg, Eric Rolfe 1945- ... 114
Greenberg, Harvey R. 1935- ... 33-36R
See also SATA 5
Greenberg, Herbert 1935- ... 25-28R
Greenberg, Ira A(rthur) 1924- ... CANR-2
Earlier sketch in CA 49-52
Greenberg, Ivan 1908-1973 ... 85-88
See also Rahv, Philip
Greenberg, Jae W. 1894(?)-1974 Obituary ... 104
Greenberg, James B(rian) 1945- ... 105
Greenberg, Jan 1942- ... JRDA
See also SATA 61
Greenberg, Jan W(eingarten) 1943- ... 118
Greenberg, Jay (R.) 1942- ... 137
Greenberg, Joanne (Goldenberg) 1932- ... CANR-69
Earlier sketches in CA 5-8R, CANR-14, 32
See also AAYA 12
See also CLC 7, 30
See also SATA 25
Greenberg, Jonathan D. 1958- ... 133
Greenberg, Joseph Harold 1915- ... 102
Greenberg, Judith Anne
See Azrael, Judith Anne
Greenberg, Kenneth R(ay) 1930- ... 57-60
Greenberg, Kenneth S. 1947- ... 124
Greenberg, Louis M. 1933- Brief entry ... 112
Greenberg, Martin 1918- ... 140

Greenberg, Martin Harry 1941- 49-52
Greenberg, Martin J. 1945- 131
Greenberg, Melanie Hope 1954- .... SATA 72
Greenberg, Milton 1927- 25-28R
Greenberg, Morrie
See Greenberg, Morris S.
Greenberg, Morris S. 1924- 33-36R
Greenberg, Moshe 1928- 13-16R
Greenberg, Norman 1945- 129
Greenberg, Paul 1937- 69-72
Greenberg, Pearl 1927- 93-96
Greenberg, Polly 1932- 85-88
See also SATA 52
See also SATA-Brief 43
Greenberg, Richard 1959(?)- 138
See also CLC 57
Greenberg, Robert Arthur 1930-1989 ..... CANR-4
Obituary 129
Earlier sketch in CA 1-4R
Greenberg, Roger P(aul) 1941- 131
Greenberg, Selig 1904- 49-52
Greenberg, Selma (Weintraub) 1930-1997 .. 29-32R
Obituary 158
Greenberg, Sidney 1917- CANR-3
Earlier sketch in CA 9-12R
Greenberg, Simon 1901-1993 .... CANR-14
Obituary 142
Earlier sketch in CA 77-80
Greenberg, Stan 1931- 119
Greenberg, Stanley Bernard 1945- 53-56
Greenberg, Uri Zvi 1898-1981 Obituary 103
Greenberger, Allen J(ay) 1937- 41-44R
Greenberger, Evelyn Barish
See Barish, Evelyn
Greenberger, Howard 1924- 45-48
Greenberger, Martin 1931- CANR-8
Earlier sketch in CA 61-64
Greenbie, Barrie B(arstow) 1920- 107
Greenbie, Marjorie Barstow
1889(?)-1976 Obituary 61-64
Greenblat, Cathy S(tein) 1940- 133
Brief entry 118
Greenblatt, Augusta 1912- CANR-6
Earlier sketch in CA 57-60
Greenblatt, Edwin 1920- 49-52
Greenblatt, M(anuel) H(arry) 1922-1972 .... CAP-2
Earlier sketch in CA 17-18
Greenblatt, Richard 1952- 130
Greenblatt, Robert Benjamin 1906-1987 .... CAP-1
Obituary 123
Earlier sketch in CA 11-12
Greenblatt, Stephen J(ay) 1943- 49-52
Greenblum, Joseph 1925- 21-24R
Greenburg, Dan 1936- CANR-25
Earlier sketches in CA 13-16R, CANR-9
See also SATA 102
Greenburger, Francis 1949- 85-88
Greenburger, Ingrid Elisabeth 1913- 104
Greene, A(lvin) C(arl) 1923- CANR-14
Earlier sketch in CA 37-40R
Greene, Adam
See Scott, Peter Dale
Greene, Anthony Hamilton Millard Kirk
See Kirk-Greene, Anthony (Hamilton Millard)
Greene, Asa 1789-1838 .... DLB 11
Greene, Belle da Costa 1883-1950 .... DLB 187
Greene, Bert 1923-1988 .... CANR-27
Obituary 125
Earlier sketches in CA 57-60, CANR-6
Greene, Bette 1934- CANR-4
Earlier sketch in CA 53-56
See also AAYA 7
See also CLC 30
See also CLR 2
See also JRDA
See also MAICYA
See also SAAS 16
See also SATA 8, 102
Greene, Bob
See Greene, Robert Bernard, Jr.
Greene, Carla 1916- CANR-1
Earlier sketch in CA 1-4R
See also SATA 1, 67
Greene, Carol 134
See also SATA 66, 102
See also SATA-Brief 44
Greene, Charles Jerome 1910-1983 Obituary .. 110
Greene, Constance C(larke) 1924- CANR-38
Earlier sketches in CA 61-64, CANR-8
See also AAYA 7
See also JRDA
See also MAICYA
See also SAAS 11
See also SATA 11, 72
Greene, David B(eckwith) 1939- 117
Greene, David H. 1913- 21-24R
Greene, David L(ouis) 1944- Brief entry 114
Greene, David M(ason) 1920- 118
Greene, Donald J(ohnson) 1916-1997 .... CANR-2
Obituary 158
Earlier sketch in CA 1-4R
Greene, Douglas G. 1944- 164
Greene, Ellin 1927- 77-80
See also SATA 23
Greene, Felix 1909-1985 .... CANR-6
Obituary 116
Earlier sketch in CA 1-4R
Greene, Fred
See Cadet, John
Greene, Gael CANR-10
Earlier sketch in CA 13-16R
See also CLC 8
Greene, Gayle 1943- 137
Greene, Graham (Henry) 1904-1991 .... CANR-61
Obituary 133
Earlier sketches in CA 13-16R, CANR-35
See also AITN 2
See also CDBLB 1945-1960
See also CLC 1, 3, 6, 9, 14, 18, 27, 37, 70, 72
See also DA
See also DAB
See also DAC
See also DAM MST, NOV
See also DLB 13, 15, 77, 100, 162, 201
See also DLBY 91
See also MTCW 1
See also SATA 20
See also SSC 29
See also WLC
Greene, Harlan 1953- 137
Greene, Harris 1921- 13-16R
Greene, Harry A. 1889- CAP-2
Earlier sketch in CA 17-18
Greene, Harry J(oseph) 1906- 57-60
Greene, Herbert 1898- CAP-1
Earlier sketch in CA 9-10
Greene, Howard R. 1937- 61-64
Greene, Hugh (Carleton) 1910-1987 102
Obituary 121
Greene, Jack P(hillip) 1931- CANR-40
Earlier sketches in CA 9-12R, CANR-3, 18
Greene, Jacqueline Dembar 1946- 144
See also SATA 76
Greene, James H. 1915- 17-20R
Greene, Janet (Churchill) 1917- 5-8R
Greene, Janice Presser
See Presser, Janice
Greene, Jay E(lihu) 1914- CANR-5
Earlier sketch in CA 5-8R
Greene, Jerry
See Greene, Charles Jerome
Greene, John C(olton) 1917- 89-92
Greene, John William, Jr. 1946- 89-92
Greene, Johnny
See Greene, John William, Jr.
Greene, Jonathan Edward 1943- CANR-12
Earlier sketch in CA 33-36R
Greene, Laura Offenhartz 1935- CANR-47
Earlier sketches in CA 107, CANR-23
See also SATA 38
Greene, Lawrence J. 1943- 113
Greene, Lee S(eifert) 1905- CANR-5
Earlier sketch in CA 13-16R
Greene, Leonard M(ichael) 1918- 109
Greene, Lorenzo Johnston
1899-1988 Obituary 124
Greene, Mabel
See Bean, Mabel Greene
Greene, Mark R. 1923- CANR-5
Earlier sketch in CA 1-4R
Greene, Maxine 1917- CANR-13
Earlier sketch in CA 21-24R
Greene, Melissa Fay 1952- 138
Greene, Mott T(uthill) 1945- CANR-28
Earlier sketch in CA 110
Greene, Naomi 1942- 45-48
Greene, Nathanael 1935- 25-28R
Greene, Owen (John) 1954- 124
Greene, Pamela
See Forman, Joan
Greene, Philip L(eon) 1924- Brief entry 113
Greene, Reynolds W(illiam), Jr. 1924- CANR-2
Earlier sketch in CA 5-8R
Greene, Rhonda Gowler 1955- 168
See also SATA 101
Greene, Richard (Thomas) 1961- 144
Greene, Richard C. 1941- 111
Greene, Richard Leighton 1904-1983 ..... CANR-2
Obituary 111
Earlier sketch in CA 5-8R
Greene, Robert
See Deindorfer, Robert Greene
Greene, Robert 1558-1592 .... DLB 62, 167
Greene, Robert Bernard, Jr. 1947- CANR-27
Earlier sketch in CA 107
Interview in CANR-27
See also DLB 185
Greene, Robert W. 1929- 104
Greene, Robert W(illiam) 1933- Brief entry 111
Greene, Ruth Altman 1896- 73-76
Greene, Sara
See Strong, June
Greene, Sheldon L. 1934- 132
Greene, Shirley E(dward) 1911- 1-4R
Greene, Stephanie 1953- 61-64
Greene, Stephen 1914-1979 Obituary 89-92
Greene, Thomas M(cLernon) 1926- 9-12R
Greene, Victor R(obert) 1933- 25-28R
Greene, Vivian .... AITN 2
Greene, Wade 1933- .... SATA 11
Greene, Walter E. 1929- 25-28R
Greene, Wilda 1911- CANR-9
Earlier sketch in CA 21-24R
Greene, William C. 1933- 13-16R
Greene, Yvonne
See Flesch, Yolande (Catarina)
Greenebaum, Louise G(uggenheim) 1919- ... 69-72
Greener, Leslie 1900-1974 .... CAP-2
Earlier sketch in CA 21-22
Greener, Michael (John) 1931- 25-28R
Greenewalt, Crawford Hallock 1902-1993 . CANR-2
Obituary 142
Earlier sketch in CA 1-4R
Greenfeder, Paul 1925(?)-1983 Obituary 109
Greenfeld, Howard CANR-19
Earlier sketch in CA 81-84
See also SATA 19
Greenfeld, Josh(ua Joseph) 1928- 140
Brief entry 116
See also SATA 62
Greenfeld, Karl Taro 1965(?)- 149
Greenfeld, Liah 1954- 138
Greenfield, Darby
See Ward, Philip
Greenfield, Edward 1928- Brief entry 110
Greenfield, Eloise 1929- CANR-43
Earlier sketches in CA 49-52, CANR-1, 19
Interview in CANR-19
See also BW 2
See also CLR 4, 38
See also JRDA
See also MAICYA
See also SAAS 16
See also SATA 19, 61
Greenfield, Gerald Michael 1943- 114
Greenfield, Harry I. 1922- 127
Brief entry 109
Greenfield, Howard 1937(?)-1986 Obituary 118
Greenfield, Irving A. 1928- 33-36R
Greenfield, James Lloyd 1924- 73-76
Greenfield, Jeanette 134
Greenfield, Jeff 1943- CANR-71
Earlier sketches in CA 37-40R, CANR-24
Greenfield, Jerome 1923- 5-8R
Greenfield, Jerry
See Greenfield, Jerome
Greenfield, Jonas Carl 1926- Brief entry 110
Greenfield, Meg 1930- 128
Brief entry 123
Greenfield, Norman S(amuel) 1923- 41-44R
Greenfield, Patricia Marks 1940- CANR-24
Earlier sketches in CA 21-24R, CANR-9
Greenfield, Sidney M(artin) 1932- 21-24R
Greenfield, Stanley B(rian) 1922- 9-12R
Greenfield, Thelma N. 1922- 25-28R
Greengold, Jane
See Stevens, Jane Greengold
Greengrass, Mark 1949- 118
Greengroin, Artie
See Brown, Harry (Peter McNab, Jr.)
Greenhalgh, P(eter) A(ndrew) L(ivsey) 1945- ......
CANR-1
Earlier sketch in CA 49-52
Greenhalgh, Paul 1955- 130
Greenhaus, Thelma Nurenberg 1903-1984 ....
CANR-42
Obituary 113
See also SATA-Obit 45
Greenhaw, H(arold) Wayne 1940- CANR-24
Earlier sketches in CA 21-24R, CANR-9
Greenhill, Basil (Jack) 1920- CANR-38
Earlier sketches in CA 5-8R, CANR-2, 17
Greenhill, Pauline 1955- 149
Greenhood, (Clarence) David 1895-1983 ..... 1-4R
Obituary 109
Greenhouse, Carol J(ane) 1950- 163
Greenhouse, Linda 1947- 77-80
Greenhow, Robert 1800-1854 .... DLB 30
Greenhut, Melvin L. 1921- 13-16R
Greening, Hamilton
See Hamilton, Charles (Harold St. John)
Greenland, Colin 1954- CANR-56
Earlier sketch in CA 117
Greenlaw, Jean-Pierre 1910- 69-72
Greenlaw, Lavinia (Elaine) 1962- 153
Greenlaw, Paul S(tephen) 1930- CANR-5
Earlier sketch in CA 1-4R
Greenleaf, Barbara Kaye 1942- 29-32R
See also SATA 6
Greenleaf, Peter 1910- 85-88
See also SATA 33
Greenleaf, Richard Edward 1930- 25-28R
Greenleaf, Robert Kiefner 1904- 125
Greenleaf, Stephen (Howell) 1942- 102
Greenleaf, William 1917- 9-12R
Greenlee, Douglas 1935-1979 45-48
Obituary 103
Greenlee, J(acob) Harold 1918- 17-20R
Greenlee, James W(allace) 1933- CANR-11
Earlier sketch in CA 69-72
Greenlee, Sam 1930- 69-72
See also BW 1
Greenlee, Sharon 1935- 145
See also SATA 77
Greenlee, William B. 1872-1953 .... DLB 187
Greenlick, Merwyn R(onald) 1935- 41-44R
Greenman, Robert 1939- CANR-38
Earlier sketch in CA 115
Greenman, Russell Lester 1904-1983 Obituary . 111
Greeno, Gayle 1949- 149
See also SATA 81
Greenough, Horatio 1805-1852 .... DLB 1
Greenough, Malcolm W(helen), Jr. 1926- 128
Greenough, Sarah 1951- 126
Greenough, William Croan 1914-1989 ...... 13-16R
Obituary 130
Greenseid, Diane 1948- .... SATA 93
Greenside, Mark 1944- 159
Greenslade, Roy 1946- 146
Greenslade, S(tanley) L(awrence)
1905-1977 Obituary 111
Greenson, Ralph R(omeo) 1911- Brief entry ... 114
Greenspan, Bud 1927- 103
Greenspan, Cappy Petrash
See Greenspan, Constance Anne Petrash
Greenspan, Charlotte L. 1921- 33-36R
Greenspan, Constance Anne Petrash
1932(?)-1983 Obituary 110
Greenspan, Elaine 1929- 110
Greenspan, Emily 1953- 124
Greenspan, Sophie 1906- 97-100
Greenspan, Stanley I(ra) 1941- 154
Greenspoon, Leonard J(ay) 1945- CANR-30
Earlier sketch in CA 111
Greenspun, Adele Aron 1938- .... SATA 76
Greenspun, H(erman) M(ilton) 1909-1989 ... CAP-2
Obituary 129
Earlier sketch in CA 21-22
See also AITN 2
Greenspun, Hank
See Greenspun, H(erman) M(ilton)
Greenspun, Roger (Austin) 1929- 102
Greenstein, Elaine 1959- .... SATA 82
Greenstein, Fred I(rwin) 1930- CANR-4
Earlier sketch in CA 49-52
Greenstein, George 1940- 130
Greenstein, Jack 1915- 130
Greenstock, David Lionel 1912- 9-12R
Greenstone, J. David 1937- 25-28R
Greenup, Ruth (Robinson)
1912(?)-1984 Obituary 113
Greenwald, G. Jonathan 1943- 142
Greenwald, Harold 1910- CANR-4
Earlier sketch in CA 1-4R
Greenwald, Jeff 1954- 153
Greenwald, Jerry 1923- 57-60
Greenwald, Sheila
See Green, Sheila Ellen
Green-Wanstall, Kenneth 1918- 13-16R
Greenway, Hugh D(avids) S(cott) 1935- 73-76
Greenway, John 1919- 9-12R
Greenway, Roger S(elles) 1934- CANR-4
Earlier sketch in CA 53-56
Greenwell, Dora 1821-1882 .... DLB 35, 199
Greenwood, Barbara 1940- 134
See also SATA 90
Greenwood, David Charles 1927-1984 61-64
Obituary 112
Greenwood, Duncan 1919- 21-24R
Greenwood, Edward Alister 1930- CANR-30
Earlier sketches in CA 29-32R, CANR-12
Greenwood, Frank 1924- CANR-10
Earlier sketch in CA 25-28R
Greenwood, Gordon 1913- CANR-9
Earlier sketch in CA 21-24R
Greenwood, Gordon E(dward) 1935- 37-40R
Greenwood, Grace
See Lippincott, Sara Jane Clarke
Greenwood, Judith Goodwin 1941- 144
Greenwood, Julia Eileen Courtney 1910- CAP-1
Earlier sketch in CA 13-14
Greenwood, Kathryn Moore 1922- 93-96
Greenwood, Lillian Bethel 1932- 104
Greenwood, Marianne (Hederstrom) 1926- ....
CANR-6
Earlier sketch in CA 9-12R
Greenwood, Ned H. 1932- Brief entry 110
Greenwood, Ted
See Greenwood, Edward Alister
Greenwood, Theresa 1936- 29-32R
Greenwood, Val D(avid) 1937- 73-76
Greenwood, Walter 1903-1974 93-96
Obituary 53-56
See also DLB 10, 191
Greer, Ann Lennarson 1944- CANR-43
Earlier sketch in CA 53-56
Greer, Art(hur Ellis, Jr.) 1929- 81-84
Greer, Ben 1948- 102
See also DLB 6
Greer, Carlotta C(herryholmes) 1879-1965 .. CAP-1
Earlier sketch in CA 13-16
Greer, Francesca
See Janas, Frankie-Lee
Greer, Georgeanna H(errmann) 1922- CANR-6
Earlier sketch in CA 57-60
Greer, Germaine 1939- CANR-70
Earlier sketches in CA 81-84, CANR-33
See also AITN 1
See also MTCW 1
Greer, Herb 1929- CANR-8
Earlier sketch in CA 5-8R
Greer, Louise 1899- CAP-1
Earlier sketch in CA 13-16
Greer, Philip 1930-1985 Obituary 116
Greer, Rebecca Ellen 1935- 103
Greer, Richard
See Garrett, (Gordon) Randall (Phillip)
and Silverberg, Robert
Greer, Rita 1942- 97-100
Greer, Scott (Allen) 1922- CANR-43
Earlier sketch in CA 45-48
Greer, Steven (Crawford) 1956- 149
Greer, Thomas H(oag) 1914- 21-24R
Greeson, Janet 1952- 121
Greet, Brian Aubrey 1922- 105
Greet, Kenneth (Gerald) 1918- CANR-25
Earlier sketches in CA 5-8R, CANR-6
Greet, T(homas) Y(oung) 1923- 13-16R
Greet, William Cabell 1901-1972 Obituary .. 37-40R
Greever, William S(t. Clair) 1916- 5-8R
Greeves, Frederic 1903-1985 Obituary 115
Greevy, David U(pton) 1953- 112
Greflinger, Georg 1620(?)-1677 .... DLB 164
Greg, W. R. 1809-1881 .... DLB 55
Greg, W. W. 1875-1959 .... DLB 201
Greger, Debora 1949- CANR-31
Earlier sketch in CA 112
Gregersen, Edgar (Alstrup) 1937- 120
Gregerson, Linda 1950- 149
Gregg, Andrew K. 1929- CANR-15
Earlier sketch in CA 29-32R
See also SATA 81
Gregg, Charles T(hornton) 1927- CANR-40
Earlier sketches in CA 81-84, CANR-14
See also SATA 65
Gregg, Davis W(einert) 1918-1993 .... 17-20R
Obituary 143
Gregg, Hubert 1916- 102

Gregg, James E(rwin) 1927- 21-24R
Gregg, James R. 1914- 21-24R
Gregg, Jess 1926- 61-64
Gregg, John E(dwin) 1925- 45-48
Gregg, Josiah 1806-1850 .... DLB 186
Gregg, Larry
See Leighton, Lauren G(ray)
Gregg, Linda (Alouise) 1942- 113
Gregg, Martin
See McNeilly, Wilfred (Glassford)
Gregg, Pauline 5-8R
Gregg, Richard A(lexander) 1927- 13-16R
Gregg, Robert J(ohn) 1912- Brief entry 110
Gregg, Walter H(arold) 1919- 73-76
See also SATA 20
Gregg, William H. 1904(?)-1983 Obituary 109
Gregor, A(nthony) James 1929- 57-60
Gregor, Arthur 1923- CANR-11
Earlier sketch in CA 25-28R
See also CAAS 10
See also CLC 9
See also SATA 36
Gregor, Carol 1943- 117
Gregor, Howard F(rank) 1920- CANR-2
Earlier sketch in CA 5-8R
Gregor, Lee
See Pohl, Frederik
Gregor, Rex H. 1922- 13-16R
Gregor-Dellin, Martin 1926- 157
Gregori, Leon 1919- .... SATA 15
Gregorian, Joyce Ballou 1946-1991 .... CANR-24
Obituary 147
Earlier sketch in CA 107
See also SATA 30
See also SATA-Obit 83
Gregorian, Vartan 1935- 29-32R
Gregorich, Barbara 1943- CANR-42
Earlier sketch in CA 117
See also SATA 66
Gregorios, Paulos Mar 1922- CANR-11
Earlier sketch in CA 25-28R
Gregorowski, Christopher 1940- CANR-15
Earlier sketch in CA 89-92
See also SATA 30
Gregory, Bettina 1946- 69-72
Gregory, Chuck
See Gnaegy, Charles
Gregory, Diana (Jean) 1933- 97-100
See also SATA 49
See also SATA-Brief 42
Gregory, Dick 1932- CANR-7
Earlier sketch in CA 45-48
Interview in CANR-7
See also BW 1
Gregory, Elizabeth
See Gilford, C(harles) B(ernard)
Gregory, Frederick 1942- 138
Gregory, Freida 1938- 69-72
Gregory, H(ollingsworth) F(ranklin) 1906- 69-72
Gregory, Harry
See Gottfried, Theodore Mark
Gregory, Hilton
See Ferguson, Charles W.
Gregory, Horace (Victor) 1898-1982 .... CANR-22
Obituary 106
Earlier sketches in CA 5-8R, CANR-3
See also DLB 48
Gregory, Isabella Augusta (Persse) 1852-1932 Brief entry 104
See also DLB 10
See also TCLC 1
Gregory, J. Dennis
See Williams, John A(lfred)
Gregory, J. S.
See Gregory, James S(tothert)
Gregory, James S(tothert) 1912-1983 77-80
Obituary 133
Gregory, Jean
See Ure, Jean
Gregory, K(enneth) J(ohn) 1938- 107
Gregory, Kenneth (Malcolm) 1921- 73-76
Gregory, Kristiana 1951- 141
See also SATA 74
Gregory, Lisa
See Camp, Candace (Pauline)
Gregory, Lydia
See Carey, Diane
Gregory, Mark
See Burch, Monte G.
Gregory, Paul Roderick 1941- 53-56
Gregory, Peter 1924- 41-44R
Gregory, Philippa 1954- 131
Gregory, R(ichard) L(angton) 1923- 57-60
Gregory, Richard Claxton
See Gregory, Dick
Gregory, Robert G(ranville) 1924- 41-44R
Gregory, Robert Lloyd 1892- 29-32R
Gregory, Ross 1933- 29-32R
Gregory, Roy 1935- 37-40R
Gregory, Ruth W(ilhelmine) 1910- 77-80
Gregory, Sara
See Gray, A(lbert) W(illiam)
Gregory, Sean
See Hossent, Harry
Gregory, Sinda 1947- 115
Gregory, Stephan
See Pendleton, Don(ald Eugene)
Gregory, Stephen
See Penzler, Otto
Gregory, Stephen 1952- 136
Gregory, Steven
See Jones, Stephen
Gregory, Susan 1945- 108
Gregory, Thomas B(ernard) 1940- 45-48
Gregory, Timothy E(dmund) 1943- 111
Gregory, Vahan 1927- 69-72
Gregory, Valiska 1940- 149
See also SATA 82
Gregory, Violet L(efler) 1907- CANR-8
Earlier sketch in CA 57-60
Gregory, William King 1876-1970 Obituary 29-32R
Gregory, Yvonne 1919(?)-1979 Obituary 89-92
Gregory of Rimini 1300(?)-1358 .... DLB 115
Gregson, Paul
See Oakley, Eric Gilbert
Gregston, Gene 1925- 81-84
Grehan, Ida 1916- 146
Greider, William (Harold) 1936- CANR-71
Earlier sketches in CA 117, CANR-41
Interview in 117
Greif, E(dwin) Charles 1915- 1-4R
Greif, Geoffrey L. 1949- 140
Greif, Martin 1938- CANR-25
Earlier sketches in CA 65-68, CANR-10
Greiff, Barrie S(anford) 1935- 134
Brief entry 114
Greiffenberg, Catharina Regina von 1633-1694 DLB 168
Greig, Cicely (?)-1983 Obituary 116
Greig, Maysie 1902-1971 102
Obituary 104
Greil, Arthur L(awrence) 1949- 139
Greimas, A. J.
See Greimas, Algirdas Julien
Greimas, Algirdas Julien 1917- 132
Greiner, Donald J(ames) 1940- CANR-37
Earlier sketches in CA 45-48, CANR-1, 16
Greinke, (Lawrence) Eric 1948- 41-44R
Greisman, Joan Ruth 1937- 103
See also SATA 31
Grekova, I.
See Ventsel, Elena Sergeevna
Grekova, Irina Nikolaevna
See Ventsel, Elena Sergeevna
Grele, Ronald J(ohn) 1934- 73-76
Gremillion, Joseph 1919- 102
Gremmels, Marion Louise Chapman 1924-1987 111
Obituary 142
Grenander, M(ary) E(lizabeth) 1918-1998 . CANR-4
Obituary 167
Earlier sketch in CA 53-56
Grendahl, J(ay) Spencer 1943- 29-32R
Grendler, Paul F(rederick) 1936- 41-44R
Grendon, Edward
See LeShan, Lawrence L(ee)
Grendon, Stephen
See Derleth, August (William)
Grene, Marjorie (Glicksman) 1910- CANR-25
Earlier sketches in CA 13-16R, CANR-8
Grenelle, Lisa
See Munroe, Elizabeth L(ee)
Grenfell, Joyce (Irene) 1910-1979 .... CANR-20
Obituary 89-92
Earlier sketch in CA 81-84
Grenfell, Wilfred Thomason 1865-1940 .... DLB 92
Grenham, John 1954- 146
Grenier, Judson A(chille) 1930- 89-92
Grenier, Mildred 1917- CANR-12
Earlier sketch in CA 29-32R
Grennan, Eamon 1941- CANR-54
Earlier sketch in CA 133
Grennan, Margaret R(ose) 41-44R
Grenville, Bryan P(eter) 1955- 117
Grenville, J(ohn) A(shley) S(oames) 1928- CANR-5
Earlier sketch in CA 9-12R
Grenville, Kate 1950- CANR-53
Earlier sketch in CA 118
See also CLC 61
Grenville, Pelham
See Wodehouse, P(elham) G(renville)
Grenyer, Norman 1913-1983 Obituary 110
Grenz, Stanley J. 1950- 163
Grescoe, Paul 1939- 165
Greshake, Gisbert 1933- 158
Gresham, Anthony
See Russell, Roy
Gresham, Claude Hamilton, Jr. 1922- CANR-8
Earlier sketch in CA 5-8R
Gresham, Elizabeth (Fenner) 1904- 81-84
Gresham, Grits
See Gresham, Claude Hamilton, Jr.
Gresham, Perry E(pler) 1907- CANR-42
Earlier sketch in CA 45-48
Gresser, Seymour 1926- 29-32R
Gresser, Sy
See Gresser, Seymour
Gressley, Gene M(aurice) 1931- CANR-10
Earlier sketch in CA 17-20R
Greteman, James 1933- 112
Greteman, Jim
See Greteman, James
Gretz, Susanna 1937- CANR-28
Earlier sketch in CA 29-32R
See also SATA 7
Gretzer, John .... SATA 18
Gretzky, Walter 1938- 120
Greulach, Victor A(ugust) 1906- 49-52
Grevatt, Wallace 1925- 129
Greve, Felix Paul (Berthold Friedrich) 1879-1948 141
Brief entry 104
See also Grove, Frederick Philip
See also DAC
See also DAM MST
Greville, Fulke 1554-1628 .... DLB 62, 172
Grew, James Hooper 1906- 103
Grew, Raymond 1930- 13-16R
Grewdead, Roy
See Gorey, Edward (St. John)
Grewer, Eira M(ary) 1931- 21-24R
Grex, Leo
See Gribble, Leonard (Reginald)
Grey, Abby (Bartlett) Weed 1903(?)-1983 Obituary 110
Grey, Anthony 1938- CANR-55
Earlier sketches in CA 29-32R, CANR-29
Grey, Belinda
See Peters, Maureen
Grey, Beryl (Elizabeth) 1927- 109
Grey, Brenda
See Mackinlay, Leila Antoinette Sterling
Grey, Carenna Jane
See Kalpakian, Laura Anne
Grey, Carol
See Lowndes, Robert A(ugustine) W(ard)
Grey, Charles
See Tubb, E(dwin) C(harles)
Grey, David Lennox 1935- 93-96
Grey, Dorothy 1913- 120
Grey, Elizabeth
See Hogg, Elizabeth (Tootill)
Grey, Georgina
See Roby, Mary Linn
Grey, Ian 1918- CANR-2
Earlier sketch in CA 5-8R
Grey, J. David 1935-1993 133
Obituary 140
Grey, Jane 1537-1554 .... DLB 132
Grey, Jerry 1926- CANR-43
Earlier sketches in CA 53-56, CANR-5, 20
See also SATA 11
Grey, Lindsey
See Peel, Colin D(udley)
Grey, Louis
See Gribble, Leonard (Reginald)
Grey, Marian Powys 1883(?)-1972 Obituary 104
Grey, Robert Waters 1943- 49-52
Grey, Robin
See Gresham, Elizabeth (Fenner)
Grey, Sir George K.C.B. 1812-1898 .... DLB 184
Grey, Vivian (Hoffman) 17-20R
Grey, Zane 1872-1939 132
Brief entry 104
See also DAM POP
See also DLB 9
See also MTCW 1
See also TCLC 6
Greybeard the Pirate
See Macintosh, Brownie
Grey Owl
See Belaney, Archibald Stansfeld
See also CLR 32
See also DLB 92
Grey Owl
See Belaney, Archibald Stansfeld
Greyser, Stephen A. 1935- 33-36R
Gri
See Denney, Diana
Gribbin, John 1946- 113
Gribbin, Lenore S. 1922- 33-36R
Gribbin, William James 1943- CANR-17
Earlier sketches in CA 45-48, CANR-1
Gribble, Charles E(dward) 1936- 41-44R
Gribble, Harry Wagstaff (Graham) 1891(?)-1981 Obituary 102
Gribble, James 1938- 29-32R
Gribble, Jennifer 1937- 116
Gribble, Leonard (Reginald) 1908- CANR-60
Earlier sketches in CA 53-56, CANR-7
Gribbons, Warren D(avid) 1921- 29-32R
Grice, Frederick 1910- CANR-3
Earlier sketch in CA 9-12R
See also SATA 6
Grice, Grimes
See Kamp, Irene Kittle
Grice, Julia (Haughey) 1940- CANR-16
Earlier sketch in CA 77-80
Gridban, Volsted
See Tubb, E(dwin) C(harles)
Gridban, Volsted
See Fearn, John Russell
Grider, Dorothy 1915- .... SATA 31
Grider, Jay
See Miller, John Grider
Gridley, Marion E(leanor) 1906-1974 45-48
Obituary 103
See also SATA 35
See also SATA-Obit 26
Gridley, Roy E. 1935- 127
Brief entry 109
Gridzewski, Mieczylawski 1895(?)-1970 Obituary 104
Grieb, Kenneth J. 1939- CANR-12
Earlier sketch in CA 29-32R
Grieb, Lyndal 1940- 61-64
Grieder, Jerome B. 1932- 130
Grieder, Josephine 1939- 53-56
Grieder, Terence 1931- CANR-35
Earlier sketch in CA 114
Grieder, Theodore 1926- 45-48
Grieder, Walter 1924- 41-44R
See also SATA 9
Grieg, Michael 1922- 17-20R
Grieg, (Johan) Nordahl (Brun) 1902-1943 Brief entry 107
See also TCLC 10
Griego, Tony A. 1955- .... SATA 77
Grier, B. R. 1913- 25-28R
Grier, Barbara G(ene Damon) 1933- 107
Grier, Edward F(rancis) 1917- 121
Grier, Eldon 1917- 113
See also DLB 88
Grier, Frances Belle Powner 1886(?)-1980(?) Obituary 104
Grier, Katherine C. 1953- 132
Grier, Roosevelt 1932- 113
Grier, Rosey
See Grier, Roosevelt
Grierson, Edward 1914-1975 .... CANR-59
Earlier sketches in CA 1-4R, CANR-4
Grierson, Francis Durham 1888-1972 Obituary . 104
Grierson, Herbert John Clifford 1886-1960 Obituary 93-96
Grierson, John 1898-1972 Obituary 116
Grierson, John 1909-1977 .... CAP-2
Obituary 69-72
Earlier sketch in CA 19-20
Grierson, (Monica) Linden 1914- CAP-1
Earlier sketch in CA 9-10
Grierson, Philip 1910- CANR-71
Earlier sketch in CA 129
Gries, Tom 1923(?)-1977 Obituary 69-72
Griese, Arnold A(lfred) 1921- CANR-1
Earlier sketch in CA 49-52
See also SATA 9
Grieson, Ronald Edward 1943- CANR-1
Earlier sketch in CA 49-52
Griesse, Carolyn 1941- 107
Griessman, Benjamin Eugene 1934- 41-44R
Griest, Guinevere L(indley) 1924- 65-68
Grieve, Andrew W. 1925- 9-12R
Grieve, C(hristopher) M(urray) 1892-1978 .... CANR-33
Obituary 85-88
Earlier sketch in CA 5-8R
See also MacDiarmid, Hugh and Pteleon
See also CLC 11, 19
See also DAM POET
See also MTCW 1
Grieves, Forest L(eslie) 1938- 53-56
Grifalconi, Ann 1929- CANR-35
Earlier sketches in CA 5-8R, CANR-9
See also CLR 35
See also MAICYA
See also SAAS 16
See also SATA 2, 66
Griff
See Fawcett, F(rank) Dubrez and McKeag, Ernest L(ionel)
Griff
See Fearn, John Russell
Griffen, Edmund
See Du Breuil, (Elizabeth) L(or)inda
Griffen, (James) Jeff(erds) 1923- 13-16R
Griffin, A(rthur) H(arold) 1911- CANR-9
Earlier sketch in CA 21-24R
Griffin, Al 1919- 33-36R
Griffin, Alice 163
Griffin, Anne J.
See Griffin, Arthur J.
Griffin, Arthur J. 1921- CANR-1
Earlier sketch in CA 49-52
Griffin, Barbara C(ook) 1945- 53-56
Griffin, Bartholomew fl. 1596- .... DLB 172
Griffin, Bryan F(rederick) 120
Brief entry 113
Interview in 120
Griffin, C. F.
See Fikso, Eunice Cleland
Griffin, C. S.
See Griffin, Clifford S(tephen)
Griffin, C(harles) W(illiam) 1925- 53-56
Griffin, Charles C(arroll) 1902-1976 Obituary . 65-68
Griffin, Charles Henry 1922- 17-20R
Griffin, Clifford S(tephen) 1929- Brief entry 111
Griffin, (George) Dan(iel) 1937-1984 Obituary . 112
Griffin, David Ray 1939- 77-80
Griffin, Donald (Redfield) 1915- CANR-15
Earlier sketch in CA 37-40R
Griffin, Dustin H(adley) 1943- 120
Griffin, Edward M(ichael) 1937- 89-92
Griffin, Elizabeth May 1985- 155
See also SATA 89
Griffin, Emilie Russell Dietrich 1936- CANR-21
Earlier sketch in CA 103
Griffin, Ernest G(eorge) 1916- 25-28R
Griffin, Gerald 1803-1840 .... DLB 159
Griffin, Gerald G(ehrig) 1933- CANR-9
Earlier sketch in CA 57-60
Griffin, Gillett Good 1928- .... SATA 26
Griffin, Glen C. 1934- CANR-17
Earlier sketch in CA 29-32R
Griffin, (Arthur) Gwyn 1922(?)-1967 Obituary . 89-92
Griffin, Jacqueline P. 1927- 33-36R
Griffin, James A. 1934- 29-32R
Griffin, Jasper 1937- 161
Griffin, Jill 1955- 164
Griffin, John Howard 1920-1980 .... CANR-2
Obituary 101
Earlier sketch in CA 1-4R
See also AITN 1
See also CLC 68
Griffin, John Q(uealy) 1948- 77-80
Griffin, Jonathan
See Griffin, Robert John Thurlow
Griffin, Judith Berry 108
See also SATA 34
Griffin, Keith B(roadwell) 1938- CANR-7
Earlier sketch in CA 57-60
Griffin, (Samuel) Marvin 1907-1982 Obituary 108
Griffin, Mary 1916-1998 61-64
Obituary 166
Griffin, Mary Claire 1924- 17-20R
Griffin, Merv(yn) Edward, Jr.) 1925- 130
Griffin, P(auline) M. 1947- 140
Griffin, Peni R(ae Robinson) 1961- 134
See also SATA 67, 99
Griffin, Peter 1942- 136
See also CLC 39
Griffin, Robert 1936- 53-56
Griffin, Robert John Thurlow 1906- 129

Griffin, Russell M(organ) 1943- ... 114
Griffin, Steven A(rthur) 1953- ... 155
See also SATA 89
Griffin, Stuart 1917- ... 5-8R
Griffin, Susan 1943- ... CANR-50
Earlier sketches in CA 49-52, CANR-3, 27
Griffin, Thomas E., Jr. 1946- ... 131
Griffin, Tom
See Griffin, Thomas E., Jr.
Griffin, W. E. B.
See Butterworth, W(illiam) E(dmund III)
Griffin, Walter 1937- ... 73-76
Griffin, (Henry) William 1935- ... 93-96
Griffin, William D(enis) 1936- ... 122
Griffin, William Lloyd 1938- ... 21-24R
Griffin-Beale, Christopher 1947-1998 ... 118
Obituary ... 167
Griffiss, James E(dward) 1928- ... 132
Brief entry ... 118
Griffith, A. Kinney 1897- ... CANR-17
Earlier sketch in CA 1-4R
Griffith, A(rthur) Leonard 1920- ... CANR-5
Earlier sketch in CA 9-12R
Griffith, Albert J(oseph, Jr.) 1932- ... 37-40R
Griffith, Benjamin Woodward, Jr. 1922- .. CANR-42
Earlier sketches in CA 1-4R, CANR-5, 20
Griffith, Bill
See Granger, Bill
Griffith, Bill 1944- ... 129
Griffith, Connie 1946- ... 155
See also SATA 89
Griffith, Corinne 1898(?)-1979 Obituary ... 89-92
Griffith, D(avid Lewelyn) W(ark) 1875(?)-1948 .. 150
Brief entry ... 119
See also TCLC 68
Griffith, Elisabeth 1947- ... 166
Griffith, Elizabeth 1727(?)-1793 ... DLB 39, 89
Griffith, Ernest S(tacey) 1896-1997 ... 13-16R
Obituary ... 156
Griffith, Francis 1906- ... 106
Griffith, G(uy) T(hompson) 1908-1985 Obituary . 117
Griffith, George
See Griffith-Jones, George Chetwynd
Griffith, George 1857-1906 ... DLB 178
Griffith, Gershom 1960- ... SATA 85
Griffith, Helen V(irginia) 1934- ... CANR-45
Earlier sketches in CA 105, CANR-22
See also SATA 39, 87
Griffith, Ivelaw L(loyd) 1955- ... 162
Griffith, Jeannette
See Eyerly, Jeannette (Hyde)
Griffith, Jerry 1932- ... 53-56
Griffith, Kathryn 1923- ... 73-76
Griffith, Kenneth 1921- ... CANR-44
Earlier sketches in CA 69-72, CANR-21
Griffith, Lawrence
See Griffith, D(avid Lewelyn) W(ark)
Griffith, Leon Odell 1921- ... CANR-2
Earlier sketch in CA 1-4R
Griffith, Lucille B(lanche) 1905- ... 17-20R
Griffith, Marlene 1928- ... 151
Griffith, Nicola 1960- ... 154
Griffith, Patricia Browning 1935- ... CANR-35
Earlier sketches in CA 77-80, CANR-13
Griffith, Paul 1921-1983 ... 21-24R
Obituary ... 109
Griffith, Richard (Edward) 1912-1969 ... CANR-6
Earlier sketch in CA 1-4R
Griffith, Robert 1940- ... 45-48
Griffith, Samuel Blair II 1906-1983 Obituary ... 109
Griffith, Thomas 1915- ... 21-24R
Griffith, Thomas Gwynfor 1926- ... 103
Griffith, William E(dgar) 1920- ... 61-64
Griffith, Winthrop 1931- ... 9-12R
Griffith-Jones, George Chetwynd 1857-1906 Brief entry ... 112
Griffith-Jones, Stephany 1947- ... CANR-53
Earlier sketch in CA 126
Griffiths, A(lan) Bede 1906- ... CANR-7
Earlier sketch in CA 13-16R
Griffiths, Alison 1953- ... 128
Griffiths, Brian 1941- ... 120
Griffiths, Bryn(lyn) David 1933- ... 101
Griffiths, Daniel E(dward) 1917- ... 25-28R
Griffiths, G. D.
See Griffiths, (Edith) Grace (Chalmers)
Griffiths, G(ordon) D(ouglas) 1910-1973 ... CAP-2
Earlier sketch in CA 21-22
See also SATA-Obit 20
Griffiths, (Edith) Grace (Chalmers) 1921- . CANR-22
Earlier sketch in CA 106
Griffiths, Helen 1939- ... CANR-51
Earlier sketches in CA 17-20R, CANR-7, 25
See also SAAS 5
See also SATA 5, 86
Griffiths, John C(harles) 1934- ... 108
Griffiths, John Gwyn 1911- ... 106
Griffiths, Kitty Anna ... 105
Griffiths, Linda 1956- ... 132
Griffiths, Louise Benckenstein 1907- ... CANR-47
Earlier sketch in CA 1-4R
Griffiths, (Thomas) Mel(vin) 1910- ... 85-88
Griffiths, Michael C(ompton) 1928- ... CANR-60
Earlier sketches in CA 37-40R, CANR-14, 31
Griffiths, Naomi 1934- ... 101
Griffiths, Paul (Anthony) 1947- ... 107
Griffiths, Percival Joseph 1899- ... 103
Griffiths, Ralph A(lan) 1937- ... CANR-45
Earlier sketches in CA 105, CANR-22
Griffiths, Richard M(athias) 1935- ... CANR-8
Earlier sketch in CA 17-20R
Griffiths, Robert David 1952- ... 118
Griffiths, Sally 1934- ... 25-28R
Griffiths, Stephen Gareth 1949- ... 131
Griffiths, Steve
See Griffiths, Stephen Gareth
Griffiths, Tom 1957- ... 160
Griffiths, Trevor 1935- ... CANR-45
Earlier sketch in CA 97-100
See also CLC 13, 52
See also DLB 13
Griffiths, Vincent Llewellyn 1902(?)-1984 Obituary ... 113
Griffy
See Griffith, Bill
Grigg, Charles M(eade) 1918- ... 13-16R
Grigg, John (Edward Poynder) 1924- ... 104
Grigg, Ray 1938- ... 149
Griggs, Barbara
See van der Zee, Barbara (Blanche)
Griggs, Charles Irwin 1902- ... 1-4R
Griggs, Earl Leslie 1899- ... 73-76
Griggs, Gary B(ruce) 1943- ... 118
Griggs, Lee 1928- ... 69-72
Griggs, Mary
See Phillips, Bluebell Stewart
Griggs, Sutton Elbert 1872-1930(?) Brief entry . 123
See also DLB 50
See also TCLC 77
Griggs, Tamar 1941- ... 77-80
Griggs, Terry 1951- ... 140
Grignon, Claude-Henri 1894-1976 ... 148
See also DLB 68
Grigoli, Valorie 1955- ... 122
Grigorenko, P. G.
See Grigorenko, Petro Grigorevich
Grigorenko, Petr Grigorevich
See Grigorenko, Petro Grigorevich
Grigorenko, Petro Grigorevich 1907-1987 ... 144
Grigorenko, Piotr Grigorevich
See Grigorenko, Petro Grigorevich
Grigorovich, Yuri Nikolayevich 1927- ... 126
Grigsby, Gordon 1927- ... CANR-19
Earlier sketch in CA 97-100
Grigson, Geoffrey (Edward Harvey) 1905-1985 ... CANR-33
Obituary ... 118
Earlier sketches in CA 25-28R, CANR-20
See also CLC 7, 39
See also DLB 27
See also MTCW 1
Grigson, Jane (McIntire) 1928-1990 ... CANR-20
Obituary ... 131
Earlier sketches in CA 49-52, CANR-1
See also SATA 63
Grill, Johnpeter Horst 1943- ... 112
Grill, Nannette L. 1935- ... 65-68
Grilli, Peter M. 1942- ... 120
Grilliot, Harold J(ohn) 1937- ... 107
Grillo, John 1942- Brief entry ... 117
Grillo, Laura S. 1956- ... 144
Grillo, Ralph David 1940- ... CANR-48
Earlier sketch in CA 49-52
Grillo, Virgil 1938- ... 53-56
Grillparzer, Franz 1791-1872 ... DLB 133
Grim, John A(llen) 1946- ... 117
Grim, Patrick 1950- ... CANR-37
Earlier sketch in CA 115
Grim, Ronald E(ugene) 1946- ... 118
Grimal, Pierre Antoine 1912- ... CANR-7
Earlier sketch in CA 13-16R
Grimaldi, J(ohn) V. 1916- ... CANR-19
Earlier sketches in CA 5-8R, CANR-3
Grimaldi, Janette Pienkny 1938- ... 139
Grimaud, Michel (Robert) 1945-1993 ... 129
Obituary ... 142
Grimault, Berthe 1940- ... 13-16R
Grimble, Ian 1921- ... CANR-39
Earlier sketches in CA 5-8R, CANR-2, 18
Grimble, Reverend Charles James
See Eliot, T(homas) S(tearns)
Grime, Harol (Riley) 1896-1984 Obituary ... 114
Grimes, Alan P. 1919- ... CANR-48
Earlier sketches in CA 1-4R, CANR-1
Grimes, (Lewis) Howard 1915- ... 25-28R
Grimes, Johnnie Marie ... 103
Grimes, Joseph E(vans) 1928- ... 37-40R
Grimes, Lee 1920- ... CANR-37
Earlier sketch in CA 61-64
See also SATA 68
Grimes, Martha ... 117
Brief entry ... 113
See also BEST 90:1
See also DAM POP
See also MTCW 1
Grimes, Nikki 1950- ... CANR-60
Earlier sketch in CA 77-80
See also CLR 42
See also SATA 93
Grimes, Orville F(rank), Jr. 1943- ... 106
Grimes, Paul 1924- ... 77-80
Grimes, Ronald L. 1943- ... CANR-17
Earlier sketches in CA 45-48, CANR-1
Grimes, Tom 1954- ... 140
Grimes, W(illiam) H(enry) 1892-1972 Obituary ... 33-36R
Grimke, Angelina (Emily) Weld 1880-1958 ... 124
See also BW 1
See also DLB 50, 54
Grimke, Charlotte L(ottie) Forten 1837(?)-1914 . 124
Brief entry ... 117
See also Forten, Charlotte L.
See also BW 1
See also DAM MULT, POET
Grimley, Mildred H(ess) 1919- ... 5-8R
Grimm, Charles John 1898(?)-1983 Obituary ... 111
Grimm, Charlie
See Grimm, Charles John
Grimm, Cherry Barbara 1930- ... 101
See also SATA-Brief 43
Grimm, Hans 1875-1959 ... DLB 66
Grimm, Harold J(ohn) 1901- ... 13-16R
Grimm, Jacob Ludwig Karl 1785-1863 ... DLB 90
See also MAICYA
See also SATA 22
Grimm, Reinhold 1931- ... CANR-47
Earlier sketches in CA 61-64, CANR-8, 23
Grimm, Wilhelm Karl 1786-1859 ... DLB 90
See also MAICYA
See also SATA 22
Grimm, William C(arey) 1907- ... CANR-34
Earlier sketch in CA 49-52
See also SATA 14
Grimmelshausen, Johann Jakob Christoffel von 1621-1676 ... DLB 168
Grimond, Joseph 1913-1993 ... 108
Obituary ... 143
Grimsdell, Jeremy 1942- ... SATA 83
Grimsditch, Herbert Borthwick 1898-1971 Obituary ... 104
Grimshaw, Allen Day 1929- ... CANR-9
Earlier sketch in CA 65-68
Grimshaw, Beatrice Ethel 1871-1953 ... DLB 174
Grimshaw, James A(lbert), Jr. 1940- ... 109
Grimshaw, Mark
See McKeag, Ernest L(ionel)
Grimshaw, Nigel (Gilroy) 1925- ... CANR-17
Earlier sketch in CA 101
See also SATA 23
Grimsley, Gordon
See Groom, Arthur William
Grimsley, Jim 1955- ... 148
Grimsley, Linda 1940- ... 81-84
Grimsley, Ronald 1915- ... CANR-3
Earlier sketch in CA 5-8R
Grimsley, Will (Henry) 1914- ... 33-36R
Grimson, Todd 1952- ... CANR-72
Earlier sketch in CA 129
Grimstead, Hettie 1903- Brief entry ... 115
Grimsted, David Allen 1935- ... 25-28R
Grimsted, Patricia Kennedy 1935- ... 77-80
Grindal, Bruce T. 1940- ... 41-44R
Grindal, Edmund 1519(?)-1583 ... DLB 132
Grindal, Gracia (Marie) 1943- ... 116
Grindal, Richard 1922- ... 167
Grinde, Donald A(ndrew), Jr. 1946- ... 141
Grindea, Miron 1909-1995 ... CANR-5
Obituary ... 150
Earlier sketch in CA 5-8R
Grindel, Carl W(illiam) 1905- ... 85-88
Grindel, Eugene 1895-1952 Brief entry ... 104
See also Eluard, Paul
Grindel, John Anthony 1937- ... 65-68
Grindell, Robert M(aclean) 1933- ... 13-16R
Grinder, Michael 1942- ... 61-64
Grindle, Carleton
See Page, Gerald W(ilburn)
Grindley, John (Thomas Ellam) 1926- ... 25-28R
Grindley, (Jane) Sally 1953- ... 121
Grindrod, Muriel (Kathleen) 1902- ... 5-8R
Gringhuis, Dirk
See Gringhuis, Richard H.
Gringhuis, Richard H. 1918-1974 ... CANR-5
Earlier sketch in CA 1-4R
See also SATA 6
See also SATA-Obit 25
Grinnell, David
See Wollheim, Donald A(llen)
Grinnell, George Bird 1849-1938 ... SATA 16
Grinnell, Isabel Hoopes 1899(?)-1988 Obituary . 124
Grinsell, Leslie Valentine 1907- ... CANR-3
Earlier sketch in CA 9-12R
Grinspoon, Lester 1928- ... 81-84
Grinstead, David 1939- ... 105
Grinstein, Alexander 1918- ... CANR-5
Earlier sketch in CA 13-16R
Gripari, Pierre 1925- ... CANR-31
Earlier sketch in CA 29-32R
Gripe, Maria (Kristina) 1923- ... CANR-39
Earlier sketches in CA 29-32R, CANR-17
See also CLR 5
See also MAICYA
See also SATA 2, 74
Grise, Jeannette
See Thomas, Jeannette Grise
Grisewood, Harman (Joseph Gerard) 1906- . CAP-2
Earlier sketch in CA 29-32
Grisez, Germain G. 1929- ... CANR-45
Earlier sketches in CA 13-16R, CANR-6, 21
Grisham, John 1955- ... CANR-69
Earlier sketches in CA 138, CANR-47
See also AAYA 14
See also CLC 84
See also DAM POP
Grisham, Noel 1916- ... CANR-10
Earlier sketch in CA 25-28R
Grispino, Joseph Aloysius 1922- ... 17-20R
Grissim, John 1941- ... 113
Grissom, Fay
See Shulman, Fay Grissom Stanley
Grissom, Ken 1945- ... 135
Griswold, Charles L., Jr. 1951- ... 123
Griswold, Erwin N(athaniel) 1904-1994 ... CAP-1
Obituary ... 147
Earlier sketch in CA 13-16
Griswold, George
See Dean, Robert George
Griswold, Jerome 1947- ... 130
Griswold, Lawrence T. 1904(?)-1984 Obituary .. 113
Griswold, Rufus Wilmot 1815-1857 ... DLB 3, 59
Griswold, Wesley S(outhmayd) 1909- ... 1-4R
Griswold del Castillo, Richard 1942- ... 101
Gritsch, Eric W. 1931- ... CANR-10
Earlier sketch in CA 21-24R
Grivas, Theodore 1922- ... 9-12R
Grizzard, Lewis (M., Jr.) 1946-1994 ... 129
Obituary ... 144
Brief entry ... 123
Interview in ... 129
See also DAM POP
See also MTCW 1
Grob, Alan 1932- Brief entry ... 113
Grob, Gerald N. 1931- ... CANR-42
Earlier sketches in CA 1-4R, CANR-5, 20
Grobel, Lawrence 1947- ... 131
Grobman, Alex 1946- ... 116
Grobsmith, Elizabeth S. 1946- ... 147
Grobsmith, Liz
See Grobsmith, Elizabeth S.
Grobstein, Clifford 1916- ... 130
Groch, Judith (Goldstein) 1929- ... 9-12R
See also SATA 25
Grode, Redway
See Gorey, Edward (St. John)
Groden, Michael (Lewis) 1947- ... 131
Grodin, Charles 1935- ... 157
Grodnick, Susan 1951- ... 122
Groemer, Gerald 1957- ... 139
Groemping, Franz A(lbert) 1909(?)-1987 Obituary ... 123
Groenbjerg, Kirsten A(ndersen) 1946- ... CANR-46
Earlier sketches in CA 85-88, CANR-15
Groene, Bertram Hawthorne 1923- ... 45-48
Groene, Janet 1936- ... 37-40R
Groener, Carl
See Lowndes, Robert A(ugustine) W(ard)
Groenewegen, Peter 1939- ... 151
Groenhoff, Edwin L. 1924- ... 57-60
Groening, Matt 1954- ... CANR-56
Earlier sketch in CA 138
See also AAYA 8
See also SATA 81
Groennings, Sven O. 1934- ... 45-48
Groenoset, Dagfinn 1920- ... 93-96
Groeschel, Benedict J(oseph) 1933- ... CANR-37
Earlier sketch in CA 115
Grof, Stanislav 1931- ... 73-76
Groff, Patrick J(ohn) 1924- ... 41-44R
Groff, Warren F(rederick) 1924- ... 53-56
Grogan, Emmett 1942-1978 ... 41-44R
Groh, Ed(win Charles) 1910- ... 49-52
Groh, George W. 1922-1984 ... CANR-47
Obituary ... 114
Earlier sketch in CA 85-88
Grohman, Joann Sills 1928- ... 107
Grohmann, Susan 1948- ... SATA 84
Grohskopf, Bernice ... CANR-3
Earlier sketch in CA 5-8R
See also SATA 7
Groia, Phil(ip) 1941- ... 53-56
Grol, Lini R(icharda) 1913- ... CANR-25
Earlier sketches in CA 61-64, CANR-8
See also SATA 9
Grollman, Earl A. 1925- ... 21-24R
See also SATA 22
Grollman, Sharon Hya 1954- ... CANR-15
Earlier sketch in CA 81-84
Grollmes, Eugene E. 1931- ... 29-32R
Gromacki, Robert Glenn 1933- ... CANR-19
Earlier sketches in CA 53-56, CANR-4
Gromada, Thaddeus V(ladimir) 1929- ... 45-48
Groman, George L. 1928- ... 21-24R
Grombach, John V(alentin) 1901- ... 103
Gromyko, Andrei (Andreevich) 1909-1989 ... 134
Gronbeck, Bruce E(lliot) 1941- ... 132
Brief entry ... 118
Gronbjerg, Kirsten A(ndersen)
See Groenbjerg, Kirsten A(ndersen)
Grondona, L(eo) St. Clare 1890-1982 ... 103
Obituary ... 108
Groneman, Chris Harold 1906- ... CANR-1
Earlier sketch in CA 1-4R
Gronert, Bernard G(eorge) 1920-1985 Obituary 116
Gronewold, Sue Ellen
See Gronewold, Susan Ellen
Gronewold, Susan Ellen 1947- ... 115
Groninger, William C. 1928(?)-1983 Obituary ... 111
Gronowicz, Antoni 1913-1985 ... CANR-45
Obituary ... 117
Earlier sketch in CA 25-28R
Groocock, J(ohn) M(ichael) 1929- ... 57-60
Groom, Arthur William 1898-1964 ... CANR-1
Earlier sketch in CA 1-4R
See also SATA 10
Groom, Bernard 1892- ... CAP-2
Earlier sketch in CA 21-22
Groom, Gloria ... 151
Groom, Nigel 1924- ... 117
Groom, Winston 1943- ... CANR-50
Earlier sketches in CA 85-88, CANR-34
Groome, Thomas H(enry) 1945- ... 110
Groopman, Jerome E. ... 168
Gropius, Walter 1883-1969 Obituary ... 25-28R
Gropman, Donald S(heldon) 1936- ... 101
Gropp, Louis (Oliver) 1935- ... 120
Gropper, William 1897-1977 ... 102
Obituary ... 89-92
Grosart, Alexander Balloch 1827-1899 ... DLB 814
Grosbard, Ulu 1929- ... 25-28R
Grose, B(url) Donald 1943- ... CANR-22
Earlier sketch in CA 45-48
Grose, Christopher (Waldo) 1939- Brief entry .. 114
Grose, Peter (Bolton) 1934- ... 149
Brief entry ... 119
Groseclose, Barbara 1944- ... 152
Groseclose, Elgin E. 1899-1983 ... CAP-2
Obituary ... 109
Earlier sketch in CA 21-22
Groseclose, Kel(vin) 1940- ... CANR-66
Earlier sketches in CA 113, CANR-32
Grosman, Brian A(llen) 1935- ... 73-76

Grosman, Ladislav 1921- ... 102
Grosman, Tatyana 1904-1982 Obituary ... 107
Grosofsky, Leslie
See Gross, Leslie
Gross, Alan 1947- ... CANR-24
Earlier sketch in CA 89-92
See also SATA 54
See also SATA-Brief 43
Gross, Albert C. 1947- ... 125
Gross, Anthony 1905-1984 Obituary ... 114
Gross, Beatrice 1935- ... 77-80
Gross, Ben Samuel 1891-1979 ... 97-100
Obituary ... 89-92
Gross, Bertram M(yron) 1912-1997 ... CANR-9
Obituary ... 157
Earlier sketch in CA 13-16R
Gross, Beverly 1938- ... 29-32R
Gross, Carl H. 1911- ... 13-16R
Gross, Daniel R(ussell) 1942- ... 53-56
Gross, David 1940- ... 140
Gross, David C(harles) 1923- ... 102
Gross, Ernest A(rnold) 1906- ... 5-8R
Gross, Ernie 1913- ... 136
See also SATA 67
Gross, Feliks 1906- ... CANR-12
Earlier sketch in CA 29-32R
Gross, Franz B(runo) 1919- ... 29-32R
Gross, Gerald 1932- ... 9-12R
Gross, Hanns 1928- ... 41-44R
Gross, Harvey S(eymour) 1922- ... CANR-8
Earlier sketch in CA 13-16R
Gross, Helen Shimota 1931- ... 9-12R
Gross, Irma H(annah) 1892- ... CAP-1
Earlier sketch in CA 13-16
Gross, James A. 1933- ... 57-60
Gross, Joel 1951- ... CANR-57
Earlier sketches in CA 29-32R, CANR-14, 31
Gross, Johannes Heinrich 1916- ... CANR-43
Earlier sketch in CA 29-32R
Gross, John (Jacob) 1935- ... CANR-39
Earlier sketch in CA 29-32R
Gross, John J. 1912-1970 ... CAP-2
Earlier sketch in CA 25-28
Gross, John Owen 1894-1971 ... CAP-2
Earlier sketch in CA 17-18
Gross, Kenneth 1954- ... 118
Gross, Kenneth G. 1939- ... 25-28R
Gross, Leonard 1928- ... 118
Brief entry ... 112
Interview in ... 118
Gross, Leslie 1927- ... 5-8R
Gross, Llewellyn (Zwicker) 1914- ... 25-28R
Gross, Martha 1931- ... 143
Gross, Martin (Arnold) 1934- ... CANR-11
Earlier sketch in CA 13-16R
Gross, Martin L(ouis) 1925- ... CANR-53
Earlier sketches in CA 9-12R, CANR-7
Gross, Mary Anne 1943- ... 49-52
Gross, Michael 1891(?)-1979 Obituary ... 97-100
Gross, Michael (Robert) 1952- ... CANR-50
Earlier sketches in CA 93-96, CANR-20
Gross, Milt 1895-1953 ... DLB 11
Gross, Milton 1912(?)-1973 Obituary ... 41-44R
See also AITN 1
Gross, Neal 1920-1981 Obituary ... 108
Gross, Philip (John) 1952- ... 131
See also SATA 84
Gross, Phyllis P(ennebaker) 1915- ... 93-96
Gross, Polly 1952- ... 128
Gross, Richard Edmund 1920- ... CANR-1
Earlier sketch in CA 1-4R
Gross, Ronald 1935- ... CANR-5
Earlier sketch in CA 5-8R
Interview in ... CANR-5
Gross, Ruth Belov 1929- ... SATA 33
Gross, S(amuel Harry) 1933- ... CANR-51
Earlier sketches in CA 45-48, CANR-27
Gross, Sarah Chokla 1906-1976 ... 61-64
Obituary ... 65-68
See also SATA 9
See also SATA-Obit 26
Gross, Seymour L. 1926- ... CANR-3
Earlier sketch in CA 1-4R
Gross, Sheldon H(arvey) 1921- ... 81-84
Gross, Shelley 1938- ... 21-24R
Gross, Shelly
See Gross, Sheldon H(arvey)
Gross, Stuart D. 1914- ... 57-60
Gross, Suzanne 1933- ... 17-20R
Gross, Terence 1947- ... 101
Gross, Theodore L(awrence) 1930- ... CANR-14
Earlier sketch in CA 41-44R
Gross, Walter 1923- ... 21-24R
Gross, William Joseph 1894- ... CAP-1
Earlier sketch in CA 11-12
Grossack, Irvin Millman 1927- ... 97-100
Grossack, Martin Myer 1928- ... CANR-6
Earlier sketch in CA 9-12R
Grossbach, Robert 1941- ... CANR-13
Earlier sketch in CA 33-36R
Grossbart, Ted A. 1946- ... 126
Grossberger, Lewis 1940(?)- Brief entry ... 121
Grosse, W. Jack 1923- ... 143
Grossen, Neal E. 1943- ... 93-96
Grosser, Alfred 1925- ... CANR-44
Earlier sketches in CA 45-48, CANR-2, 20
Grosser, Arthur E(dward) 1934- ... 116
Grosser, Morton 1931- ... CANR-17
Earlier sketch in CA 97-100
See also SATA 74
Grosser, Vicky 1958- ... SATA 83
Grosseteste, Robert 1160(?)-1253 ... DLB 115
Grossfeld, Stan 1951- ... 136
Grosshans, Henry 1921- ... 29-32R
Grossholtz, Jean 1929- ... 13-16R
Grossinger, Harvey L. 1948- ... 163
Grossinger, Richard (Selig) 1944- ... CANR-42
Earlier sketches in CA 103, CANR-19
Grossinger, Tania 1937- ... CANR-4
Earlier sketch in CA 53-56
Grosskurth, Phyllis 1924- ... CANR-42
Earlier sketches in CA 13-16R, CANR-9
Grossman, Alfred 1927- ... 5-8R
Grossman, Allen (R.) 1932- ... CANR-38
Earlier sketches in CA 1-4R, CANR-1, 16
See also DLB 193
Grossman, Bill 1948- ... SATA 72
Grossman, David 1954- ... 138
See also CLC 67
Grossman, Edith Marian 1936- ... 108
Grossman, Ellie ... 110
Grossman, Frances Kaplan 1939- ... 57-60
Grossman, Gary H(oward) 1948- ... 69-72
Grossman, Herbert 1934- ... 17-20R
Grossman, Jean Schick
1894-1972 Obituary ... 37-40R
Grossman, Joan (Adess) 1940- ... 120
Grossman, Joan Delaney 1928- ... 111
Grossman, Julian 1931- ... 53-56
Grossman, Karl (H.) 1942- ... 130
Grossman, Kurt R. 1897-1972 Obituary ... 33-36R
Grossman, Lawrence 1945- ... 65-68
Grossman, Lee 1931- ... 69-72
Grossman, Louis Irwin 1901-1988 Obituary ... 125
Grossman, Manuel Lester 1939- Brief entry ... 106
Grossman, Mark 1967- ... 147
Grossman, Martin (Allen) 1943- ... CANR-13
Earlier sketch in CA 77-80
Grossman, Martin A. 1951- ... 102
Grossman, Mary Louise 1930- ... 77-80
Grossman, Morton Charles 1919- ... CANR-2
Earlier sketch in CA 1-4R
Grossman, Nancy 1940- ... SATA 29
Grossman, Patricia 1951- ... SATA 73
Grossman, Richard L(ee) 1921- ... 97-100
Interview in ... 97-100
Grossman, Robert 1940- ... SATA 11
Grossman, Ronald P(hilip) 1934- ... 21-24R
Grossman, Samuel 1897- ... 53-56
Grossman, Sebastian P. 1934- ... 21-24R
Grossman, Shelly 1928(?)-1975 Obituary ... 57-60
Grossman, Vasily (Semenovich) 1905-1964 ... 130
Brief entry ... 124
See also CLC 41
See also MTCW 1
Grossman, Wendy ... 168
Grossman, William L(eonard) 1906-1980 ... CAP-2
Obituary ... 97-100
Earlier sketch in CA 23-24
Grossmann, Reinhardt S. 1931- ... CANR-42
Earlier sketches in CA 33-36R, CANR-20
Grossmith, Robert (Anthony) 1954- ... 134
Grossu, Sergiu 1920- ... CANR-8
Earlier sketch in CA 57-60
Grossvogel, David I. 1925- ... CANR-4
Earlier sketch in CA 1-4R
Grosswirth, Marvin 1931-1984 ... 33-36R
Obituary ... 112
Grosvenor, Donna K(erkam) 1938- ... 109
Grosvenor, Gilbert (Hovey)
1875-1966 Obituary ... 93-96
See also DLB 91
Grosvenor, Kali Diana 1960- ... 69-72
Grosvenor, Melville Bell 1901-1982 ... CANR-34
Obituary ... 106
Earlier sketch in CA 69-72
Grosvenor, Verta Mae 1938- ... CANR-42
Earlier sketch in CA 69-72
See also BW 2
Grosz, George (Ehrenfried) 1893-1959 ... 147
Grote, David (G.) 1945- ... 130
Groten, Dallas 1951- ... CANR-38
Earlier sketch in CA 115
See also SATA 64
Groth, Alexander J(acob) 1932- ... CANR-14
Earlier sketch in CA 41-44R
Groth, Janet 1936- ... 151
Groth, Jeanette L(ue) 1947- ... 111
Groth, John (August) 1908-1988 ... 101
Obituary ... 125
See also SATA 21
See also SATA-Obit 56
Groth, Klaus 1819-1899 ... DLB 129
Grothendieck, Alexander 1928- ... 164
Grotjahn, Martin 1904-1990 ... CANR-15
Obituary ... 132
Earlier sketch in CA 41-44R
Grotowski, Jerzy 1933- Brief entry ... 105
Grotpeter, John J. 1938-1993 ... 150
Groult, Benoite 1920- ... 142
Groulx, Lionel (Adolphe) 1878-1967 ... 153
See also DLB 68
Grounds, Roger (Ransford Paterson) 1938- ... 97-100
Grounds, Vernon C(arl) 1914- ... 122
Groundwater, William 1906(?)-1982 Obituary ... 106
Groupe, Darryl R.
See Bunch, David R(oosevelt)
Groussard, Serge 1921- ... 108
Grout, Donald Jay 1902-1987 ... 102
Obituary ... 121
Grout, Jack 1910- ... 69-72
Grout, Ruth E(llen) 1901- ... CAP-2
Earlier sketch in CA 17-18
Grove, Andrew S. 1936- ... 130
Grove, Fred(erick) 1913- ... CANR-37
Earlier sketches in CA 1-4R, CANR-2, 17
Grove, Frederick Philip
See Greve, Felix Paul (Berthold Friedrich)
See also DLB 92
See also TCLC 4
Grove, Jack William 1920- ... 5-8R
Grove, Lee E(dmonds) (?)-1971 Obituary ... 104
Grove, Pearce S(eymour) 1930- ... 73-76
Grove, Richard H(ugh) 1955- ... 149
Grove, Will O.
See Brister, Richard
Grovelands, Sarah
See Schneider, Myra
Grover, David H(ubert) 1925- ... 13-16R
Grover, David S(teele) 1939- ... 89-92
Grover, Jan Zita ... 165
Grover, Janice Zita
See Grover, Jan Zita
Grover, John W(agner) 1927- ... 77-80
Grover, Linda 1934- ... 29-32R
Grover, Philip 1929- ... 104
Grover, Ralph Scott 1917- ... 145
Grover, Wayne 1934- ... 137
See also SATA 69
Groves, Colin Peter 1942- ... 61-64
Groves, Don(ald) George ... 106
Groves, Francis Richard 1889- ... CAP-1
Earlier sketch in CA 13-14
Groves, Georgina
See Symons, (Dorothy) Geraldine
Groves, H(arry) E(dward) 1921- ... 5-8R
Groves, Harold M(artin) 1897-1969 ... 5-8R
Obituary ... 134
Groves, Naomi Jackson 1910- ... CANR-40
Earlier sketch in CA 117
Groves, Paul 1930- ... CANR-17
Earlier sketch in CA 93-96
Groves, Reg(inald) 1908- ... 13-16R
Groves, Ruth Clouse 1902- ... CAP-2
Earlier sketch in CA 17-18
Groves, Seli ... 145
See also SATA 77
Grow, Lawrence 1939- ... CANR-25
Earlier sketches in CA 73-76, CANR-10
Growe, Sarah Jane 1939- ... 134
Grozny, I. L.
See Berger, Ivan (Bennett)
Grub, Phillip D. 1932- ... CANR-32
Earlier sketches in CA 25-28R, CANR-14
Grubar, Francis S(tanley) 1924- ... 33-36R
Grubb
See Crumb, R(obert)
Grubb, Davis Alexander 1919-1980 ... CANR-4
Obituary ... 101
Earlier sketch in CA 1-4R
See also DLB 6
Grubb, Frederick (Crichton-Stuart) 1930- ... 101
Grubb, Kenneth George 1900-1980 ... CAP-1
Obituary ... 97-100
Earlier sketch in CA 9-10
Grubb, Michael (J.) 1960- ... 143
Grubb, Norman (Percy) 1895- ... CANR-13
Earlier sketches in CAP-1, CA 13-16
Grubb, W. Norton 1948- ... 110
Grubbs, David H(arold) 1929- ... 117
Grubbs, Donald H. 1936- ... 81-84
Grubbs, Frank Leslie, Jr. 1931- ... 29-32R
Grubbs, Robert L(owell) 1919- ... CANR-2
Earlier sketch in CA 1-4R
Grube, Georges M(aximilien) A(ntoine) 1899- ...
CAP-1
Earlier sketch in CA 13-14
Grubel, Herbert G(unter) 1934- ... CANR-5
Earlier sketch in CA 9-12R
Gruber, Frank 1904-1969 ... CANR-60
Obituary ... 25-28R
Earlier sketches in CAP-1, CA 13-14
Gruber, Frederick C(harles) 1903- ... 49-52
Gruber, Gary R. 1940- ... CANR-49
Earlier sketches in CA 53-56, CANR-9, 24
Gruber, Helmut 1928- ... 103
Gruber, Howard E(rnest) 1922- ... 119
Brief entry ... 113
Interview in ... 119
Gruber, Ira D(empsey) 1934- Brief entry ... 110
Gruber, Jacob W(illiam) 1921- ... 1-4R
Gruber, Joseph John, Jr. 1930- ... CANR-6
Earlier sketch in CA 5-8R
Gruber, Katherine 1952- ... 123
Gruber, Martin Jay 1937- ... CANR-8
Earlier sketch in CA 53-56
Gruber, Ruth ... CANR-12
Earlier sketch in CA 25-28R
Gruber, Terry (deRoy) 1953- ... 97-100
See also SATA 66
Gruber, William E. 1943- ... 150
Gruberg, Martin 1935- ... 33-36R
Grubian, Motel 1909(?)-1972 Obituary ... 104
Grudin, Louis 1898- ... 1-4R
Grudin, Robert 1938- ... 144
Gruelle, John (Barton) 1880-1938 Brief entry ... 115
See also Gruelle, Johnny
See also SATA 35
See also SATA-Brief 32
Gruelle, Johnny
See Gruelle, John (Barton)
See also CLR 34
See also DLB 22
Gruelle, Worth ... AITN 2
Gruen, Erich S(tephen) 1935- ... 131
Gruen, John 1926- ... CANR-8
Earlier sketch in CA 17-20R
Gruen, Victor (David) 1903-1980 ... CANR-10
Obituary ... 97-100
Earlier sketch in CA 13-16R
Gruen, Yetta Fisher ... 125
Gruenbaum, Adolf 1923- ... CANR-43
Earlier sketches in CA 9-12R, CANR-5, 20
Gruenbaum, Ludwig
See Gaathon, A(ryeh) L(udwig)
Gruenberg, Benj(amin) C(harles) 1875-1965 ... CAP-1
Earlier sketch in CA 13-14
Gruenberg, Sidonie Matsner 1881-1974 ... CAP-1
Obituary ... 49-52
Earlier sketch in CA 13-16
See also SATA 2
See also SATA-Obit 27
Gruenberger, Fred J(oseph) 1918- ... 118
Grueneberg, Hans 1907-1982 Obituary ... 108
Gruenfeld, Lee 1950- ... 142
Gruenhagen, Robert W. 1932- ... 29-32R
Gruening, Ernest (Henry) 1887-1974 ... CANR-34
Earlier sketch in CA 49-52
Gruenstein, Peter 1947- ... 77-80
Gruenther, Alfred M(aximilian)
1899-1983 Obituary ... 109
Gruesser, John Cullen 1959- ... 144
Gruffydd, Peter 1935- ... 104
Gruhn, Carrie Myers 1907- ... CAP-1
Earlier sketch in CA 11-12
Gruhn, George 1945- ... 150
Gruits, Patricia Beall 1923- ... 105
Grulìow, Leo 1913-1997 ... 5-8R
Obituary ... 159
Grumbach, Doris (Isaac) 1918- ... CANR-70
Earlier sketches in CA 5-8R, CANR-9, 42
Interview in ... CANR-9
See also CAAS 2
See also CLC 13, 22, 64
Grumbine, R. Edward 1953- ... 140
Grumbling Gourmet, The
See Chapman, Frank M(onroe)
Grumelli, Antonio 1928- ... 37-40R
Grumet, Robert Steven 1949- ... 102
Grumich, Charles A. 1905(?)-1981 Obituary ... 104
Grumley, Michael 1941-1988 ... 29-32R
Obituary ... 125
Grumman, Bob 1941- ... CAAS 25
Grumme, Marguerite (Evelyn) ... 5-8R
Grummer, Arnold E(dward) 1923- ... 106
See also SATA 49
Grun, Bernard 1901-1972 Obituary ... 37-40R
Grunbaum, Adolf
See Gruenbaum, Adolf
Grund, Josef Carl 1920- ... 73-76
Grundberg, Andy
See Grundberg, John Andrew
Grundberg, John Andrew 1947- ... 103
Grundlehner, Philip 1945- ... 115
Grundstein, Nathan D(avid) 1913- ... CANR-15
Earlier sketch in CA 37-40R
Grundt, Leonard 1936- ... 57-60
Grundy, J(ohn) B(rownsdon) C(lowes)
1902-1987 Obituary ... 123
Grundy, J(ohn) Owen 1911-1985 Obituary ... 114
Grundy, Joan 1920- ... 109
Grundy, Kenneth W(illiam) 1936- ... CANR-12
Earlier sketch in CA 73-76
Grundy, Lester H. 1914(?)-1985 Obituary ... 116
Grundy, Pamela C. 1962- ... 140
Grundy, Stephan 1967- ... 154
Gruneau, Richard S(teven) 1948- ... CANR-30
Earlier sketch in CA 110
Gruneberg, Hans
See Grueneberg, Hans
Gruner, Charles R. 1931- ... 167
Grunewalt, Pine
See Kunhardt, Edith
Grunfeld, Frederic V(olker) 1929-1987 ... CANR-18
Obituary ... 124
Earlier sketch in CA 73-76
Grunge
See Crumb, R(obert)
Grunlan, Stephen Arthur 1942- ... CANR-39
Earlier sketches in CA 101, CANR-18
Grunwald, Constantine de
See de Grunwald, Constantine
Grunwald, Henry Anatole 1922- ... 107
Grunwald, Joseph 1920-1997 ... 115
Obituary ... 158
Grunwald, Lisa 1959- ... 120
See also CLC 44
Grunwald, Stefan 1933- ... 29-32R
Grupp, Stanley E(ugene) 1927- ... 53-56
Grusa, Jiri 1938- ... 117
Grusd, Edward Elihu 1904- ... CAP-2
Earlier sketch in CA 19-20
Grushkin, Paul D(avid) 1951- ... 142
Grushow, Ira 1933- ... 128
Gruskin, Alan D(aniel) 1904-1970 ... CAP-1
Obituary ... 29-32R
Earlier sketch in CA 11-12
Gruson, Edward S. 1929- ... 45-48
Gruss, Edmond C(harles) 1933- ... 53-56
Grutz, Mariellen Procopio 1946- ... 93-96
Grutzmacher, Harold M(artin), Jr. 1930- ... CANR-43
Earlier sketch in CA 29-32R
Gruver, Rebecca
See Goodman, Rebecca Gruver
Gruver, William R. II 1929- ... 45-48
Gruzen, Lee Ferguson 1945- ... 128
Grylls, David (Stanway) 1947- ... 85-88
Grylls, (Mary) Rosalie Glynn 1905(?)-1988 ... 65-68
Obituary ... 127
Grynberg, Henryk 1936- ... CANR-34
Earlier sketch in CA 29-32R
Gryphius, Andreas 1616-1664 ... DLB 164
Gryphius, Christian 1649-1706 ... DLB 168
Gryski, Camilla 1948- ... SATA 72
Gryst, Edward (George) 1911- ... 1-4R
Grzimek, Bernhard (Klemens Maria H. P.)
1909-1987 ... 133
Obituary ... 121
Guadaloupe, Brother Jose de
See Mojica, Jose
Guado, Sergio
See Gerosa, Guido
Guandagnolo, Joseph F(rancis) 1912- ... 5-8R

Guandolo, John 1919- 21-24R
Guaragna, Salvatore 1893-1981 Obituary 105
Guard, Dave
See Guard, David
Guard, David 1934-1991 77-80
Obituary 134
Guardia, Ernesto de la, Jr.
See de la Guardia, Ernesto, Jr.
Guardini, Romano 1885-1968 167
Guardo, Carol Joan 1939- 103
Guare, John 1938- CANR-69
Earlier sketches in CA 73-76, CANR-21
See also CLC 8, 14, 29, 67
See also DAM DRAM
See also DLB 7
See also MTCW 1
Guarendi, Raymond N(icholas) 1952- 120
Guareschi, Giovanni 1908-1968 105
Obituary 25-28R
Guarino, Dagmar
See Guarino, Deborah
Guarino, Deborah 1954- 136
See also SATA 68
Guarino, M(artin) Vincent 1939- 41-44R
Guarnieri, Patrizia 1954- 151
Guay, Georgette (Marie Jeanne) 1952- 132
See also SATA 54
Guback, Georgia .... SATA 88
Guback, Thomas H(enry) 1937- 25-28R
Gubar, Susan (David) 1944- CANR-70
Earlier sketches in CA 108, CANR-45
See also MTCW 1
Gubern, Santiago (Garriga-Nogues) 1933- . CANR-2
Earlier sketch in CA 45-48
Gubernick, Lisa Rebecca 1955- 140
Gubert, Betty Kaplan 1934- 112
Gubrium, Jaber F(andy) 1943- CANR-4
Earlier sketch in CA 53-56
Gubser, Nicholas J. 1938- 17-20R
Guccione, Leslie Davis 1946- .... SATA 72
Guccione, Robert, Jr. .... AITN 2
Guches, Richard (Clement) 1938- 115
Guck, Dorothy 1913- 49-52
See also SATA 27
Gudde, Erwin G(ustav) 1889-1969 .... CANR-4
Earlier sketch in CA 5-8R
Gudenian, Haig (Krikor) 1918-1985(?) Obituary . 115
Guder, Eileen (Likens) 1919- 17-20R
Gudiol, Jose
See Gudiol i Ricart, Josep
Gudiol i Ricart, Josep 1904- 81-84
Gudiol Ricart, Jose M.
See Gudiol i Ricart, Josep
Gudiol Ricart, Josep
See Gudiol i Ricart, Josep
Gudjonsson, Halldor Kiljan 1902-1998 103
Obituary 164
See also Laxness, Halldor
Gudorf, Christine E. 1949- 150
Gudschinsky, Sarah C(aroline) 1919-1975 .. CAP-2
Earlier sketch in CA 33-36
Guede, Norina (Maria Esterina) Lami 1913- .. 9-12R
Guehenne, Jean
See Guehenno, Jean Marcel Jules Marie
Guehenno, Jean Marcel Jules Marie
1890-1978 Obituary 104
Guelich, Robert A(llison) 1939- CANR-17
Earlier sketches in CA 45-48, CANR-2
Guemple, Lee 1930- 41-44R
Guenderrode, Caroline von 1780-1806 .... DLB 90
Guenette, Robert (Homer) 1935- 25-28R
Guenter, Erich
See Eich, Guenter
Guenther, Charles (John) 1920- CANR-45
Earlier sketch in CA 29-32R
Guenther, Herbert V. 1917- 73-76
Guenther, John (Lewis) CANR-9
Earlier sketch in CA 5-8R
Guenther, (Robert) Wallace 1929- 65-68
Guerard, Albert Joseph 1914- CANR-69
Earlier sketches in CA 1-4R, CANR-2
See also CAAS 2
Guerin, Wilfred L(ouis) 1929- 17-20R
Guerlac, Henry (Edward) 1910-1985 Obituary .. 116
Guerlac, Rita 1916- 116
Guerney, Bernard G(uilbert), Jr. 1930- 93-96
Guerney, Bernard Guilbert
1894-1979 Obituary 85-88
Guernsey, Bruce H(ubbard) 1944- 108
Guernsey, James Lee 1923- 37-40R
Guernsey, Otis L(ove), Jr. 1918- 89-92
Guernsey, Thomas F. 1951- 146
Guerny, Gene
See Gurney, Gene
Guerra, Emilio Louis 1909-1980 Obituary ... 97-100
Guerra, Tonino 1920- .... DLB 128
Guerrant, Edward Owings 1911- 21-24R
Guerra y Sanchez, Ramiro 1880-1970 Obituary 104
Guerrero, Rogelio Diaz
See Diaz-Guerrero, Rogelio
Guerrette, Richard H(ector) 1930- 49-52
Guerrier, Dennis 1923- 29-32R
Guers-Villate, Yvonne 1924- 41-44R
Guess, Edward Preston 1925- 73-76
Guest, A(nthony) G(ordon) 1930- CANR-1
Earlier sketch in CA 1-4R
Guest, Barbara 1920- CANR-44
Earlier sketches in CA 25-28R, CANR-11
See also CLC 34
See also DLB 5, 193
Guest, Christopher 1948- 157
Guest, Edgar A(lbert) 1881-1959 168
Brief entry 112
Guest, Harry
See Guest, Henry Bayly
Guest, Henry Bayly 1932- CANR-9
Earlier sketch in CA 65-68
Guest, Ivor (Forbes) 1920- CANR-42
Earlier sketches in CA 5-8R, CANR-2, 20
Guest, Judith (Ann) 1936- CANR-15
Earlier sketch in CA 77-80
Interview in CANR-15
See also AAYA 7
See also CLC 8, 30
See also DAM NOV, POP
See also MTCW 1
Guest, Lynn 1939- 131
Guetersloh, Albert Paris 1887-1973 .... DLB 81
Guett, Dieter 1924- 65-68
Gueulette, David G(eorge) 1941- 111
Guevara, Che
See Guevara (Serna), Ernesto
See also CLC 87
See also HLC
Guevara (Serna), Ernesto 1928-1967 .... CANR-56
Obituary 111
Earlier sketch in CA 127
See also Guevara, Che
See also DAM MULT
See also HW
Guevara, Susan .... SATA 97
Guevremont, (Marianne) Germaine 1893-1968 . 148
See also DLB 68
Guffey, George
See Guffey, George Robert
Guffey, George R.
See Guffey, George Robert
Guffey, George Robert 1932- 132
Brief entry 118
Guffin, Gilbert L. 1906- 17-20R
Gugas, Chris 1921- 97-100
Gugelyk, M(yron) Ted 1938- 120
Guggenheim, Edward Armand
1901-1970 Obituary 104
Guggenheim, Hans Georg 1927- 125
Guggenheim, Harry Frank
1890-1971 Obituary 89-92
Guggenheim, Marguerite 1898-1979 Obituary .. 105
Guggenheim, Martin 1946- 129
Guggenheim, Peggy
See Guggenheim, Marguerite
Guggenheimer, Richard 1906-1977 .... 41-44R
Obituary 69-72
Guggenmos, Josef 1922- 81-84
Guggisberg, C(harles) A(lbert) W(alter) 1913- . 81-84
Gugler, Laurel Dee 160
See also SATA 95
Gugliotta, Bobette 1918- CANR-31
Earlier sketches in CA 41-44R, CANR-14
See also SATA 7
Guhin, Michael A(lan) 1940- 41-44R
Guianan, Eve 1965- .... SATA 102
Guiberson, Brenda Z. 1946- .... SATA 71
Guibert, Herve 1955-1991 155
Guice, John D(avid) W(ynne) 1931- 41-44R
Guicharnaud, June 1922-1989 93-96
Obituary 129
Guidacci, Margherita 1921-1992 .... DLB 128
Guido, Beatriz 1924-1988 153
See also HW
Guido, (Cecily) Margaret 1912- 65-68
Guignon, Charles B(urke) 1944- 145
Guild, Lurelle Van Arsdale 1898- CAP-2
Earlier sketch in CA 29-32
Guild, Nicholas M. 1944- 93-96
See also CLC 33
Guild, Thelma S(croggs) 1911- 118
Guild, Vera Palmer 1906- Brief entry 106
Guilds, John C(aldwell, Jr.) 1924- 77-80
Guiles, Fred Lawrence 1920- CANR-12
Earlier sketch in CA 25-28R
Guilford, J(oy) Paul 1897- CANR-4
Earlier sketch in CA 1-4R
Guilford, Joan S. 1928- 29-32R
Guillaume, Alfred 1888-(?) CAP-1
Earlier sketch in CA 13-16
Guillaume, Bernice F(orrest) 1950- 145
Guillaume, Jeanette G. Flierl 1899- 1-4R
See also SATA 8
Guillaumin, Colette 1934- 154
Guille, Frances V(ernor) 1908-1975 45-48
Obituary 61-64
Guillemin, Henri 1903- 81-84
Guillemin, Jacques
See Sartre, Jean-Paul
Guillen, Jorge 1893-1984 89-92
Obituary 112
See also CLC 11
See also DAM MULT, POET
See also DLB 108
See also HW
Guillen, Mauro (Federico) 1964- 134
Guillen, Michael (Arthur) 1940- 158
Guillen, Nicolas (Cristobal) 1902-1989 125
Obituary 129
Brief entry 116
See also BLC 2
See also BW 2
See also CLC 48, 79
See also DAM MST, MULT, POET
See also HLC
See also HW
See also PC 23
Guillen, Tomas 1949- 134
Guillet, Edwin C(larence) 1898-1975 107
Guillet, Jacques 1910- 102
Guillevic, (Eugene) 1907- 93-96
See also CLC 33
Guillois
See Desnos, Robert
Guillois, Valentin
See Desnos, Robert
Guillory, Dan 1944- 144
Guillot, Rene 1900-1969 .... CANR-39
Earlier sketch in CA 49-52
See also CLR 22
See also SATA 7
Guillou, Jan 1944- 143
Guilloux, Louis 1899-1980 Obituary 104
See also DLB 72
Guilmartin, John Francis, Jr. 1940- 53-56
Guimaraes, Dona 1926(?)-1989 Obituary 129
Guimary, Donald L(ee) 1932- 73-76
Guimond, James K. 1936- 25-28R
Guin, Wyman (Woods) 1915- 102
Guinagh, Kevin (Joseph) 1897- 17-20R
Guinan, Michael D(amon) 1939- 117
Guindey, Guillaume Louis 1909-1989 Obituary . 128
Guinee, Kathleen K. 1902(?)-1982 Obituary 109
Guiney, Louise Imogen 1861-1920 160
See also DLB 54
See also TCLC 41
Guiney, Mortimer 1930- 53-56
Guinier, Lani 1950- 158
Guinn, Paul (Spencer, Jr.) 1928- 13-16R
Guinness, Bryan (Walter) 1905-1992 .... CANR-46
Obituary 139
Earlier sketch in CA 102
Guinness, Desmond 1931- 141
Guinness, Jonathan (Bryan) 1930- 159
Guinness, (Ian) Os(wald) 1941- 65-68
Guinther, John 1927- CANR-56
Earlier sketches in CA 69-72, CANR-11, 28
Guion, Robert M(organ) 1924- CANR-7
Earlier sketch in CA 17-20R
Guiraldes, Ricardo (Guillermo) 1886-1927 131
See also HW
See also MTCW 1
See also TCLC 39
Guirdham, Arthur 1905- 103
Guisewite, Cathy (Lee) 1950- 113
Brief entry 111
Interview in 113
See also AAYA 2
See also SATA 57
Guisinger, Stephen Edward 1941- 103
Guitar, Mary Anne 1922- Brief entry 113
Guiterman, Arthur 1871-1943 Brief entry 120
See also DLB 11
Guither, Harold D. 1927- 29-32R
Gula, Richard M(ichael) 1947- 109
Gula, Robert J(ohn) 1941- 97-100
Gulick, Bill
Interview in CANR-17
See also Gulick, Grover C.
Gulick, Edward Vose 1915- 113
Gulick, Grover C. 1916- CANR-39
Earlier sketches in CA 33-36R, CANR-17
See also Gulick, Bill
Gulick, Robert Lee, Jr. 1912-1987 Obituary 122
Gulik, Robert H(ans) van
See van Gulik, Robert Hans
Gulker, Virgil G. 1947- 65-68
Gullace, Gino 1925- CANR-17
Earlier sketch in CA 69-72
Gullans, Charles (Bennett) 1929-1993 .... CANR-39
Obituary 141
Earlier sketches in CA 1-4R, CANR-4, 18
Gullason, Thomas A(rthur) 1924- CANR-8
Earlier sketch in CA 21-24R
Gulley, Halbert E(dison) 1919- CANR-6
Earlier sketch in CA 5-8R
Gulley, Judie 1942- .... SATA 58
Gulley, Norman 1920- 33-36R
Gullick, Charles Francis William Rowley 1907- . 5-8R
Gullick, Etta 1916- 89-92
Gullick, John M(ichael) 1916- 13-16R
Gulliford, Andrew 1953- 120
Gulliford, Ronald 1920- 13-16R
Gulliver, Harold S. 1935- 97-100
Gulliver, Lemuel
See Hastings, Macdonald
Gullotta, Thomas P. 1948- 144
Gulston, Charles 1913-1981 122
Gumilev, Nikolai (Stepanovich) 1886-1921 165
See also TCLC 60
Gummere, Richard M(ott), Jr. 1912- 45-48
Gump, Richard (Benjamin) 1906- CAP-1
Earlier sketch in CA 9-10
Gump, Sally
See Stanford, Sally
Gumpertz, Robert 1925- 69-72
Gumperz, John J(oseph) 1922- 132
Gunders, Henry 1924- 29-32R
Gundersheimer, Karen 1939- 133
See also SATA-Brief 44
Gundersheimer, Werner L. 1937- 53-56
Gunderson, Doris V. 29-32R
Gunderson, Frank L(ester) 1902-1983 Obituary 110
Gunderson, Keith (Robert) 1935- 33-36R
Gunderson, Robert Gray 1915- 1-4R
Gundrey, Elizabeth 1924- CANR-6
Earlier sketch in CA 13-16R
See also SATA 23
Gundry, Robert H(orton) 1932- 29-32R
Gundry, Stanley Norman 1937- 114
Gundulic, Ivan 1589-1638 .... DLB 147
Gundy, Elizabeth CANR-45
Earlier sketch in CA 112
Gundy, H(enry) Pearson) 1905- 45-48
Gundy, Jeff(rey Gene) 1952- 154
Gunesekera, Romesh 1954- 159
See also CLC 91
Gunetti, Daniele 1963- 159
Guney, Yilmaz 1937(?)-1984 Obituary 113
Gunji, Masakatsu 1913- 29-32R
Gunlicks, Arthur B. 1936- CANR-53
Earlier sketch in CA 126
Gunn, Bill
See Gunn, William Harrison
See also CLC 5
See also DLB 38
Gunn, Brooke
See Brooks-Gunn, Jeanne
Gunn, Christopher Eaton 1944- 117
Gunn, Diana Maureen 1926- CANR-18
Earlier sketch in CA 97-100
Gunn, Douglas 1950- 151
Gunn, Drewey Wayne 1939- 57-60
Gunn, Elizabeth
See Gunn, Diana Maureen
Gunn, Giles B(uckingham) 1938- 57-60
Gunn, Helen Montgomery
1900(?)-1987 Obituary 122
Gunn, J(ohn) A(lexander) W(ilson) 1937- . CANR-20
Earlier sketch in CA 25-28R
Gunn, James E(dwin) 1923- CANR-22
Earlier sketches in CA 9-12R, CANR-5
See also CAAS 2
See also DLB 8
See also SATA 35
Gunn, John (Charles) 1937- CANR-29
Earlier sketch in CA 49-52
Gunn, Kirsty 1960- 166
Gunn, Mrs. Aneas 1870-1961 Obituary 115
Gunn, Neil M(iller) 1891-1973 Obituary 37-40R
See also DLB 15
Gunn, Peter (Nicholson) 1914-1995 .... CANR-18
Obituary 150
Earlier sketches in CA 25-28R, CANR-10
Gunn, Robin Jones 1955- 150
See also SATA 84
Gunn, S(teven) J(ohn) 1960- 128
Gunn, Sister Agnes Marie 1928- 17-20R
Gunn, Thom(son William) 1929- CANR-33
Earlier sketches in CA 17-20R, CANR-9
Interview in CANR-33
See also CDBLB 1960 to Present
See also CLC 3, 6, 18, 32, 81
See also DAM POET
See also DLB 27
See also MTCW 1
Gunn, William Harrison 1934(?)-1989 .... CANR-25
Obituary 128
Earlier sketches in CA 13-16R, CANR-12
See also Gunn, Bill
See also AITN 1
See also BW 1
Gunnars, Kristjana 1948- 113
See also CLC 69
See also DLB 60
Gunnarsson, Gunnar 1889-1975 Obituary 61-64
Gunnell, Bryn 1933- 103
Gunnell, John G. 1933- 25-28R
Gunneweg, Antonius H. J. 1922- CANR-16
Earlier sketch in CA 89-92
Gunning, Monica Olwen 1930- 65-68
Gunning, Robert 1908-1980 .... CAP-2
Obituary 97-100
Earlier sketch in CA 25-28
Gunning, Sally (Carlson) 1951- 140
Gunsalus Gonzalez, Catherine
See Gonzalez, Catherine Gunsalus
Gunston, Bill
See Gunston, William Tudor
Gunston, William Tudor 1927- CANR-42
Earlier sketches in CA 49-52, CANR-3, 19
See also SATA 9
Gunstone, A(ntony) J. H.
1937(?)-1984 Obituary 112
Gunter, (J.) Bradley (Hunt) 1940- 29-32R
Gunter, Pete A(ddison) Y(ancey) 1936- .. CANR-34
Earlier sketches in CA 33-36R, CANR-15
Gunterman, Bertha Lisette
1886(?)-1975 Obituary 104
See also SATA-Obit 27
Gunther, A(lbert) E(verard) 1903- 29-32R
Gunther, Bernard 1929- CANR-2
Earlier sketch in CA 45-48
Gunther, Gerald 1927- CANR-13
Earlier sketch in CA 33-36R
Gunther, Johann Christian 1695-1723 .... DLB 168
Gunther, John 1901-1970 .... 9-12R
Obituary 25-28R
See also SATA 2
Gunther, Marc 1951- 129
Gunther, Max 1927- 13-16R
Gunther, Peter F. 1920- 9-12R
Gunther, Richard (Paul) 1946- 103
Gunton, Sharon R(ose) 1952- 102
Guntrip, Harry
See Guntrip, Henry James Samuel
Guntrip, Henry James Samuel 1901-1975 . CANR-5
Earlier sketch in CA 5-8R
Gunzberg, Lynn M. 1944- 143
Gunzburg, Nicholas de 1904-1981 Obituary 103
Guppy, Nicholas (Gareth Lechmere) 1925- ....
CANR-6
Earlier sketch in CA 5-8R
Guppy, Shusha 1938- 128
Guppy, Stephen (Anthony) 1951- 166
Gupta, Anil K. 1949- 144
Gupta, Brijen K(ishore) 1929- CANR-16
Earlier sketches in CA 45-48, CANR-1
Gupta, Marie (Jacqueline) 1946- 57-60
Gupta, Pranati Sen
See Sen Gupta, Pranati
Gupta, Ram Chandra 1927- CANR-13
Earlier sketch in CA 21-24R
Gupta, S(ushil) (Kumar) 1927- 57-60
Gupta, Shiv K(umar) 1930- 57-60
Gupta, Sulekh Chandra 1928- 13-16R

Gupta, Sunetra 1965- 137
Gupta, U. S. 1940- 147
Guptara, Prabhu S(iddhartha) 1949- 81-84
Guptill, Nathanael M(ann) 1917- 45-48
Gura, Philip F(rancis) 1950- CANR-47
Earlier sketch in CA 111
Guralnick, Peter 1943(?)- 147
Guravich, Dan 1918- .... SATA 74
Gurdjieff, G(eorgei) I(vanovich) 1877(?)-1949 ... 157
See also TCLC 71
Gurdus, Luba Krugman 1914- 120
Gurevich, Aaron 1924- 144
Gurevich, David 1951- 140
Gurganus, Allan 1947- 135
See also BEST 90:1
See also CLC 70
See also DAM POP
Gurik, Robert 1932- CANR-71
Earlier sketch in CA 129
See also CAAS 23
See also DLB 60
Gurin, Joel 1953- 108
Gurko, Leo 1914- CANR-5
Earlier sketch in CA 5-8R
See also SATA 9
Gurko, Miriam 1910(?)-1988 .... 1-4R
Obituary 126
See also SATA 9
See also SATA-Obit 58
Gurman, Alan S(tephen) 1945- CANR-5
Earlier sketch in CA 53-56
Gurnee, Jeanne 1926- 93-96
Gurnee, Russell H(ampton) 1922- 107
Gurney, A(lbert) R(amsdell), Jr. 1930- ... CANR-64
Earlier sketches in CA 77-80, CANR-32
See also CLC 32, 50, 54
See also DAM DRAM
Gurney, Gene 1924- CANR-9
Earlier sketch in CA 5-8R
See also SATA 65
Gurney, George 1939- 119
Gurney, Ivor (Bertie) 1890-1937 167
See also TCLC 33
Gurney, J. Eric CANR-2
Earlier sketch in CA 1-4R
Gurney, James 1958- .... SATA 76
Gurney, John Steven 1962- .... SATA 75
Gurney, Nancy Jack 1915(?)-1973 Obituary .. 45-48
Gurney, Peter
See Gurney, A(lbert) R(amsdell), Jr.
Guro, Elena 1877-1913 .... TCLC 56
Gurr, Andrew (John) 1936- 33-36R
Gurr, David 1936- 132
Brief entry 125
Interview in 132
Gurr, Ted Robert 1936- CANR-16
Earlier sketch in CA 41-44R
Gurrey, Percival 1890-1980 Obituary 97-100
Gurtov, Melvin 1941- 164
Brief entry 112
Gurval, Robert Alan 1958- 156
Gurwitsch, Aron 1901-1973 .... CAP-1
Obituary 41-44R
Earlier sketch in CA 13-16
Gusfield, Joseph R. 1923- 53-56
Gusikoff, Lynne
See Hawes, Lynne Gusikoff Salop
Guss, Donald L(eroy) 1929- 17-20R
Guss, Leonard M. 1926- 21-24R
Gussman, Boris (William) 1914- 5-8R
Gussow, Alan 1931- Brief entry 111
Gussow, Don 1907-1992 132
Obituary 136
Gussow, Joan Dye 1928- 29-32R
Gussow, Mel 1933- 107
Gustaf IV, Adolf, King of Sweden
1882-1973 Obituary 45-48
Gustafson, Alrik 1903-1970 .... 1-4R
Obituary 103
Gustafson, Anita
See Larsen, Anita
Gustafson, Anita 1942- 112
See also SATA-Brief 45
Gustafson, David A(rthur) 1946- 141
Gustafson, Donald F. 1934- CANR-36
Earlier sketch in CA 9-12R
Gustafson, James 1949- 125
Gustafson, James M(oody) 1925- CANR-37
Earlier sketch in CA 25-28R
See also CLC 100
Gustafson, Jim
See Gustafson, James
Gustafson, Paula Catherine 1941- 106
Gustafson, Ralph (Barker) 1909- CANR-45
Earlier sketches in CA 21-24R, CANR-8
See also CLC 36
See also DLB 88
Gustafson, Richard C(larence)
1933-1977 Obituary 111
Gustafson, Richard F(olke) 1934- 17-20R
Gustafson, Sarah R.
See Riedman, Sarah R(egal)
Gustafson, Scott 1956- .... SATA 34
Gustafson, Susan E(lizabeth) 1959- 152
Gustafson, W(illiam) Eric 1933- 57-60
Gustafsson, Lars 1936- 85-88
Gustaitis, Rasa 1934- 25-28R
Gustavson, Carl G(ustav) 1915- 17-20R
Guste, Roy F(rancis), Jr. 1951- 162
Gustin, Lawrence Robert 1937- CANR-37
Earlier sketch in CA 57-60
Gustkey, Earl 1940- 57-60
Gut, Gom
See Simenon, Georges (Jacques Christian)
Gutch, John 1905-1988 Obituary 124
Gutcheon, Beth R(ichardson) 1945- CANR-2
Earlier sketch in CA 49-52
Gutek, Gerald L(ee) 1935- CANR-40
Earlier sketches in CA 81-84, CANR-17
Gutenberg, Arthur W(illiam) 1920- 37-40R
Gutenberg, Beno 1889-1960 157
Guterman, Norbert 1900-1984 Obituary 113
Guterman, Simeon L(eonard) 1907- 41-44R
Guterman, Stanley S(anford) 1934- 29-32R
Guterson, David 1956- 132
See also CLC 91
Guth, Alan (Harvey) 1947- 158
Guth, DeLloyd J. 1938- 129
Gutheim, Frederick 1908-1993 .... CANR-9
Obituary 142
Earlier sketch in CA 21-24R
Guthke, Karl S(iegfried) 1933- CANR-37
Earlier sketches in CA 41-44R, CANR-15
Guthman, Edwin 1919- 33-36R
Guthman, William H(arold) 1924- CANR-37
Earlier sketch in CA 57-60
Guthmann, Harry G. 1896- 1-4R
Guthrie, A(lfred) B(ertram), Jr. 1901-1991 ....
CANR-24
Obituary 134
Earlier sketch in CA 57-60
See also CLC 23
See also DLB 6
See also SATA 62
See also SATA-Obit 67
Guthrie, Anne 1890-1979 .... 5-8R
Obituary 134
See also SATA 28
Guthrie, Arlo (Davy) 1947- CANR-53
Earlier sketch in CA 113
Guthrie, David
See Allen, H(ubert) R(aymond)
Guthrie, Donald 1916- CANR-23
Earlier sketches in CA 13-16R, CANR-7
Guthrie, Donna W. 1946- .... SATA 63
Guthrie, Harvey Henry, Jr. 1924- 13-16R
Guthrie, Hugh
See Freeman, John Crosby
Guthrie, Hunter 1901-1974 65-68
Obituary 53-56
Guthrie, Isobel
See Grieve, C(hristopher) M(urray)
Guthrie, James Shields 1931- CANR-15
Earlier sketch in CA 33-36R
Guthrie, James W. 1936- 41-44R
Guthrie, John 1908- 106
Guthrie, John A(lexander) 1907- 1-4R
Guthrie, Judith Bretherton
1905(?)-1972 Obituary 37-40R
Guthrie, Marjorie (Greenblatt Mazia)
1917-1983 Obituary 117
Guthrie, Ramon 1896-1973 .... 5-8R
Obituary 45-48
See also DLB 4
Guthrie, Randolph H. 1934- 146
Guthrie, Robert V(al) 1930- 53-56
Guthrie, Russell Dale 1936- Brief entry 106
Guthrie, T.
See Guthrie, (William) Tyrone
Guthrie, Thomas Anstey 1856-1934 Brief entry . 113
See also Anstey, F.
Guthrie, (William) Tyrone 1900-1971 123
Obituary 29-32R
Guthrie, William Keith Chambers 1906-1981 ....
CANR-11
Obituary 103
Earlier sketch in CA 65-68
Guthrie, Woodrow Wilson 1912-1967 113
Obituary 93-96
See also Guthrie, Woody
Guthrie, Woody
See Guthrie, Woodrow Wilson
See also CLC 35
Gutierrez, Donald 1932- CANR-36
Earlier sketch in CA 109
Gutierrez, Gustavo
See Gutierrez Merino, Gustavo
Gutierrez M., Gustavo
See Gutierrez Merino, Gustavo
Gutierrez Merino, Gustavo 1928- 130
See also HW
Gutierrez-Vega, Zenaida 1924- CANR-19
Earlier sketch in CA 41-44R
Gutin, Bernard 1934- 112
Gutkin, Harry 1915- 101
Gutkind, Erwin A(nton) 1886-1968 .... CANR-8
Earlier sketch in CA 5-8R
Gutkind, Lee 1943- CANR-20
Earlier sketches in CA 53-56, CANR-5
Gutkind, Peter C(laus) W(olfgang) 1925- 116
Gutman, Bill 135
See also SATA 67
See also SATA-Brief 43
Gutman, Dan 1955- 133
See also SATA 77
Gutman, David 1957- 127
Gutman, Herbert G(eorge) 1928-1985 ... CANR-36
Obituary 116
Earlier sketch in CA 65-68
Gutman, Judith Mara 1928- 21-24R
Gutman, Kellie O. 1952- 124
Gutman, Naham 1899(?)-1981 Obituary 102
See also SATA-Obit 25
Gutman, Richard J(ay) S(tephen) 1949- 101
Gutman, Robert 1926- 45-48
Gutman, Robert W. 1925- 25-28R
Gutman, Roy (W.) 1944- 131
Gutman, Stanley T. 1943- 127
Gutman, Walter
See Gutman, Walter Knowlton
Gutman, Walter Knowlton 1903-1986 Obituary . 119
Gutmann, Amy 1949- CANR-64
Earlier sketch in CA 128
Gutmann, Bessie Pease 1876-1960 .... SATA 73
Gutmann, David L(eo) 1925- 135
Gutmann, James 1897-1988 .... CAP-2
Obituary 127
Earlier sketch in CA 21-22
Gutmann, Joseph 1923- CANR-37
Earlier sketches in CA 49-52, CANR-1, 17
Gutmann, Myron P. 1949- 127
Brief entry 105
Gutnik, Martin J(erome) 1942- CANR-3
Earlier sketch in CA 49-52
Gutowski, Armin (Ferdinand) 1930-1987 136
Gutsche, Thelma 1915- 21-24R
Gutstein, Morris A(aron) 1905-1987 Obituary ... 122
Gutt, Dieter
See Guett, Dieter
Guttenberg, Barnett 89-92
Guttenberg, Virginia 1914- 81-84
Guttentag, Marcia 1932-1977 .... CANR-8
Earlier sketch in CA 57-60
Gutteridge, Anne C(hristine) 1943- 108
Gutteridge, Bernard 1916-1985 Obituary 117
Gutteridge, Don(ald George) 1937- CANR-36
Earlier sketches in CA 65-68, CANR-9
Gutteridge, Lindsay 1923- 49-52
Gutteridge, Richard (Joseph Cooke) 1911- 122
Gutteridge, Thomas G. 1942- 147
Gutteridge, William F(rank) 1919- 13-16R
Gutterson, Herbert (Lindsley, Jr.) 1915- 9-12R
Gutting, Gary (Michael) 1942- CANR-37
Earlier sketch in CA 103
Guttmacher, Alan F(rank) 1898-1974 .... CANR-6
Obituary 49-52
Earlier sketch in CA 1-4R
Guttmacher, Manfred S(chanfarber) 1898-1966 ....
CAP-1
Earlier sketch in CA 11-12
Guttmann, Alexander 29-32R
Guttmann, Allen 1932- CANR-39
Earlier sketches in CA 1-4R, CANR-1, 16
Guttmann, Hadassah 1952- 143
Guttmann, Joseph 1946- 144
Guttridge, Leonard F(rancis) 1918- 85-88
Guttsman, Wilhelm Leo 1920- 9-12R
Gutwirth, Samuel William 1903-1983 Obituary .. 111
Gutzke, Manford G(eorge) 1896- 17-20R
Gutzkow, Karl 1811-1878 .... DLB 133
Guy, Anne W(elsh) 5-8R
Guy, David 1948- 105
Guy, Harold A. 1904- 17-20R
Guy, Mary E. 1947- 138
Guy, Ray 1939- 147
See also DLB 60
Guy, Rosa (Cuthbert) 1928- CANR-34
Earlier sketches in CA 17-20R, CANR-14
See also AAYA 4
See also BW 2
See also CLC 26
See also CLR 13
See also DLB 33
See also JRDA
See also MAICYA
See also SATA 14, 62
Guyer, Paul 1948- CANR-24
Earlier sketch in CA 105
Guymer, (Wilhelmina) Mary 1909- .... SATA 50
Guyot, Arnold 1807-1884 .... DLBD 13
Guyot, James F(ranklin) 1932- 53-56
Guy-Sheftall, Beverly 1946- 142
See also BW 2
Guyth, Gabriel
See Jennings, Gary (Gayne)
Guyton, Arthur C(lifton) 1919- CANR-7
Earlier sketch in CA 17-20R
Guzie, Tad W(alter) 1934- CANR-5
Earlier sketch in CA 13-16R
Guzman (Franco), Martin Luis 1887-1976 153
See also HW
Guzman, Ralph C. 1924-1985 Obituary 117
Guzzetti, Alfred F. 1942- 136
Guzzo, Lou(is Richard) 1919- 135
Guzzo, Sandra E(lizabeth) 1941- CANR-45
Earlier sketch in CA 120
Guzzwell, John 1930- 13-16R
Gwaltney, Francis Irby 1921- CANR-2
Earlier sketch in CA 1-4R
Gwaltney, John Langston 1928- 77-80
Gwendolyn
See Bennett, (Enoch) Arnold
Gwilliam, Kenneth M(ason) 1937- 17-20R
Gwin, Lucy 1943- 109
Gwinup, Thomas 1932- 73-76
Gwirtzman, Milton S. 1933- 29-32R
Gwyn, Julian 1937- 57-60
Gwyn, Richard J. 1934- CANR-17
Earlier sketch in CA 25-28R
Gwyn, W(illiam) B(rent) 1927- CANR-36
Earlier sketches in CA 13-16R, CANR-5
Gwynelle (Dismukes) 1952- 147
Gwynn, Denis (Rolleston) 1893- CAP-1
Earlier sketch in CA 13-14
Gwynn, Mary 1952- 111
Gwynn, R(obert) S(amuel) 1948- 161
Gwynn, Robin D(avid) 1942- CANR-47
Earlier sketch in CA 121
Gwynne, Erskine 1898-1948 Brief entry 107
See also DLB 4
Gwynne, Fred(erick Hubbard) 1926-1993 113
Obituary 141
See also SATA 41
See also SATA-Brief 27
See also SATA-Obit 75
Gwynne, Oscar A.
See Ellis, Edward S(ylvester)
Gwynne, Oswald A.
See Ellis, Edward S(ylvester)
Gwynne, Peter 1941- 89-92
Gwynne-Jones, Allan 1892-1982 Obituary 107
Gwynne-Thomas, E(ric) H(ubert) 1917- 120
Gyatso, Tenzin 1935- 141
Gyftopolous, Elias Panayiotis 1927- CANR-36
Earlier sketch in CA 104
Gyldenvand, Lily M. 1917- CANR-6
Earlier sketch in CA 13-16R
Gyles, John 1680-1755 .... DLB 99
Gylfason, Thorvaldur 1951- 145
Gyllenhammar, Pehr G(ustaf) 1935- CANR-13
Earlier sketch in CA 73-76
Gyoergyi, Albert (von Nagyrapolt) Szent
See Szent-Gyoergyi, Albert (von Nagyrapolt)
Gyohten, Toyoo 1931- 140
Gyorgy, Andrew 1917- 122
Gyorgyey, Clara 1936- 77-80
Gyorgyi, Albert (von Nagyrapolt) Szent
See Szent-Gyoergyi, Albert (von Nagyrapolt)
Gysbers, Norman C(harles) 1932- 61-64
Gysin, Brion 1916-1986 117
Obituary 120
Brief entry 113
Interview in 117
See also DLB 16
Gzay, Victor
See Conquest, (George) Robert (Acworth)
Gzowski, Peter 1934- CANR-40
Earlier sketch in CA 106
Interview in 106

H

H. D.
See Doolittle, Hilda
See also CLC 3, 8, 14, 31, 34, 73
See also PC 5
H. D. P.
See Dickey, Christopher
H. de V.
See Buchan, John
H. M. S.
See Kirk-Greene, Anthony (Hamilton Millard)
Haab, Sherri 1964- .... SATA 91
Haaby, Lawrence O. 1915- 33-36R
Haac, Oscar A(lfred) 1918- 33-36R
Haack, Susan 1945- 61-64
Haaf, Beverly T(erhune) 1936- 97-100
Haaften, Julia Van
See Van Haaften, Julia
Haag, Jessie Helen 1917- CANR-5
Earlier sketch in CA 13-16R
Haagensen, Cushman D(avis)
1900-1990 Obituary 132
Haak, Bob 1926- 144
Haaker, Ann M. 25-28R
Haakonssen, Knud 1947- CANR-51
Earlier sketch in CA 124
Haan, Aubrey Edwin 1908- 1-4R
Haar, Charles M(onroe) 1920- 33-36R
Haar, Francis 1908- 53-56
Haar, Franklin B. 1906- CAP-1
Earlier sketch in CA 11-12
Haar, Jaap ter
See ter Haar, Jaap
See also CLR 15
Haar, James 1929- 21-24R
Haarer, Alec Ernest 1894-1970 .... CANR-4
Earlier sketch in CA 5-8R
Haarhoff, Theodore Johannes 1892-1971 ... CAP-1
Earlier sketch in CA 13-14
Haarsager, Sandra (L.) 1946- 146
Haas, Albert E. 1917- 21-24R
Haas, Antonio 1923- 131
Haas, Ben(jamin) L(eopold) 1926-1977 .. CANR-63
Obituary 73-76
Earlier sketches in CA 9-12R, CANR-8
Haas, Carol 1949- 146
Haas, Carolyn Buhai 1926- CANR-9
Earlier sketch in CA 65-68
See also SATA 43
Haas, Charles A. 1947- 125
Haas, Charlie 1952- 73-76
Haas, Dorothy F. CANR-44
Earlier sketches in CA 5-8R, CANR-3, 20
See also SAAS 17
See also SATA 46
See also SATA-Brief 43
Haas, Ernst 1921-1986 Obituary 120
Haas, Ernst B(ernard) 1924- 81-84
Haas, Gerda (Schild) 1922- 110
Haas, Harold I(rwin) 1925- 29-32R
Haas, Irene 1929- CANR-65
Earlier sketch in CA 97-100
See also SATA 17, 96
Haas, Irvin 1916- 41-44R
Haas, J(ohn) Eugene 1926- 41-44R
Haas, James E(dward) 1943- CANR-7
Earlier sketch in CA 61-64
See also SATA 40
Haas, Jessie 1959- 114
See also SATA 98
Haas, Kenneth B(rooks) Sr. 1898- CANR-6
Earlier sketch in CA 57-60
Haas, Kurt 53-56
Haas, LaVerne 1942- 49-52
Haas, Lawrence J. 1956- 147
Haas, Lynne 1939- 65-68
Haas, Marilyn L(oomis) 1931- 117

Haas, Mary Odin 1910- CAP-1
Earlier sketch in CA 13-14
Haas, Mary R(osamond) 1910-1996 9-12R
Obituary 152
Haas, Merle S. 1896(?)-1985 Obituary 114
See also SATA-Obit 41
Haas, Michael 1938- 53-56
Haas, Raymond Michael 1935- 37-40R
Haas, Robert Bartlett 1916- Brief entry 108
Haas, Robert Lewis 1936- 101
Haase, Ann Marie Bernazza 1942- 33-36R
Haase, Donald 1950- 148
Haase, John 1923- CANR-14
Earlier sketch in CA 5-8R
Haavikko, Paavo Juhani 1931- 106
See also CLC 18, 34
Habakkuk, John H(rothgar) 1915- 151
Habbema, Koos
See Heijermans, Herman
Habe, Hans 1911-1977 CANR-2
Obituary 73-76
Earlier sketch in CA 45-48
Habegger, Alfred (Carl) 1941- 131
Habel, Janette
See Grimaldi, Janette Pienkny
Habel, Norman C. 1932- 17-20R
Habenstreit, Barbara 1937- 29-32R
See also SATA 5
Haber, Audrey 1940- CANR-13
Earlier sketch in CA 33-36R
Haber, Carole R. 1951- 124
Haber, Eitan 1940- 104
Haber, Francis Colin 1920-1990 Obituary 131
Haber, Fritz 1868-1934 156
Haber, Heinz 1913- 73-76
Haber, Jack 1939-1984 69-72
Obituary 114
Haber, Joyce 1932-1993 65-68
Obituary 142
Haber, Karen 1955- 146
See also SATA 78
Haber, Louis 1910- 29-32R
See also SATA 12
Haber, Ralph Norman 1932- 33-36R
Haber, Samuel 1928- 9-12R
Haber, Tom Burns 1900- CAP-2
Earlier sketch in CA 17-18
Haber, William 1899- CAP-2
Earlier sketch in CA 21-22
Haberer, Joseph 1929- 65-68
Haberler, Gottfried 1900- 103
Haberly, David T(ristram) 1942- 106
Haberly, Loyd 1896-1981 105
Obituary 103
Haberman, Daniel 1933-1991 110
Obituary 135
Haberman, David A. 1928- 126
Haberman, Donald (Charles) 1933- 21-24R
Haberman, Martin 1932- 57-60
Haberman, Shelby J(oel) 1947- 103
Habermann, Helen M(argaret) 1927- 53-56
Habermas, Juergen 1929- 109
See also CLC 104
Habermas, Jurgen
See Habermas, Juergen
Habers, Walther A(drianus) 1926- 147
Haberstroh, Chadwick John 1927- 41-44R
Habgood, John Stapylton 1927- CANR-45
Earlier sketches in CA 13-16R, CANR-5, 22
Habig, Marion A(lphonse) 1901-1984 CANR-20
Obituary 114
Earlier sketches in CA 5-8R, CANR-5
Habington, William 1605-1654 DLB 126
Hablutzel, Philip 1935- 37-40R
Habsburg-Lothringen, Geza Louis Eusebius Gebhard Ralphael Albert Maria
See von Habsburg(-Lothringen), Geza Louis Eusebius Gebhard Ralphael Albert Maria
Hach, Clarence Woodrow 1917- 13-16R
Hachey, Thomas E(ugene) 1938- 37-40R
Hachten, Harva 108
Hachten, William Andrews 1924- 107
Hacikyan, A(gop) J. 1931- 33-36R
Hack, Walter G. 1925- 29-32R
Hackady, Hal Brief entry 105
Hackbarth, Steven (L.) 1945- 159
Hackelsberger, Christoph 1931- 167
Hacker, Andrew 1929- CANR-41
Earlier sketches in CA 1-4R, CANR-1
Hacker, Barton C(lyde) 1935- 150
Hacker, Carlotta 1931- 118
Hacker, Frederick J. 1914-1989 Obituary 129
Brief entry 104
Hacker, Jeffrey H. 1954- 125
Hacker, Leonard
See Hackett, Buddy
Hacker, Louis M(orton) 1899-1987 17-20R
Obituary 122
Hacker, Marilyn 1942- CANR-68
Earlier sketch in CA 77-80
See also CLC 5, 9, 23, 72, 91
See also DAM POET
See also DLB 120
Hacker, Mary Louise 1908- CAP-2
Earlier sketch in CA 17-18
Hacker, P(eter) M(ichael) S(tephen) 1939- 158
Hacker, Rose (Goldbloom) 1906- 13-16R
Hacker, Shyrle 1910- 101
Hackes, Peter Sidney 1924-1994 102
Obituary 145
Hackett, Albert (Maurice) 1900-1995 166
See also DLB 26
Hackett, Blanche Ann 1924- 73-76
Hackett, Buddy 1924- Brief entry 108
Hackett, Cecil Arthur 1908- 13-16R
Hackett, Charles J(oseph) 1915- 73-76
Hackett, Donald F. 1918- 29-32R
Hackett, Francis 1883-1962 108
Obituary 89-92
Hackett, Herbert L(ewis) 1917-1964 1-4R
Hackett, Jan Michele 1952-1996 CANR-71
Obituary 152
Earlier sketch in CA 105
See also Kerouac, Jan
Hackett, John W. 1924- 17-20R
Hackett, John Winthrop 1910-1997 CANR-49
Obituary 161
Earlier sketch in CA 89-92
See also SATA 65
Hackett, Laura Lyman 1916- 17-20R
Hackett, Lee
See Arkley, Arthur J(ames)
Hackett, Marie G. 1923- 37-40R
Hackett, Pat 105
Hackett, Paul 1920- 29-32R
Hackett, Peter 1940- Brief entry 108
Hackett, Philip 1941- 77-80
Hackett, Roger F(leming) 1922- 77-80
Hackett, William H. Y., Jr. 1921(?)-1986 Obituary 118
Hackford, Robert 1921(?)-1983 Obituary 111
Hackforth-Jones, (Frank) Gilbert 1900- 13-16R
Hacking, Ian 1936- CANR-70
Earlier sketch in CA 69-72
Hackl, Erich 1954- 137
Hackleman, Michael A(lan) 1946- 106
Hackler, James C(ourtland) 1930- 112
Hackman, J(ohn) Richard 1940- CANR-1
Earlier sketch in CA 49-52
Hackman, Martha L. 1912- 29-32R
Hackney, Alan 1924- 5-8R
Hackney, Rod(erick Peter) 1942- 135
Hackney, Sheldon 1933- 41-44R
Hackney, Vivian 1914- 21-24R
Hacks, Peter 1928- DLB 124
Hackwell, W. John 1942- 126
Hackworth, David H. 1931- 130
See also BEST 89:4
Hadamard, Jacques (Salomon) 1865-1963 158
Hadas, Moses 1900-1966 CANR-6
Obituary 25-28R
Earlier sketch in CA 1-4R
Hadas, Pamela White 1946- CANR-16
Earlier sketch in CA 93-96
Hadas, Rachel 1948- CANR-55
Earlier sketches in CA 111, CANR-29
See also CAAS 23
See also DLB 120
Hadawi, Sami 1904- CANR-13
Earlier sketch in CA 21-24R
Hadda, Janet (Ruth) 1945- 128
Haddad, Bill
See Haddad, William F(rederick)
Haddad, George M. 1910- 17-20R
Haddad, Gladys 1930- 138
Haddad, Robert M(itchell) 1930- 69-72
Haddad, William
See Haddad, William F(rederick)
Haddad, William F(rederick) 1928- 159
Brief entry 108
Haddad, Yvonne Y(azbeck) 1935- CANR-50
Earlier sketches in CA 108, CANR-25
Haddad-Garcia, George 1954- 107
Haddam, Jane
See Papazoglou, Orania
Haddan, Eugene E. 1918- Brief entry 108
Hadden, Briton 1898-1929 DLB 91
Hadden, Jeffrey K(eith) 1936- 106
Hadden, Maude Miner 1880-1967 CAP-2
Earlier sketch in CA 17-18
Haddix, Cecille
See Haddix-Kontos, Cecille P.
Haddix, Margaret Peterson 1964- 159
See also SATA 94
Haddix-Kontos, Cecille P. 1937- 69-72
Haddo, Oliver
See Puechner, Ray
Haddock, K(eith) S(tanford) 1967- 145
Haddock, Lisa (Robyn) 1960- 146
Haddock, Sally 1954- 121
Haddon, Celia 1944- 130
Haddon, Christopher
See Palmer, John (Leslie)
Haddox, John H(erbert) 1929- 45-48
Hader, Berta (Hoerner) 1890(?)-1976 73-76
Obituary 65-68
See also MAICYA
See also SATA 16
Hader, Elmer Stanley 1889-1973 73-76
See also MAICYA
See also SATA 16
Hadfield, Alice M(ary) 1908- CANR-26
Earlier sketch in CA 108
Hadfield, (Ellis) Charles (Raymond) 1909- CANR-51
Earlier sketches in CA 13-16R, CANR-7, 26
Hadfield, E. C. R.
See Hadfield, (Ellis) Charles (Raymond)
Hadfield, John (Charles Heywood) 1907- 128
Hadfield, Miles H(eywood) 1903-1982 CAP-1
Obituary 106
Earlier sketch in CA 13-16
Hadfield, Vic(tor Edward) 1940- Brief entry 106
Hadham, John
See Parkes, James William
Hadik, Laszlo 1932(?)-1973 Obituary 45-48
Hadingham, Evan 1951- 102
Hadithi, Mwenye
See Hobson, Bruce
Hadley, Arthur T. 1924- 89-92
Hadley, Charles D(avid), Jr. 1942- CANR-31
Earlier sketch in CA 110
Hadley, Eleanor M(artha) 1916- 29-32R
Hadley, Franklin
See Winterbotham, R(ussell) R(obert)
Hadley, Hamilton 1896- CAP-1
Earlier sketch in CA 9-10
Hadley, Jay 1947- 114
Hadley, Joan
See Hess, Joan
Hadley, Lee 1934-1995 CANR-36
Obituary 149
Earlier sketches in CA 101, CANR-19
See also Irwin, Hadley
See also CLR 40
See also MAICYA
See also SATA 47, 89
See also SATA-Brief 38
See also SATA-Obit 86
Hadley, Leila 1925- CANR-14
Earlier sketch in CA 41-44R
Hadley, Michael L(lewellyn) 1936- 118
Hadley, Morris 1894-1979 Obituary 85-88
Hadley, Rollin van N. 1927- 127
Hadley Chase, James
See Raymond, Rene (Brabazon)
Hadlich, Roger L(ee) 1930- Brief entry 108
Hadlow, Leonard Harold 1908- CAP-1
Earlier sketch in CA 13-14
Hadrill, Andrew (Frederic) Wallace
See Wallace-Hadrill, Andrew (Frederic)
Hadrill, John Michael Wallace
See Wallace-Hadrill, John Michael
Hadwiger, Don F. 1930- 21-24R
Haeberle, Erwin J(akob) 1936- CANR-29
Earlier sketch in CA 29-32R
Haebich, Kathryn A. 1899- 5-8R
Haeckel, Ernst Heinrich (Philipp August) 1834-1919 157
See also TCLC 83
Haedrich, Marcel 1913- CANR-44
Earlier sketch in CA 85-88
Haefele, John W(illiam) 1913- 1-4R
Haeffele, Deborah 1954- SATA 76
Haefner, Richard 1929- 108
Haeger, John Denis 1942- 137
Haegerstrand, (Stig) Torsten (Erik) 1916- Brief entry 116
Haegg, Tomas 1938- 111
Haegglund, Bengt 1920- CANR-10
Earlier sketch in CA 25-28R
Haekkerup, Per 1915-1979 Obituary 85-88
Haenel, Wolfram 1956- 155
See also SATA 89
Haenicke, Diether H. 1935- 33-36R
Haentzschel, Adolph T(heodore) 1881-1971 1-4R
Obituary 103
Haering, Bernhard 1912- CANR-9
Earlier sketch in CA 5-8R
Haering, Georg Wilhelm Heinrich
See Alexis, Willibald
Haertling, Peter 1933- CANR-48
Earlier sketches in CA 101, CANR-22
See also Hartling, Peter
See also DLB 75
See also MAICYA
See also SATA 66
Haessler, Herbert A(lfred) 1926- 125
Haessly, Jacqueline 1937- 120
Hafemeister, David W(alter) 1934- CANR-51
Earlier sketch in CA 124
Hafen, Ann Woodbury 1893-1970 Obituary 111
Hafen, Brent Q(ue) 1940- CANR-40
Earlier sketch in CA 112
Hafen, LeRoy R(euben) 1893- 65-68
Hafer, W(illiam) Keith 108
Hafertepe, Kenneth 1955- 137
Haffenden, Philip Spencer 1926- 61-64
Haffner, J. Lilliwhite
See Speed, F(rederick) Maurice
Haffner, Robert C(hristian) G(ert) 1970- 158
Hafley, James 1928- 17-20R
Hafner, Lawrence E. 1924- CANR-10
Earlier sketch in CA 25-28R
Hafner, Marylin 1925- SATA 7
Hafrey, Leigh 1951- 142
Haga, Enoch J. 1931- 25-28R
Hagan, Arthur Peter 1912- 107
Hagan, Charles B(anner) 1905- 37-40R
Hagan, Chet 1922- CANR-25
Earlier sketch in CA 107
Hagan, John T(homas) 1926- 25-28R
Hagan, Kenneth J(ames) 1936- 41-44R
Hagan, Patricia
See Howell, Patricia Hagan
Hagan, William T(homas) 1918- CANR-8
Earlier sketch in CA 5-8R
Hagar, George
See Maria Del Rey, Sister
Hagarty, Britt 1949- 110
Hagberg, David J(ames) 1942- 106
Hagbrink, Bodil 1936- 104
Hage, Jerald 1932- 37-40R
Hagedorn, Friedrich von 1708-1754 DLB 168
Hagedorn, Hermann 1882-1964 Obituary 116
Hagedorn, Jessica
See Hagedorn, Jessica T(arahata)
Hagedorn, Jessica T(arahata) 1949- CANR-69
Earlier sketch in CA 139
Hagedorn, John M. 1947- 152
Hagedorn, Robert (Bruce) 1925- CANR-28
Earlier sketch in CA 49-52
Hagee, John C(harles) 1940- CANR-3
Earlier sketch in CA 45-48
Hagelin, Aiban 1934- 145
Hagelman, Charles W(illiam), Jr. 1920- 21-24R
Hagelstange, Rudolf 1912-1984 81-84
See also DLB 69
Hageman, Howard G(arberich) 1921-1992 CANR-46
Obituary 140
Earlier sketches in CA 1-4R, CANR-5
Hagen, Clifford (Warren, Jr.) 1943- 29-32R
Hagen, Elizabeth Pauline 1915- 13-16R
Hagen, Everett E(inar) 1906- CANR-1
Earlier sketch in CA 1-4R
Hagen, John Milton 1902- 57-60
Hagen, John William 1940- 61-64
Hagen, Lorinda
See Du Breuil, (Elizabeth) L(or)inda
Hagen, Richard L(ionel) 1935- 93-96
Hagen, Uta 1919- 77-80
Hager, Alice Rogers 1894-1969 5-8R
Obituary 103
See also SATA-Obit 26
Hager, Betty 1923- 155
See also SATA 89
Hager, Henry B. 1926- 17-20R
Hager, Jean 1932- 101
Hager, Judith
See Polley, Judith (Anne)
Hager, Robert M. 1938- 65-68
Hager, Thomas Arthur 1953- 126
Hagerman, Edward 1939- 130
Hagerman, Paul Stirling 1949- 106
Hagerstrand, (Stig) Torsten (Erik)
See Haegerstrand, (Stig) Torsten (Erik)
Hagerty, James C(ampbell) 1909-1981 129
Obituary 103
Hagerty, Nancy K. 1935- 33-36R
Hagerty, Sheward 1930-1983 Obituary 109
Hagg, G. Eric 1908(?)-1979 Obituary 85-88
Hagg, Tomas
See Haegg, Tomas
Haggai, Thomas Stephens 1931- 93-96
Haggar, R. G.
See Haggar, Reginald George
Haggar, Reginald G.
See Haggar, Reginald George
Haggar, Reginald George 1905-1988 Obituary 128
Haggard, H(enry) Rider 1856-1925 148
Brief entry 108
See also DLB 70, 156, 174, 178
See also SATA 16
See also TCLC 11
Haggard, Howard W. 1902- 121
Haggard, Merle (Ronald) 1937- 156
Brief entry 112
Haggard, Paul
See Longstreet, Stephen
Haggard, Raymond (Gordon Rider) 1921- Brief entry 109
Haggard, Virginia 1915- 122
Haggard, William
See Clayton, Richard Henry Michael
See also DLBY 93
Hagger, Nicholas 1939- 149
Haggerson, Nelson L. 1927- 41-44R
Haggerty, Brian A(rthur) 1943- CANR-32
Earlier sketch in CA 113
Haggerty, James J(oseph) 1920- 41-44R
See also SATA 5
Haggerty, P(atrick) E(ugene) 1914-1980 Obituary 105
Haggett, Peter 1933- 73-76
Haggie, Paul 1949- 124
Haggin, B(ernard) H. 1900-1987 CANR-18
Obituary 122
Earlier sketch in CA 102
Hagiosy, L.
See Larbaud, Valery (Nicolas)
Hagiwara, Michio Peter 1932- CANR-13
Earlier sketch in CA 73-76
Hagiwara Sakutaro 1886-1942 PC 18
See also TCLC 60
Hagler, Erwin Harrison 1947- 120
Hagler, Skeeter
See Hagler, Erwin Harrison
Haglund, Elaine J(ean) 1937- 109
Hagman, Bette 1922- 53-56
Hagman, Donald Gerald 1932-1982 Obituary 114
Hagner, Donald Alfred 1936- 110
Hagon, Priscilla
See Allan, Mabel Esther
Hagopian, John V. 1923- 41-44R
Hagopian, Mark N. 1940- CANR-28
Earlier sketch in CA 49-52
Hagstrom, Jerry 1947- CANR-34
Earlier sketch in CA 111
Hagstrom, Julie 1950- 111
Hagstrom, Warren Olaf 1930- 21-24R
Hagstrum, Jean (Howard) 1913- 17-20R
Hague, Douglas Chalmers 1926- CANR-20
Earlier sketch in CA 69-72
Hague, Harlan 1932- CANR-40
Earlier sketch in CA 116
Hague, (Susan) Kathleen 1949- 125
See also SATA 49
See also SATA-Brief 45
Hague, Michael R. 1948- CANR-36
Brief entry 111
Earlier sketch in CA 123
See also AAYA 18
See also MAICYA
See also SATA 48, 80
See also SATA-Brief 32
Hague, Richard 1947- CANR-54
Earlier sketch in CA 126
Hague, William Edward, Jr. 1919- 85-88
Hagy, Alyson 1960- 137
Hagy, James William 1936- 143
Hagy, Ruth Geri
See Brod, Ruth Hagy
Hahm, Sung Deuk 1963- 167

Hahn, Cynthia T. 1961- ... 162
Hahn, Emily 1905-1997 ... CANR-27
Obituary ... 156
Earlier sketches in CA 1-4R, CANR-1
Interview in ... CANR-27
See also CAAS 11
See also SATA 3
See also SATA-Obit 96
Hahn, F. E.
See Hahn, Friedrich Ernest
Hahn, Fred 1906- ... 45-48
Hahn, Fred E.
See Hahn, Friedrich Ernest
Hahn, Fred Ernest
See Hahn, Friedrich Ernest
Hahn, Friedrich Ernest 1916-1989 Obituary ... 129
Hahn, Gloria 1926-1987 Obituary ... 123
Hahn, H. George 1942- ... 107
Hahn, Hannelore ... CANR-3
Earlier sketch in CA 5-8R
See also SATA 8
Hahn, Harlan 1939- ... 33-36R
Hahn, James (Sage) 1947- ... CANR-17
Earlier sketches in CA 49-52, CANR-2
See also SATA 9
Hahn, Lewis E(dwin) 1908- ... 143
Hahn, (Mona) Lynn 1949- ... CANR-17
Earlier sketches in CA 49-52, CANR-2
See also SATA 9
Hahn, Mary Downing 1937- ... CANR-48
Earlier sketch in CA 122
See also AAYA 23
See also JRDA
See also MAICYA
See also SAAS 12
See also SATA 50, 81
See also SATA-Brief 44
Hahn, Michael T. 1953- ... 156
See also SATA 92
Hahn (Garces), Oscar (Arturo) 1938- ... 131
See also HW
Hahn, Otto 1879-1968 ... 158
Obituary ... 112
Hahn, Paul H. 1932- ... 117
Hahn, Robert H. 1920- ... 123
Hahn, Robert O(scar) 1916- ... 69-72
Hahn, Roger 1932- ... 33-36R
Hahn, Steven 1951- ... 123
Hahner, June E(dith) 1940- ... CANR-11
Earlier sketch in CA 25-28R
Hahn-Hahn, Ida Graefin von 1805-1875 ... DLB 133
Hahon, James
See Swift, Patrick
Hai, Lan
See Gao, Yuan
Haiblum, Isidore 1935- ... CANR-19
Earlier sketches in CA 53-56, CANR-4
Haidu, Peter 1931- ... 37-40R
Haig, Alexander M(eigs), Jr. 1924- ... 138
Brief entry ... 124
Haig, Fenil
See Ford, Ford Madox
Haig, (Irvine Reid) Stirling 1936- ... 33-36R
Haigaz, Aram
See Chekenian, Aram Haigaz
Haig-Brown, Roderick (Langmere) 1908-1976 ... CANR-38
Obituary ... 69-72
Earlier sketches in CA 5-8R, CANR-4
See also CLC 21
See also CLR 31
See also DLB 88
See also MAICYA
See also SATA 12
Haigerty, Leo James 1924- ... 1-4R
Haigh, Christopher 1944- ... 126
Haight, Amanda 1939- ... 77-80
Haight, Anne Lyon 1895-1977 ... CAP-2
Obituary ... 73-76
Earlier sketch in CA 33-36
See also SATA-Obit 30
Haight, Gordon S(herman) 1901-1985 ... CAP-2
Obituary ... 118
Earlier sketch in CA 25-28
See also DLB 103
Haight, John McVickar, Jr. 1917- ... 29-32R
Haight, M. R. 1938- ... 124
Haight, Mabel V. Jackson
See Jackson-Haight, Mabel V.
Haight, Mary Ellen Jordan
See Jordan Haight, Mary Ellen
Haight, Sandy 1949- ... SATA 79
Hail, Marshall 1905- ... 5-8R
Haile, H(arry) G(erald) 1931- ... 65-68
Hailes, Julia 1961- ... 130
Hailey, Arthur 1920- ... CANR-36
Earlier sketches in CA 1-4R, CANR-2
See also AITN 2
See also BEST 90:3
See also CLC 5
See also DAM NOV, POP
See also DLB 88
See also DLBY 82
See also MTCW 1
Hailey, Elizabeth Forsythe 1938- ... CANR-48
Earlier sketches in CA 93-96, CANR-15
Interview in ... CANR-15
See also CAAS 1
See also CLC 40
Hailey, J. P.
See Hall, Parnell
Hailey, Johanna
See Jarvis, Sharon
Hailey, Johanna
See Howl, Marcia (Yvonne Hurt)
Hailey, (Elizabeth) Kendall 1966- ... 136
Hailey, Oliver 1932-1993 ... CANR-46
Obituary ... 140
Earlier sketches in CA 41-44R, CANR-15
Hailey, Sheila 1927- ... 85-88
Hailperin, Herman 1899-1973 ... 5-8R
Obituary ... 103
Hailstones, Thomas J(ohn) 1919- ... 41-44R
Hailwood, Mike
See Hailwood, Stanley Michael Bailey
Hailwood, Stanley Michael Bailey 1940-1981 Obituary ... 108
Haiman, Franklyn S(aul) 1921- ... 37-40R
Haiman, Robert James 1936- ... 133
Haimann, Theo 1911- ... CANR-2
Earlier sketch in CA 5-8R
Haime, Agnes Irvine Constance (Adams) 1884- ... CAP-1
Earlier sketch in CA 9-10
Haimes, Norma ... 53-56
Haimo, Ethan 1950- ... 128
Haimowitz, Morris (Loeb) 1918- ... 37-40R
Haimowitz, Natalie Reader 1923- ... 53-56
Haimson, Leopold Henri 1917- ... 126
Brief entry ... 109
Hain, Peter 1950- ... 131
Hainaux, Rene 1918- ... 73-76
Haindl, Marieluise 1901-1974 Obituary ... 49-52
See also Fleisser, Marieluise
Haine, Edgar A. 1908- ... 97-100
Haines, Carolyn 1953- ... 163
Haines, Charles 1928- ... 41-44R
Haines, Charles G(rove) 1906-1976 Obituary ... 65-68
Haines, Edward Burdette 1910-1984 Obituary ... 112
Haines, Francis 1899- ... 5-8R
Haines, Francis D., Jr. 1923- ... 53-56
Haines, Gail Kay 1943- ... CANR-31
Earlier sketches in CA 37-40R, CANR-14
See also SATA 11
Haines, George H(enry), Jr. 1937- ... 33-36R
Haines, Harry B. 1949(?)-1984 Obituary ... 112
Haines, John
See Richardson, Gladwell
Haines, John (Meade) 1924- ... CANR-34
Earlier sketches in CA 17-20R, CANR-13
See also CLC 58
See also DLB 5
Haines, Max 1931- ... CANR-15
Earlier sketch in CA 85-88
Haines, Pamela Mary 1929- ... CANR-24
Earlier sketch in CA 106
Haines, Perry Franklin 1889- ... 5-8R
Haines, Richard W. 1957- ... 146
Haines, Walter W(ells) 1918- ... 1-4R
Haines, William Wister 1908-1989 ... CAP-1
Obituary ... 130
Earlier sketch in CA 9-10
Haining, Peter 1940- ... CANR-1
Earlier sketch in CA 45-48
See also SATA 14
Hains, Harriet
See Watson, Carol
Hainsworth, D(avid) R(oger) 1931- ... 141
Hainworth, Henry Charles 1914- ... 109
Hair, Donald S(herman) 1937- ... 69-72
Hair, P(aul) E(dward) H(edley) 1926- ... 25-28R
Hair, William Ivy 1930- ... 29-32R
Haire, Wilson John 1932- ... 101
Haire-Sargeant, Lin 1946- ... 139
Hairston, William (Russell, Jr.) 1928- ... 143
See also BW 2
Haislip, Harvey (Shadle) 1889-1978 ... 1-4R
Obituary ... 103
Haislip, John 1925- ... 33-36R
Haislip, Martha Pratt 1889(?)-1984 Obituary ... 112
Haithcox, John Patrick 1933- ... 29-32R
Haizlip, Shirlee Taylor 1937- ... 146
Haj, Fareed 1935- ... 29-32R
Hajdu, David 1955- ... 166
Hake, Thomas Gordon 1809-1895 ... DLB 32
Hakeda, Yoshito S. 1924(?)-1983 Obituary ... 110
Hakeem, Wali
See Gill, Walter
Hakes, Joseph Edward 1916- ... 9-12R
Hakim, Joy 1931- ... SATA 83
Hakim, Seymour 1933- ... 65-68
Hakutani, Yoshinobu 1935- ... 101
Halabi, Rafik 1946- ... 127
Halaby, Najeeb E(lias) 1915- Brief entry ... 107
Halacy, D(aniel) S(tephen), Jr. 1919- ... CANR-9
Earlier sketch in CA 5-8R
See also Halacy, Dan
See also SATA 36
Halacy, Dan
See Halacy, D(aniel) S(tephen), Jr.
See also SAAS 8
Halal, William E. 1933- ... 123
Halam, Ann
See Jones, Gwyneth A(nn)
Halas, Celia (Mary) 1922- ... 103
Halas, George Stanley 1895-1983 Obituary ... 111
Halas, John 1912- ... 108
Halasz, Gyula 1899-1984 ... CANR-58
Obituary ... 113
Earlier sketch in CA 126
Halasz, Nicholas 1895-1985 ... 17-20R
Obituary ... 116
Halbach, Edward C(hristian), Jr. 1931- ... 93-96
Halbe, Max 1865-1944 ... DLB 118
Halberg, Arvo Kusta
See Hall, Gus
Halberstadt, John 1941- ... 49-52
Halberstadt, William Harold 1930- ... 1-4R
Halberstam, David 1934- ... CANR-69
Earlier sketches in CA 69-72, CANR-10, 45
See also BEST 89:4
Halberstam, Michael J(oseph) 1932-1980 ... CANR-10
Obituary ... 102
Earlier sketch in CA 65-68
Halbert, Frederic (Leslie) 1945- ... 122
Brief entry ... 118
Halbert, Sandra (Edith) 1943- ... 123
Halbrook, Stephen P. ... CANR-47
Earlier sketch in CA 121
Halcomb, Ruth 1936- ... 97-100
Halcrow, Harold Graham 1911- ... 17-20R
Haldane, A(rchibald) R(ichard) B(urdon) 1900-1982 ... 120
Obituary ... 108
Haldane, Charlotte 1894-1969 ... DLB 191
Haldane, J(ohn) B(urdon) S(anderson) 1892-1964 ... 101
See also DLB 160
Haldane, R(obert) A(ylmer) 1907- ... 69-72
Haldane, Roger John 1945- ... SATA 13
Haldane-Stevenson, James Patrick 1910- ... CANR-14
Earlier sketch in CA 45-48
Haldeman, Charles (Heuss) 1931- ... 5-8R
Haldeman, H(arry) R(obbins) 1926-1993 ... 81-84
Obituary ... 143
Haldeman, Jack C(arroll II) 1941- ... 148
Brief entry ... 119
Haldeman, Joe (William) 1943- ... CANR-72
Earlier sketches in CA 53-56, CANR-6, 70
Interview in ... CANR-6
See also CAAS 25
See also CLC 61
See also DLB 8
Haldeman, Linda (Wilson) 1935- ... 85-88
Halder, Ras Mohun 1905(?)-1990 Obituary ... 131
Hale, Agnes Burke 1890-1981 Obituary ... 103
Hale, Allean Lemmon 1914- ... CANR-30
Earlier sketch in CA 33-36R
Hale, Antoinette
See Stockenberg, Antoinette
Hale, Arlene 1924-1982 ... CANR-1
Earlier sketch in CA 1-4R
See also SATA 49
Hale, Bob
See Hale, Robert D(avid)
Hale, Charles A(dams) 1930- ... 25-28R
Hale, Charlotte
See Allen, Charlotte Hale
Hale, Christy
See Apostolou, Christine Hale
Hale, Clarence B(enjamin) 1905- ... 69-72
Hale, David G(eorge) 1938- ... 45-48
Hale, Dennis 1944- ... 25-28R
Hale, Douglas 1929- ... 140
Hale, Edward Everett 1822-1909 ... 160
Brief entry ... 119
See also DLB 1, 42, 74
See also SATA 16
Hale, Francesca
See Halpern, Frances J(oy)
Hale, Francis Joseph 1922- ... 53-56
Hale, Frank (Wilbur), Jr. 1927- ... 65-68
Hale, Glenn
See Walker, Robert W(ayne)
Hale, Helen
See Mulcahy, Lucille Burnett
Hale, Irina 1932- ... 105
See also SATA 26
Hale, J. Russell 1918- ... 101
Hale, Jade
See Hyatt, Betty H(ale)
Hale, Janet Campbell 1947- ... CANR-45
Earlier sketch in CA 49-52
See also DAM MULT
See also DLB 175
See also NNAL
Hale, John (Barry) 1926- ... 102
Hale, John Rigby 1923- ... CANR-19
Earlier sketch in CA 102
Hale, Judson (Drake) 1933- ... 69-72
Hale, Julian A(nthony) S(tuart) 1940- ... 41-44R
Hale, Kathleen 1898- ... 73-76
See also DLB 160
See also SATA 17, 66
Hale, Keith 1955- ... 126
Hale, Leo Thomas
See Ebon
Hale, Leon 1921- ... CANR-10
Earlier sketch in CA 17-20R
Hale, (Charles) Leslie 1902-1985 ... CAP-1
Obituary ... 116
Earlier sketch in CA 13-16
Hale, Linda (Howe) 1929- ... 5-8R
See also SATA 6
Hale, Lionel Ramsay 1909-1977 Obituary ... 107
Hale, Lucretia P.
See Hale, Lucretia Peabody
Hale, Lucretia Peabody 1820-1900 ... 136
Brief entry ... 122
See also DLB 42
See also MAICYA
See also SATA 26
Hale, Margaret
See Higonnet, Margaret Randolph
Hale, Mason E(llsworth, Jr.) 1928-1990 Obituary ... 131
Hale, Michael
See Bullock, Michael
Hale, Nancy 1908-1988 ... 5-8R
Obituary ... 126
See also DLB 86
See also DLBD 17
See also DLBY 80, 88
See also SATA 31
See also SATA-Obit 57
Hale, Nathan Cabot 1925- ... 53-56
Hale, Nathan G., Jr. 1922- ... 154
Hale, Oron James 1902-1991 ... 13-16R
Obituary ... 135
Hale, Patricia Whitaker 1922- ... 53-56
Hale, Philip
See Eastwood, C(harles) Cyril
Hale, Richard W(alden) 1909-1976 Obituary ... 65-68
Hale, Robert Beverly 1901-1985 ... 141
Obituary ... 117
Hale, Robert D(avid) 1928- ... 134
Hale, Robert William 1937- ... 114
Hale, Sarah Josepha (Buell) 1788-1879 ... DLB 1, 42, 73
Hale, Wanda
See Coutard, Wanda Lundy Hale
Hale, William 1940- ... 125
Hale, William Harlan 1910-1974 ... 93-96
Obituary ... 49-52
Hales, Ann
See Hales-Tooke, Ann (Mary Margaret)
Hales, E(dward) E(lton) Y(oung) 1908- ... 85-88
Hales, Edward John 1927- ... 106
Hales, John 1584-1656 ... DLB 151
Hales, Loyde (Wesley) 1933- ... 89-92
Hales, Norman
See Young, Vernon
Hales, Peter Bacon 1950- ... 132
Hales-Tooke, Ann (Mary Margaret) 1926- ... 123
Brief entry ... 116
Halevi, Yossi Klein 1953- ... 154
Halevi, Z'ev ben Shimon
See Kenton, Warren
Halevy, Eva Etzioni
See Etzioni-Halevy, Eva
Halevy, Ludovic 1834-1908 ... DLB 192
Haley, Alex(ander Murray Palmer) 1921-1992 ... CANR-61
Obituary ... 136
Earlier sketch in CA 77-80
See also AAYA 26
See also BLC 2
See also BW 2
See also CLC 8, 12, 76
See also DA
See also DAB
See also DAC
See also DAM MST, MULT, POP
See also DLB 38
See also MTCW 1
Haley, Andrew G(allagher) 1904- ... CAP-1
Earlier sketch in CA 13-16
Haley, Bruce Everts 1933- Brief entry ... 108
Haley, Earl. J. 1898(?)-1987 Obituary ... 122
Haley, Gail E(inhart) 1939- ... CANR-35
Earlier sketches in CA 21-24R, CANR-14
See also CLR 21
See also MAICYA
See also SAAS 13
See also SATA 43, 78
See also SATA-Brief 28
Haley, Jack, Jr.
See Haley, John J., Jr.
Haley, James L(ewis) 1951- ... 77-80
Haley, Jay 1923- ... CANR-9
Earlier sketch in CA 21-24R
Haley, John J., Jr. 1933- ... 135
Haley, Joseph E. 1915- ... 13-16R
Haley, Ken(neth) H(arold) D(obson) 1920-1997 ... 159
Haley, Margaret Angela 1861-1939 Brief entry ... 112
Haley, Michael 1952- ... 109
Haley, Neale ... 41-44R
See also SATA 52
Haley, P. Edward ... 130
Haley, (Harry) Russell 1934- ... CANR-70
Earlier sketch in CA 118
Haley, William (John) 1901-1987 Obituary ... 123
Half, Robert 1918- ... 107
Halford, Graeme S(ydney) 1937- ... 154
Haliburton, Thomas Chandler 1796-1865 ... DLB 11, 99
Halifax, Joan (Squire) 1942- ... 85-88
Halio, Jay L(eon) 1928- ... CANR-10
Earlier sketch in CA 25-28R
Halivni, David
See Halivni, David Weiss
Halivni, David Weiss 1928- ... CANR-49
Halkett, John G(eorge) 1933- ... 57-60
Halkin, Abraham S. 1903-1990 Obituary ... 131
Halkin, Shimon 1899- ... 53-56
Halkin, Simon
See Halkin, Shimon
Hall, Adam
See Trevor, Elleston
Hall, Adele 1910- ... 1-4R
See also SATA 7
Hall, Adrian 1927- ... CANR-22
Earlier sketch in CA 106
Hall, Al(fred) Rupert 1920- ... 9-12R
Hall, Alice Clay 1900- ... 73-76
Hall, Andrew 1935- ... 21-24R
Hall, Angus 1932- ... CANR-13
Earlier sketch in CA 21-24R
Hall, Ann
See Duckert, Mary
Hall, Ann C. 1959- ... 149
Hall, Anna Gertrude 1882-1967 ... CAP-1
Earlier sketch in CA 11-12
See also SATA 8
Hall, Anna Maria 1800-1881 ... DLB 159
Hall, Anthony Stewart 1945- ... 102
Hall, Ariel Perry 1906- ... 69-72
Hall, Arlene Stevens 1923- ... 17-20R
Hall, Asa Zadel 1875-1965 ... CANR-4
Earlier sketch in CA 1-4R

Hall, Austin 1882(?)-1933 160
Brief entry 114
Hall, Aylmer
See Hall, Norah E. L.
Hall, B(axter) C(larence) 1936- CANR-9
Earlier sketch in CA 57-60
Hall, Barbara 1960- 135
See also AAYA 21
See also SATA 68
Hall, Bennie Caroline (Humble) 1-4R
Hall, Bert S(tewart) 1945- 167
Hall, Beverly B. 1918- 160
See also SATA 95
Hall, Blaine H(ill) 1932- 140
Hall, Borden
See Yates, Raymond F(rancis)
Hall, Brian (Jonathan) 1959- 137
Hall, Brian P(atrick) 1935- CANR-9
Earlier sketch in CA 61-64
See also SATA 31
Hall, C(onstance) Margaret 1937- CANR-12
Earlier sketch in CA 73-76
Hall, Calvin (Springer) 1909- 13-16R
Hall, Cameron
See del Rey, Lester
Hall, Cameron P(arker) 1898- 49-52
Hall, Carl W. 1924- 135
Hall, Carolyn Vosburg 1927- 61-64
Hall, Caryl
See Hansen, Caryl (Hall)
Hall, Challis A(lva), Jr. 1917-1968 .... 1-4R
Obituary 103
Hall, Charles A(rthur) M(ann) 1924- Brief entry . 107
Hall, Clarence W(ilbur) 1902-1985 Obituary 114
Hall, Claudia
See Floren, Lee
Hall, Clifton L. 1898- CAP-1
Earlier sketch in CA 11-12
Hall, D(onald) J(ohn) 1903- 13-16R
Hall, Daniel 1952- 163
Hall, Daniel George Edward 1891-1979 103
Hall, David C. 1943- 140
Hall, David D(risko) 1936- 125
Brief entry 108
Hall, David Locke 1955- 140
Hall, Don 1929- 110
Hall, Don Alan 1938- 108
Hall, Donald (Andrew, Jr.) 1928- CANR-64
Earlier sketches in CA 5-8R, CANR-2, 44
See also CAAS 7
See also CLC 1, 13, 37, 59
See also DAM POET
See also DLB 5
See also SATA 23, 97
Hall, Donald Ray 1933- 33-36R
Hall, Dorothy Judd 122
Hall, Douglas 1931- .... SATA 43
Hall, Douglas John 1928- CANR-14
Earlier sketch in CA 69-72
Hall, Douglas Kent 1938- 33-36R
Hall, Edward 1497-1547 .... DLB 132
Hall, Edward Twitchell (Jr.) 1914- 65-68
Hall, Elizabeth 1929- CANR-60
Earlier sketches in CA 65-68, CANR-14, 31
See also SATA 77
Hall, Elizabeth Cornelia 1898- 37-40R
Hall, Elvajean 1910- CANR-8
Earlier sketch in CA 13-16R
See also SATA 6
Hall, Eric B(rinn) 1963- 149
Hall, Eric J(ohn) 1933- 97-100
Hall, Evan
See Halleran, Eugene E(dward)
Hall, F. H. 1926- 77-80
Hall, Fernau 102
Hall, Frederic Sauser
See Sauser-Hall, Frederic
Hall, Gene E(rwin) 1941- 93-96
Hall, Geoffrey Fowler 1888-1970 .... CAP-1
Earlier sketch in CA 13-14
Hall, George 1941- CANR-15
Earlier sketch in CA 85-88
Hall, George F(ridolph) 1908- CANR-22
Earlier sketch in CA 45-48
Hall, George R. 1930- 123
Hall, Georgette Brockman 1915- 57-60
Hall, Geraldine M(arion) 1935- 33-36R
Hall, Gimone 1940- CANR-33
Earlier sketches in CA 29-32R, CANR-15
Hall, Gladys 1891(?)-1977 Obituary 73-76
Hall, Gordon Langley
See Simmons, Dawn Langley
Hall, Gregory 1948- 165
Hall, Gus 1910- 137
Brief entry 108
Hall, Gwendolyn Midlo 1929- 41-44R
Hall, H(essel) Duncan 1891-1976 .... CAP-2
Obituary 65-68
Earlier sketch in CA 29-32
Hall, H(ugh) Gaston 1931- 131
Hall, Halbert Weldon 1941- 53-56
Hall, Haywood 1898- 77-80
Hall, Helen 1892- 104
Hall, Henry M(arion) 1877- 5-8R
Hall, J(ohn) C(live) 1920- 101
Hall, J(ames) Curtis 1926- 53-56
Hall, J. De P.
See McKelway, St. Clair
Hall, J. Tillman 1916- CANR-6
Earlier sketch in CA 1-4R
Hall, Jacquelyn (Dowd) 1943- 97-100
Hall, James
See Kuttner, Henry
Hall, James 1793-1868 .... DLB 73, 74
Hall, James 1918- 102
Hall, James (Herrick, Jr.) 1933- 53-56
Hall, James Andrew 1935- CANR-42
Earlier sketch in CA 118
Hall, James B(yron) 1918- CANR-42
Earlier sketches in CA 1-4R, CANR-1
See also CAAS 12
Hall, James Baker 1935- 116
Hall, James Norman 1887-1951 Brief entry 123
See also SATA 21
See also TCLC 23
Hall, James W(illiam) 1937- CANR-47
Earlier sketches in CA 45-48, CANR-22
Hall, Jay 1932- CANR-56
Earlier sketch in CA 127
Hall, Jay C.
See Hall, John C.
Hall, Jean R(ogers) 1941- 105
Hall, Jerome 1901-1992 .... CAP-1
Obituary 137
Earlier sketch in CA 11-12
Hall, Jesse
See Boesen, Victor
Hall, Joan Wylie 1947- 154
Hall, John 1937- 93-96
Hall, John C. 1915- 57-60
Hall, John F. 1919- CANR-17
Earlier sketch in CA 1-4R
Hall, John O. P. 1911- 9-12R
Hall, John Whitney 1916-1997 .... 25-28R
Obituary 162
Hall, Josef Washington 1894-1960 Obituary .. 89-92
Hall, Joseph 1574-1656 .... DLB 121, 151
Hall, Joseph (Sargent) 1906- 41-44R
Hall, Julie (Ann) 1943- Brief entry 110
Hall, Kathleen M(ary) 1924- CANR-3
Earlier sketch in CA 5-8R
Hall, Katy
See McMullan, Kate Hall
Hall, Kendall
See Heath, Harry E(ugene), Jr.
Hall, Kenneth F(ranklin) 1926- 17-20R
Hall, Kermit L(ance) 1944- 101
Hall, Kirsten Marie 1974- 135
See also SATA 67
Hall, Laurence James 1940- 97-100
Hall, Lawrence Sargent 1915- 1-4R
Hall, Lee 1934- 159
Hall, (Frederick) Leonard 1899- CANR-27
Earlier sketch in CA 65-68
Hall, Lesley A(nn) 1949- 142
Hall, Leslie 1948- 126
Hall, Linda B(iesele) 1939- CANR-23
Earlier sketch in CA 106
Hall, Livingston 1903- CAP-2
Earlier sketch in CA 21-22
Hall, Louis Brewer 1920- 110
Hall, Luella J(emima) 1890-1973 45-48
Obituary 103
Hall, Lynn 1937- CANR-37
Earlier sketches in CA 21-24R, CANR-9, 25
See also AAYA 4
See also JRDA
See also MAICYA
See also SAAS 4
See also SATA 2, 47, 79
Hall, Malcolm 1945- CANR-4
Earlier sketch in CA 49-52
See also SATA 7
Hall, Manly Palmer 1901-1990 93-96
Obituary 132
Hall, Marie Boas 1919- 9-12R
Hall, Marie-Beth 1933- 145
Hall, Marjory
See Yeakley, Marjory Hall
Hall, Mark W. 1943- 33-36R
Hall, Martha Lacy 1923- 162
Hall, Martin Hardwick 1925-1979(?) CANR-35
Earlier sketch in CA 33-36R
Hall, Mary Ann 1942- 116
Hall, Mary Bowen 1932- 21-24R
Hall, MaryAnne 1934- CANR-25
Earlier sketch in CA 29-32R
Hall, Matthew 1958- 167
Hall, Melanie 1949- .... SATA 78
Hall, Michael Garibaldi 1926- 13-16R
Hall, Monty 1924- Brief entry 108
Hall, N(orman) John 1933- CANR-57
Earlier sketches in CA 61-64, CANR-12, 31
Hall, Nancy Lee 1923- 57-60
Hall, Natalie Watson 1923- 5-8R
Hall, Neal (Gordon) 1952- 134
Hall, Noel (Frederick) 1902-1983 Obituary 109
Hall, Norah E. L. 1914- 97-100
Hall, O. M.
See Hall, Oakley (Maxwell)
Hall, Oakley (Maxwell) 1920- CANR-46
Earlier sketches in CA 9-12R, CANR-3
Hall, Parnell 1944- 166
Hall, Patrick 1932- 21-24R
Hall, Penelope C(oker) 1933- 17-20R
Hall, Peter (Reginald Frederick) 1930- 133
Hall, Peter (Geoffrey) 1932- CANR-24
Earlier sketches in CA 17-20R, CANR-8
Hall, Phil 1953- 102
Hall, R(obert) Cargill 1937- CANR-1
Earlier sketch in CA 49-52
Hall, Radclyffe 1880-1943 .... DLB 191
Hall, (Marguerite) Radclyffe 1886-1943 150
Brief entry 110
See also TCLC 12
Hall, Richard
See Bickers, Richard (Leslie) Townshend
Hall, Richard (Seymour) 1925-1997 .... CANR-9
Obituary 162
Earlier sketch in CA 17-20R
Hall, (Patrick) Richard Compton
See Compton-Hall, (Patrick) Richard
Hall, Richard H(ammond) 1934- CANR-13
Earlier sketch in CA 77-80
Hall, Richard W(alter) 1926-1992 148
Hall, Robert
See Wubbels, Lance
Hall, Robert A(nderson), Jr. 1911- CANR-5
Earlier sketch in CA 13-16R
Hall, Robert Benjamin 1918- 57-60
Hall, Robert Burnett, Jr. 1923- Brief entry 109
Hall, Robert E(lliott) 1924- CANR-13
Earlier sketch in CA 17-20R
Hall, Robert E(rnest) 1943- 114
Hall, Robert Lee 1941- 73-76
Hall, Robert T(om) 1938- Brief entry 110
Hall, Rodney 1935- CANR-69
Earlier sketch in CA 109
See also CLC 51
Hall, Roger (Wolcott) 1919- 29-32R
Hall, Roger (Leighton) 1939- 134
Hall, Roger 1945- 112
Hall, Rosalys Haskell 1914- 9-12R
See also SATA 7
Hall, Ross H(ume) 1926- 61-64
Hall, Rubylea (Ray) 1910- CAP-2
Earlier sketch in CA 17-18
Hall, Ruth 1933(?)-1981 Obituary 104
Hall, Sam 1936- 137
Hall, Sarah Ewing 1761-1830 .... DLB 200
Hall, Steffie
See Evanovich, Janet
Hall, Stephen S. 1951- CANR-72
Earlier sketch in CA 141
Hall, Steven (Leonard) 1960- 93-96
Hall, Susan 1940- 57-60
Hall, T(homas) William 1921- 118
Hall, Ted Byron 1902- CAP-2
Earlier sketch in CA 33-36
Hall, Thor 1927- 37-40R
Hall, Tom T. 1936- 102
Interview in 102
Hall, Tony
See Hall, Anthony Stewart
Hall, Tord (Erik Martin) 1910- 29-32R
Hall, Trevor H(enry) 1910-1991 .... CANR-16
Obituary 134
Earlier sketch in CA 29-32R
Hall, Van Beck 1934- 45-48
Hall, Vernon, Jr. 1913- CANR-3
Earlier sketch in CA 5-8R
Hall, Wade H. 1934- CANR-6
Earlier sketch in CA 5-8R
Hall, Walter (Earl, Jr.) 1940- CANR-13
Earlier sketch in CA 21-24R
Hall, Wayne E(dward) 1947- 105
Hall, William N(orman) 1915-1974 Obituary .. 53-56
Hall, Willis 1929- CANR-70
Earlier sketches in CA 101, CANR-36
See also MTCW 1
See also SATA 66
Hall, Wilson (Dudley) 1922-1991 69-72
Obituary 133
Halla, (Robert) Chris(tian) 1949- CANR-18
Earlier sketch in CA 77-80
Hallahan, William H(enry) Brief entry 109
Hallahmi, Benjamin Beit
See Beit-Hallahmi, Benjamin
Hallam, Arthur Henry 1811-1833 .... DLB 32
Hallam, (Samuel Benoni) Atlantis 1915- 5-8R
Hallam, Elizabeth M. 1950- CANR-50
Earlier sketch in CA 123
Hallam, H(erbert) E(noch) 1923- 21-24R
Hallam, J(ohn) Harvey 1917- 13-16R
Hallard, Peter
See Catherall, Arthur
Hallas, Richard
See Knight, Eric (Mowbray)
Hallberg, Charles William 1899- CAP-1
Earlier sketch in CA 17-18
Hallberg, Edmond C. 1931- Brief entry 111
Hallberg, Peter 1916- CANR-4
Earlier sketch in CA 53-56
Hall-Clarke, James
See Rowland-Entwistle, (Arthur) Theodore (Henry)
Halle, Jean-Claude 1939- CANR-17
Earlier sketch in CA 93-96
Halle, Katherine Murphy 1904(?)-1997 .... 41-44R
Obituary 160
Halle, Kay
See Halle, Katherine Murphy
Halle, Louis J(oseph) 1910- CANR-2
Earlier sketch in CA 1-4R
Halleck, Fitz-Greene 1790-1867 .... DLB 3
Halleck, Seymour L(eon) 1929- CANR-13
Earlier sketch in CA 21-24R
Haller, Albrecht von 1708-1777 .... DLB 168
Haller, Archibald O(rben), Jr. 1926- 45-48
Haller, Bill
See Bechko, P(eggy) A(nne)
Haller, Dorcas Woodbury 1946- 117
See also SATA 46
Haller, Ellis M(etcalf) 1915-1981 Obituary 103
Haller, John Samuel, Jr. 1940- 61-64
Haller, Mark H(ughlin) 1928- CANR-5
Earlier sketch in CA 9-12R
Haller, Mike 1945- 110
Haller, Robert S(pencer) 1933- CANR-2
Earlier sketch in CA 1-4R
Haller, Robin Meredith 1944- 65-68
Haller, William 1885-1974 Obituary 49-52
Halleran, Eugene E(dward) 1905- CANR-63
Earlier sketch in CA 1-4R
Hallet, Jean-Pierre 1927- 17-20R
Hallett, Charles A(rthur) 141
Hallett, Ellen Kathleen 1899- CAP-1
Earlier sketch in CA 13-16
Hallett, Garth L(ie) 1927- CANR-13
Earlier sketch in CA 69-72
Hallett, George H(ervey), Jr.
1895-1985 Obituary 116
Hallett, Graham 1929- CANR-16
Earlier sketch in CA 25-28R
Hallett, Judith Peller 1944- CANR-51
Earlier sketch in CA 124
Hallett, Kathryn J(osephine) 1937- 57-60
Hallett, Mark 1947- .... SATA 83
Hallett, Robin 1926- 103
Halley, Anne 1928- 121
Halley, Laurence
See O'Keeffe, Laurence
Hallgarten, George W(olfgang) F(elix)
1901-1975 65-68
Obituary 57-60
Hallgarten, Peter A(lexander) 1931- 97-100
Hallgarten, Siegfried Fritz 1902- CANR-18
Earlier sketches in CA 5-8R, CANR-3
Hallgren, Chris 1947- 115
Halliburton, David (Garland) 1933- 159
Brief entry 116
Halliburton, Richard 1900-1939(?) 135
Brief entry 114
See also SATA 81
Halliburton, Rudia, Jr. 1929- 81-84
Halliburton, Warren J. 1924- CANR-24
Earlier sketch in CA 33-36R
See also BW 2
See also SATA 19
Halliday, Brett
See Dresser, Davis
and Terrall, Robert
Halliday, David 1948- 113
Halliday, Dorothy
See Dunnett, Dorothy
Halliday, E(rnest) M(ilton) 1913- 1-4R
Halliday, Ena
See Baumgarten, Sylvia
Halliday, F(rank) E(rnest) 1903-1982 .... CANR-2
Obituary 106
Earlier sketch in CA 1-4R
Halliday, Fred 1937- 53-56
Halliday, James
See Symington, David
Halliday, Jerry 1949- 69-72
Halliday, Jon 1939- 97-100
Halliday, M(ichael) A(lexander) K(irkwood)
1925- 126
Brief entry 112
Halliday, Michael
See Creasey, John
Halliday, Nigel Vaux 1956- 140
Halliday, Richard 1905-1973 Obituary 41-44R
Halliday, Tim (Richard) 1945- 112
Halliday, William R(oss) 1926- 49-52
See also SATA 52
Hallie, Philip P(aul) 1922-1994 .... CANR-9
Obituary 146
Earlier sketch in CA 13-16R
Hallier, Amedee 1913- 73-76
Halligan, Marion (Mildred Crothall) 1940- 160
Halligan, Nicholas 1917- CANR-5
Earlier sketch in CA 13-16R
Hallin, Emily Watson CANR-26
Earlier sketches in CA 25-28R, CANR-10
See also SATA 6
Hallinan, Hazel Hunkins 1891(?)-1982 Obituary . 106
Hallinan, Nancy 1921- CANR-3
Earlier sketch in CA 9-12R
Hallinan, P(atrick) K(enneth) 1944- CANR-11
Earlier sketch in CA 69-72
See also SATA 39
See also SATA-Brief 37
Hallinan, Vincent 1896- 1-4R
Hallion, Richard P(aul, Jr.) 1948- 41-44R
Halliwell, David (William) 1936- CANR-57
Earlier sketches in CA 65-68, CANR-11, 31
Halliwell, Leslie 1929-1989 .... CANR-16
Obituary 127
Earlier sketches in CA 49-52, CANR-1
Halliwell-Phillipps, James Orchard 1820-1889 .. DLB 184
Hall-Jones, Frederick George
1891-1982 Obituary 108
Hallman, Frank Curtis 1943(?)-1975 Obituary .. 104
Hallman, G(eorge) Victor III 1930- 101
Hallman, Howard W(esley) 1928- 116
Hallman, Ralph J(efferson) 1911- 13-16R
Hallman, Ruth 1929- CANR-15
Earlier sketch in CA 85-88
See also SATA 43
See also SATA-Brief 28
Hallmann, Johann Christian c. 1640-1704(?) ... DLB 168
Hallo, William W. 1928- CANR-15
Earlier sketch in CA 37-40R
Hallock, G. B. F.
See Hallock, Gerard B(enjamin) F(leet)
Hallock, Gerard B(enjamin) F(leet) 1856-1953 Brief entry 122
Hallock, Robert Lay 1898(?)-1986 Obituary 120
Halloran, Richard (Colby) 1930- 29-32R
Halloway, Vance 1916- 53-56
Hallowell, A(lfred) Irving 1892-1974 .... 5-8R
Obituary 53-56
Hallowell, Christopher L. 1945- 93-96
Hallowell, John H(amilton) 1913- CANR-5
Earlier sketch in CA 13-16R
Hallowell, Tommy
See Hill, Thomas
Hallpike, C. R. 1938- 41-44R

Hall-Quest, (Edna) Olga W(ilbourne)
1899-1986 .... 5-8R
Obituary 118
See also SATA 11
See also SATA-Obit 47
Halls, Geraldine (Mary) 1919-1996 ...... CANR-60
Earlier sketch in CA 103
Halls, W(ilfred) D(ouglas) 1918- CANR-5
Earlier sketch in CA 1-4R
Hallstead, William F(inn III) 1924- CANR-21
Earlier sketches in CA 5-8R, CANR-6
See also SATA 11
Hallstein, Walter 1901-1982 Obituary 106
Hallstroem, Lasse 1946- 165
Hallstroem, Per (August Leonard)
1866-1960 Obituary 116
Hallstrom, Lasse
See Hallstroem, Lasse
Hallstrom, Per (August Leonard)
See Hallstroem, Per (August Leonard)
Hallus, Tak
See Robinett, Stephen (Allen)
Hallward, Michael 1889- 49-52
See also SATA 12
Hallwas, John E. 1945- 154
Halm, Ben B. 1957- 151
Halm, George N(ikolaus) 1901- 21-24R
Halman, Talat Sait 1931- CANR-4
Earlier sketch in CA 53-56
Halmi, Katherine A. 1939- 144
Halmos, Paul 1911-1977 .... CANR-8
Earlier sketch in CA 17-20R
Halper
See Halpern, Leivick
Halper, Albert 1904-1984 .... CANR-3
Obituary 111
Earlier sketch in CA 5-8R
See also DLB 9
Halper, Nathan 1908(?)-1983 Obituary 110
Halper, Sam 1916-1989 Obituary 128
Halper, Thomas 1942- 41-44R
Halperin, David M(artin) 1952- CANR-41
Earlier sketch in CA 117
Halperin, Don A(kiba) 1925- 57-60
Halperin, Edwin G. 1935(?)-1987 Obituary 123
Halperin, Irving 1922- 29-32R
Halperin, James L(ewis) 1952- 157
Halperin, Joan Ungersma 1932- 137
Halperin, John (William) 1941- CANR-57
Earlier sketches in CA 53-56, CANR-6
See also DLB 111
Halperin, Jonathan L. 1949- 132
Halperin, Mark (Warren) 1940- CANR-9
Earlier sketch in CA 65-68
Halperin, Maurice (H.) 1906-1995 73-76
Obituary 147
Halperin, Morton H. 1938- CANR-3
Earlier sketch in CA 9-12R
Halperin, S(amuel) William 1905-1979 97-100
Obituary 85-88
Halperin, Samuel 1930- CANR-1
Earlier sketch in CA 1-4R
Halperin, Wendy Anderson 1952- .... SATA 80
Halpern, A(braham) M(eyer) 1914- 17-20R
Halpern, Barbara Kerewsky
See Kerewsky-Halpern, Barbara
Halpern, Barbara Strachey 1912- 106
Halpern, Ben(jamin) 1912-1990 Obituary 131
Brief entry 115
Halpern, Cynthia Leone 1952- 147
Halpern, Daniel 1945- 33-36R
See also CLC 14
Halpern, Frances J(oy) 114
Halpern, Howard Marvin 1929- 93-96
Halpern, Joel M. 1929- CANR-3
Earlier sketch in CA 5-8R
Halpern, L.
See Halpern, Leivick
Halpern, Leivick 1888-1962 Obituary 114
Halpern, Manfred 1924- 9-12R
Halpern, Martin 1929- CANR-7
Earlier sketch in CA 5-8R
Halpern, Oscar Saul 1912-1994 97-100
Obituary 145
Halpern, Paul 1961- 141
Halpern, Paul G. 1937- 45-48
Halpern, Paul J(oseph) 1942- CANR-7
Earlier sketch in CA 57-60
Halpern, Stephen Mark 1940- 57-60
Halpern, Sue 139
Halpert, Inge D. 1926- 21-24R
Halpert, Stephen 1941- 37-40R
Halpin, Andrew W(illiams) 1911- 17-20R
Halpin, Marlene 1927- 152
See also SATA 88
Halprin, Anna Schuman 1920- 85-88
Halprin, Lawrence 1916- 41-44R
Hals, Ronald M. 1926- 33-36R
Halsall, Elizabeth 1916- 33-36R
Halsall, Eric 1920- 107
Halsband, Robert 1914-1989 .... CANR-8
Obituary 130
Earlier sketch in CA 17-20R
Halsell, Grace (Eleanor) 1923- CANR-13
Earlier sketch in CA 21-24R
See also AITN 1
See also SATA 13
Halsey, A(lbert) H(enry) 1923- CANR-7
Earlier sketch in CA 17-20R
Halsey, Elizabeth 1890- CAP-2
Earlier sketch in CA 17-18
Halsey, Elizabeth Tower
1903(?)-1976 Obituary 65-68
Halsey, George Dawson 1889-1970 .... 1-4R
Obituary 103
Halsey, Margaret (Frances) 1910-1997 81-84
Obituary 156
Halsey, Martha T. 1932- CANR-14
Earlier sketch in CA 37-40R
Halsey, William D(arrach) 1918- Brief entry 117
Halsman, Philippe 1906-1979 .... CANR-10
Obituary 89-92
Earlier sketch in CA 21-24R
Halstead, Dirck S. 1936- 133
Halstead, Murat 1829-1908 .... DLB 23
Halstead, William Perdue 1906-1982 Obituary .. 109
Halsted, Anna Roosevelt
1906-1975 Obituary 61-64
See also SATA-Obit 30
Halstock, Max
See Caulfield, Malachy Francis
Halter, Carl 1915- 17-20R
Halter, Jon C(harles) 1941- CANR-13
Earlier sketch in CA 61-64
See also SATA 22
Halter, Marek 1936- 140
Halton, David 1940- 73-76
Halton, Eugene Rochberg
See Rochberg-Halton, Eugene
Haltrecht, Montague 1932- 29-32R
Halverson, Alton C. O. 1922- 61-64
Halverson, Richard C(hristian) 1916-1995 . CANR-3
Obituary 150
Earlier sketch in CA 1-4R
Halverson, Richard P(aul) 1941- 109
Halverson, William H(agen) 1930- CANR-47
Earlier sketch in CA 37-40R
Halvorson, Arndt L(eroy) 1915- CANR-3
Earlier sketch in CA 5-8R
Halvorson, Marilyn 1948- 132
Halward, Leslie G. 1904(?)-1976 Obituary 65-68
Ham, Debra Newman 1948- 148
Ham, Wayne 1938- CANR-11
Earlier sketch in CA 21-24R
Hamachek, Don E. 1933- 17-20R
Hamada, Hirosuke 1893- 45-48
Hamady, Walter .... AITN 1
Hamalainen, Pekka Kalevi 1938- 97-100
Hamalainen, Pertti (Olavi) 1952- 138
Hamalian, Leo 1920- CANR-2
Earlier sketch in CA 5-8R
See also SATA 41
Hamamoto, Darrell Y. 1953- 151
Hamann, Johann Georg 1730-1788 .... DLB 97
Hamberg, Daniel 1924- 1-4R
Hamberger, John 1934- 69-72
See also SATA 14
Hambletonian
See Fairfax-Blakeborough, John Freeman
Hamblett, Theora 1895(?)-1977 Obituary 69-72
Hamblin, C(harles) L(eonard) 1922- 25-28R
Hamblin, Dora Jane 1920- 37-40R
See also SATA 36
Hamblin, Douglas H. 1923- 115
Hamblin, Robert L(ee) 1927- 97-100
Hamblin, Robert W(ayne) 1938- 131
Hamblin, W. K. 1928- 53-56
Hambourg, Maria Morris 1949- 130
Hambrey, Michael (John) 1948- 143
Hambrick-Stowe, Charles E(dwin) 1948- 125
Hamburg, Carl H(einz) 1915- 37-40R
Hamburg, David A(llen) 1925- Brief entry 109
Hamburg, Morris 1922- Brief entry 114
Hamburger, Ernest 1891(?)-1980 Obituary .. 97-100
Hamburger, Estelle 1898(?)-1983 Obituary 110
Hamburger, Kaete 1896- CANR-14
Earlier sketch in CA 29-32R
Hamburger, Max 1897-1970 .... CAP-2
Earlier sketch in CA 17-18
Hamburger, Michael (Peter Leopold) 1924- ....
CANR-47
Earlier sketches in CA 5-8R, CANR-2
See also CAAS 4
See also CLC 5, 14
See also DLB 27
Hamburger, Michael J(ay) 1938- CANR-3
Earlier sketch in CA 45-48
Hamburger, Philip 1914- 5-8R
Hamburger, Robert (A., Jr.) 1943- CANR-8
Earlier sketch in CA 61-64
Hamburger, Viktor 1900- 156
Hamburgh, Max 1922- 61-64
Hamby, Alonzo L. 1940- CANR-66
Earlier sketches in CA 37-40R, CANR-15
Hamel, Peter Michael 1947- 97-100
Hamel Dobkin, Kathleen
See Hamel Peifer, Kathleen
Hamelin, Louis-Edmond 1923- 110
Hamell, Patrick Joseph 1910- CAP-1
Earlier sketch in CA 13-16
Hamelman, Paul W(illiam) 1930-1976 ...... 41-44R
Hamel Peifer, Kathleen 1945- CANR-28
Earlier sketch in CA 110
Hamer, David Allan 1938- CANR-35
Earlier sketch in CA 45-48
Hamer, Forrest 1956- 152
Hamer, Frank 1929- 105
Hamer, Mick 1946- 109
Hamer, Philip (May) 1891-1971 Obituary 104
Hamermesh, Daniel S(elim) 1943- Brief entry .. 110
Hamermesh, Morton 1915- 5-8R
Hamerow, Theodore S(tephen) 1920- ... CANR-28
Earlier sketch in CA 49-52
Hamerstrom, Frances 1907- 69-72
See also SATA 24
Hames, (Alice) Inez 1892- 29-32R
Hamey, J(ohn) A(nthony) 1956- 109
Hamey, L(eonard) A(rnold) 1918- 109
Hamid, Ahmad A. 1948- 146
Hamil, Sharon Hide 1939- 122
Hamil, Thomas Arthur 1928- 73-76
See also SATA 14
Hamill, Denis 1951- 110
Hamill, Ethel
See Webb, Jean Francis
Hamill, Pete 1935- CANR-71
Earlier sketches in CA 25-28R, CANR-18
See also CLC 10
Hamill, Robert H(offman) 1912-1975 ...... CAP-2
Earlier sketch in CA 33-36
Hamill, Sam P(atrick) 1943(?)- 161
See also CAAS 15
Hamilton, A(lbert) C(harles) 1921- 133
Hamilton, Adam
See Henderson, M(arilyn) R(uth)
Hamilton, (John) Alan 1943- CANR-36
Earlier sketch in CA 115
See also SATA 66
Hamilton, Alastair 1941- 144
Hamilton, Alex John 1939- 103
Hamilton, Alexander 1712-1756 .... DLB 31
Hamilton, Alexander 1755(?)-1804 .... DLB 37
Hamilton, Alfred Starr 1914- 53-56
Hamilton, Alice
See Cromie, Alice Hamilton
Hamilton, Alice 1869-1970 156
Hamilton, Anita 1919- 156
See also SATA 92
Hamilton, B(ertram) L(awson) St. John
1914- 13-16R
Hamilton, Beth Alleman 1927- 110
Hamilton, (Arthur Douglas) Bruce
1900-1974 Obituary 109
Hamilton, Buzz
See Hemming, Roy G.
Hamilton, Carl 1914- 53-56
Hamilton, Carlos D. 1908- 69-72
Hamilton, Carol (Jean Barber) 1935- 159
See also SATA 94
Hamilton, Charles (Harold St. John) 1876-1961 ....
CANR-29
Earlier sketch in CA 73-76
See also SATA 13
Hamilton, Charles 1913-1996 .... CANR-49
Obituary 155
Earlier sketches in CA 5-8R, CANR-3, 20
See also SATA 65
See also SATA-Obit 93
Hamilton, Charles D(aniel) 1940- Brief entry ... 112
Hamilton, Charles F(ranklin) 1915- 89-92
Hamilton, Charles Granville 1905-1984 .. CANR-15
Earlier sketch in CA 41-44R
Hamilton, Charles V(ernon) 1929- CANR-42
Earlier sketch in CA 77-80
See also BW 2
Hamilton, Charles W(alter) 1890- 5-8R
Hamilton, Cicely (Mary) 1872-1952 Brief entry . 113
See also DLB 10, 197
Hamilton, Clare
See Lawless, Bettyclare Hamilton
Hamilton, Clive
See Lewis, C(live) S(taples)
Hamilton, Dave
See Troyer, Byron L(eRoy)
Hamilton, David (Boyce, Jr.) 1918- 29-32R
Hamilton, David (Peter) 1935- 119
Hamilton, David 1939- CANR-54
Earlier sketch in CA 126
Hamilton, (Charles) Denis 1918-1988 109
Obituary 125
Hamilton, Donald (Bengtsson) 1916- CANR-59
Earlier sketches in CA 1-4R, CANR-2, 18, 39
Hamilton, Dorothy (Drumm) 1906-1983 ..... 33-36R
Obituary 110
See also SATA 12
See also SATA-Obit 35
Hamilton, Earl J(efferson) 1899-1989 .... CAP-1
Obituary 128
Earlier sketch in CA 9-10
Hamilton, Edith 1867-1963 77-80
See also SATA 20
Hamilton, Edmond 1904-1977 .... CANR-3
Earlier sketch in CA 1-4R
See also CLC 1
See also DLB 8
Hamilton, Edward G. 1897- CAP-1
Earlier sketch in CA 11-12
Hamilton, Eleanor Poorman 1909- CANR-2
Earlier sketch in CA 1-4R
Hamilton, Elizabeth 1758-1816 ...... DLB 116, 158
Hamilton, (Muriel) Elizabeth (Mollie) 1906- .. CAP-1
Earlier sketch in CA 9-10
See also SATA 23
Hamilton, Elizabeth 1928- 97-100
Hamilton, Ernest
See Merril, Judith
Hamilton, Eugene (Jacob) Lee
See Lee-Hamilton, Eugene (Jacob)
Hamilton, Floyd (Garland)
1908(?)-1984 Obituary 113
Hamilton, Franklin
See Silverberg, Robert
Hamilton, Franklin Willard 1923- 33-36R
Hamilton, Gail
See Corcoran, Barbara
Hamilton, Gene 1943- 120
Hamilton, George Baillie
See Baillie-Hamilton, George
Hamilton, George Rostrevor
1888-1967 Obituary 93-96
Hamilton, Hamish 1900-1988 Obituary 125
Hamilton, Henry W. 1898- 33-36R
Hamilton, Hervey
See Robins, Denise (Naomi)
Hamilton, Holman 1910-1980 .... CANR-10
Obituary 97-100
Earlier sketch in CA 13-16R
Hamilton, Horace E(rnst) 1911- 21-24R
Hamilton, Howard Devon 1920- 13-16R
Hamilton, Hugo 1953- 138
Hamilton, Iain (Betram) 1920-1986 130
Hamilton, (Robert) Ian 1938- CANR-67
Earlier sketches in CA 106, CANR-41
See also DLB 40, 155
Hamilton, J(ames) A(lan) B(ousfield)
1899-1971 Obituary 116
Hamilton, J(ames) Scott 1956- 163
Hamilton, J(ames) Wallace 1900-1968 ..... CAP-1
Earlier sketch in CA 13-14
Hamilton, Jack
See Brannon, William T.
Hamilton, James Robertson 1921- 103
Hamilton, Jane 1957- 147
Hamilton, Janet 1795-1873 .... DLB 199
Hamilton, Janet 1951- 114
Hamilton, Jean Tyree 1909- 33-36R
Hamilton, Joan Lesley 1942- 102
Hamilton, John
See Hayden, Sterling
Hamilton, John Maxwell 1947- CANR-47
Earlier sketch in CA 121
Hamilton, Julia
See Watson, Julia
Hamilton, Katie 1945- 118
Hamilton, Kay
See DeLeeuw, Cateau
Hamilton, Kenneth (Morrison) 1917- 17-20R
Hamilton, Marshall Lee 1937- 37-40R
Hamilton, Mary (E.) 1927- 123
See also SATA 55
Hamilton, Mary Agnes 1884-1962 .... DLB 197
Hamilton, Michael (Pollock) 1927- CANR-30
Earlier sketch in CA 29-32R
Hamilton, Milton W(heaton) 1901-1989 ..... CAP-1
Obituary 128
Earlier sketch in CA 13-16
Hamilton, Mollie
See Kaye, M(ary) M(argaret)
Hamilton, Morse 1943- 108
See also SATA 35, 101
Hamilton, Nancy 1908-1985 Obituary 115
Hamilton, Neil (W.) 1945- 154
Hamilton, Neill Q. 1925- 61-64
Hamilton, (Charles) Nigel 1944- CANR-41
Earlier sketch in CA 101
Hamilton, (Anthony Walter) Patrick
1904-1962 Obituary 113
See also CLC 51
See also DLB 10
Hamilton, Patrick 1904-1962 .... DLB 191
Hamilton, Patrick Macfarlan
1892-1977 Obituary 108
Hamilton, Paul
See Dennis-Jones, H(arold)
Hamilton, Peter (Edward) 1947- 73-76
Hamilton, Peter F. 1960- 162
Hamilton, Peter N(apier)
1925(?)-1989 Obituary 128
Hamilton, Priscilla
See Gellis, Roberta L(eah Jacobs)
Hamilton, Ralph
See Stratemeyer, Edward L.
Hamilton, Raphael N(oteware) 1892- CAP-2
Earlier sketch in CA 29-32
Hamilton, Richard 1922- 159
Brief entry 116
Hamilton, Richard F(rederick) 1930- ... CANR-26
Earlier sketch in CA 108
Hamilton, Robert W. CANR-26
Earlier sketches in CAP-2, CA 19-20
Hamilton, Ronald 1909- 13-16R
Hamilton, Russell G(eorge) 1934- 61-64
Hamilton, Seena M. 1926- 17-20R
Hamilton, Sharon Jean 1944- 151
Hamilton, Virginia 1936- CANR-37
Earlier sketches in CA 25-28R, CANR-20
Interview in CANR-20
See also AAYA 2, 21
See also BW 2
See also CLC 26
See also CLR 1, 11, 40
See also DAM MULT
See also DLB 33, 52
See also JRDA
See also MAICYA
See also MTCW 1
See also SATA 4, 56, 79
Hamilton, W(illiam) B(askerville) 1908-1972 . CAP-1
Obituary 37-40R
Earlier sketch in CA 17-18
Hamilton, W(illis) D(avid) 1936- 105
Hamilton, Wade
See Floren, Lee
Hamilton, Wallace 1919-1983 .... CANR-15
Obituary 110
Earlier sketch in CA 85-88
Hamilton, Walter 1908-1988 109
Obituary 124
Hamilton, William, Jr. 1924- 53-56
Hamilton, William 1939- CANR-15
Earlier sketch in CA 69-72
Hamilton, William B(aillie) 1930- 102
Hamilton-Edwards, Gerald (Kenneth Savery) 1906-
CANR-14
Earlier sketch in CA 21-24R
Hamilton-Hill, Donald 1915-1985 Obituary 117
Hamilton-Paterson, James 1941- 137
Interview in 137
See also SATA 82
Hamizrachi, Yoram 1942- 107

Hamlet, Ova
See Lupoff, Richard A(llen)
Hamlet, Sybil E. 1913(?)-1989 Obituary....... 129
Hamley, Dennis 1935-................ CANR-26
Earlier sketches in CA 57-60, CANR-11
See also CLR 47
See also SAAS 22
See also SATA 39, 69
Hamlin, Charles Hughes 1907-............. 69-72
Hamlin, Dallas
See Schulze, Dallas
Hamlin, Gladys E(va).....................37-40R
Hamlin, Griffith Askew 1919-..............37-40R
Hamlin, Marjorie (Day) 1921-.................105
Hamlin, Peter J. 1970-.................SATA 84
Hamlin, Wilfrid G(ardiner) 1918-.............93-96
Hamlyn, D(avid) W(alter) 1924-..............132
Hamm, Charles Edward 1925-.......... CANR-72
Earlier sketch in CA 103
Hamm, Cleve 1927(?)-1984 Obituary..........112
Hamm, Diane Johnston 1949-................146
See also SATA 78
Hamm, Edward Frederick, Jr.
1908-1985 Obituary........................115
Hamm, Glenn B(ruce) 1936-1980........... 53-56
Obituary...................................125
Hamm, Jack 1916-.................... CANR-9
Earlier sketch in CA 5-8R
Hamm, Marie Roberson 1917-.............65-68
Hamm, Michael Franklin 1943-............. 89-92
Hamm, Robert M(acGowan) 1950-............116
Hamm, Russell Leroy 1926-............. CANR-2
Earlier sketch in CA 5-8R
Hamm, Thomas D. 1957-.....................137
Hammack, David C(onrad) 1941-............. 115
Hammack, James W., Jr. 1937-.............81-84
Hamman, Henry (Longley) 1946-............. 119
Hamman, Ray T(racy) 1945-............... 69-72
Hammar, Russell A(lfred) 1920-............. 104
Hammarskjoeld, Dag (Hjalmar Agne Carl)
1905-1961 77-80
Hammarskjold, Dag
See Hammarskjoeld, Dag (Hjalmar Agne Carl)
Hammel, Eric M(axwell) 1946-.......... CANR-35
Earlier sketch in CA 107
Hammel, Faye 1929-................... CANR-5
Earlier sketch in CA 1-4R
Hammell, Ian
See Emery, Clayton
Hammen, Carl Schlee 1923-............... 53-56
Hammen, Oscar J(ohn) 1907-............. CAP-2
Earlier sketch in CA 25-28
Hammer, Armand 1898-1990 Obituary........ 134
Hammer, Carl, Jr. 1910-..................53-56
Hammer, Charles 1934-.................SATA 58
Hammer, David Harry 1893(?)-1978 Obituary .81-84
Hammer, Emanuel F(rederick) 1926-.......29-32R
Hammer, Jacob
See Oppenheimer, Joel (Lester)
Hammer, Jeanne-Ruth 1912-.............. 9-12R
Hammer, Jefferson J(oseph) 1933-........ 41-44R
Hammer, Kenneth M. 1918-................85-88
Hammer, Louis (Zelig) 1931-.................139
Hammer, Reuven 1933-.............. CANR-56
Earlier sketch in CA 127
Hammer, Richard 1928-............... CANR-11
Earlier sketch in CA 25-28R
See also SATA 6
Hammer, Signe................................102
Hammerman, Donald R. 1925-............13-16R
Hammerman, Gay M(orenus) 1926-.........33-36R
See also SATA 9
Hammerschlag, Carl A(llen) 1939-............ 128
Hammerstein, Oscar (Greeley Glendenning) II
1895-1960 101
Hammes, John A(nthony) 1924-...........13-16R
Hammes, Tobi Gillian Sanders
1948(?)-1987 Obituary..................... 122
Hammett, (Samuel) Dashiell 1894-1961 .. CANR-42
Earlier sketch in CA 81-84
See also AITN 1
See also CDALB 1929-1941
See also CLC 3, 5, 10, 19, 47
See also DLBD 6
See also DLBY 96
See also MTCW 1
See also SSC 17
Hammick, Georgina 1939-.................. 126
Hammil, Joel 1909-..........................114
Hamming, Richard W(esley) 1915-1998......57-60
Obituary...................................164
Hammon, Jupiter 1711(?)-1800(?).......... BLC 2
See also DAM MULT, POET
See also DLB 31, 50
See also PC 16
Hammond, Albert L(anphier) 1892-1970...... 1-4R
Obituary...................................103
Hammond, Antony Derek 1938-.............. 114
Hammond, Brean S(imon) 1951-............. 119
Hammond, Charles Montgomery, Jr. 1922-......106
Hammond, Dorothy 1924-.................69-72
Hammond, Edwin Hughes 1919-.......... 13-16R
Hammond, Gerald (Arthur Douglas) 1926-.........
CANR-62
Earlier sketch in CA 107
Hammond, Guyton B(owers) 1930-........ 17-20R
Hammond, Herb(ert L.) 1945-................ 140
Hammond, J(ames) D(illard) 1933-...... CANR-22
Earlier sketch in CA 45-48
Hammond, J(ohn) R. 1933-.................. 130
Hammond, Jane
See Poland, Dorothy (Elizabeth Hayward)
Hammond, John (?)-1663 .... DLB 24
Hammond, John (Henry, Jr.) 1910-1987....... 106
Obituary...................................123
Hammond, Keith
See Kuttner, Henry
Hammond, Laurence........................ 104
Hammond, Lawrence 1925-................81-84
Hammond, Mac (Sawyer) 1926-...........17-20R
Hammond, Mason 1903-.................. 65-68
Hammond, N(icholas) G(eoffrey) L(empriere) 1907-.
CANR-44
Earlier sketches in CA 13-16R, CANR-5, 21
Hammond, Norman 1944-............. CANR-19
Earlier sketches in CA 49-52, CANR-3
Hammond, Paul 1947-.....................57-60
Hammond, Paul Y(oung) 1929-.......... CANR-2
Earlier sketch in CA 1-4R
Hammond, Peter B(oyd) 1928-............. 69-72
Hammond, Philip C. 1924-..................5-8R
Hammond, Phillip E(verett) 1931-........ CANR-7
Earlier sketch in CA 17-20R
Hammond, Ralph
See Hammond Innes, Ralph
Hammond, Richard J(ames) 1911-1982......61-64
Obituary...................................122
Hammond, Ross W(illiam) 1918-.......... 33-36R
Hammond, Thomas T(aylor) 1920-1993 .. CANR-46
Obituary...................................140
Earlier sketch in CA 9-12R
Hammond, W(illiam) Rogers 1920-.......... 45-48
Hammond, Wayne G(ordon) 1953-...........145
Hammond, Winifred G(raham) 1899-.......... 107
See also SATA 29
Hammond Innes, Ralph 1913-.......... CANR-52
Earlier sketches in CA 5-8R, CANR-4, 26
Hammonds, Michael (Galen) 1942-..........45-48
Hammontree, Marie (Gertrude) 1913-........ 5-8R
See also SATA 13
Hamner, Earl (Henry), Jr. 1923-............73-76
See also AITN 2
See also CLC 12
See also DLB 6
Hamner, Robert Daniel 1941-................ 106
Hamod, (Hamode) Sam(uel) 1936-...... CANR-22
Earlier sketch in CA 45-48
Hamori, Laszlo Dezso 1911-...............9-12R
Hamovitch, Mitzi Berger 1924-1992........... 112
Obituary...................................140
Hamp, Eric P(ratt) 1920-................ 17-20R
Hampden, John 1898-........................ 109
Hampden-Turner, Charles M. 1934-........33-36R
Hamper, Ben 1956(?)-........................ 138
Hampl, Patricia 1946-.................. CANR-21
Earlier sketch in CA 104
Hample, Stuart 1926-....................... 108
Hampsch, George H(arold) 1927-..........13-16R
Hampshire, Joyce Gregorian
See Gregorian, Joyce Ballou
Hampshire, Stuart (Newton) 1914-............143
Brief entry................................. 116
Hampshire, Susan 1942-............... CANR-65
Brief entry................................. 112
Earlier sketch in CA 129
See also SATA 98
Hampson, Anne.............................. 117
Brief entry................................. 111
Interview in 117
Hampson, (Margaret) Daphne 1944-.......... 165
Hampson, (Richard) Denman 1929-...... SATA 15
Hampson, Frank 1918(?)-1985 Obituary.......117
See also SATA-Obit 46
Hampson, John 1901-1955..............DLB 191
Hampson, Norman 1922-.................25-28R
Hampson, Robert (Gavin) 1948-............. 135
Hampton, Angeline A.
See Kelly, A(ngeline) A(gnes)
Hampton, Charles
See Martin, (Roy) Peter
Hampton, Christopher 1929-............ CANR-4
Earlier sketch in CA 53-56
Hampton, Christopher (James) 1946-...... 25-28R
See also CLC 4
See also DLB 13
See also MTCW 1
Hampton, David
See Fairclough, Chris
Hampton, David R(ichard) 1933-............81-84
Hampton, H(arold) Duane 1932-...........33-36R
Hampton, Henry (Eugene, Jr.) 1940-.......... 139
See also BW 2
Hampton, Jim
See Hampton, John Lewis
Hampton, John Lewis 1935-................. 133
Hampton, Kathleen 1923-.................. 1-4R
Hampton, Mark
See Norwood, Victor G(eorge) C(harles)
Hampton, Robert E. 1924-................33-36R
Hampton, William (Albert) 1929-........ CANR-13
Earlier sketch in CA 33-36R
Hamre, Leif 1914-..................... CANR-4
Earlier sketch in CA 5-8R
See also SATA 5
Hamrick, Samuel J., Jr. 1929-............... 120
Brief entry................................. 115
Interview in 120
Hamrin, Robert 1946-........................155
Hamsa, Bobbie 1944-........................ 106
See also SATA 52
See also SATA-Brief 38
Hamscher, Albert N(elson) 1946-.......... 73-76
Hamsher, J. Herbert 1938-.................57-60
Hamshere, Cyril (Eric) 1912-............. 41-44R
Hamson, C. J.
See Hamson, Charles John
Hamson, Charles John 1905-1987 Obituary....124
Hamsun, Knut
See Pedersen, Knut
See also TCLC 2, 14, 49
Hamsund, Knut Pedersen
See Pedersen, Knut
Han, Henry H. 1932-.........................125
Han, Seung Soo 1936-................. CANR-2
Earlier sketch in CA 45-48
Han, Sungjoo 1940-.......................53-56
Han, Suzanne Crowder 1953-................ 155
See also SATA 89
Hanagan, Eva (Helen) 1923-................. 101
Hanagan, Michael Patrick 1947-............. 109
Hanaghan, Jonathan 1887-1967............65-68
Hanami, Tadashi (Akamatsu) 1930-......... 89-92
Hanan, Patrick Dewes 1927-..................106
Hanau, Laia 1916-........................ 89-92
Hanawalt, Barbara A(nn) 1941-...............101
Hanbury, Victor
See Losey, Joseph (Walton)
Hanbury-Tenison, Marika 1938-1982.......... 104
Obituary...................................108
Hanbury-Tenison, (Airling) Robin 1936-...... 57-60
Hance, Kenneth G(ordon) 1903-............85-88
Hance, William A(dams) 1916-............. 9-12R
Hanchett, William 1922-..................33-36R
Hancock, Alice Van Fossen 1890-.......... 1-4R
Hancock, Carla............................ 89-92
Hancock, Carol Helen Brooks
See Hancock, Morgan
Hancock, Edward L(eslie) 1930-......... CANR-1
Earlier sketch in CA 45-48
Hancock, Geoffrey 1946-.............. CANR-19
Earlier sketch in CA 101
Hancock, Graham 1950(?)-.................. 156
Hancock, Harold B(ell) 1913-..............53-56
Hancock, Ian (Robert) 1940-................ 142
Hancock, James (A.) 1921-.................. 141
Hancock, Joy Bright 1898-1986 Obituary...... 120
Hancock, Keith
See Hancock, W(illiam) K(eith)
Hancock, Leslie 1941-................... 21-24R
Hancock, Lyn 1938-........................77-80
Hancock, M. Donald 1939-............... 33-36R
Hancock, Malcolm Cyril 1936-1993........ 25-28R
Obituary...................................140
Hancock, Mary A. 1923-..................37-40R
See also SATA 31
Hancock, Maxine 1942-................. CANR-8
Earlier sketch in CA 61-64
Hancock, Morgan 1941-......................103
Hancock, Niel (Anderson) 1941-........ CANR-58
Earlier sketches in CA 97-100, CANR-21
Hancock, Ralph Lowell 1903-............. CAP-1
Earlier sketch in CA 9-10
Hancock, Roger Nelson 1929-............ 97-100
Hancock, Sheila 1942-.................... 49-52
Hancock, Sibyl 1940-................. CANR-16
Earlier sketches in CA 49-52, CANR-1
See also SATA 9
Hancock, Taylor 1920-.................. 97-100
Hancock, W(illiam) K(eith) 1898-1988 ..... CANR-5
Obituary...................................126
Earlier sketch in CA 5-8R
Hand, Elizabeth 1957-..................... 136
Hand, G(eoffrey) J(oseph Philip Macaulay)
1931-....................................25-28R
Hand, J(oan) C(arole) 1943-...............57-60
Hand, (Andrus) Jackson 1913-.......... CANR-10
Earlier sketch in CA 61-64
Hand, John
See Pierson, John H(erman) G(roesbeck)
Hand, Richard A(llen) 1941-................ 149
Hand, Thomas A(lypius) 1915-........... 13-16R
Hand, Wayland D(ebs) 1907-1986......... 41-44R
Obituary...................................120
Handel, Gerald 1924-................. CANR-11
Earlier sketch in CA 21-24R
Handel, Michael I. 1942-................... 131
Handelman, Howard 1943-.................57-60
Handelman, John R(obert) 1948-............ 77-80
Handelman, Stephen 1947-...................152
Handelman, Susan A. 1949-.................. 137
Handel-Mazzetti, Enrica von 1871-1955 .... DLB 81
Handelsman, Judith Florence 1948-..........61-64
Handey, Jack 1949-......................... 141
Handford, Martin (John) 1956-.............. 137
See also CLR 22
See also MAICYA
See also SATA 64
Handforth, Thomas (Schofield) 1897-1948 Brief
entry......................................120
See also SATA 42
Handke, Peter 1942-................. CANR-33
Earlier sketch in CA 77-80
See also CLC 5, 8, 10, 15, 38
See also DAM DRAM, NOV
See also DLB 85, 124
See also MTCW 1
Handl, Irene 1902(?)-1987 103
Obituary...................................124
Handler, David 1952-................. CANR-72
Earlier sketch in CA 141
Handler, Evan 1961-........................ 153
Handler, Jerome S(idney) 1933-........... 53-56
Handler, Joel F. 1932- Brief entry............ 113
Handler, Julian Harris 1922-............. 21-24R
Handler, Meyer Srednick
1905-1978 Obituary.......................77-80
Handler, Milton 1903-.................... 61-64
Handler, Philip 1917-1981 ....33-36R
Obituary...................................105
Handley, Graham Roderick 1926-........ CANR-24
Earlier sketch in CA 105
Handley-Taylor, Geoffrey 1920-......... CANR-7
Earlier sketch in CA 5-8R
Handlin, Mary (Flug) 1913-1976........... CAP-2
Obituary...................................65-68
Earlier sketch in CA 33-36
Handlin, Oscar 1915-................. CANR-23
Earlier sketches in CA 1-4R, CANR-5
See also DLB 17
Handman, Herbert Ira 1932-................89-92
Handover, P(hyllis) M(argaret) 1923(?)-1974 . 9-12R
Obituary...................................53-56
Hands, D. Wade 1951-....................... 145
Handscombe, Richard 1935-..............37-40R
Handville, Robert (Tompkins) 1924-...... SATA 45
Handy, Edward Smith Craighill
1893(?)-1980 Obituary..................... 102
Handy, Lowell K. 1949-..................... 150
Handy, Robert T(heodore) 1918-......... CANR-2
Earlier sketch in CA 5-8R
Handy, Rollo 1927-........................9-12R
Handy, Toni 1930-........................97-100
Handy, W(illiam) C(hristopher) 1873-1958......167
Brief entry................................. 121
Handy, William J. 1918-.................. 45-48
Hane, Mikiso 1922-................... CANR-15
Earlier sketch in CA 81-84
Hane, Roger 1940-1974 ....SATA-Obit 20
Hanel, Wolfram
See Haenel, Wolfram
Hanenkrat, Frank (Thomas) 1939-.......... 93-96
Haner, F(rederick) T(heodore) 1929-........ 53-56
Hanes, Bailey C(ass) 1915-............... 77-80
Hanes, Elizabeth Sill 1-4R
Hanes, Frank Borden 1920-............ CANR-28
Earlier sketch in CA 1-4R
Hanes, Mary (a pseudonym) 1940(?)- Brief
entry......................................117
Haney, David P. 1938-............... CANR-21
Earlier sketches in CA 57-60, CANR-6
Haney, Eleanor H(umes) 1931- Brief entry.....114
Haney, John B. 1931-....................29-32R
Haney, Lynn 1941-.................... CANR-1
Earlier sketch in CA 49-52
See also SATA 23
Haney, Thomas K. 1936-.................13-16R
Haney, Thomas R. 45-48
Haney, William V. 1925-.................17-20R
Hanff, Helene 1916-1997 .... CANR-3
Obituary...................................157
Earlier sketch in CA 5-8R
See also SATA 11, 97
Hanfmann, George M(axim) A(nossov)
1911-1986 Obituary........................118
Brief entry................................. 117
Hanford, Lloyd D(avid) 1901-1979....... CANR-11
Earlier sketch in CA 13-16R
Hanford, S. A. 1898-1978 Obituary......... 81-84
Hang, T(ing-)Y(ung) 1908(?)-1987 Obituary.... 122
Hangen, (Putnam) Welles 1930-............9-12R
Hanh, Thich Nhat 1926-.....................167
Hanifi, M(ohammed) Jamil 1935-............61-64
Hanigan, James Patrick 1938-...............125
Haning, Bob
See Haning, James R(obert)
Haning, James R(obert) 1928-.......... CANR-2
Earlier sketch in CA 45-48
Hanke, Howard August 1911-............... 1-4R
Hanke, Lewis (Ulysses) 1905-............. 65-68
Hankey, Cyril Patrick 1886-1973............1-4R
Obituary...................................103
Hankey, Rosalie A.
See Wax, Rosalie (Amelia) H.
Hankey, Roy 1932-.......................... 108
Hankin, C(herry) A(nne) 1937-...............131
Hankin, Elizabeth Rosemary 1950-...........156
Hankin, (Edward Charles) St. John (Emile Clavering)
1869-1909 Brief entry......................110
See also DLB 10
Hankins, Clabe
See McDonald, Erwin L(awrence)
Hankins, Frank Hamilton 1877-1970 Obituary.. 104
Hankins, John Erskine 1905-..............49-52
Hankins, Norman E(lijah) 1935-......... CANR-11
Earlier sketch in CA 61-64
Hankins, Thomas Leroy 1933-............... 108
Hankinson, Alan 1926-...................... 130
Hankinson, Cyril (Francis James) 1895-...... CAP-1
Earlier sketch in CA 9-10
Hankla, Cathryn 1958-................ CANR-39
Earlier sketch in CA 116
Hanks, Lucien M(ason) 1910-............37-40R
Hanks, Stedman Shumway
1889-1979 Obituary.......................85-88
Hanle, Dorothea Zack 1917-..............13-16R
Hanley, Boniface Francis 1924-........... 9-12R
See also SATA 65
Hanley, Clifford 1922-................ CANR-69
Earlier sketches in CA 9-12R, CANR-3, 23
See also DLB 14
Hanley, Elizabeth
See Du Breuil, (Elizabeth) L(or)inda
Hanley, Evelyn A(lice) 1916-1980...........41-44R
Obituary...................................97-100
Hanley, Gerald (Anthony) 1916-1992..... CANR-6
Obituary...................................139
Earlier sketch in CA 1-4R
Hanley, Hope Anthony 1926-............ CANR-5
Earlier sketch in CA 9-12R
Hanley, James 1901-1985 .... CANR-36
Obituary...................................117
Earlier sketch in CA 73-76
See also CLC 3, 5, 8, 13
See also DLB 191
See also MTCW 1
Hanley, Katharine Rose 1932-........... 37-40R
Hanley, Michael F. IV 1941-..............65-68
Hanley, Mike
See Hanley, Michael F. IV
Hanley, Theodore Dean 1917-............. 5-8R
Hanley, Thomas O'Brien 1918-.......... CANR-1
Earlier sketch in CA 1-4R

Hanley, William 1931- ... 41-44R
Hanlon, Emily 1945- ... 77-80
See also SATA 15
Hanlon, Gregory 1953- ... 146
Hanlon, John J(oseph) 1912- ... 57-60
Hanmer, Davina
See Courtney, Nicholas (Piers)
Hann, C. M. 1953- ... CANR-47
Earlier sketch in CA 121
Hann, Jacquie 1951- ... CANR-13
Earlier sketch in CA 73-76
See also SATA 19
Hann, Judith 1942- ... 145
See also SATA 77
Hanna, Alfred Jackson 1893-1978 ... CANR-2
Earlier sketch in CA 45-48
Hanna, Bill
See Hanna, William
Hanna, Cheryl 1951- ... SATA 84
Hanna, David 1917- ... CANR-6
Earlier sketch in CA 57-60
Hanna, Frank A(llan) 1907-1978 Obituary ... 111
Hanna, J. Marshall 1907- ... CANR-24
Earlier sketch in CA 1-4R
Hanna, Jack (Bushnell) 1947- ... 141
See also SATA 74
Hanna, John Paul 1932- ... CANR-1
Earlier sketch in CA 45-48
Hanna, Lavone Agnes 1896- ... 13-16R
Hanna, Mary Carr 1905- ... 45-48
Hanna, Mary T. 1935- ... 97-100
Hanna, Nell(ie L.) 1908- ... SATA 55
Hanna, Paul R(obert) 1902-1988 ... CANR-48
Earlier sketch in CA 45-48
See also SATA 9
Hanna, S(uhail) S(alim) 1943- ... 126
Hanna, Thomas 1928- ... CANR-1
Earlier sketch in CA 1-4R
Hanna, Warren L(eonard) 1898- ... 130
Hanna, William 1910- ... SATA 51
Hanna, William John 1931- ... CANR-8
Earlier sketch in CA 61-64
Hannaford, John 1918- ... 45-48
Hannaford, Peter (Dor) 1932- ... 130
Hannah, (Juliel) Barbara 1891- ... 97-100
Hannah, Barry 1942- ... CANR-68
Brief entry ... 108
Earlier sketches in CA 110, CANR-43
Interview in ... 110
See also CLC 23, 38, 90
See also DLB 6
See also MTCW 1
Hannah, James 1951- ... 145
Hannah, Kristin 1960- ... 141
Hannah, Norman B(ritton) 1919- ... 127
Hannak, Johann Jacques 1892- ... CAP-1
Earlier sketch in CA 9-10
Hannam, Charles 1925- ... CANR-11
Earlier sketch in CA 61-64
See also SATA 50
Hannam, June 1947- ... 161
Hannan, Joseph F(rancis) 1923- ... CANR-3
Earlier sketch in CA 9-12R
Hannas, Linda 1913- ... 113
Hannau, Hans W(alter) 1904- ... CANR-10
Earlier sketch in CA 21-24R
Hannavy, John Michael 1946- ... CANR-11
Earlier sketch in CA 69-72
Hannaway, Patricia H(inman) 1929- ... 61-64
Hannaway, Patti
See Hannaway, Patricia H(inman)
Hannay, Alastair 1932- ... 130
Hannay, Allen 1946- ... 109
Hannay, Doris Fergusson
See Fergusson Hannay, Doris
Hannay, James 1827-1873 ... DLB 21
Hannay, Margaret Patterson 1944- ... CANR-44
Earlier sketches in CA 104, CANR-21
Hannelle, Pirkko
See Vainio, Pirkko
Hanneman, Audre (Louise) 1926- ... 21-24R
Hanney, Peter 1930-1976 Obituary ... 105
Hannibal
See Alexander, Stanley Walter
Hannibal, Edward 1936- ... CANR-28
Earlier sketch in CA 29-32R
Hannifin, Jerry (Bernard) 1917- ... 77-80
Hanning, Hugh 1925- ... 25-28R
Hanning, Robert William 1938- ... 93-96
Hannon, Ezra
See Hunter, Evan
Hannula, Reino 1918- ... 105
Hannum, Alberta Pierson 1906-1985 ... 65-68
Obituary ... 115
Hannum, Hurst 1945- ... 161
Hano, Arnold 1922- ... CANR-5
Earlier sketch in CA 9-12R
See also SATA 12
Hanover, Terri
See Huff, Tanya (Sue)
Hanrahan, Barbara 1939- ... 127
Brief entry ... 121
Hanrahan, John D(avid) 1938- ... CANR-15
Earlier sketch in CA 77-80
Hanrieder, Wolfram F. 1931- ... CANR-23
Earlier sketches in CA 21-24R, CANR-8
Hans, Valerie P(atricia) 1951- ... 126
Hans Abmann von, Abschatz 1646-1699 ... DLB 168
Hansberry, Lorraine (Vivian) 1930-1965 ... CANR-58
Obituary ... 25-28R
Earlier sketch in CA 109
See also CABS 3
See also AAYA 25
See also BLC 2
See also BW 1
See also CDALB 1941-1968
See also CLC 17, 62
See also DA
See also DAB
See also DAC
See also DAM DRAM, MST, MULT
See also DC 2
See also DLB 7, 38
See also MTCW 1
Hansberry, William Leo 1894-1965 ... 155
Hanscom, Leslie Rutherford 1924- ... 135
Hanscombe, Gillian E. 1945- ... 144
Hansel, C(harles) E(dward) M(ark) 1917- Brief entry ... 115
Hansel, Robert R(aymond) 1936- Brief entry ... 110
Hansell, Antonina
See Looker, Antonina (Hansell)
Hansen, Al(fred Earl) 1927- ... 17-20R
Hansen, Alvin H(arvey) 1887-1975 ... CAP-1
Obituary ... 57-60
Earlier sketch in CA 13-16
Hansen, Ann Larkin 1958- ... 161
See also SATA 96
Hansen, Anton
See Tammsaare, A(nton) H(ansen)
Hansen, Arlen J. 1936- ... 133
Hansen, Bertrand Lyle 1922- ... 9-12R
Hansen, Brooks 1965- ... CANR-56
Earlier sketch in CA 132
Hansen, Carl (Francis) 1906-1983 ... CANR-2
Obituary ... 110
Earlier sketch in CA 5-8R
Hansen, Carol
See Fenichel, Carol Hansen
Hansen, Caryl (Hall) 1929- ... 108
See also SATA 39
Hansen, Cecil
See Huffaker, Clair
Hansen, Cecil Dan
See Huffaker, Clair
Hansen, Chadwick (Clarke) 1926- ... 29-32R
Hansen, Debra Gold 1953- ... 146
Hansen, Donald A(ndrew) 1933- ... 73-76
Hansen, Donald Charles 1935- ... 33-36R
Hansen, Emmanuel 1937- ... 104
Hansen, Flemming 1938- ... 93-96
Hansen, Forest Warnyr 1931- ... 45-48
Hansen, Gary B(arker) 1935- ... CANR-21
Earlier sketches in CA 9-12R, CANR-3
Hansen, Gunnar 1947- ... 144
Hansen, Hardy 1941- ... 139
Hansen, Harry 1884-1977 ... 73-76
Obituary ... 69-72
Hansen, Joseph 1923- ... CANR-66
Earlier sketches in CA 29-32R, CANR-16, 44
Interview in ... CANR-16
See also CAAS 17
See also CLC 38
Hansen, Joyce (Viola) 1942- ... CANR-43
Earlier sketch in CA 105
See also BW 2
See also CLR 21
See also JRDA
See also MAICYA
See also SAAS 15
See also SATA 46, 101
See also SATA-Brief 39
Hansen, Karen V. 1955- ... 149
Hansen, Kenneth H(arvey) 1917- ... 13-16R
Hansen, Klaus J(uergen) 1931- ... 21-24R
Hansen, Leroy John 1922-1990 Obituary ... 132
Hansen, Maren Tonder 1952- ... 167
Hansen, Martin A(lfred) 1909-1955 ... 167
See also TCLC 32
Hansen, Mary Lewis (Patterson) 1933- ... 17-20R
Hansen, Niles M(aurice) 1937- ... CANR-30
Earlier sketches in CA 25-28R, CANR-13
Hansen, Norman J. 1918- ... 29-32R
Hansen, Poul Einer 1939- ... 141
Hansen, Richard H(erbert) 1929- ... 1-4R
Hansen, Rodney Thor 1940- ... 53-56
Hansen, Roger D(ennis) 1935-1991 ... 105
Obituary ... 133
Hansen, Ron(ald Thomas) 1947- ... CANR-63
Earlier sketches in CA 89-92, CANR-17
See also SATA 56
Hansen, Rosanna 1947- ... 105
Hansen, Terrence Leslie 1920-1974 ... 37-40R
Hansen, W(illiam) Lee 1928- ... 29-32R
Hansen, William F(reeman) 1941- ... CANR-30
Earlier sketch in CA 49-52
Hanser, Richard (Frederick) 1909-1981 ... CANR-8
Earlier sketch in CA 5-8R
See also SATA 13
Hanshew, Thomas W. 1857-1914 Brief entry ... 113
Hansi
See Hirschmann, Maria Anne
Hanson, A(lbert) H(enry) 1913-1971 ... CANR-4
Obituary ... 89-92
Earlier sketch in CA 5-8R
Hanson, Agnes O(lin) 1905- ... 107
Hanson, Anne Coffin 1921- ... 21-24R
Hanson, Anthony Tyrrell 1916-1991 ... CANR-24
Obituary ... 134
Earlier sketches in CA 21-24R, CANR-9
Hanson, Charles G(oring) 1934- ... 138
Hanson, Dirk 1950- ... 111
Hanson, E(ugene) Kenneth 1930- ... 13-16R
Hanson, Earl D(orchester) 1927-1993 ... CANR-12
Obituary ... 143
Earlier sketch in CA 73-76
Hanson, Earl Parker 1899-1978 ... 41-44R
Hanson, Elizabeth 1684-1737 ... DLB 200
Hanson, Eric O. 1942- ... 125
Hanson, F(ridolf) Allan 1939- ... 41-44R
Hanson, Harvey 1941- ... 65-68
Hanson, Howard (Harold) 1896-1981 Obituary ... 103
Hanson, Howard Gordon 1931- ... 21-24R
Hanson, Irene (Forsythe) 1898- ... 49-52
Hanson, Isabel 1929- ... 106
Hanson, James Arthur 1940- ... CANR-30
Earlier sketch in CA 49-52
Hanson, Jim 1953- ... 97-100
Hanson, Joan 1938- ... CANR-15
Earlier sketch in CA 33-36R
See also SATA 8
Hanson, Joseph E. 1894(?)-1971 Obituary ... 104
See also SATA-Obit 27
Hanson, June Andrea 1941- ... 97-100
Hanson, Kenneth O(stlin) 1922- ... CANR-7
Earlier sketch in CA 53-56
See also CLC 13
Hanson, Kristine 1958- ... 123
Hanson, Michael James 1942- ... 61-64
Hanson, Neil 1948- ... 150
Hanson, Norwood Russell 1924-1967 ... CANR-8
Earlier sketch in CA 5-8R
Hanson, Paul D(avid) 1939- ... 61-64
Hanson, Paul R. 1952- ... 134
Hanson, Pauline ... 45-48
Hanson, Peggy 1934- ... CANR-12
Earlier sketch in CA 29-32R
Hanson, Peter G. 1947- ... 145
Hanson, Philip 1936- ... 103
Hanson, R(ichard) P(atrick) C(rosland) 1916-1988 ... CANR-9
Obituary ... 127
Earlier sketch in CA 21-24R
Hanson, Richard S(imon) 1931- ... 37-40R
Hanson, Robert Carl 1926- ... 37-40R
Hanson, Robert P(aul) 1918- ... 9-12R
Hanson, Roy (Francis) 1934-1989 Obituary ... 128
Hanson, Ruth Katie 1900- ... 5-8R
Hanson, Simon
See Hanson, Richard S(imon)
Hanson, William S(tewart) 1950- ... 123
Hansson, Gunilla 1939- ... SATA 64
Hansten, Philip D. 1943- ... 33-36R
Han Suyin 1917- ... 17-20R
Hanushek, Eric Alan 1943- ... 41-44R
Hanzlicek, C(harles) G(eorge) 1942- ... CANR-12
Earlier sketch in CA 73-76
Hao, Qian
See Qian Hao
Hao, Yen-ping 1934- ... 53-56
Hapgood, Charles Hutchins 1904- ... 17-20R
Hapgood, David 1926- ... 13-16R
Hapgood, Fred 1942- ... 93-96
Hapgood, Norman 1868-1937 ... DLB 91
Hapgood, Ruth K(nott) 1920- ... 49-52
Hapke, Laura 1946- ... 138
Happe, Peter 1932- ... CANR-28
Earlier sketch in CA 45-48
Happel, Eberhard Werner 1647-1690 ... DLB 168
Happel, Robert A. 1916- ... 1-4R
Happel, Stephen 1944- ... 114
Happenstance, Aurelia
See Furdyna, Anna M.
Happold, F(rederick) C(rossfield) 1893- ... 101
Haq, Mahbub ul 1934- ... 13-16R
Harada, Masako 1939- ... 161
Harakas, Stanley Samuel 1932- ... 134
Harald, Eric
See Boesen, Victor
Haraldsson, Erlendur 1931- ... 101
Haran, Maeve 1950- ... 136
Harap, Henry 1893-1981 Obituary ... 104
Harap, Louis 1904- ... 57-60
Harari, Ehud 1935- ... 65-68
Harary, Keith 1953- ... CANR-48
Earlier sketch in CA 120
Harary, Stuart Blue
See Harary, Keith
Harasymiw, Bohdan 1936- ... 124
Haraway, Donna Jeanne 1944- ... 73-76
Harbach, Otto (Abels) 1873-1963 Obituary ... 112
Harbage, Alfred (Bennett) 1901-1976 ... CANR-58
Obituary ... 65-68
Earlier sketches in CA 5-8R, CANR-5
Harbaugh, John W(arvelle) 1926- ... CANR-30
Earlier sketch in CA 49-52
Harbaugh, William Henry 1920- ... 1-4R
Harberger, Arnold C. 1924- ... CANR-6
Earlier sketch in CA 13-16R
Harbert, Earl N(orman) 1934- ... CANR-29
Earlier sketches in CA 33-36R, CANR-13
Harbert, Mary Ann 1945- ... 61-64
Harbeson, Georgiana Brown 1894(?)-1980 Obituary ... 101
Harbeson, Gladys Evans ... 21-24R
Harbeson, John Willis 1938- ... 57-60
Harbin, Calvin E(dward) 1916- ... 21-24R
Harbin, Robert
See Williams, Ned
Harbinson, Allen
See Harbinson, W(illiam) A(llen)
Harbinson, Robert
See Bryans, Robert Harbinson
Harbinson, W(illiam) A(llen) 1941- ... CANR-72
Earlier sketches in CA 61-64, CANR-9, 25
Harbison, Frederick Harris 1912-1976 Obituary ... 65-68
Harbison, Peter 1939- ... 65-68
Harbison, Robert 1940- ... 102
Harbottle, Michael (Neale) 1917-1997 ... CANR-45
Obituary ... 157
Earlier sketch in CA 29-32R
Harbron, John D(avison) 1924- ... 9-12R
Harburg, E(dgar) Y(ipsel) 1896-1981 ... 85-88
Obituary ... 103
Harburg, Ernest 1926- ... 145
Harburg, Ernie
See Harburg, Ernest
Harburg, Yip
See Harburg, E(dgar) Y(ipsel)
Harbury, Colin (Desmond) 1922- ... 102
Harcave, Sidney S(amuel) 1916- ... 17-20R
Harcleroad, Fred F(arley) 1918- ... CANR-23
Earlier sketches in CA 17-20R, CANR-8
Harcourt, Ellen Knowles 1890(?)-1984 Obituary ... 111
See also SATA-Obit 36
Harcourt, G(eoffrey) C(olin) 1931- ... CANR-16
Earlier sketch in CA 25-28R
Harcourt, Melville 1909- ... 5-8R
Harcourt, Palma ... CANR-31
Earlier sketches in CA 77-80, CANR-14
Harcourt, Peter 1931- ... 81-84
Hard, Charlotte (Ann) 1969- ... 166
See also SATA 98
Hard, Edward W(ilhelm), Jr. 1939- ... 85-88
Hard, Frederick 1897- ... CAP-2
Earlier sketch in CA 25-28
Hard, Margaret (Steel) 1888(?)-1974 Obituary ... 49-52
Hard, T. W.
See Hard, Edward W(ilhelm), Jr.
Hard, Walter (Rice) 1882-1966 Obituary ... 116
Hardach, Gerd 1941- ... 105
Hardach, Karl 1936- ... 130
Hardaway, Francine 1941- ... 81-84
Hardcastle, Michael 1933- ... CANR-12
Earlier sketch in CA 25-28R
See also SATA 47
See also SATA-Brief 38
Hardcastle, Robert B. 1940- ... 145
Harden, Arthur 1865-1940 ... 158
Harden, Blaine 1952- ... 135
Harden, Donald B(enjamin) 1901- ... 5-8R
Harden, Edgar F(rederick) 1932- ... CANR-49
Earlier sketch in CA 123
Harden, Ian (John) 1954- ... 126
Harden, Oleta Elizabeth (McWhorter) 1935- ... 37-40R
Harden, (John) William 1903- ... 93-96
Harder, Eleanor (Loraine) 1925- ... 37-40R
Harder, Geraldine Gross 1926- ... 53-56
Harder, Kelsie B(rown) 1922- ... 139
Harder, Leland 1926- ... 143
Harder, Raymond Wymbs, Jr. 1920- ... 85-88
Hardesty, Larry (Lynn) 1947- ... 151
Hardesty, Nancy A(nn) 1941- ... CANR-23
Earlier sketches in CA 57-60, CANR-8
Hardesty, Sarah 1951- ... 126
Hardesty, Von 1939- ... CANR-46
Earlier sketch in CA 112
Hardgrave, Robert L(ewis), Jr. 1939- ... CANR-11
Earlier sketch in CA 25-28R
Hardie, Frank 1911-1989 ... 33-36R
Obituary ... 127
Hardie, Sean 1947- ... 135
Hardie, William Francis Ross 1902-1990 Obituary ... 132
Hardiman, James W. 1919- ... 33-36R
Hardin, Charles M(eyer) 1908-1997 ... CANR-30
Obituary ... 158
Earlier sketch in CA 49-52
Hardin, Clement
See Newton, D(wight) B(ennett)
Hardin, Garrett James 1915- ... CANR-9
Earlier sketch in CA 17-20R
Hardin, J. D.
See Riefe, Alan
and Sheldon, Walter J.
Hardin, James N(eal) 1939- ... CANR-35
Earlier sketch in CA 114
Hardin, Paul III 1931- ... 25-28R
Hardin, Peter
See Vaczek, Louis
Hardin, Richard F(rancis) 1937- ... 45-48
Hardin, Robert 1934- ... 77-80
Hardin, Tim 1941(?)-1981 Obituary ... 102
Hardin, Tom
See Bauer, Erwin A.
Hardin, Wes
See Keevill, Henry J(ohn)
Harding, A(nthony) F(ilmer) 1946- ... 77-80
Harding, Barbara 1926- ... 41-44R
Harding, Bertita (Leonarz de) 1902- ... 5-8R
Harding, Carl B.
See Barker, Elver A.
Harding, D(ouglas) E(dison) 1909- Brief entry ... 116
Harding, D(enys Clement) W(yatt) 1906-1993 ... CANR-16
Obituary ... 141
Earlier sketches in CAP-1, CA 13-16
Harding, D(ennis) W(illiam) 1940- ... 41-44R
Harding, Davis P. 1915(?)-1970 Obituary ... 104
Harding, Donald Edward 1916- ... CANR-4
Earlier sketch in CA 53-56
Harding, Georgina 1955- ... 133
Harding, Harold F(riend) 1903- ... 37-40R
Harding, Harry (Jr.) 1946- ... CANR-28
Earlier sketch in CA 109
Harding, Jack 1914- ... 29-32R
Harding, James 1929- ... CANR-65
Earlier sketches in CA 33-36R, CANR-14, 32
Harding, John 1948- ... 97-100
Harding, Kenneth
See Little, Paul H(ugo)

Harding, Lee 1937- 106
See also SATA 32
See also SATA-Brief 31
Harding, Maria
See Goudiss, Maria Agnes D'Elia
Harding, Matt
See Floren, Lee
Harding, Matthew Whitman
See Floren, Lee
Harding, Mildred Davis 1916- 157
Harding, Neil 1942- 125
Harding, Peter
See Burgess, Michael (Roy)
Harding, Rose
See Gemmell, David A(ndrew)
Harding, Sandra G. 1935- CANR-44
Earlier sketch in CA 120
Harding, Susan Friend 1946- 126
Harding, T(imothy) D. 1948- 85-88
Harding, Thomas G(rayson) 1937- 21-24R
Harding, Virginia Hamlet 1909- 45-48
Harding, Walter Roy 1917-1996 .... CANR-17
Obituary 151
Earlier sketches in CA 1-4R, CANR-1
See also DLB 111
Harding, Wes
See Keevill, Henry J(ohn)
Harding, William Harry 1945- 93-96
Hardinge, Helen (Mary Cecil) 1901- CAP-2
Earlier sketch in CA 29-32
Hardingham, John (Frederick Watson) 1916- CAP-1
Earlier sketch in CA 11-12
Hardison, O(sborne) B(ennett, Jr.) 1928-1990 .... CANR-40
Obituary 132
Earlier sketches in CA 5-8R, CANR-6
See also BEST 90:2
Hardman, John (David) 1944- 45-48
Hardman, Keith (Jordan) 1931- 116
Hardman, Richards Lynden 1924- 13-16R
Hardon, John A(nthony) 1914- CANR-2
Earlier sketch in CA 1-4R
Hardoy, Jorge Enrique 1926- 33-36R
Hardt, Helga Fleischhauer
See Fleischhauer-Hardt, Helga
Hardt, J(ohn) Pearce 1922- CANR-3
Earlier sketch in CA 5-8R
Hardwick, Adam
See Connor, John Anthony
Hardwick, Clyde T(homas) 1915- 5-8R
Hardwick, Elizabeth (Bruce) 1916- CANR-70
Earlier sketches in CA 5-8R, CANR-3, 32
See also CLC 13
See also DAM NOV
See also DLB 6
See also MTCW 1
Hardwick, Homer
See Rogers, Paul (Patrick)
Hardwick, J. M. D.
See Hardwick, (John) Michael (Drinkrow)
Hardwick, Joan 1940- 135
Hardwick, (John) Michael (Drinkrow) 1924-1991 .... CANR-42
Obituary 134
Earlier sketches in CA 49-52, CANR-2
Hardwick, Mollie CANR-42
Earlier sketches in CA 49-52, CANR-2
Hardwick, Richard Holmes, Jr. 1923- CANR-9
Earlier sketch in CA 5-8R
See also SATA 12
Hardwick, Sylvia
See Doherty, Ivy R. Duffy
Hardy, Adam
See Bulmer, (Henry) Kenneth
Hardy, Alan 1932- 73-76
Hardy, Alexander G(eorge)
1920-1973 Obituary 45-48
Hardy, Alice Dale CANR-26
Earlier sketches in CAP-2, CA 19-20
See also SATA 1, 67
Hardy, Alister C(lavering) 1896-1985 85-88
Obituary 116
Hardy, Antoinette
See Stockenberg, Antoinette
Hardy, B. Carmon 1934- 144
Hardy, Barbara (Gladys) 85-88
Hardy, C. Colburn 1910- CANR-47
Earlier sketches in CA 53-56, CANR-6, 21
Hardy, David A(ndrews) 1936- CANR-8
Earlier sketch in CA 61-64
See also SATA 9
Hardy, Dennis 1941- 124
Hardy, Douglas
See Andrews, (Charles) Robert Douglas (Hardy)
Hardy, Edward R(ochie) 1908- CAP-1
Earlier sketch in CA 13-16
Hardy, Eric 61-64
Hardy, Evelyn 1902- 21-24R
Hardy, Francis Joseph 1917- 154
Hardy, Frank J.
See Hardy, Francis Joseph
Hardy, G(odfrey) H(arold) 1877-1947 163
Hardy, Gayle J. 1942- 151
Hardy, Henry 1949- CANR-47
Earlier sketch in CA 113
Hardy, J(ohn) P(hillips) 1933- 25-28R
Hardy, Jason
See Oxley, William
Hardy, John Edward 1922- 13-16R
Hardy, Jon 1958- 123
See also SATA 53
Hardy, Jonathan G. Gathorne
See Gathorne-Hardy, Jonathan G.
Hardy, Laura
See Holland, Sheila
Hardy, Leroy C(lyde) 1927- 29-32R
Hardy, Lyndon (Maurice) 1941- 154
Hardy, Melissa Arnold 1952- 102
Hardy, Michael (James Langley) 1933- 25-28R
Hardy, Peter 1931- 65-68
Hardy, Richard E(arl) 1938- 37-40R
Hardy, Richard P(eter) 1940- 117
Hardy, Ronald Harold 1919- 5-8R
Hardy, Stuart
See Schisgall, Oscar
Hardy, Thomas 1840-1928 123
Brief entry 104
See also CDBLB 1890-1914
See also DA
See also DAB
See also DAC
See also DAM MST, NOV, POET
See also DLB 18, 19, 135
See also MTCW 1
See also PC 8
See also SSC 2
See also TCLC 4, 10, 18, 32, 48, 53, 72
See also WLC
Hardy, Tom 1943- 116
Hardy, W(illiam) G(eorge) 1895-1979 .... CANR-5
Earlier sketch in CA 5-8R
Hardy, Willene S(chaefer) 1937- 112
Hardy, William M(arion) 1922- CANR-2
Earlier sketch in CA 1-4R
Hardyck, Curtis D(ale) 1929- 29-32R
Hare, A(lexander) Paul 1923- CANR-2
Earlier sketch in CA 1-4R
Hare, Bill
See Hare, William Moorman
Hare, Cyril
See Clark, Alfred Alexander Gordon
See also DLB 77
Hare, Darrell T. 1930- 155
Hare, David 1947- CANR-39
Earlier sketch in CA 97-100
See also CLC 29, 58
See also DLB 13
See also MTCW 1
Hare, Douglas Robert Adams 1929- 45-48
Hare, Eric B. 1894- CAP-1
Earlier sketch in CA 13-16
Hare, F(rederick) Kenneth 1919- CANR-14
Earlier sketch in CA 37-40R
Hare, John 1935- 21-24R
Hare, Nathan 1934- CANR-24
Earlier sketch in CA 41-44R
See also BW 2
Hare, Norma Q(uarles) 1924- 101
See also SATA 46
See also SATA-Brief 41
Hare, Peter H. 1935- 33-36R
Hare, R(ichard) M(ervyn) 1919- CANR-57
Earlier sketches in CA 5-8R, CANR-2, 31
Hare, Richard (Gilbert) 1907-1966 .... CAP-1
Earlier sketch in CA 13-14
Hare, Ronald 1899- 77-80
Hare, Steve 1950- 151
Hare, Thomas Blenman
See Hare, Thomas William
Hare, Thomas William 1952- 122
Hare, Van Court, Jr. 1929- 25-28R
Hare, William 1944- CANR-28
Earlier sketch in CA 111
Hare, William Moorman 1934- 101
Hare Duke, Michael Geoffrey 1925- 111
Harel, Isser 1912- CANR-10
Earlier sketch in CA 65-68
Harer, John B. 1948- 143
Hareven, Shulamith 1931- 159
Brief entry 117
Hareven, Tamara K. 1937- CANR-30
Earlier sketches in CA 25-28R, CANR-13
Harewood, George Henry Hubert Lascelles
1923- 125
Harewood, John
See Van Druten, John (William)
Harford, David K(ennedy) 1947- 49-52
Harford, Henry
See Hudson, W(illiam) H(enry)
Hargarten, Stephen W. 1949- 162
Harger, Rolla N(eil) 1890-1983 Obituary 114
Harger, William Henderson 1936- 57-60
Hargrave, John Gordon 1894-1982 Obituary 110
Hargrave, Leonie
See Disch, Thomas M(ichael)
Hargrave, O. T. 1936- 33-36R
Hargrave, Rowena 1906- CANR-40
Earlier sketch in CA 33-36R
Hargraves, Thomas
See Ainsworth, Thomas Hargraves, Jr.
Hargreaves, Alec G(ordon) 1948- 131
Hargreaves, Harry 1922- 5-8R
Hargreaves, John D(esmond) 1924- 9-12R
Hargreaves, Mary W(ilma) M(assey) 1914- CANR-14
Earlier sketch in CA 37-40R
Hargreaves, Reginald (Charles) 1888- CAP-1
Earlier sketch in CA 9-10
Hargreaves, (Charles) Roger
1935-1988 Obituary 126
See also SATA-Obit 56
Hargreaves-Mawdsley, W(illiam) Norman
1921-1980 .... CANR-7
Earlier sketch in CA 9-12R
Hargroder, Charles M(erlin) 1926- 73-76
Hargrove, Barbara Watts 1924- 33-36R
Hargrove, Erwin C. 1930- Brief entry 111
Hargrove, Erwin C. 1930- 146
Hargrove, James 1947- 120
See also SATA 57
See also SATA-Brief 50
Hargrove, Jim
See Hargrove, James
Hargrove, Katharine T. 33-36R
Hargrove, Marion 1919- .... DLB 11
Hargrove, Merwin Matthew 1910- 9-12R
Hargrove, Nancy Duvall 1941- 97-100
Hargrove, Richard J(ohn), Jr. 1941- 116
Harik, Iliya F. 1934- CANR-16
Earlier sketch in CA 25-28R
Haring, Bernard
See Haering, Bernhard
Haring, Firth 1937- 25-28R
Haring, Jo 1934- 116
Haring, Joseph E(merick) 1931- 33-36R
Haring, Keith 1958-1990 158
See also AAYA 21
Haring, Lee 1930- 143
Haring, Norris G. 1923- CANR-2
Earlier sketch in CA 1-4R
Haring, Philip S(myth) 1915- 37-40R
Harington, Donald 1935- CANR-55
Earlier sketches in CA 13-16R, CANR-7
See also DLB 152
Hariton, Anca I. 1955- .... SATA 79
Harjo, Chinnubie
See Posey, Alexander (Lawrence)
Harjo, Joy 1951- CANR-67
Earlier sketches in CA 114, CANR-35
See also CLC 83
See also DAM MULT
See also DLB 120, 175
See also NNAL
Hark, Mildred
See McQueen, Mildred Hark
Harkabi, Yehoshafat 1921-1994 .... CANR-27
Obituary 146
Earlier sketch in CA 73-76
Harkavy, Robert E(dward) 1936- CANR-30
Earlier sketch in CA 111
Harkaway, Hal
See Stratemeyer, Edward L.
Harker, Kenneth 1927- 97-100
Harker, Ronald 1909- 77-80
Harkey, Ira B(rown), Jr. 1918- 57-60
Harkey, William G. 1914- 25-28R
Harkins, Arthur M(artin) 1936- 97-100
Harkins, Paul W(illiam) 1911- 116
Harkins, Philip 1912- 29-32R
See also SATA 6
Harkins, William E(dward) 1921- 33-36R
Harkness, Bruce 1923- 13-16R
Harkness, D(avid) W(illiam) 1937- CANR-15
Earlier sketch in CA 29-32R
Harkness, David J(ames) 1913- CANR-3
Earlier sketch in CA 9-12R
Harkness, Edward 1947- 77-80
Harkness, Georgia (Elma) 1891-1974 .... CANR-6
Obituary 53-56
Earlier sketch in CA 1-4R
Harkness, Gladys Estelle Suiter
1908(?)-1973 Obituary 41-44R
Harkness, Jack
See Harkness, John Leigh
Harkness, John Leigh 1918-1994 120
Obituary 145
Harkness, Margaret 1854-1923 .... DLB 197
Harkness, Marjory Gane 1880-(?) CAP-2
Earlier sketch in CA 23-24
Harknett, Terry 1936- CANR-21
Earlier sketches in CA 57-60, CANR-6
Harlan
See Shaw, William Harlan
Harlan, Elizabeth 1945- 111
See also SATA 41
See also SATA-Brief 35
Harlan, Glen
See Cebulash, Mel
Harlan, John Marshall 1899-1971 Obituary 33-36R
Harlan, Judith 1949- .... SATA 74
Harlan, Louis R(udolph) 1922- CANR-55
Earlier sketches in CA 21-24R, CANR-25
See also CLC 34
Harlan, William K(eith) 1938- 45-48
Harle, Elizabeth
See Roberts, Irene
Harleman, Ann 1945- 145
Harlequin
See Reed, A(lexander) W(yclif)
Harler, Ann
See Van Steenwyk, Elizabeth (Ann)
Harley, Bill 1954- 151
See also SATA 87
Harley, John
See Marsh, John
Harley, Willard F., Jr. 1941- 167
Harling, Robert 1951(?)- 147
See also CLC 53
Harling, Thomas
See Eastham, Thomas
Harlow, Enid 1939- 102
Harlow, Francis H(arvey) 1928- 57-60
Harlow, Harry F(rederick) 1905- 97-100
Harlow, Joan Hiatt 1932- 89-92
Harlow, LeRoy F(rancis) 1913- 85-88
Harlow, Lewis A(ugustus) 1901- CAP-1
Earlier sketch in CA 13-14
Harlow, Neal 1908- 109
Harlow, Robert 1923- 128
See also DLB 60
Harlow, Rosie 1961- 149
Harlow, Samuel Ralph 1885-1972 .... 1-4R
Obituary 37-40R
Harlow, W(illiam) M(orehouse) 1900-1986 .... 13-16R
Obituary 119
Harman, Alec
See Harman, Richard Alexander
Harman, Barbara Leah 1946- 126
Harman, Claire
See Schmidt, Claire Harman
Harman, David 1944- 105
Harman, Fred 1902(?)-1982 Obituary 106
See also SATA-Obit 30
Harman, Gilbert H(elms) 1938- 73-76
Harman, Harry E. III 1917- CANR-39
Earlier sketch in CA 116
Harman, Hugh 1903-1982 Obituary 108
See also SATA-Obit 33
Harman, Jane
See Harknett, Terry
Harman, Jeanne Perkins 1919- CANR-39
Earlier sketches in CA 69-72, CANR-11
Harman, Mark 1951- CANR-49
Earlier sketch in CA 118
Harman, Nicholas 1933- 101
Harman, P(eter) M(ichael) 1943- 110
Harman, R. Alec
See Harman, Richard Alexander
Harman, Richard Alexander 1917- CANR-5
Earlier sketch in CA 9-12R
Harman, Willis W(alter) 1918-1997 .... 5-8R
Obituary 156
Harmel, Robert 1950- 110
Harmelink, Barbara (Mary) 61-64
See also SATA 9
Harmer, Mabel 1894- 9-12R
See also SATA 45
Harmer, Ruth Mulvey 1919- 9-12R
Harmetz, Aljean 139
Harmin, Merrill 1928- 89-92
Harmon, A(llen) J(ackson) 1926- 21-24R
Harmon, Frederick G(ardner) 1932- 119
Harmon, Gary L. 1935- 37-40R
Harmon, Glynn 1933- 45-48
Harmon, H. H.
See Williams, Robert Moore
Harmon, James Judson 1933- 21-24R
Harmon, Jim
See Harmon, James Judson
Harmon, Lily 1912-1998 105
Obituary 166
Harmon, Lyn S. 1930- 21-24R
Harmon, Margaret 1906- 69-72
See also SATA 20
Harmon, Maurice 1930- CANR-9
Earlier sketch in CA 21-24R
Harmon, Nolan B(ailey) 1892- 89-92
Harmon, (Norman) Paul 1942- 122
Harmon, Robert Bartlett 1932- CANR-48
Earlier sketches in CA 17-20R, CANR-8, 23
Harmon, Susanna M(arie) 1940- 57-60
Harmon, William (Ruth) 1938- CANR-35
Earlier sketches in CA 33-36R, CANR-14, 32
See also CLC 38
See also SATA 65
Harms, Ernest 1895-1974 .... CAP-1
Obituary 49-52
Earlier sketch in CA 13-14
Harms, John 1900- 17-20R
Harms, Leroy Stanley 1928- CANR-8
Earlier sketch in CA 53-56
Harms, Robert T(homas) 1932- 37-40R
Harms, Valerie 1940- CANR-2
Earlier sketch in CA 49-52
Harmsel, Henrietta Ten
See Ten Harmsel, Henrietta
Harmsen, Dorothy B. Bahneman 103
Harmsen, Frieda 1931- 107
Harmston, Olivia
See Weber, Nancy
Harmsworth, Esmond Cecil
1898-1978 Obituary 89-92
Harnack, Curtis (Arthur) 1927- CANR-22
Earlier sketches in CA 1-4R, CANR-2
Harnack, R(obert) Victor 1927- 13-16R
Harnack, William J. 1953- 125
Harnan, Terry 1920- 45-48
See also SATA 12
Harnden, Ruth Peabody 73-76
Harned, David Baily 1932- 135
Brief entry 112
Harner, James L(owell) 1946- 110
Harner, Michael J(ames) 1929- 134
Brief entry 114
Harner, Stephen M. 1949- 151
Harness, Charles L(eonard) 1915- 158
Brief entry 113
See also DLB 8
Harnett, Bertram 1923- 119
Harnett, Cynthia (Mary) 1893-1981 .... CAP-1
Obituary 111
Earlier sketch in CA 9-10
See also DLB 161
See also SATA 5
See also SATA-Obit 32
Harnetty, Peter 1927- 37-40R
Harnik, Bernard 1910- 93-96
Harnois, Albert J. 1945- 151
Harnsberger, Caroline Thomas 1902-1991 61-64
Obituary 134
Harnwell, Gaylord Probasco
1903-1982 Obituary 106
Haro, Robert P(eter) 1936- 33-36R
Haroian-Guerin, Gil 1957- 163
Harold, Fred(erick) G(ordon) 1937- 118
Haroldson, William
See King, Harold
Haroutunian, Joseph 1904-1968 Obituary 111
Harp, Gillis J(ohn) 1956- 150
Harper, Anita 1943- 114
See also SATA 41
Harper, Annette
See Harper, M(eredith) A(nnette)

Harper, Bill
See Harper, William A(rthur)
Harper, Carol Ely ... 61-64
Harper, Daniel
See Brossard, Chandler
Harper, David
See Corley, Edwin (Raymond)
Harper, Donna Akiba Sullivan
See Sullivan Harper, Donna Akiba
Harper, Douglas A(lbert) 1948- ... 117
Harper, Elaine
See Hallin, Emily Watson
Harper, F. E. W.
See Harper, Frances Ellen Watkins
Harper, Fletcher 1806-1877 ... DLB 79
Harper, Floyd H(enry) 1899-1978 Obituary ... 77-80
Harper, Frances E. W.
See Harper, Frances Ellen Watkins
Harper, Frances E. Watkins
See Harper, Frances Ellen Watkins
Harper, Frances Ellen
See Harper, Frances Ellen Watkins
Harper, Frances Ellen Watkins 1825-1911 ... 125
Brief entry ... 111
See also BLC 2
See also BW 1
See also DAM MULT, POET
See also DLB 50
See also PC 21
See also TCLC 14
Harper, George Mills 1914- ... 136
Brief entry ... 114
Harper, George W(illiam) 1927- ... 113
Harper, Harold W. ... 89-92
Harper, Harry H(alsted), Jr.
1910-1983 Obituary ... 110
Harper, Howard (V.) 1904-1978 ... 17-20R
Obituary ... 133
Harper, Howard M(orrall), Jr. 1930- ... CANR-22
Earlier sketch in CA 21-24R
Harper, J(ohn) Russell 1914-1983 ... CANR-13
Earlier sketch in CA 33-36R
Harper, James E(dwin) 1927- ... 41-44R
Harper, Jo 1932- ... 163
See also SATA 97
Harper, Joan (Marie) 1932- ... 101
Harper, John C(arsten) 1924- ... 103
Harper, John Dickson 1910- ... 103
Harper, Karen 1945- ... CANR-45
Earlier sketches in CA 114, CANR-42
Harper, Kate
See Harper, Katherine E(rna)
Harper, Katherine E(rna) 1946- ... 103
Harper, M(eredith) A(nnette) 1949- ... 141
Harper, M(ichael) J(ohn) K(ennedy) 1935- ... 116
Harper, Marjory(-Ann Denoon) 1956- ... CANR-66
Earlier sketch in CA 129
Harper, Marvin Henry 1901- ... 49-52
Harper, Mary Wood
See Dixon, Jeanne
Harper, Michael 1931- ... CANR-15
Earlier sketch in CA 65-68
Harper, Michael S(teven) 1938- ... CANR-24
Earlier sketch in CA 33-36R
See also BW 1
See also CLC 7, 22
See also DLB 41
Harper, Mrs. F. E. W.
See Harper, Frances Ellen Watkins
Harper, Paula (Hays) 1938- ... 105
Harper, Robert A(lexander) 1924- ... 17-20R
Harper, Robert J(ohnston) C(raig) 1927- ... 13-16R
Harper, Stephen (Dennis) 1924- ... 97-100
Harper, Susan (Rice) 1943- ... 142
Harper, Tara K. 1961- ... 141
Harper, Tom 1923(?)-1983 Obituary ... 110
Harper, Wilhelmina 1884-1973 ... CAP-1
Earlier sketch in CA 17-18
See also SATA 4
See also SATA-Obit 26
Harper, William A(rthur) 1944- ... 77-80
Harpham, Geoffrey Galt 1946- ... 111
Harpole, Charles H(enry) 1943- ... 111
Harpole, Patricia Chayne 1933- ... 37-40R
Harpur, Patrick 1950- ... 114
Harpur, Thomas William 1929- ... 137
Harpur, Tom
See Harpur, Thomas William
Harr, Wilber C. 1908-1971 ... 1-4R
Obituary ... 103
Harraden, Beatrice 1864-1936 ... DLB 153
Harragan, Betty Lehan 1921- ... CANR-17
Earlier sketch in CA 77-80
Harrah, Barbara K. 1938- ... 107
Harrah, David 1926- ... 5-8R
Harrah, David Fletcher 1949- ... 65-68
Harrah, Michael 1940- ... 115
See also SATA 41
Harral, Stewart 1906-1964 ... 5-8R
Harrar, E(llwood) S(cott) 1905- ... CAP-1
Earlier sketch in CA 11-12
Harrar, J(acob) George 1906-1982 Obituary ... 110
Harre, John 1931- ... 21-24R
Harre, (Horace) Rom(ano) 1927- ... CANR-21
Earlier sketches in CA 5-8R, CANR-2
Harrell, Allen W(aylan) 1922- ... 29-32R
Harrell, Anne
See Neggers, Carla A(malia)
Harrell, Beatrice Orcutt 1943- ... 159
See also SATA 93
Harrell, Costen J(ordan) 1885- ... 5-8R
Harrell, David Edwin, Jr. 1930- ... CANR-34
Earlier sketches in CA 37-40R, CANR-15
Harrell, Irene B(urk) 1927- ... CANR-25
Earlier sketches in CA 21-24R, CANR-9
Harrell, Janice 1945- ... 138
See also SATA 70
Harrell, John G(rinnell) 1922- ... CANR-18
Earlier sketches in CA 9-12R, CANR-3
Harrell, Sara (Jeanne) Gordon 1940- ... 105
See also Banks, Sara (Jeanne Gordon Harrell)
Harrell, (Clyde) Stevan 1947- ... 106
Harrell, Thomas Willard 1911- ... 1-4R
Harrelson, Walter (Joseph) 1919- ... 9-12R
Harrer, Heinrich 1912- ... CANR-31
Earlier sketches in CA 17-20R, CANR-7
Harrier, Richard C(harles) 1923- ... 122
Brief entry ... 117
Harries, Joan 1922- ... 107
See also SATA 39
Harries, Karsten 1937- ... 165
Harries, Owen 1930- ... 127
Harries, Richard (Douglas) 1936- ... 116
Harriett 1905- ... 77-80
Harrigan, Anthony (Hart) 1925- ... 21-24R
Harrigan, Kathryn Rudie 1951- ... CANR-26
Earlier sketch in CA 109
Harrigan, Patrick J. 1941- ... 142
Harrigan, Stephen 1948- ... CANR-48
Earlier sketch in CA 122
Harriger, Katy J(ean) 1957- ... 143
Harrill, Ronald 1950- ... 155
See also SATA 90
Harriman, Ann 1932- ... 111
Harriman, Averell
See Harriman, W(illiam) Averell
Harriman, Edward 1922- ... 114
Harriman, Margaret 1928- ... 21-24R
Harriman, Richard L(evet) 1944- ... 33-36R
Harriman, Sarah 1942- ... 57-60
Harriman, W(illiam) Averell
1891-1986 Obituary ... 119
Brief entry ... 111
Harrington, Alan 1919-1997 ... 73-76
Obituary ... 158
Harrington, Charles (Christopher) 1942- ... CANR-9
Earlier sketch in CA 65-68
Harrington, Curtis 1928- ... 103
Harrington, Denis J(ames) 1932- ... 69-72
See also SATA 88
Harrington, Donald Szantho 1914- ... 21-24R
Harrington, Elbert W(ellington) 1901- ... 37-40R
Harrington, Evelyn Davis 1911- ... CANR-4
Earlier sketch in CA 5-8R
See also Harrington, Lyn
Harrington, Gary 1953- ... 135
Harrington, Geri ... CANR-44
Earlier sketches in CA 57-60, CANR-6, 21
Harrington, Harold David 1903-1981 ... CANR-11
Earlier sketch in CA 25-28R
Harrington, Jack 1918- ... 57-60
Harrington, Jeremy 1932- ... 41-44R
Harrington, John P. 1952- ... 138
Harrington, John W(ilbur) 1918-1986 ... 132
Harrington, Joseph Daniel 1923- ... 89-92
Harrington, K.
See Bean, Keith F(enwick)
Harrington, Kathleen ... 160
Harrington, Kent 1945- ... 141
Harrington, Lyn
See Harrington, Evelyn Davis
See also SATA 5
Harrington, Mark Raymond 1882-1971 ... CAP-2
Earlier sketch in CA 17-18
Harrington, (Edward) Michael 1928-1989 . CANR-19
Obituary ... 129
Earlier sketch in CA 17-20R
Harrington, Norman W. 1922(?)-1987 Obituary . 123
Harrington, Philip S(tuart) 1956- ... 167
Harrington, (Peter) Ty(rus) 1951- ... 102
Harrington, William 1931- ... CANR-70
Earlier sketches in CA 9-12R, CANR-4, 19, 42
Harriott, Edwin Thomas 1933- ... 117
Harriott, Peter 1927- ... 144
Harriott, Ted
See Harriott, Edwin Thomas
Harris, Alan 1928- ... 5-8R
Harris, Alan 1944- ... 139
See also SATA 71
Harris, Albert J(osiah) 1908-1990 ... CANR-5
Obituary ... 132
Earlier sketch in CA 1-4R
Harris, Alex(ander Eisemann) 1949- ... 124
Harris, Alf(red) 1928- ... 53-56
Harris, Andrea
See Connolly, Vivian
and Walker, Irma Ruth (Roden)
Harris, Andrew
See Poole, Frederick King
Harris, Anita M(arie) 1948- ... 152
Harris, Ann Sutherland 1937- ... 126
Harris, Aurand 1915-1996 ... CANR-36
Obituary ... 152
Earlier sketches in CA 93-96, CANR-16
See also SATA 37
Harris, Barbara J. 1942- ... 115
Harris, Barbara S(eger) 1927- ... 49-52
Harris, Ben(jamin) Charles 1907-1978 ... 57-60
Obituary ... 89-92
Harris, Ben(jamin) M(axwell) 1923- ... CANR-2
Earlier sketch in CA 5-8R
Harris, Benjamin (?)-1720(?) ... DLB 42, 43
Harris, Bernice K(elly) 1892-1973 ... 5-8R
Obituary ... 45-48
Harris, Bertha 1937- ... CANR-71
Earlier sketch in CA 29-32R
Harris, Beulah (?)-1970 Obituary ... 104
Harris, Bill
See Harris, William F., Jr.
Harris, Brayton 1932- ... 167
Harris, Brian
See King, Harold
Harris, Brownie 1949- ... 107
Harris, Carl V(ernon) 1937- ... 97-100
Harris, Catherine
See Ainsworth, Catherine Harris
Harris, Charlaine 1951- ... 105
Harris, Charles 1923- ... 102
Harris, Charles B(urt) 1940- ... 53-56
Harris, Charles H(ouston) III 1937- ... 13-16R
Harris, Charles Wesley 1929- ... 150
Harris, Chauncy D(ennison) 1914- ... 29-32R
Harris, Chester W(illiam) 1910- ... CAP-1
Earlier sketch in CA 11-12
Harris, Christie (Lucy) Irwin 1907- ... CANR-6
Earlier sketch in CA 5-8R
See also CLC 12
See also CLR 47
See also DLB 88
See also JRDA
See also MAICYA
See also SAAS 10
See also SATA 6, 74
Harris, Clyde E., Jr. ... 21-24R
Harris, Colver
See Colver, Anne
Harris, Curtis C(lark), Jr. 1930- ... 53-56
Harris, Cyril 1891- ... CAP-1
Earlier sketch in CA 11-12
Harris, Dale B(enner) 1914- ... 13-16R
Harris, Daniel A(rthur) 1942- ... 89-92
Harris, David (Victor) 1946- ... CANR-57
Earlier sketch in CA 69-72
Harris, David W. 1948- Brief entry ... 107
Harris, Deborah Turner 1951- ... 135
Harris, Del(mer William) 1937- ... CANR-8
Earlier sketch in CA 61-64
Harris, Donald 1931- ... 126
Harris, Dorothy Joan 1931- ... CANR-1
Earlier sketch in CA 45-48
See also SATA 13
Harris, Douglas H(ershel, Jr.) 1930- ... 25-28R
Harris, E. Lynn 1955- ... 164
Harris, Edward Arnold 1910-1976 Obituary ... 65-68
Harris, Elizabeth 1944- ... 136
Harris, Elliot 1932- ... 25-28R
Harris, Ernest E(dward) 1914- ... 33-36R
Harris, Errol E(ustace) 1908- ... CANR-41
Earlier sketches in CA 49-52, CANR-2, 18
Harris, F(rank) Brayton 1932- ... 21-24R
Harris, Francis 1957- ... 130
Harris, Frank 1856-1931 ... 150
Brief entry ... 109
See also DLB 156, 197
See also TCLC 24
Harris, Fred (Roy) 1930- ... CANR-52
Earlier sketches in CA 77-80, CANR-26
Harris, Frederick John 1943- ... 57-60
Harris, Gene Gray 1929- ... 17-20R
Harris, George A. 1950- ... 130
Harris, George Washington 1814-1869 .. DLB 3, 11
Harris, Geraldine (Rachel) 1951- ... CANR-59
Earlier sketch in CA 116
See also SATA 54
Harris, Gertrude (Margaret) 1916- ... 57-60
Harris, H(arold) A(rthur) 1902-1974 ... CANR-30
Earlier sketch in CA 49-52
Harris, H(enry) S(ilton) 1926- ... 130
Harris, Harold (Morris) 1915-1993 ... 132
Obituary ... 142
Harris, Helen(a Barbara Mary) 1927- ... 61-64
Harris, Herbert 1911- ... 102
Harris, Herbert 1914(?)-1974 Obituary ... 49-52
Harris, Hyde
See Harris, Timothy Hyde
Harris, Ian (Anthony) 1937- ... 107
Harris, Irving David 1914- ... 13-16R
Harris, Jacqueline L. 1929- ... 126
See also SATA 62
Harris, James E(dward) 1928- ... 126
Brief entry ... 110
Harris, James F. 1941- ... 146
Harris, Jana 1947- ... 105
Harris, Jane Allen 1918- ... 1-4R
Harris, Jane Gary ... 111
Harris, Janet 1932-1979 ... CANR-28
Obituary ... 93-96
Earlier sketch in CA 33-36R
See also SATA 4
See also SATA-Obit 23
Harris, Janice Hubbard 1943- ... 118
Harris, Jay S(tephen) 1938- ... 85-88
Harris, Jean (S.) 1923- ... 137
Harris, Jed
See Horowitz, Jacob
Harris, Jesse
See Standiford, Natalie
Harris, Jessica L.
See Milstead, Jessica L(ee)
Harris, Jocelyn 1939- ... 128
Harris, Joel Chandler 1848-1908 ... 137
Brief entry ... 104
See also CLR 49
See also DLB 11, 23, 42, 78, 91
See also MAICYA
See also SATA 100
See also SSC 19
See also TCLC 2
See also YABC 1
Harris, John (Roy) 1915- ... CANR-2
Earlier sketch in CA 5-8R
Harris, John 1916-1991 ... 93-96
Obituary ... 134
Harris, John (Wyndham Parkes Lucas) Beynon
1903-1969 ... 102
Obituary ... 89-92
See also Wyndham, John
Harris, John S(harp) 1917- ... 29-32R
Harris, John S(terling) 1929- ... 65-68
Harris, Jonathan 1921- ... CANR-48
Earlier sketch in CA 121
See also SATA 52
Harris, Jose ... 147
Harris, Joseph E(arl) 1929- ... 122
Brief entry ... 117
Harris, Joseph Pratt 1896-1985 ... 1-4R
Obituary ... 115
Harris, Julian (Earle) 1896-1988 ... CANR-31
Earlier sketch in CA 1-4R
Harris, Julie 1925- ... 103
Harris, Karen H(arriman) 1934- ... CANR-22
Earlier sketch in CA 103
Harris, Kathleen
See Humphries, Adelaide M.
Harris, Kathryn Gibbs
See Gibbs-Wilson, Kathryn (Beatrice)
Harris, Kenn 1947- ... 116
Harris, Kenneth 1904-1983 Obituary ... 109
Harris, Kenneth 1919- ... 129
Harris, Larry M.
See Janifer, Laurence M(ark)
Harris, Larry Vincent 1939- ... SATA 59
Harris, Lavinia
See St. John, Nicole
Harris, Leon A., Jr. 1926- ... CANR-3
Earlier sketch in CA 9-12R
See also SATA 4
Harris, Leonard 1929- ... CANR-9
Earlier sketch in CA 65-68
Harris, Lloyd J(ohn) 1947- ... 61-64
Harris, Lorle K(empe) 1912- ... 97-100
See also SATA 22
Harris, Louis 1921- ... 13-16R
Harris, Louise 1903- ... CANR-7
Earlier sketch in CA 17-20R
Harris, M(iddleton) A. 1908-1977 Obituary ... 111
Harris, MacDonald
See Heiney, Donald (William)
See also CLC 9
Harris, Madalene 1925- ... 105
Harris, Marcia Lee 1951- ... 109
Harris, Marie 1943- ... CANR-20
Earlier sketch in CA 104
Harris, Marilyn
See Springer, Marilyn Harris
Harris, Marion Rose (Young) 1925- ... CANR-57
Earlier sketches in CAP-1, CA 9-10, CANR-12, 30
Harris, Marjorie Silliman 1890- ... CAP-1
Earlier sketch in CA 13-14
Harris, Mark 1922- ... CANR-55
Earlier sketches in CA 5-8R, CANR-2
See also CAAS 3
See also CLC 19
See also DLB 2
See also DLBY 80
Harris, Mark C(harles) 1955- ... 113
Harris, Mark Jonathan 1941- ... CANR-21
Earlier sketch in CA 104
See also SATA 32, 84
Harris, Marshall (Dees) 1903- ... CANR-1
Earlier sketch in CA 1-4R
Harris, Martyn 1952-1996 ... 132
Obituary ... 154
Harris, Marvin 1927- ... 124
Brief entry ... 110
Harris, Mary (Emma) 1943- ... 135
Harris, Mary B(ierman) 1943- ... 53-56
Harris, Mary Imogene ... 49-52
Harris, Mary K. 1905-1966 ... CAP-1
Earlier sketch in CA 13-16
Harris, Mary Law 1892(?)-1980 Obituary ... 102
Harris, Maynard L(awrence)
1902-1974 Obituary ... 116
Harris, Michael (Terry) 1948- ... 125
Harris, Michael H(ope) 1941- ... 57-60
Harris, Michael R(ichard) 1936- ... 29-32R
Harris, Miles F(itzgerald) 1913- ... CANR-6
Earlier sketch in CA 5-8R
Harris, Neil 1938- ... 142
Harris, P(eter) B(ernard) 1929- ... 104
Harris, Patricia ... 57-60
Harris, Paul 1948- ... 156
Harris, Philip R(obert) 1926- ... CANR-25
Earlier sketches in CA 17-20R, CANR-8
Harris, R(ansom) Baine 1927- ... 73-76
Harris, R(obert) J(ohn) C(ecil) 1922-1980 ...
CANR-15
Earlier sketch in CA 65-68
Harris, R(obert) Laird 1911- ... CANR-1
Earlier sketch in CA 1-4R
Harris, Radie ... 65-68
Harris, Randy Allen 1956- ... 142
Harris, Raymond 1919-1989 Obituary ... 129
Harris, Rex 1904-1985 Obituary ... 118
Harris, Richard (S.) 1928(?)-1987 ... 129
Obituary ... 123
Harris, Richard 1934- ... 107
Harris, Richard 1955- ... 126
Harris, Richard Colebrook 1936- ... 97-100
Harris, Richard H. 1942- ... 103
Harris, Richard J(ohn) 1948- ... 115
Harris, Richard N(elson) 1942- ... 77-80
Harris, Ricky 1922- ... 103
Harris, Robert (Jennings) 1907- ... 5-8R
Harris, Robert (Dennis) 1957- ... 143
Harris, Robert Dalton 1921- ... 93-96
Harris, Robert Harry 1941- ... 108
Harris, Robert Samuel 1904-1983 Obituary ... 111
Harris, Robert T(aylor) 1912- ... 5-8R

Harris, Robie H. 1940- 155
See also SATA 90
See also SATA-Brief 53
Harris, Robin
See Shine, Deborah
Harris, Robin S(utton) 1919- 21-24R
Harris, Roger
See Wilson, R(oger) H(arris) L(ebus)
Harris, Ronald W(alter) 1916- 5-8R
Harris, Rosemary (Jeanne) CANR-30
Earlier sketches in CA 33-36R, CANR-13
See also CLR 30
See also SAAS 7
See also SATA 4, 82
Harris, Roy J. 1903(?)-1980 Obituary 93-96
Harris, Ruth Elwin 1935- 146
Harris, S(eymour) E(dwin) 1897-1974 65-68
Obituary 53-56
Harris, Sara Lee
See Stadelman, S(ara) L(ee)
Harris, Sheldon H(oward) 1928- 37-40R
Harris, Sherwood 1932- 97-100
See also SATA 25
Harris, Stacy 1952- 142
Harris, Stephen E. 1943- Brief entry 111
Harris, Stephen L(eRoy) 1937- 29-32R
Harris, Steve 1950- 168
Harris, Steve 1954- 165
Harris, Steven Michael 1957- 121
See also SATA 55
Harris, (William) Stewart 1922-1994 104
Obituary 147
Harris, Stuart
See Fantoni, Barry (Ernest)
Harris, Styron 1936- 112
Harris, Sydney J(ustin) 1917-1986 ..... CANR-11
Obituary 120
Earlier sketch in CA 61-64
Interview in CANR-11
Harris, T George 1924- CANR-47
Earlier sketch in CA 69-72
Harris, Thistle Y.
See Stead, Thistle Yolette
Harris, Thomas 1940(?)- CANR-35
Earlier sketch in CA 113
See also DAM POP
Harris, Thomas A(nthony) 1910-1995 93-96
Obituary 148
Harris, Thomas Cunningham
1908-1985 Obituary 114
Harris, Thomas Harold 1933- 125
Harris, Thomas J. 1892(?)-1983 Obituary 109
Harris, Thomas O(rville) 1935- 73-76
Harris, Thomas Walter 1930- 141
See also BW 2
Harris, Timothy Hyde 1946- 101
Harris, (Jonathan) Toby 1953- 118
Harris, Tom
See Harris, Thomas Cunningham
and Harris, Thomas Walter
Harris, Trudier 1948- CANR-40
Earlier sketch in CA 115
Harris, Valentina 1957- 128
Harris, Walter A. 1929- 29-32R
Harris, Warren G(ene) 1936- CANR-26
Earlier sketch in CA 77-80
Harris, Wayne T. (Sr.) 1954- 146
Harris, Wendell V. 1932- 111
Harris, William Bliss 1901(?)-1981 Obituary 104
Harris, William C. 1933- 21-24R
Harris, William F., Jr. 1933- CANR-30
Earlier sketch in CA 109
Harris, William Foster
See Foster-Harris, William
Harris, William Hamilton 1944- 111
Harris, William J(oseph) 1942- CANR-19
Earlier sketches in CA 53-56, CANR-5
Harris, William McKinley Sr. 1941- 126
Harris, (Theodore) Wilson 1921- CANR-69
Earlier sketches in CA 65-68, CANR-11, 27
See also CAAS 16
See also BW 2
See also CLC 25
See also DLB 117
See also MTCW 1
Harris, Y. L.
See Harris, Yvonne L.
Harris, Yvonne L. 138
Harris-Filderman, Diane
See Filderman, Diane E(lizabeth)
Harrison, Allan E(ugene) 1925- CANR-6
Earlier sketch in CA 57-60
Harrison, Ann Tukey 1938- 149
Harrison, Antony H. 1948- 132
Harrison, Barbara 1941- CANR-53
Earlier sketches in CA 29-32R, CANR-12, 28
Harrison, Barbara Grizzuti 1934- CANR-48
Earlier sketches in CA 77-80, CANR-15
Interview in CANR-15
Harrison, Barry (Joseph Douglas) 1935- 129
Harrison, Bennett 1942- 53-56
Harrison, Bernard 1933- 93-96
Harrison, Beverly Wildung 1932- 111
Harrison, Bill
See Harrison, William C.
Harrison, Billy R. 1937- 121
Harrison, Brian (Howard) 1937- 149
Harrison, Brian Fraser
See Fraser Harrison, Brian
Harrison, C(hester) William 1913- CANR-64
Earlier sketch in CA 107
See also SATA 35
Harrison, Carey 1944- 61-64
Harrison, Charles Yale 1898-1954 ..... DLB 68
Harrison, Chip
See Block, Lawrence
Harrison, Chip 1952- 29-32R
Harrison, Claire (E.) 1946- CANR-28
Earlier sketch in CA 111
Harrison, Colin 1960- CANR-56
Earlier sketch in CA 138
Harrison, Cynthia Ellen 1946- 57-60
Harrison, David L(akin) 1926- 117
Harrison, David L(ee) 1937- CANR-57
Earlier sketch in CA 93-96
See also SATA 26, 92
Harrison, Deloris 1938- 61-64
See also SATA 9
Harrison, Don(ald Dean) 1941- 112
Harrison, Edward Hardy 1926- CANR-39
Earlier sketch in CA 116
See also SATA 56
Harrison, Elizabeth Cavanna 1909- CANR-27
Earlier sketches in CA 9-12R, CANR-6
See also Cavanna, Betty
Harrison, Eric George William Warde
1893-1987 Obituary 124
Harrison, Everett F(alconer) 1902- CAP-1
Earlier sketch in CA 11-12
Harrison, Francis Llewelyn 1905-1987 Obituary 124
Harrison, Frank Llewelyn
See Harrison, Francis Llewelyn
Harrison, Frank R(ussell) III 1935- 53-56
Harrison, Fred
See Paine, Lauran (Bosworth)
Harrison, Fred 1917- 29-32R
Harrison, Frederic 1831-1923 ..... DLB 57, 190
Harrison, G(eorge) B(agshawe) 1894-1991 .....
CANR-3
Obituary 136
Earlier sketch in CA 1-4R
Harrison, Gary 1949- 150
Harrison, George Russell 1898-1979 ..... CANR-27
Earlier sketches in CAP-2, CA 19-20
Harrison, Hank 1940- 41-44R
Harrison, Harry (Max) 1925- CANR-21
Earlier sketches in CA 1-4R, CANR-5
See also CLC 42
See also DLB 8
See also SATA 4
Harrison, Helen Amy 1943- 114
Harrison, Helen P(atricia) 1935- 102
Harrison, Howard 1930- 5-8R
Harrison, J(ohn) F(letcher) C(lews) 1921- .....
CANR-10
Earlier sketch in CA 25-28R
Harrison, James (Ernest) 1927- 140
Harrison, James (Thomas) 1937- CANR-51
Earlier sketches in CA 13-16R, CANR-8
Interview in CANR-8
See also CLC 6, 14, 33, 66
See also DLBY 82
See also SSC 19
Harrison, James Pinckney 1932- CANR-48
Earlier sketch in CA 77-80
Harrison, Jamie (Louise) 156
Harrison, Jay S(molens) 1927-1974 Obituary 53-56
Harrison, Jeffrey (Woods) 1957- CANR-58
Earlier sketch in CA 127
Harrison, Jim
See Harrison, James (Thomas)
Harrison, Joan (Mary) 1909-1994 104
Obituary 146
Harrison, John 1924- CANR-65
Earlier sketch in CA 129
Harrison, John A(rmstrong) 1915- Brief entry 111
Harrison, John Baugham 1907- 1-4R
Harrison, John M(arshall) 1914- 25-28R
Harrison, John R(aymond) 1933- 101
See also AITN 2
Harrison, K(enneth) C(ecil) 1915- CANR-3
Earlier sketch in CA 9-12R
Harrison, Kathryn 1961- CANR-68
Earlier sketch in CA 144
See also CLC 70
Harrison, Keith Edward 1932- 73-76
Harrison, Lawrence E. 1932- 127
Harrison, Louise C(ollbran) 1908- CAP-1
Earlier sketch in CA 11-12
Harrison, Lowell H(ayes) 1922- 162
Harrison, M(ichael) John 1945- CANR-59
Earlier sketch in CA 53-56
Harrison, Marcus 1924- 102
Harrison, Marshall 1933- 138
Harrison, Martin 1930- 49-52
Harrison, Mary
See Rash, Nancy
Harrison, Max 69-72
Harrison, Michael 1907- CANR-61
Earlier sketch in CA 97-100
Harrison, Michael A. 1936- 126
Harrison, Michelle Jessica 1942- 109
Harrison, Molly 1909- 108
See also SATA 41
Harrison, Nancy 1923- 142
Harrison, Nicolas 1937(?)-1984 Obituary 114
Harrison, Paul Carter 1936- 125
Brief entry 117
Interview in 125
See also BW 2
See also DLB 38
Harrison, Paul M. 1923- 53-56
Harrison, Payne 1949- 139
Harrison, Randall P(aul) 1929- CANR-11
Earlier sketch in CA 69-72
Harrison, Ray(mond Vincent) 1928- 126
Harrison, Raymond H. 1911- 17-20R
Harrison, Reginald Carey 1908-1990 Obituary 131
Harrison, Rex
See Harrison, Reginald Carey
Harrison, Richard A(rnold) 1945- 107
Harrison, Richard John 1920- 109
Harrison, Robert (Ligon) 1932- 25-28R
Harrison, Robert Pogue 1954- 138
Harrison, Roland Kenneth 1920- CANR-48
Earlier sketch in CA 49-52
Harrison, Rosina 1899- 102
Harrison, (Thomas) Ross 1943- CANR-9
Earlier sketch in CA 61-64
Harrison, Roy M(ichael) 1948- 140
Harrison, Royden John 1927- 17-20R
Harrison, Russell (T.) 1944- 149
Harrison, S(ydney) Gerald 1924- 13-16R
Harrison, Sarah 1946- 102
See also SATA 63
Harrison, Saul I. 1925- CANR-10
Earlier sketch in CA 21-24R
Harrison, Selig S(eidenman) 1927- 85-88
Harrison, Stanley R. 1927- 41-44R
Harrison, Sue 1950- 135
Interview in 135
Harrison, Susan Frances 1859-1935 ..... DLB 99
Harrison, Suzan 1956- 166
Harrison, Ted
See Harrison, Edward Hardy
Harrison, Tony 1937- CANR-44
Earlier sketch in CA 65-68
See also CLC 43
See also DLB 40
See also MTCW 1
Harrison, Trevor (W.) 152
Harrison, Wallace (Kirkman)
1895-1981 Obituary 108
Harrison, Whit
See Whittington, Harry (Benjamin)
Harrison, Wilfrid 1909- CAP-1
Earlier sketch in CA 11-12
Harrison, William 1933- CANR-9
Earlier sketch in CA 17-20R
Harrison, William C. 1919- 25-28R
Harrison Church, Ronald James 1915- 13-16R
Harriss, C(lement) Lowell 1912- CANR-2
Earlier sketch in CA 1-4R
Harriss, Joseph 1936- 57-60
Harriss, R(obert) P(reston) 1902-1989 73-76
Obituary 129
Harriss, Will(ard Irvin) 1922- 111
See also CLC 34
Harrisse, Henry 1829-1910 ..... DLB 47
Harrity, Richard 1907-1973 Obituary 41-44R
Harrod, Leonard Montague 1905- 13-16R
Harrod, Roy Forbes 1900-1978 ..... 9-12R
Obituary 103
Harrod-Eagles, Cynthia 1948- 144
Harrold, Stanley 1946- 128
Harrold, William E(ugene) 1936- 41-44R
Harron, Don(ald) 1924- 104
Harrop-Allin, Clinton 1936- 107
Harroun, Catherine 1907- 109
Harrow, Benjamin 1888-1970 Obituary 104
Harrow, Kenneth W. 1943- 148
Harrowe, Fiona
See Hurd, Florence
Harrower, Elizabeth 1928- CANR-70
Earlier sketch in CA 101
Harrower, Molly 1906- 5-8R
Harry, Deborah Ann 1945- 129
Harry, J. S. 1939- 153
Harry, M.
See Lewis, Sasha Gregory
Harryman, Carla 1952- ..... DLB 193
Harsany, Peter 1913- CANR-56
Earlier sketch in CA 111
Harsch, Ernest 1951- 69-72
Harsch, Hilya
See Jelly, George Oliver
Harsch, Joseph C(lose) 1905- 102
Harsdoerffer, Georg Philipp 1607-1658 ..... DLB 164
Harsent, David 1942- 93-96
See also DLB 40
Harsh, Fred (T.) 1925- ..... SATA 72
Harsh, George 1908(?)-1980 Obituary 93-96
Harsh, Wayne C. 1924- CANR-15
Earlier sketch in CA 29-32R
Harshav, Barbara 1940- 157
Harshaw, Ruth H(etzel) 1890-1968 Obituary 107
See also SATA 27
Harshbarger, David Dwight 1938- 53-56
Harshman, Marc 1950- ..... SATA 71
Harson, Sley
See Ellison, Harlan (Jay)
Harss, Luis 1936- 17-20R
Harstad, Peter Tjernagel 1935- 37-40R
Harston, Ruth 1944- 41-44R
Hart, A(rthur) Tindal 1908- 9-12R
Hart, Albert Bushnell 1854-1943 Brief entry 116
See also DLB 17
Hart, Albert Gailord 1909-1997 ..... CAP-2
Obituary 161
Earlier sketch in CA 23-24
Hart, Alexandra 1939- CANR-6
Earlier sketch in CA 57-60
See also Jacopetti, Alexandra
Hart, Allan H(untley) 1935- 106
Hart, (Margaret Eleanor) Anne 141
Hart, Anne 1768-1834 ..... DLB 200
Hart, Archibald D(aniel) 1932- CANR-15
Earlier sketch in CA 93-96
Hart, Barry
See Bloom, Herman Irving
Hart, Basil Henry Liddell
See Liddell Hart, Basil Henry
Hart, Benjamin 1958- 126
Brief entry 118
Hart, Bruce 1938- 107
See also SATA 57
See also SATA-Brief 39
Hart, Carol 1944- 65-68
Hart, Carole 1943- 107
See also SATA 57
See also SATA-Brief 39
Hart, Carolyn G(impel) 1936- CANR-58
Earlier sketches in CA 13-16R, CANR-25, 41
See also SATA 74
Hart, Catherine 1948- 139
Hart, Charles (A.) 1940- 133
Hart, David 1944- 128
Hart, David K(irkwood) 1933- 123
Brief entry 117
Hart, David M(ontgomery) 1927- 136
Hart, Donald J(ohn) 1917- 9-12R
Hart, Douglas C. 1950- 101
Hart, E. Richard 1945- 152
Hart, Edward J(ack) 1941- 53-56
Hart, Edward L. 1916- CANR-14
Earlier sketch in CA 37-40R
Hart, Elizabeth 1771-1833 ..... DLB 200
Hart, Ellen 1949- 154
Hart, Ellis
See Ellison, Harlan (Jay)
Hart, Ernest H(untley) 1910- 102
Hart, Frances (Newbold) Noyes 1890-1943 Brief
entry 112
Hart, Francis
See Paine, Lauran (Bosworth)
Hart, Francis Dudley 1909- CANR-25
Earlier sketch in CA 108
Hart, Gary (Warren) 1936(?)- 124
Brief entry 114
Hart, Gavin 1939- 106
Hart, George L. III 1942- 93-96
Hart, H(erbert) L(ionel) A(dolphus) 1907-1992 .....
CANR-46
Obituary 140
Earlier sketches in CA 1-4R, CANR-2
Hart, Henry (W.) 1954- 128
Hart, Henry C(owles) 1916- 1-4R
Hart, Henry Hersch 1886-1968 ..... CAP-1
Earlier sketch in CA 9-10
Hart, Herbert Michael 1928- 9-12R
Hart, Hornell (Norris) 1888-1967 Obituary 111
Hart, James
See Hough, Harold
Hart, James D(avid) 1911-1990 ..... CANR-1
Obituary 132
Earlier sketch in CA 1-4R
Hart, Jan Siegel 1940- 147
See also SATA 79
Hart, Jane (Meyers) 1922- 107
Hart, Jeanne
See Schrager, Jeanne Hart
Hart, Jeffrey Allen 1947- 109
Hart, Jenifer 1914- 138
Hart, Jennifer B.
See Hough, Harold
Hart, Jim Allee 1914- 13-16R
Hart, John 1942- 109
Hart, John 1948- CANR-11
Earlier sketch in CA 65-68
Hart, John E(dward) 1917- 33-36R
Hart, John Fraser 1924- 37-40R
Hart, John Lewis 1931- CANR-4
Earlier sketch in CA 49-52
See also Hart, Johnny
Hart, John Mason 1935- 132
Hart, Johnny
See Hart, John Lewis
See also AITN 1
Hart, Jon
See Harvey, John (Barton)
Hart, Jonathan (Locke) 1956- 142
Hart, Joseph 1945- 85-88
Hart, Josephine 1942(?)- CANR-70
Earlier sketch in CA 138
See also CLC 70
See also DAM POP
Hart, Judith 1924- 109
Hart, Julia Catherine 1796-1867 ..... DLB 99
Hart, Kate
See Kramer, Roberta
Hart, Kevin 1954- 135
Hart, Kitty 1926- 117
Hart, Larry 1920- 33-36R
Hart, Lois B(orland) 1941- 117
Hart, Lynda 1953- 146
Hart, Marie 1932- 41-44R
Hart, Marilyn M(cGuire) 1926- 45-48
Hart, Marion Rice 1892(?)-1990 Obituary 132
Hart, Martin 1944- 129
Hart, Matthew 1945- 125
Hart, Milton R. 1896(?)-1983 Obituary 109
Hart, Moss 1904-1961 109
Obituary 89-92
See also CLC 66
See also DAM DRAM
See also DLB 7
Hart, Oliver 1723-1795 ..... DLB 31
Hart, Patricia Susan 1950- 118
Hart, Patrick 1925- 53-56
Hart, Ray L(ee) 1929- 29-32R
Hart, Richard (Harry) 1908- CAP-1
Earlier sketch in CA 9-10
Hart, Robert A(llan) 1929- Brief entry 117
Hart, Roderick P(atrick) 1945- CANR-45
Earlier sketch in CA 106
Hart, Sandra Lynn Housby 1948- CANR-50
Earlier sketches in CA 108, CANR-25
Hart, Stan 1929- 118
Hart, Stephanie 1949- 97-100
Hart, Sue
See Hart, Susanne
Hart, Susanne 1927- CANR-20
Earlier sketch in CA 102
Hart, V(orhis) Donn 1918- 13-16R

Hart, Virginia 1949- 150
See also SATA 83
Hart, W. D. 1943- 157
Hart, Walter 1906(?)-1973 Obituary 45-48
Hart, Winston Scott 1903(?)-1979 Obituary .. 89-92
Hartcup, Adeline 1918- 116
Hartcup, Guy 1919- 29-32R
Hart-Davis, Duff 1936- CANR-27
Earlier sketch in CA 29-32R
Hart-Davis, Phyllida
See Barstow, Phyllida
Hart-Davis, Rupert (Charles) 1907- 134
Brief entry 115
Hartdegen, Stephen J. 1907-1989 Obituary 130
Harte, (Francis) Bret(t) 1836(?)-1902 140
Brief entry 104
See also CDALB 1865-1917
See also DA
See also DAC
See also DAM MST
See also DLB 12, 64, 74, 79, 186
See also SATA 26
See also SSC 8
See also TCLC 1, 25
See also WLC
Harte, Edward Holmead 1922- 151
See also DLB 127
Harte, Houston Harriman 1927- 155
See also DLB 127
Harte, Marjorie
See McEvoy, Marjorie Harte
Harte, Samantha
See Hart, Sandra Lynn Housby
Harte, Thomas Joseph 1914-1974 Obituary .. 53-56
Harteis, Richard 1946- .... CAAS 26
Hartel, Klaus Dieter
See Vandenberg, Philipp
Hartendorp, A(bram) V(an) H(eyningen) 1893- .....
CAP-1
Earlier sketch in CA 13-16
Harter, Eugene C(laudius) 1926- CANR-43
Earlier sketch in CA 119
Harter, H(arman) Leon 1919- 157
Harter, Helen (O'Connor) 1905- 5-8R
Harter, Hugh A(nthony) 1922- 110
Harter, Kenneth W. 1912(?)-1984 Obituary 112
Harter, Lafayette George, Jr. 1918- 9-12R
Harter, Penny 1940- .... CAAS 28
Hartfeld, Hermann 1942- 136
Hartford, Claire 1913- 29-32R
Hartford, Ellis F(ord) 1905- CAP-1
Earlier sketch in CA 13-14
Hartford, (George) Huntington II 1911- 17-20R
Hartford, Margaret E(lizabeth) 1917- 41-44R
Hartford, Via
See Donson, Cyril
Harth, Erica 116
Harth, Erich 1919- 107
Harth, (John) Phillip 1926- Brief entry 116
Harth, Robert 1940- 33-36R
Harthan, John Plant 1916- 102
Harthoorn, A(ntonie) M(arinus) 1923- 53-56
Hartich, Alice 1888- CAP-2
Earlier sketch in CA 17-18
Hartig, John H. 1952- 143
Hartill, Rosemary (Jane) 1949- CANR-55
Earlier sketch in CA 127
Harting, Emilie Clothier 1942- 73-76
Hartje, Robert G(eorge) 1922- 25-28R
Hartje, Tod D(ale) 1968- 139
Hartjen, Clayton A(lfred) 1943- 69-72
Hartke, Vance 1919- 25-28R
Hartland, Michael 1941- 110
Hartlaub, Felix 1913(?)-1945 .... DLB 56
Hartlaub, G(ustav) F(riedrich)
1884-1963 Obituary 112
Hartle, Anthony E. 1942- 137
Hartleben, Otto Erich 1864-1905 .... DLB 118
Hartley, Cathy J. 1965- 143
Hartley, Dorothy 1893-1985 105
Obituary 118
Hartley, Ellen (Raphael) 1915-1980 .... CANR-4
Earlier sketch in CA 5-8R
See also SATA 23
Hartley, Fred Allan III 1953- 106
See also SATA 41
Hartley, Hal 1960(?)- 144
Hartley, Jean 1933- 135
Hartley, John I(rvin) 1921- 5-8R
Hartley, Keith 1940- CANR-37
Earlier sketch in CA 115
Hartley, L(eslie) P(oles) 1895-1972 .... CANR-33
Obituary 37-40R
Earlier sketch in CA 45-48
See also CLC 2, 22
See also DLB 15, 139
See also MTCW 1
Hartley, Livingston 1900- 61-64
Hartley, Lodwick (Charles) 1906-1979 .... CANR-1
Earlier sketch in CA 1-4R
Hartley, Margaret L(ohlker) 1909-1983 97-100
Obituary 110
Hartley, Marie 1905- 9-12R
Hartley, Marsden 1877-1943 Brief entry 123
See also DLB 54
Hartley, Peter (Roy) 1933- 103
Hartley, Rachel M. 1895- 5-8R
Hartley, Robert E. 1936- 130
Hartley, Robert F(rank) 1927- CANR-57
Earlier sketches in CA 69-72, CANR-11, 28
Hartley, Shirley Foster 1928- CANR-13
Earlier sketch in CA 73-76
Hartley, Steven W. 1956- 139
Hartley, Travis
See Paine, Lauran (Bosworth)
Hartley, William B(rown) 1913-1980 .... CANR-4
Earlier sketch in CA 5-8R
See also SATA 23
Hartling, Peter
See Haertling, Peter
See also CLR 29
See also DLB 75
Hartman, Berl
See Hartman, Berl Mendelson
Hartman, Berl Mendelson 1938- 122
Hartman, (Howard) Carl 1917- 122
Hartman, Carl 1928- 104
Hartman, Charles O(ssian) 1949- 108
Hartman, Chester W(arren) 1936- 57-60
Hartman, David N. 1921- 13-16R
Hartman, Donald K. 1959- 163
Hartman, Evert 1937- 113
See also SATA 38
See also SATA-Brief 35
Hartman, Geoffrey H. 1929- 125
Brief entry 117
See also CLC 27
See also DLB 67
Hartman, George E(dward) 1926- 41-44R
Hartman, Hermene D(emaris) 1948- 122
Hartman, Jan 1938- 65-68
Hartman, Jane E(vangeline) 1928- CANR-22
Earlier sketch in CA 105
See also SATA 47
Hartman, John J(acob) 1942- CANR-48
Earlier sketch in CA 49-52
Hartman, Louis F(rancis) 1901-1970 .... CAP-2
Earlier sketch in CA 23-24
See also SATA 22
Hartman, Mary S(usan) 1941- 81-84
Hartman, Nancy Carol 1942- 53-56
Hartman, Olov 1906-1982 .... CANR-14
Earlier sketch in CA 29-32R
Hartman, Patience
See Zawadsky, Patience
Hartman, Phil(ip Edward) 1948- 163
Hartman, Rachel (Frieda) 1920-1972 .... 5-8R
Obituary 33-36R
Hartman, Rhondda Evans 1934- 61-64
Hartman, Robert K(intz) 1940- 41-44R
Hartman, Robert S. 1910-1973 .... CAP-2
Obituary 45-48
Earlier sketch in CA 17-18
Hartman, Roger
See Mehta, Rustam Jehangir
Hartman, Shirley 1929- 57-60
Hartman, Victoria 1942- 155
See also SATA 91
Hartman, William E(llis) 1919-1997 69-72
Obituary 161
Hartman, William T(aylor) 1942- 117
Hartmann, Betsy
See Hartmann, Elizabeth
Hartmann, Dennis L. 1949- 148
Hartmann, Edward George 1912- 41-44R
Hartmann, Elizabeth 1951- 126
Hartmann, Ernest 1934- 21-24R
Hartmann, Franz 1838-1912 Brief entry 115
Hartmann, Frederick Howard 1922- CANR-38
Earlier sketches in CA 1-4R, CANR-1, 16
Hartmann, Heinz 1894-1970 Obituary 104
Hartmann, Helmut Henry 1931- 105
Hartmann, Klaus 1925- 21-24R
Hartmann, Michael 1944- 97-100
Hartmann, Rudolf A. 1937- Brief entry 111
Hartmann, Sadakichi 1867-1944 157
See also DLB 54
See also TCLC 73
Hartmann, Susan M(arie) 1940- 41-44R
Hartmann, William K(enneth) 1939- 69-72
Hartmann von Aue c. 1160-c. 1205 .... DLB 138
Hartnack, Justus 1912- 41-44R
Hartnett, D(avid) W(illiam) 1952- CANR-48
Earlier sketch in CA 122
Hartnett, Ken(neth Owen) 1934- 118
Hartnett, Michael 1941- 130
Hartnett, Sonya 1968- 158
See also SATA 93
Hartnoll, Phyllis (Mary) 1906-1997 81-84
Obituary 156
Hartocollis, Peter 1922- CANR-1
Earlier sketch in CA 45-48
Hartog, Diana 1942- 123
Hartog, Joseph 1933- 102
Hartoonian, Gevork 1947- 167
Hartshorn, Ruth M. 1928- .... SATA 11
Hartshorne, Charles 1897- CANR-29
Earlier sketches in CA 9-12R, CANR-4
Hartshorne, Richard 1899- 5-8R
Hartshorne, Thomas L(lewellyn) 1935- 37-40R
Hart-Smith, William 1911- CANR-11
Earlier sketch in CA 21-24R
Hartsoe, Colleen Ivey 1925- 109
Hartston, W(illiam) R(oland) 1947- 116
Hartsuch, Paul Jackson 1902- 57-60
Hartt, Julian 1916(?)-1984 Obituary 113
Hartt, Julian N(orris) 1911- 132
Hartung, Albert Edward 1923- 103
Hartung, Hans (Heinrich Ernst)
1904-1989 Obituary 130
Hartup, Willard W(ert) 1927- 25-28R
Hartwell, David G(eddes) 1941- 162
Hartwell, Dickson Jay 1906-1981 .... CAP-1
Obituary 103
Earlier sketch in CA 11-12
Hartwell, (William) Michael Berry 1911- 142
Hartwell, Nancy
See Callahan, Claire Wallis
Hartwell, Ronald Max 1921- 25-28R
Hartwick, Sylvia
See Doherty, Ivy R. Duffy
Hartwig, Manfred 1950- 149
See also SATA 81
Hartwig, Marie (Dorothy) 1906- 1-4R
Hartwig, Richard E(ric) 1942- 118
Harty, (Fredric) Russell 1934-1988 Obituary ... 125
Hartz, Fred R. 1933- 122
Hartz, Jim .... AITN 2
Hartz, Louis 1919-1986 Obituary 118
Hartzler, Daniel David 1941- 61-64
Hartzmark, Gini 167
Haruf, Kent 1943- 149
See also CLC 34
Haruki, Murakami 1949- 136
Harvard, Andrew Carson 1949- 69-72
Harvard, Charles
See Gibbs-Smith, Charles Harvard
Harvard, Stephen 1948- 57-60
Harvester, Simon
See Rumbold-Gibbs, Henry St. John Clair
Harvey, Andrew 1952- 132
Brief entry 126
Harvey, Anne 1933- CANR-48
Earlier sketch in CA 121
Harvey, Anthony Peter 1940- 106
Harvey, Barbara (Fitzgerald) 1928- 116
Harvey, Brett 1936- CANR-53
Earlier sketch in CA 126
See also SATA 61
Harvey, C(harles) J(ohn) D(errick) 1922- 9-12R
Harvey, Clay 165
Harvey, David 1935- 145
Earlier sketch in CA 123
Harvey, David Dow 1931- 65-68
Harvey, Donald J(oseph) 1922- 41-44R
Harvey, Earle (Sherburn) 1906- CANR-29
Earlier sketch in CA 109
Harvey, Edith 1908(?)-1972 Obituary 104
See also SATA-Obit 27
Harvey, Edward Burns 1939- 41-44R
Harvey, Frank 1912-1981 Obituary 105
Harvey, Frank (Laird) 1913- 5-8R
Harvey, Gabriel 1550(?)-1631 .... DLB 167
Harvey, Geoffrey 1943- 126
Harvey, Gina Cantoni 1922- CANR-33
Earlier sketch in CA 45-48
Harvey, Harriet 1924- 109
Harvey, Hazel (Mary) 1936- 145
Harvey, Ian Douglas 1914-1987 .... CAP-1
Obituary 121
Earlier sketch in CA 9-10
Harvey, Jack
See Rankin, Ian (James)
Harvey, James 1929- 135
Harvey, James C(ardwell) 1925- 45-48
Harvey, James O. 1926- 17-20R
Harvey, Jean-Charles 1891-1967 148
See also DLB 88
Harvey, Joan C. 1948- 132
Harvey, Joan M(argaret) 1918- 102
Harvey, John (Barton) 1938- CANR-56
Earlier sketch in CA 125
Harvey, John (Robert) 1942- CANR-58
Earlier sketch in CA 93-96
Harvey, John B.
See Harvey, John (Barton)
Harvey, John F(rederick) 1921- CANR-23
Earlier sketches in CA 13-16R, CANR-8
Harvey, John Hooper 1911- CANR-44
Earlier sketches in CA 5-8R, CANR-6, 21
Harvey, Jonathan 1939- 61-64
Harvey, Karen D. 1935- 152
See also SATA 88
Harvey, Karen (E.) G(iddens) 1944- 117
Harvey, Kathryn
See Wood, Barbara
Harvey, Kenneth 1919(?)-1979 Obituary 89-92
Harvey, Lashley Grey 1900- 37-40R
Harvey, Maria Luisa Alvarez 1938- 53-56
Harvey, Marian 1927- 89-92
Harvey, Michael G. 1944- 110
Harvey, Mose Lofley 1910-1985 Obituary 115
Harvey, Nancy Lenz 1935- 65-68
Harvey, Nigel 1916- CANR-57
Earlier sketches in CA 73-76, CANR-13, 30
Harvey, O. J. 1927- 37-40R
Harvey, P(aul) D(ean) A(dshead) 1930- 112
Harvey, Paul
See Aurandt, Paul Harvey
Harvey, Paulett
See Tumay, Paulett
Harvey, (Brian) Peter 1951- 135
Harvey, R. C.
See Harvey, Robert C.
Harvey, Rachel
See Bloom, Ursula (Harvey)
Harvey, Richard B(lake) 1930- 49-52
Harvey, Robert 1884- 5-8R
Harvey, Robert C. 1937- 151
Harvey, Roland 1945- .... SATA 71
Harvey, Ruth C(harlotte) 1918-1980 .... 1-4R
Obituary 102
Harvey, Stephen 1949-1993 134
Obituary 140
Harvey, Steven 1949- 163
Harvey, Van A(ustin) 1926- 33-36R
Harvey, Virginia I(sham) 1917- 57-60
Harvey, William Burnett 1922- 41-44R
Harvey-Jones, John (Henry) 1924- 140
Harvey Wood, (Elizabeth) Harriet 1934- 123
Harvie, Christopher (Thomas) 1944- 154
Harvie-Watt, George Steven 1903- 109
Harvor, Beth
See Harvor, (Erica) Elisabeth (Arendt Deichmann)
Harvor, (Erica) Elisabeth (Arendt Deichmann)
1936- 134
Harward, Donald W. 1939- 93-96
Harward, Timothy Blake 1932- 25-28R
Harwell, Ann (Manning) J. 1936- 57-60
Harwell, Ernie
See Harwell, William Earnest
Harwell, Richard Barksdale 1915- CANR-17
Earlier sketches in CA 1-4R, CANR-2
Harwell, William Earnest 1918- CANR-66
Brief entry 116
Earlier sketch in CA 128
Harwick, B. L.
See Keller, Beverly L(ou)
Harwin, Brian
See Henderson, LeGrand
Harwit, Martin Otto 1931- 105
Harwood, Alan 1935- 113
Harwood, Alice (Mary) 5-8R
Harwood, (Henry) David 1938- 104
Harwood, Edwin 1939- 29-32R
Harwood, Gina
See Battiscombe, E(sther) Georgina (Harwood)
Harwood, Gwen(doline Nessie) 1920- 97-100
Harwood, Jonathan 1943- 103
Harwood, Lee 1939- CANR-9
Earlier sketch in CA 21-24R
See also CAAS 19
See also DLB 40
Harwood, Michael 1934(?)-1989 Obituary 130
Harwood, Pearl Augusta (Bragdon) 1903- ... 13-16R
See also SATA 9
Harwood, Raymond C(harles)
1906-1987 Obituary 122
Harwood, Ronald 1934- CANR-55
Earlier sketches in CA 1-4R, CANR-4
See also CLC 32
See also DAM DRAM, MST
See also DLB 13
Harzfeld, Lois 1932- 107
Hasan, Saiyid Zafar 1930- 73-76
Hasan, Sana 128
Hasbrouck, Kenneth E(dward) Sr. 1916-1996 ......
CANR-31
Obituary 152
Earlier sketch in CA 49-52
Hasegawa, Nyozekan 1875-1969 Obituary 111
Hasegawa, Tsuyoshi 1941- 109
Hasegawa Tatsunosuke
See Futabatei, Shimei
Hasek, Jaroslav (Matej Frantisek) 1883-1923 .. 129
Brief entry 104
See also MTCW 1
See also TCLC 4
Hasel, Gerhard F(ranz) 1935- CANR-15
Earlier sketch in CA 41-44R
Haselden, John
See Forrester, Martyn (John)
Haselden, Kyle (Emerson) 1913-1968 .... 5-8R
Haseler, Stephen Michael Alan 1942- 85-88
Haseley, Dennis 1950- 162
See also SATA 57
See also SATA-Brief 44
Hasenclever, Herbert Frederick
1924-1978 Obituary 81-84
Hasford, (Jerry) Gustav 1947-1993 85-88
Obituary 140
Hashmi, Aurangzeb Alamgir 1951- CANR-48
Earlier sketches in CA 77-80, CANR-16
Haskell, Arnold L(ionel) 1903-1981(?) CANR-7
Obituary 102
Earlier sketch in CA 5-8R
See also SATA 6
Haskell, Douglas 1899-1979 Obituary 89-92
Haskell, Edward Froehlich 1906- Brief entry ... 105
Haskell, Francis (James Herbert) 1928- ... CANR-6
Earlier sketch in CA 9-12R
Haskell, Guy H. 1956- 150
Haskell, Harry 1954- CANR-65
Earlier sketch in CA 129
Haskell, John Duncan, Jr. 1941- CANR-50
Earlier sketches in CA 107, CANR-25
Haskell, Martin R(oy) 1912- 41-44R
Haskell, Molly 1939- 135
Haskett, Edythe Rance 1915- 21-24R
Haskin, Dorothy C(lark) 1905- 5-8R
Haskin, Gretchen 1936- 103
Haskins, Barbara
See Stone, Barbara Haskins
Haskins, Charles Homer 1870-1937 .... DLB 47
Haskins, George Lee 1915-1991 .... CANR-1
Obituary 135
Earlier sketch in CA 1-4R
Haskins, Ilma 1919- 45-48
Haskins, James S. 1941- CANR-48
Earlier sketches in CA 33-36R, CANR-25
See also Haskins, Jim
See also AAYA 14
See also BW 2
See also CLR 3, 39
See also JRDA
See also MAICYA
See also SATA 9, 69
Haskins, Jim
See Haskins, James S.
See also SAAS 4
Haskins, Sam(uel Joseph) 1926- 103
Haskins, Scott (M.) 1953- 153
Haslam, Gerald W. 1937- CANR-58
Earlier sketches in CA 29-32R, CANR-11, 27
Hasler, Eveline 1937- 106
Hasler, Joan 1931- 29-32R
See also SATA 28
Haslerud, George M(artin) 1906- 45-48
Hasley, Louis (Leonard) 1906- 37-40R
Hasley, Lucile (Charlotte Hardman) 1909- ... CAP-1
Earlier sketch in CA 11-12
Hasling, John 1928- 33-36R

Haslip, Joan 1912-1994 107
Obituary 145
Hasluck, Nicholas 1942- CANR-69
Earlier sketch in CA 137
Hasluck, Paul (Meernaa Caedwalla) 1905-1993 ....
CANR-46
Obituary 140
Earlier sketch in CA 109
Haspel, Eleanor C. 1944- 69-72
Hass, C(harles) Glen 1915- 17-20R
Hass, Eric 1905(?)-1980 Obituary 102
Hass, Hans 1919- 108
Hass, Robert 1941- CANR-71
Earlier sketches in CA 111, CANR-30, 50
See also CLC 18, 39, 99
See also DLB 105
See also PC 16
See also SATA 94
Hassall, Anthony J. 1939- 126
Hassall, Christopher (Vernon)
1912-1963 Obituary 89-92
Hassall, Joan 1906-1988 .... SATA 43
See also SATA-Obit 56
Hassall, Mark (William Cory) 1940- CANR-13
Earlier sketch in CA 73-76
Hassall, William Owen 1912-1994 .... 13-16R
Obituary 146
Hassam, Nick
See Crowther, Peter
Hassan, Aftab Syed 1952- 148
Hassan, Ihab Habib 1925- CANR-41
Earlier sketches in CA 5-8R, CANR-3, 19
See also CAAS 12
Hassan, Richard
See Hassan, Aftab Syed
Hassan, William Ephraim, Jr. 1923- 33-36R
Hasse, John Edward 1948- 119
Hassel, David John 1923- CANR-32
Earlier sketch in CA 113
Hassel, Odd 1897-1981 157
Obituary 108
Hassel, R. Chris, Jr. 1939- 129
Hassel, Sven 1917- 93-96
Hasselbach, Ingo 1967- 154
Hasselstrom, Linda (Michele) 1943- 153
Hassen, Philip Charles 1943- 147
Hassenger, Robert (Leo) 1937- 21-24R
Hassing, Per 1916- 37-40R
Hassinger, Edward W(esley) 1925- 125
Hassler, Donald M. (II) 1937- CANR-57
Earlier sketches in CA 41-44R, CANR-14, 31
Hassler, Jon (Francis) 1933- CANR-21
Earlier sketch in CA 73-76
Interview in CANR-2
See also SATA 19
Hassler, Warren W., Jr. 1926- 9-12R
Hassler, William T(homas) 1954- 104
Hassrick, Peter H(eyl) 1941- CANR-16
Earlier sketches in CA 49-52, CANR-1
Hast, Adele 1931- 119
Hastings, Adrian 1929- CANR-47
Earlier sketches in CA 17-20R, CANR-7, 23
Hastings, Alan
See Williamson, Geoffrey
Hastings, Arthur Claude 1935- 37-40R
Hastings, Beverly
See Barkin, Carol
and James, Elizabeth
Hastings, Brooke
See Gordon, Deborah Hannes
Hastings, Cecily Mary Eleanor 1924- 5-8R
Hastings, Graham
See Jeffries, Roderic (Graeme)
Hastings, Harrington
See Marsh, John
Hastings, Hubert de Cronin 1902-1986 109
Obituary 121
Hastings, Hudson
See Kuttner, Henry
Hastings, Ian 1912- 45-48
See also SATA 62
Hastings, Macdonald 1909- CANR-9
Earlier sketch in CA 53-56
Hastings, March
See Levinson, Leonard
Hastings, Margaret 1910- 41-44R
Hastings, (Macdonald) Max 1945- CANR-48
Earlier sketch in CA 81-84
Hastings, Michael
See Bar-Zohar, Michael
Hastings, Michael (Gerald) 1938- CANR-45
Earlier sketch in CA 97-100
Hastings, Paul G(uiler) 1914- CANR-24
Earlier sketch in CA 1-4R
Hastings, Philip Kay 1922- 102
Hastings, Phyllis (Dora Hodge) CANR-8
Earlier sketch in CA 9-12R
Hastings, Robert J. 1924- CANR-48
Earlier sketch in CA 122
Hastings, Robert Paul 1933- 73-76
Hastings, Robin Hood William Stewart
1917-1990 Obituary 131
Hastings, Roderic
See Jeffries, Graham Montague
Hastings, Selina .... CLC 44
Hastings, Susan 1942- 128
Hastings, William T(homson) 1881- 5-8R
Haston, Dougal 1940-1977 Obituary 105
Hastorf, Albert H(erman) 1920- 97-100
Hastorf, Christine Ann 1950- 146
Hasty, Olga Peters 1951- 128
Hasty, Ronald W. 1941- CANR-4
Earlier sketch in CA 53-56
Haswell, Chetwynd John Drake 1919- 41-44R
Haswell, Harold Alanson, Jr. 1912- 45-48
Haswell, Janis Tedesco 1950- 168
Haswell, Jock
See Haswell, Chetwynd John Drake
Haswell, Richard H(enry) 1940- 168
Haszard, Patricia Moyes 1923- CANR-54
Earlier sketches in CA 17-20R, CANR-13, 29
See also Moyes, Patricia
Hatab, Lawrence J. 1946- 160
Hatch, Alden 1898-1975 65-68
Obituary 57-60
Hatch, (Alden) Denison 1935- 33-36R
Hatch, Elvin (James) 1937- 45-48
Hatch, Eric S(towe) 1902(?)-1973 Obituary . 41-44R
Hatch, James V(ernon) 1928- 41-44R
Hatch, John (Charles) 1917- 9-12R
Hatch, Lynda S. 1950- 155
See also SATA 90
Hatch, Mary Cottam 1912-1970 Obituary 109
See also SATA-Brief 28
Hatch, Michael F. 1947- 162
Hatch, Mike
See Hatch, Michael F.
Hatch, Nathan O(rr) 1946- 129
Brief entry 109
Hatch, Preble D(elloss) K(ellogg) 1898- CAP-2
Earlier sketch in CA 23-24
Hatch, Raymond N(orris) 1911- 21-24R
Hatch, Richard A(llen) 1940- CANR-9
Earlier sketch in CA 21-24R
Hatch, Robert McConnell 1910- 93-96
Hatch, William H(enry) P(aine)
1875-1972 Obituary 37-40R
Hatcher, George W. 1906(?)-1983 Obituary 110
Hatcher, Harlan (Henthorne) 1898- CAP-2
Earlier sketch in CA 19-20
Hatcher, Harlan (Henthrone)
1898-1998 Obituary 165
Hatcher, John 1942- 33-36R
Hatcher, John S(outhall) 1940- 97-100
Hatcher, Larry (L.) 1956- 151
Hatcher, Nat(han) B(razzell) 1897- 1-4R
Hatcher, Robert Anthony 1937- 93-96
Hatcher, Robin Lee 1951- 154
Hatcher, William S(pottswood) 1935- 123
Hatem, Mohamed Abdel-Kader
See Hatim, Muhammad 'Abd al-Qadir
Hatfield, Antoinette Kuzmanich 1929- 85-88
Hatfield, Dorothy B(lackmon) 1921- 53-56
Hatfield, Elaine (Catherine) 1937- CANR-38
Earlier sketches in CA 25-28R, CANR-10, 17
Hatfield, Henry Caraway 1912- 65-68
Hatfield, Julie (Stockwell) 1940- 126
Hatfield, Kate
See Wright, Daphne
Hatfield, Mark O(dom) 1922- 77-80
Hatfield, Michael (Vernon) 1935- 119
Hatfield, Phyllis 1944- 146
Hathaway, Baxter L. 1909- CANR-5
Earlier sketch in CA 1-4R
Hathaway, Bo 1942- 106
Hathaway, Dale E(rnest) 1925- 9-12R
Hathaway, Jan
See Neubauer, William Arthur
Hathaway, Lulu (Bailey) 1903- 13-16R
Hathaway, Mavis
See Avery, Ira
Hathaway, Nancy 1946- 108
Hathaway, Richard Dean 1927- 125
Hathaway, Sibyl Collings 1884-1974 .... 1-4R
Obituary 103
Hathaway, Starke R(osecrans) 1903-1984 .... 5-8R
Obituary 113
Hathaway, William 1944- 73-76
See also DLB 120
Hathcock, Louise 1-4R
Hathorn, Libby 1943- .... SATA 74
Hathorn, Richmond Y(ancey) 1917- CANR-1
Earlier sketch in CA 1-4R
Hatim, Muhammad 'Abd al-Qadir 1918- 89-92
Hatkoff, Amy 141
Hatlen, Burton (Norval) 1936- 109
Hatley, George B(erton) 1924- 106
Hatlo, Jimmy 1898-1963 Obituary 93-96
See also SATA-Obit 23
Hatmon, Paul W. 1921- 106
Hatoum, Milton 1952- 156
Hatt, Harold E(rnest) 1932- 21-24R
Hatta, Mohammed 1902-1980 Obituary 97-100
Hattaway, Herman (Morell) 1938- 65-68
Hattaway, Michael 1941- CANR-39
Earlier sketch in CA 116
Hattendorf, John B(rewster) 1941- 135
Hatteras, Amelia
See Mencken, H(enry) L(ouis)
Hatteras, Owen
See Mencken, H(enry) L(ouis)
and Nathan, George Jean
See also TCLC 18
Hatteras, Owen III
See McDavid, Raven I(oor), Jr.
Hatterer, Lawrence J(ohn) 1925- Brief entry ... 118
Hattersley, Ralph (Marshall, Jr.) 1921- 103
Hattersley, Roy (Sydney George) 1932- 103
Hattersley-Smith, Geoffrey (Francis) 1923- 118
Hattery, Lowell H(arold) 1916- 17-20R
Hatton, Ragnhild Marie 1913-1995 .... CANR-12
Obituary 148
Earlier sketch in CA 25-28R
Hatton, Robert Wayland 1934- 37-40R
Hatton, Thomas J(enison) 1935- 114
Hattwick, Richard E(arl) 1938- 73-76
Hatvary, George Egon 53-56
Hatzenbuehler, Ronald L(ee) 1945- 117
Hatzfeld, Helmut A(nthony) 1892-1979 97-100
Obituary 85-88
Hauberg, Clifford A(lvin) 1906- 37-40R
Hauck, Allan 1925- 1-4R
Hauck, Paul A(nthony) 1924- CANR-14
Earlier sketch in CA 41-44R
Hauck, Richard Boyd 1936- 53-56
Haueisen, Kathryn M. 1946- 128
Haueisen, Kathy
See Haueisen, Kathryn M.
Hauerwas, Stanley Martin 1940- 57-60
Hauff, Wilhelm 1802-1827 .... DLB 90
Haug, C(harles) James 1946- CANR-38
Earlier sketch in CA 116
Haugaard, Erik Christian 1923- CANR-38
Earlier sketches in CA 5-8R, CANR-3
See also CLR 11
See also JRDA
See also MAICYA
See also SAAS 12
See also SATA 4, 68
Haugaard, William Paul 1929- 25-28R
Hauge, Ron 1955- 151
Hauge, Sharon K(aye) 1943- 116
Haugeland, John (Christian) 1945- 133
Haugen, Edmund Bennett 1913- 17-20R
Haugen, Einar (Ingvald) 1906-1994 .... CANR-25
Obituary 145
Earlier sketches in CA 21-24R, CANR-9
Haugen, Tormod 1945- 135
See also SATA 66
Haugh, Richard (Stanley) 1942- CANR-9
Earlier sketch in CA 57-60
Haugh, Robert F(ulton) 1910- 61-64
Haughey, John C. 1930- 77-80
Haughey, Thomas Brace 1943- 113
Haught, James A(lbert, Jr.) 1932- 140
Brief entry 122
Haught, John F(rancis) 1942- 85-88
Haughton, Claire Shaver 1901- 85-88
Haughton, Rosemary (Luling) 1927- CANR-35
Earlier sketch in CA 5-8R
Haughton, Sidney Henry 1888-1982 Obituary .. 107
Haughton-James, Jean Rosemary
1924-1981 Obituary 105
Haugland, Vern(on Arnold) 1908-1984 93-96
Obituary 113
Haugwitz, August Adolph von 1647-1706 .. DLB 168
Hauk, Maung
See Hobbs, Cecil (Carlton)
Haule, James M(ark) 1945- CANR-27
Earlier sketch in CA 109
Hauman, Doris 1898- .... SATA 32
Hauman, George 1890-1961 .... SATA 32
Haun, Paul 1906-1969 .... CAP-2
Earlier sketch in CA 17-18
Hau'Ofa, Epeli 1939- CANR-70
Earlier sketch in CA 124
Haupt, Christopher (Charles Herbert) Lehmann
See Lehmann-Haupt, Christopher (Charles
Herbert)
Haupt, Zygmunt 1907(?)-1975 Obituary 61-64
Hauptly, Denis J(ames) 1945- 118
See also SATA 57
Hauptman, Don 1947- 138
Hauptman, Laurence Marc 1945- 139
Hauptman, Robert 1941- 143
Hauptman, Terry 1947- 111
Hauptman, William 1942- 128
Interview in 128
Hauptmann, Carl 1858-1921 .... DLB 66, 118
Hauptmann, Gerhart (Johann Robert)
1862-1946 153
Brief entry 104
See also DAM DRAM
See also DLB 66, 118
See also TCLC 4
Haury, Emil W(alter) 1904-1992 .... CANR-49
Obituary 140
Earlier sketch in CA 65-68
Hausdorff, Don 1927- 45-48
Hausdorff, Felix 1868-1942 159
Hause, Steven C. 1942- 127
Hauser, Bengamin Gayelord
1895-1984 Obituary 114
Brief entry 111
Hauser, Carl Maria 1895-1985 Obituary 117
Hauser, Charles McCorkle 1929- 69-72
Hauser, Frank
See Wiemer, Rudolf Otto
Hauser, Gayelord
See Hauser, Bengamin Gayelord
Hauser, Hillary 1944- CANR-56
Earlier sketches in CA 69-72, CANR-11, 30
Hauser, Margaret L(ouise) 1909- CAP-1
Earlier sketch in CA 11-12
See also SATA 10
Hauser, Marianne 1910- CANR-70
Earlier sketches in CAP-1, CA 11-12, CANR-13
See also CAAS 11
See also DLBY 83
Hauser, Phillip M(orris) 1909- 17-20R
Hauser, Robert Mason 1942- 109
Hauser, Thomas 1946- CANR-45
Earlier sketch in CA 85-88
Hauser, William B(arry) 1939- 69-72
Hausherr, Rosmarie 1943- .... SATA 86
Hausknecht, Murray 1925- 37-40R
Hausknecht, Richard 1929- 121
Hausman, Gerald 1945- CANR-38
Earlier sketches in CA 45-48, CANR-2, 17
See also SATA 13, 90
Hausman, Gerry
See Hausman, Gerald
Hausman, Patricia 1953- CANR-52
Earlier sketches in CA 107, CANR-26
Hausman, Warren H. 1939- 17-20R
Hausmann, Bernard A(ndrew) 1899- CAP-2
Earlier sketch in CA 23-24
Hausmann, Manfred 1898-1986 Obituary 120
Hausmann, Winifred 1922- CANR-26
Earlier sketches in CA 21-24R, CANR-11
Hausrath, Alfred Hartmann 1901- 41-44R
Haussig, Hans Wilhelm 1916- 29-32R
Hausvater, Alexander 1948- 130
Hauth, Katherine B. 1940- 167
See also SATA 99
Hauther, Brenda 1951- 113
Hautman, Pete(r Murray) 1952- CANR-72
Earlier sketch in CA 144
See also SATA 82
Hautzig, Deborah 1956- 89-92
See also SATA 31
Hautzig, Esther Rudomin 1930- CANR-46
Earlier sketches in CA 1-4R, CANR-5, 20
See also CLR 22
See also JRDA
See also MAICYA
See also SAAS 15
See also SATA 4, 68
Hauxwell, Hannah 1926- 140
Havard, William C(lyde), Jr. 1923- CANR-5
Earlier sketch in CA 1-4R
Havel, J(ean) E(ugene Martial) 1928- 41-44R
Havel, Jennifer
See Havill, Juanita
Havel, Vaclav 1936- CANR-63
Earlier sketches in CA 104, CANR-36
See also CLC 25, 58, 65
See also DAM DRAM
See also DC 6
See also MTCW 1
Havelock, Christine Mitchell 1924- 85-88
Havelock, Eric A(lfred) 1903-1988 .... CAP-1
Obituary 125
Earlier sketch in CA 13-16
Havelock, Ronald G(eoffrey) 1935- 85-88
Haveman, Robert H. 1936- 17-20R
Havemann, Ernest (Carl) 1912-1995 .... 1-4R
Obituary 148
Havemann, Ernst 1918- 135
Havemann, Joel 1943- 85-88
Havemann, Robert (Hans Gunther)
1910-1982 Obituary 110
Havemeyer, Loomis 1886-1971 Obituary ... 33-36R
Haven, Richard 1924- 25-28R
Havens, Daniel F(rederick) 1931- 69-72
Havens, George R(emington) 1890-1977 .. CANR-4
Obituary 73-76
Earlier sketch in CA 5-8R
Havens, Gordon 1903-1983 Obituary 111
Havens, Leston Laycock 1924- CANR-43
Earlier sketch in CA 119
Havens, Murray Clark 1932- 41-44R
Havens, Shirley E(lise) 1925- 89-92
Havens, Thomas R. H. 1939- CANR-34
Earlier sketches in CA 41-44R, CANR-15
Haver, Ronald D. 1939- 109
Havergal, Frances Ridley 1836-1879 .... DLB 199
Haverkamp-Begemann, Egbert 1923- CANR-11
Earlier sketch in CA 17-20R
Haverstick, John (Mitchell) 1919- 25-28R
Haverstock, Mary Sayre 1932- 81-84
Haverstock, Nathan Alfred 1931- 53-56
Haverty, Anne 163
Havet, Jose (L.) 1937- 137
Haviaras, Stratis
See Chaviaras, Strates
See also CLC 33
Havighurst, Alfred F(reeman) 1904-1991 ... 33-36R
Obituary 133
Havighurst, Marion (M.) 1894-1974 .... CANR-29
Obituary 49-52
Earlier sketches in CAP-1, CA 13-14
Havighurst, Robert J(ames) 1900-1991 .... 21-24R
Obituary 133
Havighurst, Walter (Edwin) 1901-1994 ... CANR-29
Obituary 144
Earlier sketches in CA 1-4R, CANR-1
See also SATA 1
See also SATA-Obit 79
Haviland, Virginia 1911-1988 .... CANR-12
Obituary 124
Earlier sketch in CA 17-20R
See also SATA 6
See also SATA-Obit 54
Havill, Juanita 1949- .... SATA 74
Havill, Steven 1945- CANR-72
Earlier sketches in CA 108, CANR-25
Havis, Allan 1951- CANR-53
Earlier sketches in CA 108, CANR-28
Havlice, Patricia Pate 1943- CANR-12
Earlier sketch in CA 29-32R
Havlik, John F(ranklin) 1917-1984 .... CANR-24
Earlier sketch in CA 45-48
Havoc, June 1916- 107
Havran, Martin J. 1929- CANR-1
Earlier sketch in CA 1-4R
Havrevold, Finn 1905- 109
Havrilesky, Thomas M(ichael) 1939- CANR-19
Earlier sketches in CA 53-56, CANR-4
Haw, Richard Claude 1913- CAP-1
Earlier sketch in CA 9-10
Hawes, Evelyn (Johnson) 13-16R
See also AITN 1
Hawes, Frances Cooper (Richmond) 1897- . CAP-1
Earlier sketch in CA 9-10
Hawes, Gene R(obert) 1922- CANR-39
Earlier sketches in CA 5-8R, CANR-3, 18
Hawes, Grace M. 1926- 69-72
Hawes, Hampton 1929(?)-1977 Obituary 69-72
Hawes, John T. 1906(?)-1983 Obituary 109
Hawes, Joseph M(ilton) 1938- 53-56
Hawes, Judy 1913- 33-36R
See also SATA 4
Hawes, Louis 1931- 114

Hawes, Louise 1943- ... SATA 60
Hawes, Lynne Gusikoff Salop 1931- ... CANR-22
Earlier sketch in CA 106
Hawes, Stephen 1475(?)-1523(?) ... DLB 132
Hawes, William (Kenneth) 1931- ... 77-80
Hawgood, John Arkas 1905-1971 Obituary ... 104
Hawk, Alex
See Garfield, Brian (Wynne)
Hawk, Grace E. 1905-1983 Obituary ... 110
Hawk, Philip B(ovier) 1874-1966 Obituary ... 116
Hawke, Bob
See Hawke, Robert James Lee
Hawke, David Freeman 1923- ... CANR-18
Earlier sketch in CA 102
Hawke, Ethan 1970- ... 165
Hawke, Gary Richard 1942- ... 102
Hawke, Nancy
See Nugent, Nancy
Hawke, Robert James Lee 1929- ... 152
Hawke, Simon
See Yermakov, Nicholas
Hawken, William R. 1917- ... CANR-5
Earlier sketch in CA 9-12R
Hawker, Robert Stephen 1803-1875 ... DLB 32
Hawkes, (Charles Francis) Christopher 1905- Brief entry ... 105
Hawkes, Delmar
See Elman, Richard (Martin)
Hawkes, G(ary) W(arren) 1953- ... 138
Hawkes, Glenn R(ogers) 1919- ... 17-20R
Hawkes, J(ohn) G(regory) 1915- ... 135
Hawkes, (Jessie) Jacquetta (Hopkins) 1910-1996 ... CANR-15
Obituary ... 151
Earlier sketch in CA 69-72
Hawkes, John (Clendennin Burne, Jr.) 1925-1998 ... CANR-64
Obituary ... 167
Earlier sketches in CA 1-4R, CANR-2, 47
See also CLC 1, 2, 3, 4, 7, 9, 14, 15, 27, 49
See also DLB 2, 7
See also DLBY 80
See also MTCW 1
Hawkes, Judith 1949- ... 132
Hawkes, Kevin 1959- ... 135
See also SATA 78
Hawkes, Robert E(rnest) 1930- ... 113
Hawkes, Terence 1932- ... 17-20R
Hawkesworth, (Elizabeth) Celia 1942- ... 121
Hawkesworth, Eric 1921- ... 29-32R
See also SATA 13
Hawkesworth, John 1720-1773 ... DLB 142
Hawking, S. W.
See Hawking, Stephen W(illiam)
Hawking, Stephen W(illiam) 1942- ... CANR-48
Brief entry ... 126
Earlier sketch in CA 129
See also AAYA 13
See also BEST 89:1
See also CLC 63, 105
Hawkins, A. Desmond
See Hawkins, (Alec) Desmond
Hawkins, Angus 1953- ... 126
Hawkins, Anne Hunsaker 1944- ... 142
Hawkins, Anthony Hope
See Hope, Anthony
Hawkins, Arthur 1903- ... CANR-8
Earlier sketch in CA 21-24R
See also SATA 19
Hawkins, Bradford A(lan) 1952- ... 151
Hawkins, Brett W(illiam) 1937- ... CANR-11
Earlier sketch in CA 21-24R
Hawkins, (Alec) Desmond 1908- ... CANR-9
Earlier sketch in CA 65-68
Hawkins, Edward H. 1934- ... 85-88
Hawkins, Frances P(ockman) 1913- ... 105
Hawkins, Gary J(ames) 1937- ... 115
Hawkins, Gerald S(tanley) 1928- ... 17-20R
Hawkins, Gordon 1919- ... 41-44R
Hawkins, Harriett B(loker) 1934- Brief entry ... 112
Hawkins, Hugh (Dodge) 1929- ... CANR-57
Earlier sketches in CA 1-4R, CANR-31
Hawkins, Hunt 1943- ... 148
Hawkins, Jack
See Hawkins, John Edward
Hawkins, Jim 1944- ... 73-76
Hawkins, John 1719-1789 ... DLB 104, 142
Hawkins, John C(harles) 1948- ... 106
Hawkins, John Edward 1910-1973 ... 120
Obituary ... 111
Hawkins, John Noel 1944- ... CANR-8
Earlier sketch in CA 61-64
Hawkins, John P. 1946- ... 120
Hawkins, Joyce M(ary) 1928- ... 128
Hawkins, Laura 1951- ... SATA 74
Hawkins, Odie 1937- ... 57-60
Hawkins, Peter S(tephen) 1945- ... 110
Hawkins, (Helena Ann) Quail 1905- ... 17-20R
See also SATA 6
Hawkins, Regina Trice 1938- ... 165
Hawkins, Richard (Anthony James) 1938- ... 129
Hawkins, Robert 1923- ... CANR-14
Earlier sketch in CA 21-24R
Hawkins, Robert O(usley), Jr. 1938- ... 117
Hawkins, W(alter) Lincoln 1911-1992 ... 159
Hawkins, Walter Everette 1883(?)- ... DLB 50
Hawkins, William (Waller) 1912- ... 1-4R
Hawkinson, John (Samuel) 1912- ... 21-24R
See also SATA 4
Hawkinson, Lucy (Ozone) 1924-1971 ... 103
See also SATA 21
Hawks, Howard (Winchester) 1896-1977 ... 161
Obituary ... 73-76
Hawks, Robert 1961- ... 151
See also SATA 85
Hawksworth, Henry D. 1933- ... 73-76
Hawkwood, Allan
See Bedford-Jones, H(enry James O'Brien)
Hawley, Amos H(enry) 1910- ... 37-40R
Hawley, Beatrice
See Jagel, Beatrice Hawley
Hawley, Cameron 1905-1969 ... 1-4R
Obituary ... 25-28R
Hawley, Donald Frederick 1921- ... 108
Hawley, Donald Thomas 1923- ... CANR-11
Earlier sketch in CA 65-68
Hawley, Ellis W. 1929- ... CANR-7
Earlier sketch in CA 17-20R
Hawley, Florence M.
See Ellis, Florence Hawley
Hawley, Gessner G. 1906(?)-1983 Obituary ... 110
Hawley, Henrietta Ripperger 1890(?)-1974 Obituary ... 49-52
Hawley, Isabel (Allen) L(ockwood) 1935- ... CANR-7
Earlier sketch in CA 57-60
Hawley, Jane Stouder 1936- ... 21-24R
Hawley, John C(harles) 1947- ... 167
Hawley, John Stratton 1941- ... CANR-58
Earlier sketch in CA 110
Hawley, Mabel C. ... CANR-26
Earlier sketches in CAP-2, CA 19-20
See also SATA 1, 67
Hawley, Richard A. 1945- ... 123
Hawley, Robert C(oit) 1933- ... CANR-46
Earlier sketches in CA 57-60, CANR-7, 22
Hawley, T. M. 1953- ... 140
Hawley, Willis D(avid) 1938- ... 114
Haworth, Don 1924- ... CANR-60
Earlier sketch in CA 128
Haworth, Lawrence 1926- ... 5-8R
Haworth, Mary
See Young, Mary Elizabeth Reardon
Haworth, Walter (Norman) 1883-1950 ... 159
Haworth-Booth, Mark 1944- ... CANR-52
Earlier sketch in CA 124
Haworth-Booth, Michael 1896- ... 5-8R
Haws, Duncan 1921- ... 97-100
Hawthorn, Jeremy 1942- ... 97-100
Hawthorne, Captain R. M.
See Ellis, Edward S(ylvester)
Hawthorne, Douglas B(ruce) 1948- ... 143
Hawthorne, (Ivy Ellen) Jennie Crawley 1916- ... CAP-1
Earlier sketch in CA 9-10
Hawthorne, Julian 1846-1934 ... 165
See also TCLC 25
Hawthorne, Nathaniel 1804-1864 ... AAYA 18
See also CDALB 1640-1865
See also DA
See also DAB
See also DAC
See also DAM MST, NOV
See also DLB 1, 74
See also SSC 3, 29
See also WLC
See also YABC 2
Hawthorne, Rainey
See Riddell, Charlotte
Hawthorne, Sophia Peabody 1809-1871 ... DLB 183
Hawton, Hector 1901- ... 13-16R
Haxton, Josephine Ayres 1921- ... CANR-41
Earlier sketch in CA 115
See also Douglas, Ellen
Hay, David M(cKechnie) 1935- ... 53-56
Hay, Dennis 1952- ... 105
Hay, Denys 1915-1994 ... 13-16R
Obituary ... 146
Hay, Elizabeth (Jean) 1936- ... 131
Hay, Eloise K(napp) 1926- ... 9-12R
Hay, Jacob 1920- ... 25-28R
Hay, James G(ordon) 1936- ... CANR-4
Earlier sketch in CA 53-56
Hay, John (Milton) 1838-1905 Brief entry ... 108
See also DLB 12, 47, 189
Hay, John 1915- ... CANR-9
Earlier sketch in CA 65-68
See also SATA 13
Hay, Leon Edwards ... 25-28R
Hay, Melba Porter 1949- ... 133
Hay, Millicent V. 1945- ... 128
Hay, Peter 1935- ... 21-24R
Hay, Robert D(ean) 1921- ... CANR-8
Earlier sketch in CA 61-64
Hay, Sara Henderson 1906-1987 ... CAP-1
Obituary ... 123
Earlier sketch in CA 13-16
Hay, Stephen N(orthup) 1925- ... 5-8R
Hay, Thomas Robson 1888-1974 Obituary ... 49-52
Hay, Timothy
See Brown, Margaret Wise
Hay, Vicky
See Hay, Millicent V.
Haya de la Torre, Victor Raul 1895-1979 Obituary ... 89-92
Hayakawa, S(amuel) I(chiye) 1906-1992 ... CANR-20
Obituary ... 137
Earlier sketch in CA 13-16R
Hayami, Yujiro 1932- ... 77-80
Hayano, David M(amoru) 1942- ... 115
Hayaseca y Eizaguirre, Jorge
See Echegaray (y Eizaguirre), Jose (Maria Waldo)
Hayashi, Fumiko 1904-1951 ... 161
See also DLB 180
See also TCLC 27
Hayashi, Nancy 1939- ... 147
See also SATA 80
Hayashi, Tetsumaro 1929- ... CANR-14
Earlier sketch in CA 37-40R
Haycock, Kate 1962- ... 145
See also SATA 77
Haycock, Ken(neth) Roy 1948- ... 104
Haycock, Ronald G. 1942- ... 123
Haycraft, Anna ... 122
See also Ellis, Alice Thomas
Haycraft, Howard 1905-1991 ... 21-24R
Obituary ... 136
See also SATA 6
See also SATA-Obit 70
Haycraft, John (Stacpoole) 1926-1996 ... 133
Obituary ... 152
Haycraft, Molly Costain 1911- ... 13-16R
See also SATA 6
Hayden, Albert A(rthur) 1923- ... 33-36R
Hayden, Brian (Douglas) 1946- ... 145
Hayden, C. Gervin
See Wicker, Randolfe Hayden
Hayden, Carl T(rumbull) 1877-1972 Obituary ... 33-36R
Hayden, Dolores 1945- ... CANR-9
Earlier sketch in CA 65-68
Hayden, Donald E(ugene) 1915- ... CANR-10
Earlier sketch in CA 25-28R
Hayden, Eric W(illiam) 1919- ... CANR-2
Earlier sketch in CA 5-8R
Hayden, Gwendolen Lampshire 1904- ... SATA 35
Hayden, Howard K. 1930- ... 17-20R
Hayden, Jay
See Paine, Lauran (Bosworth)
Hayden, Jay G. 1884-1971 Obituary ... 89-92
Hayden, John O(lin) 1932- ... CANR-10
Earlier sketch in CA 25-28R
Hayden, Julia Elizabeth 1939(?)-1981 Obituary ... 104
Hayden, Julie
See Hayden, Julia Elizabeth
Hayden, Martin S(choll) 1912- ... 69-72
Hayden, (Holden) Mike 1920-1984 ... 120
Hayden, Naura 1942- ... CANR-12
Earlier sketch in CA 73-76
Hayden, Robert C(arter), Jr. 1937- ... CANR-24
Earlier sketch in CA 69-72
See also BW 1
See also SATA 47
See also SATA-Brief 28
Hayden, Robert E(arl) 1913-1980 ... CANR-24
Obituary ... 97-100
Earlier sketch in CA 69-72
See also CABS 2
See also BLC 2
See also BW 1
See also CDALB 1941-1968
See also CLC 5, 9, 14, 37
See also DA
See also DAC
See also DAM MST, MULT, POET
See also DLB 5, 76
See also MTCW 1
See also PC 6
See also SATA 19
See also SATA-Obit 26
Hayden, Sterling 1916-1986 ... 111
Obituary ... 119
Hayden, Stirling
See Hayden, Sterling
Hayden, Thomas E(mmet) 1939- ... CANR-41
Earlier sketch in CA 107
Hayden, Tom
See Hayden, Thomas E(mmet)
Hayden, Torey L(ynn) 1951- ... CANR-35
Earlier sketch in CA 103
See also SATA 65
Haydn, Hiram 1907-1973 ... CAP-1
Obituary ... 45-48
Earlier sketch in CA 9-10
Haydn, Richard 1905-1985 Obituary ... 115
Haydon, A(lbert) Eustace 1880-1975 Obituary ... 61-64
Haydon, Benjamin Robert 1786-1846 ... DLB 110
Haydon, Glen 1896-1966 ... CAP-1
Earlier sketch in CA 9-10
Haydon, June 1932- ... 109
Haydon, Roger (Malcolm) 1950- ... 118
Hayek, F(riedrich) A(ugust von) 1899-1992 ... CANR-20
Obituary ... 137
Earlier sketch in CA 93-96
See also MTCW 1
Hayes, Alden C(ary) 1916- ... 57-60
Hayes, Alfred 1911-1985 ... 106
Obituary ... 117
Interview in ... 106
Hayes, Ann L(ouise) 1924- ... 25-28R
Hayes, Anna Hansen 1886- ... 1-4R
Hayes, Bartlett (Harding, Jr.) 1904-1988 ... 77-80
Obituary ... 124
Hayes, Billy ... 97-100
Hayes, Carlton J(oseph) H(untley) 1882-1964 ... CANR-3
Earlier sketch in CA 1-4R
See also SATA 11
Hayes, Christopher L. 1958- ... 142
Hayes, Daniel 1952- ... SATA 73
Hayes, Denis A(llen) 1944- ... 132
Hayes, (Robert) Dennis 1952- ... 130
Hayes, Dorsha 1897(?)-1990 ... 77-80
Obituary ... 133
Hayes, Douglas A(nderson) 1918- ... CANR-18
Earlier sketch in CA 1-4R
Hayes, E(ugene) Nelson 1920- ... 29-32R
Hayes, Edward C(ary) 1937- ... CANR-35
Earlier sketch in CA 45-48
Hayes, Edward L(ee) 1931- ... 29-32R
Hayes, Elvin 1945- Brief entry ... 111
Hayes, Francis Clement 1904- ... CAP-2
Earlier sketch in CA 21-22
Hayes, Geoffrey 1947- ... CANR-57
Earlier sketches in CA 65-68, CANR-9, 25
See also SATA 26, 91
Hayes, Grace Person 1919- ... 33-36R
Hayes, Harold T(homas) P(ace) 1926-1989 ... CANR-22
Obituary ... 128
Earlier sketch in CA 69-72
Hayes, Helen 1900-1993 ... 138
Obituary ... 140
Hayes, James T(homas) 1923- ... 29-32R
Hayes, Joe 1945- ... 152
See also SATA 88
Hayes, John F. 1904- ... CAP-1
Earlier sketch in CA 13-14
See also SATA 11
Hayes, John H(aralson) 1934- ... CANR-21
Earlier sketch in CA 69-72
Hayes, John Michael 1919- ... 108
Interview in ... 108
See also DLB 26
Hayes, John P(hillip) 1949- ... CANR-15
Earlier sketch in CA 93-96
Hayes, John R(ichard) 1929- ... 108
Hayes, John S. 1910-1981 Obituary ... 108
Hayes, Joseph 1918- ... CANR-30
Earlier sketches in CA 17-20R, CANR-7
Hayes, Louis D. 1940- ... 29-32R
Hayes, Margaret 1925- ... 21-24R
Hayes, Mary Anne 1956- ... 105
Hayes, Mary-Rose 1939- ... 102
Hayes, N.
See DeVincentes-Hayes, Nan
Hayes, Nan
See DeVincentes-Hayes, Nan
Hayes, Nelson (Taylor) 1903-1971 ... 1-4R
Obituary ... 33-36R
Hayes, Paul J(ames) 1922- ... 57-60
Hayes, Paul Martin 1942- ... 77-80
Hayes, Penny (a pseudonym) 1940- ... CANR-47
Earlier sketch in CA 121
Hayes, Ralph E(ugene) 1927- ... CANR-15
Earlier sketch in CA 21-24R
Hayes, Robert M(ayo) 1926- ... 9-12R
Hayes, Samuel P(erkins) 1910- ... CANR-3
Earlier sketch in CA 5-8R
Hayes, Sheila 1937- ... CANR-45
Earlier sketches in CA 106, CANR-22
See also SATA 51
See also SATA-Brief 50
Hayes, Steven C(harles) 1948- ... CANR-31
Earlier sketch in CA 112
Hayes, W. Woodrow
See Hayes, Wayne Woodrow
Hayes, Wayland J(ackson) 1893-1972 ... CAP-1
Earlier sketch in CA 13-14
Hayes, Wayne Woodrow 1913-1987 Obituary ... 121
Hayes, Will ... 5-8R
See also SATA 7
Hayes, William D(imitt) 1913- ... 5-8R
See also SATA 8
Hayes, Wilson
See Gibbs-Wilson, Kathryn (Beatrice)
Hayes, Woody
See Hayes, Wayne Woodrow
Hayes, Zachary (Jerome) 1932- ... CANR-39
Earlier sketch in CA 115
Hayflick, Leonard 1928- ... 148
Hayford, Charles W. 1941- ... 136
Hayford, Fred Kwesi 1937- ... 45-48
Hayford, Harrison (Mosher) 1916- ... 118
Hayford, J(oseph) E(phraim) Casely
See Casely-Hayford, J(oseph) E(phraim)
Hayford, Taria
See Haydon, June
Haygood, Johnnie 1924- ... 167
Haygood, Wil 1954- ... 142
See also BW 2
Hayley, Barbara 1938- ... 131
Hayley, William 1745-1820 ... DLB 93, 142
Hayley Bell, Mary ... 25-28R
Haylock, John (Mervyn) 1918- ... 133
Haym, Rudolf 1821-1901 ... DLB 129
Hayman
See Peel, H(azel) M(ary)
Hayman, Carol Bessent 1927- ... 53-56
Hayman, David 1927- ... CANR-7
Earlier sketch in CA 17-20R
Hayman, John L(uther), Jr. 1929- ... 25-28R
Hayman, LeRoy 1916- ... 85-88
Hayman, Max 1908- ... 17-20R
Hayman, Richard 1959- ... 165
Hayman, Robert 1575-1629 ... DLB 99
Hayman, Ronald 1932- ... CANR-50
Earlier sketches in CA 25-28R, CANR-18
See also CLC 44
See also DLB 155
Haymes, Robert C. 1931- ... 33-36R
Haymon, S. T.
See Haymon, Sylvia (Theresa)
Haymon, Sylvia (Theresa) 1918(?)-1995 ... CANR-62
Brief entry ... 127
Earlier sketch in CA 131
Hayn, Annette 1922- ... 65-68
Haynal, Andre (Emeric) 1930- ... 120
Hayne, Paul Hamilton 1830-1886 ... DLB 3, 64, 79
Haynes, Alfred H(enry) 1910- ... 5-8R
Haynes, Anne
See Madlee, Dorothy (Haynes)
Haynes, Betsy 1937- ... CANR-67
Earlier sketches in CA 57-60, CANR-8
See also SATA 48, 94
See also SATA-Brief 37
Haynes, Brian 1939- ... 111
Haynes, C. Rayfield 1943- ... 145
Haynes, David 1955- ... 154
See also SATA 97
Haynes, Gary (Anthony) 1948- ... 143
Haynes, Glynn W(alker) 1936- ... 65-68
Haynes, James 1932- ... 110

Haynes, James Almand 1933- ... 131
Haynes, Jim
See Haynes, James Almand
Haynes, John Earl 1944- ... CANR-70
Earlier sketch in CA 143
Haynes, Jonathan 1952- ... 146
Haynes, Lincoln 1924- ... 116
Haynes, Linda
See Swinford, Betty (June Wells)
Haynes, Maria S(chnee) 1912- ... 25-28R
Haynes, Mary 1938- ... CANR-35
Earlier sketch in CA 111
See also SATA 65
Haynes, Max 1956- ... SATA 72
Haynes, Pat
See McKeag, Ernest L(ionel)
Haynes, Renee (Oriana Tickell) 1906-1992 ... CANR-34
Obituary ... 139
Earlier sketch in CA 49-52
Haynes, Richard F(rederick) 1935- ... 49-52
Haynes, Robert Talmadge, Jr. 1926- ... 1-4R
Haynes, Robert Vaughn 1929- ... 41-44R
Haynes, Sybille 1926- ... 57-60
Haynes, William Warren 1921- ... CANR-8
Earlier sketch in CA 5-8R
Haynie, Hugh 1927- ... 121
Haynie, Sandra (B.) 1943- Brief entry ... 121
Hays, (Lawrence) Brooks 1898-1981 ... CAP-1
Obituary ... 105
Earlier sketch in CA 11-12
Hays, Daniel 1960- ... 154
Hays, David G(lenn) 1928-1995 ... CANR-14
Obituary ... 149
Earlier sketch in CA 21-24R
Hays, Donald 1947- ... 132
Hays, Elinor Rice -1994 ... 1-4R
Obituary ... 144
Hays, H(offmann) R(eynolds) 1904-1980 . CANR-31
Obituary ... 105
Earlier sketch in CA 81-84
See also SATA 26
Hays, Helen Ireland 1903- ... 61-64
Hays, Kelley Ann 1960- ... 142
Hays, Mary 1760-1843 ... DLB 142, 158
Hays, Paul R. 1903-1980 ... CAP-2
Obituary ... 93-96
Earlier sketch in CA 19-20
Hays, Peter L. 1938- ... CANR-72
Earlier sketch in CA 33-36R
Hays, R. Vernon 1902- ... 89-92
Hays, Richard D. 1942- ... 37-40R
Hays, Robert Glenn 1935- ... 53-56
Hays, Samuel Pfrimmer 1921- ... 103
Hays, Terence E(ugene) 1942- ... 69-72
Hays, Thomas Anthony 1957- ... 150
See also SATA 84
Hays, Tony
See Hays, Thomas Anthony
Hays, Wilma Pitchford 1909- ... CANR-45
Earlier sketches in CA 1-4R, CANR-5
See also MAICYA
See also SAAS 3
See also SATA 1, 28
Hayslip, Le Ly 1949- ... 145
Haystead, Wes
See Haystead, Wesley
Haystead, Wesley 1942- ... CANR-45
Earlier sketches in CA 57-60, CANR-6, 22
Hayter, Adrian (Goodenough)
1914-1990 Obituary ... 131
Hayter, Alethea 1911- ... 29-32R
Hayter, Earl W(iley) 1901-1994 ... 41-44R
Obituary ... 145
Hayter, Stanley William 1901-1988 Obituary ... 125
Hayter, William Goodenough 1906-1995 .. CANR-9
Obituary ... 148
Earlier sketch in CA 21-24R
Haythornthwaite, Philip John 1951- ... CANR-42
Earlier sketches in CA 103, CANR-19
Hayton, Richard Neil 1916- ... 57-60
Hayward, Brooke 1937- ... 81-84
Hayward, Charles H(arold) 1898- ... CANR-7
Earlier sketch in CA 9-12R
Hayward, Jack 1931- ... CANR-44
Earlier sketches in CA 57-60, CANR-6, 21
Hayward, Jennifer (Poole) 1961- ... 168
Hayward, John 1905-1965 ... DLB 201
Hayward, John F(orrest) 1916-1983 ... 9-12R
Obituary ... 109
Hayward, John F(rank) 1918- ... 5-8R
Hayward, Linda 1943- ... 112
See also SATA 101
See also SATA-Brief 39
Hayward, Max 1925(?)-1979 ... 93-96
Obituary ... 85-88
Hayward, Philip 1956- ... 146
Hayward, Richard
See Kendrick, Baynard H(ardwick)
Hayward, Richard 1893- ... CAP-1
Earlier sketch in CA 9-10
Hayward, Stephen 1954- ... 133
Haywood, C. Robert 1921- ... 137
Haywood, Carolyn 1898-1990 ... CANR-20
Obituary ... 130
Earlier sketches in CA 5-8R, CANR-5
See also CLR 22
See also MAICYA
See also SATA 1, 29, 75
See also SATA-Obit 64
Haywood, Charles 1904- ... CANR-22
Earlier sketch in CA 1-4R
Haywood, Dixie 1933- ... 105
Haywood, Eliza 1693(?)-1756 ... DLB 39
Haywood, Gar Anthony 1954- ... 167
Haywood, H(erbert) Carl(ton) 1931- ... CANR-3
Earlier sketch in CA 49-52
Haywood, Harry
See Hall, Haywood
Haywood, John Alfred 1913- ... 17-20R
Haywood, Richard Mansfield 1905-1977 ... CAP-2
Obituary ... 69-72
Earlier sketch in CA 33-36
Haywood, Richard Mowbray 1933- ... 25-28R
Haywood, Stephen Patrick 1949- ... 138
Haywood, Steve
See Haywood, Stephen Patrick
Hazam, Louis J. 1911-1983 Obituary ... 110
Hazan, Marcella (Maddalena) 1924- ... CANR-71
Brief entry ... 116
Earlier sketch in CA 128
Hazan, Victor 1928- ... 114
Hazard, Ann 1952- ... 163
Hazard, David 1955- ... 116
Hazard, Harry W(illiams) 1918- ... 122
Hazard, Jack
See Booth, Edwin
Hazard, John N(ewbold) 1909-1995 ... CANR-31
Obituary ... 148
Earlier sketch in CA 1-4R
Hazard, Leland 1893-1980 ... 17-20R
Obituary ... 133
Hazard, Patrick D. 1927- ... 13-16R
Hazel, Paul 1944- ... 114
Hazelgrove, William E(lliot III) 1959- ... 138
Hazelrigg, Meredith K(ent) 1942- ... 33-36R
Hazelton, Alexander
See Armstrong, William A(lexander)
Hazelton, Fran 1947- ... 150
Hazelton, Roger 1909- ... CANR-16
Earlier sketches in CA 1-4R, CANR-1
Hazen, Allen T(racy) 1904- ... CAP-1
Earlier sketch in CA 13-14
Hazen, Barbara Shook 1930- ... CANR-46
Earlier sketches in CA 105, CANR-22
See also SATA 27, 90
Hazen, Helen 1943- ... 116
Hazen, Margaret Hindle 1948- ... 126
Hazen, Robert M(iller) 1948- ... 112
Hazlehurst, Cameron 1941- ... 103
Hazleton, Lesley 1945- ... 128
Brief entry ... 126
Hazlett, Bill
See Hazlett, William Scott
Hazlett, William Scott 1931-1983 Obituary ... 110
Hazlitt, Henry 1894-1993 ... CANR-48
Obituary ... 141
Earlier sketches in CA 5-8R, CANR-3
Hazlitt, Joseph
See Strage, Mark
Hazlitt, William 1778-1830 ... DLB 110, 158
Hazo, Robert G. 1931- ... 21-24R
Hazo, Samuel (John) 1928- ... CANR-58
Earlier sketches in CA 5-8R, CANR-8, 31
See also CAAS 11
Hazzard, Lowell B(restel)
1898-1978 Obituary ... 77-80
Hazzard, Mary 1928- ... CANR-46
Earlier sketch in CA 105
Hazzard, Shirley 1931- ... CANR-70
Earlier sketches in CA 9-12R, CANR-4
See also CLC 18
See also DLBY 82
See also MTCW 1
Heacox, Cecil E. 1903- ... 101
Heacox, Kim 1951- ... 137
Head, Alice Maud 1886-1981 Obituary ... 116
Head, Ann
See Morse, Anne Christensen
Head, Bessie 1937-1986 ... CANR-25
Obituary ... 119
Earlier sketch in CA 29-32R
See also BLC 2
See also BW 2
See also CLC 25, 67
See also DAM MULT
See also DLB 117
See also MTCW 1
Head, Constance 1939- ... 37-40R
Head, David M. 1951- ... 158
Head, Dominic 1962- ... 145
Head, Edith 1898(?)-1981 Obituary ... 105
Head, Gay
See Hauser, Margaret L(ouise)
Head, Gwen 1940- ... 89-92
Head, K(enneth) Maynard 1938- ... 110
Head, (Joanne) Lee 1931-1983 ... 65-68
Obituary ... 110
Head, Matthew
See Canaday, John E(dwin)
Head, Raymond (Victor) 1948- ... 136
Head, Richard G(lenn) 1938- ... CANR-35
Earlier sketch in CA 53-56
Head, Robert V. 1929- ... CANR-15
Earlier sketch in CA 41-44R
Head, Sydney W(arren) 1913- ... CANR-9
Earlier sketch in CA 65-68
Head, Timothy E. 1934- ... 13-16R
Headapohl, B. R.
See Headapohl, Betty R.
Headapohl, Betty R. 1940- ... 122
Headings, Mildred J. 1908- ... 37-40R
Headington, Bonnie Jay 1940- ... 114
Headington, Christopher (John Magenis)
1930-1996 ... 165
Obituary ... 151
Brief entry ... 106
Headlam, Catherine 1960- ... 139
Headley, Elizabeth
See Harrison, Elizabeth Cavanna
Headley, Gwyn 1946- ... 125
Headley, Joel T. 1813-1897 ... DLB 30
See also DLBD 13
Headley, John M. 1929- ... 130
Headley, Victor 1960- ... 146
Headon, (Nicky) Topper 1956(?)- ... CLC 30
Headrick, Daniel R. 1941- ... 145
Headstrom, (Birger) Richard 1902- ... CANR-13
Earlier sketches in CA 1-4R, CANR-2
See also SATA 8
Heady, Earl O(rel) 1916- ... CANR-8
Earlier sketch in CA 17-20R
Heady, Eleanor B(utler) 1917-1979 ... CANR-31
Earlier sketch in CA 41-44R
See also SATA 8
Heady, Harold F(ranklin) 1916- ... CANR-31
Earlier sketch in CA 53-56
Heagney, Anne 1901- ... 5-8R
Heagy, William D. 1964- ... SATA 76
Heal, Edith 1903- ... CANR-2
Earlier sketch in CA 1-4R
See also SATA 7
Heal, Gillian 1934- ... 149
See also SATA 89
Heal, Jane 1946- ... 132
Heal, Jeanne (Bennett) 1917- ... CAP-1
Earlier sketch in CA 9-10
Heald, Charles Brehmer 1882-1974 Obituary . 49-52
Heald, Edward Thornton 1885- ... 17-20R
Heald, Gordon 1941- ... 128
Heald, Morrell 1922- Brief entry ... 111
Heald, Suzette 1943- ... 132
Heald, Tim(othy Villiers) 1944- ... CANR-57
Earlier sketches in CA 49-52, CANR-2, 30
Heale, Jay (Jeremy Peter Wingfield) 1937- ... SATA 84
Healey, B. J.
See Healey, Ben (James)
Healey, Ben (James) 1908- ... CANR-17
Earlier sketch in CA 77-80
Healey, Brooks
See Albert, Burton
Healey, Denis Winston 1917- ... 110
Healey, Dorothy (Ray) 1914- ... 138
Healey, F(rancis) G(eorge) 1903- ... CAP-2
Earlier sketch in CA 21-22
Healey, James 1936- ... 53-56
Healey, James Stewart 1931- ... 57-60
Healey, Joseph G(raham) 1938- ... CANR-40
Earlier sketch in CA 116
Healey, Larry 1927- ... 101
See also SATA 44
See also SATA-Brief 42
Healey, Robert (Mathieu) 1921- ... 61-64
Healey-Kay, (Sydney Francis) Patrick (Chippendall)
1904-1983 Obituary ... 111
Healy, David F(rank) 1926- ... 17-20R
Healy, Dermot 1947- ... CANR-53
Earlier sketch in CA 114
Healy, Fleming 1911- ... 5-8R
Healy, George Robert 1923- ... 17-20R
Healy, George W(illiam), Jr. 1905-1980 ... 69-72
Obituary ... 125
Healy, Jeremiah (F. III) 1948- ... 137
Healy, John D(elaware) 1921- ... 93-96
Healy, Kent T(enney) 1902-1985 Obituary ... 114
Healy, Patrick III 1910- Brief entry ... 110
Healy, Paul F(rancis) 1915-1984 ... 17-20R
Obituary ... 114
Healy, Richard J. 1916- ... 25-28R
Healy, Sean D(esmond) 1927- ... CANR-11
Earlier sketch in CA 25-28R
Healy, Sister Kathleen ... 61-64
Healy, Sophia (Warner) 1938- ... 136
Healy, Timothy S(tafford) 1923-1992 ... CANR-46
Obituary ... 140
Earlier sketch in CA 41-44R
Heaney, John J. 1925- ... CANR-5
Earlier sketch in CA 9-12R
Heaney, Marie 1940- ... 153
Heaney, Seamus (Justin) 1939- ... CANR-48
Earlier sketches in CA 85-88, CANR-25
See also CDBLB 1960 to Present
See also CLC 5, 7, 14, 25, 37, 74, 91
See also DAB
See also DAM POET
See also DLB 40
See also DLBY 95
See also MTCW 1
See also PC 18
See also WLCS
Heany, Donald Francis 1918-1990 Obituary ... 132
Heap, Desmond 1907- ... CANR-15
Earlier sketches in CAP-1, CA 9-10
Heaps, Willard A(llison) 1908- ... 85-88
See also SATA 26
Heard, (George) Alexander 1917- ... 17-20R
Heard, Anthony Hazlitt 1937- ... 134
Heard, (Henry Fitz) Gerald 1889-1971 ... CANR-72
Obituary ... 29-32R
Earlier sketches in CAP-2, CA 21-22
Heard, H. F.
See Heard, (Henry Fitz) Gerald
Heard, J(oseph) Norman 1922- ... 9-12R
Heard, Nathan C(liff) 1936- ... CANR-25
Earlier sketch in CA 53-56
See also BW 1
See also DLB 33
Hearden, Patrick J. 1942- ... 138
Hearder, Harry 1924- ... 5-8R
Hearn, Charles R(alph) 1937- ... 77-80
Hearn, Chester G. 1932- ... 151
Hearn, Diane Dawson 1952- ... SATA 79
Hearn, Emily
See Valleau, Emily
Hearn, Janice W. 1938- ... 65-68
Hearn, John 1920- ... 97-100
Hearn, (Patricio) Lafcadio (Tessima Carlos)
1850-1904 ... 166
Brief entry ... 105
See also DLB 12, 78
See also TCLC 9
Hearn, Lafcadio 1850-1904 ... DLB 189
Hearn, M(illard) F(illmore, Jr.) 1938- ... 115
Hearn, Sneed
See Gregg, Andrew K.
Hearnden, Arthur (George) 1931- ... 65-68
Hearne, Betsy Gould 1942- ... CANR-68
Earlier sketches in CA 114, CANR-35
See also SATA 38, 95
Hearne, John (Edgar Caulwell) 1926- ... 125
Brief entry ... 116
See also BW 1
See also DLB 117
See also MTCW 1
Hearne, Samuel 1745-1792 ... DLB 99
Hearne, Vicki 1946- ... 139
See also CLC 56
Hearnshaw, Leslie Spencer 1907- ... 89-92
Hearon, Shelby 1931- ... CANR-48
Earlier sketches in CA 25-28R, CANR-18
See also AITN 2
See also CLC 63
Hearsey, John E(dward) N(icholl) 1928- ... CANR-8
Earlier sketch in CA 5-8R
Hearst, David Whitmire 1915-1986 Obituary ... 119
Hearst, George Randolph
1904-1972 Obituary ... 89-92
Hearst, James 1900-1983 ... CANR-15
Earlier sketch in CA 85-88
Hearst, Patricia Campbell 1954- ... 136
Hearst, Patty
See Hearst, Patricia Campbell
Hearst, William Randolph, Jr. 1908- ... 139
See also DLB 127
Hearst, William Randolph 1863-1951 Brief entry ... 118
See also DLB 25
Heartman, Charles Frederick 1883-1953 .. DLB 187
Heartman, Harold
See Mebane, John (Harrison)
Heasman, Kathleen Joan 1913- ... CAP-1
Earlier sketch in CA 9-10
Heater, Derek (Benjamin) 1931- ... CANR-6
Earlier sketch in CA 57-60
Heath, Catherine 1924-1991 ... CANR-30
Obituary ... 136
Earlier sketch in CA 93-96
See also DLB 14
Heath, Charles C(hastain) 1921- ... 69-72
Heath, Charles D(ickinson) 1941- ... 121
See also SATA 46
Heath, Douglas H(amilton) 1925- ... 17-20R
Heath, Dwight B(raley) 1930- ... CANR-7
Earlier sketch in CA 17-20R
Heath, Edward Richard George 1916- ... 33-36R
Heath, G. Louis 1944- ... 37-40R
Heath, Harry E(ugene), Jr. 1919- ... CANR-28
Earlier sketch in CA 85-88
Heath, (Ernest) James 1920- ... 17-20R
Heath, Jim F(rank) 1931- ... 29-32R
Heath, Lester
See Cassiday, Bruce (Bingham)
Heath, Lorraine 1954- ... 153
Heath, Malcolm (Frederick) 1957- ... 130
Heath, Mary Ellen 1928- ... 115
Heath, Monica
See Fitzgerald, Arlene J.
Heath, (Charles) Monro 1899-1966 ... CAP-1
Earlier sketch in CA 9-10
Heath, Peter (Lauchlan) 1922- ... 41-44R
Heath, Robert L. 1941- ... CANR-53
Earlier sketch in CA 126
Heath, Robert W. 1931- ... 13-16R
Heath, Roy 1917- ... 9-12R
Heath, Roy A(ubrey) K(elvin) 1926- ... CANR-53
Earlier sketches in CA 106, CANR-33
See also BW 2
See also DLB 117
See also MTCW 1
Heath, Royton E(dward) 1907- ... 9-12R
Heath, Sandra
See Wilson, Sandra
Heath, Terrence (George) 1936- ... CANR-36
Earlier sketch in CA 97-100
Heath, Veronica
See Blackett, Veronica Heath
Heath, William (Webster) 1929- ... CANR-31
Earlier sketch in CA 1-4R
Heathcott, Mary
See Keegan, Mary Heathcott
Heath-Stubbs, John (Francis Alexander) 1918- ... CANR-49
Earlier sketch in CA 13-16R
See also CAAS 21
See also DLB 27
Heat-Moon, William Least
See Trogdon, William (Lewis)
See also AAYA 9
See also CLC 29
Heaton, Charles Huddleston 1928- ... CANR-20
Earlier sketch in CA 1-4R
Heaton, Eric William 1920- ... 61-64
Heaton, Herbert 1890-1973 ... 5-8R
Obituary ... 41-44R
Heaton, Herbert 1919- ... 163
Heaton, Peter 1919- ... 104
Heaton, Rose Henniker 1884-1975 Obituary . 61-64
Heaton, Thomas Peter Starke 1928- ... 134
Heaton, Tom
See Heaton, Thomas Peter Starke
Heaton-Ward, William Alan 1919- ... 102
Heatter, Gabriel 1890-1972 Obituary ... 89-92

Heaven, Constance 1911- CANR-40
Earlier sketches in CA 49-52, CANR-2, 18
See also SATA 7
Heavysege, Charles 1816-1876 .... DLB 99
Hebard, Edna L(aura Henriksen) 1913- 9-12R
Hebb, D(onald) O(lding) 1904-1985 .... CANR-2
Obituary 118
Earlier sketch in CA 1-4R
Hebbel, Friedrich 1813-1863 .... DAM DRAM
See also DLB 129
Hebblethwaite, Brian Leslie 1939- CANR-27
Earlier sketch in CA 109
Hebblethwaite, Margaret 1951- CANR-68
Earlier sketch in CA 129
Hebblethwaite, Peter 1930-1994 .... CANR-44
Obituary 147
Earlier sketch in CA 69-72
Hebborn, Eric 1934-1996 144
Obituary 151
Hebden, Mark
See Harris, John
Hebel, Johann Peter 1760-1826 .... DLB 90
Heber, Richard 1774-1833 .... DLB 184
Heberer, Thomas 1947- 135
Hebert, Anne 1916- CANR-69
Earlier sketch in CA 85-88
See also CLC 4, 13, 29
See also DAC
See also DAM MST, POET
See also DLB 68
See also MTCW 1
Hebert, Ernest 1941- 102
See also CAAS 24
Hebert, F(elix) Edward 1901-1979 110
Obituary 106
Hebert, (Arthur) Gabriel 1886-1963 .... 1-4R
Hebert, Jacques 1923- CANR-52
Earlier sketches in CA 25-28R, CANR-11, 27
See also DLB 53
Hebert, Tom 1938- 69-72
Hebson, Ann (Hellebusch) 1925- 17-20R
Hechinger, Fred M(ichael) 1920-1995 77-80
Obituary 150
Hechinger, Grace (Bernstein) 1931- 166
Hechler, David (S.) 1950- 127
Hechler, Ken 1914- 109
Hecht, Anthony (Evan) 1923- CANR-6
Earlier sketch in CA 9-12R
See also CLC 8, 13, 19
See also DAM POET
See also DLB 5, 169
Hecht, Ben 1894-1964 85-88
See also CLC 8
See also DLB 7, 9, 25, 26, 28, 86
Hecht, George J(oseph)
1895-1980 Obituary 97-100
See also SATA-Obit 22
Hecht, Henri Joseph 1922- 29-32R
See also SATA 9
Hecht, James L(ee) 1926- 33-36R
Hecht, Jeff(rey Charles) 1947- 131
Hecht, Joseph C. 1924- 29-32R
Hecht, Marie B(ergenfeld) 1918- 21-24R
Hecht, Michael L. 1949- 145
Hecht, Robert A(nthony) 1929- 114
Hecht, Roger 1926- 17-20R
Hecht, Warren Jay 1946- 103
Hechter, Michael 1943- 69-72
Hechtkopf, Henryk 1910- .... SATA 17
Hechtlinger, Adelaide 1914- 29-32R
Heck, Alfons 1928- 131
Heck, Bessie Holland 1911- 5-8R
See also SATA 26
Heck, Frank H(opkins) 1904-1983 69-72
Obituary 126
Heck, Harold J(oseph) 1906- 41-44R
Heck, Peter J(ewell) 165
Heck, Peter M. 1937- 53-56
Heck, Suzanne Wright 1939- 53-56
Heckart, Barbara Hooper 1937- 118
Heckart, Beverly Anne 1938- 103
Heckel, Robert V. 1925- 9-12R
Heckelmann, Charles N(ewman) 1913- .. CANR-30
Earlier sketch in CA 49-52
Hecker, Isaac Thomas 1819-1888 .... DLB 1
Heckerling, Amy 1954- 139
See also AAYA 22
Heckert, Connie K(aye Delp) 1948- 149
See also SATA 82
Heckert, J(osiah) Brooks 1893- 5-8R
Heckler, Jonellen (Beth) 1943- CANR-41
Earlier sketch in CA 109
Heckman, Hazel 1904- 21-24R
Heckman, William O(scar) 1921- 21-24R
Heckmann, Wolf 1929- 114
Heckscher, August 1913-1997 .... CANR-35
Obituary 157
Earlier sketch in CA 1-4R
Heckscher, Charles 1949- 149
Hedayat, Sadeq 1903-1951 Brief entry 120
See also TCLC 21
Hedberg, Nancy 1944- 122
Hedde, Wilhelmina G(enevava) 1895- 5-8R
Hedden, Walter Page 1898(?)-1976 Obituary . 65-68
Hedden, Worth Tuttle 1896-1985 .... CAP-2
Obituary 117
Earlier sketch in CA 21-22
Hedderwick, Mairi 1939- 137
See also MAICYA
See also SATA 30, 77
Hederman, Thomas M(artin), Jr.
1911-1985 Obituary 114
Hedge, Frederic Henry 1805-1890 .... DLB 1, 59
Hedge, Leslie (Joseph) 1922- 9-12R
Hedgecoe, John 1937- 159
Hedgeman, Anna Arnold 1899-1990 .... CAP-1
Obituary 130
Earlier sketch in CA 13-16
Hedges, Bob A(tkinson) 1919- 45-48
Hedges, David (Paget) 1930- 45-48
Hedges, Elaine R(yan) 1927-1997 .... CANR-7
Obituary 158
Earlier sketch in CA 57-60
Hedges, Inez (Kathleen) 1947- 116
Hedges, Joseph
See Harknett, Terry
Hedges, Sid(ney) G(eorge) 1897-1974 .... CANR-4
Earlier sketch in CA 9-12R
See also SATA 28
Hedges, Trimble R(aymond) 1906- CAP-2
Earlier sketch in CA 21-22
Hedges, Ursula M. 1940- CANR-47
Earlier sketch in CA 29-32R
Hedges, William L(eonard) 1923- 37-40R
Hedin, Mary 103
Hedin, Robert (Alexander) 1949- 146
Hedley, George (Percy) 1899- CAP-2
Earlier sketch in CA 19-20
Hedley, (Gladys) Olwen 1912- CANR-9
Earlier sketch in CA 61-64
Hedlund, Ronald D(avid) 1941- 33-36R
Hedren, Paul L(eslie) 1949- CANR-37
Earlier sketch in CA 114
Hedrick, Addie M. 1903- CAP-2
Earlier sketch in CA 25-28
Hedrick, Basil C(alvin) 1932- CANR-21
Earlier sketch in CA 33-36R
Hedrick, Floyd D(udley) 1927- 33-36R
Hedrick, Joan D(oran) 1944- CANR-52
Earlier sketch in CA 107
Hedrick, Travis K. 1904(?)-1977 Obituary 69-72
Heefner, Wilson A. 1931- 150
Heeley, D(avid) A. 1971- 154
Heeney, Brian 1933- 89-92
Heer, David M(acAlpine) 1930- 162
Heer, John E(dward), Jr. 1921-(?) Obituary 113
Heer, Nancy Whittier 33-36R
Heerboth, Sharon
See Leon, Sharon
Heeresma, Heere 1932- CANR-48
Earlier sketch in CA 25-28R
Heeresma Inc.
See Heeresma, Heere
Heermance, J. Noel 1939- 25-28R
Heertje, Arnold 1934- 131
Heerwagen, Paul K. 1895- 29-32R
Heesterman, J(ohannes) C(ornelis) 1925- 128
Heezen, Bruce C(harles) 1924-1977 .... CANR-29
Obituary 69-72
Earlier sketch in CA 49-52
Heffer, Eric S(amuel) 1922- 123
Heffern, Richard 1950- 61-64
Heffernan, James A(nthony) W(alsh) 1939- . 25-28R
Heffernan, Michael 1942- CANR-40
Earlier sketches in CA 77-80, CANR-18
Heffernan, Nancy Coffey 1936- 146
Heffernan, Patrick
See O'Heffernan, Patrick
Heffernan, Paul 1905(?)-1983 Obituary 110
Heffernan, Thomas (Patrick Carroll) 1939- 81-84
Heffernan, Thomas Farel 1933- 107
Heffernan, Thomas J(ohn Andrew) 1944- 125
Heffernan, William A. 1937- 25-28R
Heffley, Wayne 1927- 9-12R
Heffner, Richard D(ouglas) 1925- 69-72
Heffron, Dorris 1944- CANR-36
Earlier sketch in CA 49-52
See also SATA 68
Heffron, Mary J. 1935- 135
Hefley, James C(arl) 1930- CANR-7
Earlier sketch in CA 13-16R
Heflin, Donald
See Wallmann, Jeffrey M(iner)
Hefner, Hugh (Marston) 1926- 148
Brief entry 110
See also AITN 1
See also DLB 137
Hefner, Paul
See Tabori, Paul
Hefner, Robert W(illiam) 1952- 119
Hefter, Richard 1942- CANR-47
Earlier sketches in CA 107, CANR-23
See also SATA 31
Hegarty, Edward J. 1891- CANR-5
Earlier sketch in CA 1-4R
Hegarty, Ellen 1918- 37-40R
Hegarty, Frances 1948- 135
Hegarty, Reginald Beaton 1906-1973 .... CAP-1
Obituary 41-44R
Earlier sketch in CA 13-16
See also SATA 10
Hegarty, Sister M(ary) Loyola
See Hegarty, Ellen
Hegarty, Walter 1922- 65-68
Hegel, Georg Wilhelm Friedrich 1770-1831 . DLB 90
Hegel, Richard 1927- CANR-6
Earlier sketch in CA 57-60
Hegel, Robert Earl 1943- 108
Hegeler, Sten 1923- 107
Hegeman, Elizabeth Blair 1942- 61-64
Hegenberger, John 1947- 135
Hegener, Mark Paul 1919-1988 Obituary 125
Heger, Theodore Ernest 1907- 33-36R
Hegesippus
See Schonfield, Hugh J(oseph)
Heggoy, Alf Andrew 1938- CANR-14
Earlier sketch in CA 37-40R
Hegi, Ursula 1946- 104
Heginbotham, Stanley J. 1938- Brief entry 106
Heglar, Mary Schnall 1934- 49-52
Hegner, William 1928- 93-96
Hegre, Theodore A. 1908-1984 Obituary 115
Hegstad, Roland R(ex) 1926- 57-60
Heiber, Helmut 1924- 49-52
Heiby, Walter A(lbert) 1918- 21-24R
Heichberger, Robert Lee 1930- 53-56
Heichelheim, Fritz M(oritz) 1901-1968 Obituary . 116
Heicher, Merlo K. W. 1882-1967 .... CAP-1
Earlier sketch in CA 13-14
Heidbreder, Margaret Ann
See Eastman, Ann Heidbreder
Heide, Florence Parry 1919- CANR-19
Earlier sketch in CA 93-96
See also JRDA
See also MAICYA
See also SAAS 6
See also SATA 32, 69
Heide, Kathleen M. 1954- 145
Heide, Robert 1939- CANR-20
Earlier sketch in CA 103
Heidegger, Martin 1889-1976 .... CANR-34
Obituary 65-68
Earlier sketch in CA 81-84
See also CLC 24
See also MTCW 1
Heidelberger, Michael (Johannes) 1947- 130
Heideman, Eugene P. 1929- 69-72
Heiden, Carol A. 1939- 57-60
Heiden, David 1946- 139
Heiden, Konrad 1901-1966 Obituary 116
Heidenreich, Charles A(lbert) 1917- 25-28R
Heidenry, John 1939- 142
Heidenstam, (Carl Gustaf) Verner von
1859-1940 Brief entry 104
See also TCLC 5
Heider, Karl G(ustav) 1935- 132
Heiderstadt, Dorothy 1907- CANR-1
Earlier sketch in CA 1-4R
See also SATA 6
Heidi, Gloria 69-72
Heidingsfield, Myron S(amuel) 1914-1969 ....
CANR-31
Obituary 103
Earlier sketch in CA 1-4R
Heidish, Marcy Moran 1947- 101
See also DLBY 82
Heidmann, Jean 1923- 130
Heiferman, Ronald Ian 1941- 61-64
Heifetz, Harold 1919- CANR-10
Earlier sketch in CA 25-28R
Heifetz, Milton D. 1921- 57-60
Heifner, Jack 1946- CANR-47
Earlier sketch in CA 105
See also CLC 11
Heiges, P. Myers 1887-1968 .... CAP-1
Earlier sketch in CA 13-16
Heijermans, Herman 1864-1924 Brief entry 123
See also TCLC 24
Heijke, John 1927- 21-24R
Heikal, M. Hassanein
See Heikal, Mohamed Hassanein
Heikal, Mohamed
See Heikal, Mohamed Hassanein
Heikal, Mohamed H.
See Heikal, Mohamed Hassanein
Heikal, Mohamed Hassanein 1923- 127
Brief entry 112
Heil, John 112
Heil, Ruth 1947- 112
Heilbron, J(ohn) L(ewis) 1934- CANR-41
Earlier sketches in CA 53-56, CANR-4, 19
Heilbroner, Joan Knapp 1922- 1-4R
See also SATA 63
Heilbroner, Robert L(ouis) 1919- CANR-47
Earlier sketches in CA 1-4R, CANR-4, 21
Heilbronner, Walter L(eo) 1924- 25-28R
Heilbrun, Carolyn G(old) 1926- CANR-58
Earlier sketches in CA 45-48, CANR-1, 28
See also CLC 25
Heilbrun, Lois Hussey 1922(?)-1987 Obituary .. 123
See also SATA-Obit 54
Heilbrunn, Otto 1906-1969 .... CAP-1
Earlier sketch in CA 13-16
Heilig, Matthias R. 1881-(?) CAP-2
Earlier sketch in CA 23-24
Heiliger, Edward Martin 1909- 13-16R
Heiligman, Deborah 1958- 155
See also SATA 90
Heilman, Arthur (William) 1914- CANR-5
Earlier sketch in CA 5-8R
Heilman, Grant 1919- 53-56
Heilman, Joan Rattner CANR-44
Earlier sketches in CA 57-60, CANR-6, 21
See also SATA 50
Heilman, Robert Bechtold 1906- CANR-52
Earlier sketches in CA 13-16R, CANR-9, 27
Heilman, Robert Leo 1952- 151
Heilman, Samuel C(hiel) 1946- 69-72
Heilner, Van Campen 1899-1970 Obituary .. 29-32R
Heim, Alice (Winifred) 1913- CANR-14
Earlier sketch in CA 33-36R
Heim, Bruno Bernard 1911- 89-92
Heim, Joseph A(rthur) 1949- 142
Heim, Kathleen M(cEntee) 1948- CANR-49
Earlier sketch in CA 111
Heim, Michael Henry 1943- 159
Heim, Ralph D(aniel) 1895-1983 73-76
Obituary 133
Heim, Scott 1966- 158
Heiman, Ernest J(ean) 1930- CANR-4
Earlier sketch in CA 53-56
Heiman, Grover G(eorge, Jr.) 1920- CANR-6
Earlier sketch in CA 5-8R
Heiman, Judith 1935- 1-4R
Heiman, Marcel 1909-1976 Obituary 65-68
Heimann, Robert Karl 1918-1990 Obituary 130
Heimann, Susan 1940- 33-36R
Heimarck, Theodore 1906- 5-8R
Heimbeck, Raeburne S(eeley) 1930- 29-32R
Heimberg, Marilyn Markham
See Ross, Marilyn (Ann) Heimberg
Heimdahl, Ralph 1909- 69-72
Heimer, Mel(vin Lytton) 1915-1971 .... CANR-4
Obituary 29-32R
Earlier sketch in CA 1-4R
Heimert, Alan (Edward) 1928- 5-8R
Heimler, Eugene 1922- CANR-8
Earlier sketch in CA 13-16R
Heimlich, Henry Jay 1920- 102
Heims, Steve J(oshua) 1926- 131
Heims, Steve Paul
See Heims, Steve J(oshua)
Heimsath, Charles H. 1928- 17-20R
Hein, Christoph 1944- 158
See also DLB 124
Hein, Eleanor C(harlotte) 1933- 61-64
Hein, John 1921- CANR-16
Earlier sketches in CA 45-48, CANR-1
Hein, Leonard William 1916- 53-56
Hein, Lucille Eleanor 1915- CANR-2
Earlier sketch in CA 5-8R
See also SATA 20
Hein, Marvin Lester 1925- 125
Hein, Norvin 1914- 61-64
Hein, Piet 1905- CANR-4
Earlier sketch in CA 49-52
Hein, Rolland Neal 1932- 112
Heinberg, Paul (Julius) 1924- CANR-23
Earlier sketch in CA 45-48
Heinbuch, Jean (M.) 1953- 142
Heindel, Richard Heathcote
1912-1979 Obituary 89-92
Heine, Arthur J. 1940- 138
Heine, Carl 1936- 57-60
Heine, Heinrich 1797-1856 .... DLB 90
Heine, Helme 1941- 135
See also CLR 18
See also MAICYA
See also SATA 67
Heine, Lala Koehn
See Koehn-Heine, Lala
Heine, Ralph W(illiam) 1914- 41-44R
Heine, William C(olbourne) 1919- 97-100
Heineman, Benjamin Walter, Jr. 1944- CANR-28
Earlier sketch in CA 105
Heineman, Helen 1936- 125
Heineman, Kenneth J. 1962- 144
Heinemann, George Alfred 1918- .... SATA-Brief 31
Heinemann, Katherine 1918- 77-80
Heinemann, Larry (Curtiss) 1944- CANR-31
Earlier sketch in CA 110
Interview in CANR-31
See also CAAS 21
See also CLC 50
See also DLBD 9
Heinemann, Ronald L(ynton) 1939- 112
Heinemann, Steven
See Bach, Steven
Heinen, Hubert (Plummer) 1937- 41-44R
Heinerman, John 1946- 128
Heiney, Donald (William) 1921-1993 .... CANR-58
Obituary 142
Earlier sketches in CA 1-4R, CANR-3
See also Harris, MacDonald
Heinke, Clarence H. 1912- 53-56
Heinl, Nancy G(ordon) 1916- 81-84
Heinl, Robert Debs, Jr. 1916-1979 .... CANR-4
Obituary 85-88
Earlier sketch in CA 5-8R
Heinlein, Robert A(nson) 1907-1988 .... CANR-53
Obituary 125
Earlier sketches in CA 1-4R, CANR-1, 20
See also AAYA 17
See also CLC 1, 3, 8, 14, 26, 55
See also DAM POP
See also DLB 8
See also JRDA
See also MAICYA
See also MTCW 1
See also SATA 9, 69
See also SATA-Obit 56
Heinrich, Bernd 1940- 109
Heinrich, Willi 1920- CANR-15
Earlier sketch in CA 93-96
See also DLB 75
Heinrichs, Waldo H(untley), Jr. 1925- CANR-48
Earlier sketch in CA 122
Heinrich von dem Tuerlin fl. c. 1230- .... DLB 138
Heinrich von Melk fl. 1160- .... DLB 148
Heinrich von Veldeke c. 1145-c. 1190 .... DLB 138
Heins, A(rthur) James 1931- 5-8R
Heins, Ethel L(eah) 1918-1997 102
Obituary 158
See also SATA 101
Heins, Marjorie 1946- 69-72
Heins, Paul 1909- 69-72
See also SATA 13
Heinse, Wilhelm 1746-1803 .... DLB 94
Heinsohn, A(ugereau) G(ray), Jr. 1896- CAP-1
Earlier sketch in CA 11-12
Heinsohn, Thomas William 1934- Brief entry ... 118
Heinsohn, Tommy
See Heinsohn, Thomas William
Heintz, Ann Christine 1930-1989 .... CANR-8
Obituary 127
Earlier sketch in CA 61-64
Heintz, Bonnie L(ee) 1924- 69-72
Heintz, John 1936- 45-48
Heintze, Carl 1922- 57-60
See also SATA 26
Heintzelman, Donald S(haffer) 1938- CANR-16
Earlier sketch in CA 93-96

Heinz, Brian J(ames) 1946- 160
See also SATA 95
Heinz, G.
See Gerard-Libois, Jules C.
Heinz, W(ilfred) C(harles) 1915- CANR-62
Earlier sketches in CA 5-8R, CANR-4
See also DLB 171
See also SATA 26
Heinz, William Frederick 1899-1976 .... CANR-12
Earlier sketch in CA 61-64
Heinze, Robert H(arold) 1920-1984 Obituary 113
Heinzelman, Kurt 1947- 101
Heinzen, Mildred
See Masters, Mildred
Heinzerling, Larry E(dward) 1945- 73-76
Heinzerling, Lynn Louis 1906-1983 Obituary 111
Heinzman(n), George (Melville) 1916- 1-4R
Heirich, Max 1931- 29-32R
Heise, David R(euben) 1937- 89-92
Heise, Edward Tyler 1912- 1-4R
Heise, Kenan 1933- 57-60
Heisel, Sharon E(laine) 1941- 150
See also SATA 84
Heisenberg, Werner 1901-1976 Obituary 65-68
Heiser, Charles B(ixler), Jr. 1920- 45-48
Heiser, Victor George 1893-1972 Obituary 33-36R
Heiserman, Arthur Ray 1929-1975 .... CANR-15
Obituary 103
Earlier sketch in CA 1-4R
Heiserman, David L(ee) 1940- CANR-8
Earlier sketch in CA 61-64
Heisey, Alan Milliken 1928- 57-60
Heising, Willetta L. 1947- 167
Heiskell, John Netherland
1872-1972 Obituary 89-92
See also DLB 127
Heisler, Martin O. 1938- CANR-23
Earlier sketch in CA 45-48
Heisler, Philip Samuel 1915-1988 Obituary 127
Heisner, Beverly F. 1937- 165
Heiss, Jerold (Sheldon) 1930- 126
Brief entry 111
Heissenbuettel, Helmut 1921-1996 81-84
Obituary 154
See also DLB 75
Heissenbuttel, Helmut
See Heissenbuettel, Helmut
Heisserer, Andrew Jackson 1935- 111
Heitler, Walter (Heinrich) 1904-1981 .... CANR-8
Earlier sketch in CA 13-16R
Heitman, Sidney 1924- 9-12R
Heitmiller, David A. 1945- 163
Heitner, Robert R. 1920- 5-8R
Heitschmidt, Rodney K. 1944- 142
Heitzmann, William Ray 1948- CANR-49
Earlier sketches in CA 97-100, CANR-17
See also SATA 73
Heitzmann, Wm. Ray
See Heitzmann, William Ray
Heizer, Robert Fleming 1915-1979 102
Hejinian, Lyn 153
See also DLB 165
Hekker, Terry 1932- 97-100
Hekman, Susan J(ean) 1949- 114
Helbich, Wolfgang J(ohannes) 1935- 160
Helbig, Alethea K. 1928- CANR-37
Earlier sketches in CA 97-100, CANR-17
Helbing, Terry 1951- 89-92
Helbling, Robert E(ugene) 1923- CANR-48
Earlier sketch in CA 49-52
Helck, C. Peter 1893- CANR-1
Earlier sketch in CA 1-4R
Held, David 1951- 110
Held, Jack Preston 1926- 33-36R
Held, Jacqueline 1936- CANR-14
Earlier sketch in CA 73-76
Held, Joseph 1930- 45-48
Held, Julius Samuel 1905- CANR-45
Earlier sketch in CA 103
Held, Peter
See Vance, John Holbrook
Held, R(over) Burnell 1921- 33-36R
Held, Ray E(ldred) 1918- 45-48
Held, Richard 1922- 41-44R
Held, Virginia (Potter) 1929- CANR-16
Earlier sketches in CA 1-4R, CANR-1
Helder, Dom
See Camara, Helder Pessoa
Heldman, Dan C(hristopher) 1943- 110
Heldman, Gladys M(edalie) 1922- Brief entry 111
Heldman, Robert Keith 1938- 144
Heleniak, Kathryn Moore 110
Helfen, Otto J. Maenchen
See Maenchen, Otto John
Helfert, Erich A(nton) 1931- 9-12R
Helfgott, Daniel (Andrew) 1952- CANR-46
Earlier sketches in CA 106, CANR-22
Helfgott, Roy B. 1925- 81-84
Helfman, Elizabeth S(eaver) 1911- CANR-5
Earlier sketch in CA 5-8R
See also SATA 3
Helfman, Harry 1910- 25-28R
See also SATA 3
Helforth, John
See Doolittle, Hilda
Helfritz, Hans 1902- 41-44R
Helgerson, Richard 1940- 116
Helgesen, Sally 1948- CANR-50
Earlier sketch in CA 115
Helion, Jean 1904-1987 Obituary 124
Helitzer, Florence (Saperstein) 1928- 17-20R
Hellberg, Hans-Eric 1927- CANR-18
Earlier sketch in CA 101
See also SATA 38
Helldorfer, M. C. 1954- 129
Hellegers, Andre E. 1926-1979 Obituary 85-88
Helleiner, Gerald K(arl) 1936- 140
Hellen, J(ohn) A(nthony) 1935- 61-64
Hellenga, Robert 1941- 154
Hellenhofferu, Vojtech Kapristian z
See Hasek, Jaroslav (Matej Frantisek)
Heller
See Iranek-Osmecki, Kazimierz
Heller, Abraham M. 1898-1975 Obituary 57-60
Heller, Agnes 1929- 160
Heller, Bernard 1896-1976 Obituary 65-68
Heller, Celia S(topnicka) 37-40R
Heller, David (A.) 1922-1968 .... CAP-1
Earlier sketch in CA 9-10
Heller, David 1957- CANR-52
Earlier sketch in CA 124
Heller, Dawn Hansen 1932- 125
Heller, Deane Fons 1924- 9-12R
Heller, Erich 1911-1990 .... CANR-8
Obituary 132
Earlier sketch in CA 13-16R
Heller, Francis H(oward) 1917- CANR-57
Earlier sketches in CA 1-4R, CANR-31
Heller, H(einz) Robert 1940- CANR-22
Earlier sketch in CA 69-72
Heller, Herbert L. 1908- 21-24R
Heller, Jean 1942- 73-76
Heller, John 1896(?)-1987 Obituary 124
Heller, John H(erbert) 1921- 114
Heller, Joseph 1923- CANR-66
Earlier sketches in CA 5-8R, CANR-8, 42
Interview in CANR-8
See also CABS 1
See also AAYA 24
See also AITN 1
See also CLC 1, 3, 5, 8, 11, 36, 63
See also DA
See also DAB
See also DAC
See also DAM MST, NOV, POP
See also DLB 2, 28
See also DLBY 80
See also MTCW 1
See also WLC
Heller, Keith 1949- 119
Heller, Linda 1944- 108
See also SATA 46
See also SATA-Brief 40
Heller, Mark (Francis) 1914- CANR-10
Earlier sketch in CA 61-64
Heller, Marvin J. 1940- 167
Heller, Michael (David) 1937- CANR-52
Earlier sketches in CA 45-48, CANR-26
See also DLB 165
Heller, Mike
See Hano, Arnold
Heller, Peter 1920- CANR-32
Earlier sketches in CA 41-44R, CANR-14
Heller, Rachelle S(ara) 1943- 111
Heller, Reinhold (August Friedrich) 1940- 77-80
Heller, Robert 1899(?)-1973 Obituary 41-44R
Heller, Robert (Gordon Barry) 1932- 132
Heller, Robert W(illiam) 1933- 25-28R
Heller, Ruth M. 1924- 130
See also SATA 66
Heller, Shelly
See Heller, Rachelle S(ara)
Heller, Sipa 1897(?)-1980 Obituary 97-100
Heller, Steven 1950- 160
Heller, Trudy (Marie) 1944- 115
Heller, Walter W(olfgang) 1915-1987 .... 21-24R
Obituary 122
Heller, Wilson Battin 1893-1983 Obituary 110
Hellerman, Herbert 1927- 53-56
Hellerstein, David (Joel) 1953- CANR-46
Earlier sketch in CA 120
Hellerstein, Jerome R. 1907- CAP-1
Earlier sketch in CA 13-14
Hellerstein, Kathryn (Ann) 1952- 114
Hellie, Ann 1925- CANR-15
Earlier sketch in CA 77-80
Hellie, Richard 1937- CANR-36
Earlier sketches in CA 33-36R, CANR-14
Hellinga, Lotte 1932- 129
Hellinga, Wytze (Gs) 1908-1985 Obituary 116
Hellinger, Douglas A(lan) 1948- CANR-21
Earlier sketch in CA 69-72
Hellinger, Stephen H(enry) 1948- CANR-21
Earlier sketch in CA 69-72
Hellison, Donald R(aymond) 1938- 53-56
Hellman, Arthur D(avid) 1942- 69-72
Hellman, C(larisse) Doris
1910-1973 Obituary 41-44R
Hellman, Geoffrey T(heodore) 1907-1977 ....
CANR-30
Obituary 73-76
Earlier sketch in CA 69-72
Hellman, Hal
See Hellman, Harold
Hellman, Harold 1927- CANR-10
Earlier sketch in CA 25-28R
See also SATA 4
Hellman, Hugo E. 1908- CAP-2
Earlier sketch in CA 19-20
Hellman, John 1940- 129
Hellman, Judith Adler 1945- 113
Hellman, Lillian (Florence) 1906-1984 .... CANR-33
Obituary 112
Earlier sketch in CA 13-16R
See also AITN 1, 2
See also CLC 2, 4, 8, 14, 18, 34, 44, 52
See also DAM DRAM
See also DC 1
See also DLB 7
See also DLBY 84
See also MTCW 1
Hellman, Peter 1943- 107
Hellman, Robert 1919-1984 .... 17-20R
Obituary 113
Hellman, Stephen 1943- 144
Hellmann, Anna 1902(?)-1972 Obituary 33-36R
Hellmann, Donald C(harles) 1933- CANR-28
Earlier sketch in CA 45-48
Hellmann, Ellen 1908- 106
Hellmann, John 1948- CANR-24
Earlier sketch in CA 105
Hellmuth, Jerome 1911- 13-16R
Hellmuth, William Frederick, Jr. 1920- CANR-4
Earlier sketch in CA 1-4R
Hellstrom, Ward 1930- 33-36R
Hellwig, Johann 1609-1674 .... DLB 164
Hellwig, Monika Konrad 1929- 37-40R
Helly, Dorothy O. 1931- 122
Hellyer, A(rthur) G(eorge) L(ee) 1902-1993 ....
CANR-19
Obituary 140
Earlier sketches in CA 9-12R, CANR-4
Hellyer, Arthur
See Hellyer, A(rthur) G(eorge) L(ee)
Hellyer, Clement David 1914- 118
Hellyer, David Tirrell 1913- 17-20R
Hellyer, Jill 1925- 118
Hellyer, Paul (Theodore) 1923- CANR-48
Earlier sketches in CA 69-72, CANR-14
Helm, Bertrand P. 1929- 37-40R
Helm, Ernest Eugene 1928- CANR-2
Earlier sketch in CA 1-4R
Helm, Everett 1913- 49-52
Helm, Levon 1940- 146
Helm, P(eter) J(ames) 1916- CANR-3
Earlier sketch in CA 9-12R
Helm, Robert Meredith 1917- 17-20R
Helm, Thomas (William) 1919- 5-8R
Helmer, Diana Star 1962- 151
See also SATA 86
Helmer, John 1946- 41-44R
Helmer, William F. 1926- 33-36R
Helmer, William J(oseph) 1936- 73-76
Helmericks, Bud
See Helmericks, Harmon R.
Helmericks, Constance (Chittenden)
1918-1987 .... 9-12R
Obituary 122
Helmericks, Harmon R. 1917- 29-32R
Helmering, Doris Wild 1942- 65-68
Helmers, George Dow 1906- 61-64
Helmholz, R(ichard) H(enry) 1940- CANR-29
Earlier sketch in CA 61-64
Helmi, Jack
See Sands, Leo G(eorge)
Helming, Ann 1924-(?) CANR-2
Earlier sketch in CA 1-4R
Helminiak, Daniel A. 1942- 126
Helminski, Camille Adams 1951- 140
Helmker, Judith Anne 1940- 33-36R
Helmlinger, (Benita) Trudy 1943- 69-72
Helmore, G(eoffrey) A(nthony) 1922- 29-32R
Helm-Pirgo, Marian 1897- 77-80
Helmreich, Ernst C(hristian) 1902- CANR-46
Earlier sketch in CA 1-4R
Helmreich, Jonathan Ernst 1936- Brief entry 105
Helmreich, Paul C(hristian) 1933- 53-56
Helmreich, Robert Louis 1937- 65-68
Helmreich, William B. 1945- 105
Helms, Alan 1937- 151
Helms, Christine Moss 129
Helms, Jesse (Alexander, Jr.) 1921- 152
Brief entry 124
Helms, Mary W. 1938- 151
Helms, Randel 1942- CANR-48
Earlier sketch in CA 49-52
Helms, Robert B(rake) 1940- 148
Helms, Roland Thomas, Jr. 1940- 102
Helms, Tom
See Helms, Roland Thomas, Jr.
Helmstadter, Gerald C. 1925- 13-16R
Heloise
See Reese, Heloise (Bowles)
Helper, Rose 77-80
Helpern, Milton 1902-1977 73-76
Obituary 69-72
Helprin, Mark 1947- CANR-64
Earlier sketches in CA 81-84, CANR-47
See also CLC 7, 10, 22, 32
See also DAM NOV, POP
See also DLBY 85
See also MTCW 1
Helps, Racey 1913-1971 .... CAP-2
Obituary 29-32R
Earlier sketch in CA 23-24
See also SATA 2
See also SATA-Obit 25
Helson, Harry 1898- CAP-1
Earlier sketch in CA 11-12
Helterman, Jeffrey A. 1942- 103
Helton, David (Kirby) 1940- 25-28R
Helton, Tinsley 1915- 1-4R
Helvarg, David 1951- 146
Helvick, James
See Cockburn, (Francis) Claud
Helweg, Hans H. 1917- 126
See also SATA 50
See also SATA-Brief 33
Helwig, David (Gordon) 1938- CANR-43
Earlier sketch in CA 33-36R
See also DLB 60
Helwig, Maggie
See Helwig, Sarah Magdalen
Helwig, Sarah Magdalen 1961- 130
Helyar, Jane Penelope Josephine 1933- CANR-26
Earlier sketches in CA 21-24R, CANR-10
See also Poole, Josephine
See also SATA 82
Helyar, John 1951- 140
See also BEST 90:3
Hemans, Felicia 1793-1835 .... DLB 96
Hembree, Charles R. 1938- 33-36R
Hembry, Phyllis (May) 1916- 136
Hemdahl, Reuel Gustaf 1903-1977 .... 37-40R
Hemel Dobkin, Kathleen
See Hamel Peifer, Kathleen
Hemenway, Robert 1921- 33-36R
Hemenway, Ruby 1884(?)-1987 Obituary 123
Hemery, Eric 1914- 111
Hemesath, Caroline 1899- 61-64
Hemeze
See Caballero, Manuel
Hemeze, Sebastian
See Caballero, Manuel
Hemings, T. J.
See Reiter, Victoria (Kelrich)
Hemington, Judith 1949- 129
Hemingway, Ernest (Miller) 1899-1961 .... CANR-34
Earlier sketch in CA 77-80
See also AAYA 19
See also CDALB 1917-1929
See also CLC 1, 3, 6, 8, 10, 13, 19, 30, 34, 39, 41, 44, 50, 61, 80
See also DA
See also DAB
See also DAC
See also DAM MST, NOV
See also DLB 4, 9, 102
See also DLBD 1, 15, 16
See also DLBY 81, 87, 96
See also MTCW 1
See also SSC 1, 25
See also WLC
Hemingway, Gregory H. 1931(?)- Brief entry 112
Hemingway, Leicester C. 1915-1982 Obituary 107
Hemingway, Lorian 1951- 141
Hemingway, Maggie 1946-1993 .... CANR-47
Obituary 141
Earlier sketch in CA 125
Hemingway, Mary Welsh 1908-1986 73-76
Obituary 121
Hemingway, Patricia Drake 1926-1978 69-72
Obituary 73-76
Hemingway, Taylor
See Rywell, Martin
Heminway, John (H., Jr.) 1944- 25-28R
Hemleben, Sylvester John 1902- CAP-2
Earlier sketch in CA 25-28
Hemley, Cecil Herbert 1914-1966 .... CANR-1
Obituary 25-28R
Earlier sketch in CA 1-4R
Hemley, Elaine Gottlieb
See Gottlieb, Elaine
Hemley, Robin 1958- 130
Hemlow, Joyce 1906- 5-8R
Hemmant, Lynette 1938- .... SATA 69
Hemmerechts, Kristien 1955- 133
Hemming, (Laurence) Charles 1950- 132
Hemming, John (Henry) 1935- CANR-12
Earlier sketch in CA 29-32R
Hemming, Roy G. 1928-1995 61-64
Obituary 149
See also SATA 11
See also SATA-Obit 86
Hemmings, F(rederic) W(illiam) J(ohn) 1920- ....
CANR-58
Earlier sketches in CA 97-100, CANR-27
Hemmings, Susan 1941- 118
Hemon, Louis 1880-1913 150
See also DAC
See also DLB 92
Hempel, Amy 1951- CANR-70
Brief entry 118
Earlier sketch in CA 137
See also CLC 39
Hempel, Carl G.
See Hempel, Carl Gustav
Hempel, Carl Gustav 1905-1998 Obituary 162
Brief entry 116
Hemphill, A. Marcus 1930(?)-1986 Obituary 120
Hemphill, Betty
See Hemphill, Elizabeth Anne
Hemphill, Charles F., Jr. 1917- 101
Hemphill, Christopher (Glenn)
1950-1987 Obituary 122
Hemphill, Elizabeth Anne 1920- 115
Hemphill, Essex 1956(?)- 153
See also BW 2
Hemphill, George 1922- 13-16R
Hemphill, Herbert Waide, Jr. 1929-1998 116
Obituary 167
Hemphill, John K(nox) 1919- 53-56
Hemphill, Kenneth S. 1948- 134
Hemphill, Martha Locke 1904-1973 .... 37-40R
See also SATA 37
Hemphill, Paul 1936- CANR-55
Earlier sketches in CA 49-52, CANR-12, 29
See also AITN 2
See also DLBY 87
Hemphill, W(illiam) Edwin 1912- 21-24R
Hempstone, Smith 1929- CANR-1
Earlier sketch in CA 1-4R
Hempton, David 1952- 125
Hemschemeyer, Judith 1935- 49-52
Hen, Yitzhak 1963- 154
Henaghan, Jim 1919- 102
Henahan, Donal 1921- Brief entry 111
Henault, Gilles 1920- .... DLB 88
Henault, Marie (Josephine) 1921- 33-36R
Henba, Bobbie 1926- .... SATA 87
Henbest, Nigel 1951- CANR-53
Earlier sketch in CA 124
See also SATA 55
See also SATA-Brief 52

Henbos
See Bosch, Henry G(erard)
Hench, John B(ixler) 1943- ... 131
Henchman, Daniel 1689-1761 ... DLB 24
Hencken, Hugh O'Neill 1902-1981 Obituary ... 104
Hendee, John C(lare) 1938- ... 93-96
Hendel, Charles William 1890-1982 ... CANR-13
Obituary ... 108
Earlier sketches in CAP-1, CA 13-16
Hendel, Samuel 1909-1984 ... CANR-1
Obituary ... 113
Earlier sketch in CA 1-4R
Hendelson, William H. 1904-1975 Obituary ... 104
Henderley, Brooks ... CANR-26
Earlier sketches in CAP-2, CA 19-20
See also SATA 1
Henderlite, Rachel 1905- ... 1-4R
Hendershot, Ralph 1896(?)-1979 Obituary ... 89-92
Henderson, Alexander (John) 1910- ... CAP-1
Earlier sketch in CA 13-16
Henderson, Algo D(onmyer) 1897-1988 ... CANR-1
Obituary ... 126
Earlier sketch in CA 1-4R
Henderson, Alice Corbin 1881-1949 ... DLB 54
Henderson, Archibald 1877-1963 Obituary ... 93-96
See also DLB 103
Henderson, Archibald 1916- ... 53-56
Henderson, Bert C. 1904- ... CAP-1
Earlier sketch in CA 9-10
Henderson, Bill
See Henderson, William Charles
Henderson, Brian 1941- ... 112
Henderson, Bruce B. 1946- ... 139
Henderson, C(rispin) A(listair) P(oland) 1955- ... 119
Henderson, C(elia) Nell 1959- ... 135
Henderson, C(harles) William 1925- ... 65-68
Henderson, Charles, Jr. 1923- ... 45-48
Henderson, Charles P(ackard), Jr. 1941- ... 41-44R
Henderson, Charles W(illiam) 1948- ... 135
Henderson, Dan Fenno 1921- ... 17-20R
Henderson, David 1942- ... CANR-10
Earlier sketch in CA 25-28R
See also BW 1
See also DLB 41
Henderson, Dion (Winslow) 1921-1984 ... CANR-5
Obituary ... 114
Earlier sketch in CA 9-12R
Henderson, Donald
See Laughlin, Tom
Henderson, Dwight F. 1937- ... 41-44R
Henderson, Edwin Bancroft
1883-1977 Obituary ... 116
Henderson, Eva Pendleton 1890- ... 115
Henderson, F. C.
See Mencken, H(enry) L(ouis)
Henderson, G. D. S.
See Henderson, George (David Smith)
Henderson, G(eorge) P(atrick) 1915- ... 29-32R
Henderson, G(eorge) P(oland) 1920- ... 37-40R
Henderson, George (David Smith) 1931- . CANR-27
Earlier sketch in CA 25-28R
Henderson, George L(eslie) 1925- ... 69-72
Henderson, George Wylie 1904- ... 125
See also BW 1
See also DLB 51
Henderson, Gordon 1950- ... SATA 53
Henderson, Hamish 1919- ... 153
Henderson, Harold 1948- ... 148
Henderson, Harold G(ould)
1889-1974 Obituary ... 53-56
Henderson, Harold H(ale) 1928- ... 114
Henderson, Harry B(rinton), Jr. 1914- Brief
entry ... 109
Henderson, Hazel 1933- ... 129
Henderson, Ian 1910-1969 ... CAP-2
Earlier sketch in CA 17-18
Henderson, Isabel 1933- ... 25-28R
Henderson, James 1934- ... CANR-13
Earlier sketch in CA 33-36R
Henderson, James Youngblood 1944- ... 110
Henderson, Jean Carolyn Glidden 1916- ... 102
Henderson, Jennifer 1929- ... 107
Henderson, John 1906(?)-1982 Obituary ... 108
Henderson, John 1915- ... 5-8R
Henderson, John S(teele) 1919- ... 5-8R
Henderson, John W(illiam) 1910- ... 25-28R
Henderson, K(enneth) D(avid) D(ruitt) 1903- . CAP-1
Earlier sketch in CA 13-16
Henderson, Katherine Usher 1937- ... 126
Henderson, Kathy 1949- ... CANR-67
Earlier sketch in CA 123
See also SATA 55, 95
See also SATA-Brief 53
Henderson, (Alan) Keith 1883-1982 ... 107
Obituary ... 106
Henderson, Keith M. 1934- ... 21-24R
Henderson, Laurance G.
1924(?)-1977 Obituary ... 73-76
Henderson, Laurence 1928- ... 53-56
Henderson, Lawrence W. 1921- ... 103
Henderson, LeGrand 1901-1965 ... 5-8R
See also SATA 9
Henderson, Linda Dalrymple 1948- ... 124
Henderson, Lois T(hompson) 1918- ... 81-84
Henderson, M(arilyn) R(uth) 1927- ... CANR-27
Henderson, Mary
See Mavor, Osborne Henry
Henderson, Mary C. 1928- ... 77-80
Henderson, (Andrew) Maxwell 1908- ... 132
Henderson, Michael (Douglas) 1932- ... CANR-52
Earlier sketches in CA 110, CANR-27
Henderson, Monika 1954- ... 129
Henderson, Nancy 1943- ... 41-44R
Henderson, Nancy Wallace 1916- ... 97-100
See also SATA 22
Henderson, (John) Nicholas 1919- ... 132
Henderson, Paul (III) 1939- Brief entry ... 122
Henderson, Paul III 1939- ... 144
Henderson, Peter 1904-1983 ... 108
Obituary ... 111
Henderson, Philip (Prichard) 1906-1977 .. CANR-14
Obituary ... 104
Earlier sketches in CAP-1, CA 9-10
Henderson, Randall 1888- ... CAP-1
Earlier sketch in CA 13-14
Henderson, Richard 1924- ... CANR-20
Earlier sketches in CA 13-16R, CANR-5
Henderson, Richard B(eveir) 1921- ... 77-80
Henderson, Richard I(van) 1926- ... CANR-11
Earlier sketch in CA 69-72
Henderson, Robert 1906- ... 106
Henderson, Robert M. 1926- ... 33-36R
Henderson, Robert W(augh) 1920- ... 1-4R
Henderson, Robert William
1888-1985 Obituary ... 117
Henderson, S(hirley) P(rudence) A(nn)
1929- ... 37-40R
Henderson, Stephen E. 1925- ... 29-32R
See also BW 1
Henderson, Sylvia
See Ashton-Warner, Sylvia (Constance)
Henderson, Thomas W(alter) 1949- ... 73-76
Henderson, Vivian (Wilson) 1923-1976 ... 65-68
Obituary ... 61-64
Henderson, W(illiam) O(tto) 1904- ... CANR-4
Earlier sketch in CA 1-4R
Henderson, William III 1922- ... 17-20R
Henderson, William Charles 1941- ... CANR-48
Henderson, William Darryl 1938- ... 140
Henderson, William L(eroy) 1927- ... 33-36R
Henderson, William McCranor 1943- ... CANR-72
Earlier sketch in CA 143
Henderson, Zenna (Chlarson) 1917-1983 . CANR-1
Obituary ... 133
Earlier sketch in CA 1-4R
See also DLB 8
See also SATA 5
See also SSC 29
Henderson-Howat, Gerald
See Howat, Gerald Malcolm David
Hendin, David (Bruce) 1945- ... 41-44R
Hendin, Herbert (Martin) 1926- ... 129
Brief entry ... 117
Hendin, Josephine 1946- ... 102
Hendley, Coit (Taylor), Jr. 1920-1985 Obituary . 116
Hendon, William S(cott) 1933- ... CANR-35
Earlier sketch in CA 45-48
Hendra, Tony 1941(?)- ... CANR-44
Earlier sketch in CA 102
Hendren, Ron 1945- ... 77-80
Hendrich, Paula Griffith 1928- ... CANR-1
Earlier sketch in CA 1-4R
Hendrick, George 1929- ... CANR-23
Earlier sketches in CA 13-16R, CANR-8
Hendrick, Irving G(uilford) 1936- ... 81-84
Hendrick, Ives 1898-1972 ... CAP-1
Obituary ... 33-36R
Earlier sketch in CA 11-12
Hendrick, T(homas) W(illiam) 1909- ... 108
Hendricks, Faye N(eidhold) 1913- ... 69-72
Hendricks, Frances Wade Kellam 1900- ... 37-40R
Hendricks, Gay 1945- ... 73-76
Hendricks, George D. 1913- ... 5-8R
Hendricks, J(ames) Edwin 1935- ... CANR-34
Earlier sketches in CA 41-44R, CANR-15
Hendricks, Robert J(oseph) 1944- ... 45-48
Hendricks, Vicki (Due) 1951- ... 154
Hendricks, Walter 1892-1979 Obituary ... 103
Hendricks, William Lawrence 1929- ... CANR-17
Earlier sketches in CA 49-52, CANR-2
Hendrickson, David C. 1953- ... 126
Hendrickson, Donald E(ugene) 1941- ... 93-96
Hendrickson, James E. 1932- ... 21-24R
Hendrickson, Paul 1944- ... CANR-66
Earlier sketch in CA 108
Hendrickson, Robert 1933- ... CANR-1
Earlier sketch in CA 49-52
Hendrickson, Robert A(ugustus) 1923-1996 ...
CANR-12
Obituary ... 155
Earlier sketch in CA 29-32R
Hendrickson, Walter Brookfield, Jr. 1936- . CANR-1
Earlier sketch in CA 1-4R
See also SATA 9
Hendrie, Don(ald Franz), Jr. 1942- ... CANR-18
Earlier sketches in CA 49-52, CANR-3
Hendriks, A(rthur) L(emiere) 1922- ... 97-100
Hendriksen, Eldon Sende 1917- ... 13-16R
Hendrix, Harville 1935- ... 130
Hendry, Allan 1950- ... 106
Hendry, Diana 1941- ... 136
See also SATA 68
Hendry, J(ames) F(indlay) 1912- ... 29-32R
Hendry, John (Lovat) 1952- ... 136
Hendry, Joy (McLaggan) 1953- ... 133
Hendry, Linda (Gail) 1961- ... SATA 83
Hendry, Thomas 1929- ... 69-72
Hendry, Tom
See Hendry, Thomas
Hendy, M(ichael) F(rank) 1942- ... 137
Hendy, Philip (Anstiss) 1900-1980 Obituary ... 102
Henegan, Lucius Herbert, Jr.
1902(?)-1979 Obituary ... 85-88
Heneghan, James 1930- ... 129
See also SATA 97
Heneman, Herbert Gerhard, Jr. 1916- ... CANR-1
Earlier sketch in CA 1-4R
Henfil
See Souza Filho, Henrique de
Henfrey, Colin (Vere Fleetwood) 1941- ... 13-16R
Henfrey, Norman 1929- ... 25-28R
Henggeler, Paul R. 1955- ... 149
Henggeler, Scott Walter 1950- ... 144
Henig, Gerald S(heldon) 1942- ... 57-60
Henig, Martin (Edward) 1942- ... 114
Henig, Robin Marantz 1953- ... 108
Henig, Ruth B(eatrice) 1943- ... 49-52
Henig, Suzanne 1936- ... CANR-2
Earlier sketch in CA 45-48
Henige, David 1938- ... CANR-39
Earlier sketch in CA 103
Heninger, S(imeon) K(ahn), Jr. 1922- ... CANR-1
Earlier sketch in CA 1-4R
Henisch, Bridget Ann 1932- ... CANR-56
Earlier sketch in CA 127
Henisch, Heinz K. 1922- ... CANR-70
Earlier sketch in CA 73-76
Henisch, Peter 1943- ... DLB 85
Henissart, Paul 1923- ... 29-32R
Henke, Dan (Ferdinand) 1924- ... 53-56
Henke, Emerson O(verbeck) 1916- ... CANR-12
Earlier sketch in CA 17-20R
Henkel, Barbara Osborn 1921- ... 9-12R
Henkel, Stephen C. 1933- ... 37-40R
Henkels, Robert M(acAllister), Jr. 1936- ... 57-60
Henkes, Kevin 1960- ... CANR-38
Earlier sketch in CA 114
See also CLR 23
See also MAICYA
See also SATA 43, 76
Henkes, Robert 1922- ... CANR-54
Earlier sketches in CA 33-36R, CANR-13, 29
Henkin, Harmon 1940(?)-1980 Obituary ... 101
Henkin, Joshua ... 161
Henkin, Louis 1917- ... CANR-13
Earlier sketch in CA 33-36R
Henkle, Roger B. 1935- ... 129
Henle, Faye (?)-1972 Obituary ... 37-40R
Henle, Fritz 1909-1993 ... 73-76
Obituary ... 140
Henle, James 1891(?)-1973 Obituary ... 37-40R
Henle, Jane 1913- ... 77-80
Henle, Mary 1913- ... 33-36R
Henle, Robert John 1909- ... 110
Henle, Theda O. 1918- ... 33-36R
Henley, Arthur 1921- ... 21-24R
Henley, Beth
See Henley, Elizabeth Becker
See also CABS 3
See also CLC 23
See also DC 6
See also DLBY 86
Henley, Elizabeth Becker 1952- ... CANR-32
Earlier sketch in CA 107
See also Henley, Beth
See also DAM DRAM, MST
See also MTCW 1
Henley, Gail 1952- ... CANR-21
Earlier sketch in CA 89-92
Henley, Karyn 1952- ... 102
Henley, Nancy Eloise Main 1934- Brief entry ... 106
Henley, Norman 1915- ... 17-20R
Henley, Virginia 1935- ... CANR-41
Earlier sketch in CA 109
Henley, W(illiam) Ballentine 1905- ... 61-64
Henley, Wallace (Boynton) 1941- ... CANR-14
Earlier sketch in CA 65-68
Henley, William Ernest 1849-1903 Brief entry .. 105
See also DLB 19
See also TCLC 8
Henn, Harry George 1919-1994 ... CANR-36
Obituary ... 147
Earlier sketch in CA 45-48
Henn, Henry
See Henn, Harry George
Henn, Thomas Rice 1901-1974 ... CANR-4
Earlier sketch in CA 5-8R
Hennacy, Ammon 1893-1970 Obituary ... 104
Henne, Frances E. 1906-1985 Obituary ... 118
Hennedy, Hugh L(ouis) 1929- ... 41-44R
Henneman, John Bell, Jr. 1935- ... CANR-57
Earlier sketches in CA 45-48, CANR-31
Hennesey, James J. 1926- ... 33-36R
Hennessey, Caroline
See von Block, Bela W(illiam)
and von Block, Sylvia
Hennessey, R(oger) A(nthony) S(ean)
1937- ... 29-32R
Hennessy, Bernard C. 1924- ... 13-16R
Hennessy, David James George 1932- ... CANR-22
Earlier sketch in CA 106
Hennessy, James Pope
See Pope-Hennessy, James
Hennessy, John J(oseph) 1958- ... 141
Hennessy, Jossleyn (Michael Stephen Philip)
1903- ... 9-12R
Hennessy, Mary L. 1927- ... 21-24R
Hennessy, Max
See Harris, John
Hennessy, Peter 1947- ... 123
Hennessy, Thomas C(hristopher) 1916- ... 115
Henney, Carolee Wells 1928- ... SATA 102
Hennig, Margaret (Marie) 1940- ... 81-84
Henniker, Florence 1855-1923 ... DLB 135
Henning, Ann 1948- ... 156
See also SATA 92
Henning, Basil Duke 1910-1990 Obituary ... 130
Henning, Charles N(athaniel) 1915- ... CANR-49
Earlier sketch in CA 1-4R
Henning, Daniel H(oward) 1931- ... CANR-2
Earlier sketch in CA 45-48
Henning, Edward B(urk) 1922-1993 ... CANR-49
Obituary ... 141
Earlier sketch in CA 17-20R
Henning, Standish 1932- Brief entry ... 107
Henning, Sylvie Marie Debevec
See Debevec Henning, Sylvie Marie
Henninger, G. Ross 1898-1984 Obituary ... 112
Hennings, Dorothy Grant 1935- ... CANR-4
Earlier sketch in CA 53-56
Hennings, Josephine Silva
1899(?)-1985 Obituary ... 117
Hennissart, Martha ... CANR-64
Earlier sketch in CA 85-88
See also Lathen, Emma
Henrey, Madeleine 1906- ... CANR-6
Earlier sketch in CA 13-16R
Henrey, Mrs. Robert
See Henrey, Madeleine
Henrey, Robert
See Henrey, Madeleine
Henri, Adrian (Maurice) 1932- ... CANR-34
Earlier sketches in CA 25-28R, CANR-15
See also MTCW 1
Henri, Florette 1908-1985 ... 73-76
Obituary ... 117
Henri, G.
See Clement, George H.
Henrichsen, Walt(er Arlie), Jr. 1934- ... 89-92
Henricks, Kaw
See Wolfe, Charles Keith
Henricksson, John 1926- ... 163
Henries, A. Doris Banks 1913(?)-1981 ... 125
Obituary ... 103
See also BW 1
Henries, Doris
See Henries, A. Doris Banks
Henriksen, Louise Levitas 1917- ... 128
Henriksen, Thomas H(ollinger) 1939- ... 112
Henrikson, Arthur A. 1921- ... 130
Henriod, Lorraine 1925- ... CANR-47
Earlier sketch in CA 45-48
See also SATA 26
Henriques, Veronica 1931- ... 102
Henriquez, Emile F. 1937- ... SATA 89
Henry, Alexander 1739-1824 ... DLB 99
Henry, Avril (Kay) 1935- ... 123
Henry, Bessie Walker 1921- ... 9-12R
Henry, Bill
See Henry, William Mellors
Henry, Buck 1930- ... 77-80
See also DLB 26
Henry, Carl F(erdinand) H(oward) 1913- . CANR-46
Earlier sketches in CA 13-16R, CANR-6, 21
Henry, (William) Claud 1914- ... 45-48
Henry, Daniel
See Kahnweiler, Daniel-Henry
Henry, David Dodds 1905-1995 ... 106
Obituary ... 149
Henry, David Lee
See Hill, R. Lance
Henry, Desmond Paul 1921- ... 132
Henry, DeWitt (Pawling II) 1941- ... 131
Henry, Eric P(utnam) 1943- ... 108
Henry, Faith
See Levine, Nancy D.
Henry, Fran Worden 1948- ... 111
Henry, Frances 1931- ... 77-80
Henry, Francoise 1902-1982 Obituary ... 106
Henry, Gordon D., Jr. 1955- ... 146
Henry, Harold Wilkinson 1926- ... 37-40R
Henry, Harriet
See De Steuch, Harriet Henry
Henry, James P(aget) 1914- ... 104
Henry, James S(helburne) 1950- ... 49-52
Henry, Janet Cope 1925(?)-1986 Obituary ... 118
Henry, Jeanne Heffernan 1940- ... 105
Henry, Joanne Landers 1927- ... 17-20R
See also SATA 6
Henry, John Case 1905-1990 Obituary ... 132
Henry, Joseph B. 1901- ... CAP-2
Earlier sketch in CA 17-18
Henry, Jules 1904-1969 Obituary ... 109
Henry, Kenneth 1920- ... 57-60
Henry, Laurin L(uther) 1921- ... CANR-43
Earlier sketch in CA 1-4R
Henry, Maeve 1960- ... 142
See also SATA 75
Henry, Marguerite 1902-1997 ... CANR-9
Obituary ... 162
Earlier sketch in CA 17-20R
See also CLR 4
See also DLB 22
See also JRDA
See also MAICYA
See also SAAS 7
See also SATA 100
See also SATA-Obit 99
Henry, Marie H. 1935- ... SATA 65
Henry, Marion
See del Rey, Lester
Henry, O.
See Porter, William Sydney
See also SSC 5
See also TCLC 1, 19
See also WLC
Henry, Oliver
See Porter, William Sydney
Henry, Patrick 1940- ... 145
Henry, Peter 1926- ... 109
Henry, Robert Selph 1889-1970 ... CANR-17
Obituary ... 103
Earlier sketch in CA 1-4R
See also DLB 17
Henry, Shirley 1925(?)-1972 Obituary ... 33-36R
Henry, Sondra 1930- ... CANR-49
Earlier sketch in CA 119
Henry, Stuart (Dennis) 1949- ... 143
Henry, T. E.
See Rowland-Entwistle, (Arthur) Theodore (Henry)
Henry, Vera 1909(?)-1987 ... CAP-2
Obituary ... 123
Earlier sketch in CA 21-22
Henry, W. P. 1929- ... 17-20R

Henry, Will
See Allen, Henry Wilson
Henry, William A(lfred) III 1950-1994 .... CANR-65
  Obituary 146
  Brief entry 116
  Earlier sketch in CA 130
Henry, William Earl 1917- Brief entry 108
Henry, William Mellors 1890-1970 Obituary . 89-92
Henry of Ghent 1217(?)-1293 .... DLB 115
Henryson, Robert 1430(?)-1506(?) ...... DLB 146
Henry VIII of England 1491-1547 .... DLB 132
Henschel, Elizabeth Georgie 107
  See also SATA 56
Henschke, Alfred
See Klabund
Hensey, Frederick G(erald) 1931- 89-92
Hensey, Fritz
See Hensey, Frederick G(erald)
Henshall, A(udrey) S(hore) 1927- 9-12R
Henshaw, James Ene 1924- 101
  See also BW 2
Henshaw, Richard 1945- 101
Henshaw, Tom 1924- 103
Henshel, Richard L(ee) 1939- 57-60
Hensley, Charles S(tanley) 1919- 41-44R
Hensley, Jeff (Lane) 1947- 117
Hensley, Joe L.
See Hensley, Joseph Louis
Hensley, Joseph Louis 1926- CANR-62
  Earlier sketches in CA 33-36R, CANR-14, 31, 57
  See also Hensley, Joe L.
Hensley, Sophie Almon 1866-1946 .... DLB 99
Hensley, (Malcolm) Stewart
  1914(?)-1976 Obituary 65-68
Henslin, James M(arvin) 1937- CANR-34
  Earlier sketches in CA 41-44R, CANR-15
Henson, Beth 1950- 148
Henson, Clyde E(ugene) 1914- 5-8R
Henson, James Maury 1936-1990 124
  Obituary 131
  Brief entry 106
  See also SATA 43
  See also SATA-Obit 65
Henson, Jim
See Henson, James Maury
Henson, Lance 1944- 146
  See also DLB 175
  See also NNAL
Henson, Margaret Swett 1924- CANR-50
  Earlier sketch in CA 122
Henstell, Bruce 1945- 131
Henstell, Diana
See Silber, Diana
Henstra, Friso 1928- .... SAAS 14
  See also SATA 8, 73
Henthorn, William E(llsworth) 1928- 41-44R
Hentoff, Nat(han Irving) 1925- CANR-25
  Earlier sketches in CA 1-4R, CANR-5
  Interview in CANR-25
  See also CAAS 6
  See also AAYA 4
  See also CLC 26
  See also CLR 1, 52
  See also JRDA
  See also MAICYA
  See also SATA 42, 69
  See also SATA-Brief 27
Henty, G(eorge) A(lfred) 1832-1902 Brief entry . 112
  See also DLB 18, 141
  See also SATA 64
Hentz, Caroline Lee (Whiting) 1800-1856 .... DLB 3
Henwood, James N. J. 1932- 29-32R
Henze, Donald F(rank) 1928- 21-24R
Heo, Yumi 159
  See also SATA 94
Hepburn, Andrew H. 1899(?)-1975 Obituary . 57-60
Hepburn, James Gordon 1922- CANR-29
  Earlier sketch in CA 85-88
Hepburn, Katharine (Houghton) 1909- 139
Hepburn, Ronald W(illiam) 1927- 13-16R
Heper, Metin 1940- 156
Hepner, Harry W(alker) 1893-1984 ...... 29-32R
  Obituary 114
Hepner, James O(rville) 1933- 57-60
Heppenheimer, T(homas) A(dolph) 1947- ....
  CANR-16
  Earlier sketch in CA 93-96
Heppenstall, Margit Strom 1913- 21-24R
Heppenstall, (John) Rayner 1911-1981 .. CANR-29
  Obituary 103
  Earlier sketch in CA 1-4R
  See also CLC 10
Hepple, Alex 1904(?)-1983 Obituary 111
Hepple, Bob (Alexander) 1934- CANR-12
  Earlier sketch in CA 29-32R
Hepple, Peter 1927- 81-84
Heppner, Cheryl M. 1951- 142
Heppner, Ernest G. 1921- 149
Heppner, P(uncky) Paul 1951- 141
Heppner, Sam(uel) 1913-1983 .... 25-28R
  Obituary 109
Hepworth, James B. 1910- 1-4R
Hepworth, James Michael 1938- CANR-13
  Earlier sketch in CA 73-76
Hepworth, Mike
See Hepworth, James Michael
Hepworth, (Charles) Philip 1912- 17-20R
Her
See Deal, Borden
Heraclitus c. 540B.C.-c. 450B.C. .... DLB 176
Herail, Rene James 1939- 118
Herald, Earl Stannard 1914-1973 Obituary . 112
Herald, George William 1911- 73-76
Herald, Kathleen
See Peyton, Kathleen Wendy
Heraud, Brian J(eremy) 1934- 73-76

Heraud, Javier 1942-1963 131
  See also HW
Heravi, Mehdi 1940- 29-32R
Herb, Angela M. 1970- 156
  See also SATA 92
Herber, Bernard P. 1929- 21-24R
Herber, Harold L. 1929- 108
Herber, Lewis
See Bookchin, Murray
Herberg, Will 1909-1977 73-76
  Obituary 69-72
Herberger, Charles F. 1920- 41-44R
Herbers, John N. 1923- 33-36R
Herbert, A(lan) P(atrick) 1890-1971 97-100
  Obituary 33-36R
  See also DLB 10, 191
Herbert, Agnes c. 1880-1960 .... DLB 174
Herbert, Anthony B(ernard) 1930- 77-80
Herbert, Arthur
See Shappiro, Herbert Arthur
Herbert, Brian 1947- 133
Herbert, Cecil
See Hamilton, Charles (Harold St. John)
Herbert, Cynthia Ridgeway 1943- 118
Herbert, David (Alexander Reginald)
  1908-1995 141
  Obituary 148
Herbert, David T(homas) 1935- CANR-40
  Earlier sketches in CA 49-52, CANR-2, 18
Herbert, Don(ald Jeffrey) 1917- CANR-30
  Earlier sketch in CA 29-32R
  See also SATA 2
Herbert, Edward 1583-1648 .... DLB 121, 151
Herbert, Eugenia W(arren) 1929- CANR-35
  Earlier sketch in CA 93-96
Herbert, Frank (Patrick) 1920-1986 .... CANR-43
  Obituary 118
  Earlier sketches in CA 53-56, CANR-5
  Interview in CANR-5
  See also AAYA 21
  See also CLC 12, 23, 35, 44, 85
  See also DAM POP
  See also DLB 8
  See also MTCW 1
  See also SATA 9, 37
  See also SATA-Obit 47
Herbert, George 1593-1633 ... CDBLB Before 1660
  See also DAB
  See also DAM POET
  See also DLB 126
  See also PC 4
Herbert, Gilbert 1924- CANR-47
  Earlier sketches in CA 107, CANR-23
Herbert, Helen (Jean) 1947- .... SATA 57
Herbert, Henry George Alfred Marius Victor Francis
  1898-1987 Obituary 123
Herbert, Henry William 1807-1858 ..... DLB 3, 73
Herbert, Ian 1939- 111
Herbert, (Edward) Ivor (Montgomery) 1925- ......
  CANR-19
  Earlier sketches in CA 53-56, CANR-4
Herbert, James 1943- 81-84
Herbert, Jean (Daniel Fernand) 1897-1980 ....
  CANR-9
  Earlier sketch in CA 17-20R
Herbert, John
See Brundage, John Herbert
  See also DLB 53
Herbert, John (David) 1924- CANR-13
  Earlier sketch in CA 21-24R
Herbert, Kevin (Barry John) 1921- 17-20R
Herbert, Marie 1941- 69-72
Herbert, Martin 1933- 103
Herbert, Miranda C(arleton) 1950- 97-100
Herbert, Nick 1936- 128
Herbert, Robert L(ouis) 1929- CANR-36
  Earlier sketches in CA 9-12R, CANR-5
Herbert, Sandra (Swanson) 1942- 130
Herbert, Stephen 153
Herbert, Theodore T(erence) 1942- CANR-15
  Earlier sketch in CA 65-68
Herbert, Thomas Walter, Jr. 1938- 104
Herbert, Victor 1927- 112
Herbert, Wally
See Herbert, Walter William
Herbert, Walter William 1934- CANR-15
  Earlier sketch in CA 69-72
  See also SATA 23
Herbert, William 1580-1630 .... DLB 121
Herbert, (Alfred Francis) Xavier 1901-1984 ....
  CANR-46
  Obituary 114
  Earlier sketch in CA 69-72
Herbert, Zbigniew 1924- CANR-36
  Earlier sketch in CA 89-92
  See also CLC 9, 43
  See also DAM POET
  See also MTCW 1
Herbertson, Gary J. 1938- 25-28R
Herblock
See Block, Herbert (Lawrence)
Herbrand, Jan(ice M.) 1931- 49-52
Herbruck, Christine Comstock
See Comstock, Christine
Herbst, Anthony F(rancis) 1941- CANR-35
  Earlier sketch in CA 114
Herbst, Josephine (Frey) 1897-1969 .... 5-8R
  Obituary 25-28R
  See also CLC 34
  See also DLB 9
Herbst, Judith 1926- .... SATA 74
Herbst, Jurgen (F. H.) 1928- 37-40R
Herbst, Phil(ip H.) 1944- 160
Herbst, Robert L(eroy) 1935- 61-64
Herburger, Guenter 1932- .... DLB 75, 124

Hercules, Frank (E. M.) 1917-1996 .... CANR-2
  Obituary 152
  Earlier sketch in CA 1-4R
  See also BW 1
Herd, Dale 1940- 61-64
Herd, Michael 1937- 128
Herda, D. J. 1948- 147
  See also SATA 80
Herdan, Gustav 1897- 1-4R
Herdan, Innes 1911- 142
Herdeck, Donald E. 1924- 53-56
Herdeg, Klaus 1937- 130
Herder, Johann Gottfried von 1744-1803 .. DLB 97
Herding, Klaus 1939- 140
Herdt, Gilbert H(enry) 1949- 105
Herdt, Sheryll (Enette) Patterson 1941- . 57-60
Hereford, John
See Fletcher, H(arry) L(utf) V(erne)
Heren, Louis (Philip) 1919-1995 .... CANR-12
  Obituary 147
  Earlier sketch in CA 25-28R
Herf, Jeffrey 1947- 168
Herfindahl, Orris C(lemens) 1918-1972 . 41-44R
  Obituary 37-40R
Herford, Charles Harold 1853-1931 .... DLB 149
Herge
See Remi, Georges
Hergenhahn, B(aldwin) R(oss) 1934- 123
  Brief entry 118
Hergenhan, L(aurence) T(homas) 1931- . CANR-56
  Earlier sketch in CA 127
Hergenhan, Laurie
See Hergenhan, L(aurence) T(homas)
Hergesheimer, Joseph 1880-1954 Brief entry . 109
  See also DLB 102, 9
  See also TCLC 11
Herget, Paul 1908(?)-1981 Obituary 105
Herian, V.
See Gregorian, Vartan
Heriat, Philippe
See Payelle, Raymond-Gerard
Hering, Doris (Minnie) 1920- 128
Herington, C. J(ohn) 1924- CANR-15
  Earlier sketch in CA 29-32R
Heriot, Angus 1927- 5-8R
Heritage, Martin
See Horler, Sydney
Heriteau, Jacqueline 1925- CANR-37
  Earlier sketches in CA 45-48, CANR-1, 16
Herity, Michael 1929- 49-52
Herken, Gregg (Franklin) 1947- CANR-20
  Earlier sketch in CA 104
Herkimer, L(awrence) R(ussell) 1925(?)- ... 110
  See also SATA 42
Herlihy, David (Joseph) 1930-1991 .... 41-44R
  Obituary 133
Herlihy, Dirlie Anne 1935- .... SATA 73
Herlihy, James Leo 1927-1993 .... CANR-2
  Obituary 143
  Earlier sketch in CA 1-4R
  See also CLC 6
Herlin, Hans 1925-1994 77-80
  Obituary 147
Herling, Gustaw 1919- 158
Herling, John 1907- Brief entry 112
Herling-Grudzinski, Gustaw
See Herling, Gustaw
Herm, Gerhard 1931- CANR-45
  Earlier sketches in CA 104, CANR-22
Hermalyn, Gary 1952- CANR-50
  Earlier sketch in CA 123
Herman, A(rthur) L(udwig) 1930- 65-68
Herman, Barbara 1945- 145
Herman, Ben 1927- 104
Herman, Bernard L. 1951- 140
Herman, Charlotte 1937- CANR-34
  Earlier sketches in CA 41-44R, CANR-15
  See also SATA 20, 99
Herman, Didi 1961- 164
Herman, Donald L. 1928- CANR-29
  Earlier sketches in CA 53-56, CANR-4
Herman, Ellen 1957- 149
Herman, Esther 1935- 102
Herman, George E(dward) 1920- 69-72
Herman, George R(ichard) 1925- 5-8R
Herman, Jan (Jacob) 1942- CANR-60
  Earlier sketch in CA 45-48
Herman, John R(ufus) 1928- 119
Herman, Judith 1943- 49-52
Herman, Judith Lewis 142
Herman, Justin B. 1907(?)-1983 Obituary 111
Herman, Kenneth Neil 1954- 77-80
Herman, Louis Jay 1925-1996 53-56
  Obituary 152
Herman, Marguerite Shalett 1914-1977 ... 41-44R
Herman, Masako 103
Herman, Melvin (Jerome) 1922- Brief entry . 111
Herman, Melvin 1922(?)-1983 Obituary 109
Herman, Michelle 1955- 136
Herman, Pee-Wee
See Reubens, Paul
Herman, Richard, Jr. 1939- 137
Herman, Roger E. 1943- 128
Herman, Simon N(athan) 1912- 29-32R
Herman, Sondra R(enee) 1932- 25-28R
Herman, Stanley M. 1928- 25-28R
Herman, Vic(tor J.) 1919- 107
Herman, Victor 1916(?)-1985 Obituary 115
Herman, Walter
See Wager, Walter H(erman)
Herman, William 1926- 126
Hermand, Jost 1930- CANR-57
  Earlier sketches in CA 41-44R, CANR-14, 31

Hermann, Donald H(arold) J(ames) 1943- ....
  CANR-17
  Earlier sketches in CA 45-48, CANR-2
Hermann, Edward J(ulius) 1919- 17-20R
Hermann, John 1917- 49-52
Hermann, L. William
See Licht, H. William
Hermann, Philip J(ay) 1916- CANR-41
  Earlier sketch in CA 117
Hermann, (Theodore) Placid 1909-(?) CAP-1
  Earlier sketch in CA 13-16
Hermanns, Peter
See Brannon, William T.
Hermanns, William 1895- CANR-15
  Earlier sketch in CA 37-40R
Hermann the Lame 1013-1054 .... DLB 148
Hermans, Hubert J. M. 1937- 146
Hermans, Willem Frederik 1921- CAP-1
  Earlier sketch in CA 9-10
Hermansen, Gustav 1909- 117
Hermansen, John 1918- 45-48
Hermanson, Dennis (Everett) 1947- ..... SATA 10
Hermeren, Goeran A. 1938- CANR-15
  Earlier sketch in CA 89-92
Hermes
See Flammarion, (Nicolas) Camille
Hermes, Johann Timotheus 1738-1821 ... DLB 97
Hermes, Jules 1962- 156
  See also SATA 92
Hermes, Patricia 1936- CANR-50
  Earlier sketches in CA 104, CANR-22
  See also AAYA 15
  See also SATA 31, 78
Hermlin, Stephan 1915- 153
  See also DLB 69
Hern, (George) Anthony 1916- 21-24R
Hern, Nicholas 1944- 115
Hernadi, Paul 1936- CANR-42
  Earlier sketches in CA 41-44R, CANR-15
Hernandez, Al 1909- CAP-2
  Earlier sketch in CA 21-22
Hernandez, Alfonso C. 1938- .... DLB 122
Hernandez, Amado V. 1903-1970 Obituary ... 112
Hernandez, Frances 1926- 37-40R
Hernandez, Ines 1947- .... DLB 122
Hernandez, Juana Amelia 45-48
Hernandez, Luis F. 1923- 61-64
Hernandez, Miguel 1910-1942 .... DLB 134
Hernandez, Pedro F(elix) 1925- 45-48
Hernandez Aquino, Luis 1907-(?) .... HW
Herndl, Carl G(eorge) 1956- 158
Herndl, George C. 1927- 33-36R
Herndon, Booton 1915- CANR-4
  Earlier sketch in CA 9-12R
Herndon, Ernest 155
  See also SATA 91
Herndon, James 1926- 89-92
  Interview in 89-92
Herndon, Terry (Eugene) 1939- 130
Herndon, Venable 1927- CANR-32
  Earlier sketch in CA 109
Herner, Charles H. 1930- 29-32R
Hernes, Helga Maria 1938- CANR-20
  Earlier sketch in CA 103
Hernon, Peter 1944- CANR-8
  Earlier sketch in CA 61-64
Hernton, Calvin C(oolidge) 1934- CANR-26
  Earlier sketches in CA 9-12R, CANR-3
  See also BW 1
  See also DLB 38
Hero, Alfred O(livier), Jr. 1924- 21-24R
Herodotus c. 484B.C.-429B.C. .... DLB 176
Herold, Ann Bixby 1937- .... SATA 72
Herold, Brenda 1948- 33-36R
Herold, J(ean) Christopher 1919-1964 .... CAP-1
  Earlier sketch in CA 9-10
Heron, Alasdair I(ain) C(ampbell) 1942- ... 115
Heron, Ann 1954- 147
Heron, David Winston 1920- 112
Heron, Laurence Tunstall 1902- 49-52
Heron, Patrick 1920- 109
Heron, Robert 1764-1807 .... DLB 142
Heron-Allen, Edward 1861-1943 Brief entry . 113
Herpel, George L(loyd) 1921- CANR-15
  Earlier sketch in CA 41-44R
Herr, Dan(iel J.) 1917-1990 .... 1-4R
  Obituary 132
Herr, Edwin L. 1933- 37-40R
Herr, Ethel 1936- 112
Herr, Michael 1940(?)- CANR-68
  Earlier sketch in CA 89-92
  See also DLB 185
  See also MTCW 1
Herr, Pamela (Staley) 1939- 126
Herr, Richard 1922- 1-4R
Herrera, Juan Felipe 1948- 131
  See also DLB 122
  See also HW
Herrera-Sobek, Maria 131
  See also HW
Herrera y Reissig, Julio 1875-1910 .... HW
Herrero, Stephen M(atthew) 1939- 118
Herreshoff, David 1921- 21-24R
Herreshoff, L. Francis 1890-1972 .... CAP-1
  Obituary 37-40R
  Earlier sketch in CA 13-14
Herrick, Bruce Hale 1936- CANR-7
  Earlier sketch in CA 17-20R
Herrick, Joy Field 1930- 101
Herrick, Marvin Theodore 1899-1966 ..... CANR-1
  Earlier sketch in CA 1-4R
Herrick, Neal Q(uentin) 1927- CANR-43
  Earlier sketch in CA 49-52

Herrick, Robert 1591-1674 .... DA
See also DAB
See also DAC
See also DAM MST, POP
See also DLB 126
See also PC 9
Herrick, Robert (Welch) 1868-1938 Brief entry . 119
See also DLB 9, 12, 78
Herrick, Robert L(ee) 1930- 61-64
Herrick, Tracy Grant 1933- CANR-42
Earlier sketch in CA 112
Herrick, Walter R(ussell), Jr. 1918- 21-24R
Herrick, William 1915- CANR-9
Earlier sketch in CA 21-24R
See also DLBY 83
Herridge, Robert 1914(?)-1981 Obituary 104
Herrin, Lamar 1940- 142
Herring, George C., Jr. 1936- CANR-14
Earlier sketch in CA 41-44R
Herring, Guilles
See Somerville, Edith
Herring, Hubert Clinton 1889-1967 Obituary ... 105
Herring, Jack W(illiam) 1925- 115
Herring, Peggy J. 1953- 162
Herring, Phillip F. 1936- 151
Herring, Ralph A(lderman) 1901-(?) CAP-2
Earlier sketch in CA 21-22
Herring, Reuben 1922- CANR-7
Earlier sketch in CA 17-20R
Herring, Robert H(erschel) 1938- CANR-21
Earlier sketch in CA 105
Herrington, Anne J. 1948- 145
Herrington, James L(awrence) 1928- 73-76
Herrington, Pat
See Herrington, Patricia (Murphy)
Herrington, Patricia (Murphy) 1927- 114
Herrington, Stuart A. 1941- 109
Herrington, Terri
See Blackstock, Terri
Herriot, James 1916-1995 .... CANR-40
Obituary 148
See also Wight, James Alfred
See also AAYA 1
See also CLC 12
See also DAM POP
See also SATA 86
Herriot, Peter 1939- CANR-25
Earlier sketch in CA 29-32R
Herriott, Robert E. 1929- CANR-7
Earlier sketch in CA 17-20R
Herrmann, Dorothy 1941- 107
See also CLC 44
Herrmann, Frank 1927- CANR-10
Earlier sketch in CA 21-24R
Herrmann, John 1900-1959 Brief entry 107
See also DLB 4
Herrmann, Klaus J(acob) 1929- 37-40R
Herrmann, Luke John 1932- 103
Herrmann, Nina 1943- 77-80
Herrmann, R(obert) L(awrence) 1928- 109
Herrmann, Richard K. 1952- 124
Herrmann, Robert O(mer) 1932- 41-44R
Herrmann, Taffy
See Herrmann, Dorothy
Herrmanns, Ralph 1933- CANR-18
Earlier sketches in CA 9-12R, CANR-3
See also SATA 11
Herrnstadt, Richard L. 1926- 33-36R
Herrnstein, Barbara
See Smith, Barbara Herrnstein
Herrnstein, Richard J(ulius) 1930-1994 153
Brief entry 107
Herrold, Tracey
See Dils, Tracey E.
Herron, Carolivia 1947- 141
See also BW 2
Herron, Don 1952- CANR-54
Earlier sketches in CA 111, CANR-29
Herron, Edward A(lbert) 1912- 5-8R
See also SATA 4
Herron, Ima Honaker 1899- CAP-2
Earlier sketch in CA 25-28
Herron, Lowell William 1916- 1-4R
Herron, Nancy L. 1942- 151
Herron, Orley R., Jr. 1933- CANR-12
Earlier sketch in CA 25-28R
Herron, Shaun 1912- CANR-44
Earlier sketch in CA 29-32R
Herron, William George 1933- 37-40R
Herschberger, Ruth (Margaret) 1917- 33-36R
Herschensohn, Bruce 1932- 69-72
Herscher, Uri David 1941- 107
Herschfield, Harry
See Gibson, Walter B(rown)
Herscovici, Alan 1948- 138
Hersey, George Leonard 1927- 41-44R
Hersey, Jean 1902- CANR-3
Earlier sketch in CA 9-12R
Hersey, John (Richard) 1914-1993 .... CANR-33
Obituary 140
Earlier sketch in CA 17-20R
See also CLC 1, 2, 7, 9, 40, 81, 97
See also DAM POP
See also DLB 6, 185
See also MTCW 1
See also SATA 25
See also SATA-Obit 76
Hersey, William Dearborn 1910- CAP-1
Earlier sketch in CA 11-12
Hersh, Burton 1933- 73-76
Hersh, Jacques 1935- 103
Hersh, Reuben 1927- 125
Hersh, Seymour M. 1937- CANR-15
Earlier sketch in CA 73-76
See also AITN 1
Hershan, Stella K. 1915- 33-36R
Hershatter, Richard Lawrence 1923- 81-84
Hershberg, David 1935- 45-48
Hershberger, Hazel Kuhns 5-8R
Hershberger, Priscilla (Gorman) 1951- ..... SATA 81
Hershenson, David Bert 1933- 41-44R
Hershenson, Maurice (Eugene) 1933- 41-44R
Hersher, Leonard 1925- 41-44R
Hershey, Burnet 1896-1971 .... CAP-2
Obituary 33-36R
Earlier sketch in CA 25-28
Hershey, Daniel 1931- CANR-16
Earlier sketch in CA 89-92
Hershey, Ed
See Hershey, Edward (Norman)
Hershey, Edward (Norman) 1944- Brief entry .. 118
Hershey, Gerald L. 1931- 53-56
Hershey, Kathleen M. 1934- 147
See also SATA 80
Hershey, Lenore 1919(?)-1997 104
Obituary 156
Hershey, Nathan 1930- 117
Hershey, Olive 130
Hershey, Robert Delp 1909- 69-72
Hershfield, Harry 1885-1974 Obituary 53-56
Hershhorn, Bernard S(eymour) 1928- 119
Hershkowitz, Leo 1924- 25-28R
Hershman, Marcie 1951- 141
Hershman, Morris 1926- CANR-5
Earlier sketch in CA 53-56
Hershon, Robert 1936- CANR-13
Earlier sketch in CA 33-36R
Herskovits, Frances Shapiro
1897-1972 Obituary 33-36R
Herskowitz, Herbert Bennett 1925- 17-20R
Herskowitz, Mickey 81-84
Hersom, Kathleen 1911- .... SATA 73
Herspring, Dale R. 1940- 164
Herst, Herman, Jr. 1909- CANR-2
Earlier sketch in CA 1-4R
Herstein, I(srael) N(athan) 1923-1988 Obituary . 125
Herstein, Sheila R. 1942- 119
Hertel, Francois 1905-1985 .... DLB 68
Herter, Christian A(rchibald)
1895-1966 Obituary 116
Hertling, G(unter) H. 1930- 41-44R
Hertling, James E. 1935- 93-96
Hertsens, Marcel 1918- 9-12R
Hertweck, Alma Louise 1937- 122
Hertz, Aleksander 1895-1983 Obituary 109
Hertz, David Michael 1954- CANR-52
Earlier sketch in CA 125
Hertz, Grete Janus 1915- 101
See also SATA 23
Hertz, Jackoline G. 1920- 69-72
Hertz, Jacky
See Hertz, Jackoline G.
Hertz, Karl H(erbert) 1917- 73-76
Hertz, Leah 1937-1988 Obituary 126
Hertz, Peter Donald 1933- 37-40R
Hertz, Richard C(ornell) 1916- 21-24R
Hertz, Solange (Strong) 1920- 5-8R
Hertzberg, Arthur 1921- 17-20R
Hertzberg, Hazel W(hitman) 1918-1988 73-76
Obituary 126
Hertzberg, Hendrik 1943- 126
Hertzberg, Sidney 1910-1984 Obituary 114
Hertzke, Allen D. 1950- 141
Hertzler, Daniel 1925- 115
Hertzler, Joyce O(ramel) 1895-1975 .... 1-4R
Obituary 103
Hertzler, Lois Shank 1927- 57-60
Hertzman, Lewis 1927- 9-12R
Herum, John (Maurice) 1931- 61-64
Herve, Jean-Luc
See Humbaraci, D(emir) Arslan
Herve-Bazin, Jean Pierre Marie 1911-1996 ... 81-84
Obituary 151
See also Bazin, Herve
Hervent, Maurice
See Grindel, Eugene
Hervey, Evelyn
See Keating, H(enry) R(eymond) F(itzwalter)
Hervey, Jane
See McGaw, Naomi Blanche Thoburn
Hervey, John 1696-1743 .... DLB 101
Hervey, Michael 1920- 9-12R
Herwegh, Georg 1817-1875 .... DLB 133
Herwig, Holger H(einrich) 1941- CANR-7
Earlier sketch in CA 61-64
Herz, Irene 1948- 93-96
Herz, Jerome Spencer 45-48
Herz, Jerry
See Herz, Jerome Spencer
Herz, John H(ermann) 1908- 41-44R
Herz, Martin F(lorian) 1917-1983 .... CANR-9
Obituary 111
Earlier sketch in CA 21-24R
Herz, Peggy 1936- 37-40R
Herz, Stephanie M(argarette) 1900- 101
Herzberg, Donald Gabriel 1925-1980 Obituary . 101
Herzberg, Joseph Gabriel
1907-1976 Obituary 65-68
Herzberg, Nancy K. 1951- 150
Herzberger, Maximillian Jacob
1899-1982 Obituary 106
Herzel, Catherine (Williams) 1908- 5-8R
Herzfeld, Thomas J. 1945- 107
Herzig, Alison Cragin 1935- 151
See also SATA 87
Herzinger, Kim A(llen) 1946- 114
Herzka, Heinz (Stefan) 1935- 37-40R
Herzl, Theodor 1860-1904 168
See also TCLC 36
Herzog, Arthur (III) 1927- CANR-30
Earlier sketches in CA 17-20R, CANR-9
Herzog, Chaim 1918-1997 .... CANR-42
Obituary 157
Earlier sketch in CA 103
Herzog, E.
See Maurois, Andre
Herzog, Frederick 1925- 116
Herzog, Gerard 1920- 104
Herzog, John P(hillip) 1931- 29-32R
Herzog, Kristin (K. H.) 1929- 114
Herzog, Peter Emilius 1925- 125
Herzog, Stephen J(oel) 1938- 33-36R
Herzog, Tobey C. 1946- 144
Herzog, Werner 1942- 89-92
See also CLC 16
Herzstein, Robert Edwin 1940- CANR-7
Earlier sketch in CA 57-60
Hesburgh, Theodore M(artin) 1917- 13-16R
Heschel, Abraham Joshua 1907-1972 .... CANR-4
Obituary 37-40R
Earlier sketch in CA 5-8R
Heseltine, George Coulehan
1895-1980 Obituary 97-100
Heseltine, Nigel 1916- 9-12R
Hesiod c. 8th cent. B.C.- .... DLB 176
Heskes, Irene 1928- 93-96
Hesketh, (Charles) Peter (Fleetwood) Fleetwood
See Fleetwood-Hesketh, (Charles) Peter
(Fleetwood)
Hesketh, Phoebe Rayner 1909- CANR-14
Earlier sketches in CAP-1, CA 9-10
Heskett, J(ames) L(ee) 1933- CANR-8
Earlier sketch in CA 13-16R
Hesky, Olga (?)-1974 .... CAP-2
Obituary 53-56
Earlier sketch in CA 25-28
Hesla, David H(eimarck) 1929- 33-36R
Heslep, Robert D(urham) 1930- 37-40R
Heslewood, Juliet 1951- 149
See also SATA 82
Heslin, Jo-Ann 1946- CANR-16
Earlier sketch in CA 93-96
Heslin, Richard 1936- 37-40R
Heslop, J. Malan 1923- 37-40R
Hespro, Herbert
See Robinson, Herbert Spencer
Hess, Albert G(unter) 1909- CAP-1
Earlier sketch in CA 19-20
Hess, Alexander 1898(?)-1981 Obituary 105
Hess, Bartlett L(eonard) 1910- CANR-21
Earlier sketch in CA 61-64
Hess, Beth B(owman) CANR-50
Earlier sketches in CA 65-68, CANR-9, 24
Hess, Earl J(ohn) 1955- 118
Hess, Eckhard H(einrich) 1916-1986 57-60
Obituary 118
Hess, Gary R(ay) 1937- 21-24R
Hess, Hannah S(pier) 1934- 45-48
Hess, Hans 1908-1975 Obituary 53-56
Hess, J(ohn) Daniel 1937- 116
Hess, Joan 1949- 134
Hess, John L(oft) 1917- 102
Hess, John M(ilton) 1929- 21-24R
Hess, Karen 1918- 105
Hess, Karl 1923-1994 81-84
Obituary 145
Hess, Lilo 1916- CANR-12
Earlier sketch in CA 33-36R
See also SATA 4
Hess, Margaret Johnston 1915- CANR-21
Earlier sketches in CA 57-60, CANR-6
Hess, Robert D(aniel) 1920- CANR-13
Earlier sketch in CA 21-24R
Hess, Robert L(ee) 1932-1992 .... 29-32R
Obituary 136
Hess, (Walther Richard) Rudolf
1894-1987 Obituary 123
Hess, Stephen 1933- CANR-30
Earlier sketches in CA 17-20R, CANR-10
Hess, Thomas B(aer) 1920-1978 .... CANR-45
Obituary 77-80
Earlier sketch in CA 81-84
Hess, William N. 1925- 29-32R
Hesse, Hermann 1877-1962 .... CAP-2
Earlier sketch in CA 17-18
See also CLC 1, 2, 3, 6, 11, 17, 25, 69
See also DA
See also DAB
See also DAC
See also DAM MST, NOV
See also DLB 66
See also MTCW 1
See also SATA 50
See also SSC 9
See also WLC
Hesse, Karen 1952- 168
See also AAYA 27
See also SATA 74
Hesse, Mary (Brenda) 1924- CANR-12
Earlier sketch in CA 17-20R
Hesselgesser, Debra 1939- 69-72
Hesselgrave, David J(ohn) 1924- 81-84
Hesseltine, William Best 1902-1963 .... 1-4R
Hessert, Paul 1925- 33-36R
Hessing, Dennis
See Dennis-Jones, H(arold)
Hession, Charles H(enry) 1911- 33-36R
Hession, Roy 1908- 81-84
Hessler, Gene 1928- 73-76
Hesslink, George K. 1940-1980 .... 21-24R
Obituary 120
Hessus, Eobanus 1488-1540 .... DLB 179
Hest, Amy 1950- CANR-56
Earlier sketch in CA 115
See also SATA 55, 82
Hester, Hubert Inman 1895- CANR-5
Earlier sketch in CA 5-8R
Hester, Hugh Bryan 1895-1983 Obituary 111
Hester, James J. 1931- 37-40R
Hester, Katherine L. 1964- 163
Hester, Kathleen B. 1905- CAP-2
Earlier sketch in CA 19-20
Hester, M(arvin) Thomas 1941- 131
Hester, Marcus B. 1937- 33-36R
Hester, Randolph Thompson, Jr. 1944- .. CANR-34
Earlier sketch in CA 113
Hester, Thomas R(oy) 1946- CANR-32
Earlier sketch in CA 113
Hester, William
See Hester, William C.
Hester, William C. 1934- 129
Hesterman, Vicki 1951- 112
Heston, Alan (Wiley) 1934- 97-100
Heston, Charlton 1924- CANR-57
Brief entry 108
Earlier sketch in CA 110
Interview in 110
Heston, Edward 1908(?)-1973 Obituary 45-48
Heston, Leonard L(ancaster) 1930- 101
Heth, Meir 1932- 21-24R
Hetherington, (Hector) Alastair 1919- 109
Hetherington, Eileen Mavis (Plenderleith) 1926- 115
Hetherington, Hugh W(illiam) 1903- 5-8R
Hetherington, John (Aikman) 1907-1974 93-96
Obituary 53-56
Hetherington, Norriss Swigart 1942- CANR-55
Earlier sketch in CA 126
Hetherington, Stephen Cade 1959- 158
Hethmon, Robert H(enry) 1925- 13-16R
Hettinger, Herman Strecker
1902-1972 Obituary 37-40R
Hettlinger, Richard F(rederick) 1920- CANR-7
Earlier sketch in CA 17-20R
Hetzell, Margaret Carol 1917-1978 85-88
Obituary 81-84
Hetzler, Florence M(ary) 1926- CANR-25
Earlier sketch in CA 107
Hetzler, Stanley Arthur 1919- 37-40R
Hetzron, Robert 1937- 33-36R
Heuer, John (Michael) 1941- CANR-14
Earlier sketch in CA 69-72
Heuer, Kenneth John 1927- CANR-30
Earlier sketch in CA 110
See also SATA 44
Heuman, William 1912-1971 .... CANR-64
Earlier sketches in CA 5-8R, CANR-7
See also SATA 21
Heumann, Milton 1947- 110
Heuscher, Julius E(rnst) 1918- 9-12R
Heuser, Beatrice 1961- 138
Heuss, John 1908-1966 .... CAP-1
Earlier sketch in CA 9-10
Heussler, Robert 1924- CANR-8
Earlier sketch in CA 5-8R
Heussner, Ralph C(lyde), Jr. 1949- 119
Heuterman, Thomas H(enry) 1934- 101
Heuvelmans, Bernard (Joseph Pierre) 1916- 97-100
Heuvelmans, Martin 1903- 49-52
Heuving, Jeanne 1951- 138
Heuyer, Georges 1884-1977 Obituary 73-76
Hevener, John W(atts) 1933- 103
Hevia, James L. 1947- 151
Heward, Edmund (Rawlings) 1912- 93-96
Heward, William L(ee) 1949- CANR-4
Earlier sketch in CA 53-56
Hewat, Alexander 1743(?)-1824 .... DLB 30
Hewens, Frank Edgar 1912- 45-48
Hewer, Humphrey Robert 1903-1974 Obituary . 105
Hewes, Agnes Danforth 1874-1963 Obituary ... 113
See also SATA 35
Hewes, Cady
See De Voto, Bernard (Augustine)
Hewes, Dorothy W. 1922- 37-40R
Hewes, Hayden 1943- 85-88
Hewes, Henry 1917- 13-16R
Hewes, Jeremy Joan 1944- 77-80
Hewes, Laurence (Ilsley) 1902- 105
Hewes, Leslie 1906- 41-44R
Hewett, Anita 1918- 21-24R
See also SATA 13
Hewett, Dorothy Coade 1923- CANR-69
Earlier sketch in CA 97-100
Hewett, Joan 1930- 149
See also SATA 81
Hewett, John H(arris) 1952- 115
Hewett, Richard 1929- .... SATA 81
Hewett, William S. 1924- 21-24R
Hewins, Geoffrey Shaw 1889- CAP-1
Earlier sketch in CA 9-10
Hewins, Ralph Anthony 1909-1984(?) CAP-1
Obituary 112
Earlier sketch in CA 9-10
Hewison, Robert 1943- CANR-50
Earlier sketch in CA 81-84
Hewitson, Jennifer 1961- .... SATA 97
Hewitson, John Nelson 1917- 29-32R
Hewitt, Arthur Wentworth 1883- 69-72
Hewitt, Bernard (Wolcott) 1906- 13-16R
Hewitt, Cecil Rolph 1901-1994 .... CANR-18
Obituary 144
Earlier sketch in CA 102
Hewitt, David (Sword) 1942- 118
Hewitt, Don (S.) 1922- 146
Brief entry 119
Hewitt, Emily Clark 1944- CANR-2
Earlier sketch in CA 45-48
Hewitt, Foster (William) 1903(?)-1985 Obituary . 115
Hewitt, Garnet (William) 1939- 110
Hewitt, Geof (George F.) 1943- 33-36R
Hewitt, H(erbert) J(ames) 1890- 13-16R
Hewitt, James 1928- CANR-21
Earlier sketches in CA 57-60, CANR-6

Hewitt, Jean D(aphne) 1925-1997 77-80
Obituary 156
Hewitt, John (Harold) 1907-1987 . . . . CANR-16
Obituary 123
Earlier sketch in CA 97-100
See also DLB 27
Hewitt, John P(aul) 1941- 53-56
Hewitt, Margaret 1961- . . . . SATA 84
Hewitt, Nicholas 1945- 132
Hewitt, Philip Nigel 1945- 81-84
Hewitt, Robert L. 1917(?)-1983 Obituary 111
Hewitt, Sue Whitsett 1919(?)-1984 Obituary . . . 111
Hewitt, W(arren) E(dward) 1954- 139
Hewitt, William Henry 1936- 17-20R
Hewlett, Dorothy (?)-1979 Obituary 85-88
Hewlett, Frank West 1909(?)-1983 Obituary . . . 110
Hewlett, Maurice (Henry) 1861-1923 Brief entry 121
See also DLB 34, 156
Hewlett, Richard Greening 1923- 9-12R
Hewlett, Roger S. 1911(?)-1977 Obituary 73-76
Hewlett, Sylvia Ann 1946- 123
Brief entry 118
Hewlett, Virginia B. 1912(?)-1979 Obituary . . . 85-88
Hewson, John 1930- .37-40R
Hewton, Eric 1934- 126
Hexham, Irving 1943- CANR-52
Earlier sketch in CA 125
Hexner, Ervin Paul 1893-1968 . . . . .5-8R
Obituary 103
Hext, Harrington
See Phillpotts, Eden
Hextall, David
See Phillips-Birt, Douglas Hextall Chedzey
Hexter, J(ack) H. 1910-1996 . . . . 13-16R
Obituary 155
Hey, Jeanne A. K. 1963- 154
Hey, John D(enis) 1944- 106
Hey, Nigel S(tewart) 1936- 33-36R
See also SATA 20
Hey, Robert P(ierpont) 1935- 133
Heyd, David 1945- 118
Heydenburg, Harry E. 1891(?)-1979 Obituary . 89-92
Heydenreich, Ludwig Heinrich 1903- Brief entry 105
Heydon, Peter Richard 1913-1971 . . . . CAP-1
Earlier sketch in CA 19-20
Heydron, Vicki Ann 1945- .131
Heyduck-Huth, Hilde 1929- 57-60
See also SATA 8
Heyel, Carl 1908- CANR-22
Earlier sketches in CA 17-20R, CANR-7
Heyen, William 1940- 33-36R
See also CAAS 9
See also CLC 13, 18
See also DLB 5
Heyer, Carol 1950- 130
See also SATA 74
Heyer, Georgette 1902-1974 . . . . CANR-58
Obituary 49-52
Earlier sketch in CA 93-96
See also DAM POP
See also DLB 77, 191
See also MTCW 1
Heyer, Marilee 1942- CANR-52
Earlier sketch in CA 125
See also SATA 64, 102
Heyerdahl, Thor 1914- CANR-66
Earlier sketches in CA 5-8R, CANR-5, 22
See also CLC 26
See also MTCW 1
See also SATA 2, 52
Heyes, (Nancy) Eileen 1956- 147
See also SATA 80
Heyler, David B. Sr. 1905(?)-1983 Obituary 110
Heyliger, William 1884-1955 . . . . .YABC 1
Heylin, Clinton (M.) 1960- .135
Heym, Georg (Theodor Franz Arthur) 1887-1912 Brief entry 106
See also TCLC 9
Heym, Stefan 1913- CANR-4
Earlier sketch in CA 9-12R
See also CLC 41
See also DLB 69
Heyman, Abigail 1942- 57-60
Heyman, Josiah McC(onnell) 1958- 140
Heyman, Ken(neth Louis) 1930- 112
See also SATA 34
Heyman, Neil Michael 1937- 113
Heymann, C. David
See Heymann, Clemens Claude
See also BEST 89:4
Heymann, Clemens Claude 1945- CANR-66
Earlier sketch in CA 129
See also Heymann, C. David
Heymann, Frederick Gotthold 1900-1983 Obituary 111
Heymann, Thomas N. 1958- 135
Heymann, Tom
See Heymann, Thomas N.
Heymanns, Betty 1932- 85-88
Heymanson, Randal 1903-1984 Obituary 113
Heymsfield, Steven B. 1944- 162
Heyn, Ernest V(ictor) 1904-1995 134
Obituary 149
Brief entry 111
Heyne, Paul 1931- 89-92
Heyneman, Martha (Tarpey) 1927- 142
Heynen, Jim 1940- CANR-63
Earlier sketch in CA 77-80
Heyns, Barbara 1943- 85-88
Heyrman, Christine Leigh 1950- CANR-66
Earlier sketch in CA 115
Heyse, Paul (Johann Ludwig von) 1830-1914 Brief entry 104
See also DLB 129
See also TCLC 8
Heyst, Axel
See Grabowski, Z(bigniew) Anthony
Heytesbury, William 1310(?)-1372(?) . . . . . . DLB 115
Heyward, Carter 1945- 65-68
Heyward, Dorothy (Hartzell Kuhns) 1890-1961 Obituary 112
See also DLB 7
Heyward, (Edwin) DuBose 1885-1940 157
Brief entry 108
See also DLB 7, 9, 45
See also SATA 21
See also TCLC 59
Heyward, Vivian H. 1947- .161
Heywood, Andrew 1952- 147
Heywood, Christopher 1928- 41-44R
Heywood, Colin 1947- 130
Heywood, Hugh Christopher Lempriere 1896-1987 Obituary 122
Heywood, Joe T.
See Heywood, Joseph (T.)
Heywood, Joseph (T.) 1943- 134
Brief entry 128
Interview in 134
Heywood, Karen 1946- . . . . SATA 48
Heywood, Lorimer D. 1899(?)-1977 Obituary . 73-76
Heywood, Philip 1938- 69-72
Heywood, Rosalind 1895- 89-92
Heywood, Terence CAP-1
Earlier sketch in CA 9-10
Heywood, Thomas 1573(?)-1641 . . . . . . DAM DRAM
See also DLB 62
Heyworth, Laurence 1955- .134
Heyworth, Peter (Lawrence Frederick) 1921-1991 65-68
Obituary 135
Heyworth-Dunne, James (?)-1974 Obituary . . 53-56
Hezel, Francis X(avier) 1939- CANR-42
Earlier sketch in CA 118
Hezlep, William (Earl) 1936- 152
See also SATA 88
Hiaasen, Carl 1953- CANR-65
Earlier sketches in CA 105, CANR-22, 45
Hian
See Higginson, William J(ohn)
Hiat, Elchik
See Katz, Menke
Hiatt, Howard H(aym) 1925- 133
Hibbard, George Richard 1915- 85-88
Hibbard, Howard 1928-1984 . . . . CANR-9
Obituary 114
Earlier sketch in CA 53-56
Hibben, Frank Cummings 1910- CANR-2
Earlier sketch in CA 1-4R
Hibberd, Andrew Stuart 1893-1983(?) Obituary . 111
Hibberd, Jack 1940- CANR-47
Earlier sketch in CA 103
Hibbert, Alun 1949- 130
Hibbert, Christopher 1924- CANR-2
Earlier sketch in CA 1-4R
See also SATA 4
Hibbert, Eleanor Alice Burford 1906-1993 . . . . CANR-59
Obituary 140
Earlier sketches in CA 17-20R, CANR-9, 28
See also BEST 90:4
See also CLC 7
See also DAM POP
See also SATA 2
See also SATA-Obit 74
Hibbett, Howard (Scott) 1920- 106
Hibbing, John R. 1953- 140
Hibbs, Ben 1901-1975 65-68
Obituary 104
See also DLB 137
Hibbs, Douglas A(lbert), Jr. 1944- CANR-3
Earlier sketch in CA 49-52
Hibbs, Euthymia D. 1937- .141
Hibbs, John 1925- CANR-41
Earlier sketches in CA 103, CANR-19
Hibbs, Paul 1906- CAP-1
Earlier sketch in CA 13-16
Hibdon, James E(dward) 1924- 25-28R
Hichens, Robert (Smythe) 1864-1950 162
See also DLB 153
See also TCLC 64
Hick, John (Harwood) 1922- CANR-22
Earlier sketches in CA 9-12R, CANR-6
Hickel, Walter J(oseph) 1919- 41-44R
Hicken, Mandy
See Hicken, Marilyn E.
Hicken, Marilyn E. 1937- 135
Hicken, Victor 1921- 21-24R
Hickerson, J(ohn) Mel(ancthon) 1897- 25-28R
Hickey, Edward Shelby 1928(?)-1978 85-88
Obituary 81-84
Hickey, Emily 1845-1924 . . . . .DLB 199
Hickey, Joseph J(ames) 1907- 41-44R
Hickey, Michael 1929- 102
Hickey, Neil 1931- 1-4R
Hickey, Raymond 1936- CANR-37
Earlier sketch in CA 114
Hickey, William
See Driberg, Thomas Edward Neil
Hickford, Jessie 1911- 53-56
Hickin, Norman E(rnest) 1910- CANR-15
Earlier sketch in CA 85-88
Hickinbotham, Tom 1903-1983 Obituary 111
Hickler, Holly 1923- 117
Hickling, C(harles) F(rederick) 1902-1977 Obituary 117
Hickman, Bert G(eorge), Jr. 1924- 108
Hickman, C(harles) Addison 1916- 103
Hickman, Charles 1905-1983 Obituary 109
Hickman, (Gertrud) Hannah 1928- 123
Hickman, Hoyt L(eon) 1927- CANR-47
Earlier sketch in CA 121
Hickman, Janet 1940- CANR-10
Earlier sketch in CA 65-68
See also SATA 12
Hickman, Katie 1960- 128
Hickman, Martha Whitmore 1925- CANR-52
Earlier sketches in CA 25-28R, CANR-10, 26
See also SATA 26
Hickman, Martin B(erkeley) 1925- 65-68
Hickman, Peggy 1906- 73-76
Hickman, Tracy Raye 1955- 126
Hickman, William Albert 1877-1957 . . . . DLB 92
Hickok, Dorothy Jane 1912- 73-76
Hickok, Lorena A. 1893-1968 . . . . CANR-44
Earlier sketch in CA 73-76
See also SATA 20
Hickok, Ralph 1938- 141
Hickok, Robert (Blair) 1927- 61-64
Hickok, Will
See Harrison, C(hester) William
Hicks, Charles B(alch) 1916- 5-8R
Hicks, Clifford B. 1920- CANR-24
Earlier sketches in CA 5-8R, CANR-9
See also SATA 50
Hicks, Darryl E(dwin) 1948- 120
Hicks, David E. 1931- CANR-7
Earlier sketch in CA 9-12R
Hicks, Donald A(lbert) 1947- 111
Hicks, Eleanor B.
See Coerr, Eleanor (Beatrice)
Hicks, George L(eon) 1935- 65-68
Hicks, Granville 1901-1982 . . . . CANR-13
Obituary 107
Earlier sketch in CA 9-12R
Hicks, Harvey
See Stratemeyer, Edward L.
Hicks, J. L.
See Hicks, Jim(my Lyn)
Hicks, Jack 1942- 97-100
Hicks, James L. 1915(?)-1986 Obituary 118
Hicks, Jim(my Lyn) 1937- .107
Hicks, John (Richard) 1904-1989 . . . . CANR-13
Obituary 128
Earlier sketch in CA 65-68
Hicks, John (Kenneth) 1918- 25-28R
Hicks, John D(onald) 1890-1972 . . . . CANR-2
Earlier sketch in CA 1-4R
Hicks, John Edward 1890(?)-1971 Obituary 104
Hicks, John H(arland) 1919- 45-48
Hicks, John V(ictor) 1907- CANR-56
Earlier sketches in CA 110, CANR-30
Hicks, L. Edward 1949- 150
Hicks, Raymond L. 1926- 61-64
Hicks, Robert E(lden) 1920- Brief entry 109
Hicks, Roger W(illiam) 1950- 124
Hicks, Ronald G(raydon) 1934- 73-76
Hicks, Thomas 1936- 129
Hicks, Tyler Gregory 1921- 103
Hicks, Ursula Kathleen (Webb) 1896-1985 103
Obituary 117
Hicks, Warren B(raukman) 1921- 33-36R
Hicks, Wilson 1897-1970 Obituary 29-32R
Hicky, Daniel Whitehead 1902- . . . . AITN 1
Hicyilmaz, Gay 1947- 133
See also SATA 77
Hidalgo, Jose Luis 1919-1947 . . . . DLB 108
Hidden, (Frederick) Norman 1913- 77-80
Hidore, John J. 1932- CANR-44
Earlier sketches in CA 57-60, CANR-6, 21
Hidy, Muriel E(mmie) 1906- 97-100
Hidy, Ralph W(illard) 1905- 5-8R
Hieatt, A(llen) Kent 1921- 21-24R
Hieatt, Constance B(artlett) 1928- CANR-23
Earlier sketches in CA 5-8R, CANR-8
See also SATA 4
Hiebel, Friedrich 1903- CANR-11
Earlier sketch in CA 65-68
Hiebert, Clarence 1927- 61-64
Hiebert, D(avid) Edmond 1910- 17-20R
Hiebert, Paul (Gerhardt) 1892-1987 . . . . CANR-17
Earlier sketches in CAP-2, CA 23-24
See also DLB 68
Hiebert, Ray Eldon 1932- CANR-7
Earlier sketch in CA 17-20R
See also SATA 13
Hiemstra, Marvin R. 1939- . . . . CAAS 26
Hieng, Andrej 1925- . . . . DLB 181
Hiernaux, Jean 1921- 57-60
Hieronymous, J.
See Kay, Jeremy
Hieronymus, Clara (Booth) 1913- 73-76
Hierro, Jose 1922- . . . . DLB 108
Hiers, John Turner 1945- 102
Hiers, Richard H(yde) 1932- 53-56
Hiesberger, Jean Marie 1941- 41-44R
Hiesinger, Kathryn B(loom) 1943- 119
Hiestand, Dale L(eroy) 1925- 41-44R
Hiestand, Emily (L.) 1947- 134
Hifler, Joyce (Sequichie) 1925- 21-24R
Higashiuchi, Yoshio 1915(?)-1987 Obituary 122
Higbe, (Walter) Kirby 1915-1985 Obituary 116
Higbee, Edward (Counselman) 1910- 13-16R
Higbee, Kenneth Leo 1941- 101
Higby, Mary Jane 25-28R
Higdon, David Leon 1939- 77-80
Higdon, Hal 1931- CANR-3
Earlier sketch in CA 9-12R
See also SATA 4
Higenbottam, Frank 1910-1982 . . . . 25-28R
Obituary 117
Higgie, Lincoln William 1938- 5-8R
Higginbotham, A(loysius) Leon, Jr. 1928- 110
Higginbotham, (Prieur) Jay 1937- CANR-37
Earlier sketches in CA 93-96, CANR-17
Higginbotham, John E. 1933- 29-32R
Higginbotham, R(obert) Don 1931- 17-20R
Higginbotham, Sanford Wilson 1913- Brief entry 105
Higginbotham, Virginia 1935- 115
Brief entry 110
Higginbottom, David 1923- CANR-52
See also Fisk, Nicholas
See also SATA 87
Higginbottom, J(effrey) Winslow 1945- . . . . SATA 29
Higgins, A(lbert) C(orbin) 1930- 37-40R
Higgins, A(ngus) J(ohn) B(rockhurst) 1911- . 13-16R
Higgins, Aidan 1927- CANR-70
Earlier sketch in CA 9-12R
See also DLB 14
Higgins, Alice 1924(?)-1974 Obituary 53-56
Higgins, Anna Dunlap 1962- 147
Higgins, Chester (Archer, Jr.) 1946- 73-76
Higgins, Colin 1941-1988 . . . . CANR-30
Obituary 126
Earlier sketch in CA 33-36R
See also DLB 26
Higgins, D. S(ydney) 1938- 132
Higgins, Dick
See Higgins, Richard C(arter)
See also CAAS 8
Higgins, Don 1928- CANR-14
Earlier sketch in CA 25-28R
Higgins, George V(incent) 1939- CANR-51
Earlier sketches in CA 77-80, CANR-17
Interview in CANR-17
See also CAAS 5
See also CLC 4, 7, 10, 18
See also DLB 2
See also DLBY 81
See also MTCW 1
Higgins, Gina O'Connell 1950- 151
Higgins, Ian (Kevin) 1959- 149
Higgins, Ink
See Weiss, Morris S(amuel)
Higgins, Jack
See Patterson, Harry
See also BEST 89:3
Higgins, James E(dward) 1926- 73-76
Higgins, Jean C. 1932- .29-32R
Higgins, Joan 1948- 125
Higgins, Joanna 1945- 141
Higgins, John 1934- 138
Higgins, John A(loysius) 1931- CANR-13
Earlier sketch in CA 77-80
Higgins, John C(layborn) 1934- 132
Higgins, John J(oseph) 1935- 45-48
Higgins, Judith Holden 1930- 102
Higgins, Kathleen M(arie) 1954- 138
Higgins, Lionel G(eorge) 1891-1985 123
Higgins, Marguerite 1920-1966 . . . . 5-8R
Obituary 25-28R
Higgins, Michael James 1946- 146
Higgins, Paul C. 1950- 106
Higgins, Paul Lambourne 1916- CANR-17
Earlier sketches in CA 1-4R, CANR-2
Higgins, Reynold Alleyne 1916-1993 . . . . . CANR-50
Obituary 141
Earlier sketch in CA 25-28R
Higgins, Richard C(arter) 1938- CANR-56
Earlier sketches in CA 13-16R, CANR-8, 29
See also Higgins, Dick
Higgins, Ronald 1929- 81-84
Higgins, Rosalyn (Cohen) 1937- CANR-3
Earlier sketch in CA 9-12R
Higgins, Thomas J(oseph) 1899- CANR-49
Earlier sketches in CA 1-4R, CANR-5
Higgins, Trumbull 1919-1990 . . . . .17-20R
Obituary 131
Higgins, W(illiam) Robert 1938- 37-40R
Higgins, William R(eynolds) 1935- 128
Higginsen, Vy 147
See also SATA 79
Higginson, Fred H(all) 1921- 1-4R
Higginson, Margaret V(alliant) 1923- 105
Higginson, Thomas Wentworth 1823-1911 162
See also DLB 1, 64
See also TCLC 36
Higginson, William J(ohn) 1938- 123
Higgs, David (Clive) 1939- 61-64
Higgs, E(ric) S(idney) 1908-1976 . . . . 9-12R
Obituary 69-72
Higgs, Gerald B. 1921- 106
Higgs, Gertrude Monro
See Monro-Higgs, Gertrude
Higgs, Robert J(ackson) 1932- 115
High, Dallas M. 1931- 21-24R
High, Linda Oatman 1958- .159
See also SATA 94
High, Monique Raphel 1949- CANR-21
Earlier sketch in CA 102
High, Philip E(mpson) 1914- 97-100
High, Stanley (Hoflund) 1895-1961 Obituary . . 89-92
Higham, Charles 1931- CANR-17
Earlier sketch in CA 33-36R
See also BEST 89:1
Higham, David 1895-1978 . . . . CANR-2
Earlier sketch in CA 1-4R
Higham, David (Michael) 1949- 126
See also SATA 50
Higham, Florence May Grier 1896-1980 Obituary 97-100
Higham, John 1920- CANR-6
Earlier sketch in CA 1-4R
Higham, Jon Atlas
See Higham, Jonathan Huw
Higham, Jonathan Huw 1960- 127
See also SATA 59

Higham, Robin (David Stewart) 1925- ... CANR-31
Earlier sketches in CA 1-4R, CANR-1
Higham, Roger 1935- ... 33-36R
Higham, T. F.
See Higham, Thomas Farrant
Higham, Thomas Farrant 1890-1975 Obituary ... 116
Highberger, Ruth 1917- ... 65-68
Highet, Gilbert (Arthur) 1906-1978 ... CANR-6
Obituary ... 73-76
Earlier sketch in CA 1-4R
Highet, Helen
See MacInnes, Helen (Clark)
Highfield, (John) Roger (Loxdale) 1922- ... 130
Highland, Dora
See Avallone, Michael (Angelo, Jr.)
Highland, Monica
See Espey, John (Jenkins)
and Kendall, Lisa See
and See, Carolyn (Penelope)
Highsmith, (Mary) Patricia 1921-1995 ... CANR-62
Obituary ... 147
Earlier sketches in CA 1-4R, CANR-1, 20, 48
See also CLC 2, 4, 14, 42, 102
See also DAM NOV, POP
See also MTCW 1
Highsmith, Richard M(organ), Jr. 1920- ... 37-40R
Hightower, Florence Cole 1916-1981 ... CANR-35
Obituary ... 103
Earlier sketch in CA 1-4R
See also SATA 4
See also SATA-Obit 27
Hightower, John M(urmann)
1909-1987 Obituary ... 121
Hightower, Lynn S. ... 140
Hightower, Paul
See Collins, Thomas Hightower
Highwater, Jamake (Mamake) 1942(?)- ... CANR-34
Earlier sketches in CA 65-68, CANR-10
See also CAAS 7
See also AAYA 7
See also CLC 12
See also CLR 17
See also DLB 52
See also DLBY 85
See also JRDA
See also MAICYA
See also SATA 32, 69
See also SATA-Brief 30
Highway, Tomson 1951- ... 151
See also CLC 92
See also DAC
See also DAM MULT
See also NNAL
Higley, John (Clark) 1938- Brief entry ... 116
Higman, B(arry) W(illiam) 1943- ... 81-84
Higman, Francis M(ontgomery) 1935- ... CANR-12
Earlier sketch in CA 25-28R
Hignett, Sean 1934- ... CANR-44
Earlier sketch in CA 49-52
Higon, Albert
See Jeury, Michel
Higonnet, Anne 1959- ... 139
Higonnet, Margaret Randolph 1941- ... 61-64
Higonnet, Patrice Louis-Rene 1938- ... 65-68
Higson, Charles ... 142
Higson, James D(oran) 1925- ... 49-52
Hijirida, Kyoko 1937- ... 126
Hijuelos, Oscar 1951- ... CANR-50
Earlier sketch in CA 123
See also AAYA 25
See also BEST 90:1
See also CLC 65
See also DAM MULT, POP
See also DLB 145
See also HLC
See also HW
Hikmet, Nazim 1902(?)-1963 ... 141
Obituary ... 93-96
See also CLC 40
Hilary, Christopher 1927(?)-1979 Obituary ... 89-92
Hilberg, Raul 1926- ... 33-36R
Hilberry, Conrad (Arthur) 1928- ... CANR-10
Earlier sketch in CA 25-28R
See also DLB 120
Hilbert, David 1862-1943 ... 162
Hilbert, Richard A. 1947- ... 142
Hilbert, Robert G. 1939-1993 ... 144
Hilborn, Ann 1942- ... 109
Hilborn, Harry (Warren) 1900- ... CAP-2
Earlier sketch in CA 33-36
Hilborn, Robert C. 1943- ... 149
Hild, Jack
See Preston, John
Hild, Jack
See Garside, (Clifford) Jack
Hildebidle, John 1946- ... 114
Hildebrand, Ann Meinzen 1933- ... 144
Hildebrand, George H(erbert) 1913- ... CANR-8
Earlier sketch in CA 17-20R
Hildebrand, Grant 1934- ... 57-60
Hildebrand, Joel H(enry) 1881-1983 ... CAP-1
Obituary ... 109
Earlier sketch in CA 11-12
Hildebrand, John 1949- ... 131
Hildebrand, Klaus 1941- ... 158
Hildebrand, Verna 1924- ... CANR-52
Earlier sketches in CA 33-36R, CANR-13, 28
Hildebrandt, Franz 1909-1985 ... 118
Hildebrandt, Greg 1939- ... 104
See also AAYA 12
See also SATA 55
See also SATA-Brief 33

Hildebrandt, Tim(othy) 1939- ... 122
Brief entry ... 111
See also AAYA 12
See also SATA 55
See also SATA-Brief 33
Hildebrandts, The
See Hildebrandt, Tim(othy)
Hildegard von Bingen 1098-1179 ... DLB 148
Hilder, Rowland 1905-1993 ... SATA 36
See also SATA-Obit 77
Hilderbrand, Robert Clinton 1947- ... 105
Hildesheimer, Wolfgang 1916-1991 ... 101
Obituary ... 135
See also CLC 49
See also DLB 69, 124
Hildick, E. W.
See Hildick, (Edmund) Wallace
See also SAAS 6
Hildick, (Edmund) Wallace 1925- ... CANR-49
Earlier sketch in CA 25-28R
See also Hildick, E. W.
See also MAICYA
See also SATA 2, 68
Hildreth, Gertrude Howell 1898-1984 Obituary ... 112
Hildreth, Margaret Holbrook 1927- ... 89-92
Hildreth, Richard 1807-1865 ... DLB 1, 30, 59
Hildum, Donald C(layton) 1930- ... 21-24R
Hildyard, Nicholas 1955- ... 122
Hilfer, Anthony Channell 1936- ... 73-76
Hilfiker, David 1945- ... CANR-49
Earlier sketch in CA 123
Hilgard, Ernest R(opiequet) 1904- ... CANR-32
Earlier sketch in CA 113
Hilgartner, Beth 1957- ... SATA 58
Hilgartner, Stephen 1956- ... 111
Hilger, Sister Mary Inez 1891-1977 ... 73-76
Hilken, Glen A. 1936-1976 ... 61-64
Obituary ... 134
Hill, Aaron 1685-1750 ... DLB 84
Hill, Ab
See Hill, Abram (Barrington)
Hill, Abram (Barrington) 1910(?)-1986 Obituary ... 120
Hill, Adrian Keith Graham 1895-1977 ... CANR-29
Earlier sketch in CA 77-80
Hill, Alexis
See Craig, Mary (Francis) Shura
and Glick, Ruth (Burtnick)
Hill, Alfred T(uxbury) 1908- ... 21-24R
Hill, Anita Faye 1956- ... 153
Hill, Anthony (Robert) 1942- ... 151
See also SATA 91
Hill, Archibald A(nderson) 1902- ... CANR-47
Earlier sketch in CA 49-52
Hill, Arthur Norman 1920(?)-1988 Obituary ... 125
Hill, Barrington Julian Warren 1915- ... 5-8R
Hill, Bennett D(avid) 1934- ... 111
Hill, Bob
See Hill, Robert C(ecil)
Hill, Brian (Merrikin) 1896- ... CAP-1
Earlier sketch in CA 9-10
Hill, Brian W. 1932- ... 145
Hill, Carol (Dechellis) 1942- ... CANR-69
Earlier sketch in CA 77-80
Hill, Charles 1904-1989 Obituary ... 129
Hill, Charles William, Jr. 1940- ... 125
Hill, (John Edward) Christopher 1912- ... CANR-22
Earlier sketches in CA 9-12R, CANR-4
Hill, Christopher R. 1935- ... CANR-66
Earlier sketch in CA 128
Hill, Claude 1911-1991 ... 21-24R
Obituary ... 136
Hill, Clifford S. 1927- ... CANR-27
Earlier sketches in CA 13-16R, CANR-7
Hill, Crag 1957- ... CAAS 29
Hill, Daniel G., Jr. 1896(?)-1979 Obituary ... 89-92
Hill, Dave
See Hill, David John
Hill, Dave
See Hill, David Charles
Hill, David Charles 1936- ... CANR-11
Earlier sketch in CA 17-20R
Hill, David John 1958- ... 132
Hill, Deborah 1936- ... 108
Hill, Dee
See Zucker, Dolores Mae Bolton
Hill, Denise 1919- ... CANR-23
Earlier sketch in CA 106
Hill, (Richard) Desmond 1920-1984 ... 5-8R
Obituary ... 114
Hill, Devra Z.
See Zucker, Dolores Mae Bolton
Hill, Dilys M(ary) 1935- ... 61-64
Hill, Donald (Routledge) 1922- ... 122
Hill, Donald Hamilton
See Hamilton-Hill, Donald
Hill, Donna (Marie) ... CANR-50
Earlier sketches in CA 13-16R, CANR-7, 25
See also SATA 24
Hill, Douglas (Arthur) 1935- ... CANR-4
Earlier sketch in CA 53-56
See also SATA 39, 78
Hill, Draper
See Hill, L(eroy) Draper, Jr.
Hill, Earle 1941- ... 33-36R
Hill, Edmund 1923- ... 146
Hill, Eileen
See Stack, Nicolete Meredith
Hill, Elizabeth Starr 1925- ... CANR-45
Earlier sketches in CA 17-20R, CANR-31
See also SATA 24
Hill, Ellen Wise 1942- ... 77-80
Hill, Eric 1927- ... 134
See also CLR 13
See also MAICYA
See also SATA 66
See also SATA-Brief 53

Hill, Ernest 1915- ... 53-56
Hill, Errol Gaston 1921- ... CANR-26
Earlier sketch in CA 45-48
See also BW 2
Hill, Evan 1919- ... CANR-5
Earlier sketch in CA 9-12R
Hill, Fiona
See Pall, Ellen Jane
Hill, (Charles) Fowler
1901(?)-1973 Obituary ... 37-40R
Hill, (James William) Francis
1899-1980 Obituary ... 108
Hill, Frank Ernest 1888-1969 ... 73-76
Hill, Gene (Atkins) 1928-1997 ... 97-100
Obituary ... 158
Hill, Geoffrey (William) 1932- ... CANR-21
Earlier sketch in CA 81-84
See also CDBLB 1960 to Present
See also CLC 5, 8, 18, 45
See also DAM POET
See also DLB 40
See also MTCW 1
Hill, George E(dward) 1907- ... CAP-1
Earlier sketch in CA 17-18
Hill, George Roy 1921- ... 122
Brief entry ... 110
See also CLC 26
Hill, Gerald N. 1929- ... 148
Hill, Gladwin 1914- ... 25-28R
Hill, Grace Brooks ... CANR-26
Earlier sketches in CAP-2, CA 19-20
See also SATA 1, 67
Hill, Grace Livingston 1865-1947 ... YABC 2
Hill, (Norman) Graham 1929-1975 Obituary ... 108
Hill, H. D. N.
See Disston, Harry
Hill, Hamlin (Lewis) 1931- ... CANR-18
Earlier sketches in CA 9-12R, CANR-3
Hill, Harold E(verett) 1905- ... CANR-11
Earlier sketch in CA 69-72
Hill, Helen
See Miller, Helen Hill
Hill, Helen M(orey) 1915- ... 57-60
See also SATA 27
Hill, Henry Bertram 1907- ... 1-4R
Hill, Herbert 1924- ... 65-68
Hill, Hyacinthe
See Anderson, Virginia (R. Cronin)
Hill, I(saac) William 1908- ... 65-68
Hill, J(ohn) C(ampbell) 1888- ... 37-40R
Hill, James
See Jameson, (Margaret) Storm
Hill, James N(ewlin) 1934-1997 ... 33-36R
Obituary ... 160
Hill, Jane Bowers 1950- ... 126
Hill, Jim Dan 1897- ... CAP-1
Earlier sketch in CA 11-12
Hill, John
See Koontz, Dean R(ay)
Hill, John Hugh 1905- ... CANR-5
Earlier sketch in CA 1-4R
Hill, John L. 1960- ... 124
Hill, John P(aul) 1936- ... 29-32R
Hill, John S(tanley) 1929- ... 37-40R
Hill, John Spencer 1943- ... CANR-71
Earlier sketch in CA 150
Hill, John Wiley 1890-1977 Obituary ... 69-72
Hill, Johnson
See Kunhardt, Edith
Hill, Jonathan D. 1954- ... 147
Hill, Judy I. R.
See Roberts, Judy I.
Hill, Kathleen Louise 1917- ... CANR-3
Earlier sketch in CA 9-12R
See also SATA 4
Hill, Kathleen Thompson 1941- ... 148
Hill, Kay
See Hill, Kathleen Louise
Hill, Ken(neth) 1937-1995 ... 108
Obituary ... 147
Hill, King
See Robertson, Frank C(hester)
Hill, Kirkpatrick 1938- ... SATA 72
Hill, Knox C(alvin) 1910- ... CAP-1
Earlier sketch in CA 19-20
Hill, L(eslie) A(lexander) 1918- ... CANR-48
Earlier sketch in CA 21-24R
Hill, L(eroy) Draper, Jr. 1935- ... CANR-12
Earlier sketch in CA 17-20R
Hill, Larry D(ean) 1935- ... 73-76
Hill, Lawrence 1912-1988 Obituary ... 125
Hill, Lawson (Traphagen) 1927- ... 118
Hill, Lee H(alsey) 1899-1974 ... 37-40R
Obituary ... 45-48
Hill, Lee Sullivan 1958- ... CANR-68
Earlier sketch in CA 162
See also SATA 96
Hill, Leslie Pinckney 1880-1960 ... 125
See also BW 1
See also DLB 51
Hill, Lew
See Skene-Melvin, (Lewis) David (St. Columb)
Hill, Lloyd E(rnest) 1938- ... 141
Hill, Lois
See Sternau, Cynthia
Hill, Lorna 1902- ... CANR-14
Earlier sketches in CAP-1, CA 9-10
See also SATA 12
Hill, Lowell Dean 1930- ... 114
Hill, M(elba) Anne 1953- ... CANR-50
Earlier sketch in CA 123
Hill, Malcolm R(onald) 1942- ... 130
Hill, Margaret (Ohler) 1915- ... CANR-16
Earlier sketches in CA 1-4R, CANR-1
See also SATA 36
Hill, Marnesba D. 1913- ... 101

Hill, Marvin S(idney) 1928- ... 61-64
Hill, Mary A. 1939- ... 102
Hill, Mary Raymond 1923- ... CANR-6
Earlier sketch in CA 57-60
Hill, Mary V. 1941- ... 102
Hill, Meg
See Hill, Margaret (Ohler)
Hill, Meredith
See Craig, Mary (Francis) Shura
Hill, Mike 1944- ... 122
Hill, Monica
See Watson, Jane Werner
Hill, Nancy Klenk 1936- ... 108
Hill, Napoleon 1883(?)-1970 Obituary ... 104
Hill, Nellie
See Hill, Ellen Wise
Hill, Norman Llewellyn 1895- ... 5-8R
Hill, Pamela 1920- ... CANR-37
Earlier sketches in CA 49-52, CANR-1, 16
Hill, Pati ... 69-72
Hill, Peter Proal 1926- ... 33-36R
Hill, Philip G(eorge) 1934- ... 33-36R
Hill, Polly
See Humphreys, Mary Eglantyne Hill
Hill, R(ufus) Carter 1945- ... 110
Hill, R. Lance 1943- ... CANR-11
Earlier sketch in CA 65-68
Hill, Ralph Nading 1917-1987 ... CANR-1
Obituary ... 124
Earlier sketch in CA 1-4R
See also SATA 65
Hill, Rebecca 1944- ... 111
Hill, Reginald (Charles) 1936- ... CANR-64
Earlier sketches in CA 73-76, CANR-32
Hill, Reuben (Lorenzo, Jr.) 1912-1985 ... 131
Obituary ... 117
Hill, Richard (Leslie) 1901-1996 ... CANR-1
Obituary ... 151
Earlier sketch in CA 1-4R
Hill, Richard (Fontaine) 1941- ... 33-36R
Hill, Richard E. 1920- ... 33-36R
Hill, Richard Johnson 1925- ... CANR-4
Earlier sketch in CA 9-12R
Hill, Robert A. 1943- ... 132
Hill, Robert C(ecil) 1929- ... CANR-42
Earlier sketch in CA 118
Hill, Robert S. 1954- ... 162
Hill, Robert W(hite) 1919-1982 ... 9-12R
Obituary ... 107
See also SATA 12
See also SATA-Obit 31
Hill, Roger
See Paine, Lauran (Bosworth)
Hill, Rosalind M(ary) T(heodosia) 1908-1997 ...
CAP-1
Obituary ... 156
Earlier sketch in CA 11-12
Hill, Roscoe E(arl) 1936- ... 37-40R
Hill, Rowland
See Wallace-Clarke, George
Hill, Roy Gerald 1926- ... 111
Hill, Russell 1935- ... 141
Hill, Ruth A.
See Viguers, Ruth Hill
Hill, Ruth Beebe 1913- ... 89-92
Hill, Ruth Livingston
See Munce, Ruth Hill
Hill, Samuel E(rvin) 1913- ... 17-20R
Hill, Samuel S(mythe), Jr. 1927- ... CANR-5
Earlier sketch in CA 9-12R
Hill, Sarah H. ... 163
Hill, Selima 1945- ... 117
Hill, "Sir" John 1714(?)-1775 ... DLB 39
Hill, Stephen 1946- ... 111
Hill, Susan (Elizabeth) 1942- ... CANR-69
Earlier sketches in CA 33-36R, CANR-29
See also CLC 4, 113
See also DAB
See also DAM MST, NOV
See also DLB 14, 139
See also MTCW 1
Hill, Thomas 1960- ... 135
See also SATA 82
Hill, Thomas E(nglish), Jr. 1937- ... 137
Hill, Thomas English 1909- ... 13-16R
Hill, Tobias 1970- ... 168
Hill, W. M.
See Dodd, Edward Howard, Jr.
Hill, W(illiam) Speed 1935- ... 41-44R
Hill, Walter 1942- ... 140
Brief entry ... 109
See also DLB 44
Hill, Weldon
See Scott, William R(alph)
Hill, West T(hompson), Jr. 1915- ... 37-40R
Hill, Wilhelmina 1902- ... 57-60
Hill, William Joseph 1924- ... 37-40R
Hill, Winfred F(arrington) 1929- ... 29-32R
Hillaby, John (D.) 1917-1996 Obituary ... 154
Brief entry ... 109
Hillam, Ray C. 1928- Brief entry ... 107
Hillard, Darla 1946- ... 135
Hillard, James M(ilton) 1920- ... 73-76
Hillary, Edmund (Percival) 1919- ... 112
Hillary, Peter 1954- ... 123
Hillas, Julian
See Dashwood, Robert Julian
Hillbrand, Marc 1957- ... 165
Hillbruner, Anthony 1914- ... 41-44R
Hillcourt, William 1900-1992 ... CANR-46
Obituary ... 139
Earlier sketch in CA 93-96
See also SATA 27
Hillegas, Mark R(obert) 1926- ... 33-36R
Hillel, Yehoshua Bar
See Bar-Hillel, Yehoshua

Hillenbrand, Barry R. 1941- 73-76
Hillenbrand, Martin Joseph 1915- 108
Hillenbrand, Will 1960- . . . . SATA 84
Hiller, Catherine 1946- 106
Hiller, Doris
See Nussbaum, Al(bert F.)
Hiller, Flora
See Hurd, Florence
Hiller, Herbert L. 1931- 125
Hiller, Ilo (Ann) 1938- 121
See also SATA 59
Hiller, Lejaren A(rthur), Jr. 1924-1994 . . . . 1-4R
Obituary 144
Hillerbrand, Hans J(oachim) 1931- 134
Brief entry 111
Hillerich, Robert L(ee) 1927- 112
Hillerman, Anne 1949- 118
Hillerman, Tony 1925- CANR-65
Earlier sketches in CA 29-32R, CANR-21, 42
See also AAYA 6
See also BEST 89:1
See also CLC 62
See also DAM POP
See also SATA 6
Hillers, Delbert R(oy) 1932- 77-80
Hillers, H(erman) W(illiam) 1925- 73-76
Hillert, Margaret 1920- CANR-40
Earlier sketches in CA 49-52, CANR-1, 17
See also AITN 1
See also SATA 8, 91
Hillery, George A(nthony), Jr. 1927- 25-28R
Hilles, Frederick W(hiley) 1900-1975 . . . . 5-8R
Obituary 61-64
Hilles, Robert 165
Hillesum, Etty 1914-1943 137
See also TCLC 49
Hillgarth, J(ocelyn) N(igel) 1929- 37-40R
Hillgruber, Andreas (Fritz) 1925-1989 . . . . CANR-48
Obituary 128
Earlier sketch in CA 106
Hilliard, Asa G(rant) III 1933- 153
See also BW 2
Hilliard, David 1942- 142
See also BW 2
Hilliard, Jan
See Grant, Kay
Hilliard, Noel (Harvey) 1929- CANR-69
Earlier sketches in CA 9-12R, CANR-7
See also CLC 15
Hilliard, Robert L. 1925- 107
Hilliard, Sam B(owers) 1930- 61-64
Hillier, Bevis 1940- 29-32R
Hillier, Jack R(onald) 1912-1995 . . . . CANR-3
Obituary 147
Earlier sketch in CA 5-8R
Hillier, James Martin 1941- 113
Hillier, Jim
See Hillier, James Martin
Hillier, Tristram (Paul) 1905-1983 Obituary 114
Hilliker, Grant 1921- 33-36R
Hilling, David 1935- CANR-12
Earlier sketch in CA 29-32R
Hillinger, Brad 1952- 73-76
Hillis, Bryan V. 1956- 141
Hillis, Charles Richard 1913- 13-16R
Hillis, Dave 1945- 57-60
Hillis, Dick
See Hillis, Charles Richard
Hillis, Rick 1956- 134
See also CLC 66
Hillix, W(illiam) A(llen) 1927- 89-92
Hillman, Arthur 1909-1985 Obituary 115
Hillman, Barry L(eslie) 1942- 102
Hillman, Brenda 1951- 129
Hillman, Elizabeth 1942- 142
See also SATA 75
Hillman, Howard 1934- CANR-20
Earlier sketch in CA 41-44R
Hillman, James 1926- CANR-48
Earlier sketch in CA 89-92
Hillman, Libby 1919- 146
Hillman, Martin
See Hill, Douglas (Arthur)
Hillman, Priscilla 1940- 108
See also SATA 48
See also SATA-Brief 39
Hillman, Richard S. 1943- 151
Hillman, Ruth Estelyn 1925- 53-56
Hill-Miller, Katherine C(ecelia) 1949- 139
Hillocks, George, Jr. 1934- 53-56
Hill-Reid, William Scott 1890- 5-8R
Hills, Argentina Schifano 1921- 136
See also Hills, Tina
Hills, C(harles) A(lbert) R(eis) 1955- CANR-23
Earlier sketch in CA 106
See also SATA 39
Hills, Christopher B. 1926- 114
Hills, Denis (Cecil) 1913- CANR-10
Earlier sketch in CA 65-68
Hills, George 1918- 25-28R
Hills, L(awrence) Rust 1924- 25-28R
Hills, Lawrence Donegan 1911-1990 Obituary . . 132
Hills, Lee 1906- 101
See also AITN 2
See also DLB 127
Hills, P. J.
See Hills, Philip J(ames)
Hills, Patricia Gorton Schulze 1936- 103
Hills, Philip
See Hills, Philip J(ames)
Hills, Philip J(ames) 1933- 129
Brief entry 117
Hills, Stuart Lee 1932- 33-36R
Hills, Theo(dore) L(ewis) 1925- 5-8R
Hills, Tina
See Hills, Argentina Schifano
See also AITN 2
Hillsborough, Romulus (a pseudonym) 1953- . . . 168
Hillson, Maurie 1925- 17-20R
Hillstrom, Tom 1943- 102
Hillus, Wilhelm
See Hillers, H(erman) W(illiam)
Hillway, Tyrus 1912- CANR-4
Earlier sketch in CA 1-4R
Hillyard, Brian P. 1949- 111
Hillyer, Barbara 1934- 146
Hillyer, Robert (Silliman) 1895-1961 Obituary . 89-92
See also DLB 54
Hilmes, Michele 1953- 136
Hilscher, Herb(ert H.) 1902-1987 Obituary 122
Hilsdale, (Eric) Paul 1922- 9-12R
Hilsenrath, Edgar 1926- 49-52
Hilsman, Roger 1919- 5-8R
Hilt, Douglas Richard 1932- 65-68
Hiltebeital, Alf 1942- 103
Hiltner, Seward 1909-1984 . . . . CANR-1
Obituary 114
Earlier sketch in CA 1-4R
Hilton, Alec
See Chesser, Eustace
and Fullerton, Alexander (Fergus)
Hilton, Alice Mary 1924- 29-32R
Hilton, Bruce 1930- CANR-8
Earlier sketch in CA 5-8R
Hilton, Conrad N(icholson)
1887-1979 Obituary 81-84
Hilton, Della (Marion) 1934- 69-72
Hilton, Earl (Raymond) 1914- 21-24R
Hilton, George W(oodman) 1925- CANR-4
Earlier sketch in CA 1-4R
Hilton, Howard H(oyt, Jr.) 1926- 105
Hilton, Irene Pothus 1-4R
See also SATA 7
Hilton, James 1900-1954 Brief entry 108
See also DLB 34, 77
See also SATA 34
See also TCLC 21
Hilton, John Buxton 1921-1986 . . . . CANR-58
Earlier sketches in CA 53-56, CANR-5
Hilton, Lewis B. 1920- CANR-8
Earlier sketch in CA 57-60
Hilton, Margaret Lynette 1946- 136
See also Hilton, Nette
See also SATA 68
Hilton, (Howard) Nelson 1950- 110
Hilton, Nette
See Hilton, Margaret Lynette
See also CLR 25
See also SAAS 21
Hilton, Peter 1913- 69-72
Hilton, R. H.
See Hilton, Rodney (Howard)
Hilton, Ralph 1907- 29-32R
See also SATA 8
Hilton, Richard 1894- CAP-1
Earlier sketch in CA 9-10
Hilton, Rodney (Howard) 1916- 134
Brief entry 112
Hilton, Ronald 1911- 29-32R
Hilton, Suzanne 1922- CANR-30
Earlier sketches in CA 29-32R, CANR-12
See also SATA 4
Hilton, Thomas Leonard 1924- 13-16R
Hilton, Walter (?)-1396 . . . . DLB 146
Hilton Smith, Robert D(ennis)
(?)-1974 Obituary 53-56
Hilts, Philip J(ames) 1947- 110
Hilty, James W. 1939- 163
Hilu, Virginia 1929(?)-1976 Obituary 104
Hilvert, John (Peter Paul) 1945- 124
Him
See Deal, Borden
Him, George 1900-1982 Obituary 106
See also SATA-Obit 30
Himber, Jacob 1907- 105
Himelfarb, Richard 1963- 151
Himelick, (James) Raymond 1910- 33-36R
Himelstein, Morgan Y(ale) 1926- 5-8R
Himelstein, Shmuel 1940- 150
See also SATA 83
Himes, Chester (Bomar) 1909-1984 . . . . . CANR-22
Obituary 114
Earlier sketch in CA 25-28R
See also BLC 2
See also BW 2
See also CLC 2, 4, 7, 18, 58, 108
See also DAM MULT
See also DLB 2, 76, 143
See also MTCW 1
Himes, Joseph S(andy) 1908- 25-28R
Himler, Ann 1946- 53-56
See also SATA 8
Himler, Ronald (Norbert) 1937- CANR-57
Earlier sketches in CA 53-56, CANR-5
See also SATA 6, 92
Himmel, Richard L. 1950- 149
Himmelfarb, Gertrude 1922- CANR-66
Earlier sketches in CA 49-52, CANR-28
Himmelfarb, Milton 1918- 101
Himmelheber, Diana Martin 1938- 17-20R
Himmelman, John C(arl) 1959- CANR-68
Earlier sketch in CA 114
See also SATA 47, 94
Himmelstein, Jerome L(ionel) 1948- CANR-47
Earlier sketch in CA 113
Himstreet, William Charles 1923- CANR-16
Earlier sketches in CA 1-4R, CANR-1
Hinchliff, Peter Bingham 1929-1995 102
Obituary 150
Hinchliffe, Arnold P. 1930- CANR-14
Earlier sketch in CA 77-80
Hinchman, Lewis P(atrick) 1946- 150
Hinchman, Sandra K(uracina) 1950- 149
Hinckle, Warren James III 1938- 89-92
Hinckley, Barbara 1937- 57-60
Hinckley, Helen
See Jones, Helen Hinckley
Hinckley, Ted C(harles) 1925- CANR-40
Earlier sketch in CA 57-60
Hind, Dolores (Ellen) 1931- 129
See also SATA 53
See also SATA-Brief 49
Hind, Robert James 1931- 45-48
Hinde, Richard Standish Elphinstone 1912- . CAP-1
Earlier sketch in CA 9-10
Hinde, Robert A(ubrey) 1923- CANR-57
Earlier sketches in CA 109, CANR-30
Hinde, Thomas
See Chitty, Thomas Willes
See also CLC 6, 11
Hinde, Wendy 1919- 103
Hindemith, Paul 1895-1963 Obituary 112
Hinden, Michael C(harles) 1941- 109
Hinderer, Walter (Hermann) 1934- CANR-1
Earlier sketch in CA 45-48
Hindess, Barry 1939- 153
Hindin, Nathan
See Bloch, Robert (Albert)
Hindin, Philip 1916- 166
Hinding, Andrea 1942- 126
Hindle, Brooke 1918- CANR-23
Earlier sketches in CA 13-16R, CANR-7
Hindle, Lee J(ohn) 1965- 117
Hindle, W(ilfred) H(ope) 1903-1967 . . . . CAP-2
Earlier sketch in CA 23-24
Hindley, Geoffrey 1935- 109
Hindman, Jane F(erguson) 1905- CANR-10
Earlier sketch in CA 25-28R
Hindman, Jo(sephine Long) 1910- 97-100
Hindmarch, Gladys 1940- 128
Hindmarsh, Joseph fl. 1678-1696 . . . . DLB 170
Hinds, Dudley S. 1926- 115
Hinds, E. M.
See Hinds, (Evelyn) Margery
Hinds, (Evelyn) Margery 9-12R
Hinds, Michael deCourcy
See deCourcy Hinds, Michael
Hinds, P(atricia) Mignon 165
See also SATA 98
Hindus, Maurice (Gerschon)
1891-1969 Obituary 25-28R
Hindus, Michael S(tephen) 1946- 105
Hindus, Milton Henry 1916-1998 . . . . CANR-7
Obituary 167
Earlier sketch in CA 17-20R
Hine, Al(fred Blakelee) 1915- CANR-2
Earlier sketch in CA 1-4R
Hine, Darlene Clark 1947- 143
Hine, (William) Daryl 1936- CANR-20
Earlier sketches in CA 1-4R, CANR-1
See also CAAS 15
See also CLC 15
See also DLB 60
Hine, Frederick R. 1925- 37-40R
Hine, James R. 1909- CANR-17
Earlier sketches in CA 45-48, CANR-2
Hine, Robert Van Norden, Jr. 1921- CANR-1
Earlier sketch in CA 1-4R
Hine, Sesyle Joslin 1929- 13-16R
See also Joslin, Sesyle
Hine, Thomas 1947- 123
Hine, Virginia H(aglin) 1920- 97-100
Hiner, Louis C(hase) 1919- 73-76
Hiner, N. Ray, Jr. 1937- 127
Hines, Anna G(rossnickle) 1946- CANR-67
Earlier sketches in CA 114, CANR-36
See also SAAS 16
See also SATA 51, 95
See also SATA-Brief 45
Hines, Barry (Melvin) 1939- CANR-70
Earlier sketch in CA 102
Hines, Bede F(rancis) 1918- 45-48
Hines, Donald M. 1931- 136
Hines, Earl Kenneth 1905-1983 Obituary 109
Hines, Fatha
See Hines, Earl Kenneth
Hines, Gary (Roger) 1944- . . . . SATA 74
Hines, Jeanne 1922- 140
Hines, Jerome 1921- 130
Hines, Joanna 1949- 154
Hines, John 1956- 145
Hines, Neal O(ldfield) 1908- CANR-2
Earlier sketch in CA 5-8R
Hines, Paul (David) 1934- 29-32R
Hines, Robert Stephan 1926- CANR-3
Earlier sketch in CA 9-12R
Hines, Terence (Michael) 1951- 128
Hines, Thomas S(pight) 1936- CANR-72
Earlier sketches in CA 53-56, CANR-5
Hines, William H. 1909(?)-1976 Obituary 65-68
Hinger, Charlotte 1940- 123
Hingley, Ronald F(rancis) 1920- CANR-48
Earlier sketch in CA 5-8R
See also DLB 155
Hingorani, R(up) C. 1925- CANR-26
Earlier sketch in CA 29-32R
Hinkel, John V.
See Hinkel, John Vincent
Hinkel, John Vincent 1906-1986 Obituary 121
Hinkemeyer, Michael T(homas) 1940- CANR-34
Earlier sketches in CA 69-72, CANR-11
Hinkle, Douglas P(addock) 1923- 69-72
Hinkle, Gerald H(ahn) 1931- 89-92
Hinkle, Olin Ethmer 1902- 1-4R
Hinkle, Vernon 1935- CANR-30
Earlier sketch in CA 109
Hinkson, James 1943- 69-72
Hinkson, Katharine Tynan
See Tynan, Katharine
Hinkson, Pamela 1900(?)-1982 Obituary 107
Hin-Mah-Too-Yah-Lat-Kekt
See Chief Joseph
Hinman, Charlton (Joseph Kadio) 1911-1977 . . . . . .
CANR-3
Obituary 89-92
Earlier sketch in CA 5-8R
Hinman, George W., Jr. 1891-1977 Obituary . 73-76
Hinman, Robert B(enedict) 1920- 5-8R
Hinn, Benny 1952- 142
Hinnebusch, Paul (Gerard) 1917- CANR-35
Earlier sketch in CA 114
Hinnebusch, Raymond A. 1946- 136
Hinnebusch, William A(quinas) 1908- 37-40R
Hinnells, John R(ussell) 1941- CANR-48
Earlier sketch in CA 49-52
Hinojosa, Gilberto Miguel 1942- 151
Hinojosa, Maria (de Lourdes) 1961- 152
See also SATA 88
Hinojosa(-Smith), Rolando (R.) 1929- CANR-62
Earlier sketch in CA 131
See also Hinojosa-Smith, Rolando
See also DAM MULT
See also DLB 82
See also HW
Hinojosa-S., Rolando R.
See Hinojosa(-Smith), Rolando (R.)
Hinojosa-Smith, Rolando 1929-
See Hinojosa(-Smith), Rolando (R.)
See also CAAS 16
See also HLC
Hinrichs, Ernest H(enry) 1922- 155
Hinrichsen, Max (Henry) 1901-1965 . . . . CAP-1
Earlier sketch in CA 13-14
Hinshaw, Cecil E(ugene) 1911- 13-16R
Hinshaw, H(orton) Corwin 1902- 104
Hinshaw, Randall (Weston) 1915-1997 . . . . CANR-15
Obituary 160
Earlier sketch in CA 41-44R
Hinshaw, Robert E(ugene) 1933- 57-60
Hinshaw, Seth B(ennett) 1908- 112
Hinshelwood, Cyril (Norman)
1897-1967 Obituary 116
Hinsley, F(rancis) H(arry) 1918-1998 . . . . . . 17-20R
Obituary 166
Hinsley, SirFrancis Harry
See Hinsley, F(rancis) H(arry)
Hinson, E(dward) Glenn 1931- CANR-8
Earlier sketch in CA 21-24R
Hinson, (Grady) Maurice 1930- CANR-38
Earlier sketches in CA 45-48, CANR-2, 17
Hinterhoff, Eugene 1895- CAP-1
Earlier sketch in CA 9-10
Hintikka, (Kaarlo) Jaakko (Juhani) 1929- . . CANR-2
Earlier sketch in CA 1-4R
Hinton, Ann Pearlman 1941- 108
Hinton, Bernard L. 1937- 33-36R
Hinton, Harold C(lendenin) 1924-1993 . . . . . 17-20R
Obituary 142
Hinton, John (Mark) 1926- CANR-48
Earlier sketch in CA 49-52
Hinton, Michael 1927- 149
Hinton, Milt
See Hinton, Milton John
Hinton, Milton John 1910- 134
Hinton, Nigel 1941- 85-88
Hinton, Richard W.
See Angoff, Charles
Hinton, S(usan) E(loise) 1950- CANR-62
Earlier sketches in CA 81-84, CANR-32
See also AAYA 2
See also CLC 30, 111
See also CLR 3, 23
See also DA
See also DAB
See also DAC
See also DAM MST, NOV
See also JRDA
See also MAICYA
See also MTCW 1
See also SATA 19, 58
Hinton, Sam 1917- 73-76
See also SATA 43
Hinton, Ted C. 1904(?)-1977 Obituary 73-76
Hinton, William H. 1919- CANR-40
Earlier sketches in CA 25-28R, CANR-18
Hintz, (Loren) Martin 1945- CANR-30
Earlier sketches in CA 65-68, CANR-12
See also SATA 47
See also SATA-Brief 39
Hintze, Guenther 1906- CAP-2
Earlier sketch in CA 21-22
Hintze, Naomi A. 1909- CANR-1
Earlier sketch in CA 45-48
Hinxman, Margaret 1924- 124
Hinz, Evelyn J. 1938- CANR-10
Earlier sketch in CA 65-68
Hipp, George
See Abrams, George J(oseph)
Hippel, Theodor Gottlieb von 1741-1796 . . . DLB 97
Hippisley Coxe, Antony D(acres) 1912-1988 . . . 103
Obituary 124
Hippius, Zinaida
See Gippius, Zinaida (Nikolayevna)
See also TCLC 9
Hipple, Theodore W(allace) 1935- CANR-10
Earlier sketch in CA 65-68
Hipple, Walter J(ohn), Jr. 1921- 41-44R
Hippler, Arthur E(dwin) 1935- 57-60
Hippocrates of Cos fl. c. 425B.C.- . . . . DLB 176

Hippopotamus, Eugene H.
See Kraus, (Herman) Robert
Hipps, Juanita Redmond
1913(?)-1979 Obituary ... 85-88
Hipskind, Judith 1945- ... 97-100
Hipskind, Verne K(enneth) 1925-1975 ... CAP-2
Earlier sketch in CA 21-22
Hirabayashi, Lane Ryo 1952- ... 152
Hirabayashi, Taiko 1905-1972 ... DLB 180
Hirano, Cathy 1957- ... SATA 68
Hirano, Marsha
See Hirano-Nakanishi, Marsha J(oyce)
Hirano-Nakanishi, Marsha J(oyce) 1949- ... 119
Hiraoka, Kimitake 1925-1970 ... 97-100
Obituary ... 29-32R
See also Mishima, Yukio
See also DAM DRAM
See also MTCW 1
Hiro, Dilip ... CANR-64
Earlier sketches in CA 77-80, CANR-14, 32
Hirsch, Abby 1946- ... 45-48
Hirsch, Barbara B. 1938- ... 73-76
Hirsch, Charles S. 1942- ... 105
Hirsch, David H. 1930- ... 97-100
Hirsch, E(ric) D(onald), Jr. 1928- ... CANR-51
Earlier sketches in CA 25-28R, CANR-27
Interview in ... CANR-27
See also CLC 79
See also DLB 67
See also MTCW 1
Hirsch, Edward 1950- ... CANR-42
Earlier sketches in CA 104, CANR-20
See also CLC 31, 50
See also DLB 120
Hirsch, Ernest A(lbert) 1924-1977 ... CANR-11
Earlier sketch in CA 25-28R
Hirsch, Foster (Lance) 1943- ... CANR-39
Earlier sketches in CA 45-48, CANR-2, 17
Hirsch, Fred 1931-1978 ... CANR-28
Obituary ... 77-80
Earlier sketch in CA 25-28R
Hirsch, Herbert 1941- ... CANR-15
Earlier sketch in CA 41-44R
Hirsch, Karen 1941- ... 105
See also SATA 61
Hirsch, Lester M. 1925- ... 17-20R
Hirsch, Linda 1949- ... 105
Hirsch, Marianne 1949- ... CANR-46
Earlier sketch in CA 113
Hirsch, Mark David 1910-1989 ... 89-92
Obituary ... 128
Hirsch, Miriam F. 1927- ... 106
Hirsch, Monroe J(erome) 1917-1982 ... CANR-48
Earlier sketch in CA 41-44R
Hirsch, Morris Isaac 1915- ... 103
Hirsch, Phil 1926- ... 102
See also SATA 35
Hirsch, Robin 1942- ... 154
Hirsch, S. Carl 1913- ... CANR-2
Earlier sketch in CA 5-8R
See also SAAS 7
See also SATA 2
Hirsch, Seev 1931- ... 33-36R
Hirsch, Steven R(ichard) 1937- ... CANR-32
Earlier sketch in CA 113
Hirsch, Thomas L. 1931- ... 49-52
Hirsch, Walter 1919- ... 13-16R
Hirsch, Werner Z. 1920- ... CANR-7
Earlier sketch in CA 17-20R
Hirsch, William Randolph
See Kitman, Marvin
and Lingeman, Richard R(oberts)
Hirschberg, Cornelius 1901- ... CAP-2
Earlier sketch in CA 17-18
Hirschfeld, Albert 1903- ... CANR-2
Earlier sketch in CA 1-4R
Hirschfeld, Burt 1923- ... 134
Brief entry ... 111
Hirschfeld, Charles 1913- ... 127
Brief entry ... 105
Hirschfeld, Fritz 1924- ... 167
Hirschfeld, Herman 1905- ... CAP-1
Earlier sketch in CA 13-16
Hirschfeld, Lawrence A. 1947- ... 158
Hirschfeld, Magnus 1868-1935 ... 148
Hirschfeld, Yizhar 1950- ... 143
Hirschfelder, Arlene B. 1943- ... 147
See also SATA 80
Hirschfelder, Joseph Oakland
1911-1990 Obituary ... 131
Hirschfield, Robert S(idney) 1928-1995 ... 45-48
Obituary ... 149
Hirschhorn, Clive 1940- ... CANR-9
Earlier sketch in CA 57-60
Hirschhorn, Howard H(arvey) 1931- ... CANR-42
Earlier sketches in CA 93-96, CANR-16
Hirschhorn, Joel 1937- ... 159
Hirschhorn, Richard Clark 1933- ... 69-72
Hirschi, Ron 1948- ... CANR-68
Earlier sketch in CA 120
See also SATA 56, 95
Hirschi, Travis 1935- ... CANR-13
Earlier sketch in CA 77-80
Hirschman, A. O.
See Hirschman, Albert O.
Hirschman, Albert O. 1915- ... CANR-37
Earlier sketches in CA 1-4R, CANR-1, 16
Hirschman, Jack 1933- ... CANR-22
Earlier sketch in CA 105
Hirschmann, Linda (Ann) 1941- ... 106
See also SATA 40
Hirsch-Holman, Maria Anne ... 85-88
Hirschmeier, Johannes 1921- ... CANR-5
Earlier sketch in CA 13-16R
Hirsh, James E(ric) 1946- ... 109
Hirsh, M(ary) E(lizabeth) 1947- ... 125
Hirsh, Marilyn 1944-1988 ... CANR-16
Obituary ... 126
Earlier sketches in CA 49-52, CANR-1
See also SATA 7
See also SATA-Obit 58
Hirshberg, Al(bert Simon) 1909-1973 ... CANR-4
Obituary ... 41-44R
Earlier sketch in CA 1-4R
See also SATA 38
Hirshfeld, Alan 1951- ... 141
Hirshfeld, Richard
See Hall, Richard W(alter)
Hirshfield, Daniel S. 1942- ... 29-32R
Hirshfield, Jane 1953- ... CANR-70
Earlier sketch in CA 149
Hirsh-Pasek, Kathy 1953- ... 163
Hirshson, Stanley Philip 1928- ... 1-4R
Hirst, David W(ayne) 1920- ... 37-40R
Hirst, Paul H(eywood) 1927- ... 65-68
Hirst, Paul Quentin 1946- ... 104
Hirst, Rodney Julian 1920- ... 9-12R
Hirst, Stephen M(ichael) 1939- ... 53-56
Hirst, Wilma E(llis) 1914- ... 13-16R
Hirt, Howard (Franklin) 1924-1987 ... 131
Hirt, Michael L(eonard) 1934- ... 9-12R
Hisamatsu, (Hoseki) Shin'ichi 1889- ... 81-84
Hiscock, Bruce 1940- ... CANR-49
Earlier sketch in CA 122
See also SATA 57
Hiscock, Eric 1899-1989(?) ... 109
Obituary ... 127
Hiscock, Eric C(harles) 1908-1986 ... 107
Obituary ... 120
Hiscocks, C(harles) Richard 1907- ... 53-56
Hiscoe, Helen B. 1919- ... 137
Hiser, Constance 1950- ... SATA 71
Hiser, Iona Seibert ... CANR-2
Earlier sketch in CA 1-4R
See also SATA 4
Hiskett, Mervyn 1920- ... 61-64
Hislop, Codman 1906- ... CAP-2
Earlier sketch in CA 33-36
Hislop, Julia Rose Catherine 1962- ... 141
See also SATA 74
Hisrich, Robert D(ale) 1944- ... 112
Hiss, Alger 1904-1996 ... 33-36R
Obituary ... 154
Hiss, Tony 1941- ... 77-80
Hissey, Jane (Elizabeth) 1952- ... 124
See also SATA 58
Hitchcock, Alfred (Joseph) 1899-1980 ... 159
Obituary ... 97-100
See also AAYA 22
See also CLC 16
See also SATA 27
See also SATA-Obit 24
Hitchcock, Alma Reville 1899-1982 Obituary ... 107
Hitchcock, Deborah J.
See Jessup, Deborah Hitchcock
Hitchcock, George 1914- ... CANR-13
Earlier sketch in CA 33-36R
See also CAAS 12
Hitchcock, H(ugh) Wiley 1923- ... CANR-17
Earlier sketches in CA 45-48, CANR-1
Hitchcock, Henry-Russell 1903-1987 ... 125
Obituary ... 122
Hitchcock, James 1938- ... 33-36R
Hitchcock, Raymond (John) 1922- ... 85-88
Hitchcock, Susan Tyler 1950- ... CANR-18
Earlier sketch in CA 102
Hitchcott, Nicki 1965- ... 156
Hitchens, Christopher (Eric) 1949- ... 149
Hitchens, Dolores 1908(?)-1973 Obituary ... 45-48
Hitchens, Neal 1957- ... 141
Hitchin, Martin Mewburn 1917- ... 13-16R
Hitching, (John) Francis 1933- ... 103
Hitchins, Keith 1931- ... 147
Hitchman, James H. 1932- ... 37-40R
Hitchman, Janet 1916-1980 ... 21-24R
Obituary ... 97-100
Hite, James (Cleveland) 1941- ... 53-56
Hite, Molly 1947- ... CANR-51
Earlier sketch in CA 124
Hite, Shere 1942- ... CANR-31
Earlier sketch in CA 81-84
See also MTCW 1
Hite, Sid 1954- ... 142
See also SATA 75
Hitiris, Theodore 1938- ... 41-44R
Hitler, Adolf 1889-1945 ... 147
Brief entry ... 117
See also TCLC 53
Hitrec, Joseph George 1912-1972 ... CAP-2
Earlier sketch in CA 17-18
Hitsman, J(ohn) Mackay 1917-1970 ... CAP-1
Earlier sketch in CA 17-18
Hitt, Russell T(rovillo) 1905- ... 1-4R
Hitt, William D(ee) 1929- ... 49-52
Hitte, Kathryn 1919- ... 21-24R
See also SATA 16
Hitti, Philip K(huri) 1886-1978 ... CANR-6
Obituary ... 81-84
Earlier sketch in CA 1-4R
Hittinger, (F.) Russell 1949- ... 145
Hitz, Demi 1942- ... CANR-35
Earlier sketches in CA 61-64, CANR-8
See also MAICYA
See also SATA 11, 66, 102
Hitzeroth, Deborah L. 1961- ... 146
See also SATA 78
Hitz-Holman, Betsy
See Holman, Betsy Hitz
Hively, Pete (Chester) 1934- ... 69-72
Hivnor, Robert 1916- ... CANR-28
Earlier sketch in CA 65-68
Hix, Charles (Arthur) 1942- ... CANR-21
Earlier sketch in CA 102
Hixon, Don L(ee) 1942- ... 73-76
Hixson, Joseph R(andolph) 1927- ... 65-68
Hixson, Richard F. 1932- ... 21-24R
Hixson, William B(utler), Jr. 1940- ... 37-40R
Hjelte, George 1893-1979 ... CANR-23
Earlier sketch in CA 29-32R
Hjortsberg, William (Reinhold) 1941- ... CANR-72
Earlier sketch in CA 33-36R
Hlasko, Marek 1933(?)-1969 Obituary ... 25-28R
Hlybinny, Vladimir
See Seduro, Vladimir
Hnizdovsky, Jacques 1915- ... SATA 32
Ho, Alfred K(uo-liang) 1919- ... CANR-35
Earlier sketch in CA 25-28R
Ho, Chi Minh 1890(?)-1969 Obituary ... 112
Ho, Minfong 1951- ... CANR-67
Earlier sketch in CA 77-80
See also CLR 28
See also SATA 15, 94
Ho, Ping-ti 1917- ... CANR-11
Earlier sketch in CA 5-8R
Hoa, Nguyen-Dinh
See Nguyen, Dinh Hoa
Hoadley, Irene Braden 1938- ... 29-32R
Hoadley, Walter E(vans) 1916- ... 102
Hoag, Edwin 1926- ... 13-16R
Hoag, Tami 1959- ... CANR-72
Earlier sketch in CA 138
Hoagland, Anthony Dey 1953- ... 153
Hoagland, Edward 1932- ... CANR-57
Earlier sketches in CA 1-4R, CANR-2, 31
See also CLC 28
See also DLB 6
See also SATA 51
Hoagland, Everett (III) 1942- ... CANR-25
Earlier sketch in CA 33-36R
See also BW 1
See also DLB 41
Hoagland, Jimmie Lee 1940- ... 101
Hoagland, John 1947(?)-1984 Obituary ... 112
Hoagland, Kathleen M(ary) Dooher
1909(?)-1984 ... 5-8R
Obituary ... 112
Hoagland, Mahlon B(ush) 1921- ... 85-88
Hoagland, Tony
See Hoagland, Anthony Dey
Hoang Van Chi 1915- ... CANR-7
Earlier sketch in CA 13-16R
Hoar, Jere (Richmond) 1929- ... 163
Hoar, Roger Sherman 1887-1963 ... 160
Hoare, Merval Hannah 1914- ... 103
Hoare, Philip 1958- ... 134
Hoare, Robert J(ohn) 1921-1975 ... CANR-6
Earlier sketch in CA 9-12R
See also SATA 38
Hoare, Wilber W., Jr. 1921-1976 Obituary ... 65-68
Hoban, Lillian 1925- ... CANR-23
Earlier sketch in CA 69-72
See also MAICYA
See also SATA 22, 69
Hoban, Russell (Conwell) 1925- ... CANR-66
Earlier sketches in CA 5-8R, CANR-23, 37
See also CLC 7, 25
See also CLR 3
See also DAM NOV
See also DLB 52
See also MAICYA
See also MTCW 1
See also SATA 1, 40, 78
Hoban, Tana ... CANR-23
Earlier sketch in CA 93-96
See also CLR 13
See also MAICYA
See also SAAS 12
See also SATA 22, 70
Hobart, Alice Nourse 1882-1967 ... 5-8R
Obituary ... 25-28R
Hobart, Alice Tisdale
See Hobart, Alice Nourse
Hobart, Billie 1935- ... 49-52
Hobart, Lois (Elaine) ... 5-8R
See also SATA 7
Hobb, Robin
See Lindholm, Megan
Hobbes, Thomas 1588-1679 ... DLB 151
Hobbing, Enno 1920- ... 89-92
Hobbs, Albert Hoyt 1910- ... 125
Hobbs, Anne
See Purdy, Anne S.
Hobbs, Anne Stevenson 1942- ... 133
Hobbs, Cecil (Carlton) 1907- ... 21-24R
Hobbs, Charles R(ene) 1931- ... 13-16R
Hobbs, (Carl) Fredric 1931- ... 81-84
Hobbs, Herschel Harold 1907- ... CANR-2
Earlier sketch in CA 5-8R
Hobbs, J. Kline 1928- ... 108
Hobbs, John Leslie 1916-1964 ... 5-8R
Hobbs, Mary 1923- ... 153
Hobbs, Michael 1934- ... 111
Hobbs, Perry
See Blackmur, R(ichard) P(almer)
Hobbs, Peter V(ictor) 1936- ... 53-56
Hobbs, Richard (Wright) 1931- ... 123
Brief entry ... 118
Hobbs, Robert C(arleton) 1946- ... CANR-24
Earlier sketch in CA 106
Hobbs, Valerie 1941- ... 159
See also SATA 93
Hobbs, Will 1947- ... AAYA 14
See also SATA 72
Hobbs, William (Beresford) 1939- ... 21-24R
Hobbs, Williston C. 1925(?)-1978 Obituary ... 81-84
Hobby, Bertram Maurice 1905-1983 Obituary ... 110
Hobby, Elaine (Ann) 1956- ... 130
Hobby, Gladys L(ounsbury) 1910-1993 ... 119
Obituary ... 141
Hobby, Oveta Culp 1905- ... 81-84
See also DLB 127
Hobby, William 1878-1964 ... DLB 127
Hobby, William P. 1932- ... 85-88
Hobday, Charles (Henry) 1917- ... 132
Hobday, Victor C(arr) 1914- ... 97-100
Hobel, Phil
See Fanthorpe, R(obert) Lionel
Hoben, John B. 1908- ... 37-40R
Hoberecht, Earnest 1918- ... 21-24R
Hoberman, Gerald 1943- ... 111
Hoberman, Mary Ann 1930- ... 41-44R
See also CLR 22
See also MAICYA
See also SAAS 18
See also SATA 5, 72
Hobfoll, Stevan E(arl) 1951- ... CANR-49
Earlier sketch in CA 123
Hobgood, Burnet M. 1922- ... 101
Hobhouse, Christina 1941- ... 25-28R
Hobhouse, Hermione 1934- ... CANR-15
Earlier sketch in CA 41-44R
Hobhouse, Janet 1948-1991 ... 57-60
Obituary ... 133
Hobhouse, Penelope
See Malins, Penelope
Hobkirk, Michael D(algliesh) 1924- ... 119
Hobley, Leonard Frank 1903- ... CANR-5
Earlier sketch in CA 13-16R
Hobsbaum, Philip (Dennis) 1932- ... CANR-56
Earlier sketches in CA 9-12R, CANR-3, 29
See also DLB 40
Hobsbawm, Eric J(ohn Ernest) 1917- ... CANR-56
Earlier sketches in CA 5-8R, CANR-3
Hobson, Anthony (Robert Alwyn) 1921- ... 33-36R
Hobson, Bruce 1950- ... CANR-54
Earlier sketch in CA 127
See also SATA 62
Hobson, Burton (Harold) 1933- ... CANR-2
Earlier sketch in CA 5-8R
See also SATA 28
Hobson, Charles F. 1943- ... 164
Hobson, Edmund (Schofield) 1931- ... 45-48
Hobson, Fred Colby, Jr. 1943- ... CANR-5
Earlier sketch in CA 53-56
Hobson, Geary 1941- ... 122
Hobson, Hank
See Hobson, Harry
Hobson, Harold 1904-1992 ... 81-84
Obituary ... 137
Hobson, Harry 1908- ... CAP-1
Earlier sketch in CA 9-10
Hobson, J(ohn) Allan 1933- ... 140
Hobson, Julius W(ilson) 1922(?)-1977 ... 102
See also BW 1
Hobson, Laura Z(ametkin) 1900-1986 ... CANR-55
Obituary ... 118
Earlier sketch in CA 17-20R
See also CLC 7, 25
See also DLB 28
See also SATA 52
Hobson, Mary 1926- ... 106
Hobson, Polly
See Evans, Julia (Rendel)
Hobson, Sally 1967- ... SATA 84
Hobson, William 1911- ... 103
Hoby, Thomas 1530-1566 ... DLB 132
Hobzek, Mildred J(ane) 1919- ... 101
Hoccleve, Thomas c. 1368-c. 1437 ... DLB 146
Hoch, Edward D(entinger) 1930- ... CANR-51
Earlier sketches in CA 29-32R, CANR-11, 27
Hoch, Paul L(awrence) 1942- ... CANR-27
Earlier sketch in CA 65-68
Hochbaum, H(ans) Albert 1911- ... 103
Hochfield, George 1926- ... 1-4R
Hochhuth, Rolf 1931- ... CANR-33
Earlier sketch in CA 5-8R
See also CLC 4, 11, 18
See also DAM DRAM
See also DLB 124
See also MTCW 1
Hochman, Baruch 1930- ... 128
Hochman, Elaine S(chwartz) ... 166
Hochman, Gloria 1943- ... 141
Hochman, Harold M(arvin) 1936- ... 108
Hochman, Jiri 1926- ... 141
Hochman, Sandra 1936- ... 5-8R
See also CLC 3, 8
See also DLB 5
Hochman, Shel 1944- ... 69-72
Hochman, Shirley D(ean) 1917- ... 61-64
Hochman, Stanley Richard 1928- ... CANR-48
Earlier sketch in CA 103
Hochschild, Adam 1942- ... CANR-53
Brief entry ... 121
Earlier sketch in CA 125
Interview in ... 125
Hochschild, Arlie Russell 1940- ... CANR-72
Earlier sketches in CA 57-60, CANR-45
See also BEST 89:4
See also SATA 11
Hochschild, Harold K. 1892-1981 Obituary ... 103
Hochstein, Rolaine ... CANR-23
Earlier sketch in CA 45-48
Hochstetter, Leo D. 1911(?)-1987 Obituary ... 122
Hochwaelder, Fritz 1911-1986 ... CANR-42
Obituary ... 120
Earlier sketch in CA 29-32R
See also CLC 36
See also DAM DRAM
See also MTCW 1
Hochwald, Werner 1910- ... 17-20R
Hochwalder, Fritz
See Hochwaelder, Fritz

Hockaby, Stephen
See Mitchell, Gladys (Maude Winifred)
Hocke, Martin 1938- ... 154
Hocken, Thomas Morland 1836-1910 ... DLB 184
Hockenberry, Hope
See Newell, Hope Hockenberry
Hockenberry, John 1956(?)- ... 155
Hockensmith, Sean M. 1972- ... 164
Hocker, Karla
See Hoecker, Karla
Hockett, Charles F(rancis) 1916- ... 17-20R
Hocking, Anthony 1938- ... 102
Hocking, Brian 1914-1974 ... CAP-2
Earlier sketch in CA 17-18
Hocking, Mary (Eunice) 1921- ... CANR-40
Earlier sketches in CA 101, CANR-18
See also CLC 13
Hocking, William Ernest 1873-1966 ... CAP-1
Earlier sketch in CA 13-14
Hockley, G(raham) C(harles) 1931- ... 29-32R
Hockney, David 1937- ... 150
Brief entry ... 116
See also AAYA 17
Hocks, Richard A(llen) 1936- ... 81-84
Hocquenghem, Guy 1946-1988 ... 148
Hodder-Williams, (John) Christopher (Glazebrook) 1926-1995 ... CANR-1
Obituary ... 148
Earlier sketch in CA 1-4R
Hoddinott, Ralph Field 1913- ... 127
Hodeir, Andre 1921- ... CANR-34
Earlier sketches in CA 85-88, CANR-15
Hodemart, Peter
See Audemars, Pierre
Hodes, Aubrey 1927- ... 33-36R
Hodes, Scott 1937- ... 49-52
Hodgart, Matthew (John Caldwell) 1916-1996 ... CANR-9
Obituary ... 151
Earlier sketch in CA 5-8R
Hodge, Alan 1915-1979 Obituary ... 89-92
Hodge, David W(ayne) 1935- ... 61-64
Hodge, Francis (Richard) 1915- ... CANR-12
Earlier sketch in CA 33-36R
Hodge, Gene (Meany) 1898- ... 45-48
Hodge, James L(ee) 1935- ... 41-44R
Hodge, Jane Aiken 1917- ... CANR-45
Earlier sketches in CA 5-8R, CANR-3
Hodge, Marshall Bryant 1925-(?) ... CAP-2
Earlier sketch in CA 23-24
Hodge, P. W.
See Hodge, Paul W(illiam)
Hodge, Paul W(illiam) 1934- ... CANR-42
Earlier sketches in CA 33-36R, CANR-14
See also SATA 12
Hodge, Robert 1940- ... 128
Hodge, William H(oward) 1932- ... CANR-15
Earlier sketch in CA 65-68
Hodgell, P(atricia) C(hristine) 1951- ... CANR-60
Earlier sketch in CA 109
See also SATA 42
Hodges, C(yril) Walter 1909- ... CANR-5
Earlier sketch in CA 13-16R
See also SATA 2
Hodges, Carl G. 1902-1964 ... 5-8R
See also SATA 10
Hodges, Devon Leigh 1950- ... CANR-51
Earlier sketch in CA 125
Hodges, Donald Clark 1923- ... CANR-49
Earlier sketches in CA 53-56, CANR-6, 24
Hodges, Doris M(arjorie) 1915- ... CANR-11
Earlier sketch in CA 25-28R
Hodges, Elizabeth Jamison ... 9-12R
See also SATA 1
Hodges, Gil(bert Ray) 1924-1972 Obituary ... 109
Hodges, Graham R(ushing) 1915- ... 5-8R
Hodges, H(erbert) A(rthur) 1905-1976 ... CANR-48
Obituary ... 69-72
Earlier sketch in CA 73-76
Hodges, Harold Mellor 1922- ... 17-20R
Hodges, Henry (Woolmington MacKenzie) 1920- ... 37-40R
Hodges, Henry G. 1888- ... 5-8R
Hodges, John C(unyus) 1892-1967 ... 5-8R
Obituary ... 103
Hodges, Louis W. 1933- ... 81-84
Hodges, Luther (Hartwell) 1898-1974 Obituary ... 53-56
Hodges, Margaret Moore 1911- ... CANR-30
Earlier sketches in CA 1-4R, CANR-2
See also MAICYA
See also SAAS 9
See also SATA 1, 33, 75
Hodges, Michael P. 1941- ... 136
Hodges, Richard E(dwin) 1928- ... CANR-15
Earlier sketch in CA 41-44R
Hodges, Turner
See Morehead, Albert H(odges)
Hodges, Zane Clark 1932- ... CANR-15
Earlier sketch in CA 41-44R
Hodgetts, A(lfred) Birnie 1911- ... 101
Hodgetts, Blake Christopher 1967- ... 114
See also SATA 43
Hodgetts, J(ohn) E(dwin) 1917- ... 13-16R
Hodgetts, Richard M(ichael) 1942- ... CANR-23
Earlier sketches in CA 57-60, CANR-8
Hodgins, Bruce W(illard) 1931- ... 37-40R
Hodgins, Eric 1899-1971 ... 104
Obituary ... 29-32R
Hodgins, Jack 1938- ... 93-96
See also CLC 23
See also DLB 60
Hodgins, (Ian) Philip 1959- ... 153
Hodgkin, Alan (Lloyd) 1914- ... 140
Hodgkin, Robert Allason 1916- ... 102
Hodgkin, Robin A.
See Hodgkin, Robert Allason
Hodgkin, Thomas Lionel 1910-1982 Obituary ... 115
Hodgkinson, Anthony 1916-1983 ... 126
Hodgkinson, Christopher 1928- ... 115
Hodgkinson, Edith 1959- ... 117
Hodgkinson, Liz 1943- ... 124
Hodgkinson, Marie Elisabeth 1921(?)-1983 Obituary ... 110
Hodgkiss, A(lan) G(eoffrey) 1921- ... 124
Hodgman, Helen 1945- ... 131
Brief entry ... 117
See also DLB 14
Hodgskin, Thomas 1787-1869 ... DLB 158
Hodgson, D(avid) H(argraves) 1939- ... 25-28R
Hodgson, David
See Lewis, David
Hodgson, Derek 1929- ... 118
Hodgson, Geoffrey M. 1946- ... 146
Hodgson, Godfrey (Michael Talbot) 1934- ... 25-28R
Hodgson, Harriet 1935- ... 150
See also SATA 84
Hodgson, John A(lfred) 1945- ... 125
Hodgson, Leonard 1889-1969 ... CAP-1
Earlier sketch in CA 9-10
Hodgson, Margaret
See Ballinger, (Violet) Margaret (Livingstone)
Hodgson, Marshall G. S. 1922-1968 ... CAP-2
Earlier sketch in CA 21-22
Hodgson, Martha (Keeling) 1906- ... 57-60
Hodgson, Norma
See Russell, Norma Hull Lewis
Hodgson, Pat 1928- ... CANR-7
Earlier sketch in CA 57-60
Hodgson, Peter Crafts 1934- ... CANR-15
Earlier sketch in CA 29-32R
Hodgson, Peter E(dward) 1928- ... 9-12R
Hodgson, Phyllis 1909- ... CAP-1
Earlier sketch in CA 13-14
Hodgson, Ralph 1871-1962 ... 102
See also DLB 19
Hodgson, Richard Sargeant 1924- ... CANR-7
Earlier sketch in CA 13-16R
Hodgson, Robert D(avid) 1923- ... 5-8R
Hodgson, William Hope 1877(?)-1918 ... 164
Brief entry ... 111
See also DLB 70, 153, 156, 178
See also TCLC 13
Hodin, J(osef) P(aul) 1905-1995 ... 41-44R
Obituary ... 150
Hodnett, Edward 1901-1984 ... CANR-5
Obituary ... 114
Earlier sketch in CA 13-16R
Hodsdon, Nicholas E(dward) 1941- ... 49-52
Hodsdon, Nick
See Hodsdon, Nicholas E(dward)
Hodson, Henry V(incent) 1906- ... CANR-3
Earlier sketch in CA 5-8R
Hodson, Peregrine ... 128
Hoe, Robert III 1839-1909 ... DLB 187
Hoebel, Edward Adamson 1906-1993 ... CANR-1
Obituary ... 142
Earlier sketch in CA 1-4R
Hoecker, Karla 1901- ... CANR-2
Earlier sketch in CA 49-52
Hoeg, Peter 1957- ... 151
See also CLC 95
Hoehling, A(dolph) A. 1915- ... CANR-1
Earlier sketch in CA 1-4R
Hoehling, Mary 1914- ... 93-96
Hoehn, Richard A(lbert) 1936- ... 116
Hoehne, Marcia 1951- ... 155
See also SATA 89
Hoehner, Harold W. 1935- ... 37-40R
Hoekema, Anthony A(ndrew) 1913- ... 9-12R
Hoeksema, Gertrude 1921- ... 106
Hoel, Robert F(loyd) 1942- ... 53-56
Hoelderlin, Friedrich 1770-1843 ... DLB 90
Hoelldobler, Bert(hold Karl) 1936- ... 134
Hoelterhoff, Manuela (Vali) 1949- ... 120
Brief entry ... 114
Interview in ... 120
Hoelty, Ludwig Christoph Heinrich 1748-1776 ... DLB 94
Hoelzel, Alfred 1934- ... 41-44R
Hoenig, J(ulius) 1916- ... 29-32R
Hoenig, Sidney B(enjamin) 1907-1979 ... CANR-2
Earlier sketch in CA 45-48
Hoeniger, F(rederick) David 1921- ... 41-44R
Hoenigswald, Henry M(ax) 1915- ... CANR-39
Earlier sketch in CA 13-16R
Hoepffner, Bernard 1946- ... 145
Hoepfl, Harro (Maximilian) 1943- ... 129
Hoeppner, Edward Haworth 1951- ... 150
Hoequist, Charles Ernest, Jr. 1954- ... 108
Hoerr, John P. (III) 1930- ... 135
Hoest, Bill
See Hoest, William P.
Hoest, William P. 1926-1988 ... CANR-23
Obituary ... 127
Earlier sketch in CA 69-72
Hoestlandt, Jo(celyne) 1948- ... 159
See also SATA 94
Hoetink, H(armannus) 1931- ... 21-24R
Hoeveler, Diane Long 1949- ... 102
Hoeveler, J. David, Jr. 1943- ... 129
Hoexter, Corinne K. 1927- ... CANR-27
Earlier sketch in CA 49-52
See also SATA 6
Hoey, Joanne Nobes 1936- ... 106
Hoezee, Scott E. 1964- ... 168
Hofer, Peter
See Kortner, Peter
Hofer, Philip 1898-1984 Obituary ... 114
Hoff, B. J. ... 162
Hoff, Benjamin 1946- ... 142
Hoff, Carol 1900- ... CAP-2
Earlier sketch in CA 21-22
See also SATA 11
Hoff, Ebbe Curtis 1906- ... 57-60
Hoff, H. S.
See Cooper, William
Hoff, Joan
See Wilson, Joan Hoff
Hoff, Marilyn 1942- ... CANR-7
Earlier sketch in CA 17-20R
Hoff, Mary (King) 1956- ... SATA 74
Hoff, Syd(ney) 1912- ... CANR-38
Earlier sketches in CA 5-8R, CANR-4
See also MAICYA
See also SAAS 4
See also SATA 9, 72
Hoffa, James R(iddle) 1913-1975(?) Obituary ... 109
Hoffecker, Carol E(leanor) 1938- ... 85-88
Hoffecker, (John) Savin 1908- ... 5-8R
Hoffeld, Donald R(aymond) 1933- ... 29-32R
Hoffeld, Laura 1946(?)-1982 Obituary ... 106
Hoffenberg, Jack 1906-1977 ... 81-84
Hoffenberg, Mason 1922(?)-1986 Obituary ... 119
Hoffenstein, Samuel Goodman 1890-1947 Brief entry ... 111
See also DLB 11
Hoffer, Charles R(ussell) 1929- ... CANR-22
Earlier sketches in CA 13-16R, CANR-7
Hoffer, Eric 1902-1983 ... CANR-18
Obituary ... 109
Earlier sketch in CA 13-16R
Hoffer, Peter T(homas) 1942- ... 145
Hoffer, Thomas William 1938- ... 118
Hoffer, William 1943- ... CANR-27
Earlier sketch in CA 65-68
Hofferbert, Richard I(ra) 1937- ... 29-32R
Hoffine, Lyla 1897- ... 1-4R
Hoffman, Abbie 1936-1989 ... CANR-63
Obituary ... 128
Earlier sketches in CA 21-24R, CANR-8, 35
See also MTCW 1
Hoffman, Abraham 1938- ... 106
Hoffman, Adeline M(ildred) 1908-1979 ... CANR-23
Earlier sketch in CA 29-32R
Hoffman, Alice 1952- ... CANR-66
Earlier sketches in CA 77-80, CANR-34
See also CLC 51
See also DAM NOV
See also MTCW 1
Hoffman, Andrew (Jay) 1956- ... 162
Hoffman, Andy
See Hoffman, Andrew (Jay)
Hoffman, Anita 1942- ... 69-72
Hoffman, Arthur S. 1926- ... CANR-10
Earlier sketch in CA 25-28R
Hoffman, Arthur W(olf) 1921- ... 5-8R
Hoffman, Bengt R(uno) 1913- ... 69-72
Hoffman, Bernard G(ilbert) 1925- ... 41-44R
Hoffman, Betty Hannah 1918- ... 9-12R
Hoffman, Calvin 1908(?)-1986 Obituary ... 118
Hoffman, Charles Fenno 1806-1884 ... DLB 3
Hoffman, Daniel (Gerard) 1923- ... CANR-4
Earlier sketch in CA 1-4R
See also CLC 6, 13, 23
See also DLB 5
Hoffman, David Herbert 1932(?)-1985 Obituary ... 115
Hoffman, Dominic M. 1913- ... 116
Hoffman, Donald S(tone) 1936- ... 57-60
Hoffman, Edward ... 106
Hoffman, Edwin D. ... 101
See also SATA 49
Hoffman, Elizabeth P(arkinson) 1921- ... 77-80
Hoffman, Eva 1945- ... 132
Hoffman, Frank B. 1888-1958 ... DLB 188
Hoffman, Frederick J(ohn) 1909-1967 ... CANR-6
Earlier sketch in CA 1-4R
Hoffman, Gail 1896- ... 5-8R
Hoffman, George W(alter) 1914- ... 13-16R
Hoffman, Harry G. 1911(?)-1977 Obituary ... 69-72
Hoffman, Helmut 1912- ... CANR-17
Earlier sketch in CA 1-4R
Hoffman, Herbert H(einz) 1928- ... CANR-40
Earlier sketch in CA 117
Hoffman, Hester R(osalyn) 1895- ... CAP-1
Earlier sketch in CA 9-10
Hoffman, Jo Ann S. 1942- ... 81-84
Hoffman, Jon T. 1955- ... 146
Hoffman, Joseph G(ilbert) 1909-1974 ... 65-68
Obituary ... 53-56
Hoffman, Joy 1954- ... 108
Hoffman, Julius Jennings 1895-1983 Obituary ... 110
Hoffman, L. Richard 1930- ... 13-16R
Hoffman, Lee 1932- ... CANR-68
Earlier sketches in CA 25-28R, CANR-18
Interview in ... CANR-18
See also CAAS 10
Hoffman, Lisa 1919- ... 29-32R
Hoffman, Lois Wladis 1929- ... 13-16R
Hoffman, Mark S. 1952- ... 125
Hoffman, Marshall 1942- ... 106
Hoffman, Mary (Margaret) 1945- ... CANR-68
Earlier sketch in CA 131
See also Lassiter, Mary
See also SAAS 24
See also SATA 59, 97
Hoffman, Michael Allen 1944-1990 ... 106
Obituary ... 131
Hoffman, Michael J(erome) 1939- ... 29-32R
Hoffman, Nancy Jo 1942- ... 107
Hoffman, Nina Kiriki 1955- ... 166
Hoffman, Paul 1934-1984 ... CANR-28
Obituary ... 112
Earlier sketches in CA 45-48, CANR-1
Hoffman, Philip T(homas) 1947- ... 119
Hoffman, Phyllis M(iriam) 1944- ... CANR-28
Earlier sketches in CA 29-32R, CANR-12
See also SATA 4
Hoffman, Richard L(ester) 1937-1981 ... CANR-23
Earlier sketch in CA 29-32R
Hoffman, Robert C. 1899(?)-1985 Obituary ... 116
Hoffman, Robert L. 1937- ... 37-40R
Hoffman, Ronald 1941- ... 133
Brief entry ... 112
Hoffman, Rosekrans 1926- ... CANR-15
Earlier sketch in CA 89-92
See also SATA 15
Hoffman, Ross John Swartz 1902- ... 65-68
Hoffman, Stanley 1944- ... 77-80
See also CLC 5
Hoffman, Valerie J. 1954- ... 165
Hoffman, Willa M(athews) 1914- ... 61-64
Hoffman, William 1925- ... CANR-9
Earlier sketch in CA 21-24R
Hoffman, William M(oses) 1939- ... CANR-71
Earlier sketches in CA 57-60, CANR-11
See also CLC 40
Hoffmann, Ann (Marie) 1930- ... 37-40R
Hoffmann, Banesh 1906-1986 ... CANR-3
Obituary ... 119
Earlier sketch in CA 5-8R
Hoffmann, Charles 1921- ... 106
Hoffmann, Charles G. 1921- ... 13-16R
Hoffmann, Donald 1933- ... 25-28R
Hoffmann, E(rnst) T(heodor) A(madeus) 1776-1822 ... DLB 90
See also SATA 27
See also SSC 13
Hoffmann, Eleanor 1895- ... CAP-1
Earlier sketch in CA 13-16
Hoffmann, Erik P(eter) 1939- ... CANR-29
Earlier sketches in CA 33-36R, CANR-13
Hoffmann, Felix 1911-1975 ... CAP-2
Obituary ... 57-60
Earlier sketch in CA 29-32
See also SATA 9
Hoffmann, Frank W(illiam) 1949- ... 106
Hoffmann, Hilde 1927- ... 25-28R
Hoffmann, Leon-Francois 1932- ... CANR-46
Earlier sketch in CA 49-52
Hoffmann, Malcolm A(rthur) 1912-1997 ... 65-68
Obituary ... 158
Hoffmann, Margaret Jones 1910- ... CANR-2
Earlier sketch in CA 5-8R
See also SATA 48
Hoffmann, Peggy
See Hoffmann, Margaret Jones
Hoffmann, Peter (Conrad Werner) 1930- ... CANR-14
Earlier sketch in CA 81-84
Hoffmann, Peter R. 1935- ... 108
Hoffmann, Roald 1937- ... 142
Hoffmann, Stanley (H.) 1928- ... CANR-14
Earlier sketches in CA 81-84, CANR-1
Hoffmann, Yoel 1937- ... 97-100
Hoffmannswaldau, Christian Hoffmann von 1616-1679 ... DLB 168
Hoffmeister, Adolf 1903-1973 Obituary ... 41-44R
Hoffmeister, Donald F(rederick) 1916- ... 53-56
Hoffmeister, Gerhart 1936- ... 130
Hoffnung, Michele 1944- ... 81-84
Hoff-Wilson, Joan
See Wilson, Joan Hoff
Hofheinz, Roy Mark, Jr. 1935- ... 110
Hofinger, Johannes 1905- ... CAP-1
Earlier sketch in CA 19-20
Hofling, Charles K(reimer) 1920-1980 ... CANR-34
Earlier sketch in CA 41-44R
Hofman, Anton
See Hollo, Anselm
Hofmann, Adele Dellenbaugh 1926- ... 97-100
Hofmann, Gert 1931- ... 128
See also CLC 54
Hofmann, Hans 1923- ... CANR-4
Earlier sketch in CA 1-4R
Hofmann, Melita C(ecelia) (?)-1976 ... 5-8R
Obituary ... 69-72
Hofmann, Michael 1957- ... 160
See also DLB 40
Hofmann, Paul Leopold 1912- ... 107
Hofmann, William J(ohn) 1931- ... 114
Hofmannsthal, Hugo von 1874-1929 ... 153
Brief entry ... 106
See also DAM DRAM
See also DC 4
See also DLB 81, 118
See also TCLC 11
Hofsepian, Sylvia A. 1932- ... SATA 74
Hofsinde, Robert 1902-1973 ... 73-76
Obituary ... 45-48
See also SATA 21
Hofsommer, Don(ovan) L(owell) 1938- ... CANR-49
Earlier sketches in CA 65-68, CANR-9, 24
Hofstadter, Albert 1910- ... 33-36R
Hofstadter, Douglas R(ichard) 1945- ... 105
Interview in ... 105
See also MTCW 1
Hofstadter, Richard 1916-1970 ... CANR-4
Obituary ... 29-32R
Earlier sketch in CA 1-4R
See also DLB 17
Hofstede, Geert
See Hofstede, Gerard H(endrik)
Hofstede, Geert H.
See Hofstede, Gerard H(endrik)
Hofstede, Gerard H(endrik) 1928- ... CANR-35
Earlier sketches in CA 41-44R, CANR-15
Hofstetter, Richard R(yan) 1956- ... 117
Hofvendahl, Russ(ell Lloyd) 1921- ... 116
Hogan, Bernice Harris 1929- ... CANR-7
Earlier sketch in CA 13-16R
See also SATA 12

Hogan, Chuck 1967- 156
Hogan, David Gerard 1959- 165
Hogan, Dennis P. 1950- 110
Hogan, Desmond 1950- CANR-44
Earlier sketch in CA 102
See also DLB 14
Hogan, Inez 1895- CANR-1
Earlier sketch in CA 1-4R
See also SATA 2
Hogan, J. Michael 1953- 151
Hogan, James P(atrick) 1941- CANR-58
Earlier sketches in CA 81-84, CANR-15
See also SATA 81
Hogan, John Charles 1919- 17-20R
Hogan, John D. 1927- 45-48
Hogan, Judy 1937- CANR-39
Earlier sketches in CA 77-80, CANR-16
Hogan, Lawrence D(aniel) 1944- 124
Hogan, Linda 1947- CANR-45
Earlier sketch in CA 120
See also CLC 73
See also DAM MULT
See also DLB 175
See also NNAL
Hogan, Michael 1943- CANR-34
Earlier sketches in CA 77-80, CANR-14
Hogan, Patrick Colm 1957- 134
Hogan, Paul 1927- 61-64
Hogan, (Eugene) Pendleton 1907- 127
Hogan, (Robert) Ray 1908- CANR-64
Earlier sketches in CA 9-12R, CANR-4
Hogan, Robert (Goode) 1930- CANR-41
Earlier sketches in CA 1-4R, CANR-1, 19
Hogan, Robert F(rancis) 1927- 41-44R
Hogan, Thom(as Eugene, Jr.) 1952- 103
Hogan, Ursula 1899- 5-8R
Hogan, Willard N(ewton) 1909- CAP-2
Earlier sketch in CA 21-22
Hogan, William Francis 1930- 25-28R
Hogan, William T. 1919- 97-100
Hogarth, Burne 1911-1996 93-96
Obituary 151
See also SATA 63, 89
Hogarth, Charles
See Bowen, (Ivor) Ian
and Creasey, John
Hogarth, Douglas
See Phillips-Birt, Douglas Hextall Chedzey
Hogarth, Emmett
See Polonsky, Abraham (Lincoln)
Hogarth, Grace (Weston Allen) 1905-1995 ... 89-92
Obituary 150
See also SATA 91
Hogarth, John
See Finnin, (Olive) Mary
Hogarth, Jr.
See Kent, Rockwell
Hogarth, (Arthur) Paul 1917- CANR-51
Earlier sketches in CA 49-52, CANR-27
See also SATA 41
Hogben, Lancelot T. 1895-1975 73-76
Obituary 61-64
Hogbin, H(erbert) Ian 1904- 9-12R
Hogbotel, Sebastian
See Gott, K(enneth) D(avidson)
Hoge, Cecil C(unningham) Sr. 1913- 116
Hoge, Dean R(ichard) 1937- CANR-57
Earlier sketches in CA 53-56, CANR-27
Hoge, James F(ulton), Jr. 1935- 166
Hoge, James O(tey) 1944- 89-92
Hoge, Phyllis
See Thompson, Phyllis Hoge
Hoge, Warren McClamroch 1941- 102
Hogendorn, Jan S(tafford) 1937- CANR-43
Earlier sketches in CA 37-40R, CANR-14
Hogg, Beth
See Hogg, Elizabeth (Tootill)
Hogg, Clayton L(eRoy) 1924- 104
Hogg, Elizabeth (Tootill) 1917- CANR-10
Earlier sketch in CA 5-8R
Hogg, Enderby
See Meades, Jonathan (Turner)
Hogg, Garry 1902-1976 .... CANR-10
Earlier sketch in CA 21-24R
See also SATA 2
Hogg, Helen (Battles) Sawyer 1905- 69-72
Hogg, Ian V(ernon) 1926- CANR-12
Earlier sketch in CA 29-32R
Hogg, James 1770-1835 .... DLB 93, 116, 159
Hogg, James (Dalby) 1937- 137
Hogg, Oliver Frederick Gillilan 1887-1979 ... 93-96
Obituary 85-88
Hogg, Quintin McGarel 1907- CANR-14
Earlier sketches in CAP-1, CA 11-12
Hogg, Robert (Lawrence) 1942- 53-56
Hogg, W(illiam) Richey 1921- 1-4R
Hoggart, Richard 1918- 9-12R
Hogins, James Burl 1936- 53-56
Hogner, Dorothy Childs 33-36R
See also SATA 4
Hogner, Nils 1893-1970 77-80
See also SATA 25
Hogrefe, Pearl CAP-1
Earlier sketch in CA 13-16
Hogrogian, Nonny 1932- CANR-49
Earlier sketches in CA 45-48, CANR-2
See also CLR 2
See also MAICYA
See also SAAS 1
See also SATA 7, 74
Hogue, Arthur R(eed) 1906-1986 .... 37-40R
Obituary 118
Hogue, C(harles) B(illy) 1928- 69-72
Hogue, Charles Leonard 1935- 105
Hogue, Richard 1946- 49-52
Hogue, W. Lawrence 1951- 126
Hoguet, Susan Ramsay 1945- 119
Hogwood, Brian W(alter) 1950- CANR-66
Earlier sketch in CA 128
Hogwood, Christopher (Jarvis Haley) 1941- ....
CANR-56
Brief entry 120
Earlier sketch in CA 127
Interview in 127
Hoh, Diane 1937- 120
See also SATA 52, 102
See also SATA-Brief 48
Hohberg, Wolfgang Freiherr von 1612-1688 ... DLB 168
Hohenberg, Dorothy Lannuier
1905(?)-1977 Obituary 73-76
Hohenberg, John 1906- CANR-6
Earlier sketch in CA 13-16R
Hohenberg, Paul M(arcel) 1933- 25-28R
Hohendahl, Peter Uwe 1936- CANR-40
Earlier sketches in CA 45-48, CANR-2, 17
Hohenstein, C(harles) Louis 1930- 116
Hohenstein, Henry J(ohn) 1931- 53-56
Hohenzollern, Friedrich Wilhelm (Victor Albert)
1859-1941 Brief entry 120
Hohimer, Frank 1928- 57-60
Hohl, Ludwig 1904-1980 .... DLB 56
Hohler, Robert T(illman) 1951- 123
Hohlfelder, Robert Lane 1938- CANR-45
Earlier sketch in CA 45-48
Hohlwein, Kathryn Joyce 1930- 125
Hohn, Hazel (Stamper) 5-8R
Hohnen, David 1925- 21-24R
Hohoff, Tay
See Torrey, Therese von Hohoff
Hoig, Stan(ley Warlick) 1924- CANR-1
Earlier sketch in CA 1-4R
Hoijer, Harry 1904-1976 73-76
Obituary 65-68
Hoisington, Harland 1896(?)-1973 Obituary .. 45-48
Hojman, David E(nrique) 1946- 141
Hokanson, (Anthony) Drake 1951- 162
Hoke, Helen
See Watts, Helen L. Hoke
See also SATA-Obit 65
Hoke, Helen L.
See Watts, Helen L. Hoke
Hoke, John (Lindsay) 1925- 41-44R
See also SATA 7
Holabird, Katharine 1948- 121
See also SATA 62
Holaday, Allan Gibson 1916- 37-40R
Holan, Vladimir 1905-1980 162
Obituary 114
Holbeach, Henry
See Rands, William Brighty
Holbeche, Philippa Jack 1919- CAP-1
Earlier sketch in CA 9-10
Holberg, Ruth L(angland) 1889- 5-8R
See also SATA 1
Holbik, Karel 1920- 37-40R
Holbo, Paul Sothe 1929- 25-28R
Holborn, Hajo 1902-1969 .... CAP-2
Earlier sketch in CA 25-28
Holborn, Louise W. 1898-(?) CAP-2
Earlier sketch in CA 25-28
Holborn, Mark 1949- 104
Holbrook, Bill 1921- 61-64
Holbrook, Clyde A(mos) 1911-1989 Obituary ... 130
Holbrook, David (Kenneth) 1923- CANR-43
Earlier sketches in CA 5-8R, CANR-3
See also DLB 14, 40
Holbrook, Jennifer Kearns 1931- 102
Holbrook, John
See Vance, John Holbrook
Holbrook, Peter
See Glick, Carl (Cannon)
Holbrook, Sabra
See Erickson, Sabra Rollins
Holbrook, Stewart Hall 1893-1964 .... CAP-1
Earlier sketch in CA 9-10
See also SATA 2
Holbrooke, Richard 1941- 135
Holburn, James 1900-1988 Obituary 124
Holck, Manfred, Jr. 1930- 17-20R
Holcomb, Adele M(ansfield) 1930- 113
Holcomb, Brent H. 1950- 165
Holcomb, Donald F(rank) 1925- 97-100
Holcomb, George L. 1911- 45-48
Holcomb, Jerry (Leona) 1927- 25-28R
Holcomb, Nan
See McPhee, Norma H.
Holcombe, Arthur N(orman) 1884-1977 ..... CAP-2
Obituary 73-76
Earlier sketch in CA 29-32
Holcombe, Randall G(regory) 1950- CANR-53
Earlier sketches in CA 111, CANR-29
Holcroft, Thomas 1745-1809 ...... DLB 39, 89, 158
Holden, Anthony (Ivan) 1947- CANR-68
Earlier sketch in CA 101
Holden, Anton 1934- 108
Holden, Curry
See Holden, William Curry
Holden, Dalby
See Hammond, Gerald (Arthur Douglas)
Holden, David (Shipley) 1924-1977 .... 41-44R
Holden, Donald 1931- CANR-43
Earlier sketches in CA 45-48, CANR-2, 18
Holden, Edith 1871-1920 Brief entry 113
Holden, Elizabeth Rhoda
See Lawrence, Louise
Holden, Genevieve
See Pou, Genevieve Long
Holden, George S(cott) 1926- 106
Holden, Inez 1906-1974 Obituary 53-56
Holden, Jonathan 1941- CANR-37
Earlier sketches in CA 45-48, CANR-1, 16
See also CAAS 22
See also DLB 105
Holden, Matthew
See Parkinson, Roger
Holden, Matthew, Jr. 1931- 57-60
Holden, Molly 1927-1981 .... 25-28R
Obituary 133
See also DLB 40
Holden, Paul E. 1894(?)-1976 Obituary 65-68
Holden, Peter 1948- 151
Holden, Raymond (Peckham) 1894-1972 .. CANR-4
Obituary 37-40R
Earlier sketch in CA 5-8R
Holden, Ursula 1921- CANR-22
Earlier sketch in CA 101
See also CAAS 8
See also CLC 18
Holden, Vincent F. 1911-1972 Obituary 37-40R
Holden, W. C.
See Holden, William Curry
Holden, W(illis) Sprague 1909-1973 .... 1-4R
Obituary 45-48
Holden, William Curry 1898(?)- Brief entry 117
Holder, Glenn 1906- 41-44R
Holder, Gwynneth 1943- 119
Holder, John, Jr. 1947-1985 .... CANR-42
Obituary 116
Holder, Nancy L. 1953- 164
Holder, Ray 1913- 102
Holder, William G. 1937- CANR-10
Earlier sketch in CA 25-28R
Holderlin, (Johann Christian) Friedrich
1770-1843 .... PC 4
Holdgate, Martin Wyatt 1931- 109
Holdheim, William Wolfgang 1926- CANR-2
Earlier sketch in CA 1-4R
Holding, Charles H. 1897- CAP-1
Earlier sketch in CA 11-12
Holding, Elizabeth Sanxay 1889-1955 Brief
entry 111
Holding, James (Clark Carlisle, Jr.) 1907- ... 25-28R
See also SATA 3
Holding, Vera Zumwalt 1894-1984 Obituary 114
Holditch, W(illiam) Kenneth 1933- CANR-45
Earlier sketch in CA 119
Holdren, Bob R. 1922- 37-40R
Holdren, John P(aul) 1944- 33-36R
Holdstock, Robert
See Holdstock, Robert P.
Holdstock, Robert P. 1948- 131
See also CLC 39
Holdsworth, Christopher (John) 1931- ... CANR-54
Earlier sketch in CA 124
Holdsworth, Irene CAP-1
Earlier sketch in CA 9-10
Holdsworth, Mary (Zvegintzov) 1908- CAP-1
Earlier sketch in CA 13-16
Hole, Christina 1896-1985 165
Obituary 118
Hole, Dorothy (Henrietta Field) 135
Hole, Tahu Ronald Charles Pearce
1908-1985 Obituary 118
Holeman, Linda 1949- 160
See also SATA 102
Holenstein, Elmar 1937- CANR-28
Earlier sketches in CA 65-68, CANR-11
Holford, Ingrid 1920- 102
Holford, William Graham 1907-1975 Obituary .. 108
Holiday, F(rederick) W(illiam) 1921- 25-28R
Holiday, Homer
See DeBeaubien, Philip Francis
Holinger, William (Jacques) 1944- CANR-57
Earlier sketch in CA 123
See also SATA 90
Holinshed, Raphael (?)-1580 .... DLB 167
Holisher, Desider 1901-1972 .... CAP-2
Obituary 37-40R
Earlier sketch in CA 19-20
See also SATA 6
Holl, Adelaide Hinkle 1910- CANR-2
Earlier sketch in CA 1-4R
See also SATA 8
Holl, Adolf 1930- 101
Holl, Jack M. 1937- 57-60
Holl, Kristi D(iane) 1951- CANR-48
Earlier sketch in CA 114
See also SATA 51
Holladay, Sylvia A(gnes) 1936- 57-60
Holladay, William L(ee) 1926- 53-56
Holland, Ada Morehead 1911- 122
Holland, Agnieszka 1948- 144
Holland, Alma Boice 29-32R
Holland, Barbara A(dams) 1925- 57-60
Holland, Brud
See Holland, Jerome H(eartwell)
Holland, Cecelia (Anastasia) 1943- CANR-68
Earlier sketches in CA 17-20R, CANR-9
Holland, Cecil Fletcher 1907-1978 Obituary .. 77-80
Holland, Deborah K(atherine) 1947- 57-60
Holland, DeWitte T(almage) 1923- 45-48
Holland, Elizabeth (Anne) 1928- 124
Holland, Francis Ross, Jr. 1927- 33-36R
Holland, Gail Bernice 1940- 126
Holland, Glen A. 1920- 37-40R
Holland, Harrison M(elsher) 1921- CANR-43
Earlier sketch in CA 117
Holland, Hilda 1901(?)-1975 Obituary 57-60
Holland, Isabelle 1920- CANR-47
Earlier sketches in CA 21-24R, CANR-10, 25
See also AAYA 11
See also CLC 21
See also JRDA
See also MAICYA
See also SATA 8, 70
Holland, J. G. 1819-1881 .... DLBD 13
Holland, Jack 1947- 105
Holland, Jack H. 1922- 81-84
Holland, James C(larence) 1935- 112
Holland, James Gordon 1927- 1-4R
Holland, James R. 1944- 37-40R
Holland, Janice 1913-1962 73-76
See also SATA 18
Holland, Jerome H(eartwell)
1916-1985 Obituary 114
Holland, John L(ewis) 1919- CANR-17
Earlier sketch in CA 25-28R
See also SATA 20
Holland, Joyce
See Morice, Dave
Holland, Joyce (Flint) 1921- 5-8R
Holland, Kel
See Whittington, Harry (Benjamin)
Holland, Kenneth 1948- 118
Holland, Kenneth J(ohn) 1918- 33-36R
Holland, Laurence B(edwell) 1920-1980 .... 17-20R
Obituary 102
Holland, Louise Adams 1893- 89-92
Holland, Lynda (H.) 1959- 145
See also SATA 77
Holland, Lynwood M. 1905- 41-44R
Holland, Lys
See Gater, Dilys
Holland, Marcus
See Caldwell, (Janet Miriam) Taylor (Holland)
Holland, Marion 1908-1989 61-64
Obituary 128
See also SATA 6
See also SATA-Obit 61
Holland, Max (Mendel) 1950- 135
Holland, Norman N(orwood) 1927- 17-20R
See also DLB 67
Holland, Noy 1960- 149
Holland, Patricia G. 1940- 115
Holland, Philip Welsby 1917- 109
Holland, Robert 1940- 33-36R
Holland, Sheila 1937- CANR-15
Earlier sketch in CA 85-88
Holland, Thomas E(dward) 1934- 53-56
Holland, Tim 1931- 57-60
Holland, Tom 1947- 126
Holland, Vyvyan (Beresford) 1886-1967 97-100
Obituary 25-28R
Holland, William E. 1940- 124
Hollander, A(rie) Nicolaas Jan den
See den Hollander, A(rie) Nicolaas Jan
Hollander, Anne 1930- 131
Hollander, Hans 1899-1986 103
Obituary 120
Hollander, Herbert S. 1904(?)-1976 Obituary . 69-72
Hollander, John 1929- CANR-52
Earlier sketches in CA 1-4R, CANR-1
See also CLC 2, 5, 8, 14
See also DLB 5
See also SATA 13
Hollander, Lee M(ilton) 1880- 1-4R
Hollander, Nicole 1940(?)- 162
See also SATA 101
Hollander, Paul
See Silverberg, Robert
Hollander, Paul 1932- CANR-13
Earlier sketch in CA 37-40R
Hollander, Phyllis 1928- CANR-18
Earlier sketch in CA 97-100
See also SATA 39
Hollander, Richard Isaac 1912-1985 Obituary .. 117
Hollander, Robert 1933- CANR-5
Earlier sketch in CA 13-16R
Hollander, Sophie Smith 1911- 13-16R
Hollander, Stanley C(harles) 1919- 37-40R
Hollander, Zander 1923- CANR-18
Earlier sketch in CA 65-68
See also SATA 63
Hollands, Roy (Derrick) 1924- CANR-37
Earlier sketch in CA 114
Hollandsworth, James G., Jr. 1944- 135
Hollar, David W(ason, Jr.) 1960- 144
Hollaway, Otto 1903- 69-72
Hollberg, John
See Hall, Gus
Holldobler, Bert
See Hoelldobler, Bert(hold Karl)
Holldobler, Turid 1939- .... SATA 26
Holleb, Arthur Irving 1921- 103
Holleman, Gary L. 1947- 150
Hollenberg, Donna Krolik 1942- 142
Hollender, Edward A. 1899- 105
Hollenweger, Walter J(acob) 1927- CANR-19
Earlier sketches in CA 53-56, CANR-4
Holler, Frederick L. 1921- 97-100
Holler, Ronald F. 1938- 53-56
Holleran, Andrew 1943(?)- 144
See also CLC 38
Holles, Everett R. 1904(?)-1978 Obituary 77-80
Holles, Robert Owen 1926- CANR-18
Earlier sketches in CA 5-8R, CANR-3
Holley, Bobbie Lee 1927- 33-36R
Holley, Edward Gailon 1927- CANR-6
Earlier sketch in CA 5-8R
Holley, Frederick S. 1924- 109
Holley, I(rving) B(rinton), Jr. 1919- CANR-14
Earlier sketch in CA 37-40R
Holley, Marietta 1836(?)-1926 Brief entry 118
See also DLB 11
Holli, Melvin G(eorge) 1933- CANR-26
Earlier sketches in CA 25-28R, CANR-11
Hollick, Ann L(orraine) 1941- 57-60
Holliday, Barbara Gregg 1917- 73-76
Holliday, Joe
See Holliday, Joseph

Holliday, Joseph 1910- CAP-2
Earlier sketch in CA 29-32
See also SATA 11
Hollifield, James F. 1954- 139
Hollindale, Peter 1936- 103
Holling, Holling C(lancy) 1900-1973 Obituary 106
See also CLR 50
See also MAICYA
See also SATA 15
See also SATA-Obit 26
Hollingdale, R(eginald) J(ohn) 1930- 102
Hollinghurst, Alan 1954- 114
See also CLC 55, 91
Hollings, Michael (Richard) 1921-1997 81-84
Obituary 156
Hollingshead, August deBelmont
1907-1980 13-16R
Obituary 120
Hollingshead, Greg 1947- 162
Hollingshead, (Ronald) Kyle 1941- CANR-11
Earlier sketch in CA 21-24R
Hollingsworth, Alvin C(arl) 1930- SATA 39
Hollingsworth, Brian 1923- 130
Hollingsworth, Dorothy Frances 1916- 85-88
Hollingsworth, Harold M(arvin) 1932- 53-56
Hollingsworth, J(oseph) Rogers 1932- CANR-22
Earlier sketches in CA 13-16R, CANR-7
Hollingsworth, Kent 1929- 81-84
Hollingsworth, Lyman B(urgess) 1919- 45-48
Hollingsworth, Margaret 1942- 123
See also DLB 60
Hollingsworth, Mary 1947- 155
See also SATA 91
Hollingsworth, Mary H(ead) 1910- 69-72
Hollingsworth, Michael 1950- 144
Hollingsworth, Paul M. 1932- 29-32R
Hollingworth, Clare 1911- 121
Hollinrake, Roger (Barker) 1929- 115
Hollins, Etta R(uth) 167
Hollis, C(harles) Carroll 1911- 125
Hollis, (Maurice) Christopher 1902-1977 73-76
Obituary 69-72
Hollis, Daniel W(ebster) III 1942- 118
Hollis, Daniel W(alker) 1922- 5-8R
Hollis, Florence 1907-1987 Obituary 123
Hollis, Harry Newcombe, Jr. 1938- 57-60
Hollis, Helen Rice 1908- 61-64
Hollis, James R(ussell) 1940- 41-44R
Hollis, Jim
See Summers, Hollis (Spurgeon, Jr.)
Hollis, Joseph W(illiam) 1922- 25-28R
Hollis, Lucile U(ssery) 1921- 25-28R
Hollis, Marcia 1937- 114
Hollis, Stephanie 1946- 141
Hollister, Bernard C(laiborne) 1938- CANR-3
Earlier sketch in CA 49-52
Hollister, C(harles) Warren 1930- CANR-25
Earlier sketches in CA 1-4R, CANR-1
Hollister, Charles A(mmon) 1918- 17-20R
Hollister, George E(rwin) 1905- CAP-2
Earlier sketch in CA 17-18
Hollister, Herbert A(llen) 1933- 104
Hollister, Leo E. 1920- CANR-14
Earlier sketch in CA 21-24R
Hollister, William G(ray) 1915- 122
Hollmann, Clide John 1896-1966 5-8R
Hollo, Anselm 1934- CANR-9
Earlier sketch in CA 21-24R
See also CAAS 19
See also DLB 40
Hollom, Philip Arthur Dominic 1912- 13-16R
Hollon, W. Eugene 1913- CANR-2
Earlier sketch in CA 1-4R
See also AITN 1
Hollos, Marida 1940- 139
Hollow, John Walter 1939- 111
Holloway, Brenda W(ilmar) 1908- CAP-1
Earlier sketch in CA 9-10
Holloway, David 1924- 107
Holloway, (Rufus) Emory 1885-1977 49-52
Obituary 73-76
See also DLB 103
Holloway, (Percival) Geoffrey 1918- CANR-27
Earlier sketch in CA 49-52
Holloway, George (Edward Talbot) 1921- 25-28R
Holloway, Harry (Albert) 1925- 9-12R
Holloway, James Y(oung) 1927- 53-56
Holloway, Jean
See Tobin, Jean Holloway
Holloway, John 1920- CANR-3
Earlier sketch in CA 5-8R
See also DLB 27
Holloway, Joseph E(dward) 1948- 111
Holloway, Karla F. C. 1949- 141
Holloway, Marcella M(arie) 1913- 89-92
Holloway, Mark 1917- 21-24R
Holloway, Maurice 1920- 9-12R
Holloway, Nigel 1953- 135
Holloway, Robert J. 1921- 13-16R
Holloway, Robin (Grenville) 1943- 165
Holloway, Stanley 1890-1982 Obituary 106
Holloway, Teresa (Bragunier) 1906- 17-20R
See also SATA 26
Holloway, Thomas H(alsey) 1944- 106
Holloway, W(illiam) V(ernon) 1903- CANR-2
Earlier sketch in CA 1-4R
Hollowell, John 1945- 102
Hollowood, Albert Bernard 1910-1981 9-12R
Obituary 103
Holly, Buddy 1936-1959 TCLC 65
Holly, David C. 1915- 142
Holly, Ellen (Virginia) 1931- 159
Holly, J(ohn) Fred 1915- CANR-6
Earlier sketch in CA 5-8R
Holly, Joan C(arol) 1932- CANR-1
Earlier sketch in CA 1-4R
Holly, Joan Hunter
See Holly, Joan C(arol)
Holly, Michael Ann 1944- CANR-47
Earlier sketch in CA 121
Hollyday, Frederic B(lackmar) M(umford)
1928- 45-48
Holm, (Else) Anne (Lise) 1922- 17-20R
See also MAICYA
See also SAAS 7
See also SATA 1
Holm, Bill
See Holm, Oscar William
Holm, Don(ald Raymond) 1918- 33-36R
Holm, Jeanne M(arjorie) 1921- 130
Holm, John Cecil 1904-1981 Obituary 116
Holm, Marilyn D. (Franzen) 1944- 17-20R
Holm, Oscar William 1925- Brief entry 117
Holm, Sharon Lane 1955- SATA 78
Holm, Sven (Aage) 1902- CAP-1
Earlier sketch in CA 11-12
Holman, Betsy Hitz 1951- 119
Holman, Bob
See Holman, Robert
Holman, C(larence) Hugh 1914-1981 CANR-21
Earlier sketch in CA 5-8R
Holman, Dennis (Idris) 1915- 9-12R
Holman, Felice 1919- CANR-40
Earlier sketches in CA 5-8R, CANR-3, 18
See also AAYA 17
See also SAAS 17
See also SATA 7, 82
Holman, Harriet R. 1912- 37-40R
Holman, John (William) 1951- 133
Holman, L(loyd) Bruce 1939- 61-64
Holman, Mary A(lida) 1933- 93-96
Holman, Portia Grenfell 1903-1983 Obituary 109
Holman, Robert 1936- 116
Holman, William R(oger) 1926- 49-52
Holman-Hunt, Diana
See Cuthbert, Diana Daphne Holman-Hunt
Holmans, Alan Edward 1934- 1-4R
Holme, Bryan 1913-1990 103
Obituary 132
See also SATA 26
See also SATA-Obit 66
Holme, (Edith) Constance 1880(?)-1955 Brief
entry 118
See also DLB 34
Holme, K. E.
See Hill, (John Edward) Christopher
Holme, Thea 1903- 41-44R
Holme, Timothy 19(?)-1987 158
Holmelund, Paul 1890- 5-8R
Holmer, Paul L(eroy) 1916- 37-40R
Holmes, A. R.
See Bates, Harry
Holmes, Abraham S. 1821(?)-1908 DLB 99
Holmes, Ann 1936(?)-1985 Obituary 114
Holmes, Arthur 1890-1965 Obituary 116
Holmes, Arthur F. 1924- 33-36R
Holmes, Barbara Ware 1945- 120
See also SATA 65
Holmes, Burnham 1942- 97-100
Holmes, C. Raymond 1929- 57-60
Holmes, Charles M(ason) 1923- 29-32R
Holmes, Charles S(hiveley) 1916-1976 41-44R
Obituary 61-64
Holmes, Charles Warfield 1931-1984 Obituary 112
Holmes, Colin 1938- CANR-11
Earlier sketch in CA 25-28R
Holmes, David Charles 1919- 9-12R
Holmes, David M(orton) 1929- 33-36R
Holmes, Diana 1949- 157
Holmes, Douglas 1933- 41-44R
Holmes, Edward M(orris) 1910- CANR-14
Earlier sketch in CA 37-40R
Holmes, Efner Tudor 1949- 65-68
Holmes, Eric M(ills) 1943- 121
Holmes, Frank Wakefield 1924- 109
Holmes, Frederic L(awrence) 1932- 93-96
Holmes, Geoffrey (Shorter) 1928-1993 25-28R
Obituary 143
Holmes, George (Arthur) 1927- CANR-65
Earlier sketch in CA 128
Holmes, Gordon
See Shiel, M(atthew) P(hipps)
Holmes, Grant
See Fox, James M.
Holmes, H. H.
See White, William A(nthony) P(arker)
Holmes, Jack D(avid) L(azarus) 1930- CANR-24
Earlier sketch in CA 41-44R
Holmes, Jay
See Holmes, Joseph Everett
Holmes, Jeffrey 1934- CANR-47
Earlier sketch in CA 120
Holmes, John
See Souster, (Holmes) Raymond
Holmes, John (Albert) 1904-1962 Obituary 115
Holmes, John 1913- 104
Holmes, John Clellon 1926-1988 CANR-4
Obituary 125
Earlier sketch in CA 9-12R
See also CLC 56
See also DLB 16
Holmes, John Haynes 1879-1964 Obituary 89-92
Holmes, John L. 1925- 115
Holmes, John W(endell) 1910-1989 134
Brief entry 109
Holmes, Jon 1948- 114
Holmes, Joseph Everett 1922- CANR-1
Earlier sketch in CA 1-4R
Holmes, Joseph R. 1928(?)-1983 Obituary 109
Holmes, Kenneth L(loyd) 1915- CANR-27
Earlier sketch in CA 37-40R
Holmes, Kim R(ene) 1952- 111
Holmes, Leslie (Templeman) 1948- 146
Holmes, Lowell D(on) 1925- 33-36R
Holmes, Marjorie (Rose) 1910- CANR-23
Earlier sketches in CA 1-4R, CANR-5
See also AITN 1
See also SATA 43
Holmes, Martha 1961- SATA 72
Holmes, Martin (Rivington) 1905- CANR-1
Earlier sketch in CA 49-52
Holmes, Mary Jane 1825-1907 DLB 202
Holmes, Mary Tavener 1954- 141
Holmes, Mary Z(astrow) 1943- 147
See also SATA 80
Holmes, Melody Moore 1972- 168
Holmes, (John) Michael (Aleister) 1931- 25-28R
Holmes, Michael Stephan 1942- 77-80
Holmes, Nancy 1921- 69-72
Holmes, Olive 1911- 115
Holmes, Oliver Wendell, Jr. 1841-1935 Brief
entry 114
See also TCLC 77
Holmes, Oliver Wendell 1809-1894 CDALB
1640-1865
See also DLB 1, 189
See also SATA 34
Holmes, Parker Manfred 1895- CAP-1
Earlier sketch in CA 13-14
Holmes, Paul Allen 1901-1985 CAP-2
Obituary 114
Earlier sketch in CA 19-20
Holmes, Paul Carter 1926- CANR-11
Earlier sketch in CA 21-24R
Holmes, Peggy 1898- 121
See also SATA 60
Holmes, Raymond
See Souster, (Holmes) Raymond
Holmes, Richard 1945- 133
Brief entry 126
Interview in 133
See also DLB 155
Holmes, (Edward) Richard 1946- CANR-51
Earlier sketches in CA 106, CANR-25
Holmes, Rick
See Hardwick, Richard Holmes, Jr.
Holmes, Robert A(lexander) 1943- 57-60
Holmes, Robert L(awrence) 1935- 41-44R
Holmes, Robert Merrill 1925- 89-92
Holmes, Thomas James 1874-1959 DLB 187
Holmes, Thomas K. CANR-26
Earlier sketches in CAP-2, CA 19-20
Holmes, Tiffany 1944- 97-100
Holmes, Tommy 1903-1975 Obituary 57-60
Holmes, Urban T(igner) 1900-1972 CAP-2
Earlier sketch in CA 21-22
Holmes, W(ilfred) J(ay) 1900- 29-32R
Holmes, William Kersley 1882- CAP-1
Earlier sketch in CA 9-10
Holmgren, Helen Jean 1930- 97-100
See also SATA 45
Holmgren, Norah 1939- 102
Holmgren, Sister George Ellen
See Holmgren, Helen Jean
Holmgren, Virginia C(unningham) 1909- 107
See also SATA 26
Holmquist, Anders 1933- 29-32R
Holmquist, Eve 1921- 53-56
See also SATA 11
Holmstrand, Marie Juline (Gunderson) 1908- 5-8R
Holmstrom, (John) Edwin 1898- CAP-1
Earlier sketch in CA 11-12
Holmstrom, Lynda Lytle 1939- 33-36R
Holmvik, Oyvind 1914- 17-20R
Holod, Renata O. 1942- 119
Holoien, Martin O. 1928- 112
Holquist, (James) Michael 1935- CANR-17
Earlier sketches in CA 45-48, CANR-2
Holroyd, Michael (de Courcy Fraser) 1935-
CANR-63
Earlier sketches in CA 53-56, CANR-4, 18, 35
See also DLB 155
See also MTCW 1
Holroyd, Sam
See Burton, S(amuel) H(olroyd)
Holroyd, Stuart 1933- 93-96
Holsaert, Eunice (?)-1974 Obituary 53-56
Holsinger, Jane Lumley 17-20R
Holske, Katherine (?)-1973 Obituary 104
Holsopple, Barbara 1943- 73-76
Holst, Hermann E. von 1841-1904 DLB 47
Holst, Imogen (Clare) 1907-1984 Obituary 112
Holst, Johan J(oergen) 1937-1994 CANR-11
Obituary 143
Earlier sketch in CA 25-28R
Holst, Lawrence E(berhardt) 1929- 61-64
Holstad, Scott Cameron 1966- 156
Holsti, Kalevi J(acque) 1935- 21-24R
Holsti, Ole R(udolf) 1933- CANR-52
Earlier sketches in CA 25-28R, CANR-11, 28
Holt, Andrew
See Anhalt, Edward
Holt, Conrad G.
See Fearn, John Russell
Holt, Constance Wall 1932- 147
Holt, Edgar Crawshaw 1900-1975 CANR-6
Obituary 61-64
Earlier sketch in CA 1-4R
Holt, Elizabeth B(asye) G(ilmore) 1906(?)-1987 124
Holt, Gavin
See Rodda, Charles
Holt, Georgia 1927- 129
Holt, (Wilma) Geraldene 137
Holt, Hazel 1928- 160
Holt, Helen
See Paine, Lauran (Bosworth)
Holt, (Laurence) James 1939- 25-28R
Holt, John 1721-1784 DLB 43
Holt, John (Caldwell) 1923-1985 CANR-32
Obituary 117
Earlier sketch in CA 69-72
Holt, John (Robert) 1926- CANR-11
Earlier sketch in CA 25-28R
Holt, John Agee 1920- 1-4R
Holt, Judd 1941- 141
Holt, Kaare 1917- Brief entry 111
Holt, Kare
See Holt, Kaare
Holt, L. Emmett, Jr. 1895-1974 Obituary 53-56
Holt, Lee E(lbert) 1912- 13-16R
Holt, Margaret 1937- 17-20R
See also SATA 4
Holt, Margaret Van Vechten (Saunders)
1899-1963 Obituary 111
See also SATA 32
Holt, Marilyn Irvin 1949- 144
Holt, Michael (Paul) 1929- CANR-5
Earlier sketch in CA 53-56
See also SATA 13
Holt, Michael F(itzgibbon) 1940- 81-84
Holt, Pat Mayo 1920- 111
Holt, Rackham
See Holt, Margaret Van Vechten (Saunders)
Holt, Robert R(utherford) 1917- CANR-35
Earlier sketches in CA 41-44R, CANR-15
Holt, Robert T. 1928- 37-40R
Holt, Rochelle L.
See DuBois, Rochelle (Lynn) Holt
See also SATA 41
Holt, Stephen
See Thompson, Harlan (Howard)
Holt, Tex
See Joscelyn, Archie L.
Holt, Thelma Jewett 1913- 29-32R
Holt, Thomas Charles Louis 1961- 135
Holt, Thomas J(ung) 1928- 102
Holt, Tom
See Holt, Thomas Charles Louis
Holt, Victoria
See Hibbert, Eleanor Alice Burford
Holt, Will 1929- 105
Holt, William 1897-1977 CAP-1
Obituary 69-72
Earlier sketch in CA 17-18
Holtan, Orley I. 1933- 33-36R
Holtby, Robert Tinsley 1921- 108
Holtby, Winifred 1898-1935 DLB 191
Holte, James Craig 1949- 144
Holter, Don W. 1905- 37-40R
Holthusen, Hans Egon 1913- 45-48
See also DLB 69
Holtje, Herbert F(ranklin) 1931- CANR-8
Earlier sketch in CA 61-64
Holton, Felicia Antonelli 1921- 69-72
Holton, Gerald (James) 1922- 13-16R
Holton, Leonard
See Wibberley, Leonard (Patrick O'Connor)
Holton, (William) Milne 1931- 41-44R
Holton, Richard H(enry) 1926- Brief entry 107
Holtrop, William Frans 1908- 57-60
Holtz, Avraham 1934- 29-32R
Holtz, Barry W(illiam) 1947- 109
Holtz, Herman R(alph) 1919- 105
Holtze, Sally Holmes 1952- 123
See also SATA 64
Holtzman, Abraham 1921- CANR-2
Earlier sketch in CA 1-4R
Holtzman, Elizabeth 1941- 157
Holtzman, Harry 1912-1987 Obituary 123
Holtzman, Jerome 1926- CANR-4
Earlier sketch in CA 53-56
See also SATA 57
Holtzman, Paul D(ouglas) 1918- 33-36R
Holtzman, Wayne H(arold) 1923- CANR-34
Earlier sketches in CA 37-40R, CANR-15
Holtzman, Will 1951- 102
Holub, Joan 1956- 167
See also SATA 99
Holub, Miroslav 1923- CANR-10
Earlier sketch in CA 21-24R
See also CLC 4
Holub, Robert C(harles) 1949- CANR-35
Earlier sketch in CA 114
Holum, Dianne 1951- 123
Holway, John 1929- 57-60
Holy, Ladislav 1933- 141
Holyer, Erna Maria 1925- CANR-12
Earlier sketch in CA 29-32R
See also SATA 22
Holyer, Ernie
See Holyer, Erna Maria
Holz, Arno 1863-1929 DLB 118
Holz, Loretta (Marie) 1943- CANR-10
Earlier sketch in CA 65-68
See also SATA 17
Holz, Robert K(enneth) 1930- 53-56
Holzapfel, Rudolf Patrick 1938- CAP-1
Earlier sketch in CA 11-12
Holzberger, William George 1932- 53-56
Holzel, Thomas Martin 1940- 126
Holzel, Tom
See Holzel, Thomas Martin
Holzer, Erika 1935- 141
Holzer, Hans 1920- CANR-22
Earlier sketches in CA 13-16R, CANR-7
Holzer, Harold 1949- CANR-39
Earlier sketch in CA 116
Holzman, Franklyn Dunn 1918- 61-64
Holzman, Philip Seidman 1922- 37-40R
Holzman, Red
See Holzman, William
Holzman, Robert S(tuart) 1907- CANR-2
Earlier sketch in CA 1-4R
Holzman, William 1920- 101

Holzner, Burkart 1931- ... 93-96
Hom, Ken 1949- ... CANR-26
Earlier sketch in CA 109
Hom, Marlon Kau 1947- ... 131
Homan, Robert Anthony 1929- ... 5-8R
Homan, Sidney 1938- ... 146
Homans, Abigail Adams 1879-1974 Obituary ... 104
Homans, George Caspar 1910-1989 ... 107
Obituary ... 128
Homans, Peter 1930- ... CANR-57
Earlier sketches in CA 21-24R, CANR-11, 28
Homberger, Eric (Ross) 1942- ... CANR-47
Earlier sketches in CA 106, CANR-23
Homburger, Erik
See Erikson, Erik H(omburger)
Home, Alexander Frederick (Douglas-)
1903-1995 ... 102
Obituary ... 150
Home, Charles (Cospatrick) Douglas
See Douglas-Home, Charles (Cospatrick)
Home, Henry 1696-1782 ... DLB 104
Home, Henry Douglas
See Douglas-Home, Henry
Home, John 1722-1808 ... DLB 84
Home, Michael
See Bush, Charlie Christmas
Home, Stewart 1962- ... 154
Home, William Douglas 1912-1992 ... CANR-71
Obituary ... 139
Earlier sketch in CA 102
See also DLB 13
Homel, David 1952- ... 149
See also SATA 97
Homel, Michael W. 1944- ... 126
Homer c. 8th cent. B.C.- ... DA
See also DAB
See also DAC
See also DAM MST, POET
See also DLB 176
See also PC 23
See also WLCS
Homer, Frank X. J. 1941- ... 127
Homer, Frederic D(onald) 1939- ... 65-68
Homer, Sidney 1902-1983 Obituary ... 110
Homer, Williams Innes 1929- ... 13-16R
Homer, Winslow 1836-1910 ... DLB 188
Homes, A(my) M. ... CANR-66
Earlier sketch in CA 136
Homes, Geoffrey
See Mainwaring, Daniel
Homewood, Charles H. 1914(?)-1984 Obituary . 112
Homewood, Harry
See Homewood, Charles H.
Homola, Priscilla 1947- ... 116
Homola, Samuel 1929- ... 97-100
Homolya, Istvan 1940- ... 131
Homosap
See Nuttall, Jeff
Homrighausen, Elmer George 1900- ... 45-48
Homsher, Lola Mae 1913- ... 1-4R
Homze, Alma C. 1932- ... 29-32R
See also SATA 17
Homze, Edward L. 1930- ... 33-36R
Honan, Park 1928- ... CANR-14
Earlier sketch in CA 77-80
See also DLB 111
Honan, William H(olmes) 1930- ... CANR-49
Earlier sketch in CA 123
Honce, Charles E. 1895-1975 Obituary ... 61-64
Honderich, John A. 1946- ... 128
Honderich, Ted 1933- ... CANR-35
Earlier sketches in CA 33-36R, CANR-14
Hone, Joseph 1937- ... CANR-35
Earlier sketches in CA 65-68, CANR-14
Hone, Ralph E(merson) 1913- ... CANR-9
Earlier sketch in CA 21-24R
Hone, William 1780-1842 ... DLB 110, 158
Honerkamp, Nicholas 1950- ... 138
Honey, Martha S(pencer) 1945- ... CANR-31
Earlier sketch in CA 112
Honey, P(atrick) J(ames) 1922- ... 13-16R
Honey, William (Houghton) 1910- ... 33-36R
Honeycombe, Gordon 1936- ... CANR-72
Earlier sketches in CA 77-80, CANR-15, 34
Honeycutt, Ann 1902(?)-1989 Obituary ... 129
Honeycutt, Benjamin L(awrence) 1938- ... 57-60
Honeycutt, Natalie 1945- ... 163
See also SATA 97
Honeycutt, Roy L(ee), Jr. 1926- ... 41-44R
Honeygosky, Stephen R(aymond) 1948- ... 144
Honeyman, Brenda
See Clarke, Brenda (Margaret Lilian)
Hong, Edna H. 1913- ... CANR-9
Earlier sketch in CA 21-24R
Hong, Howard V(incent) 1912- ... CANR-9
Earlier sketch in CA 21-24R
Hong, Jane Fay 1954- ... 93-96
Hong, Lily Toy 1958- ... 144
See also SATA 76
Hong, Yong Ki 1929(?)-1979 Obituary ... 85-88
Hongo, Garrett Kaoru 1951- ... 133
See also CAAS 22
See also DLB 120
See also PC 23
Honhart, Frederick L(ewis III) 1943- ... 112
Honig, Donald 1931- ... CANR-71
Earlier sketches in CA 17-20R, CANR-9, 24
See also SATA 18
Honig, Edwin 1919- ... CANR-45
Earlier sketches in CA 5-8R, CANR-4
See also CAAS 8
See also CLC 33
See also DLB 5
Honig, Louis 1911-1977 ... 77-80
Obituary ... 73-76
Honigfeld, Gilbert
See Howard, Gilbert
Honigmann, E(rnst) A(nselm) J(oachim) 1927- ... CANR-9
Earlier sketch in CA 21-24R
Honigmann, John J(oseph) 1914-1977 ... CANR-2
Earlier sketch in CA 1-4R
Honnalgere, Gopal 1944- ... 73-76
Honnef, Klaus 1939- ... 142
Honness, Elizabeth H. 1904- ... 25-28R
See also SATA 2
Honnold, John Otis, Jr. 1915- ... CANR-8
Earlier sketch in CA 13-16R
Honore, Antony Maurice 1921- ... CANR-1
Earlier sketch in CA 1-4R
Honour, Hugh 1927- ... 103
Honourable Member for X
See de Chair, Somerset (Struben)
Honri, Peter 1929- ... 103
Hoobler, Dorothy ... CANR-27
Earlier sketches in CA 69-72, CANR-11
See also SATA 28
Hoobler, Thomas ... CANR-53
Earlier sketches in CA 69-72, CANR-11, 27
See also SATA 28
Hood, Ann 1956- ... 136
Hood, Bruce 1936- ... 130
Hood, Buck 1907(?)-1983 Obituary ... 110
Hood, Daniel 1967- ... 168
Hood, David Crockett 1937- ... 37-40R
Hood, Donald W(ilbur) 1918- ... 37-40R
Hood, Dora (Ridout) 1885- ... CAP-2
Earlier sketch in CA 17-18
Hood, F(rancis) C(ampbell) 1895-1971 ... CAP-1
Earlier sketch in CA 13-14
Hood, Flora M(ae) 1898- ... 5-8R
Hood, Graham 1936- ... 77-80
Hood, Hugh (John Blagdon) 1928- ... CANR-33
Earlier sketches in CA 49-52, CANR-1
See also CAAS 17
See also CLC 15, 28
See also DLB 53
Hood, Joseph F. 1925- ... 33-36R
See also SATA 4
Hood, Lynley (Jane) 1942- ... 135
Hood, Margaret Page 1892- ... 1-4R
Hood, Mary 1946- ... 128
Hood, Robert E. 1926- ... 21-24R
See also SATA 21
Hood, Roger (Grahame) 1936- ... CANR-67
Earlier sketch in CA 128
Hood, Sarah
See Killough, (Karen) Lee
Hood, (Martin) Sinclair (Frankland) 1917- . CANR-9
Earlier sketch in CA 21-24R
Hood, Stuart (Clink) 1915- ... 152
Hood, Thomas 1799-1845 ... DLB 96
Hood, William (Joseph) 1920- ... CANR-26
Earlier sketch in CA 109
Hoodbhoy, Pervez 1950- ... 143
Hoofnagle, Keith Lundy 1941- ... 13-16R
Hoogasian-Villa, Susie 1921-1978 ... 17-20R
Obituary ... 114
Hoogenboom, Ari (Arthur) 1927- ... CANR-50
Earlier sketch in CA 45-48
Hoogenboom, Olive 1927- ... 21-24R
Hoogestraat, Wayne E. ... 5-8R
Hook, Andrew 1932- ... 53-56
Hook, Diana ffarington 1918- ... 61-64
Hook, Donald D(wight) 1928- ... CANR-4
Earlier sketch in CA 53-56
Hook, Frances 1912- ... 105
See also SATA 27
Hook, Frank S(cott) 1922- ... 21-24R
Hook, Hilary 1917-1990 Obituary ... 132
Hook, J(ulius) N(icholas) 1913- ... CANR-38
Earlier sketches in CA 5-8R, CANR-2, 17
Hook, Judith 1941(?)-1984 Obituary ... 113
Hook, Martha 1936- ... 105
See also SATA 27
Hook, Sidney 1902-1989 ... CANR-7
Obituary ... 129
Earlier sketch in CA 9-12R
Interview in ... CANR-7
Hook, Theodore 1788-1841 ... DLB 116
Hooke, Nina Warner 1907- ... 73-76
Hooke, Sylvia Denys
See Malleson, Lucy Beatrice
Hooker, C(lifford) A(lan) 1942- ... CANR-19
Earlier sketches in CA 49-52, CANR-4
Hooker, Craig Michael 1951- ... 57-60
Hooker, Frances
See Horovitz, Frances Margaret
Hooker, James Ralph 1929- ... 21-24R
Hooker, (Peter) Jeremy 1941- ... CANR-22
Earlier sketch in CA 77-80
See also CLC 43
See also DLB 40
Hooker, Richard
See Hornberger, H. Richard
Hooker, Richard
See Heinz, W(ilfred) C(harles)
Hooker, Richard 1554-1600 ... DLB 132
Hooker, Richard D., Jr. 1957- ... 145
Hooker, Richard J(ames) 1912- ... 122
Hooker, Ruth 1920- ... 69-72
See also SATA 21
Hooker, Stanley (George) 1907-1984 Obituary . 112
Hooker, Thomas 1586-1647 ... DLB 24
Hookham, Hilda Henriette (Kuttner) 1915- ... 9-12R
hooks, bell
See Watkins, Gloria
See also BLCS
See also CLC 94
Hooks, G(aylor) Eugene 1927- ... 1-4R
Hooks, Gene
See Hooks, G(aylor) Eugene
Hooks, Gregory M. 1953- ... 141
Hooks, William H(arris) 1921- ... CANR-67
Earlier sketches in CA 81-84, CANR-19
See also SATA 16, 94
Hoole, Daryl Van Dam 1934- ... 21-24R
Hoole, W(illiam) Stanley 1903- ... CANR-7
Earlier sketch in CA 17-20R
Hoon, Patricia Easterly 1954- ... SATA 90
Hooper, Biff
See Obrecht, Jas
Hooper, Byrd
See St. Clair, Byrd Hooper
Hooper, David (Vincent) 1915- ... 85-88
Hooper, Douglas 1927- ... CANR-18
Earlier sketch in CA 25-28R
Hooper, Finley (Allison) 1922- ... 123
Hooper, Hedley Colwill 1919- ... 124
Hooper, John W(illiam) 1926- ... 29-32R
Hooper, Johnson Jones 1815-1862 ... DLB 3,11
Hooper, Judith 1949- ... 136
Hooper, Kay 1957- ... CANR-66
Earlier sketch in CA 122
Hooper, Maureen Brett 1927- ... 143
See also SATA 76
Hooper, Meredith (Jean) 1939- ... CANR-47
Earlier sketches in CA 106, CANR-22
See also SATA 28, 101
Hooper, Patricia 1941- ... CANR-69
Earlier sketch in CA 127
See also SATA 95
Hooper, Paul F(ranklin) 1938- ... CANR-18
Earlier sketch in CA 101
Hooper, Peter
See Hooper, Hedley Colwill
Hooper, Walter (McGehee) 1931- ... CANR-50
Earlier sketches in CA 17-20R, CANR-7, 22
Hooper, William Loyd 1931- ... CANR-19
Earlier sketches in CA 5-8R, CANR-3
Hoopes, Clement R. 1906-1979 ... 73-76
Obituary ... 89-92
Hoopes, David S. 1928- ... CANR-42
Earlier sketch in CA 118
Hoopes, Donelson F(arquhar) 1932- ... 33-36R
Hoopes, James 1944- ... CANR-10
Earlier sketch in CA 65-68
Hoopes, John W. 1958- ... 163
Hoopes, Lyn Littlefield 1953- ... 120
See also SATA 49
See also SATA-Brief 44
Hoopes, Ned E(dward) 1932- ... 17-20R
See also SATA 21
Hoopes, Robert (Griffith) 1920- ... CANR-1
Earlier sketch in CA 1-4R
Hoopes, Roy 1922- ... CANR-15
Earlier sketch in CA 21-24R
See also SATA 11
Hoopes, Townsend Walter 1922- ... 97-100
Interview in ... 97-100
Hoople, Cheryl G. Brief entry ... 111
See also SATA-Brief 32
Hoops, Richard A(llen) 1933- ... 41-44R
Hoor, Elvie (Marie Mortensen) Ten
See Ten Hoor, Elvie (Marie Mortensen)
Hoornik, Ed(uard Jozef Antonie Marie)
1910-1970 Obituary ... 104
Hoos, Ida Russakoff 1912- ... 17-20R
Hooson, David J. M. 1926- ... 17-20R
Hooten, William J(arvis) 1900- ... 61-64
Hooton, Charles
See Rowe, Vivian C(laud)
Hooton, Joy 1935- ... 127
Hoover, Calvin Bryce 1897-1974 ... CAP-1
Obituary ... 49-52
Earlier sketch in CA 13-14
Hoover, D(onald) B(runton) 1930- ... 144
Hoover, Dorothy Estheryne 1918- ... 49-52
Hoover, Dwight W(esley) 1926- ... 33-36R
Hoover, Edgar M. 1907- ... 13-16R
Hoover, F(rancis) Louis 1913- ... 41-44R
Hoover, H(elen) M(ary) 1935- ... CANR-36
Earlier sketches in CA 105, CANR-22
See also AAYA 11
See also JRDA
See also MAICYA
See also SAAS 8
See also SATA 44, 83
See also SATA-Brief 33
Hoover, Hardy 1902- ... 29-32R
Hoover, Helen (Drusilla Blackburn)
1910-1984 ... 21-24R
Obituary ... 113
See also SATA 12
See also SATA-Obit 39
Hoover, Herbert (Clark) 1874-1964 ... 108
Obituary ... 89-92
Hoover, Herbert Theodore 1930- ... 106
Hoover, J(ohn) Edgar 1895-1972 ... CANR-2
Obituary ... 33-36R
Earlier sketch in CA 1-4R
Hoover, John P. 1910- ... 53-56
Hoover, Kenneth H(arding) 1920- ... CANR-7
Earlier sketch in CA 57-60
Hoover, Kenneth R(ay) 1940- ... 132
Hoover, Marjorie L(awson) 1910- ... 41-44R
Hoover, Mary B(idgood) 1917- ... 93-96
Hoover, Paul 1946- ... 141
Hoover, Thomas 1941- ... 102
Hopcke, Robert H(enry) 1958- ... 154
Hopcraft, Arthur 1932- ... CANR-35
Earlier sketches in CA 25-28R, CANR-14
Hope, A(lec) D(erwent) 1907- ... CANR-33
Earlier sketch in CA 21-24R
See also CLC 3, 51
See also MTCW 1
Hope, A(shley) Guy 1914-1982 ... 25-28R
Obituary ... 133
Hope, Amanda
See Lewis, Judith Mary
Hope, Andrew
See Hern, (George) Anthony
Hope, Anthony 1863-1933 ... 157
See also DLB 153, 156
See also TCLC 83
Hope, Bob 1903- ... CANR-43
Earlier sketch in CA 101
See also BEST 90:4
Hope, Brian
See Creasey, John
Hope, C(harles) E(velyn) G(raham) 1900-1971 ... CAP-1
Earlier sketch in CA 13-16
Hope, Christopher (David Tully) 1944- ... CANR-47
Earlier sketch in CA 106
See also CLC 52
See also SATA 62
Hope, David
See Fraser, Douglas
Hope, Felix
See Williamson, Claude C(harles) H.
Hope, Jack 1940- ... 81-84
Hope, Jane 1938- ... 110
Hope, Karol ... 93-96
Hope, Laura Lee ... CANR-27
Earlier sketch in CA 17-20R
See also SATA 1, 67
Hope, Margaret
See Knight, Alanna
Hope, Marjorie (Cecelia) 1923- ... 29-32R
Hope, Norman Victor 1908-1983 Obituary ... 110
Hope, Quentin M(anning) 1923- ... 13-16R
Hope, Ronald (Sidney) 1921- ... CANR-3
Earlier sketch in CA 9-12R
Hope, Welborn 1903- ... 29-32R
Hope-Jones, Arthur 1911-1984 Obituary ... 112
Hopes, David Brendan 1953- ... CANR-26
Earlier sketch in CA 109
Hope Simpson, Jacynth 1930- ... CANR-7
Earlier sketch in CA 13-16R
See also SATA 12
Hope-Wallace, Philip (Adrian)
1911-1979 Obituary ... 93-96
Hopewell, S(ydney) 1924- ... 25-28R
Hopf, Alice (Martha) L(ightner) 1904-1988 . CANR-9
Obituary ... 124
Earlier sketch in CA 17-20R
See also SATA 5
See also SATA-Obit 55
Hopke, William E. 1918- ... 21-24R
Hopkin, Alannah 1949- ... CANR-27
Earlier sketch in CA 109
Hopkins, A. T.
See Turngren, Annette
Hopkins, Antony 1921- ... CANR-17
Earlier sketch in CA 101
Hopkins, Bill 1928- ... 9-12R
Hopkins, Bruce R. 1941- ... 150
Hopkins, C(harles) Howard 1905- ... 123
Hopkins, Clark 1895-1976 ... 129
Obituary ... 109
See also SATA-Obit 34
Hopkins, David 1948- ... CANR-48
Earlier sketch in CA 122
Hopkins, Donald R(oswell) 1941- ... 123
Hopkins, Ellice 1836-1904 ... DLB 190
Hopkins, Fred W(right), Jr. 1935- ... 69-72
Hopkins, George E(mil) 1937- ... 33-36R
Hopkins, Gerard Manley 1844-1889 ... CDBLB 1890-1914
See also DA
See also DAB
See also DAC
See also DAM MST, POET
See also DLB 35, 57
See also PC 15
See also WLC
Hopkins, Harry 1913- ... 29-32R
Hopkins, J(ohn) F(eely) 1922- ... 102
Hopkins, Jack W(alker) 1930- ... 25-28R
Hopkins, Jackie (Mims) 1952- ... 156
See also SATA 92
Hopkins, James Franklin 1909- ... 1-4R
Hopkins, Jasper (Stephen, Jr.) 1936- ... CANR-57
Earlier sketches in CA 37-40R, CANR-14, 31
Hopkins, Jerry 1935- ... CANR-18
Earlier sketch in CA 25-28R
Hopkins, John (?)-1570 ... DLB 132
Hopkins, John (Richard) 1931- ... 85-88
See also CLC 4
Hopkins, John 1938- ... 165
Hopkins, Joseph G(erard) E(dward) 1909- . CANR-5
Earlier sketch in CA 1-4R
See also SATA 11
Hopkins, Joseph Martin 1919- ... 49-52
Hopkins, Keith 1934- ... 130
Hopkins, (Hector) Kenneth 1914-1988 ... CANR-1
Obituary ... 125
Earlier sketch in CA 1-4R
See also SATA-Obit 58
Hopkins, Lee (Wallace) ... 57-60
Hopkins, Lee Bennett 1938- ... CANR-55
Earlier sketches in CA 25-28R, CANR-29
See also AAYA 18
See also CLR 44
See also JRDA
See also MAICYA
See also SAAS 4
See also SATA 3, 68
Hopkins, Lemuel 1750-1801 ... DLB 37
Hopkins, Lightnin'
See Hopkins, Sam

Hopkins, Lyman
See Folsom, Franklin (Brewster)
Hopkins, Marjorie 1911- 21-24R
See also SATA 9
Hopkins, Mark W(yatt) 1931- 29-32R
Hopkins, Mary R(ice) 1956- 164
See also SATA 97
Hopkins, Milton 1906-1983 Obituary 109
Hopkins, Nicholas S(nowden) 1939- 77-80
Hopkins, Pauline Elizabeth 1859-1930 141
See also BLC 2
See also BW 2
See also DAM MULT
See also DLB 50
See also TCLC 28
Hopkins, Prynce (C.) 1885-1970 CAP-2
Earlier sketch in CA 21-22
Hopkins, Pryns
See Hopkins, Prynce (C.)
Hopkins, Raymond F(rederick) 1939- CANR-28
Earlier sketch in CA 49-52
Hopkins, Robert A. 1923- 89-92
Hopkins, Robert S(ydney) CANR-38
Earlier sketch in CA 115
Hopkins, Sam 1912-1982 Obituary 106
Hopkins, Samuel 1721-1803 DLB 31
Hopkins, Terence K(ilbourne) 1928- 9-12R
Hopkins, Thomas H(ollis) 1945- 116
Hopkins, Thomas J(ohns) 1930- 37-40R
Hopkins, Viola
See Winner, Viola Hopkins
Hopkins, Vivian C. 1909- CAP-2
Earlier sketch in CA 33-36
Hopkinson, Amanda 1948- 150
See also SATA 84
Hopkinson, Deborah 1952- CANR-72
Earlier sketch in CA 143
See also SATA 76
Hopkinson, Diana 1912- 29-32R
Hopkinson, Francis 1737-1791 DLB 31
Hopkinson, Henry Thomas 1905-1990 17-20R
Obituary 132
Hopkinson, Tom
See Hopkinson, Henry Thomas
Hopkirk, Peter 1930- 107
Hopley, George
See Hopley-Woolrich, Cornell George
Hopley-Woolrich, Cornell George 1903-1968 CANR-58
Earlier sketches in CAP-1, CA 13-14
See also Woolrich, Cornell
Hoppe, Art(hur Watterson) 1925- CANR-3
Earlier sketch in CA 5-8R
Hoppe, Eleanor Sellers 1933- 73-76
Hoppe, Emil Otho 1878- 9-12R
Hoppe, Joanne 1932- 81-84
See also SATA 42
Hoppe, Matthias 1952- 143
See also SATA 76
Hoppe, Ronald A. 1931- 45-48
Hoppen, K(arl) Theodore 1941- 119
Hoppenstedt, Elbert M. 1917- 1-4R
Hopper, Columbus B(urwell) 1931- 33-36R
Hopper, David H. 1927- 21-24R
Hopper, Dennis 1936- 114
Hopper, Grace (Brewster) Murray 1906-1992 164
Hopper, Hedda
See Furry, Elda
Hopper, John 1934- 17-20R
Hopper, Nancy J. 1937- CANR-38
Earlier sketch in CA 115
See also SATA 38
See also SATA-Brief 35
Hopper, R(obert) J(ohn) 1910-1987 123
Hopper, Robert 1945- CANR-9
Earlier sketch in CA 65-68
Hopper, Vincent Foster 1906-1976 CANR-6
Obituary 61-64
Earlier sketch in CA 1-4R
Hoppin, Augustus 1828-1896 DLB 188
Hoppin, Richard H(allowell) 1913- 41-44R
Hoppock, Robert 1901- 1-4R
Hopson, Dan, Jr. 1930- 21-24R
Hopson, Janet L(ouise) 1950- 89-92
Hopwood, Robert R. 1910- CAP-1
Earlier sketch in CA 13-14
Hora, F. Bayard 1909(?)-1984 Obituary 112
Horak, Jan-Christopher 1951- 153
Horak, M. Stephan 1920- 9-12R
Horan, Elizabeth (Rosa) 1956- 146
Horan, Francis Harding 1900-1978 Obituary 81-84
Horan, James David 1914-1981 CANR-9
Obituary 105
Earlier sketch in CA 13-16R
Horan, (Harold) Joseph Taaffe
1898(?)-1985 Obituary 117
Horan, Patrick M. 1958- 166
Horan, Richard (Vincent), (Jr.) 1957- 153
Horan, William D. 1933- 25-28R
Horat, Heinz 1948- 141
Horatio
See Proust, (Valentin-Louis-George-Eugene-) Marcel
Horatio, Algernon 89-92
Horatio, Jane
See Cudlipp, Edythe
Horbach, Michael 1924-1986 CANR-25
Obituary 120
Earlier sketch in CA 29-32R
Horchler, Richard (Thomas) 1925- 5-8R
Horchow, (Samuel) Roger 1928- 106
Hord, Frederick (Lee) 1941- 143
See also BW 2
Horder, (Thomas) Mervyn 1910- 104
Horder, (Thomas) Mervyn 1910-1997 Obituary 158
Hordern, William (Edward) 1920- 13-16R
Hordon, Harris E(ugene) 1942- 53-56
Horecky, Paul Louis 1913- CANR-2
Earlier sketch in CA 5-8R
Horelick, Arnold L(awrence) 1928- CANR-8
Earlier sketch in CA 17-20R
Horgan, Denis E. 1941- 101
Horgan, Edward R. 1934- 109
Horgan, John 1953- 162
Horgan, John J(oseph) 1910- 61-64
Horgan, John Joseph 1881-1967 Obituary 116
Horgan, Paul (George Vincent O'Shaughnessy) 1903-1995 CANR-35
Obituary 147
Earlier sketches in CA 13-16R, CANR-9
Interview in CANR-9
See also CLC 9, 53
See also DAM NOV
See also DLB 102
See also DLBY 85
See also MTCW 1
See also SATA 13
See also SATA-Obit 84
Hori, Ichiro 1910-1974 CAP-2
Earlier sketch in CA 25-28
Horie, Shigeo 1903- CAP-1
Earlier sketch in CA 13-14
Horikoshi, Jiro 1904(?)-1982 Obituary 110
Horka-Follick, Lorayne Ann 1940- 29-32R
Horkheimer, Max 1895-1973 Obituary 41-44R
Horlak, E. E.
See Tepper, Sheri S.
Horler, Sydney 1888-1954 157
See also SATA 102
Horlick, Allan S. 1941- 151
Horman, Richard E. 1945- 29-32R
Horn, D(avid) B(ayne) 1901-1969 CANR-6
Earlier sketch in CA 1-4R
Horn, Daniel 1934-1991 21-24R
Obituary 134
Horn, Edward Newman
1903(?)-1976 Obituary 65-68
Horn, Francis H(enry) 1908- 53-56
Horn, George F(rancis) 1917- CANR-8
Earlier sketch in CA 5-8R
Horn, Henry Eyster 1913- 21-24R
Horn, Jeanne P. 1925- 5-8R
Horn, John L(eonard) 1928- CANR-14
Earlier sketch in CA 37-40R
Horn, Linda L(ouise) 1947- 101
Horn, Maurice 1931- CANR-22
Earlier sketch in CA 89-92
Horn, Pamela (Lucy Ray) 1936- CANR-30
Earlier sketch in CA 69-72
Horn, Peter
See Kuttner, Henry
Horn, Peter (Rudolf Gisela) 1934- 103
Horn, Pierre L(aurence) 1942- CANR-44
Earlier sketch in CA 119
Horn, Richard 1954-1989 105
Obituary 128
Horn, Robert M. 1933- 29-32R
Horn, Siegfried H(erbert) 1908- 37-40R
Horn, Stefan F. 1900- CAP-1
Earlier sketch in CA 13-16
Horn, (John) Stephen 1931- 13-16R
Horn, Stephen (McCaffrey Moore) 1931- 45-48
Horn, Thomas D. 1918- 13-16R
Horn, Vivi 1878(?)-1971 Obituary 104
Horn, Walter (William) 1908- 21-24R
Hornback, Bert G(erald) 1935- CANR-22
Earlier sketch in CA 29-32R
Hornbaker, Alice 1927- 77-80
Hornbein, Thomas Frederic 1930- 53-56
Hornberger, H. Richard 1923(?)-1997 105
Obituary 162
Hornberger, Theodore 1906-1975 CANR-3
Earlier sketch in CA 5-8R
Hornblow, Arthur, Jr. 1893-1976 89-92
Obituary 65-68
See also SATA 15
Hornblow, Leonora (Schinasi) 1920- 73-76
See also SATA 18
Hornblower, Harry C.
See Shriver, Harry C(lair)
Hornbostel, Lloyd 1934- 159
Hornbruch, Frederick William, Jr. 1913- 109
Hornby, John (Wilkinson) 1913- 9-12R
Hornby, Leslie 1949- 103
Hornby, Nick 1957(?)- 151
Hornby, Richard 1938- 89-92
Hornby, William H(arry) 1923- 106
Horne, A(lexander) D(ouglas) 1932- 109
Horne, Aaron 1940- 138
See also BW 2
Horne, Alistair (Allan) 1925- CANR-9
Earlier sketch in CA 5-8R
Horne, Bernard Shea 1905-1970 Obituary 104
Horne, Chevis Ferber 1914- CANR-16
Earlier sketch in CA 97-100
Horne, Cynthia Miriam 1939- 5-8R
Horne, Donald (Richmond) 1921- CANR-42
Earlier sketches in CA 103, CANR-20
Horne, Elliott 1922(?)-1989 Obituary 129
Horne, Frank (Smith) 1899-1974 125
Obituary 53-56
See also BW 1
See also DLB 51
Horne, Geoffrey 1916- CANR-64
Earlier sketch in CA 9-12R
Horne, Gerald 1949- 140
See also BW 2
Horne, Howard
See Payne, (Pierre Stephen) Robert
Horne, Hugh Robert 1915- 5-8R
Horne, Kenneth 1900-1975 Obituary 115
Horne, Lewis 1932- 110
Horne, Marilyn 1934- 133
Horne, Peter 1947- 69-72
Horne, R(alph) A(lbert) 1929- 106
Horne, Richard Henry 1803-1884 DLB 32
See also SATA 29
Horne, Roman L(emuel) 1901-1987 Obituary 121
Horne, Shirley (Faith) 1919- 49-52
Hornem, Horace Esq.
See Byron, George Gordon (Noel)
Horner, Althea (Jane) 1926- 81-84
See also SATA 36
Horner, Dave 1934- 17-20R
See also SATA 12
Horner, David Stuart 1900(?)-1983(?) Obituary 111
Horner, George F(rederick) 1899-1974 CAP-2
Earlier sketch in CA 33-36
Horner, J. C.
See Horner, John Curwen
Horner, John Curwen 1922- 103
Horner, John R(obert) 1946- 168
Horner, Joyce Mary 1903-1980 Obituary 112
Horner, Kenric Lancaster 1902-1973 Obituary 111
Horner, Lance
See Horner, Kenric Lancaster
Horner, Thomas Marland 1927- 37-40R
Horner, Tom (Julian) 1913- 121
Horner, Winifred Bryan 1922- CANR-41
Earlier sketch in CA 118
Horney, Karen (Clementine Theodore Danielsen) 1885-1952 165
Brief entry 114
See also TCLC 71
Horngren, Charles T(homas) 1926- 57-60
Hornig, Doug 1943- CANR-66
Earlier sketches in CA 117, CANR-40
Hornik, Edith Lynn
See Beer, Edith Lynn
Hornik-Beer, Edith Lynn
See Beer, Edith Lynn
Horniman, Joanne 1951- 166
See also SATA 98
Horning, Alice S. 1950- 137
Hornman, Wim 1920- Brief entry 106
Hornos, Axel 1907- CAP-2
Earlier sketch in CA 29-32
See also SATA 20
Hornsby, Albert Sidney 1898(?)-1978 Obituary 104
Hornsby, Alton, Jr. 1940- 37-40R
Hornsby, Ken 1934- 105
Hornsby, Roger A. 1926- 21-24R
Hornsby-Smith, Michael P(eter) 1932- 126
Hornstein, Harvey A. 1938- 53-56
Hornstein, Lillian Herlands 1909- 45-48
Hornstein, Reuben Aaron 1912- 106
See also SATA 64
Hornung, Clarence Pearson 1899- CANR-9
Earlier sketch in CA 17-20R
Hornung, E(rnest) W(illiam) 1866-1921 160
Brief entry 108
See also DLB 70
See also TCLC 59
Hornung, Erik 1933- 117
Hornung, Maximilian 1942- 107
Horobin, Ian M. 1899-1976 Obituary 69-72
Horovitz, Frances Margaret
1938-1983 Obituary 111
Horovitz, Israel (Arthur) 1939- CANR-59
Earlier sketches in CA 33-36R, CANR-46
See also CLC 56
See also DAM DRAM
See also DLB 7
Horovitz, Michael 1935- 81-84
Horowitz, Al
See Horowitz, I(srael) A.
Horowitz, Daniel 1938- 145
Horowitz, David 1903- 69-72
Horowitz, David (Joel) 1939- CANR-68
Earlier sketch in CA 13-16R
Horowitz, David A. 1941- 89-92
Horowitz, David Charles 1937- 89-92
Horowitz, Donald L(eonard) 1939- 126
Horowitz, Edward 1904- CANR-4
Earlier sketch in CA 1-4R
Horowitz, Esther 1920- 49-52
Horowitz, Eve 1963- 139
Horowitz, Gene 1930- 77-80
Horowitz, Helen Lefkowitz 1942- CANR-58
Earlier sketch in CA 125
Horowitz, I(srael) A. 1907-1973 Obituary 41-44R
Horowitz, Ira 1934- 41-44R
Horowitz, Irving Louis 1929- CANR-50
Earlier sketch in CA 41-44R
Horowitz, Jacob 1900-1979 Obituary 89-92
Horowitz, Joseph 1948- CANR-27
Earlier sketch in CA 109
Horowitz, Laura (Godofsky)
1943-1983 Obituary 110
Horowitz, Leonard M(artin) 1937- 37-40R
Horowitz, Lois 1940- 119
Horowitz, Mardi J(on) 1934- 33-36R
Horowitz, Michael M. 1933- CANR-49
Earlier sketches in CA 41-44R, CANR-15
Horowitz, Morris A(aron) 1919- CANR-9
Earlier sketch in CA 65-68
Horowitz, Renee B(arbara) 1932- 159
Horowitz, Robert S. 1924- 9-12R
Horowitz, Shel Alan 1956- CANR-46
Earlier sketch in CA 120
See also Friedman, Alan
Horrell, C. William 1918- CANR-13
Earlier sketch in CA 61-64
Horricks, Raymond (Anthony) 1933- CANR-64
Earlier sketch in CA 129
Horrie, Chris(topher) 1956- 150
Horrock, Berta Crone 1896(?)-1983 Obituary 110
Horrock, Nicholas (Morton) 1936- 49-52
Horrocks, Brian (Gwynne) 1895-1985 Obituary 114
Horrocks, Edna M. 1908- CAP-2
Earlier sketch in CA 17-18
Horrocks, John E(dwin) 1913- 5-8R
Horsbrugh, Ian 1941- 111
Horsburgh, David Michael 1923-1984 Obituary 114
Horsburgh, H(oward) J(ohn) N(eate) 1918- 25-28R
Horsefield, J(ohn) Keith 1901-1997 5-8R
Obituary 157
Horsely, Ramsbottom
See Berne, Eric (Lennard)
Horseman, Elaine Hall 1925- 13-16R
Horsey, Miles G. 1956- 149
Horsford, Howard C(larke) 1921- 136
Horsley, David
See Bingley, David Ernest
Horsley, James (Allen) 1938- 45-48
Horsman, Reginald 1931- CANR-17
Earlier sketches in CA 1-4R, CANR-2
Horst, Irvin B(uckwalter) 1915- 41-44R
Horst, Samuel (Levi) 1919- 21-24R
Horstman, Allen (Henry) 1943- 122
Horton, Arthur MacNeill, Jr. 1947- CANR-35
Earlier sketch in CA 114
Horton, David (Edward) 1931- 164
Horton, Felix Lee
See Floren, Lee
Horton, Frank E. 1939- 29-32R
Horton, George Moses 1797(?)-1883(?) DLB 50
Horton, J(ames) Wright (Jr.) 1950- 138
Horton, James O(liver) 1943- CANR-35
Earlier sketch in CA 114
Horton, John (William) 1905- CANR-18
Earlier sketches in CA 9-12R, CANR-3
Horton, Louise (Walthall) 1916- CANR-40
Earlier sketches in CA 49-52, CANR-2
Horton, Lowell 1936- 53-56
Horton, Madelyn (Stacey) 1962- 145
See also SATA 77
Horton, Michael Scott 1964- 135
Horton, Myles 1905-1990 140
Horton, Patricia Campbell 1943- 89-92
Horton, Paul Burleigh 1916- CANR-20
Earlier sketch in CA 1-4R
Horton, Paul Chester 1942- 106
Horton, Philip C. 1911(?)-1989 Obituary 129
Horton, Rod W(illiam) 1910- 49-52
Horton, Russell M. 1946- 97-100
Horton, Stanley M(onroe) 1916- CANR-6
Earlier sketch in CA 57-60
Horton, Susan R. 1941- 109
Horton, Thomas R. 1926- 144
Horvat, Branko 1928- 53-56
Horvath, Agnes 1957- 147
Horvath, Betty 1927- 17-20R
See also SATA 4
Horvath, Janos 1921- 41-44R
Horvath, Joan 1944- 81-84
Horvath, Odon von
See Horvath, Oedoen von
See also DLB 85, 124
Horvath, Oedoen von 1901-1938 Brief entry 118
See also Horvath, Odon von
See also TCLC 45
Horvath, Polly 1957- 132
See also SATA 85
Horvath, Violet M. 1924- 29-32R
Horwich, Frances R(appaport) 1908- CAP-1
Earlier sketch in CA 13-16
See also SATA 11
Horwitt, Sanford D. 1943- 159
Horwitz, Elinor Lander CANR-13
Earlier sketch in CA 77-80
See also SATA 45
See also SATA-Brief 33
Horwitz, Julius 1920-1986 CANR-12
Obituary 119
Earlier sketch in CA 9-12R
See also CLC 14
Horwitz, Richard P(aul) 1949- CANR-48
Earlier sketch in CA 122
Horwitz, Simi L(ouise) 1949- 103
Horwitz, Sylvia L(aibman) 1911- 61-64
Horwitz, Tony 1958- 140
Horwood, Harold (Andrew) 1923- CANR-25
Earlier sketches in CA 21-24R, CANR-9
See also CAAS 15
See also DLB 60
Horwood, William 1944- 141
See also SATA 85
Hosek, Chaviva (Milada) 1946- 127
Hoselitz, Bert(hold) F(rank) 1913- CANR-1
Earlier sketch in CA 1-4R
Hosford, Bowen I. 1916- CANR-24
Earlier sketch in CA 107
Hosford, Dorothy (Grant) 1900-1952 SATA 22
Hosford, Jessie 1892- 41-44R
See also SATA 5
Hosford, Philip L(ewis) 1926- 57-60
Hosford, Ray E. 1933- 85-88
Hoshi, Shin'ichi 1926- 162
See also SATA 101
Hosie, Stanley W(illiam) 1922- 25-28R
Hosier, Helen Kooiman 1928- CANR-8
Earlier sketch in CA 61-64
Hosier, Peter
See Clark, Douglas (Malcolm Jackson)
Hosken, Fran(ziska) P(orges) 1919- CANR-6
Earlier sketch in CA 57-60
Hoskens, Jane Fenn 1693-1770(?) DLB 200
Hoskin, Cyril Henry 1911(?)-1981 Obituary 102
Hosking, Eric (John) 1909- CANR-17
Earlier sketch in CA 101
Hosking, Geoffrey A(lan) 1942- CANR-71
Earlier sketches in CA 85-88, CANR-19
Hoskins, Katharine Bail 1924- 65-68

Hoskins, Katherine (de Montalant) 1909- ... CAP-2
Earlier sketch in CA 25-28
Hoskins, Percy 1904-1989 Obituary ... 127
Hoskins, Robert 1933- ... CANR-56
Earlier sketch in CA 29-32R
Hoskins, William George 1908-1992 ... 13-16R
Obituary ... 136
Hoskyns, John 1566-1638 ... DLB 121
Hoskyns, Tam 1961- ... 164
Hoskyns-Abrahall, Clare (Constance Drury) ... 29-32R
See also SATA 13
Hosley, Richard 1921- ... CANR-8
Earlier sketch in CA 5-8R
Hosmer, Charles B(ridgham), Jr. 1932- ... 13-16R
Hosmon, Robert Stahr 1943- ... 45-48
Hosokawa, Bill
See Hosokawa, William K.
Hosokawa, William K. 1915- ... CANR-11
Earlier sketch in CA 29-32R
Hosozawa-Nagano, Elaine 1954- ... 165
Hospers, John, Jr. 1918- ... CANR-2
Earlier sketch in CA 1-4R
Hospital, Janette Turner 1942- ... CANR-48
Earlier sketch in CA 108
See also CLC 42
Hoss, Marvin Allen 1929- ... 29-32R
Hoss, Norman 1923(?)-1983 Obituary ... 111
Hossack, Joei Carlton 1944- ... 157
Hossack, Sylvia 1939- ... SATA 83
Hossack, Sylvie Adams
See Hossack, Sylvia
Hossent, Harry 1916- ... CAP-1
Earlier sketch in CA 9-10
Hostetler, Beulah Stauffer 1926- ... 126
Hostetler, Marian 1932- ... CANR-49
Earlier sketches in CA 65-68, CANR-9, 24
See also SATA 91
Hostetter, B(enjamin) Charles 1916- ... CANR-1
Earlier sketch in CA 1-4R
Hostler, Charles W(arren) 1919- ... 21-24R
Hostos, Adolfo de 1887- ... 131
See also HW
Hostos, E. M. de
See Hostos (y Bonilla), Eugenio Maria de
Hostos, Eugenio M. de
See Hostos (y Bonilla), Eugenio Maria de
Hostos, Eugenio Maria
See Hostos (y Bonilla), Eugenio Maria de
Hostos (y Bonilla), Eugenio Maria de 1839-1903 ... 131
Brief entry ... 123
See also HW
See also TCLC 24
Hostovsky, Egon 1908-1973 Obituary ... 89-92
Hostrop, Richard Winfred 1925- ... 25-28R
Hotaling, Edward 1937- ... 77-80
Hotchkiss, Bill 1936- ... 104
Hotchkiss, Jeanette 1901- ... 21-24R
Hotchkiss, Ralf D. 1947- ... 33-36R
Hotchner, A(aron) E(dward) 1920- ... CANR-56
Earlier sketches in CA 69-72, CANR-27
Hotchner, Tracy 1950- ... 102
Hothem, Lar(ry Lee) 1938- ... 106
Hothersall, David 1940- ... 111
Hotson, John H(argrove) 1930- ... 25-28R
Hotspur
See Curling, Bryan William Richard
Hottois, James W. 1943- ... 77-80
Hotz, Robert B(ergmann) 1914- ... 101
Hou, Chi-ming 1924- ... 21-24R
Hou, Fu-Wu
See Houn, Franklin W.
Houblon, Doreen (Lindsay) Archer
See Archer Houblon, Doreen (Lindsay)
Houchin, Thomas D(ouglas) 1925- ... 77-80
Houck, Carter 1924- ... CANR-14
Earlier sketch in CA 77-80
See also SATA 22
Houck, John W(illiam) 1931- ... CANR-11
Earlier sketch in CA 29-32R
Houdini
See Lovecraft, H(oward) P(hillips)
Houdini, Merlin X.
See Borgmann, Dmitri A(lfred)
Houedard, Pierre-Sylvester 1924- ... 103
Houfe, Simon (Richard) 1942- ... CANR-19
Earlier sketch in CA 103
Hougan, Carolyn 1943- ... 139
See also CLC 34
Hougan, James Richard 1942- ... 77-80
Hougan, Jim
See Hougan, James Richard
Hough, (Helen) Charlotte 1924- ... CANR-5
Earlier sketch in CA 9-12R
See also SATA 9
Hough, Denny C. 1925(?)-1983 Obituary ... 111
Hough, Emerson 1857-1923 Brief entry ... 120
See also DLB 9
Hough, George A(nthony) III 1920- ... 121
Brief entry ... 117
Hough, Graham (Goulder) 1908-1990 ... CANR-25
Obituary ... 132
Earlier sketch in CA 69-72
Hough, Harold 1952- ... 144
Hough, Henry Beetle 1896-1985 ... CANR-2
Obituary ... 116
Earlier sketch in CA 1-4R
Hough, Henry W(ade) 1906-197(?) ... 25-28R
Obituary ... 122
Hough, Hugh 1924-1986 ... 73-76
Obituary ... 119
Hough, Jerry F(incher) 1935- ... 137
Brief entry ... 114
Hough, John T., Jr. 1946- ... 33-36R
Hough, Joseph C(arl), Jr. 1933- ... 21-24R
Hough, Judy Taylor 1932- ... 124
See also SATA 56, 63
See also SATA-Brief 51
Hough, Lindy Downer 1944- ... CANR-8
Earlier sketch in CA 61-64
Hough, Louis 1914- ... 37-40R
Hough, Michael 1928- ... 133
Hough, Peter A. 1954- ... 142
Hough, Richard (Alexander) 1922- ... CANR-18
Earlier sketches in CA 5-8R, CANR-3
See also SATA 17
Hough, S(tanley) B(ennett) 1917- ... CANR-3
Earlier sketch in CA 5-8R
Houghteling, James L(awrence), Jr. 1920- ... 5-8R
Houghton, Bernard 1935- ... 77-80
Houghton, Diane 1940- ... 123
Houghton, Elizabeth
See Gilzean, Elizabeth Houghton Blanchet
Houghton, Eric 1930- ... CANR-2
Earlier sketch in CA 1-4R
See also SATA 7
Houghton, George William 1905- ... 13-16R
Houghton, J. T.
See Houghton, John T(heodore)
Houghton, SirJohn
See Houghton, John T(heodore)
Houghton, John T(heodore) 1931- ... 168
Houghton, Katharine 1945- ... 130
Houghton, Neal D(oyle) 1895- ... CAP-2
Earlier sketch in CA 25-28
Houghton, (Charles) Norris 1909- ... 21-24R
Houghton, Peter 1938- ... 119
Houghton, R(alph) E(dward) C(unliffe) 1896-1990 Obituary ... 132
Houghton, Samuel G(ilbert) 1902-1975 ... 65-68
Houghton, (William) Stanley 1881-1913 Brief entry ... 110
See also DLB 10
Houghton, Walter Edwards 1904-1983 ... CAP-1
Obituary ... 109
Earlier sketch in CA 9-10
Houk, Randy 1944- ... 151
See also Houk, Randy
See also SATA 97
Houlbrooke, Ralph (A.) 1944- ... 132
Houlden, J(ames) L(eslie) 1929- ... 77-80
Houle, Cyril O(rvin) 1913-1998 ... CANR-3
Obituary ... 167
Earlier sketch in CA 5-8R
Houlehen, Robert J. 1918- ... 49-52
See also SATA 18
Houlgate, Deke 1930- ... 61-64
Houlgate, Stephen (Glynn) 1954- ... 127
Hoult, Norah 1898-1984 Obituary ... 112
Hoult, Thomas Ford 1920- Brief entry ... 116
Houlton, Peggy Mann 1925(?)-1990 ... CANR-35
See also Mann, Peggy
Houn, Franklin W. 1920- ... 21-24R
Hounshell, David A. 1950- ... 129
Hounsome, Terry 1944- ... 109
Houpt, Katherine Albro 1939- ... 105
Hourani, A. H.
See Hourani, Albert (Habib)
Hourani, Albert (Habib) 1916(?)-1993 ... 140
Hourani, Cecil 1917- ... 129
Hourani, George F(adlo) 1913-1984 ... CANR-23
Earlier sketch in CA 45-48
Hours, Madeleine 1915- ... CANR-28
Earlier sketch in CA 49-52
Hours-Miedan, Madeleine
See Hours, Madeleine
Hours-Miedan, Magdeleine
See Hours, Madeleine
House, Anne W.
See McCauley, Elfrieda B(abnick)
House, Charles (Albert) 1916- ... 25-28R
House, Ernest R(obert) 1937- ... CANR-23
Earlier sketch in CA 45-48
House, Gloria 1941- ... CANR-41
Earlier sketch in CA 117
See also BW 2
House, H(ershel) Wayne 1948- ... 119
House, James S. 1944- ... 143
House, John William 1919-1984 ... 106
Obituary ... 112
House, Karen Elliott 1947- ... 130
Brief entry ... 125
Interview in ... 130
House, Kurt D(uane) 1947- ... 104
House, R(ichard) C(alvin) 1927- ... 142
House, Robert Burton 1892- ... CAP-1
Earlier sketch in CA 11-12
House, Robert J. 1932- ... 101
House, Robert W(illiam) 1920- ... 53-56
House, Ruth Sizemore 1946- ... 116
House, Victor 1893-1983 Obituary ... 109
Household, Geoffrey (Edward West) 1900-1988 ... CANR-58
Obituary ... 126
Earlier sketch in CA 77-80
See also CLC 11
See also DLB 87
See also SATA 14
See also SATA-Obit 59
Houselander, (Frances) Caryll 1901-1954 Brief entry ... 110
See also SATA-Brief 31
Houseman, Barton L(eroy) 1933- ... 61-64
Houseman, Gerald L. 1935- ... 108
Houseman, John 1902-1988 ... 163
Obituary ... 127
Brief entry ... 110
Housepian, Marjorie
See Dobkin, Marjorie Housepian
Houser, Caroline ... 115
Houser, Lynn Raymond 1951(?)- ... 167
Housewright, David 1955- ... 166
Housewright, Wiley L. 1913- ... 140
Housley, Norman (James) 1952- ... 108
Housman, A(lfred) E(dward) 1859-1936 ... 125
Brief entry ... 104
See also DA
See also DAB
See also DAC
See also DAM MST, POET
See also DLB 19
See also MTCW 1
See also PC 2
See also TCLC 1, 10
See also WLCS
Housman, Laurence 1865-1959 ... 155
Brief entry ... 106
See also DLB 10
See also SATA 25
See also TCLC 7
Houston, Beverle (Ann) 1936-1988 ... 89-92
Obituary ... 124
Houston, C(larence) Stuart 1927- ... 119
Houston, Cecil J(ames) 1943- ... 135
Houston, David 1938- ... 118
Houston, Dick 1943- ... SATA 74
Houston, Douglas (Norman) 1947- ... CANR-50
Earlier sketch in CA 123
Houston, Gloria ... 149
See also SATA 81
Houston, James A(rchibald) 1921- ... CANR-60
Earlier sketches in CA 65-68, CANR-38
See also AAYA 18
See also CLR 3
See also DAC
See also DAM MST
See also JRDA
See also MAICYA
See also SAAS 17
See also SATA 13, 74
Houston, James D. 1933- ... CANR-55
Earlier sketches in CA 25-28R, CANR-29
See also CAAS 16
See also SATA 78
Houston, James M(ackintosh) 1922- ... 13-16R
Houston, Jean Brief entry ... 115
Houston, Jeanne (Toyo) Wakatsuki 1934- ... CANR-29
Earlier sketch in CA 103
See also CAAS 16
See also SATA 78
Houston, Joan 1928- ... 17-20R
Houston, John Porter 1933-1987 ... CANR-3
Obituary ... 123
Earlier sketch in CA 9-12R
Houston, Neal B. 1928- ... 41-44R
Houston, Pam 1962(?)- ... 143
Houston, Peyton (Hoge) 1910-1994 ... CANR-1
Obituary ... 144
Earlier sketch in CA 49-52
Houston, R. B.
See Rae, Hugh C(rauford)
Houston, Robert 1935- ... 37-40R
Houston, Velina Hasu 1957- ... 144
Houston, W(illiam) Robert, Jr. 1928- ... CANR-40
Earlier sketches in CA 5-8R, CANR-3, 18
Houston, Will
See Paine, Lauran (Bosworth)
Houston, William Neil 1948- ... 123
Houtart, Francois 1925- ... 13-16R
Houthakker, Hendrik S(amuel) 1924- ... 17-20R
Houton, Kathleen
See Kilgore, Kathleen
Houts, Marshall (Wilson) 1919-1993 ... CANR-13
Obituary ... 143
Earlier sketch in CA 21-24R
Houts, Peter S. 1933- ... CANR-49
Earlier sketch in CA 49-52
Houwald, Ernst von 1778-1845 ... DLB 90
Hovannisian, Richard G. 1932- ... 21-24R
Hovda, Robert W(alker) 1920-1992 ... CANR-3
Obituary ... 136
Earlier sketch in CA 9-12R
Hovde, A(nnis) J(orgen) 1917- ... 112
Hovde, Christian A(rneson) 1922- ... 5-8R
Hovde, Howard 1928- ... 25-28R
Hovell, Lucille A. (Peterson) 1916- ... 5-8R
Hovell, Lucy A.
See Hovell, Lucille A. (Peterson)
Hoverland, H. Arthur 1928- ... 45-48
Hoversten, Chester E. 1922- ... 5-8R
Hovey, E(lwyn) Paul 1908- ... CANR-1
Earlier sketch in CA 1-4R
Hovey, Richard 1864-1900 ... DLB 54
Hovey, Richard B(ennett) 1917- ... 25-28R
Hovey, Sonya 1898-1960 Obituary ... 113
See also Levien, Sonya
Hoveyda, Fereydoun 1924- ... 101
Hovick, Rose Louise 1914(?)-1970 Obituary ... 113
Hoving, Thomas 1931- ... CANR-72
Earlier sketch in CA 101
Interview in ... 101
Howald, Reed Anderson 1930- ... 57-60
Howar, Barbara 1934- ... 89-92
See also AITN 1, 2
Howard, A(rthur) E(llsworth) Dick 1933- ... 13-16R
Howard, Alan 1922- ... SATA 45
Howard, Alan 1934- ... CANR-20
Earlier sketch in CA 37-40R
Howard, Alvin Wendell 1922-1975 ... 33-36R
Howard, Alyssa
See Buckholtz, Eileen (Garber)
and Glick, Ruth (Burtnick)
and Titchener, Louise
Howard, Anthony (Michell) 1934- ... 109
Howard, Audrey 1929- ... 163
Howard, Barbara 1930- ... 53-56
Howard, Ben(jamin Willis) 1944- ... 73-76
Howard, Bill
See Shannon, Mike
Howard, Bion B(radbury) 1912-1994 ... 13-16R
Obituary ... 144
Howard, Blanche 1923- ... 101
Howard, C(hester) Jeriel 1939- ... CANR-31
Earlier sketches in CA 29-32R, CANR-14
Howard, Carleton
See Howe, Charles H(orace)
Howard, Cecil
See Smith, Cecil (Howard III)
Howard, Charles Frederick 1904- ... 17-20R
Howard, Christopher 1913- ... 21-24R
Howard, Clark ... 122
Howard, Clive (?)-1974 Obituary ... 53-56
Howard, Constance (Mildred) 1910- ... CANR-11
Earlier sketch in CA 69-72
Howard, Coralie
See Cogswell, Coralie (Norris)
Howard, D(erek) L(ionel) 1930- ... CANR-8
Earlier sketch in CA 5-8R
Howard, Daniel F(rancis) 1928- ... 41-44R
Howard, David A. 1942- ... 165
Howard, David M(orris) 1928- ... CANR-10
Earlier sketch in CA 25-28R
Howard, Deborah (Janet) 1946- ... 124
Howard, Dick 1943- ... 77-80
Howard, Don (Marcel) 1940- ... CANR-22
Earlier sketch in CA 106
Howard, Donald 1927-1987 ... DLB 111
Howard, Donald R(oy) 1927-1987 ... CANR-1
Obituary ... 121
Earlier sketch in CA 1-4R
Howard, Dorothy (Arlynne) 1912- ... 65-68
Howard, Dorothy Gray 1902- ... 93-96
Howard, Edmund (Bernard Carlo) 1909- ... 85-88
Howard, Edward G(arfield) 1918(?)-1972 Obituary ... 104
Howard, Edwin 1924- ... 65-68
Howard, Edwin J(ohnston) 1901- ... CAP-1
Earlier sketch in CA 11-12
Howard, Elizabeth
See Paine, Lauran (Bosworth)
Howard, Elizabeth Fitzgerald 1927- ... CANR-60
Earlier sketch in CA 128
See also BW 2
See also SATA 74
Howard, Elizabeth Jane 1923- ... CANR-62
Earlier sketches in CA 5-8R, CANR-8
See also CLC 7, 29
Howard, Ellen 1943- ... 130
See also SATA 67, 99
Howard, Frances Minturn Brief entry ... 111
Howard, Fred D(avid) 1919- ... CANR-19
Earlier sketches in CA 1-4R, CANR-4
Howard, Frederick James 1904- ... 109
Howard, Gerald J(ohn) 1950- ... 108
Howard, Gilbert 1934- ... 49-52
Howard, Harold P. 1905- ... CAP-2
Earlier sketch in CA 33-36
Howard, Harry Nicholas 1902-1987 ... CANR-34
Obituary ... 123
Earlier sketch in CA 49-52
Howard, Hartley
See Ognall, Leopold Horace
Howard, Helen Addison 1904- ... CANR-3
Earlier sketch in CA 5-8R
Howard, Ian P. 1927- ... 21-24R
Howard, J. Grant 1929- ... 125
Howard, J. Woodford, Jr. 1931- ... 33-36R
Howard, James A(rch) 1922- ... CANR-8
Earlier sketch in CA 13-16R
Howard, James H(enri) 1925- ... 41-44R
Howard, James K(enton) 1943- ... 85-88
Howard, James T(homas) 1934- ... 101
Howard, Jane (Temple) 1935-1996 ... CANR-13
Obituary ... 152
Earlier sketch in CA 29-32R
Howard, Jane R(uble) 1924- ... 151
See also SATA 87
Howard, Jean
See MacGibbon, Jean
Howard, Jessica
See Schere, Monroe
Howard, Joan E. 1951- ... 141
Howard, John
See Hewitt, John (Harold)
Howard, John (Arnold) 1916- ... 41-44R
Howard, John R(obert) 1933- ... 53-56
Howard, John Tasker 1890-1964 Obituary ... 89-92
Howard, Joseph
See Rudnick, Paul
Howard, Joseph Leon 1917- ... CANR-1
Earlier sketch in CA 1-4R
Howard, Josephine
See Saxton, Josephine (Mary)
Howard, Joy
See Gorsky, Susan Rubinow
Howard, Joyce 1922- ... 5-8R
Howard, Kenneth I(rwin) 1932- ... 115
Howard, Kenneth Samuel 1882-1972 ... 9-12R
Obituary ... 103
Howard, Kez
See Houston, David
Howard, Lee M(ilton) 1922- ... 108
Howard, Leigh
See Lee Howard, Leon Alexander
Howard, Leon 1903-1982 ... 109
Howard, Leon Alexander Lee
See Lee Howard, Leon Alexander
Howard, Leslie G(raham) 1947- ... 114
Howard, Lowell B(ennett) 1925- ... 13-16R
Howard, M(ichael) C. 1945- ... 142
Howard, Marie
See Lena, Marie H(oward)

Howard, Mark
See Rigsby, Howard
Howard, Mary
See Mussi, Mary
Howard, Maureen 1930-.... CANR-31
Earlier sketch in CA 53-56
Interview in CANR-31
See also CLC 5, 14, 46
See also DLBY 83
See also MTCW 1
Howard, Michael (Eliot) 1922-.... CANR-2
Earlier sketch in CA 1-4R
Howard, Michael S. 1922-1974 Obituary.... 53-56
Howard, Moses L(eon) 1928-.... 109
Howard, Munroe 1913-1974.... CAP-2
Earlier sketch in CA 23-24
Howard, Nona
See Luxton, Leonora Kathrine
Howard, Norman Barry 1949-.... 155
See also SATA 90
Howard, Oliver Otis 1830-1909 Brief entry.... 109
Howard, Patricia (Lowe) 1937-.... CANR-7
Earlier sketch in CA 17-20R
Howard, Paul Jack 1908-1984 Obituary.... 113
Howard, Peter
See Koch, Howard
Howard, Peter D(unsmore) 1908-1965.... CAP-1
Earlier sketch in CA 11-12
Howard, Philip 1933-.... 65-68
Howard, Philip K. 1948-.... 153
Howard, Prosper
See Hamilton, Charles (Harold St. John)
Howard, Rhoda E. 1948-.... 157
Howard, Richard 1929-.... CANR-25
Earlier sketch in CA 85-88
Interview in CANR-25
See also AITN 1
See also CLC 7, 10, 47
See also DLB 5
Howard, Richard C. 1929-.... 53-56
Howard, Robert 1926-.... 41-44R
Howard, Robert E(rvin) 1906-1936.... 157
Brief entry.... 105
See also TCLC 8
Howard, Robert West 1908-.... CANR-1
Earlier sketch in CA 1-4R
See also SATA 5
Howard, Roger 1938-.... CANR-39
Earlier sketches in CA 93-96, CANR-17
Howard, Ron.... AAYA 8
Howard, Ronnalie Roper
See Roper, Ronnalie J.
Howard, Ross 1946-.... 120
Howard, Roy Joseph 1925-.... 112
Howard, Roy Wilson 1883-1964 Obituary.... 89-92
See also DLB 29
Howard, Sidney 1891-1939.... DLB 7, 26
Howard, Stanley E. 1888(?)-1980 Obituary.... 102
Howard, Ted
See Howard, Theodore Korner
Howard, Theodore Korner 1915-.... 103
Howard, Thomas 1930-.... 37-40R
Howard, Thomas T(rumbull) 1935-.... 111
Howard, Troy
See Paine, Lauran (Bosworth)
Howard, Vanessa 1955-.... 153
See also BW 2
Howard, Vechel
See Rigsby, Howard
Howard, Vernon (Linwood) 1918-1992.... 108
Obituary.... 139
See also SATA 40
See also SATA-Obit 73
Howard, Walter T. 1951-.... 152
Howard, Warren F.
See Pohl, Frederik
Howard, Warren Starkie 1930-.... 5-8R
Howard-Hill, Trevor Howard 1933-.... 85-88
Howard-Williams, Jeremy (Napier) 1922-. CANR-22
Earlier sketch in CA 106
Howarth, David (Armine) 1912-1991.... CANR-25
Obituary.... 134
Earlier sketches in CA 13-16R, CANR-9
See also SATA 6
See also SATA-Obit 68
Howarth, Donald 1931-.... 25-28R
Howarth, Lesley 1952-.... 153
See also SATA 94
Howarth, Pamela 1954-.... 102
Howarth, Patrick (John Fielding) 1916-.... 77-80
Howarth, Stephen (William Russell) 1953-....
CANR-25
Earlier sketch in CA 107
Howarth, T(homas) E(dward) B(rodie)
1914-1988.... 141
Obituary.... 125
Howarth, W(illiam) D(river) 1922-.... CANR-35
Earlier sketch in CA 45-48
Howarth, William Louis 1940-.... CANR-20
Earlier sketch in CA 37-40R
Howat, Gerald Malcolm David 1928-.... CANR-16
Earlier sketch in CA 93-96
Howat, John K(eith) 1937-.... 49-52
Howatch, Joseph 1935-.... 65-68
Howatch, Susan 1940-.... CANR-55
Earlier sketches in CA 45-48, CANR-24
See also AITN 1
See also DAM POP
Howe, Charles H(orace) 1912-.... 53-56
Howe, Charles L. 1932-.... 17-20R
Howe, Christine J. 1948-.... 146
Howe, Christopher (Barry) 1937-.... 121
Howe, Daniel Walker 1937-.... 29-32R
Howe, Deborah 1946-1978.... 105
See also SATA 29
Howe, Doris Kathleen.... CANR-3
Earlier sketch in CA 49-52
Howe, E. W. 1853-1937.... DLB 12, 25
Howe, Ellic (Paul) 1910-1991.... 25-28R
Obituary.... 135
Howe, Fanny (Quincy) 1940-.... CANR-70
Earlier sketch in CA 117
See also CAAS 27
See also CLC 47
See also SATA-Brief 52
Howe, Florence 1929-.... 124
Brief entry.... 109
Interview in.... 124
Howe, G(eorge) Melvyn 1920-.... 101
Howe, (Richard Edward) Geoffrey 1926-.... 150
Howe, George Frederick 1901-1988 Obituary.. 124
Howe, George Locke 1898(?)-1977 Obituary. 69-72
Howe, Helen 1905-1975.... CAP-2
Obituary.... 57-60
Earlier sketch in CA 23-24
Howe, Henry 1816-1893.... DLB 30
Howe, Hubert S(hattuck), Jr. 1942-.... 57-60
Howe, Irving 1920-1993.... CANR-50
Obituary.... 141
Earlier sketches in CA 9-12R, CANR-21
See also CLC 85
See also DLB 67
See also MTCW 1
Howe, James 1946-.... CANR-71
Earlier sketches in CA 105, CANR-22, 46
See also CLR 9
See also JRDA
See also MAICYA
See also SATA 29, 71
Howe, James Robinson 1935-.... 69-72
Howe, John F. 1957-.... SATA 79
Howe, Jonathan Trumbull 1935-.... 29-32R
Howe, Joseph 1804-1873.... DLB 99
Howe, Josephine (Mary) O'Connor
See O'Connor Howe, Josephine (Mary)
Howe, Julia Ward 1819-1910 Brief entry.... 117
See also DLB 1, 189
See also TCLC 21
Howe, Leland W(right) 1940-.... 123
Brief entry.... 118
Howe, Louise Kapp 1934-1984 Obituary.... 111
Howe, Marie 1950-.... 165
Howe, Mark Anthony DeWolfe
1864-1960 Obituary.... 89-92
Howe, Neil 1951-.... CANR-69
Earlier sketch in CA 132
Howe, Nelson 1935-.... 33-36R
Howe, Percival Presland 1886-1944.... DLB 149
Howe, Quincy 1900-1977.... 49-52
Obituary.... 69-72
Howe, Reuel L(anphier) 1905-.... 21-24R
Howe, Richard J. 1937-.... 77-80
Howe, Russell Warren 1925-.... CANR-27
Earlier sketch in CA 49-52
Howe, Susan 1937-.... 160
See also CLC 72
See also DLB 120
Howe, Tina 1937-.... 109
See also CLC 48
Howe, W(arren) Asquith 1910-.... 29-32R
Howe, William Hugh 1928-.... 65-68
Howell, Anthony 1945-.... 128
Howell, Barbara 1937-1994.... 49-52
Obituary.... 145
Howell, Benjamin Franklin
1890-1976 Obituary.... 65-68
Howell, Bette 1920-.... 130
Howell, Clark Sr. 1863-1936.... DLB 25
Howell, Clinton T(almage) 1913-1981.... 29-32R
Obituary.... 133
Howell, David
See Wynne, John (Stewart)
Howell, David Arthur Russell 1936-.... 109
Howell, Dorothy J(ulia) 1940-.... 142
Howell, Elsworth Seaman 1915-1987 Obituary. 122
Howell, Evan P(ark) 1839-1905 Brief entry.... 119
See also DLB 23
Howell, Helen (Jane) 1934-.... 57-60
Howell, James 1594(?)-1666.... DLB 151
Howell, James Edwin 1928-.... CANR-20
Earlier sketch in CA 1-4R
Howell, John
See Hall, Gus
Howell, John C(hristian) 1924-.... CANR-9
Earlier sketch in CA 21-24R
Howell, John M(ichael) 1933-.... 33-36R
Howell, Joseph T(oy III) 1942-.... CANR-24
Earlier sketch in CA 45-48
Howell, Leon 1936-.... 25-28R
Howell, Michael J. 1932(?)-1986 Obituary.... 118
Howell, Pat 1947-.... SATA 15
Howell, Patricia Hagan 1939-.... 81-84
Howell, Paul (Philip) 1917-.... 135
Howell, Peter (Adrian) 1941-.... 128
Howell, Reet 1945-.... 110
Howell, Richard W(esley) 1926-.... 57-60
Howell, Robert Lee 1928-.... 25-28R
Howell, Roger (Jr.) 1936-.... CANR-11
Earlier sketch in CA 21-24R
Howell, S.
See Styles, (Frank) Showell
Howell, Thomas 1944-.... 73-76
Howell, Virginia
See Ellison, Virginia H(owell)
Howell, Warren Richardson 1912-1984.... DLB 140
Howell, Wilbur Samuel 1904-1992.... 33-36R
Obituary.... 137
Howell, William C(arl) 1932-.... 93-96
Howells, J(ames) Harvey 1912-.... 97-100
Howells, John G(wilym) 1918-.... CANR-65
Earlier sketches in CA 21-24R, CANR-9, 24
Howells, Roscoe 1919-.... 104
Howells, W. D.
See Howells, William Dean
Howells, William D.
See Howells, William Dean
Howells, William Dean 1837-1920.... 134
Brief entry.... 104
See also CDALB 1865-1917
See also DLB 12, 64, 74, 79, 189
See also TCLC 7, 17, 41
Howells, William White 1908-.... CANR-19
Earlier sketches in CA 1-4R, CANR-2
Hower, Edward 1941-.... 106
Hower, Ralph M(erle) 1903-1973.... 1-4R
Obituary.... 45-48
Howes, Alan B(arber) 1920- Brief entry.... 112
Howes, Barbara 1914-1996.... CANR-53
Obituary.... 151
Earlier sketch in CA 9-12R
See also CAAS 3
See also CLC 15
See also SATA 5
Howes, Connie B. 1933-.... 89-92
Howes, Craig 1955-.... 148
Howes, Frank Stewart 1891-1974 Obituary.... 115
Howes, Laura L(ouise) 1956-.... 168
Howes, Michael 1904-.... 61-64
Howes, Paul Griswold 1892-1984.... 29-32R
Obituary.... 113
Howes, Raymond F(loyd) 1903-.... CAP-1
Earlier sketch in CA 17-18
Howes, Robert Gerard 1919-.... CANR-4
Earlier sketch in CA 1-4R
Howes, Royce (Bucknam) 1901-1973.... CAP-2
Obituary.... 41-44R
Earlier sketch in CA 19-20
Howes, Wright 1882-1978 Obituary.... 104
Howey, John 1933-.... 154
Howick, William Henry 1924-.... 33-36R
Howie, Carl G(ordon) 1920-.... 13-16R
Howith, Harry 1934-.... 25-28R
Howitt, Mary 1799-1888.... DLB 110, 199
Howitt, William 1792-1879.... DLB 110
Howitzer, Bronson
See Hardman, Richards Lynden
Howker, Janni 1957-.... 137
See also AAYA 9
See also CLR 14
See also JRDA
See also MAICYA
See also SAAS 13
See also SATA 72
See also SATA-Brief 46
Howkins, John 1945-.... CANR-32
Earlier sketches in CA 65-68, CANR-14
Howl, Marcia (Yvonne Hurt) 1947-.... 121
Howland, Bette 1937-.... 85-88
Howland, Harold Edward 1913-1980 Obituary.. 102
Howlett, D(onald) Roger 1945-.... 135
Howlett, Duncan 1906-.... 107
Howlett, John (Reginald) 1940-.... CANR-12
Earlier sketch in CA 69-72
Howorth, Beckett 1902-.... 114
Howorth, M. K.
See Black, Margaret K(atherine)
Howorth, Muriel.... CAP-1
Earlier sketch in CA 9-10
Howse, Ernest Marshall (Frazer) 1902-.. CANR-43
Earlier sketch in CA 49-52
Howson, Susan 1945-.... 113
Howton, F(rank) William 1925-.... 29-32R
Hoxie, Frederick E(ugene) 1947-.... 117
Hoxie, R(alph) Gordon 1919-.... 103
Hoy, Claire 1940-.... 140
Hoy, Cyrus H. 1926-.... 21-24R
Hoy, David 1930-.... 17-20R
Hoy, James F(ranklin) 1939-.... 57-60
Hoy, John C. 1933-.... CANR-9
Earlier sketch in CA 21-24R
Hoy, Linda 1946-.... 130
See also SATA 65
Hoy, Nina
See Roth, Arthur J(oseph)
Hoye, Anna Scott 1915-.... 13-16R
Hoyem, Andrew 1935-.... 9-12R
See also DLB 5
Hoyer, George W. 1919-.... CANR-4
Earlier sketch in CA 1-4R
Hoyer, H(arvey) Conrad 1907-.... 33-36R
Hoyer, Mildred N(aeher).... 57-60
Hoyers, Anna Ovena 1584-1655.... DLB 164
Hoyland, Michael 1925-.... 21-24R
Hoyle, Fred 1915-.... CANR-55
Earlier sketches in CA 5-8R, CANR-3, 29
See also MTCW 1
Hoyle, Geoffrey 1942-.... CANR-29
Earlier sketches in CA 53-56, CANR-6
See also SATA 18
Hoyle, Martha Byrd
See Byrd, Martha
Hoyle, Peter 1939-.... 124
Hoyle, Trevor 1940-.... 142
Hoyles, J(ames) Arthur 1908-.... 5-8R
Hoyningen-Huene, Paul 1946-.... 145
Hoyos, Angela de 1940(?)-.... 131
See also DLB 82
See also HW
Hoyt, Charles Alva 1931-.... 33-36R
Hoyt, Charles K(ing) 1938-.... 110
Hoyt, Clark 1942-.... 69-72
Hoyt, Edwin P(almer), Jr. 1923-.... CANR-66
Earlier sketches in CA 1-4R, CANR-1
See also SATA 28
Hoyt, Elizabeth E(llis) 1893-.... 37-40R
Hoyt, Erich 1950-.... CANR-69
Earlier sketch in CA 106
See also SATA 65
Hoyt, Herman A(rthur) 1909-.... 29-32R
Hoyt, Homer 1896-1984.... CANR-1
Obituary.... 114
Earlier sketch in CA 1-4R
Hoyt, Jo Wasson 1927-.... 21-24R
Hoyt, Joseph B(ixby) 1913-.... 5-8R
Hoyt, Kenneth B(oyd) 1924-.... CANR-1
Earlier sketch in CA 45-48
Hoyt, Mary Finch 1924(?)-.... 107
Hoyt, Murray 1904-.... 9-12R
Hoyt, Olga (Gruhzit) 1922-.... 25-28R
See also SATA 16
Hoyt, (Edwin) Palmer 1897-1979 Obituary.... 89-92
Hoyt, Palmer 1897-1979.... DLB 127
Hoyt, Richard (Duane) 1941-.... 129
Hoyt, Robert S(tuart) 1918-1971 Obituary.... 111
Hoyt, Waite (Charles) 1899-1984 Obituary.... 113
Hozeny, Tony 1946-.... 61-64
Hozjusz
See Dobraczynski, Jan
Hrabal, Bohumil 1914-1997.... CANR-57
Obituary.... 156
Earlier sketch in CA 106
See also CAAS 12
See also CLC 13, 67
Hrabanus Maurus 776(?)-856.... DLB 148
Hrdy, Sarah Blaffer 1946-.... CANR-35
Earlier sketch in CA 107
Hromadka, Josef L(ukl) 1889-1971.... CAP-1
Earlier sketch in CA 9-10
Hroswitha of Gandersheim c. 935-c. 1002. DLB 148
Hruska-Cortes, Elias 1943-.... 45-48
Hruza, Zdenek 1926-.... 61-64
Hrycej, Tomas 1954-.... 167
Hsia, Adrian (Rue Chun) 1938-.... 77-80
Hsia, C(hih)-T(sing) 1921-.... CANR-17
Earlier sketches in CA 1-4R, CANR-2
Hsia, David Yi-Yung 1925-1972 Obituary.... 33-36R
Hsia, Hsiao
See Liu, Wu-chi
Hsia, Tsi-an 1916-1965.... CAP-2
Earlier sketch in CA 25-28
Hsiang, Yeh
See Liu, Sydney (Chieh)
Hsiao, Katharine H(uei-Ying Huang) 1923-.... 77-80
Hsiao, Kung-Chuan 1897-.... 1-4R
Hsiao, Tso-liang 1910-.... 1-4R
Hsiung, James Chieh 1935-.... 37-40R
Hsu, Benedict (Pei-Hsiung) 1933-.... 69-72
Hsu, Cho-yun 1930-.... CANR-9
Earlier sketch in CA 17-20R
Hsu, Francis L(ang) K(wang) 1909-.... CANR-16
Earlier sketches in CA 1-4R, CANR-1
Hsu, Immanuel C. Y. 1923-.... 1-4R
Hsu, K.
See Hsu, Kenneth J(inghwa)
Hsu, K. J.
See Hsu, Kenneth J(inghwa)
Hsu, K. Jinghwa
See Hsu, Kenneth J(inghwa)
Hsu, Kai-yu 1922-1982.... CANR-14
Earlier sketch in CA 21-24R
Hsu, Kenneth J(inghwa) 1929-.... 135
Hsu, Madeleine (DeMory) 1938-.... 157
Hsu, Robert C. 1937-.... 141
Hsueh, Chun-tu 1922-.... CANR-34
Earlier sketches in CA 41-44R, CANR-15
Hsueh, Tien-tung 1939-.... 146
Hsun, Lu
See Lu Hsun
and Shu-Jen, Chou
Hsu Ying 1935-.... 124
Htin Aung, U.
See Aung, (Maung) Htin
Hu, Shi Ming
See Hu, Shu Ming
Hu, Shu Ming 1927-.... 85-88
Hu, Sze-Tsen 1914-.... 41-44R
Hu, Xu-wei 1928-.... 143
Hua, Gu 1942-.... 162
Hua, Jinma
See Ruan, Fang-fu
Huaco, George A. 1927-.... 17-20R
Huang, Benrei 1959-.... SATA 86
Huang, Chun-chieh 1946-.... 151
Huang, David S(hih-Li) 1930-.... 9-12R
Huang, Parker (Po-fei) 1914-.... CANR-2
Earlier sketch in CA 45-48
Huang, Philip C(hung-Chih) 1940-.... 127
Huang, Philip Chung-Chih 1940- Brief entry.... 105
Huang, Po-fei
See Huang, Parker (Po-fei)
Huang, Ray (Jen-yu) 1918-.... CANR-43
Earlier sketches in CA 61-64, CANR-8
Huang, Stanley S(hang) C(hien) 1923-.... 77-80
Huan Yue
See Shen, Congwen
Hubach, Robert R(ogers) 1916-.... 1-4R
Hubartt, Paul L(eroy) 1919-.... 5-8R
Hubback, David 1916-.... CANR-66
Earlier sketch in CA 128
Hubbard, Barbara Marx 1929-.... 103
Hubbard, D(onald) L(ee) 1929-.... 21-24R
Hubbard, David Allan 1928-1996.... CANR-40
Obituary.... 152
Earlier sketches in CA 33-36R, CANR-16
Hubbard, David G(raham) 1920-.... 33-36R
Hubbard, Dolan 1949-.... 166
Hubbard, Don 1926-.... 109
Hubbard, Edward (Horton) 1937-1989.... 124
Obituary.... 128
Hubbard, Elbert 1856-1915.... DLB 91
Hubbard, Frank T. 1921(?)-1976 Obituary.... 65-68

Hubbard, Freeman (Henry) 1894- 5-8R
Hubbard, George (Barron) 1884-1958 Brief entry 122
Hubbard, J(ake) T(imothy) W(illiam) 1935- CANR-51
Earlier sketch in CA 124
Hubbard, (Frank Mc)Kin(ney) 1868-1930 Brief entry 113
See also DLB 11
Hubbard, L(afayette) Ron(ald) 1911-1986 .... CANR-52
Obituary 118
Earlier sketch in CA 77-80
See also CLC 43
See also DAM POP
Hubbard, Lucien 1889(?)-1971 Obituary 33-36R
Hubbard, Margaret Ann
See Priley, Margaret Hubbard
Hubbard, P(hilip) M(aitland) 1910-1980 .. CANR-61
Obituary 97-100
Earlier sketch in CA 85-88
Hubbard, Paul H. 1900(?)-1983 Obituary 109
Hubbard, Preston John 1918- 5-8R
Hubbard, (Andrew) Ray 1924- 103
Hubbard, Robert Hamilton 1916- CANR-21
Earlier sketch in CA 1-4R
Hubbard, Ruth 1924- CANR-41
Earlier sketch in CA 116
Hubbard, Steve (Albert) 1957- 163
Hubbard, Susan (S.) 1951- 138
Hubbard, Thomas K. 1956- 136
Hubbard, Thomas Leslie Wallan 1905- CAP-1
Earlier sketch in CA 13-14
Hubbard, William 1621(?)-1704 .... DLB 24
Hubbard, Woodleigh Marx 165
See also SATA 98
Hubbell, Harriet Weed 1909- 5-8R
Hubbell, Harry M. 1881-1971 Obituary 29-32R
Hubbell, Jay B(roadus) 1885-1979 ...... CANR-17
Obituary 116
Earlier sketch in CA 1-4R
Hubbell, John G(erard) 1927- 65-68
Hubbell, Lindley Williams 1901- CAP-1
Earlier sketch in CA 13-16
Hubbell, Patricia 1928- 17-20R
See also SATA 8
Hubbell, Richard Whittaker 1914- 13-16R
Hubbell, Sue 1935- CANR-47
Earlier sketch in CA 120
Hubber, Therese 1764-1829 ....DLB 90
Hubbs, Carl Leavitt 1894-1979 Obituary 89-92
Hubbs, G(uy) Ward 1952- 114
Hubenka, Lloyd J(ohn) 1931-1982 ...... CANR-47
Earlier sketch in CA 49-52
Huber, Evelyne
See Stephens, Evelyne Huber
Huber, Jack T(ravis) 1918- 21-24R
Huber, Jeffrey T(odd) 1960- 144
Huber, Joan 1925- CANR-13
Earlier sketch in CA 77-80
Huber, Leonard Victor 1903- CANR-6
Earlier sketch in CA 57-60
Huber, Morton Wesley 1923- 17-20R
Huber, Peter W. 1952- 128
Huber, Richard M(iller) 1922- 33-36R
Huber, Thomas 1937- 29-32R
Huber, Thomas Michael 1944- 112
Huberman, Edward 1910- 13-16R
Huberman, Elizabeth Duncan Lyle 1915-... 13-16R
Huberman, Leo 1903-1968 .... CANR-4
Earlier sketch in CA 1-4R
Hubert, Cam
See Cameron, (Barbara) Anne
Hubert, James Lee 1947- 73-76
Hubert, Jim
See Hubert, James Lee
Hubert, Renee Riese 1916- 61-64
Hubin, Allen J. 1936- 33-36R
Hubka, Betty (Josephine Morgan) 1924- 13-16R
Hubka, Thomas C. 1946- 126
Hubler, David 1941- 110
Hubler, Edward L(orenzo) 1902-1965 ...... CAP-1
Earlier sketch in CA 13-14
Hubler, Herbert Clark 1910- 85-88
Hubler, Richard Gibson 1912- CANR-2
Earlier sketch in CA 1-4R
Hubley, Faith Elliot 1924- CANR-29
Earlier sketch in CA 81-84
See also SATA 48
Hubley, John 1914-1977 ....SATA 48
See also SATA-Obit 24
Huby, Pamela M(argaret Clark) 1922- 21-24R
Huch, Friedrich 1873-1913 .... DLB 66
Huch, Ricarda (Octavia) 1864-1947 Brief entry . 111
See also DLB 66
See also TCLC 13
Huchel, Peter 1903-1981 .... CANR-43
Earlier sketch in CA 81-84
Huck, Charlotte 1922- ....SATA 82
Huck, Gabe (Donald Joseph) 1941- CANR-30
Earlier sketch in CA 112
Huckaby, Elizabeth (Paisley) 1905- 106
Huckaby, Gerald 1933- 33-36R
Huckaby, Charles O(scar) 1919- 69-72
Hucker, Hazel 1937- 149
Huckins, Wesley C. 1918- 21-24R
Huckleberry, E(vermont) R(obbins) 1894- CANR-11
Earlier sketch in CA 61-64
Huckshorn, Robert J(ack) 1928- 97-100
Hudd, Roy 1936- 105
Huddle, David 1942- 57-60
See also CAAS 20
See also CLC 49
See also DLB 130
Huddle, Frank, Jr. 1943- 37-40R
Huddleston, Eugene L(ee) 1931- CANR-41
Earlier sketches in CA 102, CANR-19
Huddleston, Lee Eldridge 1935- 21-24R
Huddleston, Mark W. 1950- 154
Huddleston, Rodney D(esmond) 1937- 33-36R
Huddy, Delia 1934- CANR-19
Earlier sketch in CA 25-28R
Hudgens, A(lice) Gayle 1941- 37-40R
Hudgins, Andrew (Leon, Jr.) 1951- 132
See also CAAS 21
See also DLB 120
Hudgins, H(erbert) C(ornelius), Jr. 1932- 33-36R
Hudnut, Robert K(ilborne) 1934- CANR-38
Earlier sketches in CA 25-28R, CANR-17
Hudoba, Michael 1913-1984 Obituary 113
Hudon, Edward Gerard 1915- 5-8R
Hudson, Alec
See Holmes, W(ilfred) J(ay)
Hudson, Arthur Palmer 1894(?)-1978 Obituary . 111
Hudson, Charles M(elvin, Jr.) 1932- 33-36R
Hudson, Cheryl Willis 1948- .... SATA 81
Hudson, Danny L. 1940- 122
Hudson, Darril 1931- 45-48
Hudson, Derek (Rommel) 1911- 9-12R
Hudson, Geoffrey Francis 1903-1974 Obituary 49-52
Hudson, Gladys W(atts) 1926- 33-36R
Hudson, Gossie Harold 1930- 93-96
Hudson, Helen
See Lane, Helen
Hudson, Henry Norman 1814-1886 .... DLB 64
Hudson, Henry T(homas) 1932- CANR-41
Earlier sketch in CA 118
Hudson, Herman 1923- 97-100
Hudson, James A(lbert) 1924- 33-36R
Hudson, James J(ackson) 1919- 25-28R
Hudson, James R. 1933- 124
Hudson, Jan 1954-1990 136
See also AAYA 22
See also CLR 40
See also JRDA
See also SATA 77
Hudson, Jean B(arlow) 1915- 93-96
Hudson, Jeffrey
See Crichton, (John) Michael
Hudson, John A(llen) 1927- 25-28R
Hudson, John B. 1934- 142
Hudson, Kenneth 1916- 128
Brief entry 117
Hudson, (Margaret) Kirsty 1947- 107
See also SATA 32
Hudson, Liam 1933- CANR-12
Earlier sketch in CA 29-32R
Hudson, Lois Phillips 1927- CANR-64
Earlier sketch in CA 1-4R
Hudson, Marc 1947- 116
Hudson, Margaret
See Shuter, Jane Margaret
Hudson, Mark 1957- 132
Hudson, Meg
See Koehler, Margaret (Hudson)
Hudson, Michael C(raig) 1938- 37-40R
Hudson, Michael Huckleberry 1939- CANR-13
Earlier sketch in CA 33-36R
Hudson, Miles (Matthew Lee) 1925- 132
Hudson, (Arthur) Palmer 1892- CAP-2
Earlier sketch in CA 19-20
Hudson, Peggy
See Herz, Peggy
Hudson, R(obert) Lofton 1910- 13-16R
Hudson, Randolph H(oyt) 1927- 17-20R
Hudson, Richard (McLain, Jr.) 1925- 65-68
Hudson, Robert
See Oleksy, Walter
Hudson, Robert P(aul) 1926- 116
Hudson, Robert Vernon 1932- 109
Hudson, Stephen 1868(?)-1944 .... DLB 197
Hudson, Theodore R. 45-48
Hudson, W(illiam) H(enry) 1841-1922 Brief entry 115
See also DLB 98, 153, 174
See also SATA 35
See also TCLC 29
Hudson, Wade 1946- 142
See also BW 2
See also SATA 74
Hudson, Wilma J(ones) 1916- 33-36R
Hudson, Wilson Mathis 1907- 102
Hudson, Winthrop Still 1911- CANR-2
Earlier sketch in CA 1-4R
Hudspeth, Robert N. 1936- 103
Huebel, Harry Russell 1943- 77-80
Huebener, Theodore 1895-1983 Obituary 111
Huebner, Anna (Ismelda Mathews) 1877(?)-1974 Obituary 53-56
Huebner, Fredrick D. 1955- 133
Huebner, Klaus H(ermann) 1916- 126
Huebner, Kurt 1921- 132
Hueffer, Ford Madox
See Ford, Ford Madox
Hueffer, Oliver Madox 1876-1931 .... DLB 197
Huegli, A(lbert) G(eorge) 1913- 13-16R
Huelsman, Richard J(oseph) 1921- 111
Huelsmann, Carl (M.) 1914- 130
Huelsmann, Eva 1928- .... SATA 16
Huene, Paul Hoyningen
See Hoyningen-Huene, Paul
Huerlimann, Bettina 1909-1983 109
Obituary 110
See also Hurlimann, Bettina
See also MAICYA
See also SATA 34, 39
Huerlimann, Ruth 1939- 107
See also Hurlimann, Ruth
See also SATA 31, 32
Huerta, Jorge
See Huerta, Jorge A(lfonso)
Huerta, Jorge A(lfonso) 1942- 131
See also HW
Huessy, Hans R. 1921- 21-24R
Hueston, Frederick M. 1953- 153
Hueter, John E(dwin) 1918- 114
Huether, Anne Frances
See Freeman, Anne Frances
Huey, F. B., Jr. 1925- CANR-47
Earlier sketches in CA 106, CANR-23
Huey, John (Wesley, Jr.) 1948- 144
Huey, Lynda 1947- 65-68
Hufana, A(lejandrino) G. 1926- 77-80
Hufbauer, Karl (George) 1937- 109
Huff, Afton (A.) W(alker) 1928- 65-68
Huff, Barbara A. 1929- 135
See also SATA 67
Huff, Betty Tracy 25-28R
Huff, Darrell 1913- CANR-5
Earlier sketch in CA 1-4R
Huff, Richard (M.) 1962- 139
Huff, Robert 1924- CANR-6
Earlier sketch in CA 13-16R
Huff, T(om) E. 1938(?)- 93-96
See also AITN 2
Huff, T. S.
See Huff, Tanya (Sue)
Huff, Tanya (Sue) 1957- CANR-58
Earlier sketch in CA 128
See also SATA 85
Huff, Toby E. 1942- 149
Huff, Vaughn E(dward) 1935- 29-32R
Huff, Vivian 1948- ....SATA 59
Huffaker, Clair 1926(?)-1990 .... CANR-63
Obituary 131
Earlier sketch in CA 113
Huffaker, Sandy 1943- ....SATA 10
Huffard, Grace Thompson 1892- CAP-1
Earlier sketch in CA 11-12
Huffer, Lynne 1960- 143
Huffert, Anton M. 1912- 13-16R
Huffington, Arianna Stassinopoulos 1950- 129
Huffman, Carolyn 1928- 69-72
Huffman, Claire (De Cesare Licari) 116
Huffman, Franklin E(ugene) 1934- CANR-12
Earlier sketch in CA 29-32R
Huffman, James Lamar 1941- 102
Huffman, Laurie 1916- 45-48
Huffman, Phyllis
See Atwater, P(hyllis) M. H.
Huffman, Tom .... SATA 24
Hufford, Susan 1940- CANR-9
Earlier sketch in CA 57-60
Hufschmidt, Maynard Michael 1912- CANR-47
Earlier sketches in CA 41-44R, CANR-15
Hufton, Olwen H. 1938- 21-24R
Hug, Bernal D(ean) 1896- 57-60
Hugdahl, Kenneth 1948- 163
Huggan, Isabel 1943- 119
Huggett, Frank E(dward) 1924- CANR-19
Earlier sketches in CA 9-12R, CANR-3
Huggett, Joyce 1937- 126
Huggett, Richard 1929- 53-56
Huggett, William Turner 53-56
Huggins, Alice Margaret 1891-1971 .... CAP-1
Earlier sketch in CA 17-18
Huggins, Charles B(renton) 1901-1997 Obituary 156
Brief entry 115
Huggins, Nathan Irvin 1927-1989 .... CANR-25
Obituary 130
Earlier sketch in CA 29-32R
See also BW 1
See also SATA 63
Hughart, Barry 1934- 137
See also CLC 39
Hughes, Agatha C(hipley) 1924- 145
Hughes, Alan 1935- 97-100
Hughes, Alice 1899(?)-1977 Obituary 104
Hughes, Andrew 1937- 61-64
Hughes, Anthony John 1933- 9-12R
Hughes, Arthur Joseph 1928- 17-20R
Hughes, Arthur Montague D'Urban 1873-1974 Obituary 49-52
Hughes, B(asil) P(erronet) 1903- 61-64
Hughes, C(hristopher) J(ohn) 1918- 17-20R
Hughes, C. J. Pennethorne
See Hughes, (Charles James) Pennethorne
Hughes, Catharine R(achel) 1935-1987 .. CANR-27
Obituary 123
Earlier sketch in CA 41-44R
Hughes, Charles C(ampbell) 1929- 41-44R
Hughes, Charles L(loyd) 1933- CANR-11
Earlier sketch in CA 17-20R
Hughes, (John) Cledwyn 1920-1978 .... 13-16R
Obituary 126
Hughes, Colin
See Creasey, John
Hughes, Colin A(nfield) 1930- CANR-50
Earlier sketches in CA 21-24R, CANR-9, 25
Hughes, D. T.
See Hughes, Dean
Hughes, Daniel 1929- 33-36R
Hughes, Daniel T(homas) 1930- 89-92
Hughes, David (John) 1930- 129
Brief entry 116
See also CLC 48
See also DLB 14
Hughes, Dean 1943- CANR-22
Earlier sketch in CA 106
See also SATA 33, 77
Hughes, Dean Aubrey 1908(?)-1987 Obituary .. 122
Hughes, Dorothy (Berry) 1910- CAP-2
Earlier sketch in CA 33-36
Hughes, Dorothy B(elle) 1904-1993 ..... CANR-60
Obituary 141
Earlier sketch in CA 104
Hughes, Douglas A(llan) 1938- 29-32R
Hughes, Dusty
See Hughes, Richard Holland
Hughes, Eden
See Butterworth, W(illiam) E(dmund III)
Hughes, Edward James
See Hughes, Ted
See also DAM MST, POET
Hughes, Elizabeth
See Zachary, Hugh
Hughes, Emmet John 1920-1982 69-72
Obituary 107
Hughes, Erica 1931- CANR-28
Earlier sketch in CA 109
Hughes, Everett Cherrington 1897-1983 103
Obituary 108
Hughes, Felicity 1938- 33-36R
Hughes, G(eorge) E(dward) 1918- 21-24R
Hughes, Gerald (Thomas) 1930- 117
Hughes, Gervase 1905- 9-12R
Hughes, Glenn 1951- 143
Hughes, Glyn 1935- CANR-35
Earlier sketches in CA 33-36R, CANR-13
Hughes, Graham 1928- 57-60
Hughes, Gwilym Fielden 1899- 97-100
Hughes, H(enry) Stuart 1916- CANR-2
Earlier sketch in CA 1-4R
Hughes, Harold K(enneth) 1911- 9-12R
Hughes, Heather 1954- 133
Hughes, Helen (Gintz) 1928- 13-16R
Hughes, Howard (Robard) 1905-1976 Obituary . 112
Hughes, Irene Finger 103
Hughes, J(ohnson) Donald 1932- CANR-10
Earlier sketch in CA 65-68
Hughes, James Monroe 1890-1971 .... 1-4R
Obituary 103
Hughes, James Pennethorne
See Hughes, (Charles James) Pennethorne
Hughes, James Quentin 1920- CANR-6
Earlier sketch in CA 13-16R
Hughes, James W(ilfred) 1934- 77-80
Hughes, John 1677-1720 .... DLB 84
Hughes, (Robert) John 1930- CANR-4
Earlier sketch in CA 1-4R
Hughes, John 1950(?)- 129
Brief entry 124
See also AAYA 7
Hughes, John A(nthony) 1941- 41-44R
Hughes, John Jay 1928- 57-60
Hughes, John L(ewis) 1938- 77-80
Hughes, John Paul 1920-1974 .... 1-4R
Obituary 53-56
Hughes, Jonathan R(oberts) T(yson) 1928-1992 81-84
Obituary 137
Hughes, Judith M(arkham) 1941- 33-36R
Hughes, Judy 1943- 69-72
Hughes, Kathleen W. 1927(?)-1977 Obituary . 69-72
Hughes, Ken(neth) 1922- CANR-39
Earlier sketches in CA 5-8R, CANR-16
Hughes, (James) Langston 1902-1967 ... CANR-34
Obituary 25-28R
Earlier sketches in CA 1-4R, CANR-1
See also AAYA 12
See also BLC 2
See also BW 1
See also CDALB 1929-1941
See also CLC 1, 5, 10, 15, 35, 44, 108
See also CLR 17
See also DA
See also DAB
See also DAC
See also DAM DRAM, MST, MULT, POET
See also DC 3
See also DLB 4, 7, 48, 51, 86
See also JRDA
See also MAICYA
See also MTCW 1
See also PC 1
See also SATA 4, 33
See also SSC 6
See also WLC
Hughes, Leo 1908- 41-44R
Hughes, Libby .... SATA 71
Hughes, Margaret Kelly 1894(?)-1980 Obituary . 101
Hughes, Marija Matich 97-100
Hughes, Mary 1951- 122
Hughes, Mary Gray 1930- 61-64
Hughes, Mary Louise 1910- 29-32R
Hughes, Matilda
See MacLeod, Charlotte (Matilda)
Hughes, Merrit Y(erkes) 1893-1970 .... CAP-1
Earlier sketch in CA 17-18
Hughes, Monica (Ince) 1925- CANR-46
Earlier sketches in CA 77-80, CANR-23
See also AAYA 19
See also CLR 9
See also JRDA
See also MAICYA
See also SAAS 11
See also SATA 15, 70
Hughes, Nathaniel Cheairs, Jr. 1930- 17-20R
Hughes, Owain (Gardner Collingwood) 1943- 21-24R
Hughes, Patrick 1939- 61-64
Hughes, Paul L(ester) 1915- 9-12R
Hughes, (Charles James) Pennethorne 1907-1967 . CAP-2
Earlier sketch in CA 21-22
Hughes, Philip 1895-1967 .... CAP-2
Earlier sketch in CA 17-18
Hughes, Philip Edgcumbe 1915- CANR-18
Earlier sketches in CA 9-12R, CANR-3

Hughes, (James) Quentin 1920- 29-32R
Hughes, R(ichard) E(dward) 1927- CANR-6
Earlier sketch in CA 5-8R
Hughes, Richard (Arthur Warren) 1900-1976 . . . . CANR-4
Obituary 65-68
Earlier sketch in CA 5-8R
See also CLC 1, 11
See also DAM NOV
See also DLB 15, 161
See also MTCW 1
See also SATA 8
See also SATA-Obit 25
Hughes, Richard 1906-1984 Obituary 111
Hughes, Richard 1941- 107
Hughes, Richard (Edward) 1950- 156
Hughes, Richard Holland 1947- 131
Hughes, Richard T(homas) 1943- 154
Hughes, Riley 1914-1981 107
Obituary 103
Hughes, Robert 1929(?)-1972 Obituary 37-40R
Hughes, Robert (Studley Forrest) 1938(?)- 112
Brief entry 110
Hughes, Russell C. 1893(?)-1982 Obituary 108
Hughes, Russell Meriwether 1898(?)-1988 Obituary 124
Hughes, Sam
See Wilks, Brian
Hughes, Sara
See Saunders, Susan
Hughes, Sean 1965- 162
Hughes, Shirley 1927- CANR-47
Earlier sketches in CA 85-88, CANR-24
See also CLR 15
See also MAICYA
See also SATA 16, 70
Hughes, Stella 1916- 127
Hughes, Stephen Ormsby 1924- 61-64
Hughes, Ted 1930- CANR-66
Earlier sketches in CA 1-4R, CANR-1, 33
See also Hughes, Edward James
See also CLC 2, 4, 9, 14, 37
See also CLR 3
See also DAB
See also DAC
See also DLB 40, 161
See also MAICYA
See also MTCW 1
See also PC 7
See also SATA 49
See also SATA-Brief 27
Hughes, Terry A. 1933- 65-68
Hughes, Theodore E(rmond) 1942- CANR-40
Earlier sketch in CA 116
Hughes, Thomas 1822-1896 . . . . DLB 18, 163
See also SATA 31
Hughes, Thomas M(ears) 1927- 65-68
Hughes, Thomas Parke 1923- CANR-47
Earlier sketch in CA 29-32R
Hughes, Tracy
See Blackstock, Terri
Hughes, Virginia
See Campbell, Hope
Hughes, Walter (Llewellyn) 1910- CANR-1
Earlier sketch in CA 1-4R
See also SATA 26
Hughes, William J., Jr. 1897(?)-1974 Obituary 45-48
Hughes, William W(auters) 1918- 126
Hughes, Zach
See Zachary, Hugh
Hughes, Zachary
See Zachary, Hugh
Hughes-Hallett, Lucy 1951- 138
Hughey, Roberta 1942- . . . . SATA 61
Hughey, Ruth Willard 1899- 1-4R
Hugill, Stan(ley) James 1906- CAP-2
Earlier sketch in CA 23-24
Hugo, Grant
See Cable, James (Eric)
Hugo, Herbert W. 1930(?)-1979 Obituary 89-92
Hugo, Richard F(ranklin) 1923-1982 . . . . CANR-3
Obituary 108
Earlier sketch in CA 49-52
See also CLC 6, 18, 32
See also DAM POET
See also DLB 5
Hugo, Victor (Marie) 1802-1885 . . . . DA
See also DAB
See also DAC
See also DAM DRAM, MST, NOV, POET
See also DLB 119, 192
See also PC 17
See also SATA 47
See also WLC
Hugon, Anne 1965- 145
Huhne, Christopher 1954- 133
Huhta, James K(enneth) 1937- 37-40R
Huidobro, Vicente
See Huidobro Fernandez, Vicente Garcia
Huidobro Fernandez, Vicente Garcia 1893-1948 131
See also HW
See also TCLC 31
Huie, William Bradford 1910-1986 . . . . CANR-7
Obituary 121
Earlier sketch in CA 9-12R
See also AITN 1
Huie, William O(rr) 1911- 21-24R
Huisken, Ronald H(erman) 1946- 93-96
Huizenga, John R(obert) 1921- 144
Huizinga, Johan 1872-1945 161
Hula, Harold L. 1930- 25-28R
Hulbert, Ann 1956- 138
Hulbert, Jack 1892-1978 Obituary 115
Hulet, Claude Lyle 1920- CANR-9
Earlier sketch in CA 53-56
Hulicka, Irene M(ackintosh) 1927- 37-40R
Hulicka, Karel 1913- 41-44R
Huline-Dickens, Frank William 1931- 107
See also SATA 34
Hulke, Malcolm 1924- 81-84
Hull, Cary Schuler 1946- 106
Hull, Charles
See Charles, Gordon H(ull)
Hull, David L(ee) 1935- 77-80
Hull, David Stewart 1938- 25-28R
Hull, Denison Bingham 1897- 37-40R
Hull, Eleanor (Means) 1913- CANR-19
Earlier sketches in CA 9-12R, CANR-4
See also SATA 21
Hull, Eric Traviss
See Harnan, Terry
Hull, Eugene L(eslie) 1928- 37-40R
Hull, George F. 1909(?)-1974 Obituary 53-56
Hull, Gloria T(heresa Thompson) 1944- CANR-25
Earlier sketch in CA 108
See also BW 2
Hull, H. Braxton
See Jacobs, Helen Hull
Hull, Helen (Rose) 1888(?)-1971 . . . . CAP-1
Obituary 29-32R
Earlier sketch in CA 9-10
Hull, Isabel V. 1949- 156
Hull, J(ohn) H(owarth) E(ric) 1923- 25-28R
Hull, Jesse Redding
See Hull, Jessie Redding
Hull, Jessie Redding 1932- 109
See also SATA 51
Hull, John M. 1935- 137
Hull, Katharine 1921-1977 . . . . 29-32R
See also SATA 23
Hull, Lynda (K.) 1954-1994 126
Obituary 145
Hull, Marion A(da) 1911- 105
Hull, Opal
See Lehnus, Opal (Hull)
Hull, Oswald 1919- 25-28R
Hull, R(ichard) F(rancis) C(arrington) 1913(?)-1974 Obituary 53-56
Hull, Raymona E. 1907- 116
Hull, Raymond 1919-1985 . . . . CANR-11
Obituary 116
Earlier sketch in CA 25-28R
Hull, Richard 1896-1973 . . . . DLB 77
Hull, Richard W. 1940- CANR-25
Earlier sketch in CA 45-48
Hull, Roger H. 1942- 25-28R
Hull, Suzanne W(hite) 1921- 125
Hull, William (Doyle) 1918- CANR-5
Earlier sketch in CA 13-16R
Hull, William E(dward) 1930- CANR-24
Earlier sketches in CA 17-20R, CANR-7
Hulland, J(ennifer) R(osemary) 1936- 122
Hulley, Clarence C(harles) 1905- 41-44R
Hulme, Ann
See Granger, (Patricia) Ann
Hulme, Hilda Mary 1914- 77-80
Hulme, Joy N. 1922- . . . . SATA 74
Hulme, Kathryn 1900-1981 . . . . CAP-1
Obituary 104
Earlier sketch in CA 9-10
Hulme, Keri 1947- CANR-69
Earlier sketch in CA 125
Interview in 125
See also CLC 39
Hulme, T(homas) E(rnest) 1883-1917 Brief entry 117
See also DLB 19
See also TCLC 21
Hulme, William E(dward) 1920- CANR-5
Earlier sketch in CA 13-16R
Hulse, Clark 1947- 106
Hulse, Erroll 1931- CANR-21
Earlier sketch in CA 104
Hulse, James Warren 1930- 9-12R
Hulse, (Herman) LaWayne 1922- 29-32R
Hulse, Michael (William) 1955- CANR-43
Earlier sketch in CA 118
Hulse, Stewart H(arding), Jr. 1931- CANR-14
Earlier sketch in CA 33-36R
Hulsker, Jan -1907 144
Hult, Karen M(arie) 1956- 151
Hult, Ruby El 1912- 57-60
Hulteng, John L. 1921- CANR-13
Earlier sketch in CA 33-36R
Hultgren, Thor 1902- CAP-1
Earlier sketch in CA 17-18
Hultkrantz, Aake G. B. 1920- 130
Hultkrantz, Ake G. B.
See Hultkrantz, Aake G. B.
Hultman, Charles W(illiam) 1930- CANR-1
Earlier sketch in CA 1-4R
Hulton, Anne (?)-1779(?) . . . . DLB 200
Hults, Dorothy Niebrugge 1898- CAP-1
Earlier sketch in CA 9-10
See also SATA 6
Humbaraci, D(emir) Arslan 1923- 49-52
Humbard, (Alpha) Rex (Emmanuel) 1919- Brief entry 111
Humber, William 1949- CANR-51
Earlier sketch in CA 124
Humble, Richard 1945- CANR-17
Earlier sketches in CA 45-48, CANR-2
See also SATA 60
Humble, William F(rank) 1948- 21-24R
Humboldt, Alexander von 1769-1859 . . . . DLB 90
Humboldt, Wilhelm von 1767-1835 . . . . DLB 90
Hume, Arthur W. J. G. Ord
See Ord-Hume, Arthur W. J. G.
Hume, Basil
See Hume, George Haliburton
Hume, (Alexander) Brit(ton) 1943- 126
Brief entry 119
Interview in 126
Hume, David 1711-1776 . . . . DLB 104
Hume, Fergus(on Wright) 1859-1932 Brief entry 109
See also DLB 70
Hume, George Haliburton 1923- 126
Hume, John E. N., Jr. 1915-1986 Obituary 118
Hume, John Robert 1939- 106
Hume, Kathryn 1945- 57-60
Hume, L(eonard) J(ohn) 1926- 135
Hume, Lotta Carswell CAP-1
Earlier sketch in CA 9-10
See also SATA 7
Hume, Martha 1947- 112
Hume, Paul Chandler 1915- 102
Hume, Robert D. 1944- CANR-12
Earlier sketch in CA 29-32R
Hume, Ruth Fox 1922-1980 Obituary 97-100
See also SATA 26
See also SATA-Obit 22
Hume, Sophia 1702-1774 . . . . DLB 200
Hume, Stephen 1947- 125
Humes, D(ollena) Joy 1921- 1-4R
Humes, H(arold) L. 1926- 5-8R
Humes, James C. 1934- CANR-1
Earlier sketch in CA 45-48
Humes, John Portner 1921-1985 Obituary 117
Humes, Samuel 1930- 5-8R
Humez, Jean McMahon 1944- 124
Humez, Nicholas (David) 1948- 145
Humez, Nick
See Humez, Nicholas (David)
Humfrey, C.
See Osborne, C(harles) H(umfrey) C(aufeild)
Humfrey, (James) Michael 1936- 127
Hum-Ishu-Ma
See Mourning Dove
Hummel, Berta 1909-1946 . . . . SATA 43
Hummel, Charles E. 1923- 17-20R
Hummel, Jeffrey Rogers 1949- 156
Hummel, Madeline
See Moore, Madeline (Roberta)
Hummel, Monte 1946- 135
Hummel, Ray O(rvin), Jr. 1909- 33-36R
Hummel, Ruth Stevenson 1929- 5-8R
Hummel, Sister Maria Innocentia
See Hummel, Berta
Hummer, T(erry) R. 1950- 128
See also DLB 120
Humphreville, Frances Tibbetts 1909- 9-12R
Humphrey, Carol Sue 1956- 142
Humphrey, David C(hurchill) 1937- 85-88
Humphrey, Henry (III) 1930- 77-80
See also SATA 16
Humphrey, Hubert H(oratio) 1911-1978 . . . . CANR-43
Obituary 73-76
Earlier sketch in CA 69-72
Humphrey, J(ames) Edward 1918- 93-96
Humphrey, James (Earl) 1939- CANR-47
Earlier sketch in CA 45-48
Humphrey, James H(arry) 1911- CANR-48
Earlier sketches in CA 61-64, CANR-8, 23
Humphrey, Mary Ann 1943- 134
Humphrey, Michael (Edward) 1926- 29-32R
Humphrey, Paul 1915- 110
Humphrey, Robert L. 1923- 57-60
Humphrey, Sandra McLeod 1936- 160
See also SATA 95
Humphrey, William 1924-1997 . . . . CANR-68
Obituary 160
Earlier sketch in CA 77-80
See also CLC 45
See also DLB 6
Humphreys, A(rthur) R(aleigh) 1911-1988 Obituary 126
Humphreys, Alexander J(eremiah) 1913- 33-36R
Humphreys, Alice Lee 1893- 5-8R
Humphreys, (Travers) Christmas 1901-1983 77-80
Obituary 109
Humphreys, David 1752-1818 . . . . DLB 37
Humphreys, Emyr Owen 1919- CANR-24
Earlier sketches in CA 5-8R, CANR-3
See also CLC 47
See also DLB 15
Humphreys, George G(ary) 1949- 138
Humphreys, Graham 1945- . . . . SATA-Brief 32
Humphreys, J(ohn) R(ichard Adams) 1918- CANR-50
Earlier sketches in CA 1-4R, CANR-22
Humphreys, Josephine 1945- 127
Brief entry 121
Interview in 127
See also CLC 34, 57
Humphreys, (Robert Allan) Laud 1930-1988 . . . . 29-32R
Obituary 126
Humphreys, Margaret 1955- 146
Humphreys, Martha 1943- . . . . SATA 71
Humphreys, Mary Eglantyne Hill 1914- CANR-6
Earlier sketch in CA 5-8R
Humphreys, R(obert) A(rthur) 1907- 129
Humphreys, Robin A.
See Humphreys, R(obert) A(rthur)
Humphreys, Susan L.
See Lowell, Susan
Humphreyville, Theresa R. 1918- 13-16R
Humphries, Adelaide M. 1898- CAP-1
Earlier sketch in CA 13-16
Humphries, Barry 1934- 129
Humphries, Helen Speirs Dickie 1915- CAP-1
Earlier sketch in CA 9-10
Humphries, (John) Jefferson 1955- CANR-36
Earlier sketch in CA 114
Humphries, Mary 1905- 53-56
Humphries, (George) Rolfe 1894-1969 . . . . CANR-3
Obituary 25-28R
Earlier sketch in CA 5-8R
Humphries, Sydney Vernon 1907- 103
Humphry, Derek 1930- CANR-41
Earlier sketch in CA 41-44R
Humphrys, Geoffrey
See Humphrys, Leslie George
Humphrys, Leslie George 1921- 107
Humpstone, Charles Cheney 1931- 49-52
Huncke, Herbert E(dwin) 1915-1996 . . . . CANR-61
Obituary 153
Earlier sketch in CA 130
See also DLB 16
Hundert, E(dward) J. 1940- 149
Hundert, Edward M. 1956- 156
Hundert, Gershon David 1946- 146
Hundley, Joan Martin 1921- 45-48
Hundley, Norris (Cecil), Jr. 1935- CANR-8
Earlier sketch in CA 17-20R
Huneker, James Gibbons 1857-1921 . . . . DLB 71
See also TCLC 65
Huneryager, S(herwood) G(eorge) 1933- 1-4R
Hung, Chang-tai 1949- 148
Hungerford, Cy(rus Cotton) 1889(?)-1983 Obituary 109
Hungerford, Edward Buell 1900- 37-40R
Hungerford, Harold R(alph) 1928- 33-36R
Hungerford, Mary Jane 1913- 77-80
Hungerford, Pixie
See Brinsmead, H(esba) F(ay)
Hungerford, Rachael A. 145
Hungry Wolf, Adolf 1944- CANR-38
Earlier sketch in CA 115
Hungry Wolf, Beverly 1950- CANR-38
Earlier sketch in CA 117
Hunker, Henry L. 1924- 13-16R
Hunkin, Timothy Mark Trelawney 1950- 102
See also SATA 53
Hunkins, Francis P(eter) 1938- 57-60
Hunkins, Lee(cynth) 1930- 108
Hunnex, Milton D(eVerne) 1917- 29-32R
Hunnicutt, Benjamin Kline 1943- 130
Hunnings, Neville March 1929- CANR-12
Earlier sketch in CA 25-28R
Hunnisett, Basil 1923- 119
Hunold, Christian Friedrich 1681-1721 . . . . DLB 168
Hunsaker, David M(alcolm) 1944- 33-36R
Hunsberger, Edith Mae 1927- 109
Hunsberger, Warren S(eabury) 1911-1997 . . . . 41-44R
Obituary 163
Hunsehe, Raymond W. 1891(?)-1983 Obituary 111
Hunsinger, George 1945- 65-68
Hunsinger, Paul 1919- 33-36R
Hunsinger, Walter (William) 1923- 122
Hunt, Abby Campbell 1933(?)-1985 135
Obituary 116
Hunt, Angela Elwell 1957- 142
See also SATA 75
Hunt, Barbara
See Watters, Barbara H(unt)
Hunt, Bernice (Kohn) 1920- CANR-21
Earlier sketch in CA 9-12R
See also Kohn, Bernice
Hunt, Bob
See Kouf, M(arvin) James, Jr.
Hunt, Bruce J. 1956- 136
Hunt, Charles Butler 1906- 110
Hunt, Charlotte
See Hodges, Doris M(arjorie)
Hunt, Chester L. 1912- CANR-5
Earlier sketch in CA 13-16R
Hunt, Clarence
See Holman, C(larence) Hugh
Hunt, Dave
See Hunt, David C(harles Hadden)
Hunt, David (Wathen Stather) 1913- 102
Hunt, David 1942- 33-36R
Hunt, David C(harles Hadden) 1926- CANR-9
Earlier sketch in CA 57-60
Hunt, David C(urtis) 1935- CANR-38
Earlier sketches in CA 89-92, CANR-16
Hunt, Douglas 1918- 13-16R
Hunt, E(verette) Howard, (Jr.) 1918- CANR-47
Earlier sketches in CA 45-48, CANR-2
See also AITN 1
See also CLC 3
Hunt, E. K. 1937- 77-80
Hunt, Earl B. 1933- 93-96
Hunt, Earl W(ilbur) 1926- 85-88
Hunt, Edgar H(ubert) 1909- CAP-1
Earlier sketch in CA 9-10
Hunt, Elgin F(raser) 1895-1978 . . . . 1-4R
Hunt, Everett Lee 1890(?)-1984 Obituary 112
Hunt, F(lorence) V(ance) 132
Hunt, Florine E(lizabeth) 1928- 13-16R
Hunt, Francis CANR-26
Earlier sketches in CAP-2, CA 19-20
Hunt, Frazier 1885-1967 Obituary 93-96
Hunt, Garry Edward 1942- 115
Hunt, Geoffrey 1915(?)-1974 Obituary 104
Hunt, George Laird 1918- 49-52
Hunt, George W(illiam) 1937- 120
Hunt, Gill
See Tubb, E(dwin) C(harles)
Hunt, Gladys M. 1926- CANR-13
Earlier sketch in CA 29-32R
Hunt, (Leslie) Gordon 1906-1970 . . . . CAP-2
Earlier sketch in CA 29-32
Hunt, H(arry) Draper 1935- 37-40R
Hunt, Harrison
See Ballard, (Willis) Todhunter
Hunt, Herbert James 1899-1973 Obituary 89-92

Hunt, Hugh 1911-1993 .... CANR-3
Obituary 141
Earlier sketch in CA 5-8R
Hunt, Ignatius 1920- 17-20R
Hunt, Inez Whitaker 1899- CAP-1
Earlier sketch in CA 17-18
Hunt, Irene 1907- CANR-57
Earlier sketches in CA 17-20R, CANR-8
See also AAYA 18
See also CLR 1
See also DLB 52
See also JRDA
See also MAICYA
See also SATA 2, 91
Hunt, J(oseph) McVicker 1906-1991 .... 37-40R
Obituary 133
Hunt, J. William, Jr. 1930- 53-56
Hunt, James Gerald 1932- CANR-60
Earlier sketches in CA 65-68, CANR-14, 31
Hunt, Janie Louise 1963- .... SATA 102
Hunt, John
See Paine, Lauran (Bosworth)
Hunt, (Henry Cecil) John 1910- 109
Hunt, John Dixon 1936- CANR-17
Earlier sketch in CA 85-88
Hunt, John J. 1929- 33-36R
Hunt, John P(aul) 1915-1988 .... 33-36R
Obituary 124
Hunt, John W(esley) 1927- 21-24R
Hunt, Jonathan 1966- .... SATA 84
Hunt, Joyce 1927- CANR-45
Earlier sketches in CA 106, CANR-22
See also SATA 31
Hunt, June 1944- 103
Hunt, Kari (Eleanor B.) 1920- 41-44R
Hunt, Kellogg W(esley) 1912- 5-8R
Hunt, Kenneth E(dward)
1917(?)-1978 Obituary 104
Hunt, Kyle
See Creasey, John
Hunt, Lawrence J. 1920- 5-8R
Hunt, (James Henry) Leigh 1784-1859 . DAM POET
See also DLB 96, 110, 144
Hunt, (James Henry) Leigh 1784-1859 . DAM POET
Hunt, Leon (Gibson) 1931- 65-68
Hunt, Linda 1940- 106
See also SATA 39
Hunt, Lisa B(ehnke) 1967- .... SATA 84
Hunt, Lynn (Avery) 1945- 131
Hunt, Mabel Leigh 1892-1971 .... CAP-1
Obituary 106
Earlier sketch in CA 9-10
See also SATA 1
See also SATA-Obit 26
Hunt, Marsha 1946- 143
See also BW 2
See also CLC 70
Hunt, Maurice P. 1915- 25-28R
Hunt, Michael H. 1942- CANR-58
Earlier sketch in CA 127
Hunt, Morton M(agill) 1920- CANR-21
Earlier sketch in CA 5-8R
See also SATA 22
Hunt, Nan
See Ray, N(ancy) L(ouise)
Hunt, Nancy (Ridgely) 1927- 103
Hunt, Nigel
See Greenbank, Anthony Hunt
Hunt, Noel Aubrey Bonavia
See Bonavia-Hunt, Noel Aubrey
Hunt, Noreen 1931- 103
Hunt, Norman C.
See Crowther-Hunt, Norman Crowther
Hunt, Norman Crowther Crowther
See Crowther-Hunt, Norman Crowther
Hunt, Patricia 1922(?)-1983 Obituary 120
Hunt, Patricia Joan CANR-44
Earlier sketches in CA 103, CANR-21
Hunt, Penelope
See Napier, Priscilla
Hunt, Peter 1922- 5-8R
Hunt, Peter (Leonard) 1945- CANR-65
Earlier sketches in CA 113, CANR-32
See also SATA 76
Hunt, R(ichard) W(illiam) 1908-1979 141
Hunt, Ray(mond) C(hamp), Jr. 1919- 122
Hunt, Raymond G(eorge) 1928- CANR-3
Earlier sketch in CA 9-12R
Hunt, Richard (Paul) 1921-1992 73-76
Obituary 139
Hunt, Richard (Patrick) 1938- CANR-71
Earlier sketch in CA 137
Hunt, Richard N(orman) 1931- 9-12R
Hunt, Robert C(ushman) 1934- CANR-9
Earlier sketch in CA 21-24R
Hunt, Sam 1946- 110
Hunt, Stoker
See Piotrowski, Andrew
Hunt, Tim(othy A.) 1949- 121
Hunt, Todd T. 1938- 13-16R
Hunt, Tony 1944- 160
Hunt, V. Daniel 1939- 111
Hunt, Violet 1866(?)-1942 .... DLB 162, 197
See also TCLC 53
Hunt, Virginia Lloyd 1888(?)-1977 Obituary 73-76
Hunt, William 1934- CANR-3
Earlier sketch in CA 49-52
Hunt, William A(lvin) 1903-1986 Obituary 118
Hunt, William Dudley, Jr. 1922-1987 .... CANR-14
Obituary 122
Earlier sketch in CA 33-36R
Hunt, William Gibbes 1791-1833 .... DLB 73
Hunt, William R(aymond) 1929- 93-96
Hunter, A(rchibald) M(acbride) 1906- CANR-6
Earlier sketch in CA 9-12R
Hunter, Alan (James Herbert) 1922- CANR-66
Earlier sketches in CA 9-12R, CANR-3, 18, 40
Hunter, Allan A(rmstrong) 1893- 5-8R
Hunter, Anson
See Orrmont, Arthur
Hunter, Beatrice Trum 1918- CANR-50
Earlier sketches in CA 17-20R, CANR-7, 22
Hunter, Bernice Thurman 1922- CANR-52
Earlier sketch in CA 119
See also SATA 85
See also SATA-Brief 45
Hunter, Bill R. 1932(?)-1990 Obituary 131
Hunter, Bobbi Dooley 1945- .... SATA 89
Hunter, Bruce (William) 1952- CANR-58
Earlier sketch in CA 123
Hunter, C. Bruce 1917- 61-64
Hunter, Captain Marcy
See Ellis, Edward S(ylvester)
Hunter, Chris
See Gibson, Jo
Hunter, Christine
See Hunter, Maud L(ily)
Hunter, Clark 124
Hunter, Clingham M.D.
See Adams, William Taylor
Hunter, Dard 1883-1966 .... CAP-1
Obituary 25-28R
Earlier sketch in CA 13-16
Hunter, Dawe
See Downie, Mary Alice (Dawe)
Hunter, Dia
See Pace, DeWanna
Hunter, Doris A. 1929- 37-40R
Hunter, E. Waldo
See Sturgeon, Theodore (Hamilton)
Hunter, Edith Fisher 1919- 107
See also SATA 31
Hunter, Edward 1902-1978 .... 5-8R
Obituary 77-80
Hunter, Elizabeth
See de Guise, Elizabeth (Mary Teresa)
Hunter, Evan 1926- CANR-62
Earlier sketches in CA 5-8R, CANR-5, 38
Interview in CANR-5
See also CLC 11, 31
See also DAM POP
See also DLBY 82
See also MTCW 1
See also SATA 25
Hunter, Frederick J(ames) 1916- 33-36R
Hunter, Gary
See Hunter, Gwen
Hunter, Geoffrey (Basil Bailey) 1925- 33-36R
Hunter, George
See Ballard, (Willis) Todhunter
Hunter, George E.
See Ellis, Edward S(ylvester)
Hunter, Gordon C. 1924- 106
Hunter, (James) Graham 136
Hunter, Gwen 1956- 147
Hunter, Hall
See Marshall, Edison
Hunter, Henry MacGregor 1929- Brief entry 109
Hunter, Hilda 1921- 49-52
See also SATA 7
Hunter, Howard Eugene 1929- 41-44R
Hunter, J(ames) A(lston) H(ope) 1902- CANR-14
Earlier sketches in CAP-1, CA 9-10
Hunter, J(ohn) F(letcher) M(acGregor)
1924- 37-40R
Hunter, J(ames) Paul 1934- CANR-49
Earlier sketches in CA 21-24R, CANR-9, 24
Hunter, Jack D(ayton) 1921- CANR-29
Earlier sketches in CA 5-8R, CANR-6
Hunter, James H(ogg) 1890- 85-88
Hunter, Jane (Harlow) 1949- 125
Hunter, Jessie Prichard 1957(?)- 168
Hunter, Jim 1939- CANR-7
Earlier sketch in CA 9-12R
See also DLB 14
See also SATA 65
Hunter, Joan
See Yarde, Jeanne Betty Frances
Hunter, Joe
See McNeilly, Wilfred (Glassford)
Hunter, John
See Ballard, (Willis) Todhunter
and Hunter, Maud L(ily)
Hunter, John M(erlin) 1921- 13-16R
Hunter, Kim 1922- 61-64
Hunter, Kristin (Eggleston) 1931- CANR-13
Earlier sketch in CA 13-16R
Interview in CANR-13
See also AITN 1
See also BW 1
See also CLC 35
See also CLR 3
See also DLB 33
See also MAICYA
See also SAAS 10
See also SATA 12
Hunter, Leigh
See Etchison, Birdie L(ee)
Hunter, Leona Wesley
See Greif, Martin
Hunter, Leslie S(tannard) 1890-1983 .... CAP-1
Obituary 110
Earlier sketch in CA 19-20
Hunter, Lieutenant Ned
See Ellis, Edward S(ylvester)
Hunter, Louis C. 1898(?)-1984 Obituary 112
Hunter, Louise H(arris) 41-44R
Hunter, Mac
See Hunter, Henry MacGregor
Hunter, Marjorie 1922- 69-72
Hunter, Mark 1952- 128
Hunter, Marvin H(erbert) 1930- Brief entry 111
Hunter, Mary Vann 1937- 107
Hunter, Matthew
See Stone, Rodney
Hunter, Maud L(ily) 1910- CANR-4
Earlier sketch in CA 9-12R
Hunter, Mel 1927- 93-96
See also SATA 39
Hunter, Michael (Cyril William) 1949- 104
Hunter, Milton R(eed) 1902-1975 Obituary 104
Hunter, Mollie 1922- CANR-37
See also McIlwraith, Maureen Mollie Hunter
See also AAYA 13
See also CLC 21
See also CLR 25
See also DLB 161
See also JRDA
See also MAICYA
See also SAAS 7
See also SATA 54
Hunter, Ned
See Ellis, Edward S(ylvester)
Hunter, Norman (George Lorimer) 1899-1995 ....
CANR-15
Obituary 147
Earlier sketch in CA 93-96
See also SATA 26, 84
Hunter, Norman Charles
1908-1971 Obituary 29-32R
See also DLB 10
Hunter, R(ichard) L(awrence) 1953- 144
Hunter, Richard 1923-1981 Obituary 105
Hunter, Robert (Christie) 1941- 156
Hunter, Robert E(dwards) 1940- CANR-33
Earlier sketches in CA 41-44R, CANR-15
Hunter, Robert Grams 1927- 93-96
Hunter, Rodello
See Calkins, Rodello
Hunter, Sam 1923- CANR-8
Earlier sketch in CA 13-16R
Hunter, Sara Hoagland 1954- 165
See also SATA 98
Hunter, Stephen 1946- CANR-70
Earlier sketches in CA 102, CANR-19
Hunter, T. Willard 1915- 143
Hunter, Thomas 1932- 108
Hunter, Tim 1947- 85-88
Hunter, Valancy
See Meaker, Eloise
Hunter, Vickie
See Hunter, Victoria Alberta
Hunter, Victoria Alberta 1929- 5-8R
Hunter, William A(lbert) 1908- 13-16R
Hunter, William B(ridges), Jr. 1915- 77-80
Hunter Blair, Peter 1912-1982 Obituary 108
Brief entry 107
Hunter-Duvar, John 1821-1899 .... DLB 99
Hunter-Gault, Charlayne 1942- 141
See also BW 2
Huntford, Roland 1927- 142
Hunting, Constance 1925- CANR-23
Earlier sketch in CA 45-48
Huntingdon, Eugenia 1910- 127
Huntington, Anna Hyatt 1876-1973 Obituary . 45-48
Huntington, (E.) Gale 1902- 9-12R
Huntington, Harriet E(lizabeth) 1909- CANR-5
Earlier sketch in CA 5-8R
See also SATA 1
Huntington, Henry E. 1850-1927 .... DLB 140
Huntington, Henry S., Jr. 1892-1981 Obituary .. 103
Huntington, John (Willard) 1940- 112
Huntington, Madge 1937- 126
Huntington, Roy P. 1934- 166
Huntington, Samuel P(hillips) 1927- CANR-1
Earlier sketch in CA 1-4R
Huntington, Susan Mansfield 1791-1823 .. DLB 200
Huntington, Thomas W(aterman)
1893-1973 Obituary 45-48
Huntington, Vince
See Huntington, Roy P.
Huntington, Virginia 1889- 21-24R
Huntley, Chester Robert 1911-1974 97-100
Obituary 49-52
See also AITN 1
Huntley, Chet
See Huntley, Chester Robert
Huntley, Frank Livingstone 1902- 33-36R
Huntley, H(erbert) E(dwin) 1892- CAP-1
Earlier sketch in CA 13-14
Huntley, James L(ewis) 1914- 101
Huntley, James Robert 1923- CANR-12
Earlier sketch in CA 29-32R
Huntley, Timothy Wade 1939- 102
Hunton, Mary
See Gilzean, Elizabeth Houghton Blanchet
Hunton, Richard E(dwin) 1924- 21-24R
Huntress, Keith G(ibson) 1913- 5-8R
Huntsberger, John (Paul) 1931- 5-8R
Huntsberry, William E(mery) 1916- CANR-2
Earlier sketch in CA 1-4R
See also SATA 5
Hunzicker, Beatrice Plumb 1886- 5-8R
Hupchick, Dennis P(aul) 1948- 151
Hupka, Robert 1919- 61-64
Huppe, Bernard F. 1911- CANR-3
Earlier sketch in CA 5-8R
Huppert, George 1934- 29-32R
Hurd, Charles (Wesley Bolick) 1903-1968 .... CAP-1
Earlier sketch in CA 11-12
Hurd, Clement (G.) 1908-1988 .... CANR-24
Obituary 124
Earlier sketches in CA 29-32R, CANR-9
See also CLR 49
See also MAICYA
See also SATA 2, 64
See also SATA-Obit 54
Hurd, Douglas (Richard) 1930- CANR-10
Earlier sketch in CA 25-28R
Hurd, Edith (Thacher) 1910-1997 .... CANR-24
Obituary 156
Earlier sketches in CA 13-16R, CANR-9
See also CLR 49
See also MAICYA
See also SAAS 13
See also SATA 2, 64
See also SATA-Obit 95
Hurd, Florence 1918- CANR-19
Earlier sketch in CA 103
Hurd, Gale Ann 1955- 150
See also AAYA 17
Hurd, John C(oolidge), Jr. 1928- 17-20R
Hurd, Michael John 1928- CANR-12
Earlier sketch in CA 65-68
Hurd, (John) Thacher 1949- CANR-68
Earlier sketches in CA 106, CANR-24, 36
See also MAICYA
See also SATA 46, 94
See also SATA-Brief 45
Hure, Anne 1918- 9-12R
Hureau, Jean (Emile Pierre) 1915- Brief entry .. 110
Hurewitz, J(acob) C(oleman) 1914- CANR-2
Earlier sketch in CA 1-4R
Hurka, Thomas 1952- 147
hurkey, rooan
See Holzapfel, Rudolf Patrick
Hurkos, Peter 1911-1988 Obituary 125
Hurlbut, Allen F. 1910-1983 Obituary 110
Hurlbut, Cornelius S(earle), Jr. 1906- CANR-11
Earlier sketch in CA 25-28R
Hurlbutt, Robert H(arris) III 1924- 13-16R
Hurley, Alfred F(rancis) 1928- 97-100
Hurley, Ann 1947- 154
Hurley, Doran 1900-1964 .... 5-8R
Hurley, F(orrest) Jack 1940- CANR-50
Earlier sketches in CA 45-48, CANR-25
Hurley, Jane (Hezel) 1928- 13-16R
Hurley, John 1928- CANR-13
Earlier sketch in CA 33-36R
Hurley, John J(erome) 1930- 104
Hurley, Kathy 1947- 109
Hurley, Leslie J(ohn) 1911- 49-52
Hurley, Mark J(oseph, Jr.) 1919- 53-56
Hurley, Neil 1925- 29-32R
Hurley, Vic 1898-1978 .... 1-4R
Obituary 103
Hurley, W(illiam) Maurice 1916- 37-40R
Hurley, Wilfred G(eoffrey) 1895-1973 .... CAP-2
Obituary 45-48
Earlier sketch in CA 17-18
Hurley, William James, Jr. 1924- 9-12R
Hurlimann, Bettina
See Huerlimann, Bettina
See also SATA 39
See also SATA-Obit 34
Hurlimann, Ruth
See Huerlimann, Ruth
See also SATA 32
See also SATA-Brief 31
Hurlock, Elizabeth B. 1898- 41-44R
Hurlow, (Wilma) Janet 1939- 118
Hurm, Ken 1934- 106
Hurmence, Belinda 1921- 145
See also AAYA 17
See also CLR 25
See also JRDA
See also SAAS 20
See also SATA 77
Hurne, Ralph 1932- 21-24R
Hurok, Sol(omon) 1888-1974 Obituary 49-52
Hursch, Carolyn J(udge) 41-44R
Hurst, A(lexander) A(nthony) 1917- 5-8R
Hurst, Charles G., Jr. 1928- 37-40R
Hurst, Fannie 1889-1968 .... CAP-1
Obituary 25-28R
Earlier sketch in CA 13-16
See also DLB 86
Hurst, G(eorge) Cameron III 1941- 85-88
Hurst, James M(arshall) 1924- 29-32R
Hurst, James Willard 1910-1997 130
Obituary 158
Hurst, M(ichael) E(liot) Eliot
See Eliot Hurst, M(ichael) E(liot)
Hurst, Michael (Charles) 1931- 21-24R
Hurst, Norman 1944- 53-56
Hurst, Richard Maurice 1938- 101
Hurst, Virginia Radcliffe
1914(?)-1976 Obituary 69-72
Hurstfield, Joel 1911-1980 .... CANR-6
Obituary 102
Earlier sketch in CA 53-56
Hurston, Zora Neale 1903-1960 .... CANR-61
Earlier sketch in CA 85-88
See also AAYA 15
See also BLC 2
See also BW 1
See also CLC 7, 30, 61
See also DA
See also DAC
See also DAM MST, MULT, NOV
See also DLB 51, 86
See also MTCW 1
See also SSC 4
See also WLCS
Hurt, C(harlie) D(euel III) 1950- 127
Hurt, Freda M(ary) E(lizabeth) 1911- 103
Hurt, Harry III 1951- 143
Hurt, Henry 1942- 106
Hurt, James (Riggins) 1934- CANR-47
Earlier sketches in CA 45-48, CANR-23
Hurt, Ray Douglas 1946- CANR-53
Earlier sketch in CA 125
Hurtado, Albert L. 1946- 130

Hurtgen, Andre O(scar) 1932- 81-84
Hurtig, Mel 137
Hurt-Newton, Tania 1968- SATA 84
Hurvitz, Leon Nahum 1923- 106
Hurwitz, Abraham B. 1905-1981 29-32R
Obituary 133
Hurwitz, Edith F(arber) 1941- 108
Hurwitz, Howard L(awrence) 1916- 37-40R
Hurwitz, Johanna 1937- CANR-50
Earlier sketches in CA 65-68, CANR-10, 25, 44
See also JRDA
See also MAICYA
See also SAAS 18
See also SATA 20, 71
Hurwitz, Ken 1948- 33-36R
Hurwitz, Samuel J(ustin) 1912-1972 CAP-2
Earlier sketch in CA 25-28
Hurwitz, Stephan 1901-1981 Obituary 103
Hurwood, Bernhardt J. 1926-1987 CANR-43
Obituary 121
Earlier sketch in CA 25-28R
See also SATA 12
See also SATA-Obit 50
Husain, Shahrukh 1950- 168
Husar, John 1937- 81-84
Husband, William Hollow
1899(?)-1978 Obituary 81-84
Huse, Dennis P(aul) 1944- 115
Huseman, Richard C. 1939- 127
Brief entry 109
Husen, Torsten 1916- CANR-53
Earlier sketches in CA 21-24R, CANR-9, 27
Huser, (La)Verne (Carl) 1931- CANR-22
Earlier sketch in CA 106
Huskey, Eugene 1952- 145
Huson, Paul (Anthony) 1942- CANR-12
Earlier sketch in CA 29-32R
Huss, Roy 1927- CANR-47
Earlier sketch in CA 25-28R
Huss, Sandy 1953- 138
Hussein, Taha 1889-1973 Obituary 45-48
Husserl, E. G.
See Husserl, Edmund (Gustav Albrecht)
Husserl, Edmund (Gustav Albrecht) 1859-1938 133
Brief entry 116
Hussey, David Edward 1934- CANR-9
Earlier sketch in CA 57-60
Hussey, Gemma 1938- 145
Hussey, John A(dam) 1913- 61-64
Hussey, Mark 1956- 135
Hussey, Maurice Percival 1925- 9-12R
Hussey, Patricia (Ann) 1949- 143
Hussey, (John) Walter (Atherton) 1909-1985 133
Hussman, Lawrence Eugene, Jr. 1932- 115
Hussmann, Mary (Margaret) 1953- 147
Hustak, Alan (Joseph) 1944- 128
Huste, Annemarie 1943- 57-60
Husted, Darrell 1931- 81-84
Huston, Anne Marshall CANR-40
Earlier sketch in CA 116
Huston, Fran
See Miller, R. S.
Huston, James A(lvin) 1918- CANR-33
Earlier sketches in CA 41-44R, CANR-15
Huston, John (Marcellus) 1906-1987 CANR-34
Obituary 123
Earlier sketch in CA 73-76
See also CLC 20
See also DLB 26
Huston, Luther A. 1888- CAP-2
Earlier sketch in CA 21-22
Huston, Mervyn James 1912- CANR-8
Earlier sketch in CA 61-64
Huston, Nancy 1953- 145
Huston, Tony
See Huston, Walter Anthony
Huston, Walter Anthony 1950- 166
Hustvedt, Lloyd (Merlyn) 1922- 21-24R
Hustvedt, Siri 1955- 137
See also CLC 76
Huszar, George B(ernard) de 1919-(?) CAP-2
Earlier sketch in CA 19-20
Hutchcroft, Vera 1923- 102
Hutchens, Eleanor Newman 1919- 13-16R
Hutchens, John Kennedy 1905- 65-68
Hutchens, Paul 1902-1977 61-64
See also SATA 31
Hutcheon, Linda (Ann) 1947- 131
Hutcheon, Michael 1945- 158
Hutcheson, Richard G(ordon), Jr. 1921- 107
Hutchin, Kenneth Charles 1908- 110
Hutchings, Alan Eric 1910- 1-4R
Hutchings, Arthur (James Bramwell) 1906-
CANR-6
Earlier sketch in CA 5-8R
Hutchings, Bill
See Hutchings, William Bruce
Hutchings, Edward, Jr. 1912- 126
Hutchings, Margaret (Joscelyne) 1918- CANR-3
Earlier sketch in CA 9-12R
Hutchings, Monica Mary 1917- 9-12R
Hutchings, Patrick A(elfred) 1929- CANR-4
Earlier sketch in CA 53-56
Hutchings, Raymond 1924- CANR-12
Earlier sketch in CA 33-36R
Hutchings, William Bruce 1948- 111
Hutchins, Carleen Maley 1911- 17-20R
See also SATA 9
Hutchins, Charles R. 1928- 123
Hutchins, Francis Gilman 1939- 21-24R
Hutchins, Hazel J. 1952- CANR-50
Earlier sketch in CA 123
See also SAAS 24
See also SATA 81
See also SATA-Brief 51
Hutchins, Maude (Phelps McVeigh) 61-64
Hutchins, Myldred Flanigan 1910- 112
Hutchins, Pat 1942- CANR-64
Earlier sketches in CA 81-84, CANR-15, 32
See also CLR 20
See also MAICYA
See also SAAS 16
See also SATA 15, 70
Hutchins, Robert Maynard 1899-1977 69-72
Hutchins, Ross Elliott 1906- CANR-5
Earlier sketch in CA 9-12R
See also SATA 4
Hutchinson, Allan C. 1951- 154
Hutchinson, Arthur Stuart Menteth
1879-1971 Obituary 29-32R
Hutchinson, C(ecil) Alan 1914-1981 29-32R
Obituary 133
Hutchinson, D(ouglas) S(tanley) 1955- 128
Hutchinson, David (Christopher) 1960- 119
Hutchinson, Earl Ofari 1945- 138
See also BW 2
Hutchinson, Eliot Dole 1900- 61-64
Hutchinson, G(eorge) Evelyn 1903-1991 CANR-14
Obituary 134
Earlier sketches in CAP-1, CA 13-14
Hutchinson, G(regory) O(wen) 1957- 148
Hutchinson, George 1920-1980 Obituary 97-100
Hutchinson, H(ugh) Lester 1904- 17-20R
Hutchinson, John 1921- 45-48
Hutchinson, John F(ranklin) 1938- 158
Hutchinson, Joseph (Burtt) 1902-1988 109
Obituary 124
Hutchinson, Margaret Massey 1904- CAP-1
Earlier sketch in CA 13-16
Hutchinson, Mary Jane 1924- 106
Hutchinson, Michael E. 1925- 17-20R
Hutchinson, (William Patrick Henry) Pearse
1927- 103
Hutchinson, Peter 1943- CANR-8
Earlier sketch in CA 61-64
Hutchinson, Ray Coryton 1907-1975 CANR-3
Obituary 61-64
Earlier sketch in CA 1-4R
See also DLB 191
Hutchinson, Richard Wyatt 1894-1970 5-8R
Obituary 89-92
Hutchinson, Robert 1924- 13-16R
Hutchinson, Roger 1949- 156
Hutchinson, Thomas 1711-1780 DLB 30, 31
Hutchinson, Vernal 1922- 49-52
Hutchinson, Veronica S(omerville)
1895-1961 Obituary 111
Hutchinson, Warner Alton, Jr. 1929- 110
Hutchinson, William K(enneth) 1945- 102
Hutchinson, William M(iller) 1916- 112
Hutchison, (William) Bruce 1901- 103
Hutchison, Chester Smith 1902- CAP-2
Earlier sketch in CA 17-18
Hutchison, (Dorothy) Dwight
1890(?)-1975 Obituary 57-60
Hutchison, E(arl) R. 1926- CANR-10
Earlier sketch in CA 25-28R
Hutchison, Emery 1919(?)-1985 Obituary 116
Hutchison, Harold Frederick 1900- CANR-4
Earlier sketch in CA 1-4R
Hutchison, Jane Campbell 1932- 37-40R
Hutchison, John Alexander 1912- 69-72
Hutchison, Sidney C(harles) 1912- 25-28R
Hutchison, T(erence) W(ilmot) 1912- 129
Hutchison, William Robert 1930- 21-24R
Hutchisson, James M. 1961- 156
Huth, Angela 1938- CANR-20
Earlier sketch in CA 85-88
Huth, Marta 1898- Brief entry 106
Huth, Mary Jo(sephine) 1929- 103
Huth, Tom 1941- 97-100
Huthmacher, J. Joseph 1929- 21-24R
See also SATA 5
Hutin, Magdeleine 1898-1989 Obituary 130
Hutmacher (MacLean), Barbara Anne 1926- 112
Hutman, Norma Louise 1935- 25-28R
Hutschnecker, Arnold A. 1898- 81-84
Hutslar, Donald Andrew 1931- 127
Hutson, Anthony Brian Austen 1934- 93-96
Hutson, James H(oward) 1937- 85-88
Hutson, Jan 1932- 106
Hutson, Joan 1929- 89-92
Hutson, Lorna 1958- 146
Hutt, Maurice George 1928- 13-16R
Hutt, Max L. 1908- 57-60
Hutt, W(illiam) H(arold) 1899-1988 57-60
Obituary 125
Hutten, Ulrich von 1488-1523 DLB 179
Huttenback, Robert A. 1928- 25-28R
Hutter, Albert David 1941- 130
Huttig, Jack W(ilfred) 1919- 53-56
Huttner, Matthew 1915-1975 Obituary 104
Hutto, Nelson (Allen) 1904- CAP-1
Earlier sketch in CA 9-10
See also SATA 20
Hutton, Ann 1929- 108
Hutton, Barbara (Audrey) 1920- 132
Hutton, Clarke 1898- 107
Hutton, Frankie 161
Hutton, Geoffrey (William) 1909- 130
Hutton, Geoffrey 1928- 41-44R
Hutton, Ginger
See Hutton, Virginia Carol
Hutton, Harold 1912- 102
Hutton, J(oseph) Bernard 1911-(?) CANR-14
Earlier sketch in CA 21-24R
Hutton, J(ohn) H(enry) 1885-1968 CAP-1
Earlier sketch in CA 13-14
Hutton, James 1902-1980 CANR-27
Earlier sketch in CA 77-80
Hutton, John (Harwood) 1928- 107
Hutton, Kathryn 1915- SATA 89
Hutton, Malcolm 1921- CANR-24
Earlier sketch in CA 107
Hutton, Paul Andrew 1949- 133
Hutton, Richard 1949- 109
Hutton, Richard Holt 1826-1897 DLB 57
Hutton, Ronald 1953- 131
Hutton, Virginia Carol 1940- 77-80
Hutton, Warwick 1939-1994 CANR-9
Obituary 147
Earlier sketch in CA 61-64
See also SAAS 17
See also SATA 20
See also SATA-Obit 83
Hutton, Will(iam Nicholas) 1950- 130
Huus, Helen 1913- CANR-1
Earlier sketch in CA 1-4R
Huvos, Kornel 1913- 49-52
Huws, Daniel 1932- 81-84
Huxhold, Harry N(orman) 1922- 61-64
Huxley, Aldous (Leonard) 1894-1963 CANR-44
Earlier sketch in CA 85-88
See also AAYA 11
See also CDBLB 1914-1945
See also CLC 1, 3, 4, 5, 8, 11, 18, 35, 79
See also DA
See also DAB
See also DAC
See also DAM MST, NOV
See also DLB 36, 100, 162, 195
See also MTCW 1
See also SATA 63
See also WLC
Huxley, Anthony J(ulian) 1920-1992 CANR-49
Obituary 140
Earlier sketches in CA 9-12R, CANR-7, 22
Huxley, Elspeth (Josceline Grant) 1907-1997
CANR-58
Obituary 156
Earlier sketches in CA 77-80, CANR-28
See also DLB 77
See also SATA 62
See also SATA-Obit 95
Huxley, George 1932- 21-24R
Huxley, Herbert H(enry) 1916- 5-8R
Huxley, Judith 1927(?)-1983 Obituary 111
Huxley, Julian (Sorell) 1887-1975 CANR-7
Obituary 57-60
Earlier sketch in CA 9-12R
See also MTCW 1
Huxley, Laura Archera 1911- CANR-44
Earlier sketch in CA 13-16R
Huxley, T(homas) H(enry) 1825-1895 DLB 57
Huxley-Blythe, Peter J(ames) 1925- 17-20R
Huxtable, Ada Louise (Landman) 1921- 120
Huxtable, (William) John (Fairchild) 1912- 13-16R
Huy, Nguyen Ngoc
See Nguyen, Ngoc Huy
Huyck, Dorothy Boyle 1925(?)-1979 Obituary 89-92
Huyck, Margaret Hellie 1939- 49-52
Huyck, Peter H(azelwood) 1940- 107
Huyck, Willard 1945(?)- 128
Brief entry 111
Huygen, Wil(librord Joseph) 1922- CANR-15
Earlier sketch in CA 81-84
Huyghe, Patrick 1952- 135
Huyghe, Rene (Louis) 1906- CANR-20
Earlier sketch in CA 81-84
Huyghue, Douglas Smith 1816-1891 DLB 99
Huyler, Jean Wiley 1935- CANR-35
Earlier sketches in CA 69-72, CANR-13
Huynh, Quang Nhuong 1946- 107
Huyser, Robert E(rnest) 1924- 139
Huysmans, Charles Marie Georges 1848-1907
See Huysmans, Joris-Karl
Huysmans, J.-K.
See Huysmans, Joris-Karl
Huysmans, Joris-Karl 1848-1907 165
Brief entry 104
See also DLB 123
See also TCLC 7, 69
Huzar, Eleanor G(oltz) 1922- 85-88
Hvidt, Kristian 1929- 130
Hwang, David Henry 1957- 132
Brief entry 127
Interview in 132
See also CLC 55
See also DAM DRAM
See also DC 4
Hy, Ronald John 1942- 115
Hyam, Ronald 1936- 97-100
Hyams, Barry 1911-1989 13-16R
Obituary 129
Hyams, Edward (Solomon) 1910-1975 CANR-8
Obituary 61-64
Earlier sketch in CA 5-8R
Hyams, Joe
See Hyams, Joseph
Hyams, Joseph 1923- CANR-45
Earlier sketches in CA 17-20R, CANR-7, 22
Hyatt, Betty H(ale) 1927- 125
Hyatt, Carole S. 1935- 93-96
Hyatt, Daniel
See James, Daniel (Lewis)
Hyatt, I. Ralph 1927- 115
Hyatt, J(ames) Philip 1909-1972 9-12R
Obituary 134
Hyatt, Richard Herschel 1944- 101
Hybels, Bill 1951- 126
Hybels, Saundra 1938- 57-60
Hyde, Anthony 1946- 136
See also CLC 42
Hyde, Charles K(eith) 1945- 116
Hyde, Dayton O(gden) 25-28R
See also SATA 9
Hyde, Donald 1909-1966 DLB 187
Hyde, Douglas Arnold 1911-1996 156
Obituary 153
Brief entry 109
Hyde, Edward 1609-1674 DLB 101
Hyde, Eleanor (M.) 154
Hyde, Elisabeth 1953- 122
Hyde, Fillmore 1896(?)-1970 Obituary 104
Hyde, George E. 1882-1968 5-8R
Obituary 133
Hyde, H(arford) Montgomery 1907-1989 5-8R
Obituary 129
Hyde, Hawk
See Hyde, Dayton O(gden)
Hyde, Janet Shibley 1948- CANR-10
Earlier sketch in CA 65-68
Hyde, L(ouis) K(epler, Jr.) 1901- CAP-1
Earlier sketch in CA 13-14
Hyde, Laurence 1914- 17-20R
Hyde, (W.) Lewis 1945- 144
Hyde, Margaret O(ldroyd) 1917- CANR-36
Earlier sketches in CA 1-4R, CANR-1
See also CLC 21
See also CLR 23
See also JRDA
See also MAICYA
See also SAAS 8
See also SATA 1, 42, 76
Hyde, Mary (Morley Crapo) 1912- CANR-27
Earlier sketch in CA 49-52
See also DLB 187
Hyde, Nina Solomon 1932-1990 Obituary 131
Hyde, Samuel C., Jr. 1958- 168
Hyde, Shelley
See Reed, Kit
Hyde, Simeon, Jr. 1919- 21-24R
Hyde, Stuart W(allace) 1923- 61-64
Hyde, Tracy Elliot
See Venning, Corey
Hyde, Wayne Frederick 1922- 1-4R
See also SATA 7
Hyden, (Sten Gustav Vilhelm) Goeran 1938-
CANR-20
Earlier sketch in CA 103
Hyde-Price, Adrian 1957- 140
Hyder, Clyde Kenneth 1902- 33-36R
Hyder, O(liver) Quentin 1930- 127
Brief entry 105
Hyer, James Edgar 1923- 77-80
Hyer, Paul Van 1926- 104
Hyers, M. Conrad 1933- 33-36R
Hyett, Barbara Helfgott 1945- CANR-46
Earlier sketch in CA 120
Hygen, Johan B(ernitz) 1911- 21-24R
Hyink, Bernard L(ynn) 1913- CANR-49
Earlier sketch in CA 45-48
Hyland, Douglas K(irk) S(amuel) 1949- 124
Hyland, Drew A(lan) 1939- CANR-15
Earlier sketch in CA 89-92
Hyland, Jean Scammon 1926- 49-52
Hyland, Paul 1947- 121
Hyland, (Henry) Stanley 1914- 9-12R
Hyland, William G. 1929- 148
Hylander, Clarence J(ohn) 1897-1964 5-8R
See also SATA 7
Hylton, Delmer P(aul) 1920- 17-20R
Hyma, Albert 1893- 17-20R
Hyman, Alan 1910- 102
Hyman, Ann 1936- 53-56
Hyman, (Robert) Anthony 1928- 132
Hyman, B(arbara) D(avis) 1947- 125
Hyman, David N(eil) 1943- CANR-22
Earlier sketches in CA 57-60, CANR-7
Hyman, Dick 1904- CANR-7
Earlier sketch in CA 17-20R
Hyman, Frieda Clark 1913- 5-8R
Hyman, Harold M(elvin) 1924- CANR-29
Earlier sketch in CA 5-8R
Hyman, Helen Kandel 1920- 105
Hyman, Herbert H(iram) 1918-1985 21-24R
Obituary 118
Hyman, Irwin A(braham Meltzer) 1935- 93-96
Hyman, Jackie (Diamond) 1949- CANR-28
Earlier sketch in CA 108
Hyman, Jeremy (A.) 125
Hyman, Lawrence W. 1919- 41-44R
Hyman, Miranda
See Miller, Miranda
Hyman, Paula 1946- 89-92
Hyman, Richard J(oseph) 1921- CANR-1
Earlier sketch in CA 45-48
Hyman, Robin P(hilip) 1931- CANR-15
Earlier sketch in CA 41-44R
See also SATA 12
Hyman, Ronald T. 1933- CANR-50
Earlier sketches in CA 21-24R, CANR-9, 25
Hyman, Sidney 1917- 102
Hyman, Stanley Edgar 1919-1970 85-88
Obituary 25-28R
Hyman, Steven E(dward) 1952- 145
Hyman, Trina Schart 1939- CANR-70
Earlier sketches in CA 49-52, CANR-2, 36
See also CLR 50
See also DLB 61
See also MAICYA
See also SATA 7, 46, 95
Hymans, Jacques Louis 1937- 57-60
Hymes, Dell H(athaway) 1927- 13-16R
Hymes, Lucia M(anley) 1907- 5-8R
See also SATA 7
Hymoff, Edward 1924- 17-20R
Hynam, John Charles 1915-1974 158
Hynd, Alan 1904(?)-1974 Obituary 45-48
Hyndman, Donald W(illiam) 1936- CANR-51
Earlier sketches in CA 57-60, CANR-27

Hyndman, Jane Andrews Lee 1912-1978 CANR-5
Obituary 89-92
Earlier sketch in CA 5-8R
See also SATA 1, 46
See also SATA-Obit 23
Hyndman, Robert Utley 1906-1973 97-100
See also SATA 18
Hynds, Frances Jane 1929- 77-80
Hyne, C(harles) J(ohn) Cutcliffe (Wright)
1865-1944 Brief entry 111
Hynek, J(osef) Allen 1910-1986 81-84
Obituary 119
Hyneman, Charles S(hang) 1900-1985 CAP-1
Obituary 114
Earlier sketch in CA 13-14
Hynes, James 1956(?)- 164
See also CLC 65
Hynes, Pat 166
See also SATA 98
Hynes, Samuel (Lynn) 1924- CANR-32
Earlier sketch in CA 105
Hyslop, Beatrice F. 1900(?)-1973 Obituary 45-48
Hyslop, James H(ervey) 1854-1920 Brief entry 123
Hyslop, Lois Boe 1908- 41-44R
Hysom, John L(eland, Jr.) 1934- 115
Hyson, Marion C. 1942- 148
Hytier, Jean (Pierre) 1899-1983 Obituary 109
Hyun, Peter 1906-1993 136
Obituary 142

I

Iaccino, James F(rancis) 1955- 146
Iaccino, Jim
See Iaccino, James F(rancis)
Iacocca, Lee
See Iacocca, Lido Anthony
See also BEST 89:1
Iacocca, Lido Anthony 1924- 125
See also Iacocca, Lee
Iacone, Salvatore J(oseph) 1945- CANR-15
Earlier sketch in CA 85-88
Iacuzzi, Alfred 1896-1977 Obituary 73-76
Iams, Jack
See Iams, Samuel Harvey, Jr.
Iams, Samuel Harvey, Jr. 1910-1990 Obituary 130
Ian, Janis 1951- Brief entry 105
See also CLC 21
Iannelli, Richard 1949- 118
Ianni, Francis A(nthony) J(ames) 1926- CANR-28
Earlier sketch in CA 45-48
Ianniello, Lynne Young 1925- 17-20R
Iannone, Jeanne
See Balzano, Jeanne (Koppel)
See also SATA 7
Iannone, Ron(ald Vincent) 1940- 53-56
Iannuzzi, John Nicholas 1935- 93-96
Iatrides, John O(restes) 1932- CANR-10
Earlier sketch in CA 25-28R
Iavorsky, Stefan 1658-1722 DLB 150
Ibanez, Carlos G. Velez
See Velez-Ibanez, Carlos G(uillermo)
Ibanez, Vicente Blasco
See Blasco Ibanez, Vicente
Ibarbourou, Juana de 1895-1979 HW
Ibarguengoitia, Jorge 1928-1983 124
Obituary 113
See also CLC 37
See also HW
Ibarra, Crisostomo
See Yabes, Leopoldo Y(abes)
Ibbitson, John Perrie 1955- 160
See also SATA 102
Ibbotson, Eva 1925- CANR-43
Earlier sketches in CA 81-84, CANR-15
See also SATA 13
Ibbotson, M. C(hristine) 1930- 25-28R
See also SATA 5
Ibbotson, Roger G. 1943- 145
Ibele, Oscar Herman 1917- Brief entry 106
Ibingira, G(race) S(tuart) K(atebarirwe) 1932- 103
Iblacker, Reinhold A. 1930- 130
Ibn Bajja 1077(?)-1138 DLB 115
Ibn Gabirol, Solomon 1021(?)-1058(?) DLB 115
Ibrahim, Abdel-Sattar 1939- 69-72
Ibrahim, Ibrahim Abdelkader 1923- 13-16R
Ibrahim, Sami
See Moreh, Shmuel
Ibsen, Henrik (Johan) 1828-1906 141
Brief entry 104
See also DA
See also DAB
See also DAC
See also DAM DRAM, MST
See also DC 2
See also TCLC 2, 8, 16, 37, 52
See also WLC
Ibuka, Masaru 1908-1997 102
Obituary 163
Ibuse, Masuji 1898-1993 127
Obituary 141
See also CLC 22
See also DLB 180
Icaza (Coronel), Jorge 1906-1978 89-92
Obituary 85-88
See also HW
Ice, Jackson Lee 1925- 25-28R
Icenhower, Joseph Bryan 1913- CANR-5
Earlier sketch in CA 5-8R
Ichikawa, Kon 1915- 121
See also CLC 20
Ichikawa, Satomi 1949- 126
Brief entry 116
See also SATA 47, 78
See also SATA-Brief 36
Ichimura, Shinichi 1925- CANR-64
Earlier sketch in CA 129
Ichioka, Yuji 1936- 128
Icks, Robert J(oseph) 1900- 41-44R
Icolari, Daniel Leonardo 1942- 17-20R
Iddon, Don 1913(?)-1979 Obituary 89-92
Ide, Richard S(myth) 1943- 120
Idelsohn, Abraham Zevi 1882-1938 Brief entry 109
Iden, William
See Green, William M(ark)
Idinopulos, Thomas A. 1935- 141
Idle, Eric 1943- CANR-35
Earlier sketch in CA 116
See also Monty Python
See also CLC 21
Idol, John L(ane), Jr. 1932- 140
Idone, Christopher 1937- 122
Idriess, Ion L. 1891(?)-1979 Obituary 89-92
Iduarte (Foucher), Andres 1907- 33-36R
Idyll, C(larence) P(urvis) 1916- CANR-8
Earlier sketch in CA 9-12R
Ierardi, Francis B. 1886-1970 Obituary 104
Iffland, August Wilhelm 1759-1814 DLB 94
Ifft, James B(rown) 1935- 53-56
Ifkovic, Edward 1943- CANR-33
Earlier sketches in CA 61-64, CANR-8
Iggers, Georg G(erson) 1926- CANR-33
Earlier sketch in CA 25-28R
Iggers, Wilma Abeles 1921- 25-28R
Iggulden, John Manners 1917- 9-12R
Iglauer, Edith
See Daly, Edith Iglauer
Iglehart, Alfreda P(aulette) 1950- 109
Iglehart, Louis Tillman 1915-1981 Obituary 104
Iglesias, Mario 1924- CANR-50
Earlier sketches in CA 45-48, CANR-25
Iglitzin, Lynne 1931- 41-44R
Ignatieff, George 1913- 119
Ignatieff, Michael 1947- 144
Ignatiev, Noel 1940- 153
Ignatius, David 1950- CANR-71
Earlier sketch in CA 128
Ignatow, David 1914-1997 CANR-57
Obituary 162
Earlier sketches in CA 9-12R, CANR-31
See also CAAS 3
See also CLC 4, 7, 14, 40
See also DLB 5
Ignoffo, Matthew 1945- 156
See also SATA 92
Ignotus, Paul 1901-1978 CANR-8
Obituary 77-80
Earlier sketch in CA 5-8R
Igo, John N., Jr. 1927- CANR-33
Earlier sketch in CA 13-16R
Igoe, James (Thomas) 1935- 108
Igoe, (Lesly) Lynn Moody 1937- 108
Igus, Toyomi 1953- 143
See also SATA 76
Ihde, Don 1934- CANR-13
Earlier sketch in CA 33-36R
Ihimaera, Witi 1944- 77-80
See also CLC 46
Ihnat, Steve 1935(?)-1972 Obituary 33-36R
Iiams, Thomas M., Jr. 1928- CANR-35
Earlier sketch in CA 9-12R
Iida, Deborah 1956- 156
Iino, (David) Norimoto 1918- 61-64
Ike, Chukwuemeka 1931- DLB 157
Ike, Nobutaka 1916- 21-24R
Ike, Vincent Chukwuemeka 1931- 168
Ikeda, Daisaku 1928- 85-88
See also SATA 77
Ikeda, Kiyoshi 1928- Brief entry 104
Ikejiani, Okechukwu 1917- 17-20R
Ikenberry, Oliver Samuel 1908-1978 53-56
Obituary 134
Ikerman, Ruth C. (Percival) 1910- 13-16R
Ikle, Fred Charles 1924- 45-48
Iko, Momoko 1940- CANR-14
Earlier sketch in CA 77-80
Ilardi, Vincent 1925- 29-32R
Ilardo, Joseph A(nthony) 1944- 89-92
Ilchman, Warren Frederick 1934- CANR-1
Earlier sketch in CA 1-4R
Iles, Bert
See Ross, Zola Helen
Iles, Francis
See Cox, A(nthony) B(erkeley)
Iles, Greg 161
Iles, Jane 1954- 135
Ilf, Ilya
See Fainzilberg, Ilya Arnoldovich
See also TCLC 21
Ilg, Frances L(illian) 1902-1981 107
Obituary 104
Ilgen, Thomas
See Ilgen, Thomas L.
Ilgen, Thomas L. 1946- 120
Ilich, John 1933- 106
Ilie, Paul 1932- CANR-10
Earlier sketch in CA 25-28R
Illan, Jose M(anuel) 1924- 45-48
Illes, Robert E(noch) 1914- 103
Illiano, Antonio 1934- 41-44R
Illich, Ivan 1926- CANR-35
Earlier sketches in CA 53-56, CANR-10
See also AITN 2
See also MTCW 1
Illick, Joseph E. 1934- 17-20R
Illingworth, Frank (M. B.) 1908- CANR-5
Earlier sketch in CA 5-8R
Illingworth, John 1904(?)-1980 Obituary 97-100
Illingworth, Neil 1934- 13-16R
Illingworth, Ronald Stanley 1909-1990(?) CANR-3
Obituary 131
Earlier sketch in CA 9-12R
Illwitzer, Elinor G. 1934- 29-32R
Illyes, Gyula 1902-1983 114
Obituary 109
See also PC 16
Ilma, Viola 1911(?)-1989 Obituary 129
Ilowite, Sheldon A. 1931- 106
See also SATA 27
Ilsey, Dent
See Chapman, John Stanton Higham
Ilsley, Dent
See Chapman, John Stanton Higham
Ilsley, Velma (Elizabeth) 1918- CANR-3
Earlier sketch in CA 9-12R
See also SATA 12
Ilson, Robert (Frederick) 1937- 124
Ilyin, Mikhail Andreyevich 1878-1942 Brief
entry 119
Imai, Masaaki 1930- 129
Imai, Miko 1963- SATA 90
Imamura, Anne E(lizabeth Sommers) 1946- 126
Imamura, Shigeo 1922- 77-80
Imber, Gerald 1941- 89-92
Imbert, Enrique Anderson
See Anderson Imbert, Enrique
Imbrie, John 1925- Brief entry 107
Imbrie, Katherine P(almer) 1952- 104
Imbs, Bravig (Wilbur Eugene) 1904-1946 Brief
entry 107
See also DLB 4
Imbuga, Francis D. 1947- DLB 157
Imel, Dorothy Myers 1934- 149
Imershein, Betsy 1953- SATA 62
Imerti, Arthur D. 1915- 37-40R
Imes, Birney 1951- 151
Imfeld, Al 1935- CANR-29
Earlier sketches in CA 69-72, CANR-13
Imhoof, Maurice Lee 1930- Brief entry 108
Imlah, Mick 1956- 153
Immaculata, Sister
See Maxwell, Sister Mary
Immel, Mary Blair 1930- CANR-6
Earlier sketch in CA 13-16R
See also SATA 28
Immell, Myra H. 1941- 156
See also SATA 92
Immerman, Leon Andrew 1952- 103
Immerman, Richard H. 1949- 129
Immermann, Karl (Lebrecht) 1796-1840 DLB 133
Immerwahr, Sara Anderson 1914- Brief entry 108
Immoos, Thomas 1918- CANR-35
Earlier sketches in CA 85-88, CANR-15
Immroth, John Phillip 1936-1976 CAP-2
Earlier sketch in CA 33-36
Imperato, Pascal James 1937- CANR-56
Brief entry 106
Earlier sketch in CA 127
Impey, Oliver (Richard) 1936- 108
Impey, Rose 1947- 137
See also SATA 69
Impola, Richard A(arre) 1923- 139
Imrie, Richard
See Pressburger, Emeric
Imubuga, Francis D. 1947- DLB 157
Imus, (John) Don(ald) 1940- 156
Inada, Lawson Fusao 1938- CANR-59
Earlier sketch in CA 33-36R
Inalcik, Halil 1916- CANR-28
Earlier sketch in CA 49-52
Inayat-Khan, Pir Vilayat 1916- 93-96
Inbau, Fred E(dward) 1909-1998 CANR-1
Obituary 167
Earlier sketch in CA 1-4R
Inber, Vera Mikhailovna
1893-1972 Obituary 37-40R
Ince, Basil A(ndre) 1933- 57-60
Ince, Martin (Jeffrey) 1952- 110
Ince, W(alter) N(ewcombe)
1927(?)-1988 Obituary 126
Inch, Morris Alton 1925- CANR-11
Earlier sketch in CA 29-32R
Inchbald, Elizabeth 1753-1821 DLB 39, 89
Inchbald, Peter 1919- 130
Inciardi, James A(nthony) 1939- CANR-8
Earlier sketch in CA 61-64
Inclan, Ramon (Maria) del Valle
See Valle-Inclan, Ramon (Maria) del
Incogniteau, Jean-Louis
See Kerouac, Jean-Louis Lebris de
Ind, Allison 1903-1974 CAP-1
Earlier sketch in CA 13-16
Indelman, Elchanan Chonon
1908(?)-1983 Obituary 109
Indelman-Yinnon, Moshe
1895(?)-1977 Obituary 73-76
Inderlied, Mary Elizabeth 1945- 49-52
Indik, Bernard P(aul) 1932- 33-36R
Inez, Colette 1931- 37-40R
See also CAAS 10
Infante, G(uillermo) Cabrera
See Cabrera Infante, G(uillermo)
Infield, Glenn (Berton) 1920-1981 CANR-5
Obituary 103
Earlier sketch in CA 5-8R
Ing, Dean 1931- CANR-60
Earlier sketches in CA 106, CANR-23
Ingalls, Daniel H(enry) H(olmes) 1916- 17-20R
Ingalls, David Sinton 1899-1985 Obituary 116
Ingalls, Jeremy 1911- CANR-27
Earlier sketch in CA 1-4R
Ingalls, Rachel (Holmes) 1940- 127
Brief entry 123
See also CLC 42
Ingalls, Robert Paul 1941- 110
Brief entry 107
Ingamells, Reginald Charles
See Ingamells, Rex
Ingamells, Rex 1913-1955 167
See also TCLC 35
Ingard, K(arl) Uno 1921- 33-36R
Ingarden, Roman Witold 1893-1970 Obituary 113
Ingate, Mary 1912- 73-76
Ingbar, Mary Lee 1926- 41-44R
Ingberman, Sima 1947- 150
Inge, M(ilton) Thomas 1936- CANR-51
Earlier sketches in CA 17-20R, CANR-9, 25
Inge, W. R.
See Inge, William Ralph
Inge, William (Motter) 1913-1973 9-12R
See also CDALB 1941-1968
See also CLC 1, 8, 19
See also DAM DRAM
See also DLB 7
See also MTCW 1
Inge, William Ralph 1860-1954 Brief entry 116
Ingelfinger, Franz Joseph
1910-1980 Obituary 97-100
Ingelow, Jean 1820-1897 DLB 35, 163
See also SATA 33
Ingermann, Helena Antonia Maria Elisabeth Dermout
See Dermout-Ingermann, Helena Antonia Maria
Elisabeth
Ingersol, Jared
See Paine, Lauran (Bosworth)
Ingersoll, David E(dward) 1939- 41-44R
Ingersoll, Earl G(eorge) 1938- 159
Ingersoll, John H. 1925- 73-76
Ingersoll, Norman 1928- SATA 79
Ingersoll, Ralph (McAllister) 1900-1985 CAP-1
Obituary 115
Earlier sketch in CA 13-14
See also DLB 127
Ingersoll, Robert Franklin 1933- 104
Ingham, Colonel Frederic
See Hale, Edward Everett
Ingham, Daniel
See Lambot, Isobel
Ingham, Jennie 1944- 108
Ingham, John N. 1939- 138
Ingham, Kenneth 1921- 110
Brief entry 108
Ingham, (Ann) Mary 1947- 120
Ingham, Richard Arnison 1935- 104
Ingham, Robert E(dward) 1934- 108
Ingilby, Joan Alicia 1911- 9-12R
Ingle, Clifford 1915-1977 29-32R
Obituary 134
Ingle, Dwight Joyce 1907- CAP-1
Earlier sketch in CA 9-10
Ingle, Joseph B. 1946- 136
Ingle, Stephen (James) 1940- 127
Ingleby, Terry 1901- 106
Ingles, G(lenn) Lloyd 1901- CAP-1
Earlier sketch in CA 19-20
Inglis, Brian (St. John) 1916-1993 CANR-47
Obituary 140
Earlier sketches in CA 17-20R, CANR-7, 23
Inglis, David Rittenhouse 1905- CANR-5
Earlier sketch in CA 5-8R
Inglis, James 1927- 21-24R
Inglis, Janet 1946- 152
Inglis, John K(enneth) 1933- 106
Inglis, R(obert) M(orton) G(all) 1910-1975 CANR-8
Earlier sketch in CA 13-16R
Inglis, Ruth Langdon 1927- CANR-1
Earlier sketch in CA 49-52
Inglis, Stuart J(ohn) 1923- 41-44R
Ingman, Nicholas 1948- 134
See also SATA 52
Ingold, Gerard (Antoine Hubert) 1922- CANR-23
Earlier sketch in CA 106
Ingold, Klara (Schmid) 1913-1980 61-64
Obituary 134
Ingraham, Barton L(ee) 1930- CANR-43
Earlier sketch in CA 119
Ingraham, Joseph Holt 1809-1860 DLB 3
Ingraham, Leonard W(illiam) 1913- 25-28R
See also SATA 4
Ingraham, Mark H(oyt) 1896-1982 61-64
Obituary 109
Ingraham, Vernon L. 1924- 33-36R
Ingram, Anne (Whitten) Bower 1937- 102
Ingram, (Mildred Rebecca) Bowen (Prewett) 37-40R
Ingram, Collingwood 1880-1981 61-64
Obituary 103
Ingram, Derek (Thynne) 1925- 9-12R
Ingram, Forrest L(eo) 1938- 53-56
Ingram, Gregory Keith 1944- 77-80
Ingram, Helen Moyer 1937- CANR-22
Earlier sketch in CA 105
Ingram, James C(arlton) 1922- 5-8R
Ingram, (Archibald) Kenneth 1882-1965 CAP-1
Earlier sketch in CA 13-14
Ingram, Paul O. 1939- 168
Ingram, R(eginald) W(illiam) 1930-1989 129
Ingram, Scott 1948- 156
See also SATA 92
Ingram, Thomas Henry 1924- CANR-2
Earlier sketch in CA 49-52
Ingram, Tom
See Ingram, Thomas Henry
Ingram, William 1930- 41-44R
Ingram, Willis J.
See Harris, Mark

Ingrams, Doreen 1906-1997 ... CANR-12
Obituary ... 159
Earlier sketch in CA 33-36R
See also SATA 20, 97
Ingrams, Richard (Reid) 1937- ... 103
Ingrao, Charles W(illiam) 1948- ... 101
Ingstad, Helge Marcus 1899- ... 65-68
Ingves, Gunilla (Anna Maria Folkesdotter) 1939- ... 161
See also SATA 101
Ingwersen, Faith 1934- ... CANR-15
Earlier sketch in CA 69-72
Ingwersen, Niels 1935- ... CANR-15
Earlier sketch in CA 69-72
Ingwersen, Will (Alfred Theodore) 1905-1990 Obituary ... 132
Inigo, Martin
See Miles, Keith
Inkeles, Alex 1920- ... CANR-1
Earlier sketch in CA 1-4R
Inkiow, (Janakiev) Dimiter 1932- ... 101
Inkpen, Mick 1952- ... 167
See also SATA 99
Inkster, Ian 1949- ... 113
Inkster, Tim 1949- ... 163
Inlow, Gail M(aurice) 1910- ... CANR-4
Earlier sketch in CA 5-8R
Inman, Arthur Crew 1895-1963 ... 122
Inman, Billie (Jo) Andrew 1929- ... CANR-28
Earlier sketches in CA 29-32R, CANR-12
Inman, Jack (Ingles) 1919- ... 25-28R
Inman, John 1805-1850 ... DLB 73
Inman, Robert (Anthony) 1931- ... 17-20R
Inman, Will 1923- ... CANR-12
Earlier sketch in CA 25-28R
Inmerito
See Javitch, Daniel Gilbert
Inmon, W(illiam) H(arvey) 1945- ... 110
Innaurato, Albert (F.) 1948(?)- ... 122
Brief entry ... 115
Interview in ... 122
See also CLC 21, 60
Innerhofer, Franz 1944- ... 101
See also DLB 85
Innes, Brian 1928- ... CANR-14
Earlier sketch in CA 21-24R
Innes, C(atherine) L(ynette) 1940- ... 123
Innes, Christopher David 1941- ... 107
Innes, Clive 1909- ... 155
Innes, Frank C. 1934- ... 45-48
Innes, Hammond
See Hammond Innes, Ralph
Innes, Jean
See Saunders, Jean
Innes, Michael
See Stewart, J(ohn) I(nnes) M(ackintosh)
Innes, Ralph Hammond
See Hammond Innes, Ralph
Innes, Rosemary E(lizabeth Jackson) ... 25-28R
Innes, Stephen 1946- ... 116
Inness, Sherrie A. 1965- ... 161
Inness-Brown, Elizabeth (Ann) 1954- ... 156
Innis, Donald Quayle 1924- ... 41-44R
Innis, Harold Adams 1894-1952 ... DLB 88
See also TCLC 77
Innis, Mary Quayle 1899-1972 ... DLB 88
Innis, Pauline B. (Coleman) 1918- ... CANR-4
Earlier sketch in CA 1-4R
Innis, Robert E(dward) 1941- ... 130
Innocenti, Roberto 1940- ... SATA 96
Inoguchi, Takashi 1944- ... 131
Inoue, Yasushi 1907-1991 ... DLB 182
Inoue, Yukitoshi 1945- ... 25-28R
Inouye, Daniel K(en) 1924- ... 25-28R
Insall, Donald W(illiam) 1926- ... 61-64
Insana, Tino 1948- ... 123
Insel, Deborah (June) 1949- ... 110
Insight, James
See Coleman, Robert William Alfred
Insingel, Mark 1935- ... 131
Brief entry ... 110
Insolia, Anthony Edward 1926- ... 120
Intriligator, Michael D(avid) 1938- ... 53-56
Inwood, Christiane Sourvinou
See Sourvinou-Inwood, Christiane
Inwood, M(ichael) J(ames) 1944- ... 117
Inyart, Gene
See Namovicz, Gene Inyart
See also SATA 6
Ioffe, Grigory 1951- ... 167
Ionazzi, Daniel A. ... 145
Ione
See Ione, Carole
Ione, Carole 1937- ... 137
See also BW 2
Ionesco, Eugene 1909-1994 ... CANR-55
Obituary ... 144
Earlier sketch in CA 9-12R
See also CLC 1, 4, 6, 9, 11, 15, 41, 86
See also DA
See also DAB
See also DAC
See also DAM DRAM, MST
See also MTCW 1
See also SATA 7
See also SATA-Obit 79
See also WLC
Ionescu, Ghita G. 1913- ... 103
Iongh, Mary (Dows Herter Norton) Crena de
See Crena de Iongh, Mary (Dows Herter Norton)
Iorio, James 1921- ... 61-64
Iorio, John 1925- ... 49-52
Iorizzo, Luciano J(ohn) 1930- ... 73-76
Ipcar, Dahlov (Zorach) 1917- ... CANR-45
Earlier sketches in CA 17-20R, CANR-9
See also MAICYA
See also SAAS 8
See also SATA 1, 49
Ippolito, Donna 1945- ... 104
Ipsen, D(avid) C(arl) 1921- ... 33-36R
Iqbal, Afzal 1919- ... CANR-53
Earlier sketches in CA 61-64, CANR-10, 26
Iqbal, Muhammad 1873-1938 ... TCLC 28
Iqbal, Sabiha 1950- ... 111
Iranek-Osmecki, Kazimierz 1897-1984 ... 49-52
Obituary ... 113
Irby, Kenneth (Lee) 1936- ... CANR-22
Earlier sketch in CA 69-72
Ireland, Ann 1953- ... CANR-58
Earlier sketch in CA 127
Ireland, David 1927- ... CANR-29
Earlier sketch in CA 25-28R
Ireland, Earl (Crowell) 1928- ... 5-8R
Ireland, Jill (Dorothy) 1936-1990 ... 135
Ireland, Joe C. 1936- ... 73-76
Ireland, Karin ... 168
See also SATA 101
Ireland, Kevin (Mark) 1933- ... 73-76
Ireland, Norma Olin 1907- ... CANR-3
Earlier sketch in CA 9-12R
Ireland, Patricia 1945- ... 156
Ireland, Patrick
See O'Doherty, Brian
Ireland, Patrick R(ichard) 1961- ... 148
Ireland, Robert M(ichael) 1937- ... CANR-25
Earlier sketch in CA 45-48
Ireland, Sandra L(eora) Jones 1942- ... 137
Iremonger, Lucille (d'Oyen) 1915-1989(?) . CANR-6
Obituary ... 127
Earlier sketch in CA 9-12R
Iremonger, Valentin 1918- ... 101
Ireson, Barbara (Francis) 1927- ... CANR-21
Earlier sketch in CA 5-8R
Ireton, Rollo
See Shirley, Ralph
Irfani, Suroosh 1947- ... 118
Irgang, Jacob 1930- ... 85-88
Iribarne, Louis 1940- ... 123
Interview in ... 123
Irigaray, Luce 1930- ... 154
Irion, Mary Jean 1922- ... 21-24R
Irion, Paul E(rnst) 1922- ... 21-24R
Irion, Ruth (Hershey) 1921- ... 65-68
Irish, Donald P(aul) 1919- ... 49-52
Irish, Jerry ... 125
Irish, Marian D(oris) 1909- ... 9-12R
Irish, Richard K. 1932- ... 65-68
Irish, William
See Hopley-Woolrich, Cornell George
Iriye, Akira 1934- ... CANR-11
Earlier sketch in CA 25-28R
Irland, David
See Green, Julian (Hartridge)
Iron, Ralph
See Schreiner, Olive (Emilie Albertina)
Irons, Peter
See Irons, Peter H(anlon)
Irons, Peter H(anlon) 1940- ... 128
Ironside, Henry Allan 1876-1951 Brief entry ... 115
Ironside, Jetske 1940- ... SATA 60
Ironside, Virginia 1944- ... 120
Iron Thunderhorse
See Sekaxsu, Petakwonexnajunkis
Irsfeld, John H(enry) 1937- ... 65-68
Irvin, Bob
See Irvin, Robert W.
Irvin, Dona L. 1917- ... 138
Irvin, Fred 1914- ... SATA 15
Irvin, Rea 1881-1972 Obituary ... 93-96
Irvin, Robert W. 1933-1980 Obituary ... 103
Irvine, Betty Jo 1943- ... 77-80
Irvine, Demar (Buel) 1908- ... 33-36R
Irvine, Georgeanne 1955- ... SATA 72
Irvine, Janice M. 1951- ... 135
Irvine, Joan 1951- ... SATA 80
Irvine, John Henry 1951- ... 119
Irvine, Lucy 1956- ... 118
Irvine, M. Keith 1924-1994 ... 29-32R
Obituary ... 145
Irvine, R. R.
See Irvine, Robert (Ralstone)
Irvine, Reed (John) 1922- ... 128
Irvine, Robert (Ralstone) 1936- ... CANR-57
Earlier sketches in CA 81-84, CANR-15
Irvine, Sidney H(erbert) 1931- Brief entry ... 106
Irvine, William 1906-1964 Obituary ... 106
Irvine, William (Burriss III) 1958- ... 144
Irving, Alexander
See Hume, Ruth Fox
Irving, Blanche M(cDaniel) 1904- ... 114
Irving, Brian William 1932- ... 53-56
Irving, Clifford Michael 1930- ... CANR-2
Earlier sketch in CA 1-4R
See also AITN 1
Irving, Clive 1933- ... CANR-22
Earlier sketch in CA 85-88
Irving, David (John Cawdell) 1938- ... CANR-25
Earlier sketch in CA 13-16R
Irving, Edward B(urroughs), Jr. 1923- Brief entry ... 112
Irving, Gordon 1918- ... 25-28R
Irving, Henry
See Kanter, Hal
Irving, John (Winslow) 1942- ... CANR-28
Earlier sketch in CA 25-28R
See also AAYA 8
See also BEST 89:3
See also CLC 13, 23, 38, 112
See also DAM NOV, POP
See also DLB 6
See also DLBY 82
See also MTCW 1
Irving, R(obert) L(ock) Graham 1877-1969 .. CAP-1
Earlier sketch in CA 13-16
Irving, Robert
See Adler, Irving
Irving, Stephanie (Jean) 1962- ... 139
Irving, T(homas) B(allantine) 1914- ... 37-40R
Irving, Washington 1783-1859 .. CDALB 1640-1865
See also DA
See also DAB
See also DAM MST
See also DLB 3, 11, 30, 59, 73, 74, 186
See also SSC 2
See also WLC
See also YABC 2
Irwin, Ann(abelle Bowen) 1915- ... CANR-36
Earlier sketches in CA 101, CANR-19
See also Irwin, Hadley
See also CLR 40
See also MAICYA
See also SATA 44, 89
See also SATA-Brief 38
Irwin, Constance Frick 1913- ... CANR-5
Earlier sketch in CA 1-4R
See also SATA 6
Irwin, Cynthia C.
See Irwin-Williams, Cynthia (Cora)
Irwin, David 1933- ... 53-56
Irwin, Francis William 1905- Brief entry ... 105
Irwin, G. H.
See Palmer, Raymond A.
Irwin, George 1910-1971 ... 41-44R
Irwin, Grace (Lilian) 1907- ... 17-20R
See also DLB 68
Irwin, Graham W(ilkie) 1920-1991 ... 121
Obituary ... 135
Brief entry ... 118
Irwin, Hadley
See Hadley, Lee
and Irwin, Ann(abelle Bowen)
See also AAYA 13
See also CLR 40
See also SAAS 14
Irwin, Inez Haynes 1873-1970 ... 102
Irwin, James W. 1891(?)-1977 Obituary ... 73-76
Irwin, John T(homas) 1940- ... 53-56
Irwin, John V(aleur) 1915- ... CANR-1
Earlier sketch in CA 45-48
Irwin, Keith Gordon 1885-1964 ... 5-8R
See also SATA 11
Irwin, Margaret 1889-1967 Obituary ... 93-96
Irwin, P. K.
See Page, P(atricia) K(athleen)
Irwin, (Joseph) Paul 1940- ... 107
Irwin, Raymond 1902- ... CAP-1
Earlier sketch in CA 9-10
Irwin, Robert (Graham) 1946- ... CANR-48
Earlier sketch in CA 121
Irwin, Ruth Beckey 1906- ... 29-32R
Irwin, Theodore 1907- ... 65-68
Irwin, Vera Rushforth 1913- ... 33-36R
Irwin, W(illiam) R(obert) 1915- ... 65-68
Irwin, Will(iam Henry) 1873-1948 Brief entry ... 117
See also DLB 25
Irwin-Williams, Cynthia (Cora) 1936- ... CANR-1
Earlier sketch in CA 45-48
Isaac, Erich 1928- ... 45-48
Isaac, Glynn Llewelyn 1937-1985 Obituary ... 117
Isaac, Joanne 1934- ... 25-28R
See also SATA 21
Isaac, Joseph Ezra 1922- ... 115
Isaac, Paul E(dward) 1926- ... 17-20R
Isaac, Rael Jean (Isaacs) 1933- ... 17-20R
Isaac, Rhys L(lywelyn) 1937- ... 113
Isaac, Stephen 1925- ... 33-36R
Isaacs, Alan 1925- ... CANR-3
Earlier sketch in CA 9-12R
Isaacs, Anne 1949- ... 155
See also SATA 90
Isaacs, Arnold R. 1941- ... 143
Isaacs, Bernard 1924-1995 ... 107
Obituary ... 148
Isaacs, E. Elizabeth 1917- ... 5-8R
Isaacs, Edith Somborn 1884-1978 Obituary .. 77-80
Isaacs, Harold Robert 1910-1986 ... CANR-2
Obituary ... 119
Earlier sketch in CA 1-4R
Isaacs, Jacob
See Kranzler, George G(ershon)
Isaacs, Neil D. 1931- ... CANR-9
Earlier sketch in CA 5-8R
Isaacs, Norman Ellis 1908-1998 ... 81-84
Obituary ... 165
Isaacs, Ronald (Howard) 1947- ... 162
Isaacs, Stan 1929- ... 13-16R
Isaacs, Stephen D(avid) 1937- ... 81-84
Isaacs, Susan (Sutherland Fairhurst) 1885-1948 Brief entry ... 120
Isaacs, Susan 1943- ... CANR-65
Earlier sketches in CA 89-92, CANR-20, 41
Interview in ... CANR-20
See also BEST 89:1
See also CLC 32
See also DAM POP
See also MTCW 1
Isaacson, Joel 1930- Brief entry ... 114
Isaacson, Judith Magyar 1925- ... 133
Isaacson, Philip M(arshal) 1924- ... 128
See also SATA 87
Isaacson, Robert L. 1928- ... CANR-7
Earlier sketch in CA 17-20R
Isaacson, Walter (Seff) 1952- ... CANR-43
Earlier sketch in CA 112
Isaak, Robert A(llen) 1945- ... CANR-13
Earlier sketch in CA 61-64
Isadora, Rachel 1953(?)- ... 137
Brief entry ... 111
See also CLR 7
See also MAICYA
See also SATA 54, 79
See also SATA-Brief 32
Isais, Juan M. 1926- ... 29-32R
Isakovsky, Mikhail Vasilyevich 1900-1973 Obituary ... 41-44R
Isaksson, Ulla (Margareta Lundberg) 1916- Brief entry ... 109
Isard, Walter 1919- ... 114
Brief entry ... 112
Isban, Samuel 1905- ... CANR-2
Earlier sketch in CA 49-52
Isbister, Clair
See Isbister, Jean Sinclair
Isbister, Jean Sinclair 1915- ... CANR-39
Earlier sketches in CA 1-4R, CANR-1, 18
Isbister, John 1942- ... 139
Ise, John 1885-196(?) ... CAP-1
Earlier sketch in CA 13-14
Isely, Flora Kunigunde Duncan
See Duncan, Kunigunde
Isely, Helen Sue (Pearson) 1917-1978 ... 5-8R
Obituary ... 120
Iseminger, Gary 1937- ... 37-40R
Isenberg, Irwin M. 1931-1979 ... CANR-11
Earlier sketch in CA 17-20R
Isenberg, Joan P. 1941- ... 166
Isenberg, Seymour 1930- ... 33-36R
Isenberg, Sheila 1943- ... 149
Isenhour, Thomas Lee 1939- ... 57-60
Iser, Wolfgang 1926- ... 57-60
Iserson, Kenneth Victor 1949- ... 157
Ishak, Fayek (Matta) 1922- ... 41-44R
Ishak, Yusof bin 1910(?)-1970 Obituary ... 104
Isham, Charlotte H(ickock) 1912- ... 73-76
See also SATA 21
Isham, Linda (Rose) 1938- Brief entry ... 107
Ishee, John A. 1934- ... CANR-18
Earlier sketch in CA 25-28R
Isherwood, Charles 1964- ... 163
Isherwood, Christopher (William Bradshaw) 1904-1986 ... CANR-35
Obituary ... 117
Earlier sketch in CA 13-16R
See also CLC 1, 9, 11, 14, 44
See also DAM DRAM, NOV
See also DLB 15, 195
See also DLBY 86
See also MTCW 1
Isherwood, Robert M. 1935- ... 126
Ishida, Takeshi 1923- ... CANR-38
Earlier sketches in CA 97-100, CANR-16
Ishigo, Estelle 1899- ... 61-64
Ishiguro, Kazuo 1954- ... CANR-49
Earlier sketch in CA 120
See also BEST 90:2
See also CLC 27, 56, 59, 110
See also DAM NOV
See also DLB 194
See also MTCW 1
Ishihara, Shintaro 1932- ... 139
Ishikawa, Hakuhin
See Ishikawa, Takuboku
Ishikawa, Jun 1899-1987 ... DLB 182
Ishikawa, Takuboku 1886(?)-1912 ... 153
Brief entry ... 113
See also DAM POET
See also PC 10
See also TCLC 15
Ishino, Iwao 1921- ... 17-20R
Ish-Kishor, Judith 1892-1972 ... 1-4R
Obituary ... 103
See also SATA 11
Ish-Kishor, Sulamith 1896-1977 ... 73-76
Obituary ... 69-72
See also SATA 17
Ishlon, Deborah 1925- ... 1-4R
Ishmael, Woodi 1914- ... SATA 31
Ishmole, Jack 1924- ... 49-52
Ishwaran, K(arigoudar) 1922- ... 49-52
Isichei, Elizabeth 1939- ... CANR-5
Earlier sketch in CA 53-56
Isis
See Torbett, Harvey Douglas Louis
Iskander, Fazil 1929- ... 102
See also CLC 47
Islam, A(bul) K(hair) M(uhammed) Aminul 1933- ... 41-44R
Islam, Kazi Nazrul 1899(?)-1976 Obituary ... 69-72
Island, David ... 141
Islas, Arturo 1938-1991 ... 131
Obituary ... 140
See also DLB 122
See also HW
Isle, Walter (Whitfield) 1933- ... 25-28R
Isler, Alan (David) 1934- ... 156
See also CLC 91
Isler, Betty
See Isler, Elizabeth
Isler, Elizabeth 1915- ... 114
Ismach, Arnold H(arvey) 1930- ... 85-88
Ismael, Tareq Y. ... 125
Ismail, A. H. 1923- ... 25-28R
Isogai, Hiroshi 1940- ... 102

Ispahani, Mirza Abol Hassan
1902-1981 Obituary ... 108
Israel, Abby 1942- ... 107
Israel, Charles E(dward) 1920- ... 1-4R
Israel, Elaine 1945- ... CANR-9
Earlier sketch in CA 53-56
See also SATA 12
Israel, Fred L. 1934- ... CANR-12
Earlier sketch in CA 17-20R
Israel, Gerard 1928- ... 81-84
Israel, Jerry (Michael) 1941- ... 29-32R
Israel, John (Warren) 1935- ... 21-24R
Israel, Jonathan I. 1946- ... 109
Israel, Lee 1939- ... 143
Israel, Marion Louise 1882-1973 ... 1-4R
Obituary ... 103
See also SATA-Obit 26
Israel, Martin 1927- ... 109
Israel, Peter 1933- ... 128
Israel, Philip 1935- ... 133
Israel, Saul 1910-1990 ... CAP-1
Obituary ... 131
Earlier sketch in CA 13-16
Israeloff, Roberta 1952- ... 118
Israelowitz, Oscar 1949- ... CANR-32
Earlier sketch in CA 113
Israelyan, Victor (Levonov) 1919- ... 151
Issachar
See Stanford, J(ohn) K(eith)
Issawi, Charles Philip 1916- ... CANR-42
Earlier sketches in CA 5-8R, CANR-4, 20
Isser, Natalie 1927- ... 53-56
Issler, Anne Roller 1892- ... 49-52
Iswolsky, Helene 1896-1975 ... 5-8R
Obituary ... 61-64
Italiaander, Rolf (Bruno Maximilian) 1913- ...
CANR-23
Earlier sketches in CA 5-8R, CANR-6
Itani, Frances (Susan) 1942- ... 138
Iterson, S(iny) R(ose) Van
See Van Iterson, S(iny) R(ose)
Itim, Talang
See Lapena-Bonifacio, Amelia
Itse, Elizabeth M(yers) 1930- ... CANR-1
Earlier sketch in CA 49-52
Itule, Bruce D. 1947- ... 125
Itwaru, Arnold (Harrichand) 1942- ... 134
Itzin, Catherine 1944- ... CANR-14
Earlier sketch in CA 77-80
Itzkoff, Seymour W(illiam) 1928- ... 33-36R
Ivan, Martha Miller Pfaff 1909- ... CAP-2
Earlier sketch in CA 19-20
Ivancevich, John M(ichael) 1939- ... CANR-25
Earlier sketch in CA 29-32R
Ivanisevic, Drago 1907-1981 ... DLB 181
Ivanov, Miroslav 1929- ... 81-84
Ivanov, Vsevolod Vyacheslavovich
1895-1963 Obituary ... 93-96
Ivanov, Vyacheslav Ivanovich 1866-1949 Brief
entry ... 122
See also TCLC 33
Ivask, George 1910-1986 Obituary ... 118
Ivask, Ivar Vidrik 1927-1992 ... CANR-24
Obituary ... 139
Earlier sketch in CA 37-40R
See also CLC 14
Ivens, Georg Henri Anton
1898(?)-1989 Obituary ... 129
Ivens, Joris
See Ivens, Georg Henri Anton
Ivens, Michael 1924- ... 5-8R
Ivens, Virginia R(uth) 1922- ... 105
Ivers, Larry E(dward) 1936- ... 77-80
Iversen, Gudmund R(agnvaldsson) 1934- . CANR-4
Earlier sketch in CA 53-56
Iversen, Nick 1951- ... 73-76
Iverson, Eric
See Turtledove, Harry (Norman)
Iverson, Genie 1942- ... CANR-9
Earlier sketch in CA 65-68
See also SATA-Brief 52
Iverson, Jeffrey (James) 1934- ... 105
Iverson, Lucille K(arin) 1925- ... 61-64
Iverson, Peter James 1944- ... 106
Ives, Burl (Icle Ivanhoe) 1909-1995 ... 103
Obituary ... 148
Ives, Charles Edward 1874-1954 ... 149
Brief entry ... 113
Ives, Colta Feller 1943- ... 118
Ives, Edward D(awson) 1925- ... 25-28R
Ives, John
See Garfield, Brian (Wynne)
Ives, Lawrence
See Woods, Frederick
Ives, Morgan
See Bradley, Marion Zimmer
Ives, Sandy
See Ives, Edward D(awson)
Ives, Sumner 1911- ... 9-12R
Ivey, Allen E(ugene) 1933- ... CANR-2
Earlier sketch in CA 49-52
Ivey, Donald 1918- ... 89-92
Ivey, James Burnett 1925- ... 119
Ivey, Jim
See Ivey, James Burnett
Ivie, Robert L(ynn) 1945- ... 115
Ivie, Robert M. 1930- ... 9-12R
Ivins, Molly 1944(?)- ... 138
Ivnev, Riurik
See Kovalev, Mikhail A(leksandrovich)
Ivo, Ledo 1924- ... CANR-65
Earlier sketch in CA 129
Ivory, James (Francis) 1928- ... 139
Brief entry ... 109
Ivory, Judith ... 163
Ivry, Alfred Lyon 1935- ... CANR-1
Earlier sketch in CA 45-48
Ivry, Benjamin 1958- ... 144
Ivy, Ralph 1938- ... 120
Iwamatsu, Jun Atsushi 1908-1994 ... CANR-45
Obituary ... 146
Earlier sketch in CA 73-76
See also Yashima, Taro
See also MAICYA
See also SATA 14, 81
Iwamura, Kazuo 1939- ... 129
Iwaniuk, Wactaw 1915- ... 130
Iwano Homei 1873-1920 ... DLB 180
Iwao, Sumiko 1935- ... 141
Iwasaki (Matsumoto), Chihiro 1918-1974 ... CLR 18
Iwaszkiewicz, Jaroslaw 1894-1980 Obituary . 97-100
Iwata, Masakazu 1917- ... 17-20R
Iyayi, Festus 1947- ... 161
See also DLB 157
Iyengar, B(ellur) K(rishnamachar) S(undararaja)
1918- ... 97-100
Iyengar, K(odaganallur) R(amaswami) Srinivasa
1908- ... CANR-8
Earlier sketch in CA 5-8R
Iyengar, S. Kesava 1894- ... 17-20R
Iyer, Pico 1957- ... 144
Iyer, Raghavan (Narasimhan) 1930-1995 . CANR-22
Obituary ... 149
Earlier sketches in CA 57-60, CANR-6
Izant, Grace Goulder 1893- ... CAP-1
Earlier sketch in CA 9-10
Izard, Barbara 1926- ... 29-32R
Izard, Carroll E(llis) 1923- ... CANR-4
Earlier sketch in CA 49-52
Izban, Samuel
See Isban, Samuel
Izenberg, Gerald N(athan) 1939- ... 105
Izenour, George Charles 1912- ... 93-96
Izumi Kyoka 1873-1920 ... DLB 180
Izzi, Eugene 1953(?)-1996 ... 144
Obituary ... 155
See also Izzi, Eugene
Izzo, Herbert J(ohn) 1928- ... 41-44R

J

J. L.-M.
See Lees-Milne, James
J. R. S.
See Gogarty, Oliver St. John
Jaanus, Maire 1940- ... CANR-45
Earlier sketch in CA 120
Jabavu, Davidson Don Tengo 1885-1959 ... 153
See also BW 2
Jabay, Earl 1925- ... 21-24R
Jabbar, Kareem Abdul
See Abdul-Jabbar, Kareem
Jabber, Fuad (Amin)
See Jabber, Paul
Jabber, Paul 1943- ... CANR-27
Earlier sketch in CA 113
Jaber, Diana Abu
See Abu-Jaber, Diana
Jabes, Edmond 1912-1991 ... 127
Obituary ... 133
Jabez
See Nicol, Eric (Patrick)
Jabine, Thomas B(oyd) 1925- ... 141
Jablokov, Alexander 1956- ... 142
Jablon, Howard 1939- ... 116
Jablonski, Edward 1922- ... CANR-18
Earlier sketches in CA 1-4R, CANR-2
Jablonski, Ronald E. 1929- Brief entry ... 104
Jablonsky, David 1938- ... 133
Jablow, Martha M(oraghan) 1944- ... CANR-43
Earlier sketch in CA 112
Jabran, Kahlil
See Gibran, Kahlil
Jabran, Khalil
See Gibran, Kahlil
Jabs, Carolyn 1950- ... 110
Jac, Cherlyn
See Biggs, Cheryl
Jac, Lee
See Morton, Lee Jack, Jr.
Jaccottet, Philippe 1925- ... 129
Brief entry ... 116
Jack, Dana Crowley 1945- ... 141
Jack, Daniel Thomson 1901-1984 Obituary ... 115
Jack, Donald Lamont 1924- ... CANR-3
Earlier sketch in CA 1-4R
Jack, Homer A(lexander) 1916-1993 ... CANR-14
Obituary ... 142
Earlier sketch in CA 41-44R
Jack, Ian 1923- ... 57-60
Jack, R. D. S.
See Jack, Ronald D(yce) S(adler)
Jack, R(obert) Ian 1935- ... CANR-3
Earlier sketch in CA 49-52
Jack, Ronald D(yce) S(adler) 1941- ... 120
Jacka, Martin 1943- ... SATA 72
Jackall, Robert ... 135
Jackendoff, Ray S. 1945- ... CANR-6
Earlier sketch in CA 53-56
Jacker, Corinne L(itvin) 1933- ... CANR-45
Earlier sketch in CA 17-20R
Jackins, Harvey 1916- ... CANR-37
Earlier sketches in CA 49-52, CANR-1, 17
Jackley, John L. 1955- ... 158
Jacklin, Anthony 1944- ... 85-88
Jacklin, Tony
See Jacklin, Anthony
Jackman, E(dwin) R(ussell) 1894-(?) ... CAP-1
Earlier sketch in CA 13-16
Jackman, Jarrell C(lark) 1943- ... 120
Jackman, Leslie (Arthur James) 1919- ... CANR-29
Earlier sketch in CA 29-32R
Jackman, Michael R. 1952- ... 120
Jackman, Robert W(illiam) 1946- ... CANR-51
Earlier sketch in CA 124
Jackman, Stuart 1922- ... CANR-18
Earlier sketch in CA 101
Jackman, Sydney W(ayne) 1925- ... CANR-19
Earlier sketches in CA 1-4R, CANR-1
Jackont, Amnon 1948- ... 130
Jackowska, Nicki 1942- ... 119
Jacks, L(awrence) P(earsall) 1860-1955 Brief
entry ... 113
See also DLB 135
Jacks, Oliver
See Gandley, Kenneth Royce
Jackson, A(lexander) B(rooks) 1925- ... 104
Jackson, Alan 1938- ... 101
Jackson, Albert 1943- ... 93-96
Jackson, Albina
See Geis, Richard E(rwin)
Jackson, Alison 1953- ... SATA 73
Jackson, Allan 1905(?)-1976 Obituary ... 65-68
Jackson, Angela 1951- ... DLB 41
Jackson, Anna J. 1926- ... 103
Jackson, Anne
See Jackson, Anna J.
Jackson, Anne 1896(?)-1984 ... SATA-Obit 37
Jackson, Anthony 1926- ... CANR-11
Earlier sketch in CA 69-72
Jackson, Archibald Stewart 1922- ... 61-64
Jackson, Arlene M(arjorie) 1938- ... 118
Jackson, Arthur 1921- Brief entry ... 104
Jackson, B(erkley) R. 1937- ... 25-28R
Jackson, Barbara (Ward) 1914-1981 ... CANR-6
Obituary ... 103
Earlier sketch in CA 45-48
Jackson, Barbara Garvey Seagrave 1929- .. 21-24R
Jackson, Basil 1920- ... CANR-8
Earlier sketch in CA 57-60
Jackson, Blyden 1910- ... 57-60
Jackson, Bo
See Jackson, Vincent Edward
Jackson, Brian 1933(?)-1983 Obituary ... 110
Jackson, Brooks 1941- ... 97-100
Jackson, Bruce 1936- ... 89-92
Jackson, C(hester) O(scar) 1901- ... CAP-1
Earlier sketch in CA 13-16
Jackson, C(aary) Paul 1902- ... CANR-6
Earlier sketch in CA 5-8R
See also SATA 6
Jackson, Caary
See Jackson, C(aary) Paul
Jackson, Carlton (Luther) 1933- ... 21-24R
Jackson, Carole ... 104
Jackson, Charles (Reginald) 1903-1968 ... 101
Obituary ... 25-28R
Jackson, Charles O. 1935- ... 126
Brief entry ... 112
Jackson, Charlotte E. (Cobden)
1903(?)-1989 Obituary ... 128
See also SATA-Obit 62
Jackson, Christine E(lisabeth) 1936- ... CANR-47
Earlier sketch in CA 121
Jackson, Clarence J.-L.
See Bulliet, Richard W(illiams)
Jackson, Daniel
See Wingrove, David (John)
Jackson, Dave
See Jackson, J. David
Jackson, David Cooper 1931- ... 109
Jackson, Derrick 1939- ... 77-80
Jackson, Diane 1938- ... 115
Jackson, Don(ald) D(e Avila) 1920-1968 ... CAP-1
Earlier sketch in CA 11-12
Jackson, Donald (Dean) 1919-1987 ... 17-20R
Obituary ... 124
Jackson, Donald Dale 1935- ... CANR-19
Earlier sketches in CA 49-52, CANR-1
Jackson, Dorothy Virginia Steinhauer 1924- . 13-16R
Jackson, Douglas N. 1929- ... 37-40R
Jackson, E. F.
See Tubb, E(dwin) C(harles)
Jackson, Edgar (Newman) 1910- ... CANR-29
Earlier sketches in CA 77-80, CANR-13
Jackson, Elaine
See Freeman, Gillian
Jackson, Ellen B. 1943- ... 110
See also SATA 75
Jackson, Elmore 1910- ... 112
Jackson, Esther Merle 1922- ... 13-16R
Jackson, Eve 1943- ... 163
Jackson, Everatt
See Muggeson, Margaret Elizabeth
Jackson, Frank 1951- ... 120
Jackson, Franklin Jefferson
See Watkins, Mel
Jackson, G. Mark 1952- ... 132
Jackson, Gabriel 1921- ... 21-24R
Jackson, Gabriele Bernhard 1934- ... 29-32R
Jackson, Garnet Nelson 1944- ... SATA 87
Jackson, Geoffrey (Holt Seymour) 1915-1987 . 61-64
Obituary ... 123
See also SATA-Obit 53
Jackson, George (Lester) 1941-1971 ... 120
Obituary ... 111
See also BW 1
Jackson, George D. 1929- ... 81-84
Jackson, George S(tuyvesant) 1906-1976 .. CAP-1
Obituary ... 61-64
Earlier sketch in CA 17-18
Jackson, Gordon 1934- ... 104
Jackson, Graham 1949- ... 112
Jackson, Guida M. 1930- ... CANR-37
Earlier sketches in CA 93-96, CANR-16
See also SATA 71
Jackson, Harvey H(ardaway III) 1943- ... 119
Jackson, Helen Hunt 1830-1885 .. DLB 42, 47, 186,
189
Jackson, Henry 1912-1988 Obituary ... 126
Jackson, Henry F. 1939-1991 ... 129
Obituary ... 135
Jackson, Henry Martin 1912-1983 Obituary ... 110
Jackson, Herbert C(ross) 1917- ... 9-12R
Jackson, Herbert G., Jr. 1928- ... 37-40R
Jackson, Holbrook 1874-1948 ... DLB 98
Jackson, Innes
See Herdan, Innes
Jackson, J. David 1944- ... CANR-57
Earlier sketches in CA 81-84, CANR-18
See also SATA 91
Jackson, J. P.
See Atkins, (Arthur) Harold
Jackson, J(ames) R(obert) de J(ager) 1935- ... 146
Jackson, Jacqueline 1928- ... 45-48
See also SATA 65
Jackson, Jacquelyne Johnson 1932- ... 37-40R
Jackson, James Charles 1936-1979 ... 163
Obituary ... 117
Jackson, James P(ierre) 1925- ... CANR-14
Earlier sketch in CA 77-80
Jackson, Jay W. 1961- ... 139
Jackson, Jesse 1908-1983 ... CANR-27
Obituary ... 109
Earlier sketch in CA 25-28R
See also BW 1
See also CLC 12
See also CLR 28
See also MAICYA
See also SATA 2, 29
See also SATA-Obit 48
Jackson, John A. 1943- ... 138
Jackson, John Archer 1929- ... 13-16R
Jackson, John E(dgar) 1942- ... 101
Jackson, John Howard 1932- ... 41-44R
Jackson, John N(icholas) 1925- ... CANR-57
Earlier sketches in CA 37-40R, CANR-14, 31
Jackson, Jon A(nthony) 1938- ... CANR-71
Earlier sketch in CA 81-84
Jackson, Jonathan (Charles) 1966- ... 116
Jackson, Joseph 1924-1987 ... CANR-11
Obituary ... 122
Earlier sketches in CAP-1, CA 9-10
Jackson, Joseph Hollister 1912- ... 120
Jackson, Joy J(uanita) 1928- ... 29-32R
Jackson, Julia A(ndreasen) 1939- ... 119
Jackson, Karl (Dion) 1942- ... 102
Jackson, Katherine Gauss
1904-1975 Obituary ... 57-60
Jackson, Kathy Merlock 1955- ... 145
Jackson, (William) Keith 1928- ... CANR-8
Earlier sketch in CA 61-64
Jackson, Kenneth T. 1939- ... 21-24R
Jackson, Kevin 1955- ... 147
Jackson, Kevin Goldstein
See Goldstein-Jackson, Kevin
Jackson, Laura (Riding) 1901-1991 ... CANR-28
Obituary ... 135
Earlier sketch in CA 65-68
See also Riding, Laura
See also DLB 48
Jackson, Livia Bitton
See Bitton Jackson, Livia E(lvira)
Jackson, Louise A(llen) 1937- ... 93-96
Jackson, Lowell G(eorge) 1934- ... 118
Jackson, Lucille
See Strauss, (Mary) Lucille Jackson
Jackson, Lydia 1900(?)-1983 Obituary ... 110
Jackson, MacDonald P. 1938- ... CANR-51
Earlier sketch in CA 125
Jackson, Mae 1946- ... 81-84
Jackson, Mahalia 1901-1972 Obituary ... 33-36R
Jackson, Margaret Weymouth
1895-1974 Obituary ... 115
See also AITN 1
Jackson, Marian J. A.
See Rogers, Marian H.
Jackson, Mark
See Kurz, Ron
Jackson, Marni 1946- ... 149
Jackson, Martin A(lan) 1941- ... 89-92
Jackson, Mary 1924- ... 61-64
Jackson, Melvin H. 1914(?)-1983 Obituary ... 111
Jackson, Michael P. 1947- ... 125
Jackson, Mike 1946- ... 155
See also SATA 91
Jackson, Miles M(errill) 1929- ... 41-44R
Jackson, Neta J. 1944- ... CANR-57
Earlier sketches in CA 89-92, CANR-18
See also SATA 91
Jackson, Neville
See Glaskin, G(erald) M(arcus)
Jackson, Nora
See Tennant, Nora Jackson
Jackson, Norman 1932- ... CANR-17
Earlier sketch in CA 25-28R
Jackson, O. B.
See Jackson, C(aary) Paul
Jackson, Paul R. 1905- ... CAP-1
Earlier sketch in CA 13-16
Jackson, Percival Ephrates 1891-1970 ... CANR-3
Earlier sketch in CA 1-4R
Jackson, Philip W(esley) 1928- ... 21-24R
Jackson, R. E.
See Innes, Rosemary E(lizabeth Jackson)
Jackson, R(ichard) Eugene 1941- ... CANR-51
Earlier sketches in CA 109, CANR-28

Jackson, R(ichard) W(illiam) 1939- 119
Jackson, Reggie
See Jackson, Reginald Martinez
Jackson, Reginald Martinez 1946- Brief entry .. 112
Jackson, Richard 1946- 110
Jackson, Richard A(rlen) 1937- 125
Jackson, Robert 1911- 9-12R
Jackson, Robert B(lake) 1926- CANR-6
Earlier sketch in CA 5-8R
See also SATA 8
Jackson, Robert H. 1955- 148
Jackson, Robert J. 1936- 25-28R
Jackson, Robert L(owell) 1935- 73-76
Jackson, Robert Louis 1923- 109
Jackson, Robert S(umner) 1926- 29-32R
Jackson, Ruth A. 45-48
Jackson, Sally
See Kellogg, Jean (Defrees)
Jackson, Sam
See Trumbo, Dalton
Jackson, Sara
See Thomas, Sara (Sally)
and Wingrove, David (John)
Jackson, Scoop
See Jackson, Henry Martin
Jackson, Sheneska 1970(?)- 163
Jackson, Shirley 1919-1965 .... CANR-52
Obituary 25-28R
Earlier sketches in CA 1-4R, CANR-4
See also AAYA 9
See also CDALB 1941-1968
See also CLC 11, 60, 87
See also DA
See also DAC
See also DAM MST
See also DLB 6
See also SATA 2
See also SSC 9
See also WLC
Jackson, Stanley W(ebber) 1920- 124
Jackson, Stephanie
See Werner, Vivian
Jackson, Teague 1938- 93-96
Jackson, Vincent Edward 1962- 141
Jackson, W. A. Douglas
See Jackson, William Arthur Douglas
Jackson, W(illiam) G(odfrey) F(othergill)
1917- 25-28R
Jackson, W(illiam) T(homas) H(obdell) 1915-1983 ..
CANR-1
Obituary 117
Earlier sketch in CA 1-4R
Jackson, W(illiam) Turrentine 1915- 13-16R
Jackson, Wallace 1930- 114
Jackson, Wes 1936- CANR-22
Earlier sketches in CA 49-52, CANR-3
Jackson, William Arthur Douglas 1923- .. CANR-28
Earlier sketch in CA 45-48
Jackson, William J(oseph) 1943- 139
Jackson, William M. 1936- 151
Jackson, William Vernon 1926- CANR-13
Earlier sketch in CA 21-24R
Jackson, Wilma 1929- CANR-12
Earlier sketch in CA 73-76
Jackson, Woody 1948- .... SATA 92
Jackson-Haight, Mabel V. 1912- 25-28R
Jaco, E(gbert) Gartly 1923- CANR-1
Earlier sketch in CA 1-4R
Jacob, Alaric 1909- 5-8R
Jacob, Charles E. 1931- CANR-5
Earlier sketch in CA 13-16R
Jacob, Ernest Fraser 1894-1971 .... CANR-3
Earlier sketch in CA 1-4R
Jacob, Francois 1920- 102
Jacob, Fred E. 1899- 105
Jacob, Gordon (Percival Septimus)
1895-1984 Obituary 113
Jacob, Helen Pierce 1927- 69-72
See also SATA 21
Jacob, Herbert 1933- 77-80
Jacob, J. R.
See Jacob, James R.
Jacob, James R. 1940- 132
Jacob, John 1950- CANR-53
Earlier sketch in CA 126
Jacob, Joseph M. 1943- 166
Jacob, Margaret C(andee) 1943- CANR-37
Earlier sketches in CA 65-68, CANR-16
Jacob, (Cyprien-)Max 1876-1944 Brief entry ... 104
See also TCLC 6
Jacob, Merle (Lynn) 1945- 152
Jacob, Nancy L. 1943- 29-32R
Jacob, Naomi Ellington 1884(?)-1964 Obituary . 115
See also DLB 191
Jacob, Paul 1940- 103
Jacob, Philip E(rnest) 1914- CANR-4
Earlier sketch in CA 53-56
Jacobi, Carl (Richard) 1908-1997 .... CAP-1
Obituary 160
Earlier sketch in CA 13-14
Jacobi, Friedrich Heinrich 1743-1819 ...... DLB 94
Jacobi, Johann Georg 1740-1814 .... DLB 97
Jacobi, Jolande (Szekacs) 1890- 9-12R
Jacobi, Kathy .... SATA-Brief 42
Jacobowitz, Ellen 1948- 121
Jacobs, Al(bert T.) 1903-1985 Obituary 115
Jacobs, Arthur (David) 1922-1996 .... CANR-21
Obituary 155
Earlier sketches in CA 5-8R, CANR-4
Jacobs, Barbara 1947- 148
Jacobs, Barry (Douglas) 1932- 101
Jacobs, Bradford (McElderry) 1920- 121
Jacobs, Clyde E(dward) 1925- 37-40R
Jacobs, Dan(iel) N(orman) 1924- CANR-4
Earlier sketch in CA 5-8R
Jacobs, David Michael 1942- 57-60
Jacobs, Diane 1948- 73-76
Jacobs, Donald M(artin) 1937- 110
Jacobs, Flora Gill 1918- CANR-21
Earlier sketch in CA 1-4R
See also SATA 5
Jacobs, Francine 1935- CANR-18
Earlier sketches in CA 49-52, CANR-1
See also SATA 43
See also SATA-Brief 42
Jacobs, Frank 1929- CANR-6
Earlier sketch in CA 13-16R
See also SATA 30
Jacobs, G(enevieve) Walker 1948- 49-52
Jacobs, Garry (Lawrence) 1946- 120
Jacobs, Glenn 1940- 29-32R
Jacobs, Harold 1941- 45-48
Jacobs, Harvey (Collins) 1915- 21-24R
Jacobs, Harvey 1930- 29-32R
Jacobs, Hayes B(enjamin) 1919- 9-12R
Jacobs, Helen Hull 1908-1997 .... 9-12R
Obituary 159
See also SATA 12
Jacobs, Herbert (Austin) 1903-1987 .... 13-16R
Obituary 122
Jacobs, Howard 1908- 65-68
Jacobs, Jack L. 1953- 142
Jacobs, James B. 1947- CANR-39
Earlier sketches in CA 101, CANR-18
Jacobs, Jane 1916- CANR-15
Earlier sketch in CA 21-24R
Jacobs, Jerome L. 1931- 89-92
Jacobs, Jerry 1932- CANR-11
Earlier sketch in CA 29-32R
Jacobs, Jill
See Bharti, Ma Satya
Jacobs, Jim 1942- 97-100
Interview in 97-100
See also CLC 12
Jacobs, John (Kedzie) 1918- 21-24R
Jacobs, Jonnie 159
Jacobs, Joseph 1854-1916 136
Brief entry 111
See also DLB 141
See also MAICYA
See also SATA 25
Jacobs, Judy 1952- 137
See also SATA 69
Jacobs, Laurence Wile 1939- 53-56
Jacobs, Laurie A. 1956- .... SATA 89
Jacobs, Leah
See Gellis, Roberta L(eah Jacobs)
Jacobs, Leland Blair 1907-1992 73-76
Obituary 137
See also SATA 20
See also SATA-Obit 71
Jacobs, Lewis 1906-1997 77-80
Obituary 156
Jacobs, Linda
See Altman, Linda Jacobs
Jacobs, Lou(is), Jr. 1921- CANR-9
Earlier sketch in CA 21-24R
See also SATA 2
Jacobs, Louis 1920- CANR-38
Earlier sketches in CA 1-4R, CANR-1, 17
Jacobs, Melville 1902-1971 ....1-4R
Obituary 103
Jacobs, Michael (Stephen) 1955- 123
Jacobs, Michael T. 1958- 139
Jacobs, Milton 1920- 37-40R
Jacobs, Nehama 1951- 126
Jacobs, Norman (Gabriel) 1924- 77-80
Jacobs, Paul 1918-1978 ....13-16R
Obituary 73-76
Jacobs, Pepita Jimenez 1932- 17-20R
Jacobs, Philip E. 1914(?)-1985 Obituary 116
Jacobs, Renee 1962- 125
Jacobs, Robert D(urene) 1918- 41-44R
Jacobs, Roderick A(rnold) 1934- 21-24R
Jacobs, Ruth Harriet 1924- CANR-33
Earlier sketches in CA 89-92, CANR-15
Jacobs, Shannon K. 1947- 145
See also SATA 77
Jacobs, Sheldon 1931- 106
Jacobs, Sophia Yarnall 1902-1993 106
Obituary 141
Jacobs, Sue-Ellen 1936- 111
Jacobs, Susan
See Quinn, Susan
See also SATA 30
Jacobs, T. C. H.
See Pendower, Jacques
Jacobs, Travis Beal 1936- Brief entry 113
Jacobs, Vernon K(enneth) 1936- CANR-41
Earlier sketch in CA 117
Jacobs, Vivian 1916(?)-1981 Obituary 103
Jacobs, W(illiam) W(ymark) 1863-1943 167
Brief entry 121
See also DLB 135
See also TCLC 22
Jacobs, Walter Darnell 1922- 17-20R
Jacobs, Wilbur R(ipley) 1918- 13-16R
Jacobs, William Jay 1933- CANR-57
Earlier sketches in CA 57-60, CANR-7
See also SATA 28, 89
Jacobsen, Douglas G. 1951- 141
Jacobsen, Hans Jacob 1901-1987 Obituary 122
Jacobsen, Josephine 1908- CANR-48
Earlier sketches in CA 33-36R, CANR-23
See also CAAS 18
See also CLC 48, 102
Jacobsen, K(enneth) C. 1939- 133
Jacobsen, Lydik S. 1897(?)-1976 Obituary ... 69-72
Jacobsen, Lyle E. 1929- 13-16R
Jacobsen, Marion Leach 1908- 61-64
Jacobsen, O(le) Irving 1896- CAP-2
Earlier sketch in CA 25-28
Jacobsen, Phebe R(obinson) 1922- 73-76
Jacobsen, Thorkild 1904- Brief entry 105
Jacobsohn, Gary J. 1946- 89-92
Jacobson, Bernard Isaac 1936- 109
Jacobson, Beverly 1927- 113
Jacobson, Boyd 1942- 118
Jacobson, Cliff 1940- 85-88
Jacobson, Dan 1929- CANR-66
Earlier sketches in CA 1-4R, CANR-2, 25
See also CLC 4, 14
See also DLB 14
See also MTCW 1
Jacobson, Daniel 1923- 53-56
See also SATA 12
Jacobson, David B(ernard) 1928- 53-56
Jacobson, Edith 1897(?)-1978 Obituary 85-88
Jacobson, Edmund 1888- 9-12R
Jacobson, Ethel 37-40R
Jacobson, Frederick L(awrence) 1938- 49-52
Jacobson, Gary Charles 1944- 109
Jacobson, Gerald F. 1922-1987 Obituary 123
Jacobson, Harold Karan 1929- CANR-19
Earlier sketches in CA 9-12R, CANR-3
Jacobson, Helen S(altz) 1921- CANR-6
Earlier sketch in CA 57-60
Jacobson, Howard Boone 1925- 1-4R
Jacobson, Joanne 1952- 144
Jacobson, Jon 1938- 61-64
Jacobson, Julius 1922- 45-48
Jacobson, Marcia 1941- 115
Jacobson, Mark 1948- 136
Jacobson, Matthew Frye 1958- 156
Jacobson, Michael F. 1943- CANR-13
Earlier sketch in CA 77-80
Jacobson, Morris K(arl) 1906- CANR-3
Earlier sketch in CA 45-48
See also SATA 21
Jacobson, Nils Olof 1937- Brief entry 110
Jacobson, Nolan Pliny 1909- CANR-23
Earlier sketches in CA 21-24R, CANR-8
Jacobson, Robert (Marshall) 1940-1987 89-92
Obituary 122
Jacobson, Rodolfo 1915- 41-44R
Jacobson, Sheldon A(lbert) 1903- 37-40R
Jacobson, Sibyl C(hafer) 1942- 65-68
Jacobson, Stephen A. 1934- 97-100
Jacobson, Steve
See Jacobson, Stephen A.
Jacobstein, J(oseph) Myron 1920- 53-56
Jacobus, Donald L(ines) 1887-1970 ...... CANR-4
Earlier sketch in CA 5-8R
Jacobus, Elaine Wegener 1908- 33-36R
Jacobus, Lee A. 1935- CANR-57
Earlier sketches in CA 33-36R, CANR-13, 30
Jacobus, Mary 1944- 105
Jacoby, Henry 1905- 77-80
Jacoby, Joseph E. 1944- 97-100
Jacoby, Neil H(erman) 1909-1979 .... CANR-10
Obituary 89-92
Earlier sketch in CA 21-24R
Jacoby, Oswald 1902-1984 107
Obituary 113
Jacoby, Russell 1945- CANR-42
Earlier sketches in CA 77-80, CANR-15
Jacoby, Sidney B(ernard) 1908-1990 Obituary . 130
Jacoby, Stephen M(ichael) 1940- 57-60
Jacoby, Susan 108
Jacopetti, Alexandra
See Hart, Alexandra
See also SATA 14
Jacot, B. L.
See Jacot de Boinod, Bernard Louis
Jacot, Michael 1924- 104
Jacot de Boinod, Bernard Louis 1898-1977 .. 9-12R
Obituary 77-80
Jacoway, Elizabeth 1944- 110
Jacqueline
See Carpentier (y Valmont), Alejo
Jacqueney, Mona G(raubart) 41-44R
Jacqueney, Theodore 1943(?)-1979 Obituary .89-92
Jacques, Beau
See House, R(ichard) C(alvin)
Jacques, Brian 1939- CANR-68
Earlier sketch in CA 127
See also AAYA 20
See also CLR 21
See also JRDA
See also SATA 62, 95
Jacques, David (Lawson) 1948- 123
Jacques, Edwin E. 1908- 151
Jacques, Robin 1920-1995 .... MAICYA
See also SAAS 5
See also SATA 32
See also SATA-Brief 30
See also SATA-Obit 86
Jacquet, Constant Herbert, Jr. 1925- 106
Jade, Jacqueline
See Hyman, Jackie (Diamond)
Jaded Observer
See Zolf, Larry
Jados, Stanley S. 1912-1977 .... 33-36R
Jaeck, Lois Marie 1946- 137
Jaediker, Kermit 1912(?)-1986 Obituary 118
Jaeger, Cyril Karel Stuart 1912- 1-4R
Jaeger, Edmund C(arroll) 1887-1983 .... CAP-2
Obituary 110
Earlier sketch in CA 23-24
Jaeger, Harry J., Jr. 1919(?)-1979 Obituary .. 85-88
Jaeger, Lorenz Cardinal 1892-1975 Obituary . 57-60
Jaeger, Walter H(enry) E(dward)
1902(?)-1982 Obituary 108
Jaeggy, Fleur 166
Jaekel, Susan M. 1948- ....SATA 89
Jaen, Didier Tisdel 1933- 29-32R
Jaenen, Cornelius John 1927- CANR-15
Earlier sketch in CA 85-88
Jaffa, George
See Wallace-Clarke, George
Jaffa, Harry V(ictor) 1918- 33-36R
Jaffe, A(bram) J. 1912-1997 ....5-8R
Obituary 163
Jaffe, Aniela 1903- 125
Jaffe, Bernard 1896-1986 ....5-8R
Obituary 121
Jaffe, Betsy
See Jaffe, Elizabeth Latimer
Jaffe, Dan 1933- CANR-17
Earlier sketch in CA 25-28R
Jaffe, David 1911-1990 Obituary 131
Jaffe, Dennis T(heodore) 1946- CANR-32
Earlier sketches in CA 89-92, CANR-15
Jaffe, Elizabeth Latimer 1935- 135
Jaffe, Elsa
See Bartlett, Elsa Jaffe
Jaffe, Eugene D. 1937- 37-40R
Jaffe, Frederick S. 1925-1978 .... CANR-5
Earlier sketch in CA 9-12R
Jaffe, Gabriel Vivian 1923- 13-16R
Jaffe, H. L. C.
See Jaffe, Hans L(udwig) C.
Jaffe, Hans L(udwig) C. 1915-1984 144
Jaffe, Harold 1940- CANR-30
Earlier sketch in CA 29-32R
Jaffe, Hilde 1927- 105
Jaffe, Irma B(lumenthal) CANR-1
Earlier sketch in CA 45-48
Jaffe, Joseph 1924- Brief entry 113
Jaffe, Lorna S. 1941- 128
Jaffe, Louis Leventhal 1905-1996 ....21-24R
Obituary 155
Jaffe, (Andrew) Michael 1923-1997 .... 21-24R
Obituary 159
Jaffe, Nora Crow 1944- 106
Jaffe, Rona 1932- CANR-57
Earlier sketches in CA 73-76, CANR-24
Interview in CANR-24
See also AITN 1
See also BEST 90:3
See also MTCW 1
Jaffe, Sam(uel Adason) 1929(?)-1985 Obituary . 115
Jaffe, Sandra Sohn 1943- 101
Jaffe, Sherril 1945- CANR-19
Earlier sketch in CA 103
Jaffe, William 1898-1980 57-60
Obituary 122
Jaffee, Al(lan) 1921- 135
Brief entry 116
See also SATA 37, 66
Jaffee, Annette Williams 1945- 131
Jaffee, Dwight M. 1943- 57-60
Jaffee, Mary L.
See Lindsley, Mary F(rances)
Jaffin, David 1937- CANR-34
Earlier sketches in CA 65-68, CANR-15
Jaffrey, Zia 159
Jafree, Mohammed Jawaid Iqbal 1939- 164
Jagel, Beatrice Hawley 1944(?)-1985 Obituary . 116
Jagendorf, Moritz (Adolf) 1888-1981 .... 5-8R
Obituary 102
See also SATA 2
See also SATA-Obit 24
Jager, Okke 1928- CANR-23
Earlier sketches in CA 61-64, CANR-8
Jager, Ronald (Albert) 1932- 41-44R
Jaggard, Geoffrey (William) 1902-1970 ..... CAP-2
Earlier sketch in CA 21-22
Jaggard, William fl. 1591-1623 .... DLB 170
Jagger, Brenda 1936-1986 167
Jagger, John Hubert 1880- CAP-1
Earlier sketch in CA 9-10
Jagger, Mick 1944- ....CLC 17
Jagger, Peter (John) 1938- CANR-21
Earlier sketch in CA 103
Jaglom, Henry 1941- CANR-55
Earlier sketch in CA 127
Jagninski, Tom 1935- 137
Jagoda, Robert 1923- 73-76
Jahan, Rounaq 1944- CANR-29
Earlier sketch in CA 49-52
Jaher, Frederic Cople 1934- 9-12R
Jahier, Piero 1884-1966 .... DLB 114
Jahn, Ernst A(dalbert) 1929- 69-72
Jahn, Janheinz 1918-1973 Obituary 111
Jahn, Joseph C. 1914(?)-1984 Obituary 113
Jahn, Joseph Michael 1943- CANR-5
Earlier sketch in CA 49-52
See also SATA 28
Jahn, Melvin E(dward) 1938- 9-12R
Jahn, Michael
See Jahn, Joseph Michael
Jahn, Mike
See Jahn, Joseph Michael
Jahn-Clough, Lisa 1967- .... SATA 88
Jahnn, Hans Henny 1894-1959 .... DLB 56, 124
Jahoda, Gloria (Adelaide Love) 1926-1980 ....
CANR-4
Obituary 104
Earlier sketch in CA 1-4R
See also AITN 1
Jahoda, Gustav 1920- 135
Brief entry 114
Jahsmann, Allan Hart 1916- 106
See also SATA 28
Jaimes, M. Annette 1946- 137
Jaimes Freyre, Ricardo 1868-1933 ....HW
Jain, Girilal 1923-1993 .... 9-12R
Obituary 142
Jain, Rajendra K. 1951- 134
Jain, Ravindra Kumar 1937- 29-32R
Jain, Sagar C. 1930- CANR-10
Earlier sketch in CA 25-28R

Jain, Sharad Chandra 1933- ... CANR-21
Earlier sketch in CA 25-28R
Jaini, Padmanabh S. 1923- ... 103
Jaivin, Linda 1955- ... 139
Jakes, John (William) 1932- ... CANR-66
Earlier sketches in CA 57-60, CANR-10, 43
Interview in ... CANR-10
See also BEST 89:4
See also CLC 29
See also DAM NOV, POP
See also DLBY 83
See also MTCW 1
See also SATA 62
Jakle, John Allais 1939- ... 107
Jakobovits, Immanuel 1921- ... 108
Jakobovits, Leon Alex 1938- ... 25-28R
Jakobson, Michael 1939- ... 146
Jakobson, Roman 1896-1982 ... CANR-31
Obituary ... 107
Earlier sketch in CA 77-80
Jaksch, Wenzel 1896-1966 ... CAP-1
Earlier sketch in CA 13-14
Jaksic, Ivan (Andrades) 1954- ... 141
Jakubauskas, Edward B(enedict) 1930- ... 57-60
Jakubowski, Patricia (Ann) 1941- ... 65-68
Jalan, Edi Lee
See Stivender, Ed
Jalata, Asafa 1954- ... 149
Jalland, Pat(ricia) 1941- ... 133
Jalongo, Mary Renck 1950- ... 166
Jamba, Sousa 1966- ... 134
James, Alan Geoffrey 1943- ... 104
James, Allen
See Allen, James L(ovic), Jr.
James, Amalia
See Neggers, Carla A(malia)
James, Andrew
See Kirkup, James
James, Ann 1952- ... SATA 82
James, Anne Eleanor Scott
See Scott-James, Anne Eleanor
James, Anthony
See Hanna, David
James, (Eliot) Antony Brett
See Brett-James, (Eliot) Antony
James, Bernard (Joseph) 1922- Brief entry ... 110
James, Bessie (Williams) Rowland 1895-1974 ... 107
James, Bill
See James, George W(illiam)
James, Bronte
See Nash, Renea Denise
James, Bruno S(cott) 1906- ... 5-8R
James, (David) Burnett (Stephen) 1919-1987 ... 5-8R
Obituary ... 122
James, C. B.
See Coover, James B(urrell)
James, C(yril) L(ionel) R(obert) 1901-1989 ...
CANR-62
Obituary ... 128
Brief entry ... 117
Earlier sketch in CA 125
See also BLCS
See also BW 2
See also CLC 33
See also DLB 125
See also MTCW 1
James, C. W.
See Cumes, J(ames) W(illiam) C(rawford)
James, Captain Lew
See Stratemeyer, Edward L.
James, Cary A(mory) 1935- ... 29-32R
James, Charles J(oseph) 1944- ... CANR-5
Earlier sketch in CA 53-56
James, Charles L(yman) 1934- ... 29-32R
James, Clive (Vivian Leopold) 1939- ... 128
Brief entry ... 105
See also DAM POP
See also MTCW 1
James, Coy Hilton 1915- ... 103
James, Cy
See Watts, Peter Christopher
James, D(orris) Clayton 1931- ... 29-32R
James, D(avid) G(wilym) 1905-1968 ... CANR-4
Earlier sketch in CA 1-4R
James, Daniel (Lewis) 1911-1988 Obituary ... 125
See also Santiago, Danny
James, David
See Hagberg, David J(ames)
James, David 1955- ... 119
James, David N. 1952- ... 140
James, David W(illiam) 1910- ... 128
James, Deana
See Sizer, Mona Young
James, Denise ... 29-32R
James, Diana
See Gunn, Diana Maureen
James, Don(ald H.) 1905- ... CANR-2
Earlier sketch in CA 1-4R
James, Dorothy Buckton 1937- Brief entry ... 109
James, Dynely
See Mayne, William (James Carter)
James, Edgar C. 1933- ... CANR-5
Earlier sketch in CA 13-16R
James, Edward
See Masur, Harold Q.
James, Edward (Frank Willis)
1907-1984 Obituary ... 115
James, Edward T(opping) 1917- ... 33-36R
James, Edwin
See Gunn, James E(dwin)
James, Edwin Oliver 1889-1972 ... CAP-1
Earlier sketch in CA 13-16
James, Eleanor 1912- ... 41-44R
James, Elizabeth 1942- ... 121
See also SATA 39, 45, 52, 97
James, Emily
See Standiford, Natalie
James, Eric Arthur 1925- ... CAP-1
Earlier sketch in CA 9-10
James, Estelle 1935- ... 37-40R
James, F(rank) Cyril 1903-1973 Obituary ... 114
James, Fleming, Jr. 1904- ... CAP-1
Earlier sketch in CA 17-18
James, Frederick
See Martin, William
James, Gene Gray 1934- ... 114
James, George P. R. 1801-1828 ... DLB 116
James, George W(illiam) 1949- ... CANR-35
Earlier sketch in CA 109
James, H(enry) Thomas 1915- ... 25-28R
James, Harold 1956- ... 127
James, Harry Clebourne 1896-1978 ... CANR-4
Earlier sketch in CA 5-8R
See also SATA 11
James, Heather 1914- ... CANR-31
Earlier sketch in CA 45-48
James, Henry 1843-1916 ... 132
Brief entry ... 104
See also CDALB 1865-1917
See also DA
See also DAB
See also DAC
See also DAM MST, NOV
See also DLB 12, 71, 74, 189
See also DLBD 13
See also MTCW 1
See also SSC 8
See also TCLC 2, 11, 24, 40, 47, 64
See also WLC
James, Howard (Anthony, Jr.) 1935- Brief
entry ... 111
James, Hunter 1932- ... 114
James, J. Alison 1962- ... SATA 83
James, Jamie ... 163
James, Jean Rosemary Haughton
See Haughton-James, Jean Rosemary
James, (David) John ... CANR-43
Earlier sketch in CA 45-48
James, John 1633(?)-1729 ... DLB 24
James, Josef C. 1916(?)-1973 Obituary ... 45-48
James, Joseph B. 1912- ... 17-20R
James, Josephine
See Sterne, Emma Gelders
James, Judith
See Jennings, Leslie Nelson
James, Kelvin Christopher ... 138
James, Kristin
See Camp, Candace (Pauline)
James, Laurie 1930- ... 163
James, Leigh Franklin
See Little, Paul H(ugo)
James, Leonard F(rank) 1904- ... 49-52
James, Lloyd E.
See Laughlin, Tom
James, (William) Louis (Gabriel) ... CANR-6
Earlier sketch in CA 13-16R
James, Luther 1928- ... 153
See also BW 2
James, M. R.
See James, Montague (Rhodes)
See also DLB 156
James, M. R. 1940- ... 57-60
James, Margaret
See Bennetts, Pamela
James, Marlise Ann 1945- ... 57-60
James, Marquis 1891-1955 ... 144
James, Martin
See Kisner, James (Martin, Jr.)
James, Mary
See Meaker, Marijane (Agnes)
James, Matthew
See Lucey, James D(ennis)
James, Michael 1922(?)-1981 Obituary ... 104
James, Monica
See Nonhebel, Clare
James, Montague (Rhodes) 1862-1936 Brief
entry ... 104
See also DLB 201
See also SSC 16
See also TCLC 6
James, Muriel ... 85-88
James, Naomi 1949- ... 102
James, Noel David Glaves 1911- ... 107
James, Norah C(ordner) (?)-1979 ... CANR-59
Earlier sketch in CA 29-32R
James, P. D. 1920-
See White, Phyllis Dorothy James
See also BEST 90:2
See also CDBLB 1960 to Present
See also CLC 18, 46
See also DLB 87
See also DLBD 17
James, Paul
See Warburg, James Paul
James, Paul 1921- ... 125
James, Peter 1948- ... 163
James, Peter N. 1940- ... 57-60
James, Philip
See del Rey, Lester
and Moorcock, Michael (John)
James, Philip S(eaforth) 1914- ... CAP-1
Earlier sketch in CA 9-10
James, Preston
See Fearn, John Russell
James, Preston E(verett) 1899-1986 ... CANR-29
Earlier sketch in CA 45-48
James, Rebecca
See Elward, James (Joseph)
James, Robert A. 1946-1983 Obituary ... 109
James, Robert C(larke) 1918- ... 5-8R
James, Robert Leigh 1918- ... 161
James, Robert (Vidal) Rhodes
See Rhodes James, Robert (Vidal)
James, Robin
See Curtis, Sharon
James, Robin (Irene) 1953- ... 126
See also SATA 50
James, Ronald
See Preston, James
James, Russell 1942- ... 137
James, Sibyl 1946- ... 142
James, Simon
See Kunen, James Simon
James, Stanton
See Flemming, Nicholas Coit
James, Stephanie
See Krentz, Jayne Ann
James, Susan
See Griffin, Arthur J.
James, Sydney V(incent, Jr.) 1929- ... CANR-21
Earlier sketch in CA 1-4R
James, Thelma Gray 1899-1988 ... 5-8R
Obituary ... 124
James, Theodore, Jr. 1934- ... 33-36R
James, Theodore E(arle) 1913- ... 57-60
James, Thomas N.
See Neal, James T(homas)
James, Thurston 1933- ... 142
James, Trevor
See Constable, Trevor James
James, Vanessa
See Beauman, Sally
James, W(illiam) Martin (III) 1952- ... 143
James, (Arthur) Walter 1912- ... 5-8R
James, Walter S.
See Sheldon, Walter J.
James, Warren A. 1960- ... 133
James, Warren E(dward) 1922- ... 45-48
James, Weldon (Bernard) 1912- ... 1-4R
James, Will(iam Roderick) 1892-1942 ... 137
See also DLBD 16
See also MAICYA
See also SATA 19
James, William
See Craddock, William J(ames)
James, William 1842-1910 Brief entry ... 109
See also TCLC 15, 32
James, William C(losson) 1943- ... 126
James, William M.
See Harknett, Terry
and Harvey, John (Barton)
James, William Milbourne 1881- ... CAP-1
Earlier sketch in CA 11-12
James, Wilma Roberts 1905- ... 105
James, Wilmot G. 1953- ... 138
Jameson, Anna 1794-1860 ... DLB 99, 166
Jameson, Eric
See Trimmer, Eric J.
Jameson, Fredric 1934- ... DLB 67
Jameson, J. Franklin 1859-1937 ... DLB 17
Jameson, Judith
See Neyland, James (Elwyn)
Jameson, Kenneth (Ambrose) 1913- ... 77-80
Jameson, Kenneth P(eter) 1942- ... 112
Jameson, Sam 1936- ... 136
Jameson, Samuel H(aig) 1896- ... 45-48
Jameson, (Margaret) Storm 1891-1986 ... CANR-47
Obituary ... 120
Earlier sketch in CA 81-84
See also DLB 36
Jameson, Vic(tor Loyd) 1924- ... 17-20R
Jameson, W. C. 1942- ... 158
See also SATA 93
James VI of Scotland 1566-1625 ... DLB 151, 172
Jamie, Kathleen 1962- ... 128
Jamieson, Bob
See Jamieson, Robert John
Jamieson, Kathleen Hall 1946- ... 155
Jamieson, Paul F(letcher) 1903- ... CAP-1
Earlier sketch in CA 9-10
Jamieson, Robert John 1943- ... 116
Brief entry ... 110
Interview in ... 116
Jamiolkowski, Raymond M. 1953- ... 149
See also SATA 81
Jamison, A(lbert) Leland 1911- ... 89-92
Jamison, Andrew 1948- ... 29-32R
Jamison, Bill 1942- ... 153
Jamison, Cheryl Alters 1953- ... 153
Jamison, Kay Redfield ... 153
Jamme, Albert (Joseph) 1916- ... 5-8R
Jammes, Francis 1868-1938 ... TCLC 75
Jampolsky, Gerald G(ershan) 1925- ... 111
Jan
See Noble, John (Appelbe)
Jan, Emerson
See Bixby, Jerome Lewis
Jan, George P(okung) 1925- ... 21-24R
Janas, Frankie-Lee 1908- ... CANR-24
Earlier sketch in CA 106
Jancar, Barbara Wolfe 1935- Brief entry ... 111
Jancar, Drago 1948- ... DLB 181
Jance, J. A.
See Jance, J(udith) A(nn)
Jance, J(udith) A(nn) 1944- ... CANR-61
Earlier sketch in CA 118
See also SATA-Brief 50
Janda, Kenneth (Frank) 1935- ... 13-16R
Jandl, Ernst 1925- ... CLC 34
Jandl, H(enry) Ward 1946- ... 121
Jandt, Fred E(dmund) 1944- ... 53-56
Jandy, Edward Clarence
1899-1980 Obituary ... 97-100
Jane, Mary Childs 1909- ... CANR-4
Earlier sketch in CA 1-4R
See also SATA 6
Jane, Nancy 1946- ... 89-92
Janeczko, Paul B(ryan) 1945- ... CANR-49
Earlier sketches in CA 104, CANR-22
See also AAYA 9
See also CLR 47
See also SAAS 18
See also SATA 53, 98
Janello, Amy (Elizabeth) 1962- ... 136
Janes, Clara 1940- ... DLB 134
Janes, Edward C. 1908- ... 93-96
See also SATA 25
Janes, J(oseph) Robert 1935- ... CANR-49
Earlier sketch in CA 123
See also SATA 101
See also SATA-Brief 50
Janes, Percy 1922- ... 113
Janes, Regina (Mary) 1946- ... 120
Janeshutz, Patricia M(arie) 1947- ... 121
Janeshutz, Trish
See Janeshutz, Patricia M(arie)
Janevski, Slavko 1920- ... DLB 181
Janeway, Eliot 1913-1993 ... 130
Obituary ... 140
Brief entry ... 112
Interview in ... 130
Janeway, Elizabeth (Hall) 1913- ... CANR-2
Earlier sketch in CA 45-48
See also AITN 1
See also SATA 19
Janger, Allen R(obert) 1932- ... CANR-48
Earlier sketches in CA 29-32R, CANR-12
Janger, Kathleen N. 1940- ... 125
See also SATA 66
Janice
See Brustlein, Janice Tworkov
Janifer, Laurence M(ark) 1933- ... CANR-5
Earlier sketch in CA 9-12R
Janik, Allan (Stanley Peter) 1941- ... 53-56
Janik, Carolyn 1940- ... CANR-33
Earlier sketches in CA 89-92, CANR-15
Janik, Del Ivan 1945- ... 117
Janik, Phyllis 1944- ... 111
Janis, Irving L(ester) 1918- ... CANR-23
Earlier sketches in CA 17-20R, CANR-8
Janis, J(ack) Harold 1910- ... 13-16R
Janis, Sidney 1896-1989 Obituary ... 130
Janjigian, Robert 1957- ... 127
Jankelevitch, Vladimir 1903-1985 Obituary ... 117
Janko, Richard 1955- ... CANR-30
Earlier sketch in CA 111
Janko, (Kathleen) Susan 1951- ... 149
Jankowski, James P. 1937- ... 150
Jankowsky, Kurt Robert 1928- ... 37-40R
Janner, Greville Ewan 1928- ... CANR-8
Earlier sketch in CA 13-16R
Janos, Andrew C(saba) 1934- ... 106
Janos, Leo 1933- ... 127
Janosch
See Eckert, Horst
See also CLR 26
Janov, Arthur 1924- ... 116
Janov, Jill E. 1942- ... 149
Janover, Caroline (Davis) 1943- ... 155
See also SATA 89
Janovy, John, Jr. 1937- ... CANR-41
Earlier sketches in CA 97-100, CANR-19
Janowitz, Henry D. 1918- ... 145
Janowitz, Morris 1919-1988 ... 13-16R
Obituary ... 127
Janowitz, Phyllis 1940- ... CANR-45
Earlier sketch in CA 93-96
Janowitz, Tama 1957- ... CANR-52
Earlier sketch in CA 106
See also CLC 43
See also DAM POP
Janowski, Tadeus M(arian) 1923- ... 53-56
Janowsky, Oscar Isaiah 1900-1993 ... CANR-5
Obituary ... 143
Earlier sketch in CA 5-8R
Janrup, (Ruth) Birgit 1931- ... 97-100
Jans, Zephyr
See Zekowski, Arlene
Jansen, Clifford J. 1935- ... 33-36R
Jansen, G(odfrey) H(enry) 1919- ... 114
Jansen, Godfrey
See Jansen, G(odfrey) H(enry)
Jansen, Jared
See Cebulash, Mel
Jansen, John Frederick 1918- ... 21-24R
Jansen, Marius B(erthus) 1922- ... 130
Jansen, Michael (Elin) 1940- ... 130
Jansen, Robert B(ruce) 1922- ... 81-84
Jansen, Sharon L. 1951- ... 140
Jansma, Pamela E. 1958- ... 144
Janson, Anthony F(rederick) 1943- ... 121
Janson, Donald 1921- ... 5-8R
Janson, Dora Jane (Heineberg) 1916- ... 106
See also SATA 31
Janson, H(orst) W(oldemar) 1913-1982 ... CANR-4
Obituary ... 107
Earlier sketch in CA 1-4R
See also SATA 9
Janson, Hank
See Hobson, Harry
and Norwood, Victor G(eorge) C(harles)
Janson-Smith, Celina 1909-1985 Obituary ... 118
Janssen, Al(fred Guthrie) 1949- ... 121
Janssen, Lawrence H(arm) 1921- ... 13-16R
Janssen, Marian (L. M.) 1953- ... 159
Janssens, Paul Mary ... 53-56
Jansson, Tove Marika 1914- ... CANR-38
Earlier sketch in CA 17-20R
See also CLR 2
See also MAICYA
See also SATA 3, 41
Janta, Alexander 1908-1974 ... 101
Obituary ... 53-56

Jantsch, Erich 1929-1980 .... CANR-10
Earlier sketch in CA 65-68
Jantscher, Gerald R. 1939(?)-1987 Obituary ... 123
Jantzen, Hans 1881-1967 Obituary 111
Jantzen, Steven L(loyd) 1941- 77-80
Janus
See Clery, (Reginald) Val(entine)
Janus, Grete
See Hertz, Grete Janus
Janus, Sam (Shep) 1930- 134
Brief entry 111
Januz, Lauren Robert 1939- 108
Janvier, Thomas 1849-1913 .... DLB 202
Janzen, John M(arvin) 1937- 81-84
Japhson, Robert 1736-1803 .... DLB 89
Japrisot, Sebastien 1931- .... CLC 90
Jaques, Elliott 1917- CANR-6
Earlier sketch in CA 13-16R
Jaques, Faith 1923-1997 .... CANR-20
Obituary 159
Earlier sketch in CA 103
See also MAICYA
See also SATA 21, 69, 97
Jaques, Florence Page 1890-1972 103
Obituary 104
Jaques, Francis Lee 1887-1969 ..... SATA-Brief 28
Jaquette, Jane Stallmann 1942- Brief entry 105
Jaquin, Noel 1894(?)-1974 Obituary 112
Jaquith, Priscilla 1908- 121
See also SATA 51
Jaramillo, Cleofas M. 1878-1956 .... DLB 122
Jaramillo, Samuel 1925- 41-44R
Jarausch, Konrad H(ugo) 1941- 130
Jarchow, Merrill E(arl) 1910- CANR-48
Earlier sketches in CA 41-44R, CANR-14
Jardim, Anne 1936- 107
Jardim, Vasco S. 1900(?)-1983 Obituary 111
Jardin, Andre 1912- 158
Jardine, Alice (Ann) 1951- 117
Jardine, Jack 1931- 21-24R
Jareed
See Faridi, Shah Nasiruddin Mohammad
Jares, Joe 1937- CANR-12
Earlier sketch in CA 33-36R
Jarmain, W. Edwin 1938- 13-16R
Jarman, A(lfred) O(wen) H(ughes) 1911- 130
Jarman, Cosette C(otterell) 1909- CAP-2
Earlier sketch in CA 21-22
Jarman, Derek 1942-1994 144
Jarman, Douglas 1942- 133
Jarman, Mark Anthony 1955- 118
See also CAAS 22
See also DLB 120
Jarman, Rosemary Hawley 1935- CANR-59
Earlier sketches in CA 49-52, CANR-2
See also SATA 7
Jarman, Thomas Leckie 1907- CANR-4
Earlier sketch in CA 5-8R
Jarman, Walton Maxey 1904-1980 Obituary ... 108
Jarmusch, Jim 1953(?)- 132
Jarmuth, Sylvia L. 1912- 25-28R
Jarnow, Jeannette 1909- 53-56
Jaroch, F(rancis) A(nthony) Randy 1947- 89-92
Jaroch, Randy
See Jaroch, F(rancis) A(nthony) Randy
Jaroff, Leon Morton 1927- 135
Jarolimek, John 1921- Brief entry 114
Jaron, Lou
See Spender, Lynne
Jarreau, Al(wyn Lopez) 1940- 117
Brief entry 116
Jarrell, John W. 1908(?)-1978 Obituary 81-84
Jarrell, Mary Von Schrader 1914- 77-80
See also SATA 35
Jarrell, Randall 1914-1965 .... CANR-34
Obituary 25-28R
Earlier sketches in CA 5-8R, CANR-6
See also CABS 2
See also CDALB 1941-1968
See also CLC 1, 2, 6, 9, 13, 49
See also CLR 6
See also DAM POET
See also DLB 48, 52
See also MAICYA
See also MTCW 1
See also SATA 7
Jarrett, (John) Derek 1928- 57-60
Jarrett, H(arold) Reginald 1916- CANR-3
Earlier sketch in CA 9-12R
Jarrett, James Louis 1917- 53-56
Jarrett, Marjorie 1923- 105
Jarrett, Philip (Martin) 1946- 127
Jarrett, Roxanne
See Werner, Herma
Jarriel, Thomas Edwin 1934- 120
Brief entry 109
Interview in 120
Jarriel, Tom
See Jarriel, Thomas Edwin
Jarrott, Mattie L. 1881(?)-1973 Obituary 41-44R
Jarrow, Gail 1952- 150
See also SATA 84
Jarry, Alfred 1873-1907 153
Brief entry 104
See also DAM DRAM
See also DLB 192
See also SSC 20
See also TCLC 2, 14
Jarves, James Jackson 1818-1888 .... DLB 189
Jarvie, Clodagh Gibson
See Gibson-Jarvie, Clodagh
Jarvie, Gordon (Iain) 1941- 143
Jarvie, I(an) C(harles) 1937- 53-56
Jarvik, Lissy F. 128
Jarvis, Ana C(ortesi) 1936- CANR-14
Earlier sketch in CA 65-68
Jarvis, Charles E(fthemios) 1921- 111
Jarvis, E. K.
See Bloch, Robert (Albert)
and Ellison, Harlan (Jay)
and Fairman, Paul W.
and Silverberg, Robert
Jarvis, F(rank) Washington 1939- 37-40R
Jarvis, Fred(erick) G(ordon, Jr.) 1930- 33-36R
Jarvis, Howard (Arnold) 1902(?)-1986 122
Obituary 120
Brief entry 111
Jarvis, Jennifer M(ary) 1935- 13-16R
Jarvis, Martin 1941- CANR-25
Earlier sketch in CA 105
Jarvis, Rupert Charles 1899- 103
Jarvis, Sharon 1943- CANR-48
Earlier sketch in CA 119
Jarvis, Simon 1963- 150
Jarvis, William Don(ald) 1913- CAP-1
Earlier sketch in CA 13-16
Jasen, David A(lan) 1937- CANR-52
Earlier sketches in CA 29-32R, CANR-27
Jasenas, Michael 1912- Brief entry 113
Jashemski, Wilhelmina Feemster 1910- CAP-1
Earlier sketch in CA 13-16
Jasmin, Claude 1930- 123
See also DLB 60
Jasner, W. K.
See Watson, Jane Werner
Jasny, Naum 1883- CAP-1
Earlier sketch in CA 9-10
Jason
See Caballero, Manuel
and Munro, (Macfarlane) Hugh
and Stannus, (James) Gordon (Dawson)
Jason, Johnny
See Glut, Donald F(rank)
Jason, Kathrine 1953- 126
Jason, Philip K(enneth) 1941- CANR-35
Earlier sketch in CA 114
Jason, Sonya 1927- 145
Jason, Stuart
See Avallone, Michael (Angelo, Jr.)
and Floren, Lee
Jaspan, Norman 103
Jasper, David 1951- 128
Jasper, James M(acdonald) 1957- 138
Jasper, Ronald Claud Dudley
1917-1990 Obituary 131
Jaspers, Karl (Theodor) 1883-1969 122
Obituary 25-28R
Jaspersohn, William 1947- CANR-71
Earlier sketch in CA 102
Jassal, Harjinder (Singh) 1938- 111
Jassem, Kate
See Oppenheim, Joanne
Jassy, Marie-France Perrin
See Perrin Jassy, Marie-France
Jastak, Joseph Florian 1901-1979 .... CANR-4
Obituary 85-88
Earlier sketch in CA 5-8R
Jastrow, Robert 1925- CANR-18
Earlier sketch in CA 21-24R
Interview in CANR-18
Jauch, Lawrence R. 1943- 112
Jauncey, James 1949- 151
Jauncey, James H(enry) 1916- CANR-20
Earlier sketches in CA 1-4R, CANR-5
Jauss, Anne Marie 1902(?)-1991 .... CANR-4
Obituary 135
Earlier sketch in CA 1-4R
See also SATA 10
See also SATA-Obit 69
Jauss, David 1951- 121
Jaussi, Laureen Richardson 1934- 73-76
Javernick, Ellen 1938- 155
See also SATA 89
Javitch, Daniel Gilbert 1941- 103
Javits, Benjamin A(braham)
1894-1973 Obituary 41-44R
Javits, Eric Moses 1931- 1-4R
Javits, Jacob K(oppel) 1904-1986 .... CANR-17
Obituary 118
Earlier sketches in CA 1-4R, CANR-1
Javor, Frank A. 1916- 135
Jawien, Andrzej
See John Paul II, Pope
Jaworska, Wladyslawa Jadwiga 1910- 53-56
Jaworski, Francis Anthony
See Javor, Frank A.
Jaworski, Leon 1905-1982 .... CAP-1
Obituary 108
Earlier sketch in CA 13-16
Jaworskyj, Michael 1921- 61-64
Jaxon, Milt
See Kimbro, John M.
Jay, Antony (Rupert) 1930- 25-28R
Jay, Bill 1940- Brief entry 117
Jay, Charlotte
See Halls, Geraldine (Mary)
Jay, Donald
See Meyer, Charles R(obert)
Jay, Douglas (Patrick Thomas) 1907- CANR-12
Earlier sketch in CA 65-68
Jay, Elisabeth 1947- CANR-54
Earlier sketch in CA 124
Jay, Eric George 1907- 5-8R
Jay, G. M.
See Halls, Geraldine (Mary)
Jay, Gregory S. 1952- 130
Jay, Hilda L(ease) 1921- 117
Jay, James M(onroe) 1927- 53-56
Jay, John 1745-1829 .... DLB 31
Jay, Karla 1947- 85-88
Jay, M(argaret) Ellen 1946- CANR-41
Earlier sketch in CA 118
Jay, Marion
See Spalding, Ruth
Jay, Martin (Evan) 1944- 53-56
Jay, Mel
See Fanthorpe, R(obert) Lionel
Jay, Peter 1937- 109
Jay, Peter (Anthony Charles) 1945- 97-100
Jay, Peter A. 1940- 101
Jay, Robert Ravenelle 1925- Brief entry 106
Jay, Ruth I(ngrid) 1920- 93-96
Jay, Ruth Johnson
See Jay, Ruth I(ngrid)
Jay, Simon
See Alexander, Colin James
Jayawardena, Visakha Kumari 1931- CANR-59
Earlier sketch in CA 45-48
Jayme, William North 1925- 9-12R
Jayne, Lieutenant R. H.
See Ellis, Edward S(ylvester)
Jayne, Sears 1920- 13-16R
Jaynes, Clare
See Mayer, Jane Rothschild
Jaynes, Julian 1923- 41-44R
Jaynes, Richard A(ndrus) 1935- 65-68
Jaynes, Roger W. 1946- 85-88
Jaynes, Ruth 1899- CAP-2
Earlier sketch in CA 25-28
Jazayery, M(ohammad) Ali 1924- CANR-9
Earlier sketch in CA 21-24R
Jeake, Samuel, Jr.
See Aiken, Conrad (Potter)
Jeal, Tim 1945- CANR-9
Earlier sketch in CA 21-24R
Jean, Gabrielle (Lucille) 1924- CANR-14
Earlier sketch in CA 37-40R
Jean, Marcel 1900- 25-28R
Jean-Louis
See Kerouac, Jean-Louis Lebris de
Jeannerat, Pierre Gabriel 1902- 5-8R
Jeanneret, Marsh 1917-1990 132
Jeanniere, Abel 1921- CANR-28
Earlier sketch in CA 49-52
Jeans, Marylu Terral 1914- 89-92
Jeans, Michael 127
Jeans, Peter D(ouglas) 1936- 146
Jeansonne, Glen 1946- CANR-48
Earlier sketch in CA 122
Jeanty, Ninette Helene
See Raven, Ninette Helene Jeanty
Jebb, (Hubert Miles) Gladwyn 1900-1996 ... 21-24R
Obituary 154
Jedamus, Paul 1923- 37-40R
Jedlitzka, Maria
See Jeritza, Maria
Jedrey, Christopher M(ichael) 1949- 101
Jedrzejewicz, Waclaw 1893-1993 .... 25-28R
Obituary 143
Jeef, Kalle
See Tshiamala, Kabasele
Jeeves, Malcolm A(lexander) 1926- CANR-12
Earlier sketch in CA 29-32R
Jeffares, A(lexander) Norman 1920- CANR-39
Earlier sketches in CA 85-88, CANR-16
Jeffer, Marsha 1940- 41-44R
Jefferds, Vincent H(arris) 1916- 127
See also SATA 59
See also SATA-Brief 49
Jefferies, Matthew (Martin) 1962- 154
Jefferies, (John) Richard 1848-1887 ... DLB 98, 141
See also SATA 16
Jefferies, Susan Herring 1903- CAP-1
Earlier sketch in CA 13-14
Jefferies, William
See Deaver, Jeffery Wilds
Jefferis, Barbara (Tarlton) 1917- 81-84
Jefferis, H(arry) Paul 1934- CANR-71
Earlier sketches in CA 93-96, CANR-63
Jeffers, Jo
See Johnson, Joan Helen
Jeffers, Lance 1919-1985 .... CANR-25
Earlier sketch in CA 65-68
See also BW 1
See also DLB 41
Jeffers, (John) Robinson 1887-1962 ..... CANR-35
Earlier sketch in CA 85-88
See also CDALB 1917-1929
See also CLC 2, 3, 11, 15, 54
See also DA
See also DAC
See also DAM MST, POET
See also DLB 45
See also MTCW 1
See also PC 17
See also WLC
Jeffers, Susan 1942- CANR-44
Earlier sketch in CA 97-100
See also CLR 30
See also MAICYA
See also SATA 17, 70
Jefferson, Alan 1921- CANR-53
Earlier sketches in CA 33-36R, CANR-13, 29
Jefferson, Blanche (Waugaman) 1909- 5-8R
Jefferson, Carter (Alfred) 1927- 17-20R
Jefferson, Ian
See Davies, L(eslie) P(urnell)
Jefferson, Janet
See Mencken, H(enry) L(ouis)
Jefferson, Omar Xavier
See Jefferson, Xavier T(homas)
Jefferson, Roland S. 1939- CANR-35
Earlier sketch in CA 111
See also BW 2
Jefferson, Sarah
See Farjeon, (Eve) Annabel
Jefferson, Thomas 1743-1826 .. CDALB 1640-1865
See also DLB 31
Jefferson, Xavier T(homas) 1952- CANR-13
Earlier sketch in CA 73-76
Jeffery, Grant 1924- 1-4R
Jeffery, Lawrence 1953- 130
Jeffery, Ransom 1943- 21-24R
Jefferys, Allan 93-96
Jefford, Bat
See Bingley, David Ernest
Jeffress, Philip W. 1941- Brief entry 111
Jeffrey, Adi-Kent Thomas 1916- 37-40R
Jeffrey, Christopher
See Leach, Michael
Jeffrey, David Lyle 1941- CANR-49
Earlier sketches in CA 57-60, CANR-7, 24
Jeffrey, Francis 1773-1850 .... DLB 107
Jeffrey, Francis 1950- 135
Jeffrey, Julie Roy 1941- 93-96
Jeffrey, L(illian) H(amilton) 1915- 1-4R
Jeffrey, Lawrence 1953- 130
Jeffrey, Lloyd Nicholas 1918- 37-40R
Jeffrey, Mildred (Mesurac) 5-8R
Jeffrey, Richard Carl 1926- 103
Jeffrey, Ruth
See Bell, Louise Price
Jeffrey, Thomas E. 1947- 136
Jeffrey, William
See Pronzini, Bill
and Wallmann, Jeffrey M(iner)
Jeffrey, William P., Jr. 1919- 57-60
Jeffreys, Harold 1891-1989 109
Obituary 128
Jeffreys, J. G.
See Healey, Ben (James)
Jeffreys, Montagu Vaughan Castelman 1900-1985 .
CANR-4
Obituary 117
Earlier sketch in CA 5-8R
Jeffreys-Jones, Rhodri 1942- CANR-13
Earlier sketch in CA 77-80
Jeffries, Charles Joseph 1896-1972 ...... CANR-4
Earlier sketch in CA 5-8R
Jeffries, Derwin J(ames) 1915- 57-60
Jeffries, Don 1940- 137
Jeffries, Graham Montague 1900-1982 .. CANR-60
Earlier sketches in CA 77-80, CANR-25
Jeffries, Ian 1942- 143
Jeffries, John C., Jr. 1948- 145
Jeffries, John Worthington 1942- 103
Jeffries, Lewis I(ngles) 1942- 103
Jeffries, Ona (Griffin)
1893(?)-1973 Obituary 41-44R
Jeffries, Roderic (Graeme) 1926- CANR-65
Earlier sketches in CA 17-20R, CANR-9, 25, 50
See also SATA 4
Jeffries, Virginia M(urrill) 1911- 5-8R
Jeffs, Julian 1931- 37-40R
Jeffs, Rae 1921- 25-28R
Jefkins, Frank William 1920- CANR-9
Earlier sketch in CA 13-16R
Jehlen, Myra 1940- 101
Jekel, Pamela (L.) 1948- 135
Jelagin, Juri 1910-1987 Obituary 123
Jelakowitch, Ivan
See Heijermans, Herman
Jelavich, Barbara 1923- 53-56
Jelen, Ted G. 1950- 145
Jelenski, Constantin 1922- 101
Jelinek, Elfriede 1946- 154
See also DLB 85
Jelinek, Estelle C. 1935- 102
Jelinek, Hena Maes
See Maes-Jelinek, Hena
Jellema, Roderick 1927- 41-44R
Jellicoe, (Patricia) Ann 1927- 85-88
See also CLC 27
See also DLB 13
Jellicoe, Geoffrey Alan 1900-1996 .... 13-16R
Obituary 152
Jellicoe, Sidney 1906-1973 .... CAP-2
Earlier sketch in CA 33-36
Jellinek, George 1919- 89-92
Jellinek, J(oseph) Stephan 1930- 81-84
Jellinek, Paul 1897- 13-16R
Jellison, Charles Albert, Jr. 1924- CANR-27
Earlier sketch in CA 1-4R
Jellison, Katherine 1960- 147
Jelloun, Tahar ben 1944- 162
Jelly, George Oliver 1909- 103
Jemie, Onwuchekwa 1940- 89-92
Jemyma
See Holley, Marietta
Jen, Gish
See Jen, Lillian
See also CLC 70
Jen, Lillian 1956(?)- 135
See also Jen, Gish
Jena, Ruth Michaelis
See Ratcliff, Ruth
Jencks, Charles (Alexander) 1939- CANR-55
Earlier sketches in CA 49-52, CANR-2
Jencks, Christopher 1936- CANR-2
Earlier sketch in CA 49-52
Jencks, Harlan W(ardell) 1941- 111
Jenison, Don P. 1897- CANR-7
Earlier sketch in CA 17-20R
Jenkin, A(lfred) K(enneth) Hamilton
1900-1980 Obituary 102
Jenkin-Pearce, Susie 1943- .... SATA 80
Jenkins, Alan 1914- CANR-6
Earlier sketch in CA 57-60
Jenkins, Beverly 1951- 156
Jenkins, Cecil 1927- 107
Jenkins, Clive 1926- CANR-5
Earlier sketch in CA 13-16R
Jenkins, Dafydd 1911- 146

Jenkins, Dan (Thomas B.) 1929- ... 126
Brief entry ... 111
Jenkins, Daniel T(homas) 1914- ... 127
Jenkins, David 1928- ... 97-100
Jenkins, David E(dward) 1925- Brief entry ... 114
Jenkins, David L. 1931- ... 136
Jenkins, Debra Reid
See Reid Jenkins, Debra
Jenkins, Dorothy Helen
1907-1972 Obituary ... 37-40R
Jenkins, Edith A(rnstein) 1913- ... 137
Jenkins, (Margaret) Elizabeth (Heald) 1905- ... CANR-13
Earlier sketch in CA 73-76
See also DLB 155
Jenkins, Emyl 1941- ... 114
Jenkins, Ferrell 1936- ... CANR-6
Earlier sketch in CA 57-60
Jenkins, Frances Briggs 1905- ... CAP-2
Earlier sketch in CA 25-28
Jenkins, Fred W(illiam) 1957- ... 159
Jenkins, Geoffrey 1920- ... CANR-16
Earlier sketch in CA 5-8R
Jenkins, (Thomas) Gilmour
1894-1981 Obituary ... 108
Jenkins, Gladys Gardner 1901- ... CANR-4
Earlier sketch in CA 1-4R
Jenkins, Gordon (Hill) 1910-1984 Obituary ... 112
Jenkins, Greg 1952- ... 168
Jenkins, Gwyn 1919- ... 1-4R
Jenkins, Hal
See Jenkins, Harold L.
Jenkins, Harold 1909- ... 9-12R
Jenkins, Harold L. 1909(?)-1987 Obituary ... 124
Jenkins, Holt M. 1920- ... 17-20R
Jenkins, Hugh (Gater) 1908- ... 104
Jenkins, Iredell 1909- ... 106
Jenkins, James J(erome) 1923- ... 13-16R
Jenkins, Jean ... 166
See also SATA 98
Jenkins, Jerry B(ruce) 1949- ... CANR-20
Earlier sketches in CA 49-52, CANR-5
Jenkins, John (Robert Graham) 1928- ... CANR-53
Earlier sketches in CA 45-48, CANR-28
Jenkins, John A. 1950- ... 139
Jenkins, John Geraint 1929- ... 21-24R
Jenkins, John H(olmes III) 1940- ... CANR-10
Earlier sketch in CA 65-68
Jenkins, John J. 1937- ... 132
Jenkins, Kenneth V(incent) 1930- ... 53-56
Jenkins, Linda Walsh 1944- ... 111
Jenkins, Louis 1942- ... CANR-4
Earlier sketch in CA 53-56
Jenkins, Marcella 1954- ... 151
Jenkins, Marie M(agdalen) 1909- ... 41-44R
See also SATA 7
Jenkins, Mark 1958- ... 137
Jenkins, Michael (Romilly Heald) 1936- ... 25-28R
Jenkins, Nancy
See Jenkins, Nancy (Harmon)
Jenkins, Patricia 1927-1982 ... 106
Jenkins, Patrick 1955- ... SATA 72
Jenkins, Peter (George James) 1934- ... 135
Jenkins, Peter 1951- ... 89-92
Jenkins, Phyllis
See Schwalberg, Carol(yn Ernestine Stein)
Jenkins, Ray(mond Leonard) 1935- ... 103
Jenkins, Reese V(almer) 1938- ... 65-68
Jenkins, (John) Robin 1912- ... CANR-1
Earlier sketch in CA 1-4R
See also CLC 52
See also DLB 14
Jenkins, Romilly James Heald 1907-1969 ... CANR-5
Earlier sketch in CA 5-8R
Jenkins, Roy (Harris) 1920- ... CANR-30
Earlier sketches in CA 9-12R, CANR-13
Jenkins, Simon 1943- ... CANR-45
Earlier sketch in CA 81-84
Jenkins, Steven 1950- ... 162
Jenkins, T(erence) A(ndrew) 1958- ... 162
Jenkins, Virginia Scott 1948- ... 148
Jenkins, Will(iam) F(itzgerald) 1896-1975 ... CANR-63
Obituary ... 57-60
Earlier sketches in CA 9-12R, CANR-4
See also Leinster, Murray
Jenkins, William A(twell) 1922- ... 61-64
See also SATA 9
Jenkins, William Marshall, Jr. 1918- Brief entry ... 105
Jenkinson, Edward B(ernard) 1930- ... 21-24R
Jenkinson, Michael 1938- ... 25-28R
Jenks, Almet 1892-1966 ... CAP-1
Earlier sketch in CA 13-14
Jenks, C(larence) Wilfred 1909-1973 ... CANR-4
Earlier sketch in CA 9-12R
Jenks, George C(harles) 1850-1929 Brief entry 119
Jenks, James M. 1922- ... 122
Jenks, Randolph 1912- ... 9-12R
Jenks, Tom 1950- ... 137
Jenkyns, Chris 1924- ... SATA 51
Jenkyns, Richard (Henry Austen) 1949- ... 108
Jenner, Bruce 1949- ... 110
Jenner, Chrystie 1950- ... 77-80
Jenner, Delia 1944- ... 21-24R
Jenner, Heather
See James, Heather
Jenner, Philip Norman 1921- ... 89-92
Jenner, W(illiam) J(ohn) F(rancis) 1940- ... CANR-12
Earlier sketch in CA 29-32R
Jenness, Aylette 1934- ... 25-28R
Jennifer, Susan
See Hoskins, Robert
Jennings, Charles ... 162
Jennings, Coleman A(lonzo) 1933- ... CANR-51
Earlier sketch in CA 124
See also SATA 64
Jennings, Dana Andrew 1957- ... 158
See also SATA 93
Jennings, Dana Close 1923- ... 53-56
Jennings, Dean
See Frazee, Steve (Charles)
Jennings, Dean Southern
1905-1969 Obituary ... 89-92
Jennings, Edward M(orton III) 1936- ... 29-32R
Jennings, Elizabeth (Joan) 1926- ... CANR-66
Earlier sketches in CA 61-64, CANR-8, 39
See also CAAS 5
See also CLC 5, 14
See also DLB 27
See also MTCW 1
See also SATA 66
Jennings, Francis (Paul) 1918- ... 144
Jennings, Gary (Gayne) 1928- ... CANR-59
Earlier sketches in CA 5-8R, CANR-9, 29, 56
See also SATA 9
Jennings, (William) Ivor 1903-1965 ... 5-8R
Jennings, James M(urray) 1924- ... 37-40R
Jennings, Jerry (Edward) 1935- ... CANR-7
Earlier sketch in CA 53-56
Jennings, Jesse David 1909- ... CANR-13
Earlier sketch in CA 33-36R
Jennings, John (Edward, Jr.) 1906-1973 ... CAP-1
Obituary ... 45-48
Earlier sketch in CA 13-14
Jennings, Karla (Mari) 1956- ... 134
Jennings, Lane (Eaton) 1944- ... CANR-19
Earlier sketch in CA 102
Jennings, Leslie Nelson 1890-1972 ... CAP-1
Earlier sketch in CA 9-10
Jennings, Marianne Moody 1953- ... CANR-42
Earlier sketch in CA 118
Jennings, Michael Glenn 1931- ... CANR-24
Earlier sketch in CA 69-72
Jennings, Patrick
See Mayer, S(ydney) L(ouis)
Jennings, Patrick 1962- ... 161
See also SATA 96
Jennings, Paul (Francis) 1918- ... CANR-19
Earlier sketches in CA 9-12R, CANR-4
Jennings, Paul 1943- ... CLR 40
See also SATA 88
Jennings, Peter (Charles Archibald Ewart) 1938- ... CANR-69
Brief entry ... 114
Earlier sketch in CA 134
Jennings, Phillip C. 1946- ... 126
Jennings, Raymond P(olson) 1924- ... 110
Jennings, Richard (Wormington) 1907- ... 17-20R
Jennings, Robert
See Hamilton, Charles (Harold St. John)
Jennings, Robert E(dward) 1931- ... CANR-11
Earlier sketch in CA 61-64
Jennings, S. M.
See Meyer, Jerome Sydney
Jennings, Sharon (Elizabeth) 1954- ... CANR-68
Earlier sketch in CA 134
See also SATA 95
Jennings, Talbot 1895(?)-1985 Obituary ... 116
Jennings, Ted C(harles) 1949- ... 81-84
Jennings, Vivien ... 61-64
Jennings, Waylon 1937- ... CLC 21
Jennings, William Dale 1917- ... 25-28R
Jennison, C. S.
See Starbird, Kaye
Jennison, Christopher 1938- ... 53-56
Jennison, Keith Warren 1911- ... 73-76
See also SATA 14
Jennison, Peter S(axe) 1922- ... CANR-4
Earlier sketch in CA 9-12R
Jenny, Hans H(einrich) 1922- ... 103
Jenoff, Marvyne 1942- ... 117
Jens, Walter 1923- ... CANR-15
Earlier sketch in CA 89-92
See also DLB 69
Jensen, Ad(olph) E. 1899-1965 ... CAP-2
Earlier sketch in CA 19-20
Jensen, Alan F(rederick) 1938- ... 53-56
Jensen, Albert C(hristian) 1924- ... 85-88
Jensen, Andrew F(rederick), Jr. 1929- ... 57-60
Jensen, Ann ... 21-24R
Jensen, Arthur R(obert) 1923- ... CANR-2
Earlier sketch in CA 1-4R
Jensen, Clayne R. 1930- ... CANR-8
Earlier sketch in CA 17-20R
Jensen, De Lamar 1925- ... CANR-7
Earlier sketch in CA 9-12R
Jensen, Dwight 1934- ... 85-88
Jensen, Ejner J. 1937- ... 138
Jensen, Frede 1926- ... 57-60
Jensen, Gordon Duff 1926- Brief entry ... 106
Jensen, Gwendolyn Evans 1936- ... 57-60
Jensen, H. James 1933- ... 25-28R
Jensen, Irene K(hin Khin Myint) 1925- ... 69-72
Jensen, Irving L. 1920- ... CANR-7
Earlier sketch in CA 17-20R
Jensen, J(ohannes) Hans D(aniel) 1907-1973 ... 155
Jensen, J(ohn) Vernon 1922- ... 49-52
Jensen, Jo
See Pelton, Beverly Jo
Jensen, Joan M(aria) 1934- ... CANR-56
Earlier sketch in CA 127
Jensen, Johannes V. 1873-1950 ... TCLC 41
Jensen, John H(jalmar) 1929- ... 21-24R
Jensen, John Martin 1893- ... CAP-1
Earlier sketch in CA 13-16
Jensen, Julie
See McDonald, Julie
Jensen, Kathryn 1949- ... 149
See also SATA 81
Jensen, Kristine Mary 1961- ... SATA 78
Jensen, Larry Cyril 1938- ... 106
Jensen, Laura (Linnea) 1948- ... 103
See also CLC 37
Jensen, Lawrence N(eil) 1924- ... 17-20R
Jensen, Lloyd 1936- ... 61-64
Jensen, Margaret Ann 1948- ... 123
Jensen, Marlene 1947- ... 81-84
Jensen, Mary Ten Eyck Bard 1904-1970 ... 5-8R
Obituary ... 29-32R
Jensen, Maxine Dowd 1919- ... 65-68
Jensen, Merrill (Monroe) 1905-1980 ... 77-80
Obituary ... 112
See also DLB 17
Jensen, Michael C(harles) 1934- ... 127
Jensen, Michael C(ole) 1939- ... CANR-32
Earlier sketch in CA 49-52
Jensen, Muriel 1945- ... 164
Jensen, Niels 1927- ... 49-52
See also SATA 25
Jensen, Ole Klindt
See Klindt-Jensen, Ole
Jensen, Oliver (Ormerod) 1914- ... CANR-10
Earlier sketch in CA 25-28R
Jensen, Paul K. 1916- ... 17-20R
Jensen, Paul M(orris) 1944- ... 53-56
Jensen, Pauline Marie (Long) 1900- ... CAP-2
Earlier sketch in CA 17-18
Jensen, Peter
See Wallmann, Jeffrey M(iner)
Jensen, Richard C(arl) 1936- ... 49-52
Jensen, Richard J. 1941- ... 33-36R
Jensen, Robert (Earl) 1938-1990 ... 111
Obituary ... 132
Jensen, Rolf (Arthur) 1912- ... 21-24R
Jensen, Rosalie (Seymour) 1938- ... 57-60
Jensen, Vernon H(ortin) 1907- ... 106
Jensen, Vickie (Dee) 1946- ... 149
See also SATA 81
Jensen, Virginia Allen 1927- ... CANR-1
Earlier sketch in CA 45-48
See also SATA 8
Jensi, Muganwa Nsiku
See Shorter, Aylward
Jenson, Robert W(illiam) 1930- ... CANR-9
Earlier sketch in CA 5-8R
Jenson, William R(obert) 1946- ... 101
Jentleson, Bruce W. 1951- ... 124
Jentz, Gaylord A. 1931- ... CANR-31
Earlier sketches in CA 25-28R, CANR-14
Jenyns, R(oger) Soame 1904-1976 ... 73-76
Obituary ... 69-72
Jenyns, Soame
See Jenyns, R(oger) Soame
Jephcott, E(dmund) F(rancis) N(eville) 1938- Brief entry ... 115
Jeppson, J. O.
See Asimov, Janet (Jeppson)
Jepsen, Stanley M(arius) 1912- ... 77-80
Jepson, Jill 1950- ... 141
Jepson, Selwyn 1899-1989 Obituary ... 128
Jeram, Anita 1965- ... 149
See also SATA 71, 102
Jerdee, Thomas H(arlan) 1927- ... 118
Jeremias, Joachim 1900- ... CANR-11
Earlier sketch in CA 5-8R
Jeremy, David J(ohn) 1939- ... CANR-71
Earlier sketch in CA 129
Jeremy, Sister Mary ... 5-8R
Jerina, Carol 1947- ... 126
Jeritza, Maria 1887-1982 Obituary ... 107
Jermain, Clive 1966(?)-1988 Obituary ... 124
Jerman, James (Auguste) 1920- ... 123
Jerman, Jerry 1949- ... 155
See also SATA 89
Jerman, Sylvia Paul
See Cooper, Sylvia
Jernick, Ruth 1948- ... 107
Jernigan, E. Wesley 1940- ... SATA 85
Jernigan, Gisela (Evelyn) 1948- ... 151
See also SATA 85
Jerome, Jerome K(lapka) 1859-1927 Brief entry ... 119
See also DLB 10, 34, 135
See also TCLC 23
Jerome, John 1932- ... CANR-2
Earlier sketch in CA 45-48
Jerome, Joseph
See Sewell, Brocard
Jerome, Judson (Blair) 1927-1991 ... CANR-44
Earlier sketches in CA 9-12R, CANR-4, 20
See also CAAS 8
See also DLB 105
Jerome, Lawrence E(dmund) 1944- ... 77-80
Jerome, Mark
See Appleman, Mark J(erome)
Jerome, Stuart 1918(?)-1983 Obituary ... 111
Jerrold, Douglas William 1803-1857 ... DLB 158, 159
Jerrybilt
See Shields, Gerald R.
Jersild, Arthur T(homas) 1902-1994 ... CANR-21
Obituary ... 143
Earlier sketch in CA 1-4R
Jersild, P. C.
See Jersild, Per Christian
Jersild, Paul T(homas) 1931- ... 37-40R
Jersild, Per Christian 1935- ... 130
Jervell, Jacob 1925- ... CANR-23
Earlier sketches in CA 61-64, CANR-8
Jervey, Edward D(rewry) 1929- ... 133
Jervis, Robert 1940- ... 142
Jeschke, Marlin 1929- ... 45-48
Jeschke, Susan 1942- ... 77-80
See also SATA 42
See also SATA-Brief 27
Jeschke, Wolfgang 1936- ... 163
Jeske, Richard Lee 1936- ... 111
Jesmer, Elaine 1939- ... 49-52
See also AITN 1
Jespersen, James 1934- ... 103
Jesse, F(ryniwyd) Tennyson 1889-1958 Brief entry ... 112
See also DLB 77
Jesse, Michael
See Baldwin, Michael
Jessel, Camilla (Ruth) 1937- ... CANR-23
Earlier sketch in CA 104
See also SATA 29
Jessel, George (Albert) 1898-1981 ... 89-92
Obituary ... 103
Jessel, John
See Weinbaum, Stanley Grauman
Jessen, Carl A. 1887(?)-1978 Obituary ... 77-80
Jessey, Cornelia
See Sussman, Cornelia Silver
Jessner, Lucie Ney 1896-1979 Obituary ... 93-96
Jessop, Thomas Edmund 1896- ... 9-12R
Jessor, Richard 1924- ... 41-44R
Jessup, Deborah Hitchcock 1934- ... 141
Jessup, Frances
See Van Briggle, Margaret F(rances) Jessup
Jessup, John K(nox) 1907-1979 ... 101
Obituary ... 89-92
Jessup, Michael H(yle) 1937- Brief entry ... 109
Jessup, Paul F(rederick) 1939- ... 111
Jessup, Philip C(aryl) 1897-1986 ... 77-80
Obituary ... 118
Jessup, Richard 1925(?)-1982 Obituary ... 108
Jesty, P(eter) H(ugh) 1948- ... 121
Jeter, Jacky
See Jeter, Jacquelyn I.
Jeter, Jacquelyn I. 1935- ... 25-28R
Jeter, K. W. 1950- ... 158
Jett, Stephen C(linton) 1938- ... CANR-10
Earlier sketch in CA 25-28R
Jette, Fernand 1921- ... 5-8R
Jeune, Paul 1950- ... 101
Jeury, Michel 1934- ... 161
Jevons, Frederic Raphae 1929- ... 61-64
Jevons, Marshall
See Breit, William (Leo)
and Elzinga, Kenneth G(erald)
Jewell, Derek 1927-1985 ... CANR-20
Earlier sketches in CA 33-36R, CANR-13
Jewell, Edmund F. 1896(?)-1978 Obituary ... 81-84
Jewell, Malcolm E(dwin) 1928- ... CANR-5
Earlier sketch in CA 1-4R
Jewell, Nancy 1940- ... CANR-7
Earlier sketch in CA 61-64
See also SATA-Brief 41
Jewess, Kathleen
See Burk, Kathleen
Jewett, Alyce Lowrie (Williams) 1908- ... CAP-1
Earlier sketch in CA 13-14
Jewett, Ann E(lizabeth) 1921- ... 93-96
Jewett, Claudia L(owe) 1939- ... 112
Jewett, Eleanore Myers 1890-1967 ... 5-8R
See also SATA 5
Jewett, Paul King 1919-1991 ... 53-56
Obituary ... 135
Jewett, Robert 1933- ... CANR-2
Earlier sketch in CA 45-48
Jewett, (Theodora) Sarah Orne 1849-1909 ... CANR-71
Brief entry ... 108
Earlier sketch in CA 127
See also DLB 12, 74
See also SATA 15
See also SSC 6
See also TCLC 1, 22
Jewison, Norman (Frederick) 1926- ... 143
Brief entry ... 113
Jewitt, John Rodgers 1783-1821 ... DLB 99
Jewsbury, Geraldine (Endsor) 1812-1880 ... DLB 21
Jewsbury, Maria Jane 1800-1833 ... DLB 199
Jezard, Alison 1919- ... 29-32R
See also SATA 57
See also SATA-Brief 34
Jezer, Marty 1940- ... CANR-27
Earlier sketch in CA 109
Jezewski, Bohdan O(lgierd) 1900-1980 ... 5-8R
Obituary ... 103
Jha, Akhileshwar 1932- ... 107
Jha, Lakshmi Kant 1913-1988 Obituary ... 125
Jhabvala, Ruth Prawer 1927- ... CANR-51
Earlier sketches in CA 1-4R, CANR-2, 29
Interview in ... CANR-29
See also CLC 4, 8, 29, 94
See also DAB
See also DAM NOV
See also DLB 139, 194
See also MTCW 1
Jiang, Jifang
See Ruan, Fang-fu
Jiang, Ji-li 1954- ... 168
See also SATA 101
Jianou, Ionel 1905- ... CANR-9
Earlier sketch in CA 21-24R
Jibran, Kahlil
See Gibran, Kahlil
Jibran, Khalil
See Gibran, Kahlil
Jidejian, Nina 1921- ... 29-32R
Jie, Zhang
See Zhang, Jie
Jiler, John 1946- ... 114
See also SATA 42
See also SATA-Brief 35
Jiles, Paulette 1943- ... CANR-70
Earlier sketch in CA 101
See also CLC 13, 58
Jillson, Joyce 1950- ... 111

Jimenez, Francisco 1943- 131
See also HW
Jimenez, Janey (Renee) 1953- 77-80
Jimenez (Mantecon), Juan Ramon 1881-1958 131
Brief entry 104
See also DAM MULT, POET
See also DLB 134
See also HLC
See also HW
See also MTCW 1
See also PC 7
See also TCLC 4
Jimenez, Neal (Randall) 1960- 138
Jimenez, Ramon
See Jimenez (Mantecon), Juan Ramon
Jimenez Mantecon, Juan
See Jimenez (Mantecon), Juan Ramon
Jin, Ha 1956- 152
See also CLC 109
Jinks, Catherine 1963- 159
See also SATA 94
Jinks, William Howard, Jr. 1938- 41-44R
Jinpa, Geshe Thupten
See Jinpa, Thupten
Jinpa, Thupten 1958- 151
Jipson, Wayne R(ay) 1931- 45-48
Jirgens, Karl (Edward) 1952- 158
Jiskogo
See Harrington, Mark Raymond
Jo, Yung-Hwan 1932- 45-48
Joachim, Leo H. 1898-1985 Obituary 117
Joan, Polly 1933- 101
Joans, Ted 1928- CANR-25
Earlier sketches in CA 45-48, CANR-2
See also CAAS 25
See also BW 1
See also DLB 16, 41
Joas, Hans 1948- 159
Jobb, Jamie 1945- 85-88
See also SATA 29
Jobe, Brock (William) 1948- 118
Jobes, Gertrude Blumenthal 1907- CAP-1
Earlier sketch in CA 11-12
Jobling, David 168
Jobson, Gary Alan 1950- 93-96
Jobson, Hamilton 1914- 73-76
Jobson, Sandra
See Darroch, Sandra Jobson
Jocelyn, Richard
See Clutterbuck, Richard
Jochnowitz, George 1937- 49-52
Joe, Rita 1932- 153
Joedicke, Juergen 1925- 17-20R
Joel, Asher Alexander 1912- 108
Joel, Billy
See Joel, William Martin
See also CLC 26
Joel, William Martin 1949- 108
See also Joel, Billy
Joels, Merrill E. 1915- 25-28R
Joelson, Annette 1903-1971 Obituary 29-32R
Joensson, Reidar 1944- 140
Joerns, Consuelo 114
Brief entry 111
See also SATA 44
See also SATA-Brief 33
Joers, Lawrence E(ugene) C(laire) 1900- 41-44R
Joesting, Edward Henry 1925- 103
Joey D
See Macaulay, Teresa (E.)
Jofen, Jean 1922- 37-40R
Joffe, Josef 1944- 126
Joffe, Joyce 1940- 77-80
Johannes, John R. 1943- 111
Johannes, R.
See Moss, Rose
Johannesen, Richard L(ee) 1937- 17-20R
Johannesson, Olof
See Alfven, Hannes O(lof) G(oesta)
Johanningmeier, E(rwin) V(irgil) 1937- 104
Johannis, Theodore B(enjamin), Jr. 1914- 33-36R
Johannsen, Hano D. 1933- CANR-29
Earlier sketch in CA 29-32R
Johannsen, Robert Walter 1925- CANR-45
Earlier sketch in CA 1-4R
Johansen, Bruce Elliott 1950- 110
Johansen, Dorothy O. 1904- CAP-1
Earlier sketch in CA 13-14
Johanson, Donald C(arl) 1943- CANR-48
Earlier sketch in CA 107
Johanson, Stanley Morris 1933- 45-48
Johansson, Thomas (Hugo) B(ernard) 1943-
CANR-19
Earlier sketch in CA 102
John, Angela V. 1948- 125
John, B.
See John, Elizabeth Beaman
John, Betty
See John, Elizabeth Beaman
John, Colin
See Hagan, Chet
John, Dane
See Major, Alan P(ercival)
John, DeWitt 1915-1985 Obituary 117
John, Elizabeth Beaman 1907- CANR-8
Earlier sketch in CA 5-8R
John, Errol 1924-1988 Obituary 126
John, Helen James 1930- 61-64
John, Joyce SATA 59
John, Owen 1918- Brief entry 117
John, Robert 29-32R
John, Sandra D(eanne Thompson) 1951- 114
John, Vera P.
See John-Steiner, Vera P(olgar)
Johnn, David
See Engle, John D(avid), Jr.
John of Dumbleton 1310(?)-1349(?) DLB 115
John Paul I, Pope 1912-1978 CANR-29
Earlier sketch in CA 81-84
John Paul II, Pope 1920- 133
Brief entry 106
Johnpoll, Bernard K(eith) 1918- CANR-24
Earlier sketches in CA 21-24R, CANR-9
Johns, Albert Cameron 1914- CANR-6
Earlier sketch in CA 49-52
Johns, Avery
See Cousins, Margaret
Johns, Claude J., Jr. 1930- 77-80
Johns, Edward Alistair 1936- 45-48
Johns, Elizabeth 1937- 121
Johns, Elizabeth 1943- SATA 88
Johns, Eric 1907-1975 Obituary 116
Johns, Foster
See Seldes, Gilbert (Vivian)
Johns, Geoffrey
See Warner, (George) Geoffrey John
Johns, Glover S., Jr. 1911(?)-1976 Obituary 65-68
Johns, Janetta
See Quin-Harkin, Janet
Johns, John E(dwin) 1921- 9-12R
Johns, June 1925- 57-60
Johns, Kenneth
See Bulmer, (Henry) Kenneth
Johns, Linda 1945- 142
Johns, Marston
See Fanthorpe, R(obert) Lionel
Johns, Ray E(arl) 1900- 41-44R
Johns, Richard A(lton) 1929- 17-20R
Johns, Stephanie Bernardo 1947- CANR-30
Earlier sketch in CA 112
Johns, W(illiam) E(arle) 1893-1968 CANR-30
Earlier sketch in CA 73-76
See also DLB 160
See also MAICYA
See also SATA 55
Johns, Warren L. 1929- 21-24R
Johns, Whitey
See White, John I(rwin)
Johnsen, Trevor Bernard Meldal
See Meldal-Johnsen, Trevor Bernard
Johnsgard, Karin L(uisa) 1964- 118
Johnsgard, Paul A(ustin) 1931- CANR-39
Earlier sketches in CA 49-52, CANR-1, 17
Johnson, A.
See Johnson, Annabell (Jones)
Johnson, A. E.
See Johnson, Annabell (Jones)
and Johnson, Edgar (Raymond)
Johnson, A(lison) Findlay 1947- 132
Johnson, Alan P(ackard) 1929- 17-20R
Johnson, Albert (Franklin) 1904- CANR-6
Earlier sketch in CA 9-12R
Johnson, Alden Porter 1914-1972 Obituary 104
Johnson, Alexandra 1949- 164
Johnson, Alison
See Johnson, A(lison) Findlay
Johnson, Allen 85-88
Johnson, Allison H(eartz) 1910- 41-44R
Johnson, Alvin 1874-1971 Obituary 29-32R
Johnson, Amandus 1877-1974 Obituary 49-52
Johnson, Andrew 1949- 143
Johnson, Andrew N(isseu) 1887-1982 61-64
Obituary 120
Johnson, Angela 1961- 138
See also CLR 33
See also SATA 69, 102
Johnson, Ann Braden 1945- 135
Johnson, Ann Cox
See Saunders, Ann Loreille
Johnson, Annabel
See Johnson, Annabell (Jones)
Johnson, Annabell (Jones) 1921- CANR-37
Earlier sketch in CA 9-12R
See also MAICYA
See also SATA 2, 72
Johnson, Arno Hollock 1901-1985 Obituary 116
Johnson, Arnold W(aldemar) 1900- CAP-1
Earlier sketch in CA 13-14
Johnson, Arthur Menzies 1921- 21-24R
Johnson, Arthur W(illiam) 1920- CANR-41
Earlier sketch in CA 117
Johnson, Aubrey Rodway 1901-1985 Obituary 117
Johnson, Audrey P(ike) 1915- CANR-15
Earlier sketch in CA 93-96
Johnson, B(owen) C(harleston) 1945- 107
Johnson, B(urdetta) F(aye) 1920- CANR-3
Earlier sketch in CA 1-4R
See also Beebe, B(urdetta) F(aye)
Johnson, B(asil) L(eonard) C(lyde) 1919- 120
Johnson, B(ryan) S(tanley William) 1933-1973
CANR-9
Obituary 53-56
Earlier sketch in CA 9-12R
See also CLC 6, 9
See also DLB 14, 40
Johnson, Barbara F(erry) 1923-1989 CANR-44
Earlier sketch in CA 73-76
Johnson, Barclay G(iddings)
1909-1985 Obituary 116
Johnson, Barry L(ynn) 1934- 33-36R
Johnson, Barry L(ee) 1943- 61-64
Johnson, Bea (?)-1976 Obituary 65-68
Johnson, Ben E(ugene) 1940- CANR-8
Earlier sketch in CA 61-64
Johnson, Benj. F. of Boo
See Riley, James Whitcomb
Johnson, Benjamin A. 1937- CANR-9
Earlier sketch in CA 21-24R
Johnson, Benjamin F. of Boo
See Riley, James Whitcomb
Johnson, Benton 1928- 81-84
Johnson, Bernard 1933- 33-36R
Johnson, Bertha French 1906- 41-44R
Johnson, Beth 1953- 118
Johnson, Bob 1950- 130
Johnson, Bradford 1937- 57-60
Johnson, Braiden Rex
See Rex-Johnson, Braiden
Johnson, Brian (Martin) 1925- CANR-23
Earlier sketch in CA 106
Johnson, Bruce 1933- 33-36R
Johnson, Bryan 1948- 133
Johnson, Burges 1877-1963 Obituary 89-92
Johnson, Byron Lindberg 1917- 21-24R
Johnson, C. Edward
See Johnson, Carl E(dward)
Johnson, C. F.
See Goulart, Frances Sheridan
Johnson, Carl E(dward) 1937- 25-28R
Johnson, Carl G(raves) 1915- 101
Johnson, Carol
See Bolt, Carol
Johnson, Carol Virginia 1928- CANR-6
Earlier sketch in CA 9-12R
Johnson, Carroll B(ernard) 1938- 73-76
Johnson, Caryn
See Goldberg, Whoopi
Johnson, Cathy Marie 1956- 145
Johnson, Cecil Edward 1927- 33-36R
Johnson, Chalmers A(shby) 1931- CANR-6
Earlier sketch in CA 5-8R
Johnson, Charlene
See Crawford, Char
Johnson, Charles 1679-1748 DLB 84
Johnson, Charles (Richard) 1948- CANR-66
Earlier sketches in CA 116, CANR-42
See also CAAS 18
See also BLC 2
See also BW 2
See also CLC 7, 51, 65
See also DAM MULT
See also DLB 33
Johnson, Charles Benjamin 1928-1980 CANR-4
Earlier sketch in CA 5-8R
Johnson, Charles Ellicott 1920-1969 1-4R
Obituary 103
Johnson, Charles R. 1925- 65-68
See also SATA 11
Johnson, Charles S.
See Edwards, William B(ennett)
Johnson, Charles S(purgeon) 1893-1956 125
See also BW 1
See also DLB 51, 91
Johnson, Charles W(illiam) 1934- 107
Johnson, Charlotte Buel
See von Wodtke, Charlotte Buel Johnson
See also SATA 46
Johnson, Cherry L(urae) F(lake) 1968- 165
Johnson, Christine 1943- 123
Johnson, Christopher 1931- CANR-8
Earlier sketch in CA 13-16R
Johnson, Christopher Howard 1937- Brief
entry 106
Johnson, Chuck
See Johnson, Charles R.
Johnson, Clair 1915(?)-1980 Obituary 97-100
Johnson, Clarence L(eonard) 1910-1990 159
Johnson, Claudia Alta (Taylor) 1912- 89-92
Johnson, Claudia D(urst) 1938- 114
Johnson, Clive (White, Jr.) 1930- 29-32R
Johnson, Colin
See Mudrooroo (Nyoongah)
Johnson, Colin 1939- 130
Johnson, Crockett
See Leisk, David Johnson
Johnson, Curt(is Lee) 1928- 33-36R
Johnson, Curtiss Sherman 1899- CANR-45
Earlier sketch in CA 45-48
Johnson, D(onald) Barton 1933- 33-36R
Johnson, D(avid) Bruce 1942- 61-64
Johnson, D(avid) Gale 1916- 17-20R
Johnson, D(ana) William 1945- 97-100
See also SATA 23
Johnson, Dale A(rthur) 1936- 37-40R
Johnson, Dale L(eonard) 1934- 130
Johnson, Daniel M. 1940- 154
Johnson, Daniel Shahid 1954- SATA 73
Johnson, Dave W(illiam) 1931- 93-96
Johnson, David 1927- CANR-8
Earlier sketch in CA 13-16R
Johnson, David G(eorge) 1906- 9-12R
Johnson, David Lawrence 1943- 114
Johnson, David Ralph 1942- 117
Johnson, Deidre A(nn) 1953- 116
Johnson, Denis 1949- CANR-71
Brief entry 117
Earlier sketch in CA 121
See also CLC 52
See also DLB 120
Johnson, Diane 1934- CANR-62
Earlier sketches in CA 41-44R, CANR-17, 40
Interview in CANR-17
See also CLC 5, 13, 48
See also DLBY 80
See also MTCW 1
Johnson, Dick
See Johnson, Richard A.
Johnson, Dolores 1949- 137
See also SATA 69
Johnson, Don 1927- 168
Johnson, Don 1934- 116
Johnson, Donald Bruce 1921-1981 CANR-25
Earlier sketch in CA 1-4R
Johnson, Donald D. 1917- 137
Johnson, Donald M(cEwen) 1909- 1-4R
Johnson, Donald McI(ntosh) 1903- CANR-8
Earlier sketch in CA 5-8R
Johnson, Donna Kay 1935- 106
Johnson, Donovan A(lbert) 1910- CANR-5
Earlier sketch in CA 5-8R
Johnson, Doris McNeely 1941- 111
Johnson, Dorothy Biddle
1887(?)-1974 Obituary 53-56
Johnson, Dorothy E(thel) 1920- 53-56
Johnson, Dorothy M(arie) 1905-1984 CANR-63
Obituary 114
Earlier sketches in CA 5-8R, CANR-6
See also SATA 6
See also SATA-Obit 40
Johnson, Dorris 1914- 109
Johnson, Douglas W(ayne) 1934- CANR-21
Earlier sketches in CA 57-60, CANR-6
Johnson, E(dgar) A(ugustus) J(erome) 1900-1972
CAP-1
Obituary 37-40R
Earlier sketch in CA 17-18
Johnson, E(arly) Ashby 1917- 33-36R
Johnson, E(ugene) Harper SATA 44
Johnson, E. Ned
See Johnson, Enid
Johnson, E. Pauline 1861-1913 150
See also DAC
See also DAM MULT
See also DLB 92, 175
See also NNAL
Johnson, E(mil) Richard 1937- CANR-60
Earlier sketch in CA 104
Johnson, E(dward) W(arren) 1941- 29-32R
Johnson, Earl, Jr. 1933- CANR-10
Earlier sketch in CA 61-64
Johnson, Earl S.
See Johnson, Earl Shepard
Johnson, Earl Shepard 1894-1986 Obituary 119
Johnson, Earvin, Jr. 1959- 141
See also AAYA 17
Johnson, Edgar 1901-1995 9-12R
Obituary 148
See also DLB 103
Johnson, Edgar (Raymond) 1912-1990 CANR-37
Earlier sketch in CA 9-12R
See also MAICYA
See also SATA 2, 72
Johnson, Edward 1598-1672 DLB 24
Johnson, Edward A(ndrew) 1915- 37-40R
Johnson, Edwin Clark (Toby) 1945- CANR-25
Earlier sketch in CA 107
Johnson, Eleanor
See Seymour, Dorothy Jane Z(ander)
Johnson, Eleanor Murdock
1892-1987 Obituary 123
See also SATA-Obit 54
Johnson, Electa Search 1909- 1-4R
Johnson, Elizabeth 1911-1984 CANR-4
Obituary 117
Earlier sketch in CA 1-4R
See also SATA 7
See also SATA-Obit 39
Johnson, Elizabeth A. 1941- 168
Johnson, Ellen Argo 1933-1983 CANR-13
Obituary 110
Earlier sketch in CA 73-76
Johnson, Ellen H(ulda) 1910-1992 CANR-15
Obituary 137
Earlier sketch in CA 37-40R
Johnson, Elmer Douglas 1915- CANR-3
Earlier sketch in CA 9-12R
Johnson, Elmer Hubert 1917- CANR-67
Earlier sketch in CA 13-16R
Johnson, Enid 1892- 73-76
Johnson, Eola 1909- 49-52
Johnson, Eric W(arner) 1918-1994 CANR-4
Obituary 146
Earlier sketch in CA 5-8R
See also SATA 8,
See also SATA-Obit 82
Johnson, Eugene J. 1937- CANR-56
Earlier sketch in CA 127
Johnson, Evelyne 1922- CANR-21
Earlier sketch in CA 69-72
See also SATA 20
Johnson, Eyvind (Olof Verner) 1900-1976
CANR-34
Obituary 69-72
Earlier sketch in CA 73-76
See also CLC 14
Johnson, Falk S(immons) 1913- 17-20R
Johnson, Fenton 1888-1958 124
Brief entry 118
See also BLC 2
See also BW 1
See also DAM MULT
See also DLB 45, 50
Johnson, Fenton 1953- 159
Johnson, Ferd 1905-1996 69-72
Obituary 154
Johnson, Forrest B(ryant) 1935- 106
Johnson, Franklyn A(rthur) 1921- CANR-4
Earlier sketch in CA 1-4R
Johnson, Fred 19(?)-1982 SATA 63
Johnson, Frederick 1932- 73-76
Johnson, Fridolf (Lester) 1905-1988 103
Obituary 126
Johnson, Frosty
See Johnson, Forrest B(ryant)
Johnson, G(eorge) Orville 1915- CANR-4
Earlier sketch in CA 1-4R
Johnson, Gaylord 1884- CAP-1
Earlier sketch in CA 9-10
See also SATA 7
Johnson, Geoffrey 1893-1966 CAP-1
Earlier sketch in CA 13-14
Johnson, George 1917- 5-8R
Johnson, George (Laclede) 1952- 133

Johnson, Georgia Douglas (Camp) 1886-1966 .. 125
See also BW 1
See also DLB 51
Johnson, Gerald White 1890-1980 ... 85-88
Obituary ... 97-100
See also DLB 29
See also SATA 19
See also SATA-Obit 28
Johnson, Gertrude F(alk) 1929- ... 57-60
Johnson, Greer 1920(?)-1974 Obituary ... 53-56
Johnson, Greg 1953- ... 140
Johnson, H(arold) B(enjamin), Jr. 1931- ... 29-32R
Johnson, H(erbert) Webster 1906- ... CANR-4
Earlier sketch in CA 5-8R
Johnson, Halvard 1936- ... 33-36R
Johnson, Harold L. 1924- ... 13-16R
Johnson, Harold Scholl 1929- ... 37-40R
Johnson, Harold V. 1897- ... CANR-5
Earlier sketch in CA 1-4R
Johnson, Harper
See Johnson, E(ugene) Harper
Johnson, Harriett 1908-1987 Obituary ... 123
See also SATA-Obit 53
Johnson, Harry Alleyn 1921- ... CANR-31
Earlier sketch in CA 45-48
Johnson, Harry G(ordon) 1923-1977 ... CANR-29
Obituary ... 69-72
Earlier sketch in CA 5-8R
Johnson, Harry L. 1929- ... 29-32R
Johnson, Harry Morton 1917- ... 9-12R
Johnson, Harvey L(eroy) 1904- ... 37-40R
Johnson, Haynes Bonner 1931- ... CANR-48
Earlier sketches in CA 5-8R, CANR-12
Johnson, Helen (Louise) Kendrick
1844(?)-1917 Brief entry ... 123
Johnson, Helene 1907- ... DLB 51
Johnson, Henry
See Hammond, John (Henry, Jr.)
Johnson, Herbert A(lan) 1934- ... CANR-4
Earlier sketch in CA 5-8R
Johnson, Herbert J. 1933- ... 29-32R
Johnson, Hildegard Binder 1908- ... CANR-3
Earlier sketch in CA 9-12R
Johnson, Howard Albert 1915-1974 ... 1-4R
Obituary ... 49-52
Johnson, Hubert C. 1930- ... 130
Johnson, Hugh 1939- ... CANR-39
Earlier sketches in CA 93-96, CANR-16
Johnson, Humphrey Wynne
1925-1976 Obituary ... 61-64
Johnson, Irma Bolan 1903- ... CANR-1
Earlier sketch in CA 1-4R
Johnson, Irving McClure 1905-1991 ... 1-4R
Obituary ... 133
Johnson, J. R.
See James, C(yril) L(ionel) R(obert)
Johnson, J. Stewart 1925- ... 127
Johnson, Jack
See Johnson, John Arthur
Johnson, Jalmar Edwin 1905- ... 5-8R
Johnson, James A(llen) 1932- Brief entry ... 110
Johnson, James Craig 1944- ... 53-56
Johnson, James E(dgar) 1927- ... 77-80
Johnson, James H(enry) 1930- ... CANR-11
Earlier sketch in CA 25-28R
Johnson, James J(ay) 1939- ... 33-36R
Johnson, James L. 1927- ... CANR-9
Earlier sketch in CA 21-24R
Johnson, James P(earce) 1937- ... 81-84
Johnson, James Ralph 1922- ... CANR-2
Earlier sketch in CA 1-4R
See also SATA 1
Johnson, James Rosser 1916- ... 9-12R
Johnson, James Turner 1938- ... 61-64
Johnson, James Weldon 1871-1938 ... 125
Brief entry ... 104
See also BLC 2
See also BW 1
See also CDALB 1917-1929
See also CLR 32
See also DAM MULT, POET
See also DLB 51
See also MTCW 1
See also SATA 31
See also TCLC 3, 19
Johnson, James William 1927- ... 53-56
Johnson, Jane 1951- ... CANR-28
Earlier sketch in CA 110
See also SATA 48
Johnson, Jane M(axine) 1914- ... 49-52
Johnson, Janis Tyler 1930- ... 141
Johnson, Jann
See Johnson, Paula Janice
Johnson, Jay 1951(?)-1990 Obituary ... 131
Johnson, (Hettie) Jean 1937- ... 126
Johnson, Jean Dye 1920- ... 21-24R
Johnson, Jerry Mack 1927- ... CANR-4
Earlier sketch in CA 53-56
Johnson, Jim
See Johnson, James A(llen)
Johnson, Jinna
See Johnson, Virginia
Johnson, Joan D. 1929- Brief entry ... 106
Johnson, Joan Helen 1931- ... 61-64
Johnson, Joan J. 1942- ... CANR-48
Earlier sketch in CA 122
See also SATA 59
Johnson, Joe Donald 1943- ... 57-60
Johnson, John Arthur 1878-1946 Brief entry ... 115
Johnson, John Bockover, Jr.
1912-1972 Obituary ... 106
Johnson, John E(mil) 1929- ... 110
See also SATA 34
Johnson, John H(arold) 1918- ... 135
Brief entry ... 128
See also DLB 137
Johnson, John J. 1912- ... 9-12R
Johnson, John L. 1945- ... 146
Johnson, John M(yrton) 1941- ... 93-96
Johnson, Johnni 1922- ... 13-16R
Johnson, Jory (F.) 1950- ... 137
Johnson, Joseph A., Jr.
1914(?)-1979 Obituary ... 89-92
Johnson, Joseph E(arl) 1946- ... 37-40R
Johnson, Joseph M. 1883(?)-1973 Obituary ... 45-48
Johnson, Josephine W(inslow) 1910-1990 .. 25-28R
Obituary ... 131
Johnson, Joy Duvall 1932- ... 110
Johnson, Joyce 1935- ... 129
Brief entry ... 125
See also CLC 58
Johnson, Judith (Emlyn) 1936- ... 153
Johnson, Karen 1939- ... 69-72
Johnson, Kathryn 1929- ... 33-36R
Johnson, Keith B(arnard) 1933- ... 29-32R
Johnson, Kendall 1928- ... 69-72
Johnson, Kenneth G(ardner) 1922- ... 41-44R
Johnson, Kenneth M(itchell) 1903- ... 5-8R
Johnson, Kim 1955- ... 133
Johnson, Kim "Howard"
See Johnson, Kim
Johnson, Kristi Planck 1944- ... 57-60
Johnson, L. D. 1916-1981 ... CANR-28
Earlier sketch in CA 33-36R
Johnson, La Verne B(ravo) 1925- ... 65-68
See also SATA 13
Johnson, Lady Bird
See Johnson, Claudia Alta (Taylor)
Johnson, Lee Kaiser 1962- ... SATA 78
Johnson, Leland R(oss) 1937- ... 149
Johnson, Lemuel A. 1941- ... CANR-43
Earlier sketch in CA 53-56
See also BW 2
Johnson, LeRoy C. 1937- ... 126
Johnson, Lewis Kerr 1904- ... 1-4R
Johnson, Lincoln F., Jr. 1920- ... 81-84
Johnson, Linnea 1946- ... 138
Johnson, Linton Kwesi 1952- ... 153
See also DLB 157
Johnson, Lionel (Pigot) 1867-1902 Brief entry .. 117
See also DLB 19
See also TCLC 19
Johnson, Lissa H(alls) 1955- ... 136
See also SATA 65
Johnson, Loch K. 1942- ... CANR-48
Earlier sketch in CA 121
Johnson, Lois Smith 1894- ... CAP-1
Earlier sketch in CA 9-10
See also SATA 6
Johnson, Lois Walfrid 1936- ... CANR-57
Earlier sketches in CA 57-60, CANR-6
See also SATA 22, 91
Johnson, LouAnne 1953- ... 138
Johnson, Louis 1924- ... CANR-18
Earlier sketch in CA 101
Johnson, Luke Timothy 1943- ... 127
Brief entry ... 107
Johnson, Lyndon Baines 1908-1973 ... CANR-23
Obituary ... 41-44R
Earlier sketch in CA 53-56
Johnson, Lynn Eric 1932- Brief entry ... 108
Johnson, Lynn Staley
See Staley, Lynn
Johnson, M. Glen 1936- ... 41-44R
Johnson, M. L.
See Abercrombie, M(innie) L(ouie) J(ohnson)
Johnson, Magic
See Johnson, Earvin, Jr.
Johnson, Malcolm (Malone) 1904-1976 ... 69-72
Obituary ... 65-68
Johnson, Malcolm L. 1937- ... 69-72
Johnson, Manly 1920- ... 89-92
Johnson, Margaret 1926- ... 37-40R
Johnson, Margaret S(weet)
1893-1964 Obituary ... 113
See also SATA 35
Johnson, Marilue Carolyn 1931- ... CANR-1
Earlier sketch in CA 45-48
Johnson, Marilynn S. 1957- ... 164
Johnson, Marion Georgina Wikeley
1912-1980 ... 9-12R
Obituary ... 97-100
Johnson, Mark 1949- ... 115
Johnson, Marshall D. 1935- ... 33-36R
Johnson, Mary Anne 1943- ... 53-56
Johnson, Mary Ellen 1949- ... 120
Johnson, Mary Frances K.
1929(?)-1979 Obituary ... 104
See also SATA-Obit 27
Johnson, Mary Louise
See King, Mary Louise
Johnson, Mary Ritz 1904- ... CAP-1
Earlier sketch in CA 9-10
Johnson, Maryanna 1925- ... 33-36R
Johnson, Maud Battle 1918(?)-1985 Obituary .. 117
See also SATA-Obit 46
Johnson, Maurice (O.) 1913-1978 ... CANR-20
Earlier sketch in CA 1-4R
Johnson, Mauritz (Jr.) 1922- ... 41-44R
Johnson, Mel
See Malzberg, Barry N(athaniel)
Johnson, Mendal W(illiam) 1928-1976 ... 101
Johnson, Merle Allison 1934- ... 37-40R
Johnson, Michael L(illard) 1943- ... CANR-19
Earlier sketches in CA 53-56, CANR-4
Johnson, Michael P(aul) 1941- ... 132
Johnson, Mike
See Sharkey, John Michael
Johnson, Mildred D. ... 132
Johnson, Milton 1932- ... SATA 31
Johnson, Nancy 1948- ... 159
Johnson, Nancy E(dith) 1941- ... 125
Johnson, Neil 1954- ... SATA 73
Johnson, Neil (James) 1955- ... 123
Johnson, Nicholas 1934- ... 29-32R
Johnson, Niel M(elvin) 1931- ... 41-44R
Johnson, Nora 1933- ... 106
Johnson, Norman L. 1917- ... 166
Johnson, Nunnally 1897-1977 ... 81-84
Obituary ... 69-72
See also DLB 26
Johnson, Olga Weydemeyer 1901- ... CAP-2
Earlier sketch in CA 29-32
Johnson, Oliver A(dolph) 1923- ... CANR-12
Earlier sketch in CA 29-32R
Johnson, Owen (McMahon) 1878-1952 ... 159
See also DLBY 87
Johnson, Pamela 1949- ... SATA 71
Johnson, Pamela Hansford 1912-1981 .. CANR-28
Obituary ... 104
Earlier sketches in CA 1-4R, CANR-2
See also CLC 1, 7, 27
See also DLB 15
See also MTCW 1
Johnson, Patricia Polin 1956- ... 150
See also SATA 84
Johnson, Patrick Spencer 1938- ... 9-12R
Johnson, Paul (Bede) 1928- ... CANR-62
Earlier sketches in CA 17-20R, CANR-34
See also BEST 89:4
Johnson, Paul Brett 1947- ... SATA 83
Johnson, Paul C(ornelius) 1904- ... 81-84
Johnson, Paul E(manuel) 1898-1974 ... 13-16R
Obituary ... 134
Johnson, Paul Victor 1920- ... 1-4R
Johnson, Paula Janice 1946- ... 106
Johnson, Pauline B. ... 1-4R
Johnson, Penelope D(elafield) 1938- ... 124
Johnson, Peter 1930- ... 65-68
Johnson, Philip A(rthur) 1915-1991 ... 13-16R
Obituary ... 133
Johnson, Philip Cortelyou 1906- Brief entry ... 106
Johnson, Phillip E. 1940- ... 136
Johnson, Phyllis (Anne) 1937-1985 ... 126
Brief entry ... 108
Johnson, Pierce 1921- ... 41-44R
Johnson, Quentin G. 1930- ... 9-12R
Johnson, R(obbin) S(inclair) 1946- ... 29-32R
Johnson, Rachel H(arris) 1887-1983 Obituary .. 110
Johnson, Ralph W(hitney) 1923- ... 77-80
Johnson, Ray(mond Edward) 1927- ... 17-20R
Johnson, Ray DeForest 1926-1989 ... 65-68
Obituary ... 130
Johnson, Raynor C(arey) 1901- Brief entry ... 115
Johnson, Rebecca L. 1956- ... 136
See also SATA 67
Johnson, Richard
See Richey, David
Johnson, Richard
See Richardson, John
Johnson, Richard A(ugust) 1937- ... 37-40R
Johnson, Richard A. 1955- ... 135
Johnson, Richard B(righam) 1914-1977 ... 41-44R
Johnson, Richard C. 1919- ... 33-36R
Johnson, Richard D(avid) 1927- ... 109
Johnson, Richard N(ewhall)
1900-1971 Obituary ... 104
Johnson, Richard R(igby) 1942- ... 116
Johnson, Richard Tanner
See Pascale, Richard Tanner
Johnson, Rick L. 1954- ... 147
See also SATA 79
Johnson, Robert 1911(?)-1938 ... TCLC 69
Johnson, Robert A. 1921- ... 61-64
Johnson, Robert C(lyde) 1919- ... 5-8R
Johnson, Robert E. 1908(?)-1989 Obituary ... 128
Johnson, Robert Erwin 1923- ... 37-40R
Johnson, Robert I(var) 1933- ... 53-56
Johnson, Robert J. 1933- ... 21-24R
Johnson, Robert L. 1919- ... 33-36R
Johnson, Robert L(eon, Jr.) 1930- ... 33-36R
Johnson, Robert Owen 1926- ... 33-36R
Johnson, Robert Sherlaw 1932- ... 61-64
Johnson, Robert W(illard) 1921- ... 17-20R
Johnson, Roger 1942- ... 149
Johnson, Roger N(ylund) 1939- ... 53-56
Johnson, Ronald 1935-1998 ... CANR-42
Obituary ... 165
Earlier sketches in CA 9-12R, CANR-4, 20
See also CAAS 30
See also DLB 169
Johnson, Ronald C. 1927- ... 81-84
Johnson, Ronald M(aberry) 1936- ... 126
Brief entry ... 108
Johnson, Rossall J(ames) 1917- ... 21-24R
Johnson, Ruby Kelley 1928- ... 33-36R
Johnson, Ruth I.
See Jay, Ruth I(ngrid)
Johnson, (Walter) Ryerson 1901- ... CANR-2
Earlier sketch in CA 5-8R
See also SATA 10
Johnson, S(amuel) Lawrence 1909-1978 . CANR-12
Earlier sketch in CA 29-32R
Johnson, Sabina Thorne
See Thorne, Sabina
Johnson, Sam Houston 1914(?)-1978 ... 89-92
Obituary ... 81-84
Johnson, Samuel 1696-1772 ... DLB 24
Johnson, Samuel 1709-1784 ... CDBLB 1660-1789
See also DA
See also DAB
See also DAC
See also DAM MST
See also DLB 39, 95, 104, 142
See also WLC
Johnson, Samuel 1822-1882 ... DLB 1
Johnson, Samuel A(ugustus) 1895- ... 17-20R
Johnson, Scott 1952- ... 143
See also SATA 76
Johnson, Sherman E(lbridge) 1908-1993 ... 53-56
Obituary ... 141
Johnson, Sherman Ellsworth
1896-1978 Obituary ... 77-80
Johnson, Sherrie 1948- ... 151
See also SATA 87
Johnson, Shirley K(ing) 1927- ... 9-12R
See also SATA 10
Johnson, Siddie Joe 1905-1977 Obituary ... 106
See also SATA-Obit 20
Johnson, Sonia 1936- ... 118
Johnson, Spencer 1938- ... 110
See also SATA-Brief 38
Johnson, Stanley (Patrick) 1940- ... CANR-13
Earlier sketch in CA 21-24R
Johnson, Stanley J. F.
1920(?)-1978 Obituary ... 77-80
Johnson, Stanley L(ewis) 1920- ... 17-20R
Johnson, (John) Stephen 1947- ... 107
Johnson, Stephen M. ... 141
Johnson, Stephen T. 1964- ... SATA 84
Johnson, Steven F(orrest) 1954- ... 156
Johnson, (Edward) Stowers ... 5-8R
Johnson, Sue Kaiser 1963- ... SATA 78
Johnson, Susan (Ruth) 1956- ... 137
Johnson, Susan E. 1940- ... 138
Johnson, Susanna 1730-1810 ... DLB 200
Johnson, Sylvia A. ... SATA-Brief 52
Johnson, Terry 1955- ... 144
Johnson, Thomas Frank 1920- ... 9-12R
Johnson, Thomas Herbert 1902-1985 ... 124
Johnson, Thomas William 1946- Brief entry ... 110
Johnson, U(ral) Alexis 1908- ... 143
Johnson, Una E. 1905-1997 ... 134
Obituary ... 157
Brief entry ... 109
Johnson, Uwe 1934-1984 ... CANR-39
Obituary ... 112
Earlier sketches in CA 1-4R, CANR-1
See also CLC 5, 10, 15, 40
See also DLB 75
See also MTCW 1
Johnson, Van L(oran) 1908- ... 37-40R
Johnson, Vernon E(dwin) 1920- ... 93-96
Johnson, Vicki Vaughn 1948- ... 144
Johnson, Victor Hugo 1912- Brief entry ... 110
Johnson, Virginia 1914-1975 ... CAP-2
Earlier sketch in CA 33-36
Johnson, Virginia E. 1925- ... CANR-34
Earlier sketch in CA 21-24R
Johnson, Virginia W(eisel) 1910- ... 17-20R
Johnson, W. Bolingbroke
See Bishop, Morris
Johnson, W(illiam) Branch 1893- ... CANR-5
Earlier sketch in CA 5-8R
Johnson, W(illiam) E(rnest) 1858-1931 Brief
entry ... 122
Johnson, W(alter) R(alph) 1933- ... CANR-9
Earlier sketch in CA 65-68
Johnson, W(endell) Stacy 1927-1990 ... CANR-17
Obituary ... 131
Earlier sketches in CA 1-4R, CANR-2
Johnson, Walter 1915-1985 ... 89-92
Obituary ... 116
Johnson, Walter Frank, Jr. 1914- ... 5-8R
Johnson, Warren Arthur 1937- ... 33-36R
Johnson, Warren T(hurston) 1925- ... 131
Johnson, Wayne 1956- ... 135
Johnson, Wayne G(ustave) 1930- ... 113
Johnson, Wendell (Andrew Leroy) 1906-1965 ...
CANR-1
Earlier sketch in CA 1-4R
Johnson, Whittington B. 1931- ... 157
Johnson, Willard R(aymond) 1935- ... 105
Johnson, William Alexander 1932- ... 5-8R
Johnson, William C(lark, Jr.) 1945- ... CANR-8
Earlier sketch in CA 61-64
Johnson, William R. ... CANR-25
Earlier sketches in CA 17-20R, CANR-7
See also SATA 38
Johnson, William Stacy 1956- ... 156
Johnson, William Weber 1909-1992 ... CANR-46
Obituary ... 139
Earlier sketch in CA 17-20R
See also SATA 7
Johnson, Willis 1938- ... 162
Johnson, Winifred (MacNally) 1905- ... 5-8R
Johnson Abercrombie, M. L.
See Abercrombie, M(innie) L(ouie) J(ohnson)
Johnson-Marshall, Percy E(dwin) A(lan)
1915-1993 ... 21-24R
Obituary ... 142
John-Steiner, Vera P(olgar) ... 121
Johnston, A(aron) Montgomery 1915- ... CANR-11
Earlier sketch in CA 29-32R
Johnston, Agnes Christine
See Dazey, Agnes J(ohnston)
Johnston, Alan (William) 1942- ... 103
Johnston, Albert H. 1914- ... 69-72
Johnston, Angus James II 1916- ... 9-12R
Johnston, Annie Fellows 1863-1931 Brief
entry ... 116
See also DLB 42
See also SATA 37
Johnston, (William) Arnold 1942- ... 77-80
Johnston, Arthur 1924- ... 21-24R
Johnston, Arvin Harry 1906- ... 1-4R
Johnston, Barbara Rose 1957- ... 150
Johnston, Basil H. 1929- ... CANR-66
Earlier sketches in CA 69-72, CANR-11, 28
See also DAC
See also DAM MULT
See also DLB 60
See also NNAL

Johnston, Bernard 1934- 17-20R
Johnston, Bernice Houle 1914-1971 .... CAP-2
Earlier sketch in CA 33-36
Johnston, Brenda A(rlivia) 1944- 57-60
Johnston, Brian 1932- 65-68
Johnston, Bruce F(oster) 1919- CANR-14
Earlier sketch in CA 41-44R
Johnston, Charles (Hepburn) 1912-1986 .. CANR-5
Obituary 119
Earlier sketch in CA 13-16R
Johnston, Colin 1946- 108
Johnston, Dan 1912- 123
Johnston, David (Cay Boyle) 1948- 131
Johnston, David Claypoole 1798(?)-1865 .. DLB 188
Johnston, (William) Denis 1901-1984 .... CAP-2
Obituary 113
Earlier sketch in CA 21-22
See also DLB 10
Johnston, Donald J(ames) 1936- 162
Johnston, Dorothy Grunbock 1915-1979 .. CANR-5
Earlier sketch in CA 5-8R
See also SATA 54
Johnston, Ellen 1835-1873 .... DLB 199
Johnston, Ellen Turlington 1929- 65-68
Johnston, Fran(ces Jonsson) 1925- 13-16R
Johnston, Francis E. 1931- CANR-4
Earlier sketch in CA 53-56
Johnston, George 1913- CANR-15
Earlier sketch in CA 89-92
Johnston, George (Benson) 1913- CANR-20
Earlier sketches in CA 1-4R, CANR-5
See also CLC 51
See also DLB 88
Johnston, George Burke 1907- CAP-1
Earlier sketch in CA 17-18
Johnston, Ginny 1946- .... SATA 60
Johnston, Gordon (Frederick) 1920-1983 122
Johnston, H(ugh) A(nthony) S(tephen) 1913-1967 ..
CAP-2
Earlier sketch in CA 21-22
See also SATA 14
Johnston, H(ugh) J(ames) M(orton) 1939- .. 41-44R
Johnston, Hank
See Johnston, Henry
Johnston, SirHarry 1858-1927 .... DLB 174
Johnston, Henry 1922- 25-28R
Johnston, Herbert (Leo) 1912- 5-8R
Johnston, Hugh Buckner 1913- 69-72
Johnston, Janet 1944- .... SATA 71
Johnston, Jennifer 1930- 85-88
See also CLC 7
See also DLB 14
Johnston, Jill 1929- CANR-44
Earlier sketch in CA 53-56
Johnston, Joan 1948- 147
Johnston, Johanna 1914(?)-1982 .... CANR-7
Obituary 108
Earlier sketch in CA 57-60
See also SATA 12
See also SATA-Obit 33
Johnston, John H(ubert) 1921- 9-12R
Johnston, John M. 1898(?)-1979 Obituary ... 89-92
Johnston, Joni E. 1960- 148
Johnston, Julie 1941- CANR-69
Earlier sketch in CA 146
See also AAYA 27
See also CLR 41
See also SAAS 24
See also SATA 78
Johnston, Kenneth R(ichard) 1938- 121
Johnston, Leonard 1920- CANR-11
Earlier sketch in CA 13-16R
Johnston, Lynn (Beverley) 1947- 110
See also AAYA 12
Johnston, Marguerite 1917- 138
Johnston, Mary 1870-1936 Brief entry 109
See also DLB 9
Johnston, Mary E(lizabeth)
1919-1989 Obituary 128
Johnston, Minton C(oyne) 1900- 5-8R
Johnston, Mireille 1940- 49-52
Johnston, Norma
See St. John, Nicole
See also AAYA 12
See also JRDA
See also SATA 29
Johnston, Norman (Bruce) 1921- CANR-18
Earlier sketch in CA 93-96
Johnston, Norman J. 1918- 120
Johnston, Portia
See Takakjian, Portia
Johnston, R(onald) J(ohn) 1941- CANR-40
Earlier sketches in CA 101, CANR-18
Johnston, Randolph W(ardell) 1904- CANR-15
Earlier sketch in CA 85-88
Johnston, Richard 1948- 164
Johnston, Richard Malcolm 1822-1898 .... DLB 74
Johnston, Richard W(yckoff)
1915-1981 Obituary 104
Johnston, Robert Kent 1945- 104
Johnston, Ronald 1926- 13-16R
Johnston, Ronald Carlyle 1907-1990 Obituary .. 131
Johnston, Russell G. 1933- 118
Johnston, S(amuel) Paul 1899-1985 Obituary .. 117
Johnston, Stanley H(oward), Jr. 1946- 137
Johnston, Susan Taylor 1942- CANR-15
Earlier sketch in CA 41-44R
See also Johnston, Tony
See also SATA 83
Johnston, Terry C(onrad) 1947- CANR-63
Earlier sketch in CA 113
Johnston, Thomas 1945- 104
Johnston, Thomas E. 1931- 13-16R
Johnston, Tony
See Johnston, Susan Taylor
See also SATA 8
Johnston, Velma B. 1912(?)-1977 Obituary .. 69-72
Johnston, Wayne 1958- 125
Johnston, William 1924- 85-88
Johnston, William 1925- 33-36R
Johnston, William M(urray) 1936- 37-40R
Johnstone, Charles 1719(?)-1800(?) .... DLB 39
Johnstone, D(onald) Bruce 1909- 104
Johnstone, Henry W(ebb), Jr. 1920- 1-4R
Johnstone, Iain 1943- 108
Johnstone, Kathleen Yerger 1906- 9-12R
Johnstone, Keith 129
Johnstone, Lammy Olcott 1949- CANR-14
Earlier sketch in CA 81-84
Johnstone, Parker Lochiel 1903- 69-72
Johnstone, Rex
See Chapman, Frank M(onroe)
Johnstone, Robert 1951- 118
Johnstone, Robert Morton, Jr. 1939- 81-84
Johnstone, T(homas) M(uir)
1924-1983 Obituary 114
Johnstone, Ted
See McDaniel, David (Edward)
Johnstone, William D(avid) G(ordon) 1935- ... 77-80
Johnston-Saint, Peter 1889-1974 Obituary ... 53-56
John XXIII, Pope 1881-1963 134
Obituary 113
Johst, Hanns 1890-1978 .... DLB 124
Joiner, Charles A(drian) 1932- 77-80
Joiner, Charles W(ycliffe) 1916- CANR-1
Earlier sketch in CA 1-4R
Joiner, Edward Earl 1924- 49-52
Joiner, Verna J(ones) 1896- 1-4R
Jokemeisters
See Krauzer, Steven M(ark)
Joki, Virginia (Carville) 1909(?)-1986 Obituary .. 120
Jolas, Eugene 1894-1952 166
Brief entry 107
See also DLB 4, 45
Joliat, Eugene 1910- 49-52
Joliffe, John E(dward) A(ustin) 1891-1964 .... 5-8R
Jolin, Stephen Towne 1941- 45-48
Jolivet, R(egis) 1891-1966 .... CAP-1
Earlier sketch in CA 9-10
Joll, (Dowrish) Evelyn (Louis) 1925- 101
Joll, James (Bysse) 1918- CANR-7
Earlier sketch in CA 5-8R
Jolley, (Monica) Elizabeth 1923- CANR-59
Earlier sketch in CA 127
See also CAAS 13
See also CLC 46
See also SSC 19
Jolley, (Stephen) Nicholas 1948- 120
Jolliffe, H(arold) R(ichard) 1904-1978 .... 1-4R
Obituary 103
Jolliffe, John (Hedworth) 1935- 133
Jolly, Alison 1937- CANR-15
Earlier sketch in CA 41-44R
Jolly, Clifford J. 1939- Brief entry 108
Jolly, Cyril Arthur 1910- CAP-1
Earlier sketch in CA 9-10
Jolly, Hugh R. 1918-1986 85-88
Obituary 118
Jolly, Roslyn 1963- 152
Jolly, W(illiam) P(ercy) 1922- CANR-4
Earlier sketch in CA 53-56
Jolly Cholly
See Grimm, Charles John
Jolson, Marvin A(rnold) 1922- CANR-1
Earlier sketch in CA 49-52
Joly, Cyril Bencraft 1918- CAP-1
Earlier sketch in CA 9-10
Jomo
See Raskin, Jonah (Seth)
Jonaitis, Aldona 1948- 139
Jonas, A(dolphe) David 1913- 107
Jonas, Ann 1919- 105
Jonas, Ann 1932- 136
Brief entry 118
See also CLR 12
See also MAICYA
See also SATA 50
See also SATA-Brief 42
Jonas, Arthur 1930- 13-16R
Jonas, Carl 1913-1976 .... 9-12R
Obituary 69-72
Jonas, Doris F(rances) 1916- CANR-8
Earlier sketch in CA 61-64
Jonas, George 1935- CANR-32
Earlier sketch in CA 29-32R
Jonas, Gerald 1935- 65-68
Jonas, Hans 1903-1993 .... CANR-23
Obituary 140
Earlier sketches in CA 61-64, CANR-7
Jonas, Ilsedore B. 1920- 33-36R
Jonas, Klaus W(erner) 1920- CANR-2
Earlier sketch in CA 1-4R
Jonas, Manfred 1927- CANR-8
Earlier sketch in CA 21-24R
Jonas, Norman N. 1931-1988 Obituary 125
Jonas, Paul 1922- CANR-13
Earlier sketch in CA 73-76
Jonas, Steven 1936- 89-92
Jonas, Susan 1938- 146
Jonasdottir, Anna G(udrun) 1942- 146
Jonassen, Christen T(onnes) 1912- 41-44R
Joncich, Geraldine
See Clifford, Geraldine Joncich
Jones, A(rnold) H(ugh) M(artin)
1904-1970 Obituary 89-92
Jones, A(rthur) Morris 1899- CAP-1
Earlier sketch in CA 13-14
Jones, Adam Mars
See Mars-Jones, Adam
Jones, Adrienne 1915- CANR-28
Earlier sketch in CA 33-36R
See also SAAS 10
See also SATA 7, 82
Jones, Alan Griffith 1943- CANR-19
Earlier sketch in CA 103
Jones, Alan Moore, Jr. 1942- 53-56
Jones, Alan William 1940- 117
Jones, Alex S. 1946- 135
Jones, Alexander 1906-1970 .... CANR-2
Obituary 103
Earlier sketch in CA 1-4R
Jones, Alfred Winslow 1900-1989 Obituary 128
Jones, Alice C. 1853-1933 .... DLB 92
Jones, Allan Gwynne
See Gwynne-Jones, Allan
Jones, Amelia 1961- 146
Jones, Andrew 1921- 93-96
Jones, Andrew (Eric) 1950- 111
Jones, Ann (Maret) 1937- 156
Jones, Annabel
See Lewis, Mary (Christianna)
Jones, Anne Hudson 1944- 135
Jones, Antony Armstrong
See Armstrong-Jones, Antony (Charles Robert)
Jones, Archer 1926- CANR-18
Earlier sketches in CA 1-4R, CANR-4
Jones, Archie N(eff) 1900- CAP-1
Earlier sketch in CA 13-16
Jones, Arthur F(rederick) 1945- 81-84
Jones, Arthur Glyn Prys
See Prys-Jones, Arthur Glyn
Jones, (Alun) Arthur Gwynne 1919- 128
Brief entry 120
Jones, Arthur Hope
See Hope-Jones, Arthur
Jones, Arthur (Mervyn) Keppel
See Keppel-Jones, Arthur (Mervyn)
Jones, Arthur Llewellyn 1863-1947 Brief entry .. 104
See also Machen, Arthur
Jones, Aubrey 1911- 103
Jones, Barbara (Mildred) 1917(?)-1978 ... CANR-4
Obituary 81-84
Earlier sketch in CA 1-4R
Jones, Bessie 1902-1984 Obituary 114
Jones, Betty Millsaps 1940- 109
See also SATA 54
Jones, Bill
See Jones, William David Anthony
Jones, Billy M(ac) 1925- CANR-25
Earlier sketches in CA 21-24R, CANR-10
Jones, Bob
See Jones, Robert Reynolds, Jr.
Jones, Bobby
See Jones, Robert Tyre, Jr.
Jones, Bobi
See Jones, R(obert) M(aynard)
Jones, Brennon 1945- 136
Jones, Brian 1938- 153
Brief entry 119
Jones, Bridget 1955- 141
Jones, Bryan D(avidson) 1944- 139
Jones, Bryan L. 1945- 110
Jones, C(lifton) Clyde 1922- 109
Jones, C. M.
See Jones, C(larence) M(edleycott)
Jones, C(larence) M(edleycott) 1913(?)-1986 ... 164
Obituary 118
Jones, C(harles) Robert 1932- CANR-66
Earlier sketch in CA 129
Jones, Calico
See Richardson, Gladwell
Jones, Candy 1925-1990 107
Obituary 130
Jones, Capt. Wilbur
See Edwards, William B(ennett)
Jones, Carol 1942- .... SATA 79
Jones, Carolyn (Sue) 1933-1983 .... 29-32R
Obituary 110
Jones, Charles 1910- CAP-1
Earlier sketch in CA 9-10
Jones, Charles Alfred 1921-1982 Obituary 107
Jones, Charles C., Jr. 1831-1893 .... DLB 30
Jones, Charles Edwin 1932- CANR-47
Earlier sketches in CA 49-52, CANR-23
Jones, Charles M(artin) 1912- 129
See also Jones, Chuck
See also SATA 53
Jones, Charles O(scar) 1931- CANR-7
Earlier sketch in CA 17-20R
Jones, Charles W(illiams) 1905- 13-16R
Jones, Charlotte Foltz 1945- 145
See also SATA 77
Jones, Cheslyn Peter Montague
1918-1987(?) Obituary 125
Jones, Christina Hendry 1896- 73-76
Jones, (Audrey) Christine 1937- 61-64
Jones, Christopher 1937- 21-24R
Jones, Chuck
See Jones, Charles M(artin)
See also AAYA 2
Jones, Clifford M(erton) 1902- 17-20R
Jones, Craig 1945- CANR-34
Earlier sketch in CA 81-84
Jones, Cranston E(dward) 1918-1991 ... CANR-26
Obituary 134
Earlier sketch in CA 1-4R
Jones, Cyril Meredith 1904- CAP-2
Earlier sketch in CA 23-24
Jones, D(ennis) F(eltham) 1917-1981 163
Brief entry 111
Jones, D(ouglas) G(ordon) 1929- CANR-13
Earlier sketch in CA 29-32R
See also CLC 10
See also DLB 53
Jones, D(avid) Gareth 1940- 106
Jones, D(onald) L(ewis) 1925- 25-28R
Jones, D(avid) Mervyn 1922- 21-24R
Jones, D. S. 1922- 141
Jones, Daisy (Marvel) 1906- 17-20R
Jones, Dan Burne 1908- 65-68
Jones, Daniel 1881-1967 .... CANR-6
Earlier sketch in CA 5-8R
Jones, Daryl (Emrys) 1946- 134
Jones, David (Michael) 1895-1974 .... CANR-28
Obituary 53-56
Earlier sketch in CA 9-12R
See also CDBLB 1945-1960
See also CLC 2, 4, 7, 13, 42
See also DLB 20, 100
See also MTCW 1
Jones, David Arthur 1946- CANR-13
Earlier sketch in CA 73-76
Jones, David (Erik) Hay 1959- 133
Jones, David Lee 1948- 149
Jones, David Pryce
See Pryce-Jones, David
Jones, David Rhodes 1932- 101
Jones, David Richard 1942- 125
Jones, David Robert 1947- 103
See also Bowie, David
Jones, David W(yn) 1950- 131
Jones, Dennis 1945- 143
Jones, Diana Wynne 1934- CANR-56
Earlier sketches in CA 49-52, CANR-4, 26
See also AAYA 12
See also CLC 26
See also CLR 23
See also DLB 161
See also JRDA
See also MAICYA
See also SAAS 7
See also SATA 9, 70
Jones, Dolores Blythe 1947- 120
Jones, Don 1924- 125
Jones, (Gene) Donald 1931- CANR-34
Earlier sketches in CA 85-88, CANR-15
Jones, Donald (Lawrence) 1938- 17-20R
Jones, Dorothy 1948- 146
Jones, Dorothy Holder 1925(?)-1991 .... 9-12R
Obituary 134
Jones, Dorothy V. 1927- 138
Jones, Douglas C(lyde) 1924- CANR-48
Earlier sketches in CA 21-24R, CANR-12
See also SATA 52
Jones, DuPre Anderson 1937- 21-24R
Jones, Dylan 1960- 142
Jones, E(li) Stanley 1884-1973 93-96
Obituary 41-44R
Jones, E(ndsley) Terrence 1941- 33-36R
Jones, E(lbert) Winston 1911- 13-16R
Jones, Ebenezer 1820-1860 .... DLB 32
Jones, (Hilary) Edgar 1953- 118
Jones, Edgar A(llen), Jr. 1921- 89-92
Jones, Edward A(llen) 1903-1981 .... 25-28R
Obituary 134
Jones, Edward E(llsworth) 1926-1993 .... 17-20R
Obituary 142
Jones, Edward H(arral), Jr. 1922- 13-16R
Jones, Edward P. 1950- 142
See also BW 2
See also CLC 76
Jones, Eileen 1952- 147
Jones, Eldred D(urosimi) 1925- CANR-30
Earlier sketch in CA 45-48
Jones, Elizabeth B(rown) 1907- 61-64
Jones, Elizabeth Orton 1910- 77-80
See also SATA 18
Jones, Elwyn 1923-1982 .... CANR-21
Obituary 106
Earlier sketch in CA 69-72
Jones, Emlyn (David) 1912-1975 .... CAP-2
Earlier sketch in CA 23-24
Jones, Emrys 1920- 17-20R
Jones, Enid (Mary) Huws 1911- 49-52
Jones, Eric Lionel 1936- 104
Jones, Ernest 1819-1868 .... DLB 32
Jones, (Alfred) Ernest 1879-1958 Brief entry ... 121
Jones, Eva (Eleonore) 1913-1996 131
Obituary 151
Jones, Evan 1915-1996 .... CANR-6
Obituary 151
Earlier sketch in CA 9-12R
See also SATA 3
Jones, Evan David 1903-1987 Obituary 122
Jones, Eve (Spiro-John) 1924- 1-4R
Jones, Everett L(ee) 1915-1990 .... 13-16R
Obituary 131
Jones, Ezra Earl 1939- 57-60
Jones, F(rank) Lancaster 1937- 29-32R
Jones, Faustine Childress
See Jones-Wilson, Faustine C(hildress)
Jones, Felix Edward Aylmer 1889- CAP-1
Earlier sketch in CA 9-10
Jones, Francis P(rice) 1890- 9-12R
Jones, Frank 1937- CANR-43
Earlier sketch in CA 119
Jones, Frank E(dward) 1917- 13-16R
Jones, Frank Pierce 1905-1975 Obituary 110
Jones, Franklin Ross 1921- 53-56
Jones, Frederic J. 1925- 149
Jones, Frederick George Hall
See Hall-Jones, Frederick George
Jones, G. Brian 1935- 128
Jones, G(eorge) Curtis 1911- CANR-3
Earlier sketch in CA 5-8R
Jones, G(wyn) O(wain) 1917- 25-28R
Jones, G(eorge) William 1931- CANR-11
Earlier sketch in CA 21-24R
Jones, Gareth (Elwyn) 1939- CANR-41
Earlier sketches in CA 102, CANR-19
Jones, Garth N(elson) 1925- 81-84

Jones, Gary M(artin) 1925- ... 17-20R
Jones, Gayl 1949- ... CANR-66
  Earlier sketches in CA 77-80, CANR-27
  See also BLC 2
  See also BW 2
  See also CLC 6, 9
  See also DAM MULT
  See also DLB 33
  See also MTCW 1
Jones, Gene 1928- ... 21-24R
Jones, Geoffrey (Gareth) 1952- ... CANR-48
  Earlier sketch in CA 122
Jones, George 1800-1870 ... DLB 183
Jones, George (Glenn) 1931- ... 159
Jones, George Chetwynd Griffith
  See Griffith-Jones, George Chetwynd
Jones, George Fenwick 1916- ... CANR-7
  Earlier sketch in CA 13-16R
Jones, George Hilton 1924- ... 33-36R
Jones, George Thaddeus 1917- ... 53-56
Jones, Geraldine
  See McCaughrean, Geraldine
Jones, Gillingham
  See Hamilton, Charles (Harold St. John)
Jones, (Morgan) Glyn 1905- ... CANR-3
  Earlier sketch in CA 9-12R
  See also DLB 15
Jones, Gordon W(illis) 1915- ... 45-48
Jones, Goronwy J(ohn) 1915- ... 9-12R
Jones, Grant D(rummond) 1941- ... 129
Jones, Guy Salisbury
  See Salisbury-Jones, Guy
Jones, Gwen 1951(?)-1988 Obituary ... 124
Jones, Gwendolyn ... 33-36R
Jones, Gwilym Peredur 1892-1975 Obituary ... 57-60
Jones, Gwyn 1907- ... 124
  Brief entry ... 117
  See also DLB 15, 139
Jones, Gwyneth A(nn) 1952- ... CANR-58
  Earlier sketch in CA 107
Jones, H(ouston) G(wynne) 1924- ... CANR-13
  Earlier sketch in CA 33-36R
Jones, H(enry) John F(ranklin) 1924- ... 9-12R
Jones, Hardin Blair 1914-1978 Obituary ... 77-80
Jones, Harold
  See Page, Gerald W(ilburn)
Jones, Harold 1904-1992 ... CANR-49
  Obituary ... 139
  Earlier sketches in CA 85-88, CANR-15
  See also SATA 14
  See also SATA-Obit 72
Jones, Harriet
  See Marble, Harriet Clement
Jones, Harry Lee 1921(?)-1983 Obituary ... 110
Jones, Helen 1917- ... 105
Jones, Helen Hinckley 1903- ... CANR-5
  Earlier sketch in CA 5-8R
  See also SATA 26
Jones, Helen L(ouise) 1903-1973 Obituary ... 104
  See also SATA-Obit 22
Jones, (Max Him) Henri 1921- ... 41-44R
Jones, Henry Albert 1889-1981 Obituary ... 103
Jones, Henry Arthur 1851-1929 Brief entry ... 110
  See also DLB 10
Jones, Hettie 1934- ... 81-84
  See also SATA 42
  See also SATA-Brief 27
Jones, Hortense P. 1918- ... 61-64
  See also SATA 9
Jones, Howard 1940- ... 85-88
Jones, Howard Mumford 1892-1980 ... 85-88
  Obituary ... 97-100
Jones, Howard P(alfry) 1899-1973 Obituary ... 111
Jones, Hugh 1692(?)-1760 ... DLB 24
Jones, Iris Sanderson 1932- ... 73-76
Jones, J. Barrie 1946- ... 131
Jones, J. Farragut
  See Levinson, Leonard
  and Streib, Dan(iel Thomas)
Jones, J. Gwynfor 1936- ... 146
Jones, J(ohn) Ithel 1911- ... CAP-2
  Earlier sketch in CA 25-28
Jones, J(on) Sydney 1948- ... 168
  See also SATA 101
Jones, Jack
  See Jones, James Larkin
Jones, Jack 1884-1970 Obituary ... 115
Jones, Jack 1913-1984 Obituary ... 113
  Brief entry ... 109
Jones, Jack 1924- ... 85-88
Jones, Jack P(ayne) 1928- ... 168
Jones, Jacqueline 1948- ... 122
  See also BW
Jones, James 1921-1977 ... CANR-6
  Obituary ... 69-72
  Earlier sketch in CA 1-4R
  See also AITN 1, 2
  See also CLC 1, 3, 10, 39
  See also DLB 2, 143
  See also DLBD 17
  See also MTCW 1
Jones, James C(linton) 1922- ... 69-72
Jones, James Earl 1931- ... 146
Jones, James Henry 1907(?)-1977 Obituary ... 73-76
Jones, James Larkin 1913- ... CANR-27
  Earlier sketch in CA 109
Jones, James T. 1948- ... 124
Jones, Jeanie Schmit Kayser
  See Kayser-Jones, Jeanie Schmit
Jones, Jeanne 1937- ... CANR-28
  Earlier sketches in CA 61-64, CANR-12
Jones, Jeannette 1944- ... 110
Jones, Jenkin Lloyd 1911- ... 9-12R
  See also DLB 127
Jones, Jennifer (Berry) 1947- ... SATA 90
Jones, Jenny 1954- ... 155
Jones, Jessie Mae Orton
  1887(?)-1983 Obituary ... 111
  See also SATA-Obit 37
Jones, Jimmy
  See Jones, C(larence) M(edleycott)
Jones, Jo ... 33-36R
Jones, Joanna
  See Burke, John (Frederick)
Jones, Johanna 1909- ... 118
Jones, (Harry) John (Franklin) 1924- ... 158
Jones, John (Henry) 1942- ... 140
Jones, John Beauchamp 1810-1866 ... DLB 202
Jones, John Bush 1940- ... 33-36R
Jones, John F(inbar) 1929- ... 130
Jones, John Griffin 1955- ... 113
Jones, John J.
  See Lovecraft, H(oward) P(hillips)
Jones, John Paul, Jr. 1912- ... CANR-11
  Earlier sketch in CA 69-72
Jones, John Philip 1930- ... 130
Jones, John R(obert) 1926- ... 116
  See also SATA 76
Jones, Joseph Jay 1908- ... CANR-16
  Earlier sketches in CA 1-4R, CANR-1
Jones, Joseph L. 1897-1980 Obituary ... 102
Jones, Joseph Marion, Jr. 1908-1990 Obituary ... 132
Jones, Judith Paterson 1938- ... 106
Jones, K. Westcott
  See Westcott-Jones, K(enneth)
Jones, Karen Midkiff 1948- ... 104
Jones, Katharine M(acbeth) 1900- ... 5-8R
Jones, Kathleen 1922- ... CANR-48
  Earlier sketch in CA 81-84
Jones, Kathleen Eve 1944- ... CANR-46
  Earlier sketch in CA 102
Jones, Kaylie (Ann) 1960- ... 123
Jones, Ken D(uane) 1930- ... CANR-31
  Earlier sketch in CA 49-52
Jones, Kenley 1935- ... 69-72
Jones, Kenneth E(ffner) 1920- ... 57-60
Jones, Kenneth Glyn 1915- ... 115
Jones, Kenneth LaMar 1931- ... 53-56
Jones, Kenneth S. 1919- ... 21-24R
Jones, Kenneth W. 1934- Brief entry ... 113
Jones, Landon Y(oung) 1943- ... 105
Jones, Laurie Beth 1952- ... 155
Jones, Lawrence K. 1940- ... 143
Jones, Leon 1936-1992 ... 101
  Obituary ... 137
Jones, Leonidas M(onroe) Sr. 1923- ... CANR-46
  Earlier sketch in CA 45-48
Jones, LeRoi
  See Baraka, Amiri
  See also CLC 1, 2, 3, 5, 10, 14
Jones, Leroy P. 1941- ... 118
Jones, Lewis 1897-1939 ... DLB 15
Jones, Lewis Pinckney 1916- ... 61-64
Jones, Linda Phillips
  See Phillips-Jones, Linda
Jones, Lisa 1961- ... 130
Jones, Lloyd S(cott) 1931- ... CANR-4
  Earlier sketch in CA 1-4R
Jones, Louis B. ... 141
  See also CLC 65
Jones, Louis C(lark) 1908-1990 ... 5-8R
  Obituary ... 133
Jones, Lyndon Hamer 1927- ... CANR-45
  Earlier sketches in CA 103, CANR-22
Jones, M(arjorie) L(ilian) Glynne
  See Glynne-Jones, M(arjorie) L(ilian)
Jones, Madeline Adams 1913- ... 21-24R
Jones, Madison (Percy, Jr.) 1925- ... CANR-54
  Earlier sketches in CA 13-16R, CANR-7
  See also CAAS 11
  See also CLC 4
  See also DLB 152
Jones, Major J. 1919- ... 33-36R
Jones, Major Joseph
  See Thompson, William Tappan
Jones, Malcolm V(ince) 1940- ... CANR-48
  Earlier sketch in CA 103
Jones, Maldwyn Allen 1922- ... CANR-4
  Earlier sketch in CA 1-4R
Jones, Marc Edmund 1888- ... 33-36R
Jones, Marcia Thornton 1958- ... SATA 73
Jones, Margaret Boone ... 25-28R
Jones, Margaret C. 1949- ... 146
Jones, Margaret E. W. 1938- ... 37-40R
Jones, Marvin 1886-1976 Obituary ... 65-68
Jones, Mary (Elizabeth) 1942- ... 120
Jones, Mary Alice 1898(?)-1980 ... 17-20R
  Obituary ... 118
  See also SATA 6
Jones, Mary Brush 1925- ... 25-28R
Jones, Mary Voell 1933- ... 21-24R
Jones, Maxwell (Shaw) 1907- ... 25-28R
Jones, Maynard Benedict
  1904-1972 Obituary ... 93-96
Jones, McClure ... 112
  See also SATA 34
Jones, Merry Bloch 1948- ... 140
Jones, Mervyn 1922- ... CANR-1
  Earlier sketch in CA 45-48
  See also CAAS 5
  See also CLC 10, 52
  See also MTCW 1
Jones, Michael (Christopher Emlyn) 1940- ... CANR-42
  Earlier sketches in CA 104, CANR-20
Jones, Michael Owen 1942- ... 101
Jones, Mick 1956(?)- ... CLC 30
Jones, Miriam
  See Schuchman, Joan
Jones, Morris Val 1914- ... 5-8R
Jones, Nancy L.
  See Holder, Nancy L.
Jones, Naomi Brooks 1941- ... 145
Jones, Nard
  See Jones, Maynard Benedict
Jones, Neil R(onald) 1909-1988 ... 160
Jones, Nettie (Pearl) 1941- ... 137
  See also CAAS 20
  See also BW 2
  See also CLC 34
Jones, Noel 1939- ... 81-84
Jones, Norman (Leslie) 1951- ... 146
Jones, O(wen) R(ogers) 1922- ... 1-4R
Jones, Oakah L., Jr. 1930- ... CANR-8
  Earlier sketch in CA 17-20R
Jones, Orlando
  See Looker, Antonina (Hansell)
Jones, P(eter) M(ichael) 1949- ... CANR-48
  Earlier sketch in CA 122
Jones, Pamela M. 1953- ... 146
Jones, Pat
  See Jones, Virgil Carrington
Jones, Paul Davis 1940- ... 49-52
Jones, Paul J. 1897(?)-1974 Obituary ... 53-56
Jones, Pearl Binder Elwyn
  See Elwyn-Jones, Pearl Binder
Jones, Peggy 1947- ... 109
Jones, Penelope 1938- ... CANR-14
  Earlier sketch in CA 81-84
  See also SATA 31
Jones, Peter 1802-1856 ... NNAL
Jones, Peter 1920- ... 103
Jones, Peter 1921- ... 5-8R
Jones, Peter (Austin) 1929- ... CANR-4
  Earlier sketch in CA 53-56
Jones, Peter d'Alroy 1931- ... CANR-20
  Earlier sketches in CA 5-8R, CANR-3
Jones, Peter Gaylord 1929- ... 73-76
Jones, Philip Howard 1937- ... 102
Jones, Phillip L. 1928(?)-1979 Obituary ... 89-92
Jones, Pirkle 1914- ... 29-32R
Jones, Preston 1936-1979 ... 73-76
  Obituary ... 89-92
  See also CLC 10
  See also DLB 7
Jones, R(ichard) Ben(jamin) 1933- ... CANR-12
  Earlier sketch in CA 25-28R
Jones, R. D.
  See Jones, Dennis
Jones, R(obert) M(aynard) 1929- ... 152
Jones, R(oger) W(illiam) 1941- ... 128
Jones, Ray O. 1930- ... 89-92
Jones, Raymond F. 1915- ... 156
  Brief entry ... 106
Jones, Rebecca C(astaldi) 1947- ... CANR-50
  Earlier sketches in CA 106, CANR-22
  See also SATA 33, 99
Jones, Reginald L(anier) 1931- ... CANR-48
  Earlier sketch in CA 45-48
Jones, Reginald Victor 1911-1997 ... 103
  Obituary ... 163
Jones, Richard 1926- ... CANR-2
  Earlier sketch in CA 49-52
Jones, Richard 1953- ... 121
Jones, Richard Allan 1943- ... 103
Jones, Richard Granville 1926- ... 112
Jones, Richard H(utton) 1914- ... 49-52
Jones, Richard M(atthew) 1925- ... 93-96
Jones, Robert B(rinkley) 1942- ... 114
Jones, Robert Emmet 1928- ... CANR-2
  Earlier sketch in CA 1-4R
Jones, Robert Epes 1908- ... CAP-1
  Earlier sketch in CA 13-14
Jones, Robert F(rancis) 1934- ... CANR-61
  Earlier sketches in CA 49-52, CANR-2
  See also CLC 7
Jones, Robert Godwin
  See Godwin-Jones, Robert
Jones, Robert H(uhn) 1927- ... CANR-2
  Earlier sketch in CA 5-8R
Jones, Robert O(wen) 1928- ... 29-32R
Jones, Robert R(ussell) 1927- ... 69-72
Jones, Robert Reynolds, Jr. 1911-1997 ... CANR-11
  Obituary ... 162
  Earlier sketch in CA 25-28R
Jones, Robert Tyre, Jr. 1902-1971 Obituary ... 113
Jones, Robin D(orothy) 1959- ... 147
  See also SATA 80
Jones, Robin Lloyd
  See Lloyd-Jones, Robin
Jones, Rod 1953- ... 128
  See also CLC 50
Jones, Rodney 1950- ... CANR-64
  Earlier sketch in CA 133
  See also DLB 120
Jones, Rodney W(illiam) 1943- ... CANR-33
  Earlier sketch in CA 113
Jones, Roger (Winston) 1939- ... 101
Jones, Roger Stanley 1934- ... 113
Jones, Royston Oscar 1925-1974 ... 85-88
Jones, Ruby Aileen Hiday 1908- ... CAP-1
  Earlier sketch in CA 11-12
Jones, Russell 1918-1979 ... 106
  Obituary ... 89-92
Jones, Russell Bradley 1894- ... 1-4R
Jones, Ruth Ann 1928- ... 107
Jones, Ruth Dorval ... 93-96
Jones, Sally Roberts 1935- ... 102
Jones, Sandra (Redmond) 1937- ... 132
Jones, Sandra L.
  See Ireland, Sandra L(eora) Jones
Jones, Sandy 1943- ... CANR-15
  Earlier sketch in CA 85-88
Jones, Sanford W.
  See Thorn, John
Jones, Scott N. 1929- ... 29-32R
Jones, Seaborn (Gustavus), Jr. 1942- ... 104
Jones, Simmons 1920- ... 136
Jones, Simon (C.) 1957- ... 128
Jones, Sonia 1938- ... 127
Jones, Stacy V(anderhoof) 1894-1989 ... 1-4R
  Obituary ... 127
Jones, Stanley L(lewellyn) 1918- ... 9-12R
Jones, Stephen (Phillip) 1935- ... CANR-2
  Earlier sketch in CA 49-52
Jones, Stephen 1953- ... 134
Jones, Stephen D(wight) 1948- ... 112
Jones, Steve 1961- ... 143
Jones, Stuart 1933- ... 146
Jones, Susan Mann
  See Mann, Susan
Jones, T(homas) Anthony 1940- ... 110
Jones, Tad
  See Jones, Thaddeus B.
Jones, Ted
  See Jones, Theador Edward
Jones, Terence Graham Parry 1942- ... CANR-35
  Brief entry ... 112
  Earlier sketch in CA 116
  Interview in ... 116
  See also Jones, Terry
  and Monty Python
  See also CLC 21
Jones, Terry
  See Jones, Terence Graham Parry
  See also SATA 67
  See also SATA-Brief 51
Jones, Thaddeus B. 1952- ... 125
Jones, Theador Edward 1937- ... 138
Jones, Thom 1945(?)- ... 157
  See also CLC 81
Jones, Thomas B. 1929- ... 25-28R
Jones, Thomas M(artin) 1916- ... 29-32R
Jones, Thomas W(arren) 1947- ... 53-56
Jones, Tim(othy) Wynne
  See Wynne-Jones, Tim(othy)
Jones, Tom 1928- ... CANR-6
  Earlier sketch in CA 53-56
  Interview in ... CANR-6
Jones, Tony Armstrong
  See Armstrong-Jones, Antony (Charles Robert)
Jones, Trevor Arthur 1936- ... 105
Jones, Trevor David 1908-1984 Obituary ... 114
Jones, Tristan 1924-1995 ... 73-76
  Obituary ... 148
Jones, Turkel
  See McKimmey, James
Jones, Vane A. 1917- ... 21-24R
Jones, Vernon 1897- ... 53-56
Jones, (Charles) Victor 1919- ... 5-8R
Jones, Virgil Carrington 1906- ... CANR-2
  Earlier sketch in CA 1-4R
Jones, Volcano
  See Mitchell, Adrian
Jones, W(alton) Glyn 1928- ... CANR-56
  Earlier sketches in CA 49-52, CANR-29
Jones, W(illiam) J(ohn) 1932- ... 129
Jones, W(alter) Paul 1891- ... CAP-1
  Earlier sketch in CA 11-12
Jones, W(illiam) T(homas) 1910- ... 37-40R
Jones, Walter Benton 1893- ... 1-4R
Jones, Webb
  See Henley, Arthur
Jones, Weyman (B.) 1928- ... 17-20R
  See also SAAS 11
  See also SATA 4
Jones, Wilbur Devereux 1916- ... CANR-2
  Earlier sketch in CA 1-4R
Jones, William 1746-1794 ... DLB 109
Jones, William Alfred 1817-1900 ... DLB 59
Jones, William David Anthony 1946- ... 113
Jones, William Glynne
  See Glynne-Jones, William
Jones, William H(ugh) 1939-1982 ... 112
  Obituary ... 108
Jones, William M(cKendrey) 1927- ... CANR-7
  Earlier sketch in CA 61-64
Jones, William Monarch
  See Guthrie, Thomas Anstey
Jones, William P(owell) 1901- ... 1-4R
Jones, William R(onald) 1933- ... 104
Jones, Willis Knapp 1895- ... 13-16R
Jones, Zelda
  See Schuchman, Joan
Jones-Evans, Eric 1898- ... 21-24R
Jones-Jackson, Pat
  See Jones-Jackson, Patricia
Jones-Jackson, Patricia 1946-1986 Obituary ... 124
Jones-Ryan, Maureen 1943- ... 93-96
Jones-Wilson, Faustine C(hildress) 1927- ... CANR-27
  Earlier sketch in CA 77-80
Jong, Erica 1942- ... CANR-52
  Earlier sketches in CA 73-76, CANR-26
  Interview in ... CANR-26
  See also AITN 1
  See also BEST 90:2
  See also CLC 4, 6, 8, 18, 83
  See also DAM NOV, POP
  See also DLB 2, 5, 28, 152
  See also MTCW 1
Jongeward, Dorothy 1925- ... CANR-3
  Earlier sketch in CA 49-52
Jonk, Clarence 1906- ... 5-8R
  See also SATA 10
Jonke, Gert F 1946- ... DLB 85
Jonnes, Jill 1952- ... 121
Jonsen, Albert R(upert) 1931- ... CANR-28
  Earlier sketches in CA 25-28R, CANR-11

Jonson, Ben(jamin) 1572(?)-1637 ... CDBLB Before 1660
See also DA
See also DAB
See also DAC
See also DAM DRAM, MST, POET
See also DC 4
See also DLB 62, 121
See also PC 17
See also WLC
Jonsson, Reidar
See Joensson, Reidar
Jonsson, Snaebjorn 1888(?)-1978 Obituary .. 81-84
Joos, Francoise 1956- .... SATA 78
Joos, Frederic 1953- .... SATA 78
Joos, Martin (George) 1907- CAP-1
Earlier sketch in CA 13-16
Joosse, Barbara M(onnot) 1949- CANR-48
Earlier sketch in CA 109
See also SATA 52, 96
Joost, Nicholas (Teynac) 1916-1980 .... 13-16R
Obituary 97-100
Joplin, Scott 1868-1917 Brief entry 123
Jopp, Hal
See Jopp, Harold Dowling, Jr.
Jopp, Harold Dowling, Jr. 1946- 57-60
Joppke, Christian 1959- 145
Joralemon, Ira B(eaman)
1884-1975 Obituary 61-64
Joravsky, David 1925- CANR-2
Earlier sketch in CA 1-4R
Jordan, Alexis Hill
See Glick, Ruth (Burtnick)
and Titchener, Louise
Jordan, Alma Theodora 1929- 33-36R
Jordan, Amos A(zariah) 1922- 33-36R
Jordan, Anne Devereaux 1943- 135
See also SATA 80
Jordan, Barbara (Charline) 1936-1996 123
Obituary 151
Brief entry 113
See also BW 1
Jordan, Bill
See Jordan, William
Jordan, Borimir 1933- 89-92
Jordan, Carrie
See Cudlipp, Edythe
Jordan, Clarence L(eonard) 1912-1969 ..... CAP-2
Earlier sketch in CA 23-24
Jordan, Claudia E. 1954- 163
Jordan, Constance 168
Jordan, Dale R(oderick) 1931- CANR-46
Earlier sketch in CA 45-48
Jordan, Daniel P(orter), Jr. 1938- 130
Jordan, David C. 1935- 146
Jordan, David K. 1942- 61-64
Jordan, David M(alcolm) 1935- 33-36R
Jordan, David P(aul) 1939- 57-60
Jordan, David William 1940- 93-96
Jordan, Don
See Howard, Vernon (Linwood)
Jordan, Donald A. 1936- 65-68
Jordan, E(mil) L(eopold) 1900- ...... SATA-Brief 31
Jordan, Emma Coleman 1946- 153
Jordan, Franklin Everard
1904(?)-1983 Obituary 110
Jordan, Gail
See Dern, Erolie Pearl Gaddis
Jordan, Gerald Ray 1896-1964 .... CAP-1
Earlier sketch in CA 13-14
Jordan, Gilbert John 1902- CANR-28
Earlier sketch in CA 49-52
Jordan, Gill
See Gilbert, George
Jordan, Grace Edgington CANR-2
Earlier sketch in CA 1-4R
Jordan, Hope Dahle 1905- CANR-13
Earlier sketch in CA 77-80
See also SATA 15
Jordan, Jael (Michal) 1949- .... SATA 30
Jordan, John 1930- 103
Jordan, John E(mory) 1919- CANR-20
Earlier sketch in CA 1-4R
Jordan, June 1936- CANR-70
Earlier sketches in CA 33-36R, CANR-25
See also AAYA 2
See also BLCS
See also BW 2
See also CLC 5, 11, 23
See also CLR 10
See also DAM MULT, POET
See also DLB 38
See also MAICYA
See also MTCW 1
See also SATA 4
Jordan, Laura
See Brown, Sandra
Jordan, Lee
See Scholefield, Alan
Jordan, Leonard
See Levinson, Leonard
Jordan, Lewis 1912-1983 Obituary 111
Jordan, Lois B(reedlove) 1912- 57-60
Jordan, Martin George 1944- .... SATA 84
Jordan, Michael (Jeffrey) 1963- 149
Jordan, Mildred
See Bausher, Mildred Jordan
Jordan, Mildred Arlene 1918- 110
Jordan, Monica
See Caruba, Alan
Jordan, Neil (Patrick) 1950- CANR-54
Brief entry 124
Earlier sketch in CA 130
Interview in 130
See also CLC 110
Jordan, Norman 1938- 33-36R
Jordan, Pascual 1902-1982(?) Obituary 112
Jordan, Pat(rick M.) 1941- 33-36R
See also CLC 37
Jordan, Penny 1946- 163
Jordan, Philip D(ean) 1940- 110
Jordan, Philip Dillon 1903- 9-12R
Jordan, Robert
See Rigney, James Oliver, Jr.
See also AAYA 26
Jordan, Robert B. 1939- 141
Jordan, Robert Paul 1921- 29-32R
Jordan, Robert S(mith) 1929- CANR-1
Earlier sketch in CA 45-48
Jordan, Robin 1947- 65-68
Jordan, Ruth 1926-1994 .... CANR-7
Obituary 144
Earlier sketch in CA 57-60
Jordan, Sherryl 1949- .... SAAS 23
See also SATA 71
Jordan, Stello 1914- 29-32R
Jordan, Tanis 1946- .... SATA 84
Jordan, Terry G(ilbert) 1938- CANR-9
Earlier sketch in CA 21-24R
Jordan, Thomas E(dward) 1929- 120
Jordan, Thurston C., Jr. 1940- 25-28R
Jordan, Wayne 1903(?)-1979 Obituary 85-88
Jordan, Weymouth T(yree) 1912-1968 ...... CAP-2
Earlier sketch in CA 17-18
Jordan, Wilbur K(itchener) 1902-1980 .... CANR-5
Obituary 97-100
Earlier sketch in CA 5-8R
Jordan, William 1941- Brief entry 118
Jordan, William A. 1928- 33-36R
Jordan, William H., Jr. 1944- 114
Jordan, William J(ohnston) 1924- CANR-39
Earlier sketch in CA 114
Jordan, William S(tone), Jr. 1917- 13-16R
Jordan, Winthrop D(onaldson) 1931- 25-28R
Jordan, Z(bigniew) A(ntoni) 1911-1977 ..... 25-28R
Obituary 89-92
Jordan Haight, Mary Ellen 1927- 136
Jordan-Smith, Paul 1885(?)-1971 Obituary 104
Jorden, Eleanor Harz CANR-8
Earlier sketch in CA 5-8R
Jorden, William John 1923- 140
Jordy, William H(enry) 1917-1997 .... CANR-25
Obituary 160
Earlier sketch in CA 1-4R
Jorgens, Jack J(ohnstone) 1943- 65-68
Jorgensen, Christine 1926-1989 Obituary 128
Jorgensen, Ivar
See Ellison, Harlan (Jay)
and Garrett, (Gordon) Randall (Phillip)
Jorgensen, James (Aleck) 1931- CANR-19
Earlier sketch in CA 103
Jorgensen, James D(ale) 1932- 41-44R
Jorgensen, Joseph G(ilbert) 1934- CANR-7
Earlier sketch in CA 61-64
Jorgensen, Mary Venn CANR-1
Earlier sketch in CA 1-4R
See also SATA 36
Jorgensen, Neil 1934- 53-56
Jorgenson, Allen
See Stine, Henry Eugene
Jorgenson, Ivar
See Silverberg, Robert
Jorgenson, Lloyd P. 1912- 125
Jorn, Asger 1914-1973 Obituary 41-44R
Jorstad, Erling (Theodore) 1930- CANR-30
Earlier sketches in CA 29-32R, CANR-12
Joscelyn, Archie L. 1899- CANR-63
Earlier sketches in CA 1-4R, CANR-5
Jose, F(rancisco) Sionil
See Sionil Jose, F(rancisco)
Jose, James R(obert) 1939- 29-32R
Josefowitz, Natasha 1926- CANR-40
Earlier sketch in CA 114
Josefsberg, Milt 1911-1987 .... CANR-29
Obituary 124
Earlier sketch in CA 81-84
Joselovitz, Ernest A. 1942- 108
Joselow, Beth Baruch 1948- CANR-36
Earlier sketch in CA 114
Joseph, Alexander 1907-1976 .... 13-16R
Obituary 120
Joseph, Anne
See Coates, Anna
Joseph, Anne
See Coates, Anna
Joseph, Bertram L(eon) 1915-1981 .... CANR-6
Obituary 104
Earlier sketch in CA 5-8R
Joseph, David I(glauer) 1941- 9-12R
Joseph, Dov 1899-1980 Obituary 93-96
Joseph, Franz
See Schnaubelt, Franz Joseph
Joseph, Helen (Beatrice May) 1905-1992 128
Obituary 140
Joseph, Henry 1948- 153
Joseph, James (Herz) 1924- CANR-2
Earlier sketch in CA 1-4R
See also SATA 53
Joseph, Jenny 1932- CANR-60
Earlier sketches in CA 107, CANR-25
See also DLB 40
Joseph, Joan 1939- CANR-17
Earlier sketch in CA 25-28R
See also SATA 34
Joseph, John 1923- 1-4R
Joseph, Jonathan
See Fineman, Irving
Joseph, Joseph M(aron) 1903-1979 .... 5-8R
See also SATA 22
Joseph, Lawrence 1948- 165
Joseph, M(ichael) K(ennedy) 1914-1981 .. CANR-6
Earlier sketch in CA 9-12R
Joseph, Marie CANR-59
Earlier sketch in CA 109
Joseph, Marjory L(ockwood) 1917- 77-80
Joseph, Mark (Chester) 1946- 120
Joseph, R. F.
See Joseph, Robert Farras
Joseph, Richard 1910-1976 .... CANR-6
Obituary 69-72
Earlier sketch in CA 1-4R
Joseph, Robert F.
See Joseph, Robert Farras
Joseph, Robert Farras 1935- 129
Joseph, Stephen 1921-1967 .... 9-12R
Obituary 103
Joseph, Stephen M. 1938- 25-28R
Joseph, William A(llen) 1947- CANR-41
Earlier sketch in CA 118
Josephs, Arthur
See Gottlieb, Arthur
Josephs, Ray 1912- 9-12R
Josephs, Rebecca
See Talbot, Toby
See also SATA 14
Josephs, Stephen
See Dolmatch, Theodore B(ieley)
Josephson, Clifford A. 1922- 17-20R
Josephson, Elmer A. 1909- CANR-49
Earlier sketch in CA 121
Josephson, Halsey D. 1906(?)-1977 Obituary 69-72
Josephson, Hannah 1900-1976 .... CAP-2
Obituary 69-72
Earlier sketch in CA 29-32
Josephson, Harold 1942- 61-64
Josephson, Matthew 1899-1978 81-84
Obituary 77-80
See also DLB 4
Joseph the Younger
See Chief Joseph
Josephy, Alvin M., Jr. 1915- CANR-48
Earlier sketches in CA 17-20R, CANR-8
Josey, E(lonnie) J(unius) 1924- CANR-42
Earlier sketch in CA 29-32R
See also BW 2
Josh
See Clemens, Samuel Langhorne
Joshee, O(m) K(umar) 1934- 117
Joshi, Arun 1939- 160
Joshi, Irene M(arian) 1934- 110
Joshi, S(unand) T(ryambak) 1958- 131
Joshi, Shivkumar 1916- 77-80
Joshua, Wynfred 1930- 29-32R
Josiah Allen's Wife
See Holley, Marietta
Josipovici, Gabriel 1940- CANR-47
Earlier sketch in CA 37-40R
See also CAAS 8
See also CLC 6, 43
See also DLB 14
Joskow, Paul L. 1947- 124
Joslin, Sesyle
See Hine, Sesyle Joslin
See also SATA 2
Jospe, Alfred 1909-1994 106
Obituary 147
Joss, John 1934- 101
Josselson, Ruthellen (Lefkowitz) 1946- 139
Josselyn, John (?)-1675 .... DLB 24
Josten, Josef 1913-1985 Obituary 118
Jotischky, Andrew 1965- 133
Joubert, Andre J. 1924- 49-52
Joubert, Ingrid 1942- 110
Joudry, Patricia 1921- 65-68
See also DLB 88
Jouhandeau, Marcel Henri
1888-1979 Obituary 85-88
Jourard, Sidney M(arshall) 1926-1974 .... CANR-6
Obituary 53-56
Earlier sketch in CA 5-8R
Jourdain, Alice M. 1923- 53-56
Jourdain, Robert 1950- 163
Jourdain, Rose (Leonora) 1932- 89-92
Journet, Charles 1891-1975 65-68
Obituary 57-60
Journlet, Marie de
See Little, Paul H(ugo)
Jouve, Pierre Jean 1887-1976 Obituary 65-68
See also CLC 47
Jouvenel, Bertrand de
See de Jouvenel des Ursins, Edouard Bertrand
Jouvet, Jean
See Strich, Christian
Jovanovich, William (Iliya) 1920- 107
Jovanovski, Meto 1928- 142
Jovine, Francesco 1902-1950 .... TCLC 79
Jovine, Giuseppe 1922- .... DLB 128
Jowett, Garth Samuel 1940- CANR-10
Earlier sketch in CA 65-68
Jowett, Paul (Melville) 1959- 120
Jowitt, Deborah 1934- 103
Joy, Barbara Ellen 1898- 5-8R
Joy, David Anthony Welton 1942- CANR-20
Earlier sketch in CA 103
Joy, Donald Marvin 1928- 13-16R
Joy, Edward T(homas) 1909- 9-12R
Joy, Kenneth Ernest 1908- CAP-2
Earlier sketch in CA 23-24
Joy, Thomas Alfred 1904- 102
Joyaux, Julia
See Kristeva, Julia
Joyaux, Philippe
See Sollers, Philippe
Joyce, Adrien
See Eastman, Carol
Joyce, Bill
See Joyce, William
Joyce, Brian T(homas) 1938- 106
Joyce, Bruce R(ogers) 1930- Brief entry 114
Joyce, Christopher 1950- 140
Joyce, Davis D. 1940- 149
Joyce, Donald Franklin 1938- 139
See also BW 2
Joyce, Ernest 1899-1975 .... CAP-2
Earlier sketch in CA 33-36
Joyce, Graham 1954- 151
Joyce, J(ames) Avery 1902-1987 .... CANR-10
Obituary 121
Earlier sketch in CA 65-68
See also SATA 11
See also SATA-Obit 50
Joyce, James (Augustine Aloysius) 1882-1941 . 126
Brief entry 104
See also CDBLB 1914-1945
See also DA
See also DAB
See also DAC
See also DAM MST, NOV, POET
See also DLB 10, 19, 36, 162
See also MTCW 1
See also PC 22
See also SSC 3, 26
See also TCLC 3, 8, 16, 35, 52
See also WLC
Joyce, James Daniel 1921- 9-12R
Joyce, Jon L(oyd) 1937- CANR-10
Earlier sketch in CA 65-68
Joyce, Joyce Ann 1949- 137
Joyce, Julia
See Tetel, Julie
Joyce, Mary Rosera 1930- 29-32R
Joyce, Michael 1945- 148
Joyce, Patrick 1945- 128
Joyce, R(oger) B(ilbrough) 1924- CANR-1
Earlier sketch in CA 45-48
Joyce, Robert E(dward) 1934- 29-32R
Joyce, Rosemary A. 1956- 141
Joyce, Thomas
See Cary, (Arthur) Joyce (Lunel)
Joyce, William 1959(?)- 124
See also CLR 26
See also SATA 72
See also SATA-Brief 46
Joyce, William L(eonard) 1942- 111
Joyce, William W(alter) 1934- CANR-15
Earlier sketch in CA 85-88
Joyner, Charles W. 1935- 37-40R
Joyner, Jerry 1938- 107
See also SATA 34
Joyner, Stephen Christopher 1967- 144
Joyner, Tim(othy) 1922- 141
Joyner, William T. 1934- 21-24R
Joynson, R(obert) B(illington) 1922- 57-60
Joynt, Carey Bonthron 1924- 124
Joynt, Robert R(ichard) 1915- 106
Jozsef, Attila 1905-1937 Brief entry 116
See also TCLC 22
Juarroz, Roberto 1925- 131
See also HW
Jucker, Sita 1921- CANR-12
Earlier sketch in CA 29-32R
See also SATA 5
Jucovy, Milton Edward 1918- 109
Juda, L(yon) 1923- 9-12R
Judah, Aaron 1923- 103
Judah, J(ay) Stillson 1911- 21-24R
Judd, Alan 1946- 139
Judd, Cyril
See Kornbluth, C(yril) M.
and Merril, Judith
and Pohl, Frederik
Judd, Deane B(rewster) 1900-1972 .... CAP-1
Earlier sketch in CA 13-14
Judd, Denis (O'Nan) 1938- CANR-49
Earlier sketches in CA 25-28R, CANR-13
See also SATA 33
Judd, Dennis R. 1943- CANR-16
Earlier sketch in CA 93-96
Judd, Frances K. CANR-27
Earlier sketches in CAP-2, CA 19-20
See also Benson, Mildred (Augustine Wirt)
See also SATA 1
Judd, Frederick Charles 1914- CANR-6
Earlier sketch in CA 5-8R
Judd, Gerrit P(armele) 1915-1971 .... 5-8R
Obituary 29-32R
Judd, H(oward) Stanley 1936- CANR-21
Earlier sketch in CA 69-72
Judd, Harrison
See Daniels, Norman
Judd, Larry R. 1937- 45-48
Judd, Margaret Haddican 1906- 5-8R
Judd, Naomi 1946- 146
Judd, Robert 1939- CANR-38
Earlier sketch in CA 85-88
Judd, Sara (Hutton) Bowen
See Bowen-Judd, Sara (Hutton)
Judd, Sylvester 1813-1853 .... DLB 1
Jude, Conny .... SATA 81
Judelle, Beatrice 1908- 33-36R
Judge, Edward H. 1945- 145
Judge, Harry George 1928- 124
Judge, Mike 1963(?)- 156
See also AAYA 20
Judis, John B. 1941- 140
Judkins, Phil(lip Edward) 1947- 142
Judovitz, Dalia 1951- 130
Judson, Clara Ingram 1879-1960 137
See also MAICYA
See also SATA 38
See also SATA-Brief 27
Judson, David (Malcolm) 1941- 93-96
Judson, Don 1950- 155
Judson, Edward Zane Carroll 1821-1886 .. DLB 186

Judson, Horace Freeland 1931- ... 89-92
Judson, John 1930- ... CANR-12
Earlier sketch in CA 13-16R
Judson, Lewis Van Hagen
1893-1973 Obituary ... 41-44R
Judson, Margaret Atwood 1899-1991 ... 102
Obituary ... 134
Judson, Sylvia Shaw 1897-1978 ... 41-44R
Obituary ... 133
Judson, William
See Corley, Edwin (Raymond)
Judy, Marvin T(hornton) 1911- ... 33-36R
Judy, Stephen
See Tchudi, Stephen N.
Judy, Stephen N.
See Tchudi, Stephen N.
Judy, Susan J(ane) 1944- ... 107
Judy, Will(iam Lewis) 1891- ... 5-8R
Juel, Donald H. 1942- ... CANR-35
Earlier sketch in CA 114
Juel-Nielsen, Niels 1920- ... 106
Juengel, Eberhard 1934- Brief entry ... 118
Juenger, Ernst 1895-1998 ... CANR-47
Obituary ... 167
Earlier sketches in CA 101, CANR-21
See also DLB 56
Juergens, George Ivar 1932- ... 109
Juergensen, Hans 1919- ... CANR-48
Earlier sketches in CA 21-24R, CANR-8
Juergensmeyer, Jane Stuart
See Stuart, (Jessica) Jane
Juergensmeyer, John Eli 1934- ... 41-44R
Juergensmeyer, Mark (Karl) 1940- ... 129
Jugenheimer, Donald W(ayne) 1943- ... CANR-52
Earlier sketch in CA 125
Juhasz, Anne McCreary 1922- ... 53-56
Juhasz, Leslie A.
See Shepard, Leslie Albert
Juhasz, Suzanne 1942- ... 85-88
Jukes, (James Thomas) Geoffrey 1928- ... 29-32R
Jukes, Mavis 1947- ... 127
Brief entry ... 121
Interview in ... 127
See also MAICYA
See also SAAS 12
See also SATA 72
See also SATA-Brief 43
Jukic, Ilija 1901-1977 ... 49-52
Obituary ... 103
Julesberg, Elizabeth Rider Montgomery 1902-1985 . CANR-42
Obituary ... 115
See also Montgomery, Elizabeth Rider
Jules-Rosette, Bennetta (Washington) 1948- ... 112
Julian, Jane
See Wiseman, David
Julian of Norwich 1342(?)-1416(?) ... DLB 146
Juliard, Pierre 1939- ... 41-44R
Julie
See Robbins, June
Julien, Charles-Andre 1891- ... 103
Julie of Colorado Springs
See Robbins, June
Julier, Virginia Cheatham 1918- ... 5-8R
Julin, Joseph R. 1926- ... 37-40R
Juline, Ruth Bishop
See Ritchie, Ruth
Julitte, Pierre (Gaston Louis) 1910- ... 37-40R
Julius
See Curling, Bryan William Richard
Jullian, Philippe 1919-1977 ... 73-76
Julty, Sam 1927- ... 61-64
July, Robert W(illiam) 1918- ... 41-44R
Jumper, Andrew Albert 1927- ... 17-20R
Jumpp, Hugo
See MacPeek, Walter G.
Jumsai, Sumet 1939- ... 129
Jun, Jong S(up) 1936- ... 53-56
June, Jennie
See Croly, Jane Cunningham
Jung, C(arl) G(ustav) 1875-1961 ... 117
See also MTCW 1
Jung, Franz 1888-1963 ... DLB 118
Jung, Hwa Yol 1932- ... 37-40R
Jung, John A. 1937- ... 17-20R
Jung, Leo 1892-1987 Obituary ... 124
Junge, Mark G(ene) 1943- ... CANR-48
Earlier sketch in CA 122
Jungel, Eberhard
See Juengel, Eberhard
Junger, Ernst
See Juenger, Ernst
Junger, Sebastian 1962- ... 165
See also CLC 109
Jungk, Robert 1913- ... 85-88
Jungle Doctor
See White, Paul Hamilton Hume
Jungmann, Joseph Andreas 1889-1975 ... 165
Jungreis, Esther 1936- ... 110
Jung-Stilling, Johann Heinrich 1740-1817 ... DLB 94
Juniper, Alex
See Hospital, Janette Turner
Juniper, D(ean) F(rancis) 1929- ... CANR-18
Earlier sketch in CA 97-100
Junius
See Luxemburg, Rosa
Junker, Karin Stensland 1916- ... CANR-3
Earlier sketch in CA 9-12R
Junkins, Donald 1931- ... 33-36R
Junkyard Moondog
See Dwyer, Jim
Junor, John 1919-1997 ... 108
Obituary ... 158
Jupo, Frank J. 1904- ... CANR-2
Earlier sketch in CA 5-8R
See also SATA 7
Jupp, James 1932- ... CANR-11
Earlier sketch in CA 21-24R
Jupp, Kenneth 1939- ... 65-68
Juptner, Joseph Paul 1913- ... 5-8R
Jur, Jerzy
See Lerski, George Jan
Jurek, Martin 1942- ... 77-80
Jurgela, Constantine R. 1904-1988 Obituary ... 124
Jurgens, Curt 1912-1982 Obituary ... 107
Jurgens, W(illiam) A(nthony) 1928- ... 41-44R
Jurgensen, Barbara (Bitting) 1928- ... 17-20R
Juris, Hervey A(sher) 1938- ... CANR-5
Earlier sketch in CA 53-56
Jurjevich, Ratibor-Ray (Momchila) 1915- ... 37-40R
Jurji, Edward J. 1907-1990 ... 13-16R
Obituary ... 132
Jurkevich, Gayana 1953- ... 139
Jurmain, Suzanne 1945- ... 133
See also SATA 72
Jurnak, Sheila
See Raeschild, Sheila
Jussawalla, Adil (Jehangir) 1940- ... 153
Jussawalla, Feroza 1953- ... 165
Jussim, Estelle 1927- ... CANR-29
Earlier sketch in CA 81-84
Just, Ward (Swift) 1935- ... CANR-32
Earlier sketch in CA 25-28R
Interview in ... CANR-32
See also CLC 4, 27
Juster, F. Thomas 1926- ... CANR-2
Earlier sketch in CA 45-48
Juster, Norton 1929- ... CANR-44
Earlier sketches in CA 13-16R, CANR-13
See also JRDA
See also MAICYA
See also SATA 3
Justice, Blair 1927- ... CANR-1
Earlier sketch in CA 45-48
Justice, Donald (Rodney) 1925- ... CANR-54
Earlier sketches in CA 5-8R, CANR-26
Interview in ... CANR-26
See also CLC 6, 19, 102
See also DAM POET
See also DLBY 83
Justice, William G(ross), Jr. 1930- ... CANR-20
Earlier sketches in CA 53-56, CANR-5
Justiciar
See Powell-Smith, Vincent (Walter Francis)
Justman, Robert H. 1926- ... 155
Justus, May 1898- ... 9-12R
See also SATA 1
Justus, Moeser 1720-1794 ... DLB 97
Juta, Jan 1895- ... 49-52
Juta, Rene
See Juta, Jan
Jute, Andre 1945- ... 131
Jutikkala, Eino Kaarlo Ilmari 1907- ... CAP-1
Earlier sketch in CA 9-10
Jutson, Mary Carolyn Hollers
See George, Mary Carolyn Hollers Jutson
Juvenilia
See Taylor, Ann
Juvenis
See Bourne, Randolph S(illiman)
Juviler, Peter H(enry) 1926- ... 77-80
Jwaideh, Nizar 1933(?)-1988 Obituary ... 124

K

Kaapu, Myrtle King 1898-1985 Obituary ... 119
Kaba, Lansine 1941- ... 61-64
Kabadi, Sunder 1898(?)-1983 Obituary ... 111
Kabaker, Ray 1934(?)-1990 Obituary ... 132
Kabal, A. M.
See Bhabra, H(argurchet) S(ingh)
Kabaphe, Konstantinos Petrou
See Kavafis, Konstantinos Petrou
Kabaphes, Konstantinos Petrou
See Kavafis, Konstantinos Petrou
Kabasele, Joseph
See Tshiamala, Kabasele
Kabat-Zinn, Jon ... 153
Kabbani, Rana 1958- ... 125
Kabdebo, Tamas
See Kabdebo, Thomas
Kabdebo, Thomas 1934- ... CANR-23
Earlier sketches in CA 53-56, CANR-7
See also SATA 10
Kabibble, Ish
See Bogue, Merwyn (Alton)
Kabibble, Osh
See Jobb, Jamie
Kabira, Wanjiku Mukabi ... 168
Kabotie, Fred 1900- ... 118
Kabraji, Fredoon 1897- ... CAP-1
Earlier sketch in CA 13-14
Kac, Arthur W(ayne) 1904- ... 117
Kac, Mark 1914-1984 Obituary ... 114
Kacapyr, Elia 1956- ... 158
Kacew, Romain 1914-1980 ... 108
Obituary ... 102
See also Gary, Romain
Kacew, Roman
See Kacew, Romain
Kachru, Braj B(ehari) 1932- ... CANR-49
Earlier sketches in CA 61-64, CANR-8, 23
Kachur, Lewis ... 142
Kack-Brice, Valerie 1950- ... 150
Kaczer, Illes 1887- ... CAP-1
Earlier sketch in CA 9-10
Kadai, Heino Olavi 1931- ... 21-24R
Kadans, Joseph M(ichael) 1912- ... 118
Kadare, Ismail 1936- ... 161
See also CLC 52
Kadel, Andrew 1954- ... 154
Kadesch, Robert R(udstone) 1922- ... 57-60
See also SATA 31
Kadic, Ante 1910- Brief entry ... 107
Kadir, Djelal 1946- ... 147
Kadish, Alon 1950- ... 131
Kadish, Ferne 1940- ... 61-64
Kadish, Mortimer Raymond 1916- Brief entry ... 106
Kadler, Eric H(enry) 1922- ... 29-32R
Kadohata, Cynthia ... 140
See also CLC 59
Kadushin, Alfred 1916- ... 25-28R
Kadushin, Charles 1932- ... 25-28R
Kaegi, Walter Emil, Jr. 1937- ... CANR-10
Earlier sketch in CA 25-28R
Kael, Pauline 1919- ... CANR-70
Earlier sketches in CA 45-48, CANR-6, 44
Interview in ... CANR-6
Kaelbling, Rudolf 1928- ... 17-20R
Kaelin, Eugene F(rancis) 1926- ... 45-48
Kaellberg, Sture 1928- ... CANR-50
Earlier sketches in CA 107, CANR-25
Kaemmer, John E. 1928- ... 145
Kaempfer, William H. 1951- ... 144
Kaempfert, Wade
See del Rey, Lester
Kaempffert, Waldemar (Bernhard) 1877-1956 Brief entry ... 113
Kaeppler, Adrienne Lois 1935- Brief entry ... 107
Kaese, Harold 1909(?)-1975 Obituary ... 57-60
Kaestle, Carl F(rederick) 1940- ... 85-88
Kaestner, Dorothy 1920- ... 61-64
Kaestner, Erich 1899-1974 ... CANR-40
Obituary ... 49-52
Earlier sketch in CA 73-76
See also CLR 4
See also DLB 56
See also MAICYA
See also SATA 14
Kaeuper, Richard W(illiam) 1941- Brief entry ... 115
Kafe, Joseph Kofi Thompson 1933- ... 49-52
Kafka, Barbara 1933- ... 136
Kafka, F(rancis) L. 1926- ... 139
Kafka, Franz 1883-1924 ... 126
Brief entry ... 105
See also DA
See also DAB
See also DAC
See also DAM MST, NOV
See also DLB 81
See also MTCW 1
See also SSC 5, 29
See also TCLC 2, 6, 13, 29, 47, 53
See also WLC
Kafka, Sherry 1937- ... 21-24R
Kafka, Vincent W(infield) 1924- ... 61-64
Kafker, Frank A. 1931- ... 37-40R
Kafu
See Nagai Sokichi
Kagan, Abram S. 1889(?)-1983 Obituary ... 111
Kagan, Andrew 1947- ... 123
Kagan, Benjamin 1914- ... 21-24R
Kagan, Donald 1932- ... CANR-9
Earlier sketch in CA 21-24R
Kagan, Elaine ... 147
Kagan, Janet 1945- ... 162
Kagan, Jerome 1929- ... CANR-49
Earlier sketches in CA 5-8R, CANR-2, 24
Kagan, Norman 1931- ... 153
Kagan, Richard (Lauren) 1943- ... 57-60
Kagan, Richard C(lark) 1938- ... 53-56
Kagan, Robert A. 1938- ... 126
Kagan-Kans, Eva 1928- ... 49-52
Kaganoff, Nathan M. 1926- ... 126
Brief entry ... 108
Kagarlitsky, Boris 1958- ... 134
Kagy, Frederick D(avid) 1917- ... 13-16R
Kahan, Alan S. 1959- ... 139
Kahan, Arcadius 1920-1982 ... 135
Kahan, Gerald 1923- ... 33-36R
Kahan, Stanley 1931- ... 5-8R
Kahan, Stuart 1936- ... 93-96
Kahane, Claire 1935- ... CANR-53
Earlier sketch in CA 126
Kahane, Howard 1928- ... CANR-1
Earlier sketch in CA 49-52
Kahane, Meir (David) 1932-1990 ... 133
Brief entry ... 112
Kahanovitsch, Pinkhes
See Der Nister
Kahari, Victoria A(nn) 1952- ... 137
Kahin, Audrey R. 1934- ... 121
Kahin, George McTurnan 1918- ... 144
Kahl, Ann Hammel 1929- ... 17-20R
Kahl, Jonathan (D.) 1959- ... 145
See also SATA 77
Kahl, Joseph A(lan) 1923- Brief entry ... 109
Kahl, M(arvin) P(hilip) 1934- ... 107
See also SATA 37
Kahl, Virginia 1919- ... CANR-2
Earlier sketch in CA 49-52
See also SATA 48
See also SATA-Brief 38
Kahle, Roger (Raymond) 1943- ... 33-36R
Kahlenberg, Mary Hunt 1940- ... CANR-2
Earlier sketch in CA 45-48
Kahlenberg, Richard D(awson) 1963- ... 138
Kahler, Erich Gabriel 1885-1970 ... CANR-7
Obituary ... 29-32R
Earlier sketch in CA 5-8R
Interview in ... CANR-7
Kahler, Hugh (Torbert) MacNair 1883-1969 ... 102
Kahler, Woodland 1895- ... 1-4R
Kahlo, Frida 1907-1954 ... 153
Kahm, H(arold) S. ... 101
Kahn, Albert E(ugene) 1912-1979 ... 118
Obituary ... 89-92
Kahn, Alfred E(dward) 1917- ... 41-44R
Kahn, Alfred J. 1919- ... CANR-66
Earlier sketches in CA 5-8R, CANR-15, 32
Kahn, Alice 1943- ... 119
Kahn, Arnold Dexter 1939- ... 101
Kahn, Balthazar
See Carlisle, Thomas (Fiske)
Kahn, Charles H(enry) 1928- ... 132
Kahn, Coppelia 1939- ... 129
Kahn, Dan 1933(?)-1989 Obituary ... 129
Kahn, David 1930- ... CANR-12
Earlier sketch in CA 25-28R
Kahn, E(ly) J(acques), Jr. 1916-1994 ... 65-68
Obituary ... 145
Kahn, Ely Jacques 1884-1972 Obituary ... 37-40R
Kahn, Frank J(ules) 1938- ... 33-36R
Kahn, Gilbert 1912-1971 ... CANR-6
Earlier sketch in CA 1-4R
Kahn, Grace Leboy 1891-1983 Obituary ... 109
Kahn, Hannah 1911- ... CANR-14
Earlier sketch in CA 77-80
See also AITN 2
Kahn, Herman 1922-1983 ... CANR-44
Obituary ... 110
Earlier sketch in CA 65-68
Kahn, Herta Hess 1919- ... 25-28R
Kahn, James 1947- ... CANR-27
Earlier sketch in CA 109
Kahn, James M. 1903(?)-1978 Obituary ... 77-80
Kahn, Joan 1914-1994 ... 77-80
Obituary ... 146
See also SATA 48
See also SATA-Obit 82
Kahn, John (Ellison) 1950- ... 135
Kahn, Judd 1940- ... 101
Kahn, Katherine Janus 1942- ... SATA 90
Kahn, Kathy 1945- ... 41-44R
Kahn, Lawrence E(dwin) 1937- ... 103
Kahn, Lothar 1922- ... 25-28R
Kahn, Louis I. 1901-1974 Obituary ... 49-52
Kahn, Ludwig W(erner) 1910- ... 41-44R
Kahn, Madeleine (H.) 1955- ... 137
Kahn, Margaret 1949- ... 101
Kahn, Michael A. 1952- ... CANR-71
Earlier sketch in CA 138
Kahn, Michael D. 1936- ... CANR-27
Earlier sketch in CA 109
Kahn, Michele 1940- ... 130
Kahn, Peggy
See Katz, Bobbi
Kahn, Richard (Ferdinand Karn) 1905-1989 . 97-100
Obituary ... 128
Kahn, Robert I(rving) 1910- ... 5-8R
Kahn, Robert L(ouis) 1918- ... CANR-10
Earlier sketch in CA 17-20R
Kahn, Roger 1927- ... CANR-69
Earlier sketches in CA 25-28R, CANR-44
See also CLC 30
See also DLB 171
See also SATA 37
Kahn, Samuel 1897-1981 Obituary ... 106
Kahn, Sanders A(rthur) 1919-1987 ... 89-92
Obituary ... 121
Kahn, Sandra S(utker) 1942- ... 106
Kahn, Sholom J(acob) 1918- ... 102
Kahn, Si(mon) 1944- ... 33-36R
Kahn, Stephen 1940-1988 ... 5-8R
Obituary ... 127
Kahn, Steve
See Kahn, Stephen
Kahn, Sy M. 1924- ... CANR-10
Earlier sketch in CA 25-28R
Kahn, Theodore C(harles) 1912- ... 33-36R
Kahne, Joseph 1964- ... 162
Kahn-Fogel, Daniel (Mark) 1948- ... 97-100
Kahn-Freund, Otto 1900-1979 Obituary ... 108
Kahnweiler, Daniel-Henry 1884-1979 ... 29-32R
Obituary ... 85-88
Kahrl, George M(orrow) 1904- ... 105
Kahrl, Stanley J. 1931- ... 9-12R
Kahrl, William L. 1946- ... 109
Kaid, Lynda Lee 1948- ... CANR-16
Earlier sketch in CA 89-92
Kaikini, P(rabhakar) R(amrao) 1912- ... 61-64
Kaikkonen, Gus 1951- ... 129
Kaiko, Takeshi 1930- ... 104
See also DLB 182
Kaim-Caudle, Peter Robert 1916- ... 21-24R
Kain, John F(orrest) 1935- ... 29-32R
Kain, Malcolm
See Oglesby, Joseph
Kain, Philip J(oseph) 1943- ... 132
Kain, Richard M(organ) 1908-1990 ... CANR-2
Obituary ... 131
Earlier sketch in CA 5-8R
Kain, Richard Y(erkes) 1936- ... 37-40R
Kain, Saul
See Sassoon, Siegfried (Lorraine)
Kains, Josephine
See Goulart, Ron(ald Joseph)
Kainsdatter, Marianne
See Madsen, Svend Aage
Kainz, Howard Paul 1933- ... CANR-35
Earlier sketch in CA 114
Kairys, Anatolijus 1914- ... CANR-32
Earlier sketch in CA 102
Kairys, David 1943- ... 142
Kaisari, Uri 1899(?)-1979 Obituary ... 85-88
Kaiser, Artur 1943- ... 97-100
Kaiser, Bill
See Sumner, David (W. K.)
Kaiser, Charles 1950- ... 163

Kaiser, Christopher B(arina) 1941-...... CANR-47
Earlier sketch in CA 114
Kaiser, Daniel H. 1945-...... CANR-53
Earlier sketch in CA 126
Kaiser, David E. 1947-...... 144
Kaiser, Edward J(ohn) 1935-...... 93-96
Kaiser, Edwin George 1893-1984...... 45-48
Obituary...... 114
Kaiser, Ernest 1915-...... CANR-16
Earlier sketches in CA 49-52, CANR-1
Kaiser, Frances E(lkan) 1922-...... 57-60
Kaiser, Georg 1878-1945 Brief entry...... 106
See also DLB 124
See also TCLC 9
Kaiser, Harvey H. 1936-...... CANR-14
Earlier sketch in CA 81-84
Kaiser, Leo M(ax) 1918-...... 116
Kaiser, Otto 1924-...... 85-88
Kaiser, Philip M. 1913-...... 141
Kaiser, Robert Blair 1930-...... 9-12R
Kaiser, Robert G(reeley) 1943-...... CANR-31
Earlier sketch in CA 65-68
Kaiser, Walter (Jacob) 1931-...... CANR-36
Earlier sketches in CA 37-40R, CANR-15
Kaiser, Walter Christian, Jr. 1933-...... CANR-43
Earlier sketch in CA 114
Kaiser, Ward L(ouis) 1923-...... 53-56
Kaiser Wilhelm II
See Hohenzollern, Friedrich Wilhelm (Victor Albert)
Kaitz, Edward M. 1928-...... CANR-13
Earlier sketch in CA 29-32R
Kaizuki, Kiyonori 1950-...... SATA 72
Kajencki, Francis C(asimir) 1918-...... CANR-38
Earlier sketch in CA 115
Kakar, Sudhir 1938-...... 33-36R
Kaki
See Heinemann, Katherine
Kakimoto, Kozo 1915-...... SATA 11
Kakonen, Ulla
See Anobile, Ulla (Kakonen)
Kakonis, Thomas E. 1930-...... CANR-48
Earlier sketch in CA 57-60
Kakonis, Tom E.
See Kakonis, Thomas E.
Kakugawa, Frances H(ideko) 1936-...... 77-80
Kaland, William J. 1915(?)-1983 Obituary...... 111
Kalashnikoff, Nicholas 1888-1961...... 73-76
See also SATA 16
Kalb, Bernard 1932- Brief entry...... 109
Kalb, Jonah 1926-...... CANR-4
Earlier sketch in CA 53-56
See also SATA 23
Kalb, Jonathan 1959-...... 135
Kalb, Marvin L(eonard) 1930-...... CANR-45
Earlier sketch in CA 5-8R
Kalb, S(am) William 1897-...... 33-36R
Kalbacken, Joan 1925-...... 161
See also SATA 96
Kalberer, Augustine 1917-...... 61-64
Kalberg, Stephen...... 154
Kalcheim, Lee 1938-...... 85-88
Kaldor, Mary 1946-...... 93-96
Kaldor, Nicholas 1908-1986...... 134
Kale, Arvind and Shanta
See Gantzer, Hugh
Kale, Steven D(avid) 1957-...... 144
Kaleb, Vjekoslav 1905-1997...... DLB 181
Kalechofsky, Roberta 1931-...... CANR-57
Earlier sketches in CA 49-52, CANR-2
See also DLB 28
See also SATA 92
Kaledin, Eugenia 1929-...... 109
Kalem, T(heodore) E(ustace)
1919-1985 Obituary...... 116
Kalemkerian, Zarouhi 1874(?)-1971 Obituary...... 104
Kalenik, Sandra 1945-1993...... 73-76
Obituary...... 140
Kaler, Anne K(atherine) 1935-...... 138
Kaler, James Otis 1848-1912 Brief entry...... 120
See also DLB 42
See also SATA 15
Kales, Emily Fox 1944-...... 21-24R
Kaleta, Kenneth C. 1948-...... 146
Kaletski, Alexander 1946-...... 143
Brief entry...... 118
See also CLC 39
Kalfatovic, Martin R. 1961-...... 141
Kalfus, Melvin 1931-...... 134
Kalia, Narendra Nath 1942-...... CANR-30
Earlier sketch in CA 112
Kalia, Ravi 1947-...... 161
Kalich, Jacob 1891-1975 Obituary...... 89-92
Kalich, Richard 1947-...... CANR-55
Earlier sketch in CA 127
Kalich, Robert 1947-...... 106
Kalicki, Jan H(enryk) 1948-...... 65-68
Kalidasa fl. c. 400-...... PC 22
Kalijarvi, Thorsten V(alentine) 1897-1980...... CAP-1
Obituary...... 97-100
Earlier sketch in CA 19-20
Kalin, Martin (Gregory) 1943-...... 53-56
Kalin, Robert 1921-...... CANR-8
Earlier sketch in CA 61-64
Kalin, Rudolf 1938-...... 45-48
Kalina, Sigmund 1911-1977...... CANR-3
Earlier sketch in CA 49-52
Kalins, Dorothy (G.) 1942-...... CANR-17
Earlier sketch in CA 25-28R
Kalinsky, George 1936-...... CANR-2
Earlier sketch in CA 49-52
Kalish, Betty McKelvey 1913-1997...... 45-48
Obituary...... 157
Kalish, Claire M. 1947-...... SATA 92
Kalish, Donald 1919-...... 9-12R
Kalish, Richard A(llan) 1930-...... CANR-25
Earlier sketches in CA 5-8R, CANR-10
Kalisher, Simpson 1926-...... 17-20R
Kallas, James (Gus) 1928-...... CANR-10
Earlier sketch in CA 17-20R
Kallaus, Norman F. 1924-...... 33-36R
Kallberg, Sture
See Kaellberg, Sture
Kallen, (Marc) Christian 1950-...... 120
Kallen, Horace M(eyer) 1882-1974...... 93-96
Obituary...... 49-52
Kallen, Laurence 1944-...... 41-44R
Kallen, Lucille...... 97-100
Kallen, Stuart A(rnold) 1955-...... 151
See also SATA 86
Kallenbach, Joseph E(rnest) 1903-...... 77-80
Kallenbach, W(illiam) Warren 1926-...... 9-12R
Kallesser, Michael 1886(?)-1975 Obituary...... 61-64
Kallet, Arthur 1902-1972 Obituary...... 33-36R
Kallet, Marilyn 1946-...... 104
Kallgren, Beverly Hayes 1925-...... 146
Kallich, Martin 1918-...... CANR-2
Earlier sketch in CA 5-8R
Kallifatides, Theodor 1938-...... CANR-43
Earlier sketches in CA 85-88, CANR-15
Kallir, Jane K(atherine) 1954-...... CANR-52
Earlier sketches in CA 109, CANR-25
Kallir, Otto 1894-1978...... 49-52
Obituary...... 81-84
Kallman, Chester (Simon) 1921-1975...... CANR-3
Obituary...... 53-56
Earlier sketch in CA 45-48
See also CLC 2
Kallmann, Helmut Max 1922-...... 108
Kallsen, T(heodore) J(ohn) 1915-...... 5-8R
Kalman, Bobbie 1947-...... SATA 63
Kalman, Harold David 1943-...... 103
Kalman, Laura 1955-...... 140
Kalman, Maira 1949(?)-...... 161
See also CLR 32
See also SATA 96
Kalme, Egils 1909-...... 81-84
Kalmijn, Jo 1905-...... CAP-2
Earlier sketch in CA 21-22
Kalmus, Ain
See Mand, Ewald
Kalmus, Hans 1906(?)-1988 Obituary...... 128
Kalnay, Francis 1899-...... 49-52
See also SATA 7
Kalnoky, Ingeborg L(ouise) 1909-...... 61-64
Kaloustian, Rosanne 1955-...... SATA 93
Kalow, Gert 1921-...... 29-32R
Kalow, Gisela 1946-...... 107
See also SATA 32
Kalpakian, Laura Anne 1945-...... CANR-15
Earlier sketch in CA 81-84
Kals, W(illiam) S(teven) 1910-...... CANR-24
Earlier sketch in CA 45-48
Kalson, Albert E(ugene) 1932-...... 132
Kalstone, David (Michael) 1932-1986...... 166
Obituary...... 119
Kalstone, Shirlee A(nn) 1932-...... CANR-8
Earlier sketch in CA 61-64
Kalt, Bryson R. 1934-...... 33-36R
Kalt, Jeannette Chappell
1898(?)-1976 Obituary...... 69-72
Kaltenborn, Hans Von 1878-1965 Obituary...... 93-96
Kalter, Joanmarie 1951-...... 102
Kalu, Ogbu Uke 1944-...... 93-96
Kaluger, George 1921-...... 29-32R
Kaluger, Meriem Fair 1921-...... 81-84
Kalven, Harry, Jr. 1914-1974...... 162
Obituary...... 53-56
Kalyanaraman, Aiyaswamy 1903-...... CAP-2
Earlier sketch in CA 33-36
Kamakahi, Jeffrey J(on) 1960-...... 139
Kamal, Aleph 1950-...... 134
Kamarck, Andrew M(artin) 1914-...... CANR-10
Earlier sketch in CA 21-24R
Kamarck, Lawrence 1927-...... CANR-32
Earlier sketch in CA 73-76
Kamath, M(adhav) V(ithal) 1921-...... CANR-21
Earlier sketch in CA 69-72
Kamau, Kwadwo Agymah...... 164
Kamboureli, Smaro 1955-...... CANR-56
Earlier sketch in CA 127
Kambu, Joseph
See Amamoo, Joseph Godson
Kamen, Betty 1925-...... CANR-43
Earlier sketch in CA 114
Kamen, Gloria 1923-...... CANR-35
Earlier sketch in CA 114
See also SATA 9, 98
Kamen, Henry Arthur 1936-...... CANR-7
Earlier sketch in CA 5-8R, 163
Kamen, Isai
See Stein, Jess
Kamen, Martin D(avid) 1913-...... 118
Kamen, Paula 1967-...... 137
Kamen, Si 1920-...... 114
Kamenetsky, Ihor 1927-...... CANR-4
Earlier sketch in CA 1-4R
Kamenetz, Rodger 1950-...... CANR-47
Earlier sketches in CA 112, CANR-30
Kamenka, Eugene 1928-...... CANR-2
Earlier sketch in CA 5-8R
Kamerlingh Onnes, Heike 1853-1926...... 155
Kamerman, Jack B. 1940-...... 115
Kamerman, Sheila B(rody) 1928-...... CANR-10
Earlier sketch in CA 65-68
Kamerman, Sylvia E.
See Burack, Sylvia K.
Kamerschen, David R(oy) 1937-...... 53-56
Kamien, Marcia 1940-...... CANR-45
Earlier sketches in CA 105, CANR-22
Kamieniecki, Sheldon...... 156
Kamil, Alan C(urtis) 1941-...... 134
Brief entry...... 109
Kamil, Jill 1930-...... CANR-7
Earlier sketch in CA 57-60
Kamin, Leon J. 1927-...... 103
Kamin, Nick
See Antonick, Robert J.
Kaminer, Wendy 1950(?)-...... 162
Kamins, Jeanette...... 5-8R
Kamins, Robert Martin 1918- Brief entry...... 105
Kaminska, Ida 1899-1980 Obituary...... 97-100
Kaminskaya, Dina 1920-...... 115
Kaminski, Margaret (Joan) 1944-...... CANR-8
Earlier sketch in CA 61-64
Kaminsky, Alice R....... 33-36R
Kaminsky, Howard 1940-...... 105
Interview in...... 105
Kaminsky, Jack 1922-...... 21-24R
Kaminsky, Marc 1943-...... CANR-24
Earlier sketches in CA 53-56, CANR-5
Kaminsky, Melvin 1926-...... CANR-16
Earlier sketch in CA 65-68
See also Brooks, Mel
Kaminsky, Peretz 1916-...... 33-36R
Kaminsky, Stuart M(elvin) 1934-...... CANR-53
Earlier sketches in CA 73-76, CANR-29
See also CLC 59
Kaminsky, Susan Stanwood 1937-...... 115
Brief entry...... 110
Kamisar, Yale 1929-...... CANR-13
Earlier sketch in CA 69-72
Kamitses, Zoe 1941-...... 111
Kamm, Antony 1931-...... CANR-41
Earlier sketch in CA 117
Kamm, (Jan) Dorinda 1952-...... CANR-14
Earlier sketch in CA 37-40R
Kamm, Henry 1925-...... 151
Kamm, Herbert 1917-...... 69-72
Kamm, Jacob Oswald 1918-...... 5-8R
Kamm, Josephine (Hart) 1905-...... CANR-5
Earlier sketch in CA 9-12R
See also SATA 24
Kamm, Phyllis S. 1918-...... 112
Kamman, Madeleine M(arguerite Pin) 1930-...... 85-88
Kamman, William 1930-...... 25-28R
Kammen, Michael G(edaliah) 1936-...... CANR-63
Earlier sketches in CA 25-28R, CANR-22, 34
See also CAAS 23
See also MTCW 1
Kammerer, Gladys M. 1909-1970...... CANR-16
Obituary...... 103
Earlier sketch in CA 1-4R
Kammeyer, Kenneth C(arl) W(illiam) 1931-...... 29-32R
Kamp, Irene Kittle 1910-1985 Obituary...... 116
Kampelman, Max M. 1920-...... 41-44R
Kampen, Irene Trepel 1922-1998...... CANR-1
Obituary...... 166
Earlier sketch in CA 1-4R
Kampen, Michael Edwin 1939- Brief entry...... 110
Kampf, Abraham 1920-...... 21-24R
Kampf, Avram
See Kampf, Abraham
Kampf, Louis 1929-...... 33-36R
Kamphoefner, Walter D. 1948-...... 137
Kampov, Boris Nikolayevich 1908-1981...... 108
Obituary...... 104
Kampowski, Walter 1929-...... DLB 75
Kamrany, Nake M. 1934-...... CANR-14
Earlier sketch in CA 37-40R
Kamstra, Leslie D. 1920-...... 69-72
Kan, Sergei 1953-...... 137
Kanahele, George Sanford 1930-...... 102
Kanazawa, Masakata 1934-...... 25-28R
Kanazawa, Roger
See Kanazawa, Masakata
Kanchier, Carole...... 132
Kandall, Stephen R. 1940-...... 163
Kandaouroff, Berice 1912-...... 33-36R
Kandel, Denise Bystryn 1933-...... 13-16R
Kandel, I(saac) L(eon) 1881-1965...... CANR-3
Earlier sketch in CA 1-4R
Kandel, Lenore 1932-...... DLB 16
Kandel, Michael 1941-...... 159
See also SATA 93
Kandel, Thelma E. 1932-...... 111
Kandell, Alice S. 1938-...... CANR-13
Earlier sketch in CA 33-36R
See also SATA 35
Kandinsky, Nina 1896(?)-1980...... 101
Kandinsky, Wassily 1866-1944...... 155
Brief entry...... 118
Kando, Thomas M. 1941-...... CANR-2
Earlier sketch in CA 49-52
Kane, Aarno
See Kagan, Andrew
Kane, Alex
See Lazuta, Gene
Kane, Basil G(odfrey) 1931-...... CANR-24
Earlier sketch in CA 69-72
Kane, Bob...... 163
See also AAYA 8
Kane, Dennis Cornelius 1918-...... 41-44R
Kane, E. B. 1944-...... 57-60
Kane, Edward J(ames) 1935-...... 41-44R
Kane, Elizabeth 1942-...... 136
Kane, Francis
See Robbins, Harold
Kane, Frank 1912-1968...... CANR-58
Obituary...... 25-28R
Earlier sketch in CA 5-8R
Kane, Frank R. 1925-...... 77-80
Kane, George 1916-...... 103
Kane, Gerard Thomas Matthew 1946-...... 133
Kane, Gordon L. 1937-...... 149
Kane, H. Victor 1906-...... 29-32R
Kane, Harnett T(homas) 1910-1984 Obituary...... 113
Kane, Henry 1918-...... 156
See also McKay, Kenneth R.
Kane, Henry Bugbee 1902-1971...... 73-76
See also SATA 14
Kane, J. Herbert 1910-...... 97-100
Kane, Jack
See Baker, (Allen) Albert
Kane, James
See Germano, Peter B.
Kane, Jim
See Germano, Peter B.
Kane, John 1946-...... 167
Kane, John Joseph 1909-...... CAP-2
Earlier sketch in CA 13-14
Kane, Julia
See Robins, Denise (Naomi)
Kane, L. A.
See Mannetti, Lisa
Kane, Leslie 1945-...... 140
Kane, Pablo
See Zachary, Hugh
Kane, Paul
See Simon, Paul (Frederick)
Kane, Penelope Susan 1945-...... 131
Kane, Penny
See Kane, Penelope Susan
Kane, Peter E(vans) 1932-...... CANR-31
Earlier sketch in CA 112
Kane, Robert S. 1925-1997...... CANR-48
Obituary...... 162
Earlier sketches in CA 9-12R, CANR-7, 23
Kane, Robert W. 1910-...... SATA 18
Kane, Rod
See Kane, Gerard Thomas Matthew
Kane, Thomas S. 1925-...... 114
Kane, William Everett 1943-...... 49-52
Kane, Wilson
See Bloch, Robert (Albert)
Kanellos, Nicolas 1945-...... 131
See also HW
Kanerova, Mita Castle
See Castle-Kanerova, Mita
Kanes, Eveline L. 1929-...... 141
Kanet, Roger E(dward) 1936-...... CANR-49
Earlier sketches in CA 33-36R, CANR-14
Kanetzke, Howard W(illiam) 1932-...... 112
See also SATA 38
Kanfer, Allen 1905(?)-1983 Obituary...... 110
Kanfer, Frederick H. 1925-...... CANR-32
Earlier sketches in CA 41-44R, CANR-15
Kanfer, Stefan 1933-...... 103
Interview in...... 103
Kang, K. Connie 1942-...... 152
Kang, Shin T. 1935-...... 33-36R
Kang, Younghill 1903-1972 Obituary...... 37-40R
Kanigel, Robert 1946-...... CANR-69
Earlier sketch in CA 132
Kanin, Garson 1912-...... CANR-7
Earlier sketch in CA 5-8R
See also AITN 1
See also CLC 22
See also DLB 7
Kanin, Michael 1910-1993...... CANR-46
Obituary...... 140
Earlier sketch in CA 61-64
Kanin, Ruth 1920-...... 107
Kanitz, Walter 1910-...... 97-100
Kaniuk, Yoram 1930-...... 134
See also CLC 19
Kaniut, Larry (LeRoy) 1942-...... 114
Kann, Mark E. 1947-...... 130
Kann, Robert A. 1906-1981 Obituary...... 105
Kann, Robert A(dolf) 1906-1981...... 129
Kannappan, Subbiah 1927-...... 93-96
Kanner, Catherine 1954-...... 123
Kanner, Leo 1894-1981...... 17-20R
Obituary...... 103
Kanof, Abram 1903-...... 29-32R
Kanon, Joseph A. 1946-...... 163
Kanovsky, Eliyahu 1922-...... 33-36R
Kanoza, Muriel Canfield 1935-...... SATA 94
Kansil, Joli 1943-...... 81-84
Kant, Hermann 1926-...... 159
See also DLB 75
Kant, Immanuel 1724-1804...... DLB 94
Kantar, Edwin B(ruce) 1932-...... 41-44R
Kantaris, Sylvia 1936-...... 139
Kantarizis, Sylvia
See Kantaris, Sylvia
Kantemir, Antiokh Dmitrievich 1708-1744...... DLB 150
Kanter, Arnold 1945-...... 89-92
Kanter, Hal 1918-...... 81-84
Kanter, Lynn 1954-...... 164
Kanter, Rosabeth Moss 1943-...... CANR-14
Earlier sketch in CA 77-80
Kanto, Peter
See Zachary, Hugh
Kantonen, T(aito) A(lmar) 1900-...... 33-36R
Kantor, Hal 1924-...... 77-80
Kantor, Harry 1911-...... CANR-2
Earlier sketch in CA 1-4R
Kantor, Herman I. 1909-...... 57-60
Kantor, James 1927-1974...... CAP-2
Earlier sketch in CA 21-22
Kantor, Leonard 1924(?)-1984 Obituary...... 112
Kantor, MacKinlay 1904-1977...... CANR-63
Obituary...... 73-76
Earlier sketches in CA 61-64, CANR-60
See also CLC 7
See also DLB 9, 102
Kantor, Marvin 1934-...... CANR-2
Earlier sketch in CA 49-52
Kantor, Seth 1926-1993...... 81-84
Obituary...... 142
Kantor, Tim 1932-...... 128
Kantor-Berg, Friedrich 1908-1979...... 133
Obituary...... 89-92
See also Torberg, Friedrich

Kantorovich, Leonid V(italevich) 1912-1986 ... 164
Obituary ... 119
Kantowicz, Edward Robert 1943- ... 114
Kantrowitz, Arnie 1940- ... 77-80
Kantrowitz, Joanne Spencer 1931- ... 81-84
Kantzer, Kenneth S(ealer) 1917- ... 106
Kanungo, R(abindra) N. 1935- ... 135
Kanwar, Mahfooz A. 1939- ... 37-40R
Kany, Charles E(mil) 1895-1968 ... CANR-3
Earlier sketch in CA 1-4R
Kanya, Maria
See Green, Maria A.
Kanya-Forstner, A(lexander) S(ydney) 1940- ... CANR-17
Earlier sketch in CA 25-28R
Kanza, Thomas R. (Nsenga) 1933- ... CANR-5
Earlier sketch in CA 53-56
Kanzawa, Toshiko
See Furukawa, Toshi
Kanze, Edward (J. III) 1956- ... 139
Kanzer, Mark 1908- ... 37-40R
Kao, Charles C. L. 1932- ... 85-88
Kao, George 1912- ... 132
Kao Hsiao-sheng
See Gao Xiaosheng
Kapel, Andrew
See Burgess, Michael (Roy)
Kapel, David E(dward) 1932- ... 125
Kapel, Saul M.D.
See Schanche, Don(ald) A(rthur)
Kapelner, Alan ... 5-8R
Kapelrud, Arvid Schou 1912- ... 102
Kapfer, Miriam B(ierbaum) 1935- ... 33-36R
Kapfer, Philip G(ordon) 1936- ... 33-36R
Kapferer, Jean-Noel 1948- ... 147
Kapitsa, Pyotr L(eonidovich) 1894-1984 Obituary ... 112
Kaplan, Abraham 1918-1993 ... CANR-48
Obituary ... 141
Earlier sketch in CA 13-16R
Kaplan, Alice Y.
See Kaplan, Alice Yaeger
Kaplan, Alice Yaeger 1954- ... 153
Kaplan, Allan 1932- ... 33-36R
Kaplan, Andrew (Gary) 1941- ... 125
Kaplan, Andrew 1960- ... 146
See also SATA 78
Kaplan, Anne Bernays 1930- ... CANR-72
Earlier sketches in CA 1-4R, CANR-5
See also SATA 32
Kaplan, Arthur 1925- ... 5-8R
Kaplan, Barbara Beigun 1943- ... 146
Kaplan, Benjamin 1911- ... CANR-47
Earlier sketch in CA 1-4R
Kaplan, Bernard 1944- ... CANR-2
Earlier sketch in CA 49-52
Kaplan, Berton H(arris) 1930- ... 61-64
Kaplan, Bess 1927- ... 85-88
See also SATA 22
Kaplan, Boche 1926- ... CANR-10
Earlier sketch in CA 21-24R
See also SATA 24
Kaplan, Charles 1919- ... 9-12R
Kaplan, David Gordon 1908- ... 61-64
Kaplan, David Michael 1946- ... CLC 50
Kaplan, Doris
See Willens, Doris
Kaplan, E(lizabeth) Ann 1936- ... 127
Kaplan, Edward 1946- ... CANR-11
Earlier sketch in CA 69-72
Kaplan, Elizabeth (A.) 1956- ... 150
See also SATA 83
Kaplan, Eugene H(erbert) 1932- ... 81-84
Kaplan, Flora S(tewart) ... 109
Kaplan, Fred
See Kaplan, Fred Michael
Kaplan, Fred 1937- ... CANR-48
Earlier sketches in CA 41-44R, CANR-14
See also DLB 111
Kaplan, Fred M.
See Kaplan, Fred Michael
Kaplan, Fred Michael 1954- ... 127
Brief entry ... 121
Kaplan, Frederick I(srael) 1920- ... 21-24R
Kaplan, H. Roy 1944- ... 89-92
Kaplan, Harold 1916- ... 17-20R
Kaplan, Helen Singer 1929-1995 ... 102
Obituary ... 149
See also AITN 1
Kaplan, Howard 1950- ... 69-72
Kaplan, Howard B(ernard) 1932- ... CANR-22
Earlier sketches in CA 61-64, CANR-8
Kaplan, Hymen R. 1910- ... 102
Kaplan, Irma 1900- ... 29-32R
See also SATA 10
Kaplan, Jack A(rnold) 1947- ... 57-60
Kaplan, Jacob J. 1920- ... CANR-10
Earlier sketch in CA 21-24R
Kaplan, James 1951- ... 135
See also CLC 59
Kaplan, Janet A(nn) 1945- ... 130
Kaplan, Janice Ellen 1955- ... CANR-67
Earlier sketch in CA 117
Kaplan, Jean Caryl Korn 1926- ... 5-8R
See also SATA 10
Kaplan, Jeffrey 1954- ... 165
Kaplan, Jerry 1952- ... 152
Kaplan, Jim 1944- ... 126
Kaplan, Joel 1956- ... 134
Kaplan, Johanna 1942- ... 77-80
See also DLB 28
Kaplan, John 1929-1989 Obituary ... 130
Kaplan, Joseph 1916(?)-1980 Obituary ... 97-100
Kaplan, Justin 1925- ... CANR-8
Earlier sketch in CA 17-20R
See also DLB 111
Kaplan, Lawrence Jay 1915- ... 21-24R
Kaplan, Lawrence S(amuel) 1924- ... 33-36R
Kaplan, Leonard 1918(?)-1977 Obituary ... 69-72
Kaplan, Louise J. 1929- ... 141
Kaplan, Marion A. 1946- ... 142
Kaplan, Martin (Harold) 1950- ... 65-68
Kaplan, Martin F(rancis) 1940- ... 93-96
Kaplan, Max 1911- ... CANR-20
Earlier sketches in CA 1-4R, CANR-5
Kaplan, Milton 1910- ... 65-68
Kaplan, Milton 1918-1988 Obituary ... 127
Kaplan, Mordecai M(enahem) 1881-1983 Obituary ... 111
Kaplan, Morton A. 1921- ... CANR-7
Earlier sketch in CA 5-8R
Kaplan, Nelly 1936- ... 144
Kaplan, Norman Mayer 1931- ... 110
Kaplan, Philip 1916- ... 13-16R
Kaplan, Rachel ... 166
Kaplan, Richard 1929- ... 73-76
Kaplan, Robert B. 1928- ... CANR-22
Earlier sketches in CA 13-16R, CANR-7
Kaplan, Robert D. 1952- ... 142
Kaplan, S(aul) Howard 1938- ... 25-28R
Kaplan, Samuel 1935- ... 21-24R
Kaplan, Sidney 1913-1993 ... CANR-47
Obituary ... 141
Earlier sketch in CA 85-88
Kaplan, Stephen 1940- ... 142
Kaplan, Steven B. 1953- ... 135
Kaplan, Steven M. 1960- ... 166
Kaplan, Stuart R(onald) 1932- ... CANR-21
Earlier sketches in CA 49-52, CANR-2
Kaplan, Sydney Janet 1939- ... 110
Kaplan, William 1957- ... CANR-53
Earlier sketch in CA 126
Kaplar, Richard T. 1951- ... 154
Kapler, Aleksei (Yakovlevich) 1904(?)-1979 Obituary ... 89-92
Kaplon, Morton F(ischel) 1921- ... 21-24R
Kaplow, Herb(ert Elias) 1927- ... 119
Brief entry ... 110
Interview in ... 119
Kaplow, Jeffry 1937- ... 17-20R
Kaplow, Robert 1954- ... 138
See also SATA 70
Kapnist, Vasilii Vasil'evich 1758(?)-1823 ... DLB 150
Kapoor, Ashok 1940- ... 85-88
Kapoor, L(achman) D(as) 1916- ... 21-24R
Kapoor, Sukhbir Singh 1937- ... CANR-56
Earlier sketches in CA 109, CANR-29
Kapp, Colin 1928(?)- ... 132
Kapp, K(arl) William 1910-1976 ... CANR-8
Obituary ... 65-68
Earlier sketch in CA 5-8R
Kapp, Reginald Otto 1885-1966 ... 5-8R
Kapp, Yvonne (Mayer) 1903- ... 103
Kappauf, William Emil (Jr.) 1913- ... 106
Kappel, Philip 1901- ... CAP-1
Earlier sketch in CA 13-16
Kappelman, Murray M(artin) 1931- ... 73-76
Kappel-Smith, Diana 1951- ... 121
Kappen, Charles Vaughan 1910- ... 9-12R
Kappes, Marcia Ann 1947- ... 151
Kappes, Sister Marcianne
See Kappes, Marcia Ann
Kaprow, Allan 1927- ... 105
Kapsis, Robert E. 1943- ... 141
Kapsner, Oliver L(eonard) 1902- ... 116
Kapstein, I(srael) J(ames) 1904-1983 Obituary ... 110
Kaptchuk, Ted J(ack) 1947- ... CANR-27
Earlier sketch in CA 110
Kapur, Harish 1929- ... CANR-34
Earlier sketches in CA 85-88, CANR-15
Kapur, L. D.
See Kapoor, L(achman) D(as)
Kapur, Rajiv A. 1951- ... 136
Kapur, Sudarshan 1940- ... 142
Kapuscinski, Ryszard 1932- ... 114
Kapusta, Paul
See Bickers, Richard (Leslie) Townshend
Karadzic, Vuk Stefanovic 1787-1864 ... DLB 147
Karageorge, Michael
See Anderson, Poul (William)
Karageorghis, Vassos 1929- ... CANR-33
Earlier sketches in CA 81-84, CANR-15
Karamanski, Theodore J. 1953- ... 126
Karamzin, Nikolai Mikhailovich 1766-1826 ... DLB 150
Karan, Pradyumna P(rasad) 1930- ... CANR-35
Earlier sketch in CA 114
Karanikas, Alexander 1916- ... 33-36R
Karapanou, Margarita 1946- ... 101
See also CLC 13
Karas, Jim 1949-1981 ... 126
Obituary ... 108
Karas, Joza 1926- ... 124
Karas, Phyllis 1944- ... 105
Karasu, Toksoz B(yram) 1935- ... 105
Karasz, Ilonka 1896-1981 ... SATA-Obit 29
Karbo, Joe 1925(?)-1980 Obituary ... 115
Karbo, Karen (Lee) 1956(?)- ... 141
Kardiner, Abram 1891-1981 ... 107
Obituary ... 104
Kardish, Laurence 1945- ... CANR-30
Earlier sketch in CA 49-52
Kardouche, G(eorge) Khalil 1935- ... 17-20R
Karel, Leonard 1912- ... 49-52
Karen
See Aldrich, Sandra Picklesimer
Karen, Robert L(e Roy) 1925- ... 73-76
Karen, Ruth 1922-1987 ... CANR-11
Obituary ... 123
Earlier sketch in CA 17-20R
See also SATA 9
See also SATA-Obit 54
Karg, Elissa Jane 1951- ... 21-24R
Karger, Delmar William 1913- ... CANR-8
Earlier sketch in CA 17-20R
Kargon, Robert Hugh 1938- ... CANR-28
Earlier sketch in CA 45-48
Kari, Daven M(ichael) 1953- ... 156
Kariel, Henry S. 1924- ... 13-16R
Karier, Thomas 1956- ... 148
Karin, Sidney 1943- ... 126
Karina
See Goud, Anne
Karinthy, Frigyes 1887-1938 ... TCLC 47
Kariuki, Josiah Mwangi 1929- ... 107
Kark, Nina Mary (Mabey)
See Bawden, Nina (Mary Mabey)
See also SATA 4
Karkala, John A.
See Alphonso-Karkala, John B.
Karkala, John B. A.
See Alphonso-Karkala, John B.
Karkhanis, Sharad 1935- ... 110
Karkoschka, Erhard 1923- ... 45-48
Karl, Barry D(ean) 1927- ... 102
Karl, Dennis (R.) 1954-1992 ... 134
Obituary ... 139
Karl, Frederick R(obert) 1927- ... CANR-44
Earlier sketches in CA 5-8R, CANR-3
See also CLC 34
Karl, Herb 1938- ... SATA 73
Karl, Jean E(dna) 1927- ... CANR-12
Earlier sketch in CA 29-32R
See also SAAS 10
See also SATA 34
Karl, Roger
See Trouve, Roger
Karlan, Richard 1919- ... 17-20R
Karle, Hellmut (William Arthur) 1932- ... 142
Karlen, Arno 1937- ... CANR-5
Earlier sketch in CA 1-4R
Karlen, Delmar 1912-1988 ... CANR-2
Obituary ... 127
Earlier sketch in CA 5-8R
Karlen, Neal (Stuart) 1959- ... 154
Karlgren, (Klas) Bernhard (Johannes) 1889- ... CAP-1
Earlier sketch in CA 9-10
Karlin, Bernie 1927- ... 136
See also SATA 68
Karlin, Daniel 1953- ... 139
Karlin, Eugene 1918- ... SATA 10
Karlin, Jules 1899- ... CAP-2
Earlier sketch in CA 25-28
Karlin, Muriel S.
See Trachman, Muriel Karlin
Karlin, Nurit ... SATA 63
Karlin, Robert 1918- ... 9-12R
Karlin, Samuel 1924- ... 148
Karlin, Wayne (Stephen) 1945- ... 133
Karlins, Marvin 1941- ... CANR-17
Earlier sketch in CA 25-28R
Karlowich, Robert A. 1927- ... 125
Karlsson, Elis (Viktor) 1905- ... CAP-1
Earlier sketch in CA 13-16
Karlsson, T. Edward 1915(?)-1984 Obituary ... 113
Karma Karen
See Kent, Karen
Karman, James W. 1947- ... 126
Karman, Mal 1944- ... 103
Karmel, Alex 1931- ... 21-24R
Karmel, Roberta S(arah) 1937- ... 108
Karmel-Wolfe, Henia 1923- ... 49-52
Karmen, Roman Lazarevich 1906-1978 Obituary ... 77-80
Karmi, Abdul Karim 1907(?)-1980 Obituary ... 102
Karmi, Hasan Said 1908- ... 45-48
Karmiloff-Smith, Annette Dionne 1938- ... 143
Karmin, Monroe William 1929- ... 101
Karnad, Girish 1938- ... 65-68
Karnes, Merle B(riggs) 1916- ... 85-88
Karnes, Thomas L(indas) 1914- ... 21-24R
Karney, Beulah Mullen ... 13-16R
Karniewski, Janusz
See Wittlin, Thaddeus (Andrew)
Karno, Bung
See Sukarno, (Ahmed)
Karnos, David D. 1947- ... 141
Karnow, Stanley 1925- ... CANR-64
Earlier sketches in CA 57-60, CANR-31
See also MTCW 1
Karodia, Farida 1942- ... 168
Karol, Alexander
See Kent, Arthur William Charles
Karol, K. S.
See Kewes, Karol
Karolevitz, Bob
See Karolevitz, Robert F.
Karolevitz, Robert F. 1922- ... CANR-22
Earlier sketches in CA 17-20R, CANR-7
Karolides, Nicholas J(ames) 1928- ... 21-24R
Karolyi, Catherine (Andrassy) 1898-1985 Obituary ... 116
Karon, Bertram Paul 1930- ... CANR-7
Earlier sketch in CA 61-64
Karp, Abraham J. 1921- ... CANR-40
Earlier sketches in CA 5-8R, CANR-3, 18
Karp, Alan 1947- ... 107
Karp, Carl 1954- ... 139
Karp, David 1922- ... CANR-1
Earlier sketch in CA 1-4R
Karp, Ivan C. 1926- ... 17-20R
Karp, Laurence E(dward) 1939- ... 77-80
Karp, Lila 1933- ... 25-28R
Karp, Mark 1922- ... 1-4R
Karp, Naomi J. 1926- ... 81-84
See also SATA 16
Karp, Robert J. 1941- ... 151
Karp, Stephen A(rnold) 1928- ... CANR-6
Earlier sketch in CA 1-4R
Karp, Walter 1934(?)-1989 Obituary ... 129
Karpat, Kemal H(asim) 1925- ... CANR-11
Earlier sketch in CA 69-72
Karpatkin, Marvin M. 1926-1975 Obituary ... 53-56
Karpau, Uladzimir
See Karpov, Vladimir
Karpel, Bernard 1911-1986 ... 106
Obituary ... 118
Karpel, Craig S. 1944- ... 65-68
Karpeles, Maud 1885- ... 25-28R
Karpf, Holly W. 1946- ... 37-40R
Karpin, Fred L(eon) 1913-1986 ... CANR-9
Obituary ... 119
Earlier sketch in CA 13-16R
Karpinski, J. Rick
See Karpinski, John Eric
Karpinski, John Eric 1952- ... SATA 81
Karpinski, Rick
See Karpinski, John Eric
Karplus, Walter J. 1927- ... 21-24R
Karpman, Harold L(ew) 1927- ... 77-80
Karpov, Vladimir 1912(?)-1977 Obituary ... 73-76
Karr, E(arl) R(alph) 1918- ... 1-4R
Karr, Kathleen 1946- ... 149
See also SATA 82
Karr, Mary 1954(?)- ... 151
Karr, Phyllis Ann 1944- ... CANR-40
Earlier sketches in CA 101, CANR-18
Karras, Alex(ander G.) 1935- ... 107
Karrass, Chester L. 1923- ... 101
Karren, Keith J(ohn) 1943- ... CANR-40
Earlier sketch in CA 116
Karrer, Paul 1889-1971 Obituary ... 113
Karris, Robert J(oseph) 1938- ... CANR-5
Earlier sketch in CA 53-56
Karsavina, Jean (Faterson) 1908- ... 101
Karsavina, Tamara 1885-1978 Obituary ... 77-80
Karsch, Anna Louisa 1722-1791 ... DLB 97
Karsch, Robert F(rederick) 1909- ... 77-80
Karsen, Sonja (Petra) 1919- ... 41-44R
Karsh, Bernard 1921- ... 103
Karsh, Yousuf 1908- ... 33-36R
Karshner, Roger 1928- ... 33-36R
Karst, Kenneth L(eslie) 1929- ... 132
Karsten, Peter 1938- ... CANR-13
Earlier sketch in CA 37-40R
Karta, Nat
See Norwood, Victor G(eorge) C(harles)
Karta, Nat
See Fearn, John Russell
Kartiganer, Donald M. 1937- ... 97-100
Karttunen, Frances 1942- ... 138
Karu, Baruch 1899-1972 Obituary ... 104
Karve, Dinakar Dhondo 1899-1980 ... 5-8R
Obituary ... 103
Karve, Irawati (Karmarkar) 1905-1970 ... CAP-1
Earlier sketch in CA 19-20
Kary, Elizabeth N. (a pseudonym) 1947- ... 122
Kasabov, Nikola K(irilov) 1948- ... 168
Kasack, Hermann 1896-1966 ... DLB 69
Kasai Zenzo 1887-1927 ... DLB 180
Kasarda, John Dale 1945- ... 103
Kaschak, Ellyn 1943- ... 139
Kaschnitz, Marie Luise
See von Kaschnitz-Weinberg, Marie Luise
See also DLB 69
Kasdan, Lawrence 1949- ... 109
Interview in ... 109
Kasdan, Sara (Moskovitz) 1911- ... 1-4R
Kasdorf, Hans 1928- ... 116
Kasdorf, Julia 1962- ... 139
Kase, Francis J(oseph) 1910- ... 21-24R
Kaselow, Joseph 1912-1986 Obituary ... 119
Kaser, David 1924- ... 17-20R
Kaser, Michael (Charles) 1926- ... CANR-10
Earlier sketch in CA 17-20R
Kaser, Paul 1944- ... 104
Kash, Don E(ldon) 1934- ... CANR-9
Earlier sketch in CA 21-24R
Kasha, Lawrence N(athan) 1934(?)-1990 Obituary ... 132
Kashdan, Isaac 1905-1985 Obituary ... 115
Kashima, Tetsuden 1940- ... 81-84
Kashiwagi, Isami 1925- ... SATA 10
Kashner, Rita 1942- ... CANR-27
Earlier sketch in CA 105
Kasinitz, Philip 1957- ... 137
Kasischke, Laura 1961- ... 154
Kaske, Robert Earl 1921-1989 Obituary ... 129
Kaslow, Florence (Whiteman) 1930- ... CANR-41
Earlier sketches in CA 45-48, CANR-1, 18
Kasparov, G. K.
See Kasparov, Gary (Kimovich)
Kasparov, Gari
See Kasparov, Gary (Kimovich)
Kasparov, Garry
See Kasparov, Gary (Kimovich)
Kasparov, Gary (Kimovich) 1963- ... 139
Kasper, Shirl(ey Elaine) 1948- ... 137
Kasper, Sydney H. 1911- ... 1-4R
Kasper, Walter 1933- ... 130
Kasperson, Roger E. 1938- ... 29-32R
Kasrils, Ronald 1938- ... 29-32R
Kass, Edward H(arold) 1917- ... 129
Kass, Jerome 1923(?)-1973 Obituary ... 104
Kass, Jerome 1937- ... 57-60
Kass, Linda Stern 1953- ... 138
Kass, Norman 1934- ... 29-32R
Kass, Ray 1944- ... 118
Kassalow, Everett M(alcolm) 1918-1995 ... CANR-25
Obituary ... 149
Earlier sketch in CA 45-48
Kassebaum, Gene G(irard) 1929- ... 17-20R

Kassem, Lou 1931- CANR-62
Earlier sketch in CA 128
See also SATA 62
See also SATA-Brief 51
Kassewitz, Jack 1914(?)-1984 Obituary 112
Kassis, Hanna (Emmanuel) 1932- 125
Kassler, J. C.
See Kassler, Jamie C(roy)
Kassler, Jamie C(roy) 1938- 135
Kassof, Allen 1930- 21-24R
Kasson, John F(ranklin) 1944- 81-84
Kassorla, Irene Chamie 1931- 110
Kast, Fremont E. 1926- 21-24R
Kastan, David Scott 1946- 109
Kastein, Shulamith 1903-1983 105
Obituary 110
Kastel, Warren
See Silverberg, Robert
Kastelan, Jure 1919-1990 DLB 147
Kastely, James L. 1947- 166
Kastenbaum, Robert (Jay) 1932- CANR-9
Earlier sketch in CA 13-16R
Kaster, Joseph 1912-(?) CAP-1
Earlier sketch in CA 19-20
Kastl, Albert J(oseph) 1939- 57-60
Kastl, Lena 1942- 61-64
Kastle, Herbert D(avid) 1924-1987 CANR-1
Obituary 123
Earlier sketch in CA 1-4R
Kastner, Jill (Marie) 1964- SATA 70
Kastner, Jonathan 1937- 25-28R
Kastner, Joseph 1907-1997 CANR-71
Obituary 156
Earlier sketch in CA 85-88
Kastner, Marianna 1940- 25-28R
Kastner, Patricia Wilson
See Wilson-Kastner, Patricia
Kasulis, T(homas) P(atrick) 1948- 124
Kasuya, Masahiro 1937- CANR-29
Earlier sketch in CA 110
See also SATA 51
Kaszner, Kurt
See Serwicher, Kurt
Kaszubski, Marek 1951- 105
Kataev, Evgeny Petrovich 1903-1942 Brief entry 120
See also Petrov, Evgeny
Katahn, Martin 1928- 114
Katan, Norma-Jean 1936- 113
Kataphusin
See Ruskin, John
Katayev, Valentin (Petrovich) 1897-1986 131
Obituary 119
Brief entry 117
Katcha, Vahe
See Katchadourian, Vahe
Katchadourian, Herant A(ram) 1933- CANR-42
Earlier sketches in CA 103, CANR-20
Katchadourian, Vahe 1928- CANR-25
Earlier sketch in CA 29-32R
Katchen, Carole 1944- 61-64
See also SATA 9
Katchmer, George Andrew 1916- 1-4R
Kateb, George (Anthony) 1931- 123
Brief entry 118
Katen, Thomas Ellis 1931- 53-56
Kater, Michael H(ans) 1937- CANR-69
Earlier sketch in CA 114
Kates, Brian 1946- 119
Kates, Carol A. 1943- 115
Kates, Gary (Richard) 1952- 125
Kates, Robert W. 1929- CANR-24
Earlier sketches in CA 17-20R, CANR-8
Kathman, Michael D(ennis) 1943- 109
Kathryn
See Searle, Kathryn Adrienne
Kati
See Rekai, Kati
Katicic, Radoslav 1930- 37-40R
Katkov, George 1903-1985 Obituary 115
Katkov, Norman 1918- 13-16R
Kato, Hidetoshi 1930- 115
Kato, Shuichi 1919- 37-40R
Kato, Tosio 1917- 161
Kato, Tsuyoski 1943- CANR-56
Earlier sketch in CA 126
Katona, Edita 1913- 69-72
Katona, George 1901-1981 128
Obituary 104
Katona, Robert 1949- SATA 21
Katope, Christopher G. 1918- 21-24R
Katoppo, (Henriette) Marianne 1943- 123
Katrovas, Richard 1953- CANR-55
Earlier sketch in CA 126
Katsarakis, Joan Harries
See Harries, Joan
Katsaros, Thomas 1926- 57-60
Katsh, Abraham I(saac) 1908- CANR-8
Earlier sketch in CA 5-8R
Katsh, M. Ethan 1945- 133
Katsh, Salem M(ichael) 1948- 110
Kattan, Naim 1928- CANR-44
Earlier sketches in CA 69-72, CANR-11
See also DLB 53
Katterjohn, Arthur D. 1930(?)-1980 Obituary 93-96
Katz, Abraham 1926- 49-52
Katz, Albert M(ichael) 1938- 93-96
Katz, Alfred
See Allan, Alfred K.
Katz, Alfred 1938- 77-80
Katz, Arthur M. 1942- 124
Katz, Barbara 1956- 142
Katz, Basho
See Gatti, Arthur Gerard
Katz, Benjamin 1904-1985 Obituary 115
Katz, Bobbi 1933- CANR-37
Earlier sketches in CA 37-40R, CANR-16
See also SATA 12
Katz, Carol 1939- 115
Katz, Daniel 1903-1998 41-44R
Obituary 166
Katz, Elia (Jacob) 1948- 151
Katz, Elias 1912- 29-32R
Katz, Ellis 1938- 29-32R
Katz, Eve 1938- CANR-1
Earlier sketch in CA 45-48
Katz, Fred(eric Phillip) 1938- 49-52
See also SATA 6
Katz, Fred E(mil) 1927- 77-80
Katz, Friedrich 1927- 134
Brief entry 113
Katz, Gloria 1945(?)- 107
Katz, Herbert Melvin 1930- 103
Katz, Irving I. 1907- 1-4R
Katz, Jack 1944- 111
Katz, Jacob 1904- CANR-4
Earlier sketch in CA 1-4R
Katz, Jane B(resler) 1934- 85-88
See also SATA 33
Katz, Jay 1922- 118
Katz, John Stuart 1938- CANR-14
Earlier sketch in CA 37-40R
Katz, Jon 165
Katz, Jonathan 1938- 85-88
Katz, Josef 1918- 53-56
Katz, Joseph 1910- CANR-2
Earlier sketch in CA 1-4R
Katz, Judith 1951- 139
Katz, Judith Milstein 1943- 106
Katz, Lawrence S(anford) 1947- 154
Katz, Leon 1919- CANR-20
Earlier sketches in CA 49-52, CANR-4
Katz, Leonard 1926- 21-24R
Katz, Lewis R(obert) 1938- CANR-46
Earlier sketch in CA 116
Katz, Lilian G(onshaw) 1932- 111
Katz, Marjorie P.
See Weiser, Marjorie P(hillis) K(atz)
Katz, Marshall P. 1939- 153
Katz, Martin 1929- 21-24R
Katz, Marvin C(harles) 1930- 25-28R
Katz, Menke 1906-1991 CANR-11
Obituary 134
Earlier sketch in CA 13-16R
Interview in CANR-11
See also CAAS 9
Katz, Michael B(arry) 1939- CANR-48
Earlier sketches in CA 33-36R, CANR-13
Katz, Michael M. 1956(?)-1988 Obituary 126
Katz, Michael Ray 1944- CANR-39
Earlier sketches in CA 102, CANR-18
Katz, Mickey
See Katz, Myron Meyer
Katz, Milton 1907-1995 CAP-1
Obituary 149
Earlier sketch in CA 11-12
Katz, Mort 1925- CANR-11
Earlier sketch in CA 61-64
Katz, Myron Meyer 1909-1985 81-84
Obituary 116
Katz, Robert 1933- CANR-11
Earlier sketch in CA 25-28R
Katz, Robert L. 1917- 9-12R
Katz, Samuel 1914- CANR-12
Earlier sketch in CA 25-28R
Katz, Sanford N. 1933- CANR-13
Earlier sketch in CA 33-36R
Katz, Shmuel
See Katz, Samuel
Katz, Stan
See Chapman, Frank M(onroe)
Katz, Stanley Nider 1934- 9-12R
Katz, Steve 1935- CANR-12
Earlier sketch in CA 25-28R
See also CAAS 14, 64
See also CLC 47
See also DLBY 83
Katz, Steven T(heodore) 1944- 132
Katz, Susan 1944(?)-1982 Obituary 107
Katz, Welwyn Wilton 1948- 154
See also AAYA 19
See also CLR 45
See also JRDA
See also SATA 62, 96
Katz, William 1940- 85-88
See also SATA 98
Katz, William A(rmstrong) 1924- CANR-10
Earlier sketch in CA 25-28R
Katz, William Loren 1927- CANR-9
Earlier sketch in CA 21-24R
See also SATA 13
Katzander, Howard L. 1911(?)-1983 Obituary 110
Katzen, Mollie 1950- 165
Katzenbach, John 1950- 119
Katzenbach, Maria 1953- 77-80
Katzenbach, William E. 1904-1975 Obituary 61-64
Katzenstein, Mary Fainsod 1945- 93-96
Katzenstein, Peter J(oachim) 1945- CANR-17
Earlier sketch in CA 93-96
Ka-Tzetnik 135633 CANR-27
Earlier sketch in CA 29-32R
Katzman, Allen 1937- CANR-43
Earlier sketch in CA 29-32R
Katzman, Anita 1920- 57-60
Katzman, David Manners 1941- CANR-5
Earlier sketch in CA 53-56
Katzman, Martin T(heodore) 1941- 111
Katzman, Melanie A. 1958- 151
Katznelson-Shazar, Rachel
1888-1975 Obituary 61-64
Katzner, Kenneth 1930- 5-8R
Kau, Michael Y. M.
See Kau, Ying-mao
Kau, Ying-mao 1934- Brief entry 114
Kauder, Emil 1901- 17-20R
Kaufelt, David Allan 1939- CANR-71
Earlier sketches in CA 45-48, CANR-1, 16, 38
Kauffeld, Carl F. 1911-1974 Obituary 49-52
Kauffman, Bill 1959- 156
Kauffman, Christmas Carol 1902- 1-4R
Kauffman, Christopher J. 1936- 107
Kauffman, Donald T(homas) 1920- CANR-11
Earlier sketch in CA 25-28R
Kauffman, Dorotha S(trayer) 1925- 17-20R
Kauffman, Draper L. 1946- 108
Kauffman, George B(ernard) 1930- 17-20R
Kauffman, Henry J. 1908- 13-16R
Kauffman, J. Howard 1919- 145
Kauffman, James M(ilton) 1940- CANR-7
Earlier sketch in CA 57-60
Kauffman, Janet 1945- CANR-43
Earlier sketch in CA 117
See also CLC 42
See also DLBY 86
Kauffman, Joseph F(rank) 1921- CANR-1
Earlier sketch in CA 45-48
Kauffman, Milo (Franklin) 1898- 89-92
Kauffman, Stuart Alan 1939- 153
Kauffmann, C. Michael 1931- 125
Kauffmann, Georg (Friedrich) 1925- 49-52
Kauffmann, Lane 1921- 17-20R
Kauffmann, (Franklin) Lane
1922(?)-1988 Obituary 125
Kauffmann, Samuel Hay 1898-1971 Obituary 89-92
See also DLB 127
Kauffmann, Stanley 1916- CANR-6
Earlier sketch in CA 5-8R
Interview in CANR-6
Kaufman, Alan 1952- 128
Kaufman, Arnold S. 1927- 25-28R
Kaufman, Arthur 1934- CANR-25
Earlier sketch in CA 107
Kaufman, Barry Neil 1942- CANR-17
Earlier sketch in CA 97-100
Kaufman, Bel CANR-13
Earlier sketch in CA 13-16R
See also AAYA 4
See also SATA 57
Kaufman, Bob (Garnell) 1925-1986 CANR-22
Obituary 118
Earlier sketch in CA 41-44R
See also BW 1
See also CLC 49
See also DLB 16, 41
Kaufman, Burton I. 1940- 33-36R
Kaufman, Daniel 1949- 85-88
Kaufman, Debra Renee 1941- 109
Kaufman, Donald D(avid) 1933- 29-32R
Kaufman, Edmund George 1891- 73-76
Kaufman, George S. 1889-1961 108
Obituary 93-96
Interview in 108
See also CLC 38
See also DAM DRAM
See also DLB 7
Kaufman, Gerald (Bernard) 1930- 21-24R
Kaufman, Gershen 1943- 117
Kaufman, Gloria Joan Frances (Shapiro) 1929- CANR-47
Earlier sketch in CA 122
Kaufman, Gordon Dester 1925- CANR-7
Earlier sketch in CA 13-16R
Kaufman, H(arold) G(erson) 1939- 69-72
Kaufman, Herbert 1922- 137
Brief entry 115
Kaufman, I(sadore) 1892-1978 Obituary 77-80
Kaufman, Irving 1920- 21-24R
Kaufman, Jacob J(oseph) 1914- 41-44R
Kaufman, Jeff 1955- SATA 84
Kaufman, Joe 1911- 107
See also SATA 33
Kaufman, Lloyd 1927- 93-96
Kaufman, Martin 1940- CANR-54
Earlier sketches in CA 109, CANR-28
Kaufman, Menahem 1921- 138
Kaufman, Mervyn D. 1932- 5-8R
See also SATA 4
Kaufman, Paul 1886-1979 Obituary 89-92
Kaufman, Paula T. 1946- 126
Kaufman, Philip 1936- 121
Brief entry 112
Kaufman, Polly W(elts) 1929- 114
Kaufman, Robert 1931- CANR-25
Earlier sketch in CA 17-20R
Kaufman, Roger (Alexander) 1932- CANR-9
Earlier sketch in CA 53-56
Kaufman, Rosamond (Arleen) V(an) P(oznak)
1923- CANR-7
Earlier sketch in CA 9-12R
Kaufman, Sherwin A. 1920- CANR-10
Earlier sketch in CA 25-28R
Kaufman, Shirley 1923- 49-52
Kaufman, Sidney 1910-1983 Obituary 110
Kaufman, Stuart Bruce 1942-1997 CANR-50
Obituary 156
Earlier sketch in CA 123
Kaufman, Sue
See Barondess, Sue K(aufman)
See also CLC 3, 8
Kaufman, Wallace 1939- CANR-46
Earlier sketches in CA 25-28R, CANR-10
Kaufman, William I(rving) 1922-1995 CANR-24
Obituary 149
Earlier sketches in CA 13-16R, CANR-7
Kaufman, Wolfe 1905(?)-1970 Obituary 29-32R
Kaufmann, Angelika 1935- SATA 15
Kaufmann, Edgar, Jr. 1910-1989 Obituary 129
Kaufmann, Harry 1927- 45-48
Kaufmann, Helen L(oeb) 1887- CANR-7
Earlier sketch in CA 5-8R
Kaufmann, Henry William 1913- 41-44R
Kaufmann, John 1931- 81-84
See also SATA 18
Kaufmann, Myron S. 1921- 25-28R
Kaufmann, R(alph) James 1924- 13-16R
Kaufmann, Thomas DaCosta 1948- 129
Kaufmann, U(rlin) Milo 1934- 41-44R
Kaufmann, Ulrich George 1920- 21-24R
Kaufmann, Walter 1921-1980 CANR-1
Obituary 101
Earlier sketch in CA 1-4R
Kaufmann, Walter 1933- 61-64
Kaufmann, William J(ohn) III 1942- 93-96
Kaufmann, William W. 1918- 13-16R
Kaul, Donald 1934- 65-68
Kaula, Edna Mason 1906- 5-8R
See also SATA 13
Kaumeyer, Mary Leta Dorothy
See Lamour, Dorothy
Kaumeyer, Mary Leta Dorothy
See Lamour, Dorothy
Kaunda, K. D.
See Kaunda, Kenneth David
Kaunda, Kenneth
See Kaunda, Kenneth David
Kaunda, Kenneth D.
See Kaunda, Kenneth David
Kaunda, Kenneth David 1924- 133
Kauper, Paul Gerhardt 1907-1974 CANR-6
Obituary 49-52
Earlier sketch in CA 1-4R
Kaur, Sardarni Premka 1943- 77-80
Kaurismaki, Aki 1957- 140
Kaur Khalsa, Dayal 1943(?)-1989 Obituary 129
Kaus, Mickey 1951- 142
Kausler, Donald H(arvey) 1927- 17-20R
Kauth, Benjamin 1914- 5-8R
Kautsky, Karl (Johann) 1854-1938 Brief entry 123
Kauvar, Gerald B(luestone) 1938- 45-48
Kavafis, Konstantinos Petrou 1863-1933 Brief entry 104
See also Cavafy, C(onstantine) P(eter)
Kavaler, Lucy 1930- CANR-48
Earlier sketches in CA 57-60, CANR-7, 22
See also SATA 23
Kavaler, Rebecca 1932- CANR-16
Earlier sketch in CA 89-92
Kavan, Anna 1901-1968 CANR-57
Earlier sketches in CA 5-8R, CANR-6
See also CLC 5, 13, 82
See also MTCW 1
Kavanagh, Aidan 1929- 112
Kavanagh, Dan
See Barnes, Julian (Patrick)
Kavanagh, Dan(iel) 1946- 125
Kavanagh, Jack 1920- 151
See also SATA 85
Kavanagh, James H. 1948- 126
Kavanagh, Jennifer 1947- 119
Kavanagh, Julie 1952- 163
Kavanagh, Michael 1945- 118
Kavanagh, P(atrick) J(oseph Gregory) 1931- CANR-45
Earlier sketch in CA 81-84
See also DLB 40
Kavanagh, Patrick (Joseph) 1904-1967 123
Obituary 25-28R
See also CLC 22
See also DLB 15, 20
See also MTCW 1
Kavanagh, Paul
See Block, Lawrence
Kavanagh, Peter 1916- 132
Kavanaugh, Andrea L(ee) 1951- 165
Kavanaugh, Cynthia
See Daniels, Dorothy
Kavanaugh, Ian
See Webb, Jean Francis
Kavanaugh, James J(oseph) 1934- CANR-38
Earlier sketches in CA 13-16R, CANR-17
Kavanaugh, John F(rancis) 1941- 115
Kavanaugh, Kieran 1928- 25-28R
Kavanaugh, Robert E. 1926- 29-32R
Kavasch, E(lizabeth) Barrie 1942- 110
Kavenagh, W(illiam) Keith 1926- 37-40R
Kavesh, Robert A(llyn) 1927- 17-20R
Kavet, Robert 1924- 37-40R
Kavifis, Konstantinos Petrou
See Kavafis, Konstantinos Petrou
Kavli, Guthorm 1917- CAP-1
Earlier sketch in CA 9-10
Kavner, Richard S. 1936- 93-96
Kavolis, Vytautas 1930- 25-28R
Kawabata, Yasunari 1899-1972 93-96
Obituary 33-36R
See also CLC 2, 5, 9, 18, 107
See also DAM MULT
See also DLB 180
See also SSC 17
Kawahito, Kiyoshi 1939- 37-40R
Kawai, Kazuo 1904-1963 1-4R
Kawakami, Barbara Fusako 1921- 146
Kawakami, Tovo S(uvemoto) 1916- 33-36R
Kawatski, Deanna 1951- 146
Kawin, Bruce F. 1945- CANR-13
Earlier sketch in CA 37-40R
Kawin, Ethel (?)-1969 CAP-1
Earlier sketch in CA 11-12
Kay, Barbara Ann 1929- 13-16R
Kay, Brian Ross 1924- 1-4R
Kay, David A(llen) 1940- 154
Brief entry 114
Kay, Donald 1939- 57-60

Kay, E(lizabeth) Alison 1928- 65-68
Kay, Ellen
See DeMille, Nelson (Richard)
Kay, Ernest 1915- CANR-24
Earlier sketches in CA 13-16R, CANR-6
Kay, George
See Lambert, Eric
Kay, George 1936- 21-24R
Kay, Guy Gavriel 1954- 134
Kay, Harry 1919- 25-28R
Kay, Helen
See Goldfrank, Helen Colodny
Kay, J(ohn) A(nderson) 1948- 119
Kay, Jackie
See Kay, Jacqueline Margaret
Kay, Jacqueline Margaret 1961- 153
See also SATA 97
Kay, Jane Holtz 1938- CANR-22
Earlier sketch in CA 106
Kay, Jeremy 1942- 156
Kay, Kenneth (Edmond) 1915- CANR-6
Earlier sketch in CA 9-12R
Kay, Mara CANR-2
Earlier sketch in CA 5-8R
See also SATA 13
Kay, Mary
See Ash, Mary Kay (Wagner)
Kay, Norman (Forber) 1929- 45-48
Kay, (Sydney Francis) Patrick (Chippendall) Healey
See Healey-Kay, (Sydney Francis) Patrick (Chippendall)
Kay, Paul 1934- 41-44R
Kay, Reed 1925- 77-80
Kay, Ronald
See Knox-Mawer, Ronald
Kay, Susan 1952- 144
Kay, Terence 1918- 17-20R
Kay, Teresa
See de Kerpely, Theresa
Kay, Terry
See Kay, Terence
Kay, Terry (Winter) 1938- 110
Kay, Thomas O(bed) 1932- 1-4R
Kay, (Albert) William 1930-1976 ..... CAP-2
Earlier sketch in CA 29-32
Kay, Zell
See Kemp, Roy Z(ell)
Kayal, Joseph M(itchell) 1942- 57-60
Kayal, Philip M(itchell) 1943- 57-60
Kayden, Xandra 1939- 127
Kaye, Alan
See Horowitz, Shel Alan
Kaye, Barbara
See Muir, Marie
Kaye, Bruce (Norman) 1939- 93-96
Kaye, Buddy 1918- 81-84
Kaye, Danny 1913-1987 Obituary 121
See also SATA-Obit 50
Kaye, Elizabeth 1945- 152
Kaye, Evelyn 1937- 57-60
Kaye, Geraldine (Hughesdon) 1925- CANR-46
Earlier sketches in CA 13-16R, CANR-7, 22
See also SATA 10, 85
Kaye, H. R.
See Knox, Hugh (Randolph)
Kaye, Harvey E(arle) 1927- 101
Kaye, Harvey J(ordan) 1949- CANR-47
Earlier sketch in CA 121
Kaye, Hilary 1950- 116
Kaye, Howard L. 1951- 126
Kaye, Joanne
See Payes, Rachel C(osgrove)
Kaye, Judy
See Baer, Judy
Kaye, Julian B(ertram) 1925- 1-4R
Kaye, Kenneth Peter 1946- 111
Kaye, Lenny 1946- Brief entry 121
Kaye, M(ary) M(argaret) 1909- CANR-60
Earlier sketches in CA 89-92, CANR-24
See also CLC 28
See also MTCW 1
See also SATA 62
Kaye, Marilyn 1949- CANR-49
Earlier sketches in CA 107, CANR-24
See also SATA 56
Kaye, Marvin (Nathan) 1938- CANR-41
Earlier sketches in CA 53-56, CANR-5, 19
Kaye, Melanie
See Kaye-Kantrowitz, Melanie
Kaye, Mollie
See Kaye, M(ary) M(argaret)
Kaye, Myrna 1930- 57-60
Kaye, Peggy 1948- 116
Kaye, Philip A. 1920- 37-40R
Kaye, Phyllis Johnson 102
Kaye-Kantrowitz, Melanie 1945- 141
Kaye-Smith, Sheila 1887-1956 Brief entry 118
See also DLB 36
See also TCLC 20
Kayira, Legson Didimu 1942- 17-20R
See also BW 1
Kaymor, Patrice Maguilene
See Senghor, Leopold Sedar
Kaynak, Erdener 1947- 149
Kaysen, Carl 1920- CANR-11
Earlier sketch in CA 17-20R
Kaysen, Susanna 1948- 144
Kayser, Elmer Louis 1896-1985 ..... 37-40R
Obituary 116
Kayser, Hugh F. 1926- 107
Kayser-Jones, Jeanie Schmit 1935- 105
Kaysing, Bill
See Kaysing, William C.
Kaysing, William C. 1922- 33-36R
Kayyali, Abdul-Wahhab (Said)
1939-1981 Obituary 108
Kazakov, Yuri Pavlovich 1927-1982 ..... CANR-36
Earlier sketch in CA 5-8R
See also MTCW 1
Kazamias, Andreas M. 1927- 17-20R
Kazan, Elia 1909- CANR-32
Earlier sketch in CA 21-24R
See also CLC 6, 16, 63
Kazan, Frances 1946- 125
Kazantzakis, Nikos 1883(?)-1957 132
Brief entry 105
See also MTCW 1
See also TCLC 2, 5, 33
Kazantzis, Judith 1940- 144
Kazarian, Edward A(rshak) 1931- 53-56
Kazdin, Alan E(dward) 1945- 104
Kazee, Buell H(ilton) 1900-1976 Obituary 111
Kazemzadeh, Firuz 1924- 21-24R
Kazhdan, Alexander P(etrovich) 1922-1997 138
Obituary 158
Kazickas, Jurate C(atherine) 1943- 102
Kazimiroff, Theodore L. 1941- 109
Kazin, Alfred 1915- CANR-45
Earlier sketches in CA 1-4R, CANR-1
See also CAAS 7
See also CLC 34, 38
See also DLB 67
Kazin, Michael 1948- 127
Kazis, Richard 1952- 112
Kazmer, Daniel (Raphael) 1947- 102
Kazmier, Leonard J(ohn) 1930- 107
Kazziha, Walid W. 1941- 65-68
Keach, Richard L(eroy) 1919- 89-92
Kealey, Edward J(oseph) 1936- CANR-14
Earlier sketch in CA 37-40R
Kealy, Sean P(atrick) 1937- 114
Kean, Benjamin Harrison 1912-1993 103
Obituary 142
Kean, Charles Duell 1910-1963 ..... 5-8R
Kean, Edmund (Stanley) 1915- 102
Keane, Betty Winkler 1914- 93-96
Keane, Bil 1922- CANR-13
Earlier sketch in CA 33-36R
See also SATA 4
Keane, John 1949- 148
Keane, John B(rendan) 1928- CANR-42
Earlier sketch in CA 29-32R
See also DLB 13
Keane, Mary Nesta (Skrine) 1904-1996 114
Obituary 151
Brief entry 108
See also Keane, Molly
Keane, Molly
Interview in 114
See also Keane, Mary Nesta (Skrine)
See also CLC 31
Keane, Noel 1938- 133
Keane, Patrick J(oseph) 1939- CANR-1
Earlier sketch in CA 45-48
Keaney, Marian 1944- 103
Kearey, Charles 1916- 45-48
Kearley, F(loyd) Furman 1932- 57-60
Kearney, Hugh Francis 1924- 5-8R
Kearney, James R(obert III) 1929- 25-28R
Kearney, Jean Nylander 1923- 65-68
Kearney, Robert N(orman) 1930- 81-84
Kearney, Ruth Elizabeth
See Carlson, Ruth (Elizabeth) Kearney
Kearns, Doris Helen
See Goodwin, Doris (Helen) Kearns
Kearns, Francis E(dward) 1931- 29-32R
Kearns, Frank 1917(?)-1986 Obituary 119
Kearns, Frank T. 1903-1984 Obituary 111
Kearns, James A(loysius) III 1949- 29-32R
Kearns, Lionel 1937- CANR-11
Earlier sketch in CA 17-20R
See also DLB 13
Kearns, Martha 1945- 57-60
Kearns, Michael S. 1947- 126
Kearns, Sheila M. 1955- 156
Kearns, Edward N. III 1936- 29-32R
Kearny, Jillian
See Goulart, Ron(ald Joseph)
Kearse, Amalya (Lyle) 1937- 155
Kearsley, Edward
See Mitchell, S(ilas) Weir
Keary, Annie 1825-1879 ..... DLB 163
Keasey, Carol Tomlinson
See Tomlinson-Keasey, Carol
Keast, James D. 1930- 25-28R
Keast, William R(ea) 1914- 13-16R
Keates, Jonathan 1946(?)- 163
See also CLC 34
Keating, AnaLouise 1961- 162
Keating, AnnLouise
See Keating, AnaLouise
Keating, Bern
See Keating, Leo Bernard
Keating, Charlotte Matthews 1927- 33-36R
Keating, Diane 1940- CANR-18
Earlier sketch in CA 101
Keating, Edward M. 1925- 13-16R
Keating, H(enry) R(eymond) F(itzwalter) 1926- CANR-64
Earlier sketches in CA 33-36R, CANR-18, 34
Interview in CANR-18
See also CAAS 8
See also DLB 87
See also MTCW 1
Keating, John J. 1918(?)-1975 Obituary 61-64
Keating, L(ouis) Clark 1907- 21-24R
Keating, Lawrence A. 1903-1966 ..... 5-8R
See also SATA 23
Keating, Leo Bernard 1915- 29-32R
See also SATA 10
Keating, Michael (F.) 1932- 49-52
Keating, Michael (Irvine) 1943- CANR-64
Earlier sketch in CA 129
Keating, Micheline 1904(?)-1989 Obituary 127
Keating, Tom 1917-1984 Obituary 112
Keaton, Buster 1895-1966 ..... CLC 20
Keats, Charles B. 1905- CAP-1
Earlier sketch in CA 13-16
Keats, Emma 1899(?)-1979(?) 135
See also SATA 68
Keats, Ezra Jack 1916-1983 77-80
Obituary 109
See also AITN 1
See also CLR 1, 35
See also DLB 61
See also MAICYA
See also SATA 14, 57
See also SATA-Obit 34
Keats, John 1795-1821 ..... CDBLB 1789-1832
See also DA
See also DAB
See also DAC
See also DAM MST, POET
See also DLB 96, 110
See also PC 1
See also WLC
Keats, John (C.) 1920- 73-76
Keats, Mark 1905- 77-80
Keaveney, Arthur 1951- 124
Keaveney, Sydney Starr 1939- 53-56
Keay, Frederick 1915- 33-36R
Keay, John (Stanley Melville) 1941- 65-68
Kebbe, Charles Maynard 1913- 114
Kebin, Jodi
See Lawrence, Jodi
Keble, John 1792-1866 ..... DLB 32, 55
Kebschull, Harvey G(ustav) 1932- 41-44R
Keck, Leander Earl 1928- 104
Keddell, Georgina (Murray) 1913- 25-28R
Keddie, Nikki R(agozin) 1930- CANR-56
Earlier sketches in CA 25-28R, CANR-13
Kedgley, Susan (Jane) 1948- 61-64
Kedourie, Elie 1926-1992 ..... CANR-31
Obituary 139
Earlier sketches in CA 21-24R, CANR-10
Kedzie, Daniel Peter 1930- 17-20R
Kee, (Alexander) Alistair 1937- 89-92
Kee, Howard Clark 1920- CANR-10
Earlier sketch in CA 21-24R
Kee, Robert 1919- 130
Brief entry 113
Keeble, John 1944- CANR-14
Earlier sketch in CA 29-32R
See also DLBY 83
Keeble, Neil H(oward) 1944- 135
Keech, Thomas (Walton) 1946- 149
Keech, William J(ohn) 1904- CAP-1
Earlier sketch in CA 9-10
Keech, William R(obertson) 1939- 25-28R
Keedy, Mervin L(averne) 1920- CANR-5
Earlier sketch in CA 53-56
Keefe, Carolyn 1928- 57-60
Keefe, Donald Joseph 1924- 37-40R
Keefe, John Edwin 1942- 107
Keefe, Michael 1946- 93-96
Keefe, Richard S(tanley) E(dwards) 1958- 148
Keefe, Robert 1938- 89-92
Keefe, Susan E. 1947- 126
Keefe, Terry 1940- 125
Keefer, Catherine
See Ogan, George F.
and Ogan, Margaret E. (Nettles)
Keefer, Janice Kulyk
See Kulyk Keefer, Janice
Keefer, T(ruman) Frederick 1930- 21-24R
Keeffe, Barrie (Colin) 1945- 144
Brief entry 116
See also DLB 13
Keegan, Frank L. 1925- 45-48
Keegan, John (Desmond Patrick) 1934- 136
Brief entry 130
Interview in 136
See also BEST 90:3
Keegan, John E. 1943- 146
Keegan, Marcia 1943- CANR-32
Earlier sketch in CA 49-52
See also SATA 9
Keegan, Mary Heathcott 1914- CANR-3
Earlier sketch in CA 5-8R
Keegan, Terence J(ames) 1939- 117
Keegan, Warren J(oseph) 1936- 57-60
Keegan, William (James Gregory) 1938- 161
Keehn, Sally M. 1947- 137
See also SATA 87
Keel, Frank
See Keeler, Ronald F(ranklin)
Keel, John A.
See Kiehle, John Alva
Keele, Alan (Frank) 1942- 152
Keele, Kenneth D(avid) 1909- 5-8R
Keele, Reba Lou 1941- Brief entry 106
Keeler, Mary Frear 1904- 77-80
Keeler, Ronald F(ranklin) 1913-1983 107
See also SATA 47
Keeley, Edmund (Leroy) 1928- CANR-22
Earlier sketches in CA 1-4R, CANR-1
Keeley, James 1867-1934 ..... DLB 25
Keeley, Joseph C(harles) 1907- 25-28R
Keeley, Steve 1949- 93-96
Keeling, Clinton Harry 1932- CANR-7
Earlier sketch in CA 9-12R
Keeling, E. B.
See Curl, James Stevens
Keeling, Jill Annette (Shaw) 1923- CANR-12
Earlier sketches in CAP-1, CA 9-10
Keely, Charles C(larke), Jr.
1934-1985 Obituary 116
Keely, Harry Harris 1904- 65-68
Keely, Jane 1922- 107
Keen, Benjamin 1913- 136
Brief entry 114
Keen, (John) Ernest 1937- 33-36R
Keen, Geraldine
See Norman, Geraldine (Lucia)
Keen, M. H.
See Keen, Maurice Hugh
Keen, Martin L. 1913- 33-36R
See also SATA 4
Keen, Maurice
See Keen, Maurice Hugh
Keen, Maurice Hugh 1933- 122
Keen, Sam 137
Keen, Tommy 1923- 108
Keenan, Angela Elizabeth 1890-1983 61-64
Obituary 111
Keenan, Boyd R(aymond) 1928- 17-20R
Keenan, Brian 1950- 145
Keenan, Deborah (Anne) 1950- CANR-56
Earlier sketches in CA 69-72, CANR-11, 30
Keenan, Desmond (Joseph) 1933- 125
Keenan, Joseph H(enry) 1900-1977 Obituary 73-76
Keenan, Martha 1927- 77-80
Keenan, Sheila 1953- 160
See also SATA 95
Keene, Ann T(odd) 1940- 151
See also SATA 86
Keene, Burt
See Bickers, Richard (Leslie) Townshend
Keene, Carolyn CANR-56
Earlier sketches in CA 17-20R, CANR-27
See also McFarlane, Leslie (Charles)
See also JRDA
See also MAICYA
See also SATA 65, 100
Keene, Dennis 1934- 144
Keene, Donald 1922- CANR-5
Earlier sketch in CA 1-4R
See also CLC 34
Keene, J(ames) Calvin 1908- CAP-1
Earlier sketch in CA 17-18
Keene, James A(llen) 1932- CANR-43
Earlier sketch in CA 109
Keene, John (R.), (Jr.) 1965- 151
Keene, R. D.
See Keene, Raymond D(ennis)
Keene, Ray
See Keene, Raymond D(ennis)
Keene, Raymond D(ennis) 1948- 158
Brief entry 112
Keener, Frederick M(ichael) 1937- CANR-43
Earlier sketches in CA 53-56, CANR-15
Keeney, Charles James 1912- 5-8R
Keeney, Chuck
See Keeney, Charles James
Keeney, Ralph L(yons) 1944- CANR-16
Earlier sketch in CA 97-100
Keeney, William (Echard) 1922- CANR-15
Earlier sketch in CA 41-44R
Keenleyside, Hugh Llewellyn 1898- CAP-1
Earlier sketch in CA 17-18
Keenleyside, T(erence) A(shley) 1940- 77-80
Keens-Douglas, Richardo 1953- 160
See also SATA 95
Keeny, S. M.
See Keeny, Spurgeon Milton
Keeny, Spurgeon Milton 1893-1988 Obituary 126
Keep, Carolyn 1940- 65-68
Keep, David (John) 1936- 61-64
Keep, John (Leslie Howard) 1926- 9-12R
Keeping, Charles (William James) 1924-1988 ..... CANR-43
Obituary 125
Earlier sketches in CA 21-24R, CANR-11
See also AAYA 26
See also CLR 34
See also MAICYA
See also SATA 9, 69
See also SATA-Obit 56
Keery, Sam 1929- 124
Kees, Beverly (Ann) 1941- 81-84
Keese, Parton 1926- 109
Keesecker, William Francis 1918- 33-36R
Keeshan, Robert J. 1927- CANR-5
Earlier sketch in CA 5-8R
See also SATA 32
Keesing, Nancy (Florence) 1923-1995 ..... CANR-27
Obituary 149
Earlier sketches in CA 9-12R, CANR-6
Keeslar, Oreon 1907- CAP-1
Earlier sketch in CA 13-14
Keeter, (Charles) Scott 1951- 160
Keeton, Elizabeth B(aker) 1919- 29-32R
Keeton, George Williams 1902- 13-16R
Keeton, Kathy 1939-1997 125
Obituary 161
See also AITN 2
Keeton, Morris Teuton 1917- CANR-4
Earlier sketch in CA 1-4R
Keeton, Robert E(rnest) 1919- CANR-2
Earlier sketch in CA 5-8R
Keeton, William T(insley) 1933-1980 124
Obituary 105
Keever, Jack 1938- 53-56
Keevill, Henry J(ohn) 1914-1978 ..... CANR-63
Earlier sketches in CAP-1, CA 9-10
Keezer, Dexter Merriam 1895- 1-4R
Kefala, Antigone 1935- 153
Kefferstan, Jean
See Pedrick, Jean
Kegan, Adrienne Koch 1912-1971 Obituary 33-36R
Kegel, Charles H(erbert) 1924- CANR-45
Earlier sketch in CA 1-4R
Kegley, Charles W(illiam), Jr. 1944- CANR-36
Earlier sketch in CA 114

Kegley, Charles William 1912- ... CANR-2
Earlier sketch in CA 5-8R
Kehayan, V. Alex 1944- ... 110
Kehde, Ned 1940- ... 143
Kehl, D(elmar) G(eorge) 1936- ... 33-36R
Kehl, James Arthur 1922- ... 112
Kehle, Roberta L(unsford) 1936- ... 116
Kehm, Freda (Irma) S(amuels) ... CAP-2
Earlier sketch in CA 29-32
Kehoe, Constance (DeMuzio) 1933- ... 13-16R
Kehoe, Monika 1909- ... 21-24R
Kehoe, Patricia D. 1951- ... 132
Kehoe, Patrick E(mmett) 1941- ... 57-60
Kehoe, William F. 1933- ... 13-16R
Kehrer, Daniel M(ark) 1953- ... 120
Kehrer, James P(aul) 1951- ... 117
Kehret, Peg 1936- ... SATA 73
Keidel, Eudene 1921- ... 109
Keidel, Levi (Jr.) 1927- ... 115
Keifetz, Norman 1932- ... 89-92
Keiger, John F(rederick) V(ictor) 1952- ... 125
Keightley, David N(oel) 1932- ... 97-100
Keil, (Harold) Bill 1926- ... 81-84
Keil, Charles 1939- ... 140
Keil, Sally Van Wagenen 1946- ... 89-92
Keillor, Garrison
See Keillor, Gary (Edward)
See also AAYA 2
See also BEST 89:3
See also CLC 40
See also DLBY 87
See also SATA 58
Keillor, Gary (Edward) 1942- ... CANR-59
Brief entry ... 111
Earlier sketches in CA 117, CANR-36
See also Keillor, Garrison
See also DAM POP
See also MTCW 1
Keillor, Steven J(ames) 1948- ... 151
Keilstrup, Margaret 1945- ... 138
Keim, Charles J. 1921- ... CANR-13
Earlier sketch in CA 33-36R
Keimberg, Allyn
See Kimbro, John M.
Kein, Sybil 1939- ... 163
Keinzley, Frances 1922- ... 85-88
Keir, Christine
See Popescu, Christine
Keir, David E(dwin) 1906-1969 ... CAP-1
Earlier sketch in CA 9-10
Keir, David Lindsay 1895-1973 ... CAP-2
Earlier sketch in CA 21-22
Keirstead, Burton Seely 1907- ... 5-8R
Keiser, Bea(trice) 1931- ... 97-100
Keiser, Norman F(red) 1930- ... 13-16R
Keislar, Evan R(ollo) 1913- ... 21-24R
Keisling, Bill
See Keisling, William
Keisling, William 1958- ... 113
Keisman, Michael E(dward) 1932- ... 25-28R
Keister, Douglas 1948- ... SATA 88
Keister, Elinore
See Dobson, Elinore (Lucille)
Keitges, Julie 1940- ... 110
Keith, Agnes Newton 1901- ... 17-20R
Keith, Carlton
See Robertson, Keith (Carlton)
Keith, Caroline H(elen) 1940- ... 139
Keith, David
See Steegmuller, Francis
Keith, Donald
See Monroe, Keith
Keith, Doug 1952- ... SATA 81
Keith, Elmer (Merrifield) 1899- ... 101
Keith, Eros 1942- ... 114
See also SATA 52
Keith, Hal 1934- ... SATA 36
Keith, Hamish
See Chapman, James (Keith)
Keith, Harold Verne 1903- ... CANR-48
Earlier sketches in CA 5-8R, CANR-2
See also JRDA
See also MAICYA
See also SATA 2, 74
Keith, Herbert F. 1895- ... 37-40R
Keith, J. Kilmeny
See Malleson, Lucy Beatrice
Keith, Jean E. 1921-1979 Obituary ... 85-88
Keith, Jennie 1942- ... 116
Keith, Judith 1923- ... 49-52
Keith, Julie (Houghton) 1940- ... 151
Keith, K. Wymand 1924- ... 33-36R
Keith, Larry Ficquette 1947- ... 97-100
Keith, Lee
See Sunners, William
Keith, Leigh
See Gold, H(orace) L(eonard)
Keith, Marian
See MacGregor, Mary Esther
Keith, Marian 1874(?)-1961 ... DLB 92
Keith, Michael
See Hubbard, L(afayette) Ron(ald)
Keith, Michael C(urtis) 1945- ... 132
Keith, Nancy 1916-1990 ... 138
Keith, Noel L(eonard) 1903-1981 ... 57-60
Obituary ... 133
Keith, Robert
See Applebaum, Stan
Keith, Ronald (A.) 1914(?)-1985 Obituary ... 117
Keith, Sam 1921- ... 65-68
Keith, Slim
See Keith, Nancy
Keith, Stuart 1931- ... 126
Keith, W(illiam) J(ohn) 1934- ... CANR-11
Earlier sketch in CA 17-20R
Keithley, Erwin M. 1905- ... 73-76
Keithley, George 1935- ... 37-40R
Keith-Lucas, Alan 1910- ... CANR-42
Earlier sketches in CA 5-8R, CANR-2, 20
Keith-Lucas, Bryan 1912- ... 107
Keith-Spiegel, Patricia 1939- ... 41-44R
Keith X
See Armstrong, Keith F(rancis) W(hitfield)
Kekes, John 1936- ... 65-68
Kekkonen, Sylvi 1900(?)-1974 Obituary ... 53-56
Kelber, Magda 1908- ... 5-8R
Kelch, Ray Alden 1923- ... 85-88
Kelder, Diane 1934- ... CANR-40
Earlier sketches in CA 25-28R, CANR-18
Keldysh, Mstislav V(sevolodovich)
1911-1978 Obituary ... 77-80
Kele, Max H(erschel) 1936- Brief entry ... 114
Keleher, Will(iam Aloysius)
1886-1972 Obituary ... 37-40R
Keleinikov, Andrei 1924- ... SATA 65
Keleman, Stanley 1931- ... CANR-49
Earlier sketches in CA 81-84, CANR-14
Kelemen, Julie 1959- ... 146
See also SATA 78
Kelemen, Pal 1894- ... 104
Kelen, Emery 1896-1978 ... 9-12R
Obituary ... 103
See also SATA 13
See also SATA-Obit 26
Kelen, Stephen 1912- ... 107
Kelf-Cohen, Reuben 1895- ... 49-52
Kelikian, Hampar 1899(?)-1983 Obituary ... 110
Kell, Joseph
See Wilson, John (Anthony) Burgess
Kell, Richard (Alexander) 1927- ... CANR-8
Earlier sketch in CA 5-8R
Kellam, Sheppard (Gordon) 1931- ... 73-76
Kelland, Clarence Budington
1881-1964 Obituary ... 89-92
Kellar, Kenneth C(hambers) 1906- ... 45-48
Kellaway, Frank (Gerald) 1922- ... 9-12R
Kellaway, George P(ercival) 1909- ... CAP-2
Earlier sketch in CA 23-24
Kelleam, Joseph E(veridge) 1913-1975 ... 107
See also SATA 31
Kelleher, Catherine McArdle 1939- ... CANR-53
Brief entry ... 115
Earlier sketch in CA 125
Kelleher, Daria Valerian 1955- ... 147
See also SATA 79
Kelleher, Patrick J(oseph) 1917-1985 Obituary . 116
Kelleher, Stephen J(oseph) 1915- ... 69-72
Kelleher, Victor (Michael Kitchener) 1939- ...
CANR-56
Earlier sketch in CA 126
See also CLR 36
See also SATA 75
See also SATA-Brief 52
Kellenberger, James 1938- ... 155
Keller, Allan 1904-1981 ... CANR-29
Earlier sketch in CA 29-32R
Keller, Betty 1930- ... 121
Keller, Beverly L(ou) ... CANR-57
Earlier sketches in CA 49-52, CANR-1, 17, 38
See also SATA 13, 91
Keller, Charles 1942- ... CANR-43
Earlier sketches in CA 49-52, CANR-2
See also SATA 8, 82
Keller, Clair W(ayne) 1932- ... 53-56
Keller, David H(enry) 1880-1966 ... 161
Keller, Dean H(oward) 1933- ... 53-56
Keller, Debra 1958- ... 159
See also SATA 94
Keller, Dick 1923- ... SATA 36
Keller, Dolores Elaine 1926- ... 104
Keller, Edward A(nthony) 1942- ... 73-76
Keller, Emily ... 161
See also SATA 96
Keller, Evelyn Fox 1936- ... CANR-51
Earlier sketch in CA 125
Keller, Frances Richardson 1914- ... 81-84
Keller, Franklin J. 1887(?)-1976 Obituary ... 65-68
Keller, Fred S(immons) 1899-1996 ... CANR-11
Obituary ... 151
Earlier sketch in CA 69-72
Keller, Gail Faithfull
See Faithfull, Gail
Keller, Gary D. 1943- ... 131
See also DLB 82
See also HW
Keller, George 1928- ... 123
Keller, Gottfried 1819-1890 ... DLB 129
See also SSC 26
Keller, Helen (Adams) 1880-1968 ... 101
Obituary ... 89-92
See also MTCW 1
Keller, Holly 1942- Brief entry ... 118
See also CLR 45
See also SATA 76
See also SATA-Brief 42
Keller, Howard H(ughes) 1941- ... 45-48
Keller, Irene (Barron) 1927- ... 116
See also SATA 36
Keller, James Gregory 1900-1977 Obituary .. 69-72
Keller, John E(sten) 1917- ... 45-48
Keller, Karl 1933- ... CANR-12
Earlier sketch in CA 57-60
Keller, Laurent 1961- ... 148
Keller, Marti 1948- ... 97-100
Keller, Mitzie Stuart ... 111
Keller, Mollie ... SATA-Brief 50
Keller, Morton 1929- ... 5-8R
Keller, Nora Okja ... CLC 109
Keller, Sharon R. ... 142
Keller, Suzanne 1930- ... 65-68
Keller, Thomas F(ranklin) 1931- ... CANR-3
Earlier sketch in CA 9-12R
Keller, W(alter) D(avid) 1900- ... 41-44R
Keller, Werner (Rudolf August Wolfgang) 1909-(?) .
CANR-13
Earlier sketch in CA 21-24R
Kellerman, Barbara 1939- ... 110
Kellerman, Faye 1952- ... CANR-60
Earlier sketch in CA 120
Kellerman, Jonathan 1949- ... CANR-51
Earlier sketches in CA 106, CANR-29
Interview in ... CANR-29
See also BEST 90:1
See also CLC 44
See also DAM POP
Kellermann, Bernhard 1879-1951 ... 165
Kellert, Stephen R. 1944- ... 147
Kellett, Arnold 1926- ... CANR-41
Earlier sketches in CA 103, CANR-19
Kelley, Alden D(rew) 1903- ... 1-4R
Kelley, Alec E(rvin) 1923- ... 143
Kelley, Alice van Buren 1944- ... 81-84
Kelley, (Kathleen) Alita 1932- ... 143
Kelley, Allen C(harles) 1937- ... 104
Kelley, Arleon L(eigh) 1935- ... 115
Kelley, (Albert) Ben 1936- ... 45-48
Kelley, Brooks Mather 1929- ... 111
Kelley, Cecil B. Sr. 1911(?)-1987 Obituary ... 123
Kelley, Clarence M(arion) 1911-1997 ... 127
Obituary ... 160
Kelley, Dean M(aurice) 1926-1997 ... 81-84
Obituary ... 158
Kelley, Donald R(eed) 1931- ... CANR-12
Earlier sketch in CA 29-32R
Kelley, Earl Clarence 1895- ... 5-8R
Kelley, Edith Summers 1884-1956 Brief entry .. 109
See also DLB 9
Kelley, Eugene J(ohn) 1922- ... 13-16R
Kelley, H. N. 1911- ... 45-48
Kelley, Hubert (Williams), Jr. 1926- ... 5-8R
Kelley, J(ohn) Charles 1913- ... 97-100
Kelley, Jane Holden 1928- ... 45-48
Kelley, Joanna (Elizabeth) 1910- ... CAP-2
Earlier sketch in CA 23-24
Kelley, Jonathan ... 107
Kelley, Joseph J(ohn), Jr. 1914- ... CANR-8
Earlier sketch in CA 61-64
Kelley, Kevin J. 1948- ... 120
Kelley, Kitty 1942- ... CANR-27
Earlier sketch in CA 81-84
Interview in ... CANR-27
Kelley, Leo P(atrick) 1928- ... CANR-24
Earlier sketch in CA 107
See also SATA 32
See also SATA-Brief 31
Kelley, Mary 1943- ... CANR-52
Earlier sketch in CA 124
Kelley, Maurice (Willyle) 1903- ... 119
Kelley, Page H(utto) 1924- ... 25-28R
Kelley, Patte 1947- ... SATA 93
Kelley, Ray
See Paine, Lauran (Bosworth)
Kelley, Robert 1925- ... 25-28R
Kelley, Robert E(mmett) 1938- ... 53-56
Kelley, Ruby M.
See Johnson, Ruby Kelley
Kelley, Stanley, Jr. 1926- ... 13-16R
Kelley, True (Adelaide) 1946- ... CANR-47
Earlier sketches in CA 105, CANR-23
See also SATA 41, 92
See also SATA-Brief 39
Kelley, William 1929- ... CANR-6
Earlier sketch in CA 5-8R
Kelley, William Melvin 1937- ... CANR-27
Earlier sketch in CA 77-80
See also BW 1
See also CLC 22
See also DLB 33
Kelley, William T(homas) 1917- ... 37-40R
Kelley, Win 1923- ... 89-92
Kellin, Sally Moffet 1932- ... 61-64
See also SATA 9
Kelling, Furn L. 1914- ... 17-20R
See also SATA 37
Kelling, George W(alton) 1944- ... CANR-9
Earlier sketch in CA 57-60
Kelling, Hans-Wilhelm 1932- ... 37-40R
Kellison, Stephen G. 1942- ... 53-56
Kellman, Steven G. 1947- ... CANR-53
Earlier sketches in CA 112, CANR-29
Kellner, Bruce 1930- ... CANR-27
Earlier sketches in CA 29-32R, CANR-11
Kellner, Douglas Mackay 1943- ... 116
Kellner, Esther ... 13-16R
Kellner, L. 1904- ... 5-8R
Kellock, Archibald P.
See Mavor, Osborne Henry
Kellogg, Alfred Latimer 1915- ... 41-44R
Kellogg, Ansel Nash 1832-1886 ... DLB 23
Kellogg, Charles Edwin 1902-1980 Obituary 97-100
Kellogg, Charles Flint 1909- ... CAP-2
Earlier sketch in CA 23-24
Kellogg, Frederick 1929- ... 150
Kellogg, Gene
See Kellogg, Jean (Defrees)
Kellogg, James C. III 1915-1980 Obituary ... 103
Kellogg, Jean (Defrees) 1916-1978 ... CANR-7
Earlier sketch in CA 9-12R
See also SATA 10
Kellogg, M. Bradley
See Kellogg, Marjorie Bradley
Kellogg, Marion S(chuyler) 1920- ... 120
Kellogg, Marjorie 1922- ... 81-84
See also CLC 2
Kellogg, Marjorie B.
See Kellogg, Marjorie Bradley
Kellogg, Marjorie Bradley 1946- ... 164
Kellogg, Marne Davis 1946- ... 152
Kellogg, Mary Alice 1948- ... 81-84
Kellogg, Steven 1941- ... CANR-1
Earlier sketch in CA 49-52
See also CLR 6
See also DLB 61
See also MAICYA
See also SATA 8, 57
Kellogg, Virginia 1907-1981 Obituary ... 108
Kellogg, Winthrop N(iles) 1898-1971 ... 1-4R
Kellough, Richard Dean 1935- ... 53-56
Kellow, Kathleen
See Hibbert, Eleanor Alice Burford
Kellow, Norman B. 1914- ... 21-24R
Kellum, D(avid) F(ranklin) 1936- ... 61-64
Kelly, A(ngeline) A(gnes) 1924- ... 128
Kelly, Alfred H. 1907-1976 ... 5-8R
Obituary ... 65-68
Kelly, Alison 1913- ... 105
Kelly, Balmer H(ancock) 1914- ... 17-20R
Kelly, Brian 1954- ... 158
Kelly, C(harles) Brian 1935- ... 89-92
Kelly, C. M. O.
See Gibbs, (Cecilia) May
Kelly, Carla 1947- ... 118
Kelly, Catriona (Helen Moncrieff) 1959- ... 147
Kelly, Charles E. 1920(?)-1985 Obituary ... 114
Kelly, Charles M. 1932- ... 128
Kelly, Charles Patrick Bernard
1891(?)-1971 Obituary ... 29-32R
Kelly, Chris 1940- ... 154
Kelly, Clarence 1941- ... 61-64
Kelly, Commando
See Kelly, Charles E.
Kelly, Dave
See Kelly, David M(ichael)
Kelly, David M(ichael) 1938- ... CANR-12
Earlier sketch in CA 29-32R
Kelly, Deirdre M. 1959- ... 146
Kelly, Edward H(anford) 1930- ... 37-40R
Kelly, Emmett (Leo) 1898-1979 Obituary ... 85-88
Kelly, Eric Philbrook 1884-1960 Obituary ... 93-96
See also MAICYA
See also YABC 1
Kelly, Erin E. 1972- ... 149
Kelly, Faye L(ucius) 1914- ... 21-24R
Kelly, Fiona
See Welford, Sue
Kelly, Frank K. 1914- ... CANR-39
Earlier sketches in CA 1-4R, CANR-1, 16
Kelly, Franklin (Wood) 1953- ... 139
Kelly, Frederic Joseph 1922- ... 53-56
Kelly, Gail P(aradise) 1940-1991 ... 81-84
Obituary ... 133
Kelly, Gary F(rank) 1943- ... 89-92
Kelly, Gene 1912-1996 ... 159
Kelly, George A(nthony) 1916- ... CANR-43
Earlier sketches in CA 17-20R, CANR-11
Kelly, George Armstrong 1932-1987 Obituary .. 125
Kelly, George E. 1887-1974 Obituary ... 49-52
See also AITN 1
See also DLB 7
Kelly, George V(incent) 1919- ... 93-96
Kelly, George W. 1894- ... CANR-9
Earlier sketch in CA 65-68
Kelly, Gerald R(ay) 1930- ... 29-32R
Kelly, Grace (Patricia) 1929-1982 Obituary ... 107
Kelly, Guy
See Moore, Nicholas
Kelly, H(enry) A(nsgar) 1934- ... CANR-57
Earlier sketches in CA 25-28R, CANR-30
Kelly, Hugh 1739-1777 ... DLB 89
Kelly, Ian
See Kelly, John Spence
Kelly, J(ohn) M(aurice) 1931-1991 ... 109
Obituary ... 133
Kelly, James B(urton) 1905- ... 49-52
Kelly, James Patrick 1951- ... 135
Kelly, James Plunkett 1920- ... 53-56
See also Plunkett, James
Kelly, Jeff
See Kelly, Jeffrey
Kelly, Jeffrey 1946- ... 136
See also SATA 65
Kelly, Jeffrey A(llen) 1948- ... 114
Kelly, Joan 1928(?)-1982 Obituary ... 107
Kelly, Joan Berlin 1939- ... 107
Kelly, Joanne (W.) 1934- ... 151
See also SATA 87
Kelly, John 1921- ... 73-76
Kelly, John 1943- ... 127
Kelly, John M., Jr. 1919- ... 13-16R
Kelly, John N(orman) D(avidson) 1909- ... CANR-5
Earlier sketch in CA 5-8R
Kelly, John Rivard 1939- ... 103
Kelly, John Spence 1934- ... 125
Kelly, Joyce 1933- ... 106
Kelly, Karen 1935- ... 101
Kelly, Kate 1958- ... 155
See also SATA 91
Kelly, Kathleen M. 1964- ... SATA 71
Kelly, Kathleen Sheridan White 1945- ... 49-52
Kelly, Kevin 1934- ... 130
Kelly, Kevin (J.) 1952- ... 149
Kelly, L(ouis) G(erard) 1935- ... 107
Kelly, Laurence 1933- ... CANR-15
Earlier sketch in CA 81-84
Kelly, Lawrence C(harles) 1932- ... CANR-8
Earlier sketch in CA 21-24R
Kelly, Leo J. 1925- ... 41-44R
Kelly, (Alison) Linda 1936- ... 103
Kelly, M(ilton) T(erry) 1947- ... CANR-43
Earlier sketches in CA 97-100, CANR-19
See also CAAS 22
See also CLC 55
Kelly, Maeve ... 144
Kelly, Mahlon (George) 1939- ... 53-56

Kelly, Marguerite (Lelong) 1932- 65-68
Kelly, Martha Rose 1914-1983 69-72
See also SATA 37
Kelly, Marty
See Kelly, Martha Rose
Kelly, Mary (Theresa Coolican) 1927- CANR-66
Earlier sketches in CA 1-4R, CANR-2
Kelly, Mary J(osephine) 1944- 117
Kelly, Maurice Anthony 1931- 53-56
Kelly, Maurice N. 1919- 21-24R
Kelly, Nora (Hickson) 1910- 101
Kelly, Patrick
See Allbeury, Theodore Edward le Bouthillier
Kelly, Paula 1949- 114
Kelly, Pauline Agnes 1936- 45-48
Kelly, Philip John 1896-1972 5-8R
Obituary 37-40R
Kelly, R. M.
See Kelly, Ronald
Kelly, Ralph
See Geis, Darlene Stern
Kelly, Ray
See Paine, Lauran (Bosworth)
Kelly, Regina Z(immerman) 1898- CANR-2
Earlier sketch in CA 1-4R
See also SATA 5
Kelly, Richard (Michael) 1937- CANR-72
Earlier sketches in CA 107, CANR-34
Kelly, Richard J(ohn) 1938- 41-44R
Kelly, Rita Mae 1939- 81-84
Kelly, Robert 1935- CANR-47
Earlier sketch in CA 17-20R
See also CAAS 19
See also DLB 5, 130, 165
Kelly, Robert Glynn 1920- 1-4R
Kelly, Robert J. 1938- 164
Kelly, Ronald 1959- 154
Kelly, Rosalie (Ruth) CANR-11
Earlier sketch in CA 61-64
See also SATA 43
Kelly, Russell 1949- 123
Kelly, Sean C. 1940- 145
Kelly, Stan
See Kelly-Bootle, Stan
Kelly, Stephen E(ugene) 1919-1978 110
Obituary 104
Kelly, Susan Croce 1947- 129
Kelly, Thomas 1909- CAP-1
Earlier sketch in CA 9-10
Kelly, Thomas 1929- 109
Kelly, Tim 1935- CANR-47
Earlier sketch in CA 13-16R
Kelly, Timothy Michael 1947- 133
Kelly, Walt(er Crawford) 1913-1973 73-76
Obituary 45-48
See also SATA 18
Kelly, William Leo 1924- 13-16R
Kelly, William W(atkins) 1928- 9-12R
Kelly-Benjamin, Kathleen 140
Kelly-Bootle, Stan 1929- 110
Kelly-Gadol, Joan 61-64
Kelm, Karlton 1908(?)-1987 Obituary 121
Kelman, Charles D. 1930- 110
Kelman, Herbert C(hanoch) 1927- 13-16R
Kelman, James 1946- 148
See also CLC 58, 86
See also DLB 194
Kelman, Judith (Ann) 1945- 166
Kelman, Mark 1951- 93-96
Kelman, Steven 1948- CANR-12
Earlier sketch in CA 29-32R
Kelner, Toni L. P. 166
Kelsay, Isabel Thompson 1905- 121
Kelsen, Hans 1881-1973 Obituary 115
Kelsey, Alice Geer 1896- 5-8R
See also SATA 1
Kelsey, Joan Marshall 1907-1989 CANR-58
Earlier sketch in CA 5-8R
Kelsey, Morton T(rippe) 1917- CANR-26
Earlier sketches in CA 21-24R, CANR-10
Kelsey, Robert J(ohn) 1927- 103
Kelso, Louis O(rth) 1913-1991 25-28R
Obituary 133
Kelso, Ruth 1885-1986 Obituary 119
Kelson, Allen H(oward) 1940- CANR-13
Earlier sketch in CA 77-80
Keltner, John W(illiam) 1918- 29-32R
Kelton, Elmer 1926- CANR-36
Earlier sketches in CA 21-24R, CANR-12
See also AITN 1
Kelvin, Norman 1924- 164
Brief entry 118
Kemal, Salim 1948- 125
Kemal, Yashar 1923- CANR-44
Earlier sketch in CA 89-92
See also CLC 14, 29
Kemble, E. W. 1861-1933 DLB 188
Kemble, Fanny 1809-1893 DLB 32
Kemble, James CAP-2
Earlier sketch in CA 29-32
Kemelman, Harry 1908-1996 CANR-71
Obituary 155
Earlier sketches in CA 9-12R, CANR-6
See also AITN 1
See also CLC 2
See also DLB 28
Kemeny, Jean A(lexander) 1930- 117
Kemeny, John G(eorge) 1926-1992 CANR-46
Obituary 140
Earlier sketch in CA 33-36R
Kemeny, Peter 1938-1975 53-56
Obituary 89-92
Kemerer, Frank R(obert) 1940- CANR-54
Earlier sketches in CA 65-68, CANR-10, 26
Kemery, Mary Alice
See Goodman, Linda
Kemmerer, Donald L(orenzo) 1905- 1-4R
Kemmis, Daniel (Orra) 1945- 161
Kemp, Anthony 1939- CANR-51
Earlier sketches in CA 105, CANR-25
Kemp, Arnold 1938- Brief entry 110
Kemp, Bernard Peter 1942- 107
Kemp, Betty 1916- 9-12R
Kemp, Charles F. 1912- CANR-5
Earlier sketch in CA 9-12R
Kemp, Diana Moyle 1919- CAP-1
Earlier sketch in CA 9-10
Kemp, Edward C. 1929- 81-84
Kemp, Gene 1926- CANR-12
Earlier sketch in CA 69-72
See also CLR 29
See also MAICYA
See also SATA 25, 75
Kemp, Jack (French) 1935- 109
Kemp, Jerrold E(dwin) 1921- 77-80
Kemp, John C(rocker) 1942- 93-96
Kemp, Kenny 1955- 168
Kemp, Lysander (Schaffer, Jr.) 1920- CANR-1
Earlier sketch in CA 45-48
Kemp, Martin (John) 1942- 108
Kemp, Patrick S(amuel) 1932- 53-56
Kemp, Penny 1944- 130
Kemp, Peter (Mant Macintyre) 1915-1993 25-28R
Obituary 143
Kemp, Robert 1908-1967 CAP-1
Earlier sketch in CA 13-16
Kemp, Roger L. 1946- 154
Kemp, Roy Z(ell) 1910- 9-12R
Kemp, Tom 1921-1993 25-28R
Obituary 143
Kempe, C(harles) Henry 1922-1984 122
Kempe, Frederick 1954- 138
Kempe, Margery 1373(?)-1440(?) DLB 146
Kemper, Donald J. 1929- 21-24R
Kemper, Inez 1906- CAP-1
Earlier sketch in CA 13-14
Kemper, Kathi J. 1957- 156
Kemper, R. Crosby (III)' 1951- 153
Kemper, Rachel H. 1931- 102
Kemper, Robert V(an) 1945- 104
Kemper, Troxey 1915- 136
Kemperman, Steve (Richard) 1955- 108
Kempfer, Lester Leroy 1932- 49-52
Kempher, Ruth Moon 1934- CANR-17
Earlier sketch in CA 25-28R
Kempner, Friederike 1836-1904 DLB 129
Kempner, Mary Jean 1913-1969 CAP-2
Earlier sketch in CA 29-32
See also SATA 10
Kempner, S. Marshall 1898- 85-88
Kempowski, Walter 1929- 158
Brief entry 122
Kemprecos, Paul 166
Kempson, Rachel 1910- 130
Kempster, Mary Yates 1911- CAP-1
Earlier sketch in CA 9-10
Kempster, Norman 1936- 77-80
Kempton, James Murray, Jr.
1945(?)-1971 Obituary 33-36R
Kempton, Jean Goldschmidt
1946(?)-1971 Obituary 33-36R
Kempton, Jean Welch 1914- 49-52
See also SATA 10
Kempton, (James) Murray 1918-1997 CANR-51
Obituary 158
Earlier sketch in CA 97-100
Kempton, Richard 1935- 106
Kemske, Floyd 1947- 151
Kemsley, Viscount
See Berry, James Gomer
Kemsley, William George, Jr. 1928- 85-88
Kenan, Randall (G.) 1963- 142
See also BW 2
Kenda, Margaret 1942- SATA 71
Kendal, Geoffrey
See Bragg, Richard Geoffrey
Kendal, Wallis 1937- 107
Kendall, Alan 1939- 131
Kendall, Aubyn 1919- 107
Kendall, Carol (Seeger) 1917- CANR-25
Earlier sketches in CA 5-8R, CANR-7
See also MAICYA
See also SAAS 7
See also SATA 11, 74
Kendall, David Evan 1944- 29-32R
Kendall, Dorothy Steinbomer 1912- 57-60
Kendall, E(dith) Lorna 1921- 5-8R
Kendall, Edward C(alvin) 1886-1972 Obituary 111
Kendall, Elaine (Becker) 1929- 17-20R
Kendall, Elizabeth B(emis) 1947- 81-84
Kendall, Gordon
See Lewitt, Shariann (N.)
Kendall, Henry Madison 1901-1966 5-8R
Kendall, Jane (F.) 1952- 137
Kendall, Kenneth E(verett) 1913- 45-48
Kendall, Lace
See Stoutenburg, Adrien (Pearl)
Kendall, Laurel 1947- 121
Kendall, Lisa See 1955- CANR-25
Earlier sketch in CA 111
Kendall, Lyle H(arris), Jr. 1919- 17-20R
Kendall, Marjorie 1930- 121
Kendall, Martha E. SATA 87
Kendall, Maurice (George) 1907-1983 Obituary 109
Kendall, Patricia Louise 1921-1990 Obituary 131
Kendall, Paul Murray 1911-1973 CAP-1
Earlier sketch in CA 13-16
Kendall, R(obert) T(illman) 1935- 93-96
Kendall, Robert 1934- CANR-6
Earlier sketch in CA 13-16R
Kendall, Russ 1957- SATA 83
Kendall, T(homas) Robert 1935- 69-72
Kendall, Willmoore 1909-1967 CANR-6
Earlier sketch in CA 5-8R
Kendle, John Edward 1937- 61-64
Kendler, Howard H(arvard) 1919- 17-20R
Kendrake, Carleton
See Gardner, Erle Stanley
Kendrick, Alexander 1911(?)-1991 143
Kendrick, Baynard H(ardwick) 1894-1977
CANR-60
Obituary 69-72
Earlier sketches in CA 1-4R, CANR-4
Kendrick, David Andrew 1937- CANR-9
Earlier sketch in CA 21-24R
Kendrick, Frank J(enness) 1928- 41-44R
Kendrick, John (Stafford) 1917- 121
Kendrick, John W(hitefield) 1917- 127
Brief entry 110
Kendrick, Thomas Downing 1895- 81-84
Kendrick, Walter 1947- 112
Kendricks, James
See Fox, G(ardner) F(rancis)
Kendris, Christopher 1923- CANR-24
Earlier sketches in CA 5-8R, CANR-7
Keneally, Thomas (Michael) 1935- CANR-50
Earlier sketches in CA 85-88, CANR-10
See also CLC 5, 8, 10, 14, 19, 27, 43
See also DAM NOV
See also MTCW 1
Kenealy, James P. 1927- 93-96
See also SATA 52
See also SATA-Brief 29
Kenealy, Jim
See Kenealy, James P.
Keneas, Alexander 1938(?)-1984 Obituary 113
Kenelly, John W(illis Jr.) 1935- 25-28R
Kenen, Isaiah Leo 1905- 107
Kenen, Peter B(ain) 1932- CANR-22
Earlier sketches in CA 5-8R, CANR-7
Kenesson, Frank G. 1913(?)-1985 Obituary 119
Kenez, Peter 1937- 29-32R
Kenian, Paul Roger
See Clifford, Martin
Kenin, Richard (Metz) 1947-1983 Obituary 111
Kenison, Katrina 1958- 138
Keniston, Kenneth 1930- 25-28R
Kenjo, Takashi 1940- 137
Kenkel, William F(rancis) 1925- 61-64
Kenna, Peter 1930- 61-64
Kennamer, Lorrin, Jr. 1924- CANR-6
Earlier sketch in CA 5-8R
Kennan, George 1845-1924 DLB 189
Kennan, George Frost 1904- CANR-39
Earlier sketches in CA 1-4R, CANR-2
Kennan, Kent (Wheeler) 1913- 1-4R
Kennard, George (Arnold Ford) 1915- 134
Kennard-Davis, Arthur (Shelley) 1910- CAP-1
Earlier sketch in CA 9-10
Kennaway, Adrienne 1945- SATA 60
Kennaway, James (Peebles Ewing) 1928-1968 103
Obituary 89-92
Kenneally, Michael 1945- 133
Kennealy, Jerry 1938- 142
Kennealy (Morrison), Patricia 1946- 120
Kennebeck, Edwin 1924-1996 41-44R
Obituary 152
Kennebeck, Paul 1943- 53-56
Kennecott, G. J.
See Viksnins, George J(uris)
Kennedy, A(lison) L. 168
Kennedy, Adam 1920(?)-1997 CANR-24
Obituary 162
Earlier sketch in CA 107
See also AITN 1
Kennedy, Adrienne (Lita) 1931- CANR-53
Earlier sketches in CA 103, CANR-26
See also CAAS 20
See also BLC 2
See also BW 2
See also CABS 3
See also CLC 66
See also DAM MULT
See also DC 5
See also DLB 38
Kennedy, Andrew (Karpati) 1931- 61-64
Kennedy, Betty 1926- 121
Kennedy, Brendan 1970- 123
See also SATA 57
Kennedy, Bruce M. 1929- 57-60
Kennedy, Carol CANR-21
Earlier sketch in CA 105
Kennedy, Caroline 1944- 125
Kennedy, Caroline (Bouvier) 1957- 140
Kennedy, Charles J(oseph)
1935-1984 Obituary 114
Kennedy, Chuck
See Kennedy, Charles J(oseph)
Kennedy, Cody, Jr.
See Reese, John (Henry)
Kennedy, D. James 1930- 61-64
Kennedy, Dana Forrest 1917- SATA 74
Kennedy, Dane K(eith) 1951- CANR-56
Earlier sketch in CA 126
Kennedy, David M. 1941- CANR-13
Earlier sketch in CA 29-32R
Kennedy, Dennis (Edward) 1940- CANR-46
Earlier sketch in CA 120
Kennedy, Don H(enry) 1911- 61-64
Kennedy, Dorothy M(intzlaff) 1931- CANR-40
Earlier sketch in CA 116
See also SATA 53
Kennedy, Douglas 1955- 158
Kennedy, Eddie C. 1910- 89-92
Kennedy, Edward Moore 1932- 110
Kennedy, Edward R(idgway)
1923(?)-1975 Obituary 104
Kennedy, Elliot
See Godfrey, Lionel (Robert Holcombe)
Kennedy, (Robert) Emmet (Jr.) 1941- 132
Kennedy, Eugene C(ullen) 1928- CANR-44
Earlier sketch in CA 25-28R
Kennedy, Florynce (Rae) 1916- 155
Kennedy, Gail 1900-1972 Obituary 33-36R
Kennedy, Gavin 1940- CANR-9
Earlier sketch in CA 61-64
Kennedy, George 1899(?)-1977 Obituary 73-76
Kennedy, George (Alexander) 1928- CANR-2
Earlier sketch in CA 5-8R
Kennedy, Gerald (Hamilton) 1907- CANR-6
Earlier sketch in CA 5-8R
Kennedy, Gerald Studdert
See Studdert-Kennedy, (William) Gerald
Kennedy, Harold J. 1915(?)-1988 Obituary 124
Kennedy, Hubert (Collings) 1931- 93-96
Kennedy, Hugh 1947- 127
Kennedy, J. Gerald 1947- 127
Kennedy, J(ames) Hardee 1915- 13-16R
Kennedy, James
See Monahan, James (Henry Francis)
Kennedy, James G(ettier) 1932- 81-84
Kennedy, James William 1905- CANR-1
Earlier sketch in CA 1-4R
Kennedy, James Y(oung) 1916- 77-80
Kennedy, Jimmy 1903(?)-1984 Obituary 112
Kennedy, John C. 1943- 152
Kennedy, John Fitzgerald 1917-1963 CANR-1
Earlier sketch in CA 1-4R
See also MTCW 1
See also SATA 11
Kennedy, John J(oseph) 1914- 57-60
Kennedy, John Pendleton 1795-1870 DLB 3
Kennedy, Joseph Charles 1929- CANR-40
Earlier sketches in CA 1-4R, CANR-4, 30
See also Kennedy, X. J.
See also SATA 14, 86
Kennedy, Judith M(ary) 1935- 41-44R
Kennedy, Kathleen 1947(?)-1975 Obituary 57-60
Kennedy, Kenneth A(drian) R(aine) 1930- CANR-1
Earlier sketch in CA 45-48
Kennedy, Kieran A. 1935- 37-40R
Kennedy, L. D. 1924- 45-48
Kennedy, Lawrence W. 1952- 141
Kennedy, Leigh 1951- 122
Kennedy, Lena
See Smith, Lena (Kennedy)
Kennedy, Leo 1907- DLB 88
Kennedy, Leonard Anthony 1922- 37-40R
Kennedy, Leonard M(ilton) 1925- 73-76
Kennedy, Liv 1934- 140
Kennedy, Ludovic (Henry Coverley) 1919-
CANR-46
Earlier sketch in CA 65-68
Kennedy, Malcolm D(uncan) 1895- 9-12R
Kennedy, Margaret 1896-1967 Obituary 25-28R
See also DLB 36
Kennedy, Marilyn Moats 1943- CANR-32
Earlier sketch in CA 109
Kennedy, Mary 102
Kennedy, Michael 1926- CANR-47
Earlier sketches in CA 13-16R, CANR-5, 23
Kennedy, Moorhead 1930- 123
Kennedy, Nigel (Paul) 1956- 140
Kennedy, P(eter) J(ohn) 1925- 123
Kennedy, Pagan
See Kennedy, Pamela
Kennedy, Pamela 1946- 151
See also SATA 87
Kennedy, Pamela 1962- 146
Kennedy, Patrick 1801-1873 DLB 159
Kennedy, Paul (Michael) 1945- CANR-30
Earlier sketches in CA 65-68, CANR-9
See also BEST 89:1
Kennedy, Paul E(dward) 1929- SATA 33
Kennedy, Paul M.
See Kennedy, Paul (Michael)
Kennedy, Ralph Dale 1897-1965 1-4R
Kennedy, Randall 1954- 162
Kennedy, Raymond A. 1934- 5-8R
Kennedy, Richard (Pitt) 1910-1989 102
Obituary 127
See also SATA-Obit 60
Kennedy, (Jerome) Richard 1932- CANR-26
Earlier sketches in CA 57-60, CANR-7
See also SATA 22
Kennedy, Richard S(ylvester) 1920- CANR-56
Earlier sketches in CA 5-8R, CANR-3, 29
See also DLB 111
Kennedy, Robert 1938- SATA 63
Kennedy, Robert E(mmet), Jr. 1937- 37-40R
Kennedy, Robert F(rancis), Jr. 1954- 110
Kennedy, Robert F(rancis) 1925-1968 CANR-1
Earlier sketch in CA 1-4R
Kennedy, Robert L(ee) 1930- 57-60
Kennedy, Robert Woods 1911- 49-52
Kennedy, Roger G(eorge) 1926- 115
Kennedy, Rose (Elizabeth Fitzgerald)
1890-1995 53-56
Obituary 147
Kennedy, Sighle Aileen 1919- 53-56
Kennedy, Stetson 1916- CANR-45
Earlier sketch in CA 5-8R
Kennedy, Susan Estabrook 1942- CANR-43
Earlier sketch in CA 45-48
Kennedy, T(eresa) A. 1953- 114
See also SATA 42
See also SATA-Brief 35
Kennedy, T(homas) F(illans) 1921- 53-56
Kennedy, Ted
See Kennedy, Edward Moore
Kennedy, Teresa
See Kennedy, T(eresa) A.
Kennedy, Theodore Reginald 1936- 105

Kennedy, Thomas 1920- ... 116
Kennedy, Thomas C. 1937- ... 125
Kennedy, William 1928- ... CANR-31
Earlier sketches in CA 85-88, CANR-14
Interview in ... CANR-31
See also AAYA 1
See also CLC 6, 28, 34, 53
See also DAM NOV
See also DLB 143
See also DLBY 85
See also MTCW 1
See also SATA 57
Kennedy, William B(ean) 1926- ... 116
Kennedy, William J(ohn) 1942- ... 117
Kennedy, X. J.
See Kennedy, Joseph Charles
See also CAAS 9
See also CLC 8, 42
See also CLR 27
See also DLB 5
See also SAAS 22
Kennedy-Martin, Ian 1936- ... 101
Kenneggy, Richard
See Nettell, Richard (Geoffrey)
Kennel, LeRoy E(ldon) 1930- ... 77-80
Kennell, Nigel M. 1955- ... 155
Kennell, Ruth Epperson 1893-1977 ... CAP-2
Earlier sketch in CA 29-32
See also SATA 6
See also SATA-Obit 25
Kennelly, Brendan 1936- ... CANR-5
Earlier sketch in CA 9-12R
See also DLB 40
Kenner, Charles Leroy 1933- ... 25-28R
Kenner, (William) Hugh 1923- ... CANR-28
Earlier sketch in CA 21-24R
See also DLB 67
Kennerly, David Hume 1947- ... 101
See also AITN 2
Kennerly, Karen 1940- ... 33-36R
Kennett, Audrey 1905- ... 147
Kennett, (Houn) Jiyu 1924- ... 93-96
Kennett, Lee 1931- ... 21-24R
Kennett, Peggy Teresa Nancy
See Kennett, (Houn) Jiyu
Kenney, Alice P(atricia) 1937-1985 ... CANR-10
Obituary ... 115
Earlier sketch in CA 25-28R
Kenney, Catherine (McGehee) 1948- ... 135
Kenney, Charles 1950- ... 135
Kenney, Douglas C. 1947(?)-1980 ... 107
Obituary ... 101
Kenney, Edwin James, Jr. 1942- ... 53-56
Kenney, George Churchill 1889- ... CAP-1
Earlier sketch in CA 11-12
Kenney, John Paul 1920- ... 17-20R
Kenney, Lona B(ronberg) 1921- ... 115
Kenney, Richard (L.) 1948- ... 134
Kenney, Susan (McIlvaine) 1941- ... CANR-37
Earlier sketch in CA 115
Kenney, Sylvia W. 1922-(?) ... CAP-1
Earlier sketch in CA 19-20
Kennick, W(illiam) E(lmer) 1923- ... 13-16R
Kennington, (Gilbert) Alan 1906-1986 Obituary ... 121
Kennington, Alice Eve 1935- ... 119
Kennon, Donald R. 1948- ... 122
Kenny, Anthony
See Kenny, Anthony John Patrick
Kenny, Anthony John Patrick 1931- ... CANR-23
Earlier sketch in CA 101
Kenny, Charles J.
See Gardner, Erle Stanley
Kenny, Ellsworth Newcomb 1909-1971 ... 5-8R
Obituary ... 103
See also SATA-Obit 26
Kenny, Herbert Andrew 1912- ... 41-44R
See also SATA 13
Kenny, James Andrew 1933- ... CANR-51
Earlier sketches in CA 107, CANR-26
Kenny, Jean
See Freeman, Jean Kenny
Kenny, John P. 1909- ... 17-20R
Kenny, John Peter 1916- ... CANR-1
Earlier sketch in CA 45-48
Kenny, Kathryn
See Bowden, Joan Chase
and Krull, Kathleen
and Sanderlin, Owenita (Harrah)
and Stack, Nicolete Meredith
Kenny, Kevin
See Krull, Kathleen
Kenny, Mary 1936- ... 108
Kenny, Maurice (Francis) 1929- ... 144
See also CAAS 22
See also CLC 87
See also DAM MULT
See also DLB 175
See also NNAL
Kenny, Michael 1923- ... CANR-5
Earlier sketch in CA 1-4R
Kenny, Nicholas Napoleon
1895-1975 Obituary ... 89-92
Kenny, Nick
See Kenny, Nicholas Napoleon
Kenny, Shirley (Elise) Strum 1934- ... CANR-31
Earlier sketch in CA 45-48
Kenny, Vincent 1919- ... 45-48
Kenny, W. Henry 1918- ... 37-40R
Kenofer, C(harles) Louis 1923- ... 69-72
Kenoyer, Natlee Peoples 1907- ... CANR-5
Earlier sketch in CA 5-8R
Kenrick, Donald Simon 1929- ... 81-84
Kenrick, Tony 1935- ... 104
Kenshalo, Daniel R(alph) 1922- ... 41-44R
Kensinger, George
See Fichter, George S.
Kent, Alexander
See Reeman, Douglas Edward
Kent, Allegra 1938(?)- ... CANR-72
Brief entry ... 105
Earlier sketch in CA 126
Kent, Allen 1921- ... CANR-39
Earlier sketches in CA 9-12R, CANR-3, 18
Kent, Arden
See Marion, Frieda
Kent, Arthur William Charles 1925- ... 102
Kent, Bill
See Kent, Carleton Volney, Jr.
Kent, Carleton Volney, Jr. 1909-1985 Obituary ... 114
Kent, Christopher 1940- ... 129
Kent, Cromwell
See Sparshott, Francis (Edward)
Kent, David
See Lambert, David (Compton)
Kent, Deborah Ann 1948- ... 103
See also SATA 47
See also SATA-Brief 41
Kent, Donald P(eterson) 1916-1972 ... 17-20R
Obituary ... 120
Kent, Edward Allen 1933- ... 45-48
Kent, Ernest W(illiam) 1940- ... 104
Kent, Fortune
See Toombs, John
Kent, Frank (Richardson, Jr.)
1907(?)-1978 Obituary ... 81-84
Kent, Frank R(ichardson) 1877-1958 Brief
entry ... 121
See also DLB 29
Kent, George O(tto) 1919- ... 37-40R
Kent, George W. 1928- ... 25-28R
Kent, Harold W(infield) 1900- ... 65-68
Kent, Helen
See Polley, Judith (Anne)
Kent, Homer A(ustin), Jr. 1926- ... CANR-3
Earlier sketch in CA 9-12R
Kent, Jack
See Kent, John Wellington
Kent, James M. 1956- ... 139
Kent, John Henry Somerset 1923- ... 9-12R
Kent, John Wellington 1920-1985 ... CANR-16
Obituary ... 117
Earlier sketch in CA 85-88
Interview in ... CANR-16
See also SATA 24
See also SATA-Obit 45
Kent, Karen 1941- ... 159
Kent, Katherine
See Dial, Joan
Kent, Katie
See Green, Kay
Kent, Kelvin
See Kuttner, Henry
Kent, Leonard J. 1927- ... 77-80
Kent, Lisa 1942- ... 155
See also SATA 90
Kent, Louise Andrews 1886-1969 ... CANR-4
Obituary ... 25-28R
Earlier sketch in CA 1-4R
Kent, Malcolm 1932- ... 45-48
Kent, Mallory
See Lowndes, Robert A(ugustine) W(ard)
Kent, Margaret 1894- ... CAP-2
Earlier sketch in CA 25-28
See also SATA 2
Kent, Neil (Lowell) 1951- ... 129
Kent, Noel J(ay) 1944- ... 111
Kent, Nora 1899- ... CAP-1
Earlier sketch in CA 9-10
Kent, Pete
See Richardson, Gladwell
Kent, Philip
See Bulmer, (Henry) Kenneth
Kent, Rockwell 1882-1971 ... CANR-4
Obituary ... 29-32R
Earlier sketch in CA 5-8R
See also SATA 6
Kent, Sherman 1903-1986 ... 53-56
Obituary ... 118
See also SATA 20
See also SATA-Obit 47
Kent, Sherry 1955- ... 128
Kent, Simon
See Catto, Max(well Jeffrey)
Kent, Stella
See Phillips, Stella
Kent, Tony
See Crechales, Anthony George
Kent, Valerie 1947- ... 114
Kentfield, Calvin 1924- ... 5-8R
Kentfield, J(ohn) A(lan) C. 1930- ... 165
Kenton, Leslie 1941- ... 113
Kenton, Maxwell
See Hoffenberg, Mason
and Southern, Terry
Kenton, Warren 1933- ... CANR-29
Earlier sketch in CA 29-32R
Kenward, James (Macara) 1908- ... 5-8R
Kenward, Jean 1920- ... 108
See also SATA 42
Kenward, Michael 1945- ... 103
Kenworthy, Brian J(ohn) 1920- ... 103
Kenworthy, Eldon (G.) 1935- ... 154
Kenworthy, Leonard S. 1912- ... CANR-1
Earlier sketch in CA 1-4R
See also SATA 6
Kenyatta, Jomo 1891(?)-1978 ... 124
Obituary ... 113
See also BW 1
See also MTCW 1
Kenyon, Bernice
See Gilkyson, Bernice Kenyon
Kenyon, Ernest M(onroe) 1920- ... 85-88
Kenyon, F(rank) W(ilson) 1912- ... CANR-1
Earlier sketch in CA 1-4R
Kenyon, J(ohn) P(hilipps) 1927-1996 ... CANR-45
Obituary ... 151
Earlier sketches in CA 9-12R, CANR-3
Kenyon, James William 1910- ... CAP-1
Earlier sketch in CA 9-10
Kenyon, Jane 1947-1995 ... CANR-69
Obituary ... 148
Earlier sketches in CA 118, CANR-44
See also DLB 120
Kenyon, John R(obert) 1948- ... CANR-55
Earlier sketch in CA 127
Kenyon, Karen 1938- ... 106
Kenyon, Kate
See Adorjan, Carol (Madden)
and Ransom, Candice F.
Kenyon, Kathleen Mary 1906-1978 ... CANR-13
Earlier sketch in CA 21-24R
Kenyon, Ley 1913- ... 13-16R
See also SATA 6
Kenyon, Michael 1931- ... CANR-12
Earlier sketch in CA 13-16R
Kenyon, Mildred Adams 1894-1980 ... 108
Obituary ... 105
Kenyon, Paul
See Freedland, Nat(haniel)
Kenyon, Robert O.
See Kuttner, Henry
Kenyon, W. A.
See Kenyon, Walter Andrew
Kenyon, Walter
See Kenyon, Walter Andrew
Kenyon, Walter A.
See Kenyon, Walter Andrew
Kenyon, Walter Andrew 1917-1986 Obituary ... 121
Kenzer, Robert C. 1955- ... 126
Keogh, Dermot (Francis) 1945- ... 126
Keogh, James 1916- ... 45-48
Keogh, Lilian Gilmore 1927- ... 9-12R
Keohane, Dan 1941- ... 146
Keohane, Nannerl O(verholser) 1940- ... 106
Keohane, Robert O(wen) 1941- ... CANR-33
Earlier sketch in CA 45-48
Keough, Hugh Edmund 1864-1912 ... DLB 171
Keown, Elizabeth ... SATA 78
Kepel, Gilles 1955- ... 149
Kepes, Gyorgy 1906- ... 101
Kepes, Juliet A(ppleby) 1919- ... 69-72
See also SATA 13
Kephart, Horace 1862-1931 Brief entry ... 119
Kephart, Newell C. 1911-1973 ... CAP-2
Earlier sketch in CA 17-18
Kephart, William M. 1921- ... 41-44R
Kepler, Thomas Samuel 1897-1963 ... 1-4R
Keppel, Charlotte
See Torday, Ursula
Keppel, Sonia 1900-1986 ... 107
Obituary ... 120
Keppel-Jones, Arthur (Mervyn) 1909- ... 118
Kepple, Ella Huff 1902- ... CAP-2
Earlier sketch in CA 17-18
Keppler, Ann B(lystad) 1946- ... 117
Keppler, C(arl) F(rancis) 1909- ... 17-20R
Keppler, Herbert 1925- ... 85-88
Keppler, Victor 1904-1987 Obituary ... 124
Ker, Jill
See Conway, Jill K(er)
Ker, Neil Ripley 1908-1982 Obituary ... 107
See also DLB 201
Ker, William Paton 1855-1923 Brief entry ... 121
Kerbel, Matthew Robert 1958- ... 148
Kerber, August Frank 1917- ... 21-24R
Kerber, Linda K(aufman) 1940- ... 160
Brief entry ... 115
Kerby, Anthony Paul 1953- ... 141
Kerby, Bill 1937- ... 104
Kerby, Joe Kent 1933- ... 53-56
Kerby, Mona 1951- ... 142
See also SATA 75
Kerby, Philip Pearce 1911- Brief entry ... 116
Kerby, Robert L(ee) 1934- ... 41-44R
Kerby, Susan Alice
See Burton, (Alice) Elizabeth
Kercheval, Jesse Lee 1956- ... CANR-53
Earlier sketch in CA 126
Kerckhoff, Alan C(hester) 1924- ... CANR-67
Earlier sketches in CA 113, CANR-32
Kerek, Andrew 1936- ... 102
Kerekes, Tibor 1893-1969 ... CAP-2
Earlier sketch in CA 17-18
Kerensky, Alexandr Fedorovich
1881-1970 Obituary ... 113
Kerensky, Oleg 1930-1993 ... CANR-12
Obituary ... 141
Earlier sketch in CA 29-32R
Kerensky, V(asil) M(ichael) 1930- ... 53-56
Keres, Paul (Petrovich) 1916-1975 Obituary ... 57-60
Kerestesi, Michael 1929- ... 109
Kereszty, Roch A(ndrew) 1933- ... 29-32R
Kerewsky-Halpern, Barbara 1931- ... 102
Kerferd, G(eorge) B(riscoe) 1915- ... 132
Kerigan, Florence 1896- ... 29-32R
See also SATA 12
Kerin, Roger A(nthony) 1947- ... CANR-26
Earlier sketch in CA 109
Kerina, Mburumba 1932- ... CANR-71
Earlier sketch in CA 129
Kerkvliet, Benedict J(ohn) 1943- ... 93-96
Kerlan, Irvin 1912-1963 ... 5-8R
See also DLB 187
Kerlinger, Fred N(ichols) 1910- ... CANR-2
Earlier sketch in CA 49-52
Kerman, Cynthia Earl 1923- ... 57-60
Kerman, Gertrude
See Furman, Gertrude Lerner Kerman
Kerman, Gertrude Lerner 1909- ... 5-8R
See also SATA 21
Kerman, Joseph Wilfred 1924- ... CANR-15
Earlier sketch in CA 65-68
Kerman, Judith (Berna) 1945- ... 77-80
Kerman, Sheppard 1928- ... CANR-26
Earlier sketch in CA 85-88
Kermani, Taghi Thomas 1929- ... 25-28R
Kermode, (John) Frank 1919- ... CANR-47
Earlier sketches in CA 1-4R, CANR-1
Kern, Alfred 1924- ... 33-36R
Kern, Canyon
See Raborg, Frederick A(shton), Jr.
Kern, E. R.
See Kerner, Fred
Kern, Edith 1912- ... 113
Kern, Gary 1938- ... 65-68
Kern, Gregory
See Tubb, E(dwin) C(harles)
Kern, Janet (Rosalie) 1924-1998 ... 5-8R
Obituary ... 166
Kern, Jean B(ordner) 1913- ... 85-88
Kern, Jerome 1885-1945 ... DLB 187
Kern, Mary Margaret 1906- ... 101
Kern, Robert W(illiam) 1934- ... CANR-7
Earlier sketch in CA 61-64
Kern, Seymour 1913- ... 93-96
Kern, Stephen 1943- ... 69-72
Kern, Walter O(tto) 1930- ... 117
Kernaghan, Eileen 1939- ... CANR-54
Earlier sketches in CA 111, CANR-28
Kernan, Alvin B(ernard) 1923- ... CANR-33
Earlier sketch in CA 49-52
Kernan, Jerome B(ernard) 1932- ... 25-28R
Kernan, Julia K. 1901(?)-1988 Obituary ... 125
Kernan, Michael 1927- ... 81-84
Kerner, Fred 1921- ... CANR-47
Earlier sketches in CA 9-12R, CANR-6, 22
Kerner, Justinus 1786-1862 ... DLB 90
Kernfeld, Barry (Dean) 1950- ... 161
Kernochan, Sarah 1947- ... 73-76
Kernodle, George R(iley) 1907- ... 65-68
Kerns, Daniel R.
See Lichtenberg, Jacqueline
Kerns, Frances Casey 1937- ... 81-84
Kerns, J(ames) Alexander 1894-1975 Obituary ... 104
Kerns, Robert Louis 1929- ... 77-80
Kerouac, Jack
See Kerouac, Jean-Louis Lebris de
See also AAYA 25
See also CDALB 1941-1968
See also CLC 1, 2, 3, 5, 14, 29, 61
See also DLB 2, 16
See also DLBD 3
See also DLBY 95
Kerouac, Jan
See Hackett, Jan Michele
See also DLB 16
Kerouac, Jean-Louis Lebris de 1922-1969 ...
CANR-54
Obituary ... 25-28R
Earlier sketches in CA 5-8R, CANR-26
See also Kerouac, Jack
See also AITN 1
See also DA
See also DAB
See also DAC
See also DAM MST, NOV, POET, POP
See also MTCW 1
See also WLC
Kerouac, John
See Kerouac, Jean-Louis Lebris de
Kerpelman, Larry C(yril) 1939- ... 37-40R
Kerr, Alex(ander McBride) 1921- ... 61-64
Kerr, Alex A. 1922- ... 125
Kerr, Andrea Moore 1940- ... 141
Kerr, Andy
See Kerr, Alex A.
Kerr, Ann Zwicker 1934- ... 148
Kerr, Barbara 1913- ... 89-92
Kerr, Ben
See Ard, William (Thomas)
Kerr, Carole
See Carr, Margaret
Kerr, Catherine 1945- ... 102
Kerr, Clark 1911- ... CANR-22
Earlier sketches in CA 45-48, CANR-1
Kerr, D(onald) G(ordon) G(rady) 1913-1976 ...
CANR-6
Earlier sketch in CA 1-4R
Kerr, Donna H(anneman) 1944- ... 112
Kerr, E. Bartlett 1924- ... 139
Kerr, Elizabeth M. 1905- ... 37-40R
Kerr, Frederick
See Kerner, Fred
Kerr, Graham 1934- ... 108
Kerr, Harry P(rice) 1928- ... 5-8R
Kerr, Homer L(ee) 1921- ... 120
Kerr, Howard Hastings 1931- ... 103
Kerr, Hugh Thomson 1909-1992 ... 103
Obituary ... 137
Kerr, James Lennox 1899-1963 ... 102
Kerr, James Stolee 1928- ... 17-20R
Kerr, Jean 1923- ... CANR-7
Earlier sketch in CA 5-8R
Interview in ... CANR-7
See also CLC 22
Kerr, Jessica 1901- ... CAP-2
Earlier sketch in CA 29-32
See also SATA 13
Kerr, Joan P(aterson) 1921-1996 ... 81-84
Obituary ... 154
Kerr, John 1950- ... 149
Kerr, (Anne-) Judith 1923- ... 93-96
See also SATA 24
Kerr, K(athel) Austin 1938- ... 25-28R

Kerr, Katharine 1944- ... 155
Kerr, M. E.
See Meaker, Marijane (Agnes)
See also AAYA 2, 23
See also CLC 12, 35
See also CLR 29
See also SAAS 1
Kerr, Malcolm (Hooper) 1931-1984 ... 97-100
Obituary ... 111
Kerr, Norman D.
See Sieber, Sam Dixon
Kerr, Orpheus C.
See Newell, Robert Henry
Kerr, Philip 1956- ... 159
Kerr, Phyllis Forbes 1942- ... 120
See also SATA 72
Kerr, Robert ... CLC 55
Kerr, Robert (a pseudonym) 1899- ... 69-72
Kerr, Rose Netzorg 1892-1974 ... CAP-2
Earlier sketch in CA 23-24
Kerr, Stanley E. 1894(?)-1976 Obituary ... 69-72
Kerr, Tom 1950- ... SATA 77
Kerr, Walter (Francis) 1913-1996 ... CANR-7
Obituary ... 154
Earlier sketch in CA 5-8R
Kerrigan, (Thomas) Anthony 1918- ... CANR-4
Earlier sketch in CA 49-52
See also CAAS 11
See also CLC 4, 6
Kerrigan, Catherine 1939- ... 117
Kerrigan, Kate Lowe
See Rickett, Frances
Kerrigan, William J(oseph) ... CANR-2
Earlier sketch in CA 49-52
Kerry, Frances
See Kerigan, Florence
Kerry, Lois
See Duncan, Lois
Kersaudy, Francois 1948- ... 144
Kersell, John E(dgar) 1930- ... 45-48
Kersenboom, Saskia 1953- ... 152
Kersey, Katharine C(lark) 1935- ... CANR-38
Earlier sketch in CA 116
Kersey, Tanya-Monique 1961- ... 138
See also BW 2
Kersh, Cyril 1925-1993 ... CANR-47
Obituary ... 141
Earlier sketch in CA 104
Kersh, Gerald 1911-1968 Obituary ... 25-28R
Kershaw, Alister (Nasmyth) 1921- ... CANR-41
Earlier sketches in CA 5-8R, CANR-3, 19
Kershaw, Gordon Ernest 1928- ... 85-88
Kershaw, Ian 1943- ... 137
Kershaw, John (Hugh D'Allenger) ... 73-76
Kershen, (L.) Michael 1982- ... 149
See also SATA 82
Kershner, Howard E(ldred) 1891- ... 73-76
Kershner, Richard B(randon) 1913-1982 Obituary ... 110
Kerslake, Susan 1943- ... CANR-17
Earlier sketch in CA 93-96
Kersnowski, Frank L. 1934- ... 41-44R
Kertes, Joseph ... 166
Kertess, Klaus 1940- ... 162
Kertesz, Andre 1894-1985 ... 85-88
Obituary ... 117
Kertesz, Louise 1939- ... 102
Kertesz, Stephen D(enis) 1904- ... CAP-2
Earlier sketch in CA 21-22
Kertzer, David I(srael) 1948- ... CANR-44
Earlier sketch in CA 106
Kertzer, Morris Norman 1910-1983 ... CANR-1
Obituary ... 111
Earlier sketch in CA 1-4R
Kerven, Rosalind 1954- ... 150
See also SATA 83
Ker Wilson, Barbara 1929- ... CANR-7
Earlier sketch in CA 5-8R
See also SAAS 18
See also SATA 20, 70
Kerwood, John R. 1942- ... 53-56
Kesey, Ken (Elton) 1935- ... CANR-66
Earlier sketches in CA 1-4R, CANR-22, 38
See also AAYA 25
See also CDALB 1968-1988
See also CLC 1, 3, 6, 11, 46, 64
See also DA
See also DAB
See also DAC
See also DAM MST, NOV, POP
See also DLB 2, 16
See also MTCW 1
See also SATA 66
See also WLC
Keshet, Harry F(inkelstein) 1940- ... 109
Keshishian, John M. 1923- ... 25-28R
Kesich, Veselin 1921- Brief entry ... 111
Kesler, (William) Jackson (II) 1938- ... 102
Kesler, Jay 1935- ... CANR-51
Earlier sketches in CA 61-64, CANR-8, 26
See also SATA 65
Kess, Joseph Francis 1942- ... 65-68
Kessel, Dmitri 1902- ... 120
Kessel, John (Joseph Vincent) 1950- ... 120
Kessel, John H(oward) 1928- ... CANR-46
Earlier sketches in CA 21-24R, CANR-21
Kessel, Joseph (Elie) 1898-1979 ... 105
Obituary ... 89-92
See also DLB 72
Kessel, Joyce Karen 1937- ... 105
See also SATA 41
Kessel, Lipmann 1914- ... 13-16R
Kessel, Martin 1901- ... DLB 56
Kessell, John L(ottridge) 1936- ... 93-96
Kesselman, Judi R.
See Kesselman-Turkel, Judi
Kesselman, Louis Coleridge 1919-1974 Obituary ... 110
Kesselman, Mark J. ... CANR-14
Earlier sketch in CA 37-40R
Kesselman-Turkel, Judi 1934- ... CANR-37
Kesselring, Joseph (Otto) 1902-1967 ... 150
See also CLC 45
See also DAM DRAM, MST
Kessen, William 1925- ... CANR-1
Earlier sketch in CA 1-4R
Kessler, Diane Cooksey 1947- ... 57-60
Kessler, Edward 1927- ... 61-64
Kessler, Ethel 1922- ... CANR-48
Brief entry ... 115
Earlier sketch in CA 121
See also SATA 44
See also SATA-Brief 37
Kessler, Francis P(aschal) 1944- ... 109
Kessler, Frank
See Kessler, Francis P(aschal)
Kessler, Gail 1937- ... 65-68
Kessler, Henry H(oward) 1896-1978 Obituary 73-76
Kessler, Herbert L(eon) 1941- ... CANR-51
Earlier sketch in CA 125
Kessler, Jascha (Frederick) 1929- ... CANR-48
Earlier sketches in CA 17-20R, CANR-8
See also CLC 4
Kessler, Judy 1947- ... 146
Kessler, Julia Braun 1926- ... CANR-70
Earlier sketch in CA 144
Kessler, Kaye (Warren) 1923- ... 112
Kessler, Lauren J. 1950- ... CANR-54
Earlier sketch in CA 127
Kessler, Leonard P. 1921- ... 77-80
See also SATA 14
Kessler, Merle (Bruce) 1949- ... 128
Kessler, Milton 1930- ... CANR-2
Earlier sketch in CA 1-4R
Kessler, Rod 1949- ... 117
Kessler, Ronald (Borek) 1943- ... CANR-55
Earlier sketches in CA 69-72, CANR-13, 28
Kessler, Sheila ... 57-60
Kessler, Suzanne J. 1946- ... 167
Kessler, Walter R. 1913-1978 Obituary ... 81-84
Kessler-Harris, Alice 1941- ... CANR-65
Earlier sketch in CANR-32
Kessner, Lawrence 1957- ... 109
Kessner, Thomas 1946- ... CANR-11
Earlier sketch in CA 69-72
Kesteloot, Lilyan 1931- ... CANR-41
Earlier sketches in CA 73-76, CANR-19
Kesten, Hermann 1900- ... DLB 56
Kester, Dana R(ay) 1943- ... 116
Kesterson, David B(ert) 1938- ... 41-44R
Kesterton, Wilfred (Harold) 1914- ... 41-44R
Kesteven, G. R.
See Crosher, G. R.
Kestler, Frances Roe 1929- ... 135
Kestner, Joseph A(loysius) 1943- ... 89-92
Ketch, Jack
See Tibbetts, John C(arter)
Ketcham, Carl H(untington) 1923- ... 29-32R
Ketcham, Charles B(rown) 1926- ... 29-32R
Ketcham, Hank
See Ketcham, Henry King
Ketcham, Henry King 1920- ... 105
See also SATA 28
See also SATA-Brief 27
Ketcham, Howard 1902-1982 Obituary ... 106
Ketcham, Katherine 1949- ... 118
Ketcham, Orman W(eston) 1918- ... CANR-9
Earlier sketch in CA 21-24R
Ketcham, Ralph (Louis) 1927- ... CANR-4
Earlier sketch in CA 9-12R
Ketcham, Rodney K(enneth) 1909- ... CANR-4
Earlier sketch in CA 1-4R
Ketchum, Carlton Griswold 1892- ... 85-88
Ketchum, Cliff
See Paine, Lauran (Bosworth)
Ketchum, Creston Donald 1922- ... 9-12R
Ketchum, Frank
See Paine, Lauran (Bosworth)
Ketchum, J.
See Frentzen, Jeffrey
Ketchum, Jack
See Paine, Lauran (Bosworth)
Ketchum, Marshall D(ana) 1905- ... CAP-1
Earlier sketch in CA 17-18
Ketchum, Richard M(alcolm) 1922- ... 25-28R
Ketchum, Robert Glenn 1947- ... CANR-23
Earlier sketch in CA 107
Ketchum, William C(larence), Jr. 1931- ... CANR-55
Earlier sketches in CA 33-36R, CANR-12, 28
Keteyian, Armen 1953- ... 122
Ketner, Kenneth Laine (Sr.) 1939- ... 139
Ketner, Mary Grace 1946- ... SATA 75
Ketron, Larry 1947- ... 141
Kets de Vries, Manfred F. R. 1942- ... 111
Kett, Joseph F. 1938- ... 25-28R
Kettani, M. Ali 1941- ... 133
Kettelhack, Guy 1951- ... 134
Kettelkamp, Larry (Dale) 1933- ... CANR-16
Earlier sketch in CA 29-32R
See also CLC 12
See also SAAS 3
See also SATA 2
Ketteman, Helen 1945- ... SATA 73
Ketterer, David (Anthony Theodor) 1942- ... CANR-46
Earlier sketches in CA 53-56, CANR-4, 21
Ketterman, Grace H(orst) 1926- ... CANR-22
Earlier sketch in CA 106
Kettl, Donald F. 1952- ... CANR-34
Earlier sketch in CA 111
Kettle, Arnold (Charles) 1916-1986 ... CANR-6
Obituary ... 121
Earlier sketch in CA 9-12R
Kettle, Jocelyn Pamela 1934- ... 25-28R
Kettle, Pamela
See Kettle, Jocelyn Pamela
Kettle, Peter
See Glover, Denis (James Matthews)
Kettner, Elmer Arthur 1906-1964 ... 1-4R
Kettner, James H(arold) 1944- ... 89-92
Ketton-Cremer, Robert Wyndham 1906-1969 Obituary ... 106
Keucher, William F. 1918- ... 49-52
Keuls, Eva C(lara) 1928- ... 123
Keuls, Hans 1910-1985 Obituary ... 117
Keun, Irmgard 1905-1982 ... DLB 69
Kevan, Martin 1949- ... CANR-27
Earlier sketch in CA 110
Keve, Paul W(illard) 1913- ... CANR-6
Earlier sketch in CA 9-12R
Kevern, Barbara
See Shepherd, Donald (Lee)
Keveson, Peter 1919-1986 Obituary ... 118
Kevill-Davies, Sally 1945- ... 138
Kevin, Jodi
See Lawrence, Jodi
Kevles, Barbara (Lynne) 1940- ... 128
Kevles, Bettyann Holtzmann 1938- ... CANR-72
Earlier sketches in CA 69-72, CANR-11, 27
See also SATA 23
Kevles, Daniel J(erome) 1939- ... CANR-27
Earlier sketch in CA 85-88
Kevorkian, Jack 1928- ... 161
Kew, Stephen 1947- ... 103
Kewes, Karol 1924- ... 9-12R
Key, Alexander (Hill) 1904-1979 ... CANR-6
Obituary ... 89-92
Earlier sketch in CA 5-8R
See also SATA 8
See also SATA-Obit 23
Key, Ellen 1849-1926 ... TCLC 65
Key, Jack D(ayton) 1934- ... CANR-30
Earlier sketch in CA 112
Key, Mary Ritchie 1924- ... CANR-38
Earlier sketches in CA 45-48, CANR-1, 16
Key, Ted
See Key, Theodore
Key, Theodore 1912- ... 13-16R
Key, V(aldimer) O(rlando), Jr. 1908-1963 ... 1-4R
Key, William H(enry) 1919- ... 45-48
Key, Wilson Bryan 1925- ... CANR-2
Earlier sketch in CA 49-52
Keyber, Conny
See Fielding, Henry
Keyes, Alan L(ee) 1950- ... 155
Keyes, Claire J. 1938- ... 126
Keyes, Daniel 1927- ... CANR-54
Earlier sketches in CA 17-20R, CANR-10, 26
See also AAYA 23
See also CLC 80
See also DA
See also DAC
See also DAM MST, NOV
See also SATA 37
Keyes, Edward 1927- ... 103
Keyes, Evelyn 1919(?)- ... 85-88
Keyes, Fenton 1915- ... 107
See also SATA 34
Keyes, Frances Parkinson 1885-1970 ... CANR-59
Obituary ... 25-28R
Earlier sketches in CA 5-8R, CANR-7
Keyes, Jessica 1950- ... 145
Keyes, Kenneth S(cofield), Jr. 1921-1995 ... CANR-24
Obituary ... 150
Earlier sketches in CA 17-20R, CANR-8
Keyes, Langley Carleton, Jr. 1938- ... 25-28R
Keyes, Margaret Frings 1929- ... 57-60
Keyes, Noel
See Keightley, David N(oel)
Keyes, Ralph 1945- ... CANR-47
Earlier sketches in CA 49-52, CANR-3
Keyfitz, Nathan 1913- ... CANR-10
Earlier sketch in CA 25-28R
Keyhoe, Donald E(dward) 1897-1988 Obituary . 127
Keyishian, Harry 1932- ... 61-64
Keylock, Leslie R(obert) 1933- ... 117
Keylor, Arthur (W.) 1920(?)-1981 Obituary ... 104
Keylor, William R(obert) 1944- ... 89-92
Keyne, Gordon
See Bedford-Jones, H(enry James O'Brien)
Keynes, Edward 1940- ... 120
Keynes, SirGeoffrey Langdon 1887-1982 ... 103
Obituary ... 107
See also DLB 201
Keynes, John Maynard 1883-1946 ... 163
Brief entry ... 114
Earlier sketch in CA 162
See also DLBD 10
See also TCLC 64
Keynes, Richard Darwin 1919- ... 114
Keys, Ancel 1904- ... 61-64
Keys, Donald (Fraser) 1924- ... 115
Keys, Ivor Christopher Banfield 1919- ... 103
Keys, John D. 1938- ... 9-12R
Keys, Kerry Shawn 1946- ... 145
Keys, Thomas Edward 1908- ... CAP-1
Earlier sketch in CA 11-12
Keyser, Daniel J. 1935- ... 121
Keyser, (George) Gustave 1910- ... 77-80
Keyser, Lester Joseph 1943- ... 105
Keyser, Marcia 1933- ... 116
See also SATA 42
Keyser, Samuel Jay 1935- ... 106
Keyser, Sarah
See McGuire, Leslie (Sarah)
Keyser, William R(ussell) 1916- ... 69-72
Keyserling, Eduard von 1855-1918 ... DLB 66
Keyserling, Leon H. 1908-1987 ... 61-64
Obituary ... 123
Keyserlingk, Robert H. 1933- ... 131
Keyssar, Alexander 1947- ... 121
Keyt, David (Alan) 1930- ... 1-4R
Kezdi, Paul 1914- ... 77-80
Kezys, Algimantas 1928- ... CANR-31
Earlier sketches in CA 81-84, CANR-14
Kgositsile, Aneb
See House, Gloria
Kgositsile, Keorapetse (William) 1938- ... CANR-25
Earlier sketch in CA 77-80
See also BW 2
Khadduri, Majid 1909- ... CANR-2
Earlier sketch in CA 1-4R
Khaketla, B. M.
See Khaketla, B(ennett) Makalo
Khaketla, B(ennett) Makalo 1913- Brief entry .. 113
Khalatbari, Adel-Sultan 1901(?)-1977 Obituary ... 69-72
Khalid, Farooq 1950- ... 159
Khalid, Mansour 1931- ... 160
Khalsa, Dayal Kaur 1943-1989 ... 137
See also CLR 30
See also MAICYA
See also SATA 62
Khalvati, Mimi 1944- ... 142
Khan, Adib 1949- ... 168
Khan, Badrul H(uda) 1958- ... 168
Khan, Hasan-Uddin 1947- ... 157
Khan, Hassina
See Ali Khan, Shirley
Khan, Ismith 1925- ... DLB 125
Khan, Lurey 1927- ... 97-100
Khan, Mahmood H(asan) 1937- ... 143
Khan, Mohammed Masud R. 1927(?)-1989 ... 129
Khan, (Chaudhri) Muhammad Zafrulla 1893-1985 Obituary ... 117
Khan, Pir Vilayat Inayat
See Inayat-Khan, Pir Vilayat
Khan, Riaz M. 1945- ... 142
Khan, Shirley Ali
See Ali Khan, Shirley
Khan, Taidje 1920(?)-1985 Obituary ... 117
Khan, Zillur Rahman 1938- ... CANR-14
Earlier sketch in CA 41-44R
Khanna, J(aswant) L(al) 1925- ... 21-24R
Khanshendel, Chiron
See Rose, Wendy
Kharasch, Robert Nelson 1926- ... 103
Khare, Narayan Bhaskar 1882- ... CAP-1
Earlier sketch in CA 11-12
Kharitonov, Yevgeny 1941(?)-1981 Obituary ... 104
Khatchadourian, Haig 1925- ... 53-56
Khatena, Joe
See Khatena, Joseph
Khatena, Joseph 1925- ... CANR-39
Earlier sketch in CA 116
Khaytov, Nikolay 1919- ... DLB 181
Khayyam, Omar 1048-1131 ... DAM POET
See also PC 8
Khazanov, Anatoly M. 1937- ... 154
Khazzoom, J. Daniel 1932- ... 17-20R
Khedouri, Franklin 1944- ... 101
Kheirabadi, Masoud 1951- ... 142
Khemir, Sabiha ... SATA 87
Khemnitser, Ivan Ivanovich 1745-1784 ... DLB 150
Kher, Inder Nath 1933- ... 93-96
Khera, S(ucha) S(ingh) 1903- ... 13-16R
Kheraskov, Mikhail Matveevich 1733-1807 ... DLB 150
Kherdian, David 1931- ... CANR-39
Earlier sketch in CA 21-24R
See also CAAS 2
See also CLC 6, 9
See also CLR 24
See also JRDA
See also MAICYA
See also SATA 16, 74
Khilnani, Sunil 1960- ... 149
Khlebnikov, Velimir
See Khlebnikov, Viktor Vladimirovich
See also TCLC 20
Khlebnikov, Viktor Vladimirovich 1885-1922 Brief entry ... 117
See also Khlebnikov, Velimir
Khodasevich, Vladislav (Felitsianovich) 1886-1939 Brief entry ... 115
See also TCLC 15
Khomaini, Ayatullah Sayyed Ruholla Mousavi
See Khomeini, Ruhollah (Mussavi)
Khomeini, Ayatollah
See Khomeini, Ruhollah (Mussavi)
Khomeini, Ayatollah Ruhollah
See Khomeini, Ruhollah (Mussavi)
Khomeini, Imam
See Khomeini, Ruhollah (Mussavi)
Khomeini, Ruhollah (Mussavi) 1900(?)-1989 ... CANR-43
Obituary ... 128
Earlier sketch in CA 117
Khornak, Lucille 1953- ... 110
Khoroche, Peter (Andrew) 1947- ... 136
Khosla, G(opal) D(as) 1901- ... 113
Khouri, Fred J(ohn) 1916- ... 25-28R
Khouri, Mounah A(bdallah) 1918- ... 114
Khristov, Boris 1945- ... DLB 181
Khrushchev, Nikita Sergeyevich 1894-1971 ... 112
Khrushchev, Sergei (Nikitich) 1935- ... 136
Khubchandani, Lachman M(ulchand) 1932- ... 128
Khumeini, Ruhollah
See Khomeini, Ruhollah (Mussavi)
Khush, Gurdev S. 1935- ... 155
Khvostov, Dmitrii Ivanovich 1757-1835 ... DLB 150

Khwaja, Waqas Ahmad 1952-...160
Kiam, Victor K(ermit) (II) 1926-...158
Kiang, Ying-cheng...17-20R
Kianto, Ilmari 1874-1970 Obituary...29-32R
Kibbe, Pat (Hosley)...125
See also SATA 60
Kibbee, Roland 1914-1984 Obituary...113
Kibera, Leonard 1940(?)-...153
See also BW 2
Kiberd, Declan 1951-...157
Kibler, James Everett, Jr. 1944-...CANR-46
Earlier sketches in CA 105, CANR-22
Kibler, Robert J(oseph) 1934-...29-32R
Kibler, William W. 1942-...37-40R
Kibre, Pearl 1902(?)-1985...165
Obituary...116
Kicknosway, Faye 1936-...CANR-7
Earlier sketch in CA 57-60
Kicza, John E(dward) 1947-...120
Kidd, Adam 1802(?)-1831...DLB 99
Kidd, Aline H(alstead) 1922-...17-20R
Kidd, Charles (William) 1952-...134
Kidd, David Lundy 1926-...CANR-1
Earlier sketch in CA 1-4R
Kidd, Elisabeth
See Triegel, Linda (Jeanette)
Kidd, Harry 1917-...29-32R
Kidd, I(an) G(ray) 1922-...132
Kidd, J(ames) R(obbins) 1915-...CANR-3
Earlier sketch in CA 5-8R
Kidd, J. Roby
See Kidd, J(ames) R(obbins)
Kidd, Janet (Gladys) Aitken
1908(?)-1988 Obituary...127
Kidd, Paul 1963-...150
Kidd, Ronald 1948-...CANR-39
Earlier sketch in CA 116
See also SATA 42, 92
Kidd, Russ
See Donson, Cyril
Kidd, Virginia 1921-...CANR-10
Earlier sketch in CA 65-68
Kidd, Walter E. 1917-...21-24R
Kiddell, John 1922-...29-32R
See also SATA 3
Kiddell-Monroe, Joan 1908-...CAP-1
Earlier sketch in CA 13-14
See also SATA 55
Kidder, Barbara (Ann) 1933-...41-44R
Kidder, J(onathan) Edward (Jr.) 1922-...107
Kidder, Rushworth M(oulton) 1944-...77-80
Kidder, Tracy 1945-...CANR-61
Earlier sketches in CA 109, CANR-40
Interview in...109
See also BEST 90:1
See also DLB 185
See also MTCW 1
Kiddle, Lawrence B(ayard) 1907-...33-36R
Kidman, Fiona (Judith) 1940-...159
Kidner, (Frank) Derek 1913-...41-44R
Kidney, Dorothy Boone 1919-...CANR-3
Earlier sketch in CA 9-12R
Kidney, Walter C(urtis) 1932-...CANR-19
Earlier sketches in CA 53-56, CANR-4
Kido, Koichi 1890(?)-1977 Obituary...69-72
Kidwell, Carl 1910-...SATA 43
Kidwell, Catherine (Arthelia) 1921-...109
Kidwell, Clara Sue 1941-...150
Kieckhefer, Richard 1946-...93-96
Kiefer, Bill
See Kiefer, Tillman W.
Kiefer, Christie Weber 1937-...103
Kiefer, Frederick (Paul) 1945-...114
Kiefer, Irene 1926-...CANR-11
Earlier sketch in CA 69-72
See also SATA 21
Kiefer, Louis Sr. 1936-...131
Kiefer, Tillman W. 1898-...CAP-2
Earlier sketch in CA 29-32
Kiefer, Warren 1929-...77-80
Kiefer, William Joseph 1925-...1-4R
Kiehle, John Alva 1930- Brief entry...115
Kiehtreiber, Albert Conrad
See Guetersloh, Albert Paris
Kiell, Norman 1916-...CANR-5
Earlier sketch in CA 13-16R
Kiell, Paul J(acob) 1930-...124
Brief entry...118
Kielland, Alexander Lange 1849-1906 Brief
entry...104
See also TCLC 5
Kiely, Benedict 1919-...CANR-2
Earlier sketch in CA 1-4R
See also CLC 23, 43
See also DLB 15
Kiely, Robert (James) 1931-...131
Kiemel, Ann
See Anderson, Ann Kiemel
Kieniewicz, Stefan 1907-...29-32R
Kienzle, William X(avier) 1928-...CANR-59
Earlier sketches in CA 93-96, CANR-9, 31
Interview in...CANR-31
See also CAAS 1
See also CLC 25
See also DAM POP
See also MTCW 1
Kiepper, Shirley Morgan 1933-...37-40R
See also Morgan, Shirley
Kieran, John Francis 1892-1981...CANR-62
Obituary...105
Earlier sketch in CA 101
See also DLB 171
Kieran, Sheila 1930-...97-100
Kierland, Joseph Scott 1937-...61-64
Kierman, Frank Algerton, Jr. 1914-...125
Kiernan, Ben 1953-...147
Kiernan, Brian 1937-...107
Kiernan, Robert F(rancis) 1940-...115
Kiernan, Thomas...113
Kiernan, (E.) V(ictor) G(ordon) 1913-...CANR-11
Earlier sketch in CA 25-28R
Kiernan, Walter 1902-1978 Obituary...73-76
Kies, Cosette (Nell) 1936-...124
Kieschnick, Michael Hall 1953-...139
Kiesel, Stanley 1925-...104
See also SATA 35
Kieser, Rolf 1936-...77-80
Kiesler, Charles A(dolphus) 1934-...CANR-10
Earlier sketch in CA 25-28R
Kiesler, Kate (A.) 1971-...SATA 90
Kiesler, Sara B(eth) 1940-...CANR-16
Earlier sketch in CA 25-28R
Kiesling, Christopher (Gerald) 1925-1986 CANR-12
Obituary...120
Earlier sketch in CA 29-32R
Kiesling, Herbert J. 1934-...45-48
Kieslowski, Krzysztof 1941-1996...147
Obituary...151
Kiessling, Nicolas K. 1936-...151
Kiester, Edwin, Jr. 1927-...110
Kieszak, Kenneth 1939-...89-92
Kiev, Ari 1933-...CANR-3
Earlier sketch in CA 9-12R
Kiev, I. Edward 1905-1975 Obituary...104
Kiger, Joseph Charles 1920-...125
Kihl, Armand
See Ald, Roy A(llison)
Kihl, Young Whan 1932-...127
Kihlman, Christer Alfred 1930-...159
Kihss, Peter (Frederick) 1912(?)-1984 Obituary...114
Kijewski, Karen 1943-...161
Kijima Hajime
See Kojima Shozo
Kikel, Rudy (John) 1942-...117
Kiker, B(ill) F(razier) 1937-...61-64
Kiker, Douglas 1930-1991...65-68
Obituary...135
Kikukawa, Cecily H(arder) 1919-...113
See also SATA 44
See also SATA-Brief 35
Kilander, H(olger) Frederick 1900-1969...CAP-2
Earlier sketch in CA 17-18
Kilborne, Virginia Wylie 1912-...21-24R
Kilbourn, Jonathan 1916(?)-1976 Obituary...65-68
Kilbourn, William (Morley) 1926-...CANR-11
Earlier sketch in CA 21-24R
Kilbracken, John (Raymond Godley) 1920-...5-8R
Kilburn, Henry
See Rigg, H(enry Hemmingway) K(ilburn)
Kilburn, Robert E(dward) 1931-...17-20R
Kilby, Clyde Samuel 1902-1986...CANR-9
Obituary...120
Earlier sketch in CA 13-16R
Kilby, Peter 1935-...CANR-17
Earlier sketch in CA 25-28R
Kildahl, John P. 1927-...89-92
Kildahl, Phillip A. 1912-...21-24R
Kildare, Maurice
See Richardson, Gladwell
Kilduff, (Mary) Dorrell 1901-...5-8R
Kile, Joan 1940-...SATA 78
Kiley, Dan (Edward) 1942-1996...132
Obituary...151
Brief entry...125
Interview in...132
Kiley, Frederick 1932-...CANR-15
Earlier sketch in CA 37-40R
Kiley, Jed
See Kiley, John Gerald
See also DLB 4
Kiley, John Gerald 1889-1962 Obituary...112
See also Kiley, Jed
Kiley, Margaret A(nn) 1920-...53-56
Kilgallen, Dorothy (Mae) 1913-1965 Obituary...89-92
Kilgallen, James L. 1888(?)-1982 Obituary...108
Kilgo, James 1941-...127
Kilgore, Bernard 1908-1967...DLB 127
Kilgore, James C(olumbus) 1928-1988...33-36R
Obituary...127
Kilgore, John
See Paine, Lauran (Bosworth)
Kilgore, Kathleen 1946-...CANR-27
Earlier sketch in CA 109
See also SATA 42
Kilgore, William J(ackson) 1917-...45-48
Kilgour, John Graham 1937-...105
Kilgour, Raymond L(incoln) 1903-...CAP-1
Earlier sketch in CA 13-16
Kilian, Crawford 1941-...CANR-56
Earlier sketches in CA 105, CANR-22
See also SATA 35
Kilina, Patricia
See Warren, Patricia Nell
Kiljunen, Kimmo (Roobert) 1951-...132
Killam, (Gordon) Douglas 1930-...CANR-3
Earlier sketch in CA 49-52
Killan, Gerald 1945-...147
Killanin, Lord
See Morris, Michael
Killdeer, John
See Mayhar, Ardath
Kille, Mary F. 1948-...33-36R
Killebrew, Harmon (Clayton, Jr.) 1936-...159
Killeen, Jacqueline 1931-...61-64
Killen, Linda 1945-...118
Killenberg, George A(ndrew) 1917-...77-80
Killens, John Oliver 1916-1987...CANR-26
Obituary...123
Earlier sketch in CA 77-80
See also CAAS 2
See also BW 2
See also CLC 10
See also DLB 33
Killham, Edward L(eo) 1926-...147
Killian, Ida F(aith) 1910-...65-68
Killian, James R(hyne), Jr. 1904-1988...97-100
Obituary...124
Killian, Larry
See Wellen, Edward (Paul)
Killian, Lewis M(artin) 1919-...9-12R
Killian, Ray A. 1922-...21-24R
Killien, Christi 1956-...SATA 73
Killigrew, Anne 1660-1685...DLB 131
Killigrew, Thomas 1612-1683...DLB 58
Killilea, Marie (Lyons) 1913-...5-8R
See also SATA 2
Killingback, Julia 1944-...SATA 63
Killinger, George G(lenn) 1908-...102
Killinger, John 1933-...81-84
Killingley, Carl A(rthur) 1918-...118
Killingsworth, Frank R.
1873(?)-1976 Obituary...65-68
Killion, Katheryn L. 1936-...17-20R
Killion, Ronald G(ene) 1931-...61-64
Killorin, Joseph I(gnatius) 1926-...111
Killough, (Karen) Lee 1942-...CANR-66
Earlier sketches in CA 89-92, CANR-15, 32
See also SATA 64
Killy, Jean-Claude 1943- Brief entry...115
Kilmann, Peter R(ichard) 1945-...118
Kilmartin, Edward J(ohn) 1923-...17-20R
Kilmer, (Alfred) Joyce 1886-1918 Brief entry...120
See also DLB 45
Kilmer, Kenton 1909-1995...1-4R
Obituary...148
Kilmer, Nicholas (John) 1941-...CANR-56
Earlier sketch in CA 129
Kilmer, Val 1959-...160
Kilmister, C(live) W(illiam) 1924-...119
Kilodney, Crad 1948-...CANR-37
Earlier sketch in CA 115
Kilpatrick, Andrew 1943-...140
Kilpatrick, Carroll 1913-...69-72
Kilpatrick, F(ranklin) P(eirce) 1920-...21-24R
Kilpatrick, James Jackson 1920-...CANR-1
Earlier sketch in CA 1-4R
See also AITN 1, 2
Kilpatrick, Nancy 1946-...150
Kilpatrick, Sarah
See Underwood, Mavis Eileen
Kilpatrick, Terrence 1920-...81-84
Kilreon, Beth
See Walker, Barbara (Jeanne) K(erlin)
Kilroy, James F(rancis) 1935-...133
Kilroy, Thomas 1934-...53-56
Kilson, Marion 1936-...37-40R
Kilson, Martin Luther, Jr. 1931-...103
Kilvert, B. Cory, Jr. 1930-...45-48
Kilwardby, Robert 1215(?)-1279...DLB 115
Kilworth, Garry (D.) 1941-...CANR-67
Earlier sketch in CA 128
See also SATA 94
Kim
See Simenon, Georges (Jacques Christian)
Kim, Byoung-lo Philo 1960-...143
Kim, C(hong-) I(k) Eugene 1930-...37-40R
Kim, Chin W. 1936-...37-40R
Kim, Chong Lim 1937-...114
Kim, Choong Soon 1938-...116
Kim, David U(ngchon) 1932-...109
Kim, Elaine H(aikyung) 1942-...130
Kim, Hakjoon 1943-...147
Kim, Hee-Jin 1927-...106
Kim, Helen 1899-1970...CAP-1
Earlier sketch in CA 13-16
See also SATA 98
Kim, Hyung-chan 1938-...57-60
Kim, Hyun-Hee 1962-...164
Kim, Ilpyong J(ohn) 1931-...53-56
Kim, In S(oo) 1943-...164
Kim, Jung-Gun 1933-...53-56
Kim, K(wan) H(o) 1936-...29-32R
Kim, Kwan-Bong 1936-...37-40R
Kim, Kyung-Won 1936-...29-32R
Kim, Richard C(hong) C(hin) 1923-...29-32R
Kim, Richard E. 1932-...5-8R
Kim, Samuel S(oonki) 1935-...104
Kim, Se-Jin 1933-...53-56
Kim, Seung Hee 1936-...29-32R
Kim, Sung Bok 1932- Brief entry...113
Kim, Yong Choon 1935-...57-60
Kim, Yong-ik 1920-...17-20R
Kim, Yoon Hough 1934-1976...33-36R
Kim, Young Hum 1920-...21-24R
Kimball, Arthur G(ustaf) 1927-...41-44R
Kimball, Dean 1912-...69-72
Kimball, Frank
See Paine, Lauran (Bosworth)
Kimball, Gayle 1943-...CANR-58
Earlier sketch in CA 107
See also SATA 90
Kimball, George 1943-...53-56
Kimball, John P. 1941-...CANR-2
Earlier sketch in CA 45-48
Kimball, John W(ard) 1931-...CANR-15
Earlier sketch in CA 93-96
Kimball, Meredith M. 1944-...154
Kimball, Michael 1949-...120
Kimball, Nancy
See Upson, Norma
Kimball, Penn T(ownsend) 1915-...CANR-18
Earlier sketch in CA 102
Kimball, Philip 1941-...117
Kimball, Ralph
See Paine, Lauran (Bosworth)
Kimball, Richard B(urleigh) 1816-1892...DLB 202
Kimball, Richard Laurance 1939-...CANR-7
Earlier sketch in CA 53-56
Kimball, Robert (Eric) 1939-...159
Brief entry...106
Kimball, Roger 1953-...CANR-64
Earlier sketch in CA 136
Kimball, Solon T(oothaker) 1909-...21-24R
Kimball, Spencer L(evan) 1918-...CANR-1
Earlier sketch in CA 1-4R
Kimball, Spencer W(oolley) 1895-1985...CANR-39
Obituary...117
Earlier sketch in CA 45-48
Kimball, Stanley B(uchholz) 1926-...CANR-26
Earlier sketches in CA 17-20R, CANR-10
Kimball, Warren F. 1935-...25-28R
Kimball, Yeffe 1914-1978...SATA 37
Kimberley, Hugh
See Morland, Nigel
Kimberly, Gail...81-84
Kimble, Daniel Porter 1934-...41-44R
Kimble, David 1921-...13-16R
Kimble, George H(erbert) T(inley) 1908-...108
Kimble, Gregory A(dams) 1917-...21-24R
Kimbrell, Grady 1933-...33-36R
Kimbro, Harriet
See Kofalk, Harriet
Kimbro, Jean
See Kimbro, John M.
Kimbro, John M. 1929-...CANR-2
Earlier sketch in CA 45-48
Kimbrough, Emily 1899-1989...17-20R
Obituary...127
See also SATA 2
See also SATA-Obit 59
Kimbrough, Katheryn
See Kimbro, John M.
Kimbrough, Ralph B(radley) 1922-...73-76
Kimbrough, Richard B(enito) 1931-...41-44R
Kimbrough, Robert (Alexander III) 1929-...CANR-6
Earlier sketch in CA 9-12R
Kimbrough, Sara Dodge 1901-...93-96
Kimche, David...103
Kimenye, Barbara 1940(?)-...101
Kimes, Beverly Rae 1939-...CANR-47
Brief entry...107
Earlier sketch in CA 122
Kimmel, Arthur S(andor) 1930-...41-44R
Kimmel, Douglas C(harles) 1943-...53-56
Kimmel, Eric A. 1946-...CANR-3
Earlier sketch in CA 49-52
See also SATA 13, 80
Kimmel, Jo 1931-...CANR-4
Earlier sketch in CA 53-56
Kimmel, Margaret Mary 1938-...124
See also SATA 43
See also SATA-Brief 33
Kimmel, Melvin 1930-...25-28R
Kimmel, Michael S(cott) 1951-...153
Kimmel, Stanley (Preston)
1894(?)-1982 Obituary...109
Kimmel, William (Breyfogel)
1908-1982 Obituary...109
Kimmelman, Elaine 1925-...111
Kimmelman, Leslie (Grodinsky) 1958-...132
See also SATA 85
Kimmens, Andrew C(harles) 1942-...124
Kimmerling, Baruch 1939-...141
Kimmey, John Lansing 1922- Brief entry...108
Kimmich, Christoph M(artin) 1939-...69-72
Kimmich, Flora (Graham Horne) 1939-...106
Kimpel, Ben D(rew) 1915-...57-60
Kimpel, Ben F(ranklin) 1905-...1-4R
Kimrey, Grace (Evelyn) Saunders 1910-...CANR-24
Earlier sketch in CA 45-48
Kim Ronyoung
See Hahn, Gloria
Kimura, Jiro 1949-...85-88
Kincaid, Alan
See Rikhoff, James C.
Kincaid, Jamaica 1949-...CANR-59
Earlier sketches in CA 125, CANR-47
See also AAYA 13
See also BLC 2
See also BW 2
See also CLC 43, 68
See also DAM MULT, NOV
See also DLB 157
Kincaid, James R(ussell) 1937-...CANR-15
Earlier sketch in CA 65-68
Kincaid, Suzanne (Moss) 1936-...9-12R
Kinch, Sam E., Jr. 1940-...45-48
Kincheloe, Raymond McFarland 1909-...61-64
Kincher, Jonni 1949-...147
See also SATA 79
Kincl, (Gladys) Kay Owens 1955-...106
Kindall, Alva Frederick 1906-...1-4R
Kindem, Gorham A(nders) 1948-...CANR-51
Earlier sketch in CA 125
Kinder, Faye 1902-...5-8R
Kinder, Gary 1946-...109
Kinder, James S. 1895-...13-16R
Kinder, Kathleen
See Potter, Kathleen Jill
Kinder, Marsha 1940-...CANR-15
Earlier sketch in CA 41-44R
Kinderlehrer, Jane 1913-...106
Kindl, Patrice 1951-...149
See also SATA 82
Kindleberger, Charles P(oor) II 1910-...CANR-36
Earlier sketches in CA 73-76, CANR-12

Kindley, Jeffrey (Bowman) 1945- ... 130
Brief entry ... 125
Interview in ... 130
Kindred, Alton R(ichard) 1922- ... 109
Kindred, Leslie W(ithrow) 1905- ... 41-44R
Kindred, Wendy (Good) 1937- ... 37-40R
See also SATA 7
Kindregan, Charles P(eter) 1935- ... CANR-10
Earlier sketch in CA 21-24R
Kinealy, Christine 1956- ... 149
Kineji, Maborushi
See Gibson, Walter B(rown)
Kiner, Ralph (McPherran) 1922- ... 161
Kinert, Reed (Charles) 1911(?)- ... 107
Kines, Pat Decker 1937- ... 65-68
See also SATA 12
Kines, Thomas Alvin 1922- ... 13-16R
Kines, Tom
See Kines, Thomas Alvin
King, Adam
See Hoare, Robert J(ohn)
King, Adele Cockshoot 1932- ... CANR-8
Earlier sketch in CA 13-16R
King, Alan 1927- ... 89-92
King, Alec Hyatt
See King, Alexander Hyatt
King, Alexander 1909- ... 110
King, Alexander Hyatt 1911-1995 ... 124
Obituary ... 148
King, Alfred M. 1933- ... 25-28R
King, Algin B(raddy) 1927- ... CANR-15
Earlier sketch in CA 41-44R
King, Alison
See Martini, Teri
King, Alvy L(eon) 1932- ... 33-36R
King, (Maria) Anna 1964- ... SATA 72
King, Annette 1941- ... 33-36R
King, Anthony (Stephen) 1934- ... 17-20R
King, Archdale Arthur 1890-1972 ... CAP-1
Earlier sketch in CA 17-18
King, Ben F(rank) 1937- ... 57-60
King, Bernard 1946- ... 156
King, Bert T(homas) 1927- ... 45-48
King, Betty (Alice) 1919- ... 103
King, Betty Patterson 1925- ... 9-12R
King, Billi
See Caulder, Colline
King, Billie Jean 1943- ... CANR-10
Earlier sketch in CA 53-56
See also SATA 12
King, Bruce (?)-1976 Obituary ... 61-64
King, Bruce A(lvin) 1933- ... CANR-41
Earlier sketches in CA 53-56, CANR-4, 19
King, C(lyde) Richard 1924- ... CANR-11
Earlier sketch in CA 69-72
King, Captain Charles
See King, Charles
King, Carol Soucek 1943- ... 145
King, Cecil
See King, Cecil H(armsworth)
King, Cecil H(armsworth) 1901-1987 ... 110
Obituary ... 122
King, Charles 1844-1933 Brief entry ... 122
See also DLB 186
King, Charles (Lester) 1922- ... 57-60
King, Charles R. 1947- ... 148
King, Christopher (L.) 1945- ... SATA 84
King, Clarence (Rivers) 1842-1901 Brief entry ... 110
See also DLB 12
King, Clarence 1884(?)-1974 Obituary ... 53-56
King, (David) Clive 1924- ... 104
See also SATA 28
King, Clyde S(tuart) 1919- ... 17-20R
King, Colin 1943- ... SATA 76
King, Coretta Scott 1927- ... CANR-27
Earlier sketch in CA 29-32R
See also BW 1
King, Cynthia 1925- ... CANR-36
Earlier sketch in CA 29-32R
See also SATA 7
King, Daniel P(atrick) 1942- ... CANR-4
Earlier sketch in CA 53-56
King, David 1943- ... 168
King, Deborah 1950- ... CANR-31
Earlier sketch in CA 112
King, (William) Dennis 1941- ... 130
King, Donald B. 1913- ... 13-16R
King, Edith W(eiss) 1930- ... CANR-14
Earlier sketch in CA 33-36R
King, Edmund J(ames) 1914- ... CANR-2
Earlier sketch in CA 5-8R
King, Edmund L(udwig) 1914- ... CANR-49
Earlier sketches in CA 33-36R, CANR-13
King, Edward L. 1928- ... 81-84
King, Elizabeth 1953- ... SATA 83
King, Elizabeth A.
See Abravanel, Elizabeth
King, Florence 1936- ... CANR-41
Earlier sketches in CA 57-60, CANR-7
See also AITN 1
See also DLBY 85
King, Francis (Henry) 1923- ... CANR-33
Earlier sketches in CA 1-4R, CANR-1
See also CLC 8, 53
See also DAM NOV
See also DLB 15, 139
See also MTCW 1
King, Francis Edward 1931- ... 61-64
King, Francis P(aul) 1922- ... 13-16R
King, Frank A.
See King, Franklin Alexander
King, Frank H(enry) H(aviland) 1926- ... CANR-44
Earlier sketch in CA 119
King, Frank O. 1883-1969 Obituary ... 89-92
See also SATA-Obit 22
King, Franklin Alexander 1923- ... 45-48
King, Frederick Murl 1916- ... CANR-2
Earlier sketch in CA 5-8R
King, General Charles
See King, Charles
King, Glen D. 1925- ... 9-12R
King, Grace (Elizabeth) 1852(?)-1932 Brief entry ... 116
See also DLB 12, 78
King, Graham (Peter) 1930- ... 132
King, Harold 1898-1990 Obituary ... 132
King, Harold 1945- ... CANR-7
Earlier sketch in CA 57-60
King, Harriet Hamilton 1840-1920 ... DLB 199
King, Hedley 1949- ... 141
King, Helen H(ayes) 1937- ... 33-36R
King, Henry 1592-1669 ... DLB 126
King, Homer W. 1907- ... CAP-1
Earlier sketch in CA 13-16
King, Horace Maybray
See Maybray-King, Horace
King, Irving H(enry) 1935- ... 89-92
King, Ivan R(obert) 1927- ... 89-92
King, Jack
See Dowling, Allen
King, James 1942- ... CANR-49
Earlier sketch in CA 121
King, James Cecil 1924- ... CANR-14
Earlier sketch in CA 41-44R
King, James G. 1898(?)-1979 Obituary ... 89-92
King, James T(errell) 1933- ... 37-40R
King, James W. 1920- ... 9-12R
King, Janet Kauffman 1935- Brief entry ... 110
King, Jere Clemens 1910- ... 5-8R
King, Jerome Babcock 1927- ... 103
King, (Frederick) Jerry 1941- ... 97-100
King, Jerry P. 1935- ... 139
King, Joan (M.) 1930- ... 123
King, Joe 1909(?)-1979 Obituary ... 85-88
King, John
See McKeag, Ernest L(ionel)
King, John Edward 1947- ... 102
King, John L(afayette) 1917- ... 41-44R
King, John N. 1945- ... CANR-32
Earlier sketch in CA 113
King, John O(zias) 1923- Brief entry ... 108
King, John Q. Taylor 1921- ... 25-28R
King, Jonny 1965- ... 162
King, Josie
See Germany, (Vera) Jo(sephine)
King, Joyce
See Ching, Julia (Chia-yi)
King, K. DeWayne (Dewey) 1925- ... 13-16R
King, Katherine Callen 1942- ... CANR-56
Earlier sketch in CA 127
King, Kathleen (Marie) 1948- ... 114
King, Kennedy
See Brown, George Douglas
King, Kimball 1934- ... CANR-57
Earlier sketches in CA 110, CANR-31
King, Larry 1933- ... 139
Brief entry ... 111
King, Larry L. 1929- ... CANR-24
Earlier sketch in CA 13-16R
See also MTCW 1
See also SATA 66
King, Laurie R. 1952- ... CANR-63
Earlier sketch in CA 140
See also SATA 88
King, Leila Pier 1882-1981 Obituary ... 105
King, Leslie John 1934- Brief entry ... 106
King, Lester S(now) 1908- ... 33-36R
King, Louise W(ooster) ... CANR-7
Earlier sketch in CA 13-16R
King, Marcet (Alice Hines) 1922- ... 25-28R
King, Margaret L(eah) 1947- ... CANR-50
Earlier sketch in CA 123
King, Marian 1900(?)-1986 ... CANR-2
Obituary ... 118
Earlier sketch in CA 5-8R
See also SATA 23
See also SATA-Obit 47
King, Marjorie Cameron 1909- ... 33-36R
King, Mark 1945- ... 61-64
King, Martha L. 1918- ... 127
Brief entry ... 109
King, Martin Luther Sr. 1899-1984 ... 125
Obituary ... 117
See also BW 1
King, Martin Luther, Jr. 1929-1968 ... CANR-44
Earlier sketches in CAP-2, CA 25-28, CANR-27
See also BLC 2
See also BW 2
See also CLC 83
See also DA
See also DAB
See also DAC
See also DAM MST, MULT
See also MTCW 1
See also SATA 14
See also WLCS
King, Mary (Elizabeth) 1940- ... 160
King, Mary Ellen 1958- ... 158
See also SATA 93
King, Mary Louise 1911- ... 21-24R
King, Michael
See Buse, Renee
and Kahane, Meir (David)
King, Michael J(ulius) 1941- ... 119
King, Morton Brandon 1913- ... 102
King, Noel Q(uixote) 1922- ... CANR-19
Earlier sketches in CA 1-4R, CANR-4
King, Norman A.
See Tralins, S(andor) Robert
King, O. H. P. 1902- ... 1-4R
King, Patricia 1930- ... 5-8R
King, Paul
See Drackett, Phil(ip Arthur)
King, Paula
See Downing, Paula E.
King, Pauline 1917- ... 119
King, Peggy Cameron
See King, Marjorie Cameron
King, Peter 1925- ... 125
King, Peter (John) 1940-1989 Obituary ... 127
King, Philip 1904- ... 103
King, Philip B(urke) 1903-1987 ... 125
Obituary ... 122
King, Philip J. 1925- ... 149
King, Preston (Theodore) 1936- ... CANR-26
Earlier sketches in CA 21-24R, CANR-10
King, Ray A(iken) 1933- ... 21-24R
King, Richard A(ustin) 1929- ... 21-24R
King, Richard G. 1922- ... 37-40R
King, Richard H. 1942- ... CANR-40
Earlier sketch in CA 77-80
King, Richard L(ouis) 1937- ... CANR-1
Earlier sketch in CA 45-48
King, Robert B. 1949- ... 125
King, Robert Charles 1928- ... 17-20R
King, Robert G. 1929- ... 21-24R
King, Robert H(arlen) 1935- ... 45-48
King, Robert L. 1950- ... 77-80
King, Robert R(ay) 1942- ... CANR-8
Earlier sketch in CA 61-64
King, Robin 1919- ... 5-8R
King, Roger (Frank Graham) 1947- ... 139
King, Roma Alvah, Jr. 1914- ... CANR-1
Earlier sketch in CA 1-4R
King, Ronald (Wilfred) 1914- ... 107
King, Rufus 1917- ... 25-28R
King, Ruth Rodney
See Manley, Ruth Rodney King
King, Spencer B(idwell), Jr. 1904- ... CAP-1
Earlier sketch in CA 17-18
King, Stanley H(all) 1921- Brief entry ... 110
King, Stella ... 69-72
King, Stephen (Edwin) 1947- ... CANR-52
Earlier sketches in CA 61-64, CANR-1, 30
See also AAYA 1, 17
See also BEST 90:1
See also CLC 12, 26, 37, 61, 113
See also DAM NOV, POP
See also DLB 143
See also DLBY 80
See also JRDA
See also MTCW 1
See also SATA 9, 55
See also SSC 17
King, Stephen W(illiam) 1947- ... 61-64
King, Steve
See King, Stephen (Edwin)
King, T(homas) J(ames) 1925- ... 37-40R
King, Tabitha (Jane) 1949- ... CANR-30
Earlier sketch in CA 105
King, Teri 1940- ... 89-92
King, Terry Johnson 1929-1978 ... 17-20R
Obituary ... 77-80
King, Thomas 1943- ... 144
See also CLC 89
See also DAC
See also DAM MULT
See also DLB 175
See also NNAL
See also SATA 96
King, Thomas M(ulvihill) 1929- ... 57-60
King, Tony 1947- ... 109
See also SATA 39
King, Veronica
See King, Florence
King, Vincent
See Vinson, Rex Thomas
King, Willard L. 1893-1981 ... 1-4R
Obituary ... 103
King, William Donald Aelian 1910- ... 89-92
King, William R(ichard) 1938- ... CANR-8
Earlier sketch in CA 21-24R
King, Wilma 1942- ... 141
King, Winston L(ee) 1907- ... 41-44R
King, Woodie, Jr. 1937- ... CANR-25
Earlier sketch in CA 103
See also BW 2
See also DLB 38
Kingdon, Frank 1894-1972 Obituary ... 33-36R
Kingdon, John W(ells) 1940- ... 25-28R
Kingdon, Robert M(cCune) 1927- ... 21-24R
Kingdon, Roger 1891-1984 Obituary ... 113
Kingery, Robert E(rnest) 1913-1978 ... 9-12R
Obituary ... 103
King-Farlow, John 1932- ... 111
King-Hall, Magdalen 1904-1971 ... CAP-1
Obituary ... 29-32R
Earlier sketch in CA 9-10
King-Hall, (William) Stephen (Richard) 1893-1966 ... 5-8R
King-Hamilton, Alan 1904- ... 130
King-Hele, Desmond (George) 1927- ... CANR-66
Earlier sketches in CA 29-32R, CANR-14, 32
Kinghorn, A(lexander) M(anson) 1926- ... 93-96
Kinghorn, Kenneth Cain 1930- ... CANR-57
Earlier sketches in CA 41-44R, CANR-14, 31
Kinglake, Alexander William 1809-1891 ... DLB 55, 166
Kingley, Charles 1819-1875 ... DLB 178
Kingman, Dong (Moy Shu) 1911- ... 112
See also SATA 44
Kingman, Lee
See Natti, (Mary) Lee
See also CLC 17
See also SAAS 3
See also SATA 1, 67
Kingman, Russ 1917- ... CANR-17
Earlier sketch in CA 101
Kingry, Philip L. 1942- ... 53-56
Kingsbury, Arthur 1939- ... 29-32R
Kingsbury, Donald (MacDonald) 1929- ... 124
Kingsbury, Jack Dean 1934- ... 37-40R
Kingsbury, John M(erriam) 1928- ... CANR-6
Earlier sketch in CA 13-16R
Kingsbury, Robert C(arrick) 1924- ... CANR-2
Earlier sketch in CA 1-4R
Kingsbury-Smith, Joseph 1908- ... 133
Kingsland, Leslie William 1912- ... 69-72
See also SATA 13
Kingsland, Sharon E. 1951- ... 124
Kingsley, April 1941- ... 140
Kingsley, Charles 1819-1875 . DLB 21, 32, 163, 190
See also YABC 2
Kingsley, Charlotte Mary
See Hanshew, Thomas W.
Kingsley, Daniel T(hain) 1932- ... 117
Kingsley, Emily Perl 1940- ... 107
See also SATA 33
Kingsley, G. Thomas 1936- ... 149
Kingsley, Henry 1830-1876 ... DLB 21
Kingsley, Mary Henrietta 1862-1900 ... DLB 174
Kingsley, Michael J. 1918(?)-1972 Obituary . 37-40R
Kingsley, Sidney 1906-1995 ... 85-88
Obituary ... 147
See also CLC 44
See also DLB 7
Kingsley-Smith, Terence 1940- ... 57-60
Kingsmill, Hugh 1889-1949 ... DLB 149
King-Smith, Dick 1922- ... CANR-48
Earlier sketches in CA 105, CANR-22
See also CLR 40
See also MAICYA
See also SATA 47, 80
See also SATA-Brief 38
Kingsnorth, George W(illiam) 1924- ... 5-8R
Kingsolver, Barbara 1955- ... CANR-60
Brief entry ... 129
Earlier sketch in CA 134
Interview in ... 134
See also AAYA 15
See also CLC 55, 81
See also DAM POP
Kingston, Albert J(ames) 1917- ... 21-24R
Kingston, Jeremy
See Betancourt, John (Gregory)
Kingston, Jeremy Henry Spencer 1931- ... 103
Kingston, Maxine (Ting Ting) Hong 1940- ... CANR-38
Earlier sketches in CA 69-72, CANR-13
Interview in ... CANR-13
See also AAYA 8
See also CLC 12, 19, 58
See also DAM MULT, NOV
See also DLB 173
See also DLBY 80
See also MTCW 1
See also SATA 53
See also WLCS
Kingston, Syd
See Bingley, David Ernest
Kingston, (Frederick) Temple 1925- ... CANR-12
Earlier sketch in CA 33-36R
Kingston, William Henry Giles 1814-1880 . DLB 163
Kingston-Mann, Esther ... 112
King-Stoops, Joyce 1923- ... 81-84
Kington, Miles (Beresford) 1941- ... 130
Kininmonth, Christopher 1917- ... 53-56
Kinkade, Richard P(aisley) 1939- ... CANR-31
Earlier sketches in CA 37-40R, CANR-14
Kinkaid, Matt
See Adams, Clifton
Kinkaid, Wyatt E.
See Jennings, Michael Glenn
Kinkead, Eugene (Francis) 1906- ... CANR-1
Earlier sketch in CA 1-4R
Kinkead, Gwen 1951- ... 144
Kinkead-Weekes, Mark 1931- ... CANR-56
Earlier sketch in CA 124
Kinkley, Jeffrey C(arroll) 1948- ... CANR-57
Earlier sketch in CA 125
Kinley, Phyllis (Elaine Gillespie) 1930- ... 1-4R
Kinloch, A. Murray 1923- ... 103
Kinmonth, Earl H. 1946- ... 107
Kinnaird, Clark 1901-1983 ... CANR-1
Obituary ... 111
Earlier sketch in CA 45-48
Kinnaird, John (William) 1924-1980 ... 124
Obituary ... 97-100
Kinnaird, William M(cKee) 1928- ... 101
Kinnamon, Keneth 1932- ... 37-40R
Kinnan, Mary Lewis 1763-1848 ... DLB 200
Kinnane, John F. 1921-1987 Obituary ... 123
Kinnard, Douglas 1921- ... CANR-14
Earlier sketch in CA 77-80
Kinnear, Elizabeth K. 1902- ... CAP-2
Earlier sketch in CA 33-36
Kinnear, Michael 1937- ... 37-40R
Kinneavy, James Louis 1920- ... 69-72
Kinneir, (Richard) Jock 1917- ... 121
Kinnell, Galway 1927- ... CANR-66
Earlier sketches in CA 9-12R, CANR-10, 34
Interview in ... CANR-34
See also CLC 1, 2, 3, 5, 13, 29
See also DLB 5
See also DLBY 87
See also MTCW 1
Kinney, Arthur F(rederick) 1933- ... CANR-14
Earlier sketch in CA 37-40R
Kinney, C. Cle(land) 1915- ... 9-12R
See also SATA 6
Kinney, Francis S(herwood) 1915-1993 ... 106
Obituary ... 140

Kinney, Harrison 1921- CANR-52
Earlier sketch in CA 1-4R
See also SATA 13
Kinney, James (Joseph) 1942- 120
Kinney, James R(oser)
1902(?)-1978 Obituary 81-84
Kinney, Jean Stout 1912- 9-12R
See also SATA 12
Kinney, John F. 1914- 150
Kinney, Lucien Blair 1895-1971 .... CAP-2
Earlier sketch in CA 23-24
Kinney, Peter 1943- 73-76
Kinney, Richard 1924(?)-1979 Obituary 85-88
Kinnicutt, Susan Sibley 1926- 77-80
Kinnison, William A(ndrew) 1932- 21-24R
Kinor, Jehuda
See Rothmuller, Aron Marko
Kinoshita Junji 1914- 124
Kinoy, Arthur 1920- 143
Kinross, Lord
See Balfour, (John) Patrick Douglas
Kinsbruner, Jay 1939- 25-28R
Kinsel, Paschal 1895(?)-1976 Obituary 69-72
Kinsella, James 1959- 134
Kinsella, Paul L. 1923- 21-24R
Kinsella, Thomas 1928- CANR-15
Earlier sketch in CA 17-20R
See also CLC 4, 19
See also DLB 27
See also MTCW 1
Kinsella, W(illiam) P(atrick) 1935- CANR-66
Earlier sketches in CA 97-100, CANR-21, 35
Interview in CANR-21
See also CAAS 7
See also AAYA 7
See also CLC 27, 43
See also DAC
See also DAM NOV, POP
See also MTCW 1
Kinsey, Alfred C(harles) 1894-1956 Brief entry . 115
Kinsey, Barry Allan 1931- 17-20R
Kinsey, Elizabeth
See Clymer, Eleanor
Kinsey, Helen 1948- .... SATA 82
Kinsey-Jones, Brian
See Ball, Brian N(eville)
Kinsey-Warnock, Natalie 1956- .... SATA 71
Kinsley, D(aniel) A(llan) 1939- 45-48
Kinsley, James 1922-1984 .... CANR-2
Obituary 114
Earlier sketch in CA 1-4R
Kinsolving, Charles McIlvaine
1893-1984 Obituary 114
Kinstler, Clysta (Joyce) 1931- 154
Kinstler, Everett Raymond 1926- 33-36R
Kinter, Judith 1928- 109
Kintgen, Eugene R(obert), Jr. 1942- 116
Kintner, Earl W(ilson) 1912- CANR-1
Earlier sketch in CA 45-48
Kintner, Robert Edmonds 1909-1980 Obituary . 103
Kintner, William R(oscoe) 1915-1997 ..... CANR-6
Obituary 156
Earlier sketch in CA 5-8R
Kinton, Jack F(ranklin) 1939- CANR-7
Earlier sketch in CA 57-60
Kintsch, Walter 1932- 29-32R
Kinyatti, Maina wa
See wa Kinyatti, Maina
Kinzel, Dorothy 1950- .... SATA 57
Kinzel, Dottie
See Kinzel, Dorothy
Kinzer, Betty 1922- 21-24R
Kinzer, Donald Louis 1914- 53-56
Kinzer, H(arless) M(ahlon)
1923(?)-1975 Obituary 57-60
Kinzer, Nora Scott 1936- 126
Brief entry 106
Kinzer, Stephen 1951- 142
Kinzie, Mary 1944- 133
Kiparsky, Valentin (Julius Alexander) 1904- . 17-20R
Kipfer, Barbara Ann 1954- 134
Kiple, Kenneth F(ranklin) 1939- CANR-46
Earlier sketch in CA 120
Kipling, (Joseph) Rudyard 1865-1936 .... CANR-33
Brief entry 105
Earlier sketch in CA 120
See also CDBLB 1890-1914
See also CLR 39
See also DA
See also DAB
See also DAC
See also DAM MST, POET
See also DLB 19, 34, 141, 156
See also MAICYA
See also MTCW 1
See also PC 3
See also SATA 100
See also SSC 5
See also TCLC 8, 17
See also WLC
See also YABC 2
Kiplinger, Austin H(untington) 1918- 57-60
Kiplinger, Willard Monroe
1891-1967 Obituary 89-92
Kipnis, Aaron R. 1948- 137
Kipnis, Claude 1938-1981 107
Obituary 103
Kipnis, Kenneth 1943- 129
Kipp, Rita Smith 1948- 147
Kippax, Frank
See Needle, Jan
Kippax, Janet 1926- 97-100
Kippax, John
See Hynam, John Charles
Kippenhahn, Rudolf 1926- 130
Kipphardt, Heinar 1922-1982 89-92
Obituary 108
See also DLB 124
Kippley, John F(rancis) 1930- 29-32R
Kippley, Sheila K. 1939- 61-64
Kipps, Harriet C(lyde) 1926- 124
Kiraly, Bela (Kalman) 1912- CANR-8
Earlier sketch in CA 61-64
Kiraly, Marie
See Bergstrom, Elaine
Kiraly, Sherwood 1949- 158
Kiratli, Cemile
See Schimmel, Annemarie (Brigitte)
Kirby, (George) Blaik 1928- 77-80
Kirby, D(avid) P(eter) 1936- 25-28R
Kirby, David G. 1942- 101
Kirby, David K(irk) 1944- 53-56
See also SATA 78
Kirby, Douglas J. 1929- 25-28R
Kirby, E(dward) Stuart 1909- CANR-22
Earlier sketches in CA 13-16R, CANR-7
Kirby, Emily B(aruch) 1929- 117
Kirby, F(rank) E(ugene) 1928- 65-68
Kirby, Gilbert W(alter) 1914- 103
Kirby, Jack Temple 1938- 25-28R
Kirby, James
See Kirby, James C(ordell), Jr.
Kirby, James C(ordell), Jr. 1928-1989 Obituary . 130
Kirby, Jean
See Robinson, Chaille Howard (Payne)
Kirby, Jean
See McDonnell, Virginia B(leecker)
Kirby, John B(yron) 1938- 105
Kirby, John R. 1951- 146
Kirby, M(ary) Sheelah Flanagan 1916- 5-8R
Kirby, Margaret
See Bingley, Margaret (Jane)
Kirby, Margaret
See Bingley, Margaret (Jane)
Kirby, Mark
See Floren, Lee
Kirby, Rollin 1875-1952 Brief entry 118
Kirby, Susan E. 1949- .... SATA 62
Kirby, Thomas Austin 1904- 5-8R
Kirby, William 1817-1906 .... DLB 99
Kirch, Patrick V(inton) 1950- 143
Kircher, Athanasius 1602-1680 .... DLB 164
Kirchhofer, Alfred H. 1892(?)-1985 Obituary ... 117
Kirchhoff, Frederick (Thomas) 1942- 111
Kirchner, Audrey Burie 1937- CANR-12
Earlier sketch in CA 73-76
Kirchner, Emil J. 1942- 130
Kirchner, Glenn 1930- 29-32R
Kirchner, Walther 1905- CANR-1
Earlier sketch in CA 1-4R
Kirchwey, Freda 1893-1976 93-96
Obituary 61-64
Kirdar, Uner 1933- 21-24R
Kireevsky, Ivan Vasil'evich 1806-1856 .... DLB 198
Kirgis, Frederic L(ee), Jr. 1934- 125
Kiriakopoulos, George C. 1925- 161
Kirk, Alexandra
See Woods, Sherryl
Kirk, Clara M(arburg) 1898-1976 .... CAP-1
Obituary 69-72
Earlier sketch in CA 17-18
Kirk, Cooper 1920- 116
Kirk, David 1935- 29-32R
Kirk, Donald 1938- 37-40R
Kirk, Donald R. 1935- CANR-47
Earlier sketch in CA 57-60
Kirk, Elizabeth D(oan) 1937- 53-56
Kirk, G(eoffrey) S(tephen) 1921- CANR-2
Earlier sketch in CA 5-8R
Kirk, George (Eden) 1911- 1-4R
Kirk, H(enry) David 1918- CANR-11
Earlier sketch in CA 17-20R
Kirk, Irene 1926- CANR-6
Earlier sketch in CA 5-8R
Kirk, Irina
See Kirk, Irene
Kirk, James A(lbert) 1929- 37-40R
Kirk, Janice E(mily) 1935- 146
Kirk, Jeremy
See Powell, Richard (Pitts)
Kirk, Jerome (Richard) 1937- 49-52
Kirk, John Esben 1905-1975 Obituary 57-60
Kirk, John Foster 1824-1904 .... DLB 79
Kirk, John T(homas) 1933- 49-52
Kirk, John W. 1932- 129
Kirk, Lydia (Chapin) 1896-1984 Obituary 114
Kirk, Marshall (Kenneth) 1957- 135
Kirk, Mary Wallace 1889- 57-60
Kirk, Matthew
See Wells, Angus
Kirk, Michael
See Knox, William
Kirk, Pauline (M.) 1942- 157
Kirk, Philip
See Levinson, Leonard
Kirk, R.
See Dietrich, Richard V(incent)
Kirk, Richard (Edmund) 1931- 13-16R
Kirk, Robert Warner (?)-1980 .... 9-12R
Obituary 103
Kirk, Roger E(dward) 1930- 41-44R
Kirk, Rudolf 1898-1989 Obituary 130
Kirk, Russell (Amos) 1918-1994 .... CANR-60
Obituary 145
Earlier sketches in CA 1-4R, CANR-1, 20
Interview in CANR-20
See also CAAS 9
See also AITN 1
See also MTCW 1
Kirk, Ruth (Kratz) 1925- CANR-9
Earlier sketch in CA 13-16R
See also SATA 5
Kirk, Samuel A(lexander) 1904-1996 ...... CANR-1
Obituary 152
Earlier sketch in CA 45-48
Kirk, T(homas) H(obson) 1899- CAP-2
Earlier sketch in CA 23-24
Kirk, Ted
See Bank, Theodore P(aul) II
Kirk, Wayne
See Kock, Winston E(dward)
Kirkaldy, John F(rancis) 1908-1990 Obituary ... 132
Kirkbride, Norma Jean 1924(?)-1983 Obituary .. 111
Kirkbride, Ronald (de Levington) 1912- ... CANR-2
Earlier sketch in CA 1-4R
Kirkconnell, Watson 1895-1977 125
Obituary 108
See also DLB 68
Kirkendall, Don(ald M.) 1923- 49-52
Kirkendall, Lester A(llen) 1903- CANR-5
Earlier sketch in CA 1-4R
Kirkendall, Richard Stewart 1928- 77-80
Kirk-Greene, Anthony (Hamilton Millard) 1925- .....
CANR-54
Earlier sketches in CA 61-64, CANR-11, 27
Kirk-Greene, Anthony H. M.
See Kirk-Greene, Anthony (Hamilton Millard)
Kirk-Greene, Christopher Walter Edward
1926- 13-16R
Kirkham, E. Bruce 1938- 37-40R
Kirkham, George L. 1941- 77-80
Kirkham, Michael 1934- 25-28R
Kirkland, Bryant M(ays) 1914- 21-24R
Kirkland, Caroline M. 1801-1864 ..... DLB 3, 73, 74
See also DLBD 13
Kirkland, Edward Chase 1894-1975 ...... CANR-6
Obituary 104
Earlier sketch in CA 1-4R
Kirkland, Joseph 1830-1893 .... DLB 12
Kirkland, Martha 166
Kirkland, Sally 1912-1989 Obituary 129
Kirkland, Wallace W. 1891(?)-1979 Obituary . 89-92
Kirkland, Will
See Hale, Arlene
Kirkman, Francis fl. 1652-1680 .... DLB 170
Kirkman, James S(pedding) 1906-1989 93-96
Obituary 128
Kirkpatrick, Clayton 1915- .... DLB 127
Kirkpatrick, Diane 1933- 53-56
Kirkpatrick, Donald L(ee) 1924- 41-44R
Kirkpatrick, Doris (Upton) 1902- 93-96
Kirkpatrick, Dow (Napier) 1917- 21-24R
Kirkpatrick, Evron M(aurice) 1911- 57-60
Kirkpatrick, Frank 1924- 108
Kirkpatrick, Ivone Augustine 1897-1964 .... CAP-1
Earlier sketch in CA 9-10
Kirkpatrick, Jean 1923- 81-84
Kirkpatrick, Jeane D(uane) J(ordan) 1926- . CANR-7
Earlier sketch in CA 53-56
Kirkpatrick, John 1905-1991 45-48
Obituary 136
Kirkpatrick, Lyman B(ickford), Jr. 1916- 33-36R
Kirkpatrick, Oliver (Austin) 1911- 49-52
Kirkpatrick, Ralph 1911-1984 49-52
Obituary 112
Kirkpatrick, Samuel A(lexander) III 1943- ... 41-44R
Kirkpatrick, Sidney D(ale) 1955- 136
Kirkpatrick, Smith 1922- 49-52
Kirkup, James 1918- CANR-2
Earlier sketch in CA 1-4R
See also CAAS 4
See also CLC 1
See also DLB 27
See also SATA 12
Kirkus, Virginia
See Glick, Virginia Kirkus
Kirkwood, Annie 1937- 154
Kirkwood, Byron (Ray) 1946- 141
Kirkwood, Ellen Swan 1904- 25-28R
Kirkwood, G(ordon) M(acdonald) 1916- 93-96
Kirkwood, James 1930(?)-1989 .... CANR-40
Obituary 128
Earlier sketches in CA 1-4R, CANR-6
See also AITN 2
See also CLC 9
Kirkwood, Kenneth P. 1899-1968 .... 37-40R
Kirn, Ann Minette 1910- 93-96
Kirn, Walter 1962- 142
Kirp, David L(eslie) 1944- 109
Kirsch, Anthony Thomas 1930- 103
Kirsch, Arthur C(lifford) 1932- 13-16R
Kirsch, Charlotte 1942- 109
Kirsch, George B(enson) 1945- 151
Kirsch, Herbert 1924(?)-1978 Obituary 104
Kirsch, Irving 1943- 136
Kirsch, James Isaac 1901-1989 Obituary 128
Kirsch, Jonathan 1949- 164
Kirsch, Leonard Joel 1934-1977 .... 37-40R
Kirsch, Paul John 1914- 108
Kirsch, Robert R. 1922-1980 .... CANR-13
Obituary 102
Earlier sketch in CA 33-36R
Kirsch, Sarah 1935- .... DLB 75
Kirschen, Leonard 1908-1983 Obituary 109
Kirschenbaum, Aaron 1926- 33-36R
Kirschenbaum, Howard 1944- 89-92
Kirschner, Allen 1930- 29-32R
Kirschner, Don S(tuart) 1928- 148
Kirschner, Fritz
See Bickers, Richard (Leslie) Townshend
Kirschner, Joseph 1930- 121
Kirschner, Linda Rae 1939- 33-36R
Kirschten, Ernest 1902-1974 .... CAP-1
Obituary 49-52
Earlier sketch in CA 11-12
Kirshenbaum, Binnie .... SATA 79
Kirshenbaum, Jerry 1938- 107
Kirshenblatt-Gimblett, Barbara 1942- CANR-15
Earlier sketch in CA 81-84
Kirshner, Gloria Ifland 41-44R
Kirshner, Sidney
See Kingsley, Sidney
Kirsner, Douglas 1947- 77-80
Kirsner, Robert 1921- 21-24R
Kirst, Hans Hellmut 1914-1989 104
Obituary 128
See also DLB 69
Kirst, Michael W(eile) 1939- CANR-49
Earlier sketches in CA 45-48, CANR-24
Kirstein, George G(arland) 1909-1986 Obituary . 118
Kirstein, Lincoln (Edward) 1907-1996 128
Obituary 151
Brief entry 117
Kirsten, Grace 1900- 104
Kirtland, G. B.
See Hine, Al(fred Blakelee)
and Hine, Sesyle Joslin
Kirtland, Helen Johns 1890(?)-1979 Obituary . 89-92
Kirtland, Kathleen 1945- 65-68
Kirvan, John J. 1932- CANR-10
Earlier sketch in CA 21-24R
Kirwan, Albert D(ennis) 1904-1971 .... CANR-4
Earlier sketch in CA 1-4R
Kirwan, Laurence Patrick 1907- CANR-70
Earlier sketch in CA 1-4R
Kirwan, Molly (Morrow) 1906- CAP-1
Earlier sketch in CA 13-14
Kirwin, Harry Wynne 1911-1963 .... 1-4R
Kirzner, Israel M(ayer) 1930- CANR-3
Earlier sketch in CA 1-4R
Kis, Danilo 1935-1989 .... CANR-61
Obituary 129
Brief entry 109
Earlier sketch in CA 118
See also CLC 57
See also DLB 181
See also MTCW 1
Kisamore, Norman D(ale) 1928- 5-8R
Kiser, Clyde V(ernon) 1904- 25-28R
Kiser, Lisa J. 1949- 114
Kish, Eleanor M(ary) 1924- .... SATA 73
Kish, Ely
See Kish, Eleanor M(ary)
Kish, G. Hobab
See Kennedy, Gerald (Hamilton)
Kish, George 1914- CANR-1
Earlier sketch in CA 1-4R
Kish, Kathleen Vera 1942- CANR-12
Earlier sketch in CA 69-72
Kish, Leslie 1910- CAP-1
Earlier sketch in CA 19-20
Kishel, Patricia G(unter) 1948- 117
Kishida, Eriko 1929- CANR-7
Earlier sketch in CA 53-56
See also SATA 12
Kishon, Ephraim 1924- CANR-2
Earlier sketch in CA 49-52
Kishtainy, Khalid 1929- 115
Kisiel, Marie 1929- 112
Kisinger, Grace Gelvin (Maze) 1913-1965 ... CAP-1
Earlier sketch in CA 13-14
See also SATA 10
Kisker, George W. 1912- 21-24R
Kismaric, Carole 1942- CANR-23
Earlier sketches in CA 33-36R, CANR-8
Kisner, James (Martin, Jr.) 1947- CANR-35
Earlier sketch in CA 113
Kisor, Henry (Du Bois) 1940- 73-76
Kissam, Edward 1943- 61-64
Kissane, John M(ichael) 1928- 53-56
Kissane, Leedice McAnelly 1905- CAP-2
Earlier sketch in CA 25-28
Kissel, Susan S. 1943- 162
Kissen, Fan(ny) 1904- CAP-1
Earlier sketch in CA 13-16
Kissick, Gary 1946- 118
Kissin, Eva H. 1923- 29-32R
See also SATA 10
Kissinger, Henry A(lfred) 1923- CANR-66
Earlier sketches in CA 1-4R, CANR-2, 33
See also MTCW 1
Kissinger, Warren S(tauffer) 1922- 116
Kissling, Dorothy (Hight) 1904-1969 Obituary .. 105
Kissling, Fred R., Jr. 1930- 21-24R
Kiste, Robert Carl 1936- 61-64
Kister, Kenneth F. 1935- 25-28R
Kistiakowsky, George B(ogdan)
1900-1982 Obituary 108
Kistiakowsky, Vera 1928- 21-24R
Kistler, Mark O(liver) 1918- 77-80
Kistner, Robert William 1917- CANR-13
Earlier sketch in CA 61-64
Kita, Morio 1927- .... DLB 182
Kitagawa, Daisuke 1910- CAP-2
Earlier sketch in CA 17-18
Kitagawa, Joseph M. 1915- CANR-2
Earlier sketch in CA 1-4R
Kitamura, Satoshi 1956- 165
See also SATA 62, 98
Kitano, Harry H. L. 1926- 29-32R
Kitao, T(imothy) Kaori 1933- 106
Kitcat, Mabel Greenhow 1859-1922 ...... DLB 135
Kitch, Sally L. 1946- 140
Kitchel, Denison 1908- 105
Kitchell, Webster (Lardner) 1931- 165
Kitchen, Bert
See Kitchen, Herbert Thomas
Kitchen, Helen (Angell) CANR-47
Earlier sketches in CA 9-12R, CANR-8, 23
Kitchen, Herbert Thomas 1940- 138
See also SATA 70

Kitchen, Herminie B(roedel) 1901-1973 ..... CAP-1
Earlier sketch in CA 17-18
Kitchen, Judith 1941- 147
Kitchen, Martin 1936- CANR-51
Earlier sketches in CA 61-64, CANR-10, 26
Kitchen, Paddy 1934- CANR-21
Earlier sketch in CA 25-28R
Kitchener, Richard Frank 1941- 124
Kitcher, Philip 1947- 113
Kitchin, C. H. B. 1895-1967 ..... DLB 77
Kitchin, Laurence 1913- 104
Kite, Larry
See Schneck, Stephen
Kite, Pat 1940- 119
See also Kite, (L.) Patricia
See also SATA 78
Kite, (L.) Patricia 1940-
See Kite, Pat
See also SATA 78
Kiteley, Brian 1956- 132
Kitfield, James C. 1956- 147
Kitman, Marvin 1929- 101
Kitson, Jack William 1940- 25-28R
Kitson Clark, George Sydney Roberts 1900-1975 .. CANR-14
Earlier sketch in CA 21-24R
Kitt, Eartha (Mae) 1928- 77-80
Kitt, Sandra (E.) 1947- 146
Kitt, Tamara
See de Regniers, Beatrice Schenk (Freedman)
Kittelson, David James 1931-1989 119
Obituary 142
Kittinger, Jo S(usenbach) 1955- 161
See also SATA 96
Kittler, Glenn D. 1920(?)-1986 Obituary 119
Kitto, Crispin 1951- 119
Kitto, H(umphrey) D(avy) F(indley) 1897-1982 ..... CAP-1
Obituary 105
Earlier sketch in CA 11-12
Kittredge, William 1932- CANR-44
Earlier sketch in CA 111
Kittrie, Nicholas N(orbert Nehemiah) 1928- ... 81-84
Kitts, Thomas M(ichael) 1955- 155
Kituomba
See Odaga, Asenath (Bole)
Kitzinger, Ernst 1912- 108
Kitzinger, Sheila 1929- 37-40R
See also SATA 57
Kitzinger, U(we) W(ebster) 1928- CANR-1
Earlier sketch in CA 1-4R
Kivenson, Gilbert 1920- 112
Kivy, Peter Nathan 1934- 103
Kiyota, Minoru 1923- CANR-61
Earlier sketches in CA 113, CANR-32
Kizaki, Satoko
See Harada, Masako
Kizer, Carolyn (Ashley) 1925- CANR-70
Earlier sketches in CA 65-68, CANR-24
See also CAAS 5
See also CLC 15, 39, 80
See also DAM POET
See also DLB 5, 169
Kjelgaard, James Arthur 1910-1959 137
Brief entry 109
See also Kjelgaard, Jim
See also MAICYA
See also SATA 17
Kjelgaard, Jim
See Kjelgaard, James Arthur
See also JRDA
Kjome, June C(reola) 1920- 5-8R
Klaas, Joe 1920- CANR-12
Earlier sketch in CA 29-32R
Klaassen, Leo(nardus) H(endrik) 1920- .. CANR-26
Earlier sketches in CA 21-24R, CANR-11
Klaassen, Walter 1926- 115
Klabund 1890-1928 162
See also DLB 66
See also TCLC 44
Kladstrup, Don(ald) 1943- 77-80
Klafs, Carl E. 1911- 13-16R
Klagsbrun, Francine (Lifton) 21-24R
See also SATA 36
Klaiber, Jeffrey L. 1943- 85-88
Klaich, Dolores 1936- 49-52
Klaidman, Stephen 1938- 125
Klainikite, Anne
See Gehman, Betsy Holland
Klaits, Barrie 1944- 73-76
See also SATA 52
Klaits, Joseph (Aaron) 1942- 126
Klaj, Johann 1616-1656 ..... DLB 164
Klamer, Arjo 1953- 116
Klamkin, Charles 1923- 61-64
Klamkin, Lynn 1950- 45-48
Klamkin, Marian 1926- CANR-1
Earlier sketch in CA 49-52
Klammer, Martin (P.) 1957- 151
Klaniczay, Tibor 1923- 132
Klann, Margaret L. 1911- 77-80
Klaperman, Gilbert 1921- 49-52
See also SATA 33
Klaperman, Libby Mindlin 1921-1982 ..... 9-12R
Obituary 107
See also SATA 33
See also SATA-Obit 31
Klapp, Orrin E. 1915- 9-12R
Klapper, Charles F(rederick) 1905- CAP-1
Earlier sketch in CA 9-10
Klapper, Joseph T(homas) 1917-1984 Obituary 112
Klapper, M(olly) Roxana 1937- 53-56
Klapper, Marvin 1922- 17-20R
Klappert, Peter 1942- 33-36R
See also CLC 57
See also DLB 5
Klappholz, Kurt 1913-1975 Obituary 61-64
Klapthor, Margaret B(rown) 1922- 119
Klare, George R(oger) 1922- 5-8R
Klare, Hugh J(ohn) 1916- 103
Klare, Michael T(homas) 1942- 130
Klaren, Peter F(lindell) 1938- 57-60
Klarsfeld, Beate 1939- 65-68
Klarsfeld, Serge 1935- 115
Klass, Allan Arnold 1907- 65-68
Klass, David 1960- 152
See also AAYA 26
See also SATA 88
Klass, Morton 1927- CANR-5
Earlier sketch in CA 1-4R
See also SATA 11
Klass, Perri 1958- 126
Interview in 126
Klass, Philip J. 1919- 25-28R
Klass, Sheila Solomon 1927- CANR-37
Earlier sketches in CA 37-40R, CANR-13
See also SAAS 26
See also SATA 45, 99
Klass, Sholom 1916- 21-24R
Klassen, Albert D(ale, Jr.) 1931- 133
Klassen, Frank Roy 1910- 113
Klassen, Peter J(ames) 1930- CANR-1
Earlier sketch in CA 45-48
Klassen, Randolph Jacob 1933- 61-64
Klassen, Walter
See Klaassen, Walter
Klassen, William 1930- CANR-10
Earlier sketch in CA 25-28R
Klauber, John 1917-1981 Obituary 104
Klauber, Laurence M(onroe) 1883-1968 Obituary 105
Klauck, Daniel L. 1947- 69-72
Klauder, Francis John 1918- 53-56
Klaue, Lola Shelton 1903- 5-8R
Klause, Annette Curtis 1953- 147
See also AAYA 27
See also SATA 79
Klause, John L(ouis) 1943- 118
Klausler, Alfred P(aul) 1910- 21-24R
Klausmeier, Herbert J. 1915- CANR-20
Earlier sketches in CA 1-4R, CANR-5
Klausner, Abraham J. 1915- 108
Klausner, Lawrence D(avid) 1939- 110
Klausner, Margot 1905-1976(?) Obituary 61-64
Klausner, Samuel Z(undel) 1923- 17-20R
Klavans, J(odie) K(ay) 1956- 118
Klaveness, Jan O'Donnell 1939- 151
See also SATA 86
Klaw, Spencer 1920- 25-28R
Klawans, Harold L(eo) 1937-1998 106
Obituary 166
Klayman, Maxwell Irving 1917- 29-32R
Klebe, Charles Eugene 1907- CAP-2
Earlier sketch in CA 23-24
Klebe, Gene
See Klebe, Charles Eugene
Kleberger, Ilse 1921- CANR-39
Earlier sketches in CA 41-44R, CANR-15
See also SATA 5
Kleck, Gary 1951- 140
Klee, James B(utt) 1916- 109
Klee, Paul 1879-1940 155
Kleeberg, Irene (Flitner) Cumming 1932- . CANR-35
Earlier sketches in CA 61-64, CANR-12
See also SATA 65
Kleeblatt, Norman L(eslie) 1948- 128
Kleene, Stephen Cole 1909-1994 ..... 41-44R
Obituary 143
Klees, Fredric (Spang) 1901- CAP-2
Earlier sketch in CA 19-20
Klehr, Harvey 1945- CANR-69
Earlier sketches in CA 111, CANR-48
Kleiler, Frank Munro 1914- 89-92
Kleiman, Ed 1932- 135
Kleiman, Mark A. R. 1951- 138
Kleiman, Robert 1918- 13-16R
Klein, A(braham) M(oses) 1909-1972 101
Obituary 37-40R
See also CLC 19
See also DAB
See also DAC
See also DAM MST
See also DLB 68
Klein, Aaron E. 1930- CANR-19
Earlier sketch in CA 25-28R
See also SATA 45
See also SATA-Brief 28
Klein, Alan F(redric) 1911- 57-60
Klein, Alexander 1918- CANR-14
Earlier sketch in CA 5-8R
Klein, Allen 1938- 131
Klein, Anne Carolyn 148
Klein, Arnold William 1945- 37-40R
Klein, Bernard 1921- 17-20R
Klein, Bill 1945- ..... SATA 89
Klein, Carole (Doreen Honig) 1934- 168
Brief entry 118
Klein, Charlotte 1925- 101
Klein, Cornelis 1937- 145
Klein, Daniel M(artin) 1939- CANR-28
Earlier sketches in CA 61-64, CANR-11
Klein, Dave 1940- 89-92
Klein, David 1919- CANR-40
Earlier sketches in CA 1-4R, CANR-1, 18
See also SATA 59
Klein, David Ballin 1897- 41-44R
Klein, Donald C(harles) 1923- 25-28R
Klein, Donald F. 1928- 146
Klein, Donald W(alker) 1929- Brief entry 114
Klein, Doris F.
See Jonas, Doris F(rances)
Klein, Edward 1936- 69-72
Klein, Elizabeth 1939- 110
Klein, Erica Levy 1966- 151
Klein, Ernest 1899- CAP-2
Earlier sketch in CA 21-22
Klein, Fannie J. 1903-1984 Obituary 113
Klein, Fred 1932- Brief entry 115
Klein, Frederic Shriver 1904- 13-16R
Klein, Gene 1921- 126
Klein, George 1925- 140
Klein, Gerard 1937- CANR-48
Earlier sketch in CA 49-52
Klein, Gerda Weissmann 1924- 116
See also SATA 44
Klein, H(erbert) Arthur 13-16R
See also SATA 8
Klein, Herbert G(eorge) 1918- 165
Klein, Herbert Sanford 1936- CANR-37
Earlier sketches in CA 93-96, CANR-17
Klein, Heywood 1954(?)-1984 Obituary 111
Klein, Holger Michael 1938- 65-68
Klein, Isaac 1905- 57-60
Klein, Jeffrey B. 1948- 77-80
Klein, Joe
See Klein, Joseph
Klein, John J(acob) 1929- 17-20R
Klein, Joseph 1946- CANR-55
Earlier sketch in CA 85-88
Klein, Josephine (F. H.) 1926- 1-4R
Klein, Julius 1901-1984 Obituary 112
Klein, K. K.
See Turner, Robert (Harry)
Klein, Karl
See Sala, Charles
Klein, Kathleen Gregory 1946- 130
Klein, Lawrence R(obert) 1920- 152
Brief entry 116
Klein, Leonore (Glotzer) 1916- CANR-1
Earlier sketch in CA 1-4R
See also SATA 6
Klein, Marcus 1928- 9-12R
Klein, Martin A. 1934- 21-24R
Klein, Marymae E. 1917- CANR-40
Earlier sketch in CA 97-100
Klein, Maury 1939- 33-36R
Klein, Maxine 1934- CANR-10
Earlier sketch in CA 61-64
Klein, Melanie 1882-1960 Obituary 111
Klein, Milton M(artin) 1917- 93-96
Klein, Mina C(ooper) 1906-1979 ..... 37-40R
Obituary 133
See also SATA 8
Klein, Muriel Walzer 1920- 29-32R
Klein, Norma 1938-1989 ..... CANR-37
Obituary 128
Earlier sketches in CA 41-44R, CANR-15
Interview in CANR-15
See also AAYA 2
See also CLC 30
See also CLR 2, 19
See also JRDA
See also MAICYA
See also SAAS 1
See also SATA 7, 57
Klein, Philip A(lexander) 1927- 17-20R
Klein, Philip Shriver 1909-1993 ..... CANR-1
Obituary 140
Earlier sketch in CA 1-4R
Klein, Rachel S. 1953- 165
Klein, Randolph Shipley 1942- 73-76
Klein, Richard 1941- 158
Klein, Richard C. 1916(?)-1983 Obituary 111
Klein, Richard G. 1941- 120
Klein, Richard M. 1923- CANR-25
Earlier sketch in CA 108
Klein, Robin 1936- CANR-40
Earlier sketch in CA 116
See also AAYA 21
See also CLR 21
See also JRDA
See also MAICYA
See also SATA 55, 80
See also SATA-Brief 45
Klein, Rose (Shweitzer) 1918- 21-24R
Klein, Sherwin 1932- 147
Klein, Stanley 1930- 57-60
Klein, Stanley D. 1936- 77-80
Klein, Stuart M(arc) 1932- 134
Brief entry 111
Klein, Suzanne Marie 1940- 57-60
Klein, T(heodore) E(ibon) D(onald) 1947- CANR-44
Earlier sketch in CA 119
See also CLC 34
Klein, Ted U. 1926- 25-28R
Klein, Thomas D(icker) 1941- 61-64
Klein, Walter J(ulian) 1923- 69-72
Klein, Woody 1929- 13-16R
Klein, Zachary 1948- 135
Kleinbauer, W(alter) Eugene 1937- 37-40R
Kleinbaum, Abby Wettan 1943- 113
Kleinberg, Aviad M. 1957- 141
Kleinberg, Seymour 1933- 105
Kleine, Glen 1936- 73-76
Kleine-Ahlbrandt, W(illiam) Laird 1932- 29-32R
Kleiner, Art 1954- 124
Kleiner, Diana E. E. 1947- 144
Kleiner, Dick
See Kleiner, Richard Arthur
Kleiner, Fred S. 1948- 163
Kleiner, Richard Arthur 1921- 129
Kleinfeld, Gerald R. 1936- 103
Kleinfeld, Judith S. 1944- CANR-15
Earlier sketch in CA 77-80
Kleinfeld, Vincent A. 1907-1993 ..... CANR-10
Obituary 143
Earlier sketch in CA 17-20R
Kleinfield, N(athan) R(ichard) 1950- CANR-18
Earlier sketch in CA 97-100
Kleinfield, Sonny
See Kleinfield, N(athan) R(ichard)
Kleinhans, Theodore John 1924- 5-8R
Kleinke, Chris (Lynn) 1944- CANR-15
Earlier sketch in CA 89-92
Kleinman, Arthur (Michael) 1941- CANR-22
Earlier sketch in CA 105
Kleinman, Philip (Julian) 1932- 131
Kleinman, Ruth 1929- 125
Kleinmann, Jack H(enry) 1932- 21-24R
Kleinmuntz, Benjamin 1930- 33-36R
Kleinsasser, Lois 168
Kleinsmith, Bruce John 1942- 132
Kleinzahler, August 1949- CANR-51
Earlier sketch in CA 125
Kleiser, Randal 1946- 166
Kleist, Ewald von 1715-1759 ..... DLB 97
Kleist, Heinrich von 1777-1811 ..... DAM DRAM
See also DLB 90
See also SSC 22
Klejment, Anne M. 1950- CANR-17
Earlier sketch in CA 101
Klem, Kaye Wilson 1941- 89-92
Klement, Frank L(udwig) 1908- 9-12R
Klemer, Richard Hudson 1918-1972 ..... CANR-4
Obituary 37-40R
Earlier sketch in CA 5-8R
Klemesrud, Judy 1939(?)-1985 89-92
Obituary 117
Klemin, Diana 49-52
See also SATA 65
Klemke, E(lmer) D. 1926- CANR-10
Earlier sketch in CA 25-28R
Klemm, Edward G., Jr. 1910- 57-60
See also SATA 30
Klemm, Roberta K(ohnhorst) 1884- 61-64
See also SATA 30
Klemm, W(illiam) R(obert) 1934- 93-96
Klemperer, Otto 1885-1973 Obituary 116
Klempner, Irving M(ax) 1924- 53-56
Klempner, John 1898(?)-1972 Obituary 37-40R
Klempner, Joseph T(eller) 1940- 151
Klenbort, Charlotte
See Sempell, Charlotte
Klenicki, Leon 1930- 106
Klenk, Robert W(illiam) 1934- 29-32R
Klenz, William 1915- 5-8R
Klerer, Melvin 1926- 21-24R
Klerman, Lorraine V(ogel) 1929- CANR-15
Earlier sketch in CA 81-84
Klett, Guy S(oulliard) 1897- CAP-1
Earlier sketch in CA 13-14
Kleuser, Louise C(aroline) 1889(?)-1976 Obituary 65-68
Kleven, Elisa 1958- 143
See also SATA 76
Klevin, Jill Ross 1935- 111
See also SATA 39
See also SATA-Brief 38
Klewin, W(illiam) Thomas 1921- 29-32R
Kleyman, Paul (Fred) 1945- 57-60
Kleypas, Lisa 1964- 127
Kliban, B(ernard) 1935-1990 106
Obituary 132
See also SATA 35
See also SATA-Obit 66
Klibansky, Raymond 1905- Brief entry 117
Klieman, Charles 1940- 140
Klier, John Doyle 1944- 141
Kliever, Lonnie D(ean) 1931- CANR-47
Earlier sketch in CA 29-32R
Kliewer, Evelyn 1933- 101
Kliewer, Warren 1931- CANR-2
Earlier sketch in CA 45-48
Kliger, Hannah 1953- 149
Kligerman, Jack 1938- 85-88
Kligman, Ruth 1930- 101
Klima, Ivan 1931- CANR-50
Earlier sketches in CA 25-28R, CANR-17
See also CLC 56
See also DAM NOV
Kliman, Bernice W. 1933- 162
Kliman, Gilbert W(allace) 1929- 117
Klimas, Antanas 1924- 41-44R
Klimas, John E(dward) 1927-1975 Obituary 111
Klimek, David E(rnest) 1941- 89-92
Klimenko, Michael 1924- 73-76
Klimentov, Andrei Platonovich 1899-1951 Brief entry 108
See also Platonov, Andrei
Klimisch, Sister Mary Jane 1920- 17-20R
Klimo, Jake
See Klimo, Vernon
Klimo, Vernon 1914- 101
Klimowicz, Barbara 1927- 21-24R
See also SATA 10
Klin, George 1931- 53-56
Klinck, Carl Frederick 1908- 17-20R
Klinck, George Alfred 1903-1973 ..... 9-12R
Obituary 103
Klindt-Jensen, Ole 1918-1980 ..... CANR-10
Obituary 101
Earlier sketch in CA 21-24R
Kline, Christina Baker 1964- 161
See also SATA 101
Kline, George L(ouis) 1921- CANR-9
Earlier sketch in CA 17-20R
Kline, Linda 1940- 126
Kline, Lloyd W. 1931- 33-36R
Kline, Morris 1908-1992 ..... CANR-46
Obituary 139
Earlier sketches in CA 5-8R, CANR-2
Kline, Nancy Meadors 1946- 57-60

Kline, Nathan S(chellenberg) 1916-1983 . CANR-36
Obituary ... 109
Earlier sketch in CA 81-84
Kline, Otis Adelbert 1891-1946 ... 162
Kline, Peter 1936- ... 25-28R
Kline, Ronald R. 1947- ... 148
Kline, Stephen Edward 1945- ... 132
Kline, Steve
See Kline, Stephen Edward
Kline, Suzy 1943- ... 120
See also SATA 67, 99
See also SATA-Brief 48
Kline, Thomas J(efferson) 1942- ... 85-88
Klineberg, Stephen L(ouis) 1940- ... 77-80
Klinefelter, Walter 1899- ... CANR-3
Earlier sketch in CA 9-12R
Klineman, George A(lfred) 1947- ... 107
Kling, Robert E(dward), Jr. 1920- ... 29-32R
Kling, Simcha 1922- ... 13-16R
Kling, Woody 1926(?)-1988 Obituary ... 125
Klingelhofer, E(dwin) L(ewis) 1920- ... CANR-51
Earlier sketch in CA 124
Klingenstein, Susanne (Schloetelburg) 1959- ... 140
Klinger, Eric 1933- ... CANR-29
Earlier sketches in CA 33-36R, CANR-13
Klinger, Friedrich Maximilian von 1752-1831 ... DLB 94
Klinger, Kurt 1914- ... 17-20R
Klinghoffer, Arthur Jay 1941- ... 65-68
Klingman, Lawrence (Lewis)
1918-1986 Obituary ... 120
Klingsor the Magician
See Hartmann, Sadakichi
Klingstedt, Joe Lars 1938- ... 53-56
Klink, Johanna L. 1918- ... CANR-8
Earlier sketch in CA 61-64
Klinkenborg, Verlyn 1953- ... 139
Klinkowitz, Jerome 1943- ... CANR-1
Earlier sketch in CA 45-48
See also CAAS 9
Klipper, Miriam Z(eldner) ... 108
Klise, Eugene Storm 1908- ... 5-8R
Klise, Thomas S. 1928-1978 ... 57-60
Obituary ... 134
Klitzman, Robert (L.) 1958- ... 135
Klobuchar, James John 1928- ... 73-76
Klobuchar, Jim
See Klobuchar, James John
Kloepfer, Marguerite (Fonnesbeck) 1916- ... 97-100
Kloesel, Christian Johannes Wilhelm 1942- ... 113
Kloetzli, Walter, (Jr.) 1921- ... 1-4R
Klonglan, Gerald E(dward) 1936- ... 41-44R
Klonis, N. I.
See Clones, N(icholas) J.
Klonsky, Milton 1921(?)-1981 Obituary ... 105
Kloos, Peter 1936- ... 93-96
Klooster, Fred H. 1922- ... 1-4R
Klopf, Donald W(illiam) 1923- ... CANR-34
Earlier sketches in CA 89-92, CANR-15
Klopfer, Donald S(imon) 1902-1986 Obituary ... 119
See also DLBY 97
Klopfer, Peter H(ubert) 1930- ... 85-88
Klopfer, Walter G(eorge) 1923- ... 89-92
Kloppenburg, Boaventura 1919- ... CANR-15
Earlier sketch in CA 65-68
Klopstock, Friedrich Gottlieb 1724-1803 ... DLB 97
Klopstock, Meta 1728-1758 ... DLB 97
Klos, Frank W(illiam), Jr. 1924- ... 13-16R
Klose, Kevin 1940- ... 53-56
Klose, Norma Cline 1936- ... 17-20R
Klosinski, Emil 1922- ... 65-68
Kloss, Phillips 1902- ... CAP-1
Earlier sketch in CA 13-16
Kloss, Robert J(ames) 1935- ... 45-48
Kloss, Robert Marsh 1938- ... 65-68
Klosty, James (Michael) 1943- Brief entry ... 112
Klotman, Phyllis Rauch ... 93-96
Klotman, Robert Howard 1918- ... 53-56
Klots, Alexander Barrett 1903-1989 ... 107
Obituary ... 128
See also SATA-Obit 62
Klotter, James C(hristopher) 1947- ... 77-80
Klotter, John C(harles) 1918- ... 93-96
Klotz, Lynn C(harles) 1940- ... 116
Klubertanz, George Peter 1912- ... 5-8R
Kluckhohn, Frank L. 1907-1970 ... 5-8R
Obituary ... 29-32R
Klueger, Ruth
See Kluger, Ruth
Klug, Eugene F(rederick Adolf) 1917- ... CANR-1
Earlier sketch in CA 45-48
Klug, Ron(ald) 1939- ... CANR-24
Earlier sketch in CA 107
See also SATA 31
Kluge, Alexander 1932- ... 81-84
See also DLB 75
Kluge, Eike-Henner W. 1942- ... 61-64
Kluge, P(aul) F(rederick) 1942- ... CANR-37
Earlier sketches in CA 73-76, CANR-16
Kluger, James R. 1939- ... 29-32R
Kluger, Richard 1934- ... CANR-54
Earlier sketches in CA 9-12R, CANR-6, 28
Kluger, Ruth 1914-1980 ... 116
Obituary ... 108
Kluger, Steve 1952- ... 138
Klugh, Henry E(licker III) 1927- ... 53-56
Klugman, Edgar 1925- ... 132
Kluver, Billy
See Kluver, J. Wilhelm
Kluver, J. Wilhelm 1927- ... 133
Kluwe, Mary Jean 1905-1975 ... CAP-2
Earlier sketch in CA 23-24
Klyza, Christopher McGrory 1959- ... 150
Kmoch, Hans 1897(?)-1973 Obituary ... 41-44R
Knaack, Twila 1944- ... 119
Knaak, Richard A(llen) 1961- ... CANR-58
Earlier sketch in CA 128
See also SATA 86
Knachel, Philip A(therton) 1926- ... 21-24R
Knack, Martha C(arol) 1948- ... 118
Knaplund, Paul (Alexander) 1885-1964 ... CAP-1
Earlier sketch in CA 11-12
Knapp, Bettina (Liebowitz) ... CANR-44
Earlier sketches in CA 13-16R, CANR-6, 21
Knapp, Caroline 1959- ... 154
See also CLC 99
Knapp, David A(llan) 1938- ... 41-44R
Knapp, Edward
See Kunhardt, Edith
Knapp, Herbert W. 1931- ... 105
Knapp, J(ohn) Merrill 1914-1993 ... 53-56
Obituary ... 140
Knapp, James F(ranklin) 1940- ... 107
Knapp, John (Allen) II 1940- ... 116
Knapp, Joseph G(rant) 1900-1983 ... 37-40R
Obituary ... 110
Knapp, Joseph G(eorge) 1924- ... 41-44R
Knapp, Joseph Palmer 1864-1951 ... DLB 91
Knapp, Lewis M(ansfield) 1894- ... 21-24R
Knapp, Mark L(ane) 1938- ... 81-84
Knapp, Mary L. 1931- ... 105
Knapp, Peggy A(nn) 1937- ... 119
Knapp, Robert Hampden 1915-1974 ... CAP-2
Obituary ... 53-56
Earlier sketch in CA 13-14
Knapp, Ron 1952- ... 103
See also SATA 34
Knapp, Ronald Gary 1940- ... CANR-56
Earlier sketches in CA 112, CANR-30
Knapp, Ronald J(ames) 1935- ... 119
Knapp, Samuel Lorenzo 1783-1838 ... DLB 59
Knapp, Sara D. 1936- ... 143
Knapp, William R. 1920(?)-1990 Obituary ... 132
Knapper, Christopher (Kay) 1940- ... CANR-12
Earlier sketch in CA 29-32R
Knapton, Ernest John 1902- ... CANR-1
Earlier sketch in CA 1-4R
Knaub, Richard K. 1928- ... 41-44R
Knauft, Bruce M. 1954- ... 146
Knaus, William A. 1946- ... 105
Knauss, Peter R(ichard) 1937-1990 Obituary ... 131
Knauth, Percival Roediger
See Knauth, Percy
Knauth, Percy 1914-1995 ... 57-60
Obituary ... 147
Knauth, Victor W. 1895(?)-1977 Obituary ... 73-76
Kneale, Matthew (Nicholas Kerr) 1960- ... CANR-52
Earlier sketch in CA 125
Kneale, (Thomas) Nigel 1922- ... 132
Knebel, Fletcher 1911-1993 ... CANR-36
Obituary ... 140
Earlier sketches in CA 1-4R, CANR-1
See also CAAS 3
See also AITN 1
See also CLC 14
See also SATA 36
See also SATA-Obit 75
Knecht, Robert (Jean) 1926- ... CANR-46
Earlier sketches in CA 33-36R, CANR-13
Knechtges, David R(ichard) 1942- ... 65-68
Kneebone, Geoffrey Thomas 1918- ... 5-8R
Kneeland, Linda Clarke 1947- ... 159
See also SATA 94
Kneese, Allen V(ictor) 1930- ... CANR-8
Earlier sketch in CA 13-16R
Knef, Hildegard 1925- ... CANR-4
Earlier sketch in CA 45-48
Kneller, John W(illiam) 1916- ... 17-20R
Kneller, Marianna 1942- ... 153
Knelman, Fred H. 1919- ... 102
Knelman, Martin 1943- ... 73-76
Knepler, Henry (William) 1922- ... 21-24R
Knevitt, Charles (Philip Paul) 1952- ... 132
Knezevich, Stephen J(oseph) 1920- ... CANR-10
Earlier sketch in CA 5-8R
Kniazhnin, Iakov Borisovich 1740-1791 ... DLB 150
Knickerbocker, Charles H(errick) 1922- ... 13-16R
Knickerbocker, Cholly
See Cassini, Igor (Loiewski)
Knickerbocker, Diedrich
See Irving, Washington
Knickerbocker, Kenneth L(eslie) 1905- ... 5-8R
Knickmeyer, Steve 1944- ... 85-88
Knies, Elizabeth 1941- ... 109
Knifesmith
See Cutler, Ivor
Kniffen, Fred B(owerman) 1900- ... CANR-47
Earlier sketch in CA 1-4R
Knigge, Adolph Franz Friedrich Ludwig Freiherr von 1752-1796 ... DLB 94
Knigge, Robert (R.) 1921(?)-1987 Obituary ... 121
See also SATA 50
Knight, Adam
See Lariar, Lawrence
Knight, Alan 1946- ... 125
Knight, Alanna ... CANR-33
Earlier sketches in CA 81-84, CANR-15
Knight, Alice Valle 1922- ... 81-84
Knight, Amarantha
See Kilpatrick, Nancy
Knight, Amy 1946- ... CANR-60
Earlier sketch in CA 128
Knight, Anne (Katherine) 1946- ... SATA 34
Knight, Arthur 1916-1991 ... 41-44R
Obituary ... 135
Knight, Arthur Winfield 1937- ... CANR-41
Earlier sketches in CA 53-56, CANR-4, 19
See also CAAS 27
Knight, B(etty) Carolyn 1944- ... 118
Knight, Bernard 1931- ... CANR-2
Earlier sketch in CA 49-52
Knight, Bertram 1904- ... 103
Knight, Charles 1910- ... 109
Knight, Charles Landon ... AITN 2
Knight, Charles W. 1891- ... CAP-1
Earlier sketch in CA 9-10
Knight, Christopher G. 1943- ... SATA 96
Knight, Clayton 1891-1969 ... CAP-1
Earlier sketch in CA 9-10
Knight, Damon (Francis) 1922- ... CANR-36
Earlier sketches in CA 49-52, CANR-3, 17
See also CAAS 10
See also DLB 8
See also SATA 9
Knight, David
See Prather, Richard S(cott)
Knight, David C(arpenter) 1925- ... 73-76
See also CLR 38
See also SATA 14
Knight, David Marcus 1936- ... CANR-7
Earlier sketch in CA 57-60
Knight, Denis 1921- ... 137
Knight, Doug(las E.) 1925- ... 85-88
Knight, Douglas M(aitland) 1921- ... CANR-2
Earlier sketch in CA 49-52
Knight, Eric (Mowbray) 1897-1943 ... 137
See also JRDA
See also MAICYA
See also SATA 18
Knight, Etheridge 1931-1991 ... CANR-23
Obituary ... 133
Earlier sketch in CA 21-24R
See also BLC 2
See also BW 1
See also CLC 40
See also DAM POET
See also DLB 41
See also PC 14
Knight, Everett 1919- ... 33-36R
Knight, Francis Edgar 1905- ... 73-76
See also SATA 14
Knight, Frank
See Knight, Francis Edgar
Knight, Frank H(yneman)
1885-1972 Obituary ... 33-36R
Knight, Franklin Willis 1942- ... 101
Knight, Frida 1910-1996 ... CANR-2
Obituary ... 154
Earlier sketch in CA 49-52
Knight, G(ilfred) Norman 1891-1978 ... CANR-17
Earlier sketch in CA 25-28R
Knight, G(eorge) Wilson 1897-1985 ... CANR-10
Obituary ... 115
Earlier sketch in CA 13-16R
Knight, Gareth
See Wilby, Basil Leslie
Knight, Geoffrey Egerton 1921- ... 122
Knight, George A(ngus) F(ulton) 1909- ... CANR-42
Earlier sketch in CA 1-4R
Knight, Glee 1947-1975 ... 57-60
Obituary ... 120
Knight, H(erbert) Ralph 1895- ... CAP-2
Earlier sketch in CA 25-28
Knight, Harold V(incent) 1907- ... 21-24R
Knight, Harry Adam
See Brosnan, John
Knight, Hattie M. 1908-1976 ... CAP-2
Earlier sketch in CA 29-32
Knight, Hilary 1926- ... 73-76
See also MAICYA
See also SATA 15, 69
Knight, Hugh McCown 1905- ... 5-8R
Knight, Ione Kemp 1922- ... 37-40R
Knight, Isabel F(rances) 1930- ... 25-28R
Knight, James
See Schneck, Stephen
Knight, James A(llen) 1918- ... CANR-6
Earlier sketch in CA 13-16R
Knight, Janet M(argaret) 1940- ... 93-96
Knight, Jesse F. 1946- ... 129
Knight, Joan (M.) ... 149
See also SATA 82
Knight, John S. III ... AITN 2
Knight, John Shively 1894-1981 ... 93-96
Obituary ... 103
Interview in ... 93-96
See also AITN 2
See also DLB 29
Knight, Julia 1957- ... 143
Knight, K(enneth) G(raham) 1921- ... 25-28R
Knight, Karl F. 1930- ... 17-20R
Knight, Kathryn Lasky
See Lasky, Kathryn
Knight, Mallory T.
See Hurwood, Bernhardt J.
Knight, Margaret K(ennedy) Horsey 1903- ... CAP-1
Earlier sketch in CA 9-10
Knight, Max 1909-1993 ... CANR-40
Obituary ... 142
Earlier sketch in CA 93-96
Knight, Maxwell 1900- ... CAP-1
Earlier sketch in CA 13-14
Knight, Michael E(mery) 1935- ... 105
Knight, Norman L(ouis) 1895- ... CAP-2
Earlier sketch in CA 23-24
Knight, Oliver (Holmes) 1919- ... 21-24R
Knight, Paul Emerson 1925- ... 13-16R
Knight, R(oy) C(lement) 1907- ... 13-16R
Knight, Richard S. 1936- ... 115
Knight, Robin 1943- ... 73-76
Knight, Roderic C(opley) 1942- ... 61-64
Knight, Ruth Adams 1898-1974 ... 5-8R
Obituary ... 49-52
See also SATA-Obit 20
Knight, Sarah Kemble 1666-1727 ... DLB 24, 200
Knight, Stephen 1951-1985 ... CANR-34
Obituary ... 117
Earlier sketch in CA 69-72
Knight, Theodore O. 1946- ... 145
See also SATA 77
Knight, Thomas J(oseph) 1937- ... 102
Knight, Thomas S(tanley, Jr.) 1921- ... 17-20R
Knight, Vick (Ralph) Sr. 1908-1984 Obituary ... 112
Knight, Vick R(alph), Jr. 1928- ... CANR-37
Earlier sketches in CA 45-48, CANR-1, 16
Knight, W(illiam) Nicholas 1939- ... 37-40R
Knight, Walker L(eigh) 1924- ... CANR-13
Earlier sketch in CA 37-40R
Knight, Wallace E(dward) 1926- ... CANR-11
Earlier sketch in CA 65-68
Knight, William E. 1922- ... CANR-66
Earlier sketch in CA 128
Knight-Bruce, G. W. H. 1852-1896 ... DLB 174
Knightley, Phillip 1929- ... 25-28R
Knight-Patterson, W. M.
See Kulski, Wladyslaw W(szebor)
Knights, John Keell 1930(?)-1981 Obituary ... 102
Knights, L(ionel) C(harles) 1906- ... CANR-43
Earlier sketches in CA 5-8R, CANR-3
Knights, Peter R(oger) 1938- ... 37-40R
Knights, Ward A(rthur), Jr. 1927- ... 97-100
Knigin, Michael Jay 1942- ... 85-88
Kniker, Charles Robert 1936- ... 77-80
Knipe, Humphry 1941- ... 37-40R
Knipe, Wayne Bishop III 1946- ... 53-56
Knipschield, Don(ald Harold) 1940- ... 5-8R
Kniskern, David Paul 1948- ... 112
Knister, Raymond 1899-1932 ... DLB 68
See also TCLC 56
Knittel, John (Herman Emanuel)
1891-1970 Obituary ... 104
Knitter, Paul F(rancis) 1939- ... 129
Knobel, Lance 1956- ... 121
Knoblauch, C(yril) H. 1945- ... CANR-53
Earlier sketch in CA 124
Knobler, Nathan 1926- ... 33-36R
Knobler, Peter (Stephen) 1946- ... CANR-44
Earlier sketch in CA 97-100
Knobloch, Dorothea 1951- ... 152
See also SATA 88
Knoblock, Edward 1874-1945 Brief entry ... 108
See also DLB 10
Knock, Thomas J. 1950- ... 141
Knock, Warren 1932- ... 65-68
Knoebl, Kuno 1936- ... 25-28R
Knoepfle, John 1923- ... CANR-53
Earlier sketches in CA 13-16R, CANR-12, 29
See also SATA 66
Knoepflmacher, U(lrich) C(amillus) 1931- . CANR-10
Earlier sketch in CA 13-16R
Knoerle, Jeanne 1928- ... 45-48
Knoke, David (Harmon) 1947- ... CANR-51
Earlier sketches in CA 65-68, CANR-10, 26
Knoles, George Harmon 1907- ... 5-8R
Knoll, Erwin 1931- ... 89-92
Knoll, Gerald M. 1942- ... 29-32R
Knoll, Paul W(endell) 1937- ... 107
Knoll, Robert Edwin 1922- ... CANR-5
Earlier sketch in CA 1-4R
Knollenberg, Bernhard 1892-1973 ... CAP-2
Obituary ... 41-44R
Earlier sketch in CA 21-22
Knoop, Faith Yingling 1896- ... 97-100
Knop, Werner 1912(?)-1970 Obituary ... 29-32R
Knopf, Alfred A. 1892-1984 ... 106
Obituary ... 113
See also DLBY 84
Knopf, Edwin H. 1899-1982(?) Obituary ... 105
Knopf, Irwin J(ay) 1924- ... 119
Knopf, Kenyon A(lfred) 1921- ... 77-80
Knopf, Marcy 1969- ... 142
Knopf, Terry Ann 1940- ... CANR-17
Earlier sketch in CA 25-28R
Knopp, Josephine Zadovsky 1941- ... 103
Knopp, Lisa 1956- ... 158
Knorr, Albert Scofield 1929- ... 25-28R
Knorr, Dandi 1949- ... 112
Knorr, K. E.
See Knorr, Klaus E(ugene)
Knorr, Klaus
See Knorr, Klaus E(ugene)
Knorr, Klaus E(ugene) 1911-1990 ... 134
Obituary ... 131
Brief entry ... 113
Knorr, Marian L(ockwood) 1910- ... 102
Knorr von Rosenroth, Christian 1636-1689 ... DLB 168
Knott, Bill
See Knott, William C(ecil, Jr.)
Knott, John R(ay), Jr. 1937- ... 57-60
Knott, Kim 1955- ... 124
Knott, Leonard L(ewis) 1905- ... 107
Knott, Will C.
See Knott, William C(ecil, Jr.)
Knott, William C(ecil, Jr.) 1927- ... CANR-63
Earlier sketches in CA 5-8R, CANR-7, 22
See also DAM POP
See also SATA 3
Knotts, Howard (Clayton, Jr.) 1922- ... CANR-11
Earlier sketch in CA 69-72
See also SATA 25
Knowland, A(nthony) S(tephen) 1919- ... 116
Knowland, William Fife 1908-1974 Obituary ... 89-92
Knowler, John 1933(?)-1979 Obituary ... 85-88
Knowles, A(lbert) Sidney, Jr. 1926- ... 101
Knowles, Alison 1933- ... CANR-29
Earlier sketches in CA 17-20R, CANR-8
Knowles, Anne 1933- ... 102
See also SATA 37
Knowles, Asa S(mallidge) 1909-1990 ... 29-32R
Obituary ... 132

Knowles, Clayton 1908-1978 81-84
Obituary 73-76
Knowles, (Michael Clive) David 1896-1974 .... CANR-4
Obituary 53-56
Knowles, David 1966- 152
Knowles, Dorothy 1906- 25-28R
Knowles, Henry P(aine) 1912- 61-64
Knowles, John 1926- CANR-40
Earlier sketch in CA 17-20R
See also AAYA 10
See also CDALB 1968-1988
See also CLC 1, 4, 10, 26
See also DA
See also DAC
See also DAM MST, NOV
See also DLB 6
See also MTCW 1
See also SATA 8, 89
Knowles, John H(ilton) 1926-1979 101
Obituary 85-88
Knowles, Joseph W(illiam) 1922- 21-24R
Knowles, Louis L(eonard) 1947- 29-32R
Knowles, Mabel Winifred 1875-1949 Brief entry 122
Knowles, Malcolm Shepherd 1913-1997 .. CANR-5
Obituary 162
Earlier sketch in CA 5-8R
Knowles, Valerie (J.) 1934- CANR-59
Earlier sketch in CA 128
Knowles, Yereth K(ahn) 1920- 93-96
Knowlton, Derrick 1921- CANR-6
Earlier sketch in CA 57-60
Knowlton, Edgar C(olby), Jr. 1921- 41-44R
Knowlton, James 1943- 120
Knowlton, Robert A(lmy) 1914-1968 .... 1-4R
Obituary 103
Knowlton, William H. 1927- 17-20R
Knox, Alan B. 1931- 147
Knox, Alexander 1907-1995 81-84
Obituary 148
Knox, Bernard M(acGregor) W(alker) 1914- 128
Brief entry 117
Knox, Bill
See Knox, William
Knox, Calvin M.
See Silverberg, Robert
Knox, Caroline 1938- 120
Knox, Cleone
See King-Hall, Magdalen
Knox, Collie T. 1897-1977 77-80
Obituary 73-76
Knox, David H., Jr. 1943- 41-44R
Knox, Donald E(dward) 1936-1986 ...... CANR-39
Obituary 119
Earlier sketch in CA 45-48
Knox, Edmund George Valpy 1881-1971 112
Obituary 29-32R
Knox, (Mary) Eleanor Jessie 1909- .... MAICYA
See also SATA 30, 59
Knox, Elizabeth (Fiona) 1959- 159
Knox, Frank 1874-1944 .... DLB 29
Knox, George 1922- 138
Knox, George A(lbert) 1918- 121
Knox, Gilbert
See Macbeth, Madge (Hamilton)
Knox, Henry M(acdonald) 1916- 13-16R
Knox, Hugh (Randolph) 1942- 103
Knox, Israel 1906-1986 Obituary 119
Knox, James
See Brittain, William (E.)
Knox, John c. 1505-1572 .... DLB 132
Knox, John 1900-1990 .... 13-16R
Obituary 132
Knox, John Armory 1850-1906 .... DLB 23
Knox, John Ballenger 1909- CAP-1
Earlier sketch in CA 9-10
Knox, Jolyne 1937- .... SATA 76
Knox, Katharine McCook 1890(?)-1983 Obituary 110
Knox, (Thomas) Malcolm 1900-1980 103
Obituary 97-100
Knox, Melissa 1957- 149
Knox, Robert Buick 1918- 25-28R
Knox, Ronald A(rbuthnott) 1888-1957 Brief entry 111
See also DLB 77
Knox, Sanka (Lutins) 1906-1984 Obituary 112
Knox, Thomas Wallace 1835-1896 .... DLB 189
Knox, Vera Huntingdon 9-12R
Knox, Warren Barr 1925- 49-52
Knox, William 1928- CANR-47
Earlier sketches in CA 1-4R, CANR-1
Knox-Johnston, Robin 1939- CANR-15
Earlier sketch in CA 29-32R
Knox-Mawer, June 1930- 151
Knox-Mawer, Ronald 1925- 123
Knox-Mawer, Ronnie
See Knox-Mawer, Ronald
Knudbucker, Homer T., Jr.
See Garfinkle, Adam M.
Knudsen, Hans August Heinrich 1886-1971 Obituary 29-32R
Knudsen, James 1950- CANR-47
Earlier sketch in CA 111
See also SATA 42
Knudson, Danny (Alan) 1940- CANR-11
Earlier sketch in CA 61-64
Knudson, R. R.
See Knudson, Rozanne
See also AAYA 20
See also SAAS 18
Knudson, Richard L(ewis) 1930- CANR-20
Earlier sketch in CA 104
See also SATA 34
Knudson, Rozanne 1932- CANR-35
Earlier sketches in CA 33-36R, CANR-15
See also Knudson, R. R.
See also SATA 7, 79
Knudtson, Peter M(ichael) 1947- CANR-68
Earlier sketch in CA 129
Knuemann, Carl H(einz) 1922- 77-80
Knusel, Jack L(eonard) 1923- 25-28R
Knuth, Donald E. 1938- 163
Knuth, Helen 1912- 53-56
Knutson, Donald C. 1931(?)-1990 Obituary 131
Knutson, Harold Christian 1928- 112
Knutson, Jeanne N(ickell) 1934- 41-44R
Knutson, Kent S(iguart) 1924-1973 .... CAP-2
Obituary 41-44R
Earlier sketch in CA 33-36
Knutson, Roger M. 1933- 126
Knye, Cassandra
See Disch, Thomas M(ichael)
Ko, Kanzein
See Isogai, Hiroshi
Ko, Won 1925- 61-64
Kobal, John 1943(?)-1991 .... CANR-11
Obituary 135
Earlier sketch in CA 61-64
Kobayashi, Koji 1907- 133
Kobayashi, Masako Matsuno 1935- CANR-31
Earlier sketches in CA 5-8R, CANR-13
See also Matsuno, Masako
Kobayashi, Noritake 1932- 53-56
Kobayashi, Tetsuya 1926- 69-72
Kobayashi Takiji 1903-1933 .... DLB 180
Kober, Arthur 1900-1975 .... CAP-1
Obituary 57-60
Earlier sketch in CA 13-14
See also DLB 11
Kobler, Arthur L(eon) 1920- 13-16R
Kobler, (Albert) John (Jr.) 1910- 65-68
Kobler, (Mary) Turner S. 1930- 37-40R
Kobrak, Peter 1936- 104
Kobre, Sidney 1907- 65-68
Kobrin, David 1941- 41-44R
Kobrin, Janet 1942- 57-60
Kobryn, A(llen) P(aul) 1949- 93-96
Kocbek, Edvard 1904-1981 .... DLB 147
Koch, C(hristopher) J(ohn) 1932- 127
See also CLC 42
Koch, Charlotte 85-88
Koch, Christopher
See Koch, C(hristopher) J(ohn)
Koch, Claude (F.) 1918- 9-12R
Koch, Dorothy Clarke 1924- 5-8R
See also SATA 6
Koch, Edward I(rving) 1924- 113
Koch, Eric 1919- 69-72
Koch, H(annsjoachim) W(olfgang) 1933- . CANR-15
Earlier sketch in CA 93-96
Koch, Hans-Gerhard 1913- 17-20R
Koch, Helen L(ois) 1895- CAP-2
Earlier sketch in CA 21-22
Koch, Howard 1902-1995 73-76
Obituary 149
See also DLB 26
Koch, James Harold 1926- 106
Koch, Joanne 1940- CANR-32
Earlier sketches in CA 69-72, CANR-15
Koch, Kenneth 1925- CANR-57
Earlier sketches in CA 1-4R, CANR-6, 36
Interview in CANR-36
See also CLC 5, 8, 44
See also DAM POET
See also DLB 5
See also SATA 65
Koch, Kurt E(mil) 1913-1987 107
Obituary 122
Koch, Lew(is) Z. 1935- 69-72
Koch, Michael 1916(?)-1981 Obituary 103
Koch, Raymond -1994 85-88
Obituary 145
Koch, Richard 1921- 29-32R
Koch, Robert 1918- 9-12R
Koch, Stephen 1941- 77-80
Koch, Thilo 1920- CANR-11
Earlier sketch in CA 25-28R
Koch, Thomas J(ohn) 1947- 61-64
Koch, Thomas Walter 1933- 17-20R
Koch, William H., Jr. 1923- 17-20R
Kochan, Lionel 1922- 105
Kochan, Miriam (Louise) 1929- 103
Kochan, Paul C(ranston) 1906- 45-48
Kochan, Thomas A(nton) 1947- 123
Kochanek, Stanley A(nthony) 1934- CANR-38
Earlier sketch in CA 116
Kochen, Manfred 1928- 21-24R
Kochenburger, Ralph J. 1919- 53-56
Kochendoerfer, Violet A. 1912- 159
Kocher, Eric 1912- 57-60
Kocher, Paul H(arold) 1907- 65-68
Kochetov, Vsevolod A(nisimovich) 1912-1973 Obituary 45-48
Kochiss, John (Matthew) 1926- 97-100
Kochka, Mary Murray 1894(?)-1984 Obituary ... 112
Kochman, Thomas 1936- 37-40R
Kock, Winston E(dward) 1909-1982 110
Kocka, Juergen 1941- 133
Kocka, Jurgen
See Kocka, Juergen
Kockelmans, Joseph J(ohn) 1923- CANR-41
Brief entry 113
Earlier sketch in CA 117
Kocsis, J. C.
See Paul, James
Kocsis, Robert
See Kossez, Robes
Koda-Callan, Elizabeth 1944- 136
See also SATA 67
Kodaira, Kunihiko 1915- 164
Kodaly, Zoltan 1882-1967 Obituary 112
Kodama, Sanehide 1932- 120
Kodanda Rao, Pandurangi 1889- 13-16R
Koda Rohan 1867-1947
See Koda Shigeyuki
See also DLB 180
Koda Shigeyuki 1867-1947 Brief entry 121
See also Koda Rohan
and Rohan, Koda
Kodera, Takashi James 1945- 111
Koegler, Hans-Herbert 1960- 165
Koehler, Alan (Robert) 1928- 13-16R
Koehler, Frank
See Paine, Lauran (Bosworth)
Koehler, G(eorge) Stanley 1915- 37-40R
Koehler, George E. 1930- 25-28R
Koehler, Ludmila 1917- 53-56
Koehler, Lyle P(eter) 1944- 109
Koehler, Margaret (Hudson) CANR-30
Earlier sketch in CA 85-88
Koehler, Nikki 1951- 25-28R
Koehler, Phoebe 1955- 132
See also SATA 85
Koehler, W(illiam) R. 1914- 9-12R
Koehler, Wolfgang 1887-1967 Obituary 111
Koehler-Pentacoff, Elizabeth 1957- 161
See also SATA 96
Koehn, Ilse
See Van Zwienen, Ilse Charlotte Koehn
Koehn, Lala
See Koehn-Heine, Lala
Koehn-Heine, Lala 1936- 112
Koelb, Clayton T. 1942- 132
Koelsch, William Alvin 1933- 104
Koen, Ross Y. 1918- 1-4R
Koenig, Allen Edward 1939- 21-24R
Koenig, C(lyde) Eldo 1919- 21-24R
Koenig, Duane (Walter) 1918- 37-40R
Koenig, Franz 1905- 101
Koenig, Fritz H(ans) 1940- 53-56
Koenig, John (Thomas) 1938- 102
Koenig, Karl P. 1938- 148
Koenig, Laird CANR-32
Earlier sketch in CA 29-32R
Koenig, Linda Lee 1948- 113
Koenig, Louis William 1916- CANR-48
Earlier sketch in CA 1-4R
Koenig, Rene 1906- CANR-15
Earlier sketch in CA 81-84
Koenig, Samuel 1899-1972 .... CAP-2
Obituary 37-40R
Earlier sketch in CA 17-18
Koenig, Viviane 1950- 147
See also SATA 80
Koenig, Walter 1936- 104
Koenigsberg, Moses 1879-1945 .... DLB 25
Koenigsberger, H(elmut) G(eorg) 1918- 33-36R
Koenigswald, (Gustav Heinrich) Ralph von
See von Koenigswald, (Gustav Heinrich) Ralph
Koenker, Diane 1947- 112
Koenker, Ernest Benjamin 1920- Brief entry ... 106
Koenner, Alfred 1921- CANR-40
Earlier sketches in CA 101, CANR-18
Koepf, Michael 1940- 81-84
Koepke, Paul 1918- 114
Koepke, Wulf 1928- CANR-39
Earlier sketches in CA 93-96, CANR-16
Koepp, David 1964(?)- 156
Koeppel, Gary 1938- 49-52
Koeppen, Wolfgang 1906- .... DLB 69
Koering, Ursula 1921-1976 .... SATA 64
Koerner, James D. 1923- 9-12R
Koerner, Joseph Leo 1958- 146
Koerner, Stephan 1913- 1-4R
Koerner, Theodor 1791-1813 .... DLB 90
Koerner, W(illiam) H(enry) D(avid) 1878-1938 . SATA 21
Koerte, Mary Norbert 1934- 103
Koertge, Noretta 1935- CANR-22
Earlier sketch in CA 106
Koertge, Ronald 1940- CANR-58
Earlier sketches in CA 65-68, CANR-9, 25
See also AAYA 12
See also DLB 105
See also SATA 53, 92
Koestenbaum, Peter 1928- CANR-13
Earlier sketch in CA 29-32R
Koestenbaum, Phyllis 1930- CANR-25
Earlier sketch in CA 107
Koestenbaum, Wayne 1958- 134
Koester, Helmut 1926- 110
Koestler, Arthur 1905-1983 .... CANR-33
Obituary 109
Earlier sketches in CA 1-4R, CANR-1
See also CDBLB 1945-1960
See also CLC 1, 3, 6, 8, 15, 33
See also DLBY 83
See also MTCW 1
Koestler, Cynthia 1928(?)-1983 Obituary 114
Koethe, John (Louis) 1945- 49-52
Koetzsch, Ronald E. 1944- 164
Kofalk, Harriet 1937- CANR-30
Earlier sketch in CA 112
Koff, Richard Myram 1926- CANR-15
Earlier sketch in CA 89-92
See also SATA 62
Koffinke, Carol 1949- 149
See also SATA 82
Kofoed, Jack
See Kofoed, John C.
Kofoed, John C. 1894-1979 .... 5-8R
Obituary 93-96
Koford, Kenneth J. 1948- 140
Kofsky, Frank (Joseph) 1935-1997 57-60
Obituary 162
Kogan, Bernard Robert 1920- 9-12R
Kogan, Deborah
See Kogan Ray, Deborah
See also SATA 50
Kogan, Herman 1914-1989 .... CANR-20
Obituary 128
Earlier sketches in CA 9-12R, CANR-5
Kogan, Judith 1956- 126
Kogan, Leonard S(aul) 1919-1976 Obituary .. 65-68
Kogan, Maurice 1930- 107
Kogan, Norman 1919- 1-4R
Kogan Ray, Deborah 1940- CANR-22
Earlier sketches in CA 57-60, CANR-7
See also Kogan, Deborah
and Ray, Deborah
Kogawa, Joy Nozomi 1935- CANR-62
Earlier sketches in CA 101, CANR-19
See also CLC 78
See also DAC
See also DAM MST, MULT
See also SATA 99
Koger, Lisa (Jan) 1953- 133
Kogiku, K(iichiro) C(hris) 1927- 33-36R
Koginos, Manny T. 1933- 21-24R
Kogos, Frederick 1907-1974 .... CAP-2
Obituary 53-56
Earlier sketch in CA 29-32
Koh, Byung Chul 1936- 17-20R
Koh, Sung Jae 1917- 17-20R
Kohak, Erazim V. 1933- CANR-31
Earlier sketches in CA 37-40R, CANR-14
Kohake, Rosanne 1951- 114
Kohan, Rhea 89-92
Kohanski, Alexander S(iskind) 1902-1987 108
Obituary 123
Kohavi, Y.
See Stern, Jay B(enjamin)
Kohen-Raz, Reuven 1921- 37-40R
Kohfeldt, Mary Lou (Stevenson) 1939- ... CANR-44
Earlier sketch in CA 119
Kohl, Benjamin G. 1938- CANR-56
Earlier sketch in CA 126
Kohl, Herbert 1937- CANR-14
Earlier sketch in CA 65-68
See also SATA 47
Kohl, Irene C(aistor) 1927- 119
Kohl, James (Virgil) 1942- 57-60
Kohl, James Vaughn 1951- 157
Kohl, Marvin 1932- 85-88
Kohl, MaryAnn F. 1947- .... SATA 74
Kohlberg, Lawrence 1927-1987 125
Obituary 122
Kohlenberg, Robert J(oseph) 1937- 111
Kohler, Foy D(avid) 1908-1990 .... 29-32R
Obituary 133
Kohler, Heinz 1934- 21-24R
Kohler, Julilly H(ouse) 1908-1976 77-80
Obituary 69-72
See also SATA-Obit 20
Kohler, Mary Conway 1903-1986 135
Obituary 119
Kohler, Saul 1928- 69-72
Kohler, Sheila (May) 1941- 137
Kohler, Sister Mary Hortense 1892- 5-8R
Kohler, Wolfgang
See Koehler, Wolfgang
Kohlmeier, Louis M(artin), Jr. 1926- 49-52
Kohls, R. L.
See Kohls, Richard L(ouis)
Kohls, Richard L(ouis) 1921- 126
Brief entry 106
Kohlstedt, Sally Gregory 1943- 69-72
Kohmescher, Matthew Franklin 1921- 113
Kohn, Alan J(acobs) 1931- 146
Kohn, Alexander 1919- 123
Kohn, Alfie 1957- 122
Kohn, Bernice
See Hunt, Bernice (Kohn)
See also SATA 4
Kohn, Clyde Frederick 1911-1989 Obituary 130
Brief entry 109
Kohn, Eugene 1887-1977 Obituary 69-72
Kohn, George C(hilds) 1940- CANR-42
Earlier sketches in CA 103, CANR-19
Kohn, Hans 1891-1971 .... CANR-4
Obituary 29-32R
Earlier sketch in CA 1-4R
Kohn, Howard 1947- 124
Kohn, Jacob 1881-1968 .... 5-8R
Obituary 103
Kohn, John S. (Van E.) 1906-1976 Obituary ... 104
See also DLB 187
Kohn, Livia 1956- 139
Kohn, Marek (Czeslaw Patrick) 1958- 128
Kohn, Melvin L(ester) 1928- 41-44R
Kohn, Richard H(enry) 1940- CANR-37
Earlier sketch in CA 115
Kohn, Rita (T.) 1933- .... SATA 89
Kohn, Walter S(amuel) G(erst) 1923- 107
Kohner, Frederick 1905-1986 .... CANR-1
Obituary 119
Earlier sketch in CA 1-4R
See also SATA 10
See also SATA-Obit 48
Kohon, Gregorio 1943- 159
Kohout, Pavel 1928- CANR-3
Earlier sketch in CA 45-48
See also CLC 13
Kohr, Louise Hannah 1903- 41-44R
Kohs, Samuel C(almin) 1890-1984 Obituary ... 111
Koht, Halvdan 1873-1965 85-88
Kohut, Heinz 1913-1981 .... CANR-1
Obituary 105
Earlier sketch in CA 45-48
Kohut, Les
See Kohut, Nester C(larence)

Kohut, Nester C(larence) 1925- 45-48
Kohut, Thomas A. 1950- 142
Koidahl, Ilona 1924- 97-100
Koide, Tan 1938-1986 132
See also SATA 50
Koi Hai
See Palmer, (Nathaniel) Humphrey
Koike, Kay 1940- ....SATA 72
Koilpillai, (Jesudas) Charles 41-44R
Koilpillai, Das
See Koilpillai, (Jesudas) Charles
Koinange, Mbiyu (Peter) 1907-1981 Obituary ...108
Koiner, Richard B. 1929- 17-20R
Koizumi, Yakumo
See Hearn, (Patricio) Lafcadio (Tessima Carlos)
Koja, Kathe 1960- 147
Kojecky, Roger 1943- 85-88
Kojima, Naomi 1950- 109
Kojima, Takashi 1902- CAP-1
Earlier sketch in CA 9-10
Kojima Shozo 1928- 69-72
Kokoschka, Oskar 1886-1980 109
Obituary 93-96
See also DLB 124
Kokyshev, Lazor 1933(?)-1975 Obituary 104
Kolaja, Jiri Thomas 1919- 9-12R
Kolakowski, Leszek 1927- 49-52
Kolars, Frank 1899-1973 ....5-8R
Obituary 37-40R
Kolasky, John 1915- 25-28R
Kolatch, Alfred Jacob 1916- 107
Kolatch, Jonathan 1943- 41-44R
Kolatkar, Arun (Balkrishna) 1932- 153
Kolb, Annette 1870-1967 ....DLB 66
Kolb, Carolyn 1942- 89-92
Kolb, David A(llen) 1939- CANR-15
Earlier sketch in CA 65-68
Kolb, Erwin J(ohn) 1924- 37-40R
Kolb, Gwin Jackson 1919- 1-4R
Kolb, Harold H(utchinson), Jr. 1933- CANR-12
Earlier sketch in CA 29-32R
Kolb, (Gwin) Jack (II) 1946- 125
Kolb, John F. 1916(?)-1974 Obituary 53-56
Kolb, Ken(neth) 1926- 21-24R
Kolb, Lawrence 1911-1972 Obituary 37-40R
Kolb, Philip 1907-1992 ....CANR-4
Obituary 139
Earlier sketch in CA 53-56
Kolba, St. Tamara 97-100
See also SATA 22
Kolbas, Grace Holden 1914- 93-96
Kolbe, Henry E(ugene) 1907- 5-8R
Kolbenheyer, Erwin Guido 1878-1962 . DLB 66, 124
Kolbenschlag, Madonna (Claire) 1935- Brief entry 115
Kolbrek, Loyal 1914- 29-32R
Kolchin, Peter 1943- 41-44R
Kolde, Endel Jakob 1917- CANR-1
Earlier sketch in CA 45-48
Kolenda, Konstantin 1923- 13-16R
Kolers, Paul A. 1926- 97-100
Kolesar, Paul 1927- 105
Kolesnik, Walter B(ernard) 1923- CANR-2
Earlier sketch in CA 5-8R
Kolevzon, Edward R. 1913(?)-1976 Obituary . 69-72
Kolin, Philip C(harles) 1945- CANR-43
Earlier sketch in CA 119
Kolins, William 1926(?)-1973 Obituary 104
Kolinski, Charles J(ames) 1916- 17-20R
Kolinsky, Martin 1936- CANR-8
Earlier sketch in CA 61-64
Koljevic, Svetozar 1930- CANR-7
Earlier sketch in CA 17-20R
Kolker, Robert Phillip 1940- 112
Kolko, Gabriel 1932- CANR-4
Earlier sketch in CA 5-8R
Kolko, Joyce 1933- 130
Kolkowicz, Roman 1929- 154
Brief entry 116
Kollat, David T(ruman) 1938- 41-44R
Kollek, Teddy
See Kollek, Theodore
Kollek, Theodore 1911- CAP-2
Earlier sketch in CA 29-32
Koller, Ann Marie 128
Koller, Charles W. 1896(?)-1983 61-64
Obituary 109
Koller, Jackie French 1948- ....SATA 72
Koller, James 1936- CANR-39
Earlier sketches in CA 49-52, CANR-2, 18
See also CAAS 5
Koller, John M. 1938- 33-36R
Koller, Larry
See Koller, Lawrence Robert
Koller, Lawrence Robert 1912-1967 ....CANR-6
Earlier sketch in CA 1-4R
Koller, Marvin Robert 1919- 13-16R
Kolleritsch, Alfred 1931- ....DLB 85
Kollmar, Dick
See Kollmar, Richard Tompkins
Kollmar, Richard Tompkins 1910-1971 Obituary 89-92
Kollock, Will(iam Raymond) 1940- 33-36R
Kollontai, Alexandra (Mikhailovna Domantovich) 1872-1952 154
Brief entry 112
Kollstedt, Paula Lubke 1946- 113
Kolmar, Gertrud 1894-1943 167
See also TCLC 40
Kolmerten, Carol A. 1946- 135
Kolmogorov, Andrei Nikolayevich 1903-1987 Obituary 123
Kolnai, Aurel (Thomas) 1900-1973 103
Kolodin, Irving 1908-1988 93-96
Obituary 125
Kolodny, Annette 1941- CANR-8
Earlier sketch in CA 61-64
See also DLB 67
Kolodny, Nancy J. 1946- 143
See also SATA 76
Kolodny, Ralph (Leonard) 1923- 116
Kolodziej, Edward Albert 1935- CANR-45
Earlier sketch in CA 97-100
Kolon, Nita
See Onadipe, (Nathaniel) Kola(wole)
Kolosimo, Peter 1922- CANR-7
Earlier sketch in CA 53-56
Kolpen, Jana (Fayne) 1958- 156
Kolsky, Thomas A. 1942- 135
Kolson, Clifford J(ohn) 1920- 9-12R
Kolstoe, Oliver P(aul) 1920- 17-20R
Koltes, Bernard-Marie 1948-1989 Obituary 128
Koltun, Frances Lang 69-72
Kolumban, Nicholas 1937- CANR-56
Earlier sketch in CA 111
Kolve, Carolee Nance 1946- 122
Kolyer, John (McNaughton) 1933- CANR-39
Earlier sketches in CA 69-72, CANR-11
Komai, Akira 1908(?)-1983 Obituary 111
Komaiko, Jean R. 1922(?)-1984 Obituary 114
Komaiko, Leah 1954- 164
See also SATA 97
Komar, Kathleen L(enore) 1949- 128
Komarnicki, Tytus 1896- CAP-1
Earlier sketch in CA 9-10
Komarov, Matvei c. 1730-1812 ....DLB 150
Komarovsky, Mirra CAP-1
Earlier sketch in CA 17-18
Komatsu Sakyo 1931- 162
Brief entry 113
Kome, Penney 1948- 116
Komenich, Kim 1956- 160
Komer, Robert W(illiam) 1922- 108
Kometani, Foumiko 1930- 135
Komisar, Lucy 1942- 33-36R
See also SATA 9
Kommers, Donald P. 1932- 116
Komoda, Beverly 1939- 85-88
See also SATA 25
Komoda, Kiyo 1937- ....SATA 9
Komroff, Manuel 1890-1974 ....CANR-4
Obituary 53-56
Earlier sketch in CA 1-4R
See also DLB 4
See also SATA 2
See also SATA-Obit 20
Komunyakaa, Yusef 1947- 147
See also BLCS
See also CLC 86, 94
See also DLB 120
Konadu, Asare
See Konadu, S(amuel) A(sare)
Konadu, S(amuel) A(sare) 1932- CANR-26
Earlier sketch in CA 21-24R
See also BW 2
Konchalovsky, Andrei
See Mikhalkov-Konchalovsky, Andrei (Sergeyevich)
Konczacki, Zbigniew Andrzej 1917- CANR-10
Earlier sketch in CA 21-24R
Kondoleon, Harry 1955-1994 112
Obituary 144
Kondracke, Morton 1939- 127
Brief entry 119
Interview in 127
Kondrashin, Kiril (Petrovich) 1914-1981 Obituary 108
Kondrashov, Stanislav (Nikolaevich) 1928- CANR-40
Earlier sketch in CA 69-72
Konecky, Edith 1922- 69-72
Konefsky, Samuel J. 1915-1970 Obituary ...29-32R
Konek, Carol (Wolfe) 1934- Brief entry 114
Koner, Marvin 1921(?)-1983 Obituary 109
Koner, Pauline 1912- 132
Koneski, Blaze 1921-1993 ....DLB 181
Kong, Shiu Loon 1934- 108
Konick, Marcus 1914- 37-40R
Konig, David Thomas 1947- 97-100
Konig, Franz
See Koenig, Franz
Konig, Fritz H(ans)
See Koenig, Fritz H(ans)
Konig, Rene
See Koenig, Rene
Konigsberg, Conrad Isidore 1916-1976 ....21-24R
Obituary 134
Konigsburg, E(laine) L(obl) 1930- CANR-59
Earlier sketches in CA 21-24R, CANR-17, 39
Interview in CANR-17
See also AAYA 3
See also CLR 1, 47
See also DLB 52
See also JRDA
See also MAICYA
See also MTCW 1
See also SATA 4, 48, 94
Koning, Hans 1924- CANR-48
See also Koningsberger, Hans
Koningsberger, Hans
See Koning, Hans
See also SATA 5
Konkel, Wilbur Stanton 1912- 111
Konkle, Janet Everest 1917- 1-4R
See also SATA 12
Konner, Alfred
See Koenner, Alfred
Konner, Linda 1951- 102
Konner, Melvin Joel 1946- Brief entry 116
Konnyu, Leslie 1914- CANR-7
Earlier sketch in CA 13-16R
Konopka, Gisela 1910- 9-12R
Konovalov, Sergey 1899-1982 Obituary 106
Konrad, Evelyn 1931- CANR-45
Earlier sketch in CA 33-36R
Konrad, George
See Konrad, Gyoergy
Konrad, Gyoergy 1933- 85-88
See also CLC 4, 10, 73
Konrad, James
See Maclean, Charles
Konrad von Wuerzburg c. 1230-1287 ....DLB 138
Konstan, David 1940- CANR-68
Earlier sketches in CA 113, CANR-32
Konstantinov, Aleko 1863-1897 ....DLB 147
Kontos, Cecille
See Haddix-Kontos, Cecille P.
Kontos, Peter G(eorge) 1935-1977 ....CANR-17
Obituary 115
Earlier sketch in CA 25-28R
Konvitz, Jeffrey 1944- CANR-7
Earlier sketch in CA 53-56
Konvitz, Milton Ridvas 1908- CANR-4
Earlier sketch in CA 1-4R
Konwicki, Tadeusz 1926- CANR-59
Earlier sketches in CA 101, CANR-39
See also CAAS 9
See also CLC 8, 28, 54
See also MTCW 1
Konz, Helen S. 1922- 145
Koo, Anthony Y(ing) C(hang) 1918- 57-60
Koo, Samuel 1941- 77-80
Koo, V(i) K(yuin) Wellington 1888-1985 81-84
Obituary 117
Koob, C(harles) Albert 1920- 41-44R
Koob, Derry D(elos) 1933- 37-40R
Koob, Joseph E. II 1948- 121
Koob, Theodora (J. Foth) 1918- 5-8R
See also SATA 23
Kooiker, Leonie
See Kooyker-Romijn, Johanna Maria
Kooiman, Gladys 1927- 89-92
Kooiman, Helen W.
See Hosier, Helen Kooiman
Kooistra, Paul G. 1952- 141
Koolmatrie, Wanda
See Carmen, Leon
Koon, George William 1942- 116
Koon, Helene Wickham 1924-1996 120
Obituary 161
Koonce, Ray F. 1913- 9-12R
Koons, Carolyn 136
Koons, James
See Pernu, Dennis
Koonts, Jones Calvin 1924- 49-52
Koontz, Dean R(ay) 1945- CANR-52
Earlier sketches in CA 108, CANR-19, 36
See also AAYA 9
See also BEST 89:3, 90:2
See also CLC 78
See also DAM NOV, POP
See also MTCW 1
See also SATA 92
Koontz, Harold 1908-1984 ....41-44R
Obituary 112
Koontz, Robin Michal 1954- 138
See also SATA 70
Koonz, Claudia
See Koonz, Claudia Ann
Koonz, Claudia Ann 131
Brief entry 126
Interview in 131
Koop, Katherine C. 1923- 17-20R
Koop, Theodore Frederick 1907(?)-1988 Obituary 126
Koopman, LeRoy George 1935- 101
Koopmans, Tjalling (Charles) 1910-1985 Obituary 115
Koopowitz, Harold 1940- 114
Kooser, Ted
See Kooser, Theodore
See also DLB 105
Kooser, Theodore 1939- CANR-15
Earlier sketch in CA 33-36R
See also Kooser, Ted
Kootz, Samuel Melvin 1898-1982 Obituary 107
Kooyker-Romijn, Johanna Maria 1927- CANR-34
Earlier sketch in CA 107
See also SATA 48
Kooyker-Romyn, Johanna Maria
See Kooyker-Romijn, Johanna Maria
Kopal, Zdenek 1914-1993 93-96
Obituary 141
Kopelev, Lev (Zinovievich) 1912-1997 123
Obituary 159
Kopelev, Raissa (Davydovna) Orlova
See Orlova-Kopelev, Raissa (Davydovna)
Kopelman, Arie 1937- 113
Kopelnitsky, Raimonda 1977- 151
Kopernik, Mikolaj
See Copernicus, Nicolaus
Koperwas, Sam 1948- CANR-22
Earlier sketch in CA 105
Kopf, David 1930- 89-92
Kopff, E(dward) Christian 1946- 117
Kopinak, Kathryn 166
Kopit, Arthur (Lee) 1937- 81-84
See also CABS 3
See also AITN 1
See also CLC 1, 18, 33
See also DAM DRAM
See also DLB 7
See also MTCW 1
Kopkind, Andrew D(avid) 1935-1994 ....29-32R
Obituary 147
Koplewicz, Harold S. 1953- 156
Koplin, H(arry) T(homas) 1923- 33-36R
Koplinka, Charlotte
See Lukas, Charlotte Koplinka
Koplitz, Eugene D(e Vere) 1928- 37-40R
Kopman, H(enri Marshall) 1918- 89-92
Kopp, Anatole 1915-1990 ....CANR-45
Earlier sketches in CA 29-32R, CANR-12
Kopp, Harriet Green 41-44R
Kopp, O(swald) W. 1918- 33-36R
Kopp, Richard L. 1934- CANR-13
Earlier sketch in CA 33-36R
Kopp, Sheldon B(ernard) 1929- 37-40R
Kopp, William LaMarr 1930- 65-68
Koppel, Lillian 1926- 108
Koppel, Shelley R(uth) 1951- 108
Koppel, Ted 1940(?)- 103
Kopper, Edward A(nthony), Jr. 1937- CANR-33
Earlier sketches in CA 69-72, CANR-15
Kopper, Lisa (Esther) 1950- ....SATA-Brief 51
Kopper, Philip (Dana) 1937- CANR-47
Earlier sketch in CA 97-100
Kopperman, Paul Edward 1945- 69-72
Koppeschaar, Carl (Egon) 1953- 154
Koppett, Leonard 1923- CANR-11
Earlier sketch in CA 25-28R
Koppitz, Elizabeth M(unsterberg) 1919-1983 ....CANR-14
Obituary 111
Earlier sketch in CA 13-16R
Koppman, Lionel 1920- CANR-6
Earlier sketch in CA 9-12R
Kops, Bernard 1926- 5-8R
See also CLC 4
See also DLB 13
Kopulos, Stella 1906- 49-52
Kopycinski, Joseph V(alentine) 1923- 33-36R
Korach, Mimi 1922- ....SATA 9
Koralek, Jenny 1934- ....SATA 71
Koran, Dennis 1947- 120
Korb, Lawrence J(oseph) 1939- 77-80
Korbel, John 1918- 9-12R
Korbel, Josef 1909-1977 ....37-40R
Obituary 73-76
Korbonski, Andrzej 1927- 9-12R
Korbonski, Stefan 1903-1989 ....CANR-5
Obituary 128
Earlier sketch in CA 5-8R
Korchilov, Igor 1941- 159
Korczak, Janusz
See Goldszmit, Henryk
See also SATA 65
Korda, Michael (Vincent) 1933- CANR-39
Earlier sketch in CA 107
See also BEST 89:3
Kordel, Lelord 1904- 106
Korder, Howard 1958(?)- 153
Korelitz, Jean Hanff 1961- 132
Koren, Edward 1935- CANR-11
Earlier sketch in CA 25-28R
See also SATA 5
Koren, Henry J(oseph) 1912- CANR-35
Earlier sketch in CA 9-12R
Korenbaum, Myrtle 1915- 57-60
Korenblit, Joan B(ravo) 1952- 113
Korey, William 1922- Brief entry 112
Korfker, Dena 1908- CANR-17
Earlier sketch in CA 1-4R
Korg, Jacob 1922- CANR-2
Earlier sketch in CA 5-8R
Korges, James 1930-1975 ....CAP-2
Earlier sketch in CA 25-28
Korinets, Iurii Iosifovich
See Korinetz, Yuri (Iosifovich)
Korinetz, Yuri (Iosifovich) 1923- CANR-11
Earlier sketch in CA 61-64
See also CLR 4
See also SATA 9
Korman, A. Gerd 1928- CANR-35
Earlier sketch in CA 53-56
Korman, Bernice 1937- 146
See also SATA 78
Korman, Gordon (Richard) 1963- CANR-56
Earlier sketches in CA 112, CANR-34
See also AAYA 10
See also CLR 25
See also JRDA
See also MAICYA
See also SATA 49, 81
See also SATA-Brief 41
Korman, Justine 1958- 138
See also SATA 70
Korman, Keith 1956- 102
Kormendi, Ferenc 1900-1972 Obituary 37-40R
Kormondy, Edward J(ohn) 1926- CANR-13
Earlier sketch in CA 33-36R
Korn, Alfons L(udwig) 1906-1986 ....CANR-34
Obituary 119
Earlier sketch in CA 93-96
Korn, Bertram Wallace 1918-1979 ....CANR-1
Earlier sketch in CA 1-4R
Korn, David A(dolph) 1930- 139
Korn, Frank J(ames) 1935- 115
Korn, Henry (James) 1945- CANR-47
Earlier sketch in CA 69-72
Korn, Noel 1923- 73-76
Korn, Peggy
See Liss, Peggy K(orn)
Korn, Walter 1908- 73-76
Kornai, J(anos) 1928- CANR-56
Earlier sketches in CA 13-16R, CANR-35
Kornblatt, Joyce Reiser 1944- CANR-27
Earlier sketch in CA 106
Kornblatt, Judith Deutsch 1955- 141
Kornblatt, Marc 1954- 150
See also SATA 84
Kornblith, Hilary 1954- 144
Kornbluh, Marvin 1927-1987 Obituary 124

Kornblum, Allan 1949- ... CANR-54
Earlier sketch in CA 69-72
Kornblum, Cinda 1950- ... 69-72
Kornblum, Sylvan 1927- ... 41-44R
Kornbluth, C(yril) M. 1923-1958 ... 160
Brief entry ... 105
See also DLB 8
See also TCLC 8
Kornbluth, Jesse 1946- ... CANR-17
Earlier sketch in CA 25-28R
Korneichuk, Aleksandr Y.
1905-1972 Obituary ... 33-36R
Korner, Stephan
See Koerner, Stephan
Kornfeld, Anita Clay 1928- ... 97-100
Kornfeld, Paul 1889-1942 ... DLB 118
Kornfeld, Robert J(onathan) 1919- ... 104
Kornhauser, David H(enry) 1918- ... CANR-14
Earlier sketch in CA 41-44R
Kornhauser, Jincy
See Willett, Jincy
Kornhauser, William 1925- ... 1-4R
Kornheiser, Tony 1948- ... 138
Kornrich, Milton 1933- ... 17-20R
Korol, Alexander G. 1900- ... 5-8R
Korolenko, V. G.
See Korolenko, Vladimir Galaktionovich
Korolenko, Vladimir
See Korolenko, Vladimir Galaktionovich
Korolenko, Vladimir G.
See Korolenko, Vladimir Galaktionovich
Korolenko, Vladimir Galaktionovich 1853-1921 Brief entry ... 121
See also TCLC 22
Korotkin, Judith 1931- ... 53-56
Korr, Charles Paul 1939- ... 112
Kors, Alan Charles 1943- ... 77-80
Kort, Carol 1945- ... 106
Kort, Wesley A(lbert) 1935- ... CANR-34
Earlier sketch in CA 37-40R
Korte, Gene J. 1950- ... SATA 74
Korte, Mary Norbert
See Koerte, Mary Norbert
Korten, David C(raig) 1937- ... CANR-34
Earlier sketches in CA 41-44R, CANR-15
Kortepeter, C(arl) Max 1928- ... CANR-26
Earlier sketch in CA 41-44R
Korth, Francis N(icholas) 1912- ... 25-28R
Korth, Philip A. 1936- ... 137
Kortner, Peter 1924-1991 ... 33-36R
Obituary ... 133
Korty, Carol 1937- ... 77-80
See also SATA 15
Korty, John Van Cleave 1936- ... 106
Kory, Robert B(ruce) 1950- ... 65-68
Korzenik, Diana 1941- ... 133
Korzenny, Felipe 1947- ... 116
Korzybski, Alfred (Habdank Skarbek)
1879-1950 ... 160
Brief entry ... 123
See also TCLC 61
Kos, Erih 1913- Brief entry ... 106
Kosa, John 1914-1972 ... CANR-34
Earlier sketch in CA 5-8R
Kosch, Erich
See Kos, Erih
Koschade, Alfred 1928- ... 21-24R
Koscielniak, Bruce 1947- ... 134
See also SATA 67, 99
Kosel, Janice E. 1948- ... 116
Koshetz, Herbert 1907(?)-1977 Obituary ... 73-76
Koshi, George M. 1911- ... CAP-2
Earlier sketch in CA 29-32
Koshin, Alexander (A.) 1952- ... SATA 86
Koshland, Ellen 1947- ... CANR-13
Earlier sketch in CA 33-36R
Kosinski, Dorothy M. 1953- ... 145
Kosinski, Jerzy (Nikodem) 1933-1991 ... CANR-46
Obituary ... 134
Earlier sketches in CA 17-20R, CANR-9
See also CLC 1, 2, 3, 6, 10, 15, 53, 70
See also DAM NOV
See also DLB 2
See also DLBY 82
See also MTCW 1
Kosinski, Leonard V. 1923- ... 25-28R
Koskenmaki, Rosalie
See Maggio, Rosalie
Koski, Mary B(ernadette) 1951- ... 167
Koskoff, David E(lihu) 1939- ... 49-52
Koslow, Jules 1916- ... CANR-6
Earlier sketch in CA 1-4R
Kosmac, Ciril 1910-1980 ... DLB 181
Kosmala, Hans 1904(?)-1981 Obituary ... 104
Kosof, Anna 1945- ... CANR-35
Earlier sketch in CA 85-88
Kosovel, Srecko 1904-1926 ... DLB 147
Koss, Joan
See Koss-Chioino, Joan D.
Koss, Stephen E(dward) 1940-1984 ... CANR-48
Obituary ... 114
Earlier sketch in CA 25-28R
Koss-Chioino, Joan D. 1935- ... 144
Kosser, Mike 1941- ... 145
Kossez, Robes 1935- ... CANR-12
Earlier sketch in CA 29-32R
Kossin, Sandy (Sanford) 1926- ... SATA 10
Kosslyn, Stephen Michael 1948- ... CANR-40
Earlier sketch in CA 117
Kossman, Nina 1959- ... 150
See also SATA 84
Kossmann, Rudolf R(ichard) 1934- ... 37-40R
Kossoff, David 1919- ... CANR-35
Earlier sketch in CA 61-64
Kost, Mary Lu 1924- ... 45-48
Kost, Robert John 1913- ... 1-4R
Kostash, Myrna 1944- ... 65-68
Koste, Robert Francis 1933- ... 81-84
Kostelanetz, Andre 1901-1980 ... 165
Obituary ... 107
Kostelanetz, Richard (Cory) 1940- ... CANR-38
Earlier sketch in CA 13-16R
See also CAAS 8
See also CLC 28
Kosten, Andrew 1921- ... 1-4R
Koster, Donald N(elson) 1910- ... 52-56
Koster, John (Peter, Jr.) 1945- ... CANR-5
Earlier sketch in CA 53-56
Koster, R(ichard) M(orton) 1934- ... 37-40R
Kosters, Marvin H(oward) 1933- ... 143
Kostich, Dragos D. 1921- ... CANR-10
Earlier sketch in CA 5-8R
Kostis, Nicholas ... 103
Kostiuk, Hryhory 1902- ... 77-80
Kostka, Edmund Karl 1915- ... 17-20R
Kostrov, Ermil Ivanovich 1755-1796 ... DLB 150
Kostrowitzki, Wilhelm Apollinaris de
1880-1918 Brief entry ... 104
See also Apollinaire, Guillaume
Kostrubala, Thaddeus 1930- ... 101
Kostyu, Frank A(lexander) 1919- ... CANR-1
Earlier sketch in CA 49-52
Kosygin, Alexei Nikolayevich
1904-1980 Obituary ... 102
Kot, Stanislaw 1886(?)-1976 Obituary ... 65-68
Kotarba, Joseph A(nthony) 1947- ... 111
Kotarbinski, Tadeusz (Marian)
1886-1981 Obituary ... 105
Kotcheff, Ted
See Kotcheff, William Theodore
Kotcheff, William Theodore 1931- ... 115
Kothari, Rajni 1928- ... CANR-35
Earlier sketch in CA 33-36R
Kotin, Armine Avakian
See Mortimer, Armine Kotin
Kotker, Norman 1931- ... CANR-35
Earlier sketches in CA 25-28R, CANR-10
Kotker, Zane 1934- ... CANR-3
Earlier sketch in CA 49-52
Kotler, Milton 1935- ... CANR-25
Earlier sketch in CA 29-32R
Kotler, Neil G. 1941- ... 146
Kotler, Philip 1931- ... CANR-13
Earlier sketch in CA 33-36R
Kotlowitz, Alex 1955(?)- ... 138
Kotlowitz, Robert 1924- ... CANR-36
Earlier sketch in CA 33-36R
See also CLC 4
Kotowska, Monika 1942- ... 93-96
Kotowski, Joanne 1930- ... 57-60
Kotre, John N(icholas) 1940- ... 81-84
Kotrozo, Carol Donnell
See Donnell-Kotrozo, Carol
Kotschevar, Lendal H(enry) 1908- ... CANR-10
Earlier sketch in CA 17-20R
Kotschnig, Walter M(aria) 1901-1985 Obituary . 117
Kotsilibas-Davis, James 1940- ... 106
Kotsuji, Abraham S(etsuzau) 1899-1973 ... CAP-1
Obituary ... 45-48
Earlier sketch in CA 13-16
Kott, Jan 1914- ... 13-16R
Kottler, Dorothy 1918- ... 97-100
Kottler, Jeffrey (A.) 1951- ... 136
Kottman, Richard N(orman) 1932- ... 25-28R
Kotto, Yaphet (Fredrick) 1944(?)- ... 166
Kotz, David M(ichael) 1943- ... 81-84
Kotz, Mary Lynn 1936- ... 104
Kotz, Nick 1932- ... CANR-32
Earlier sketch in CA 29-32R
Kotz, Samuel 1930- ... CANR-34
Earlier sketches in CA 13-16R, CANR-7
Kotzebue, August (Friedrich Ferdinand) von
1761-1819 ... DLB 94
Kotzin, Michael C(harles) 1941- ... 37-40R
Kotzwinkle, William 1938- ... CANR-44
Earlier sketches in CA 45-48, CANR-3
See also CLC 5, 14, 35
See also CLR 6
See also DLB 173
See also MAICYA
See also SATA 24, 70
Koubourlis, Demetrius J(ohn) 1938- ... 57-60
Kouf, Jim
See Kouf, M(arvin) James, Jr.
Kouf, M(arvin) James, Jr. 1951- ... 141
Koufax, Sandy
See Koufax, Sanford
Koufax, Sanford 1935- ... 89-92
Kouhi, Elizabeth 1917- ... 126
See also SATA 54
See also SATA-Brief 49
Koulack, David 1938- ... 102
Koumoulides, John (Thomas Anastassios) 1938- ... CANR-34
Earlier sketch in CA 41-44R
Koupal, Nancy Tystad 1947- ... 158
Koupernik, Cyrille 1917- ... CANR-35
Earlier sketch in CA 57-60
Kourdakov, Sergei 1951-1973 Obituary ... 115
Kourilsky, Francoise 1933- ... 148
Kourouma, Ahmadou 1940- ... 143
See also BW 2
Kourvetaris, George A.
See Kourvetaris, Yorgos A.
Kourvetaris, Yorgos A. 1933- ... 127
Kousoulas, D(imitrios) George 1923- ... 17-20R
Kousser, J(oseph) Morgan 1943- ... CANR-32
Earlier sketch in CA 57-60
Koutoukas, H. M. 1947- ... CANR-47
Earlier sketch in CA 69-72
Kouts, Anne 1945- ... 29-32R
See also SATA 8
Kouts, Hertha Pretorius 1922-1973 ... 1-4R
Obituary ... 103
Kouwenhoven, John A(tlee) 1909-1990 ... 1-4R
Obituary ... 132
Kouyoumdjian, Dikran
See Arlen, Michael
Kovach, Barbara L(usk) Forisha
See Forisha-Kovach, Barbara L(usk)
Kovach, Bill 1932- ... CANR-11
Earlier sketch in CA 69-72
Kovach, Francis J(oseph) 1918- ... CANR-35
Earlier sketch in CA 61-64
Kovach, Gay H(aff) 1956- ... 149
Kovach, Kenneth A. 1946- ... 144
Kovach, Thomas A(llen) 1949- ... 129
Kovacic, Ante 1854-1889 ... DLB 147
Kovacs, Alexander 1930(?)-1977 Obituary ... 73-76
Kovacs, Deborah 1954- ... 148
See also SATA 79
Kovacs, Imre 1913-1980 ... CANR-34
Obituary ... 102
Earlier sketch in CA 21-24R
Kovacs, Steven 1946- ... 130
Kovaleff, Theodore Philip 1943- ... 116
Kovalev, Mikhail A(leksandrovich)
1893-1981 Obituary ... 108
Kovalik, Nada 1926- ... 25-28R
Kovalik, Vladimir 1928- ... 25-28R
Kovalski, Maryann 1951- ... 163
See also CLR 34
See also SAAS 21
See also SATA 58, 97
Kovarik, Bill
See Kovarik, William
Kovarik, William 1951- ... 113
Kovarsky, Irving 1918- ... 29-32R
Kovel, Joel S. 1936- ... CANR-66
Earlier sketches in CA 29-32R, CANR-14, 32
Kovel, Ralph ... CANR-48
Earlier sketches in CA 17-20R, CANR-8, 23
Kovel, Terry 1928- ... CANR-48
Earlier sketches in CA 17-20R, CANR-8, 23
Koves, Andras 1938- ... 145
Kovic, Kajetan 1931- ... DLB 181
Kovic, Ron 1946- ... 138
Kovner, Aba 1918-1987 Obituary ... 123
Kovner, B.
See Adler, Jacob
Kovrig, Bennett 1940- ... CANR-12
Earlier sketch in CA 29-32R
Kowaleski, Maryanne 1952- ... 150
Kowalewski, David 1943- ... 112
Kowalewski, Michael (John) 1956- ... 140
Kowalke, Kim H. 1948- ... 132
Kowalski, Frank 1907- ... 37-40R
Kowalski, Kathiann M. 1955- ... 161
See also SATA 96
Kowet, Don 1937- ... CANR-35
Earlier sketches in CA 57-60, CANR-10
Kowit, Steve 1938- ... 118
Kowitt, Sylvia
See Crosbie, Sylvia Kowitt
Kowitz, Gerald T(homas) 1928- ... 33-36R
Kowna, Stancy
See Szymborska, Wislawa
Kownslar, Allan O(wen) 1935- ... CANR-35
Earlier sketch in CA 61-64
Koya, Tatsuhito 1964- ... 144
Koyama, Kosuke 1929- ... CANR-35
Earlier sketches in CA 57-60, CANR-7
Koykka, Arthur S(idney) 1937- ... 116
Koyre, Alexandre 1892-1964 Obituary ... 111
Kozak, Jan B(lahoslav)
1889(?)-1974 Obituary ... 45-48
Kozak, Roman 1948(?)-1988 Obituary ... 126
Kozar, Andrew Joseph 1930- ... 103
Kozelka, Paul 1909- ... CAP-2
Earlier sketch in CA 25-28
Kozer, Jose 1940- ... CANR-34
Earlier sketches in CA 49-52, CANR-2
See also CAAS 29
Kozicki, Henry 1924- ... 103
Kozicki, Richard J(oseph) 1929- ... 125
Brief entry ... 118
Koziebrodzki, Leopold B(olesta) 1906- ... 41-44R
Kozintsev, Grigori (Mikhailovich) 1905-1973 .. 53-56
Kozlenko, William 1917- ... 57-60
Kozloff, Max 1933- ... 127
Brief entry ... 114
Kozloski, Lillian D. 1934- ... 150
Kozlow, Mark J.
See Newton, Michael
Kozlowski, Theodore T(homas) 1917- ... CANR-19
Earlier sketches in CA 9-12R, CANR-4
Kozol, Jonathan 1936- ... CANR-45
Earlier sketches in CA 61-64, CANR-16
See also CLC 17
Kozoll, Michael 1940(?)- ... CLC 35
Kozulin, Alex 1949- ... 122
Kpomassie, Tete-Michel 1941- ... 123
Kra, Siegfried J. 1930- ... CANR-67
Earlier sketch in CA 129
Kraay, Colin M(ackennal) 1918-1982 Obituary .. 116
Kracmar, John Z. 1916- ... 37-40R
Krader, Lawrence 1919- ... 21-24R
Kraditor, Aileen S. 1928- ... CANR-35
Earlier sketch in CA 13-16R
Kraehe, Enno E(dward) 1921- ... CANR-35
Earlier sketch in CA 9-12R
Kraemer, Kenneth L(eo) 1936- ... CANR-35
Earlier sketch in CA 111
Kraemer, Richard H(oward) 1920- ... CANR-35
Earlier sketches in CA 53-56, CANR-4
Kraenzel, Carl F(rederick) 1906- ... 73-76
Kraenzel, Margaret (Powell) 1899- ... 1-4R
Kraeuter, David W. 1941- ... 143
Kraf, Elaine 1946- ... CANR-11
Earlier sketch in CA 65-68
See also DLBY 81
Krafft, C(onrad) James 1923- ... 119
Krafft, Jim
See Krafft, C(onrad) James
Krafft, Maurice 1946-1991 ... CANR-10
Obituary ... 134
Earlier sketch in CA 65-68
Krafsur, Richard Paul 1940- ... 103
Kraft, Barbara 1939- ... 97-100
Kraft, Betsy Harvey 1937- ... 89-92
Kraft, Charles H(oward) 1932- ... CANR-16
Earlier sketches in CA 45-48, CANR-1
Kraft, Charlotte 1922- ... 103
Kraft, Dean 1950- ... 114
Kraft, Eric (Lance) 1944- ... 108
Kraft, Hy(man Solomon) 1899-1975 ... CANR-36
Obituary ... 57-60
Earlier sketch in CA 41-44R
Kraft, Joseph 1924-1986 ... CANR-34
Obituary ... 118
Earlier sketch in CA 9-12R
Kraft, Ken(neth) 1907- ... CANR-1
Earlier sketch in CA 1-4R
Kraft, Kenneth H. Sr. 1896-1983 Obituary ... 111
Kraft, Leo 1922- ... 41-44R
Kraft, Leonard E(dward) 1923- ... 29-32R
Kraft, Robert Alan 1934- ... 37-40R
Kraft, Stephanie (Barlett) 1944- ... 105
Kraft, Virginia 1932- ... 21-24R
Kraft, Walter Andreas
See Friedlander, Walter A(ndreas)
Kraft, William F. 1938- ... 33-36R
Kragen, Jinx
See Morgan, Judith A(dams)
Krahn, Fernando 1935- ... CANR-11
Earlier sketch in CA 65-68
See also CLR 3
See also SATA 49
See also SATA-Brief 31
Kraig, Bruce 1939- ... CANR-18
Earlier sketch in CA 102
Krailsheimer, Alban John 1921- ... CANR-2
Earlier sketch in CA 5-8R
Kraines, Oscar 1916- ... 97-100
Kraines, Samuel H(enry) 1906- ... 77-80
Kraizer, Sherryll Kerns 1948- ... 164
Krajenke, Robert William 1939- ... 29-32R
Krajewski, Frank R. 1938- ... CANR-10
Earlier sketch in CA 65-68
Krajewski, Robert J(oseph) 1940- ... 97-100
Krakauer, Hoong Yee Lee 1955- ... SATA 86
Krakauer, Jon ... 153
See also AAYA 24
Krakel, Dean (Fenton) 1923- ... CANR-47
Earlier sketch in CA 45-48
Krakowski, Lili 1930- ... 85-88
Kramarz, Joachim 1931- ... 25-28R
Kramer, A(lfred) T(heodore) 1892- ... CAP-1
Earlier sketch in CA 11-12
Kramer, Aaron 1921-1997 ... CANR-12
Obituary ... 157
Earlier sketch in CA 21-24R
Kramer, Anthony ... SATA-Brief 42
Kramer, Bernard M(ordecai) 1923- ... 77-80
Kramer, Charles 1915-1988 Obituary ... 125
Kramer, Dale 1936- ... CANR-5
Earlier sketch in CA 53-56
Kramer, Daniel C(aleb) 1934- ... 53-56
Kramer, Douglas 1950- ... 138
Kramer, Edith 1916- ... 33-36R
Kramer, Edna E.
See Kramer-Lassar, Edna Ernestine
Kramer, Edward (E.) 1961- ... 146
Kramer, Eugene F(rancis) 1921- ... 37-40R
Kramer, Frank Raymond 1908- ... CAP-1
Earlier sketch in CA 11-12
Kramer, Fritz W. 1941- ... 147
Kramer, Gene 1927- ... 69-72
Kramer, George
See Heuman, William
Kramer, Helen 1946- ... 146
Kramer, Hilton 1928- ... 113
Brief entry ... 109
Kramer, Jack N. 1923-1983 ... CANR-47
Earlier sketch in CA 41-44R
Kramer, Jane 1938- ... CANR-68
Earlier sketch in CA 102
Interview in ... 102
See also DLB 185
Kramer, Joel (Herbert) 1937- ... 97-100
Kramer, John Eichholtz, Jr. 1935- ... 108
Kramer, Jonathan D. 1942- ... 130
Kramer, Jonathan M. 1946- ... 121
Kramer, Judith Rita 1933-1970 ... 1-4R
Obituary ... 103
Kramer, Kathryn 19(?)- ... CLC 34
Kramer, Larry 1935- ... CANR-60
Brief entry ... 124
Earlier sketch in CA 126
See also CLC 42
See also DAM POP
See also DC 8
Kramer, Lawrence (Eliot) 1946- ... CANR-45
Earlier sketch in CA 120
Kramer, Leonie Judith 1924- ... CANR-39
Earlier sketches in CA 81-84, CANR-17
Kramer, Linda Konheim 1939- ... 146
Kramer, Lloyd S. 1949- ... 165
Kramer, Lotte (Karoline) 1923- ... 153
Kramer, Mark (William) 1944- ... CANR-68
Earlier sketches in CA 97-100, CANR-17
See also DLB 185
Kramer, Martin 1954- ... 160
Kramer, Milton D. 1915-1973 Obituary ... 37-40R

Kramer, Nancy 1942- ... 101
Kramer, Nora 1896(?)-1984 ... 107
Obituary ... 113
See also SATA 26
See also SATA-Obit 39
Kramer, (Simon) Paul 1914- ... 21-24R
Kramer, Paul J(ackson) 1904-1995 ... CANR-1
Obituary ... 149
Earlier sketch in CA 45-48
Kramer, Peter (D.) 1948- ... 145
Kramer, Remi (Thomas) 1935- ... SATA 90
Kramer, Rita 1929- ... CANR-57
Earlier sketches in CA 69-72, CANR-31
Kramer, Roberta 1935- ... 103
Kramer, Roland Laird 1898- ... 5-8R
Kramer, Samuel Noah 1897-1990 ... 9-12R
Obituary ... 133
Kramer, Ted
See Steward, Samuel M(orris)
Kramer, Victor A. 1939- ... CANR-16
Earlier sketch in CA 85-88
Kramer-Lassar, Edna Ernestine 1902-1984 ... 107
Obituary ... 113
Kramish, Arnold 1923- ... CANR-7
Earlier sketch in CA 5-8R
Krammer, Arnold Paul 1941- ... CANR-27
Earlier sketches in CA 61-64, CANR-11
Kramnick, Isaac 1938- ... 139
Kramon, Florence 1920- ... 25-28R
Kramrisch, Stella 1896(?)-1993 ... CAP-2
Obituary ... 142
Earlier sketch in CA 21-22
Kranidas, Kathleen
See Collins, Kathleen
Kranjcevic, Silvije Strahimir 1865-1908 ... DLB 147
Krantz, Grover S. 1931- ... 146
Krantz, Hazel (Newman) ... CANR-40
Earlier sketches in CA 1-4R, CANR-1, 16
See also SATA 12
Krantz, Judith 1927- ... CANR-66
Earlier sketches in CA 81-84, CANR-11, 33
See also BEST 89:1
See also DAM NOV, POP
See also MTCW 1
Krantz, Les(lie Jay) 1945- ... 120
Krantz, Steven G. 1951- ... 165
Kranz, E(dwin) Kirker 1949- ... 33-36R
Kranz, Stewart D(uane) 1924- ... 101
Kranzberg, Melvin 1917-1995 ... CANR-11
Obituary ... 150
Earlier sketch in CA 21-24R
Kranzler, David 1930- ... 93-96
Kranzler, George G(ershon) 1916- ... CANR-12
Earlier sketch in CA 57-60
See also SATA 28
Kranzler, Gershon
See Kranzler, George G(ershon)
Krapf, Norbert 1943- ... 117
Krapp, R. M.
See Adams, Robert Martin
Krar, Stephen Frank 1924- ... CANR-42
Earlier sketches in CA 53-56, CANR-4, 20
Kraselchik, R.
See Dyer, Charles (Raymond)
Krashen, Stephen D. 1941- ... 132
Krasilovsky, M(arvin) William 1926- ... 61-64
Krasilovsky, Phyllis 1926- ... CANR-45
Earlier sketches in CA 29-32R, CANR-11
See also MAICYA
See also SAAS 5
See also SATA 1, 38
Kraske, Robert Brief entry ... 116
See also SATA-Brief 36
Kraslow, David 1926- ... 29-32R
Krasna, Norman 1909-1984 Obituary ... 114
See also DLB 26
Krasna, Norman 1909-1984 ... 164
Krasne, Betty
See Levine, Betty K(rasne)
Krasner, Jack Daniel 1921-1978 ... CANR-3
Earlier sketch in CA 49-52
Krasner, Leonard 1924- ... 33-36R
Krasner, Stephen D(avid) 1942- ... CANR-15
Earlier sketch in CA 85-88
Krasner, William 1917- ... CANR-35
Earlier sketches in CA 37-40R, CANR-15
Krasney, Samuel A. 1922- ... 1-4R
Krasnov, Vladislav Georgievich 1937- ... 132
Krasnow, Erwin G(ilbert) 1936- ... 103
Krasnow, Iris 1954(?)- ... 163
Krasovskaya, Vera (Mikhailovna) 1915- ... 130
Brief entry ... 106
Krass, Alfred C(harles) 1936- ... 116
Krasser, Wilhelm 1925(?)-1979 Obituary ... 89-92
Krassner, Paul 1932- ... CANR-11
Earlier sketch in CA 21-24R
Krasso, Miklos 1929(?)-1986 Obituary ... 118
Kratcoski, Peter C(harles) 1936- ... 111
Kratochvil, Paul 1932- ... 25-28R
Kratos
See Power, Norman S(andiford)
Kratovil, Robert 1910- ... CANR-5
Earlier sketch in CA 5-8R
Kratz, Martin P. J. 1955- ... 143
Kratzenstein, Jossef J. 1904- ... CAP-2
Earlier sketch in CA 17-18
Krauch, Velma 1916- ... 37-40R
Kraues, Judith E. ... 101
Kraus, Albert L(awson) 1920-1996 ... 41-44R
Obituary ... 151
Kraus, Barbara 1929-1977 ... 102
Kraus, Bruce R. 1954- ... 97-100
Kraus, C(lyde) Norman 1924- ... CANR-33
Earlier sketches in CA 41-44R, CANR-15
Kraus, Charles E. 1946- ... 111
Kraus, Constantine Raymond 1900- ... 129
Kraus, George 1930- ... 25-28R
Kraus, H. P.
See Kraus, Hans P(eter)
Kraus, Hans P(eter) 1907-1988 ... CAP-2
Obituary ... 127
Earlier sketch in CA 29-32
See also DLB 187
Kraus, Joanna Halpert 1937- ... CANR-44
Earlier sketches in CA 104, CANR-21
See also SATA 87
Kraus, Joe 1939- ... CANR-15
Earlier sketch in CA 89-92
Kraus, Joseph 1925- ... CANR-4
Earlier sketch in CA 53-56
Kraus, Karl 1874-1936 Brief entry ... 104
See also DLB 118
See also TCLC 5
Kraus, Michael 1901-1990 ... 5-8R
Obituary ... 132
Kraus, Richard G(ordon) 1923- ... CANR-11
Earlier sketch in CA 13-16R
Kraus, (Herman) Robert 1925- ... CANR-54
Earlier sketch in CA 33-36R
See also MAICYA
See also SAAS 11
See also SATA 4, 65, 93
Kraus, Sidney 1927- ... CANR-10
Earlier sketch in CA 5-8R
Kraus, W. Keith 1934- ... 21-24R
Krause, David 1917- ... 168
Krause, Frank H(arold) 1942- ... 104
Krause, Harry D(ieter) 1932- ... 33-36R
Krause, Herbert (Arthur) 1905-1976 ... CANR-63
Obituary ... 103
Earlier sketch in CA 49-52
Krause, Jill A.
See Steans, Jill A.
Krause, Lawrence Berle 1929- ... 113
Krause, Pat 1930- ... CANR-37
Earlier sketch in CA 114
Krause, Paul 1951- ... 139
Krause, Shari Stamford
See Stamford Krause, Shari
Krause, Sydney J(oseph) 1925- ... 21-24R
Krause, Walter 1917- ... CANR-1
Earlier sketch in CA 1-4R
Kraushaar, John L. 1917- ... 45-48
Kraushaar, Otto F(rederick) 1901- ... 37-40R
Krauskopf, Konrad B(ates) 1910- ... 77-80
Krauss, Bob
See Krauss, Robert G.
Krauss, Bruno
See Bulmer, (Henry) Kenneth
Krauss, Clifford 1953- ... 136
Krauss, Ellis S(aunders) 1944- ... CANR-8
Earlier sketch in CA 61-64
Krauss, Herbert Harris 1940- ... 85-88
Krauss, Lawrence M. 1954- ... 147
Krauss, Paul Gerhardt 1905- ... 1-4R
Krauss, Robert G. 1924- ... CANR-2
Earlier sketch in CA 1-4R
Krauss, Robert M. 1931- ... 17-20R
Krauss, Rosalind E(pstein) 1940- ... 81-84
Krauss, Ruth (Ida) 1911-1993 ... CANR-47
Obituary ... 141
Earlier sketches in CA 1-4R, CANR-1, 13
See also CLR 42
See also DLB 52
See also MAICYA
See also SATA 1, 30
See also SATA-Obit 75
Krausz, Ernest 1931- ... 104
Krausz, Michael 1942- ... CANR-4
Earlier sketch in CA 53-56
Krausz, Norman G(eorge) P(hilip) 1920- ... 41-44R
Kraut, Benny 1947- ... 113
Kraut, Richard 1944- ... 130
Krauthammer, Charles 1950- ... 127
Brief entry ... 121
Interview in ... 127
Krautheimer, Richard 1897-1994 ... 103
Obituary ... 147
Krautter, Elisa (Bialk) 1912(?)-1990 ... CANR-1
Obituary ... 131
Earlier sketch in CA 1-4R
See also SATA 1
See also SATA-Obit 65
Krautwurst, Terry 1946- ... SATA 79
Krauze, Andrzej 1947- ... SATA-Brief 46
Krauzer, Steven M(ark) 1948- ... CANR-51
Earlier sketches in CA 109, CANR-25
Kravetz, Nathan 1921- ... 9-12R
Kravis, Irving B(ernard) 1916- ... CANR-7
Earlier sketch in CA 17-20R
Kravitz, Nathan
See Kravitz, Nathaniel
Kravitz, Nathaniel 1905- ... 49-52
Krawiec, Richard 1952- ... 122
Krawiec, T(heophile) S(tanley) 1913- ... CANR-10
Earlier sketch in CA 25-28R
Krawitz, Henry 1947- ... 45-48
Krawitz, Herman E(verett) 1925- ... 61-64
Krawitz, Ruth (Lifshitz) 1929- ... 9-12R
Kray, Robert Clement 1930- ... SATA 82
Kraybill, Donald B(rubaker) 1945- ... 69-72
Krebs, Alfred H. 1920- ... 21-24R
Krebs, Hans (Adolf) 1900-1981 ... 129
Obituary ... 108
Krech, David 1909-1977 Obituary ... 73-76
Krech, Shepard III 1944- ... 119
Kredel, Fritz 1900-1973 Obituary ... 41-44R
See also SATA 17
Kredenser, Gail 1936- ... 21-24R
Kreeft, Peter 1937- ... CANR-57
Earlier sketches in CA 81-84, CANR-14, 31
Krefetz, Gerald 1932- ... CANR-15
Earlier sketch in CA 33-36R
Krefetz, Ruth 1931-1972 ... CAP-2
Obituary ... 37-40R
Earlier sketch in CA 33-36
Kregel, J(an) A(llen) 1944- ... 41-44R
Kreh, Bernard 1925- ... 57-60
Kreider, Barbara 1942- ... 41-44R
Kreider, Carl 1914- ... 37-40R
Kreider, Jan F(rederick) 1942- ... 111
Kreidl, John Francis 1939- ... 81-84
Kreig, Margaret B. (Baltzell) 1922-1998 ... 13-16R
Obituary ... 164
Kreikemeier, Gregory Scott 1965- ... SATA 85
Krein, David F(rederick) 1942- ... 85-88
Kreindler, Lee (Stanley) 1924- ... 17-20R
Kreingold, Shana 1889(?)-1972 Obituary ... 37-40R
Kreinin, Mordechai 1930- ... 9-12R
Kreisel, Henry 1922-1991 ... CANR-42
Earlier sketch in CA 61-64
See also DAC
See also DAM MST
See also DLB 88
Kreiser, B(ernard) Robert 1943- ... 116
Kreisler, Fritz 1875-1962 Obituary ... 115
Kreisman, Leonard T(heodore) 1925- ... 13-16R
Kreisman, Marvin 1933(?)-1979(?) Obituary ... 102
Kreitler, Hans 1916- ... 45-48
Kreitler, Shulamith 1938- ... 45-48
Krejci, Jaroslav 1916- ... CANR-57
Earlier sketches in CA 41-44R, CANR-14, 31
Kremen, Bennett 1936- ... 57-60
Kremenliev, Boris A(ngeloff) 1911-1988 ... 45-48
Obituary ... 125
Krementz, Jill 1940- ... CANR-46
Earlier sketches in CA 41-44R, CANR-23
Interview in ... CANR-23
See also AITN 1, 2
See also CLR 5
See also MAICYA
See also SAAS 8
See also SATA 17, 71
Kremer, Laura Evelyn 1921- ... 103
Kremer, Marcie
See Sorenson, Margo
Kremer, Rudiger
See Kremer, Ruediger
Kremer, Ruediger 1942- ... 139
Kremer, William F. 1919- ... 69-72
Kreml, Anne Lee 1930- ... 21-24R
Kreml, William P. 1941- ... 165
Krempel, Daniel S(partakus) 1926- ... 33-36R
Kren, George M. 1926- ... 102
Krenek, Ernst 1900-1991 ... 57-60
Obituary ... 136
Krenina, Katya 1968- ... SATA 101
Krenkel, John H(enry) 1906- ... CAP-2
Earlier sketch in CA 33-36
Krensky, Stephen (Alan) 1953- ... CANR-67
Earlier sketches in CA 73-76, CANR-13, 46
See also SATA 47, 93
See also SATA-Brief 41
Krentel, Mildred White 1921- ... 5-8R
Krents, Harold Eliot 1944-1987 ... 37-40R
Obituary ... 121
Krentz, Edgar (Martin) 1928- ... 21-24R
Krentz, Jayne Ann 1948- ... CANR-63
Earlier sketch in CA 139
Krepon, Michael 1946- ... 128
Krepps, Robert W(ilson) 1919-1980 ... CANR-1
Earlier sketch in CA 1-4R
Kreps, Juanita M(orris) 1921- ... 130
Kresge, George Joseph, Jr.
See Kreskin
Kresh, Paul 1919-1997 ... CANR-13
Obituary ... 156
Earlier sketch in CA 13-16R
See also SATA 61
See also SATA-Obit 94
Kreskin 1935- ... 101
Kress, Nancy 1948- ... CANR-60
Earlier sketch in CA 126
See also SATA 85
Kress, Paul F(rederick) 1935- ... 29-32R
Kress, Robert (Lee) 1932- ... CANR-8
Earlier sketch in CA 61-64
Kress, Roy A(lfred) 1916- ... 107
Kress, Stephen W. 1945- ... 122
Kressel, Kenneth 1942- ... 119
Kressel, Neil J. 1957- ... 152
Kressy, Michael 1936- ... CANR-8
Earlier sketch in CA 61-64
Kretsch, Robert W. 1913(?)-1979 Obituary ... 89-92
Kretzmann, Adalbert Raphael 1903- ... CAP-1
Earlier sketch in CA 13-16
Kretzmann, Norman 1928- ... 49-52
Kretzmer, Herbert 1925- ... 105
Kreuder, Ernst 1903-1972 ... DLB 69
Kreuger, Miles 1934- ... 81-84
Kreusler, Abraham A(rthur) 1897- ... 65-68
Kreuter, Kent 1932- ... 29-32R
Kreuzer, James R. 1913-1971 ... CAP-1
Earlier sketch in CA 11-12
Kreve (Mickevicius), Vincas 1882-1954 ... TCLC 27
Krevitsky, Nathan I. 1914- ... 9-12R
Krevitsky, Nik
See Krevitsky, Nathan I.
Krevolin, Nathan 1927- ... CANR-14
Earlier sketch in CA 41-44R
Krewer, Semyon E(fimovich) 1915- ... 105
Kreyche, Gerald F. 1927- ... 37-40R
Kreyche, Robert J(oseph) 1920-1974 ... 13-16R
Obituary ... 133
Kreymborg, Alfred 1883-1966 Obituary ... 25-28R
See also DLB 4, 54
Krich, A. M.
See Krich, Aron
Krich, Aron 1916- ... 120
Krich, Aron M.
See Krich, Aron
Krich, John 1951- ... 108
Krich, Rochelle Majer ... 166
Krieg, Joann P(eck) 1932- ... 143
Krieg, Robert Anthony 1946- ... 145
Krieg, Saul 1917- ... 81-84
Kriegel, Gail 1942- ... 108
Kriegel, Harriet ... 104
Kriegel, Leonard 1933- ... CANR-12
Earlier sketch in CA 33-36R
Krieger, Frieda Frome 1925- ... 128
Krieger, Leonard 1918-1990 ... CANR-7
Obituary ... 132
Earlier sketch in CA 17-20R
Krieger, Martin H. 1944- ... 138
Krieger, Melanie ... 161
See also SATA 96
Krieger, Michael J. 1940- ... 146
Krieger, Murray 1923- ... CANR-50
Earlier sketches in CA 1-4R, CANR-2
See also DLB 67
Krieghbaum, Hillier (Hiram) 1902- ... CANR-2
Earlier sketch in CA 5-8R
Kriegman, Oscar M(arvin) 1930- ... 9-12R
Kriensky, Morris (Edward) 1917-1998 ... 57-60
Obituary ... 166
Krier, James E(dward) 1939- ... 81-84
Kriesberg, Louis 1926- ... CANR-12
Earlier sketch in CA 29-32R
Krikorian, Yervant H(ovhannes) 1892-1977 ... CANR-2
Obituary ... 73-76
Earlier sketch in CA 45-48
Krim, Seymour 1922-1989 ... CANR-4
Obituary ... 129
Earlier sketch in CA 5-8R
See also DLB 16
Krimerman, Leonard Isaiah 1934- ... 17-20R
Krims, Milton Robert 1904(?)-1988 Obituary ... 126
Krimsky, George A. 1942- ... 156
Krimsky, Joseph (Hayylm) 1883(?)-1971 Obituary ... 104
Krimsky, Sheldon 1941- ... CANR-33
Earlier sketch in CA 113
Krin, Sylvie
See Fantoni, Barry (Ernest)
Kring, Hilda Adam 1921- ... 77-80
Kring, Walter Donald 1916- ... 116
Kringle, Karen 1947- ... 140
Krinsky, Carol Herselle 1937- ... 37-40R
Kripalani, J(iwatram) B(hagwandas) 1888-1982 Obituary ... 110
Kripke, Dorothy Karp ... 17-20R
See also SATA 30
Kripke, Saul A(aron) 1940- ... 130
Krippendorff, Klaus 1932- ... 77-80
Krippner, Stanley (Curtis) 1932- ... CANR-68
Earlier sketches in CA 81-84, CANR-15, 32
Krisch, Henry 1931- ... 134
Brief entry ... 111
Krise, Raymond (Owens, Jr.) 1949- ... 109
Krisher, Bernard 1931- ... CANR-18
Earlier sketch in CA 77-80
Krisher, Trudy (B.) 1946- ... 151
See also SATA 86
Krishna, Gopi
See Shivpuri, Gopi Krishna
Krishnamurti, Jiddu 1895-1986 ... CANR-69
Obituary ... 118
Earlier sketches in CA 61-64, CANR-11, 39
Krislov, Alexander
See Lee Howard, Leon Alexander
Krislov, Joseph 1927- ... 41-44R
Krislov, Samuel 1929- ... CANR-18
Earlier sketches in CA 9-12R, CANR-3
Krispyn, Egbert 1930- ... 13-16R
Kriss, Ronald P(aul) 1934- ... 69-72
Krist, Gary (Michael) 1957- ... 132
Kristein, Marvin M(ichael) 1926- ... 29-32R
Kristeller, Paul Oskar 1905- ... CANR-6
Earlier sketch in CA 9-12R
Kristensen, Thorkil 1899-1989 ... 130
Kristeva, Julia 1941- ... 154
See also CLC 77
Kristian, Hans
See Neerskov, Hans Kristian
Kristof, Agota 1935- ... 168
Kristof, Jane 1932- ... 29-32R
See also SATA 8
Kristof, Ladis K(ris) D(onabed) 1918- ... 61-64
Kristof, Nicholas D(onabet) 1959- ... CANR-53
Earlier sketch in CA 126
Kristofferson, Kris 1936- ... 104
See also CLC 26
Kristol, Irving 1920- ... CANR-28
Earlier sketch in CA 25-28R
Kritsick, Stephen M(ark) 1951-1994 ... 112
Obituary ... 143
Kritz, Mary M. ... 138
Kritzeck, James 1930- ... 5-8R
Kritzer, Amelia Howe 1947- ... 146
Kriyananda
See Walters, J. Donald
Kriyananda, S.
See Walters, J. Donald
Kriyananda, Sri
See Walters, J. Donald
Kriyananda, Swami
See Walters, J. Donald
Krizanc, John 1956- ... CLC 57
Krizay, John 1926- ... 61-64

Krleza, Miroslav 1893-1981 .... CANR-50
Obituary 105
Earlier sketch in CA 97-100
See also CLC 8
See also DLB 147
Krmpotic, Vesna 1932- CANR-44
Earlier sketches in CA 102, CANR-20
Kroc, Ray(mond Albert) 1902-1984 118
Obituary 111
Kroch, Adolph A. 1882-1978 Obituary 81-84
Krochmal, Arnold 1919- CANR-14
Earlier sketch in CA 69-72
Krochmal, Connie 1949- 41-44R
Krock, Arthur 1887-1974 .... CAP-2
Obituary 49-52
Earlier sketch in CA 33-36
See also AITN 1
See also DLB 29
Krodel, Gerhard 1926- 61-64
Kroeber, A(lfred) L(ouis) 1876-1960 129
Obituary 110
Kroeber, Clifton B(rown) 1921- CANR-32
Earlier sketch in CA 110
Kroeber, Donald W(alter) 1934- 115
Kroeber, Karl 1926- CANR-66
Earlier sketches in CA 57-60, CANR-32
Kroeber, Theodora (Kracaw) 1897-1979 . CANR-32
Obituary 89-92
Earlier sketches in CA 5-8R, CANR-5
See also Quinn, Theodora K.
See also SATA 1
Kroeger, Arthur 1908- 13-16R
Kroeger, Brooke 1949- 146
Kroeger, Frederick P(aul) 1921- 33-36R
Kroeger, Mary Kay 1950- .... SATA 92
Kroepcke, Karol
See Krolow, Karl (Gustav Heinrich)
Kroetsch, Robert 1927- CANR-38
Earlier sketches in CA 17-20R, CANR-8
See also CLC 5, 23, 57
See also DAC
See also DAM POET
See also DLB 53
See also MTCW 1
Kroetz, Franz
See Kroetz, Franz Xaver
Kroetz, Franz Xaver 1946- 130
See also CLC 41
Kroger, William S. 1906- CAP-1
Earlier sketch in CA 13-14
Krohn, Claus-Dieter 1941- 146
Krohn, Ernst C(hristopher) 1888-1975 .... 37-40R
See also AITN 1
Krohn, Katherine E(lizabeth) 1961- 150
See also SATA 84
Krohn, Norman Odya 1920- 116
Krohn, Robert 1937- 45-48
Kroker, Arthur (W.) 1945- 161
See also CLC 77
Krok-Paszkowski, Jan 1925- 130
Kroll, Burt
See Rowland, D(onald) S(ydney)
Kroll, Ernest 1914- 97-100
Kroll, Francis Lynde 1904-1973 .... CAP-1
Earlier sketch in CA 13-16
See also SATA 10
Kroll, John (Leon) 1925-1986 Obituary 119
Kroll, Judith 1943- 65-68
Kroll, Morton 1923- 49-52
Kroll, Steven 1941- CANR-50
Earlier sketches in CA 65-68, CANR-9, 25, 35
See also SAAS 7
See also SATA 19, 66
Kroll, Virginia L(ouise) 1948- 143
See also SATA 76
Kroller, Eva-Marie 1949- 128
Krolow, Karl (Gustav Heinrich) 1915- 81-84
Kromer, Helen CANR-34
Earlier sketch in CA 93-96
Kromm, David E. 1938- 144
Komminga, John H(enry) 1918- 77-80
Krondorfer, Bjorn 1959- 151
Kronegger, Maria Elisabeth 1932- 25-28R
Kronen, Steve 1953- 140
Kronenberg, Henry Harold 1902- 1-4R
Kronenberg, Maria Elizabeth
1881(?)-1970 Obituary 104
Kronenberger, Louis 1904-1980 .... CANR-2
Obituary 97-100
Earlier sketch in CA 1-4R
Kronenfeld, Jennie J(acobs) 1949- 146
Kronenwetter, Michael 1943- .... SATA 62
Kroner, Richard 1884- 9-12R
Kronhausen, Eberhard W(ilhelm) 1915- ... CANR-6
Earlier sketch in CA 9-12R
Kronhausen, Phyllis C(armen) 1929- CANR-6
Earlier sketch in CA 9-12R
Kronick, David A(braham) 1917- 9-12R
Kronick, Joseph G. 1953- 122
Kroninger, Robert H(enry) 1923- 13-16R
Kroniuk, Lisa
See Berton, Pierre (Francis Demarigny)
Kronk, Gary (Wayne) 1956- 115
Kronman, Anthony T(ownsend) 1945- 113
Kronstadt, Henry L(ippin) 1915- 73-76
Kronus, Sidney J., Jr. 1937- Brief entry 107
Krook, Dorothea 1920- 123
Krooss, Herman E. 1912-1975 .... CAP-2
Obituary 57-60
Earlier sketch in CA 17-18
Krooth, Dick
See Krooth, Richard
Krooth, Richard 1935- 146
Kropf, Linda S(toddart) 1947- 49-52
Kropf, Richard W(illiam Bartlett) 1932- ... CANR-10
Earlier sketch in CA 65-68
Kropotkin, Peter (Aleksieevich) 1842-1921 Brief entry 119
See also TCLC 36
Kropp, Lloyd 25-28R
Kropp, Paul (Stephan) 1948- 112
See also SATA 38
See also SATA-Brief 34
Krosby, H(ans) Peter 1929- 89-92
Krosney, Mary Stewart 1939- 17-20R
Krotki, Karol J(ozef) 1922- 41-44R
Krotkov, Yuri 1917- 102
See also CLC 19
Krout, John Allen 1896-1979 97-100
Obituary 85-88
Krstic, Radivoj V(ase) 1935- 142
Kruchkow, Diane 1947- 69-72
Kruck, William E(vert) 1942- 114
Kruckeberg, Arthur R(ice) 1920- 137
Krueger, Anne O. 1934- CANR-32
Earlier sketches in CA 37-40R, CANR-15
Krueger, Arnd
See Kruger, Arnd
Krueger, Christoph 1937- 33-36R
Krueger, Hardy 1928- 77-80
Krueger, Henrik S. 1938- 130
Krueger, John R(ichard) 1927- CANR-33
Earlier sketches in CA 21-24R, CANR-10
Krueger, Lorenz 1932- 136
Krueger, Marj 158
Krueger, Ralph R. 1927- CANR-2
Earlier sketch in CA 49-52
Krueger, Robert B(lair) 1928- 57-60
Krueger, Thomas A. 1936- 21-24R
Kruell, Marianne 1936- 132
Kruess, James 1926- CANR-5
Earlier sketch in CA 53-56
See also Kruss, James
See also MAICYA
See also SATA 8
Krug, Edward August 1911-1980 .... CANR-4
Earlier sketch in CA 5-8R
Krug, Mark M. 1915- Brief entry 109
Krug, Samuel E(dward) 1943- 121
Kruger, Arnd 1944- 163
Kruger, Arthur N(ewman) 1916- CANR-1
Earlier sketch in CA 1-4R
Kruger, Daniel H(erschel) 1922- 25-28R
Kruger, Hardy
See Krueger, Hardy
Kruger, Lorenz
See Krueger, Lorenz
Kruger, Mollee (Coppel) 1929- CANR-45
Earlier sketches in CA 69-72, CANR-21
Kruger, Paul
See Sebenthall, R(oberta) E(lizabeth)
Kruger, (Charles) Rayne 5-8R
Kruglak, Haym 1909- 53-56
Kruh, David (S.) 1956- 138
Kruh, Louis 1923- 138
Kruise, Carol Sue 1939- 125
Krukowski, Lucian 1929- 125
Krulewitch, Melvin Levin 1895-1978 103
Krulik, Stephen 1933- CANR-8
Earlier sketch in CA 17-20R
Krull, Felix
See White, Stanley
Krull, Kathleen 1952- 106
See also CLR 44
See also SATA 52, 80
See also SATA-Brief 39
Krull, Marianne
See Kruell, Marianne
Kruman, Marc W. 1949- 166
Krumb
See Crumb, R(obert)
Krumboltz, John D(wight) 1928- Brief entry 110
Krumgold, Joseph (Quincy) 1908-1980 .... CANR-7
Obituary 101
Earlier sketch in CA 9-12R
See also CLC 12
See also MAICYA
See also SATA 1, 48
See also SATA-Obit 23
Krumm, John McGill 1913-1995 109
Obituary 150
Krummel, Donald William 1929- 106
Krump, John M. 1929(?)-1990 Obituary 132
Krumpelmann, John T(heodore) 1892- 41-44R
Krumwitz
See Crumb, R(obert)
Krupat, Arnold 1941- 126
Krupat, Edward 1945- 77-80
Krupinski, Loretta 1940- .... SATA 67, 102
Krupnick, Karen 1947- 155
See also SATA 89
Krupnick, Mark L. 1939- 130
Krupnik, Baruch
See Karu, Baruch
Krupp, E(dwin) C(harles) 1944- CANR-21
Earlier sketch in CA 105
See also SATA 53
Krupp, Nate 1935- CANR-10
Earlier sketch in CA 21-24R
Krupp, Robin Rector 1946- 135
See also SATA 53
Krupp, Sherman Roy 1926-1988 .... 1-4R
Obituary 125
Krusch, Werner E. 1927- 5-8R
Kruschke, Earl R(oger) 1934- 41-44R
Kruse, Alexander Z. 1888(?)-1972 Obituary . 33-36R
Kruse, Harry D(ayton) 1900-1977 Obituary ... 73-76
Kruse, John 1919- CANR-35
Earlier sketch in CA 114
Krush, Beth 1918- .... MAICYA
See also SATA 18
Krush, Joe 1918- .... MAICYA
See also SATA 18
Krusich, Walter S(teve) 1922- 49-52
Kruskal, William H(enry) 1919- 33-36R
Kruss, James
See Kruess, James
See also CLR 9
Kruszewski, Z. Anthony 1928- 134
Brief entry 113
Krutch, Joseph Wood 1893-1970 .... CANR-4
Obituary 25-28R
Earlier sketch in CA 1-4R
See also CLC 24
See also DLB 63
Krutilla, John Vasil 1922- CANR-9
Earlier sketch in CA 21-24R
Krutzch, Gus
See Eliot, T(homas) S(tearns)
Kruuk, Hans 1937- 61-64
Kruzas, Anthony T(homas) 1914- CANR-17
Earlier sketches in CA 1-4R, CANR-2
Krykorka, Vladyana 1945- .... SATA 96
Krylov, Ivan Andreevich 1768(?)-1844 .... DLB 150
Krymow, Virginia P(auline) 1930- 69-72
Krypton
See Graham, Lloyd M.
Krysl, Marilyn 1943- 105
Krythe, Maymie Richardson 17-20R
Krzywan, Jozef
See Krotki, Karol J(ozef)
Krzyzaniak, Marian 1911- 9-12R
Krzyzanowski, Jerzy R(oman) 1922- 37-40R
Krzyzanowski, Ludwik 1907(?)-1986 Obituary .. 118
Kselman, Thomas A. 1948- 110
K-Turkel, Judi
See Kesselman-Turkel, Judi
Kubal, David L(awrence) 1936- 45-48
Kubat, Daniel 1928- Brief entry 114
Kubeck, James (Ernest) 1920- 17-20R
Kubek, Anthony 1920- 104
Kubelka, Susanna 1942- 113
Kube-McDowell, Michael P(aul) 1954- 119
Kuberski, Philip 1952- 145
Kubey, Robert W(illiam) 1952- 165
Kubiak, Greg D. 1960- 147
Kubiak, T(imothy) J(ames) 1942- 61-64
Kubiak, William J. 1929- 33-36R
Kubicek, Robert V(incent) 1935- CANR-47
Earlier sketch in CA 29-32R
Kubie, Eleanor Gottheil
See Kubie, Nora Gottheil Benjamin
Kubie, Lawrence S. 1896(?)-1973 Obituary ... 45-48
Kubie, Nora Benjamin
See Kubie, Nora Gottheil Benjamin
Kubie, Nora Gottheil Benjamin 1899-1988 .... 5-8R
Obituary 126
See also SATA 39
See also SATA-Obit 59
Kubin, Alfred (Leopold Isidor) 1877-1959 149
Brief entry 112
See also DLB 81
See also TCLC 23
Kubinyi, Laszlo 1937- CANR-68
Earlier sketch in CA 85-88
See also SATA 17, 94
Kubis, Pat 1928- 25-28R
Kubler, George (Alexander) 1912-1996 .... 9-12R
Obituary 154
Kubler-Ross, Elisabeth
See Kuebler-Ross, Elisabeth
Kublin, Hyman 1919- 9-12R
Kubly, Herbert (Oswald Nicholas) 1915-1996 .... CANR-44
Obituary 153
Earlier sketches in CA 5-8R, CANR-4
Kubo, Sakae 1926- CANR-7
Earlier sketch in CA 57-60
Kubose, Gyomay M(asao) 1905- 49-52
Kubota, Akira 1932- 37-40R
Kubrick, Stanley 1928- CANR-33
Earlier sketch in CA 81-84
See also CLC 16
See also DLB 26
Kucera, Henry 1925- 21-24R
Kucharek, Casimir (Anthony) 1928- 57-60
Kucharski, Kasimir
See Koch, Kurt E(mil)
Kucharsky, David (Eugene) 1931- 65-68
Kucherov, Alexander 1927-1985 Obituary 117
Kucich, John (Richard) 1952- 112
Kuczkir, Mary 1933- CANR-42
Brief entry 111
Earlier sketch in CA 115
Interview in 115
Kuczmarski, Susan Smith 1951- 150
Kuczmarski, Thomas D(ale) 1951- 150
Kuczynski, Pedro-Pablo 1938- 77-80
Kudian, Mischa 107
Kudrle, Robert Thomas 1942- 112
Kuebler-Ross, Elisabeth 1926- 25-28R
Kuebrich, David 1943- 134
Kuehl, John 1928- 21-24R
Kuehl, Linda 1939(?)-1978 Obituary 104
Kuehl, Stefan 1966- 146
Kuehl, Warren F(rederick) 1924- CANR-7
Earlier sketch in CA 17-20R
Kuehn, Dorothy Dalton
See Dalton, Dorothy
Kuehn, Heinz R(ichard) 1919- 130
Kuehn, Thomas James 1950- 116
Kuehnelt-Leddihn, Erik (Maria) Ritter von 1909- CANR-44
Earlier sketches in CA 9-12R, CANR-3, 20
Kuemmerly, Walter 1903- 49-52
Kuen, Alfred (F.) 1921- CANR-53
Earlier sketches in CA 107, CANR-25
Kuenan, Philip Henry 1902-1976 Obituary 116
Kueng, Hans 1928- CANR-66
Earlier sketch in CA 53-56
See also MTCW 1
Kuenne, Robert E(ugene) 1924- 5-8R
Kuenstler, Morton 1927- .... SATA 10
Kuenzli, Alfred E(ugene) 1923- 17-20R
Kuernberger, Ferdinand 1821-1879 .... DLB 129
Kuesel, Harry N. 1892(?)-1977 Obituary 73-76
Kuester, David 1938- 53-56
Kuether, Edith Lyman 1915- 49-52
Kufeldt, George 1923- 37-40R
Kuffler, Stephen 1913-1980 Obituary 105
Kufner, Herbert L(eopold) 1927- 5-8R
Kugel, James 1945- 29-32R
Kugelman, Richard 1908- 41-44R
Kugelmass, J. Alvin 1910-1972 .... CANR-4
Obituary 33-36R
Earlier sketch in CA 5-8R
Kugi, Constance Todd 1939- 127
Kuh, Charlotte 1892(?)-1985 Obituary 115
See also SATA-Obit 43
Kuh, Edwin 1925-1986 .... CANR-36
Obituary 119
Earlier sketch in CA 21-24R
Kuh, Frederick Robert 1895-1978 Obituary ... 89-92
Kuh, Katharine (W.) 1904-1994 .... 13-16R
Obituary 143
Kuh, Richard H. 1921- 21-24R
Kuhatschek, Jack 1949- 122
Kuhfeld, Mary Pulver 1943- 128
Kuhl, Ernest Peter 1881-1981 .... CANR-39
Obituary 133
Earlier sketch in CA 41-44R
Kuhl, Stefan
See Kuehl, Stefan
Kuhlken, Ken(neth Wayne) 1945- 102
Kuhlman, James A(llen) 1941- 85-88
Kuhlman, John M(elville) 1923- 17-20R
Kuhlman, Kathryn 1910(?)-1976 .... CANR-12
Obituary 65-68
Earlier sketch in CA 57-60
Kuhlmann, Quirinus 1651-1689 .... DLB 168
Kuhlmann, Susan
See Lohafer, Susan
Kuhn, Alfred 1914-1981 .... CANR-37
Earlier sketches in CA 9-12R, CANR-3
Kuhn, Annette 1945- CANR-53
Earlier sketches in CA 111, CANR-29
Kuhn, Bowie (Kent) 1926- 126
Kuhn, Delia (Wolf) 1903-1989 130
Kuhn, Edward, Jr. 1924(?)-1979 102
Obituary 93-96
Kuhn, Ferdinand 1905-1978 .... CANR-36
Obituary 81-84
Earlier sketch in CA 5-8R
Kuhn, Harold B(arnes) 1911- 49-52
Kuhn, Heinz R(ichard)
See Kuehn, Heinz R(ichard)
Kuhn, Irene Corbally CAP-1
Earlier sketch in CA 9-10
Kuhn, Karl F(rancis) 1939- CANR-37
Earlier sketch in CA 65-68
Kuhn, Maggie
See Kuhn, Margaret E.
Kuhn, Margaret E. 1905-1995 Obituary 148
Brief entry 109
Kuhn, Martin A(rno) 1924- 9-12R
Kuhn, Reinhard (Clifford) 1930-1980 .... CANR-34
Earlier sketch in CA 45-48
Kuhn, Thomas S(amuel) 1922-1996 .... CANR-11
Obituary 152
Earlier sketch in CA 21-24R
Kuhn, Tillo E. 1919- 5-8R
Kuhn, William Ernst 1922- 37-40R
Kuhn, Wolfgang Erasmus 1914- 5-8R
Kuhnau, Johann 1660-1722 .... DLB 168
Kuhne, Cecil 1952- 93-96
Kuhne, Marie (Ahnighito Peary)
1893-1978 Obituary 77-80
Kuhner, Herbert 1935- 25-28R
Kuhns, Dennis R(ay) 1947- 113
Kuhns, Dorothy
See Heyward, Dorothy (Hartzell Kuhns)
Kuhns, Grant (Wilson) 1929- 9-12R
Kuhns, Richard F(rancis, Jr.) 1924- CANR-36
Earlier sketch in CA 37-40R
Kuhns, William 1943- 21-24R
Kuhre, W. Lee 1947- 154
Kuhse, Helga 1940- CANR-47
Earlier sketch in CA 122
Kuic, Vukan 1923- 37-40R
Kuiper, Gerard Peter 1905-1973 .... CAP-2
Obituary 45-48
Earlier sketch in CA 17-18
Kuisel, Richard F(rancis) 1935- 21-24R
Kuist, J(ames) M(arquis) 1935- 124
Kuitert, H(arminus) Martinus 1924- CANR-37
Earlier sketch in CA 25-28R
Kujawa, Duane 1938- 33-36R
Kujoth, Jean Spealman 1935-1975 .... CAP-2
Earlier sketch in CA 25-28
See also SATA-Obit 30
Kukla, Robert J(ohn) 1932- 49-52
Kuklick, Bruce 1941- 41-44R
Kuklin, Susan 1941- CANR-67
Earlier sketch in CA 130
See also AAYA 27
See also CLR 51
See also SATA 63, 95
Kukreja, Veena 1960- 143
Kula, Witold 1916-1988 159
Kuleshov, Arkady A. 1914-1978 Obituary 77-80
Kulick, John
See Pinchot, Ann (Kramer)
Kulka, Richard A. 1945- 130

Kulkarni, Hemant B(alvantrao) 1916- CANR-1
Earlier sketch in CA 45-48
Kulkarni, R(amchandra) G(anesh) 1931- 29-32R
Kulkarni, Venkatesh S(rinivas) 1945- 113
Kulkin, Mary-Ellen
See Siegel, Mary-Ellen (Kulkin)
Kull, A. Stoddard
See Kull, Andrew
Kull, Andrew 1947- 138
Kull, Steven 1951- 128
Kulling, Monica 1952- 155
See also SATA 89
Kullman, Colby H(aight) 1945- 165
Kullman, Harry 1919-1982 .... CANR-39
Earlier sketch in CA 93-96
See also SATA 35
Kulshrestha, Chirantan 1946- 107
Kulski, Julian (Eugeniusz) 1929- CANR-14
Earlier sketch in CA 21-24R
Kulski, Wladyslaw W(szebor) 1903- CANR-37
Earlier sketch in CA 5-8R
Kulstein, David J. 1916-1974 .... CAP-2
Earlier sketch in CA 25-28
Kultermann, Udo 1927- 85-88
Kulukundis, Elias 1937- 21-24R
Kulyk Keefer, Janice 1952- 127
Kumar, Alok 1954- 142
Kumar, (Jagdish) Krishan 1942- 130
Kumar, Krishna 1942- CANR-45
Earlier sketch in CA 109
Kumar, Satish 1933- 112
Kumar, Shiv K(umar) 1921- CANR-7
Earlier sketch in CA 9-12R
Kumar, Udaya 1960- 142
Kumbel
See Hein, Piet
Kumin, Maxine (Winokur) 1925- CANR-69
Earlier sketches in CA 1-4R, CANR-1, 21
See also CAAS 8
See also AITN 2
See also CLC 5, 13, 28
See also DAM POET
See also DLB 5
See also MTCW 1
See also PC 15
See also SATA 12
Kummel, Bernhard 1919- 33-36R
Kummerly, Walter
See Kuemmerly, Walter
Kun, Michael (Stuart) 1962- 132
Kunce, Joseph T(yree) 1928- 41-44R
Kuncewicz, Maria (Szczepanska) 1899- CAP-1
Earlier sketch in CA 9-10
Kuncewiczowa, Maria
See Kuncewicz, Maria (Szczepanska)
Kunda, Gideon 1952- 141
Kundera, Milan 1929- CANR-52
Earlier sketches in CA 85-88, CANR-19
See also AAYA 2
See also CLC 4, 9, 19, 32, 68
See also DAM NOV
See also MTCW 1
See also SSC 24
Kundsin, Ruth Blumfeld 1916- 106
Kunen, James Simon 1948- 25-28R
Kunene, Mazisi (Raymond) 1930- 125
See also BW 1
See also CLC 85
See also DLB 117
Kuner, M(ildred) C(hristophe) 1922- 41-44R
Kunert, Guenter 1929- .... DLB 75
Kung, Hans
See Kueng, Hans
Kung, Shien Woo 1905- 1-4R
Kunhappa, Murkot 1905- 69-72
Kunhardt, Dorothy (Meserve) 1901-1979 107
Obituary 93-96
See also SATA 53
See also SATA-Obit 22
Kunhardt, Edith 1937- 134
See also SATA 67
Kunhardt, Philip B(radish) Jr. 1928- CANR-37
Earlier sketch in CA 85-88
Kunhi Krishnan, T(aramal) V(anmeri) 1919- ... 61-64
Kuniczak, W(ieslaw) S(tanislaw) 1930- ... CANR-42
Earlier sketch in CA 85-88
Kuniholm, Bruce Robellet 1942- CANR-27
Earlier sketch in CA 93-96
Kuniholm, Whitney 1954- 112
Kunikida Doppo 1869-1908 .... DLB 180
Kunin, Madeleine May 1933- 93-96
Kunin, Richard A(llen) 1932- 107
Kunitz, Joshua 1896(?)-1980 Obituary 97-100
Kunitz, Stanley (Jasspon) 1905- CANR-57
Earlier sketches in CA 41-44R, CANR-26
Interview in CANR-26
See also CLC 6, 11, 14
See also DLB 48
See also MTCW 1
See also PC 19
Kunjufu, Jawanza 1953- .... SATA 73
Kunjufu, Johari M. Amini 1935- 41-44R
See also Amini, Johari M.
See also BW 1
Kunkel, Francis L(eo) 1921- 45-48
Kunnes, Richard 1941- 33-36R
Kuno, Susumu 1933- 41-44R
Kunreuther, Howard Charles 1938- CANR-37
Earlier sketch in CA 25-28R
Kunst, David W(illiam) 1939- 85-88
Kunstler, James Howard 1948- CANR-18
Earlier sketch in CA 101
Kunstler, Morton
See Kuenstler, Morton
Kunstler, William M(oses) 1919-1995 ..... CANR-5
Obituary 149
Earlier sketch in CA 9-12R
Interview in CANR-5
Kuntz, J(ohn) Kenneth 1934- CANR-9
Earlier sketch in CA 21-24R
Kuntz, J(ohn) L. 1947- 155
See also SATA 91
Kuntz, Kenneth A. 1916- 1-4R
Kuntz, Paul G. 1915- 5-8R
Kuntzleman, Charles T(homas) 1940- ... CANR-22
Earlier sketches in CA 57-60, CANR-7
Kunz, Kathleen 1935- 143
Kunz, Marji 1939(?)-1979 Obituary 89-92
Kunz, Phillip Ray 1936- CANR-41
Earlier sketches in CA 37-40R, CANR-19
Kunz, Roxane (Brown) 1932- 121
See also SATA-Brief 53
Kunz, Virginia B(rainard) 1921- CANR-37
Earlier sketch in CA 21-24R
Kunze, Reiner 1933- 93-96
See also CLC 10
See also DLB 75
Kunzle, David Mark 1936- CANR-36
Earlier sketches in CA 53-56, CANR-5
Kunzur, Sheela
See Geis, Richard E(rwin)
Kuo, Mo-Jo 1892-1978 Obituary 77-80
Kuo, Ping-chia 1908- 5-8R
Kuo, Shirley W. Y. 1930- 115
Kuo, Ting-yee 1904(?)-1975 Obituary 61-64
Kup, Alexander Peter 1924- CANR-9
Earlier sketch in CA 13-16R
Kup, Karl 1903-1981 Obituary 104
Kupcinet, Irv(ing) 1912- 166
Kuper, Adam (Jonathan) 1941- CANR-42
Earlier sketches in CA 103, CANR-20
Kuper, Hilda Beemer 1911- CANR-2
Earlier sketch in CA 1-4R
Kuper, Jack 1932- 21-24R
Kuper, Leo 1908-1994 .... CANR-35
Obituary 145
Earlier sketches in CA 21-24R, CANR-11
Kuper, Yuri
See Kuperman, Yuri
Kuperman, Yuri 1940- 102
Kupfer, Fern 1946- CANR-36
Earlier sketch in CA 106
Kupferberg, Herbert 1918- 29-32R
See also SATA 19
Kupferberg, Naphtali 1923- CANR-13
Earlier sketch in CA 21-24R
See also Kupferberg, Tuli
Kupferberg, Tuli
See Kupferberg, Naphtali
See also DLB 16
Kupperman, Joel J. 1936- CANR-36
Earlier sketch in CA 33-36R
Kupperman, Karen O(rdahl) 1939- 111
Kuppner, Frank 1951- 153
Kuprin, Aleksandr Ivanovich 1870-1938 Brief
entry 104
See also TCLC 5
Kurahashi, Yumiko 1935- .... DLB 182
Kuralt, Charles (Bishop) 1934-1997 ..... CANR-43
Obituary 159
Earlier sketch in CA 89-92
Kurath, Gertrude Prokosch 1903- 13-16R
Kurath, Hans 1891- 9-12R
Kuratomi, Chizuko 1939- CANR-10
Earlier sketch in CA 21-24R
See also CLR 32
See also SATA 12
Kurdi, Abdulrahman Abdulkadir 1941- 133
Kurdsen, Stephen
See Noon, Brian
Kureishi, Hanif 1954(?)- 139
See also CLC 64
See also DLB 194
Kurelek, William 1927-1977 .... CANR-3
Earlier sketch in CA 49-52
See also CLR 2
See also JRDA
See also MAICYA
See also SATA 8
See also SATA-Obit 27
Kurian, George 1928- 107
See also SATA 65
Kuriansky, Judith (Anne Brodsky) 1947- 132
Kurien, C(hristopher) T(homas) 1931- CANR-13
Earlier sketch in CA 33-36R
Kurihara, Kenneth Kenkichi 1910-1972 ... CANR-6
Obituary 37-40R
Earlier sketch in CA 1-4R
Kurkjian, Stephen A(noosh) 1943- 129
Brief entry 116
Kurkul, Edward 1916- 25-28R
Kurland, Gerald 1942- CANR-14
Earlier sketch in CA 41-44R
See also SATA 13
Kurland, Michael (Joseph) 1938- CANR-11
Earlier sketch in CA 61-64
See also SATA 48
Kurland, Philip B. 1921-1996 .... CANR-7
Obituary 151
Earlier sketch in CA 9-12R
Kurlansky, Mark 1948- 163
Kurman, George 1942- 53-56
Kurnitz, Harry 1909-1968 Obituary 25-28R
Kuroda, Yasumasa 1931- CANR-35
Earlier sketch in CA 45-48
Kurokawa, Mitsuhiro 1954- 152
See also SATA 88
Kuropas, Myron B(ohdon) 1932- 45-48
Kurosawa, Akira 1910- CANR-46
Earlier sketch in CA 101
See also AAYA 11
See also CLC 16
See also DAM MULT
Kurowski, Eugeniusz
See Dobraczynski, Jan
Kurrik, Maire Jaanus 1940- 101
Kursh, Charlotte Olmsted 1912- 9-12R
Kursh, Harry 1919- 9-12R
Kurten, Bjorn (Olof) 1924-1988 .... CANR-56
Earlier sketches in CA 25-28R, CANR-20
See also SATA 64
Kurth, Peter 1953- 139
Kurth-Voigt, Lieselotte E. 1923- Brief entry 110
Kurtis, Arlene Harris 1927- 25-28R
Kurtis, Bill
See Kurtis, William Horton
Kurtis, William Horton 1940- 133
Brief entry 124
Interview in 133
Kurtz, C(larence) Gordon 1902- 65-68
Kurtz, David L(ee) 1941- 41-44R
Kurtz, Don 1951- 152
Kurtz, Donn M. II 168
Kurtz, Donna Carol 1943- 93-96
Kurtz, Ernest 1935- 112
Kurtz, Harold 1913- 17-20R
Kurtz, Howard 1953- 141
Kurtz, Irma 1935- 118
Kurtz, Jane 1952- 155
See also SATA 91
Kurtz, Katherine (Irene) 1944- CANR-50
Earlier sketches in CA 29-32R, CANR-25
See also AAYA 21
See also SATA 76
Kurtz, Kenneth H(assett) 1928- 33-36R
Kurtz, Lester R. 1949- 126
Kurtz, Michael L(ouis) 1941- CANR-36
Earlier sketch in CA 107
Kurtz, Paul 1925- CANR-25
Earlier sketches in CA 13-16R, CANR-5
Kurtz, Stephen G(uild) 1926- 9-12R
Kurtzman, Jeffrey G(ordon) 1940- 110
Kurtzman, Joel 1947- CANR-30
Earlier sketch in CA 29-32R
Kurtz-Phelan, James L(anham) 1946- 49-52
Kuryluk, Ewa 1946- 135
Kurys, Diane 1949- CANR-59
Earlier sketch in CA 125
Kurz, Artur R.
See Scortia, Thomas N(icholas)
Kurz, Isolde 1853-1944 .... DLB 66
Kurz, Mordecai 1934- CANR-12
Earlier sketch in CA 29-32R
Kurz, Otto 1908-1975 107
Obituary 104
Kurz, Paul Konrad 1927- CANR-48
Earlier sketch in CA 29-32R
Kurz, Ron 1940- CANR-14
Earlier sketch in CA 81-84
Kurz, Rudolf 1952- .... SATA 95
Kurzer, Siegmund F. 1907(?)-1973 Obituary ... 104
Kurzman, Dan 1927- CANR-32
Earlier sketches in CA 69-72, CANR-14
Kurzman, Paul A(lfred) 1938- CANR-13
Earlier sketch in CA 33-36R
Kurzweg, Bernhard F. 1926- 17-20R
Kurzweil, Allen 1961(?)- 168
Kurzweil, Arthur 1951- 97-100
Kurzweil, Edith 110
Kurzweil, Raymond (C.) 1948- 134
Kurzweil, Zvi Erich 1911- CANR-36
Earlier sketches in CAP-1, CA 11-12
Kurzydlowski, Krzysztof Jan 1954- 155
Kusan, Ivan 1933- CANR-6
Earlier sketch in CA 9-12R
Kusano Shimpei 1903-1988 167
Kusche, Larry
See Kusche, Lawrence David
Kusche, Lawrence David 1940- CANR-5
Earlier sketch in CA 53-56
Kusenberg, Kurt 1904-1983 .... DLB 69
Kushel, Gerald 1930- CANR-11
Earlier sketch in CA 25-28R
Kushigian, Julia A. 1950- 143
Kushlan, James A. 1947- 142
Kushner, Carol 1950- 133
Kushner, David Z(arkeri) 1935- 53-56
Kushner, Donn (J.) 1927- CANR-35
Earlier sketch in CA 113
See also SATA 52
Kushner, Ellen (Ruth) 1955- .... SATA 98
Kushner, Harold S(amuel) 1935- CANR-36
Earlier sketch in CA 107
See also BEST 90:2
Kushner, Harvey W(olf) 1941- 110
Kushner, Howard Irvin 1943- 81-84
Kushner, Irving 1929- 119
Kushner, James A(lan) 1945- 132
Kushner, Jill Menkes 1951- .... SATA 62
Kushner, Lawrence 1943- 150
See also SATA 83
Kushner, Malcolm 1952- 134
Kushner, Rose 1929-1990 61-64
Obituary 130
Kushner, Sam 1915(?)-1987 Obituary 123
Kushner, Tony 1957(?)- 144
See also CLC 81
See also DAM DRAM
Kusin, Vladimir V(ictor) 1929- CANR-13
Earlier sketch in CA 33-36R
Kuske, Martin 1940- 97-100
Kuskin, Karla (Seidman) 1932- CANR-41
Earlier sketches in CA 1-4R, CANR-4, 22
See also CLR 4
See also MAICYA
See also SAAS 3
See also SATA 2, 68
Kuslan, Louis I(saac) 1922- CANR-1
Earlier sketch in CA 45-48
Kusmer, Kenneth Leslie 1945- 102
Kusnet, David 1951- 160
Kusnick, Barry A. 1910- CANR-37
Earlier sketch in CA 53-56
Kusniewicz, Andrzej 1904- 107
Kuspit, Donald B(urton) 1935- CANR-37
Earlier sketch in CA 97-100
Kussmaul, Ann (Sturm) 1945- 110
Kustermeir, Rudolf 1893(?)-1977 Obituary ... 73-76
Kustow, Michael (David) 1939- Brief entry 106
Kusturica, Emir 1955- 156
Kusz, Natalie 1962- 141
Kutash, Samuel Benjamin 1912-1979 ..... CANR-2
Earlier sketch in CA 1-4R
Kuten, Jay 1935- Brief entry 108
Kuter, Laurence S(herman)
1905-1979 Obituary 113
Kutler, Laurence 1953- 142
Kutler, Stanley I. 1934- CANR-36
Earlier sketch in CA 21-24R
Kutner, Luis 1908-1993 109
Obituary 140
Kutner, Nanette 1906(?)-1962 .... 1-4R
Kutsche, Paul 1927- 114
Kutscher, Charles L(awrence) 1936- 77-80
Kutsky, Roman Joseph 1922- Brief entry 110
Kuttna, Mari 1934-1983 Obituary 109
Kuttner, Henry 1915-1958 157
Brief entry 107
See also Vance, Jack
See also DLB 8
See also TCLC 10
Kuttner, Paul 1922- CANR-56
Earlier sketches in CA 77-80, CANR-13, 30
See also SATA 18
Kuttner, Robert 168
Kutty, Madhavi
See Das, Kamala
Kutz, LeRoy M. 1922- 13-16R
Kutza, Elizabeth Ann 111
Kuvshinoff, Boris W. 1922- 146
Kuwayama, George 1925- CANR-39
Earlier sketch in CA 116
Kuyk, Dirk (A., Jr.) 1934- 135
Kuykendall, Eleanor 1938- Brief entry 109
Kuykendall, Jack L(awrence) 1940- 57-60
Kuykendall, Ralph S(impson) 1885-1963 ...... 1-4R
Kuzma, Greg 1944- CANR-70
Earlier sketch in CA 33-36R
See also CLC 7
Kuzma, Kay 1941- CANR-23
Earlier sketch in CA 106
See also SATA 39
Kuzmich, Natalie 1932- 127
Kuzmin, Mikhail 1872(?)-1936 .... TCLC 40
Kuznets, Simon (Smith) 1901-1985 158
Obituary 116
Brief entry 108
Kuznetsov, (Edward) 1939- CANR-39
Earlier sketch in CA 57-60
Kuznetsov, Anatoli 1929-1979 Obituary 89-92
Kuznetsov, Nickolaj 1955- 158
Kuzniewski, Anthony J(oseph) 1945- 107
Kuzwayo, Ellen (Kate) 1914- 134
Kvale, Velma R(uth) 1898- CAP-2
Earlier sketch in CA 25-28
See also SATA 8
Kvam, Wayne (Eugene) 1938- 45-48
Kvasnicka, Robert M(ichael) 1935- 97-100
Kvasnosky, Laura McGee 1951- 159
See also SATA 93
Kwabena Nketia, J. H.
See Nketia, J(oseph) H(anson) Kwabena
Kwamena-Poh, M(ichael Albert) 1932- 132
Kwan, Kian M(oon) 1929- 17-20R
Kwant, R. C.
See Kwant, Remigius C(ornelis)
Kwant, Remigius C(ornelis) 1918- CANR-18
Earlier sketches in CA 9-12R, CANR-3
Kwant, Remy C.
See Kwant, Remigius C(ornelis)
Kwanten, Luc 1944- 93-96
Kwavnick, David 1940- 45-48
Kweder, Adele 1910- 5-8R
Kweder, David James 1905- 5-8R
Kweit, Robert W(illiam) 1946- CANR-37
Earlier sketch in CA 112
Kwiatkowska, Hanna Yaxa
1907(?)-1980 Obituary 97-100
Kwitny, Jonathan 1941- CANR-23
Earlier sketches in CA 49-52, CANR-1
Kwolek, Constance
See Porcari, Constance Kwolek
Kyburg, Henry (Guy) E(ly), Jr. 1928- CANR-36
Earlier sketches in CA 5-8R, CANR-8
Kyd, Thomas
See Harbage, Alfred (Bennett)
Kyd, Thomas 1558-1594 .... DAM DRAM
See also DC 3
See also DLB 62
Kydd, Sam(uel) 1917-1982 109
Obituary 106
Kyemba, Henry 1939- 81-84
Kyes, Robert L(ange) 1933- CANR-37
Earlier sketch in CA 49-52

Kyger, Joanne (Elizabeth) 1934- CANR-40
Earlier sketches in CA 101, CANR-17
See also CAAS 16
See also DLB 16
Kyle, Benjamin
See Gottfried, Theodore Mark
Kyle, Duncan
See Broxholme, John Franklin
Kyle, Elisabeth
See Dunlop, Agnes M. R.
Kyle, Keith 1925- 137
Kyle, Marlaine
See Hager, Jean
Kyle, Molly M. 1959- 146
Kyle, Robert
See Terrall, Robert
Kyle, Sefton
See Vickers, Roy
Kyle, Susan (Spaeth) 1946- 141
Kyle, Susan S.
See Kyle, Susan (Spaeth)
Kyme, Ernest Hector 1906- 103
Kynaston, SirFrancis 1587-1642 .... DLB 121
Kyndrup, Morten 1952- 140
Kyne, Peter B. 1880-1957 .... DLB 78
Kynett, Harold Havelock 1889-1973 Obituary .. 106
Kyper, Frank 1940- 85-88
Kyprianos, Iossif
See Samarakis, Antonis
Kyre, Joan Randolph 1935- 25-28R
Kyre, Martin (Theodore, Jr.) 1928- 25-28R
Kyrle, Roger (Ernie) Money
See Money-Kyrle, Roger (Ernie)
Kysar, Robert (Dean) 1934- CANR-22
Earlier sketch in CA 69-72
Kyselka, Will 1921- 106
Kyte, Kathy S. 1946- .... SATA 50
See also SATA-Brief 44
Kytle, Elizabeth 112
Kytle, Ray(mond) 1941- 29-32R
Kyvig, David E(dward) 1944- CANR-36
Earlier sketch in CA 101

L

L., Tommy
See Lorkowski, Thomas V(incent)
Laake, Deborah 1954(?)- 167
La-Anyane, Seth 1922- 9-12R
Laas, Virginia J(eans) 1943- 139
Laas, William M. 1910(?)-1975 Obituary 61-64
Laband, John (Paul Clow) 1947- 145
Labanyi, Jo 1946- 154
LaBar, Tom 1937- 25-28R
Labaree, Benjamin Woods 1927- CANR-6
Earlier sketch in CA 9-12R
Labaree, Leonard W(oods) 1897-1980 73-76
Obituary 97-100
Labarge, Margaret Wade 1916- CANR-11
Earlier sketch in CA 25-28R
LaBarge, William Howard 1948- 116
La Barr, Creighton
See von Block, Bela W(illiam)
La Barre, Weston 1911- CANR-22
Earlier sketch in CA 1-4R
LaBastille, Anne 1938- CANR-8
Earlier sketch in CA 57-60
L'Abate, Luciano 1928- 111
Labatut, Jean 1899-1986 Obituary 121
Labbe, John T. CANR-17
Earlier sketch in CA 97-100
La Beau, Dennis (George) 1941- 97-100
LaBelle, Maurice Marc 1939- 113
Laber, Jeri 1931- CANR-9
Earlier sketch in CA 65-68
Laberge, Albert 1871-1960 .... DLB 68
La Berge, Ann F. 1944- 143
Laberge, Marie 1950- .... DLB 60
Labiche, Eugene 1815-1888 .... DLB 192
LaBier, Douglas 1944- 124
Labin, Suzanne (Devoyon) 1913- CANR-32
Earlier sketches in CA 29-32R, CANR-14
Laboda, Lawrence R. 1952- 150
Labor, Earle G. 1928- 21-24R
LaBorde, Rene
See Neuffer, Irene LaBorde
Labovitz, I(srael) M(ilton) 1907- 5-8R
Labrador, James
See Hamel Peifer, Kathleen
Labrador, Judy
See Hamel Peifer, Kathleen
LaBrecque, Claude X. 85-88
La Brie, Henry George III 1946- 57-60
Labrie, Roger P(aul) 1952- 113
Labro, Philippe (Christian) 1936- 167
Labroca, Mario 1897(?)-1973 Obituary 41-44R
Labus, Marta Haake 1943- 109
Labuta, Joseph A(nthony) 1931- 57-60
Labuz, Ronald M. 1953- 123
Labys, Walter C(arl) 1937- CANR-34
Earlier sketch in CA 73-76
La Camera, Anthony 1914(?)-1984 Obituary ... 114
Lacan, Jacques (Marie Emile) 1901-1981 121
Obituary 104
See also CLC 75
LaCapra, Dominick 1939- CANR-52
Earlier sketches in CA 109, CANR-28
La Capria, Raffaele 1922- CANR-4
Earlier sketch in CA 9-12R
See also DLB 196
Lacarriere, Jacques 1925- Brief entry 125
La Casce, Steward 1935- 37-40R
Laccetti, (Silvio) Richard 1941- CANR-13
Earlier sketch in CA 37-40R
Lace, O(live) Jessie 1906- 17-20R
Lacerda, Carlos 1914-1977 Obituary 69-72
Lacey, A(lan) R(obert) 1926- 112
Lacey, Archie L(ouis) 1923- 9-12R
Lacey, Douglas R(aymond) 1913-1973 ..... 29-32R
Obituary 134
Lacey, Earnest Edward 1939- 163
Lacey, Elizabeth A. 1954- 132
Lacey, Jeannette F. 77-80
Lacey, John
See Alexander, Boyd
Lacey, Louise 1940- 81-84
Lacey, Nicola 1958- 130
Lacey, Paul A. 1934- 41-44R
Lacey, Peter 1929- 21-24R
Lacey, Robert 1944- CANR-43
Earlier sketches in CA 33-36R, CANR-16
Interview in CANR-16
Lacey, W(alter) K(irkpatrick) 1921- CANR-11
Earlier sketch in CA 25-28R
Lach, Donald F(rederick) 1917- 102
La Chapelle, Mary 1955- 132
La Charite, Virginia Anding 1937- 29-32R
Lachenbruch, David 1921-1996 89-92
Obituary 154
Lachenmeyer, Charles W(illiam) 1943- 105
Lachman, Barbara 1938- 163
Lachman, Marvin 166
Lachman, Seymour P. 1933- 154
Lachmann, Frank M(ichael) 1929- 103
Lachner, Dorothea
See Knobloch, Dorothea
Lachs, John 1934- 21-24R
Lack, David Lambert 1910-1973 .... CANR-4
Obituary 89-92
Earlier sketch in CA 5-8R
Lack, Paul D. 1944- 140
Lackey, Douglas Paul 1945- 103
Lackey, Kris 1953- 162
Lackey, Mercedes R(itchie) 1950- CANR-51
Earlier sketch in CA 126
See also AAYA 13
See also SATA 81
Lackmann, Ron(ald) 1934- CANR-13
Earlier sketch in CA 29-32R
Lackner, Stephan 1910- CANR-15
Earlier sketch in CA 29-32R
Lacks, Cecilia 1945- 69-72
Lacks, Cissy
See Lacks, Cecilia
Lacks, Roslyn 1933- 102
La Clair, Earl E. 1916- 21-24R
La Claustra, Vera Berneicia (Derrick) 1903- .. 53-56
LaCocque, Andre (Marie) 1927- CANR-31
Earlier sketch in CA 112
Lacocque, Pierre-Emmanuel 1952- 112
Lacoe, Addie .... SATA 78
Lacolere, Francois
See Aragon, Louis
La Colere, Francois
See Aragon, Louis
Lacombe, Gabriel 1905(?)-1973 Obituary ... 37-40R
Lacome, Julie 1961- .... SATA 80
LaCoste, Lilly
See Harris, Yvonne L.
Lacoste, Paul 1923- CANR-1
Earlier sketch in CA 45-48
La Coste, Warren 1941- 141
Lacouture, Jean Marie Gerard 1921- CANR-43
Earlier sketch in CA 101
Lacretelle, Jacques de 1888-1985 .... DLB 65
La Croix, I(sobyl) F. 1933- 142
Lacroix, Louise
See Swift, Helen C(ecilia)
LaCroix, Mary 1937- CANR-22
Earlier sketch in CA 106
Lacroix, Ramon
See McKeag, Ernest L(ionel)
LaCrosse, E. Robert 1937- 33-36R
Lacy, A(lexander) D(acre) 1894-1969 ...... CAP-2
Earlier sketch in CA 25-28
Lacy, Allen 1935- 159
Lacy, Charles
See Hippisley Coxe, Antony D(acres)
Lacy, Creighton (Boutelle) 1919- 13-16R
Lacy, Dan (Mabry) 1914- 37-40R
Lacy, Donald Charles 1933- CANR-59
Earlier sketch in CA 105
Lacy, Eric Russell 1933- 17-20R
Lacy, Gene M(elvin) 1934- 53-56
Lacy, Gerald M(orris) 1940- 77-80
Lacy, Leslie Alexander 1937- 33-36R
See also SATA 6
Lacy, Mary Lou (Pannill) 1914- 17-20R
Lacy, Norris J(oiner) 1940- CANR-23
Earlier sketches in CA 61-64, CANR-8
Lacy, Sam 1903- .... DLB 171
Lacy, Tira
See Estrada, Rita Clay
Ladany, L.
See Ladany, Laszlo
Ladany, Laszlo 1914-1990 Obituary 132
Ladas, Alice Kahn 129
Ladas, Gerasimos 1937- 53-56
Ladas, Stephen P(ericles) 1898-1976 102
Ladd, Brian 1957- 137
Ladd, Bruce 1936- 25-28R
Ladd, Edward T(aylor) 1918-1973 .... CANR-4
Earlier sketch in CA 5-8R
Ladd, Everett Carll, Jr. 1937- CANR-11
Earlier sketch in CA 25-28R
Ladd, George E(ldon) 1911- CANR-5
Earlier sketch in CA 5-8R
Ladd, Helen F. 1945- 111
Ladd, Jerrold J. 1970- 145
Ladd, John 1917- 81-84
Ladd, Joseph Brown 1764-1786 .... DLB 37
Ladd, Louise 1943- 154
See also SATA 97
Ladd, Veronica
See Miner, Jane Claypool
Ladell, John L. 1924- 147
Laden, Nina 1962- .... SATA 85
Ladenson, Alex 1907- 17-20R
Ladenson, Robert Franklin 1943- 113
Lader, Lawrence 1919- CANR-2
Earlier sketch in CA 1-4R
See also SATA 6
Laderman, Carol (C.) CANR-47
Earlier sketch in CA 121
La Deshabilleuse
See Simenon, Georges (Jacques Christian)
Ladman, Jerry R. 1935- 128
Ladner, Joyce A(nn) 1943- 124
Brief entry 122
See also BW 2
Ladner, Kurt
See DeMille, Nelson (Richard)
Ladner, Mildred D. 1918- 97-100
Lado, Robert 1915- CANR-7
Earlier sketch in CA 9-12R
LaDoux, Rita C. 1951- .... SATA 74
LaDuke, Betty 1933- 143
Laduke, Winona 1959- 168
Ladurie, Emmanuel Le Roy
See Le Roy Ladurie, Emmanuel (Bernard)
Lady, A
See Taylor, Ann
Lady Culross
See Melville, Elizabeth
Lady Gregory
See Gregory, Isabella Augusta (Persse)
Ladyman, Phyllis 103
Lady Mears
See Tempest, Margaret Mary
Lady of Quality, A
See Bagnold, Enid
Lael, Richard L(ee) 1946- 111
Laemmar, Jack W. 1909- 1-4R
Laertes, Joseph
See Saltzman, Joseph
Laestadius, Lars-Levi 1909-1982 Obituary 107
Laeuchli, Samuel 1924- CANR-4
Earlier sketch in CA 5-8R
Laevastu, Taivo 1923- CANR-15
Earlier sketch in CA 41-44R
LaFantasie, Glenn W(arren) 1949- 125
La Farge, Oliver (Hazard Perry) 1901-1963 ....
CANR-30
Earlier sketch in CA 81-84
See also DLB 9
See also SATA 19
La Farge, Phyllis 73-76
See also SATA 14
Lafarge, Rene 1902- CAP-2
Earlier sketch in CA 29-32
LaFauci, Horatio M(ichael) 1917- 33-36R
LaFaye, A(lexandria R. T.) 1970- 162
Lafayette, Carlos
See Boiles, Charles Lafayette (Jr.)
Lafayette, Rene
See Hubbard, L(afayette) Ron(ald)
LaFeber, Walter (Fredrick) 1933- CANR-48
Earlier sketches in CA 9-12R, CANR-5
Laferriere, Daniel
See Rancour-Laferriere, Daniel
Laferriere, Dany 1953- 142
Laffal, Julius 1920- 49-52
Laffan, Kevin (Barry) 1922- 37-40R
Lafferty, Perry (Francis) 1917- CANR-6
Earlier sketch in CA 9-12R
Lafferty, R(aphael) A(loysius) 1914- CANR-32
Earlier sketches in CA 57-60, CANR-12
See also DLB 8
Laffin, John (Alfred Charles) 1922- CANR-23
Earlier sketches in CA 53-56, CANR-7
See also SATA 31
Laffont, Jean-Pierre 1935- 115
Laffrado, Laura 1959- 138
LaFitte, Pat Chew 1950- 107
La Flesche, Francis 1857(?)-1932 144
See also DLB 175
See also NNAL
LaFleur, William R. 1936- 115
La Follette, Marcel (Evelyn) Chotkowski 1944- . 114
La Follette, Suzanne 1894(?)-1983 Obituary ... 109
LaFontaine, Blanche
See Schwalberg, Carol(yn Ernestine Stein)
LaFontaine, Charles Vivian 1936- 57-60
La Fontaine, Jean de 1621-1695 .... MAICYA
See also SATA 18
Lafore, Laurence Davis 1917-1985 .... 13-16R
Obituary 118
Laforest, Guy 1955- 149
Laforgue, Jules 1860-1887 .... PC 14
See also SSC 20
LaForte, Robert Sherman 1933- 57-60
La Fountaine, George 1934- CANR-41
Earlier sketches in CA 57-60, CANR-7
Lafourcade, Bernard 1934-1986 115
Obituary 118
LaFraniere, Sharon 1955- 136
La Freniere, (B. Marie) Celine 1950- 132
Lafreniere, Gyslaine F. 1948- 116
Lagace, Louise Lambert
See Lambert-Lagace, Louise
LaGattuta, Margo 1942- CANR-38
Earlier sketch in CA 115
Lagemann, Ellen Condliffe 1945- 128
Lager, Claude
See Lapp, Christiane (Germain)
Lager, Fred "Chico" 1955(?)- 168
Lager, Marilyn 1939- 121
See also SATA 52
Lagercrantz, Rose (Elsa) 1947- 108
See also SATA 39
Lagerkvist, Paer (Fabian) 1891-1974 85-88
Obituary 49-52
See also Lagerkvist, Par
See also CLC 7, 10, 13, 54
See also DAM DRAM, NOV
See also MTCW 1
Lagerkvist, Par
See Lagerkvist, Paer (Fabian)
See also SSC 12
Lagerloef, Selma (Ottiliana Lovisa) 1858-1940 Brief
entry 108
See also Lagerlof, Selma (Ottiliana Lovisa)
See also SATA 15
See also TCLC 4, 36
Lagerlof, Selma (Ottiliana Lovisa)
See Lagerloef, Selma (Ottiliana Lovisa)
See also CLR 7
See also SATA 15
Lagerwall, Edna 45-48
Lagerwerff, Ellen Best 1919- 85-88
Lagevi, Bo
See Blom, Karl Arne
Lago, Mary M(cClelland) 1919- CANR-15
Earlier sketch in CA 85-88
Lagorio, Gina 1922- .... DLB 196
LaGrand, Louis E. 1935- 33-36R
La Grange, Henry Louis De
See De La Grange, Henry Louis
La Greca, Annette M(arie) 1950- 142
LaGuardia, David M(ichael) 1943- 118
La Guardia, Fiorello (Henry) 1882-1947 168
Brief entry 120
Laguerre, Andre 1915(?)-1979 97-100
Obituary 85-88
Laguerre, Enrique A(rturo) 1906- 131
See also HW
Laguerre, Michel S(aturnin) 1945- 115
La Guma, (Justin) Alex(ander) 1925-1985 ....
CANR-25
Obituary 118
Earlier sketch in CA 49-52
See also BLCS
See also BW 1
See also CLC 19
See also DAM NOV
See also DLB 117
See also MTCW 1
La Gumina, Salvatore John 1928- 77-80
LaHaye, Tim 1926- CANR-9
Earlier sketch in CA 65-68
Lahee, Frederic Henry 1884-1968 .... CAP-2
Earlier sketch in CA 19-20
Lahey, Edwin A(loysius) 1902-1969 Obituary ... 115
Lahontan, Louis-Armand de Lom d'Arce Baron
1666-1715(?) .... DLB 99
LaHood, Marvin J(ohn) 1933- CANR-10
Earlier sketch in CA 25-28R
Lahr, John (Henry) 1941- CANR-21
Earlier sketch in CA 25-28R
Lahr, Raymond M(errill)
1914-1973 Obituary 41-44R
Lahue, Kalton C. 1934- CANR-7
Earlier sketch in CA 13-16R
Lai, David Chuenyan 1937- 138
Lai, Larissa 1967- 157
Lai, T'ien-Ch'ang 1921- CANR-11
Earlier sketch in CA 69-72
Lai, Violet Lau 1916- 119
Laidlaw, A. K.
See Grieve, C(hristopher) M(urray)
Laidlaw, Harry Hyde, Jr. 1907- 5-8R
Laidlaw, Marc 1960- CANR-45
Earlier sketch in CA 119
Laidlaw, Ross 1931- CANR-44
Earlier sketch in CA 118
Laidlaw, W(illiam) A(llison) 1898-1983 Obituary . 109
Laidler, Harry W(ellington) 1884-1970 ..... CANR-5
Obituary 29-32R
Earlier sketch in CA 5-8R
Laiken, Deirdre S(usan) 1948- 104
See also SATA 48
See also SATA-Brief 40
Laikin, Paul 1927- 5-8R
Laimgruber, Monika 1946- .... SATA 11
Lain, Anna
See Lamb, Nancy
Laine, Barry 1951-1987 Obituary 123
Laine, Gloria
See Hanna, David
Lainez, Manuel Mujica
See Mujica Lainez, Manuel
See also HW
Laing, Alastair 1944- 127
Laing, Alexander (Kinnan) 1903-1976 ..... CANR-4
Obituary 65-68
Earlier sketch in CA 5-8R
Laing, Anne C.
See Schachterle, Nancy (Lange)
Laing, Frederick 105
Laing, Jennifer 1948- 106
Laing, Lloyd (Robert) 1944- CANR-5
Earlier sketch in CA 53-56
Laing, Martha
See Celestino, Martha Laing
Laing, R(onald) D(avid) 1927-1989 ...... CANR-34
Obituary 129
Earlier sketch in CA 107
See also CLC 95
See also MTCW 1

Laingen, L(owell) Bruce 1922- 139
Lair, Jacqueline Carey 1930- 119
Lair, Jess K. 1926- CANR-14
Earlier sketch in CA 41-44R
Lair, Robert L(eland) 1932- 53-56
Laird, Betty A(nn) 1925- CANR-33
Earlier sketches in CA 33-36R, CANR-15
Laird, Brian Andrew 1964- 151
Laird, Carobeth 1895-1983 .... CANR-8
Obituary 110
Earlier sketch in CA 61-64
See also DLBY 82
Laird, Charlton G(rant) 1901- 13-16R
Laird, Christa 1944- .... SAAS 26
Laird, David
See Laird, W(ilbur) David, Jr.
Laird, Donald A(nderson) 1897-1969 .... 5-8R
Obituary 25-28R
Laird, Dorothy
See Carr, Dorothy Stevenson Laird
Laird, Dugan 1920- CANR-12
Earlier sketch in CA 73-76
Laird, Eleanor Childs 1908- 73-76
Laird, Elizabeth (Mary Risk) 1943- CANR-65
Earlier sketch in CA 128
See also SATA 77
Laird, Helen 1933- 122
Laird, J(ohn) T(udor) 1921- 69-72
Laird, Jean E(louise) 1930- CANR-6
Earlier sketch in CA 9-12R
See also SATA 38
Laird, Melvin R(obert) 1922- 65-68
Laird, Robbin F. 1946- 113
Laird, Roy D(ean) 1925- CANR-33
Earlier sketches in CA 33-36R, CANR-15
Laird, W(ilbur) David, Jr. 1937- 113
Lait, Robert 1921- CANR-2
Earlier sketch in CA 1-4R
Laite, Gordon 1925- .... SATA 31
Laite, William Edward, Jr. 1932- 37-40R
Laithwaite, Eric Roberts 1921- 103
Laitin, Joseph 1914- 136
Laitin, Ken 1963- 102
Laitin, Lindy 1968- 108
Laitin, Steve 1965- 102
Lajoie, Antoine Gerin 1824-1882 .... DLB 99
Lajolo, Davide 1913(?)-1984 Obituary 113
Lakatos, Imre 1922-1974 Obituary 116
Lake, Alice (Dannenberg) 1916-1990 Obituary 131
Lake, Carolyn 1932- 25-28R
Lake, David J. 1929- CANR-41
Earlier sketches in CA 65-68, CANR-10
Lake, Frank 1914-1982 .... CANR-10
Earlier sketch in CA 21-24R
Lake, Harriet
See Taylor, Paula (Wright)
Lake, Kenneth R(obert) 1931- CANR-5
Earlier sketch in CA 53-56
Lake, Timothy
See Bates, Tom
Lakeland, Paul 1946- 137
Lakeman, Enid 1903- 107
Laken, Bob
See Holman, Robert
Laker, Rosalind
See Ovstedal, Barbara
Lakey, George (Russell) 1937- CANR-7
Earlier sketch in CA 17-20R
Lakhu
See Khubchandani, Lachman M(ulchand)
Lakin, Martin 1925- 73-76
Laklan, Carli 1907- CANR-1
Earlier sketch in CA 1-4R
See also SATA 5
Lakoff, George 1941- CANR-27
Earlier sketch in CA 29-32R
Lakoff, Robin Tolmach 1942- CANR-27
Earlier sketch in CA 103
Lakoff, Sanford A(llan) 1931- CANR-1
Earlier sketch in CA 1-4R
Lakos, Amos 1946- 143
Lakritz, Esther Himmelman 1928- 1-4R
Lal, Brij V. 1952- 139
Lal, Gobind Behari 1890(?)-1982 Obituary 106
Lal, Kishori Saran 1920- 21-24R
Lal, P. 1929- CANR-9
Earlier sketch in CA 13-16R
Laliberte, Norman 1925- 104
Lalic, Ivan V. 1931-1996 .... DLB 181
Lalic, Mihailo 1914-1992 .... DLB 181
Lalicki, Barbara 119
See also SATA 61
Lalita, K. 1953- 144
Lalley, Joseph M. 1897(?)-1980 Obituary 102
Lalli, Judy 1949- 110
Lally, Michael (David) 1942- CANR-32
Earlier sketches in CA 77-80, CANR-14
La Londe, Bernard J. 1933- 33-36R
Lalonde, Michele 1937- .... DLB 60
Lalonde, Robert 1947- 109
Laluah, Aquah
See Casely-Hayford, Gladys May
Lalumia, Joseph 1916- 21-24R
Lam, Charlotte (Dawson) 1924- 37-40R
Lam, Truong Buu 1933- 25-28R
Laman, Russell 1907- CAP-1
Earlier sketch in CA 9-10
LaMancusa, Katherine C.
See Koop, Katherine C.
Lamanna, Dolores B. 1930-1980 .... 9-12R
Obituary 97-100
Lamantia, Philip 1927- 117
Brief entry 111
See also DLB 16
Lamar, Howard R(oberts) 1923- 17-20R
Lamar, Jake 1961- 137
Lamar, Lavoisier 1907- 5-8R
Lamar, Nedra Newkirk 69-72
Lamarque, Peter 1948- 120
LaMarre, Virgil E. 1910(?)-1985 Obituary 115
LaMarsh, Judy
See LaMarsh, Julia Verlyn
LaMarsh, Julia Verlyn 1924-1980 .... CANR-13
Obituary 105
Earlier sketch in CA 29-32R
Lamartine, Alphonse (Marie Louis Prat) de 1790-1869 .... DAM POET
See also PC 16
Lamb, Andrew (Martin) 1942- 137
Lamb, Antonia 1943- 21-24R
Lamb, Beatrice Pitney 1904- 5-8R
See also SATA 21
Lamb, Charles 1775-1834 .... CDBLB 1789-1832
See also DA
See also DAB
See also DAC
See also DAM MST
See also DLB 93, 107, 163
See also SATA 17
See also WLC
Lamb, Charles Bentall 1914-1981 102
Obituary 105
Lamb, Charles M(oody) 1945- 124
Lamb, Charlotte
See Holland, Sheila
Lamb, Christina 1965- 140
Lamb, Connie 1947- 139
Lamb, Dana S(torrs) 1900-1986 134
Obituary 120
Lamb, David 1940- 110
Lamb, Edward 1902-1987 108
Obituary 122
Lamb, Eleanor 1917- 69-72
Lamb, Elizabeth Searle 1917- 33-36R
See also SATA 31
Lamb, F(rank) Bruce 1913- 33-36R
Lamb, G(eoffrey) F(rederick) CANR-41
Earlier sketches in CA 53-56, CANR-4, 19
See also SATA 10
Lamb, H(ubert) H(orace) 1913- 21-24R
Lamb, Harold (Albert) 1892-1962 101
Obituary 89-92
See also SATA 53
Lamb, Helen B.
See Lamont, Helen Lamb
Lamb, Hugh 1946- CANR-1
Earlier sketch in CA 49-52
Lamb, James B(arrett) 1919- 133
Lamb, Karl A(llen) 1933- CANR-18
Earlier sketches in CA 5-8R, CANR-3
Lamb, Lady Caroline 1785-1828 .... DLB 116
Lamb, Lawrence E(dward) 1926- 97-100
Lamb, Lynton (Harold) 1907-1977 .... CANR-4
Earlier sketch in CA 1-4R
See also SATA 10
Lamb, Marion M(inerva) 1905- 5-8R
Lamb, Mary Ann 1764-1847 .... DLB 163
See also SATA 17
Lamb, Nancy 1939- 148
See also SATA 80
Lamb, Patricia Frazer 1931- 126
Lamb, Robert (Boyden) 1941- CANR-35
Earlier sketch in CA 29-32R
See also SATA 13
Lamb, Ruth S(tanton) CANR-21
Earlier sketch in CA 45-48
Lamb, Sydney M(acDonald) 1929- 33-36R
Lamb, Wally 1950- 140
Lamb, Walter
See Lamb, Wally
Lamb, William
See Jameson, (Margaret) Storm
Lamb, William Kaye 1904- 81-84
Lambasa, Frank Slavko 1921-1987 Obituary 123
Lambdin, Dewey (W.) 1945- 140
Lambdin, William 1936- 102
Lambec, Zoltan
See Kimbro, John M.
Lamberg, Robert F(elix) 1929- 65-68
Lamberg-Karlovsky, Clifford Charles 1937- 85-88
Lambert, Angela Maria 1940- 138
Lambert, B. Geraldine 1922- 41-44R
Lambert, Betty
See Lambert, Elizabeth (Minnie)
See also DLB 60
Lambert, Byron Cecil 1923- 97-100
Lambert, Darwin (Seymour) 1916- CANR-2
Earlier sketch in CA 5-8R
Lambert, David (Compton) 1932- 122
See also SATA 84
See also SATA-Brief 49
Lambert, Derek 1929- CANR-69
Earlier sketches in CA 25-28R, CANR-17
Lambert, Eleanor 102
Lambert, Elisabeth
See Ortiz, Elisabeth Lambert
Lambert, Elizabeth (Minnie) 1933-1983 102
See also Lambert, Betty
Lambert, Eric 1918-1966 .... CAP-1
Earlier sketch in CA 13-14
Lambert, Gavin 1924- CANR-1
Earlier sketch in CA 1-4R
Lambert, Hazel Margaret (?)-1968 .... 1-4R
Lambert, Herbert H. 1929- 69-72
Lambert, J(ack) W(alter) 1917-1986 108
Obituary 120
Lambert, Jacques Edward 1901- CAP-2
Earlier sketch in CA 23-24
Lambert, Janet 1895(?)-1973 Obituary 41-44R
See also SATA 25
Lambert, John (Robin) 1936- CANR-8
Earlier sketch in CA 5-8R
Lambert, Mark 1942- 73-76
Lambert, Page 1952- 154
Lambert, Ronald Dick 1936- 108
Lambert, Roy Eugene 1918- 37-40R
Lambert, Royston James 1932-1982 Obituary 108
Lambert, Saul 1928- 106
See also SATA 23
Lambert, Sheila 1926- 85-88
Lambert, William Wilson 1919- 9-12R
Lamberti, Marjorie 1937- 103
Lambert-Lagace, Louise 1941- CANR-29
Earlier sketch in CA 111
Lamberton, Donald McLean 1927- 103
Lamberts, J(acob) J. 1910- 37-40R
Lambeth, Edmund Barry 1932- 123
Lambi, Ivo Nikolai 1931- 132
Lambley, Peter 1946- 109
Lambo, Thomas Adeoye 1923- 29-32R
Lamborn, LeRoy L(eslie) 1937- 21-24R
Lambot, Isobel 1926- 73-76
Lambourne, John
See Lamburn, John Battersby Crompton
Lambrecht, Frank L. 1915- 164
Lambrick, Hugh Trevor 1904- CANR-6
Earlier sketch in CA 9-12R
Lambright, William Henry 1939- 103
Lambro, Donald (Joseph) 1940- CANR-25
Earlier sketches in CA 57-60, CANR-7
Lambton, Anne (Patricia St. Clair) 1918- 85-88
Lamburn, John Battersby Crompton 1893- CAP-1
Earlier sketch in CA 9-10
Lamburn, Richmal Crompton 1890-1969 .... CAP-1
Obituary 25-28R
Earlier sketch in CA 9-10
See also Crompton, Richmal
See also SATA 5
Lame Deer 1895(?)-1976 Obituary 69-72
See also NNAL
Lamensdorf, Leonard 1930- 29-32R
La Meri
See Hughes, Russell Meriwether
L'Ami, Charles Ernest 1896- 102
Lamirande, Emilien 1926- CANR-8
Earlier sketch in CA 17-20R
Lamis, Alexander P. 1946- CANR-52
Earlier sketch in CA 125
Lamm, Joyce 1933- 57-60
Lamm, Leonard Jonathan 1945- 146
Lamm, Maurice 1930- 17-20R
Lamm, Norman 1927- CANR-28
Earlier sketch in CA 49-52
Lamme, Linda Leonard 1942- 102
Lammers, Wayne P. 1951- 140
Lamming, George (William) 1927- CANR-26
Earlier sketch in CA 85-88
See also BLC 2
See also BW 2
See also CLC 2, 4, 66
See also DAM MULT
See also DLB 125
See also MTCW 1
Lamming, R. M. 1949- 125
Brief entry 119
Interview in 125
Lammon, Martin 1958- 162
Lamon, Lester C(rawford) 1942- 89-92
Lamond, Henry George 1885-1969 Obituary 25-28R
Lamont, Corliss 1902-1995 .... CANR-11
Obituary 148
Earlier sketch in CA 13-16R
Lamont, Douglas Felix 1937- 41-44R
Lamont, Helen Lamb 1906(?)-1975 Obituary 61-64
Lamont, Lansing 1930- CANR-11
Earlier sketch in CA 17-20R
Lamont, Marianne
See Rundle, Anne
Lamont, Michele 1957- 143
Lamont, N. B.
See Barnitt, Nedda Lemmon
Lamont, Nedda
See Barnitt, Nedda Lemmon
Lamont, Rosette C(lementine) 33-36R
Lamont, William D(awson) 1901-1982 .... CAP-1
Obituary 108
Earlier sketch in CA 11-12
Lamont-Brown, Raymond 1939- CANR-66
Earlier sketches in CA 73-76, CANR-14, 32
Lamorisse, Albert (Emmanuel) 1922-1970 101
See also SATA 23
Lamott, Anne 1954- 144
Lamott, Kenneth (Church) 1923-1979 .... 25-28R
Obituary 89-92
Lamotte, Etienne 1904(?)-1983 Obituary 109
Lamour, Dorothy 1914-1996 134
Brief entry 105
L'Amour, Louis (Dearborn) 1908-1988 .... CANR-40
Obituary 125
Earlier sketches in CA 1-4R, CANR-3, 25
See also AAYA 16
See also AITN 2
See also BEST 89:2
See also CLC 25, 55
See also DAM NOV, POP
See also DLBY 80
See also MTCW 1
Lamparski, Richard 21-24R
Lampe, David 1923- CANR-1
Earlier sketch in CA 1-4R
Lampedusa, Giuseppe (Tomasi) di 1896-1957 164
See also Tomasi di Lampedusa, Giuseppe
See also DLB 177
See also TCLC 13
Lampell, Millard 1919-1997 .... 9-12R
Obituary 162
Lampert, Emily 1951- 121
See also SATA 52
See also SATA-Brief 49
Lampert, Hope 1960- 143
Lamphear, John 1941- 147
Lamphere, Louise (Anne) 1940- 89-92
Lampitt, Dinah 1937- 132
Lampkin, William R(obert) 1932- 106
Lampl, Paul 1915- Brief entry 104
Lamplugh, Lois 1921- CANR-24
Earlier sketches in CA 13-16R, CANR-9
See also SATA 17
Lampman, Archibald 1861-1899 .... DLB 92
Lampman, Ben Hur 1886-1954 Brief entry 111
Lampman, Evelyn Sibley 1907-1980 .... CANR-11
Obituary 101
Earlier sketch in CA 13-16R
See also SATA 4, 87
See also SATA-Obit 23
Lampman, Robert James 1920-1997 103
Obituary 157
Lampo, Hubert 1920- Brief entry 105
Lamport, Felicia 1916- 1-4R
Lamppa, William R(ussell) 1928- 53-56
Lamprecht, Sterling P(ower) 1890-1973 .... CAP-1
Earlier sketch in CA 17-18
Lamprey, Louise 1869-1951 Brief entry 117
See also YABC 2
Lampson, Robin 1900-1978 Obituary 77-80
Lampton, Chris
See Lampton, Christopher F.
Lampton, Christopher
See Lampton, Christopher F.
Lampton, Christopher F. CANR-37
Earlier sketch in CA 125
See also SATA 67
See also SATA-Brief 47
Lamsa, George M(amishisho) 1892-1975 .... CANR-9
Earlier sketches in CAP-2, CA 23-24
Lamson, Peggy 1912- 25-28R
La Mure, Pierre 1909-1976 Obituary 104
Lan, David 1952- CANR-24
Earlier sketch in CA 97-100
Lana, Robert E(dward) 1932- 33-36R
Lancaster, Bob 1943- 111
Lancaster, Bruce 1896-1963 .... CANR-70
Earlier sketches in CAP-1, CA 9-10
See also CLC 36
See also SATA 9
Lancaster, Burt(on Stephen) 1913-1994 122
Obituary 147
Brief entry 116
Lancaster, Clay 1917- CANR-8
Earlier sketch in CA 5-8R
Lancaster, David
See Heald, Tim(othy Villiers)
Lancaster, Evelyn
See Sizemore, Chris(tine) Costner
Lancaster, F. Donald
See Fredriksson, Don
Lancaster, F(rederick) Wilfrid 1933- CANR-42
Earlier sketches in CA 53-56, CANR-4, 19
Lancaster, Jane F(airchild) 1940- 150
Lancaster, Kelvin (John) 1924- 33-36R
Lancaster, Lydia
See Meaker, Eloise
Lancaster, Marie-Jaqueline 1922- 25-28R
Lancaster, Matthew 1973(?)-1983 Obituary 117
See also SATA-Obit 45
Lancaster, Michael (L.) 1928- 154
Lancaster, Osbert 1908-1986 105
Obituary 119
Lancaster, Otis Ewing 1909- 103
Lancaster, Richard 21-24R
Lancaster, Roger N(elson) 1959- 143
Lancaster, Sheila
See Holland, Sheila
Lancaster-Brown, Peter 1927- CANR-19
Earlier sketches in CA 53-56, CANR-4
Lance, Derek (Paul) 1932- CANR-9
Earlier sketch in CA 13-16R
Lance, H(ubert) Darrell 1935- 115
Lance, James Waldo 1926- 65-68
Lance, Kathryn 1943- 122
See also SATA 76
Lance, LaBelle D(avid) 1931- 81-84
Lance, Leslie
See Swatridge, Charles (John)
Lancer, Jack CANR-27
Earlier sketch in CAP-2
Lanchester, Elsa 1902-1986 134
Obituary 121
Lanchester, John .... CLC 99
Lanciano, Claude O(lwen), Jr. 1922- CANR-1
Earlier sketch in CA 45-48
Lancour, Gene
See Fisher, Gene L(ouis)
Lancour, (Adlore) Harold 1908-1981 .... 21-24R
Obituary 105
Lancy, David F(alcon) 1945- 110
Land
See Landry, Robert John
Land, Aubrey C(hristian) 1912- 41-44R
Land, Barbara (Neblett) 1923- 81-84
See also SATA 16
Land, Ben
See Rosenberg, Robert
Land, (Reginald) Brian 1927- 101
Land, Edwin H(erbert) 1909-1991 155
Land, George T(homas) Lock 1933- 53-56
Land, Jane
See Borland, Kathryn Kilby
and Speicher, Helen Ross S(mith)
Land, Myrick (Ebben) 1922- CANR-11
Earlier sketch in CA 13-16R
See also SATA 15

Land, Ross
See Borland, Kathryn Kilby
and Speicher, Helen Ross S(mith)
Landar, Herbert (Jay) 1927- ... 33-36R
Landau, Elaine 1948- ... CANR-5
Earlier sketch in CA 53-56
See also SATA 10, 94
Landau, Genevieve Millet 1927-1993 ... 107
Obituary ... 141
Landau, Jacob 1917- ... SATA 38
Landau, Jacob M. 1924- ... CANR-24
Earlier sketches in CA 17-20R, CANR-8
Landau, Lev Davidovich 1908-1968 ... 158
Obituary ... 113
Landau, Mark Alexandrovich
See Aldanov, Mark (Alexandrovich)
Landau, Martin 1921- ... 45-48
Landau, Paul Stuart 1962- ... 153
Landau, Rom 1899-1974 ... CANR-4
Obituary ... 49-52
Earlier sketch in CA 1-4R
Landau, Saul (I.) 1936- ... 130
Landau, Sidney I(van) 1933- ... CANR-7
Earlier sketch in CA 57-60
Landau, Sol 1920- ... CANR-31
Earlier sketch in CA 49-52
Landau, Susan 1954- ... 166
Landau-Aldanov, Mark Alexandrovich
See Aldanov, Mark (Alexandrovich)
Landauer, Carl 1891-1983 ... CANR-21
Earlier sketch in CA 1-4R
Landauer, Jerry Gerd 1932-1981 ... 109
Obituary ... 103
Lande, Henry F(rank) 1920- ... 29-32R
Lande, Lawrence (Montague) 1906- ... 105
Lande, Nathaniel 1939- ... 104
Landeck, Beatrice 1904- ... 73-76
See also SATA 15
Landecker, Manfred 1929- ... 29-32R
Landeen, William M. 1891-1982 Obituary ... 109
Landeira, Ricardo L(opez) 1917- ... 81-84
Landen, Robert Geran 1930- ... 21-24R
Lander, Ernest McPherson, Jr. 1915- ... CANR-4
Earlier sketch in CA 1-4R
Lander, Jack Robert 1921- ... 101
Lander, Jeannette 1931- ... 33-36R
Lander, Louise 1938- ... 85-88
Lander, Mamie Stubbs
1891(?)-1975 Obituary ... 53-56
Landers, Ann
See Lederer, Esther Pauline
Landers, Gunnard W(illiam) 1944- ... 93-96
Landes, David S(aul) 1924- ... CANR-22
Earlier sketch in CA 103
Landes, Marie Gisele
See Landes-Fuss, Marie-Gisele
Landes, Richard 1949- ... 154
Landes, Ruth 1908-1991 ... CAP-2
Obituary ... 133
Earlier sketch in CA 29-32
Landes, Sonia 1925- ... CANR-22
Earlier sketch in CA 104
Landes-Fuss, Marie-Gisele 1936- ... 129
Landesman, Charles 1932- ... 85-88
Landesman, Fran(ces) 1927- ... CANR-55
Brief entry ... 120
Earlier sketch in CA 127
See also DLB 16
Landesman, Jay (Irving) 1919- ... 127
Brief entry ... 118
See also DLB 16
Landesman, Peter 1965- ... 154
Landgrebe, Ludwig 1902- ... 142
Landgren, Marchal E. 1907(?)-1983 Obituary ... 109
Landi, Ferruccio Rossi
See Rossi-Landi, Ferruccio
Landin, Les 1923- ... 5-8R
See also SATA 2
Landis, Benson Y. 1897-1966 ... CAP-1
Earlier sketch in CA 13-14
Landis, Dennis Channing 1947- ... 110
Landis, Fred S(imon) 1943- ... 107
Landis, Geoffrey A(lan) 1955- ... 159
Landis, J(ames) D(avid) 1942- ... 126
See also SATA 60
See also SATA-Brief 52
Landis, Jerry
See Simon, Paul (Frederick)
Landis, Jessie Royce 1904-1972 Obituary ... 33-36R
Landis, Jill Marie 1948- ... 161
See also SATA 101
Landis, John 1950- ... 122
Brief entry ... 112
See also CLC 26
Landis, Judson R(ichard) 1935- ... 33-36R
Landis, Lincoln 1922- ... 45-48
Landis, Marie A. ... 161
Landis, Paul H(enry) 1901- ... CANR-5
Earlier sketch in CA 5-8R
Landman, David 1917- ... CANR-11
Earlier sketch in CA 69-72
Landman, Jessica C. 1955- ... 149
Lando, Barry Mitchell 1939- ... 77-80
Landolfi, Tommaso 1908-1979 ... 127
Obituary ... 117
See also CLC 11, 49
See also DLB 177
Landon, Donald D. 1930- ... 25-28R
Landon, H(oward) C(handler) Robbins 1926- ...
CANR-34
Earlier sketches in CA 77-80, CANR-13
Landon, Letitia Elizabeth 1802-1838 ... DLB 96
Landon, Lucinda 1950- ... 123
See also SATA 56
See also SATA-Brief 51
Landon, Margaret (Dorothea Mortenson)
1903-1993 ... CAP-1
Obituary ... 143
Earlier sketch in CA 13-14
See also SATA 50
Landon, Michael de L(aval) 1935- ... CANR-57
Earlier sketches in CA 29-32R, CANR-30
Landor, Walter Savage 1775-1864 ... DLB 93, 107
Landorf, Joyce 1932- ... 124
See also AITN 1
Landow, George P(aul) 1940- ... CANR-41
Earlier sketches in CA 53-56, CANR-4, 19
Landowska, Wanda (Aleksandra) 1879-1959 Brief
entry ... 122
Landreth, Bill 1964- ... 138
Landreth, Catherine 1899- ... 77-80
Landreth, Marsha Ann 1947- ... 140
Landrith, Harold Fochone 1919- ... 103
Landrum, Gene N. 1935- ... 147
Landrum, Graham (Gordon) 1922- ... 148
Landrum, Phil 1939- ... 81-84
Landry, Hilton (James) 1924- ... 13-16R
Landry, Napoleon-P. 1884-1956 ... DLB 92
Landry, Robert John 1903-1991 ... 69-72
Obituary ... 134
Landry, Tom 1924- ... 141
Landsberg, Brian K. 1937- ... 165
Landsberg, Hans H. 1913- ... CANR-10
Earlier sketch in CA 17-20R
Landsberg, Helmut Erich 1906-1985 ... 107
Obituary ... 118
Landsberg, Melvin 1926- ... 142
Landsberg, Michele 1939- ... 123
Landsbergis, Algirdas J. 1924- ... CANR-45
Earlier sketches in CA 33-36R, CANR-13
Landsburg, Alan William 1933- ... 103
Landsburg, Sally (Breit) 1933- ... 57-60
Landsburg, Steven E(lliot) 1954- ... 168
Landshoff, Fritz Helmut 1901-1988 Obituary ... 125
Landshoff, Ursula 1908- ... 29-32R
See also SATA 13
Landskroner, Ronald A. 1946- ... 165
Landsman, Ned C. 1951- ... 126
Landsteiner, Karl (Otto) 1868-1943 ... 158
Landstrom, Bjorn O(lof) 1917- ... 13-16R
Landsverk, O(le) G(odfred) 1901- ... 61-64
Landvater, Dorothy 1927- ... 103
Landwehr, Arthur J. II 1934- ... 37-40R
Landwirth, Heinz 1927- ... CANR-7
Earlier sketch in CA 9-12R
See also Lind, Jakov
Landy, David 1917- ... 77-80
Landy, Eugene E(llsworth) 1934- ... 41-44R
Landy, John (Michael) 1930- ... 128
Landy, Marcia 1931- ... 168
Landynski, Jacob W. 1930- ... 21-24R
Lane, Abbe 1935- ... 140
Lane, Allen 1902-1970 Obituary ... 29-32R
Lane, Ann J(udith) 1931- ... 126
Brief entry ... 110
Lane, Anthony 1916- ... 13-16R
Lane, Arthur (Ernest) 1937- ... 41-44R
Lane, Carl D(aniel) 1899- ... 105
Lane, Carolyn 1926- ... CANR-12
Earlier sketch in CA 29-32R
See also SATA 10
Lane, Charles
See Gatti, Arthur Gerard
Lane, Charles 1800-1870 ... DLB 1
Lane, Dakota 1959- ... 162
Lane, David (Stuart) ... CANR-39
Earlier sketches in CA 29-32R, CANR-17
Lane, Dixie
See Salazar, Dixie
Lane, E(ugene Numa) 1936- ... 37-40R
Lane, Frank Walter 1908- ... 9-12R
Lane, Frederic C(hapin) 1900-1984 ... 105
Obituary ... 114
Lane, Gary 1943- ... 37-40R
Lane, Hana Umlauf 1946- ... 118
Lane, Harlan (Lawson) 1936- ... 126
Brief entry ... 111
Lane, Helen 1920- ... 123
Lane, Helen R(uth) ... CANR-2
Earlier sketch in CA 45-48
Lane, Irving M(ark) 1944- ... 53-56
Lane, Jack C(onstant) 1932- ... CANR-4
Earlier sketch in CA 53-56
Lane, James B(uchanan) 1942- ... 93-96
Lane, Jane
See Dakers, Elaine Kidner
Lane, Jan-Erik 1946- ... 138
Lane, Jerry
See Martin, Patricia Miles
Lane, John (Richard) 1932- ... 106
See also SATA 15
Lane, Laura Gordon 1913- ... 102
Lane, Laurence W. 1890-1967 ... DLB 91
Lane, M(illicent) Travis 1934- ... CANR-44
Earlier sketch in CA 112
See also DLB 60
Lane, Marc J(ay) 1946- ... CANR-46
Earlier sketches in CA 105, CANR-21
Lane, Margaret 1907-1994 ... CANR-29
Obituary ... 144
Earlier sketches in CA 25-28R, CANR-13
See also SATA 65
See also SATA-Brief 38
See also SATA-Obit 79
Lane, Mark 1927- ... CANR-21
Earlier sketch in CA 61-64
Lane, Mary (Lois) B(eauchamp) 1911- ... CANR-9
Earlier sketch in CA 13-16R
Lane, Mary D.
See Delaney, Mary Murray
Lane, Michael (John) 1941- ... 85-88
Lane, Nancy 1947- ... 147
Lane, Patrick 1939- ... CANR-54
Earlier sketch in CA 97-100
Interview in ... 97-100
See also CLC 25
See also DAM POET
See also DLB 53
Lane, Pinkie Gordon 1923- ... CANR-25
Earlier sketch in CA 41-44R
See also BW 2
See also DLB 41
Lane, Raymond A. 1894(?)-1974 Obituary ... 53-56
Lane, Richard 1926- ... CANR-10
Earlier sketch in CA 21-24R
Lane, Robert E(dwards) 1917- ... CANR-6
Earlier sketch in CA 1-4R
Lane, Roger 1934- ... 105
Lane, Ronnie M(ack) 1949- ... 41-44R
Lane, Rose Wilder 1887-1968 ... CANR-63
Earlier sketch in CA 102
See also SATA 29
See also SATA-Brief 28
Lane, Roumelia
See Green, Kay
Lane, Sherry
See Smith, Richard Rein
Lane, Sylvia 1916- ... CANR-8
Earlier sketch in CA 5-8R
Lane, Terry 1939- ... 165
Lane, Thomas A(lphonsus) 1906-1975 ... 13-16R
Obituary ... 125
Lane, Wheaton J. 1902-1983 Obituary ... 111
Lane, William G(uerrant) 1919- ... 25-28R
Lane, William L(ister) 1931- ... CANR-27
Earlier sketch in CA 29-32R
Lane, Yoti ... 1-4R
Lanegran, David A(ndrew) 1941- ... CANR-37
Earlier sketches in CA 89-92, CANR-16
Lanes, Selma Gordon 1929- ... 25-28R
See also SATA 3
Laney, Al 1896-1988 ... CANR-62
Earlier sketch in CA 108
See also DLB 171
Laney, J(ohn) Carl 1948- ... CANR-35
Earlier sketch in CA 114
Laney, James Thomas 1927- ... 103
Lanford, H(orace) W(haley) 1919- ... 41-44R
Lanfredi, Judy 1964- ... SATA 83
Lang, Allen Kim 1928- ... 17-20R
Lang, Andrew 1844-1912 ... 137
Brief entry ... 114
See also DLB 98, 141, 184
See also MAICYA
See also SATA 16
See also TCLC 16
Lang, Barbara 1935- ... 9-12R
Lang, Berel 1933- ... CANR-34
Earlier sketches in CA 41-44R, CANR-15
Lang, Daniel 1915-1981 ... CANR-4
Obituary ... 105
Earlier sketch in CA 5-8R
Lang, David 1913- ... 106
Lang, David Marshall 1924-1991 ... CANR-17
Obituary ... 134
Earlier sketches in CA 5-8R, CANR-2
Lang, Derek 1913- ... 102
Lang, Frances
See Mantle, Winifred (Langford)
Lang, Fritz 1890-1976 ... CANR-30
Obituary ... 69-72
Earlier sketch in CA 77-80
See also CLC 20, 103
Lang, George 1924- ... 101
Lang, Gottfried O(tto) 1919- ... 45-48
Lang, Grace
See Floren, Lee
Lang, Gregor
See Birren, Faber
Lang, H. Jack 1904- ... 115
Lang, Jack (Frederick) 1921- ... 5-8R
Lang, Jeannie
See Brewer, Jeannie A.
Lang, Jenifer Harvey 1951- ... 138
Lang, Jovian Peter 1919- ... CANR-15
Earlier sketch in CA 41-44R
Lang, Judith 1939- ... 165
Lang, King
See Tubb, E(dwin) C(harles)
Lang, Kurt 1924- ... 33-36R
Lang, Mabel L(ouise) 1917- ... 126
Brief entry ... 106
Lang, Martin
See Birren, Faber
Lang, Martin A(ndrew) 1930- ... 115
Lang, Maud
See Williams, Claerwen
Lang, Michel (Jules Jean Marcel) 1939- ... 129
Lang, Miriam (Milman) 1915- ... 5-8R
Lang, Nancy M.
See Mace, Nancy L(awson)
Lang, Ned
See Sheckley, Robert
Lang, Paul 1948- ... 150
See also SATA 83
Lang, Paul Henry 1901-1991 ... 103
Obituary ... 135
Lang, Robert (Peregrine) 1912- ... 41-44R
Lang, Ronald William 1933- ... 103
Lang, Rupert
See Turner, E(rnest) S(ackville)
Lang, Susan S. 1950- ... 136
See also SATA 68
Lang, T. T.
See Taylor, Theodore
Lang, William L. 1942- ... 165
Lang, William Rawson 1909- ... CANR-21
Earlier sketch in CA 103
Langa, Mandla 1950- ... 168
Langacker, Ronald W(ayne) 1942- ... 21-24R
Langan, Ruth Ryan 1937- ... CANR-24
Earlier sketch in CA 107
Langan, Thomas 1929- ... CANR-17
Earlier sketch in CA 1-4R
Langart, Darrell T.
See Garrett, (Gordon) Randall (Phillip)
Langbaum, Robert (Woodrow) 1924- ... CANR-1
Earlier sketch in CA 45-48
Langbein, John H(arriss) 1941- ... CANR-53
Earlier sketch in CA 124
Langdale, Cecily 1939- ... CANR-53
Earlier sketch in CA 126
Langdale, Eve
See Craig, E(velyn) Quita
Langdon, Charles 1934- ... 77-80
Langdon, E(sther) Jean Matteson 1944- ... 146
Langdon, Frank C(orriston) 1919- ... 21-24R
Langdon, George D(orland), Jr. 1933- ... 21-24R
Langdon, Grace 1889- ... 1-4R
Langdon, John 1913- ... 5-8R
Langdon, Margaret Hoffmann (Storms) 1926- Brief
entry ... 107
Langdon, Philip 1947- ... CANR-66
Earlier sketch in CA 129
Langdon, Robert Adrian 1924- ... CANR-42
Earlier sketches in CA 104, CANR-20
Lange, Arthur D. 1952- ... 145
Lange, Dorothea 1895-1965 ... 148
Obituary ... 107
See also AAYA 14
Lange, Frederick Douglas
See Lange, Tom
Lange, Gerald 1946- ... 69-72
Lange, James E(dward) T(homas) ... 142
Lange, John
See Crichton, (John) Michael
Lange, John Frederick, Jr. 1931- ... CANR-54
Earlier sketches in CA 97-100, CANR-8, 25
Lange, (Leo) Joseph (Jr.) 1932- ... CANR-8
Earlier sketch in CA 17-20R
Lange, Kelly ... 89-92
Lange, Martin 1955- ... 130
Lange, Oliver (a pseudonym) 1927- ... CANR-23
Earlier sketch in CA 103
Lange, Oskar (Richard) 1904-1965 Obituary ... 116
Lange, Suzanne 1945- ... 29-32R
See also SATA 5
Lange, Tom 1945- ... 158
Lange, (Hermann Walter) Victor 1908-1996 ... 9-12R
Obituary ... 152
Langendoen, D(onald) Terence 1939- ... 33-36R
Langer, Elinor 1939- ... 121
See also CLC 34
Langer, Ellen J(ane) 1947- ... CANR-72
Earlier sketches in CA 49-52, CANR-30
Langer, Erick D. 1955- ... 137
Langer, Jonas 1936- ... 33-36R
Langer, Lawrence L(ee) 1929- ... CANR-41
Earlier sketches in CA 65-68, CANR-11
Langer, Marshall J. 1928- ... 105
Langer, Susanne (Katherina) K(nauth) 1895-1985 ..
CANR-34
Obituary ... 116
Earlier sketch in CA 41-44R
See also MTCW 1
Langer, Sydney 1914- ... 109
Langer, Thomas Edward 1929- ... 5-8R
Langer, Walter Charles 1899-1981 ... 102
Obituary ... 104
Langer, William L(eonard) 1896-1977 ... CANR-14
Obituary ... 73-76
Earlier sketch in CA 29-32R
Langevin, Andre 1927- ... DLB 60
Langevin, Sister Jean Marie 1917- ... 53-56
Langford, Alec J. 1926- ... 97-100
Langford, David 1953- ... 135
Langford, Gary R(aymond) 1947- ... CANR-45
Earlier sketches in CA 103, CANR-20
Langford, George 1939- ... 53-56
Langford, Gerald 1911- ... CANR-32
Earlier sketch in CA 1-4R
Langford, James R(ouleau) 1937- ... 53-56
Langford, Jane
See Mantle, Winifred (Langford)
Langford, Jerome J.
See Langford, James R(ouleau)
Langford, Thomas Anderson 1929- ... 9-12R
Langford, Walter McCarty 1908- ... 33-36R
Langgaesser, Elisabeth (Maria) 1899-1950 Brief
entry ... 121
See also Langgasser, Elisabeth (Maria)
See also DLB 69
Langgasser, Elisabeth (Maria)
See Langgaesser, Elisabeth (Maria)
See also DLB 69
Langguth, A(rthur) J(ohn) 1933- ... CANR-30
Earlier sketch in CA 61-64
Langhoff, Severin Peter, Jr.
1910-1987 Obituary ... 122
Langholm, Neil
See Bulmer, (Henry) Kenneth
Langhorne, Elizabeth (Coles) 1909- ... CANR-40
Earlier sketch in CA 49-52
Langhorne, John 1735-1779 ... DLB 109
Langhorne, Richard (Tristan Bailey) 1940- ... 122
Langiulli, Nino 1932- ... 53-56
Langlais, Jacques 1921- ... 141
Langland, Elizabeth 1948- ... 112
Langland, Joseph (Thomas) 1917- ... CANR-8
Earlier sketch in CA 5-8R

Langland, William 1330(?)-1400(?) .... DA
See also DAB
See also DAC
See also DAM MST, POET
See also DLB 146
Langley, Adria (Locke) 1899(?)-1983 Obituary .. 110
Langley, Bob 1936- 85-88
Langley, Dorothy
See Kissling, Dorothy (Hight)
Langley, Gill(ian Rose) 1952- 133
Langley, Harold D. 1925- 21-24R
Langley, Helen
See Rowland, D(onald) S(ydney)
Langley, James Maydon 1916-1983 102
Obituary 109
Langley, Lee 1932- 159
Langley, Lester D(anny) 1940- CANR-41
Earlier sketches in CA 102, CANR-19
Langley, Michael (John) 1933- 97-100
Langley, Noel 1911-1980 .... CANR-30
Obituary 102
Earlier sketch in CA 13-16R
See also SATA-Obit 25
Langley, Raymond J. 1935- Brief entry 108
Langley, Roger 1930- 73-76
Langley, Stephen G(ould) 1938-1997 .... 41-44R
Obituary 159
Langley, Tania
See Armstrong, Tilly
Langley, Wright 1935- 57-60
Langlois, Walter G(ordon) 1925- CANR-9
Earlier sketch in CA 21-24R
Langman, Ida Kaplan 1904- CAP-1
Earlier sketch in CA 13-16
Langman, Larry 1930- 109
Langner, Lawrence 1890-1962 Obituary 116
Langner, Nola
See Malone, Nola Langner
See also SATA 8
Langone, John (Michael) 1929- CANR-1
Earlier sketch in CA 49-52
See also SATA 46
See also SATA-Brief 38
Langsam, Walter Consuelo 1906-1985 .... CANR-2
Obituary 117
Earlier sketch in CA 1-4R
Langsen, Richard C. 1953- 160
See also SATA 95
Lang-Sims, Lois Dorothy 1917- 106
Langsley, Donald G(ene) 1925- CANR-4
Earlier sketch in CA 53-56
Langstaff, J(ohn) Brett 1889-1985 .... CANR-29
Obituary 115
Earlier sketch in CA 1-4R
Langstaff, John (Meredith) 1920- CANR-49
Earlier sketches in CA 1-4R, CANR-4
See also CLR 3
See also MAICYA
See also SATA 6, 68
Langstaff, Josephine
See Herschberger, Ruth (Margaret)
Langstaff, Launcelot
See Irving, Washington
Langstaff, Nancy 1925- CANR-12
Earlier sketch in CA 73-76
Langton, Anne 1804-1893 .... DLB 99
Langton, Clair V(an Norman) 1895- 5-8R
Langton, Daniel J(oseph) 1927- 93-96
Langton, Jane (Gillson) 1922- CANR-40
Earlier sketches in CA 1-4R, CANR-1, 18
See also CLR 33
See also MAICYA
See also SAAS 5
See also SATA 3, 68
Langton, Kenneth P(atrick) 1933- 25-28R
Languirand, Jacques 1931- 166
Langum, David J. 1940- 141
Langwill, Lyndesay Graham 1897- 13-16R
Langworth, Richard M(ichael) 1941- 73-76
Langworthy, Harry W(ells III) 1939- 57-60
Lanham, Charles Trueman
1902-1978 Obituary 81-84
Lanham, Edwin (Moultrie) 1904-1979 .... 9-12R
Obituary 89-92
See also DLB 4
Lanham, Frank W(esley) 1914- CANR-6
Earlier sketch in CA 1-4R
Lanham, Richard Alan 1936- CANR-10
Earlier sketch in CA 25-28R
Lanham, Url(ess Norton) 1918- 25-28R
Lanier, Alison Raymond 1917-1993 .... CANR-12
Obituary 142
Earlier sketch in CA 17-20R
Lanier, Sidney 1842-1881 .... DAM POET
See also DLB 64
See also DLBD 13
See also MAICYA
See also SATA 18
Lanier, Sterling E(dmund) 1927- 162
Brief entry 118
Lanigan, Catherine 1947- 108
Laning, Edward 1906- 53-56
Lank, Edith H(andleman) 1926- 109
Lanker, Brian T(imothy) 1947- 134
Lankevich, George J(ohn) 1939- CANR-13
Earlier sketch in CA 77-80
Lankford, John (Errett) 1934- 17-20R
Lankford, Mary D. 1932- 145
See also SATA 77
Lankford, Mike 1951- 163
Lankford, Nelson D. 1948- 138
Lankford, Philip Marlin 1945- CANR-7
Earlier sketch in CA 57-60
Lankford, T(homas) Randall 1942- 65-68
Lanks, Herbert C(harles) 1899-1987 Obituary .. 122
Lanne, William F.
See Leopold, Nathan F.
Lanner, Ronald Martin 1930- 107
Lanning, Edward P(utnam) 1930- 17-20R
Lanning, George (William), Jr. 1925- 9-12R
Lanning, John Tate 1902-1976 Obituary 108
Lannoy, Violet Dias 1925-1973 168
Lanoil, Georgia Hope Witkin
See Witkin-Lanoil, Georgia Hope
Lanoue, Fred Richard 1908-1965 .... CAP-1
Earlier sketch in CA 13-14
La Noue, George R(ichard) 1937- 73-76
Lanouette, William (John) 1940- 136
Lanoux, Armand 1913-1983 Obituary 109
Lansbury, Angela 1946- 81-84
Lansbury, Coral 1933-1991 143
Lansdale, Edward Geary 1908-1987 Obituary .. 121
Lansdale, Joe R(ichard) 1951- CANR-50
Earlier sketches in CA 113, CANR-32
Lansdale, Robert Tucker 1900-1980 Obituary .. 103
Lansdowne, J(ames) F(enwick) 1937- ... CANR-30
Earlier sketch in CA 49-52
Lanser, Susan Sniader 107
Lansing, Alfred 1921-1975 .... 13-16R
Obituary 61-64
See also SATA 35
Lansing, Elisabeth Hubbard 1911- 5-8R
Lansing, Gerrit (Yates) 1928- 73-76
Lansing, Henry
See Rowland, D(onald) S(ydney)
Lansing, John B(elcher) 1919-1970 Obituary ... 108
Lansing, Karen E. 1954- .... SATA 71
Lansky, Bruce 1941- CANR-29
Earlier sketch in CA 109
Lansky, Vicki 1942- CANR-53
Earlier sketches in CA 81-84, CANR-26
Lanson, Lucienne (Therese) 1930- Brief entry .. 108
Lant, Harvey
See Rowland, D(onald) S(ydney)
Lant, Jeffrey Ladd 1947- CANR-30
Earlier sketch in CA 109
Lanterman, Ray(mond E.) 1916- 106
Lantier-Sampon, Patricia 1952- 156
See also SATA 92
Lantis, David W(illiam) 1917- 13-16R
Lantis, Margaret (Lydia) 1906- CAP-2
Earlier sketch in CA 29-32
Lantry, Mike
See Tubb, E(dwin) C(harles)
Lantz, Fran
See Lantz, Francess L(in)
Lantz, Francess L(in) 1952- CANR-39
Earlier sketch in CA 115
See also SATA 63
Lantz, Herman R. 1919-1987 .... 37-40R
Obituary 122
Lantz, Louise K. 1930- 45-48
Lantz, Paul 1908- .... SATA 45
Lantz, Walter 1900-1994 Obituary 144
Brief entry 108
See also SATA 37
See also SATA-Obit 79
Lanyer, Aemilia 1569-1645 .... DLB 121
Lanyon, Carla 1906-1971 .... CAP-1
Earlier sketch in CA 13-14
Lanza, Barbara 1945- .... SATA 101
Lanza, Joseph 1955- 154
Lanzillotti, Robert F(ranklin) 1921- 77-80
Lanzmann, Claude 1925- 139
Lao, Kan 1907- 41-44R
Lao She
See Shu, Ch' ing-ch'un
Lapage, Geoffrey 1888- CAP-1
Earlier sketch in CA 9-10
La Pallo, A. Elise 128
La Palombara, Joseph 1925- CANR-57
Earlier sketches in CA 1-4R, CANR-6, 31
Lapaquellerie, Yvon
See Bizardel, Yvon
Lapati, Americo D. 1924- CANR-1
Earlier sketch in CA 1-4R
La Patra, Jack W(illiam) 1927- 93-96
Lape, Esther Everett 1881-1981 Obituary 108
Lape, Fred 1900- 102
Lapedes, Daniel N. 1913(?)-1979 Obituary ... 93-96
Lapena-Bonifacio, Amelia 1930- 130
LaPenta, Anthony V(incent), Jr. 1943- 69-72
Lapeza, David (Henry) 1950- 73-76
Lapham, Arthur L(owell) 1922- 49-52
Lapham, Lewis H(enry) 1935- CANR-33
Earlier sketch in CA 77-80
Interview in CANR-33
Lapham, Maxwell E(dward)
1900(?)-1983 Obituary 110
Lapham, Samuel, Jr. 1892-1972 Obituary 106
Lapide, Phinn E.
See Lapide, Pinchas E.
Lapide, Pinchas E. 1922- CANR-13
Earlier sketch in CA 21-24R
Lapides, Robert 1940- 145
Lapidus, Elaine 1939- 21-24R
Lapidus, Jacqueline (Anita) 1941- 97-100
Lapidus, Morris 1902- 77-80
Lapierre, Dominique 1931- CANR-42
Earlier sketches in CA 69-72, CANR-19
LaPierre, Laurier L. 1929- 164
Brief entry 107
La Pietra, Mary 1929- 61-64
Lapin, Howard S(idney) 1922- 17-20R
Lapin, Jackie 1951- 85-88
Lapine, James (Elliot) 1949- CANR-54
Brief entry 123
Earlier sketch in CA 130
Interview in 130
See also CLC 39
Lapinski, Susan 1948- 115
La Place, John 1922- 103
LaPointe, Frank 1936- 93-96
Lapointe, (Joseph-) Gatien (-Fernand)
1931-1983 148
See also DLB 88
Lapointe, Paul-Marie 1929- Brief entry 109
See also DLB 88
Laponce, Jean Antoine 1925- 53-56
Laporte, Jean 1924- 41-44R
Laporte, Maurice 1901(?)-1987 Obituary 123
LaPorte, Robert, Jr. 1940- 41-44R
Lapp, Charles (Leon) 1914- CANR-1
Earlier sketch in CA 45-48
Lapp, Christiane (Germain) 1948- .... SATA 74
Lapp, Chuck
See Lapp, Charles (Leon)
Lapp, Eleanor J. 1936- 69-72
Lapp, Eunice Willis Bodine 1905- 123
Lapp, John Allen 1933- 41-44R
Lapp, John Clarke 1917-1977 85-88
Lapp, Ralph Eugene 1917- 81-84
Lapp, Rudolph M(athew) 1915- 113
Lappe, Frances Moore 1944- 37-40R
Lappe, Marc 1943- CANR-56
Earlier sketch in CA 126
Lappin, Ben
See Lappin, Bernard William
Lappin, Bernard William 1916- 9-12R
Lappin, Peter 1911- CANR-50
Earlier sketches in CA 57-60, CANR-7, 25
See also SATA 32
Lapping, Brian 1937- 25-28R
Laprade, William Thomas
1883-1975 Obituary 89-92
LaPray, (Margaret) Helen 1916- CANR-7
Earlier sketch in CA 53-56
Lapsley, James N(orvell) 1930- 25-28R
La Puma, Salvatore 1929- 136
Laqueur, Walter (Ze'ev) 1921- CANR-23
Earlier sketch in CA 5-8R
See also CAAS 19
Laquian, Aprodicio A(rcilla) 1935- CANR-26
Earlier sketch in CA 29-32R
Lara
See Griffith-Jones, George Chetwynd
Lara, Agustin 1900-1970 Obituary 104
Lara, Jan
See Hinkemeyer, Michael T(homas)
Laramore, Darryl 1928- 101
Larangeira, Crispin 1940- 129
Larbaud, Valery (Nicolas) 1881-1957 152
Brief entry 106
See also TCLC 9
Larco, Isabel Granda 1911(?)-1983 Obituary ... 109
Lardas, Konstantinos 1927- 13-16R
Lardner, George, Jr. 1934- 73-76
Lardner, James 1948- 118
Lardner, John (Abbott) 1912-1960 Obituary .. 93-96
See also DLB 171
Lardner, Ring
See Lardner, Ring(gold) W(ilmer)
Lardner, Ring(gold Wilmer), Jr. 1915- CANR-13
Earlier sketch in CA 25-28R
Interview in CANR-13
See also DLB 26, 171
Lardner, Ring W., Jr.
See Lardner, Ring(gold) W(ilmer)
Lardner, Ring(gold) W(ilmer) 1885-1933 131
Brief entry 104
See also CDALB 1917-1929
See also DLB 11, 25, 86
See also DLBD 16
See also MTCW 1
See also TCLC 2, 14
Lardner-Burke, Desmond William
1909-1984 Obituary 114
Lardy, Nicholas R. 1946- 140
Laredo, Betty
See Codrescu, Andrei
Laredo, Johnny
See Caesar, (Eu)Gene (Lee)
La Reyniere
See Courtine, Robert
Large, David C.
See Large, David Clay
Large, David Clay 1945- 140
Large, E(rnest) C(harles) (?)-1976 160
Large, Peter Somerville
See Somerville-Large, Peter
Large, R(ichard) Geddes 1901- 102
Large, Stephen S(toker) 1942- 120
Largo, Michael 1950- 73-76
Lariar, Lawrence 1908- CAP-1
Earlier sketch in CA 9-10
Larimore, Bertha B(urnham) 1915- 61-64
La Rivers, Ira II 1915-1977 .... 41-44R
Larkey, Patrick Darrel 1943- 85-88
Larkin, Amy
See Burns, Olive Ann
Larkin, Emmet 1927- CANR-9
Earlier sketch in CA 13-16R
Larkin, John A(lan) 1936- 41-44R
Larkin, John Day 1897-1986 Obituary 118
Larkin, Maia
See Wojciechowska, Maia (Teresa)
Larkin, Maurice (John Milner) 1932- 102
Larkin, Miriam Therese 1930- Brief entry 108
Larkin, Oliver Waterman 1896-1970 .... 1-4R
Obituary 29-32R
Larkin, Philip (Arthur) 1922-1985 .... CANR-62
Obituary 117
Earlier sketches in CA 5-8R, CANR-24
See also CDBLB 1960 to Present
See also CLC 3, 5, 8, 9, 13, 18, 33, 39, 64
See also DAB
See also DAM MST, POET
See also DLB 27
See also MTCW 1
See also PC 21
Larkin, R. T.
See Larkin, Rochelle
Larkin, Rochelle 1935- CANR-13
Earlier sketch in CA 33-36R
Larkin, Sarah
See Loening, Sarah (Elizabeth) Larkin
Larlham, Hattie 1914- 113
Larminie, Margaret Beda 1924- CANR-59
Earlier sketches in CA 5-8R, CANR-2, 18
Larmore, Lewis 1915- 45-48
Larn, Richard (James Vincent) 1930- CANR-20
Earlier sketch in CA 103
Larnach, Rupert
See Nevill, Barry St-John
Larner, Christina (Ross) (?)-1983 Obituary 115
Larner, Jeremy 1937- 9-12R
Larner, John (Patrick) 1930- 81-84
Larneuil, Michel
See Batbedat, Jean
Laroche, Giles 1956- .... SATA 71
Laroche, Rene
See McKeag, Ernest L(ionel)
La Roche, Sophie von 1730-1807 .... DLB 94
Larock, Bruce Edward 1940- 53-56
La Rocque, Gilbert 1943-1984 148
See also DLB 60
Larom, Henry V. 1903(?)-1975 Obituary 61-64
See also SATA-Obit 30
Laroque, Francois G. 1948- 140
Laroque de Roquebrune, Robert
See Roquebrune, Robert (Laroque) de
La Rosa, Pablo 1944- 161
La Rosa, Paul (Frank) 1953- 113
Larose, Paul 1947- 114
LaRouche, Lyndon H(ermyle), Jr. 1922- 138
Brief entry 124
Larrabee, Carroll Burton 1896-1983 Obituary .. 110
Larrabee, Eric 1922-1990 .... CANR-1
Obituary 133
Earlier sketch in CA 1-4R
Larrabee, Harold A(tkins) 1894-1979 .... CAP-1
Obituary 85-88
Earlier sketch in CA 11-12
Larrabee, Lisa 1947- 150
See also SATA 84
Larranaga, Robert O. 1940- 49-52
Larrea, Jean-Jacques 1960- 45-48
Larrecq, John M(aurice) 1926-1980 ...... SATA 44
See also SATA-Obit 25
Larrick, Nancy 1910- CANR-1
Earlier sketch in CA 1-4R
See also DLB 61
See also SATA 4
Larrie, Reginald R. 1928- 123
Brief entry 118
Larrison, Earl J(unior) 1919- CANR-9
Earlier sketch in CA 57-60
Larrowe, Charles P(atrick) 1916- 41-44R
Larry
See Parkes, Terence
Larsen, Anita 1942- .... SATA 78
Larsen, Beverly (Namen) 1929- 17-20R
Larsen, Carl 1934- CANR-27
Earlier sketch in CA 77-80
Larsen, Charles E(dward) 1923- 33-36R
Larsen, David C(harles) 1944- 73-76
Larsen, E(gner) John 1926- CANR-16
Earlier sketch in CA 25-28R
Larsen, Egon 1904- CANR-3
Earlier sketch in CA 9-12R
See also SATA 14
Larsen, Elyse 1957- 41-44R
Larsen, Eric 1941- 132
See also CLC 55
Larsen, Erik 1911- 41-44R
Larsen, Erling 1909- 13-16R
Larsen, Ernest 1946- 106
Larsen, Gaylord 1932- CANR-30
Earlier sketch in CA 112
Larsen, J(akob) A(all) O(tteson)
1888-1974 Obituary 111
Larsen, Jack Lenor 1927- 126
Larsen, Jeanne (Louise) 1950- 134
Larsen, Jens Peter 1902-1988 Obituary 126
Larsen, Kalee 1952- 41-44R
Larsen, Knud S(onderhede) 1938- 53-56
Larsen, Lawrence H. 1931- 21-24R
Larsen, Nella 1891-1964 125
See also BLC 2
See also BW 1
See also CLC 37
See also DAM MULT
See also DLB 51
Larsen, Otto N. 1922- CANR-2
Earlier sketch in CA 1-4R
Larsen, Paul E(manuel) 1933- 93-96
Larsen, Peter 1933- CANR-22
Earlier sketch in CA 29-32R
Larsen, Rebecca 1944- 122
See also SATA 54
Larsen, Ronald J(ames) 1948- 41-44R
Larsen, Roy E(dward) 1899-1979 Obituary ... 89-92
Larsen, Stephen 1941- 69-72
Larsen, Susan C(arol) 1946- 105
Larsen, Tony 1949- 107
Larsen, Torben B. 1944- 143

Larsen, Wendy Wilder 1940- ... 120
Larsen, William E(dward) 1936- ... 17-20R
Larsgaard, Mary L(ynette) 1946- ... 122
Larson, Albert J. 1934- ... 112
Larson, Andrew Karl 1899- ... CAP-2
Earlier sketch in CA 33-36
Larson, (Lewis) Arthur 1910-1993 ... CANR-1
Obituary ... 141
Earlier sketch in CA 1-4R
Larson, Bob 1944- ... CANR-5
Earlier sketch in CA 53-56
Larson, Bruce 1925- ... CANR-56
Earlier sketches in CA 57-60, CANR-13, 30
Larson, Bruce L(lewellyn) 1936- ... 85-88
Larson, Calvin J(ames) 1933- ... CANR-31
Earlier sketch in CA 49-52
Larson, Carl M. 1916- ... 41-44R
Larson, Carole 1940- ... 147
Larson, Cedric Arthur 1908- ... 65-68
Larson, Charles 1922- ... 25-28R
Larson, Charles R(aymond) 1938- ... CANR-4
Earlier sketch in CA 53-56
See also CLC 31
Larson, Charles U(rban) 1940- ... 97-100
Larson, Clem
See Fearn, John Russell
Larson, Clinton F(oster) 1919- ... 57-60
Larson, Donald (Norman) 1925- ... 57-60
Larson, Doran 1957- ... 124
Larson, E. Richard 1944- ... 105
Larson, Edward J(ohn) 1953- ... 158
Larson, Esther Elisabeth 1908-1978 ... 17-20R
Obituary ... 134
Larson, Eve
See St. John, Wylly Folk
Larson, Gary 1950- ... CANR-60
Earlier sketches in CA 118, CANR-41
See also AAYA 1
See also DAM POP
See also SATA 57
Larson, Gary O(tto) 1949- ... 115
Larson, George C(harles) 1942- ... CANR-9
Earlier sketch in CA 65-68
Larson, Gerald James 1938- ... 93-96
Larson, Glen A. 1937(?)- Brief entry ... 115
Larson, Gustive O(lof) 1897-1978 ... 29-32R
Obituary ... 125
Larson, Harold J. 1934- ... 53-56
Larson, Henrietta M(elia) 1894-1983 ... CAP-2
Obituary ... 110
Earlier sketch in CA 23-24
Larson, Ingrid D(ana) 1965- ... 156
See also SATA 92
Larson, James F(rederick) 1947- ... 115
Larson, Janet Karsten 1945- ... 104
Larson, Jean Russell 1930- ... 21-24R
Larson, Jeanne 1920- ... 57-60
Larson, Jennifer 1965- ... 152
Larson, Jonathan 1961-1996 ... 156
See also CLC 99
Larson, Kirby 1954- ... 161
See also SATA 96
Larson, Knute (G.) 1919- ... 9-12R
Larson, Kris 1953- ... 77-80
Larson, Magali Sarfatti 1936- ... 97-100
Larson, Martin Alfred 1897- ... CANR-2
Earlier sketch in CA 5-8R
Larson, Mel(vin Gunnard) 1916- ... 5-8R
Larson, Muriel 1924- ... CANR-49
Earlier sketches in CA 21-24R, CANR-9, 24
Larson, Norita D(ittberner) 1944- ... 105
See also SATA 29
Larson, Orvin Prentiss 1910- ... 77-80
Larson, P(aul) Merville 1903- ... 41-44R
Larson, Peggy (Ann Pickering) 1931- ... 81-84
Larson, Reed (W.) 1950- ... 128
Larson, Richard Francis 1931- ... CANR-15
Earlier sketch in CA 41-44R
Larson, Robert H(erbert) 1942- ... 113
Larson, Robert W. 1927- ... 85-88
Larson, Sidner J. 1949- ... 149
Larson, Simeon 1925- ... 61-64
Larson, Stephanie Greco 1960- ... 144
Larson, T(aft) A(lfred) 1910- ... 33-36R
Larson, Thomas B(ryan) 1914- ... 25-28R
Larson, Victor E. 1898-1981 ... 25-28R
Obituary ... 134
Larson, William H. 1938- ... 21-24R
See also SATA 10
Larsson, Carl (Olof) 1853-1919 Brief entry ... 115
See also SATA 35
Larsson, Flora (Benwell) 1904- ... 93-96
Lartigue, Jacques-Henri 1894-1986 ... 33-36R
Obituary ... 120
La Rue, Daniel Wolford, Jr.
1878-1969 Obituary ... 116
Larue, Gerald A(lexander) 1916- ... 21-24R
LaRue, L. H. 1938- ... 135
LaRusso, Dominic A(nthony) 1924- ... 33-36R
Lary, N(ikita) M(ichael) 1940- ... 61-64
Larzelere, Alex 1936- ... 166
Lasagna, Louis (Cesare) 1923- Brief entry ... 106
LaSalle, Charles A.
See Ellis, Edward S(ylvester)
LaSalle, Charles E.
See Ellis, Edward S(ylvester)
La Salle, Donald (Philip) 1933- ... 29-32R
La Salle, Dorothy (Marguerite) 1895-1980 ... 5-8R
Obituary ... 126
LaSalle, Peter 1947- ... 103
La Salle, Victor
See Fanthorpe, R(obert) Lionel
Lasater, Alice E(lizabeth) 1936- ... 57-60
Lasby, Clarence G(eorge) 1933- ... 105
Lasch, Christopher 1932-1994 ... CANR-25
Obituary ... 144
Earlier sketch in CA 73-76
See also CLC 102
See also MTCW 1
Lasch, Robert 1907-1998 ... 102
Obituary ... 167
Laschever, Barnett D. 1924- ... CANR-6
Earlier sketch in CA 1-4R
LaScola, Ray(mond) L. 1915- ... 1-4R
Lasdun, James 1958- ... 137
Lasdun, Susan 1929- ... 111
Lasell, Elinor H. 1929- ... CANR-7
Earlier sketch in CA 5-8R
See also SATA 19
Lasell, Fen H.
See Lasell, Elinor H.
Lasenby, Jack 1931- ... 130
See also SATA 65
Laser, Marvin 1914- ... 9-12R
Lash, Jeffrey N. 1949- ... 136
Lash, Jennifer 1938-1993 ... 168
Lash, Joseph P. 1909-1987 ... CANR-16
Obituary ... 123
Earlier sketch in CA 17-20R
See also SATA 43
Lash, Nicholas (Langrishe Alleyne) 1934- ... 144
Lasher, Albert C. 1928- ... 25-28R
Lasher, Faith B. 1921- ... 37-40R
See also SATA 12
Lashner, William 1956(?)- ... CANR-71
Earlier sketch in CA 152
Laska
See Laska, P(eter) J(erome)
Laska, P(eter) J(erome) 1938- ... CANR-15
Earlier sketch in CA 65-68
Laska, Vera
See Laska, Vera O(ravec)
Laska, Vera O(ravec) 1923- ... 119
Lasker, David 1950- ... 112
See also SATA 38
Lasker, Edward 1885-1981 ... 5-8R
Obituary ... 103
Lasker, Gabriel Ward 1912- ... 1-4R
Lasker, Joe
See Lasker, Joseph Leon
See also SAAS 17
See also SATA 83
Lasker, Joseph Leon 1919- ... CANR-38
Earlier sketches in CA 49-52, CANR-1
See also Lasker, Joe
See also SATA 9
Lasker, Judith N. 1947- ... 130
Lasker, Lawrence 1949- ... 166
Lasker, Michael
See Elman, Richard (Martin)
Lasker-Schueler, Else 1869-1945 ... DLB 66, 124
See also TCLC 57
Laski, Harold 1893-1950 ... TCLC 79
Laski, Marghanita 1915-1988 ... 105
Obituary ... 124
See also SATA 55
Laskier, Michael M. 1949- ... 142
Laskin, Bora 1912-1984 Obituary ... 112
Laskin, David 1953- ... 146
Laskin, Pamela L. 1954- ... 142
See also SATA 75
Lasko, Peter (Erik) 1924- ... 150
Laskowski, Jerzy 1919- ... 77-80
Lasky, Betty 1927- ... 119
Lasky, Jesse Louis, Jr. 1910- ... CANR-20
Earlier sketches in CA 1-4R, CANR-4
See also AITN 1
Lasky, Kathryn 1944- ... CANR-11
Earlier sketch in CA 69-72
See also AAYA 19
See also CLR 11
See also JRDA
See also MAICYA
See also SATA 13, 69
Lasky, Melvin J(onah) 1920- ... 53-56
Lasky, Victor 1918-1990 ... CANR-10
Obituary ... 131
Earlier sketch in CA 5-8R
Interview in ... CANR-10
See also AITN 1
Lasky, William R(aymond) 1921- ... 97-100
Laslett, John H(enry) M(artin) 1933- ... CANR-12
Earlier sketch in CA 29-32R
Laslett, Peter 1915- ... CANR-12
Earlier sketch in CA 73-76
Lasley, Jack
See Lasley, John Wayne III
Lasley, John Wayne III 1925- ... 17-20R
Lasnier, Rina 1915- ... DLB 88
LaSor, William Sanford 1911-1991 ... CANR-21
Obituary ... 133
Earlier sketches in CA 1-4R, CANR-2
La Sorte, A(ntonio) Michael 1931- ... 13-16R
La Spina, (Fanny) Greye 1880- ... CAP-1
Earlier sketch in CA 13-14
Lass, Abraham H(arold) 1907- ... 9-12R
Lass, Betty (Lipschitz)
1908(?)-1976 Obituary ... 69-72
Lass, Roger 1937- ... 132
Lass, William E(dward) 1928- ... CANR-2
Earlier sketch in CA 1-4R
Lass, William M. 1910(?)-1975 Obituary ... 104
Lassaigne, Jacques 1910(?)-1982 ... 129
Lassalle, C. E.
See Ellis, Edward S(ylvester)
Lassalle, Ferdinand 1825-1864 ... DLB 129
Lassam, Robert (Errington) 1914- ... 112
Lassen-Willems, James
See Willems, J. Rutherford
Lasserre, Philippe 1939- ... 159
Lassers, Willard J. 1919- ... 17-20R
Lassimonne, Denise ... 25-28R
Lassiter, Adam
See Krauzer, Steven M(ark)
Lassiter, Isaac Steele 1941- ... 33-36R
Lassiter, Mary
See Hoffman, Mary (Margaret)
See also SATA 59
Lassiter, (Albin) Perry (Jr.) 1935- ... 97-100
Lassiter, Roy L(eland), Jr. 1927- ... 21-24R
Lassner, Jacob 1935- ... CANR-42
Earlier sketches in CA 29-32R, CANR-20
Lasson, Kenneth (Lee) 1943- ... CANR-13
Earlier sketch in CA 33-36R
Lasswell, Harold D. 1902-1978 Obituary ... 104
Lasswell, Marcia 1927- ... 97-100
Lasswell, Thomas Ely 1919- ... 17-20R
Lasswitz, Kurd 1848-1910 ... 168
Last, Jef
See Last, Josephus Carel Franciscus
Last, Joan 1908- ... 107
Last, Josephus Carel Franciscus 1898-1972 ...
CAP-2
Earlier sketch in CA 33-36
Laster, Ann A(ppleton) 1936- ... 29-32R
Laszlo, Ervin 1932- ... 41-44R
Laszlo, Miklos 1904(?)-1973 Obituary ... 41-44R
Latane, Bibb 1937- ... 37-40R
Latch, William 1950(?)-1985 Obituary ... 117
Latchaw, Marjorie Elizabeth 1914- ... 5-8R
Lateef, Tolen S.
See Sanders, Clinton R.
Lateiner, Donald 1944- ... 135
Latham, Aaron 1943- ... 33-36R
Latham, Barbara 1896- ... SATA 16
Latham, Caroline S. 1940- ... 125
Latham, Donald Crawford 1932- ... 9-12R
Latham, Earl Ganson 1907- ... 103
Latham, Frank B(rown) 1910- ... 49-52
See also SATA 6
Latham, Harold Strong 1887-1969 ... CAP-1
Earlier sketch in CA 9-10
Latham, Ian 1956- ... 109
Latham, Jean Lee 1902-1995 ... CANR-7
Earlier sketch in CA 5-8R
See also AITN 1
See also CLC 12
See also CLR 50
See also MAICYA
See also SATA 2, 68
Latham, John H. 1917- ... 5-8R
Latham, Joyce 1943- ... 73-76
Latham, Lenn Learner 1901-197(?) ... 1-4R
Obituary ... 135
Latham, Lorraine 1948- ... 65-68
Latham, Marte Hooper 1924- ... 9-12R
Latham, Mavis
See Clark, Mavis Thorpe
Latham, Peter 1910- ... CAP-1
Earlier sketch in CA 11-12
Latham, Philip
See Richardson, Robert S(hirley)
Latham, Robert 1912-1995 ... DLB 201
Latham, Robert C(lifford) 1912- ... 158
Latham, Roger M. 1914(?)-1979 Obituary ... 85-88
Lathen, Emma
See Hennissart, Martha
and Latsis, Mary J(ane)
See also CLC 2
Lather, Patti 1948- ... 163
Lathrop, Dorothy P(ulis) 1891-1980 ... 73-76
Obituary ... 102
See also DLB 22
See also MAICYA
See also SATA 14
See also SATA-Obit 24
Lathrop, Francis
See Leiber, Fritz (Reuter, Jr.)
Lathrop, George Parsons 1851-1898 ... DLB 71
Lathrop, Irvin T(unis) 1927- ... CANR-22
Earlier sketch in CA 45-48
Lathrop, JoAnna 1931- ... 61-64
Lathrop, John, Jr. 1772-1820 ... DLB 37
Latimer, Dean 1945- ... 129
See also AAYA 2
Latimer, H(enry) C. 1893- ... 29-32R
Latimer, Jim 1943- ... SATA 80
Latimer, Jonathan (Wyatt) 1906-1983 Obituary ... 110
Latman, Alan 1930-1984 Obituary ... 113
Latner, Helen (Stambler) 1918- ... 106
Latner, Pat Wallace
See Strother, Pat Wallace
Latorre, Dolores L(aguarta Blasco) 1903- ... 65-68
Latorre, Felipe A(ugusto) 1907- ... 65-68
La Tour du Pin, Patrice de 1911-1975 Obituary ... 115
Latourelle, Rene 1918- ... 130
La Tourette, Aileen 1946- ... 119
Latourette, Kenneth Scott 1884-1967 ... CAP-2
Earlier sketch in CA 23-24
La Tourrette, Jacqueline 1926- ... CANR-34
Earlier sketch in CA 49-52
Latow, (Muriel) Roberta 1931- ... CANR-40
Earlier sketch in CA 116
Latsis, Mary J(ane) 1927(?)-1997 ... 85-88
Obituary ... 162
See also Lathen, Emma
Latta, Richard 1946- ... CANR-41
Earlier sketches in CA 53-56, CANR-4, 19
Latta, William (Charlton, Jr.) 1929- ... 115
Lattimer, John Kingsley 1914- ... 106
Lattimore, Eleanor Frances 1904-1986 ... CANR-6
Obituary ... 119
Earlier sketch in CA 9-12R
See also SATA 7
See also SATA-Obit 48
Lattimore, Jessie
See Dresser, Norine
and Fontes, Montserrat
Lattimore, Owen 1900-1989 ... 97-100
Obituary ... 128
Lattimore, Richmond (Alexander) 1906-1984 ...
CANR-1
Obituary ... 112
Earlier sketch in CA 1-4R
See also CLC 3
Lattin, Ann
See Cole, Lois Dwight
Lattin, Harriet Pratt 1898- ... 33-36R
Lattis, James M. 1954- ... 150
Latukefu, Sione 1927- ... 73-76
Latymer, William 1498-1583 ... DLB 132
Latzer, Beth Good 1911- ... 65-68
Lau, Charles Richard 1933-1984 Obituary ... 112
Lau, Charley
See Lau, Charles Richard
Lau, Evelyn 1970- ... 155
Lau, Joseph S(hui) M(ing) 1934- ... 77-80
Laub, (Martin) Julian 1929- ... 37-40R
Laubach, Frank Charles 1884-1970 ... CAP-1
Earlier sketch in CA 9-10
Laube, Clifford J(ames) 1891-1974 Obituary ... 53-56
Laube, Heinrich 1806-1884 ... DLB 133
Laubenbacher, Reinhard C. 1954- ... 148
Laubenthal, Sanders Anne 1943- ... 61-64
Lauber, Lynn 1952- ... 133
Lauber, Patricia (Grace) 1924- ... CANR-38
Earlier sketches in CA 9-12R, CANR-6, 24
See also CLR 16
See also JRDA
See also MAICYA
See also SATA 1, 33, 75
Lauber, Volkmar 1944- ... 132
Laubin, Gladys (Winifred) ... 111
Laubin, Reginald K(arl) ... 111
Laucanno, Christopher Sawyer
See Sawyer-Laucanno, Christopher
Lauck, Carol 1934- ... 93-96
Laudan, Larry L. 1941- ... 129
Lauder, George
See Dick-Lauder, George (Andrew)
Lauder, George (Andrew) Dick
See Dick-Lauder, George (Andrew)
Lauder, Phyllis 1898- ... 93-96
Lauder, Robert E(dward) 1934- ... 134
Lauderdale, Pat 1944- ... 101
Laudicina, Paul A(ndrew) 1949- ... 93-96
Laudin, Harvey 1922- ... 77-80
Laue, Max Theodor Felix von
1879-1960 Obituary ... 113
Lauer, Evelyn G(erda) 1938- ... 29-32R
Lauer, Jeanette C(arol) 1935- ... CANR-43
Earlier sketches in CA 104, CANR-19
Lauer, Jean-Philippe 1902- ... 85-88
Lauer, (Joseph) Quentin 1917- ... 152
Lauer, Robert H(arold) 1933- ... CANR-43
Earlier sketches in CA 53-56, CANR-4, 19
Lauer, Rosemary Zita 1919- ... 5-8R
Lauer, Theodore E. 1931- ... 37-40R
Lauerman, David A(nthony) 1931- ... 17-20R
Lauersen, Niels H(elth) 1939- ... CANR-33
Earlier sketches in CA 85-88, CANR-15
Lauf, Detlef I. Charles 1936- ... 103
Laufe, Abe 1906- ... 17-20R
Laufenberg, Cindy 1965- ... 147
Laufer, Leopold 1925- ... 21-24R
Laufer, Robert S. 1942(?)-1989 Obituary ... 129
Lauffer, Armand A(lbert) 1933- ... CANR-19
Earlier sketches in CA 53-56, CANR-5
Laugesen, Mary E(akin) 1906- ... CAP-2
Earlier sketch in CA 29-32
See also SATA 5
Laughbaum, Steve 1945- ... SATA 12
Laughlin, Clarence John 1905-1985 Obituary ... 114
Laughlin, Florence Young 1910- ... 9-12R
See also SATA 3
Laughlin, Henry Prather 1916- ... CANR-8
Earlier sketch in CA 61-64
Laughlin, James 1914-1997 ... CANR-47
Obituary ... 162
Earlier sketches in CA 21-24R, CANR-9
See also CAAS 22
See also CLC 49
See also DLB 48
See also DLBY 96, 97
Laughlin, Ledlie Irwin 1890-1977 ... 37-40R
Laughlin, P. S.
See Shea, Patrick
Laughlin, Tom 1938(?)- ... 138
Brief entry ... 116
Laughton, Bruce (Kyle Blake) 1928- ... 133
Laughton, Tom 1904(?)-1984 Obituary ... 112
Laugier, Odile 1956- ... 108
Laugier, R.
See Cumberland, Marten
Laumann, Edward O. 1938- ... 33-36R
Laumer, (John) Keith 1925-1993 ... CANR-51
Earlier sketches in CA 9-12R, CANR-7
See also DLB 8
Launay, Andre (Joseph) 1930- ... 25-28R
Launay, Droo
See Launay, Andre (Joseph)
Laune, Paul Sidney 1899- ... 17-20R
Launer, Donald 1926- ... 162
Launitz-Schurer, Leopold (Sidney), Jr. 1942- ... 103
Launius, Roger D. 1954- ... 154
Launko, Okinba
See Osofisan, Femi
Laurance, Alfred D.
See Tralins, S(andor) Robert
Laurance, Alice (a pseudonym) 1938- ... 101

Laure, Ettagale
See Blauer, Ettagale
Laure, Jason 1940- ... 104
See also SATA 50
See also SATA-Brief 44
Laurel, Alicia Bay 1949- ... 41-44R
Lauremberg, Johann 1590-1658 ... DLB 164
Lauren, Linda
See Bunce, Linda Susan (Staines)
Laurence, Dan H. 1920- ... CANR-66
Earlier sketches in CA 17-20R, CANR-13, 32
Laurence, Ester Hauser 1935- ... 29-32R
See also SATA 7
Laurence, Gerald (Robert) 1948- ... 131
Laurence, Janet 1937- ... 140
Laurence, John 1939- ... 69-72
Laurence, (Jean) Margaret (Wemyss) 1926-1987 ... CANR-33
Obituary ... 121
Earlier sketch in CA 5-8R
See also CLC 3, 6, 13, 50, 62
See also DAC
See also DAM MST
See also DLB 53
See also MTCW 1
See also SATA-Obit 50
See also SSC 7
Laurence, Michael M(arshall) 1940- ... 33-36R
Laurence, Will
See Smith, Willard L(aurence)
Laurence, William Leonard 1888-1977 ... 77-80
Obituary ... 69-72
Laurens, Jeannine 1950- ... 151
Laurent, Antoine 1952- ... CLC 50
Laurent, Lawrence (Bell) 1925- ... 69-72
Laurenti, Joseph L(ucian) 1931- ... CANR-57
Earlier sketches in CA 49-52, CANR-31
Laurentin, Rene 1917- ... CANR-48
Earlier sketch in CA 106
Laurentius von Schnuffis 1633-1702 ... DLB 168
Laurents, Arthur 1918- ... CANR-8
Earlier sketch in CA 13-16R
Interview in ... CANR-8
See also DLB 26
Lauria, Frank (Jonathan) 1935- ... 103
Laurie, Annie
See Black, Winifred
and Scarberry, Alma Sioux
Laurie, Bruce 1943- ... 115
Laurie, Clayton D. 1954- ... 153
Laurie, Edward J(ames) 1925- ... CANR-8
Earlier sketch in CA 17-20R
Laurie, Harry C.
See Cahn, Zvi
Laurie, Hugh 1959- ... 164
Laurie, James 1947- ... 69-72
Laurie, Michael M. 1932- ... 126
Laurie, Peter 1937- ... 158
Laurie, Rona ... CANR-33
Laurie, Rona 1916- ... CANR-15
Earlier sketch in CA 85-88
See also SATA 55
Laurin, Anne
See McLaurin, Anne
Lauritsen, John (Phillip) 1939- ... 57-60
Lauritzen, Elizabeth Moyes 1909- ... CAP-1
Earlier sketch in CA 13-16
Lauritzen, Jonreed 1902- ... 5-8R
See also SATA 13
Lauri-Volpi, Giacomo 1893(?)-1979 Obituary ... 85-88
Lauro, Shirley (Shapiro) Mezvinsky 1933- ... 126
Interview in ... 126
Laursen, John Christian 1952- ... 145
Laury, Jean Ray 1928- ... 77-80
Lauscher, Hermann
See Hesse, Hermann
Laut, Agnes Christina 1871-1936 ... DLB 92
Lautenbach, Renee 1932- ... 110
Lautens, Gary 1928-1993(?) ... 144
Lauter
See Chamson, Andre J(ules) L(ouis)
Lauter, Geza Peter 1932- ... 41-44R
Lauter, Paul 1932- ... 13-16R
Lauterbach, Albert 1904- ... CANR-1
Earlier sketch in CA 1-4R
Lauterbach, Ann 1942- ... DLB 193
Lauterborn, Robert F. 1936- ... 146
Lauterstein, Ingeborg 1935- ... 130
Lautreamont, Comte de 1846-1870 ... SSC 14
Lauture, Denize 1946- ... 152
See also SATA 86
Lauwerys, Joseph (Albert) 1902-1981 ... 13-16R
Obituary ... 104
Laux, Connie
See Laux, Constance
Laux, Constance 1952- ... 151
See also SATA 97
Laux, Dorothy 1920- ... 61-64
See also SATA 49
Laux, James M(ichael) 1927- ... 33-36R
Laux, P(eter) J(ohn) 1922- ... 25-28R
Lavagnino, Allessandra 1927- ... CANR-2
Earlier sketch in CA 45-48
LaValle, Irving H(oward) 1939- ... 33-36R
Lavallee, Barbara 1941- ... SATA 74
Lavan, Spencer 1937- ... CANR-8
Earlier sketch in CA 57-60
Lavater, Johann Kaspar 1741-1801 ... DLB 97
Lave, Lester B(ernard) 1939- ... CANR-33
Earlier sketches in CA 41-44R, CANR-15
Lavelle, Mike 1933- ... 65-68
Lavelle, Sheila 1939- ... 109
Lavender, Abraham D(onald) 1940- ... 151
Lavender, David (Sievert) 1910- ... CANR-40
Earlier sketches in CA 1-4R, CANR-2, 18
See also SATA 64, 97
Lavender, William 1921- ... CANR-10
Earlier sketch in CA 65-68
Lavenson, James H. 1919- ... 103
Lavenson, Jim
See Lavenson, James H.
Laver, James 1899-1975 ... CANR-3
Obituary ... 57-60
Earlier sketch in CA 1-4R
Laver, Michael (John) 1949- ... CANR-46
Earlier sketches in CA 107, CANR-23
Laver, Rod(ney George) 1938- Brief entry ... 112
La Verdiere, Eugene Armand 1936- ... CANR-19
Earlier sketch in CA 102
Lavers, Annette 1932- ... 130
Lavers, Norman 1935- ... 104
Laverty, Carroll D(ee) 1906- ... 77-80
Laverty, Donald
See Blish, James (Benjamin)
and Knight, Damon (Francis)
Lavery, David 1949- ... 163
Lavery, Emmet (Godfrey) 1902-1986 Obituary ... 118
Laves, Walter H(erman) C(arl) 1902-1983 Obituary ... 111
La Vey, (Howard) Anton Szandor 1930-1997 ... 158
Obituary ... 162
Brief entry ... 109
Lavigne, Louis-Dominique ... 165
Lavin, David E(dwin) 1931- ... CANR-2
Earlier sketch in CA 1-4R
Lavin, Henry St. C. 1921-1985 Obituary ... 114
Lavin, Irving 1927- ... 158
Lavin, J(oseph) A(nthony) 1932- ... 33-36R
Lavin, Marilyn Aronberg 1925- ... 106
Lavin, Mary 1912-1996 ... CANR-33
Obituary ... 151
Earlier sketch in CA 9-12R
See also CLC 4, 18, 99
See also DLB 15
See also MTCW 1
See also SSC 4
Lavin, Maud 1954- ... 142
Lavin, Sylvia 1960- ... 142
Lavine, David 1928- ... SATA 31
Lavine, Harold 1915-1984 ... 41-44R
Obituary ... 113
Lavine, Richard A. 1917- ... 21-24R
Lavine, Sigmund Arnold 1908- ... CANR-41
Earlier sketches in CA 1-4R, CANR-4, 19
See also CLR 35
See also SATA 3, 82
Lavine, Steven D(avid) 1947- ... 139
Lavington, H(arold) Dude 1907- ... 117
Lavinson, Joseph
See Kaye, Marvin (Nathan)
Laviolette, Emily A. 1923(?)-1975 ... SATA-Brief 49
Lavitt, Wendy (Adler) 1939- ... 127
Lavond, Paul Dennis
See Kornbluth, C(yril) M.
and Lowndes, Robert A(ugustine) W(ard)
and Pohl, Frederik
Lavori, Nora 1950- ... 93-96
Lavrentiev, Alexander (Nikolaevich) 1954- ... 135
Lavrin, Janko Matthew 1887-1986 ... 9-12R
Obituary ... 120
Law, Alexander 1904- ... 128
Law, Carol Russell ... 106
Law, Elizabeth
See Peters, Maureen
Law, Howard W(illiam) 1919- ... 21-24R
Law, Janice
See Trecker, Janice Law
Law, John
See Harkness, Margaret
Law, John 1946- ... 145
Law, Jonathan 1961- ... 154
Law, Marie Hamilton 1884-1981 Obituary ... 106
Law, Richard 1901-1980 Obituary ... 105
Law, Virginia W.
See Shell, Virginia Law
Lawder, Douglas W(ard) 1934- ... CANR-1
Earlier sketch in CA 45-48
Lawes, Henry 1596-1662 ... DLB 126
Lawford, J(ames) P(hilip) 1915-1977 ... CANR-28
Earlier sketch in CA 33-36R
Lawford, Paula Jane 1960- ... 125
See also Martyr, Paula (Jane)
See also SATA-Brief 53
Lawhead, Stephen R. 1950- ... 155
Lawhead, Victor B(ernard) 1919- ... 41-44R
Lawhorne, Clifton O. 1927-1983 ... 104
Obituary ... 110
Lawler, Donald L(ester) 1935- ... 105
Lawler, James R. 1929- ... 57-60
Lawler, Lillian B. 1898- ... 13-16R
Lawler, Patrick 1948- ... 136
Lawler, Philip F(rederick) 1950- ... 110
Lawler, Raymond Evenor 1922- ... 103
See also CLC 58
Lawler, Ronald (David) 1926- ... 126
Brief entry ... 110
Lawless, Anthony
See MacDonald, Philip
Lawless, Bettyclare Hamilton 1915- ... 61-64
Lawless, Dorothy (Mae) Kennedy 1906- ... 5-8R
Lawless, Edward W(illiam) 1931- ... 114
Lawless, Elaine J. 1947- ... CANR-53
Earlier sketch in CA 126
Lawless, Gary 1951- ... CANR-13
Earlier sketch in CA 73-76
Lawless, John
See Best, Don(ald M.)
Lawlor, Florine 1925- ... 65-68
Lawlor, John (James) 1918- ... 5-8R
Lawlor, Laurie 1953- ... SATA 80
Lawlor, Monica (Mary) 1926- ... 9-12R
Lawlor, Pat
See Lawlor, Patrick Anthony
Lawlor, Patrick Anthony 1893- ... CAP-1
Earlier sketch in CA 9-10
Lawlor, Rob(ert Thomas) 1936- ... 127
Lawner, Lynne 1935- ... 9-12R
Lawrence, A. R.
See Foff, Arthur R(aymond)
Lawrence, Alexander Atkinson 1906-1979 ... 102
Lawrence, Ann (Margaret) 1942-1987 ... 104
See also SATA 41
See also SATA-Obit 54
Lawrence, Ariadne
See Ling, Amy
Lawrence, Berta ... 73-76
Lawrence, Bill 1930- ... 25-28R
Lawrence, C(lifford) H(ugh) 1921- ... 132
Lawrence, D. Baloti 1950- ... CANR-32
Earlier sketch in CA 113
Lawrence, D(avid) H(erbert Richards) 1885-1930 ... 121
Brief entry ... 104
See also CDBLB 1914-1945
See also DA
See also DAB
See also DAC
See also DAM MST, NOV, POET
See also DLB 10, 19, 36, 98, 162, 195
See also MTCW 1
See also SSC 4, 19
See also TCLC 2, 9, 16, 33, 48, 61
See also WLC
Lawrence, Daniel 1940- ... 57-60
Lawrence, David, Jr. 1942- ... 73-76
Lawrence, David 1888-1973 ... CANR-70
Obituary ... 41-44R
Earlier sketch in CA 102
See also DLB 29
Lawrence, E. S.
See Bradburne, E(lizabeth) S.
Lawrence, Eddie
See Eisler, Lawrence
Lawrence, Edward
See Eisler, Lawrence
Lawrence, Elizabeth L. 1904-1985 ... 124
Lawrence, Emeric Anthony 1908- ... CANR-5
Earlier sketch in CA 1-4R
Lawrence, Francis L(eo) 1937- ... 49-52
Lawrence, Gale 1941- ... 126
Lawrence, George H(ill Mathewson) 1910-1978 Obituary ... 81-84
Lawrence, H(enry) L(ionel) 1908- ... CAP-1
Earlier sketch in CA 9-10
Lawrence, Irene
See Marsh, John
Lawrence, Isabelle (Wentworth) ... SATA-Brief 29
Lawrence, J. D.
See Lawrence, James Duncan
Lawrence, J. T.
See Rowland-Entwistle, (Arthur) Theodore (Henry)
Lawrence, Jack
See Fitzgerald, Lawrence P(ennybaker)
Lawrence, James Duncan 1918- ... CANR-27
Earlier sketch in CA 17-20R
Lawrence, Jerome 1915- ... CANR-44
Earlier sketch in CA 41-44R
See also SATA 65
Lawrence, Jim
See Lawrence, James Duncan
Lawrence, Jock
See Lawrence, Justus Baldwin
Lawrence, Jodi 1938- ... CANR-3
Earlier sketch in CA 45-48
Lawrence, John
See Lawrence, Jodi
Lawrence, John (Waldemar) 1907- ... 81-84
Lawrence, John 1933- ... CANR-24
Earlier sketch in CA 107
See also SATA 30
Lawrence, John A. 1908-1976 Obituary ... 65-68
Lawrence, John S(helton) 1938- ... 123
Brief entry ... 107
Lawrence, Joseph D(ouglas) 1895- ... 126
Lawrence, Josephine 1890(?)-1978 ... 77-80
See also SATA-Obit 24
Lawrence, Justus Baldwin 1903-1987 Obituary ... 122
Lawrence, Karen 1949- ... 126
Lawrence, Karen 1951- ... 126
Lawrence, Karl
See Foff, Arthur R(aymond)
Lawrence, Kathleen Rockwell 1945- ... 136
Lawrence, Kathy
See Martin, Kat
Lawrence, Kenneth G.
See Ringgold, Gene
Lawrence, Lesley
See Lewis, Lesley
Lawrence, Louise 1943- ... 97-100
See also SATA 38, 78
Lawrence, Louise de Kiriline 1894- ... 25-28R
See also SATA 13
Lawrence, Lynn
See Garland, Sherry
Lawrence, Lynn
See Garland, Sherry
Lawrence, Margaret Morgan 1914- ... 33-36R
Lawrence, Margot ... 132
Lawrence, Marjorie 1907-1979 Obituary ... 85-88
Lawrence, Martha C. 1956- ... 165
Lawrence, Martin
See Greif, Martin
and Grow, Lawrence
Lawrence, Mary
See Young, Mary Lou Daves
Lawrence, Mary Margaret 1920- ... 93-96
Lawrence, Melinda
See Weinhouse, Beth (R)
Lawrence, Merle 1915- ... 21-24R
Lawrence, Michael
See Lariar, Lawrence
Lawrence, Mildred Elwood 1907- ... CANR-5
Earlier sketch in CA 1-4R
See also SATA 3
Lawrence, Nathaniel (Morris) 1917-1986 ... CANR-22
Earlier sketch in CA 45-48
Lawrence, P.
See Tubb, E(dwin) C(harles)
Lawrence, Paul Frederic 1912- ... 153
See also BW 2
Lawrence, Paul Roger 1922- ... 158
Lawrence, Peter 1921-1988 Obituary ... 124
Lawrence, R(onald) D(ouglas) 1921- ... CANR-51
Earlier sketches in CA 65-68, CANR-11
See also SATA 55
Lawrence, Richard A.
See Leopold, Nathan F.
Lawrence, Robert
See Beum, Robert (Lawrence)
Lawrence, Robert 1912(?)-1981 Obituary ... 105
Lawrence, Robert A(llen) 1948- ... 118
Lawrence, Roy 1930- ... 45-48
Lawrence, Samuel A. 1928- ... 21-24R
Lawrence, Seymour 1926-1994 ... DLBY 94
Lawrence, Sharon 1945- ... 65-68
Lawrence, Starling ... 165
Lawrence, Steven C.
See Murphy, Lawrence A(gustus)
Lawrence, T(homas) E(dward) 1888-1935 ... 167
Brief entry ... 115
See also Dale, Colin
See also DLB 195
See also TCLC 18
Lawrence, Thomas
See Roberts, Thom(as Sacra)
Lawrence, Vera Brodsky 1909-1996 Brief entry 109
Lawrence, William Howard 1916-1972 Obituary ... 33-36R
Lawrence, William J(ohn) C(ooper) 1899(?)-1985 Obituary ... 118
Lawrence of Arabia
See Lawrence, T(homas) E(dward)
Lawrenson, Helen 1907-1982 ... 117
Obituary ... 106
Lawrenson, Thomas Edward 1918-1982 Obituary ... 106
Lawry, Jon Sherman 1924- ... 5-8R
Laws, G(eorge) Malcolm, Jr. 1919- ... 37-40R
Laws, Priscilla W(atson) 1940- ... 73-76
Laws, Stephen 1952- ... 168
Lawshe, C(harles) H(ubert) 1908- ... CAP-2
Earlier sketch in CA 23-24
Lawson, (Richard) Alan 1934- ... 53-56
Lawson, Annetta 1939- ... 116
Lawson, Annette 1936- ... 129
Lawson, Carol (Antell) 1946- ... SATA 42
Lawson, Chet
See Tubb, E(dwin) C(harles)
Lawson, David 1927- ... 57-60
Lawson, Don(ald Elmer) 1917-1990 ... CANR-26
Earlier sketches in CA 1-4R, 130, CANR-2
See also SATA 9
Lawson, Donna Roberta 1937- ... 41-44R
Lawson, E(verett) LeRoy 1938- ... CANR-19
Earlier sketches in CA 53-56, CANR-4
Lawson, Evelyn 1917- ... 57-60
Lawson, F(loyd) Melvyn 1907- ... 53-56
Lawson, Frederick Henry 1897-1983 Obituary ... 109
Lawson, Greg 1944- ... 164
Lawson, H(orace) L(owe) 1900- ... 5-8R
Lawson, H. Lowe
See Lawson, H(orace) L(owe)
Lawson, Henry (Archibald Hertzberg) 1867-1922 Brief entry ... 120
See also SSC 18
See also TCLC 27
Lawson, Jacob
See Burgess, Michael (Roy)
Lawson, James 1938- ... 65-68
Lawson, Joan 1906- ... 103
See also SATA 55
Lawson, John (?)-1711 ... DLB 24
Lawson, John 1909- ... CANR-3
Earlier sketch in CA 1-4R
Lawson, John Howard 1894-1977 ... CAP-1
Obituary ... 73-76
Earlier sketch in CA 13-16
Lawson, Julie 1947- ... SATA 79
Lawson, Kay 1933- ... 104
Lawson, Lewis A. 1931- ... 21-24R
Lawson, Linda 1952- ... 148
Lawson, M. C.
See Lawson, H(orace) L(owe)
Lawson, Marion Tubbs 1896- ... CAP-1
Earlier sketch in CA 9-10
See also SATA 22
Lawson, Mark 1962- ... 139
Lawson, Michael
See Ryder, M(ichael) L(awson)
Lawson, Philip 1949- ... 146
Lawson, Philip J. 1908(?)-1978 Obituary ... 77-80
Lawson, (Philippe) Reed 1929- ... 5-8R
Lawson, Richard H(enry) 1919- ... CANR-8
Earlier sketch in CA 17-20R
Lawson, Robert 1892-1957 ... 137
Brief entry ... 118
See also CLR 2
See also DLB 22
See also MAICYA
See also SATA 100
See also YABC 2
Lawson, Robert G. 1938- ... 118

Lawson, Ronald (Lynton) 1940- ... 126
Lawson, Ruth C(atherine) 1911- ... 9-12R
Lawson, S. Alexander 1912- ... 57-60
Lawson, Sarah (Anne) 1943- ... CANR-45
Earlier sketch in CA 120
Lawson, Steve
See Turner, Robert (Harry)
Lawson, Steven F(red) 1945- ... CANR-48
Earlier sketch in CA 122
Lawson, Victor F. 1850-1925 ... DLB 25
Lawson, W. B.
See Jenks, George C(harles)
Lawton, Barbara (Perry) 1930- ... 144
Lawton, Charles
See Heckelmann, Charles N(ewman)
Lawton, David 1943- ... 156
Lawton, Dennis
See Faust, Frederick (Schiller)
Lawton, Harry Wilson 1927- ... 33-36R
Lawton, John 1949- ... 168
Lawton, Manny
See Lawton, Marion R(ussell)
Lawton, Marion R(ussell) 1918-1986 ... 118
Lawton, Paul 1924- ... 148
Lawton, Sherman P(axton) 1908- ... CAP-2
Earlier sketch in CA 19-20
Lawyer, Annabel Glenn
1906(?)-1974 Obituary ... 53-56
Law Yone, Edward Michael
1911(?)-1980 Obituary ... 101
Lax, Eric 1944- ... 138
Lax, Robert 1915- ... CANR-27
Earlier sketches in CA 25-28R, CANR-11
Laxalt, Robert P(eter) 1923- ... CANR-38
Earlier sketch in CA 13-16R
Laxness, Halldor
See Gudjonsson, Halldor Kiljan
See also CLC 25
Lay, Bennett 1910- ... CAP-1
Earlier sketch in CA 11-12
Lay, Bierne, Jr. 1909-1982 Obituary ... 107
Lay, Daniel W(ayne) 1914- ... 118
Lay, Nancy Duke S. 1938- ... CANR-21
Earlier sketch in CA 105
Lay, Norvie L(ee) 1940- ... 49-52
Lay, S(amuel) Houston 1912- ... 33-36R
Lay, Shawn 1953- ... 124
Layamon fl. c. 1200- ... DLB 146
Layard, (Peter) Richard (Grenville) 1934- ... 128
Layard, Sir Austen Henry 1817-1894 ... DLB 166
Laybourne, Lawrence E.
1914(?)-1976 Obituary ... 65-68
Laycock, Ellen (Mae) 1921- ... 112
Laycock, George (Edwin) 1921- ... CANR-41
Earlier sketches in CA 5-8R, CANR-4, 19
See also SATA 5
Laycock, Harold R. (I. O.) 1916- ... 5-8R
Laye, Camara 1928-1980 ... CANR-25
Obituary ... 97-100
Earlier sketch in CA 85-88
See also BLC 2
See also BW 1
See also CLC 4, 38
See also DAM MULT
See also MTCW 1
Layman, Carol Spurlock 1937- ... 140
Layman, Constance 1943- ... 111
Layman, Emma McCloy 1910- ... 81-84
Layman, Richard 1947- ... CANR-35
Earlier sketch in CA 65-68
Laymon, Charles Martin 1904- ... CANR-7
Earlier sketch in CA 9-12R
Layne, Bobby
See Layne, Robert Lawrence
Layne, Laura
See Knott, William C(ecil, Jr.)
Layne, Robert Lawrence 1927-1986 Obituary ... 121
Layton, Andrea
See Bancroft, Iris (May Nelson)
Layton, Aviva 1933- ... 116
Layton, Edwin T(homas), Jr. 1928- ... 29-32R
Layton, Felix 1910- ... CAP-2
Earlier sketch in CA 23-24
Layton, Irving (Peter) 1912- ... CANR-66
Earlier sketches in CA 1-4R, CANR-2, 33, 43
See also CLC 2, 15
See also DAC
See also DAM MST, POET
See also DLB 88
See also MTCW 1
Layton, Marilyn Smith 1941- ... 114
Layton, Max 1946- ... 128
Layton, Robert 1930- ... 21-24R
Layton, Thomas Arthur 1910- ... 9-12R
Layton, Wilbur L. 1922- Brief entry ... 106
Layton, William (Isaac) 1913- ... 17-20R
Lazar, Irving (Paul) 1907-1993 ... 149
Lazar, Swifty
See Lazar, Irving (Paul)
Lazar, Wendy 1939- ... 104
Lazare, Daniel (Henry) 1950- ... 154
Lazare, Gerald John 1927- ... SATA 44
Lazare, Jerry
See Lazare, Gerald John
Lazareff, Pierre 1907-1972 Obituary ... 33-36R
Lazareth, William Henry 1928- ... CANR-16
Earlier sketches in CA 1-4R, CANR-1
Lazarevic, Laza K. 1851-1890 ... DLB 147
Lazarevich, Mila 1942- ... SATA 17
Lazaron, Hilda R(othschild) 1895- ... 49-52
Lazarre, Jane D(eitz) 1943- ... 101
Lazarsfeld, Paul F(elix) 1901-1976 ... CANR-29
Obituary ... 69-72
Earlier sketch in CA 73-76
Lazarus, A(rnold) L(eslie) 1914- ... CANR-11
Earlier sketch in CA 25-28R
Lazarus, Arnold A(llan) 1932- ... CANR-14
Earlier sketch in CA 41-44R
Lazarus, Arthur 1892(?)-1978 Obituary ... 77-80
Lazarus, Edward H. 1959- ... 122
Lazarus, Felix
See Cable, George Washington
Lazarus, George 1904-1997 ... DLB 201
Lazarus, Harold 1927- ... 21-24R
Lazarus, Henry
See Slavitt, David R(ytman)
Lazarus, John 1947- ... 132
Lazarus, Keo Felker 1913- ... 41-44R
See also SATA 21
Lazarus, Marguerite 1916- ... 106
Lazarus, Mell 1927- ... CANR-11
Earlier sketch in CA 17-20R
Lazarus, Pat 1935- ... 130
Lazarus, Paul N. 1913- ... 126
Lazarus, Richard S(tanley) 1922- ... CANR-5
Earlier sketch in CA 1-4R
Lazarus, Simon 1941- ... 57-60
Lazarus-Black, Mindie ... 151
Lazear, Edward P. 1948- ... CANR-65
Earlier sketch in CA 129
LaZebnik, Edith 1897- ... 85-88
Lazell, James Draper, Jr. 1939- ... 65-68
Lazenby, Edith P. 1945- ... 161
Lazenby, J(ohn) F(rancis) 1934- ... 147
Lazenby, Walter S(ylvester), Jr. 1930- ... 65-68
Lazer, Hank 1950- ... CAAS 27
Lazer, William 1924- ... CANR-19
Earlier sketches in CA 1-4R, CANR-4
Lazere, Donald 1935- ... 105
Lazerowitz, Alice Ambrose 1906- ... CANR-17
Earlier sketches in CA 49-52, CANR-1
Lazerowitz, Morris 1907- ... CANR-17
Earlier sketches in CA 9-12R, CANR-3
Lazerson, Joshua N(athaniel) 1959- ... 148
Lazhechnikov, Ivan Ivanovich 1790(?)-1869 ... DLB 198
Lazlo, Kate
See Angus, Sylvia
Lazo, Hector 1899-1965 ... CANR-3
Earlier sketch in CA 1-4R
Lazreg, Marnia 1941- ... 69-72
Lazuta, Gene 1959- ... CANR-71
Earlier sketch in CA 148
Le, Duan 1908(?)-1986 Obituary ... 119
Lea, Alec 1907- ... 73-76
See also SATA 19
Lea, David A(lexander) M(aclure) 1934- ... CANR-10
Earlier sketch in CA 21-24R
Lea, F(rank) A(lfred) 1915-1977 ... CANR-3
Earlier sketch in CA 1-4R
Lea, Frederick (Measham) 1900-1984 Obituary ... 113
Lea, Henry Charles 1825-1909 Brief entry ... 122
See also DLB 47
Lea, James F(ranklin) 1945- ... 130
Lea, Joan
See Neufeld, John (Arthur)
Lea, John Sedgwick 1910(?)-1987 Obituary ... 124
Lea, Kathleen M(arguerite) 1903- ... 119
Lea, Sydney (L. Wright, Jr.) 1942- ... CANR-70
Earlier sketches in CA 106, CANR-22
See also DLB 120
Lea, Timothy
See Wood, Christopher (Hovelle)
Lea, Tom 1907- Brief entry ... 115
See also DLB 6
Leab, Daniel Josef 1936- ... CANR-11
Earlier sketch in CA 29-32R
Leabo, Dick A. 1921- ... 9-12R
Leacacos, John P. 1908-1986 ... 25-28R
Obituary ... 121
Leach, Aroline Beecher 1899- ... 61-64
Leach, Barry Arthur 1930- ... 102
Leach, Bernard Howell 1887-1979 ... 97-100
Obituary ... 85-88
Leach, Douglas Edward 1920- ... 17-20R
Leach, E. R.
See Leach, Edmund Ronald
Leach, Edmund
See Leach, Edmund Ronald
Leach, Edmund R.
See Leach, Edmund Ronald
Leach, Edmund Ronald 1910-1989 Obituary ... 127
Leach, Eleanor Winsor 1937- ... 103
Leach, Gerald Adrian 1933- ... CANR-21
Earlier sketch in CA 5-8R
Leach, Graham (John) 1948- ... 122
Leach, John Robert 1922- ... 21-24R
Leach, Joseph (Lee) 1921- ... 29-32R
Leach, Maria 1892-1977 ... 53-56
Obituary ... 69-72
See also SATA 39
See also SATA-Brief 28
Leach, Marjorie S. 1911- ... 142
Leach, (Richard) Max(well) 1909- ... 41-44R
Leach, Michael 1940- ... 73-76
Leach, Paul Roscoe 1890-1977 Obituary ... 73-76
Leach, Penelope (Jane) 1937- ... CANR-44
Earlier sketches in CA 97-100, CANR-21
Leach, Richard H(eald) 1922- ... 127
Brief entry ... 113
Leach, Robert J. 1916- ... 29-32R
Leach, (Carson) Wilford 1932(?)-1988 ... CANR-2
Obituary ... 125
Earlier sketch in CA 45-48
Leach, William 1944- ... 146
Leachman, Robert Briggs 1921- ... 104
Leacock, Eleanor Burke 1922-1987 ... CANR-15
Obituary ... 122
Earlier sketch in CA 37-40R
Leacock, John 1729-1802 ... DLB 31
Leacock, Ruth 1926- ... 37-40R
Leacock, Stephen (Butler) 1869-1944 ... 141
Brief entry ... 104
See also DAC
See also DAM MST
See also DLB 92
See also TCLC 2
Leacroft, Helen (Mabel Beal) 1919- ... CANR-2
Earlier sketch in CA 5-8R
See also SATA 6
Leacroft, Richard (Vallance Becher) 1914- ... CANR-2
Earlier sketch in CA 5-8R
See also SATA 6
Lead, Jane Ward 1623-1704 ... DLB 131
Leadbetter, Eric 1892(?)-1971 Obituary ... 104
Leadbitter, Mike 1942- ... 41-44R
Leader, (Evelyn) Barbara (Blackburn) 1898- ... 61-64
Leader, Charles
See Smith, Robert Charles
Leader, Darian ... 161
Leader, Mary 1948- ... 159
Leader, Mary (Bartelt) 1948- ... 85-88
Leader, Ninon 1933- ... 21-24R
Leader, Shelah Gilbert 1943- ... CANR-27
Earlier sketch in CA 110
Leader, Zachary 1946- ... 138
Leaf, David 1952- ... 117
Leaf, Margaret P. 1909(?)-1988 Obituary ... 124
See also SATA-Obit 55
Leaf, (Wilbur) Munro 1905-1976 ... CANR-29
Obituary ... 69-72
Earlier sketch in CA 73-76
See also CLR 25
See also MAICYA
See also SATA 20
Leaf, Murray J(ohn) 1939- ... CANR-1
Earlier sketch in CA 45-48
Leaf, Paul 1929- ... 132
Leaf, Russell C(harles) 1935- ... 21-24R
Leaf, VaDonna Jean 1929- ... 57-60
See also SATA 26
Leagans, John Paul 1911- ... 103
Leahy, James E. 1919- ... 138
Leahy, Syrell Rogovin 1935- ... CANR-56
Earlier sketches in CA 57-60, CANR-12, 29
Leake, Chauncey D(epew) 1896-1978 ... CANR-3
Obituary ... 73-76
Earlier sketch in CA 49-52
Leake, Jane Acomb 1928- ... 21-24R
Leakey, Louis S(eymour) B(azett)
1903-1972 ... 97-100
Obituary ... 37-40R
See also MTCW 1
Leakey, Mary (Douglas Nicol) 1913-1996 CANR-60
Obituary ... 155
Earlier sketches in CA 97-100, CANR-18
Leakey, Richard E(rskine Frere) 1944- ... CANR-18
Earlier sketch in CA 93-96
See also SATA 42
Leal, Luis 1907- ... 131
See also HW
Leale, B(arry) C(avendish) 1930- ... 132
Leaman, David R(ay) 1947- ... 115
Leamer, Edward E(mery) 1944- ... 29-32R
Leamer, Laurence Allen 1941- ... CANR-35
Earlier sketches in CA 65-68, CANR-13
Leaming, Barbara ... CANR-50
Earlier sketches in CA 107, CANR-25
Lean, Arthur E(dward) 1909- ... 73-76
Lean, David 1908-1991 ... 134
Brief entry ... 111
Lean, E(dward) Tangye 1911-1974 Obituary ... 53-56
Lean, Garth Dickinson 1912-1993 ... CANR-17
Obituary ... 143
Earlier sketch in CA 29-32R
Leander, Ed
See Richelson, Geraldine
Leaney, Alfred Robert Clare 1909-1995 ... CANR-2
Obituary ... 148
Earlier sketch in CA 5-8R
Leaning, Jennifer 1945- ... 132
Leap, Harry P(atrick) 1908-1976 ... 1-4R
Obituary ... 103
Leapman, Michael (Henry) 1938- ... CANR-41
Earlier sketch in CA 109
Leapor, Mary 1722-1746 ... DLB 109
Lear, Edward 1812-1888 ... CLR 1
See also DLB 32, 163, 166
See also MAICYA
See also SATA 18, 100
Lear, Floyd Seyward 1895- ... CAP-1
Earlier sketch in CA 17-18
Lear, John 1909- ... 37-40R
Lear, Linda J(ane) 1940- ... 166
Lear, Martha Weinman 1930- ... CANR-9
Earlier sketch in CA 9-12R
Lear, Melva Gwendoline Bartlett 1917- ... 5-8R
Lear, Norman (Milton) 1922- ... 73-76
See also CLC 12
Lear, Patricia 1944- ... 150
Lear, Peter
See Lovesey, Peter (Harmer)
Leard, G(eorge) Earl 1918- ... 9-12R
Leard, John E. 1916- ... 73-76
Learmonth, Andrew Thomas Amos 1916- ... 13-16R
Learned, Edmund Philip 1900- ... 104
Learning, Walter J. 1938- ... 130
Leary, David E. 1945- ... CANR-51
Earlier sketch in CA 124
Leary, Denis 1958- ... 154
Leary, Edward A(ndrew) 1913- ... CANR-12
Earlier sketch in CA 29-32R
Leary, James F. 1942- ... 126
Leary, John P(atrick) 1919- ... 9-12R
Leary, Lewis (Gaston) 1906-1990 ... CANR-4
Obituary ... 131
Earlier sketch in CA 1-4R
Leary, Paris 1931- ... 17-20R
Leary, Timothy (Francis) 1920-1996 ... 107
Obituary ... 152
Interview in ... 107
See also DLB 16
See also MTCW 1
Leary, William G(ordon) 1915- ... CANR-31
Earlier sketch in CA 49-52
Leary, William M., Jr. 1934- ... 93-96
Leas, Speed 1937- ... CANR-30
Earlier sketch in CA 49-52
Lease, Benjamin 1917- Brief entry ... 114
Lease, Gary 1940- ... CANR-38
Earlier sketch in CA 45-48
Leasher, Evelyn M(arie) 1941- ... 115
Leask, Ian Graham 1951- ... 138
Leask, Nigel 1958- ... 145
Leaska, Mitchell A(lexander) 1934- ... CANR-39
Earlier sketches in CA 77-80, CANR-13
Leasor, (Thomas) James 1923- ... CANR-2
Earlier sketch in CA 1-4R
See also SATA 54
Least Heat Moon, William
See Trogdon, William (Lewis)
Leasure, Robert E. 1921- ... 112
Leather, Edwin (Hartley Cameron) 1919- ... 97-100
Leather, George
See Swallow, Norman
Leatherbarrow, W(illiam) J(ohn) 1947- ... 145
Leatherman, LeRoy 1922-1984 ... 21-24R
Obituary ... 112
Leatherwood, (James) Stephen 1943- ... 146
Leaton, Anne 1932- ... 130
Leautaud, Paul 1872-1956 ... DLB 65
See also TCLC 83
Leavell, Landrum P(inson) II 1926- ... 89-92
Leavell, Linda 1954- ... 154
Leavenworth, Carol 1940- ... CANR-14
Earlier sketch in CA 81-84
Leavenworth, James Lynn 1915- ... 21-24R
Leaver, Robin Alan 1939- ... CANR-9
Earlier sketch in CA 61-64
Leavey, John P(eter), Jr. 1951- ... 127
Leavis, F(rank) R(aymond) 1895-1978 ... CANR-44
Obituary ... 77-80
Earlier sketch in CA 21-24R
See also CLC 24
See also MTCW 1
Leavis, Q(ueenie) D(orothy) 1906-1981 ... 97-100
Obituary ... 108
Leavitt, Caroline 1952- ... 150
Leavitt, David 1961- ... CANR-62
Brief entry ... 116
Earlier sketches in CA 122, CANR-50
Interview in ... 122
See also CLC 34
See also DAM POP
See also DLB 130
Leavitt, Harold J(ack) 1922- ... 125
Brief entry ... 117
Leavitt, Hart Day 1909- ... 13-16R
Leavitt, Harvey R(obert) 1934- ... 65-68
Leavitt, Jack 1931- ... 97-100
Leavitt, Jerome E(dward) 1916- ... CANR-17
Earlier sketches in CA 1-4R, CANR-1
See also SATA 23
Leavitt, Judith A(nn) 1947- ... CANR-27
Earlier sketch in CA 110
Leavitt, Judith Walzer 1940- ... 158
Leavitt, Richard Freeman 1929- ... 89-92
Leavitt, Ruby R.
See Rohrlich, Ruby
Leavitt, William J. 1928-1984 Obituary ... 112
Leavy, Barbara Fass 1936- ... 145
Leavy, Stanley A(rnold) 1915- ... 120
LeBar, Lois E. 1907- ... 21-24R
LeBar, Mary E(velyn) 1910-1982 ... CANR-25
Earlier sketch in CA 107
See also SATA 35
LeBaron, Charles W. 1943- ... CANR-9
Earlier sketch in CA 61-64
LeBeau, Roy
See Smith, Mitchell
Lebeaux, Richard 1946- ... CANR-12
Earlier sketch in CA 73-76
Lebedoff, David (Michael) 1938- ... 126
Leber, George L. 1917(?)-1976 Obituary ... 61-64
Lebergott, Stanley 1918- ... 103
Lebert, Randy
See Brannon, William T.
Lebesgue, Henri (Leon) 1875-1941 ... 155
Lebeson, Anita Libman 1896-1987 ... 29-32R
Obituary ... 121
LeBlanc, Annette M. 1965- ... SATA 68
LeBlanc, L(ee) 1913- ... SATA 54
Leblanc, Maurice (Marie Emile) 1864-1941 Brief entry ... 110
See also TCLC 49
LeBlanc, Rena Dictor 1938- ... 104
Leblon, Jean (Marcel Jules) 1928- ... 41-44R
Le Blond, Aubrey 1861-1934 ... DLB 174
Lebo, Dell 1922- ... 57-60
LeBoeuf, Michael 1942- ... CANR-15
Earlier sketch in CA 93-96
Le Boutillier, Cornelia Geer
1894(?)-1973 Obituary ... 45-48
Lebovich, William Louis 1948- ... CANR-37
Earlier sketch in CA 115
Lebovitz, Harold Paul 1916- ... 77-80
Lebow, Eileen F. 1925- ... 132
Lebow, Jeanne 1951- ... 135
Lebow, Richard Ned 1942- ... 129

Lebow, Victor 1902-1980 37-40R
Obituary 133
Lebowitz, Alan 1934- 25-28R
Lebowitz, Albert 1922- 73-76
Lebowitz, Fran(ces Ann) 1951(?)- CANR-70
Earlier sketches in CA 81-84, CANR-14, 60
Interview in CANR-14
See also CLC 11, 36
See also MTCW 1
Lebowitz, Naomi 1932- 37-40R
Leboyer, Frederick 1918- 106
Lebra, Joyce C(hapman) CANR-1
Earlier sketch in CA 45-48
Lebra, Takie Sugiyama 1930- 77-80
Lebra, William P(hilip) 1922- 33-36R
Lebrecht, Norman 1948- 117
Lebrecht, Peter
See Tieck, (Johann) Ludwig
Lebreo, Steward
See Weiner, Stewart
Lebreo, Stewart
See Weiner, Stewart
Le Breton, Auguste
See Montfort, Auguste
Le Breton, Binka 1942- 142
Lebreton, J(ean) D(ominique) 1950- 146
Le Bris, Michel 1944- 131
Le Brown, Andreas
See Brown, Andreas Le
Lebrun, Claude 1929- 136
See also SATA 66
LeBrun, Gautier
See Gibson, Walter B(rown)
LeBrun, George P. 1862-1966 5-8R
Lebrun, Richard Allen 1931- 41-44R
Lebsock, Suzanne (Dee) 1949- 153
le Cagat, Benat
See Whitaker, Rod(ney)
Le Cain, Errol (John) 1941-1989 CANR-42
Obituary 127
Earlier sketches in CA 33-36R, CANR-13
See also MAICYA
See also SATA 6, 68
See also SATA-Obit 60
Lecale, Errol
See McNeilly, Wilfred (Glassford)
Lecar, Helene Lerner 1938- 25-28R
le Carre, John
See Cornwell, David (John Moore)
See also BEST 89:4
See also CDBLB 1960 to Present
See also CLC 3, 5, 9, 15, 28
See also DLB 87
Lecavele, Roland
See Dorgeles, Roland
Le Chanois, Jean-Paul
See Drefus, Jean-Paul Etienne
Lechleidner, Mary L. 1947- 149
Lechlitner, Ruth N. 1901- 105
See also DLB 48
Lechner, Robert F(irman) 1918- 33-36R
Lecht, Charles Philip 1933- 21-24R
Lecht, Leonard A. 1920- CANR-28
Earlier sketches in CA 25-28R, CANR-11
Lechtenberg, Richard 1947- 125
Lecker, Robert 1951- CANR-28
Earlier sketch in CA 111
Leckey, Dolores (Conklin) 1933- 109
Leckie, Keith (Ross) 1952- 130
Leckie, Robert (Hugh) 1920- 13-16R
Leckie, Ross 1957- 157
Leckie, Shirley A(nne) 1937- 146
Leckie, William H. 1915- 21-24R
LeClair, Thomas 1944- CANR-43
Earlier sketch in CA 113
LeClair, Tom
See LeClair, Thomas
LeClaire, Anne D(ickinson) 1942- 150
LeClaire, Gordon 1905- 69-72
Leclant, Jean 1920- 132
Leclerc, Felix 1914- DLB 60
Leclerc, Ivor 1915- 33-36R
Leclerc, Victor
See Parry, Albert
Le Clercq, Jacques Georges Clemenceau
1898-1972 Obituary 37-40R
Leclercq, Jean 1911-1993 149
Le Clezio, J(ean) M(arie) G(ustave) 1940- 128
Brief entry 116
See also CLC 31
See also DLB 83
Le Cocq, Rhoda P(riscilla) 1921- 73-76
Lecoin, Louis 1888(?)-1971 Obituary 33-36R
Lecomber, Brian 1945- CANR-13
Earlier sketch in CA 73-76
LeCompte, (Nancy) Jane 1948- 133
Lecompte, Janet 1923- 122
LeCompte, Mary Lou 1935- 146
Le Comte, Edward (Semple) 1916- CANR-5
Earlier sketch in CA 1-4R
Lecomte du Nouey
See Lecomte du Nouey, Pierre (-Andre-Leon)
Lecomte du Nouey, P.
See Lecomte du Nouey, Pierre (-Andre-Leon)
Lecomte du Nouey, Pierre (-Andre-Leon)
1883-1947 Brief entry 119
Lecomte du Nouy, Pierre (-Andre-Leon)
See Lecomte du Nouey, Pierre (-Andre-Leon)
Le Coq, Monsieur
See Simenon, Georges (Jacques Christian)
Lecourt, Nancy (Hoyt) 1951- SATA 73
LeCroy, Anne K(ingsbury) 1930- CANR-16
Earlier sketch in CA 41-44R
LeCroy, Ruth Brooks 45-48
Ledbetter, J(ack) T(racy) 1934- 73-76
Ledbetter, Jack Wallace 1930- 5-8R
Ledbetter, Joe O(verton) 1927- 45-48
Ledbetter, Ken(neth Lee) 1931- CANR-40
Earlier sketch in CA 117
Ledbetter, Les 1941(?)-1985 Obituary 116
Ledbetter, Suzann 1953- 144
Ledbetter, Virgil C. 1918-(?) CAP-1
Earlier sketch in CA 13-16
Ledderose, Lothar 1942- 85-88
Leddy, Mary Jo 1946- 164
Ledeen, Michael A(rthur) 1941- 144
Leder, Jane Mersky 1945- 117
See also SATA 61
See also SATA-Brief 51
Leder, Lawrence H. 1927- 25-28R
Leder, Rudolf
See Hermlin, Stephan
Lederberg, Joshua 1925- 156
Lederer, Charles 1910-1976 Obituary 65-68
See also DLB 26
Lederer, Chloe 1915- 77-80
Lederer, Edith Madelon 1943- 97-100
Lederer, Esther Pauline 1918- 89-92
Lederer, Ivo J(ohn) 1929- 9-12R
Lederer, Jiri 1922-1983 Obituary 111
Lederer, Joseph 1927- 73-76
Lederer, Lajos 1904-1985 Obituary 118
Lederer, Laura 1951- 121
Lederer, Muriel 1929- 77-80
See also SATA 48
Lederer, Paul Joseph 1944- 111
Lederer, Rhoda Catharine (Kitto) 1910- CANR-22
Earlier sketches in CA 9-12R, CANR-6
Lederer, Richard 1938- 132
Lederer, William J(ulius) 1912- CANR-5
Earlier sketch in CA 1-4R
See also SATA 62
Lederman, Leonard L(awrence) 1931- 61-64
Ledermann, Erich Kurt 1908- 107
Ledermann, Walter 1911- CANR-30
Earlier sketch in CA 49-52
Ledesert, (Dorothy) Margaret 1916- CANR-28
Earlier sketch in CA 45-48
Ledesert, R(ene) P(ierre) L(ouis) 1913-1984
CANR-28
Obituary 114
Earlier sketch in CA 45-48
Le Doeuff, Michele 1948- 143
Ledoux, Paul (Martin) 1949- 131
Le Duc, Don R(aymond) 1933- CANR-31
Earlier sketch in CA 49-52
Leduc, Violette 1907-1972 CANR-69
Obituary 33-36R
Earlier sketches in CAP-1, CA 13-14
See also CLC 22
Ledwidge, Francis 1887(?)-1917 Brief entry 123
See also DLB 20
See also TCLC 23
Ledwidge, William (Bernard) John 1915- 103
Ledwith, Frank 1907- 103
Ledyard, Gleason H(ines) 1919- 5-8R
Lee, A. R.
See Ash, Rene Lee
Lee, A(rthur) Robert 1941- 130
Lee, Addison E(arl) 1914- 9-12R
Lee, Adrian Iselin, Jr. 1920- 89-92
Lee, Al(fred Matthew) 1938- 45-48
Lee, Alfred McClung 1906-1992 CANR-19
Obituary 137
Earlier sketches in CA 1-4R, CANR-3
Lee, Alvin A. 1930- 33-36R
Lee, Amanda
See Baggett, Nancy
and Buckholtz, Eileen (Garber)
and Glick, Ruth (Burtnick)
Lee, Amber
See Baldwin, Faith
Lee, Andrea
See Toona, Elin(-Kai)
Lee, Andrea 1953- 125
See also BLC 2
See also BW 1
See also CLC 36
See also DAM MULT
Lee, Andrew
See Auchincloss, Louis (Stanton)
Lee, Ang 1954- 157
Lee, Arthur M(atthias) 1918- 41-44R
Lee, Asher 1909- 73-76
Lee, Audrey 25-28R
Lee, Austin 1904-(?) CAP-1
Earlier sketch in CA 13-16
Lee, Barbara 1932- 109
Lee, Barbara (Moore) 1934- CANR-9
Earlier sketch in CA 53-56
Lee, Barbara A(nne) 1949- 128
Lee, Benjamin 1921- 104
See also SATA 27
Lee, Bernie 1926- 144
Lee, Betsy 1949- 106
See also SATA 37
Lee, Betty
See Lambert, Elizabeth (Minnie)
Lee, Betty 1921- 103
Lee, Bill
See Lee, William Saul
Lee, Bob
See McGrath, Robert L(ee)
Lee, Brother Basil Leo 1909-1974 Obituary 53-56
Lee, C(live) H(oward) 1942- 126
Lee, C(larence) P(endleton) 1913- 49-52
Lee, Calvin B. T. 1934- 33-36R
Lee, Carol
See Fletcher, Helen Jill
Lee, Carolina
See Dern, Erolie Pearl Gaddis
Lee, Carvel (Bigham) 1910- CAP-1
Earlier sketch in CA 13-14
Lee, Chang-rae 1965- 148
See also CLC 91
Lee, Charles 1913- 33-36R
Lee, Charles Robert, Jr. 1929- 5-8R
Lee, Charlotte I(rene) 1909- 21-24R
Lee, Chin-Chuan 1946- 150
Lee, Chong-Sik 1931- CANR-15
Earlier sketch in CA 41-44R
Lee, Christine Eckstrom 1952- 110
Lee, Christopher 1941- 149
Lee, Christopher Frank Carandini 1922- 73-76
Lee, Cora
See Anderson, Catherine Corley
Lee, C(hin)-Y(ana) 1917- 9-12R
Lee, David 1944- CANR-29
Earlier sketch in CA 111
Lee, David Dale 1948- 117
Lee, Deemer 1905-1979 111
Lee, Dennis (Beynon) 1939- CANR-61
Earlier sketches in CA 25-28R, CANR-11, 31, 57
See also CLR 3
See also DAC
See also DLB 53
See also MAICYA
See also SATA 14, 102
Lee, Derek 1937- 107
Lee, (Henry) Desmond (Pritchard) 1908- 102
Lee, Devon
See Pohle, Robert W(arren), Jr.
Lee, Dom 1959- SAAS 26
See also SATA 83
Lee, Don L.
See Madhubuti, Haki R.
See also CLC 2
Lee, Doris Emrick 1905-1983 Obituary 110
See also SATA 44
See also SATA-Obit 35
Lee, Dorris M(ay Potter) 1905- 13-16R
Lee, Douglas A(llen) 1932- 53-56
Lee, Dwight E(rwin) 1898- 5-8R
Lee, Eddie H. 1917- 69-72
Lee, Edward Edson 1884-1944 128
See also AITN 1
Lee, Edward N(icholls) 1935- 29-32R
Lee, Elizabeth Briant 1908- 37-40R
Lee, Elizabeth Rogers 1940- SATA 90
Lee, Elsie 1912- 85-88
Lee, Eric
See Lee, Fleming
and Page, Gerald W(ilburn)
Lee, Essie E. 1920- CANR-4
Earlier sketch in CA 49-52
Lee, Eugene (Huey) 1941- 49-52
Lee, Fleming 1933- CANR-7
Earlier sketch in CA 9-12R
Lee, Florence Henry 1910- CAP-1
Earlier sketch in CA 17-18
Lee, Francis Nigel 1934- CANR-8
Earlier sketch in CA 57-60
Lee, Frank F(reeman) 1920- 1-4R
Lee, Fred 1927- 109
Lee, G. Avery 1916- 104
Lee, Gentry 1942- 140
Lee, George J. 1920(?)-1976 Obituary 65-68
Lee, George Leslie
See Lee, Brother Basil Leo
Lee, George W(ashington) 1894-1976 125
See also BLC 2
See also BW 1
See also CLC 52
See also DAM MULT
See also DLB 51
Lee, Gerard (Majella) 1951- 93-96
Lee, Ginffa 1900(?)-1976 Obituary 69-72
Lee, Gordon C(anfield) 1916-1972 13-16R
Obituary 135
Lee, Gus 1947- 142
Lee, Gypsy Rose
See Hovick, Rose Louise
Lee, H. Alton 1942- 81-84
Lee, Hahn-Been 1921- CANR-11
Earlier sketch in CA 25-28R
Lee, Harold N(ewton) 1899- 37-40R
Lee, (Nelle) Harper 1926- CANR-51
Earlier sketch in CA 13-16R
See also AAYA 13
See also CDALB 1941-1968
See also CLC 12, 60
See also DA
See also DAB
See also DAC
See also DAM MST, NOV
See also DLB 6
See also MTCW 1
See also SATA 11
See also WLC
Lee, Harriet 1757-1851 DLB 39
Lee, Harry J., Jr. 1914-1985 Obituary 118
Lee, Hector (Haight) 1908- 97-100
Lee, Helen Clara 1919- 49-52
Lee, Helen Elaine 1959(?)- 148
See also CLC 86
Lee, Helen Jackson 1908- 81-84
Lee, Henry (Walsh) 1911-1993 5-8R
Obituary 142
Lee, Henry C(hang-Yuh) 1938- 161
Lee, Henry F(oster) 1913- 89-92
Lee, Herbert d'H.
See Kastle, Herbert D(avid)
Lee, Hermione 1948- CANR-15
Earlier sketch in CA 73-76
Lee, Howard
See Goulart, Ron(ald Joseph)
Lee, Irvin H. 1932-1980 21-24R
Obituary 133
Lee, J. Cleo
See Johnson, Leland R(oss)
Lee, J(erry) W(allace) 1932- 93-96
Lee, James A(lvin) 1922- CANR-53
Earlier sketch in CA 126
Lee, James F. 1905(?)-1975 Obituary 61-64
Lee, James Michael 1931- CANR-30
Earlier sketches in CA 17-20R, CANR-13
Lee, James W. 1931- 25-28R
Lee, Janet 1904-1988 Obituary 127
Lee, Janice (Jeanne) 1944- 33-36R
Lee, Jennie
See Lee, Janet
Lee, Joe Won 1921- 41-44R
Lee, John (Darrell) 1931- CANR-9
Earlier sketch in CA 25-28R
Lee, John A(lexander) 1891- CANR-7
Earlier sketch in CA 53-56
Lee, John Eric 1919- 33-36R
Lee, John Michael 1932- CANR-6
Earlier sketch in CA 13-16R
Lee, John R(obert) 1923-1976 57-60
Obituary 120
See also SATA 27
Lee, Jordan
See Scholefield, Alan
Lee, Judith Yaross 1949- 137
Lee, Judy
See Carlson, Judith Lee
Lee, Julian
See Latham, Jean Lee
Lee, Jung Young 1935- 33-36R
Lee, Kay
See Kelly, Karen
Lee, L(awrence) L(ynn) 1924- 73-76
Lee, Lamar, Jr. 1911- 17-20R
Lee, Lance 1942- CANR-13
Earlier sketch in CA 77-80
Lee, Larry
See Lee, Lawrence
Lee, Laurel 1945- 138
Brief entry 113
Lee, Laurie 1914-1997 CANR-33
Obituary 158
Earlier sketch in CA 77-80
See also CLC 90
See also DAB
See also DAM POP
See also DLB 27
See also MTCW 1
Lee, Lawrence 1903- CANR-44
Earlier sketch in CA 25-28R
Lee, (Enoch) Lawrence 1912- 13-16R
Lee, Lawrence 1941-1990 CANR-43
Obituary 131
See also CLC 34
Lee, Leo Ou-fan 1939- 102
Lee, Lincoln 1922- 9-12R
Lee, Linda 1947- CANR-13
Earlier sketch in CA 77-80
Lee, Li-Young 1957- 153
See also DLB 165
Lee, Liz
See Lee, Elizabeth Rogers
Lee, Loyd Ervin 1939- 102
Lee, Lucy
See Talbot, Charlene Joy
Lee, M(ark) Owen 1930- 33-36R
Lee, Mabel 1886-1985 134
Lee, Mabel Barbee 1886(?)-1978 Obituary 85-88
Lee, Malka 1905(?)-1976 Obituary 65-68
Lee, Manfred B(ennington) 1905-1971 CANR-2
Obituary 29-32R
Earlier sketch in CA 1-4R
See also Queen, Ellery
See also CLC 11
See also DLB 137
Lee, Manning de Villeneuve
1894-1980 Obituary 104
See also SATA 37
See also SATA-Obit 22
Lee, Maria Berl 1924- CANR-9
Earlier sketch in CA 61-64
Lee, Marian
See Clish, (Lee) Marian
Lee, Marie G. 1964- CANR-71
Earlier sketch in CA 149
See also AAYA 27
See also SATA 81
Lee, Marjorie 1921- CANR-4
Earlier sketch in CA 1-4R
Lee, Mark W. 1923- CANR-18
Earlier sketches in CA 9-12R, CANR-3
Lee, Martha F(rances) 1962- 160
Lee, Martin A. 1954- CANR-47
Earlier sketch in CA 121
Lee, Mary 1949- 29-32R
Lee, Mary Price 1934- CANR-24
Earlier sketches in CA 57-60, CANR-9
See also SATA 8, 82
Lee, Maryat 1923-1989 25-28R
Obituary 129
Lee, Matt
See Merwin, Sam(uel Kimball), Jr.
Lee, Maurice (duPont), Jr. 1925- CANR-21
Earlier sketch in CA 45-48
Lee, Meredith 1945- 93-96
Lee, Mildred
See Scudder, Mildred Lee
See also SAAS 12
See also SATA 6
Lee, Molly K(yung) S(ook) C(hang) 1934- 53-56
Lee, Muna 1895-1965 Obituary 25-28R

Lee, Nata
See Frackman, Nathaline
Lee, Nathaniel 1645(?)-1692 ... DLB 80
Lee, Norma E. 1924- ... 65-68
Lee, Oliver M(inseem) 1927- ... 41-44R
Lee, Pali Jae 1929- ... CANR-31
Earlier sketches in CA 29-32R, CANR-13
Lee, Parker
See Turner, Robert (Harry)
Lee, Patricia 1941- ... 115
Lee, Patrick C(ornelius) 1936- ... 65-68
Lee, Peter 1947- ... 127
Lee, Peter H(acksoo) 1929- ... CANR-3
Earlier sketch in CA 9-12R
Lee, Philip J. 1932- ... 124
Lee, Philip Randolph 1924- ... 149
Lee, Polly Jae
See Lee, Pali Jae
Lee, R(oy) Alton 1931- ... 21-24R
Lee, Raymond 1910(?)-1974 Obituary ... 49-52
Lee, Raymond L(awrence) 1911- ... 41-44R
Lee, Rebecca Smith 1894- ... 5-8R
Lee, Rensselaer W(right) 1898-1984 Obituary ... 114
Lee, Richard
See Lee, Richard B(orshay)
Lee, Richard B(orshay) 1937- ... CANR-20
Earlier sketch in CA 45-48
Lee, Richard S. 1927- ... SATA 82
Lee, Robert
See Fairman, Paul W.
Lee, Robert 1929- ... CANR-3
Earlier sketch in CA 5-8R
Lee, Robert C. 1931- ... CANR-10
Earlier sketch in CA 25-28R
See also SATA 20
Lee, Robert E(arl) 1906- ... 53-56
See also AITN 1
Lee, Robert E(dwin) 1918-1994 ... CANR-2
Obituary ... 146
Earlier sketch in CA 45-48
See also SATA 65
See also SATA-Obit 82
Lee, Robert E. A. 1921- ... 9-12R
Lee, Robert Edson 1921- ... 25-28R
Lee, Robert Edward 1912- ... 111
Lee, Robert Greene 1886-(?) ... CANR-3
Earlier sketch in CA 1-4R
Lee, Robert J. 1921- ... SATA 10
Lee, Roberta
See McGrath, Robert L(ee)
Lee, Ronald 1934- ... 37-40R
Lee, Rowena
See Bartlett, Marie (Swan)
Lee, Roy
See Hopkins, Clark
Lee, Roy Stuart 1899- ... CAP-1
Earlier sketch in CA 9-10
Lee, Russel V(an Arsdale) 1895-1982 Obituary ... 110
Lee, Ruth (Wile) 1892- ... CAP-2
Earlier sketch in CA 23-24
Lee, S(amuel) E(dgar) 1894- ... 73-76
Lee, S(idney) G(illmore) M(cKenzie) 1920-1973 ...
CAP-2
Earlier sketch in CA 33-36
Lee, Sally 1943- ... 134
See also SATA 67
Lee, Samuel J(ames) 1906- ... CAP-2
Earlier sketch in CA 29-32
Lee, Sandra
See Cusick, Heidi Haughy
Lee, Sharon 1952- ... 166
Lee, Shelton Jackson 1957(?)- ... CANR-42
Earlier sketch in CA 125
See also Lee, Spike
See also BLCS
See also BW 2
See also CLC 105
See also DAM MULT
Lee, Sherman Emery 1918- ... CANR-1
Earlier sketch in CA 1-4R
Lee, Sidney 1859-1926 ... DLB 149, 184
Lee, Sky 1952- ... 161
Lee, Sophia 1750-1824 ... DLB 39
Lee, Spike
See Lee, Shelton Jackson
See also AAYA 4
Lee, Stan 1922- ... 111
Brief entry ... 108
Interview in ... 111
See also AAYA 5
See also CLC 17
Lee, Stewart M(unro) 1925- ... 57-60
Lee, Susan ... 135
Lee, Susan 1944- ... 110
Lee, Susan Dye 1939- ... 85-88
Lee, Tammie
See Townsend, Thomas L.
Lee, Tanith 1947- ... CANR-53
Earlier sketch in CA 37-40R
See also AAYA 15
See also CLC 46
See also SATA 8, 88
Lee, Terence R(ichard) 1938- ... 29-32R
Lee, Tom(my L.) 1950- ... 65-68
Lee, Vernon
See Paget, Violet
See also DLB 57, 153, 156, 174, 178
See also TCLC 5
Lee, Virginia 1905(?)-1981 Obituary ... 105
Lee, Virginia (Yew) 1927- ... 9-12R
Lee, W. Storrs
See Lee, William Storrs
Lee, Walt(er William, Jr.) 1931- ... 61-64
Lee, Warner
See Battin, B(rinton) W(arner)
Lee, Warren M. 1908- ... 77-80
Lee, Wayne C. 1917- ... CANR-41
Earlier sketches in CA 1-4R, CANR-2, 17
Lee, William
See Burroughs, William S(eward)
Lee, William R(owland) 1911- ... CANR-42
Earlier sketches in CA 9-12R, CANR-4, 19
Lee, William Saul 1938- ... 104
Lee, William Storrs 1906- ... CANR-1
Earlier sketch in CA 1-4R
Lee, Willy
See Burroughs, William S(eward)
Lee, Yur Bok 1934- ... 29-32R
Leech, Alfred B. 1918(?)-1974 Obituary ... 49-52
Leech, Bryan Jeffery 1931- ... 93-96
Leech, Clifford 1909-1977 ... CANR-4
Earlier sketch in CA 1-4R
Leech, Geoffrey N(eil) 1936- ... CANR-53
Earlier sketches in CA 29-32R, CANR-12, 29
Leech, John 1925- ... 139
Leech, Kenneth 1939- ... 103
Leech, Margaret (Kernochan) 1893-1974 ... 93-96
Obituary ... 49-52
Leecing, Walden A. 1932- ... 33-36R
Leed, Eric J. 1942- ... 89-92
Leed, Jacob R. 1924- ... CANR-7
Earlier sketch in CA 17-20R
Leed, Richard L. 1929- ... 13-16R
Leed, Theodore W(illiam) 1927- ... 126
Brief entry ... 106
Leeder, Elaine J. 1944- ... 147
Leedham, Charles 1926- ... 13-16R
Leedham, John 1912- ... CANR-13
Earlier sketch in CA 21-24R
Leeds, Anthony 1925- ... 17-20R
Leeds, Barry H. 1940- ... 29-32R
Leeds, Morton (Harold) 1921- ... 13-16R
Leeds, Patricia (Miriam) 1920(?)-1985 Obituary ... 114
Leedy, Jack J. 1921- ... 21-24R
Leedy, Loreen (Janelle) 1959- ... CANR-48
Earlier sketch in CA 122
See also SATA 54, 84
See also SATA-Brief 50
Leedy, Paul D. 1908- ... CANR-1
Earlier sketch in CA 1-4R
Leefeldt, Christine 1941- ... 93-96
Lee-Hamilton, Eugene (Jacob) 1845-1907 Brief entry ... 117
See also TCLC 22
Lee-Hostetler, Jeri 1940- ... SATA 63
Lee Howard, Leon Alexander
1914-1979(?) Obituary ... 104
Leek, Margaret
See Bowen-Judd, Sara (Hutton)
Leek, Sybil 1923-1982 ... 102
Obituary ... 108
Leekley, Richard N. 1912-1976 Obituary ... 69-72
Leekley, Thomas B(riggs) 1910- ... 5-8R
See also SATA 23
Leeman, Wayne A(lvin) 1924- ... 13-16R
Leeming, David Adams 1937- ... 49-52
Leeming, Donald 1944- ... 114
Leeming, Glenda 1943- ... CANR-4
Earlier sketch in CA 53-56
Leeming, Jo Ann
See Leeming, Joseph
Leeming, John F(ishwick) 1900- ... CAP-1
Earlier sketch in CA 9-10
Leeming, Joseph 1897-1968 ... 73-76
See also SATA 26
Leeming, Owen (Alfred) 1930- ... CANR-15
Earlier sketch in CA 65-68
Leemis, Ralph B. 1954- ... SATA 72
Leenhouts, Keith J(ames) 1925- ... 61-64
Leepa, Allen 1919- ... 45-48
Leeper, Sarah (Lou) H(ammond) 1912-1992 ... 57-60
Obituary ... 139
Leepson, Marc 1945- ... 111
Leer, Norman Robert 1937- ... 17-20R
Leerburger, Benedict A., Jr. 1932- ... 9-12R
Lees, Andrew 1940- ... 122
Lees, Carlton Brown 1924- ... 103
Lees, Charles J. 1919- ... 25-28R
Lees, Dan 1927- ... CANR-13
Earlier sketch in CA 33-36R
Lees, Francis A(nthony) 1931- ... CANR-9
Earlier sketch in CA 65-68
Lees, Gene 1928- ... CANR-49
Earlier sketches in CA 21-24R, CANR-9, 24
Lees, Hannah
See Fetter, Elizabeth Head
Lees, Hilda Frances 1900-1983 Obituary ... 111
Lees, John D(avid) 1936- ... 53-56
Lees, John G(arfield) 1931- ... 57-60
Lees, Lynn Hollen 1941- ... 113
Lees, Ray 1931- ... CANR-8
Earlier sketch in CA 61-64
Lees, Richard 1948- ... CANR-26
Earlier sketch in CA 108
Lees, Stella 1931- ... 150
Leese, Elizabeth 1937- ... 85-88
Lee Six, Abigail (Etta) 1960- ... 132
Lees-Milne, James 1908-1997 ... CANR-31
Obituary ... 163
Earlier sketches in CA 9-12R, CANR-13
Leeson, C(harles) Roland 1926- ... 93-96
Leeson, Howard A(lfred) 1942- ... 118
Leeson, Muriel 1920- ... SATA 54
Leeson, R. A.
See Leeson, Robert (Arthur)
Leeson, Robert (Arthur) 1928- ... CANR-46
Earlier sketches in CA 105, CANR-22
See also MAICYA
See also SATA 42, 76
Leeson, Ted 1954- ... 145
Leet, Judith 1935- ... CLC 11
Leevy, Carroll (Moton) 1920- ... 158
Le Fanu, Joseph Sheridan 1814-1873 ... DAM POP
See also DLB 21, 70, 159, 178
See also SSC 14
LeFanu, Sarah 1953- ... 149
Lefco, Helene 1922- ... 53-56
Lefcoe, George 1938- ... 21-24R
Lefcourt, Peter 1941- ... 140
Lefcowitz, Barbara F(reedgood) 1935- ... 104
Lefebure, Leo D. 1952- ... 150
Lefebure, Marcus 1933- ... 113
Lefebure, Molly ... 57-60
Lefebvre, Henri 1901- ... CANR-11
Earlier sketch in CA 25-28R
Lefebvre d'Argence, Rene-Yvon 1928- ... CANR-11
Earlier sketch in CA 21-24R
Le Feuvre, Amy (?)-1929 Brief entry ... 111
Lefever, D(avid) Welty 1901- ... 49-52
Lefever, Ernest W(arren) 1919- ... CANR-1
Earlier sketch in CA 1-4R
Lefevere, Andre A. 1945- ... 151
LeFevre, Adam 1950- ... 81-84
Lefevre, Carl A(nthony) 1913- ... CANR-7
Earlier sketch in CA 9-12R
Lefevre, Gui
See Bickers, Richard (Leslie) Townshend
Lefevre, Helen (Elveback) ... 17-20R
LeFevre, Perry D(eyo) 1921- ... CANR-25
Earlier sketches in CA 21-24R, CANR-10
LeFevre, Robert (Thomas) 1911-1986 ... CANR-9
Obituary ... 119
Earlier sketch in CA 57-60
Leff, Arthur A(llen) 1935-1981 Obituary ... 105
Leff, Gordon 1926- ... CANR-3
Earlier sketch in CA 9-12R
Leff, Leonard J. 1942- ... 128
Leff, Nathaniel H. 1938- ... 25-28R
Leffelaar, Hendrik Louis 1929-1980 ... 5-8R
Obituary ... 145
Lefferts, George 1921- ... CANR-14
Earlier sketch in CA 69-72
Leffland, Ella 1931- ... CANR-35
Earlier sketch in CA 29-32R
Interview in ... CANR-35
See also CLC 19
See also DLBY 84
See also SATA 65
Leffler, Melvyn Paul 1945- ... 89-92
Lefkoe, Morty R. 1937- ... 29-32R
Lefkowitz, Annette S(ara) 1922- ... 17-20R
Lefkowitz, Bernard 1937- ... CANR-30
Earlier sketch in CA 29-32R
Lefkowitz, Joel M. 1940- ... 45-48
Lefkowitz, Mary Rosenthal 1935- ... CANR-41
Earlier sketches in CA 103, CANR-19
Lefkowitz, R(obert) J. 1942- ... 45-48
Leflar, Robert A(llen) 1901- ... 29-32R
Le Fleming, Christopher (Kaye)
1908-1985 Obituary ... 117
Lefler, Hugh Talmage 1901- ... 5-8R
Lefler, Irene (Whitney) 1917- ... CANR-1
Earlier sketch in CA 45-48
See also SATA 12
LeFlore, Ron(ald) 1948(?)- Brief entry ... 115
Le Fontaine, Joseph (Raymond) 1927- ... 106
le Fort, Gertrud (Petrea) von 1876-1971 ... CANR-31
Obituary ... 33-36R
Earlier sketch in CA 69-72
See also DLB 66
Lefranc, Pierre 1927- ... 41-44R
Lefrancois, Guy R(enald) 1940- ... CANR-18
Earlier sketches in CA 45-48, CANR-2
Lefton, Robert Eugene 1931- ... CANR-31
Earlier sketch in CA 49-52
Leftwich, James (Adolf) 1902- ... CANR-15
Earlier sketch in CA 41-44R
Leftwich, Jim 1956- ... CAAS 25
Leftwich, Joseph 1892-1983 ... 5-8R
Obituary ... 109
Leftwich, Richard Henry 1920- ... CANR-5
Earlier sketch in CA 13-16R
LeGalley, Donald P(aul) 1901- ... CAP-2
Earlier sketch in CA 17-18
Le Gallienne, Eva 1899-1991 ... 45-48
Obituary ... 134
See also SATA 9
See also SATA-Obit 68
Le Gallienne, Richard 1866-1947 Brief entry ... 107
See also DLB 4
Legany, Dezso 1916- ... 157
Legare, Hugh Swinton 1797-1843 ... DLB 3, 59, 73
Legare, James Mathewes 1823-1859 ... DLB 3
Legaret, Jean 1913-1976 ... CAP-2
Earlier sketch in CA 29-32
Legarreta, Dorothy 1926- ... 118
Legat, Michael (Ronald) 1923- ... 122
Legault, Albert 1938- ... 53-56
Leger, Alexis
See Leger, (Marie-Rene Auguste) Alexis
Saint-Leger
Leger, (Marie-Rene Auguste) Alexis Saint-Leger
1887-1975 ... CANR-43
Obituary ... 61-64
Earlier sketch in CA 13-16R
See also CLC 4, 11, 46
See also DAM POET
See also MTCW 1
See also PC 23
Leger, Antoine-J 1880-1950 ... DLB 88
Leger, Fernand 1881-1955 ... 165
Brief entry ... 123
Leger, Saintleger
See Leger, (Marie-Rene Auguste) Alexis
Saint-Leger
Legeza, (Ireneus) Laszlo 1934- ... CANR-32
Earlier sketch in CA 65-68
Legg, Sarah Martha Ross Bruggeman
(?)-1982 ... SATA-Obit 40
Legg, (Francis) Stuart 1910-1988 Obituary ... 126
Leggatt, Alexander (Maxwell) 1940- ... 97-100
Legge, Elisabeth Schwarzkopf
See Schwarzkopf-Legge, Elisabeth
Legge, J(ohn) D(avid) 1921- ... CANR-2
Earlier sketch in CA 1-4R
Legge, M(ary) Dominica 1905-1986 Obituary ... 121
Legge-Bourke, (Edward Alexander) Henry
1914-1973 ... CAP-1
Earlier sketch in CA 9-10
Leggett, B(obby) J(oe) 1938- ... 53-56
Leggett, Eric
See Rimel, Duane (Weldon)
Leggett, Glenn 1918- ... CANR-5
Earlier sketch in CA 13-16R
Leggett, John (Ward) 1917- ... CANR-2
Earlier sketch in CA 1-4R
Leggett, John C. 1930- ... 25-28R
Leggett, Linda 1941- ... 108
Leggett, Stephen 1949- ... 77-80
Leggitt, (Samuel) Hunter (Jr.) 1935- ... 65-68
Legh, Kathleen Louise Wood
See Wood-Legh, Kathleen Louise
Legler, Gretchen 1960- ... 166
Legler, Henry M. 1897- ... 97-100
Legler, Philip 1928- ... 9-12R
Legman, G(ershon) 1917- ... CANR-15
Earlier sketch in CA 21-24R
LeGrand
See Henderson, LeGrand
Legrand, Catherine Carlisle 1947- ... 126
Legrand, Lucien 1926- ... 5-8R
Legrand, Michel (Jean) 1932- Brief entry ... 114
Legters, Lyman H(oward) 1928- ... CANR-15
Earlier sketch in CA 33-36R
Le Guin, Ursula K(roeber) 1929- ... CANR-52
Earlier sketches in CA 21-24R, CANR-9, 32
Interview in ... CANR-32
See also AAYA 9, 27
See also AITN 1
See also CDALB 1968-1988
See also CLC 8, 13, 22, 45, 71
See also CLR 3, 28
See also DAB
See also DAC
See also DAM MST, POP
See also DLB 8, 52
See also JRDA
See also MAICYA
See also MTCW 1
See also SATA 4, 52, 99
See also SSC 12
Legum, Colin 1919- ... CANR-4
Earlier sketch in CA 1-4R
See also SATA 10
Legvold, Robert 1940- ... 85-88
Lehan, Richard (D'Aubin Daniel) 1930- ... 21-24R
Lehane, Brendan 1936- ... CANR-26
Earlier sketches in CA 21-24R, CANR-10
Lehane, Dennis 1965- ... CANR-72
Earlier sketch in CA 154
Lehiste, Ilse 1922- ... 37-40R
Lehman, Anita Jacobs 1920- ... 21-24R
Lehman, Bob ... SATA 91
Lehman, Celia 1928- ... CANR-1
Earlier sketch in CA 49-52
Lehman, Chester K. 1895-1980 ... CANR-1
Earlier sketch in CA 1-4R
Lehman, Dale 1920- ... 9-12R
Lehman, David 1948- ... CANR-24
Earlier sketches in CA 57-60, CANR-8
Lehman, Donna (Jean) 1940- ... 143
Lehman, Elaine ... SATA 91
Lehman, Ernest Paul 1915- ... CANR-69
Earlier sketch in CA 85-88
See also DLB 44
Lehman, F(rederick) K. 1924- ... 9-12R
Lehman, Godfrey ... 25-28R
Lehman, Harold D(aniel) 1921- ... 81-84
Lehman, John F(rancis), Jr. 1942- ... 13-16R
Lehman, John H. 1932- ... 141
Lehman, Milton 1917-1966 ... CAP-1
Earlier sketch in CA 13-14
Lehman, Peter 1944- ... 115
Lehman, Sam 1899- ... 49-52
Lehman, Warren (Winfred, Jr.) 1930- ... 21-24R
Lehman, Yvonne 1936- ... CANR-12
Earlier sketch in CA 29-32R
Lehmann, A(ndrew) George 1922- ... CANR-4
Earlier sketch in CA 1-4R
Lehmann, Arno 1901- ... CAP-2
Earlier sketch in CA 29-32
Lehmann, Geoffrey (John) 1940- Brief entry ... 107
Lehmann, Irving J(ack) 1927- ... 53-56
Lehmann, Johannes 1929- ... CANR-14
Earlier sketch in CA 37-40R
Lehmann, (Rudolph) John (Frederick) 1907-1987 ...
CANR-8
Obituary ... 122
Earlier sketch in CA 9-12R
Interview in ... CANR-8
See also DLB 27, 100
Lehmann, Linda 1906- ... 85-88
Lehmann, Lotte 1888-1976 ... 73-76
Obituary ... 69-72
Lehmann, Martin Ernest 1915- ... 5-8R
Lehmann, Michael Boas 1941- ... 119
Lehmann, Paul Louis 1906-1994 ... 85-88
Obituary ... 144
Lehmann, Peter 1938- ... 57-60
Lehmann, Robert A(rthur) 1932- ... 57-60

Lehmann, Rosamond (Nina) 1901-1990 ... CANR-8
Obituary ... 131
Earlier sketch in CA 77-80
See also CLC 5
See also DLB 15
Lehmann, Theo 1934- ... 41-44R
Lehmann, Wilhelm 1882-1968 ... DLB 56
Lehmann, Winfred P(hilipp) 1916- ... 33-36R
Lehmann-Haupt, Christopher (Charles Herbert) 1934- ... 109
Interview in ... 109
Lehmann-Haupt, Hellmut (Emile) 1903-1992 . 9-12R
Obituary ... 137
Lehmberg, Paul 1946- ... 102
Lehmberg, Stanford Eugene 1931- ... CANR-2
Earlier sketch in CA 1-4R
Lehn, Cornelia 1920- ... CANR-12
Earlier sketch in CA 29-32R
See also SATA 46
Lehne, Judith Logan 1947- ... 158
See also SATA 93
Lehner, Christine (Reine) 1952- ... 109
Lehnert, Herbert (Hermann) 1925- ... 41-44R
Lehning, James R(obert) 1947- ... 105
Lehninger, Albert L(ester) 1917-1986 ... 153
Obituary ... 119
Lehnus, Donald James 1934- ... CANR-9
Earlier sketch in CA 57-60
Lehnus, Opal (Hull) 1920- ... 9-12R
Lehovich, Eugenie Ouroussow
See Ouroussow, Eugenie
Lehr, Delores 1920- ... 17-20R
See also SATA 10
Lehr, Norma 1930- ... SATA 71
Lehr, Paul E(dwin) 1918- ... 65-68
Lehr, Robert 1919- ... 153
Lehrack, Otto J(ohn III) 1938- ... 139
Lehrer, Adrienne (Joyce) 1937- ... 29-32R
Lehrer, James (Charles) 1934- ... CANR-43
Brief entry ... 109
Earlier sketch in CA 114
Lehrer, Jim
See Lehrer, James (Charles)
Lehrer, Kate 1939- ... 138
Lehrer, Keith 1936- ... 17-20R
Lehrer, Robert N(athaniel) 1922- ... 61-64
Lehrer, Stanley 1929- ... CANR-2
Earlier sketch in CA 5-8R
Lehrer, Thomas Andrew 1928- ... 123
Lehrer, Tom
See Lehrer, Thomas Andrew
Lehrman, Harold Arthur 1911-1988 Obituary ... 127
Lehrman, Liza
See Williams, Liza
Lehrman, Nat 1929- ... 93-96
Lehrman, Robert L(awrence) 1921- ... CANR-7
Earlier sketch in CA 5-8R
Lehrman, Simon Maurice 1900- ... CAP-1
Earlier sketch in CA 9-10
Lehrmann, Chanan
See Lehrmann, Charles C(uno)
Lehrmann, Charles C(uno) 1905-1977 ... 33-36R
Lehrmann, Cuno Chanan
See Lehrmann, Charles C(uno)
Leib, Amos Patten 1917-1977 ... 45-48
Obituary ... 133
Leib, Franklin A(llen) 1944- ... 138
Leibbrand, Kurt 1914- ... 45-48
Leibel, Charlotte P(ollack) 1899- ... 33-36R
Leibenguth, Charla Ann
See Banner, Charla Ann Leibenguth
Leibenstein, Harvey 1922-1994 ... 103
Obituary ... 144
Leiber, Fritz (Reuter, Jr.) 1910-1992 ... CANR-40
Obituary ... 139
Earlier sketches in CA 45-48, CANR-2
See also CLC 25
See also DLB 8
See also MTCW 1
See also SATA 45
See also SATA-Obit 73
Leiber, Justin Fritz 1938- ... CANR-39
Earlier sketches in CA 97-100, CANR-17
Leibert, Julius A(mos) 1888- ... CAP-2
Earlier sketch in CA 17-18
Leibniz, Gottfried Wilhelm von 1646-1716 . DLB 168
Leibold, Jay 1957- ... 123
See also SATA 57
See also SATA-Brief 52
Leibold, (William) John 1926- ... 37-40R
Leibovitz, Annie 1949- ... 140
See also AAYA 11
Leibowitz, Herbert A. 1935- ... 25-28R
Leibowitz, Herschel W. 1925- ... CANR-8
Earlier sketch in CA 17-20R
Leibowitz, Irving 1922-1979 ... 9-12R
Obituary ... 85-88
Leibowitz, Rene 1913-1972 Obituary ... 37-40R
Leibson, Jacob J. 1883(?)-1971 Obituary ... 33-36R
Leiby, Adrian C(oulter) 1904-1976 ... CAP-1
Obituary ... 65-68
Earlier sketch in CA 9-10
Leiby, James 1924- ... 33-36R
Leichman, Seymour 1933- ... 25-28R
See also SATA 5
Leichter, Otto 1898(?)-1973 Obituary ... 41-44R
Leiden, Carl 1922- ... 5-8R
Leider, Emily Wortis 1937- ... CANR-72
Earlier sketch in CA 81-84
Leider, Frida 1888-1975 Obituary ... 57-60
Leier, Mark 1956- ... 164
Leigh, Carolyn 1926-1983 Obituary ... 111
Leigh, David 1946- ... 144
Leigh, Egbert Giles, Jr. 1940- ... 57-60
Leigh, Eugene
See Seltzer, Leon E(ugene)
Leigh, James L(eighton) 1930- ... 9-12R
Leigh, Janet
See Morrison, Jeanette Helen
Leigh, Matthew Andrew
See Chervokas, John V(incent)
Leigh, Michael 1914- ... 13-16R
Leigh, Mike 1943- ... CANR-68
Earlier sketches in CA 109, CANR-31
Leigh, Nila K. 1981- ... 149
See also SATA 81
Leigh, Palmer
See Palmer, Pamela Lynn
Leigh, Ralph Alexander 1915-1987 Obituary ... 124
Leigh, Richard (Harris) 1943- ... 140
Leigh, Robert
See Randisi, Robert J(oseph)
Leigh, Robin
See Hatcher, Robin Lee
Leigh, Spencer 1945- ... 102
Leigh, Stephen (W.) 1951- ... 135
Leigh, Susannah 1938- ... CANR-15
Earlier sketch in CA 81-84
Leigh, Tom 1947- ... SATA 46
Leigh, W. R. 1866-1955 ... DLB 188
Leigh Fermor, Patrick (Michael) 1915- ... CANR-35
Earlier sketch in CA 81-84
See also MTCW 1
Leigh-Pemberton, John 1911- ... 108
See also SATA 35
Leight, Robert L(ewis) 1932- ... 110
Leighton, Albert C(hester) 1919- ... 37-40R
Leighton, Alexander H(amilton) 1908- ... 41-44R
Leighton, Ann
See Smith, Isadore Leighton Luce
Leighton, Clare (Veronica Hope) 1899- ... 108
See also SATA 37
Leighton, David S(truan) R(obertson) 1928- ... CANR-2
Earlier sketch in CA 5-8R
Leighton, Frances Spatz ... CANR-58
Earlier sketches in CA 81-84, CANR-30
Leighton, Jack Richard 1918- ... 1-4R
Leighton, Lauren G(ray) 1934- ... 118
Leighton, Lee
See Overholser, Wayne D.
Leighton, Margaret (Carver) 1896-1987 ... 9-12R
Obituary ... 123
See also SATA 1
See also SATA-Obit 52
Leiken, Robert S. 1939- ... 145
Leikind, Morris C. 1906(?)-1976 Obituary ... 65-68
Leimbach, Martha 1963- ... 130
See also Leimbach, Marti
Leimbach, Marti
See Leimbach, Martha
See also CLC 65
Leimbach, Patricia Penton 1927- ... 57-60
Leimberg, Stephan R(obert) 1943- ... 117
Leimert, Lucille 1895(?)-1983 Obituary ... 110
Lein, Glenna R. Schroeder
See Schroeder-Lein, Glenna R(uth)
Leinbach, Esther V(ashti) 1924- ... 61-64
Leiner, Al(an) 1938- ... SATA 83
Leiner, Katherine 1949- ... CANR-61
Earlier sketch in CA 132
See also SATA 93
Leinfellner, Werner (Hubertus) 1921- ... CANR-5
Earlier sketch in CA 53-56
Leininger, Madeleine M. 1925- ... 33-36R
Leino, Eino
See Loennbohm, Armas Eino Leopold
See also TCLC 24
Leinsdorf, Erich 1912-1993 ... 119
Obituary ... 142
Brief entry ... 112
Leinster, Murray
See Jenkins, Will(iam) F(itzgerald)
See also DLB 8
Leinwand, Gerald 1921- ... CANR-9
Earlier sketch in CA 5-8R
Leip, Hans 1893-1983 Obituary ... 110
Leipart, Charles 1944- ... 108
Leiper, Henry Smith 1891-1975 Obituary ... 53-56
Leipold, L. Edmond 1902- ... 69-72
See also SATA 16
Leiris, Michel (Julien) 1901-1990 ... 128
Obituary ... 132
Brief entry ... 119
See also CLC 61
Leiser, Burton M. 1930- ... CANR-42
Earlier sketches in CA 29-32R, CANR-12
Leiser, Erwin (Moritz) 1923- ... CANR-14
Earlier sketch in CA 29-32R
Leiser, Gary 1946- ... 153
Leiserson, Michael 1939- ... 37-40R
Leisewitz, Johann Anton 1752-1806 ... DLB 94
Leishman, J(ames) Blair 1902-1963 ... CANR-6
Earlier sketch in CA 5-8R
Leishman, Thomas L. 1900-1978 Obituary ... 81-84
Leisk, David Johnson 1906-1975 ... 9-12R
Obituary ... 57-60
See also MAICYA
See also SATA 1, 30
See also SATA-Obit 26
Leiss, William 1939- ... 41-44R
Leister, Mary 1917- ... CANR-11
Earlier sketch in CA 65-68
See also SATA 29
Leistritz, F(redrick) Larry 1945- ... 104
Leisy, James (Franklin) 1927- ... CANR-20
Earlier sketches in CA 9-12R, CANR-4
Leitch, Adelaide 1921- ... 101
Leitch, D(avid) B(ruce) 1940- ... 57-60
Leitch, Maurice 1933- ... CANR-40
Earlier sketch in CA 102
See also DLB 14
Leitch, Patricia 1933- ... CANR-9
Earlier sketch in CA 61-64
See also SATA 11, 98
Leitch, Vincent Barry 1944- ... 113
Leitenberg, Milton 1933- ... CANR-19
Earlier sketch in CA 101
Leiter, Louis (Henry) 1921- ... 37-40R
Leiter, Marcia 1942- ... 116
Leiter, Robert D(avid) 1922-1976 ... CANR-4
Obituary ... 69-72
Earlier sketch in CA 5-8R
Leiter, Samuel L(ouis) 1940- ... CANR-56
Earlier sketches in CA 93-96, CANR-31
Leiter, Sharon 1942- ... 57-60
Leites, Edmund 1939- ... 126
Leites, Nathan Constantin 1912-1987 ... 126
Obituary ... 122
Leith, (James) Andrew 1931- ... CANR-20
Earlier sketch in CA 45-48
Leith, J(ames) Clark 1937- ... 57-60
Leith, John H. 1919- ... CANR-3
Earlier sketch in CA 5-8R
Leith, Linda 1949- ... 131
Leithauser, Brad 1953- ... CANR-27
Earlier sketch in CA 107
See also CLC 27
See also DLB 120
Leithauser, Gladys Garner 1925- ... CANR-27
Earlier sketch in CA 13-16R
Leith-Ross, Prudence 1922- ... 132
Leitmann, George 1925- ... 53-56
Leitner, Isabella 1924- ... 152
See also SATA 86
Leitner, Moses J. 1908- ... CAP-1
Earlier sketch in CA 13-16
Leitz, Robert C(harles) III 1944- ... 133
Leivick, H.
See Halpern, Leivick
Leivick, Halper
See Halpern, Leivick
Lekachman, Robert 1920-1989 Obituary ... 127
Brief entry ... 106
Lekai, J(ulius) Louis 1916- ... 33-36R
Lekis, Lisa 1917- ... 9-12R
Lekson, Stephen H(enry) 1950- ... CANR-48
Earlier sketch in CA 122
Leland, Bob 1956- ... SATA 92
Leland, Charles G(odfrey) 1824-1903 Brief entry ... 118
See also DLB 11
Leland, Christopher Towne 1951- ... 108
Leland, Henry 1923- ... CANR-18
Earlier sketch in CA 89-92
Leland, Jeremy (Francis David) 1932- ... CANR-13
Earlier sketch in CA 33-36R
Leland, Robert E.
See Leland, Bob
Leland, Timothy 1937- ... 102
Lelchuk, Alan 1938- ... CANR-70
Earlier sketches in CA 45-48, CANR-1
See also CAAS 20
See also CLC 5
Lele, Uma 1941- ... 73-76
Leliaert, Richard Maurice 1940- ... 101
le Lievre, Audrey 1923- ... 132
Lellenberg, Jon L. 1946- ... 165
Lelouch, Claude (Barruck Joseph) 1937- Brief entry ... 113
LeLoup, Lance T. 1949- ... 110
Lelyveld, Arthur J(oseph) 1913-1996 ... 25-28R
Obituary ... 152
Lelyveld, Joseph (Salem) 1937- ... 126
Brief entry ... 117
Interview in ... 126
Lem, Stanislaw 1921- ... CANR-32
Earlier sketch in CA 105
See also CAAS 1
See also CLC 8, 15, 40
See also MTCW 1
Lemagny, Jean-Claude 1931- ... 136
LeMahieu, D(an) L(loyd) 1945- ... 69-72
LeMair, H(enriette) Willebeek 1889-1966 ... SATA-Brief 29
LeMaire, H. Paul 1933- ... 113
Lemaitre, Georges E(douard) 1898-1972 ... CAP-2
Obituary ... 37-40R
Earlier sketch in CA 25-28
Lemann, Bernard 1905- ... CANR-21
Earlier sketch in CA 41-44R
Lemann, Nancy 1956- ... 136
Brief entry ... 118
See also CLC 39
Lemann, Nicholas 1954- ... 138
Lemarchand, Elizabeth (Wharton) 1906- . CANR-64
Earlier sketches in CA 25-28R, CANR-10, 26
Lemarchand, Rene 1932- ... 13-16R
LeMaster, Carolyn Gray ... 150
LeMaster, J(immie) R(ay) 1934- ... CANR-30
Earlier sketches in CA 33-36R, CANR-13
LeMaster, Leslie Jean 1943- ... 125
LeMay, Alan 1899-1964 Obituary ... 115
Lemay, Harding 1922- ... CANR-21
Earlier sketches in CA 45-48, CANR-1
Lemay, J(oseph) A(lberic) Leo 1935- ... CANR-49
Earlier sketches in CA 17-20R, CANR-9, 24
Lemay, Pamphile 1837-1918 ... DLB 99
le May, Reginald Stuart 1885- ... 5-8R
Lembark, Connie W. 1934- ... 144
Lembeck, Ruth (Louise) 1919- ... 105
Lember, Barbara Hirsch 1941- ... SATA 92
Lembke, Janet (Nutt) 1933- ... 45-48
Lembo, Diana L.
See Spirt, Diana L(ouise)
Lembo, John M(ario) 1937- ... 29-32R
Lembourn, Hans Joergen 1923- ... 105
Lemco, Jonathan 1956- ... 139
Lemelin, Roger 1919- ... DLB 88
Lemelle, Wilbert J. 1931- ... 45-48
Lemercier, Louis-Jean-Nepomucene 1771-1840 ... DLB 192
Lemerle, Paul (Emile) 1903-1989 Obituary ... 129
Lemert, Charles C(lay) 1937- ... 111
Lemert, Edwin M(cCarty) 1912- ... 93-96
Lemert, James B(olton) 1935- ... 73-76
Lemert, Jim
See Lemert, James B(olton)
Lemesurier, Peter
See Britton, Peter Ewart
LeMieux, A(nne) C(onnelly) 1954- ... 155
See also SATA 90
Lemieux, Joanne (Hero) 1946- ... 114
Lemieux, Lucien 1934- ... 41-44R
Lemieux, Marc 1948- ... 102
Lemir, Andre
See Rimel, Duane (Weldon)
Lemire, Beverly 1950- ... 141
Le Mire, Eugene D(ennis) 1929- ... 41-44R
Lemire, Robert A(rthur) 1933- ... 101
Lemish, John 1921- ... 5-8R
Lemke, Horst 1922- ... 107
See also SATA 38
Lemlin, Jeanne 1953- ... 150
Lemme, Janet E(llen) 1941- ... 29-32R
Lemmon, David (Hector) 1931- ... 131
Lemmon, Kenneth 1911- ... 65-68
Lemmon, Sarah McCulloh 1914- ... 21-24R
Lemmons, Thom 1955- ... 134
Lemoine, Ernest
See Roy, Ewell Paul
Le Moine, James MacPherson 1825-1912 .. DLB 99
LeMon, Cal 1945- ... 53-56
Lemon, James Thomas 1929- ... 37-40R
Lemon, Lee T(homas) 1931- ... 17-20R
LeMon, Lynn
See Wert, Lynette L(emon)
Lemon, Mark 1809-1870 ... DLB 163
LeMond, Alan 1938- ... CANR-9
Earlier sketch in CA 61-64
Lemonnier, (Antoine Louis) Camille 1844-1913 Brief entry ... 121
See also TCLC 22
Lemons, J. Stanley 1938- ... 37-40R
Lemont, George 1927- ... 65-68
Lemos, Ramon M(arcelino) 1927- ... 37-40R
Le Moyne, Jean 1913-1996 ... 163
See also DLB 88
Lemperly, Paul 1858-1939 ... DLB 187
Lena, Dan 1955- ... 134
Lena, Marie
See Lena, Marie H(oward)
Lena, Marie H(oward) 1956- ... 134
Lenanton, Carola Mary Anima Oman
See Oman, Carola (Mary Anima)
Lenarcic, R(aymond) J(ames) 1942- ... 49-52
Lenard, Alexander 1910-1972 ... CANR-4
Obituary ... 89-92
Earlier sketch in CA 5-8R
See also SATA-Obit 21
Lenard, Yvone 1921- ... CANR-7
Earlier sketch in CA 53-56
Lenardon, Robert J(oseph) 1928- ... 33-36R
Lenburg, Greg 1956- ... 105
Lenburg, Jeff 1956- ... CANR-20
Earlier sketch in CA 104
Lenczowski, George 1915- ... CANR-4
Earlier sketch in CA 1-4R
Lendon, Kenneth Harry 1928- ... 9-12R
Lendvai, Paul 1929- ... CANR-33
Earlier sketches in CA 85-88, CANR-15
Lenehan, William T. 1930- ... 21-24R
L'Enfant, Julie 1944- ... 109
Lenfestey, (William Frederick) Thompson 1925- ... 153
Leng, Russell J. 1938- ... 144
Lengel, Frances
See Trocchi, Alexander
Lengle, James I(rvin) 1949- ... 106
L'Engle, Madeleine (Camp Franklin) 1918- ... CANR-66
Earlier sketches in CA 1-4R, CANR-3, 21, 39
See also AAYA 1
See also AITN 2
See also CLC 12
See also CLR 1, 14
See also DAM POP
See also DLB 52
See also JRDA
See also MAICYA
See also MTCW 1
See also SAAS 15
See also SATA 1, 27, 75
Lengyel, Alfonz 1921- ... 116
Lengyel, Cornel Adam 1915- ... CANR-24
Earlier sketches in CA 1-4R, CANR-1
See also SATA 27
Lengyel, Emil 1895-1985 ... CANR-3
Obituary ... 115
Earlier sketch in CA 9-12R
See also SATA 3
See also SATA-Obit 42
Lengyel, Jozsef 1896-1975 ... CANR-71
Obituary ... 57-60
Earlier sketch in CA 85-88
See also CLC 7
Lengyel, Melchior 1879(?)-1974 Obituary ... 53-56
Lenhoff, Alan (Stuart) 1951- ... 73-76
Lenier, Sue 1957- ... 120
Lenihan, John (Howard) 1941- ... 105
Lenihan, Kenneth J. 1928-1998 ... 97-100
Obituary ... 167

Lenin 1870-1924 168
Brief entry 121
See also Lenin, V. I.
Lenin, N.
See Lenin
Lenin, Nikolai
See Lenin
Lenin, V. I.
See Lenin
See also TCLC 67
Lenin, Vladimir I.
See Lenin
Lenin, Vladimir Ilyich
See Lenin
Lenn, Theodore I. 1914- 45-48
Lennard, John (Chevening) 1964- 137
Lennart, Isobel 1915-1971 Obituary 29-32R
See also DLB 44
Lenneberg, Eric H. 1921-1975 .... CANR-7
Obituary 57-60
Earlier sketch in CA 53-56
Lennig, Arthur 1933- 57-60
Lennon, Donald R. 1938- 139
Lennon, Florence Becker (Tanenbaum)
1895- 13-16R
Lennon, Helen M.
See Goulart, Frances Sheridan
Lennon, John (Ono) 1940-1980 102
See also CLC 12, 35
Lennon, Joseph Luke 1919- 33-36R
Lennon, Nigey 1954- 109
Lennon, Sister M. Isidore 1901- 41-44R
Lennon, Thomas M. 1942- CANR-56
Earlier sketch in CA 125
Lennox, Charlotte Ramsay 1729(?)-1804 ... DLB 39
Lennox, Terry
See Harvey, John (Barton)
Lennox-Short, Alan 1913- 102
Lennox-Smith, Judith (Elizabeth) 1953- 134
Leno, Jay 1950- 159
LeNoir, Janice 1941- 155
See also SATA 89
Lenox, James 1800-1880 .... DLB 140
Lens, Sidney 1912-1986 .... CANR-17
Obituary 119
Earlier sketches in CA 1-4R, CANR-1
See also SATA 13
See also SATA-Obit 48
Lensen, George Alexander 1923-1980 .... CANR-2
Earlier sketch in CA 1-4R
Lensink, Judy Nolte 1948- 127
Lenski, Gerhard Emmanuel, Jr. 1924- 1-4R
Lenski, Lois 1893-1974 .... CANR-41
Obituary 53-56
Earlier sketches in CAP-1, CA 13-14
See also CLR 26
See also DLB 22
See also MAICYA
See also SATA 1, 26, 100
Lenson, David (Rollar) 1945- 73-76
Lent, Blair CANR-11
Earlier sketch in CA 21-24R
See also MAICYA
See also SATA 2
Lent, D(ora) Geneva 1904- 5-8R
Lent, Henry Bolles 1901-1973 73-76
See also SATA 17
Lent, John A(nthony) 1936- CANR-57
Earlier sketches in CA 29-32R, CANR-12, 30
Lentfoehr, Therese 1902- 97-100
Lentilhon, Robert Ward 1925- 9-12R
Lentin, Antony 1941- 103
Lentner, Howard H(enry) 1931- 106
Lenton, Henry Trevor 1924- 103
Lentricchia, Frank (Jr.) 1940- CANR-19
Earlier sketch in CA 25-28R
See also CLC 34
Lentz, Donald A. 1910- 17-20R
Lentz, Harold H(erbert) 1910- 57-60
Lentz, John C(layton), Jr. 1957- 146
Lentz, Perry 1943- 21-24R
Lenz, Carolyn Ruth Swift
See Swift, Carolyn Ruth
Lenz, Elinor 1928- 145
Lenz, Frederick (P.), (Jr.) 1950-1998 .... CANR-52
Obituary 167
Earlier sketch in CA 97-100
Lenz, Hermann 1913- .... DLB 69
Lenz, J. M. R. 1751-1792 .... DLB 94
Lenz, Siegfried 1926- 89-92
See also CLC 27
See also DLB 75
Lenz, William E(rnest) 1950- 118
Lenzner, Robert 1935- 145
Leo, Mabel R. 1937- 166
Leo, Richard C. 1952- 139
Leodhas, Sorche Nic
See Alger, Leclaire (Gowans)
LeoGrande, William M(ark) 1949- 122
Leokum, Arkady 1916(?)- 116
See also SATA 45
Leon, Frances
See Swadesh, Frances Leon
Leon, Henry Cecil 1902-1976 Obituary 115
Leon, Nick
See Grant, Graeme
Leon, Pierre R. 1926- CANR-43
Earlier sketches in CA 45-48, CANR-1, 17
Leon, Sharon 1959- 148
See also SATA 79
Leon, Vicki 1942- 132
Leonard, Alison 1944- 138
See also SATA 70
Leonard, Calista V(erne) 1919- 21-24R
Leonard, Charlene M(arie) 1928- 33-36R
Leonard, Constance (Brink) 1923- CANR-28
Earlier sketch in CA 49-52
See also SATA 42
See also SATA-Brief 40
Leonard, Diana 1941- 137
Leonard, Edith Marian CAP-1
Earlier sketch in CA 13-16
Leonard, Elmore (John, Jr.) 1925- CANR-53
Earlier sketches in CA 81-84, CANR-12, 28
Interview in CANR-28
See also AAYA 22
See also AITN 1
See also BEST 89:1, 90:4
See also CLC 28, 34, 71
See also DAM POP
See also DLB 173
See also MTCW 1
Leonard, Eugenie Andruss 1888-1980 .... CAP-2
Obituary 97-100
Earlier sketch in CA 17-18
Leonard, Frances 1939- 141
Leonard, Frank G. 1935(?)-1974 Obituary 49-52
Leonard, George (Jay) 1946- 112
Leonard, George B(urr) 1923- CANR-20
Earlier sketches in CA 9-12R, CANR-3
Leonard, George E(dward) 1931- 21-24R
Leonard, George H. 1921- 65-68
Leonard, George K., Jr. 1915- 17-20R
Leonard, Gladys Osborne 1882-1968 Obituary . 112
Leonard, Graham Douglas 1921- 103
Leonard, Hugh
See Byrne, John Keyes
See also CLC 19
See also DLB 13
Leonard, Irving A(lbert) 1896- CANR-5
Earlier sketch in CA 5-8R
Leonard, J. S.
See Leonard, James S.
Leonard, James S. 1947- 142
Leonard, Jason
See Escott, Jonathan
Leonard, John 1939- CANR-12
Earlier sketch in CA 13-16R
Leonard, Jonathan N(orton) 1903-1975 61-64
Obituary 57-60
See also SATA 36
Leonard, Joseph T. 1916- 9-12R
Leonard, Justin W(ilkinson) 1909- CAP-1
Earlier sketch in CA 19-20
Leonard, Karen Isaksen 1939- 144
Leonard, Laura 1923- 142
See also SATA 75
Leonard, Lawrence 1928- CANR-47
Earlier sketch in CA 121
Leonard, Leo D(onald) 1938- CANR-5
Earlier sketch in CA 53-56
Leonard, Maurice 1939- 107
Leonard, Neil 1927- 1-4R
Leonard, Phyllis B. 1929- 117
Leonard, Phyllis G(rubbs) 1924- CANR-12
Earlier sketch in CA 69-72
Leonard, Richard 1954- 141
Leonard, Richard Anthony
1900(?)-1979 Obituary 85-88
Leonard, Robert 1928-1984 Obituary 112
Leonard, Robert C(arl) 1928- 45-48
Leonard, Roger Ashley 1940- 25-28R
Leonard, Ruth S(haw) 1906- CAP-2
Earlier sketch in CA 23-24
Leonard, Stephen J. 1941- 147
Leonard, Thomas C(harles) 1944- CANR-53
Earlier sketch in CA 77-80
Leonard, Thomas M. 1937- CANR-48
Earlier sketch in CA 122
Leonard, Tom 1944- CANR-31
Earlier sketches in CA 77-80, CANR-13
Leonard, V. A. 1898- CANR-15
Earlier sketch in CA 37-40R
Leonard, William Ellery 1876-1944 .... DLB 54
Leonard, William N. 1912- 37-40R
Leonard, William Torbert 1918- 107
Leonard-Barton, Dorothy 1942- 155
Leonardi, Susan J. 1946- 131
Leondes, Cornelius Thomas 1927- 17-20R
Leone, Bruno 1939- 110
Leone, Daniel 1969- 165
Leone, Leonard 1914- 115
Leone, Mark P(aul) 1940- 93-96
Leone, Robert A. 1945- 122
Leone, Sergio 1929(?)-1989 123
Obituary 128
Leong, Charles L. 1911(?)-1984 Obituary 112
Leong, Gor Yun
See Ellison, Virginia H(owell)
Leong, Russell (C.) 1950- 142
Leonhard, Charles 1915- 5-8R
Leonhard, Wolfgang 1921- 144
Leonhardt, Fritz 1909- CANR-49
Earlier sketch in CA 123
Leonhardt, Rudolf Walter 1921- CANR-3
Earlier sketch in CA 9-12R
Leoni, Edgar (Hugh) 1925- CANR-38
Earlier sketch in CA 125
Leonov, Leonid (Maximovich) 1899-1994 129
See also CLC 92
See also DAM NOV
See also MTCW 1
Leonowens, Anna 1834-1914 .... DLB 99, 166
Leon-Portilla, Miguel 1926- CANR-32
Earlier sketches in CA 21-24R, CANR-11
See also HW
Leontiades, Milton 1932- 110
Leontief, Wassily 1906- CAP-1
Earlier sketch in CA 17-18
Leontyev, Lev Abramovich
1901-1974 Obituary 49-52
Leopold, A(ldo) Starker 1913-1983 Obituary 110
Leopold, Aldo 1886-1948 141
Leopold, Allison Kyle 1955- 112
Leopold, Carolyn Clugston 1923- 73-76
Leopold, Christopher
See Synge, Allen
Leopold, Luna B(ergere) 1915- CANR-31
Earlier sketch in CA 49-52
Leopold, Nathan F. 1904-1971 .... CAP-1
Obituary 29-32R
Earlier sketch in CA 13-16
Leopold, Richard William 1912- CANR-2
Earlier sketch in CA 1-4R
Leopold, Werner F. 1896- 45-48
Leopold III 1901-1983 Obituary 110
Lepage, Robert 1957- 162
Le Pan, Douglas (Valentine) 1914- 129
Brief entry 117
See also DLB 88
Le Patourel, John Herbert 1909-1981 .... CAP-1
Obituary 104
Earlier sketch in CA 9-10
Lepawsky, Albert 1908- 45-48
Le Pelley, Guernsey 1910- 81-84
Lepetit, Charles
See Sala, Charles
Lepidus, Henry 1916(?)-1983 Obituary 110
Lepko, E.
See Kopelev, Lev (Zinovievich)
Lepley, Jean Elizabeth 1934- 69-72
Lepley, Paul M(ichael) 1933- 53-56
Le Poer Trench, (William Francis) Brinsley
1911- Brief entry 116
Lepore, D(ominick) J(ames) 1911- 45-48
Le Poulain, Jean 1924-1988 Obituary 125
Lepovitz, Helena Waddy 1945- 135
Lepp, Henry 1922- 53-56
Leppmann, Peter K. 1931- 25-28R
Leppmann, Wolfgang Arthur 1922- CANR-37
Earlier sketch in CA 1-4R
Leppzer, Robert 1958- 105
Leprohon, Pierre 1903- CANR-1
Earlier sketch in CA 45-48
Leprohon, Rosanna Eleanor 1829-1879 .... DLB 99
Le Quesne, A(lfred) L(aurence) 1928- 116
Le Quesne, Laurence
See Le Quesne, A(lfred) L(aurence)
Le Queux, William (Tufnell) 1864-1927 Brief
entry 109
See also DLB 70
Lerangis, Peter 1955- .... SATA 72
Lerbinger, Otto 1925- 21-24R
Lerche, Charles O(lsen), Jr. 1918-1966 .... 5-8R
Le Reveler
See Artaud, Antonin (Marie Joseph)
le Riche, William Harding 1916- 107
Lerman, Eleanor 1952- CANR-69
Earlier sketch in CA 85-88
See also CLC 9
Lerman, Leo 1914-1994 45-48
Obituary 146
Lerman, Paul 1926- 97-100
Lerman, Rhoda 1936- CANR-70
Earlier sketch in CA 49-52
See also CLC 56
Lermontov, Mikhail Yuryevich 1814-1841 .... PC 18
Lernat-Holenia, Alexander 1898(?)-1976 ... DLB 85
Lerner, Aaron Bunsen 1920- 108
See also SATA 35
Lerner, Abba P(tachya) 1903-1982 .... CANR-2
Obituary 108
Earlier sketch in CA 1-4R
Lerner, Alan Jay 1918-1986 .... CANR-31
Obituary 119
Earlier sketch in CA 77-80
Lerner, Andrea 1954- 134
Lerner, Arthur 1915-1998 102
Obituary 167
Lerner, Carol 1927- CANR-70
Earlier sketch in CA 102
See also CLR 34
See also SAAS 12
See also SATA 33, 86
Lerner, Daniel 1917-1980 .... CANR-6
Obituary 97-100
Earlier sketch in CA 1-4R
Lerner, Eugene Max 1928- 17-20R
Lerner, Gerda 1920- CANR-70
Earlier sketches in CA 25-28R, CANR-26, 45
See also SATA 65
Lerner, Harriet 1944- 168
See also SATA 101
Lerner, Herbert J. 1933- 53-56
Lerner, I. Michael 1910- 41-44R
Lerner, Janet W(eiss) 1926- CANR-7
Earlier sketch in CA 57-60
Lerner, Joel J. 1936- 53-56
Lerner, Laurence (David) 1925- CANR-20
Earlier sketches in CA 5-8R, CANR-3
Lerner, Lily Gluck 1928- 117
Lerner, Linda 73-76
Lerner, Louis A. 1935-1984 Obituary 114
Lerner, Marguerite Rush 1924-1987 .... 13-16R
Obituary 122
See also SATA 11
See also SATA-Obit 51
Lerner, Martin 1936- 141
Lerner, Maura 1953- 97-100
Lerner, Max(well Alan) 1902-1992 .... CANR-25
Obituary 137
Earlier sketch in CA 13-16R
See also AITN 1
See also DLB 29
Lerner, Michael G(ordon) 1943- 49-52
Lerner, Michael P(hillip) 1943- 45-48
Lerner, Richard E(dward) 1941- 73-76
Lerner, Richard M(artin) 1946- 93-96
Lerner, Robert E. 1940- CANR-8
Earlier sketch in CA 21-24R
Lerner, Sharon (Ruth) 1938-1982 .... CANR-3
Obituary 106
Earlier sketch in CA 5-8R
See also SATA 11
See also SATA-Obit 29
Lerner, Steve 1946- 167
Lerner, Warren 1929- 29-32R
Lernet-Holenia, Alexander
1898(?)-1976 Obituary 65-68
Lernoux, Penny (Mary) 1940-1989 77-80
Obituary 129
Leroe, Ellen W(hitney) 1949- CANR-40
Earlier sketch in CA 116
See also SATA 61, 99
See also SATA-Brief 51
Le Roi, David (de Roche) 1905- CANR-3
Earlier sketch in CA 9-12R
Leroi-Gourhan, Andre (Georges Leandre)
1911-1986 Obituary 118
Le Rossignol, James 1866-1969 148
See also DLB 92
Leroux, Etienne
See Leroux, S(tephanus) P(etrus) D(aniel)
Leroux, Gaston 1868-1927 .... CANR-69
Brief entry 108
Earlier sketch in CA 136
See also SATA 65
See also TCLC 25
Leroux, S(tephanus) P(etrus) D(aniel) 1922- ....
CANR-2
Earlier sketch in CA 49-52
Le Roy, Bruce Murdock 1920- Brief entry 106
LeRoy, Dave
See LeRoy, (Lemuel) David
LeRoy, (Lemuel) David 1920- 81-84
LeRoy, Douglas 1943- CANR-18
Earlier sketches in CA 49-52, CANR-3
LeRoy, Gaylord C. 1910- 37-40R
LeRoy, Gen 134
Brief entry 115
See also SATA 52
See also SATA-Brief 36
Leroy, Gilles 1958- 157
Leroy, Maurice (A. L.) 1909- 25-28R
LeRoy, Mervyn 1900-1987 166
Obituary 123
Brief entry 108
Le Roy Ladurie, Emmanuel (Bernard) 1929- ....
CANR-49
Earlier sketch in CA 113
Lerrigo, Marion Olive 1898-1968 Obituary 109
See also SATA-Obit 29
Lerro, Anthony Joseph 1932- 33-36R
Lerski, George Jan 1917- 73-76
Lerteth, Oban
See Fanthorpe, R(obert) Lionel
Lerude, Warren (Leslie) 1937- 146
Brief entry 122
Le Sage, Laurent 1913- CANR-25
Earlier sketch in CA 1-4R
Lescarbot, Marc c. 1570-1642 .... DLB 99
Lesch, David W. 1960- 167
Lesch, John E(mmett) 1945- 132
Leschak, Peter M. 1951- CANR-52
Earlier sketch in CA 126
Lescoe, Francis J(oseph) 1916- 61-64
Lescroart, John T. 1948- CANR-61
Earlier sketch in CA 122
Lesesne, J(oab) Mauldin 1899- CAP-2
Earlier sketch in CA 33-36
LeShan, Eda J(oan) 1922- CANR-21
Earlier sketch in CA 13-16R
See also CLR 6
See also SATA 21
LeShan, Lawrence L(ee) 1920- CANR-21
Earlier sketch in CA 17-20R
Le Shana, David C(harles) 1932- 29-32R
Lesher, Phyllis A(senath Bayers) 1912- .. CANR-17
Earlier sketch in CA 25-28R
Lesher, Stephan 1935- 103
Leshoai, Benjamin Letholoa 1920- 153
See also BW 2
LeSieg, Theo.
See Geisel, Theodor Seuss
Lesieur, Henry R(ichard) 1946- 77-80
Lesikar, Raymond Vincent 1922- CANR-2
Earlier sketch in CA 1-4R
Lesikin, Joan 1947- 93-96
Lesins, Knuts 1909- 73-76
Lesko, George 1932- 17-20R
Lesko, Leonard Henry 1938- CANR-8
Earlier sketch in CA 61-64
Lesko, Wendy
See Schaetzel, Wendy
Lesky, Albin (Hans) 1896- 85-88
Leslau, Wolf 1906- 104
Lesley, Blake
See Duckworth, Leslie Blakey
Lesley, Cole
See Cole, Leonard Leslie
Leslie, A. L.
See Lazarus, A(rnold) L(eslie)
Leslie, Aleen 5-8R
Leslie, Anita 1914-1985 .... CANR-32
Obituary 117
Earlier sketch in CA 49-52
Leslie, Anne
See Leslie, Anita
Leslie, Cecilie 1914- 17-20R
Leslie, Charles M. 1923- 5-8R
Leslie, Clare Walker 1947- 108
Leslie, Conrad 1923- 29-32R
Leslie, Desmond 1921- 9-12R

Leslie, Donald Daniel 1922- ... 102
Leslie, Doris
See Fergusson Hannay, Doris
Leslie, Eliza 1787-1858 ... DLB 202
Leslie, F(rederic) Andrew 1927- ... CANR-7
Earlier sketch in CA 17-20R
Leslie, Frank 1821-1880 ... DLB 43, 79
Leslie, Gerald R(onnell) 1925- ... 17-20R
Leslie, Jane
See Coade, Jessie
Leslie, John 1944- ... CANR-71
Earlier sketch in CA 148
Leslie, John Andrew 1940- ... CANR-56
Earlier sketches in CA 112, CANR-30
Leslie, Josephine Aimee Campbell
1898-1979 ... 85-88
Leslie, Kenneth 1892-1974 ... 93-96
Obituary ... 53-56
Leslie, (Virginia) Kent A(nderson) 1942- ... 149
Leslie, Michael 1952- ... 118
Leslie, O. H.
See Slesar, Henry
Leslie, Phil 1909(?)-1988 Obituary ... 126
Leslie, Richard
See Bickers, Richard (Leslie) Townshend
Leslie, Robert B.
See Wooley, John (Steven)
Leslie, Robert C(ampbell) 1917- ... 33-36R
Leslie, Robert Franklin 1911- ... CANR-28
Earlier sketch in CA 49-52
See also SATA 7
Leslie, Rochelle
See Diamond, Graham
Leslie, Roy F. 1922- ... 41-44R
Leslie, S(amuel) Clement 1898- ... 85-88
Leslie, San
See Crook, Bette (Jean)
Leslie, Sarah
See McGuire, Leslie (Sarah)
Leslie, Seymour 1890(?)-1979 Obituary ... 89-92
Leslie, (John Randolph) Shane
1885-1971 Obituary ... 33-36R
Leslie, Sir Shane
See Leslie, (John Randolph) Shane
Leslie, Ward S.
See Ward, Elizabeth Honor (Shedden)
Leslie, Warren III 1927- ... 9-12R
Leslie-Melville, Betty 1929- ... 81-84
Leslie-Melville, Jock
See Leslie-Melville, John D.
Leslie-Melville, John D. 1933-1984 ... 81-84
Obituary ... 112
Lesly, Philip 1918- ... CANR-44
Earlier sketches in CA 81-84, CANR-14
Lesniak, Rose 1955- ... 147
Lesnoff-Caravaglia, Gari ... 41-44R
LeSourd, Catherine
See Marshall, (Sarah) Catherine (Wood)
LeSourd, Leonard (Earle) 1919-1996 ... 135
Obituary ... 151
Lesourne, Jacques 1928- ... 142
Lesowitz, Robert I(rwin) 1939- ... 57-60
Lesperance, John 1835(?)-1891 ... DLB 99
L'Esperance, Wilford L(ouis) III 1930-1982 ...
CANR-27
Earlier sketch in CA 33-36R
Lessa, William A(rmand) 1908- ... 61-64
Lessac, Arthur 1910- Brief entry ... 110
Lessac, Frane 1954- ... 127
See also SATA 61
Lessard, Michel 1942- ... 104
Lessard, Suzannah ... 166
Lessel, William M. 1906- ... CAP-2
Earlier sketch in CA 33-36
Lessem, Don 1951- ... 164
See also SATA 97
Lesser, Alexander 1902-1982 ... CANR-28
Obituary ... 107
Earlier sketch in CA 49-52
Lesser, Charles H(uber) 1944- ... 73-76
Lesser, Eugene (Bernard) 1936- ... 49-52
Lesser, Gerald S(amuel) 1926- ... 97-100
Lesser, Margaret 1899(?)-1979 Obituary ... 93-96
See also SATA-Obit 22
Lesser, Michael 1939- ... 102
Lesser, Milton
See Marlowe, Stephen
Lesser, R(oger) H(arold) 1928- ... CANR-14
Earlier sketch in CA 73-76
Lesser, Rika 1953- ... 118
See also SATA 53
Lesser, Robert C. 1933- ... 104
Lesser, Wendy 1952- ... 140
Lessere, Samuel E. 1892- ... CAP-2
Earlier sketch in CA 21-22
Lessing, Bruno 1870-1940 ... DLB 28
Lessing, Doris (May) 1919- ... CANR-54
Earlier sketches in CA 9-12R, CANR-33
See also CAAS 14
See also CDBLB 1960 to Present
See also CLC 1, 2, 3, 6, 10, 15, 22, 40, 94
See also DA
See also DAB
See also DAC
See also DAM MST, NOV
See also DLB 15, 139
See also DLBY 85
See also MTCW 1
See also SSC 6
See also WLCS
Lessing, Gotthold Ephraim 1729-1781 ... DLB 97
Lessiter, Mike (J.) 1969- ... 135
Lessler, Richard Sigmund 1924- ... 1-4R
Lessmann, Paul G. 1919- ... 17-20R
LesStrang, Jacques 1926- ... CANR-17
Earlier sketch in CA 65-68
Lester, Alison 1952- ... CANR-52
Earlier sketch in CA 125
See also SATA 50, 90
Lester, Andrew D(ouglas) 1939- ... CANR-54
Earlier sketches in CA 109, CANR-26
Lester, Anthony 1936- ... 37-40R
Lester, David 1942- ... CANR-57
Earlier sketches in CA 33-36R, CANR-12, 31
Lester, Frank
See Usher, Frank (Hugh)
Lester, Gene
See Mercer, Jean
Lester, Godfrey Allen 1943- ... CANR-28
Earlier sketch in CA 111
Lester, Helen 1936- ... CANR-58
Earlier sketches in CA 115, CANR-38
See also SATA 46, 92
Lester, James
See Blake, L(eslie) J(ames)
Lester, James D. 1935- ... CANR-15
Earlier sketch in CA 89-92
Lester, James P(inkney) 1944- ... CANR-35
Earlier sketch in CA 114
Lester, John
See Werner, Vivian
Lester, Julius (Bernard) 1939- ... CANR-43
Earlier sketches in CA 17-20R, CANR-8, 23
See also AAYA 12
See also BW 2
See also CLR 2, 41
See also JRDA
See also MAICYA
See also SATA 12, 74
Lester, Margot Carmichael 1962- ... 164
Lester, Mark
See Russell, Martin
Lester, Reginald Mounstephens 1896- ... CAP-1
Earlier sketch in CA 9-10
Lester, Richard 1932- ... CLC 20
Lester, Richard A(llen) 1908-1997 ... 102
Obituary ... 163
Lester, Robert C(arlton) 1933- ... 73-76
Lester, Tanya 1956- ... 138
Lester, William ... 57-60
Lester-Rands, A.
See Judd, Frederick Charles
LeStourgeon, Diana E. 1927- ... 13-16R
L'Estrange, Anna
See Ellerbeck, Rosemary (Anne L'Estrange)
Le Sueur, Lucille 1908(?)-1977 Obituary ... 111
Le Sueur, Meridel 1900-1996 ... CANR-30
Obituary ... 154
Earlier sketches in CA 49-52, CANR-2
See also SATA 6
LeSueur, Stephen C. 1952- ... 133
LeSueur, William Dawson 1840-1917 ... DLB 92
Lesure, Francois 1923- Brief entry ... 108
Lesure, Thomas B(arbour) 1923- ... 102
Leszlei, Marta
See Dosa, Marta Leszlei
L'Etang, Hugh J(oseph) C(harles) J(ames)
1917- ... 45-48
LeTarte, Clyde E(dward) 1938- ... 53-56
Letellier, Robert Ignatius 1953- ... 151
Leterman, Elmer G. 1897- ... 25-28R
Letessier, Dorothee 1953- ... 158
Lethbridge, Rex
See Meyers, Roy (Lethbridge)
Lethbridge, Robert (David) 1947- ... 135
Lethbridge, T(homas) C(harles) 1901-1971 ... CAP-2
Earlier sketch in CA 29-32
Lethem, Jonathan (Allen) 1964- ... 150
Letiche, John M(arion) 1918- ... 49-52
Letley, Emma 1949- ... 131
Letnanova, Elena 1942- ... 140
Le Tord, Bijou 1945- ... CANR-68
Earlier sketches in CA 65-68, CANR-31
See also SATA 49, 95
LeTourneau, Richard (Howard) 1925- ... CANR-23
Earlier sketches in CA 53-56, CANR-7
Letrusco
See Martini, Virgilio
Lettau, Reinhard 1929-1996 ... CANR-70
Earlier sketches in CA 17-20R, CANR-9
See also DLB 75
Lette, Kathy 1958- ... 136
Letterman, David (Michael) 1947- ... 139
See also AAYA 10
Letterman, Edward John 1926- ... 29-32R
Lettis, Richard 1928- ... 5-8R
Letts, Billie 1938- ... 151
Lettvin, Maggie 1927- ... 73-76
Letwin, Shirley Robin 1924-1993 ... 17-20R
Obituary ... 141
Letwin, William L(ouis) 1922- ... 9-12R
Leuba, Clarence J(ames) 1899- ... 37-40R
Leubsdorf, Carl P(hilipp) 1938- ... 73-76
Leuchtenburg, William E(dward) 1922- ... CANR-12
Earlier sketch in CA 5-8R
Leuci, Bob
See Leuci, Robert
Leuci, Robert 1940- ... CANR-50
Earlier sketch in CA 125
Leuck, Laura 1962- ... SATA 85
Leukel, Francis 1922- ... 53-56
Leung, John K(ong-cheong) 1949- ... 127
Leupp, Gary P. 1956- ... 144
Leuthner, Stuart 1939- ... 125
Leuthold, David Allen 1932- ... 21-24R
Leutscher, Alfred (George) 1913- ... 73-76
See also SATA 23
Lev, Daniel S(aul) 1933- ... 41-44R
Lev, Peter 1948- ... 146
Levack, Brian P(aul) 1943- ... 53-56
Levai, Blaise 1919- ... 108
See also SATA 39
Levant, Howard 1929- ... 89-92
Levant, Oscar 1906-1972 Obituary ... 37-40R
Levant, Victor 1947- ... CANR-52
Earlier sketch in CA 126
Levantrosser, William F(rederick) 1925- ... 21-24R
Levanway, Russell W(ilford) 1919- Brief entry ... 107
Levarie, Siegmund 1914- ... 13-16R
Le Vay, David 1915- ... 89-92
LeVay, Simon 1943- ... 142
Levell, Byrd 1911(?)-1979 Obituary ... 89-92
Levelt, Willem J(ohannes) M(aria) 1938- ... 133
Leven, Charles L(ouis) 1928- ... CANR-14
Earlier sketch in CA 41-44R
Leven, Jeremy 1941- ... 102
Levendosky, Charles (Leonard) 1936- ... CANR-12
Earlier sketch in CA 29-32R
Levene, Malcolm 1937- ... 45-48
Levene, Mark 1953- ... 142
Levenkron, Steven 1941- ... CANR-52
Earlier sketch in CA 109
See also SATA 86
Levenson, Alan Ira 1935- ... 45-48
Levenson, Alec R. 1966- ... 150
Levenson, Christopher 1934- ... 29-32R
Levenson, Dorothy (Perkins) 1927- ... 9-12R
Levenson, Edgar A. 1924- ... 128
Brief entry ... 108
Levenson, J(acob) C(lavner) 1922- ... 25-28R
Levenson, Jordan 1936- ... CANR-23
Earlier sketches in CA 57-60, CANR-7
Levenson, Joseph Richmond 1920-1969 ... CANR-6
Earlier sketch in CA 1-4R
Levenson, Myron H(erbert) 1926-1974 ... 53-56
Levenson, Sam(uel) 1911-1980 ... CANR-26
Obituary ... 101
Earlier sketch in CA 65-68
See also AITN 1
Levenson, William B. 1907- ... CAP-2
Earlier sketch in CA 25-28
Levenstein, Aaron 1910-1986 ... CAP-1
Obituary ... 119
Earlier sketch in CA 19-20
Levenstein, Harvey A(llan) 1938- ... 106
Levenstein, Sidney 1917- ... 9-12R
Leventhal, Albert Rice 1907-1976 ... 65-68
Obituary ... 61-64
Leventhal, Bennett (L.) 1949- ... 135
Leventhal, Donald B(ecker) 1930- ... 45-48
Leventhal, Fred Marc 1938- Brief entry ... 109
Leventhal, Herbert 1941- ... 69-72
Leventhal, Lance A. 1945- ... CANR-27
Earlier sketch in CA 110
Leventman, Seymour 1930- ... CANR-1
Earlier sketch in CA 1-4R
Lever, Charles (James) 1806-1872 ... DLB 21
Lever, (Tresham) Christopher (Arthur Lindsay)
1932- ... 136
Lever, J(ulius) W(alter) 1913-1975 ... CAP-2
Obituary ... 61-64
Earlier sketch in CA 23-24
Lever, Janet 1946- ... 85-88
Lever, Judy 1947- ... 107
Lever, Katherine 1916- ... 17-20R
Lever, Tresham (Joseph Philip) 1900-1975 ... 13-16R
Obituary ... 57-60
Lever, Walter
See Lever, J(ulius) W(alter)
Levere, Trevor H(arvey) 1944- ... 147
Leverence, William John 1946- ... 102
Leverich, Kathleen 1948- ... 137
Levering, Frank (Graham) 1952- ... CANR-43
Earlier sketch in CA 119
Levering, Ralph (Brooks) 1947- ... 85-88
Levering, Robert 1944- ... 160
Leverson, Ada 1865(?)-1936(?) Brief entry ... 117
See also Elaine
See also DLB 153
See also TCLC 18
LeVert, (William) John 1946- ... 122
See also SATA 55
Levert, Liberte E.
See Bleiler, Everett F(ranklin)
Levertov, Denise 1923-1997 ... CANR-50
Obituary ... 163
Earlier sketches in CA 1-4R, CANR-3, 29
Interview in ... CANR-29
See also CAAS 19
See also CLC 1, 2, 3, 5, 8, 15, 28, 66
See also DAM POET
See also DLB 5, 165
See also MTCW 1
See also PC 11
Levesque, John 1953- ... 165
Levesque, Rene 1922-1987 Obituary ... 125
Levey, Martin 1913-1970 ... CANR-10
Earlier sketch in CA 13-16R
Levey, Michael (Vincent) 1927- ... CANR-25
Earlier sketches in CA 5-8R, CANR-4
Levey, Samuel 1932- ... CANR-2
Earlier sketch in CA 45-48
Levi, Albert William 1911- Brief entry ... 107
Levi, Anthony H(erbert) T(igar) 1929- ... CANR-24
Earlier sketches in CA 13-16R, CANR-9
Levi, Barbara Goss 1943- ... 144
Levi, Carlo 1902-1975 ... CANR-10
Obituary ... 53-56
Earlier sketch in CA 65-68
Levi, Darrell E(rville) 1940- ... 131
Levi, Edward H(irsch) 1911- ... CANR-2
Earlier sketch in CA 49-52
Levi, Gershon
See Levi, S(amuel) Gershon
Levi, Hans 1935- ... 41-44R
Levi, Helen I(sabel) 1929- ... 117
Levi, Isaac 1930- ... 97-100
Levi, Jonathan ... CLC 76
Levi, Julian (Edwin) 1900-1982 Obituary ... 106
Levi, Lennart 1930- ... CANR-8
Earlier sketch in CA 17-20R
Levi, Maurice (David) 1945- ... CANR-43
Earlier sketch in CA 111
Levi, Peter (Chad Tigar) 1931- ... CANR-34
Earlier sketch in CA 5-8R
See also CLC 41
See also DLB 40
Levi, Primo 1919-1987 ... CANR-70
Obituary ... 122
Earlier sketches in CA 13-16R, CANR-12, 33, 61
See also CLC 37, 50
See also DLB 177
See also MTCW 1
See also SSC 12
Levi, S(amuel) Gershon 1908-1990 Obituary ... 131
Levi, Vicki Gold 1941- ... 101
Levi, Werner 1912- ... CANR-37
Earlier sketches in CA 25-28R, CANR-16
Levi, Y. Leo 1926- ... CANR-36
Earlier sketch in CA 114
Leviatin, David 1961- ... 130
Levi-Civita, Tullio 1873-1941 ... 163
Levi D'Ancona, Mirella
See D'Ancona, Mirella Levi
LeVie, Donn, Jr. 1951- ... 134
Levien, Sonya
See Hovey, Sonya
See also DLB 44
Levi-Montalcini, Rita 1909- ... 149
Levin, Alexandra Lee 1912- ... 9-12R
Levin, Alfred 1908- ... 13-16R
Levin, Alvin Irving 1921- ... CANR-1
Earlier sketch in CA 45-48
Levin, Amy K. 1957- ... 145
Levin, Beatrice Schwartz 1920- ... CANR-18
Earlier sketches in CA 9-12R, CANR-3
Levin, Benjamin H. ... 49-52
Levin, Betty 1927- ... CANR-53
Earlier sketches in CA 65-68, CANR-9, 25, 50
See also AAYA 23
See also SAAS 11
See also SATA 19, 84
Levin, Bob
See Levin, Robert A.
Levin, Dan 1914- Brief entry ... 108
Levin, David 1924- ... CANR-8
Earlier sketch in CA 5-8R
Levin, Donna 1954- ... 134
Levin, Doron P. 1950- ... 130
Levin, Gail 1948- ... CANR-53
Earlier sketch in CA 102
Levin, Gerald H(enry) 1929- ... CANR-33
Earlier sketches in CA 33-36R, CANR-15
Levin, Harold L(eonard) 1929- ... 93-96
Levin, Harry (Tuchman) 1912-1994 ... CANR-2
Obituary ... 145
Earlier sketch in CA 1-4R
Levin, Harry 1925- ... 109
Levin, Harvey J(oshua) 1924-1992 ... 9-12R
Obituary ... 137
Levin, Henry M(ordecai) 1938- ... 122
Levin, Igor 1931- ... 144
Levin, Ira 1929- ... CANR-44
Earlier sketches in CA 21-24R, CANR-17
See also CLC 3, 6
See also DAM POP
See also MTCW 1
See also SATA 66
Levin, Irina 1937- ... 144
Levin, Jack 1941- ... CANR-41
Earlier sketches in CA 53-56, CANR-4, 19
Levin, James (Benesch) 1940- ... 111
Levin, Jane Whitbread 1914- Brief entry ... 106
Levin, Jenifer 1955- ... CANR-26
Earlier sketch in CA 108
Levin, John 1944- ... 107
Levin, Jonathan V(ictor) 1927- ... 9-12R
Levin, Kenneth 1944- Brief entry ... 115
Levin, Kim ... 73-76
Levin, Kristine Cox 1944- ... 65-68
Levin, Marcia Obrasky 1918- ... 13-16R
See also SATA 13
Levin, Marlin 1921- ... CANR-9
Earlier sketch in CA 65-68
Levin, Meyer 1905-1981 ... CANR-15
Obituary ... 104
Earlier sketch in CA 9-12R
See also AITN 1
See also CLC 7
See also DAM POP
See also DLB 9, 28
See also DLBY 81
See also SATA 21
See also SATA-Obit 27
Levin, Michael (Graubart) 1958- ... 135
Levin, Michael Eric 1943- ... 131
Levin, Milton 1925- ... 25-28R
Levin, Miriam (Ramsfelder) 1962- ... 164
See also SATA 97
Levin, Molly Apple ... 61-64
Levin, N. Gordon, Jr. 1935- ... 25-28R
Levin, Nora 1916-1989 ... 25-28R
Obituary ... 130
Levin, Richard Louis 1922- ... 1-4R
Levin, Robert A. 1942- ... 81-84
Levin, Robert E. 1955- ... 160
Levin, Robert J. 1921(?)-1976 Obituary ... 65-68
Levin, Saul 1921- ... 13-16R
Levin, William C. 1946- ... 105
Levine, A(aron) L(awrence) 1925- ... 21-24R
Levine, Abby 1943- ... 126
See also SATA 54
See also SATA-Brief 52
Levine, Adeline 1925- ... 49-52

Levine, Allan 1956- ... 135
Levine, Andrew 1944- ... 65-68
Levine, Arthur E(lliott) 1948- ... 73-76
Levine, Barbara Hoberman 1937- ... 139
Levine, Barry B(ernard) 1941- ... 101
Levine, Bernard 1934- ... 29-32R
Levine, Betty K(rasne) 1933- ... 93-96
See also SATA 66
Levine, Bob
See Levine, Robert
Levine, Caroline Anne 1942- ... 89-92
Levine, Charles H(oward) 1939-1988 ... CANR-35
Obituary ... 126
Earlier sketches in CA 89-92, CANR-15
Levine, Daniel 1934- ... 13-16R
Levine, Daniel H(arris) 1942- ... 73-76
Levine, Daniel Urey 1935- ... 57-60
Levine, David 1926- ... 116
Brief entry ... 113
See also SATA 43
See also SATA-Brief 35
Levine, David 1928- ... 17-20R
Levine, David O(scar) 1955- ... 124
Levine, Donald N(athan) 1931- ... 53-56
Levine, Edna S(imon) ... 85-88
See also SATA 35
Levine, Edward M(onroe) 1924- ... 21-24R
Levine, Edwin Burton 1920- ... 25-28R
Levine, Ellen 1939- ... CANR-22
Earlier sketch in CA 69-72
Levine, Erwin L(eon) 1926- ... 9-12R
Levine, Evan 1962- ... 145
See also SATA 74, 77
Levine, Faye (Iris) 1944- ... CANR-3
Earlier sketch in CA 49-52
Levine, Frederick S(pencer) 1945- ... 120
Levine, Gail Carson 1947- ... 166
See also SATA 98
Levine, Gary 1938- ... 61-64
Levine, Gene N(orman) 1930- ... 5-8R
Levine, George 1931- ... CANR-42
Earlier sketches in CA 25-28R, CANR-20
Levine, George R. 1929- ... 21-24R
Levine, Gustav 1926- ... 149
Levine, Herbert S(amuel) 1928- ... 128
Brief entry ... 107
Levine, I(srael) E. 1923- ... CANR-1
Earlier sketch in CA 1-4R
See also SATA 12
Levine, Irving R(askin) 1922- ... 13-16R
Levine, Isaac Don 1892-1981 ... CANR-11
Obituary ... 103
Earlier sketch in CA 13-16R
Levine, Isidore N. 1909-1972 ... 41-44R
Levine, Israel 1893(?)-1988(?) Obituary ... 125
Levine, Jeffrey P. 1957- ... 168
Levine, Joan Goldman ... 61-64
See also SATA 11
Levine, Joel S. 1942- ... 165
Levine, John R. 1954- ... 150
Levine, Joseph 1910- ... 108
See also SATA 33
Levine, Judith 1952- ... 139
Levine, Laurence William 1931- ... 103
Levine, Lawrence 1916- ... 9-12R
Levine, Lawrence W(illiam) 1933- ... 145
Brief entry ... 115
Levine, Lois (Elaine) L. 1931- ... 106
Levine, Louis 1921- Brief entry ... 116
Levine, Marge 1934- ... SATA 81
Levine, Mark Lee 1943- ... CANR-2
Earlier sketch in CA 49-52
Levine, Marvin J. 1930- ... CANR-21
Earlier sketch in CA 45-48
Levine, Maurice 1902-1971 ... 85-88
Levine, Michael 1939- ... 133
Levine, Michael 1954- ... 89-92
Levine, Milton I(sra) 1902-1993 ... 109
Obituary ... 143
Levine, Miriam 1939- ... 116
Levine, Mortimer 1922- ... 17-20R
Levine, Murray 1928- ... CANR-29
Earlier sketch in CA 49-52
Levine, Nancy D. 1955- ... 146
Levine, Norman 1924- ... CANR-70
Earlier sketches in CA 73-76, CANR-14
See also CAAS 23
See also CLC 54
See also DLB 88
Levine, Norman D(ion) 1912- ... 85-88
Levine, Paul (J.) 1948- ... CANR-72
Earlier sketch in CA 137
Levine, Peter D. 1944- ... CANR-52
Earlier sketch in CA 126
Levine, Philip 1928- ... CANR-52
Earlier sketches in CA 9-12R, CANR-9, 37
See also CLC 2, 4, 5, 9, 14, 33
See also DAM POET
See also DLB 5
See also PC 22
Levine, Rhoda ... 73-76
See also SATA 14
Levine, Robert 1944- ... 121
LeVine, Robert A(lan) 1932- ... CANR-13
Earlier sketch in CA 21-24R
Levine, Robert M. 1910(?)-1981 Obituary ... 108
Levine, Robert M. 1941- ... CANR-11
Earlier sketch in CA 21-24R
Levine, Sarah 1970- ... 125
See also SATA 57
Levine, Saul V. 1938- ... 123
Levine, Sol 1914-1987 ... 9-12R
Obituary ... 124
Levine, Solomon B. 1920- ... 104
Levine, Stacey 1960- ... 145
Levine, Stephen 1937- ... CANR-35
Earlier sketch in CA 45-48
Levine, Stuart (George) 1932- ... 17-20R
Levine, Suzanne Jill 1946- ... CANR-31
Earlier sketches in CA 49-52, CANR-13
LeVine, Victor T(heodore) 1928- ... 13-16R
Levine-Freidus, Gail
See Provost, Gail Levine
Levine-Shneidman, Conalee 1930- ... 119
Levinger, George 1927- ... CANR-2
Earlier sketch in CA 49-52
Levins, Richard 1930- ... 119
Levinsohn, Florence H(amlish) 1926- ... 132
Levinson, Alan 1943- ... 150
Levinson, Barry 1942- ... 149
See also AAYA 25
Levinson, Boris M(ayer) 1907-1984 ... CANR-13
Obituary ... 112
Earlier sketch in CA 33-36R
Levinson, Charles 1920- ... CANR-21
Earlier sketch in CA 45-48
Levinson, Daniel Jacob 1920-1994 ... 102
Obituary ... 145
Levinson, Deirdre 1931- ... CANR-70
Earlier sketch in CA 73-76
See also CLC 49
Levinson, Harold M(yer) 1919- ... 21-24R
Levinson, Harry 1922- ... CANR-29
Earlier sketches in CA 1-4R, CANR-1
Levinson, Henry Samuel 1948- ... CANR-26
Earlier sketch in CA 109
Levinson, Horace C(lifford) 1895-(?) ... CAP-1
Earlier sketch in CA 19-20
Levinson, Irene
See Zahava, Irene
Levinson, Jerrold 1948- ... 156
Levinson, Leonard 1935- ... CANR-31
Earlier sketches in CA 77-80, CANR-14
Levinson, Leonard L. 1905(?)-1974 Obituary ... 45-48
Levinson, Marjorie 1951- ... 127
Levinson, Nancy Smiler 1938- ... CANR-47
Earlier sketches in CA 107, CANR-23
See also SATA 33, 80
Levinson, Olga May ... 103
Levinson, Richard (Leighton) 1934-1987 ... CANR-41
Obituary ... 121
Earlier sketches in CA 73-76, CANR-13
Levinson, Riki ... CANR-37
Earlier sketch in CA 121
See also MAICYA
See also SATA 52, 99
See also SATA-Brief 49
Levinson, Robert E. 1925- ... 132
Levinthal, Charles F(rederick) 1945- ... CANR-54
Earlier sketch in CA 127
Levinthal, Israel Herbert 1888- ... 13-16R
Levis, Donald J(ames) 1936- ... 41-44R
Levis, Larry (Patrick) 1946-1996 ... CANR-71
Obituary ... 152
Earlier sketch in CA 77-80
See also CAAS 23
See also DLB 120
Levison, Andrew 1948- ... 93-96
Levi-Strauss, Claude 1908- ... CANR-57
Earlier sketches in CA 1-4R, CANR-6, 32
See also CLC 38
See also MTCW 1
Levit, Herschel 1912- ... 111
Levit, Martin 1918- ... 45-48
Levit, Rose 1922- ... 73-76
Levitan, Donald 1928- ... 104
Levitan, Max 1921- ... 53-56
Levitan, Sar A. 1914-1994 ... CANR-3
Obituary ... 145
Earlier sketch in CA 9-12R
Levitan, Tina (Nellie) 1928- ... 9-12R
Levitas, Gloria B(arach) 1931- ... CANR-21
Earlier sketch in CA 45-48
Levitas, Louise
See Henriksen, Louise Levitas
Levitas, Maurice 1917- ... 77-80
Levitch, Joel A. 1942- ... 37-40R
Levith, Murray J(ay) 1939- ... 81-84
Levitin, Sonia (Wolff) 1934- ... CANR-32
Earlier sketches in CA 29-32R, CANR-14
See also AAYA 13
See also CLC 17
See also JRDA
See also MAICYA
See also SAAS 2
See also SATA 4, 68
Levitine, George 1916- ... 41-44R
Levitsky, David A(aron) 1942- ... 116
Levitt, B. Blake 1948- ... 139
Levitt, I(srael) M(onroe) 1908- ... 45-48
Levitt, Jesse 1919- ... 45-48
Levitt, Leonard 1941- ... 104
Levitt, Morris J(acob) 1938- ... CANR-15
Earlier sketch in CA 41-44R
Levitt, Mortimer 1907- ... 118
Levitt, Morton 1920- ... 61-64
Levitt, Morton P(aul) 1936- ... CANR-43
Earlier sketch in CA 111
Levitt, Saul 1911-1977 ... 81-84
Obituary ... 73-76
Levitt, Sidney (Mark) 1947- ... SATA 68
Levitzky, Sergei A. 1909-1983 Obituary ... 110
Levon, Fred
See Ayvazian, L. Fred
Levon, O. U.
See Kesey, Ken (Elton)
Le Vot, Andre 1921- ... 130
Levoy, Myron ... CANR-40
Earlier sketches in CA 93-96, CANR-18
See also AAYA 19
See also SATA 49
See also SATA-Brief 37
Levtzion, Nehemia 1935- ... CANR-4
Earlier sketch in CA 53-56
Levy, Alan 1932- ... CANR-46
Earlier sketches in CA 9-12R, CANR-6, 21
Levy, Amy 1861-1889 ... DLB 156
Levy, Babette May 1907-1977 ... 81-84
Obituary ... 73-76
Levy, Benn W(olfe) 1900-1973 ... 101
Obituary ... 45-48
See also DLB 13
See also DLBY 81
Levy, Bernard 1907- ... 61-64
Levy, Bernard-Henri 1949- ... 122
Levy, Bill
See Levy, William V.
Levy, Charles K(ingsley) 1924- ... 120
Levy, Claude 1924- ... 129
Levy, Constance 1931- ... SAAS 22
See also SATA 73
Levy, D(arryl) A(llen) 1942-1968 ... CAP-2
Earlier sketch in CA 19-20
Levy, Daniel S. 1959- ... 167
Levy, Darline Gay Shapiro 1939- ... 102
Levy, David 1913- ... 13-16R
Levy, David A(rthur) 1955- ... 108
Levy, David M(ordecai) 1892-1977 ... 73-76
Obituary ... 69-72
Levy, David N(eil) L(aurence) 1945- ... 119
Levy, David W(illiam) 1937- ... 41-44R
Levy, Deborah 1959- ... 147
Levy, Donald 1936- ... 164
Levy, Elizabeth 1942- ... CANR-34
Earlier sketches in CA 77-80, CANR-15
See also MAICYA
See also SAAS 18
See also SATA 31, 69
Levy, Emanuel 1947- ... CANR-26
Earlier sketch in CA 108
Levy, Eugene Donald 1933- ... 102
Levy, Faye 1951- ... CANR-51
Earlier sketch in CA 125
Levy, Fred D(avid), Jr. 1937- ... CANR-14
Earlier sketch in CA 37-40R
Levy, G(ertrude) Rachel 1883-1966 ... 5-8R
Levy, Harold B(ernard) 1918- ... 73-76
Levy, Harry L(ouis) 1906-1981 ... 33-36R
Obituary ... 103
Levy, Helen Fiddyment 1937- ... 142
Levy, Herta Hess
See Kahn, Herta Hess
Levy, Howard S(eymour) 1923- ... CANR-25
Earlier sketches in CA 17-20R, CANR-10
Levy, Hyman 1889-1975 Obituary ... 57-60
Levy, Isaac Jack 1928- ... 41-44R
Levy, Jack Steven 1948- ... 115
Levy, JoAnn 1941- ... 134
Levy, John 1954- ... 128
Levy, Jonathan 1935- ... CANR-10
Earlier sketch in CA 61-64
Levy, Joseph V(ictor) 1928- ... 106
Levy, Julien 1906-1981 Obituary ... 103
Levy, Leonard W(illiams) 1923- ... CANR-69
Earlier sketches in CA 1-4R, CANR-1, 20
Levy, Lester S(tern) 1896- ... 61-64
Levy, Lillian (Rae Berliner) 1918-1986 ... 17-20R
Obituary ... 120
Levy, Lorelei
See Schwalberg, Carol(yn Ernestine Stein)
Levy, Marilyn 1937- ... 135
See also SATA 67
Levy, Marion Joseph, Jr. 1918- ... 73-76
Levy, Matthys 1929- ... 139
Levy, Michael E(rnst) 1929- ... CANR-2
Earlier sketch in CA 5-8R
Levy, Michael R(ichard) 1946- ... 77-80
Levy, Morton 1930- ... 77-80
Levy, Nathan 1945- ... SATA 63
Levy, Owen 1948- ... 118
Levy, Peter B. 1956- ... 168
Levy, Raphael 1900-1969 ... CAP-1
Earlier sketch in CA 13-16
Levy, Reynold 1945- ... 97-100
Levy, Richard C. 1947- ... 73-76
Levy, Robert 1926- ... 77-80
Levy, Robert 1945- ... 149
See also SATA 82
Levy, Robert Calmann
See Calmann-Levy, Robert
Levy, Robert J(oseph) 1931- ... 37-40R
Levy, Roger (P.) 1950- ... 134
Levy, Rosalie Marie 1889- ... CAP-1
Earlier sketch in CA 9-10
Levy, S Jay 1922- ... 108
Levy, Sidney Jay 1921- Brief entry ... 106
Levy, Stephen 1947- ... 105
Levy, Steven 1951- ... 149
Levy, Sue 1936- ... CANR-8
Earlier sketch in CA 57-60
Levy, Wilbert J. 1917- ... CANR-6
Earlier sketch in CA 57-60
Levy, William Turner 1922- ... 25-28R
Levy, William V. 1930- ... 9-12R
Levytskyj, Borys 1915- ... 65-68
Lewald, Fanny 1811-1889 ... DLB 129
Lewald, H(erald) Ernest 1922-1982 ... 21-24R
Obituary ... 114
Lewald, (Theo) Roon 1942- ... 93-96
Lewallen, John 1942- ... 69-72
Lewalski, Barbara Kiefer 1931- ... 104
Lewandowski, Dan 1947- ... 77-80
Lewandowski, Stephen 1947- ... 93-96
Lewanski, Richard C(asimir) 1918- ... 17-20R
LeWarne, Charles P(ierce) 1930- ... 57-60
Lewbin, Hyman J(oseph) 1894- ... 61-64
Lewcock, Ronald (B.) 1929- ... CANR-46
Earlier sketch in CA 121
Lewees, John
See Stockton, Francis Richard
Lewellen, T(ed) C(harles) 1940- ... CANR-6
Earlier sketch in CA 13-16R
Lewels, Francisco J(ose), Jr. 1944- ... 104
Lewenstein, Morris R. 1923- ... 13-16R
Lewes, Darby 1946- ... 153
Lewes, George Henry 1817-1878 ... DLB 55, 144
Lewes, Lettie
See Cleveland, Philip Jerome
Lewesdon, John
See Daniell, Albert Scott
Lewiecki-Wilson, Cynthia 1948- ... 147
Lewin, Bertram D(avid) 1896-1971 ... 65-68
Lewin, Betsy 1937- ... CANR-58
Earlier sketch in CA 104
See also SATA 32, 90
Lewin, C. L.
See Brister, Richard
Lewin, Ellen 1946- ... 156
Lewin, Elsa ... 118
Lewin, Esther 1922- ... 61-64
Lewin, Hugh 1939- ... CANR-38
Earlier sketch in CA 113
See also CLR 9
See also MAICYA
See also SATA 72
See also SATA-Brief 40
Lewin, L.
See Lewin, Leonard
Lewin, Leonard 1919- ... CANR-28
Earlier sketch in CA 49-52
Lewin, Leonard C(ase) 1916- ... 17-20R
Lewin, Michael Zinn 1942- ... CANR-59
Earlier sketch in CA 73-76
Lewin, Moshe 1921- ... 152
Lewin, Nathan 1936- ... 101
Lewin, Rhoda G. 1929- ... 135
Lewin, Roger A. 1946- ... 161
Lewin, (George) Ronald 1914-1984 ... CANR-13
Obituary ... 111
Earlier sketch in CA 25-28R
Lewin, Ted 1935- ... CANR-50
Earlier sketches in CA 69-72, CANR-25
See also SATA 21, 76
Lewine, Richard 1910- ... 81-84
Lewing, Anthony Charles 1933- ... 81-84
Lewinson, Paul 1900-1988 Obituary ... 127
LeWinter, Oswald 1931- ... 1-4R
Lewis, A(rthur) J(ames) 1914- ... 5-8R
Lewis, A(drian) S(teven) 1945- ... 116
Lewis, Adele
See Corwin, Adele Beatrice Lewis
Lewis, Agnes Smith 1843-1926 ... DLB 174
Lewis, Albert 1885(?)-1978 Obituary ... 77-80
Lewis, Alfred Allan 1929- ... CANR-15
Earlier sketch in CA 73-76
Lewis, Alfred E. 1912-1968 Obituary ... 111
See also SATA-Brief 32
Lewis, Alfred Henry 1857-1914 Brief entry ... 120
See also DLB 25, 186
Lewis, Alice C. 1936- ... SATA 46
Lewis, Alice Hudson 1895(?)-1971 Obituary ... 109
See also SATA-Obit 29
Lewis, Allan 1905- ... 13-16R
Lewis, Alun 1915-1944 Brief entry ... 104
See also DLB 20, 162
See also TCLC 3
Lewis, Amanda 1955- ... SATA 80
Lewis, (Joseph) Anthony 1927- ... 9-12R
See also SATA 27
Lewis, Anthony Carey 1915-1983 Obituary ... 110
Lewis, Archibald Ross 1914-1990 ... 81-84
Obituary ... 130
Lewis, Arnold 1930- ... 166
Lewis, Arthur H. 1906- ... CANR-1
Earlier sketch in CA 1-4R
Lewis, Arthur O(rcutt), Jr. 1920- ... 9-12R
Lewis, Arthur William 1905-1970 ... CAP-1
Earlier sketch in CA 9-10
Lewis, Barbara 1928-1984 Obituary ... 113
Lewis, Barbara A. 1943- ... SATA 73
Lewis, Benjamin F. 1918- ... 45-48
Lewis, Bernard 1916- ... CANR-44
Brief entry ... 113
Earlier sketch in CA 118
Interview in ... 118
Lewis, Beth Irwin 1934- ... 33-36R
Lewis, Beverly 1949- ... 148
See also SATA 80
Lewis, Bill
See Lewis, William
Lewis, Bill H. 1927- ... 1-4R
Lewis, Brad (Alan) 1954- ... 127
Lewis, Brenda Ralph 1932- ... SATA 72
Lewis, C. Day
See Day Lewis, C(ecil)
Lewis, C(larence) I(rving) 1883-1964 ... 5-8R

Lewis, C(live) S(taples) 1898-1963 ...... CANR-71
Earlier sketches in CA 81-84, CANR-33
See also AAYA 3
See also CDBLB 1945-1960
See also CLC 1, 3, 6, 14, 27
See also CLR 3, 27
See also DA
See also DAB
See also DAC
See also DAM MST, NOV, POP
See also DLB 15, 100, 160
See also JRDA
See also MAICYA
See also MTCW 1
See also SATA 13, 100
See also WLC
Lewis, Charles
See Dixon, Roger
Lewis, Charles Bertrand 1842-1924 Brief entry . 114
See also DLB 11
Lewis, Claude A. 1934- 9-12R
Lewis, Claudia (Louise) 1907- CANR-6
Earlier sketch in CA 5-8R
See also SATA 5
Lewis, Clay(ton Wilson) 1936- 101
Lewis, Craig A. 1955- 132
Lewis, D. B.
See Bixby, Jerome Lewis
Lewis, D(ominic) B(evan) Wyndham
1894-1969 Obituary 25-28R
Lewis, D(es) F. 1948- 152
Lewis, Dave
See Lewis, David V.
Lewis, David 1909-1981 104
Lewis, David 1922- 41-44R
Lewis, David 1942- CANR-12
Earlier sketch in CA 69-72
Lewis, David B(enjamin) 1965- 111
Lewis, David Kellogg 1941- CANR-33
Earlier sketches in CA 81-84, CANR-15
Lewis, David L(anier) 1927- 69-72
Lewis, David L(evering) 1936- CANR-50
Earlier sketches in CA 45-48, CANR-2
Lewis, David Marshall
See Cook, Michael Lewis
Lewis, David T(revor) 1920- 45-48
Lewis, David V. 1923- 5-8R
Lewis, Derek 1946- 164
Lewis, Diane 1936- 129
Lewis, Donald Earle 1925- 5-8R
Lewis, Dorothy Roe 1904-1985 Obituary 115
Lewis, E(arl) B(radley) 1956- .... SATA 93
Lewis, E. M. 69-72
See also SATA 20
Lewis, Edith 1882(?)-1972 Obituary 111
Lewis, Edward W(illiams) 1899-1986 Obituary .. 118
Lewis, Edwin C(lark) 1933- 25-28R
Lewis, Eils Moorhouse 1919- 106
Lewis, Elizabeth Foreman 1892-1958 137
See also MAICYA
See also YABC 2
Lewis, Elliott (Bruce) 1917-1990 .... CANR-22
Obituary 131
Earlier sketch in CA 104
Lewis, Eugene 1940- CANR-4
Earlier sketch in CA 53-56
Lewis, (E.) Faye (Cashatt) 1896-1982 ...... 25-28R
Obituary 135
Lewis, Felice (Elizabeth) Flanery 1920- 73-76
Lewis, Finlay 1938- 101
Lewis, Flora 127
Brief entry 119
Lewis, Francine
See Wells, Helen
Lewis, Francis Ames
See Ames-Lewis, Francis
Lewis, Freeman 1908-1976 Obituary 69-72
Lewis, Fulton, Jr. 1903-1966 Obituary 89-92
Lewis, G(ranville) Douglass 1934- 106
Lewis, Gene D. 1931- 45-48
Lewis, Geoffrey (Lewis) 1920- 13-16R
Lewis, George 1941- 29-32R
Lewis, George 1943- 77-80
Lewis, George H(allam) 1943- 53-56
Lewis, George L. 1916- CANR-3
Earlier sketch in CA 45-48
Lewis, George Q. 1916-1979 .... 21-24R
Obituary 135
Lewis, Gilbert Newton 1875-1946 160
Lewis, Gordon R(ussell) 1926- CANR-50
Earlier sketches in CA 21-24R, CANR-10, 25
Lewis, Gregg (Allan) 1951- 141
Lewis, Grover Virgil 1934-1995 106
Obituary 148
Lewis, H(ywel) D(avid) 1910- CANR-3
Earlier sketch in CA 9-12R
Lewis, H. W. 1923- 167
Lewis, H. Warren 1924- 29-32R
Lewis, Harold M. 1891(?)-1973 Obituary 45-48
Lewis, Harry 1917- 109
Lewis, Harry 1942- CANR-3
Earlier sketch in CA 49-52
Lewis, Helen (Lillian) Block 1913-1987 110
Obituary 121
Lewis, Henry Clay 1825-1850 .... DLB 3
Lewis, Henry T(rickey) 1928- 73-76
Lewis, Herbert S(amuel) 1934- 17-20R
Lewis, Hilda (Winifred) 1896-1974 93-96
Obituary 49-52
See also SATA-Obit 20
Lewis, Horacio D(elano) 1944- 57-60
Lewis, Howard R(obert) 1934- CANR-10
Earlier sketch in CA 25-28R
Lewis, Hunter 1947- 109
Lewis, I(oan) M(yrddin) 1930- CANR-21
Earlier sketches in CA 9-12R, CANR-5
Lewis, Ian
See Bensman, Joseph
Lewis, J. Patrick 1942- 138
See also SATA 69
Lewis, J. R.
See Lewis, (John) Roy(ston)
Lewis, Jack P(earl) 1919- CANR-34
Earlier sketch in CA 37-40R
See also SATA 65
Lewis, James, Jr. 1930- CANR-12
Earlier sketch in CA 29-32R
Lewis, James 1935- 65-68
Lewis, Jan (Ellen) 1949- 115
Lewis, Janet 1899- CANR-63
Earlier sketches in CAP-1, CA 9-12R, CANR-29
See also Winters, Janet Lewis
See also CLC 41
See also DLBY 87
Lewis, Jean 1924- CANR-28
Earlier sketches in CA 21-24R, CANR-11
See also SATA 61
Lewis, Jerry 1926- 121
Brief entry 113
Lewis, Johanna Miller 1961- 151
Lewis, John 1889- CANR-5
Earlier sketch in CA 5-8R
Lewis, John (Noel Claude) 1912- CANR-19
Earlier sketch in CA 102
Lewis, (F.) John 1916- 133
Lewis, John D(onald) 1905-1988 65-68
Obituary 124
Lewis, John E(arl) 1931- CANR-44
Earlier sketches in CA 57-60, CANR-6, 21
Lewis, John P(rior) 1921- 9-12R
Lewis, John Parry 1927- 107
Lewis, John W(ilson) 1930- 9-12R
Lewis, Joseph 1889-1968 .... CAP-1
Earlier sketch in CA 13-14
Lewis, Judith Mary 1921- 97-100
Lewis, Judy 1935- 152
Lewis, Julian Herman 1891-1989 161
Lewis, Julinda
See Lewis-Ferguson, Julinda
Lewis, June E(thelyn) 1905- CAP-2
Earlier sketch in CA 29-32
Lewis, Kim 1951- .... SATA 84
Lewis, Lange
See Brandt, Jane Lewis
Lewis, Larry L(ynn) 1935- 115
Lewis, Lawrence E(dwin) 1928- 69-72
Lewis, Leon 1904- CAP-1
Earlier sketch in CA 13-16
Lewis, Leon Ray 1883- CAP-1
Earlier sketch in CA 9-10
Lewis, Lesley 1909- 102
Lewis, Linda 1927- 93-96
Lewis, Linda (Joy) 1946- 135
See also SATA 67
Lewis, Lionel Stanley 1933- CANR-5
Earlier sketch in CA 53-56
Lewis, Lucia Z.
See Anderson, Lucia (Lewis)
Lewis, Margaret (B.) 1942- 135
Lewis, Margie M. 1923- 101
Lewis, Marianna Olmstead 1923- 9-12R
Lewis, Marjorie 1929- 108
See also SATA 40
See also SATA-Brief 35
Lewis, Martha E(llen) 1941- CANR-10
Earlier sketch in CA 25-28R
Lewis, Martin W. 1956- 139
Lewis, Martyn (John Dudley) 1945- 141
Lewis, Marvin 1923-1971 .... CAP-2
Earlier sketch in CA 21-22
Lewis, Mary (Christianna) 1907(?)-1988 .. CANR-43
Obituary 125
Earlier sketches in CA 77-80, CANR-13
See also SATA 64
See also SATA-Obit 56
Lewis, Mary F. W.
See Bond, Mary Fanning Wickham
Lewis, Matthew Gregory 1775-1818 .. DLB 39, 158, 178
Lewis, Maynah 1919- CANR-16
Earlier sketch in CA 25-28R
Lewis, Meriwether 1774-1809 .... DLB 186
Lewis, Mervyn
See Frewer, Glyn (M.)
Lewis, Mervyn K(eith) 1941- CANR-51
Earlier sketch in CA 125
Lewis, Michael
See Untermeyer, Louis
Lewis, Michael 1937- CANR-1
Earlier sketch in CA 45-48
Lewis, Michael 1960- 140
See also BEST 90:2
Lewis, Michael Arthur 1890-1970 .... CANR-5
Obituary 29-32R
Earlier sketch in CA 5-8R
Lewis, Mildred D. 1912- 13-16R
Lewis, Mort(imer) R(eis) 1908-1991 105
Obituary 134
Lewis, Naomi 143
See also SATA 76
Lewis, Naphtali 1911- 110
Lewis, Nigel (Stephen) 1948- 116
Lewis, Nolan D(on) C(arpenter) 1889- 5-8R
Lewis, Norman 1912- CANR-3
Earlier sketch in CA 9-12R
Lewis, Norman 1918- 129
Brief entry 112
See also MTCW 1
Lewis, Norman 1940- 136
Lewis, Oren Ritter 1902-1983 Obituary 110
Lewis, Oscar 1893-1992 .... CANR-46
Obituary 139
Earlier sketch in CA 5-8R
Lewis, Oscar 1914-1970 .... CAP-1
Obituary 29-32R
Earlier sketch in CA 19-20
Lewis, Padmore
See Lewis, Sandra Padmore
Lewis, Patricia Ann 1933- 112
Lewis, Paul
See Gerson, Noel Bertram
Lewis, Paul H. 1937- 73-76
Lewis, Peirce F(ee) 1927- 41-44R
Lewis, Peter
See Lewis, Peter Elvet (Elfed)
Lewis, Peter 1922- 9-12R
Lewis, Peter 1938- CANR-21
Earlier sketch in CA 45-48
Lewis, Peter Elvet (Elfed) 1937- 133
Lewis, Philip 1913- 1-4R
Lewis, R. Duffy 1908- CAP-1
Earlier sketch in CA 11-12
Lewis, R(ichard) W(arrington) B(aldwin) 1917- CANR-71
Earlier sketch in CA 102
See also DLB 111
Lewis, Ralph F(erguson) 1918-1979 .... 29-32R
Obituary 89-92
Lewis, Ralph L(oren) 1919- 117
Lewis, Richard 1700(?)-1734 .... DLB 24
Lewis, Richard 1935- CANR-45
Earlier sketches in CA 9-12R, CANR-5
See also SATA 3
Lewis, Richard S. 1916- CANR-9
Earlier sketch in CA 57-60
Lewis, Rob 1962- .... SATA 72
Lewis, Robert 1932- 97-100
Lewis, Robert T(urner) 1923- 85-88
Lewis, Robert W. 1930- 143
Lewis, Roger
See Zarchy, Harry
Lewis, Ronello B. 1909- CAP-1
Earlier sketch in CA 17-18
Lewis, (Ernest Michael) Roy 1913- CANR-3
Earlier sketch in CA 5-8R
Lewis, (John) Roy(ston) 1933- CANR-64
Earlier sketch in CA 105
Lewis, Rupert 1947- 142
Lewis, Samella S(anders) 1924- Brief entry 112
Lewis, Sandra Padmore 1957- 153
Lewis, Sasha Gregory 1947- CANR-15
Earlier sketch in CA 85-88
Lewis, Saunders 1893-1985 Obituary 117
Lewis, Sean Day
See Day-Lewis, Sean (Francis)
Lewis, Selma S. 1921- 123
Lewis, Shari 1934- CANR-19
Earlier sketch in CA 89-92
See also SATA 35
See also SATA-Brief 30
Lewis, Sherry 166
Lewis, (Harry) Sinclair 1885-1951 133
Brief entry 104
See also CDALB 1917-1929
See also DA
See also DAB
See also DAC
See also DAM MST, NOV
See also DLB 9, 102
See also DLBD 1
See also MTCW 1
See also TCLC 4, 13, 23, 39
See also WLC
Lewis, Stephen 1947(?)-1981 Obituary 103
See also AITN 1
Lewis, Stephen Richmond, Jr. 1939- 41-44R
Lewis, Sylvan R.
See Aronson, Virginia
Lewis, T(heodore) G(yle) 1941- 111
Lewis, Ted
See Lewis, Edward W(illiams)
Lewis, Theophilus 1891-1974 125
See also BW 1
Lewis, Therese 1912(?)-1984 Obituary 113
Lewis, Thomas A. 1942- 128
Lewis, Thomas H. 1919- 141
Lewis, Thomas P(arker) 1936- CANR-45
Earlier sketch in CA 29-32R
See also SATA 27
Lewis, Thomas S(pottswood) W(ellford) 1942- CANR-31
Earlier sketch in CA 49-52
Lewis, Tom 1940- 105
Lewis, Tony 1938- 122
Lewis, Trudy 1961- 147
Lewis, Voltaire
See Ritchie, Edwin
Lewis, W(illiam) Arthur 1915-1991 .... CANR-13
Obituary 134
Brief entry 111
Earlier sketch in CA 17-20R
Lewis, W(alter) David 1931- CANR-9
Earlier sketch in CA 13-16R
Lewis, Walker 1904- CAP-2
Earlier sketch in CA 19-20
Lewis, Ward B., (Jr.) 1938- 168
Lewis, Warren 1940- 115
Lewis, William 1946- 120
Lewis, William Hubert 1928- 13-16R
Lewis, Willie Newbury 1891-1985 93-96
Obituary 116
Lewis, Wilmarth Sheldon 1895-1979 ..... CANR-15
Obituary 89-92
Earlier sketch in CA 65-68
See also DLB 140
Lewis, (Percy) Wyndham 1882(?)-1957 157
Brief entry 104
See also DLB 15
See also TCLC 2, 9
Lewis-Ferguson, Julinda 1955- 152
See also SATA 85
Lewisohn, Ludwig 1883-1955 Brief entry 107
See also DLB 4, 9, 28, 102
See also TCLC 19
Lewisohn, Mark 1958- 130
Lewiston, Robert R(ueben) 1909- CAP-2
Earlier sketch in CA 23-24
Lewis-Williams, J(ames) David 1934- CANR-41
Earlier sketch in CA 117
Lewiton, Mina 1904-1970 .... CAP-2
Obituary 29-32R
Earlier sketch in CA 23-24
See also SATA 2
Lewitt, Shariann (N.) 1954- 119
Lewittes, Mordecai Henry
See Lewittes, Morton H(enry)
Lewittes, Morton H(enry) 1911-1990 .... 25-28R
Obituary 133
Lewontin, Richard Charles 1929- 104
Lewontin, Timothy (Andrew) 1955- 130
Lewsen, Phyllis 1916- 109
Lewton, Val 1904-1951 .... TCLC 76
Lewton-Brain, James 1923- 97-100
Lewty, Marjorie 1906- CAP-1
Earlier sketch in CA 9-10
Lewy, Guenter 1923- CANR-21
Earlier sketches in CA 9-12R, CANR-3
Lexau, Joan M. CANR-11
Earlier sketch in CA 17-20R
See also SATA 1, 36
Ley, Alice Chetwynd 1913- CANR-44
Earlier sketches in CA 13-16R, CANR-6, 21
Ley, Arthur Gordon 1911-1968 Obituary 102
Ley, Charles David 1913- 9-12R
Ley, Ralph 1929- 41-44R
Ley, Robert Arthur
See Ley, Arthur Gordon
Ley, Sandra 1944- 57-60
Ley, Willy 1906-1969 .... 9-12R
Obituary 25-28R
See also SATA 2
Leyburn, Ellen Douglass 1907-1966 .... CAP-2
Earlier sketch in CA 25-28
Leyburn, James G(raham) 1902- 5-8R
Leyda, Jay 1910-1988 108
Obituary 124
Leydet, Francois G(uillaume) 1927- 9-12R
Leydon, Rita (Floden) 1949- .... SATA 21
Leyendecker, J. C. 1874-1951 .... DLB 188
Leyhart, Edward
See Edwards, Elwyn Hartley
Leyland, Eric (Arthur) 1911- .... SATA 37
Leyland, Mal(colm Rex) 1944- 108
Leyland, Winston 1940- CANR-71
Earlier sketch in CA 107
Leynard, Martin
See Berger, Ivan (Bennett)
Leyner, Mark 1956- CANR-53
Earlier sketches in CA 110, CANR-28
See also CLC 92
Leypoldt, Martha M. 1918-1975 .... CAP-2
Earlier sketch in CA 23-24
Leys, Mary Dorothy Rose 1890- 5-8R
Leys, Simon
See Ryckmans, Pierre
Leys, Wayne A(lbert) R(isser) 1905-1973 ... CAP-1
Earlier sketch in CA 17-18
Leyser, Karl Joseph 1920-1992 112
Obituary 137
Leyton, Elliott (Hastings) 1939- 120
Leyton, Sophie
See Walsh, Sheila
Leyva, Ricardo
See Valdes, Nelson P.
Lezama Lima, Jose 1910-1976 .... CANR-71
Earlier sketch in CA 77-80
See also CLC 4, 10, 101
See also DAM MULT
See also DLB 113
See also HW
Lezra, Grizzella Paull 1934- 61-64
Lhamon, W(illiam) T(aylor), Jr. 1945- 65-68
L'Heureux, Bill
See L'Heureux, W(illard) J(oseph)
L'Heureux, John (Clarke) 1934- CANR-45
Earlier sketches in CA 13-16R, CANR-23
See also CLC 52
L'Heureux, W(illard) J(oseph) 1918- 5-8R
L'Hommedieu, Dorothy Keasley
1885-1961 Obituary 109
See also SATA-Obit 29
Li, C(hing) C(hun) 1912- 17-20R
Li, Chiang-Kwang 1915- 73-76
Li, Choh Hao 1913-1987 164
Li, Choh-Ming 1912- 1-4R
Li, David H(siang-fu) 1928- 13-16R
Li, Fang Kuei 1902- 112
Li, Hui-Lin 1911- CANR-15
Earlier sketch in CA 85-88
Li, Leslie 1945- 148
Li, Shu Hua 1890(?)-1979 Obituary 89-92
Li, Tien-yi 1915- 37-40R
Li, Tze-chung 1927- CANR-14
Earlier sketch in CA 41-44R
Li, Xiao Jun 1952- .... SATA 86
Li, Xueqin 1933- 136
Li, Yao-wen 1924- 106
Li, Zhisui 1919- 152
Liang, Chin-tung 1893- 81-84
Liang, Heng 1954- 142
Liang, Ssu-ch'eng 1901-1972 162

Liang, Yen 1908- ... 5-8R
Liao, David C. E. 1925- ... 41-44R
Lias, Edward J(ohn) 1934- ... 120
Lias, Godfrey ... 5-8R
Libbey, Elizabeth 1947- ... 110
Libbey, James K(eith) 1942- ... 81-84
Libby, Anthony 1942- ... 118
Libby, Bill
See Libby, William M.
Libby, Leona Marshall 1919-1986 ... 101
Obituary ... 121
Libby, Ronald T(heodore) 1941- ... 135
Libby, Violet K(elway) 1892(?)-1981 Obituary ... 105
Libby, Willard F(rank) 1908-1980 ... 160
Obituary ... 113
Libby, William C(harles) ... 104
Libby, William M. 1927-1984 ... CANR-10
Obituary ... 113
Earlier sketch in CA 25-28R
See also SATA 5
See also SATA-Obit 39
Liberace
See Liberace, Wladziu Valentino
Liberace, Wladziu Valentino 1919-1987 ... CANR-22
Obituary ... 121
Earlier sketch in CA 89-92
Liberman, Alexander 1912- Brief entry ... 113
Liberman, Anatoly 1937- ... CANR-40
Earlier sketch in CA 116
Liberman, Evsei Grigorevich
1897-1983 Obituary ... 109
Liberman, Judith 1929- ... 73-76
Liberman, M(yron) M(andell) 1921- ... 57-60
Liberman, Robert Paul 1937- ... CANR-49
Earlier sketches in CA 61-64, CANR-7, 22
Liberman, Yevsei Grigorievich
See Liberman, Evsei Grigorevich
Libersat, Henry 1934- ... 53-56
Liberty, Gene 1924- ... CANR-8
Earlier sketch in CA 5-8R
See also SATA 3
Libin, Laurence (Elliot) 1944- ... 119
Liblit, Jerome ... 13-16R
Libman, Carol 1928- ... 113
Libo, Kenneth (Harold) 1937- ... 133
Brief entry ... 109
Libo, Lester M(artin) 1923- ... 77-80
Libov, Charlotte 1950- ... 145
Librach, Jan 1904(?)-1973 Obituary ... 41-44R
LiBretto, Ellen V. 1947- ... 110
Lich, G(len) E(rnst) 1948- ... 139
Lichbach, Mark Irving 1951- ... 152
Lichello, Robert 1926- ... 13-16R
Lichfield I, Leonard fl. 1671-1685 ... DLB 170
Lichine, Alexis 1913-1989 ... 9-12R
Obituary ... 128
Licht, Fred (Stephen) 1928- ... 101
Licht, H. William 1915- ... 145
Licht, Sidney Herman 1907-1979 Obituary ... 108
Lichtblau, Myron Ivor 1925- ... 17-20R
Lichten, Joseph I. 1906(?)-1987 Obituary ... 125
Lichtenberg, Elisabeth Jacoba 1913- ... 13-16R
Lichtenberg, Georg Christoph 1742-1799 ... DLB 94
Lichtenberg, Jacqueline 1942- ... CANR-59
Earlier sketch in CA 73-76
Lichtenberg, Peter A. 1959- ... 149
Lichtenberg, Philip 1926- ... CANR-13
Earlier sketch in CA 37-40R
Lichtenstadter, Ilse 1907-1991 ... CANR-13
Obituary ... 134
Earlier sketch in CA 33-36R
Lichtenstein, Aharon 1933- ... 17-20R
Lichtenstein, Grace 1941- ... CANR-22
Earlier sketches in CA 49-52, CANR-2
Lichtenstein, Nelson 1944- ... 155
Lichtheim, George 1912-1973 Obituary ... 41-44R
Lichtman, Allan J. 1947- ... 124
Lichtman, Celia S(chmukler) 1932- ... 41-44R
Lichtman, Wendy 1946- ... 114
Lichty, George M(aurice) 1905-1983 ... 104
Obituary ... 110
Lichty, Lawrence W(ilson) 1937- ... 53-56
Lichty, Ron 1950- ... CANR-18
Earlier sketch in CA 101
Licklider, Roy E(ilers) 1941- ... 33-36R
Lickona, Thomas Edward 1943- ... 113
Lida, Denah (Levy) 1923- ... 21-24R
Lidchi, Maggi
See Lidchi Grassi, Maggi
Lidchi Grassi, Maggi 1930- ... 132
Liddell, Brendan E(dwin) A(lexander) 1927- ... 29-32R
Liddell, C. H.
See Kuttner, Henry
Liddell, Kenneth 1912-1975 ... SATA 63
Liddell, (John) Robert 1908-1992 ... CANR-46
Obituary ... 139
Earlier sketch in CA 13-16R
Liddell Hart, Basil Henry 1895-1970 ... 103
Obituary ... 89-92
Lidderdale, Halliday Adair 1917- ... 21-24R
Liddicoat, Richard T., Jr. 1918- ... 45-48
Liddle, Peter Hammond 1934- ... CANR-18
Earlier sketch in CA 102
See also DLBY 97
Liddle, William 1925- ... 77-80
Liddy, G(eorge) Gordon (Battle) 1930- ... CANR-66
Earlier sketch in CA 114
Interview in ... 114
Liddy, James (Daniel Reeves) 1934- ... CANR-43
Earlier sketches in CA 13-16R, CANR-5, 20
See also AITN 2
Lide, David R. 1928- ... 146
Lide, Mary ... 132
Brief entry ... 127
Interview in ... 132
Lidman, David 1905- ... 69-72
Lidoff, Joan (Ilene) 1944-1989 ... 115
Obituary ... 130
Lidtke, Vernon L. 1930- ... 21-24R
Lidz, Theodore 1910- ... 29-32R
Lie, John 1959- ... 152
Lie, Jonas (Lauritz Idemil) 1833-1908(?) Brief entry ... 115
See also TCLC 5
Lie, Trygve (Halvdan) 1896-1968 Obituary ... 113
Lieb, Fred(erick George) 1888-1980 ... CANR-62
Obituary ... 97-100
Earlier sketch in CA 69-72
See also DLB 171
Lieb, Irwin Chester 1925- Brief entry ... 105
Lieb, Michael 1940- ... 65-68
Lieb, Robert C. 1944- ... 37-40R
Lieb, Sandra ... 112
Liebenow, J. Gus 1925-1993 ... 45-48
Obituary ... 141
Lieber, Arnold L(ou) 1937- Brief entry ... 113
Lieber, Joel 1937-1971 ... 73-76
Obituary ... 29-32R
See also CLC 6
Lieber, Robert J(ames) 1941- ... CANR-57
Earlier sketches in CA 29-32R, CANR-12, 30
Lieber, Stanley Martin
See Lee, Stan
Lieber, Todd M(ichael) 1944- ... 45-48
Lieberg, Owen S. 1896-1973 ... CAP-2
Earlier sketch in CA 25-28
Lieberman, Arnold (Leo) 1903- ... CAP-1
Earlier sketch in CA 19-20
Lieberman, Donald 1927- ... 111
Lieberman, E(dwin) James 1934- ... CANR-22
Earlier sketch in CA 45-48
See also SATA 62
Lieberman, Elias 1883- ... 5-8R
Lieberman, Fredric 1940- ... CANR-7
Earlier sketch in CA 53-56
Lieberman, Gerald F. 1923-1986 ... 85-88
Obituary ... 119
Lieberman, Herbert (Henry) 1933- ... CANR-19
Earlier sketches in CA 9-12R, CANR-5
Interview in ... CANR-19
Lieberman, J. Ben 1914-1984 Obituary ... 113
Lieberman, Jethro K(oller) 1943- ... CANR-10
Earlier sketch in CA 21-24R
Lieberman, Joseph I. 1942- ... 17-20R
Lieberman, Laurence (James) 1935- ... CANR-36
Earlier sketches in CA 17-20R, CANR-8
See also CLC 4, 36
Lieberman, Mark 1942- ... 29-32R
Lieberman, Mendel Halliday 1913- ... 106
Lieberman, Morton A(lexander) 1931- ... 41-44R
Lieberman, Myron 1919- ... CANR-8
Earlier sketch in CA 5-8R
Lieberman, Philip 1934- ... 93-96
Lieberman, Robert (Howard) 1941- ... CANR-10
Earlier sketch in CA 57-60
See also AITN 1
Lieberman, Rosalie ... 9-12R
Lieberman, Samuel 1911-1981 ... 17-20R
Obituary ... 134
Lieberman, Saul 1898-1983 Obituary ... 109
Liebers, Arthur 1913- ... CANR-3
Earlier sketch in CA 5-8R
See also SATA 12
Liebers, Ruth 1910- ... CAP-1
Earlier sketch in CA 9-10
Lieberson, Goddard 1911- ... CAP-2
Earlier sketch in CA 25-28
Lieberson, Jonathan 1949(?)-1989 Obituary ... 128
Lieberson, Stanley 1933- ... CANR-38
Earlier sketches in CA 1-4R, CANR-1, 17
Lieberstein, Stanley H. 1934- ... 105
Liebert, Burt 1925- ... 33-36R
Liebert, Doris 1934- ... 105
Liebert, Robert M. 1942- ... 41-44R
Liebert, Robert S. 1930-1988 Obituary ... 125
Lieberthal, Kenneth G. 1943- ... 130
Lieberthal, Milton M(orton) 1911- ... 117
Liebeschuetz, Hans
1893(?)-1978(?) Obituary ... 85-88
Liebeschuetz, John Hugo W(olfgang) G(ideon)
1927- ... 141
Liebhafsky, Herbert Hugo 1919- ... 5-8R
Liebhafsky, Herman A(lfred) 1905- ... 53-56
Liebich, Andre 1948- ... 166
Lieblich, Amia 1939- ... 93-96
Lieblich, Irene 1923- ... SATA 22
Liebling, A(bbott) J(oseph) 1904-1963 ... CANR-63
Obituary ... 89-92
Earlier sketch in CA 104
See also DLB 4, 171
Liebman, Arthur 1926- ... CANR-6
Earlier sketch in CA 57-60
Liebman, Charles S(eymour) 1934- ... 61-64
Liebman, Marcel 1930(?)-1986 Obituary ... 118
Liebman, Ron(ald S.) 1943- ... 120
Liebman, Seymour B(ertrand) 1907-1986 ... CANR-7
Obituary ... 120
Earlier sketch in CA 17-20R
Liebow, Averill A(braham) 1911-1978 Obituary ... 111
Liebowitz, Daniel 1921- ... 164
Liederbach, Clarence Andrew 1910- ... 93-96
Liederman, Judith 1927- ... 85-88
Liedholm, Carl (Edward) 1940- ... 41-44R
Liedloff, Jean ... 81-84
Liedtke, Kurt E(rnst) H(einrich) 1919- ... 17-20R
Lief, Judith L. 1946- ... 162
Lief, N. H.
See Bayes, Ronald H(omer)
Lief, Nina R. 1907- ... 118
Lief, Philip 1947- ... 107
Liehm, Antonin J. 1924- ... 102
Lieksman, Anders
See Haavikko, Paavo Juhani
Liem, Nguyen Dang 1936- ... 57-60
Lien, Arnold J. 1920-1979 ... 21-24R
Obituary ... 122
Lienhard, John H(enry IV) 1930- ... CANR-4
Earlier sketch in CA 53-56
Lientz, Bennet Price 1942- ... CANR-8
Earlier sketch in CA 61-64
Liepmann, Hans Wolfgang (Leopold Edmund Eugen
1914- ... 155
Liepolt, Werner 1944- ... 25-28R
Liers, Emil E(rnest) 1890-1975 ... 107
See also SATA 37
Liesner, Hans Hubertus (Karl Kurt Otto) 1929- ... 104
Liestman, Vicki 1961- ... SATA 72
Lietaer, Bernard A(rthur) 1942- ... 33-36R
Lietaert Peerbolte, Maarten 1905- ... 102
Lietz, Gerald S. 1918- ... SATA 11
Lieuwen, Edwin 1923- ... CANR-5
Earlier sketch in CA 1-4R
Lieven, Anatol 1960- ... 145
Liew, Kit Siong 1932- ... 77-80
Lifar, Serge 1905-1986 Obituary ... 121
Lifchitz, Boris 1895-1984 Obituary ... 114
Life, Kay (Guinn) 1930- ... SATA 83
Li Fei-kan 1904- ... 105
See also Pa Chin
Liffring, Joan Louise 1929- ... 17-20R
Lifshin, Lyn (Diane) 1944- ... CANR-50
Earlier sketches in CA 33-36R, CANR-8, 25
See also CAAS 10
Lifson, David S. 1908-1996 ... CANR-32
Obituary ... 154
Earlier sketch in CA 33-36R
Lifton, Betty Jean ... CANR-27
Earlier sketches in CA 5-8R, CANR-12
See also SATA 6
Lifton, Robert Jay 1926- ... CANR-27
Earlier sketch in CA 17-20R
Interview in ... CANR-27
See also CLC 67
See also SATA 66
Lifton, Walter M. 1918- ... CANR-16
Earlier sketch in CA 33-36R
Liggero, John 1921- ... 25-28R
Liggett, Clayton E(ugene) 1930- ... 29-32R
Liggett, Hunter
See Paine, Lauran (Bosworth)
Liggett, John 1923- ... 57-60
Liggett, Thomas 1918- ... 5-8R
Light, Albert 1927- ... 93-96
Light, Ivan 1941- ... 73-76
Light, James F. 1921- ... CANR-1
Earlier sketch in CA 1-4R
Light, Martin 1927- ... 53-56
Light, P(aul) H. 1947- ... 128
Light, Patricia Kahn 1939- ... 61-64
Lightbody, Charles Wayland 1904- ... 5-8R
Lightbody, Donna Mae 1920-1976 Obituary ... 110
Lightbown, Ronald William 1932- ... 104
Lightburn, Ron 1954- ... SATA 91
Lightburn, Sandra 1955- ... 155
See also SATA 91
Lighter, J(onathan) E. 1949(?)- ... 147
Lightfoot, Alfred 1936- ... CANR-4
Earlier sketch in CA 53-56
Lightfoot, Claude M. 1910- ... 123
See also BW 1
Lightfoot, D. J.
See Sizemore, Deborah Lightfoot
Lightfoot, David (William) 1945- ... 116
Lightfoot, Gordon 1938- Brief entry ... 109
See also CLC 26
Lightfoot, Neil R(oland) 1929- ... 81-84
Lightfoot, Paul 1946- ... 110
Lightfoot, Sara Lawrence ... 142
See also BW 2
Lighthall, William Douw 1857-1954 ... DLB 92
Lightman, Alan P(aige) 1948- ... CANR-63
Earlier sketch in CA 141
See also CLC 81
Lightman, Bernard 1950- ... 116
Lightner, A. M.
See Hopf, Alice (Martha) L(ightner)
Lightner, Alice
See Hopf, Alice (Martha) L(ightner)
Lightner, Robert P(aul) 1931- ... CANR-37
Earlier sketches in CA 49-52, CANR-1, 16
Lightner, Theodore 1893(?)-1981 Obituary ... 113
Lightwood, Martha B. 1923- ... 33-36R
Lignell, Lois 1911- ... SATA 37
Ligomenides, Panos A. 1928- ... 29-32R
Ligon, Ernest M(ayfield) 1897- ... CAP-1
Earlier sketch in CA 9-10
Ligotti, Thomas (Robert) 1953- ... CANR-49
Earlier sketch in CA 123
See also CLC 44
See also SSC 16
Liguori, Frank E. 1917-1980 ... 21-24R
Obituary ... 134
Lihani, John 1927- ... CANR-14
Earlier sketch in CA 37-40R
Lihn, Enrique 1929-1988 ... CANR-32
Earlier sketch in CA 104
See also HW
Li Ho 791-817 ... PC 13
Lijphart, Arend 1936- ... CANR-50
Earlier sketches in CA 21-24R, CANR-10, 25
Likeness, George C(lark) 1927- ... 17-20R
Likert, Rensis 1903- ... 93-96
Likhovski, Eliahou 1927- ... 45-48
Lila, Kim 1966- ... 165
Liles, Bruce (Lynn) 1934- ... 53-56
Liles, Maurine Walpole 1935- ... 149
See also SATA 81
Liley, Helen Margaret Irwin 1928- ... 25-28R
Liliencron, (Friedrich Adolf Axel) Detlev von
1844-1909 Brief entry ... 117
See also TCLC 18
Lilienfeld, Abraham M(orris)
1920-1984 Obituary ... 113
Lilienfeld, Robert Henry 1927- ... CANR-1
Earlier sketch in CA 1-4R
Lilienheim, Henry 1908- ... 150
Lilienthal, Alfred M(orton) 1913- ... 37-40R
Lilienthal, David E(li) 1899-1981 ... CANR-3
Obituary ... 102
Earlier sketch in CA 5-8R
Li Ling-Ai ... 77-80
Lilje, Hanns 1899-1977 Obituary ... 69-72
Lillard, Charles (Marion) 1944- ... CANR-8
Earlier sketch in CA 61-64
Lillard, Paula Polk 1931- ... 73-76
Lillard, Richard G(ordon) 1909-1990 ... 21-24R
Obituary ... 131
Liller, William 1927- ... 145
L'Illettre
See Bernard, Harry
Lilley, Dorothy B(race) 1914- ... 113
Lilley, Peter 1943- ... 77-80
Lilley, Stephen R(ay) 1950- ... 164
See also SATA 97
Lillibridge, G(eorge) D(onald) 1921- ... 13-16R
Lillich, Meredith Parsons 1932- Brief entry ... 105
Lillich, Richard B(onnot) 1933-1996 ... 119
Obituary ... 153
Lillie, Beatrice (Gladys) 1894(?)-1989 Obituary ... 127
Lillie, Helen 1915- ... 65-68
Lillie, John Adam 1884-1983 Obituary ... 110
Lillie, Ralph D(ougall) 1896-1979 Obituary ... 89-92
Lillie, William 1899- ... 5-8R
Lillington, Kenneth (James) 1916- ... CANR-3
Earlier sketch in CA 5-8R
See also SATA 39
Lillo, George 1691-1739 ... DLB 84
Lilly, Charles ... SATA-Brief 33
Lilly, Doris 1926-1991 ... CANR-11
Obituary ... 135
Earlier sketch in CA 29-32R
Lilly, Eli 1885-1977 Obituary ... 69-72
Lilly, J. K., Jr. 1893-1966 ... DLB 140
Lilly, John C(unningham) 1915- ... CANR-1
Earlier sketch in CA 1-4R
Lilly, Mark 1950- ... 136
Lilly, Ray
See Curtis, Richard (Alan)
Lilly, Ray
See Fisher, David
Lily, William c. 1468-1522 ... DLB 132
Lim, Catherine 1942(?)- ... 160
Lim, Genny 1946- ... CANR-39
Earlier sketch in CA 116
Lim, John 1932- ... 116
See also SATA 43
Lim, Paul Stephen 1944- ... CANR-25
Earlier sketch in CA 108
Lim, Shirley Geok-lin 1944- ... 140
Lima, Carolyn W(omack) 1938- ... 118
Lima, Frank 1939- ... 73-76
Lima, Jose Lezama
See Lezama Lima, Jose
Lima, Robert 1935- ... 9-12R
Lima Barreto, Afonso Henrique de 1881-1922 Brief entry ... 117
See also TCLC 23
Liman, Claude Gilbert 1943- ... 57-60
Liman, Ellen (Fogelson) 1936- ... CANR-13
Earlier sketch in CA 61-64
See also SATA 22
Limb, Sue 1946- ... CANR-37
Earlier sketch in CA 115
Limbacher, James L. 1926- ... CANR-17
Earlier sketches in CA 5-8R, CANR-2
Limbaugh, Rush H. III 1951(?)- ... 142
Limburg, James 1935- ... CANR-46
Earlier sketch in CA 112
Limburg, Peter R(ichard) 1929- ... 33-36R
See also SATA 13
Limentani, Uberto 1913-1989(?) ... 17-20R
Obituary ... 129
Limerick, Jeffrey W. 1948- ... 102
Limmer, Ruth 1927- ... CANR-1
Earlier sketch in CA 45-48
Limon, Jerzy 1950- ... 153
Limon, Martin 1948- ... 163
Limonov, Edward 1944- ... 137
See also CLC 67
Limpert, John A. 1934- ... 77-80
Lin, Adet J(usu) 1923- ... 5-8R
Lin, Florence (Shen) ... CANR-12
Earlier sketch in CA 61-64
Lin, Frank
See Atherton, Gertrude (Franklin Horn)
Lin, Jami 1956- ... 164
Lin, Julia C(hang) 1928- ... 73-76
Lin, Maya 1959- ... AAYA 20
Lin, Nan 1938- ... 73-76
Lin, Robert K(wan-Hwan) 1937- ... CANR-10
Earlier sketch in CA 65-68
Lin, San-su C(hen) 1916- ... 17-20R
Lin, Tai-yi 1926- ... 9-12R
Lin, Tan (Anthony) 1957- ... 161
Lin, Wallace
See Leong, Russell (C.)
Lin, Yu-sheng 1934- ... 89-92
Lin, Yutang 1895-1976 ... CANR-2
Obituary ... 65-68
Earlier sketch in CA 45-48
Linamen, Harold Frederick 1921- ... 17-20R
Linaweaver, Brad 1952- ... 156
Lincecum, Jerry Bryan 1942- ... 168

Lincicome, Bernard Wesley
See Lincicome, Bernie
Lincicome, Bernie 1941- ... 136
Linck, Orville F. 1906- ... 5-8R
Lincke, Jack 1909- ... CAP-2
Earlier sketch in CA 29-32
Lincoff, Gary Henry 1942- ... 112
Lincoln, Alan Jay 1945- ... 123
Lincoln, Bruce 1948- ... CANR-45
Earlier sketches in CA 105, CANR-22
Lincoln, C(harles) Eric 1924- ... CANR-27
Earlier sketches in CA 1-4R, CANR-1
See also BW 2
See also SATA 5
Lincoln, Edith Maas 1891-1977 Obituary ... 73-76
Lincoln, G(eorge) Gould 1880-1974 Obituary ... 113
See also AITN 1
Lincoln, George Arthur 1907-1975 ... 1-4R
Obituary ... 57-60
Lincoln, Harry B. 1922- ... 25-28R
Lincoln, Henry ... 110
Lincoln, James Finney 1883-1965 ... 1-4R
Lincoln, James H. 1916- ... 25-28R
Lincoln, Kenneth Robert 1943- ... CANR-36
Earlier sketch in CA 114
Lincoln, Les
See Swatridge, Charles (John)
Lincoln, Murray D. 1892-1966 ... CAP-2
Earlier sketch in CA 19-20
Lincoln, Roger J(ohn) 1942- ... 117
Lincoln, Victoria 1904-1981 ... CAP-1
Obituary ... 104
Earlier sketch in CA 17-18
Lincoln, W(illiam) Bruce 1938- ... CANR-29
Earlier sketch in CA 85-88
Lind, Alan R(obert) 1940- ... CANR-12
Earlier sketch in CA 61-64
Lind, Andrew W(illiam) 1901- ... CANR-21
Earlier sketch in CA 45-48
Lind, Jakov
See Landwirth, Heinz
See also CAAS 4
See also CLC 1, 2, 4, 27, 82
Lind, L(evi) R(obert) 1906- ... CANR-4
Earlier sketch in CA 5-8R
Lind, Michael 1962- ... 152
Lind, Millard C. 1918- ... 115
Lind, Sidney Edmund 1914- ... 37-40R
Lind, William S(turgiss) 1947- ... CANR-49
Earlier sketch in CA 123
Lindaman, Edward B. 1920-1982 ... 77-80
Obituary ... 107
Lindars, Barnabas 1923-1991 ... CANR-27
Obituary ... 135
Earlier sketches in CA 25-28R, CANR-11
Lindau, Joan
See Alden, Joan
Lindauer, John Howard 1937- ... 21-24R
Lindauer, Lois Lyons 1933- ... CANR-35
Earlier sketch in CA 49-52
Lindauer, Martin 1918- ... 5-8R
Linday, Ryllis Elizabeth Paine 1919- ... 13-16R
Lindbeck, (K.) Assar (E.) 1930- ... 37-40R
Lindberg, Carter 1937- ... CANR-47
Earlier sketch in CA 112
Lindberg, David C. 1935- ... CANR-11
Earlier sketch in CA 69-72
Lindberg, Gary H(ans) 1941- ... 65-68
Lindberg, Gladys 1905(?)-1990 Obituary ... 131
Lindberg, Leon N. 1932- ... 33-36R
Lindberg, Lucile 1913- ... 37-40R
Lindberg, Paul M(artin) 1905- ... 5-8R
Lindberg, Richard 1953- ... CANR-52
Earlier sketches in CA 110, CANR-27
Lindberg, Stanley W(illiam) 1939- ... 112
Lindbergh, Anne
See Sapieyevski, Anne Lindbergh
See also SATA 81
Lindbergh, Anne (Spencer) Morrow 1906- ... CANR-16
Earlier sketch in CA 17-20R
See also CLC 82
See also DAM NOV
See also MTCW 1
See also SATA 33
Lindbergh, Charles A(ugustus, Jr.) 1902-1974 ... CANR-16
Obituary ... 53-56
Earlier sketch in CA 93-96
See also SATA 33
Lindberg-Seyersted, Brita 1923- ... 111
Lindblom, Charles E(dward) 1917- ... CANR-1
Earlier sketch in CA 1-4R
Lindblom, (Christian) Johannes 1882-1974 Obituary ... 53-56
Lindblom, Steven (Winther) 1946- ... CANR-47
Earlier sketches in CA 106, CANR-23
See also SATA 42, 94
See also SATA-Brief 39
Linde, Gunnel 1924- ... CANR-27
Earlier sketches in CA 21-24R, CANR-11
See also SATA 5
Linde, Nancy 1949- ... 160
Linde, Shirley Motter 1929- ... CANR-18
Earlier sketches in CA 45-48, CANR-1
Lindeburg, Franklin Alfred 1918- ... 5-8R
Lindeman, Jack 1924- ... 21-24R
Lindemann, Albert S(hirk) 1938- ... 49-52
Lindemann, Constance 1923- ... 61-64
Lindemann, Herbert Fred 1909- ... 29-32R
Linden, Catherine 1939- ... 110
Linden, George William 1938- ... 65-68
Linden, Kathryn (Wolaver) 1925- ... 37-40R
Linden, Oliver
See Abrahams, Doris Caroline
Linden, Patricia
See Nutting, Patricia Fink
Linden, Sara
See Bartlett, Marie (Swan)
Lindenau, Judith Wood 1941- ... 77-80
Lindenbaum, Pija 1955- ... 145
See also SATA 77
Lindenberger, Herbert (Samuel) 1929- ... CANR-3
Earlier sketch in CA 5-8R
Lindenfeld, David Frank 1944- ... 106
Lindenfeld, Frank 1934- ... 33-36R
Lindenmeyer, Otto J. 1936- ... 77-80
Linder, Bertram L. 1931- ... CANR-2
Earlier sketch in CA 49-52
Linder, Bill R. 1937- ... 112
Linder, Darwyn E(llsworth) 1939- ... 57-60
Linder, Erich 1925(?)-1983 Obituary ... 109
Linder, Ivan H. 1894- ... CAP-1
Earlier sketch in CA 9-10
Linder, Leslie (?)-1973 Obituary ... 41-44R
Linder, Marc 1946- ... 142
Linder, Mark 1944- ... 120
Linder, Norma West 1928- ... 97-100
Linder, Robert D(ean) 1933- ... 41-44R
Linder, Staffan B.
See Linder, Staffan Burenstam
Linder, Staffan Burenstam 1931- ... 152
Brief entry ... 105
Linder, Steven 1953- ... 112
Linderman, Earl W. 1931- ... 33-36R
Linderman, Gerald F(loyd) 1934- ... 85-88
Linderman, Lawrence 1940- ... 128
Linderman, Winifred B. ... CAP-2
Earlier sketch in CA 25-28
Lindesmith, Alfred Ray 1905- ... CAP-1
Earlier sketch in CA 9-10
Lindey, Christine 1947- ... CANR-53
Earlier sketch in CA 126
Lindfors, Judith Wells 1937- ... 117
Lindfors, Viveca 1920- ... 128
Lindgren, Alvin J. 1917- ... CANR-8
Earlier sketch in CA 17-20R
Lindgren, Astrid (Ericsson) 1907- ... CANR-39
Earlier sketch in CA 13-16R
See also CLR 1, 39
See also MAICYA
See also SATA 2, 38
Lindgren, Barbro 1937- ... 149
See also CLR 20
See also SATA 63
See also SATA-Brief 46
Lindgren, Ernest H. 1910-1973 ... CAP-1
Earlier sketch in CA 13-14
Lindgren, Ethel John
See Lindgren-Utsi, E(thel) J(ohn)
Lindgren, Henry Clay 1914- ... CANR-1
Earlier sketch in CA 1-4R
Lindgren, James M. 1950- ... 146
Lindgren, Torgny 1938- ... 136
Lindgren-Utsi, E(thel) J(ohn) 1905-1988 Obituary ... 125
Lindheim, Irma Levy 1886-1978 ... 5-8R
Obituary ... 77-80
Lindholdt, Paul J. 1954- ... 137
Lindholm, Charles T. 1946- ... 134
Lindholm, Megan 1952- ... 155
Lindholm, Richard W(adsworth) 1914- ... CANR-5
Earlier sketch in CA 1-4R
Lindisfarne, Nancy 1944- ... 143
Lindisfarne-Tapper, Nancy
See Lindisfarne, Nancy
Lindley, Betty G(rimes) 1900(?)-1976 Obituary ... 65-68
Lindley, Denver 1904-1982 Obituary ... 106
Lindley, Erica
See Quigley, Aileen
Lindley, Ernest K(idder) 1899-1979 Obituary ... 89-92
Lindley, Hilda 1919(?)-1980 Obituary ... 102
Lindley, Kenneth (Arthur) 1928- ... CANR-10
Earlier sketch in CA 5-8R
Lindman, Maj (Jan) 1886-1972 ... SATA 43
Lindner, D. Berry
See Du Breuil, (Elizabeth) L(or)inda
Lindner, Edgar T(heodore) 1911- ... 57-60
Lindner, Koenraad J(an) 1941- ... 165
Lindop, Audrey (Beatrice Noel) Erskine
See Erskine-Lindop, Audrey (Beatrice Noel)
Lindop, Christine (Robin) 1949- ... 128
Lindop, Edmund 1925- ... CANR-38
Earlier sketches in CA 5-8R, CANR-2, 17
See also SATA 5
Lindop, Grevel 1948- ... CANR-29
Earlier sketches in CA 61-64, CANR-13
Lindow, John Frederick 1946- ... 113
Lindow, Wesley 1910- ... 45-48
Lindquist, Donald 1930- ... 65-68
Lindquist, E(veret) F(ranklin) 1901-1978 Obituary ... 77-80
Lindquist, Emory Kempton 1908-1992 ... CANR-31
Obituary ... 136
Earlier sketch in CA 49-52
Lindquist, Jennie Dorothea 1899-1977 ... 73-76
Obituary ... 69-72
See also SATA 13
Lindquist, John H(enry) 1931- ... 41-44R
Lindquist, Mark 1959- ... 136
Lindquist, Ray (Irving) 1941- ... 45-48
Lindquist, Rowena Cory 1958- ... 165
Lindquist, Rowena Cory 1958- ... SATA 98
Lindquist, Willis 1908- ... 73-76
See also SATA 20
Lindsay, Alexander William 1812-1880 ... DLB 184
Lindsay, Caroline Blanche Elizabeth Fitzroy Lindsay
See Lindsay, Lady
Lindsay, Catherine Brown 1928- ... 21-24R
Lindsay, Cressida 1934- ... 21-24R
Lindsay, David c. 1485-1555 ... DLB 132
Lindsay, David 1878-1945 Brief entry ... 113
See also TCLC 15
Lindsay, Dorothy 1902(?)-1983 Obituary ... 110
Lindsay, Frank Whiteman 1909- ... 104
Lindsay, Frederic 1933- ... 143
Lindsay, Harold Arthur 1900- ... 5-8R
Lindsay, Howard 1889-1968 Obituary ... 25-28R
Lindsay, Ian G(ordon) 1906-1966 ... CAP-1
Earlier sketch in CA 9-10
Lindsay, Inabel (Frances) B(urns) 1900-1983 Obituary ... 110
Lindsay, J(ohn) Robert 1925- ... 13-16R
Lindsay, Jack 1900-1990 ... CANR-11
Obituary ... 131
Earlier sketch in CA 9-12R
See also Preston, Richard
See also DLBY 84
Lindsay, James Martin 1924- ... 29-32R
Lindsay, Jean 1926- ... CANR-11
Earlier sketch in CA 25-28R
Lindsay, Jeanne Warren 1929- ... CANR-22
Earlier sketch in CA 106
Lindsay, John
See Ladell, John L.
Lindsay, John (Joseph) 1921-1988 Obituary ... 127
Lindsay, John Vliet 1921- ... 101
Lindsay, Kenneth C(lement) 1919- ... 112
Lindsay, Lady 1844-1912 ... DLB 199
Lindsay, Loelia (Mary) 1902-1993 ... 133
Obituary ... 143
Lindsay, Martin Alexander 1905-1981 Obituary ... 103
Lindsay, Mary
See Nonhebel, Clare
Lindsay, (John) Maurice 1918- ... CANR-47
Earlier sketches in CA 9-12R, CANR-6, 22
Lindsay, Merrill K(irk) 1915-1985 ... 73-76
Obituary ... 115
Lindsay, Michael (Francis Morris) 1909-1994 ... CANR-1
Obituary ... 144
Earlier sketch in CA 45-48
Lindsay, Norman Alfred William 1879-1969 ... 102
See also CLR 8
See also SATA 67
Lindsay, Perry
See Dern, Erolie Pearl Gaddis
Lindsay, R(obert) Bruce 1900- ... CANR-8
Earlier sketch in CA 13-16R
Lindsay, Rae ... 109
Lindsay, Robert 1924- ... 77-80
Lindsay, Thomas Fanshawe 1910- ... 21-24R
Lindsay, (Nicholas) Vachel 1879-1931 ... 135
Brief entry ... 114
See also CDALB 1865-1917
See also DA
See also DAC
See also DAM MST, POET
See also DLB 54
See also PC 23
See also SATA 40
See also TCLC 17
See also WLC
Lindsay, Zaidee 1923- ... 29-32R
Lindsell, Harold 1913-1998 ... CANR-5
Obituary ... 164
Earlier sketch in CA 13-16R
Lindsey, Alfred J. 1931- ... 41-44R
Lindsey, Almont 1906- ... 1-4R
Lindsey, Alton A(nthony) 1907- ... 131
Lindsey, David 1914- ... 9-12R
Lindsey, David L. 1944- ... 162
Lindsey, George R(oy) 1920- ... 65-68
Lindsey, Hal ... CANR-22
Earlier sketch in CA 104
Lindsey, Jim 1957- ... 65-68
Lindsey, (Helen) Johanna 1952- ... CANR-66
Earlier sketches in CA 73-76, CANR-18, 40
Interview in ... CANR-18
Lindsey, Karen 1944- ... 73-76
Lindsey, Robert (Hughes) 1935- ... CANR-50
Earlier sketches in CA 97-100, CANR-22
Interview in ... CANR-22
Lindskold, Jane M. 1962- ... 147
Lindskoog, Kathryn (Ann) 1934- ... CANR-50
Earlier sketches in CA 65-68, CANR-10, 25
Lindsley, Mary F(rances) ... CANR-30
Earlier sketches in CA 61-64, CANR-9
Lindstrom, Carl E(inar) 1896-1969 ... 1-4R
Obituary ... 103
Lindstrom, Lamont (Carl) 1953- ... 143
Lindstrom, Naomi (Eva) 1950- ... CANR-30
Earlier sketch in CA 112
Lindstrom, Thais (Stakhy) 1917- ... 21-24R
Lindt, Gillian 1932- ... 107
Lindvall, Michael L(loyd) 1947- ... 146
Line, David
See Davidson, Lionel
Line, Les 1935- ... 73-76
See also SATA 27
Line, Maurice Bernard 1928- ... 107
Lineaweaver, Thomas H(astings) III 1926- ... 73-76
Lineback, Richard H(arold) 1936- ... CANR-31
Earlier sketch in CA 29-32R
Linebarger, J(ames) M(orris) 1934- ... CANR-2
Earlier sketch in CA 49-52
Linebarger, Paul M(yron) A(nthony) 1913-1966 ... CANR-6
Earlier sketch in CA 5-8R
See also Smith, Cordwainer
Lineberry, John H(arvey) 1926- ... 1-4R
Lineberry, Robert L(eon) 1942- ... CANR-18
Earlier sketch in CA 73-76
Linecar, Howard (Walter Arthur) 1912- ... 110
Linedecker, Clifford L. 1931- ... 73-76
Linen, James A. III 1912-1988 Obituary ... 124
Linenthal, Edward Tabor 1947- ... CANR-30
Earlier sketch in CA 112
Lines, Kathleen Mary 1902-1988 Obituary ... 127
See also SATA-Obit 61
Linet, Beverly 1929- ... CANR-22
Earlier sketch in CA 89-92
Linett, Deena 1938- ... 113
Linfield, Esther ... 112
See also SATA 40
Ling, Amy 1939- ... 137
Ling, Arthur (William) 1901- ... 5-8R
Ling, Cyril Curtis 1936- ... 17-20R
Ling, Dwight L(eroy) 1923- ... CANR-11
Earlier sketch in CA 21-24R
Ling, H(sien) C(hang) 1910- ... 57-60
Ling, Hung-hsun 1894(?)-1981 Obituary ... 105
Ling, Jack (Chieh Sheng) 1930- ... 25-28R
Ling, Mona ... 9-12R
Ling, Peter J(ohn) 1956- ... 135
Ling, Roger (John) 1942- ... CANR-41
Earlier sketches in CA 103, CANR-19
Ling, Trevor 1920- ... CANR-11
Earlier sketch in CA 21-24R
Lingard, Joan 1932- ... CANR-40
Earlier sketches in CA 41-44R, CANR-18
See also JRDA
See also MAICYA
See also SAAS 5
See also SATA 8, 74
Lingeman, Richard R(oberts) 1931- ... CANR-11
Earlier sketch in CA 17-20R
Lingenfelter, Richard Emery 1934- ... CANR-5
Earlier sketch in CA 13-16R
Lingenfelter, Sherwood Galen 1941- ... 53-56
Lingis, Alphonso Frank 1933- ... CANR-15
Earlier sketch in CA 37-40R
Lings, Martin 1909- ... 57-60
Linhart, Robert 1944- ... 130
Linington, (Barbara) Elizabeth 1921-1988 ... CANR-65
Obituary ... 125
Earlier sketches in CA 1-4R, CANR 1, CANR-20
Link, Arthur S(tanley) 1920-1998 ... CANR-3
Obituary ... 165
Earlier sketch in CA 1-4R
See also DLB 17
Link, Edwin A(lbert) 1904-1981 Obituary ... 108
Link, Eugene P(erry) 1907- ... 37-40R
Link, Frederick M(artin) 1930- ... CANR-4
Earlier sketch in CA 53-56
Link, (S.) Gordden 1907-1986 ... 120
Link, Howard Anthony 1934- ... 127
Link, John R(einhardt) 1907- ... 17-20R
Link, Mark J(oseph) 1924- ... CANR-42
Earlier sketches in CA 13-16R, CANR-5, 20
Link, Martin 1934- ... 106
See also SATA 28
Link, Matthew 1969- ... 167
Link, (Eugene) Perry (Jr.) 1944- ... 105
Link, Robert G(rant) 1918-1984 Obituary ... 113
Link, Ruth 1923- ... 29-32R
Link, Theodore Carl 1905(?)-1974 Obituary ... 104
Link, William 1933- ... CANR-41
Earlier sketches in CA 73-76, CANR-13
Linke, Maria (Zeitner) 1908- ... 65-68
Linke-Poot
See Doeblin, Alfred
Linker, Robert White 1905- ... 104
Linklater, Andro ... 168
Linklater, Eric (Robert Russell) 1899-1974 ... CAP-2
Obituary ... 53-56
Earlier sketch in CA 13-14
Linklater, Magnus (Duncan) 1942- ... 131
Linklater, Richard 1962(?)- ... 152
Linkletter, Art(hur Gordan) 1912- ... CANR-4
Earlier sketch in CA 9-12R
Interview in ... CANR-4
Linkletter, John A(ustin) 1923-1985 ... 69-72
Obituary ... 115
Links, Bo 1949- ... 150
Links, J(oseph) G(luckenstein) 1904-1997 ... 81-84
Obituary ... 162
Linkugel, Wil(mer) A(lbert) 1929- ... CANR-13
Earlier sketch in CA 17-20R
Linley, John (William) 1916- ... 41-44R
Lin Mao
See Shen, Congwen
Linn, Bill
See Linn, William J(oseph)
Linn, Charles F. 1930- ... 85-88
Linn, Edward Allen 1922- ... 97-100
Linn, John Blair 1777-1804 ... DLB 37
Linn, John Gaywood 1917- ... 25-28R
Linn, Karen 1957- ... 139
Linn, William J(oseph) 1943- ... 117
Linnea, Ann 1949- ... 151
Linnea, Sharon 1956- ... 149
See also SATA 82
Linnell, Charles Lawrence Scruton 1915- ... 5-8R
Linnell, David 1928- ... 146
Linnell, Robert H(artley) 1922- ... 53-56
Linneman, Robert E. 1928- ... 29-32R
Linneman, William R(ichard) 1926- ... 125
Brief entry ... 118
Linner, Birgitta 1920- ... CANR-10
Earlier sketch in CA 21-24R
Linney, Peter 1931- ... 145
Linney, Romulus 1930- ... CANR-44
Earlier sketches in CA 1-4R, CANR-40
See also CLC 51
Linowes, David F(rancis) 1917- ... 49-52
Lins, Osman 1924- Brief entry ... 105
See also DLB 145
Linscomb, Shadrach 1971- ... 164
Linscott, Gillian 1944- ... 128

Linsenmeyer, Helen Walker 1906- CANR-1
Earlier sketch in CA 45-48
Linsky, Leonard 1922- 134
Brief entry 112
Linsley, William A(llan) 1933- 25-28R
Linstone, Harold A(drian) 1924- 112
Linstrum, Derek 1925- 107
Linthicum, Robert Charles 1936- 65-68
Lintner, John (Virgil) 1916-1983 104
Obituary 110
Linton, Barbara Leslie 1945- 33-36R
Linton, Calvin D(arlington) 1914- CANR-5
Earlier sketch in CA 13-16R
Linton, David (Hector) 1923- 9-12R
Linton, Eliza Lynn 1822-1898 DLB 18
Linton, James M(ichael) 1946- 123
Linton, Robert R. 1909(?)-1979 Obituary 89-92
Linton, Ron(ald) M. 1929- 41-44R
Linton, William James 1812-1897 DLB 32
Lintot, Barnaby Bernard fl. 1699-1736 DLB 170
Lintott, Andrew (William) 1936- 116
Lintrey, Alan R.
See Gordon, W. Terrence
Lintz, Harry McCormick 1-4R
Linzee, David (Augustine Anthony) 1952- 73-76
Linzey, Andrew 1952- 149
Linzey, Donald Wayne 1939- CANR-13
Earlier sketch in CA 61-64
Lionberger, Herbert F(rederick) 1912- 73-76
Lionel, Robert
See Fanthorpe, R(obert) Lionel
Lionni, Leo(nard) 1910- CANR-38
Earlier sketch in CA 53-56
See also CLR 7
See also DLB 61
See also MAICYA
See also SATA 8, 72
Liotta, P. H. 1956- 136
Liou, K(uo-) N(an) 1943- 145
Lipe, Dewey 1933- 85-88
Lipetz, Ben-Ami 1927- 33-36R
Lipez, Richard 1938- CANR-18
Earlier sketch in CA 101
Lipham, James Maurice 1927- 81-84
Lipinsky de Orlov, Lino S. 1908- SATA 22
Lipkin, Gladys B(albus) 1925- CANR-2
Earlier sketch in CA 49-52
Lipkin, Mack, Jr. 1943- CANR-18
Earlier sketch in CA 101
Lipkina, Lawrence (Irwin) 1934- 41-44R
Lipkind, William 1904-1974 101
Obituary 53-56
See also SATA 15
Lipking, Lawrence 1934- 130
Lipkowitz, Myron A. 1938- 149
Lipman, Aaron 1925- 21-24R
Lipman, Burton E(llis) 1931- 109
Lipman, David 1931- 21-24R
See also SATA 21
Lipman, Elinor 1950- 136
Lipman, Eugene Jay 1919-1994 9-12R
Obituary 143
Lipman, Ira A 1940- 65-68
Lipman, Jean CANR-28
Earlier sketches in CA 21-24R, CANR-10
Lipman, Marilyn 1938- 69-72
Lipman, Matthew 1923- CANR-32
Earlier sketches in CA 33-36R, CANR-13
See also SATA 14
Lipman, Maureen (Diane) 1946- 141
Lipman, Samuel 1934-1994 77-80
Obituary 147
Lipman, Vivian David 1921-1990 9-12R
Obituary 131
Lipmann, Fritz Albert 1899-1986 Obituary 119
Lipmann, Fritz Albert 1899-1986 159
Lipp, Frederick (John) 1916- 106
Lipp, Martin R(obert) 1940- 106
Lipp, Solomon 1913- Brief entry 111
Lippard, George 1822-1854 DLB 202
Lippard, Lucy R. 1937- CANR-20
Earlier sketch in CA 25-28R
Lipper, Arthur III 1931- 127
Lippert, Clarissa Start 1917- 77-80
Lipphard, William B(enjamin) 1886-1971 CAP-2
Earlier sketch in CA 29-32
Lippincott, Bertram 1898(?)-1985 Obituary 115
See also SATA-Obit 42
Lippincott, David (McCord) 1925- CANR-9
Earlier sketch in CA 61-64
Lippincott, Gary A. 1953- SATA 73
Lippincott, Joseph W(harton) 1887-1976 73-76
Obituary 69-72
See also SATA 17
Lippincott, Sara Jane Clarke 1823-1904 Brief entry 120
See also DLB 43
Lippincott, Sarah Lee 1920- 17-20R
See also SATA 22
Lippitt, Gordon L(eslie) 1920- CANR-12
Earlier sketch in CA 29-32R
Lippitt, Ronald O. 1914- 37-40R
Lippman, Edward A. 1920- 122
Lippman, Leopold 1919- 49-52
Lippman, Peter J. 1936- CANR-26
Earlier sketch in CA 108
See also SATA 31
Lippman, Theo, Jr. 1929- 33-36R
Lippmann, Walter 1889-1974 CANR-61
Obituary 53-56
Earlier sketches in CA 9-12R, CANR-6
See also AITN 1
See also DLB 29
See also MTCW 1
Lippy, Charles H(oward) 1943- 138
Lipschutz, Ilse Hempel 1923- 41-44R
Lipscomb, Commander F. W.
See Lipscomb, F(rank) W(oodgate)
Lipscomb, David M(ilton) 1935- CANR-1
Earlier sketch in CA 49-52
Lipscomb, Elizabeth J(ohnston) 1938- 115
Lipscomb, F(rank) W(oodgate) 1903-1983 29-32R
Obituary 126
Lipscomb, James 1926- 85-88
Lipsen, Charles B. 1925- 73-76
Lipset, David 1951- 129
Lipset, Seymour Martin 1922- CANR-69
Earlier sketches in CA 1-4R, CANR-1
Lipsett, Laurence Cline 1915- 9-12R
Lipsett, Suzanne 1943- 132
Lipsey, David (Lawrence) 1948- 130
Lipsey, Richard A(llan) 1930- CANR-23
Earlier sketch in CA 107
Lipsey, Richard G(eorge) 1928- CANR-17
Earlier sketch in CA 97-100
Lipsey, Robert E(dward) 1926- CANR-40
Earlier sketches in CA 5-8R, CANR-2, 18
Lipsitz, George R(aymond) 1947- CANR-32
Earlier sketch in CA 113
Lipsitz, Lou 1938- CANR-18
Earlier sketch in CA 101
Lipska, Ewa 1945- 132
Lipski, Alexander 1919- CANR-28
Earlier sketch in CA 49-52
Lipsky, David Bruce 1939- 103
Lipsky, Eleazar 1911- Brief entry 115
Lipsky, Michael 1940- 61-64
Lipsky, Mortimer 1915- 73-76
Lipson, Charles 1948- CANR-49
Earlier sketch in CA 123
Lipson, Goldie 1905- 33-36R
Lipson, Harry A(aron, Jr.) 1919- 61-64
Lipson, Leon Samuel 1921-1996 104
Obituary 153
Lipson, Leslie (Michel) 1912- 106
Lipson, Milton 1913- 65-68
Lipson, Shelley 1948- 119
Lipstadt, Deborah E(sther) 1947- 111
Lipstein, Kurt 1909- 117
Lipstreu, Otis 1919-1970 CAP-1
Earlier sketch in CA 13-16
Lipsyte, Marjorie (Rubin) 1932- 105
Lipsyte, Robert (Michael) 1938- CANR-57
Earlier sketches in CA 17-20R, CANR-8
See also AAYA 7
See also CLC 21
See also CLR 23
See also DA
See also DAC
See also DAM MST, NOV
See also JRDA
See also MAICYA
See also SATA 5, 68
Lipton, David R(obert) 1947- 97-100
Lipton, Dean 1919- CANR-31
Earlier sketch in CA 29-32R
Lipton, Eunice 140
Lipton, Lawrence 1898-1975 93-96
Obituary 57-60
See also DLB 16
Lipton, Lenny 1940- 101
Lipton, Peter 1954- 138
Liptzin, Sol(omon) 1901-1995 9-12R
Obituary 150
Liquori, Martin William, Jr. 1949- 130
Liquori, Marty
See Liquori, Martin William, Jr.
Liroff, Richard A(llan) 1948- CANR-11
Earlier sketch in CA 69-72
Lisagor, Peter 1915-1976 Obituary 69-72
Lisandrelli, Elaine Slivinski 1951- 159
See also SATA 94
Lisboa, Maria Manuel 1963- 157
Lisca, Peter 1925- 37-40R
Lischer, Richard 1943- 101
Lisci, Leonardo Ginori
See Ginori Lisci, Leonardo
Liscomb, Kathlyn Maurean 1950- 145
Liscombe, R. M.
See Windsor-Liscombe, Rhodri
Liscombe, R. W.
See Windsor-Liscombe, Rhodri
Liscow, Christian Ludwig 1701-1760 DLB 97
Lish, Gordon (Jay) 1934- 117
Brief entry 113
Interview in 117
See also CLC 45
See also DLB 130
See also SSC 18
Lishka, Gerald R 1949- 89-92
Lisi, Albert 1929- 25-28R
Lisio, Donald J(ohn) 1934- 124
Lisk, Jill 1938- 25-28R
Liska, Edward G. 1914(?)-1984 Obituary 113
Liska, George 1922- 104
Lisker, Sonia O. 1933- CANR-2
Earlier sketch in CA 49-52
See also SATA 44
Lisle, Holly 1960- 157
See also SATA 98
Lisle, Janet Taylor 1947- 153
See also SAAS 14
See also SATA 59, 96
See also SATA-Brief 47
Lisle, Laurie 1942- 133
Lisle, Seward D.
See Ellis, Edward S(ylvester)
Lison-Tolosana, Carmelo 1929- CANR-13
Earlier sketch in CA 21-24R
Lisowski, Gabriel 1946- 97-100
See also SATA 47
See also SATA-Brief 31
Lispector, Clarice 1925(?)-1977 CANR-71
Obituary 116
Earlier sketch in CA 139
See also CLC 43
See also DLB 113
Liss, Howard 1922-1995 CANR-16
Obituary 147
Earlier sketch in CA 25-28R
See also SATA 4
See also SATA-Obit 84
Liss, Jerome 1938- 53-56
Liss, Peggy K(orn) 1927- 41-44R
Liss, Robert E. 1945(?)-1979 Obituary 115
Liss, Sheldon B. 1936-1994 21-24R
Obituary 147
Lissak, Moshe (Avraham) 1928- 97-100
Lissakers, Karin 1944- 141
Lissim, Simon 1900-1981 Obituary 109
See also SATA-Brief 28
Lissitzyn, Oliver J(ames) 1912- 45-48
Lissner, Will 1908- 101
Lisson, Deborah 1941- SATA 71
List, Ilka Katherine 1935- 37-40R
See also SATA 6
List, Jacob Samuel 1896-1967 CAP-1
Earlier sketch in CA 19-20
List, Robert Stuart 1903-1983 Obituary 109
List, Shelley Steinmann 1930-1996 144
Obituary 152
Lister, Eric 1926(?)-1988(?) Obituary 125
Lister, Hal
See Lister, Harold
Lister, Harold 1922- 73-76
Lister, Laurier L. 1907-1986 Obituary 120
Lister, R(ichard) P(ercival) 1914- CANR-5
Earlier sketch in CA 9-12R
Lister, Raymond (George) 1919- CANR-49
Earlier sketches in CA 13-16R, CANR-8, 24
Listfield, Emily 1957- 127
Liston, Jack
See Maloney, Ralph Liston
Liston, Mary Dawn 1936- 53-56
Liston, Robert A. 1927- CANR-30
Earlier sketches in CA 17-20R, CANR-12
See also SATA 5
Listowel, Judith (de Marffy-Mantuano) 1904- 13-16R
Litan, Robert E(li) 1950- 131
Litchfield, Ada B(assett) 1916- CANR-10
Earlier sketch in CA 25-28R
See also SATA 5
Litchfield, Harry R(obert) 1898-1973 Obituary 41-44R
Litchfield, Robert O(rbin) (?)-1977 Obituary 73-76
Lite, Jams
See Schneck, Stephen
Lithman, Yngve Georg 1943- 132
Lithwick, Norman Harvey 1938- 61-64
Litoff, Judy Barrett 1944- 85-88
Litowinsky, Olga (Jean) 1936- 81-84
See also SATA 26
Litsey, Sarah 5-8R
Littauer, Florence 1928- 115
Littauer, Raphael (Max) 1925- Brief entry 109
Littauer, Vladimir S. 1893-1989 Obituary 129
Littell, Eliakim 1797-1870 DLB 79
Littell, Franklin H(amlin) 1917- 134
Brief entry 112
Littell, Robert 1896-1963 Obituary 93-96
Littell, Robert 1935(?)- CANR-64
Brief entry 109
Earlier sketch in CA 112
See also CLC 42
Littell, Robert S. 1831-1896 DLB 79
Litten, Julian (William Sebastian) 1947- 136
Litterer, Joseph A(ugust) 1926- CANR-35
Earlier sketches in CA 9-12R, CANR-3
Littke, Lael J. 1929- CANR-33
Earlier sketches in CA 85-88, CANR-15
See also SATA 51, 83
Little, A. Edward
See Klein, Aaron E.
Little, Alan M(acNaughton) G(ordon) 1901-1987 Obituary 124
Little, Bentley 1960- 164
Little, Bryan (Desmond Greenway) 1913- CANR-22
Earlier sketch in CA 104
Little, Charles E. 1931- 128
Little, David 1933- CANR-48
Earlier sketch in CA 29-32R
Little, Douglas 1942- 161
See also SATA 96
Little, Elbert L(uther), Jr. 1907- 57-60
Little, Elbert Payson 1912(?)-1983 Obituary 110
Little, Geraldine C(linton) 109
Little, Ian M(alcolm) D(avid) 1918- CANR-34
Earlier sketches in CA 21-24R, CANR-15
Little, Jack
See Little, John D(utton)
Little, Jane Sneddon 1942- Brief entry 113
Little, (Flora) Jean 1932- CANR-66
Earlier sketches in CA 21-24R, CANR-42
See also CLR 4
See also DAC
See also DAM MST
See also JRDA
See also MAICYA
See also SAAS 17
See also SATA 2, 68
Little, John D(utton) 1894- 65-68
Little, Kenneth
See Scotland, James
Little, Kenneth L(indsay) 1908- 17-20R
Little, Lawrence Calvin 1897-1976 CANR-3
Earlier sketch in CA 1-4R
Little, Lessie Jones 1906-1986 101
Obituary 121
See also SATA 60
See also SATA-Obit 50
Little, Lester Knox 1935- 103
Little, Loyd (Harry), Jr. 1940- 81-84
Little, Malcolm 1925-1965 125
Obituary 111
See also Malcolm X
See also BW 1
See also DA
See also DAB
See also DAC
See also DAM MST, MULT
See also MTCW 1
Little, Mary E. 1912- 105
See also SATA 28
Little, Nina Fletcher 1903- 127
Brief entry 106
Little, Paul E. 1928-1975 CAP-2
Earlier sketch in CA 21-22
Little, Paul H(ugo) 1915-1987 CANR-13
Obituary 122
Earlier sketch in CA 17-20R
Little, Paula
See Little, Paul H(ugo)
Little, Pippa 1958- 123
Little, Ray 1918(?)-1980 Obituary 102
Little, Richard 1944- 114
Little, Roger W(illiam) 1922- 29-32R
Little, Royal (D.) 1896-1989 106
Obituary 127
Little, S. George 1903-1974 Obituary 49-52
Little, Sara (Pamela) 1919- 116
Little, Stuart W. 1921- CANR-1
Earlier sketch in CA 45-48
Little, Thomas Russell 1911- 13-16R
Little, Tom
See Little, Thomas Russell
Little, William Alfred
See Little, Wm. A.
Little, Wm. A. 1929- 57-60
Littleboy, Sheila M.
See Ary, Sheila M(ary Littleboy)
Littlechild, George 1958- SATA 85
Littledale, Freya (Lota) -1992 CANR-25
Earlier sketches in CA 21-24R, CANR-10
See also SATA 2, 74
Littledale, Harold (Aylmer) 1927- 5-8R
Littlefair, Duncan (Elliot) 1912- 45-48
Littlefield, Bill 1948- 150
See also SATA 83
Littlefield, David Joseph 1928- 41-44R
Littlefield, Holly 1963- 164
See also SATA 97
Littlefield, James Edward 1932- 53-56
Littlehawk, Jay
See Goingback, Owl
Littlejohn, (Cameron) Bruce 1913- 61-64
Littlejohn, David 1937- CANR-14
Earlier sketch in CA 41-44R
Littlejohn, Duffy 1953- 146
Littleton, C(ovington) Scott 1933- 21-24R
Littleton, Harvey K(line) 1922- 53-56
Littleton, Mark (R.) 1950- 155
See also SATA 89
Littlewit, Humphrey Gent.
See Lovecraft, H(oward) P(hillips)
Littlewood, Joan (Maud) 1914- 149
Brief entry 116
See also DLB 13
Littlewood, Robert Percy 1910- 5-8R
Littlewood, Thomas B. 1928- 29-32R
Littman, Jonathan (Russell) 1958- 153
Littman, Robert J. 1943- 81-84
Litto, Fredric M. 1939- 25-28R
Litto, Gertrude 1929- 69-72
Litvag, Irving 1928- 57-60
Litvak, Isaiah A(llan) 1936- 13-16R
Litvinoff, Barnet 1917- 17-20R
Litvinoff, Emanuel 1915- 129
Brief entry 117
Litvinoff, Saul 1925- 41-44R
Litvinov, Ivy 1890(?)-1977 Obituary 69-72
Litvinov, Pavel 1940- 89-92
Litwack, Leon F(rank) 1929- CANR-1
Earlier sketch in CA 1-4R
Litwak, Eugene 1925- Brief entry 114
Litwak, Leo (E.) 1924- CANR-22
Earlier sketch in CA 5-8R
Litweiler, John (Berkey) 1940- 142
Litwos
See Sienkiewicz, Henryk (Adam Alexander Pius)
Litz, A(rthur) Walton (Jr.) 1929- 33-36R
Litzel, Otto 1901- 57-60
Litzinger, Boyd (A., Jr.) 1929- CANR-20
Earlier sketches in CA 13-16R, CANR-5
Liu, Aimee E. 1953- CANR-49
Earlier sketch in CA 89-92
Liu, Alan P(ing-) L(in) 1937- 61-64
Liu, Da 1910- 85-88
Liu, E 1857-1909 Brief entry 115
See also TCLC 15
Liu, Eric 1968- 146
Liu, James J(o) Y(u) 1926- CANR-7
Earlier sketch in CA 5-8R
Liu, James T(zu) C(hien) 1919- 21-24R
Liu, Jung-Chao 1929- 29-32R
Liu, Leo Yueh-yun 1940- 41-44R
Liu, Sarah 1943- CANR-38
Earlier sketch in CA 115
Liu, Sydney (Chieh) 1920- 103
Liu, Tzu-chien
See Liu, James T(zu) C(hien)
Liu, William T(homas) 1930- CANR-13
Earlier sketch in CA 21-24R

Liu, Wu-chi 1907- CANR-50
Earlier sketches in CA 13-16R, CANR-10, 25
Liu, Yong
See Liu, William T(homas)
Liu Binyan 1925- 136
Liu Zongren 1940- 116
Livant, Rose Adleman 1899(?)-1986 Obituary .. 120
Lively, Adam 1961- 147
Lively, Penelope (Margaret) 1933- CANR-67
Earlier sketches in CA 41-44R, CANR-29
See also CLC 32, 50
See also CLR 7
See also DAM NOV
See also DLB 14, 161
See also JRDA
See also MAICYA
See also MTCW 1
See also SATA 7, 60, 101
Lively, Walter
See Elliott, Bruce (Walter Gardner Lively Stacy)
Liverani, Giuseppe 1903- CANR-6
Earlier sketch in CA 5-8R
Liverani, Mary Rose 1939- 104
Livergood, Norman D(avid) 1933- 37-40R
Livermore, Jean
See Sanville, Jean
Livermore, Seward W. 1901(?)-1984 Obituary .. 112
Livermore, Shaw 1902- CAP-2
Earlier sketch in CA 19-20
Liversidge, (Henry) Douglas 1913- CAP-1
Earlier sketch in CA 9-10
See also SATA 8
Liversidge, Joan (Eileen Annie) 1915(?)-1984 .. 103
Obituary 112
Liverton, Joan 1913- CAP-1
Earlier sketch in CA 9-10
Livesay, Dorothy (Kathleen) 1909- CANR-67
Earlier sketches in CA 25-28R, CANR-36
See also CAAS 8
See also AITN 2
See also CLC 4, 15, 79
See also DAC
See also DAM MST, POET
See also DLB 68
See also MTCW 1
Livesay, Florence Randal 1874-1953 .... DLB 92
Livesey, Claire Warner 1927- 29-32R
Livgren, Kerry 1949- 114
Livia, Anna 1955- CANR-71
Earlier sketch in CA 119
Livie-Noble, Frederick Stanley 1899-1970 ... CAP-1
Earlier sketch in CA 9-10
Livingood, James W(eston) 1910- CANR-32
Earlier sketches in CA 17-20R, CANR-8
Livings, Henry 1929-1998 .... CANR-71
Earlier sketch in CA 13-16R
See also DLB 13
Livingston, A(lfred) D(elano) 1932- CANR-13
Earlier sketch in CA 17-20R
Livingston, Anne Home 1763-1841 .... DLB 37, 200
Livingston, Bernard 1911- 81-84
Livingston, Carole 1941- 105
See also SATA 42
Livingston, Dorothy Michelson 1906- 49-52
Livingston, Elizabeth J(ane) 1952- 113
Livingston, George Herbert 1916- 53-56
Livingston, Gordon (S.) 1938- 149
Livingston, Harold 1924- 1-4R
Livingston, J(oseph) A(rnold) 1905-1989 .... 1-4R
Obituary 130
Livingston, James C(raig) 1930- CANR-21
Earlier sketch in CA 45-48
Livingston, Jane S(helton) 1944- 107
Livingston, Jayson 1965- 136
Livingston, John A. 1937- 166
Livingston, Jon 1944- 49-52
Livingston, M. Jay
See Livingston, Myran Jabez, Jr.
Livingston, Martha 1945- 115
Livingston, Myra Cohn 1926-1996 .... CANR-58
Obituary 153
Earlier sketches in CA 1-4R, CANR-1, 33
Interview in CANR-33
See also CLR 7
See also DLB 61
See also MAICYA
See also SAAS 1
See also SATA 5, 68,
See also SATA-Obit 92
Livingston, Myran Jabez, Jr. 1934- CANR-22
Earlier sketch in CA 105
Livingston, Nancy 1935-1994 .... CANR-62
Earlier sketch in CA 134
Livingston, Paisley 1951- 136
Livingston, Peter Van Rensselaer
See Townsend, James B(arclay) J(ermain)
Livingston, Richard R(oland) 1922- 45-48
See also SATA 8
Livingston, Robert B(urr) 1918- 97-100
Livingston, Robert Henry 1934- 134
Livingston, William 1723-1790 .... DLB 31
Livingston, William S. 1920- CANR-3
Earlier sketch in CA 9-12R
Livingstone, Angela 1934- 119
Livingstone, Bernard L. 1907(?)-1984 Obituary . 112
Livingstone, David 1813-1873 .... DLB 166
Livingstone, Douglas (James) 1932- CANR-20
Earlier sketches in CA 13-16R, CANR-5
Livingstone, Harrison Edward 1937- CANR-52
Earlier sketch in CA 33-36R
Livingstone, J(ohn) Leslie 1932- 73-76
Livingstone, Leon 1912- 33-36R
Livingstone, Marco (Eduardo) 1952- CANR-49
Earlier sketches in CA 107, CANR-24
Livo, Norma J. 1929- CANR-49
Earlier sketch in CA 123
See also SATA 76
Livoni, Cathy 1956- 113
Livsey, Clara G(rabois) 1924- 107
Livson, Norman 1924- 49-52
Li Yikai 1932- 141
Liyong, Taban lo 1938- 105
See also BW 2
Lizardi, Joseph 1941- 129
See also HW
Lizarraga, Sylvia S. 1925- .... DLB 82
Lizotte, Ken 1948- 126
Ljoka, Daniel J. 1935- 49-52
Ljubomir, Simovic 1935- .... DLB 181
Llano, George A(lbert) 1911- 125
Lleo, Manuel Urrutia
See Urrutia Lleo, Manuel
Llerena, Mario 1913- 81-84
Llerena Aguirre, Carlos (Antonio) 1952- 77-80
See also SATA 19
Llewellyn, Claire 1954- .... SATA 77
Llewellyn, D(avid) W(illiam) Alun 1903- 57-60
Llewellyn, Edward
See Llewellyn-Thomas, Edward
Llewellyn, Kate 1940- 153
Llewellyn, Richard
See Llewellyn Lloyd, Richard Dafydd Vivian
See also DLB 15
Llewellyn, Sam 1948- 140
See also SATA 95
Llewellyn-Jones, Derek 1923- CANR-34
Earlier sketches in CA 37-40R, CANR-15
Llewellyn Lloyd, Richard Dafydd Vivian 1906-1983 .
CANR-71
Obituary 111
Earlier sketches in CA 53-56, CANR-7
See also Llewellyn, Richard
See also CLC 7, 80
See also SATA 11
See also SATA-Obit 37
Llewellyn-Thomas, Edward 1917- 104
Llewellyn-Williams, Hilary (Maria) 1951- 127
Llewelyn, T. Harcourt
See Hamilton, Charles (Harold St. John)
Llewelyn-Davies, Richard 1912-1981 .... 13-16R
Obituary 105
Llewelyn-Owens, Joan (Margaret) 1919- . CANR-36
Llorens, Vicente 1906-1979 Obituary 89-92
LLorens, Washington 1900- .... HW
Llorens, Washington 1900- 153
Lloret, Antoni 1935- 29-32R
Llosa, (Jorge) Mario (Pedro) Vargas
See Vargas Llosa, (Jorge) Mario (Pedro)
Llosa, Ricardo Pau
See Pau-Llosa, Ricardo
Lloyd, A(lan) R(ichard) 1927- 155
See also SATA 97
Lloyd, Adrien
See Gelb, Alan Lloyd
Lloyd, Alan
See Lloyd, A(lan) R(ichard)
Lloyd, Alan C(hester) 1915- CANR-1
Earlier sketch in CA 1-4R
Lloyd, Albert Lancaster 1908-1982 Obituary ... 107
Lloyd, Charles
See Birkin, Charles (Lloyd)
Lloyd, (Charles) Christopher
1906-1986 Obituary 119
Lloyd, Christopher 1921- CANR-46
Earlier sketch in CA 120
Lloyd, Craig 1940- 61-64
Lloyd, Cynthia B(rown) 1943- CANR-8
Earlier sketch in CA 61-64
Lloyd, David 1946- 89-92
Lloyd, David Demarest 1911-1962 .... CAP-1
Earlier sketch in CA 11-12
Lloyd, Dennis 1915- 13-16R
Lloyd, E. James
See James, Elizabeth
Lloyd, Elisabeth A. 1956- 139
Lloyd, Errol 1943- 101
See also SATA 22
Lloyd, Francis V(ernon), Jr. 1908- CAP-2
Earlier sketch in CA 21-22
Lloyd, G(eoffrey) E(rnest) R(ichard) 1933- 57-60
Lloyd, Howell Arnold 1937- 103
Lloyd, Hugh
See Fitzhugh, Percy Keese
Lloyd, Hugh (Pughe) 1894-1981 Obituary 108
Lloyd, J. Ivester 1905- 13-16R
Lloyd, Jack Ivester
See Lloyd, J. Ivester
Lloyd, James
See James, Elizabeth
Lloyd, James Barlow 1945- 112
Lloyd, John Ivester
See Lloyd, J. Ivester
Lloyd, John S. B. Selwyn
See Selwyn-Lloyd, John S. B.
Lloyd, Levanah
See Peters, Maureen
Lloyd, Lisa
See Lloyd, Elisabeth A.
Lloyd, Manda
See Mander, (Mary) Jane
Lloyd, Margaret Glynne 1946- 130
Lloyd, Marjorie 1909- CANR-8
Earlier sketch in CA 5-8R
Lloyd, Megan 1958- .... SATA 77
Lloyd, Norman 1909-1980 .... CANR-28
Obituary 101
Earlier sketch in CA 37-40R
See also SATA-Obit 23
Lloyd, (Mary) Norris 1908-1993 .... CANR-1
Obituary 140
Earlier sketch in CA 1-4R
See also SATA 10
See also SATA-Obit 75
Lloyd, Peter C(utt) 1927- CANR-11
Earlier sketch in CA 25-28R
Lloyd, Peter Edward 1938- 107
Lloyd, Robin 1925- 73-76
Lloyd, Ronald
See Friedland, Ronald Lloyd
Lloyd, Rosemary (Helen) 1949- 116
Lloyd, Sarah
See Cox, Jennifer Lloyd
Lloyd, Seton (Howard Frederick) 1902-1996 ... 132
Obituary 151
Lloyd, Stephanie
See Golding, Morton J(ay)
Lloyd, Trevor (Owen) 1934- 25-28R
Lloyd Evans, Barbara 1924- CANR-37
Earlier sketch in CA 93-96
Lloyd Evans, Gareth 1923-1984 Obituary 117
Lloyd George (of Dwyor), Frances (Louise
1888(?)-1972 Obituary 37-40R
Lloyd-Jones, Esther McDonald 1901- 13-16R
Lloyd-Jones, (Peter) Hugh (Jefferd) 1922- ....
CANR-21
Earlier sketches in CA 5-8R, CANR-4
Lloyd-Jones, Robin 1934- 111
Lloyd Owen, David Lanyon 1917- 117
Lloyd-Thomas, Catherine 1917- 65-68
Lloyd Webber, Andrew 1948- 149
Brief entry 116
See also Webber, Andrew Lloyd
See also AAYA 1
See also DAM DRAM
See also SATA 56
Llywelyn, Morgan 1937- CANR-16
Earlier sketch in CA 81-84
Interview in CANR-16
Llywelyn-Williams, Alun 1913- CAP-1
Earlier sketch in CA 9-10
Lo, Irving Yucheng 1922- 57-60
Lo, Ruth Earnshaw 1910- 106
Lo, Samuel E. 1931- 29-32R
Lo, Steven C. 1949- 132
Lo, Winston W. 1938- 133
Loader, William Reginald 1916- 1-4R
Loades, David Michael 1934- 17-20R
Loane, Marcus L(awrence) 1911- CANR-2
Earlier sketch in CA 1-4R
Loasby, Brian John 1930- 93-96
Lobb, Charlotte 1935- CANR-15
Earlier sketch in CA 65-68
Lobb, Ebenezer
See Upward, Allen
Lobban, Carolyn Fluehr
See Fluehr-Lobban, Carolyn
Lobban, Richard A., Jr. 1943- 144
Lobdell, Helen 1919- 9-12R
Lobdell, Jared C(harles) 1937- CANR-28
Earlier sketch in CA 49-52
Lobel, Anita (Kempler) 1934- CANR-68
Earlier sketches in CA 53-56, CANR-9, 33
See also MAICYA
See also SATA 6, 55, 96
Lobel, Arnold (Stark) 1933-1987 .... CANR-33
Obituary 124
Earlier sketches in CA 1-4R, CANR-2
See also AITN 1
See also CLR 5
See also DLB 61
See also MAICYA
See also SATA 6, 55
See also SATA-Obit 54
Lobel, Brana 1942- 97-100
Lobel, Edgar 1889-1982 Obituary 107
Lobel, Stanley 1937- 111
Lo Bello, Nino 1921- CANR-53
Earlier sketches in CA 29-32R, CANR-12, 28
Loberg, Mary Alice 1943- 29-32R
Lobkowicz, Nicholas 1931- CANR-32
Earlier sketches in CA 21-24R, CANR-10
Lobley, Robert (John) 1934- CANR-29
Earlier sketch in CA 29-32R
Lobo, Anthony S(avio) 1937- 49-52
Lobsenz, Amelia 13-16R
See also SATA 12
Lobsenz, Norman M(itchell) 1919- CANR-4
Earlier sketch in CA 9-12R
See also SATA 6
Loch, Joice N(anKivell) 1893-1982 .... 25-28R
Obituary 108
Lochak, Michele 1936- 106
See also SATA 39
Lochard, Metz T(ullus) P(aul)
1896-1984 Obituary 112
Lochbiler, Don 1908- 49-52
Locher, Dick
See Locher, Richard (Earl)
Locher, Frances C(arol) CANR-17
Earlier sketch in CA 97-100
Locher, Richard (Earl) 1929- CANR-16
Earlier sketch in CA 85-88
Lochhead, Douglas (Grant) 1922- CANR-39
Earlier sketches in CA 45-48, CANR-1, 16
Lochhead, Liz 1947- 81-84
Lochhead, Marion Cleland 1902-1985 101
Obituary 115
Lochlons, Colin
See Jackson, C(aary) Paul
Lochman, Jan Milic 1922- CANR-28
Earlier sketches in CA 29-32R, CANR-12
Lochnan, Katharine A. 1946- 127
Lochner, Louis P(aul) 1887-1975 65-68
Obituary 53-56
Lochridge, Betsy Hopkins
See Fancher, Betsy
Lochte, Dick
See Lochte, Richard S(amuel)
Lochte, Richard S(amuel) 1944- CANR-66
Earlier sketches in CA 105, CANR-23, 47
LoCicero, Donald 1937- 25-28R
Lock, C(lara) B(eatrice) Muriel 1914- 49-52
Lock, C. J. S.
See Lock, Charles (John Somerset)
Lock, Charles (John Somerset) 1955- 146
Lock, Dennis (Laurence) 1929- CANR-32
Earlier sketches in CA 41-44R, CANR-14
Lock, F(rederick) P(eter) 1948- 118
Lock, Fred
See Lock, F(rederick) P(eter)
Lock, Joan 1933- 132
Lock, Margaret M. 1936- 126
Lockard, Craig Alan 1942- 122
Lockard, (Walter) Duane 1921- 17-20R
Lockard, Isabel 1915- 141
Lockard, Leonard
See Thomas, Theodore L.
Locke, Alain (Le Roy) 1886-1954 124
Brief entry 106
See also BLCS
See also BW 1
See also DLB 51
See also TCLC 43
Locke, Charles O. 1896(?)-1977 Obituary 69-72
Locke, Clinton W. CANR-26
Earlier sketches in CAP-2, CA 19-20
See also SATA 1
Locke, David M(illard) 1929- 41-44R
Locke, David Ross 1833-1888 .... DLB 11, 23
Locke, Duane CANR-1
Earlier sketch in CA 49-52
Locke, Edwin A. III 1938- 13-16R
Locke, Elsie 1912- CANR-53
Earlier sketches in CA 25-28R, CANR-11, 26
See also SATA 87
Locke, Frederick W. 1918- 13-16R
Locke, Hubert G. 1934- 29-32R
Locke, John 1632-1704 .... DLB 101
Locke, Louis G(lenn) 1912- 33-36R
Locke, Lucie 1904- 53-56
See also SATA 10
Locke, Martin
See Duncan, W(illiam) Murdoch
Locke, Maryel 144
Locke, Michael (Stephen) 1943- 73-76
Locke, Peter
See McCutchan, J(ohn) Wilson
Locke, R. E.
See Raffelock, David
Locke, Ralph P(aul) 1949- CANR-53
Earlier sketch in CA 124
Locke, Richard Adams 1800-1871 .... DLB 43
Locke, Robert 1944- 129
See also Bess, Clayton
See also SATA 63
Locke, Robert R. 1932- 163
Locke, Steven E(lliot) 1945- 127
Locke, Wende 1945- 33-36R
Locke-Elliott, Sumner
See Elliott, Sumner Locke
Locker, Thomas 1937- CANR-66
Earlier sketch in CA 128
See also CLR 14
See also MAICYA
See also SATA 59
Lockerbie, D(onald) Bruce 1935- CANR-14
Earlier sketch in CA 37-40R
Lockerbie, Jeanette W. Honeyman CANR-5
Earlier sketch in CA 9-12R
Lockerbie, Jeannie 1938- CANR-13
Earlier sketch in CA 73-76
Locker-Lampson, Frederick 1821-1895 .... DLB 35, 184
Lockert, (Charles) Lacy (Jr.) 1888-1974 ..... CAP-2
Earlier sketch in CA 25-28
Lockert, Lucia (Alicia Ungaro Fox) 1928- . CANR-14
Earlier sketch in CA 73-76
Lockett, Reginald (Franklin) 1947- .... BW 2
Lockett, Reginald (Franklin) 1947- 153
Lockhard, Leonard
See Harness, Charles L(eonard)
Lockhart, (Jeanne) Aileene Simpson 1911- . 13-16R
Lockhart, Freda Bruce 1909-1987 Obituary 124
Lockhart, Jack Herbert 1909-1985 Obituary 117
Lockhart, John Gibson 1794-1854 ... DLB 110, 116, 144
Lockhart, Robert (Hamilton) Bruce
1886-1970 Obituary 89-92
Lockhart, Russell A(rthur) 1938- CANR-21
Earlier sketch in CA 45-48
Locklair, Wriston 1924(?)-1984 Obituary 112
Lockley, Lawrence Campbell 1899-1969 .... CAP-1
Earlier sketch in CA 11-12
Lockley, Ronald M(athias) 1903- CANR-22
Earlier sketches in CA 9-12R, CANR-5
Locklin, Gerald (Ivan) 1941- CANR-32
Earlier sketches in CA 37-40R, CANR-14
Locklin, (David) Philip 1897- 1-4R
Lockmann, Ronald F(rederick) 1942- 117
Lockmiller, David A(lexander) 1906- 77-80
Lockridge, Ernest (Hugh) 1938- 25-28R
See also AITN 1
Lockridge, Frances Louise (?)-1963 Obituary . 93-96
Lockridge, Hildegarde (Dolson) 1908-1981 ....
CANR-3
Obituary 102
Earlier sketch in CA 5-8R
See also Dolson, Hildegarde
Lockridge, Kenneth A(lan) 1940- 134
Brief entry 107

Lockridge, Laurence S(hockley) 1942- ... 130
Lockridge, Norman
See Roth, Samuel
Lockridge, Richard 1898-1982 ... CANR-62
Obituary ... 107
Earlier sketch in CA 85-88
Lockridge, Ross (Franklin), Jr. 1914-1948 ... 145
Brief entry ... 108
See also DLB 143
See also DLBY 80
Lockspeiser, Edward 1905-1973 ... CANR-6
Earlier sketch in CA 5-8R
Lockwood, Allison 1920- ... 115
Lockwood, C. C. 1949- ... CANR-41
Earlier sketch in CA 117
Lockwood, Charles Andrews 1890-1967 ... 1-4R
Lockwood, Douglas (Wright) 1918- ... 21-24R
Lockwood, Guy C. 1943- ... 65-68
Lockwood, Lee 1932- ... 37-40R
Lockwood, M(ichael) J(ohn) 1950- ... 128
Lockwood, Margo 1939- ... CANR-41
Earlier sketch in CA 117
Lockwood, Mary
See Spelman, Mary
Lockwood, Michael 1944- ... 122
Lockwood, Theodore Davidge 1924- ... CANR-1
Earlier sketch in CA 1-4R
Lockwood, W(illiam) B(urley) 1917- ... 29-32R
Lockwood, William W(irt) 1906- ... CAP-2
Earlier sketch in CA 23-24
Lockyer, Herbert 1888(?)-1984 Obituary ... 115
Lockyer, Judith 1949- ... 138
Lockyer, Roger 1927- ... CANR-12
Earlier sketch in CA 17-20R
Locre, Peter E.
See Cole, E(ugene) R(oger)
Lodder, Christina (Anne) 1948- ... 125
Lode, Rex
See Goldstein, William Isaac
Loden, Barbara (Ann) 1937-1980 Obituary ... 101
Loder, John 1898-1988 Obituary ... 128
Lodge, Bernard 1933- ... 107
See also SATA 33
Lodge, David (John) 1935- ... CANR-53
Earlier sketches in CA 17-20R, CANR-19
Interview in ... CANR-19
See also BEST 90:1
See also CLC 36
See also DAM POP
See also DLB 14, 194
See also MTCW 1
Lodge, George Cabot 1873-1909 Brief entry ... 123
See also DLB 54
Lodge, George Cabot 1927- ... 17-20R
Lodge, Henry Cabot 1850-1924 ... DLB 47
Lodge, Henry Cabot (Jr.) 1902-1985 ... 53-56
Obituary ... 115
Lodge, Jeff 1952- ... 164
Lodge, Oliver (Joseph) 1851-1940 Brief entry ... 117
Lodge, Orlan Robert 1917-1975 Obituary ... 57-60
Lodge, Thomas 1558-1625 ... DLB 172
Lodrick, Deryck O(scar) 1942- ... 106
Loeb, Arthur L. 1923- ... 145
Loeb, Benjamin S. 1914- ... 128
Loeb, Catherine (Roberta) 1949- ... 89-92
Loeb, Gerald M(artin) 1899-1974 ... CAP-1
Obituary ... 49-52
Earlier sketch in CA 13-16
Loeb, Harold A(lbert) 1891-1974 ... 106
Obituary ... 45-48
See also DLB 4
Loeb, Jacques 1859-1924 ... 161
Loeb, Jeffrey 1946- ... 123
See also SATA 57
Loeb, Karen 1946- ... 144
Loeb, Madeleine H. 1905(?)-1974 Obituary ... 45-48
Loeb, Marshall Robert 1929- ... 21-24R
Loeb, Paul Rogat 1952- ... 109
Loeb, Robert F(rederick) 1895-1973 Obituary ... 45-48
Loeb, Robert H., Jr. 1917- ... CANR-12
Earlier sketch in CA 29-32R
See also SATA 21
Loeb, William 1905-1981 ... CANR-71
Obituary ... 104
Earlier sketch in CA 93-96
Interview in ... 93-96
See also DLB 127
Loebl, Eugen 1907-1987 Obituary ... 123
Loebl, Suzanne ... 69-72
Loeffelholz, Mary 1958- ... 141
Loefgren, Ulf 1931- ... CANR-16
Earlier sketch in CA 25-28R
See also SATA 3
Loefstedt, Bengt 1931- ... CANR-1
Earlier sketch in CA 45-48
Loehlin, John C(linton) 1926- ... 21-24R
Loemker, Leroy E(arl) 1900- ... 41-44R
Loen, Raymond O(rdell) 1924- ... 146
Loengard, John 1934- ... 133
Loening, Grover C. 1889(?)-1976 Obituary ... 65-68
Loening, Sarah (Elizabeth) Larkin 1896-1988 ... CANR-21
Obituary ... 124
Earlier sketch in CA 45-48
Loennbohm, Armas Eino Leopold 1878-1926 Brief entry ... 123
See also Leino, Eino
Loeoef, Jan 1940- ... 81-84
Loeper, John J(oseph) 1929- ... CANR-12
Earlier sketch in CA 29-32R
See also SATA 10
Loertscher, David V. 1940- ... 126
Loesch, Juli(anne) 1951- ... 89-92
Loescher, Ann Dull 1942- ... CANR-9
Earlier sketch in CA 61-64
See also SATA 20
Loescher, Gil(burt Damian) 1945- ... CANR-9
Earlier sketch in CA 61-64
See also SATA 20
Loeschke, Maravene Sheppard 1947- ... 115
Loeser, Herta 1921- ... 57-60
Loeser, Katinka 1913-1991 ... 17-20R
Obituary ... 133
Loesser, Francis Henry 1910-1969 Obituary ... 112
Loesser, Frank
See Loesser, Francis Henry
Loether, Herman J(ohn) 1930- ... 21-24R
Loetscher, Lefferts A(ugustine) 1904- ... 5-8R
Loevinger, Jane 1918- ... 41-44R
Loevinger, Lee 1913- ... CANR-15
Earlier sketch in CA 81-84
Loew, Ralph William 1907- ... CAP-1
Earlier sketch in CA 19-20
Loew, Sebastian 1939- ... CANR-19
Earlier sketch in CA 103
Loewald, Hans W. 1906-1993 ... CANR-46
Obituary ... 140
Earlier sketch in CA 101
Loewe, Michael 1922- ... 133
Loewe, Ralph E. 1923- ... 21-24R
Loewe, Raphael J(ames) 1919- ... CANR-42
Earlier sketch in CA 118
Loewen, James W. 1942- ... CANR-50
Earlier sketches in CA 37-40R, CANR-14
Loewenberg, Bert James 1905-1974 ... CANR-5
Earlier sketch in CA 9-12R
Loewenberg, Frank M(eyer) 1925- ... CANR-2
Earlier sketch in CA 45-48
Loewenberg, Gerhard 1928- ... CANR-9
Earlier sketch in CA 21-24R
Loewenberg, J(orn) Joseph 1933- ... 33-36R
Loewenberg, Peter J(acob) 1933- ... 109
Loewenberg, Robert J(ames) 1938- Brief entry ... 114
Loewenfeld, Claire 1899-1974 ... CAP-2
Earlier sketch in CA 23-24
Loewenstein, Bernice ... SATA-Brief 40
Loewenstein(-Wertheim-Freudenberg), Hubertus (Friedrich Maria Johannes Leopold Ludwig) 1906-1984 ... CANR-29
Obituary ... 114
Earlier sketches in CA 5-8R, CANR-4
Loewenstein, Joseph 1952- ... 124
Loewenstein, Karl 1891-1973 Obituary ... 41-44R
Loewenstein, Louis Klee 1927- ... 37-40R
Loewenstein, Prince Hubertus (F. zu)
See Loewenstein(-Wertheim-Freudenberg), Hubertus (Friedrich Maria Johannes Leopold Ludwig)
Loewenstein, Rudolph M(aurice) 1898-1976 ... CAP-2
Obituary ... 65-68
Earlier sketch in CA 21-22
Loewenthal, L(eonard) J(oseph) A(lfonso) ... 61-64
Loewer, Jean
See Jenkins, Jean
Loewer, Peter 1934- ... 138
See also SATA 98
Loewinsohn, Ron(ald William) 1937- ... CANR-71
Earlier sketch in CA 25-28R
See also CLC 52
Loewith, Karl 1897-1973 Obituary ... 116
Loewy, Ariel G(ideon) 1925- ... 89-92
Loewy, Erich H. 1927- ... 139
Loewy, Raymond Fernand 1893-1986 ... 104
Obituary ... 119
LoFaro, Jerry 1959- ... SATA 77
Lofaro, Michael Anthony 1948- ... 89-92
Lofas, Jeannette 1940- ... 157
Lofland, John (Franklin) 1936- ... CANR-12
Earlier sketch in CA 33-36R
Lofland, Lyn (Hebert) 1937- ... 61-64
Lofstedt, Bengt
See Loefstedt, Bengt
Loftas, Tony 1940- ... 21-24R
Lofthouse, Jessica 1916-1988 ... 29-32R
Obituary ... 125
Lofthus, Myrna 1935- ... 115
Lofting, Hugh (John) 1886-1947 ... 137
Brief entry ... 109
See also CLR 19
See also DLB 160
See also MAICYA
See also SATA 15, 100
Loftis, Anne 1922- ... 45-48
Loftis, John (Clyde, Jr.) 1919- ... CANR-3
Earlier sketch in CA 1-4R
Lofton, John (Marion) 1919- ... CANR-6
Earlier sketch in CA 9-12R
Lofts, Norah (Robinson) 1904-1983 ... CANR-6
Obituary ... 110
Earlier sketch in CA 5-8R
Interview in ... CANR-6
See also AITN 2
See also SATA 8
See also SATA-Obit 36
Loftus, Elizabeth F. 1944- ... 105
Loftus, Ernest Achey 1884-1987 Obituary ... 123
Loftus, John (Joseph) 1950- ... 117
Loftus, Richard J. 1929- ... 13-16R
Logan, Albert Boyd 1909- ... 53-56
Logan, Cait
See Kleinsasser, Lois
Logan, Daniel 1936- ... 25-28R
Logan, Deborah Norris 1761-1839 ... DLB 200
Logan, Don
See Crawford, William (Elbert)
Logan, Elizabeth D(ulaney) 1914- ... 61-64
Logan, F(rancis) Donald 1930- ... 45-48
Logan, Ford
See Newton, D(wight) B(ennett)
Logan, Frank A(nderson) 1924- ... 41-44R
Logan, Gene A(dams) 1922- ... CANR-7
Earlier sketch in CA 9-12R
Logan, George M(eredith) 1941- ... 131
Logan, Gerald E(lton) 1924- ... 73-76
Logan, Jake
See Knott, William C(ecil, Jr.)
and Krepps, Robert W(ilson)
and Pearl, Jacques Bain
and Riefe, Alan
and Rifkin, Shepard
and Smith, Martin Cruz
Logan, James 1674-1751 ... DLB 24, 140
Logan, James Phillips 1921- ... 37-40R
Logan, Jane
See Gardner, Virginia (Marberry)
Logan, John (Burton) 1923-1987 ... CANR-45
Obituary ... 124
Earlier sketch in CA 77-80
See also CLC 5
See also DLB 5
Logan, John A(rthur), Jr. 1923- ... 1-4R
Logan, Joshua (Lockwood) 1908-1988 ... 89-92
Obituary ... 126
Interview in ... 89-92
See also AITN 1
Logan, Lillian M(ay) 1909- ... CANR-1
Earlier sketch in CA 1-4R
Logan, Mark
See Nicole, Christopher (Robin)
Logan, Martha Daniell 1704(?)-1779 ... DLB 200
Logan, Michael F. 1950- ... 157
Logan, Onnie Lee 1910(?)-1995 ... 144
Obituary ... 149
Logan, Rayford W(hittingham) 1897-1982 ... CANR-25
Obituary ... 108
Earlier sketches in CA 1-4R, CANR-1
See also BW 1
Logan, Sara
See Haydon, June
and Simpson, Judith H(olroyd)
Logan, Shirley Wilson 1943- ... 151
Logan, Sister Mary Francis Louise 1928- ... 5-8R
Logan, Spencer 1912(?)-1980 Obituary ... 93-96
Logan, Terence P(atrick) 1936- ... 57-60
Logan, Virgil G(lenn) 1904- ... 21-24R
Logan, William 1950- ... 136
See also DLB 120
Loganbill, G. Bruce 1938- ... 37-40R
Logelin, Warren E. 1940(?)-1985 Obituary ... 117
Loggins, Vernon 1893-1968 ... 5-8R
Loggins, William Kirk 1946- ... 77-80
Logsdon, John M(ortimer III) 1937- Brief entry ... 115
Logsdon, Joseph 1938- ... 25-28R
Logsdon, Richard Henry 1912- ... CANR-2
Earlier sketch in CA 5-8R
Logsdon, Thomas S(tanley) 1937- ... CANR-46
Earlier sketches in CA 57-60, CANR-6, 21
Logsdon, Tom
See Logsdon, Thomas S(tanley)
Logue, Cal(vin McLeod) 1935- ... 127
Brief entry ... 105
Logue, Christopher 1926- ... CANR-42
Earlier sketches in CA 9-12R, CANR-3
See also DLB 27
See also SATA 23
Logue, Jeanne 1921- ... 89-92
Logue, John 1933- ... 126
Logue, John A(lan) 1947- ... 141
Logue, William (Herbert) 1934- ... 45-48
Loh, Jules 1931- ... 33-36R
Loh, Morag 1935- ... SATA 73
Loh, Pichon P(ei) Y(ung) 1928- ... 17-20R
Loh, Robert 1924- ... 17-20R
Loh, Sandra Tsing 1962- ... 166
Lohafer, Susan 1942- ... CANR-37
Lohans, Alison 1949- ... 160
See also SATA 101
Lohenstein, Daniel Casper von 1635-1683 DLB 168
Lohf, Kenneth A. 1925- ... CANR-3
Earlier sketch in CA 9-12R
Lohman, Joseph D(ean) 1910-1968 ... CAP-2
Earlier sketch in CA 23-24
Lohnes, Walter F. W. 1925- ... CANR-29
Earlier sketch in CA 49-52
Lohr, Thomas F. 1926- ... 77-80
Lohrer, M(ary) Alice 1907- ... 17-20R
Lohrli, Anne 1906- ... 111
Lohrman, Paul
See Fairman, Paul W.
Lohse, Eduard 1924- ... CANR-46
Earlier sketch in CA 107
Lois, George 1931- ... 127
Loisy, Alfred (Firmin) 1857-1940 Brief entry ... 120
Lo-Johansson, (Karl) Ivar 1901-1990 ... CANR-20
Obituary ... 131
Earlier sketch in CA 102
Loken, Newton Clayton 1919- ... 1-4R
See also SATA 26
Loki
See Pearson, Karl
Lokken, Roy N(orman) 1917- ... 53-56
Lokos, Lionel 1928- ... 25-28R
Loll, Leo M(arius), Jr. 1923-1968 ... CAP-2
Earlier sketch in CA 25-28
Lollar, Coleman Aubrey (Jr.) 1946-1993 ... 49-52
Obituary ... 141
Lolli, Giorgio 1905-1979 ... CANR-2
Obituary ... 85-88
Earlier sketch in CA 1-4R
Lollis, Lorraine 1911- ... CAP-2
Earlier sketch in CA 29-32
Lolos, Kimon 1917- ... 1-4R
Lom, Herbert 1917- ... 166
Lomas, Charles W(yatt) 1907- ... CAP-1
Earlier sketch in CA 13-14
Lomas, Derek 1933- ... 29-32R
Lomas, Geoffrey (Robert) 1950- ... 93-96
Lomas, Herbert 1924- ... 144
Lomas, Peter 1923- ... 21-24R
Lomas, Steve
See Brennan, Joseph Lomas
Lomask, Milton (Nachman) 1909-1991 ... CANR-44
Obituary ... 135
Earlier sketches in CA 1-4R, CANR-1
See also SATA 20
Lomax, Alan 1915- ... CANR-1
Earlier sketch in CA 1-4R
Lomax, Bliss
See Drago, Harry Sinclair
Lomax, Derek W(illiam) 1933-1992 ... 130
Obituary ... 137
Lomax, John A(lbert) 1930- ... 61-64
Lomax, Louis E(manuel) 1922-1970 ... CAP-2
Earlier sketch in CA 25-28
See also BW 1
Lomax, Marion 1953- ... 133
Lomax, Pearl
See Cleage, Pearl (Michelle)
Lombard, C(harles) M(orris) 1920- ... CANR-1
Earlier sketch in CA 49-52
Lombard, Helen
See Vischer, Helen (Cassin Lombard) Carusi
Lombard, Lawrence Brian 1944- ... 124
Lombard, Nap
See Johnson, Pamela Hansford
Lombardi, John V(incent) 1942- ... CANR-20
Earlier sketches in CA 53-56, CANR-5
Lombardi, Mary 1940- ... 61-64
Lombardo, Josef Vincent 1908- ... 5-8R
LoMedico, Brian T.
See Monteleone, Thomas F(rancis)
Lomer, Mary
See Lide, Mary
Lommasson, Robert C(urtis) 1917- ... 41-44R
Lomnitz, Cinna 1925- ... 150
Lomnitz, Larissa Adler
See Adler, Larissa
LoMonaco, Palmyra 1932- ... SATA 102
Lomonosov, Mikhail Vasil'evich 1711-1765 ... DLB 150
Lomosia, Andrew
See Stern, Jay B(enjamin)
Lomperis, Timothy J. 1947- ... CANR-52
Earlier sketch in CA 126
Lomupo, Brother Robert 1939- ... 13-16R
London, Artur 1915-1986 ... CANR-12
Obituary ... 120
Earlier sketch in CA 65-68
London, Cait
See Kleinsasser, Lois
London, Carolyn 1918- ... 57-60
London, Ephraim 1911-1990 Obituary ... 131
London, Fritz Wolfgang 1900-1954 ... 161
London, H(oyt) H(obson) 1900- ... 49-52
London, Hannah R. 1894- ... 29-32R
London, Herbert I(ra) 1939- ... CANR-12
Earlier sketch in CA 33-36R
London, Jack
See London, John Griffith
See also AAYA 13
See also AITN 2
See also CDALB 1865-1917
See also DLB 8, 12, 78
See also SATA 18
See also SSC 4
See also TCLC 9, 15, 39
See also WLC
London, Jack 1915-1988 ... CANR-25
Obituary ... 126
Earlier sketch in CA 89-92
London, Jane
See Geis, Darlene Stern
London, Joan 1901-1971 ... CAP-2
Earlier sketch in CA 25-28
London, John Griffith 1876-1916 ... 119
Brief entry ... 110
See also London, Jack
See also DA
See also DAB
See also DAC
See also DAM MST, NOV
See also JRDA
See also MAICYA
See also MTCW 1
London, Jonathan (Paul) 1947- ... SATA 74
London, Julius 1917- ... 118
London, Kurt L(udwig) 1900- ... CANR-6
Earlier sketch in CA 1-4R
London, Laura
See Curtis, Sharon
and Curtis, Thomas Dale
London, Lawrence Steven 1950- ... 146
London, Mel 1923- ... CANR-49
Earlier sketches in CA 107, CANR-24
London, Perry 1931-1992 ... CANR-49
Obituary ... 139
Earlier sketch in CA 45-48
London, Roy (Laird) 1943-1993 ... 108
Obituary ... 142
Londre, Felicia Hardison 1941- ... CANR-21
Earlier sketch in CA 105
Lonergan, Bernard J(oseph) F(rancis) 1904-1984 ... CANR-11
Obituary ... 114
Earlier sketch in CA 53-56
Lonergan, (Pauline) Joy (MacLean) 1909- ... 1-4R
See also SATA 10
Lonesome Cowboy
See White, John I(rwin)

Lone Star Ranger
See White, John I(rwin)
Lonette, Reisie (Dominee) 1924- ... SATA 43
Loney, Glenn (Meredith) 1928- ... CANR-14
Earlier sketch in CA 33-36R
Loney, Martin 1944- ... CANR-18
Earlier sketch in CA 102
Long, A(nthony) A(rthur) 1937- ... CANR-29
Earlier sketches in CA 33-36R, CANR-13
Long, Ann Marie
See Jensen, Pauline Marie (Long)
Long, Cathryn J. 1946- ... 155
See also SATA 89
Long, Charles 1938- ... 65-68
Long, Charles R(ussell) 1904- ... CAP-1
Earlier sketch in CA 11-12
Long, Chester Clayton 1932- ... 25-28R
Long, Clayton
See Long, Chester Clayton
Long, Cynthia 1956- ... 126
Long, D. Stephen 1960- ... 151
Long, David 1948- ... CANR-56
Earlier sketch in CA 127
Long, David E(dwin) 1937- ... 89-92
Long, David F(oster) 1917- ... CANR-8
Earlier sketch in CA 61-64
Long, E(verette) B(each) 1919-1981 ... CANR-1
Obituary ... 103
Earlier sketch in CA 1-4R
Long, Earlene (Roberta) 1938- ... 126
See also SATA 50
Long, Edward LeRoy, Jr. 1924- ... CANR-22
Earlier sketches in CA 5-8R, CANR-7
Long, Emmett
See Leonard, Elmore (John, Jr.)
Long, Esmond R(ay) 1890-1979 Obituary ... 89-92
Long, Eugene Thomas (III) 1935- ... 25-28R
Long, Father Valentine W. 1902- ... 17-20R
Long, Fern ... CAP-2
Earlier sketch in CA 23-24
Long, Frank Belknap 1903-1994 ... CANR-16
Obituary ... 143
Earlier sketch in CA 81-84
Long, Franklin A. 1910- ... 127
Long, Frederick Lawrence 1917- ... 9-12R
Long, Haniel (Clark) 1888-1956 Brief entry ... 122
See also DLB 45
Long, Helen Beecher ... CANR-26
Earlier sketches in CAP-2, CA 19-20
See also SATA 1
Long, Howard Rusk 1906- ... CANR-3
Earlier sketch in CA 5-8R
Long, Huey P(ierce) 1893-1935 ... 166
Brief entry ... 115
Long, J(ohn) C(uthbert) 1892- ... CAP-1
Earlier sketch in CA 9-10
Long, James M. 1907-1979 Obituary ... 85-88
Long, John D(ouglas) 1920- ... 17-20R
Long, John H(enderson) 1916- ... 13-16R
Long, John L(atham) 1932- ... 111
Long, Judith Elaine 1953- ... 65-68
See also SATA 20
Long, Judy
See Long, Judith Elaine
Long, Kim 1949- ... 129
See also SATA 69
Long, Laura Mooney 1892-1967 Obituary ... 109
See also SATA-Obit 29
Long, Lois 1901-1974 Obituary ... 104
Long, Louise ... 37-40R
Long, Lucile
See Brandt, Lucile (Long Strayer)
Long, Luman H(arrison) 1907-1971 ... 108
Obituary ... 104
Long, Lyda Belknap
See Long, Frank Belknap
Long, M(olly) 1916- ... 21-24R
Long, Naomi Cornelia
See Madgett, Naomi Long
Long, Norton E. 1910- ... 45-48
Long, Priscilla 1943- ... 29-32R
Long, Ralph B(ernard) 1906- ... 5-8R
Long, Ray 1878-1935 ... DLB 137
Long, Richard A(lexander) 1927- ... CANR-42
Earlier sketches in CA 37-40R, CANR-24
See also BW 2
Long, Robert 1954- ... CANR-30
Earlier sketch in CA 110
Long, Robert Emmet 1934- ... CANR-48
Earlier sketch in CA 122
Long, Steven 1944- ... 125
Long, T(heodore) Dixon 1933- ... 121
Brief entry ... 118
Long, Theodore E(dward) 1944- ... 126
Long, Thomas (Joseph) 1938- ... 119
Long, Wesley
See Smith, George O(liver)
Long, William Stuart
See Stuart, (Violet) Vivian (Finlay)
Longacre, Edward G(eorge) 1946- ... CANR-22
Earlier sketches in CA 53-56, CANR-5
Longacre, Robert E(dmondson) 1922- ... CANR-19
Earlier sketches in CA 53-56, CANR-4
Longacre, William A(tlas) II 1937- ... CANR-12
Earlier sketch in CA 29-32R
Longaker, Richard P(ancoast) 1924- ... CANR-1
Earlier sketch in CA 1-4R
Longbaugh, Harry
See Goldman, William (W.)
Longbeard, Frederick
See Longyear, Barry Brookes
Longeaux y Vasquex, Enriqueta 1930- ... 57-60
Longenbach, James 1959- ... 127
Longenecker, Justin G. 1917- ... CANR-1
Earlier sketch in CA 1-4R
Longenecker, Richard N(orman) 1930- ... 13-16R
Longest, George C(alvin) 1938- ... 107
Longfellow, Henry Wadsworth 1807-1882 .. CDALB 1640-1865
See also DA
See also DAB
See also DAC
See also DAM MST, POET
See also DLB 1, 59
See also SATA 19
See also WLCS
Longfellow, Layne (A.) 1937- ... SATA 102
Longfellow, Samuel 1819-1892 ... DLB 1
Longfield, Bradley J(ames) 1955- ... 139
Longford, Elizabeth (Harmon Pakenham) 1906- ... CANR-46
Earlier sketch in CA 5-8R
See also DLB 155
Longford, Frank
See Pakenham, Francis Aungier
Longgood, William (Frank) 1917- ... CANR-17
Earlier sketch in CA 1-4R
Longhurst, Henry Carpenter 1909-1978 ... 85-88
Obituary ... 81-84
Longino, Charles F(reeman), Jr. 1938- ... CANR-24
Earlier sketches in CA 53-56, CANR-7
Longinus c. 1st cent. - ... DLB 176
Longland, Jean R(ogers) 1913- ... CANR-10
Earlier sketch in CA 21-24R
Longleigh, Peter J., Jr.
See Korges, James
Longley, John Lewis, Jr. 1920- ... 5-8R
Longley, Lawrence D(ouglas) 1939- ... 41-44R
Longley, Michael 1939- ... 102
See also CLC 29
See also DLB 40
Longley, Richmond W(ilberforce) 1907- ... 73-76
Longley, W. B.
See Randisi, Robert J(oseph)
Longman, Harold S. 1919- ... 25-28R
See also SATA 5
Longman, Lester Duncan 1905-1987 Obituary . 121
Longman, Mark Frederic Kerr 1916-1972 Obituary ... 37-40R
Longmate, Norman Richard 1925- ... CANR-28
Earlier sketches in CA 9-12R, CANR-6
Longmore, George 1793(?)-1867 ... DLB 99
Longmore, Laura ... 5-8R
Long-Neck Woman
See Cheatham, K(aryn) Follis
Longo, Lucas 1919- ... 25-28R
Longrigg, Jane Chichester 1929- ... 9-12R
Longrigg, Roger (Erskine) 1929- ... CANR-3
Earlier sketch in CA 1-4R
Longrigg, Stephen Hemsley 1893-1979 Obituary ... 89-92
Longstreet, Augustus Baldwin 1790-1870 ... DLB 3, 11, 74
Longstreet, Stephen 1907- ... CANR-7
Earlier sketch in CA 9-12R
Longstreet, Wilma S. 1935- ... 93-96
Longstreth, Edward 1894-(?) ... CAP-1
Earlier sketch in CA 13-16
Longstreth, Richard 1946- ... 132
Longstreth, T(homas) Morris 1886- ... 5-8R
Longstreth, W(illiam) Thacher 1920- ... 134
Longsworth, Polly 1933- ... 106
See also SATA 28
Longsworth, Robert M. 1937- ... 21-24R
Longtemps, Kenneth 1933- ... SATA 17
Longway, A. Hugh
See Lang, Andrew
Longworth, Alice Lee (Roosevelt) 1884-1980 Obituary ... 93-96
Longworth, I(an) H(eaps) 1935- ... 120
Longworth, Philip 1933- ... CANR-28
Earlier sketches in CA 21-24R, CANR-10
Longworth, Richard C(ole) 1935- ... 85-88
Longyard, William H(enry) 1958- ... 152
Longyear, Barry Brookes 1942- ... 102
Longyear, Christopher R(udston) 1929- ... 105
Longyear, Marie Marcia Bernstein 1928- ... 115
Longyear, Rey M(organ) 1930- ... CANR-22
Earlier sketch in CA 45-48
Lonnbohm, Armas Eino Leopold
See Loennbohm, Armas Eino Leopold
Lonsdale, Adrian L. 1927- ... 13-16R
Lonsdale, Frederick 1881-1954 Brief entry ... 109
See also DLB 10
Lonsdale, Gordon Arnold 1923(?)-1970 Obituary ... 104
Lonsdale, Kathleen (Yardley) 1903-1971 ... 5-8R
Obituary ... 33-36R
Lonsdale, Richard E. 1926- ... CANR-13
Earlier sketch in CA 21-24R
Lonsdale, Steven (Hancock) 1952- ... CANR-36
Earlier sketch in CA 114
Look, Al 1893- ... 57-60
Look, Dennis 1949- ... 73-76
Looker, Antonina (Hansell) ... 29-32R
Looker, (Reginald) Earle 1895-1976 ... CAP-2
Obituary ... 65-68
Earlier sketch in CA 29-32
Lookout
See Noble, John (Appelbe)
Lookstein, Haskel 1932- ... 119
Loomans, Diane 1955- ... 155
See also SATA 90
Loomba, N(arendra) Paul 1927- ... 57-60
Loomes, Brian 1938- ... CANR-56
Earlier sketches in CA 69-72, CANR-12, 30
Loomie, Albert Joseph 1922- ... 5-8R
Loomis, Albertine (G.) 1895-1985 ... 93-96
Obituary ... 117
Loomis, Burdett A. 1945- ... CANR-65
Earlier sketch in CA 129
Loomis, Charles P(rice) 1905- ... CANR-13
Earlier sketch in CA 21-24R
Loomis, Chauncey C(hester), Jr. 1930- ... 33-36R
Loomis, Edward 1924- ... CANR-2
Earlier sketch in CA 1-4R
Loomis, Jennifer A. 1942- ... 168
See also SATA 101
Loomis, Noel M(iller) 1905-1969 ... CANR-68
Obituary ... 25-28R
Earlier sketch in CA 1-4R
Loomis, Rae
See Steger, Shelby
Loomis, Robert D. ... 17-20R
See also SATA 5
Loomis, Roger Sherman 1887-1966 ... CANR-8
Earlier sketch in CA 5-8R
Loomis, Stanley 1922-1972 ... CAP-1
Obituary ... 37-40R
Earlier sketch in CA 11-12
Loomis, Susan Herrmann 1955- ... 140
Loomis, Zona Kemp 1911- ... 45-48
Looney, Douglas S. 1942- ... 144
Looney, Robert E(dward) 1941- ... 104
Loori, John Daido 1931- ... 154
Loory, Stuart H. 1932- ... 25-28R
Loos, Anita 1893(?)-1981 ... CANR-26
Obituary ... 104
Earlier sketch in CA 21-24R
See also AITN 1
See also DLB 11, 26
See also DLBY 81
Loos, Mary ... AITN 1
Loose, Gerhard 1907- ... 45-48
Loose, H.
See Lourie, Dick
Loosley, William Robert
See Langford, David
Loots, Barbara Kunz 1946- ... 57-60
Loovis, David (Mactavish) 1926- ... CANR-1
Earlier sketch in CA 1-4R
Lopach, James J. 1942- ... 135
Lopata, Helena Znaniecka 1925- ... 104
Lopate, Carol
See Ascher, Carol
Lopate, Phillip 1943- ... 97-100
Interview in ... 97-100
See also CLC 29
See also DLBY 80
Lopatin, Judy 1954- ... 124
Loper, William C. 1927- ... 13-16R
Lopes, Dominic (M. McIver) 1964- ... 157
Lopes, Henri (Marie-Joseph) 1937- ... 132
See also BW 2
Lopes, Michael 1943- ... 57-60
Lopez, Adalberto 1943- ... 103
Lopez, Andrew 1910-1986 Obituary ... 120
Lopez, Angelo (Cayas) 1967- ... SATA 83
Lopez, Barry Holstun 1945- ... CANR-68
Earlier sketches in CA 65-68, CANR-7, 23, 47
Interview in ... CANR-23
See also AAYA 9
See also MTCW 1
See also SATA 67
Lopez, Cecilia L(uisa) 1941- ... 53-56
Lopez, Claude-Anne 1920- ... 104
Lopez, Diana 1948- ... 153
See also HW
Lopez, Ella B. 1900(?)-1978 Obituary ... 81-84
Lopez, Enrique 1921(?)-1985 Obituary ... 117
Lopez, Felix Manuel, Jr. 1917- ... 13-16R
Lopez, Laura 1957- ... 136
Lopez, Manuel Dennis 1934- ... CANR-22
Earlier sketch in CA 105
Lopez, Nancy (Marie) 1957- Brief entry ... 113
Lopez, Robert S(abatino) 1910-1986 Obituary .. 119
Brief entry ... 112
Lopez, Vincent (Joseph) 1895-1975 Obituary . 61-64
Lopez-Morillas, Frances M. 1918- ... 149
Lopez-Morillas, Juan 1913- ... CANR-1
Earlier sketch in CA 1-4R
Lopez Portillo (y Pacheco), Jose 1920- ... 129
See also CLC 46
See also HW
Lopez-Rey, Jose 1905- ... 37-40R
Lopez-Rey (y Arrojo), Manuel 1902-1987 ... 29-32R
Obituary ... 124
Lopez Suria, Violeta 1926- ... HW
Lopez y Fuentes, Gregorio 1897(?)-1966 ... 131
See also CLC 32
See also HW
Lopez Y Rivas, Gilberto 1943- ... 97-100
LoPiccolo, Joseph 1943- ... CANR-15
Earlier sketch in CA 81-84
Lo Pinto, Maria 1900(?)-1970 Obituary ... 104
Lopreato, Joseph 1928- ... 33-36R
Lopresti, Robert 1954- ... 137
Lopshire, Robert M(artin) 1927- ... CANR-30
Earlier sketches in CA 5-8R, CANR-8
See also SATA 6
Lopukhov, Fyodor V(asilevich) 1886-1973 Obituary ... 41-44R
Lora, Josephine
See Alexander, Josephine
Lora, Ronald 1938- ... 41-44R
Lorac, E. C. R.
See Rivett, Edith Caroline
Loram, Ian Craig 1917- ... 5-8R
Loran, Martin
See Baxter, John
Lorand, (Alexander) Sandor 1893(?)-1987 .. CAP-1
Obituary ... 123
Earlier sketch in CA 9-10
Lorang, Ruth Mary
See Lorang, Sister Mary Corde
Lorang, Sister Mary Corde 1904- ... 49-52
Loranger, Jean-Aubert 1896-1942 ... DLB 92
Lorant, Stefan 1901-1997 ... CANR-9
Obituary ... 162
Earlier sketch in CA 5-8R
See also AITN 1
Lorayne, Harry 1926- ... 41-44R
Lorber, Judith 1931- ... 150
Lorberg, Aileen Dorothy 1910- ... CANR-2
Earlier sketch in CA 5-8R
Lorca, Federico Garcia
See Garcia Lorca, Federico
Lorca de Tagle, Lillian 1914- ... 145
Lorch, Edgar R(aymond) 1907-1990 Obituary .. 131
Lorch, Robert Stuart 1925- ... 73-76
Lord, Albert Bates 1912-1991 ... 103
Obituary ... 135
Lord, Alison
See Ellis, Julie
Lord, Athena V. 1932- ... CANR-46
Earlier sketch in CA 109
See also SATA 39
Lord, Beman 1924-1991 ... 33-36R
Obituary ... 135
See also SATA 5
See also SATA-Obit 69
Lord, Bette Bao 1938- ... CANR-41
Earlier sketch in CA 107
Interview in ... 107
See also BEST 90:3
See also CLC 23
See also SATA 58
Lord, Chalfont
See Jones, (Alun) Arthur Gwynne
Lord, Clifford L(ee) 1912-1980 ... CANR-8
Obituary ... 102
Earlier sketch in CA 13-16R
Lord, Donald Charles 1930- ... 37-40R
Lord, Douglas
See Cooper, Douglas
Lord, (Doreen Mildred) Douglas 1904- ... CAP-1
Earlier sketch in CA 13-14
See also SATA 12
Lord, Eda 1907-1976 Obituary ... 104
Lord, Edith Elizabeth 1907- ... 41-44R
Lord, Eugene Hodgdon 1894- ... 1-4R
Lord, Francis A. 1911- ... 17-20R
Lord, Frederic Mather 1912- ... 37-40R
Lord, Gabrielle 1946- ... 106
Lord, George deF(orest) 1919- ... CANR-25
Earlier sketches in CA 65-68, CANR-10
Lord, Graham 1943- ... CANR-4
Earlier sketch in CA 53-56
Lord, Jeffrey
See Green, Roland (James)
and Nelson, R(adell) Faraday
Lord, Jeremy
See Redman, Ben Ray
Lord, Jess R. 1911- ... 65-68
Lord, John Keast 1818-1872 ... DLB 99
Lord, John Vernon 1939- ... 53-56
See also SATA 21
Lord, M(ary) G(race) 1955- ... 127
Lord, Mary Stinson Pillsbury 1904-1978 ... 85-88
Obituary ... 81-84
Lord, Nancy
See Titus, Eve
Lord, Patricia C. 1927-1988 ... SATA-Obit 58
Lord, Phillips H.
See Yolen, Will(iam Hyatt)
Lord, Priscilla Sawyer 1908- ... 9-12R
Lord, Robert (Needham) 1945- ... 61-64
Lord, Shirley
See Rosenthal, Shirley Lord
Lord, Vivian
See Strother, Pat Wallace
Lord, Walter 1917- ... CANR-22
Earlier sketches in CA 1-4R, CANR-5
See also SATA 3
Lord, William Jackson, Jr. 1926- ... 5-8R
Lord Altrincham
See Grigg, John (Edward Poynder)
Lordan, (Ellenora) Beth 1948- ... 130
Lord Astor of Hever
See Astor, Gavin
Lord Auch
See Bataille, Georges
Lord Beveridge
See Beveridge, William (Henry)
Lord Blake
See Blake, Robert (Norman William)
Lord Boyle of Handsworth
See Boyle, Edward Charles Gurney
Lord Brooke
See Greville, Fulke
Lord Butler of Saffron Walden
See Butler, Richard Austen
Lord Byron
See Byron, George Gordon (Noel)
Lord Chalfont
See Jones, (Alun) Arthur Gwynne
Lord Crowther-Hunt
See Crowther-Hunt, Norman Crowther
Lord Denning
See Denning, Alfred Thompson
Lord Dunsany
See Dunsany, Edward John Moreton Drax Plunkett
Lorde, Audre (Geraldine) 1934-1992 ... CANR-46
Obituary ... 142
Earlier sketches in CA 25-28R, CANR-16, 26
See also BLC 2
See also BW 1
See also CLC 18, 71
See also DAM MULT, POET
See also DLB 41
See also MTCW 1
See also PC 12

Lord Energlyn
See Evans, William David
Lord Evans of Hungershall
See Evans, Benjamin Ifor
Lord Francis Williams
See Williams, Edward Francis
Lord George-Brown
See George-Brown, George Alfred
Lord Hailsham of St. Marylebone
See Hogg, Quintin McGarel
Lord Herbert of Cherbury, Edward 1582-1648 .. DLB 151
Lord Home
See Home, Alexander Frederick (Douglas-)
Lord Houghton
See Milnes, Richard Monckton
Lord Howe of Aberon
See Howe, (Richard Edward) Geoffrey
Lordi, Robert J(oseph) 1923- ... 89-92
Lord Jeffrey
See Jeffrey, Francis
Lord Kames
See Home, Henry
Lord Killanin
See Morris, Michael
Lord Longford
See Pakenham, Francis Aungier
Lord Mancroft
See Mancroft, Stormont Mancroft Samuel
Lord Moran
See Wilson, (Richard) John (McMoran)
Lord Mountbatten
See Mountbatten, Louis (Francis Albert Victor Nicholas)
Lord Pakenham
See Pakenham, Francis Aungier
Lord Rhyl
See Birch, (Evelyn) Nigel (Chetwode)
Lord Rothschild
See Rothschild, Nathaniel Mayer Victor
Lord Snowdon
See Armstrong-Jones, Antony (Charles Robert)
Lord Strange
See Drummond, John
Lord Thomas
See Thomas, (William) Miles (Webster)
Lord Windlesham
See Hennessy, David James George
Loree, Kate (Lambie) 1920- ... 21-24R
Lorek, Daniel N. 1958(?)-1983 Obituary ... 110
Loren, Sophia 1936- ... 142
Brief entry ... 111
Lorence, James J(ohn) 1937- ... 148
Lorens, M. K.
See Keilstrup, Margaret
Lorenz, Alfred Lawrence 1937- ... 45-48
Lorenz, Edward N(orton) 1917- ... 162
Lorenz, J(ames) D(ouglas) 1938- ... 102
Lorenz, Konrad Zacharias 1903-1989 ... CANR-61
Obituary ... 128
Earlier sketches in CA 61-64, CANR-35
See also MTCW 1
Lorenz, Lee (Sharp) 1932- ... 150
Brief entry ... 124
See also SATA-Brief 39
Lorenz, Sarah E.
See Winston, Sarah
Lorenzen, Coral Elsie 1925- ... 113
Lorenzen, David N(eal) 1940- ... 33-36R
Lorenzini, Carlo 1826-1890
See Collodi, Carlo
See also MAICYA
See also SATA 29, 100
Lorenzo, Carol Lee 1939- ... CANR-50
Earlier sketch in CA 53-56
Lorenzo, Heberto Padilla
See Padilla (Lorenzo), Heberto
Lorenzo, Orestes ... 148
Loreto, Charles A. 1903(?)-1990 Obituary ... 132
Loria, Jeffrey H. 1940- ... 17-20R
Lorie, James Hirsch 1922- ... 103
Lorig, Kate R. 1942- ... 117
Lorimer, Frank 1894-1985 Obituary ... 116
Lorimer, George Horace 1867-1937 ... DLB 91
Lorimer, James 1942- ... 123
Lorimer, Janet 1941- ... SATA 60
Lorimer, Lawrence T(heodore) 1941- ... CANR-6
Earlier sketch in CA 57-60
Lorimer, Scat
See Fuentes, Martha Ayers
Loring, Ann 1915- ... 97-100
Loring, Emilie (Baker) 1864(?)-1951 ... SATA 51
Loring, J. M.
See Warner-Crozetti, R(uth G.)
Loring, Murray 1917- ... CANR-22
Earlier sketch in CA 45-48
Loring, Peter
See Shellabarger, Samuel
Lorion, R(aymond) P(aul) 1946- ... 85-88
Loris
See Hofmannsthal, Hugo von
Loris, Joseph James 1943-1987 Obituary ... 125
Lorkowski, Thomas V(incent) 1950- ... SATA 92
Lorkowski, Tom
See Lorkowski, Thomas V(incent)
Lorme, Anna
See Markowa, Nina Alexandrovna
Lornquest, Olaf
See Rips, Ervine M(ilton)
Lorrah, Jean ... CANR-41
Earlier sketches in CA 103, CANR-19
Lorraine, Paul
See Fearn, John Russell
Lorraine, Walter (Henry) 1929- ... SATA 16
Lorrance, Arleen 1939- ... 85-88
Lorrimer, Claire 1921- ... CANR-42
Lorsch, Jay William 1932- ... 97-100
Lorsch, Susan E. 1950- ... 116
Lortie, Dan C(lement) 1926- ... 115
Lortz, Richard 1917-1980 ... CANR-11
Obituary ... 102
Earlier sketch in CA 57-60
Lorusso, Edward N. S. 1949- ... 133
Lorwin, Val Rogin 1907-1982 Obituary ... 111
Lory, Robert (Edward) 1936- ... CANR-10
Earlier sketch in CA 53-56
Los, George
See Amabile, George
Losada (Goya), Jose Manuel 1962- ... 168
Losang, Rato Khyongla Ngawang 1923- ... 81-84
Lose, M(argaret) Phyllis 1925- ... CANR-18
Earlier sketch in CA 101
Losev, S(ergei) A(ndreevich) 1927-1988 Obituary ... 126
Losey, Joseph (Walton) 1909-1984 Obituary ... 113
Losey, Patricia 1930- ... 144
Loshak, David (Leslie Ivor) 1933- ... 41-44R
Loshitzky, Yosefa ... 158
Losoncy, Lawrence J. 1941- ... CANR-32
Earlier sketches in CA 37-40R, CANR-14
Losoncy, Mary Jan 1942- ... 37-40R
los Rios, Francisco Giner de
See Giner de los Rios, Francisco
Loss, Joan 1933- ... SATA 11
Loss, Louis 1914-1997 ... CANR-2
Obituary ... 163
Earlier sketch in CA 5-8R
Loss, Richard (Archibald John) 1938- ... 65-68
Losse, Deborah N(ichols) 1944- ... 147
Lossing, Benson J. 1813-1891 ... DLB 30
Lossky, Andrew 1917- ... 93-96
Lossy, Rella 1934- ... 81-84
Lotchin, Roger W. 1935- ... 139
Loth, Calder 1943- ... 73-76
Loth, David 1899-1988 ... CANR-1
Obituary ... 125
Earlier sketch in CA 1-4R
Lothar, Ernst 1890-1974 ... DLB 81
Lothian, John Maule 1896-1970 ... CAP-1
Earlier sketch in CA 9-10
Lothringen, Geza Louis Eusebius Gebhard Ralphael Albert Maria
See von Habsburg(-Lothringen), Geza Louis Eusebius Gebhard Ralphael Albert Maria
Lothrop, Harriet Mulford Stone 1844-1924 .. DLB 42
See also SATA 20
Lothstein, Leslie Martin 1942- ... 126
Loti, Pierre
See Viaud, (Louis Marie) Julien
See also DLB 123
See also TCLC 11
Lott, Arnold S(amuel) 1912-1992 ... CANR-46
Obituary ... 139
Earlier sketch in CA 13-16R
Lott, Bret 1958- ... 126
Lott, Davis Newton 1913- ... CANR-10
Earlier sketch in CA 21-24R
Lott, Emmeline ... DLB 166
Lott, Eric 1959- ... 149
Lott, Milton 1919- ... CANR-64
Earlier sketch in CA 17-20R
Lott, Monroe
See Howard, Edwin
Lott, Robert E(ugene) 1926- ... CANR-4
Earlier sketch in CA 5-8R
Lottich, Kenneth V(erne) 1904- ... 17-20R
Lottie
See Grimke, Charlotte L(ottie) Forten
Lottinville, Savoie 1906- ... 105
Lottman, Eileen 1927- ... CANR-56
Earlier sketches in CA 57-60, CANR-12, 30
Lottman, Herbert R. 1927- ... CANR-71
Earlier sketch in CA 105
Interview in ... 105
See also CAAS 12
LoTurco, Laura 1963- ... SATA 84
Lotz, Anne Graham 1948- ... 165
Lotz, David W(alter) 1937- Brief entry ... 115
Lotz, James Robert 1929- ... CANR-14
Earlier sketches in CA 37-40R, CANR-31
Lotz, Jim
See Lotz, James Robert
Lotz, John 1913-1973 Obituary ... 45-48
Lotz, Wolfgang 1912-1981 ... CANR-34
Earlier sketch in CA 81-84
See also SATA 65
Lotze, Dieter P(aul) 1933- ... 132
Loubere, Leo A(lbert) 1923- ... 130
Louch, A(lfred) R(ichard) 1927- ... 17-20R
Louchheim, Kathleen 1903-1991 ... 21-24R
Obituary ... 133
Louchheim, Katie
See Louchheim, Kathleen
Loucks, William Negele 1899- ... 1-4R
Loud, G(raham) A(nthony) 1953- ... 136
Loud, Pat(ricia Russell) 1926- Brief entry ... 114
Loud, Patricia C(ummings) ... 135
Louden, J(ames) Keith 1905- ... 132
Louden, Robert B. 1953- ... 139
Louden, Robert Stuart 1912- ... 5-8R
Loudon, David L. 1944- ... 142
Loudon, Irvine 1924- ... CANR-53
Earlier sketch in CA 126
Lougee, Robert Wayne 1919- ... 5-8R
Loughary, John W(illiam) 1930- ... 41-44R
Loughery, John 1953- ... 138
Loughhead, LaRue A(lvin) 1927- ... 61-64
Loughlin, Caroline 1940- ... 126
Loughlin, James 1948- ... 153
Loughlin, Richard L(awrence) 1907- ... CANR-21
Earlier sketch in CA 45-48
Loughmiller, Campbell 1906- ... CANR-13
Earlier sketch in CA 77-80
Loughran, Bernice B(ingham) 1919- ... 5-8R
Loughran, Peter 1938- ... 25-28R
Lougy, Robert E. 1940- ... 118
Louie, Ai-Ling 1949- ... 112
See also SATA 40
See also SATA-Brief 34
Louie, Andréa 1966- ... 152
Louie, David Wong 1954- ... 139
See also CLC 70
Louis, Adrian C. ... NNAL
Louis, Arthur M(urray) 1938- ... 106
Louis, David
See Carroll, David L.
Louis, Debbie 1945- ... 29-32R
Louis, Father M.
See Merton, Thomas
Louis, J(ack) C(harles), Jr. 1949- ... 105
Louis, Joe
See Barrow, Joseph Louis
Louis, Murray 1926- ... 126
Louis, Pat
See Francis, Dorothy Brenner
Louis, Paul P(anickavede) 1918- ... CANR-12
Earlier sketch in CA 61-64
Louis, Pierre(-Felix) 1870-1925 Brief entry ... 105
See also Louys, Pierre
Louis, Ray Baldwin 1949- ... 65-68
Louis, Tobi 1940- ... 57-60
Louis, Valerie
See Salvatore, Diane
Louisburgh, Sheila Burnford
See Burnford, Sheila (Philip Cochrane Every)
Louisell, David William 1913-1977 ... CANR-4
Obituary ... 73-76
Earlier sketch in CA 1-4R
Loukes, Harold 1912- ... 17-20R
Lounsberry, Barbara 1946- ... 138
Lounsbury, Myron O. 1940- ... 37-40R
Lounsbury, Thomas R. 1838-1915 ... DLB 71
Loup, Jacques 1942- ... 120
Lourdeaux, Lee 1951- ... 136
Louria, Donald B(ruce) 1928- ... 107
Lourie, Dick 1937- ... 33-36R
Lourie, Helen
See Storr, Catherine (Cole)
Lourie, Peter (King) 1952- ... 137
See also SATA 82
Lourie, Richard 1940- ... 131
Brief entry ... 125
Interview in ... 131
Loury, Glenn C(artman) 1948- ... 152
Lousley, J(ob) E(dward) 1907-1976 Obituary ... 104
Louthan, Robert 1951- ... 109
Louv, Richard 1949- ... 154
Louviere, Vernon Ray 1920- ... 108
Louvish, Misha 1909- ... CANR-1
Earlier sketch in CA 45-48
Louvish, Simon 1947- ... 121
Louw, Nicholaas Petrus Van Wyk 1906-1970 Obituary ... 89-92
Loux, Ann Kimble 1943- ... 168
Loux, Michael Joseph 1942- ... 103
Louys, Pierre
See Louis, Pierre(-Felix)
See also DLB 123
Lovaas, O(le) Ivar 1927- ... CANR-22
Earlier sketch in CA 45-48
Lovasik, Lawrence George 1913- ... CANR-20
Earlier sketches in CA 1-4R, CANR-1
Lovatt, Edwin A(lbert) 1944- ... 119
Love, Alan C(arson) 1937- ... 53-56
Love, (Kathleen) Ann 1947- ... 148
See also SATA 79
Love, Barbara J. 1937- ... 37-40R
Love, Charles (Ross) 1932- ... 25-28R
Love, Charles K.
See Swicegood, Thomas L. P.
Love, D. Anne 1949- ... 149
See also SATA 96
Love, Douglas 1967- ... 156
See also SATA 92
Love, Edmund G(eorge) 1912-1990 ... CANR-4
Obituary ... 132
Earlier sketch in CA 1-4R
Love, Glen A. 1932- ... 29-32R
Love, Iris Cornelia 1933- ... 29-32R
Love, Janet
See Ferrier, Janet Mackay
Love, Jean O. 1920- ... 29-32R
Love, Joseph L., (Jr.) 1938- ... 29-32R
Love, Katherine (Isabel) 1907- ... SATA 3
Love, Kennett 1924- ... 77-80
Love, Philip H(ampton) 1905-1977 ... 77-80
Obituary ... 73-76
Love, Richard S. 1923- ... 81-84
Love, Sandra (Weller) 1940- ... CANR-11
Earlier sketch in CA 69-72
See also SATA 26
Love, Susan M. ... 168
Love, Sydney F(rancis) 1923- ... 81-84
Love, Thomas Teel 1931- ... 13-16R
Love, William F. 1932- ... 132
Lovecraft, H(oward) P(hillips) 1890-1937 ... 133
Brief entry ... 104
See also AAYA 14
See also DAM POP
See also MTCW 1
See also SSC 3
See also TCLC 4, 22
Lovegrove, Philip
See Ray, John (Philip)
Lovehill, C. B.
See Beaumont, Charles
Lovejoy, Bahija Fattuhi 1914- ... 5-8R
Lovejoy, Clarence Earle 1894-1974 ... 5-8R
Obituary ... 45-48
Lovejoy, David Sherman 1919- ... 103
Lovejoy, Elijah P(arish) 1940- ... 45-48
Lovejoy, Jack 1937- ... CANR-35
Earlier sketch in CA 114
Lovejoy, L(awrence) C(lark) 1893- ... 1-4R
Lovejoy, Paul E(llsworth) 1943- ... 115
Lovejoy, Thomas E. 1941- ... 143
Lovelace, Delos Wheeler 1894-1967 ... 5-8R
Obituary ... 25-28R
See also SATA 7
Lovelace, Earl 1935- ... CANR-72
Earlier sketches in CA 77-80, CANR-41
See also BW 2
See also CLC 51
See also DLB 125
See also MTCW 1
Lovelace, Linda
See Marchiano, Linda Boreman
Lovelace, Marc Hoyle 1920- ... 37-40R
Lovelace, Maud Hart 1892-1980 ... CANR-39
Obituary ... 104
Earlier sketch in CA 5-8R
See also MAICYA
See also SATA 2
See also SATA-Obit 23
Lovelace, Merline (A.) 1946- ... 158
Lovelace, Richard 1618-1657 ... DLB 131
Lovelace, Richard Franz 1930- ... 101
Loveland, Anne C(arol) 1938- ... CANR-56
Brief entry ... 114
Earlier sketch in CA 126
Loveless, E(dward) E. 1919- ... 57-60
Lovell, Ann 1933- ... CANR-41
Earlier sketches in CA 97-100, CANR-19
Lovell, (Alfred Charles) Bernard 1913- ... CANR-6
Earlier sketch in CA 13-16R
Lovell, Colin Rhys 1917- ... 5-8R
Lovell, Ernest J(ames), Jr. 1918-1975 ... 1-4R
Obituary ... 103
Lovell, Glenville 1955- ... 166
Lovell, Ingraham
See Bacon, Josephine Dodge (Daskam)
Lovell, John, Jr. 1907-1974 ... CAP-2
Obituary ... 49-52
Earlier sketch in CA 33-36
Lovell, John P(hilip) 1932- ... CANR-15
Earlier sketch in CA 29-32R
Lovell, Marc
See McShane, Mark
Lovell, Mark 1934- ... CANR-8
Earlier sketch in CA 61-64
Lovell, Mary S(ybilla) 1941- ... 140
Lovell, Michael Christopher 1930- ... 33-36R
Lovell, Ronald P. 1937- ... CANR-13
Earlier sketch in CA 73-76
Lovell, Stanley P(latt) 1890- ... 5-8R
Lovelock, J. E.
See Lovelock, James (Ephraim)
Lovelock, James (Ephraim) 1919- ... 123
Loveman, Brian E(lliot) 1944- ... CANR-17
Earlier sketch in CA 89-92
Loveman, Samuel 1885(?)-1976 Obituary ... 65-68
Lovenstein, Meno 1909- ... CANR-3
Earlier sketch in CA 5-8R
Lovequist, Gwendlelynn
See Stafford, Linda (Crying Wind)
Lover, Samuel 1797-1868 ... DLB 159, 190
Loverde, Lorin (James Bell) 1943- ... 45-48
Loveridge, Ronald O. 1938- ... 33-36R
Lovering, Joseph Paul 1921- ... 104
Loverseed, Amanda (Jane) 1965- ... 142
See also SATA 75
Lovesey, Peter (Harmer) 1936- ... CANR-59
Earlier sketches in CA 41-44R, CANR-28
See also DLB 87
See also MTCW 1
Lovestrand, Harold 1925- ... 21-24R
Lovett, A(lbert) W(inston) 1944- ... 124
Lovett, Clara Maria 1939- ... CANR-16
Earlier sketch in CA 93-96
Lovett, Gabriel H(arry) 1921- ... 65-68
Lovett, Margaret (Rose) 1915- ... 61-64
See also SATA 22
Lovett, Robert W. 1913- ... 33-36R
Lovin, Clifford R(amsey) 1937- ... 37-40R
Lovin, Roger Robert 1941- ... CANR-6
Earlier sketch in CA 57-60
Loving, Jerome MacNeill 1941- ... CANR-56
Earlier sketches in CA 112, CANR-30
Lovins, Amory B(loch) 1947- ... CANR-32
Earlier sketch in CA 69-72
Lovoll, Odd Sverre 1934- ... CANR-7
Earlier sketch in CA 61-64
Lovoos, Janice
See Garbutt, Janice (D.) Lovoos
Low, Alfred D(avid) 1913- ... 33-36R
Low, Alice 1926- ... CANR-8
Earlier sketch in CA 61-64
See also SATA 11, 76
Low, Ann Marie 1912- ... 118
Low, Anthony 1935- ... CANR-13
Earlier sketch in CA 37-40R
Low, D(onald) A(nthony) 1927- ... 73-76
Low, David (Alexander Cecil) 1891-1963 Obituary ... 89-92
Low, Dorothy Mackie
See Low, Lois Dorothea
Low, Elizabeth Hammond 1898- ... CAP-2
Earlier sketch in CA 19-20
See also SATA 5
Low, Francis 1893-1972 Obituary ... 115
Low, Gardner
See Rodda, Charles
Low, George M(ichael) 1926-1984 Obituary ... 113

Low, Ivy
See Litvinov, Ivy
Low, Joseph 1911- CANR-49
Earlier sketches in CA 85-88, CANR-15
See also MAICYA
See also SATA 14
Low, Kathleen 153
Low, Lois Dorothea 1916- CANR-15
Earlier sketch in CA 37-40R
Low, Rachael 1923- 125
Low, Samuel 1765-(?) DLB 37
Low, Setha M. 1948- 156
Low, Victor N. 1931- CANR-1
Earlier sketch in CA 49-52
Lowance, Mason I(ra), Jr. 1938- 57-60
Lowbury, Edward (Joseph Lister) 1913- CANR-54
Earlier sketches in CA 29-32R, CANR-12, 29
Lowden, Desmond 1937- 53-56
Lowder, Jerry 1932- 65-68
Lowder, Paul D(aniel) 1929- 93-96
Lowdermilk, W(alter) C(lay)
1888-1974 Obituary 49-52
Lowe, A(lfred) Mifflin 1948- 128
Lowe, Alfonso
See Loewenthal, L(eonard) J(oseph) A(lfonso)
Lowe, Ben(no P.) 1956- 163
Lowe, C(arrington) Marshall 1930- 29-32R
Lowe, Carl 1949- 125
Lowe, Corke
See Pepper, Choral
Lowe, David A(llan) 1948- CANR-29
Earlier sketch in CA 111
Lowe, David Garrard 1933- CANR-47
Earlier sketches in CA 104, CANR-22
Lowe, Donald M. 1928- 21-24R
Lowe, Gordon R(obb) 1928- 49-52
Lowe, Gustav E. 1901- CAP-2
Earlier sketch in CA 23-24
Lowe, James 1941- 151
Lowe, Jay, Jr.
See Loeper, John J(oseph)
Lowe, Jeanne R. 1924(?)-1972 Obituary 33-36R
Lowe, John (Evelyn) 1928- CANR-49
Earlier sketch in CA 123
Lowe, John W(esley) G(uinn) 1946- 121
Lowe, Judah
See Lyon, Christopher (Leslie)
Lowe, Marjorie G(riffiths) Lowe 1909- 1-4R
Lowe, Michael Ellenwood
See Lowe, Mick
Lowe, Mick 1947- 165
Lowe, Richard Barrett 1902-1972 Obituary 33-36R
Lowe, Richard G. 1942- CANR-49
Earlier sketch in CA 123
Lowe, Robert W. 1910- CAP-1
Earlier sketch in CA 13-14
Lowe, Roberta (Justine) 1940- CANR-24
Earlier sketches in CA 61-64, CANR-8
Lowe, Rodney 1946- 146
Lowe, Sam Jack
See Rummel, (Louis) Jack(son)
Lowe, Sarah M. 1956- 153
Lowe, Sue Davidson 1922- 118
Lowe, Victor (Augustus) 1907-1988 17-20R
Obituary 127
Lowe, Victoria Lincoln
See Lincoln, Victoria
Lowe, William T(ebbs) 1929- 73-76
Lowe-Evans, Mary 1941- 145
Lowell, Amy 1874-1925 151
Brief entry 104
See also DAM POET
See also DLB 54, 140
See also PC 13
See also TCLC 1, 8
Lowell, C. Stanley 1909- CANR-6
Earlier sketch in CA 5-8R
Lowell, Elizabeth
See Maxwell, Ann (Elizabeth)
Lowell, James Russell 1819-1891 CDALB 1640-1865
See also DLB 1, 11, 64, 79, 189
Lowell, Jon 1938- 97-100
Interview in 97-100
Lowell, Juliet 1901- CANR-1
Earlier sketch in CA 1-4R
Lowell, Mildred Hawksworth 1905-1974 CAP-2
Earlier sketch in CA 33-36
Lowell, Robert (Traill Spence, Jr.) 1917-1977 CANR-60
Obituary 73-76
Earlier sketches in CA 9-12R, CANR-26
See also CABS 2
See also CLC 1, 2, 3, 4, 5, 8, 9, 11, 15, 37
See also DA
See also DAB
See also DAC
See also DAM MST, NOV
See also DLB 5, 169
See also MTCW 1
See also PC 3
See also WLC
Lowell, Susan 1950- 126
See also SATA 81
Lowell, Tex
See Turner, George E(ugene)
Lowen, Alexander 1910- 17-20R
Lowenberg, Anton D(avid) 1957- 144
Lowenberg, Carlton 1919- 146
Lowenberg, Susan 1957- 146
Lowenfeld, Andreas F(rank) 1930- CANR-8
Earlier sketch in CA 61-64
Lowenfeld, Berthold 1901- 17-20R
Lowenfels, Walter 1897-1976 CANR-3
Obituary 65-68
Earlier sketch in CA 1-4R
See also DLB 4
Lowenfish, Lee (Elihu) 1942- 106
Lowenkopf, Shelly A(lan) 1931- CANR-4
Earlier sketch in CA 49-52
Lowens, Irving 1916-1983 CANR-11
Obituary 111
Earlier sketch in CA 17-20R
Lowenstein, Dyno 1914- 9-12R
See also SATA 6
Lowenstein, Michael W. 1942- 154
Lowenstein, Ralph Lynn 1930- 17-20R
Lowenstein, Sharon R. 1937- 122
Lowenstein, Tom 1941- 93-96
Lowenthal, Abraham F(rederic) 1941- 127
Lowenthal, Cynthia J. 1952- 145
Lowenthal, David 1923- CANR-69
Earlier sketches in CA 115, CANR-41
Lowenthal, Leo 1900-1993 CANR-46
Obituary 140
Earlier sketches in CA 1-4R, CANR-5, 20
Lowenthal, Marjorie Fiske
See Fiske, Marjorie
Lowenthal, Michael (Francis) 1969- 150
Lower, Arthur R(eginald) M(arsden) 1889-1988 CANR-4
Obituary 124
Earlier sketch in CA 9-12R
Lower, J(oseph) Arthur 1907- 21-24R
Lowerre, Susan (K.) 1962- 134
Lowery, Bruce Arlie 1931- CANR-1
Earlier sketch in CA 1-4R
Lowery, Daniel L(orne) 1929- 113
Lowery, James L(incoln), Jr. 1932- 45-48
Lowery, Linda 1949- 141
See also SATA 74
Lowery, Lynn 1949- 93-96
Lowery, Robert G. 1941- 130
Lowery, Thomas V(incent) 1919- 37-40R
Lowi, Theodore J(ay) 1931- 37-40R
Lowidski, Witt
See Clinton, (Lloyd) D(eWitt)
Lowing, Anne
See Geach, Christine
Lowinsky, Edward E(lias) 1908-1985 CAP-1
Obituary 117
Earlier sketch in CA 13-14
Lowith, Karl
See Loewith, Karl
Lowitz, Anson C. 1901(?)-1978 81-84
Obituary 73-76
See also SATA 18
Lowitz, Leza 1962- CAAS 26
Lowitz, Sadyebeth Heath 1901-1969 85-88
See also SATA 17
Lowman, Charles LeRoy
1880(?)-1977 Obituary 69-72
Lowman, Eleanor B(arry) 1906-1983 Obituary 110
Lowman, Josephine (Cherry)
1899(?)-1983 Obituary 110
Lowndes, Betty 1929- 61-64
Lowndes, George Alfred Norman 1897- 5-8R
Lowndes, Marie Adelaide (Belloc) 1868-1947 Brief entry 107
See also DLB 70
See also TCLC 12
Lowndes, Robert A(ugustine) W(ard) 1916- 128
Brief entry 113
Lowndes, William 1914- 13-16R
Lowndes, William Thomas 1798-1843 DLB 184
Lownes, Humphrey fl. 1590-1630 DLB 170
Lowney, Paul Benjamin 1922- CANR-17
Earlier sketch in CA 93-96
Lowrey, Janette Sebring 1892- 13-16R
See also SATA 43
Lowrey, Kathleen 1943- 57-60
Lowrey, P(errin) H(olmes) 1923-1965 CAP-1
Earlier sketch in CA 11-12
Lowrey, Sara 1897- 17-20R
Lowrie, Donald A(lexander) 1889-1974 5-8R
Obituary 53-56
Lowrie, Jean E(lizabeth) 1918- 45-48
Lowry, Albert J(ames) 1927- 129
Brief entry 118
Lowry, Bates 1923- CANR-1
Earlier sketch in CA 1-4R
Lowry, Beverly (Fey) 1938- 101
Lowry, Bullitt 1936- 165
Lowry, Charles W(esley) 1905- 37-40R
Lowry, Fern 1896(?)-1983 Obituary 111
Lowry, Joan (Catlow) 1911- 13-16R
Lowry, Lois 1937- CANR-70
Earlier sketches in CA 69-72, CANR-13, 43
Interview in CANR-13
See also AAYA 5
See also CLR 6, 46
See also DLB 52
See also JRDA
See also MAICYA
See also SAAS 3
See also SATA 23, 70
Lowry, (Clarence) Malcolm 1909-1957 CANR-62
Brief entry 105
Earlier sketch in CA 131
See also CDBLB 1945-1960
See also DLB 15
See also MTCW 1
See also SSC 31
See also TCLC 6, 40
Lowry, Martin John Clement 1940- 107
Lowry, Mina Gertrude 1882-1966 113
See also Loy, Mina
Lowry, Nan
See MacLeod, Ruth
Lowry, Peter 1953- 49-52
See also SATA 7
Lowry, Ritchie P(eter) 1926- 17-20R
Lowry, Robert (James Collas) 1919- 61-64
Lowry, S(tanley) Todd 1927- 126
Lowry, Shirley Park 1933- 109
Lowry, Thomas P. 1932- 21-24R
Lowry, William R. 1953- 142
Lowther, George F. 1913-1975 Obituary 57-60
See also SATA-Obit 30
Lowther, Kevin G(eorge) 1941- 81-84
Lowther, Pat 1935-1975 153
See also DLB 53
Lowther, William (Anthony) 1942- 136
Lowy, George 1924- 17-20R
Loxsmith, John
See Brunner, John (Kilian Houston)
Loxterkamp, David 166
Loxton, (Charles) Howard 1934- CANR-27
Earlier sketches in CA 25-28R, CANR-11
Loy, J(ohn) Robert 1918- Brief entry 108
Loy, Jane M.
See Rausch, Jane M(eyer)
Loy, Mina
See Lowry, Mina Gertrude
See also CLC 28
See also DAM POET
See also DLB 4, 54
See also PC 16
Loy, Rosetta 1931- 138
Loyd, Marianne 1955- 115
Loye, David (Elliot) 1925- 33-36R
Loyn, H(enry) R(oyston) 1922- CANR-41
Earlier sketch in CA 117
Loyn, Henry
See Loyn, H(enry) R(oyston)
Loyn, Henry R.
See Loyn, H(enry) R(oyston)
Loyson-Bridet
See Schwob, Marcel (Mayer Andre)
Lozano, Wendy 1941- 102
Lozansky, Edward D. 1941- SATA 62
Lozeau, Albert 1878-1924 DLB 92
Lozier, Herbert 1915- 49-52
See also SATA 26
Lozowick, Lee 1943- 160
Lozowick, Louis 1892-1973 Obituary 107
Lu, David J(ohn) 1928- CANR-5
Earlier sketch in CA 9-12R
Lu, K'uan-yu
See Luk, Charles
Lu, Paul Hsien 1926- 41-44R
Luard, (David) Evan (Trant) 1926- CANR-1
Earlier sketch in CA 1-4R
Luard, Nicholas 1937- CANR-70
Earlier sketch in CA 85-88
Lubalin, Herb(ert Frederick)
1918-1981 Obituary 104
Lubans, John, Jr. 1941- 57-60
Lubar, Joel F. 1938- 37-40R
Lubar, Robert 1920-1995 73-76
Obituary 148
Lubbe, Catherine Case AITN 1
Lubbock, (Mary Katherine) Adelaide 1906- 29-32R
Lubbock, Mark Hugh 1898-1986 Obituary 121
Lubbock, Percy 1879-1965 CANR-72
Earlier sketch in CA 85-88
See also DLB 149
Lubchenco, Jane 1947- 161
Lubeck, Steven G. 1944- 29-32R
Lubell, Cecil 1912- CANR-4
Earlier sketch in CA 9-12R
See also SATA 6
Lubell, Harold 1925- 9-12R
Lubell, Samuel 1911-1987 13-16R
Obituary 123
Lubell, Winifred (A. Milius) 1914- CANR-4
Earlier sketch in CA 49-52
See also SATA 6
Lubenow, William (Cornelius) 1939- Brief entry 107
Luber, Philip 1948- 124
Lubetski, Edith 1940- 112
Lubetski, Meir 1938- 112
Lubin, Bernard 1923- CANR-9
Earlier sketch in CA 21-24R
Lubin, David M. 1950- 120
Lubin, Ernest 1916-1977 41-44R
Lubin, Isador 1896-1978 Obituary 77-80
Lubin, Leonard
See Lubin, Leonard B.
Lubin, Leonard B. 1943- CANR-38
Brief entry 115
Earlier sketch in CA 125
See also MAICYA
See also SATA 45
See also SATA-Brief 37
Lubis, Mochtar 1922- 29-32R
Lubitz, Raymond 1937-1984 Obituary 113
Lubove, Roy 1934- 21-24R
Lubow, Arthur 1952- 140
Lubow, Robert E. 1932- 77-80
Lubowe, Irwin I(rville) 1905- 53-56
Lubrano, Linda L. 1943- 126
Brief entry 108
Lucado, Max (Lee) 1955- 163
Lucas, Alec 1913- 101
Lucas, Barbara
See Wall, Barbara
Lucas, Bryan Keith
See Keith-Lucas, Bryan
Lucas, C. Payne 1933- 85-88
Lucas, Carol 1929- 17-20R
Lucas, Cedric 1962- SATA 101
Lucas, Celia 1938- CANR-24
Earlier sketch in CA 107
Lucas, Christopher J(ohn) 1940- 25-28R
Lucas, Craig 1951- CANR-71
Earlier sketch in CA 137
See also CLC 64
Lucas, D(onald) W(illiam) 1905-1985 CAP-1
Obituary 116
Earlier sketch in CA 13-14
Lucas, Darrel B(laine) 1902- CAP-1
Earlier sketch in CA 9-10
Lucas, Dione (Narnona Margaris Wilson)
1909-1971 Obituary 104
Lucas, E(dna) Louise 1899-1970 CAP-2
Earlier sketch in CA 25-28
Lucas, E(dward) V(errall) 1868-1938 DLB 98, 149, 153
See also SATA 20
See also TCLC 73
Lucas, Eileen 1956- 143
See also SATA 76
Lucas, F(rank) L(aurence) 1894-1967 CANR-4
Obituary 25-28R
Earlier sketch in CA 1-4R
Lucas, George 1944- CANR-30
Earlier sketch in CA 77-80
See also AAYA 1, 23
See also CLC 16
See also SATA 56
Lucas, Hans
See Godard, Jean-Luc
Lucas, Henry C(ameron), Jr. 1944- CANR-52
Earlier sketches in CA 109, CANR-28
Lucas, J. K.
See Paine, Lauran (Bosworth)
Lucas, J(ohn) R(andolph) 1929- CANR-35
Earlier sketches in CA 21-24R, CANR-11
Lucas, J(ames) R(aymond) 1950- CANR-42
Earlier sketch in CA 118
Lucas, Jason 1904- CAP-1
Earlier sketch in CA 9-10
Lucas, Jeremy 1953- 108
Lucas, Jerry 1940- 108
See also SATA 33
Lucas, Jim Griffing 1914-1970 Obituary 104
Lucas, John 1937- CANR-69
Earlier sketches in CA 37-40R, CANR-14, 32
Lucas, John A. 1927- 143
Lucas, Joseph 1928- 69-72
Lucas, Joyce 1927- 57-60
Lucas, Lawrence E(dward) 1933- 65-68
Lucas, Marion B(runson) 1935- 81-84
Lucas, Martin 1944- 111
Lucas, N. B. C. 1901- 81-84
Lucas, Noah 1927- 57-60
Lucas, Robert 1904-1984 101
Obituary 111
Lucas, Robert Emerson, Jr. 1937- 107
Lucas, Robert Harold 1933- 37-40R
Lucas, Russell 1930- 137
Lucas, Ruth (Baxendale) 1909- CAP-2
Earlier sketch in CA 19-20
Lucas, Scott 1937- 93-96
Lucas, Stephen E. 1946- 125
Lucas, T(homas) E(dward) 1919- 77-80
Lucas, Victoria
See Plath, Sylvia
Lucas, W(ilmer) F(rancis, Jr.) 1927- 77-80
See also BW 1
Lucash, Frank S. 1938- 120
Lucas Phillips, C(ecil) E(rnest) 1897-1984 CANR-3
Obituary 112
Earlier sketch in CA 1-4R
Luccarelli, Vincent 1923- 155
See also SATA 90
Lucchesi, Aldo
See von Block, Bela W(illiam)
Luce, Celia (Geneva Larsen) 1914- 61-64
See also SATA 38
Luce, Clare Boothe 1903-1987 45-48
Obituary 123
Luce, Don 1934- CANR-12
Earlier sketch in CA 29-32R
Luce, Gay Gaer 1930- 103
Luce, Henry R(obinson) 1898-1967 104
Obituary 89-92
See also MTCW 1
Luce, J(ohn) V(ictor) 1920- 61-64
Luce, T(orry) James, (Jr.) 1932- 129
Luce, Willard (Ray) 1914- 61-64
See also SATA 38
Luce, William (Aubert) 1931- CANR-25
Earlier sketches in CA 65-68, CANR-11
Lucente, Gregory L. 1948- 120
Lucentini, Mauro 1924- 69-72
Lucero, Roberto
See Meredith, Robert C(hidester)
Lucey, James D(ennis) 1923- 25-28R
Luchetti, Cathy 162
Lu-ch'iao
See Wu, Nelson I(kon)
Luchins, Abraham S(amuel) 1914- CANR-11
Earlier sketch in CA 69-72
Luchins, Edith H(irsch) 1921- CANR-11
Earlier sketch in CA 17-20R
Luchsinger, Elaine King 1902- CAP-2
Earlier sketch in CA 17-18
Lucht, Irmgard 1937- SATA 82
Lucia, Ellis (Joel) 1922- CANR-22
Earlier sketches in CA 1-4R, CANR-4
Lucia, Salvatore Pablo 1901-1984 13-16R
Obituary 112
Lucian c. 120-c. 180 DLB 176
Luciani, Vincent 1906- 61-64
Lucid, Robert F(rancis) 1930- 25-28R
Lucie-Smith, (John) Edward (McKenzie) 1933- CANR-7
Earlier sketch in CA 13-16R
See also DLB 40

Lucini, Gian Pietro 1867-1914 ... DLB 114
Luciuk, Lubomyr Y(aroslav) 1953- ... 132
Luck, David Johnston 1912- ... CANR-4
Earlier sketch in CA 53-56
Luck, G(eorge) Coleman 1913- ... 13-16R
Luck, George Hans 1926- ... 5-8R
Luck, Thomas Jefferson 1922- ... 5-8R
Luckert, Karl W(ilhelm) 1934- ... 81-84
Luckett, Hubert Pearson 1916- ... 77-80
Luckett, Karen Beth 1944- ... 77-80
Luckey, Eleanore Braun 1915- ... 33-36R
Luckhardt, C(harles) Grant 1943- ... 93-96
Luckhardt, Mildred Corell 1898- ... 13-16R
See also SATA 5
Luckless, John
See Burkholz, Herbert
and Irving, Clifford Michael
Luckmann, Thomas 1927- ... CANR-44
Earlier sketches in CA 101, CANR-19
Luckmann, William H. 1926- ... 153
Luckock, Elizabeth 1914- ... 21-24R
Luckovich, Mike 1960(?)- ... 144
Luckyj, George S(tephen) N(estor) 1919- CANR-46
Earlier sketches in CA 45-48, CANR-21
Lucretius
See Lucretius
Ludden, Allen (Ellsworth)
1918(?)-1981 Obituary ... 104
See also SATA-Obit 27
Ludden, David 1948- ... 127
Ludel, Jacqueline 1945- ... 111
See also SATA 64
Luder, Peter c. 1415-1472 ... DLB 179
Luder, William Fay 1910- ... 29-32R
Ludington, (Charles) Townsend 1936- ... CANR-25
Earlier sketches in CA 45-48, CANR-9
Ludlam, Charles 1943-1987 ... CANR-72
Obituary ... 122
Earlier sketch in CA 85-88
See also CLC 46, 50
Ludlow, Geoffrey
See Meynell, Laurence Walter
Ludlow, George
See Kay, Ernest
Ludlow, Howard T(homas) 1921- ... 21-24R
Ludlow, James Minor 1917-1974 Obituary ... 53-56
Ludlum, Mabel Cleland
See Widdemer, Mabel Cleland
Ludlum, Robert 1927- ... CANR-68
Earlier sketches in CA 33-36R, CANR-25, 41
See also AAYA 10
See also BEST 89:1, 90:3
See also CLC 22, 43
See also DAM NOV, POP
See also DLBY 82
See also MTCW 1
Ludlum, Robert P(hillips) 1909-1987 ... CAP-1
Obituary ... 122
Earlier sketch in CA 13-16
Ludmerer, Kenneth M. 1947- ... CANR-27
Earlier sketch in CA 45-48
Ludovici, Anthony M(ario) 1882-(?) ... CAP-1
Earlier sketch in CA 11-12
Ludovici, L. J.
See Ludovici, Lorenz James
Ludovici, Laurence James
See Ludovici, Lorenz James
Ludovici, Lorenz James 1910- ... CANR-10
Earlier sketch in CA 21-24R
Ludowyk, E(velyn) F(rederick) C(harles) 1906-1985
CAP-1
Obituary ... 117
Earlier sketch in CA 11-12
Ludtke, James Buren 1924- ... 1-4R
Ludvigsen, Karl (Eric) 1934- ... 73-76
Ludvigson, Susan 1942- ... CANR-71
Earlier sketches in CA 57-60, CANR-7
See also DLB 120
Ludwickson, John 1948- ... 144
Ludwig, Charles Shelton 1918- ... CANR-42
Earlier sketches in CA 9-12R, CANR-5, 20
Ludwig, Ed(ward William) 1920- ... 97-100
Ludwig, Eric
See Grunwald, Stefan
Ludwig, Frederic
See Grunwald, Stefan
Ludwig, Helen ... SATA 33
Ludwig, Jack 1922- ... CANR-72
Earlier sketches in CA 1-4R, CANR-1
See also DLB 60
Ludwig, Jerry 1934- ... 81-84
Ludwig, Ken ... CLC 60
Ludwig, Lyndell 1923- ... CANR-38
Earlier sketch in CA 115
See also SATA 63
Ludwig, Myles Eric 1942- ... 25-28R
Ludwig, Otto 1813-1865 ... DLB 129
Ludwig, Richard M(ilton) 1920- ... 17-20R
Ludwigson, Kathryn Romaine 1921- ... CANR-6
Earlier sketch in CA 53-56
Ludwikowski, Rett R. 1943- ... 139
Luebbermann, Mimi 1945- ... 150
Luebke, Frederick Carl 1927- ... CANR-12
Earlier sketch in CA 33-36R
Luecke, Janemarie 1924- ... CANR-21
Earlier sketch in CA 104
Lueders, Edward (George) 1923- ... CANR-5
Earlier sketch in CA 13-16R
See also SATA 14
Luedtke, Kurt (Mamre) 1939- ... 111
Brief entry ... 109
Interview in ... 111
Lueker, Erwin L(ouis) 1914- ... CANR-23
Earlier sketches in CA 17-20R, CANR-8
Luellen, Valentina
See Polley, Judith (Anne)
Luening, Otto 1900-1996 ... 102
Obituary ... 153
Luenn, Nancy 1954- ... CANR-39
Earlier sketch in CA 116
See also SATA 51, 79
Luera, Yolanda 1953- ... DLB 122
Lueschen, Guenther R(udolf) 1930- ... CANR-4
Earlier sketch in CA 53-56
Luescher, Max 1923- ... 101
Luetgen, Kurt (Bodo Heinrich) 1911- ... 108
Luethi, Max 1909- ... 29-32R
Luetzelschwab, John (William) 1940- ... 121
Brief entry ... 118
Lufburrow, William 1931(?)-1986 Obituary ... 118
Luff, S(tanley) G(eorge) A(nthony) 1921- ... 9-12R
Lufkin, Raymond H. 1897- ... SATA 38
Luft, David Sheers 1944- ... 106
Luft, Lya 1938- ... DLB 145
Lugansky, Kazak Vladimir
See Dal', Vladimir Ivanovich
Lugard, Flora Louisa Shaw 1852-1929 ... SATA 21
Luger, Harriett Mandelay 1914- ... CANR-1
Earlier sketch in CA 45-48
See also SATA 23
Lugg, George Wilson 1902- ... 105
Lugger, Phyllis M. 1954- ... 142
Lugo, Ariel E(milio) 1943- ... 41-44R
Lugo, James O. 1928- ... 29-32R
Lugones, Leopoldo 1874-1938 ... 131
Brief entry ... 116
See also HW
See also TCLC 15
Lugt, Herbert Vander
See Vander Lugt, Herbert
Luhr, William 1946- ... 106
Luhrmann, T(anya) M(arie) 1959- ... 130
Luhrmann, Winifred B(ruce) 1934- ... 61-64
See also SATA 11
Lu Hsun 1881-1936
See Shu-Jen, Chou
See also SSC 20
See also TCLC 3
Luick, John F(rancis) 1920- ... 25-28R
Luis, Earlene W. 1929- ... 61-64
See also SATA 11
Luisada, Aldo A(ugusto) 1901-1987 Obituary ... 124
Luisi, Billie M(eisner) 1940- ... 73-76
Lujan, Leonardo Lopez 1964- ... 148
Luk, Charles 1898- ... 9-12R
Luka, Ronald 1937- ... 61-64
Lukach, Joan M(ickelson) 1935- ... 118
Lukacher, Ned 1950- ... CANR-46
Earlier sketch in CA 120
Lukacs, George
See Lukacs, Gyorgy (Szegeny von)
See also CLC 24
Lukacs, George
See Lukacs, Gyorgy (Szegeny von)
Lukacs, Gyorgy (Szegeny von) 1885-1971 ...
CANR-62
Obituary ... 29-32R
Earlier sketch in CA 101
See also Lukacs, George
Lukacs, John (Adalbert) 1923- ... CANR-17
Earlier sketches in CA 1-4R, CANR-1
Lukaczer, Moses 1911-1984 Obituary ... 112
Lukas, Charlotte Koplinka 1954- ... 93-96
Lukas, Ellen ... 97-100
Lukas, J(ay) Anthony 1933-1997 ... CANR-19
Obituary ... 159
Earlier sketches in CA 49-52, CANR-2
See also MTCW 1
Lukas, Mary ... 101
Lukas, Richard C. 1937- ... 33-36R
Lukas, Susan 1940- ... 53-56
Lukashevich, Stephen 1931- ... 33-36R
Luke, Hugh J(ay) 1932- ... 89-92
Luke, Mary M(unger) 1919-1993 ... CANR-14
Obituary ... 143
Earlier sketch in CA 21-24R
Luke, Peter (Ambrose Cyprian) 1919-1995 ...
CANR-72
Obituary ... 147
Earlier sketch in CA 81-84
See also CLC 38
See also DLB 13
Luke, Thomas
See Masterton, Graham
Lukenbill, Willis B(ernard) 1939- ... 103
Luker, Kristin Carol 1946- ... 61-64
Luker, Nicholas (John Lydgate) 1945- ... 130
Luker, Ralph E(dlin) 1940- ... 139
Lukes, Steven (Michael) 1941- ... CANR-53
Earlier sketches in CA 93-96, CANR-16
Lukins, Sheila 1942- ... 139
Lukodianov, Isai (Borisovich) 1913- ... 101
Lukonin, Mikhail K. 1920(?)-1977 Obituary ... 69-72
Lum, Peter
See Crowe, Bettina Lum
Lumian, Norman C. 1928- ... 29-32R
Lumiansky, R(obert) M(ayer)
1913-1987 Obituary ... 122
Lumley, Brian 1937- ... CANR-54
Brief entry ... 120
Earlier sketch in CA 132
See also DAM POP
Lummis, Charles F. 1859-1928 ... DLB 186
Lummis, Keith 1904- ... 104
Lumpkin, Angela 1950- ... CANR-32
Earlier sketch in CA 112
Lumpkin, Betty S(tewart) 1934- ... 146
Lumpkin, Grace ... 69-72
Lumpkin, Henry H(ope) 1913- ... 122
Lumpkin, William Latane 1916- ... CANR-4
Earlier sketch in CA 1-4R
Lumsden, Charles J(ohn) 1949- ... CANR-29
Earlier sketch in CA 111
Lumsden, D(an) Barry 1939- ... CANR-21
Earlier sketch in CA 45-48
Lunan, Duncan (Alasdair) 1945- ... 107
Lunar, Dennis
See Mungo, Raymond
Lunch, Lydia 1959- ... CANR-38
Earlier sketch in CA 115
Lund, A. Morten 1926- ... 13-16R
Lund, Doris Herold 1919- ... 17-20R
See also SATA 12
Lund, Gerald N. 1939- ... CANR-13
Earlier sketch in CA 33-36R
Lund, Gilda E. 1909- ... 5-8R
Lund, Herb(ert Frederick) 1926- ... 45-48
Lund, James
See Stonehouse, John (Thomson)
Lund, Michael 1945- ... 145
Lund, Philip R(eginald) 1938- ... 57-60
Lund, Robert P. 1915- ... 1-4R
Lund, Robert T. 1924- ... 126
Lund, Thomas A. 1922- ... 33-36R
Lundahl, Gene 1933- ... 21-24R
Lundberg, Dan
See Lundberg, Daniel
Lundberg, Daniel 1912-1986 ... 114
Obituary ... 119
Lundberg, Donald E(mil) 1916- ... CANR-12
Earlier sketch in CA 33-36R
Lundberg, Erik F(ilip) 1907-1987 ... CANR-38
Earlier sketches in CA 25-28R, CANR-17
Lundberg, (Edgar) Ferdinand 1905-1995 ... CAP-1
Obituary ... 148
Earlier sketch in CA 9-10
Lundberg, Margaret (Jessie) 1919- ... 61-64
Lundborg, Louis B(illings) 1906- ... 81-84
Lunde, David (Eric) 1941- ... 158
Lunde, Donald T(heodore) 1937- ... 101
Lunde, Karl (Roy) 1931- ... 122
Lunden, Joan 1950- ... 145
Lunden, Walter A(lbin) 1899- ... 21-24R
Lundgren, Paul Arthur 1925-1981 Obituary ... 103
Lundgren, William R. 1918- ... 13-16R
Lundin, Robert W(illiam) 1920- ... 1-4R
Lundkvist, Artur (Nils) 1906- Brief entry ... 117
See also DAM POET
Lundkvist, (Nils) Artur 1906-1991(?) ... 147
Lundman, Richard J. 1944- ... 138
Lundquist, James (Carl) 1941- ... 65-68
Lundquist, Leslie (Dwynn Heeler) ... 154
Lundqvist, Lennart J. 1939- ... 129
Lundsgaarde, Henry P(eder) 1938- ... CANR-14
Earlier sketch in CA 73-76
Lundsteen, Sara W. ... 109
Lundstrom, David E. 1929- ... 126
Lundstrom, John B(ernard) 1948- ... 148
Lundwall, Sam J(errie) 1941- ... CANR-37
Earlier sketches in CA 49-52, CANR-1, 17
Lundy, Robert F(ranklin) 1937- ... 5-8R
Lunenfeld, Marvin C. 1934- ... 61-64
Lung, Chang
See Rigney, James Oliver, Jr.
Lunin, Lois F(ranklin) ... 102
Lunn, Arnold 1888-1974 ... 81-84
Obituary ... 49-52
Lunn, Carolyn (Kowalczyk) 1960- ... 136
See also SATA 67
Lunn, Eugene 1941- ... 45-48
Lunn, Janet (Louise Swoboda) 1928- ... CANR-22
Earlier sketch in CA 33-36R
See also CLR 18
See also JRDA
See also MAICYA
See also SAAS 12
See also SATA 4, 68
Lunn, John Edward 1930- ... 41-44R
Lunsford, Cin Forshay
See Forshay-Lunsford, Cin
Lunt, Elizabeth Graves 1922- ... 33-36R
Lunt, Horace G(ray) 1918- ... 134
Brief entry ... 107
Lunt, James D(oiran) 1917- ... CANR-3
Earlier sketch in CA 1-4R
Lunt, Lois
See Metz, Lois Lunt
Lunt, Richard D(eForest) 1933- ... 13-16R
Luoma, Jon R. 1951- ... 127
Luomala, Katharine 1907- ... 37-40R
Luongo, C. Paul 1930- ... 105
Luongo, Edward Parker 1912(?)-1989 Obituary ... 128
Luper, Harold L(ee) 1924- ... 17-20R
Luper, Steven 1956- ... 162
Lupica, Michael Thomas
See Lupica, Mike
Lupica, Mike 1952- ... 142
Lupo, Alan 1938- ... 41-44R
Lupoff, Dick
See Lupoff, Richard A(llen)
Lupoff, Richard A(llen) 1935- ... CANR-50
Earlier sketches in CA 21-24R, CANR-9, 25
See also SATA 60
Lupold, Harry F. 1936- ... 139
Lupul, Manoly R(obert) 1927- ... 127
Brief entry ... 106
Lupus of Ferrieres c. 805-c. 862 ... DLB 148
Luraghi, Raimondo 1921- ... 164
Lurgan, Lester
See Knowles, Mabel Winifred
Luria, Alexander R(omanovich) 1902-1977 ...
CANR-33
Obituary ... 73-76
Earlier sketch in CA 25-28R
See also MTCW 1
Luria, Maxwell Sidney 1932- ... 37-40R
Luria, S(alvador) E(dward) 1912-1991 ... 61-64
Obituary ... 133
Lurie, Alison 1926- ... CANR-50
Earlier sketches in CA 1-4R, CANR-2, 17
See also CLC 4, 5, 18, 39
See also DLB 2
See also MTCW 1
See also SATA 46
Lurie, Edward 1927- ... CANR-7
Earlier sketch in CA 9-12R
Lurie, Harry L. 1892(?)-1973 Obituary ... 41-44R
Lurie, Jonathan 1939- ... 132
Lurie, Morris 1938- ... 133
See also SATA 72
Lurie, Nancy Oestreich 1924- ... CANR-16
Earlier sketch in CA 1-4R
Lurie, Ranan R(aymond) 1932- ... 57-60
Lurie, Richard G. 1919- ... 21-24R
Lurie, Toby 1925- ... 45-48
Luriya, Aleksander Romanovich
See Luria, Alexander R(omanovich)
Luschei, Eugene C(harles) 1928- ... 37-40R
Luscher, Max
See Luescher, Max
Luscombe, David Edward 1938- ... 41-44R
Luscombe, William 1912- ... 5-8R
Lusinchi, Victor 1912-1985 Obituary ... 115
Luskin, Bernard J(ay) 1937- ... 33-36R
Luskin, John 1908- ... 45-48
Lussert, Anneliese 1929- ... 168
See also SATA 101
Lussier, (Joseph) Ernest 1911-1979 ... CANR-9
Earlier sketch in CA 57-60
Lussu, Joyce (Salvadori) 1912- ... CANR-14
Earlier sketch in CA 29-32R
Lust, John (Benedict) 1920- ... 116
Lust, Peter 1911- ... 103
Lustbader, Eric Van 1946- ... CANR-66
Earlier sketches in CA 85-88, CANR-14, 42
Interview in ... CANR-14
See also BEST 90:2
See also DAM POP
Lustgarten, Edgar (Marcus) 1907-1978 ... CANR-60
Earlier sketches in CA 25-28R, CANR-22
Lustgarten, Karen 1944- ... 85-88
Lustick, Ian Steven 1949- ... CANR-40
Earlier sketch in CA 117
Lustig, Arnost 1926- ... CANR-47
Earlier sketch in CA 69-72
See also AAYA 3
See also CLC 56
See also SATA 56
Lustig, Loretta 1944- ... SATA 46
Lustig, Nora Claudia 1951- ... 145
Lustig, R(ichard) Jeffrey 1943- ... 112
Lustig, T(imothy) J(ohn) 1961- ... 150
Lustig-Arecco, Vera 1942- ... 101
Lutes, Catherine Urell 1900(?)-1983 Obituary ... 110
Lutetius
See Stearns, Harold Edmund
Lutgen, Kurt
See Luetgen, Kurt (Bodo Heinrich)
Luthans, Fred 1939- ... 29-32R
Luther, Edward T(urner) 1928- ... 77-80
Luther, Frank 1905-1980 Obituary ... 102
See also SATA-Obit 25
Luther, James W(allace) 1940- ... 69-72
Luther, Jim
See Luther, James W(allace)
Luther, Martin 1483-1546 ... DLB 179
Luther, Ray
See Ley, Arthur Gordon
Luther, Rebekah (Lyn) S(tiles) 1960- ... 155
See also SATA 90
Luthi, Max
See Luethi, Max
Luthuli, A. J.
See Luthuli, Albert John
Luthuli, Albert John 1898(?)-1967 ... 153
Obituary ... 113
See also BW 2
Lutin, Michael 1940- ... 89-92
Luttbeg, Norman R. 1938- ... CANR-10
Earlier sketch in CA 25-28R
Luttmann, Gail
See Damerow, Gail (Jane)
Luttrell, Guy L. 1938- ... 97-100
See also SATA 22
Luttrell, Ida (Alleene) 1934- ... CANR-52
Earlier sketches in CA 110, CANR-27
See also SATA 40, 91
See also SATA-Brief 35
Luttrell, Mark H. 1914- ... 97-100
Luttwak, Edward N(icholae) 1942- ... CANR-48
Earlier sketches in CA 25-28R, CANR-11
Lutwack, Leonard 1917- ... 41-44R
Lutyens, (Agnes) Elisabeth
1906-1983 Obituary ... 109
Lutyens, Mary 1908- ... 25-28R
Lutz, Alma 1890-1973 ... CAP-1
Obituary ... 45-48
Earlier sketch in CA 9-10
Lutz, Catherine A. 1952- ... CANR-66
Earlier sketch in CA 145
Lutz, Charles P(aul) 1931- ... 115
Lutz, Cora Elizabeth 1906-1985 ... 102
Obituary ... 115
Lutz, Frank W. 1928- ... 33-36R
Lutz, Gertrude May 1899- ... 33-36R
Lutz, Harley L. 1882-1975 Obituary ... 53-56
Lutz, Jerry 1939- ... 89-92
Lutz, Jessie Gregory 1925- ... 13-16R
Lutz, John (Thomas) 1939- ... CANR-49
Earlier sketches in CA 65-68, CANR-9, 24
Lutz, Paul E(ugene) 1934- ... 61-64
Lutz, William D. 1940- ... 33-36R

Lutz, William W(alter) 1919- 49-52
Lutze, Karl E(rnst) 1920- 89-92
Lutzeier, Elizabeth 1952- SATA 72
Lutzer, Erwin W(esley) 1941- CANR-2
Earlier sketch in CA 45-48
Lutzker, Edythe 1904-1991 37-40R
Obituary 135
See also SATA 5
Luvaas, Jay 1927- 13-16R
Luvaas, William 1945- 121
Lux, Jimmy
See Obrecht, Jas
Lux, Thomas 1946- CANR-53
Earlier sketch in CA 41-44R
Luxemburg, Rosa 1870(?)-1919 Brief entry 118
See also TCLC 63
Luxenburg, Norman 1927- 41-44R
Luxon, Thomas H. 1954- 155
Luxton, Leonora Kathrine 1895- 85-88
Luxton, Richard (Neil) 1950- 110
Luyben, Helen L. 1932- 17-20R
Luytens, David (Edwin) Bulwer 1929- 13-16R
Luza, Radomir 1922- CANR-24
Earlier sketches in CA 9-12R, CANR-9
Luzadder, Patrick 1954- SATA 89
Luzbetak, Louis J(oseph) 1918- 33-36R
Luzi, Mario 1914- CANR-70
Earlier sketches in CA 61-64, CANR-9
See also CLC 13
See also DLB 128
Luzma
See Umpierre (Herrera), Luz Maria
Luzwick, Dierdre 1945- 65-68
Luzzati, Emanuele 1921- 29-32R
See also SATA 7
Luzzatto, Paola Caboara 1938- 112
See also SATA 38
L'vov, Nikolai Aleksandrovich 1751-1803 DLB 150
Lwoff, Andre Michel 1902- 160
Lyall, Gavin (Tudor) 1932- CANR-59
Earlier sketches in CA 9-12R, CANR-4, 26
See also DLB 87
Lyall, Katharine Elizabeth 1928- CANR-7
Earlier sketch in CA 5-8R
Lyall, Leslie T(heodore) 1905- 13-16R
Lyandres, Yulian Semenovich 1931-1993 CANR-35
Obituary 142
Lybbert, Tyler 1970- SATA 88
Lycan, Gilbert L(ester) 1909- CAP-2
Earlier sketch in CA 33-36
Lyday, Leon F(aidherbee) III 1939- 33-36R
Lydecker, Beatrice 1938- 106
Lyden, Fremont J(ames) 1926- 25-28R
Lyden, Jacki 1954- 162
Lydenberg, John 1913- 37-40R
Lydgate, John c. 1370-1450 DLB 146
Lydolph, Paul E. 1924- 13-16R
Lydon, James G(avin) 1927- 126
Brief entry 105
Lydon, John (Joseph) 1956- 158
Lydon, Michael 1942- 85-88
See also SATA 11
Lydon, Susan Gordon 1943- 152
Lyfick, Warren
See Reeves, Lawrence F.
Lyford, Joseph Philip 1918-1992 37-40R
Obituary 140
Lyford-Pike, Margaret (Prudence) 1911- 109
Lyftogt, Kenneth L. 1951- 150
Lygre, David G(erald) 1942- 93-96
Lykiard, Alexis (Constantine) 1940- 81-84
Lykins, Jenny 168
Lykken, David Thoreson 1928- 105
Lyle, Albert Walter 1944- 124
Brief entry 117
Lyle, David 1927- 118
Lyle, Guy R(edvers) 1907- 61-64
Lyle, Jack 1929- 13-16R
Lyle, Jerolyn R(oss) 1937- 89-92
Lyle, Katie Letcher 1938- CANR-53
Earlier sketches in CA 49-52, CANR-29
See also SATA 8
Lyle, Sparky
See Lyle, Albert Walter
Lyles, Vina Honish 1935- 9-12R
Lyles, William H(using) 1946- 111
Lyle-Smythe, Alan 1914- 103
Lyly, John 1554(?)-1606 DAM DRAM
See also DC 7
See also DLB 62, 167
L'Ymagier
See Gourmont, Remy (-Marie-Charles) de
Lyman, Albert Robison 1880-1973 CAP-1
Earlier sketch in CA 13-16
Lyman, Darryl (Dean) 1944- 151
Lyman, Francesca 1951- 133
Lyman, Helen (Lucille) Huguenor 1910- 65-68
Lyman, Howard B(urbeck) 1920- 41-44R
Lyman, Irene (Vera) Ponting 5-8R
Lyman, Lauren D(wight) 1891-1972 Obituary 89-92
Lyman, Marilyn F(lorence) 1925- 93-96
Lyman, Mary Ely 1887-1975 Obituary 53-56
Lyman, Stanford M(orris) 1933- CANR-32
Earlier sketches in CA 29-32R, CANR-12
Lyman, Susan Elizabeth 1906-1976 Obituary 69-72
Lymington, John
See Chance, John Newton
Lynch, Allen C. 1955- 145
Lynch, B. Suarez
See Bioy Casares, Adolfo
and Borges, Jorge Luis
Lynch, Benito 1885-1951 HW
Lynch, Charles B. 1919- 137
Lynch, Chris 1962- 154
See also AAYA 19
See also SATA 95
Lynch, Daniel 1946- 139
Lynch, David (K.) 1946- 129
Brief entry 124
See also CLC 66
Lynch, Edith M. (Carstensen) 1912-1986 105
Obituary 119
Lynch, Eric
See Bingley, David Ernest
Lynch, Etta Lee 1924- 69-72
Lynch, Frances
See Compton, D(avid) G(uy)
Lynch, Hayden Wood 1927(?)-1979 Obituary 89-92
Lynch, Henry T(homson) 1928- 89-92
Lynch, Hollis Ralph 1935- CANR-1
Earlier sketch in CA 45-48
Lynch, J(ohn) Joseph 1894-1987 Obituary 123
Lynch, James
See Andreyev, Leonid (Nikolaevich)
Lynch, James 1936- CANR-40
Earlier sketches in CA 101, CANR-18
Lynch, James F. 1919(?)-1985 Obituary 117
Lynch, James J(oseph) 1938- 73-76
Lynch, Jennifer 1968- 142
Lynch, John 1927- 85-88
Lynch, Kathleen M(artha) 1898- 73-76
Lynch, Kevin (Andrew) 1918-1984 CANR-3
Obituary 112
Earlier sketch in CA 5-8R
Lynch, Lorenzo 1932- 29-32R
See also SATA 7
Lynch, Malcolm 1922- 119
Lynch, Marietta 1947- 106
See also SATA 29
Lynch, Marilyn 1938- 89-92
Lynch, Owen M(artin) 1931- CANR-11
Earlier sketch in CA 29-32R
Lynch, P. J. 1962- SATA 79
Lynch, Patricia (Nora) 1898-1972 CANR-70
Earlier sketches in CAP-1, CA 11-12
See also DLB 160
See also SATA 9
Lynch, Patrick
See Sington, Philip
Lynch, Patrick B(eavis) 1927- 9-12R
Lynch, Peter S. 1944- 154
Lynch, Thomas 1948- 164
Lynch, Thomas Francis 1938- 45-48
Lynch, W(illiam) E(dward) 1930- CANR-10
Earlier sketch in CA 17-20R
Lynch, W. Ware 1914(?)-1989 Obituary 128
Lynch, William F. 1908-1987 CANR-3
Obituary 121
Earlier sketch in CA 1-4R
Lynch Davis, B.
See Bioy Casares, Adolfo
and Borges, Jorge Luis
Lynche, Richard fl. 1596-1601 DLB 172
Lynch-Fraser, Diane 1953- 111
Lynch-Watson, Janet 1936- 93-96
Lynd, Barry
See Cannell, Charles (Henry)
Lynd, Helen Merrell 1896-1982 Obituary 105
Lynd, Robert 1879-1949 DLB 98
Lynd, Robert S. 1892-1970 Obituary 29-32R
Lynd, Staughton (Craig) 1929- 133
Brief entry 112
Lynde, Stan 1931- 65-68
Lynden, Patricia 1937- 73-76
Lyndon, Amy
See Radford, Richard F(rancis), Jr.
Lyndon, Diana
See Anthony, Diana
Lynds, Dennis 1924- CANR-22
Earlier sketches in CA 1-4R, CANR-6
See also SATA 47
See also SATA-Brief 37
Lynds, Gayle (Hallenbeck) 160
Lyne, John Alexander 1909- 97-100
Lyneis, Richard George 1935- 81-84
Lynen, John Fairbanks 1924- CANR-2
Earlier sketch in CA 1-4R
Lynes, (Joseph) Russell (Jr.) 1910-1991 CANR-3
Obituary 135
Earlier sketch in CA 1-4R
Lyngseth, Joan
See Davies, Joan
Lyngstad, Alexandra Halina 1925- 37-40R
Lyngstad, Sverre 1922- CANR-37
Earlier sketches in CA 37-40R, CANR-16
Lynk, Miles V(andahurst) 1871-1956 155
Lynn
See Brown, Velma Darbo
Lynn, Adele B. 1953- 167
Lynn, Arthur D(ellert), Jr. 1921- CANR-10
Earlier sketch in CA 25-28R
Lynn, Conrad J. 1908-1995 CAP-2
Obituary 150
Earlier sketch in CA 23-24
Lynn, David B(randon) 1925- 57-60
Lynn, Edward S(hird) 1919- 57-60
Lynn, Edwin Charles 1935- 45-48
Lynn, Elizabeth A(nne) 1946- CANR-58
Earlier sketch in CA 81-84
See also SATA 99
Lynn, Frank
See Leisy, James (Franklin)
Lynn, Irene
See Rowland, D(onald) S(ydney)
Lynn, Janet
See Salomon, Janet Lynn (Nowicki)
Lynn, Jeannette Murphy 1905- CAP-2
Earlier sketch in CA 21-22
Lynn, (Dorcas) Joanne (Harley) 1951- CANR-53
Earlier sketch in CA 125
Lynn, John A(lbert) 1943- 146
Lynn, Jonathan 1943- 104
Lynn, Kenneth S(chuyler) 1923- CANR-65
Earlier sketches in CA 1-4R, CANR-3, 27
See also CLC 50
Lynn, Laurence Edwin, Jr. 1937- 105
Lynn, Loretta (Webb) 1932(?)- 81-84
Lynn, Margaret
See Battye, Gladys Starkey
Lynn, Mary
See Brokamp, Marilyn
Lynn, Naomi B. 1933- 61-64
Lynn, Patricia
See Watts, Mabel Pizzey
Lynn, Richard 1930- CANR-64
Earlier sketch in CA 37-40R
Lynn, Roa 1937- 101
Lynn, Robert A(than) 1930- 17-20R
Lynn, Robert Wood 1925- 21-24R
Lynn, Ruth Nadelman 1948- 103
Lynne, Becky
See Zawadsky, Patience
Lynne, James Broom 1920- 77-80
Lynskey, Winifred 1904- CAP-2
Earlier sketch in CA 23-24
Lynton, Ann
See Rayner, Claire (Berenice)
Lynton, Harriet Ronken 1920- 73-76
Lynton, Mark (Oliver Lawrence) 1920- 150
Lynx
See West, Rebecca
Lyon, Bentley 1929- 140
Lyon, Bryce Dale 1920- CANR-52
Brief entry 106
Earlier sketch in CA 126
Lyon, Buck
See Paine, Lauran (Bosworth)
Lyon, Christopher (Leslie) 1949- 132
Brief entry 118
Lyon, David 1948- 148
Lyon, E(lijah) Wilson 1904-1989 97-100
Obituary 128
Lyon, Elinor 1921- 25-28R
See also SATA 6
Lyon, Eugene 1929- 106
Lyon, George Ella 1949- CANR-46
Earlier sketch in CA 120
See also SATA 68
Lyon, Harold C(lifford), Jr. 1935- 41-44R
Lyon, James K(arl) 1934- CANR-1
Earlier sketch in CA 45-48
Lyon, Jeff(rey R.) 1943- 130
Interview in 130
Lyon, Jessica
See DeLeeuw, Cateau
Lyon, John 1932- CANR-15
Earlier sketch in CA 41-44R
Lyon, Katherine
See Mix, Katherine Lyon
Lyon, Linda Gale
See Van Voorhis, Linda Lyon
Lyon, Lyman R.
See de Camp, L(yon) Sprague
Lyon, Matthew 1749-1822 DLB 43
Lyon, Melvin (Ernest) 1927- 33-36R
Lyon, Peter 1915-1996 CANR-5
Obituary 154
Earlier sketch in CA 5-8R
Lyon, Peyton V(aughan) 1921- CANR-3
Earlier sketch in CA 9-12R
Lyon, Quinter M(arcellus) 1898- CAP-1
Earlier sketch in CA 19-20
Lyon, Thomas Edgar, Jr. 1939- 37-40R
Lyon, William Henry 1926- 13-16R
Lyon, Winston
See Woolfolk, William
Lyons, Albert S. 1912- 126
Lyons, Arthur (Jr.) 1946- CANR-61
Earlier sketches in CA 29-32R, CANR-12, 35
Lyons, Augusta Wallace 85-88
Lyons, Barbara (Baldwin) 1912- 93-96
Lyons, Catherine 1944- 85-88
Lyons, Christine 1943- 136
Lyons, Daniel 1920- 41-44R
Lyons, David (Barry) 1935- 33-36R
Lyons, Delphine C.
See Smith, Evelyn E.
Lyons, Dorothy M(arawee) 1907- CANR-24
Earlier sketch in CA 1-4R
See also SATA 3
Lyons, Elena
See Fairburn, Eleanor
Lyons, Enid (Muriel) 1897-1981 21-24R
Obituary 108
Lyons, Eugene 1898-1985 9-12R
Obituary 114
Lyons, F(rancis) S(tewart) L(eland) 1923-1983 29-32R
Obituary 110
Lyons, Gene 1943- 126
Lyons, Grant 1941- CANR-15
Earlier sketch in CA 41-44R
See also SATA 30
Lyons, Ivan 1934- CANR-45
Earlier sketches in CA 101, CANR-19
Lyons, J. B. 1922- CANR-17
Earlier sketch in CA 97-100
Lyons, James
See Loewen, James W.
Lyons, John 1932- 132
Lyons, John O(rmsby) 1927- 1-4R
Lyons, John T. 1926- 29-32R
Lyons, Joseph 1918- 13-16R
Lyons, Len 1942- 93-96
Lyons, Leonard 1906-1976 Obituary 69-72
Lyons, Louis 1937- 143
Lyons, Louis M. 1897-1982 Obituary 106
Lyons, Marcus
See Blish, James (Benjamin)
Lyons, Mark Joseph 1910- 5-8R
Lyons, Mary E(velyn) 1947- 159
See also AAYA 26
See also SATA 93
Lyons, Nan 1935- CANR-45
Earlier sketches in CA 101, CANR-19
Lyons, Nick 1932- CANR-4
Earlier sketch in CA 53-56
Lyons, Paul 1942- 162
Lyons, Phyllis I. 1942- 126
Lyons, Richard D(aniel) 1928- 69-72
Lyons, Richard E(ugene) 1920- CANR-21
Earlier sketch in CA 45-48
Lyons, Sister Jeanne Marie 1904- CAP-1
Earlier sketch in CA 11-12
Lyons, Thomas Tolman 1934- CANR-3
Earlier sketch in CA 9-12R
Lyons, Timothy J(ames) 1944- 73-76
Lyons, Tom W(allace) 1943- 116
Ly-Qui, Chung 1940- 29-32R
Lyre, Pinchbeck
See Sassoon, Siegfried (Lorraine)
Lys, Daniel 1924- 21-24R
Lysaght, Averil M(argaret) 85-88
Lysaught, Jerome Paul 1930- CANR-6
Earlier sketch in CA 5-8R
Lysenko, T(rofim) D(enisovich) 1898-1976 Obituary 69-72
Lysias c. 459B.C.-c. 380B.C. DLB 176
Lysons, Kenneth 1923- CANR-33
Earlier sketches in CA 85-88, CANR-15
Lystad, Mary (Hanemann) 1928- CANR-26
Earlier sketches in CA 65-68, CANR-10
See also SATA 11
Lystad, Robert A(rthur) 1920- 13-16R
Lyte, Charles 1935- 104
Lyte, Richard
See Whelpton, (George) Eric
Lytle, Andrew (Nelson) 1902-1995 CANR-70
Obituary 150
Earlier sketch in CA 9-12R
See also CLC 22
See also DLB 6
See also DLBY 95
Lytle, Clifford M(erle) 1932- 93-96
Lytle, Elizabeth Stewart 1949- 148
See also SATA 79
Lytle, Guy Fitch (III) 1944- 118
Lytle, Ruby (Coker) 1917-(?) CAP-1
Earlier sketch in CA 13-16
Lyttelton, George (William) 1883-1962 134
Lyttelton, Humphrey (Richard Adeane) 1921- 129
Brief entry 118
Lyttle, Charles Harold 1885(?)-1980 109
Obituary 97-100
Lyttle, G(erald) R(oland) 1908- CAP-1
Earlier sketch in CA 9-10
Lyttle, Jean
See Garrett, Eileen J(eanette)
Lyttle, Richard B(ard) 1927- CANR-13
Earlier sketch in CA 33-36R
See also SATA 23
Lytton, Edward G(eorge) E(arle) L(ytton) Bulwer-Lytton Baron 1803-1873 SATA 23
Lytton, Edward Robert Bulwer 1831-1891 DLB 32
Lytton, Hugh 1921- 45-48
Lytton, Noel (Anthony Scawen) 1900-1985 CAP-1
Obituary 115
Earlier sketch in CA 9-10
Lytton-Sells, Iris (Esther) 1903- 29-32R
Lyudvinskaya, Tatyana 1885(?)-1976 Obituary 65-68

M

Ma, John T(a-jen) 1920- CANR-31
Earlier sketch in CA 49-52
Ma, Nancy Chih 1919- CANR-10
Earlier sketch in CA 65-68
Ma, Pearl (Pik Chun) 1928(?)-1989 Obituary 130
Ma, Wenhai 1954- SATA 84
Ma, Yinchu 1882-1982 Obituary 110
Maakestad, William J(ohn) 1951- 126
Maar, Leonard (Frank, Jr.) 1927- 106
See also SATA 30
Maartens, Maretha 1945- SATA 73
Maas, Audrey Gellen 1936-1975 CAP-2
Obituary 57-60
Earlier sketch in CA 23-24
Maas, Henry 1929- 25-28R
Maas, Jeremy (Stephen) 1928- CANR-32
Earlier sketch in CA 29-32R
Maas, Peter 1929- 93-96
Interview in 93-96
See also CLC 29
Maas, Selve 69-72
See also SATA 14
Maas, Virginia H(argrave) 1913- 105
Maas, Willard 1911-1971 CAP-1
Obituary 29-32R
Earlier sketch in CA 13-14
Maasarani, Aly Mohamed 1927- 49-52
Maass, Arthur 1917- Brief entry 105
Maass, Joachim 1901-1972 Obituary 37-40R
See also DLB 69
Maass, John 1918- Brief entry 108

Maathai, Wangari (Muta) 1940- ... 155
Mabberley, D(avid) J(ohn) 1948- ... 122
Mabbett, I(an) W(illiam) 1939- ... 29-32R
Mabbott, John David 1898-1988 ... 13-16R
Obituary ... 124
Mabee, Carleton 1914- ... CANR-21
Earlier sketch in CA 1-4R
Maberly, Allan 1922-1977 ... 103
Maberly, Norman C(harles) 1926- ... 33-36R
Mabery, D. L. 1953- ... 121
See also SATA-Brief 53
Mabey, Richard (Thomas) 1941- ... CANR-26
Earlier sketches in CA 21-24R, CANR-9
Mabie, Hamilton Wright 1845-1916 ... DLB 71
Mabie, Margot C(auldwell) J(ones) 1944- ... 125
Mabley, Edward (Howe) 1906-1984 ... 29-32R
Obituary ... 114
Mabley, Jack 1915- ... 105
Mabogunje, Akin(lawon) L(adipo) 1931- ... CANR-16
Earlier sketch in CA 77-80
Mabon, John Scott 1910(?)-1980 Obituary ... 104
Mabry, Bevars Dupre 1928- ... 45-48
Mabry, Donald J(oseph) 1941- ... CANR-37
Earlier sketch in CA 49-52
Mabry, Marcus 1967- ... 152
Mac
See Maccari, Ruggero
and MacManus, Seumas
Mac, Carm
See Armstrong, Keith F(rancis) W(hitfield)
MacAdam, Eve
See Leslie, Cecilie
MacAdam, Preston
See Preston, John
MacAdams, Lewis (Perry, Jr.) 1944- ... 97-100
MacAdams, William 1944- ... 150
MacAfee, Norman 1943- ... 122
MacAgy, Douglas G(uernsey) 1913-1973 ... 102
Macainsh, Noel Leslie 1926- ... 103
MacAlan, Peter
See Ellis, Peter Berresford
MacAlister, Ian
See Albert, Marvin H(ubert)
MacAlpin, Rory
See Mackinnon, Charles Roy
MacAlpine, Margaret H(esketh Murray) 1907- ... CAP-1
Earlier sketch in CA 11-12
Macan, T(homas) T(ownley) 1910- ... 107
MacAndrew, Elizabeth 1924-1983(?) ... 126
Macao, Marshall
See Tuleja, Thaddeus F(rancis)
MacAodhagain, Eamon
See Egan, E(dward) W(elstead)
MacApp, C. C.
See Capps, Carroll M.
Macarov, David 1918- ... CANR-53
Earlier sketches in CA 29-32R, CANR-12, 28
MacArthur, Charles 1895-1956 Brief entry ... 108
See also DLB 7, 25, 44
MacArthur, D(avid) Wilson 1903- ... CANR-5
Earlier sketch in CA 9-12R
MacArthur, Douglas 1880-1964 Obituary ... 113
MacArthur, John F., Jr. 1939- ... 81-84
MacArthur, John R. 1956- ... 140
MacArthur, Robert H(elmer) 1930-1972 ... 167
Obituary ... 37-40R
MacArthur-Onslow, Annette Rosemary 1933- ... 102
See also SATA 26
Macartney, (Carlile) Aylmer 1895-1978 ... 17-20R
Obituary ... 125
Macaulay, Catherine 1731-1791 ... DLB 104
Macaulay, David (Alexander) 1946- ... CANR-34
Earlier sketches in CA 53-56, CANR-5
Interview in ... CANR-34
See also AAYA 21
See also BEST 89:2
See also CLR 3, 14
See also DLB 61
See also MAICYA
See also SATA 46, 72
See also SATA-Brief 27
Macaulay, John (Ure) 1925- ... 107
Macaulay, Neill (Webster, Jr.) 1935- ... 21-24R
Macaulay, Ronald K. S. 1927- ... 146
Macaulay, Rose 1881-1958 Brief entry ... 104
See also DLB 36
See also TCLC 7, 44
Macaulay, Stewart 1931- ... 77-80
Macaulay, Susan Schaeffer 1941- ... 120
Macaulay, Teresa (E.) 1947- ... 160
See also SATA 95
Macaulay, Thomas Babington 1800-1859 ... CDBLB 1832-1890
See also DLB 32, 55
Macauley, Robie Mayhew 1919-1995 ... CANR-3
Obituary ... 150
Earlier sketch in CA 1-4R
MacAusland, Earle R(utherford) 1893-1980 Obituary ... 101
MacAvoy, Paul W(ebster) 1934- ... 126
Brief entry ... 105
MacAvoy, Roberta Ann 1949- ... CANR-59
Earlier sketch in CA 113
MacBean, Dilla Whittemore 1895- ... 5-8R
MacBeth, George (Mann) 1932-1992 ... CANR-66
Obituary ... 136
Earlier sketches in CA 25-28R, CANR-61
See also CLC 2, 5, 9
See also DLB 40
See also MTCW 1
See also SATA 4
See also SATA-Obit 70
Macbeth, Madge (Hamilton) 1880(?)-1965 ... 148
See also DLB 92
Macbeth, Norman 1910- ... CAP-2
Earlier sketch in CA 33-36
MacBride, Robert O(liver) 1926- ... 17-20R
MacBride, Roger Lea 1929-1995 ... 81-84
Obituary ... 147
See also SATA 85
MacBride, Sean 1904-1988 Obituary ... 124
MacCaffrey, Isabel Gamble 1924-1978 ... 81-84
Obituary ... 77-80
MacCaffrey, Wallace T(revethic) 1920- ... 134
Brief entry ... 112
MacCaig, Norman (Alexander) 1910- ... CANR-34
Earlier sketches in CA 9-12R, CANR-3
See also CLC 36
See also DAB
See also DAM POET
See also DLB 27
MacCall, Libby
See Machol, Libby
MacCallum, Hugh R. 1928- ... 127
MacCallum Scott, John H. 1911- ... 25-28R
MacCampbell, James C(urtis) 1916- ... 9-12R
MacCann, Donnarae 1931- ... CANR-1
Earlier sketch in CA 45-48
MacCann, Richard Dyer 1920- ... CANR-5
Earlier sketch in CA 9-12R
MacCannell, Juliet Flower 1943- ... CANR-56
Earlier sketch in CA 127
Maccari, Ruggero 1919(?)-1989 Obituary ... 128
MacCarter, Don 1944- ... SATA 91
MacCarthy, Sir(Charles Otto) Desmond 1877-1952 ... 167
See also TCLC 36
MacCarthy, Fiona 1940- ... CANR-48
Earlier sketch in CA 105
MacCarthy, J(oseph) A(idan) 1913- ... 107
MacCauley, Sister Rose Agnes 1911- ... 37-40R
Macchiarola, Frank Joseph 1941- ... 145
Macciocchi, Maria Antoinetta 1922- ... 73-76
MacClancy, Jeremy 1953- ... 144
MacClintock, Dorcas 1932- ... CANR-6
Earlier sketch in CA 57-60
See also SATA 8
MacCloskey, Monro 1902- ... CANR-5
Earlier sketch in CA 9-12R
Maccoby, Eleanor E(mmons) 1917- Brief entry ... 113
Maccoby, Hyam 1924- ... 143
Maccoby, Michael 1933- ... CANR-14
Earlier sketch in CA 33-36R
MacCollam, Joel A(llan) 1946- ... 105
MacCombie, John 1932- ... 37-40R
MacCorkle, Stuart A(lexander) 1903- ... 17-20R
MacCormac, Earl Ronald 1935- ... 85-88
MacCormack, Sabine G(abriele) 1941- ... 106
MacCormick, Austin H(arbutt) 1893-1979 Obituary ... 93-96
MacCormick, (Donald) Neil 1941- ... 129
MacCorquodale, Patricia (Lee) 1950- ... 101
MacCoun, Catherine 1953- ... 131
MacCracken, Calvin D(odd) 1919- ... 116
MacCracken, Henry Noble 1880-1970 ... CAP-1
Obituary ... 29-32R
Earlier sketch in CA 19-20
MacCracken, Mary 1926- ... CANR-30
Earlier sketch in CA 49-52
MacCraig, Hugh
See Ward, Craig
MacCulloch, Diarmaid 1951- ... 125
MacCullum, Hugh R. 1928- ... 127
MacCurdy, Raymond R(alph, Jr.) 1916- ... 41-44R
MacDermot, Thomas Henry 1870-1933 ... 167
MacDermott, Mercia 1927- ... 106
MacDiarmid, Hugh
See Grieve, C(hristopher) M(urray)
See also CDBLB 1945-1960
See also CLC 2, 4, 11, 19, 63
See also DLB 20
See also PC 9
MacDonagh, Donagh 1912-1968 Obituary ... 93-96
MacDonald, Aeneas
See Thomson, George Malcolm
Macdonald, Aeneas
See Thompson, George Malcolm
Macdonald, Alastair (A.) 1920- ... 136
MacDonald, Amy 1951- ... 135
See also SATA 76
MacDonald, Anne Elizabeth Campbell Bard
See MacDonald, Betty
See also MAICYA
Macdonald, Anne L. 1920- ... 136
MacDonald, Anson
See Heinlein, Robert A(nson)
MacDonald, Bernell 1948- ... 113
MacDonald, Betty 1908-1958 ... 136
See also MacDonald, Anne Elizabeth Campbell Bard
See also YABC 1
Macdonald, Blackie
See Emrich, Duncan (Black Macdonald)
MacDonald, Bonnie 1941- ... 117
MacDonald, Callum A. 1947- ... 144
Macdonald, Caroline 1948- ... 152
See also SATA 86
MacDonald, Charles B(rown) 1922-1990 ... CANR-23
Obituary ... 133
Earlier sketches in CA 9-12R, CANR-6
Macdonald, Coll 1924- ... 17-20R
Macdonald, Copthorne 1936- ... 145
MacDonald, Craig 1949- ... CANR-9
Earlier sketch in CA 57-60
Macdonald, Cynthia 1928- ... CANR-44
Earlier sketches in CA 49-52, CANR-4
See also CLC 13, 19
See also DLB 105
Macdonald, David W(hyte) 1951- ... 106
MacDonald, Dennis Ronald 1946- ... CANR-47
Earlier sketch in CA 111
Macdonald, Douglas J. 1947- ... 138
Macdonald, Dwight 1906-1982 ... 29-32R
Obituary ... 108
See also SATA 29
See also SATA-Obit 33
MacDonald, Edgar E(dgeworth) 1919- ... 115
MacDonald, Edwin A(nderson) 1907- ... 41-44R
Macdonald, Eleanor 1910- ... CAP-1
Earlier sketch in CA 9-10
Macdonald, Elisabeth 1926- ... 65-68
Macdonald, Finlay J. 1925- ... 132
MacDonald, George 1824-1905 ... 137
Brief entry ... 106
See also DLB 18, 163, 178
See also MAICYA
See also SATA 33, 100
See also TCLC 9
Macdonald, Gerard 1940- ... 119
MacDonald, Golden
See Brown, Margaret Wise
MacDonald, Gordon (James Fraser) 1929- ... 155
Macdonald, Gordon A(ndrew) 1911-1978 ... CANR-15
Earlier sketch in CA 65-68
Macdonald, H(enry) Malcolm 1914- ... 17-20R
MacDonald, Hope 1928- ... 135
Macdonald, J. Fred(erick) 1941- ... 130
Brief entry ... 117
MacDonald, Jake (M.) 1949- ... 126
Macdonald, James D. 1954-
See Appleton, Victor
See also SATA 81
MacDonald, Jerry (Paul) 1953- ... 150
Macdonald, John
See Millar, Kenneth
Macdonald, John (Barfoot) 1918- ... CANR-1
Earlier sketch in CA 49-52
MacDonald, John D(ann) 1916-1986 ... CANR-60
Obituary ... 121
Earlier sketches in CA 1-4R, CANR-1, 19
See also CLC 3, 27, 44
See also DAM NOV, POP
See also DLB 8
See also DLBY 86
See also MTCW 1
Macdonald, John M. ... CANR-2
Earlier sketch in CA 1-4R
Macdonald, John Ross
See Millar, Kenneth
Macdonald, Julie 1926- ... 17-20R
Macdonald, Kenneth 1905- ... 73-76
Macdonald, Malcolm
See Ross-Macdonald, Malcolm J(ohn)
MacDonald, Malcolm John 1901-1981 ... 9-12R
Obituary ... 102
MacDonald, Malcolm M(urdoch) 1935- ... 41-44R
Macdonald, Marcia
See Hill, Grace Livingston
MacDonald, Margaret Read 1940- ... CANR-56
Earlier sketches in CA 110, CANR-27
See also SATA 94
Macdonald, Mary
See Gifford, Griselda
MacDonald, Maryann 1947- ... SATA 72
MacDonald, Marylee 1945- ... 144
Macdonald, Nancy (Gardiner Rodman) 1910-1996 ... 126
Obituary ... 155
Macdonald, Neil (William) 1936- ... 89-92
Macdonald, Nina Hansell
See Looker, Antonina (Hansell)
MacDonald, Norman Malcolm 1927- ... 130
MacDonald, Philip 1896-1980 ... CANR-58
Earlier sketch in CA 81-84
See also DLB 77
Macdonald, R. Ross 1923(?)-1983 Obituary ... 110
Macdonald, Robert M(unro) 1923- ... 9-12R
Macdonald, Robert S. 1925- ... 13-16R
Macdonald, Robert W. 1922- ... 17-20R
MacDonald, Ron(ald) 1932- ... 149
Macdonald, Ronald St. John 1928- ... 103
Macdonald, Ross
See Millar, Kenneth
See also CLC 1, 2, 3, 14, 34, 41
See also DLBD 6
MacDonald, Ruby (DeAngelo Norton) 1930- ... 115
MacDonald, Sandy 1949- ... 103
Macdonald, Shelagh 1937- ... 97-100
See also SATA 25
MacDonald, Simon G(avin) G(eorge) 1923- ... 53-56
MacDonald, Suse 1940- ... CANR-70
Earlier sketch in CA 125
See also SATA 54
See also SATA-Brief 52
MacDonald, Timothy I(gnatius) 1941- ... 121
MacDonald, William L. 1921- ... 21-24R
MacDonald, Wilson (Pugsley) 1880-1967 ... 148
See also DLB 92
Macdonald, Zillah K(atherine) 1885- ... CAP-1
Earlier sketch in CA 9-10
See also SATA 11
Macdonnell, James Edmond 1917- ... CANR-8
Earlier sketch in CA 5-8R
MacDonnell, Kevin 1919- ... CANR-31
Earlier sketch in CA 45-48
MacDonnell, Megan
See Stevens, Serita (Deborah)
MacDonogh, Giles 1955- ... 132
MacDonogh, Steve 1949- ... 145
MacDouall, Robertson
See Mair, George Brown
MacDougal, Bonnie 1953- ... 164
MacDougal, John
See Blish, James (Benjamin)
MacDougal, Sheila X.
See Manly, Peter L.
MacDougall, A(llan) Kent 1931- ... CANR-29
Earlier sketch in CA 45-48
MacDougall, Curtis D(aniel) 1903-1985 ... CANR-29
Obituary ... 117
Earlier sketch in CA 53-56
MacDougall, (George) Donald (Alastair) 1912- ... 106
MacDougall, Fiona
See MacLeod, Robert F.
MacDougall, Malcolm D(ouglas) 1928- Brief entry ... 110
MacDougall, Mary Katherine ... CANR-12
Earlier sketch in CA 29-32R
MacDougall, Ruth Doan 1939- ... CANR-8
Earlier sketch in CA 17-20R
MacDowell, Douglas M(aurice) 1931- ... CANR-6
Earlier sketch in CA 5-8R
MacDowell, John
See Parks, Tim(othy Harold)
Mace, C(ecil) Alec 1894- ... CAP-1
Earlier sketch in CA 13-14
Mace, Carroll Edward 1926- ... 41-44R
Mace, David Robert 1907-1990 ... CANR-23
Obituary ... 133
Earlier sketches in CA 57-60, CANR-7
Mace, Don 1899(?)-1983 Obituary ... 109
Mace, Elisabeth 1933- ... CANR-23
Earlier sketch in CA 77-80
See also SATA 27
Mace, Elizabeth Rhoda 1943- ... CANR-38
Mace, Myles L(a Grange) 1911- Brief entry ... 110
Mace, Nancy L(awson) 1941- ... 119
Mace, Varian 1938- ... SATA 49
Mace, Vera C(hapman) 1902- ... 113
MacEachern, Diane 1952- ... 133
Macedo, Stephen 1957- ... 138
MacEoin, Denis 1949- ... 141
MacEoin, Gary 1909- ... CANR-2
Earlier sketch in CA 1-4R
Macer-Story, E(ugenia) 1945- ... CANR-23
Earlier sketch in CA 107
Macesich, George 1927- ... 13-16R
MacEwan, J(ohn) W(alter) Grant 1902- ... 41-44R
MacEwan, Paul W. 1943- ... CANR-7
Earlier sketch in CA 61-64
MacEwen, Gwendolyn (Margaret) 1941-1987 ... CANR-22
Obituary ... 124
Earlier sketches in CA 9-12R, CANR-7
See also CLC 13, 55
See also DLB 53
See also SATA 50
See also SATA-Obit 55
MacEwen, Malcolm 1911-1996 ... 110
Obituary ... 152
Macey, Samuel L(awson) 1922- ... 102
Macfadden, Bernarr 1868-1955 ... DLB 25, 91
MacFadden, Bruce J. 1949- ... 146
MacFall, Russell P(atterson) 1903-1983 ... CAP-1
Obituary ... 110
Earlier sketch in CA 11-12
Macfarlan, Allan A. 1892-1982 ... 107
See also SATA 35
Macfarlane, (Robert) Gwyn 1907-1987 ... 131
Obituary ... 122
MacFarlane, Iris 1922- ... 89-92
See also SATA 11
MacFarlane, James Douglas 1916- ... 132
MacFarlane, Kenneth
See Walker, Kenneth Macfarlane
Macfarlane, Leslie John 1924- ... 21-24R
MacFarlane, Louise 1917(?)-1979 Obituary ... 89-92
MacFarlane, Neil 1936- ... 127
MacFarlane, Stephen
See Cross, John Keir
MacFarquhar, Roderick 1930- ... CANR-13
Earlier sketch in CA 21-24R
MacFee, Maxwell
See Rennie, James Alan
MacGaffey, Wyatt 1932- ... 73-76
MacGibbon, Jean 1913- ... 97-100
MacGill, Patrick 1890(?)-1963 ... 116
MacGill-Callahan, Sheila 1926- ... 146
See also SATA 78
MacGillivray, John H(enry) 1899- ... CAP-2
Earlier sketch in CA 25-28
MacGorman, J(ohn) W(illiam) 1920- ... 102
MacGowan, Christopher (John) 1948- ... 133
Macgowan, Jonathan
See Thurlow, David (Michael)
Macgowan, Kenneth 1888-1963 Obituary ... 93-96
MacGoye, Marjorie (King) Oludhe 1928- ... 168
MacGraw, Ali 1939- ... 139
MacGregor, Alasdair Alpin (Douglas) 1899-1970 ... CAP-1
Obituary ... 29-32R
Earlier sketch in CA 11-12
MacGregor, Bruce (Alan) 1945- ... 77-80
MacGregor, David Roy 1925- ... 93-96
MacGregor, Ellen 1906-1954 ... 137
Brief entry ... 111
See also MAICYA
See also SATA 39
See also SATA-Brief 27
Macgregor, Frances Cooke ... CANR-1
Earlier sketch in CA 1-4R
MacGregor, (John) Geddes 1909- ... CANR-45
Earlier sketches in CA 1-4R, CANR-2, 21
Macgregor, James (Murdoch) 1925- ... CANR-5
Earlier sketch in CA 13-16R
MacGregor, James G(rierson) 1905- ... CANR-10
Earlier sketch in CA 25-28R
MacGregor, John 1825-1892 ... DLB 166
MacGregor, John M. 1941- ... 133
MacGregor, Loren J. 1950- ... 126

MacGregor, Malcolm D(ouglas) 1945- 102
MacGregor, Mary Esther 1876-1961 158
MacGregor, Neil 1946- 145
MacGregor, Robert Mercer
1911-1974 Obituary 104
MacGregor, T. J.
See Janeshutz, Patricia M(arie)
MacGregor-Hastie, Roy (Alasdhair Niall) 1929- ....
CANR-20
Earlier sketches in CA 1-4R, CANR-2
See also SATA 3
Macgregor-Morris, Pamela 1925- CANR-25
Earlier sketch in CA 29-32R
MacGuigan, Mark R(udolph) 1931- 21-24R
MacGuire, James 1952- 142
Mach, Elyse (Janet) 1941- 131
Machado (y Ruiz), Antonio 1875-1939 Brief
entry 104
See also DLB 108
See also TCLC 3
Machado, Eduardo 1953- 131
See also HW
Machado, Manuel 1874-1947 .... DLB 108
Machado, Manuel Anthony, Jr. 1939- 29-32R
Machado de Assis, Joaquim Maria 1839-1908 .. 153
Brief entry 107
See also BLC 2
See also SSC 24
See also TCLC 10
Machan, Tibor R(ichard) 1939- CANR-1
Earlier sketch in CA 45-48
Machann, Clinton (John) 1947- 131
Machar, Agnes Maule 1837-1927 .... DLB 92
MacHardy, Charles 1926- 104
Machen, Arthur
See Jones, Arthur Llewellyn
See also DLB 36, 156, 178
See also SSC 20
See also TCLC 4
Machetanz, Frederick 1908- .... SATA 34
Machetanz, Sara Burleson 1918- 1-4R
Machiavelli
See McCready, Warren T(homas)
Machiavelli, Niccolo 1469-1527 .... DA
See also DAB
See also DAC
See also DAM MST
See also WLCS
Machin, G(eorge) Ian T(hom) 1937- 13-16R
Machin Goodall, Daphne (Edith) CANR-7
Earlier sketch in CA 5-8R
See also SATA 37
Machlin, Milton Robert 1924- CANR-2
Earlier sketch in CA 1-4R
Machlis, Joseph 1906- CANR-22
Earlier sketches in CA 1-4R, CANR-2
Interview in CANR-22
Machlowitz, Marilyn M(arcia) 1952- 101
Machlup, Fritz 1902-1983 .... CANR-6
Obituary 109
Earlier sketch in CA 1-4R
Machol, Libby 1916- 21-24R
Machol, Robert E(ngel) 1917- 37-40R
Macholtz, James Donald 1926- 53-56
Machor, James L(awrence) 1950- 140
MacHorton, Ian
See Machorton, Ian (Duncan)
Machorton, Ian (Duncan) 1923- CANR-8
Earlier sketch in CA 17-20R
Machotka, Otakar (Richard) 1899-1970 ..... CAP-1
Obituary 29-32R
Earlier sketch in CA 13-16
Machotka, Pavel 1936- 161
Macht, Joel 1938- 57-60
Machung, Anne 1947- 133
Macia, Rafael 1946- 97-100
Maciel, Judi(th Anne) 1942- 33-36R
MacInnes, Colin 1914-1976 .... CANR-21
Obituary 65-68
Earlier sketch in CA 69-72
See also CLC 4, 23
See also DLB 14
See also MTCW 1
MacInnes, Helen (Clark) 1907-1985 ..... CANR-58
Obituary 117
Earlier sketches in CA 1-4R, CANR-1, 28
See also CLC 27, 39
See also DAM POP
See also DLB 87
See also MTCW 1
See also SATA 22
See also SATA-Obit 44
MacInnes, Mairi 1925- 141
MacInnes, Patricia 1954- 148
MacInnis, Donald E(arl) 1920- 41-44R
Macintosh, Brownie 1950- 166
See also SATA 98
MacIntosh, J(ohn) J(ames) 1934- 37-40R
MacIntosh, Joan 1924- 107
MacIntosh, Keitha 1954- 112
MacIntosh, Robert 1923- 137
MacIntyre, Alasdair (Chalmers) 1929- 128
Brief entry 118
Macintyre, Angus (Donald) 1935- 118
Macintyre, Ben 1963- CANR-70
Earlier sketch in CA 143
MacIntyre, Christine Melba
1939-1987 Obituary 123
Macintyre, Donald George (Frederick Wyville)
1904- 5-8R
MacIntyre, Elisabeth 1916- CANR-5
Earlier sketch in CA 9-12R
See also SATA 17
MacIntyre, Michael 1939- 131
MacIntyre, Rod(erick Peter) 1947- 132
Macintyre, Stuart (Forbes) 1947- 131
MacIre, Esor B.
See Ambrose, Eric (Samuel)
MacIsaac, David 1935- CANR-31
Earlier sketches in CA 77-80, CANR-14
MacIsaac, Sharon 57-60
Maciuszko, Jerzy J. 1913- 25-28R
Maciuszko, Kathleen L(ynn) 1947- 113
MacIver, Robert M(orrison) 1882-1970 ..... CAP-1
Obituary 25-28R
Earlier sketch in CA 11-12
Mack, Arien 1931- 141
Mack, Beverly (B.) 1952- 143
Mack, Carol K. 130
Mack, Charles R. 1940- 126
Mack, Dana 165
Mack, Edward C. 1905(?)-1973 Obituary 45-48
Mack, Evalina
See McNamara, Lena Brooke
Mack, Gerstle 1894-1983 129
Obituary 109
Mack, J. A. 1906- 65-68
Mack, James D(ecker) 1916- 21-24R
Mack, Jerry
See Johnson, Jerry Mack
Mack, John E(dward) 1929- 106
Mack, Karin E(ileen) 1946- 97-100
Mack, Kirby
See McEvoy, Harry K(irby)
Mack, Marjorie
See Dixon, Marjorie (Mack)
Mack, Mary Peter 1927-1973 .... 1-4R
Obituary 103
Mack, Max Noble 1916- 61-64
Mack, Maynard 1909- CANR-50
Earlier sketches in CA 9-12R, CANR-25
See also DLB 111
Mack, Raymond (Wright) 1927- 13-16R
Mack, Stan(ley) 85-88
See also SATA 17
Mack, Walter Staunton 1895- 109
Mack, William P. 1915- 127
Mackal, Roy P(aul) 1925- 73-76
Mackall, Leonard L. 1879-1937 .... DLB 140
Mackaman, Frank H(indes) II 1950- 111
Mackarness, Richard 1916- 103
Mackay, Alan L(indsay) 1926- 137
MacKay, Alfred F(arnum) 1938- 104
MacKay, Alistair McColl 1931- 81-84
Mackay, Barbara E. 1944- 77-80
Mackay, Claire 1930- CANR-50
Earlier sketches in CA 105, CANR-22
See also CLR 43
See also SATA 40, 97
Mackay, Constance D'Arcy (?)-1966 102
MacKay, D(onald) I(ain) 1937- CANR-24
Earlier sketch in CA 29-32R
Mackay, Donald (Alexander) 1914- CANR-55
Earlier sketch in CA 136
See also SATA 81
MacKay, Donald 1925- 144
MacKay, Donald M(acCrimmon) 1922-1987 ....
CANR-13
Obituary 121
Earlier sketch in CA 29-32R
Mackay, Harvey (B.) 1933(?)- 130
See also BEST 89:3
MacKay, Isabel Ecclestone 1875-1928 ..... DLB 92
Mackay, James (Alexander) 1936- CANR-23
Earlier sketches in CA 53-56, CANR-7
Mackay, Jane 1920-1986 .... CANR-45
Mackay, John Alexander 1889-1983 Obituary .. 110
MacKay, Joy 1918- 65-68
Mackay, Malcolm George 1919- 108
Mackay, Mary 1855-1924 Brief entry 118
See also Corelli, Marie
Mackay, Mercedes (Isabelle) 1906- CAP-1
Earlier sketch in CA 11-12
MacKay, Robert A(lexander) 1894- 9-12R
MacKay, Ruddock F(inlay) 1922- 102
Mackay, Shena 1944- 104
MacKay, William 1943(?)- Brief entry 110
MacKaye, Benton 1879-1975 Obituary 61-64
MacKaye, Milton 1901-1979 93-96
Obituary 85-88
MacKaye, Percy (Wallace) 1875-1956 Brief
entry 113
See also DLB 54
See also SATA 32
MacKaye, William Ross 1934- Brief entry 109
MacKeever, Maggie
See Clark, Gail
MacKeith, Ronald Charles
1908-1977 Obituary 77-80
MacKellar, William 1914- CANR-13
Earlier sketch in CA 33-36R
See also SATA 4
Mackelworth, R(onald) W(alter) 1930- 29-32R
Macken, Walter 1915-1967 .... CAP-1
Obituary 25-28R
Earlier sketch in CA 13-14
See also DLB 13
See also SATA 36
Mackendrick, John 1946- 81-84
MacKendrick, Paul Lachlan 1914- CANR-1
Earlier sketch in CA 1-4R
MacKenna, John 1952- 149
MacKenney, Richard 1953- 157
Mackensen, Heinz Friedrich 1921- Brief entry .. 107
Mackenzie, Alastair (Ian Folliott) 1933- 118
Mackenzie, Alexander 1763-1820 .... DLB 99
MacKenzie, Andrew (Carr) 1911- CANR-29
Earlier sketch in CA 49-52
Mackenzie, Basil William Sholto
1900-1983 Obituary 111
MacKenzie, Christine Butchart 1917- 13-16R
Mackenzie, Compton (Edward Montague)
1883-1972 .... CAP-2
Obituary 37-40R
Earlier sketch in CA 21-22
See also CLC 18
See also DLB 34, 100
MacKenzie, David 1927- 21-24R
MacKenzie, Donald 1918-1993 .... CANR-60
Obituary 142
Earlier sketches in CA 25-28R, CANR-21
MacKenzie, Donald (Angus) 1950- 166
MacKenzie, Fred 1905- CAP-2
Earlier sketch in CA 25-28
MacKenzie, Garry 1921- .... SATA-Brief 31
Mackenzie, Henry 1745-1831 .... DLB 39
MacKenzie, Jean 1928- 93-96
MacKenzie, (Daisy) Jeanne 1922-1986 130
Obituary 120
MacKenzie, Jill (Kelly) 1947- 142
See also SATA 75
MacKenzie, John P(ettibone) 1930- 65-68
Mackenzie, Kathleen Guy 1907- 5-8R
Mackenzie, Kenneth (Ivo) 1913-1955 Brief
entry 122
Mackenzie, Kenneth Donald 1937- 37-40R
MacKenzie, Lewis (Wharton) 1940- 155
Mackenzie, Locke L. 1900(?)-1977 Obituary .. 69-72
MacKenzie, Louise (Wilks) 1920- 29-32R
Mackenzie, Manfred 1934- 65-68
MacKenzie, Norman (Ian) 1921- 130
MacKenzie, Norman H(ugh) 1915- 21-24R
MacKenzie, Ossian 1907-1980 .... 25-28R
Obituary 120
MacKenzie, R(oderick) A(ndrew) F(rancis)
1911- 5-8R
Mackenzie, R. Alec
See Mackenzie, Richard Alexander
MacKenzie, Rachel 1909-1980 102
Obituary 97-100
Mackenzie, Richard Alexander 1923- 109
Mackenzie, Seaforth
See Mackenzie, Kenneth (Ivo)
Mackenzie, Suzanne 1950- 136
MacKenzie, W(illiam) J(ames) M(illar) 1909- 104
Mackenzie, William 1758-1828 .... DLB 187
Mackenzie-Grieve, Averil (Salmond) 1903- ... 9-12R
Mackerras, Colin Patrick 1939- CANR-33
Earlier sketches in CA 85-88, CANR-15
Mackesy, Piers G(erald) 1924- CANR-3
Earlier sketch in CA 9-12R
MacKethan, Lucinda Hardwick 1945- 102
Mackey, Ernan
See McInerny, Ralph
Mackey, Helen T. 1918- 5-8R
Mackey, J(ames) P(atrick) 1934- CANR-9
Earlier sketch in CA 65-68
Mackey, Louis H(enry) 1926- 33-36R
Mackey, Mary 1945- CANR-50
Earlier sketches in CA 77-80, CANR-15
See also CAAS 27
Mackey, Nathaniel (Ernest) 1947- 153
See also DLB 169
Mackey, Sandra 1937- CANR-54
Earlier sketch in CA 127
Mackey, William Francis 1918- 37-40R
Mackey, William J., Jr.
1902(?)-1972 Obituary 37-40R
Mackey, William Wellington 1937- 124
Brief entry 120
See also BW 1
See also DLB 38
Mackie, Alastair 1925- 17-20R
Mackie, Albert D(avid) 1904- CAP-1
Earlier sketch in CA 9-10
Mackie, J(ohn) L(eslie) 1917- CANR-7
Earlier sketch in CA 57-60
Mackie, (Benjamin) James 1932- 41-44R
Mackie, John
See Levinson, Leonard
Mackie, Margaret Davidson 1914- 102
Mackie, Maron
See McNeely, Jeannette
Mackie, Philip 1918-1985 103
Obituary 118
Mackiewicz, Jozef 1902-1985 Obituary 116
Mackillop, Ian D(uncan) 166
MacKillop, James (John) 1939- 113
Mackin, Anita
See Donson, Cyril
Mackin, Catherine (Patricia) 1939-1982 109
Obituary 108
Mackin, Cooper R(icherson) 1933- 41-44R
Mackin, Dorothy (May Mabee) 1917- 107
Mackin, Edward
See McInerny, Ralph
Mackin, Jeanne 1951- 134
Mackin, John H(oward) 1921- 33-36R
Mackin, Theodore 1922- 116
Mackinlay, Leila Antoinette Sterling 1910- ....
CANR-24
Earlier sketches in CAP-1, CA 11-12
Mackinlock, Duncan
See Watts, Peter Christopher
MacKinnon, Bernie 1957- 137
See also SATA 69
MacKinnon, Catharine A. 1946- 132
Brief entry 128
Mackinnon, Charles Roy 1924- CANR-7
Earlier sketch in CA 9-12R
MacKinnon, Edward M(ichael) 1928- CANR-12
Earlier sketch in CA 61-64
MacKinnon, Frank 1919- 49-52
MacKinnon, John Ramsay 1947- 103
Mackinnon, Marianne 1925- 128
MacKinnon, Stephen Robert 1940- CANR-36
Earlier sketch in CA 107
MacKinnon Groomer, Vera 1915- .... SATA 57
MacKinstry, Elizabeth 1879-1956 .... SATA 42
Mackintosh, Athole S(palding) 1926-1977 ..... 5-8R
Obituary 134
Mackintosh, Elizabeth 1896(?)-1952 Brief entry 110
See also Daviot, Gordon
and Tey, Josephine
MacKintosh, Graham (D.) 1951- 132
MacKintosh, Ian 1940- 73-76
Mackintosh, James 1765-1832 .... DLB 158
Mackintosh, John (Pitcairn) 1929-1978 103
Mackintosh, (John) Malcolm 1921- 5-8R
Mackintosh, N(icholas) J(ohn) 1935- 124
Mackintosh, Prudence 1944- 124
Mackle, Jeff
See McLeod, John F(reeland)
Mackler, Bernard 1934- 21-24R
Mackley, George 1900-1983 Obituary 109
Macklin, Barbara J(une) 1925- Brief entry 118
Macklin, Charles 1699-1797 .... DLB 89
Macklin, Elizabeth 1952- 141
Macklin, June
See Macklin, Barbara J(une)
MacKnight, Nancy (Margaret) 1940- 118
Mackowski, Richard M(artin) 1929- 106
Macksey, (Catherine Angela) Joan 1925- 65-68
Macksey, Kenneth J. 1923- CANR-56
Earlier sketches in CA 25-28R, CANR-11, 30
Macksey, Major K. J.
See Macksey, Kenneth J.
Macksey, Richard (Alan) 1930- 101
Mack Smith, Denis 1920- CANR-39
Earlier sketches in CA 21-24R, CANR-17
Mackworth, Cecily 57-60
Mackworth, Jane F. 1917- 37-40R
Macky, Peter W(allace) 1937- 53-56
MacLachlan, James Angell 1891-1967 ..... CAP-2
Earlier sketch in CA 19-20
Maclachlan, Lewis 1894-1980 .... CANR-6
Earlier sketch in CA 5-8R
MacLachlan, Patricia 1938- 136
Brief entry 118
See also AAYA 18
See also CLR 14
See also JRDA
See also MAICYA
See also SATA 62
See also SATA-Brief 42
Maclagan, Bridget
See Borden, Mary
Maclagan, Michael 1914- 5-8R
MacLaine, Allan H(ugh) 1924- 13-16R
MacLaine, Shirley 1934- CANR-32
Earlier sketch in CA 103
MacLane, Jack
See Crider, (Allen) Bill(y)
MacLane, Mary 1881-1929 156
Mac Lane, Saunders 1909- 158
MacLaren, A. Allan 1938- 106
Maclaren, Colin Shaw 1898-1985 Obituary 116
MacLaren, James
See Grieve, C(hristopher) M(urray)
MacLaren, Sherrill M. 1939- 124
Mac Laverty, Bernard 1942- CANR-43
Brief entry 116
Earlier sketch in CA 118
Interview in 118
See also CLC 31
Maclay, George 1943- 45-48
Maclay, Joanna Hawkins 1938- 112
Maclean, Alasdair 1926- Brief entry 113
MacLean, Alistair (Stuart) 1922(?)-1987 .. CANR-61
Obituary 121
Earlier sketches in CA 57-60, CANR-28
See also CLC 3, 13, 50, 63
See also DAM POP
See also MTCW 1
See also SATA 23
See also SATA-Obit 50
Maclean, Arthur
See Tubb, E(dwin) C(harles)
MacLean, Barbara Anne Hutmacher
See Hutmacher (MacLean), Barbara Anne
Maclean, Charles 1946- 109
Maclean, Donald Duart 1913-1983 Obituary ... 109
Maclean, Fitzroy (Hew) 1911-1996 ...... CANR-31
Obituary 152
Earlier sketches in CA 29-32R, CANR-14
MacLean, Frederick
See MacDonald, Wilson (Pugsley)
MacLean, Harry N(orman) 1942- 130
See also BEST 90:3
MacLean, Jane 1935- 101
MacLean, Janet Rockwood 1917- 33-36R
MacLean, Katherine 1925- 33-36R
See also DLB 8
Maclean, Lady
See Maclean, Veronica
Maclean, Norman (Fitzroy) 1902-1990 ... CANR-49
Obituary 132
Earlier sketch in CA 102
See also CLC 78
See also DAM POP
See also SSC 13
Maclean, Rory Howe 1954- 168
MacLean, Sorley 1911- 154
Maclean, Una 1925- 69-72
Maclean, Veronica 1920- 144
MacLeish, Andrew 1923- 17-20R

MacLeish, Archibald 1892-1982 .... CANR-63
Obituary 106
Earlier sketches in CA 9-12R, CANR-33
See also CLC 3, 8, 14, 68
See also DAM POET
See also DLB 4, 7, 45
See also DLBY 82
See also MTCW 1
MacLeish, Kenneth 1917-1977 81-84
Obituary 73-76
MacLeish, Rod(erick) 1926- 41-44R
MacLeish, William H(itchcock) 1928- CANR-46
Earlier sketch in CA 120
MacLennan, David Alexander 1903-1978 . CANR-2
Earlier sketch in CA 1-4R
MacLennan, (John) Hugh 1907-1990 .... CANR-33
Obituary 142
Earlier sketch in CA 5-8R
See also CLC 2, 14, 92
See also DAC
See also DAM MST
See also DLB 68
See also MTCW 1
MacLennan, Toby 1939- 115
Macleod, Alison 1920- 53-56
MacLeod, Alistair 1936- 123
See also CLC 56
See also DAC
See also DAM MST
See also DLB 60
MacLeod, Ann 1940- 138
MacLeod, Beatrice (Beach) 1910- CAP-1
Earlier sketch in CA 19-20
See also SATA 10
MacLeod, Celeste (Lipow) 1931- 105
MacLeod, Charlotte (Matilda) 1922- CANR-66
Earlier sketches in CA 21-24R, CANR-18, 40
See also SATA 28
Macleod, David I(rving, Jr.) 1943- 123
Macleod, Donald 1914- 17-20R
MacLeod, Doug 1959- 112
See also SATA 60
MacLeod, Duncan J(ohn) 1939- 61-64
MacLeod, Earle Henry 1907- CAP-1
Earlier sketch in CA 9-10
MacLeod, Ellen Jane (Anderson) 1916- ... CANR-3
Earlier sketch in CA 5-8R
See also SATA 14
Macleod, Fiona
See Sharp, William
MacLeod, Ian R. 1959- 158
MacLeod, Jay 1961- 126
MacLeod, Jean Sutherland 1908- CANR-3
Earlier sketch in CA 9-12R
Macleod, Jennifer Selfridge 1929- 102
MacLeod, Joan 1954- 165
Macleod, Joseph (Todd Gordon)
1903-1984(?) 65-68
Obituary 112
Macleod, Norman (Wicklund) 1906-1985 73-76
Obituary 116
See also DLB 4
MacLeod, Robert
See Knox, William
MacLeod, Robert F. 1917- 77-80
MacLeod, Roderick 1892(?)-1984 Obituary 113
MacLeod, Ruth 1903- 93-96
MacLeod, Sheila 1939- 162
Mac Liammhoir, Micheal
See Mac Liammoir, Micheal
Mac Liammhoir, Micheal
See Mac Liammoir, Micheal
Mac Liammoir, Micheal 1899-1978 .... CANR-3
Obituary 77-80
Earlier sketch in CA 45-48
Mac Low, Jackson 1922- 81-84
See also DLB 193
Maclure, (John) Stuart 1926- 61-64
MacLysaght, Edward Anthony 1887-1986 . CANR-1
Obituary 118
Earlier sketch in CA 1-4R
Macmahon, Arthur W(hittier) 1890-1980 .... 17-20R
Obituary 135
MacMahon, Bryan (Michael) 1909- CANR-47
Earlier sketches in CA 41-44R, CANR-23
MacMahon, Candace W(addell) 1950- 112
Macmann, Elaine
See Willoughby, Elaine Macmann
MacManus, James
See MacManus, Seumas
MacManus, Seumas 1869-1960 102
Obituary 93-96
See also SATA 25
Macmanus, Sheila 1946- 111
MacManus, Susan A(nn) 1947- CANR-40
Earlier sketch in CA 116
MacManus, Yvonne 1931- CANR-45
Earlier sketches in CA 25-28R, CANR-11
MacMaster, Eve (Ruth) B(owers) 1942- 112
See also SATA 46
MacMaster, Richard Kerwin 1935- 115
Mac Master, Robert E(llsworth) 1919- 33-36R
MacMillan, Annabelle
See Quick, Annabelle
Macmillan, C(harles) J(ames) B(arr) 1935- .. 21-24R
MacMillan, Cecile 1898(?)-1986 Obituary 120
Macmillan, David S(tirling) 1925- 113
MacMillan, Dianne M(arie) 1943- 150
See also SATA 84
MacMillan, Donald L(ee) 1940- 57-60
MacMillan, (John) Duncan 1939- 142
MacMillan, Gail 1944- 97-100
Macmillan, (Maurice) Harold 1894-1986 128
Obituary 121
Brief entry 113
Macmillan, James
See Brown, Hamish M.
Macmillan, Maurice Victor 1921-1984 Obituary . 112
Macmillan, Mona 1908- 33-36R
MacMillan, Norma 1947- 149
Macmillan, Norman 1892-1976 .... CAP-1
Obituary 69-72
Earlier sketch in CA 11-12
Macmillan, William Miller 1885-1974 ...... CANR-9
Obituary 53-56
Earlier sketches in CAP-1, CA 11-12
MacMullan, Charles Walden Kirkpatrick
1889-1973 Obituary 89-92
MacMullen, Ramsay 1928- CANR-13
Earlier sketch in CA 21-24R
Macnab, Francis Auchline 1931- 25-28R
MacNab, P(eter) A(ngus) 1903- 33-36R
Macnab, Roy 1923- 65-68
MacNalty, Arthur (Salusbury) 1880-1969 .. CANR-5
Earlier sketch in CA 5-8R
MacNamara, Brinsley
See Weldon, John
See also DLB 10
Mac Namara, Desmond 1918- 146
Mac Namara, Donal E(oin) J(oseph) 1916- ....
CANR-14
Earlier sketch in CA 33-36R
Macnamara, Ellen 1924- 103
Macnamara, John (Theodore) 1929- CANR-13
Earlier sketch in CA 21-24R
Macnaughton, William R(obert) 1939- 119
MacNeice, Jill 1956- 115
MacNeice, (Frederick) Louis 1907-1963 .. CANR-61
Earlier sketch in CA 85-88
See also CLC 1, 4, 10, 53
See also DAB
See also DAM POET
See also DLB 10, 20
See also MTCW 1
MacNeil, Duncan
See McCutchan, Philip (Donald)
Macneil, Ian R(oderick) 1929- 33-36R
MacNeil, Neil
See Ballard, (Willis) Todhunter
MacNeil, Neil 1891-1969 .... CAP-1
Obituary 29-32R
Earlier sketch in CA 19-20
MacNeil, Robert (Breckenridge Ware) 1931- ....
CANR-53
Brief entry 108
Earlier sketch in CA 114
Interview in 114
See also BEST 89:3
MacNeill, Alastair (John) 1960- 130
MacNeill, Dand
See Fraser, George MacDonald
MacNeill, Earl S(chwom)
1893-1972 Obituary 37-40R
Macneill, Janet
See McNeely, Jeannette
Macneill, Norma 1922- 117
MacNeish, Richard S(tockton) 1918- 37-40R
Macnell, James
See Macdonnell, James Edmond
MacNelly, C(larence) L(amont)
1920(?)-1986 Obituary 118
MacNelly, Jeff(rey Kenneth) 1947- 102
MacNib
See Mackie, Albert D(avid)
MacNicholas, John (Malcolm) 1943- 123
Brief entry 118
Macnicol, Eona K(athleen) Fraser 1910- 9-12R
MacNutt, Francis S. 1925- CANR-12
Earlier sketch in CA 73-76
Macomber, Daria
See Robinson, Patricia Colbert
Macomber, William (Butts, Jr.) 1921- 61-64
Mac Orlan, Pierre
See Dumarchais, Pierre
Macourek, Milos 1926- 140
MacPeek, Walter G. 1902-1973 .... CAP-2
Obituary 41-44R
Earlier sketch in CA 29-32
See also SATA 4
See also SATA-Obit 25
Macphail, Andrew 1864-1938 .... DLB 92
MacPhearson, James
See Wright, John L.
MacPhee, Ross D(ouglas) E(arle) 1949- 149
Macpherson, C(rawford) Brough 1911-1987 ....
CANR-2
Obituary 123
Earlier sketch in CA 5-8R
Macpherson, James 1736-1796
See Ossian
See also DLB 109
Macpherson, James (Campbell) 1942- 136
Macpherson, (Jean) Jay 1931- 5-8R
See also CLC 14
See also DLB 53
Macpherson, Jeanie 1884-1946 Brief entry 123
See also DLB 44
Macpherson, Kenneth
1903(?)-1971 Obituary 29-32R
MacPherson, Malcolm C(ook) 1943- CANR-24
Earlier sketch in CA 102
MacPherson, Margaret 1908- 49-52
See also SAAS 4
See also SATA 9
MacPherson, Thomas George 1915-1976 . CANR-4
Earlier sketch in CA 1-4R
See also SATA-Obit 30
Macquarrie, Alan (Denis) 1954- 122
Macquarrie, Heath Nelson 1919- CANR-20
Earlier sketch in CA 41-44R
Macquarrie, John 1919- CANR-29
Earlier sketches in CA 1-4R, CANR-1
Macqueen, James G(alloway) 1932- 17-20R
MacQueen, John 1929- 133
MacQueen, Winifred (Wallace) 1928- 133
MacQuitty, William CANR-7
Earlier sketch in CA 17-20R
MacRae, C(hristopher) Fred(erick) 1909- 45-48
MacRae, Donald E. 1907- 93-96
MacRae, Donald G. 1921-1997 .... 13-16R
Obituary 167
MacRae, Duncan (Jr.) 1921- 21-24R
MacRae, George W(insor) 1928-1985 Obituary . 117
Macrae, John, Jr. 1898(?)-1983 Obituary 111
Macrae, Marjorie Knight (?)-1973 Obituary .. 41-44R
Macrae, Norman 1923- CANR-22
Earlier sketch in CA 106
Macrae, Travis
See Feagles, Anita M(acRae)
MacRaois, Cormac 1944- .... SATA 72
Macridis, Roy C(onstantine) 1918-1991 115
Obituary 136
Macro, Eric 1920- CANR-32
Earlier sketch in CA 29-32R
Macrorie, Ken(neth) 1918- 65-68
Macrow, Brenda G(race Joan) Barton 1916- . 9-12R
MacShane, Denis 1948- 109
MacShane, Frank 1927- CANR-33
Earlier sketches in CA 9-12R, CANR-3
See also CLC 39
See also DLB 111
MacStiofain, Sean
See Stephenson, John Edward Drayton
MacSweeney, Barry 1948- CANR-20
Earlier sketch in CA 25-28R
MacTaggart, Morna Doris
See Brown, Morna Doris
MacThomais, Ruaraidh
See Thomson, Derick S(mith)
Macu, Pavel
See Magocsi, Paul Robert
Macumber, Mari
See Sandoz, Mari(e Susette)
Macura, Paul 1924- CANR-8
Earlier sketch in CA 17-20R
MacVane, John (Franklin) 1912-1984 .... CANR-16
Obituary 111
Earlier sketch in CA 65-68
Macvaugh, Gilbert S(tillman)
1902-1990 Obituary 131
MacVeagh, Lincoln 1890-1972 Obituary 33-36R
MacVean, Jean 131
Macvey, John W(ishart) 1923- CANR-7
Earlier sketch in CA 17-20R
MacVicar, Angus 1908- CANR-30
Earlier sketches in CA 13-16R, CANR-10
Macy, Helen 1904(?)-1978 Obituary 81-84
Macy, Joanna Rogers 1929- CANR-52
Earlier sketch in CA 125
Macy, John W(illiams), Jr. 1917-1986 ...... 33-36R
Obituary 121
Macy, Mike 1951- 122
Macy, Sue 1954- 152
See also SATA 88
Madachy, Joseph S(teven) 1927- 5-8R
Madame Simone
See Porche, Simone (Benda)
Madan, T(riloki) N(ath) 1931- CANR-7
Earlier sketch in CA 17-20R
Madaras, Area 1969- 116
Madaras, Lynda 1947- 107
Madariaga, Isabel de
See de Madariaga, Isabel
Madariaga (Y Rojo), Salvador de 1886-1978 ......
CANR-32
Obituary 81-84
Earlier sketches in CA 9-12R, CANR-6
See also HW
Maday, Bela C(harles) 1912- 41-44R
Madden, Arthur Gerard 1911- 1-4R
Madden, Betty I(senbarger) 1915- 57-60
Madden, Bill 1945- 133
Madden, Carl H(alford) 1920-1978 .... 41-44R
Obituary 81-84
Madden, Cecil (Charles) 1902-1987 Obituary .. 122
Madden, Charles F(rank) 1921- 25-28R
Madden, Daniel Michael 1916- 65-68
Madden, (Jerry) David 1933- CANR-45
Earlier sketches in CA 1-4R, CANR-4
See also CAAS 3
See also CLC 5, 15
See also DLB 6
See also MTCW 1
Madden, Deirdre 1960- CANR-59
Earlier sketch in CA 133
Madden, Don 1927- 25-28R
See also SATA 3
Madden, Donald L(eo) 1937- CANR-4
Earlier sketch in CA 53-56
Madden, E(dward) S(tanislaus) 1919- 9-12R
Madden, Edward H. 1925- CANR-1
Earlier sketch in CA 1-4R
Madden, Henry Miller 1912-1982 Obituary 108
Madden, Myron C(rowson) 1918- 115
Madden, Peter 1939- 115
Madden, Richard Raymond 1924- 5-8R
Madden, Sir Frederick 1801-1873 .... DLB 184
Madden, Susan
See Johnson, Susan E.
Madden, Tara Roth 1942- 126
Madden, W. C. 1947- 166
Madden, Warren
See Cameron, Kenneth Neill
Madden, William A. 1923- 21-24R
Maddern, Al(an)
See Ellison, Harlan (Jay)
Madderom, Gary 1937- 45-48
Maddex, Jack P(endleton), Jr. 1941- Brief
entry 111
Maddi, Salvatore R(ichard) 1933- 13-16R
Maddison, Angela Mary 1923- 53-56
See also Banner, Angela
See also SATA 10
Maddison, Angus 1926- CANR-10
Earlier sketch in CA 13-16R
Maddison, Carol Hopkins 1923- 17-20R
Maddock, Brent 1950- 81-84
Maddock, Kenneth (?)-1971 Obituary 104
Maddock, Larry
See Jardine, Jack
Maddock, Mary (Denise Catharine Majdak)
1951- 116
Maddock, Reginald (Bertram) 1912- 81-84
See also SATA 15
Maddocks, Margaret (Kathleen Avern) 1906- ... 116
Maddocks, Morris Henry St. John 1928- 116
Maddow, Ben 1909- .... DLB 44
Maddox, Brenda 1932- CANR-22
Earlier sketch in CA 97-100
Maddox, Carl
See Tubb, E(dwin) C(harles)
Maddox, Conroy 1912- 101
Maddox, Gaynor 9-12R
Maddox, George L(amar), Jr. 1925- 17-20R
Maddox, James G(ray) 1907-1973 .... CAP-2
Obituary 45-48
Earlier sketch in CA 21-22
Maddox, Jerrold (Warren) 1932- 17-20R
Maddox, Lester (Garfield) 1915- Brief entry 112
Maddox, Marion Errol 1910- 21-24R
Maddox, Rebecca 1953- 152
Maddox, Robert James 1931- 33-36R
Maddox, Russell W(ebber), Jr. 1921- 1-4R
Maddox, Sara Higgins Sturm
See Sturm-Maddox, Sara Higgins
Maddux, Rachel 1912- CANR-5
Earlier sketch in CA 1-4R
See also DLBY 93
Madeleva, Sister Mary
See Wolff, Mary Evaline
Madelung, A. Margaret (Arent) 1926- 13-16R
Madenski, Melissa (Ann) 1949- 146
See also SATA 77
Mader, (Stanley) Chris(topher, Jr.)
1943(?)-1980 Obituary 103
Mader, Katherine 1948- 126
Madge, Charles Henry 1912- 97-100
Madge, John (Hylton) 1914-1968 .... CAP-1
Earlier sketch in CA 9-10
Madge, Nicola 1949- 130
Madge, Violet 1916-(?) CAP-2
Earlier sketch in CA 21-22
Madgett, Naomi Long 1923- CANR-29
Earlier sketches in CA 33-36R, CANR-13
See also CAAS 23
See also BW 2
See also DLB 76
Madgwick, P(eter) J(ames) 1925- CANR-24
Earlier sketch in CA 29-32R
Madhubuti, Haki R. 1942- CANR-51
Earlier sketches in CA 73-76, CANR-24
See also Lee, Don L.
See also BLC 2
See also BW 2
See also CLC 6, 73
See also DAM MULT, POET
See also DLB 5, 41
See also DLBD 8
See also PC 5
Madian, Jon 1941- 61-64
See also SATA 9
Madigan, Brian 1949- 165
Madigan, Marian East 1898- CAP-2
Earlier sketch in CA 19-20
Madigan, Mark J. 1961- 147
Madigan, Mary Jean Smith 1941- 110
Madigan, Patrick 1945- 144
Madison, Alfreda Louise 1911-1989 Obituary .. 129
Madison, Arnold 1937- CANR-9
Earlier sketch in CA 21-24R
See also SATA 6
Madison, Charles A(llan) 1895-1970 .... CANR-1
Earlier sketch in CA 1-4R
Madison, Frank
See Hutchins, Francis Gilman
Madison, Gary (Brent) 1940- 131
Madison, Hank
See Rowland, D(onald) S(ydney)
Madison, James 1751-1836 .... DLB 37
Madison, James H. 1944- 138
Madison, Jane
See Horne, Hugh Robert
Madison, Joyce
See Mintz, Joyce Lois
Madison, Peter 1918- 9-12R
Madison, Russ 1929- 25-28R
Madison, Thomas A(lvin) 1926- 57-60
Madison, Tom
See Madison, Thomas A(lvin)
Madison, Winifred 37-40R
See also SATA 5
Madle, Dorothy
See Madlee, Dorothy (Haynes)
Madlee, Dorothy (Haynes) 1917-1980 ... CANR-10
Earlier sketch in CA 17-20R
Madonna 1958- 143
Madott, Darlene (Patrice) 1952- 123
Madow, Leo 1915- CANR-13
Earlier sketch in CA 33-36R
Madow, Pauline (Reichberg) 9-12R
Madrigal, Margarita 1912(?)-1983 Obituary 110
Madruga, Lenor 1942- 102

Madsen, Axel 1930- CANR-33
Earlier sketch in CA 25-28R
Madsen, Borge Gedso 1920- 1-4R
Madsen, Brigham Dwaine 1914- 103
Madsen, David Lawrence 1929- 21-24R
Madsen, (Mark) Hunter 1955- 133
Madsen, Richard (Paul) 1941- CANR-50
Earlier sketch in CA 123
Madsen, Ross Martin 1946- 149
See also SATA 82
Madsen, Roy Paul 1928- 89-92
Madsen, Susan A(rrington) 1954- 155
See also SATA 90
Madsen, Svend Aage 1939- 150
Madsen, Truman Grant 1926- Brief entry 106
Madubuike, Ihechukwu (Chiedozie) 1943- 134
Maduell, Charles Rene, Jr. 1918- 73-76
Mae, Eydie
See Hunsberger, Edith Mae
Maeder, Thomas 1951- 132
Maedke, Wilmer O(tto) 1922- 57-60
Maehl, William H(arvey) 1915- 89-92
Maehl, William Henry, Jr. 1930- 21-24R
Maehlqvist, (Karl) Stefan 1943- CANR-50
Earlier sketches in CA 107, CANR-24
See also Mahlqvist, (Karl) Stefan
See also SATA 30
Maenchen, Otto John 1894-1969 Obituary 109
Maenchen-Helfen, Otto J.
See Maenchen, Otto John
Maend, Evald
See Mand, Ewald
Maepenn, Hugh
See Kuttner, Henry
Maepenn, K. H.
See Kuttner, Henry
Maeroff, Gene I(rving) 1939- 61-64
Maertz, Richard Charles 1935- 73-76
Maes-Jelinek, Hena 1929- 107
Maestro, Betsy C(rippen) 1944- CANR-37
Earlier sketches in CA 61-64, CANR-8, 23
See also CLR 45
See also MAICYA
See also SATA 59
See also SATA-Brief 30
Maestro, Giulio 1942- CANR-37
Earlier sketches in CA 57-60, CANR-8, 23
See also CLR 45
See also MAICYA
See also SATA 8, 59
Maeterlinck, Maurice 1862-1949 136
Brief entry 104
See also DAM DRAM
See also DLB 192
See also SATA 66
See also TCLC 3
Maffei, Paolo 1926- CANR-25
Earlier sketch in CA 108
Maffi, Mario 1947- 153
Mafham, Rod Preston
See Preston-Mafham, Rod(ney Arthur)
Magalaner, Marvin 1920- CANR-1
Earlier sketch in CA 1-4R
Magaret, Helene 1906- 1-4R
Magarshack, David 1899-1977 .... CANR-29
Earlier sketch in CA 5-8R
Magary, Alan 1944- CANR-8
Earlier sketch in CA 61-64
Magary, James F(rederick) 1933- 25-28R
Magary, Kerstin Fraser 1947- CANR-12
Earlier sketch in CA 61-64
Magdalany, Philip 1936(?)-1985 Obituary 117
Magdol, Edward 1918- CANR-9
Earlier sketch in CA 21-24R
Magee, Bryan 1930- CANR-2
Earlier sketch in CA 5-8R
Magee, David (Bickersteth) 1905-1977 81-84
Obituary 73-76
See also DLB 187
Magee, Doug 1947- 146
See also SATA 78
Magee, John 1901-1987 Obituary 122
Magee, Wes 1939- CANR-23
Earlier sketch in CA 107
See also SATA 64
Mager, George C(lyde) 1937- 49-52
Mager, Nathan H. 1912-1986 .... CANR-18
Earlier sketches in CA 45-48, CANR-2
Maggal, Moshe M(orris) 1908- CAP-2
Earlier sketch in CA 23-24
Maggin, Elliot S. 1950- 102
Maggio, Joe 1938- CANR-1
Earlier sketch in CA 45-48
Maggio, Rosalie 1943- 130
See also SATA 69
Maggiolo, Marcio E. Veloz
See Veloz Maggiolo, Marcio E.
Maggiolo, Walter A(ndrew) 1908- 85-88
Maggs, Peter B(lount) 1936- CANR-46
Earlier sketches in CA 17-20R, CANR-8, 23
Maggs, Will(iam) Colston 1912- 13-16R
Magid, Ken(neth Marshall) 128
See also SATA 65
Magida, Arthur J. 1945- 163
Magidoff, Robert 1905-1970 .... CAP-1
Earlier sketch in CA 19-20
Magidson, Herbert (Adolph)
1906-1986 Obituary 118
Magill, Frank N(orthen) 1907-1997 .... CANR-6
Obituary 158
Earlier sketch in CA 5-8R
Magill, Kathleen 1948- 116
Magill, Marcus
See Hill, Brian (Merrikin)
Magill, Robert S(amuel) 1941- 89-92
Maginn, Simon 1961- 150
Maginn, William 1794-1842 .... DLB 110, 159
Maginnis, Andrew Francis 1923- 45-48
Magister, Joseph
See Grant, Louis T(heodore)
Magistrale, Tony 1952- 144
Magloire-Saint-Aude, Clement 1912- 13-16R
Magnarella, Paul J(oseph) 93-96
Magnarelli, Sharon 1946- 147
Magner, James A. 1901- CAP-1
Earlier sketch in CA 13-14
Magner, James Edmund, Jr. 1928- CANR-7
Earlier sketch in CA 17-20R
Magner, Lois N. 1943- 143
Magner, Thomas F(reeman) 1918- 17-20R
Magnin, Cyril I(saac) 1899-1988 107
Obituary 125
Magnus, Erica 1946- 145
See also SATA 77
Magnus, Philip
See Magnus-Allcroft, Philip (Montefiore)
Magnus, Samuel Woolf 1910- CAP-1
Earlier sketch in CA 9-10
Magnus-Allcroft, Philip (Montefiore) 1906-1988 ....
CAP-1
Obituary 127
Earlier sketch in CA 11-12
Magnuson, Don(ald Hammer)
1911-1979 Obituary 89-92
Magnuson, Edward F. 1926- 102
Magnuson, Keith (Arlen) 1947- 93-96
Magnuson, Paul 1939- 69-72
Magnuson, Paul Budd 1884-1968 Obituary 106
Magnuson, Warren G(rant) 1905- 85-88
Magnussen, Daniel Osar 1919- 65-68
Magnusson, Magnus 1929- CANR-23
Earlier sketch in CA 105
Magocsi, Paul Robert 1945- 148
Magog, Paul Dowsey
See Dowsey-Magog, Paul
Magoon, Robert A(rnold) 1922- CANR-24
Earlier sketch in CA 107
Magorian, Christopher 1959- 111
Magorian, James 1942- CANR-58
Earlier sketches in CA 102, CANR-18, 40
See also SATA 32, 92
Magorian, Michelle 1947- 135
See also JRDA
See also MAICYA
See also SATA 67
Magoun, F(rederick) Alexander 1896- CAP-2
Earlier sketch in CA 17-18
Magoun, Francis P(eabody), Jr. 1895-1979(?) .. 107
Magowan, Robin 1936- CANR-20
Earlier sketches in CA 9-12R, CANR-4
Magrath, Allan J. 1949- 142
Magrath, C(laude) Peter 1933- 17-20R
Magrid, Henry M. 1918(?)-1979 Obituary 89-92
Magriel, Paul (David) 1906(?)-1990 Obituary ... 132
Magris, Claudio 1939- 133
Magruder, Jeb Stuart 1934- 101
Magsam, Charles Michael 1907- CAP-1
Earlier sketch in CA 13-16
Magubane, Bernard (Makhosezwe) 1930- 93-96
Maguen, David
See Markish, David
Maguinness, W(illiam) Stuart 1903-1982 .... CAP-1
Obituary 108
Earlier sketch in CA 13-16
Maguire, Anne
See Nearing, Penny
Maguire, Daniel Charles 1931- CANR-32
Earlier sketch in CA 49-52
Maguire, Francis T(homas)
1911-1976 Obituary 69-72
Maguire, Gregory (Peter) 1954- CANR-53
Earlier sketch in CA 81-84
See also AAYA 22
See also SAAS 22
See also SATA 28, 84
Maguire, Henry Pownall 1943- 111
Maguire, Jack 1920- 81-84
See also SATA 74
Maguire, Jessie
See Smith, Sherwood
Maguire, John David 1932- CANR-9
Earlier sketch in CA 21-24R
Maguire, John T(homas) 1917- 1-4R
Maguire, Michael 1945- 104
Maguire, R(obert) A(ugustine) J(oseph) 1898- . 5-8R
Maguire, Robert A(lan) 1930- 73-76
Magun, Carol 1949- 147
Magwood, John McLean 1912- 106
Mahaffey, Vicki 1952- 133
Mahajan, Vidya Dhar 1913- CANR-29
Earlier sketches in CA 25-28R, CANR-11
Mahajani, Usha 1933- 53-56
Mahan, Alfred Thayer 1840-1914 ....DLB 47
Mahan, Bill
See Mahan, William Allen
Mahan, Pat
See Wheat, Patte
Mahan, Patte Wheat
See Wheat, Patte
Mahan, William Allen 1930- CANR-15
Earlier sketch in CA 85-88
Mahapatra, Jayanta 1928- CANR-66
Earlier sketches in CA 73-76, CANR-15, 33
See also CAAS 9
See also CLC 33
See also DAM MULT
Mahar, J. Michael 1929- 13-16R
Maharani of Jaipur
See Devi, Gayatri
Maharidge, Dale (Dimitro) 1956- 148
Mahdi, Muhsin S(ayyid) 1926- CANR-3
Earlier sketch in CA 1-4R
Maher, Bill 1956- 154
Maher, Brendan A(rnold) 1924- 25-28R
Maher, James T(homas) 1917- 65-68
Maher, John E. 1925- 17-20R
Maher, Mary 1940- 140
Maher, Mary Z. 1941- 163
Maher, Peter Kevin 1960- 166
Maher, Ramona 1934- CANR-9
Earlier sketch in CA 21-24R
See also SATA 13
Maher, Robert F. 1922- 17-20R
Maher, Trafford P(atrick) 1914- 21-24R
Maheshwari, Shriram 1931- CANR-30
Earlier sketches in CA 21-24R, CANR-11
Maheux-Forcier, Louise 1929- 162
See also DLB 60
Mahfouz, Naguib (Abdel Aziz Al-Sabilgi) 1911(?)- ...
CANR-55
Earlier sketch in CA 128
See also Mahfuz, Najib
See also BEST 89:2
See also DAM NOV
See also MTCW 1
Mahfuz, Najib
See Mahfouz, Naguib (Abdel Aziz Al-Sabilgi)
See also CLC 52, 55
See also DLBY 88
Mahin, John Lee 1902(?)-1984 Obituary 112
See also DLB 44
Mahindra, Indira 1926- 136
Mahl, George F(ranklin) 1917- 93-96
Mahl, Mary R. 1914- 25-28R
Mahlendorf, Ursula R. 1929- 49-52
Mahler, Gregory S. 1950- CANR-50
Earlier sketch in CA 123
Mahler, Jane Gaston 1906- 37-40R
Mahler, Margaret S(choenberger) 1897-1985 ... 103
Obituary 117
Mahlqvist, (Karl) Stefan
See Maehlqvist, (Karl) Stefan
See also SATA 30
Mahmood, Mamdani 1946- 105
Mahmoody, Betty 1945(?)- 142
Mahmud, Shabana 144
Maholick, Leonard T(homas) 1921- CANR-1
Earlier sketch in CA 1-4R
Mahon, Derek 1941- 128
Brief entry 113
See also CLC 27
See also DLB 40
Mahon, John K(eith) 1912- 17-20R
Mahon, Julia C(unha) 1916- 61-64
See also SATA 11
Mahon, Thomas (Cavan) 1944- 119
Mahoney, Dan 1947- 141
Mahoney, Irene 1921- 61-64
Mahoney, J. Daniel 1931- 61-64
Mahoney, John (Francis) 1929- 41-44R
Mahoney, John Leo 1928- CANR-14
Earlier sketch in CA 33-36R
Mahoney, John Thomas 1905-1981 .... CAP-1
Obituary 104
Earlier sketch in CA 11-12
Mahoney, Michael J(ohn) 1946- CANR-8
Earlier sketch in CA 53-56
Mahoney, Olivia 1952- 133
Mahoney, Patrick 1927- 81-84
Mahoney, Paul F. 1938- 155
Mahoney, Robert F. 1914- 13-16R
Mahoney, Rosemary 1961- 135
Mahoney, Thomas Arthur 1928- 1-4R
Mahoney, Thomas H(enry) D(onald)
1913-1997 ....13-16R
Obituary 157
Mahoney, Tim 1947- 123
Mahoney, Tom
See Mahoney, John Thomas
Mahony, Devin (Adair) 1963- 130
Mahony, Elizabeth Winthrop 1948- 41-44R
See also Winthrop, Elizabeth
See also SATA 8
Mahony, Patrick
See O'Mahony, Patrick
Mahony, Patrick J(oseph) 1932- 162
Mahony, Peter (Bernard) 1931- 118
Mahood, Kenneth 1930- 103
See also SATA 24
Mahood, Ruth I. 1908- CAP-1
Earlier sketch in CA 19-20
Mahowald, Mary Briody 1935- 146
Mahrer, Alvin R(aymond) 1927- 21-24R
Mahy, Margaret 1936- CANR-38
Earlier sketches in CA 69-72, CANR-13, 30
See also AAYA 8
See also CLR 7
See also JRDA
See also MAICYA
See also SATA 14, 69
Mai, Ludwig H(ubert) 1898- 73-76
Maibaum, Richard 1909-1991 102
Obituary 133
Interview in 102
Maiden, Cecil (Edward) 1902-1981 73-76
See also SATA 52
Maiden, Jennifer 1949- 154
Maidoff, Ilka
See List, Ilka Katherine
Maier, Anne McDonald 1954- 142
Maier, Charles S(teven) 1939- CANR-66
Earlier sketch in CA 69-72
Maier, Ernest L(ouis) 1938- 105
Maier, Howard 1906(?)-1983 Obituary 109
Maier, Joseph (Ben) 1911- 21-24R
Maier, Norman R(aymond) F(rederick) 1900-1977 ..
CANR-4
Obituary 73-76
Earlier sketch in CA 1-4R
Maier, Paul L(uther) 1930- CANR-2
Earlier sketch in CA 5-8R
Maier, Pauline (Rubbelke) 1938- 37-40R
Maier, Thomas 1956- 148
Maier, (Henry) William (Jr.) 1901- 1-4R
Maifair, Linda Lee 1947- 150
See also SATA 83
Maik, Henri
See Hecht, Henri Joseph
Maikov, Vasilii Ivanovich 1728-1778 ...... DLB 150
Mailer, Adele 166
Mailer, Norman 1923- CANR-28
Earlier sketch in CA 9-12R
See also CABS 1
See also AITN 2
See also CDALB 1968-1988
See also CLC 1, 2, 3, 4, 5, 8, 11, 14, 28, 39, 74, 111
See also DA
See also DAB
See also DAC
See also DAM MST, NOV, POP
See also DLB 2, 16, 28, 185
See also DLBD 3
See also DLBY 80, 83
See also MTCW 1
Maillard, Keith 1942- 93-96
Maillart, Ella 1903-1997 158
See also DLB 195
Maillet, Adrienne 1885-1963 .... DLB 68
Maillet, Antonine 1929- CANR-46
Brief entry 115
Earlier sketch in CA 120
Interview in 120
See also CLC 54
See also DAC
See also DLB 60
Mailloux, Steven 1950- CANR-53
Earlier sketches in CA 107, CANR-25
Maillu, David G. 1939- .... DLB 157
Mails, Thomas E. 1920(?)- 134
Brief entry 111
Maiman, Jaye 1957- CANR-72
Earlier sketch in CA 145
Maimon, Morton A. 1931- 33-36R
Maimonides, Moses 1138-1204 .... DLB 115
Main, Gloria (Jean) L(und) 1933- 112
Main, Jackson Turner 1917- CANR-1
Earlier sketch in CA 1-4R
Main, Mildred Miles 1898- CAP-1
Earlier sketch in CA 13-16
Maine, Charles Eric
See McIlwain, David
Maine, David
See Avice, Claude (Pierre Marie)
Maine, Trevor
See Catherall, Arthur
Maingot, Anthony P. 1937- 151
Maingot, Rodney 1893-1982 Obituary 105
Mainland, William Faulkner
1905-1988(?) Obituary 125
Mainprize, Don 1930- CANR-7
Earlier sketch in CA 17-20R
Mains, David R(andall) 1936- 93-96
Mains, Randolph P. 1946- 148
See also SATA 80
Mainstone, Rowland J(ohnson) 1923- ... CANR-23
Earlier sketch in CA 107
Mainwaring, Daniel 1902-1977 .... DLB 44
Mainwaring, Marion CANR-3
Earlier sketch in CA 1-4R
Mainwaring, Scott 1954- 145
Maiolo, Joseph 1938- 49-52
Maiorano, Robert 1946- 116
See also SATA 43
Mair, Alistair 1924- 9-12R
Mair, Charles 1838-1927 .... DLB 99
Mair, (Alexander) Craig 1948- 102
Mair, George Brown 1914- CANR-12
Earlier sketch in CA 13-16R
Mair, George F(isk) 1922-1978 Obituary 111
Mair, George L. 1929- 129
Mair, Lucy Philip 1901-1986 Obituary 119
Mair, Margaret
See Crompton, Margaret (Norah Mair)
Mair, Victor H(enry) 1943- CANR-32
Earlier sketch in CA 113
Mairowitz, David Zane 1943- CANR-48
Earlier sketch in CA 122
Mairs, Nancy 1943- 136
Mais, Roger 1905-1955 124
Brief entry 105
See also BW 1
See also DLB 125
See also MTCW 1
See also TCLC 8
Mais, S(tuart) P(etre) B(rodie) 1885-1975 69-72
Obituary 57-60
Maisel, Herbert 1930- 53-56
Maisel, Louis Sandy 1945- 117
Maisel, Sherman J(oseph) 1918- CANR-19
Earlier sketches in CA 5-8R, CANR-4
Maisels, Maxine S. 1939- 49-52
Maisky, Ivan (Mikhailovich) 1884-1975 65-68
Obituary 61-64
Maisner, Heather 1947- ....SATA 89
Maison, Della
See Katz, Bobbi
Maison, Margaret M(ary Bowles) 1920- 17-20R
Maissi, Elie 1911(?)-1983 Obituary 110
Maital, Sharone L(evow) 1947- 131

Maital, Shlomo 1942- CANR-52
Earlier sketches in CA 108, CANR-25
Maitland, Antony Jasper 1935- 101
See also SATA 25
Maitland, Barbara .... SATA 102
Maitland, David J(ohnston) 1922- CANR-38
Earlier sketch in CA 116
Maitland, Derek 1943- CANR-23
Earlier sketch in CA 29-32R
Maitland, Frederic 1850-1906 .... TCLC 65
Maitland, Margaret
See Du Breuil, (Elizabeth) L(or)inda
and Wallmann, Jeffrey M(iner)
Maitland, Sara (Louise) 1950- CANR-59
Earlier sketches in CA 69-72, CANR-13
See also CLC 49
Maitra, Priyatosh 1930- 107
Maizel, C. L.
See Maizel, Clarice Matthews
Maizel, Clarice Matthews 1919- 9-12R
Maizel, Leah
See Maizel, Clarice Matthews
Maizels, John 1945- 157
Maja-Pearce, Adewale 1953- 126
Majault, Joseph 1916- 101
Majerus, Janet 1936- 65-68
Majeski, Bill
See Majeski, William
Majeski, William 1927- CANR-18
Earlier sketch in CA 25-28R
Majka, Linda C. 1947- 124
Majonica, Ernst 1920- 29-32R
Major, Alan P(ercival) 1929- CANR-7
Earlier sketch in CA 57-60
Major, Andre 1942- 166
See also DLB 60
Major, Charles 1856-1913 .... DLB 202
Major, Clarence 1936- CANR-53
Earlier sketches in CA 21-24R, CANR-13, 25
See also CAAS 6
See also BLC 2
See also BW 2
See also CLC 3, 19, 48
See also DAM MULT
See also DLB 33
major, devorah 1952- 158
Major, Geraldyn Hodges 1894-1984 85-88
Obituary 113
Major, Gerri
See Major, Geraldyn Hodges
Major, H. M.
See Jarvis, Sharon
Major, Henriette 1933- 109
Major, J(ames) Russell 1921- CANR-2
Earlier sketch in CA 5-8R
Major, Jean-Louis 1937- CANR-40
Earlier sketches in CA 49-52, CANR-2, 18
Major, John M(cClellan) 1918- 13-16R
Major, Kevin (Gerald) 1949- CANR-38
Earlier sketches in CA 97-100, CANR-21
Interview in CANR-21
See also AAYA 16
See also CLC 26
See also CLR 11
See also DAC
See also DLB 60
See also JRDA
See also MAICYA
See also SATA 32, 82
Major, Mabel 1893- 45-48
Major, Mark Imre 1923- 65-68
Major, Ralph Hermon 1884-1970 .... CAP-1
Earlier sketch in CA 9-10
Major, Reginald W. 1926- 29-32R
Major-Ball, Terry 1932- 153
Major-General of Marsland
See Duncan, Ronald
Major-Poetzl, Pamela 1943- 116
Majors, Richard G. III 148
Majors, Simon
See Fox, G(ardner) F(rancis)
Majumdar, R(amesh) C(handra) 1888- 33-36R
Majumder, Sanat K(umer) 1929- 33-36R
Majure, Janet 1954- 161
See also SATA 96
Makanowitzky, Barbara
See Norman, Barbara
Makarova, Marina 1942- 120
Makarova, Natalia 1940- 113
Makary
See Iranek-Osmecki, Kazimierz
Makavejev, Dusan 1946- 157
Makaveli
See Shakur, Tupac (Amaru)
Makdisi, Jean Said 155
Makeba, (Zensi) Miriam 1932- 104
See also BW 1
Makely, William O(rson) 1932- 53-56
Makemie, Francis 1658(?)-1708 .... DLB 24
Makepeace, Joanna
See York, Margaret Elizabeth
Makepeace, R(oyston) W(illiam) 1950- 116
Makerney, Edna Smith 1921- 61-64
Maki, James
See Ozu, Yasujiro
Maki, John M(cGilvrey) 1909- 109
Makie, Pam 1943- .... SATA 37
Makin, Peter (Julian) 1946- 93-96
Makinen, Merja 1953- 156
Makino, Seiichi 1935- 113
Makins, Clifford 1924-1990 Obituary 132
Makins, Roger Mellor 1904- 111
Makkai, Adam 1935- CANR-10
Earlier sketch in CA 57-60
Makkreel, Rudolf A. 1939- CANR-48
Earlier sketch in CA 122
Makow, Henry 1949- 5-8R
Makower, Addie (Gertrude Leonaura) 1906- 65-68
Makower, Joel 1952- 124
Makowski, Silk
See Makowski, Silvia Ann
Makowski, Silvia Ann 1940- 168
See also SATA 101
Makowsky, Veronica A(nn) 1954- CANR-38
Earlier sketch in CA 116
Maksimov, Vladimir (Yemelyanovich)
See Maximov, Vladimir (Yemelyanovich)
Maksimovic, Desanka 1898-1993 .... DLB 147
Maktari, Abdulla M. A. 1936- 37-40R
Maktos, John 1902-1977 Obituary 69-72
Makumi, Joel 1945(?)- .... BW 2
Mal
See Hancock, Malcolm Cyril
Malabaila, Damiano
See Levi, Primo
Malabre, Alfred L(eopold), Jr. 1931- CANR-28
Earlier sketches in CA 65-68, CANR-12
Malam, John 1957- .... SATA 89
Malamud, Bernard 1914-1986 .... CANR-62
Obituary 118
Earlier sketches in CA 5-8R, CANR-28
See also CABS 1
See also AAYA 16
See also CDALB 1941-1968
See also CLC 1, 2, 3, 5, 8, 9, 11, 18, 27, 44, 78, 85
See also DA
See also DAB
See also DAC
See also DAM MST, NOV, POP
See also DLB 2, 28, 152
See also DLBY 80, 86
See also MTCW 1
See also SSC 15
See also WLC
Malamud, Phyllis Carole 1938- 125
Malamud, Randy 1962- 142
Malamud-Goti, Jaime 1943- 147
Malan, Herman
See Bosman, Herman Charles
and Bosman, Herman Charles
Malan, Rian 1954- 133
See also BEST 90:3
Malan, Roy Mark 1911- 41-44R
Maland, David 1929- 103
Malanga, Gerard (Joseph) 1943- 128
Brief entry 112
See also CAAS 17
Malanos, George J(ohn) 1919-1962 .... 1-4R
Obituary 103
Malanowski, Jamie 1953- 140
Malaparte, Curzio 1898-1957 .... TCLC 52
Malarek, Victor 1948- 123
Malatesta, Peter J. 1932-1990 Obituary 130
Malavie, M. J. 1920- 29-32R
Malbin, Michael J(acob) 1943- CANR-17
Earlier sketch in CA 73-76
Malcolm, Andrew (Ian) 1927- 97-100
Malcolm, Andrew H(ogarth) 1943- 53-56
Malcolm, Dan
See Silverberg, Robert
Malcolm, Donald 1932(?)-1975 Obituary 104
Malcolm, Ian
See Malcolm, Andrew (Ian)
Malcolm, Janet 123
Malcolm, John
See Andrews, John Malcolm
Malcolm, Joyce Lee 1942- 152
Malcolm, Margaret
See Kuether, Edith Lyman
Malcolm, Noel 159
Malcolm, Norman (Adrian) 1911-1990 .... 37-40R
Obituary 132
Malcolmson, Anne
See von Storch, Anne B.
Malcolmson, David 1899- 5-8R
See also SATA 6
Malcolmson, Robert W(illiam) 1943- CANR-19
Earlier sketch in CA 103
Malcolm X
See Little, Malcolm
See also BLC 2
See also CLC 82
See also WLCS
Malcom, Robert E. 1933- 17-20R
Malcomson, R(osalie) M(ary) 1925- 119
Malcomson, Scott L. 1961- 137
Malcomson, William L. 1932- 25-28R
Malcoskey, Edna Walker 17-20R
Maldonado-Denis, Manuel 1933- 131
Brief entry 113
See also HW
Male, Belkis Cuza
See Cuza Male, Belkis
Male, David Arthur 1928- 57-60
Male, Roy R(aymond) 1919- 104
Malecki, Edward S(tanley) 1938- 41-44R
Malefakis, Edward E(manuel) 1932- 29-32R
Malefijt, Annemarie de Waal
See de Waal Malefijt, Annemarie
Malek, Frederic Vincent 1937- 81-84
Malek, James S(tanley) 1941- 57-60
Malenbaum, Wilfred 1913- CANR-1
Earlier sketch in CA 1-4R
Malerba, Luigi 1927- 142
See also DLB 196
Malerich, Edward P. 1940- 33-36R
Maleska, Eugene Thomas 1916-1993 .... CANR-1
Obituary 142
Earlier sketch in CA 1-4R
Malet, B(aldwyn) Hugh G(renville) 1928- 17-20R
Malet, Lucas 1852-1931 .... DLB 153
Malgonkar, Manohar (Dattatray) 1913- CANR-40
Earlier sketches in CA 1-4R, CANR-1, 18
Malherbe, Abraham J(ohannes) 1930- CANR-1
Earlier sketch in CA 49-52
Malherbe, Ernst Gideon 1895- CAP-1
Earlier sketch in CA 13-14
Malherbe, Janie Antonia (Nel) 1897- CAP-1
Earlier sketch in CA 13-16
Malhotra, Ashok Kumar 1940- 110
Malhotra, Inder 1930- 135
Mali, Jane Lawrence 1937-1995 .... CANR-36
Obituary 149
Earlier sketch in CA 114
See also SATA 51
See also SATA-Brief 44
See also SATA-Obit 86
Mali, Paul 1926- CANR-8
Earlier sketch in CA 57-60
Malia, Martin (Edward) 1924- 148
Malick, Terrence 1943- 101
Malick, Terry
See Malick, Terrence
Malickson, David L. 1928- 110
Malik, Charles Habib 1906-1987 .... CANR-7
Obituary 124
Earlier sketch in CA 45-48
Malik, Hafeez 1930- CANR-21
Earlier sketch in CA 77-80
Malik, Yogendra K(umar) 1929- 81-84
Malikin, David 1913- 77-80
Malimoto
See Puri, Shamlal
Malin, David (Frederick) 1941- 118
Malin, Irving 1934- CANR-6
Earlier sketch in CA 13-16R
Malin, James Claude 1893-1979 Obituary 113
Malin, Peter
See Conner, Patrick Reardon
Malina, Bruce J(ohn) 1933- 112
Malina, Frank J(oseph) 1912-1981 93-96
Obituary 108
Malina, Judith 1926- CANR-18
Earlier sketch in CA 102
Maling, Arthur (Gordon) 1923- CANR-22
Earlier sketches in CA 49-52, CANR-3
Malinin, Theodore I 1933- 93-96
Malino, Frances 1940- 115
Malinowitz, Harriet 160
Malinowski, Bronislaw (Kasper) 1884-1942 Brief entry 114
Malins, Edward (Greenway) 1910- 103
Malins, Penelope 1929- 126
Malipiero, Gian Francesco
1882-1973 Obituary 45-48
Malkiel, Burton Gordon 1932- CANR-57
Earlier sketches in CA 49-52, CANR-31
Malkiel, Yakov 1914- 25-28R
Malkiewicz, J(an) Kris 1931- 57-60
Malkin, Lawrence 1930- 126
Malkin, Maurice L. 1900- 49-52
Malkin, Michael R(obert) 1943- 129
Malkin, Sol(omon) M. 1910-1986 Obituary 118
Malkmus, Lizbeth 1937- 139
Malkoff, Karl 1938- 17-20R
Malkus, Alida Wright 1899- 5-8R
Mall, E. Jane 1920- CANR-13
Earlier sketch in CA 21-24R
Mall, Viktor
See Beskow, Bo
Mallaby, (Howard) George 1902-1978 Obituary 108
Mallaby, Sebastian 1964- 138
Mallalieu, John Percival William 1908-1980 129
Obituary 97-100
Mallan, Lloyd 1914- 5-8R
Mallarme, Stephane 1842-1898 .... DAM POET
See also PC 4
Malle, Louis 1932-1995 101
Obituary 150
Mallea, Eduardo 1903-1982(?) 153
Obituary 114
See also HW
Mallen, Bruce E. 1937- CANR-14
Earlier sketch in CA 21-24R
Mallery, David 1923- 5-8R
Malleson, Andrew (Graeme) 1931- Brief entry 112
Malleson, Lucy Beatrice 1899-1973 .... CANR-59
Obituary 49-52
Earlier sketch in CA 97-100
See also Gilbert, Anthony
Mallet-Joris, Francoise 1930- CANR-17
Earlier sketch in CA 65-68
See also CLC 11
See also DLB 83
Mallett, Anne 1913- 49-52
Mallett, Daryl F(urumi) 1969- 149
Mallett, Jerry J. 1939- .... SATA 76
Malley, Ern
See McAuley, James Phillip
and Stewart, Harold Frederick
Mallick, Ross 153
Mallin, Jay 1927- 17-20R
Mallin, Tom 1927(?)-1978 Obituary 89-92
Mallinson, George Greisen 1918- CANR-1
Earlier sketch in CA 1-4R
Mallinson, Jeremy (John Crosby) 1937- CANR-6
Earlier sketch in CA 57-60
Mallinson, Vernon 1910- 5-8R
Malliol, William
See McInenly, William T(homas)
Mallis, Jackie
See Mallis, Jacqueline
Mallis, Jacqueline 1922- 113
Malloch, Peter
See Duncan, W(illiam) Murdoch
Mallock, W. H. 1849-1923 .... DLB 18, 57
Mallon, Bill 1952- 119
Mallon, Thomas 1951- CANR-57
Earlier sketches in CA 110, CANR-29
Mallone, George 1944- 115
Mallone, Ronald Stephen 1916- CAP-1
Earlier sketch in CA 9-10
Mallonee, Richard C(arvel) II 1923- 109
Mallory, Bob F(ranklin) 1932- 89-92
Mallory, Drew
See Garfield, Brian (Wynne)
Mallory, Enid Lorraine 1938- 105
Mallory, James Patrick 1945- 136
Mallory, Kenneth 1945- 124
Mallory, Mark
See Reynolds, Dallas McCord
Mallory, Walter Hampton 1892-1980 .... 9-12R
Obituary 101
Mallough, Don 1914- 21-24R
Mallow, Judy M(ofield) 1949- 163
Mallowan, Agatha Christie
See Christie, Agatha (Mary Clarissa)
Mallowan, Max (Edgar Lucien) 1904-1978 .... CANR-21
Obituary 81-84
Earlier sketch in CA 69-72
Mallows, (Edward) Wilfrid (Nassau) 1905- 119
Malloy, Jerry 1946- 152
Malloy, Ruth Lor 1932- CANR-22
Earlier sketch in CA 69-72
Malloy, Terry 1950- 69-72
Mally, E(mma) Louise 1908- 33-36R
Malm, F(inn) T(heodore) 1919- 17-20R
Malm, William P(aul) 1928- 9-12R
Malmberg, Carl 1904- 33-36R
See also SATA 9
Malmgren, Dallin 1949- 133
See also SATA 65
Malmgren, Harald B(ernard) 1935- CANR-27
Earlier sketch in CA 45-48
Malmo, Robert Beverley 1912- 61-64
Malmont, Valerie S(kuse) 1937- 150
Malmstroem, Vincent H(erschel)
See Malmstrom, Vincent H(erschel)
Malmstrom, Jean 1908- 53-56
Malmstrom, Vincent H(erschel) 1926- 112
Malo, John W. 1911- CANR-12
Earlier sketch in CA 33-36R
See also SATA 4
Malocsay, Zoltan 1946- 81-84
Malof, Joseph F(etler) 1934- 29-32R
Maloff, Chalda (Irene) 1946- 129
Maloff, Saul 1922- 33-36R
See also CLC 5
Malone, Bill C(harles) 1934- 65-68
Malone, Colonel Dick
See Malone, Richard S(ankey)
Malone, Dick
See Malone, Richard S(ankey)
Malone, Dumas 1892-1986 .... CANR-2
Obituary 121
Earlier sketch in CA 1-4R
See also DLB 17
Malone, Edmond 1741-1812 .... DLB 142
Malone, Elmer Taylor, Jr. 1943- CANR-17
Earlier sketches in CA 49-52, CANR-1
Malone, Hank 1940- 158
Malone, James Hiram 1930- 157
See also SATA 84
Malone, Joseph James 1924-1983 Obituary 111
Malone, Kemp 1889-1971 Obituary 89-92
Malone, Louis
See MacNeice, (Frederick) Louis
Malone, Margaret Gay 1939- 112
Malone, Mary CANR-2
Earlier sketch in CA 1-4R
Malone, Michael (Christopher) 1942- CANR-57
Earlier sketches in CA 77-80, CANR-14, 32
See also CLC 43
Malone, Michael P. 1940- CANR-12
Earlier sketch in CA 29-32R
Malone, Nola Langner 1930- CANR-41
Earlier sketches in CA 37-40R, CANR-15
See also Langner, Nola
Malone, Paul B. III 1929- 166
Malone, Paul Scott 1952- 150
Malone, R. S.
See Malone, Richard S(ankey)
Malone, Richard S(ankey) 1909-1985 129
Obituary 116
Brief entry 107
Malone, Ruth 1918- 93-96
Malone, Susan (Mary) 1957- 150
Malone, Ted
See Malone, Elmer Taylor, Jr.
Malone, Wex S(mathers) 1906- 9-12R
Maloney, Arnold Hamilton 1888-1955 162
Maloney, Frank E(dward) 1918-1980 73-76
Obituary 97-100
Maloney, George A(nthony) 1924- CANR-8
Earlier sketch in CA 21-24R
Maloney, J(oseph) J(ohn) 1940- 109
Maloney, Joan M(arie) 1931- 37-40R
Maloney, Pat
See Markun, Patricia Maloney
Maloney, Ralph Liston 1927-1973 .... CANR-3
Obituary 45-48
Earlier sketch in CA 1-4R
Maloney, Ray 1951- 133
Malony, H(enry) Newton 1931- 104

Malory, (Sir) Thomas 1410(?)-1471(?) ...... CDBLB Before 1660
See also DA
See also DAB
See also DAC
See also DAM MST
See also DLB 146
See also SATA 59
See also SATA-Brief 33
See also WLCS
Malouf, (George Joseph) David 1934- ... CANR-50
Earlier sketch in CA 124
See also CLC 28, 86
Malouf, Pyrrha 1929- 117
Malpas, J(effery) E(dward) 1958- 144
Malpass, E(ric) L(awson) 1910-1996 ..... CANR-18
Obituary 154
Earlier sketches in CA 9-12R, CANR-3
Malpass, Leslie F(rederick) 1922- CANR-8
Earlier sketch in CA 17-20R
Malpede, Karen (Sophia) 1945- CANR-26
Earlier sketch in CA 45-48
Malpott, Virgule
See Ghnassia, Maurice (Jean-Henri)
Malquiades
See Hayes, (Robert) Dennis
Malraux, (Georges-)Andre 1901-1976 .... CANR-58
Obituary 69-72
Earlier sketches in CAP-2, CA 21-22, CANR-34
See also CLC 1, 4, 9, 13, 15, 57
See also DAM NOV
See also DLB 72
See also MTCW 1
Malraux, Clara (Goldschmidt) 1897(?)-1982 Obituary 108
Malraux-Goldschmidt, Clara
See Malraux, Clara (Goldschmidt)
Malta, Demetrio Aguilera
See Aguilera Malta, Demetrio
Maltby, Arthur 1935- CANR-10
Earlier sketch in CA 25-28R
Maltby, William S(aunders) 1940- 152
Brief entry 113
Malten, William 1902- CAP-2
Earlier sketch in CA 23-24
Maltese, John Anthony 1960- 143
Maltese, Michael 1909(?)-1981 Obituary 103
See also SATA-Obit 24
Malthus, Thomas Robert 1766-1834 . DLB 107, 158
Maltin, Leonard 1950- CANR-28
Earlier sketches in CA 29-32R, CANR-12
Maltman, Kim 1950- 112
Maltz, Albert 1908-1985 .... 41-44R
Obituary 115
See also DLB 102
Maltz, Maxwell 1899-1975 65-68
Obituary 57-60
Maltz, Stephen 1932- 57-60
Maluf, Chafic 1905(?)-1976 Obituary 69-72
Malveaux, Julianne M(arie) 1953- CANR-23
Earlier sketch in CA 105
Malvern, Corinne 1905-1956 Brief entry 115
See also SATA 34
Malvern, Gladys (?)-1962 73-76
See also SATA 23
Malville, J. McKim
See Malville, John McKim
Malville, John McKim 1934- 120
Malville, Kim
See Malville, John McKim
Maly, Eugene H. 1920-1981 .... CANR-14
Earlier sketch in CA 21-24R
Malz, Betty 1929- CANR-32
Earlier sketch in CA 113
Malzahn, Manfred 1955- 146
Malzberg, Barry N(athaniel) 1939- CANR-16
Earlier sketch in CA 61-64
See also CAAS 4
See also CLC 7
See also DLB 8
Malzberg, Benjamin 1893-1975 .... CAP-1
Obituary 57-60
Earlier sketch in CA 13-16
Mama G.
See Davis, Grania
Mama G.
See Davis, Grania
Mamalakis, Markos J(ohn) 1932- CANR-52
Earlier sketches in CA 45-48, CANR-27
Maman, Andre 1927- 73-76
Mamatey, Victor S(amuel) 1917- 9-12R
Mamedov, Seville 1964- 150
Mamet, David (Alan) 1947- CANR-72
Earlier sketches in CA 81-84, CANR-15, 41, 67
See also CABS 3
See also AAYA 3
See also CLC 9, 15, 34, 46, 91
See also DAM DRAM
See also DC 4
See also DLB 7
See also MTCW 1
Mamis, Justin E. 1929- 9-12R
Mamleev, Yury
See Mamleyev, Yuri
Mamleyev, Yuri 1931- 85-88
Mamonova, Tatyana 1943- 114
See also SATA 93
Mamoulian, Rouben (Zachary) 1897-1987 .. 25-28R
Obituary 124
See also CLC 16
Man, Felix H.
See Baumann, Hans Felix S(iegismund)
Man, John 1941- CANR-16
Earlier sketch in CA 93-96
Manach, Jorge 1898(?)-1961 Obituary 111
Manaka, Matsemela 1956- 140
See also BW 2
See also DLB 157
Manard, Barbara Bolling 1945- 121
Manarin, Louis H(enry) 1932- 21-24R
Manaster, Benjamin 1938- 149
Mana-Zucca
See Cassel, Mana-Zucca
Mancewicz, Bernice Winslow 1917- 37-40R
Manch, Joseph (Rodman) 1910- 53-56
Manchee, Fred B. 1903(?)-1981 Obituary 105
Manchel, Frank 1935- CANR-14
Earlier sketch in CA 37-40R
See also SATA 10
Manchester, Harland 1898-1977 .... 1-4R
Obituary 73-76
Manchester, Paul T(homas) 1893- 61-64
Manchester, William (Raymond) 1922- ... CANR-59
Earlier sketches in CA 1-4R, CANR-3, 31
See also AITN 1
See also BEST 89:2
See also DAM POP
See also MTCW 1
See also SATA 65
Mancini, Anthony 1939- 73-76
Mancini, Pat McNees
See McNees, Pat
Mancke, Richard B(ell) 1943- 81-84
Mancroft, Stormont Mancroft Samuel 1914- CANR-28
Earlier sketch in CA 49-52
Mancusi-Ungaro, Harold R(aymond), Jr. 1947- 97-100
Mancuso, Joe
See Mancuso, Joseph R.
Mancuso, Joseph R. 1941- 93-96
Mand, Ewald 1906- 17-20R
Mandel, Adrienne Schizzano 1934- 37-40R
Mandel, (Mark) Babaloo 1949(?)- 154
Mandel, Benjamin 1891(?)-1973 Obituary 45-48
Mandel, Bernard 1920- 1-4R
Mandel, Brett H. 1969- 161
Mandel, Charlotte 1925- 140
Mandel, Eli(as Wolf) 1922- CANR-43
Earlier sketches in CA 73-76, CANR-15
See also DLB 53
Mandel, Ernest 1923- CANR-15
Earlier sketch in CA 37-40R
Mandel, George 1920- 1-4R
Mandel, Jerome 1937- 37-40R
Mandel, Leon 1928- CANR-13
Earlier sketch in CA 77-80
Mandel, Loring 1928- 73-76
Mandel, Morris 1911- CANR-6
Earlier sketch in CA 5-8R
Mandel, Oscar 1926- CANR-48
Earlier sketches in CA 1-4R, CANR-2, 21
Mandel, Peter (Bevan) 1957- 152
See also SATA 87
Mandel, Ruth Blumenstock 1938- 105
Mandel, Sally Elizabeth 1944- 102
See also SATA 64
Mandel, Sheila 1930(?)-1987 Obituary 124
Mandel, Sidney Albert 1923- 93-96
Mandel, Siegfried 1922- CANR-20
Earlier sketches in CA 1-4R, CANR-5
Mandel, William M(arx) 1917- 9-12R
Mandela, Nelson R(olihlahla) 1918- CANR-59
Earlier sketches in CA 125, CANR-43
See also BW 2
See also DAM MULT
Mandela, (Nomzamo) Winnie (Madikileza) 1936- 125
See also BW 1
Mandelbaum, Allen 111
Mandelbaum, Bernard 1922- 130
Mandelbaum, David G(oodman) 1911-1987 . 41-44R
Obituary 122
Mandelbaum, Maurice (H.) 1908-1987 131
Obituary 121
Brief entry 113
Mandelbaum, Michael 1946- 101
Mandelbaum, Seymour J. 1936- 17-20R
Mandelbrot, Benoit B. 1924- 161
Mandelker, Amy 1953- 149
Mandelker, Daniel Robert 1926- CANR-43
Earlier sketches in CA 1-4R, CANR-5, 20
Mandelkorn, Eugenia Miller 1916- 9-12R
Mandell, Arnold Joseph 1934- 101
Mandell, Betty Reid 1924- CANR-8
Earlier sketch in CA 61-64
Mandell, Fran Gare 1939- 115
Mandell, Gail Porter 1940- 123
Mandell, Maurice I(ra) 1925- CANR-11
Earlier sketch in CA 25-28R
Mandell, Mel 1926- 41-44R
Mandell, Muriel (Hortense Levin) 1921- 9-12R
See also SATA 63
Mandell, Richard Donald 1929- CANR-10
Earlier sketch in CA 25-28R
Mandelshtam, Nadezhda
See Mandelstam, Nadezhda (Yakovlevna)
Mandelstam, Nadezhda (Yakovlevna) 1899-1980 110
Obituary 102
Mandelstam, Osip (Emilievich) 1891(?)-1938(?) . 150
Brief entry 104
See also PC 14
See also TCLC 2, 6
Mandelstamm, Allan B(eryle) 1928- 41-44R
Mander, A(lfred) E(rnest) 1894- CAP-1
Earlier sketch in CA 11-12
Mander, Anica Vesel 1934- CANR-8
Earlier sketch in CA 61-64
Mander, Christine 136
Mander, Gertrud 1927- 93-96
Mander, (Mary) Jane 1877-1949 162
See also TCLC 31
Mander, Jerry 1936- 81-84
Mander, Raymond (Josiah Gale) 1911(?)-1983 . 101
Obituary 111
Mander, Rosalie Grylls 5-8R
Mandeville, Bernard 1670-1733 .... DLB 101
Mandeville, John fl. 1350- .... DLB 146
Mandiargues, Andre Pieyre de
See Pieyre de Mandiargues, Andre
See also CLC 41
See also DLB 83
Mandino, Augustine A.
See Mandino, Og
Mandino, Og 1923-1996 103
Obituary 153
Mandler, George 1924- CANR-19
Earlier sketches in CA 1-4R, CANR-4
Mandler, Jean Matter 1929- CANR-19
Earlier sketch in CA 13-16R
Mandler, Peter 1958- 165
Mandrake, Ethel Belle
See Thurman, Wallace (Henry)
Mandrell, Barbara (Ann) 1948- 139
Mandrepelias, Loizos
See Hartocollis, Peter
Mane, Robert 1926- 37-40R
Manea, Norman 1936- 142
Manella, Raymond L(awrence) 1917- 17-20R
Maner, Martin 1946- 135
Manes, Christopher 1957- 133
Manes, Stephen 1949- 97-100
See also SATA 42, 99
See also SATA-Brief 40
Manfred, Frederick (Feikema) 1912-1994 .... CANR-25
Obituary 146
Earlier sketches in CA 9-12R, CANR-5
See also CAAS 18
See also DLB 6
See also SATA 30
Manfred, Freya 1944- 69-72
Manfred, Robert
See Marx, Erica Elizabeth
Manfredi, Gianfranco 1948- .... DLB 196
Manfredi, John Francis 1920- 109
Manfredi, Renee 144
Manfredi, V.
See Musciano, Walter A.
Mang, Karl 1922- 101
Mangalam, J(oseph) J(oseph) 1924- 37-40R
Mangan, James J. 1907- 139
Mangan, James Thomas 1896- CAP-2
Earlier sketch in CA 19-20
Mangan, (John Joseph) Sherry 1904-1961 Obituary 112
See also DLB 4
Manganelli, Giorgio 1922-1990 .... DLB 196
Manganiello, Dominic 1951- 124
Mangat, J(agjit) S(ingh) 1937- 73-76
Mangin, Marie France 1940- .... SATA 59
Mangini (Gonzalez), Shirley 1946- 149
Mangione, Geraldo 1909- CANR-42
See also Mangione, Jerre
Mangione, Jerre
See Mangione, Geraldo
See also SATA 6
Mango, Cyril (Alexander) 1928- 109
Mango, Karin N. 1936- CANR-50
Earlier sketch in CA 123
See also SATA 52
Mangold, Tom 1934- 69-72
Mangua, Charles 168
Manguel, Alberto (Adrian) 1948- CANR-44
Earlier sketch in CA 131
See also HW
Mangum, Garth L(eroy) 1926- 81-84
Mangurian, David 1938- CANR-10
Earlier sketch in CA 57-60
See also SATA 14
Manhattan, Avro 1914- CANR-30
Earlier sketches in CA 9-12R, CANR-5
Manheim, Emanuel 1897-1988 Obituary 125
Manheim, Jarol B(ruce) 1946- CANR-21
Earlier sketches in CA 57-60, CANR-6
Manheim, Leonard (Falk) 1902- CAP-2
Earlier sketch in CA 21-22
Manheim, Michael 1928- 81-84
Manheim, Ralph 1907(?)- 159
Brief entry 115
Manheim, Sylvan D. 1897-1977 Obituary 73-76
Manheim, Theodore 1921- Brief entry 108
Manheim, Werner 1915- 53-56
Manhire, Bill 1946- CANR-20
Earlier sketch in CA 103
Manhoff, Bill
See Manhoff, Wilton
Manhoff, Wilton 1919-1974 Obituary 49-52
Mania, Cathy 1950- .... SATA 102
Mania, Robert (C.) 1952- .... SATA 102
Maniates, Maria Rika 1937- 113
Maniatty, Taramesha 1978- .... SATA 92
Maniaty, Anthony 1949- 119
Maniaty, Tony
See Maniaty, Anthony
Manicas, Peter T(heodore) 1934- 53-56
Maniere, J.-E.
See Giraudoux, (Hippolyte) Jean
Manifold, J(ohn) S(treeter) 1915- CANR-24
Earlier sketch in CA 69-72
Manigault, Edward 1897(?)-1983 Obituary 109
Manilla, James 97-100
Manis, Jerome G. 1917- 25-28R
Manis, Melvin 1931- 21-24R
Maniscalco, Joseph 1926- CANR-8
Earlier sketch in CA 5-8R
See also SATA 10
Manjon, Maite
See Manjon De Read, Maria Teresa
Manjon De Read, Maria Teresa 1931- ... CANR-38
Mank, Gregory William 1950- 89-92
Mankekar, D. R. 1910- CANR-13
Earlier sketch in CA 21-24R
Mankiewicz, Don M(artin) 1922- 13-16R
Mankiewicz, Frank (Fabian) 1924- 89-92
Mankiewicz, Herman (Jacob) 1897-1953 Brief entry 120
See also DLB 26
Mankiewicz, Joseph L(eo) 1909-1993 73-76
Obituary 140
See also DLB 44
Mankiewicz, Thomas F. 1942- 128
Brief entry 124
Mankiewicz, Tom
See Mankiewicz, Thomas F.
Mankiller, Wilma (Pearl) 1945- 146
Mankin, Paul A. 1924- 37-40R
Mankoff, Allan H. 1935- 45-48
Mankowitz, Wolf 1924- CANR-5
Earlier sketch in CA 5-8R
See also DLB 15
Mankowska, Joyce Kells Batten 1919- CAP-1
Earlier sketch in CA 9-10
Manley, Deborah 1932- CANR-22
Earlier sketch in CA 105
See also SATA 28
Manley, (Mary) Delariviere 1672(?)-1724 ... DLB 39, 80
Manley, Frank 1930- 5-8R
Manley, Joey 1965- 138
Manley, John F(rederick) 1939- 77-80
Manley, Lawrence (Gordon) 1949- 109
Manley, Michael Norman 1924-1997 .... CANR-27
Obituary 157
Earlier sketch in CA 85-88
Manley, Ruth Rodney King 1907(?)-1973 Obituary 41-44R
Manley, Seon 1921- 85-88
See also CLR 3
See also SAAS 2
See also SATA 15
Manley-Tucker, Audrie 1924(?)-1983(?) Obituary 108
Manlove, Colin Nicholas 1942- CANR-32
Earlier sketch in CA 113
Manly, Peter L. 1945- 144
Mann, A. Philo
See Ald, Roy A(llison)
Mann, Abby 1927- 109
Interview in 109
See also DLB 44
Mann, Abel
See Creasey, John
Mann, (Francis) Anthony 1914- CAP-1
Earlier sketch in CA 9-10
Mann, Arthur 1922-1993 109
Obituary 140
Mann, Avery
See Breetveld, Jim Patrick
Mann, Bob 1948- 61-64
Mann, Catherine 1943- 139
Mann, Charles F. 1946- 149
Mann, Charles W., Jr. 1929- 41-44R
Mann, Chris(topher Michael Zithulele) 1948- ... 126
Mann, (Robert Francis) Christopher Stephen 1917- 89-92
Mann, D. J.
See Freeman, James Dillet
Mann, Dale 1938- 61-64
Mann, David Douglas 1934- CANR-52
Earlier sketches in CA 49-52, CANR-28
Mann, Dean Edson 1927- CANR-5
Earlier sketch in CA 9-12R
Mann, Deborah
See Bloom, Ursula (Harvey)
Mann, Donald Nathaniel 1920-1985 Obituary .. 114
Mann, Edward
See Fried, Emanuel
Mann, Edward Andrew 1932- 103
Mann, Emily 1952- CANR-55
Earlier sketch in CA 130
See also DC 7
Mann, Erika 1905-1969 Obituary 25-28R
Mann, Esther Kingston
See Kingston-Mann, Esther
Mann, Floyd C(hristopher) 1917- 1-4R
Mann, Georg K(arl) F(riedrich) 1913- 1-4R
Mann, Golo 1909-1994 97-100
Obituary 145
Mann, Harold W(ilson) 1925- 17-20R
Mann, (Luiz) Heinrich 1871-1950 164
Brief entry 106
See also DLB 66
See also TCLC 9
Mann, Heinrich 1871-1950 .... DLB 118
Mann, Horace 1796-1859 .... DLB 1
Mann, Jack
See Cannell, Charles (Henry)
Mann, Jack 1917(?)- 143
Mann, Jackie
See Mann, Jack
Mann, James
See Harvey, John (Barton)
Mann, Jessica 1937- CANR-60
Earlier sketches in CA 49-52, CANR-2, 24
Mann, John H. 1928- 85-88
Mann, Josephine
See Pullein-Thompson, Josephine (Mary Wedderburn)
Mann, Judy 1943- 146

Mann, Julia de Lacy 1891-1985 Obituary ... 116
Mann, Katharina 1883(?)-1980 Obituary ... 97-100
Mann, Kenneth Walker 1914- ... 29-32R
Mann, Kenny 1946- ... 155
See also SATA 91
Mann, Klaus 1906-1949 ... DLB 56
Mann, Lucile Q.
See Mann, Lucile Quarry
Mann, Lucile Quarry 1897(?)-1986 Obituary ... 121
Mann, Marty 1904-1980 ... 103
Obituary ... 101
Mann, Michael 1919-1977 ... CANR-3
Obituary ... 69-72
Earlier sketch in CA 49-52
Mann, Michael K. 1943- ... 134
Brief entry ... 120
Mann, Milton B(ernard) 1937- ... 45-48
Mann, Pamela 1946- ... 155
See also SATA 91
Mann, Patrick
See Waller, Leslie
Mann, Paul (James) 1947- ... 143
Mann, Peggy
See Houlton, Peggy Mann
See also SATA 6
Mann, Peter (Clifford) 1948- ... 93-96
Mann, Peter H. 1926- ... CANR-12
Earlier sketch in CA 25-28R
Mann, Philip A(lan) 1934- ... 73-76
Mann, Ralph 1943- ... 112
Mann, Richard G(eorge) 1949- ... 124
Mann, Robert 1958- ... 140
Mann, Sunnie 1914(?)-1992 ... 143
Mann, Susan 1943- ... 128
Mann, (Paul) Thomas 1875-1955 ... 128
Brief entry ... 104
See also DA
See also DAB
See also DAC
See also DAM MST, NOV
See also DLB 66
See also MTCW 1
See also SSC 5
See also TCLC 2, 8, 14, 21, 35, 44, 60
See also WLC
Mann, W(illiam) Edward 1918- ... CANR-28
Earlier sketch in CA 49-52
Mann, William D'Alton 1839-1920 ... DLB 137
Mann, William J. 1963- ... 162
Mann, William S(omervell) 1924-1989 ... 109
Obituary ... 129
Mann, Zane B. 1924- ... 101
Manne, Henry G. 1928- ... 33-36R
Mannello, George Jr. 1913- ... 33-36R
Mannering, Julia
See Bingham, Madeleine (Mary Ebel)
Manners, Alexandra
See Rundle, Anne
Manners, Ande Miller 1923(?)-1975 Obituary ... 57-60
Manners, David X. 1912- ... CANR-46
Earlier sketch in CA 106
Manners, Elizabeth (Maude) 1917- ... 49-52
Manners, Gerald 1932- ... 37-40R
Manners, John (Errol) 1914- ... 106
Manners, Julia
See Greenaway, Gladys
Manners, Robert A(lan) 1913-1996 ... 33-36R
Obituary ... 152
Manners, William 1907- ... 65-68
Mannes, Marya 1904-1990 ... CANR-3
Obituary ... 132
Earlier sketch in CA 1-4R
Mannetti, Lisa 1953- ... 125
See also SATA 57
See also SATA-Brief 51
Manngian, Peter
See Monger, (Ifor) David
Mannheim, Grete (Salomon) 1909- ... 9-12R
See also SATA 10
Mannheim, Karl 1893-1947 ... TCLC 65
Manniche, Lise 1943- ... CANR-25
Earlier sketch in CA 107
See also SATA 31
Mannin, Ethel (Edith) 1900-1984 ... CANR-8
Obituary ... 114
Earlier sketch in CA 53-56
See also DLB 191, 195
Manning, Ambrose N(uel) 1922- ... 114
Manning, Bayless Andrew 1923- ... CANR-9
Earlier sketch in CA 13-16R
Manning, Beverley J(ane) 1942- ... 109
Manning, Clarence A(ugustus)
1893-1972 Obituary ... 37-40R
Manning, David
See Faust, Frederick (Schiller)
Manning, David John 1938- ... 103
Manning, Frank E(dward) 1944- ... CANR-7
Earlier sketch in CA 53-56
Manning, Frederic 1887(?)-1935 Brief entry ... 124
See also TCLC 25
Manning, Harvey (Hawthorne) 1925- ... CANR-56
Earlier sketches in CA 112, CANR-30
Manning, Helen Taft 1891(?)-1987 Obituary ... 121
Manning, Jack 1920- ... 69-72
Manning, Laurence (Edward) 1899-1972 ... 160
Manning, Margaret Raymond
1921-1984 Obituary ... 114
Manning, Marie 1873(?)-1945 ... DLB 29
Manning, Marsha
See Grimstead, Hettie
Manning, Martha M. 1952- ... 149
Manning, Martin
See Smith, R(eginald) D(onald)
Manning, Mary Louise
See Cameron, Lou
Manning, Matthew 1955- Brief entry ... 111
Manning, Michael 1940- ... 65-68
Manning, Olivia 1915-1980 ... CANR-29
Obituary ... 101
Earlier sketch in CA 5-8R
See also CLC 5, 19
See also MTCW 1
Manning, Paul 1912- ... 107
Manning, Peter J. 1942- ... CANR-56
Earlier sketch in CA 125
Manning, Peter K(irby) 1940- ... CANR-34
Earlier sketches in CA 37-40R, CANR-14
Manning, Philip 1930(?)-1983 Obituary ... 110
Manning, Phyllis A(nne) Sergeant 1903- ... 5-8R
Manning, Preston 1942- ... 141
Manning, Reg(inald West) 1905-1986 Obituary ... 118
Manning, Robert (Joseph) 1919- ... 69-72
Manning, Roberta Thompson 1940- ... 130
Manning, Rosemary
See Cole, Margaret Alice
Manning, Rosemary (Joy) 1911-1988 ... CANR-70
Earlier sketches in CA 1-4R, CANR-1, 25
See also SATA 10
Manning, Stanley Arthur 1921- ... 110
Manning, Sylvia 1943- ... 81-84
Manning, Thomas Davys 1898-1972 ... CAP-1
Earlier sketch in CA 19-20
Manning-Sanders, Ruth 1895(?)-1988 ... CANR-41
Obituary ... 126
Earlier sketch in CA 73-76
See also MAICYA
See also SATA 15, 73
See also SATA-Obit 57
Mannion, John J(oseph) 1941- ... 73-76
Mannix, Edward 1928- ... 13-16R
Mannon, James M(onroe) 1942- ... 110
Mannon, Warwick
See Hopkins, (Hector) Kenneth
Mannoni, Octave 1899- ... 102
Mannyng, Robert fl. 1303-1338 ... DLB 146
Mano, D. Keith 1942- ... CANR-57
Earlier sketches in CA 25-28R, CANR-26
See also CAAS 6
See also CLC 2, 10
See also DLB 6
Mano, M(oshe) Morris 1927- ... 103
Manocchia, Benito 1934- ... 69-72
Manoff, Robert Karl 1944- ... 126
Manogaran, Chelvadurai 1935- ... 124
Manolson, Frank 1925- ... 17-20R
Manoni, Mary H(allahan) 1924- ... CANR-4
Earlier sketch in CA 49-52
Manoogian, Haig P. 1916(?)-1980 Obituary ... 97-100
Manor, Jason
See Hall, Oakley (Maxwell)
Manos, Charley 1923-1985 ... 29-32R
Obituary ... 116
Manosevitz, Martin 1938- ... 29-32R
Manrique (Ardila), Jaime 1949- ... 139
Manross, William Wilson 1905- ... 57-60
Manry, Robert 1918-1971 ... CAP-2
Obituary ... 29-32R
Earlier sketch in CA 21-22
Mansbach, Richard W(allace) 1943- ... 53-56
Mansberg, Ruth 1924- ... 130
Mansbridge, Francis 1943- ... 133
Mansbridge, John 1901(?)-1981 Obituary ... 105
Manschreck, Clyde Leonard 1917- ... CANR-5
Earlier sketch in CA 9-12R
Mansell, Darrel (Lee, Jr.) 1934- ... 57-60
Mansell, Gerard (Evelyn Herbert) 1921- ... 130
Manser, Martin H(ugh) 1952- ... CANR-42
Earlier sketch in CA 118
Mansergh, (Philip) Nicholas (Seton) 1910-1991 ... 105
Obituary ... 133
Mansfield, Bruce Edgar 1926- ... 103
Mansfield, Comins 1896-1984 Obituary ... 112
Mansfield, Edwin 1930-1997 ... CANR-18
Obituary ... 162
Earlier sketches in CA 9-12R, CANR-3
Mansfield, Elizabeth
See Schwartz, Paula
Mansfield, Harold H. 1912- ... 17-20R
Mansfield, Harvey C(laflin) 1905-1988 ... 1-4R
Obituary ... 125
Mansfield, Howard 1957- ... 146
Mansfield, Irving 1908(?)-1988 Obituary ... 126
Mansfield, John M(aurice) 1936- ... 29-32R
Mansfield, Katherine
See Beauchamp, Kathleen Mansfield
See also DAB
See also DLB 162
See also SSC 9, 23
See also TCLC 2, 8, 39
See also WLC
Mansfield, Libby
See Schwartz, Paula
Mansfield, Norman
See Gladden, E(dgar) Norman
Mansfield, Peter 1928-1996 ... 65-68
Obituary ... 151
Mansfield, Roger (Ernest) 1939- ... CANR-11
Earlier sketch in CA 25-28R
Manship, David 1927- ... 25-28R
Manski, Charles F. 1948- ... 138
Manso, Peter 1940- ... CANR-44
Earlier sketch in CA 29-32R
See also CLC 39
Manson, Beverlie 1945- ... 113
See also SATA 57
See also SATA-Brief 44
Manson, Richard 1939- ... 29-32R
Mansoor, Menahem 1911- ... CANR-15
Earlier sketch in CA 41-44R
Mansur, Ina 1910-1988 ... CANR-38
Earlier sketch in CA 116
Mantecon, Juan Jimenez
See Jimenez (Mantecon), Juan Ramon
Mantel, Hilary (Mary) 1952- ... CANR-54
Earlier sketch in CA 125
Mantel, Samuel J(oseph), Jr. 1921- ... 13-16R
Mantell, Leroy H. 1919- ... 37-40R
Mantell, Martin E(den) 1936- ... 45-48
Manternach, Janaan 1927- ... 116
Mantey, Julius Robert 1890- ... CAP-1
Earlier sketch in CA 11-12
Mantinband, Gerda (B.) 1917- ... SATA 74
Mantle, Jonathan 1954- ... 129
Mantle, Mickey (Charles) 1931-1995 ... 89-92
Obituary ... 149
Mantle, Winifred (Langford) ... CANR-6
Earlier sketch in CA 13-16R
Manton, Jo
See Gittings, Jo (Grenville) Manton
Manton, Kenneth G. 1947- ... 143
Manton, Peter
See Creasey, John
Manton, Sidnie Milana 1902-1979 ... 167
Mantovano
See Spagnola, Giovanni Battista
Mantyla, Martti 1955- ... 161
Manuel, E(spiridion) Arsenio 1909- ... 118
See also CAAS 9
Manuel, Frank Edward 1910- ... CANR-53
Earlier sketches in CA 9-12R, CANR-6, 29
Manuel, George 1921- ... 107
Manuel, Lynn 1948- ... SATA 99
Manuel, Niklaus c. 1484-1530 ... DLB 179
Manus, Mavis 1929- ... 116
Manus, Willard 1930- ... CANR-53
Earlier sketches in CA 108, CANR-28
Manushkin, Fran(ces) 1942- ... CANR-61
Earlier sketches in CA 49-52, CANR-1
See also SATA 7, 54, 93
Manvell, (Arnold) Roger 1909-1987 ... CANR-23
Obituary ... 124
Earlier sketches in CA 1-4R, CANR-6
Manville, W(illiam) H(enry) 1930- ... 93-96
Interview in ... 93-96
Manwell, Reginald D. 1897- ... 37-40R
Man Without a Spleen, A
See Chekhov, Anton (Pavlovich)
Man Xibo
See Porkert, Manfred (Bruno)
Many, Seth E(dward) 1939- ... 97-100
Manyan, Gladys 1911- ... 57-60
Manzalaoui, Mahmoud (Ali) 1924- ... CANR-12
Earlier sketch in CA 29-32R
Manzella, David (Bernard) 1924- ... 5-8R
Manzini, Gianna 1899-1974 Obituary ... 53-56
See also DLB 177
Manzoni, Pablo Michelangelo 1939- Brief entry ... 106
Mao, James C. T. 1925- ... 37-40R
Mao, Tse-tung 1893-1976 ... CANR-46
Obituary ... 69-72
Earlier sketch in CA 73-76
See also MTCW 1
Mapanje, (John Alfred Clement) Jack 1944(?)- ... 166
See also DLB 157
Mapel, William 1902-1984 Obituary ... 112
Mapes, Arthur Franklin 1913-1986 Obituary ... 118
Mapes, Mary A.
See Ellison, Virginia H(owell)
Maple, Eric William 1915- ... CANR-6
Earlier sketch in CA 53-56
Maple, Marilyn 1931- ... 148
See also SATA 80
Maple, Terry 1946- ... CANR-1
Earlier sketch in CA 49-52
Maples, Evelyn Palmer 1919- ... CANR-17
Earlier sketches in CA 5-8R, CANR-2
Mapp, Alf J(ohnson), Jr. 1925- ... CANR-1
Earlier sketch in CA 1-4R
Mapp, Edward C(harles) ... 33-36R
Maquet, Jacques Jerome Pierre 1919- ... CANR-29
Earlier sketches in CA 61-64, CANR-8
Mara, Barney
See Roth, Arthur J(oseph)
Mara, Jeanette
See Cebulash, Mel
Mara, Sally
See Queneau, Raymond
Mara, Thalia 1911- ... 9-12R
Marable, Manning 1950- ... 110
Maracle, Lee 1950- ... 149
See also NNAL
Marahiman, Ismail 1934- ... 136
Marai, Sandor 1900-1989 Obituary ... 128
Maraini, Dacia 1936- ... CANR-11
Earlier sketch in CA 5-8R
See also DLB 196
Maraini, Fosco 1912- Brief entry ... 116
Marais, Josef 1905-1978 Obituary ... 77-80
See also SATA-Obit 24
Maran, Rene 1887-1960 ... 125
Obituary ... 107
See also BW 1
Maran, Stephen P(aul) 1938- ... 57-60
Maranda, Elli Kongas 1932- Brief entry ... 107
Maranda, Pierre 1930- ... 37-40R
Maranell, Gary M. 1932- ... 37-40R
Marangell, Virginia J(ohnson) 1924- ... 93-96
Maraniss, David 1949- ... 147
Maraniss, James (Elliott) 1945- ... 139
Maranto, Gina (Lisa) 1955- ... 154
Marantz, Kenneth A. 1927- ... 142
Marantz, Sylvia S. 1929- ... 142
Maras, Karl
See Bulmer, (Henry) Kenneth
Marasmus, Seymour
See Rivoli, Mario
Marath, Laurie
See Roberts, Suzanne
Marath, Sparrow
See Roberts, Suzanne
Maravich, Pete(r Press) 1947(?)-1988 Obituary ... 124
Marazzi, Rich(ard Thomas) 1943- ... 102
Marbach, Ethel
See Pochocki, Ethel (Frances)
Marberry, M. M(arion) 1905-1968 ... CAP-2
Earlier sketch in CA 21-22
Marble, Allan Everett 1939- ... 147
Marble, Harriet Clement 1903-1975 ... 73-76
Marble, Samuel D(avey) 1915- ... 106
Marbrook, Del
See Marbrook, Djelloul
Marbrook, Djelloul 1934- ... 73-76
Marbut, F(rederick) B(rowning) 1905- ... 33-36R
Marc
See Boxer, (Charles) Mark (Edward)
Marc, David 1951- ... 138
Marcal, Annette B.
See Callaway, Bernice (Anne)
Marcantel, Pamela 1949- ... 162
Marcatante, John 1930- ... CANR-10
Earlier sketch in CA 25-28R
Marceau, Felicien
See Carette, Louis
Marceau, LeRoy 1907- ... CAP-1
Earlier sketch in CA 19-20
Marceau, Marcel 1923- ... 85-88
Marcel, Gabriel Honore 1889-1973 ... 102
Obituary ... 45-48
See also CLC 15
See also MTCW 1
Marcelin, Pierre 1908- ... 106
Marcelino
See Agnew, Edith J(osephine)
Marcell, David Wyburn 1937- ... 41-44R
Marcellino, Fred 1939- ... SATA 68
Marcello, Ronald E. 1939- ... 144
March, Andrew Lee 1932- ... 110
March, Anthony 1912-1973 Obituary ... 45-48
March, Bill
See March, William Joseph
March, Carl
See Fleischman, (Albert) Sid(ney)
March, Hilary
See Adcock, Almey St. John
March, James Gardner 1928- ... 13-16R
March, Jessica
See Africano, Lillian
March, Joseph Moncure 1899-1977 ... 149
Obituary ... 69-72
March, Josie
See Titchener, Louise
March, Robert H(erbert) 1934- ... 61-64
March, Valerie
See Beecher, Maureen Ursenbach
March, William
See Campbell, William Edward March
See also DLB 9, 86
March, William J. 1915- ... 13-16R
March, William Joseph 1941-1990 Obituary ... 132
Marchaj, C(zeslaw) A(ntony) 1918- ... CANR-5
Earlier sketch in CA 9-12R
Marchak, M(aureen) Patricia 1936- ... CANR-54
Earlier sketches in CA 111, CANR-29
Marchak, Maureen
See Marchak, M(aureen) Patricia
Marcham, Frederick George 1898-1992 ... 13-16R
Obituary ... 140
Marchand, C(harles) Roland 1933- Brief entry ... 110
Marchand, Leslie A(lexis) 1900- ... CANR-12
Earlier sketch in CA 65-68
See also DLB 103
Marchand, Philip (Edward) 1946- ... 130
Marchant, Anyda 1911- ... CANR-53
Earlier sketches in CA 13-16R, CANR-29
Marchant, Bessie 1862-1941 ... DLB 160
See also YABC 2
Marchant, Catherine
See Cookson, Catherine (McMullen)
Marchant, Herbert S(tanley) ... 106
Marchant, John H. 1951- ... 125
Marchant, Leslie R(onald) 1924- Brief entry ... 110
Marchant, Maurice P(eterson) 1927- ... 110
Marchant, R(ex) A(lan) 1933- ... 13-16R
Marchant, William 1923-1995 ... 69-72
Obituary ... 150
Marchbanks, Samuel
See Davies, (William) Robertson
Marchenko, Anatoly (Timofeevich)
1938-1986 ... 25-28R
Obituary ... 121
Marcher, Marion Walden 1890- ... 1-4R
See also SATA 10
Marchessault, Jovette 1938- ... 161
See also DLB 60
Marchetti, Albert 1947- ... 89-92
Marchetti, Victor Brief entry ... 108
Marchi, Giacomo
See Bassani, Giorgio
Marchiano, Linda Boreman 1949(?)- ... 129
Brief entry ... 114
Marchione, Margherita (Frances) 1922- ... CANR-15
Earlier sketch in CA 37-40R
Marciniak, Ed(ward) 1917- ... 29-32R
Marcinko, Richard 1940- ... 143
Marckwardt, Albert H(enry) 1903-1975 ... CANR-4
Obituary ... 61-64
Earlier sketch in CA 1-4R
Marco
See Mountbatten, Louis (Francis Albert Victor Nicholas)
Marco
See Charlier, Roger H(enri)

Marco, Anton N(icholas) 1943- 110
Marco, Barbara (Starkey) 1934- 9-12R
Marco, Guy A(nthony) 1927- 118
Marco, Lou
See Gottfried, Theodore Mark
Marcombe, Edith Marion
See Shiffert, Edith (Marcombe)
Marconi, Guglielmo 1874-1937 160
Marcos, Ferdinand E(dralin) 1917-1989 130
Marcosson, Isaac Frederick
1877-1961 Obituary 89-92
Marcot, Bruce G. 1953- 145
Marcotte, Gilles 1925- 166
Marcovich, Miroslav 1919- 115
Marcson, Simon 1910- 49-52
Marcum, John A(rthur) 1927- CANR-14
Earlier sketch in CA 25-28R
Marcus, Aaron 1943- 53-56
Marcus, Adrianne 1935- CANR-1
Earlier sketch in CA 45-48
Marcus, Alan I. 1949- 163
Marcus, Alfred A(llen) 1950- CANR-43
Earlier sketch in CA 118
Marcus, Anne M(ulkeen) 1927- 73-76
Marcus, Ben 1967- 165
Marcus, Betty Blum 1923-1984 Obituary 113
Marcus, David 1926- 134
Brief entry 110
Marcus, Donald (Edwin) 1946- 134
Marcus, Edward 1918- CANR-14
Earlier sketch in CA 21-24R
Marcus, Ellis 1918(?)-1990 Obituary 132
Marcus, Frank 1928-1996 CANR-2
Obituary 153
Earlier sketch in CA 45-48
See also DLB 13
Marcus, Fred H(arold) 1921- 104
Marcus, Genevieve Grafe 1932- 111
Marcus, George E. 1946- CANR-52
Earlier sketch in CA 124
Marcus, George H. 1939- 120
Marcus, Greil (Gerstley) 1945- 122
Marcus, Harold G. 1936- 37-40R
Marcus, Irwin M. 1919- 45-48
Marcus, Jacob Rader 1896-1995 CANR-28
Obituary 152
Earlier sketch in CA 21-24R
Marcus, Jana 1962- 165
Marcus, Jerry 1924- 97-100
Marcus, Joanna
See Andrews, Lucilla (Mathew)
Marcus, Joe 1933- 65-68
Marcus, K(aren) Melissa 1956- 153
Marcus, Larry
See Marcus, Lawrence B.
Marcus, Laurence R. 1947- 135
Marcus, Lawrence B. 1925- 133
Marcus, Leonard S. 1950- 134
Marcus, Lyn
See LaRouche, Lyndon H(ermyle), Jr.
Marcus, Maeva 1941- Brief entry 108
Marcus, Martin 1933- 25-28R
Marcus, Mildred Rendl 1928- CANR-2
Earlier sketch in CA 1-4R
Marcus, Millicent 1946- 146
Marcus, Mordecai 1925- CANR-38
Earlier sketches in CA 77-80, CANR-17
Marcus, Morton 1936- 105
Marcus, Paul 1953- 149
See also SATA 82
Marcus, Phillip L. 1941- 134
Brief entry 111
Marcus, Rebecca B(rian) 1907- CANR-1
Earlier sketch in CA 5-8R
See also SATA 9
Marcus, Robert D. 1936- Brief entry 110
Marcus, Ruth Barcan 1921- 41-44R
Marcus, Sheldon 1937- Brief entry 106
Marcus, Stanley 1905- 53-56
Marcus, Steven 1928- 41-44R
Marcus Aurelius
See Antoninus, Marcus Aurelius
Marcuse, Aida E. 1934- 155
See also SATA 89
Marcuse, F(rederick) L(awrence) 1916- 9-12R
Marcuse, Gary 1949- 154
Marcuse, Herbert 1898-1979 Obituary 89-92
Marcuse, Ludwig 1894-1971 Obituary 33-36R
Marden, Charles F(rederick) 1902- 37-40R
Marden, Orison Swett 1850-1924 DLB 137
Marden, William (Edward) 1947- 61-64
Marder, Arthur (Jacob) 1910-1980 105
Obituary 102
Marder, Daniel 1923- 21-24R
Marder, Herbert 1934- 69-72
Marder, Louis 1915- 5-8R
Marder, Norma 1934- 144
Mardock, Robert W(inston) 1921- 17-20R
Mardon, Austin Albert 1962- 164
Mardon, Ernest George 1928- 168
Mardon, Michael (Claude) 1919- 13-16R
Mardor, Munya Meir 1913- 17-20R
Mardus, Elaine Bassler 1914- 9-12R
Mare, W(illiam) Harold 1918- 105
Marechal, Leopoldo 1900-1970 153
See also HW
Marechera, Dambudzo 1952-1987 166
See also DLB 157
Marei, Sayed (Ahmed) 1913- 73-76
Marein, Shirley 1926- CANR-1
Earlier sketch in CA 45-48
Marek, George R(ichard) 1902-1987 CANR-1
Obituary 121
Earlier sketch in CA 49-52
Marek, Hannelore M(arie) C(harlotte) 1926- 13-16R
Marek, Kurt W(illi) 1915-1972 CAP-2
Obituary 33-36R
Earlier sketch in CA 17-18
Marek, Margot L. 1934(?)-1987 Obituary 123
See also SATA-Obit 54
Marek, Richard (William) 1933- 126
Marelli, Leonard R(ussell) 1933-1973 CAP-1
Earlier sketch in CA 13-16
Maremaa, Thomas 1945- 85-88
Marenbon, John (Alexander) 1955- 131
Marenco, Ethne (Elsie) K(aplan) 1925- 103
Marer, Paul 1936- 105
Mares, E. A. 1938- DLB 122
Mares, F(rancis) H(ugh) 1925- 25-28R
Mares, Michael A. 1945- 138
Maresca, Thomas Edward 1938- 85-88
Mareth, Glenville
See Gilbert, Willie
Marett, Robert Hugh Kirk 1907- 25-28R
Marevna
See Vorobeva, Maria
Margadant, Ted W(inston) 1941- 93-96
Margalith, Pinhas Z(alman) 1926- 110
Margaret, Karla
See Andersdatter, Karla M(argaret)
Margenau, Henry 1901-1997 CANR-14
Obituary 156
Earlier sketch in CA 37-40R
Marger, Mary Ann 1934- 93-96
Margerson, David
See Davies, David Margerison
Margetson, Stella 1912- CANR-40
Earlier sketches in CA 33-36R, CANR-13
Marghieri, Clotilde 1901(?)-1981 Obituary 105
Margold, Stella 81-84
Margolies, Alan 1933- 125
Margolies, Edward 1925- CANR-11
Earlier sketch in CA 65-68
Margolies, Joseph A(aron) 1889-1982 Obituary 108
Margolies, Luise 1945- 102
Margolies, Marjorie 1942- CANR-13
Earlier sketch in CA 65-68
Margolin, Edythe 69-72
Margolin, Judith B(elle) 1946- 117
Margolin, Malcolm 1940- 57-60
Margolin, Phillip (Michael) 1944- 145
Margolin, Victor 1941- 65-68
Margolis, Anne T(hrone) 1949- 128
Margolis, Diane Rothbard 1933- 97-100
Margolis, Ellen (Edelman) 1934- 1-4R
Margolis, Gary 1945- 73-76
Margolis, Howard 1932- 130
Margolis, Jack S 1934- 69-72
Margolis, Jeffrey A. 1948- 168
Margolis, John D(avid) 1941- 134
Brief entry 113
Margolis, Jonathan 1955- 139
Margolis, Joseph 1924- 37-40R
Margolis, Julius 1920- Brief entry 109
Margolis, Maxine L(uanna) 1942- 53-56
Margolis, Michael (Stephen) 1940- 93-96
Margolis, Nadia 1949- 140
Margolis, Richard J(ules) 1929-1991 CANR-25
Obituary 134
Earlier sketch in CA 29-32R
See also SATA 4, 86
See also SATA-Obit 67
Margolis, Seth J(acob) 166
Margolis, Susan Spector 1941- 81-84
Margolis, Susanna 1944- 107
Margolis, Vivienne 1922- SATA 46
Margolius, Sidney (Senier) 1911-1980 CANR-11
Obituary 93-96
Earlier sketch in CA 21-24R
Margon, Lester 1892- CAP-1
Earlier sketch in CA 13-16
Margoshes, Dave 1941- CANR-54
Earlier sketches in CA 111, CANR-29
Margroff, Robert E. 1930- 134
Margulies, Donald CLC 76
Margulies, Harry D. 1907(?)-1980 Obituary 97-100
Margulies, Herbert F(elix) 1928- 77-80
Margulies, Jimmy 1951- 133
Margulies, Leo 1900-1975 Obituary 61-64
Margulies, Newton 1932- 61-64
Margulis, Lynn 1938- CANR-4
Earlier sketch in CA 53-56
Margull, Hans J(ochen) 1925- 9-12R
Marhoefer, Barbara (McGeary) 1936- 61-64
Maria Del Rey, Sister 1908- 5-8R
Mariah, Paul 1937- CANR-4
Earlier sketch in CA 53-56
Mariana
See Foster, Marian Curtis
Mariani, John Francis 1945- CANR-41
Earlier sketch in CA 117
Mariani, Paul L(ouis) 1940- CANR-12
Earlier sketch in CA 29-32R
See also DLB 111
Mariano, Frank 1931(?)-1976 Obituary 69-72
Marias, Javier 1951- 167
Marias (Aguilera), Julian 1914- CANR-48
Earlier sketches in CA 9-12R, CANR-5, 22
Marie, Beverly Sainte
See Sainte-Marie, Beverly
Marie, Buffy Sainte
See Sainte-Marie, Beverly
Marie, Geraldine 1949- 108
See also SATA 61
Marie, Jeanne
See Wilson, Marie B(eatrice)
Marie-Andre du Sacre-Coeur, Sister 1899- 5-8R
Marie de France c. 12th cent. - PC 22
Marien, Michael 1938- CANR-16
Earlier sketches in CA 49-52, CANR-1
Marier, Captain Victor
See Griffith, D(avid Lewelyn) W(ark)
Marie Therese, Mother 1891- CAP-1
Earlier sketch in CA 13-14
Marie-Victorin, Frere 1885-1944 DLB 92
Maril, Nadja 1954- CANR-17
Earlier sketch in CA 85-88
Marill, Alvin H(erbert) 1934- CANR-12
Earlier sketch in CA 73-76
Marilla, E(smond) L(inworth) 1900- CAP-2
Earlier sketch in CA 23-24
Marilue
See Johnson, Marilue Carolyn
Marimow, William K. 1947- 93-96
Marin, A. C.
See Coppel, Alfred
Marin, Biagio 1891-1985 DLB 128
Marin, Cheech
See Marin, Richard Anthony
Marin, Diego 1914- 17-20R
Marin, Luis Munoz
See Munoz Marin, (Jose) Luis (Alberto)
Marin, Mindy 1960- 163
Marin, Richard Anthony 1946- 148
Brief entry 112
Marinacci, Barbara 1933- CANR-9
Earlier sketch in CA 21-24R
Marinaccio, Anthony 1912- 53-56
Marine, David 1880(?)-1976 Obituary 69-72
Marine, Gene 1926- 65-68
Marine, Nick
See Oursler, Will(iam Charles)
Marineau, Michele 1955- 166
Marinelli, Peter V(incent) 1933- 41-44R
Mariner, David
See Smith, David MacLeod
Mariner, Scott
See Pohl, Frederik
Marinetti, Filippo Tommaso 1876-1944 Brief entry 107
See also DLB 114
See also TCLC 10
Maring, Joel M(arvin) 1935- 49-52
Maring, Norman H(ill) 1914- 17-20R
Marini, Frank N(ick) 1935- 45-48
Marinkovic, Ranko 1913- DLB 147
Marino, Carolyn Fitch 1942- 110
Marino, Dorothy Bronson 1912- 73-76
See also SATA 14
Marino, John J. 1948- 106
Marino, Joseph D. 1912(?)-1983 Obituary 109
Marino, Susan
See Ellis, Julie
Marino, Trentino J(oseph) 1917- 65-68
Marinoni, Rosa Zagnoni 1888-1970 CAP-1
Earlier sketch in CA 13-14
Marion, Frances 1886-1973 Obituary 41-44R
See also DLB 44
Marion, Frieda 1912- CANR-8
Earlier sketch in CA 61-64
Marion, Henry
See del Rey, Lester
Marion, John Francis 1922- CANR-3
Earlier sketch in CA 5-8R
Marion, Robert W. 1952- 130
Mariotti, (Raffaello) Marcello 1938- 29-32R
Marique, Joseph M(arie-) F(elix) 1899- 33-36R
Maris, Roger (Eugene) 1934-1985 Obituary 118
Maris, Ron SATA 71
See also SATA-Brief 45
Marisa
See Nucera, Marisa Lonette
Mariscal, Richard N(orth) 1935- 53-56
Maritain, Jacques 1882-1973 85-88
Obituary 41-44R
Maritano, Nino 1919- 13-16R
Marius, Richard (Curry) 1933- CANR-56
Earlier sketches in CA 25-28R, CANR-29
See also DLBY 85
Marivaux, Pierre Carlet de Chamblain de
1688-1763 DC 7
Mariz, Linda 1948- 139
Marjolin, Robert (Ernest) 1911-1986 154
Obituary 119
Marjoram, J.
See Mottram, R(alph) H(ale)
Mark, Charles Christopher 1927-1998 CANR-1
Obituary 165
Earlier sketch in CA 1-4R
Mark, David 1922- 1-4R
Mark, Edwina
See Fadiman, Edwin, Jr.
Mark, Irving 1908-1987 CAP-1
Obituary 121
Earlier sketch in CA 19-20
Mark, Jan(et Marjorie) 1943- CANR-42
Earlier sketches in CA 93-96, CANR-17
See also CLR 11
See also MAICYA
See also SATA 22, 69
Mark, Joan 1937- 130
Mark, Jon
See Du Breuil, (Elizabeth) L(or)inda
Mark, Julius 1898-1977 81-84
Obituary 73-76
Mark, Matthew
See Babcock, Frederic
Mark, Max 1910- 73-76
Mark, Michael L(aurence) 1936- 93-96
Mark, Norman (Barry) 1939- 113
Mark, Pauline (Dahlin) 1913- CANR-7
Earlier sketch in CA 17-20R
See also SATA 14
Mark, Polly
See Mark, Pauline (Dahlin)
Mark, Rebecca 1955- 150
Mark, Robert 1930- 110
Mark, Shelley M(uin) 1922- CANR-1
Earlier sketch in CA 1-4R
Mark, Steven Joseph 1913- 17-20R
Mark, Ted
See Gottfried, Theodore Mark
Mark, Theonie Diakidis 1938- 69-72
Mark, Yudel 1897-1975 Obituary 61-64
Markandaya, Kamala
See Taylor, Kamala (Purnaiya)
See also CLC 8, 38
Markbreit, Jerry 1935- 49-52
Marke, Julius J(ay) 1913- 17-20R
Markel, Geraldine (Ponte) 1939- 108
Markel, Helen 1919(?)-1990 Obituary 130
Markel, Howard 1960- 154
Markel, Lester 1894-1977 37-40R
Obituary 73-76
Markels, Julian 1925- 25-28R
Marken, Jack W(alter) 1922- CANR-31
Earlier sketch in CA 49-52
Marker, Frederick (Joseph, Jr.) 1936- CANR-39
Earlier sketches in CA 41-44R, CANR-16
Marker, Gary 1948- 125
Marker, Lise-Lone (Christensen) 1934- CANR-39
Earlier sketches in CA 61-64, CANR-8
Marker, Rita 1940- 148
Marker, Sherry 1941- 143
See also SATA 76
Markert, Jennifer 1965- 150
See also SATA 83
Markert, Jenny
See Markert, Jennifer
Market Man
See Lake, Kenneth R(obert)
Markevitch, Igor 1912-1983 Obituary 109
Markey, Dorothy
See Page, Myra
Markey, Gene 1895-1980 CAP-1
Obituary 97-100
Earlier sketch in CA 11-12
Markey, Kevin 1965- 143
Markfield, Wallace 1926- 69-72
See also CAAS 3
See also CLC 8
See also DLB 2, 28
Markgraf, Carl 1928- CANR-57
Earlier sketches in CA 49-52, CANR-31
Markham, Beryl 1902-1986 Obituary 119
Markham, Clarence M(atthew), Jr. 1911- 69-72
Markham, Dewey 1904-1981 Obituary 108
Markham, E(dward) A(rchibald) 1939- 154
Markham, Edwin 1852-1940 160
See also DLB 54, 186
See also TCLC 47
Markham, Felix (Maurice Hippisley) 1908-1992
CAP-1
Obituary 139
Earlier sketch in CA 11-12
Markham, Gervase 1568(?)-1637 DLB 121
Markham, Ian Stephen 1962- 154
Markham, James M(orris IV) 1943-1989 93-96
Obituary 129
Markham, James W(alter) 1910-1972 CAP-2
Earlier sketch in CA 21-22
Markham, Jesse William 1916- 9-12R
Markham, Lynne 1947- SATA 102
Markham, Marion M. 1929- 129
See also SATA 60
Markham, Meeler 1914- CANR-12
Earlier sketch in CA 25-28R
Markham, Pigmeat
See Markham, Dewey
Markham, Reed 1957- 110
Markham, Robert
See Amis, Kingsley (William)
Marki, Ivan 1934- 97-100
Markides, Constantinos C. 1960- 162
Markides, Kyriacos (Costa) 1942- 81-84
Markie, Peter J(oseph) 1950- CANR-50
Earlier sketch in CA 123
Markins, W. S.
See Jenkins, Marie M(agdalen)
Markish, David 1938- 69-72
Markle, Fletcher 1921- DLB 68
See also DLBY 91
Markle, Joyce B(onners) 1942- 69-72
Markle, Sandra L(ee) 1946- CANR-58
Earlier sketch in CA 111
See also SATA 57, 92
See also SATA-Brief 41
Markley, Kenneth A(lan) 1933- 61-64
Markley, R(ayner) W(are) 1934- 111
Marklin, Megan
See Harrington, William
Markman, Howard (Joel) 1950- 69-72
Markman, Ronald A. 1936- 145
Markman, Sherwin J. 1929- 104
Markman, Sidney David 1911- CAP-2
Earlier sketch in CA 33-36
Markmann, Charles Lam 1913- 13-16R
Marko, Katherine D(olores) CANR-15
Earlier sketch in CA 29-32R
See also SATA 28
Markoe, Glenn E. 1951- 162
Markoe, Karen 1942- 81-84
Markoff, John 1949- 160
Markoosie
See Markoosie, Patsauq
See also CLR 23
See also DAM MULT
See also NNAL
Markoosie, Patsauq 1942- 101
See also Markoosie
Markov, Andrei Andreevich 1856-1922 161
Markov, Georgi 1929(?)-1978 Obituary 104

Markov, Vladimir 1920- ... 17-20R
Markova, Alicia 1910- ... CAP-2
Earlier sketch in CA 19-20
Markovic, Mihailo (M.) 1923- ... 131
Markovic, Miroslav
See Marcovich, Miroslav
Markovic, Vida E. 1916- ... 33-36R
Markovitz, Irving Leonard 1934- ... 33-36R
Markowa, Nina Alexandrovna 1925- ... 142
Markowitz, Norman Daniel 1943- ... 45-48
Marks, Alan 1957- ... 145
See also SATA 77
Marks, Alfred H(arding) 1920- ... CANR-47
Earlier sketches in CA 45-48, CANR-23
Marks, Barry A(lan) 1926- ... 17-20R
Marks, Bayly Ellen 1943- ... 115
Marks, Burton 1930- ... 107
See also SATA 47
See also SATA-Brief 43
Marks, Charles 1922- ... CANR-5
Earlier sketch in CA 53-56
Marks, Claude (Mordecai) 1915-1991 ... 61-64
Obituary ... 134
Marks, Copeland H. 1921- ... 167
Marks, David (Francis) 1945- ... 132
Marks, Edith Bobroff 1924- ... 17-20R
Marks, Edward S(tanford) 1936- ... 45-48
Marks, Elaine 1930- ... CANR-23
Earlier sketches in CA 17-20R, CANR-7
Marks, Eli S(amplin) 1911-1991 ... 85-88
Obituary ... 133
Marks, Frederick (William III) 1940- ... 97-100
Marks, Geoffrey 1906- ... 33-36R
Marks, Gil(bert S.) 1952- ... 168
Marks, Hannah K.
See Trivelpiece, Laurel
Marks, Henry S(eymour) 1933- ... 73-76
Marks, J
See Highwater, Jamake (Mamake)
Marks, J(ames) M(acdonald) 1921- ... 61-64
See also SATA 13
Marks, James R(obert) 1932- ... 17-20R
Marks, Jane (A. Steinberg) 1943- ... 113
Marks, John 1943- ... 110
Marks, John David 1909-1985 Obituary ... 117
Marks, John H(enry) 1923- ... 17-20R
Marks, Johnny
See Marks, John David
Marks, Kathy (L.) 1953- ... 153
Marks, Laurie J. 1957- ... 135
See also SATA 68
Marks, (Amelia) Lee 1948- ... 137
Marks, Margaret L. 1911(?)-1980 Obituary ... 101
See also SATA-Obit 23
Marks, Marjorie
See Bitker, Marjorie M(arks)
Marks, Mickey Klar ... CANR-6
Earlier sketch in CA 1-4R
See also SATA 12
Marks, Mitchell Lee 1955- ... 165
Marks, Norton E(lliott) 1932- ... 21-24R
Marks, Pat R.
See Feinman, Jeffrey
Marks, Paula Mitchell 1951- ... 135
Marks, Peter
See Smith, Robert Kimmel
Marks, Richard Lee 1923(?)- ... 140
Marks, Rita 1938- ... 106
See also SATA 47
Marks, Sally (Jean) 1931- ... 102
Marks, Sema 1942- ... 29-32R
Marks, Stan(ley) ... CANR-57
Earlier sketches in CA 29-32R, CANR-12, 31
See also SATA 14
Marks, Stuart A. 1939- ... 69-72
Marks, Thomas A. 1950- ... 164
Marks, Vic(tor James) 1955- ... 118
Marksberry, Mary Lee ... 13-16R
Marks-Highwater, J
See Highwater, Jamake (Mamake)
Markson, David M(errill) 1927- ... CANR-1
Earlier sketch in CA 49-52
See also CLC 67
Markstein, David L. 1920- ... 29-32R
Markstein, George 1929-1987 Obituary ... 121
Markun, Alan Fletcher 1925- ... 45-48
Markun, Patricia Maloney 1924- ... CANR-4
Earlier sketch in CA 5-8R
See also SATA 15
Markus, Julia 1939- ... 105
Interview in ... 105
Markus, R(obert) A(ustin) 1924- ... CANR-16
Earlier sketch in CA 65-68
Markusen, Ann Roell 1946- ... 142
Markusen, Eric 1946- ... 156
Marland, Christina
See Pemberton, Margaret
Marland, Edward Allen 1912- ... 17-20R
Marland, Michael 1934- ... 103
Marland, Sidney P(ercy, Jr.) 1914-1992 ... 53-56
Obituary ... 137
Marlatt, Daphne (Buckle) 1942- ... CANR-39
Earlier sketches in CA 25-28R, CANR-17
See also DLB 60
Marlborough
See Oaksey, John
Marlette
See Marlette, Doug(las Nigel)
Marlette, Doug(las Nigel) 1949- ... 145
Marley, Augusta Anne (?)-1973 Obituary ... 41-44R
Marley, Bob
See Marley, Robert Nesta
See also CLC 17
Marley, Robert Nesta 1945-1981 ... 107
Obituary ... 103
See also Marley, Bob
Marley, Stephen 1946- ... 155
Marlin, Alice Tepper 1944- ... 123
Marlin, Henry
See Giggal, Kenneth
Marlin, Hilda
See Van Stockum, Hilda
Marlin, Jeannie
See Woods, Jeannie Marlin
Marlin, Jeffrey 1940- ... 45-48
Marlin, John Tepper 1942- ... 124
Marling, Karal Ann 1943- ... 148
Marling, William 1951- ... 123
Marling, Yvonne Rodd
See Rodd-Marling, Yvonne
Marlitt, E. 1825-1887 ... DLB 129
Marlo, John A. 1934- ... 29-32R
Marlor, Clark Strang 1922- ... 37-40R
Marlot, Raymond
See Angremy, Jean-Pierre
Marlow, Cecilia Ann 1952- ... 121
Marlow, David 1943- ... 107
Marlow, Edwina
See Huff, T(om) E.
Marlow, Joyce
See Connor, Joyce Mary
Marlow, Louis
See Wilkinson, Louis (Umfreville)
Marlow, Max
See Nicole, Christopher (Robin)
Marlowe, Alan Stephen 1937- ... 21-24R
Marlowe, Amy Bell ... CANR-26
Earlier sketches in CAP-2, CA 19-20
See also SATA 1, 67
Marlowe, Christopher 1564-1593 ... CDBLB Before 1660
See also DA
See also DAB
See also DAC
See also DAM DRAM, MST
See also DC 1
See also DLB 62
See also WLC
Marlowe, Dan J(ames) 1914-1987 ... CANR-60
Earlier sketches in CA 1-4R, CANR-1
Marlowe, Derek 1938- ... CANR-59
Earlier sketches in CA 17-20R, CANR-11
Marlowe, Don ... 61-64
Marlowe, Hugh
See Patterson, Harry
Marlowe, Katherine
See Allen, Charlotte Vale
Marlowe, Katherine
See Allen, Charlotte Vale
Marlowe, Kenneth 1926- ... 13-16R
Marlowe, Stephen 1928- ... CANR-55
Earlier sketches in CA 13-16R, CANR-6
See also Queen, Ellery
Marlowe, Webb
See McComas, J(esse) Francis
Marlyn, John 1912- ... 9-12R
See also DLB 88
Marmion, Harry A. 1931- ... 25-28R
Marmion, Shakerley 1603-1639 ... DLB 58
Marmon, William F., Jr. 1942- ... 77-80
Marmor, J(udd) 1910- ... CANR-12
Earlier sketch in CA 25-28R
Marmor, T(heodore) R(ichard) 1939- ... CANR-52
Earlier sketches in CA 29-32R, CANR-27
Marmur, Dow 1935- ... CANR-47
Earlier sketch in CA 121
Marmur, Jacland 1901- ... 9-12R
Marmur, Mildred 1930- ... 5-8R
Marnell, William H. 1907- ... 21-24R
Marner, Der c. 1230-c. 1287 ... DLB 138
Marney, (Leonard) Carlyle 1916-1978 ... 57-60
Obituary ... 135
Marney, Dean 1952- ... CANR-52
Earlier sketches in CA 110, CANR-28
Marney, Dean 1952- ... SATA 90
Marney, John 1933- ... 69-72
Marnham, Patrick 1943- ... CANR-46
Earlier sketch in CA 102
Marokvia, Artur 1909- ... SATA 31
Marokvia, Mireille (Journet) 1918- ... 29-32R
See also SATA 5
Marol, Jean-Claude 1946- ... 130
Maron, Margaret ... CANR-66
Earlier sketches in CA 122, CANR-44, 50
Maroon, Fred J. 1924- ... 132
Marossi, Ruth
See Krefetz, Ruth
Marot, Marc
See Koch, Kurt E(mil)
Marple, Allen Clark 1901(?)-1968 Obituary ... 106
Marple, Hugo D(ixon) 1920- ... 53-56
Marples, William F(rank) 1907- ... CAP-1
Earlier sketch in CA 13-16
Marquand, John P(hillips) 1893-1960 ... 85-88
See also CLC 2, 10
See also DLB 9, 102
Marquand, Josephine
See Gladstone, Josephine
Marquand, Robert 1957- ... 136
Marquard, Leo(pold) 1897- ... 5-8R
Marquardt, Dorothy Ann 1921- ... 13-16R
Marquardt, Virginia C. Hagelstein 1945- ... 168
Marques, Rene 1919-1979 ... 97-100
Obituary ... 85-88
See also CLC 96
See also DAM MULT
See also DLB 113
See also HLC
See also HW
Marquess, Harlan E(arl) 1931- ... 49-52
Marquess, William Henry 1954- ... 126
Marquess of Anglesey
See Paget, George Charles Henry Victor
Marquez, Gabriel (Jose) Garcia
See Garcia Marquez, Gabriel (Jose)
Marquez, Robert 1942- ... 53-56
Marquis, Alice Goldfarb 1930- ... 156
Marquis, Arnold ... 57-60
Marquis, Dave 1951- ... 113
Marquis, Don(ald Robert Perry) 1878-1937 ... 166
Brief entry ... 104
See also DLB 11, 25
See also TCLC 7
Marquis, Donald G(eorge)
1908-1973 Obituary ... 45-48
Marquis, G(eorge) Welton 1916- ... 17-20R
Marquis, Max ... CANR-69
Earlier sketch in CA 136
Marqusee, Mike 1953- ... 148
Marr, David G(eorge) 1937- ... CANR-28
Earlier sketch in CA 33-36R
Marr, James Pratt 1898-1986 Obituary ... 121
Marr, John S(tuart) 1940- ... 81-84
See also SATA 48
Marranca, Bonnie 1947- ... CANR-9
Earlier sketch in CA 65-68
Marreco, Anne
See Wignall, Anne
Marric, J. J.
See Butler, William (Arthur) Vivian
and Creasey, John
Marrin, Albert 1936- ... CANR-58
Earlier sketches in CA 49-52, CANR-30
See also SATA 53, 90
See also SATA-Brief 43
Marriner, Brian 1937- ... 141
Marriner, Ernest (Cummings) 1891-1983 ... CANR-28
Obituary ... 109
Earlier sketch in CA 37-40R
Marriner Tomey, Ann 1943- ... 168
Marrington, Pauline 1921- ... CANR-10
Earlier sketch in CA 65-68
Marriott, Alice Lee 1910-1992 ... 57-60
Obituary ... 137
See also SATA 31
See also SATA-Obit 71
Marriott, (Joyce) Anne 1913- ... CANR-18
Earlier sketch in CA 102
See also DLB 68
Marriott, Pat(ricia) 1920- ... SATA 35
Marriott, William H. 1909(?)-1986 Obituary ... 118
Marriott-Watson, Nan 1899-1982 Obituary ... 107
Marris, Peter (Horsey) 1927- ... CANR-29
Earlier sketch in CA 111
Marris, Robin Lapthorn 1924- ... CANR-8
Earlier sketch in CA 5-8R
Marris, Ruth 1948- ... 106
Marrison, L(eslie) W(illiam) 1901- ... 29-32R
Marr-Johnson, Diana (Maugham) 1908- ... 13-16R
Marrocco, W(illiam) Thomas 1909- ... 9-12R
Marron, Kevin (Christopher Gerard) 1947- ... 127
Marrone, Robert 1941- ... 77-80
Marrone, Steven P(hillip) 1947- ... 130
Marroquin, Patricio
See Markun, Patricia Maloney
Marrow, Alfred J. 1905-1978 ... 81-84
Obituary ... 77-80
Marrow, Stanley B. 1931- ... CANR-26
Earlier sketches in CA 25-28R, CANR-10
Marrs, Edwin W(ilson), Jr. 1928- ... 25-28R
Marrs, Jim 1943- ... 139
Marrus, Michael R(obert) 1941- ... CANR-12
Earlier sketch in CA 33-36R
Marryat, Frederick 1792-1848 ... DLB 21, 163
Mars, Alastair 1915-1985 Obituary ... 116
Mars, Florence L. 1923- ... 101
Mars, Gerald 1933- ... 132
Mars, Jean Price
See Price-Mars, Jean
Mars, Kasey
See Martin, Kat
Mars, W. T.
See Mars, Witold Tadeusz J.
Mars, Witold Tadeusz J. 1912- ... 25-28R
See also SATA 3
Marsa, Linda J. 1948- ... 161
Marsack, Robyn (Louise) 1953- ... CANR-54
Earlier sketch in CA 127
Marsano, Ramon
See Dinges, John (Charles)
Marsden, Alexander
See Waddington, Patrick (Haynes)
Marsden, George (Mish) 1939- ... CANR-12
Earlier sketch in CA 73-76
Marsden, James
See Creasey, John
Marsden, John 1950- ... 135
See also AAYA 20
See also CLR 34
See also SAAS 22
See also SATA 66, 97
Marsden, Lorna R(uth) 1942- ... 85-88
Marsden, Malcolm Morse 1922- ... 5-8R
Marsden, Peter (Richard Valentine) 1940- ... CANR-47
Earlier sketches in CA 77-80, CANR-14
Marsden, Philip Kitson 1916-1984 Obituary ... 113
Marsden-Smedley, Hester 1901-1982 Obituary ... 107
Marsden-Smedley, Philip 1961- ... 135
Marsella, Anne (Francesca) 1964- ... 146
Marsh, Analyticus
See Morrison, Marsh
Marsh, Andrew
See O'Donovan, John
Marsh, Clifton E. 1946- ... 77-80
Marsh, Corinna (Reiman) 1891-1990 Obituary ... 132
Marsh, Dave 1950- ... CANR-41
Earlier sketches in CA 97-100, CANR-17
See also SATA 66
Marsh, David Charles 1917- ... 103
Marsh, Edwin
See Schorb, E(dwin) M(arsh)
Marsh, George Perkins 1801-1882 ... DLB 1, 64
Marsh, Henry
See Saklatvala, Beram
Marsh, Irving T. 1907-1982 ... 9-12R
Obituary ... 107
Marsh, J. E.
See Marshall, Evelyn
Marsh, James 1794-1842 ... DLB 1, 59
Marsh, James 1946- ... SATA 73
Marsh, Jan 1942- ... 145
Marsh, Jean
See Marshall, Evelyn
Marsh, Jeanne C(ay) 1948- ... 111
Marsh, Jeri 1940- ... 85-88
Marsh, Joan
See Marsh, John
Marsh, Joan F. 1923- ... 150
See also SATA 83
Marsh, John 1904- ... CAP-1
Earlier sketch in CA 9-10
Marsh, John 1904-1994 Obituary ... 144
Marsh, John 1907-1997 ... CANR-60
Earlier sketches in CAP-1, CA 13-16
Marsh, John L(eslie) 1927- ... CANR-1
Earlier sketch in CA 45-48
Marsh, Leonard (Charles) 1906- ... 37-40R
Marsh, Leonard (George) 1930- ... CANR-13
Earlier sketch in CA 73-76
Marsh, Margaret Sammartino 1945- ... 106
Marsh, Mary Val 1925- ... CANR-52
Earlier sketches in CA 69-72, CANR-11, 26
Marsh, Meredith 1946- ... 77-80
Marsh, (Edith) Ngaio 1899-1982 ... CANR-58
Earlier sketches in CA 9-12R, CANR-6
See also CLC 7, 53
See also DAM POP
See also DLB 77
See also MTCW 1
Marsh, Norman Stayner 1913- ... 117
Marsh, Patrick O(tis) 1928- ... 25-28R
Marsh, Paul
See Hopkins, (Hector) Kenneth
Marsh, Peter T(imothy) 1935- ... 33-36R
Marsh, Philip M(errill) 1893- ... 9-12R
Marsh, Rebecca
See Neubauer, William Arthur
Marsh, Robert (Harrison) 1926-1979 ... 17-20R
Obituary ... 134
Marsh, Robert C(harles) 1924- ... 13-16R
Marsh, Robert M(ortimer) 1931- ... CANR-2
Earlier sketch in CA 1-4R
Marsh, Ronald (James) 1914- ... 13-16R
Marsh, Rosalind
See Marsh, Rosalind J(udith)
Marsh, Rosalind J(udith) 1950- ... 132
Marsh, Spencer 1931- ... 61-64
Marsh, Susan (Sherry Raymond) 1914- ... 9-12R
Marsh, Susan H. 1926- ... 148
Marsh, U(lysses) Grant 1911- ... 57-60
Marsh, Valerie 1954- ... SATA 89
Marsh, Willard 1922-1970 ... CAP-2
Earlier sketch in CA 25-28
Marshak, Robert Eugene 1916-1992 ... 107
Obituary ... 140
Marshak, Samuil Yakovlevich
1887-1964 Obituary ... 111
Marshall, Alan 1902- ... 85-88
Marshall, Alfred 1884-1965 ... 5-8R
Marshall, Annie Jessie 1922- ... CAP-1
Earlier sketch in CA 9-10
Marshall, Anthony D(ryden) 1924- ... 29-32R
See also SATA 18
Marshall, (Charles) Arthur (Bertram)
1910-1989 Obituary ... 127
Marshall, Bill 1937- ... CANR-17
Earlier sketch in CA 65-68
Marshall, Bruce 1899-1987 ... 5-8R
Obituary ... 123
Marshall, Burke 1922- ... 13-16R
Marshall, Byron K. 1936- ... 33-36R
Marshall, (Sarah) Catherine (Wood) 1914-1983 ... CANR-57
Obituary ... 109
Earlier sketches in CA 17-20R, CANR-8
See also SATA 2
See also SATA-Obit 34
Marshall, Charles Burton 1908- ... 37-40R
Marshall, Charles F(rancis) 1915- ... 146
Marshall, Charles Wheeler 1906- ... 110
Marshall, D(onald) Bruce 1931- ... 65-68
Marshall, David F(ranklin) 1938- ... 25-28R
Marshall, Don
See Marshall, Donovan
Marshall, Donald G. 1943- ... 145
Marshall, Donald R. 1934- ... 93-96
Marshall, Donald S(tanley) 1919- ... 29-32R
Marshall, Donovan 1908- ... 117
Marshall, Dorothy 1900-1994 ... CAP-1
Obituary ... 144
Earlier sketch in CA 13-14
Marshall, Douglas
See McClintock, Marshall
Marshall, E(dmund) Jesse 1888- ... CAP-1
Earlier sketch in CA 11-12
Marshall, Edison 1894-1967 ... CAP-1
Obituary ... 29-32R
Earlier sketch in CA 9-10
See also DLB 102
Marshall, Edmund
See Hopkins, (Hector) Kenneth

Marshall, Edward
See Marshall, James (Edward)
Marshall, Edward 1932- DLB 16
Marshall, Emily
See Hall, Bennie Caroline (Humble)
Marshall, Emma 1828-1899 DLB 163
Marshall, Evelyn 1897- CANR-18
Earlier sketches in CA 5-8R, CANR-2
See also SATA 11
Marshall, F(reddie) Ray 1928- CANR-8
Earlier sketch in CA 17-20R
Marshall, Garry 1934- 111
See also AAYA 3
See also CLC 17
See also SATA 60
Marshall, George C(atlett), Jr. 1880-1959 Brief entry 115
Marshall, George N(ichols) 1920(?)-1993 CANR-46
Obituary 140
Earlier sketch in CA 77-80
Marshall, George O(ctavius), Jr. 1922- 17-20R
Marshall, H. H.
See Jahn, Joseph Michael
Marshall, Helen E(dith) 1899- 37-40R
Marshall, Helen Lowrie 1904-1975 103
Marshall, Herbert (Percival James) 1906- CANR-29
Earlier sketch in CA 25-28R
Marshall, Herbert Hedley 1909(?)-1982 Obituary 112
Marshall, Hermine H(alprin) 1935- CANR-14
Earlier sketch in CA 41-44R
Marshall, Howard D(rake) 1924-1972 CAP-2
Obituary 37-40R
Earlier sketch in CA 23-24
Marshall, Howard Wight 1944- 107
Marshall, Hubert (Ray) 1920- 21-24R
Marshall, I(an) Howard 1934- CANR-50
Earlier sketch in CA 122
Marshall, I. N. 1931- 134
Marshall, J(ohn) D(uncan) 1919- CANR-31
Earlier sketch in CA 73-76
Marshall, Jack 1937- 97-100
Marshall, James 1896-1986 41-44R
Obituary 120
Marshall, James (Edward) 1942-1992 CANR-38
Obituary 139
Earlier sketch in CA 41-44R
See also CLR 21
See also DLB 61
See also MAICYA
See also SATA 6, 51, 75
Marshall, James M(orse) 1924- 120
Marshall, James Vance
See Payne, Donald Gordon
Marshall, James Vance 1887-1964 CAP-1
Earlier sketch in CA 11-12
Marshall, Janet (Perry) 1938- 164
See also SATA 97
Marshall, Jeff
See Laycock, George (Edwin)
Marshall, Joanne
See Rundle, Anne
Marshall, John 1905(?)-1985(?) Obituary 116
Marshall, John 1922- CANR-43
Earlier sketches in CA 89-92, CANR-15
Marshall, John David 1928- CANR-41
Earlier sketches in CA 9-12R, CANR-3, 19
Marshall, John Douglas 1947- 145
Marshall, John Ross 1912- 109
Marshall, John S(edberry) 1898- CAP-1
Earlier sketch in CA 19-20
Marshall, Joyce 1913- 102
See also DLB 88
Marshall, Kathryn 1951- 57-60
See also AITN 1
Marshall, Kim
See Marshall, Michael (Kimbrough)
Marshall, Lenore Guinzburg 1899-1971 CAP-2
Obituary 33-36R
Earlier sketch in CA 25-28
Marshall, Lovat
See Duncan, W(illiam) Murdoch
Marshall, Margaret 1901(?)-1974 Obituary 104
Marshall, Margaret Wiley 1908- CAP-1
Earlier sketch in CA 9-10
Marshall, Martin V(ivan) 1922- 1-4R
Marshall, Max Lawrence 1922- 17-20R
Marshall, Max S(kidmore) 1897- CAP-1
Earlier sketch in CA 13-14
Marshall, Megan 1954- 124
Marshall, Mel(vin D.) 1911- CANR-12
Earlier sketch in CA 29-32R
Marshall, Michael (Kimbrough) 1948- CANR-3
Earlier sketch in CA 49-52
See also SATA 37
Marshall, Muriel 106
Marshall, Natalie J(unemann) 1929- 41-44R
Marshall, Norman 1901-1980 Obituary 108
Marshall, Owen 1941- 160
Marshall, Paul A. 1948- 165
Marshall, Paule 1929- CANR-25
Earlier sketch in CA 77-80
See also BLC 3
See also BW 2
See also CLC 27, 72
See also DAM MULT
See also DLB 157
See also MTCW 1
See also SSC 3
Marshall, Penny 1943- AAYA 10
Marshall, Percy
See Young, Percy M(arshall)
Marshall, Peter 1902-1949 Brief entry 112
Marshall, Peter (H.) 1946- 140
Marshall, Ray
See Marshall, F(reddie) Ray
Marshall, Raymond
See Raymond, Rene (Brabazon)
Marshall, Richard (D.) 1947- 125
Marshall, Robert G. 1919- 37-40R
Marshall, Robert L(ewis) 1939- 104
Marshall, Roderick 1903-1975 Obituary 53-56
Marshall, Ronald 1905- CAP-2
Earlier sketch in CA 33-36
Marshall, Rosalind Kay CANR-41
Earlier sketches in CA 53-56, CANR-4, 19
Marshall, S(amuel) L(yman) A(twood) 1900-1977 81-84
Obituary 73-76
See also SATA 21
Marshall, Shirley E(velyn) 1925- 21-24R
Marshall, Sybil Mary (Edwards) 1913- CANR-1
Earlier sketch in CA 1-4R
Marshall, T(homas) H(umphrey) 1893-1981 109
Obituary 105
Marshall, Thomas Archibald 1938- CANR-38
Earlier sketches in CA 49-52, CANR-1, 17
See also Marshall, Tom
Marshall, Thomas F(rederic) 1908- CAP-2
Earlier sketch in CA 23-24
Marshall, Thomas R. 1949- 115
Marshall, Tom
See Marshall, Thomas Archibald
See also DLB 60
Marshall, Tyler 1941- 136
Marshall, W. Gerald 1948- 145
Marshall, William
See Marshall, William Leonard
Marshall, William H(arvey) 1925-1968 CAP-1
Earlier sketch in CA 11-12
Marshall, William Leonard 1944- CANR-62
Brief entry 127
Earlier sketch in CA 133
Interview in 133
Marshall-Cornwall, James (Handyside) 1887-1985 107
Obituary 118
Marshallik
See Zangwill, Israel
Marshburn, Joseph Hancock 1890-1975 109
Obituary 106
Marshner, Connaught Coyne 1951- CANR-16
Earlier sketch in CA 93-96
Marsilius of Padua 1275(?)-1342(?) DLB 115
Mars-Jones, Adam 1954- CANR-27
Earlier sketch in CA 109
Marsland, Amy 1924- CANR-19
Earlier sketch in CA 103
Marsoli, Lisa Ann 1958- 120
See also SATA 101
See also SATA-Brief 53
Marson, Philip 1892- 9-12R
Marson, Una 1905-1965 DLB 157
Marsteller, Bill
See Marsteller, William A.
Marsteller, William A. 1914-1987 Obituary 123
Marsten, Richard
See Hunter, Evan
Marston, David W(eese) 1942- 125
Marston, Edward
See Miles, Keith
Marston, Elsa 1933- CANR-32
Earlier sketch in CA 113
Marston, Hope Irvin 1935- 101
See also SATA 31
Marston, John 1576-1634 DAM DRAM
See also DLB 58, 172
Marston, John E. 1911- 5-8R
Marston, Philip Bourke 1850-1887 DLB 35
Marston, Thomas Ewart 1904-1984 Obituary 112
Marszalek, John F(rancis, Jr.) 1939- CANR-45
Earlier sketches in CA 37-40R, CANR-14
Martchenko, Michael 1942- 160
See also SATA 50, 95
Marte, Fred
See Marte, Leonard Ferdinand
Marte, Leonard Ferdinand 1942- 156
Marteka, Vincent (James) 1936- 13-16R
Martel, Jane G. 1926- 57-60
Martel, Leon C. 1933- 125
Martel, Suzanne 1924- 160
See also SATA 99
Martel, Yann 1963- 146
Martell, James
See Bingley, David Ernest
Martell, Paul 1921(?)-1985 Obituary 116
Martellaro, Joseph A. 1924- 17-20R
Martelli, Leonard J. 1938(?)-1988 Obituary 125
Marten, Jacqueline (Lee) 1923- 141
Marten, Michael 1947- 132
Martens, E. A.
See Martens, Elmer A(rthur)
Martens, Elmer A(rthur) 1930- CANR-54
Earlier sketch in CA 127
Martens, Kurt 1870-1945 DLB 66
Martens, Lorna 1946- 157
Martens, Margaret Hosmer 1942- 151
Marter, Joan M. 1946- CANR-52
Earlier sketch in CA 124
Marth, Del 1925- 61-64
Martha, Henry
See Harris, Mark
Marti, Fritz 1894- 107
Marti, Jose 1853-1895 DAM MULT
See also HLC
Martial c. 40-c. 104 PC 10
Martianoff, Nicholas 1893-1984 Obituary 112
Martien, Jerry 1939- 154
Martignoni, Margaret E. 1908(?)-1974 Obituary 104
See also SATA-Obit 27
Marti-Ibanez, Felix 1912(?)-1972 Obituary 33-36R
Martin, Albert
See Mehan, Joseph Albert and Nussbaum, Al(bert F.)
Martin, Albro 1921- 77-80
Martin, Alex 1953- 137
Martin, Alfred 1916- 117
Martin, Alfred Manuel 1928-1989 108
Obituary 130
Martin, Allie Beth 1914-1976 Obituary 65-68
Martin, Anamae 1919- 9-12R
Martin, Andre
See Jacoby, Henry
Martin, Andrew 1906-1985 137
Obituary 115
Martin, Andrew 1952- 137
Martin, Andy
See Martin, Andrew
Martin, Ann Bodenhamer 1927- CANR-11
Earlier sketch in CA 69-72
Martin, Ann M(atthews) 1955- CANR-32
Earlier sketch in CA 111
Interview in CANR-32
See also AAYA 6
See also CLR 32
See also JRDA
See also MAICYA
See also SATA 44, 70
See also SATA-Brief 41
Martin, April
See Sherrill, Dorothy
Martin, Arlan Stone 1932- 69-72
Martin, Augustine 1935- 93-96
Martin, Barclay (Cluck) 1923- 73-76
Martin, Ben(jamin S.) 1921- 1-4R
Martin, Benjamin F(ranklin, Jr.) 1947- 89-92
Martin, Bernard (Davis) 1897- CAP-1
Earlier sketch in CA 9-10
Martin, Bernard 1905- CAP-1
Earlier sketch in CA 11-12
Martin, Bernard 1928- CANR-4
Earlier sketch in CA 53-56
Martin, Betty
See Martin, Elizabeth DuVernet
Martin, Bill
See Martin, William Ivan
Martin, Bill, Jr.
See Martin, William Ivan
See also SATA 67
See also SATA-Brief 40
Martin, Billy
See Martin, Alfred Manuel
Martin, Boyd A(rcher) 1911- 37-40R
Martin, Brian P(hilip) 1947- CANR-38
Earlier sketch in CA 116
Martin, Bruce
See Paine, Lauran (Bosworth)
Martin, Bruce 1922- 168
Martin, C(arol) Dianne 1943- 113
Martin, C(harles) Leslie 1897- 5-8R
Martin, C. Lewis 1915- 25-28R
Martin, Calvin (L.) 1948- Brief entry 113
Martin, Carol A. 1941- 149
Martin, Carter W(illiams) 1933- 25-28R
Martin, Charles 1906- 1-4R
Martin, Charles 1942- DLB 120
Martin, Charles B(asil) 1930- 93-96
Martin, Charles Burton 1924- 25-28R
Martin, Charles E.
See Mastrangelo, Charles E.
See also SATA 69, 70
Martin, Charles-Noel 1923- 29-32R
Martin, Chip
See Martin, Stoddard (Hammond), Jr.
Martin, Christopher
See Hoyt, Edwin P(almer), Jr.
Martin, Chryssee MacCasler Perry 1940- CANR-56
Earlier sketch in CA 126
Martin, Claire 1914- 164
See also DLB 60
Martin, Claire 1933- 143
See also SATA 76
Martin, Constance R. 1923- 158
Martin, Cort
See Sherman, Jory (Tecumseh)
Martin, Curtis 1915- 53-56
Martin, Dannie M. 1939- 145
Martin, David 1915- CANR-49
Earlier sketches in CA 103, CANR-24
Martin, David (Lozell) 1946- CANR-27
Earlier sketch in CA 89-92
Martin, David Alfred 1929- 107
Martin, David C(lark) 1943- 102
Martin, David Grant 1939- 65-68
Martin, David L(incoln) 1947- 119
Martin, David S. 1937- 142
Martin, David Stone 1913- SATA 39
Martin, Del
See Martin, Dorothy L.
Martin, Don 1931- 101
Martin, Don W. 1934- CANR-52
Earlier sketch in CA 126
Martin, Donald
See Honig, Donald
Martin, Donald Franklin 1944- 65-68
Martin, Donald L(loyd) 1939- 111
Martin, Dorothy 1921- CANR-6
Earlier sketch in CA 57-60
See also SATA 47
Martin, Dorothy L. 1921- 138
Martin, Douglas (Ivor) 1939- 133
Martin, Dwight 1921-1978 Obituary 77-80
Martin, E(rnest) W(alter) 1914- CANR-20
Earlier sketches in CA 9-12R, CANR-5
Martin, Earl S(auder) 1944- 102
Martin, Edward A(lexander) 1927- 120
Martin, Elizabeth A(nn) 1945- 132
Martin, Elizabeth DuVernet 1910- 103
Martin, Ellis
See Ryan, Marah Ellis
Martin, Emily 1944- CANR-27
Earlier sketch in CA 49-52
Martin, Esmond Bradley 1941- CANR-16
Earlier sketch in CA 93-96
Martin, Eugene CANR-26
Earlier sketches in CAP-2, CA 19-20
See also SATA 1
Martin, Eva M. 1939- 126
See also SATA 65
Martin, F(rancis) David 1920- 33-36R
Martin, F(rancis) X(avier) 1922- CANR-30
Earlier sketches in CA 21-24R, CANR-13
Martin, Fenton S(trickland) 1943- 157
Martin, Frances M(cEntee) 1906- 61-64
See also SATA 36
Martin, Francesca 1947- 168
See also SATA 101
Martin, Francis
See Reid, Charles (Stuart)
Martin, Frederick M(orris) 1923-1985 Obituary 115
Martin, Fredric
See Christopher, Matt(hew Frederick)
Martin, G(eoffrey) H(oward) 1928- 5-8R
Martin, Gary M. 1936- 89-92
Martin, Ged
See Martin, Gerald Warren
Martin, Geoffrey John 1934- CANR-14
Earlier sketch in CA 37-40R
Martin, George (Whitney) 1926- CANR-44
Earlier sketches in CA 9-12R, CANR-3, 21
Martin, George E. 1932- 143
Martin, George R(aymond) R(ichard) 1948- 81-84
Martin, Gerald Warren 1945- CANR-38
Earlier sketches in CA 45-48, CANR-1, 17
Martin, Graham Dunstan 1932- CANR-47
Earlier sketches in CA 106, CANR-23
Martin, Greg
See Miller, George Louquet
Martin, Harold Clark 1917- 9-12R
Martin, Harold Harber 1910-1994 CANR-7
Obituary 146
Earlier sketch in CA 61-64
Martin, Harold S(heaffer) 1930- 57-60
Martin, Herbert 1913- 29-32R
Martin, Herbert Woodward 1933- CANR-52
Earlier sketches in CA 73-76, CANR-27
See also BW 1
Martin, Hubert M., Jr. 1932- 103
Martin, Ian Kennedy
See Kennedy-Martin, Ian
Martin, Ira Jay III 1911- 53-56
Martin, J(ohn) P(ercival) 1880(?)-1966 81-84
See also SATA 15
Martin, Jack
See Etchison, Dennis (William)
Martin, Jacqueline Briggs 1945- 165
Martin, Jacqueline Briggs 1945- SATA 98
Martin, James 1921- 119
Martin, James (Thomas) 1933- 134
Brief entry 112
Martin, James Alfred, Jr. 1917- 73-76
Martin, James Gilbert 1926- 9-12R
Martin, James J(oseph) 1916- CANR-8
Earlier sketch in CA 5-8R
Martin, James Kirby 1943- CANR-53
Earlier sketch in CA 125
Martin, James L. 1948- 81-84
Martin, James Perry 1923- 5-8R
Martin, Jane Read 1957- 150
See also SATA 84
Martin, Jane Roland 1929- CANR-43
Earlier sketch in CA 119
Martin, Janet
See Garfinkel, Bernard Max
Martin, Jay
See Golding, Morton J(ay)
Martin, Jay (Herbert) 1935- CANR-21
Earlier sketch in CA 5-8R
See also DLB 111
Martin, Jeremy
See Levin, Marcia Obrasky
Martin, John 1893-1985 Obituary 116
Martin, John B.
See Martin, Bruce
Martin, John Bartlow 1915-1987 CANR-8
Obituary 121
Earlier sketch in CA 13-16R
Martin, John Hanbury 1892-1983 Obituary 109
Martin, John Henry 1915- 102
Martin, John Rupert 1916- 17-20R
Martin, John Sayre 1921- 103
Martin, John Stuart 1900-1977 9-12R
Obituary 69-72
Martin (Montes), Jose L(uis) 1921- CANR-12
Earlier sketch in CA 61-64
See also HW
Martin, Josef
See Bauer, Henry H.
Martin, Joseph George 1915-1981 108
Obituary 102
Martin, Joy 1922- 57-60
Martin, Judith (Sylvia) 1938- CANR-12
Earlier sketch in CA 97-100
Interview in CANR-12
Martin, Julie (Breyer) 1938- 133
Martin, June Hall
See McCash, June Hall
Martin, Kat 1947- 150
Martin, Kathryn 1908- 108
Martin, Ken
See Hubbard, L(afayette) Ron(ald)

Martin, Kenneth R(obert) 1938- CANR-38
Earlier sketches in CA 45-48, CANR-1, 17
Martin, Kevin
See Pelton, Robert W(ayne)
Martin, (Basil) Kingsley 1897-1969 ...... CANR-11
Obituary 25-28R
Earlier sketch in CA 5-8R
Martin, L(eslie) John 1921- CANR-46
Earlier sketches in CA 57-60, CANR-6, 22
Martin, Laura C(oogle) 1952- 117
Martin, Laurence W(oodward) 1928- CANR-7
Earlier sketch in CA 5-8R
Martin(-Berg), Laurey K(ramer) 1950- 143
Martin, Lawrence 1895- CAP-1
Earlier sketch in CA 9-10
Martin, Lee
See Wingate, (Martha) Anne (Guice)
Martin, Lee Nicholson 1916(?)-1987 Obituary .. 124
Martin, Les
See Schulman, L(ester) M(artin)
Martin, Linda 1961- .... SATA 82
Martin, Linda G. 1947- 128
Martin, Lucien
See Gabel, Joseph
Martin, Luis 1927- 131
See also HW
Martin, Luther H(oward), Jr. 1937- 124
Martin, Lynne 1923- 65-68
See also SATA 21
Martin, M(arilynn) Kay 1942- 65-68
Martin, Malachi CANR-70
Earlier sketch in CA 81-84
See also AITN 1
Martin, Marcia
See Levin, Marcia Obrasky
Martin, Margaret Joan 1928- 69-72
Martin, Marie-Louise 1912- 69-72
Martin, Mario, Jr.
See Monteleone, Thomas F(rancis)
Martin, Marjorie 1942- 53-56
Martin, Marta San
See San Martin, Marta
Martin, Mary 1913(?)-1990 113
Obituary 132
Brief entry 111
Martin, Mary Steichen
See Calderone, Mary S(teichen)
Martin, Maurice 1946- 115
Martin, Melanie
See Pellowski, Michael (Joseph)
Martin, Michael L. 1932- 17-20R
Martin, Michael William 1946- CANR-47
Earlier sketch in CA 121
Martin, Michelle 1957- 119
Martin, Mike W.
See Martin, Michael William
Martin, Milward Wyatt 1895-1974 .... CAP-1
Earlier sketch in CA 19-20
Martin, Morgan 1921- 17-20R
Martin, Murray S(impson) 1928- 112
Martin, Nancy
See Salmon, Annie Elizabeth
Martin, Noah S(ensenig) 1940- 69-72
Martin, Norma F(rances) 1936- 113
Martin, Oliver
See Smith, R(eginald) D(onald)
Martin, Ovid A. 1904-1979 Obituary 89-92
Martin, Patricia Miles 1899-1986 .... CANR-37
Obituary 119
Earlier sketches in CA 1-4R, CANR-2
See also MAICYA
See also SATA 1, 43
See also SATA-Obit 48
Martin, Paul
See Deale, Kenneth Edwin Lee
Martin, Paul Sidney 1899-1974 .... CANR-8
Earlier sketch in CA 5-8R
Martin, Pete
See Martin, William Thorton
Martin, Peter
See Chaundler, Christine
Martin, (Roy) Peter 1931- CANR-63
Brief entry 120
Earlier sketch in CA 125
Interview in 125
Martin, Peter W(illiam) 1939- 89-92
Martin, Philip (John Talbot) 1931- CANR-24
Earlier sketches in CA 61-64, CANR-9
Martin, Phyllis Cook 1908- 5-8R
Martin, Phyllis R(odgers) 130
Martin, Quinn 1922-1987 Obituary 123
Martin, R. Johnson
See Mehta, Rustam Jehangir
Martin, R(ichard) M(ilton) 1916- CANR-15
Earlier sketch in CA 41-44R
Martin, Ralph 1942- CANR-9
Earlier sketch in CA 57-60
Martin, Ralph C. 1924- 9-12R
Martin, Ralph G(uy) 1920- CANR-50
Earlier sketch in CA 5-8R
Martin, Ralph P(hilip) CANR-9
Earlier sketch in CA 65-68
Martin, Reginald 1956- 126
See also BW 2
Martin, Rene 1891-1977 .... SATA 42
See also SATA-Obit 20
Martin, Renee C(ohen) 1928- 49-52
Martin, Rhona 1922- 121
Brief entry 116
Martin, Richard
See Creasey, John
Martin, Richard 1946- 124
Martin, Robert (Lee) 1908-1976 .... 1-4R
Obituary 103
Martin, Robert A(llen) 1930- 110
Martin, Robert Bernard 1918- CANR-25
Earlier sketches in CA 1-4R, CANR-2
Martin, Robert K(essler) 1941- 102
Martin, Robert M. 1942- 143
Martin, Robert Sidney 1949- 122
Martin, Robert W.
See Pelton, Robert W(ayne)
Martin, Roderick 1940- CANR-12
Earlier sketch in CA 29-32R
Martin, Roger H(arry) 1943- 132
Martin, Ron 1941- 122
Martin, Ronald E(dward) 1933- 17-20R
Martin, Roscoe C(oleman) 1903-1972 ...... CAP-1
Obituary 33-36R
Earlier sketch in CA 19-20
Martin, Rupert (Claude) 1905- .... SATA 31
Martin, Russell 1952- 143
Martin, Ruth
See Rayner, Claire (Berenice)
Martin, Sam
See Moskowitz, Sam
Martin, Samuel Elmo 1924- Brief entry 105
Martin, Stefan 1936- .... SATA 32
Martin, Stella
See Heyer, Georgette
Martin, Stephen-Paul 1949- 145
Martin, Steve 1945- CANR-30
Earlier sketch in CA 97-100
See also CLC 30
See also MTCW 1
Martin, Stoddard (Hammond), Jr. 1948- 117
Martin, Susan B(oyles) 1959- 128
Martin, Susan Ehrlich 1940- 124
Martin, Sylvia (Pass) 1913-1981 .... 17-20R
Obituary 135
Martin, Taffy 1945- 125
Martin, Thom(as) Francis 1934- 5-8R
Martin, Thomas Lyle, Jr. 1921- 9-12R
Martin, Timothy (Peter) 1950- 138
Martin, Tom
See Paine, Lauran (Bosworth)
Martin, Tony 1942- CANR-52
Earlier sketches in CA 57-60, CANR-6, 26
See also BW 2
Martin, Valerie 1948- CANR-49
Earlier sketch in CA 85-88
See also BEST 90:2
See also CLC 89
Martin, Vance G(regory) 1949- 114
Martin, Vernon N(orthfleet) 1930- 45-48
Martin, Vicky
See Storey, Victoria Carolyn
Martin, Violet Florence 1862-1915 .... TCLC 51
Martin, Wallace 1933- 122
Martin, Walter Ralston 1928-1989 Obituary 129
Martin, Walter T(ilford) 1917- 9-12R
Martin, Warren Bryan 1925- CANR-20
Earlier sketch in CA 41-44R
Martin, Webber
See Silverberg, Robert
Martin, Wendy
See Martini, Teri
Martin, Wendy 1940- 37-40R
Martin, Wilfred B(enjamin) W(eldon) 1940- 116
Martin, William 1950- 140
Martin, William C. 1937- CANR-41
Earlier sketches in CA 77-80, CANR-14
Martin, William Ivan 1916- 130
Brief entry 117
See also Martin, Bill, Jr.
See also MAICYA
See also SATA 40
Martin, William Keble 1877-1969 Obituary 104
Martin, William Thorton 1901(?)-1980 Obituary . 102
Martinac, Paula 1954- 164
Martinco, John P. 1917(?)-1986 Obituary 118
Martindale, Charles (Anthony) 1949- 124
Martindale, Colin (Eugene) 1943- 61-64
Martindale, Don (Albert) 1915- CANR-6
Earlier sketch in CA 13-16R
Martindale, Patrick Victor
See White, Patrick (Victor Martindale)
Martin du Gard, Roger 1881-1958 Brief entry .. 118
See also DLB 65
See also TCLC 24
Martine
See Woolfolk, Joanna Martine
Martine, James J(ohn) 1937- 57-60
Martineau, Gilbert CANR-17
Earlier sketch in CA 29-32R
Martineau, Harriet 1802-1876 ..... DLB 21, 55, 159, 163, 166, 190
See also YABC 2
Martineau, James 1805-1900 Brief entry 122
Martineau, Robert Arnold Schurhoff 1913- 106
Martine-Barnes, Adrienne 1942- 110
Martinelli, Ricardo
See Brandon, Johnny
Martines, Julia
See O'Faolain, Julia
Martines, Lauro 1927- CANR-12
Earlier sketch in CA 25-28R
Martinet, Andre 1908- CAP-1
Earlier sketch in CA 11-12
Martinet, Jeanne 1958- 148
See also SATA 80
Martinetti, Ronald 1945- 57-60
Martinetz, V(ivian) L. 1927- 61-64
Martinez, Al 1929- 57-60
Martinez, Ed(ward) 1954- .... SATA 98
Martinez, Eliud 1935- .... DLB 122
Martinez, Elizabeth Coonrod 1954- 152
See also SATA 85
Martinez, Elizabeth Sutherland 1925- 121
Martinez, Enrique Gonzalez
See Gonzalez Martinez, Enrique
Martinez, Jacinto Benavente y
See Benavente (y Martinez), Jacinto
Martinez, Joseph G. R. 145
Martinez, Julio A(ntonio) 1931- CANR-18
Earlier sketch in CA 101
See also HW
Martinez, Max(imiano) 1943- 131
See also DLB 82
See also HW
Martinez, Nancy C. 145
Martinez, Orlando 1924- 138
Martinez, Oscar J(aquez) 1943- 120
Martinez, Rafael Arevalo
See Arevalo Martinez, Rafael
Martinez, Rafael V. 1923- 9-12R
Martinez, Raymond J(oseph) 1889- 61-64
Martinez, S(ally) A. 1938- 81-84
Martinez, Tomas Eloy CANR-62
Earlier sketch in CA 131
See also HW
Martinez, Victor .... SATA 95
Martinez, Victor 1954- 159
Martinez Moreno, Carlos 1917-1986 131
See also HW
Martinez Ruiz, Jose 1873-1967 93-96
See also Azorin
and Ruiz, Jose Martinez
See also HW
Martinez Sierra, Gregorio 1881-1947 Brief entry 115
See also TCLC 6
Martinez Sierra, Maria (de la O'LeJarraga) 1874-1974 Obituary 115
See also TCLC 6
Marting, Diane E. 1952- 138
Martini, Steve(n Paul) 1946- CANR-62
Earlier sketch in CA 140
Martini, Teri 1930- CANR-2
Earlier sketch in CA 5-8R
See also SATA 3
Martini, Therese
See Martini, Teri
Martini, Virgilio 1903- 37-40R
Martino, Bill 1933- 57-60
Martino, Joseph P(aul) 1931- 61-64
Martino, Rocco L(eonard) 1929- 13-16R
Martin-Perdue, Nancy J(ean) 1934- 164
Martins, Maria 1898(?)-1973 Obituary 41-44R
Martins, Maria Isabel Barreno de Faria 1939- .. 105
See also Barreno, Maria Isabel
Martins, Peter 1946- 113
Martins, Wilson 1921- 17-20R
Martinsen, Ella Barbara Lung 1901-1977 103
Martinsen, Martin
See Follett, Ken(neth Martin)
Martinson, David (Keith) 1946- CANR-1
Earlier sketch in CA 45-48
Martinson, Floyd M(ansfield) 1916- 93-96
Martinson, Harry (Edmund) 1904-1978 ... CANR-34
Earlier sketch in CA 77-80
See also CLC 14
Martinson, Ida M(arie) 1936- 157
Martinson, Robert M. 1927- 41-44R
Martinson, Ruth A(lice) 1915- CANR-17
Earlier sketch in CA 25-28R
Martinson, Tom L. 1941- 77-80
Martinson, William D. 1924-1979 .... 21-24R
Obituary 135
Martland, Thomas R(odolphe) 1926- 5-8R
Marton, Beryl M(itchell) 1922- CANR-11
Earlier sketch in CA 69-72
Marton, Endre 1910- 37-40R
Marton, George 1900- 29-32R
Marton, Jirina 1946- 160
See also SATA 95
Marton, Kati (Ilona) 1949- 140
Martone, John 1952- .... CAAS 30
Martone, Michael 1955- CANR-56
Brief entry 118
Earlier sketch in CA 124
Interview in 124
Martos, Borys 1879-1977 Obituary 73-76
Martos, Joseph (John) 1943- 105
Martson, Del
See Lupoff, Richard A(llen)
Marty, Martin E(mil) 1928- CANR-49
Earlier sketches in CA 5-8R, CANR-21
Interview in CANR-21
Marty, Myron A. 1932- CANR-11
Earlier sketch in CA 25-28R
Marty, Sid 1944- 108
Martyn, Edward 1859-1923 .... DLB 10
Martyn, Howe 1906-1989 .... 9-12R
Obituary 129
Martyn, J(ames) Louis 1925- 126
Brief entry 105
Martyn, Kenneth A(lfred) 1926- 21-24R
Martynov, Leonid (Nikolaevich) 1905- Brief entry 116
Martyr, Paula (Jane)
See Lawford, Paula Jane
See also SATA 57
Martz, John D(anhouse) 1934- CANR-1
Earlier sketch in CA 45-48
Martz, Lawrence J. 1933- 69-72
Martz, Linda 1939- 135
Martz, Louis L(ohr) 1913- CANR-5
Earlier sketch in CA 13-16R
Martz, Sandra (Haldeman) 1944- 149
Martz, William J. 1928- CANR-9
Earlier sketch in CA 21-24R
Maruki, Toshi 1912- .... CLR 19
Marut, Ret
See Traven, B.
Marut, Robert
See Traven, B.
Maruya, Saiichi 1925- 135
Maruyama, Masao 1914-1996 .... 13-16R
Obituary 153
Marvel, Thomas S. 1935- 145
Marvel, Tom 1901-1970 Obituary 104
Marvel, William 1949- 139
Marvell, Andrew 1621-1678 ..... CDBLB 1660-1789
See also DA
See also DAB
See also DAC
See also DAM MST, POET
See also DLB 131
See also PC 10
See also WLC
Marvick, Elizabeth Wirth 1925- CANR-41
Earlier sketch in CA 117
Marvin, Burton Wright 1913-1979 Obituary ... 85-88
Marvin, David Keith 1921- 13-16R
Marvin, Dorothy Betts 1894(?)-1975 Obituary . 57-60
Marvin, Garry 1952- 127
Marvin, Harold Myers 1893-1977 .... 5-8R
Obituary 73-76
Marvin, Isabel R(idout) 1924- 150
See also SATA 84
Marvin, John R(obert) 1923- 117
Marvin, John T. 1906- 17-20R
Marvin, Julie
See Ellis, Julie
Marvin, Philip (Roger) 1916- CANR-13
Earlier sketch in CA 37-40R
Marvin, Richard
See Ellis, Julie
Marvin, Susan
See Ellis, Julie
Marvin, W. R.
See Cameron, Lou
Marvin X
See El Muhajir
See also DLB 38
Marwell, Gerald 1937- 41-44R
Marwick, Arthur 1936- CANR-57
Earlier sketches in CA 29-32R, CANR-13, 30
Marwick, Helen
See Lillie, Helen
Marwick, Lawrence 1909-1981 Obituary 106
Marwick, M(axwell) G(ay) 1916- 37-40R
Marwil, Jonathan L(evy) 1940- CANR-35
Earlier sketch in CA 114
Marwood, William
See Morton, James (Severs)
Marx, Anne CANR-56
Earlier sketches in CA 29-32R, CANR-12, 30
Marx, Anthony W. 1959- 143
Marx, Arthur 1893-1964 Obituary 113
Marx, Arthur 1921- CANR-24
Earlier sketch in CA 81-84
Marx, Erica Elizabeth 1909-1967 .... CAP-1
Earlier sketch in CA 13-14
Marx, Gary T. 1938- CANR-32
Earlier sketches in CA 37-40R, CANR-14
Marx, Groucho
See Marx, Julius Henry
Marx, Harpo
See Marx, Arthur
Marx, Herbert L(ewis), Jr. 1922- CANR-6
Earlier sketch in CA 9-12R
Marx, Jenifer (Grant) 1940- 101
Marx, Jerry
See Bernstein, Jerry Marx
Marx, Julius Henry 1890-1977 81-84
Obituary 73-76
Marx, Karl (Heinrich) 1818-1883 .... DLB 129
Marx, Kenneth S(amuel) 1939- 69-72
Marx, Leo 1919- 126
Marx, Melvin H(erman) 1919- CANR-6
Earlier sketch in CA 5-8R
Marx, Paul 1920- 37-40R
Marx, Robert F(rank) 1936- CANR-6
Earlier sketch in CA 9-12R
See also SATA 24
Marx, Samuel 1902-1992 103
Obituary 137
Marx, Werner 1910- 81-84
Marx, Wesley 1934- CANR-12
Earlier sketch in CA 21-24R
Marxhausen, Joanne G. 1935- 37-40R
Mary Agnes Therese, Sister 1910- 1-4R
Mary Francis, Mother
See Aschmann, Alberta
Mary Kay
See Ash, Mary Kay (Wagner)
Mary Madeleine, Sister 1916-1974 .... CAP-1
Earlier sketch in CA 13-16
Marzan, Julio 1946- 131
Brief entry 113
See also HW
Marzani, Carl (Aldo) 1912- 61-64
See also SATA 12
Marzials, Theo 1850-1920 .... DLB 35
Marzolf, Marion Tuttle 1930- CANR-52
Brief entry 114
Earlier sketch in CA 124
Marzollo, Jean 1942- CANR-15
Earlier sketch in CA 81-84
See also SAAS 15
See also SATA 29, 77
Masalha, Nur 1957- 143
Masani, Shakuntala 112
Masani, Zareer 1947- 97-100
Masannat, George S. 1933- 25-28R
Masao, Maruyama 1914- 107
Masaoka Shiki
See Masaoka Tsunenori
See also TCLC 18
Masaoka Tsunenori 1867-1902 Brief entry 117
See also Masaoka Shiki

Masatsugu, Mitsuyuki 1924-...129
Mascall, Eric L(ionel) 1905-...5-8R
Masciangelo, Bill
See Masciangelo, William R., Jr.
Masciangelo, William R., Jr. 1944-...139
Mascott, Trina...81-84
Masefield, Geoffrey Bussell 1911-...5-8R
Masefield, John (Edward) 1878-1967...CANR-33
Obituary...25-28R
Earlier sketches in CAP-2, CA 19-20
See also CDBLB 1890-1914
See also CLC 11, 47
See also DAM POET
See also DLB 10, 19, 153, 160
See also MTCW 1
See also SATA 19
Masefield, (John) Richard (William) 1943-...119
Maser, Chris 1938-...132
Maser, Edward A(ndrew) 1923-1988...CANR-28
Obituary...126
Earlier sketch in CA 45-48
Maser, Jack D(avid) 1937-...57-60
Masey, Mary Lou(ise) 1932-1991...21-24R
Obituary...134
Masha
See Stern, Marie
Masheck, Joseph (Daniel) 1942-...105
Masia, Seth 1948-...CANR-28
Earlier sketch in CA 110
Masini, Eleonora Barbieri 1928-...130
Masinton, Charles G(erald) 1938-...77-80
Maskarinec, Gregory G. 1951-...150
Maskinen, Oskari
See Hamalainen, Pertti (Olavi)
Maslach, Christina 1946-...111
Maslenikov, Oleg A(lexander)
1907-1972 Obituary...111
Maslin, Alice 1914(?)-1981 Obituary...104
Maslin, Bonnie L(ynn) 1947-...107
Maslow, Abraham H. 1908-1970...CANR-4
Obituary...29-32R
Earlier sketch in CA 1-4R
See also MTCW 1
Maslow, Jonathan Evan 1948-...CANR-63
Earlier sketch in CA 126
Maslowski, Peter 1944-...97-100
Maslowski, Raymond M(arion) 1931-...93-96
Maslowski, Stanley 1937-...21-24R
Masnata, Albert 1900-...93-96
Maso, Carole 19(?)-...CLC 44
Mason, A. E. W. 1865-1948...DLB 70
Mason, Alpheus Thomas 1899-1989...CANR-32
Obituary...130
Earlier sketch in CA 1-4R
Mason, Anita 1942-...139
Mason, Betty (Oxford) 1930-...37-40R
Mason, Bobbie Ann 1940-...CANR-58
Earlier sketches in CA 53-56, CANR-11, 31
Interview in...CANR-31
See also AAYA 5
See also CLC 28, 43, 82
See also DLB 173
See also DLBY 87
See also MTCW 1
See also SSC 4
Mason, Bruce B(onner) 1923-...9-12R
Mason, Bruce Edward George 1921-1982...129
Obituary...110
Mason, Carola
See Zentner, Carola
Mason, Chuck
See Rowland, D(onald) S(ydney)
Mason, Clarence (Eugene), Jr. 1904-...57-60
Mason, Connie 1930-...164
Mason, David 1951-...147
Mason, David 1954-...166
Mason, David E(rnest) 1928-...21-24R
Mason, Douglas R(ankine) 1918-...CANR-17
Earlier sketches in CA 49-52, CANR-1
Mason, Edmund (John) 1911-...103
Mason, Edward S(agendorph) 1899-1992...73-76
Obituary...137
Mason, Edwin A. 1905-1979...CAP-2
Obituary...89-92
Earlier sketch in CA 25-28
See also SATA-Obit 32
Mason, Ellsworth (Goodwin) 1917-...126
Mason, Ernst
See Pohl, Frederik
Mason, Eudo C(olecestra) 1901-1969...CAP-1
Earlier sketch in CA 9-10
Mason, F(rancis) van Wyck 1901-1978...CANR-58
Obituary...81-84
Earlier sketches in CA 5-8R, CANR-8
See also SATA 3
See also SATA-Obit 26
Mason, Francis K(enneth) 1928-...103
Mason, Frank Earl 1893-1979 Obituary...89-92
Mason, Frank W.
See Mason, F(rancis) van Wyck
Mason, Gabriel Richard 1884-1979 Obituary...85-88
Mason, Gene (William) 1928-...89-92
Mason, George E(van) 1932-...CANR-30
Earlier sketches in CA 29-32R, CANR-12
Mason, George Frederick 1904-...73-76
See also SATA 14
Mason, Harry M. 1908-...139
Mason, Haydn T(revor) 1929-...CANR-3
Earlier sketch in CA 9-12R
Mason, Herbert Molloy, Jr. 1927-...CANR-6
Earlier sketch in CA 13-16R
Mason, Herbert Warren, Jr. 1932-...CANR-38
Earlier sketches in CA 85-88, CANR-16
Mason, James (Neville) 1909-1984...146
Mason, Jim 1940-...145
Mason, John Brown 1904-...49-52
Mason, Joseph B(igsbee) 1903-...125
Mason, Julian D(ewey) Jr. 1931-...37-40R
Mason, Lee W.
See Malzberg, Barry N(athaniel)
Mason, Lowell Blake 1893-1983 Obituary...110
Mason, Madeline 1913-...9-12R
Mason, Marilyn (J.) 1933-...159
Mason, Mark 1953-...163
Mason, Mark 1955-...138
Mason, Michael 1939-...120
Mason, Michael Henry 1900-1982 Obituary...108
Mason, Mike 1952-...126
Mason, Miriam E(vangeline) 1900-1973...CANR-15
Obituary...103
Earlier sketch in CA 1-4R
See also SATA 2
See also SATA-Obit 26
Mason, Nicholas (Charles Sheppard) 1938-...CANR-24
Earlier sketch in CA 104
Mason, Nick 1945-...CLC 35
Mason, Pamela 1918(?)-1996 Obituary...152
Brief entry...105
Mason, Paul T(aylor) 1937-...33-36R
Mason, Peter (Geoffrey) 1914-...CANR-35
Earlier sketch in CA 114
Mason, Philip 1906-...CANR-3
Earlier sketch in CA 9-12R
Mason, Philip (Parker) 1927-...CANR-38
Earlier sketch in CA 17-20R
Mason, R(ichard) A(nthony) 1932-...119
Mason, R(onald) A(lison) K(ells)
1905-1971 Obituary...89-92
Mason, Raymond 1926-...9-12R
Mason, Richard (Lakin) 1919-1997...9-12R
Obituary...162
Mason, Robert C(averly) 1942-...134
Brief entry...128
Interview in...134
Mason, Robert E(mmett) 1914-...CANR-17
Earlier sketch in CA 1-4R
Mason, Ronald (Charles) 1912-...CANR-24
Earlier sketch in CA 13-16R
Mason, Ronald M. 1949-...111
Mason, Ruth Fitch 1890-1974 Obituary...53-56
Mason, Sarah J. 1949-...167
Mason, Stephen F(inney) 1923-...141
Mason, Tally
See Derleth, August (William)
Mason, Ted
See Mason, Theodore C(harles)
Mason, Theodore C(harles) 1921-...109
Mason, Thomas A(lexander) 1944-...120
Mason, Tyler
See Mason, Madeline
Mason, Van Wyck
See Mason, F(rancis) van Wyck
Mason, Will Edwin 1912-...5-8R
Mason, William 1725-1797...DLB 142
Masotti, Louis H(enry) 1934-...41-44R
Mass, Jeffrey P(aul) 1940- Brief entry...111
Mass, William
See Gibson, William
Massa, Ann 1940-...29-32R
Massa, Richard W(ayne) 1932-...57-60
Massad, (Leslie) Stewart (Jr.) 1958-...144
Massanari, Jared (Dean) 1943-...65-68
Massaquoi, Hans J(urgen) 1926-...69-72
Massarik, Fred 1926-...CANR-35
Earlier sketch in CA 1-4R
Massel, Mark S. 1910-...CAP-1
Earlier sketch in CA 11-12
Masselink, Ben 1919-...17-20R
Masselman, George 1897-1971...9-12R
See also SATA 19
Massengale, John (Edward) Montague 1951-...125
Masserman, Jules H(oman) 1905-...69-72
Massey, Calvin R(andolph) 1949-...152
Massey, Ellen Gray 1921-...CANR-42
Earlier sketch in CA 118
Massey, Erika 1900-...61-64
Massey, Floyd, Jr. 1915-...65-68
Massey, Gerald 1828-1907...DLB 32
Massey, Gerald J. 1934-...89-92
Massey, Harrie Stewart Wilson
1908-1983 Obituary...111
Massey, Irving (Joseph) 1924-...77-80
Massey, James A(ldege) 1939-...121
Massey, James Earl 1930-...CANR-12
Earlier sketch in CA 29-32R
Massey, Joseph Earl 1897-...29-32R
Massey, Linton R. 1900-1974...DLB 187
Massey, Mary Elizabeth 1915-197(?)...CAP-2
Earlier sketch in CA 23-24
Massey, Raymond (Hart) 1896-1983...104
Obituary...110
Interview in...104
Massey, Reginald 1932-...21-24R
Massialas, Byron G. 1929-...CANR-8
Earlier sketch in CA 21-24R
Massie, Allan (Johnstone) 1938-...145
Massie, Diane Redfield...81-84
See also SATA 16
Massie, Joseph Logan 1921-...CANR-2
Earlier sketch in CA 1-4R
Massie, Robert K(inloch) 1929-...CANR-40
Earlier sketches in CA 77-80, CANR-14
Interview in...CANR-14
Massie, Suzanne 1931-...142
Massine, Leonide
See Myassin, Leonid Fedorovich
Massing, Hede 1899-1981 Obituary...108
Massinger, Philip 1583-1640...DLB 58
Massingham, Harold William 1932-...65-68
Massis, Henri 1886-1970 Obituary...29-32R
Massman, Patti 1945-...CANR-41
Earlier sketch in CA 117
Massman, Virgil Frank 1929-...37-40R
Masson, Andre (Aime Rene)
1896-1987 Obituary...124
Masson, David 1822-1907...DLB 144
Masson, David I(rvine) 1915-...CANR-59
Earlier sketch in CA 25-28R
Masson, Georgina
See Johnson, Marion Georgina Wikeley
Masson, J. Moussaieff
See Masson, Jeffrey Moussaieff
Masson, Jeffrey M.
See Masson, Jeffrey Moussaieff
Masson, Jeffrey Moussaieff 1941-...122
Masson, Loyes 1915-1969...CAP-1
Earlier sketch in CA 13-14
Masson, Paul R(obert) 1946-...142
Masson, Rosalind...89-92
Massy, William F(rancis) 1934-...41-44R
Mast, Gerald 1940-1988...CANR-12
Obituary...126
Earlier sketch in CA 69-72
Mast, Russell L. 1915-...13-16R
Masterman, John Cecil 1891-1977...CANR-64
Obituary...69-72
Earlier sketches in CA 9-12R, CANR-6
Masterman-Smith, Virginia 1937-...110
Master of Life, The
See Olisah, Sunday Okenwa
Masters, Anthony...CANR-45
Earlier sketch in CA 25-28R
Masters, Anthony 1948(?)-1985 Obituary...115
Masters, Brian 1939-...CANR-43
Earlier sketch in CA 118
Masters, Dexter (Wright) 1908-1989 Obituary...127
Masters, Edgar Lee 1868-1950...133
Brief entry...104
See also CDALB 1865-1917
See also DA
See also DAC
See also DAM MST, POET
See also DLB 54
See also MTCW 1
See also PC 1
See also TCLC 2, 25
See also WLCS
Masters, Elaine 1932-...57-60
Masters, G(eorge) Mallary 1936-...25-28R
Masters, Hardin (Wallace)
1899(?)-1979 Obituary...89-92
Masters, Hilary 1928-...CANR-47
Earlier sketches in CA 25-28R, CANR-13
See also CLC 48
Masters, John 1914-1983...110
Brief entry...108
Interview in...110
Masters, Kelly R. 1897-...1-4R
See also SATA 3
Masters, Mildred 1932-...110
See also SATA 42
Masters, Nicholas A. 1929-...13-16R
Masters, Olga 1919-1986...121
Obituary...135
Masters, Roger D(avis) 1933-...21-24R
Masters, Susan Rowan 1943-...156
Masters, William
See Cousins, Margaret
Masters, William H(owell) 1915-...CANR-34
Earlier sketch in CA 21-24R
See also AITN 1
Masters, Zeke
See Bensen, Donald R.
and Goulart, Ron(ald Joseph)
Masterson, B. L. H.
See Sternau, Cynthia
Masterson, Dan 1934-...81-84
Masterson, Daniel M. 1945-...140
Masterson, Dave 1951-...118
Masterson, J. B.
See Edmondson, G. C.
Masterson, James F(rancis) 1925-...69-72
Masterson, Patrick 1936-...73-76
Masterson, Peter 1934-...153
Masterson, Thomas R(obert) 1915-...25-28R
Masterson, Whit
See Miller, (H.) Bill(y)
and Wade, Robert (Allison)
Masterson, William Henry 1914-1983...123
Masterton, Elsie (Lipstein) 1914-1966...5-8R
Masterton, Graham 1946-...CANR-45
Earlier sketches in CA 105, CANR-22
Masthay, Carl (David) 1941-...142
Mastny, Vojtech 1936-...CANR-29
Earlier sketches in CA 33-36R, CANR-13
Maston, T(homas) B(uford) 1897-1988...CANR-18
Obituary...128
Earlier sketches in CA 5-8R, CANR-2
Mastrangelo, Charles E. 1910-...113
See also Martin, Charles E.
Mastro, Susan (Duff) 1945-...69-72
Mastronardi, Lucio 1930-1979...DLB 177
Mastrosimone, William 19(?)-...CLC 36
Masuccio Salernitano
See dei Guardati, Tommaso
Masud
See Choudhury, Masudul Alam
Masuda, Takeshi 1944-...CANR-50
Earlier sketch in CA 123
See also Aska, Warabe
Masuda, Yoneji 1909-...109
Masumoto, David Mas 1954-...150
Masur, Gerhard Strassman 1901-1975...CANR-4
Earlier sketch in CA 1-4R
Masur, Harold Q. 1909-...CANR-65
Earlier sketches in CA 77-80, CANR-13
Masur, Jenny 1948-...65-68
Mata, Daya 1914-...77-80
Matalin, Mary 1953(?)-...147
Matanzo, Jane Brady 1940-...103
Matarazzo, James M. 1941-...CANR-49
Earlier sketches in CA 37-40R, CANR-14
Matarazzo, Joseph D(ominic) 1925-...57-60
Matas, Carol 1949-...158
See also AAYA 22
See also CLR 52
See also SATA 93
Matas, David 1943-...156
Matatu, Michael
See Puri, Shamlal
Matcha, Jack 1919-...CANR-2
Earlier sketch in CA 1-4R
Matchett, William H(enry) 1923-...13-16R
Matchette, Katharine E. 1941-...53-56
See also SATA 38
Matczak, Sebastian A(lexander) 1914-...9-12R
Matejic, Mateja 1924-...CANR-56
Earlier sketches in CA 112, CANR-30
Matejka, Ladislav 1919-...73-76
Matejko, Alexander J. 1924-...CANR-49
Earlier sketches in CA 57-60, CANR-6, 22
Matek, Ord 1922-...89-92
Matenko, Percy 1901-...CANR-1
Earlier sketch in CA 45-48
Mateosian, S. Richard 1941-...111
Materer, Timothy (John) 1940-...89-92
Mates, Julian 1927-...CANR-31
Earlier sketch in CA 1-4R
Mates, Susan Onthank 1950-...148
Matesky, Ralph 1913-...5-8R
Matevski, Mateja 1929-...DLB 181
Math, Irwin 1940-...112
See also SATA 42
Mathabane, Mark 1960-...CANR-51
Earlier sketch in CA 125
See also AAYA 4
See also BW 2
See also DAM MULT
Mathai, M. O. 1909-1981 Obituary...108
Mathay, Francis 1925-...57-60
Mathe, Albert
See Camus, Albert
Matheny, Albert R(alston III) 1950-...152
Mather, Berkely
See Davies, John Evan Weston
Mather, Bertrand 1914-...CAP-1
Earlier sketch in CA 9-10
Mather, Bob
See Mather, Robert E(dward)
Mather, Cotton 1663-1728...CDALB 1640-1865
See also DLB 24, 30, 140
Mather, Eleanore Price 1910-...116
Mather, Increase 1639-1723...DLB 24
Mather, Jean 1946-...115
Mather, June 1924-...107
Mather, Kenneth 1911-1990 Obituary...131
Mather, Kirtley F(letcher) 1888-1978...CANR-35
Earlier sketch in CA 17-20R
See also SATA 65
Mather, Melissa
See Brown, Melissa Mather
Mather, Richard 1596-1669...DLB 24
Mather, Richard B(urroughs) 1913-...73-76
Mather, Robert E(dward) 1945-...115
Mathers, Michael 1945-...65-68
Mathers, Peter 1931-...130
Brief entry...116
Mathes, Charles (Elliott) 1949-...141
Mathes, J(ohn) C(harles) 1931-...49-52
Mathes, W(illiam) Michael 1936-...CANR-52
Earlier sketches in CA 61-64, CANR-8, 26
Matheson, Ann 1940-...133
Matheson, Don(ald S.) 1948-...126
Matheson, Joan (Transue) 1924-...97-100
Matheson, John Ross 1917-...CANR-23
Earlier sketch in CA 106
Matheson, Richard Burton 1926-...97-100
Interview in...97-100
See also CLC 37
See also DLB 8, 44
Matheson, Sylvia A.
See Schofield, Sylvia Anne
Matheson, William H(oward) 1929-...21-24R
Matheus, John F(rederick) 1887-1983...124
See also BW 1
See also DLB 51
Mathew, David 1902-1975...CAP-2
Earlier sketch in CA 25-28
Mathew, (Anthony) Gervase 1905-...9-12R
Mathew, Ray(mond Frank) 1929-...17-20R
Mathews, Aidan (Carl) 1956(?)-...152
Mathews, Anthony Stuart 1930-...93-96
Mathews, Arthur 1903(?)-1980 Obituary...102
Mathews, Cornelius 1817(?)-1889...DLB 3, 64
Mathews, Denise
See Mathews, Patricia J.
Mathews, Donald G. 1932-...17-20R
Mathews, Donald K(enneth) 1923-...57-60
Mathews, Eleanor Muth 1923-...13-16R
Mathews, Evelyn Craw 1906-...CAP-2
Earlier sketch in CA 19-20
Mathews, F(rancis) X. 1935-...25-28R
Mathews, H(arry) Lee 1939-...37-40R
Mathews, Harry 1930-...CANR-40
Earlier sketches in CA 21-24R, CANR-18
See also CAAS 6
See also CLC 6, 52
Mathews, J(oseph) Howard 1881-1970...9-12R
Obituary...103
Mathews, Jackson 1907(?)-1978 Obituary...104
Mathews, Jane DeHart 1936-...21-24R

Mathews, Janet 1914- 115
See also SATA 41
Mathews, (Thomas) Jay (II) 1945- 147
Mathews, John Joseph 1894-1979 .... CANR-45
Obituary 142
Earlier sketches in CAP-2, CA 19-20
See also CLC 84
See also DAM MULT
See also DLB 175
See also NNAL
Mathews, Judith
See Goldberger, Judith M.
See also SATA 80
Mathews, Louise
See Tooke, Louise Mathews
Mathews, Marcia Mayfield 9-12R
Mathews, Mitford M(cLeod)
1891-1985 Obituary 115
Mathews, Nieves 1917- 156
Mathews, Patricia J. 1929(?)-1983 Obituary 109
Mathews, Richard (Barrett) 1944- CANR-1
Earlier sketch in CA 45-48
Mathews, Russell Lloyd 1921- 109
Mathews, Thomas G(eorge) 1925- 49-52
Mathews, Virginia H(opper) 1925- 121
Mathews, Walter M(ichael) 1942- 110
Mathewson, Rufus Wellington, Jr.
1919(?)-1978 Obituary 81-84
Mathewson, William (Glen, Jr.) 1940- 106
Mathias, Frank Furlong 1925- CANR-12
Earlier sketch in CA 61-64
Mathias, Peter 1928- 17-20R
Mathias, Roland (Glyn) 1915- CANR-41
Earlier sketches in CA 97-100, CANR-19
See also CLC 45
See also DLB 27
Mathias, Sean (Gerard) 1956- 158
Mathiesen, Egon 1907-1976 Obituary 109
See also SATA-Obit 28
Mathiesen, Thomas J(ames) 1947- CANR-34
Earlier sketch in CA 113
Mathieson, John A(ndrew) 1949- 111
Mathieson, Theodore 1913- 9-12R
Mathieu, Beatrice 1904-1976 Obituary 65-68
Mathieu, Bertrand 1936- 73-76
Mathieu, Joe
See Mathieu, Joseph P.
Mathieu, Joseph P. 1949- CANR-68
Brief entry 117
Earlier sketch in CA 125
See also SATA 43, 94
See also SATA-Brief 36
Mathieu, Noel Jean 1916-1984 130
Obituary 113
Mathis, (Byron) Claude 1927- 45-48
Mathis, Cleopatra 1947- 104
Mathis, (Luster) Doyle 1936- 45-48
Mathis, Edward 1927- 119
Mathis, F(erdinand) John 1941- 37-40R
Mathis, James L. 1925- 105
Mathis, June 1892-1927 .... DLB 44
Mathis, (Gerald) Ray 1937-1981 .... CANR-31
Obituary 113
Earlier sketch in CA 37-40R
Mathis, Sharon Bell 1937- 41-44R
See also AAYA 12
See also BW 2
See also CLR 3
See also DLB 33
See also JRDA
See also MAICYA
See also SAAS 3
See also SATA 7, 58
Mathison, Melissa 1950- 165
Mathison, Richard Randolph 1919-1980 .. CANR-3
Earlier sketch in CA 1-4R
Mathison, Stuart L. 1942- 29-32R
Mathur, Dinesh C(handra) 1918- 41-44R
Mathur, Y. B. 1930- 49-52
Matias, Waldemar 1934- 5-8R
Matilal, Bimal Krishna 1935-1991 .... CANR-30
Obituary 134
Earlier sketches in CA 21-24R, CANR-13
Matilsky, Sarah
See Ruthchild, Rochelle Goldberg
Matisoff, James A(lan) 1937- 103
Matisoff, Susan 1940- 104
Matisse, Henri (Emile Benoit) 1869-1954 Brief
entry 122
Matkovic, Marijan 1915-1985 .... DLB 181
Matlaw, Myron 1924- 33-36R
Matlaw, Ralph E. 1927-1990 Obituary 131
Matlin, David 1944- 141
Matlin, Margaret White 1944- CANR-44
Earlier sketch in CA 119
Matlock, Jack F., Jr. 1929- 153
Matloff, Gregory 1945- .... SATA 73
Matloff, Maurice 1915-1993 .... CANR-6
Obituary 141
Earlier sketch in CA 13-16R
Matney, Bill
See Matney, William C., Jr.
Matney, William C., Jr. 1924- 69-72
Matos, Antun Gustav 1873-1914 .... DLB 147
Matos, Luis Pales
See Pales Matos, Luis
Matos Paoli, Francisco
See Matos Paoli, Francisco
See also HW
Matos Paoli, Francisco 1915- 131
See also Matos Paoli, Francisco
See also HW
Matossian, Mary Kilbourne 1930- 125
Matossian, Nouritza 1945- 124
Matranga, Frances Carfi 1922- 146
See also SATA 78
Matrat, Jean 1915- 61-64
Matray, James I(rving) 1948- 135
Matschat, Cecile H. 1895(?)-1976 Obituary .. 65-68
Matsen, Bradford (Conway) 1944- 144
Matsen, Herbert Stanley 1926- 57-60
Matson, Albert Thomas 1915(?)-1987 Obituary . 124
Matson, Clive 1941- 129
Matson, Emerson N(els) 1926- 45-48
See also SATA 12
Matson, Floyd W(illiam) 1921- 13-16R
Matson, Molly 1921- 139
Matson, Suzanne 1959- 144
Matson, Theodore E. 1906- 1-4R
Matson, Virginia (Mae) Freeberg 1914- 33-36R
Matson, Wallace I(rving) 1921- 13-16R
Matsuba, Moshe 1917- 37-40R
Matsuda, Mari J. 140
Matsui, Tadashi 1926- 41-44R
See also SATA 8
Matsumoto, Seicho 1909-1992 .... DLB 182
Matsumoto, Toru 1914(?)-1979 Obituary 89-92
Matsumura, Takao 1942- 132
Matsunaga, Alicia 1936- 29-32R
Matsunaga, Daigan Lee 1941- 41-44R
Matsunaga, Spark M(asayuki) 1916-1990 128
Obituary 131
Matsuno, Masako
See Kobayashi, Masako Matsuno
See also SATA 6
Matsuo Basho 1644-1694 .... DAM POET
See also PC 3
Matsushita, Konosuke 1894-1989 Obituary 128
Matsutani, Miyoko 1925- 69-72
Matsuura, Kumiko 1955- 140
Matt, Daniel C(hanan) 1950- 116
Matt, Paul R(obert) 1926- 33-36R
Mattam, Donald 1909- 45-48
Matte, (Encarnacion) L'Enc 1936- .... SATA 22
Matte, Robert G., Jr. 1948- CANR-16
Earlier sketch in CA 65-68
Matteo, P. B., Jr.
See Ringgold, Gene
Matteo, Sherri 1951- 141
Matter, Joseph Allen 1901- 29-32R
Mattera, John 1953- 131
Mattera, Philip 1953- 133
Mattersdorf, Leo 1903-1985 Obituary 117
Mattes, Merrill J(ohn) 1910-1996 .... 41-44R
Obituary 152
Matteson, Michael T(ownsend) 1943- CANR-16
Earlier sketch in CA 89-92
Matteson, Stefanie (Newton) 1946- 160
Mattessich, Richard V(ictor) 1922- CANR-9
Earlier sketch in CA 13-16R
Matthaei, Julie Ann 1951- 110
Matthau, Carol 1932- 139
Matthee, Dalene 1938- 141
Mattheson, Rodney
See Creasey, John
Matthew, Christopher C(harles) F(orrest) 1939- ....
CANR-69
Brief entry 116
Earlier sketch in CA 129
Matthew, Donald J(ames) A(lexander) 1930- ....
CANR-15
Earlier sketch in CA 5-8R
Matthew, Henry Colin Gray 1941- 53-56
Matthews, Alex 168
Matthews, Anne 1957- 141
Matthews, Anthony
See Barker, Dudley
Matthews, Bonnye L. 1943- 145
Matthews, Brad
See DeMille, Nelson (Richard)
Matthews, Brander 1852-1929 .... DLB 71, 78
See also DLBD 13
Matthews, C(onstance) M(ary) 1908- 25-28R
Matthews, Carola 1937- 25-28R
Matthews, Carole Smith 1943- 111
Matthews, Clayton (Hartley) 1918- CANR-25
Earlier sketches in CA 53-56, CANR-9
Matthews, Clyde 1917- 103
Matthews, (Robert) Curt(is, Jr.) 1934- 73-76
Matthews, Denis (James) 1919-1988 103
Obituary 127
Matthews, Desmond S. 1922- 21-24R
Matthews, Donald Rowe 1925- CANR-2
Earlier sketch in CA 1-4R
Matthews, Downs 1925- .... SATA 71
Matthews, Elizabeth W(oodfin) 1927- 161
Matthews, Ellen
See Bache, Ellyn
Matthews, Ellen 1950- 89-92
See also SATA 28
Matthews, Elmora Messer 1925- 21-24R
Matthews, Gareth B(lanc) 1929- 135
Matthews, Geoffrey M. 1920-1984 Obituary 115
Matthews, Glenna C. 1938- 126
Matthews, Greg 1949- 135
See also CLC 45
Matthews, Harry G(len) 1939- 73-76
Matthews, Herbert Lionel 1900-1977 .... CANR-2
Obituary 73-76
Earlier sketch in CA 1-4R
Matthews, Honor 1901- CAP-2
Earlier sketch in CA 23-24
Matthews, J(ohn) H(erbert) 1930- CANR-20
Earlier sketches in CA 13-16R, CANR-5
Matthews, Jack
See Matthews, John H(arold)
See also DLB 6
Matthews, Jack 1917- 9-12R
Matthews, Jack 1925- .... CAAS 15
Matthews, Jacklyn Meek
See Meek, Jacklyn O'Hanlon
Matthews, Jessie 1907-1981 Obituary 108
Matthews, Joan E(thel) 1914- 21-24R
Matthews, John (Pengwerne) 1927- CANR-41
Earlier sketch in CA 118
Matthews, John H(arold) 1925- CANR-15
Earlier sketch in CA 33-36R
See also Matthews, Jack
Matthews, Kathy 1949- CANR-27
Earlier sketch in CA 110
Matthews, Kevin
See Fox, G(ardner) F(rancis)
Matthews, L(eonard) Harrison 1901-1986 . CANR-4
Obituary 121
Earlier sketch in CA 53-56
Matthews, Liz
See Pellowski, Michael (Joseph)
Matthews, Lloyd J. 1929- 141
Matthews, Morgan
See Pellowski, Michael (Joseph)
Matthews, Patricia (Anne) 1927- CANR-25
Earlier sketches in CA 29-32R, CANR-9
Interview in CANR-25
See also DAM POP
See also MTCW 1
See also SATA 28
Matthews, Ralph 1904(?)-1978 85-88
Obituary 81-84
Matthews, Richard K(evin) 1952- 117
Matthews, Robert J(ames) 1926- 65-68
Matthews, Roy A(nthony) 1927- CANR-13
Earlier sketch in CA 33-36R
Matthews, Roy T(homas) 1932- 109
Matthews, Rupert O(liver) 1961- 118
Matthews, Stanley 1915- 134
Brief entry 115
Matthews, Stanley G(oodwin) 1924- 21-24R
Matthews, T(homas) S(tanley) 1901-1991 ....
CANR-18
Obituary 133
Earlier sketches in CAP-1, CA 11-12
Matthews, Tom
See Klewin, W(illiam) Thomas
Matthews, Victor Monroe 1921- 93-96
Matthews, Victoria (Ann) 1941- 163
Matthews, Walter Robert 1881-1973 .... CAP-1
Earlier sketch in CA 13-14
Matthews, William (Richard) 1905-1975 61-64
Obituary 57-60
Matthews, William (Procter, III) 1942-1997 ....
CANR-57
Obituary 162
Earlier sketches in CA 29-32R, CANR-12
See also CAAS 18
See also CLC 40
See also DLB 5
Matthews, William Henry III 1919- 9-12R
See also SATA 45
See also SATA-Brief 28
Matthews-Simonton, Stephanie 1947- 132
Matthias, Catherine 1945- 110
See also SATA-Brief 41
Matthias, John (Edward) 1941- CANR-56
Earlier sketch in CA 33-36R
See also CLC 9
Matthiessen, F. O. 1902-1950 .... DLB 63
Matthiessen, Peter 1927- CANR-50
Earlier sketches in CA 9-12R, CANR-21
See also AAYA 6
See also BEST 90:4
See also CLC 5, 7, 11, 32, 64
See also DAM NOV
See also DLB 6, 173
See also MTCW 1
See also SATA 27
Matthis, Raimund Eugen 1928- 37-40R
Mattick, Paul 1904-1981 Obituary 115
Mattil, Edward La Marr 1918- 127
Brief entry 106
Mattill, A(ndrew) J(acob), Jr. 1924- CANR-58
Earlier sketches in CA 37-40R, CANR-14, 31
Mattingley, Christobel (Rosemary) 1931- . CANR-47
Earlier sketches in CA 97-100, CANR-20
See also CLR 24
See also MAICYA
See also SAAS 18
See also SATA 37, 85
Mattingly, Garrett 1900-1962 Obituary 111
Mattingly, George E. 1950- 105
Mattingly, Paul H(avey) 1941- 129
Mattioli, Raffaele 1895-1973 Obituary 45-48
Mattis, George 1905- CAP-2
Earlier sketch in CA 29-32
Mattison, Alice 1942- 110
Mattison, Christopher 1949- 125
Mattison, Judith 1939- CANR-24
Earlier sketches in CA 61-64, CANR-8
Mattlin, Paula Plotnick 1934(?)-1981 Obituary .. 104
Mattson, George E(dward) 1937- 5-8R
Mattson, Kevin 1966- 162
Mattson, Lloyd 1923- CANR-17
Earlier sketch in CA 93-96
Mattusch, Carol C. 1947- 163
Matulay, Laszlo 1912- .... SATA 43
Matulka, Jan 1890-1972 .... SATA-Brief 28
Matura, Mustapha 1939- CANR-63
Earlier sketches in CA 65-68, CANR-12
Matura, Thaddee 1922- 132
Maturin, Charles Robert 1780(?)-1824 .... DLB 178
Matus, Greta 1938- 93-96
See also SATA 12
Matus, Irvin Leigh 1941- 129
Matusow, Allen J(oseph) 1937- 142
Matusow, Barbara 1938- 143
Matuszak, John (Daniel) 1950-1989 Obituary .. 130
Matute (Ausejo), Ana Maria 1925- 89-92
See also CLC 11
See also MTCW 1
Mau, Ernest E(ugene) 1945- 112
Mau, James A. 1935- 25-28R
Mauceri, Philip 1961- 163
Mauch, Christof 1960- 163
Mauchline, Mary 1915- 53-56
Maud, John P. R.
See Redcliffe-Maud, John Primatt
Maud, John Primatt Redcliffe
See Redcliffe-Maud, John Primatt
Maud, Ralph (Noel) 1928- 129
Maude, George 1931- CANR-33
Earlier sketch in CA 113
Maude, H(enry) E(vans) 1906- 103
Maududi, Maulana Abdul Ala
1903(?)-1979 Obituary 89-92
Maue, Kenneth 1947- 97-100
Mauermann, Mary Anne 1927- 33-36R
Maugham, Diana
See Marr-Johnson, Diana (Maugham)
Maugham, Robert Cecil Romer 1916-1981 ....
CANR-40
Obituary 103
Earlier sketch in CA 9-12R
Maugham, Robin
See Maugham, Robert Cecil Romer
Maugham, W. S.
See Maugham, W(illiam) Somerset
Maugham, W(illiam) Somerset 1874-1965 ....
CANR-40
Obituary 25-28R
Earlier sketch in CA 5-8R
See also CDBLB 1914-1945
See also CLC 1, 11, 15, 67, 93
See also DA
See also DAB
See also DAC
See also DAM DRAM, MST, NOV
See also DLB 10, 36, 77, 100, 162, 195
See also MTCW 1
See also SATA 54
See also SSC 8
See also WLC
Maugham, William Somerset
See Maugham, W(illiam) Somerset
Maughan, A(nne) M(argery) 53-56
Maughan, Jackie Johnson 1948- 153
Mauldin, Bill
See Mauldin, William Henry
Mauldin, William Henry 1921- Brief entry 111
Maule, Christopher J(ohn) 1934- 37-40R
Maule, Hamilton Bee 1915- CANR-3
Earlier sketch in CA 1-4R
Maule, Harry E(dward) 1886-1971 Obituary 104
Maule, Henry (Ramsay) 1915-1981 133
Maule, Tex
See Maule, Hamilton Bee
Maultsby, Maxie C(larence), Jr. 1932- 81-84
Maund, Alfred (Thomas, Jr.) 1923- 1-4R
Maunder, Elwood R(ondeau) 1917- 85-88
Maunder, W(illiam) J(ohn) 1932- 33-36R
Maung, Mya 1933- 37-40R
Maupassant, (Henri Rene Albert) Guy de
1850-1893 .... DA
See also DAB
See also DAC
See also DAM MST
See also DLB 123
See also SSC 1
See also WLC
Maupin, Armistead 1944- CANR-58
Brief entry 125
Earlier sketch in CA 130
Interview in 130
See also CLC 95
See also DAM POP
Maura, Sister
See Eichner, Maura
Maureen, Sister Mary 1924- 21-24R
Maurensig, Paolo 1943- 168
Maurer, Armand A(ugustine) 1915- 21-24R
Maurer, Charles Benes 1933- 33-36R
Maurer, Daphne (Jean) 1946- 128
Maurer, David J(oseph) 1935- 102
Maurer, David W(arren) 1906-1981 .... 17-20R
Obituary 104
Maurer, Diane Philippoff
See Maurer-Mathison, Diane V(ogel)
Maurer, Diane Vogel
See Maurer-Mathison, Diane V(ogel)
Maurer, Joan Howard 1927- 119
Maurer, John G. 1937- 37-40R
Maurer, Otto
See Mason, Eudo C(olecestra)
Maurer, Rose
See Somerville, Rose M(aurer)
Maurer, Warren R(ichard) 1929- 146
Maurer-Mathison, Diane V(ogel) 1944- 155
See also SATA 89
Maurhut, Richard
See Traven, B.
Mauriac, Claude 1914-1996 89-92
Obituary 152
See also CLC 9
See also DLB 83
Mauriac, Francois (Charles) 1885-1970 .... CAP-2
Earlier sketch in CA 25-28
See also CLC 4, 9, 56
See also DLB 65
See also MTCW 1
See also SSC 24
Maurice, David (John Kerr) 1899- CAP-1
Earlier sketch in CA 11-12
Maurice, Frederick Denison 1805-1872 .... DLB 55
Maurice, Roger
See Asselineau, Roger (Maurice)
Mauricio, Victoria Courtney 1928- 106

Maurina, Zenta 1897-1978 Obituary 85-88
Maurois, Andre 1885-1967 .... CAP-2
Obituary 25-28R
Earlier sketch in CA 21-22
See also DLB 65
See also MTCW 1
Mauron, Charles (Paul) 1899-1966 .... CAP-1
Earlier sketch in CA 9-10
Maury, Inez 1909- 61-64
Maury, James 1718-1769 .... DLB 31
Maury, Reuben 1899-1981 Obituary 103
Mauser, Ferdinand F. 1914- CANR-2
Earlier sketch in CA 1-4R
Mauser, Patricia Rhoads 1943- CANR-22
Earlier sketch in CA 106
See also SATA 37
Mauskopf, Seymour Harold 1938- 104
Mauss, Armand L(ind) 1928- 111
Mautner, Franz H(einrich) 1902- CANR-12
Earlier sketch in CA 61-64
Mautner, Thomas 1935- 151
Mauzey, Merritt 1897-1975 102
Mauzy, Peter
See Burgess, Michael (Roy)
Maves, Carl (Edwin) 1940- 69-72
Maves, Karl
See Maves, Carl (Edwin)
Maves, Mary Carolyn 1916- 49-52
See also SATA 10
Maves, Paul B(enjamin) 1913- CANR-17
Earlier sketches in CA 45-48, CANR-1
See also SATA 10
Mavin, John
See Rickword, (John) Edgell
Mavis, Walter Curry 1905- 5-8R
Mavity, Hubert
See Bond, Nelson S(lade)
Mavor, Elizabeth (Osborne) 1927- 107
See also DLB 14
Mavor, Osborne Henry 1888-1951 Brief entry .. 104
See also Bridie, James
Mavrodes, George I(on) 1926- 21-24R
Mavrogordato, J(ohn) G(eorge)
1905-1987 Obituary 122
Mavrogordato, Jack G.
See Mavrogordato, J(ohn) G(eorge)
Mavrogordatos, George T(hemistocles) 1945- .. 115
Mawby, Janet
See Garton, Janet
Mawdsley, Norman
See Hargreaves-Mawdsley, W(illiam) Norman
Mawer, June
See Knox-Mawer, June
Mawer, Ronald Knox
See Knox-Mawer, Ronald
Mawer, Ronnie Knox
See Knox-Mawer, Ronald
Mawicke, Tran 1911- .... SATA 15
Max
See Diop, Birago (Ismael)
Max, Nicholas
See Asbell, Bernard
Max, Peter 1939- 116
See also SATA 45
Maxa, Rudolph Joseph, Jr. 1949- 65-68
Maxa, Rudy
See Maxa, Rudolph Joseph, Jr.
Maxcy, Spencer J. 1939- 110
Maxey, Chester Collins 1890- CAP-1
Earlier sketch in CA 13-16
Maxey, David R(oy) 1936-1984 73-76
Obituary 112
Maxfield, Doris Morris 1953- 129
Maxfield, Elizabeth
See Miller, Elizabeth Maxfield
Maxford, Howard 1964- 165
Maxhim, Tristan
See Jones, (Max Him) Henri
Maxim, John R. 1937- CANR-70
Earlier sketch in CA 118
Maximov, Vladimir (Yemelyanovich) 1930-1995 . 104
Obituary 148
Maxmen, Jerrold S(amuel) 1942- CANR-27
Earlier sketch in CA 106
Maxner, Joyce (Karen Leopold) 1929- 133
Maxon, Anne
See Best, (Evangel) Allena Champlin
Maxon, John 1916-1977 Obituary 69-72
Maxon, Lou R(ussell) 1900-1971 Obituary 116
Maxton, Hugh
See McCormack, W(illiam) J(ohn)
Maxtone Graham, James Anstruther 1924- .. 69-72
Maxtone-Graham, John 1929- 69-72
Maxwell, A. E.
See Maxwell, Ann (Elizabeth)
Maxwell, A(lbert) E(rnest) 1916- 5-8R
Maxwell, Ann (Elizabeth) 1944- CANR-58
Earlier sketch in CA 105
Maxwell, Arthur S. 1896-1970 .... CAP-1
Earlier sketch in CA 9-10
See also SATA 11
Maxwell, Cassandre 1942- 117
Maxwell, Catherine (Fern) 1953- 160
See also Maxwell, Cathy
Maxwell, Cathy
See Maxwell, Catherine (Fern)
Maxwell, Colin 1956- 132
Maxwell, D(esmond) E(rnest) S(tewart)
1925- 33-36R
Maxwell, Edith 1923- 49-52
See also SATA 7
Maxwell, Edward
See Allan, Ted
Maxwell, Elisabeth (Meynard) 1921- 151
Maxwell, Elsa 1883-1963 Obituary 89-92
Maxwell, Gavin 1914-1969 .... CANR-61
Obituary 25-28R
Earlier sketch in CA 5-8R
See also MTCW 1
See also SATA 65
Maxwell, Gilbert 1910-1979 .... CAP-1
Obituary 93-96
Earlier sketch in CA 9-10
Maxwell, Glyn 1962- 154
Maxwell, Grant
See Richardson, Gladwell
Maxwell, Grover (Edward) 1918-1981 .... CANR-9
Earlier sketch in CA 5-8R
Maxwell, Jack
See McKeag, Ernest L(ionel)
Maxwell, James A. 1912- 13-16R
Maxwell, John
See Freemantle, Brian (Harry)
Maxwell, Kenneth (Robert) 1941- CANR-33
Earlier sketches in CA 85-88, CANR-15
Maxwell, Kenneth E(ugene) 1908- 73-76
Maxwell, Margaret F(inlayson) 1927- 109
Maxwell, Maurice 1910-1982 Obituary 107
Maxwell, Neville (George Anthony) 1926- . CANR-4
Earlier sketch in CA 49-52
Maxwell, Nicholas 1937- 132
Maxwell, Nicole (Hughes) 1905(?)-1998 .... 1-4R
Obituary 167
Maxwell, Patricia 1942- CANR-52
Earlier sketches in CA 29-32R, CANR-12, 28
Maxwell, Rhonda 1950- 112
Maxwell, Richard 1948- 152
Maxwell, Richard C(allender) 1919- 41-44R
Maxwell, (Ian) Robert 1923-1991 .... 9-12R
Obituary 135
Maxwell, Robert S(idney) 1911- 57-60
Maxwell, Robin 1948- 162
Maxwell, Ronald
See Smith, Ronald Gregor
Maxwell, Sister Mary 1913- 37-40R
Maxwell, Vicky
See Worboys, Anne(tte Isobel) Eyre
Maxwell, W(illiam) David 1926- 61-64
Maxwell, William
See Allan, Ted
Maxwell, William (Keepers, Jr.) 1908- CANR-54
Earlier sketch in CA 93-96
Interview in 93-96
See also CLC 19
See also DLBY 80
Maxwell-Hudson, (Rachel) Clare 1946- 69-72
Maxwell-Lefroy, Cecil Anthony 1907- CAP-1
Earlier sketch in CA 13-16
May, Allan 1923- 85-88
May, Arthur James 1899-1968 .... CAP-1
Earlier sketch in CA 11-12
May, Brian 1959- 165
May, Charles E(dward) 1941- CANR-41
Earlier sketch in CA 117
May, Charles Paul 1920- CANR-5
Earlier sketch in CA 1-4R
See also SATA 4
May, Clifford D. 1951- 136
May, Daryl (Alden) 1936- 139
May, Dean E(dward) 1944- 57-60
May, Derwent (James) 1930- CANR-28
Earlier sketches in CA 25-28R, CANR-11
May, Edgar 1929- 9-12R
May, Elaine 1932- 142
Brief entry 124
See also CLC 16
See also DLB 44
May, Elaine Tyler 1947- CANR-57
Earlier sketches in CA 111, CANR-30
May, Elizabeth 1907- CAP-2
Earlier sketch in CA 19-20
May, Ernest R(ichard) 1928- CANR-22
Earlier sketches in CA 1-4R, CANR-6
May, Eugene 1906- 1-4R
May, Florissa
See Green, Kay
May, Francis Barns 1915- 9-12R
May, George S(mith) 1924- 65-68
May, Georges Claude 1920- CANR-6
Earlier sketch in CA 13-16R
May, Gerald G(ordon) 1940- Brief entry 112
May, Gita 1929- CANR-13
Earlier sketch in CA 29-32R
May, H(enry) J(ohn) 1903- 13-16R
May, Henry F(arnham) 1915- 9-12R
May, Herbert Gordon 1904-1977 .... CANR-6
Obituary 89-92
Earlier sketch in CA 5-8R
May, Irvin M(arion), Jr. 1939- 123
May, J. C.
See May, Julian
May, Jacques M. 1896-1975 Obituary 57-60
May, James Boyer 1904- CAP-1
Earlier sketch in CA 11-12
May, John D(ickinson) 1932- 45-48
May, John R(ichard) 1931- CANR-18
Earlier sketches in CA 45-48, CANR-2
May, Judy Gail 1943- 57-60
May, Julian 1931- CANR-54
Earlier sketches in CA 1-4R, CANR-6
See also AAYA 17
See also SATA 11
May, Karl 1842-1912 .... DLB 129
May, Kenneth Ownsworth
1915-1977 Obituary 73-76
May, Lary L. 1944- 130
May, Lawrence Alan 1948- 106
May, Philip Radford 1928- 45-48
May, Robert E(van) 1943- 57-60
May, Robert Lewis 1905-1976 Obituary 104
See also SATA-Obit 27
May, Robert M(cCredie) 1936- 69-72
May, Robert Stephen 1929- CANR-30
Earlier sketches in CA 29-32R, CANR-13
See also SATA 46
May, Robin
See May, Robert Stephen
May, Rollo (Reece) 1909-1994 111
Obituary 147
Interview in 111
May, Sophie
See Clarke, Rebecca Sophia
May, Stephen 1946- 124
May, Steven W. 1941- 141
May, Thomas 1595(?)-1650 .... DLB 58
May, Timothy C(laude) 1940- 73-76
May, Todd Gifford 1955- 145
May, William E(ugene) 1928- CANR-14
Earlier sketch in CA 41-44R
Mayakovski, Vladimir (Vladimirovich)
1893-1930 158
Brief entry 104
See also TCLC 4, 18
Mayall, David 1953- 119
Mayall, R(obert) Newton 1904- CAP-1
Earlier sketch in CA 11-12
Maybaum, Ignaz 1897- CAP-1
Earlier sketch in CA 9-10
Mayberry, Florence V(irginia) Wilson 9-12R
See also SATA 10
Mayberry, Genevieve 1900- CAP-1
Earlier sketch in CA 19-20
Maybray-King, Horace 1901-1986 .... 29-32R
Obituary 120
Maybury, Anne
See Buxton, Anne (Arundel)
Maybury, Richard J. 1946- .... SATA 72
Maybury-Lewis, David H(enry) P(eter) 1929- 17-20R
Maye, Patricia 1940- 53-56
Mayer, Adrian C(urtius) 1922- 1-4R
Mayer, Agatha
See Maher, Ramona
Mayer, Albert 1897-1981 73-76
Obituary 105
Mayer, Albert Ignatius, Jr. 1906-1960 Obituary . 109
See also SATA-Obit 29
Mayer, Alfred 1903(?)-1984 Obituary 114
Mayer, (Henri) Andre (Van Huysen) 1946- 110
Mayer, Ann M(argaret) 1938- 57-60
See also SATA 14
Mayer, Arno J. 1926- 85-88
Mayer, Arthur L(oeb) 1886-1981 Obituary 108
Mayer, Barbara 1939- 145
Mayer, Bernadette 1945- CANR-70
Earlier sketch in CA 33-36R
See also DLB 165
Mayer, Bob 1959- 137
Mayer, Carl J. 1959- 122
Mayer, Charles Leopold 1881- CANR-6
Earlier sketch in CA 1-4R
Mayer, Christa Charlotte
See Thurman, Christa C(harlotte) Mayer
Mayer, Clara Woollie 1895- CAP-2
Earlier sketch in CA 19-20
Mayer, Debby
See Mayer, Deborah Anne
Mayer, Deborah Anne 1946- 109
Mayer, Ellen Moers
See Moers, Ellen
Mayer, Fanny (Alice) Hagin 1899- 118
Mayer, Gary (Richard) 1945- 53-56
Mayer, Gerda (Kamilla) 1927- 106
Mayer, Hannelore Valencak 1929- 116
See also Valencak, Hannelore
Mayer, Hans (Heinrich) 1907- 133
Brief entry 113
Mayer, Harold M(elvin) 1916- 41-44R
Mayer, Harry F(rederick) 1912- 101
Mayer, Henry 1941- 122
Mayer, Herbert Carleton 1893-1978 .... 41-44R
Mayer, Herbert T. 1922- 33-36R
Mayer, Jane 158
Mayer, Jane Rothschild 1903- 9-12R
See also SATA 38
Mayer, Jean 1920-1993 129
Obituary 140
Brief entry 117
Mayer, Lawrence C(lark) 1936- 97-100
Mayer, Leo V. 1936- 73-76
Mayer, Lynne Rhodes 1926- 73-76
Mayer, Marianna 1945- 93-96
See also SATA 32, 83
Mayer, Martin (Prager) 1928- 5-8R
Mayer, Mercer 1943- CANR-38
Earlier sketch in CA 85-88
See also CLR 11
See also DLB 61
See also MAICYA
See also SATA 16, 32, 73
Mayer, Michael F. 1917- 13-16R
Mayer, Milton (Sanford) 1908-1986 .... 37-40R
Obituary 119
Mayer, Musa 1943- 135
Mayer, Orlando Benedict 1818-1891 .... DLB 3
Mayer, Philip 1910- 49-52
Mayer, Ralph 1895-1979 .... CANR-28
Obituary 89-92
Earlier sketch in CA 29-32R
Mayer, Raymond Richard 1924- 1-4R
Mayer, Robert 1879-1985 Obituary 115
Mayer, Robert 1939- 136
Mayer, S(ydney) L(ouis) 1937- 103
Mayer, Sigrid 1933- 121
Mayer, Thomas 1927- CANR-9
Earlier sketch in CA 21-24R
Mayer, Tom 1943- 9-12R
Mayers, Daniel E. 1933(?)-1988 Obituary 129
Mayers, David (Allan) 1951- 131
Mayers, Lewis 1890-1975 Obituary 61-64
Mayers, Marvin K(eene) 1927- CANR-43
Earlier sketch in CA 41-44R
Mayerson, Charlotte Leon 13-16R
See also SATA 36
Mayerson, Evelyn Wilde 1935- 101
See also SATA 55
Mayerson, Philip 1918- 41-44R
Mayer-Thurman, Christa C.
See Thurman, Christa C(harlotte) Mayer
Mayes, Edythe Beam 1902- CANR-7
Earlier sketch in CA 53-56
Mayes, Frances 81-84
Mayes, Herbert R(aymond) 1900-1987 105
Obituary 124
See also DLB 137
Mayes, Stanley (Herbert) 1911- 1-4R
Mayes, Wendell 1919(?)-1992 103
Obituary 137
Interview in 103
See also DLB 26
Mayeux, Peter E(dmond) 1942- 119
Mayfair, Bertha
See Raborg, Frederick A(shton), Jr.
Mayfair, Franklin
See Mendelsohn, Felix, Jr.
Mayfield, Chris 1951- 107
Mayfield, Guy 1905-1976 .... 5-8R
Obituary 122
Mayfield, Jack
See Cooper, Parley J(oseph)
Mayfield, James Bruce 1934- 69-72
Mayfield, John S. 1904-1983 Obituary 109
Mayfield, Julia
See Hastings, Phyllis (Dora Hodge)
Mayfield, Julian (Hudson) 1928-1984 .... CANR-26
Obituary 114
Earlier sketch in CA 13-16R
See also BW 1
See also DLB 33
See also DLBY 84
Mayfield, L(afayette) H(enry) II 1910- CAP-2
Earlier sketch in CA 19-20
Mayfield, Marlys 1931- CANR-27
Earlier sketches in CA 25-28R, CANR-10
Mayfield, Robert C(harles) 1928- 37-40R
Mayfield, Sara (Martin) 1905-1979 .... 25-28R
Obituary 85-88
Mayfield, Sue 1963- .... SATA 72
Mayhall, Jane (Francis) 1921- CANR-8
Earlier sketch in CA 17-20R
Mayhall, Mildred P(ickle) 1902- CANR-1
Earlier sketch in CA 1-4R
Mayhar, Ardath 1930- CANR-42
Earlier sketches in CA 103, CANR-19
See also SATA 38
Mayhew, Christopher Paget 1915- Brief entry .. 106
Mayhew, David R(aymond) 1937- 17-20R
Mayhew, Edgar deNoailles 1913- 37-40R
Mayhew, Elizabeth
See Bear, Joan
Mayhew, Henry 1812-1887 .... DLB 18, 55, 190
Mayhew, James (John) 1964- .... SATA 85
Mayhew, Jonathan 1720-1766 .... DLB 31
Mayhew, Lenore 1924- 49-52
Mayhew, Lewis B. 1917- CANR-4
Earlier sketch in CA 1-4R
Mayhue, Richard L(ee) 1944- 116
Mayle, Peter 1939(?)- CANR-64
Earlier sketch in CA 139
See also CLC 89
Mayleas, William 1927- 120
Mayman, Martin 1924- 9-12R
Maynard, Alan (Keith) 1944- CANR-7
Earlier sketch in CA 57-60
Maynard, Chris
See Maynard, Christopher
Maynard, Christopher 1949- Brief entry 118
See also SATA-Brief 43
Maynard, Fredelle (Bruser) 1922- 85-88
Maynard, Geoffrey W(alter) 1921- 5-8R
Maynard, Harold Bright 1902-1975 .... 9-12R
Obituary 103
Maynard, Isabelle 1929- 162
Maynard, John (Rogers) 1941- CANR-40
Earlier sketch in CA 65-68
Maynard, Joyce 1953- CANR-64
Brief entry 111
Earlier sketch in CA 129
See also CLC 23
Maynard, Olga 1920- 114
See also SATA 40
Maynard, Richard Allen 1942- 33-36R
Maynard, Robert C(lyve) 1937-1993 115
Obituary 142
Brief entry 110
Interview in 115
Mayne, Ethel Colburn 1865-1941 .... DLB 197
Mayne, Jasper 1604-1672 .... DLB 126
Mayne, Richard (John) 1926- CANR-6
Earlier sketch in CA 13-16R
Mayne, Seymour 1944- CANR-47
Earlier sketches in CA 101, CANR-18
See also DLB 60
Mayne, William (James Carter) 1928- CANR-37
Earlier sketch in CA 9-12R
See also AAYA 20
See also CLC 12
See also CLR 25
See also JRDA
See also MAICYA
See also SAAS 11
See also SATA 6, 68
Maynes, E(dwin) Scott 1922- CANR-30
Earlier sketch in CA 45-48

Maynes, J. O. Rocky, Jr.
See Maynes, J. Oscar, Jr.
Maynes, J. Oscar, Jr. 1929-..................115
See also SATA 38
Mayo, Bernard 1902-1979 Obituary.........89-92
Mayo, C(atherine) M(ansell) 1961-............154
Mayo, Charles G(eorge) 1931-1985 Obituary...116
Mayo, E(dward) L(eslie) 1904-..........97-100
Mayo, Gretchen Will 1936-..............SATA 84
Mayo, James
See Coulter, Stephen
Mayo, Janet 1949-..........................121
Mayo, Jim
See L'Amour, Louis (Dearborn)
Mayo, Lida (Smith) 1904-1978 Obituary.......112
Mayo, Lucy Graves 1909-1963...............5-8R
Mayo, Margaret (Mary) 1935-...........CANR-68
Earlier sketch in CA 107
See also SATA 38, 96
Mayo, Margot 1910-.....................CAP-1
Earlier sketch in CA 13-16
Mayo, Mark
See Lane, Yoti
Mayo, Nick 1922-1983......................103
Obituary..................................110
Mayo, Patricia Elton 1915-.................103
Mayo, Wendell 1953-........................161
Mayo, William L. 1931-...................17-20R
Mayor, A(lpheus) Hyatt 1901-1980.......CANR-1
Obituary...............................97-100
Earlier sketch in CA 45-48
Mayor, Alfred Hyatt 1934-..................65-68
Mayor, Archer
See Mayor, Archer H(untington)
Mayor, Archer H(untington) 1950-.......CANR-65
Earlier sketch in CA 134
Mayor, Beatrice (?)-1971.................CAP-1
Earlier sketch in CA 9-10
Mayor, Federico 1934-......................154
Mayor, Flora Macdonald 1872-1932.......DLB 36
Mayor, Stephen (Harold) 1927-...........21-24R
Mayotte, Judy A. 1937-.....................144
Mayoux, Jean-Jacques
1901(?)-1987(?) Obituary...................125
Mayr, Ernst 1904-.......................CANR-2
Earlier sketch in CA 5-8R
Mayrant, Drayton
See Simons, Katherine Drayton Mayrant
Mayrocker, Friederike 1924-..............DLB 85
Mays, Benjamin E(lijah) 1894-1984......CANR-25
Obituary...................................112
Earlier sketch in CA 45-48
See also BW 1
Mays, Buddy (Gene) 1943-...............CANR-30
Earlier sketches in CA 73-76, CANR-12
Mays, Cedric Wesley 1907-...............29-32R
Mays, James A(rthur) 1939-.............CANR-25
Earlier sketch in CA 57-60
See also BW 1
Mays, John Barron 1914-1987 Obituary.......123
Mays, John Bentley 1941-...................164
Mays, Lucinda L(a Bella) 1924-.............101
See also SATA 49
Mays, Spike
See Mays, Cedric Wesley
Mays, (Lewis) Victor (Jr.) 1927-........25-28R
See also SATA 5
Mays, Willie (Howard, Jr.) 1931-...........105
Mayshark, Cyrus 1926-1976...............17-20R
Obituary...................................134
Maysi, Kadra
See Simons, Katherine Drayton Mayrant
Maysles, Albert 1926-...................29-32R
See also CLC 16
Maysles, David 1932-....................CLC 16
Maytham, Thomas N(orthrup) 1931-...........103
Maza, Regino Sainz de la
See Sainz de la Maza, Regino
Maze, Edward 1925-.......................5-8R
Mazer, Anne 1953-..........................135
See also SATA 67
Mazer, Harry 1925-.....................CANR-32
Earlier sketch in CA 97-100
Interview in............................97-100
See also AAYA 5
See also CLR 16
See also JRDA
See also MAICYA
See also SAAS 11
See also SATA 31, 67
Mazer, Milton 1911-......................85-88
Mazer, Norma Fox 1931-.................CANR-66
Earlier sketches in CA 69-72, CANR-12, 32
See also AAYA 5
See also CLC 26
See also CLR 23
See also JRDA
See also MAICYA
See also SAAS 1
See also SATA 24, 67
Mazia, Marjorie
See Guthrie, Marjorie (Greenblatt Mazia)
Maziarz, Edward A(nthony) 1915-.........37-40R
Mazille, Capucine 1953-..................SATA 96
Mazlish, Bruce 1923-....................CANR-2
Earlier sketch in CA 5-8R
Mazmanian, Arthur B(arkev) 1931-..........77-80
Mazmanian, Daniel (Aram) 1945-.........CANR-5
Earlier sketch in CA 53-56
Mazo, Earl 1919-........................37-40R
Mazo, Joseph H(enry) 1938-.................69-72
Mazonowicz, Douglas 1920-.................57-60
Mazour, Anatole G. 1900-................13-16R
Mazow, Julia Wolf 1937-....................103
Mazrui, Ali A(l'Amin) 1933-............CANR-13
Earlier sketch in CA 21-24R
See also BW 2
See also DLB 125
Mazumdar, Maxim 1952(?)-1988 Obituary.....125
Mazur, Allan Carl 1939-....................105
Mazur, Gail 1937-..........................77-80
Mazur, Laurie Ann 1961-....................150
Mazur, Paul M(yer) 1892-1979...............102
Obituary..................................89-92
Mazur, Ronald Michael 1934-.............25-28R
Mazuranic, Ivan 1814-1890...............DLB 147
Mazurkiewicz, Albert J. 1926-..........CANR-3
Earlier sketch in CA 9-12R
Mazursky, Paul 1930-...................CANR-24
Earlier sketch in CA 77-80
See also DLB 44
Mazza, Adriana 1928-...................CANR-4
Earlier sketch in CA 1-4R
See also SATA 19
Mazza, Cris 1956-..........................132
Mazzarins, Laimdota 1945-..................159
Mazzaro, Jerome 1934-..................CANR-45
Earlier sketches in CA 33-36R, CANR-13
Mazze, Edward M(ark) 1941-.............CANR-5
Earlier sketch in CA 13-16R
Mazzei, George 1941-.......................117
Mazzeo, Guido E(ttore) 1914-1984.......CANR-28
Obituary...................................113
Earlier sketch in CA 45-48
Mazzeo, Joseph Anthony 1923-...........17-20R
Mazzetti, Lorenza 1933-...................9-12R
Mazzio, Joann 1926-.....................SATA 74
Mazzotta, Giuseppe 1942-...............CANR-37
Earlier sketches in CA 93-96, CANR-16
Mazzulla, Fred 1903-....................CAP-2
Earlier sketch in CA 29-32
Mbaye, Marietou (Bileoma) 1948-............139
Mberi, Antar Sudan Katara 1949-..........81-84
Mbiti, John S(amuel) 1931-.............CANR-11
Earlier sketch in CA 21-24R
See also BW 1
Mbuende, Kaire (Munionganda) 1953-.........155
Mbugua, Kioi Wa 1962-...................SATA 83
McAdam, Charles Vincent 1892-1985 Obituary.116
McAdam, Doug 1951-.....................CANR-55
Earlier sketch in CA 126
Mc Adam, Robert E(verett) 1920-..........81-84
McAdams, Dan P. 1954-......................141
McAdoo, Henry Robert 1916-.................107
McAfee, Carol 1955-........................149
See also SATA 81
McAfee, John P. 1947-......................141
McAfee, (James) Thomas 1928-...........CANR-1
Earlier sketch in CA 45-48
McAfee, Ward M(erner) 1939-...............57-60
McAleavey, David 1946-....................65-68
McAleavy, Henry 1912-1968...............CAP-2
Earlier sketch in CA 21-22
McAleer, John J(oseph) 1923-...........CANR-13
Earlier sketch in CA 21-24R
McAleer, Neil 1942-........................119
McAlester, A(rcie) Lee 1933-...............118
McAlester, Lee
See McAlester, A(rcie) Lee
McAlester, Virginia 1943-..................120
McAlindon, Thomas 1932-..................97-100
McAlister, Luther Durwood 1927-............134
McAlister, Neil Harding 1952-..............110
McAlister, W(alter) Robert 1930-..........69-72
McAll, Christopher 1948-...................137
McAllaster, Elva 1922-..................33-36R
McAllen, Jack 1929-........................145
McAllen, John Banks
See McAllen, Jack
McAllister, Alister 1877-1943 Brief entry.......121
McAllister, Amanda
See Dowdell, Dorothy (Florence) Karns
and Hager, Jean
and Meaker, Eloise
McAllister, Annie Laurie
See Cassiday, Bruce (Bingham)
McAllister, Bruce (Hugh) 1946-..........33-36R
McAllister, Casey
See Battin, B(rinton) W(arner)
McAllister, Harry E(dward)................5-8R
McAllister, Ian 1950-......................128
McAllister, Lester G(rover) 1919-.......41-44R
McAlmon, Robert (Menzies) 1895-1956.......168
Brief entry................................107
See also DLB 4, 45
See also DLBD 15
McAlpin, Heller 1955-......................109
McAlpine, Alistair 1942-...................167
McAnally, Mary E(llen) 1939-...........CANR-46
Earlier sketches in CA 105, CANR-21
McAndrew, John 1904-1978 Obituary.......77-80
McAndrews, John
See Steward, Samuel M(orris)
McAnelly, James R. 1932-..................57-60
McArdle, Catherine
See Kelleher, Catherine McArdle
McArdle, Hugh M(c Lure) 1905-..............107
McArdle, Karen 1936-.......................129
McArdle, Phil 1939-........................129
McArdle, William D(aniel) 1939-............110
McArthur, Benjamin 1951-...................167
McArthur, Charles C(ampbell) 1920-......41-44R
McArthur, Edwin Douglas 1907-1987.......17-20R
Obituary...................................121
McArthur, Harvey K(ing) 1912-...........25-28R
McArthur, John
See Wise, Arthur
McArthur, Nancy............................161
See also SATA 96
McArthur, Peter 1866-1924...............DLB 92
McAulay, John D(avid) 1912-.............13-16R
McAuley, James J(ohn) 1936-...............77-80
McAuley, James Phillip 1917-1976........97-100
See also CLC 45
McAuley, Patricia Ann Calistro
See Calistro McAuley, Patricia Ann
McAuley, Paul J. 1955-.....................157
McAuliffe, Clarence 1903-...............CAP-2
Earlier sketch in CA 19-20
McAuliffe, Kevin Michael 1949-............81-84
McAuliffe, Mary Sperling 1943-............81-84
McAvoy, Thomas T(imothy) 1903-1969 ..CANR-15
Earlier sketch in CA 1-4R
McBain, Donald J(ames) 1945-..............45-48
McBain, Ed
See Hunter, Evan
McBain, Gordon D(uncan) III 1946-..........106
McBain, John M(aurice) 1921-............41-44R
McBain, Laurie 1949-.....................97-100
McBath, James Harvey 1922-..............17-20R
McBee, Mary Louise 1924-...................103
McBratney, Sam 1943-.......................155
See also CLR 44
See also SATA 89
McBrearty, James C(onnell) 1941- Brief entry..113
McBreen, Joan 1944-........................151
McBriar, Alan M(arne) 1918-...............5-8R
McBride, Alfred 1928-..................CANR-6
Earlier sketch in CA 13-16R
McBride, (Mary) Angela Barron 1941-.....CANR-1
Earlier sketch in CA 49-52
McBride, Chris(topher James) 1941-........81-84
McBride, David P(aul) 1947-................116
McBride, Donald O(pie) 1903-1978 Obituary.77-80
McBride, Earl Duwain 1891-..............CAP-1
Earlier sketch in CA 13-14
McBride, Genevieve G. 1949-................149
McBride, James C. 1957-....................153
McBride, James H(ubert) 1924-...........25-28R
McBride, Jim 1941-.........................157
McBride, John Cosgrove 1911-1983 Obituary..110
McBride, John G. 1919-....................9-12R
McBride, Joseph (Pierce) 1947-..........41-44R
McBride, Jule 1959-........................166
McBride, Katharine 1904-1976 Obituary.....65-68
McBride, Mary Margaret 1899-1976..........69-72
Obituary..................................65-68
McBride, Patricia
See Bartz, Patricia McBride
McBride, Richard William 1928-..........17-20R
McBride, Robert 1941- Brief entry..........116
McBride, Robert H(enry) 1918-1983..........107
Obituary...................................111
McBride, Stephen 1947-.....................148
McBride, Theresa Marie 1947-...............112
McBride, William Leon 1938-............CANR-6
Earlier sketch in CA 57-60
McBrien, Richard P(eter) 1936-.........CANR-10
Earlier sketch in CA 17-20R
McBrien, William Augustine 1930-...........107
See also CLC 44
McBroom, R. Curtis 1910-................CAP-2
Earlier sketch in CA 21-22
McBurney, James H(oward) 1905-..........17-20R
McCabe, Bernard P(atrick), Jr. 1933-......53-56
McCabe, Cameron
See Borneman, Ernest
McCabe, Charles B. 1899-1970 Obituary....89-92
McCabe, Charles Raymond
1915-1983 Obituary.........................109
McCabe, Cynthia Jaffee 1943-1986...........117
Obituary...................................120
McCabe, David Aloysius
1884(?)-1974 Obituary.....................45-48
McCabe, Eugene 1930-.......................158
McCabe, Herbert 1926-...................13-16R
McCabe, James P(atrick) 1937-..............101
McCabe, John Charles III 1920-.........CANR-1
Earlier sketch in CA 1-4R
McCabe, Joseph E. 1912-.................17-20R
McCabe, Patrick 1955-..................CANR-50
Earlier sketch in CA 130
See also DLB 194
McCabe, Peter 1945-........................140
McCabe, Sybil Anderson 1902-............CAP-1
Earlier sketch in CA 13-16
McCabe, Victoria 1948-..................29-32R
McCafferty, Jane 1960-.....................141
McCafferty, Jim 1954-......................150
See also SATA 84
McCafferty, Lawrence....................25-28R
McCafferty, (Barbara) Taylor 1946-.........134
McCaffery, Dan 1952-.......................129
McCaffery, Janet 1936-..................SATA 38
McCaffery, John K(erwin) M(ichael)
1914(?)-1983 Obituary......................111
McCaffery, Larry 1946-.....................115
McCaffery, Margo (Smith) 1938-..........37-40R
McCaffery, Steve 1947-.....................154
McCaffrey, Anne (Inez) 1926-...........CANR-55
Earlier sketches in CA 25-28R, CANR-15, 35
See also AAYA 6
See also AITN 2
See also BEST 89:2
See also CLC 17
See also CLR 49
See also DAM NOV, POP
See also DLB 8
See also JRDA
See also MAICYA
See also MTCW 1
See also SAAS 11
See also SATA 8, 70
McCaffrey, Donald W. 1926- Brief entry.......114
McCaffrey, James M. 1946-..................143
McCaffrey, Joseph A. 1940-..............37-40R
McCaffrey, Lawrence John 1925-..........25-28R
McCaffrey, Mary
See Szudek, Agnes S(usan) P(hilomena)
McCaffrey, Phillip 1945-...............CANR-15
Earlier sketch in CA 77-80
McCagg, William O., Jr. 1930-.............93-96
McCaghy, Charles H(enry) 1934-..........25-28R
McCague, James (P.) 1909-1977..........CANR-2
Earlier sketch in CA 1-4R
McCahill, Thomas 1907(?)-1975 Obituary......104
McCaig, Donald 1940-...................CANR-47
Earlier sketches in CA 104, CANR-14
McCaig, Robert Jesse 1907-1982.........CANR-64
Earlier sketches in CA 1-4R, CANR-1
McCaig, Snee
See McCaig, Donald
McCain, Murray (David, Jr.) 1926-1981..CANR-15
Obituary...................................105
Earlier sketch in CA 1-4R
See also SATA 7
See also SATA-Obit 29
McCaleb, Robert Bruce 1950-................111
McCaleb, Walter Flavius 1873-1967.......CAP-1
Earlier sketch in CA 9-10
McCall, Anthony
See Kane, Henry
McCall, Christina 1935-....................162
McCall, Dan (Elliott) 1940-................135
Brief entry................................113
McCall, Daniel F(rancis) 1918-..........17-20R
McCall, Dorothy Lawson 1889(?)-1982........109
Obituary...................................106
McCall, Edith (Sansom) 1911-...........CANR-43
Earlier sketches in CA 1-4R, CANR-4, 19
See also SATA 6
McCall, George J(ohn) 1939-............CANR-9
Earlier sketch in CA 21-24R
McCall, Grant 1943-........................107
McCall, John Corey
See Morland, Nigel
McCall, John R(obert) 1920-............CANR-1
Earlier sketch in CA 45-48
McCall, Marsh H(oward), Jr. 1939-.......29-32R
McCall, Mary C(aldwell), Jr.
1904-1986 Obituary.........................118
McCall, Nathan 1955(?)-....................146
See also CLC 86
McCall, Robert B(ooth) 1940-...........CANR-14
Earlier sketch in CA 33-36R
McCall, Storrs 1930-.......................147
McCall, Thomas (Lawson) 1913-1983 Obituary.108
McCall, Thomas S(creven) 1936-.........CANR-1
Earlier sketch in CA 49-52
McCall, Tom
See McCall, Thomas (Lawson)
McCall, Vincent
See Morland, Nigel
McCall, Virginia Nielsen 1909-.........CANR-39
Earlier sketches in CA 1-4R, CANR-1, 17
See also SATA 13
McCall, Wendell
See Pearson, Ridley
McCall, William A(nderson) 1891-........CAP-1
Earlier sketch in CA 19-20
McCalley, John W(allace) 1916-1983.........110
McCall-Newman, Christina
See McCall, Christina
McCall Smith, Alexander 1948-...........SATA 73
McCallum, George E(dward) 1931-.........37-40R
McCallum, Ian R(obert) M(ore) 1919-1987...13-16R
Obituary...................................124
McCallum, James Dow 1893-1971 Obituary...104
McCallum, John D(ennis) 1924-1988......CANR-4
Obituary...................................127
Earlier sketch in CA 53-56
McCallum, Neil 1916-....................13-16R
McCallum, Phyllis 1911-................CANR-4
Earlier sketch in CA 53-56
See also SATA 10
McCallum, Ronald Buchanan 1898-1973.....5-8R
Obituary..................................89-92
McCallum, Stephen 1960-.................SATA 91
McCallum, Taffy Gould 1942-................141
McCamant, John F. 1933-.................25-28R
McCammon, Robert R(ick) 1952-.........CANR-40
Earlier sketch in CA 81-84
See also AAYA 17
See also DAM POP
McCampbell, Darlene Z. 1942-............SATA 83
McCampbell, James M. 1924-................49-52
McCamy, James L(ucian) 1906-..............5-8R
McCandless, Anthony
See McConville, Michael (Anthony)
McCandless, George T., Jr. 1947-...........139
McCandless, Hugh (Douglas) 1907-..........5-8R
McCandless, Perry 1917-................CANR-1
Earlier sketch in CA 49-52
McCandless, Ruth Strout 1909-..............128
McCandlish, George E(dward) 1914-1975.....65-68
Obituary..................................61-64
McCanles, Michael (Frederick) 1936-.......69-72
McCann, Arthur
See Campbell, John W(ood, Jr.)
McCann, Colum 1965-........................152
McCann, Coolidge
See Fawcett, F(rank) Dubrez
McCann, Dennis P(atrick) 1945-.............115
McCann, Eamonn 1943- Brief entry...........117
McCann, Edson
See del Rey, Lester
and Pohl, Frederik
McCann, Francis Daniel, Jr. 1938-......CANR-43
Earlier sketch in CA 117
McCann, Frank D., Jr.
See McCann, Francis Daniel, Jr.
McCann, Gerald 1916-....................SATA 41

McCann, Graham 1961- ... 134
McCann, Helen 1948- ... 142
See also SATA 75
McCann, Jim 1951- ... 168
McCann, Kevin 1904-1981 Obituary ... 103
McCann, Sean 1929- ... 134
Brief entry ... 115
McCann, Thomas 1934- ... 73-76
McCannon, Dindga ... 114
See also SATA 41
McCannon, John 1967- ... 158
McCants, Olga 1901- ... CANR-14
Earlier sketch in CA 73-76
McCants, Sister Dorothea Olga
See McCants, Olga
McCants, William D. 1961- ... 149
See also SATA 82
McCardell, John (Malcolm, Jr.) 1949- ... 101
McCardle, Carl W(esley) 1904(?)-1972 ... 37-40R
McCardle, Dorothy Bartlett 1904-1978 ... 85-88
Obituary ... 81-84
McCarey, Peter 1956- ... 138
McCargar, James (Goodrich) 1920- ... 137
McCarr, Ken(neth George) 1903-1977 ... 109
Obituary ... 106
McCarrick, Earlean M. 1930- ... 103
McCarriston, Linda 1943- ... CAAS 28
McCarroll, Marion C(lyde)
1893(?)-1977 Obituary ... 73-76
McCarroll, Tolbert (Henry) 1931- ... 110
McCarry, Charles 1930- ... CANR-41
Earlier sketch in CA 103
McCarten, John (Bernard Francis James)
1916(?)-1974 Obituary ... 115
McCarter, Alan 1943- ... 107
McCarter, Neely Dixon 1929- ... 109
See also SATA 47
McCarter, P(ete) Kyle (Jr.) 1945- ... 105
McCarthy, Agnes 1933- ... 17-20R
See also SATA 4
McCarthy, Barry (Wayne) 1943- ... CANR-61
Earlier sketches in CA 113, CANR-32
McCarthy, Cavan 1943- ... 61-64
McCarthy, Charlene B(arbara) 1929- ... 41-44R
McCarthy, Charles, Jr. 1933- ... CANR-69
Earlier sketch in CANR-42
See also McCarthy, Cormac
See also DAM POP
McCarthy, Clarence F. 1909- ... 29-32R
McCarthy, Colin (John) 1951- ... 145
See also SATA 77
McCarthy, Cormac 1933-
See McCarthy, Charles, Jr.
See also CLC 4, 57, 59, 101
See also DLB 6, 143
McCarthy, Darry 1930- ... CANR-35
Earlier sketch in CA 5-8R
McCarthy, David (Edgar) 1925- ... 1-4R
McCarthy, David Seymour 1935- ... 115
McCarthy, Dennis John 1924- ... 21-24R
McCarthy, E(dmund) Jerome 1928- Brief entry . 112
McCarthy, Edward V., Jr. 1924- ... 93-96
McCarthy, Emily J(eannette) 1945- ... CANR-32
Earlier sketch in CA 113
McCarthy, Eugene J(oseph) 1916- ... CANR-2
Earlier sketch in CA 1-4R
McCarthy, Gary 1943- ... CANR-64
Earlier sketches in CA 69-72, CANR-22
McCarthy, Harold T. 1920- ... 127
McCarthy, James J(erome) 1927- ... 41-44R
McCarthy, Jenny 1972- ... 167
McCarthy, Joe
See McCarthy, Joseph Weston
McCarthy, John 1898- ... 45-48
McCarthy, John J(oseph) 1909- ... 130
McCarthy, John P(atrick) 1938- ... 97-100
McCarthy, Joseph M(ichael) 1940- ... 97-100
McCarthy, Joseph Raymond 1909-1957 Brief
entry ... 111
McCarthy, Joseph Weston 1915-1980 ... CANR-1
Obituary ... 97-100
Earlier sketch in CA 1-4R
McCarthy, Justin 1945- ... 163
McCarthy, Kevin M. 1940- ... CANR-45
Earlier sketch in CA 120
McCarthy, Kyle 1954- ... CANR-54
Earlier sketch in CA 127
McCarthy, Martha M(ay) 1945- ... CANR-31
Earlier sketch in CA 111
McCarthy, Marvin 1902-1983 Obituary ... 110
McCarthy, Mary (Therese) 1912-1989 ... CANR-64
Obituary ... 129
Earlier sketches in CA 5-8R, CANR-16, 50
Interview in ... CANR-16
See also CLC 1, 3, 5, 14, 24, 39, 59
See also DLB 2
See also DLBY 81
See also MTCW 1
See also SSC 24
McCarthy, Michael 1939- ... 127
McCarthy, Mignon ... 138
McCarthy, Nan(cy J.) 1961- ... 160
McCarthy, Patrick A. 1945- ... 145
McCarthy, Patrick Joseph 1922- ... 9-12R
McCarthy, Paul Eugene 1921- ... 103
McCarthy, R. Delphina (Polley) 1894- ... CAP-1
Earlier sketch in CA 13-16
McCarthy, Ralph F. 1950- ... 145
McCarthy, Ray 1920(?)-1984 Obituary ... 112
McCarthy, Richard D(ean Max) 1927- ... 41-44R
McCarthy, Shaun (Lloyd) 1928- ... CANR-65
Earlier sketches in CA 9-12R, CANR-6
McCarthy, Teresa
See Anderson, Teresa
McCarthy, Thomas 1954- ... 133
McCarthy, Thomas N. 1927- ... 37-40R
McCarthy, Thomas P. 1920- ... 13-16R
McCarthy, Timothy G. 1929- ... 158
McCarthy, (Daniel) Todd 1950- ... 105
McCarthy, Wil 1966- ... 166
McCarthy, William E(dward) J(ohn) 1925- . CANR-6
Earlier sketch in CA 9-12R
McCarthy-Tucker, Sherri N. 1958- ... 151
See also SATA 83
McCartney, Christine Maye 1949- ... 116
McCartney, James H(arold) 1925- ... 73-76
McCartney, Mike
See McCartney, Peter Michael
McCartney, (James) Paul 1942- ... 146
See also CLC 12, 35
McCartney, Peter Michael 1944- ... 109
McCartney, Scott 1960- ... 138
McCarty, Clifford 1929- ... 17-20R
McCarty, Doran Chester 1931- ... CANR-31
Earlier sketches in CA 65-68, CANR-10
McCarty, Frederick H.
See McCarty, Hanoch
McCarty, Hanoch 1940- ... 161
McCarty, Maclyn 1911- ... 120
McCarty, Norma
See Crandall, Norma
McCarty, Rega Kramer 1904- ... 5-8R
See also SATA 10
McCary, James Leslie 1919-1978 ... 85-88
McCash, June Hall 1938- ... 37-40R
McCasland, S(elby) Vernon 1896- ... 5-8R
McCaslin, Nellie 1914- ... 33-36R
See also SATA 12
McCaslin, Richard B(ryan) 1961- ... 144
McCaughey, Ellen
See Koshland, Ellen
McCaughey, Robert A(nthony) 1939- ... 77-80
McCaughrean, Geraldine 1951- ... CANR-52
Earlier sketch in CA 117
See also AAYA 23
See also CLR 38
See also SATA 87
McCaughren, Tom 1936- ... 142
See also SATA 75
McCauley, Carole Spearin 1939- ... CANR-50
Earlier sketches in CA 57-60, CANR-8, 25
McCauley, Elfrieda B(abnick) 1915- ... 9-12R
McCauley, Leon 1908(?)-1984 Obituary ... 112
McCauley, Martin 1934- ... CANR-46
Earlier sketches in CA 107, CANR-23
McCauley, Michael F(rederick) 1947- ... CANR-9
Earlier sketch in CA 61-64
McCauley, Michael J. 1961- ... 138
McCauley, Stephen (D.) 1955- ... 141
See also CLC 50
McCauley, Sue 1941- ... 140
McCaull, M. E.
See Bohlman, (Mary) Edna McCaull
McCaw, Kenneth Malcolm 1907- ... 109
McCaw, Mabel Niedermeyer 1899- ... CAP-2
Earlier sketch in CA 19-20
McCay, Winsor 1871-1934 ... DLB 22
See also SATA 41
McChesney, Kathryn 1936- ... 115
McClain, Alva J. 1888-1968 ... 65-68
McClain, Carl S. 1899- ... 37-40R
McClain, John O. 1942- ... CANR-30
Earlier sketch in CA 110
McClain, Leanita 1952(?)-1984 Obituary ... 112
McClain, Russell H(arding) 1910- ... CAP-2
Earlier sketch in CA 21-22
McClane, A(lbert) J(ules) 1922-1991 ... 126
Obituary ... 136
Brief entry ... 106
See also DLB 171
McClane, Kenneth Anderson, Jr. 1951- ... CANR-21
Earlier sketches in CA 57-60, CANR-6
McClary, Andrew 1927- ... 61-64
McClary, Ben Harris 1931- ... CANR-3
Earlier sketch in CA 9-12R
McClary, Jane Stevenson 1919-1990 ... CANR-1
Obituary ... 130
Earlier sketch in CA 1-4R
See also SATA-Obit 64
McClary, Susan 1946- ... 154
McClatchy, C. K. 1858-1936 ... DLB 25
McClatchy, Eleanor Grace
1895(?)-1980 Obituary ... 102
McClatchy, J(oseph) D(onald, Jr.) 1945- . CANR-44
Earlier sketch in CA 105
McClaurin, Irma Pearl 1952- ... 57-60
McClay, Wilfred M(ark) 1951- ... 149
McClean, Joseph Lucius 1919- ... CAP-1
Earlier sketch in CA 9-10
McCleary, Elliott H(arold) 1927- ... 57-60
McCleary, Robert A(ltwig) 1923-1973 ... 17-20R
Obituary ... 134
McCleary, William J(ames) 1938- ... 119
McCleery, Patsy R. 1925- ... 160
See also SATA 88
McCleery, William (Thomas) 1911- ... CANR-5
Earlier sketch in CA 1-4R
McClellan, A(rchibald) W(illiam) 1908- ... 77-80
McClellan, Albert (Alfred) 1922- ... 122
McClellan, Edwin 1925- Brief entry ... 115
McClellan, George Marion 1860-1934 ... 125
See also BW 1
See also DLB 50
McClellan, Grant S(amuel) 1914- Brief entry ... 114
McClellan, James (Paul) 1937- ... 21-24R
McClellan, James Edward, Jr. 1922- ... 25-28R
McClellan, Norris 1905-1984 Obituary ... 116
McClellan, Robert F., Jr. 1934- ... 33-36R
McClellan, Stephen T. 1942- ... 133
McClelland, Charles A. 1917- ... 85-88
McClelland, Charles E(dgar III) 1940- ... 33-36R
McClelland, David C(larence) 1917-1998 ... 25-28R
Obituary ... 165
McClelland, Diane Margaret 1931- ... CANR-59
Earlier sketch in CA 105
McClelland, Doug 1934- ... CANR-57
Earlier sketches in CA 41-44R, CANR-14, 31
McClelland, Ivy Lilian 1908- ... 29-32R
McClelland, Lucille Hudlin 1920- ... 21-24R
McClelland, Vincent Alan 1933- ... 103
McClendon, James William, Jr. 1924- ... CANR-49
Earlier sketches in CA 9-12R, CANR-5
McClendon, Lise (Webb) 1952- ... 146
McClendon, Sarah 1910- ... 73-76
McClennen, Sandra Elaine 1942- ... 103
McClintick, David 1940- ... 146
McClintock, Barbara 1902-1992 ... 161
McClintock, Barbara 1955- ... 160
See also SATA 57, 95
McClintock, Marshall 1906-1967 ... CAP-1
Earlier sketch in CA 9-10
See also SATA 3
McClintock, May Garelick
See Garelick, May
McClintock, Mike
See McClintock, Marshall
McClintock, Robert (Mills) 1909- ... CAP-2
Earlier sketch in CA 21-22
McClintock, Theodore 1902-1971 ... 73-76
Obituary ... 33-36R
See also SATA 14
McClinton, Katharine Morrison 1899-1993 . CANR-5
Obituary ... 140
Earlier sketch in CA 1-4R
McClinton, Leon 1933- ... 65-68
See also SATA 11
McClory, Robert J(oseph) 1932- ... CANR-13
Earlier sketch in CA 77-80
McCloskey, Deirdre N(ansen) 1942- ... CANR-31
Earlier sketches in CA 57-60, CANR-8
McCloskey, Donald N.
See McCloskey, Deirdre N(ansen)
McCloskey, Eunice (Loncoske) 1906- ... 9-12R
McCloskey, H(enry) J(ohn) 1925- ... 110
McCloskey, Kevin 1951- ... SATA 79
McCloskey, Mark 1938- ... CANR-1
Earlier sketch in CA 45-48
McCloskey, Maxine E(laine) 1927- ... 33-36R
McCloskey, Patrick 1948- ... CANR-38
Earlier sketch in CA 115
McCloskey, Paul N., Jr. 1927- ... 37-40R
McCloskey, (John) Robert 1914- ... CANR-47
Earlier sketch in CA 9-12R
See also CLR 7
See also DLB 22
See also MAICYA
See also SATA 2, 39, 100
McCloskey, William B(ertine), Jr. 1928- ... 101
McCloud, Jed
See Fearn, John Russell
McCloud, Scott
See McLeod, Scott Willard
McCloy, Helen (Worrell Clarkson) 1904- . CANR-44
Earlier sketch in CA 25-28R
McCloy, James F(loyd) 1941- ... 103
See also SATA 59
McCloy, Shelby Thomas 1898-(?) ... CAP-2
Earlier sketch in CA 23-24
McClung, Floyd, Jr. 1945- ... 61-64
McClung, Nellie Letitia 1873-1951 ... DLB 92
McClung, Patricia A. 1950- ... 119
McClung, Robert M(arshall) 1916- ... CANR-46
Earlier sketches in CA 13-16R, CANR-6, 21
See also AITN 2
See also CLR 11
See also MAICYA
See also SAAS 15
See also SATA 2, 68
McClung, William Alexander 1944- ... 113
McClure, Arthur F(rederick) II 1936- ... CANR-10
Earlier sketch in CA 65-68
McClure, Charles R(obert) 1949- ... CANR-53
Earlier sketches in CA 111, CANR-29
McClure, Gillian Mary 1948- ... 103
See also SATA 31
McClure, Grace 1918- ... 123
McClure, Hal 1921- ... 81-84
McClure, James (Howe) 1939- ... CANR-66
Earlier sketches in CA 69-72, CANR-44
McClure, Joanna 1930- Brief entry ... 116
See also DLB 16
McClure, John A. 1945- ... 132
McClure, Larry 1941- ... CANR-26
Earlier sketch in CA 69-72
McClure, Michael (Thomas) 1932- ... CANR-46
Earlier sketches in CA 21-24R, CANR-17
See also CLC 6, 10
See also DLB 16
McClure, Ron 1941- ... 37-40R
McClure, Ruth Koonz ... 107
McClure, S. S. 1857-1949 ... DLB 91
McClure, Sandy 1948- ... 154
McCluskey, John (A.), Jr. 1944- ... CANR-24
Earlier sketches in CA 57-60, CANR-7
See also BW 1
See also DLB 33
McCluskey, Neil Gerard 1921- ... CANR-12
Earlier sketch in CA 25-28R
McCole, John 1954- ... 148
McColgan, John (Joseph) 1946- ... 132
McCollam, James Graham 1913- ... CANR-4
Earlier sketch in CA 45-48
McCollam, Jim
See McCollam, James Graham
McColley, Diane Kelsey 1934- ... 130
McColley, Kevin 1961- ... 148
See also SAAS 23
See also SATA 80
McColley, Robert (McNair) 1933- ... 13-16R
McCollough, Albert W. 1917- ... 102
McCollough, Celeste 1926- ... 13-16R
McCollough, Charles R(andolph) 1934- ... CANR-42
Earlier sketch in CA 118
McCollum, Audrey T(almage) 1924- ... 107
McCollum, Elmer Verner 1879-1967 ... CAP-1
Earlier sketch in CA 13-14
McCollum, Michael (Allen) 1946- ... 147
McComas, Annette Peltz 1911- ... 109
McComas, J(esse) Francis
1911-1978 Obituary ... 104
McComb, David G(lendinning) 1934- ... CANR-28
Earlier sketches in CA 29-32R, CANR-12
McComb, K(atherine Woods) 1895- ... 13-16R
McCombs, Don 1948- ... 115
McCombs, Judith 1939- ... 102
McCombs, Maxwell E(lbert) 1938- ... CANR-58
Earlier sketches in CA 73-76, CANR-12, 31
McCombs, Philip A(lgie) 1944- ... 49-52
McConagha, Alan 1932- ... 77-80
McConahay, John B. 1938- ... 110
McCondach, J. P. 1912- ... 117
McConduit, Denise Walter 1950- ... 155
See also SATA 89
McCone, R(obert) Clyde 1915- ... 77-80
McConica, James Kelsey 1930- ... CANR-44
Earlier sketches in CA 33-36R, CANR-13
McConkey, Clarence 1925- ... 29-32R
McConkey, Dale Durant 1928- ... 93-96
McConkey, James (Rodney) 1921- ... CANR-41
Earlier sketch in CA 17-20R
McConkie, Bruce R(edd) 1915-1985 Obituary .. 115
McConnel, Patricia 1931- ... 133
McConnell, Allen 1923- ... 77-80
McConnell, Campbell R(obertson) 1928- ... 5-8R
McConnell, Dorothy 1900(?)-1989 Obituary ... 129
McConnell, Frank D(eMay) 1942- ... CANR-70
Earlier sketch in CA 104
McConnell, Grant 1915- ... 65-68
McConnell, James Douglas Rutherford 1915-1988 .
CANR-22
Obituary ... 125
Earlier sketches in CA 9-12R, CANR-6
See also SATA 40
See also SATA-Obit 56
McConnell, James V(ernon) 1925-1990 ... 5-8R
Obituary ... 131
McConnell, Jean 1928- ... CANR-39
Earlier sketches in CA 85-88, CANR-16
McConnell, John Lithgow Chandos 1918- ... 53-56
McConnell, John W(ilkinson) 1907- ... 107
McConnell, Jon Patrick 1928- ... 21-24R
McConnell, Malcolm 1939- ... 106
McConnell, Marie Antoinette 1939- ... 163
McConnell, Raymond A(rnott)
1915-1979 Obituary ... 89-92
McConnell, Roland C(alhoun) 1910- ... 73-76
McConnell, T. R.
See McConnell, Thomas Raymond
McConnell, Terrance C(allihan) 1948- ... 110
McConnell, Thomas Raymond 1901- ... 118
McConnell, Virginia (McCorison) 1928- ... 13-16R
McConnell, William C 1917- ... DLB 88
McConnell, William T(ate) 1941- ... 115
McConnor, Vincent ... CANR-23
Earlier sketch in CA 106
McConville, Michael (Anthony) 1925- ... 144
McConville, Sean 1943- ... 137
McCord, Anne 1942- ... 109
See also SATA 41
McCord, Arline F(ujii) 1934- ... CANR-1
Earlier sketch in CA 45-48
McCord, David (Thompson Watson) 1897-1997 ...
CANR-38
Obituary ... 157
Earlier sketch in CA 73-76
See also CLR 9
See also DLB 61
See also MAICYA
See also SATA 18
See also SATA-Obit 96
McCord, Guy
See Reynolds, Dallas McCord
McCord, Howard 1932- ... CANR-40
Earlier sketches in CA 9-12R, CANR-4, 18
See also CAAS 9
McCord, James I(ley) 1919- ... 21-24R
McCord, James W(alter), Jr. 1918(?)- ... AITN 1
McCord, Jean 1924- ... 49-52
See also SATA 34
McCord, John H(arrison) 1934- ... CANR-17
Earlier sketch in CA 25-28R
McCord, Margaret 1916- ... 161
McCord, Whip
See Norwood, Victor G(eorge) C(harles)
McCord, William Maxwell 1930-1992 ... CANR-46
Earlier sketches in CA 1-4R, 139, CANR-1
McCorduck, Pamela (Ann) 1940- ... CANR-36
Earlier sketches in CA 81-84, CANR-15
McCorison, Marcus Allen 1926- ... 33-36R
McCorkle, Chester O(liver), Jr. 1925- ... 110
McCorkle, Jill (Collins) 1958- ... 121
See also CLC 51
See also DLBY 87
McCorkle, Samuel Eusebius 1746-1811 ... DLB 37
McCormac, John W. 1926- ... 41-44R
McCormack, Arthur Gerard 1911-1992 ... CANR-47
Obituary ... 140
Earlier sketch in CA 5-8R
McCormack, Gavan Patrick 1937- ... CANR-22
Earlier sketch in CA 105

McCormack, Mark H(ume) 1930- CANR-17
Earlier sketch in CA 49-52
McCormack, S(usan) Allison 1943- 111
McCormack, W(illiam) J(ohn) 1947- 145
McCormack, William A. 1932- 25-28R
McCormick, Anita Louise 1957- 146
McCormick, Anne (Elizabeth) O'Hare
1882(?)-1954 Brief entry 118
See also DLB 29
McCormick, Brooks
See Adams, William Taylor
McCormick, Claire
See Labus, Marta Haake
McCormick, Dell J. 1892-1949 SATA 19
McCormick, Diana Festa
See Festa-McCormick, Diana
McCormick, (George) Donald (King) 1911-
CANR-65
Earlier sketches in CA 73-76, CANR-14, 32
See also SATA 14
McCormick, E(dward) Allen 1925- 107
McCormick, E(ric) H(all) 1906- 103
McCormick, Edgar L(indsley) 1914- 5-8R
McCormick, Edith (Joan) 1934- SATA 30
McCormick, Ernest J(ames) 1911- 93-96
McCormick, Jack (Sovern) 1929-1979 CANR-5
Obituary 85-88
Earlier sketch in CA 9-12R
McCormick, James (Phillip) 1920- 25-28R
McCormick, James P(atton)
1911-1988 Obituary 125
McCormick, John O(wen) 1918- 17-20R
McCormick, Kenneth Dale 1906-1997 DLBY 97
McCormick, Mary
See McCormick, Sister Rose M(atthew)
McCormick, Merla Jean 1938- 97-100
McCormick, Mona 77-80
McCormick, Peter J(oseph) 1940- 112
McCormick, Richard Arthur 1922- CANR-22
Earlier sketch in CA 105
McCormick, Richard P(atrick) 1916- 9-12R
McCormick, Robert (K.) 1911-1985 115
Obituary 117
McCormick, Robert R. 1880-1955 DLB 29
McCormick, Scott, Jr. 1929- 17-20R
McCormick, Sister Rose M(atthew) 1914- 21-24R
McCormick, Theresa E. 1939- 150
McCormick, Theresa Mickey
See McCormick, Theresa E.
McCormick, Wilfred 1903- CANR-1
Earlier sketch in CA 1-4R
McCormmach, Russell (Keith) 1933- 118
Brief entry 112
McCorquodale, Barbara
See Cartland, Barbara (Hamilton)
McCorquodale, Robin (Hunt) 121
McCorry, Vincent P(atrick) 1909-1990 Obituary 131
McCorvey, Norma (Leah) 1947- 147
McCourt, Edward (Alexander) 1907-1972 9-12R
Obituary 103
See also DLB 88
See also SATA-Obit 28
McCourt, Frank 1930- 157
See also CLC 109
McCourt, James 1941- 57-60
See also CLC 5
McCowen, Alec
See McCowen, Alexander Duncan
McCowen, Alexander Duncan 1925- 129
McCowen, George S(mith), Jr. 1935- 89-92
McCown, Edna 1947- 140
McCown, James H. 1911- 89-92
McCown, Wayne (Gordon) 1942- 111
McCoy, Alfred W. 1945- CANR-17
Earlier sketch in CA 29-32R
McCoy, Andrew 117
McCoy, Arch
See Miller, Victor (Brooke)
McCoy, Charles A(llan) 1920- CANR-16
Earlier sketch in CA 65-68
McCoy, D(onald) E(dward) 1923- 37-40R
McCoy, Donald R(ichard) 1928-1996 CANR-2
Obituary 154
Earlier sketch in CA 5-8R
McCoy, Edain
See Taylor, Carol MacKenzie
McCoy, Elaine 1945- 119
McCoy, Esther 1904-1989 Obituary 130
McCoy, F(lorence) N(ina) 1925- 65-68
McCoy, Horace (Stanley) 1897-1955 155
Brief entry 108
See also DLB 9
See also TCLC 28
McCoy, Iola Fuller 13-16R
See also SATA 3
McCoy, J(oseph) J(erome) 1917- CANR-6
Earlier sketch in CA 13-16R
See also SATA 8
McCoy, John P(leasant)
1906(?)-1974 Obituary 49-52
McCoy, Joseph A(loysius) 1911- 1-4R
McCoy, Karen Kawamoto 1953- SATA 82
McCoy, Kathleen 1945- CANR-47
Earlier sketches in CA 81-84, CANR-22
McCoy, Kathy
See McCoy, Kathleen
McCoy, Lois (Rich) 1941- CANR-22
Earlier sketch in CA 101
See also SATA 38
McCoy, Malachy
See Caulfield, Malachy Francis
McCoy, Marjorie Casebier 1934-1985 Obituary 114
McCoy, Maureen 1949- 119
McCoy, Max 1958- 153
McCoy, Mike
See Fearn, John Russell
McCoy, Ralph E(dward) 1915- 37-40R
McCoy, Ronald 1947- 81-84
McCoy, Roy 1935- 29-32R
McCoy, Samuel (Duff) 1882-1964 Obituary 93-96
McCoy, Tim(othy John Fitzgerald) 1891-1978 81-84
Obituary 77-80
McCracken, (James) David 1939- 119
McCracken, Elizabeth 1966- 167
McCracken, Esther 1902-1971 Obituary 33-36R
McCracken, George E(nglert) 1904- 17-20R
McCracken, Glenn 1908- 5-8R
McCracken, Harold 1894- 107
McCracken, J(ohn) L(eslie) 1914- 25-28R
McCracken, James (Eugene)
1926-1988 Obituary 126
McCracken, Karen Harden 1905- 122
McCracken, Kay
See McCracken, Karen Harden
McCracken, Kenneth David
1901-1983 Obituary 109
McCracken, Mary Lou 1943- 61-64
McCracken, Paul Winston 1915- CANR-6
Earlier sketch in CA 5-8R
McCracken, Samuel 111
McCrackin, Mark (Owens) 1949- 107
McCrady, Lady 1951- 93-96
See also SATA 16
McCrae, John 1872-1918 Brief entry 109
See also DLB 92
See also TCLC 12
McCrank, Lawrence J(oseph) 1945- CANR-29
Earlier sketch in CA 110
McCrary, (James) Peyton 1943- 85-88
McCraw, James Edward 1943- 101
McCraw, Louise Harrison 1893-1975 1-4R
Obituary 103
McCraw, Thomas K(incaid) 1940- CANR-17
Earlier sketch in CA 33-36R
McCray, Mike
See Preston, John
McCrea, James (Craig, Jr.) 1920- CANR-8
Earlier sketch in CA 5-8R
See also SATA 3
McCrea, Joan Marie Ryan 1922- 57-60
McCrea, Ruth (Pirman) 1921- CANR-8
Earlier sketch in CA 5-8R
See also SATA 3
McCrea, William Hunter 1904- 107
McCreadie, Marsha A. 1943- 111
McCready, Jack
See Powell, Talmage
McCready, Warren T(homas) 1915- 21-24R
McCreary, Alf(red) 1940- CANR-31
Earlier sketch in CA 69-72
McCreary, W. Burgess 1894- CAP-1
Earlier sketch in CA 19-20
McCreery, Charles (Anthony Selby) 1942- 25-28R
McCreigh, James
See Pohl, Frederik
McCrimmon, Barbara (Smith) 1918- 108
McCrimmon, James M(cNab) 1908- 9-12R
McCrindle, Joseph F(eder) 1923- 29-32R
McCrohan, Donna 1947- 111
McCrone, John (Robert) 1957- 139
McCrone, Kathleen E. 1941- 130
McCrorey, Sanders
See Counselman, Mary Elizabeth
McCrorie, Edward (P.) 1936- 153
McCrory, Moy (Ellen) 1953- 130
McCroskey, James C(layborne) 1936- CANR-13
Earlier sketch in CA 77-80
McCrossen, V(incent) A(loysius) 1918- 53-56
McCrosson, Doris Ross 1923- 17-20R
McCrum, Robert 1953- 101
McCrumb, Sharyn 168
See also AAYA 27
McCuaig, Ronald 1908- 114
McCue, Frances 1962- 139
McCue, George R(obert) 1910- 110
McCue, Lillian Bueno 1902-1993 CANR-63
Obituary 142
Earlier sketches in CA 1-4R, CANR-2
McCue, Lisa (Emiline) 1959- 136
See also SATA 65
McCuen, Jo Ray 1929- 85-88
McCuen, John J(oachim) 1926- 21-24R
McCullagh, Joseph B. 1842-1896 DLB 23
McCullagh, Sheila K(athleen) 1920- 110
McCullagh, Suzanne Folds 1951- 127
McCullar, Michael 1951- 122
McCullers, (Lula) Carson (Smith) 1917-1967
CANR-18
Obituary 25-28R
Earlier sketch in CA 5-8R
See also CABS 1, 3
See also AAYA 21
See also CDALB 1941-1968
See also CLC 1, 4, 10, 12, 48, 100
See also DA
See also DAB
See also DAC
See also DAM MST, NOV
See also DLB 2, 7, 173
See also MTCW 1
See also SATA 27
See also SSC 9, 24
See also WLC
McCulley, Johnston 1883-1958 Brief entry 115
McCullin, Don(ald) 1935- 141
Brief entry 106
McCulloch, Alan McLeod 1907- 104
McCulloch, Derek (Ivor Breashur)
1897-1967 Obituary 109
See also SATA-Obit 29
McCulloch, Frank E(liot) 1898- 112
McCulloch, John I(rvin) B(eggs)
1909(?)-1983 Obituary 110
McCulloch, John Tyler
See Burroughs, Edgar Rice
McCulloch, Joseph 1908-1990 Obituary 131
McCulloch, Sarah
See Ure, Jean
McCulloch, Thomas 1776-1843 DLB 99
McCulloch, Warren S(turgis) 1898-1969 CAP-2
Earlier sketch in CA 21-22
McCulloh, William Ezra 1931- 49-52
McCullough, Bonnie Runyan 1944- CANR-18
Earlier sketch in CA 102
McCullough, Colleen 1938(?)- CANR-67
Earlier sketches in CA 81-84, CANR-17, 46
See also CLC 27, 107
See also DAM NOV, POP
See also MTCW 1
McCullough, Constance Mary 1912- CANR-5
Earlier sketch in CA 1-4R
McCullough, Dale Richard 1933- 125
McCullough, David (Gaub) 1933- CANR-53
Earlier sketches in CA 49-52, CANR-2, 31
See also SATA 62
McCullough, David Willis 1937- 143
McCullough, Donald W. 1949- 130
McCullough, Edo
See McCullough, Edward Joseph Tilyou
McCullough, Edward Joseph Tilyou
1901(?)-1987 Obituary 123
McCullough, Frances Monson 1938- 41-44R
See also SATA 8
McCullough, Helen Craig 1918- 151
McCullough, John Gerard 1917-1984 Obituary 111
McCullough, Ken(neth Douglas) 1943- CANR-22
Earlier sketch in CA 45-48
McCullough, W. S.
See McCullough, W(illiam) Stewart
McCullough, W(illiam) Stewart 1902-1982 21-24R
Obituary 135
McCully, Emily Arnold
See Arnold, Emily
See also CLR 46
See also SAAS 7
See also SATA 5
McCully, Ethel Walbridge 1896-1980 Obituary 103
McCully, Helen 1902(?)-1977 81-84
Obituary 73-76
McCully, Robert (Stephen) 1921- 53-56
McCune, Dan
See Haas, Dorothy F.
McCune, Shannon (Boyd-Bailey) 1913-1993
CANR-46
Obituary 140
Earlier sketches in CA 77-80, CANR-13
McCunn, Ruthanne Lum 1946- CANR-43
Earlier sketch in CA 119
See also SATA 63
McCurdy, Charles Robert 1926- 5-8R
McCurdy, Frances Lea 1906- 41-44R
McCurdy, Harold Grier 1909- CANR-7
Earlier sketch in CA 17-20R
McCurdy, Howard E(arl) 1941- 81-84
McCurdy, Jack 1933- 69-72
McCurdy, Michael 1942- CANR-50
Earlier sketches in CA 69-72, CANR-25
See also SATA 13, 82
McCurley, Foster R., Jr. 1937- 134
Brief entry 107
McCusker, John J(ames) 1939- 102
McCutchan, J(ohn) Wilson 1909- 5-8R
McCutchan, Philip (Donald) 1920- CANR-66
Earlier sketches in CA 9-12R, CANR-5, 22, 46
McCutchen, Samuel Proctor 1909-1966 CAP-1
Earlier sketch in CA 9-10
McCutcheon, Elsie (Mary Jackson) 1937- 133
See also SATA 60
McCutcheon, Hugh Davie-Martin 1909- CANR-5
Earlier sketch in CA 9-12R
McCutcheon, James
See Lundgren, Paul Arthur
McCutcheon, James M(iller) 1932- 45-48
McCutcheon, John 1952- 164
See also SATA 97
McCutcheon, John Tinney, Jr. 1917- 69-72
McCutcheon, Lynn E(llis) 1944- 57-60
McCutcheon, W(illiam) A(lan) 1934- 53-56
McCutcheon, W(illiam) J(ohn) 1928- 41-44R
McDade, Thomas M. 1907- CAP-1
Earlier sketch in CA 13-16
McDaniel, Becky Bring 1953- 117
See also SATA 61
McDaniel, C. Yates 1907(?)-1983 Obituary 109
McDaniel, David (Edward) 1939-1977 CANR-10
Earlier sketch in CA 21-24R
McDaniel, Elsiebeth 65-68
McDaniel, Eugene B(arker) 1931- 65-68
McDaniel, George William 1944- 116
McDaniel, Gerald G(reen) 1945- 122
McDaniel, Herman 1938- 111
McDaniel, John N(oble) 1941- 57-60
McDaniel, Joseph Milton, Jr.
1902-1980 Obituary 97-100
McDaniel, Lurlene 1944- 148
See also AAYA 15
See also SATA 71
McDaniel, Roderick D. 1927- 37-40R
McDaniel, Ruel 1896- CAP-1
Earlier sketch in CA 13-14
McDaniel, Walton Brooks 1871-1978 77-80
Obituary 81-84
McDaniels, Carl 1930- 93-96
McDarrah, Fred W(illiam) 1926- CANR-49
Earlier sketches in CA 81-84, CANR-24
McDavid, John E., Jr. 1934- 37-40R
McDavid, John W(alter, Jr.) 1933- 41-44R
McDavid, Raven I(oor), Jr. 1911-1984 41-44R
Obituary 114
McDavid, Virginia (Glenn) 1926- 37-40R
McDearmon, Kay CANR-11
Earlier sketch in CA 69-72
See also SATA 20
McDermott, A(gnes) Charlene Senape 1937- 77-80
McDermott, Alice 1953- CANR-40
Earlier sketch in CA 109
See also CLC 90
McDermott, Beatrice Schmulling 17-20R
McDermott, Beverly Brodsky 1941- CANR-16
Earlier sketch in CA 65-68
See also SATA 11
McDermott, Catherine 1952- 125
McDermott, Charles J(ames) 1905- CAP-1
Earlier sketch in CA 13-16
McDermott, Geoffrey (Lyster) 1912- 73-76
McDermott, Gerald 1941- 85-88
See also AITN 2
See also CLR 9
See also MAICYA
See also SATA 16, 74
McDermott, John F(rancis), Jr. 1929- Brief
entry 114
McDermott, John Francis (III) 1902-1981 CANR-6
Earlier sketch in CA 5-8R
McDermott, John J(oseph) 1932- 73-76
McDermott, John R(alph)
1921-1977 Obituary 69-72
McDermott, Michael 1962- SATA 76
McDermott, Robert
See Hawley, Donald Thomas
McDermott, Robert A(nthony) 1939- 57-60
McDermott, Sister Maria Concepta 1913- 17-20R
McDermott, Thomas J. 1915- 9-12R
McDermott, Walsh 1909-1981 Obituary 105
McDevitt, Jack 1935- 149
McDevitt, John Charles 1935-
See McDevitt, Jack
See also SATA 94
McDill, Edward L. 1930- 77-80
McDole, Carol
See Farley, Carol
McDollu, Michael A. 1946- DLBY 87
McDonagh, Don(ald Francis) 1932- CANR-1
Earlier sketch in CA 49-52
McDonagh, Enda 1930- 101
McDonagh, John Michael 1944- 109
McDonald, Alan (Patrick) 1949- 124
McDonald, Angus Henry
1904(?)-1990 Obituary 130
McDonald, Angus W(illiam), Jr. 1941- 105
McDonald, Archie P(hilip) 1935- CANR-15
Earlier sketch in CA 81-84
McDonald, Christie (V.) 1942- 144
McDonald, Claude C(omstock), Jr. 1925- 29-32R
McDonald, Collin 1943- 148
See also SATA 79
McDonald, David J(ohn) 1902-1979 45-48
Obituary 125
McDonald, Dianna
See Shomaker, Dianna
McDonald, Elvin 1937- CANR-34
Earlier sketches in CA 5-8R, CANR-8
McDonald, Erwin L(awrence) 1907- 73-76
McDonald, Eva (Rose) CANR-6
Earlier sketch in CA 13-16R
McDonald, Forrest 1927- CANR-5
Earlier sketch in CA 9-12R
See also DLB 17
McDonald, Frank J(ames) 1941- 97-100
McDonald, Gerald D(oan) 1905-1970 CAP-1
Earlier sketch in CA 11-12
See also SATA 3
Mcdonald, Gregory (Christopher) 1937- CANR-42
Earlier sketches in CA 5-8R, CANR-3
McDonald, Hugh C(hisholm) 1913- 65-68
McDonald, Hugh Dermot 1910- CANR-3
Earlier sketch in CA 9-12R
McDonald, Ian A(rchie) 1933- CANR-52
Earlier sketches in CA 29-32R, CANR-26
McDonald, Iverach 1908- 138
McDonald, J. I(an) H. 1933- 148
McDonald, James Robert 1934- 41-44R
McDonald, Jamie
See Heide, Florence Parry
McDonald, Jerry N(ealon) 1944- CANR-31
Earlier sketch in CA 105
McDonald, Jill (Masefield) 1927-1982 CANR-12
Obituary 105
Earlier sketch in CA 65-68
See also SATA 13
See also SATA-Obit 29
McDonald, John D(ennis) 1906- CAP-2
Earlier sketch in CA 19-20
McDonald, Joyce 1946- 168
See also SATA 101
McDonald, Julie 1929- CANR-43
Earlier sketches in CA 29-32R, CANR-12
McDonald, Julie Jensen
See McDonald, Julie
McDonald, Kay L(aureen) 1934- 57-60
McDonald, Lee Cameron 1925- 5-8R
McDonald, Linda 1939- CANR-4
Earlier sketch in CA 49-52
McDonald, Lucile Saunders 1898- CANR-18
Earlier sketches in CA 1-4R, CANR-4
See also SATA 10
McDonald, (Mary) Lynn 1940- 101
McDonald, Mary Ann 1956- SATA 84
McDonald, Mary Reynolds 1888- CAP-1
Earlier sketch in CA 13-16
McDonald, Megan 1959- 135
See also SATA 67, 99

McDonald, Mercedes 1956- 164
See also SATA 97
McDonald, Nicholas 1923- 13-16R
McDonald, Paula 1939(?)- .... AITN 1
McDonald, Pauline 1907- 33-36R
McDonald, (Duncan) Peter 1962- 124
McDonald, Richard C. 1935(?)- .... AITN 1
McDonald, Robert 1943- 115
McDonald, Roger 1941- 101
McDonald, Stephen L(ee) 1924- 89-92
McDonald, Walter (Robert) 1934- CANR-58
Earlier sketches in CA 73-76, CANR-12, 31
See also DLB 105
See also DLBD 9
McDonald, William Andrew 1913- 41-44R
McDonald, William Francis 1898-1976 ..... 37-40R
McDonald, William U(lma), Jr. 1927- 17-20R
McDonell, J. M. 149
McDonnell, Christine 1949- CANR-23
Earlier sketch in CA 107
See also SATA 34
McDonnell, Flora (Mary) 1963- ....SATA 90
McDonnell, Helen M(argaret) 1923- CANR-13
Earlier sketch in CA 33-36R
McDonnell, Jinny
See McDonnell, Virginia B(leecker)
McDonnell, Kilian (Perry) 1921- CANR-34
Earlier sketch in CA 33-36R
McDonnell, Lois Eddy 1914- 5-8R
See also SATA 10
McDonnell, Rea 1942- 127
McDonnell, Robert F. 1928- 17-20R
McDonnell, Virginia B(leecker) 1917- CANR-8
Earlier sketch in CA 21-24R
McDonogh, Gary Wray 1952- 127
McDonough, George Edward 1924- 41-44R
McDonough, Jack 1944- 125
McDonough, James Lee 1934- 73-76
McDonough, James R(ichard) 1946- 146
McDonough, Jerome 1946- CANR-27
Earlier sketch in CA 109
McDonough, Jerry
See McDonough, Jerome
McDonough, Kaye 1943- .... CAAS 29
McDonough, Nancy 1935- 57-60
McDonough, Peter 1939- 138
McDonough, Sheila 1928- 77-80
McDonough, Thomas E(dmund) 1929- 21-24R
McDonough, William K. 1900- CAP-1
Earlier sketch in CA 9-10
McDonough, Yona Zeldis 1957- .... SATA 73
McDormand, Thomas Bruce 1904- CAP-1
Earlier sketch in CA 19-20
McDougal, Myres Smith 1906- CANR-6
Earlier sketch in CA 5-8R
McDougal, Stan
See Diamant, Lincoln
McDougal, Stuart Y(eatman) 1942- CANR-13
Earlier sketch in CA 73-76
McDougall, Anne 1926- 104
McDougall, Bonnie S. 1941- 127
McDougall, Colin (Malcolm) 1917-1984 153
See also DLB 68
McDougall, Donald 1907- 81-84
McDougall, Gay J. 1947- 155
McDougall, John Lorne 1900- 37-40R
McDougall, Joyce 1926- CANR-36
Earlier sketches in CA 25-28R, CANR-11
McDougall, Marina 1945- 97-100
McDougall, Walter A(llan) 1946- 126
Brief entry 121
Interview in 126
McDow, Gerald
See Scortia, Thomas N(icholas)
McDowall, Robert William 1914-1987 Obituary . 123
McDowall, Roddy 1928-1998 167
McDowell, (Ho)Bart (Kelliston, Jr.) 1923- ... 25-28R
McDowell, Charles (Rice), Jr. 1926- 1-4R
McDowell, Crosby
See Freeman, John Crosby
McDowell, David 1918(?)-1985 Obituary 115
McDowell, Dimmes 1925(?)-1976 Obituary ... 69-72
McDowell, Edward Allison, Jr. 1898- CAP-2
Earlier sketch in CA 21-22
McDowell, Edwin (Stewart) 1935- 9-12R
McDowell, Elizabeth Tibbals 1912- 5-8R
McDowell, Frank 1911- 53-56
McDowell, Frederick P(eter) W(oll) 1915- .. CANR-5
Earlier sketch in CA 1-4R
McDowell, Gary L. 1949- 145
McDowell, John (Henry) 1942- 103
McDowell, John Holmes 1946- 97-100
McDowell, Margaret B(laine) 1923- 69-72
McDowell, Michael 1950- CANR-29
Earlier sketch in CA 93-96
McDowell, Michael P(aul) Kube
See Kube-McDowell, Michael P(aul)
McDowell, Robert 1953- 127
McDowell, Robert Emmett 1914-1975 .... 1-4R
Obituary 103
McDowell, Virginia (Duncan) H(ecker) 1933- .. 85-88
McEachern, Theodore 1928- 21-24R
McEachin, James 160
McElaney, (Joseph) Paul 1922- 9-12R
McElderry, Bruce R., Jr. 1900-1970 .... CAP-1
Earlier sketch in CA 13-14
McEldowney, (Richard) Dennis 1926- 103
McEldowney, Eugene 1943- 158
McEleney, Neil Joseph 1927- 115
McElfresh, (Elizabeth) Adeline 1918- 1-4R
McElhaney, James W(illson) 1937- 85-88
McElhanon, K(enneth) A(ndrew) 1939- CANR-5
Earlier sketch in CA 53-56
McEllhenney, John Galen 1934- 53-56
McElmeel, Sharron L. 1942- 145
McElrath, Damian (Edmund) 1928- Brief entry .. 111
McElrath, Dennis Cornealius 1929- 45-48
McElrath, Joseph R(ichard), Jr. 1945- 65-68
McElrath, William N. 1932- CANR-35
Earlier sketch in CA 77-80
See also SATA 65
McElrath-Eslick, Lori 1960- ....SATA 96
McElroy, Bernard (Patrick, Jr.) 1938-1991 61-64
Obituary 136
McElroy, Colleen J(ohnson) 1935- CANR-38
Earlier sketches in CA 49-52, CANR-2, 17
See also CAAS 21
See also BW 2
McElroy, Davis Dunbar 1917- 37-40R
McElroy, Elam E. 1922- 57-60
McElroy, John Alexander 1913- 17-20R
McElroy, Joseph 1930- 17-20R
See also CLC 5, 47
McElroy, Lee
See Kelton, Elmer
McElroy, Paul Simpson 1902- 5-8R
McElroy, Thomas P(arker), Jr. 1914- 73-76
McElroy, Wendy 152
McElvaine, Robert S(tuart) 1947- 114
McElwee, William (Lloyd) 1907-1979 57-60
Obituary 104
McEnery, John H. 1925- 134
McEnroe, Colin (Welles) 1954- 127
McEntee, Dorothy (Layng) 1902- ....SATA 37
McEntire, Reba (Nell) 1954(?)- 147
McEvedy, Colin (Peter) 1930- 97-100
McEvilley, Thomas 1939- 140
McEvoy, Dennis 1918- 73-76
McEvoy, Harry K(irby) 1910- 17-20R
McEvoy, Hubert 1899- 5-8R
McEvoy, James III 1940-1976 .... CAP-2
Earlier sketch in CA 33-36
McEvoy, Marjorie Harte CANR-40
Earlier sketches in CA 5-8R, CANR-2, 18
McEwan, Barbara 1926- 139
McEwan, Ian (Russell) 1948- CANR-69
Earlier sketches in CA 61-64, CANR-14, 41
See also BEST 90:4
See also CLC 13, 66
See also DAM NOV
See also DLB 14, 194
See also MTCW 1
McEwan, Jenny 1951- 124
McEwan, Keith 1926- 21-24R
McEwan, (John) Neil 1946- 130
McEwan, Peter J(ames) M(ichael) 1924- . CANR-17
Earlier sketch in CA 25-28R
McEwen, Christian 1956- 162
McEwen, Robert (Lindley) 1926-1980 Obituary . 101
See also SATA-Obit 23
McFadden, Charles Joseph 1909- 77-80
McFadden, Cyra 1937- 77-80
McFadden, David 1940- 104
Interview in 104
See also CLC 48
See also DLB 60
McFadden, Dorothy Loa 1902- 17-20R
McFadden, George 1916- 111
McFadden, James A., Jr. 1913- 17-20R
McFadden, Kevin Christopher 1961(?)- ... CANR-66
Earlier sketch in CA 136
See also AAYA 13
See also CLR 29
See also JRDA
See also SATA 68
McFadden, Maggie
See McFadden, Margaret
McFadden, Margaret 1941- 115
McFadden, Robert D(ennis) 1937- CANR-15
Earlier sketch in CA 85-88
McFadden, Roy 1921- 144
Brief entry 111
McFadden, Steven (S. H.) 1948- 138
McFadden, Thomas M(ore) 1935- 89-92
McFadyean, Melanie 1950- 127
McFague, Sallie 1933- CANR-11
Earlier sketch in CA 21-24R
McFall, Christie 1918- 5-8R
See also SATA 12
McFall, Frances Elizabeth Clarke
See Grand, Sarah
McFarlan, Donald M(aitland) 1915- CANR-10
Earlier sketch in CA 65-68
See also SATA 59
McFarlan, F. Warren 1937- 17-20R
McFarland, Andrew S(tuart) 1940- CANR-13
Earlier sketch in CA 25-28R
McFarland, C(harles) K(eith) 1934- 29-32R
McFarland, Carl 1904-1979 Obituary 85-88
McFarland, Dalton E(dward) 1919- CANR-2
Earlier sketch in CA 5-8R
McFarland, Dennis 1950- 165
See also CLC 65
McFarland, Dorothy Tuck 1938- 9-12R
McFarland, Ernest W(illiam)
1894-1984 Obituary 114
McFarland, Gerald Ward 1938- 85-88
McFarland, John 1943- 116
McFarland, Keith D(onavon) 1940- 57-60
McFarland, Kenton D(ean) 1920- 61-64
See also SATA 11
McFarland, M(alcolm) Carter 1912- 85-88
McFarland, Marvin W(ilks) 1919-1985 Obituary . 115
McFarland, Philip (James) 1930- CANR-12
Earlier sketch in CA 73-76
McFarland, Ron(ald Earl) 1942- CANR-69
Earlier sketches in CA 113, CANR-32
McFarland, Ross A(rmstrong) 1901- CAP-2
Earlier sketch in CA 21-22
McFarland, Stephen L. 1950- 139
McFarland, Thomas (Alfred, Jr.) 1926- 41-44R
McFarlane, Alexander C. 1952- 157
McFarlane, Brian 1931- 122
McFarlane, Bruce John 1936- CANR-16
Earlier sketch in CA 81-84
McFarlane, I(an) D(alrymple) 1915- 107
McFarlane, James Walter 1920- CANR-5
Earlier sketch in CA 1-4R
McFarlane, K. B. 1903-1966 Obituary 114
McFarlane, Leslie (Charles) 1902-1977 .. CANR-37
Earlier sketch in CA 112
See also DLB 88
See also MAICYA
See also SATA 31
McFarlane, Peter (William) 1940- 160
See also SATA 95
McFarlane, Sheryl P. 1954- .... SATA 86
McFate, Patricia Ann 1932- 103
McFather, Nelle 1936- CANR-4
Earlier sketch in CA 49-52
McFeat, Tom Farrar Scott 1919- 103
McFee, J. Scott
See Johnson, Don
McFee, June King 1917- CANR-16
Earlier sketch in CA 81-84
McFee, Michael 1954- CANR-57
Earlier sketches in CA 112, CANR-30
McFee, Oonah 1922- 116
McFee, William (Morley Punshon)
1881-1966 Obituary 116
See also DLB 153
McFeely, Mary Drake 1932- CANR-27
Earlier sketch in CA 110
McFeely, William S(hield) 1930- CANR-50
Earlier sketches in CA 33-36R, CANR-15
McFerran, Ann
See Townsend, Doris McFerran
McFerran, Doris
See Townsend, Doris McFerran
McFerran, Douglass David 1934- 65-68
McGaa, Ed 1936- 97-100
McGaffin, William 1910-1975 .... CAP-2
Earlier sketch in CA 25-28
McGahan, Andrew 1967- 168
McGahern, John 1934- CANR-68
Earlier sketches in CA 17-20R, CANR-29
See also CLC 5, 9, 48
See also DLB 14
See also MTCW 1
See also SSC 17
McGahey, Michael J(oseph) 1948- 116
McGann, George T(homas) 1913- 93-96
McGann, Jerome J(ohn) 1937- CANR-14
Earlier sketches in CA 45-48, CANR-1
McGann, Michael
See Naha, Ed
McGann, Thomas F. 1920- 13-16R
McGannon, J(ohn) Barry 1924- 13-16R
McGarey, Gladys T(aylor) 1920- 57-60
McGarey, William A. 1919- 57-60
McGarrigle, Francis Joseph 1888- 5-8R
McGarrity, Mark 1943- CANR-63
Earlier sketches in CA 45-48, CANR-1, 17, 37
McGarry, Daniel D(oyle) 1907- CAP-1
Earlier sketch in CA 11-12
McGarry, Jean 1952- 126
McGarry, Kevin J(ohn) 1935- 102
McGarry, Michael B(rett) 1948- 102
McGarvey, Robert 1948- 113
McGaugh, James L(afayette) 1931- CANR-7
Earlier sketch in CA 57-60
McGaughey, (Florence) Helen 1904- 37-40R
McGaughey, Neil 1951- CANR-70
Earlier sketch in CA 152
McGavin, E(lmer) Cecil 1900- CAP-1
Earlier sketch in CA 11-12
McGavran, Donald (Anderson)
1897-1990(?) 13-16R
Obituary 132
McGaw, Charles James 1910-1978 Obituary ... 106
McGaw, Jessie Brewer 1913- 1-4R
See also SATA 10
McGaw, Naomi Blanche Thoburn 1920- 9-12R
McGaw, William C(ochran) 1914- 101
McGeachy, D(aniel) P(atrick) III 1929- CANR-8
Earlier sketch in CA 61-64
McGear, Mike
See McCartney, Peter Michael
McGee, Barbara 1943- 25-28R
See also SATA 6
McGee, (Doctor) Frank 1921-1974 105
Obituary 89-92
McGee, Harold 1951- 118
McGee, Mark
See McGee, Mark T(homas)
McGee, Mark T(homas) 1947- 134
McGee, Reece (Jerome) 1929- CANR-17
Earlier sketches in CA 5-8R, CANR-2
McGee, Robert W(illiam) 1947- 112
McGee, Spike
See Moody, Fred
McGee, T. D.
See Savage, Teresa
McGee, T(erence) G(ary) 1936- CANR-10
Earlier sketch in CA 21-24R
McGee, Thomas D'Arcy 1825-1868 ....DLB 99
McGee, Victor (Errol) 1935- 41-44R
McGeehan, Robert 1933- 33-36R
McGeehan, W. O. 1879-1933 .... DLB 25, 171
McGeeney, Patrick John 1918- 5-8R
McGeezer, Mark
See McGee, Mark T(homas)
McGehee, Nicole 1956- 141
McGehee, Ralph W(alter) 1928- 112
McGeown, Patrick 1897- CAP-2
Earlier sketch in CA 23-24
McGerr, Patricia 1917-1985 .... CANR-61
Obituary 116
Earlier sketches in CA 1-4R, CANR-1
See also AITN 1
McGhan, Barry (Robert) 1939- 69-72
McGhee, George (Crews) 152
McGhie, Andrew 1926- 97-100
McGiffert, Michael 1928- 13-16R
McGiffert, Robert C(arnahan) 1922- 49-52
McGiffin, (Lewis) Lee (Shaffer) 1908- CAP-1
Earlier sketch in CA 13-16
See also SATA 1
McGilchrist, Iain 1953- 132
McGill, Dan M(ays) 1919- 134
Brief entry 107
McGill, Ian
See Allegro, John Marco
McGill, Leonard J(ames) 1956- 115
McGill, Ormond 1913- CANR-58
Earlier sketches in CA 49-52, CANR-2
See also SATA 92
McGill, Ralph (Emerson) 1898-1969 ....5-8R
Obituary 25-28R
See also DLB 29
McGill, Thomas E(merson) 1930- 17-20R
McGilligan, Patrick (Michael) 1951- CANR-10
Earlier sketch in CA 65-68
McGilvery, Laurence 1932- 33-36R
McGimsey, Charles Robert III 1925- 37-40R
McGinley, Patrick (Anthony) 1937- CANR-56
Brief entry 120
Earlier sketch in CA 127
Interview in 127
See also CLC 41
McGinley, Phyllis 1905-1978 .... CANR-19
Obituary 77-80
Earlier sketch in CA 9-12R
See also CLC 14
See also DLB 11, 48
See also SATA 2, 44
See also SATA-Obit 24
McGinn, Bernard John 1937- 113
McGinn, Donald Joseph 1905- CAP-2
Earlier sketch in CA 23-24
McGinn, Elinor Myers 1923- 149
McGinn, John T. 1900(?)-1972 Obituary 33-36R
McGinn, Matt 1928-1977 106
McGinn, Maureen Ann
See Sautel, Maureen Ann
McGinn, Noel F(rancis) 1934- 73-76
McGinn, Richard 1939- 126
McGinnies, Elliott M(orse) 1921- 77-80
McGinnies, W(illiam) G(rovenor) 1899- CANR-7
Earlier sketch in CA 57-60
McGinnis, Bruce 1941- 97-100
McGinnis, Dorothy Jean 1920- 29-32R
McGinnis, Duane
See Niatum, Duane
McGinnis, K. K.
See Page, Grover, Jr.
McGinnis, Lila S(prague) 1924- 93-96
See also SATA 44
McGinnis, Marilyn 1939- 57-60
McGinnis, Robert 1927- 45-48
McGinnis, Thomas C(harles) 1925-1987 65-68
Obituary 123
McGinniss, Joe 1942- CANR-70
Earlier sketches in CA 25-28R, CANR-26
Interview in CANR-26
See also AITN 2
See also BEST 89:2
See also CLC 32
See also DLB 185
McGirk, Tim(othy Stephen) 1952- 136
McGirt, Dan(iel) 1967- 155
McGirt, James E(phraim) 1874-1930 153
See also BW 2
See also DLB 50
McGivering, John H. 1923- 25-28R
McGivern, Maureen Daly
See Daly, Maureen
McGivern, William P(eter) 1922-1982 .... CANR-62
Obituary 108
Earlier sketches in CA 49-52, CANR-7
McGlade, Francis S(tanley) 1930- 41-44R
McGlamry, Beverly 1932- CANR-43
Earlier sketch in CA 119
McGlashan, Alan (Fleming) 1898-1997 ..... 41-44R
Obituary 158
McGlennon, John J(oseph) 1949- 119
McGlinchee, Claire CAP-2
Earlier sketch in CA 23-24
McGlinn, Dwight
See Brannon, William T.
McGloin, John Bernard 1912- 33-36R
McGloin, Joseph T(haddeus) 1917- CANR-39
Earlier sketches in CA 1-4R, CANR-1, 18
McGlone, Edward Leon 1941- Brief entry 108
McGlothlen, Ronald L(ee) 1947- 143
McGlothlin, William J(oseph) 1908- CAP-2
Earlier sketch in CA 19-20
McGlynn, Christopher
See Ginder, Richard
McGlynn, James V(incent) 1919-1973 .... 1-4R
Obituary 103
McGoey, John Heck 1915- CANR-21
Earlier sketches in CA 9-12R, CANR-6
McGoldrick, Desmond Francis 1919- 17-20R
McGoldrick, Edward J., Jr. 1909-1967 ...... CAP-1
Earlier sketch in CA 19-20
McGoldrick, Joseph D. 1901-1978 Obituary . 97-100
McGoldstein, Paddy
See Page, William
McGonigle, Thomas 1944- 137
McGoogan, Ken 1947- 144
McGoon, Clifford D. 1939- 113

McGough, Elizabeth (Hemmes) 1934- 107
See also SATA 33
McGough, Roger 1937- CANR-44
Earlier sketch in CA 105
See also DLB 40
McGovern, Ann 1930- CANR-44
Earlier sketches in CA 49-52, CANR-2
See also CLR 50
See also MAICYA
See also SAAS 17
See also SATA 8, 69, 70
McGovern, Arthur F(rancis) 1929- CANR-40
Earlier sketch in CA 116
McGovern, Constance M(adeline) 1938- 120
McGovern, George S(tanley) 1922- CANR-63
Earlier sketches in CA 45-48, CANR-8
McGovern, James (Walter) 1923-1989 .... CANR-7
Obituary 129
Earlier sketch in CA 17-20R
McGovern, James R(ichard) 1928- 108
McGovern, John P(hillip) 1921- CANR-44
Earlier sketches in CA 21-24R, CANR-13
McGovern, Robert 1927- CANR-28
Earlier sketch in CA 49-52
McGowan, Jack 1896(?)-1977 Obituary 69-72
McGowan, James A(lfred) 1932- 97-100
McGowan, Joe A., Jr.
See McGowan, Joseph A., Jr.
McGowan, John J. 1936(?)-1982 Obituary 106
McGowan, John P. 1953- 135
McGowan, Joseph A., Jr. 1931- 133
McGowan, Margaret M(ary) 69-72
McGowen, Charles H(ammond) 1936- 69-72
McGowen, Thomas E. 1927- CANR-50
Earlier sketches in CA 21-24R, CANR-8, 25
See also SATA 2
McGowen, Tom
See McGowen, Thomas E.
McGrade, Arthur Stephen 1934- 25-28R
McGrady, Donald Lee 1935- 25-28R
McGrady, Mike 1933- CANR-2
Earlier sketch in CA 49-52
See also SATA 6
McGrady, Patrick M(ichael), Jr. 1932- CANR-12
Earlier sketch in CA 29-32R
McGrady, Patrick Michael Sr. 1908-1980 103
Obituary 97-100
McGrail, Joie 1922(?)-1977 Obituary 69-72
McGrane, Bernard 1947- 133
McGrath, Alice (Greenfield) 1917- 112
McGrath, Alister E(dgar) 1953- 134
Mcgrath, Campbell 1962- 164
McGrath, Dennis 1946- 139
McGrath, Doyle
See Schorb, E(dwin) M(arsh)
McGrath, Eamonn 1929- 139
McGrath, Earl James 1902-1993 .... CAP-1
Obituary 140
Earlier sketch in CA 19-20
McGrath, Edward G(orham) 1917- 25-28R
McGrath, Francis E. 1903(?)-1976 Obituary 61-64
McGrath, J. H. 1923- 29-32R
McGrath, James Bernard, Jr. 1917- 5-8R
McGrath, Joan Rosita (Torr)
1895(?)-1967 Obituary 116
See also Forbes, Rosita
McGrath, John (Peter) 1935- 145
Brief entry 112
McGrath, Kristina 1950- 148
McGrath, Lee Parr 1933- 29-32R
McGrath, Patrick 1950- CANR-65
Earlier sketch in CA 136
See also CLC 55
McGrath, Robert L(ee) 1920- 97-100
McGrath, Roger D. 1947- 118
McGrath, Sean
See Douglas, John (Frederick James)
McGrath, Susan 1955- 121
McGrath, Sylvia Wallace 1937- 61-64
McGrath, Thomas (Matthew) 1916-1990 .... CANR-33
Obituary 132
Earlier sketches in CA 9-12R, CANR-6
See also CLC 28, 59
See also DAM POET
See also MTCW 1
See also SATA 41
See also SATA-Obit 66
McGrath, Tom 1940- 130
McGrath, William J(ames) 1937- 85-88
McGrath, William Thomas 1917- 103
McGratty, Arthur R. 1909-1975 Obituary 53-56
McGraw, Eloise Jarvis 1915- CANR-36
Earlier sketches in CA 5-8R, CANR-4, 19
See also MAICYA
See also SAAS 6
See also SATA 1, 67
McGraw, Erin 1957- 158
McGraw, Harold Whittlesey Sr.
1890(?)-1970 Obituary 29-32R
McGraw, James (Paul) 1913-1977 .... 1-4R
McGraw, James R. 1935- 93-96
McGraw, Walter John, Jr.
1919(?)-1978 Obituary 81-84
McGraw, William Corbin 1916- CANR-36
Earlier sketch in CA 29-32R
See also SATA 3
McGreal, Elizabeth
See Yates, Elizabeth
McGreal, Ian Philip 1919- 77-80
McGreevey, William Paul 1938- CANR-11
Earlier sketch in CA 69-72
McGreevy, Susan Brown 1934- 126
McGregor
See Hurley, Doran
McGregor, Barbara 1959- .... SATA 82
McGregor, Craig 1933- CANR-13
Earlier sketch in CA 21-24R
See also SATA 8
McGregor, Iona 1929- 105
See also SATA 25
McGregor, James H. 1946- 138
McGregor, John C(harles) 1905- CAP-1
Earlier sketch in CA 19-20
McGregor, Malcolm Francis 1910- 45-48
McGregor, Rob Roy, Jr. 1929- 108
McGregor, Tom
See Grant, Graeme
McGrew, William W. 1933- 122
McGrory, Mary 1918- 106
Interview in 106
See also AITN 2
McGuane, Thomas (Francis III) 1939- CANR-49
Earlier sketches in CA 49-52, CANR-5, 24
Interview in CANR-24
See also AITN 2
See also CLC 3, 7, 18, 45
See also DLB 2
See also DLBY 80
See also MTCW 1
McGuckian, Medbh 1950- 143
See also CLC 48
See also DAM POET
See also DLB 40
McGuffey, Alexander Hamilton 1816-1896 .... SATA 60
McGuffey, William Holmes 1800-1873 .... DLB 42
McGuffie, Tom H(enderson) 1902- CAP-2
Earlier sketch in CA 19-20
McGuffin, Mark
See McGee, Mark T(homas)
McGuigan, Dorothy Gies 1914-1982 .... CANR-11
Earlier sketch in CA 21-24R
McGuigan, F(rank) J(oseph) 1924- CANR-8
Earlier sketch in CA 5-8R
McGuinness, Arthur E(dward) 1936- 25-28R
McGuire, Don 1919-1979 167
McGuire, E(dward) Patrick 1932- 25-28R
McGuire, Edna 1899- CANR-2
Earlier sketch in CA 5-8R
See also SATA 13
McGuire, Frances Margaret (Cheadle) CAP-1
Earlier sketch in CA 9-10
McGuire, James Dean 1936- 21-24R
McGuire, Jerry 1934- 93-96
McGuire, Joseph William 1925- 9-12R
McGuire, Leslie (Sarah) 1945- CANR-69
Earlier sketch in CA 107
See also SATA 52, 94
See also SATA-Brief 45
McGuire, Martin C. 1933- 37-40R
McGuire, Martin Rawson Patrick
1897-1969 Obituary 111
McGuire, Meredith Anne (Black) 1944- 118
McGuire, Michael Terrance 1929- 41-44R
McGuire, Richard L(en) 1940- 57-60
McGuire, Robert G. (III)
1938(?)-1975 Obituary 61-64
McGuire, Thomas (Vertin) 1945- 73-76
McGuire, Thomas G. 1950- 111
McGuire, William 1917- 143
McGuirk, Bernard 1949- 129
McGurk, Patrick (Maurice) 1928- 118
McGurk, Slater
See Roth, Arthur J(oseph)
McGurn, Barrett 1914- CANR-1
Earlier sketch in CA 1-4R
McGurn, James (Edward) 1953- 136
McGurn, William 1958- 126
McGwire, Michael 1924- 128
McHale, John 1922-1978 .... CANR-17
Earlier sketch in CA 61-64
McHale, Philip John 1928- 103
McHale, Tom 1942(?)-1982 77-80
Obituary 106
See also AITN 1
See also CLC 3, 5
McHale, Vincent E(dward) 1939- 112
McHam, David 1933- 73-76
McHaney, Thomas L(afayette) 1936- CANR-24
Earlier sketches in CA 65-68, CANR-9
McHarg, Ian L(ennox) 1920- CANR-66
Earlier sketch in CA 29-32R
McHargue, Georgess 1941- CANR-24
Earlier sketch in CA 25-28R
See also CLR 2
See also JRDA
See also SAAS 5
See also SATA 4, 77
McHenry, Dean E(ugene) 1910-1998 109
Obituary 167
McHenry, James 1785-1845 .... DLB 202
McHenry, Leemon B. 1956- 140
McHenry, Paul G(raham), Jr. 1924- 61-64
McHugh, Arona (Lipman) 1924-1996 .... 5-8R
Obituary 152
McHugh, Edna 69-72
McHugh, (Berit) Elisabet 1941- CANR-32
Earlier sketch in CA 113
See also SATA 55
See also SATA-Brief 44
McHugh, Heather 1948- CANR-55
Earlier sketches in CA 69-72, CANR-11, 28
McHugh, John (Francis) 1927- 103
McHugh, Leroy 1891(?)-1975 Obituary 104
McHugh, Mary 1928- 85-88
McHugh, Maureen F. 139
McHugh, Maxine Davis
1899(?)-1978 Obituary 77-80
McHugh, P(atrick) J(oseph) 1922- 21-24R
McHugh, Roger Joseph 1908- 5-8R
McHugh, Roland 1945- CANR-10
Earlier sketch in CA 65-68
McHugh, Ruth Nelson
See Nelson, Ruth
McHugh, Stuart
See Rowland, D(onald) S(ydney)
McHugh, Thomas Cannell 1926- 103
McHugh, Tom
See McHugh, Thomas Cannell
McHugh, Vincent 1904-1983 Obituary 109
McIlhany, William H(erbert) II 1951- CANR-6
Earlier sketch in CA 57-60
McIlroy, Thad 1956- 122
McIlvaine, Betsy 1945- 123
McIlvaine, Jane
See McClary, Jane Stevenson
McIlvanney, William 1936- CANR-61
Earlier sketch in CA 25-28R
See also CLC 42
See also DLB 14
McIlwain, Charles Howard 1871-1968 102
McIlwain, David 1921- 109
McIlwain, William (Franklin, Jr.) 1925- CANR-1
Earlier sketch in CA 1-4R
McIlwraith, Jean Newton 1859-1938 .... DLB 92
McIlwraith, Maureen Mollie Hunter
See Hunter, Mollie
See also SATA 2
McInerny, William T(homas) 1932- 124
McInerney, Jay 1955- CANR-68
Brief entry 116
Earlier sketches in CA 123, CANR-45
Interview in 123
See also AAYA 18
See also CLC 34, 112
See also DAM POP
McInerney, Judith W(hitelock) 1945- 118
See also SATA 49
See also SATA-Brief 46
McInerny, Dennis Q(uentin) 1936- 97-100
McInerny, Ralph 1929- CANR-63
Earlier sketches in CA 21-24R, CANR-12, 34
See also SATA 93
McInnes, Edward 1935- 109
McInnes, Graham (Campbell) 1912-1970 .... CAP-2
Earlier sketch in CA 25-28
McInnes, Ian (Andrew Stuart Fraser) 1925- 25-28R
McInnes, Neil 1924- 77-80
McInnis, Edgar Wardwell 1899- 5-8R
McInnis, Noel F. 1936- CANR-14
Earlier sketch in CA 33-36R
McInnis, Raymond G(eorge) 1936- 110
McIntire, C(arl) T(homas) 1939- 130
McIntire, Roger W(arren) 1935- 53-56
McIntosh, Alexander 1947- CANR-2
Earlier sketch in CA 45-48
McIntosh, Carey 1934- 77-80
McIntosh, Christopher 1943- 33-36R
McIntosh, Dave
See McIntosh, David Norman
McIntosh, David Norman 1921- 142
McIntosh, Donal W. 1919- 69-72
McIntosh, Douglas M. 1909- CAP-1
Earlier sketch in CA 13-14
McIntosh, E. 1894(?)-1970 Obituary 104
McIntosh, J. T.
See Macgregor, James (Murdoch)
McIntosh, James (Henry) 1934- 104
McIntosh, John 1930-1970 .... CAP-2
Earlier sketch in CA 21-22
McIntosh, Kinn Hamilton 1930- CANR-58
Earlier sketches in CA 25-28R, CANR-27
McIntosh, Louis
See Johnson, Christopher
McIntosh, Marjorie Keniston 1940- 144
McIntosh, Michael (Scott) 1945- 107
McIntosh, Peter Chisholm 1915- 102
McIntosh, Sandy
See McIntosh, Alexander
McInturff, Roy A(rthur) 1905- 53-56
McIntyre, Dennis 1943(?)-1990 Obituary 130
McIntyre, Ian (James) 1931- 157
McIntyre, James 1827-1906 .... DLB 99
McIntyre, John A(rmin) 1920- 57-60
McIntyre, Kenneth E. 1918- CANR-9
Earlier sketch in CA 21-24R
McIntyre, Lee C(ameron) 1962- 163
McIntyre, Michael P(erry) 1921- 41-44R
McIntyre, O. O. 1884-1938 .... DLB 25
McIntyre, Thomas (Alfred) 1952- 120
McIntyre, Thomas J(ames) 1915- Brief entry 114
McIntyre, Vonda N(eel) 1948- CANR-69
Earlier sketches in CA 81-84, CANR-17, 34
See also CLC 18
See also MTCW 1
McIntyre, W(illiam) David 1932- CANR-51
Earlier sketches in CA 21-24R, CANR-10, 26
McIntyre, William (Alexander) 1916- 37-40R
McIver, J(ohn) R(abie) 1931- 25-28R
McIver, Ray 1913- 25-28R
McIver, Stuart B(etts) 1921- 69-72
McJimsey, George T(ilden) 1936- 93-96
McJimsey, Harriet Tilden 1902- 5-8R
McKain, David W. 1937- CANR-5
Earlier sketch in CA 9-12R
See also CAAS 14
McKale, Donald M(arshall) 1943- CANR-70
Earlier sketches in CA 53-56, CANR-5
McKane, William 1921- 117
McKaughan, Larry (Scott) 1941- 142
See also SATA 75
McKay, Alexander G(ordon) 1924- 37-40R
McKay, (Herbert) Alwyn (Cochrane) 1913- 119
McKay, Arthur R(aymond) 1918- 5-8R
McKay, Claude
See McKay, Festus Claudius
See also BLC 3
See also DAB
See also DLB 4, 45, 51, 117
See also PC 2
See also TCLC 7, 41
McKay, Derek 1942- 81-84
McKay, Don(ald) 1932- 33-36R
McKay, Don 1942- 163
McKay, Donald 1895- .... SATA 45
McKay, Douglas R(ich) 1936- CANR-7
Earlier sketch in CA 57-60
McKay, Ernest A. 1918- 21-24R
McKay, Festus Claudius 1889-1948 124
Brief entry 104
See also McKay, Claude
See also BW 1
See also DA
See also DAC
See also DAM MST, MULT, NOV, POET
See also MTCW 1
See also WLC
McKay, George Frederick 1899-1970 Obituary 106
McKay, Hilary 1959- 156
See also SAAS 23
See also SATA 92
McKay, Jim
See McManus, James Kenneth
McKay, John H(arvey) 1923- Brief entry 115
McKay, John P(atrick) 1938- 29-32R
McKay, Kenneth R.
See Kane, Henry
McKay, Quinn G(unn) 1926- 57-60
McKay, Robert B(udge) 1919-1990 57-60
Obituary 132
McKay, Robert W. 1921- CANR-10
Earlier sketch in CA 13-16R
See also SATA 15
McKay, Ron 1949- 156
McKay, Simon
See Nicole, Christopher (Robin)
McKay, Vernon 1912- 5-8R
McKay, William Paul 1951- 116
McKeachie, Wilbert J(ames) 1921- 21-24R
McKeag, Ernest L(ionel) 1896- CAP-1
Earlier sketch in CA 13-16
McKean, Charles (Alexander) 1946- 137
McKean, Dayton D(avid) 1904- CAP-1
Earlier sketch in CA 19-20
McKean, Gil(bert S.) 1918- 5-8R
McKean, Hugh Ferguson 1908-1995 102
Obituary 148
McKean, John (Maule) 1943- 107
McKean, John Richard 1939- 33-36R
McKean, Keith F. 1915- 37-40R
McKean, Margaret A(nne) 1946- 108
McKean, Robert B. 1943- 135
McKean, Robert C(laud) 1920- 13-16R
McKean, Roland N(eely) 1917- 33-36R
McKean, William V. 1820-1903 .... DLB 23
McKeating, Eileen 1957- .... SATA 81
McKeating, Henry 1932- 37-40R
McKeay, Eileen
See McKeag, Ernest L(ionel)
McKechnie, Paul (Richard) 1957- 137
McKee, Alasdair 1963- 132
McKee, Alexander (Paul Charrier) 1918- CANR-11
Earlier sketch in CA 9-12R
McKee, Barbara H(astings) 1902- 57-60
McKee, Christopher (Fulton) 1935- 77-80
McKee, David (John) 1935- 137
See also CLR 38
See also MAICYA
See also SATA 70
McKee, Edwin D(inwiddie) 1906- 57-60
McKee, Eric
See McKee, J. E. G.
McKee, J. E. G. (?)-1983 Obituary 111
McKee, John DeWitt 1919- 41-44R
McKee, LaVonne L. 1932- 145
McKee, Louis 1951- CANR-46
Earlier sketch in CA 110
McKee, Paul Gordon 1897- CAP-1
Earlier sketch in CA 11-12
McKeefery, William James 1918-1987 Obituary 123
McKeen, William 1954- 145
McKeever, James Ross 1909(?)-1986 Obituary 120
McKeever, Marcia
See Laird, Jean E(louise)
McKelvey, Blake F. 1903- 17-20R
McKelvey, Carole A. 1942- 135
See also SATA 78
McKelvey, James Lee 1934- 45-48
McKelvey, John J(ay), Jr. 1917- CANR-8
Earlier sketch in CA 61-64
McKelvy, Natalie 1950- 138
McKelway, Alexander J(effery) 1932- 13-16R
McKelway, Benjamin M. 1895-1976 Obituary 69-72
McKelway, St. Clair 1905-1980 .... 5-8R
Obituary 93-96
McKemy, Kay 1924- 29-32R
McKendrick, (Hector) Fergus 1933- 115
McKendrick, Melveena (Christine) 1941- CANR-37
Earlier sketches in CA 93-96, CANR-17
See also SATA 55
McKendry, John (Joseph)
1933-1975 Obituary 61-64
McKenna, A. Daniel
See Corson-Finnerty, Adam Daniel
McKenna, Colleen O'Shaughnessy 1948- 143
See also SATA 76
McKenna, Evelyn
See Joscelyn, Archie L.
McKenna, F(rancis) E(ugene)
1921-1978 Obituary 85-88

McKenna, George 1937- CANR-14
Earlier sketch in CA 81-84
McKenna, J(ane) J(essica) 1945- 93-96
McKenna, J(ohn) W(illiam) 1938- 37-40R
McKenna, Marian Cecilia 1926- CANR-22
Earlier sketch in CA 1-4R
McKenna, Michael C(layton) 1947- 116
McKenna, Richard (Milton) 1913-1964 CANR-13
Earlier sketch in CA 5-8R
McKenna, Sister Margaret Mary 1930- 21-24R
McKenna, Sister Mary Lawrence
See McKenna, Sister Margaret Mary
McKenna, Stephen 1888-1967 CAP-1
Earlier sketch in CA 9-10
See also DLB 197
McKenna, Terry 1949- 109
McKenney, Kenneth 1929- 69-72
McKenney, Mary 1946- 61-64
McKenney, Ruth 1911-1972 93-96
Obituary 37-40R
McKennon, Joe
See McKennon, Joseph W(esley)
McKennon, Joseph W(esley) 1907- CANR-2
Earlier sketch in CA 49-52
Mc Kenny, Margaret 73-76
McKenzie, Barbara 1934- 21-24R
McKenzie, Dorothy Clayton 1910-1981 SATA-Obit 28
McKenzie, Doug
See Thomas, Dave
McKenzie, Ellen Kindt 1928- SATA 80
McKenzie, Evan 1951- 148
McKenzie, Garry D(onald) 1941- 41-44R
McKenzie, George W(ashington) 1939- 69-72
McKenzie, John D. 1924- 156
McKenzie, John L(awrence) 1910-1991 9-12R
Obituary 133
McKenzie, Leon R(oy) 1932- 29-32R
McKenzie, Michael 1954- 127
McKenzie, Paige
See Blood, Marje
McKenzie, Robert T(relford) 1917-1981 17-20R
Obituary 105
McKenzie, William P. 1954- 130
McKeon, Richard P(eter) 1900-1985 Obituary 115
McKeon, Zahava Karl 1927- 126
McKeown, Charles 165
McKeown, James E(dward) 1919- 13-16R
McKeown, Thomas 1912-1988 Obituary 125
McKeown, Tom 1937- CANR-20
Earlier sketches in CA 45-48, CANR-2
McKercher, Berneth N(oble) 1915- 53-56
McKern, Leo
See McKern, Reginald
McKern, Reginald 1920- 134
McKern, Sharon S(mith) 1941- 37-40R
McKernan, John J(oseph) 1942- 110
McKernan, John R(ettie), Jr. 1948- 151
McKernan, Victoria 1957- 140
McKerrow, Mary 1915- 132
McKerrow, R. B. 1872-1940 DLB 201
McKersie, R. B.
See McKersie, Robert Bruce
McKersie, Robert Bruce 1929- Brief entry 116
McKhann, Charles Fremont 1930- 112
McKibben, Bill
See McKibben, William (Ernest)
McKibben, William (Ernest) 1960- CANR-66
Earlier sketch in CA 130
McKibbin, Alma E(stelle Baker) 1871-1974 CAP-1
Earlier sketch in CA 19-20
McKibbin, Frank L(owell) 1917- 65-68
McKibbin, Jean 1919- 65-68
McKie, Ronald (Cecil Hamlyn) 1909- CANR-6
Earlier sketch in CA 9-12R
McKillen, Elizabeth 1957- 156
McKillip, Patricia A(nne) 1948- CANR-63
Earlier sketches in CA 49-52, CANR-4, 18
Interview in CANR-18
See also AAYA 14
See also JRDA
See also MTCW 1
See also SATA 30, 80
McKillop, Alan D(ugald) 1892-1974 CAP-1
Obituary 53-56
Earlier sketch in CA 19-20
McKillop, Menzies 1929- 77-80
McKillop, Norman 1892-1974 5-8R
McKillop, Susan Regan 1929- CANR-8
Earlier sketch in CA 61-64
McKim, Audrey Margaret 1909- CANR-4
Earlier sketch in CA 1-4R
See also SATA 47
McKim, Donald K(eith) 1950- CANR-17
Earlier sketch in CA 93-96
McKimmey, James 1923- CANR-22
Earlier sketch in CA 85-88
McKinlay, Brian John 1933- CANR-19
Earlier sketch in CA 103
McKinley, Daniel (Lawson) 1924- 25-28R
McKinley, David Hopwood 1906- CAP-2
Earlier sketch in CA 33-36
McKinley, James (Courtright) 1935- 69-72
McKinley, (Jennifer Carolyn) Robin 1952- CANR-64
Earlier sketches in CA 107, CANR-31
See also AAYA 4
See also CLR 10
See also DLB 52
See also JRDA
See also MAICYA
See also SATA 50, 89
See also SATA-Brief 32
McKinnell, James 1933- CANR-12
Earlier sketch in CA 61-64
McKinnell, Robert Gilmore 1926- 102
McKinney, D. J.
See Cooper, Parley J(oseph)
McKinney, David Walter, Jr. 1920- 37-40R
McKinney, Don(ald Lee) 1923- 73-76
McKinney, Donald 1909- CANR-7
Earlier sketch in CA 57-60
McKinney, Eleanor Ruth 1918- 33-36R
McKinney, Eugene 1922- CANR-15
Earlier sketch in CA 73-76
McKinney, Fred 1908-1981 17-20R
Obituary 135
McKinney, Gene
See McKinney, Eugene
McKinney, George Dallas, Jr. 1932- 5-8R
McKinney, George W(esley), Jr. 1922- 57-60
McKinney, Gordon B(artlett) 1943- 85-88
McKinney, H(enry) Lewis 1935- 41-44R
McKinney, Jack
See Daley, Brian
McKinney, John William 1908- 1-4R
McKinney, Kathleen 1954- 139
McKinney, Meagan 1961- 139
McKinney, Nadine 1938- 155
See also SATA 91
McKinney, Sally (Brown) 1933- 149
McKinney, Virginia (Marie) 1940- 57-60
McKinney, William 1946- 121
McKinnon, Alastair Thomson 1925- 102
McKinnon, James 1932- 128
McKinnon, Robert Scott 1937- 37-40R
McKinnon, Ronald I(an) 1935- 131
McKinsey, Elizabeth 1947- 139
McKinzie, Richard D. 1936- 77-80
McKisack, May 1900-1981 107
Obituary 103
McKissack, Fredrick L(emuel) 1939- CANR-49
Earlier sketch in CA 120
See also SATA 73
See also SATA-Brief 53
McKissack, Patricia (L'Ann) C(arwell) 1944- CANR-38
Earlier sketch in CA 118
See also BW 2
See also CLR 23
See also JRDA
See also MAICYA
See also SATA 51, 73
McKissick, Floyd Bixler 1922-1991 49-52
Obituary 134
McKitrick, Eric Louis 1919- 21-24R
McKittrick, David 1938- 61-64
McKivigan, John R(aymond) 1949- 119
McKnight, Allan Douglas 1918- 104
McKnight, Brian Emerson 1938- 106
McKnight, C. A.
See Russell, Rosalind
McKnight, C(olbert) A(ugustus) 1916-1986 Obituary 120
McKnight, Edgar V(ernon) 1931- 21-24R
McKnight, Gerald 1919- 13-16R
McKnight, John P(roctor) 1908(?)-1987 Obituary 123
McKnight, Linton W. 1942- 159
McKnight, Reginald 129
McKnight, Stephen A. 1944- 143
McKnight, Thomas Lee
See McKnight, Tom Lee
McKnight, Tom Lee 1928- CANR-5
Earlier sketch in CA 9-12R
McKowen, Clark 1929- 41-44R
McKown, Dave Ross 1895- 97-100
McKown, Delos B. 1930- 141
McKown, Robert 1908-1973 Obituary 104
McKown, Robin (?)-1976 CANR-1
Earlier sketch in CA 1-4R
See also SATA 6
McKuen, Rod 1933- CANR-40
Earlier sketch in CA 41-44R
See also AITN 1
See also CLC 1, 3
McKusick, Marshall Bassford 1930- CANR-9
Earlier sketch in CA 13-16R
McLachlan, Alexander 1818-1896 DLB 99
McLachlan, Ian 1938- 69-72
McLaglen, John J.
See Harvey, John (Barton)
McLanathan, Richard 1916- 81-84
McLandress, Herschel
See Galbraith, John Kenneth
McLane, Charles B(ancroft) 1919- 25-28R
McLane, Helen J. CANR-4
Earlier sketch in CA 9-12R
McLane, John R. 1935- 97-100
McLane, Paul Elliott 1907- CAP-1
Earlier sketch in CA 9-10
McLaren, Clemence 1938- 164
McLaren, Colin Andrew 1940- CANR-27
Earlier sketch in CA 106
McLaren, Floris (Marion) Clark 1904-1978 148
See also DLB 68
McLaren, Homer D. 1887- CAP-2
Earlier sketch in CA 29-32
McLaren, Ian A. 1928- 103
McLaren, Ian Francis 1912- CANR-24
Earlier sketch in CA 106
McLaren, John (David) 1932- 29-32R
McLaren, Moray (David Shaw) 1901-1971 103
McLaren, N(orman) Loyall 1892(?)-1977 Obituary 73-76
McLaren, Philip 1943- 168
McLaren, Robert Bruce 1923- 29-32R
McLarey, Myra 1942- 150
McLarry, Newman R(ay) 1923- 13-16R
McLaughlin, Andree N.
See McLaughlin, Andree Nicola
McLaughlin, Andree Nicola 1948- 133
McLaughlin, Ann L. 1928- 135
McLaughlin, Arthur Leo 1921- 17-20R
McLaughlin, Bill
See Phillips, James W.
McLaughlin, Brian P. 1949- 141
McLaughlin, Charles Bernard 1937- 61-64
McLaughlin, Corinne 1947- 147
McLaughlin, Curtis P. 1932- CANR-5
Earlier sketch in CA 53-56
McLaughlin, David J(ohn) 1936- 73-76
McLaughlin, Dean (Jr.) 1931- 9-12R
McLaughlin, Elizabeth Taylor 1923- 93-96
McLaughlin, Emma Maude 1901- 65-68
McLaughlin, Frank 1934- SATA 73
McLaughlin, Jack
See McLaughlin, John Joseph
McLaughlin, John Joseph 1926- CANR-65
Earlier sketch in CA 129
McLaughlin, Joseph 1940- CANR-20
Earlier sketches in CA 45-48, CANR-4
McLaughlin, Joseph F., Jr. 1919-1978 Obituary 77-80
McLaughlin, Kathleen 1898-1990 Obituary 132
McLaughlin, Lorrie (Bell) 1924-1971 CANR-5
Earlier sketch in CA 5-8R
McLaughlin, Michael 1949- 141
McLaughlin, Mignon 9-12R
McLaughlin, Robert (Emmet) 1908-1973 1-4R
Obituary 45-48
McLaughlin, Robert William 1900- 1-4R
McLaughlin, Samuel Clarke 1924- 89-92
McLaughlin, Sister Raymond 1897- 25-28R
McLaughlin, Ted J(ohn) 1921- 13-16R
McLaughlin, Terence (Patrick) 1928- 33-36R
McLaughlin, Virginia Yans
See Yans-McLaughlin, Virginia
McLaughlin, William (DeWitt) 1918- 107
McLaughlin, William Raffian Davidson 1908- CAP-1
Earlier sketch in CA 11-12
McLaurin, Anne 1953- 106
See also SATA 27
McLaurin, Melton A(lonza) 1941- CANR-28
Earlier sketch in CA 81-84
McLaurin, R(onald) D(e) 1944- CANR-17
Earlier sketch in CA 65-68
McLaverty, Michael 1904- CAP-1
Earlier sketch in CA 13-14
See also DLB 15
McLean, Alan A(ngus) 1925- 157
McLean, Albert F(orbes), Jr. 1928- 17-20R
McLean, Allan Campbell 1922- CANR-4
Earlier sketch in CA 1-4R
McLean, Anne (Julia) 1951- 120
McLean, Antonio (Maxwell) 1919- 130
McLean, Beth Bailey 1892- CAP-2
Earlier sketch in CA 19-20
McLean, Don(ald George) 1932- 122
McLean, Donald 1905-1975 CANR-4
Earlier sketch in CA 1-4R
McLean, Duncan 1964- 149
McLean, George 1905(?)-1983 Obituary 109
McLean, George F(rancis) 1929- CANR-6
Earlier sketch in CA 13-16R
McLean, Gordon R(onald) 1934- CANR-2
Earlier sketch in CA 49-52
McLean, Hugh 1925- 65-68
McLean, Iain (S.) 1946- 135
McLean, J. Sloan
See Gillette, Virginia M(ary)
and Wunsch, Josephine (McLean)
McLean, J. W. 1922- 143
McLean, Janice W(alker) 1944- 119
McLean, John R. 1848-1916 DLB 23
McLean, Joseph E(rigina) 1915-1985 Obituary 118
McLean, Kathryn (Anderson) 1909-1966 CAP-2
Obituary 25-28R
Earlier sketch in CA 21-22
See also SATA 9
McLean, Malcolm Dallas 1913- CANR-39
Earlier sketches in CA 93-96, CANR-16
McLean, Robert 1891-1980 Obituary 103
McLean, Robert Colin 1927- 17-20R
McLean, Ruari 1917- CANR-10
Earlier sketch in CA 21-24R
McLean, Sammy Kay 1929- 37-40R
McLean, Susan 1937- 106
McLean, Teresa 1951- 143
McLean, Virginia Overton 1946- 155
See also SATA 90
McLean, William L. 1852-1931 DLB 25
McLeave, Hugh George 1923- CANR-27
Earlier sketches in CA 5-8R, CANR-6
McLeavy, Gus 1951- 105
McLees, Ainslie Armstrong 1947- 135
McLeish, Garen
See Stine, Whitney Ward
McLeish, John 1917- CANR-7
Earlier sketch in CA 57-60
McLeish, Kenneth 1940- CANR-45
Earlier sketches in CA 29-32R, CANR-13
See also SATA 35
McLellan, David 1940- CANR-33
Earlier sketches in CA 33-36R, CANR-15
McLellan, David S(tanley) 1924- 103
McLellan, Diana 1937- 114
Interview in 114
McLellan, Robert 1907-1985 41-44R
Obituary 115
McLemore, S(amuel) Dale 1928- 9-12R
McLendon, Gloria H(ouston) 1940- 112
McLendon, Gordon (Barton) 1921-1986 133
Obituary 120
McLendon, Jacquelyn Y. 1943- 167
McLendon, James (Nelson) 1942-1982 41-44R
Obituary 106
McLendon, Jonathon C(ollins) 1919-1977 17-20R
Obituary 134
McLendon, Will L(oving) 1925- 9-12R
McLendon, Winzola Poole 93-96
McLenighan, Valjean 1947- 108
See also SATA 46
See also SATA-Brief 40
McLennan, Barbara N(ancy) 1940- 85-88
McLennan, Will
See Wisler, G(ary) Clifton
McLennan, William 1856-1904 DLB 92
McLeod, Alan L(indsey) 1928- 9-12R
McLeod, Chum 1955- SATA 95
McLeod, Emilie Warren 1926-1982 33-36R
Obituary 108
See also SATA 23
See also SATA-Obit 31
McLeod, Enid (Devoge) 1896-1985 134
Obituary 116
McLeod, Grover S(tephen) 1929- 143
McLeod, Jack (T.) 1932- 129
McLeod, James R(ichard) 1942- 41-44R
McLeod, John F(reeland) 1917-1989 69-72
Obituary 128
McLeod, Joseph (Bertram) 1929- 156
McLeod, Kirsty
See Hudson, (Margaret) Kirsty
McLeod, Malcolm Donald 1941- 110
McLeod, Margaret Vail
See Holloway, Teresa (Bragunier)
McLeod, Mary Alice 1937- 112
McLeod, Raymond, Jr. 1932- CANR-19
Earlier sketches in CA 49-52, CANR-3
McLeod, Ross
See Feldman, Herbert (H. S.)
McLeod, Scott Willard 1960- 148
McLeod, Wallace (Edmond) 1931- CANR-57
Earlier sketches in CA 37-40R, CANR-14, 31
McLerran, Alice 1933- 136
See also SATA 68
McLin, Jon (Blythe) 1938- 102
McLin, Ruth (Arlene) 1924- 61-64
McLoughlin, John C. 1949- 108
See also SATA 47
McLoughlin, Leslie J. 1935- 146
McLoughlin, R. B.
See Mencken, H(enry) L(ouis)
McLoughlin, William G. 1922-1993 CANR-6
Obituary 140
Earlier sketch in CA 13-16R
McLouth, Gary (Michael) 1944- 119
McLowery, Frank
See Keevill, Henry J(ohn)
McLuhan, (Thomas) Eric (Marshall) 1942- 130
McLuhan, (Herbert) Marshall 1911-1980 CANR-61
Obituary 102
Earlier sketches in CA 9-12R, CANR-12, 34
Interview in CANR-12
See also CLC 37, 83
See also DLB 88
See also MTCW 1
McLure, Charles E., Jr. 1940- CANR-58
Earlier sketches in CA 57-60, CANR-8, 28
McMahan, Ian SATA-Brief 45
McMahon, Bob 1943- 111
McMahon, Bryan T(homas) 1950- CANR-35
Earlier sketch in CA 45-48
McMahon, Charles P. 1916(?)-1983 Obituary 109
McMahon, Dorothy 1912-1984 Obituary 112
McMahon, Ed(ward Leo Peter, Jr.) 1923- 89-92
McMahon, Edwin Mansfield 1930- 126
McMahon, Eileen M. 1957- 151
McMahon, Francis E(lmer) 1906-1987 Obituary 123
McMahon, Jeremiah 1919- 109
McMahon, Joseph H(enry) 1930-1987 9-12R
Obituary 124
McMahon, Michael 1943- 69-72
McMahon, Pat
See Hoch, Edward D(entinger)
McMahon, Robert
See Weverka, Robert
McMahon, Robert J. 1949- 109
McMahon, Thomas 1923(?)-1972 Obituary 37-40R
McMahon, Thomas (Arthur) 1943- CANR-45
Earlier sketches in CA 33-36R, CANR-15
McManis, Douglas R. 69-72
McManners, (Joseph) Hugh 1952- 132
McManners, John 1916- CANR-14
Earlier sketch in CA 37-40R
McManus, Edgar J. 1924- 97-100
McManus, Frederick R(ichard) 1923- 1-4R
McManus, James 1951- CANR-67
Earlier sketch in CA 117
McManus, James Kenneth 1921- 85-88
McManus, Jason 1934- 125
McManus, Marjorie 1950- 73-76
McManus, Patrick (Francis) 1933- 105
See also SATA 46
McMaster, Beth 1935- CANR-30
Earlier sketch in CA 112
McMaster, John Bach 1852-1932 DLB 47
McMaster, Juliet 1937- 37-40R
McMaster, Rhyll 1947- 154
McMath, Robert C(arroll), Jr. 1944- 129
McMeekin, Clark
See McMeekin, Isabel McLennan
McMeekin, Dorothy 1932- 125
McMeekin, Isabel McLennan 1895- 5-8R
See also SATA 3
McMenemey, William Henry 1905- CAP-1
Earlier sketch in CA 11-12
McMenemy, Nickie 1925- 97-100
McMichael, George 1927- 103
McMichael, James 1939- 69-72
McMichael, Joan K(atharine) 1906- 107
McMillan, Alan D. 1945- 130

McMillan, Bruce 1947- CANR-35
Earlier sketches in CA 73-76, CANR-13
See also CLR 47
See also MAICYA
See also SATA 22, 70
McMillan, Colin 1923- 29-32R
McMillan, Constance (VanBrunt Johnson)
1949- 85-88
McMillan, George 1913-1987 102
Obituary 123
McMillan, Ian 1956- 132
McMillan, James B. 1907- 85-88
McMillan, James F(rancis) 1948- 122
McMillan, John 1951- 138
McMillan, Naomi
See Grimes, Nikki
McMillan, Polly Miller 1920- 1-4R
McMillan, Priscilla Johnson 1928- 41-44R
McMillan, Roddy 1923-1979 Obituary 109
McMillan, Sally 1929- 145
McMillan, Terry (L.) 1951- CANR-60
Earlier sketch in CA 140
See also AAYA 21
See also BLCS
See also BW 2
See also CLC 50, 61, 112
See also DAM MULT, NOV, POP
McMillen, Howard 1938- 57-60
McMillen, Neil R(aymond) 1939- 33-36R
McMillen, S(im) I. (Socrates) 1898- 5-8R
McMillen, Sally G(regory) 1944- 133
McMillen, Wheeler 1893- 33-36R
McMillin, (Joseph) Laurence (Jr.) 1923- .. 33-36R
McMillin, (Harvey) Scott 1934- 126
McMillion, Bonner 1921- 13-16R
McMorey, James L.
See Moyer, Terry J.
McMorran, Susan
See Beattie, Susan
McMorrow, Fred 1925- 57-60
McMullan, Frank (Alonzo) 1907- 5-8R
McMullan, Gordon 1962- 149
McMullan, Jim 1934- .... SATA 87
McMullan, Kate
See McMullan, Kate Hall
McMullan, Kate Hall 1947- 123
See also SATA 52, 87
See also SATA-Brief 48
McMullan, Margaret 1960- 145
McMullen, Jay L. 1921-1992 118
Obituary 137
Brief entry 114
Interview in 118
McMullen, Jeremy (John) 1948- 103
McMullen, Lorraine 1926- CANR-41
Earlier sketch in CA 117
McMullen, Mary
See Reilly, Mary
McMullen, Roy 1911-1984 .... 25-28R
Obituary 113
McMullen, Sean (Christopher) 1948- 161
McMullen, William Wallace 1952- 151
McMullin, Ernan 1924- CANR-49
Earlier sketches in CA 13-16R, CANR-6, 22
McMullin, Ruth R(oney) 1942- 61-64
McMurdie, Annie Laurie
See Cassiday, Bruce (Bingham)
McMurray, George R(ay) 1925- 103
McMurray, Nancy A(rmistead) 1936- 41-44R
McMurrin, Sterling M(oss) 1914-1996 ...... 29-32R
Obituary 152
McMurry, James Burton 1941- 69-72
McMurry, Linda O. 1945- 106
McMurry, Richard M. 1939- 132
McMurry, Robert N(oleman) 1901- 17-20R
McMurry, Sarah L. 1944- 123
McMurtrey, Martin A(loysias) 1921- 69-72
See also SATA 21
McMurtry, Jo 1937- 89-92
McMurtry, Larry (Jeff) 1936- CANR-64
Earlier sketches in CA 5-8R, CANR-19, 43
See also AAYA 15
See also AITN 2
See also BEST 89:2
See also CDALB 1968-1988
See also CLC 2, 3, 7, 11, 27, 44
See also DAM NOV, POP
See also DLB 2, 143
See also DLBY 80, 87
See also MTCW 1
McMurtry, R(obert) Gerald 1906-1988 ...... CAP-1
Obituary 127
Earlier sketch in CA 11-12
McNab, Oliver
See Frede, Richard
McNab, Thomas 1933- 108
McNab, Tom
See McNab, Thomas
McNail, Eddie Gathings 1905- CANR-6
Earlier sketch in CA 57-60
McNair, Clement John 1915-1989 Obituary .. 129
McNair, Kate 17-20R
See also SATA 3
McNair, Malcolm P(errine) 1894-1985 ...... CAP-1
Obituary 117
Earlier sketch in CA 11-12
McNair, Marie 1900(?)-1989 Obituary 130
McNair, Philip Murray Jourdan 1924- 21-24R
McNair, Sylvia 1924- 121
See also SATA 74
McNair Scott, Ronald (Guthrie) 1906-1995 . 111
Obituary 148
McNairy, Philip F(rederick) 1911- 17-20R
McNall, P(reston) E(ssex) 1888-1981 ...... 29-32R
Obituary 135
McNall, Scott G(rant) 1941- CANR-11
Earlier sketch in CA 25-28R
McNally, Curtis
See Birchall, Ian H(arry)
McNally, Dennis 1949- 103
McNally, Gertrude Bancroft
1908(?)-1985 Obituary 115
McNally, John 1914- 17-20R
McNally, Raymond T. 1931- CANR-14
Earlier sketch in CA 37-40R
McNally, Robert 1946- 107
McNally, Robert E(dward) 1917-1978 .... CANR-11
Earlier sketch in CA 21-24R
McNally, T. M. 1961- .... CLC 82
McNally, Terrence 1939- CANR-56
Earlier sketches in CA 45-48, CANR-2
See also CLC 4, 7, 41, 91
See also DAM DRAM
See also DLB 7
McNally, Tom 1923- 85-88
McNamara, Brooks 1937- 25-28R
McNamara, Dennis L. 1945- 136
McNamara, Eugene (Joseph) 1930- CANR-53
Earlier sketches in CA 21-24R, CANR-10, 26
McNamara, Jo Ann 1931- CANR-15
Earlier sketch in CA 85-88
McNamara, John J(oseph), Jr. 1932-1986 ... 41-44R
Obituary 120
McNamara, John S. 1908(?)-1977 Obituary .. 69-72
McNamara, Kevin (John) 1926-1987 .... 25-28R
Obituary 122
McNamara, Lena Brooke 1891- CAP-1
Earlier sketch in CA 11-12
McNamara, Margaret C(raig) 1915-1981 . SATA-Obit 24
McNamara, Michael M. 1940-1979 Obituary .. 89-92
McNamara, Robert S(trange) 1916- CANR-63
Brief entry 112
Earlier sketch in CA 129
McNamara, Sister Marie Aquinas
See Schaub, Marilyn McNamara
McNamara, William E. 1926- CANR-4
Earlier sketch in CA 1-4R
McNamee, Eoin 1961- 152
McNamee, James 1904- 5-8R
McNamee, Lawrence F. 1917- 25-28R
McNamee, Maurice B(asil) 1909- 5-8R
McNamee, Thomas 1947- 125
McNamer, Deirdre 1950- .... CLC 70
McNarie, Alan Decker 1954- 143
McNaron, Toni (A. H.) 1937- 139
McNaspy, Clement James 1915- CANR-2
Earlier sketch in CA 5-8R
McNaught, Brian Robert 1948- 105
McNaught, Harry 106
See also SATA 32
McNaught, Judith 1944- 138
McNaught, Kenneth (William Kirkpatrick)
1918- 29-32R
McNaughton, Arnold 1930- 57-60
McNaughton, Colin 1951- CANR-47
Earlier sketch in CA 112
See also SATA 39, 92
McNaughton, Frank 1906(?)-1978 Obituary .. 81-84
McNaughton, Howard (Douglas) 1945- 57-60
McNaughton, Wayne L. 1902- 1-4R
McNaughton, William (Frank) 1933- 41-44R
McNeal, Patricia 1942- 144
McNeal, Robert H(atch) 1930- 9-12R
McNear, Robert 1930(?)-1985 Obituary 117
McNeely, Jeannette 1918- 41-44R
See also SATA 25
McNeely, Jerry Clark 1928- Brief entry ... 115
McNeer, May (Yonge) 1902-1994 .... CANR-2
Obituary 146
Earlier sketch in CA 5-8R
See also SATA 1, 81
McNees, Pat 1940- CANR-7
Earlier sketch in CA 57-60
McNeil, Art 1944- 124
McNeil, Barbara L(aurie) 1951- 97-100
McNeil, Bill
See McNeil, William Russell
McNeil, Elton B(urbank) 1924-1974 .... CAP-2
Earlier sketch in CA 25-28
McNeil, Florence 1940- 116
See also DLB 60
McNeil, John 1939- 131
McNeil, Legs
See McNeil, Roderick Edward
McNeil, Mary 134
McNeil, Maureen (Christena) 1948- 128
McNeil, Roderick Edward 1956- 168
McNeil, W. K. 1940- 154
McNeil, William F. 1932- 166
McNeil, William Russell 1924- 133
McNeile, Herman Cyril 1888-1937
See Sapper
See also DLB 77
McNeill, Anthony 1941- 97-100
See also BW 2
McNeill, Christine 1953- 153
McNeill, Daniel 1947- 141
McNeill, Donald P(aul) 1936- 107
McNeill, Elisabeth
See Taylor, Elisabeth (D.)
McNeill, J(ohn) R(obert) 144
McNeill, Janet 1907-1994
See Alexander, Janet
See also SATA 1, 97
McNeill, John J. 1925- 65-68
McNeill, John Thomas 1885-1975 .... CANR-10
Obituary 57-60
Earlier sketches in CAP-1, CA 11-12
McNeill, Louise 1911- 139
McNeill, Robert B(lakely) 1915- 17-20R
McNeill, Stuart 1942- 65-68
McNeill, William H(ardy) 1917- CANR-2
Earlier sketch in CA 5-8R
McNeilly, Wilfred (Glassford) 1921- CANR-28
Earlier sketch in CA 29-32R
McNeir, Waldo F(orest) 1908- 17-20R
McNeish, James 1931- CANR-29
Earlier sketches in CA 69-72, CANR-12
McNelly, Theodore (Hart) 1919- 5-8R
McNelly, Willis E(verett) 1920- 107
McNew, Ben(nie) B(anks) 1931- CANR-3
Earlier sketch in CA 9-12R
McNickle, (William) D'Arcy 1904-1977 ..... CANR-45
Obituary 85-88
Earlier sketches in CA 9-12R, CANR-5
See also CLC 89
See also DAM MULT
See also DLB 175
See also NNAL
See also SATA-Obit 22
McNicoll, Alan (Wedel Ramsay)
1908-1987 Obituary 124
McNicoll, Robert E. 1907- 37-40R
McNicoll, Sylvia (Marilyn) 1954- 163
McNiece, Harold Francis
1923-1972 Obituary 37-40R
McNierney, Mary Alice 9-12R
McNiff, William John 1899-1987 Obituary .. 122
McNitt, Gale 1921- 57-60
McNiven, Malcolm A(lbert) 1929- 29-32R
McNown, John S(tephenson) 1916- 57-60
McNulty, Edward N. 1936- CANR-25
Earlier sketches in CA 65-68, CANR-10
McNulty, Faith 1918- CANR-25
Earlier sketches in CA 49-52, CANR-1
See also SATA 12, 84
McNulty, James Edmund, Jr. 1924-1965 ..... 1-4R
Obituary 103
McNulty, James Francis 1934-1979 Obituary 113
McNutt, Dan James 1938- 61-64
McNutt, James (Allen) 1944- 49-52
McNutt, Patrick A. 1957- 165
McOwan, Rennie 1933- CANR-37
Earlier sketch in CA 115
McPhail, David M(ichael) 1940- CANR-56
Earlier sketches in CA 85-88, CANR-22, 38
See also MAICYA
See also SATA 47, 81
See also SATA-Brief 32
McPharlin, Paul 1903-1948 Brief entry 110
See also SATA-Brief 31
McPhaul, Jack
See McPhaul, John J.
McPhaul, John J. 1904-1983 .... 9-12R
Obituary 110
McPhee, Arthur G(ene) 1945- Brief entry .. 116
McPhee, John (Angus) 1931- CANR-69
Earlier sketches in CA 65-68, CANR-20, 46, 64
See also BEST 90:1
See also CLC 36
See also DLB 185
See also MTCW 1
McPhee, Martha (A.) 1957- 165
McPhee, Norma H. 1928- 160
See also SATA 95
McPhee, Richard B(yron) 1934- 111
See also SATA 41
McPhee, William N(orvell) 1921- 17-20R
McPherson, Anna Talbott 1904- CANR-19
Earlier sketches in CA 1-4R, CANR-4
McPherson, Gertrude H(untington) 1923- ... 45-48
McPherson, Harry Cummings, Jr. 1929- 104
McPherson, Holt 1907(?)-1979 Obituary 89-92
McPherson, Hugo (Archibald) 1921- 29-32R
McPherson, James Alan 1943- CANR-24
Earlier sketch in CA 25-28R
See also CAAS 17
See also BLCS
See also BW 1
See also CLC 19, 77
See also DLB 38
See also MTCW 1
McPherson, James Lowell 1921- 13-16R
McPherson, James M(unro) 1936- CANR-31
Earlier sketch in CA 9-12R
Interview in CANR-31
See also MTCW 1
See also SATA 16
McPherson, John 1925- 119
McPherson, Sandra 1943- CANR-70
Earlier sketches in CA 29-32R, CANR-12
See also CAAS 23
See also DLBY 86
McPherson, Thomas Herdman 1925- 17-20R
McPherson, William (Alexander) 1933- CANR-28
Earlier sketch in CA 69-72
Interview in CANR-28
See also CLC 34
McPherson, William 1939- 57-60
McPhie, Walter E(van) 1926- 29-32R
McQuade, Ann Aikman 1928- CANR-34
Earlier sketch in CA 1-4R
McQuade, De Rosset Morrissey
1934(?)-1978 Obituary 81-84
McQuade, Donald A(nthony) 1941- CANR-16
Earlier sketch in CA 65-68
McQuade, Walter 1922- 103
McQuaid, Kim 1947- CANR-49
Earlier sketches in CA 107, CANR-24
McQuaig, Jack Hunter 9-12R
McQuaig, Linda 1951- 127
McQueen, Cilla 1949- 154
McQueen, Cyrus B. 1951- 135
McQueen, Ian 1930- 104
McQueen, Lucinda 1950- .... SATA 58
See also SATA-Brief 48
McQueen, Mildred Hark 1908- CAP-1
Earlier sketch in CA 9-10
See also SATA 12
McQueen, William A. 1926- 21-24R
McQuigg, R. Bruce 1927- 17-20R
McQuilkin, Frank 1936- CANR-13
Earlier sketch in CA 33-36R
McQuillan, Karin 1950- 133
McQuin, Susan Coultrap
See Coultrap-McQuin, Susan (M.)
McQuiston, Joanne W(orth)
1922(?)-1985 Obituary 117
McQuown, F(rederic) R(ichard) 1907- 9-12R
McQuown, Judith H(ershkowitz) 1941- 107
McQuown, Norman A(nthony) 1914- 126
Brief entry 106
McRae, Barry (Donald) 1935- 136
McRae, Hamish (Malcolm Donald) 1943- 57-60
McRae, Kenneth D(ouglas) 1925- CANR-17
Earlier sketch in CA 1-4R
McRae, Lindsay
See Sowerby, A(rthur) L(indsay) M(cRae)
McRae, Robert (Forbes) 1914- 77-80
McRae, Russell (William) 1934- 129
See also SATA 63
McRae, William John 1933- 106
McReynolds, David 1929- 29-32R
McReynolds, Edwin C(larence) 1890-1967 .. CAP-1
Earlier sketch in CA 19-20
McReynolds, Ronald W(eldon) 1934- 49-52
McRoberts, Agnesann
See Meek, Pauline Palmer
McRoberts, R(obert) Lewis 1944- 33-36R
McShan, James 1937- 69-72
McShane, Fred
See Elman, Richard (Martin)
McShane, Joseph M(ichael) 1949- 127
McShane, Mark 1930- CANR-61
Earlier sketches in CA 17-20R, CANR-7, 22
McShane, Philip 1932- 69-72
McShean, Gordon 1936- 108
See also SATA 41
McSherry, Frank D(avid), Jr. 1927- CANR-47
Earlier sketches in CA 107, CANR-23
McSherry, James E(dward) 1920- CANR-28
Earlier sketch in CA 49-52
McShine, Kynaston
See McShine, Kynaston L(eigh)
McShine, Kynaston L(eigh) 1935- 134
Brief entry 115
McSorley, Jean Sarah 1958- 133
McSorley, Joseph 1874-1963 .... CAP-1
Earlier sketch in CA 13-16
McSweeny, Maxine 1905- 61-64
Mc Swigan, Marie 1907-1962 73-76
See also SATA 24
McTaggart, Fred 1939- 65-68
McTaggart, J. McT. Ellis
See McTaggart, John McTaggart Ellis
McTaggart, John McTaggart Ellis 1866-1925 Brief entry ... 120
McTaggart, Lynne (Ann) 1951- 145
Brief entry 113
McTeer, Wilson 1905- 41-44R
McVaugh, Michael R(ogers) 1938- 147
McVay, Gordon 1941- 73-76
McVean, James
See Luard, Nicholas
McVeigh, Malcolm J(ames) 1931- 61-64
McVey, Ruth T(homas) 1930- 109
McVey, Vicki 1946- 148
See also SATA 80
McVickar, Elinor Guthrie
1902(?)-1982 Obituary 106
McVicker, Charles (Taggart) 1930- .... SATA 39
McVicker, Chuck
See McVicker, Charles (Taggart)
McVicker, Daphne Alloway
1895-1979 Obituary 85-88
McWaters, Barry 1937- 108
McWhiney, Grady 1928- CANR-6
Earlier sketch in CA 5-8R
McWhinney, Edward Watson 1926- CANR-52
Earlier sketches in CA 29-32R, CANR-12, 28
McWhinnie, Donald 1920-1987 Obituary 123
McWhirter, A(lan) Ross 1925-1975 .... CANR-46
Obituary 61-64
Earlier sketch in CA 17-20R
See also SATA 37
See also SATA-Obit 31
McWhirter, George 1939- CANR-13
Earlier sketch in CA 77-80
See also DLB 60
McWhirter, Glenna S. 1929- 89-92
McWhirter, Nickie
See McWhirter, Glenna S.
McWhirter, Norris Dewar 1925- CANR-50
Earlier sketch in CA 13-16R
See also SATA 37
McWilliam, Candia 1955- 136
McWilliams, Carey 1905-1980 .... CANR-2
Obituary 101
Earlier sketch in CA 45-48
See also DLB 137
McWilliams, John P(robasco), Jr. 1940- .. CANR-28
Earlier sketch in CA 49-52
McWilliams, Karen 1943- 133
See also SATA 65
McWilliams, Margaret (Ann Edgar) 1929- .. CANR-26
Earlier sketches in CA 17-20R, CANR-8
McWilliams, Peter 1949- CANR-72
Earlier sketch in CA 41-44R
McWilliams, Wilson Carey 1933- CANR-40
Earlier sketches in CA 103, CANR-19
Mdurvwa, Hajara E. 1962- 156
See also SATA 92

Meacham, Beth 1951- 166
Meacham, Ellis K. 1913- 25-28R
Meacham, Harry M(onroe) 1901-1975 .... CAP-2
Earlier sketch in CA 25-28
Meacham, Margaret 1952- CANR-42
Earlier sketch in CA 118
See also SATA 95
Meacham, Standish (Jr.) 1932- 135
Brief entry 110
Meacher, Michael Hugh 1939- 109
Meachum, Virginia 1918- 151
See also SATA 87
Mead, Alice 1952- 159
See also SATA 94
Mead, Chris 1959- 142
Mead, Christopher Curtis 1953- 140
Mead, D(onald) Eugene 1934- 65-68
Mead, Edgar T(horn), Jr. 1922- 113
Mead, Frank Spencer 1898-1982 .... CANR-9
Obituary 107
Earlier sketches in CAP-1, CA 19-20
Mead, G(eorge) R(obert) S(tow) 1863-1933 Brief entry 122
Mead, Harold C(harles) H(ugh) 1910- CAP-1
Earlier sketch in CA 13-14
Mead, Jude 1919- 25-28R
Mead, Margaret 1901-1978 .... CANR-4
Obituary 81-84
Earlier sketch in CA 1-4R
See also AITN 1
See also CLC 37
See also MTCW 1
See also SATA-Obit 20
Mead, Matthew 1924- 101
See also CAAS 13
See also DLB 40
Mead, Peter (Willan) 1911- 116
Mead, Philip (Stirling) 1953- 154
Mead, Robert Douglas 1928-1983 .... 41-44R
Obituary 110
Mead, Russell
See Koehler, Margaret (Hudson)
Mead, Russell (M., Jr.) 1935- 9-12R
See also SATA 10
Mead, (Edward) Shepherd 1914- 9-12R
Mead, Sidney E(arl) 1904- CAP-1
Earlier sketch in CA 9-10
Mead, Sidney Moko 1927- CANR-49
Earlier sketches in CA 106, CANR-23
Mead, Stella (?)-1981 Obituary 103
See also SATA-Obit 27
Mead, Taylor 1931(?)- 126
Brief entry 116
See also DLB 16
Mead, Walter B(ruce) 1934- 37-40R
Mead, William B(owmar) 1934- CANR-32
Earlier sketches in CA 85-88, CANR-15
Mead, William Richard 1915- 103
Meade, Bill C.
See Rogers, Paul T(aylor)
Meade, Dorothy (Joan Sampson) 1923- 9-12R
Meade, Elizabeth Thomasina 1854(?)-1914(?) Brief entry 112
See also Meade, L. T.
Meade, Ellen
See Roddick, Ellen
See also SATA 5
Meade, Everard 1914- 25-28R
Meade, James Edward 1907-1995 .... CANR-2
Obituary 150
Earlier sketch in CA 1-4R
Meade, L. T.
See Meade, Elizabeth Thomasina
See also DLB 141
Meade, Marion 1934- CANR-53
Earlier sketches in CA 49-52, CANR-1
See also SATA 23
Meade, Mary
See Church, Ruth Ellen (Lovrien)
Meade, Richard
See Haas, Ben(jamin) L(eopold)
Meade, Richard A(ndrew) 1911- 45-48
Meade, Robert Douthat 1903-197(?) CAP-2
Earlier sketch in CA 25-28
Meader, Stephen W(arren) 1892- 5-8R
See also SATA 1
Meades, Jonathan (Turner) 1947- 130
Meadmore, Susan
See Sallis, Susan (Diana)
Meador, Roy 1929- CANR-11
Earlier sketch in CA 69-72
Meadow, Barry 1947- 125
Meadow, Charles T(roub) 1929- CANR-15
Earlier sketch in CA 29-32R
See also SATA 23
Meadow, Kathryn Pendleton 1929- CANR-7
Earlier sketch in CA 57-60
Meadowcroft, Enid LaMonte
See Wright, Enid Meadowcroft (LaMonte)
Meadowes, Alicia
See Burak, Linda (Gallina)
and Zieg, Joan (Gallina)
Meadows, A(rthur) J(ack) 1934- 137
Meadows, Audrey 1922(?)-1996 160
Meadows, Eddie S(pencer) 1939- 109
Meadows, Edward 1944- 101
Meadows, Jack
See Meadows, A(rthur) J(ack)
Meadows, Paul 1913- 41-44R
Meadows, Peter
See Lindsay, Jack
Meagher, John C. 1935- CANR-11
Earlier sketch in CA 17-20R
Meagher, Paul Kevin 1907-1976 Obituary 69-72
Meagher, Robert E(mmett) 1943- CANR-10
Earlier sketch in CA 25-28R
Meagher, Robert F. 1927- 41-44R
Meaker, Eloise 1915- CANR-28
Earlier sketch in CA 105
Meaker, M. J.
See Meaker, Marijane (Agnes)
Meaker, Marijane (Agnes) 1927- CANR-63
Earlier sketches in CA 107, CANR-37
Interview in 107
See also Kerr, M. E.
See also JRDA
See also MAICYA
See also MTCW 1
See also SATA 20, 61, 99
Meakin, David 1943- 69-72
Means, Florence Crannell 1891-1980 .... CANR-37
Obituary 103
Earlier sketch in CA 1-4R
See also MAICYA
See also SATA 1
See also SATA-Obit 25
Means, Gardiner C(oit) 1896-1988 Obituary 124
Means, Gordon P(aul) 1927- 33-36R
Means, Howard 1944- 141
Means, John Barkley 1939- 33-36R
Means, Louis Edgar 1902- CANR-2
Earlier sketch in CA 5-8R
Means, Marianne Hansen 1934- 9-12R
Means, Richard K(eith) 1929- CANR-17
Earlier sketches in CA 5-8R, CANR-2
Means, Russell (Charles) 1939- 158
Meany, George 1894-1980 Obituary 97-100
Meany, Tom 1903-1964 .... DLB 171
Meara, (Mary) Jane (Frances) Cavolina 1954- .. 120
Meara, Mary Jane Frances Cavolina
See Meara, (Mary) Jane (Frances) Cavolina
Meares, Ainslie Dixon 1910- CANR-11
Earlier sketch in CA 25-28R
Mearian, Judy Frank 1936- 101
See also SATA 49
Mearns, Barbara (Crawford) 1955- 132
Mearns, David Chambers 1899-1981 .... 1-4R
Obituary 104
Mearns, Richard (James) 1950- 132
Mears, Brainerd, Jr. 1921- 53-56
Mears, Gillian 1964- 168
Mears, Richard Chase 1935- 101
Mears, Walter R(obert) 1935- 113
Brief entry 111
Interview in 113
Mearsheimer, John J(oseph) 1947- 117
Measday, George
See Soderberg, Percy Measday
Measham, D(onald) C. 1932- 21-24R
Measures, (William) Howard 1894- CAP-1
Earlier sketch in CA 13-14
Meath, Michael
See Marquis, Max
Mebane, John (Harrison) 1909- 13-16R
Mebane, Mary E(lizabeth) 1933- CANR-30
Earlier sketch in CA 73-76
Mech, Dave
See Mech, L(ucyan) David
Mech, L(ucyan) David 1937- CANR-14
Earlier sketch in CA 33-36R
Mecham, John Lloyd 1893- 1-4R
Mechanic, David 1936- CANR-19
Earlier sketches in CA 5-8R, CANR-3
Mechanic, Sylvia (Gertrude) 1920- 69-72
Mechin, Jacques Benoist
See Benoist-Mechin, Jacques
Mechthild von Magdeburg c. 1207-c. 1282 .... DLB 138
Meckel, Richard A(lan) 1948- 135
Meckier, Jerome (Thomas) 1941- 33-36R
Meckler, Alan Marshall 1945- 57-60
Meckley, Richard F(rederick) 1928- 37-40R
Mecklin, John Martin 1918-1971 Obituary 33-36R
Meckstroth, Jacob A. 1887(?)-1985 Obituary 115
Meckstroth, Jake
See Meckstroth, Jacob A.
Medalia, Leon S. 1881- 85-88
Medary, Marjorie 1890- 73-76
See also SATA 14
Medawar, Jean 1913- 134
Medawar, Peter Brian 1915-1987 97-100
Obituary 123
Medd, Charles Leighton 1928-1989 Obituary 130
Medd, Patrick 1919-1995 150
Meddaugh, Susan 1944- 106
See also SATA 29, 84
Meddis, Ray 1944- 77-80
Medea, Andra 1953- 57-60
Medearis, Angela Shelf 1956- .... SATA 72
Medearis, Mary 1915- 69-72
See also SATA 5
Medeiros, Earl Caton 1933- 89-92
Medeiros, Teresa 1962- 142
Medhin, Tsegaye (Kawessa) Gabre
See Gabre-Medhin, Tsegaye (Kawessa)
Medhurst, Joan
See Liverton, Joan
Medhurst, Martin J. 1952- 161
Medicine-Eagle, Brooke 1943- 140
Medicus II
See Philipp, Elliot Elias
Medill, Joseph 1823-1899 .... DLB 43
Medina, Jeremy T(yler) 1942- CANR-11
Earlier sketch in CA 69-72
Medina, Robert C. 1924- 153
See also HW
Medina, William A.
See Medina, William Antonio
Medina, William Antonio 1935-1985 Obituary .. 117
Medley, Anne
See Borchard, Ruth (Berendsohn)
Medley, (Rachel) Margaret 1918- 13-16R
Medley, Morris L(ee) 1942- 57-60
Medlicott, Alexander G(uild), Jr. 1927- 37-40R
Medlicott, Margaret P(aget) 1913- 29-32R
Medlicott, Mary 1946- 152
See also SATA 88
Medlicott, William Norton 1900-1987 .... 9-12R
Obituary 123
Medlin, Virgil D(ewain) 1943- 57-60
Mednick, Murray 1939- 21-24R
Medoff, Jeslyn 1951- 128
Medoff, Jillian 1963- 166
Medoff, Mark (Howard) 1940- CANR-5
Earlier sketch in CA 53-56
Interview in CANR-5
See also AITN 1
See also CLC 6, 23
See also DAM DRAM
See also DLB 7
Medsger, Betty (Louise) 1942- 113
Medsker, Leland L. 1905- CANR-2
Earlier sketch in CA 1-4R
Medved, Diane 1951- 132
Medved, Harry 1961(?)- 93-96
Medved, Michael 1948- CANR-45
Earlier sketches in CA 65-68, CANR-11
Medvedev, Grigori 1933- 141
Medvedev, P. N.
See Bakhtin, Mikhail Mikhailovich
Medvedev, Roy (Alexandrovich) 1925- 81-84
Medvedev, Zhores A(leksandrovich) 1925- 69-72
Medwed, Mameve 160
Mee, Charles L., Jr. 1938- CANR-50
Earlier sketches in CA 45-48, CANR-3
See also SATA 8, 72
Mee, Fiona 1946(?)-1978 Obituary 104
Mee, John F(ranklin) 1908- CAP-1
Earlier sketch in CA 9-10
Mee, Susie (B.) 1938- 154
Meechan, Hugh L(awrence) 1933- 17-20R
Meehan, Daniel Joseph 1930-1978 Obituary . 77-80
Meehan, Danny
See Meehan, Daniel Joseph
Meehan, Eugene J(ohn) 1923- CANR-14
Earlier sketch in CA 37-40R
Meehan, Francis X(avier) 1937- 116
Meehan, Paula 1955- 154
Meehan, Richard Lawrence 1939- 107
Meehan, Thomas Edward 1932- CANR-28
Earlier sketch in CA 29-32R
Meehl, Paul E(verett) 1920- 93-96
Meek, Alexander Beaufort 1814-1865 .... DLB 3
Meek, Forrest B(urns) 1928- 110
Meek, H(arold) A(lan) 1922- CANR-71
Earlier sketch in CA 129
Meek, Jacklyn O'Hanlon 1933- 77-80
See also SATA 51
See also SATA-Brief 34
Meek, Jay 1937- CANR-25
Earlier sketch in CA 107
Meek, Joseph
See Randisi, Robert J(oseph)
Meek, Lois Hayden
See Stolz, Lois Meek
Meek, Loyal George 1918- 73-76
Meek, M(argaret) R(eid) D(uncan) 1918- . CANR-66
Earlier sketch in CA 142
Meek, Margaret
See Meek Spencer, Margaret (Diston)
Meek, Pauline Palmer 1917- 106
Meek, Ronald L(indley) 1917-1978 .... CANR-6
Earlier sketch in CA 9-12R
Meek, S(terner St.) P(aul) 1894-1972 .... 1-4R
Obituary 103
See also SATA-Obit 28
Meeke, Mary (?)-1816(?) .... DLB 116
Meeker, Alice (MacCutcheon) 1904- CAP-2
Earlier sketch in CA 25-28
Meeker, Clare Hodgson 1952- 161
See also SATA 96
Meeker, Joseph W(arren) 1932- CANR-28
Earlier sketch in CA 49-52
Meeker, Mary Nacol 1928- 53-56
Meeker, Oden 1919(?)-1976 73-76
Obituary 65-68
See also SATA 14
Meeker, Richard
See Brown, Fornan
Meeker, Richard Kilburn 1925-(?) CAP-2
Earlier sketch in CA 19-20
Meeks, Esther MacBain 1-4R
See also SATA 1
Meeks, John E. 33-36R
Meeks, Linda A.
See Brower, Linda A.
Meeks, M(errill) Douglas 1941- 93-96
Meeks, Wayne A. 1932- CANR-54
Earlier sketches in CA 13-16R, CANR-5, 28
Meek Spencer, Margaret (Diston) 1925- . CANR-21
Earlier sketch in CA 105
Meen, Victor Ben 1910-1971 Obituary 106
Meenan, James F(rancis) 1910-1987 124
Meer, Fatima 1929- 73-76
Meerhaeghe, M(arcel) A(lfons) G(ilbert) Van
See Van Meerhaeghe, M(arcel) A(lfons) G(ilbert)
Meerloo, Joost A(braham) M(aurits) 1903-1976 .... CANR-4
Obituary 69-72
Earlier sketch in CA 1-4R
Meeropol, Abel 1903(?)-1986 Obituary 121
Meese, Elizabeth Ann 1943- 122
Meeter, Glenn 1934- CANR-12
Earlier sketch in CA 33-36R
Meeth, Louis Richard 1934- 17-20R
Meeuse, Bastiaan (Jacob Dirk) 1916- 119
Meezan, William 1947- 117
Megargee, Edwin I(nglee) 1937- CANR-7
Earlier sketch in CA 17-20R
Megarry, Tim 1941- 162
Meged, Aharon
See Megged, Aharon
Meged, Aron
See Megged, Aharon
Megged, Aharon 1920- CANR-1
Earlier sketch in CA 49-52
See also CAAS 13
See also CLC 9
Meggendorfer, Lothar 1847-1925 Brief entry 115
See also SATA-Brief 36
Meggers, Betty J(ane) 1921- 17-20R
Meggitt, M(ervyn) J(ohn) 1924- 13-16R
Meggs, Brown (Moore) 1930-1997 .... CANR-7
Obituary 162
Earlier sketch in CA 61-64
Meggs, Philip B(axter) 1942- 116
Meggyesy, Dave
See Meggyesy, David M.
Meggyesy, David M. 1941- 33-36R
Megill, Kenneth Alden 1939- Brief entry 106
Megivern, James J(oseph) 1931- 167
Meglin, Nick 1935- CANR-45
Earlier sketches in CA 69-72, CANR-21
Meglitsch, Paul A(llen) 1914- 53-56
Mego, Al
See Roberts, Arthur O.
Megrah, Maurice Henry 1896-1985 Obituary 116
Megson, Barbara 1930- 29-32R
Mehaffey, Karen Rae 1959- 140
Mehaffy, Robert E(ugene) 1935- 113
Mehan, Joseph Albert 1929- 101
Mehdevi, Alexander (Sinclair) 1947- 49-52
See also SATA 7
Mehdevi, Anne (Marie) Sinclair 1947- 5-8R
See also SATA 8
Mehdi, M(ohammed) T(aki) 1928-1998 .... CANR-8
Obituary 167
Earlier sketch in CA 17-20R
Mehegan, John (Francis) 1920(?)-1984 .... 5-8R
Obituary 112
Meher Baba
See Baba, Meher
Mehl, Roger 1912- CANR-21
Earlier sketches in CA 9-12R, CANR-6
Mehlinger, Howard D(ean) 1931- CANR-6
Earlier sketch in CA 9-12R
Mehlmann, Marilyn 1939- 119
Mehnert, Klaus 1906-1984 .... CANR-2
Obituary 111
Earlier sketch in CA 1-4R
Mehr, Joseph (John) 1941- Brief entry 113
Mehrabian, Albert 1939- 33-36R
Mehrens, William A(rthur) 1937- 37-40R
Mehring, Walter 1896-1981 Obituary 105
Mehrotra, Arvind Krishna 1947- 154
Mehrotra, S(ri) Ram 1931- CANR-8
Earlier sketch in CA 13-16R
Mehrtens, Susan E(mily) 1945- 53-56
Mehta, Gaganvihari L(allubhai) 1900-1974 Obituary 49-52
Mehta, J. L. 1912(?)-1988 Obituary 126
Mehta, Rustam Jehangir 1912- 9-12R
Mehta, Shahnaz 106
Mehta, Ved (Parkash) 1934- CANR-69
Earlier sketches in CA 1-4R, CANR-2, 23
See also CLC 37
See also MTCW 1
Mei, Ko-Wang 1918- CANR-2
Earlier sketch in CA 45-48
Meidell, Sherry 1951- .... SATA 73
Meiden, Walter 1907- CANR-8
Earlier sketch in CA 13-16R
Meier, August 1923- CANR-3
Earlier sketch in CA 9-12R
Meier, C(arl) A(lfred) 1905- 130
Meier, Gerald M(arvin) 1923- CANR-56
Earlier sketches in CA 112, CANR-30
Meier, Heinz K(arl) 1929- 61-64
Meier, Joel F(rancis) 1940- 109
Meier, Matt S(ebastian) 1917- CANR-43
Earlier sketches in CA 41-44R, CANR-14
Meier, Minta 1906- .... SATA 55
Meier, Paul D. 136
Meier, Richard (Alan) 1934- 143
Meier, Richard L(ouis) 1920- 17-20R
Meierhenry, Wesley Carl 1915- 41-44R
Meiggs, Russell 1902-1989 103
Obituary 129
Meighan, Donald Charles 1929- CANR-49
Earlier sketches in CA 107, CANR-24
See also SATA 30
Meigs, Alexander James 1921- 104
Meigs, Cornelia Lynde 1884-1973 .... 9-12R
Obituary 45-48
See also JRDA
See also MAICYA
See also SATA 6
Meigs, Mary 1917- 132
Meigs, Peveril 1903-1979 .... 37-40R
Obituary 133
Meigs, Walter B(erkeley) 1912- 21-24R
Meij, Jacob L(ouis) 1900- 5-8R
Meijer, M(arinus) J(ohan) 1912- 69-72
Meikle, Clive
See Brooks, Jeremy
Meikle, Jeffrey L(ee) 1949- CANR-64
Earlier sketch in CA 101
Meiklejohn, Alexander 1872-1964 Obituary 111
Meilach, Dona Z(weigoron) 1926- CANR-22
Earlier sketches in CA 9-12R, CANR-5
See also SATA 34
Meilach, Michael D(avid) 1932- CANR-2
Earlier sketch in CA 5-8R

Meilaender, Gilbert 1946- 109
Meilen, Bill 1932- 69-72
Meillassoux, Claude 1925- 25-28R
Meilman, Philip W(arren) 1951- 148
See also SATA 79
Mein, Margaret 61-64
Meine, Curt 1958- 126
Meiners, R(oger) K(eith) 1932- CANR-3
Earlier sketch in CA 5-8R
Meiners, Roger Evert 1948- 110
Meinig, Donald William 1924- 112
Meinke, Peter 1932- CANR-53
Earlier sketches in CA 25-28R, CANR-29
See also DLB 5
Meinkoth, Norman A(ugust) 1913- 113
Meintjes, Johannes 1923-1980 .... CANR-8
Earlier sketch in CA 17-20R
Meir, Avinoam 1946- 168
Meir, Golda 1898-1978 89-92
Obituary 81-84
Meiring, Desmond
See Rice, Desmond Charles
Meiring, Jane (Muriel) 1920- CANR-20
Earlier sketch in CA 103
Meisch, Lynn A. 1945- 105
Meisch, Richard A(lden) 1943- 33-36R
Meisel, Anthony C(lark) 1943- 105
Meisel, Gerald Stanley 1937- 9-12R
Meisel, John 1923- 17-20R
Meisel, Martin 1931- CANR-15
Earlier sketch in CA 5-8R
Meisel, Perry 1949- 102
Meisel, Tony
See Meisel, Anthony C(lark)
Meiselas, Susan 1948- 106
Meiselman, David I(srael) 1924- 13-16R
Meisenholder, Robert 1915- 37-40R
Meisler, Richard 1940- 124
Meisler, Stanley 1931- CANR-51
Earlier sketch in CA 73-76
Meisner, Maurice 1931- 21-24R
Meiss, Millard (Lazare) 1904-1975 61-64
Obituary 57-60
Meissner, Hans-Otto 1909- CANR-2
Earlier sketch in CA 49-52
Meissner, Kurt 1885-1976 .... CAP-2
Earlier sketch in CA 29-32
Meissner, W(illiam) W. 1931- CANR-29
Earlier sketches in CA 33-36R, CANR-13
Meister, Anton D(iderik) 1944- 118
Meister, Barbara 1932- 102
Meister, Richard J(ulius) 1938- 57-60
Meister, Robert 1926- CANR-9
Earlier sketch in CA 5-8R
Meixner, John A(lbert) 1925- 5-8R
Mejia, Arthur, Jr. 1934- 81-84
Mejia Vallejo, Manuel 1923- .... DLB 113
Mekas, Jonas 1922- Brief entry 113
Meketa, Jacqueline
See Meketa, Jacqueline Dorgan
Meketa, Jacqueline Dorgan 1926- 125
Mekler, Eva 1945- 158
Melady, John 1938- CANR-49
Earlier sketch in CA 122
See also SATA-Brief 49
Melady, Thomas Patrick 1927- CANR-5
Earlier sketch in CA 9-12R
Melahn, Martha 1924- 107
Melamed, Leo 1932- 162
Melamid, Alexander 1914- 45-48
Melanchthon, Philipp 1497-1560 .... DLB 179
Melancon, Robert 1947- .... DLB 60
Meland, Bernard Eugene 1899- 17-20R
Melanson, Richard A(llen) 1944- 113
Melanter
See Blackmore, R(ichard) D(oddridge)
Melantzon, Ricardo Aguilar
See Aguilar Melantzon, Ricardo
Melaragno, Michele G. 1928- 163
Melaro, Constance L(oraine) 1929- 17-20R
Melas, Evi 1930- 65-68
Melber, Jehuda 1916- 29-32R
Melbin, Murray 1927- 45-48
Melbo, Irving Robert 1908-1995 49-52
Obituary 148
Melby, Ernest O(scar) 1891-1987 Obituary 121
Melby, John Fremont 1913- Brief entry 106
Melcher, Daniel 1912-1985 .... CANR-49
Obituary 116
Earlier sketch in CA 33-36R
See also SATA-Obit 43
Melcher, Frederic Gershom
1879-1963 Obituary 89-92
See also SATA-Obit 22
Melcher, Marguerite Fellows 1879-1969 .... 5-8R
See also SATA 10
Melcher, Robert Augustus 1910- 17-20R
Melchert, Norman Paul 1933- 25-28R
Melchett, Sonia
See Sinclair, Sonia
Melchinger, Siegfried 1906- 81-84
Melchior, Ib (Jorgen) 1917- CANR-22
Earlier sketches in CA 45-48, CANR-2
Melchiori, Barbara Arnett 1926- 142
Meldal-Johnsen, Trevor Bernard 1944- .. CANR-19
Earlier sketch in CA 101
Melden, A(braham) I(rving) 1910- 17-20R
Melder, Keith E(ugene) 1932- 81-84
Meldrum, James
See Broxholme, John Franklin
Mele, Alfred R. 1951- 138
Mele, Frank Michael 1935- 53-56
Mele, Jim 1950- 113
Melendez (Ramirez), Concha 1892- .... HW
Melendez, Conchita
See Melendez (Ramirez), Concha
Melendez, Edwin 1951- 142
Melendez, Francisco 1964- .... SATA 72
Melendy, H(oward) Brett 1924- CANR-23
Earlier sketches in CA 17-20R, CANR-8
Meleski, Patricia F(erguson) 1935- 61-64
Melezh, Ivan 1921(?)-1976 Obituary 69-72
Melfi, Leonard 1935- 73-76
Melfi, Mary 1951- CANR-71
Earlier sketches in CA 113, CANR-32
Melford, Austin (Alfred) 1884-1971 Obituary 115
Melges, Buddy
See Melges, Harry C., Jr.
Melges, Harry C., Jr. 1930- 130
Melhem, D(iana) H(elen) CANR-42
Earlier sketches in CA 49-52, CANR-2
Melhorn, Charles M(ason) 1918-1983 57-60
Obituary 111
Melhuish, George (William Seymour)
1916-1985 Obituary 117
Melich, Tanya 1936- 154
Melick, Arden Davis 1940- 106
Melies, Georges 1861-1938 .... TCLC 81
Melikow, Loris
See Hofmannsthal, Hugo von
Melin, Grace Hathaway 1892-1973 .... CAP-2
Obituary 45-48
Earlier sketch in CA 21-22
See also SATA 10
Melion, Walter S. 1952- 144
Mell
See Lazarus, Mell
Mell, Donald C(harles), Jr. 1931- 115
Mell, Max 1882-1971 .... DLB 81, 124
Mellaart, James 1925- 161
Brief entry 118
Mellan, Eleanor 1905- 5-8R
Mellan, Ibert 1901- 5-8R
Mellan, Olivia 1946- 146
Mellanby, Kenneth 1908-1993 85-88
Obituary 143
Mellander, Gustavo Adolfo 1935- 33-36R
Mellard, James Milton 1938- 105
Mellen, Ida M(ay) 1877- 5-8R
Mellen, Joan 1941- CANR-11
Earlier sketch in CA 65-68
Mellencamp, Virginia Lynn 1917- 9-12R
Meller, Norman 1913- 25-28R
Mellers, Wilfrid (Howard) 1914- CANR-4
Earlier sketch in CA 5-8R
Mellersh, H(arold) E(dward) L(eslie) 1897- . CANR-9
Earlier sketch in CA 53-56
See also SATA 10
Mellert, Robert B(oros) 1937- 61-64
Mellichamp, Josephine 1923- 93-96
Mellin, Jeanne 1929- CANR-24
Earlier sketch in CA 49-52
Melling, O. R.
See Whelan, G(eraldine) V(alerie)
Melling, Orla
See Whelan, G(eraldine) V(alerie)
Mellinger, Philip J. 1940- 156
Mellini, Peter 1935- 93-96
Mellinkoff, David 1914- 13-16R
Mellinkoff, Ruth 1924- CANR-14
Earlier sketch in CA 37-40R
Mellins, Thomas 1957- CANR-49
Earlier sketch in CA 122
Mellizo (Cuadrado), Carlos 1942- 130
See also HW
Mellon, Constance A. 1938- 123
Mellon, James R(oss) 1942- 69-72
Mellon, John C(raig) 1933- Brief entry 107
Mellon, Knox
See Mellon, William Knox, Jr.
Mellon, Matthew T(aylor) 1897- 29-32R
Mellon, Stanley 1927- Brief entry 108
Mellon, William Knox, Jr. 1925- 37-40R
Mellor, Anne Kostelanetz 1941- 45-48
Mellor, J(ohn) Leigh 1928- 17-20R
Mellor, John W(illiams) 1928- 33-36R
Mellor, William Bancroft 1906- 61-64
Mellors, John (Parkin) 1920- 65-68
Mellors, Samantha
See Lottman, Eileen
Mellow, James R(obert) 1926-1997 .... CANR-29
Obituary 162
Earlier sketch in CA 105
See also DLB 111
Mellown, Elgin W(endell, Jr.) 1931- 17-20R
Mellows, Joan 77-80
Melly, Diana 1937- 130
Melly, George 1926- 81-84
Melman, Seymour 1917- CANR-4
Earlier sketch in CA 1-4R
Melman, Yossi (Bili) 1950- 140
Melmoth, Sebastian
See Wilde, Oscar (Fingal O'Flahertie Wills)
Melnick, Donald 1926-1977 Obituary 69-72
Melnick, Jack 1929- 89-92
Melnick, Ralph 1946- 167
Melnikoff, Pamela (Rita) 164
See also SATA 97
Melnitz, William W(olf) 1900-1989 Obituary 127
Melnyczuk, Askold 1954- 146
Melnyk, Steven A. 1953- 142
Melnyk, Z(inowii) Lew 1928- 41-44R
Meloan, Taylor Wells 1919- CANR-29
Earlier sketch in CA 45-48
Melone, Albert P(hilip) 1942- CANR-52
Earlier sketches in CA 109, CANR-27
Melone, Joseph J(ames) 1931- 13-16R
Meloney, Franken
See Franken, Rose (Dorothy)
Meloney, William Brown 1905-1971 Obituary 104
Meloon, Marion 1921- 65-68
Melosh, Barbara 1950- 130
Melosi, Martin Victor 1947- CANR-13
Earlier sketch in CA 77-80
Melot, Michel 1943- 132
Melrose, Andrea La Sonde
See Anastos, Andrea La Sonde (Melrose)
Melsa, James L(ouis) 1938- 104
Melson, Robert 1937- 85-88
Melton, David 1934- CANR-22
Earlier sketch in CA 69-72
Melton, J(ohn) Gordon 1942- 110
Melton, John L. 1920- 9-12R
Melton, Julius W(emyss), Jr. 1933- 21-24R
Melton, William 1920- 37-40R
Meltsner, Arnold J(erry) 1931- 57-60
Meltsner, Michael (Charles) 1937- Brief entry .. 108
Meltzer, Allan H. 1928- CANR-39
Earlier sketches in CA 5-8R, CANR-3, 18
Meltzer, Bernard N(athan) 1916- 21-24R
Meltzer, Brad 1970- 167
Meltzer, David 1937- CANR-35
Earlier sketches in CA 9-12R, CANR-6
See also CAAS 26
See also DLB 16
Meltzer, Jack 1921- 119
Meltzer, Milton 1915- CANR-38
Earlier sketch in CA 13-16R
See also AAYA 8
See also CLC 26
See also CLR 13
See also DLB 61
See also JRDA
See also MAICYA
See also SAAS 1
See also SATA 1, 50, 80
Meltzer, Morton F. 1930- 21-24R
Meltzer, Peter D. 1951- 120
Meltzoff, Julian 1921- 21-24R
Meltzoff, Nancy 1952- 93-96
Meluch, R(ebecca) M. 1956- CANR-56
Earlier sketch in CA 109
Melvill, Harald 1895- 5-8R
Melville, A(lan) D(avid) 1912- 137
Melville, Alan
See Caverhill, William Melville
Melville, Annabelle McConnell 1910- 5-8R
Melville, Anne
See Potter, Margaret (Newman)
Melville, Arabella 1948- 130
Melville, Charles (Peter) 1951- 138
Melville, Elizabeth c. 1585-1640 .... DLB 172
Melville, Herman 1819-1891 .... AAYA 25
See also CDALB 1640-1865
See also DA
See also DAB
See also DAC
See also DAM MST, NOV
See also DLB 3, 74
See also SATA 59
See also SSC 1, 17
See also WLC
Melville, J. Keith 1921- 53-56
Melville, James
See Martin, (Roy) Peter
Melville, Jennie
See Butler, Gwendoline Williams
Melville, Jock Leslie
See Leslie-Melville, John D.
Melville, John D. Leslie
See Leslie-Melville, John D.
Melville, Joy 1932- 85-88
Melville, Keith 1945- 41-44R
Melvin, A(rthur) Gordon 1894- 9-12R
Melvin, Ann (Patricia) Skene
See Skene-Melvin, Ann (Patricia)
Melvin, (Lewis) David (St. Columb) Skene
See Skene-Melvin, (Lewis) David (St. Columb)
Melvin, Herman 1819-1891 .... DLB 3
Melwani, Murli Das 1939- 61-64
Melwood, Mary
See Lewis, E. M.
Melzack, Ronald 1929- CANR-15
Earlier sketch in CA 41-44R
See also SATA 5
Melzer, John Henry 1908-1967 .... CAP-1
Earlier sketch in CA 13-14
Melzi, Robert C. 1915- 37-40R
Memling, Carl 1918-1969 .... CANR-4
Earlier sketch in CA 1-4R
See also SATA 6
Memmi, Albert 1920- CANR-32
Earlier sketches in CA 81-84, CANR-14
Memmott, David R. 1948- 159
Mena, Janet Gonzalez
See Gonzalez-Mena, Janet
Menacker, Julius 1933- 41-44R
Menaker, Daniel 1941- 65-68
See also DLBY 97
Menander c. 342B.C.-c. 292B.C. .... DAM DRAM
See also DC 3
See also DLB 176
Menard, H(enry) William 1920-1986 .... 37-40R
Obituary 118
Menard, Jean 1930(?)-1977 Obituary 69-72
Menard, Orville D. 1933- 21-24R
Menard, Russell 1942- 126
Menasco, Norman
See Guin, Wyman (Woods)
Menashe, Louis 1935- 21-24R
Menashe, Samuel 1925- 115
Brief entry 111
Interview in 115
See also CAAS 11
Mencher, Melvin 1927- 73-76
Menchin, Robert S(tanley) 1923- CANR-13
Earlier sketch in CA 21-24R
Mencke, Johann Burckhard 1674-1732 .... DLB 168
Mencken, H(enry) L(ouis) 1880-1956 125
Brief entry 105
See also CDALB 1917-1929
See also DLB 11, 29, 63, 137
See also MTCW 1
See also TCLC 13
Menczer, Bela 1902-1983 Obituary 110
Mendel, Arthur 1905-1979 .... CANR-29
Obituary 89-92
Earlier sketch in CA 41-44R
Mendel, Arthur P(aul) 1927-1988 .... 13-16R
Obituary 124
Mendel, Douglas H(eusted), Jr. 1921- 17-20R
Mendel, Jo
See Bond, Gladys Baker
and Gilbertson, Mildred Geiger
Mendel, Sydney 1925- Brief entry 109
Mendel, Werner M(ax) 1927- CANR-11
Earlier sketch in CA 21-24R
Mendele mocher seforim
See Abramowitz, Shalom Jacob
Mendell, Clarence W(hittlesey) 1883-1970 .. CAP-1
Earlier sketch in CA 19-20
Mendeloff, Henry 1917-1984 Obituary 113
Mendelowitz, Daniel M(arcus) 1905-1980 .... 9-12R
Obituary 135
Mendels, Joseph 1937- 29-32R
Mendels, Ora 1936- 124
Mendelsohn, Allan R(obert) 1928- 45-48
Mendelsohn, Everett (Irwin) 1931- CANR-28
Earlier sketches in CA 17-20R, CANR-11
Mendelsohn, Ezra 1940- 130
Mendelsohn, Felix, Jr. 1906- 29-32R
Mendelsohn, Harold 1923- 49-52
Mendelsohn, Jack 1918- CANR-1
Earlier sketch in CA 1-4R
Mendelsohn, Jane 1965(?)- 154
See also CLC 99
Mendelsohn, Martin 1935- CANR-13
Earlier sketch in CA 33-36R
Mendelsohn, Michael John 1931- 85-88
Mendelsohn, Oscar (Adolf) 1896-1978 .... CANR-22
Earlier sketch in CA 9-12R
Mendelsohn, Pamela 1944- 101
Mendelsohn, Robert S(aul)
1926-1988 Obituary 125
Mendelsohn, Stefan 1930(?)-1987(?) Obituary . 122
Mendelson, Edward 1946- CANR-11
Earlier sketch in CA 65-68
Mendelson, Lee 1933- 33-36R
Mendelson, Mary Adelaide (Jones) 1917- 85-88
Mendelson, Morris 1922- CANR-2
Earlier sketch in CA 5-8R
Mendelson, Sara Heller 1947- 126
Mendelson, Steven T. 1958-1995 .... SATA 86
Mendelson, Wallace 1911- 1-4R
Mendelssohn, Kurt (Alfred Georg) 1906-1980 ....
CANR-7
Obituary 105
Earlier sketch in CA 53-56
Mendelssohn, Moses 1729-1786 .... DLB 97
Mendenhall, Corwin (Guy, Jr.) 1916- 134
Mendenhall, George E(mery) 1916- 33-36R
Mendenhall, James Edgar
1903-1971 Obituary 33-36R
Mendenhall, John D(ale)
1911(?)-1983 Obituary 110
Mendenhall, Ruth Dyar 1912-1989 65-68
Obituary 128
Mendenhall, Thomas C(orwin II) 1910- 115
Mender, Mona (Siegler) 1926- 141
Mendes France, Pierre 1907-1982 .... CANR-43
Obituary 108
Earlier sketch in CA 81-84
Mendez, Charlotte (Walker) 1935- 120
Mendez, Eugenio Fernandez
See Fernandez Mendez, Eugenio
Mendez, Miguel 1930- CANR-66
Earlier sketch in CA 131
See also DAM MULT
See also DLB 82
See also HW
Mendez, Raymond A. 1947- .... SATA 66
Mendl, Robert William Sigismund
1892-1983 Obituary 111
Mendlovitz, Saul H. 1925- 21-24R
Mendonca, Susan
See Smith, Susan Vernon
See also SATA-Brief 45
Mendonsa, Eugene L(ouis) 1942- 109
Mendoza, George 1934- 73-76
See also SAAS 7
See also SATA 41
See also SATA-Brief 39
Mendoza, Manuel G. 1936- 53-56
Mendoza, Tony 1941- 128
Mendoza, Vincent L. 1947- 162
Mendras, Henri 1927- CANR-13
Earlier sketch in CA 73-76
Mendus, Susan 1951- 123
Mendyk, Stan A. E. 1953- 135
Menefee, Sarah 1946- .... CAAS 26
Menen, (Salvator) Aubrey (Clarence) 1912-1989 ...
CANR-2
Obituary 127
Earlier sketch in CA 1-4R
Menendez, Albert J(ohn) 1942- CANR-46
Earlier sketches in CA 53-56, CANR-7, 22
Menendez Pidal, Ramon 1869-1968 153
Obituary 116
See also HW
Meneses, Enrique 1929- CANR-27
Earlier sketches in CA 25-28R, CANR-11
Meng, Heinz (Karl) 1924- 69-72
See also SATA 13
Meng, John J(oseph) 1906-1988 Obituary 124

Menges, Karl (Heinrich) 1908- 37-40R
Menhennet, Alan 1933- 97-100
Menikoff, Barry 1939- 37-40R
Menkiti, Ifeanyi 1940- 65-68
Menkus, Belden 1931- CANR-58
Earlier sketches in CA 17-20R, CANR-31
Mennel, Robert McKisson 1938- Brief entry ... 109
Mennell, Stephen (John) 1944- 107
Mennen, Ingrid 1954- ....SATA 85
Menning, J(ack) H(arwood) 1915-1973 ..... 21-24R
Obituary 134
Menninger, Edwin A(rnold) 1896- CANR-29
Earlier sketch in CA 9-12R
Menninger, Karl A(ugustus) 1893-1990 .. CANR-61
Obituary 132
Earlier sketches in CA 17-20R, CANR-29
See also MTCW 1
Menninger, W(illiam) Walter 1931- 111
Menninger, Walt
See Menninger, W(illiam) Walter
Menninger, William C(laire)
1899-1966 Obituary 25-28R
Mennis, Bernard 1938- 41-44R
Menolascino, Frenk J(oseph) 1930- 73-76
Menon, Dilip M(adhav) 1962- 147
Menon, K(umara) P(admanabha) S(ivasankara)
1898-1982 .... CANR-5
Obituary 108
Earlier sketch in CA 5-8R
Menon, R(amakrishna) Rabindranath 1927- ....
CANR-11
Earlier sketch in CA 65-68
Menon, Ritu 1948- 167
Menotti, Gian Carlo 1911- 104
See also SATA 29
Menshikov, Marina 1928(?)-1979 Obituary ... 93-96
Mensoian, Michael G(eorge), Jr. 1927- 85-88
Menton, Seymour 1927- CANR-31
Earlier sketch in CA 45-48
Mentor
See Lake, Kenneth R(obert)
Mentschikoff, Soia 1915-1984 Obituary 113
Mentzer, Michael J(ohn) 1949- 118
Mentzer, Raymond A. 1945- 148
Menuhin, Hephzibah 1920-1981 Obituary 108
Menuhin, Yehudi 1916- CANR-2
Earlier sketch in CA 45-48
See also SATA 40
Menut, Albert D(ouglas Bartlett) 1894-1981 . 25-28R
Obituary 135
Menville, Douglas 1935- 57-60
See also SATA 64
Menyuk, Paula 1929- 37-40R
Menzel, Barbara Jean 1946- 114
See also SATA 63
Menzel, Donald H(oward) 1901-1976 .... CAP-2
Obituary 69-72
Earlier sketch in CA 21-22
Menzel, Johanna
See Meskill, Johanna Menzel
Menzel, Paul T(heodore) 1942- 53-56
Menzel, Roderich 1907- 93-96
Menzies, Edna O(live) 1921- 116
Menzies, Elizabeth G(rant) C(ranbrook)
1915- 17-20R
Menzies, Robert Gordon 1894-1978 81-84
Obituary 77-80
Menzies, William W(atson) 1931- Brief entry 110
Meo, Lucy Dorothy 1920- 25-28R
Meras, Phyllis 1931- CANR-37
Earlier sketches in CA 41-44R, CANR-16
Merbaum, Michael 1933- 65-68
Mercatante, Anthony Stephen 1940- 41-44R
Mercer, Blaine (Eugene) 1921- CANR-2
Earlier sketch in CA 1-4R
Mercer, Cecil William 1885-1960 Obituary 114
See also Yates, Dornford
Mercer, Charles (Edward) 1917-1988 ..... CANR-2
Obituary 127
Earlier sketch in CA 1-4R
See also SATA 16
See also SATA-Obit 61
Mercer, Colin 1952- 117
Mercer, David 1928-1980 .... CANR-23
Obituary 102
Earlier sketch in CA 9-12R
See also CLC 5
See also DAM DRAM
See also DLB 13
See also MTCW 1
Mercer, Derrik 1944- 130
Mercer, James L(ee) 1936- CANR-56
Earlier sketches in CA 112, CANR-30
Mercer, Jane R. 45-48
Mercer, Jean 1941- CANR-13
Earlier sketch in CA 33-36R
Mercer, Jessie CANR-2
Earlier sketch in CA 1-4R
See also Shannon, Terry
Mercer, Joan Bodger 1923- 101
Mercer, John 1704-1768 .... DLB 31
Mercer, Johnny 1906-1976 Obituary 65-68
Mercer, Judy 166
Mercer, Marilyn 1923- Brief entry 107
Mercer, Paul 1950- 111
Mercer, Virginia Fletcher 1916- 5-8R
Mercey, Arch Andrew 1906-1980 Obituary 102
Merchant, Carolyn 1936- 113
Merchant, Jane (Hess) 1919-1972 .... CANR-4
Obituary 33-36R
Earlier sketch in CA 1-4R
Merchant, Larry 1931- 102
Merchant, Paul
See Ellison, Harlan (Jay)
Mercie, Jean-Luc Henri 1939- 49-52
Mercier, Jean Doyle 1916- 1-4R
Mercier, Vivian (Herbert Samuel) 1919-1989 .. 81-84
Obituary 130
Mercouri, Melina 1925-1994 Obituary 144
Brief entry 106
Mercury
See Allen, Cecil J(ohn)
Meredith, Anne
See Malleson, Lucy Beatrice
Meredith, Arnold
See Hopkins, (Hector) Kenneth
Meredith, Burgess 1909(?)-1997 147
Obituary 162
Meredith, Char(lotte) 1921- 106
Meredith, Christopher (Laurence) 1954- 126
Meredith, D(oris) R. 1944- 128
Meredith, David William
See Miers, Earl Schenck
Meredith, Dean
See Dean, Edith M(ae)
Meredith, Don 1938- 102
Meredith, George 1828-1909 153
Brief entry 117
See also CDBLB 1832-1890
See also DAM POET
See also DLB 18, 35, 57, 159
See also TCLC 17, 43
Meredith, George (Marlor) 1923- CANR-4
Earlier sketch in CA 9-12R
Meredith, George Patrick 1904-1978 Obituary .. 108
Meredith, James Howard 1933- 77-80
Meredith, Joel L(yman) 1935- 116
Meredith, Joseph C(harlton) 1914- 53-56
Meredith, Louisa Anne 1812-1895 .... DLB 166
Meredith, Nicolete
See Stack, Nicolete Meredith
Meredith, Owen
See Lytton, Edward Robert Bulwer
Meredith, Richard C(arlton) 1937- 85-88
Meredith, Robert (King) 1923- 5-8R
Meredith, Robert C(hidester) 1921- 5-8R
Meredith, Roy 1914(?)-1984 Obituary 111
Meredith, Scott 1923-1993 .... CANR-3
Obituary 140
Earlier sketch in CA 9-12R
Meredith, William (Morris) 1919- CANR-40
Earlier sketches in CA 9-12R, CANR-6
See also CAAS 14
See also CLC 4, 13, 22, 55
See also DAM POET
See also DLB 5
Merewitz, Leonard (Alan) 1943- 69-72
Merezhkovsky, Dmitry Sergeyevich
1865-1941 .... TCLC 29
Merezhkovsky, Zinaida
See Gippius, Zinaida (Nikolayevna)
Mergen, Bernard 1937- 112
Merians, Linda E. 1955- 168
Merick, Wendell S. 1928(?)-1988 Obituary 124
Merideth, Robert 1935- 49-52
Merillat, Herbert C(hristian) L(aing) 1915- ... 29-32R
Merimee, Prosper 1803-1870 .... DLB 119, 192
See also SSC 7
Merin, Peter
See Bihalji-Merin, Oto
Meringoff, Laurene Krasny
See Brown, Laurene Krasny
Merino, Gustavo Gutierrez
See Gutierrez Merino, Gustavo
Meritt, Lucy Shoe 1906- 37-40R
Merivale, John Herman 1779-1844 .... DLB 96
Merivale, Patricia 1934- 29-32R
Meriwether, James B. 1928- 13-16R
Meriwether, Lee 1862-1966 Obituary 116
Meriwether, Louise 1923- 77-80
See also BW 1
See also DLB 33
See also SATA 52
See also SATA-Brief 31
Merk, Frederick 1887-1977 .... 41-44R
Obituary 73-76
Merkel, Miles Adair 1929- 53-56
Merkhofer, Miley W(esson Lee) 1947- 147
Merkin, Daphne 1954- 123
See also CLC 44
Merkin, Donald H. 1945- 69-72
Merkin, Robert (Bruce) 1947- 109
Merkl, Peter H(ans) 1932- CANR-49
Earlier sketches in CA 5-8R, CANR-7, 24
Merkle, Edgar A. 1900(?)-1984 Obituary 113
Merkle, Judith A(stria) 105
See also Riley, Judith (Astria) Merkle
Merklinghaus, Michele 1965- 116
Merle, Robert (Jean Georges) 1908- 93-96
Merleau-Ponty, Maurice 1908-1961 114
Obituary 89-92
Merli, Frank J(ohn) 1929- Brief entry 113
Merlin, Arthur
See Blish, James (Benjamin)
Merlin, Christina
See Heaven, Constance
Merlin, David
See Moreau, David Merlin
Merlin, Jan 1925- 108
Merlin, Mark D(avid) 118
Merlin, Samuel 1910- 115
Merlis, George 1940- 33-36R
Merliss, Reuben 1915- 17-20R
Merman, Ethel
See Zimmermann, Ethel Agnes
Mermin, Samuel 1912- 53-56
Merne, Oscar James 1943- 102
Mernissi, Fatima 152
Mernit, Susan 1953- 69-72
Meroff, Deborah 1948- 89-92
Meron, Theodor 1930- 138
Merquior, J(ose) G(uilherme) 1941- 143
Merrell, James H. 1953- 127
Merrell, James L(ee) 1930- 17-20R
Merrell, Jo Ann 1945- 113
Merrell, Karen Dixon 1936- CANR-6
Earlier sketch in CA 13-16R
Merrell, V(ictor) Dallas 1936- 9-12R
Merrens, H(arry) Roy 1931- 9-12R
Merrett, Christopher 1951- 151
Merrett, Robert James 1944- 111
Merriam, Alan P(arkhurst) 1923-1980 ..... CANR-1
Earlier sketch in CA 1-4R
Merriam, Eve 1916-1992 .... CANR-29
Obituary 137
Earlier sketch in CA 5-8R
See also CLR 14
See also DLB 61
See also MAICYA
See also SATA 3, 40, 73
Merriam, Harold G(uy) 1883-1981 .... CANR-10
Earlier sketch in CA 61-64
Merriam, Robert E(dward) 1918- 5-8R
Merriam, Sharan B. 1943- 135
Merrick, Gordon 1916-1988 .... CANR-11
Obituary 125
Earlier sketch in CA 13-16R
Merrick, Hugh
See Meyer, H(arold) A(lbert)
Merrick, William 1916-1969 .... CAP-1
Earlier sketch in CA 11-12
Merril, Judith 1923-1997 .... CANR-15
Obituary 161
Earlier sketch in CA 13-16R
Interview in CANR-15
See also MTCW 1
Merrill, Antoinette June 1912- 45-48
Merrill, Arch 1895(?)-1974 Obituary 49-52
Merrill, Bob
See Merrill, Robert Alexander
Merrill, Boynton, Jr. 1925- 69-72
Merrill, Christopher (Lyall) 1957- 130
Merrill, David W. 1928- 108
Merrill, Dean 1943- CANR-27
Earlier sketches in CA 61-64, CANR-8
Merrill, Dick
See Merrill, Henry Tindall
Merrill, Edward C(lifton), Jr. 1920- 21-24R
Merrill, Edward H. 1903- CAP-1
Earlier sketch in CA 13-16
Merrill, Francis E(llsworth) 1904-1969 ...... CAP-1
Earlier sketch in CA 19-20
Merrill, Frederick Thayer 1905-1974 Obituary .53-56
Merrill, Gary (Franklin) 1915(?)-1990 Obituary .. 131
Merrill, Harwood F(erry) 1904-1984 Obituary ... 114
Merrill, Henry Tindall 1897-1982 Obituary 108
Merrill, Hugh (Davis) (III) 1942- 151
Merrill, James (Ingram) 1926-1995 ...... CANR-63
Obituary 147
Earlier sketches in CA 13-16R, CANR-10, 49
Interview in CANR-10
See also CLC 2, 3, 6, 8, 13, 18, 34, 91
See also DAM POET
See also DLB 5, 165
See also DLBY 85
See also MTCW 1
Merrill, James M(ercer) 1920- 9-12R
Merrill, Jane 1946- .... SATA 42
Merrill, Jean (Fairbanks) 1923- CANR-38
Earlier sketches in CA 1-4R, CANR-4
See also CLR 52
See also MAICYA
See also SATA 1, 82
Merrill, John Calhoun 1924- CANR-13
Earlier sketch in CA 73-76
Merrill, John N(igel) 1943- CANR-22
Earlier sketch in CA 103
Merrill, M. David 1937- CANR-16
Earlier sketch in CA 41-44R
Merrill, P. J.
See Roth, Holly
Merrill, Phil
See Filstrup, Jane (Merrill)
Merrill, Robert 1919- 81-84
Merrill, Robert 1944- 89-92
Merrill, Robert Alexander 1958- 136
Merrill, Thomas F. 1932- 29-32R
Merrill, Toni
See Merrill, Antoinette June
Merrill, Walter M. 1915- CANR-13
Earlier sketch in CA 21-24R
Merrill, Wilfred K. 1903- 9-12R
Merrill, William C. 1934- 29-32R
Merriman, Alex
See Silverberg, Robert
Merriman, Ann Lloyd 1934- 77-80
Merriman, Beth
See Taylor, Demetria
Merriman, Catherine 1949- 140
Merriman, Jerry Johnson 1939- 25-28R
Merriman, John 1924-1974 Obituary 104
Merriman, Marion 1909- 133
Merriman, Pat
See Atkey, Philip
Merriman, Rachel 1971- .... SATA 98
Merrin, Jeredith 1944- 160
Merrit, Elizabeth
See Goudge, Eileen
Merrit, Elizabeth
See Goudge, Eileen
Merritt, A.
See Merritt, A(braham P.)
Merritt, A(braham P.) 1884-1943 167
Brief entry 120
Merritt, Dixon Lanier 1879-1972 Obituary ... 33-36R
Merritt, Don 1945- CANR-22
Earlier sketch in CA 106
Merritt, E. B.
See Waddington, Miriam
Merritt, Helen Henry 1920- 17-20R
Merritt, James D. 1934- 33-36R
Merritt, LeRoy Charles 1912-1970 .... CAP-2
Earlier sketch in CA 33-36
Merritt, Miriam 1925- 17-20R
Merritt, Muriel 1905- 69-72
Merritt, Ray E(merson), Jr. 1948- 73-76
Merritt, Raymond H(arland) 1936- 85-88
Merritt, Richard L(awrence) 1933- 41-44R
Merritt, William E. 1945- 132
Merry, Henry J(ohn) 1908- 37-40R
Merry, Robert William 1946- 153
Mersand, Joseph 1907- CANR-1
Earlier sketch in CA 1-4R
Merser, Cheryl 1951- 141
Mersereau, John, Jr. 1925- CANR-2
Earlier sketch in CA 1-4R
Mersky, Roy M. 1925- 37-40R
Mersmann, James Frederick 1938- 61-64
Mertens, Lawrence E(dwin) 1929- 85-88
Mertens, Thomas R(obert) 1930- CANR-6
Earlier sketch in CA 57-60
Mertes, Kate 1955- 129
Mertins, Herman, Jr. 1931- 41-44R
Mertins, (Marshall) Louis 1885-1973 .... 41-44R
Merton, Andrew H(arris) 1944- 107
Merton, Giles
See Curran, Mona (Elisa)
Merton, Robert K(ing) 1910- CANR-31
Earlier sketch in CA 41-44R
Merton, Stephen 1912- 21-24R
Merton, Thomas 1915-1968 .... CANR-53
Obituary 25-28R
Earlier sketches in CA 5-8R, CANR-22
See also CLC 1, 3, 11, 34, 83
See also DLB 48
See also DLBY 81
See also MTCW 1
See also PC 10
Mertvago, Peter 1946- 154
Mertz, Barbara (Gross) 1927- CANR-63
Earlier sketches in CA 21-24R, CANR-11, 36
Interview in CANR-36
See also AAYA 24
See also BEST 90:4
See also SATA 49
Mertz, Richard R(olland) 1927- 21-24R
Merullo, Roland 1953- 136
Merwe, A. v. d.
See Geyl, Pieter (Catharinus Arie)
Merwin, Decie 1894-1961 Obituary 111
See also SATA-Brief 32
Merwin, Sam(uel Kimball), Jr. 1910- 131
Merwin, W(illiam) S(tanley) 1927- CANR-51
Earlier sketches in CA 13-16R, CANR-15
Interview in CANR-15
See also CLC 1, 2, 3, 5, 8, 13, 18, 45, 88
See also DAM POET
See also DLB 5, 169
See also MTCW 1
Mery, Fernand 1897-1984 .... CANR-29
Earlier sketch in CA 105
Merz, Charles 1893-1977 Obituary 73-76
Merzer, Meridee 1947- 102
Mesa-Lago, Carmelo 1934- CANR-53
Earlier sketches in CA 25-28R, CANR-10, 26
Meschel, Susan V. 1936- .... SATA 83
Meserve, Walter Joseph, Jr. 1923- CANR-1
Earlier sketch in CA 1-4R
Meshack, B(illie) A(ugusta) 1922- 93-96
Meshenberg, Michael J(ay) 1942- CANR-16
Earlier sketch in CA 93-96
Meske, Eunice Boardman 1926- CANR-4
Earlier sketch in CA 9-12R
Meskill, Johanna Menzel 1930- 17-20R
Meskill, Robert 1918(?)-1970 Obituary 104
Mesle, C. Robert 1949- 147
Mesquita, Bruce James Bueno de
See Bueno de Mesquita, Bruce James
Messager, Charles 1882-1971 Obituary 93-96
Messdeck Annie
See Coade, Jessie
Messegue, Maurice 1921- 103
Messel, Harry 1922- CANR-21
Earlier sketch in CA 103
Messenger, Charles (Rynd Milles) 1942- . CANR-31
Earlier sketches in CA 73-76, CANR-13
See also SATA 59
Messenger, Christian K(arl) 1943- CANR-56
Earlier sketch in CA 132
Messenger, Elizabeth Margery (Esson) 1908- ......
CAP-1
Earlier sketch in CA 11-12
Messenger, Phyllis (E.) Mauch 1950- 132
Messent, Peter Ronald 1949- 106
Messer, Alfred A(mes) 1922- 29-32R
Messer, Donald E(dward) 1941- 138
Messer, Richard 1965- 147
Messer, Ronald Keith 1942- 57-60
Messer, Sarah Carlin 1924(?)-1984 Obituary ... 112
Messer, Thomas M. 1920- 111
Brief entry 106
Messerer, Asaf Mikhailovich 1903-1992 104
Obituary 137
Messerli, Douglas 1947- CANR-39
Earlier sketch in CA 116
Messerli, Jonathan C. 1926- 41-44R
Messerly, John G. 1955- 165
Messick, Dale 1906- .... SATA 64
See also SATA-Brief 48
Messick, Hank
See Messick, Henry H(icks)
Messick, Henry H(icks) 1922- CANR-2
Earlier sketch in CA 45-48

Messieres, Nicole de
See de Messieres, Nicole
Messing, Shep 1949- Brief entry 111
Messing, Simon D(avid) 1922- 57-60
Messinger, C. F. 1913- 21-24R
Messinger, Sheldon L(eopold) 1925- 25-28R
Messmer, Otto 1892(?)-1983 Obituary 111
See also SATA 37
Messner, Fred(rick) R(ichard) 1926- 13-16R
Messner, Gerald 1935- 29-32R
Messner, Johannes 1891-1984 Obituary 112
Messner, Michael A. 1952- 138
Messner, Reinhold 1944- CANR-35
Earlier sketches in CA 81-84, CANR-15
Messner, Stephen Dale 1936- 21-24R
Mesta, Perle 1893(?)-1975 Obituary 57-60
Mester, Terri A. 1948- 165
Mesthene, Emmanuel George 1920- 77-80
Meston, John 1915(?)-1979 Obituary 85-88
Mestrovic, Stjepan G. 1955- 168
Meszaros, Istvan 1930- CANR-9
Earlier sketch in CA 57-60
Meszaros, Marta 1931- 127
Meta
See Tomkiewicz, Mina
Metalious, Grace (de Repentigny) 1924-1964 .... CAP-2
Earlier sketch in CA 21-22
Metaxas, B(asil) N(icolas) 1925- 37-40R
Metcalf, Alida C. 1954- 143
Metcalf, Doris H(unter) .... SATA 91
Metcalf, E(ugene) W(esley) 1945- 65-68
Metcalf, George R. 1914- 25-28R
Metcalf, John 1938- 113
See also CLC 37
See also DLB 60
Metcalf, Kenneth N(olan) 1923-1965 .... 5-8R
Metcalf, Keyes DeWitt 1889-1983 .... 17-20R
Obituary 111
Metcalf, Lawrence E(ugene) 1915- 21-24R
Metcalf, Paul 1917- CANR-39
Earlier sketches in CA 45-48, CANR-1, 17
Metcalf, Peter 116
Metcalf, Suzanne
See Baum, L(yman) Frank
Metcalf, Thomas R. 1934- 13-16R
Metcalf, Vicky 1901- 89-92
Metcalfe, John Wallace 1901-1982 Obituary 107
Metcalfe, Philip (Earle) 1946- 149
Metcalfe, Steve 1953- 108
Metchnikoff, Elie 1845-1916 160
Metereau, Rebecca Bell
See Bell-Metereau, Rebecca
Metesky, George
See Hoffman, Abbie
Methold, Kenneth (Walter) 1931- CANR-32
Earlier sketch in CA 13-16R
Methvin, Eugene H. 1934- 29-32R
Metos, Thomas H(arry) 1932- 93-96
See also SATA 37
Metraux, Guy S(erge) 1917- 9-12R
Metraux, Rhoda 1914- 57-60
Metress, James F.
See Metress, Seamus P.
Metress, Seamus P. 1933- CANR-44
Earlier sketches in CA 57-60, CANR-6, 21
Metropolis, Nicholas Constantine 1915- 110
Mets, David Raymond 1928- 118
Metter, Bert(ram Milton) 1927- .... SATA 56
Mettler, George B(arry) 1934- 93-96
Metwally, M(okhtar) M(ohamed) 1939- CANR-15
Earlier sketch in CA 65-68
Metz, Don 1940- 135
Metz, Donald L(ehman) 1935- 21-24R
Metz, Donald S(hink) 1916- 45-48
Metz, Jerred 1943- CANR-22
Earlier sketch in CA 104
Metz, Leon C(laire) 1930- CANR-36
Earlier sketches in CA 45-48, CANR-1, 16
Metz, Lois Lunt 1906- CAP-1
Earlier sketch in CA 9-10
Metz, Mary (Seawell) 1937- 53-56
Metz, Mary Haywood 1939- CANR-15
Earlier sketch in CA 85-88
Metz, Robert (Henry) 1928- CANR-13
Earlier sketch in CA 61-64
Metz, William 1918- 77-80
Metzdorf, Robert F(rederic)
1912-1975 Obituary 57-60
Metzger, Barbara 1944- 110
Metzger, Bruce Manning 1914- CANR-4
Earlier sketch in CA 9-12R
Metzger, Charles R(eid) 1921- 25-28R
Metzger, Deena P. 1936- 130
Metzger, Erika A(lma) 1933- 33-36R
Metzger, H(owell) Peter 1931- Brief entry 111
Metzger, Michael M(oses) 1935- 21-24R
Metzger, Norman 1924- CANR-9
Earlier sketch in CA 53-56
Metzger, Philip W. 1931- 45-48
Metzger, Robert 1950- 117
Metzger, Stanley D. 1916- 9-12R
Metzger, Thomas A(lbert) 1933- 97-100
Metzger, Walter P. 1922- CANR-17
Earlier sketch in CA 61-64
Metzker, Isaac 1901- 45-48
Metzler, Ken(neth Theodore) 1929- CANR-4
Earlier sketch in CA 53-56
Metzler, Lloyd A(ppleton) 1913- 104
Metzler, Paul 1914- CANR-6
Earlier sketch in CA 57-60
Metzner, Ralph 1936- 69-72
Metzner, Seymour 1924- 21-24R
Meudt, Edna Kritz 1906- CANR-9
Earlier sketch in CA 13-16R
Meurant, Georges 1948- 135
Meurice, Blanca
See von Block, Bela W(illiam)
Meux, Milton O(tto) 1930- 45-48
Meves, Christa 1925- CANR-49
Earlier sketches in CA 93-96, CANR-24
Mew, Charlotte (Mary) 1870-1928 Brief entry 105
See also DLB 19, 135
See also TCLC 8
Mewburn, Martin
See Hitchin, Martin Mewburn
Mewhinney, Bruce 1949- 118
Mews, Hazel 1909-1975 .... CAP-2
Earlier sketch in CA 29-32
Mews, Siegfried 1933- CANR-45
Earlier sketches in CA 57-60, CANR-7, 22
Mewshaw, Michael 1943- CANR-47
Earlier sketches in CA 53-56, CANR-7
See also CLC 9
See also DLBY 80
Mey, Jacob Lovis
See Meij, Jacob L(ouis)
Meyen, Edward L. 1937- 33-36R
Meyendorff, John 1926-1992 .... CANR-47
Obituary 138
Earlier sketches in CA 21-24R, CANR-9
Meyer, Agnes E(lizabeth Ernst)
1887-1970 Obituary 29-32R
Meyer, Albert Julius 1919-1983 Obituary 111
Meyer, Alfred (Herman) 1893- CAP-1
Earlier sketch in CA 13-14
Meyer, Alfred George 1920- 17-20R
Meyer, Anthony 1920- 134
Meyer, Armin Henry 1914- 85-88
Meyer, Barbara 1939- .... SATA 77
Meyer, Ben F(ranklin) 1927- CANR-43
Earlier sketches in CA 37-40R, CANR-14
Meyer, Bernard C. 1910- 73-76
Meyer, Bernard F. 1891(?)-1975 Obituary 57-60
Meyer, Carl S(tamm) 1907-1972 .... CAP-1
Earlier sketch in CA 13-16
Meyer, Carol H. 1924-1996 .... CANR-13
Obituary 155
Earlier sketch in CA 73-76
Meyer, Carolyn (Mae) 1935- CANR-57
Earlier sketches in CA 49-52, CANR-2
See also AAYA 16
See also JRDA
See also MAICYA
See also SAAS 9
See also SATA 9, 70
Meyer, Charles R. 1920- 33-36R
Meyer, Charles R(obert) 1926- 69-72
Meyer, Clarence 1903- 97-100
Meyer, Conrad Ferdinand 1825-1905 .... DLB 129
Meyer, Cord, Jr. 1920- 144
Meyer, D. Swing 1938- 17-20R
Meyer, David R. 1943- 65-68
Meyer, Donald (Burton) 1923- 21-24R
Meyer, Donald H(arvey) 1935- Brief entry 113
Meyer, Doris (L.) 1942- CANR-33
Earlier sketch in CA 89-92
See also HW
Meyer, Duane Gilbert 1926- 5-8R
Meyer, E. Y. 1946- .... DLB 75
Meyer, Edith Patterson 1895- CANR-1
Earlier sketch in CA 1-4R
See also SATA 5
Meyer, Elizabeth C(ooper) 1958- 69-72
Meyer, Ellen Hope 1928- 119
Meyer, Erika 1904- 73-76
Meyer, Ernst Hermann 1905-1988(?) Obituary 127
Meyer, Eugene 1875-1959 .... DLB 29
Meyer, Eugene L. 1942- 135
Meyer, F(ranklyn) E(dward) 1932- 1-4R
See also SATA 9
Meyer, Frank S(traus) 1909-1972 .... CAP-1
Obituary 33-36R
Earlier sketch in CA 9-10
Meyer, Fred(erick Robert) 1922-1985 57-60
Obituary 117
Meyer, George H(erbert) 1928- 116
Meyer, Gladys (Eleanor) 1908-1986 166
Obituary 118
Meyer, H(arold) A(lbert) 1898-1980 .... CANR-4
Obituary 102
Earlier sketch in CA 5-8R
Meyer, H. K. Houston
See Meyer, Heinrich
Meyer, Harding 1928- 130
Meyer, Harold D(iedrich) 1892-1974(?) CAP-2
Earlier sketch in CA 19-20
Meyer, Harold G. 1909(?)-1986 Obituary 118
Meyer, Heinrich 1904-1977 49-52
Obituary 85-88
Meyer, Herbert W(alter) 1892- CAP-2
Earlier sketch in CA 33-36
Meyer, Herman 1911- 21-24R
Meyer, Howard N(icholas) 1914- 13-16R
Meyer, Jean Shepherd .... SATA 11
Meyer, Jerome Sydney 1895-1975 .... CANR-4
Obituary 57-60
Earlier sketch in CA 1-4R
See also SATA 3
See also SATA-Obit 25
Meyer, Joachim-Ernst 1917- 57-60
Meyer, John Robert 1927- CANR-9
Earlier sketch in CA 13-16R
Meyer, June
See Jordan, June
Meyer, Karl E(rnest) 1928- CANR-1
Earlier sketch in CA 1-4R
Meyer, Lawrence (Robert) 1941- CANR-34
Earlier sketch in CA 73-76
Meyer, Leisa D. 159
Meyer, Leonard B. 1918- 13-16R
Meyer, Lillian Nicholson 1917(?)-1983 Obituary 109
Meyer, Linda D(oreen) 1948- CANR-37
Earlier sketches in CA 93-96, CANR-16
Meyer, Louis A(lbert) 1942- 37-40R
See also SATA 12
Meyer, Lynn
See Slavitt, David R(ytman)
Meyer, Lysle E(dward) 1932- 144
Meyer, Mabel H. 1890(?)-1976 Obituary 61-64
Meyer, Marie-Louise 1936- 97-100
Meyer, Mary Keysor 1919- 102
Meyer, Michael (Leverson) 1921- CANR-64
Earlier sketches in CA 25-28R, CANR-13
See also DLB 155
Meyer, Michael A. 1937- 21-24R
Meyer, Michael C. 1935- CANR-10
Earlier sketch in CA 21-24R
Meyer, Michael J. 1956- 139
Meyer, Nicholas 1945- CANR-7
Earlier sketch in CA 49-52
Meyer, Peter (Barrett) 1950- 141
Meyer, Philip (Edward) 1930- CANR-10
Earlier sketch in CA 65-68
Meyer, Renate 1930- 53-56
See also SATA 6
Meyer, Richard E. 1939- 150
Meyer, Robert H. 1934- 37-40R
Meyer, Ronald 1952- 135
Meyer, Roy W(illard) 1925- 17-20R
Meyer, Ruth F(ritz) 1910- CAP-2
Earlier sketch in CA 23-24
Meyer, Stewart (Martin) 1947- 118
Meyer, Susan E. 1940- CANR-19
Earlier sketches in CA 45-48, CANR-2
See also SATA 64
Meyer, Thomas 1947- CANR-1
Earlier sketch in CA 49-52
Meyer, William Eugene 1923- 45-48
Meyer, William R(obert) 1949- 77-80
Meyer de Schauensee, Rodolphe
See De Schauensee, Rodolphe Meyer
Meyerhof, Otto Fritz 1884-1951 162
Meyerhoff, Arthur E(dward)
1895-1986 Obituary 120
Meyerhoff, Howard A(ugustus) 1899- CAP-2
Earlier sketch in CA 19-20
Meyering, Ralph A. 1930- 29-32R
Meyering, Sheryl L. 1948- 148
Meyer-Meyrink, Gustav 1868-1932 Brief entry 117
See also Meyrink, Gustav
Meyerowitz, Eva (Leonie) L(ewin-) R(ichter) 9-12R
Meyerowitz, Joanne 1954- 146
Meyerowitz, Patricia 1933- 21-24R
Meyers, Albert L. 1904(?)-1981 Obituary 102
Meyers, Annette (Brafman) 1934- 132
Meyers, Bert(ram) 1928-1979 101
Meyers, Carlton R(oy) 1922- 57-60
Meyers, Carol L(yons) 1942- CANR-32
Earlier sketch in CA 113
Meyers, Carole Terwilliger 1945- 69-72
Meyers, Cecil H(arold) 1920- 29-32R
Meyers, David W. 1942- 29-32R
Meyers, Edward 1934- 101
Meyers, Eric M(ark) 1940- 110
Meyers, Gertrude Barlow 1902- 1-4R
Meyers, Jeffrey 1939- CANR-54
Earlier sketch in CA 73-76
See also CLC 39
See also DLB 111
Meyers, Joan Simpson 1927- CANR-14
Earlier sketch in CA 17-20R
Meyers, Lawrence Stanley 1943- 57-60
Meyers, Mann
See Meyers, Martin
Meyers, Martin 1934- 146
Meyers, Marvin 1921- Brief entry 108
Meyers, Mary Ann 1937- 116
Meyers, Michael Jay 1946- 65-68
Meyers, Nancy 1950- 138
Meyers, Odette 1934- 164
Meyers, Robert Rex 1923- 17-20R
Meyers, Roy (Lethbridge) 1910-1974 .... CAP-2
Earlier sketch in CA 25-28
Meyers, Ruth S(chlaff) 1923- 117
Meyers, Susan
See Falk, Susan Meyers
Meyers, Susan 1942- CANR-13
Earlier sketch in CA 21-24R
See also SATA 19
Meyers, Walter E(arl) 1939- CANR-6
Earlier sketch in CA 53-56
Meyerson, Adam 1953- 128
Meyerson, Edward L(eon) 1904-1980 .... CANR-12
Earlier sketch in CA 61-64
Meyerson, Martin 1922- Brief entry 115
Meynell, Alice (Christina Gertrude Thompson)
1847-1922 Brief entry 104
See also DLB 19, 98
See also TCLC 6
Meynell, Alix (Hester M.) 1903- 128
Meynell, Francis Meredith Wilfrid 1891-1975 .... CAP-2
Obituary 57-60
Earlier sketch in CA 19-20
Meynell, Hugo A. 1936- 130
Meynell, Laurence Walter 1899-1989 .... CANR-15
Obituary 128
Earlier sketch in CA 81-84
See also SATA-Obit 61
Meynell, Viola 1885-1956 .... DLB 153
Meyners, J. Robert 1922- 104
Meynier, Yvonne (Pollet) 1908- 73-76
See also SATA 14
Meyrink, Gustav
See Meyer-Meyrink, Gustav
See also DLB 81
See also TCLC 21
Meyrink, Gustav Meyer
See Meyer-Meyrink, Gustav
Meza, Pedro Thomas 1941- 37-40R
Mezerick, Avrahm G. 1901-1986 Obituary 119
Mezey, Michael L(loyd) 1943- 118
Mezey, Robert 1935- CANR-7
Earlier sketch in CA 57-60
See also SATA 33
Mezvinsky, Edward M. 1937- 103
Mezvinsky, Shirley
See Lauro, Shirley (Shapiro) Mezvinsky
Mezzrow, Mezz
See Mezzrow, Milton
Mezzrow, Milton 1890(?)-1972 .... 37-40R
Miall, Robert
See Burke, John (Frederick)
Mian, Mary (Lawrence Shipman) 1902- .... SATA-Brief 47
Micale, Albert 1913- .... SATA 22
Micallef, Benjamin A(nthony) 1925-1980 53-56
Obituary 103
Micallef, John 1923- 25-28R
Micaud, Charles Antoine 1910- 5-8R
Miceli, Frank 1932- 57-60
Miceli, Vincent P(eter) 1915- Brief entry 114
Michael, Colette V(erger) 1937- 139
Michael, David J. 1944- 29-32R
Michael, Franz H(enry) 1907- CANR-4
Earlier sketch in CA 5-8R
Michael, George 1919- 41-44R
Michael, Henry N(athaniel) 1913- 33-36R
Michael, Ian (Lockie) 1915- 104
Michael, James
See Scagnetti, Jack
Michael, John A(rthur) 1921- 133
Michael, Judith
See Barnard, Judith
Michael, Manfred
See Winterfeld, Henry
Michael, Paul Martin 1934- CANR-10
Earlier sketch in CA 17-20R
Michael, Phyllis C(allender) 1908- CANR-2
Earlier sketch in CA 5-8R
Michael, S(tanley) T(heodore) 1912- 13-16R
Michael, Thomas A. 1933- 33-36R
Michael, Tom
See Michael, Thomas A.
Michael, William B(urton) 1922- 45-48
Michael, Wolfgang F(riedrich) 1909- CANR-14
Earlier sketch in CA 41-44R
Michaeles, M. M.
See Golding, Morton J(ay)
Michaelides, Constantine E. 1930- 25-28R
Michaelis, David (Tead) 1957- 114
Michaelis, John U(dell) 1912- 69-72
Michaelis-Jena, Ruth
See Ratcliff, Ruth
Michaels, Anne 1958- 157
Michaels, Barbara
See Mertz, Barbara (Gross)
Michaels, Carolyn Leopold
See Leopold, Carolyn Clugston
Michaels, Dale
See Rifkin, Shepard
Michaels, Fern
See Anderson, Roberta
and Kuczkir, Mary
Michaels, J. Ramsey 1931- CANR-38
Earlier sketch in CA 116
Michaels, Joanne 1950- CANR-23
Earlier sketch in CA 107
Michaels, Joanne Louise
See Teitelbaum, Michael
Michaels, Joe
See Saltzman, Joseph
Michaels, Kasey
See Seidick, Kathryn A(melia)
Michaels, Kristin
See Williams, Jeanne
Michaels, Leonard 1933- CANR-62
Earlier sketches in CA 61-64, CANR-21
See also CLC 6, 25
See also DLB 130
See also MTCW 1
See also SSC 16
Michaels, Lorne 1944- 142
See also AAYA 12
Michaels, Lynn
See Strongin, Lynn
Michaels, Molly
See Untermeyer, Louis
Michaels, Neal
See Teitelbaum, Michael
Michaels, Norman 97-100
Michaels, Philip
See Magocsi, Paul Robert
and van Rjndt, Philippe
Michaels, Ralph
See Filicchia, Ralph
Michaels, Sidney R(amon) 1927- 17-20R
Michaels, Ski
See Pellowski, Michael (Joseph)
Michaels, Steve
See Avallone, Michael (Angelo, Jr.)
Michaels, Steve 1955- .... SATA 71
Michaels, William M. 1917- .... SATA 77
Michaelson, L(ouis) W. 1917- CANR-14
Earlier sketch in CA 77-80
Michaely, Michael 1928- 103
Michalczyk, John Joseph 1941- 104
Michalopoulos, Andre 1897- CAP-2
Earlier sketch in CA 23-24
Michalos, Alex C. 1935- 37-40R
Michalowski, Kazimierz 1901-1981 Obituary 108
Michalski, John 1934- 25-28R
Michalson, Carl (Donald, Jr.) 1915-1965 .... 1-4R

Michaud, Charles Regis 1910- ... CAP-2
Earlier sketch in CA 19-20
Michaud, Stephen G(age) 1948- ... 109
Michaux, Henri 1899-1984 ... 85-88
Obituary ... 114
See also CLC 8, 19
Michaux, William W(hitehead) 1919- ... 41-44R
Miche, Giuseppe
See Bochenski, Joseph M.
Micheaux, Oscar 1884-1951 ... DLB 50
See also TCLC 76
Micheels, Peter A. 1945- ... 132
Michel, Anna 1943- ... 85-88
See also SATA 49
See also SATA-Brief 40
Michel, Beth
See Dubus, Elizabeth Nell
Michel, Francois 1948- ... SATA 82
Michel, Georges 1926- ... CANR-31
Earlier sketch in CA 25-28R
Michel, Henri (Jules) 1907- ... CANR-19
Earlier sketches in CA 53-56, CANR-4
Michel, Joseph 1922- ... CANR-13
Earlier sketch in CA 25-28R
Michel, Michel Georges
See Georges-Michel, Michel
Michel, Pierre 1934- ... 57-60
Michel, Sandra (Seaton) 1935- ... 77-80
Michel, Sandy
See Michel, Sandra (Seaton)
Michel, (Milton) Scott 1916- ... 1-4R
Michel, Walter 1922- ... 81-84
Micheli, Lyle Joseph 1940- ... CANR-20
Earlier sketch in CA 97-100
Micheline, Jack 1929-1998 ... 122
Obituary ... 165
Brief entry ... 114
Interview in ... 122
See also DLB 16
Michell, John (F.) 1933- ... CANR-23
Earlier sketch in CA 107
Michelman, Herbert 1913-1980 Obituary ... 102
Michelman, Irving S(imon) 1917- ... 69-72
Michelmore, Peter 1930- ... CANR-7
Earlier sketch in CA 5-8R
Michel of Northgate, Dan c. 1265-c. 1340 . DLB 146
Michelon, L. C. 1918- ... CANR-1
Earlier sketch in CA 45-48
Michels, Caroll Chesy 1943- ... 117
Michelson, Albert (Abraham) 1852-1931 ... 163
Michelson, Bruce (N.) 1948- ... 139
Michelson, Edward J(ulias) 1915- ... 77-80
Michelson, Florence B. ... CAP-2
Earlier sketch in CA 21-22
Michelson, Peter 1937- ... CANR-1
Earlier sketch in CA 45-48
Michelson, Stephan 1938- ... 93-96
Michelson, William M. 1940- ... 33-36R
Michener, Charles D(uncan) 1918- ... 117
Michener, Charles Thomson 1940- ... 104
Michener, James A(lbert) 1907(?)-1997 .. CANR-68
Obituary ... 161
Earlier sketches in CA 5-8R, CANR-21, 45
See also AAYA 27
See also AITN 1
See also BEST 90:1
See also CLC 1, 5, 11, 29, 60, 109
See also DAM NOV, POP
See also DLB 6
See also MTCW 1
Michie, Allan (Andrew) 1915-1973 Obituary .. 45-48
Michie, Donald 1923- ... 121
Michie, James 1927- ... 164
Brief entry ... 116
Michie, Jonathan 1957- ... 132
Michman, Ronald D(avid) 1931- ... CANR-7
Earlier sketch in CA 57-60
Michod, Richard E. 1951- ... 147
Micich, Paul ... SATA 74
Mickel, Emanuel John, Jr. 1937- ... 37-40R
Mickelbury, Penny 1948- ... 146
Mickelsen, A(nton) Berkeley 1920- ... 9-12R
Mickelsen, Olaf 1912- ... 17-20R
Mickelson, Monty (Phillip) 1956- ... 141
Mickelson, Sig 1913- ... 111
Micken, Charles M. 1918- ... 13-16R
Mickey, Paul A(lbert) 1937- ... CANR-1
Earlier sketch in CA 49-52
Mickiewicz, Ellen Propper 1938- ... CANR-49
Earlier sketches in CA 21-24R, CANR-9, 24
Mickle, Shelley Fraser 1944- ... 132
Micklejohn, George 1717(?)-1818 ... DLB 31
Micklem, Nathaniel 1888-1976 ... 103
Mickler, Ernest M(atthew)
1940(?)-1988 Obituary ... 127
Micklish, Rita 1931- ... 49-52
See also SATA 12
Mickolus, Edward F(rancis) 1950- ... 106
Micks, Marianne H(offman) 1923- ... CANR-12
Earlier sketch in CA 17-20R
Micou, Paul 1959- ... 140
Micucci, Charles (Patrick, Jr.) 1959- ... 137
See also SATA 82
Micunovic, Veljko 1916-1982 ... 109
Obituary ... 107
Midda, Sara 1951- ... 135
Middeldorf, Ulrich Alexander
1901-1983 Obituary ... 109
Middendorf, John Harlan 1922- ... 104
Middlebrook, Christina 1941- ... 156
Middlebrook, David
See Rosenus, Alan (Harvey)
Middlebrook, Diane Wood 1939- ... CANR-15
Earlier sketch in CA 81-84
Middlebrook, Jonathan 1940- ... 65-68
Middlebrook, (Norman) Martin 1932- ... CANR-57
Earlier sketches in CA 37-40R, CANR-14, 31
Middlekauff, Robert (Lawrence) 1929- ... 130
Brief entry ... 112
Middleman, Ruth J. Rosenbloom 1923- ... 104
Middlemas, Keith
See Middlemas, Robert Keith
Middlemas, Robert Keith 1935- ... CANR-12
Earlier sketch in CA 29-32R
Middlemiss, Robert (William) 1938- ... CANR-12
Earlier sketch in CA 73-76
Middleton, Bernard C(hester) 1924- ... 41-44R
Middleton, Christopher 1926- ... CANR-54
Earlier sketches in CA 13-16R, CANR-29
See also CLC 13
See also DLB 40
Middleton, Darren J. N. 1966- ... 157
Middleton, David L. 1940- ... 37-40R
Middleton, Drew 1914(?)-1990 Obituary ... 130
Brief entry ... 110
Middleton, George 1880-1967 Obituary ... 25-28R
Middleton, Haydn 1955- ... 132
See also SATA 85
Middleton, Michael (Humfrey) 1917- ... CANR-51
Earlier sketch in CA 124
Middleton, Michael L. 1945- ... 145
Middleton, Nigel (Gordon) 1918- ... CANR-25
Earlier sketch in CA 45-48
Middleton, O(sman) E(dward) 1925- ... 81-84
Middleton, Richard (Barham) 1882-1911 .. DLB 156
See also TCLC 56
Middleton, Richard 1945- ... 109
Middleton, Roger 1955- ... 126
Middleton, Stanley 1919- ... CANR-46
Earlier sketches in CA 25-28R, CANR-21
See also CAAS 23
See also CLC 7, 38
See also DLB 14
Middleton, Stephen 1954- ... 144
Middleton, Thomas 1580-1627 .. DAM DRAM, MST
See also DC 5
See also DLB 58
Middleton-Murry, Colin
See Middleton-Murry, John (Jr.)
Middleton-Murry, John (Jr.) 1926- ... CANR-3
Earlier sketch in CA 5-8R
Middleton Murry, Mary
See Murry, Mary Middleton
Midelfort, H(ans) C(hristian) Erik 1942- ... CANR-26
Earlier sketch in CA 45-48
Midgett, Elwin W. 1911- ... CAP-2
Earlier sketch in CA 29-32
Midgett, Wink
See Midgett, Elwin W.
Midgley, David A(lan) 1898- ... 17-20R
Midgley, E(rnest) B(rian) F(rancis) 1927- ... 93-96
Midgley, Graham 1923- ... 73-76
Midgley, Louis C(asper) 1931- ... 41-44R
Midgley, Mary 1919- ... CANR-43
Earlier sketches in CA 89-92, CANR-20
Midlarsky, Manus I(ssacher) 1937- ... 57-60
Midler, Bette 1945- ... 106
Midtlyng, Joanna 1927- ... 61-64
Midwinter, E(ric) C(lare) 1932- ... CANR-26
Earlier sketch in CA 29-32R
Mieczkowski, Bogdan 1924- ... 111
Miegel, Agnes 1879-1964 ... DLB 56
Miel, Alice Marie 1906-1998 ... CANR-20
Obituary ... 164
Earlier sketches in CA 1-4R, CANR-5
Mielke, Arthur W(illard) 1912-1978 ... CANR-4
Earlier sketch in CA 1-4R
Mielziner, Jo 1901-1976 ... 45-48
Obituary ... 65-68
Miernyk, William Henry 1918- ... 17-20R
Miers, Earl Schenck 1910-1972 ... CANR-2
Obituary ... 37-40R
Earlier sketch in CA 1-4R
See also SATA 1
See also SATA-Obit 26
Miers, Suzanne (Doyle) 1922- ... 61-64
Mierzenski, Stanislaw 1903-1964 ... 1-4R
Miesel, Sandra (Louise) 1941- ... 120
Miethe, Terry Lee 1948- ... 105
Miewald, Robert D(ale) 1938- ... 117
Migdal, Joel S(amuel) 1945- ... CANR-6
Earlier sketch in CA 57-60
Migdale, Lawrence 1951- ... SATA 89
Migdalski, Edward C(harles) 1918- ... CANR-4
Earlier sketch in CA 9-12R
Migel, Parmenia
See Ekstrom, Parmenia Migel
Mighetto, Lisa 1955- ... 141
Mighton, John 1957- ... 166
Migliore, R. Henry 1940- ... 110
Migliorini, Bruno 1896-1975 Obituary ... 116
Miglis, John 1950- ... CANR-20
Earlier sketch in CA 81-84
Mignani, Rigo 1921- ... 37-40R
Migueis, Jose Rodrigues 1901- ... CLC 10
Miguez-Bonino, Jose 1924- ... 49-52
Mihailovic, Dragoslav 1930- ... DLB 181
Mihailovich, Vasa D. 1926- ... CANR-14
Earlier sketch in CA 41-44R
Mihajlov, Mihajlo 1934- ... 130
Brief entry ... 105
Mihalas, Dimitri M(anuel) 1939- ... CANR-4
Earlier sketch in CA 53-56
Mihalic, Slavko 1928- ... DLB 181
Mihaly, Mary E(llen) 1950- ... 97-100
Mihanovich, Clement Simon 1913- ... 5-8R
Mijuskovic, Ben Lazare 1937- ... 132
Mikaelsen, Ben(jamin John) 1952- ... 139
See also SATA 73
Mikalson, Jon D. 1943- ... 140
Mikan, Baron
See Barba, Harry
Mikdashi, Zuhayr 1933- ... CANR-39
Earlier sketches in CA 89-92, CANR-17
Mikes, George 1912-1987 ... CANR-6
Obituary ... 123
Earlier sketch in CA 9-12R
Mikesell, Arthur M. 1932- ... 13-16R
Mikesell, John L(ee) 1942- ... 102
Mikesell, Marvin Wray 1930- ... CANR-4
Earlier sketch in CA 1-4R
Mikesell, Raymond F(rech) 1913- ... CANR-41
Earlier sketches in CA 1-4R, CANR-4, 19
Mikesell, Rufus Merrill 1893-1972 ... CAP-2
Earlier sketch in CA 25-28
Mikesell, William H(enry) 1887-1969 ... CAP-2
Earlier sketch in CA 19-20
Mikhail, E(dward) H(alim) 1926- ... CANR-58
Earlier sketches in CA 37-40R, CANR-14, 31
Mikhailov, M.
See Mihajlov, Mihajlo
Mikhalkov, Sergei Vladimirovich 1913- Brief entry ... 116
Mikhalkov-Konchalovsky, Andrei (Sergeyevich)
1937- ... 127
Miki, Chihan
See Naruse, Mikio
Mikkelsen, Ejnar 1881(?)-1971 Obituary ... 29-32R
Miklowitz, Gloria D. 1927- ... CANR-51
Earlier sketches in CA 25-28R, CANR-10, 26
See also AAYA 6
See also JRDA
See also MAICYA
See also SAAS 17
See also SATA 4, 68
Mikolaycak, Charles 1937-1993 ... CANR-38
Obituary ... 141
Earlier sketches in CA 61-64, CANR-8, 23
See also MAICYA
See also SAAS 4
See also SATA 9, 78
See also SATA-Obit 75
Mikolyzk, Thomas A. 1953- ... 138
Mikszath, Kalman 1847-1910 ... TCLC 31
Mikulas, William Lee 1942- ... 53-56
Mikus, Joseph A(ugust) 1909- ... 61-64
Milano, Paolo 1904-1988 Obituary ... 125
Milberg, Warren H(oward) 1941- ... 109
Milbrath, Lester W(alter) 1925- ... CANR-4
Earlier sketch in CA 9-12R
Milburn, George 1906-1966 Obituary ... 109
Milburn, Josephine F(ishel) 1928- ... CANR-13
Earlier sketch in CA 21-24R
Milburn, Joyce 1953- ... 114
Milburn, Robert (Leslie Pollington) 1907- ... 130
Milch, Robert J(effrey) 1938- ... 25-28R
Milcsik, Margie 1950- ... 110
Mild, Warren (Paul) 1922- ... CANR-8
Earlier sketch in CA 21-24R
See also SATA 41
Mildner, Gerard C. S. 1959- ... 138
Mileck, Joseph 1922- ... 107
Milenkovitch, Michael M. 1932- ... 37-40R
Milenski, Paul Edward 1942- ... 128
Miles, Angela R(ose) 1946- ... 122
Miles, Barry 1943- ... 134
Miles, (Louise) Bebe 1924-1980 ... CANR-9
Earlier sketch in CA 61-64
Miles, Bernard 1907- ... 133
Miles, Betty 1928- ... CANR-48
Earlier sketches in CA 1-4R, CANR-5, 20
See also JRDA
See also SAAS 9
See also SATA 8, 78
Miles, Beverly Parkhurst 1940- ... 107
Miles, Charles 1894- ... 5-8R
Miles, David H(olmes) 1940- ... 57-60
Miles, Dorien K(lein) 1915- ... CANR-8
Earlier sketch in CA 61-64
Miles, Dudley (Robert Alexander) 1947- ... 131
Miles, Edwin A(rthur) 1926- ... 1-4R
Miles, Elliot
See Ludvigsen, Karl (Eric)
Miles, Elton (Roger) 1917- ... 37-40R
Miles, Gary Britten 1940- ... 102
Miles, George C(arpenter)
1904-1975 Obituary ... 61-64
Miles, Herbert J(ackson) 1907- ... 21-24R
Miles, Ian (Douglas) 1948- ... 115
Miles, Jack ... CLC 100
Miles, John
See Bickham, Jack M(iles)
Miles, Josephine (Louise) 1911-1985 ... CANR-55
Obituary ... 116
Earlier sketches in CA 1-4R, CANR-2
See also CLC 1, 2, 14, 34, 39
See also DAM POET
See also DLB 48
Miles, Joyce C(rudgington) 1927- ... 105
Miles, Judith Mary (Huhta) 1937- ... 65-68
Miles, Keith 1940- ... 139
Miles, Leland (Weber, Jr.) 1924- ... 13-16R
Miles, Margaret R(uth) 1937- ... 117
Miles, Mary Lillian (Brown) 1908- ... 13-16R
Miles, Matthew B(ailey) 1926- ... CANR-36
Earlier sketches in CA 81-84, CANR-15
Miles, Michael W. 1945- ... 33-36R
Miles, Miska
See Martin, Patricia Miles
Miles, O. Thomas 1923- ... 21-24R
Miles, (Mary) Patricia 1930- ... CANR-27
Earlier sketches in CA 69-72, CANR-11
See also SATA 29
Miles, Patricia A.
See Martin, Patricia Miles
Miles, Peter
See Miles, Richard
Miles, Richard 1938- ... 105
Miles, Robert H. 1944- ... 118
Miles, Robert L(ee) 1939- ... 107
Miles, Russell Hancock 1895- ... CAP-1
Earlier sketch in CA 9-10
Miles, Stanley 1911-1987 Obituary ... 123
Miles, Sylva
See Miles, Dorien K(lein)
and Mularchyk, Sylva
Miles, T(homas) R(ichard) 1923- ... CANR-38
Earlier sketches in CA 49-52, CANR-1, 17
Miles, William F. S. 1955- ... 151
Milestone, Lewis 1895-1980 Obituary ... 101
Miletich, Leo N(ick) 1946- ... 148
Miletus, Rex
See Burgess, Michael (Roy)
Milford, D(avid) S(umner) 1905-1984 Obituary .. 113
Milford, Nancy 1938- ... 29-32R
Milgate, Rodney Armour 1934- ... 107
Milgram, Gail Gleason 1942- ... 29-32R
Milgram, Morris 1916-1997 ... 73-76
Obituary ... 159
Milgram, Stanley 1933-1984 ... CANR-29
Obituary ... 114
Earlier sketch in CA 105
Milgrom, Harry 1912- ... CANR-3
Earlier sketch in CA 1-4R
See also SATA 25
Milgrom, Jacob 1923- ... 53-56
Milhaud, Darius 1892-1974 Obituary ... 49-52
Milhaven, John Giles 1927- ... 29-32R
Milhorn, H(oward) Thomas, Jr. 1936- ... 146
Milhous, Judith 1946- ... 129
Milhous, Katherine 1894-1977 Obituary ... 104
See also SATA 15
Milhouse, Paul W(illiam) 1910- ... CANR-27
Earlier sketches in CA 25-28R, CANR-11
Mili, Gjon 1904-1984 Obituary ... 112
Milic, Louis T(onko) 1922- ... 21-24R
Milio, Nancy 1938- ... CANR-13
Earlier sketch in CA 29-32R
Milios, Rita 1949- ... 148
See also SATA 79
Milis, Ludo(vicus) J. R. 1940- ... 145
Militant
See Sandburg, Carl (August)
Militello, Pietro
See Natali, Alfred Maxim
Milius, John 1945- ... 101
Interview in ... 101
See also DLB 44
Miljkovic, Branko 1934-1962 ... DLB 181
Milkomane, George Alexis Milkomanovich 1903- ... CANR-20
Earlier sketch in CA 104
Milks, Harold Keith 1908-1979 ... 108
Obituary ... 93-96
Mill, C. R.
See Crnjanski, Milos
Mill, James 1773-1836 ... DLB 107, 158
Mill, John Stuart 1806-1873 ... CDBLB 1832-1890
See also DLB 55, 190
Millais, Raoul 1901- ... SATA 77
Milland, Jack
See Milland, Ray
Milland, Ray 1908(?)-1986 Obituary ... 118
Brief entry ... 113
Millar, Barbara F. 1924- ... 25-28R
See also SATA 12
Millar, Fergus 1935- ... CANR-20
Earlier sketches in CA 13-16R, CANR-5
Millar, George Reid 1910- ... 73-76
Millar, Gilbert John 1939- ... 104
Millar, J(ohn) Halket 1899- ... 9-12R
Millar, James Primrose Malcolm 1893- ... CAP-1
Earlier sketch in CA 9-10
Millar, James R(obert) 1936- ... 29-32R
Millar, Jeff(ery Lynn) 1942- ... CANR-11
Earlier sketch in CA 69-72
Millar, (Minna Henrietta) Joy 1914- ... 93-96
Millar, Kenneth 1915-1983 ... CANR-63
Obituary ... 110
Earlier sketches in CA 9-12R, CANR-16
See also Macdonald, Ross
See also CLC 14
See also DAM POP
See also DLB 2
See also DLBD 6
See also DLBY 83
See also MTCW 1
Millar, Margaret (Ellis Sturm) 1915-1994 . CANR-44
Obituary ... 144
Earlier sketches in CA 13-16R, CANR-16
See also SATA 61
See also SATA-Obit 79
Millar, Oliver (Nicholas) 1923- ... 142
Millar, Ronald (Graeme) 1919-1998 ... 73-76
Obituary ... 167
Millar, T(homas) B(ruce) ... CANR-26
Earlier sketch in CA 29-32R
Millard, A(lan) R(alph) 1937- ... CANR-11
Earlier sketch in CA 25-28R
Millard, Andre 1947- ... 136
Millard, Charles W(arren III) 1932- ... 153
Brief entry ... 115
Millard, Gregory B. 1947(?)-1984 Obituary ... 114
Millard, Joe
See Millard, Joseph (John)
Millard, Joseph (John) 1908- ... CANR-71
Earlier sketch in CA 13-16R
Millay, E. Vincent
See Millay, Edna St. Vincent

Millay, Edna St. Vincent 1892-1950 ... 130
Brief entry ... 104
See also CDALB 1917-1929
See also DA
See also DAB
See also DAC
See also DAM MST, POET
See also DLB 45
See also MTCW 1
See also PC 6
See also TCLC 4, 49
See also WLCS
Millbank, Captain H. R.
See Ellis, Edward S(ylvester)
Millburn, Cynthia
See Brooks, Anne Tedlock
Milldyke, (John) William 1937-1983 ... 77-80
Obituary ... 111
Millen, Clifford H. 1901(?)-1972 Obituary ... 104
Millender, Dharathula H(ood) 1920- ... 17-20R
Miller, Abraham H(irsh) 1940- ... 104
Miller, Al 1936- ... 65-68
Miller, Alan Robert 1929- ... 73-76
Miller, Alan S. 1949- ... 147
Miller, Alan W. 1926- ... 29-32R
Miller, Albert G(riffith) 1905-1982 ... CANR-1
Obituary ... 107
Earlier sketch in CA 1-4R
See also SATA 12
See also SATA-Obit 31
Miller, Albert Jay 1928- ... CANR-1
Earlier sketch in CA 45-48
Miller, Alden D(ykstra) 1940(?)-1984 Obituary ... 113
Miller, Alden Holmes 1906-1965 Obituary ... 109
Miller, Alfred W. 1893(?)-1983 Obituary ... 111
Miller, Alice ... 142
Miller, Alice P(atricia McCarthy) ... CANR-44
Earlier sketch in CA 29-32R
See also SATA 22
Miller, Alicia (Metcalf) 1939- ... 127
Miller, Andrew M. 1960- ... 159
Miller, Anesa 1954- ... 156
Miller, Anita 1926- ... CANR-53
Earlier sketches in CA 111, CANR-29
Miller, Ann
See Collier, Lucille Ann
Miller, Arthur 1915- ... CANR-54
Earlier sketches in CA 1-4R, CANR-2, 30
See also CABS 3
See also AAYA 15
See also AITN 1
See also CDALB 1941-1968
See also CLC 1, 2, 6, 10, 15, 26, 47, 78
See also DA
See also DAB
See also DAC
See also DAM DRAM, MST
See also DC 1
See also DLB 7
See also MTCW 1
See also WLC
Miller, Arthur B(urton) 1922- ... 37-40R
Miller, Arthur R(aphael) 1934- ... 150
Brief entry ... 114
Miller, Arthur S(elwyn) 1917-1988 ... CANR-11
Obituary ... 125
Earlier sketch in CA 69-72
Miller, Barbara D(iane) 1948- ... CANR-23
Earlier sketch in CA 106
Miller, Barbara S(toler) 1940-1993 ... CANR-47
Obituary ... 141
Earlier sketches in CA 25-28R, CANR-11, 27
Miller, Barry 1946- ... 33-36R
Miller, Benj.
See Loomis, Noel M(iller)
Miller, Benjamin F(rank) 1907-1971 ... CANR-4
Obituary ... 29-32R
Earlier sketch in CA 1-4R
Miller, Bernard S. 1920- ... 106
Miller, Beth 1941- ... 136
Miller, Beulah Montgomery 1917- ... 61-64
Miller, (H.) Bill(y) 1920-1961 ... CANR-62
Earlier sketch in CA 108
Miller, Bill D. 1936- ... 102
Miller, Blair 1955- ... 153
Miller, Brent C(arlton) 1947- ... 112
Miller, (Harvey) Brown 1943- ... 101
Miller, Byron Strongman
1912(?)-1978 Obituary ... 77-80
Miller, C(larence) William 1914- ... 53-56
Miller, Calvin 1936- ... CANR-13
Earlier sketch in CA 21-24R
Miller, Caroline 1903- ... DLB 9
Miller, Carroll H(iram) 1907-197(?) ... CAP-1
Earlier sketch in CA 19-20
Miller, Casey (Geddes) 1919-1997 ... 69-72
Obituary ... 156
Miller, Cecilia Parsons 1909- ... CANR-12
Earlier sketch in CA 21-24R
Miller, Cecille (Boyd) 1908- ... 9-12R
Miller, Char
See Miller, Frank L(ubbock) IV
Miller, Charles 1918- ... 77-80
Miller, Charles A. 1937- ... 29-32R
Miller, Charles D(avid) 1942- ... CANR-32
Earlier sketch in CA 69-72
Miller, Charles E. 1929- ... 33-36R
Miller, Charles Henderson 1905- ... CAP-2
Earlier sketch in CA 19-20
Miller, Charles Leslie 1908- ... 49-52
Miller, Christian 1920- ... 108
Miller, Clarence H(arvey) 1930- ... 102
Miller, Clarence J(ohn) 1916- ... CANR-13
Earlier sketch in CA 21-24R
Miller, Clement (Albin) 1915- ... 41-44R
Miller, Conrad
See Strung, Norman
Miller, D(ean) A(rthur) 1931- ... 21-24R
Miller, Daniel Adlai II 1918- ... 37-40R
Miller, Danny 1947- ... CANR-53
Earlier sketch in CA 126
Miller, Danny L(ester) 1949- ... 166
Miller, Darlis A(nn) 1939- ... 125
Miller, David (Leslie) 1946- ... 130
Miller, David 1950- ... CAAS 30
Miller, David C. 1951- ... 147
Miller, David E(ugene) 1909-1978 ... 45-48
Obituary ... 103
Miller, David Harry 1938- ... 57-60
Miller, David L(eroy) 1936- ... 49-52
Miller, David Lee 1951- ... 122
Miller, David Louis 1903-1986 ... 21-24R
Obituary ... 118
Miller, David Merlin 1934- ... 93-96
Miller, David W. 1940- ... 49-52
Miller, Debbie (S.) 1951- ... 133
Miller, Deborah Uchill 1944- ... 116
See also SATA 61
Miller, Delbert C(harles) 1913- ... 25-28R
Miller, Don 1923- ... SATA 15
Miller, Donald 1893-1986 Obituary ... 119
Miller, Donald 1934- ... 97-100
Miller, Donald C(urtis) 1933- ... CANR-6
Earlier sketch in CA 57-60
Miller, Donald Eugene 1929- ... CANR-24
Earlier sketch in CA 106
Miller, Donald George 1909- ... CANR-4
Earlier sketch in CA 5-8R
Miller, Donald L(ane) 1918- ... 17-20R
Miller, Doris R.
See Mosesson, Gloria R(ubin)
Miller, Dorothy (Ryan)
See Ryan, Dorothy (Barger)
Miller, Douglas T(aylor) 1937- ... 21-24R
Miller, E(ugene) Ethelbert 1950- ... 143
See also BW 2
See also DLB 41
Miller, E. F.
See Pohle, Robert W(arren), Jr.
Miller, E(dwin) S(hepard) 1904- ... 45-48
Miller, E(ugene) Willard 1915- ... CANR-40
Earlier sketches in CA 5-8R, CANR-2, 17
Miller, Ed(die) L(eRoy) 1937- ... 37-40R
Miller, Eddie
See Miller, Edward
Miller, Edna Anita 1920- ... 112
See also SATA 29
Miller, Edward 1905-1974 ... CAP-2
Earlier sketch in CA 25-28
See also SATA 8
Miller, Edward G. 1958- ... 150
Miller, Edwin Haviland 1918- ... 110
Miller, Elizabeth 1933- ... 117
See also SATA 41
Miller, Elizabeth Kubota 1932- ... 13-16R
Miller, Elizabeth Maxfield 1910- ... 45-48
Miller, Ella May 1915- ... CANR-11
Earlier sketch in CA 21-24R
Miller, Ellanita 1957- ... SATA 87
Miller, Elmer S(chaffner) 1931- ... 152
Miller, Elwood E. 1925- ... 122
Miller, Ethel Prince 1893- ... CAP-1
Earlier sketch in CA 13-14
Miller, Eugene 1925- ... 101
See also SATA 33
Miller, Eugene E. 1930- ... 135
Miller, Eugenia
See Mandelkorn, Eugenia Miller
Miller, F(rederick) W(alter) G(ascoyne) 1904- ... CANR-11
Earlier sketch in CA 25-28R
Miller, Florence B. 1895(?)-1976 Obituary ... 69-72
Miller, Floyd C. 1912- ... CANR-2
Earlier sketch in CA 1-4R
Miller, Forrestt A. 1931- ... 25-28R
Miller, Frances A. 1937- ... 123
See also SATA 52
See also SATA-Brief 46
Miller, Francis Pickens 1895-1978 ... 69-72
Obituary ... 135
Miller, Frank
See Loomis, Noel M(iller)
Miller, Frank 1925-1983 Obituary ... 109
Miller, Frank L(ubbock) IV 1951- ... CANR-34
Earlier sketch in CA 113
Miller, Fred D., Jr. 1944- ... 129
Miller, G. R.
See Judd, Frederick Charles
Miller, Gabriel 1948- ... 115
Miller, Gary M(ichael) 1941- ... 113
Miller, Gene Edward 1928- ... 97-100
Miller, Genevieve 1914- ... 17-20R
Miller, Geoffrey 1921-1984 Obituary ... 112
Miller, Geoffrey Samuel 1945- ... 104
Miller, George (Eric) 1943- ... CANR-14
Earlier sketch in CA 73-76
Miller, George 1945- ... 157
Miller, George A(rmitage) 1920- ... CANR-1
Earlier sketch in CA 1-4R
Miller, George H(all) 1919- ... 33-36R
Miller, George Louquet 1934- ... 89-92
Miller, Gerald 1928(?)-1970 Obituary ... 104
Miller, Gerald R(aymond) 1931- ... CANR-16
Earlier sketch in CA 93-96
Miller, Glenn T(homas) 1942- Brief entry ... 110
Miller, Gordon W(esley) 1918- ... 89-92
Miller, Gus
See Miller, Gustavus Hindman
Miller, Gustavus Hindman 1857-1929 Brief entry ... 120
Miller, H. Orlo
See Miller, Hanson Orlo
Miller, Hanson Orlo 1911- ... 138
Miller, Haskell M(orris) 1910- ... CAP-2
Earlier sketch in CA 23-24
Miller, Heather Ross 1939- ... CANR-5
Earlier sketch in CA 13-16R
See also DLB 120
Miller, Helen Hill 1899-1995 ... 9-12R
Obituary ... 150
Miller, Helen M(arkley) ... CANR-2
Earlier sketch in CA 1-4R
See also SATA 5
Miller, Helen Topping 1884-1960 Obituary ... 109
See also SATA-Obit 29
Miller, Henry (Valentine) 1891-1980 ... CANR-64
Obituary ... 97-100
Earlier sketches in CA 9-12R, CANR-33
See also CDALB 1929-1941
See also CLC 1, 2, 4, 9, 14, 43, 84
See also DA
See also DAB
See also DAC
See also DAM MST, NOV
See also DLB 4, 9
See also DLBY 80
See also MTCW 1
See also WLC
Miller, Henry Knight 1920- ... CANR-2
Earlier sketch in CA 1-4R
Miller, Herbert E(lmer) 1914- ... CANR-11
Earlier sketch in CA 17-20R
Miller, Hope Ridings ... 25-28R
Miller, Howard S(mith) 1936- ... 29-32R
Miller, Hubert John 1927- ... 37-40R
Miller, Hugh 1802-1856 ... DLB 190
Miller, Hugh 1897(?)-1979 Obituary ... 89-92
Miller, Hugh 1937- ... CANR-12
Earlier sketch in CA 61-64
Miller, Hugh Milton 1908- ... 33-36R
Miller, Ian
See Milne, John
Miller, Isabel
See Routsong, Alma
Miller, J(ohn) D(onald) B(ruce) 1922- ... CANR-13
Earlier sketch in CA 73-76
Miller, J. Dale 1923- ... 105
Miller, J(oseph) Hillis 1928- ... 85-88
See also DLB 67
Miller, J. Innes 1892-1976 ... CAP-2
Earlier sketch in CA 29-32
Miller, J(ames) Maxwell 1937- ... 110
Miller, J(ames) P(inckney) 1919- ... CANR-49
Earlier sketch in CA 25-28R
See also AITN 1, 2
Miller, J(ohn) Robert 1913- ... 45-48
Miller, Jake C. 1929- ... 126
Miller, James 1947- ... 137
Miller, James A. 1957- ... 126
Miller, James C(lifford) III 1942- ... CANR-10
Earlier sketch in CA 25-28R
Miller, James Edward 1945- ... 135
Miller, James Edwin (Jr.) 1920- ... CANR-1
Earlier sketch in CA 1-4R
Miller, James G(rier) 1916- ... 21-24R
Miller, Jane (Judith) 1925-1989 ... CANR-34
Earlier sketches in CA 77-80, CANR-13
See also SATA 15
Miller, Jane 1949- ... 146
Miller, Jason 1939(?)- ... 73-76
See also AITN 1
See also CLC 2
See also DLB 7
Miller, Jay W(ilson) 1893- ... CAP-1
Earlier sketch in CA 13-14
Miller, Jean Baker 1927- ... 154
Brief entry ... 108
Miller, Jeffrey G. 1941- ... 144
Miller, Jerome G. 1931- ... 139
Miller, Jerome K. 1931- ... CANR-44
Earlier sketch in CA 105
Miller, Jewel 1956- ... SATA 73
Miller, Jim Wayne 1936- ... CANR-45
Earlier sketches in CA 49-52, CANR-1, 20
See also CAAS 15
Miller, Joan I(rene) 1944- ... CANR-41
Earlier sketch in CA 117
Miller, Joan M(ary) 1941- ... 108
Miller, Joaquin 1839-1913 ... DLB 186
Miller, John
See Samachson, Joseph
Miller, John (Laurence) 1947- ... 93-96
Miller, John C. 1916(?)-1979 Obituary ... 89-92
Miller, John Chester 1907-1991 ... 73-76
Obituary ... 136
Miller, John Grider 1935- ... 133
Miller, John Harold 1925- ... 5-8R
Miller, John N. 1933- ... 33-36R
Miller, John P(earse, Jr.) 1943- ... CANR-27
Earlier sketch in CA 69-72
Miller, Johnny
See Miller, John (Laurence)
Miller, Jolonda 1945- ... 108
Miller, Jon (Gordon) 1921- ... 53-56
Miller, Jonathan (Wolfe) 1934- ... 115
Brief entry ... 110
Miller, Jordan Y(ale) 1919- ... CANR-2
Earlier sketch in CA 1-4R
Miller, Joseph C(alder) 1939- ... 93-96
Miller, Judi 1941- ... 106
Miller, Judith 1948- ... CANR-61
Earlier sketch in CA 140
Miller, Judith von Daler 1940- ... 69-72
Miller, Julian M. 1922-1976 Obituary ... 69-72
Miller, June 1923- ... 89-92
Miller, K(eith) Bruce 1927- ... 33-36R
See also AITN 1
Miller, Karl (Fergus Connor) 1931- ... 145
Brief entry ... 107
Miller, Katherine C. Hill
See Hill-Miller, Katherine C(ecelia)
Miller, Keith G.
See Graber Miller, Keith Allen
Miller, Kenneth Dexter 1887- ... CAP-1
Earlier sketch in CA 13-14
Miller, Kenneth E(ugene) 1926- ... 21-24R
Miller, Kent S(amuel) 1927- Brief entry ... 109
Miller, Kerby A. 1944- ... 132
Miller, Kristie 1944- ... 142
Miller, Lanora 1932- ... 61-64
Miller, Lee 1907-1977 ... 149
Miller, Lenore 1924- ... 107
Miller, Leon Gordon 1917- ... 104
Miller, Levi 1944- ... 113
Miller, Lewis (Ames) 1928- ... 93-96
Miller, Liam 1924(?)-1987 Obituary ... 122
Miller, Libuse (Lukas) 1915-1973 ... 1-4R
Obituary ... 103
Miller, Lillian B(eresnack) 1923-1997 ... CANR-52
Obituary ... 162
Earlier sketches in CA 21-24R, CANR-9, 25
Miller, Lily Poritz 1938- ... 126
Miller, Linda B. 1937- ... 21-24R
Miller, Linda Lael 1949- ... CANR-30
Earlier sketch in CA 110
Miller, Linda Patterson 1946- ... 135
Miller, Louise (Rolfe) 1940- ... 143
See also SATA 76
Miller, Luree 1926-1996 ... 93-96
Obituary ... 152
Miller, Lyle L. 1919- ... CANR-6
Earlier sketch in CA 13-16R
Miller, Lynn F(ieldman) 1938- ... 109
Miller, Lynn H(ellwarth) 1937- ... 37-40R
Miller, Lynne (Ellen) 1945- ... 89-92
Miller, M. Hughes 1913-1989 Obituary ... 130
Miller, M. L. ... SATA 85
Miller, Madelaine Hemingway 1904- ... 103
See also AITN 2
Miller, Madge 1918- ... 123
Brief entry ... 117
See also SATA 63
Miller, Mara (Jayne) 1944- ... 97-100
Miller, Marc S(cott) 1947- ... CANR-31
Earlier sketch in CA 105
Miller, Margaret J.
See Dale, Margaret J(essy) Miller
Miller, Margery
See Welles, Margery Miller
Miller, Marilyn (Jean) 1925- ... SATA 33
Miller, Marilyn McMeen
See Brown, Marilyn McMeen Miller
Miller, Marjorie M. 1922- ... 101
Miller, Marshall Lee 1942- ... CANR-9
Earlier sketch in CA 57-60
Miller, Martha
See Ivan, Martha Miller Pfaff
Miller, Martha Porter 1897(?)-1983 Obituary ... 109
Miller, Martin A. 1938- ... 65-68
Miller, Marvin ... 133
See also SATA 65
Miller, Mary
See Northcott, (William) Cecil
Miller, Mary Agnes 1888(?)-1973 Obituary ... 45-48
Miller, Mary Beth 1942- ... 61-64
See also SATA 9
Miller, Mary Britton 1883-1975 ... CANR-16
Obituary ... 57-60
Earlier sketch in CA 1-4R
Miller, Maryann 1943- ... SATA 73
Miller (Riis), Maurine 1910- ... 118
Miller, Max (Carlton) 1899-1967 ... CANR-16
Obituary ... 25-28R
Earlier sketch in CA 1-4R
Miller, May 1899- ... 142
See also BW 2
See also DLB 41
Miller, Melvin H(ull) 1920- ... 13-16R
Miller, Merl Kem 1942- ... 111
Miller, Merle 1919-1986 ... CANR-4
Obituary ... 119
Earlier sketch in CA 9-12R
See also AITN 1
Miller, Merton Howard 1923- ... 134
Brief entry ... 109
Miller, Michael M. 1910(?)-1977 Obituary ... 73-76
Miller, Milt 1916- ... 117
Miller, Minnie M. 1899-1983 ... CAP-2
Obituary ... 110
Earlier sketch in CA 21-22
Miller, Miranda 1950- ... 132
Miller, Morris 1914- ... 17-20R
Miller, Muriel
See Minor, Muriel Miller
Miller, N(ewton) Edd 1920- ... 25-28R
Miller, Naomi 1928- ... 111
Miller, Natalie 1917-1976 ... SATA 35
Miller, Nathan 1927- ... CANR-4
Earlier sketch in CA 53-56
Miller, Neal E(lgar) 1909- ... 81-84
Miller, Nicole Puleo 1944- ... 49-52
Miller, Nina Hull 1894-1974 ... CAP-1
Earlier sketch in CA 9-10
Miller, Nolan 1912- ... 9-12R
Miller, Norman 1933- ... 37-40R
Miller, Norman C(harles) 1934- ... 37-40R
Miller, Nyle H. 1907- ... CAP-2
Earlier sketch in CA 23-24
Miller, Olga K(omarkova) 1908- ... 107
Miller, Orlo
See Miller, Hanson Orlo

Miller, Orson K., Jr. 1930- ... 126
Brief entry ... 110
Miller, Osborn (Maitland)
1896(?)-1979 Obituary ... 89-92
Miller, Oscar J. 1913- ... 37-40R
Miller, Patrick Dwight, Jr. 1935- ... 112
Miller, Paul 1906-1991 ... DLB 127
Miller, Paul Martin 1914- ... CANR-10
Earlier sketch in CA 17-20R
Miller, Paul R(ichard) 1929- ... 21-24R
Miller, Paul William 1926- ... 41-44R
Miller, Perry (Gilbert Eddy)
1905-1963 Obituary ... 93-96
See also DLB 17, 63
Miller, (Mitchell) Peter 1934- ... 37-40R
Miller, Peter G. 1945- ... 129
Miller, Peter M(ichael) 1942- ... CANR-25
Earlier sketch in CA 69-72
Miller, Philip L(ieson) 1906-1996 ... CAP-1
Earlier sketch in CA 11-12
Miller, Phyllis (Steinfurth) 1920- ... 131
Miller, R(onald) Baxter 1948- ... 115
Miller, R. Craig 1946- ... 135
Miller, R. S. 1936- ... 45-48
Miller, Randall Martin 1945- ... CANR-34
Earlier sketches in CA 81-84, CANR-15
Miller, Randolph Crump 1910- ... CANR-1
Earlier sketch in CA 1-4R
Miller, Raymond W(iley) 1895-1988 Obituary ... 124
Miller, Rene Fueloep
See Fueloep-Miller, Rene
Miller, Rene Fulop
See Fueloep-Miller, Rene
Miller, Rex 1929- ... CANR-30
Earlier sketch in CA 110
Miller, Richard
See Pietschmann, Richard John III
Miller, Richard (Connelly) 1925- ... CANR-26
Earlier sketch in CA 17-20R
Miller, Richard B. 1927- ... 146
Miller, Richard I(rwin) 1924- ... 41-44R
Miller, Richard Lawrence 1949- ... 134
Miller, Richard S(herwin) 1930- ... 21-24R
Miller, Richard Ulric 1932- ... CANR-17
Earlier sketch in CA 41-44R
Miller, Rob(ert) Hollis 1944- ... 37-40R
Miller, Robert A(llen) 1932- ... 33-36R
Miller, Robert H(enry) 1889- ... 33-36R
Miller, Robert H. 1944- ... 155
See also SATA 91
Miller, Robert Henry 1938- ... 110
Miller, Robert Keith 1949- ... CANR-35
Earlier sketch in CA 114
Miller, Robert L. 1928- ... 25-28R
Miller, Robert Moats 1924- Brief entry ... 105
Miller, Robert Ryal 1923- ... 41-44R
Miller, Robin Feuer 1947- ... 130
Miller, Roger LeRoy 1943- Brief entry ... 107
Miller, Ron 1947- ... 117
Miller, Ronald E(ugene) 1933- ... 5-8R
Miller, Roy Andrew 1924- ... CANR-40
Earlier sketches in CA 5-8R, CANR-2, 18
Miller, Ruby 1890(?)-1976 Obituary ... 65-68
Miller, Ruby M. 1911- ... 141
Miller, Russell 1938- ... 133
Miller, Russell E(lliott) 1916- Brief entry ... 117
Miller, Ruth
See Jacobs, Ruth Harriet
Miller, Ruth 1921- Brief entry ... 106
Miller, Ruth White
See White, Ruth C.
Miller, S(eymour) M(ichael) 1922- ... 17-20R
Miller, Sally M. 1937- ... CANR-51
Earlier sketches in CA 45-48, CANR-26
Miller, Samuel Jefferson 1919- ... 53-56
Miller, Sandra (Peden) 1948- ... CANR-38
Earlier sketch in CA 115
See also Miller, Sandy (Peden)
Miller, Sandy (Peden) 1948-
See Miller, Sandra (Peden)
See also SATA 41
See also SATA-Brief 35
Miller, Seumas 1953- ... 141
Miller, Shane 1907- ... CAP-2
Earlier sketch in CA 21-22
Miller, Shirley 1920- ... 93-96
Miller, Sigmund Stephen 1917- ... CANR-4
Earlier sketch in CA 1-4R
Miller, Stanley 1916(?)-1977 Obituary ... 69-72
Miller, Stanley L(loyd) 1930- ... 45-48
Miller, Stanley S. 1924- ... 13-16R
Miller, Stephen J(ohn) 1936- ... 33-36R
Miller, Steve(n R.) 1950- ... 165
Miller, Stuart 1937- ... 41-44R
Miller, Stuart Creighton 1927- ... 33-36R
Miller, Sue 1943- ... CANR-59
Earlier sketch in CA 139
See also BEST 90:3
See also CLC 44
See also DAM POP
See also DLB 143
Miller, Susan 1944- ... 107
Miller, Teresa 1952- ... 105
Miller, Thomas Lloyd 1913- ... 25-28R
Miller, Thomas W. 1943- ... 167
Miller, Tice L. 1938- ... 143
Miller, Timothy (Alan) 1944- ... CANR-56
Earlier sketch in CA 126
Miller, Tom 1947- ... CANR-14
Earlier sketch in CA 73-76
Miller, Tony
See Penrose, Antony
Miller, Vassar 1924- ... CANR-4
Earlier sketch in CA 9-12R
See also DLB 105
Miller, Victor (Brooke) 1940- ... 107
Miller, Virginia
See Austin, Virginia
Miller, Wade
See Miller, (H.) Bill(y)
and Wade, Robert (Allison)
Miller, Walter James 1918- ... 81-84
Miller, Walter M(ichael, Jr.) 1923- ... 85-88
See also CLC 4, 30
See also DLB 8
Miller, Warren 1921-1966 ... 143
Obituary ... 25-28R
See also BW 2
Miller, Warren E. 1924- ... CANR-11
Earlier sketch in CA 13-16R
Miller, Wayne Charles 1939- ... CANR-1
Earlier sketch in CA 45-48
Miller, Webb 1892-1940 ... DLB 29
Miller, William (Moseley) 1909-1989 ... 81-84
Obituary ... 129
Miller, William Alvin 1931- ... CANR-17
Earlier sketches in CA 49-52, CANR-1
Miller, William D. 1916- ... 13-16R
Miller, William Hugh 1905-1975 ... 1-4R
Miller, William Ian 1946- ... 163
Miller, William J. 1913(?)-1989 Obituary ... 128
Miller, William L. 1943- ... 130
Miller, William Lee 1926- ... CANR-65
Earlier sketch in CA 127
Miller, William McElwee 1892- ... CANR-6
Earlier sketch in CA 57-60
Miller, William Robert 1927-1970 ... CAP-1
Obituary ... 29-32R
Earlier sketch in CA 11-12
Miller, Wilma H(ildruth) 1936- ... CANR-58
Earlier sketches in CA 33-36R, CANR-12, 30
Miller, Wright (Watts) 1903-1974 ... 17-20R
Obituary ... 120
Miller, Zane L. 1934- ... CANR-27
Earlier sketches in CA 25-28R, CANR-12
Miller-Pogacar, Anesa
See Miller, Anesa
Millerson, Geoffrey L. 1931- ... 17-20R
Millet, Lydia 1968- ... 152
Millet, Stanton 1931- ... 25-28R
Millett, Allan R(eed) 1937- ... 21-24R
Millett, Fred B(enjamin) 1890-1976 Obituary ... 61-64
Millett, John (Antill) 1922- ... CANR-43
Earlier sketches in CA 103, CANR-20
Millett, John D(avid) 1912-1993 ... 104
Obituary ... 143
Millett, Kate 1934- ... CANR-53
Earlier sketches in CA 73-76, CANR-32
See also AITN 1
See also CLC 67
See also MTCW 1
Millett, Martin 1955- ... 133
Millett, Richard L(eroy) 1938- ... 117
Millezr, William Lee 1926- ... 127
Millgate, Jane 1937- ... 57-60
Millgate, Michael (Henry) 1929- ... CANR-48
Earlier sketches in CA 29-32R, CANR-28
Millgram, Abraham E(zra) 1901- ... 33-36R
Millham, C(harles) B(lanchard) 1936- ... 37-40R
Millhauser, Milton 1910- ... CAP-1
Earlier sketch in CA 13-16
Millhauser, Steven (Lewis) 1943- ... CANR-63
Brief entry ... 110
Earlier sketch in CA 111
Interview in ... 111
See also CLC 21, 54, 109
See also DLB 2
Millhiser, Marlys (Joy) 1938- ... 53-56
Millican, Arthenia Jackson Bates 1920- ... 105
See also BW 2
See also DLB 38
Millicent
See Jordan, Mildred Arlene
Millichap, Joseph R(obert) 1940- ... 116
Millies, Suzanne 1943- ... 49-52
Milligan, Edward Archibald 1903-1977 ... 41-44R
Milligan, Spike
See Milligan, Terence Alan
Milligan, Terence Alan 1918- ... CANR-64
Earlier sketches in CA 9-12R, CANR-4, 33
See also MTCW 1
See also SATA 29
Millikan, Ruth Garrett 1933- ... 128
Milliken, Ernest Kenneth 1899- ... 5-8R
Milliken, Stephen F(rederick) 1928- ... 93-96
Milliken, William Mathewson 1889- ... CAP-2
Earlier sketch in CA 23-24
Millimaki, Robert H. 1931- ... 57-60
Millin, Sarah Gertrude 1889-1968 ... 102
Obituary ... 93-96
See also CLC 49
Milling, Michael C. Crowley
See Crowley-Milling, Michael C.
Millington, Ada
See Deyneka, Anita
Millington, Barry 1951- ... CANR-43
Earlier sketch in CA 119
Millington, Frances Ryan
1899-1977 Obituary ... 69-72
Millington, Patrick 1910-1982 Obituary ... 107
Millington, Roger 1939- ... 65-68
Millinship, William 1929- ... 145
Million, Elmer M(ayse) 1912- ... 41-44R
Millis, Walter 1899-1968 ... CAP-1
Obituary ... 37-40R
Earlier sketch in CA 9-10
Millman, Joan (M.) 1931- ... 135
Millman, Lawrence 1946- ... CANR-38
Earlier sketches in CA 93-96, CANR-17
Millner, Cork 1931- ... 134
Millon, Henry (Armand) 1927- ... 97-100
Millon, Rene 1921- ... 116
Brief entry ... 113
Millon, Robert Paul 1932- ... 21-24R
Millon, Theodore 1929- ... 57-60
Mills, A(nthony) D(avid) 1935- ... 145
Mills, Alison 1951- ... 53-56
Mills, Barriss 1912- ... CANR-12
Earlier sketch in CA 25-28R
Mills, Belen Collantes 1930- ... 37-40R
Mills, Betty (Lidstrom) 1926- ... 9-12R
Mills, Brenda J. 1940- ... 120
Mills, C(harles) Wright 1916-1962 Obituary ... 107
Mills, Carley 1897-1962 ... 1-4R
Obituary ... 103
Mills, Clarence A(lonzo) 1891-1974 ... CAP-1
Obituary ... 53-56
Earlier sketch in CA 13-16
Mills, Claudia 1954- ... CANR-58
Earlier sketches in CA 109, CANR-27
See also SATA 44, 89
See also SATA-Brief 41
Mills, Constance (Quinby) 1898-1987 Obituary ... 122
Mills, Daniel Quinn 1941- ... CANR-57
Earlier sketches in CA 112, CANR-30
Mills, David Harlow 1932- ... 104
Mills, Dorothy
See Howard, Dorothy Gray
Mills, Edward D(avid) 1915-1998 ... CANR-19
Obituary ... 164
Earlier sketches in CA 5-8R, CANR-4
Mills, Elaine (Rosemary) 1941- ... SATA 72
Mills, G(len) E(arl) 1908- ... CAP-1
Earlier sketch in CA 13-14
Mills, Gary B(ernard) 1944- ... 81-84
Mills, George S(torginne) 1906- ... 97-100
Mills, Gordon H(arrison) 1914-1978 Obituary ... 117
Mills, Helen 1923- ... CANR-16
Earlier sketch in CA 97-100
Mills, Hilary (Paterson) 1950- ... 115
Mills, Irving 1894-1985 Obituary ... 115
Mills, J(anet) M(elanie) A(ilsa) 1894- ... 69-72
Mills, James R(obert) 1927- ... 85-88
Mills, Jane (Kathryn) 1948- ... 139
Mills, Jeannie 1939- ... 93-96
Mills, John 1908- ... 108
Mills, John 1930- ... 81-84
Mills, John FitzMaurice 1917- ... 103
Mills, John W(illiam) 1933- ... 69-72
Mills, Joyce C. 1944- ... SATA 102
Mills, Kathi
See Mills, Kathleen Lorraine
Mills, Kathleen Lorraine 1948- ... 131
Mills, Leonard Russell 1917- ... 45-48
Mills, Liston O. 1928- ... 107
Mills, Margaret A(nn) 1946- ... 141
Mills, (William) Mervyn 1906- ... CAP-1
Earlier sketch in CA 11-12
Mills, Patricia J(agentowicz) 1944- ... 151
Mills, Ralph J(oseph), Jr. 1931- ... CANR-39
Earlier sketches in CA 9-12R, CANR-3, 18
Mills, Richard W. 1945- Brief entry ... 112
Mills, Robert P(ark) 1920-1986 ... 97-100
Obituary ... 118
Mills, Stephanie 1948- ... 149
Mills, Stephen (Paul) 1952- ... 130
Mills, Terry Kenneth 1949- ... 107
Mills, Theodore M(ason) 1920- ... 21-24R
Mills, Watson Early 1939- ... CANR-48
Earlier sketch in CA 57-60
Mills, William 1935- Brief entry ... 118
Mills, William Donald 1925- ... 33-36R
Mills, Yaroslava Surmach 1925- ... SATA 35
Millspaugh, Ben P. 1936- ... 145
See also SATA 77
Millstead, Thomas E. ... 106
See also SATA 30
Millstein, Rose Silverman
1903(?)-1975 Obituary ... 61-64
Millu, Liana 1915- ... 141
Millum, Trevor 1945- ... CANR-44
Earlier sketches in CA 104, CANR-21
Millward, Celia M(cCullough) 1935- ... 53-56
Millward, Eric (Geoffrey William) 1935- ... 65-68
Millward, John S(candrett) 1924- ... 13-16R
Milman, Donald S. 1924- ... 134
Brief entry ... 111
Milman, Henry Hart 1796-1868 ... DLB 96
Milman, Miriam 1928- ... 112
Milne, A(lan) A(lexander) 1882-1956 ... 133
Brief entry ... 104
See also CLR 1, 26
See also DAB
See also DAC
See also DAM MST
See also DLB 10, 77, 100, 160
See also MAICYA
See also MTCW 1
See also SATA 100
See also TCLC 6
See also YABC 1
Milne, Antony 1942- ... 101
Milne, Christopher (Robin) 1920-1996 ... CANR-27
Obituary ... 152
Earlier sketches in CA 61-64, CANR-11
See also AITN 2
Milne, Edward Arthur 1896-1950 ... 158
Milne, Edward James 1915-1983 Obituary ... 109
Milne, Evander Mackay 1920- ... 5-8R
Milne, (Charles) Ewart 1903-1987 ... CANR-16
Obituary ... 121
Earlier sketch in CA 97-100
Milne, G(eorge) W. A. 1937- ... 154
Milne, (William) Gordon 1921- ... 21-24R
Milne, Jean (Killgrove) 1920- ... 17-20R
Milne, John 1952- ... CANR-66
Earlier sketch in CA 143
Milne, Lorus J. ... CANR-14
Earlier sketch in CA 33-36R
See also CLR 22
See also SAAS 18
See also SATA 5
Milne, Margery ... CANR-14
Earlier sketch in CA 33-36R
See also CLR 22
See also SAAS 18
See also SATA 5
Milne, Roseleen 1945- ... CANR-13
Earlier sketch in CA 73-76
Milne, Seumas 1958- ... 135
Milne, Terry
See Milne, Theresa Ann
Milne, Theresa Ann 1964- ... SATA 84
Milner, Christina 1942- ... 49-52
Milner, Clyde A. II 1948- ... CANR-26
Earlier sketch in CA 108
Milner, Esther 1918- ... 21-24R
Milner, Ian Frank George 1911- ... 104
Milner, Jay
See Morton, James (Severs)
Milner, Jay (Dunston) 1926- ... 1-4R
Milner, Lucille Bernheimer
1888(?)-1975 Obituary ... 61-64
Milner, Marion (Blackett) 1900- ... 9-12R
Milner, Michael
See Cooper, Saul
Milner, Murray, Jr. 1935- ... 41-44R
Milner, Neal A(lan) 1941- Brief entry ... 112
Milner, Richard B(ruce) 1941- ... 49-52
Milner, Ron(ald) 1938- ... CANR-24
Earlier sketch in CA 73-76
See also AITN 1
See also BLC 3
See also BW 1
See also CLC 56
See also DAM MULT
See also DLB 38
See also MTCW 1
Milnes, Eric Charles 1912-1984 Obituary ... 112
Milnes, Irma McDonough 1924- ... 168
See also SATA 101
Milnes, Richard Monckton 1809-1885 . DLB 32, 184
Milnor, John (Willard) 1931- ... 161
Milns, R(obert) D(avid) 1938- ... 33-36R
Milo, Ronald D(mitri) 1935- ... 25-28R
Milofsky, Carl 1948- ... 139
Milonas, Rolf
See Myller, Rolf
Miloradovich, Milo 1901(?)-1972 Obituary ... 37-40R
Milord, Susan 1954- ... SATA 74
Milosh, Joseph E(dmund) 1936- ... 21-24R
Miloslavsky, Nikolai Dimitrievich Tolstoy
See Tolstoy (-Miloslavsky), Nikolai (Dimitrievich)
Milosz, Czeslaw 1911- ... CANR-51
Earlier sketches in CA 81-84, CANR-23
See also CLC 5, 11, 22, 31, 56, 82
See also DAM MST, POET
See also MTCW 1
See also PC 8
See also WLCS
Milotte, Alfred G(eorge) 1904-1989 ... CAP-1
Obituary ... 128
Earlier sketch in CA 19-20
See also SATA 11
See also SATA-Obit 62
Milotte, Elma (Moore) 1908(?)-1989 Obituary ... 128
Milsen, Oscar
See Mendelsohn, Oscar (Adolf)
Milson, Fred(erick William) 1912- ... 73-76
Milstead, Jessica L(ee) 1939- ... CANR-14
Earlier sketch in CA 33-36R
Milstead, John 1924- ... 49-52
Milsted, David 1954- ... 132
Milstein, Linda 1954- ... SATA 80
Milstein, Mike M(yron) 1937- ... 81-84
Miltner, Robert F. 1949- ... 168
Milton, Arthur 1922- ... CANR-27
Earlier sketch in CA 109
Milton, Charles R(udolph) 1925- ... 53-56
Milton, David Scott 1934- ... CANR-13
Earlier sketch in CA 73-76
Milton, Hilary (Herbert) 1920- ... CANR-21
Earlier sketches in CA 57-60, CANR-6
See also SATA 23
Milton, Jack
See Kimbro, John M.
Milton, John 1608-1674 ... CDBLB 1660-1789
See also DA
See also DAB
See also DAC
See also DAM MST, POET
See also DLB 131, 151
See also PC 19
See also WLC
Milton, John R(onald) 1924- ... 33-36R
See also SATA 24
Milton, Joyce 1946- ... 106
See also SATA 52, 101
See also SATA-Brief 41
Milton, Mark
See Pelton, Robert W(ayne)
Milton, Oliver
See Hewitt, Cecil Rolph
Milunsky, Aubrey 1936- ... 103
Milverton, Charles A.
See Penzler, Otto
Milvy, Paul 1931-1989 Obituary ... 129
Milward, Alan S. 1935- ... CANR-45
Earlier sketch in CA 45-48
Milward, Peter 1925- ... 101
Mims, Forrest M(arion) III 1944- ... CANR-39
Earlier sketches in CA 97-100, CANR-16
Mims, George L. 1934- ... 129

Mims, Lambert C. 1930- ... 29-32R
Mims, Roddey Earl 1936(?)-1982 Obituary ... 108
Min, Anchee 1957- ... 146
See also CLC 86
Min, Tu-ki 1932- ... 138
Minadeo, Richard (William) 1929- ... 25-28R
Minahan, John 1933- ... CANR-2
Earlier sketch in CA 45-48
Minahan, John A. 1956- ... 142
See also SATA 92
Minale, Marcello 1938- ... 108
Minar, Barbra (Goodyear) 1940- ... 148
See also SATA 79
Minar, David W(illiam) 1925-1973 Obituary ... 111
Minard, Rosemary 1939- ... SATA 63
Minarik, Else Holmelund 1920- ... CANR-48
Earlier sketch in CA 73-76
See also CLR 33
See also MAICYA
See also SATA 15
Minarik, John Paul 1947- ... CANR-13
Earlier sketch in CA 73-76
Minc, Alain J. R. 1949- ... 146
Mincer, Jacob 1922- Brief entry ... 114
Minchin, Timothy J. 1969- ... 166
Minchinton, W(alter) E(dward) 1921- ... CANR-29
Earlier sketches in CA 29-32R, CANR-12
Mincieli, Rose Laura 1912- ... CANR-4
Earlier sketch in CA 5-8R
Minckler, (Sherwood) Leon 1906- ... 57-60
Minczeski, John 1947- ... 137
Mindel, Eugene D. 1934- ... 41-44R
Mindell, Earl L(awrence) 1940- ... 105
Mindlin, Michael 1923- ... 133
Mindlin, Murray 1924(?)-1987 Obituary ... 122
Mindszenty, Jozsef 1892-1975 ... 65-68
Obituary ... 57-60
Mindt, Heinz R. 1940- Brief entry ... 115
Minear, Paul Sevier 1906- ... CANR-3
Earlier sketch in CA 1-4R
Minear, Richard H(offman) 1938- ... 33-36R
Minehaha, Cornelius
See Wedekind, (Benjamin) Frank(lin)
Mineka, Francis Edward 1907- Brief entry ... 106
Miner, Caroline Eyring 1907- ... CANR-27
Earlier sketches in CA 25-28R, CANR-11
Miner, Charles S(ydney) 1906- ... CAP-1
Earlier sketch in CA 19-20
Miner, Dwight Carroll 1904-1978 Obituary ... 81-84
Miner, Earl (Roy) 1927- ... CANR-1
Earlier sketch in CA 1-4R
Miner, Ellis D(evere, Jr.) 1937- ... 144
Miner, H. Craig 1944- ... CANR-16
Earlier sketches in CA 45-48, CANR-1
Miner, (Opal) Irene Sevrey (Frazine) 1906- ... 5-8R
Miner, Jane Claypool 1933- ... CANR-27
Earlier sketch in CA 106
See also SATA 38
See also SATA-Brief 37
Miner, John B(urnham) 1926- ... CANR-20
Earlier sketches in CA 9-12R, CANR-5
Miner, Joshua L. 1920- ... 106
Miner, Lewis S. 1909- ... CAP-1
Earlier sketch in CA 11-12
See also SATA 11
Miner, Mary Green 1928- ... 69-72
Miner, Matthew
See Wallmann, Jeffrey M(iner)
Miner, Valerie 1947- ... CANR-59
Earlier sketch in CA 97-100
See also CLC 40
Miner, Ward L(ester) 1916- ... 9-12R
Minerbrook, Scott 1951- ... 156
Mines, Jeanette (Marie) 1948- ... 119
See also SATA 61
Mines, Samuel 1909- ... CANR-1
Earlier sketch in CA 45-48
Mines, Stephanie 1944- ... 77-80
Minetree, Harry 1935- ... 93-96
Minford, John (Michael) 1946- ... 130
Mingay, G(ordon) E(dmund) 1923- ... CANR-45
Earlier sketches in CA 17-20R, CANR-11
Minge, Ward Alan 1924- ... 97-100
Minghella, Anthony 1954- ... 165
Minghi, Julian V(incent) 1933- ... 29-32R
Mingi, Akili
See Puri, Shamlal
Mingione, Enzo 1947- ... 141
Mingus, Charles 1922-1979 ... 93-96
Obituary ... 85-88
Minhinnick, Robert 1952- ... 126
Minichiello, Sharon ... 126
Minick, Michael 1945- ... 65-68
Minier, Nelson
See Stoutenburg, Adrien (Pearl)
Minifie, James MacDonald 1900-1974 ... 49-52
Minihan, Janet
See Oppenheim, Janet
Minimo, Duca
See D'Annunzio, Gabriele
Minio-Paluello, Lorenzo 1907-1986 Obituary ... 119
Minirth, Frank B. ... 136
Minium, Edward W(headon) 1917- ... 29-32R
Mink, JoAnna Stephens 1947- ... 138
Mink, Louis Otto, Jr. 1921-1983 ... 104
Obituary ... 109
Mink, Nelson G. 1907- ... 123
Minkler, Meredith 1946- ... 162
Minkoff, Randy 1949- ... 141
Minkovitz, Moshe
See Shokeid, Moshe
Minkow, Rosalie 1927- ... 135
Minnelli, Vincente 1913(?)-1986 ... 153
Obituary ... 119
Brief entry ... 117
Minney, R(ubeigh) J(ames) 1895- ... CANR-5
Earlier sketch in CA 5-8R
Minnich, Elizabeth (Anne) Kamarck ... 158
Minnich, Helen Benton 1892- ... CAP-1
Earlier sketch in CA 9-10
Minnick, Wayne C. 1915- ... 25-28R
Minnick, Wendell L. 1962- ... 144
Minnigerode, Meade 1887-1967 Obituary ... 116
Minnion, John (Lawrence) 1939- ... 130
Minns, Susan 1839-1938 ... DLB 140
Minock, Daniel 1944- ... 165
Minogue, Kenneth R(obert) 1930- ... 5-8R
Minogue, Valerie Pearson 1931- ... 132
Minor, Andrew Collier 1918- ... 13-16R
Minor, Anthropopagus
See Conniff, James C(lifford) G(regory)
Minor, Audax
See Ryall, George (Francis Trafford)
Minor, Edward Orville 1920- ... 9-12R
Minor, Marz 1928- ... 103
Minor, Muriel Miller 1908-1987 Obituary ... 122
Minor, Nono 1932- ... 103
Minor, Wendell G. 1944- ... SATA 78
Minot, Stephen 1927- ... CANR-17
Earlier sketch in CA 13-16R
Minot, Susan 1956- ... 134
See also CLC 44
Minott, Rodney G(lisan) 1928- ... 9-12R
Minow, Martha 1954- ... 137
Minow, Newton N(orman) 1926- ... CANR-55
Earlier sketch in CA 13-16R
Minrath, William R(ichard) 1900-1971 ... CAP-1
Obituary ... 89-92
Earlier sketch in CA 9-10
Minshall, Merlin (Theodore)
1906-1987 Obituary ... 123
Minshall, Vera (Wild) 1924- ... 13-16R
Minshull, Evelyn 1929- ... 37-40R
Minshull, Roger (Michael) 1935- ... 21-24R
Minsky, Betty Jane (Toebe) 1932- ... 5-8R
Minsky, Hyman P(hilip) 1919-1996 ... 85-88
Obituary ... 154
Minsky, Marvin (Lee) 1927- ... 21-24R
Minsky, Morton 1902-1987 ... 135
Obituary ... 122
Minta, Stephen 1947- ... 132
Minter, David L. 1935- ... CANR-12
Earlier sketch in CA 25-28R
Minter, William 1942- ... 124
Minters, Arthur Herman 1932- ... 102
Minto-Cowen, Frances
See Munthe, Frances
Minton, Henry L. 1934- ... 138
Minton, Lynn ... 107
Minton, Madge Rutherford 1920- ... 45-48
Minton, Paula
See Little, Paul H(ugo)
Minton, Robert 1918- ... 57-60
Minton, Sherman A(nthony), Jr. 1919- ... 45-48
Mintonye, Grace ... 25-28R
See also SATA 4
Minturn, Leigh 1928- ... 21-24R
Minty, Judith 1937- ... CANR-21
Earlier sketches in CA 49-52, CANR-2
Mintz, Alan L. ... 139
Mintz, Barbara 1931- ... 110
Mintz, Donald E(dward) 1932- ... 17-20R
Mintz, Elizabeth E(mmons) 1913-1997 ... 73-76
Obituary ... 159
Mintz, Joel A(lan) 1949- ... 167
Mintz, Joyce Lois 1933- ... 65-68
Mintz, Lannon W. 1938-1988 ... 126
Mintz, Leigh W(ayne) 1939- ... 57-60
Mintz, Max M. 1919- ... 33-36R
Mintz, Morton A. 1922- ... 13-16R
Mintz, Norman N(elson) 1934- ... 41-44R
Mintz, Ruth Finer 1919- ... 13-16R
Mintz, Samuel I(saiah) 1923- ... 5-8R
Mintz, Sidney W(ilfred) 1922- ... CANR-21
Earlier sketches in CA 1-4R, CANR-5
Mintz, Steven (Harry) 1953- ... 118
Mintz, Thomas 1931- ... 108
Mintzberg, Henry 1939- ... CANR-1
Earlier sketch in CA 45-48
Mintzer, Yvette 1947- ... 77-80
Minuchin, Salvador 1921- ... 144
Minus, Ed 1938- ... CLC 39
Minus, Paul M(urray, Jr.) 1935- ... 118
Minyard, John Douglas 1943-1990 ... 120
Obituary ... 145
Miola, Robert S(teven) 1951- ... 129
Mirabehn
See Slade, Madeleine
Mirabelli, Eugene (Jr.) 1931- ... 25-28R
Miracle, Andrew W., (Jr.) 1945- ... 146
Miracle, Gordon E. 1930- ... 33-36R
Miracle, Marvin P(reston) 1933- ... 17-20R
Miranda, Anne 1954- ... SATA 71
Miranda, Javier
See Bioy Casares, Adolfo
Mirande, Alfredo M(anuel) 1940- ... 115
Mirbeau, Octave 1848-1917 ... DLB 123, 192
See also TCLC 55
Mireaux, Emile 1885(?)-1969 Obituary ... 104
Mireles, Marina 1927(?)-1986 Obituary ... 119
Mirelman, Victor A. 1943- ... 136
Mirenburg, Barry (Leonard Steffan) 1952- ... 101
Mirepoix, Camille 1926- ... 105
Mirk, John (?)-c. 1414 ... DLB 146
Mirkin, Gabe 1935- ... 129
Miro (Ferrer), Gabriel (Francisco Victor)
1879-1930 Brief entry ... 104
See also TCLC 5
Miro, Joan 1893-1983 ... 121
Obituary ... 111
Miron, Dan 1934- ... 77-80
Miron, Gaston 1928- ... DLB 60
Miron, Murray S(amuel) 1932- ... 81-84
Miron, Salvador Diaz
See Diaz Miron, Salvador
Mirow, Kurt Rudolf 1936- ... 130
Mirrlees, Hope 1887-1978 ... 155
Mirsky, Jeannette 1903-1987 ... CAP-2
Obituary ... 122
Earlier sketch in CA 19-20
See also SATA 8
See also SATA-Obit 51
Mirsky, Mark Jay 1939- ... CANR-44
Earlier sketch in CA 25-28R
See also CAAS 30
Mirsky, Reba Paeff 1902-1966 ... 1-4R
See also SATA 1
Mirsky, Stanley 1929- ... 110
Mirvish, Robert Franklin 1921- ... 1-4R
Misbin, Robert I. 1947- ... 146
Miscall, Peter D(arwin) 1943- ... 111
Misch, Robert J(ay) 1905- ... 21-24R
Mische, Gerald F(rederick) 1926- ... 97-100
Mische, Patricia M(ary) 1939- ... CANR-16
Earlier sketch in CA 93-96
Mischke, Bernard Cyril 1926- ... 13-16R
Mischke, Fridolin 1916- ... 117
Mischke, Fritz
See Mischke, Fridolin
Mises, Ludwig (Edler) von 1881-1973 ... CANR-19
Obituary ... 45-48
Earlier sketch in CA 5-8R
Mises, Margit von 1896- ... CANR-19
Earlier sketch in CA 89-92
Mish, Charles C(arroll) 1913-1992 ... 33-36R
Obituary ... 140
Mishael, Bert
See Mishael, Herbert Stanley
Mishael, Herbert Stanley
1900(?)-1985 Obituary ... 117
Mishan, E(zra) J(oshua) 1917- ... CANR-30
Earlier sketches in CA 73-76, CANR-13
Misheiker, Betty Fairly 1919- ... 9-12R
Mishica, Clare 1960- ... 155
See also SATA 91
Mishima, Yukio 1925-1970
See Hiraoka, Kimitake
See also CLC 2, 4, 6, 9, 27
See also DC 1
See also DLB 182
See also SSC 4
Mishkin, Paul J. 1927- ... 17-20R
Mishler, Clayton (R.) 1908-1992 ... 146
Mishler, William (Thomas Earle II) 1947- ... CANR-52
Earlier sketch in CA 125
Mishne, Judith 1932- ... 162
Mishra, Sudesh (Raj) 1962- ... 154
Mishra, Vishwa Mohan 1937- ... 61-64
Misiak, Henryk 1911- ... CANR-5
Earlier sketch in CA 1-4R
Misiunas, Romuald John 1945- ... 109
Miskimin, Harry A(lvin, Jr.) 1932- Brief entry ... 109
Miskovits, Christine 1939- ... 53-56
See also SATA 10
Misner, Arthur J(ack) 1921- ... 21-24R
Misner, Paul 1936- ... 138
Misra, Bankey Bihari 1909- ... 104
Miss C. L. F.
See Grimke, Charlotte L(ottie) Forten
Miss Elbee
See Baker, Lillian (L.)
Missen, Leslie R(obert) 1897-1983 Obituary ... 110
Miss Frances
See Horwich, Frances R(appaport)
Missildine, (Whitney) Hugh 1915- ... 77-80
Missinne, Leo E(miel) 1927- ... CANR-39
Earlier sketch in CA 116
Missiroli, Mario 1886-1974 Obituary ... 53-56
Miss Lou
See Bennett-Coverley, Louise
Miss Manners
See Martin, Judith (Sylvia)
Miss Read
See Saint, Dora Jessie
Mister Rogers
See Rogers, Fred McFeely
Mister X
See Hoch, Edward D(entinger)
Mistral, Frederic 1830-1914 Brief entry ... 122
See also TCLC 51
Mistral, Gabriela
See Godoy Alcayaga, Lucila
See also HLC
See also TCLC 2
Mistry, Rohinton 1952- ... 141
See also CLC 71
See also DAC
Misurella, Fred 1940- ... 143
Mitcalfe, Barry 1930- ... 110
Mitcham, Carl 1941- ... CANR-37
Earlier sketches in CA 85-88, CANR-16
Mitcham, Gilroy
See Newton, William Simpson
Mitcham, Samuel W(ayne), Jr. 1949- ... 106
Mitchard, Jacquelyn 1953- ... 157
See also SATA 98
Mitchel, Jonathan 1624-1668 ... DLB 24
Mitchell, Adam
See Pyle, Hilary
Mitchell, Adrian 1932- ... 33-36R
See also DLB 40
Mitchell, Alan 1922- ... CANR-27
Earlier sketches in CA 57-60, CANR-8
Mitchell, Alexander Ross Kerr 1934- ... 73-76
Mitchell, Allan 1933- ... 102
Mitchell, Allison
See Butterworth, W(illiam) E(dmund III)
Mitchell, Andrew W. 1953- ... 124
Mitchell, Arnold 1918- ... 131
Mitchell, Arthur A(ustin) 1926- ... 9-12R
Mitchell, Austin (Vernon) 1934- ... CANR-12
Earlier sketch in CA 25-28R
Mitchell, B(rian) R(edman) 1929- ... 49-52
Mitchell, Barbara 1941- ... 117
Mitchell, Barbara A. 1939- ... 25-28R
Mitchell, Basil George 1917- ... 104
Mitchell, Betty L(ou) 1947- ... 107
Mitchell, Bonner 1929- ... 25-28R
Mitchell, Breon 1942- ... 112
Mitchell, Broadus 1892-1988 ... CANR-5
Obituary ... 125
Earlier sketch in CA 1-4R
Mitchell, Burroughs 1914(?)-1979 ... 129
Obituary ... 89-92
Mitchell, Carlton
See Marshall, Mel(vin D.)
Mitchell, Charles 1912-1995 ... 9-12R
Obituary ... 150
Mitchell, Clyde
See Ellison, Harlan (Jay)
and Garrett, (Gordon) Randall (Phillip)
and Silverberg, Robert
Mitchell, Colin W(are) 1927-1996 ... 73-76
Obituary ... 152
Mitchell, Curtis Cornelius, Jr. 1927- ... 105
Mitchell, Cynthia 1922- ... 106
See also SATA 29
Mitchell, Daniel J(esse) B(rody) 1942- ... CANR-50
Earlier sketch in CA 123
Mitchell, David (John) 1924- ... CANR-12
Earlier sketch in CA 53-56
Mitchell, Don(ald Earl) 1947- ... CANR-31
Earlier sketches in CA 33-36R, CANR-14
Mitchell, Donald (Charles Peter) 1925- ... 103
Mitchell, Donald Grant 1822-1908 ... DLB 1
See also DLBD 13
Mitchell, Edgar D(ean) 1930- ... 53-56
Mitchell, Edward B. 1937- ... 21-24R
Mitchell, Elizabeth P(ryse) 1946- ... 101
Mitchell, Ellinor R. 1930- ... 159
Mitchell, (Sibyl) Elyne (Keith) 1913- ... CANR-44
Earlier sketches in CA 53-56, CANR-5, 21
See also SATA 10
Mitchell, Emerson Blackhorse Barney 1945- ... 45-48
See also NNAL
Mitchell, Erica
See Posner, Richard
Mitchell, Ewan
See Janner, Greville Ewan
Mitchell, Fay Langellier 1884-1964 ... 5-8R
Mitchell, Frank
See Mitchell, George Francis
Mitchell, Frank Vincent 1919-(?) ... 9-12R
Mitchell, Franklin D. 1932- Brief entry ... 118
Mitchell, G(eoffrey) Duncan 1921- ... CANR-11
Earlier sketch in CA 29-32R
Mitchell, George Francis 1912- ... 77-80
Mitchell, George J(ohn) 1933- ... 141
Mitchell, Giles 1928- ... 93-96
Mitchell, Gladys (Maude Winifred) 1901-1983 ...
CANR-63
Obituary ... 110
Earlier sketches in CA 9-12R, CANR-9
See also DLB 77
See also SATA 46
See also SATA-Obit 35
Mitchell, Greg 1947- ... CANR-70
Earlier sketch in CA 73-76
Mitchell, Harold P(aton) 1900-1983 ... 9-12R
Obituary ... 109
Mitchell, (Arthur) Harris 1916- ... 119
Mitchell, Helen S(wift) 1895-1984 ... 25-28R
Obituary ... 114
Mitchell, Henry (Clay II) 1923-1993 ... 130
Obituary ... 143
Mitchell, Henry H(eywood) 1919- ... CANR-10
Earlier sketch in CA 57-60
Mitchell, (William) Hobart 1908- ... 119
Mitchell, Howard E(still) 1921- ... 108
Mitchell, J(ames) Clyde 1918- ... CANR-9
Earlier sketch in CA 13-16R
Mitchell, Jack 1925- ... 9-12R
Mitchell, Jackson
See Matcha, Jack
Mitchell, James 1926- ... CANR-66
Earlier sketches in CA 13-16R, CANR-12
Mitchell, James (Alexander Hugh)
1939-1985 Obituary ... 115
Mitchell, James Leslie 1901-1935 Brief entry ... 104
See also Gibbon, Lewis Grassic
See also DLB 15
Mitchell, Jay
See Roberson, Jennifer
Mitchell, Jay P. 1940- ... 145
Mitchell, Jeremy 1929- ... 41-44R
Mitchell, Jerome 1935- ... 25-28R
Mitchell, Jerry 1905(?)-1972 Obituary ... 33-36R
Mitchell, Joan Cattermole 1920- ... CAP-1
Earlier sketch in CA 9-10
Mitchell, John 1930- ... 143
Mitchell, John Ames 1845-1918 ... DLB 79
Mitchell, John D(ietrich) 1917- ... 49-52
Mitchell, John D(avid) B(awden)
1917-1980 Obituary ... 105
Mitchell, John Hanson 1940- ... 142
Mitchell, John Howard 1921- ... 9-12R
Mitchell, John J(oseph) 1941- ... CANR-1
Earlier sketch in CA 45-48
Mitchell, Joni 1943- ... 112
See also CLC 12

Mitchell, Joseph (Quincy) 1908-1996 CANR-69
Obituary 152
Earlier sketch in CA 77-80
See also CLC 98
See also DLB 185
See also DLBY 96
Mitchell, Joseph B(rady) 1915-1993 9-12R
Obituary 140
Mitchell, Joyce Slayton 1933- CANR-15
Earlier sketch in CA 65-68
See also SATA 46
See also SATA-Brief 43
Mitchell, Judith Paige CANR-40
Earlier sketches in CA 85-88, CANR-18
Interview in CANR-18
Mitchell, (Charles) Julian (Humphrey) 1935- CANR-39
Earlier sketches in CA 5-8R, CANR-5
See also DLB 14
Mitchell, Julie 1959- 128
Mitchell, Juliet (Constance Wyatt) 1940- CANR-29
Earlier sketch in CA 45-48
Mitchell, K. L.
See Lamb, Elizabeth Searle
Mitchell, Kathy 1948- SATA 59
Mitchell, Ken(neth Ronald) 1940- CANR-37
Earlier sketches in CA 93-96, CANR-16
See also DLB 60
Mitchell, Kenneth R. 1930- 17-20R
Mitchell, Kerry
See Wilkes-Hunter, R(ichard)
Mitchell, Kirk (John) 1950- 128
Mitchell, Lane 1907- CAP-1
Earlier sketch in CA 19-20
Mitchell, Langdon (Elwyn) 1862-1935 Brief entry 120
See also DLB 7
Mitchell, Larry 1938- 152
Mitchell, Lee M(ark) 1943- CANR-1
Earlier sketch in CA 49-52
Mitchell, Leeds 1912- 89-92
Mitchell, Leonel Lake 1930- 89-92
Mitchell, Leslie (Scott Falconer) 1905-1985 156
Obituary 118
Mitchell, Lionel H. 1942- 106
Mitchell, Loften 1919- CANR-26
Earlier sketch in CA 81-84
See also BW 1
See also DLB 38
Mitchell, Marcia L(ouise) 1942- 113
Mitchell, Margaree King 1953- 150
See also SATA 84
Mitchell, Margaret (Munnerlyn) 1900-1949 CANR-55
Brief entry 109
Earlier sketch in CA 125
See also AAYA 23
See also DAM NOV, POP
See also DLB 9
See also MTCW 1
See also TCLC 11
Mitchell, Margaretta K. 1935- CANR-14
Earlier sketch in CA 29-32R
Mitchell, Marianne Helen 1937- 85-88
Mitchell, Mark 1961- 156
Mitchell, Memory F(armer) 1924- 37-40R
Mitchell, Otis C. 1935- CANR-13
Earlier sketch in CA 37-40R
Mitchell, P(hilip) M(arshall) 1916- CANR-43
Earlier sketches in CA 104, CANR-20
Mitchell, Paige
See Mitchell, Judith Paige
Mitchell, Pamela Holsclaw 1940- CANR-6
Earlier sketch in CA 57-60
Mitchell, Peggy
See Mitchell, Margaret (Munnerlyn)
Mitchell, Peter M(cQuilkin) 1934- 85-88
Mitchell, Reid 1955- 140
Mitchell, Rhonda SATA 89
Mitchell, Richard H(anks) 1931- 21-24R
Mitchell, Robert H(ughes) 1921- 117
Mitchell, Roger (Sherman) 1935- 25-28R
Mitchell, Ruth K. 33-36R
Mitchell, S. Valentine
See Gammell, Susanna Valentine Mitchell
Mitchell, S(ilas) Weir 1829-1914 165
See also DLB 202
See also TCLC 36
Mitchell, Sally 1937- 110
Mitchell, Scott
See Godfrey, Lionel (Robert Holcombe)
Mitchell, Sidney Alexander 1895-1966 5-8R
Obituary 134
Mitchell, Stephen 1948- 146
Mitchell, Stephen A. 1946- 133
Mitchell, Stephen Arnold 1903-1974 Obituary 49-52
Mitchell, Stephen O. 1930- 13-16R
Mitchell, Susan 1944- 154
Mitchell, Susanna (Ryland) 1941- 161
Mitchell, Thomas N(oel) 1939- 103
Mitchell, W. J. T. 1942- CANR-14
Earlier sketch in CA 81-84
Mitchell, W(illiam) O(rmond) 1914-1998 CANR-43
Obituary 165
Earlier sketches in CA 77-80, CANR-15
See also CLC 25
See also DAC
See also DAM MST
See also DLB 88
Mitchell, William 1879-1936 TCLC 81
Mitchell, William E(dward) 1927- 81-84
Mitchell, William E. 1936- 93-96
Mitchell, William Hamilton 1907(?)-1982 Obituary 107
Mitchell, William J. 1944- 146
Mitchell, William P. 1937- 141
Mitchell, Yvonne 1925-1979 CANR-10
Obituary 85-88
Earlier sketch in CA 17-20R
See also SATA-Obit 24
Mitchelson, Marvin M. 1928- 104
Mitchenson, Francis Joseph Blackett 1911-1992 101
Obituary 139
Mitchenson, Joe
See Mitchenson, Francis Joseph Blackett
Mitchison, (Sonja) Lois 1-4R
Mitchison, Naomi Margaret (Haldane) 1897- CANR-15
Earlier sketch in CA 77-80
See also DLB 160, 191
See also SATA 24
Mitchison, Rosalind (Mary) 1919- 33-36R
Mitchll, John
See Slater, Patrick
Mitchner, Stuart 1938- 61-64
Mitchnik, Helen 1901- 117
See also SATA 41
See also SATA-Brief 35
Mitchum, Hank
See Knott, William C(ecil, Jr.)
and Newton, D(wight) B(ennett)
and Sherman, Jory (Tecumseh)
Mitelman, Bonnie Cossman 1941- 111
Mitford, Jessica 1917-1996 CANR-60
Obituary 152
Earlier sketches in CA 1-4R, CANR-1
See also CAAS 17
Mitford, Mary Russell 1787-1855 DLB 110, 116
Mitford, Nancy 1904-1973 9-12R
See also CLC 44
See also DLB 191
Mitgang, Herbert 1920- CANR-4
Earlier sketch in CA 9-12R
Mitgang, Lee D. 1949- 77-80
Mitgutsch, Ali 1935- 143
See also SATA 76
Mitrany, David 1888-1975 65-68
Obituary 61-64
Mitrokhina, Yelena
See Costa, (Elena) Alexandra
Mitscherlich, Alexander Joseph 1908-1982 Obituary 107
Mitson, Eileen N(ora) 1930- 25-28R
Mitsuhashi, Yoko SATA 45
See also SATA-Brief 33
Mittelholzer, Edgar Austin 1909-1965 CAP-1
Earlier sketch in CA 13-14
See also BW 1
See also DLB 117
Mittelman, James H(oward) 1944- CANR-13
Earlier sketch in CA 73-76
Mitterer, Erika 1906- DLB 85
Mitterer, Felix 1948- DLB 124
Mitterling, Philip Ira 1926- 102
Mittermeier, Russell (Alan) 1949- 161
Mittermeyer, Helen (Hayton Monteith) 1930- 124
Mitternacht, Johann Sebastian 1613-1679 DLB 168
Mittlebeeler, Emmet V(aughn) 1915- 57-60
Mittman, Stephanie 1950- 167
Mitton, Bruce H(arold) 1950- 108
Mitton, Charles Leslie 1907- CANR-4
Earlier sketch in CA 1-4R
Mitton, Jacqueline 1948- 97-100
See also SATA 66
Mitton, Simon 1946- 97-100
See also SATA 66
Mittra, S(id) 1930- 41-44R
Mitzman, Arthur Benjamin 1931- 104
Mitzman, Max E. 1908- 97-100
Miura, Akira 1927- 117
Miura, Ayako 1922- 73-76
Miura, Chizuko 1931- 133
See also Sono, Ayako
Miura, Hiroshi 1944- 164
Mix, C(larence) Rex 1935- 29-32R
Mix, Katherine Lyon 53-56
Mix, Paul E(merson) 1934- 45-48
Mix, Susan Shank 1943- 29-32R
Mixon, Laura J. 165
Mixter, Elisabeth W.
See Morss, Elisabeth W.
Mixter, Keith Eugene 1922- 41-44R
Mixter, Russell Lowell 1906- CAP-1
Earlier sketch in CA 13-16
Miyakawa, T(etsuo) Scott 1906- 17-20R
Miyamoto, Kazuo 1900- CAP-1
Earlier sketch in CA 11-12
Miyamoto, Yuriko 1899-1951 DLB 180
See also TCLC 37
Miyazawa, Kenji 1896-1933 157
See also TCLC 76
Miyoshi, Masao 1928- 29-32R
Mizejewski, Linda 1952- 144
Mizener, Arthur (Moore) 1907-1988 CANR-5
Obituary 124
Earlier sketch in CA 5-8R
See also DLB 103
Mizner, Elizabeth Howard 1907- 13-16R
See also SATA 27
Mizoguchi, Kenji 1898-1956 167
See also TCLC 72
Mizruchi, Ephraim H(arold) 1926- 41-44R
Mizruchi, Mark S(heldon) 1953- CANR-30
Earlier sketch in CA 110
Mizumura, Kazue 85-88
See also SATA 18
Mjelde, Michael Jay 1938- 69-72
Mnacko, Ladislav 1919- CANR-31
Earlier sketch in CA 29-32R
Mnookin, Robert H(arris) 1942- 140
Mo, Timothy (Peter) 1950(?)- 117
See also CLC 46
See also DLB 194
See also MTCW 1
Moak, Lennox L. 1912- 21-24R
Moak, Samuel K(uhn) 1929- 37-40R
Moan, Terrence 1947- 97-100
Moat, John 1936- CANR-29
Earlier sketches in CA 33-36R, CANR-13
Moats, Alice-Leone 1908(?)-1989 CAP-1
Obituary 128
Earlier sketch in CA 13-16
Moberg, David O(scar) 1922- CANR-18
Earlier sketches in CA 1-4R, CANR-2
Moberg, (Carl Arthur) Vilhelm 1898-1973 97-100
Obituary 45-48
Moberly, R(obert) B(asil) 1920- 29-32R
Moberly, Walter (Hamilton) 1881-1974 CAP-2
Earlier sketch in CA 29-32
Moberly-Bell, Enid 1881- 5-8R
Mobley, Charles M(urray) 1954- 139
Mobley, Harris W(itsel) 1929- 37-40R
Mobley, James Bryce 1934- CANR-48
Mobley, Joe A. 1945- 155
See also SATA 91
Mobley, Tony Allen 1938- 102
Mobley, Walt
See Burgess, Michael (Roy)
Moche, Dinah (Rachel) L(evine) 1936- CANR-57
Earlier sketch in CA 89-92
See also SATA 44
See also SATA-Brief 40
Mochi, Ugo (A.) 1889-1977 SATA 38
Mochizuki, Ken 1954- 149
See also SAAS 22
See also SATA 81
Mock, Edward J(oseph) 1934- 21-24R
Mocker, Donald W(ilbur) 1935- 102
Mockler, Anthony 1937- 69-72
Mockler, Mike 1945- 109
Mockler, Robert J. 1932- 33-36R
Mockridge, Norton 1915- Brief entry 110
Mocsy, Andras 1929- 65-68
Modak, Manorama Ramkrishna 1895- 97-100
Modarressi, Taghi (M.) 1931- 134
Brief entry 121
Interview in 134
See also CLC 44
Mode, Heinz (Adolf) 1913- Brief entry 111
Model, Lisette 1906-1983 Obituary 109
Modell, Frank B. 1917- CANR-39
Earlier sketch in CA 116
See also SATA 39
See also SATA-Brief 36
Modell, John 1941- 93-96
Modell, Judith Schachter 1941- 111
Modelski, George 1926- CANR-2
Earlier sketch in CA 49-52
Modert, (Betty) Jo 1921- 132
Modesitt, Jeanne 1953- SATA 92
Modesitt, L(eland) E(xton), Jr. 1943- CANR-58
Earlier sketches in CA 109, CANR-27
See also SATA 91
Modgil, Celia 1937- 124
Modgil, Sohan (Lal) 1938- 124
Modiano, Patrick (Jean) 1945- CANR-40
Earlier sketches in CA 85-88, CANR-17
See also CLC 18
See also DLB 83
Modigliani, Andre 1940- 53-56
Modigliani, Jeanne 1918(?)-1984 Obituary 113
Modinos, Antonis 1938- 160
Modisane, Bloke
See Modisane, William
Modisane, William 1923-1986 Obituary 118
Modley, Rudolph 1906-1976 Obituary 69-72
Modras, Ronald E(dward) 1937- CANR-9
Earlier sketch in CA 21-24R
Modrell, Dolores 1933- SATA 72
Moe, Barbara 1937- 69-72
See also SATA 20
Moe, Christian (Hollis) 1929- 41-44R
Moe, Edith Monroe 1896(?)-1987 Obituary 122
Moe, Richard 1936- 145
Moehlman, Arthur H(enry) 1907- 9-12R
Moehlmann, F. Herbert 1893- 93-96
Moelleken, Wolfgang W. 1934- 33-36R
Moeller, Charles 1912- 73-76
Moeller, Dade W. 1927- 138
Moeller, Dorothy W(ilson) 1902- 45-48
Moeller, Helen (Elaine) 1921- CANR-13
Earlier sketch in CA 21-24R
Moellering, Ralph L(uther) 1923- 13-16R
Moellhausen, Balduin 1825-1905 DLB 129
Moen, Matthew C. 1958- 143
Moenkemeyer, Heinz 1914- 102
Moenssens, Andre A. 1930- 29-32R
Moeran, Brian 1944- 127
Moerbeek, Kees 1955- 166
See also SATA 98
Moerck, Paal
See Roelvaag, O(le) E(dvart)
Moeri, Louise 1924- CANR-61
Earlier sketches in CA 65-68, CANR-9
See also SAAS 10
See also SATA 24, 93
Moerk, Ernst L(orenz) 1937- 126
Moerman, Daniel E(llis) 1941- 105
Moerman, Michael (Harris) 1934- 25-28R
Moerner, Magnus 1924- 132
Moers, Ellen 1928-1979 CANR-59
Obituary 89-92
Earlier sketch in CA 9-12R
Moes, Joh(a)n E(rnst) 1926- 1-4R
Moeser, John V(ictor) 1942- 116
Moffat, Abbot Low 1901- 1-4R
Moffat, Alexander W(hite) 1891- 69-72
Moffat, Anne Simon 1947- 107
Moffat, Frances 1912- 97-100
Moffat, Gwen 1924- CANR-66
Earlier sketches in CA 13-16R, CANR-10, 27, 52
Moffat, John Lawrence 1916- 103
Moffat, Mary Jane 1933- CANR-17
Earlier sketch in CA 97-100
Moffatt, Doris 1919- 105
Moffatt, (Marston) Michael 1944- CANR-20
Earlier sketch in CA 85-88
Moffett, Eileen Flower 1928- 123
Moffett, George D(inwiddie) III 1943- 118
Moffett, Hugh (Oliver) 1910-1985 73-76
Obituary 115
Moffett, Jami 1952- SATA 84
Moffett, Judith 1942- CANR-48
Earlier sketches in CA 69-72, CANR-14
Moffett, Kenworth W(illiam) 1934- 167
Brief entry 118
Moffett, Marian (Scott) 1949- 149
Moffett, Martha (Leatherwood) 1934- 37-40R
See also SATA 8
Moffett, Samuel Hugh 1916- CANR-5
Earlier sketch in CA 9-12R
Moffett, (Anthony) Toby 1944- 85-88
Moffitt, Donald (Anthony) 1936- Brief entry 111
Moffitt, John 1908- CANR-10
Earlier sketch in CA 25-28R
Moffitt, Peggy 1937- 138
Moffitt, Phillip 1946- 114
Brief entry 110
Interview in 114
Moffitt, William J. 1930- 57-60
Mofolo, Thomas (Mokopu) 1875(?)-1948 153
Brief entry 121
See also BLC 3
See also DAM MULT
See also TCLC 22
Mofsie, Louis B. 1936- SATA-Brief 33
Mogal, Doris P(ick) 1918- 69-72
Mogan, Joseph J(ohn), Jr. 1924- 49-52
Mogel, Leonard Henry 1922- 104
Moger, Allen W(esley) 1905- CAP-2
Earlier sketch in CA 25-28
Moger, Art 1911- 120
Moggach, Deborah 1948- CANR-18
Earlier sketch in CA 89-92
Moggridge, D(onald) E(dward) 1943- 29-32R
Moghadam, Valentine M. 1952- 146
Moglen, Helene 1936- 65-68
Mogulof, Melvin B(ernard) 1926- 105
Mohamed
See Muhammad
Mohammed Riza Pahlevi
See Pahlevi, Mohammed Riza
Mohan, Beverly Moffett 1918- 5-8R
Mohan, Brij 1939- CANR-57
Earlier sketches in CA 110, CANR-29
Mohan, Peter John 1930- CANR-10
Earlier sketch in CA 61-64
Mohan, Rakesh 1948- 151
Mohan, Robert Paul 1920- 41-44R
Mohanti, Prafulla 1936- 134
Mohanty, Jitendra N(ath) 1928- 117
Moher, Francis Anthony Peter 1955- 133
Moher, Frank
See Moher, Francis Anthony Peter
Mohl, Raymond A(llen) 1939- CANR-30
Earlier sketches in CA 33-36R, CANR-13
Mohl, Ruth 1891- CAP-1
Earlier sketch in CA 13-16
Mohle, Robert L. 1949- 167
Mohlenbrock, Robert H. 1931- CANR-5
Earlier sketch in CA 53-56
Mohler, Charles 1913- 29-32R
Mohler, James A(ylward) 1923- CANR-47
Earlier sketches in CA 21-24R, CANR-8, 23
Mohn, Peter B(urnet) 1934- 106
See also SATA 28
Mohn, Viola Kohl 1914- SATA 8
Mohr, Charles (Henry) 1929-1989 Obituary 128
Mohr, Clarence L(ee) 1946- 137
Mohr, Gordon 1916- CANR-12
Earlier sketch in CA 25-28R
Mohr, Jack
See Mohr, Gordon
Mohr, James C(rail) 1943- 73-76
Mohr, Nicholasa 1938- CANR-64
Earlier sketches in CA 49-52, CANR-1, 32
See also AAYA 8
See also CLC 12
See also CLR 22
See also DAM MULT
See also DLB 145
See also HLC
See also HW
See also JRDA
See also SAAS 8
See also SATA 8, 97
Mohr, Richard D(rake) 1950- 140
Mohrenschildt, Dimitri Sergius Von
See Von Mohrenschildt, Dimitri Sergius
Mohrhardt, Foster E(dward) 1907- CAP-1
Earlier sketch in CA 13-16
Mohrmann, Christine A(ndrina) E(lisabeth) M(aria) 1903- CAP-1
Earlier sketch in CA 9-10
Mohrt, Michel 1914- 13-16R
Moi, Toril 1953- 154
Moir, Alfred 1924- CANR-49
Earlier sketches in CA 21-24R, CANR-9, 24
Moir, Duncan Wilson 1930-1983 Obituary 110
Moir, John S(argent) 1926- 41-44R
Moir, May A(rstad) 1907- 111
Moir, Ronald Eugene 1928- 29-32R

Moise, Edwin E(variste) 1946- 130
Moise, Lotte E(lla) 1917- 103
Moissan, (Ferdinand Frederic) Henri
1852-1907 168
Moix, Ana Maria 1947- .... DLB 134
Mojica, Jose 1896-1974 Obituary 53-56
Mojtabai, A(nn) G(race) 1938- 85-88
See also CLC 5, 9, 15, 29
Mok, Esther 1953- 159
See also SATA 93
Mok, Paul P. 1934- 9-12R
Mokashi-Punekar, Shankar 1925- 97-100
Mokgatle, (Monyadio Moreleba) Naboth 1911-1985
CAP-2
Obituary 115
Earlier sketch in CA 33-36
Mokgatle, Naboth Nyadioe
See Mokgatle, (Monyadio Moreleba) Naboth
Mokgatle, Nyadioe Naboth
See Mokgatle, (Monyadio Moreleba) Naboth
Mokres, James A(llen) 1945- 49-52
Mokyr, Joel 1946- 136
Mol, Hans
See Mol, J(ohannis) J(acob)
Mol, J(ohannis) J(acob) 1922- CANR-43
Earlier sketches in CA 49-52, CANR-2, 18
Molan, Christine 1943- .... SATA 84
Molan, Dorothy L(ennon) 1911- 9-12R
Molan, Pat Carlson 1941- 112
Molarsky, Osmond 1909- CANR-48
Earlier sketch in CA 25-28R
See also SATA 16
Moldafsky, Annie 1930- 61-64
Moldea, Dan E. 1950- 122
Moldenhauer, Hans 1906- CANR-3
Earlier sketch in CA 1-4R
Moldenhauer, Joseph J(ohn) 1934- 33-36R
Moldenhauer, Rosaleen 1926- 97-100
Moldon, Peter L(eonard) 1937- 121
See also SATA 49
Moldovsky, Joel S(amuel) 1939- 97-100
Mole, John 1941- CANR-41
Earlier sketches in CA 101, CANR-18
See also SATA 36
Mole, Robert L. 1923- 29-32R
Molen, Ronald Lowry 1929- 65-68
Molenaar, Dee 1918- 37-40R
Moler, Kenneth Lloyd 1938- 89-92
Molesworth, Carl 1947- 147
Molesworth, Charles 1941- CANR-18
Earlier sketch in CA 77-80
Molesworth, Mary Louisa 1839-1921 165
See also DLB 135
See also SATA 98
Molette, Barbara Jean 1940- CANR-56
Earlier sketches in CA 45-48, CANR-26
See also BW 1
Molette, Carlton W(oodard) II 1939- CANR-25
Earlier sketches in CA 45-48, CANR-1
See also BW 1
Moley, Raymond (Charles) 1886-1975 61-64
Molho, Anthony 1939- Brief entry 106
Moliere 1622-1673 .... DA
See also DAB
See also DAC
See also DAM DRAM, MST
See also WLC
Molin, Charles
See Mayne, William (James Carter)
Molin, Sven Eric 1929- 17-20R
Molina, Enrique 1910- .... HW
Molina, Silvia 1946- 151
See also SATA 97
Molinaro, Julius A(rthur) 1918- 41-44R
Molinaro, Matie A. 1922- 128
Molinaro, Ursule CANR-48
Earlier sketch in CA 69-72
Moline, Jon Nelson 1937- 111
Moline, Mary 1932- CANR-7
Earlier sketch in CA 57-60
Molinsky, Joan Sandra 1933- 123
Brief entry 116
Molk, Laurel 1957- .... SATA 92
Moll, Elick 1907- CANR-2
Earlier sketch in CA 1-4R
Molland, Einar 1908- 53-56
Mollegen, Albert Theodore
1906-1984 Obituary 111
Mollegen, Anne Rush
See Smith, Anne Mollegen
Mollel, Tololwa M. 1952- 137
See also SATA 88
Mollenhoff, Clark R(aymond) 1921-1991 . CANR-13
Obituary 133
Earlier sketch in CA 17-20R
Mollenkott, Virginia R(amey) 1932- CANR-12
Earlier sketch in CA 33-36R
Moller, Richard Jay 1952- 106
Mollinger, Robert N. 1945- 106
Mollo, Andrew 1940- CANR-15
Earlier sketch in CA 65-68
Mollo, Terry (Madeline) 1949- 102
Mollo, Victor 1909-1987 .... CANR-20
Obituary 123
Earlier sketches in CA 9-12R, CANR-5
Molloy, Anne Baker 1907- 13-16R
See also SATA 32
Molloy, Frances
See Brady, Ann
Molloy, John T. 1937(?)- 81-84
Molloy, Johnny 1961- 168
Molloy, Julia Sale 1905-1983 .... CANR-1
Obituary 110
Earlier sketch in CA 1-4R
Molloy, M(ichael) J(oseph) 1917- 103
Molloy, Paul (George) 1924- CANR-17
Earlier sketch in CA 1-4R
See also SATA 5
Molloy, Robert (William) 1906-1977 .... CAP-2
Obituary 69-72
Earlier sketch in CA 29-32
Molloy, Tom 1948- 107
Molnar, Ferenc 1878-1952 153
Brief entry 109
See also DAM DRAM
See also TCLC 20
Molnar, Imre
See Lakatos, Imre
Molnar, Maria 1910(?)-1985 Obituary 117
Molnar, Michael 1946- 147
Molnar, Thomas 1921- CANR-42
Earlier sketches in CA 1-4R, CANR-3, 19
Molody, Konan Trofimovich
See Lonsdale, Gordon Arnold
Moloney, James 1954- 159
See also SATA 94
Molotch, Harvey L(uskin) 1940- CANR-15
Earlier sketch in CA 41-44R
Molotov, V.
See Molotov, Viacheslav Mikhailovich
Molotov, V. M.
See Molotov, Viacheslav Mikhailovich
Molotov, Viacheslav Mikhailovich
1890-1986 Obituary 121
Molt, Cynthia Marylee 1957- 138
Moltmann, Juergen 1926- 93-96
Molton, Stephen 1951- 127
Molumby, Lawrence E. 1932- 21-24R
Molz, (Redmond) Kathleen 1928- 49-52
Momaday, N(avarre) Scott 1934- CANR-68
Earlier sketches in CA 25-28R, CANR-14, 34
Interview in CANR-14
See also AAYA 11
See also CLC 2, 19, 85, 95
See also DA
See also DAB
See also DAC
See also DAM MST, MULT, NOV, POP
See also DLB 143, 175
See also MTCW 1
See also NNAL
See also SATA 48
See also SATA-Brief 30
See also WLCS
Momboisse, Raymond M. 1927- 29-32R
Momen, Moojan 1950- CANR-48
Earlier sketch in CA 122
Moment, David 1925- 9-12R
Momigliano, Arnaldo (Dante)
1908-1987 Obituary 123
Mommsen, Hans 1930- 164
Mommsen, Katharina 1925- 69-72
Mommsen, Wolfgang J(ustin) 1930- 101
Monaco, James 1942- CANR-33
Earlier sketches in CA 69-72, CANR-15
Monaco, Richard 1940- CANR-33
Earlier sketches in CA 65-68, CANR-15
Monad, Jacques 1910-1976 Obituary 65-68
Monagan, Charles A(ndrew) 1950- 109
Monagan, John S(tephen) 1911- 126
Monaghan, David (Mark) 1944- 133
Monaghan, E(dith) Jennifer 1933- 115
Monaghan, (James) Jay (IV) 1891-1981 .... 41-44R
Obituary 103
Monaghan, (Mary) Patricia 1946- CANR-23
Earlier sketch in CA 107
Monaghan, Patrick C.
1903(?)-1972 Obituary 37-40R
Monahan, Arthur P(atrick) 1928- 57-60
Monahan, Brent J(effrey) 1948- 93-96
Monahan, James (Henry Francis)
1912-1985 Obituary 118
Monahan, John
See Burnett, W(illiam) R(iley)
Monahan, John 1946- 149
Monahan, Kaspar .... AITN 1
Monahan, Patrick J. 1954- 148
Monahan, William G(regory) 1927(?)- 132
Monas, Sidney 1924- 13-16R
Monaster, Nathan 1916(?)-1990 Obituary 131
Monath, Elizabeth 1907- 5-8R
Monbeck, Michael E(ugene) 1942- CANR-2
Earlier sketch in CA 49-52
Monbiot, George (Joshua) 1963- 132
Monclova, Lidio Cruz
See Cruz Monclova, Lidio
Moncreiffe, (Rupert) Iain (Kay)
1919-1985 Obituary 115
Moncrieff, David (William Hardy) Scott
See Scott-Moncrieff, David (William Hardy)
Moncrieff, Earnest
See Chi, Richard Hu See-Yee
Moncrieff, Elspeth 1959- 160
Moncrieff, Martha Christian Scott
See Scott Moncrieff, Martha Christian
Moncure, Jane Belk 1926- CANR-6
Earlier sketch in CA 9-12R
See also SATA 23
Mondadori, Alberto 1914(?)-1976 Obituary 65-68
Mondadori, Arnoldo 1889-1971 Obituary 29-32R
Mondale, Joan Adams 1930- 41-44R
Mondale, Walter F(rederick) 1928- 65-68
Monday, James 1951- 61-64
Monday, Michael
See Ginder, Richard
Mondey, David (Charles) 1917- 93-96
Mondor, Henri 1885(?)-1962 Obituary 111
Monegal, Emir Rodriquez
See Rodriguez Monegal, Emir
Monelli, Paolo 1894(?)-1984 Obituary 114
Mones, Paul 138
Monesson, Harry S. 1935- 133
Monet, Claude 1840-1926 .... AAYA 25
Monet, Dorothy 1927- 81-84
Monet, Jacques 1930- CANR-11
Earlier sketch in CA 65-68
Monet, Jean 1932- 167
Monette, Paul 1945-1995 139
Obituary 147
See also CLC 82
Money, David Charles 1918- 107
Money, James (Henry) 1918- 133
Money, John (William) 1921- CANR-41
Earlier sketches in CA 45-48, CANR-1, 18
Money, Keith 1935- 107
Moneyhon, Carl H. 1944- CANR-46
Earlier sketch in CA 120
Money-Kyrle, Roger (Ernie)
1898-1980 Obituary 101
Monfalcone, Wesley R. 1942- 109
Monfolo, Rodolpho 1899(?)-1976 Obituary 69-72
Monfredo, Miriam Grace 166
Monger, Christopher 1950- 158
Monger, (Ifor) David 1908- 5-8R
Mongre, Dr. Paul
See Hausdorff, Felix
Monguio, Luis 1908- 5-8R
Monheim, Leonard M. 1911-1971 Obituary . 33-36R
Monhoff, June Hildegarde Flanner
1899-1987 Obituary 122
See also Flanner, Hildegarde
Monhollon, Michael L. 1959- 168
Monie, Willis J. 1945- 112
Moniere, Denis 1947- 167
Monier-Williams, Randall Herbert
1892(?)-1984 Obituary 113
Monig, Christopher
See Crossen, Kendell Foster
Monjo, F(erdinand) N(icholas III) 1924-1978 ....
CANR-37
Earlier sketch in CA 81-84
See also CLR 2
See also MAICYA
See also SATA 16
Monk, Alan
See Kendall, Willmoore
Monk, Galdo
See Riseley, Jerry B(urr, Jr.)
Monk, Janice J(ones) 1937- 93-96
Monk, Lorraine (Althea Constance) 101
Monk, Raymond 1925- 136
Monk, Robert C(larence) 1930- 21-24R
Monka, Paul 1935- 29-32R
Monkhouse, Alan 1858-1936 .... DLB 10
Monkhouse, Francis John 1914-1975 .... CANR-10
Obituary 57-60
Earlier sketch in CA 13-16R
Monkkonen, Eric H(enry) 1942- 61-64
Monkman, Leslie
See Monkman, Leslie G.
Monkman, Leslie G. 1946- CANR-52
Earlier sketch in CA 125
Monmonier, Mark Stephen 1943- CANR-27
Earlier sketch in CA 109
Monnet, Jean (Omer Marie) 1888-1979 102
Monnier, Genevieve 1939- 156
Monninger, Joseph 1953- 121
Monnow, Peter
See Croudace, Glynn
Monod, Jacques 1910-1976 69-72
Monod, Rene
See Koch, Kurt E(mil)
Monod, Sylvere 1921- 21-24R
Monod, (Andre) Theodore 1902- 65-68
Monongo
See Clytus, John
Monro, Gavin
See Monro-Higgs, Gertrude
Monro, Harold 1879-1932 .... DLB 19
Monro, Isabel S(tevenson) 1884- CAP-2
Earlier sketch in CA 19-20
Monro, Kate M. 1883-(?) CAP-2
Earlier sketch in CA 19-20
Monroe, Alan D(ouglas) 1944- 57-60
Monroe, Alan Houston 1903- 5-8R
Monroe, Bill
See Monroe, William Blanc, Jr.
Monroe, Carole 1944- 105
Monroe, Charles R(exford) 1905- 73-76
Monroe, Debra 1958- 134
Monroe, Elizabeth 1905-1986 .... 13-16R
Obituary 118
Monroe, Frank
See Chapman, Frank M(onroe)
Monroe, Harriet 1860-1936 Brief entry 109
See also DLB 54, 91
See also TCLC 12
Monroe, Jonathan B(eck) 1954- 126
Monroe, Keith 1917- CANR-2
Earlier sketch in CA 5-8R
Monroe, Lyle
See Heinlein, Robert A(nson)
Monroe, (Marilyn) Lynn Lee 1935- 53-56
Monroe, Margaret Ellen 1914- 5-8R
Monroe, Marilyn
See Baker, Norma Jean
Monroe, Marion
See Cox, Marion Monroe
See also SATA-Obit 34
Monroe, William Blanc, Jr. 1920- 108
Interview in 108
Monro-Higgs, Gertrude 1905- 105
Monsaingeon, Bruno 1943- 142
Monsarrat, Ann Whitelaw 1937- 73-76
Monsarrat, Nicholas (John Turney) 1910-1979 ....
CANR-3
Earlier sketch in CA 1-4R
See also DLB 15
Monsell, Helen Albee 1895-1971 .... CAP-1
Earlier sketch in CA 9-10
See also SATA 24
Monsen, R(aymond) Joseph, Jr. 1931- 9-12R
Monsey, Derek 1921-1979 .... CANR-2
Obituary 85-88
Earlier sketch in CA 1-4R
Monshipouri, Mahmood 1952- 151
Monsivais, Carlos 1938- 161
Monsky, Mark 1941- 65-68
Monsma, James E. 1929- 29-32R
Monsma, Stephen V(os) 1936- 33-36R
Monsman, Gerald Cornelius 1940- CANR-8
Earlier sketch in CA 21-24R
Monson, Charles H., Jr. 1924- 5-8R
Monson, Ingrid (T.) 1955- 165
Monson, Karen Ann 1945-1988 .... CANR-20
Obituary 124
Earlier sketch in CA 97-100
Monsour, Sally A. 1929- 21-24R
Montag, Thomas 1947- 103
Montag, Tom
See Montag, Thomas
Montagnes, Ian 1932- 45-48
Montagnier, Luc 1932- 160
Montagu, Ashley 1905- CANR-5
Earlier sketch in CA 5-8R
Interview in CANR-5
Montagu, Elizabeth 1917- 9-12R
Montagu, Ewen (Edward Samuel) 1901-1985 . 77-80
Obituary 116
Montagu, Ivor (Goldsmid Samuel)
1904-1984 .... 13-16R
Obituary 114
Montagu, Jeremy (Peter Samuel) 1927- 93-96
Montagu, Mary (Pierrepont) Wortley
1689-1762 .... DLB 95, 101
See also PC 16
Montagu, Robert 1949- 128
Montagu, W. H.
See Coleridge, Samuel Taylor
Montague, C. E. 1867-1928 .... DLB 197
Montague, Gene Bryan 1928- 93-96
Montague, George T(homas) 1929- 133
Montague, Jeanne
See Yarde, Jeanne Betty Frances
Montague, Joel B(enjamin), Jr. 1912- 5-8R
Montague, John (Patrick) 1929- CANR-69
Earlier sketches in CA 9-12R, CANR-9
See also CLC 13, 46
See also DLB 40
See also MTCW 1
Montague, Lisa
See Shulman, Sandra (Dawn)
Montague, Peter Gunn 1938- 85-88
Montague-Smith, Patrick Wykeham 1920- 107
Montagu of Beaulieu, Edward John Barrington
1926- CANR-6
Earlier sketch in CA 9-12R
Montaigne, Michel (Eyquem) de 1533-1592 .... DA
See also DAB
See also DAC
See also DAM MST
See also WLC
Montaigne, Sanford H(oward) 1935- 65-68
Montalbano, William D(aniel) 1940-1998 . CANR-22
Obituary 167
Earlier sketch in CA 105
Montalcini, Rita Levi
See Levi-Montalcini, Rita
Montale, Eugenio 1896-1981 .... CANR-30
Obituary 104
Earlier sketch in CA 17-20R
See also CLC 7, 9, 18
See also DLB 114
See also MTCW 1
See also PC 13
Montana, Bob 1920-1975 Obituary 89-92
See also SATA-Obit 21
Montana, Patrick J(oseph) 1937- CANR-10
Earlier sketch in CA 25-28R
Montanari, A(delio) J(oseph) 1917- 104
Montandon, Pat 57-60
Montapert, Alfred Armand 1906- 108
Montapert, William D(avid) 1930- 107
Montauredes, Rita 165
Montclair, Dennis
See Sladen, Norman St. Barbe
Montecino, Marcel 1945- 137
Brief entry 131
Montefiore, Hugh (William) 1920- 133
Montefiore, Simon Sebag
See Sebag-Montefiore, Simon
Monteilhet, Hubert 1928- Brief entry 117
Monteiro, George 1932- CANR-7
Earlier sketch in CA 17-20R
Monteiro, Luis (Infante de la Cerda) de Sttau
1926-1993 .... CANR-10
Obituary 142
Earlier sketch in CA 13-16R
Monteith, Hayton
See Mittermeyer, Helen (Hayton Monteith)
Montejo, Victor (D.) 1951- 139
Monteleone, Thomas F(rancis) 1946- CANR-50
Brief entry 109
Earlier sketch in CA 113
Interview in 113
Montell, William Lynwood 1931- CANR-11
Earlier sketch in CA 29-32R
Montemayor, Carlos 1947- 152
Montenegro, Laura Nyman 1953- 160
See also SATA 95

Monter, E. William 1936- 21-24R
Montero, Darrel Martin 1946- 101
Monterosso, Carlo 1921- 29-32R
Monterroso, Augusto 1921- 153
See also DLB 145
See also HW
Montes, Antonio Llano 1924- CANR-14
Earlier sketch in CA 69-72
Montes de Oca, Marco Antonio 1932- 114
See also HW
Montesi, Albert Joseph 1921- 37-40R
Montessori, Maria 1870-1952 147
Brief entry 115
Monteux, Doris (Hodgkins) 1894-1984 CAP-2
Obituary 112
Earlier sketch in CA 19-20
Montey, Vivian M(arie) 1956- 105
Montfort, Auguste 1913- CANR-41
Earlier sketches in CA 101, CANR-18
Montgomerie, Alexander 1550(?)-1598 DLB 167
Montgomerie, Norah (Mary) 1913- 105
See also SATA 26
Montgomery, Albert A. 1929- 13-16R
Montgomery, Bernard Law 1887-1976 69-72
Obituary 65-68
Montgomery, Brian (Frederick) 1903-1989 53-56
Obituary 128
Montgomery, (Robert) Bruce
1921-1978 Obituary 104
See also Crispin, Edmund
Montgomery, Charles F(ranklin) 1910-1978 81-84
Obituary 77-80
Montgomery, Constance
See Cappel, Constance
Montgomery, David 1927- 81-84
Montgomery, David 1928- 148
Montgomery, David Bruce 1938- 29-32R
Montgomery, Diane 1940- 162
Montgomery, Edward F(inley) 1918- 9-12R
Montgomery, Elizabeth
See Julesberg, Elizabeth Rider Montgomery
Montgomery, Elizabeth Rider
See Julesberg, Elizabeth Rider Montgomery
See also SATA 3, 34
See also SATA-Obit 41
Montgomery, Elizabeth Wakefield 1891- 41-44R
Montgomery, Helen
See Gunn, Helen Montgomery
Montgomery, Herbert J. 1933- CANR-40
Earlier sketches in CA 49-52, CANR-3, 18
Montgomery, Horace 1906- 9-12R
Montgomery, James 1771-1854 DLB 93, 158
Montgomery, John (McVey) 1919- 25-28R
See also DLB 16
Montgomery, John D(ickey) 1920- CANR-18
Earlier sketches in CA 5-8R, CANR-3
Montgomery, John Warwick 1931- CANR-25
Earlier sketches in CA 21-24R, CANR-10
Montgomery, L(ucy) M(aud) 1874-1942 137
Brief entry 108
See also AAYA 12
See also CLR 8
See also DAC
See also DAM MST
See also DLB 92
See also DLBD 14
See also JRDA
See also MAICYA
See also SATA 100
See also TCLC 51
See also YABC 1
Montgomery, M(aurice) R(ichard) 1938- 143
Montgomery, Marion H., Jr. 1925- CANR-48
Earlier sketches in CA 1-4R, CANR-3
See also AITN 1
See also CLC 7
See also DLB 6
Montgomery, Max
See Davenport, Guy (Mattison, Jr.)
Montgomery, Michael B. 1950- 122
Montgomery, Nancy S(chwinn) 93-96
Montgomery, Raymond A. (Jr.) 1936- CANR-16
Earlier sketch in CA 97-100
See also SATA 39
Montgomery, Robert 1904-1981 Obituary 108
Montgomery, Robert L(angford), Jr. 1927- 5-8R
Montgomery, Ruth Shick CANR-17
Earlier sketches in CA 1-4R, CANR-2
See also AITN 1
Montgomery, Rutherford George 1894-1985
CANR-70
Earlier sketch in CA 9-12R
See also SATA 3
Montgomery, Sy 1958- 135
Montgomery, Thomas (Andrew) 1925- 49-52
Montgomery, Tommie Sue 1942- 112
Montgomery, Vivian 102
See also SATA 36
Monthan, Doris Born 1924- CANR-37
Earlier sketch in CA 115
Montherlant, Henry (Milon) de 1896-1972 85-88
Obituary 37-40R
See also CLC 8, 19
See also DAM DRAM
See also DLB 72
See also MTCW 1
Monti, Laura V(irginia) 1930- 111
Monti, Nicolas 1956- 128
Montias, John Michael 1928- CANR-2
Earlier sketch in CA 1-4R
Monticello, Roberto 1954- 142
Monticone, Ronald Charles 1937- 73-76
Montier, Jean-Pierre 1956- 165
Montigny, Louvigny de 1876-1955 DLB 92
Montini, Giovanni Battista (Enrico Antonio Maria)
1897-1978 CANR-30
Obituary 77-80
Earlier sketch in CA 81-84
Montoya, Jose 1932- 131
See also DLB 122
See also HW
Montpetit, Charles 1958- 160
See also SATA 101
Montresor, Beni 1926- CANR-28
Earlier sketch in CA 29-32R
See also MAICYA
See also SAAS 4
See also SATA 3, 38
Montreuil, Claire
See Martin, Claire
Montrose, Graham
See Mackinnon, Charles Roy
Montrose, James St. David
See Appleman, John Alan
Montross, David
See Backus, Jean L(ouise)
Monty, Jeanne R(uth) 1935- 49-52
Monty Python
See Chapman, Graham
and Cleese, John (Marwood)
and Gilliam, Terry (Vance)
and Idle, Eric
and Jones, Terence Graham Parry
and Palin, Michael (Edward)
See also AAYA 7
Mood, Alexander M(cFarlane) 1913- 53-56
Mood, John J(ordan) L(indemann) 1932- 57-60
Mood, Terry Ann 1945- 154
Moodie, Graeme C(ochrane) 1924- CANR-2
Earlier sketch in CA 1-4R
Moodie, John Wedderburn Dunbar 1797-1869 DLB 99
Moodie, Susanna (Strickland) 1803-1885 DLB 99
Moodie, T(homas) Dunbar 1940- 77-80
Moody, Anne 1940- 65-68
See also BW 1
Moody, Bill 1941- 154
Moody, Dale 1915- 17-20R
Moody, Eric N(elson) 1946- 116
Moody, Ernest A(ddison) 1903-1975 13-16R
Obituary 61-64
Moody, Fred 1949- 153
Moody, G. F.
See Hamel Peifer, Kathleen
Moody, Hiram F. III 1961- CANR-64
Earlier sketch in CA 138
Moody, J. Carroll 1934- 33-36R
Moody, Jess C. 1925- 21-24R
Moody, John (Henry) 1953- 138
Moody, Joseph Nestor 1904-1994 CANR-1
Obituary 145
Earlier sketch in CA 49-52
Moody, Joshua 1633(?)-1697 DLB 24
Moody, Mary 1950- 144
Moody, Paul Amos 1903- 53-56
Moody, Paul E(lliot) 1936- 118
Moody, Peter R(ichard, Jr.) 1943- 130
Brief entry 107
Moody, R. Bruce 1933- 17-20R
Moody, Ralph Owen 1898- CAP-1
Earlier sketch in CA 9-10
See also SATA 1
Moody, Raymond Avery, Jr. 1944- 93-96
Moody, Richard 1911-1996 33-36R
Obituary 151
Moody, Rick
See Moody, Hiram F. III
Moody, Ron 1924- 108
Moody, T(heodore) W(illiam) 1907- 13-16R
Moody, William Vaughn 1869-1910 Brief entry 110
See also DLB 7, 54
Mookerjee, Ajit 1915- 157
Mookerjee, Ajitcoomar
See Mookerjee, Ajit
Mookini, Esther T. 1928- 135
Moolb, Leinad
See Bloom, Daniel Halevi
Moolson, Melusa
See Solomon, Samuel
Moomaw, Ira W. 1894- CAP-1
Earlier sketch in CA 13-14
Moon, Carl 1879-1948 Brief entry 111
See also SATA 25
Moon, Douglas Mark 1937- 17-20R
Moon, Elaine Latzman 1939- 147
Moon, Elizabeth 1945- 134
Moon, G(eoff) J. H. 1915- 105
Moon, Grace Purdie 1877(?)-1947 Brief entry 113
See also SATA 25
Moon, Harold K(ay) 1932- 53-56
Moon, Henry Lee 1901-1985 Obituary 116
Moon, Jeremy 1955- 149
Moon, Michael E(lliott) 1948- 85-88
Moon, Nicola 1952- 148
See also SATA 96
Moon, (Edward) Penderel 1905-1987 145
Obituary 122
Moon, Rexford G(eorge), Jr. 1922- 41-44R
Moon, Robert 1925- 73-76
Moon, Sheila (Elizabeth) 1910- 25-28R
See also SATA 5
Moon, Warren G. 1946- 125
Moonblood, Q.
See Stallone, Sylvester (Enzio)
Mooney, Bel 1946- CANR-69
Earlier sketch in CA 138
See also SATA 95
Mooney, Bill
See Mooney, William F.
Mooney, Booth 1912-1977 CANR-3
Obituary 69-72
Earlier sketch in CA 49-52
Mooney, Canice (Albert James) 1911-1963 5-8R
Mooney, Chase C(urran) 1913-1972 CAP-2
Earlier sketch in CA 19-20
Mooney, Christopher F(rancis) 1925-1993
CANR-14
Obituary 142
Earlier sketch in CA 37-40R
Mooney, Edward 1951- 130
See also Mooney, Ted
Mooney, Elizabeth C(omstock) 1918-1986 CANR-9
Obituary 119
Earlier sketch in CA 61-64
See also SATA-Obit 48
Mooney, Eugene F. 1930- 17-20R
Mooney, George A(ustin)
1911-1979 Obituary 89-92
Mooney, Harry J(ohn), Jr. 1927- 5-8R
Mooney, Michael M.
See Mooney, Michael Macdonald
Mooney, Michael Macdonald 1930-1985 CANR-21
Obituary 117
Earlier sketch in CA 65-68
Mooney, Patrick 1937- 115
Mooney, Ted
See Mooney, Edward
See also CLC 25
Mooney, William F. 1919(?)-1985 Obituary 116
Mooneyham, W(alter) Stanley 1926-1991 CANR-6
Obituary 134
Earlier sketch in CA 13-16R
Moonitz, Maurice 1910- CANR-2
Earlier sketch in CA 5-8R
Moonman, Eric 1929- 103
Mooradian, Karlen 1935- 97-100
Moorcock, Michael (John) 1939- CANR-64
Earlier sketches in CA 45-48, CANR-2, 17, 38
See also CAAS 5
See also AAYA 26
See also CLC 5, 27, 58
See also DLB 14
See also MTCW 1
See also SATA 93
Moore, Acel 1940- 69-72
Moore, Alan 1960- 123
Moore, Alexis 1951- 162
Moore, Alice Ruth
See Nelson, Alice Ruth Moore Dunbar
Moore, Alison 1951- 153
Moore, Allan F. 1954- 146
Moore, Alma Chesnut 1901- CAP-1
Earlier sketch in CA 13-14
Moore, Amos
See Hubbard, George (Barron)
Moore, Andrew
See Binder, Frederick Moore
Moore, Anne Carroll 1871-1961 73-76
See also SATA 13
Moore, Archie Lee 1916- 33-36R
Moore, Arthur 1906(?)-1977 Obituary 69-72
Moore, Arthur James 1888-1974 5-8R
Obituary 49-52
Moore, Austin
See Muir, (Charles) Augustus (Carlow)
Moore, Barbara
See Lee, Barbara (Moore)
Moore, Barrington, Jr. 1913- 117
Moore, Basil John 1933- 21-24R
Moore, Bernard 1904- CANR-13
Earlier sketch in CA 69-72
Moore, Bidwell 1917- 33-36R
Moore, Bob 1948- 61-64
Moore, Brenda L(ee) 1950- 159
Moore, Brian 1921- CANR-63
Earlier sketches in CA 1-4R, CANR-1, 25, 42
See also CLC 1, 3, 5, 7, 8, 19, 32, 90
See also DAB
See also DAC
See also DAM MST
See also MTCW 1
Moore, C(atherine) L(ucile) 1911- 104
Interview in 104
See also DLB 8
Moore, Carey Armstrong 1930- 37-40R
Moore, Carl L(eland) 1921- CANR-15
Earlier sketch in CA 5-8R
Moore, Carman L(eroy) 1936- 61-64
Moore, Cassandra Chrones 166
Moore, Charles
See Moore, Reg(inald Charles Arthur)
Moore, Charles A(lexander) 1901-1967 CANR-3
Earlier sketch in CA 1-4R
Moore, Charles Garrett Ponsonby 1910- 108
Moore, Charlotte E(mma) 1898-1990 160
Moore, Chauncey O. 1895-1965 CAP-1
Earlier sketch in CA 11-12
Moore, Christine Palamidessi 1951- 151
Moore, Christopher (Hugh) 1950- 119
Moore, Clayton
See Brandner, Gary (Phil)
and Henderson, M(arilyn) R(uth)
Moore, Clement Clarke 1779-1863 DLB 42
See also MAICYA
See also SATA 18
Moore, Clyde B. 1886-1973 CANR-4
Earlier sketch in CA 1-4R
Moore, Colleen 1902(?)-1988 Obituary 124
Moore, Cora R. 1902- CAP-2
Earlier sketch in CA 25-28
Moore, Cory
See Sturgeon, Wina
Moore, Cyd 1957- SATA 83
Moore, Dan Tyler 1908- 5-8R
Moore, Daniel G(eorge) 1899-1977 57-60
Obituary 126
Moore, David G. 1918- CANR-2
Earlier sketch in CA 1-4R
Moore, David Moresby 1933- 112
Moore, Deborah Dash 1946- 108
Moore, Dick
See Moore, John Richard, Jr.
Moore, Dinty W. 1955- 150
Moore, Don W. 1905(?)-1986 Obituary 119
See also SATA-Obit 48
Moore, Donald Joseph 1929- 57-60
Moore, Dora Mavor 1888-1979 148
See also DLB 92
Moore, Doris Langley 1903(?)-1989 CANR-1
Obituary 128
Earlier sketch in CA 1-4R
Moore, Dorothea (Mary) 1881-1933 Brief entry 121
Moore, Dorothy N(elson) 1915- CANR-44
Earlier sketches in CA 89-92, CANR-21
Moore, Douglas Stuart 1893-1969 CAP-1
Earlier sketch in CA 13-16
Moore, Dudley 1935- 167
Moore, E(velyn) Garth 1906- CAP-1
Earlier sketch in CA 11-12
Moore, Edmund A(rthur) 1903- 5-8R
Moore, Edward
See Muir, Edwin
Moore, Edward C(arter) 1917- CANR-5
Earlier sketch in CA 1-4R
Moore, Edward J(ames) 1935- 65-68
Moore, Edward M(umford) 1940- 57-60
Moore, Elaine 1944- 151
See also SATA 86
Moore, Elizabeth
See Atkins, Meg Elizabeth
Moore, Ethel Pauline Perry 1902- CAP-1
Earlier sketch in CA 11-12
Moore, Eva 1942- 45-48
See also SATA 20
Moore, Everett T(homson) 1909- CAP-1
Earlier sketch in CA 11-12
Moore, Fenworth CANR-26
Earlier sketches in CAP-2, CA 19-20
Moore, Francis D(aniels) 1913- Brief entry 113
Moore, Francis Edward 1898- CAP-1
Earlier sketch in CA 9-10
Moore, Frank Harper 1920- 5-8R
Moore, Frank Ledlie 1923- 5-8R
Moore, Franklin G. 1905- 1-4R
Moore, G(ranville) Alexander Jr. 1937- 21-24R
Moore, Gary T(homas) 1945- CANR-15
Earlier sketch in CA 85-88
Moore, Gene D. 1919- 21-24R
Moore, Geoffrey H(oyt) 1914- CANR-41
Earlier sketches in CA 81-84, CANR-19
Moore, Geoffrey Herbert 1920- 109
Moore, George Augustus 1852-1933 Brief
entry 104
See also DLB 10, 18, 57, 135
See also SSC 19
See also TCLC 7
Moore, George Ellis 1916- 5-8R
Moore, Gerald 1899-1987 CANR-5
Obituary 122
Earlier sketch in CA 1-4R
Moore, Glover 1911- 107
Moore, Gwyneth
See Bannister, Patricia Valeria
Moore, (David) Harmon 1911- 13-16R
Moore, Harold A. 1913- 33-36R
Moore, Harold G(regory, Jr.) 1922- 144
Moore, Harris
See Harris, Alf(red)
Moore, Harry Estill 1897- CAP-1
Earlier sketch in CA 13-14
Moore, Harry T(hornton) 1908-1981 CANR-3
Obituary 103
Earlier sketch in CA 5-8R
Moore, Henry (Spencer) 1898-1986 126
Obituary 121
Moore, Honor 1945- 85-88
Moore, J(ohn) Preston 1906- 65-68
Moore, J. Stuart 1953- 147
Moore, J(ohn) William 1928- 5-8R
Moore, Jack (William) 1941- 112
See also SATA 46
See also SATA-Brief 32
Moore, Jack B(ailey) 1933- 33-36R
Moore, Jack L(ynne) 1920- 89-92
Moore, James 1928- 97-100
Moore, James R(ichard) 1947- CANR-22
Earlier sketch in CA 105
Moore, James T. III 1939- CANR-31
Earlier sketch in CA 29-32R
Moore, James T(almadge) 1936- 139
Moore, James Tice 1945- 73-76
Moore, Jane Ann 1931- 37-40R
Moore, Janet Gaylord 1905- 77-80
See also SATA 18
Moore, Jean S. 130
Moore, Jenny 1923-1973 Obituary 45-48
Moore, Jerome (Aaron) 1903- 81-84
Moore, Jerrold Northrup 1934- 104
Moore, Jessie Eleanor 1886-(?) CAP-1
Earlier sketch in CA 19-20
Moore, Jim 1946- SATA 42
Moore, Jimmy
See Moore, James T. III
Moore, John (Cecil) 1907- 5-8R
Moore, John A.
See Moore, John Allen
Moore, John A(lexander) 1915- CANR-55
Earlier sketches in CA 45-48, CANR-26
Moore, John A(ndrew) 1918-1972 Obituary 37-40R
Moore, John Allen 1912- 119

Moore, John C(lare) 1933- 49-52
Moore, John H. 1935- 118
Moore, John Hammond 1924- 57-60
Moore, John Hebron 1920- 21-24R
Moore, John Michael 1935- 104
Moore, John Norton 1937- CANR-14
Earlier sketch in CA 37-40R
Moore, John R(obert) 1928- CANR-3
Earlier sketch in CA 1-4R
Moore, John Rees 1918- 33-36R
Moore, John Richard, Jr. 1925- 17-20R
Moore, John Robert 1890-1973 CAP-1
Earlier sketch in CA 9-10
Moore, John Travers 1908- CANR-3
Earlier sketch in CA 5-8R
See also SATA 12
Moore, Judith 1940- 159
Moore, Judith K. 1939- 158
Moore, Julia A. (Davis) 1847-1920 Brief entry 116
Moore, Katharine 1898- CANR-20
Earlier sketch in CA 89-92
Moore, Katherine Davis 1915- 13-16R
Moore, Kay 1948- 130
Moore, Keith L(eon) 1925- 69-72
Moore, Kenneth Clark 1943- 102
Moore, Kenneth E(ugene) 1930- 73-76
Moore, Kenny
See Moore, Kenneth Clark
Moore, L(ittleton) Hugh 1935- 49-52
Moore, L. Silas (Jr.) 1936- 41-44R
Moore, Lamont 1909- SATA-Brief 29
Moore, Lander
See Fensch, Thomas
Moore, Lester L(ee) 1924- 33-36R
Moore, Lilian 1909- CANR-38
Earlier sketch in CA 103
See also CLR 15
See also MAICYA
See also SATA 52
Moore, Lillian 1917-1967 CANR-2
Earlier sketch in CA 1-4R
Moore, Linda Perigo 1946- CANR-28
Earlier sketch in CA 107
Moore, Lisa
See Chater, Elizabeth (Eileen)
Moore, Lorrie
See Moore, Marie Lorena
See also CLC 39, 45, 68
Moore, Louis 1946- 130
Moore, Madeline (Roberta) 1934- 124
Moore, Marcia 1928- CANR-13
Earlier sketch in CA 61-64
Moore, Margaret A.
See Moore-Hart, Margaret A.
Moore, Margaret R(umberger) 1903- 9-12R
See also SATA 12
Moore, Marianne (Craig) 1887-1972 CANR-61
Obituary 33-36R
Earlier sketches in CA 1-4R, CANR-3
See also CDALB 1929-1941
See also CLC 1, 2, 4, 8, 10, 13, 19, 47
See also DA
See also DAB
See also DAC
See also DAM MST, POET
See also DLB 45
See also DLBD 7
See also MTCW 1
See also PC 4
See also SATA 20
See also WLCS
Moore, Marie Drury 1926- 33-36R
Moore, Marie Lorena 1957- CANR-39
Earlier sketch in CA 116
See also Moore, Lorrie
Moore, Marna
See Reynolds, (Marjorie) Moira Davison
Moore, Martha 1950- 152
Moore, (Georgina) Mary (Galbraith) 1930- Brief entry 112
Moore, Mary Tyler 1936- 165
Moore, Maureen (Audrey) 1943- 135
Moore, (James) Mavor 1919- 132
See also DLB 88
Moore, Maxine 1927- 73-76
Moore, Michael
See Harris, Herbert
Moore, Michael 1954- 166
Moore, Nicholas 1918- 69-72
Moore, P(eter) G(erald) 1928- CANR-26
Earlier sketch in CA 45-48
Moore, Pamela 1937-1964 1-4R
Moore, Pat(ricia A.) 1952- 144
Moore, Patrick (Alfred Caldwell) 1923- CANR-57
Earlier sketches in CA 13-16R, CANR-8
See also SAAS 8
See also SATA 49
See also SATA-Brief 39
Moore, Paul, Jr. 1919- 89-92
Moore, Paul L. 1917-1976 1-4R
Obituary 103
Moore, Peter D(ale) 1942- CANR-58
Earlier sketch in CA 127
Moore, R(obert) Laurence 1940- 29-32R
Moore, Ray (S.) 1905(?)-1984 Obituary 111
See also SATA-Obit 37
Moore, Ray 1941(?)-1989 Obituary 127
Moore, Rayburn Sabatzky 1920- CANR-37
Earlier sketches in CA 1-4R, CANR-2, 17
Moore, Raylyn 1928- 29-32R
Moore, Raymond Arthur, Jr. 1925- 5-8R
Moore, Raymond Cecil 1892-1974 156
Moore, Raymond S. 1915- CANR-49
Earlier sketches in CA 29-32R, CANR-21
Moore, Reg(inald Charles Arthur) 1930- 104
Moore, Regina
See Dunne, Mary Collins
Moore, Richard (Thomas) 1927- CANR-65
Earlier sketches in CA 33-36R, CANR-20
See also DLB 105
Moore, Richard B. 1893(?)-1978 Obituary 81-84
Moore, Richard H(arlan) 1945- 121
Moore, Richard R. 1934- 105
Moore, Robert
See Williams, Robert Moore
Moore, Robert (Samuel) 1936- CANR-11
Earlier sketch in CA 25-28R
Moore, Robert E(verett) 1914- 57-60
Moore, Robert Etheridge 1919- 61-64
Moore, Robert Hamilton 1913-1984 Obituary 114
Moore, Robert L(owell), Jr. 1925- 13-16R
See also AITN 1
Moore, Robin
See Moore, Robert L(owell), Jr.
Moore, Robin 1950- 134
Moore, Roger George 1927- 109
Moore, Rosalie (Gertrude) 1910- CANR-3
Earlier sketch in CA 5-8R
See also Brown, Rosalie
Moore, Roy L. 1947- 147
Moore, Russell Franklin 1920- CANR-6
Earlier sketch in CA 9-12R
Moore, Ruth (Ellen) 1908-1989 CANR-6
Obituary 127
Earlier sketch in CA 1-4R
See also SATA 23
Moore, Ruth Nulton 1923- CANR-15
Earlier sketch in CA 81-84
See also SATA 38
Moore, S(arah) E. CANR-2
Earlier sketch in CA 49-52
See also SATA 23
Moore, Sally Falk 1924- CANR-6
Earlier sketch in CA 57-60
Moore, Samuel Taylor 1893-1974 Obituary 53-56
Moore, Sandra Crockett 1945- 139
Moore, Sebastian 1917- 21-24R
Moore, Sonia 1902- CANR-2
Earlier sketch in CA 45-48
Moore, Steven 1951- 123
Moore, Susanna 1948- CANR-52
Earlier sketch in CA 109
Moore, T. Inglis
See Moore, Tom Inglis
Moore, T(homas) Sturge 1870-1944 Brief entry 118
See also DLB 19
Moore, Tara 1950- CANR-38
Earlier sketch in CA 116
See also SATA 61
Moore, Thomas 1779-1852 DLB 96, 144
Moore, Thomas (William) 1940- CANR-57
Earlier sketch in CA 132
Moore, Thomas Gale 1930- CANR-12
Earlier sketch in CA 29-32R
Moore, Thomas S(cott) 1945- 160
Moore, Tom 1950- CANR-18
Earlier sketch in CA 101
Moore, Tom Inglis 1901-1978(?) 21-24R
Obituary 135
Moore, Trevor Wyatt 1924- CANR-12
Earlier sketch in CA 29-32R
Moore, Tui De Roy 1953- 107
Moore, Vardine (Russell) 1906- 41-44R
Moore, Virginia Dryden 1911- 17-20R
Moore, W(illiam) Glenn 1925- 49-52
Moore, Walter (John) 1918- 131
Moore, Walter Lane 1905- CAP-1
Earlier sketch in CA 19-20
Moore, Ward 1903-1978 CAP-2
Obituary 113
Earlier sketch in CA 29-32
See also DLB 8
Moore, Warner O(land),, Jr. 1942-1992(?) 167
Moore, Warren (M., Jr.) 1923- 25-28R
Moore, Wilbert E(llis) 1914- CANR-5
Earlier sketch in CA 1-4R
Moore, Wilfred George 1907- CANR-4
Earlier sketch in CA 9-12R
Moore, William Howard 1942- 73-76
Moore, William L(eonard, Jr.) 1943- 93-96
Moore, Yvette 1958- 135
See also JRDA
See also SATA 69, 70
Moore-Colyer, Richard 1945- 141
Moore-Gilbert, Bart 1952- 158
Moore-Hart, Margaret A. 1946- 151
Moorehead, Agnes 1906-1974 Obituary 49-52
Moorehead, Alan (McCrae) 1910-1983 CANR-6
Obituary 110
Earlier sketch in CA 5-8R
Moorehead, Caroline 1944- CANR-39
Earlier sketches in CA 101, CANR-18
Moore-Rinvolucri, Mina Josephine 1902- 107
Moores, Dick
See Moores, Richard (Arnold)
Moores, Richard (Arnold) 1909-1986 69-72
Obituary 119
See also SATA-Obit 48
Moore-Sitterly, Charlotte Emma
See Moore, Charlotte E(mma)
Moorey, P(eter) R(oger) S(tuart) 1937- 132
Moorey, Roger
See Moorey, P(eter) R(oger) S(tuart)
Moorhead, Diana 1940- 105
Moorhead, Hugh S. 1922- 130
Moorhead, James H(owell) 1947- 124
Moorhead, John (Anthony) 1948- 142
Moorhead, Max L(eon) 1914-1981 21-24R
Obituary 135
Moorhouse, Charles Edmund 1911- 108
Moorhouse, Frank 1938- 118
Moorhouse, Geoffrey 1931- CANR-49
Earlier sketch in CA 25-28R
Moorhouse, Hilda Vansittart CAP-1
Earlier sketch in CA 11-12
Moorman, Charles (Wickliffe) 1925- Brief entry 114
Moorman, John Richard Humpidge 1905- CANR-2
Earlier sketch in CA 1-4R
Moorman, Mary C. 1905-1994 DLB 155
Moorshead, Henry
See Pine, Leslie Gilbert
Moorsom, Sasha 1931- CANR-14
Earlier sketch in CA 69-72
Moorsteen, Richard H.
1926(?)-1975 Obituary 57-60
Moos, Malcolm C(harles) 1916-1982 37-40R
Obituary 105
Moos, Rudolf H. 1934- CANR-1
Earlier sketch in CA 49-52
Moosa, Matti 1924- CANR-55
Earlier sketch in CA 127
Moose, Ruth 1938- 101
Mooser, Stephen 1941- CANR-15
Earlier sketch in CA 89-92
See also SATA 28, 75
Moote, A(lanson) Lloyd 1931- 33-36R
Moquin, Wayne-(Francis) 1930- 33-36R
Mora, Carl J(ose) 1936- 109
Mora, Francisco X(avier) 1952- SATA 90
Mora, George 1923- CANR-1
Earlier sketch in CA 45-48
Mora, Pat(ricia) 1942- CANR-57
Earlier sketch in CA 129
See also DAM MULT
See also HLC
See also HW
See also SATA 92
Morabito, Rocco 1920- 134
Morace, Robert A(nthony) 1947- 113
Moraes, Dom(inic F.) 1938- 25-28R
Moraes, Frank Robert 1907-1974 CAP-1
Obituary 49-52
Earlier sketch in CA 13-14
Moraes, (Marcus) Vinicius (Cruz) de (Mello)
1913-1980 Obituary 101
Moraga, Cherrie 1952- CANR-66
Earlier sketch in CA 131
See also DAM MULT
See also DLB 82
See also HW
Morain, Lloyd L. 1917- 69-72
Morais, Vamberto 1921- 69-72
Morales, Alejandro 1944- 131
See also DLB 82
See also HW
Morales, Angel Luis 1919- 49-52
See also HW
Morales, Edmundo 1943- 153
Morales, Jorge Luis 1930(?)- 153
See also HW
Morales, Mario Roberto 1947- DLB 145
Morales, Rafael 1919- DLB 108
Morales, Rebecca (Hope) 147
Morales, Waltraud Queiser 1947- 144
Morales Carrion, Arturo 1914(?)-1989 131
Obituary 129
See also HW
Moramarco, Fred Stephen 1938- 57-60
Moran, Barbara B. 1944- 124
Moran, Charles 1936- 144
Moran, Charles McMoran Wilson
See Wilson, Charles McMoran
Moran, Daniel
See Vardeman, Robert E(dward)
Moran, Emilio F(ederico) 1946- 117
Moran, Gabriel 1935- CANR-4
Earlier sketch in CA 53-56
Moran, George 1942- 115
Moran, Hugh Anderson 1881-1977 Obituary 73-76
Moran, J. L.
See Whitaker, Rod(ney)
Moran, James P. 1958- 146
Moran, James Sterling 1909- CANR-12
Earlier sketch in CA 9-12R
Moran, Jim
See Moran, James Sterling
Moran, John 1930- 45-48
Moran, John C(harles) 1942- CANR-27
Earlier sketch in CA 110
Moran, Mary Hurley 1947- 148
Moran, Michael G. 1947- 138
Moran, Mike
See Ard, William (Thomas)
Moran, Patrick Alfred Pierce 1917- 9-12R
Moran, Richard (Jerome) 1942- 121
Moran, Ronald (Wesson, Jr.) 1936- 37-40R
Moran, Tom 1943- CANR-29
Earlier sketch in CA 111
See also SATA 60
Moran, Victoria 1950- 160
Moran, William E(dward), Jr. 1916- 13-16R
Morand, Paul 1888-1976 Obituary 69-72
See also CLC 41
See also DLB 65
See also SSC 22
Morano, Donald V(ictor) 1934- 45-48
Morante, Elsa 1918-1985 CANR-35
Obituary 117
Earlier sketch in CA 85-88
See also CLC 8, 47
See also DLB 177
See also MTCW 1
Morantz, Regina Markell
See Morantz-Sanchez, Regina (Ann) Markell
Morantz-Sanchez, Regina (Ann) Markell 1943- 124
Morash, Christopher 1963- 151
Morasky, Robert Louis 1940- 105
Morata, Olympia Fulvia 1526-1555 DLB 179
Moraud, Marcel I(an) 1917- 53-56
Moravec, Hans P(eter) 1948- 142
Moravec, Ivo 1948- 168
Moravia, Alberto 1907-1990
See Pincherle, Alberto
See also CLC 2, 7, 11, 27, 46
See also DLB 177
See also SSC 26
Morawetz, Thomas H(ubert) 1942- 101
Morawski, Stefan T(adeusz) 1921- 81-84
Moray, Helga 89-92
Moray, Neville (Peter) 1935- 29-32R
Moray Williams, Ursula 1911- CANR-26
Earlier sketch in CA 111
See also Williams, Ursula Moray
See also MAICYA
See also SAAS 9
See also SATA 73
Morcom, John Brian 1925- 5-8R
Mordaunt, Elinor 1872(?)-1942 DLB 174
Mordden, Ethan (Christopher) 1947- CANR-65
Earlier sketch in CA 73-76
Mordecai, Pamela (Claire) 1942- 134
Mordechai, Ben
See Gerber, Israel J(oshua)
Mordock, John B. 1938- 61-64
Mordvinoff, Nicolas 1911-1973 73-76
Obituary 41-44R
See also SATA 17
More, Caroline
See Cone, Molly Lamken
and Strachan, Margaret Pitcairn
More, Daphne 1929- 65-68
More, Hannah 1745-1833 DLB 107, 109, 116, 158
More, Harry W(illiam) 1929- CANR-44
Earlier sketches in CA 53-56, CANR-4, 20
More, Henry 1614-1687 DLB 126
More, Jasper 1907-1987 CAP-1
Obituary 124
Earlier sketch in CA 9-10
More, Julian 1928- 144
More, Kenneth 1914-1982 Obituary 107
Moreas, Jean
See Papadiamantopoulos, Johannes
See also TCLC 18
Moreau, Daniel 1949- 125
Moreau, David Merlin 1927- 93-96
Moreau, John Adam 1938- 37-40R
Moreau, Jules Laurence 1917-1971 1-4R
Obituary 103
Moreau, Reginald E(rnest) 1897-1970 Obituary 104
Morecambe, Eric 1926-1984 Obituary 112
Moreh, Shmuel 1932- 141
Morehead, Albert H(odges) 1909-1966 CAP-1
Earlier sketch in CA 13-14
Morehead, James B. 1916- 166
Morehead, Joe
See Morehead, Joseph H(yde), Jr.
Morehead, Joseph H(yde), Jr. 1931- CANR-27
Earlier sketches in CA 57-60, CANR-6
Morehouse, Clifford P(helps) 1904-1977 9-12R
Obituary 134
Morehouse, Laurence E(nglemohr) 1913- CANR-4
Earlier sketch in CA 9-12R
Morehouse, Thomas A(lvin) 1937- 124
Morehouse, Ward 1899(?)-1966 Obituary 25-28R
Morel, Dighton
See Warner, Kenneth (Lewis)
Morel, Nina
See Markowa, Nina Alexandrovna
Moreland, Lois B. 45-48
Moreland, Richard C. 1953- 135
Morell, David 1939- 110
Morell, James B. 1956- 144
Morell, Virginia 1949- 156
Morella, Joe
See Morella, Joseph (James)
Morella, Joseph (James) 1949- CANR-48
Earlier sketch in CA 104
Morello, Karen Berger 1949- 126
Moremen, Grace E(llen Partin) 1930- CANR-1
Earlier sketch in CA 45-48
Moren, Sally M(oore) 1947- 97-100
Morency, Pierre 1942- DLB 60
Moreno, Antonio Elosequi 1918- 33-36R
Moreno, Baldomero Fernandez
See Fernandez Moreno, Baldomero
Moreno, Carlos Martinez
See Martinez Moreno, Carlos
Moreno, Cesar Fernandez
See Fernandez Moreno, Cesar
Moreno, Dorinda 1939- DLB 122
Moreno, Francisco Jose 1934- 29-32R
Moreno, Jacob L. 1892-1974 CAP-2
Obituary 49-52
Earlier sketch in CA 19-20
Moreno, Jose A. 1928- 25-28R
Moreno, Martin
See Swartz, Harry (Felix)
Moreno, Pedro R. 1947- 69-72
Morentz, Ethel Irene 29-32R
Morentz, Pat
See Morentz, Ethel Irene
Morenus, Constance Gay
1895(?)-1985 Obituary 117
Moreton, John
See Cohen, Morton N(orton)
Moreton, N. Edwina 1950- 135
Moretti, Marino 1885(?)-1979 Obituary 89-92
See also DLB 114
Morewedge, Parviz 1934- 93-96
Morey, Ann-Janine 1951- 144
Morey, Charles
See Fletcher, Helen Jill

Morey, Robert A(lbert) 1946- CANR-32
Earlier sketch in CA 113
Morey, Roy D. 1937- 17-20R
Morey, Walt(er Nelson) 1907-1992 CANR-31
Obituary 136
Earlier sketch in CA 29-32R
See also JRDA
See also MAICYA
See also SAAS 9
See also SATA 3, 51
See also SATA-Obit 70
Morey-Gaines, Ann-Janine
See Morey, Ann-Janine
Morford, Mark P(ercy) O(wen) 1929- Brief entry 111
Morgan, Al(bert Edward) 1920- CANR-1
Earlier sketch in CA 45-48
Morgan, Alfred P(owell) 1889-1972 107
See also SATA 33
Morgan, Alison 1959- 137
Morgan, Alison Mary 1930- CANR-51
Earlier sketches in CA 49-52, CANR-1, 18
See also SATA 30, 85
Morgan, Alyssa
See Delatush, Edith G.
Morgan, Angela
See Paine, Lauran (Bosworth)
Morgan, Ann Lee 1941- 125
Morgan, Anne Hodges 1940- 117
Morgan, Arlene
See Paine, Lauran (Bosworth)
Morgan, Arthur Ernest 1878-1975 CANR-3
Obituary 61-64
Earlier sketch in CA 5-8R
Morgan, Austen 1949- 130
Morgan, B(ayard) Q(uincy) 1883-1967 CAP-1
Earlier sketch in CA 11-12
Morgan, Barton 1889- CAP-1
Earlier sketch in CA 9-10
Morgan, Berry 1919- 49-52
See also CLC 6
See also DLB 6
Morgan, Bill 1949- CANR-30
Earlier sketch in CA 110
Morgan, Brian 1919- 5-8R
Morgan, Bryan S(tanford) 1923-1976 CANR-9
Earlier sketch in CA 5-8R
Morgan, By
See Morgan, Byron
Morgan, Byron 1921- 165
Morgan, Cary
See Cutler, Roland
Morgan, Charles, Jr. 1930- CANR-13
Earlier sketch in CA 17-20R
Morgan, Charles 1894-1958 DLB 34, 100
Morgan, Charles H(ill) 1902-1984 37-40R
Obituary 112
Morgan, Chester A(lan) 1914- 17-20R
Morgan, Christine 1904-1996 166
Morgan, Christopher 1952- CANR-48
Earlier sketch in CA 105
Morgan, Claire
See Highsmith, (Mary) Patricia
Morgan, Clifford T(homas) 1915-1976 CANR-4
Obituary 65-68
Earlier sketch in CA 1-4R
Morgan, Dale L. 1914-1971 Obituary 104
Morgan, Dan 1925- CANR-14
Earlier sketch in CA 37-40R
Morgan, Dan 1937- 143
Morgan, Daniel C(roxton), Jr. 1931- 17-20R
Morgan, Dareion
See Walz, Marjorie A.
Morgan, Darold H. 1924- 21-24R
Morgan, David (Rhys) 1937- CANR-45
Earlier sketch in CA 45-48
Morgan, David P(age) 1927- 123
Brief entry 118
Morgan, David T(aft, Jr.) 1937- 69-72
Morgan, Dewi (Lewis) 1916- CANR-1
Earlier sketch in CA 1-4R
Morgan, Donald G(rant) 1911- 17-20R
Morgan, Donn F(arley) 1943- 113
Morgan, Edmund S(ears) 1916- CANR-49
Earlier sketches in CA 9-12R, CANR-4
See also DLB 17
Morgan, Edward James Ranembe 1900-1978 Obituary 108
Morgan, Edward P(addock) 1910-1993 CAP-1
Obituary 140
Earlier sketch in CA 19-20
Morgan, Edwin (George) 1920- CANR-43
Earlier sketches in CA 5-8R, CANR-3
See also CLC 31
See also DLB 27
Morgan, Elaine (Neville) 1920- 41-44R
Morgan, Elizabeth 1947- 108
Interview in 108
Morgan, Ellen
See Bumstead, Kathleen Mary
Morgan, Emanuel
See Bynner, Witter
Morgan, Fidelis 1952- CANR-57
Earlier sketch in CA 127
Morgan, Frank
See Paine, Lauran (Bosworth)
Morgan, Fred Bruce, Jr. 1919-1975 65-68
Obituary 61-64
Morgan, Fred Troy 1926- 89-92
Morgan, (George) Frederick 1922- CANR-21
Earlier sketch in CA 17-20R
See also CLC 23
Morgan, G. J.
See Rowland, D(onald) S(ydney)
Morgan, Geoffrey 1916- 21-24R
See also SATA 46
Morgan, Gerald 1925- 41-44R
Morgan, Glebe
See Rowland, D(onald) S(ydney)
Morgan, Glenn G(uy) 1926- 9-12R
Morgan, Gwen 101
Morgan, Gwyneth
See Beal, Gwyneth
Morgan, H(oward) Wayne 1934- CANR-40
Earlier sketches in CA 5-8R, CANR-2, 18
Morgan, Hal
See Morgan, Henry A.
Morgan, Harriet
See Mencken, H(enry) L(ouis)
Morgan, Helen (Gertrude Louise) 1921- 57-60
See also SATA 29
Morgan, Henry
See von Ost, Henry Lerner
Morgan, Henry A. 1954- 112
Morgan, Hilda Campbell 1892-1985 Obituary 118
Morgan, Irvonwy 1907-1982 Obituary 107
Morgan, J(ill) M(eredith) 1946- 137
Morgan, James N(ewton) 1918- 21-24R
Morgan, Jane
See Cooper, James Fenimore
and Franklin, Jane (Morgan)
and Moren, Sally M(oore)
Morgan, Janet 1945- 65-68
See also CLC 39
Morgan, Jean (Werner) 1922- 102
Morgan, Jeanne
See Zarucchi, Jeanne Morgan
Morgan, (Walter) Jefferson 1940- CANR-29
Earlier sketches in CA 73-76, CANR-12
Morgan, Jim 1950- 45-48
Morgan, Joan 1905- 5-8R
Morgan, Joe Warner 1912- 9-12R
Morgan, John
See Paine, Lauran (Bosworth)
Morgan, John A(ndrew), Jr. 1935- 49-52
Morgan, John Medford
See Fox, G(ardner) F(rancis)
Morgan, John Pierpont, Jr. 1867-1943 DLB 140
Morgan, John Pierpont 1837-1913 DLB 140
Morgan, John S. 1921- 13-16R
Morgan, Joseph G. 1953- 167
Morgan, Joy Elmer 1889-1986 Obituary 119
Morgan, Judith A(dams) 1939- 49-52
Morgan, Kathryn L. 117
Morgan, Kay Summersby 1909-1975 Obituary 53-56
Morgan, Kenneth Owen 1934- CANR-23
Earlier sketches in CA 13-16R, CANR-7
Morgan, Kenneth R(emsen) 1916- 13-16R
Morgan, Lady 1776(?)-1859 DLB 116, 158
Morgan, Lael 1936- CANR-5
Earlier sketch in CA 53-56
Morgan, Lenore H. 1908-1976 CAP-2
Earlier sketch in CA 33-36
See also SATA 8
Morgan, Louise 9-12R
Morgan, Lucy 1940- 108
Morgan, M(argaret) Ruth 1942(?)-1983 Obituary 109
Morgan, Marabel 1937- CANR-2
Earlier sketch in CA 49-52
See also AITN 1
Morgan, Marion (Nora Eluned) 1942- CANR-46
Earlier sketch in CA 120
Morgan, Marjorie
See Chibnall, Marjorie (McCallum)
Morgan, Mark
See Overholser, Wayne D.
Morgan, Mary 1943- 132
See also SATA 81
Morgan, McKayla
See Basile, Gloria Vitanza
Morgan, Memo
See Avallone, Michael (Angelo, Jr.)
Morgan, Meredith
See Morgan, J(ill) M(eredith)
Morgan, Michael Croke 1911- 93-96
Morgan, Michaela
See Basile, Gloria Vitanza
Morgan, Murray 1916- 107
Morgan, Neil 1924- CANR-2
Earlier sketch in CA 5-8R
Morgan, Nicholas
See Morgan, Thomas Bruce
Morgan, Nicholas H. 1953- 144
Morgan, Patricia 1944- 89-92
Morgan, Patrick M. 1940- 37-40R
Morgan, Paul 1928- 61-64
Morgan, (Colin) Pete(r) 1939- 133
Morgan, Peter F(rederick) 1930- 113
Morgan, Pierr 1952- 145
See also SATA 77
Morgan, Raleigh, Jr. 1916- 41-44R
Morgan, Rebecca
See Forrest, Richard (Stockton)
Morgan, Rhodri 1939- 162
Morgan, Richard E(rnest) 1937- CANR-15
Earlier sketch in CA 41-44R
Morgan, Robert
See Turner, Robert (Harry)
Morgan, Robert 1921- CANR-42
Earlier sketches in CA 103, CANR-20
Morgan, Robert (R.) 1944- CANR-21
Earlier sketch in CA 33-36R
See also CAAS 20
See also DLB 120
Morgan, Robert C. 1943- 148
Morgan, Roberta 1953- CANR-15
Earlier sketch in CA 93-96
Morgan, Robin (Evonne) 1941- CANR-68
Earlier sketches in CA 69-72, CANR-29
See also CLC 2
See also MTCW 1
See also SATA 80
Morgan, Roger P(earce) 1932- CANR-12
Earlier sketch in CA 17-20R
Morgan, Rosemarie (Anne Louise) 131
Morgan, Roy A(mos) 1916- 41-44R
Morgan, Ruth P. 1934- 37-40R
Morgan, Sally (Jane) 1951- 134
Morgan, Sarah (Williams) 1901- CAP-1
Earlier sketch in CA 9-10
Morgan, Sarah (Nicola) 1959- 136
See also SATA 68
Morgan, Scott
See Kuttner, Henry
Morgan, Seth 1949(?)-1990 Obituary 132
See also CLC 65
Morgan, Sharon A(ntonia) 1951- 61-64
Morgan, Shirley
See Kiepper, Shirley Morgan
See also SATA 10
Morgan, Speer 1946- 97-100
Morgan, Stanley 1929- 69-72
Morgan, Steven Michael 1942- 115
Morgan, Stevie
See Davies, Nicola
Morgan, Susan 1943- 137
Morgan, Ted 1932- CANR-3
See also CAAS 4
Morgan, (Joseph) Theodore 1910- 17-20R
See also CAAS 3
Morgan, Thomas (Bruce) 1885(?)-1972 Obituary 37-40R
Morgan, Thomas Bruce 1926- 13-16R
Morgan, Thomas Hunt 1866-1945 156
Morgan, Tom 1942- 108
See also SATA 42
Morgan, Valerie
See Paine, Lauran (Bosworth)
Morgan, Virginia
See Mundis, Hester
Morgan, Wesley
See Bennett, Isadora
Morgan, William 1944- 109
Morgan-Grenville, Gerard (Wyndham) 1931- 57-60
Morgan-Witts, Max 1931- CANR-40
Earlier sketch in CA 29-32R
Morgello, Clemente Frank 1923- 103
Morgenroth, Barbara Brief entry 117
See also SATA-Brief 36
Morgenstein, Gary 1952- 116
Morgenstern, Christian 1871-1914 Brief entry 105
See also TCLC 8
Morgenstern, Dan (Michael) 1929- 127
Brief entry 111
Morgenstern, Julian 1881-1976 CAP-1
Obituary 89-92
Earlier sketch in CA 19-20
Morgenstern, Oskar 1902-1977 CANR-5
Obituary 73-76
Earlier sketch in CA 9-12R
Morgenstern, S.
See Goldman, William (W.)
Morgenstern, Soma 1891(?)-1976 Obituary 65-68
Morgenthau, Hans Joachim 1904-1980 9-12R
Obituary 101
Morgenthau, Henry, Jr. 1891-1967 Obituary 116
Morghen, Raffaello 1896-1983 Obituary 109
Morgner, Irmtraud 1933- DLB 75
Morgulas, Jerrold 1934- CANR-13
Earlier sketch in CA 21-24R
Morhaim, Victoria Kelrich 1937- 1-4R
Morhof, Daniel Georg 1639-1691 DLB 164
Mori, Hana 1909-1990(?) SATA 88
Mori, Kyoko 1957(?)- 153
See also AAYA 25
See also SAAS 26
Mori, Kyozo 1907(?)-1984 Obituary 112
Mori, Ogai 1862-1922 164
See also DLB 180
Mori, Rintaro Brief entry 110
See also Mori, Ogai
Mori, Toshio 1910- Brief entry 116
Moriarty, Alice Marie Ewell 1917- 21-24R
Moriarty, Christopher 1936- 81-84
Moriarty, Florence Jarman 104
Moriarty, Frederick Leo 1913- CANR-2
Earlier sketch in CA 5-8R
Moriarty, Marilyn F(rances) 1953- 168
Moriarty, Michael 1941- 163
Moriarty, Tim 1923- 61-64
Morice, Anne
See Shaw, Felicity
Morice, Dave 1946- CANR-61
Earlier sketch in CA 109
See also SATA 93
Morich, Stanton
See Griffith-Jones, George Chetwynd
Morick, Harold 1933- 25-28R
Moricz, Zsigmond 1879-1942 165
See also TCLC 33
Morier, James Justinian 1782(?)-1849 DLB 116
Morike, Eduard (Friedrich) 1804-1875 DLB 133
Morillas, Frances M. Lopez
See Lopez-Morillas, Frances M.
Morillo, Stephen (Reeder) 1958- 156
Morimoto, Anri 1956- 154
Morin, Claire
See Dore, Claire (Morin)
Morin, Edgar 1921- 107
Morin, Paul 1889-1963 DLB 92
Morin, Relman George 1907-1973 CANR-4
Obituary 41-44R
Earlier sketch in CA 1-4R
Morin, William J(ames) 1939- 111
Morine, Hoder
See Conroy, John Wesley
Moringstar, Mildred 1912- 127
Morini, Simona 1932- 110
Morinis, Alan 1949- 143
Morisey, A. Alexander 1913-1979 Obituary 89-92
Morison, David Lindsay 1920- 13-16R
Morison, Samuel Eliot 1887-1976 CANR-4
Obituary 65-68
Earlier sketch in CA 1-4R
See also DLB 17
Morison, Stanley 1889-1967 DLB 201
Morisseau, James J(oseph) 1929- 41-44R
Morita, James R. 1931- 103
Morita, Yuzo 1940- CANR-1
Earlier sketch in CA 45-48
Moritz, A(lbert) F(rank) 1947- 110
Moritz, Charles Fredric 1917- 118
Moritz, Karl Philipp 1756-1793 DLB 94
Moritz, Theresa
See Moritz, Theresa Anne
Moritz, Theresa Anne 1948- 127
Morken, Lucinda Oakland 1906- 61-64
Morkovin, Bela V.
See Morkovin, Boris V(ladimir)
Morkovin, Boris V(ladimir) 1882-1968 CAP-1
Earlier sketch in CA 19-20
Morlan, George K(olmer) 1904- 29-32R
Morlan, John E(dmund) 1930- 9-12R
Morlan, Robert L(oren) 1920-1985 17-20R
Obituary 118
Morland, Dick
See Hill, Reginald (Charles)
Morland, Howard 1942- 107
Morland, (John) Kenneth 1916- 41-44R
Morland, Nigel 1905-1986 CANR-63
Obituary 119
Earlier sketch in CA 53-56
Morland, Peter Henry
See Faust, Frederick (Schiller)
Morle, Albert Henry George 1919- 5-8R
Morley, Christopher (Darlington) 1890-1957 Brief entry 112
See also DLB 9
Morley, David 1923- 108
Morley, Don 1937- 108
Morley, Felix M(uskett) 1894-1982 166
Obituary 106
Morley, Frank V(igor) 1899-1980 105
Obituary 102
Morley, (John) Geoffrey (Nicholson) 1905-1983 Obituary 109
Morley (Wolpe), Hilda 1916(?)-1998 147
Obituary 167
Morley, Hugh 1908(?)-1978 Obituary 77-80
Morley, James William 1921- 13-16R
Morley, John 1838-1923 DLB 57, 144, 190
Morley, John(athan) David 1948- 126
Morley, John F(rancis) 1936- 132
Morley, Margaret 1941- 140
Morley, Patricia (Ann) 1929- 73-76
Morley, R.
See Morley, Robert (Adolph Wilton)
Morley, Robert (Adolph Wilton) 1908-1992 130
Obituary 137
Brief entry 113
Morley, S(ylvanus) Griswold 1878- 5-8R
Morley, Samuel A. 1934- 37-40R
Morley, Sheridan 1941- 29-32R
Morley, Steve 1953- 132
Morley, Susan
See Cross, John Keir
Morley, Wilfred Owen
See Lowndes, Robert A(ugustine) W(ard)
Morman, Jean Mary 1925- 61-64
Morn, Frank T(homas) 1937- 107
Morneau, Robert Fealey 1938- 113
Mornell, Pierre 1935- 131
Morner, Magnus
See Moerner, Magnus
Morninghouse, Sundaira
See Wilson, Carletta
Morningstar, Connie 1927- 69-72
Morningstar, Mildred 1912- SATA 61
Moro, Cesar 1903-1956 131
See also HW
Morone, James A. 1951- 142
Moroney, John R. 1939- CANR-17
Earlier sketch in CA 41-44R
Morowitz, Harold Joseph 1927- 104
Morpurgo, J(ack) E(ric) 1918- CANR-4
Earlier sketch in CA 9-12R
Morpurgo, Michael 1943- 158
See also CLR 51
See also SATA 93
Morra, Marion Eleanor 104
Morra, Umberto (?)-1981 Obituary 105
Morrah, Dave
See Morrah, David Wardlaw, Jr.
Morrah, David Wardlaw, Jr. 1914-1991 1-4R
Obituary 134
See also SATA 10
Morrah, Dermot (Michael Macgregor) 1896-1974 CAP-2
Obituary 53-56
Earlier sketch in CA 29-32
Morrall, John B. 1923- 25-28R
Morray, Joseph Parker 1916- 5-8R
Morreale, Ben 1924- 57-60
Morreim, E. Haavi 1950- 156
Morrell, David 1943- CANR-43
Earlier sketches in CA 57-60, CANR-7
Morrell, David C. 1929- 81-84
Morrell, Robert E(llis) 1930- 121

Morrell, William Parker 1899- ... CANR-1
Earlier sketch in CA 1-4R
Morren, Lee Fishman
See Fishman, Lisa
Morren, Theophil
See Hofmannsthal, Hugo von
Morressy, John 1930- ... CANR-52
Earlier sketches in CA 21-24R, CANR-8, 28
See also SATA 23
Morrice, J(ames) K(enneth) W(att) 1924- . CANR-41
Earlier sketch in CA 118
Morrice, Ken
See Morrice, J(ames) K(enneth) W(att)
Morrie
See Turner, Morris
Morrill, Allen C(onrad) 1904- ... 101
Morrill, Claire 1900(?)-1981 Obituary ... 103
Morrill, Eleanor D(unlap) 1907- ... 101
Morrill, George Percival 1920- ... 33-36R
Morrill, John S. 1946- ... 130
Morrill, Leslie H(olt) 1934- ... MAICYA
See also SAAS 22
See also SATA 48
See also SATA-Brief 33
Morrill, Richard
See Schreck, Everett M.
Morrill, Richard L(eland) 1934- ... CANR-35
Earlier sketch in CA 29-32R
Morris, A(ndrew) J(ames) A(nthony) 1936- ... CANR-12
Earlier sketch in CA 73-76
Morris, Adalaide K(irby) 1942- ... 57-60
Morris, Alan 1955- ... 156
Morris, Aldyth V. 1901- ... 29-32R
Morris, Alton C(hester) 1903- ... 13-16R
Morris, Ben(jamin Stephen) 1910-1990 ... 113
Obituary ... 132
Morris, Berenice Robinson
1909(?)-1990 Obituary ... 132
Morris, Bernadine (Taub) 1925- ... 102
Morris, Bertram 1908- ... CANR-18
Earlier sketch in CA 1-4R
Morris, Bill 1952- ... CLC 76
Morris, Brian 1930- ... CANR-18
Earlier sketch in CA 29-32R
Morris, Bruce R(obert) 1909- ... 5-8R
Morris, C(harles) R(ichard) 1898-1990 Obituary 131
Morris, Celia 1935- ... 138
Morris, Charles (William) 1901-1979 ... 13-16R
Obituary ... 135
Morris, Charles Lee 1943(?)-1986 Obituary ... 118
Morris, Chris(topher Crosby) 1946- ... 133
See also SATA 66
Morris, Christopher 1938- ... 21-24R
Morris, Christopher W. 1949- ... 147
Morris, Clyde M(cMahon) 1921- ... 93-96
Morris, (Edward) Craig 1939- ... 123
Morris, Cynthia Taft 1928- ... 25-28R
Morris, Dan (H.) 1912- ... 21-24R
Morris, David 1945- ... 85-88
Morris, David Brown 1942- ... CANR-48
Earlier sketches in CA 105, CANR-22
Morris, Deborah 1956- ... 155
See also SATA 91
Morris, Desmond (John) 1928- ... CANR-62
Earlier sketches in CA 45-48, CANR-2, 18, 38
See also MTCW 1
See also SATA 14
Morris, Dick 1948- ... 160
Morris, Don 1954- ... SATA 83
Morris, Donald R. 1924- ... 17-20R
Morris, Edgar Poe
See Kinnaird, Clark
Morris, Edita (deToll) ... CANR-1
Earlier sketch in CA 1-4R
Morris, Edmund 1940- ... 89-92
Morris, (Murrell) Edward 1935- ... CANR-31
Earlier sketches in CA 69-72, CANR-14
Morris, Edwin Bateman 1881-1971 Obituary ... 112
Morris, Eric 1940- ... 81-84
Morris, Everett B. 1899-1967 ... CAP-1
Earlier sketch in CA 9-10
Morris, Frances 1959- ... 144
Morris, Freda 1933- ... CANR-4
Earlier sketch in CA 53-56
Morris, Gareth (Charles Walter) 1920- ... 144
Morris, George Pope 1802-1864 ... DLB 73
Morris, Gilbert (Leslie) 1929- ... 117
Morris, Grant Harold 1940- ... 29-32R
Morris, Gregory L(ynn) 1950- ... 119
Morris, Harry (Caesar) 1924- ... 9-12R
Morris, Harvey 1946- ... 134
Morris, Helen 1909- ... CANR-18
Earlier sketch in CA 101
Morris, Henry M(adison, Jr.) 1918- ... CANR-29
Earlier sketches in CA 37-40R, CANR-13
Morris, Herbert 1928- ... CANR-1
Earlier sketch in CA 1-4R
Morris, Ira (Victor) 1903- ... 9-12R
Morris, Ivan (Ira Esme) 1925-1976 ... CANR-11
Obituary ... 65-68
Earlier sketch in CA 9-12R
Morris, J(ohn) H(umphrey) C(arlile) 1910- ... 5-8R
Morris, J(ames) Kenneth 1896- ... 5-8R
Morris, J. R. 1914(?)-1977 Obituary ... 73-76
Morris, Jackson E(dgar) 1918- ... 17-20R
Morris, James (Humphrey)
See Morris, Jan
Morris, James A(lvin) 1938- ... CANR-46
Earlier sketch in CA 120
Morris, James E(lliot) 1942- ... 112
Morris, James M(atthew) 1935- ... 89-92
Morris, Jan 1926- ... CANR-61
Earlier sketches in CA 1-4R, CANR-1
See also MTCW 1
Morris, Jane
See Ardmore, Jane Kesner
Morris, Janet (Ellen) 1946- ... CANR-35
Earlier sketches in CA 73-76, CANR-13
See also SATA 66
Morris, Jay
See Tatham, Julie Campbell
Morris, (Margaret) Jean 1924- ... 153
Brief entry ... 116
See also SATA 98
Morris, Jeffrey B(randon) 1941- ... 156
See also SATA 92
Morris, Jerrold 1911- ... CANR-11
Earlier sketch in CA 21-24R
Morris, Joan 1901- ... 45-48
Morris, Joe A(lex) 1904-1990 ... 65-68
Obituary ... 130
Morris, Joe Alex, Jr. 1927- ... 73-76
Morris, John
See Hearne, John (Edgar Caulwell)
Morris, John 1895-1980 Obituary ... 102
Morris, John D(avid) 1946- ... 111
Morris, John N(elson) 1931- ... 33-36R
See also CAAS 13
Morris, John O(sgood) 1918- ... 41-44R
Morris, John W(esley) 1907- ... CANR-6
Earlier sketch in CA 13-16R
Morris, Jonas 1933- ... 117
Morris, Juddi ... 152
See also SATA 85
Morris, Judy K. 1936- ... 116
See also SATA 61
Morris, Julian
See West, Morris L(anglo)
Morris, Katharine ... CAP-1
Earlier sketch in CA 13-16
Morris, Kenneth Earl 1955- ... 127
Morris, Kenneth T(hompson) 1941- ... 57-60
Morris, Kevin L. 1954- ... 129
Morris, Leon (Lamb) 1914- ... CANR-43
Earlier sketches in CA 9-12R, CANR-4, 20
Morris, Lewis 1833-1907 ... DLB 35
Morris, Loverne Lawton 1896- ... 5-8R
Morris, Lynn ... 167
Morris, M.
See Thibaudeau, Colleen
Morris, Margaret 1737-1816 ... DLB 200
Morris, Margaret 1891-1980 Obituary ... 97-100
Morris, Margaret Francine 1938- ... 57-60
Morris, Marilyn (A.) 1957- ... 167
Morris, Mark ... 150
Morris, Mary (Elizabeth Davis) 1913-1986 ... 53-56
Obituary ... 121
Morris, Mary 1947- ... CANR-71
Earlier sketch in CA 132
Morris, Mary Lee ... 120
Morris, Mary (Joan) McGarry 1943- ... 139
Morris, Max 1913- ... 109
Morris, Mel (Merrill) 1930- ... 69-72
Morris, Mervyn 1937- ... 154
Morris, Michael 1914- ... CANR-5
Earlier sketch in CA 5-8R
Morris, Michael (Spence Lowdell) 1940- . CANR-23
Earlier sketch in CA 107
Morris, Michelle 1941- ... 108
Morris, Milton D(onald) 1939- ... 57-60
Morris, Monica B. 1928- Brief entry ... 113
Morris, Nobuko
See Albery, Nobuko
Morris, Norman S. 1931- ... 33-36R
Morris, Norval 1923- ... 37-40R
Morris, Phyllis 1894-1982 Obituary ... 106
Morris, Phyllis Sutton 1931- ... 104
Morris, R(oger) J(ohn) B(owring) 1946- ... 93-96
Morris, Raymond N. 1936- ... 25-28R
Morris, Raymond Philip 1904- ... 45-48
Morris, Richard (Ward) 1939- ... CANR-39
Earlier sketches in CA 45-48, CANR-1, 18
Morris, Richard B(randon) 1904-1989 ... CANR-2
Obituary ... 128
Earlier sketch in CA 49-52
See also DLB 17
Morris, Richard J(ules) 1942- ... CANR-16
Earlier sketch in CA 89-92
Morris, Richard K(nowles) 1915- ... 21-24R
Morris, Robert 1910- ... CANR-16
Earlier sketch in CA 89-92
Morris, Robert (Lyle) 1942- Brief entry ... 116
Morris, Robert A(da) 1933- ... 49-52
See also SATA 7
Morris, Robert C. 1942- ... 135
Morris, Robert Kerwin 1933- ... 33-36R
Morris, Roger 1938- ... 140
Morris, Ruby Turner 1908- ... CANR-1
Earlier sketch in CA 1-4R
Morris, Ruth
See Webb, Ruth Enid Borlase Morris
Morris, Sara
See Burke, John (Frederick)
Morris, Sarah M(iller) 1906- ... 81-84
Morris, Scot 1942- ... 101
Morris, Stephen 1935- ... CANR-20
Earlier sketch in CA 103
Morris, Steveland Judkins 1950(?)- Brief entry . 111
See also Wonder, Stevie
Morris, Suzanne 1944- ... CANR-17
Earlier sketch in CA 89-92
Morris, T(homas) B(aden) 1900- ... CANR-2
Earlier sketch in CA 5-8R
Morris, Taylor 1923- ... 103
Morris, Terry Lesser 1914-1993 ... 9-12R
Obituary ... 142
Morris, Thomas D(ean) 1938- Brief entry ... 112
Morris, Thomas Victor 1952- ... CANR-46
Earlier sketch in CA 120
Morris, Timothy 1959- ... 150
Morris, Tina 1941- ... CANR-12
Earlier sketch in CA 29-32R
Morris, W. R. 1936- ... 77-80
Morris, William 1834-1896 ... CDBLB 1832-1890
See also DLB 18, 35, 57, 156, 178, 184
Morris, William 1913-1994 ... CANR-12
Obituary ... 143
Earlier sketch in CA 17-20R
See also SATA 29
Morris, William E(dgar) 1926- ... 9-12R
Morris, William O. 1922- ... 37-40R
Morris, William Sparkes 1916-1983 ... 141
Morris, William T(homas) 1928- ... 17-20R
Morris, Willie 1934- ... CANR-13
Earlier sketch in CA 17-20R
See also AITN 2
See also DLBY 80
Morris, Wright 1910-1998 ... CANR-21
Obituary ... 167
Earlier sketch in CA 9-12R
See also CLC 1, 3, 7, 18, 37
See also DLB 2
See also DLBY 81
See also MTCW 1
Morrisey, George L(ewis) 1926- ... CANR-14
Earlier sketch in CA 73-76
Morris-Goodall, Vanne 1909- ... 29-32R
Morrish, (Ernest) Ivor (James) 1914- ... 33-36R
Morris-Jones, W(yndraeth) H(umphreys) 1918- ... CANR-11
Earlier sketch in CA 21-24R
Morrison, Arnold Telford 1928- ... 110
Morrison, Arthur 1863-1945 ... 157
Brief entry ... 120
See also DLB 70, 135, 197
See also TCLC 72
Morrison, Bill 1935- ... 135
Brief entry ... 115
See also SATA 66
See also SATA-Brief 37
Morrison, (Philip) Blake 1950- ... 138
Morrison, Bruce 1904(?)-1983 Obituary ... 109
Morrison, Carl V(incent) 1908- ... 93-96
Morrison, Charles Clayton
1874-1966 Obituary ... 89-92
See also DLB 91
Morrison, Cheryl 1947- ... 107
Morrison, Chloe Anthony Wofford
See Morrison, Toni
Morrison, Claudia C(hristopherson) 1936- ... 29-32R
Morrison, Clinton (Dawson, Jr.) 1924- ... 13-16R
Morrison, David (Douglas) 1940- ... CANR-30
Earlier sketch in CA 112
Morrison, Denton E(dward) 1932- ... CANR-6
Earlier sketch in CA 57-60
Morrison, Donald George 1938- ... 85-88
Morrison, Dorothy Nafus ... CANR-49
Earlier sketches in CA 61-64, CANR-8, 24
See also SATA 29
Morrison, Edward
See Humphrey, Paul
Morrison, Eleanor S(helton) 1921- ... CANR-1
Earlier sketch in CA 49-52
Morrison, Eula Atwood 1911- ... 25-28R
Morrison, Frank G. 1894(?)-1983 Obituary ... 111
Morrison, Frank M. 1914- ... 37-40R
Morrison, Fred L. 1939- Brief entry ... 112
Morrison, G. F.
See Bernstein, Gerry
Morrison, Gertrude W. ... CANR-26
Earlier sketches in CAP-2, CA 19-20
Morrison, Gordon 1944- ... SATA 87
Morrison, Hobe 1904- ... 77-80
Morrison, Howard A(lexander) 1955- ... 118
Morrison, Ida Edith ... 1-4R
Morrison, J. S.
See Morrison, John (Sinclair)
Morrison, Jack 1912- ... 105
Morrison, James (Harris) 1918- ... 73-76
Morrison, James (Ryan) 1924- ... 105
Morrison, James Douglas 1943-1971 ... CANR-40
Earlier sketch in CA 73-76
See also Morrison, Jim
Morrison, James F(rederic) 1937- ... 25-28R
Morrison, James L(unsford), Jr. 1923- ... 57-60
Morrison, James R(oy) 1940- ... 123
Brief entry ... 118
Morrison, Jeanette Helen 1927- ... 134
Morrison, Jim
See Morrison, James Douglas
See also CLC 17
Morrison, Joan 1922- ... 133
See also SATA 65
Morrison, John (Sinclair) 1913- ... CANR-48
Earlier sketch in CA 122
Morrison, John 1949- ... 137
Morrison, John Gordon 1904- ... 103
Morrison, Joseph L(ederman) 1918-1970 ... 5-8R
Obituary ... 122
Morrison, Keith 1942- ... 155
Morrison, Kristin (Diane) 1934- ... CANR-14
Earlier sketch in CA 37-40R
Morrison, Lester M(arvin) 1907-1991 ... CAP-1
Obituary ... 134
Earlier sketch in CA 13-16
Morrison, Lillian 1917- ... CANR-22
Earlier sketches in CA 9-12R, CANR-7
See also SATA 3
Morrison, Lucile Phillips 1896- ... SATA 17
Morrison, Margaret Mackie
19(?)-1973 Obituary ... 41-44R
Morrison, Marsh 1902- ... CANR-10
Earlier sketch in CA 61-64
Morrison, Martha A. 1948- ... 145
See also SATA 77
Morrison, Meighan 1966- ... SATA 90
Morrison, N(ancy Agnes) Brysson (Inglis)
(?)-1986 ... 13-16R
Obituary ... 118
Morrison, Paul Fix 1902-1983 Obituary ... 111
Morrison, Peggy
See Morrison, Margaret Mackie
Morrison, Perry 1959- ... 134
Morrison, Philip 1915- Brief entry ... 106
Morrison, Phylis 1927- ... 117
Morrison, R(obert) H(ay) 1915- ... 135
Morrison, Richard
See Lowndes, Robert A(ugustine) W(ard)
Morrison, Robert
See Lowndes, Robert A(ugustine) W(ard)
Morrison, Robert H(aywood) 1927- ... 5-8R
Morrison, Robert S(tanley) 1909- ... 65-68
Morrison, Roberta
See Webb, Jean Francis
Morrison, Susan Dudley
See Gold, Susan Dudley
Morrison, Taylor 1971- ... 160
See also SATA 95
Morrison, Theodore 1901-1988 ... CANR-1
Obituary ... 127
Earlier sketch in CA 1-4R
Morrison, Toni 1931- ... CANR-67
Earlier sketches in CA 29-32R, CANR-27, 42
See also AAYA 1, 22
See also BLC 3
See also BW 2
See also CDALB 1968-1988
See also CLC 4, 10, 22, 55, 81, 87
See also DA
See also DAB
See also DAC
See also DAM MST, MULT, NOV, POP
See also DLB 6, 33, 143
See also DLBY 81
See also MTCW 1
See also SATA 57
Morrison, Tony 1936- ... 81-84
Morrison, Van 1945- ... 168
Brief entry ... 116
See also CLC 21
Morrison, Velma Ford 1909- ... 9-12R
See also SATA 21
Morrison, Victor
See Glut, Donald F(rank)
Morrison, Wilbur Howard 1915- ... CANR-1
Earlier sketch in CA 1-4R
See also SATA 64
Morrison, William
See Samachson, Joseph
Morrison, William R(obert) 1942- ... 124
Morrison-Reed, Mark D(ouglas) 1949- ... 116
Morrisroe, Patricia 1951- ... 154
Morriss, Frank 1923- ... CANR-3
Earlier sketch in CA 5-8R
Morriss, James E(dward) 1932- ... 57-60
See also SATA 8
Morriss, J.-H.
See Ghnassia, Maurice (Jean-Henri)
Morriss, Mack 1920(?)-1976 Obituary ... 65-68
Morrissette, Bruce A(rcher) 1911- ... 17-20R
Morrissey, Charles Thomas 1933- ... 108
Morrissey, Kevin L. 1952- ... 154
Morrissey, L(eroy) J(ohn) 1935- ... CANR-1
Earlier sketch in CA 49-52
Morrissey, Leonard E., Jr. 1925- ... 9-12R
Morrissey, Stephen 1950- ... 115
Morris-Suzuki, Tessa 1951- ... 123
Morrissy, Mary 1958- ... CLC 99
Morritt, Hope 1930- ... CANR-16
Earlier sketch in CA 97-100
Morrow, Ann Patricia ... 130
Morrow, Baker H(arrison) 1946- ... 127
Morrow, Barry (Nelson) 1948- ... 166
Morrow, Betty
See Bacon, Elizabeth
Morrow, Bradford 1951- ... CANR-32
Earlier sketch in CA 113
Morrow, Charlotte
See Kirwan, Molly (Morrow)
Morrow, Dennis 1952- ... 132
Morrow, E(verett) Frederic 1909-1994 ... CANR-2
Obituary ... 146
Earlier sketch in CA 5-8R
See also BW 1
Morrow, Felix 1906- ... 107
Morrow, Glenn R(aymond) 1895-197(?) ... CAP-1
Earlier sketch in CA 19-20
Morrow, James (Kenneth) 1947- ... CANR-55
Earlier sketch in CA 108
Morrow, John Howard, Jr. 1944- ... 113
Morrow, John Howard 1910- ... 25-28R
Morrow, Lance 1939- ... 153
Brief entry ... 119
Morrow, Mable 1892-1977 Obituary ... 106
Morrow, Mark 1952- ... 167
Morrow, Mary Lou 1926- ... 61-64
Morrow, Patrick David 1940- ... CANR-8
Earlier sketch in CA 61-64
Morrow, Skip
See Morrow, Dennis
Morrow, Stephen 1939- ... 73-76
Morrow, William L(ockhart) 1935- ... 33-36R
Mors, Victor
See Roeseler, W(olfgang) G(uenter)
Mors, Wallace P. 1911- ... 17-20R
Morsberger, Katharine M. 1931- ... 105
Morsberger, Robert Eustis 1929- ... CANR-3
Earlier sketch in CA 5-8R
Morscher, Betsy 1939- ... 115
Morse, A. Reynolds 1914- ... CANR-7
Earlier sketch in CA 17-20R
Morse, Anne Christensen 1915- ... 1-4R

Morse, Arthur David 1920-1971 Obituary ... 29-32R
Morse, B. J. (?)-1977 Obituary ... 73-76
Morse, Carol
See Yeakley, Marjory Hall
Morse, Chandler 1906- ... 5-8R
Morse, Charles A. 1898- ... CAP-1
Earlier sketch in CA 19-20
Morse, David 1940- ... 37-40R
Morse, Donald E. 1936- ... 37-40R
Morse, Donald R(oy) 1931- ... CANR-21
Earlier sketch in CA 105
Morse, Dorothy B(ayley) 1906-1979 .. SATA-Obit 24
Morse, Edward Lewis 1942- ... CANR-7
Earlier sketch in CA 57-60
Morse, Flo 1921- ... 106
See also SATA 30
Morse, Grant W(esley) 1926- ... 17-20R
Morse, H(enry) Clifton IV 1924- ... 9-12R
Morse, Harold Marston 1892-1977 Obituary .. 69-72
Morse, Hermann Nelson 1887-1977 Obituary 73-76
Morse, J(osiah) Mitchell 1912- ... 65-68
Morse, James Herbert 1841-1923 ... DLB 71
Morse, Jedidiah 1761-1826 ... DLB 37
Morse, John D. 1906- ... 104
Morse, John T., Jr. 1840-1937 ... DLB 47
Morse, L(arry) A(lan) 1945- ... 107
Morse, Melvin (L.) 1953- ... 144
Morse, Peter 1935- ... CANR-14
Earlier sketch in CA 73-76
Morse, Philip M(cCord) 1903-1985 ... 108
Obituary ... 117
Morse, Richard M(cGee) 1922- ... CANR-10
Earlier sketch in CA 13-16R
Morse, Roger A(lfred) 1927- ... CANR-47
Earlier sketches in CA 57-60, CANR-8, 23
Morse, Samuel French 1916- ... CANR-4
Earlier sketch in CA 9-12R
Morse, Theresa Adler 1901-1980 ... 89-92
Obituary ... 97-100
Morse, Thomas S(purr) 1925- ... 109
Morse, Wayne (Lyman) 1900-1974 Obituary .. 49-52
Morse-Boycott, Desmond (Lionel) 1892-1979 .. 107
Obituary ... 104
Morselli, Guido 1912-1973 ... DLB 177
Morsey, Royal J(oseph) 1910- ... 73-76
Morshead, Ian 1922- ... 111
Morshiel, George
See Shiels, George
Morsi, Pamela 1951- ... CANR-70
Earlier sketch in CA 145
Morson, Gary S(aul) 1948- ... CANR-70
Earlier sketch in CA 121
Morson, Ian (Nairne) ... 165
Morss, Elisabeth W. 1918- ... 41-44R
Morsy, Magali 1933- ... 132
Mort, Vivian
See Cromie, Alice Hamilton
Mortensen, Ben(jamin) F. 1928- ... 104
Mortensen, C. David 1939- ... 37-40R
Morthland, John 1947- ... 129
Mortimer, Anthony 1936- ... 116
Mortimer, Armine Kotin 1943- ... CANR-41
Earlier sketch in CA 117
Mortimer, Chapman
See Chapman-Mortimer, William Charles
Mortimer, Favell Lee 1802-1878 ... DLB 163
Mortimer, John (Clifford) 1923- ... CANR-69
Earlier sketches in CA 13-16R, CANR-21
Interview in ... CANR-21
See also CDBLB 1960 to Present
See also CLC 28, 43
See also DAM DRAM, POP
See also DLB 13
See also MTCW 1
Mortimer, John L(ynn) 1908-1977 ... 69-72
Obituary ... 135
Mortimer, Mary H.
See Coury, Louise Andree
Mortimer, Penelope (Ruth) 1918- ... CANR-45
Earlier sketch in CA 57-60
See also CLC 5
Mortimer, Peter
See Roberts, Dorothy James
Mortimore, Olive 1890- ... 49-52
Mortlake, G. N.
See Stonov, Natasha
Mortman, Doris Brief entry ... 129
See also BEST 89:4
Mortmane, J. D.
See Kiefer, Louis Sr.
Morton, A(rthur) L(eslie) 1903-1987 ... 9-12R
Obituary ... 124
Morton, A(ndrew) Q(ueen) 1919- ... 105
Morton, Adam 1945- ... 128
Morton, Alexander C(lark) 1936- ... CANR-12
Earlier sketch in CA 25-28R
Morton, Andrew 1953- ... 141
Morton, Anthony
See Creasey, John
Morton, Brian 1942- ... 167
Morton, C(lement) Manly 1884-1976 ... CAP-2
Earlier sketch in CA 29-32
Morton, Carlos 1947- ... CANR-32
Earlier sketch in CA 73-76
See also DLB 122
See also HW
Morton, Desmond 1937- ... CANR-32
Earlier sketches in CA 29-32R, CANR-15
Morton, Donald E(dward) 1938- ... 57-60
Morton, Frederic 1924- ... CANR-43
Earlier sketches in CA 1-4R, CANR-3, 20
Morton, Gregory 1911-1986 ... 102
Obituary ... 118
Morton, H(enry Canova) V(ollam) 1892-1979 ... 103
Obituary ... 89-92
See also DLB 195
Morton, Harry 1925- ... CANR-15
Earlier sketch in CA 81-84
Morton, Henry W(alter) 1929- ... 13-16R
Morton, James (Severs) 1938- ... 133
Morton, Jane 1931- ... 93-96
See also SATA 50
Morton, Jocelyn 1912- ... 73-76
Morton, John (Cameron Andrieu) Bingham (Michael)
1893-1979 ... 93-96
Obituary ... 85-88
Morton, Joseph
See Richmond, Al
Morton, Lee Jack, Jr. 1928- ... SATA 32
Morton, Lena Beatrice 1901- ... 17-20R
Morton, Louis 1913-1976 ... CANR-21
Obituary ... 65-68
Earlier sketch in CA 69-72
Morton, Lucie T. 1950- ... 118
Morton, Lynne 1952- ... 106
Morton, Marcia Colman 1927- ... 73-76
Morton, Marian J(ohnson) 1937- ... 77-80
Morton, Miriam 1918(?)-1985 ... CANR-2
Obituary ... 117
Earlier sketch in CA 49-52
See also SATA 9
See also SATA-Obit 46
Morton, Nathaniel 1613-1685 ... DLB 24
Morton, Newton 1901-1967 ... CAP-1
Earlier sketch in CA 19-20
Morton, Patricia
See Golding, Morton J(ay)
Morton, Phyllis Digby (?)-1984 Obituary ... 113
Morton, R(obert) S(teel) 1917- ... 49-52
Morton, Richard (Everett) 1930- ... 37-40R
Morton, Richard Lee 1889-1974 ... CANR-16
Obituary ... 53-56
Earlier sketch in CA 1-4R
Morton, Robert 1934- ... 69-72
Morton, Robert L(ee) 1889-1976 ... 45-48
Obituary ... 134
Morton, Sarah Wentworth 1759-1846 ... DLB 37
Morton, Stanley
See Freedgood, Morton
Morton, T(homas) Ralph 1900- ... 29-32R
Morton, Thomas 1579(?)-1647(?) ... DLB 24
Morton, W(illiam) L(ewis) 1908- ... CAP-1
Earlier sketch in CA 19-20
Morton, W(illiam) Scott 1908- ... 81-84
Morton, Ward McKinnon 1907- ... 1-4R
Morton, William C(uthbert) 1875-1971 ... CAP-2
Earlier sketch in CA 25-28
Morwood, James 1943- ... 124
Mosby, Aline 1922- ... 130
Mosca, Gaetano 1858-1941 ... TCLC 75
Moscati, Sabatino 1922-1997 ... 77-80
Obituary ... 161
Moschella, David C. 1954- ... 165
Moscherosch, Johann Michael 1601-1669 . DLB 164
Mosco, Vincent 1948- ... CANR-35
Earlier sketch in CA 114
Moscoe, Mike ... 166
Moscotti, Albert D(ennis) 1920- ... 65-68
Moscovitch, Allan 1946- ... 111
Moscovitz, Judy 1942- ... CANR-50
Earlier sketch in CA 123
Moscow, Alvin 1925- ... CANR-45
Earlier sketches in CA 1-4R, CANR-4
See also SATA 3
Moscow, Henry (I.) 1904(?)-1983 Obituary ... 108
Moscow, Warren 1908- ... 21-24R
Moscowitz, Raymond 1938- ... 111
Mosel, Arlene (Tichy) 1921- ... 49-52
See also SATA 7
Mosel, Tad 1922- ... 73-76
Moseley, David (Victor) 1939- ... 97-100
Moseley, Edward H(olt) 1931- ... 132
Moseley, Edwin M(aurice) 1916-1978 ... CANR-8
Earlier sketch in CA 5-8R
Moseley, George (V. H. III) 1931- ... 49-52
Moseley, Humphrey fl. 1627-1661 ... DLB 170
Moseley, J(oseph) Edward 1910-1973 ... 37-40R
Moseley, James G(wyn) 1946- ... CANR-38
Earlier sketch in CA 116
Moseley, Michael E(dward) 1941- ... 139
Moseley, Ray 1932- ... 85-88
Moseley, Spencer A(ltemont) 1925- ... 93-96
Moseley, Virginia D(ouglas) 1917- ... 21-24R
Moseley, Philip Edward 1905-1972 Obituary . 33-36R
Moseng, Elisabeth 1967- ... SATA 90
Moser, Barry 1940- ... CLR 49
See also MAICYA
See also SAAS 15
See also SATA 56, 79
Moser, Charles A. 1935- ... 29-32R
Moser, Don(ald Bruce) 1932- ... 106
See also SATA 31
Moser, Edward P. 1958- ... 152
Moser, Lawrence E. 1939- ... 33-36R
Moser, Mary Beck 1924- ... 122
Moser, Norman Calvin 1931- ... CANR-10
Earlier sketch in CA 57-60
Moser, Paul K. 1957- ... 145
Moser, Reta C(arol) 1936- ... 13-16R
Moser, Shia 1906- ... CAP-2
Earlier sketch in CA 25-28
Moser, Thomas (Colborn) 1923- ... 5-8R
Moses, Anna Mary Robertson
1860-1961 Obituary ... 93-96
Moses, Claire Goldberg 1941- ... CANR-43
Earlier sketch in CA 113
Moses, Daniel David 1952- ... NNAL
Moses, Elbert R(aymond), Jr. 1908- ... CAP-1
Earlier sketch in CA 13-16
Moses, Gerald Robert 1938- ... 57-60
Moses, Grandma
See Moses, Anna Mary Robertson
Moses, (Russell) Greg(ory) 1954- ... 168
Moses, Joel C(harles) 1944- ... CANR-10
Earlier sketch in CA 65-68
Moses, Robert 1888-1981 ... 45-48
Obituary ... 104
Moses, W(illiam) R(obert) 1911- ... 9-12R
Moses, Wilson Jeremiah 1942- ... 85-88
Mosesson, Gloria R(ubin) ... 41-44R
See also SATA 24
Mosey, Anne Cronin 1938- ... 49-52
Moshe, David
See Winkelman, Donald M.
Mosher, Arthur Theodore 1910- ... 85-88
Mosher, Frederick C(amp) 1913-1990 ... 37-40R
Obituary ... 131
Mosher, Howard Frank 1943- ... CANR-65
Earlier sketch in CA 139
See also CLC 62
Mosher, Ralph Lamont 1928- ... CANR-7
Earlier sketch in CA 17-20R
Mosher, Richard ... 165
Mosher, Steven W(estley) 1948- ... 116
Mosher, (Christopher) Terry 1942- ... 93-96
Moshier, W(illiam) Franklyn 1929- ... 97-100
Moshiri, Farrokh 1961- ... 142
Mosiman, Billie Sue (Stahl) 1947- ... 119
Mosimann, Anton 1947- ... 141
Mosk
See Moskowitz, Gene
Moskin, J(ohn) Robert 1923- ... 17-20R
Moskin, Marietta D(unston) 1928- ... CANR-13
Earlier sketch in CA 73-76
See also SATA 23
Moskof, Martin Stephen 1930- ... 29-32R
See also SATA 27
Moskos, Charles C. 1934- ... CANR-56
Earlier sketches in CA 25-28R, CANR-10, 26
Moskow, Michael H. 1938- ... CANR-14
Earlier sketch in CA 37-40R
Moskow, Shirley Blotnick 1935- ... CANR-55
Earlier sketch in CA 127
Moskowitz, Anita F(iderer) 1937- ... 150
Moskowitz, Faye (Stollman) 1930- ... 146
Moskowitz, Gene 1921(?)-1982 Obituary ... 108
Moskowitz, Ira 1912- ... 102
Moskowitz, Moses 1911(?)-1990 Obituary ... 131
Brief entry ... 114
Moskowitz, Robert (A.) 1946- ... CANR-57
Earlier sketch in CA 109
Moskowitz, Sam 1920-1997 ... CANR-4
Obituary ... 157
Earlier sketch in CA 5-8R
Interview in ... CANR-4
Moskvitin, Jurij 1938- ... 93-96
Mosley, Charlotte 1952- ... 145
Mosley, Diana 1910- ... 106
Mosley, Francis 1957- ... SATA 57
Mosley, J(ohn) Brooke (Jr.)
1915-1988 Obituary ... 125
Mosley, Jean Bell 1913- ... 9-12R
Mosley, Leonard O(swald) 1913-1992 ... 109
Obituary ... 139
Brief entry ... 108
Interview in ... 109
Mosley, Nicholas 1923- ... CANR-60
Earlier sketches in CA 69-72, CANR-41
See also CLC 43, 70
See also DLB 14
Mosley, Oswald (Ernald) 1896-1980 ... CAP-2
Obituary ... 102
Earlier sketch in CA 25-28
Mosley, Philip 1947- ... 130
Mosley, Steven 1952- ... 133
Mosley, Walter 1952- ... CANR-57
Earlier sketch in CA 142
See also AAYA 17
See also BLCS
See also BW 2
See also CLC 97
See also DAM MULT, POP
Moss, Arthur 1889-1969 Obituary ... 112
See also DLB 4
Moss, Barbara 1946- ... 116
Moss, Bernard H(aym) 1943- Brief entry ... 115
Moss, Bobby Gilmer 1932- ... 49-52
Moss, C(laude) Scott 1924- ... CANR-8
Earlier sketch in CA 17-20R
Moss, Carolyn (J.) 1932- ... 163
Moss, Cynthia F. 1957- ... 163
Moss, Cynthia J(ane) 1940- ... CANR-12
Earlier sketch in CA 65-68
Moss, Don(ald) 1920- ... SATA 11
Moss, Elaine (Dora) 1924- Brief entry ... 110
See also SATA 57
See also SATA-Brief 31
Moss, Frank Edward 1911- ... CANR-13
Earlier sketch in CA 61-64
Moss, Gordon E(rvin) 1937- ... 57-60
Moss, Howard 1922-1987 ... CANR-44
Obituary ... 123
Earlier sketches in CA 1-4R, CANR-1
See also CLC 7, 14, 45, 50
See also DAM POET
See also DLB 5
Moss, J. Joel 1922- ... 45-48
Moss, James A(llen) 1920- ... 33-36R
Moss, Jeff(rey) ... 140
See also SATA 73
Moss, John 1940- ... CANR-17
Earlier sketch in CA 97-100
Moss, Leonard (Jerome) 1931- ... 25-28R
Moss, Marissa 1959- ... SATA 71
Moss, Michael (Stanley) 1947- ... 108
Moss, Miriam 1955- ... 143
See also SATA 76
Moss, Nancy
See Moss, Robert (Alfred)
Moss, Norman 1928- ... 49-52
Moss, (Victor) Peter (Cannings) 1921- ... CANR-2
Earlier sketch in CA 49-52
Moss, Ralph W(alter) 1943- ... 101
Moss, Robert (Alfred) 1903- ... CAP-1
Earlier sketch in CA 11-12
Moss, Robert (John) 1946- ... 146
Brief entry ... 118
Moss, Robert F. 1942- ... CANR-20
Earlier sketch in CA 81-84
Moss, Roberta
See Moss, Robert (Alfred)
Moss, Roger 1951- ... 124
Moss, Rosalind (Louisa Beaufort)
1890-1990 Obituary ... 131
Moss, Rose 1937- ... 49-52
Moss, Sanford Alexander III 1939- ... 118
Moss, Sidney P(hil) 1917- ... 5-8R
Moss, Stanley 1925- ... 97-100
Moss, Stephen Joseph 1935- ... 103
Moss, Stirling 1929- ... 5-8R
Moss, Thylias 1954- ... DLB 120
Moss, Walter (Gerald) 1938- ... 65-68
Mosse, George L(achmann) 1918- ... CANR-52
Earlier sketches in CA 5-8R, CANR-12, 28
Mosse, Werner E(ugen Emil) 1918- ... 9-12R
Mossgiel, Rab
See Burns, Robert
Mossiker, Frances (Sanger) 1906-1985 ... 9-12R
Obituary ... 116
Mossman, Burt
See Keevill, Henry J(ohn)
Mossman, Dow 1943- ... 45-48
Mossman, Frank H(omer) 1915- ... CANR-5
Earlier sketch in CA 1-4R
Mossman, Jennifer 1944- ... CANR-38
Earlier sketches in CA 97-100, CANR-17
Mossner, Ernest C(ampbell) 1907-1986 ... 123
Obituary ... 120
Mossop, D(eryk) J(oseph) 1919- ... 1-4R
Mossop, Irene
See Swatridge, Irene Maude (Mossop)
Most, Bernard 1937- ... CANR-52
Earlier sketches in CA 104, CANR-27
See also SATA 48, 91
See also SATA-Brief 40
Most, Glenn W(arren) 1952- ... 112
Most, Kenneth S. 1924- ... 144
Most, William G(eorge) 1914- ... 49-52
Mostel, Kate
See Mostel, Kathryn Harkin
Mostel, Katherine Harkin
See Mostel, Kathryn Harkin
Mostel, Kathryn Harkin 1918-1986 ... 81-84
Obituary ... 118
Mostel, Samuel Joel 1915-1977 ... 89-92
Mostel, Zero
See Mostel, Samuel Joel
Mosteller, (Charles) Frederick 1916- ... CANR-23
Earlier sketches in CA 17-20R, CANR-7
Mostert, Noel 1929- ... 105
Mostofsky, David I(saac) 1931- ... 17-20R
Mostyn, Trevor 1946- ... CANR-66
Earlier sketch in CA 129
Mota, Avelino Teixeira da
See Teixeira da Mota, Avelino
Motchenbacher, C(urt) D. 1931- ... 146
Mother Mary Anthony
See Weinig, Jean Maria
Mothershead, Harmon Ross 1931- ... 33-36R
Mother Teresa 1910-1997 ... 164
Motherwell, Cathryn 1957- ... 132
Mothner, Ira S(anders) 1932- ... CANR-13
Earlier sketch in CA 21-24R
Motion, Andrew (Peter) 1952- ... 146
See also CLC 47
See also DLB 40
Motley, Arthur H(arrison) 1900-1984 Obituary .. 112
See also AITN 2
Motley, John Lothrop 1814-1877 ... DLB 1, 30, 59
Motley, Mary
See De Reneville, Mary Margaret Motley Sheridan
Motley, Mary Penick 1920- ... 73-76
Motley, Red
See Motley, Arthur H(arrison)
Motley, Willard (Francis) 1909-1965 ... 117
Obituary ... 106
See also BW 1
See also CLC 18
See also DLB 76, 143
Motley, Wilma E(lizabeth) 1912- ... 41-44R
Motmot, Snik P.
See Tompkins, Everett Thomas
Motoyama, Hiroshi 1925- ... 110
Mott, Evelyn Clarke 1962- ... SATA 75
Mott, Frank Luther 1886-1964 ... 1-4R
Mott, George Fox 1907-1987 ... 13-16R
Obituary ... 123
Mott, Michael (Charles Alston) 1930- ... CANR-29
Earlier sketches in CA 5-8R, CANR-7
See also CAAS 7
See also CLC 15, 34
Mott, N(evill) F(rancis) 1905-1996 ... 129
Obituary ... 153
Mott, Paul E. ... 103
Mott, Robert L. ... 144
Mott, Sir Nevill
See Mott, N(evill) F(rancis)
Mott, Stephen Charles 1940- ... CANR-38
Earlier sketch in CA 116
Mott, Vincent Valmon 1916- ... 41-44R
Motta, Dick 1931- ... 134
Brief entry ... 111

Mottahedeh, Roy Parviz 1940- CANR-21
Earlier sketch in CA 104
Mottelson, Ben R. 1926- 168
Motter, Alton M(yers) 1907- CAP-1
Earlier sketch in CA 11-12
Motteux, Peter Anthony 1663-1718 .... DLB 80
Motto, Anna Lydia 41-44R
Motto, Carmine J. 1914- 33-36R
Mottram, Anthony John 1920- 5-8R
Mottram, (Vernon) Henry 1882-(?) CAP-1
Earlier sketch in CA 11-12
Mottram, R(alph) H(ale) 1883-1971 108
Obituary 29-32R
See also DLB 36
Mottram, Tony
See Mottram, Anthony John
Motyl, Alexander J(ohn) 1953- 144
Motz, Lloyd 1909- CANR-4
Earlier sketch in CA 9-12R
See also SATA 20
Mouat, Kit
See Mackay, Jane
Moulakis, Athanasios 1945- 147
Mould, Daphne D(esiree) C(harlotte) Pochin 1920- CANR-4
Earlier sketch in CA 9-12R
Mould, Edwin
See Whitlock, Ralph
Mould, George 1894- 57-60
Moule, C(harles) F(rancis) D(igby) 1908- CANR-5
Earlier sketch in CA 1-4R
Moulier, (Antoine) Fernand 1913- 81-84
Moulin, Annie 1946- 140
Moulin, Marie-Annie
See Moulin, Annie
Moult, Edward (Walker) 1926-1986 Obituary 120
Moult, Ted
See Moult, Edward (Walker)
Moult, Thomas 1895-1974 Obituary 89-92
Moulton, Edward C. 1936- 77-80
Moulton, Eugene R(ussell) 1916-1981 .... CANR-11
Earlier sketch in CA 21-24R
Moulton, Forest Ray 1872-1952 159
Moulton, Gary E(van) 1942- 115
Moulton, Harland B. 1925- 37-40R
Moulton, J(ames) L(ouis) 1906- 21-24R
Moulton, Nancy 1946- 116
Moulton, Phillips P(rentice) 1909- 37-40R
Moulton, William G(amwell) 1914- 9-12R
Mouly, George J(oseph) 1915- CANR-17
Earlier sketch in CA 1-4R
Mounce, R(obert H.) 1921- CANR-2
Earlier sketch in CA 1-4R
Mount, Charles Merrill 1928- 13-16R
Mount, Elisabeth
See Dougherty, Betty
Mount, Ellis 1921- CANR-39
Earlier sketch in CA 116
Mount, (William Robert) Ferdinand 1939- CANR-11
Earlier sketch in CA 21-24R
Mount, Marshall Ward 1927- 73-76
Mountain, Julian
See Cowie, Donald
Mountain, Marian
See Wisberg, Marian Aline
Mountain, Robert
See Montgomery, Raymond A. (Jr.)
Mountain Wolf Woman 1884-1960 144
See also CLC 92
See also NNAL
Mountbatten, Louis (Francis Albert Victor Nicholas) 1900-1979 133
Obituary 113
Mountbatten, Richard
See Wallmann, Jeffrey M(iner)
Mountfield, David
See Grant, Neil
Mountfield, Stuart 1903(?)-1984 Obituary 115
Mountfort, Guy 1905- 17-20R
Mountjoy, Christopher
See Miles, Keith
Mountjoy, Roberta Jean
See Sohl, Jerry
Mountrose, Phillip 1950- 163
Mountsier, Robert 1888(?)-1972 Obituary 37-40R
Mourant, John A(rthur) 1903- CAP-1
Earlier sketch in CA 9-10
Moure, Erin 1955- 113
See also CLC 88
See also DLB 60
Mourelatos, Alexander P(hoebus) D(ionysiou) 1936- 29-32R
Mourier, Marguerite
See Boulton, Marjorie
Mourning Dove 1888(?)-1936 144
See also DAM MULT
See also DLB 175
See also NNAL
Moursund, David G. 1936- CANR-30
Earlier sketches in CA 25-28R, CANR-12
Moursund, Janet (Peck) 1936- CANR-30
Earlier sketch in CA 45-48
Moussa, Pierre L(ouis) 1922- 13-16R
Moussard, Jacqueline 1924- CANR-8
Earlier sketch in CA 61-64
See also SATA 24
Mouton, Jane Srygley 1930- 123
Moutoux, John T. 1901(?)-1979 Obituary 89-92
Mouzelis, Nicos P. 1939- 33-36R
Mouzon, Olin T(errell) 1912- 5-8R
Mow, Anna Beahm 1893- CANR-3
Earlier sketch in CA 9-12R
Mowat, C(harles) L(och) 1911-1970 .... CAP-1
Earlier sketch in CA 13-16
Mowat, Claire (Angel Wheeler) 1933- 131
Mowat, David 1943- 77-80
Mowat, Farley (McGill) 1921- CANR-68
Earlier sketches in CA 1-4R, CANR-4, 24, 42
Interview in CANAR-24
See also AAYA 1
See also CLC 26
See also CLR 20
See also DAC
See also DAM MST
See also DLB 68
See also JRDA
See also MAICYA
See also MTCW 1
See also SATA 3, 55
Mowat, R(obert) C(ase) 1913- 29-32R
Mowatt, Ian 1948- 41-44R
Mowitt, John 1952- 140
Mowitz, Robert J(ames) 1920- CANR-3
Earlier sketch in CA 5-8R
Mowrer, Edgar Ansel 1892-1977 .... CAP-1
Obituary 69-72
Earlier sketch in CA 13-16
See also DLB 29
Mowrer, Lilian Thomson 1889(?)-1990 65-68
Obituary 132
Mowrer, O(rval) Hobart 1907- CANR-1
Earlier sketch in CA 1-4R
Mowrer, Paul Scott 1887-1971 .... CANR-4
Obituary 29-32R
Earlier sketch in CA 5-8R
See also DLB 29
Mowry, George E(dwin) 1909-1984 .... CANR-17
Earlier sketch in CA 1-4R
Mowry, Jess 1960- 133
Mowshowitz, Abbe 1939- 109
Moxham, Robert Morgan 1919-1978 Obituary 77-80
Moxley, Sheila 1966- 163
See also SATA 96
Moxon, Joseph fl. 1647-1684 .... DLB 170
Moy, James S. 1948- 146
Moyano, Daniel 1930- 131
See also HW
Moye, Catherine 1960- 136
Moyer, Carolyn
See Swayze, Carolyn (Norma)
Moyer, Claire B. (Inch) 1905- CAP-2
Earlier sketch in CA 19-20
Moyer, Elgin Sylvester 1890- 5-8R
Moyer, Kenneth E(van) 1919- CANR-13
Earlier sketch in CA 33-36R
Moyer, Kermit 1943- 136
Moyer, Terry J. 1937- 159
See also SATA 94
Moyers, Bill 1934- CANR-52
Earlier sketches in CA 61-64, CANR-31
See also AITN 2
See also CLC 74
Moyes, John Stoward 1884- CAP-1
Earlier sketch in CA 13-14
Moyes, Norman Barr 1931- 37-40R
Moyes, Patricia 1923-
See Haszard, Patricia Moyes
See also SATA 63
Moyler, Alan (Frank Powell) 1926- .... SATA 36
Moyles, R(obert) Gordon 1939- CANR-17
Earlier sketch in CA 65-68
Moynahan, John F. 1912-1985 Obituary 115
Moynahan, Julian (Lane) 1925- CANR-1
Earlier sketch in CA 1-4R
Moynahan, Molly 1957- 133
Moyne, Ernest J(ohn) 1916-1976 .... CAP-2
Earlier sketch in CA 25-28
Moynihan, Daniel P(atrick) 1927- CANR-43
Earlier sketch in CA 5-8R
Moynihan, John Dominic 1932- 103
Moynihan, Maurice (Gerard) 1902- 107
Moynihan, Ruth B(arnes) 1933- CANR-41
Earlier sketch in CA 117
Moynihan, William T. 1927- 21-24R
Moyse-Bartlett, Hubert 1902(?)-1973(?) Obituary 104
Moyser, George H. 1945- 134
Mozley, Charles 1915- .... SATA 43
See also SATA-Brief 32
Mphahlele, Es'kia
See Mphahlele, Ezekiel
See also DLB 125
Mphahlele, Ezekiel 1919-1983 .... CANR-26
Earlier sketch in CA 81-84
See also Mphahlele, Es'kia
See also BLC 3
See also BW 2
See also CLC 25
See also DAM MULT
Mqhayi, S(amuel) E(dward) K(rune Loliwe) 1875-1945 153
See also BLC 3
See also DAM MULT
See also TCLC 25
Mr. Cleveland
See Seltzer, Louis B(enson)
Mr. Kenneth
See Marlowe, Kenneth
Mr. McGillicuddy
See Abisch, Roslyn Kroop
Mr. Metropolitan Opera
See Robinson, Francis (Arthur)
Mr. Sniff
See Abisch, Roslyn Kroop
Mr. Tivil
See Lorkowski, Thomas V(incent)
Mr. Wizard
See Herbert, Don(ald Jeffrey)
Mrabet, Mohammed
See el Hajjam, Mohammed ben Chaib
Mrazek, James E(dward) 1914- 33-36R
Mrosovsky, Kitty 128
Mrozek, Donald J(ohn) 1945- 107
Mrozek, Slawomir 1930- CANR-29
Earlier sketch in CA 13-16R
See also CAAS 10
See also CLC 3, 13
See also MTCW 1
Mrs. Belloc-Lowndes
See Lowndes, Marie Adelaide (Belloc)
Mrs. Bishop
See Bishop, Isabella Lucy (Bird)
Mrs. Fairstar
See Horne, Richard Henry
Mrs. G.
See Griffiths, Kitty Anna
Mrs. Miggy
See Krentel, Mildred White
Mrs. R. F. D.
See Peden, Rachel (Mason)
M'Taggart, John M'Taggart Ellis
See McTaggart, John McTaggart Ellis
M'Timkulu, Donald (Guy Sidney) 1910- 97-100
Mtshali, Oswald Mbuyiseni 1940- 142
See also BW 2
See also DLB 125
Mtwa, Percy (?)- .... CLC 47
Mu, Yang
See Wang, C(hing) H(sien)
Mucha, Jiri 1915-1991 .... CANR-26
Obituary 134
Earlier sketches in CA 21-24R, CANR-11
Muchnic, Helen (Lenore) 1903- CANR-5
Earlier sketch in CA 1-4R
Mudd, Emily Hartshorne 1898- 13-16R
Mudd, Harvey (Seeley II) 1940- 130
Mudd, Roger H(arrison) 1928- 105
Mudd, Stuart 1893-1975 .... 9-12R
Obituary 57-60
Muddiman, John 1947- 136
Mude, O.
See Gorey, Edward (St. John)
Mudford, William 1782-1848 .... DLB 159
Mudge, Jean McClure 1933- CANR-6
Earlier sketch in CA 5-8R
Mudge, Lewis Seymour 1929- 89-92
Mudgeon, Apeman
See Mitchell, Adrian
Mudgett, Herman W.
See White, William A(nthony) P(arker)
Mudie, Ian (Mayelston) 1911-1976 .... 25-28R
Obituary 135
Mudimbe, V. Y. 1941- 141
See also BW 2
Mudrick, Marvin 1921- CANR-20
Earlier sketch in CA 25-28R
Mudrooroo (Nyoongah) 1938- 154
Muecke, D(ouglas) C(olin) 1919- 53-56
Muehl, Lois Baker 1920- CANR-18
Earlier sketch in CA 1-4R
Muehl, (Ernest) William 1919- 45-48
Muehlbach, Luise 1814-1873 .... DLB 133
Muehlen, Norbert 1909-1981 69-72
Obituary 104
Muehsam, Gerd 1913(?)-1979 Obituary 93-96
Muelder, Walter George 1907- CAP-1
Earlier sketch in CA 13-14
Mueller, Amelia 1911- 57-60
Mueller, Barbara R(uth) 1925- 9-12R
Mueller, Charles S(teinkamp) 1929- CANR-20
Earlier sketches in CA 13-16R, CANR-5
Mueller, Claus 1941- CANR-60
Earlier sketches in CA 65-68, CANR-31
Mueller, David L. 1929- 29-32R
Mueller, Dennis C(ary) 1940- CANR-39
Earlier sketch in CA 116
Mueller, Dorothy 1901- 102
Mueller, Dorothy 1949(?)-1989 Obituary 130
Mueller, Erwin W. 1911-1977 Obituary 69-72
Mueller, Gerald F(rancis) 1927- 13-16R
Mueller, Gerhard G(ottlob) 1930- CANR-36
Earlier sketches in CA 25-28R, CANR-12
Mueller, Gerhard O. W. 1926- CANR-44
Earlier sketches in CA 1-4R, CANR-5, 20
Mueller, Gerhardt
See Bickers, Richard (Leslie) Townshend
Mueller, Gustav Emil 1898- CANR-7
Earlier sketch in CA 17-20R
Mueller, Heiner 1929- .... DLB 124
Mueller, Ingo 1942- 142
Mueller, James R. 1951- 138
Mueller, James W(illiam) 1941- 57-60
Mueller, Janel M(ulder) 1938- 132
Mueller, Joachim W(ilhelm) 1953- 139
Mueller, Joerg 1942- 136
See also CLR 43
See also SATA 67
Mueller, John E(rnest) 1937- CANR-56
Earlier sketches in CA 37-40R, CANR-14
Mueller, Kate Hevner 1898- 41-44R
Mueller, Klaus Andrew 1921- CANR-4
Earlier sketch in CA 49-52
Mueller, Lisel 1924- 93-96
See also CLC 13, 51
See also DLB 105
Mueller, M(ax) G(erhard) 1925- 17-20R
Mueller, Maler 1749-1825 .... DLB 94
Mueller, Marlies K(uhfuss) 1937- 114
Mueller, Merrill 1916-1980 Obituary 103
Mueller, Red
See Mueller, Merrill
Mueller, Reuben Herbert 1897-1982 Obituary 107
Mueller, Robert E(mmett) 1925- 1-4R
Mueller, Robert Kirk 1913- CANR-12
Earlier sketch in CA 73-76
Mueller, Virginia 1924- CANR-57
Earlier sketches in CA 65-68, CANR-10, 27
See also SATA 28
Mueller, Wilhelm 1794-1827 .... DLB 90
Mueller, Willard Fritz 1925- 17-20R
Mueller, William R(andolph) 1916- CANR-2
Earlier sketch in CA 1-4R
Mueller-Vollmer, Kurt 1928- 126
Muenchen, Al(fred) 1917- 49-52
Muesing, Edith E(lizabeth)
See Muesing-Ellwood, Edith E(lizabeth)
Muesing-Ellwood, Edith E(lizabeth) 1947- 114
Muffett, D(avid) J(oseph) M(ead) 1919- 45-48
Muggeridge, Malcolm (Thomas) 1903-1990 .... CANR-63
Earlier sketches in CA 101, CANR-33
See also AITN 1
See also MTCW 1
Muggeson, Margaret Elizabeth 1942- 103
Muggs
See Watkins, Lois
Mugny, Gabriel 1949- 140
Mugo, Micere Githae 1942- 164
Muhajir, Nazzam Al Fitnah
See El Muhajir
Muhammad 570-632 .... DA
See also DAB
See also DAC
See also DAM MST
See also WLCS
Muheim, Harry Miles 1920- 85-88
Muhlen, Norbert
See Muehlen, Norbert
Muhlenfeld, Elisabeth 1944- CANR-24
Earlier sketch in CA 108
Muhlhausen, John Prague 1940- 61-64
Muhlstein, Anka 1935- 114
Mui, Hoh-cheung 1916- 45-48
Mui, Lorna H(olbrook) 1915- 133
Muileman, Kathryn Saltzman 1946- 85-88
Muilenburg, Grace (Evelyn) 1913- 61-64
Muir, (Charles) Augustus (Carlow) 1893(?)-1989 .... 13-16R
Obituary 128
Muir, Barbara K(enrick Gowing) 1908- 9-12R
Muir, Dexter
See Gribble, Leonard (Reginald)
Muir, Edwin 1887-1959 Brief entry 104
See also DLB 20, 100, 191
See also TCLC 2
Muir, Frank (Herbert) 1920-1998 .... CANR-29
Obituary 164
Earlier sketch in CA 81-84
See also SATA 30
Muir, Helen 1911(?)- .... AITN 2
Muir, Helen 1937- 130
See also DLB 14
See also SATA 65
Muir, James A.
See Wells, Angus
Muir, Jane
See Petrone, Jane Muir
Muir, Jean 1906-1973 .... CAP-2
Obituary 41-44R
Earlier sketch in CA 29-32
Muir, John 1838-1914 165
See also DLB 186
See also TCLC 28
Muir, Kenneth (Arthur) 1907-1996 .... CANR-44
Obituary 153
Earlier sketches in CA 1-4R, CANR-4
Muir, Lynette R(oss) 1930- CANR-48
Earlier sketch in CA 122
Muir, Malcolm, Jr. 1915-1984 Obituary 113
Muir, Malcolm 1885-1979 93-96
Obituary 85-88
Muir, Marie 1904- CANR-5
Earlier sketch in CA 1-4R
Muir, Percival H(orace) 1894-1979 .... CANR-5
Obituary 97-100
Earlier sketch in CA 9-12R
See also DLB 201
Muir, Percy H.
See Muir, Percival H(orace)
Muir, Richard 1943- CANR-23
Earlier sketch in CA 106
Muir, Rory 1962- 156
Muir, William Ker, Jr. 1931- 53-56
Muirhead, Ian A(dair) 1913- 13-16R
Muirhead, Thorburn 1899- 5-8R
Mujica, Barbara 1943- 138
Mujica Lainez, Manuel 1910-1984 .... CANR-32
Obituary 112
Earlier sketch in CA 81-84
See also Lainez, Manuel Mujica
See also CLC 31
See also HW
Mukerji, Chandra 1945- 113
Mukerji, Dhan Gopal 1890-1936 136
Brief entry 119
See also CLR 10
See also MAICYA
See also SATA 40
Mukerji, Kshitimohon 1920- 17-20R
Mukherjee, Bharati 1940- CANR-72
Earlier sketches in CA 107, CANR-45
See also BEST 89:2
See also CLC 53
See also DAM NOV
See also DLB 60
See also MTCW 1
Mukherjee, Meenakshi 1937- 65-68
Mukherjee, Ramkrishna 1919- CANR-7
Earlier sketch in CA 57-60
Mula, Frank (Charles) 158

Mulac, Margaret E(lizabeth) 1912- CANR-2
Earlier sketch in CA 5-8R
Mulaisho, Dominic (Chola) 1933- 97-100
Mularchyk, Sylva 93-96
Mulay, Larry L. 1904(?)-1987 Obituary 122
Mulcahy, Greg 145
Mulcahy, Lucille Burnett 5-8R
See also SATA 12
Mulcaster, Richard c. 1531-1611 DLB 167
Mulchrone, Vincent 1919(?)-1977 Obituary 73-76
Mulder, John M(ark) 1946- Brief entry 112
Muldoon, Paul 1951- CANR-52
Brief entry 113
Earlier sketch in CA 129
Interview in 129
See also CLC 32, 72
See also DAM POET
See also DLB 40
Muldoon, Roland W. 1941- 105
Muldowny, John 1931- 127
Mule, Marty 1944- 108
Mulesko, Angelo
See Oglesby, Joseph
Mulford, David Campbell 1937- 9-12R
Mulford, Philippa G(reene) 1948- 116
See also SATA 43
Mulgan, Catherine 1931- CANR-11
Earlier sketch in CA 25-28R
See also Gough, Catherine
Mulgrew, Peter David 1927- 13-16R
Mulhauser, Ruth (Elizabeth) 1913-1980 CANR-7
Earlier sketch in CA 5-8R
Mulhearn, John 1932- 65-68
Mulholland, Jim 1949- CANR-48
Earlier sketch in CA 61-64
Mulholland, John 1898-1970 5-8R
Obituary 89-92
Mulholland, John F(ield) 1903- 41-44R
Mulisch, Harry 1927- CANR-56
Earlier sketches in CA 9-12R, CANR-6, 26
See also CLC 42
Mulkeen, Anne
See Marcus, Anne M(ulkeen)
Mulkeen, Thomas P(atrick) 1923- 85-88
Mulkerne, Donald James Dennis 1921- 9-12R
Mull, Martin 1943- 105
See also CLC 17
Mullally, Frederic 1920- CANR-1
Earlier sketch in CA 1-4R
Mullaly, Edward (Joseph) 1941- 41-44R
Mullan, Bob 1950- 123
Mullan, David George 1951- 130
Mullan, Fitzhugh 1942- 69-72
Mullan, Robert 1950- CANR-50
Mullane, (R.) Mike 1945- 143
Mullaney, Marie Marmo 1953- 112
Mullaney, Thomas E. 1922(?)-1978 93-96
Obituary 81-84
Mullard, Chris(topher Paul) 1944- Brief entry 112
Mullay, Alexander John 1947- 168
Mullay, Sandy
See Mullay, Alexander John
Mullen, Barbara 1914-1979 Obituary 85-88
Mullen, C. J. J.
See Mullen, Cyril J.
Mullen, Cyril J. 1908- 61-64
Mullen, Dore
See Mullen, Dorothy
Mullen, Dorothy 1933- 104
Mullen, Edward John, Jr. 1942- CANR-17
Earlier sketches in CA 49-52, CANR-2
Mullen, Harris H. 1924- 69-72
Mullen, James H. 1924- 1-4R
Mullen, Michael 1937- CANR-39
Earlier sketch in CA 116
Mullen, Patrick B. 1941- 143
Mullen, Robert R(odolph) 1908- CAP-1
Earlier sketch in CA 19-20
Mullen, Thomas J(ames) 1934- CANR-5
Earlier sketch in CA 9-12R
Mullen, William Charles 1944- 73-76
Mullenbach, Philip 1912-1989 Obituary 128
Mullendore, William Clinton
1892-1983 Obituary 111
Muller, Alexander V(ilhelm) 1932- 45-48
Muller, Billex
See Ellis, Edward S(ylvester)
Muller, Charles G(eorge Geoffrey) 1897- CANR-2
Earlier sketch in CA 1-4R
Muller, Charles Geoffrey
See Muller, Charles G(eorge Geoffrey)
Muller, Dorothy
See Mueller, Dorothy
Muller, Edward John 1916- 57-60
Muller, Gilbert H(enry) 1941- CANR-14
Earlier sketch in CA 41-44R
Muller, Herbert J(oseph) 1905- CANR-1
Earlier sketch in CA 1-4R
Muller, Herman J(oseph) 1909- 73-76
Muller, Hermann Joseph 1890-1967 161
Obituary 106
Muller, Hilgard 1914-1985 Obituary 117
Muller, Ingo
See Mueller, Ingo
Muller, James W(aldemar) 1953- 132
Muller, Jerry Z(ucker) 1954- 144
Muller, Joachim W.
See Mueller, Joachim W(ilhelm)
Muller, John E.
See Fanthorpe, R(obert) Lionel
Muller, John P(aul) 1940- 103
Muller, Jorg
See Mueller, Joerg
Muller, Leo C., Jr. 1924- 5-8R
Muller, Marcia 1944- CANR-62
Earlier sketches in CA 81-84, CANR-41
See also AAYA 25
Muller, Peter O. 1942- CANR-45
Earlier sketch in CA 110
Muller, Priscilla E(lkow) 1930- 61-64
Muller, Robert George 1923- 103
Muller, (Lester) Robin 1953- CANR-52
Earlier sketch in CA 127
See also SATA 86
Muller, Ronald E(rnst) 1939- 107
Muller, Siegfried H(ermann) 1902-1965 CAP-1
Earlier sketch in CA 11-12
Mulligan, Hugh A. 1925- CANR-11
Earlier sketch in CA 21-24R
Mulligan, James J. 1936- 45-48
Mulligan, John Joseph 1918- 33-36R
Mulligan, Raymond A(lexander) 1914- 37-40R
Mulligan, Robert S(mith) 1941- 65-68
Mulliken, Robert Sanderson 1896-1986 109
Obituary 120
Mullin, Chris(topher John) 1947- 132
Mullin, Michael 1944- 103
Mullin, Robert N(orville) 1893- 89-92
Mullin, Willard 1902-1978 Obituary 89-92
Mullings, Llewellyn M. 1932- 37-40R
Mullins, (George) Aloysius 1910- CAP-1
Earlier sketch in CA 13-14
Mullins, Ann
See Dally, Ann
Mullins, Carolyn J(ohns) 1940- CANR-10
Earlier sketch in CA 65-68
Mullins, Claud 1887-1968 CAP-1
Earlier sketch in CA 13-14
Mullins, Edward S(wift) 1922- 17-20R
See also SATA 10
Mullins, Edwin (Brandt) 1933- CANR-46
Earlier sketches in CA 53-56, CANR-4, 22
Mullins, Helene 1899- 77-80
Mullins, Hilary 1962- 150
See also SATA 84
Mullins, June B(onner) 1927- 126
Mullins, Larry E(dward) 1935- 117
Mullins, Nicholas C(reed) 1939- 33-36R
Mullins, Pat(rick Joseph) 1923- CANR-66
Earlier sketch in CA 128
Mullins, Vera (Annie) Cooper 1903- 61-64
Mulloy, Elizabeth D(ibert) 1945- 93-96
Mulock, Dinah Maria
See Craik, Dinah Maria (Mulock)
Multhauf, Robert P(hilip) 1919- 93-96
Mulvaney, Robert J(oseph) 1937- 126
Mulvanity, George 1903(?)-1976 Obituary 69-72
Mulvey, Ruth Watt
See Harmer, Ruth Mulvey
Mulvihill, Edward Robert 1917- 9-12R
Mulvihill, Maureen E. 1944- 135
Mulvihill, William Patrick 1923- 1-4R
See also SATA 8
Mulville, Frank 1924- 107
Mumey, Glen A(llen) 1933- 73-76
Mumford, Bob 1930- 103
Mumford, Emily (Hamilton) 1920(?)-1987 57-60
Obituary 123
Mumford, Erika 1935(?)-1988 Obituary 126
Mumford, Lewis 1895-1990 CANR-5
Obituary 130
Earlier sketch in CA 1-4R
See also DLB 63
Mumford, Ruth 1919- CANR-51
See also SATA 86
Mumms, Hardee
See McLellan, Diana
Mun
See Leaf, (Wilbur) Munro
Munari, Bruno 1907- CANR-38
Earlier sketch in CA 73-76
See also CLR 9
See also MAICYA
See also SATA 15
Munby, A(lan) N(oel) L(atimer)
1913-1974 Obituary 53-56
See also DLB 201
Munby, Arthur Joseph 1828-1910 DLB 35
Munby, D(enys) L(awrence) 1919-1976 CANR-2
Earlier sketch in CA 1-4R
Munce, Ruth Hill 1898- CAP-1
Earlier sketch in CA 9-10
See also SATA 12
Munch, Peter A(ndreas) 1908-1984 29-32R
Obituary 111
Munch, Theodore W(illiam) 1919- 57-60
Muncy, Raymond Lee 1928- 49-52
Mund, Vernon A(rthur) 1906- CANR-20
Earlier sketch in CA 1-4R
Munday, Anthony 1560-1633 DLB 62, 172
Mundel, Marvin E(verett) 1916- 21-24R
Mundell, Robert A(lexander) 1932- CANR-2
Earlier sketch in CA 45-48
Mundell, William Daniel 1913-1997 73-76
Obituary 163
Mundis, Hester 1938- CANR-34
Earlier sketches in CA 69-72, CANR-15
Mundis, Jerrold 1941- CANR-11
Earlier sketch in CA 69-72
Mundlak, Max 1899- CAP-1
Earlier sketch in CA 9-10
Mundt, Clara
See Muehlbach, Luise
Mundt, Theodor 1808-1861 DLB 133
Mundy, John Hine 1917- CANR-45
Earlier sketch in CA 45-48
Mundy, Max
See Schofield, Sylvia Anne
Mundy, Simon (Andrew James Hainault) 1954-
CANR-65
Earlier sketch in CA 128
See also SATA 64
Mundy, Talbot 1879-1940 155
Munford, Robert 1737(?)-1783 DLB 31
Munford, W(illiam) A(rthur) 1911- 116
Mungello, David Emil 1943- 110
Munger, Al
See Unger, Maurice Albert
Munger, Frank James 1929-1981 CANR-1
Obituary 116
Earlier sketch in CA 1-4R
Munger, Hortense Roberta
See Roberts, Hortense Roberta
Munger, Robert Boyd 1910- 77-80
Mungo, Raymond 1946- CANR-2
Earlier sketch in CA 49-52
See also CLC 72
Mungoshi, Charles L. 1947- 168
See also DLB 157
Munhall, Edgar 1933- 150
Munholland, John K(im) 1934- CANR-25
Earlier sketch in CA 29-32R
Munif, Abdelrahman 1933- 144
Munir, Muhammad 1895-1981 Obituary 108
Munitz, Milton K(arl) 1913-1995 CANR-36
Obituary 149
Earlier sketches in CA 93-96, CANR-16
Muniz, Angelina 1936- 131
See also HW
Munk, Arthur W. 1909- CANR-7
Earlier sketch in CA 13-16R
Munk, Christian
See Weisenborn, Guenther
Munk, Erika 1939- 17-20R
Munker, Dona 1945- 138
Munn, Geoffrey C(harles) 1953- CANR-47
Earlier sketch in CA 118
Munn, Glenn (Gaywaine)
1890(?)-1977 Obituary 73-76
Munn, H(arold) Warner 1903-1981 CANR-11
Earlier sketch in CA 21-24R
Munnecke, Wilbur C(heney)
1906-1984 Obituary 112
Munnell, Alicia H(aydock) 1942- CANR-30
Earlier sketches in CA 73-76, CANR-13
Munonye, John 1929- 103
See also DLB 117
Munowitz, Ken 1935-1977 SATA 14
Munoz, Braulio 1946- 110
Munoz, Heraldo 1948- 111
Munoz, William 1949- SATA 42, 92
Munoz Marin, (Jose) Luis (Alberto) 1898-1980 153
Obituary 97-100
See also HW
Munro, Alice 1931- CANR-53
Earlier sketches in CA 33-36R, CANR-33
See also AITN 2
See also CLC 6, 10, 19, 50, 95
See also DAC
See also DAM MST, NOV
See also DLB 53
See also MTCW 1
See also SATA 29
See also SSC 3
See also WLCS
Munro, Bertha 1887-1983 45-48
Munro, C. K.
See MacMullan, Charles Walden Kirkpatrick
Munro, Dana Gardner 1892-1990 1-4R
Obituary 131
Munro, David
See Devine, D(avid) M(cDonald)
Munro, Donald J(acques) 1931- 133
Munro, Duncan H.
See Russell, Eric Frank
Munro, Eleanor 1928- 1-4R
See also SATA 37
Munro, H(ector) H(ugh) 1870-1916 130
Brief entry 104
See also Saki
See also CDBLB 1890-1914
See also DA
See also DAB
See also DAC
See also DAM MST, NOV
See also DLB 34, 162
See also MTCW 1
See also WLC
Munro, Hector H.
See Munro, H(ector) H(ugh)
Munro, (Macfarlane) Hugh 9-12R
Munro, Ian S. 29-32R
Munro, James
See Cave, Roderick (George James Munro)
and Mitchell, James
Munro, Jane 1943- 112
Munro, John (Henry Alexander) 1938- 41-44R
Munro, John M(urchinson) 1932- CANR-11
Earlier sketch in CA 69-72
Munro, Leslie Knox 1901-1974 Obituary 49-52
Munro, Mary
See Howe, Doris Kathleen
Munro, Neil 1864-1930 DLB 156
Munro, Roxie 1945- SATA 58
Munro, Thomas 1897-1974 CANR-3
Earlier sketch in CA 5-8R
Munroe, Elizabeth L(ee) 1900- CANR-2
Earlier sketch in CA 17-20R
Munroe, John A(ndrew) 1914- 49-52
Munroe, Kirk 1850-1930 Brief entry 123
See also DLB 42
Munrow, David John 1942-1976 103
Obituary 106
Munsch, Robert (Norman) 1945- CANR-37
Earlier sketch in CA 121
See also CLR 19
See also MAICYA
See also SATA 50, 83
See also SATA-Brief 48
Munsell, F(loyd) Darrell 1934- 129
Munsey, Cecil (Richard, Jr.) 1935- CANR-17
Earlier sketch in CA 41-44R
Munsey, Frank A(ndrew) 1854-1925 Brief entry 116
See also DLB 25, 91
Munshi, Kiki Skagen 1943- CANR-15
Earlier sketch in CA 37-40R
Munshi, Shehnaaz
See Munshi, Kiki Skagen
Munshower, Suzanne 1945- 97-100
Munsinger, Harry 1935- 45-48
Munsinger, Lynn 1951- SATA 33, 94
Munslow, Barry 1950- CANR-41
Earlier sketch in CA 117
Munson, Amelia H. (?)-1972 Obituary 33-36R
Munson, Byron Edwin 1921- 41-44R
Munson, Charlie E(llis) 1877-1975 57-60
Obituary 134
Munson, Don 1908-1978 73-76
Obituary 133
Munson, Fred C(aleb) 1928- 33-36R
Munson, Gorham B(ert) 1896-1969 CAP-1
Earlier sketch in CA 11-12
Munson, Harold L(ewis) 1923- 29-32R
Munson, Henry (Lee), Jr. 1946- CANR-40
Earlier sketch in CA 115
Munson, James (Edward Bradbury) 1944- 124
Munson, Kenneth (George) 1929- 127
Brief entry 111
Munson, Lou
See Munson, Mary Lou (Easley)
Munson, Mary Lou (Easley) 1935- 9-12R
Munson, Thomas N(olan) 1924- CANR-20
Earlier sketch in CA 1-4R
Munson, Thurman (Lee) 1947-1979 108
Obituary 89-92
Munson-Benson, Tunie 1946- 77-80
See also SATA 15
Munsterberg, Hugo 1916- CANR-2
Earlier sketch in CA 5-8R
Munsterberg, Peggy 1921- SATA 102
Munsterhjelm, Erik 1905- 49-52
Munter, Robert (L.) 1926- 21-24R
Munthe, Adam John 1946- 107
Munthe, Frances 1915- 9-12R
Munthe, Malcolm Grane 1920- 5-8R
Munthe, Nelly 1947- 117
See also SATA 53
Munting, Roger 1945- 127
Munton, Alan (Guy) 1945- CANR-24
Earlier sketch in CA 107
Muntyan, Miodrag 1914-1985 Obituary 117
Muntz, (Isabelle) Hope 1907- 13-16R
Muntz, James
See Crowcroft, Peter
Munves, James (Albert) 1922- CANR-3
Earlier sketch in CA 5-8R
See also SATA 30
Munz, Peter 1921- 13-16R
Munz, Philip Alexander 1892- 5-8R
Munzer, Martha E. 1899- CANR-4
Earlier sketch in CA 1-4R
See also SATA 4
Mura, David (Alan) 1952- 138
Mura, Toshio 1925- 144
Murad, Anatol 1904- 73-76
Murad, Gauhar-i
See Sa'ldi, Ghulam Husayn
Murakami, Haruki 1949- 165
See also DLB 182
Murakami, Ryu(nosuke) 1952- 162
Murari, Timeri N(rupendra) 1941- 102
Murarka, Shyam P. 1940- 144
Murat, Ines 1939- 130
Murata, Kiyoaki 1922- 130
Muravchik, Joshua 1947- 136
Murav'ev, Mikhail Nikitich 1757-1807 DLB 150
Muravin, Victor 1929- 85-88
Murawski, Benjamin J(oseph) 1926- 45-48
Murbarger, Nell Lounsberry 1909- CAP-1
Earlier sketch in CA 13-16
Murch, Edward (William Lionel) 1920- 61-64
Murch, James DeForest 1892-1973 CANR-4
Earlier sketch in CA 5-8R
Murch, Mel
See Manes, Stephen
Murchie, Guy 1907-1997 CANR-27
Obituary 159
Earlier sketch in CA 1-4R
See also CAAS 19
Murchison, Thomas Moffat
1907-1984 Obituary 111
Murchison, William 1942- 147
Murchland, Bernard 1929- 112
Murcott, Anne 147
Murden, Forrest D(ozier), Jr.
1921-1977 Obituary 73-76
Murdick, Robert Gordon 1920- CANR-6
Earlier sketch in CA 5-8R
Murdin, Paul 1942- CANR-23
Earlier sketch in CA 106
Murdoch, Brian (Oliver) 1944- 141
Murdoch, David H. 1937- 161
See also SATA 96
Murdoch, (Henry) Derrick 1909-1985 89-92
Obituary 116

Murdoch, (Jean) Iris 1919- ... CANR-68
Earlier sketches in CA 13-16R, CANR-8, 43
Interview in ... CANR-8
See also CDBLB 1960 to Present
See also CLC 1, 2, 3, 4, 6, 8, 11, 15, 22, 31, 51
See also DAB
See also DAC
See also DAM MST, NOV
See also DLB 14, 194
See also MTCW 1
Murdoch, J. Campbell
See Wells, John Campbell
Murdoch, Joseph S(impson) F(erguson) 1919- . 102
Murdoch, Norman H. 1939- ... 154
Murdoch, (Keith) Rupert 1931- Brief entry ... 111
See also DLB 127
Murdock, Eugene C(onverse) 1921- ... CANR-48
Earlier sketches in CA 33-36R, CANR-13
Murdock, George Peter 1897- ... CAP-1
Earlier sketch in CA 13-14
Murdock, Kenneth Ballard 1895-1975 ... 65-68
Obituary ... 61-64
Murdock, Laurette P. 1900- ... 101
Murdock, M(elinda) S(eabrooke) 1947- .. CANR-32
Earlier sketch in CA 113
Murdock, Myrtle Cheney
1886(?)-1980 Obituary ... 97-100
Murdy, Louise Baughan 1935- ... 33-36R
Mure, David (William Alexander) 1912-1986 ... 134
Obituary ... 120
Mure, G(eoffrey) R(eginald) G(ilchrist)
1893-1979 ... 107
Murena, H. A.
See Alvarez Murena, Hector Alberto
Murena, Hector Alberto Alvarez
See Alvarez Murena, Hector Alberto
Murfin, James Vernon 1930(?)-1987 Obituary .. 122
Murfin, Ross C. 1948- ... 125
Murfree, Mary Noailles 1850-1922 Brief entry .. 122
See also DLB 12, 74
See also SSC 22
Murie, Margaret Elizabeth 1902- ... 110
Murnane, Gerald 1939- ... 164
Murnau, Friedrich Wilhelm
See Plumpe, Friedrich Wilhelm
Murner, Thomas 1475-1537 ... DLB 179
Murnion, Philip (Joseph) 1938- ... 116
Muro, Amado (Jesus)
See Seltzer, Chester E.
See also DLB 82
Muro, Diane Patricia 1940- ... 65-68
Muro, James J(oseph) 1934- ... 33-36R
Murphet, Howard 1906- ... 61-64
Murphey, Murray Griffin 1928- ... CANR-6
Earlier sketch in CA 5-8R
Murphey, Rhoads 1919- ... 33-36R
Murphey, Robert W(entworth) 1916- ... 13-16R
Murphy, Agnes Louise Keating 1912- ... 1-4R
Murphy, Annie 1948(?)- ... 145
Murphy, Arthur 1727-1805 ... DLB 89, 142
Murphy, Arthur Lister 1906- ... 77-80
Murphy, Arthur Richard, Jr.
1915-1987 Obituary ... 123
Murphy, Barbara Beasley 1933- ... CANR-20
Earlier sketch in CA 41-44R
See also SATA 5
Murphy, Beatrice M. 1908-1992 ... CANR-9
Obituary ... 137
Earlier sketch in CA 53-56
See also BW 2
See also DLB 76
Murphy, Brenda C(arol) 1950- ... 120
Murphy, Brian (Michael) 1931- ... CANR-13
Earlier sketch in CA 21-24R
Murphy, Brian 1939- ... 108
Murphy, Buck
See Whitcomb, Ian
Murphy, C. L.
See Murphy, Charlotte A(lice)
and Murphy, Lawrence A(gustus)
Murphy, Charles J(ohn) V(incent)
1904-1987 Obituary ... 124
Murphy, Charlotte A(lice) 1924- ... 105
Murphy, Claire Rudolf 1951- ... 143
See also SATA 76
Murphy, Cornelius Francis, Jr. 1933- ... 89-92
Murphy, Cullen 1952- ... 143
Murphy, Dervla (Mary) 1931- ... CANR-21
Earlier sketch in CA 103
Murphy, Dorothy Dey 1911(?)-1983 Obituary ... 110
Murphy, E(mmett) Jefferson 1926- ... 25-28R
See also Murphy, Pat
See also SATA 4
Murphy, Earl Finbar 1928- ... 13-16R
Murphy, Ed
See Murphy, Edward Francis
Murphy, Edward Francis 1914- ... 102
Murphy, Edward J. 1927- ... 37-40R
Murphy, Emily 1868-1933 ... DLB 99
Murphy, Emmy Lou Osborne 1910- ... 5-8R
Murphy, Francis 1932- ... CANR-7
Earlier sketch in CA 13-16R
Murphy, Francis X(avier) 1914- ... 154
Murphy, Frank Hughes 1940- ... 61-64
Murphy, Fred P. 1889-1979 Obituary ... 89-92
Murphy, Gardner 1895-1979 ... 93-96
Obituary ... 85-88
Murphy, George E(dward), Jr. 1948- ... CANR-13
Earlier sketch in CA 77-80
Murphy, George G(regory) S(tanislaus)
1924- ... 21-24R
Murphy, George Lloyd 1902- ... 45-48
Murphy, Geraldine (Joanne)
1920-1990 Obituary ... 131
Murphy, Grace E. Barstow
1888-1975 Obituary ... 57-60
Murphy, Haughton
See Duffy, James H(enry)
Murphy, Hazel
See Thurston, Hazel (Patricia)
Murphy, Herta A(lbrecht) 1908- ... 49-52
Murphy, Irene L(yons) 1920- ... 53-56
Murphy, J(ohn) Carter 1921- ... 13-16R
Murphy, James Bernard 1958- ... 146
Murphy, James F(redrick) 1943- ... CANR-8
Earlier sketch in CA 61-64
Murphy, James J(erome) 1923- ... CANR-27
Earlier sketches in CA 33-36R, CANR-12
Murphy, James M(artin) 1917- ... 29-32R
Murphy, James M(aurice) 1932-1966(?) ... CAP-1
Earlier sketch in CA 11-12
Murphy, James S. 1934- ... 134
Murphy, Jane Brevoort Walden
1902(?)-1980 Obituary ... 97-100
Murphy, Jeffrie G(uy) 1940- Brief entry ... 118
Murphy, Jill (Frances) 1949- ... CANR-50
Earlier sketches in CA 105, CANR-44
See also CLR 39
See also MAICYA
See also SATA 37, 70
Murphy, Jim 1947- ... 111
See also AAYA 20
See also SATA 37, 77
See also SATA-Brief 32
Murphy, John
See Grady, Ronan Calistus, Jr.
Murphy, John C. 1947- ... 165
Murphy, John H. III 1916- ... DLB 127
Murphy, John L(awrence) 1924- ... CANR-20
Earlier sketch in CA 1-4R
Murphy, John W(illiam) 1948- ... CANR-30
Earlier sketch in CA 112
Murphy, Joseph E., Jr. 1930- ... 156
Earlier sketch in CA 133
See also SATA 65
Murphy, Karen A(lee) 1945- ... 115
Murphy, Larry
See Murphy, Lawrence R(ichard)
Murphy, Lawrence A(gustus) 1924- ... CANR-64
Earlier sketch in CA 104
Murphy, Lawrence R(ichard) 1942- ... 105
Murphy, Lois Barclay 1902- ... CANR-41
Earlier sketches in CA 1-4R, CANR-4, 19
Murphy, Louis J.
See Hicks, Tyler Gregory
Murphy, Mario
See Edmondson, G. C.
Murphy, Marion Fisher 1902- ... 53-56
Murphy, Martha W(atson) 1951- ... 136
Murphy, (Gavin) Martin (Hedd) 1934- ... 132
Murphy, Michael 1930- ... 73-76
Murphy, N(orman) T. P. 1933- ... 125
Murphy, Nonie Carol
See Caroll, Nonie
Murphy, P(eter) J(ohn) 1946- ... 136
Murphy, Pat 1955- ... 137
See also Murphy, E(mmett) Jefferson
Murphy, Patrick T(homas) 1939- ... 108
Murphy, Patrick V(incent) 1920- ... 105
Murphy, Paul 1917(?)-1983 Obituary ... 111
Murphy, Paul J(ames) 1943- ... 112
Murphy, Paul L(loyd) 1923- ... CANR-7
Earlier sketch in CA 17-20R
Murphy, Peter 1956- ... 163
Murphy, Rae Allan 1935- ... 142
Murphy, Raymond E(dward) 1898- ... 41-44R
Murphy, Reg 1934- ... 33-36R
Murphy, Richard 1927- ... 29-32R
See also CLC 41
See also DLB 40
Murphy, Richard T. A. 1908- ... CANR-1
Earlier sketch in CA 1-4R
Murphy, Robert (William) 1902-1971 ... CAP-1
Obituary ... 29-32R
Earlier sketch in CA 9-10
See also SATA 10
Murphy, Robert 1947- ... 144
Murphy, Robert Cushman 1887-1973 ... CAP-2
Obituary ... 41-44R
Earlier sketch in CA 23-24
Murphy, Robert D(aniel) 1894-1978 ... CAP-1
Obituary ... 73-76
Earlier sketch in CA 9-10
Murphy, Robert F(rancis) 1924- ... 118
Murphy, Roland Edmund 1917- ... CANR-6
Earlier sketch in CA 5-8R
Murphy, Romaine 1941- ... 77-80
Murphy, Shane M. 1957- ... 150
Murphy, Sharon M. 1940- ... 77-80
Murphy, Sheila E. 1951- ... CAAS 26
Murphy, Shirley Rousseau 1928- ... CANR-56
Earlier sketches in CA 21-24R, CANR-13, 29
See also JRDA
See also MAICYA
See also SAAS 18
See also SATA 36, 71
Murphy, Sylvia 1937- ... 121
See also CLC 34
Murphy, Terrence J. 1921- ... 5-8R
Murphy, Thomas (Bernard) 1935- ... 101
See also CLC 51
Murphy, Thomas Basil, Jr. 1935- ... CANR-11
Earlier sketch in CA 69-72
Murphy, Thomas P(atrick) 1931- ... CANR-16
Earlier sketch in CA 41-44R
Murphy, Tom
See Murphy, Thomas Basil, Jr.
Murphy, Vi 1924(?)-1987 Obituary ... 124
Murphy, Walter F(rancis) 1929- ... CANR-2
Earlier sketch in CA 1-4R
Murphy, Warren B. 1933- ... CANR-31
Earlier sketches in CA 33-36R, CANR-13
Murphy, William Francis 1906- ... 17-20R
Murphy, William M(ichael) 1916- ... 85-88
Murphy-O'Connor, Jerome James 1935- .. CANR-5
Earlier sketch in CA 13-16R
Murra, John V(ictor) 1916- ... CANR-1
Earlier sketch in CA 45-48
Murrah, David Joe 1941- ... 106
Murray, Adrian
See Curran, Mona (Elisa)
Murray, Albert L. 1916- ... CANR-52
Earlier sketches in CA 49-52, CANR-26
See also BW 2
See also CLC 73
See also DLB 38
Murray, Andrew Evans 1917- ... 25-28R
Murray, Beatrice
See Posner, Richard
Murray, Bruce C(hurchill) 1931- ... 103
Murray, Charles (Alan) 1943- ... CANR-63
Earlier sketch in CA 147
Murray, Christopher 1940- ... 117
Murray, Clara Elizabeth 1894- ... CAP-1
Earlier sketch in CA 9-10
Murray, Cromwell
See Morgan, Murray
Murray, D. Stark
See Murray, David Stark
Murray, Daniel E(dward) 1925- ... 45-48
Murray, David (J.) 1945- ... 133
Murray, David Stark 1900-1977 Obituary ... 111
Murray, Dick 1924- ... 106
Murray, Don(ald Patrick) 1929- ... 156
Murray, Donald M(orison) 1924- ... CANR-17
Earlier sketch in CA 1-4R
Murray, Dorothy Garst 1915- ... 21-24R
Murray, Edmund P(atrick) 1930- ... 81-84
Murray, Edna
See Rowland, D(onald) S(ydney)
Murray, Edward (James, Jr.) 1928- ... CANR-1
Earlier sketch in CA 49-52
Murray, Edward J(ames) 1928- ... 13-16R
Murray, Elaine 1941- ... 144
Murray, Elwood 1897- ... 73-76
Murray, Eugene Bernard 1927- ... 104
Murray, Fiona
See Bevan, Gloria (Isabel)
Murray, Frances
See Booth, Rosemary Frances
Murray, G(erald) E(dward, Jr.) 1945- ... CANR-5
Earlier sketch in CA 53-56
Murray, G. T. 1927- ... 145
Murray, Gale Barbara 1945- ... 140
Murray, George (McIntosh) 1900-1970 ... CAP-1
Earlier sketch in CA 13-14
Murray, (Jesse) George 1909- ... 17-20R
Murray, (George) Gilbert (Aime) 1866-1957 Brief
entry ... 110
See also DLB 10
Murray, Glen 1955- ... 168
Murray, Hallard T(homas), Jr. 1937- ... 17-20R
Murray, Henry A(lexander) 1893-1988 Obituary . 125
Brief entry ... 116
Murray, Irene
See Witherspoon, Irene Murray
Murray, J(ohn) Alex ... 41-44R
Murray, J. Harley 1910(?)-1977 Obituary ... 73-76
Murray, J(ohn) Joseph 1915- ... CANR-4
Earlier sketch in CA 5-8R
Murray, James 1946- ... CANR-1
Earlier sketch in CA 49-52
Murray, James Patrick 1919- ... CANR-34
Earlier sketches in CA 65-68, CANR-15
Murray, Janet Horowitz 1946- ... 144
Murray, Jean Shaw 1927(?)-1985 Obituary ... 116
Murray, Jerome T(homas) 1928- ... 33-36R
Murray, Jim
See Murray, James Patrick
Murray, Joan 1943- ... 124
Murray, Joan 1945- ... 77-80
Murray, Joan E. 1941- ... 81-84
Murray, Jocelyn (Margaret) 1929- ... 113
Murray, John 1923- ... CANR-19
Earlier sketches in CA 5-8R, CANR-4
See also SATA 39
Murray, John A. 1954- ... 138
Murray, John Bernard 1915- ... 41-44R
Murray, John Courtney 1904-1967 Obituary ... 106
Murray, John E(dward), Jr. 1932- ... CANR-31
Earlier sketch in CA 45-48
Murray, John F(rancis) 1923-1977 ... CAP-2
Obituary ... 69-72
Earlier sketch in CA 29-32
Murray, John L(arry) 1937- ... 108
Murray, John MacDougall 1910- ... 33-36R
Murray, Judith Sargent 1751-1820 ... DLB 37, 200
Murray, K. F.
See Carlisle, Fred
Murray, K(atherine) M(aud) Elisabeth 1909-1998 ...
CANR-70
Earlier sketch in CA 77-80
Murray, Keith A. 1910- ... CAP-2
Earlier sketch in CA 33-36
Murray, Ken
See Turner, Robert (Harry)
Murray, Ken 1903-1988 Obituary ... 126
Murray, Les(lie) A(llan) 1938- ... CANR-56
Earlier sketches in CA 21-24R, CANR-11, 27
See also CLC 40
See also DAM POET
Murray, Lieutenant
See Ballou, Maturin Murray
Murray, Linda Charlton 1936(?)-1986 Obituary . 118
Murray, Lois Smith 1906- ... 37-40R
Murray, Margaret Alice 1863-1963 ... 5-8R
Murray, Marguerite 1917- ... SATA 63
Murray, Marian ... 41-44R
See also SATA 5
Murray, Martin J(ulius) 1945- ... 132
Murray, Mary (Morrison) 1925- ... 25-28R
Murray, Maynard 1911(?)-1983 Obituary ... 110
Murray, Merrill G. 1900(?)-1976 Obituary ... 69-72
Murray, Michael
See McLaren, Moray (David Shaw)
Murray, Michael V(ivian) 1906- ... 5-8R
Murray, (Judith) Michele (Freedman)
1933-1974 ... 49-52
See also SATA 7
Murray, Ossie 1938- ... SATA 43
Murray, Paul T(hom, Jr.) 1944- ... 146
Murray, (Anna) Pauli(ne) 1910-1985 ... 125
Obituary ... 116
See also BW 2
See also DLB 41
Murray, Peter
See Hautman, Pete(r Murray)
Murray, Peter (John) 1920-1992 ... CANR-10
Obituary ... 137
Earlier sketch in CA 13-16R
Murray, Philip 1924- ... 65-68
Murray, Ralph L(a Verne) 1921- ... 13-16R
Murray, Raymond C. 1929- ... 142
Murray, Rebecca (Jean) 1936- ... 57-60
Murray, Robert A. 1929- ... 29-32R
Murray, Robert Keith 1922- ... 53-56
Murray, Robin 1940- ... CANR-55
Earlier sketch in CA 126
Murray, Roger N(icholas) 1932- ... 21-24R
Murray, Rona 1924- ... 154
Murray, Ruth Lovell 1900- ... 103
Murray, Sinclair
See Sullivan, (Edward) Alan
Murray, Sister Mary Verona 1909- ... 17-20R
Murray, Sonia Bennett 1936- ... 65-68
Murray, Thomas J(oseph) 1943- ... 77-80
Murray, W(illiam) H(utchison) 1913-1996 .. CANR-4
Obituary ... 151
Earlier sketch in CA 9-12R
Murray, Walter I(saiah) 1910-1978 ... 85-88
Obituary ... 73-76
Murray, William Cotter 1929- ... 53-56
Murray, William J(oseph) III 1946- ... CANR-46
Earlier sketch in CA 110
Murray-Brown, Jeremy 1932- ... 77-80
Murray-Smith, Stephen 1922- ... 103
Murrell, Elsie Kathleen Seth-Smith 1883- ... CAP-1
Earlier sketch in CA 9-10
Murrell, Jim
See Murrell, Vernon James
Murrell, K(eith) F(rank) H(ywel)
1908(?)-1984 Obituary ... 112
Murrell, Vernon James 1934- ... 132
Murren, Doug(las) 1951- ... 136
Murrett, John Charles 1892- ... 1-4R
Murrow, Casey 1945- ... 97-100
Murrow, Edward R(oscoe) 1908-1965 ... 103
Obituary ... 89-92
Murrow, Liza Ketchum 1946- ... 146
Murrow, Liza Ketchum 1946- ... SATA 78
Murry, J. Middleton
See Murry, John Middleton
Murry, John Middleton 1889-1957 Brief entry .. 118
See also DLB 149
See also TCLC 16
Murry, Katherine Middleton 1925- ... 133
Murry, Mary Middleton 1897-1983 Obituary ... 110
Murstein, Bernard I(rving) 1929- ... CANR-3
Earlier sketch in CA 9-12R
Murtagh, John M(artin) 1911-1976 ... 17-20R
Obituary ... 61-64
Murtagh, William J. 1923- ... 25-28R
Murton, Jessie Wilmore ... 5-8R
Murton, Mary 1933- ... 117
Murton, Thomas O'Rhelius
1929-1990 Obituary ... 132
Murton, Tom
See Murton, Thomas O'Rhelius
Musa, Mark 1934- ... 13-16R
Musacchio, George 1938- ... 143
Musaeus, Johann Karl August 1735-1787 .. DLB 97
Musafir
See Tagore, Amitendranath
Musaphia, Joseph 1935- ... CANR-17
Earlier sketch in CA 97-100
Musarurwa, Willie 1928(?)-1990 Obituary ... 131
Muscat, Robert J. 1931- ... 17-20R
Muscatine, Charles 1920- ... 21-24R
Muscatine, Doris (Corn) 1926- ... 9-12R
Muschamp, Thomas
See Lloyd-Thomas, Catherine
Muschenheim, Carl 1905-1977 Obituary ... 69-72
Muschenheim, William (Emil) 1902-1990 ... CAP-1
Obituary ... 130
Earlier sketch in CA 13-16
Muschg, Adolf 1934- ... DLB 75
Musciano, Walt
See Musciano, Walter A.
Musciano, Walter A. 1922- ... 121
Muse, Beatriz de Regil 1901(?)-1983 Obituary . 109
Muse, Benjamin 1898- ... CANR-1
Earlier sketch in CA 1-4R
Muse, Clarence 1889-1979 Obituary ... 104
Muse, Daphne P. 1944- ... 112
Muse, Ken 1925- ... 111
Muse, Patricia (Alice) 1923- ... 69-72
Muses, C. A.
See Muses, Charles Arthur
Muses, Charles Arthur 1919- ... 135
Brief entry ... 115
Musetto, Andrew P(aul) 1945- ... 111
Musgrave, Barbara S(tewart) 1913- ... 5-8R
Musgrave, Clifford 1904-1982 Obituary ... 107

Musgrave, Florence 1902- ... CAP-1
Earlier sketch in CA 13-14
See also SATA 3
Musgrave, Gerald L. 1942- ... 143
Musgrave, Richard Abel 1910- ... 113
Musgrave, Susan 1951- ... CANR-45
Earlier sketch in CA 69-72
See also CLC 13, 54
Musgraves, Don 1935- ... 65-68
Musgrove, Frank 1922- ... CANR-6
Earlier sketch in CA 13-16R
Musgrove, Margaret Wynkoop 1943- ... 65-68
See also SATA 26
Musgrove, Philip 1940- ... CANR-11
Earlier sketch in CA 29-32R
Musgrove, Stanley (E.) 1924-1986 ... 108
Obituary ... 118
Mushabac, Jane 1944- ... 108
Mushkat, Jerome 1931- ... 81-84
Mushkat, Mari'on 1919- ... 120
Mushkin, Selma J. 1913-1979 Obituary ... 93-96
Musial, Joe 1905(?)-1977 Obituary ... 69-72
Musial, Stan(ley Frank) 1920- ... 93-96
Musicant, Elke (Alice) 1919- ... 107
Musicant, Ivan 1943- ... 168
Musicant, Tobias (Ted) 1921- ... 108
Musiker, Reuben 1931- ... 57-60
Musil, Robert (Edler von) 1880-1942 ... CANR-55
Brief entry ... 109
See also DLB 81, 124
See also SSC 18
See also TCLC 12, 68
Muske, Carol 1945-
See Muske-Dukes, Carol (Anne)
See also CLC 90
Muske, Irmgard (Gertrud) 1912- ... CANR-18
Earlier sketch in CA 25-28R
Muske-Dukes, Carol (Anne) 1945- ... CANR-70
Earlier sketches in CA 65-68, CANR-32
See also Muske, Carol
Muskie, Edmund S(ixtus) 1914-1996 ... CANR-2
Obituary ... 151
Earlier sketch in CA 49-52
Musmanno, Michael A(ngelo) (?)-1968 ... CAP-1
Earlier sketch in CA 9-10
Musolf, Lloyd D(aryl) 1919- ... CANR-9
Earlier sketch in CA 17-20R
Musselman, George Paul 1895-1987 Obituary . 123
Musselman, Vernon A(rmor) 1912- ... 37-40R
Mussen, Paul Henry 1922- ... 159
Brief entry ... 114
Musser, Joe
See Musser, Joseph L.
Musser, Joseph L. 1936- ... CANR-12
Earlier sketch in CA 29-32R
Musset, (Louis Charles) Alfred de 1810-1857 .. DLB 192
Mussey, Virginia Howell
See Ellison, Virginia H(owell)
Mussey, Virginia T.H.
See Ellison, Virginia H(owell)
Mussi, Mary 1907- ... CANR-6
Earlier sketch in CA 53-56
Mussoff, Lenore 1927- ... 21-24R
Mussolini, Benito (Amilcare Andrea)
1883-1945 Brief entry ... 116
Mussolini, Rachele Guidi 1890-1979 Obituary .. 111
Mussulman Joseph A(gee) 1928- ... 37-40R
Mustafa, Zaki 1934- ... 41-44R
Muste, John M(artin) 1927- ... 21-24R
Musteikis, Antanas 1914- ... 45-48
Musto, Barry 1930- ... 106
Musto, David Franklin 1936- ... 104
Musto, Michael 1955- ... 132
Musto, Ronald G. 1948- ... 127
Musurillo, Herbert (Anthony Peter) 1917-1974 ... CAP-1
Obituary ... 49-52
Earlier sketch in CA 13-14
Mutafchieva, Vera 1929- ... DLB 181
Mutchler, David E(dward) 1941- ... 33-36R
Mutel, Cornelia F. 1947- ... SATA 74
Muth, John F(raser) 1930- ... 13-16R
Muth, Richard F(erris) 1927- ... 13-16R
Mutharika, B(rightson) W(ebster) T(hom) 1934- ... CANR-46
Earlier sketch in CA 41-44R
Muthesius, Stefan 1939- ... CANR-50
Earlier sketch in CA 61-64
Mutis, Alvaro 1923- ... 149
See also HW
Mutke, Peter H(ans) C(hristoph) 1927- ... 93-96
Muto, Susan Annette 1942- ... CANR-53
Earlier sketches in CA 110, CANR-29
Mutton, Alice F. A. 1908- ... 5-8R
Mutz
See Kuenstler, Morton
Muus, Bent J(oergen) 1926- ... 103
Muus, Flemming B(ruun) 1907-1982 Obituary .. 110
Muuss, Rolf E(duard Helmut) 1924- ... 9-12R
Muzumdar, Ammu Menon 1919- ... 21-24R
Mwangi, Meja 1948- ... 143
See also BW 2
See also DLB 125
Myassin, Leonid Fedorovich 1895-1979 ... 97-100
Obituary ... 85-88
My Brother's Brother
See Chekhov, Anton (Pavlovich)
Mycue, Edward 1937- ... CANR-45
Earlier sketches in CA 53-56, CANR-4
Mydans, Carl ... 97-100
Mydans, Shelley Smith 1915- ... 145
Brief entry ... 105
Myddleton, Robert
See Hebblethwaite, Peter
Myer, Dillon S(eymour) 1891-1982 ... CAP-2
Obituary ... 116
Earlier sketch in CA 29-32
Myer, John Colby 1912- ... 45-48
Myer, John Randolph 1927- ... 5-8R
Myerhoff, Barbara G. 1936(?)-1985 Obituary ... 114
Myers, A(lexander) J(ohn) William 1877- ... CAP-1
Earlier sketch in CA 11-12
Myers, Albert M(orris) 1917- ... 118
Myers, Alec Reginald
See Myers, Alexander Reginald
Myers, Alexander Reginald 1912-1980 ... CANR-10
Earlier sketch in CA 13-16R
Myers, Alonzo F(ranklin) 1895-1970 Obituary .. 104
Myers, Andrew Breen 1920- ... 61-64
Myers, Arthur 1917- ... CANR-58
Earlier sketches in CA 17-20R, CANR-7
See also SATA 35, 91
Myers, Arthur 1917- ... CANR-58
Earlier sketches in CA 17-20R, CANR-7
See also SATA 35, 91
Myers, Arthur Sim 1928-1984 Obituary ... 113
Myers, Bernard S(amuel) 1908-1993 ... CANR-48
Obituary ... 140
Earlier sketch in CA 65-68
Myers, Bernice ... CANR-55
Earlier sketches in CA 61-64, CANR-8
See also SATA 9, 81
Myers, Bettye (Blanche) 1926- Brief entry ... 107
Myers, Bill 1953- ... 163
Myers, C. F.
See Fairbanks, Carol
Myers, C(hauncie) Kilmer 1916-1981 Obituary .. 108
Myers, Carol Fairbanks
See Fairbanks, Carol
Myers, Caroline Elizabeth Clark 1887-1980 . 29-32R
Obituary ... 134
See also SATA 28
Myers, Charles A(ndrew) 1913- ... 85-88
Myers, Charles B(ennett) 1939- ... 57-60
Myers, David G. 1942- ... CANR-46
Earlier sketches in CA 106, CANR-22
Myers, (Eugene Victor) Debs
1911-1971 Obituary ... 104
Myers, Desaix B. III 1945- ... 104
Myers, Drew(fus Young, Jr.) 1946- ... 145
Myers, Edward 1950- ... CANR-50
Earlier sketch in CA 116
See also SATA 96
Myers, Elisabeth P(erkins) 1918- ... CANR-3
Earlier sketch in CA 5-8R
See also SATA 36
Myers, Eugene A(braham) 1910- ... 45-48
Myers, Francis Milton 1917- ... 5-8R
Myers, Frederic W. H. 1843-1901 ... DLB 190
Myers, Gail E(ldridge) 1923- ... CANR-1
Earlier sketch in CA 49-52
Myers, Garry Cleveland 1884-1971 ... CAP-2
Earlier sketch in CA 29-32
Myers, Gay Nagle 1943- ... 102
Myers, George (Francis), Jr. 1953- ... 119
Myers, Gerald E(ugene) 1923- ... 29-32R
Myers, Gustavus 1872-1942 Brief entry ... 123
See also DLB 47
Myers, Harriet Kathryn
See Whittington, Harry (Benjamin)
Myers, Helen ... 145
Myers, (Mary) Hortense (Powner) 1913-1987 ... CANR-2
Obituary ... 123
Earlier sketch in CA 1-4R
See also SATA 10
Myers, Irma A(shley) 1924- ... 112
Myers, J(ohn) William 1919- ... CANR-57
Earlier sketches in CA 33-36R, CANR-12, 30
Myers, Jack 1913- ... 150
See also SATA 83
Myers, (Elliott) Jack 1941- ... 73-76
Myers, Jacob M(artin) 1904- ... 17-20R
Myers, John Bernard 1920(?)-1987 Obituary ... 123
Myers, John H(olmes) 1915-1993 ... 9-12R
Obituary ... 143
Myers, John L. 1958- ... 141
Myers, John Myers 1906- ... CANR-65
Earlier sketches in CA 1-4R, CANR-1
Myers, Katherine 1952- ... CANR-28
Earlier sketch in CA 110
Myers, L(eopold) H(amilton) 1881-1944 ... 157
See also DLB 15
See also TCLC 59
Myers, L(ouis) M(cCorry) 1901- ... 21-24R
Myers, Lois E. 1946- ... 139
Myers, Lonny 1922- ... 65-68
Myers, Lou(is) 1915- ... CANR-55
Earlier sketch in CA 136
See also SATA 81
Myers, M(arvin) Scott 1922- ... 69-72
Myers, Martin 1927- ... CANR-20
Earlier sketch in CA 29-32R
Myers, Mary Ruth 1947- ... CANR-16
Earlier sketch in CA 85-88
Myers, Mike 1963- ... 165
Myers, Minor, Jr. 1942- ... 133
Myers, Neil 1930- ... 105
Myers, Norma 1929- ... 61-64
Myers, Norman 1934- ... CANR-20
Earlier sketches in CA 49-52, CANR-1
Myers, Patricia 1929- ... 37-40R
Myers, Paul 1932- ... 123
Myers, R(obert) E(ugene) 1924- ... CANR-47
Earlier sketches in CA 77-80, CANR-23
Myers, Ramon H. 1929- ... 113
Myers, Raymond E(dward) 1902- ... CAP-1
Earlier sketch in CA 13-16
Myers, Robert J(ulius) 1912- ... CANR-6
Earlier sketch in CA 13-16R
Myers, Robert J(ohn) 1924- ... CANR-27
Earlier sketch in CA 107
Myers, Robert Manson 1921- ... 37-40R
Myers, Rollo Hugh 1892-1984(?) ... 17-20R
Obituary ... 115
Myers, Samuel 1897(?)-1983 Obituary ... 109
Myers, Tamar 1948- ... 154
Myers, Vernon C. 1911-1990 Obituary ... 130
Myers, W. David 1956- ... 159
Myers, Walter Dean 1937- ... CANR-67
Earlier sketches in CA 33-36R, CANR-20, 42
Interview in ... CANR-20
See also AAYA 4, 23
See also BLC 3
See also BW 2
See also CLC 35
See also CLR 4, 16, 35
See also DAM MULT, NOV
See also DLB 33
See also JRDA
See also MAICYA
See also SAAS 2
See also SATA 41, 71
See also SATA-Brief 27
Myers, Walter M.
See Myers, Walter Dean
Myers, Wayne A(lan) 1931- ... 138
Myers, William 1939- ... 132
Myerscough-Walker, Raymond
1912-1984 Obituary ... 113
Myerson, Bess 1924- ... 108
Myerson, Joel 1945- ... CANR-41
Earlier sketches in CA 102, CANR-19
Myerson, Michael 1940- ... 73-76
Myhers, John 1921-1992 ... 105
Obituary ... 137
Myhill, Henry (James) 1925-1977 ... 103
Mykle, Agrar 1915- ... 13-16R
Mylander, Maureen 1937- ... CANR-5
Earlier sketch in CA 53-56
Myler, Joseph L. 1905(?)-1973 Obituary ... 41-44R
Myles, Eileen 1949- ... 148
See also DLB 193
Myles, Eugenie Louise (Butler) 1905- ... CAP-1
Earlier sketch in CA 11-12
Myles, Symon
See Follett, Ken(neth Martin)
Myller, Rolf 1926- ... CANR-8
Earlier sketch in CA 5-8R
See also SATA 27
Mylonas, George Emmanuel
1898-1988 Obituary ... 125
Mylroie, Laurie 1953- ... 139
Mynors, Roger A(ubrey) B(askerville)
1903-1989 ... 5-8R
Obituary ... 129
Myra, Harold L(awrence) 1939- ... CANR-8
Earlier sketch in CA 61-64
See also SATA 46
See also SATA-Brief 42
Myrdal, Alva Reimer 1902-1986 ... 69-72
Obituary ... 118
Myrdal, (Karl) Gunnar 1898-1987 ... CANR-4
Obituary ... 122
Earlier sketch in CA 9-12R
Myrdal, Jan 1927- ... 132
Brief entry ... 117
Myrer, Anton (Olmstead) 1922-1996 ... CANR-3
Obituary ... 151
Earlier sketch in CA 1-4R
Myres, J(ohn) N(owell) L(inton) 1902-1989 ... 123
Myres, J(ohn) N(owell) L(inton)
1902-1989 Obituary ... 129
Myres, Sandra Lynn 1933- ... CANR-14
Earlier sketch in CA 33-36R
Myrick, David F. ... CANR-6
Earlier sketch in CA 13-16R
Myrick, Robert D(eWayne) 1935- ... CANR-17
Earlier sketch in CA 41-44R
Myrick, William J(ennings, Jr.) 1932- ... 73-76
Myrland, Doug 1952- ... 117
Myron, Robert 1926- ... 13-16R
Myrsiades, Kostas J. 1940- ... CANR-52
Earlier sketches in CA 109, CANR-27
Myrus, Donald (Richard) 1927- ... CANR-4
Earlier sketch in CA 1-4R
See also SATA 23
Mysak, Edward D(amien) 1930-1989 Obituary .. 130
Myss, Caroline 1953(?)- ... 168

N

Naamani, Israel T(arkow) 1913(?)- ... 124
Brief entry ... 106
Naar, Jon 1920- ... 102
Nabbes, Thomas 1605(?)-1641 ... DLB 58
Nabhan, Gary Paul 1952- ... 143
Nabholtz, John R(obert) 1931- ... 65-68
Nabl, Franz 1883-1974 ... DLB 81
Nabokov, Dmitri 1934- ... 132
Nabokov, Nicolas 1903-1978 ... 85-88
Obituary ... 77-80
Nabokov, Peter (Francis) 1940- ... CANR-27
Earlier sketches in CA 21-24R, CANR-9
Nabokov, Vladimir (Vladimirovich) 1899-1977 ... CANR-20
Obituary ... 69-72
Earlier sketch in CA 5-8R
See also CDALB 1941-1968
See also CLC 1, 2, 3, 6, 8, 11, 15, 23, 44, 46, 64
See also DA
See also DAB
See also DAC
See also DAM MST, NOV
See also DLB 2
See also DLBD 3
See also DLBY 80, 91
See also MTCW 1
See also SSC 11
See also WLC
Nacci, Chris (Natale) 1909- ... 41-44R
Nachbar, Herbert 1930(?)-1980 Obituary ... 97-100
Nachbar, Jack 1941- ... 53-56
Nachman, Gerald 1938- ... CANR-37
Earlier sketches in CA 65-68, CANR-16
Nachtigal, Paul M. 1930- ... 112
Nachtigall, Lila Ehrenstein 1934- Brief entry ... 105
Nachtmann, Francis Weldon 1913-1982 ... 37-40R
Obituary ... 133
Nadan, Paul 1933(?)-1978 Obituary ... 104
Nadas, Peter 1942- ... 166
Naddor, Eliezer 1920- ... 21-24R
Nadeau, Adel 1940- ... 168
Nadeau, Maurice 1911- ... 49-52
Nadeau, R(aymond) E(rnest) 1913- Brief entry . 107
Nadeau, Ray E.
See Nadeau, R(aymond) E(rnest)
Nadeau, Remi A(llen) 1920- ... CANR-2
Earlier sketch in CA 1-4R
Nadeau, Roland 1928- ... CANR-4
Earlier sketch in CA 53-56
Nadel, Frances 1905(?)-1977 Obituary ... 69-72
Nadel, Gerald H. 1944-1977 ... 81-84
Obituary ... 73-76
Nadel, Ira Bruce 1943- ... CANR-39
Earlier sketches in CA 102, CANR-18
Nadel, Jennifer 1962- ... 144
Nadel, Laurie 1948- ... SATA 74
Nadel, Mark V(ictor) 1943- ... 33-36R
Nadel, Norman (Sanford) 1915- ... 106
Nadelhoffer, Hans (L.) 1940-1988 ... 137
Nadelmann, Ethan A. 1957- ... 150
Naden, Constance 1858-1889 ... DLB 199
Naden, Corinne J. 1930- ... 148
See also SATA 79
Nader, George 1921- Brief entry ... 109
Nader, George Albert 1940- ... 111
Nader, Laura 1930- ... CANR-7
Earlier sketch in CA 17-20R
Nader, Ralph 1934- ... 77-80
Nadezhdin, Nikolai Ivanovich 1804-1856 .. DLB 198
Nadich, Judah 1912- ... CANR-55
Earlier sketch in CA 127
Nadler, Harvey 1933- ... 13-16R
Nadler, Leonard 1922- ... CANR-20
Earlier sketches in CA 53-56, CANR-5
Nadler, Paul S(tephen) 1930- ... 25-28R
Nadler, Susan
See Gantry, Susan Nadler
Nadler, Zeace 1925- ... 121
Naef, Weston J(ohn) 1942- Brief entry ... 111
Naeslund, Erik 1948- ... 103
Naess, Harald Sigurd 1925- ... 41-44R
Naether, Carl (Albert) 1892- ... 25-28R
Naff, Clayton 1956- ... 146
Naftali, Timothy ... 166
Nafziger, E(stel) Wayne 1938- ... 85-88
Nafziger, George F(rancis) 1949- ... 132
Nag
See Grauer, Neil A(lbert)
Nag, Moni 1925- ... 41-44R
Nagahiro, Toshio 1905- ... 158
Nagai Berthrong, Evelyn 1946- ... 115
Nagai Kafu 1879-1959
See Nagai Sokichi
See also DLB 180
See also TCLC 51
Nagai Sokichi 1879-1959 Brief entry ... 117
See also Nagai Kafu
Nagara, Susumu 1932- ... CANR-3
Earlier sketch in CA 45-48
Nagatsu, Toshiharu 1930- ... 107
Nagatsuka, Ryuji 1924- Brief entry ... 125
na gCopaleen, Myles
See O Nuallain, Brian
Nagel, Andreas Fischer
See Fischer-Nagel, Andreas
Nagel, Ernest 1901-1985 ... 93-96
Obituary ... 117
Nagel, Heiderose Fischer
See Fischer-Nagel, Heiderose
Nagel, James (Edward) 1940- ... CANR-27
Earlier sketch in CA 29-32R
Nagel, Otto 1894-1967 Obituary ... 106
Nagel, Paul C(hester) 1926- ... CANR-22
Earlier sketches in CA 9-12R, CANR-5
Nagel, Shirley 1922- ... 93-96
Nagel, Stuart S(amuel) 1934- ... CANR-33
Earlier sketches in CA 33-36R, CANR-14
Nagel, Thomas 1937- ... CANR-4
Earlier sketch in CA 53-56
Nagel, William G(eorge) 1916- ... 49-52
Nagem, Monique F. 1941- ... 140
Nagenda, John 1938- ... 142
See also BW 2
Nagenda, Musa
See Howard, Moses L(eon)
Nagera, Humberto 1927- ... 57-60
Nagi, Mostafa H. 1934- ... 33-36R
Nagi, Saad Z. 1925- ... 29-32R

Nagle, James J. 1909-1978 ... 85-88
Obituary ... 81-84
Naglee, David Ingersoll 1930- ... 53-56
Nagler, Alois Maria 1907-1993 ... CANR-19
Obituary ... 141
Earlier sketch in CA 103
Nagler, Barney 1912-1990 ... 17-20R
Obituary ... 132
Nagler, Michael N(icholas) 1937- ... CANR-13
Earlier sketch in CA 73-76
na Gopaleen, Myles
See O Nuallain, Brian
Nagorski, Andrew 1947- ... 93-96
Nagorski, Zygmunt, Jr. 1912- ... 73-76
Nagorski, Zygmunt 1885(?)-1973 Obituary ... 41-44R
Nagourney, Peter (Jon) 1940- ... 37-40R
Nagrin, Daniel 1917- ... 148
Naguib, Mohammed 1902(?)-1984 Obituary ... 113
Nagy, Ferenc 1903-1979 Obituary ... 89-92
Nagy, Gil D. 1933- ... 25-28R
Nagy, Gloria ... 148
Nagy, Gregory 1942- ... 102
Nagy, Imre 1895(?)-1958 Brief entry ... 118
Nagy, Laszlo 1925-1978 ... 129
Obituary ... 112
See also CLC 7
Nagy-Talavera, Nicholas M(anuel) 1929- ... 33-36R
Naha, Ed 1950- ... CANR-57
Earlier sketch in CA 109
Nahal, Chaman 1927- ... CANR-17
Earlier sketch in CA 37-40R
Nahas, Gabriel G(eorges) 1920- ... CANR-17
Earlier sketches in CA 49-52, CANR-1
Nahas, Rebecca 1946- ... 69-72
Nahem, Joseph 1917- ... 113
Nahm, Milton C(harles) 1903-1991 ... 13-16R
Obituary ... 133
Nahum, Lucien 1930(?)-1983 Obituary ... 111
Naidis, Mark 1918- ... 33-36R
Naidoo, Beverley 1943- ... 160
See also AAYA 23
See also CLR 29
See also SATA 63
Naidu, Prabhakar S. 1937- ... 163
Naidu, Sarojini 1879-1943 ... TCLC 80
Naifeh, Steven Woodward 1952- ... CANR-40
Earlier sketch in CA 102
Naik, Madhukar Krishna 1926- ... CANR-25
Earlier sketches in CA 21-24R, CANR-10
Naim, C(houdhri) M(ohammed) 1936- Brief entry ... 112
Naiman, Arthur 1941- ... CANR-29
Earlier sketch in CA 108
Naimy, Mikhail 1889-1988 Obituary ... 124
Naipaul, Shiva(dhar Srinivasa) 1945-1985 ... CANR-33
Obituary ... 116
Brief entry ... 110
Earlier sketch in CA 112
See also CLC 32, 39
See also DAM NOV
See also DLB 157
See also DLBY 85
See also MTCW 1
Naipaul, V(idiadhar) S(urajprasad) 1932- ... CANR-51
Earlier sketches in CA 1-4R, CANR-1, 33
See also CDBLB 1960 to Present
See also CLC 4, 7, 9, 13, 18, 37, 105
See also DAB
See also DAC
See also DAM MST, NOV
See also DLB 125
See also DLBY 85
See also MTCW 1
Nairn, Ian (Douglas) 1930-1983 Obituary ... 110
Nairn, Ronald C(harles) 1922- ... 21-24R
Nairne, Katharine Davina 1949- ... 128
Nairne, Kathy
See Nairne, Katharine Davina
Naisawald, L. Van Loan 1920- ... CANR-6
Earlier sketch in CA 5-8R
Naisbitt, John 1929- ... 128
Brief entry ... 113
See also BEST 90:3
Naismith, Grace (Akin) 1904-1983 ... CANR-20
Obituary ... 111
Earlier sketch in CA 65-68
Naismith, Helen 1929- ... 69-72
Naismith, Horace
See Helmer, William J(oseph)
Naismith, James 1861-1939 Brief entry ... 118
Naismith, Marion (Overend) 1922- ... 29-32R
Naismith, Robert J. 1916- ... CANR-47
Earlier sketch in CA 121
Naj, Amal K. 1951- ... 140
Najafi, Najmeh ... 25-28R
Najarian, Nevart 1901(?)-1985 Obituary ... 117
Najder, Zdzislaw 1930- ... 17-20R
Najemy, John Michael 1943- ... 118
Nakadate, Neil Edward 1943- ... 115
Nakae, Noriko 1940- ... 49-52
See also SATA 59
Nakagami, Kenji 1946-1992 ... DLB 182
Nakamura, Hajime 1912- ... CANR-10
Earlier sketch in CA 53-56
Nakamura, James I. 1919- ... 21-24R
Nakamura, Yasuo 1919- ... 45-48
Nakanishi, Don T(oshiaki) 1949- ... 114
Nakanishi, Marsha
See Hirano-Nakanishi, Marsha J(oyce)
Nakanishi, Marsha J(oyce) Hirano
See Hirano-Nakanishi, Marsha J(oyce)
Nakano, Desmond ... 134
Nakano, Hirotaka 1942- ... 33-36R
Nakarai, Toyozo W(ada) 1898- ... 41-44R
Nakashima, George Katsutoshi 1905- ... 106
Nakatani, Chiyoko 1930-1981 ... 77-80
See also CLR 30
See also SATA 55
See also SATA-Brief 40
Nakayama, Shigeru 1928- ... 29-32R
Nakdimon, Shlomo 1936- ... CANR-60
Earlier sketch in CA 128
Nakhimovsky, Alice Stone 1950- ... 139
Nakhleh, Emile A. 1938- ... 77-80
Nakhnikian, George 1920- ... CANR-2
Earlier sketch in CA 1-4R
Nakos, Lilika 1899(?)- ... CLC 29
Nalder, Eric C(hristopher) 1946- ... 89-92
Nale, Sharon Anne 1944- ... 108
Nall, Barry T(homas) 1948- ... 141
Nall, Hiram Abiff 1950- ... 57-60
Nall, T(orney) Otto 1900- ... 17-20R
Nallin, Walter E. 1917(?)-1978 Obituary ... 77-80
Nally, Susan W. 1947- ... 155
See also SATA 90
Nalty, Bernard Charles 1931- ... CANR-18
Earlier sketch in CA 102
Nam, Charles B(enjamin) 1926- ... CANR-10
Earlier sketch in CA 65-68
Nam, Koon Woo 1928- ... 61-64
Namath, Joe
See Namath, Joseph William
Namath, Joseph William 1943- ... 89-92
Namba, Toshio 1910-1987 Obituary ... 124
Nambiar, O. K. 1910- ... 13-16R
Nameroff, Rochelle 1943- ... 41-44R
Namias, June 1941- ... 81-84
Namier, Julia 1893-1977 ... 61-64
Obituary ... 120
Namier, Lewis Bernstein 1888-1960 Obituary ... 113
Namikawa, Banri 1931- ... CANR-8
Earlier sketch in CA 53-56
Namikawa, Ryo 1905- ... 93-96
Namioka, Lensey 1929- ... CANR-52
Earlier sketches in CA 69-72, CANR-11, 27
See also AAYA 27
See also CLR 48
See also SAAS 24
See also SATA 27, 89
Namir, Mordecai 1897-1975 Obituary ... 57-60
Namjoshi, Suniti 1941- ... CANR-59
Earlier sketch in CA 113
Namora, Fernando (Goncalves) 1919-1989 Obituary ... 127
Namovicz, Gene Inyart 1927- ... 17-20R
See also Inyart, Gene
Nanassy, Louis C(harles) 1913- ... CANR-41
Earlier sketches in CA 53-56, CANR-4, 19
Nance, Guinevera Ann 1939- ... 106
Nance, James Clark 1893(?)-1984 Obituary ... 113
Nance, John J. 1946- ... 137
Nance, Joseph Milton 1913- ... CANR-1
Earlier sketch in CA 1-4R
Nanda, B(al) R(am) 1917- ... CANR-47
Earlier sketches in CA 13-16R, CANR-7, 23
Nandakumar, Prema 1939- ... 9-12R
Nandy, Pritish 1947- ... CANR-12
Earlier sketch in CA 65-68
Nangia, Sudesh 1942- ... CANR-22
Earlier sketches in CA 53-56, CANR-4
NanKivell, Joice M.
See Loch, Joice N(anKivell)
Nannes, Caspar Harold 1906-1978 ... 9-12R
Obituary ... 81-84
Nanogak Agnes 1925- ... SATA 61
Nanry, Charles (Anthony) 1938- ... 73-76
Nanus, Burt 1936- ... 115
Napier, B(unyan) Davie 1915- ... CANR-4
Earlier sketch in CA 1-4R
Napier, Bill 1940- ... 130
Napier, Geraldine
See Glemser, Bernard
Napier, Mark
See Laffin, John (Alfred Charles)
Napier, Mary
See Wright, (Mary) Patricia
Napier, Nancy J. 1945- ... 144
Napier, Priscilla 1908- ... 21-24R
Napier, William
See Seymour, William Napier
Napjus, Alice James 1913- ... 21-24R
Napjus, James
See Napjus, Alice James
Napley, David 1915-1994 ... 129
Obituary ... 146
Napley, Sir David
See Napley, David
Napoleon, Art
See Sudhalter, Richard M(errill)
Napoli, Donna Jo 1948- ... 156
See also AAYA 25
See also CLR 51
See also SAAS 23
See also SATA 92
Napolitan, Joseph 1929- ... 37-40R
Napolitane, Catherine A(nn) Durrum 1936- ... 85-88
Naraghi, Ehsan 1926- ... 147
Narahashi, Keiko 1959- ... SATA 79
Narain, Jai Prakash
See Narayan, Jayaprakash
Narang, Gopi Chand 1931- ... CANR-31
Earlier sketches in CA 29-32R, CANR-14
Naranjo, Carmen 1930- ... DLB 145
Naranjo, Claudio 1932- ... 147
Narasimhachar, K. T.
See Narasimha Char, K. T.
Narasimha Char, K. T. 1903- ... CANR-5
Earlier sketch in CA 53-56
Narasimhan, Chakravarthi V. 1915- ... 17-20R
Narayan, Jayaprakash 1902-1979 ... 97-100
Obituary ... 89-92
Narayan, Ongkar 1926- ... 103
Narayan, R(asipuram) K(rishnaswami) 1906- ... CANR-61
Earlier sketches in CA 81-84, CANR-33
See also CLC 7, 28, 47
See also DAM NOV
See also MTCW 1
See also SATA 62
See also SSC 25
Narayn, Deane 1929- ... 1-4R
Nardi, James B. 1948- ... 127
Nardi, Peter M. 1947- ... 144
Nardin, Terry 1942- ... 41-44R
Narell, Irena 1923- ... CANR-1
Earlier sketch in CA 1-4R
Naremore, James 1941- ... CANR-11
Earlier sketch in CA 69-72
Narezhny, Vasilii Trofimovich 1780-1825 ... DLB 198
Naroll, Raoul 1920-1985 ... 33-36R
Obituary ... 116
Narrache, Jean
See Coderre, Emile
See also DLB 92
Narramore, Stanley Bruce 1941- ... 57-60
Naruse, Mikio 1905-1969 ... 118
Narveson, Jan F(redric) 1936- ... CANR-24
Earlier sketches in CA 21-24R, CANR-9
Nasar, Jack L. 1947- ... 164
Nasatir, A(braham) P(hineas) 1904- ... CANR-5
Earlier sketch in CA 9-12R
Nasatir, David 1934- ... 41-44R
Nasaw, David 1945- ... 116
Nasaw, Jonathan Lewis 1947- ... CANR-63
Earlier sketch in CA 61-64
Nasby, A(sher Gordon) 1909-1983 Obituary ... 109
Nasby, Petroleum Vesuvius
See Locke, David Ross
Nash, Alanna 1950- ... 129
Nash, Allan N(ylin) 1932- ... 41-44R
Nash, Bruce M(itchell) 1947- ... CANR-15
Earlier sketch in CA 85-88
See also SATA 34
Nash, Daniel
See Loader, William Reginald
Nash, David T(heodore) 1929- ... 93-96
Nash, Elizabeth (Hamilton) 1934- ... 142
Nash, Eno
See Stevens, Austin N(eil)
Nash, Ethel Miller 1909- ... CAP-1
Earlier sketch in CA 13-16
Nash, Father Stephen
See Kavanaugh, James J(oseph)
Nash, Gary B. 1933- ... 37-40R
Nash, George (E.) 1948- ... 138
Nash, Gerald D(avid) 1928- ... CANR-8
Earlier sketch in CA 21-24R
Nash, Howard P(ervear), Jr. 1900-1981 ... 73-76
Obituary ... 133
Nash, Isabel
See Eberstadt, Isabel
Nash, J(essie) Madeleine 1943- ... 69-72
Nash, James E(dward) 1933- ... 29-32R
Nash, Jay Robert 1937- ... 21-24R
Nash, June (Caprice) 1927- ... 29-32R
Nash, (Cyril) Knowlton 1927- ... 135
Nash, Lee (Marten) 1927- ... 41-44R
Nash, Linell
See Smith, Linell Nash
Nash, Manning 1924- ... 17-20R
Nash, Mary (Hughes) 1925- ... 5-8R
See also SATA 41
Nash, Mary 1947- ... 163
Nash, Michael R. 1951- ... 148
Nash, N. Richard 1913- ... CANR-14
Earlier sketch in CA 85-88
Interview in ... CANR-14
Nash, Nancy 1943- ... 21-24R
Nash, Newlyn
See Howe, Doris Kathleen
Nash, (Fredric) Ogden 1902-1971 ... CANR-61
Obituary ... 29-32R
Earlier sketches in CAP-1, CA 13-14, CANR-34
See also CLC 23
See also DAM POET
See also DLB 11
See also MAICYA
See also MTCW 1
See also PC 21
See also SATA 2, 46
Nash, Padder
See Sewart, Alan
Nash, Paul 1924- ... 17-20R
Nash, Ralph (Lee) 1925- ... 17-20R
Nash, Ray 1905-1982 Obituary ... 106
Nash, Renea Denise 1963- ... 149
See also SATA 81
Nash, Robert 1902- ... CAP-1
Earlier sketch in CA 9-10
Nash, Roderick 1939- ... 17-20R
Nash, Ronald H. 1936- ... CANR-49
Earlier sketches in CA 5-8R, CANR-8, 23
Nash, Simon
See Chapman, Raymond
Nash, Stan
See Nash, Stanley D.
Nash, Stanley D. 1946- ... 147
Nash, Susan Smith 1958- ... CAAS 25
Nash, William (Wray), Jr. 1928- ... 85-88
Nashe, Thomas 1567-1601(?) ... DLB 167
Naske, Claus-M(ichael) 1935- ... CANR-57
Earlier sketches in CA 77-80, CANR-13, 31
Naslund, Erik
See Naeslund, Erik
Nason, Alvin 1919-1978 Obituary ... 77-80
Nason, Donna 1944- ... 97-100
Nason, Leonard H(astings) 1895-1970 Obituary ... 114
Nason, Leslie J. ... 5-8R
Nason, Tema ... 138
Nason, Thelma
See Nason, Tema
Nasr, Kameel 1949- ... 141
Nasr, Seyyed Hossein 1933- ... CANR-10
Earlier sketch in CA 21-24R
Nass, Elyse (Linda) 1947- ... 111
Nass, Stanley 1940- ... 115
Nassaar, Christopher S(uhayl) 1944- ... 97-100
Nassar, Eugene Paul 1935- ... 33-36R
Nassau, Wilhelmina Helena Pauline Maria 1880-1962 Obituary ... 113
Nassauer, Rudolf 1924- ... 105
Nasser, Gamal Abdel 1918-1970 Obituary ... 113
Nassivera, John 1950- ... 109
Nasson, Bill 1952- ... 139
Nassour, Ellis (Michael) 1941- ... CANR-43
Earlier sketch in CA 119
Nast, Conde 1873-1942 ... DLB 91
Nast, Elsa Ruth
See Watson, Jane Werner
Nast, Thomas 1840-1902 Brief entry ... 112
See also DLB 188
See also SATA 51
See also SATA-Brief 33
Nastasijevic, Momcilo 1894-1938 ... DLB 147
Nastick, Sharon 1954- ... 114
See also SATA 41
Natale, Samuel M(ichael) 1943- ... 116
Natali, Alfred Maxim 1915- ... 57-60
Natanson, George 1928- ... 73-76
Natanson, Maurice (Alexander) 1924-1996 ... CANR-12
Obituary ... 153
Earlier sketch in CA 17-20R
Natchez, Gladys W. 1915-1994 ... CANR-4
Obituary ... 145
Earlier sketch in CA 9-12R
Natella, Arthur A(ristides), Jr. 1941- ... CANR-43
Earlier sketches in CA 89-92, CANR-15
Nathan, Adele (Gutman) 1900(?)-1986 ... 73-76
Obituary ... 119
See also SATA-Obit 48
Nathan, Andrew J(ames) 1943- ... 65-68
Nathan, Daniel
See Dannay, Frederic
Nathan, David 1926- ... CANR-12
Earlier sketch in CA 29-32R
Nathan, Debbie ... 160
Nathan, Dorothy (Goldeen) (?)-1966 ... 81-84
See also SATA 15
Nathan, George Jean 1882-1958 Brief entry ... 114
See also Hatteras, Owen
See also DLB 137
See also TCLC 18
Nathan, Hans 1910- ... CANR-1
Earlier sketch in CA 1-4R
Nathan, James A. 1942- ... CANR-16
Earlier sketch in CA 85-88
Nathan, Jean
See Levinsohn, Florence H(amlish)
Nathan, Joan 1943- ... 61-64
Nathan, Joe 1948- ... 115
Nathan, Leonard E(dward) 1924- ... CANR-69
Earlier sketches in CA 5-8R, CANR-7
Nathan, Norman 1915- ... CANR-1
Earlier sketch in CA 1-4R
Nathan, Otto 1893-1987 Obituary ... 121
Nathan, Paul S. 1913- ... 148
Brief entry ... 116
Nathan, Peter E. 1935- ... 73-76
Nathan, Richard P(erle) 1935- ... CANR-7
Earlier sketch in CA 57-60
Nathan, Robert (Gruntal) 1894-1985 ... CANR-55
Obituary ... 116
Earlier sketches in CA 13-16R, CANR-6
See also DLB 9
See also SATA 6
See also SATA-Obit 43
Nathan, Robert Stuart 1948- ... 81-84
Nathanson, Carol (Edna) 1922- ... 132
Nathanson, Jerome 1908-1975 Obituary ... 57-60
Nathanson, Laura Walther 1941- ... 123
See also SATA 57
Nathanson, Leonard 1933- ... 21-24R
Nathanson, Nathaniel L(ouis) 1908-1983 ... 89-92
Obituary ... 111
Nathanson, Paul 1947- ... 140
Nathanson, Yale S(amuel) 1895- ... 77-80
Nathiri, N. Y. 1948- ... 141
Nations, Opal (Louis) 1941- ... 112
Natkin, Rick 1952- ... 129
Natoli, Joseph
See Natoli, Joseph P.
Natoli, Joseph P. 1943- ... 132
Natow, Annette 1933- ... 114
Natsume, Kinnosuke 1867-1916 Brief entry ... 104
See also Natsume, Soseki
Natsume, Soseki 1867-1916
See Natsume, Kinnosuke
See also DLB 180
See also TCLC 2, 10
Natta, Giulio 1903-1979 Obituary ... 113
Natti, (Mary) Lee 1919- ... CANR-2
Earlier sketch in CA 5-8R
See also Kingman, Lee
Natti, Susanna 1948- ... SATA 32
Nattiez, Jean-Jacques 1945- ... 146
Natusch, Sheila (Ellen) 1926- ... CANR-44
Earlier sketches in CA 103, CANR-20
Natwar-Singh, K. 1931- ... 13-16R
Nau, Erika S(chwager) 1918- ... 65-68
Nau, Henry R(ichard) 1941- ... 135

Naude, (Aletta) Adele da Fonseca-Wollheim
1910- 9-12R
Nauer, Barbara Joan 1932- Brief entry 105
Naughton, Bill
See Naughton, William John (Francis)
Naughton, James Franklin 1957- 132
See also SATA 85
Naughton, Jim
See Naughton, James Franklin
Naughton, John 1933- 57-60
Naughton, William John (Francis) 1910-1992 ....
CANR-61
Obituary 136
Earlier sketches in CA 105, CANR-36
See also DLB 13
See also MTCW 1
See also SATA 86
Naugle, Helen Harrold 1920- 53-56
Naugle, John E(arl) 1923- 65-68
Nauheim, Ferd(inand Alan) 1909- CANR-16
Earlier sketches in CA 49-52, CANR-1
Nauman, St. Elmo, Jr. 1935- 53-56
Naumann, Anthony Frank 1921-1971 .... 21-24R
Obituary 89-92
Naumann, Marina 1938- 93-96
Naumann, Oscar E(dward) 1912- 77-80
Naumann, Rose 1919- 65-68
Naumburg, Margaret 1890-1983 Obituary 109
Naumoff, Lawrence 1946- CANR-66
Earlier sketch in CA 128
Naureckas, Jim 1964- 154
Nauticus
See Waltari, Mika (Toimi)
Nava, Gregory 1949- 131
See also HW
Nava, Julian 1927- 61-64
See also HW
Nava, Michael 1954- 124
Nava, Roberto 1906(?)-1983 Obituary 111
Navarra, Fernand Jean 1915- 108
Navarra, John Gabriel 1927- 41-44R
See also SATA 8
Navarra, Tova 1948- 149
Navarre, Yves (Henri Michel) 1940-1994 133
Obituary 143
Navarro, Antonio 1922- 107
Navarro (Gerassi), Marysa 1934- 106
Navarro, Peter 1949- 118
Navarro, Yvonne 1957- 168
Navas, Deborah 1943- 112
Navasky, Victor S. 1932- CANR-10
Earlier sketch in CA 21-24R
Interview in CANR-10
Navas-Ruiz, Ricardo 1932- Brief entry 107
Navone, John J(oseph) 1930- CANR-52
Earlier sketches in CA 21-24R, CANR-10, 28
Navrozov, Andrei 1956- 144
Navrozov, Lev 1928- 61-64
Naydler, Merton 1920- 45-48
Naylor, Chris(topher Michael) 1947- 118
Naylor, Eric W(oodfin) 1936- 45-48
Naylor, Gloria 1950- CANR-51
Earlier sketches in CA 107, CANR-27
See also AAYA 6
See also BLC 3
See also BW 2
See also CLC 28, 52
See also DA
See also DAC
See also DAM MST, MULT, NOV, POP
See also DLB 173
See also MTCW 1
See also WLCS
Naylor, Harriet H. 1915- CANR-9
Earlier sketch in CA 21-24R
Naylor, James C(harles) 1932- CANR-1
Earlier sketch in CA 45-48
Naylor, John 1920- 93-96
Naylor, Margot Ailsa (Lodge) 1907-1972 .... 9-12R
Obituary 134
Naylor, Penelope 1941- 37-40R
See also SATA 10
Naylor, Phyllis (Reynolds) 1933- CANR-59
Earlier sketches in CA 21-24R, CANR-8, 24
See also AAYA 4
See also CLR 17
See also JRDA
See also MAICYA
See also SAAS 10
See also SATA 12, 66, 102
Nayman, Michele 147
Nazareth, Peter 1940- 101
Nazarian, Nikki
See Nichols, Cecilia Fawn
Nazaroff, Alexander I. 1898- 33-36R
See also SATA 4
Nazor, Vladimir 1876-1949 .... DLB 147
Nazzaro, Anthony M. 1927- Brief entry 106
Ndebele, Njabulo 1948- .... DLB 157
Neagle, Anna 1904-1986 Obituary 119
Neagley, Ross Linn 1907- 106
Neagoe, Anna (Frankel)
1885(?)-1986 Obituary 120
Neagoe, Peter 1881-1960 105
See also DLB 4
Neal, Alfred C. 1912- 121
Neal, Ann Parker 1934- 158
Brief entry 114
Neal, Arminta Pearl 1921- 85-88
Neal, Bruce W(alter) 1931- 21-24R
Neal, Charles Dempsey 1908- CANR-5
Earlier sketch in CA 5-8R
Neal, Emily Gardiner CANR-3
Earlier sketch in CA 5-8R
Neal, Ernest G(ordon) 1911-1998 .... 13-16R
Obituary 165
Neal, Fred Warner 1915- CANR-2
Earlier sketch in CA 5-8R
Neal, Harry
See Bixby, Jerome Lewis
Neal, Harry Edward 1906-1993 .... CANR-2
Obituary 141
Earlier sketch in CA 5-8R
See also SATA 5
See also SATA-Obit 76
Neal, Helen Keating 1907-1987 124
Obituary 122
Neal, Hilary
See Norton, Olive (Claydon)
Neal, James M(adison) 1925- 73-76
Neal, James T(homas) 1936- 57-60
Neal, John 1793-1876 .... DLB 1, 59
Neal, Joseph C. 1807-1847 .... DLB 11
Neal, Julia 1905- 69-72
Neal, Larry
See Neal, Lawrence (P.)
See also DLB 38
Neal, Lawrence (P.) 1937-1981 81-84
Obituary 102
See also Neal, Larry
See also BW 1
Neal, Marie Augusta 1921- CANR-35
Earlier sketches in CA 114, CANR-32
Neal, Michael
See Teitelbaum, Michael
Neal, Nelson 1921(?)-1983 Obituary 109
Neal, Patsy 1938- 61-64
Neal, W(illiam) Keith 1905-1990 Obituary 131
Neale, Gay Weeks 1935- 113
Neale, John E(rnest) 1890-1975 65-68
Obituary 61-64
Neale, R(onald) S(tanley) 1927-1985 157
Neale, Robert George 1919- Brief entry 108
Neale, Walter Castle 1925- CANR-7
Earlier sketch in CA 5-8R
Neale-Silva, Eduardo 1905- Brief entry 106
Nealon, Eleanor 103
Nealon, Thomas E. 1933- 33-36R
Neaman, Judith S(ilverman) 1936- 61-64
Neame, Alan John 1924- CANR-2
Earlier sketch in CA 1-4R
Near, Holly 1949- 143
Nearing, Guy 1890-1986 Obituary 118
Nearing, Helen K(nothe) 1904-1995 .... CANR-11
Obituary 149
Earlier sketch in CA 29-32R
Nearing, Penny 1916- 81-84
See also SATA 47
See also SATA-Brief 42
Nearing, Scott 1883-1983 .... CANR-11
Obituary 110
Earlier sketch in CA 41-44R
Neary, John (Anthony, Jr.) 1937- Brief entry 107
Neatby, H(erbert) Blair 1924- Brief entry 111
Neatby, Leslie Hamilton 1902- CANR-3
Earlier sketch in CA 5-8R
Neate, Frank Anthony 1928- 105
Neave, Airey (Middleton Sheffield) 1916-1979 85-88
Neavles, Janet Talmadge 1919- 5-8R
Nebel, Gustave E. .... SATA 45
See also SATA-Brief 33
Nebel, Mimouca
See Nebel, Gustave E.
Nebenzahl, Kenneth 1927- 111
Brief entry 109
Nebrensky, Alex
See Cooper, Parley J(oseph)
Nebylitsyn, Vladimir Dmitrievich
1930(?)-1972 Obituary 37-40R
Nechas, Eileen (T.) 1944- 146
Necheles, Ruth F. 1936- 41-44R
Necker, Claire (Kral) 1917- 33-36R
Nederhood, Joel H(oman) 1930- 29-32R
Nee, Brett de Bary 1943- 101
Nee, Kay Bonner CANR-31
Earlier sketches in CA 49-52, CANR-2
See also SATA 10
Needham, David C. 1929- 118
Needham, (Noel) Joseph (Terence Montgomery)
1900-1995 .... CANR-34
Obituary 148
Earlier sketches in CA 9-12R, CANR-5
Needham, Kate 1962- 160
See also SATA 95
Needham, Richard (John) 1912- 101
Needham, Rodney 1923- CANR-15
Earlier sketch in CA 81-84
Needham, (Amy) Violet 1876-1967 Obituary 116
Needle, Jan 1943- CANR-28
Earlier sketch in CA 106
See also AAYA 23
See also CLR 43
See also SAAS 23
See also SATA 30, 98
Needleman, Jacob 1934- CANR-12
Earlier sketch in CA 29-32R
See also SATA 6
Needleman, Morriss H. 1907- 25-28R
Needler, Howard I(an) 1937- 111
Needler, Martin C(yril) 1933- CANR-18
Earlier sketches in CA 5-8R, CANR-2
Needles, Robert Johnson 1903- CAP-1
Earlier sketch in CA 11-12
Neef, Elton T.
See Fanthorpe, R(obert) Lionel
Neel, (Louis) Boyd 1905-1981 Obituary 108
Neel, David 1960- .... SATA 82
Neel, Janet
See Cohen, Janet
Neel, Jasper 1946- 151
Neel, Joanne Loewe 1920- 25-28R
Neel, Louis (Eugene Felix) 1904- 167
Neel, Preston 1959- .... SATA 93
Neeld, Elizabeth Harper 1940- 141
Neely, Bill 1930- CANR-28
Earlier sketches in CA 33-36R, CANR-13
Neely, Carol Thomas 1939- 128
Brief entry 107
Neely, James C. 1926- 109
Neely, Mark E(dward), Jr. 1944- CANR-25
Earlier sketch in CA 106
Neely, Martina 1939- 61-64
Neely, Richard (Forlani) 1941- CANR-28
Earlier sketch in CA 107
Neenan, Colin 1958- 151
Neenan, William B(raunger) 1929- 41-44R
Neeper, Carolyn 1937- 57-60
Neeper, Cary
See Neeper, Carolyn
Neerskov, Hans Kristian 1932- 65-68
Nees, Lawrence 1949- 139
Nef, Evelyn Stefansson 1913- CANR-20
Earlier sketch in CA 49-52
Nef, John Ulric 1899-1988 .... CANR-20
Obituary 127
Earlier sketch in CA 1-4R
Nefedova, Tatyana 1949- 166
Neff, Alan (Henry) 1949- 117
Neff, Donald (Lloyd) 1930- CANR-28
Earlier sketch in CA 77-80
Neff, Emery E. 1892-1983 .... 5-8R
Obituary 109
Neff, H(arry) Richard 1933- 33-36R
Neff, Hildegard
See Knef, Hildegard
Neff, John C. 1913- 17-20R
Neff, Kirk Powis 1950- 163
Neff, Miriam 1945- 115
Neff, Renfreu (de St. Laurence) 1938- 29-32R
Neff, Robert W(ilbur) 1936- 106
Neff, Walter S(cott) 1910- CAP-2
Earlier sketch in CA 25-28
Neff, William Lee 1906-1973 .... 1-4R
Obituary 103
Neft, David S(amuel) 1937- 41-44R
Negandhi, A(nant) R(anchoddas) 1933- 33-36R
Neggers, Carla A(malia) 1955- CANR-30
Earlier sketch in CA 112
Negley, Glenn (Robert) 1907-1988 .... 17-20R
Obituary 125
Negri, Ada 1870-1945 .... DLB 114
Negri, Rocco 1932- .... SATA 12
Negroponte, Nicholas Peter 1943- 29-32R
Negus, Arthur George 1903-1985 Obituary 116
Negus, Kenneth George 1927- 17-20R
Nehamas, Alexander 1946- 126
Neher, Andre 1914- CANR-26
Earlier sketch in CA 109
Neher, Clark D(umont) 1938- 118
Neher, Erwin 1944- 156
Neher, Jack 1918- 118
Nehring, James 1958- 140
Nehrling, Arno H. 1886-1974 .... 9-12R
Obituary 53-56
Nehrling, Irene Dahlberg 1900- 9-12R
Nehrt, Lee Charles 1926- CANR-13
Earlier sketch in CA 21-24R
Nehru, Jawaharlal 1889-1964 .... CANR-34
Earlier sketch in CA 85-88
See also MTCW 1
Neiburg, Gladys Eudas 1898- 61-64
Neider, Charles 1915- CANR-24
Earlier sketch in CA 17-20R
Interview in CANR-24
Neiderman, Andrew 1940- CANR-13
Earlier sketch in CA 33-36R
Neidermyer, Dan 1947- CANR-24
Earlier sketch in CA 45-48
Neidhardt, W(ilfried) S(teffen) 1941- 65-68
Neidhart von Reuental c. 1185-c. 1240 .... DLB 138
Neidpath, James
See Charteris, James Donald
Neier, Aryeh 1937- 57-60
See also SATA 59
Neighbour, Ralph W(ebster) 1906- CANR-1
Earlier sketch in CA 1-4R
Neighbour, Rhona M.
See Martin, Rhona
Neighbours, Kenneth Franklin 1915- 61-64
Neigoff, Anne 41-44R
See also SATA 13
Neigoff, Mike 1920- CANR-2
Earlier sketch in CA 5-8R
See also SATA 13
Neihardt, John Gneisenau 1881-1973 .... CANR-65
Earlier sketches in CAP-1, CA 13-14
See also CLC 32
See also DLB 9, 54
Neikirk, William (Robert) 1938- 117
Neil, Hugh Michael 1930- Brief entry 109
Neil, J. Meredith 1937- 33-36R
Neil, Randolph L. 1941- 93-96
Neil, Randy
See Neil, Randolph L.
Neil, William 1909-1979 .... CANR-6
Obituary 93-96
Earlier sketch in CA 9-12R
Neilan, Sarah 69-72
Neilands, J(ohn) B(rian) 1921- 97-100
Neill, A(lexander) S(utherland) 1883-1973 101
Obituary 45-48
Neill, Christopher Harry Douglas 1955- 117
Neill, Stephen Charles 1900-1984 .... CANR-7
Obituary 113
Earlier sketch in CA 9-12R
Neill, Thomas Patrick 1915-1970 .... CANR-3
Earlier sketch in CA 5-8R
Neilson, Andrew 1946- CANR-27
Earlier sketch in CA 110
Neilson, Frances Fullerton (Jones) 1910- 73-76
See also SATA 14
Neilson, James Warren 1933- 1-4R
Neilson, Marguerite
See Tompkins, Julia (Marguerite Hunter Manchee)
Neilson, Melany 1958- 132
Neilson, N(eils) P. 1895- CANR-2
Earlier sketch in CA 5-8R
Neiman, David 1921- 69-72
Neiman, Fraser 1911- 25-28R
Neiman, Morris 1910(?)-1989 Obituary 130
Neimark, Anne E. 1935- CANR-36
Earlier sketches in CA 29-32R, CANR-16
See also SATA 4
Neimark, Edith D(eborah) 1928- 41-44R
Neimark, Paul G. 1934- 135
Brief entry 115
See also SATA 80
See also SATA-Brief 37
Neipris, Janet
See Wille, Janet Neipris
Neisser, Hans P(hilip) 1895-1975 .... CAP-1
Obituary 53-56
Earlier sketch in CA 13-16
Neisser, Ulric 1928- CANR-55
Earlier sketches in CA 108, CANR-26
Neitzel, Shirley 1941- .... SATA 77
Nekrasov, Viktor (Platonovich)
1911-1987 Obituary 123
Nekrich, Aleksandr M(oisei) 1920- 81-84
Neledinsky-Meletsky, Iurii Aleksandrovich
1752-1828 .... DLB 150
Neligan, David 1899- CAP-2
Earlier sketch in CA 29-32
Nelkin, Dorothy 1933- CANR-31
Earlier sketches in CA 41-44R, CANR-14
Nell
See Hanna, Nell(ie L.)
Nell, Edward John 1935- 65-68
Nell, Victor 1935- 136
Nelles, Henry Vivian 1942- 103
Nelli, Humbert S(teven) 1930- CANR-14
Earlier sketch in CA 41-44R
Nelligan, Emile 1879-1941 Brief entry 114
See also DLB 92
See also TCLC 14
Nellis, Muriel 102
Nellist, John B(owman) 1923- 25-28R
Nelms, C(larice) E. 1919- 25-28R
Nelms, Henning C(unningham)
1900-1986 Obituary 119
Nelsen, Anne Kusener 1942- 97-100
Nelsen, Hart M(ichael) 1938- CANR-8
Earlier sketch in CA 53-56
Nelson, A(ndrew) Thomas 1933- 5-8R
Nelson, Alan H(olm) 1938- 104
Nelson, Alice Fray 1911(?)-1983 Obituary 110
Nelson, Alice Ruth Moore Dunbar 1875-1935 124
Brief entry 122
See also BW 1
See also DLB 50
See also MTCW 1
Nelson, Alvin F(redolph) 1917-1973 .... CAP-2
Earlier sketch in CA 25-28
Nelson, Amirtharaj 1934- 57-60
Nelson, Andrew N(athaniel) 1893-1975 .... CANR-3
Earlier sketch in CA 5-8R
Nelson, Anne 1954- 123
Nelson, Antonya 1961- 138
Nelson, Benjamin N. 1911-1977 .... CANR-28
Obituary 73-76
Earlier sketch in CA 81-84
Nelson, Benjamin N(athaniel) 1935- CANR-1
Earlier sketch in CA 1-4R
Nelson, Beth
See Nelson, Mary Elizabeth
Nelson, Betty Palmer 1938- 134
Nelson, C(arl) Ellis 1916- 108
Nelson, Carl Leroy 1910- 104
Nelson, Carnot E(dward) 1941- 37-40R
Nelson, Carolyn W(illiamson) 1942- 150
Nelson, Cary (Robert) 1946- 49-52
Nelson, Catherine Chadwick 1926- .... SATA 87
Nelson, Charles Lamar 1917- 69-72
Nelson, Charles R(owe) 1942- 37-40R
Nelson, Cholmondeley M. 1903- 5-8R
Nelson, Claudia (Bedell) 1960- 150
Nelson, Clifford Ansgar 1906- CAP-1
Earlier sketch in CA 11-12
Nelson, Conny E(dwin) 1933- Brief entry 108
Nelson, Cordner (Bruce) 1918- 29-32R
See also SATA 54
See also SATA-Brief 29
Nelson, Dalmas H(ildor) 1925- 119
Nelson, Daniel 1941- 25-28R
Nelson, David Moir 1920- CANR-38
Earlier sketches in CA 1-4R, CANR-17
Nelson, Donald F. 1929- 37-40R
Nelson, Drew 1952- 145
See also SATA 77
Nelson, E(ugene) Clifford 1911- 13-16R
Nelson, Edna Deu Pree 5-8R
Nelson, Elof G. 1924- CANR-35
Earlier sketch in CA 21-24R
Nelson, Emmanuel S(ampath) 1954- 142
Nelson, Eric Hilliard 1940-1985 Obituary 118
Nelson, Esther L. 1928- CANR-53
Earlier sketches in CA 69-72, CANR-11, 28
See also SATA 13
Nelson, Ethel Florence 1913- CANR-6
Earlier sketch in CA 53-56
Nelson, Eugene 1929- 61-64
Nelson, F(rancis) William 1922- 13-16R

Nelson, Geoffrey K(enneth) 1923- ... CANR-49
Earlier sketches in CA 29-32R, CANR-24
Nelson, George (H.) 1908-1986 ... 81-84
Obituary ... 118
Nelson, George (Carl) E(dward) 1900-1982 ... CANR-24
Earlier sketch in CA 45-48
Nelson, Gideon E(dmund, Jr.) 1924- ... 53-56
Nelson, Harold A(lfred) 1932- ... 114
Nelson, Harold L(ewis) 1917- ... 93-96
Nelson, Herbert B(enjamin) 1903- ... CAP-2
Earlier sketch in CA 19-20
Nelson, Howard 1947- ... 136
Nelson, Indiana 1940- ... 97-100
Nelson, J. Bryan 1932- ... CANR-10
Earlier sketch in CA 25-28R
Nelson, J(oseph) Raleigh 1873-1961 Obituary . 110
Nelson, J(ohn) Robert 1920- ... CANR-19
Earlier sketches in CA 9-12R, CANR-3
Nelson, Jack
See Nelson, John Howard
Nelson, Jack L. 1932- ... CANR-10
Earlier sketch in CA 25-28R
Nelson, Jacquelyn S. 1950- ... 137
Nelson, James B(ruce) 1930- ... CANR-17
Earlier sketches in CA 49-52, CANR-1
Nelson, James C(ecil) 1908- ... CANR-13
Earlier sketch in CA 77-80
Nelson, James G(raham) 1929- ... 9-12R
Nelson, James L. 1962- ... 159
Nelson, Jan Alan 1935- ... 41-44R
Nelson, Jane Armstrong 1927- Brief entry ... 105
Nelson, Janet 1930- ... 115
Nelson, Jean Erichsen
See Erichsen-Nelson, Jean
Nelson, Jill 1952- ... 163
Nelson, John Charles 1925- ... 49-52
Nelson, John Howard 1929- ... 29-32R
Nelson, John Oliver 1909-1990 ... 37-40R
Obituary ... 131
Nelson, Joseph Schieser 1937- ... 73-76
Nelson, June Kompass 1920- ... 73-76
Nelson, Katherine Shaw 1926- ... 110
Nelson, Kay Shaw
See Nelson, Katherine Shaw
Nelson, Keith L(ebahn) 1932- Brief entry ... 113
Nelson, Kent 1943- ... 77-80
Nelson, L(ester) Ivar 1941- ... 119
Nelson, Lawrence E(rnest) 1928-1977 ... 53-56
Obituary ... 103
See also SATA-Obit 28
Nelson, Lawrence Emerson 1893-1978 ... 17-20R
Obituary ... 134
Nelson, Lois (Ney) 1930- ... 61-64
Nelson, Lowry, Jr. 1926- ... CANR-39
Earlier sketch in CA 5-8R
Nelson, Malcolm A. 1934- ... 45-48
Nelson, Marg (Raibley) 1899- ... CANR-2
Earlier sketch in CA 1-4R
Nelson, Marguerite
See Floren, Lee
Nelson, Mariah Burton 1956- ... 146
Nelson, Marilyn ... CANR-51
See also Waniek, Marilyn Nelson
See also CAAS 23
Nelson, Marion Harvey 1925- ... 9-12R
Nelson, Martha 1923- ... 29-32R
Nelson, Mary Carroll 1929- ... CANR-16
Earlier sketches in CA 49-52, CANR-1
See also SATA 23
Nelson, Mary Elizabeth 1926- ... 93-96
Nelson, Michael Harrington 1921- ... CANR-2
Earlier sketch in CA 5-8R
Nelson, Nina
See Nelson, Ethel Florence
Nelson, O. Terry 1941- ... SATA 62
Nelson, Oliver W(endell) 1904- ... 29-32R
Nelson, Oswald George 1907-1975 ... 93-96
Obituary ... 57-60
Nelson, Ozzie
See Nelson, Oswald George
Nelson, P. 1945- ... 145
Nelson, Paul David 1941- ... CANR-45
Earlier sketch in CA 120
Nelson, Peter
See Solow, Martin
Nelson, Peter 1940- ... CANR-12
Earlier sketch in CA 61-64
Nelson, Peter N. 1953- ... 140
See also SATA 73
Nelson, Philip Bradford 1951- ... 113
Nelson, R(adell) Faraday 1931- ... CANR-26
Earlier sketch in CA 69-72
Nelson, Rachel W(est) 1955- ... 117
Nelson, Ralph 1916-1987 ... 49-52
Obituary ... 124
Nelson, Ralph C(arl) 1927- ... 53-56
Nelson, Randy F(ranklin) 1948- ... 125
Brief entry ... 110
Nelson, Ray
See Nelson, R(adell) Faraday
Nelson, Raymond S(tanley) 1921- ... CANR-36
Earlier sketches in CA 45-48, CANR-1, 16
Nelson, Richard 1950- ... 129
Brief entry ... 123
Interview in ... 129
Nelson, Richard K(ing) 1941- ... CANR-30
Earlier sketches in CA 29-32R, CANR-12
See also SATA 65
Nelson, Richard R(obinson) 1930- ... CANR-16
Earlier sketch in CA 97-100
Nelson, Rick
See Nelson, Eric Hilliard
Nelson, Ricky
See Nelson, Eric Hilliard
Nelson, Robert James 1925- ... CANR-8
Earlier sketch in CA 5-8R
Nelson, Robert M(cDowell, Jr.) 1945- ... 146
Nelson, Rosanne E(ierdanz) 1939- ... 49-52
Nelson, Rowland Whiteway 1902-1979 Obituary ... 105
Nelson, Roy Paul 1923- ... CANR-45
Earlier sketches in CA 17-20R, CANR-7, 22
See also SATA 59
Nelson, Ruben F(rederick) W(erthenbach) 1939- ... CANR-58
Earlier sketches in CA 112, CANR-31
Nelson, Ruth 1914- ... 41-44R
Nelson, Ruth Youngdahl 1904(?)-1984 Obituary ... 112
Nelson, Severing E. 1896- ... 5-8R
Nelson, Sharlene (P.) 1933- ... 161
See also SATA 96
Nelson, Sharon H. 1948- ... 113
Nelson, Stanley 1933- ... CANR-39
Earlier sketches in CA 49-52, CANR-1, 18
Nelson, T. G. A. 1940- ... 154
Nelson, Ted (W.) 1931- ... 161
See also SATA 96
Nelson, Theresa 1948- ... 148
See also AAYA 25
See also SATA 79
Nelson, Thomas P. 1925(?)-1983 Obituary ... 110
Nelson, Truman (John Seymour) 1911-1987 ... CANR-1
Obituary ... 123
Earlier sketch in CA 1-4R
Nelson, W(esley) Dale 1927- ... 77-80
Nelson, Walter Henry 1928- ... CANR-7
Earlier sketch in CA 13-16R
Nelson, Warren L. 1940- ... 89-92
Nelson, William 1908-1978 ... 49-52
Obituary ... 103
See also DLB 103
Nelson, William R(ichard) 1924- ... 25-28R
Nelson, William Rockhill 1841-1915 ... DLB 23
Nelson, Willie 1933- ... 107
See also CLC 17
Nelton, Sharon (Lee) 1937- ... 123
Nemanic, Gerald Carl 1941- ... 107
Nemec, David 1938- ... CANR-2
Earlier sketch in CA 49-52
Nemerov, Howard (Stanley) 1920-1991 .. CANR-53
Obituary ... 134
Earlier sketches in CA 1-4R, CANR-1, 27
Interview in ... CANR-27
See also CABS 2
See also CLC 2, 6, 9, 36
See also DAM POET
See also DLB 5, 6
See also DLBY 83
See also MTCW 1
Nemeshegyi, Peter 1923- ... 130
Nemeth, Laszlo 1901-1975 ... 93-96
Obituary ... 57-60
Nemir, Alma 1902-1971 ... CAP-2
Earlier sketch in CA 29-32
Nemiro, Beverly Anderson 1925- ... CANR-5
Earlier sketch in CA 53-56
Nemiroff, Robert Brief entry ... 116
See also AITN 2
Nemirow, Steven 1949- ... 110
Nemmers, Erwin Esser 1916- ... 9-12R
Nemoianu, Virgil (Petre) 1940- ... 130
Nemow, A.
See Neznansky, Friedrich
Nemser, Cindy 1937- ... 61-64
Nena
See Saarikoski, Pentti (Ilmari)
Nenae
See Saarikoski, Pentti (Ilmari)
Nenni, Pietro 1891-1980 Obituary ... 105
Nepaulsingh, Colbert I(vor) 1943- ... 155
Nerbovig, Marcella H. 1919- ... 89-92
Nerburn, Kent Michael 1946- ... 166
Nere, Jacques 1917- ... 57-60
Nerhood, Harry W(arren) 1910- ... 29-32R
Nerin, William F. 1926- ... 142
Nerlich, Graham ... 73-76
Nerlove, Marc L(eon) 1933- ... 104
Nerlove, Miriam 1959- ... 121
See also SATA 53
See also SATA-Brief 49
Nernst, (Hermann) Walther 1864-1941 ... 157
Nersessian, Edward 1944- ... 162
Neruda, Pablo 1904-1973 ... CAP-2
Obituary ... 45-48
Earlier sketch in CA 19-20
See also CLC 1, 2, 5, 7, 9, 28, 62
See also DA
See also DAB
See also DAC
See also DAM MST, MULT, POET
See also HLC
See also HW
See also MTCW 1
See also PC 4
See also WLC
Nerval, Gaston
See Diez de Medina, Raul
Nerval, Gerard de 1808-1855 ... PC 13
See also SSC 18
Nervi, Pier Luigi 1891-1979 Obituary ... 113
Nervo, (Jose) Amado (Ruiz de) 1870-1919 ... 131
Brief entry ... 109
See also HW
See also TCLC 11
Nesaule, Agate 1938- ... 159
Nesbin, Esther W(inter) 1910- ... 41-44R
Nesbit, Andrew
See Kelly, Ronald
Nesbit, E(dith) 1858-1924 ... 137
Brief entry ... 118
See also CLR 3
See also DLB 141, 153, 178
See also MAICYA
See also SATA 100
See also YABC 1
Nesbit, Molly 1952- ... 142
Nesbit, Robert C(arrington) 1917- ... 45-48
Nesbit, Troy
See Folsom, Franklin (Brewster)
Nesbitt, Cathleen 1888-1982 Obituary ... 107
Nesbitt, Elizabeth 1897(?)-1977 Obituary ... 73-76
Nesbitt, George L(yman) 1903- ... 41-44R
Nesbitt, John D. 1948- ... 153
Nesbitt, Paul H(omer) 1904- ... 77-80
Nesbitt, Ralph Beryl 1891(?)-1975 Obituary .. 61-64
Nesbitt, Rosemary (Sinnett) 1924- ... 81-84
Neshamith, Sara
See Dushnitzky-Shner, Sara
Nesmith, Robert I. 1891-1972 ... CANR-15
Obituary ... 103
Earlier sketch in CA 1-4R
Nesovich, Peter
See Naumoff, Lawrence
Nespojohn, Katherine V(eronica) 1912- ... 37-40R
See also SATA 7
Ness, Evaline (Michelow) 1911-1986 ... CANR-37
Obituary ... 120
Earlier sketches in CA 5-8R, CANR-5
See also CLR 6
See also DLB 61
See also MAICYA
See also SAAS 1
See also SATA 1, 26
See also SATA-Obit 49
Ness, Gayl D(eForrest) 1929- ... 29-32R
Ness, John H., Jr. 1919- ... 21-24R
Nesse, Randolph M. 1948- ... 150
Nessen, (Lewis) Robert 1932- ... 107
Nessen, Ron(ald Harold) 1934- Brief entry ... 106
Nesset, Kirk 1957- ... 150
Nessi, Pio Baroja y
See Baroja (y Nessi), Pio
Nester, William R. 1956- ... 146
Nestle, John Francis 1912- ... 89-92
Nestler, Eric J. 1954- ... 145
Nestor, William P(rodromos) 1947- ... CANR-26
Earlier sketch in CA 109
See also SATA 49
Nestroy, Johann 1801-1862 ... DLB 133
Nesvadba, Josef 1926- ... 97-100
Netanyahu, B(enzion) 1910- ... CANR-52
Earlier sketch in CA 61-64
Netanyahu, Benjamin 1949- ... 152
Netanyahu, Binyamin
See Netanyahu, Benjamin
Netanyahu, Jonathan 1946(?)-1976 Obituary ... 114
Netanyahu, Yonatan
See Netanyahu, Jonathan
Netboy, Anthony 1906- ... CANR-7
Earlier sketch in CA 17-20R
Neter, John 1923- ... 53-56
Netherclift, Beryl (Constance) 1911- ... 93-96
Nethercot, Arthur H(obart) 1895- ... CANR-28
Earlier sketch in CA 1-4R
Nethery, Mary ... 159
See also SATA 93
Netifnet, Dadisi Mwende 1959- ... 145
Netland, Dwayne 1932- ... 110
Neto, Antonio Agostinho 1922-1979 ... 101
Obituary ... 89-92
Nettel, Reginald 1899- ... 13-16R
Nettelbeck, F(red) A(rthur) 1950- ... 118
Nettell, Richard (Geoffrey) 1907- ... CAP-2
Earlier sketch in CA 25-28
Nettels, Curtis Putnam 1898- ... CANR-1
Earlier sketch in CA 1-4R
Nettels, Elsa 1931- ... 77-80
Netter, (Jean) Patrick 1952- ... 119
Netterville, Luke
See O'Grady, Standish (James)
Netting, Robert M(cCorkle) 1934- ... 61-64
Nettis, Joseph 1928- ... 9-12R
Nettl, Bruno 1930- ... 17-20R
Nettl, J(ohn) P(eter) 1926-1968 ... CAP-2
Earlier sketch in CA 23-24
Nettl, Paul 1889-1972 ... CAP-1
Obituary ... 33-36R
Earlier sketch in CA 9-10
Nettleford, Rex M. ... 37-40R
Nettler, Gwynn 1913- ... 33-36R
Nettles, Thomas Julian 1946- ... 117
Nettles, Tom
See Nettles, Thomas Julian
Netzer, Dick 1928- Brief entry ... 112
Netzer, Lanore A. 1916- ... 17-20R
Neu, Charles E. 1936- ... 21-24R
Neu, Jerome 1947- ... 138
Neubauer, Alex(ander) 1959- ... 135
Neubauer, David William 1944- ... 65-68
Neubauer, John 1933- ... 101
Neubauer, William Arthur 1916- ... 9-12R
Neubeck, Gerhard 1918- ... 41-44R
Neuberger, Egon 1925- ... CANR-30
Earlier sketch in CA 25-28R
Neuberger, Julia 1950- ... 135
See also SATA 78
Neuberger, Richard Lewis 1912-1960 Obituary ... 89-92
Neubert, Christopher J. 1948- ... 106
Neuburg, Paul 1939- ... 45-48
Neuburg, Victor E. 1924- ... 33-36R
Neuenschwander, John A. 1941- Brief entry ... 113
Neufeld, Elizabeth F(ondal) 1928- ... 161
Neufeld, James (E.) 1944- ... 164
Neufeld, John (Arthur) 1938- ... CANR-56
Earlier sketches in CA 25-28R, CANR-11, 37
See also AAYA 11
See also CLC 17
See also CLR 52
See also MAICYA
See also SAAS 3
See also SATA 6, 81
Neufeld, Maurice Frank 1910- ... 1-4R
Neufeld, Michael J. 1951- ... 148
Neufeld, Peter Lorenz 1931- ... 25-28R
Neufeld, Rose 1924- ... 29-32R
Neufelder, Jerome M(ichael) 1929- ... 115
Neufeldt, Leonard N(ick) 1937- ... 108
Neufer Emswiler, Sharon
See Emswiler, Sharon Neufer
Neuffer, Claude Henry 1911- ... 41-44R
Neuffer, Irene LaBorde 1919- ... 61-64
Neugeboren, Jay (Michael) 1938- ... CANR-21
Earlier sketch in CA 17-20R
Interview in ... CANR-21
See also DLB 28
Neuharth, Allen ... AITN 2
Neuhaus, David 1958- ... SATA 83
Neuhaus, Denise ... 152
Neuhaus, Richard (John) 1936- ... 33-36R
Neuhaus, Ruby (Hart) 1932- ... 103
Neukirch, Benjamin 1665-1729 ... DLB 168
Neulinger, John 1924-1991 ... CANR-16
Obituary ... 134
Earlier sketch in CA 41-44R
Neuls-Bates, Carol 1939- ... 114
Neuman, Abraham A(aron) 1890-1970 Obituary ... 104
Neuman, Betty Mavine 1924- ... 33-36R
Neuman, E(rnst) Jack 1921- Brief entry ... 127
Neuman, Fredric (Jay) 1934- ... CANR-20
Earlier sketch in CA 97-100
Neuman, Ladd A. 1942- ... 97-100
Neuman, Shirley Carol 1946- ... CANR-48
Earlier sketch in CA 121
Neuman, William Frederick 1919-1981 Obituary ... 103
Neumann, Alfred 1895-1952 ... DLB 56
Neumann, Emanuel 1893-1980 Obituary ... 105
Neumann, Gareth William 1930- ... 61-64
Neumann, Gerhard 1917- ... 132
Neumann, John von
See von Neumann, John
Neumann, Jonathan 1950- ... 85-88
Neumann, Robert 1897-1975 ... 103
Obituary ... 89-92
Neumann, Robert G(erhard) 1916- ... 5-8R
Neumann, William Louis 1915-1971 ... CAP-1
Obituary ... 33-36R
Earlier sketch in CA 11-12
Neumark, Georg 1621-1681 ... DLB 164
Neumeister, Erdmann 1671-1756 ... DLB 168
Neumeyer, Alfred 1900(?)-1973 Obituary ... 41-44R
Neumeyer, Ken(neth Walter) 1953- ... 107
Neumeyer, M(artin) Henry 1892- ... CAP-2
Earlier sketch in CA 19-20
Neumeyer, Peter F(lorian) 1929- ... CANR-30
Earlier sketch in CA 33-36R
See also SATA 13
Neurath, Marie (Reidemeister) 1898- ... 13-16R
See also SATA 1
Neurath, Otto 1882-1945 Brief entry ... 117
Neuschel, Richard F(rederick) 1915- ... 13-16R
Neuschuetz, Karin 1946- ... 116
Neuschutz, Karin
See Neuschuetz, Karin
Neuse, Erna Kritsch 1923- ... 105
Neusner, Jacob 1932- ... CANR-22
Earlier sketches in CA 13-16R, CANR-7
See also SATA 38
Neustadt, Bertha C(ummings) 1921(?)-1984 Obituary ... 112
Neustadt, Egon 1898(?)-1984 Obituary ... 112
Neustadt, Richard E(lliott) 1919- ... CANR-27
Earlier sketch in CA 9-12R
Neustadt, Richard M(itchells) 1948- ... CANR-27
Earlier sketch in CA 45-48
Neutra, Richard Joseph 1892-1970 ... CANR-5
Obituary ... 29-32R
Earlier sketch in CA 5-8R
Neutrelle, Dale 1937- ... 61-64
Neuville, H(enry) Richmond, Jr. 1937- ... 21-24R
Nevai, Lucia 1945- ... 166
Neve, Herbert T(heodore) 1931- ... 25-28R
Neve, Lloyd 1923- ... 53-56
Nevell, Dick
See Nevell, Richard (William Babcock)
Nevell, Richard (William Babcock) 1947- ... 102
Nevelson, Louise 1900(?)-1988 ... 108
Obituary ... 125
Neveux, Georges 1900-1982 Obituary ... 108
Nevill, Barry St-John 1941- ... 119
Neville, Anna
See Fairburn, Eleanor
Neville, B(arbara) Alison (Boodson) 1925- ... CANR-11
Earlier sketch in CA 5-8R
Neville, Charles
See Bodsworth, (Charles) Fred(erick)
Neville, Emily Cheney 1919- ... CANR-37
Earlier sketches in CA 5-8R, CANR-3
See also CLC 12
See also JRDA
See also MAICYA
See also SAAS 2
See also SATA 1
Neville, Gwen Kennedy 1938- ... CANR-35
Earlier sketch in CA 114
Neville, Heather Buckley
See Buckley Neville, Heather

Neville, James Edmund Henderson
1897-1982 Obituary....................107
Neville, Jill 1932-....................21-24R
Neville, Joyce.......................115
Neville, Kris (Ottman) 1925-1980..........132
Obituary..............................117
Neville, Mary
See Woodrich, Mary Neville
Neville, Pauline 1924-..................29-32R
Neville, Richard F. 1931-.................85-88
Neville, Robert 1905-1970 Obituary..........104
Neville, Robert C(ummings) 1939-........ CANR-29
Earlier sketches in CA 25-28R, CANR-11
Neville, Susan 1951-.....................119
Nevin, David 1927-.......................121
Nevin, Evelyn C. 1910-..................17-20R
Nevins, Albert (Francis) J(erome) 1915-1997......
CANR-41
Obituary..............................163
Earlier sketches in CA 5-8R, CANR-5, 19
See also SATA 20
Nevins, (Joseph) Allan 1890-1971...... CANR-30
Obituary..............................29-32R
Earlier sketch in CA 5-8R
See also DLB 17
See also DLBD 17
Nevins, Deborah 1947-....................105
Nevins, Edward M(ichael) 1938-...........29-32R
Nevins, Francis M(ichael), Jr. 1943-..... CANR-43
Earlier sketches in CA 41-44R, CANR-16
Nevinson, C(hristopher) R(ichard) W(ynne)
1889-1946 Brief entry.....................120
Nevinson, Henry Woodd 1956-1941...... DLB 135
Nevitt, H(enry) J(ohn) Barrington 1908-.. CANR-14
Earlier sketch in CA 37-40R
Nevius, Blake (Reynolds) 1916-...........17-20R
Nevo, Ruth 1924-........................61-64
New, Anthony (Sherwood Brooks) 1924-. CANR-23
Earlier sketch in CA 107
New, Christopher.........................116
New, Melvyn 1938-........................142
New, William Herbert 1938-................148
Brief entry...............................114
Newall, Christopher 1951-..................128
Newall, Venetia 1935-...................37-40R
Newberger, Devra
See Speregen, Devra Newberger
Newberry
See Vellacott, Jo
Newberry, Clare Turlay 1903-1970......... CAP-2
Earlier sketch in CA 19-20
See also SATA 1
See also SATA-Obit 26
Newberry, Lida 1909-..................97-100
Newberry, Vellacott
See Vellacott, Jo
Newberry, Wilma (Jean) 1927-.............73-76
Newbery, John 1713-1767...............MAICYA
See also SATA 20
Newbigin, (James Edward) Lesslie 1909- CANR-26
Earlier sketches in CA 13-16R, CANR-10
Newbill, James Guy 1931-.................61-64
Newbold, H(erbert) L(eon, Jr.) 1921-..... CANR-5
Earlier sketch in CA 1-4R
Newbold, Robert T(homas, Jr.) 1920-........89-92
Newbold, Stokes
See Adams, Richard N(ewbold)
Newbolt, Henry (John) 1862-1938 Brief entry.. 118
See also DLB 19
Newborn, Jud 1952-........................125
Newbound, Bernard Slade 1930-....... CANR-49
Earlier sketch in CA 81-84
See also Slade, Bernard
See also DAM DRAM
Newbury, Colin (Walter) 1929-........... CANR-8
Earlier sketch in CA 5-8R
Newbury, Will 1912-......................45-48
Newby, Eric 1919-.................... CANR-44
Earlier sketch in CA 5-8R
Newby, I(dus) A. 1931-..................17-20R
Newby, James R(ichard) 1949-...............112
Newby, Leroy Winfred 1921-.................114
Newby, P(ercy) H(oward) 1918-1997.... CANR-67
Obituary..............................161
Earlier sketches in CA 5-8R, CANR-32
See also CLC 2, 13
See also DAM NOV
See also DLB 15
See also MTCW 1
Newcomb, Benjamin H. 1938-...............45-48
Newcomb, Charles King 1820-1894.........DLB 1
Newcomb, Covelle 1908-.................. CAP-2
Earlier sketch in CA 19-20
Newcomb, Duane G(raham) 1929-....... CANR-5
Earlier sketch in CA 53-56
Newcomb, Ellsworth
See Kenny, Ellsworth Newcomb
Newcomb, Franc(es Lynette) J(ohnson)
1887-..................................17-20R
Newcomb, John (Robert) 1937-..............123
Newcomb, Kerry 1946-................ CANR-10
Earlier sketch in CA 65-68
Newcomb, Norma
See Neubauer, William Arthur
Newcomb, Richard F(airchild) 1913-......... 1-4R
Newcomb, Robert N(orman) 1925-........ 21-24R
Newcomb, Simon 1835-1909 Brief entry....... 108
Newcomb, Theodore Mead 1903-1984.......33-36R
Obituary..............................114
Newcomb, Wilburn Wendell 1935-.........17-20R
Newcomb, William W(ilmon), Jr. 1921-........ 102
Newcombe, Eugene A. 1923-1990...... CANR-42
Obituary..............................130
See also Newcombe, Jack
Newcombe, Jack
See Newcombe, Eugene A.
See also SATA 45
See also SATA-Brief 33
Newcombe, John (David) 1944-........ CANR-25
Earlier sketch in CA 69-72
Newcombe, Park Judson 1930-.............. 106
Newcome, Robert 1955-..................... 155
See also SATA 91
Newcome, Zita 1959-................... SATA 88
Newcomer, James (William) 1912-...... CANR-15
Earlier sketch in CA 41-44R
Newcomer, Robert (J.) 1943-............... 168
Newell, Allen 1927-.......................104
Newell, Arlo F(rederic) 1926-...............114
Newell, Barbara Warne 1929-...............1-4R
Newell, Charles J. 1956-................... 149
Newell, Crosby
See Bonsall, Crosby Barbara (Newell)
Newell, D. A.
See Musciano, Walter A.
Newell, David McCheyne
1898(?)-1986 Obituary..................... 120
Newell, Edythe W(eatherford) 1910-.........65-68
See also SATA 11
Newell, Fred D(elmer) 1912-............. 97-100
Newell, Gordon 1913-................ CANR-20
Earlier sketches in CA 9-12R, CANR-4
Newell, Helen M(arie) 1909-...............93-96
Newell, Homer E(dward) 1915-1983........97-100
Obituary..............................110
Newell, Hope Hockenberry 1896-1965.......73-76
See also SATA 24
Newell, Kenneth B(ernard) 1930-..........41-44R
Newell, Linda King 1941-...................156
Newell, Norman Dennis 1909-......... CANR-21
Earlier sketch in CA 104
Newell, Peter (Sheaf Hersey) 1862-1924 Brief
entry....................................122
See also DLB 42
Newell, Peter F(rancis) 1915-............ 13-16R
Newell, Richard S. 1933-...................134
Brief entry...............................112
Newell, Robert Henry 1836-1901 Brief entry... 111
See also DLB 11
Newell, Rosemary 1922-...................49-52
Newell, William H(are) 1922-................103
Newell, William T(hrift) 1929-............ 37-40R
Newey, Vincent 1943-......................132
Newfeld, Frank 1928-......................105
See also SATA 26
Newfield, Jack 1939-................. CANR-13
Earlier sketch in CA 21-24R
Newhafer, Richard L. 1922-..............13-16R
Newhall, Beaumont 1908-1993......... CANR-47
Obituary..............................140
Earlier sketch in CA 9-12R
Newhall, David S(owle) 1929-............... 140
Newhall, Nancy 1908-1974 Obituary........ 49-52
Newhall, Richard A. 1888-1973 Obituary... 41-44R
Newhouse, Edward 1911-.................. 97-100
Newhouse, Joseph P. 1942-................. 111
Newhouse, Neville H. 1919-.............. 21-24R
Newhouse, Norman N(athan)
1906-1988 Obituary........................127
Newhouse, Samuel I(rving)
1895-1979 Obituary........................89-92
See also DLB 127
Newick, John 1919-.......................CAP-1
Earlier sketch in CA 11-12
Newkirk, Glen A. 1931-..................37-40R
Newland, Kathleen 1951-..................97-100
Newland, T. Ernest 1903-...................105
Newlands, George (McLeod) 1941-...........129
Newley, Anthony (George) 1931-............ 105
Newlin, Dika 1923-........................ 107
Newlin, Margaret Rudd 1925-............ CANR-1
Earlier sketch in CA 49-52
Newlon, (Frank) Clarke 1905(?)-1982.... CANR-10
Obituary..............................108
Earlier sketch in CA 49-52
See also SATA 6
See also SATA-Obit 33
Newlove, Donald 1928-................ CANR-25
Earlier sketch in CA 29-32R
See also CLC 6
Newlove, John (Herbert) 1938-......... CANR-25
Earlier sketches in CA 21-24R, CANR-9
See also CLC 14
Newlyn, Lucy 1956-........................150
Newlyn, Walter T(essier) 1915-............21-24R
Newman, Adrien Ann 1941-..................102
Newman, Albert H. 1913(?)-1987 Obituary.....122
Newman, Alyse 1953-......................107
Newman, Andrea 1938-.................... 73-76
Newman, Andrew 1948-.....................144
Newman, Arnold 1941-.....................137
Newman, Arthur J. 1939-...................117
Newman, Aubrey N(orris) 1927-........ CANR-25
Earlier sketch in CA 29-32R
Newman, Barbara
See Newman, Mona Alice Jean
Newman, Barbara (Pollock) 1939-............ 132
Newman, Barclay M., Jr. 1931-.......... CANR-9
Earlier sketch in CA 17-20R
Newman, Bernard (Charles) 1897-1968.....97-100
Obituary..............................25-28R
Newman, Cecil Earl 1903-1976.......... DLB 127
Newman, Charles 1900-1989 Obituary......... 129
Newman, Charles 1938-....................21-24R
See also CLC 2, 8
Newman, Charles L. 1923-............. CANR-6
Earlier sketch in CA 13-16R
Newman, Christina McCall 1935-............ 112
Newman, Coleman J. 1935-................77-80
Newman, Daisy 1904-1994............... 37-40R
Obituary..............................143
See also SATA 27
See also SATA-Obit 78
Newman, David 1937-..................... 102
Interview in..............................102
See also DLB 44
Newman, Debra Lynn
See Ham, Debra Newman
Newman, E. J. 1943-......................61-64
Newman, Edwin (Harold) 1919-.......... CANR-5
Earlier sketch in CA 69-72
See also AITN 1
See also CLC 14
Newman, Elmer S(imon) 1919-...............106
Newman, Eric P. 1911-.....................5-8R
Newman, Ernest
See Roberts, William
Newman, Frances 1883(?)-1928 Brief entry....110
See also DLBY 80
Newman, Francis William 1805-1897..... DLB 190
Newman, Frank
See Abrams, Sam(uel)
Newman, G(ordon) F. 1942-............ CANR-61
Earlier sketch in CA 104
Newman, George 1936-.....................106
Newman, Gerald 1939-......................101
See also SATA 46
See also SATA-Brief 42
Newman, Greatrex 1892-1984(?) Obituary..... 112
Newman, Harold 1899-................ CANR-10
Earlier sketch in CA 65-68
Newman, Harold 1927-.....................53-56
Newman, Herbert Ellis 1914-..............25-28R
Newman, Howard 1911-1977...............57-60
Obituary..............................73-76
Newman, Isadore 1942-.....................163
Newman, Jacob 1914-.......................9-12R
Newman, James L. 1939-.................... 151
Newman, Jay 1948-........................ 168
Newman, Jay Hartley 1951-............. CANR-9
Earlier sketch in CA 65-68
Newman, Jeremiah Joseph 1926-......... CANR-8
Earlier sketch in CA 5-8R
Newman, Jerry 1935-....................... 149
See also SATA 82
Newman, John Henry 1801-1890... DLB 18, 32, 55
Newman, John Kevin 1928-............ CANR-50
Earlier sketch in CA 123
Newman, Jon O(rmond) 1932-............. 21-24R
Newman, Joseph 1912-1995............ CANR-17
Obituary..............................148
Earlier sketch in CA 89-92
Newman, Joseph W(illiam) 1918-..........37-40R
Newman, Judie 1950-.................. CANR-40
Earlier sketch in CA 117
Newman, Katharine D. 1911-............. 37-40R
Newman, Katherine S. 1953-................152
Newman, Kim (James) 1959-........... CANR-61
Earlier sketch in CA 119
Newman, L(eonard) Hugh 1909-............9-12R
Newman, Lea Bertani Vozar 1926-............120
Newman, Lee Scott 1953-.............. CANR-15
Earlier sketch in CA 65-68
Newman, Leslea 1955-......................126
See also SATA 71
Newman, Loretta Marie 1911-.............. 45-48
Newman, Louis Israel 1893-1972.......... CAP-1
Obituary..............................33-36R
Earlier sketch in CA 19-20
Newman, Matthew (Harrison) 1955-...... SATA 56
Newman, Michael 1946-................ CANR-40
Earlier sketch in CA 116
Newman, Mona Alice Jean.............. CANR-31
Earlier sketch in CA 102
Newman, Oscar 1935-...................... 102
Newman, P(aul) B(aker) 1919-............ 33-36R
Newman, Parley Wright 1923- Brief entry......106
Newman, Peter (Kenneth) 1928-........... 17-20R
Newman, Peter C(harles) 1929-......... CANR-29
Earlier sketches in CA 9-12R, CANR-3
Newman, Philip L(ee) 1931-............... 17-20R
Newman, Phyllis 1933-......................134
Newman, Ralph Abraham 1892-.......... CANR-6
Earlier sketch in CA 1-4R
Newman, Ralph G(eoffrey) 1911-....... CANR-25
Earlier sketch in CA 45-48
Newman, Randolph H. 1904-1975 Obituary.. 61-64
Newman, Richard (Alan) 1930-...............110
Newman, Robert (Howard) 1909-1988... CANR-51
Obituary..............................127
Earlier sketches in CA 1-4R, CANR-4, 19
See also SATA 4, 87
See also SATA-Obit 60
Newman, Robert Chapman 1941-........... 115
Newman, Robert D(ouglas) 1951-........... 120
Newman, Robert P(reston) 1922-............ 1-4R
Newman, Robert S. 1935-.................. 65-68
Newman, Ruth (May) G(allert) 1914-......... 105
Newman, Sharan 1949-................ CANR-25
Earlier sketch in CA 106
Newman, Shirlee P(etkin) 1924-........ CANR-59
Earlier sketch in CA 5-8R
See also SATA 10, 90
Newman, Shirley S. 1924-.................. 123
Newman, Stephen A(aron) 1946-.......... 97-100
Newman, Stephen L. 1952-..................132
Newman, Stewart A(lbert) 1907-.......... CAP-2
Earlier sketch in CA 23-24
Newman, Terence 1927-.................... 5-8R
Newman, Terry
See Newman, Terence
Newman, Thelma R(ita) 1925-1978....... CANR-7
Obituary..............................81-84
Earlier sketch in CA 13-16R
Newman, Walter (Brown)
1916(?)-1993 Obituary..................... 143
Brief entry...............................110
Newman, William H(erman) 1909-....... CANR-19
Earlier sketches in CA 5-8R, CANR-3
Newman, William Mark 1943-............. 57-60
Newman, William S(tein) 1912-.......... CANR-3
Earlier sketch in CA 1-4R
Newmar, Rima
See Wagman, Naomi
Newmark, Joseph 1943-...................53-56
Newmark, Leonard 1929-..................17-20R
Newmyer, R. Kent 1930-..................77-80
Newport, Cris 1960-........................ 168
Newport, John P(aul) 1917-........... CANR-29
Earlier sketches in CA 33-36R, CANR-13
Newport, John Paul, Jr. 1954-...............135
Newquist, Jerreld L. 1919-1976........... 17-20R
Obituary..............................134
Newquist, Roy 1925-.....................13-16R
Newsham, Ian (Alan) 1953-.................115
Newsham, Wendy (Elizabeth) 1952-...........117
Newsholme, Christopher (Mansford) 1920-.....146
Newsom, Carol 1948-................SATA 40, 92
Newsom, Carroll V(incent) 1904-1990...... CAP-2
Obituary..............................130
Earlier sketch in CA 17-18
Newsom, Doug(las Ann) 1934-............. 73-76
Newsom, Tom 1944-.....................SATA 80
Newsome, Arden J(eanne) 1932-...........29-32R
Newsome, David Hay 1929-............ CANR-17
Earlier sketch in CA 89-92
Newsome, Effie Lee 1885-1979.......... DLB 76
Newsome, George L(ane), Jr. 1923-...... 29-32R
Newsome, Walter L(ee) 1941-................105
Newson, Elizabeth (Palmer) 1929-....... CANR-5
Earlier sketch in CA 9-12R
Newson, John 1925-.......................9-12R
Newson, Tony 1953-........................124
Newth, Rebecca 1940-...................33-36R
Newton, A. Edward 1864-1940...........DLB 140
Newton, Brian 1928-...................... 49-52
Newton, Byron Louis 1913-................ 53-56
Newton, Candelas 1948-.................... 153
Newton, D(wight) B(ennett) 1916-....... CANR-17
Earlier sketches in CA 5-8R, CANR-2
Newton, David C.
See Chance, John Newton
Newton, David E(dward) 1933-............... 135
See also SATA 67
Newton, Derek A(rnold) 1930-...............120
Newton, Douglas 1920-..................... 104
Newton, Earle Williams 1917-.............41-44R
Newton, Eric 1893-1965................. CAP-1
Earlier sketch in CA 13-16
Newton, Esther 1940-.......................149
Newton, Francis
See Hobsbawm, Eric J(ohn Ernest)
Newton, Huey P(ercy) 1942-1989 Obituary.... 129
Brief entry...............................114
Newton, Ian 1940-..........................123
Newton, Ivor 1892-1981 Obituary............108
Newton, James R(obert) 1935-...............101
See also SATA 23
Newton, Kenneth 1940-............... CANR-16
Earlier sketch in CA 29-32R
Newton, Lionel 1961(?)-..................... 152
Newton, Macdonald
See Newton, William Simpson
Newton, Maxwell 1929-..................... 126
Newton, Merlin Owen 1935-................. 150
Newton, Michael 1951-......................108
Newton, Norman (Lewis) 1929-.............9-12R
Newton, Norman Thomas 1898-...............104
Newton, Peter 1906-..................... CAP-1
Earlier sketch in CA 9-10
Newton, Peter A(nthony) 1935-1987 Obituary.. 124
Newton, Ray C(lyde) 1935-................. 77-80
Newton, Robert (Henry) G(erald) 1903-..... CAP-1
Earlier sketch in CA 9
Newton, Robert P(arr) 1929-................ 113
Newton, Roger G(erhard) 1924-.............. 146
Newton, Roy 1904(?)-1974 Obituary.......... 104
Newton, Stu
See Whitcomb, Ian
Newton, Suzanne 1936-................ CANR-14
Earlier sketch in CA 41-44R
See also CLC 35
See also JRDA
See also SATA 5, 77
Newton, Verne W. 1944-.................... 141
Newton, Virgil Miller, Jr. 1904-1977.......... 1-4R
Obituary..............................103
Newton, William Simpson 1923-......... CANR-7
Earlier sketch in CA 53-56
Nexo, Martin Andersen 1869-1954....... TCLC 43
Ney, James W(alter) 1932-............ CANR-15
Earlier sketch in CA 41-44R
Ney, John 1923-........................... 115
See also SATA 43
See also SATA-Brief 33
Ney, Patrick
See Bolitho, (Henry) Hector
Ney, Richard 1917(?)-.....................AITN 1
Ney, Ronald E., (Jr.) 1936-................. 151
Ney, Virgil 1905-1979 Obituary............. 85-88
Neyland, James (Elwyn) 1939-............... 103
Neyman, Jerzy 1894-1981 Obituary...........108
Neyrey, Jerome H(enry) 1940-............... 126
Neznansky, Friedrich 1932-..................128
Nezval, Vitezslav 1900-1958 Brief entry...... 123
See also TCLC 44
Ng, David 1934-...........................115
Ng, Fae Myenne 1957(?)-.................... 146
See also CLC 81

Ng, Franklin 149
See also SATA 82
Ng, Larry K. Y. 1940- CANR-9
Earlier sketch in CA 17-20R
Ng, Man-lun 1946- 168
Nga, Tran Thi
See Tran Thi Nga
Ngagoyeanes, Nicholas 1939- 49-52
Ngara, Emmanuel 1947- 109
Ngcobo, Lauretta 1931- 165
Ngema, Mbongeni 1955- 143
See also BW 2
See also CLC 57
Ngoc, Nguyen Huy
See Nguyen, Ngoc Huy
Ngor, Haing S. 1947(?)-1996 159
Ngubane, Jordan K(hush) 1917- 121
Ngugi, James T(hiong'o)
See Ngugi wa Thiong'o
See also CLC 3, 7, 13
Ngugi wa Thiong'o 1938- CANR-58
Earlier sketches in CA 81-84, CANR-27
See also Ngugi, James T(hiong'o)
See also BLC 3
See also BW 2
See also CLC 36
See also DAM MULT, NOV
See also DLB 125
See also MTCW 1
Nguyen, Dinh Hoa 1924- CANR-10
Earlier sketch in CA 21-24R
Nguyen, Ngoc Huy 1924- 126
Nguyen, Vuong Hung 1922(?)-1985 Obituary 118
Nguyen huong
See Nguyen-Vo, Thu-huong
Nguyen Ngoc Bich 1937- CANR-15
Earlier sketch in CA 81-84
Nguyen-Vo, Thu-huong 1962- 146
Ni, Hua-Ching 1925- 164
Niall, Sean
See Mangan, (John Joseph) Sherry
Nias, D(avid) K(enneth) B(oydell) 1940- 105
Niatum, Duane 1938- CANR-45
Earlier sketches in CA 41-44R, CANR-21
See also DLB 175
See also NNAL
Niblett, W(illiam) R(oy) 1906- CANR-3
Earlier sketch in CA 1-4R
Niccolini, Dianora 1936- 113
Nice, David C. 1952- 148
Nice, Jill 1940- 138
Nice, Margaret Morse 1883-1974 156
Nicely, Thomas S(hryock), Jr. 1939- 93-96
Nicely, Tom
See Nicely, Thomas S(hryock), Jr.
Nichelson, F(loyd) Patrick 1942- 33-36R
Nichol, B(arrie) P(hillip) 1944-1988 53-56
See also CLC 18
See also DLB 53
See also SATA 66
Nichol, John Thomas 1928- 17-20R
Nicholas, Anna Katherine 1917- 93-96
Nicholas, Barry 1919- 5-8R
Nicholas, David M(ansfield) 1939- 49-52
Nicholas, Donald 1909- 5-8R
Nicholas, Elizabeth 1915-1985 Obituary 117
Nicholas, Herbert George 1911- CANR-26
Earlier sketch in CA 1-4R
Nicholas, John (Morton) 1944- 118
Nicholas, Laura F(arnsworth) 1960- 158
Nicholas, Leslie 1913- 81-84
Nicholas, Robert L(eon) 1937- 53-56
Nicholas, Sian (Helen) 1964- 168
Nicholas, Ted
See Peterson, Ted Nicholas
Nicholas, Tracy (Christine) 1952- 121
Nicholas, William
See Thimmesch, Nicholas Palen
Nicholas of Cusa 1401-1464 .... DLB 115
Nicholds, Elizabeth (Beckwith) CAP-1
Earlier sketch in CA 11-12
Nicholl, Louise Townsend 1890(?)-1981 97-100
Obituary 105
Nicholls, C(hristine) S(tephanie) 1943- 133
Nicholls, David 1948- 97-100
Nicholls, Elizabeth L. 1946- 168
Nicholls, F(rederick) F(rancis) 1926- 5-8R
Nicholls, Judith (Ann) 1941- CANR-47
Earlier sketch in CA 121
See also SATA 61
Nicholls, Mark
See Frewin, Leslie Ronald
Nicholls, Peter (Douglas) 1939- 105
Nicholls, (C. G.) William 1921- 17-20R
Nichols, Adelaide
See Baker, Adelaide N(ichols)
Nichols, Albert L. 1951- 122
Nichols, Beverley 1893-1983 .... DLB 191
Nichols, (John) Beverley 1898-1983 .... CANR-62
Obituary 110
Earlier sketches in CA 93-96, CANR-17
Nichols, Bill
See Nichols, William James
Nichols, Cecilia Fawn 1906- CAP-1
Earlier sketch in CA 13-16
See also SATA 12
Nichols, Charles H(arold) 1919- CANR-6
Earlier sketch in CA 53-56
See also BW 1
Nichols, Dale (William) 1904- CAP-2
Earlier sketch in CA 17-18
Nichols, Dave
See Frost, Helen
Nichols, David 1956- 133
Nichols, David A(llen) 1939- 104
Nichols, Dudley 1895-1960 Obituary 89-92
See also DLB 26
Nichols, Edward J(ay) 1900- 5-8R
Nichols, Eve K(aufman) 1952- 128
Nichols, Fred Joseph 1939- 114
Nichols, Frederick Adams 1907-1983 Obituary 111
Nichols, Grace 1950- 154
See also DLB 157
See also SATA 98
Nichols, Harold 1903- CAP-1
Earlier sketch in CA 13-16
Nichols, Irby C(oghill), Jr. 1926- 41-44R
Nichols, J(ohn) G(ordon) 1930- 33-36R
See also CAAS 2
Nichols, Jack 1938- 41-44R
Nichols, James Hastings 1915- Brief entry 114
Nichols, James R(ichard) 1938- 105
Nichols, Janet (Louise) 1952- 135
See also SATA 67
Nichols, Jeannette 1931- 77-80
Nichols, Jeannette Paddock 1890-1982 .... 9-12R
Obituary 107
Nichols, John (Treadwell) 1940- CANR-70
Earlier sketches in CA 9-12R, CANR-6
See also CAAS 2
See also CLC 38
See also DLBY 82
Nichols, Joseph C. 1905(?)-1984 Obituary 114
Nichols, K(enneth) D(avid) 1907- 126
Nichols, Leigh
See Koontz, Dean R(ay)
Nichols, Lewis 1903-1982 Obituary 106
Nichols, Maggie
See Nichols, Margaret
Nichols, Margaret 1931- 81-84
Nichols, Marie Hochmuth 1908-1978 103
Nichols, Marion 1921- 102
Nichols, Mary Sargeant (Neal) Gove
1810-1884 .... DLB 1
Nichols, Nichelle 1933(?)- 155
Nichols, Nina (Marianna) da Vinci 1932- CANR-14
Earlier sketch in CA 73-76
Nichols, Paul
See Hawks, Robert
Nichols, Paul D(yer) 1938- 109
Nichols, Peter
See Youd, (Christopher) Samuel
Nichols, Peter (Richard) 1927- CANR-33
Earlier sketch in CA 104
See also CLC 5, 36, 65
See also DLB 13
See also MTCW 1
Nichols, Peter 1928-1989 Obituary 127
Nichols, R(oy) Eugene 1914- 29-32R
Nichols, Robert (Molise Bowyer) 1919- 93-96
Nichols, Roger 1939- 108
Nichols, Roger L(ouis) 1933- CANR-5
Earlier sketch in CA 13-16R
Nichols, Roy F(ranklin) 1896-1973 .... CANR-3
Obituary 37-40R
Earlier sketch in CA 5-8R
See also DLB 17
Nichols, (Joanna) Ruth 1948- CANR-37
Earlier sketches in CA 25-28R, CANR-16
See also DLB 60
See also JRDA
See also SATA 15
Nichols, Scott
See Scortia, Thomas N(icholas)
Nichols, Stephen G(eorge, Jr.) 1936- CANR-31
Earlier sketch in CA 45-48
Nichols, Sue 9-12R
Nichols, Victoria (Sorensen) 1944- 132
Nichols, William James 1942- 93-96
Nichols, William Thomas 1927- 41-44R
Nicholsen, Margaret E(sther) 1904- 29-32R
Nicholson, Arnold 1902- CAP-2
Earlier sketch in CA 19-20
Nicholson, Ben 1894-1982 Obituary 110
Nicholson, C(harles) A. III 1922- 41-44R
Nicholson, C. R.
See Nicole, Christopher (Robin)
Nicholson, Charles (Edward) 1946- 136
Nicholson, Christina
See Nicole, Christopher (Robin)
Nicholson, Colin 1944- 150
Nicholson, Dorothy Nelis 1923- Brief entry 109
Nicholson, Edward Williams Byron 1849-1912 .... DLB 184
Nicholson, Geoff 1953- 130
Nicholson, Geoffrey (George) 1929- CANR-8
Earlier sketch in CA 5-8R
Nicholson, Gerald W(illiam) L(ingen)
1902-1980 101
Nicholson, Hubert 1908-1996 .... 13-16R
Obituary 151
Nicholson, Jack 1937- 143
Brief entry 116
Nicholson, Jane
See Steen, Marguerite
Nicholson, Joe
See Nicholson, Joseph Hugh, Jr.
Nicholson, John Greer 1929-1995 45-48
Obituary 148
Nicholson, Joseph Hugh, Jr. 1943- 81-84
Nicholson, Joyce Thorpe 1919- CANR-5
Earlier sketch in CA 9-12R
See also SATA 35
Nicholson, Lois P. 1949- 152
See also SATA 88
Nicholson, Mavis 1930- 150
Nicholson, (Edward) Max 1904- Brief entry 106
Nicholson, Norman (Cornthwaite) 1914-1987 .... CANR-24
Obituary 122
Earlier sketches in CA 9-12R, CANR-3
See also DLB 27
Nicholson, Norman L(eon) 1919- CANR-3
Earlier sketch in CA 9-12R
Nicholson, Patrick J(ames) 1920- CANR-45
Earlier sketch in CA 120
Nicholson, Paul (Joseph), Jr. 1937- 73-76
Nicholson, Ranald (George) 1931- 37-40R
Nicholson, Robert Lawrence 1908-1985 53-56
Obituary 117
Nicholson, Robin
See Nicole, Christopher (Robin)
Nicholson, Shirley J. 1925- CANR-55
Earlier sketches in CA 29-32R, CANR-26
Nicholson, Simon 1934- 114
Nicholson, W(illiam) G(eorge) 1935- 93-96
Nicholson, William 1872-1949 .... DLB 141
Nichter, Mark (Andrew) 1949- 144
Nichter, Rhoda 1926- 81-84
Nichtern, Sol 1920-1988 .... 17-20R
Obituary 126
Ni Chuilleanain, Eilean 1942- CANR-53
Earlier sketch in CA 126
See also DLB 40
Nickel, Herman 1928- 73-76
Nickel, Mildred L(ucille) 1912- 108
Nickell, Joe 1944- CANR-46
Earlier sketch in CA 110
See also SATA 73
Nickell, Lesley J(acqueline) 1944- 103
Nickels, William G(eorge) 1939- 108
Nickelsburg, George W(illiam) E(lmer), Jr. 1934- CANR-19
Earlier sketches in CA 53-56, CANR-5
Nickelsburg, Janet 1893- 65-68
See also SATA 11
Nickerson, Betty 1922- 77-80
See also Nickerson, Elizabeth
Nickerson, Clarence B(entley) 1906- 5-8R
Nickerson, Elizabeth
See Nickerson, Betty
See also SATA 14
Nickerson, Jan 1-4R
Nickerson, Jane Soames (Bon) 1900-1988 .... CANR-28
Obituary 124
Earlier sketch in CA 77-80
Nickerson, John Mitchell 1937- 53-56
Nickerson, Joseph 1914-1990 Obituary 131
Nickerson, Roy 1927- CANR-35
Earlier sketch in CA 114
Nickerson, Sheila B(unker) 1942- CANR-43
Earlier sketch in CA 118
Nickerson, William (Ernest) 1908- 1-4R
Nickl, Barbara (Elisabeth) 1939-
See Schroeder, Binette
See also SATA 56
Nicklanovich, Michael David 1941- 107
Nicklaus, Carol .... SATA 62
See also SATA-Brief 33
Nicklaus, (Charles) Frederick 1936- 37-40R
Nicklaus, Jack (William) 1940- CANR-39
Earlier sketches in CA 89-92, CANR-16
Nickle, Keith Fullerton 1933- 115
Nickless, Will 1902- 81-84
See also SATA 66
Nickson, J. Richard 1917- 129
Niclas, Yolla 1900- 25-28R
Nic Leodhas, Sorche
See Alger, Leclaire (Gowans)
Nicol, Abioseh
See Nicol, Davidson (Sylvester Hector Willoughby)
Nicol, Ann
See Turnbull, Ann (Christine)
Nicol, Charles (David) 1940- 115
Nicol, D(onald) M(acGillivray) 1923- CANR-4
Earlier sketch in CA 53-56
Nicol, Davidson (Sylvester Hector Willoughby)
1924-1994 .... CANR-26
Obituary 147
Earlier sketch in CA 61-64
See also BW 1
Nicol, Eric (Patrick) 1919- CANR-36
Earlier sketches in CA 49-52, CANR-1, 16
See also DLB 68
Nicol, Jean 1919- 21-24R
Nicola, Andree
See McLaughlin, Andree Nicola
Nicolaeff, Ariadne 1915- 57-60
Nicolai, Friedrich 1733-1811 .... DLB 97
Nicolaisen, (Agnes) Ida (Benedicte) 1940- 148
Nicolas
See Mordvinoff, Nicolas
Nicolas, Claire
See White, Claire Nicolas
Nicolas, F. R. E.
See Freeling, Nicolas
Nicolay, Helen 1866-1954 Brief entry 121
See also YABC 1
Nicolay, John G(eorge) 1832-1901 Brief entry 122
See also DLB 47
Nicolaysen, Bruce 1934- 105
Nicole, Christopher (Robin) 1930- CANR-68
Earlier sketches in CA 13-16R, CANR-45
See also SATA 5
Nicoll, (John Ramsay) Allardyce 1894-1976 .... CANR-5
Obituary 65-68
Earlier sketch in CA 9-12R
Nicoll, Bruce H. 1913(?)-1983 Obituary 111
Nicoll, Helen 1937- CANR-51
Earlier sketch in CA 122
See also SATA 87
Nicolle, Jacques Maurice Raoul 1901- 9-12R
Nicoloff, Philip Loveless 1926- 1-4R
Nicolson, (Lionel) Benedict 1914-1978 .... CANR-6
Earlier sketch in CA 13-16R
Nicolson, Catherine 121
Nicolson, Harold George 1886-1968 .... CAP-1
Earlier sketch in CA 13-16
See also DLB 100, 149
Nicolson, I(an) F(erguson) 1921- 29-32R
Nicolson, James R(obert) 1934- CANR-9
Earlier sketch in CA 65-68
Nicolson, Marjorie Hope 1894-1981 .... 9-12R
Obituary 103
Nicolson, Nigel 1917- 101
See also DLB 155
Nicosia, Francesco M(ichael) 1933- 81-84
Nicosia, Franco M.
See Nicosia, Francesco M(ichael)
Nicosia, Gerald (Martin) 1949- 115
See also CAAS 28
Nida, Eugene A(lbert) 1914- CANR-17
Earlier sketches in CA 1-4R, CANR-1
Niddith, Peter (Harold) 1928-1983 Obituary 109
Niddrie, David Lawrence 1917- 25-28R
Nideffer, Robert M(orse) 1942- CANR-9
Earlier sketch in CA 65-68
Nidetch, Jean 1923- 89-92
Ni Dhuibhne, Eilis 1954- 155
See also SATA 91
Niditch, Susan 1950- 143
Nie, Norman H. 1943- CANR-15
Earlier sketch in CA 65-68
Niebuhr, Gary Warren 1954- 146
Niebuhr, H(elmut) Richard 1894-1962 Obituary 116
Niebuhr, Reinhold 1892-1971 .... 41-44R
Obituary 29-32R
See also DLB 17
See also DLBD 17
Niebuhr, Richard R. 1926- 77-80
Niebuhr, Ursula 1907-1997 89-92
Obituary 156
Nieburg, H(arold) L. 1927- 9-12R
Niedecker, Lorine 1903-1970 .... CAP-2
Earlier sketch in CA 25-28
See also CLC 10, 42
See also DAM POET
See also DLB 48
Niederauer, David J(ohn) 1924- 45-48
Niederhoffer, Arthur 1917-1981 Obituary 103
Niederland, William G(ugliemo) 1904-1993 81-84
Obituary 142
Niedzielski, Henri 1931- 49-52
Nieh, Hualing 1925- 81-84
Niehans, Juerg 1919- 133
Niehans, Jurg
See Niehans, Juerg
Niehoff, Arthur H. 1921- CANR-67
Earlier sketch in CA 21-24R
Nielander, William Ahlers 1901- 5-8R
Nield, Howard (Kingsley) 1949- 135
Nielsen, Aage Rosendal 1921- 25-28R
Nielsen, Aldon Lynn 1950- 136
Nielsen, Dulcimer 1943- 93-96
Nielsen, Eduard 1923- 29-32R
Nielsen, Gary (Elton) 1939- 97-100
Nielsen, Helen Berniece 1918- CANR-61
Earlier sketches in CA 1-4R, CANR-1
Nielsen, Jean Sarver 1922- 5-8R
Nielsen, Kay (Rasmus) 1886-1957 .... CLR 16
See also MAICYA
See also SATA 16
Nielsen, Knut Schmidt
See Schmidt-Nielsen, Knut
Nielsen, Laura F(arnsworth) 1960- 158
See also SATA 93
Nielsen, Margaret A(nne) 105
Nielsen, Nancy J. 1951- 145
See also SATA 77
Nielsen, Niels Christian, Jr. 1921- CANR-3
Earlier sketch in CA 9-12R
Nielsen, Niels Juel
See Juel-Nielsen, Niels
Nielsen, Oswald 1904- CAP-2
Earlier sketch in CA 19-20
Nielsen, Robert F. 1937- 122
Nielsen, Sven Sigurd 1901-1976 Obituary 104
Nielsen, Torben 1918- Brief entry 114
Nielsen, Veneta Leatham 1909- 89-92
Nielsen, Virginia
See McCall, Virginia Nielsen
Nielsen, Waldemar August 1917- 103
Nielsen Hayden, Patrick 1959- 163
Nielson, James 1958- 154
Nielssen, Eric
See Ludvigsen, Karl (Eric)
Nieman, Egbert William 1909- CAP-1
Earlier sketch in CA 11-12
Nieman, Lucius W. 1857-1935 .... DLB 25
Niemann, Linda (Grant) 1946- 133
Niemeier, Jean (Gilbreath) 1912- 25-28R
Niemela, Pirkko 1939- 146
Niemeyer, Eberhardt Victor, Jr. 1919- 102
Niemeyer, Gerhart 1907-1997 .... CANR-30
Obituary 159
Earlier sketch in CA 1-4R
Niemeyer, Roy K(urt) 1922- 1-4R
Niemi, Albert (William), Jr. 1942- 73-76
Niemi, John A. 1932- 77-80
Niemi, Richard G(ene) 1941- 41-44R
Niemoeller, (Friedrich Gustav Emil) Martin
1892-1984 Obituary 112
Niemoller, Ara
See Llerena, Mario
Niemoller, (Friedrich Gustav Emil) Martin
See Niemoeller, (Friedrich Gustav Emil) Martin
Nienhauser, William H., Jr. 1943- 125

Nierenberg, Gerard I. 1923- 25-28R
Nierman, M. Murray 1918- 1-4R
Nies, Judith 1941- 77-80
Niesewand, Peter 1944-1983 101
Obituary 109
Niess, Robert Judson 1911- CAP-2
Earlier sketch in CA 29-32
Niethammer, Carolyn 1944- 85-88
Nietz, John Alfred 1888- 1-4R
Nietzke, Ann 1945- 105
Nietzsche, Friedrich (Wilhelm) 1844-1900 121
Brief entry 107
See also DLB 129
See also TCLC 10, 18, 55
Nievergelt, Jurg 1938- CANR-26
Earlier sketch in CA 29-32R
Nievo, Stanislao 1928- DLB 196
Niewyk, Donald L. 1940- 33-36R
Nigg, Joe
See Nigg, Joseph E(ugene)
Nigg, Joseph E(ugene) 1938- CANR-35
Earlier sketch in CA 114
Niggli, Josefina (Maria) 1910- CANR-32
Earlier sketches in CAP-2, CA 23-24R
See also DLBY 80
See also HW
Nighbert, David F(ranklin) 1948- CANR-70
Earlier sketch in CA 141
Nightingale, Anne Redmon 1943- 103
See also Redmon, Anne
Nightingale, Benedict 1939- 132
Nightingale, Earl (Clifford) 1921-1989 Obituary 128
Nightingale, Elena O(ttolenghi) 1932- 123
Nightingale, Florence 1820-1910 DLB 166
Nightingale, Pamela 1938- 158
Nightingale, Sandy 1953- SATA 76
Nightingale, Sir Geoffrey (Slingsby) 1904- CAP-1
Earlier sketch in CA 13-14
Nightrate, Emil
See Spielmann, Peter James
Nigro, Felix A(nthony) 1914- CANR-14
Earlier sketch in CA 37-40R
Nihal Singh, Surendra 1929- 93-96
Niizaka, Kazuo 1943- 77-80
Nijinska, Bronislava 1891-1972 117
Nijinsky, Romola Flavia 1891-1978 Obituary 81-84
Nijinsky, Vaslav (Fomitch) 1888-1950 168
Brief entry 115
Nik. T. O.
See Annensky, Innokenty (Fyodorovich)
Nikelly, Arthur G(eorge) 1927- 17-20R
Nikkel, David H. 1952- 165
Niklas, Gerald R. 1933- 118
Niklas, Karl J(oseph) 1948- 145
Niklaus, Robert 1910- 9-12R
Niklaus, Thelma (Jones) 1912-1970 9-12R
Obituary 134
Nikolaev, Vsevolod A(postolov) 1909- 130
Nikola-Lisa, W. 1951- SATA 71
Nikolay, Michael 1941- 97-100
Nikolev, Nikolai Petrovich 1758-1815 DLB 150
Nikolic, Mile
See Djilas, Milovan
Niland, D'Arcy Francis 1920-1967 CANR-3
Earlier sketch in CA 1-4R
Niland, Deborah 1951- 106
See also SATA 27
Niland, Kilmeny SATA 75
Niland, Powell 1919- 21-24R
Nile, Dorothea
See Avallone, Michael (Angelo, Jr.)
Niles, D(aniel) T(hambyrajah)
1908-1970 Obituary 29-32R
Niles, Douglas 160
Niles, Gwendolyn 1914- 9-12R
Niles, Hezekiah 1777-1839 DLB 43
Niles, John D(eWitt) 1945- 125
Niles, John Jacob 1892-1980 CANR-33
Obituary 97-100
Earlier sketch in CA 41-44R
Nill, Michael 1942- 124
Nilles, Jack M(athias) 1932- 108
Nilsen, Alleen Pace 1936- 112
Nilsen, Anna
See Bassil, Andrea
Nilsen, Don L(ee) F(red) 1934- CANR-15
Earlier sketch in CA 41-44R
Nilsson, Birgit (Marta) 1918- 129
Nilsson, Eleanor 1939- 149
See also SAAS 23
See also SATA 81
Nilsson, Jenny Lind 165
Nilsson, Usha Saksena 1930- 41-44R
Niman, Michael I. 1957- 164
Nimble, Jack B.
See Burgess, Michael (Roy)
Nimeth, Albert J. 1918-1984 25-28R
Obituary 114
Nimitz, Chester W(illiam) 1885-1966 Obituary 113
Nimmer, Melville B(ernard) 1923-1985 49-52
Obituary 117
Nimmo, Dan D(ean) 1933- CANR-7
Earlier sketch in CA 13-16R
Nimmo, Derek (Robert) 1933- CANR-28
Earlier sketch in CA 109
Nimmo, Jenny 1942- CANR-52
Earlier sketch in CA 108
See also CLR 44
See also SATA 87
Nimnicht, Nona 1930- 73-76
Nimocks, Walter 1930- 41-44R
Nimoy, Leonard 1931- CANR-25
Earlier sketch in CA 57-60
Nims, Charles F(rancis) 1906-1988 17-20R
Obituary 127
Nims, John Frederick 1913- CANR-35
Earlier sketches in CA 13-16R, CANR-6
See also CAAS 17
See also DLB 5
Nin, Anais 1903-1977 CANR-53
Obituary 69-72
Earlier sketches in CA 13-16R, CANR-22
See also AITN 2
See also CLC 1, 4, 8, 11, 14, 60
See also DAM NOV, POP
See also DLB 2, 4, 152
See also MTCW 1
See also SSC 10
Nineham, Dennis (Eric) 1921- 85-88
Ningkun, Wu 1921- 140
Ninh, Bao 1952(?)- 152
Nininger, H(arvey) H(arlow) 1887-1986 21-24R
Obituary 118
Ninkovich, Thomas 1943- 137
Ninkovich, Tom
See Ninkovich, Thomas
Nino, Carlos Santiago 1943- 141
Nioche, Brigitte 109
Niosi, Jorge 1945- CANR-65
Earlier sketch in CA 129
See also HW
Nir, Yehuda 1930- 107
Nirenberg, Jesse S(tanley) 1921- 69-72
Nirmala-Kumara, V
See Bose, N(irmal) K(umar)
Nirodi, Hira 1930- 5-8R
Nisbet, Ada Blanche 1907- 41-44R
Nisbet, Robert A(lexander) 1913-1996 CANR-17
Obituary 153
Earlier sketch in CA 25-28R
Interview in CANR-17
Nisbet, Stanley (Donald) 1912- CAP-1
Earlier sketch in CA 13-14
Nisbett, (Thomas) Alec 1930- CANR-22
Earlier sketch in CA 81-84
Nisbett, Richard E. 1941- 37-40R
Nisetich, Frank Joseph 1942- 97-100
Nish, Ian Hill 1926- CANR-17
Earlier sketch in CA 21-24R
Nishida, Kitaro 1870-1945 TCLC 83
Nishihara, Masashi 1937- CANR-12
Earlier sketch in CA 69-72
Nishio, Suehiro 1891-1981 Obituary 108
Nishiwaki, Junzaburo 1894-1982 Obituary 107
See also PC 15
Nishiyama, Chiaki 1924- Brief entry 110
Niskanen, William Arthur, Jr. 1933- CANR-54
Earlier sketch in CA 41-44R
Nissen, Lowell A(llen) 1932- 33-36R
Nissenbaum, Stephen 1941- 77-80
Nissenson, Hugh 1933- CANR-27
Earlier sketch in CA 17-20R
See also CLC 4, 9
See also DLB 28
Nissenson, Marilyn 1939- 146
Nissman, Albert 1930- 37-40R
Nissman, Blossom S. 1928- CANR-19
Earlier sketch in CA 37-40R
Nist, John (Albert) 1925-1981 CANR-11
Earlier sketch in CA 21-24R
Nitchie, George W(ilson) 1921- 9-12R
Nitske, W(illiam) Robert 1909- CANR-5
Earlier sketch in CA 13-16R
Nittler, Alan H(opkins) 1918- CANR-13
Earlier sketch in CA 61-64
Nityanandan, P(erumpilavil) M(adhava Menon)
1926- 9-12R
Nitze, Paul H(enry) 1907- 140
Nitzsche, Jane Chance 1945- CANR-8
Earlier sketch in CA 57-60
Niven, Alastair 1944- CANR-16
Earlier sketch in CA 81-84
Niven, Alexander Curt 1920- CANR-2
Earlier sketch in CA 5-8R
Niven, (James) David (Graham) 1910-1983
CANR-31
Obituary 110
Earlier sketch in CA 77-80
Niven, Frederick John 1878-1944 DLB 92
Niven, John 1921- 65-68
Niven, Larry
See Niven, Laurence Van Cott
See also AAYA 27
See also CLC 8
See also DLB 8
Niven, Laurence Van Cott 1938- CANR-66
Earlier sketches in CA 21-24R, CANR-14, 44
See also Niven, Larry
See also CAAS 12
See also DAM POP
See also MTCW 1
See also SATA 95
Niven, Marian
See Alston, Mary Niven
Niven, (Cecil) Rex 1898- 120
Niven, Vern
See Grier, Barbara G(ene Damon)
Nivens, Beatryce 1948- 114
Niver, Garry 1938- 138
Nivison, David Shepherd 1923- 103
Nivola, Claire A. 1947- SATA 84
Niwa, Tamako 1922- Brief entry 106
Niwano, Nikkyo 1906- 130
Nix, Garth 1963- 164
See also AAYA 27
See also SATA 97
Nixon, Agnes Eckhardt 1927- 110
See also CLC 21
Nixon, Allan 1918-1995 17-20R
Obituary 148
Nixon, Clarence H., Jr. 1908(?)-1990 Obituary 130
Nixon, Edna (Mary) 5-8R
Nixon, George 1924- 49-52
Nixon, Hershell Howard 1923- 89-92
See also SATA 42
Nixon, Howard Millar 1909-1983 Obituary 109
See also DLB 201
Nixon, Ivor Gray 1905- CAP-2
Earlier sketch in CA 29-32
Nixon, Joan Lowery 1927- CANR-38
Earlier sketches in CA 9-12R, CANR-7, 24
See also AAYA 12
See also CLR 24
See also JRDA
See also MAICYA
See also SAAS 9
See also SATA 8, 44, 78
Nixon, John Erskine 1917- 101
Nixon, K.
See Nixon, Kathleen Irene (Blundell)
Nixon, Kathleen Irene (Blundell)
1894-1988(?) 73-76
Obituary 126
See also SATA 14
See also SATA-Obit 59
Nixon, Lucille M. 1908-1963 5-8R
Nixon, Marion 1930- 49-52
Nixon, Richard M(ilhous) 1913-1994 CANR-61
Obituary 147
Earlier sketches in CA 73-76, CANR-33
See also BEST 90:3
See also MTCW 1
Nixon, Robert E(arl, Jr.) 1918- 5-8R
Nixon, St. John Cousins 1885- 5-8R
Nixon, William R(ussell) 1918- 29-32R
Nixson, Frederick Ian 1943- CANR-44
Earlier sketches in CA 104, CANR-20
Nizan, Paul 1905-1940 161
See also DLB 72
See also TCLC 40
Nizer, Louis 1902-1994 53-56
Obituary 147
Njau, Rebecca
See Njau, Rebeka
Njau, Rebeka 1932- 142
See also BW 2
Njegos, Petar II Petrovic 1813-1851 DLB 147
Njeri, Itabari (Lord) CANR-71
Earlier sketch in CA 139
See also BW 2
Njoroge, J(ames) K(ingangi) 1933- 153
See also BW 2
Njururi, Ngumbu 1930- 17-20R
Nketia, J(oseph) H(anson) Kwabena 1921-
CANR-7
Earlier sketch in CA 9-12R
Nkosi, Lewis 1936- CANR-27
Earlier sketch in CA 65-68
See also BLC 3
See also BW 1
See also CLC 45
See also DAM MULT
See also DLB 157
Nkrumah, Kwame 1909-1972 132
Obituary 113
See also BW 2
Nnadozie, Emmanuel 1956- 164
Noad, Frederick (McNeill) 1929- CANR-4
Earlier sketch in CA 9-12R
Noah, Harold J(ulius) 1925- CANR-30
Earlier sketches in CA 33-36R, CANR-13
Noah, Joseph W(atson) 1928- 81-84
Noah, Robert 1926- 168
Noakes, Jeremy 1941- 101
Noakes, Vivien 1937- 65-68
Noall, Roger 1935- 9-12R
Noam, Eli Michael 1946- 145
Nobbs, David 1935- 138
Nobile, Philip 1941- 152
Nobile, Umberto 1885-1978 Obituary 81-84
Nobisso, Josephine 1953- 146
See also SATA 78
Noble, Allen G(eorge) 1930- 116
Noble, Charles
See Pawley, Martin Edward
Noble, David Watson 1925- CANR-1
Earlier sketch in CA 49-52
Noble, Dudley (Henry) 1893(?)-1970 Obituary 104
Noble, Elizabeth Marian 1945- CANR-9
Earlier sketch in CA 65-68
Noble, G(eorge) Bernard 1892-1972 CAP-2
Obituary 37-40R
Earlier sketch in CA 33-36
Noble, Iain (Andrew) 1949- 128
Noble, Iris (Davis) 1922-1986 CANR-2
Obituary 120
Earlier sketch in CA 1-4R
See also SATA 5
See also SATA-Obit 49
Noble, J(ames) Kendrick, Jr. 1928- 17-20R
Noble, J(ames) Kendrick
1896(?)-1978 Obituary 104
Noble, Jeanne L(aveta) 1926- Brief entry 112
Noble, John (Appelbe) 1914- CANR-1
Earlier sketch in CA 45-48
Noble, John 1923- 45-48
Noble, John Wesley 1913- 9-12R
Noble, Joseph Veach 1920- 61-64
Noble, June (Solveig) 1924-1984 CANR-18
Earlier sketch in CA 97-100
Noble, Kathleen 1950- 146
Noble, Marguerite (Buchanan) 1910- 105
Noble, Marty 1947- SATA 97
Noble, Stanley R(odman)
1904(?)-1977 Obituary 104
Noble, Trinka Hakes Brief entry 116
See also SATA-Brief 37
Noble, William Charles 1935- 107
Noble, William P(arker) 1932- CANR-39
Earlier sketches in CA 101, CANR-18
Nochlin, Linda Weinberg 1931- CANR-6
Earlier sketch in CA 9-12R
Nock, Albert Jay 1870(?)-1945 166
Brief entry 122
Nock, Francis J. 1905-1969 CAP-1
Earlier sketch in CA 13-14
Nock, O(swald) S(tevens) 1905- CANR-16
Earlier sketch in CA 85-88
Nockolds, Harold 1907-1982 Obituary 108
Noddings, Nel 1929- CANR-48
Earlier sketch in CA 115
Noddings, Thomas C. 1933- CANR-2
Earlier sketch in CA 49-52
Nodel, Sol 1912-1976 Obituary 107
Nodelman, Perry 1942- 160
See also SATA 101
Nodier, (Jean) Charles (Emmanuel) 1780-1844 DLB 119
Nodset, Joan L.
See Lexau, Joan M.
Noe, Kenneth W. 1957- 150
Noe, Thomas R. 1947- 112
Noe, Tom
See Noe, Thomas R.
Noel, Christopher 1960- 127
Noel, Daniel C(alhoun) 1936- 101
Noel, Hilda Bloxton, Jr.
See Schroetter, Hilda Noel
Noel, John
See Bird, Dennis L(eslie)
Noel, John V(avasour), Jr. 1912- CANR-15
Earlier sketch in CA 21-24R
Noel, Roden 1834-1894 DLB 35
Noel, Roger Arthur 1942- 144
Noel, Ruth (Swycaffer) 1947- 69-72
Noel, Sterling 1903-1984 Obituary 114
Noel, Thomas Jacob 1945- CANR-49
Earlier sketches in CA 107, CANR-24
Noel-Baker, Philip John 1889-1982 Obituary 108
Noel Hume, Ivor 1927- CANR-12
Earlier sketch in CA 13-16R
See also SATA 65
Noer, David M. 1939- 145
Noer, Thomas John 1944- 102
Noestlinger, Christine 1936- CANR-38
Brief entry 115
Earlier sketch in CA 123
See also CLR 12
See also MAICYA
See also SATA 64
See also SATA-Brief 37
Noether, Emiliana P. 101
Nof, Shimon Y. 1946- 135
Nofi, Albert A(urelio) 1944- 112
Nofziger, Lyn (C.) 1924- 145
Nofziger, Margaret 1946- CANR-30
Earlier sketch in CA 110
Nogami Yaeko 1885-1985 DLB 180
Nogee, Joseph Lippman 1929- 17-20R
Noggle, Burl L. 1924- 134
Brief entry 107
Nogo, Rajko Petrov 1945- DLB 181
Noguchi, Hideyo Seisaku 1876-1928 162
Noguchi, Rick 1967- 162
Noguchi, Yone 1875-1947 TCLC 80
Noguere, Suzanne 1947- 107
See also SATA 34
Nohl, Frederick 1927- CANR-3
Earlier sketch in CA 5-8R
Nohrnberg, James (Carson) 1941- 69-72
Nojiri, Kiyohiko 1897-1973 93-96
Obituary 41-44R
Nokes, David 1948- 141
Nokes, Gerald Dacre 1899-1971 Obituary 104
Nolan, Alan T. 1923- 1-4R
Nolan, Albert 1934- 117
Nolan, Bob 1908(?)-1980 Obituary 101
Nolan, Brian
See O Nuallain, Brian
Nolan, Carroll A(nthony) 1906- 17-20R
Nolan, Christopher 1965- 111
See also CLC 58
Nolan, Chuck
See Edson, J(ohn) T(homas)
Nolan, David (Joseph) 1946- 132
Nolan, Dennis 1945- CANR-59
Earlier sketches in CA 112, CANR-32
See also SATA 42, 92
See also SATA-Brief 34
Nolan, Edward Francis 1915- Brief entry 108
Nolan, Frederick William 1931- 147
Nolan, James 1947- CANR-5
Earlier sketch in CA 53-56
Nolan, Janne E. 140
Nolan, Jeannette Covert 1897-1974 CANR-4
Obituary 53-56
Earlier sketch in CA 5-8R
See also SATA 2
See also SATA-Obit 27
Nolan, Keith W(illiam) 1964- CANR-36
Earlier sketch in CA 114
Nolan, Madeena Spray 1943- 89-92
Nolan, Michael 1940- 126
Nolan, Paul T(homas) 1919- CANR-2
Earlier sketch in CA 5-8R
See also SATA 48
Nolan, Richard Thomas 1937- CANR-10
Earlier sketch in CA 25-28R
Nolan, Tom 1948- 77-80

Nolan, William F(rancis) 1928- CANR-63
Earlier sketches in CA 1-4R, CANR-1
See also CAAS 16
See also DLB 8
See also SATA 88
See also SATA-Brief 28
Nolan, Winefride (Bell) 1913- 13-16R
Noland, C. F. M. 1810(?)-1858 .... DLB 11
Noland, Ronald G(ene) 1936- 41-44R
Nolde, O(tto) Frederick 1899-1972 .... CAP-2
Obituary 37-40R
Earlier sketch in CA 29-32
Nolen, Barbara 1902- 104
Nolen, Claude H. 1921- 21-24R
Nolen, William A(nthony) 1928-1986 .... CANR-15
Obituary 121
Earlier sketch in CA 77-80
Nolin, Bertil 1926- CANR-52
Earlier sketch in CA 65-68
Noling, A(lfred) W(ells) 1899- CAP-2
Earlier sketch in CA 29-32
Noll, Bink
See Noll, Lou Barker
Noll, Lou Barker 1927- 5-8R
Noll, Mark A(llan) 1946- CANR-38
Earlier sketch in CA 115
Noll, Martin
See Buxbaum, Martin (David)
Noll, Peter 1926-1982 142
Noll, Richard 1959- 134
Noll, Roger G(ordon) 1940- CANR-55
Earlier sketches in CA 53-56, CANR-8, 27
Noll, Sally 1946- .... SATA 82
Nollau, Gunther 1911- 5-8R
Nollen, Stanley D(ale) 1940- 110
Nolletti, Arthur (E., Jr.) 1941- 145
Nolte, Carl William 1933- 77-80
Nolte, Elleta 1919- 61-64
Nolte, M(ervin) Chester 1911- 9-12R
Nolte, William H(enry) 1928- 33-36R
Nolting, Frederick (Ernest, Jr.)
1911-1989 Obituary 130
Nolting, Orin F(rederyc) 1903- 29-32R
Noltingk, B(ernard) E(dward) 1918- 17-20R
Noma, Hiroshi 1915-1991 .... DLB 182
Noma, Koremichi 1938(?)-1987 Obituary 122
Noma, Shoichi 1911-1984 Obituary 113
Nomad, Max 1880(?)-1973 Obituary 41-44R
Nomura, Masayasu 1927- 164
Noname
See Senarens, Luis P(hilip)
Nonas, Elisabeth 1949- 119
Nonet, Philippe 1939- 57-60
Nonhebel, Clare 1953- 119
Noon, Brian 1919- 49-52
Noon, Jeff 1957- 148
See also CLC 91
Noon, William T(homas) 1912-1975 65-68
Obituary 53-56
Noonan, John Ford 1943- 85-88
Noonan, John T(homas), Jr. 1926- CANR-13
Earlier sketch in CA 13-16R
Noonan, Julia 1946- CANR-65
Earlier sketch in CA 33-36R
See also SATA 4, 95
Noonan, Lowell G(erald) 1922- 29-32R
Noonan, Michael John 1921- 21-24R
Noonan, Miles
See McConville, Michael (Anthony)
Noonan, Peggy 1950- 132
See also BEST 90:3
Noonan, Robert Phillipe
See Tressell, Robert
Noonan, Tom 1951- 158
Noone, Edwina
See Avallone, Michael (Angelo, Jr.)
Noone, John 1936- Brief entry 109
See also DLB 14
Noone, Richard 1918(?)-1973 Obituary 104
Noorbergen, Rene 1928- 77-80
Nooteboom, Cees 1933- 130
Brief entry 124
Nora, Eugenio de 1923- .... DLB 134
Nora, James Jackson 1928- CANR-42
Earlier sketches in CA 104, CANR-20
Norall, Frank 1918- 133
Norback, Craig T(homas) 1943- 113
Norbeck, Edward 1915- CANR-1
Earlier sketch in CA 1-4R
Norberg-Schulz, Christian 1926- 81-84
Norbu, Thubten Jigme
See Thubten, Sigme Norbu
Norcross, John
See Conroy, John Wesley
Norcross, Lisabet
See Gladstone, Arthur M.
Norcutt, Bill
See Norcutt, William E.
Norcutt, William E. 1946- Brief entry 118
Nord, Ole C. 1935- 13-16R
Nord, Paul 1900(?)-1981 Obituary 103
Nord, Walter R(obert) 1939- 37-40R
Nordan, Lewis (Alonzo) 1939- CANR-72
Earlier sketches in CA 117, CANR-40
Nordberg, H(arold) Orville 1916- 1-4R
Nordberg, Robert B. 1921- 13-16R
Nordby, Vernon James 1945- 57-60
Nordell, (Hans) Roderick 1925- 104
Norden, Albert 1904-1982 Obituary 107
Norden, Charles
See Durrell, Lawrence (George)
Norden, Denis 1922- CANR-29
Earlier sketch in CA 104
Norden, Heinz 1905- 53-56
Norden, Helen Brown
See Lawrenson, Helen
Nordham, George Washington 1929- CANR-47
Earlier sketches in CA 106, CANR-23
Nordhaug, Odd 1953- 140
Nordhaus, William D(awbney) 1941- 97-100
Nordhoff, Charles (Bernard) 1887-1947 Brief
entry 108
See also DLB 9
See also SATA 23
See also TCLC 23
Nordholm, Harriet 1912- 29-32R
Nordicus
See Snyder, Louis L(eo)
Nordin, D(ennis) Sven 1942- 61-64
Nordland, Gerald John 1927- 104
Nordland, Rod(ney Lee) 1949- 118
Nordlicht, Lillian 105
See also SATA 29
Nordlinger, Eric A. 1939- 77-80
Nordloh, David J(oseph) 1942- 137
Nordmann, Joseph (Behrens) 1922- 25-28R
Nordness, Lee 1924- 9-12R
Nordoff, Paul 1909-1977 102
Nordquist, Barbara K(ay) 1940- 77-80
Nordskog, John Eric 1893-1974 .... 1-4R
Obituary 120
Nordstrom, Ursula 1910-1988 .... 13-16R
Obituary 126
See also SATA 3
See also SATA-Obit 57
Nordtvedt, Matilda 1926- 124
See also SATA 67
Nordyke, Eleanor C(ole) 1927- 107
Nordyke, James W(alter) 1930- 49-52
Noreen, Robert Gerald 1938- 77-80
Norelli, Martina R(oudabush) 1942- 73-76
Noren, Catherine (Hanf) 1938- CANR-16
Earlier sketch in CA 65-68
Noren, Paul Harold Andreas 1910- CAP-1
Earlier sketch in CA 11-12
Norfleet, Barbara P. 1926- Brief entry 107
Norfleet, Mary Crockett 1919- 1-4R
Norfolk, Lawrence 1963- 144
See also CLC 76
Norgate, Matthew 1901- 103
Norgay, Tenzing 1914-1986 Obituary 119
Nori, Claude 1949- CANR-18
Earlier sketch in CA 101
Noriega, Chon A. 1961- 141
Norinsky, Marvin 1927- 130
Norland, Howard Bernett 1932- 49-52
Norling, Bernard 1924- 29-32R
Norling, Jo(sephine Stearns) 1-4R
Norling, Rita 61-64
Norman, Adrian R(oger) D(udley) 1938- CANR-26
Earlier sketch in CA 29-32R
Norman, Alexander Vesey Bethune 1930- CANR-9
Earlier sketch in CA 21-24R
Norman, Barbara 33-36R
Norman, Barry 151
Norman, Bruce 1936- 61-64
Norman, C. J.
See Barrett, Norman (S.)
Norman, Cecilia 1927- CANR-23
Earlier sketches in CA 57-60, CANR-7
Norman, Charles 1904-1996 107
Obituary 153
See also DLB 111
See also SATA 38
See also SATA-Obit 92
Norman, Diana 1935- 135
Norman, Don(ald) Cleveland
1909(?)-1979 Obituary 89-92
Norman, Donald A(rthur) 1935- CANR-1
Earlier sketch in CA 49-52
Norman, Dorothy 1905-1997 .... 25-28R
Obituary 157
Norman, E. D.
See Goodwin, Bennie Eugene II
Norman, Edward (Robert) 1938- CANR-27
Earlier sketches in CA 17-20R, CANR-10
Norman, Frank 1930-1980 .... CANR-6
Obituary 102
Earlier sketch in CA 1-4R
Norman, Geraldine (Lucia) 1940- 93-96
Norman, Greg(ory John) 1955- 133
Norman, Hilary 126
Norman, Howard
See Norman, Howard A.
Norman, Howard A. 1949- 137
Brief entry 129
Interview in 137
See also SATA 81
Norman, James
See Schmidt, James Norman
Norman, Jillian 1940- 25-28R
Norman, Joe
See Heard, J(oseph) Norman
Norman, John
See Lange, John Frederick, Jr.
Norman, John 1912- 17-20R
Norman, Joyce Ann 1937- 65-68
Norman, Kerry
See Le Pelley, Guernsey
Norman, Lilith 1927- CANR-52
Earlier sketches in CA 45-48, CANR-1
See also SATA 86
Norman, Lloyd (Henry) 1913-1987 102
Obituary 124
Norman, Louis
See Whittemore, Don
Norman, Marc 1941- 49-52
Norman, Marsha 1947- CANR-41
Earlier sketch in CA 105
See also CABS 3
See also CLC 28
See also DAM DRAM
See also DC 8
See also DLBY 84
Norman, Mary 1931- .... SATA 36
Norman, Maxwell H(erbert) 1917- 29-32R
Norman, Michael 1947- 129
Norman, Nicole
See Cudlipp, Edythe
Norman, Philip 1943- 156
Norman, Rick (J.) 1954- 137
Norman, Ruth 1903(?)-1977 Obituary 73-76
Norman, Steve
See Pashko, Stanley
Norman, Sylva 1901- CAP-1
Earlier sketch in CA 13-14
Norman, Theodore 1910-1987 124
Obituary 122
Norman, Vesey
See Norman, Alexander Vesey Bethune
Norman, W. S.
See Wilson, N(orman) Scarlyn
Norman, Yvonne
See Seely, Norma
Norment, Lisa 1966- 155
See also SATA 91
Normyx
See Douglas, (George) Norman
Norodom Sihanouk (Varman), Samdech Preah
1922- 129
Brief entry 106
Norquest, Carrol 1901-1981 .... 41-44R
Obituary 133
Norquist, Richard F(ranklin) 1933- 113
Norrander, Barbara 1954- 141
Norrell, Gregory T. 1960- 160
Norrell, Robert J(efferson) 1952- 139
Norrie, Ian 1927- CANR-49
Earlier sketches in CA 106, CANR-23
Norris, Charles G(ilman Smith) 1881-1945 155
Brief entry 118
See also DLB 9
Norris, Christopher (Charles) 1947- CANR-53
Earlier sketches in CA 111, CANR-29
Norris, Christopher Neil Foxley
See Foxley-Norris, Christopher Neil
Norris, Clarence 1912-1989 Obituary 127
Norris, Donald F(ranklin) 1942- CANR-2
Earlier sketch in CA 49-52
Norris, Dorothy E. Koch 1907- CAP-2
Earlier sketch in CA 21-22
Norris, Edgar Poe
See Kinnaird, Clark
Norris, Francis Hubert 1909- 5-8R
Norris, Frank 1870-1902
See Norris, (Benjamin) Frank(lin, Jr.)
See also CDALB 1865-1917
See also DLB 12, 71, 186
See also SSC 28
Norris, (Benjamin) Frank(lin, Jr.) 1870-1902 160
Brief entry 110
See also Norris, Frank
See also TCLC 24
Norris, Frank C(allan) 1907-1967 Obituary 25-28R
Norris, Gunilla Brodde 1939- 93-96
See also SATA 20
Norris, H. T. 160
Norris, Harold 1918- 108
Norris, Hoke 1913-1977 .... 9-12R
Obituary 73-76
Norris, J(ames) A(lfred) 1929- 25-28R
Norris, James Donald 1930- 17-20R
Norris, Joan 1943- 73-76
Norris, John 1925- 9-12R
Norris, Kathleen (Thompson)
1880-1966 Obituary 25-28R
Norris, Kathleen 1947- 160
Norris, Ken 1951- 113
Norris, Kenneth S(tafford) 1924- 77-80
Norris, Leslie 1921- CANR-14
Earlier sketches in CAP-1, CA 11-12
See also CLC 14
See also DLB 27
Norris, Louanne 1930- CANR-20
Earlier sketch in CA 53-56
Norris, Louis William 1906- CAP-1
Earlier sketch in CA 9-10
Norris, Maureen
See Cudlipp, Edythe
Norris, Nigel (Harold) 1943- 65-68
Norris, Pippa 1953- 134
Norris, Richard A(lfred), Jr. 1930- 17-20R
Norris, Ronald V. 1940- 116
Norris, Ruby Turner
See Morris, Ruby Turner
Norris, Russell Bradner (Jr.) 1942- 53-56
Norris, Theo L. 1926- 21-24R
Norse, Harold (George) 1916- CANR-4
Earlier sketch in CA 53-56
See also CAAS 18
See also DLB 16
Norst, Joel
See Mitchell, Kirk (John)
North, Alvin J(ohn) 1917- 49-52
North, Andrew
See Norton, Andre
North, Anthony
See Koontz, Dean R(ay)
North, Captain George
See Stevenson, Robert Louis (Balfour)
North, Carol S. 1954- 128
North, Charles W.
See Bauer, Erwin A.
North, Christopher
See Wilson, John
North, Christopher R(ichard)
1888-1975 Obituary 61-64
North, Colin
See Bingley, David Ernest
North, Darian 166
North, Edmund H(all) 1911-1990 121
Obituary 132
North, Eleanor B(eryl) 1898- 49-52
North, Elizabeth 1932- 81-84
North, Gary 1942- CANR-38
Earlier sketches in CA 65-68, CANR-16
North, Gil
See Horne, Geoffrey
North, Helen Florence 1921- 104
North, Howard
See Trevor, Elleston
North, Joan 1920- 13-16R
See also SATA 16
North, John (Francis Allen) 1894-1973 107
Obituary 104
North, John (David) 1934- 148
North, Joseph 1904-1976 .... CANR-4
Obituary 69-72
Earlier sketch in CA 1-4R
North, Marianne 1830-1890 .... DLB 174
North, Mark
See Miller, Wright (Watts)
North, Milou
See Erdrich, Louise
North, Morgan 1915(?)-1978 Obituary 104
North, Oliver L(aurence) 1943- 142
North, Rick
See Brenner, Mayer Alan
North, Robert
See Withers, Carl A.
North, Robert Carver 1914- CANR-4
Earlier sketch in CA 5-8R
North, Robert Grady 1916- 17-20R
North, Sara
See Bonham, Barbara Thomas
and Hager, Jean
North, Sterling 1906-1974 .... CANR-40
Obituary 53-56
Earlier sketch in CA 5-8R
See also JRDA
See also MAICYA
See also SATA 1, 45
See also SATA-Obit 26
North, Wheeler James 1922- 101
Northam, Ray M(ervyn) 1929- 73-76
Northart, Leo J(oseph) 1929- 69-72
Northcote, Peter
See Cotes, Peter
Northcott, (William) Cecil 1902-1987 .... 9-12R
Obituary 124
See also SATA-Obit 55
Northcott, Kenneth J(ames) 1922- CANR-29
Earlier sketch in CA 45-48
Northcutt, Wayne 1944- 138
Northedge, Frederick Samuel 1918-1985 104
Obituary 115
Northen, Helen 1914- CANR-13
Earlier sketch in CA 33-36R
Northen, Henry T(heodore) 1908-1979 97-100
Northen, Rebecca Tyson 1910- 105
Northgrave, Anne
See Tibble, Anne
Northmore, Elizabeth Florence 1906-1974 .... CAP-2
Earlier sketch in CA 19-20
Northouse, Cameron (George) 1948- 81-84
Northrop, Filmer S(tuart) C(uckow) 1893-1992 ....
CANR-17
Obituary 139
Earlier sketch in CA 1-4R
Northrop, J. H.
See Northrop, John H(oward)
Northrop, John H(oward) 1891-1987 Obituary 123
Northrup, B. A.
See Hubbard, L(afayette) Ron(ald)
Northrup, Herbert Roof 1918- 9-12R
North Staffs
See Hulme, T(homas) E(rnest)
Northumbrian Gentleman, The
See Tegner, Henry (Stuart)
Northway, Mary L(ouise) 1909- 45-48
Northwood, Lawrence K(ing) 1917- 13-16R
Nortje, Arthur 1942- .... DLB 125
Nortje, (Kenneth) Arthur 1942-1970 141
See also BW 2
Norton, Alan (Lewis) 1926- CANR-15
Earlier sketch in CA 81-84
Norton, Alden H(olmes) 1903- 101
Norton, Alice 1926- 33-36R
Norton, Alice Mary
See Norton, Andre
See also MAICYA
See also SATA 1, 43
Norton, Andre 1912- CANR-68
Earlier sketch in CA 1-4R
See also Norton, Alice Mary
See also AAYA 14
See also CLC 12
See also CLR 50
See also DLB 8, 52
See also JRDA
See also MTCW 1
See also SATA 91
Norton, Andrews 1786-1853 .... DLB 1
Norton, Augustus Richard 1946- CANR-48
Earlier sketch in CA 113
Norton, Bess
See Norton, Olive (Claydon)
Norton, Bettina A(ntonia) 1936- 93-96
Norton, Boyd 1936- 37-40R

Norton, Bram
See Bramesco, Norton J.
Norton, Browning
See Norton, Frank R. B(rowning)
Norton, Bryan G(eorge) 1944- ... 143
Norton, Caroline 1808-1877 ... DLB 21, 159, 199
Norton, Charles A(lbert) 1920- ... 109
Norton, Charles Eliot 1827-1908 ... DLB 1, 64
Norton, David Fate 1937- ... 107
Norton, David L. 1930- ... 37-40R
Norton, (William) Elliot 1903- Brief entry ... 109
Norton, Frank R. B(rowning) 1909- ... 61-64
See also SATA 10
Norton, Frederick H. 1896- ... 61-64
Norton, Glyn P(eter) 1941- ... 122
Norton, Harry N(eugebauer) 1922- ... 142
Norton, Herman A. 1921- ... CANR-7
Earlier sketch in CA 5-8R
Norton, Howard Melvin 1911-1994 ... CANR-3
Obituary ... 144
Earlier sketch in CA 1-4R
Norton, Hugh S(tanton) 1921- ... 9-12R
Norton, John 1606-1663 ... DLB 24
Norton, Joseph L(ouis) 1918- ... 29-32R
Norton, Lucy 1902-1989 Obituary ... 129
Norton, M. D. Herter
See Crena de Iongh, Mary (Dows Herter Norton)
Norton, Mary 1903-1992 ... 139
Earlier sketch in CA 97-100
See also CLR 6
See also DLB 160
See also MAICYA
See also SATA 18, 60
See also SATA-Obit 72
Norton, Mary Beth 1943- ... CANR-5
Earlier sketch in CA 49-52
Norton, Mary E(lizabeth) 1913- ... 41-44R
Norton, Olive (Claydon) 1913-1973 ... 9-12R
Norton, Paul Foote 1917- ... 41-44R
Norton, Perry L. 1920- ... 13-16R
Norton, Peter (John) 1913-1995 ... 13-16R
Obituary ... 148
Norton, Philip 1951- ... 143
Norton, Rictor 1945- ... 165
Norton, Robert L. 1939- ... 143
Norton, Roger C(ecil) 1921- ... 114
Norton, Thomas 1532-1584 ... DLB 62
Norton, Thomas Elliot 1942- ... 61-64
Norton, Victor 1906-1983 Obituary ... 109
Norton, Wesley 1923- ... 114
Norton-Smith, John 1931-1988 ... 107
Obituary ... 127
Norton-Taylor, Duncan 1904-1982 ... 102
Obituary ... 107
Norvil, Manning
See Bulmer, (Henry) Kenneth
Norville, Warren 1923- ... 73-76
Norwak, Mary 1929- ... 109
Norway, Kate
See Norton, Olive (Claydon)
Norway, Nevil Shute 1899-1960 ... 102
Obituary ... 93-96
See also Shute, Nevil
Norwich, (Lord) John Julius (Cooper) 1929- ... CANR-60
Earlier sketches in CA 49-52, CANR-5, 29
Norwich, William 1954- ... 157
Norwood, Fred W(ayland) 1920- Brief entry ... 112
Norwood, Frederick Abbott 1914- ... CANR-42
Earlier sketches in CA 1-4R, CANR-5, 20
Norwood, Gilbert 1880-1954 Brief entry ... 116
Norwood, John
See Stark, Raymond
Norwood, Paul
See Nettl, J(ohn) P(eter)
Norwood, Robert (Winkworth) 1874-1932 ... 155
See also DLB 92
Norwood, Robin ... 128
Norwood, Victor G(eorge) C(harles) 1920-1983 ... CANR-64
Earlier sketches in CA 21-24R, CANR-10
Norwood, Warren C. 1945- ... 112
Nosaka, Akiyuki 1930- ... DLB 182
Nosanow, Barbara Shissler 1931- ... CANR-28
Earlier sketch in CA 29-32R
Nosco, Peter 1950- ... 93-96
Nosille, Nabrah
See Ellison, Harlan (Jay)
Noss, John Boyer 1896- ... 85-88
Noss, Luther (Melancthon) 1907- ... 5-8R
Nossack, Hans Erich 1901-1978 ... 93-96
Obituary ... 85-88
See also CLC 6
See also DLB 69
Nossal, Frederick (Christian) 1927-1979 ... 5-8R
Obituary ... 89-92
Nossal, Gustav Joseph Victor 1931- ... 109
Nossiter, Bernard D(aniel) 1926-1992 ... CANR-47
Obituary ... 138
Earlier sketch in CA 41-44R
Nostrand, Howard Lee 1910- ... 9-12R
Nostwich, T(heodore) D. ... 127
Nosu, Chuji
See Ozu, Yasujiro
Notar, Stephen 1926- ... 119
Notarius
See Martin, Andrew
Notehelfer, F(red) G(eorge) 1939- ... 81-84
Notenburg, Eleanora (Genrikhovna) von
See Guro, Elena
Notestein, Frank Wallace 1902-1983 Obituary ... 109
Notestein, Wallace 1878-1969 ... CAP-1
Earlier sketch in CA 9-10
Noth, Martin D. 1902-1968 ... CAP-2
Earlier sketch in CA 21-22
Nothing Venture
See Finney, Humphrey S.
Notker Balbulus c. 840-912 ... DLB 148
Notker III of Saint Gall c. 950-1022 ... DLB 148
Notker von Zwiefalten (?)-1095 ... DLB 148
Notlep, Robert
See Pelton, Robert W(ayne)
Notley, Alice 1945- ... 154
Brief entry ... 124
See also CAAS 27
Noto, Lore(nzo) 1923- ... 134
Nott, David 1928- ... 45-48
Nott, Kathleen Cecilia ... CANR-3
Earlier sketch in CA 1-4R
Notterman, Joseph M(elvin) 1923- ... 17-20R
Nottingham, Elizabeth K. 1900- ... 93-96
Nottingham, William Jesse 1927- ... 25-28R
Notz, Rebecca Love 1888-1974 Obituary ... 104
Nourbese Philip, M(arlene)
See Philip, M(arlene) Nourbese
Nourie, Alan (Raymond) 1942- ... 138
Nourie, Barbara (Livingston) 1947- ... 138
Nourissier, Francois 1927- ... 81-84
Nourse, Alan E(dward) 1928-1992 ... CANR-45
Obituary ... 145
Earlier sketches in CA 1-4R, CANR-3, 21
See also CLR 33
See also DLB 8
See also SATA 48
Nourse, Edwin G(riswold) 1883-1974 Obituary ... 49-52
Nourse, Hugh O(liver) 1933- Brief entry ... 107
Nourse, James G(regory) 1947- ... 105
Nourse, Joan Thellusson 1921- ... 9-12R
Nourse, Mary Augusta 1880(?)-1971 Obituary ... 33-36R
Nourse, Robert Eric Martin 1938- ... 21-24R
Nouveau, Arthur
See Whitcomb, Ian
Nouwen, Henri J(osef Machiel) 1932-1996 ... 73-76
Obituary ... 153
Nova, Craig 1945- ... CANR-53
Earlier sketches in CA 45-48, CANR-2
See also CLC 7, 31
Novack, Evelyn Reed 1906(?)-1979 Obituary ... 85-88
Novack, George (Edward) 1905-1992 ... CANR-47
Obituary ... 139
Earlier sketch in CA 49-52
Novak, Barbara ... 97-100
Novak, Bogdan C(yril) 1919- ... 33-36R
Novak, David 1941- ... 93-96
Novak, Jane Dailey 1917- ... 105
Novak, Joe
See Novak, Joseph
Novak, Joseph
See Kosinski, Jerzy (Nikodem)
Novak, Joseph 1898- ... CAP-1
Earlier sketch in CA 11-12
Novak, Lorna 1927- ... 17-20R
Novak, Matt 1962- ... 125
See also SATA 60
See also SATA-Brief 52
Novak, Maximillian E(rwin) 1930- ... CANR-12
Earlier sketch in CA 33-36R
Novak, Michael 1933- ... CANR-30
Earlier sketches in CA 1-4R, CANR-1
Novak, Michael Paul 1935- ... 49-52
Novak, Robert
See Levinson, Leonard
Novak, Robert D(avid) 1931- ... CANR-12
Earlier sketch in CA 13-16R
Novak, Rose 1940- ... CANR-22
Earlier sketch in CA 105
Novak, Slobodan 1924- ... DLB 181
Novak, Stephen R(obert) 1922- ... 85-88
Novak, Vjenceslav 1859-1905 ... DLB 147
Novak, William (Arnold) 1948- ... CANR-26
Earlier sketch in CA 93-96
Novakovich, Josip 1956- ... 149
Novalis 1772-1801 ... DLB 90
Novaro, Mario 1868-1944 ... DLB 114
Novarr, David 1917- ... 17-20R
Novas, Himilce 1944- ... 156
Novas Calvo, Lino 1905-1983 ... DLB 145
See also HW
Nove, Alec 1915-1994 ... CANR-3
Obituary ... 145
Earlier sketch in CA 1-4R
Novelli, Florence 1931- ... 112
Novelli, Luca 1947- ... SATA 61
Novello, Don 1943- ... CANR-44
Earlier sketch in CA 107
Noventa, Giacomo 1898-1960 ... DLB 114
Nover, Barnet 1899-1973 Obituary ... 41-44R
Noverr, Douglas A(rthur) 1942- ... 102
Novick, David 1906- ... 33-36R
Novick, Julius Lerner 1939- ... 103
Novick, Marian 1951- ... 123
Novick, Paul 1891-1989 Obituary ... 130
Novick, Sheldon M. 1941- ... 144
Novik, Mary 1945- ... 61-64
Novikov, Nikolai Ivanovich 1744-1818 ... DLB 150
Novins, Stuart 1914(?)-1989 Obituary ... 130
Novis, Emile
See Weil, Simone (Adolphine)
Novitski, Joseph (W. D.) 1940- ... 124
Novitz, Charles R. 1934- ... 69-72
Novitz, David 1945- ... 139
Novo, Salvador 1904-1974 ... 131
Obituary ... 110
See also HW
Novoa, John David Bruce
See Bruce-Novoa, Juan D.
Novoa, Juan Bruce
See Bruce-Novoa, Juan D.
Novogrod, R(eevan) Joseph 1916- ... 29-32R
Novomesky, Ladislav 1904-1976 Obituary ... 69-72
Novotny, Ann M. 1936-1982 ... 25-28R
Obituary ... 108
Novotny, Fritz 1903-(?) ... CANR-18
Earlier sketch in CA 65-68
Novotny, Louise Miller 1889- ... CAP-2
Earlier sketch in CA 23-24
Novy, Marianne (Lucille) 1945- ... 118
Nowacki, Walenty 1906- ... 37-40R
Nowak, Jan 1913- ... 143
Nowak, Mariette 1941- ... 102
Nowakowski, Marek 1935- ... 119
Nowell, Elizabeth Cameron ... CANR-1
Earlier sketch in CA 1-4R
See also SATA 12
Nowlan, Alden (Albert) 1933-1983 ... CANR-5
Earlier sketch in CA 9-12R
See also CLC 15
See also DAC
See also DAM MST
See also DLB 53
Nowlan, James Dunlap 1941- Brief entry ... 105
Nowlan, Philip Francis 1888-1940 ... 164
Brief entry ... 108
Nowlan, Robert Anthony, Jr. 1934- ... CANR-32
Earlier sketch in CA 113
Nowlis, Helen H(oward) 1913- Brief entry ... 111
Noxon, James Herbert 1924- ... 85-88
Noyce, Gaylord B. 1926- ... CANR-53
Earlier sketches in CA 37-40R, CANR-13, 29
Noyes, Alfred 1880-1958 Brief entry ... 104
See also DLB 20
See also TCLC 7
Noyes, Charles Edmund 1904-1972 ... 37-40R
Noyes, Crosby S. 1825-1908 ... DLB 23
Noyes, Crosby S(tuart) 1921-1988 Obituary ... 125
Noyes, David 1898(?)-1981 Obituary ... 104
Noyes, Henry (Halsey) 1910- ... 133
Noyes, James H(oyt) 1927- ... 118
Noyes, Jeanice W. 1914- ... 25-28R
Noyes, Joan 1935- ... 115
Noyes, Kathryn Johnston 1930- ... 17-20R
Noyes, Morgan Phelps 1891-1972 ... CAP-1
Obituary ... 37-40R
Earlier sketch in CA 11-12
Noyes, Nell Braly 1921- ... 37-40R
Noyes, Nicholas 1647-1717 ... DLB 24
Noyes, Peter R. 1930- ... 49-52
Noyes, Russell 1901- ... 25-28R
Noyes, Stanley 1924- ... CANR-35
Earlier sketches in CA 45-48, CANR-1
Noyes, Theodore W. 1858-1946 ... DLB 29
Noyes-Kane, Dorothy 1906- ... CAP-1
Earlier sketch in CA 13-14
Noyle, Ken(neth Alfred Edward) 1922- ... 85-88
Nozick, Martin 1917- ... 37-40R
Nozick, Robert 1938- ... 61-64
Nriagu, Jerome O. 1942- ... 135
Nsarkoh, J. K(wasi) 1931- ... 13-16R
Nucera, Marisa Lonette 1959- ... 17-20R
Nuchtern, Jean 1939- ... 25-28R
Nuckolls, James L(awton) 1938-1987 Obituary ... 123
Nudel, Adele Rice 1927- ... 124
Nudel, Ida 1931- ... 134
Nudelman, Jerrold 1942- ... 33-36R
Nuechterlein, Donald Edwin 1925- ... CANR-1
Earlier sketch in CA 1-4R
Nuelle, Helen S(hearman) 1923- ... CANR-12
Earlier sketch in CA 61-64
Nuernberger, Phil 1942- ... CANR-35
Earlier sketch in CA 114
Nuessel, Frank H(enry) 1943- ... CANR-56
Earlier sketches in CA 111, CANR-31
Nuetzel, Charles (Alexander) 1934- ... 105
Nugent, Bruce
See Nugent, Richard Bruce
Nugent, (Donald) Christopher 1930- ... 139
Nugent, Donald G(ene) 1930- ... 45-48
Nugent, Elliott (John) 1899-1980 ... 5-8R
Obituary ... 101
Nugent, Frances Roberts 1904-1964(?) ... 5-8R
Nugent, Frank 1908-1965 ... DLB 44
Nugent, Jeffrey B(ishop) 1936- ... 93-96
Nugent, John Peer 1930- ... 13-16R
Nugent, Nancy 1938- ... CANR-16
Earlier sketch in CA 65-68
Nugent, Neill 1947- ... 133
Nugent, Nicholas 1949- ... SATA 73
Nugent, Richard Bruce 1906(?)- ... 125
See also BW 1
See also DLB 51
Nugent, Robert 1920- ... 61-64
Nugent, Tom 1943- ... 49-52
Nugent, Vincent Joseph 1913- ... 41-44R
Nugent, Walter T(erry) K(ing) 1935- ... CANR-5
Earlier sketch in CA 5-8R
Null, Gary ... CANR-17
Earlier sketch in CA 65-68
Nulman, Macy 1923- ... 57-60
Nulty, William H(arry) 1932- ... 136
Numbers, Ronald L(eslie) 1942- ... CANR-18
Earlier sketch in CA 101
Numeroff, Laura Joffe 1953- ... CANR-58
Earlier sketch in CA 106
See also SATA 28, 90
Nummi, Seppo (Antero Yrjoepoika) 1932-1981 Obituary ... 108
Nunan, Desmond J. 1927- ... 17-20R
Nunes, Claude 1924- ... 134
Brief entry ... 112
Nunes, Lygia Bojunga 1932- ... 142
See also SATA 75
Nunes, Rhoda (Gwylleth) 1938- Brief entry ... 113
Nunez, Ana Rosa 1926- ... CANR-14
Earlier sketch in CA 69-72
Nunis, Doyce B(lackman), Jr. 1924- ... CANR-42
Earlier sketches in CA 5-8R, CANR-3, 19
Nunley, Maggie Rennert
See Rennert, Maggie
Nunn, Frederick M. 1937- ... 33-36R
Nunn, G(odfrey) Raymond 1918- ... CANR-55
Earlier sketches in CA 33-36R, CANR-13
Nunn, Henry L(ightfoot) 1878-1972 Obituary ... 37-40R
Nunn, John 1955- ... 115
Nunn, Kem ... 159
See also CLC 34
Nunn, Marshall E(arl) 1928- ... 112
Nunn, Walter (Harris) 1942- ... CANR-23
Earlier sketch in CA 45-48
Nunn, William Curtis 1908- ... CANR-1
Earlier sketch in CA 1-4R
Nunnally, Tiina 1952- ... 158
Nunnerley, (Gould) David 1947- ... 45-48
Nuquist, Andrew E(dgerton) 1905-1975 Obituary ... 61-64
Nuraini
See Sim, Katharine (Thomasset)
Nurcombe, Barry 1933- ... 65-68
Nurenberg, Thelma
See Greenhaus, Thelma Nurenberg
Nurge, Ethel 1920- ... 33-36R
Nurmi, Martin Karl 1920- ... CANR-17
Earlier sketch in CA 1-4R
Nurnberg, Maxwell 1897-1984 ... CANR-2
Obituary ... 114
Earlier sketch in CA 5-8R
See also SATA 27
See also SATA-Obit 41
Nurnberg, Walter 1907- ... 13-16R
Nurse, Malcolm Ivan Meredith 1903-1959 Brief entry ... 119
Nurse, Peter H(arold) 1926- ... 9-12R
Nusbaum, N. Richard
See Nash, N. Richard
Nusbaum, Rosemary 1907- ... 113
Nusic, Branislav 1864-1938 ... DLB 147
Nussbaum, Aaron 1910-1981 ... 49-52
Obituary ... 104
Nussbaum, Al(bert F.) 1934- ... 85-88
Nussbaum, Martha Craven 1947- ... 134
Nussbaumer, Paul (Edmund) 1934- ... 93-96
See also SATA 16
Nusser, J(ames) L(ivingston) 1925- ... 1-4R
Nute, Grace Lee 1895-1990 Obituary ... 131
Nute, Kevin 1958- ... 145
Nutini, Hugo G(ino) 1928- ... 155
Brief entry ... 109
Nutt, Grady 1934- ... 97-100
Nutt, Ken 1951- ... SATA 97
Nutt, Paul C. 1939- ... 142
Nuttall, A(nthony) D(avid) 1937- ... CANR-11
Earlier sketch in CA 21-24R
Nuttall, Geoffrey Fillingham 1911- ... CANR-25
Earlier sketches in CA 13-16R, CANR-10
Nuttall, Jeff 1933- ... CANR-14
Earlier sketch in CA 29-32R
Nuttall, Kenneth 1907- ... 17-20R
Nuttall-Smith, Margaret Emily Noel 1919- ... CANR-45
Earlier sketch in CA 104
See also Fortnum, Peggy
Nutter, G(ilbert) Warren 1923-1979 ... CANR-2
Obituary ... 85-88
Earlier sketch in CA 1-4R
Nuttgens, Patrick 1930- ... 128
Nutting, (Harold) Anthony 1920- ... CANR-7
Earlier sketch in CA 5-8R
Nutting, Patricia Fink 1926- ... 129
Nutting, Willis D(wight) 1900-1975 ... CAP-2
Earlier sketch in CA 25-28
Nutzle, Futzie
See Kleinsmith, Bruce John
Nuwer, Hank
See Nuwer, Henry
Nuwer, Henry 1946- ... CANR-57
Earlier sketch in CA 128
Nuygen, Mathieu 1967- ... SATA 80
Nuytten, Bruno 1945- ... 153
Nwankwo, Nkem 1936- ... 65-68
See also BW 2
Nwapa, Flora 1931- ... 143
See also BLCS
See also BW 2
See also DLB 125
Nwoauau, Edwin Ifeanyichukwu 1933- ... 17-20R
Nyabongo, Akiki K. 1905-1975 Obituary ... 61-64
Nyad, Diana 1949- ... 136
Brief entry ... 111
Nyagumbo, Maurice (Tapfumaneyi) 1924-1989 Obituary ... 128
Nyanaponika 1901- ... CAP-1
Earlier sketch in CA 9-10
Nybakken, Elizabeth I. 1940- ... 114
Nybakken, Oscar Edward 1904- ... 93-96
Nyberg, David (Alan) 1943- ... 107
Nyberg, Kathleen Neill 1919- ... 21-24R
Nyberg, (Everett Wayne) Morgan 1944- ... 127
See also SATA 87
Nyce, (Nellie) Helene von Strecker 1885-1969 ... SATA 19
Nyce, Vera 1862-1925 ... SATA 19
Nye, Bill
See Nye, Edgar Wilson
Nye, Doug(las Charles) 1945- Brief entry ... 114
Nye, Edgar Wilson 1850-1896 ... DLB 11, 23, 186
Nye, F(rancis) Ivan 1918- ... CANR-21
Earlier sketches in CA 9-12R, CANR-6
Nye, Hermes 1908- ... CAP-2
Earlier sketch in CA 19-20

Nye, Joseph S(amuel), Jr. 1937- CANR-35
Earlier sketches in CA 25-28R, CANR-12
Nye, Loyal 1921- 106
Nye, Miriam (Maurine Hawthorn) Baker 1918- 85-88
Nye, Naomi Shihab 1952- CANR-70
Earlier sketch in CA 146
See also AAYA 27
See also DLB 120
See also SATA 86
Nye, Nelson C(oral) 1907- CANR-4
Earlier sketch in CA 5-8R
Nye, Robert 1939- CANR-67
Earlier sketches in CA 33-36R, CANR-29
See also CLC 13, 42
See also DAM NOV
See also DLB 14
See also MTCW 1
See also SATA 6
Nye, Robert D(onald) 1934- 73-76
Nye, Robert Evans 1911- CANR-1
Earlier sketch in CA 1-4R
Nye, Russel B(laine) 1913-1993 CANR-4
Obituary 142
Earlier sketch in CA 1-4R
Nye, Simon (Beresford) 1958- 131
Nye, Vernice Trousdale 1913- CANR-1
Earlier sketch in CA 1-4R
Nye, Wilbur S. 1898-1970 CANR-15
Obituary 103
Earlier sketch in CA 1-4R
Nyenhuis, Jacob E(ugene) 1935- Brief entry 117
Nyerere, Julius K(ambarage) 1922- 125
Brief entry 105
See also BW 2
Nygaard, Anita 1934- 65-68
Nygaard, Norman E. 1897-1971 CANR-2
Earlier sketch in CA 1-4R
Nygard, Roald 1935- 103
Nygren, Anders T(heodor) S(amuel) 1890- 9-12R
Nyhart, Nina 1934- 135
Nykoruk, Barbara (Christine) 1949- Brief entry 115
Nylander, Carl 1932- 33-36R
Nylander, Jane C. 1938- 143
Nynych, Stephanie J.
See Caulder, Colline
Nyquist, Ewald B(erger) 1914- Brief entry 113
Nyquist, Thomas E. 1931- 41-44R
Nyren, Dorothy Elizabeth 1927- CANR-5
Earlier sketch in CA 1-4R
Nyren, Karl 1922(?)-1988 Obituary 126
Nyro, Laura 1947- CLC 17
Nystrom, Carolyn 1940- CANR-37
Earlier sketch in CA 114
See also SATA 67
Nzekwu, Onuora 1928- BW 2
Nzimiro, Ikenna 1927- CANR-2
Earlier sketch in CA 45-48

O

O(rdonez), Jaime E(dmundo) Rodriguez
See Rodriguez O(rdonez), Jaime E(dmundo)
Oak, Liston M. 1895-1970 Obituary 104
Oakes, James 1953- 107
Oakes, John Bertram 1913- 13-16R
Oakes, Philip (Barlow) 1928- CANR-29
Earlier sketches in CA 53-56, CANR-4
See also CAAS 25
Oakes, Urian 1631(?)-1681 DLB 24
Oakes, Vanya 1909-1983 33-36R
Obituary 111
See also SATA 6
See also SATA-Obit 37
Oakeshott, Michael (Joseph) 1901-1990 CANR-64
Obituary 133
Earlier sketches in CA 1-4R, CANR-27
Oakeshott, Walter (Fraser) 1903-1987 13-16R
Obituary 123
Oakie, Jack
See Offield, Lewis Delaney
Oakland, Thomas David 1939- 53-56
Oakley, Allen 1943- CANR-53
Earlier sketch in CA 126
Oakley, Ann (Rosamund) 1944- CANR-50
Earlier sketches in CA 57-60, CANR-6, 25
Oakley, Barry K(ingham) 1931- 104
Oakley, Charles Allen 1900- 108
Oakley, Don(ald G.) 1927- 29-32R
See also SATA 8
Oakley, Eric Gilbert 1916- 9-12R
Oakley, Francis (Christopher) 1931- 13-16R
Oakley, Giles (Francis) 1946- 103
Oakley, Graham 1929- CANR-54
Earlier sketches in CA 106, CANR-38
See also CLR 7
See also MAICYA
See also SATA 30, 84
Oakley, Helen (McKelvey) 1906- 17-20R
See also SATA 10
Oakley, J. Ronald 1941- 121
Oakley, John H. 1945- 165
Oakley, Josephine 1903(?)-1978 Obituary 81-84
Oakley, K. P.
See Oakley, Kenneth Page
Oakley, Kenneth P.
See Oakley, Kenneth Page
Oakley, Kenneth Page 1911-1981 122
Obituary 108
Oakley, Mary Ann B. 1940- 45-48
Oakley, Stewart P(hilip) 1931- 21-24R
Oakley, Violet 1874-1961 DLB 188
Oakman, Barbara F(rances) 1931- 57-60
Oaks, Dallin H(arris) 1932- 25-28R
Oaksey, John 1929- 105
Oana, Katherine 1929- 108
See also SATA 53
See also SATA-Brief 37
Oates, Eddie H. 1943- SATA 88
Oates, Jeannette 1912(?)-1984 Obituary 112
Oates, John (Frederick) 1944- 69-72
Oates, John F. 1934- 17-20R
Oates, Joyce Carol 1938- CANR-45
Earlier sketches in CA 5-8R, CANR-25
Interview in CANR-25
See also AAYA 15
See also AITN 1
See also BEST 89:2
See also CDALB 1968-1988
See also CLC 1, 2, 3, 6, 9, 11, 15, 19, 33, 52, 108
See also DA
See also DAB
See also DAC
See also DAM MST, NOV, POP
See also DLB 2, 5, 130
See also DLBY 81
See also MTCW 1
See also SSC 6
See also WLC
Oates, Stephen B(aery) 1936- CANR-50
Earlier sketches in CA 9-12R, CANR-4, 26
Interview in CANR-26
See also SATA 59
Oates, Wallace Eugene 1937- CANR-14
Earlier sketch in CA 37-40R
Oates, Wayne Edward 1917- 85-88
Oates, Whitney J(ennings) 1904-1973 CANR-3
Obituary 45-48
Earlier sketch in CA 5-8R
Oathout, John D(avid) 1913- 111
Oatley, Keith 1939- 45-48
Oatman, Eric F(urber) 1939- CANR-19
Earlier sketch in CA 103
Oatts, Balfour
See Oatts, Lewis Balfour
Oatts, Henry Augustus 1898-1980 5-8R
Obituary 103
Oatts, Lewis Balfour 1902- 110
Oba, Minako 1930- DLB 182
Obach, Robert 1939- 106
Obaldia, Rene de 1918- 133
Brief entry 116
O'Ballance, Edgar 1918- CANR-7
Earlier sketch in CA 5-8R
O'Banion, Terry 1936- 33-36R
O'Bannon, Dan(iel Thomas) 1946- 138
O'Barr, Jean (Fox) 1942- 163
O'Barr, William M(cAlston) 1942- 49-52
Obed, Ellen Bryan 1944- SATA 74
O'Beirne, T(homas) H(ay) 1915-1982 17-20R
Obituary 120
Obele, Norma Taylor 1933- 104
Obenchain, Anne DeCroes
1914(?)-1984 Obituary 112
Obenhaus, Victor 1903-1994 CAP-1
Obituary 145
Earlier sketch in CA 13-14
Ober, Frederick Albion 1849-1913 DLB 189
Ober, Richard 1960- 150
Ober, Stuart Alan 1946- 103
Ober, Warren U(pton) 1925- 13-16R
Ober, William DLBY 93
Oberdorf, Charles (Donnell) 1941- 126
Oberdorfer, Don 1931- 129
Oberg, Alcestis R. 1949- 128
Oberg, Arthur K. 1938-1977 Obituary 112
Oberg, James E(dward) 1944- CANR-56
Earlier sketches in CA 108, CANR-26
Oberhansli, Trudi
See Schlapbach-Oberhansli, Trudi
Oberhelman, Harley D(ean) 1928- 53-56
Oberholtzer, Ellis Paxton 1868-1936 DLB 47
Oberholtzer, Peter
See Brannon, William T.
Oberholtzer, W(alter) Dwight 1939- 101
Oberholzer, Emil, Jr. 1926(?)-1981 Obituary 102
Oberle, Joseph 1958- 136
See also SATA 69
Oberman, Heiko Augustinus 1930- CANR-25
Earlier sketches in CA 5-8R, CANR-7
Oberman, Sheldon 1949- 152
See also SAAS 26
See also SATA 85
Obermann, C. Esco 1904- 53-56
Obermayer, Herman J. 1924- 65-68
Obermeyer, Barrett John 1937- 5-8R
Obermeyer, Henry 1899- CAP-2
Earlier sketch in CA 29-32
Obermeyer, Marion Barrett 5-8R
Oberndorf, Charles G. 1959- 165
Oberschall, Antony R. 1936- 97-100
Obert, John C. 1924-1987 Obituary 122
Oberth, Hermann Julius 1894-1979(?) Obituary 113
Obey, Andre 1892-1975 97-100
Obituary 57-60
Obichere, Boniface Ihewunwa 1932- 41-44R
Obiechina, Emmanuel Nwanonye 1933- CANR-15
Earlier sketch in CA 41-44R
Obika, Akili Addae 1969- 150
O'Biso, Carol (Anne) 1953- 133
Obligado, Lilian (Isabel) 1931- 134
See also SATA 61
See also SATA-Brief 45
Oboe, Peter
See Jacobs, Walter Darnell
Obojski, Robert 1929- CANR-49
Earlier sketches in CA 108, CANR-24
Obolensky, Dimitri 1918- CANR-25
Earlier sketch in CA 45-48
Oboler, Arch 1909(?)-1987 Obituary 122
Brief entry 105
Oboler, Eli M(artin) 1915-1983 CANR-6
Obituary 110
Earlier sketch in CA 57-60
Obourn, Ellsworth Scott 1897- CAP-2
Earlier sketch in CA 17-18
Obradovic, Dositej 1740(?)-1811 DLB 147
O'Brady, Frederic Michel Maurice 1903- CANR-3
Earlier sketch in CA 9-12R
Obrant, Susan 1946- SATA 11
O'Brawes, Tarnel
See La Barre, Weston
Obrecht, James Carlton
See Obrecht, Jas
Obrecht, Jas 1952- 135
Obregon, Mauricio 1921- CANR-1
Earlier sketch in CA 45-48
O'Brian, Frank
See Garfield, Brian (Wynne)
O'Brian, Jack 1921- 103
O'Brian, John Lord 1874-1973 Obituary 41-44R
O'Brian, Patrick 1914- 144
O'Briant, Walter H(erbert) 1937- 25-28R
O'Brien, Andrew William 1910- CANR-17
Earlier sketch in CA 25-28R
O'Brien, Andy
See O'Brien, Andrew William
O'Brien, Anne Sibley 1952- 122
See also SATA 53, 80
See also SATA-Brief 48
O'Brien, Conor Cruise 1917- CANR-47
Earlier sketch in CA 65-68
O'Brien, Cyril C(ornelius) 1906- 53-56
O'Brien, D(enis) P(atrick) 1939- 158
O'Brien, Dan(iel) 1947- 160
O'Brien, Darcy 1939-1998 CANR-59
Obituary 167
Earlier sketches in CA 21-24R, CANR-8
See also CLC 11
O'Brien, David J(oseph) 1938- 25-28R
O'Brien, David M(ichael) 1951- 143
O'Brien, Dean D.
See Binder, Otto O(scar)
O'Brien, Des(mond John) 1930- 114
O'Brien, E. G.
See Clarke, Arthur C(harles)
O'Brien, Edna 1936- CANR-65
Earlier sketches in CA 1-4R, CANR-6, 41
See also CDBLB 1960 to Present
See also CLC 3, 5, 8, 13, 36, 65
See also DAM NOV
See also DLB 14
See also MTCW 1
See also SSC 10
O'Brien, Edward C.
See Schrodt, Philip A(ndrew)
O'Brien, Elmer 1911- 17-20R
O'Brien, Esse Forrester
1895(?)-1975 Obituary 61-64
See also SATA-Obit 30
O'Brien, Fitz-James 1828-1862 DLB 74
O'Brien, Flann
See O Nuallain, Brian
See also CLC 1, 4, 5, 7, 10, 47
O'Brien, Frances (Kelly) 1906- CAP-2
Earlier sketch in CA 17-18
O'Brien, Francis J(oseph) 1903- 81-84
O'Brien, Geoffrey 1948- 106
O'Brien, George 1945- 131
O'Brien, George Dennis 1931- 103
O'Brien, Gregory (C., Jr.) 1945- 117
O'Brien, J(ohn) W(ilfrid) 1931- 13-16R
O'Brien, Jacqueline Robin 1949- 105
O'Brien, James A(loysius) 1936- Brief entry 110
O'Brien, James J. 1929- CANR-9
Earlier sketch in CA 17-20R
O'Brien, John 1953- 132
O'Brien, John Anthony 1893-1980 CANR-1
Obituary 97-100
Earlier sketch in CA 1-4R
O'Brien, John J(oseph) 1937- 111
O'Brien, Justin (McCortney) 1906-1968 CANR-5
Earlier sketch in CA 5-8R
O'Brien, K.
See O'Brien, Katherine
O'Brien, Kate 1897-1974 93-96
Obituary 53-56
See also DLB 15
O'Brien, Katherine 1915-1982 Obituary 118
O'Brien, Kevin P. 1922- 53-56
O'Brien, Lawrence Francis 1917- 57-60
O'Brien, Lee 1948- 61-64
O'Brien, Lucy 1961- 152
O'Brien, Marian P(lowman) 1915- 53-56
O'Brien, Michael 1943- 126
O'Brien, Michael 1948- 121
O'Brien, Michael J. 1920- 25-28R
O'Brien, (William Joseph) Pat(rick)
1899-1983 Obituary 111
O'Brien, Patrick 1932- 21-24R
O'Brien, Richard 1934- 73-76
O'Brien, Richard 1942- 124
See also CLC 17
O'Brien, Robert C.
See Conly, Robert Leslie
See also AAYA 6
See also CLR 2
O'Brien, Robert W(illiam) 1907- CANR-25
Earlier sketch in CA 45-48
O'Brien, Saliee
See Janas, Frankie-Lee
O'Brien, Sean 1952- 154
O'Brien, Sister Mary Celine 1922- 21-24R
O'Brien, Thomas C(lement) 1938- 106
See also SATA 29
O'Brien, (William) Tim(othy) 1946- CANR-58
Earlier sketches in CA 85-88, CANR-40
See also AAYA 16
See also CLC 7, 19, 40, 103
See also DAM POP
See also DLB 152
See also DLBD 9
See also DLBY 80
O'Brien, Vincent 1916- 9-12R
O'Brien, William V(incent) 1923- 13-16R
O'Broin, Leon 1902- CANR-8
Earlier sketch in CA 61-64
O'Brynt, Jon
See Barnum, W(illiam) Paul
Observer
See Velikovsky, Immanuel
Obst, Frances Melanie 17-20R
Obstfeld, Raymond 1952- 116
Obstfelder, Sigbjoern 1866-1900 Brief entry 123
See also TCLC 23
Oca, Marco Antonio Montes de
See Montes de Oca, Marco Antonio
O'Callaghan, Denis F(rancis) 1931- 17-20R
O'Callaghan, Joseph F(rancis) 1928- 81-84
O'Callaghan, Julie 1954- 117
O'Callahan, Jay 1938- 152
See also SATA 88
Ocampo, Silvina 1906-1993 131
See also HW
Ocampo, Victoria 1891-1979 105
Obituary 85-88
See also HW
O'Carroll, Ryan
See Markun, Patricia Maloney
O'Casey, Eileen (Kathleen Reynolds)
1903-1995 133
Obituary 148
Brief entry 112
O'Casey, Sean 1880-1964 CANR-62
Earlier sketch in CA 89-92
See also CDBLB 1914-1945
See also CLC 1, 5, 9, 11, 15, 88
See also DAB
See also DAC
See also DAM DRAM, MST
See also DLB 10
See also MTCW 1
See also WLCS
O'Cathasaigh, Donal
See Casey, Daniel J(oseph)
O'Cathasaigh, Sean
See O'Casey, Sean
Occom, Samson 1723-1792 DLB 175
See also NNAL
Occomy, Marita (Odette) Bonner 1899(?)-1971 142
See also BW 2
See also DLB 51
Ocean, Julian
See de Mesne, Eugene (Frederick Peter Cheshire)
O Ceithearnaigh, Seumas
See Carney, James (Patrick)
Ochester, Ed(win Frank) 1939- CANR-51
Earlier sketches in CA 45-48, CANR-25
Ochiltree, Thomas H 1912- 77-80
Ochoa, Holly Byers 1951- 149
Ochojski, Paul M(aximilian) 1916-1983 CANR-20
Earlier sketch in CA 25-28R
Ochorowicz, Julian 1850-1917 Brief entry 114
Ochs, Adolph S(imon) 1858-1935 Brief entry 118
See also DLB 25
Ochs, Carol (Rebecca) 1939- CANR-36
Earlier sketch in CA 114
Ochs, Donovan J(oseph) 1938- 45-48
Ochs, Michael 1943- CANR-43
Earlier sketch in CA 119
Ochs, Phil 1940-1976 Obituary 65-68
See also CLC 17
Ochs, Robert J. 1930- 29-32R
Ochs, Vanessa (L.) 1953- 134
Ochse, Orpha Caroline 1925- 93-96
Ochsenschlager, Edward L(loyd) 1932- 17-20R
Ochsner, (Edward William) Alton
1896-1981 17-20R
Obituary 105
Ochsner, Jeffrey Karl 1950- 111
Ochs-Oakes, George Washington 1861-1931 DLB 137
Ockenga, Harold John 1905-1985 CANR-1
Obituary 115
Earlier sketch in CA 1-4R
Ockenga, Starr 1938- 134
Ockham, Joan Price
See Price, Joan
Ockham, William of 1285(?)-1347 DLB 115
O'Clair, Robert M. 1923- 77-80
O'Clery, Helen (Gallagher) 1910- 9-12R
O'Collins, Gerald Glynn 1931- CANR-34
Earlier sketches in CA 85-88, CANR-15
O'Connell, Brian (Vincent) J(ohn) 1923- Brief entry 113
O'Connell, Carol 1947- 152
O'Connell, Caroline 1953- 139
O'Connell, Daniel Patrick 1924-1979 CANR-25
Obituary 89-92
Earlier sketch in CA 29-32R
O'Connell, David 1940- 102
O'Connell, Frank 1892- 5-8R
O'Connell, Jack 1959- 137
O'Connell, Jeffrey 1928- CANR-11
Earlier sketch in CA 25-28R
O'Connell, Jeremiah Joseph 1932- CANR-7
Earlier sketch in CA 13-16R
O'Connell, John James III 1921-1982 Obituary 107
O'Connell, Laurence J. 1945- 157

O'Connell, Margaret F(orster) 1935-1977 73-76
See also SATA 30
See also SATA-Obit 30
O'Connell, Marvin R(ichard) 1930- 134
Brief entry 111
O'Connell, Maurice R. 1922- 17-20R
O'Connell, Michael (William) 1943- 101
O'Connell, P. J. 1935- 144
O'Connell, Peg
See Ahern, Margaret McCrohan
O'Connell, Richard L(eo), Jr. 1912-1975 .... 41-44R
O'Connell, Timothy E(dward) 1943- CANR-12
Earlier sketch in CA 73-76
O'Connell, Walter E(dward) 1925- 41-44R
O'Conner, Bert
See Paine, Lauran (Bosworth)
O'Conner, Clint
See Paine, Lauran (Bosworth)
O'Conner, R(ay) L. 1928- 17-20R
O'Connor, A(nthony) M(ichael) 1939- CANR-11
Earlier sketch in CA 21-24R
O'Connor, Alan 1955- 133
O'Connor, Anthony (?)-1983(?) Obituary 109
O'Connor, Colin 1928- 150
O'Connor, Daniel William 1925- 33-36R
O'Connor, David 1949- 110
O'Connor, Dick 1930- 97-100
O'Connor, Edward Dennis 1922- 41-44R
O'Connor, Edwin (Greene) 1918-1968 93-96
Obituary 25-28R
See also CLC 14
O'Connor, Egan 1937- 119
O'Connor, Elizabeth (Anita) 1921- CANR-30
Earlier sketch in CA 25-28R
O'Connor, (Mary) Flannery 1925-1964 ... CANR-41
Earlier sketches in CA 1-4R, CANR-3
See also AAYA 7
See also CDALB 1941-1968
See also CLC 1, 2, 3, 6, 10, 13, 15, 21, 66, 104
See also DA
See also DAB
See also DAC
See also DAM MST, NOV
See also DLB 2, 152
See also DLBD 12
See also DLBY 80
See also MTCW 1
See also SSC 1, 23
See also WLC
O'Connor, Francine M(arie) 1930- CANR-59
Earlier sketch in CA 111
See also SATA 90
O'Connor, Francis V(alentine) 1937- CANR-13
Earlier sketch in CA 21-24R
O'Connor, Frank
See O'Donovan, Michael John
See also CLC 23
See also DLB 162
See also SSC 5
O'Connor, Garry 1938- CANR-45
Earlier sketches in CA 89-92, CANR-20
O'Connor, Genevieve A. 1914- .... SATA 75
O'Connor, Harvey 1897-1987 .... 5-8R
Obituary 123
O'Connor, Jack
See O'Connor, John Woolf
O'Connor, James I(gnatius) 1910-1988 ..... CAP-1
Obituary 126
Earlier sketch in CA 13-16
O'Connor, Jane 1947- 124
See also SATA 59
See also SATA-Brief 47
O'Connor, John (Morris) 1937- 29-32R
O'Connor, John E. 1943- 127
Brief entry 109
O'Connor, John J(oseph) 1918- 73-76
O'Connor, John Joseph 1904-1978 Obituary . 77-80
O'Connor, John P. 1892-1986 Obituary 119
O'Connor, John Woolf 1902-1978 .... CANR-64
Obituary 77-80
Earlier sketches in CA 5-8R, CANR-3
O'Connor, June (Elizabeth) 1941- 114
O'Connor, Karen 1938- CANR-59
Earlier sketches in CA 89-92, CANR-28
See also SATA 34, 89
O'Connor, Leo F. 1936- 141
O'Connor, Lillian M. 1894(?)-1987 Obituary 122
O'Connor, M.
See O'Connor, Michael Patrick
O'Connor, Mallory McCane 1943- 151
O'Connor, Mark 1945- CANR-31
Earlier sketches in CA 65-68, CANR-11
O'Connor, Marty 1924(?)-1990 Obituary 131
O'Connor, Mary 1947- 133
O'Connor, Michael Patrick 1950- CANR-45
Earlier sketch in CA 113
O'Connor, Pat 1950- 143
O'Connor, Patricia Walker 1931- CANR-38
Earlier sketches in CA 37-40R, CANR-17
O'Connor, Patrick 77-80
O'Connor, Patrick
See Wibberley, Leonard (Patrick O'Connor)
O'Connor, Patrick 1949- 130
O'Connor, Patrick J(oseph) 1947- 113
O'Connor, Patrick Joseph 1924- 53-56
O'Connor, Philip F(rancis) 1932- CANR-28
Earlier sketch in CA 33-36R
O'Connor, Philip Marie Constant Bancroft
1916- 9-12R
O'Connor, Raymond G(ish) 1915- CANR-4
Earlier sketch in CA 5-8R
O'Connor, Richard 1915-1975 61-64
Obituary 57-60
See also SATA-Obit 21
O'Connor, Robert 1959- 140
O'Connor, Robert F. 1943- 128
O'Connor, Rory 1951- 109
O'Connor, Sister Mary Catharine CAP-2
Earlier sketch in CA 17-18
O'Connor, Thomas Henry 1922- 33-36R
O'Connor, Timothy Edward 1951- 145
O'Connor, Ulick 1928- CANR-4
Earlier sketch in CA 9-12R
O'Connor, William E(dmund) 1922- 37-40R
O'Connor, William P., Jr. 1916- 9-12R
O'Connor, William Van 1915-1966 .... CANR-1
Obituary 25-28R
Earlier sketch in CA 1-4R
O'Connor Howe, Josephine (Mary) 1924- 119
O'Conor, Jane 1958- .... SATA 78
O'Conor, John F(rancis) 1918- 33-36R
October, John
See Portway, Christopher (John)
Octopus
See Drachman, Julian M(oses)
O Cuilleanain, Cormac 1950- 146
Oculi, Okello 1942- 143
See also BW 2
Ocvirk, Otto G(eorge) 1922- 61-64
Oda, Makoto 1932- 139
Oda, Sakunosuke 1913-1947 .... DLB 182
Odaga, Asenath (Bole) 1937- CANR-43
Earlier sketch in CA 124
See also BW 2
See also MAICYA
See also SAAS 19
See also SATA 67
Odahl, Charles Matson 1944- 37-40R
Odajnyk, Walter 1938- 13-16R
O'Daly, William 1951- 137
O Danachair, Caoimhin
See Danaher, Kevin
O'Daniel, Janet 1921- 29-32R
See also SATA 24
O'Daniel, Therman B(enjamin) 1908-1986 45-48
Obituary 133
See also BW 1
O'Day, Alan (Earl) 143
O'Day, Cathy
See Crane, Barbara (Joyce)
O'Day, Edward Francis 1925- 29-32R
O'Day, Rey 1947- 105
Odber (de Baubeta), Patricia (Anne) 1953- 168
Odd, Gilbert E(dward) 1902- 110
Oddner, Georg 1923- 129
Oddo, Gilbert L. 1922- CANR-1
Earlier sketch in CA 1-4R
Oddo, Sandra (Schmidt) 1937- 65-68
O'Dea, Agnes C. 1911- 124
O'Dea, Thomas F(rancis) 1915-1974 .... CAP-2
Obituary 53-56
Earlier sketch in CA 23-24
Odean, Kathleen 1953- 128
Odegaard, Charles Edwin 1911- Brief entry 106
Odegard, Douglas Andrew 1935- 108
Odegard, Holtan Peter 1923- 61-64
Odeku, Emmanuel Latunde 1927- 153
See also BW 2
O'Dell, Andrew C(harles) 1909-1966 .... CAP-1
Earlier sketch in CA 13-16
Odell, George H. 1942- 160
Odell, Gill
See Gill, Traviss
Odell, Jonathan 1737-1818 .... DLB 31, 99
Odell, Ling Chung 1945- 45-48
O'Dell, M(ary) E(lise) 9-12R
Odell, Peter R(andon) 1930- 97-100
Odell, Rice 1928- 77-80
Odell, Robin 1935- CANR-12
Earlier sketch in CA 73-76
O'Dell, Scott 1898-1989 .... CANR-30
Obituary 129
Earlier sketches in CA 61-64, CANR-12
See also AAYA 3
See also CLC 30
See also CLR 1, 16
See also DLB 52
See also JRDA
See also MAICYA
See also SATA 12, 60
O'Dell, William F(rancis) 1909- CANR-12
Earlier sketch in CA 25-28R
Odem, J.
See Rubin, Jacob A.
Oden, Clifford 1916- 65-68
Oden, Gloria (Catherine) 1923- CANR-25
Earlier sketch in CA 108
Oden, Marilyn Brown 1937- 33-36R
Oden, Thomas C(lark) 1931- CANR-43
Earlier sketches in CA 9-12R, CANR-5, 19
Oden, William E(ugene) 1923- 37-40R
Odenwald, Neil G. 1935- 141
Odenwald, Robert P(aul) 1899-1965 .... 1-4R
See also SATA 11
Oderman, Stuart (Douglas) 1940- 148
Odescalchi, Esther Kando 1938- 69-72
Odets, Clifford 1906-1963 .... CANR-62
Earlier sketch in CA 85-88
See also CLC 2, 28, 98
See also DAM DRAM
See also DC 6
See also DLB 7, 26
See also MTCW 1
Odets, Walt (Whitman) 1947- 151
Odgers, Merle Middleton 1900-1983 Obituary .. 110
Odgers, Sally Farrell 1957- .... SATA 72
Odier, Daniel 1945- CANR-29
Earlier sketch in CA 29-32R
Odiorne, George Stanley 1920-1992 ...... CANR-1
Obituary 136
Earlier sketch in CA 1-4R
Odishaw, Hugh 1916-1984 Obituary 112
Odle, Joe T(aft) 1908-1980 .... 33-36R
Obituary 97-100
Odling-Smee, John (Charles) 1943- 112
Odlum, Doris Maude 1890-1985 .... CAP-1
Obituary 118
Earlier sketch in CA 13-14
Odoevsky, Vladimir Fedorovich 1804(?)-1869 .. DLB 198
O'Doherty, Brian 1934- 105
See also CLC 76
O'Doherty, E(amonn) F(elchin) 1918- 37-40R
O'Doire, Annraoi
See Beechhold, Henry F(rank)
Odom, William E(ldridge) 1932- 73-76
O'Donnell, Bernard 1929-1983 .... 41-44R
Obituary 133
O'Donnell, Brennan (Patrick) 1958- 156
O'Donnell, Cyril 1900- CAP-1
Earlier sketch in CA 11-12
O'Donnell, Dick
See Lupoff, Richard A(llen)
and Thompson, Don(ald Arthur)
O'Donnell, Donat
See O'Brien, Conor Cruise
O'Donnell, Elliott 1872-1965 .... CAP-1
Earlier sketch in CA 13-16
O'Donnell, Francis (?)-1984 Obituary 114
O'Donnell, Harry J(ames) 1914-1985 Obituary . 117
O'Donnell, James H(owlett) III 1937- CANR-27
Earlier sketch in CA 45-48
O'Donnell, James J(oseph, Jr.) 1950- ... CANR-16
Earlier sketch in CA 89-92
O'Donnell, James Kevin 1951- CANR-6
Earlier sketch in CA 57-60
O'Donnell, James P(reston)
1917-1990 Obituary 131
O'Donnell, Jim
See O'Donnell, James Kevin
O'Donnell, John A. 1916- 17-20R
O'Donnell, John P. 1923- 17-20R
O'Donnell, K. M.
See Malzberg, Barry N(athaniel)
O'Donnell, (Philip) Kenneth 1924-1977 81-84
Obituary 73-76
O'Donnell, Kenneth P.
See O'Donnell, (Philip) Kenneth
O'Donnell, Kevin, Jr. 1950- CANR-23
Earlier sketch in CA 106
O'Donnell, Lawrence
See Kuttner, Henry
and Moore, C(atherine) L(ucile)
O'Donnell, Lawrence F(rancis), Jr. 1951- 117
O'Donnell, Lillian Udvardy 1926- CANR-60
Earlier sketches in CA 5-8R, CANR-3, 18
O'Donnell, Margaret Jane 1899- 5-8R
O'Donnell, Mark 1954- CANR-45
Earlier sketches in CA 104, CANR-21
O'Donnell, Patrick (James) 1948- 114
O'Donnell, Peadar 1893-1986 135
Obituary 119
O'Donnell, Peter 1920- CANR-71
Brief entry 114
Earlier sketch in CA 117
Interview in 117
See also DLB 87
O'Donnell, Red
See O'Donnell, Francis
O'Donnell, Thomas Francis 1915- CANR-1
Earlier sketch in CA 1-4R
O'Donnell, Thomas J(oseph) 1918- 65-68
O'Donnell, William H. 1940- 128
O'Donnevan, Finn
See Sheckley, Robert
O'Donoghue, Bernard 1945- 137
O'Donoghue, Bryan 1921- 77-80
O'Donoghue, Gregory 1951- 114
Brief entry 109
O'Donoghue, Joseph 1931- 21-24R
O'Donoghue, Michael 1940-1994 128
Obituary 147
O'Donohoe, Nicholas Benjamin
See O'Donohoe, Nick
O'Donohoe, Nick 1952- 167
O'Donovan, John 1921- CANR-11
Earlier sketch in CA 25-28R
O'Donovan, Katherine 1942- 123
O'Donovan, Michael John 1903-1966 93-96
See also O'Connor, Frank
See also CLC 14
O'Dor, Ronald Keith 1944- 163
Odor, Ruth Shannon 1926- 120
See also SATA-Brief 44
O'Dowd, Liam 1947- 116
O'Driscoll, Dennis 1954- CANR-54
Earlier sketch in CA 127
O'Driscoll, Gerald P(atrick), Jr. 1947- 133
O'Driscoll, Robert 1938- CANR-35
Earlier sketch in CA 53-56
O'Dwyer, James F. 1939- 33-36R
O'Dwyer, Paul 1907- 97-100
O'Dwyer, Tess 1966- 147
Odysseus
See Johnson, Donald McI(ntosh)
Oe, Kenzaburo 1935- CANR-50
Earlier sketches in CA 97-100, CANR-36
See also CLC 10, 36, 86
See also DAM NOV
See also DLB 182
See also DLBY 94
See also MTCW 1
See also SSC 20
Oechsli, Kelly 1918- CANR-16
Earlier sketch in CA 97-100
See also SATA 5
Oehmke, T(homas) H(arold) 1947- CANR-11
Earlier sketch in CA 65-68
Oehser, Paul H(enry) 1904-1996 .... CANR-12
Obituary 155
Earlier sketch in CA 29-32R
Oeksenholt, Svein 1925- Brief entry 106
Oelschlaeger, Max 1943- 141
Oenslager, Donald (Mitchell) 1902-1975 61-64
Obituary 57-60
Oepik, Ernst Julius 1893-1985 Obituary 118
Oerkeny, Istvan
See Orkeny, Istvan
Oerum, Poul (Erik) 1919- CANR-32
Earlier sketches in CA 65-68, CANR-13
Oesterle, John A(rthur) 1912- 5-8R
Oesterle, Virginia Rorby
See Rorby, Ginny
Oesterreicher, John M(aria) 1904-1993 .. CANR-26
Obituary 141
Earlier sketch in CA 29-32R
Oettinger, Anthony Gervin 1929- CANR-31
Earlier sketch in CA 1-4R
Oettinger, Elmer R(osenthal, Jr.) 1913- 29-32R
O'Faolain, Julia 1932- CANR-61
Earlier sketches in CA 81-84, CANR-12
See also CAAS 2
See also CLC 6, 19, 47, 108
See also DLB 14
See also MTCW 1
O'Faolain, Sean 1900-1991 .... CANR-66
Obituary 134
Earlier sketches in CA 61-64, CANR-12
See also CLC 1, 7, 14, 32, 70
See also DLB 15, 162
See also MTCW 1
See also SSC 13
Ofari, Earl 1945- 41-44R
O'Farrell, Patrick (James) 1933- CANR-42
Earlier sketches in CA 103, CANR-20
Ofek, Uriel 1926- CANR-18
Earlier sketch in CA 101
See also CLR 28
See also SATA 36
Offen, Karen (Marie Stedtfeld) 1939- CANR-34
Earlier sketch in CA 113
Offen, Neil 1946- 49-52
Offen, Ron 1930- 45-48
Offenbacher, Ami 1958- 155
See also SATA 91
Offer, Daniel 1930- CANR-11
Earlier sketch in CA 21-24R
Offerle, Mildred 1912- 77-80
Offield, Lewis Delaney 1903-1978 Obituary 111
Offiong, Daniel A(sukwo) 1942- 118
Offit, Avodah K(omito) 1931- CANR-13
Earlier sketch in CA 77-80
Offit, Sidney 1928- CANR-1
Earlier sketch in CA 1-4R
See also SATA 10
Offner, Arnold A. 1937- 25-28R
Offner, Eric D(elmonte) 1928- CANR-9
Earlier sketch in CA 17-20R
Offord, Carl Ruthven 1910- 142
See also BW 2
See also DLB 76
Offord, Lenore Glen 1905- 77-80
Offutt, Andrew J(efferson V) 1934(?)- CANR-55
Earlier sketches in CA 41-44R, CANR-15
Offutt, Chris 1958- 154
O Fiaich, Tomas (Seamus) 1923-1990 103
Obituary 131
O'Finn, Thaddeus
See McGloin, Joseph T(haddeus)
O'Flaherty, James C(arneal) 1914- 21-24R
O'Flaherty, Liam 1896-1984 .... CANR-35
Obituary 113
Earlier sketch in CA 101
See also CLC 5, 34
See also DLB 36, 162
See also DLBY 84
See also MTCW 1
See also SSC 6
O'Flaherty, Louise 1920- CANR-6
Earlier sketch in CA 57-60
O'Flaherty, Terrence 1917- 73-76
O'Flaherty, Wendy Doniger 1940- CANR-23
Earlier sketch in CA 65-68
O'Flynn, Peter
See Fanthorpe, R(obert) Lionel
Ofomata, G(odfrey) E(zediaso) K(ingsley)
1936- 93-96
Oforiwaa, Yaa 1949- 152
Ofosu-Appiah, L(awrence) H(enry) 1920- ... 33-36R
See also SATA 13
Ofshe, Richard 1941- 89-92
Og, Liam
See O'Neill, William
Ogali, Ogali A(gu) 1931- 153
See also BW 2
O'Gallagher, Liam 1917- 45-48
Ogan, George F. 1912- CANR-4
Earlier sketch in CA 9-12R
See also SATA 13
Ogan, M. G.
See Ogan, George F.
and Ogan, Margaret E. (Nettles)
Ogan, Margaret E. (Nettles) 1923-1979 ... CANR-4
Earlier sketch in CA 9-12R
See also SATA 13
O'Gara, James Vincent, Jr. 1918-1979 69-72
Obituary 85-88
Ogata, Sadako (Nakamura) 1927- CANR-9
Earlier sketch in CA 17-20R
Ogawa, Dennis Masaaki 1943- 37-40R
Ogawa, Tetsuro 1912-1978 .... 41-44R
Ogbaa, Kalu 1945- 141
See also BW 2
Ogbu, John U(zor) 1939- 93-96

Ogburn, Charlton (Jr.) 1911- ... CANR-3
Earlier sketch in CA 5-8R
See also SATA 3
Ogburn, W. F.
See Ogburn, William Fielding
Ogburn, William F.
See Ogburn, William Fielding
Ogburn, William Fielding 1886-1959 Brief entry . 122
Ogden, Chris 1945- ... 133
Ogden, Daniel M(iller), Jr. 1922- ... 9-12R
Ogden, Dunbar H. ... 53-56
Ogden, Gina 1935- ... 81-84
Ogden, Howard
See Winokur, Jon
Ogden, Margaret Sinclair 1909- Brief entry ... 107
Ogden, (John) Michael (Hubert) 1923- ... 13-16R
Ogden, Samuel R(obinson) 1896- ... 29-32R
Ogden, Schubert Miles 1928- ... CANR-45
Earlier sketches in CA 104, CANR-21
Ogden, Scott 1957- ... 138
Ogg, Oscar (John) 1908-1971 ... CAP-1
Obituary ... 33-36R
Earlier sketch in CA 11-12
Ogilvie, Elisabeth May 1917- ... CANR-42
Earlier sketches in CA 103, CANR-19
See also SATA 40
See also SATA-Brief 29
Ogilvie, Gordon (Bryant) 1934- ... CANR-8
Earlier sketch in CA 61-64
Ogilvie, Lloyd John 1930- ... 73-76
Ogilvie, Mardel 1910- ... CANR-29
Earlier sketch in CA 1-4R
Ogilvie, Robert Maxwell 1932-1981 ... CANR-6
Obituary ... 105
Earlier sketch in CA 13-16R
Ogilvie, William G(eorge) 1899- ... 130
Ogilvy, C(harles) Stanley 1913- ... CANR-4
Earlier sketch in CA 5-8R
Ogilvy, David Mackenzie 1911- Brief entry ... 105
Ogilvy, Eliza 1822-1912 ... DLB 199
Ogilvy, Gavin
See Barrie, J(ames) M(atthew)
Ogilvy, Stewart Marks 1914-1985(?) Obituary .. 118
Oglanby, Elva
See Clairmont, Elva
Ogle, James Lawrence 1911- ... 5-8R
Ogle, Jim
See Ogle, James Lawrence
Ogle, Lucille Edith 1904-1988 ... SATA-Obit 59
Ogle, Robert 1926(?)-1984 Obituary ... 112
Oglesby, Joseph 1931- ... CANR-17
Earlier sketch in CA 97-100
Oglesby, Richard E(dward) 1931- ... CANR-6
Earlier sketch in CA 9-12R
Oglesby, William B(arr), Jr. 1916- ... 25-28R
Ogletree, Earl Joseph 1930- ... CANR-10
Earlier sketch in CA 65-68
Ogletree, Thomas W(arren) 1933- ... 17-20R
Ognall, Leopold Horace 1908-1979 ... CANR-60
Earlier sketches in CA 9-12R, CANR-12
Ognibene, Peter J(ohn) 1941- ... 110
O'Gorman, Edward Charles 1929- ... 81-84
O'Gorman, Frank 1940- ... 61-64
O'Gorman, Gerald 1916- ... 21-24R
O'Gorman, Hubert J(oseph)
1925-1990 Obituary ... 131
O'Gorman, James F(rancis) 1933- ... 53-56
O'Gorman, John
See MacGill, Patrick
O'Gorman, Ned
See O'Gorman, Edward Charles
O'Gorman, Richard F. 1928- ... 37-40R
O'Gorman, Samuel F.
See Cusack, Michael J(oseph)
Ogot, Grace 1930- ... 142
See also BW 2
See also DLB 125
O'Grada, Sean
See O'Grady, John (Patrick)
O'Grady, Anne ... 53-56
O'Grady, Desmond (James Bernard) 1935- ...
CANR-38
Earlier sketches in CA 25-28R, CANR-14
See also DLB 40
O'Grady, Francis Dominic 1909- ... CAP-1
Earlier sketch in CA 9-10
O'Grady, Frank
See O'Grady, Francis Dominic
O'Grady, John (Patrick) 1907- ... 104
O'Grady, John F(rancis) 1939- ... 93-96
O'Grady, John P. 1958- ... 145
O'Grady, Joseph P(atrick) 1934- ... 41-44R
O'Grady, Rohan
See Skinner, June O'Grady
O'Grady, Ron 1930- ... 114
O'Grady, Standish (James) 1846-1928 ... 157
Brief entry ... 104
See also TCLC 5
O'Grady, Timothy 1951- ... 138
See also CLC 59
O'Grady, Tony
See Clemens, Brian (Horace)
Ogram, Ernest W(illiam), Jr. 1928- ... 57-60
O'Green, Jennifer
See Roberson, Jennifer
O'Green, Jennifer Roberson
See Roberson, Jennifer
Ogrin, Dusan 1929- ... 151
Ogul, Morris S(amuel) 1931- ... 13-16R
Ogundipe-Leslie, 'Molara ... 154
Ogunyemi, Chikwenye Okonjo 1939- ... 168
Ogunyemi, Wale 1939(?)- ... 153
See also BW 2
See also DLB 157
Oh, John Kie-chiang 1930- ... 29-32R
O'Hagan, Caroline 1946- ... 111
See also SATA 38
O'Hagan, Howard 1902-1982 ... 1-4R
See also DLB 68
O'Hagan, Joan 1926- ... 132
O'Hair, Madalyn (Mays) Murray 1919- ... CANR-44
Earlier sketches in CA 61-64, CANR-12
O'Hallion, Sheila
See Allen, Sheila Rosalynd
O'Halpin, Eunan 1954- ... 128
O'Hanlon, Daniel John 1919-1992 ... CANR-47
Obituary ... 139
Earlier sketch in CA 61-64
O'Hanlon, Jacklyn
See Meek, Jacklyn O'Hanlon
O'Hanlon, Redmond (Douglas) 1947- ... 123
O'Hanlon, Thomas J(oseph) 1933- ... 61-64
Ohanneson, Joan 1930- ... 130
O'Hara, Charles E. 1912-1984 ... 29-32R
Obituary ... 125
O'Hara, Dale
See Gillese, John Patrick
O'Hara, Elizabeth
See Ni Dhuibhne, Eilis
O'Hara, Frank 1926-1966 ... CANR-33
Obituary ... 25-28R
Earlier sketch in CA 9-12R
See also CLC 2, 5, 13, 78
See also DAM POET
See also DLB 5, 16, 193
See also MTCW 1
O'Hara, Frederic James 1917- ... 103
O'Hara, Georgina 1956- ... 126
O'Hara, John (Henry) 1905-1970 ... CANR-60
Obituary ... 25-28R
Earlier sketches in CA 5-8R, CANR-31
See also CDALB 1929-1941
See also CLC 1, 2, 3, 6, 11, 42
See also DAM NOV
See also DLB 9, 86
See also DLBD 2
See also MTCW 1
See also SSC 15
O'Hara, Kenneth
See Morris, (Margaret) Jean
O'Hara, Kevin
See Cumberland, Marten
O'Hara, Marjorie (Doreen) 1928- ... 135
O'Hara, Mary
See Alsop, Mary O'Hara
Ohashi, Wataru 1944- ... 73-76
O'Hayre, John 1923-1986 Obituary ... 121
O'hearn, Peter J(oseph) T(homas) 1917- ... 17-20R
O'Heffernan, Patrick 1944- ... 117
O'Hegarty, P. S. 1879-1955 ... DLB 201
O Hehir, Diana 1922- ... 93-96
See also CLC 41
O hEithir, Breandan 1930-1990 Obituary ... 132
Ohi, Ruth 1964- ... SATA 95
O'Higgins, Donal Peter 1922-1984 ... 77-80
Obituary ... 112
O'Higgins, Paul 1927- ... 130
Ohira, Masayoshi 1910-1980 Obituary ... 105
Ohkawa, Kazushi 1908- ... 85-88
Ohl, (Mary) Suzanne Sickler 1923- ... 69-72
Ohles, John Ford 1920- ... 57-60
Ohlig, Karl-Heinz 1938- ... CANR-13
Earlier sketch in CA 69-72
Ohlin, Bertil 1899(?)-1979 Obituary ... 89-92
Ohlin, Lloyd E(dgar) 1918- ... 104
Ohlinger, Gustavus 1877-1972 Obituary ... 37-40R
Ohlmeyer, Jane H. 1962- ... 149
Ohlsen, Merle M(arvel) 1914- ... CANR-15
Earlier sketch in CA 37-40R
Ohlsson, Ib 1935- ... SATA 7
Ohmae, Kenichi 1943- ... 152
Ohman, Jack 1960- ... 110
Brief entry ... 108
Interview in ... 110
Ohmann, Carol Burke 1929(?)-1989 Obituary .. 129
Ohmann, Richard (Malin) 1931- ... 13-16R
Ohmer, Merlin M(aurice) 1923- ... 57-60
Ohon
See Barba, Harry
Ohsberg, H(arry) Oliver 1926- ... 114
Ohtomo, Yasuo 1946- ... SATA 37
Oinas, Felix J(ohannes) 1911- ... CANR-54
Earlier sketches in CA 33-36R, CANR-13, 29
Oison
See O'Neill, Joseph James
Oiwa, Keibo ... 138
Oja, Carol J. 1953- ... 135
Ojany, Francis Frederick 1935- ... 77-80
Ojo, G. J. Afolabi 1930- ... 25-28R
Oka, Takashi 1924- ... 135
Okada, Sumie 1940- ... 132
Okai, John 1967- ... 154
Okamoto, Shumpei 1932- ... 29-32R
O'Kane, James M. 1941- ... 143
O'Kane, Rosemary H(eather) T(eresa) 1947- ... 143
Okara, Gabriel Imomotimi Gbaingbain 1921- ... 105
See also BW 1
See also DLB 125
Okasha, Elisabeth 1942- ... 45-48
Oke, Janette 1935- ... CANR-58
Earlier sketch in CA 111
See also SATA 97
O'Keefe, Bernard J(oseph) 1919-1989 ... 120
Obituary ... 129
O'Keefe, Daniel Lawrence 1928- Brief entry ... 116
O'Keefe, M(aurice) Timothy 1943- ... 77-80
O'Keefe, Patrick E.
See Grace, John Patrick
O'Keefe, Paul 1900(?)-1976 Obituary ... 65-68
O'Keefe, Richard R(obert) 1934- ... 57-60
O'Keefe, Sister Maureen 1917- ... 5-8R
O'Keeffe, Frank 1938- ... 160
See also SATA 99
O'Keeffe, Georgia 1887-1986 ... 156
Obituary ... 118
Earlier sketch in CA 110
See also AAYA 20
O'Keeffe, John 1747-1833 ... DLB 89
O'Keeffe, Laurence 1931- ... 122
Okeke, Uchefuna 1933- ... 97-100
O'Kelley, Mattie Lou 1908-1997 ... 116
Obituary ... 159
See also SATA 36, 97
O'Kelly, Charlotte G. 1946- ... 111
O'Kelly, Elizabeth 1915- ... CANR-20
Earlier sketch in CA 103
Oken, Alan C(harles) 1944- ... 45-48
Okenfuss, Max J. 1938- ... 156
Okes, Nicholas fl. 1607-1645 ... DLB 170
O'Key
See Radwanski, Pierre A(rthur)
Okigbo, Christopher (Ifenayichukwu)
1932-1967 ... 77-80
See also BLC 3
See also BW 1
See also CLC 25, 84
See also DAM MULT, POET
See also DLB 125
See also MTCW 1
See also PC 7
Okigbo, P(ius) N(wabufo) C. 1924- ... 17-20R
Okihiro, Gary Y(ukio) 1945- ... CANR-45
Earlier sketch in CA 120
Okimoto, Jean Davies 1942- ... CANR-37
Earlier sketches in CA 97-100, CANR-16
See also SATA 34
Okin, Susan Moller 1946- ... 93-96
Okker, Patricia 1960- ... 151
Oklahoma Peddler
See Gilles, Albert S(imeon) Sr.
Okner, Benjamin A. 1936- ... 21-24R
Okomfo, Amasewa
See Cousins, Linda
Okonjo, Chukuka 1928- ... 29-32R
Okpaku, Joseph (Ohiomogben) 1943- ... 29-32R
See also BW 1
Okpara, Mzee Lasana
See Hord, Frederick (Lee)
Okpewho, Isidore 1941- ... CANR-3
Earlier sketch in CA 49-52
See also DLB 157
Okrent, Daniel 1948- ... CANR-45
Earlier sketches in CA 105, CANR-22
Okri, Ben 1959- ... CANR-65
Brief entry ... 130
Earlier sketch in CA 138
Interview in ... 138
See also BW 2
See also CLC 87
See also DLB 157
Oksenberg, Michel Charles 1938- ... 111
Oksenholt, Svein
See Oeksenholt, Svein
Okubo, Genji 1915- ... 25-28R
Okudzhava, Bulat Shalvovich 1924-1997 ... 129
Obituary ... 159
Brief entry ... 116
Okun, Arthur M. 1928-1980 ... CANR-11
Obituary ... 97-100
Earlier sketch in CA 61-64
Okun, Lawrence E(ugene) 1929- ... 101
Olafson, Frederick A(rlan) 1924- ... 17-20R
Olafsson, Olafur Johann 1962- ... 146
Olaleye, Isaac O. 1941- ... 145
See also SAAS 23
See also SATA 96
Olan, Ben 1923- ... 111
Olan, Levi Arthur 1903- ... 109
O'Laoghaire, Liam
See O'Leary, Liam
Olasky, Marvin 1950- ... 139
Olbricht, Thomas H. 1929- ... 33-36R
Olby, Robert C(ecil) 1933- ... 21-24R
Olcheski, Bill 1925- ... CANR-8
Earlier sketch in CA 61-64
Olcott, Anthony 1950- ... 106
Olcott, Frances Jenkins 1872(?)-1963 ... SATA 19
Olcott, Henry Steel 1832-1907 Brief entry ... 118
Olcott, Jack 1932- ... 53-56
Old, Bruce S(cott) 1913- ... CANR-17
Earlier sketch in CA 1-4R
Old Boy
See Hughes, Thomas
Oldenburg, Carl
See Oldenburg, Ray
Oldenburg, Claes (Thure) 1929- ... 121
Brief entry ... 117
Oldenburg, E(gbert) William 1936-1974 ... 105
See also SATA 35
Oldenburg, Ray 1932- ... 132
Older, Fremont 1856-1935 ... DLB 25
Older, Julia 1941- ... CANR-14
Earlier sketch in CA 73-76
Olderman, Murray 1922- ... CANR-1
Earlier sketch in CA 45-48
Olderman, Raymond M. 1937- ... 41-44R
Olderr, Steven 1943- ... 146
Old Fag
See Bell, Robert S(tanley) W(arren)
Oldfeld, Peter
See Bartlett, (Charles) Vernon (Oldfield)
Oldfield, A(rthur) Barney 1909- ... 105
Oldfield, J(ohn) R(ichard) 1953- ... 151
Oldfield, James E(dmund) 1921- ... 89-92
Oldfield, Margaret J(ean) 1932- ... SATA 56
Oldfield, Michael 1950- ... 135
Oldfield, Mike
See Oldfield, Michael
Oldfield, Pamela 1931- ... SATA 86
Oldfield, R(ichard) C(harles) 1909-1972 ... CAP-2
Earlier sketch in CA 25-28
Oldfield, Ruth L(atzer) 1922- ... 13-16R
Oldham, Frank 1903- ... 9-12R
Oldham, John 1653-1683 ... DLB 131
Oldham, John (M.) 1940- ... 138
Oldham, June ... 138
See also SATA 70
Oldham, Mary 1944- ... 109
See also SATA 65
Oldham, Perry (Donald) 1943- ... 107
Oldham, W(illiam) Dale 1903- ... 9-12R
Old Jowett
See Fantoni, Barry (Ernest)
Oldman, C. B. 1894-1969 ... DLB 201
Oldman, Oliver 1920- ... 33-36R
Oldroyd, Harold 1913- ... 77-80
Olds, Bruce 1951- ... 152
Olds, Elizabeth 1896-1991 ... 5-8R
Obituary ... 133
See also SATA 3
See also SATA-Obit 66
Olds, Elizabeth Fagg 1913-1995 ... 123
Obituary ... 149
Olds, Helen Diehl 1895-1981 ... CANR-3
Obituary ... 103
Earlier sketch in CA 1-4R
See also SATA 9
See also SATA-Obit 25
Olds, Sally Wendkos 1933- ... CANR-39
Earlier sketches in CA 45-48, CANR-1, 18
Olds, Sharon 1942- ... CANR-66
Earlier sketches in CA 101, CANR-18, 41
See also CLC 32, 39, 85
See also DAM POET
See also DLB 120
See also PC 22
Old Settler, The
See Lyman, Albert Robison
Oldsey, Bernard 1923- ... CANR-7
Earlier sketch in CA 5-8R
Oldson, William O(rville) 1940- ... 53-56
Old Stager
See Gore, John Francis
Oldstyle, Jonathan
See Irving, Washington
Olea, Maria Florencia Varas 1938- ... 105
Olearius, Adam 1599-1671 ... DLB 164
O'Leary, A. P. 1950- ... 161
O'Leary, Brian (Todd) 1940- ... CANR-20
Earlier sketch in CA 33-36R
See also SATA 6
O'Leary, Chester F.
See Kuehnelt-Leddihn, Erik (Maria) Ritter von
O'Leary, Frank(lin) J. 1922- ... 5-8R
O'Leary, K. Daniel 1940- ... 41-44R
O'Leary, Les
See O'Leary, A. P.
O'Leary, Liam 1910- ... 109
O'Leary, Patrick 1920- ... 134
O'Leary, Patsy B(aker) 1937- ... 164
See also SATA 97
O'Leary, Rosemary 1955- ... 149
O'Leary, Thomas V(incent) 1910- ... 5-8R
Oleck, Howard L(eoner) 1911- ... CANR-4
Earlier sketch in CA 9-12R
Oleksiw, Susan (Prince) 1945- ... 141
Oleksy, Walter 1930- ... CANR-17
Earlier sketches in CA 45-48, CANR-1
Olen, Jeffrey 1946- ... 112
Olendorf, Bill
See Olendorf, William
Olendorf, William 1924- ... CANR-41
Earlier sketch in CA 117
Olesha, Yuri (Karlovich) 1899-1960 ... 85-88
See also CLC 8
Oleszek, Walter J(oseph) 1941- ... 120
O'Levenson, Jordan
See Levenson, Jordan
Oleyar, Rita Balkey
See Balkey, Rita
Olford, Stephen F(rederick) 1918- ... 17-20R
Olfson, Lewy 1937- ... 93-96
Olgyay, Victor 1910-1970 ... 5-8R
Obituary ... 103
Oliansky, Joel 1935- ... 133
Olien, Diana Davids 1943- ... CANR-32
Earlier sketch in CA 113
Olien, Michael D(avid) 1937- ... CANR-3
Earlier sketch in CA 49-52
Olien, Roger M. 1938- ... 113
Olin, John C(harles) 1915- ... CANR-52
Earlier sketch in CA 126
Olin, Spencer C(arl), Jr. 1937- ... 93-96
Olin, William 1929- ... 106
Oliner, Samuel P. 1930- ... 129
Olins, Wally 1930- ... 120
Oliphant, B. J.
See Tepper, Sheri S.
Oliphant, Dave (Edward Davis) 1939- ... 151
Oliphant, J(ames) Orin 1894-1979 Obituary .. 85-88
Oliphant, Laurence 1829(?)-1888 ... DLB 18, 166
Oliphant, Margaret (Oliphant Wilson)
1828-1897 ... DLB 18, 159, 190
See also SSC 25
Oliphant, Patrick (Bruce) 1935- ... 101
Interview in ... 101
Oliphant, Robert (Thompson) 1924- ... 102
Olisah, Sunday Okenwa 1936-1964(?) ... 153
See also BW 2
Olitzky, Kerry M. 1954- ... 143
Oliva, L(awrence) Jay 1933- ... 13-16R

Oliva, Leo E. 1937- CANR-49
Earlier sketches in CA 21-24R, CANR-9, 24
Oliva, Pavel 1923- 132
Olivares, Julian (Jr.) 1940- CANR-42
Earlier sketch in CA 118
Oliveira, Antonio Ramos
See Ramos-Oliveira, Antonio
Oliveira Salazar, Antonio de
See Salazar, Antonio de Oliveira
Olivella, Manuel Zapata
See Zapata Olivella, Manuel
Olivelle, Patrick 1942- 138
Oliven, John F. 1915(?)-1975 Obituary 53-56
Oliver, A. Richard 1912- 13-16R
Oliver, Amy Roberta
See Ruck, Amy Roberta
Oliver, Andrew 1906-1981 109
Obituary 105
Oliver, Anthony 1923-1995 CANR-60
Earlier sketches in CA 103, CANR-20
Oliver, Bernard John Jr. 1918-1966 5-8R
Oliver, Burton
See Burt, Olive Woolley
Oliver, Carl Russell 1941- 106
Oliver, Chad
See Oliver, Symmes C(hadwick)
Oliver, Chad 1928- DLB 8
Oliver, Covey T(homas) 1913- 111
Oliver, Dawn 1942- 123
Oliver, Douglas 1937- CAAS 27
Oliver, Douglas Llewellyn 1913- 97-100
Oliver, E(dward) J(ames) 1911- 9-12R
Oliver, Egbert S(amuel) 1902- 103
Oliver, G(uillaume) Raymond 1909- CAP-2
Earlier sketch in CA 25-28
Oliver, George
See Onions, (George) Oliver
Oliver, H(arold) J(ames) 1916-1982 Obituary 111
Oliver, Herman 1885- CAP-1
Earlier sketch in CA 11-12
Oliver, James A(rthur) 1914-1981 Obituary 106
Oliver, James Henry 1905- CANR-17
Earlier sketch in CA 1-4R
Oliver, Jane
See Rees, Helen Christina Easson (Evans)
Oliver, John Edward 1933- 33-36R
See also SATA 21
Oliver, Kenneth A(rthur) 1912- 53-56
Oliver, Lawrence J. 1949- 159
Oliver, Marie
See Beck, K(athrine) K(ristine)
Oliver, Marilyn Tower 1935- 155
See also SATA 89
Oliver, Mark
See Tyler-Whittle, Michael Sidney
Oliver, Mary 1935- CANR-43
Earlier sketches in CA 21-24R, CANR-9
See also CLC 19, 34, 98
See also DLB 5, 193
Oliver, Mary Hempstone
1885(?)-1973 Obituary 41-44R
Oliver, Paul (Hereford) 1927- CANR-1
Earlier sketch in CA 1-4R
Oliver, R(ichard) A(lexander) C(avaye) 1904-
CAP-1
Earlier sketch in CA 11-12
Oliver, Raymond (Guillaume)
1909-1990 Obituary 132
Oliver, Raymond (Davies) 1936- CANR-26
Earlier sketch in CA 109
Oliver, Revilo P(endleton) 1910- 121
Oliver, Richard (Bruce) 1942-1985 116
Oliver, Robert (Shelton) 1934- 105
Oliver, Robert T(arbell) 1909- CANR-41
Earlier sketches in CA 5-8R, CANR-4, 19
Oliver, Robert W. 1922- 135
Oliver, Roland Anthony 1923- CANR-12
Earlier sketch in CA 73-76
Oliver, Rupert
See Matthews, Rupert O(liver)
Oliver, Shirley (Louise Dawkins) 1958- SATA 74
Oliver, Smith Hempstone 1912- 25-28R
Oliver, Symmes C(hadwick) 1928-1993 113
See also SATA 101
Oliver, (McWhorter) Thomas 1950- 127
Oliver, W. Andrew 1941- 37-40R
Oliver, William Irvin 1926- 17-20R
Olivera, Otto 1919- 49-52
Oliveri, Mario 1944- 107
Olivier, Charles P(ollard) 1884-1975 Obituary 61-64
Olivier, Laurence (Kerr) 1907-1989 150
Obituary 129
Brief entry 111
See also CLC 20
Olivier, Robert L(ouis) 1903- 93-96
Oliviero, Jamie 1950- SATA 84
Olivova, Vera 1926- 81-84
Olkes, Cheryl 1948- 127
Olkowski, Helga 1931- 85-88
Olkowski, William 1941- 97-100
Ollard, Richard (Laurence) 1923- CANR-20
Earlier sketch in CA 93-96
Oller, John W(illiam), Jr. 1943- CANR-5
Earlier sketch in CA 53-56
Ollerenshaw, Kathleen (Mary) 1912- Brief
entry 107
Ollestad, Norman (Tennyson) 1935- 21-24R
Olli, John B. 1893(?)-1984 Obituary 112
Ollier, Claude 1922- DLB 83
Ollier, Cliff(ord) David 1931- 61-64
Ollif, Lorna (Anne) 1918- 93-96
Olliff, Donathan C(arnes) 1933- 115
Ollman, Bertell 1935- CANR-16
Earlier sketch in CA 85-88
Olm, Kenneth W(illiam) 1924- 21-24R
Olmert, Michael 1940- 140
Olmstead, Alan H. 1907(?)-1980 Obituary 101
Olmstead, Andrea (Louise) 1948- 127
Olmstead, Clifton Earl 1926-1962 1-4R
Olmstead, Earl P. 1920- 137
Olmstead, Robert 1954- 129
Olmsted, Charlotte
See Kursh, Charlotte Olmsted
Olmsted, Frederick Law 1822-1903 Brief entry 120
Olmsted, John Charles 1942- 93-96
Olmsted, Lorena Ann 1890- 29-32R
See also SATA 13
Olmsted, Robert W(alsh) 1936- 41-44R
Olmsted, Sterling P(itkin) 1915- 25-28R
Olney, James 1933- 77-80
Olney, Ross R. 1929- CANR-7
Earlier sketch in CA 13-16R
See also SATA 13
Olorunsola, Victor A. 1939- CANR-7
Earlier sketch in CA 57-60
O'Loughlin, Carleen CAP-2
Earlier sketch in CA 25-28
Olowu, (Claudius) Dele 1952- 135
O.L.S.
See Russell, George William
Olscamp, Paul James 1937- 104
Olschewski, Alfred 1920- 41-44R
See also SATA 7
Olschki, G. Cesare 1890-1971 Obituary 104
Olsen, Alfa-Betty 1947- 103
Olsen, Alfred Johannes, Jr. 1884-1956 Brief
entry 113
Olsen, Bob
See Olsen, Alfred Johannes, Jr.
Olsen, Carol 1945- SATA 89
Olsen, Donald J(ames) 1929-1997 13-16R
Obituary 158
Olsen, Edward G(ustave) 1908- CANR-11
Earlier sketches in CAP-1, CA 9-10
Olsen, Gary 1948- 160
Olsen, Hans Christian, Jr. 1929- Brief entry 106
Olsen, Ib Spang 1921- CANR-56
Earlier sketches in CA 49-52, CANR-3, 37
See also MAICYA
See also SATA 6, 81
Olsen, Jack
See Olsen, John Edward
Olsen, James 1933- 49-52
Olsen, John Edward 1925- CANR-55
Earlier sketches in CA 17-20R, CANR-9, 29
Olsen, Larry Dean 1939- 69-72
Olsen, Marvin E(lliott) 1936- CANR-26
Earlier sketch in CA 29-32R
Olsen, Otto H(arald) 1925- 33-36R
Olsen, R(obert) Arthur 1910- CAP-2
Earlier sketch in CA 23-24
Olsen, Richard E(llison) 1941- 81-84
Olsen, Stein Haugom 1946- 128
Olsen, T(heodore) V(ictor) 1932- CANR-39
Earlier sketches in CA 1-4R, CANR-3, 18
Olsen, Tillie 1913- CANR-43
Earlier sketches in CA 1-4R, CANR-1
See also CLC 4, 13
See also DA
See also DAB
See also DAC
See also DAM MST
See also DLB 28
See also DLBY 80
See also MTCW 1
See also SSC 11
Olsen, V(iggo) Norskov 1916- 53-56
Olsen, Violet (Mae) 1922-1991 113
Obituary 134
See also SATA 58
Olsen, William 1954- 128
Olshaker, Bennett 1921- Brief entry 108
Olshaker, Mark 1951- 73-76
Olshaker, Thelma 114
Olshan, Joseph 1956- 128
Olshan, Neal H(ugh) 1947- 119
Olshen, Barry N(eil) 1944- 89-92
Olshewsky, Thomas M(ack) 1934- 37-40R
Olson, Alan M(elvin) 1939- CANR-8
Earlier sketch in CA 61-64
Olson, Alison Gilbert 1931- Brief entry 109
Olson, (Elizabeth) Ann 1953- 126
Olson, Arielle North 1932- 134
See also SATA 67
Olson, Arnold O(rville) 1917- 45-48
Olson, Bernhard Emanuel 1910-1975 CANR-24
Obituary 61-64
Earlier sketch in CA 45-48
Olson, Carl 1941- CANR-36
Earlier sketch in CA 114
Olson, Charles (John) 1910-1970 CANR-61
Obituary 25-28R
Earlier sketches in CAP-1, CA 13-16, CANR-35
See also CABS 2
See also CLC 1, 2, 5, 6, 9, 11, 29
See also DAM POET
See also DLB 5, 16, 193
See also MTCW 1
See also PC 19
Olson, Clair C(olby) 1901-1972 41-44R
Olson, (Carl Bernard) David 1904- 61-64
Olson, David F. 1938- 49-52
Olson, David John 1941- 53-56
Olson, David R(ichard) 1935- 33-36R
Olson, Donald 1938- 65-68
Olson, Elder (James) 1909-1992 CANR-31
Obituary 139
Earlier sketches in CA 5-8R, CANR-6
See also CAAS 12
See also DLB 48, 63
Olson, Eric 1944- 53-56
Olson, Everett C. 1910-1993 53-56
Obituary 143
Olson, Gary A. 1954- 148
Olson, Gene 1922- 106
See also SATA 32
Olson, Harry E(dwin), Jr. 1932- 61-64
Olson, Harry F(erdinand) 1901- 37-40R
Olson, Harvey S(tuart) 1908-1985 CANR-1
Obituary 118
Earlier sketch in CA 1-4R
Olson, Helen Kronberg CANR-12
Earlier sketch in CA 29-32R
See also SATA 48
Olson, Herbert Waldo 1927- 1-4R
Olson, James C(lifton) 1917- 37-40R
Olson, James R(obert) 1938- 49-52
Olson, Jane Virginia 1916- 89-92
Olson, Keith W(aldemar) 1931- 49-52
Olson, Ken(neth John) 1930- 97-100
Olson, Lawrence Alexander
1918-1992 Obituary 137
Brief entry 110
Olson, Lester C. 1955- 142
Olson, Linda Steffel 1949- 167
Olson, Lois Ellen 1941- 105
Olson, Mancur, Jr. 1932-1998 13-16R
Obituary 165
Olson, McKinley C(lar) 1931- 110
Olson, Mildred Thompson 1922- 21-24R
Olson, Paul R(ichard) 1925- 21-24R
Olson, Philip G(ilbert) 1934- 9-12R
Olson, Richard G(eorge) 1940- CANR-17
Earlier sketch in CA 89-92
Olson, Richard Paul 1934- CANR-49
Earlier sketches in CA 61-64, CANR-8, 24
Olson, Robert G(oodwin) 1924- 29-32R
Olson, Robert W(illiam) 1940- 136
Olson, Sidney 1908- CAP-1
Earlier sketch in CA 11-12
Olson, Sigurd F(erdinand) 1899-1982 CANR-1
Obituary 105
Earlier sketch in CA 1-4R
Olson, Stanley 1948-1989 89-92
Obituary 130
Olson, Steven 1950- 149
Olson, Ted
See Olson, Theodore B.
Olson, Theodore B. 1899- 49-52
Olson, Toby 1937- CANR-31
Earlier sketches in CA 65-68, CANR-9
See also CLC 28
Olson, Walter K. 1954- 135
Olson, Willard Clifford 1899-1978 Obituary 111
Olsson, Axel Adolf 1889-1977 Obituary 73-76
Olsson, Jennifer 1959- 157
Olsson, Karl A(rthur) 1913- CANR-4
Earlier sketch in CA 5-8R
Olsson, Nils 1909- 73-76
Olstad, Charles (Frederick) 1932-1976 17-20R
Obituary 134
Olthuis, James H(erman) 1938- 61-64
Oltmans, Willem L(eonard) 1925- 57-60
Olton, Charles S(haw) 1938- Brief entry 108
Olton, Roy 1922- 103
Oludhe-Macgoye, Marjorie 1928- 133
Olugebefola, Ademole 1941- SATA 15
Olyesha, Yuri
See Olesha, Yuri (Karlovich)
Olzendam, Roderic Marble
1892-1986 Obituary 121
O'Mahoney, Rich
See Warner-Crozetti, R(uth G.)
O'Mahony, Patrick 1911- 13-16R
O'Malley, Brian (Jack Morgan)
1918(?)-1980 Obituary 101
O'Malley, Charles Donald 1907-1970 Obituary 109
O'Malley, Frank
See O'Rourke, Frank
O'Malley, J(ohn) Steven 1942- 53-56
O'Malley, John W(illiam) 1927- Brief entry 114
O'Malley, Joseph James 1930- 37-40R
O'Malley, Kevin
See Hossent, Harry
O'Malley, Lady Mary Dolling (Sanders) 1889-1974
CANR-59
Earlier sketch in CA 65-68
See also DLB 191
O'Malley, Mary Brief entry 110
O'Malley, Mary Josephine 1941- 156
O'Malley, Michael (Anthony) 1-4R
O'Malley, Padraig 139
O'Malley, Patrick
See O'Rourke, Frank
O'Malley, Richard K(ilroy) 1911- 97-100
O'Malley, Suzanne 1951- 110
O'Malley, William J(ohn) 1931- CANR-31
Earlier sketches in CA 73-76, CANR-12
Oman, Carola (Mary Anima) 1897-1978 CANR-4
Earlier sketch in CA 5-8R
See also SATA 35
Oman, Charles Chichele 1901-1982 103
Obituary 105
Oman, Julia Trevelyan 1930- 126
Omang, Joanne (Brenda) 1943- 135
Omansky, Dorothy Linder
1905(?)-1977 Obituary 73-76
O Maolain, Ciaran 1958- 123
O'Maonaigh, Cainneach
See Mooney, Canice (Albert James)
Omari, T(hompson) Peter 1930- 29-32R
O'Marie, Carol Anne 1933- CANR-63
Earlier sketch in CA 136
Omarr, Sydney Brief entry 116
O'Meally, Robert G(eorge) 1948- 130
O'Meara, John J. 1915- CANR-3
Earlier sketch in CA 1-4R
O'Meara, Patrick 1938- 113
O'Meara, Thomas F(ranklin) 1935- 110
O'Meara, Walter (Andrew) 1897-1989 13-16R
Obituary 129
See also SATA 65
Omer, Garth St.
See St. Omer, Garth
Ommanney, F(rancis) D(ownes) 1903-1980
CANR-7
Obituary 101
Earlier sketch in CA 13-16R
See also SATA 23
Ommundsen, Wenche 1952- 147
O'More, Peggy
See Blocklinger, Peggy O'More
O'Morrison, Kevin CANR-9
Earlier sketch in CA 53-56
Omotoso, Kole 1943- 143
See also BW 2
See also DLB 125
O Mude
See Gorey, Edward (St. John)
O'Mullane, Tess De Araugo
See De Araugo, Tess (S.)
Onacewicz, Wlodzimierz
1893(?)-1986 Obituary 120
Onadipe, (Nathaniel) Kola(wole) 1922- 101
O'Nair, Mairi
See Evans, Constance May
O'Nan, Stewart 1961- 146
Onate, Andres David 1940- Brief entry 112
Ondaatje, Christopher 1933- 49-52
Ondaatje, (Philip) Michael 1943- CANR-42
Earlier sketch in CA 77-80
See also CLC 14, 29, 51, 76
See also DAB
See also DAC
See also DAM MST
See also DLB 60
O'Neal, Bill
See O'Neal, John W(illiam)
O'Neal, Charles E. 1904-1996 CAP-2
Obituary 153
Earlier sketch in CA 19-20
O'Neal, Cothburn M(adison) 1907- 1-4R
Oneal, Elizabeth 1934- CANR-28
Earlier sketch in CA 106
See also Oneal, Zibby
See also MAICYA
See also SATA 30, 82
O'Neal, Forest Hodge 1917- 5-8R
O'Neal, Glenn (Franklin) 1919- 49-52
O'Neal, Hank 1940- 134
O'Neal, John W(illiam) 1942- 89-92
O'Neal, Reagan
See Rigney, James Oliver, Jr.
O'Neal, William B(ainter) 1907- 73-76
Oneal, Zibby
See Oneal, Elizabeth
See also AAYA 5
See also CLC 30
See also CLR 13
See also JRDA
O'Neil, Daniel J. 1936- 89-92
O'Neil, Dennis 1939- 97-100
O'Neil, Eric
See Barnum, W(illiam) Paul
O'Neil, Isabel MacDonald
1908(?)-1981 Obituary 105
O'Neil, Paul E. 1909(?)-1988 Obituary 125
O'Neil, Robert M(archant) 1934- 106
O'Neil, Terry 1949- 61-64
O'Neil, W(illiam) M(atthew) 1912- CANR-32
Earlier sketch in CA 113
O'Neil, Will(iam Daniel III) 1938- 101
O'Neill, Archie
See Henaghan, Jim
O'Neill, Barbara Powell 1929- 17-20R
O'Neill, Brian Juan 1950- 153
O'Neill, Carlota 1918- 101
O'Neill, Carlotta Monterey
1888-1970 Obituary 29-32R
O'Neill, Charles Edwards 1927- CANR-9
Earlier sketch in CA 21-24R
O'Neill, Cherry Boone 1954- 112
O'Neill, Daniel Joseph 1905- Brief entry 106
O'Neill, David P(atrick) 1918- 17-20R
O'Neill, Dennis (Bernard) 1947- 114
O'Neill, E. Bard 1941- 85-88
O'Neill, Egan
See Linington, (Barbara) Elizabeth
O'Neill, Eugene (Gladstone) 1888-1953 132
Brief entry 110
See also AITN 1
See also CDALB 1929-1941
See also DA
See also DAB
See also DAC
See also DAM DRAM, MST
See also DLB 7
See also MTCW 1
See also TCLC 1, 6, 27, 49
See also WLC
O'Neill, Eugene 1922- 77-80
O'Neill, Frank (Quale) 1943- 120
O'Neill, Frank F. 1926(?)-1983 Obituary 109
O'Neill, George 1921(?)-1980 Obituary 102
See also AITN 1
O'Neill, Gerard (Michael) 1942- 69-72
O'Neill, Gerard K(itchen) 1927-1992 CANR-21
Obituary 137
Earlier sketch in CA 93-96
See also SATA 65
O'Neill, James E(dward) 1929-1987 117
Obituary 121
O'Neill, John 1933- 53-56

O'Neill, John Joseph 1920- 21-24R
O'Neill, Joseph 1964- 164
O'Neill, Joseph Harry 1915- 13-16R
O'Neill, Joseph James 1878-1952 162
O'Neill, Judith (Beatrice) 1930- CANR-51
Earlier sketches in CA 109, CANR-26
See also SATA 34
O'Neill, Mary L(e Duc) 1908(?)-1990 ...... CANR-4
Obituary 130
Earlier sketch in CA 5-8R
See also SATA 2
See also SATA-Obit 64
O'Neill, Michael 1953- 133
O'Neill, Michael J. 104
O'Neill, Michael J. 1913- 13-16R
O'Neill, Michael J(ames) 1922- 112
Brief entry 108
Interview in 112
O'Neill, Nena .... AITN 1
O'Neill, Olivia
See Barstow, Phyllida
O'Neill, Patrick Geoffrey 1924- 21-24R
O'Neill, Paul 1928- 107
O'Neill, Reginald F. 1915- 1-4R
O'Neill, Richard W(inslow) 1925- Brief entry ... 107
O'Neill, Robert J(ohn) 1936- 25-28R
O'Neill, Seosamh
See O'Neill, Joseph James
O'Neill, Shane
See O'Neill, William
O'Neill, Terence Marne 1914- 108
O'Neill, Thomas Philip, Jr. 1912-1994 159
O'Neill, Tim 1918- 1-4R
O'Neill, Timothy J. 1949- 153
O'Neill, Timothy P. 1941- 85-88
O'Neill, Timothy R. 1943- 128
O'Neill, Tip
See O'Neill, Thomas Philip, Jr.
O'Neill, William 1927- 37-40R
O'Neill, William F. 1931- 29-32R
O'Neill, William L. 1935- CANR-34
Earlier sketches in CA 21-24R, CANR-12
O'Neill of the Maine, Baron of Ahoghill
See O'Neill, Terence Marne
O'Nell, Carl William 1925- 73-76
Onetti, Juan Carlos 1909-1994 .... CANR-63
Obituary 145
Earlier sketches in CA 85-88, CANR-32
See also CLC 7, 10
See also DAM MULT, NOV
See also DLB 113
See also HW
See also MTCW 1
See also SSC 23
Ong, Walter J(ackson) 1912- CANR-21
Earlier sketches in CA 1-4R, CANR-4
Ongaro, Alberto 1925- 25-28R
O'Niell, C. M.
See Wilkes-Hunter, R(ichard)
Onions, Charles Talbut 1873-1965 Obituary ... 107
Onions, Oliver
See Oliver, George
Onions, (George) Oliver 1872-1961 166
See also DLB 153
Onley, David C(harles) 1950- 112
Onlooker
See Grange, Cyril
Onnes, Heike Kamerlingh
See Kamerlingh Onnes, Heike
Ono, Chiyo 1941- CANR-12
Earlier sketch in CA 29-32R
Onoda, Hiroo 1922(?)- Brief entry 108
Onofri, Arturo 1885-1928 .... DLB 114
O'Nolan, Brian
See O Nuallain, Brian
Onopa, Robert 1943- 112
Onorato, Richard James 1933- Brief entry 108
Onslow, Annette Rosemary MacArthur
See MacArthur-Onslow, Annette Rosemary
Onslow, John 1906-1985 Obituary 118
See also SATA-Obit 47
Onstott, Kyle 1887-1966 .... 5-8R
Obituary 126
Ontoya, Jose 1932- 131
O Nuallain, Brian 1911-1966 .... CAP-2
Obituary 25-28R
Earlier sketch in CA 21-22
See also O'Brien, Flann
Onwueme, Tess Akaeke 1954- 168
Onwueme, Tess Osonye
See Onwueme, Tess Akaeke
Onyeama, (Charles) Dillibe 1951- 125
See also BW 1
Onyefulu, Ifeoma 1959- .... SATA 81
Ooi Jin-Bee 1931- 73-76
Ooiman, Jo Ann
See Robinson, Jo Ann Ooiman
Oost, Stewart Irvin 1921-1981 .... 29-32R
Obituary 135
Oosterman, Gordon 1927- 49-52
Oosterwal, Gottfried 1930- 93-96
Oosthuizen, G(erhardus) C(ornelis) 1922- ....
CANR-52
Earlier sketches in CA 29-32R, CANR-27
Oparin, Aleksandr (Ivanovich)
1894-1980 Obituary 108
Opdahl, Keith Michael 1934- 61-64
Opdahl, Richard D(ean) 1924- 21-24R
Opgenoorth, Winfried 1939- .... SATA-Brief 50
Ophuls, Max 1902-1957 Brief entry 113
See also TCLC 79
Ophuls, Patrick 1934- 135
Ophuls, William
See Ophuls, Patrick
Opie, Amelia 1769-1853 .... DLB 116, 159
Opie, Anne 1946- 145
Opie, Iona 1923- 61-64
See also SAAS 6
See also SATA 3, 63
Opie, John 1934- 29-32R
Opie, Peter (Mason) 1918-1982 .... CANR-2
Obituary 106
Earlier sketch in CA 5-8R
See also SATA 3, 63
See also SATA-Obit 28
Opie, Redvers 1900-1984 Obituary 112
Opik, E.
See Oepik, Ernst Julius
Opik, Ernst
See Oepik, Ernst Julius
Opik, Ernst J.
See Oepik, Ernst Julius
Opik, Ernst Julius
See Oepik, Ernst Julius
Opitz, Edmund A. 1914- 29-32R
Opitz, Martin 1597-1639 .... DLB 164
Opitz, May
See Ayim, May
Opland, Jeff 1943- 106
Opler, Marvin K(aufmann) 1914-1981 ...... 21-24R
Obituary 133
Opler, Morris E(dward) 1907- CANR-29
Earlier sketch in CA 45-48
Opotowsky, Stan(ford L.) 1923-1997 ..... CANR-1
Obituary 161
Earlier sketch in CA 1-4R
Oppel, Kenneth 1967- 160
See also SATA 99
Oppelt, Norman T. 1930- 139
Oppen, George 1908-1984 .... CANR-8
Obituary 113
Earlier sketch in CA 13-16R
See also CLC 7, 13, 34
See also DLB 5, 165
Oppen, Mary 1908-1990 119
Obituary 131
Oppenheim, A(dolph) Leo
1904-1974 Obituary 49-52
Oppenheim, E(dward) Phillips 1866-1946 Brief
entry 111
See also DLB 70
See also TCLC 45
Oppenheim, Felix E(rrera) 1913- 1-4R
Oppenheim, Frank Mathias 1925- 116
Oppenheim, Irene 1928- 77-80
Oppenheim, James 1882-1932 .... DLB 28
Oppenheim, Janet 1948- 117
Oppenheim, Joanne 1934- CANR-50
Earlier sketches in CA 21-24R, CANR-9, 25
See also SATA 5, 82
Oppenheim, Lois Hecht 1948- 149
Oppenheim, Lois Susan
See Oppenheim, Lois Hecht
Oppenheim, Micha Falk 1937- 147
Oppenheim, Michael 1940- 138
Oppenheim, Paul 1885(?)-1977 Obituary 69-72
Oppenheim, Philip 1956- 138
Oppenheim, S(aul) Chesterfield
1897-1988 Obituary 124
Oppenheim, Shulamith (Levey) 1930- 73-76
Oppenheimer, Andres 1951- 145
Oppenheimer, Evelyn 1907- CANR-3
Earlier sketch in CA 1-4R
Oppenheimer, George 1900-1977 .... 13-16R
Obituary 73-76
Oppenheimer, Gregg 1951- 160
Oppenheimer, Harold L. 1919- 17-20R
Oppenheimer, J(ulius) Robert 1904-1967 CANR-34
Earlier sketch in CA 103
See also MTCW 1
Oppenheimer, Jess 1913(?)-1988 Obituary 127
Oppenheimer, Joan L(etson) 1925- CANR-37
Earlier sketches in CA 37-40R, CANR-17
See also SATA 28
Oppenheimer, Joe A(llan) 1941- 111
Oppenheimer, Joel (Lester) 1930-1988 .. CANR-21
Obituary 126
Earlier sketches in CA 9-12R, CANR-4
See also DLB 5, 193
Oppenheimer, Martin 1930- 29-32R
Oppenheimer, Max, Jr. 1917- 17-20R
Oppenheimer, Paul 1939- 21-24R
Oppenheimer, Samuel P(hilip) 1903- 33-36R
Opper, F.
See Opper, Frederick (Burr)
Opper, Frederick (Burr) 1857-1937 Brief entry .. 118
See also AITN 1
Opper, Jacob 1935- 49-52
Opperby, Preben 1924- 110
Oppersdorff, Tony 1945- 137
Oppitz, Rene 1905(?)-1976 Obituary 65-68
Oppong, Christine 1940- CANR-7
Earlier sketch in CA 57-60
Optic, Oliver
See Adams, William Taylor
and Stratemeyer, Edward L.
Opton, Edward M., Jr. 1936- CANR-11
Earlier sketch in CA 21-24R
Opuls, Max
See Ophuls, Max
O'Quill, Scarlett
See Mossman, Dow
O'Quinn, Garland 1935- 21-24R
O'Quinn, Hazel Hedick 37-40R
Orage, A(lfred) R(ichard) 1873-1934 Brief
entry 122
Oraison, Marc 1914- 85-88
Oram, Hiawyn 1946- 106
See also SATA 56, 101
Oram, Malcolm 1944(?)-1976 Obituary 104
O'Ramus, Seamus
See O'Neill, William
O'Rand, Angela M(etropulos) 1945- 104
Oras, Ants 1900- CAP-1
Earlier sketch in CA 13-16
Orbaan, Albert F. CANR-8
Earlier sketch in CA 5-8R
Orbach, Ruth Gary 1941- 65-68
See also SATA 21
Orbach, Susie 1946- CANR-42
Earlier sketches in CA 85-88, CANR-19
Orbach, William W(olf) 1946- 73-76
Orbell, Margaret 1934- 158
Orben, Robert 1927- CANR-70
Earlier sketches in CA 81-84, CANR-31
Orbis, Victor
See Powell-Smith, Vincent (Walter Francis)
Orcutt, Georgia 1949- 112
Orczy, Emma Magdalena Rosalia Maria Josefa
See Orczy, BaronessEmmuska
Orczy, Emmuska
See Orczy, BaronessEmmuska
Orczy, BaronessEmmuska 1865-1947 167
Brief entry 104
See also Orczy, Emmuska
See also DLB 70
See also SATA 40
Ord, John E. 1917- 81-84
Orde, A. J.
See Tepper, Sheri S.
Orde, Lewis 1943- CANR-28
Earlier sketch in CA 109
Ord-Hume, Arthur W. J. G. 101
Ordish, (Francis) George 1908(?)-1991 ... CANR-9
Obituary 133
Earlier sketch in CA 61-64
Ordover, Sondra T. 1929-1988 Obituary 127
Ordway, Frederick I(ra) III 1927- CANR-49
Earlier sketches in CA 5-8R, CANR-5, 20
Ordway, Sally 1939- 57-60
Ore, Rebecca 1948- 164
O'Regan, Richard Arthur 1919- 73-76
O'Reilly, Don 1913- 111
O'Reilly, Jackson
See Rigney, James Oliver, Jr.
O'Reilly, Jane 1936- CANR-31
Earlier sketch in CA 73-76
O'Reilly, John (Thomas) 1945- 29-32R
O'Reilly, Kenneth 1951- 155
O'Reilly, Montagu
See Andrews, Wayne
O'Reilly, Robert P. 1936- 29-32R
O'Reilly, Timothy 1954- CANR-23
Earlier sketch in CA 106
O'Reilly, Victor 1944- 156
Orel, Harold 1926- CANR-43
Earlier sketches in CA 5-8R, CANR-3, 19
Orellana, Sandra L. 1941- 126
O'Relley, Z(oltan) Edward 1940- 119
Orem, R(eginald) C(alvert) 1931- 17-20R
Oren, Dan A. 1958- 138
Oren, Uri 1931- 65-68
Orengo, Charles 1913(?)-1974 Obituary 104
Orenstein, Denise Gosliner 1950- 110
Orenstein, Frank (Everett) 1919- CANR-54
Earlier sketches in CA 111, CANR-30
Orenstein, Gloria Feman 1938- 65-68
Orenstein, Henry 1924- 13-16R
Orenstein, Peggy 1961- 147
Orent, Norman B. 1920- 17-20R
Oreshnik, A. F.
See Nussbaum, Al(bert F.)
Oresick, Peter (Michael) 1955- CANR-56
Earlier sketches in CA 73-76, CANR-13, 30
Orest
See Bedrij, Orest (John)
Orewa, George Oka 1928- 5-8R
Orfalea, Gregory (M.) 1949- 128
Orff, Carl 1895-1982 Obituary 106
Orfield, Olivia 1922- 103
Orga, Ates 1944- 93-96
Organ, John 1925- CANR-7
Earlier sketch in CA 5-8R
Organ, Troy Wilson 1912- 37-40R
Organski, A(bramo) F(imo) K(enneth) 1923- 103
Orgel, Doris 1929- CANR-2
Earlier sketch in CA 45-48
See also AITN 1
See also CLR 48
See also SAAS 19
See also SATA 7, 85
Orgel, Joseph Randolph 1902-1987 .... CAP-1
Obituary 123
Earlier sketch in CA 11-12
Orgel, Stephen (Kitay) 1933- CANR-14
Earlier sketch in CA 73-76
Orgill, Douglas 1922-1984 .... CANR-29
Earlier sketch in CA 81-84
Orgill, Michael (Thomas) 1946- 61-64
Orians, George H(arrison) 1900- 49-52
Orians, Gordon H(owell) 1932- CANR-30
Earlier sketch in CA 45-48
Oriard, Michael (Vincent) 1948- 110
Origo, Iris (Margaret Cutting) 1902-1988 . CANR-47
Earlier sketch in CA 105
See also DLB 155
O'Riley, Warren
See Richardson, Gladwell
Oring, Elliott 1945- 111
Oriolo, Joe
See Oriolo, Joseph D.
Oriolo, Joseph D. 1913-1985 Obituary 118
See also SATA-Obit 46
Orion
See Naylor, John
O'Riordan, Robert (Garrett) 1943- 119
Orjuela, Hector H(ugo) 1930- CANR-32
Earlier sketches in CA 45-48, CANR-2
See also HW
Orkeny, Antal 1954- 143
Orkeny, Istvan 1912-1979 103
Obituary 89-92
Orkin, Harvey 1918(?)-1975 Obituary 61-64
Orkin, Ruth 1921-1985 119
Obituary 114
Orlando, Guido 1908(?)-1988 Obituary 126
Orlans, Harold 1921- CANR-15
Earlier sketch in CA 33-36R
Orlean, Susan 1955- 134
Orleans, Ilo 1897-1962 .... CANR-15
Earlier sketch in CA 1-4R
See also SATA 10
Orleans, Leo A(nton) 1924- CANR-32
Earlier sketches in CA 41-44R, CANR-15
Orleck, Annelise 1959- 149
Orledge, Robert (Nicholas) 1948- 113
Orlen, Steve 1942- 101
Orlev, Uri 1931- CANR-34
Earlier sketch in CA 101
See also AAYA 20
See also CLR 30
See also SAAS 19
See also SATA 58
Orlich, Donald C(harles) 1931- CANR-45
Earlier sketches in CA 13-16R, CANR-7, 22
Orlick, Terrance D(ouglas) 1945- CANR-45
Earlier sketches in CA 57-60, CANR-6, 21
Orlick, Terry
See Orlick, Terrance D(ouglas)
Orlicky, Joseph A. 1922- 25-28R
Orlier, Blaise
See Sylvestre, (Joseph Jean) Guy
Orlinsky, Harry M(eyer) 1908-1992 85-88
Obituary 137
Orlob, Helen Seaburg 1908- 5-8R
Orlock, Carol (Ellen) 1947- CANR-48
Earlier sketch in CA 122
Orloff, Ed(gar Sam) 1923-1983 69-72
Obituary 110
Orloff, Judith 1951- 155
Orloff, Max
See Crowcroft, Peter
Orlofsky, Myron 1928(?)-1976 Obituary 69-72
Orloski, Richard J(ohn) 1947- 97-100
Orlova, Alexandra (Anatol'evna) 1911- 133
Orlova, R.
See Orlova-Kopelev, Raissa (Davydovna)
Orlova, R. D.
See Orlova-Kopelev, Raissa (Davydovna)
Orlova, Raisa
See Orlova-Kopelev, Raissa (Davydovna)
Orlova-Kopelev, Raissa (Davydovna) 1918- 123
Orlovitz, Gil 1918-1973 77-80
Obituary 45-48
See also CLC 22
See also DLB 2, 5
Orlovsky, Peter 1933- CANR-9
Earlier sketch in CA 13-16R
See also DLB 16
Orlow, Dietrich 1937- 65-68
Ormai, Stella .... SATA 57
See also SATA-Brief 48
Orme, Antony R(onald) 1936- CANR-35
Earlier sketch in CA 73-76
Ormerod, Jan(ette Louise) 1946- CANR-35
Earlier sketch in CA 113
See also CLR 20
See also MAICYA
See also SATA 55, 70
See also SATA-Brief 44
Ormerod, Roger 1920- CANR-63
Earlier sketches in CA 77-80, CANR-15, 35
Ormes, Jackie
See Ormes, Zelda J.
Ormes, Robert M. 1904- CAP-1
Earlier sketch in CA 11-12
Ormes, Robert Verner 1921-1984 Obituary 112
Ormes, Zelda J. 1914-1986 Obituary 118
See also SATA-Obit 47
Ormesson, Jean (Bruno Waldemar Francois-de-Paule
Lefevre) d'
See d'Ormesson, Jean (Bruno Waldemar
Francois-de-Paule Lefevre)
Ormesson, Wladimir d' 1888-1973 Obituary .. 45-48
Ormiston, Roberta
See Fletcher, Adele (Whitely)
Ormond, (Willard) Clyde 1906-1985 ..... CANR-36
Obituary 115
Earlier sketch in CA 9-12R
Ormond, Frederic
See Dey, Frederic (Merrill) Van Rensselaer
Ormond, John 1923- CANR-32
Earlier sketch in CA 65-68
See also DLB 27
Ormond, Leonee (Jasper) 1940- 85-88
Ormond, Richard (Louis) 1939- CANR-35
Earlier sketches in CA 41-44R, CANR-15
Ormondroyd, Edward 1925- 73-76
See also SATA 14
Ormont, Louis Robert 1918- CANR-35
Earlier sketch in CA 13-16R
Ormrod, Richard (James) 1946- 119
Ormsbee, David
See Longstreet, Stephen
Ormsby, Frank 1947- CANR-23
Earlier sketch in CA 107
Ormsby, Virginia H(aire) 9-12R
See also SATA 11
Ormsby, William (George) 1921- 73-76
Orna, Mary Virginia 1934- 29-32R

Ornati, Oscar A(braham) 1922-1991 ..... CANR-14
Obituary 136
Earlier sketch in CA 37-40R
Ornis
See Winchester, Clarence
Ornish, Dean 1953- CANR-70
Earlier sketch in CA 142
Ornitz, Samuel (Badisch) 1890-1957 Brief entry 117
See also DLB 28, 44
Ornstein, Allan C(harles) 1941- CANR-4
Earlier sketch in CA 53-56
Ornstein, Dolph 1947- 77-80
Ornstein, J. L.
See Ornstein-Galicia, J(acob) L(eonard)
Ornstein, Jack H(ervey) 1938- 103
Ornstein, Norman J(ay) 1948- 93-96
Ornstein, Robert 1925- 1-4R
Ornstein, Robert E. 1942- CANR-35
Earlier sketch in CA 53-56
Ornstein-Galicia, J(acob) L(eonard) 1915- 93-96
Oropeza, Renato Prada
See Prada Oropeza, Renato
O'Rourke, Andrew P(atrick) 1933- 126
O'Rourke, Edward William 1917- 112
O'Rourke, Frank 1916-1989 ..... CANR-65
Obituary 128
Brief entry 114
Earlier sketch in CA 118
Interview in 118
O'Rourke, John James Joseph 1926- 33-36R
O'Rourke, John T(homas) 1900-1983 Obituary . 111
O'Rourke, Lawrence Michael 1938- CANR-35
Earlier sketch in CA 69-72
O'Rourke, P(atrick) J(ake) 1947- CANR-67
Earlier sketches in CA 77-80, CANR-13, 41
See also DAM POP
See also DLB 185
O'Rourke, Terrence James 1932-1992 ..... 41-44R
Obituary 136
O'Rourke, Timothy G(erald) 1949- 111
O'Rourke, William (Andrew) 1945- CANR-35
Earlier sketches in CA 45-48, CANR-1
Orozco, Olga 1920- ..... HW
Orpaz, Yitzhak 1923- 101
Orpen, Eve 1926(?)-1978 Obituary 104
Orpen, Neil (Newton D'Arcy) 1913- 120
Orpen, Neil D.
See Orpen, Neil (Newton D'Arcy)
Orr, Bobby
See Orr, Robert Gordon
Orr, Daniel 1933- 29-32R
Orr, David 1929- 33-36R
Orr, Gregory 1947- CANR-45
Earlier sketches in CA 105, CANR-22
Orr, Helen Frances Burton 1913-1989 Obituary 129
Orr, J(ames) Edwin 1912- CANR-4
Earlier sketch in CA 9-12R
Orr, John Boyd 1880-1971 Obituary 113
Orr, Katherine S(helley) 1950- ..... SATA 72
Orr, Linda 1943- CANR-35
Earlier sketch in CA 97-100
Orr, Mary
See Denham, Mary Orr
Orr, Mary E. E. McCombe 1917- 5-8R
Orr, Oliver H(amilton), Jr. 1921- 1-4R
Orr, Robert Gordon 1948- 112
Orr, Robert R(ichmond) 1930- 25-28R
Orr, Robert T. 1908-1994 ..... 33-36R
Obituary 146
Orr, Wendy 1953- 155
See also SATA 90
Orr, William F(ridell) 1907- 108
Orrell, John (Overton) 1934- CANR-35
Earlier sketches in CA 37-40R, CANR-15
Orris
See Ingelow, Jean
Orrmont, Arthur 1922- CANR-35
Earlier sketches in CA 1-4R, CANR-4
Orsborn, Carol 1948- 124
Orsini, Gian Napoleone Giordano 1903-(?) 5-8R
Orsini, Joseph E(mmanuel) 1937- 37-40R
Orso, Kathryn Wickey 1921-1979 57-60
Obituary 85-88
Orsy, Ladislas M. 1921- 25-28R
Orszagh, Laszlo 1907-1984 Obituary 112
Ort, Ana
See Andrews, Arthur (Douglas, Jr.)
Ortega, James M. 1932- 144
Ortega y Gasset, Jose 1883-1955 130
Brief entry 106
See also DAM MULT
See also HLC
See also HW
See also MTCW 1
See also TCLC 9
Ortego, Philip D.
See Ortego y Gasca, Philip D.
Ortego y Gasca, Philip D. 1926- 131
See also HW
Ortenberg, Veronica 1961- 139
Ortese, Anna Maria 1914- ..... CLC 89
See also DLB 177
Orth, Charles D. III 1921- 5-8R
Orth, Penelope 1938- 45-48
Orth, Ralph H(arry) 1930- 21-24R
Orth, Richard
See Gardner, Richard (M.)
Orthwine, Rudolf 1900(?)-1970 Obituary 104
Ortiz, Adalberto 1914- 131
See also HW
Ortiz, Alfonso A(lex) 1939-1997 ..... 29-32R
Obituary 156
Ortiz, Elisabeth Lambert 1928- CANR-35
Earlier sketch in CA 97-100
Ortiz, Simon J(oseph) 1941- CANR-69
Earlier sketch in CA 134
See also CLC 45
See also DAM MULT, POET
See also DLB 120, 175
See also NNAL
See also PC 17
Ortiz, Victoria 1942- 107
Ortiz de Montellano, Thelma 1906- 162
Ortiz y Pino, Jose III 1932- 112
Ortlund, Anne 1923- 106
Ortlund, Raymond C(arl) 1923- 114
Ortman, E(lmore) Jan 1884- CAP-2
Earlier sketch in CA 25-28
Ortman, Elmer John
See Ortman, E(lmore) Jan
Ortner, Donald John 1938- 117
Ortner, Robert 1927- 135
Ortner, Sherry B(eth) 1941- 130
Ortner, Toni 1941- CANR-42
Ortner-Zimmerman, Toni
See Ortner, Toni
Orton, Alvin E. 1906-1987 Obituary 122
Orton, Anthony 1937- 163
Orton, Barry 1949- 111
Orton, Harold 1898-1975 Obituary 57-60
Orton, Joe
See Orton, John Kingsley
See also CDBLB 1960 to Present
See also CLC 4, 13, 43
See also DC 3
See also DLB 13
Orton, John Kingsley 1933-1967 ..... CANR-66
Earlier sketches in CA 85-88, CANR-35
See also Orton, Joe
See also DAM DRAM
See also MTCW 1
Orton, Lawrence D(wayne) 1941- Brief entry ... 118
Orton, Vrest (Teachout) 1897-1986 ..... CANR-35
Obituary 121
Earlier sketch in CA 33-36R
Ortzen, Len
See Ortzen, Leonard Edwin
Ortzen, Leonard Edwin 1912-1979 118
Brief entry 114
Orum, Anthony M(endl) 1939- 41-44R
Orvell, Miles 1944- 41-44R
Orwell, George
See Blair, Eric (Arthur)
See also CDBLB 1945-1960
See also DAB
See also DLB 15, 98, 195
See also TCLC 2, 6, 15, 31, 51
See also WLC
Orwell, Sonia 1919(?)-1980 Obituary 102
Orwen, (Phillips) Gifford 37-40R
Ory, Carlos Edmundo de 1923- ..... DLB 134
Ory, Edward 1886-1973 Obituary 41-44R
Ory, Kid
See Ory, Edward
Ory, Marcia G. 1950- 141
Ory, Robert L(ouis) 1925- 142
Orzeck, Arthur Z(alman) 1921- CANR-1
Earlier sketch in CA 45-48
Osa, Osayimwense 1951- 152
Osanka, Franklin Mark 1936- 5-8R
Osaragi, Jiro
See Nojiri, Kiyohiko
Osbeck, Kenneth W. 1924- CANR-41
Earlier sketches in CA 1-4R, CANR-3, 19
Osbey, Brenda Marie 1957- ..... DLB 120
Osbon, B. S. 1827-1912 ..... DLB 43
Osborn, Albert D. 1896(?)-1972 Obituary 104
Osborn, Alex(ander) F(aickney) 1888-1966 Obituary 106
Osborn, Arthur W(alter) 1891- 21-24R
Osborn, Barbara M(onroe)
See Henkel, Barbara Osborn
Osborn, Carolyn 1934- 93-96
Osborn, Catherine B. 1914- 29-32R
Osborn, E. Margaret 1912- 165
Osborn, Eric (Francis) 1922- 65-68
Osborn, Frederic J(ames) 1885-1978 ..... CANR-5
Earlier sketch in CA 5-8R
Osborn, Frederick (Henry) 1889-1981 ..... 25-28R
Obituary 102
Osborn, George C(oleman) 1904-1982 .. CANR-19
Earlier sketch in CA 25-28R
Osborn, Ian 1946- 167
Osborn, James M(arshall) 1906-1976 ..... CAP-2
Obituary 69-72
Earlier sketch in CA 25-28
Osborn, John Jay, Jr. 1945- CANR-6
Earlier sketch in CA 57-60
Osborn, Karen 1954- 162
Osborn, Lois D(orothy) 1915- 116
See also SATA 61
Osborn, Margot
See Osborn, E. Margaret
Osborn, Mary Elizabeth 1898- 5-8R
Osborn, Merton B(idwell) 1908- 25-28R
Osborn, Paul 1901-1988 112
Obituary 125
Brief entry 108
Interview in 112
Osborn, Percy George 1899(?)-1972 Obituary .. 104
Osborn, Robert (Chesley) 1904- 13-16R
Osborn, Robert T(appan) 1926- 21-24R
Osborn, Ronald E(dwin) 1917- 13-16R
Osborn, Sarah 1714-1796 ..... DLB 200
Osborn, Stella Brunt
See Osborn, Stellanova
Osborn, Stellanova 1894-1988 Obituary 125
Osborn, Susan (E.) 1954- 139
Osborn, Thomas Noel II 1940- 114
Osborne, Adam 1939- 109
Osborne, (Reginald) Arthur 1906-1970 ..... 17-20R
Obituary 125
Osborne, Betsy
See Boswell, Barbara (S.)
Osborne, C(harles) H(umfrey) C(aufeild) 1891- 5-8R
Osborne, Cecil G. 1904- CANR-1
Earlier sketch in CA 45-48
Osborne, Charles 1927- CANR-34
Earlier sketches in CA 13-16R, CANR-13
See also SATA 59
Osborne, Chester G(orham) 1915- CANR-35
Earlier sketches in CA 21-24R, CANR-9
See also SATA 11
Osborne, Dan 1948(?)-1983 Obituary 110
Osborne, David
See Silverberg, Robert
Osborne, David (E.) 1923- 134
Brief entry 109
Osborne, Dorothy (Gladys) Yeo 1917- 9-12R
Osborne, Elsie L(etitia) 1924-1995 118
Obituary 151
Osborne, Ernest (Glenn) 1903-1963 ..... 5-8R
Osborne, G(erald) S(tanley) 1926- 21-24R
Osborne, Geoffrey 1930- 110
Osborne, George
See Silverberg, Robert
Osborne, George E(dward) 1893- CAP-2
Earlier sketch in CA 23-24
Osborne, Harold 1905-1987 ..... CANR-6
Obituary 122
Earlier sketch in CA 13-16R
Osborne, Harold W(ayne) 1930- 57-60
Osborne, Helena
See Moore, (Georgina) Mary (Galbraith)
Osborne, J(ulius) K(enneth) 1941- 33-36R
Osborne, John (Franklin) 1907-1981 ..... CANR-10
Obituary 108
Earlier sketch in CA 61-64
Osborne, John (James) 1929-1994 ..... CANR-56
Obituary 147
Earlier sketches in CA 13-16R, CANR-21
See also CDBLB 1945-1960
See also CLC 1, 2, 5, 11, 45
See also DA
See also DAB
See also DAC
See also DAM DRAM, MST
See also DLB 13
See also MTCW 1
See also WLC
Osborne, John W(alter) 1927- 33-36R
Osborne, Juanita Tyree 1916- CANR-23
Earlier sketches in CA 61-64, CANR-8
Osborne, Lawrence 1958- ..... CLC 50
Osborne, Leone Neal 1914- 21-24R
See also SATA 2
Osborne, Linda Barrett 1949- 65-68
Osborne, Maggie
See Osborne, Margaret Ellen
Osborne, Margaret 1909- 13-16R
Osborne, Margaret Ellen 1941- CANR-40
Earlier sketches in CA 102, CANR-18
Osborne, Martha Lee 1928- 113
Osborne, Mary Pope 1949- CANR-62
Earlier sketches in CA 111, CANR-29
See also SATA 41, 55, 98
Osborne, Maureen 1924- 109
Osborne, Milton Edgeworth 1936- CANR-9
Earlier sketch in CA 13-16R
Osborne, Richard 1943- 123
Osborne, Richard Horsley 1925- 21-24R
Osborne, Will 1949- 132
Osborne, William (Terry, Jr.) 1934- 25-28R
Osborne, William A(udley) 1919- 61-64
Osborne, William S(tewart) 1923- 53-56
Osbourn, R(ichard) A(lton) 1930- 120
Osbourne, Ivor Livingstone 1951- 108
Osburn, Charles B(enjamin) 1939- CANR-13
Earlier sketch in CA 33-36R
Osceola
See Blixen, Karen (Christentze Dinesen)
Osen, Lynn M(oses) 1920- 65-68
Osenenko, John 1918-1983 Obituary 109
Oser, Jacob 1915- CANR-2
Earlier sketch in CA 5-8R
Osers, Ewald 1917- 139
Osgood, Charles
See Wood, Charles Osgood III
Osgood, Charles E(gerton) 1916- 17-20R
Osgood, Charles Grosvenor 1871-1964 ... CANR-4
Earlier sketch in CA 5-8R
Osgood, Cornelius 1905-1985 Obituary 114
Osgood, David William 1940- 89-92
Osgood, Don(ald W.) 1930- CANR-11
Earlier sketch in CA 61-64
Osgood, Ernest S(taples) 1888- CAP-1
Earlier sketch in CA 11-12
Osgood, Herbert L(evi) 1855-1918 Brief entry ... 122
See also DLB 47
Osgood, Lawrence 1929- 85-88
Osgood, Robert Endicott 1921-1986 ..... CANR-3
Obituary 121
Earlier sketch in CA 1-4R
Osgood, Samuel M(aurice) 1920-1975 ..... 33-36R
Osgood, William E(dward) 1926- 33-36R
See also SATA 37
O'Shaughnessy, Arthur 1844-1881 ..... DLB 35
O'Shaughnessy, Brian 1925- 132
O'Shaughnessy, Ellen Cassels 1937- 146
See also SATA 78
O'Shea, (Martin) Lester 1938- 108
O'Shea, (Catherine) Pat(ricia Shiels) 1931- 145
See also CLR 18
See also SATA 87
O'Shea, Sean
See Tralins, S(andor) Robert
Osherow, Jacqueline 1956- 137
Oshima, Nagisa 1932- 121
Brief entry 116
See also CLC 20
Oshinsky, David M. 1944- 165
O'Siadhail, Micheal 1947- 158
Osiek, Betty Tyree 1931- 45-48
Osing, Gordon T. 1937- 136
O Siochain, P(adraig) A(ugustine) 1905- CAP-2
Earlier sketch in CA 17-18
Osipov, Nikolai Petrovich 1751-1799 ..... DLB 150
Osipow, Samuel H(erman) 1934- CANR-1
Earlier sketch in CA 49-52
Osis, Karlis 1917- 85-88
Oskam, Bob
See Oskam, Robert T(heo)
Oskam, Robert T(heo) 1945- 108
Oskamp, Stuart 1930- CANR-12
Earlier sketch in CA 29-32R
Oski, Frank A(ram) 1932-1996 119
Obituary 155
Oskison, John Milton 1874-1947 144
See also DAM MULT
See also DLB 175
See also NNAL
See also TCLC 35
Osler, Margaret Jo 1942- 126
Osler, Robert Willard 1911-1984 ..... CANR-17
Obituary 114
Earlier sketch in CA 1-4R
Osler, Sir William 1849-1919 ..... DLB 184
Osley, A(rthur) S(idney) 1917-1987 125
Oslin, George P(oer) 1899-1996 143
Obituary 154
Osman, Betty B(arshad) 1929- CANR-35
Earlier sketch in CA 93-96
Osman, Jack D(ouglas) 1943- CANR-35
Earlier sketches in CA 61-64, CANR-11
Osman, John 1907(?)-1978 Obituary 77-80
Osmanczyk, Edmund Jan 1913-1989 Obituary . 130
Osmer, Margaret 93-96
Osmond, Andrew 1938- 25-28R
Osmond, Edward 1900- CAP-1
Earlier sketch in CA 13-14
See also SATA 10
Osmond, Humphrey (Fortescue) 1917- .. CANR-28
Earlier sketch in CA 21-24R
Osmond, John 1946- 154
Osmond, Jonathan 1953- 146
Osmond, Marie 1959- 134
Brief entry 112
Osmond-Smith, David 1946- CANR-45
Earlier sketch in CA 120
Osmun, Mark 1952- 93-96
Osmunson, Robert Lee 1924- 9-12R
Osofisan, Femi 1946- 142
See also BW 2
See also DLB 125
Osofsky, Gilbert 1935-1974 65-68
Obituary 53-56
Osserman, Richard A. 1930- 29-32R
Osserman, Robert 1926- 150
Ossian c. 3rd cent. -
See Macpherson, James
Osslinger, Kurt
See Allen, Bob
Ossman, David (H.) 1936- 9-12R
Ossoli, Sarah Margaret (Fuller marchesa d') 1810-1850
See Fuller, Margaret
See also SATA 25
Ossorgin, Mikhail
See Ilyin, Mikhail Andreyevich
Ossowska, Maria 1896- 29-32R
Ossowski, Stanislaw 1897-1963 ..... CAP-1
Earlier sketch in CA 13-14
Ost, David H(arry) 1940- CANR-6
Earlier sketch in CA 53-56
Ost, John William Philip 1931- 37-40R
Osten, Gar 1923- 65-68
Ostendorf, (Arthur) Lloyd (Jr.) 1921- CANR-6
Earlier sketch in CA 1-4R
See also SATA 65
Ostenso, Martha 1900-1963 ..... CANR-67
Earlier sketches in CAP-1, CA 13-16
See also DLB 92
Oster, Clinton Victor, Jr. 1947- 139
Oster, Jerry 1943- CANR-35
Earlier sketch in CA 77-80
Oster, Ludwig (Friedrich) 1931- 53-56
Oster, Patrick (Ralph) 1944- 131
Osterbrock, Donald E. 1924- 165
Osterburg, James W(illiam) 1917- 45-48
Ostergaard, G(eoffrey) N(ielsen) 1926-1990 . 25-28R
Obituary 131
Osterhaven, M(aurice) Eugene 1915- 49-52
Osterhoudt, Robert G(erald) 1942- CANR-35
Earlier sketch in CA 53-56
Osterlund, Steven 1943- 77-80
Osterritter, John F. 1923- 45-48
Osterweis, Rollin G(ustav) 1907-1982(?) 41-44R
Obituary 106
Ostheimer, John 1938- 41-44R
Ostle, Bernard 1921- 5-8R
Ostlere, Gordon (Stanley) 1921- 107
Ostling, Richard N(eil) 1940- CANR-35
Earlier sketch in CA 53-56
Ostow, Mortimer 1918- CANR-35
Earlier sketch in CA 49-52
Ostrander, Gilman Marston 1923- 65-68
Ostriker, Alicia (Suskin) 1937- CANR-62
Earlier sketches in CA 25-28R, CANR-10, 30
See also CAAS 24
See also DLB 120
Ostrinsky, Meir Simha 1906- CAP-2
Earlier sketch in CA 29-32

Ostroff, Anthony J(ames) 1923-1978 ..... CANR-3
Obituary 77-80
Earlier sketch in CA 5-8R
Ostrom, Alan (Baer) 1925- 21-24R
Ostrom, Hans 1954- 139
Ostrom, John Ward 1903- 1-4R
Ostrom, Thomas M. 1936- 37-40R
Ostrom, Vincent (Alfred) 1919- Brief entry 113
Ostrov, Eric 1941- CANR-34
Earlier sketch in CA 113
Ostrovsky, Eugene 1938- 147
Ostrovsky, Victor 1949- 140
Ostrow, Joanna 1938- 29-32R
Ostrow, Ronald J. 1931- 130
Ostrower, Alexander 1901-1979 ..... 17-20R
Obituary 120
Ostrower, Gary B. 1939- 154
Ostrowsky
See Holmquist, Anders
Ostry, Sylvia 1927- CANR-15
Earlier sketch in CA 41-44R
Ostwald, Martin 1922- CANR-35
Earlier sketch in CA 33-36R
Ostwald, Peter F(rederic) 1928-1996 ..... 17-20R
O Suilleabhain, Sean 1903- CANR-18
Earlier sketch in CA 25-28R
O'Sullivan, Gerry 1959- 135
O'Sullivan, Joan (D'Arcy) 77-80
O'Sullivan, John 1942- 132
O'Sullivan, John J. 1939- Brief entry 114
O'Sullivan, Judith 1942- 120
O'Sullivan, P. Michael 1940- 93-96
O'Sullivan, Sean
See O Suilleabhain, Sean
O'Sullivan, Vincent (Gerard) 1937- CANR-35
Earlier sketch in CA 97-100
Osundare, Niyi 1947- ..... DLB 157
Osusky, Stefan 1889-1973 Obituary 45-48
Oswald, Eleazer 1755-1795 ..... DLB 43
Oswald, Ian 1929- CANR-13
Earlier sketch in CA 17-20R
Oswald, J(oseph) Gregory 1922- 104
Oswald, Russell G. 1908- 45-48
Oswalt, John N(ewell) 1940- 117
Oswalt, Sabine
See MacCormack, Sabine G(abriele)
Oswalt, Wendell H(illman) 1927- CANR-35
Earlier sketches in CA 17-20R, CANR-12
Otake, Sadao 1913(?)-1983 Obituary 109
Otchis, Ethel (Herberg) 1920- 13-16R
Otero, Blas de 1916-1979 89-92
See also CLC 11
See also DLB 134
Otero, Miguel Antonio (II) 1859-1944 153
See also DLB 82
See also HW
Otero Silva, Miguel 1908-1985 ..... DLB 145
Otfinoski, Steven 1949- ..... SATA 56
Otfried von Weissenburg c. 800-c. 875(?) . DLB 148
Otis, George
See Mellen, Ida M(ay)
Otis, Jack 1923- 1-4R
Otis, James
See Kaler, James Otis
Otis, James, Jr. 1725-1783 ..... DLB 31
Otis, Johnny 1921- 147
O'Toole, G(eorge) J(oseph) A(nthony) 1936- ... 141
O'Toole, James (Joseph) 1945- 126
O'Toole, Judith Hansen 1953- 142
O'Toole, Peter (Seamus) 1932- 160
O'Toole, Rex
See Tralins, S(andor) Robert
O'Toole, Thomas 1941- ..... SATA 71
O'Trigger, Sir Lucius
See Horne, Richard Henry
Ott, Attiat F(arag) 1935- CANR-10
Earlier sketch in CA 21-24R
Ott, David Jackson 1934-1975 ..... CANR-8
Earlier sketch in CA 5-8R
Ott, Maggie Glen
See Ott, Virginia
Ott, Peter
See von Hildebrand, Dietrich
Ott, Thomas O(liver) III 1938- 49-52
Ott, Virginia 1917- 77-80
Ott, William Griffith 1909- CANR-1
Earlier sketch in CA 1-4R
Ottaway, James 1911- ..... DLB 127
Ottaway, Marina (Seassaro) 1943- 142
Ottemiller, John H(enry) 1916-1968 ..... CAP-2
Earlier sketch in CA 17-18
Otten, Anna 21-24R
Otten, C. Michael 1934- 33-36R
Otten, Charlotte F(ennema) 1926- 131
See also SATA 98
Otten, Charlotte M(arie) 1915- CANR-35
Earlier sketch in CA 29-32R
Otten, Terry (Ralph) 1938- CANR-35
Earlier sketches in CA 37-40R, CANR-15
Ottenberg, Miriam 1914-1982 ..... CANR-10
Obituary 108
Earlier sketch in CA 5-8R
Ottenberg, Simon 1923- CANR-35
Earlier sketch in CA 33-36R
Ottendorfer, Oswald 1826-1900 Brief entry 123
See also DLB 23
Otter, Anthony 1896-1986 Obituary 118
Otterbein, Keith Frederick 1936- CANR-35
Earlier sketch in CA 21-24R
Ottersen, (John) Ottar 1918- 33-36R
Ottesen, Thea Tauber 1913- 5-8R
Otteson, Schuyler Franklin 1917- Brief entry ... 106
Ottieri, Ottiero 1924- ..... DLB 177
Ottley, Matt 1962- ..... SATA 102
Ottley, Reginald Leslie 1909-1985 ..... CANR-34
Earlier sketch in CA 93-96
See also CLR 16
See also MAICYA
See also SATA 26
Ottley, Roi (Vincent) 1906-1960 153
Obituary 89-92
See also BW 2
Ottlik, Geza 1912-1990 ..... CANR-39
Obituary 132
Earlier sketch in CA 17-20R
Ottman, Robert W(illiam) 1914- CANR-3
Earlier sketch in CA 1-4R
Otto, Calvin P. 1930- 29-32R
Otto, Henry J. 1901- CAP-2
Earlier sketch in CA 13-14
Otto, Herbert Arthur 1922- CANR-1
Earlier sketch in CA 45-48
Otto, Lon 1948- 130
Otto, Luther B(enedict) 1937- 133
Otto, Margaret Glover 1909-1976 Obituary ... 61-64
See also SATA-Obit 30
Otto, Svend
See Soerensen, Svend Otto
Otto, Wayne (R.) 1931- CANR-11
Earlier sketch in CA 29-32R
Otto, Whitney 1955- 140
See also CLC 70
Otto-Peters, Louise 1819-1895 ..... DLB 129
Ottum, Bob
See Ottum, Robert K., Jr.
Ottum, Robert K., Jr. 1925(?)-1986 Obituary ... 119
Otway, Thomas 1652-1685 ..... DAM DRAM
See also DLB 80
Otway-Ruthven, Jocelyn 1909-1989 Obituary .. 128
Otway-Ward, Patricia
See Weenolsen, Patricia
Otwell, John H(erbert) 1915- 73-76
Ouchi, William G(eorge) 1943- 129
Oudaii, Hashmi el
See McGirk, Tim(othy Stephen)
Ouellette, Fernand 1930- CANR-17
Earlier sketches in CA 49-52, CANR-2
See also CAAS 13
See also DLB 60
Ouellette, Pierre 1945- 166
Oughton, Frederick 1923- CANR-29
Earlier sketch in CA 1-4R
Oughton, Jerrie 1937- 143
See also SATA 76
Ouida
See De La Ramee, (Marie) Louise
See also DLB 18, 156
See also TCLC 43
Ouimette, Victor 1944- 73-76
Oulahan, Richard 1918-1985 ..... CANR-36
Obituary 117
Earlier sketch in CA 33-36R
Oulanoff, Hongor 1929- 25-28R
Ouologuem, Yambo 1940- Brief entry 111
Ouroussoff, Peter Sergeivich
1900(?)-1984 Obituary 114
Ouroussow, Eugenie 1908-1975 Obituary 53-56
Oursler, Fulton, Jr. 1932- Brief entry 116
Oursler, (Charles) Fulton 1893-1952 Brief
entry 108
Oursler, Will(iam Charles) 1913-1985 ..... CANR-35
Obituary 115
Earlier sketches in CA 5-8R, CANR-2
Ousby, Ian (Vaughan Kenneth) 1947- CANR-35
Earlier sketch in CA 89-92
Ouseley, Gideon
See Paranjape, Makarand (Ramachandra)
Ousley, Odille 1896- CAP-1
Earlier sketch in CA 11-12
See also SATA 10
Ousmane, Sembene 1923- 125
Brief entry 117
See also BLC 3
See also BW 1
See also CLC 66
See also MTCW 1
Ouston, Philip (Anfield)
1924(?)-1988(?) Obituary 125
Outerbridge, David E(ugene) 1933- CANR-38
Earlier sketches in CA 93-96, CANR-16
Outhwaite, Leonard 1892- 53-56
Outhwaite, (Richard) William 1949- 130
Outka, Gene 1937- 41-44R
Outland, Charles (Faulkner) 1910-1988 .. CANR-40
Earlier sketch in CA 9-12R
Outler, Albert C(ook) 1908- CANR-1
Earlier sketch in CA 1-4R
Outram, Dorinda 1949- 132
Out to Lunch
See Watson, Ben
Ouverson, Marlin D(ean) 1952- 111
Ovard, Glen F. 1928- 33-36R
Ove, Robert S. 1927- 164
Oved, Iaacov
See Oved, Yaacov
Oved, Yaacov 1929- 159
Overacker, Louise 1891- CAP-2
Earlier sketch in CA 29-32
Overall, Christine (Dorothy) 1949- 138
Overbeck, Pauletta 1915- 97-100
Overbeek, J(ohannes) 1932- 73-76
Overberg, Kenneth R(ichard) 1944- CANR-35
Earlier sketch in CA 114
Overbury, Stephen 1954- 119
Overbury, Thomas c. 1581-1613 ..... DLB 151
Overbye, Dennis 1944- 142
Overgard, William (Thomas, Jr.) 1926-1990 ... 138
Obituary 131
Overholser, Stephen 1944- CANR-16
Earlier sketch in CA 97-100
Overholser, Wayne D. 1906- CANR-64
Earlier sketches in CA 5-8R, CANR-2, 16
Overholt, Thomas (William) 1935- 163
Overholt, William H. 1945- 117
Overman, Michael 1920- 108
Overmeyer, Eric 1952(?)- 153
Overmyer, James E. 1946- 152
See also SATA 88
Overstreet, Bonaro (Wilkinson) 1902-1985 142
Obituary 117
Overstreet, Harry Allen 1875-1970 ..... CAP-1
Obituary 29-32R
Earlier sketch in CA 13-16
Overton, Jenny (Margaret Mary) 1942- 57-60
See also SATA 52
See also SATA-Brief 36
Overton, Richard Cleghorn 1907- 108
Overton, Robert
See Knox-Mawer, Ronald
Overton, Ron 1943- 147
Overy, Paul 1940- CANR-35
Earlier sketch in CA 29-32R
Overy, R(ichard) J(ames) 1947- 119
Ovesen, Ellis
See Smith, Shirley M(ae)
Ovid 43B.C.-18(?) ..... DAM POET
See also PC 2
Ovington, Mary White 1865-1951 166
Ovstedal, Barbara 130
Ovsyanikov, Nikita 1952- 162
Owen, Alan Robert George 1919- 9-12R
Owen, Alun (Davies) 1925-1994 ..... CANR-34
Obituary 147
Earlier sketch in CA 5-8R
Owen, Annie 1949- ..... SATA 75
Owen, Bob
See Geis, Richard E(rwin)
Owen, Bruce M(anning) 1943- CANR-35
Earlier sketch in CA 57-60
Owen, Caroline Dale
See Snedeker, Caroline Dale (Parke)
Owen, Charles A(braham), Jr. 1914- CANR-36
Earlier sketch in CA 53-56
Owen, Clifford
See Hamilton, Charles (Harold St. John)
Owen, D(enis) F(rank) 1931- CANR-35
Earlier sketches in CA 53-56, CANR-4
Owen, David (Edward) 1898-1968 ..... CANR-36
Earlier sketches in CAP-1, CA 13-16
Owen, David (Anthony Llewellyn) 1938- .. CANR-65
Earlier sketch in CA 129
Owen, David E(lystan) 1912-1987 124
Owen, David Lanyon Lloyd
See Lloyd Owen, David Lanyon
Owen, Dilys
See Gater, Dilys
Owen, Dolores B(ullock) CANR-34
Earlier sketch in CA 53-56
Owen, Douglas David Roy 1922- CANR-35
Earlier sketch in CA 89-92
Owen, Edmund
See Teller, Neville
Owen, (Benjamin) Evan 1918-1984 109
See also SATA 38
Owen, Frank 1907(?)-1979 Obituary 85-88
Owen, G(ail) L(ee) 1937- 45-48
Owen, G(eorge) Vale 1869-1931 Brief entry ... 119
Owen, Gail R.
See Owen-Crocker, Gale R(edfern)
Owen, Gareth 1936- 150
See also CLR 31
See also SAAS 14
See also SATA 83
Owen, George Earle 1908- 77-80
Owen, Guy (Jr.) 1925-1981 ..... CANR-36
Obituary 104
Earlier sketches in CA 1-4R, CANR-3
See also DLB 5
Owen, Gwilym Ellis Lane 1922-1982 Obituary .. 107
Owen, (William) Harold 1897-1971 ..... 13-16R
Obituary 89-92
Owen, Henry 1920- Brief entry 111
Owen, Howard (Wayne) 1949- 141
Owen, Hugh
See Faust, Frederick (Schiller)
Owen, Irvin 1910- 97-100
Owen, Jack 1929- CANR-37
Earlier sketch in CA 33-36R
Owen, Jan 1940- 154
Owen, Jennifer 1936- CANR-38
Earlier sketch in CA 116
Owen, John 1564-1622 ..... DLB 121
Owen, John E. 1919- CANR-4
Earlier sketch in CA 9-12R
Owen, Lewis 1915- 29-32R
Owen, Lewis J(ames) 1925- Brief entry 116
Owen, Marsha
See Stanford, Sally
Owen, Norman G. 1944- 126
Owen, Oliver S. 1920- 104
Owen, Philip
See Philips, Judson (Pentecost)
Owen, Reginald 1887-1972 Obituary 37-40R
Owen, Richard 1947- 127
Owen, Robert 1771-1858 ..... DLB 107, 158
Owen, Robert N.
See Geis, Richard E(rwin)
Owen, Roderic
See Fenwick-Owen, Roderic (Franklin Rawnsley)
Owen, Roderic Fenwick
See Fenwick-Owen, Roderic (Franklin Rawnsley)
Owen, Roger C(orey) 1928- CANR-37
Earlier sketch in CA 77-80
Owen, Thomas Richard 1918- CANR-10
Earlier sketch in CA 21-24R
Owen, Tobias Chant 1936- CANR-29
Earlier sketch in CA 111
Owen, Tom
See Watts, Peter Christopher
Owen, W(arwick) J(ack) B(urgoyne) 1916- 134
Brief entry 111
Owen, Wilfred (Edward Salter) . 1893-1918 141
Brief entry 104
See also CDBLB 1914-1945
See also DA
See also DAB
See also DAC
See also DAM MST, POET
See also DLB 20
See also PC 19
See also TCLC 5, 27
See also WLC
Owen, Wilfred 1912- CANR-36
Earlier sketch in CA 37-40R
Owen, William Vern 1894- CAP-2
Earlier sketch in CA 17-18
Owen, Wyn F(oster) 1923- Brief entry 115
Owen-Crocker, Gale R(edfern) 1947- 128
Owendoff, Robert S(cott) 1945- 17-20R
Owens, Agnes 1926- CANR-60
Earlier sketch in CA 128
Owens, Bill 1938- 73-76
Owens, Carole (Ehrlich) 1942- 116
Owens, Carolyn 1946- 109
Owens, Craig 1950-1990 Obituary 132
Owens, E(dwin) J(ohn) 1950- 139
Owens, Edgar (Leonard) 1924-1987 Obituary .. 124
Owens, Gail 1939- ..... SATA 54
Owens, Gary 1936- 97-100
Owens, Jesse 1913-1980 110
Owens, John E. 1948- 162
Owens, John R(obert) 1926- 77-80
Owens, Joseph 1908- CANR-20
Earlier sketches in CA 5-8R, CANR-5
Owens, Kenneth N. 1933- 147
Owens, Louis (D.) 1948- CANR-71
Earlier sketch in CA 137
See also CAAS 24
See also NNAL
Owens, Pat(rick) J. 1929- 73-76
Owens, Richard Meredith 1944- CANR-37
Earlier sketch in CA 61-64
Owens, Robert Goronwy 1923- CANR-28
Earlier sketch in CA 29-32R
Owens, Rochelle 1936- CANR-39
Earlier sketch in CA 17-20R
See also CAAS 2
See also CLC 8
Owens, Thelma 1905- 69-72
Owens, Thomas S(heldon) 1960- 151
See also SATA 86
Owens, Tom
See Owens, Thomas S(heldon)
Owens, Virginia Stem 1941- CANR-14
Earlier sketch in CA 81-84
Owens, William A. 1905-1990 ..... CANR-36
Obituary 133
Earlier sketch in CA 9-12R
Ower, John 1942- 77-80
Owings, Loren C(lyde) 1928- 37-40R
Owings, Mark (Samuel) 1945- Brief entry 114
Owings, Nathaniel Alexander 1903-1984 . CANR-35
Obituary 113
Earlier sketch in CA 61-64
Owomoyela, Oyekan 1938- 112
Owsley, Frank L(awrence) 1890-1956 Brief
entry 116
See also DLB 17
Owsley, Harriet Chappell 1901- 81-84
Oxenbury, Helen 1938- CANR-35
Earlier sketch in CA 25-28R
See also CLR 22
See also MAICYA
See also SATA 3, 68
Oxendine, Bess Holland 1933- 155
See also SATA 90
Oxenham, Elsie J.
See Dunkerley, Elsie Jeanette
Oxenhandler, Neal 1926- CANR-6
Earlier sketch in CA 13-16R
Oxenhorn, Harvey 1952(?)-1990 Obituary 131
Oxford, Cheryl 1955- 148
Oxhorn, Philip D. 151
Oxley, Dorothy (Anne) 1948- 116
Oxley, William 1939- 73-76
Oxnam, Robert B(romley) 1942- CANR-5
Earlier sketch in CA 53-56
Oxnard, Charles (Ernest) 1933- CANR-42
Earlier sketches in CA 45-48, CANR-1, 16
Oxorn, Harry 1920- CANR-42
Earlier sketch in CA 111
Oxtoby, Willard Gurdon 1933- CANR-37
Earlier sketch in CA 49-52
Oyen, Else (Sjorup) 165
Oyle, Irving 1925- CANR-6
Earlier sketch in CA 57-60
Oyler, Philip (Tom) 1879- CAP-1
Earlier sketch in CA 9-10
Oy-Vik
See Holmvik, Oyvind
Oz, Amos 1939- CANR-65
Earlier sketches in CA 53-56, CANR-27, 47
See also CLC 5, 8, 11, 27, 33, 54
See also DAM NOV
See also MTCW 1
Oz, Frank (Richard) 1944- ..... SATA 60
Ozaki, Robert S(higeo) 1934- CANR-35
Earlier sketch in CA 49-52
Ozawa, Terutomo 1935- CANR-34
Earlier sketch in CA 85-88
Ozbudun, Ergun 1937- 126

Ozer, Jerome S. 1927- ... 107
See also SATA 59
Ozer, Mark N(orman) 1932- ... CANR-30
Earlier sketch in CA 112
Ozerov, Vladislav Aleksandrovich 1769-1816 .. DLB 150
Ozick, Cynthia 1928- ... CANR-58
Earlier sketches in CA 17-20R, CANR-23
Interview in ... CANR-23
See also BEST 90:1
See also CLC 3, 7, 28, 62
See also DAM NOV, POP
See also DLB 28, 152
See also DLBY 82
See also MTCW 1
See also SSC 15
Ozinga, James Richard 1932- ... CANR-37
Earlier sketch in CA 97-100
Ozment, Robert V. 1927- ... 17-20R
Ozment, Steven E(dgar) 1939- ... CANR-35
Earlier sketch in CA 108
Ozmon, Howard A. ... 25-28R
Ozu, Yasujiro 1903-1963 ... 112
See also CLC 16
Ozy
See Rosset, B(enjamin) C(harles)

P

P. L. K.
See Kirk-Greene, Anthony (Hamilton Millard)
P. Q.
See Quennell, Peter (Courtney)
Paak, Carl Erich 1922- ... 106
Paananen, Eloise (Katherine) 1923- ... CANR-18
Earlier sketches in CA 1-4R, CANR-2
See also Engle, Eloise
Paananen, Victor Niles 1938- ... 73-76
Paarlberg, Don 1911- ... 21-24R
Paasche, Carol L(evine) 1937- ... 5-8R
Paauw, Douglas Seymour 1921- ... 103
Pab
See Blooman, Percy A.
Paca, Lillian Grace (Baker) 1883- ... CAP-1
Earlier sketch in CA 11-12
Pacaut, Marcel 1920- ... 29-32R
Pace, C(harles) Robert 1912- ... 81-84
Pace, David 1944- ... 130
Pace, Denny F. 1925- ... 49-52
Pace, DeWanna 1954- ... 162
Pace, Donald Metcalf 1906-1982 Obituary ... 108
Pace, Eric 1936- ... 45-48
Pace, J. Blair 1916- ... 69-72
Pace, Mildred Mastin 1907- ... CANR-5
Earlier sketch in CA 5-8R
See also SATA 46
See also SATA-Brief 29
Pace, Nathaniel 1925- ... 110
Pace, Peter
See Burnett, David (Benjamin Foley)
Pace, R(alph) Wayne 1931- ... CANR-1
Earlier sketch in CA 45-48
Pace, Richard 1482(?)-1536 ... DLB 167
Pace, Robert Lee 1924- ... 1-4R
Pacernick, Gary 1941- ... 73-76
Pacey, (William Cyril) Desmond 1917-1975 ... CANR-4
Earlier sketch in CA 5-8R
See also DLB 88
Pachai, Bridglal 1927- ... CANR-17
Earlier sketch in CA 93-96
Pacheco, C.
See Pessoa, Fernando (Antonio Nogueira)
Pacheco, Catherine Chapman 1927- ... 130
Pacheco, Ferdie 1927- ... 81-84
Pacheco, Henricus Luis
See Pacheco, Henry L(uis)
Pacheco, Henry L(uis) 1947- ... 49-52
See also HW
Pacheco, Jose Emilio 1939- ... CANR-65
Brief entry ... 111
Earlier sketch in CA 131
See also DAM MULT
See also HLC
See also HW
Pa Chin
See Li Fei-kan
See also CLC 18
Pachmuss, Temira 1927- ... CANR-44
Earlier sketches in CA 9-12R, CANR-4, 20
Pachter, Hedwig (?)-1988 ... SATA 63
Pachter, Henry M(aximillian) 1907- ... 9-12R
Pachter, Josh 1951- ... 132
Pacifici, Sergio 1925- ... CANR-3
Earlier sketch in CA 1-4R
Pacifico, Carl 1921- ... 21-24R
Pack, Janet 1952- ... 145
See also SATA 77
Pack, Robert 1929- ... CANR-44
Earlier sketches in CA 1-4R, CANR-3
See also CLC 13
See also DLB 5
Pack, Roger A(mbrose) 1907- ... CAP-1
Earlier sketch in CA 13-16
Pack, S(tanley) W(alter) C(roucher) 1904-1977 ... 13-16R
Obituary ... 125
Pack, Spencer J. 1953- ... 140
Packard, Andrew 1929- ... 1-4R
Packard, Cindy
See Richmond, Cindy Packard
Packard, Edward 1931- ... CANR-59
Earlier sketch in CA 114
See also SATA 47, 90
Packard, Frederick Clifton, Jr. 1899-1985 Obituary ... 116
Packard, George R(andolph) III 1932- ... 127
Brief entry ... 112
Packard, Jerrold M(ichael) 1943- ... CANR-23
Earlier sketch in CA 106
Packard, Karl 1911(?)-1977 Obituary ... 69-72
Packard, Reynolds 1903-1976 ... 73-76
Obituary ... 69-72
Packard, Robert 1916- ... 134
Packard, Robert G(eorge) 1933- ... 57-60
Packard, Rosa Covington 1935- ... 97-100
Packard, Rosalie ... 1-4R
Packard, Russell C. 1946- ... 119
Packard, Sidney R(aymond) 1893- ... 61-64
Packard, Vance (Oakley) 1914-1996 ... CANR-7
Obituary ... 155
Earlier sketch in CA 9-12R
See also AITN 1
Packard, William 1933- ... CANR-7
Earlier sketch in CA 13-16R
Packenham, Robert Allen 1937- ... 73-76
Packer, Arnold H. 1935- ... 37-40R
Packer, B(arbara) L(ee) 1947- ... 133
Packer, Bernard J(ules) 1934- ... CANR-19
Earlier sketch in CA 65-68
Packer, David W(illiam) 1937- ... 9-12R
Packer, Herbert L(eslie) 1925-1972 ... 37-40R
Packer, J(ames) I(nnell) 1926- ... CANR-37
Earlier sketches in CA 49-52, CANR-1, 16
Packer, Joan Garrett 1947- ... 139
Packer, Joy (Petersen) 1905-1977 ... CANR-3
Earlier sketch in CA 1-4R
Packer, Lady
See Packer, Joy (Petersen)
Packer, Nancy Huddleston 1925- ... 65-68
Packer, Rod Earle 1931- ... 109
Packer, Vin
See Meaker, Marijane (Agnes)
Packman, David 1949- ... 123
Pacosz, Christina V(ivian) 1946- ... 77-80
Pacyga, Dominic A. 1949- ... 128
Pad, Peter
See Stratemeyer, Edward L.
Padberg, Daniel I(van) 1931- ... 33-36R
Padberg, John W(illiam) 1926- ... 25-28R
Padden, R(obert) C(harles) 1922- ... 21-24R
Paddison, Ronan 1945- ... 117
Paddison, Sara 1953- ... 143
Paddleford, Clementine Haskin 1900-1967 Obituary ... 89-92
Paddock, John 1918- ... 17-20R
Paddock, Paul (Ezekiel, Jr.) 1907-1975 ... CAP-2
Obituary ... 61-64
Earlier sketch in CA 21-22
Paddock, William (Carson) 1921- ... 21-24R
Pade, Victoria 1953- ... 113
Padel, Ruth 1946- ... 134
Paden, William D(oremus, Jr.) 1941- ... 124
Paden, William E. 1939- ... 142
Padev, Michael Alexander 1915-1989 Obituary ... 128
Padfield, Harland (Irvine) 1926- Brief entry ... 112
Padfield, Peter 1932- ... CANR-26
Earlier sketch in CA 101
Padgett, (Mary) Abigail 1942- ... CANR-66
Earlier sketch in CA 141
Padgett, Desmond
See von Block, Bela W(illiam)
Padgett, Dora 1893(?)-1976 Obituary ... 61-64
Padgett, Lewis
See Kuttner, Henry
and Moore, C(atherine) L(ucile)
Padgett, Ron 1942- ... CANR-57
Earlier sketches in CA 25-28R, CANR-12, 30
See also DLB 5
Padgett, Stephen 1951- ... 139
Padilla, Ernesto Chavez 1944- ... DLB 122
Padilla, Genaro M(iguel) 1949- ... 128
Padilla (Lorenzo), Heberto 1932- ... 131
Brief entry ... 123
See also AITN 1
See also CLC 38
See also HW
Padilla, Raymond V. 1944- ... 130
See also HW
Padilla, Victoria 1907-1986 ... 103
Obituary ... 120
Padley, Walter Ernest 1916-1984 Obituary ... 112
Padmore, George
See Nurse, Malcolm Ivan Meredith
Padoa-Schioppa Rostoris, Fiorella 1945- ... CANR-54
Earlier sketch in CA 148
Padovano, Anthony T(homas) 1934- ... CANR-45
Earlier sketches in CA 17-20R, CANR-7, 22
Padover, Saul K(ussiel) 1905-1981 ... CANR-2
Obituary ... 103
Earlier sketch in CA 49-52
Padwick, E(ric) W(illiam) 1923- ... 119
Pae, Sung Moon 1939- ... 146
Paesler, Michael 1946- ... 158
Paetro, Maxine 1946- ... 123
Paffard, Michael Kenneth 1928- ... 103
Pafford, John Henry Pyle 1900-1996 ... CANR-21
Obituary ... 151
Earlier sketch in CA 104
Pagan Ferrer, Gloria M. 1921-
See Palma, Marigloria
See also HW
Pagden, Anthony 1945- ... 101
Page, Benjamin I(ngrim) 1940- ... 112
Page, Carl 1957- ... 154
Page, Carole Gift 1942- ... 117
Page, Charles H(unt) 1909-1992 ... CANR-4
Obituary ... 136
Earlier sketch in CA 5-8R
Page, Christopher H. 1952- ... 137
Page, Clarence 1947- ... 145
Page, Curtis C(arling) 1914- ... 21-24R
Page, Diana (Preuthun) 1946- ... 126
Page, Dorothy Myra
See Page, Myra
Page, Drew 1905- ... 105
Page, Eileen
See Heal, Edith
Page, Eleanor
See Coerr, Eleanor (Beatrice)
Page, Ellis Batten 1924- ... 13-16R
Page, Emma
See Tirbutt, Honoria
Page, Evelyn 1902- ... 5-8R
Page, G. S.
See Galbraith, Georgie Starbuck
Page, Geoff(rey Donald) 1940- ... 133
Page, Gerald W(ilburn) 1939- ... 93-96
Page, Grover, Jr. 1918- ... 17-20R
Page, Harry Robert 1915- ... 9-12R
Page, Homer (Gordon) 1918-1985 Obituary ... 117
Page, Jake
See Page, James K(eena), Jr.
Page, James A(llen) 1918- ... 107
Page, James D. 1910- ... 73-76
Page, James K(eena), Jr. 1936- ... CANR-35
Earlier sketch in CA 97-100
See also SATA 81
Page, Jimmy 1944- ... CLC 12
Page, Joseph A(nthony) 1934- ... CANR-65
Earlier sketches in CA 81-84, CANR-14
Page, Katherine Hall 1947- ... 136
Page, Kathy 1958- ... 133
Page, Lorna
See Rowland, D(onald) S(ydney)
Page, Lou Williams 1912- ... CANR-5
Earlier sketch in CA 5-8R
See also SATA 38
Page, Louise 1955- ... 140
See also CLC 40
Page, Malcolm 1935- ... CANR-31
Earlier sketch in CA 45-48
Page, Marian ... 69-72
Page, Martin 1938- ... CANR-12
Earlier sketch in CA 17-20R
Page, Mary
See Heal, Edith
Page, Myra 1897-1993 ... 166
Page, N. Wooten
See Page, Norvell W(ooten)
Page, Norman 1930- ... CANR-31
Earlier sketches in CA 61-64, CANR-8
Page, Norvell W(ooten) 1904-1961 ... 155
Page, P(atricia) K(athleen) 1916- ... CANR-65
Earlier sketches in CA 53-56, CANR-4, 22
See also CLC 7, 18
See also DAC
See also DAM MST
See also DLB 68
See also MTCW 1
See also PC 12
Page, Penny B(ooth) 1949- ... 140
Page, Reba Neukom 1942- ... 139
Page, Robert Collier 1908-1977 Obituary ... 73-76
Page, Robert J(effress) 1922- ... 17-20R
Page, Robert Morris 1903- ... CAP-2
Earlier sketch in CA 17-18
Page, Robin 1943- ... 103
Page, Roch 1939- ... 33-36R
Page, Russell 1906-1985 Obituary ... 114
Page, Stanton
See Fuller, Henry Blake
Page, Thomas 1942- ... 81-84
Page, Thomas Nelson 1853-1922 Brief entry .. 118
See also DLB 12, 78
See also DLBD 13
See also SSC 23
Page, Thornton (Leigh) 1913- ... CANR-2
Earlier sketch in CA 5-8R
Page, Vicki
See Avey, Ruby
Page, Walter Hines 1855-1918 ... DLB 71, 91
Page, Warren (Kempton) 1910-1977 Obituary .. 111
Page, William 1929- ... CANR-35
Earlier sketch in CA 114
Page, William 1946- ... 115
Page, William Roberts 1904- ... 21-24R
Pagel, Walter T. U. 1898-1983 ... 129
Obituary ... 109
Pagels, Elaine Hiesey 1943- ... CANR-51
Earlier sketches in CA 45-48, CANR-2, 24
See also CLC 104
Pagels, Heinz R(udolf) 1939-1988 ... CANR-23
Obituary ... 126
Earlier sketch in CA 107
Pages, Pedro
See Alba, Victor
Paget, Francis Edward 1806-1882 ... DLB 163
Paget, George Charles Henry Victor 1922- .. 17-20R
Paget, John
See Aiken, John (Kempton)
Paget, Julian 1921- ... 21-24R
Paget, Margaret
See Medlicott, Margaret P(aget)
Paget, Violet 1856-1935 ... 166
Brief entry ... 104
See also Lee, Vernon
Paget-Fredericks, Joseph E. P. Rous-Marten 1903-1963 ... SATA-Brief 30
Paget-Lowe, Henry
See Lovecraft, H(oward) P(hillips)
Paglia, Camille (Anna) 1947- ... CANR-72
Earlier sketch in CA 140
See also CLC 68
Pagliarani, Elio 1927- ... DLB 128
Paglin, Morton 1922- ... 97-100
Pagnol, Marcel (Paul) 1895-1974 ... 128
Obituary ... 49-52
See also MTCW 1
Pagnucci, Susan 1944- ... SATA 90
Pagonis, William G. 1941- ... 139
Pagter, Carl R(ichard) 1934- ... CANR-54
Earlier sketch in CA 127
Paher, Stanley W(illiam) 1940- ... 29-32R
Pahl, R(aymond) E(dward) 1935- ... 25-28R
Pahlavi, Mohammed Riza
See Pahlevi, Mohammed Riza
Pahlen, Kurt 1907- ... CANR-7
Earlier sketch in CA 13-16R
Pahlevi, Mohammed Riza 1919-1980 Obituary . 106
Pahor, Boris 1913- ... 156
Pahz, (Anne) Cheryl Suzanne 1949- ... CANR-8
Earlier sketch in CA 53-56
See also SATA 11
Pahz, James Alon 1943- ... CANR-8
Earlier sketch in CA 53-56
See also SATA 11
Pai, Anna C(hao) 1935- ... 89-92
Pai, Young 1929- ... 33-36R
Paice, Eric 1927(?)-1989 Obituary ... 129
Paice, Margaret 1920- ... CANR-20
Earlier sketch in CA 29-32R
See also SATA 10
Paier, Robert (David) 1943- ... 89-92
Paiewonsky, Michael 1939- ... 137
Paige, Connie 1945- ... 130
Paige, David
See Whittingham, Richard
Paige, Glenn D(urland) 1929- ... 25-28R
Paige, Harry W(orthington) 1922- ... CANR-32
Earlier sketch in CA 113
See also SATA 41
See also SATA-Brief 35
Paige, Leo
See Cochrane, William E.
Paige, Leroy Robert 1907(?)-1982 Obituary ... 107
Paige, Michele Anna 1969- ... 141
Paige, Richard
See Koontz, Dean R(ay)
Paige, Richard E(aton) 1904-1988 ... 111
Obituary ... 126
Paige, Robin
See Albert, Susan Wittig
Paige, Satchel
See Paige, Leroy Robert
Paikeday, Thomas M. 1926- ... CANR-65
Earlier sketch in CA 128
Pailin, David A. 1936- ... 129
Pain, Barry (Eric Odell) 1864-1928 Brief entry .. 109
See also DLB 135, 197
Pain, Philip (?)-1666(?) ... DLB 24
Paine, Albert Bigelow 1861-1937 Brief entry ... 108
Paine, J. Lincoln
See Kramish, Arnold
Paine, Lauran (Bosworth) 1916- ... CANR-31
Earlier sketches in CA 45-48, CANR-7
Paine, Penelope Colville 1946- ... SATA 87
Paine, Philbrook 1910- ... CAP-1
Earlier sketch in CA 11-12
Paine, R(ussell) Howard 1922- ... 5-8R
Paine, Robert Treat, Jr. 1773-1811 ... DLB 37
Paine, Roberta M. 1925- ... 33-36R
See also SATA 13
Paine, Roger W(arde) III 1942- ... 65-68
Paine, Sheila 1929- ... 146
Paine, Stephen William 1908- ... 1-4R
Paine, Thomas 1737-1809 ... CDALB 1640-1865
See also DLB 31, 43, 73, 158
Painter, Charlotte ... CANR-3
Earlier sketch in CA 1-4R
Painter, Daniel
See Burgess, Michael (Roy)
Painter, George D(uncan) 1914- ... 101
See also DLB 155
Painter, Helen W(elch) 1913- ... 33-36R
Painter, John 1935- ... 166
Painter, Nell Irvin 1942- ... CANR-19
Earlier sketch in CA 65-68
See also BW 1
Painter, Pamela 1941- ... 122
Pairault, Pierre 1922- ... 53-56
Pairo, Preston (A. III) 1958- ... CANR-70
Earlier sketch in CA 142
Pais, Abraham 1918- ... 109
Paish, F(rank) W(alter) 1898-1988 ... 17-20R
Obituary ... 125
Paisley, Melvyn 1924- ... 139
Paisley, Tom 1932- ... CANR-15
Earlier sketch in CA 61-64
See also Bethancourt, T. Ernesto
See also SATA 78
Paisley, Vicki ... 139
Paisner, Milton 1915- ... 113
Pak Chong-Hui
See Park Chung Hee
Pakenham, Antonia
See Fraser, (Lady) Antonia (Pakenham)
Pakenham, Edward Arthur Henry 1902-1961 Obituary ... 114
Pakenham, Elizabeth
See Longford, Elizabeth (Harmon Pakenham)
Pakenham, Elizabeth
See Longford, Elizabeth (Harmon Pakenham)
Pakenham, Francis Aungier 1905- ... CANR-46
Earlier sketch in CA 109
Pakenham, Frank
See Pakenham, Francis Aungier

Pakenham, Simona Vere 1916- CANR-3
Earlier sketch in CA 1-4R
Pakenham, Thomas (Frank Dermot) 1933- CANR-46
Earlier sketch in CA 109
Interview in 109
Paker, Saliha 143
Pakula, Alan J(ay) 1928- 130
Brief entry 124
Pakula, Hannah (Cohn) 1933- CANR-55
Earlier sketch in CA 139
Pakula, Marion Broome 1926- CANR-7
Earlier sketch in CA 57-60
Pal, Pratapaditya 1935- 37-40R
Palais, James B. 1934- 165
Palamas, Kostes 1859-1943 Brief entry 105
See also TCLC 5
Palamountain, Joseph Cornwall, Jr. 1920-1987 45-48
Obituary 124
Palandri, Angela (Chin-ying) Jung 1926- 37-40R
Palange, Anthony (Jr.) 1942- 37-40R
Palau, Luis (Jr.) 1934- CANR-39
Earlier sketch in CA 116
Palazchenko, Pavel 1949- 168
Palazzeschi, Aldo 1885-1974 89-92
Obituary 53-56
See also CLC 11
See also DLB 114
Palazzo, Anthony D.
See Palazzo, Tony
Palazzo, Tony 1905-1970 .... CANR-4
Obituary 29-32R
Earlier sketch in CA 5-8R
See also SATA 3
Palazzolo, Daniel J. 139
Palda, Filip 1962- 148
Palder, Edward L. 1922- .... SATA 5
Paldiel, Mordecai 1937- 145
Palecek, Josef 1932- .... SATA 56
Palecek, Libuse 1937- 155
See also SATA 89
Paleckis, Justas (Ignovich) 1899-1980 Obituary 105
Palen, J(oseph) John 1939- CANR-15
Earlier sketch in CA 41-44R
Palen, Jennie M. 5-8R
Palencia, Elaine Fowler 1946- 142
Palermo, David Stuart 1929- 17-20R
Pales Matos, Luis 1898-1959 .... HW
Palestrant, Simon S. 1907- CAP-1
Earlier sketch in CA 9-10
Paley, Alan L(ouis) 1943- 69-72
Paley, Grace 1922- CANR-46
Earlier sketches in CA 25-28R, CANR-13
Interview in CANR-13
See also CLC 4, 6, 37
See also DAM POP
See also DLB 28
See also MTCW 1
See also SSC 8
Paley, Maggie 1939- 121
Paley, Morton D(avid) 1935- CANR-13
Earlier sketch in CA 33-36R
Paley, Nicholas M(iroslav) 1911- CANR-15
Earlier sketch in CA 41-44R
Paley, Vivian Gussin 1929- CANR-58
Earlier sketches in CA 93-96, CANR-30
Paley, William S(amuel) 1901-1990 110
Obituary 132
Palffy-Alpar, Julius 1908- CAP-2
Earlier sketch in CA 23-24
Palfrey, John Gorham 1796-1881 .... DLB 1, 30
Palfrey, Thomas R(ossman) 1895- 61-64
Palgrave, Francis Turner 1824-1897 .... DLB 35
Palin, Michael (Edward) 1943- CANR-35
Earlier sketch in CA 107
See also Monty Python
See also CLC 21
See also SATA 67
Palinchak, Robert S(tephen) 1942- 49-52
Paling, Chris 1956- 156
Palinurus
See Connolly, Cyril (Vernon)
Palisca, Claude V. 1921- 17-20R
Palkovic, Mark 1954- 137
Pall, Ellen Jane 1952- CANR-59
Earlier sketch in CA 93-96
Palladini, David (Mario) 1946- .... MAICYA
See also SATA 40
See also SATA-Brief 32
Pallas, Dorothy Constance 1933-1971 Obituary 33-36R
Pallas, Norvin 1918- CANR-3
Earlier sketch in CA 1-4R
See also SATA 23
Pallavera, Franco
See Soldati, Mario
Palle, Albert 1916- 13-16R
Pallenberg, Corrado 1912- 13-16R
Palley, Julian I(rving) 1925- 73-76
Palley, Marian Lief 1939- CANR-8
Earlier sketch in CA 61-64
Palli, Pitsa
See Hartocollis, Peter
Pallidini, Jodi
See Robbin, (Jodi) Luna
Palling, (Studley) Bruce 1949- 155
Pallis, Alexander (Anastasius) 1883-1975 Obituary 61-64
Palliser, Charles 1947- 136
See also CLC 65
Pallister, Janis L(ouise) 1926- CANR-14
Earlier sketch in CA 41-44R
Pallister, John C(lare) 1891-1980 .... 5-8R
Obituary 103
See also SATA-Obit 26
Pallone, Dave 1951- 140
Pallone, Nathaniel John 1935- CANR-29
Earlier sketches in CA 21-24R, CANR-10
Palm, Goeran 1931- 29-32R
Palm, Goran
See Palm, Goeran
Palm, John Daniel 1924- Brief entry 106
Palma, Marigloria
See Pagan Ferrer, Gloria M.
See also HW
Palma, Ricardo 1833-1919 168
See also TCLC 29
Palmatier, Robert Allen 1926- 37-40R
Palmedo, Roland 1895-1977 53-56
Obituary 69-72
Palmer, Alan Warwick 1926- CANR-6
Earlier sketch in CA 13-16R
Palmer, Archie M(acInnes) 1896-1985 .... 13-16R
Obituary 116
Palmer, Arnold (Daniel) 1929- 85-88
Palmer, B. C.
See Schmidt, Laura M(arie)
Palmer, Bernard 1914- CANR-64
Earlier sketches in CA 57-60, CANR-7, 12
See also SATA 26
Palmer, Beverly Wilson 1936- 148
Palmer, Brooks 1900(?)-1974 Obituary 45-48
Palmer, Bruce (Hamilton) 1932- CANR-3
Earlier sketch in CA 1-4R
Palmer, Bryan D(ouglas) 1951- 151
Palmer, C(yril) Everard 1930- 41-44R
See also BW 1
See also SATA 14
Palmer, C(edric) King 1913- 13-16R
Palmer, (Ruth) Candida 1926- 61-64
See also SATA 11
Palmer, (John) Carey (Bowden) 1943- 103
Palmer, Charles Earl 1919- 13-16R
Palmer, (Thomas) Cruise 1917- 69-72
Palmer, Dave Richard 1934- CANR-1
Earlier sketch in CA 45-48
Palmer, David (Walter) 1928- CANR-28
Earlier sketch in CA 21-24R
Palmer, Diana
See Kyle, Susan (Spaeth)
Palmer, Don
See Benson, Mildred (Augustine Wirt)
Palmer, Donald C. 1934- 53-56
Palmer, Dorothy Ann 1935- 57-60
Palmer, E(dgar) P(oole), Jr. 1938- 116
Palmer, Earl Frank 1931- 113
Palmer, Edgar Z(avitz) 1898-1977 .... 21-24R
Obituary 135
Palmer, Edward L. 1938- 101
Palmer, Elizabeth 1942- 142
Palmer, Elsie Pavitt 1922- 5-8R
Palmer, Eve 1916- 21-24R
Palmer, Everett W(alter) 1906-1970 .... CAP-2
Earlier sketch in CA 17-18
Palmer, Frank 1933- CANR-69
Earlier sketch in CA 139
Palmer, Frank R. 1922- 17-20R
Palmer, Gabrielle G. 1938- 128
Palmer, George 1915(?)-1986 Obituary 119
Palmer, George E. 1908- 1-4R
Palmer, George Herbert 1842-1933 Brief entry 121
Palmer, Gerald Eustace Howell 1904-1984 Obituary 112
Palmer, (James) Gregory 1938- 121
Palmer, Hap 1942- 136
See also SATA 68
Palmer, Heidi 1948- .... SATA 15
Palmer, Helen H. 1911- 21-24R
Palmer, Helen Marion
See Geisel, Helen
Palmer, Henry R(obinson), Jr. 1911- 21-24R
Palmer, (Nathaniel) Humphrey 1930- CANR-31
Earlier sketches in CA 29-32R, CANR-12
Palmer, James B. 1929- 25-28R
Palmer, Jerome Robert 1904- 45-48
Palmer, Jim
See Palmer, James B.
Palmer, Joe H. 1904-1952 .... DLB 171
Palmer, John (Leslie) 1885-1944 Brief entry 121
Palmer, John A(lfred)
See Lacey, Douglas R(aymond)
Palmer, John A(lfred) 1926-1982 .... 29-32R
Palmer, John D. 1932- 158
Palmer, John L(ogan) 1943- 73-76
Palmer, Joseph (Mansergh) 1912- 5-8R
Palmer, Juliette 1930- 81-84
See also SATA 15
Palmer, Kate Salley 1946- 163
See also SATA 97
Palmer, Kenneth T. 1937- 77-80
Palmer, L(eonard) R(obert) 1906-1984 .... 25-28R
Obituary 114
Palmer, Larry Garland 1938- 17-20R
Palmer, Laura
See Schmidt, Laura M(arie)
Palmer, Lilli
See Peiser, Maria Lilli
Palmer, Lynn
See Palmer, Pamela Lynn
Palmer, Madelyn 1910- 103
Palmer, Maria
See Strachan, Ian
Palmer, Marian 1930- 53-56
Palmer, Marjorie 1919- CANR-12
Earlier sketch in CA 57-60
Palmer, Michael (Stephen) 1942- CANR-35
Earlier sketch in CA 114
See also DAM POET
See also DLB 169
Palmer, Michael D. 1933- 37-40R
Palmer, Nicholas 1950- CANR-15
Earlier sketch in CA 89-92
Palmer, Norman D(unbar) 1909- CANR-41
Earlier sketches in CA 1-4R, CANR-3, 19
Palmer, Pamela Lynn 1951- CANR-4
Earlier sketch in CA 53-56
Palmer, Parker J. 1939- CANR-38
Earlier sketch in CA 115
Palmer, Pete
See Palmer, E(dgar) P(oole), Jr.
Palmer, Peter
See Palmer, Elsie Pavitt
Palmer, Peter John 1932- CANR-42
Earlier sketches in CA 103, CANR-20
Palmer, R(obert) R(oswell) 1909- 13-16R
Palmer, Ralph Simon 1914- 73-76
Palmer, Randy 1953- 164
Palmer, Raymond A. 1910-1977 Obituary 111
Palmer, Raymond Edward 1927- 77-80
Palmer, Richard 1904- 97-100
Palmer, Richard Edward 1933- CANR-1
Earlier sketch in CA 45-48
Palmer, Richard Phillips 1921- 57-60
Palmer, Robert (Franklin, Jr.) 1945-1997 128
Obituary 162
Brief entry 121
Palmer, Robert C(harles) 1947- 113
Palmer, Robert E(verett) A(llen) 1932- Brief entry 114
Palmer, Robin 1911- 109
See also SATA 43
Palmer, Roy (Ernest) 1932- CANR-23
Earlier sketches in CA 61-64, CANR-8
Palmer, Spencer J(ohn) 1927- CANR-10
Earlier sketch in CA 61-64
Palmer, Stanley H. 1944- 135
Palmer, Stuart 1924- CANR-3
Earlier sketch in CA 1-4R
Palmer, Susann(a Louisa) 1923- 132
Palmer, Thomas (Coryell) 1955- CANR-39
Earlier sketch in CA 109
Palmer, Tim 1948- 121
Palmer, Tobias
See Weathers, Winston
Palmer, Tony 1941- Brief entry 111
Palmer, William J. 1943- CANR-72
Earlier sketch in CA 134
Palmer, Winthrop Bushnell 1899-1988 65-68
Obituary 126
Palmieri, Anthony Francis 1920- 114
Palmore, Erdman B. 1930- 37-40R
Palms, Roger C(urtis) 1936- CANR-38
Earlier sketches in CA 93-96, CANR-17
Paloczi-Horvath, George 1908-1973 .... 5-8R
Obituary 37-40R
Palombo, Stanley R(obert) 1934- 122
Palomo, G(aspar) J(esus) 1952- 61-64
Palovic, Clara Lora 1918- 25-28R
Paltenghi, Madeleine
See Anderson, Madeleine Paltenghi
Paltock, Robert 1697-1767 .... DLB 39
Paltrowitz, Donna (Milman) 1950- 119
See also SATA 61
See also SATA-Brief 50
Paltrowitz, Stuart 1946- 118
See also SATA 61
See also SATA-Brief 50
Paludan, (Stig Henning) Jacob (Puggaard) 1896-1975 Obituary 115
Paludan, Phillip S(haw) 1938- 73-76
Paludi, Michele A. 1954- 140
Paluello, Lorenzo Minio
See Minio-Paluello, Lorenzo
Palumbo, Dennis J(ames) 1929- CANR-55
Earlier sketches in CA 29-32R, CANR-28
Palusci, Larry 1916- 29-32R
Paluszny, Maria Janina 1939- 103
Palyi, Melchior 1892(?)-1970 Obituary 104
Pampel, Fred C. 1950- 141
Pamuk, Orhan 1952- 142
Pan, Peter
See Bartier, Pierre
Pan, Stephen C(hao) Y(ing) 1915- 45-48
Panaev, Ivan Ivanovich 1812-1862 .... DLB 198
Panagariya, Arvind 1952- 167
Panagopoulos, Epaminondas Peter 1915- 13-16R
Panama, Norman 1920- 104
See also DLB 26
Panassie, Hugues (Louis Marie Henri) 1912-1974 97-100
Obituary 53-56
Panati, Charles 1943- 81-84
See also SATA 65
Panayi, Panikos 1962- 143
Pancake, Breece Dexter 1952-1979 123
Obituary 109
See also Pancake, Breece D'J
Pancake, Breece D'J
See Pancake, Breece Dexter
See also CLC 29
See also DLB 130
Pancake, John S(ilas) 1920- 53-56
Pandey, B(ishwa) N(ath) 1929-1982 .... CANR-20
Obituary 108
Earlier sketch in CA 25-28R
Pandit, Vijaya Lakshmi 1900- 104
Panek, LeRoy Lad 1943- CANR-32
Earlier sketch in CA 113
Panella, Vincent 1939- 97-100
Panero, Leopoldo 1909-1962 .... DLB 108
Panetta, George 1915-1969 81-84
See also SATA 15
Panetta, Joseph N. 1953- 161
See also SATA 96
Panetta, Leon Edward 1938- 101
Pang, May 1950- 118
Pangborn, Edgar 1909-1976 .... CANR-4
Earlier sketch in CA 1-4R
See also DLB 8
Panger, Daniel 1926- 93-96
Panglaykim, J(usuf Pangestu) 1922- CANR-15
Earlier sketch in CA 21-24R
Pangle, Thomas L(ee) 1944- CANR-1
Earlier sketch in CA 49-52
Pangrazzi, Arnaldo 1947- 115
Paniagua Bermudez, Domingo 1880(?)-1973 Obituary 41-44R
Panichas, George A(ndrew) 1930- CANR-25
Earlier sketches in CA 25-28R, CANR-10
Panik, Sharon 1952- 149
See also SATA 82
Paniker, Raimundo
See Panikkar, Raimon
Panikkar, K(avalam) Madhava 1895-1963 .... CAP-1
Earlier sketch in CA 13-16
Panikkar, Raimon 1918- CANR-51
Earlier sketches in CA 81-84, CANR-25
Panikkar, Raymond
See Panikkar, Raimon
Panin, Dimitri (Mikhailovich) 1911-1987 Obituary 124
Panitch, Leo (Victor) 1945- 119
Panitt, Merrill 1917- 106
Panitz, Esther L(eah) CANR-40
Earlier sketch in CA 116
Panizzi, Sir Anthony 1797-1879 .... DLB 184
Pankey, Eric 1959- 120
Pankhurst, Emmeline (Goulden) 1858-1928 Brief entry 116
Pankhurst, Helen 1964- 143
Pankhurst, Richard (Keir Pethick) 1927- CANR-44
Earlier sketches in CA 9-12R, CANR-6, 21
Pankin, Robert M. 1935- 114
Panko, Rudy
See Gogol, Nikolai (Vasilyevich)
Pannabecker, Samuel Floyd 1896- 65-68
Pannell, Anne Gary 1910- CAP-2
Earlier sketch in CA 23-24
Pannenberg, Wolfhart (Ulrich) 1928- CANR-48
Earlier sketches in CA 25-28R, CANR-11
Panneton, Philippe 1895-1960 148
See also Ringuet
Pannick, David 1956- 130
Panning, Anne 1966- 138
Pannor, Reuben 1922- 61-64
Pannwitz, Rudolf 1881-1969 Obituary 89-92
Pano, Nicholas C(hristopher) 1934- 37-40R
Panofsky, Erwin 1892-1968 117
Obituary 113
Panos, Chris(tos) 1935- 65-68
Panos, Louis G. 1925- 136
Panourgia, Neni K(onstantinou) 1958- 154
Panourgia, Nenny
See Panourgia, Neni K(onstantinou)
Panov, Valery (Shulman) 1938- 102
Panova, Vera (Fedorovna) 1905-1973 102
Obituary 89-92
See also MTCW 1
Panowski, Eileen Thompson 1920- 5-8R
See also SATA 49
Panshin, Alexei 1940- 57-60
See also DLB 8
Panshin, Cory (Seidman) 1947- Brief entry 112
Pansy
See Alden, Isabella (Macdonald)
Pantell, Dora (Fuchs) 111
See also SATA 39
Panter, Carol 1936- 49-52
See also SATA 9
Panter, Gideon G. 1935- 77-80
Panter-Downes, Mollie Patricia 1906-1997 101
Obituary 156
Panting, Phyllis
See Morton, Phyllis Digby
Panych, Morris 166
Panzarella, Andrew 1940- 25-28R
Panzarella, Joseph John, Jr. 1919- 85-88
Panzer, Pauline (Richman) 1911(?)-1972 Obituary 37-40R
Pao, Ping-Nie 1922- 103
Paoletti, John T(homas) 1939- 112
Paoli, Pia 1930- 25-28R
Paolini, Gilberto 1928- CANR-45
Earlier sketches in CA 45-48, CANR-22
Paolucci, Anne (Attura) CANR-47
Earlier sketch in CA 73-76
Paolucci, Henry 1921- 102
Paone, Anthony J(oseph) 1913- 5-8R
Paor, Richard de
See Power, Richard
Papachristou, Judy 1930- 93-96
Papadiamantis, Alexandros 1851-1911 168
See also TCLC 29
Papadiamantopoulos, Johannes 1856-1910 Brief entry 117
See also Moreas, Jean
Papadimitriou, Dimitri B. 1946- 147
Papaleo, Joseph 1925- 25-28R
Papandreou, Andreas G(eorge) 1919-1996 .... 37-40R
Obituary 152
Papandreou, Margaret C. 1923- 29-32R
Papanek, Ernst 1900-1973 .... CANR-4
Earlier sketch in CA 1-4R
Papanek, Gustav F(ritz) 1926- CANR-1
Earlier sketch in CA 45-48
Papanicolaou, George (Nicholas) 1883-1962 167
Papanikolas, Zeese 1942- 156
Papantonio, Michael 1907-1978 .... DLB 187
Papas, William 1927- CANR-12
Earlier sketch in CA 25-28R
See also SATA 50

Papashvily, George 1898-1978 81-84
Obituary 77-80
See also SATA 17
Papashvily, Helen (Waite) 1906- 81-84
See also SATA 17
Papazian, Dennis R(ichard) 1931- 45-48
Papazoglou, Orania 1951- CANR-65
Earlier sketch in CA 126
Pape, D. L.
See Pape, Donna (Lugg)
Pape, Donna (Lugg) 1930- CANR-50
Earlier sketches in CA 21-24R, CANR-9, 25
See also SATA 2, 82
Pape, Gordon 1936- CANR-25
Earlier sketch in CA 105
Pape, Greg 1947- 113
Papenfuse, Edward C(arl), Jr. 1943- CANR-8
Earlier sketch in CA 57-60
Paper, Herbert H(arry) 1925- CANR-1
Earlier sketch in CA 45-48
Paper, Lewis Jay 1946- 146
Brief entry 114
Paperny, Myra (Green) 1932- 69-72
See also SATA 51
See also SATA-Brief 33
Papert, Emma N. 1926- 101
Papi, G(iuseppe) Ugo 1893- 25-28R
Papich, Stephen 1925- 69-72
Papier, Judith Barnard 1932- 21-24R
Papin, Joseph 1914- 65-68
Papineau, David 1947- 130
Papini, Giovanni 1881-1956 Brief entry 121
See also TCLC 22
Papp, Charles Steven 1917- CANR-15
Earlier sketch in CA 41-44R
Pappageotes, George C(hristos) 1926-1963 ....
CANR-2
Earlier sketch in CA 1-4R
Pappas, George 1929- 29-32R
Pappas, Lou Seibert 1930- CANR-47
Earlier sketches in CA 61-64, CANR-8, 23
Pappworth, M(aurice) H(enry) 1910- 21-24R
Paprika
See Holmvik, Oyvind
Papus
See Encausse, Gerard (Anaclet Vincent)
Paquet, Alfons 1881-1944 ....DLB 66
Paracelsus 1493-1541 ....DLB 179
Paradeise, Catherine 1946- 138
Paradis, Adrian A(lexis) 1912- CANR-40
Earlier sketches in CA 1-4R, CANR-3, 18
See also SAAS 8
See also SATA 1, 67
Paradis, James G(ardiner) 1942- 93-96
Paradis, Marjorie Bartholomew 1886(?)-1970 . 73-76
Obituary 29-32R
See also SATA 17
Paradis, Suzanne 1936- ....DLB 53
Paradise, Louis V(incent) 1946- 114
Paradise, Paul R. 1950- 137
Parakh, Jal Sohrab 1932- Brief entry 105
Parandowski, Jan 1895- CAP-1
Earlier sketch in CA 11-12
Paranjape, Makarand (Ramachandra) 1960- ... 150
Parasol, Peter
See Stevens, Wallace
Parasuram, T(attamangalam) V(iswanatha Iyer)
1923- 106
Paratore, Angela 1912- 13-16R
Paravisini-Gebert, Lizabeth 1953- 139
Parberry, Ian 1959- 150
Parchman, William E(ugene) 1936- 93-96
Pardee, Michael 1945- 113
Pardey, Larry
See Pardey, Lawrence Fred
Pardey, Lawrence Fred 1939- 93-96
Pardey, (Mary) Lin 1944- 93-96
Pardo Bazan, Emilia 1851-1921 ....SSC 30
Pardoe, Julia 1804-1862 ....DLB 166
Paredes, Americo 1915- 37-40R
See also HW
Pareek, Udai (Narain) 1925- CANR-53
Earlier sketches in CA 21-24R, CANR-11, 28
Pareja Diezcanseco, Alfredo 1908-1993 ...DLB 145
Parelius, Ann Parker 1943- 81-84
Parelius, Robert J. 1941- 81-84
Parens, Henri 1928- 89-92
Parent, David J(oseph) 1931- CANR-9
Earlier sketch in CA 57-60
Parent, Gail 1940- 101
Interview in 101
Parent, Ronald 1937-1982 Obituary 107
Parent, William A. 1944- 127
Parente, Pascal P(rosper) 1890-1971 ...... CAP-1
Obituary 33-36R
Earlier sketch in CA 17-18
Parenteau, Shirley Laurolyn 1935- CANR-71
Earlier sketches in CA 85-88, CANR-15, 33
See also SATA 47
See also SATA-Brief 40
Parenti, Michael 1933- 73-76
Pares, Marion (Stapylton) 1914- CANR-12
Earlier sketch in CA 17-20R
Paret, Peter 1924- Brief entry 114
Pareto, Vilfredo 1848-1923 ....TCLC 69
Paretsky, Sara 1947- CANR-59
Brief entry 125
Earlier sketch in CA 129
Interview in 129
See also BEST 90:3
See also DAM POP
Paretti, Sandra 1935(?)-1994 .... CANR-7
Obituary 144
Earlier sketch in CA 53-56
Parezo, Nancy Jean 1951- 114
Parfenie, Maria
See Codrescu, Andrei
Parfit, Michael 1947- 119
Parfitt, George (Albert Ekins) 1939- CANR-26
Earlier sketch in CA 109
Parfitt, Tudor (Vernon) 1944- 123
Pargeter, Edith Mary 1913-1995 .... CANR-41
Obituary 149
Earlier sketches in CA 1-4R, CANR-4, 24
See also MTCW 1
Parham, Joseph Byars 1919-1980 65-68
Obituary 135
Parham, Robert Randall 1943- 57-60
Parham, William 1914- 103
Parham, William Thomas 1913- CANR-20
Earlier sketch in CA 103
Parini, Jay (Lee) 1948- CANR-32
Earlier sketch in CA 97-100
See also CAAS 16
See also CLC 54
Parins, James William 1939- 109
Paris, Arthur E. 127
Paris, Barry 153
Paris, Bernard J. 1931- CANR-7
Earlier sketch in CA 17-20R
Paris, David C. 1949- 154
Paris, Erna 1938- 105
Paris, Ginette 1946- 123
Paris, I. Mark 1950- 141
Paris, Jeanne 1918- 1-4R
Paris, Michael 1949- 135
Paris, Mike
See Paris, Michael
Parise, Goffredo 1929-1986 132
Obituary 120
See also DLB 177
Pariseau, Earl J(oseph) 1928- 9-12R
Parish, Charles 1927- 25-28R
Parish, David 1932- CANR-14
Earlier sketch in CA 73-76
Parish, Helen Rand 1912- Brief entry 115
Parish, James 1904-1973 Obituary 114
Parish, James Robert 1944- CANR-37
Earlier sketch in CA 33-36R
Parish, Margaret Cecile 1927-1988 ...... CANR-38
Obituary 127
Earlier sketches in CA 73-76, CANR-18
See also Parish, Peggy
See also MAICYA
See also SATA 73
Parish, Margaret Holt
See Holt, Margaret
Parish, Peggy
See Parish, Margaret Cecile
See also CLR 22
See also SATA 17
See also SATA-Obit 59
Parish, Peter J(oseph) 1929- 57-60
Parish, Steven M. 1953- 157
Parish, Townsend
See Pietschmann, Richard John III
Parisi, Joseph 1944- 93-96
Parizeau, Alice (Poznanska) 1930- 157
See also DLB 60
Park, Barbara 1947- 113
See also CLR 34
See also SATA 40, 78
See also SATA-Brief 35
Park, Bert Edward 1947- 128
Park, Bill
See Park, W(illiam) B(ryan)
See also SATA 22
Park, Charles F(rederick), Jr. 1903- 57-60
Park, Clara Claiborne 1923- CANR-39
Earlier sketch in CA 21-24R
Park, D. U.
See Woods, Clee
Park, David 1919- 105
Park, Ed 1930- 73-76
Park, Edwards 1917- CANR-49
Earlier sketch in CA 123
Park, Elm
See Dunbar, Charles Stuart
Park, George 1925- 77-80
Park, James (Robert) 1956- 120
Park, James William 1936- 121
Park, Joe 1913- 21-24R
Park, Jordan
See Kornbluth, C(yril) M.
and Pohl, Frederik
Park, Joseph H. 1890(?)-1979 Obituary 89-92
Park, Keith K. H. 1964- 143
Park, Maeva
See Dobner, Maeva Park
Park, O'Hyun 1940- 53-56
Park, Paul (Claiborne) 1954- 128
Park, Peter 1929- 29-32R
Park, Richard L(eonard) 1920- 77-80
Park, Robert E(zra) 1864-1944 165
Brief entry 122
See also TCLC 73
Park, Robert L. 1932- 89-92
Park, Roberta J. 1931- 159
Park, (Rosina) Ruth (Lucia) CANR-65
Earlier sketch in CA 105
See also CLR 51
See also SATA 25, 93
Park, Sung-Bae 1933- 115
Park, W(illiam) B(ryan) 1936- CANR-39
Earlier sketches in CA 97-100, CANR-17
See also Park, Bill
See also SATA 22
Park, William John 1930- 49-52
Park Chung Hee 1917-1979 .... CANR-10
Obituary 97-100
Earlier sketch in CA 61-64
Parke, Herbert William 1903- 105
Parke, John 1754-1789 .... DLB 31
Parke, Lawrence 1922- 149
Parke, Margaret Bittner 1901- 89-92
Parke, Marilyn 1928- 149
See also SATA 82
Parke, Richard H. 1909(?)-1989 Obituary 128
Parke, Ross D(uke) 1938- CANR-38
Earlier sketches in CA 45-48, CANR-1, 16
Parker, Adrian David 1947- 103
Parker, Alexander A(ugustine) 1908- CANR-16
Earlier sketch in CA 21-24R
Parker, Alfred Browning 1916- 17-20R
Parker, Angela
See Thirkell, Angela (Margaret)
Parker, Ann
See Neal, Ann Parker
Parker, Arthur C(aswell) 1881-1955 Brief entry . 115
Parker, Barbara J. 160
Parker, Barry (Richard) 1935- CANR-57
Earlier sketches in CA 112, CANR-31
Parker, Beatrice
See Huff, T(om) E.
Parker, Bert
See Ellison, Harlan (Jay)
Parker, Bertha Morris 1890-1980 .... CANR-5
Obituary 102
Earlier sketch in CA 5-8R
Parker, Betty June 1929- CANR-22
Earlier sketches in CA 57-60, CANR-7
Parker, Beulah 1912- 81-84
Parker, Brant Julian 1920- Brief entry 114
Parker, Brother Michael
See Parker, Kenneth L(eroy)
Parker, Clifford S(tetson) 1891- 5-8R
Parker, Clyde A. 1927- 41-44R
Parker, D(avid) C. 1953- 167
Parker, David 1941- 132
Parker, David B. 1956- 135
Parker, David L(ambert) 1935- 108
Parker, David Marshall 1929- 77-80
Parker, Dee
See Parker, David L(ambert)
Parker, (William George) Derek 1932- CANR-49
Earlier sketches in CA 29-32R, CANR-23
Parker, Don(ald) H(enry) 1912- CANR-6
Earlier sketch in CA 5-8R
Parker, Donald Dean 1899-1983 .... CANR-34
Earlier sketch in CA 37-40R
Parker, Donn B(lanchard) 1929- CANR-9
Earlier sketch in CA 65-68
Parker, Dorian Leigh 1920- 145
Parker, Dorothy (Rothschild) 1893-1967 .... CAP-2
Obituary 25-28R
Earlier sketch in CA 19-20
See also CLC 15, 68
See also DAM POET
See also DLB 11, 45, 86
See also MTCW 1
See also SSC 2
Parker, Dorothy 1922- 93-96
Parker, Dorothy Mills CANR-11
Earlier sketch in CA 21-24R
Parker, Douglas Hugh 1926- 1-4R
Parker, Edna Jean 1935- 101
Parker, Edwin B(urke) 1932- 13-16R
Parker, Elinor Milnor 1906- CANR-3
Earlier sketch in CA 1-4R
See also SATA 3
Parker, Elliott S(evern) 1939- 103
Parker, Francis H(oward) 1920- 21-24R
Parker, Frank J(oseph) 1940- 49-52
Parker, Frank R. 1940-1997 136
Obituary 159
Parker, Franklin 1921- CANR-22
Earlier sketches in CA 33-36R, CANR-7
Parker, Franklin D(allas) 1918- 13-16R
Parker, Gail Thain 1943- 104
Parker, Geoffrey 1933- 49-52
Parker, Gilbert 1860-1932 ....DLB 99
Parker, Gordon 1940- 103
Parker, Gwendolyn M(cDougand) 1950- 155
Parker, H(enry) M(ichael) D(enne)
1896(?)-1971 Obituary 104
Parker, Harold T(albot) 1907- CANR-9
Earlier sketch in CA 21-24R
Parker, Hershel 1935- CANR-57
Earlier sketches in CA 33-36R, CANR-13, 30
Parker, Howard J(ohn) 1948- 57-60
Parker, J(ohn) Carlyle 1931- CANR-50
Earlier sketches in CA 57-60, CANR-7, 24
Parker, Jack Horace 1914- 113
Parker, James
See Newby, Eric
Parker, James 1714(?)-1770 ....DLB 43
Parker, James Reid 1909-1984 Obituary 111
Parker, Jean
See Sharat Chandra, G(ubbi) S(hankara Chetty)
Parker, Joan H. 1932- 85-88
Parker, John
See Wyatt, John
Parker, (Herbert) John (Harvey) 1906-1987 ....
CANR-34
Obituary 124
Earlier sketch in CA 5-8R
Parker, John 1923- CANR-5
Earlier sketch in CA 5-8R
Parker, John Thomas 1950- CANR-41
Earlier sketch in CA 118
Parker, Julia (Louise) 1932- CANR-48
Earlier sketches in CA 101, CANR-23
Parker, Julie F. 1961- 156
See also SATA 92
Parker, Kenneth L(eroy) 1954- 132
Parker, Kristy 1957- 126
See also SATA 59
Parker, Laura
See Castoro, Laura A(nn)
Parker, Lois M(ay) 1912- CANR-39
Earlier sketches in CA 69-72, CANR-11
See also SATA 30
Parker, Margot M. 1937- 122
See also SATA 52
Parker, Marsha Zurich 1952- 107
Parker, Mary Jessie 1948- .... SATA 71
Parker, Michael 1959- 140
Parker, Nancy Winslow 1930- CANR-49
Earlier sketches in CA 49-52, CANR-1, 22
See also MAICYA
See also SAAS 20
See also SATA 10, 69
Parker, Nathan Carlyle 1960- 102
Parker, Noel
See Shreffler, Philip A.
Parker, Pat 1944-1989 .... CANR-42
Earlier sketch in CA 57-60
See also BW 2
Parker, Percy Spurlark 1940- 53-56
See also BW 2
Parker, Peter (Robert Nevill) 1954- 136
Parker, Richard 1915- 73-76
See also SATA 14
Parker, Robert
See Boyd, Waldo T.
Parker, Robert 1920- CANR-13
Earlier sketch in CA 77-80
Parker, Robert Allerton
1889(?)-1970 Obituary 29-32R
Parker, Robert B(rown) 1932- CANR-52
Earlier sketches in CA 49-52, CANR-1, 26
Interview in CANR-26
See also BEST 89:4
See also CLC 27
See also DAM NOV, POP
See also MTCW 1
Parker, Robert Miles 1939- 118
Parker, Robert Stewart 1915- 103
Parker, Rolland (Sandau) 1928- CANR-2
Earlier sketch in CA 45-48
Parker, Ron
See Parker, Ronald B(ruce)
Parker, Ronald B(ruce) 1932- 117
Parker, Ronald K(eith) 1939- 108
Parker, Rowland 1912-1989 .... CANR-10
Obituary 128
Earlier sketch in CA 65-68
Parker, Sanford S. 1919(?)-1980 Obituary .. 97-100
Parker, Scott 1950- 113
Parker, Stanley R(obert) 1927- CANR-19
Earlier sketch in CA 103
Parker, Stephen Jan 1939- 118
Parker, (James) Stewart 1941-1988 ..... CANR-32
Obituary 127
Earlier sketch in CA 103
Parker, T(homas) H(enry) L(ouis) 1916- ... CANR-6
Earlier sketch in CA 5-8R
Parker, Theodore 1810-1860 .... DLB 1
Parker, Thomas F(rancis) 1932- 73-76
Parker, Thomas Maynard 1906- CAP-2
Earlier sketch in CA 17-18
Parker, Tom
See Parker, John Thomas
Parker, Tom 1943- 130
Parker, Trey 1969- 168
See also AAYA 27
Parker, Una-Mary 1930- 140
Parker, W(illiam) H(enry) 1912- CANR-13
Earlier sketch in CA 33-36R
Parker, W(ilford) Oren 1911- 41-44R
Parker, Watson 1924- 106
Parker, William Riley 1906-1968 .... CAP-2
Earlier sketch in CA 17-18
See also DLB 103
Parker, Willie J. 1924- 77-80
Parker, Wyman W(est) 1912- 13-16R
Parkerson, Donald H. 1946- 151
Parkerson, John 1885(?)-1978 Obituary 77-80
Parkerson, Michelle (Denise) 1953- 153
See also BW 2
Parkes, Colin Murray 1928- 81-84
Parkes, Graham 1949- CANR-58
Earlier sketch in CA 127
Parkes, Henry B. 1904-1972 Obituary 33-36R
Parkes, James William 1896-1981 Obituary 104
Parkes, K. Stuart 1943- 127
Parkes, Lucas
See Harris, John (Wyndham Parkes Lucas)
Beynon
Parkes, M(alcolm) B(eckwith) 1930- 145
Parkes, (Grahem) Roger 1933- 53-56
Parkes, Terence 1927- 104
Parkes, Walter F. 1951- 167
Parket, I(rwin) Robert 1931- 114
Parkhill, Forbes 1892- 1-4R
Parkhill, John
See Cox, William R(obert)
Parkhill, Wilson 1901- 5-8R
Parkhurst, Helen 1887-1973 Obituary 41-44R
Parkhurst, Louis Gifford, Jr. 1946- 113
Parkhurst, Winthrop 1892(?)-1983 Obituary 110
Parkin, Alan 1934- 29-32R
Parkin, David 1940- CANR-30
Earlier sketches in CA 25-28R, CANR-13
Parkin, Frank 1940- 147
See also CLC 43
Parkin, G(eorge) Raleigh
1896-1977(?) Obituary 106
Parkin, Molly 1932- 104
Parkin, Peter Hubert 1917-1984 Obituary 113
Parkin, Sara (Lamb) 1946- 153

Parkinson, C(yril) Northcote 1909-1993 .. CANR-59
Obituary ... 140
Earlier sketches in CA 5-8R, CANR-5
Parkinson, (Frederick) Charles Douglas 1916- CAP-1
Earlier sketch in CA 11-12
Parkinson, Claire L(ucille) 1948- ... CANR-49
Earlier sketch in CA 120
Parkinson, Cornelia M. 1925- ... CANR-15
Earlier sketch in CA 81-84
Parkinson, David 1961- ... 145
Parkinson, Ethelyn M(inerva) 1906- ... CANR-1
Earlier sketch in CA 49-52
See also SATA 11
Parkinson, J(ohn) R(ichard) 1922- ... 102
Parkinson, Kathryn N. 1954- ... CANR-49
Earlier sketch in CA 120
See also Parkinson, Kathy
Parkinson, Kathy
See Parkinson, Kathryn N.
See also SATA 71
Parkinson, Michael 1944- ... CANR-27
Earlier sketch in CA 29-32R
Parkinson, Roger 1939-1978 ... 106
Parkinson, Stanley 1941- ... 149
Parkinson, Thomas (Francis) 1920-1992 .. CANR-3
Obituary ... 136
Earlier sketch in CA 5-8R
Parkinson, Thomas P(aul) ... 102
Parkinson, Tom
See Parkinson, Thomas P(aul)
Parkman, Francis, Jr. 1823-1893 ... DLB 1, 30, 186
Parks, Aileen Wells 1901- ... 5-8R
Parks, Arva Moore 1939- ... 103
Parks, David 1944- ... 25-28R
Parks, Deborah A. 1948- ... 155
See also SATA 91
Parks, Douglas R(ichard) 1942- ... 111
Parks, Edd Winfield 1906-1968 ... 5-8R
See also SATA 10
Parks, Edmund 1911- ... 69-72
Parks, Edna D(orintha) 1910- ... 13-16R
Parks, Gordon (Alexander Buchanan) 1912- CANR-66
Earlier sketches in CA 41-44R, CANR-26
See also AITN 2
See also BLC 3
See also BW 2
See also CLC 1, 16
See also DAM MULT
See also DLB 33
See also SATA 8
Parks, Joseph Howard 1903- ... 1-4R
Parks, Lloyd Clifford 1922- ... 57-60
Parks, Michael 1943- ... 126
Parks, Pat 1918- ... 61-64
Parks, Robert James 1940- ... 65-68
Parks, Rosa (Louise Lee) 1913- ... 150
See also SATA 83
Parks, Stephen Robert 1940- ... 65-68
Parks, Tim(othy Harold) 1954- ... 131
Brief entry ... 126
Interview in ... 131
Parks, Van Dyke 1943- ... SATA 62
Parks, William 1698(?)-1750 ... DLB 43
Parksmith, George
See Bush, George S(idney)
Parlakian, Nishan 1925- ... 133
Parlato, Salvatore J(oseph), Jr. 1936- ... 73-76
Parlett, David (Sidney) 1939- ... CANR-20
Earlier sketch in CA 103
Parley, Peter
See Goodrich, Samuel Griswold
Parlin, Bradley W(illiam) 1938- ... 69-72
Parlin, John
See Graves, Charles Parlin
Parloff, Roger (Harris) 1955- ... 159
Parma, Clemens
See Menzel, Roderich
Parman, Donald L(ee) 1932- ... 65-68
Parmelee, Alice 1903- ... CAP-2
Earlier sketch in CA 21-22
Parmelee, David Freeland 1924- ... 143
Parmenides c. 515B.C.-c. 450B.C. ... DLB 176
Parmenter, Ross 1912- ... 17-20R
Parmer, J(ess) Norman 1925- ... 5-8R
Parmet, Herbert S. 1929- ... CANR-11
Earlier sketch in CA 21-24R
Parmet, Robert D(avid) 1938- ... 77-80
Parmet, Simon 1897- ... CAP-1
Earlier sketch in CA 13-14
Parnaby, Owen Wilfred 1921- ... 9-12R
Parnall, Peter 1936- ... 81-84
See also MAICYA
See also SAAS 11
See also SATA 16, 69
Parnas, Raymond I. 1937- ... 33-36R
Parnell, Mary Davies 1936- ... 140
Parnell, Michael
See Elman, Richard (Martin)
Parnell, (David) Michael 1934- ... 130
Parnell, Peter 1953- ... 143
Parnell, Thomas 1679-1718 ... DLB 94
Parnes, Herbert S(aul) 1919- ... CANR-34
Earlier sketches in CA 41-44R, CANR-15
Parnes, Sidmore 1928-1984 Obituary ... 113
Parnes, Sidney J. 1922- ... CANR-10
Earlier sketch in CA 21-24R
Parnok, Sophia (Yakovlevna) 1885-1932 ... 148
Paroissien, David (Harry) 1939- ... 111
Parot, Joseph (John) 1940- ... 126
Parotti, Phillip (Elliott) 1941- ... 161
Parque, Richard (Anthony) 1935- ... 124
Parr, A. H.
See Parr, Adolf Henry
Parr, Adolf Henry 1900-1990 Obituary ... 132
Parr, Charles McKew 1884- ... CAP-1
Earlier sketch in CA 11-12
Parr, Delia
See Lechleidner, Mary L.
Parr, James A(llan) 1936- ... 49-52
Parr, John (Lloyd) 1928- ... 102
Parr, Letitia (Evelyn) 1906- ... 103
See also SATA 37
Parr, Lucy 1924- ... 29-32R
See also SATA 10
Parr, Michael 1927- ... 17-20R
Parra, Nicanor 1914- ... CANR-32
Earlier sketch in CA 85-88
See also CLC 2, 102
See also DAM MULT
See also HLC
See also HW
See also MTCW 1
Parramore, Thomas C(ustis) 1932- ... 112
Parrinder, E(dward) Geoffrey 1910- ... CANR-10
Earlier sketch in CA 21-24R
Parrinder, (John) Patrick 1944- ... 127
Parrington, Vernon L(ouis) 1871-1929 Brief entry ... 113
See also DLB 17, 63
Parrini, Carl P. 1933- Brief entry ... 107
Parrino, John J(oseph) 1942- ... 101
Parrino, Michael 1915(?)-1976 Obituary ... 65-68
Parriott, Sara 1953- ... 107
Parris, Addison W(ilson) 1923-1975 ... CAP-2
Earlier sketch in CA 25-28
Parris, Guichard 1903-1990 ... 81-84
Obituary ... 133
Parris, Judith (Ann) H(eimlich) 1939- ... 57-60
Parris, Matthew (Francis) 1949- ... 134
Parrish, Anne 1888-1957 Brief entry ... 115
See also SATA 27
Parrish, Bernard P. 1936- ... 103
Parrish, Bernie
See Parrish, Bernard P.
Parrish, Carl (George) 1904-1965 ... 5-8R
Parrish, Eugene
See Harding, Donald Edward
Parrish, John A(lbert) 1939- ... 37-40R
Parrish, Louis 1927- Brief entry ... 107
Parrish, Mary
See Cousins, Margaret
Parrish, Mary Frances
See Fisher, M(ary) F(rances) K(ennedy)
Parrish, (Frederick) Maxfield 1870-1966 ... SATA 14
Parrish, Maxfield 1870-1966 ... DLB 188
Parrish, Michael E(merson) 1942- ... CANR-43
Earlier sketch in CA 29-32R
Parrish, Patt
See Bucheister, Patt
Parrish, Richard ... 168
Parrish, Robert (Reese) 1916-1995 ... 81-84
Obituary ... 150
Parrish, Stephen Maxfield 1921- ... 104
Parrish, T(homas) Michael 1953- ... 143
Parrish, Thomas (Douglas) 1927- ... 93-96
Parrish, Wayland Maxfield 1887-(?) ... CAP-2
Earlier sketch in CA 23-24
Parrish, Wendy (Louise) 1950-1977 ... 73-76
Obituary ... 133
Parrish, William E(arl) 1931- ... CANR-3
Earlier sketch in CA 1-4R
Parronchi, Alessandro 1914- ... DLB 128
Parrott, Bruce 1945- ... 128
Parrott, Cecil (Cuthbert) 1909-1984 ... 103
Obituary ... 113
Parrott, Fred J(ames) 1913- ... 41-44R
Parrott, Ian 1916- ... CANR-2
Earlier sketch in CA 5-8R
Parrott, (Alonzo) Leslie 1922- ... 97-100
Parrott, Lindesay 1901-1987 Obituary ... 123
Parrott, Lora Lee 1923- ... 25-28R
Parry, Albert 1901- ... CANR-6
Earlier sketch in CA 1-4R
Parry, Caroline (Balderston) 1945- ... 128
Parry, Clive 1917-1982 Obituary ... 107
Parry, David 1908- ... 113
Parry, Ellwood C(omly) III 1941- ... 93-96
Parry, Graham 1940- ... 162
Parry, Hugh J(ones) 1916- ... 13-16R
Parry, J(ohn) H(orace) 1914- ... CANR-6
Earlier sketch in CA 5-8R
Parry, John
See Whelpton, (George) Eric
Parry, Linda (Alberta) 1945- ... 111
Parry, Marian 1924- ... 41-44R
See also SATA 13
Parry, Michael Patrick 1947- ... 101
Parry, Richard (Gittings) 1942- ... 162
Parry, Thomas H. 1904-1985 Obituary ... 116
Parry-Jones, Daniel 1891- ... 13-16R
Parseghian, Ara (Raoul) 1923- Brief entry ... 105
Parsegian, V(ozcan) Lawrence 1908-1996 ... 57-60
Obituary ... 152
Parsifal
See Curl, James Stevens
Parsloe, Guy Charles 1900- ... CAP-1
Earlier sketch in CA 13-14
Parson
See Coleridge, Samuel Taylor
Parson, Ann B(olton) 1950- ... 153
Parson, Mary Jean 1934- ... 133
Parson, Ruben L(eRoy) 1907- ... 13-16R
Parson Lot
See Kingsley, Charles
Parson-Nesbitt, Julie 1957- ... 153
Parsons, Alexandra 1947- ... 156
See also SATA 92
Parsons, C(hristopher) J(ames) 1941- ... 103
Parsons, Charles (Dacre) 1933- ... 45-48
Parsons, Charles H(enry III) 1940- ... 134
Parsons, Coleman O(scar) 1905-1991 ... CAP-1
Obituary ... 134
Earlier sketch in CA 13-16
Parsons, Cynthia 1926- ... CANR-45
Earlier sketches in CA 45-48, CANR-21
Parsons, Denys 1914- ... CANR-12
Earlier sketch in CA 13-16R
Parsons, Ellen
See Dragonwagon, Crescent
Parsons, Elmer E. 1919- ... 25-28R
Parsons, Frances M. 1923- ... 129
Parsons, Geoffrey 1908-1981 Obituary ... 105
Parsons, George W. 1927- ... 156
Parsons, Harriet Oettinger 1906(?)-1983(?) Obituary ... 108
Parsons, Howard L(ee) 1918- ... CANR-17
Earlier sketches in CA 49-52, CANR-1
Parsons, Ian (Macnaghten) 1906-1980 ... 97-100
Obituary ... 102
Parsons, Jack 1920- ... 104
Parsons, James Bunyan 1921- ... 29-32R
Parsons, John (Anthony) 1938- ... CANR-45
Earlier sketch in CA 120
Parsons, Kermit Carlyle 1927- ... 29-32R
Parsons, Kitty (?)-1976 ... 13-16R
Obituary ... 120
Parsons, Louella (Oettinger) 1881-1972 ... 93-96
Obituary ... 37-40R
Parsons, Malcolm Barningham 1919- Brief entry ... 108
Parsons, Martin 1907- ... 53-56
Parsons, Michael L. 1940- ... 151
Parsons, Paul 1952- ... 132
Parsons, R(ichard) A(ugustus) ... 101
Parsons, Stanley B., Jr. 1927- ... CANR-21
Earlier sketch in CA 45-48
Parsons, Talcott 1902-1979 ... CANR-35
Obituary ... 85-88
Earlier sketches in CA 5-8R, CANR-4
See also MTCW 1
Parsons, Thornton H(arris) 1921- ... 73-76
Parsons, Tom
See MacPherson, Thomas George
Parsons, William Edward, Jr. 1936- ... 21-24R
Parsons, William T(homas) 1923- ... 65-68
Partain, Floydene 1924- ... 114
Partch, Virgil Franklin II 1916-1984 ... 108
Obituary ... 113
See also SATA 39
See also SATA-Obit 39
Parthasarathy, R(ajagopal) 1934- ... 154
Partington, F. H.
See Yoxall, Harry W(aldo)
Partington, Martin 1944- ... 124
Partington, Susan Trowbridge 1924- ... 9-12R
Partlow, Vern 1910(?)-1987 Obituary ... 121
Partner, Peter (David) 1924- ... 85-88
Partnow, Elaine 1941- ... 147
Parton, Anthony 1959- ... 133
Parton, Dolly (Rebecca) 1946- ... 150
See also SATA 94
Parton, James 1822-1891 ... DLB 30
Parton, Margaret 1915- ... 97-100
Parton, Sara Payson Willis 1811-1872 .. DLB 43, 74
Partridge, Anthony
See Oppenheim, E(dward) Phillips
Partridge, Astley Cooper 1901- ... 103
Partridge, Benjamin W(aring), Jr. 1915- ... 25-28R
See also SATA 28
Partridge, Derek 1945- ... 135
Partridge, Edward B(ellamy) 1916- ... 65-68
Partridge, Elinore Hughes 1937- ... 115
Partridge, Eric (Honeywood) 1894-1979 ... CANR-3
Obituary ... 85-88
Earlier sketch in CA 1-4R
Partridge, Ernest 1935- ... 115
Partridge, Frances (Catherine) 1900- ... CANR-30
Earlier sketch in CA 29-32R
Partridge, Jenny (Lilian) 1947- ... CANR-26
Earlier sketch in CA 109
See also SATA 52
See also SATA-Brief 37
Partridge, Larry (Harold) 1949- ... 114
Partridge, Norman 195(?)- ... 166
Partridge, William L(ee) 1944- ... CANR-1
Earlier sketch in CA 45-48
Parulski, George R(ichard), Jr. 1954- ... CANR-17
Earlier sketch in CA 97-100
Parun, Vesna 1922- ... DLB 181
Parvin, Betty 1916- ... CANR-17
Earlier sketch in CA 97-100
Parx, C. C.
See Gilmore, Christopher Cook
Parzen, Herbert 1896- ... 25-28R
Pasachoff, Jay M(yron) 1943- ... CANR-40
Earlier sketch in CA 117
Pasamanik, Luisa 1930- ... 101
Pasarell, Emilio J(ulio) 1891-(?) ... HW
Pascal, Anthony H(enry) 1933- ... CANR-16
Earlier sketch in CA 29-32R
Pascal, David 1918- ... 9-12R
See also SATA 14
Pascal, Francine 1938- ... CANR-50
Brief entry ... 115
Earlier sketches in CA 123, CANR-39
See also AAYA 1
See also CLR 25
See also JRDA
See also MAICYA
See also SATA 51, 80
See also SATA-Brief 37
Pascal, Gerald Ross 1907-1984 ... 37-40R
Obituary ... 133
Pascal, John Robert 1932(?)-1981 Obituary ... 102
Pascal, Paul 1925- ... 21-24R
Pascal, Roy 1904-1980 ... CANR-6
Earlier sketch in CA 5-8R
Pascale, Richard Tanner 1938- ... CANR-25
Earlier sketch in CA 53-56
Pascarella, Perry (James) 1934- ... 93-96
Paschal, George H., Jr. 1925- ... 29-32R
Paschal, Nancy
See Trotter, Grace V(iolet)
Paschall, H. Franklin 1922- ... 25-28R
Pascoe, Elaine 1946- ... 124
Pascoe, Elizabeth Jean ... 69-72
Pascoe, John (Dobree) 1908-1972 ... CAP-1
Earlier sketch in CA 13-14
Pascoe, Peggy 1954- ... 136
Pascoli, Giovanni 1855-1912 ... TCLC 45
Pascu, Stefan 1914- ... 117
Pascudniak, Pascal
See Lupoff, Richard A(llen)
Pasewark, William R(obert) 1924- ... CANR-35
Earlier sketches in CA 33-36R, CANR-15
Pashko, Stanley 1913- ... 97-100
See also SATA 29
Pashman, Susan 1942- ... 162
Pasick, Robert 1946- ... 134
Pasinetti, P(ier-) M(aria) 1913- ... 73-76
See also DLB 177
Pask, Gordon 1928- ... 111
Pask, Raymond (Frank) 1944- ... CANR-22
Earlier sketch in CA 105
Paskowicz, Patricia
See Molan, Pat Carlson
Pasley, Virginia Schmitz 1905-1986 Obituary ... 119
Pasmanik, Wolf 1924- ... 101
Pasolini, Pier Paolo 1922-1975 ... CANR-63
Obituary ... 61-64
Earlier sketch in CA 93-96
See also CLC 20, 37, 106
See also DLB 128, 177
See also MTCW 1
See also PC 17
Pasqua, Thomas M(ario), Jr. 1938- ... 131
Pasqua, Tom
See Pasqua, Thomas M(ario), Jr.
Pasquier, Marie-Claire 1933- ... 29-32R
Pasquini
See Silone, Ignazio
Pass, Gail 1940- ... 65-68
Passage, Charles Edward 1913-1983 ... 33-36R
Obituary ... 110
Passailaigue, Thomas E.
See Paisley, Tom
Passantino, Gretchen 1953- ... 110
Passantino, Robert Louis 1951- ... 108
Passaro, Maria (C. Pastore) 1948- ... 165
Passel, Anne W(onders) 1918- ... CANR-11
Earlier sketch in CA 29-32R
Passell, Peter 1944- ... CANR-2
Earlier sketch in CA 45-48
Passerin D'Entreves, Alessandro 1902- ... 69-72
Passeron, Jean-Claude 1930- ... 151
Passeron, Rene (Jean) 1920- ... CANR-17
Earlier sketch in CA 97-100
Passes(-Pazolski), Alan 1943- ... 85-88
Passin, Herbert 1916- ... CANR-20
Earlier sketches in CA 45-48, CANR-1
Passman, Brian 1934- ... 25-28R
Passmore, John (Arthur) 1914- ... CANR-6
Earlier sketch in CA 13-16R
Passmore, Richard E. (?)-1982 Obituary ... 107
Passonneau, Joseph Russell 1921- ... 17-20R
Passow, A(aron) Harry 1920- ... CANR-3
Earlier sketch in CA 1-4R
Passwater, Richard (Albert) 1937- ... CANR-19
Earlier sketch in CA 97-100
Past, Ray(mond Edgar) 1918- ... 29-32R
Pastan, Linda (Olenik) 1932- ... CANR-61
Earlier sketches in CA 61-64, CANR-18, 40
See also CLC 27
See also DAM POET
See also DLB 5
Pasternack, Stefan Alan 1939- Brief entry ... 108
Pasternak, Boris (Leonidovich) 1890-1960 ... 127
Obituary ... 116
See also CLC 7, 10, 18, 63
See also DA
See also DAB
See also DAC
See also DAM MST, NOV, POET
See also MTCW 1
See also PC 6
See also SSC 31
See also WLC
Pasternak, Burton 1933- ... 127
Brief entry ... 109
Pasternak, Velvel 1933- ... 73-76
Pastine, Maureen (Diane) 1944- ... CANR-8
Earlier sketch in CA 57-60
Paston, George 1860-1936 ... DLB 149, 197
Paston, Herbert S. 1928- ... 49-52
Pastor, Robert (Alan) 1947- ... 105
Pastore, Arthur R(alph), Jr. 1922- ... 17-20R
Pastore, Nicholas 1916- ... 29-32R
Pastorius, Francis Daniel 1651-1720(?) ... DLB 24
Pastor X
See Johnson, Merle Allison
Pastos, Spero 1940- ... 126
Paszkowski, Jan Krok
See Krok-Paszkowski, Jan
Patai, Daphne 1943- ... CANR-33
Earlier sketch in CA 113
Patai, Raphael 1910-1996 ... CANR-33
Obituary ... 152
Earlier sketches in CA 29-32R, CANR-20
Pataky, Denes 1921- ... 13-16R
Patanne, Maria
See La Pietra, Mary

Patapoff, Elizabeth 1917- ... 29-32R
Patchen, Kenneth 1911-1972 ... CANR-35
Obituary ... 33-36R
Earlier sketches in CA 1-4R, CANR-3
See also CLC 1, 2, 18
See also DAM POET
See also DLB 16, 48
See also MTCW 1
Patchen, Martin 1932- ... 57-60
Patchett, Ann 1963- ... CANR-64
Earlier sketch in CA 139
Patchett, Mary (Osborne) Elwyn 1897- ... CANR-3
Earlier sketch in CA 5-8R
Pate, Billie 1932- ... 61-64
Pate, J'Nell L(aVerne) 1938- ... 139
Pate, Martha B. Lucas 1912-1983 Obituary ... 110
Patel, Gieve 1940- ... 154
Patel, Harshad C(hhotabhia) 1934- ... 53-56
Patel, I(ndraprasad) G(ordhanbhai) 1924- ... 126
Pateman, Carole 1940- ... 85-88
Pateman, Kim
See Levin, Kim
Pateman, Robert 1954- ... SATA 84
Pateman, Trevor 1947- ... 49-52
Patent, Dorothy Hinshaw 1940- ... CANR-24
Earlier sketches in CA 61-64, CANR-9
See also CLR 19
See also MAICYA
See also SAAS 13
See also SATA 22, 69
Pater, Walter (Horatio) 1839-1894 ... CDBLB 1832-1890
See also DLB 57, 156
Paterek, Josephine 1916- ... 148
Paterson, A(ndrew) B(arton) 1864-1941 ... 155
See also SATA 97
See also TCLC 32
Paterson, Alistair (Ian Hughes) 1929- ... 107
Paterson, Allen P(eter) 1933- ... 139
Patersbn, Ann 1916- ... 33-36R
Paterson, Barbara (Olive) 1933- ... 112
Paterson, Diane (R. Cole) 1946- ... 101
See also SATA 59
See also SATA-Brief 33
Paterson, Don(ald) 1963- ... 154
Paterson, George W(illiam) 1931- ... 103
Paterson, Hugh
See Bower, Ursula Violet Graham
Paterson, Huntley
See Ludovici, Anthony M(ario)
Paterson, Janet M. 1944- ... 151
Paterson, John 1887- ... CAP-1
Earlier sketch in CA 13-14
Paterson, John Harris 1923- ... CANR-6
Earlier sketch in CA 5-8R
Paterson, Judith
See Jones, Judith Paterson
Paterson, Katherine (Womeldorf) 1932- ... CANR-59
Earlier sketches in CA 21-24R, CANR-28
See also AAYA 1
See also CLC 12, 30
See also CLR 7, 50
See also DLB 52
See also JRDA
See also MAICYA
See also MTCW 1
See also SATA 13, 53, 92
Paterson, (James Edmund) Neil 1916- ... 13-16R
Paterson, R(onald) W(illiam) K(eith) 1933- ... 33-36R
Paterson, Richard 1947- ... 148
Paterson, Thomas G(raham) 1941- ... CANR-16
Earlier sketches in CA 45-48, CANR-1
Paterson, William E(dgar) 1941- ... CANR-13
Earlier sketch in CA 61-64
Paterson-Jones, Judith
See Jones, Judith Paterson
Patience, John 1949- ... 155
See also SATA 90
Patinkin, Don 1922-1995 ... CANR-10
Obituary ... 149
Earlier sketch in CA 17-20R
Patinkin, Mark 1953- ... 133
Patka, Frederick 1922- ... 9-12R
Patman, (John William) Wright 1893-1976 ... 109
Obituary ... 107
Patmore, Coventry Kersey Dighton 1823-1896 . DLB 35, 98
Patmore, Derek Coventry 1908-1972 ... 5-8R
Obituary ... 103
Patmore, John Allan 1931- ... 104
Patneaude, David 1944- ... 151
See also SATA 85
Patner, Andrew 1959- ... 128
Paton, Alan (Stewart) 1903-1988 ... CANR-22
Obituary ... 125
Earlier sketches in CAP-1, CA 13-16
See also AAYA 26
See also CLC 4, 10, 25, 55, 106
See also DA
See also DAB
See also DAC
See also DAM MST, NOV
See also DLBD 17
See also MTCW 1
See also SATA 11
See also SATA-Obit 56
See also WLC
Paton, David Macdonald 1913-1992 ... CANR-47
Obituary ... 139
Earlier sketch in CA 114
Paton, George (Whitecross) 1902- ... CAP-1
Earlier sketch in CA 11-12
Paton, Herbert James 1887-1969 ... CAP-1
Earlier sketch in CA 13-14
Paton, Jane (Elizabeth) 1934- ... SATA 35
Paton, Joseph Noel 1821-1901 ... DLB 35
Paton, Priscilla 1952- ... 166
See also SATA 98
Paton, Steven C. 1928(?)-1980 Obituary ... 97-100
Paton Walsh, Gillian 1937- ... CANR-38
See also Walsh, Jill Paton
See also JRDA
See also MAICYA
See also SAAS 3
See also SATA 4, 72
Paton Walsh, Jill
See Paton Walsh, Gillian
Patoski, Joe Nick 1951- ... 141
Patoski, Margaret (Nancy Pearson) 1930- ... 69-72
Patra, Atul Chandra 1915- ... 57-60
Patras, Louis 1931- ... CANR-15
Earlier sketch in CA 85-88
Patrice, Ann
See Galbraith, Georgie Starbuck
Patrick, Alison (Mary Houston) 1921- ... 49-52
Patrick, Clarence H(odges) 1907- ... 33-36R
Patrick, Cuthbert Melvin 1914-1985 Obituary ... 116
Patrick, Douglas Arthur 1905- ... 17-20R
Patrick, Edwin Hill 1901-1964 ... DLB 137
Patrick, Hugh 1930- ... 41-44R
Patrick, J(ohn) Max 1911- ... CANR-5
Earlier sketch in CA 5-8R
Patrick, James (Arthur) 1933- ... CANR-20
Earlier sketch in CA 104
Patrick, John 1905-1995 ... 89-92
Obituary ... 150
Interview in ... 89-92
See also DLB 7
Patrick, Johnstone G(illespie) 1918- ... CANR-2
Earlier sketch in CA 5-8R
Patrick, Leal
See Stone, Patti
Patrick, Lilian
See Keogh, Lilian Gilmore
Patrick, Martha 1956- ... 109
Patrick, Maxine
See Maxwell, Patricia
Patrick, Q.
See Wheeler, Hugh (Callingham)
Patrick, Rembert Wallace 1909-1967 ... 5-8R
Obituary ... 134
Patrick, Robert 1937- ... CANR-57
Earlier sketches in CA 45-48, CANR-1, 30
See also AITN 2
Patrick, Ruth 1907- ... 156
Patrick, Vincent 1935- ... CANR-22
Earlier sketch in CA 104
Interview in ... CANR-22
Patrick, Walton Richard 1909- ... 37-40R
Patrides, C(onstantinos) A(postolos) 1930- ... CANR-20
Earlier sketches in CA 13-16R, CANR-5
Patrikeyev
See Healey-Kay, (Sydney Francis) Patrick (Chippendall)
Patron, Susan 1948- ... 143
See also SATA 76
Patrouch, Joseph F(rancis), Jr. 1935- ... 49-52
Patry, Jean-Luc (P.) 1947- ... 143
Patsouras, Louis
See Patras, Louis
Patt, Richard B. 1954- ... 145
Pattee, Fred Lewis 1863-1950 ... DLB 71
Pattee, Howard Hunt, Jr. 1926- Brief entry ... 109
Pattemore, Arnel W(ilfred) 1934- ... 53-56
Patten, Bebe H(arrison) 1913- ... 61-64
Patten, Brian 1946- ... CANR-43
Earlier sketch in CA 25-28R
See also SATA 29
Patten, Lewis B(yford) 1915-1981 ... CANR-21
Obituary ... 103
Earlier sketch in CA 25-28R
Patten, Nigel 1940- ... 25-28R
Patten, Priscilla C(arla) 1950- ... 117
Patten, (Bebe) Rebecca 1950- ... 117
Patten, Robert L(owry) 1939- ... 109
Patten, Thomas H., Jr. 1929- ... 21-24R
Patterson, A(lfred) Temple 1902-1983 ... 103
Obituary ... 111
Patterson, Alicia Brooks 1906-1963 Obituary . 89-92
See also DLB 127
Patterson, Barbara 1944- ... 110
Patterson, Benton Rain 1929- ... 122
Patterson, Bradley H., Jr. 1921- ... 136
Patterson, C(ecil) H(olden) 1912- ... CANR-16
Earlier sketch in CA 21-24R
Patterson, Carolyn Bennett 1921- ... 106
Patterson, Charles 1935- ... CANR-41
Earlier sketch in CA 117
See also SATA 59
Patterson, Charles D(arold) 1928- ... 122
Patterson, Charles E(dwin), Jr. 1934- ... 41-44R
Patterson, Charles H(enry) 1896- ... 37-40R
Patterson, Charlotte (Buist) 1942- ... 29-32R
Patterson, Craig E(ugene) 1945- ... 93-96
Patterson, David S(ands) 1937- ... 65-68
Patterson, E. Britt 1954- ... 142
Patterson, Edwin W(ilhite) 1889-1965 ... CANR-27
Earlier sketch in CA 1-4R
Patterson, Eleanor Medill 1881(?)-1948 Brief entry ... 118
See also DLB 29
Patterson, Elinor Josephine
See Patterson, Eleanor Medill
Patterson, Elizabeth C. ... 29-32R
Patterson, Emma L. 1904-1984 ... CAP-2
Obituary ... 135
Earlier sketch in CA 25-28
Patterson, Eric James 1891-1972 ... CAP-1
Earlier sketch in CA 11-12
Patterson, Eugene 1923- ... DLB 127
Patterson, Evelyn Roelofs 1917- ... 5-8R
Patterson, Francine (G.) 1947- ... 147
Patterson, Frank Harmon 1912- Brief entry ... 109
Patterson, Frank M(organ) 1931- ... CANR-25
Earlier sketch in CA 45-48
Patterson, Franklin (Kessel) 1916- ... 45-48
Patterson, Frederick D(ouglass) 1901-1988 ... 155
Patterson, Gardner 1916- Brief entry ... 106
Patterson, Geoffrey 1943- ... 103
See also SATA 54
See also SATA-Brief 44
Patterson, George N(eilson) 1920- ... 137
Patterson, Gerald R. 1926- ... 41-44R
Patterson, Glenn 1961- ... 154
Patterson, Harriet-Louise H(olland) 1903- ... CAP-1
Earlier sketch in CA 13-16
Patterson, Harry 1929- ... CANR-63
Earlier sketches in CA 13-16R, CANR-33
See also Higgins, Jack
See also DAM POP
Patterson, Henry
See Patterson, Harry
Patterson, Horace L. 1947- ... 145
Patterson, James (Tyler) 1935- ... 21-24R
Patterson, James (B.) 1947- ... CANR-72
Earlier sketch in CA 133
See also AAYA 25
Patterson, Jane
See Britton, Mattie Lula Cooper
Patterson, Janet McFadden 1915- ... 89-92
Patterson, Jefferson 1891-1977 Obituary ... 115
Patterson, Jerry E(ugene) 1931- Brief entry ... 107
Patterson, Jerry L. 1934- ... 145
Patterson, John McCready 1913-1983 Obituary ... 109
Patterson, Joseph Medill 1879-1946 Brief entry ... 118
See also DLB 29
Patterson, June (Marie) 1924- ... 126
Patterson, K(arl) David 1941- ... 65-68
Patterson, Kevin 1956(?)-1988 Obituary ... 126
Patterson, L(loyd) G(eorge), Jr. 1929- ... 41-44R
Patterson, L(yman) Ray 1929- ... 33-36R
Patterson, Lawrence Thomas II 1937- ... 104
Patterson, Letha L(emon) 1913- ... 5-8R
Patterson, Lillie G. ... 73-76
See also SATA 14, 88
Patterson, Lindsay 1942- ... 77-80
See also BW 1
Patterson, Margaret C(leveland) 1923- ... CANR-7
Earlier sketch in CA 57-60
Patterson, Mary H(agelin) 1928-1973 Obituary ... 37-40R
Patterson, Michael 1939- ... 111
Patterson, (James) Milton 1927- ... 53-56
Patterson, Nancy Ruth 1944- ... SATA 72
Patterson, Olive
See Rowland, D(onald) S(ydney)
Patterson, (Horace) Orlando (Lloyd) 1940- ... CANR-27
Earlier sketch in CA 65-68
See also BLCS
See also BW 1
Patterson, (Leighton) Paige 1942- ... CANR-10
Earlier sketch in CA 25-28R
Patterson, Paul 1909- ... 85-88
Patterson, Peter
See Terson, Peter
Patterson, Raymond R. 1929- ... 29-32R
Patterson, Rebecca Elizabeth Coy 1911-1975 ... 103
Patterson, Richard 1908(?)-1976 Obituary ... 69-72
Patterson, Richard North 1947- ... CANR-41
Earlier sketch in CA 85-88
Patterson, Robert B(enjamin) 1934- ... 73-76
Patterson, Robert Leet 1893- ... 17-20R
Patterson, Ruth P(olk) 1930- ... 119
Patterson, Samuel C(harles) 1931- ... CANR-22
Earlier sketches in CA 17-20R, CANR-7
Patterson, Samuel White 1883-1975 ... CAP-2
Obituary ... 61-64
Earlier sketch in CA 17-18
Patterson, Sheila Caffyn 1918- ... 9-12R
Patterson, Sylvia W(iese) 1940- ... 61-64
Patterson, Tom 1920- ... 128
Patterson, Virginia 1931- ... 102
Patterson, W. M(acLean) 1912(?)-1976 Obituary ... 69-72
Patterson, W. Morgan 1925- ... 65-68
Patterson, Walter C(ram) 1936- ... CANR-20
Earlier sketch in CA 103
Patterson, Ward L(amont) 1933- ... CANR-23
Earlier sketches in CA 57-60, CANR-8
Patterson, Wayne 1946- ... CANR-16
Earlier sketch in CA 85-88
Patterson, Webster T. 1920- ... 25-28R
Patterson, William Dudley 1910-1986 Obituary . 119
Patterson, William L(orenzo) 1890-1980 ... 41-44R
Obituary ... 97-100
Patti, Archimedes L(eonida) A(ttilio) 1913- ... 106
Patti, Ercole 1904(?)-1976 Obituary ... 69-72
Patti, Paul 1956- ... 136
Pattie, Alice 1906- ... CAP-2
Earlier sketch in CA 29-32
Pattillo, Henry 1726-1801 ... DLB 37
Pattillo, James W(ilson) 1937- ... CANR-11
Earlier sketch in CA 17-20R
Pattillo, Manning M., Jr. 1919- ... 21-24R
Pattinson, Nancy Evelyn Brief entry ... 117
Pattison, Darcy (S.) 1954- ... SATA 72
Pattison, O(live) R(uth) B(rown) 1916- ... 29-32R
Pattison, Robert 1945- ... 129
Pattison, Walter Thomas 1903- ... 81-84
Patton, Alva Rae 1908- ... 5-8R
Patton, Arch 1908-1996 ... CAP-1
Obituary ... 154
Earlier sketch in CA 13-16
Patton, Bobby R(ay) 1935- ... CANR-17
Earlier sketches in CA 45-48, CANR-1
Patton, Brian (Lee) 1943- ... 123
Patton, Frances Gray 1906- ... 101
Patton, Frank
See Palmer, Raymond A.
and Shaver, Richard S(harpe)
Patton, George S. 1885-1945 ... TCLC 79
Patton, Gerald W(ilson) 1947- ... 112
Patton, James W(elch) 1900- ... CAP-1
Earlier sketch in CA 11-12
Patton, Kenneth L(eo) 1911- ... CANR-7
Earlier sketch in CA 17-20R
Patton, Oliver B(eirne) 1920- ... 81-84
Patton, Phil 1952- ... 133
Patton, Rob(ert Warren) 1943- ... 37-40R
Pattullo, George 1879-1967 Obituary ... 115
Pattullo, Polly 1946- ... 162
Patty, C. Robert 1925- ... CANR-10
Earlier sketch in CA 25-28R
Patty, Ernest N(ewton) 1894-1976 ... CAP-2
Earlier sketch in CA 25-28
Patty, James S(ingleton) 1925- ... 53-56
Paturi, Felix R.
See Mindt, Heinz R.
Patzert, Rudolph W. 1911- ... 146
Pauck, Wilhelm 1901-1981 ... CANR-28
Obituary ... 104
Earlier sketch in CA 81-84
Pauk, Walter 1914- ... CANR-39
Earlier sketches in CA 5-8R, CANR-2, 18
Pauker, Guy J(ean) 1916- ... CANR-1
Earlier sketch in CA 45-48
Pauker, John 1920-1991 ... 25-28R
Obituary ... 133
Pauker, Samuel L. 1948- ... 127
Pauker, Ted
See Conquest, (George) Robert (Acworth)
Paul, Aileen 1917- ... CANR-19
Earlier sketch in CA 41-44R
See also SATA 12
Paul, Ann Whitford 1941- ... 143
See also SATA 76
Paul, Anthony (Marcus) 1937- ... 77-80
Paul, (John) Anthony 1941- ... 77-80
Paul, Auren
See Uris, Auren
Paul, Barbara
See Ovstedal, Barbara
Paul, Barbara 1931- ... CANR-62
Earlier sketch in CA 132
Paul, Celeste 1952- ... 140
Paul, Charles B. 1931- ... 105
Paul, Charlotte 1916-1989 ... CANR-7
Obituary ... 129
Earlier sketch in CA 5-8R
Paul, Daniel
See Kessel, Lipmann
Paul, Danielle
See Mittermeyer, Helen (Hayton Monteith)
Paul, David (Tyler) 1934-1988 Obituary ... 125
See also SATA-Obit 56
Paul, David W(arren) 1944- ... 107
Paul, Elizabeth
See Crow, Donna Fletcher
Paul, Elliot (Harold) 1891-1958 Brief entry ... 107
See also DLB 4
Paul, Emily
See Eicher, (Ethel) Elizabeth
Paul, F. W.
See Fairman, Paul W.
Paul, Florrie 1928- ... 61-64
Paul, Geoffrey John 1921-1983 Obituary ... 110
Paul, George F(ranklin) 1954- ... 167
Paul, Gordon L. 1935- ... CANR-7
Earlier sketch in CA 17-20R
Paul, Grace 1908- ... 17-20R
Paul, Hugo
See Little, Paul H(ugo)
Paul, I(rving) H. 1928- ... 103
Paul, James 1936- ... SATA 23
Paul, Jordan 1936- ... 97-100
Paul, Judith Edison 1939- ... CANR-16
Earlier sketch in CA 29-32R
Paul, Leslie (Allen) 1905-1985 ... CANR-3
Obituary ... 117
Earlier sketch in CA 1-4R
Paul, Louis
See Placet, Leroi
Paul, Margaret 1939- ... 97-100
Paul, Norman L(eo) 1926- ... 61-64
Paul, Raymond 1940- ... 106
Paul, Robert
See Roberts, John G(aither)
Paul, Robert S(idney) 1918- ... CANR-3
Earlier sketch in CA 1-4R
Paul, Rodman Wilson 1912-1987 ... CANR-3
Obituary ... 122
Earlier sketch in CA 1-4R
Paul, Roland A(rthur) 1937- ... 41-44R
Paul, Sheri
See Resnick, Sylvia (Safran)
Paul, Sherman 1920-1995 ... CANR-3
Obituary ... 148
Earlier sketch in CA 5-8R
Paul, William
See Eicher, (Ethel) Elizabeth
Paulden, Sydney (Maurice) 1932- ... CANR-12
Earlier sketch in CA 29-32R
Paulding, James Kirke 1778-1860 ... DLB 3, 59, 74
Pauley, Barbara Anne 1925- ... CANR-61
Earlier sketch in CA 89-92
Pauley, Bruce F. 1937- ... 41-44R
Pauley, (Margaret) Jane 1950- ... 106
Paulhan, Jean 1884-1968 Obituary ... 25-28R

Pauli, Hertha (Ernestine) 1909-1973 ... CANR-2
Obituary ... 41-44R
Earlier sketch in CA 1-4R
See also SATA 3
See also SATA-Obit 26
Paulin, Thomas Neilson 1949- ... 128
Brief entry ... 123
See also Paulin, Tom
Paulin, Tom
See Paulin, Thomas Neilson
See also CLC 37
See also DLB 40
Pauling, Linus (Carl) 1901-1994 ... CANR-68
Obituary ... 146
Brief entry ... 110
Earlier sketches in CA 116, CANR-45
Interview in ... 116
See also MTCW 1
Paull, Grace A. 1898- ... SATA 24
Paull, Raymond Allan 1906-1972 ... CAP-1
Earlier sketch in CA 9-10
Pau-Llosa, Ricardo 1954- ... 111
See also HW
Paulon, Flavia 1907(?)-1987 Obituary ... 122
Paulos, John Allen 1945- ... 136
Brief entry ... 128
Interview in ... 136
See also BEST 89:3
Pauls, John P. 1916- ... 45-48
Paulsell, William Oliver 1935- ... 111
Paulsen, F(rank) Robert 1922- ... 21-24R
Paulsen, Gary 1939- ... CANR-54
Earlier sketches in CA 73-76, CANR-30
See also AAYA 2, 17
See also CLR 19
See also JRDA
See also MAICYA
See also SATA 22, 50, 54, 79
Paulsen, Lois (Thompson) 1905- ... CAP-2
Earlier sketch in CA 19-20
Paulsen, Wolfgang 1910- ... CANR-11
Earlier sketch in CA 17-20R
Paulson, Belden 1927- ... 21-24R
Paulson, Jack
See Jackson, C(aary) Paul
Paulson, Michael G. 1945- ... 139
Paulson, Morton C. 1923- ... 111
Paulson, Ronald (Howard) 1930- ... CANR-33
Earlier sketches in CA 17-20R, CANR-15
Paulson, Terry L. 1945- ... 136
Paulsson, Bjoern 1932- ... 61-64
Paulsson, Martin W. 1942- ... 149
Paulsson, Thomas A(lfred) 1923- ... 9-12R
Paulston, Christina Bratt ... CANR-10
Earlier sketch in CA 65-68
Paulston, Rolland G(lenn) 1929- ... CANR-13
Earlier sketch in CA 33-36R
Paulu, Burton 1910- ... 13-16R
Paulus, John Douglas 1917- ... 69-72
Paul VI, Pope
See Montini, Giovanni Battista (Enrico Antonio Maria)
Pauly, Rebecca M. 1942- ... 147
Pauly, Thomas H(arry) 1940- ... 115
Paun, Maggie
See Voysey, Margaret
Pauquet, Gina Ruck
See Ruck-Pauquet, Gina
Pausacker, Jenny 1948- ... SAAS 23
See also SATA 72
Paustovsky, Konstantin (Georgievich) 1892-1968 ... 93-96
Obituary ... 25-28R
See also CLC 40
Pautler, Albert J., Jr. 1935- ... 33-36R
Pauw, Berthold Adolf 1924- ... 9-12R
Pauwels, Louis 1920- Brief entry ... 111
Pavalko, Ronald M(ichael) 1934- ... 57-60
Pavarotti, Luciano 1935- Brief entry ... 112
Pavel, Frances 1907- ... 21-24R
See also SATA 10
Pavenstedt, Eleanor 1903- ... 21-24R
Pavese, Cesare 1908-1950 Brief entry ... 104
See also DLB 128, 177
See also PC 13
See also SSC 19
See also TCLC 3
Pavey, Don 1922- ... 107
Pavic, Milorad 1929- ... 136
See also CLC 60
See also DLB 181
Pavitranda, Swami 1896(?)-1977 Obituary ... 73-76
Pavlakis, Christopher 1928- ... 73-76
Pavletich, Aida ... 101
Pavlik, Evelyn Marie 1954- ... 97-100
Pavlik, John V. ... 154
Pavlov, Ivan Petrovich 1849-1936 Brief entry ... 118
Pavlov, Konstantin 1933- ... DLB 181
Pavlov, Nikolai Filippovich 1803-1864 ... DLB 198
Pavlovic, Miodrag 1928- ... DLB 181
Pavlowitch, Stevan K. 1933- ... CANR-53
Earlier sketches in CA 33-36R, CANR-13, 29
Pavord, Anna 1940- ... CANR-37
Earlier sketch in CA 115
Pawel, Ernst 1920- ... 131
Pawelczynska, Anna 1922- ... 101
Pawlak, Mark 1948- ... 145
Pawle, Gerald Strachan 1913-1991 ... 5-8R
Obituary ... 135
Pawley, Bernard C(linton) 1911-1981 ... 25-28R
Obituary ... 105
Pawley, Martin Edward 1938- ... 101
Pawley, Thomas Desire III 1917- ... 29-32R
Pawlick, Thomas F(rancis) 1941- ... 119
Pawlicki, T(homas) B(ert) 1930- ... 109
Pawlikowski, John T. 1940- ... CANR-24
Earlier sketches in CA 21-24R, CANR-9
Pawlowicz, Sala Kaminska 1925- ... 5-8R
Pawlowski, Gareth L(ee) 1939-1995 ... 29-32R
Obituary ... 148
Pawson, G(eoffrey) P(hilip) H(enry) 1904- ... 5-8R
Pax, Clyde 1928- ... 49-52
Paxman, Jeremy Dickson 1950- ... 108
Paxson, Diana L(ucile) 1943- ... 157
Paxson, Ethel 1885- ... 25-28R
Paxton, Dr. John
See Lawton, Sherman P(axton)
Paxton, Jack
See Lawton, Sherman P(axton)
Paxton, Jack 1939-1985 Obituary ... 117
Paxton, John 1911-1985 Obituary ... 114
See also DLB 44
Paxton, John 1923- ... CANR-67
Earlier sketch in CA 129
Paxton, Lois
See Low, Lois Dorothea
Paxton, Mary Jean Wallace 1930- ... 109
Paxton, Robert O(wen) 1932- ... CANR-42
Earlier sketch in CA 73-76
Paxton, Thomas R. 1937- ... CANR-44
Earlier sketch in CA 105
See also Paxton, Tom
Paxton, Tom
See Paxton, Thomas R.
See also SATA 70
Payack, Paul J. J. 1950- ... CANR-31
Earlier sketch in CA 69-72
Paye, Robert
See Campbell, (Gabrielle) Margaret (Vere)
Payelle, Raymond-Gerard 1898-1971 Obituary ... 33-36R
Payer, Cheryl Ann 1940- ... 61-64
Payer, Lynn (Jeanine) 1945- ... 128
Payes, Rachel C(osgrove) 1922- ... CANR-16
Earlier sketches in CA 49-52, CANR-1
Payn, James 1830-1898 ... DLB 18
Payne, A. J.
See Payne, Anthony
Payne, Alan
See Jakes, John (William)
Payne, Alma Smith
See Ralston, Alma (Smith Payne)
Payne, Anthony 1952- ... CANR-56
Earlier sketch in CA 125
Payne, B(en) Iden 1888-1976 ... 73-76
Obituary ... 65-68
Payne, Basil 1928- ... 81-84
Payne, Bernal C., Jr. 1941- ... SATA 60
Payne, Bruce 1911- ... 9-12R
Payne, Charles 1909- ... 103
Payne, Daniel G. 1958- ... 167
Payne, Darwin 1937- ... 143
Payne, (William) David 1955- ... 154
Payne, David A(llen) 1935- ... 25-28R
Payne, Deborah C. 1952- ... 150
Payne, Donald Gordon 1924- ... CANR-24
Earlier sketches in CA 13-16R, CANR-9
See also SATA 37
Payne, Emmy
See West, Emily Govan
Payne, Eric Francis Jules 1895- ... 57-60
Payne, Ernest A(lexander) 1902-1980 ... CANR-9
Obituary ... 105
Earlier sketch in CA 9-12R
Payne, F(rances) Anne 1932- ... 73-76
Payne, J(ohn) Barton 1922- ... CANR-3
Earlier sketch in CA 1-4R
Payne, J(ames) Gregory 1949- ... 123
Payne, Jack 1926- ... 33-36R
Payne, James L. 1939- ... 33-36R
Payne, Joan Balfour (?)-1973 Obituary ... 41-44R
Payne, John 1842-1916 ... DLB 35
Payne, John Howard 1791-1852 ... DLB 37
Payne, Karen 1951- ... 111
Payne, Ladell 1933- ... 134
Brief entry ... 111
Payne, Laurence 1919- ... CANR-63
Earlier sketch in CA 5-8R
Payne, LaVeta Maxine 1916- ... 37-40R
Payne, Leanne 1932- ... CANR-37
Earlier sketch in CA 115
Payne, Leigh A. 1956- ... 147
Payne, Michael 1941- ... CANR-12
Earlier sketch in CA 29-32R
Payne, Mildred Y(ounger) 1906- ... 41-44R
Payne, Neil F. 1939- ... 149
Payne, Peggy 1949- ... 128
Payne, Richard A. 1934- ... 97-100
Payne, (Pierre Stephen) Robert 1911-1983 ... CANR-31
Obituary ... 109
Earlier sketch in CA 25-28R
Payne, Robert O. 1924- ... 97-100
Payne, Ronald 1926- ... 97-100
Payne, Stanley G(eorge) 1934- ... CANR-3
Earlier sketch in CA 1-4R
Payne-Gaposchkin, Cecilia (Helena) 1900-1979 167
Paynter, David H. 1921- ... 135
Paynter, Will(iam) 1903-1984 Obituary ... 115
Paynter, William Henry 1901- ... 13-16R
Paynton, Clifford T. 1929- ... 37-40R
Payro, Roberto J(orge) 1867-1928 ... HW
Payson, Dale 1943- ... CANR-3
Earlier sketch in CA 49-52
See also SATA 9
Payson, Herb(ert III) 1927- ... 115
Payton, Rodney J. 1940- ... 144
Payzant, Charles ... SATA 18
Paz, A.
See Pahz, James Alon
Paz, Carlos F(ernando) 1937- ... 109
Paz, Gil
See Lugones, Leopoldo
Paz, Octavio 1914-1998 ... CANR-65
Obituary ... 165
Earlier sketches in CA 73-76, CANR-32
See also CLC 3, 4, 6, 10, 19, 51, 65
See also DA
See also DAB
See also DAC
See also DAM MST, MULT, POET
See also DLBY 90
See also HLC
See also HW
See also MTCW 1
See also PC 1
See also WLC
Paz, Zan
See Pahz, (Anne) Cheryl Suzanne
Pazder, Lawrence Henry 1936- ... 107
Pazzi, Roberto 1946- ... DLB 196
p'Bitek, Okot 1931-1982 ... 124
Obituary ... 107
See also BLC 3
See also BW 2
See also CLC 96
See also DAM MULT
See also DLB 125
See also MTCW 1
Peabody, Barbara 1933- ... 122
Peabody, Elizabeth Palmer 1804-1894 ... DLB 1
Peabody, Oliver William Bourn 1799-1848 .. DLB 59
Peabody, Richard (Myers, Jr.) 1951- ... 143
Peabody, Robert Lee 1931- ... 9-12R
Peabody, Velton 1936- ... 53-56
Peace, Mary
See Finley, Mary Peace
Peace, Richard (Arthur) 1933- ... 131
Peace, Richard 1938- ... CANR-14
Earlier sketch in CA 25-28R
Peace, Roger Craft 1899-1968 Obituary ... 89-92
See also DLB 127
Peach, Lawrence du Garde 1890-1974 ... 101
Peach, William Bernard 1918- ... 127
Peach, William Nelson 1912- ... 21-24R
Peacham, Henry 1578-1644(?) ... DLB 151
Peacham the Elder, Henry 1547-1634 ... DLB 172
Peacher, Georgiana M(elicent) 1919- ... 25-28R
Peachey, Laban 1927- ... 17-20R
Peacock, Alan T(urner) 1922- ... CANR-3
Earlier sketch in CA 1-4R
Peacock, Basil 1898- ... 103
Peacock, Carlos (Charles Hanbury) ... 132
Peacock, D(avid) P(hilip) S(pencer) 1939- ... 123
Peacock, Daniel J. 1919- ... 125
Peacock, Dick
See Peacock, Richard
Peacock, James Craig 1888(?)-1977 Obituary ... 73-76
Peacock, James L(owe) 1937- Brief entry ... 113
Peacock, L(elon) J(ames) 1928- ... 21-24R
Peacock, Mary (Willa) 1942- ... 69-72
Peacock, Mary Reynolds (Bradshaw) 1916- .. 57-60
Peacock, Molly 1947- ... CANR-52
Earlier sketch in CA 103
See also CAAS 21
See also CLC 60
See also DLB 120
Peacock, Richard 1933- ... 107
Peacock, Ronald 1907-1993 ... CANR-5
Obituary ... 141
Earlier sketch in CA 53-56
Peacock, Thomas Love 1785-1866 ... DLB 96, 116
Peacock, Wilbur Scott 1915(?)-1979 Obituary ... 89-92
Peacocke, A(rthur) R(obert) 1924- ... 41-44R
Peacocke, Christopher 1950- ... 124
Peacocke, Isabel Maud 1881-1973 Obituary ... 116
Pead, Deuel (?)-1727 ... DLB 24
Peairs, Lillian Gehrke 1925- ... 103
Peairs, Richard Hope 1929- Brief entry ... 105
Peak, David 1953- ... 133
Peak, John A. ... 168
Peake, C(harles) H. 1920(?)-1988 Obituary ... 124
Peake, Lilian (Margaret) 1924- Brief entry ... 115
Peake, Mervyn 1911-1968 ... CANR-3
Obituary ... 25-28R
Earlier sketch in CA 5-8R
See also CLC 7, 54
See also DLB 15, 160
See also MTCW 1
See also SATA 23
Peake, Miriam Morrison 1901- ... 57-60
Peaker, G(ilbert) F. 1903(?)-1983(?) Obituary .. 109
Peale, Norman Vincent 1898-1993 ... CANR-55
Obituary ... 143
Earlier sketches in CA 81-84, CANR-29
See also AITN 1
See also MTCW 1
See also SATA 20
See also SATA-Obit 78
Peale, Rembrandt 1778-1860 ... DLB 183
Peale, Ruth Stafford 1906- ... CANR-29
Earlier sketch in CA 73-76
Peano, Giuseppe 1858-1932 ... 163
Pear, David (Adrian) 1957- ... 141
Pear, Lillian Myers ... 73-76
Pearce, Ann Philippa
See Christie, (Ann) Philippa
Pearce, Arthur Williams 1913(?)-1983 Obituary . 111
Pearce, Brian Louis 1933- ... CANR-42
Earlier sketches in CA 103, CANR-19
Pearce, Charles A. 1906-1970 Obituary ... 104
Pearce, David (Robert) 1937- ... 126
Pearce, David W(illiam) 1941- ... 146
Pearce, Dick
See Pearce, Richard Elmo
Pearce, Donald R(oss) 1917- ... 119
Pearce, Donn 1928- ... 13-16R
Pearce, Frank 1909- ... 109
Pearce, J(ohn) Kenneth 1898- ... 45-48
Pearce, J. Winston 1907-(?) ... 130
Brief entry ... 106
Pearce, Janice 1931- ... 61-64
Pearce, John Kingston 1925- ... 118
Pearce, Kenneth 1921- ... 120
Pearce, Mary E(mily) 1932- ... CANR-31
Earlier sketch in CA 69-72
Pearce, Moira ... 103
Pearce, Philippa
See Christie, (Ann) Philippa
See also CLC 21
See also CLR 9
See also DLB 161
See also MAICYA
See also SATA 1, 67
Pearce, Richard 1932- ... 41-44R
Pearce, Richard Elmo 1909- ... 1-4R
Pearce, Roy Harvey 1919- ... CANR-3
Earlier sketch in CA 1-4R
Pearce, Thomas Matthews 1902- ... CANR-7
Earlier sketch in CA 17-20R
Pearce, William M(artin) 1913- ... 9-12R
Pearcy, G(eorge) Etzel 1905-1980 ... CANR-3
Earlier sketch in CA 1-4R
Peardon, Thomas Preston 1899-1985 Obituary . 116
Peare, Catherine Owens 1911- ... 5-8R
See also SATA 9
Pearl, Arthur 1922- ... 13-16R
Pearl, Chaim 1919- ... 49-52
Pearl, Cyril (Altson) 1906-1987(?) Obituary ... 122
Pearl, David 1944- ... 133
Pearl, Eric
See Elman, Richard (Martin)
Pearl, Esther Elizabeth
See Ritz, David
Pearl, Hal 1914(?)-1975 Obituary ... 61-64
Pearl, Jack
See Pearl, Jacques Bain
Pearl, Jacques Bain 1923- ... CANR-60
Earlier sketches in CA 5-8R, CANR-23
Pearl, Joseph L. 1886(?)-1974 Obituary ... 53-56
Pearl, Leon 1922- ... 5-8R
Pearl, Leonard 1911- ... CAP-2
Earlier sketch in CA 33-36
Pearl, Minnie
See Cannon, Sarah Ophelia Colley
Pearl, Ralph 1910- ... 73-76
Pearl, Richard M(axwell) 1913- ... CANR-3
Earlier sketch in CA 9-12R
Pearl, Virginia L(ou) 1930- ... 61-64
Pearlman, Daniel (David) 1935- ... CANR-24
Earlier sketches in CA 61-64, CANR-9
Pearlman, Daniel D. 1935- ... 158
Pearlman, Maurice 1911- ... CANR-6
Earlier sketch in CA 5-8R
Pearlman, Mickey 1938- ... 134
Pearlman, Moshe
See Pearlman, Maurice
Pearlstein, Howard J. 1942- ... 57-60
Pearman, Jean R(ichardson) 1915- ... 49-52
Pears, Charles 1873-1958 Brief entry ... 114
See also SATA-Brief 30
Pears, David Francis 1921- ... 65-68
Pears, Iain (George) 1955- ... CANR-71
Earlier sketch in CA 130
Pears, Tim 1956- ... 143
Pearsall, Derek (Albert) 1931- ... CANR-49
Earlier sketches in CA 107, CANR-24
Pearsall, (F.) Paul ... CANR-55
Earlier sketch in CA 126
Pearsall, Robert Brainard 1920- ... CANR-2
Earlier sketch in CA 45-48
Pearsall, Ronald 1927- ... CANR-31
Earlier sketches in CA 21-24R, CANR-14
Pearsall, Thomas E. 1925- ... 25-28R
Pearsall, William Harold 1891-1964 Obituary ... 106
Pearse, Peter H(ector) 1932- ... 138
Pearson, Andrew Russell 1897-1969 ... CANR-6
Obituary ... 25-28R
Earlier sketch in CA 5-8R
See also MTCW 1
Pearson, B(enjamin) H(arold) 1893- ... 65-68
Pearson, Bill
See Pearson, William Harrison
Pearson, Bruce L. 1932- ... 73-76
Pearson, Carol 1944- ... 57-60
Pearson, Carol Lynn 1939- ... 133
Pearson, David E. 1953- ... 127
Pearson, Diane
See McClelland, Diane Margaret
Pearson, Drew
See Pearson, Andrew Russell
Pearson, Frederic S(tephen) 1944- ... 113
Pearson, Gayle 1947- ... 122
See also SATA 53
Pearson, (Edward) Hesketh (Gibbons) 1887-1964 ... 5-8R
See also DLB 149
Pearson, James Larkin 1879-1981 Obituary ... 104
Pearson, Jim Berry 1924- ... 17-20R
Pearson, John 1934- ... CANR-4
Earlier sketch in CA 49-52
Pearson, Karl 1857-1936 Brief entry ... 119
Pearson, Kit 1947- ... CANR-71
Earlier sketch in CA 145
See also AAYA 19
See also CLR 26
See also JRDA
See also SATA 77
Pearson, Lester B(owles) 1897-1972 ... 121
Obituary ... 37-40R
Pearson, (Edith) Linnea 1942- ... 65-68

Pearson, Lionel (Ignatius Cusack) 1908-1988 . 1-4R
Obituary 126
Pearson, Lon
See Pearson, Milo Lorentz
Pearson, M(ichael) N(aylor) 1941- Brief entry .. 118
Pearson, Michael 102
Pearson, Milo Lorentz 1939- 73-76
Pearson, Neville P(ershing) 1917- 45-48
Pearson, Norman Holmes 1909-1975 ...... CAP-1
Obituary 61-64
Earlier sketch in CA 13-16
Pearson, R(obert) A(rthur) 1945- 128
Pearson, Richard Joseph 1938- 65-68
Pearson, Ridley 1953- CANR-71
Earlier sketch in CA 135
Pearson, Robert Paul 1938- 65-68
Pearson, Ronald Hooke 1915- 13-16R
Pearson, Roy 1914- 1-4R
Pearson, Scott Roberts 1938- CANR-11
Earlier sketch in CA 29-32R
Pearson, Susan 1946- CANR-58
Earlier sketches in CA 65-68, CANR-14
See also SATA 39, 91
See also SATA-Brief 27
Pearson, Sybille 1937- 156
Pearson, T(homas) R(eid) 1956- 130
Brief entry 120
Interview in 130
See also CLC 39
Pearson, Thomas S(pencer) 1949- 132
Pearson, Tracey Campbell 1956- .... SATA 64
Pearson, William Harrison 1922- 57-60
Peary, Dannis 1949- CANR-27
Earlier sketch in CA 109
Peary, Danny
See Peary, Dannis
Peary, Marie Ahnighito
See Kuhne, Marie (Ahnighito Peary)
Peascod, Bill
See Peascod, William
Peascod, William 1920(?)-1985 Obituary 116
Pease, Dorothy Wells 1896- 5-8R
Pease, (Clarence) Howard 1894-1974 ... CANR-41
Obituary 106
Earlier sketch in CA 5-8R
See also MAICYA
See also SATA 2
See also SATA-Obit 25
Pease, Jane H(anna) 1929- CANR-4
Earlier sketch in CA 9-12R
Pease, Louise
See McNeill, Louise
Pease, Victor Philip 1938- 107
Pease, William H(enry) 1924- CANR-4
Earlier sketch in CA 9-12R
Peaston, Monroe 1914- 49-52
Peat, F. David 1938- 132
Peate, Iorwerth C.
See Peate, Iorwerth Cyfeiliog
Peate, Iorwerth Cyfeiliog 1901-1982 120
Obituary 108
Peate, Patricia Flynn 1911(?)-1983 Obituary ... 111
Peatman, John Gray 1904-1997 .... 5-8R
Obituary 157
Peattie, Donald Culross 1898-1964 102
Peattie, Lisa Redfield 1924- CANR-10
Earlier sketch in CA 25-28R
Peattie, Mark R(obert) 1930- CANR-8
Earlier sketch in CA 61-64
Peavler, Terry J. 1942- 135
Peavy, Charles D(ruery) 1931- 25-28R
Peavy, John W(esley) III 1944- 119
Peavy, Linda 1943- CANR-31
Earlier sketch in CA 109
See also SATA 54
Pebworth, Ted-Larry 1936- 121
Peccei, Aurelio 1908-1984 Obituary 112
Peccorini, Francisco L(etona) 1915- CANR-25
Earlier sketch in CA 45-48
Pech, Stanley Z. 1924- 33-36R
Pechel, Peter (Rudolf) 1920- 135
Pechman, Joseph A(aron) 1918-1989 85-88
Obituary 129
Pecht, Michael G. 1952- 145
Pechter, Edward 1941- 85-88
Peck, Abe 1945- 73-76
Peck, Anne Merriman 1884- 77-80
See also SATA 18
Peck, Beth 1957- .... SATA 79
Peck, Dale 1967- CANR-72
Earlier sketch in CA 146
See also CLC 81
Peck, David R. 1938- 143
Peck, David W(arner) 1902-1990 .... 1-4R
Obituary 132
Peck, Ellen 1942- Brief entry 113
Peck, Frederic Taylor 1920(?)-1983 Obituary ... 110
Peck, George (Willis) 1931-1990 Obituary 130
Peck, George W(ilbur) 1840-1916 Brief entry .. 115
See also DLB 23, 42
Peck, Harry Thurston 1856-1914 .... DLB 71, 91
Peck, Helen E(stelle) 1910- 5-8R
Peck, Ira 1922- 77-80
Peck, Jane Cary 1932-1990 Obituary 132
Peck, John 1941- CANR-3
Earlier sketch in CA 49-52
See also CLC 3
Peck, John B. 1918(?)-1973 Obituary 104
Peck, Kathryn Blackburn 1904-1975 .... CAP-2
Earlier sketch in CA 25-28
Peck, M(organ) Scott 1936- CANR-66
Earlier sketches in CA 89-92, CANR-20, 45
See also BEST 89:2
See also DAM POP
Peck, Marshall III 1951- .... SATA 92
Peck, Merton J(oseph) 1925- 13-16R
Peck, Paula 1927(?)-1972 Obituary 104
Peck, Ralph H(arold-Henry) 1926- CANR-22
Earlier sketch in CA 69-72
Peck, Richard (Wayne) 1934- CANR-38
Earlier sketches in CA 85-88, CANR-19
Interview in CANR-19
See also AAYA 1, 24
See also CLC 21
See also CLR 15
See also JRDA
See also MAICYA
See also SAAS 2
See also SATA 18, 55, 97
Peck, Richard E(arl) 1936- CANR-31
Earlier sketch in CA 81-84
Peck, Robert F. 1919- 13-16R
Peck, Robert McCracken 1952- 112
Peck, Robert Newton 1928- CANR-63
Earlier sketches in CA 81-84, CANR-31
See also AAYA 3
See also CLC 17
See also CLR 45
See also DA
See also DAC
See also DAM MST
See also JRDA
See also MAICYA
See also SAAS 1
See also SATA 21, 62
Peck, Robert S(tephen) 1953- 141
Peck, Russell A(lbert) 1933- 108
Peck, Ruth L. 1915- 29-32R
Peck, Seymour 1917-1985 Obituary 114
Peck, Sidney M. 1926- 5-8R
Peck, Stacey 1925- 123
Peck, Suzy
See Carlson, Maureen
Peck, Sylvia 1953- 135
Peck, Theodore P(arker) 1924- 103
Peckenpaugh, Angela J(ohnson) 1942- 104
Peckham, Howard Henry 1910- 9-12R
Peckham, James O. 1903(?)-1984 Obituary 113
Peckham, Lawton (Parker Greenman)
1904-1979 Obituary 89-92
Peckham, Morse 1914- CANR-1
Earlier sketch in CA 1-4R
Peckham, Richard
See Holden, Raymond (Peckham)
Peckinpah, (David) Sam(uel) 1925-1984 109
Obituary 114
See also CLC 20
Pecsok, Mary Bodell 1919- 5-8R
Peddicord, Jo (Anne) 1925- 154
Peden, Margaret Sayers 1927- CANR-14
Earlier sketch in CA 37-40R
Peden, Rachel (Mason) 1901- 110
Peden, W. Creighton 1935- 144
Peden, William (Harwood) 1913- 21-24R
Pedersen, Elsa Kienitz 1915- CANR-2
Earlier sketch in CA 1-4R
Pedersen, (Thelma) Jean J(orgenson) 1934- ......
CANR-21
Earlier sketches in CA 57-60, CANR-6
Pedersen, Knut 1859-1952 .... CANR-63
Brief entry 104
Earlier sketch in CA 119
See also Hamsun, Knut
See also MTCW 1
Pedersen, Paul B(odholdt) 1936- 41-44R
Pederson, Jay P(orter) 1961- 165
Pederson, Kern O(wen) 1910- 102
Pederson, Sharleen
See Collicott, Sharleen
Pedicord, Harry William 1912- 33-36R
Pedler, Christopher Magnus Howard 1927- .. 97-100
Pedler, Frederick Johnson 1908-1991 107
Obituary 134
Pedler, Kit
See Pedler, Christopher Magnus Howard
Pedley, Robin 1914-1988 .... 9-12R
Obituary 127
Pedoe, Daniel 1910- 65-68
Pedolsky, Andrea 1951- CANR-38
Earlier sketch in CA 115
Pedrazas, Allan 168
Pedrick, Jean 1922- CANR-6
Earlier sketch in CA 57-60
Pedrosa, Carmen Navarro 1941- 128
Peebles, Anne
See Galloway, Priscilla
Peebles, Dick 1918-1980 77-80
Obituary 97-100
Peek, Bertrand Meigh 1891-1964 Obituary 111
Peek, Merle 1938- CANR-22
Earlier sketch in CA 105
See also SATA 39
Peek, Walter W(illiam) 1922- 45-48
Peel, Bruce Braden 1916- 17-20R
Peel, Colin D(udley) 1936- 119
Peel, Edwin A(rthur) 1911-1992 .... 13-16R
Obituary 139
Peel, H(azel) M(ary) 1930- CANR-4
Earlier sketch in CA 9-12R
Peel, J(ohn) D(avid) Y(eadon) 1941- 33-36R
Peel, John 1954- .... SATA 79
Peel, John Donald 1908- 33-36R
Peel, Kendal J(ohn) 1940- 116
Peel, Malcolm Lee 1936- 29-32R
Peel, Norman Lemon
See Hirsch, Phil
Peel, Robert 1909-1992 77-80
Obituary 136
Peel, Ronald Francis (Edward Waite)
1912-1985 Obituary 117
Peel, Wallis
See Peel, H(azel) M(ary)
Peele, David A(rnold) 1929-1985 102
Obituary 118
Peele, George 1556-1596 .... DLB 62, 167
Peele, Stanton 1946- 57-60
Peelor, Harry N. 1922- 17-20R
Peeples, Edwin A(ugustus, Jr.) 1915- 9-12R
See also SATA 6
Peer, Lyndon A. 1899(?)-1977 Obituary 73-76
Peeradina, Saleem 1944- 154
Peerbolte, Maarten Lietaert
See Lietaert Peerbolte, Maarten
Peerce, Jan 1904-1984 101
Obituary 114
Peerman, Dean G(ordon) 1931- 13-16R
Peers, William R(aymond) 1914-1984 ...... 13-16R
Obituary 112
Peery, Janet 1948- 157
Peery, Nelson 1923- 149
Peery, Paul D(enver) 1906- CAP-2
Earlier sketch in CA 29-32
Peeslake, Gaffer
See Durrell, Lawrence (George)
Peet, Bill
See Peet, William Bartlett
See also CLR 12
Peet, C(harles) Donald, Jr. 1927- 13-16R
Peet, Creighton B. 1899-1977 106
Obituary 69-72
See also SATA 30
Peet, Louise Jenison 1885- 5-8R
Peet, William Bartlett 1915- CANR-38
Earlier sketch in CA 17-20R
See also Peet, Bill
See also MAICYA
See also SATA 2, 41, 78
Peffer, Randall S(cott) 1948- 101
Pegge, C(ecil) Denis 1902- CAP-1
Earlier sketch in CA 13-16
Pegis, Anton Charles 1905- Brief entry 106
Pegis, Jessie Corrigan 1907- CAP-1
Earlier sketch in CA 13-14
Pegler, (James) Westbrook 1894-1969 .. CANR-62
Obituary 89-92
Earlier sketch in CA 103
See also DLB 171
Pegram, Marjorie Anne (Dykes) 1925- 9-12R
Pegram, Thomas R. 1955- 143
Pegrum, Dudley F(rank) 1898- 33-36R
Pegues, Franklin J(ohnson) 1924- 5-8R
Peguy, Charles Pierre 1873-1914 Brief entry ... 107
See also TCLC 10
Pehnt, Wolfgang 1931- CANR-24
Earlier sketch in CA 107
Pehrson, Justine Davis Randers
See Randers-Pehrson, Justine Davis
Pei, Mario A(ndrew) 1901-1978 .... CANR-5
Obituary 77-80
Earlier sketch in CA 5-8R
Peierls, Rudolf (Ernst) 1907-1995 128
Obituary 149
Peierls, Rudolf E.
See Peierls, Rudolf (Ernst)
Peifer, Claude J(ohn) 1927- 17-20R
Peifer, Kathleen Hamel
See Hamel Peifer, Kathleen
Peikoff, Leonard 1933- 108
Peil, Margaret 1929- CANR-8
Earlier sketch in CA 61-64
Peirce, Charles Sanders 1839-1914 ...... TCLC 81
Peirce, J(ames) F(ranklin) 1918- 41-44R
Peirce, Neal R. 1932- CANR-21
Earlier sketch in CA 25-28R
Peirce, Waldo 1884-1970 .... SATA-Brief 28
Peiris, Denzil 1918(?)-1985 Obituary 116
Peiser, Maria Lilli 1914-1986 116
Obituary 118
Brief entry 110
Peissel, Michel (Francois) 1937- CANR-30
Earlier sketches in CA 25-28R, CANR-12
Peitchinis, Stephen G(abriel) 1925- CANR-49
Earlier sketches in CA 45-48, CANR-24
Pejovich, Svetozar 1931- CANR-12
Earlier sketch in CA 17-20R
Pejovich, Ted
See Pejovich, Theodore Peter
Pejovich, Theodore Peter 1945- 131
Pekarik, Andrew J(oseph) 1946- 112
Pekarkova, Iva 1963- 147
Pekic, Borislav 1930-1992 .... CANR-47
Obituary 139
Earlier sketch in CA 69-72
See also DLB 181
Pekkanen, John 1939- 153
Peladeau, Marius B(eaudoin) 1935- 73-76
Pelaez, Jill 1924- 33-36R
See also SATA 12
Pelavin, Cheryl 1946- 106
Pelecanos, George P. 1957- 138
Peleg, Ilan 1944- 161
Pelenski, Jaroslaw 1929- 153
Brief entry 111
Pelevin, Victor 1962- 154
Pelfrey, William 1947- 33-36R
Pelger, Lucy J. 1913-1971 .... CAP-2
Earlier sketch in CA 21-22
Pelham, David 1938- 138
See also SATA 70
Peli, Pinchas H(acohen)
1930(?)-1989 Obituary 128
Pelikan, Jaroslav Jan 1923- CANR-41
Earlier sketches in CA 1-4R, CANR-1
Pelissier, Anthony 1912-1988 Obituary 125
Pelissier, Roger 1924-1972 .... CAP-2
Obituary 37-40R
Earlier sketch in CA 23-24
Pell, Arthur R. 1920- CANR-51
Earlier sketches in CA 29-32R, CANR-11, 26
Pell, Claiborne (de Borda) 1918- 49-52
Pell, Derek 1947- 77-80
Pell, Eve 1937- 33-36R
Pell, John (Howland Gibbs)
1904-1987 Obituary 123
Pell, Olive Bigelow 1886-1980 Obituary 103
Pell, Robert
See Hagberg, David J(ames)
Pell, Walden II 1902-1983 Obituary 109
Pella, Milton O(rville) 1914- 17-20R
Pellegreno, Ann Holtaren 33-36R
Pellegrini, Angelo 1904-1991 .... CANR-40
Earlier sketch in CA 17-20R
See also CAAS 11
Pellegrini, Anthony D(avid) 1949- 117
Pellegrino, Charles R. 1953- 136
Pellegrino, Victoria Y(urasits) 1944- 107
Peller, Sigismund 1890-1985 Obituary 116
Pellerano, Maria B. 1957- 133
Pelletier, Cathie 1953(?)- 146
Pelletier, Ingrid 1912- 29-32R
Pelletier, Kenneth R. 1946- CANR-29
Earlier sketches in CA 69-72, CANR-11
Pelletier, Nancy 1923- 136
Pelletreau, John 1925(?)-1983 Obituary 111
Pellew, Jill (Hosford) 1942- 109
Pelli, Moshe 1936- 132
Pellicer, Carlos 1900(?)-1977 153
Obituary 69-72
See also HW
Pelling, Henry Mathison 1920- 61-64
Pellow, Deborah 1945- CANR-13
Earlier sketch in CA 73-76
Pellowski, Anne 1933- CANR-9
Earlier sketch in CA 21-24R
See also SATA 20
Pellowski, Michael (Joseph) 1949- CANR-29
Earlier sketch in CA 110
See also SATA 88
See also SATA-Brief 48
Pellowski, Michael Morgan
See Pellowski, Michael (Joseph)
Pells, Richard Henry 1941- 53-56
Pelly, David F. 1948- 124
Pelshe, Arvid Yanovich 1899-1983 Obituary ... 109
Pelta, Kathy 1928- 85-88
See also SATA 18
Peltason, J(ack) W(alter) 1923- CANR-4
Earlier sketch in CA 1-4R
Peltier, Leslie C(opus) 1900- 17-20R
See also SATA 13
Pelto, Bert
See Pelto, Pertti J(uho)
Pelto, Pertti J(uho) 1927- 97-100
Pelton, Alan R. 1953- 145
Pelton, Barry C(lifton) 1935- 61-64
Pelton, Beverly Jo 1939- 49-52
Pelton, Joseph N(eal) 1943- 107
Pelton, Robert D(oane) 1935- 103
Pelton, Robert Stuart 1921- 5-8R
Pelton, Robert W(ayne) 1934- CANR-28
Earlier sketch in CA 29-32R
Pelton, Warren J. 1923- 133
Peltz, Mary Ellis 1896-1981 85-88
Obituary 105
Peluso, Joseph L(ouis) 1929- 97-100
Pelz, Lotte A(uguste) Hensl 1924- 9-12R
Pelz, Stephen Ernest 1942- 114
Brief entry 110
Pelz, Werner 1921- 9-12R
Peman, Jose Maria 1897-1981 Obituary 104
Pemberton, Gayle Renee 1948- 143
See also BW 2
Pemberton, John E(dward) 1930- 33-36R
Pemberton, John Leigh
See Leigh-Pemberton, John
Pemberton, Madge 188(?)-1970 Obituary ... 29-32R
Pemberton, Margaret 1943- CANR-38
Earlier sketches in CA 93-96, CANR-17
Pemberton, Max 1863-1950 Brief entry 120
See also DLB 70
Pemberton, Nan
See Pykare, Nina
Pemberton, William Baring 1897- 5-8R
Pemberton, William E(rwin) 1940- 97-100
Pembrook, Linda 1942- 61-64
Pembrooke, Kenneth
See Page, Gerald W(ilburn)
Pembury, Bill
See Groom, Arthur William
Pempel, T. J. 1942- CANR-30
Earlier sketch in CA 112
Pemsteen, Hans
See Manes, Stephen
Pen, Jan 1921- CANR-17
Earlier sketch in CA 1-4R
Pena, Humberto J(ose) 1928- 73-76
Pena, Milagros 1955- 152
Pena, Ramon del Valle y
See Valle-Inclan, Ramon (Maria) del
Pencavel, John (H.) 1943- 140
Pendar, Kenneth 1906-1972 Obituary 37-40R
Pendarvis, China Clark
See Clark-Pendarvis, China
Pendell, Elmer 1894- CAP-1
Earlier sketch in CA 11-12
Pendennis, Arthur Esquir
See Thackeray, William Makepeace
Pender, Lex
See Pendower, Jacques
Pender, Lydia Podger 1907- CANR-2
Earlier sketch in CA 5-8R
See also SATA 61

Pender, Marilyn
See Pendower, Jacques
Pendergast, Charles 1950- 65-68
Pendergast, Chuck
See Pendergast, Charles
Pendergast, Richard J. 1927- 93-96
Pendery, Rosemary (Schmitz) 53-56
See also SATA 7
Pendle, Alexy 1943- .... SATA 29
Pendle, George 1906-1977 .... 5-8R
Obituary 103
See also SATA-Obit 28
Pendle, Karin 1939- 141
Pendlebury, B(evis) J(ohn) 1898- CAP-2
Earlier sketch in CA 33-36
Pendleton, Conrad
See Kidd, Walter E.
Pendleton, Don
See Cunningham, Chet
and Garside, (Clifford) Jack
and Jagninski, Tom
and Obstfeld, Raymond
Pendleton, Don(ald Eugene) 1927-1995 . CANR-55
Obituary 150
Earlier sketch in CA 33-36R
Pendleton, James D(udley) 1930- 107
Pendleton, Mary 65-68
Pendleton, Winston K. 1910- CAP-1
Earlier sketch in CA 13-16
Pendo, Stephen 1947- 65-68
Pendower, Jacques 1899-1976 .... 9-12R
Obituary 89-92
Pendray, Edward
See Pendray, George Edward
Pendray, G. Edward
See Pendray, George Edward
Pendray, George Edward 1901-1987 Obituary .. 123
Pene du Bois, William (Sherman) 1916-1993 ......
CANR-41
Earlier sketches in CA 5-8R, CANR-17
See also CLR 1
See also DLB 61
See also MAICYA
See also SATA 4, 68
See also SATA-Obit 74
Penelope
See Boyden, Sarah B.
Penelope, Julia 1941- 145
Penfield, Edward 1866-1925 .... DLB 188
Penfield, Thomas 1903- 5-8R
Penfield, Wilder (Graves) 1891-1976 ..... CANR-3
Obituary 65-68
Earlier sketch in CA 5-8R
Pengelley, Eric T. 1919- 89-92
Penick, Harvey 1904-1995 147
Penick, James (Lal), Jr. 1932- 33-36R
Penn, Anne
See Pendower, Jacques
Penn, Arthur (Hiller) 1922- 130
Brief entry 112
Penn, Asher 1908(?)-1979 Obituary 93-96
Penn, Audrey 1950- CANR-13
Earlier sketch in CA 77-80
See also Zellan, Audrey Penn
Penn, Christopher
See Lawlor, Patrick Anthony
Penn, David
See Balsiger, David (Wayne)
Penn, John
See Harcourt, Palma
Penn, Margaret (?)-1981 Obituary 105
Penn, Richard
See Sproat, Iain (MacDonald)
Penn, Ruth Bonn
See Rosenberg, Ethel (Clifford)
Penn, Sean 1960- 163
Penn, W(illiam) S. 1949- 145
Penn, William 1644-1718 .... DLB 24
Penna, Sandro 1906-1977 .... DLB 114
Pennac, Daniel 1944- 168
Pennage, E. M.
See Finkel, George (Irvine)
Pennar, Jaan 1924- Brief entry 115
Pennekamp, John (David)
1897-1978 Obituary 89-92
See also AITN 2
Pennell, Joseph 1857-1926 .... DLB 188
Penner, Fred (Ralph Cornelius) 1946- 136
See also SATA 67
Penner, Jonathan 1940- CANR-39
Earlier sketches in CA 97-100, CANR-17
See also DLBY 83
Penner, Peter 1925- 129
Penney, Annette Culler 1916- 45-48
Penney, Edmund F. 1926- 132
Penney, Grace Jackson 1904- 5-8R
See also SATA 35
Penney, Ian 1960- .... SATA 76
Penney, J(ames) C(ash)
1875-1971 Obituary 29-32R
Penney, Jennifer 1946- 122
Penney, Sue 1957- .... SATA 102
Pennick, Nigel Campbell 1946- CANR-28
Earlier sketch in CA 110
Pennie, Hester
See Taylor, Elisabeth (D.)
Penniman, Clara 1914- Brief entry 111
Penniman, Howard R(ae) 1916- CANR-12
Earlier sketch in CA 13-16R
Penniman, Thomas Kenneth
1896(?)-1977 Obituary 69-72
Penninger, F(rieda) Elaine 1927- 57-60
Penningroth, Paul W(illiam) 1901-1974 49-52
Obituary 103
Penning-Rowsell, Edmund 1913- 127
Pennington, Albert Joe 1950- 57-60
Pennington, Anne (Elizabeth)
1934-1981 Obituary 114
Pennington, Chester Arthur 1916- 104
Pennington, Donald Henshaw 1919- 5-8R
Pennington, Eunice 1923- 57-60
See also SATA 27
Pennington, Howard (George) 1923- 49-52
Pennington, John Selman
1924(?)-1980 Obituary 102
Pennington, Lee 1939- CANR-67
Earlier sketches in CA 69-72, CANR-31
See also DLBY 82
Pennington, Lillian Boyer 1904- .... SATA 45
Pennington, Lucinda 1945- 117
Pennington, M. (Robert John) Basil 1931- ....
CANR-37
Earlier sketches in CA 93-96, CANR-16
Pennington, Penny
See Galbraith, Georgie Starbuck
Pennington, Robert (Roland) 1927- 73-76
Pennington, Stuart
See Galbraith, Georgie Starbuck
Pennington, W(eldon) J(erry)
1919-1985 Obituary 115
Pennink, (John Jacob) Frank 1913- 5-8R
Pennock, J(ames) Roland 1906-1995 .... CANR-29
Obituary 148
Earlier sketches in CA 33-36R, CANR-13
Penny, J. Leith 1955- 127
Penny, Julie 1945- 117
Penny, Prudence
See Goldberg, Hyman
Penny, Ruthanna (Merrick) 1914- 17-20R
Pennycuick, John 1943- 97-100
Penrod, James 1934- 77-80
Penrose, Antony 1947- 137
Penrose, Boies 1902-1976 Obituary 65-68
Penrose, Edith Tilton 1914-1996 .... 25-28R
Obituary 154
Penrose, Gordon 1925- 127
See also SATA 66
Penrose, Harald 1904- CANR-44
Earlier sketches in CA 13-16R, CANR-6, 21
Penrose, Margaret CANR-27
Earlier sketches in CAP-2, CA 19-20
Penrose, Roger 1931- 139
See also BEST 90:2
Penrose, Roland (Algernon) 1900-1984 85-88
Obituary 112
Pensack, Robert Jon 1951- 148
Pensky, Max 1961- 144
Penslar, Derek J(onathan) 1958- 136
Penson, Mary E. 1917- 146
See also SATA 78
Pentecost, Edward C(lyde) 1917- 57-60
Pentecost, Hugh
See Philips, Judson (Pentecost)
Pentecost, J(ohn) Dwight 1915- CANR-2
Earlier sketch in CA 5-8R
Pentecost, Martin
See Hearn, John
Pentony, DeVere Edwin 1924- CANR-8
Earlier sketch in CA 5-8R
Pentreath, A(rthur Godolphin) Guy C(arleton)
1902-1985 .... CAP-1
Obituary 118
Earlier sketch in CA 13-14
Pentz, Croft Miner CANR-9
Earlier sketch in CA 5-8R
Pentz, Lundy H(urd) 1951- 116
Penuel, Arnold M(cCoy) 1936- 57-60
Penuelas, Marcelino C. 1916- 25-28R
Penycate, John (Vincent George) 1943- 144
Penzel, Frederick 1948- 85-88
Penzik, Irena
See Narell, Irena
Penzl, Herbert 1910- CANR-24
Earlier sketch in CA 45-48
Penzler, Otto 1942- CANR-35
Earlier sketch in CA 81-84
See also DLBY 96
See also SATA 38
Peoples, Morgan D. 1919- 133
Pepe, John Frank 1920- 9-12R
Pepe, Phil(ip) 1935- CANR-18
Earlier sketch in CA 25-28R
See also SATA 20
PEPECE
See Prado (Calvo), Pedro
Pepelasis, Adam(antios) A. 1923- CANR-2
Earlier sketch in CA 1-4R
Peper, George Frederick 1950- CANR-25
Earlier sketch in CA 108
Pepin, Jacques (Georges) 1935- CANR-25
Earlier sketch in CA 103
Pepinsky, Harold E(ugene) 1945- 119
Pepitone, Albert (Davison) 1923- 9-12R
Pepitone, Joe 1940- Brief entry 109
Pepitone, Joseph Anthony
See Pepitone, Joe
Peploe, Mark 164
Peppard, Murray B(isbee) 1917-1974 .... CAP-2
Obituary 53-56
Earlier sketch in CA 21-22
Peppe, Rodney 1934- 33-36R
See also MAICYA
See also SAAS 10
See also SATA 4, 74
Pepper, Adeline 41-44R
Pepper, Art(hur Edward) 1925-1982 Obituary .. 107
Pepper, Choral 1918- 25-28R
Pepper, Claude Denson 1900-1989 Obituary ... 128
Pepper, Curtis Bill
See Pepper, Curtis G.
Pepper, Curtis G. 1920- CANR-10
Earlier sketch in CA 21-24R
Pepper, Frank S. 1910-1988 Obituary 127
See also SATA-Obit 61
Pepper, Joan
See Wetherell-Pepper, Joan Alexander
Pepper, John 1942- 117
Pepper, Martin
See Krich, John
Pepper, Stephen C(oburn) 1891-1972 ... CANR-32
Obituary 103
Earlier sketch in CA 1-4R
Pepper, Thomas 1939- CANR-16
Earlier sketch in CA 97-100
Pepper, William M(ullin), Jr. 1903-1975 97-100
Obituary 57-60
Peppercorn, David 1931- 118
Peppercorn, Lisa M(argot) 1913- 138
Peppiatt, Michael 1941- CANR-42
Earlier sketch in CA 118
Peppin, Brigid (Mary) 1941- 65-68
Peppler, Alice Stolper 1934- 53-56
Pepys, Samuel 1633-1703 ...... CDBLB 1660-1789
See also DA
See also DAB
See also DAC
See also DAM MST
See also DLB 101
See also WLC
Peradotto, John Joseph 1933- 41-44R
Perceval-Maxwell, M(ichael) 1933- 53-56
Percival, Alicia C(onstance) 1903- 9-12R
Percival, John 1927- 33-36R
Percival, Walter 1896- CAP-1
Earlier sketch in CA 11-12
Percy
See Walton, Priscilla L.
Percy, Charles H(arting) 1919- 65-68
Percy, Charles Henry
See Smith, Dorothy Gladys
Percy, Douglas Cecil 1914- CANR-3
Earlier sketch in CA 5-8R
Percy, Herbert R(oland) 1920- 5-8R
Percy, John R(ees) 1941- 140
Percy, Rachel 1930- .... SATA 63
Percy, Thomas 1729-1811 .... DLB 104
Percy, Walker 1916-1990 .... CANR-64
Obituary 131
Earlier sketches in CA 1-4R, CANR-1, 23
See also CLC 2, 3, 6, 8, 14, 18, 47, 65
See also DAM NOV, POP
See also DLB 2
See also DLBY 80, 90
See also MTCW 1
Percy, William 1575-1648 .... DLB 172
Percy, William A., Jr. 1933- 29-32R
Percy, William Alexander 1885-1942 163
See also TCLC 84
Perdrizet, Marie-Pierre 1952- 148
See also SATA 79
Perdue, Charles L., Jr. 1930- 135
Perdue, Theda 1949- CANR-16
Earlier sketch in CA 93-96
Perdurabo, Frater
See Crowley, Edward Alexander
Perec, Georges 1936-1982 141
See also CLC 56
See also DLB 83
Pereda (y Sanchez de Porrua), Jose Maria de
1833-1906 Brief entry 117
See also TCLC 16
Pereda y Porrua, Jose Maria de
See Pereda (y Sanchez de Porrua), Jose Maria de
Peregoy, George Weems
See Mencken, H(enry) L(ouis)
Peregrine
See Deutscher, Isaac
Pereira, Harold Bertram 1890- 9-12R
Pereira, Sam 1949- 111
Pereira, W(ilfred) D(ennis) 1921- CANR-42
Earlier sketches in CA 104, CANR-20
Pereira Carneiro, Maurina
1899(?)-1983 Obituary 111
Perel, William M. 1927- 33-36R
Perella, Nicholas James 1927- 73-76
Perelman, Bob 1947- 154
See also DLB 193
Perelman, Chaim 1912- 103
Perelman, Lewis J(oel) 1946- 73-76
Perelman, Michael 1939- 111
Perelman, S(idney) J(oseph) 1904-1979 . CANR-18
Obituary 89-92
Earlier sketch in CA 73-76
See also AITN 1, 2
See also CLC 3, 5, 9, 15, 23, 44, 49
See also DAM DRAM
See also DLB 11, 44
See also MTCW 1
Perenyi, Constance (Marie) 1954- 159
See also SATA 93
Perenyi, Eleanor (Spencer Stone) 1918- 133
Brief entry 113
Perera, Gretchen G(ifford) 1940- 93-96
Perera, Thomas Biddle 1938- CANR-48
Earlier sketches in CA 37-40R, CANR-21
See also SATA 13
Perera, Victor 1934- 29-32R
Peres, Richard 1947- 93-96
Peres, Shimon 1923- 85-88
Peret, Benjamin 1899-1959 Brief entry 117
See also TCLC 20
Peretti, Burton W(illiam) 1961- 144
Peretti, Frank E. 1951- CANR-65
Earlier sketch in CA 136
See also SATA 80
Peretz, Don 1922- CANR-41
Earlier sketches in CA 9-12R, CANR-4, 19
Peretz, Isaac Loeb 1851(?)-1915 Brief entry ... 109
See also SSC 26
See also TCLC 16
Peretz, Yitzkhok Leibush
See Peretz, Isaac Loeb
Pereyra, Lillian A(nita) 1920- 21-24R
Perez, Joseph F(rancis) 1930- CANR-36
Earlier sketches in CA 29-32R, CANR-16
Perez, Louis A., Jr. 1943- 121
Perez, Louis C(elestino) 1923- 77-80
Perez, Raymundo "Tigre" 1946- .... DLB 122
Perez, Rolando 1957- 160
Perez, Sofia A(na) 1963- 168
Perez de Ayala, Ramon 1881-1962 Obituary . 93-96
Perez-Firmat, Gustavo (Francisco) 1949- . CANR-49
Earlier sketch in CA 123
Perez Galdos, Benito 1843-1920 153
Brief entry 125
See also HW
See also TCLC 27
Perez-Gomez, Alberto 1949- 130
See also HW
Perez Lopez, Francisco 1916- 49-52
Perez-Marchand, Monelisa L(ina) 1918- 153
See also HW
Perez-Reverte, Arturo 1951- 163
Perez-Stable, Marifeli 1949(?)- 151
Perfetti, Charles A. 1940- 139
Perham, Margery (Freda) 1895-1982 ..... CANR-1
Obituary 106
Earlier sketch in CA 1-4R
Pericoli, Ugo 1923- 97-100
Perigoe, J. Rae 1910- 61-64
Perillo, Joseph M. 1933- 17-20R
Perin, Constance 29-32R
Perin, Roberto 1948- 133
Perinbanayagam, Robert S(idharthan) 1934- .. 109
Perino, Joseph 1946- 106
Perino, Sheila C. 1948- 106
Peripatus
See Whittington-Egan, Richard
Peri Rossi, Cristina 1941- CANR-59
Earlier sketch in CA 131
See also DLB 145
See also HW
Peristiany, John G(eorge) 1911-1987 ...... 17-20R
Obituary 124
Peritz, Rene 1933- 45-48
Perkes, Dan 1931- CANR-21
Earlier sketch in CA 69-72
Perkin, Harold (James) 1926- CANR-14
Earlier sketch in CA 77-80
Perkin, J(ames) R(ussell) C(onway) 1928- 113
Perkin, Joan 1926- 131
Perkin, Robert L(yman) 1914-1978 Obituary .. 77-80
Perkins, Agnes (Regan) 1926- CANR-10
Earlier sketch in CA 57-60
Perkins, Al(bert Rogers) 1904-1975 107
Obituary 57-60
See also SATA 30
Perkins, Ann (Louise) 1915- Brief entry 113
Perkins, Bradford 1925- 1-4R
Perkins, Carl (Lee) 1932-1998 102
Obituary 164
Perkins, David 1928- 77-80
Perkins, David (Lee) 1939- CANR-13
Earlier sketch in CA 73-76
Perkins, Dexter 1889-1984 .... 5-8R
Obituary 113
Perkins, Dwight Heald 1934- CANR-22
Earlier sketches in CA 17-20R, CANR-7
Perkins, E(rnest) Benson 1881-1964 .... 5-8R
Obituary 134
Perkins, Edward A., Jr. 1928- CANR-14
Earlier sketch in CA 21-24R
Perkins, Edwin Judson 1939- 106
Perkins, (Useni) Eugene 1932- 142
See also BW 2
See also DLB 41
Perkins, Faith
See Bramer, Jennie (Perkins)
Perkins, George (Burton, Jr.) 1930- 13-16R
Perkins, Hugh V(ictor) 1918-1988 93-96
Obituary 124
Perkins, James Alfred 1911- 108
Perkins, James Ashbrook 1941- 73-76
Perkins, James Oliver Newton 1924- 9-12R
Perkins, James S(cudday) 1899- 89-92
Perkins, John (William) 1935- CANR-13
Earlier sketch in CA 73-76
Perkins, John Allen 1919- 114
Perkins, John Bryan Ward
See Ward-Perkins, John Bryan
Perkins, Ken 1926- 137
Perkins, Lawrence A. 1917(?)-1979 Obituary . 89-92
Perkins, Lucy Fitch 1865-1937 137
Brief entry 122
See also MAICYA
See also SATA 72
Perkins, (Richard) Marlin 1905-1986 103
Obituary 119
See also SATA 21
See also SATA-Obit 48
Perkins, Merle Lester 1919- 45-48
Perkins, Michael 1942- CANR-8
Earlier sketch in CA 17-20R
Perkins, Mitali 1963- 152
See also SATA 88
Perkins, Newton Stephens 1925- 49-52
Perkins, Ralph 1913- 13-16R
Perkins, Robert L(ee) 1930- 25-28R
Perkins, Rollin M(orris) 1889- 53-56
Perkins, Steve
See Perkins, Newton Stephens
Perkins, Van L. 1930- Brief entry 106

Perkins, Virginia Chase 1902- CAP-2
Earlier sketch in CA 33-36
Perkins, Whitney Trow 1921- 106
Perkins, William H(ughes) 1923- 53-56
Perkins, Wilma Lord 1897-1976 Obituary 104
Perkinson, Henry J(oseph) 1930- CANR-12
Earlier sketch in CA 17-20R
Perkoff, Stuart Z. 1930-1974 Obituary 113
See also DLB 16
Perkowski, Jan Louis 1936- CANR-2
Earlier sketch in CA 45-48
Perl, Arnold 1914-1971 Obituary 33-36R
Perl, Jeffrey M(ichael) 1952- 138
Perl, Lila 33-36R
See also JRDA
See also SATA 6, 72
Perl, Ruth June 1929- 25-28R
Perl, Susan 1922-1983 CANR-11
Obituary 110
Earlier sketch in CA 17-20R
See also SATA 22
See also SATA-Obit 34
Perl, Teri (Hoch) 1926- CANR-42
Earlier sketches in CA 93-96, CANR-19
Perl, William R. 1906- 126
Perlberg, Deborah 1948- 118
Perlberg, Mark 1929- 37-40R
Perle, George 1915- CANR-3
Earlier sketch in CA 1-4R
Perles, Alfred 1897-1990(?) Obituary 130
Perles, Benjamin Max 1922- 45-48
Perley, Michael 1946- 114
Perley, Moses Henry 1804-1862 DLB 99
Perlin, John 1944- 134
Perlin, Seymour 1925- 121
Perlinski, Jerome 1940- 112
Perlis, Vivian 1928- 85-88
Perlman, Bennard B(loch) 1928- 89-92
Perlman, Helen Harris 1905- CANR-3
Earlier sketch in CA 1-4R
Perlman, Janice E(laine) 1943- 61-64
Perlman, Jess 1891- 89-92
Perlman, John N(iels) 1946- CANR-12
Earlier sketch in CA 33-36R
Perlman, Mark 1923- CANR-57
Earlier sketches in CA 1-4R, CANR-3, 19
Perlman, Samuel 1905-1975 CAP-2
Earlier sketch in CA 33-36
Perlmutter, Emanuel 1907(?)-1986 Obituary 118
Perlmutter, Jerome H. 1924- 17-20R
Perlmutter, Nathan 1923-1987 CANR-49
Obituary 123
Earlier sketch in CA 13-16R
Perlmutter, O(scar) William 1920-1975 57-60
See also SATA 8
Perlmutter, Ruth Ann 1924- 109
Perlo, Victor 1912- CANR-2
Earlier sketch in CA 5-8R
Perloff, Harvey S(tephen) 1915-1983 129
Obituary 110
Perloff, Marjorie G(abrielle) 1931- CANR-49
Earlier sketches in CA 57-60, CANR-7, 22
Perloff, Richard M. 1951- 146
Perlongo, Bob 1933- 112
Perls, Eugenia Soderberg
1904(?)-1973 Obituary 37-40R
Perls, Frederick S(alomon) 1893-1970 101
Perls, Fritz
See Perls, Frederick S(alomon)
Perls, Hugo 1886(?)-1977 Obituary 73-76
Perlstein, Gary R(obert) 1940- 57-60
Permal, Lindy
See Palmer, Randy
Perman, Dagmar Horna
1926(?)-1978 Obituary 77-80
Perman, Michael 1942- Brief entry 113
Pern, Stephen (Antony Nigel) 1950- 128
Pernet, A(nn) 1940- 107
Perniciaro, Tony 1917- 41-44R
Pernick, Martin S(teven) 1948- CANR-67
Earlier sketch in CA 128
Pernoud, Regine 1909- 102
Pernu, Dennis 1970- 152
See also SATA 87
Peroff, Nicholas C(arl) 1944- 113
Peron, Juan (Domingo) 1895-1974 Obituary 49-52
Perosa, Sergio 1933- CAP-1
Earlier sketch in CA 13-16
Perot, H(enry) Ross 1930- 142
Peroutka, Ferdinand 1895(?)-1978 Obituary 77-80
Perovsky, Aleksei Alekseevich 1787-1836 DLB 198
Perowne, Barry
See Atkey, Philip
Perowne, Stewart Henry 1901-1989 CANR-3
Obituary 128
Earlier sketch in CA 1-4R
Perrault, Charles 1628-1703 MAICYA
See also SATA 25
Perreard, Suzanne Louise Butler 1919- SATA-Brief 29
Perreault, John 1937- CANR-1
Earlier sketch in CA 45-48
Perreault, William D(aniel), Jr. 1948- 110
Perrella, Robert 1917- 61-64
Perrenod, Virginia Marion (Lacy) 1928- 117
Perret, Gene (Richard) 1937- CANR-49
Brief entry 114
Earlier sketch in CA 117
Interview in 117
See also SATA 76
Perret, Patti 1955- 168
Perrett, Bryan 1934- CANR-48
Earlier sketches in CA 29-32R, CANR-20
Perrett, Geoffrey 1940- CANR-63
Earlier sketches in CA 53-56, CANR-4
Perriam, Wendy 1940- 136
Perrigo, Lynn I(rwin) 1904- 33-36R
Perrin, Alice 1867-1934 DLB 156
Perrin, Blanche Chenery 1894-1973 5-8R
Obituary 41-44R
Perrin, Don 1964- 158
Perrin, Gail 1938- 136
Perrin, Noel 1927- CANR-57
Earlier sketches in CA 13-16R, CANR-31
Perrin, (Horace) Norman 1920-1976 CANR-11
Earlier sketch in CA 13-16R
Perrin, Porter Gale 1896-1962 Obituary 113
Perrin, Robert 1939- 97-100
Perrin, Robert G(eorge) 1945- 111
Perrin, Ursula 1935- CANR-57
Earlier sketch in CA 101
Perrine, Laurence 1915- CANR-3
Earlier sketch in CA 1-4R
Perrine, Mary 1913- 25-28R
See also SATA 2
Perrin Jassy, Marie-France 1942- 93-96
Perrins, Lesley 1953- 123
See also SATA 56
Perrone, Charles A. 1951- 132
Perrott, John (R.) 1932- 139
Perrotta, Tom 1961- 162
Perrottet, Philippe (Louis Gaston)
1921-1982 25-28R
Obituary 122
Perroy, Edouard (Marie Joseph)
1901-1974 Obituary 53-56
Perrucci, Robert 1931- CANR-34
Earlier sketches in CA 85-88, CANR-15
Perruchot, Henri 1917-1967 CAP-1
Earlier sketch in CA 9-10
Perry, Anne 1938- CANR-50
Earlier sketches in CA 101, CANR-22
Perry, Barbara Fisher
See Fisher, Barbara
Perry, Ben Edwin 1892-1968 CAP-2
Earlier sketch in CA 23-24
Perry, Bernard (Berenson) 1910-1985 Obituary 117
Perry, Bliss 1860-1954 DLB 71
Perry, Brighton
See Sherwood, Robert E(mmet)
Perry, Carmen AITN 2
Perry, Charles 1941- 124
Perry, Charles Edward AITN 2
Perry, Charner M(arquis) 1902-1985 Obituary 117
Perry, Collin 1949- 108
Perry, David L. 1931- 33-36R
Perry, David Thomas 1946- 37-40R
Perry, Dick 1922- 13-16R
Perry, Edgar C(loud) 1900- 117
Perry, Eleanor (Rosenfeld Bayer) 1915(?)-1981 111
Obituary 103
See also DLB 44
Perry, Elisabeth Israels 1939- 111
Perry, Elizabeth Jean 1948- 104
Perry, Erma (Jackson McNeil) 89-92
Perry, Gaylord (Jackson) 1938- Brief entry 113
Perry, George 1935- CANR-26
Earlier sketch in CA 103
Perry, Gordon Arthur 1914- 108
Perry, Grace 1927- CANR-20
Earlier sketch in CA 102
Perry, Helen Swick 1911- 148
Perry, Henry Ten Eyck 1890-1973 CAP-2
Earlier sketch in CA 19-20
Perry, Huey 1936- 49-52
Perry, James M(oorhead) 1927- 13-16R
Perry, Jim (Angelo) 1942- 53-56
Perry, John 1914- CANR-6
Earlier sketch in CA 5-8R
Perry, John Curtis 1930- 104
Perry, John D(elbert), Jr. 1940- 25-28R
Perry, John Oliver 1929- 93-96
Perry, Joseph M(cGarity) 1936- 37-40R
Perry, Kenneth F(rederick) 1902-1974 CAP-2
Earlier sketch in CA 19-20
Perry, Kenneth I. 1929- 29-32R
Perry, Kenneth W(ilbur) 1919- 57-60
Perry, Lewis (Curtis) 1938- CANR-1
Earlier sketch in CA 45-48
Perry, Linette (Purbi) 108
Perry, Lloyd M(erle) 1916-1998 CANR-9
Obituary 165
Earlier sketch in CA 21-24R
Perry, Louis B(arnes) 1918- CAP-1
Earlier sketch in CA 13-14
Perry, Margaret 1933- 89-92
See also BW 1
Perry, Matthew 1794-1858 DLB 183
Perry, Michael (Charles) 1933- 101
Perry, Milton F(reeman) 1926- 13-16R
Perry, Nicolette E. 1949- 119
Perry, Octavia Jordan 1894- CAP-1
Earlier sketch in CA 13-14
Perry, Patricia 1949- 106
See also SATA 30
Perry, Paul 1950- 140
Perry, Peter John 1937- 49-52
Perry, Phillip M. 1948- 29-32R
Perry, Phyllis J. 1933- 168
See also SATA 60, 101
Perry, Ralph Barton 1876-1957 Brief entry 123
Perry, Regenia (Alfreda) 1941- 126
Perry, Richard 41-44R
Perry, Richard 1944- 115
See also BW 1
Perry, Richard S. 1924- 13-16R
Perry, Ritchie (John Allen) 1942- CANR-61
Earlier sketches in CA 45-48, CANR-1, 21
Perry, Robin 1917- 65-68
Perry, Roger 1933- CANR-14
Earlier sketch in CA 77-80
See also SATA 27
Perry, Rosalie Sandra 1945- 53-56
Perry, Rufus
See Gibson, Walter B(rown)
Perry, Ruth (Fuller) 1892- 131
Perry, Ruth 1943- 118
Perry, Sampson 1747-1823 DLB 158
Perry, Shauneille 1930- 113
Perry, Steve 1947- 143
See also SATA 76
Perry, Stewart E(dmond) 1928- 17-20R
Perry, (Charles) Stuart 1908- 107
Perry, Susan
See Perry, Susan M.
Perry, Susan M. 1950- 124
Perry, T. Anthony 1938- 81-84
Perry, Thomas Brief entry 123
Perry, Thomas 1947- CANR-64
Earlier sketch in CA 130
Perry, Thomas Whipple 1925- 9-12R
Perry, Troy D(eroy) 1940- Brief entry 109
Perry, Walter (Laing Macdonald) 1921- 113
Perry, Will 1933- 65-68
Perry, William E(dward) 1931- 111
Perry, Wilma I. 1912- 105
Perse, St.-John
See Leger, (Marie-Rene Auguste) Alexis Saint-Leger
Pershall, Mary K. 1951- 138
See also SATA 70
Pershing, Marie
See Schultz, Pearle Henriksen
Persichetti, Vincent 1915-1987 Obituary 124
Persico, Joseph E(dward) 1930- CANR-21
Earlier sketch in CA 93-96
Persinger, Michael A. 1945- 69-72
Persis
See Haime, Agnes Irvine Constance (Adams)
Persius
See Flaccus, Alus Persius
Perske, Robert 1927- 106
See also SATA 57
Persky, Mordecai 1931- 81-84
Persky, Mort
See Persky, Mordecai
Persky, Stan 1941- CANR-39
Earlier sketches in CA 101, CANR-18
Person, Amy L. 1896- CAP-2
Earlier sketch in CA 23-24
Person, Bernard 1895(?)-1981 Obituary 103
Person, Peter P. 1889- CAP-1
Earlier sketch in CA 11-12
Persons, Robert H(odge), Jr. 1922- CANR-13
Earlier sketch in CA 17-20R
Persons, Stow Spaulding 1913- 103
Pertinax
See Geraud, (Charles Joseph) Andre and Haws, Duncan
Pertschuk, Michael 1933- CANR-26
Earlier sketch in CA 109
Pertwee, Michael (Henry Roland) 1916-1991 154
Brief entry 124
Pertwee, Roland 1885-1963 Obituary 93-96
Perutz, Kathrin 1939- CANR-3
Earlier sketch in CA 1-4R
Perutz, Leo 1882-1957 DLB 81
See also TCLC 60
Perutz, Leo(pold) 1882-1957 147
Perutz, Max 1914- 156
Pervin, Lawrence A. 1936- CANR-8
Earlier sketch in CA 21-24R
Pescadero, Joey
See Obrecht, Jas
Pescadero, Julia
See Obrecht, Jas
Peschel, Enid Rhodes 1943- 110
Pescow, Jerome K(enneth) 1929- 45-48
Peseenz, Tulio F.
See Lopez y Fuentes, Gregorio
Pesek, Boris P(eter) 1926- 21-24R
Pesek, Ludek 1919- 29-32R
Pesetsky, Bette 1932- 133
See also CLC 28
See also DLB 130
Peshkin, Alan 1931- 81-84
Peshkov, Alexei Maximovich 1868-1936 141
Brief entry 105
See also Gorky, Maxim
See also DA
See also DAC
See also DAM DRAM, MST, NOV
Pesin, Harry 1919- 29-32R
Peskett, William 1952- 154
Peskin, Allan 1933- Brief entry 109
Pesnot, Patrick 1943- 101
Pessen, Beth 1943- 97-100
Pessen, Edward 1920-1992 CANR-14
Obituary 140
Earlier sketch in CA 37-40R
Pesseo, Fernando (Antonio Nogueira)
1888-1935 DAM MULT
Pessina, Giorgio 1902(?)-1977 Obituary 73-76
Pessino, Clara Park 1899(?)-1985 Obituary 116
Pesso, Albert 1929- 73-76
Pessoa, Fernando (Antonio Nogueira)
1898-1935 Brief entry 125
See also HLC
See also PC 20
See also TCLC 27
Pestalozzi, Johann Heinrich 1746-1827 DLB 94
Pestana, Carla Gardina 1958- 141
Pestelli, Giorgio 1938- 124
Pestieau, Phyllis Smith 1946- 97-100
Petacco, Arrigo 1929- CANR-21
Earlier sketch in CA 103
Petacque, Art 1924- 136
Petaja, Emil (Theodore) 1915- 25-28R
Peter
See Stratemeyer, Edward L.
Peter, Armistead (III) 1896(?)-1983 Obituary 111
Peter, James (Fletcher) 1919- 17-20R
Peter, John (Desmond) 1921- CANR-3
Earlier sketch in CA 1-4R
Peter, Laurence J(ohnston) 1919-1990 CANR-17
Obituary 130
Earlier sketch in CA 17-20R
See also DLB 53
Peterfreund, Sheldon P(aul) 1917- 21-24R
Peterfreund, Stuart (Samuel) 1945- CANR-58
Earlier sketches in CA 33-36R, CANR-13, 30
Peterkiewicz, Jerzy 1916- CANR-5
Earlier sketch in CA 5-8R
Peterkin, Julia Mood 1880-1961 102
See also CLC 31
See also DLB 9
Peterman, Michael A(lan) 1942- 111
Peterman, Ruth 1924- 57-60
Peter of Spain 1205(?)-1277 DLB 115
Peters, Alexander
See Hollander, Zander
Peters, Arthur Anderson 1913-1979 Obituary 93-96
Peters, Arthur King 1919- 104
Peters, Barney
See Bauer, Erwin A.
Peters, Caroline
See Betz, Eva Kelly
Peters, Catherine 1930- 127
Peters, Charles (Given, Jr.) 1926- 122
Brief entry 116
Peters, Christina 1942- 85-88
Peters, Curtis H. 1942- 147
Peters, Daniel (James) 1948- CANR-39
Earlier sketches in CA 85-88, CANR-15
Peters, David 1954- SATA 72
Peters, David A(lexander) 1923- 25-28R
Peters, Donald L. 1925- 21-24R
Peters, Edward (Murray) 1936- CANR-40
Earlier sketches in CA 101, CANR-18
Peters, Elizabeth
See Mertz, Barbara (Gross)
Peters, Ellis
See Pargeter, Edith Mary
Peters, Eugene H(erbert) 1929- 41-44R
Peters, F(rancis) E(dward) 1927- CANR-12
Earlier sketch in CA 73-76
Peters, Frederick George 1935- 104
Peters, Fritz
See Peters, Arthur Anderson
Peters, Geoffrey
See Palmer, Madelyn
Peters, George W(illiam) 1907- CANR-24
Earlier sketch in CA 45-48
Peters, H. Frederick 1910- 73-76
Peters, J. Ross 1936- 29-32R
Peters, Jean (Rae) 1935- 116
Peters, Joan K(aren) 1945- 158
See also CLC 39
Peters, Julie Anne 1952- 149
See also SATA 82
Peters, Ken(neth Walter) 1929- 17-20R
Peters, Lane
See Lapidus, Elaine
Peters, Lawrence
See Davies, L(eslie) P(urnell)
Peters, Lenrie (Wilfred Leopold) 1932- 108
See also BW 1
See also DLB 117
Peters, Leslie
See Peters, Donald L.
Peters, Linda
See Catherall, Arthur
Peters, Lisa Westberg 1951- 141
See also SATA 74
Peters, Ludovic
See Brent, Peter (Ludwig)
Peters, Marcia
See Gouled, Vivian G(loria)
Peters, Margaret Evelyn 1936- 53-56
Peters, Margot 1933- CANR-12
Earlier sketch in CA 73-76
Peters, Maureen 1935- CANR-65
Earlier sketch in CA 33-36R
Peters, Max S(tone) 1920- 57-60
Peters, Michael
See Hornsby-Smith, Michael P(eter)
Peters, Michael (Adrian) 1948- 163
Peters, Michael Bartley 1943- 110
Brief entry 108
Interview in 110
Peters, Mike
See Peters, Michael Bartley
Peters, Natasha
See Cleaver, Anastasia N.
Peters, Nell
See Pietila, Nellie
Peters, Patricia 1953- SATA 84
Peters, R(ichard) S(tanley) 1919- CANR-16
Earlier sketch in CA 21-24R
Peters, Ralph 1952- 140
Peters, Richard Dorland 1910-1984 Obituary 114
Peters, Robert Anthony 1926- 49-52
Peters, Robert Henry 1946- 143
Peters, Robert L(ouis) 1924- 13-16R
See also CAAS 8
See also CLC 7
See also DLB 105
Peters, Ronald M., Jr. 1947- 85-88
Peters, Russell M. 1929- 146
See also SATA 78
Peters, Ruth Marie 1913(?)-1978 Obituary 104
Peters, S. H.
See Porter, William Sydney and Proffitt, Nicholas (Charles)

Peters, S. T.
See Brannon, William T.
Peters, Stephen 1907(?)-1990 Obituary 130
Peters, Steven
See Geiser, Robert L(ee)
Peters, Ted
See Peters, Theodore F(rank)
Peters, Theodore F(rank) 1941- 81-84
Peters, Thomas J. 1942- CANR-71
Brief entry 123
Earlier sketch in CA 135
See also Peters, Tom
Peters, Tom
See Peters, Thomas J.
See also BEST 89:1
Peters, Victor 1915- 17-20R
Peters, Virginia Bergman 1918- 93-96
Peters, William 1921- CANR-20
Earlier sketches in CA 9-12R, CANR-3
Petersen, Arnold 1885-1976 Obituary 65-68
Petersen, Carol Otto 1914- 57-60
Petersen, Clarence G. 1933- 77-80
Petersen, David 1946- ....SATA 62
Petersen, David M(uir) 1939- 41-44R
Petersen, Donald 1928- 13-16R
Petersen, E. Allen 1903(?)-1987 Obituary 122
Petersen, Gwenn Boardman 1924- CANR-2
Earlier sketch in CA 45-48
See also Boardman, Gwenn R.
See also SATA 61
Petersen, James R(eeve) 1948- 114
Petersen, Karen Daniels 1910- 73-76
Petersen, Mark E. 1900-1984 132
Obituary 111
Petersen, Melba F(rances) Runtz 1919- 5-8R
Petersen, P(eter) J(ames) 1941- CANR-30
Earlier sketch in CA 112
See also JRDA
See also MAICYA
See also SATA 48
See also SATA-Brief 43
Petersen, P(eter) J(ames) 1941- .... SATA 83
Petersen, Palle 1943- .... SATA 85
Petersen, Peter (Barron) 1932- 57-60
Petersen, Sigurd Damskov 1904- 9-12R
Petersen, William 1912- CANR-3
Earlier sketch in CA 1-4R
Petersen, William J. 1929- CANR-9
Earlier sketch in CA 21-24R
Petersen, William John 1901- 5-8R
Petersham, Maud (Sylvia Fuller) 1890-1971 ....
CANR-29
Obituary 33-36R
Earlier sketch in CA 73-76
See also CLR 24
See also DLB 22
See also MAICYA
See also SATA 17
Petersham, Miska 1888-1960 .... CANR-29
Earlier sketch in CA 73-76
See also CLR 24
See also DLB 22
See also MAICYA
See also SATA 17
Peterson, A(lexander) D(uncan) C(ampbell)
1908-1988 108
Obituary 126
Peterson, Agnes F(ischer) 1923- 29-32R
Peterson, Arthur L(aVerne) 1926- 9-12R
Peterson, Audrey 131
Peterson, Brent D(an) 1942- 120
Peterson, Carl 1896(?)-1983 Obituary 110
Peterson, Carolyn Sue 1938- CANR-12
Earlier sketch in CA 73-76
Peterson, Carroll V(alleen) 1929- 45-48
Peterson, Charles 1900(?)-1976 Obituary 69-72
Peterson, Charles Jacobs 1819-1887 ...... DLB 79
Peterson, Charles S. 1927- 49-52
Peterson, Chris(tine Louise) 1957- 141
Peterson, Christian A. 1953- 144
Peterson, Christmas
See Christmas, Joyce
Peterson, Cris 1952- 150
See also SATA 84
Peterson, Dale 1944- 109
Peterson, Dawn 1934- ....SATA 86
Peterson, Donald 1956- 135
Peterson, Donald R(obert) 1923- 25-28R
Peterson, Douglas L(ee) 1924- 41-44R
Peterson, Edward N(orman) 1925- 29-32R
Peterson, Edwin (Lewis)
1904-1972 Obituary 37-40R
Peterson, Edwin Loose 1915- 5-8R
Peterson, Eldridge 1905(?)-1977 Obituary 73-76
Peterson, Eleanor M. 1912- 25-28R
Peterson, Elmer 1930- 37-40R
Peterson, Esther (Allen) 1934- CANR-16
Earlier sketch in CA 89-92
See also SATA 35
Peterson, Evan T(ye) 1925- 45-48
Peterson, F. Ross 1941- 97-100
Peterson, Forrest H(arold) 1912- CANR-25
Earlier sketch in CA 45-48
Peterson, Franklynn 1938- CANR-37
Earlier sketch in CA 110
Peterson, Fred W. 1932- 140
Peterson, Frederick Alvin 1920- 49-52
Peterson, Gilbert Allan 1935- CANR-35
Earlier sketch in CA 114
Peterson, Hans 1922- CANR-1
Earlier sketch in CA 49-52
See also SATA 8
Peterson, Harold 1939- 29-32R
Peterson, Harold F(erdinand) 1900- 5-8R
Peterson, Harold L(eslie) 1922-1978 ...... CANR-4
Obituary 73-76
Earlier sketch in CA 1-4R
See also SATA 8
Peterson, Helen Stone 1910- 37-40R
See also SATA 8
Peterson, Houston 1897-1981 107
Obituary 103
Peterson, Ivars 168
Peterson, James
See Zeiger, Henry A(nthony)
Peterson, James Alfred 1913-1992 104
Obituary 137
Peterson, James Allan 1932- 29-32R
Peterson, Jeanne Whitehouse
See Whitehouse, Jeanne
Peterson, Jim
See Crawford, William (Elbert)
Peterson, John Eric 1933- 53-56
Peterson, John J. 1918- 53-56
Peterson, John W(illard) 1921- 97-100
Peterson, Kenneth G(erard) 1927- 33-36R
Peterson, Len 1917- ....DLB 88
Peterson, Levi S(avage) 1933- CANR-51
Earlier sketches in CA 109, CANR-26
Peterson, Linda H(aenlein) 1948- CANR-46
Earlier sketch in CA 121
Peterson, Lloyd R(ichard) 1922- Brief entry 107
Peterson, Lorraine 1940- 113
See also SATA 56
See also SATA-Brief 44
Peterson, Louis (Stamford), (Jr.) 1922-1998 153
Obituary 166
See also BW 2
See also DLB 76
Peterson, M(ildred) Jeanne 1937- 103
Peterson, Marilyn Ann 1933- 57-60
Peterson, Martin Severin 1897- CANR-3
Earlier sketch in CA 1-4R
Peterson, Melvin N. A. 1929-1995 144
Obituary 149
Peterson, Mendel (Lazear) 1918- 73-76
Peterson, Merrill D(aniel) 1921- CANR-44
Earlier sketches in CA 1-4R, CANR-3, 19
Peterson, Michael L. 1950- 148
Peterson, Nancy L(ee) 1939- 105
Peterson, Norma Lois 1922- 13-16R
Peterson, Ottis 1907- 21-24R
Peterson, Owen M. 1924- CANR-51
Earlier sketches in CA 108, CANR-26
Peterson, Paul E(lliott) 1940- CANR-24
Earlier sketch in CA 45-48
Peterson, Peter G. 1926- 151
Peterson, R(odney) D(elos) 1932- 41-44R
Peterson, Reona 1941- 73-76
Peterson, Richard A(ustin) 1932- 25-28R
Peterson, Richard F(rank) 1939- 128
Peterson, Richard H(ermann) 1942- 137
Peterson, Richard S(cot) 1938- 133
Peterson, Robert 1924- CANR-17
Earlier sketch in CA 25-28R
Peterson, Robert E(ugene) 1928- 13-16R
Peterson, Robert W. 1925- 33-36R
Peterson, Roger Tory 1908-1996 .... CANR-1
Obituary 152
Earlier sketch in CA 1-4R
Peterson, Russell Arthur 1922- 33-36R
Peterson, Simone
See Thomson, Daisy H(icks)
Peterson, Steven A. 1947- 138
Peterson, Susan (Annette) H(arnly) 1925- 57-60
Peterson, Ted Nicholas 1934- 121
Peterson, Theodore (Bernard) 1918-1997 ....9-12R
Obituary 160
Peterson, Trudy H(uskamp) 1945- 116
Peterson, V. Spike 1946- 144
Peterson, Virgil W(allace) 1904-1989 Obituary . 127
Peterson, Virgilia 1904-1966 Obituary 25-28R
Peterson, Wallace Carroll 1921- 5-8R
Peterson, Walter Scott 1944- 21-24R
Peterson, Wilferd Arlan 1900- CANR-6
Earlier sketch in CA 9-12R
Peterson, Willard James 1938- 103
Peterson, William R. 1943-1990 Obituary 132
Peterson, William S(amuel) 1939- CANR-11
Earlier sketch in CA 29-32R
Petersson, Robert T. 1918- 45-48
Peterzell, Jay 1952- 118
Petesch, Natalie L(evin) M(aines) 1924- . CANR-21
Earlier sketches in CA 57-60, CANR-6
See also CAAS 12
Petgen, Dorothea 1903(?)-1985 Obituary 115
Petgen, Dorothy
See Petgen, Dorothea
Pethybridge, Roger 1934- 5-8R
Petie, Haris
See Petty, Roberta
See also SATA 10
Petievich, Gerald 1944- CANR-62
Earlier sketch in CA 105
Petiot, Henri Jules Charles
1901-1965 Obituary 114
Petit, Gaston 1930- 73-76
Petit, Susan 1945- 142
Petitclair, Pierre 1813-1860 ....DLB 99
Petitclerc, Denne Bart 1929- 93-96
Petite, Irving (Laurence) 1920- Brief entry 113
Petitfils, Pierre (Robert) 1908- 137
Petkas, Peter (James) 1945- 37-40R
Petkovsek, Marko 1955- 165
Petmecky, Ben (Joe) 1922- 1-4R
Peto
See White, Stanley
Peto, James
See White, Stanley
Petrakis, Harry Mark 1923- CANR-30
Earlier sketches in CA 9-12R, CANR-4
See also CLC 3
Petranek, Stephen Lynn 1944- 133
Petrarch 1304-1374 ....DAM POET
See also PC 8
Petras, James Frank 1937- CANR-47
Earlier sketches in CA 61-64, CANR-7, 22
Petras, John W. 1940- 29-32R
Petrement, Simone 1907- 77-80
Petres, Robert E(van) 1939- 104
Petric, Vlada
See Petric, Vladimir
Petric, Vladimir 1928- 129
Petrich, Patricia Barrett 1942- 61-64
Petrides, Avra 123
Petrides, George Athan 1916- Brief entry 106
Petrides, Heidrun 1944- ....SATA 19
Petrie, Alexander 1881- CAP-1
Earlier sketch in CA 13-16
Petrie, Asenath 1914- 21-24R
Petrie, Catherine 1947- 109
See also SATA 52
See also SATA-Brief 41
Petrie, Charles (Alexander) 1895-1977 .... CANR-8
Obituary 89-92
Earlier sketch in CA 17-20R
Petrie, Duncan 1963- 164
Petrie, Mildred McClary 1912- 21-24R
Petrie, Paul J(ames) 1928- CANR-18
Earlier sketches in CA 9-12R, CANR-3
Petrie, Rhona
See Buchanan, Marie
Petrie, Sidney 1923- 21-24R
Petrinovich, Lewis 1930- 41-44R
Petro, Nicolai N. 1958- 135
Petro, Peter 1946- 144
Petro, Sylvester 1917- 1-4R
Petrocelli, Orlando R(alph) 1930- CANR-1
Earlier sketch in CA 45-48
Petrone, Jane Muir 1929- 5-8R
Petroni, Frank A. 1936- 85-88
Petropoulos, Jonathan G. 1961- 153
Petropulos, John A(nthony) 1929- 25-28R
Petroski, Catherine (Ann Groom) 1939- .. CANR-22
Earlier sketch in CA 106
See also SATA 48
Petrou, David Michael 1949- 73-76
Petrov, Aleksander 1938- .... DLB 181
Petrov, Evgeny
See Kataev, Evgeny Petrovich
See also TCLC 21
Petrov, Fyodor 1877(?)-1973 Obituary 41-44R
Petrov, Gavriil 1730-1801 .... DLB 150
Petrov, Michel
See Visson, Lynn
Petrov, Valeri 1920- .... DLB 181
Petrov, Vasilii Petrovich 1736-1799 .... DLB 150
Petrov, Victor P. 1907- CANR-51
Earlier sketches in CA 21-24R, CANR-10, 26
Petrov, Vladimir 1915- 21-24R
Petrova, Olga 1884(?)-1977 Obituary 73-76
Petrovic, Rastko 1898-1949 .... DLB 147
Petrovich, Michael B(oro) 1922- 108
See also SATA 40
Petrovska, Marija 1926- 107
Petrovskaya, Kyra
See Wayne, Kyra Petrovskaya
Petrovsky, Boris
See Beauchamp, Kathleen Mansfield
Petrovsky, N.
See Poltoratzky, N(ikolai) P(etrovich)
Petrucci, Armando 1932- 159
Petrucci, Kenneth R(occo) 1947- 57-60
Petruccio, Steven James 1961- ....SATA 67
Petry, Alice Hall 1951- 130
Petry, Ann (Lane) 1908-1997 .... CANR-46
Obituary 157
Earlier sketches in CA 5-8R, CANR-4
See also CAAS 6
See also BW 1
See also CLC 1, 7, 18
See also CLR 12
See also DLB 76
See also JRDA
See also MAICYA
See also MTCW 1
See also SATA 5
See also SATA-Obit 94
Petry, Carl Forbes 1943- 106
Petry, R(ay) C. 1903- 5-8R
Pettas, Mary 1918- 25-28R
Pettee, George S(awyer)
1904(?)-1989 Obituary 130
Petterson, Henry William 1922- 9-12R
Petterson, Steve D. 1948- 138
Petterssen, Sverre 1898-1974 Obituary 53-56
Pettersson, Karl-Henrik 1937- 65-68
Pettes, Dorothy E. CANR-12
Earlier sketch in CA 25-28R
Pettifer, James 1949- 146
Pettifer, Julian 1935- 136
Pettigrew, Thomas Fraser 1931- CANR-30
Earlier sketches in CA 33-36R, CANR-13
Pettingill, Amos
See Harris, William Bliss
Pettingill, Olin Sewall, Jr. 1907- CANR-1
Earlier sketch in CA 45-48
Pettit, Arthur G. 1938-1977 53-56
Obituary 135
Pettit, Clyde Edwin 1932- 65-68
Pettit, Henry (Jewett) 1906- 1-4R
Pettit, Lawrence K. 1937- 33-36R
Pettit, Michael (Edwin) 1950- 114
Pettit, Norman 1929- 17-20R
Pettit, Philip 1945- CANR-37
Earlier sketches in CA 97-100, CANR-17
Pettitt, George A(lbert) 1901-1976 .... CAP-2
Earlier sketch in CA 29-32
Pettoello, Decio (Egberto Saadi)
1886-1984 Obituary 113
Petty, Anne C(otton) 1945- 115
Petty, Mary 1899-1976 Obituary 65-68
Petty, Norman 1927(?)-1984 Obituary 113
Petty, Roberta 1915- CANR-10
Earlier sketch in CA 61-64
See also Petie, Haris
Petty, Walter T. 1918- CANR-9
Earlier sketch in CA 21-24R
Petty, William Henry 1921- 65-68
Petuchowski, Jakob Josef 1925-1991 ... CANR-18
Obituary 136
Earlier sketches in CA 1-4R, CANR-3
Petulla, Joseph M. 1932- CANR-9
Earlier sketch in CA 21-24R
Petzinger, Thomas, Jr. 1955- 136
Petzold, Paul 1940- CANR-9
Earlier sketch in CA 61-64
Petzoldt, Paul Kiesow 1908- 57-60
Petzoldt, Richard 1907-1974 Obituary 111
Peukert, Detlev
See Peukert, Detlev J(ulio) K.
Peukert, Detlev J(ulio) K. 1950- 133
Pevsner, Nikolaus (Bernhard Leon) 1902-1983 ....
CANR-64
Obituary 110
Earlier sketches in CA 9-12R, CANR-7
See also MTCW 1
Pevsner, Stella CANR-27
Earlier sketch in CA 57-60
See also AAYA 15
See also JRDA
See also SAAS 14
See also SATA 8, 77
Peychinovich
See Vazov, Ivan (Minchov)
Peyer, Bernd C. 1946- 166
Peyo
See Culliford, Pierre
Peyre, Henri (Maurice) 1901-1988 .... CANR-3
Obituary 127
Earlier sketch in CA 5-8R
Peyrefitte, Alain Antoine 1925- 85-88
Peyrefitte, (Pierre) Roger 1907- CANR-47
Earlier sketch in CA 65-68
Peyser, Joan 1931- Brief entry 112
Peyton, A(nthony) J(oseph) 1962- 147
Peyton, K. M.
See Peyton, Kathleen Wendy
See also AAYA 20
See also CLR 3
See also DLB 161
See also SAAS 17
Peyton, Karen (Hansen) 1897-196(?) CAP-1
Earlier sketch in CA 9-10
Peyton, Kathleen Wendy 1929- CANR-69
Earlier sketches in CA 69-72, CANR-32
See also Peyton, K. M.
See also JRDA
See also MAICYA
See also SATA 15, 62
Peyton, Myron A(lvin) 1909- Brief entry 114
Peyton, Patrick J(oseph) 1909-1992 .... CAP-2
Obituary 137
Earlier sketch in CA 23-24
Pezzullo, Ralph 1951- 135
Pezzulo, Ted 1936(?)-1979 Obituary 89-92
Pezzuti, Thomas Alexander 1936- 61-64
Pfadt, Robert Edward 1915- 73-76
Pfaff, Daniel W. 1940- 136
Pfaff, Richard W(illiam) 1936- CANR-61
Earlier sketch in CA 128
Pfaff, William (Wendle III) 1928- CANR-49
Earlier sketches in CA 5-8R, CANR-24
Pfaffe Konrad fl. c. 1172- ....DLB 148
Pfaffe Lamprecht fl. c. 1150- ....DLB 148
Pfaffenberger, Bryan 1949- 118
Pfaffenberger, Clarence J. 1889-1967 .... CAP-1
Earlier sketch in CA 13-14
Pfahl, John K(erch) 1927- CANR-1
Earlier sketch in CA 1-4R
Pfaltz, Marilyn 1933- 103
Pfaltzgraff, Robert L., Jr. 1934- CANR-24
Earlier sketches in CA 21-24R, CANR-9
Pfanner, Helmut Franz 1933- 57-60
Pfanner, (Anne) Louise 1955- 136
See also SATA 68
Pfanz, Harry W. 1921- CANR-60
Earlier sketch in CA 128
Pfarrer, Donald 1934- 111
Pfatteicher, Philip H(enry) 1935- 114
Pfau, Hugo 1908- 29-32R
Pfau, Richard Anthony 1942- 120
Pfeffer, J(ay) Alan 1907- CANR-3
Earlier sketch in CA 1-4R
Pfeffer, Jeffrey 1946- 109
Pfeffer, Leo 1910- CANR-22
Earlier sketches in CA 13-16R, CANR-7
Pfeffer, Rose 1908-1985 Obituary 115
Pfeffer, Susan Beth 1948- CANR-58
Earlier sketches in CA 29-32R, CANR-31
See also AAYA 12
See also CLR 11
See also JRDA
See also SAAS 17
See also SATA 4, 83
Pfeffer, Wendy 1929- 146
See also SATA 78
Pfefferle, Seth 1955- 128
Pfeffermann, Guy 1941- 25-28R
Pfeifer, Carl J(ames) 1929- 49-52

Pfeifer, Luanne 1928- CANR-16
Earlier sketch in CA 89-92
Pfeiffer, Bruce Brooks 1930- CANR-46
Earlier sketch in CA 121
Pfeiffer, C(urtis) Boyd 1937- 57-60
Pfeiffer, Carl Curt 1908- 101
Pfeiffer, Charles F. 1919-1976 CANR-4
Obituary 65-68
Earlier sketch in CA 1-4R
Pfeiffer, Emily 1827-1890 DLB 199
Pfeiffer, Eric 1935- CANR-10
Earlier sketch in CA 13-16R
Pfeiffer, Janet (B.) 1949- 161
See also SATA 96
Pfeiffer, John E(dward) 1914- 101
Pfeiffer, Karl G(raham) 1-4R
Pfeiffer, Marcella
See Syracuse, Marcella Pfeiffer
Pfeil, (John) Fred(erick) 1949- 133
Pfeilschifter, Boniface 1900- CAP-2
Earlier sketch in CA 19-20
Pferd, William (III) 1922(?)-1987 Obituary 121
Pfiffner, John M(cDonald) 1893- 5-8R
Pfingston, Roger 1940- CANR-20
Earlier sketch in CA 104
Pfister, Arthur 1949- 45-48
Pfister, Marcus CLR 42
See also SATA 83
Pfister, Patrick 1949- 153
Pflanze, Otto (Paul) 1918- 5-8R
Pflaum, Irving Peter 1906-1985 13-16R
Obituary 115
Pflaum, Melanie L(oewenthal) 1909- CANR-6
Earlier sketch in CA 13-16R
Pflaum, Susanna Whitney 1937- 110
Brief entry 106
Pflaum-Connor, Susanna
See Pflaum, Susanna Whitney
Pflieger, Elmer F. 1908- 17-20R
Pflieger, Pat 1955- 150
See also SATA 84
Pflum, John (Edward) 1934- Brief entry 107
Pfordresher, John 1943- 65-68
Pforzheimer, Carl H. 1879-1957 DLB 140
Pfouts, Ralph W(illiam) 1920- 41-44R
Pfoutz, Shirley Eclov 1922- 1-4R
Pfriem, John E. 1923(?)-1983 Obituary 110
Pfuetze, Paul E(ugene) 1904-1985 1-4R
Obituary 118
Phaer, Thomas 1510(?)-1560 DLB 167
Phair, Judith Turner 1946- 61-64
Phalle, Thibaut de Saint
See de Saint Phalle, Thibaut
Phan, Peter C(ho) 1943- 114
Phares, Donald 1942- 81-84
Phares, Ross (Oscar) 1908- CAP-1
Earlier sketch in CA 11-12
Phares, Timothy B. 1954- 97-100
Pharr, Emory Charles 1896(?)-1981 Obituary 104
Pharr, Robert Deane 1916-1992 CANR-27
Obituary 137
Earlier sketch in CA 49-52
See also BW 1
See also DLB 33
Pharr, Susan J(ane) 1944- 105
Phathanothai, Sirin 1947- 147
Phelan, Anna Hamilton 165
Phelan, Francis (Joseph) 1925- CANR-36
Earlier sketch in CA 5-8R
Phelan, James 1912-1997 144
Obituary 161
Phelan, James Pius X 1951- CANR-35
Earlier sketch in CA 114
Phelan, John Leddy 1924-1976 CANR-12
Earlier sketch in CA 21-24R
Phelan, John Martin 1932- 73-76
Phelan, Josephine 1905- SATA-Brief 30
Phelan, Mary Kay 1914- CANR-4
Earlier sketch in CA 1-4R
See also SATA 3
Phelan, Mary Michenfelder 1936- 97-100
Phelan, Nancy 1913- 101
Phelan, Shane 1956- 137
Phelan, Terry Wolfe 1941- 97-100
See also SATA 56
Phelan, Tom 1940- 161
Phelge, Nanker
See Richards, Keith
Phelps, Arthur Warren 1909- 49-52
Phelps, Ashton 1913-1983 Obituary 109
Phelps, Barry 1941- 140
Phelps, D(udley) Maynard 1897- CAP-2
Earlier sketch in CA 25-28
Phelps, Digger
See Phelps, Richard
Phelps, Donald (Norman) 1929- CANR-25
Earlier sketch in CA 45-48
Phelps, Edmund S. 1933- 166
Phelps, Elizabeth Stuart 1815-1852 DLB 202
Phelps, Elizabeth Stuart 1844-1911 DLB 74
Phelps, Ethel Johnston 1914- 106
See also SATA 35
Phelps, Frederic
See McCulley, Johnston
Phelps, Gilbert (Henry, Jr.) 1915-1993 CANR-47
Obituary 141
Earlier sketches in CA 5-8R, CANR-7, 26
Phelps, Humphrey 1927- 111
Phelps, J(oseph) Alfred 1927- 135
Phelps, Jack 1926- 29-32R
Phelps, O(rme) Wheelock 1906- 1-4R
Phelps, Phelps 1897-1981 Obituary 104
Phelps, Richard 103
Phelps, Robert 1922-1989 CANR-19
Obituary 129
Earlier sketch in CA 17-20R
Phelps, Roger P(aul) 1920- 49-52
Phelps, Thomas Ross 1929- 61-64
Phenix, Philip Henry 1915- 5-8R
Pheto, Molefe 1935- 118
Phialas, Peter George 1914- 25-28R
Phibbs, Brendan (Pearse) 1916- 33-36R
Phifer, Kenneth G. 1915- 17-20R
Philbrick, Allen Kellogg 1914- 117
Philbrick, Charles (Horace) II 1922-1971 CANR-4
Earlier sketch in CA 1-4R
Philbrick, Helen L. 1910- 103
Philbrick, Joseph Lawrence 1927- 45-48
Philbrook, Clem(ent E.) 1917- 104
See also SATA 24
Philby, H. St. John B. 1885-1960 DLB 195
Philby, Harold Adrian Russell
1912-1988 Obituary 125
Philby, Kim
See Philby, Harold Adrian Russell
Philip, Cynthia Owen 1928- 49-52
Philip, George 1951- 156
Philip, J(ames) A(llenby) 1901- CAP-2
Earlier sketch in CA 23-24
Philip, John Robert 1927- 108
Philip, Leila 1961- 137
Philip, Lotte Brand
See Foerster, Lotte B(rand)
Philip, M(arlene) Nourbese 1947- 163
See also DLB 157
Philipp, Elliot Elias 1915- CANR-3
Earlier sketch in CA 9-12R
Philippatos, George Crito 1938- Brief entry 106
Philippe, Charles-Louis 1874-1909 DLB 65
Philippe-Auguste, Jean-Marie Mathias
1838-1889 DLB 192
Philippi, Donald L. 1930- 108
Philips, Cyril Henry 1912- 103
Philips, G(eorge) Edward 1926- 41-44R
Philips, J. Stanley
See Gibilisco, Stan
Philips, John 1676-1708 DLB 95
Philips, Judson (Pentecost) 1903-1989 CANR-72
Obituary 128
Earlier sketches in CA 89-92, CANR-14
Interview in CANR-14
See also AITN 1
Philips, Katherine 1632-1664 DLB 131
Philips, Michael 1942- 125
Philips, Thomas
See Davies, L(eslie) P(urnell)
Philipsen, Dirk 1959- 139
Philipson, Morris H. 1926- CANR-4
Earlier sketch in CA 1-4R
See also CLC 53
Philipson, Susan Sacher 1934-1994 9-12R
Obituary 146
Philliber, William W(esley) 1943- 111
Phillifent, John Thomas 1916-1976 Obituary 102
Phillippi, Wendell Crane 1918- 136
Phillipps, Sir Thomas 1792-1872 DLB 184
Phillips, Aileen Paul
See Paul, Aileen
Phillips, Alan
See Stauderman, Albert P(hilip)
Phillips, Alan Meyrick Kerr 1916- 5-8R
Phillips, Alice H(erz) 1909- 114
Phillips, Allen
See Allen, (Evelyn) Elizabeth
Phillips, Almarin 1925- CANR-1
Earlier sketch in CA 1-4R
Phillips, Anne G(arvey) 1929- 73-76
Phillips, (Elizabeth Margaret Ann) Barty 1933- CANR-24
Earlier sketches in CA 61-64, CANR-8
Phillips, Beeman N(oal) 1927- 122
Phillips, Bernard S. 1931- CANR-12
Earlier sketch in CA 25-28R
Phillips, Bernice Maxine 1925- 45-48
Phillips, Betty Lou
See Phillips, Elizabeth Louise
Phillips, Billie M(cKindra) 1925- 102
Phillips, Bluebell
See Phillips, Bluebell Stewart
Phillips, Bluebell S.
See Phillips, Bluebell Stewart
Phillips, Bluebell Stewart 1904- 131
Phillips, Bob 1940- CANR-68
Earlier sketch in CA 69-72
See also SATA 95
Phillips, C(ecil) E(rnest) Lucas
See Lucas Phillips, C(ecil) E(rnest)
Phillips, Cabell (Beverly Hatchett)
1904-1975 97-100
Obituary 61-64
Phillips, Carla Rahn 1943- CANR-60
Earlier sketch in CA 128
Phillips, Carole 1938- 108
Phillips, Caryl 1958- CANR-63
Earlier sketch in CA 141
See also BLCS
See also BW 2
See also CLC 96
See also DAM MULT
See also DLB 157
Phillips, Cecil R(andolph) 1933- 13-16R
Phillips, Celeste R(ose Nagel) 1933- 110
Phillips, Charles F(ranklin), Jr. 1934- CANR-2
Earlier sketch in CA 5-8R
Phillips, Charles F(ranklin, Jr.) 1910-1998 85-88
Obituary 167
Phillips, Claude S., Jr. 1923- 9-12R
Phillips, Clifton J(ackson) 1919- 37-40R
Phillips, (Preswly) Craig 1922- 9-12R
Phillips, D(ennis) J(ohn Andrew) 1924- CANR-60
Earlier sketches in CA 13-16R, CANR-10
Phillips, David Atlee 1922-1988 CANR-12
Obituary 126
Earlier sketch in CA 69-72
Phillips, David Graham 1867-1911 Brief entry 108
See also DLB 9, 12
See also TCLC 44
Phillips, Debora R(othman) 1939- 93-96
Phillips, Dennis
See Phillips, D(ennis) J(ohn Andrew)
Phillips, Dennis 1951- 141
Phillips, Derek L(ee) 1934- CANR-18
Earlier sketch in CA 33-36R
Phillips, Dewi Zephaniah 1934- CANR-51
Earlier sketches in CA 17-20R, CANR-9, 25
Phillips, Dorothy
See Garlock, Dorothy
Phillips, Dorothy S(anborn)
1893-1972 Obituary 37-40R
Phillips, Dorothy W. 1906-1977 Obituary 73-76
Phillips, E(lmo) Bryant 1905-1975 CANR-6
Earlier sketch in CA 5-8R
Phillips, E(wing) Lakin 1915-1994 37-40R
Obituary 144
Phillips, E(ugene) Lee 1941- CANR-40
Earlier sketch in CA 115
Phillips, Edward O. 1931- 124
Phillips, Edwin A(llen) 1915- 53-56
Phillips, Elizabeth C(row) 1906- 41-44R
Phillips, Elizabeth Louise SATA 48, 58
Phillips, Emma Julia 1900- CAP-1
Earlier sketch in CA 13-14
Phillips, Frances Lucas 1896-1986 Obituary 119
Phillips, Frank
See Nowlan, Philip Francis
Phillips, Gary 1955- 161
Phillips, Gene D(aniel) 1935- CANR-38
Earlier sketches in CA 45-48, CANR-1, 17
Phillips, George H(oward) 1907- 112
Phillips, Gerald M. 1928- CANR-29
Earlier sketches in CA 33-36R, CANR-13
Phillips, Gordon Lewis 1911-1982 Obituary 108
Phillips, Herbert P. 1929- 13-16R
Phillips, Hiram Stone 1912(?)-1979 85-88
Phillips, Hugh D. 1952- 139
Phillips, Irv(ing W.) 1905- CANR-31
Earlier sketch in CA 65-68
See also SATA 11
Phillips, J(ohn) B(ertram) 1906-1982 106
Obituary 108
Phillips, Jack
See Sandburg, Carl (August)
Phillips, James E(merson, Jr.)
1912-1979 Obituary 89-92
Phillips, James Emerson, Jr. 1912-1979 101
Phillips, James M(cJunkin) 1929- 106
Phillips, James W. 1922- 33-36R
Phillips, Jayne Anne 1952- CANR-50
Earlier sketches in CA 101, CANR-24
Interview in CANR-24
See also CLC 15, 33
See also DLBY 80
See also MTCW 1
See also SSC 16
Phillips, Jerome C.
See Cleveland, Philip Jerome
Phillips, Jewell Cass 1900- CAP-2
Earlier sketch in CA 33-36
Phillips, Jill (Meta) 1952- CANR-39
Earlier sketches in CA 65-68, CANR-14
Phillips, Johanna
See Garlock, Dorothy
Phillips, John 1914-1996 147
Obituary 153
Phillips, John A(llen) 1949- 133
Phillips, John L(awrence), Jr. 1923- 33-36R
Phillips, Josephine E(lvira Frye) 1896-1975 5-8R
Obituary 61-64
Phillips, Julia (Miller) 1944- 140
Phillips, Julien L(ind) 1945- 77-80
Phillips, Kate 1966- 157
Phillips, Kathleen C(oleman) 1920- CANR-39
Earlier sketch in CA 116
Phillips, Keith W(endall) 1946- 102
Phillips, Kenneth J. H. 1946- 143
Phillips, Kevin (Price) 1940- CANR-40
Earlier sketch in CA 65-68
Phillips, Klaus (Peter) 1947- 116
Phillips, L(ouis) C(hristopher) 1939- 57-60
Phillips, Laughlin 1924- 102
Phillips, Leon
See Gerson, Noel Bertram
Phillips, Leona Rasmussen 1925- CANR-14
Earlier sketch in CA 65-68
Phillips, Lisa 1956- 139
Phillips, Lois (Elisabeth) 1926- Brief entry 114
Phillips, Loretta (Hosey) 1893- CAP-1
Earlier sketch in CA 13-16
See also SATA 10
Phillips, Louis 1942- CANR-20
Earlier sketches in CA 49-52, CANR-3
See also SATA 8, 102
Phillips, Mac
See Phillips, Maurice J(ack)
Phillips, Margaret 1892(?)-1985 Obituary 116
Phillips, Margaret Mann 1906-1987 13-16R
Obituary 123
Phillips, Margaret McDonald
1910(?)-1978 Obituary 77-80
Phillips, Marjorie (Fell) 5-8R
Phillips, Mark
See Garrett, (Gordon) Randall (Phillip)
and Janifer, Laurence M(ark)
Phillips, Mary Geisler 1881-1964 5-8R
See also SATA 10
Phillips, Mary L. 1930- 116
Phillips, Maurice J(ack) 1914-1976 5-8R
Obituary 103
Phillips, Melicia 1960- 149
Phillips, Michael
See Nolan, William F(rancis)
Phillips, Michael 1938- 108
Phillips, Michael Joseph 1937- CANR-18
Earlier sketches in CA 49-52, CANR-3
Phillips, Michael R(ay) 1946- 114
See also Phillips, Mike
Phillips, (Holly) Michelle 1944- 137
Phillips, Mickey
See Phillips, Alan Meyrick Kerr
Phillips, Mike 147
See also Phillips, Michael R(ay)
Phillips, O(wen) Hood 1907- CANR-2
Earlier sketch in CA 5-8R
Phillips, O(wen) M(artin) 1930- 89-92
Phillips, Osborne
See Barcynski, Leon Roger
Phillips, Patricia 1935- 103
Phillips, Paul 1938- CANR-14
Earlier sketch in CA 73-76
Phillips, Paul T(homas) 1942- 138
Phillips, Pauline (Esther Friedman) 1918- CANR-19
Earlier sketch in CA 1-4R
Phillips, Prentice 1894- CAP-1
Earlier sketch in CA 13-16
See also SATA 10
Phillips, R. Hart
See Phillips, Ruby Hart
Phillips, Rachel 1934- 49-52
Phillips, Ray C. 1922- CANR-10
Earlier sketch in CA 25-28R
Phillips, Richard
See Dick, Philip K(indred)
Phillips, Richard C(laybourne) 1934- 65-68
Phillips, Robert (Schaeffer) 1938- CANR-8
Earlier sketch in CA 17-20R
See also CAAS 13
See also CLC 28
See also DLB 105
Phillips, Robert L(eRoy), Jr. 1940- 77-80
Phillips, Roderick (Goler) 1947- 131
Phillips, Ruby Hart 1902-1985 Obituary 117
Phillips, Samantha
See Gelles-Cole, Sandi
Phillips, Sky 1921- 140
Phillips, Stella 1927- CANR-11
Earlier sketch in CA 21-24R
Phillips, Stephen 1864-1915 Brief entry 111
See also DLB 10
Phillips, Stephen H. 1950- 160
Phillips, Steve
See Whittington, Harry (Benjamin)
Phillips, Steven 1947- 103
Phillips, Susan Elizabeth 142
Phillips, Susan S. 1954- 154
Phillips, Tom
See Drotning, Phillip T(homas)
Phillips, Tom 1937- 128
Phillips, Ulrich B. 1877-1934 DLB 17
Phillips, Velma 1894- CAP-2
Earlier sketch in CA 19-20
Phillips, Vic 1941- 128
Phillips, Ward
See Lovecraft, H(oward) P(hillips)
Phillips, Warren (Henry) 1926- 107
Interview in 107
Phillips, Wendell 1921-1975 CAP-2
Obituary 61-64
Earlier sketch in CA 23-24
Phillips, Willard 1784-1873 DLB 59
Phillips, William 1907- CANR-35
Earlier sketch in CA 29-32R
See also DLB 137
Phillips, William G. 1924(?)-1990 Obituary 130
Phillips-Birt, Douglas Hextall Chedzey 1920-1977 CANR-1
Earlier sketch in CA 1-4R
Phillips-Jones, Linda 1943- CANR-26
Earlier sketch in CA 109
Phillipson, David 1930- 57-60
Phillipson, David W(alter) 1942- 107
Phillipson, Michael 1940- 133
Phillpotts, (Mary) Adelaide Eden 1896-1993 CANR-37
Earlier sketch in CA 115
See also DLB 191
Phillpotts, Eden 1862-1960 102
Obituary 93-96
See also DLB 10, 70, 135, 153
See also SATA 24
Philmus, Robert M. 1943- 33-36R
Philo c. 20B.C.-c. 50 DLB 176
Philomythes
See Dewart, Leslie
Philp, Howard Littleton 1902- 5-8R
Philp, Kenneth R(oy) 1941- 65-68
Philp, (Dennis Alfred) Peter 1920- 5-8R
Philp, Richard B(lain) 1934- 154
Philp, Richard Nilson 1943- CANR-11
Earlier sketch in CA 69-72
Philpott, David G(oodwin) 1927- 123
Philpott, Kent 1942- 61-64
Phin
See Thayer, Ernest Lawrence
Phipps, Christine 1945- 123
Phipps, Frances (Lucille Walker)
1924(?)-1986 Obituary 119
Phipps, Grace May Palk 1901- CANR-4
Earlier sketch in CA 9-12R
Phipps, Joe (Kenneth) 1921- 139
Phipps, Joyce 1942- 49-52
Phipps, Nicholas 1913-1980 Obituary 97-100

Phipps, William E(ugene) 1930- CANR-30
Earlier sketches in CA 29-32R, CANR-12
Phipson, Joan
See Fitzhardinge, Joan Margaret
See also AAYA 14
See also CLR 5
See also SAAS 3
Phiz
See Browne, Hablot Knight
Phleger, Fred B. 1909- CANR-21
Earlier sketch in CA 1-4R
See also SATA 34
Phleger, Marjorie Temple 1908(?)-1986 ..... 9-12R
Obituary 118
See also SATA 1
See also SATA-Obit 47
Phoenix, John
See Derby, George Horatio
Phoenix, Pat
See Pilkington, Pat
Phypers, David (John) 1939- 114
Physick, John Frederick 1923- 114
Phythian, B(rian) A(rthur) 1932- CANR-10
Earlier sketch in CA 21-24R
Piaf, Edith 1915-1963 Obituary 113
Piaget, Jean 1896-1980 ..... CANR-31
Obituary 101
Earlier sketch in CA 21-24R
See also MTCW 1
See also SATA-Obit 23
Pian, Rulan Chao 1922- 21-24R
Piano, Celeste
See Lykiard, Alexis (Constantine)
Piasecki, Bruce 1955- CANR-12
Earlier sketch in CA 69-72
Piatigorsky, Alexander 1929- 124
Piatigorsky, Gregor 1903-1976 Obituary 69-72
Piatt, Bill
See Piatt, Robert William, Jr.
Piatt, Robert William, Jr. 1950- 146
Piatti, Celestino 1922- 73-76
See also SATA 16
Piazza, Ben 1934- 9-12R
Piazza, Tom 1955- 155
Picano, Felice 1944- CANR-52
Earlier sketches in CA 69-72, CANR-11, 27
See also CAAS 13
See also DAM POP
Picard, Barbara Leonie 1917- CANR-58
Earlier sketches in CA 5-8R, CANR-2
See also MAICYA
See also SAAS 10
See also SATA 2, 89
Picard, Elizabeth 1944- 158
Picard, Robert G(eorge) 1951- 127
Picasso, Pablo (Ruiz) 1881-1973 97-100
Obituary 41-44R
See also AAYA 10
Picazo, Jose 1910- CAP-1
Earlier sketch in CA 13-14
Piccard, Auguste 1884-1962 157
Obituary 113
Piccard, Betty
See Piccard, Elizabeth J(ane)
Piccard, Elizabeth J(ane) 1925- 65-68
Piccard, Jacques 1922- 65-68
Piccard, Joan Russell 29-32R
Picchio, Riccardo 1923- CANR-24
Earlier sketch in CA 45-48
Piccolo, Lucio 1901-1969 97-100
See also CLC 13
See also DLB 114
Pichaske, David Richard 1943- CANR-1
Earlier sketch in CA 45-48
Pichois, Claude 1925- 132
Pick, Hella 160
Pick, J(ohn) B(arclay) 1921- CANR-5
Earlier sketch in CA 1-4R
Pick, John 1911- CAP-2
Earlier sketch in CA 33-36
Pick, (Frederick) Michael 1949- 123
Pick, Robert 1898-1978 ..... CANR-8
Obituary 77-80
Earlier sketch in CA 17-20R
Pickard, Charles 1932- ..... SATA 36
Pickard, Dorothea Wilgus 1902- 21-24R
Pickard, John Benedict 1928- 1-4R
Pickard, Nancy 1945- 153
Pickard, Tom 1946- CANR-44
Earlier sketch in CA 81-84
See also DLB 40
Pickell, Charles N(orman) 1927- 17-20R
Pickem, Peter
See Stearns, Harold Edmund
Picken, Mary Brooks 1886(?)-1981 Obituary 103
Picken, Stuart D(onald) B(lair) 1942- 106
Pickens, Donald Kenneth 1934- 53-56
Pickens, Robert S. 1900(?)-1978 Obituary 81-84
Pickens, Roy 1939- 57-60
Pickens, T. Boone, Jr. 1928- 147
Picker, Fred 1927- 81-84
Picker, Ingrid 1932- 25-28R
Picker, Martin 1929- CANR-7
Earlier sketch in CA 17-20R
Pickerell, Albert G(eorge) 1912- 25-28R
Pickerill, Don 1928- 77-80
Pickering, David (Hugh) 1958- 139
Pickering, Ernest 1893(?)-1974 Obituary 53-56
Pickering, Frederick Pickering 1909- 105
Pickering, George (White) 1904-1980 73-76
Obituary 105
Pickering, George W. 1937- 136
Pickering, James H(enry) 1937- CANR-53
Earlier sketches in CA 33-36R, CANR-13, 29
Pickering, James Sayre 1897-1969 ..... CANR-16
Obituary 103
Earlier sketch in CA 1-4R
See also SATA 36
See also SATA-Obit 28
Pickering, Jerry V(ane) 1931- 57-60
Pickering, Paul 1952- 138
Pickering, Percival
See Stirling, Anna Maria Diana Wilhelmina (Pickering)
Pickering, R(obert) E(aston) 1934- 21-24R
Pickering, Robert B. 1950- 158
See also SATA 93
Pickering, Samuel Francis, Jr. 1941- 104
Pickering, Stephen 1947- 57-60
Pickersgill, J(ohn) W(hitney) 1905- 45-48
Pickett, Calder M. 1921- 53-56
Pickett, Carla 1944- 37-40R
Pickett, J(arrell) Waskom 1890- CAP-1
Earlier sketch in CA 13-16
Pickett, Robert S. 1931- 33-36R
Pickford, Cedric Edward 1926-1983 107
Obituary 109
Pickford, Mary 1893-1979 Obituary 85-88
Pickle, Hal B(rittain) 1929- CANR-21
Earlier sketches in CA 57-60, CANR-6
Pickles, (Maud) Dorothy 1903- 77-80
Pickles, M(abel) Elizabeth 1902- CAP-1
Earlier sketch in CA 9-10
Pickles, Wilfred 1904-1978(?) 108
Pickoff, David 1930(?)-1986 Obituary 118
Pickover, Clifford A. 1957- 141
Pickrel, Paul (Murphy) 1917- 9-12R
Pickthall, Marjorie L(owry) C(hristie) 1883-1922 Brief entry 107
See also DLB 92
See also TCLC 21
Pickthorn, Helen 1927- 25-28R
Pico, Rafael 1912- 45-48
Picon, Molly 1898- 104
Picot, Derek 1952- 151
Picott, J(ohn) Rupert 1916(?)-1989 Obituary 129
Picou, Alphonse
See Ghnassia, Maurice (Jean-Henri)
Picoult, Jodi 1966- 138
Picton, Bernard
See Knight, Bernard
Pidal, Ramon Menendez
See Menendez Pidal, Ramon
Pidgeon, Mary E. 1890(?)-1979 Obituary 89-92
Piechocki, Joachim von Lang
See von Lang-Piechocki, Joachim
Piediscalzi, Nicholas 1931- 122
Brief entry 112
Pied Piper
See Mallalieu, John Percival William
Piehl, Mel (Willis) 1946- 111
Piehler, Paul 1929- Brief entry 111
Piekalkiewicz, Jaroslaw A. 1926- 81-84
Piel, Gerard 1915- 57-60
See also DLB 137
Pielmeier, John 1949- 132
Brief entry 125
Interview in 132
Pienkowski, Jan (Michal) 1936- CANR-38
Earlier sketches in CA 65-68, CANR-11
See also CLR 6
See also MAICYA
See also SATA 6, 58
Pieper, Josef 1904- CANR-44
Earlier sketch in CA 119
Piepkorn, Arthur Carl 1907-1973 ..... 41-44R
Pier, Arthur Stanhope 1874(?)-1966 Obituary 25-28R
Pierard, Richard Victor 1934- CANR-38
Earlier sketches in CA 29-32R, CANR-17
Pieratt, Asa B. 1938- 77-80
Pierce, Arthur 1959- 154
Pierce, Arthur Dudley 1897-1967 ..... 1-4R
Obituary 103
Pierce, Bessie Louise 1888-1974 Obituary 53-56
Pierce, David 1947- 141
Pierce, E(ugene) 1924- 13-16R
Pierce, Edith Gray 1893-1977 61-64
See also SATA 45
Pierce, Edward T. 1917(?)-1978 Obituary 77-80
Pierce, F(ranklin) David 1947- 153
Pierce, George Gilbert 1923- 5-8R
Pierce, Gerald S(wetnam) 1933- 45-48
Pierce, Glenn
See Dumke, Glenn S.
Pierce, James Smith 1930- 21-24R
Pierce, Janis V(aughn) 1934- 45-48
Pierce, Joe E. 1924- 33-36R
Pierce, John Leonard, Jr. 1921- 9-12R
Pierce, John Robinson 1910- 17-20R
Pierce, Katherine
See St. John, Wylly Folk
Pierce, Lawrence C(olman) 1936- 85-88
Pierce, Meredith Ann 1958- CANR-48
Earlier sketches in CA 108, CANR-26
See also AAYA 13
See also CLR 20
See also JRDA
See also MAICYA
See also SATA 67
See also SATA-Brief 48
Pierce, Michael D(ale) 1940- 142
Pierce, Milton Plotz 1933- 106
Pierce, Ovid Williams 1910- CANR-4
Earlier sketch in CA 1-4R
Pierce, Patricia (May) 1943- 120
Pierce, Patricia Jobe 1943- 148
Pierce, Paul 1910- 69-72
Pierce, Philip E(arly) 1912- 110
Pierce, Richard A(ustin) 1918- CANR-2
Earlier sketch in CA 5-8R
Pierce, Robert N(ash) 1931- 104
Pierce, Ronald K. 1944- 142
Pierce, Roy 1923- 37-40R
Pierce, Ruth (Ireland) 1936- 29-32R
See also SATA 5
Pierce, Tamora 1954- CANR-69
Earlier sketch in CA 118
See also AAYA 26
See also SATA 51, 96
See also SATA-Brief 49
Pierce, Willard Bob 1914- 13-16R
Piercy, Josephine Ketcham 1895- CAP-1
Earlier sketch in CA 13-16
Piercy, Marge 1936- CANR-66
Earlier sketches in CA 21-24R, CANR-13, 43
See also CAAS 1
See also CLC 3, 6, 14, 18, 27, 62
See also DLB 120
See also MTCW 1
Pierik, Robert 1921- 37-40R
See also SATA 13
Pierman, Carol J 1947- 77-80
Pierotti, John 1911-1987 133
Obituary 122
Pierpoint, Katherine 1961- 153
Pierpoint, Robert (Charles) 1925- 107
Interview in 107
Pierre, Andrew J. 1934- CANR-1
Earlier sketch in CA 45-48
Pierre, Clara 1939- 65-68
Pierre, Jose 1927- 143
Pierro, Albino 1916- ..... DLB 128
Pierrot, George Francis 1898-1980 ..... 5-8R
Obituary 103
See also AITN 2
Piers, Maria W(eigl) 1911-1997 ..... CANR-8
Obituary 158
Earlier sketch in CA 21-24R
Piers, Robert
See Anthony, Piers
Piersen, William D. 1942- CANR-53
Earlier sketch in CA 126
Pierson, Christopher 1956- 149
Pierson, Frank
See Pierson, Frank R(omer)
Pierson, Frank R(omer) 1925- 123
Brief entry 114
Interview in 123
Pierson, G(eorge) W(ilson) 1904-1993 ..... CANR-3
Obituary 143
Earlier sketch in CA 9-12R
Pierson, Howard 1922- 49-52
Pierson, Jan 1937- 112
Pierson, John H(erman) G(roesbeck) 1906- CANR-4
Earlier sketch in CA 9-12R
Pierson, Paul Everett 1927- 108
Pierson, Peter O'Malley 1932- 97-100
Pierson, Robert H. 1911- 21-24R
Pierson, Stanley 1925- 85-88
Pierson, William H(arvey), Jr. 1911- 122
Piet, John H(enry) 1914- 29-32R
Pietila, Nellie 1932- 156
Pietri, Arturo Uslar
See Uslar Pietri, Arturo
Pietri, Pedro (Juan) 1943- CANR-32
Earlier sketch in CA 97-100
See also HW
Pietrofesa, John J(oseph) 1940- 57-60
Pietropinto, Anthony 1938- 89-92
Pietrusza, David 1949- 135
Pietsch, Paul Andrew 1929- 104
Pietschmann, Richard John III 1940- 69-72
Pieyre de Mandiargues, Andre 1909-1991 ..... CANR-22
Obituary 136
Earlier sketch in CA 103
See also Mandiargues, Andre Pieyre de
Pifer, Alan J(ay Parrish) 1921- 127
Pifer, Ellen 1942- CANR-23
Earlier sketch in CA 106
Pig, Edward
See Gorey, Edward (St. John)
Pigg, Kenneth E. 1945- 139
Piggott, C. M.
See Guido, (Cecily) Margaret
Piggott, (Alan) Derek 1923- CANR-37
Earlier sketch in CA 115
Piggott, Stuart 1910- 134
Pigman, William Ward 1910-1977 Obituary 73-76
Pigney, Joseph Pape 1908- 1-4R
Pignotti, Lamberto 1926- ..... DLB 128
Pihera, Larry 1933- CANR-1
Earlier sketch in CA 45-48
Pihl, Marshall R(alph) 1933- 49-52
Piirto, Jane 1941- 144
Pijewski, John 1952- 111
Piji
See Williams, Ann, Jr.
Pike, Albert 1809-1891 ..... DLB 74
Pike, B(arry) A(ustin) 1935- 150
Pike, Bob
See Pike, Robert W(ilson)
Pike, Burton 1930- CANR-33
Earlier sketch in CA 1-4R
Pike, Charles R.
See Bulmer, (Henry) Kenneth and Harknett, Terry
Pike, Charles R.
See Wells, Angus
Pike, Christopher CANR-66
See also McFadden, Kevin Christopher
Pike, Dag 1933- 69-72
Pike, Deborah 1951- ..... SATA 89
Pike, Diane Kennedy 1938- 37-40R
Pike, Douglas Eugene 1924- 153
Pike, E(dgar) Royston 1896-1980 ..... 9-12R
Obituary 125
See also SATA 22
See also SATA-Obit 56
Pike, Eunice V(ictoria) 1913- CANR-20
Earlier sketch in CA 97-100
Pike, James A(lbert) 1913-1969 ..... CANR-4
Obituary 25-28R
Earlier sketch in CA 1-4R
Pike, Kenneth Lee 1912- CANR-46
Earlier sketch in CA 120
Pike, Margaret (Prudence) Lyford
See Lyford-Pike, Margaret (Prudence)
Pike, Nelson C. 1930- Brief entry 111
Pike, Norman 1901- CAP-2
Earlier sketch in CA 25-28
Pike, R. William 1956- 156
See also SATA 92
Pike, Robert E(vording) 1905-1997 ..... 5-8R
Obituary 160
Pike, Robert L.
See Fish, Robert L(loyd)
Pike, Robert W(ilson) 1931- ..... SATA 102
Pike, Ruth 1931- 134
Brief entry 112
Pike, William H. 1943- 115
Pike, Zebulon Montgomery 1779-1813 ..... DLB 183
Pikelny, Philip S. 1951- 107
Pikoulis, John 1941- 115
Pikunas, Justin 1920- 25-28R
Pilapil, Vicente R. 1941- 37-40R
Pilarski, Laura 1926- 29-32R
See also SATA 13
Pilat, O. R.
See Pilat, Oliver (Ramsay)
Pilat, Oliver (Ramsay) 1903-1987 ..... 5-8R
Obituary 123
Pilbrow, Richard (Hugh) 1933- 29-32R
Pilcer, Sonia 1949- CANR-13
Earlier sketch in CA 89-92
Interview in CANR-13
Pilch, John J(oseph) 1936- CANR-25
Earlier sketch in CA 108
Pilch, Judah 1902- CANR-6
Earlier sketch in CA 5-8R
Pilcher, George William 1935- 105
Pilcher, Rosamunde 1924- CANR-58
Earlier sketches in CA 57-60, CANR-27
Interview in CANR-27
See also BEST 89:1, 90:4
See also DAM POP
See also MTCW 1
Pilcher, William W. 1930- 45-48
Pilditch, James (George Christopher) 1929- 9-12R
Pile, John F(rederick) 1924- CANR-36
Earlier sketches in CA 93-96, CANR-16
Pileggi, Nicholas 1933- CANR-52
Earlier sketch in CA 124
Pilger, John Richard 1939- 141
Pilgrim, Anne
See Allan, Mabel Esther
Pilgrim, David
See Palmer, John (Leslie) and Saunders, Hilary Aidan St. George
Pilgrim, David 1950- 120
Pilgrim, Geneva Hanna 1914- 25-28R
Pilgrim, Walter E(dward) 1934- 113
Piliawsky, Monte 1944- 111
Pilinszky, Janos 1921-1981 142
Obituary 104
Pilio, Gerone
See Whitfield, John Humphreys
Pilipp, Frank 1961- 141
Pilisuk, Marc 1934- 29-32R
Pilk, Henry
See Campbell, Ken
Pilkey, Dav 1966- 136
See also CLR 48
See also SATA 68
Pilkey, Orrin H. 1934- CANR-40
Earlier sketch in CA 97-100
Pilkington, Betty 69-72
Pilkington, Cynthia
See Horne, Cynthia Miriam
Pilkington, E(dward) C(ecil) A(rnold) 1907- CAP-2
Earlier sketch in CA 25-28
Pilkington, Francis Meredyth 1907- CAP-2
Earlier sketch in CA 25-28
See also SATA 4
Pilkington, John, Jr. 1918- 17-20R
Pilkington, Pat 1923-1986 123
Obituary 120
Pilkington, Roger (Windle) 1915- CANR-5
Earlier sketch in CA 1-4R
See also SATA 10
Pilkington, Walter (?)-1983 Obituary 109
Pilkington, William T(homas, Jr.) 1939- CANR-8
Earlier sketch in CA 61-64
Pill, Erastes
See Madsen, (Mark) Hunter
Pill, Virginia 1922- 61-64
Pillai, Karnam Chengalvaroya 1901- 5-8R
Pillar, James Jerome 1928- 13-16R
Pillin, William 1910-1985 ..... 9-12R
Obituary 116
Pilling, Arnold R(emington) 1926- CANR-3
Earlier sketch in CA 1-4R
Pilling, Christopher Robert 1936- CANR-44
Earlier sketches in CA 101, CANR-19
Pilling, John 1946- 153
Pillinger, Douglass 1906(?)-1983 Obituary 111
Pillon, Nancy Bach 1917- 110

Pilnyak, Boris
See Vogau, Boris Andreyevich
See also TCLC 23
Pilo, Giuseppe Maria 1929- CANR-5
Earlier sketch in CA 9-12R
Pilon, Jean-Guy 1930- 161
See also DLB 60
Pilon, Juliana Geran 1947- 97-100
Pilou
See Bardot, Louis
Pilpel, Harriet F(leischl) CAP-2
Earlier sketch in CA 21-22
Pilpel, Robert H(arry) 1943- CANR-9
Earlier sketch in CA 65-68
Pimentel, David 1925- 167
Pimlott, Ben 1945- 144
Pimm, Stuart L(eonard) 1949- 142
Pimsleur, Meira Goldwater 1905(?)-1979 ... 13-16R
Obituary 89-92
Pimsleur, Paul 1927-1976 .... CAP-2
Obituary 65-68
Earlier sketch in CA 33-36
Pina, Laura (?)-1984 Obituary 113
Pina, Leslie A. 1947- 138
Pina-Cabral, Joao de 1954- 136
Pinar, William 1947- 57-60
Pinard, (J. L.-M.) Maurice 1929- 41-44R
Pinch, Richard G. E. 1954- 145
Pinch, Trevor (John) 1952- 147
Pincher, H(enry) Chapman 1914- CANR-34
Earlier sketches in CA 13-16R, CANR-12
Pincherle, Alberto 1907-1990 .... CANR-63
Obituary 132
Earlier sketches in CA 25-28R, CANR-33
See also Moravia, Alberto
See also CLC 11, 18
See also DAM NOV
See also MTCW 1
Pincherle, Marc 1888-1974 Obituary 49-52
Pinchin, Jane Lagoudis 1942- 69-72
Pinchot, Ann (Kramer) CANR-4
Earlier sketch in CA 1-4R
Pinchot, David 1914(?)-1983 Obituary 109
See also SATA-Obit 34
Pinckney, Catherine L(arkum) 17-20R
Pinckney, Cathey
See Pinckney, Catherine L(arkum)
Pinckney, Darryl 1953- 143
See also BW 2
See also CLC 76
Pinckney, Edward R(obert) 1924- 17-20R
Pinckney, Eliza Lucas 1722-1793 .... DLB 200
Pinckney, Josephine (Lyons Scott) 1895-1957 Brief entry 107
See also DLB 6
Pincus, Edward R. 1938- CANR-12
Earlier sketch in CA 33-36R
Pincus, Gregory Goodwin 1903-1967 Obituary . 113
Pincus, Harriet 1938- 102
See also SATA 27
Pincus, Joseph 1919- 25-28R
Pincus, Lily 1898-1981 .... CANR-5
Obituary 105
Earlier sketch in CA 53-56
Pinczes, Elinor J(ane) 1940- 149
See also SATA 81
Pindar 518B.C.-446B.C. .... DLB 176
See also PC 19
Pindar, Peter
See Wolcot, John
Pindell, Terry 1947- 133
Pinder, John H(umphrey) M(urray) CANR-39
Earlier sketches in CA 9-12R, CANR-3, 18
Pinder, Leslie Hall
See Hall, Leslie
Pindyck, Robert (Stephen) 1945- 89-92
Pine, Leslie Gilbert 1907-1987 .... 13-16R
Obituary 122
Pine, Nicholas 1951- 155
See also SATA 91
Pine, Robert 1928- 129
Pine, Theodore
See Petaja, Emil (Theodore)
Pine, Tillie S(chloss) 1896- 69-72
See also SATA 13
Pine, William
See Harknett, Terry
Pineau, Roger 1916-1993 .... 25-28R
Obituary 143
Pineda, Cecile 1942- 118
See also CLC 39
Pineiro, R. J. 1961- 152
Pinera, Virgilio 1912- 131
See also HW
Pinero, Arthur Wing 1855-1934 153
Brief entry 110
See also DAM DRAM
See also DLB 10
See also TCLC 32
Pinero, Miguel (Antonio Gomez) 1946-1988 .... CANR-29
Obituary 125
Earlier sketch in CA 61-64
See also CLC 4, 55
See also HW
Pines, Maya 13-16R
Pines, Paul (Andre) 1941- 112
Ping, Charles J. 1930- 17-20R
Pinget, Robert 1919-1997 85-88
Obituary 160
See also CLC 7, 13, 37
See also DLB 83
Pini, Richard (Alan) 1950- 150
See also AAYA 12
See also SATA 89
Pini, Wendy 1951- 150
See also AAYA 12
See also SATA 89
Pinion, F(rancis) B(ertram) 1908- CANR-52
Earlier sketches in CA 25-28R, CANR-12, 28
Pinka, Patricia G(arland) 1935- 126
Pinker, Steven Arthur 1954- 150
Pinkerton, Edward C(askin) 1911- 108
Pinkerton, James R(onald) 1932- CANR-24
Earlier sketch in CA 45-48
Pinkerton, Jan 1934- Brief entry 112
Pinkerton, Joan Trego 1928- 107
Pinkerton, Kathrene Sutherland (Gedney) 1887-1967 .... 1-4R
Obituary 103
See also SATA-Obit 26
Pinkerton, Marjorie Jean 1934- 45-48
Pinkerton, Robert E(ugene) 1882-1970 Obituary 29-32R
Pinkerton, Todd 1917- 69-72
Pinkerton, W. Anson
See Steele, Henry
Pinkett, Harold T(homas) 1914- 29-32R
Pinkett, Jada 1971- 163
Pink Floyd
See Barrett, (Roger) Syd
and Gilmour, David
and Mason, Nick
and Waters, Roger
and Wright, Rick
Pinkham, Mary Ellen 101
Pinkney, Alphonso 1929- 25-28R
Pinkney, (Jerry) Brian 1961- .... SATA 74
Pinkney, David H(enry) 1914-1993 .... 9-12R
Obituary 146
Pinkney, Gloria Jean 1941- .... SATA 85
Pinkney, J. Brian
See Pinkney, (Jerry) Brian
Pinkney, Jerry 1939- .... CLR 43
See also MAICYA
See also SAAS 12
See also SATA 41, 71
See also SATA-Brief 32
Pinkney, John 164
See also SATA 97
Pinkowski, Edward 1916- 9-12R
Pinkston, Joe M. 1931- 5-8R
Pinkus, Oscar 1927- CANR-27
Earlier sketch in CA 5-8R
Pinkus, Philip 1922- Brief entry 113
Pinkwater, Daniel Manus 1941- CANR-38
Earlier sketches in CA 29-32R, CANR-12
See also Pinkwater, Manus
See also AAYA 1
See also CLC 35
See also CLR 4
See also JRDA
See also MAICYA
See also SAAS 3
See also SATA 46, 76
Pinkwater, Manus
See Pinkwater, Daniel Manus
See also SATA 8
Pinn, Anthony B(ernard) 1964- 162
Pinna, Giovanni 1939- CANR-4
Earlier sketch in CA 49-52
Pinner, David 1940- CANR-19
Earlier sketch in CA 25-28R
Pinner, Erna 1896- CAP-1
Earlier sketch in CA 11-12
Pinner, Joma
See Werner, Herma
Pinney, Lucy (Catherine) 1952- 136
Pinney, Peter (Patrick) 1922- 25-28R
Pinney, Roy 1911- CANR-6
Earlier sketch in CA 5-8R
Pinney, Thomas 1932- CANR-21
Earlier sketch in CA 85-88
Pinney, Wilson G(ifford) 1929- 45-48
Pino, E.
See Wittermans, Elizabeth (Pino)
Pino, Jose Ortiz y III
See Ortiz y Pino, Jose III
Pinoak, Justin Willard
See Prosser, H(arold) L(ee)
Pinon, Nelida 1935- .... DLB 145
Pinsdorf, Marion K(atheryn) 1932- 124
Pinsent, Arthur 1888- CAP-2
Earlier sketch in CA 29-32
Pinsent, Gordon (Edward) 1930- 106
Pinsker, Sanford 1941- CANR-60
Earlier sketches in CA 33-36R, CANR-12, 31
Pinsky, Robert 1940- CANR-58
Earlier sketch in CA 29-32R
See also CAAS 4
See also CLC 9, 19, 38, 94
See also DAM POET
See also DLBY 82
Pinson, Hermine (Dolorez) 1953- 153
See also BW 2
Pinson, William M(eredith), Jr. 1934- CANR-9
Earlier sketch in CA 17-20R
Pinta, Harold
See Pinter, Harold
Pintak, Larry 1955- 132
Pintauro, Joseph 1930- 81-84
Pintel, Gerald 1922- CANR-4
Earlier sketch in CA 49-52
Pinter, Harold 1930- CANR-65
Earlier sketches in CA 5-8R, CANR-33
See also CDBLB 1960 to Present
See also CLC 1, 3, 6, 9, 11, 15, 27, 58, 73
See also DA
See also DAB
See also DAC
See also DAM DRAM, MST
See also DLB 13
See also MTCW 1
See also WLC
Pinter, Walter S. 1928- 102
Pintner, Walter McKenzie 1931- 21-24R
Pinto, David 1937- 61-64
Pinto, Edward Henry 1901-1972 .... CAP-1
Earlier sketch in CA 13-14
Pinto, John A. 1948- CANR-54
Earlier sketch in CA 127
Pinto, Peter
See Berne, Eric (Lennard)
Pinto, Vivian de Sola 1895-1969 .... CANR-10
Earlier sketch in CA 5-8R
Pintoff, Ernest 1931- 17-20R
Pintoro, John 1947- 103
Pinxten, Rik 1947- 131
Pioneer
See Yates, Raymond F(rancis)
Piontek, Heinz 1925- CANR-34
Earlier sketches in CA 25-28R, CANR-13
See also DLB 75
Piore, Michael J(oseph) 1940- 130
Piotrow, Phyllis Tilson 1933- 122
Piotrowski, Andrew 1939- 131
Piotrowski, Tadeusz 1940- 151
Piovene, Guido 1907-1974 97-100
Obituary 53-56
Piowaty, Kim Kennelly 1957- 115
See also SATA 49
Piozzi, Hester Lynch (Thrale) 1741-1821 .. DLB 104, 142
Pipa, Arshi 1920- CANR-10
Earlier sketch in CA 25-28R
Piper, Anson C(onant) 1918- 41-44R
Piper, David (Towry) 1918-1990 147
Piper, Don Courtney 1932- CANR-15
Earlier sketch in CA 41-44R
Piper, Eileen 1906- 122
Piper, H(enry) Beam 1904-1964 117
Obituary 110
See also DLB 8
Piper, H(erbert) W(alter) 1915- 5-8R
Piper, Henry Dan 1918- 17-20R
Piper, Jim 1937- 97-100
Piper, Jon Kingsbury 1957- 140
Piper, Otto A. 1891- 5-8R
Piper, Roger
See Fisher, John (Oswald Hamilton)
Piper, Watty 137
See also DLB 22
See also MAICYA
Piper, William Bowman 1927- CANR-12
Earlier sketch in CA 61-64
Pipes, Daniel 1949- 145
Pipes, Richard (Edgar) 1923- 158
Pipher, Mary (Bray) 1947- CANR-72
Earlier sketch in CA 145
Pippert, Wesley Gerald 1934- 53-56
Pippett, (Winifred) Aileen 1895- CAP-1
Earlier sketch in CA 13-14
Pippin, Frank Johnson 1906-1968 .... CAP-2
Earlier sketch in CA 19-20
Pippin, Robert B. 1948- 130
Pipping, Ella (Geologica) 1897- 61-64
Piquet, Howard S(amuel) 1903-1983 .... CANR-16
Obituary 111
Earlier sketches in CAP-2, CA 19-20
Piquet-Wicks, Eric 1915- 5-8R
Pirages, Dennis (Clark) 1942- 116
Pirandello, Luigi 1867-1936 153
Brief entry 104
See also DA
See also DAB
See also DAC
See also DAM DRAM, MST
See also DC 5
See also SSC 22
See also TCLC 4, 29
See also WLC
Pirckheimer, Caritas 1467-1532 .... DLB 179
Pirckheimer, Willibald 1470-1530 .... DLB 179
Pires, Joe
See Stout, Robert Joe
Pirie, David (Tarbat) 1946- CANR-21
Earlier sketch in CA 97-100
Pirie, N(orman) W(ingate) 1907- 29-32R
Pirie-Gordon, (Charles) Harry (Clinton) 1883(?)-1969 Obituary 104
Pirmantgen, Pat
See Pirmantgen, Patricia H.
Pirmantgen, Patricia H. 1933- 45-48
Pirner, Connie White 1955- .... SATA 72
Piro, Richard 1934- 49-52
See also SATA 7
Pirogov, Peter A. 1920-1987 Obituary 121
Pirone, Pascal P(ompey) 1907- 9-12R
Pirosh, Robert 1910-1989 Obituary 130
Pirot, Alison Lohans
See Lohans, Alison
Pirsig, Robert M(aynard) 1928- CANR-42
Earlier sketch in CA 53-56
See also CLC 4, 6, 73
See also DAM POP
See also MTCW 1
See also SATA 39
Pirson, Sylvain J. 1905- 5-8R
Pirtle, Caleb (Jackson) III 1941- CANR-26
Earlier sketches in CA 69-72, CANR-11
Pisano, Ronald G(eorge) 1948- CANR-44
Earlier sketches in CA 102, CANR-20
Pisar, Samuel 1929- CANR-27
Earlier sketch in CA 29-32R
See also DLBY 83
Piserchia, Doris (Elaine) 1928- 125
Brief entry 107
Pishkin, Vladimir 1931- CANR-24
Earlier sketch in CA 45-48
Pisk, Paul A(madeus) 1893- CAP-1
Earlier sketch in CA 13-14
Pismire, Osbert
See Hivnor, Robert
Pisor, Robert (Louis) 1939- 109
Pistole, Elizabeth (Smith) 1920- CANR-8
Earlier sketch in CA 17-20R
Piston, Walter 1894-1976 Obituary 69-72
Pitavy, Francois L(ouis) 1934- 73-76
Pitcairn, Frank
See Cockburn, (Francis) Claud
Pitcairn, Leonora 1912- 21-24R
Pitcher, Caroline (Nell) 1948- 132
Pitcher, Evelyn G(oodenough) 1915- 17-20R
Pitcher, George (Willard) 1925- 21-24R
Pitcher, Gladys 1890- CAP-1
Earlier sketch in CA 9-10
Pitcher, Harvey (John) 1936- CANR-3
Earlier sketch in CA 45-48
Pitcher, Oliver 1923(?)- 153
See also BW 2
Pitcher, Robert W(alter) 1918- 29-32R
Pitchford, Kenneth S(amuel) 1931- 104
Pitino, Rick 1952- 165
Pitkin, Dorothy (Horton) 1899(?)-1972 Obituary 37-40R
Pitkin, Hanna Fenichel 1931- 122
Brief entry 111
Pitkin, Thomas M(onroe) 1901- 17-20R
Pitkin, Timothy 1766-1847 .... DLB 30
Pitkin, Walter, Jr. 1913- 13-16R
Pitman, (Isaac) James 1901-1985 .... CAP-2
Obituary 117
Earlier sketch in CA 29-32
See also SATA-Obit 46
Pitre, Felix 1949- .... SATA 84
Pitrone, Jean Maddern 1920- CANR-8
Earlier sketch in CA 17-20R
See also SATA 4
Pitseolak, Peter 1902-1973 93-96
Pitsula, James (Michael) 1950- 137
Pitt, Barrie (William Edward) 1918- CANR-20
Earlier sketch in CA 5-8R
Pitt, David C(harles) 1938- CANR-37
Earlier sketches in CA 29-32R, CANR-16
Pitt, David G(eorge) 1921- 126
Pitt, Jeremy
See Wynne-Tyson, (Timothy) Jon (Lyden)
Pitt, Peter (Clive Crawford) 1933- 33-36R
Pitt, Valerie Joan 1925- 5-8R
Pitt-Aikens, Tom 1940- 131
Pittenger, W(illiam) Norman 1905-1997 .. CANR-20
Obituary 159
Earlier sketches in CA 1-4R, CANR-5
Pitter, Ruth 1897-1992 .... CAP-1
Obituary 137
Earlier sketch in CA 13-14
See also DLB 20
Pitt-Kethley, Fiona 1954- 129
Pittman, David J(oshua) 1927- CANR-6
Earlier sketch in CA 5-8R
Pittman, Helena Clare 1945- .... SATA 71
Pittock, Joan (Hornby) 1930- CANR-26
Earlier sketch in CA 107
Pittock, Murray (G. H.) 1962- 138
Pitt-Rivers, Julian Alfred 1919- 101
Pitts, Denis (Trewin) 1930-1994 65-68
Obituary 145
Pitts, Michael R. 1947- 146
Pitts, Robert F. 1908-1977 Obituary 69-72
Pittwood, James Beattie
See Ritchie, (Harry) Ward
Pitz, Henry C(larence) 1895-1976 .... CANR-9
Obituary 69-72
Earlier sketch in CA 9-12R
See also SATA 4
See also SATA-Obit 24
Pitzer, Sara 1938- 107
Pivar, David J. 1933- 45-48
Piven, Frances Fox 1932- 49-52
Piver, M. Steven 1934- 138
Pix, Mary (Griffith) 1666-1709 .... DLB 80
Pixerecourt, (Rene Charles) Guilbert de 1773-1844 .... DLB 192
Pixley, Jorge V. 1937- CANR-37
Earlier sketches in CA 45-48, CANR-1, 16
Pizarro, Agueda 1941- 131
See also HW
Pizer, Donald 1929- 9-12R
Pizer, Harry F(rancis) 1947- 101
Pizer, John 1953- 152
Pizer, Vernon 1918- CANR-4
Earlier sketch in CA 1-4R
See also SATA 21
Pizzat, Frank J(oseph) 1924- 49-52
Pizzey, Erin 1939- CANR-61
Earlier sketch in CA 81-84
Pizzo, Peggy 1946- 118
Pjerrou, Mary 1945- 137
Pla, Josep 1897-1981 Obituary 103
Plaatje, Sol(omon) T(shekisho) 1876-1932 141
See also BLCS
See also BW 2
See also TCLC 73

Place, Irene Magdaline (Glazik) 1912- CANR-1
  Earlier sketch in CA 1-4R
Place, Janey Ann 1946- 73-76
Place, Marian T(empleton) 1910- CANR-20
  Earlier sketches in CA 1-4R, CANR-5
  See also SATA 3
Place, Milner 1930- 150
Place, Robin (Mary) 1926- .... SATA 71
Placere, Morris N.
  See Gupta, S(ushil) (Kumar)
Placet, Leroi 1901-1970 Obituary 29-32R
Placksin, Sally 1948- 111
Placzek, Adolf Kurt 1913- 112
Plagemann, (William) Bentz 1913-1991 .... CANR-4
  Obituary 134
  Earlier sketch in CA 1-4R
Plagens, Peter (L.) 1941- Brief entry 107
Plager, Sheldon J. 1931- 25-28R
Plaidy, Jean
  See Hibbert, Eleanor Alice Burford
Plain, Belva 1919- CANR-53
  Earlier sketches in CA 81-84, CANR-14, 29
  Interview in CANR-29
  See also BEST 89:4
  See also DAM POP
  See also SATA 62
Plaine, Alfred R. 1898(?)-1981 Obituary 105
  See also SATA-Obit 29
Plaister, Theodore H. 1923- Brief entry 113
Plaja, Guillermo Diaz
  See Diaz Plaja, Guillermo
Plamenatz, John Petrov 1912-1975 .... CANR-5
  Earlier sketch in CA 13-16R
Planck, Annika 1941- 139
Planck, Carolyn H(eine) 1910- 73-76
Planck, Charles Evans 1896-1987 73-76
  Obituary 121
Planck, Max (Karl Ernst Ludwig) 1858-1947 Brief entry 115
Plank, Emma N(uschi) 1905- CAP-2
  Earlier sketch in CA 33-36
Plank, Robert 1907-1983 .... CANR-12
  Earlier sketch in CA 25-28R
Plano, Jack Charles 1921- CANR-39
  Earlier sketches in CA 5-8R, CANR-2, 17
Plant, Marcus L. 1911- 1-4R
Plant, Raymond 1945- CANR-21
  Earlier sketch in CA 29-32R
Plant, Robert 1948- .... CLC 12
Plante, David (Robert) 1940- CANR-58
  Earlier sketches in CA 37-40R, CANR-12, 36
  Interview in CANR-12
  See also CLC 7, 23, 38
  See also DAM NOV
  See also DLBY 83
  See also MTCW 1
Plante, (Joseph) Jacques (Omer) 1929-1986 Obituary 118
  Brief entry 108
Plante, Julian G(erard) 41-44R
Plantinga, Alvin C. 1932- CANR-11
  Earlier sketch in CA 21-24R
Plantinga, Leon B(rooks) 1935- 21-24R
Planz, Allen 1937- 53-56
Plaskow, Judith (Ellen) 1947- CANR-53
  Brief entry 108
  Earlier sketch in CA 126
Plastaras, James C(onstantine) 1931- 21-24R
Plate, Andrea 1952- 130
Plate, Andrea Darvi
  See Plate, Andrea
Plate, Robert 1918- 17-20R
Plate, Thomas 1944- CANR-46
  Earlier sketches in CA 69-72, CANR-23
Platen, August von 1796-1835 .... DLB 90
Plater, Alan (Frederick) 1935- 85-88
Plater, William M(armaduke) 1945- 85-88
Plath, David W(illiam) 1930- CANR-3
  Earlier sketch in CA 9-12R
Plath, Sylvia 1932-1963 .... CANR-34
  Earlier sketches in CAP-2, CA 19-20
  See also AAYA 13
  See also CDALB 1941-1968
  See also CLC 1, 2, 3, 5, 9, 11, 14, 17, 50, 51, 62, 111
  See also DA
  See also DAB
  See also DAC
  See also DAM MST, POET
  See also DLB 5, 6, 152
  See also MTCW 1
  See also PC 1
  See also SATA 96
  See also WLC
Platig, E(mil) Raymond 1924- 37-40R
Plato 428(?)B.C.-348(?)B.C. .... DA
  See also DAB
  See also DAC
  See also DAM MST
  See also DLB 176
  See also WLCS
Platon 1737-1812 .... DLB 150
Platonov, Andrei
  See Klimentov, Andrei Platonovich
  See also TCLC 14
Platov, Mariquita (Villard) 1905- 5-8R
Platt, Anthony M. 1942- 25-28R
Platt, Charles 1945- CANR-24
  Earlier sketch in CA 21-24R
Platt, Christopher
  See Platt, D(esmond) C(hristopher St.) M(artin)
Platt, Colin (Peter Sherard) 1934- 152
Platt, D(esmond) C(hristopher St.) M(artin) 1934-1989 Obituary 129
  Brief entry 109
Platt, David 1903-1992 152
Platt, Eugene Robert 1939- CANR-3
  Earlier sketch in CA 49-52
Platt, Frederick 1946- 61-64
Platt, Gerald M. 1933- CANR-17
  Earlier sketch in CA 97-100
Platt, Harlan D. 1950- 123
Platt, Harrison Gray 1902- 41-44R
Platt, Jennifer (Ann) 1937- 29-32R
Platt, John Rader 1918-1992 .... 17-20R
  Obituary 138
Platt, Kin 1911- CANR-11
  Earlier sketch in CA 17-20R
  See also AAYA 11
  See also CLC 26
  See also JRDA
  See also SAAS 17
  See also SATA 21, 86
Platt, Lyman De 1943- 102
Platt, Michael 1942- 122
Platt, Randall (Beth) 1948- 144
  See also SATA 95
Platt, Rutherford 1894-1975 Obituary 61-64
Platt, Rutherford H. 1940- 148
Platt, Washington 1890-1965 .... 1-4R
  Obituary 120
Platten, Thomas George 1899- CAP-1
  Earlier sketch in CA 11-12
Platts, Beryl 1918- 61-64
Plauger, P(hillip) J(ames) 1944- 57-60
Plaut, Allene Talmey 1903-1986 Obituary 118
Plaut, Eric A. 1927- 147
Plaut, Joshua Eli 1957- 157
Plaut, Thomas F(ranz) A(lfred) 1925- 25-28R
Plaut, W(olf) Gunther 1912- CANR-17
  Earlier sketches in CA 5-8R, CANR-2
Plautus c. 251B.C.-184B.C. .... DC 6
Plawin, Paul 1938- 89-92
Player, Gary (Jim) 1935- 101
Player, Ian 1927- 49-52
Playfair, Giles 1910- 133
Playfair, Guy Lyon 1935- CANR-47
  Earlier sketches in CA 106, CANR-23
Playfellow, Robin
  See Ellis, Edward S(ylvester)
Playford, John fl. 1647-1684 .... DLB 170
Playsted, James
  See Wood, James Playsted
Pleasants, Henry, Jr. 1884-1963 .... 1-4R
Pleasants, Henry 1910- 107
Pleasants, Samuel A(ugustus III) 1918- 77-80
Plecas, Jennifer 1966- .... SATA 84
Plecas, Jennifer 1966- .... SATA 84
Pleck, Elizabeth
  See Pleck, Elizabeth Hafkin
Pleck, Elizabeth H.
  See Pleck, Elizabeth Hafkin
Pleck, Elizabeth Hafkin 1945- 129
  Brief entry 115
Pleck, Joseph H(ealy) 1946- CANR-23
  Earlier sketches in CA 57-60, CANR-7
Pleier, Der fl. c. 1250- .... DLB 138
Pleijel, Agneta (Christina) 1940- 142
Plekker, Robert J(ohn) 1929- 69-72
Plendello, Leo
  See Saint, Andrew (John)
Plender, Richard O(wen) 1945- 101
Plenzdorf, Ulrich 1934- .... DLB 75
Plesko, Les 1954- 147
Pless, Vera 1931- 161
Plessen, Elisabeth 1944- .... DLB 75
Plesset, Isabel R(osahoff) 1912- 103
Plesur, Milton 1927-1987 .... CANR-24
  Earlier sketch in CA 45-48
Pletcher, Barbara A. 1946- 123
Pletcher, David M(itchell) 1920- 1-4R
Pletcher, Eldon L(ee) 1922- 133
Pletsch, Carl (Erich) 1943- 137
Pleydell, Susan
  See Senior, Isabel J(anet Couper Syme)
Plick et Plock
  See Simenon, Georges (Jacques Christian)
Plievier, Theodor 1892-1955 .... DLB 69
Plimmer, Charlotte 1916- 104
Plimmer, Denis 1914- 104
Plimpton, George (Ames) 1927- CANR-70
  Earlier sketches in CA 21-24R, CANR-32
  See also AITN 1
  See also CLC 36
  See also DLB 185
  See also MTCW 1
  See also SATA 10
Plimpton, Ruth Talbot 1916- 13-16R
Pliny the Younger
  See Secundus, Gaius Plinius Caecilius
Plischke, Elmer 1914- CANR-40
  Earlier sketches in CA 1-4R, CANR-2, 18
Plochmann, George Kimball 1914- 5-8R
Ploeg, Johannes P(etrus) M(aria) van der
  See van der Ploeg, Johannes P(etrus) M(aria)
Plog, Fred (Thomas III) 1944- CANR-12
  Earlier sketch in CA 25-28R
Plog, Stanley C. 1930- CANR-15
  Earlier sketch in CA 41-44R
Ploghoft, Milton E(rnest) 1923- 104
Plomer, William Charles Franklin 1903-1973 .... CANR-34
  Earlier sketches in CAP-2, CA 21-22
  See also CLC 4, 8
  See also DLB 20, 162, 191
  See also MTCW 1
  See also SATA 24
Plomley, Roy 1914-1985 Obituary 116
  Brief entry 107
Plommer, (William) Hugh (?)-1983 Obituary 109
Plopper, Julie Jynelle 1916- 69-72
Ploscowe, Morris 1904-1975 .... CANR-2
  Obituary 61-64
  Earlier sketch in CA 45-48
Ploss, Sidney I. 1932- 13-16R
Plossl, George W. 1918- 21-24R
Plotinus 204-270 .... DLB 176
Plotnick, Alan R(alph) 1926- 17-20R
Plotnick, Charles K(eith) 1931- 114
Plotnicov, Leonard 1930- 21-24R
Plotnik, Arthur 1937- CANR-20
  Earlier sketch in CA 69-72
Plotz, Helen Ratnoff 1913- CANR-8
  Earlier sketch in CA 9-12R
  See also SATA 38
Plous, Scott 1959- 144
Plowden, Alison 1931- CANR-15
  Earlier sketch in CA 33-36R
Plowden, David 1932- 33-36R
  See also SATA 52
Plowden, G(eoffrey) F(rank) C(hichele) 1929- 116
Plowden, Gene 1906-1985 .... 21-24R
  Obituary 117
Plowden, Martha Ward 1948- 166
  See also SATA 98
Plowhead, Ruth Gipson 1877-1967 .... SATA 43
Plowman, E(dward) Grosvenor 1899- 13-16R
Plowman, Edward E(arl) 1931- 37-40R
Plowman, Piers
  See Kavanagh, Patrick (Joseph)
Plowman, Stephanie 1922- CANR-5
  Earlier sketch in CA 53-56
  See also SATA 6
Pluckrose, Henry (Arthur) 1931- 33-36R
  See also SATA 13
Pluff, Barbara Littlefield 1926- 5-8R
Plum, J.
  See Wodehouse, P(elham) G(renville)
Plum, Jennifer
  See Kurland, Michael (Joseph)
Plum, Lester Virgil 1906-1972 .... 1-4R
  Obituary 37-40R
Plum, Patrick
  See McConville, Michael (Anthony)
Plumb, Barbara Louise Brown 1934- CANR-15
  Earlier sketch in CA 89-92
Plumb, Beatrice
  See Hunzicker, Beatrice Plumb
Plumb, Charles P. 1900(?)-1982 Obituary 105
  See also SATA-Obit 29
Plumb, Charlie
  See Plumb, Joseph Charles, Jr.
Plumb, J(ohn) H(arold) 1911- CANR-3
  Earlier sketch in CA 5-8R
Plumb, Joseph Charles, Jr. 1942- CANR-3
  Earlier sketch in CA 49-52
Plume, Ilse .... SATA-Brief 43
Plumly, Stanley (Ross) 1939- 110
  Brief entry 108
  Interview in 110
  See also CLC 33
  See also DLB 5, 193
Plumme, Don E.
  See Katz, Bobbi
Plummer, Alfred 1896- 29-32R
Plummer, Ben
  See Bingley, David Ernest
Plummer, Beverly J. 1918- 29-32R
Plummer, Catharine 1922- 21-24R
Plummer, Clare (Emsley) 1912- 25-28R
Plummer, Kenneth 1946- 73-76
Plummer, L. Gordon 1904- CAP-2
  Earlier sketch in CA 33-36
Plummer, Margaret 1911- CAP-2
  Earlier sketch in CA 25-28
  See also SATA 2
Plummer, Mark A(llen) 1929- 37-40R
Plummer, William (Halsey Jr.) 1945- 102
Plummer, William J(oseph) 1927- 53-56
Plumpe, Friedrich Wilhelm 1888-1931 Brief entry 112
  See also TCLC 53
Plumpp, Sterling D(ominic) 1940- CANR-24
  Earlier sketch in CA 45-48
  See also CAAS 21
  See also BW 1
  See also DLB 41
Plumptre, Arthur Fitzwalter Wynne 1907-1977 109
  Obituary 106
Plumstead, A(rthur) William 1933- CANR-11
  Earlier sketch in CA 25-28R
Plunket, Robert 1945- 115
Plunkett, James
  See Kelly, James Plunkett
  See also DLB 14
Plunkett, Thomas J. 1921- 33-36R
Plutarch c. 46-c. 120 .... DLB 176
Plutchik, Robert 1927- CANR-11
  Earlier sketch in CA 21-24R
Pluto, Terry 1955- 107
Plutonius
  See Mehta, Rustam Jehangir
Plutschow, Herbert Eugen 1939- CANR-18
  Earlier sketch in CA 102
Plutzik, Roberta Ann 1948- 110
Plymell, Charles 1935- CANR-11
  Earlier sketch in CA 21-24R
  See also CAAS 11
  See also DLB 16
Plympton, Bill
  See Plympton, William M.
Plympton, William M. 1946- 110
Poag, James F(itzgerald) 1934- Brief entry 107
Poage, Godfrey Robert 1920- 5-8R
Poage, Scott T(abor) 1931- 53-56
Poague, Leland A(llen) 1948- CANR-6
  Earlier sketch in CA 57-60
Pobo, Kenneth 1954- 104
Pochin, Edward (Eric) 1909-1990 Obituary 130
Pochmann, Henry A(ugust) 1901-1973 .... 37-40R
Pochmann, Ruth Fouts 1903- CAP-2
  Earlier sketch in CA 25-28
Pochocki, Ethel (Frances) 1925- 143
  See also SATA 76
Pocius, Gerald L(ewis) 1950- 137
Pocock, Douglas C. D. 1935- 129
Pocock, H(ugh) R(aymond) S(pilsbury) 1904- 25-28R
Pocock, Nick 1934- 53-56
Pocock, Thomas Allcot Guy 1925- CANR-49
  Earlier sketches in CA 103, CANR-23
Pocock, Tom
  See Pocock, Thomas Allcot Guy
Podbielski, Gisele 1918- 53-56
Podell, Diane K(opperman) 1931- 149
Podell, Janet 1954- 124
Podendorf, Illa (E.) 1903(?)-1983 .... CANR-28
  Obituary 110
  Earlier sketch in CA 81-84
  See also SATA 18
  See also SATA-Obit 35
Podeschi, John B(attista) 1942- 110
Podhajsky, Alois 1898-1973 69-72
Podhoretz, Norman 1930- CANR-7
  Earlier sketch in CA 9-12R
Podhradsky, Gerhard 1929- 21-24R
Podlecki, Anthony J(oseph) 1936- CANR-3
  Earlier sketch in CA 49-52
Podmarsh, Rollo
  See Salter, Donald P. M.
Podoliak, Boris
  See Kostiuk, Hryhory
Podro, Michael (Isaac) 1931- 132
Podulka, Fran 1933- 49-52
Poduschka, Walter 1922- 107
Podwal, Mark 1945- 147
  See also SATA 101
Poe, Charlsie 1909- CAP-2
  Earlier sketch in CA 23-24
Poe, Edgar Allan 1809-1849 .... AAYA 14
  See also CDALB 1640-1865
  See also DA
  See also DAB
  See also DAC
  See also DAM MST, POET
  See also DLB 3, 59, 73, 74
  See also PC 1
  See also SATA 23
  See also SSC 1, 22
  See also WLC
Poe, James 1921-1980 113
  Obituary 93-96
  See also DLB 44
Poe, Ty (Christopher) 1975- .... SATA 94
Poen, Monte Mac 1930- 107
Poeppel, Ernst 1940- 158
Poern, Ingmar 1935- 33-36R
Poesch, Jessie (J.) 1922- CANR-62
  Earlier sketch in CA 128
Poetker, Frances Jones 1912- 85-88
Poet of Titchfield Street, The
  See Pound, Ezra (Weston Loomis)
Poetzl, Pamela Major
  See Major-Poetzl, Pamela
Poewe, Karla 1941- 124
Poganski, Donald J(ohn) 1928- 25-28R
Pogany, Andras H(enrik) 1919- 21-24R
Pogany, Hortenzia Lers 21-24R
Pogany, William Andrew 1882-1955
  See Pogany, Willy
  See also SATA 44
Pogany, Willy
  See Pogany, William Andrew
  See also SATA-Brief 30
Poggi, Emil J. 1928- 29-32R
Poggi, Gianfranco 1934- 85-88
Poggi, Jack
  See Poggi, Emil J.
Poggie, John J(oseph), Jr. 1937- Brief entry 107
Poggioli, Renato 1907-1963 .... CANR-2
  Earlier sketch in CA 1-4R
Pogodin, Mikhail Petrovich 1800-1875 .... DLB 198
Pogorel'sky, Antonii 1787-1836
  See Perovsky, Aleksei Alekseevich
Pogrebin, Letty Cottin 1939- CANR-33
  Earlier sketches in CA 29-32R, CANR-15
Pogue, Bill
  See Pogue, William R.
Pogue, Charles (Edward), Jr. 1950- 164
Pogue, Forrest Carlisle 1912-1996 .... CANR-3
  Obituary 154
  Earlier sketch in CA 5-8R
Pogue, William R. 1930- 137
Poh, Caroline (Anne) 1938- 61-64
Pohanka, Brian C. 165
Pohl, Frederick Julius 1889- CANR-27
  Earlier sketches in CA 1-4R, CANR-5
Pohl, Frederik 1919- CANR-37
  Earlier sketches in CA 61-64, CANR-11
  Interview in CANR-11
  See also CAAS 1
  See also AAYA 24
  See also CLC 18
  See also DLB 8
  See also MTCW 1
  See also SATA 24
  See also SSC 25
Pohle, Linda C(arol) 1947- 45-48
Pohle, Robert W(arren), Jr. 1949- 81-84
Pohlman, Edward 1933- 33-36R
Pohlmann, Lillian (Grenfell) 1902- 9-12R
  See also SATA 11

Pohndorf, Richard Henry
1916-1977 Obituary ... 73-76
Pohrt, Tom ... SATA 67
Poignant, Raymond 1917- ... 29-32R
Poincelot, Raymond P. 1944- ... 122
Poindexter, Clarence Albert
1902(?)-1984 Obituary ... 111
Poindexter, David 1929- ... 29-32R
Poindexter, Hally Beth Walker 1927- Brief entry ... 110
Poindexter, Marian J(ean) 1929- ... 29-32R
Poinsett, Alex(ander) Ceasar 1926- ... 29-32R
Pointer, Larry 1940- ... 101
Pointer, Michael 1927- ... 57-60
Pointer, Richard W(ayne) 1955- ... 131
Pointon, Marcia R(achel) 1943- ... 33-36R
Pointon, Robert
See Rooke, Daphne (Marie)
Poirier, Frank E(ugene) 1940- ... CANR-3
Earlier sketch in CA 49-52
Poirier, Louis 1910- ... 126
Brief entry ... 122
See also Gracq, Julien
Poirier, Normand 1928(?)-1981 Obituary ... 102
Poirier, Philip P(atrick) 1920-1979 ... 133
Brief entry ... 113
Poirier, Richard 1925- ... CANR-40
Earlier sketches in CA 1-4R, CANR-3
Poirier-Bures, Simone 1944- ... 153
Pois, Joseph 1905- ... CAP-1
Earlier sketch in CA 13-16
Poitier, Sidney 1927- ... 117
See also BW 1
See also CLC 26
Pokagon, Simon 1830-1899 ... DAM MULT
See also NNAL
Pok Chong-Hui
See Park Chung Hee
Pokrovsky, Boris Aleksandrovich 1912- Brief entry ... 109
POLA
See Watson, Pauline
Polacco, Patricia 1944- ... CLR 40
See also SATA 74
Polach, Jaroslav G(eorge) 1914- ... 9-12R
Polack, Albert Isaac 1892- ... CAP-1
Earlier sketch in CA 9-10
Polak, Ada Buch 1914- Brief entry ... 111
Polak, Jacques Jacobus 1914- ... 104
Polakoff, Keith Ian 1941- ... 49-52
Polakoff, Murray Emanuel 1922- Brief entry ... 114
Polakow, Valerie (Suransky) 1950- ... 111
Polanco, Vincente Geigel
See Geigel Polanco, Vicente
Poland, Dorothy (Elizabeth Hayward) 1937- ... CANR-20
Earlier sketch in CA 103
Poland, Larry 1939- ... 101
Polanski, Roman 1933- ... 77-80
See also CLC 16
Polansky, Norman A. 1918- ... 85-88
Polansky, Ronald M. 1948- ... 144
Polanyi, Michael 1891-1976 ... CANR-28
Obituary ... 65-68
Earlier sketch in CA 81-84
See also DLB 100
Polatnick, Florence T. 1923- ... 29-32R
See also SATA 5
Polcher, Egon
See Anschel, Eugene
Polder, Markus
See Kruess, James
Poldervaart, Arie 1909-1969 ... 1-4R
Obituary ... 103
Pole, J(ack) R(ichon) 1922- ... CANR-8
Earlier sketch in CA 17-20R
Pole, Reginald 1500-1558 ... DLB 132
Polebaum, Elliot E(dward) 1950- ... 107
Poleman, Thomas T(heobald) 1928- ... 13-16R
Polenberg, Richard 1937- ... 21-24R
Polese, Carolyn 1947- ... 127
See also SATA 58
Polese, James 1914- ... 152
See also SATA 87
Polese, Marcia Ann 1949- ... 65-68
Polette, Nancy (Jane) 1930- ... CANR-45
Earlier sketches in CA 57-60, CANR-6, 21
See also SATA 42
Polevoi, Boris
See Kampov, Boris Nikolayevich
Polevoi, Nikolai Alekseevich 1796-1846 ... DLB 198
Polhamus, Jean Burt 1928- ... 103
See also SATA 21
Polhemus, Robert M(ackinlay) 1935- ... 130
Poli, Bernard 1929- ... 21-24R
Poliakoff, Michael B. 1953- ... 127
Poliakoff, Stephen 1952- ... 106
See also CLC 38
See also DLB 13
Poliakov, Leon 1910-1997 ... 104
Obituary ... 163
Police Captain Howard
See Senarens, Luis P(hilip)POLICE
Police, The
See Copeland, Stewart (Armstrong)
and Summers, Andrew James
and Sumner, Gordon Matthew
Policoff, Stephen Phillip 1948- ... 145
See also SATA 77
Polidori, John William 1795-1821 ... DLB 116
Polier, Justine Wise 1903-1987 ... 104
Obituary ... 123
Polikoff, Barbara G(arland) 1929- ... 145
See also SATA 77
Polin, Raymond 1918- ... 37-40R
Poling, Daniel Alfred 1884-1968 Obituary ... 93-96
Poling, David 1928- ... 85-88
Poling(-Kempes), Lesley 1954- ... 136
Polinger, Elliot Hirsch 1898-1970 Obituary ... 104
Polis, A(lbert) Richard 1937- ... CANR-6
Earlier sketch in CA 57-60
Polisar, Barry Louis 1954- ... 145
See also SATA 77
Polisensky, Josef V. 1915- Brief entry ... 107
Polish, David 1910-1995 ... 13-16R
Obituary ... 148
Polishook, Irwin H. 1935- ... 21-24R
Polite, Carlene Hatcher 1932- ... CANR-25
Earlier sketch in CA 21-24R
See also BW 1
See also DLB 33
Polite, Frank (C.) 1936- ... 125
Politella, Dario 1921- ... 13-16R
Politella, Joseph 1910- ... CAP-2
Earlier sketch in CA 21-22
Politi, Leo 1908-1996 ... CANR-47
Obituary ... 151
Earlier sketches in CA 17-20R, CANR-13
See also CLR 29
See also MAICYA
See also SATA 1, 47
See also SATA-Obit 88
Politicus
See Kulski, Wladyslaw W(szebor)
Polito, Robert 1951- ... 152
Politzer, Heinrich 1910-1978 ... CANR-3
Obituary ... 81-84
Earlier sketch in CA 5-8R
Politzer, Heinz
See Politzer, Heinrich
Politzer, Robert L. 1921- ... 5-8R
Polivy, Janet 1951- ... 115
Polizzotti, Mark 1957- ... 152
Poljanski, Hristo Andonov
See Andonov-Poljanski, Hristo
Polk, Cara Saylor 1945- ... CANR-38
Earlier sketch in CA 116
Polk, Dora (Beale) 1923- ... 49-52
Polk, Edwin Weiss 1916- ... 37-40R
Polk, James 1939- ... CANR-23
Earlier sketch in CA 105
Polk, James R. 1937- ... 69-72
Polk, Judd (Knox) 1913(?)-1975 Obituary ... 57-60
Polk, Kenneth 1935- ... CANR-1
Earlier sketch in CA 1-4R
Polk, Mary 1898- ... CAP-1
Earlier sketch in CA 11-12
Polk, Noel E(arl) 1943- ... CANR-49
Earlier sketch in CA 123
Polk, Ralph Lane, Jr. 1940-1985 Obituary ... 118
Polk, Ralph Weiss 1890-1978 ... 37-40R
Obituary ... 77-80
Polk, Stella Gipson 1901- ... CANR-16
Earlier sketch in CA 93-96
Polk, William R(oe) 1929- ... 25-28R
Polking, Kirk 1925- ... CANR-30
Earlier sketches in CA 29-32R, CANR-12
See also SATA 5
Polkingharn, Anne T(oogood) 1937- ... 109
Polkinhorn, Harry 1945- ... 159
See also CAAS 25
Poll, Richard Douglas 1918- ... 101
Pollack, Cecelia 1909- ... 29-32R
Pollack, Dale 1950- ... 130
Pollack, Eileen 1956- ... 138
Pollack, Ervin H(arold) 1913-1972 ... CAP-1
Earlier sketch in CA 13-16
Pollack, (Wilburt) Erwin 1935- ... 49-52
Pollack, Harvey 1913- ... 5-8R
Pollack, Herman 1907- ... 69-72
Pollack, Howard 1952- ... 145
Pollack, Jack H(arrison) 1915(?)-1984 Obituary ... 113
Pollack, Jill S. 1963- ... 152
See also SATA 88
Pollack, Merrill S. 1924-1988 ... 5-8R
Obituary ... 124
See also SATA-Obit 55
Pollack, Norman 1933- ... 13-16R
Pollack, Peter 1911-1978 ... 81-84
Obituary ... 77-80
Pollack, Rachel (Grace) 1945- ... CANR-99
Earlier sketch in CA 157
Pollack, Reginald 1924- ... 37-40R
Pollack, Robert (Elliot) 1940- ... 159
Pollack, Robert H(arvey) 1927- ... 49-52
Pollack, Sandra (Barbara) 1937- ... CANR-43
Earlier sketch in CA 119
Pollack, Seymour V(ictor) 1933- ... 25-28R
Pollak, Felix 1909- ... CANR-10
Earlier sketch in CA 25-28R
Pollak, Kurt 1919- ... 29-32R
Pollak, Louis Heilprin 1922- ... 17-20R
Pollak, Martha D. 1941- ... 140
Pollak, Michael 1918- ... CANR-48
Earlier sketch in CA 122
Pollak, Richard 1934- Brief entry ... 111
Pollak, Vivian R. 1938- ... 136
Polland, Barbara K(ay) 1939- ... 73-76
See also SATA 44
Polland, Madeleine A(ngela Cahill) 1918- ... CANR-37
Earlier sketches in CA 5-8R, CANR-3
See also MAICYA
See also SAAS 8
See also SATA 6, 68
Pollard, A(nthony) J(ames) 1941- ... 132
Pollard, Alfred W. 1859-1944 ... DLB 201
Pollard, David 1942- ... 123
Pollard, Edward A. 1832-1872 ... DLB 30
Pollard, (Henry) Graham 1903-1976 Obituary ... 69-72
See also DLB 201
Pollard, Helen Perlstein 1946- ... 146
Pollard, Irina 1939- ... 150
Pollard, Jack 1926- ... CANR-58
Earlier sketches in CA 29-32R, CANR-30
Pollard, James E(dward) 1894-1979 ... CAP-1
Obituary ... 89-92
Earlier sketch in CA 13-16
Pollard, John (Richard Thornhill) 1914- ... 5-8R
Pollard, Percival 1869-1911 ... DLB 71
Pollard, Sidney 1925- ... CANR-44
Earlier sketches in CA 17-20R, CANR-13
Pollard, T(homas) E(van) 1921- ... 29-32R
Pollard, William G(rosvenor) 1911- ... CANR-6
Earlier sketch in CA 13-16R
Pollen, Daniel A. 1935- ... 144
Polley, Judith (Anne) 1938- ... 129
Polley, Robert L. 1933- ... 17-20R
Pollin, Burton R(alph) 1916- ... CANR-67
Earlier sketch in CA 129
Pollinger, Kenneth Joseph 1933- ... 57-60
Pollini, Francis 1930- ... CANR-1
Earlier sketch in CA 1-4R
Pollio, Howard R. 1937- ... 37-40R
Pollitt, Jerome J(ordan) 1934- ... 21-24R
Pollitt, Katha 1949- ... CANR-66
Brief entry ... 120
Earlier sketch in CA 122
See also CLC 28
See also MTCW 1
Pollitt, Michael G(erald) 1967- ... 162
Pollitt, Ronald 1939- ... 122
Pollitz, Edward A(lan), Jr. 1937- ... 127
Pollock, Bruce 1945- ... CANR-23
Earlier sketches in CA 57-60, CANR-7
See also SATA 46
Pollock, David H(arold) 1922- ... 49-52
Pollock, George 1938- ... 61-64
Pollock, Harry 1920- ... 89-92
Pollock, James K(err) 1898-1968 ... CAP-2
Obituary ... 29-32R
Earlier sketch in CA 21-22
Pollock, John (Charles) 1923- ... CANR-40
Earlier sketches in CA 5-8R, CANR-2, 18
Pollock, John L(eslie) 1940- ... 37-40R
Pollock, Lansing R. 1943- ... 162
Pollock, Leland W(ells) 1943- ... 162
Pollock, Linda A(nne) 1955- ... CANR-39
Earlier sketch in CA 116
Pollock, Mary
See Blyton, Enid (Mary)
Pollock, Nancy J. 1934- ... 139
Pollock, Norman H(all), Jr. 1909- ... CAP-2
Earlier sketch in CA 33-36
Pollock, Penny 1935- ... 101
See also SATA 44
See also SATA-Brief 42
Pollock, Robert 1930- ... 45-48
Pollock, Seton 1910- ... 5-8R
Pollock, (Mary) Sharon 1936- ... 141
See also CLC 50
See also DAC
See also DAM DRAM, MST
See also DLB 60
Pollock, Ted 1929- ... 85-88
Pollock, Thomas Clark 1902-1988 ... CAP-2
Obituary ... 125
Earlier sketch in CA 21-22
Pollock, William 1899-1982 Obituary ... 110
Pollowitz, Melinda Kilborn 1944- ... CANR-13
Earlier sketch in CA 77-80
See also SATA 26
Polmar, Norman 1938- ... 49-52
Polnaszek, Frank P(aul) 1947- ... 107
Polner, Murray 1928- ... CANR-49
Earlier sketches in CA 13-16R, CANR-5, 23
See also SATA 64
Poloma, Margaret Mary 1943- ... CANR-58
Earlier sketches in CA 111, CANR-30
Polome, Edgar (Ghislain) C(harles) 1920- ... CANR-13
Earlier sketch in CA 29-32R
Polon, Linda Beth 1943- ... CANR-46
Earlier sketches in CA 103, CANR-20
Polonsky, Abraham (Lincoln) 1910- ... 104
Interview in ... 104
See also CLC 92
See also DLB 26
Polonsky, Antony Barry 1940- ... 73-76
Polonsky, Arthur 1925- ... SATA 34
Polonsky, Michael Jay 1959- ... 154
Polony, Raymond
See Machan, Tibor R(ichard)
Polos, Nicholas C(hristopher) 1917- ... 17-20R
Polotsky, Simeon 1629-1680 ... DLB 150
Pols, Edward 1919- ... 9-12R
Polsby, Nelson W(oolf) 1934- ... CANR-23
Earlier sketches in CA 53-56, CANR-5
Polselli, Joseph 1950- ... 122
Polseno, Jo ... 81-84
See also SATA 17
Polsky, Abe 1935- ... 109
Polsky, Andrew J. 1955- ... 139
Polsky, Howard W. 1928- ... 25-28R
Polsky, Ned 1928- ... 25-28R
Polster, James 1947- ... 152
Poltawska, Wanda (Wiktoria) 1921- ... 136
Poltoratzky, N(ikolai) P(etrovich) 1921- ... 73-76
Poltroon, Milford
See Bascom, David
Polukhina, Valentina 1936- ... 135
Polunin, Nicholas (Vladimir) 1909- ... 65-68
Polunin, Oleg 1914-1985 ... 85-88
Obituary ... 117
Polya, George 1887-1985 Obituary ... 117
Polya, Gyorgy
See Polya, George
Polyanin, Andrey
See Parnok, Sophia (Yakovlevna)
Polybius c. 200B.C.-c. 118B.C. ... DLB 176
Pomada, Elizabeth 1940- ... CANR-8
Earlier sketch in CA 61-64
Pomerance, Bernard 1940- ... CANR-49
Earlier sketch in CA 101
See also CLC 13
See also DAM DRAM
Pomerans, Arno
See Pomerans, Arnold J(ulius)
Pomerans, Arnold J(ulius) 1920- ... 129
Pomerantz, Charlotte 1930- ... CANR-38
Earlier sketches in CA 85-88, CANR-16
See also SATA 20, 80
Pomerantz, Edward 1934- ... 65-68
Pomerantz, Joel 1930- ... 29-32R
Pomerantz, Sidney I(rving)
1909-1975 Obituary ... 61-64
Pomeranz, Virginia E. 1925(?)-1986 ... 134
Obituary ... 120
Pomerleau, Cynthia S(todola) 1943- ... 73-76
Pomerleau, Ovide F(elix) 1940- ... CANR-13
Earlier sketch in CA 73-76
Pomeroy, Charles A. 1930- ... 25-28R
Pomeroy, Earl 1915- ... 17-20R
Pomeroy, Elizabeth W(right) 1938- ... CANR-32
Earlier sketch in CA 113
Pomeroy, Florence Mary
See Powley, Florence Mary Pomeroy
Pomeroy, Hub(bard)
See Claassen, Harold
Pomeroy, John H(oward) 1918-1985 Obituary ... 115
Pomeroy, Kenneth B(rownridge)
1907-1975 Obituary ... 61-64
Pomeroy, Pete
See Roth, Arthur J(oseph)
Pomeroy, Sarah B(erman) 1938- ... 65-68
Pomeroy, Wardell B. 1913- ... CANR-1
Earlier sketch in CA 1-4R
Pomeroy, William J(oseph) 1916- ... 85-88
Pomfret, Baron
See Dame, Lawrence
Pomfret, John Edwin 1898-1981 ... CANR-3
Obituary ... 105
Earlier sketch in CA 1-4R
Pomfret, Richard 1948- ... CANR-42
Earlier sketch in CA 112
Pomilio, Mario 1921-1990 ... DLB 177
Pommer, Henry F(rancis) 1918- ... CANR-20
Earlier sketch in CA 1-4R
Pommer, Richard 1930- ... 137
Pommery, Jean 1932- ... 101
Pomorska, Krystyna 1928-1986 ... CANR-31
Earlier sketch in CA 41-44R
Pompa, Leon 1933- ... CANR-7
Earlier sketch in CA 57-60
Pomper, Gerald M(arvin) 1935- ... CANR-41
Earlier sketches in CA 9-12R, CANR-5, 19
Pomper, Philip 1936- ... 77-80
Pompian, Richard O(wen) 1935- ... CANR-11
Earlier sketch in CA 29-32R
Pompidou, Georges (Jean Raymond)
1911-1974 Obituary ... 49-52
Pomrenke, Norman E. 1930- ... 21-24R
Pomroy, Martha 1943- ... 101
Ponce, Juan Garcia
See Garcia Ponce, Juan
Ponce, Mary Helen 1938- ... DLB 122
Ponce de Leon, Jose Luis S. 1931- ... 49-52
Ponce-Montoya, Juanita 1949- ... DLB 122
Pond, Alonzo W(illiam) 1894- ... CANR-1
Earlier sketch in CA 1-4R
See also SATA 5
Pond, Elizabeth (Ann) ... 129
Pond, Grace (Isabelle) 1910- ... CANR-5
Earlier sketch in CA 13-16R
Pond, L. W.
See Chute, Robert M.
Ponder, Catherine 1927- ... CANR-17
Earlier sketches in CA 1-4R, CANR-1
Ponder, James A(lton) 1933- ... 69-72
Ponder, Patricia
See Maxwell, Patricia
Pondrom, Cyrena N(orman) 1938- Brief entry ... 111
Poneman, Daniel 1956- ... 130
Ponet, John 1516(?)-1556 ... DLB 132
Pong, David (B. P. T.) 1939- ... 149
Ponge, Francis (Jean Gaston Alfred) 1899-1988 ... CANR-40
Obituary ... 126
Earlier sketch in CA 85-88
See also CLC 6, 18
See also DAM POET
Poniatowska, Elena 1933- ... CANR-66
Earlier sketches in CA 101, CANR-32
See also DAM MULT
See also DLB 113
See also HLC
See also HW
Ponicsan, Darryl 1938- ... CANR-21
Earlier sketch in CA 29-32R
Ponnamperuma, Cyril A. 1923- ... 101
Pons, Maurice 1927- ... CANR-5
Earlier sketch in CA 53-56
Ponsard, Francois 1814-1867 ... DLB 192
Ponsonby, D(oris) A(lmon) 1907- ... CANR-59
Earlier sketches in CA 5-8R, CANR-2
Ponsonby, Frederick Edward Neuflize
1913-1993 ... 13-16R
Obituary ... 143
Ponsonby, Laura 1935- ... 140
Ponsonby, William fl. 1577(?)-1604 ... DLB 170
Ponsot, Marie Birmingham ... 9-12R
Pont, Clarice Holt 1907- ... 5-8R
Ponte, Lowell (Alton) 1946- ... 57-60
Ponte, Pierre Viansson
See Viansson-Ponte, Pierre

Pontes, Paulo 1941(?)-1976 Obituary ... 69-72
Pontiero, Giovanni 1932- ... CANR-45
Earlier sketch in CA 29-32R
Pontiflet, Ted 1932- ... 105
See also SATA 32
Pontiggia, Giuseppe 1934- ... DLB 196
Ponting, Kenneth 1913-1983 Obituary ... 109
Pontney, Jack A(rthur) 1931- ... 21-24R
Pontoppidan, Henrik 1857-1943 ... TCLC 29
Ponty, Maurice Merleau
See Merleau-Ponty, Maurice
Pool, David de Sola 1885-1970 Obituary ... 29-32R
Pool, Elizabeth 1914- ... 114
Pool, Eugene (Hillhouse) 1943- ... 85-88
Pool, Ithiel de Sola 1917-1984 ... CANR-14
Obituary ... 112
Earlier sketch in CA 17-20R
Pool, Phoebe Dorothy 1913- ... 5-8R
Pool, Tamar de Sola 1891(?)-1981 Obituary ... 104
Poole, Ernest 1880-1950 Brief entry ... 109
See also DLB 9
Poole, Frederick King 1934- ... 25-28R
Poole, Gary Thomas 1931- ... 107
Poole, Gray Johnson 1906- ... CANR-6
Earlier sketch in CA 5-8R
See also SATA 1
Poole, Herbert (Leslie) ... 103
Poole, Herbert Edmund 1912-1984 Obituary ... 115
Poole, Josephine
See Helyar, Jane Penelope Josephine
See also CLC 17
See also SAAS 2
See also SATA 5
Poole, Lynn 1910-1969 ... 5-8R
See also SATA 1
Poole, Peggy 1925- ... CANR-49
Earlier sketches in CA 107, CANR-24
See also SATA 39
Poole, Peter A(ndrews) ... 113
Poole, Richard 1945- ... 135
Poole, Robert W(illiam), Jr. 1944- ... 112
Poole, Roger 1939- ... 102
Poole, Scott 1951- ... 147
Poole, Seth
See Riemer, George
Poole, Sophia 1804-1891 ... DLB 166
Poole, Susan 1926- ... 114
Poole, Victoria (Simes) 1927- ... 102
Pooler, Victor H(erbert), Jr. 1924- ... 13-16R
Pooley, Beverley J(ohn) 1934- ... 45-48
Pooley, Robert C(ecil) 1898-1978 ... CANR-7
Earlier sketch in CA 5-8R
Pooley, Roger 1947- ... 115
Poolla, Tirupati Raju
See Raju, Poolla Tirupati
Poor, Harold Lloyd 1935- ... 45-48
Poor, Henry Varnum 1914(?)-1972 Obituary 37-40R
Porere, Benjamin Perley 1820-1887 ... DLB 23
Poore, Charles (Graydon)
1902-1971 Obituary ... 29-32R
Poorman, Paul Arthur 1930-1992 ... 106
Obituary ... 136
Poortvliet, Rien 1932- ... 136
See also SATA 65
See also SATA-Brief 37
Poos, L. R. 1954- ... 141
Poots-Booby, Edna
See Larsen, Carl
Poovey, W(illiam) A(rthur) 1913- ... CANR-10
Earlier sketch in CA 21-24R
Popa, Vasko 1922-1991 ... 148
Brief entry ... 112
See also CLC 19
See also DLB 181
Popcorn, Faith (Beryl) 1947(?)- ... 145
Pope, Abbie Hanscom 1858-1894 ... DLB 140
Pope, Alexander 1688-1744 ... CDBLB 1660-1789
See also DA
See also DAB
See also DAC
See also DAM MST, POET
See also DLB 95, 101
See also WLC
Pope, Arthur Upham 1881-1969 Obituary ... 25-28R
Pope, Carl 1945- ... 113
Pope, Clifford Hillhouse 1899-1974 ... 1-4R
Obituary ... 103
Pope, Daniel 1946- ... 111
Pope, Deborah ... 136
Pope, Dudley (Bernard Egerton) 1925-1997 ...
CANR-59
Obituary ... 157
Earlier sketches in CA 5-8R, CANR-2
Pope, Edwin 1928- ... 73-76
Pope, Elizabeth Marie 1917- ... 49-52
See also SATA 38
See also SATA-Brief 36
Pope, Generoso Paul, Jr. 1927-1988 Obituary ... 126
Pope, Harrison (Graham), Jr. 1947- ... 41-44R
Pope, James S. Sr. 1900(?)-1985 Obituary ... 118
Pope, John Alexander 1906-1982 Obituary ... 107
Pope, Joya 1943- ... 124
Pope, Katherine Victoria 1939- ... 111
Pope, Maurice (Wildon Montague) 1926- ... 69-72
Pope, Michael James 1940- ... 101
Pope, Phyllis Ackerman
1894(?)-1977 Obituary ... 69-72
Pope, Ray 1924- ... 29-32R
Pope, Rebecca A. 1955- ... 167
Pope, Richard Martin 1916- ... 17-20R
Pope, Robert G(ardner) 1936- ... 29-32R
Pope, Robert H. 1925- ... 33-36R
Pope, Thomas Harrington 1913- ... 73-76
Pope, Whitney 1935- ... 69-72
Pope, Willard Bissell 1903-1988 Obituary ... 127
Pope-Hennessy, James 1916-1974 ... 97-100
Obituary ... 45-48
Pope-Hennessy, John W(yndham) 1913-1994 ...
CANR-35
Obituary ... 147
Earlier sketches in CA 1-4R, CANR-1
Popenoe, David 1932- ... CANR-54
Earlier sketches in CA 29-32R, CANR-12, 28
Popenoe, Paul (Bowman) 1888- ... CANR-27
Earlier sketch in CA 1-4R
Popescu, Christine 1930- ... CANR-20
Earlier sketches in CA 13-16R, CANR-7
See also Pullein-Thompson, Christine
See also SATA 82
Popescu, D. R.
See Popescu, Dumitru Radu
Popescu, Dumitru Radu 1935- Brief entry ... 122
Popescu, Julian (John Hunter) 1928- ... CANR-20
Earlier sketches in CA 1-4R, CANR-1
Popham, Arthur Ewart 1889-1970 Obituary ... 111
Popham, Estelle I. 1906- ... CANR-5
Earlier sketch in CA 1-4R
Popham, Hugh 1920- ... CANR-6
Earlier sketch in CA 5-8R
Popham, Margaret Evelyn
1895(?)-1982 Obituary ... 106
Popham, Melinda 1944- ... 49-52
Popham, Peter (Nicholas Home) 1952- ... 121
Popiel, Elda S(taver) 1915- ... 57-60
Popkin, Debra 1944- ... 118
Popkin, Jeremy D(avid) 1948- ... 102
Popkin, John William 1909- ... CAP-1
Earlier sketch in CA 13-14
Popkin, Richard H(enry) 1923- ... 77-80
Popkin, Roy 1921- ... 25-28R
Popkin, Samuel L(ewis) 1942- ... 163
Popkin, Zelda F. 1898-1983 ... 25-28R
Obituary ... 109
Poploff, Michelle 1956- ... 135
See also SATA 67
Popov, Dusko 1912(?)-1981 Obituary ... 105
Popov, Haralan (Ivanov) 1907-1988 ... 21-24R
Obituary ... 127
Popov, Mikhail Ivanovich 1742-c. 1790 ... DLB 150
Popovic, Aleksander 1929-1996 ... DLB 181
Popovic, Nenad D(ushan) 1909-1997 ... CAP-2
Earlier sketch in CA 29-32
Popovic, Tanya
See Popovic, Tatyana (Vladana)
Popovic, Tatyana (Vladana) 1928- ... 130
Popovsky, Mark 1922- ... CANR-41
Earlier sketches in CA 102, CANR-19
Popowski, Bert (John) 1904- ... CANR-17
Earlier sketch in CA 1-4R
Popp, K. Wendy ... SATA 91
Poppe, Fred C(hristoph) 1923- ... CANR-35
Earlier sketch in CA 114
Poppe, Nicholas N. 1897- ... 73-76
Poppel, Ernst
See Poeppel, Ernst
Poppel, Hans 1942- ... SATA 71
Poppema, Suzanne T. 1948- ... 154
Popper, Frank J. 1944- ... CANR-12
Earlier sketch in CA 29-32R
Popper, Karl R(aimund) 1902-1994 ... CANR-61
Obituary ... 146
Earlier sketches in CA 5-8R, CANR-3, 20
See also MTCW 1
Popperwell, Ronald G(eorge) (?)-1983 ... 153
Obituary ... 111
Poppino, Rollie E(dward) 1922- ... 13-16R
Popple, James 1927- ... 107
Poppleton, Marjorie 1895- ... CAP-1
Earlier sketch in CA 13-14
Popplewell, Jack 1911-1996 ... 9-12R
Obituary ... 154
Porada, Edith 1912-1994 ... 103
Obituary ... 144
Porath, Jonathan David 1944- ... 118
Porcari, Constance Kwolek 1933- ... 33-36R
Porcel, Baltasar 1937- ... 154
Porch, Douglas 1944- ... 107
Porche, Simone (Benda)
1877(?)-1985 Obituary ... 118
Porcher, Mary F. Wickham
See Bond, Mary Fanning Wickham
Porcino, Jane 1923- ... 116
Pore, Renate (Elfriede) 1943- ... 113
Porell, Bruce 1947- ... 102
Porges, Paul Peter 1927- ... 124
Poriss, Martin 1948- ... 81-84
Poritz, Lily
See Miller, Lily Poritz
Porkert, Manfred (Bruno) 1933- ... 131
Porlock, Martin
See MacDonald, Philip
Porosky, P. H. ... 45-48
Porqueras-Mayo, Alberto 1930- ... CANR-49
Earlier sketches in CA 45-48, CANR-24
Porsche, Ferdinand (Anton Ernst) 1909-1998 .89-92
Obituary ... 165
Porsche, Ferry
See Porsche, Ferdinand (Anton Ernst)
Port, M(ichael) H. 1930- ... 69-72
Port, Wymar
See Judy, Will(iam Lewis)
Porta, Antonio 1935-1989 ... DLB 128
Portal, Colette 1936- ... 53-56
See also SATA 6
Portal, Ellis
See Powe, Bruce
Portal, Francis Spencer 1903-1984 Obituary ... 114
Porte, Barbara Ann 1943- ... 159
See also SATA 57, 93
See also SATA-Brief 45
Porte, Joan 1955- ... 154
Porte, Joel (Miles) 1933- ... CANR-24
Earlier sketches in CA 17-20R, CANR-8
Porten, Bezalel 1931- ... CANR-11
Earlier sketch in CA 25-28R
Porteous, (Leslie) Crichton 1901- ... 5-8R
Porter, A(nthony) P(eyton) 1945- ... 136
See also SATA 68
Porter, Alan
See Clark, Ruth C(ampbell)
Porter, Alan L(eslie) 1945- ... 115
Porter, Albert Wright 1923- ... 107
Porter, Alvin
See Rowland, D(onald) S(ydney)
Porter, Andrew 1928- ... CANR-23
Earlier sketches in CA 53-56, CANR-5
Porter, Anna ... CANR-71
Earlier sketch in CA 130
Porter, Anna Maria 1780-1832 ... DLB 116, 159
Porter, Arthur T(homas) 1924- ... 5-8R
Porter, Barbara Nevling 1946- ... 152
Porter, Bern(ard Harden) 1911- ... CANR-24
Earlier sketches in CA 21-24R, CANR-9
Porter, Bernard (John) 1941- ... CANR-49
Earlier sketches in CA 107, CANR-24
Porter, Brian (Ernest) 1928- ... 25-28R
Porter, Bruce 1938- ... 124
Porter, Burton F(rederick) 1936- ... 106
Porter, C(edric) L(ambert) 1905- ... CAP-2
Earlier sketch in CA 23-24
Porter, Carolyn (Jane) 1946- ... 131
Porter, Charles A(llan) 1932- ... 21-24R
Porter, Cole 1893-1964 Obituary ... 93-96
Porter, Connie (Rose) 1959(?)- ... 142
See also BW 2
See also CLC 70
See also SATA 81
Porter, Darwin (Fred) 1937- ... CANR-56
Earlier sketches in CA 69-72, CANR-13, 30
Porter, David 1780-1843 ... DLB 183
Porter, David L(indsey) 1941- ... CANR-50
Earlier sketches in CA 107, CANR-24
Porter, David T. 1928- ... 17-20R
Porter, Donald 1939- ... CANR-19
Earlier sketch in CA 103
Porter, Donald Clayton
See Gerson, Noel Bertram
Porter, Edgar A(dwell) 1949- ... 168
Porter, Edward A. 1936- ... 21-24R
Porter, Eleanor H(odgman) 1868-1920 Brief
entry ... 108
See also DLB 9
Porter, Elias H(ull) 1914- ... 9-12R
Porter, Eliot (Furness) 1901-1990 ... CANR-42
Obituary ... 132
Earlier sketch in CA 5-8R
Porter, Ernest Graham 1889- ... 1-4R
Porter, Ethel K. 1901- ... CAP-2
Earlier sketch in CA 21-22
Porter, Fairfield 1907-1975 Obituary ... 61-64
Porter, Frank W(illiam) III 1947- ... 97-100
Porter, Gareth 1942- ... 130
Porter, Gene L. 1935- ... 25-28R
Porter, Gene(va Grace) Stratton 1863(?)-1924 Brief
entry ... 112
See also TCLC 21
Porter, George 1920- ... 107
Porter, Glenn 1944- ... 73-76
Porter, H(arry) Boone 1923- ... CANR-8
Earlier sketch in CA 5-8R
Porter, H(arry) C(ulverwell) 1927- ... 33-36R
Porter, Hal 1911-1984 ... CANR-60
Obituary ... 114
Earlier sketches in CA 9-12R, CANR-3
Porter, Henry ... DLB 62
Porter, J(ene) M(iles) 1937- ... CANR-21
Earlier sketch in CA 103
Porter, J(oshua) R(oy) 1921- ... CANR-5
Earlier sketch in CA 53-56
Porter, Jack Nusan 1944- ... CANR-44
Earlier sketches in CA 41-44R, CANR-20
Porter, James A(rmer), Jr. 1922- ... 121
Porter, James A(mos) 1905-1970 ... 155
Porter, Jane 1776-1850 ... DLB 116, 159
Porter, Janice Lee 1953- ... SATA 68
Porter, Joe Ashby 1942- ... CANR-12
Earlier sketch in CA 73-76
Porter, John 1919- ... 21-24R
Porter, Jonathan 1938- ... 77-80
Porter, Joseph C(harles) 1946- ... 116
Porter, Joyce 1924-1990 ... CANR-60
Obituary ... 133
Earlier sketches in CA 17-20R, CANR-8
Porter, Judith D(eborah) R(evitch) 1940- ... 81-84
Porter, Katherine Anne 1890-1980 ... CANR-65
Obituary ... 101
Earlier sketches in CA 1-4R, CANR-1
See also AITN 2
See also CLC 1, 3, 7, 10, 13, 15, 27, 101
See also DA
See also DAB
See also DAC
See also DAM MST, NOV
See also DLB 4, 9, 102
See also DLBD 12
See also DLBY 80
See also MTCW 1
See also SATA 39
See also SATA-Obit 23
See also SSC 4, 31
Porter, Kathryn
See Swinford, Betty (June Wells)
Porter, Kenneth Wiggins 1905- ... CANR-2
Earlier sketch in CA 5-8R
Porter, Laurence M(inot) 1936- ... CANR-47
Earlier sketches in CA 107, CANR-23
Porter, Lyman W(illiam) 1930- ... 21-24R
Porter, M. Gilbert 1937- ... 129
Porter, Margaret Eudine 1905-1975 ... CANR-8
Earlier sketch in CA 57-60
Porter, Mark
See Cox, James Anthony
and Leckie, Robert (Hugh)
Porter, McKenzie 1911- ... 69-72
Porter, Melinda Camber 1953- ... 127
Porter, Michael E. 1947- ... CANR-47
Earlier sketches in CA 105, CANR-22
Porter, Michael Leroy 1947- ... 118
Porter, Monica 1952- ... 107
Porter, Peter (Neville Frederick) 1929- ... 85-88
See also CLC 5, 13, 33
See also DLB 40
Porter, Philip W(iley) 1900-1985 ... 69-72
Obituary ... 116
Porter, R(obert) Russell 1908-1986 Obituary ... 120
Porter, Raymond J(ames) 1935- ... 85-88
Porter, Richard C(orbin) 1931- ... 9-12R
Porter, Robert 1946- ... CANR-48
Earlier sketch in CA 122
Porter, Roger B. 1946- ... 131
Porter, Sheena 1935- ... 81-84
See also SAAS 10
See also SATA 24
Porter, Sue
See Limb, Sue
Porter, Sue 1951- ... 143
See also SATA 76
Porter, Susan L(oraine) 1941- ... 142
Porter, Sylvia F(ield) 1913-1991 ... 81-84
Obituary ... 134
Porter, Theodore M(ark) 1953- ... CANR-50
Earlier sketch in CA 123
Porter, Thomas E. 1928- ... 29-32R
Porter, W(alter) Thomas, Jr. 1934- ... 29-32R
Porter, Willard H(all) 1920- ... 57-60
Porter, William E. 1918- ... CANR-13
Earlier sketch in CA 69-72
Porter, William Sydney 1862-1910 ... 131
Brief entry ... 104
See also Henry, O.
See also CDALB 1865-1917
See also DA
See also DAB
See also DAC
See also DAM MST
See also DLB 12, 78, 79
See also MTCW 1
See also YABC 2
Porter, William Trotter 1809-1858 ... DLB 3, 43
Porterfield, Amanda 1947- ... 138
Porterfield, Bruce 1925- ... 21-24R
Porterfield, Nolan 1936- ... 33-36R
Portes, Alejandro 1944- ... CANR-36
Earlier sketches in CA 93-96, CANR-16
Porteus, Stanley D(avid) 1883- ... CANR-17
Earlier sketch in CA 1-4R
Portillo (y Pacheco), Jose Lopez
See Lopez Portillo (y Pacheco), Jose
Portillo Trambley, Estela 1936- ... CANR-32
See also DAM MULT
See also HLC
See also HW
Portis, Charles (McColl) 1933- ... CANR-64
Earlier sketches in CA 45-48, CANR-1
See also DLB 6
Portisch, Hugo 1927- ... CANR-36
Earlier sketch in CA 21-24R
Portland, Charles 1952- ... 163
Portlock, Rob 1952- ... 128
Portman, David N(athan) 1937- ... 45-48
Portner, Hans O. 1955- ... 161
Portnoy, Howard N. 1946- ... 81-84
Portoghesi, Paolo 1931- ... 108
Portteus, Eleanora Marie Manthei
(?)-1983 ... SATA-Obit 36
Portugal, Franklin H. 1940- Brief entry ... 116
Portuges, Paul 1945- ... 77-80
Portway, Christopher (John) 1923- ... 57-60
Porush, David H(illel) 1952- ... CANR-17
Earlier sketch in CA 93-96
Porzelt, Paul 1902- ... 108
Posell, Elsa Z. ... CANR-20
Earlier sketches in CA 1-4R, CANR-4
See also SATA 3
Posen, Barry R. 1952- ... 137
Posener, Georges (Henri) 1906-1988 Obituary ... 125
Posey, Alexander (Lawrence) 1873-1908 ... 144
See also DAM MULT
See also DLB 175
See also NNAL
Posey, Carl A(lfred, Jr.) 1933- ... CANR-30
Earlier sketch in CA 111
Posey, Sam 1944- ... 93-96
Posey, Walter B(rownlow) 1900- ... CAP-1
Earlier sketch in CA 13-16
Posin, Daniel Q. 1909- ... CAP-1
Earlier sketch in CA 13-14
Posin, Jack A. 1900- ... 13-16R
Posnack, Emanuel R. 1897-1989 Obituary ... 128
Posner, Alice
See Fins, Alice
Posner, Barry Z(ane) 1949- ... CANR-54
Earlier sketch in CA 111
Posner, David Louis 1938-1985 ... 106
Obituary ... 117
Posner, Donald 1931- Brief entry ... 115
Posner, Ernst (Maximilian) 1892-1980 ... 41-44R
Obituary ... 97-100
Posner, Gerald L. 1954- ... 147
Posner, Mitchell Jay 1949- ... 110
Posner, Richard 1944- ... CANR-20
Earlier sketches in CA 53-56, CANR-5
Posner, Richard A. 1939- ... 135

Posner, Steve 1953- 127
Pospelov, Pyotr Nikolayevich
1898-1979 Obituary 85-88
Pospesel, Howard Andrew 1937- 73-76
Pospielovsky, Dimitry V. 1935- 29-32R
Pospisil, J(aroslav) Leopold 1923- 13-16R
Possony, Stefan T(homas)
1913-1995 Obituary 148
Brief entry 117
Post, Austin 1922- 85-88
Post, C(harles) Gordon 1903- CAP-1
Earlier sketch in CA 11-12
Post, Elizabeth L(indley) 1920- 49-52
Post, Emily Price 1873-1960 103
Obituary 89-92
Post, Felix 1913- 21-24R
Post, Gaines, Jr. 1937- CANR-12
Earlier sketch in CA 73-76
Post, Gaines 1902- CAP-1
Earlier sketch in CA 13-14
Post, Henry 1948- 61-64
Post, Homer A(very) 1888- CAP-2
Earlier sketch in CA 25-28
Post, J(eremiah) B(enjamin) 1937- 97-100
Post, Jeffrey E. 1954- 167
Post, John F(rederic) 1936- 127
Post, Jonathan F(rench) S(cott) 1947- CANR-37
Earlier sketch in CA 115
Post, Joyce A(rnold) 1939- CANR-8
Earlier sketch in CA 61-64
Post, Marie J. 1919- 111
Post, Melville Davisson 1869-1930 Brief entry 110
See also TCLC 39
Post, Robert C(harles) 1937- 148
Post, Steve(n A.) 1944- 103
Postal, Bernard 1905-1981 CANR-2
Obituary 103
Earlier sketch in CA 5-8R
Postan, Michael Moissey 1899-1981 Obituary 105
Postans, Marianne c. 1810-1865 DLB 166
Posten, Margaret L(ois) 1915- 29-32R
See also SATA 10
Poster, Carol 1956- 118
Poster, Cyril D(ennis) 1924- CANR-7
Earlier sketch in CA 13-16R
Poster, John B. 1939- 29-32R
Poster, Mark 1941- 33-36R
Posteuca, Vasile 1912-1972 Obituary 37-40R
Postgate, John (Raymond) 1922- 148
Postgate, Raymond (William) 1896-1971 CANR-3
Obituary 89-92
Earlier sketch in CA 5-8R
Posthumus, Cyril 1918- 104
Postl, Carl
See Sealsfield, Charles
Postlethwait, S(amuel) N(oel) 1918- CANR-8
Earlier sketch in CA 17-20R
Postma, Johannes Menne 1935- 135
Postma, Lidia 1952- 101
Postma, Magdalena Jacomina 1908- 65-68
Postma, Minnie
See Postma, Magdalena Jacomina
Postman, Andrew 1961- 147
Postman, Neil 102
Poston, Larry (A.) 1952- 138
Poston, Richard W(averly) 1914- 65-68
Poston, Ted
See Poston, Theodore Roosevelt Augustus Major
See also DLB 51
Poston, Theodore Roosevelt Augustus Major
1906-1974 125
Obituary 104
See also Poston, Ted
See also BW
Posvar, Wesley W(entz) 1925- 17-20R
Posy, Arnold 1894- 9-12R
Potash, Betty 1933- 122
Potash, P. Jeffrey 1953- 142
Potash, Robert A(aron) 1921- CANR-19
Earlier sketch in CA 102
Poteet, G(eorge) Howard 1935- CANR-53
Earlier sketches in CA 33-36R, CANR-13, 29
Pothan, Kap 1929- 29-32R
Potholm, Christian Peter II 1940- 29-32R
Potichnyj, Peter J(oseph) 1930- 41-44R
Potiphar
See Hern, (George) Anthony
Potok, Andrew 1931- 139
Potok, Chaim 1929- CANR-64
Earlier sketches in CA 17-20R, CANR-19, 35
Interview in CANR-19
See also AAYA 15
See also AITN 1, 2
See also CLC 2, 7, 14, 26, 112
See also DAM NOV
See also DLB 28, 152
See also MTCW 1
See also SATA 33
Potoker, Edward M(artin) 1931- 33-36R
Pottebaum, Gerald A. 1934- CANR-5
Earlier sketch in CA 9-12R
Potter, A(lfred) Neal 1915- 13-16R
Potter, (Helen) Beatrix 1866-1943 137
Brief entry 108
See also CLR 1, 19
See also DLB 141
See also SATA 100
See also YABC 1
Potter, (Helen) Beatrix 1866-1943
See Webb, (Martha) Beatrice (Potter)
See also MAICYA
Potter, Beverly A(nn) 1944- CANR-43
Earlier sketch in CA 119
Potter, Carol 1950- 152
Potter, Carole A. 1940- 123
Potter, Charles E(dward) 1916-1979 61-64
Obituary 135
Potter, Clare J. 1946- 122
Potter, Dan (Scott) 1932- 33-36R
Potter, David 1915- 29-32R
Potter, David Morris 1910-1971 108
See also DLB 17
Potter, Dennis (Christopher George) 1935-1994
CANR-61
Obituary 145
Earlier sketches in CA 107, CANR-33
See also CLC 58, 86
See also MTCW 1
Potter, Douglas A. 1956- 141
Potter, E. B. 1908- 37-40R
Potter, Eloise Fretz 1931- CANR-21
Earlier sketch in CA 105
Potter, Faith
See Toperoff, Sam
Potter, Frank N(ewton) 1911- 130
Potter, G(eorge) W(illiam, Jr.) 1930- 1-4R
Potter, Gail M(ac Leod) 1914- 25-28R
Potter, George Richard 1900- 5-8R
Potter, Harry (D.) 1954- 143
Potter, J(im) 1922- 21-24R
Potter, Jack M(ichael) 1936- 41-44R
Potter, James Gerrard 1944- 97-100
Potter, James H(arry) 1912-1978 Obituary 77-80
Potter, James L(ane) 1922- 107
Potter, Jennifer 1949- 156
Potter, (Ronald) Jeremy 1922-1997 CANR-58
Obituary 162
Earlier sketches in CA 53-56, CANR-30
Potter, John Mason 1907- CAP-1
Earlier sketch in CA 11-12
Potter, Joy Hambuechen 1935- 123
Potter, Karl Harrington 1927- 5-8R
Potter, Kathleen 1929(?)-1987 Obituary 122
Potter, Kathleen Jill 1932- 104
Potter, Lois 1941- CANR-15
Earlier sketch in CA 41-44R
Potter, Loren D(avid) 1918- 121
Potter, M(aurice) David 1900- CAP-2
Earlier sketch in CA 23-24
Potter, Margaret (Newman) 1926- CANR-44
Earlier sketches in CA 13-16R, CANR-6, 21
See also SATA 21
Potter, Marian 1915- CANR-1
Earlier sketch in CA 49-52
See also SATA 9
Potter, Miriam Clark 1886-1965 5-8R
See also SATA 3
Potter, Philip 1907-1988 Obituary 125
Potter, Robert Alonzo 1934- CANR-1
Earlier sketch in CA 45-48
Potter, Robert D(ucharme)
1905-1978 Obituary 77-80
Potter, Simeon 1898-1976 CANR-4
Earlier sketch in CA 5-8R
Potter, Stephen 1900-1969 101
Obituary 25-28R
See also MTCW 1
Potter, Sulamith Heins 1944- 81-84
Potter, Van Rensselaer 1911- 37-40R
Potter, Vincent G. 1928- 25-28R
Potter, William Hotchkiss 1914- 1-4R
Potterton, Gerald 1931- 49-52
Potterton, Homan 1946- CANR-25
Earlier sketch in CA 108
Pottker, Janice Marie 1948- CANR-42
Earlier sketch in CA 118
Pottle, Frederick A(lbert) 1897-1987 CANR-3
Obituary 122
Earlier sketch in CA 5-8R
See also DLB 103
See also DLBY 87
Potts, Albert M(intz) 1914- 116
Potts, Charles 1943- 105
Potts, E(li) Daniel 1930- 25-28R
Potts, Eve 1929- 103
Potts, George Chapman 1898- CAP-1
Earlier sketch in CA 11-12
Potts, Jean 1910- CANR-63
Earlier sketches in CA 5-8R, CANR-2
Potts, Paul (Hugh Patrick Howard)
1911-1990 Obituary 132
Potts, Ralph Bushnell 1901- 57-60
Potts, Richard 1938- 103
Potts, Stephen W(ayne) 1949- 149
Potts, Willard (Charles) 1929- 123
Potvin, Denis (Charles) 1953- Brief entry 113
Potvin, Georges C. 1928- 45-48
Potvin, Raymond H(erve) 1924- 21-24R
Pou, Genevieve Long 1919- Brief entry 114
Poucher, William Arthur 1891- CAP-1
Earlier sketch in CA 11-12
Pough, Frederick Harvey 1906- 81-84
Pouillon, Fernand 1912- 29-32R
Poulakidas, Andreas K. 1934- 45-48
Poulet, Georges 1902- 13-16R
Poulin, A(lfred A.), Jr. 1938-1996 CANR-32
Obituary 152
Earlier sketches in CA 21-24R, CANR-12
Poulin, Jacques 1937- 165
See also DLB 60
Poulin, Stephane 1961- 165
See also CLR 28
See also SATA 98
Poullada, Leon B(aqueiro) 1913-1987 Obituary 123
Poulos, Constantine 1916(?)-1986 Obituary 119
Poulter, S(cott) L(arry) 1943- 49-52
Poultney, David 1939- 141
Poulton, Edith Eleanor (Diana) Chloe 1903- 85-88
Poulton, Helen Jean 1920-1971 CAP-2
Earlier sketch in CA 33-36
Poulton, Richard (Christopher) 1938- 107
Pound, Arthur 1884-1966 Obituary 89-92
Pound, Ezra (Weston Loomis) 1885-1972
CANR-40
Obituary 37-40R
Earlier sketch in CA 5-8R
See also CDALB 1917-1929
See also CLC 1, 2, 3, 4, 5, 7, 10, 13, 18, 34, 48, 50, 112
See also DA
See also DAB
See also DAC
See also DAM MST, POET
See also DLB 4, 45, 63
See also DLBD 15
See also MTCW 1
See also PC 4
See also WLC
Pound, Merritt B(loodworth) 1898-1970 CAP-2
Earlier sketch in CA 19-20
Pound, Omar S(hakespear) 1926- CANR-45
Earlier sketches in CA 49-52, CANR-1, 16
Pound, Roscoe 1870-1964 Obituary 111
Pounds, Norman John Greville 1912- CANR-4
Earlier sketch in CA 1-4R
Pounds, Ralph Linnaeus 1910- 5-8R
Poundstone, William 1955- 151
Pournelle, Jerry (Eugene) 1933- CANR-30
Earlier sketch in CA 77-80
See also SATA 26, 91
Poussaint, Alvin F(rancis) 1934- 53-56
Povelite, Kay 1955- SATA 102
Povenmire, (Edward) King(sley) 1904- 61-64
Poverman, C. E. 1944- Brief entry 115
Povey, John F. 1929- 85-88
Povich, Maury 1939- 138
Povich, Shirley 1905- DLB 171
Povod, Reinaldo 1959-1994 136
Obituary 146
See also CLC 44
Pow, Tom 1950- 134
Powdermaker, Hortense 1900-1970 CAP-1
Obituary 29-32R
Earlier sketch in CA 13-14
Powe, B(ruce) W. 1955- 133
Powe, Bruce 1925- 53-56
Powe, Lucas A., Jr. 1943- 155
Powell, A. M.
See Morgan, Alfred P(owell)
Powell, Adam Clayton, Jr. 1908-1972 102
Obituary 33-36R
See also BLC 3
See also BW 1
See also CLC 89
See also DAM MULT
Powell, Alan 1936- 158
Powell, Ann 1951- SATA-Brief 51
Powell, Anthony (Dymoke) 1905- CANR-62
Earlier sketches in CA 1-4R, CANR-1, 32
See also CDBLB 1945-1960
See also CLC 1, 3, 7, 9, 10, 31
See also DLB 15
See also MTCW 1
Powell, Ardal 1958- 142
Powell, Barbara 1929- 119
Powell, Barry B. 1942- 136
Powell, Brian S(harples) 1934- 25-28R
Powell, Cecil Frank 1903-1969 157
Obituary 113
Powell, Clarence Alva 1905- CAP-1
Earlier sketch in CA 11-12
Powell, Clilan B. 1894-1977 Obituary 73-76
Powell, Colin L(uther) 1937- 158
Powell, (John) Craig 1940- 77-80
Powell, D. A. 1963- 168
Powell, Dannye Romine 1941- 147
Powell, David 1925- 142
Powell, David A. 1952- 146
Powell, Dawn 1897-1965 5-8R
See also CLC 66
See also DLBY 97
Powell, Donald M. 1914- 13-16R
Powell, Dorothy Baden
See Baden-Powell, Dorothy
Powell, Dorothy M. 1914- 106
Powell, (Drexel) Dwane (Jr.) 1944- 89-92
Powell, E. Sandy 1947- SATA 72
Powell, Elwin H(umphreys) 1925- 81-84
Powell, Eric F(rederick) W(illiam) 1899- CANR-6
Earlier sketch in CA 5-8R
Powell, Evan Arnold 1937- CANR-21
Earlier sketch in CA 69-72
Powell, Fern 1942- 25-28R
Powell, G. Bingham, Jr. 1942- CANR-11
Earlier sketch in CA 29-32R
Powell, Geoffrey Stewart 1914- 61-64
Powell, Gordon (George) 1911- 1-4R
Powell, Grosvenor (Edward) 1932- 129
Powell, Ivor 1910- CANR-38
Earlier sketches in CA 1-4R, CANR-17
Powell, J(ohn) Enoch 1912- 97-100
Powell, James 1932- CANR-65
Earlier sketch in CA 107
Powell, James M(atthew) 1930- CANR-8
Earlier sketch in CA 5-8R
Powell, James V(irgil) 1938- 104
Powell, John Roland 1889- CAP-1
Earlier sketch in CA 13-14
Powell, John Wesley 1834-1902 DLB 186
Powell, L(awrence) F(itzroy)
1881-1975 Obituary 57-60
Powell, Larson Merrill 1932- 103
Powell, Lawrence Clark 1906- CANR-25
Earlier sketches in CA 21-24R, CANR-8
Powell, Lawrence N(elson) 1943- 104
Powell, Lily
See Froissard, Lily Powell
Powell, Marcia (Leonora) 108
Powell, Margaret 1907(?)-1984 CANR-15
Obituary 112
Earlier sketch in CA 29-32R
Powell, Marvin 1924- CANR-8
Earlier sketch in CA 21-24R
Powell, Meredith (Ann) 1936- 37-40R
Powell, Michael (Latham) 1905-1990 150
Obituary 130
Powell, Milton Bryan 1934- 21-24R
Powell, Neil
See Innes, Brian
Powell, Neil 1948- CANR-34
Earlier sketches in CA 85-88, CANR-15
Powell, (Caryll) Nicolas (Peter) 1920- CANR-12
Earlier sketch in CA 61-64
Powell, Norman J(ohn) 1908-1974 CAP-2
Obituary 49-52
Earlier sketch in CA 21-22
Powell, Padgett 1952- CANR-63
Earlier sketch in CA 126
See also CLC 34
Powell, Pamela 1960- 146
See also SATA 78
Powell, Paul W. 1933- 116
Powell, Peter 1908-1985 Obituary 116
Powell, Peter John 1928- 33-36R
Powell, Philip Wayne 1913- 85-88
Powell, Ralph L. 1917-1975 Obituary 57-60
Powell, Raymond P(ark)
1922-1980 Obituary 97-100
Powell, Reed M(adsen) 1921- 29-32R
Powell, Richard (Pitts) 1908- CANR-4
Earlier sketch in CA 1-4R
Powell, Richard Stillman
See Barbour, Ralph Henry
Powell, Robert (Stephenson Smyth) Baden
See Baden-Powell, Robert (Stephenson Smyth)
Powell, Robert Richard 1909- 5-8R
Powell, Ronald R(owe) 1944- 114
Powell, Shirley 1931- 106
Powell, Sidney W. 5-8R
Powell, Simon G. 1960- 144
Powell, Stephanie 1953- 158
See also SATA 93
Powell, Sumner Chilton 1924- 5-8R
Powell, Talmage 1920- CANR-2
Earlier sketch in CA 5-8R
Powell, Terry 1949- 103
Powell, Theodore 1919- 1-4R
Powell, Thomas F. 1933- 25-28R
Powell, Victor M(organ) 1919- 45-48
Powell, Violet Georgiana 1912- 103
Powell, William S(tevens) 1919- 69-72
Powell-Smith, Vincent (Walter Francis) 1939-
CANR-30
Earlier sketch in CA 25-28R
Powelson, John Palen 1920- CANR-41
Earlier sketches in CA 1-4R, CANR-4, 19
Power, Arthur
See Dudden, Arthur P(ower)
Power, Brian 1918- 139
Power, Catherine
See Du Breuil, (Elizabeth) L(or)inda
Power, Edward John 1921- CANR-2
Earlier sketch in CA 5-8R
Power, Eileen (Edna Le Poer) 1889-1940 154
Power, Francis C. 1909(?)-1987 Obituary 124
Power, John 1927- 61-64
Power, Jonathan 1941- 107
Power, M(aurice) S(tephen) 1935- 130
Power, Margaret (M.) SATA 75
Power, Margaret 1950- CANR-54
Earlier sketch in CA 127
Power, Michael 1933- CAP-1
Earlier sketch in CA 11-12
Power, Nancy Goslee 1942- 154
Power, Norman S(andiford) 1916- CANR-10
Earlier sketch in CA 65-68
Power, Patrick C(arthage) 1928- 146
Power, Paul F(rederick) 1925- 41-44R
Power, Richard 1928-1970 CAP-1
Earlier sketch in CA 9-10
Power, Susan 1961- CLC 91
Power, Tyrone
See Guthrie, (William) Tyrone
Power, (Patrick) Victor 1930- CANR-13
Earlier sketch in CA 77-80
Power-Ross, Robert W. 1922- 102
Powers, Alan 1955- 140
Powers, Andy 1896- CANR-6
Earlier sketch in CA 57-60
Powers, Anne
See Schwartz, Anne Powers
Powers, Barbara Hudson
See Dudley, Barbara Hudson
Powers, Bill 1931- 77-80
See also SATA 52
See also SATA-Brief 31
Powers, Bob
See Powers, Robert L(eroy)
and Repp, William
Powers, David Guy 1911-1967 CAP-2
Earlier sketch in CA 19-20
Powers, Doris Cooper 1918- 105
Powers, Edward A(lvin) 1941- 77-80
Powers, Edward Alton 1927- 53-56
Powers, Edward D(oyle) 1900- 45-48
Powers, Edwin 1896- 73-76
Powers, Francis Gary 1929-1977 Obituary 109
Powers, George
See Infield, Glenn (Berton)
Powers, Georgia Davis 1923- 150
Powers, Helen 1925- 97-100

Powers, J(ames) F(arl) 1917- CANR-61
Earlier sketches in CA 1-4R, CANR-2
See also CLC 1, 4, 8, 57
See also DLB 130
See also MTCW 1
See also SSC 4
Powers, Jeffrey W(ells) 1950- 61-64
Powers, John J(ames) 1945- 69-72
See also Powers, John R.
Powers, John R.
See Powers, John J(ames)
See also CLC 66
Powers, Joseph M(ichael) 1926- 85-88
Powers, Lyall H(arris) 1924- 145
Brief entry 115
Powers, M. L.
See Tubb, E(dwin) C(harles)
Powers, Mala 1931- 129
Powers, Margaret
See Heal, Edith
Powers, Mark James 1940- 110
Powers, Meredith A(nn) 1949- 140
Powers, Nora
See Pykare, Nina
Powers, Patrick W(illiam) 1924- 13-16R
Powers, Richard (S.) 1957- 148
See also CLC 93
Powers, Richard M. Gorman 1921- 21-24R
Powers, Robert L(eroy) 1924- 93-96
Powers, Robert M(aynard) 1942- CANR-14
Earlier sketch in CA 77-80
Powers, Ron(ald Dean) 1941- CANR-56
Earlier sketch in CA 97-100
Powers, Steve 1934- 145
Powers, Thomas (Moore) 1940- CANR-17
Earlier sketch in CA 37-40R
Interview in CANR-17
Powers, Tim 1952- 134
Powers, Treval C(lifford) 1900- 158
Powers, William 1930- 45-48
Powers, William Edwards 1902- CAP-2
Earlier sketch in CA 19-20
Powers, William K(eegan) 1934- 25-28R
Powers, William T(reval) 1926- 111
Powers, Willow Roberts 1943- 127
Powerscourt, Sheila
See Wingfield, Sheila (Claude)
Power-Waters, Alma Shelley 1896-1983 . CANR-18
Earlier sketch in CA 1-4R
Power-Waters, Brian 1922- CANR-18
Earlier sketch in CA 93-96
Powicke, Michael Rhys 1920- CANR-8
Earlier sketch in CA 5-8R
Powledge, Fred 1935- CANR-58
Earlier sketches in CA 21-24R, CANR-9, 27
See also SATA 37
Powles, William E(arnest) 1919- 144
Powley, Edward Barzillai 1887-1968 .... CAP-1
Earlier sketch in CA 13-14
Powley, Florence Mary Pomeroy 1892- CAP-1
Earlier sketch in CA 13-16
Powling, Chris 1943- CANR-49
Earlier sketch in CA 121
Pownall, David 1938- CANR-49
Earlier sketch in CA 89-92
See also CAAS 18
See also CLC 10
See also DLB 14
Powrie, Peter James 1927- 21-24R
Powys, John Cowper 1872-1963 85-88
See also CLC 7, 9, 15, 46
See also DLB 15
See also MTCW 1
Powys, Llewelyn 1884-1939 .... DLB 98
Powys, T(heodore) F(rancis) 1875-1953 Brief entry 106
See also DLB 36, 162
See also TCLC 9
Poyer, David 1949- CANR-30
Earlier sketch in CA 111
Poyer, Joe
See Poyer, Joseph John (Jr.)
Poyer, Joseph John (Jr.) 1939- CANR-40
Earlier sketches in CA 49-52, CANR-1, 17
Poynor, Robin 1942- 150
Poynter, Dan(iel Frank) 1938- CANR-49
Earlier sketches in CA 89-92, CANR-24
Poynter, Margaret 1927- CANR-36
Earlier sketches in CA 93-96, CANR-16
See also SATA 27
Poynter, Nelson 1903-1978 Obituary 77-80
See also DLB 127
Pozner, Vladimir 1934- 136
See also BEST 90:3
Pozzessere, Heather Graham 141
Pozzetta, George Enrico 1942- CANR-29
Earlier sketch in CA 111
Prabhavananda, Swami 1893-1976 .... CANR-8
Obituary 65-68
Earlier sketch in CA 17-20R
Prabhu, Pandharinath H. 1911- CANR-7
Earlier sketch in CA 13-16R
Prabhupada, A. C. Bhaktivedanta 1896-1977 .... CANR-14
Earlier sketch in CA 73-76
Prabhupada, A. C. Bhaktivedanta Swami
See Prabhupada, A. C. Bhaktivedanta
Prada, Manuel Gonzalez
See Gonzalez Prada, Manuel
Prada Oropeza, Renato 1937- CANR-32
Earlier sketch in CA 41-44R
See also HW
Prado, C(arlos) G(onzalez) 1937- CANR-52
Earlier sketches in CA 110, CANR-27
Prado (Calvo), Pedro 1886-1952 131
See also HW
See also TCLC 75
Prados, Emilio 1899-1962 .... DLB 134
Prados, John 1951- 106
Praed, Winthrop Mackworth 1802-1839 .... DLB 96
Praetorius, Johannes 1630-1680 .... DLB 168
Prager, Arthur CANR-12
Earlier sketch in CA 29-32R
See also SATA 44
Prager, Emily 1952- .... CLC 56
Prager, Jonas 1938- 105
Prager, Karsten 1936-1998 73-76
Obituary 166
Prago, Albert 1911- 29-32R
Prain, Ronald (Lindsay) 1907- 109
Prall, Stuart E(dward) 1929- 21-24R
Pramoedya, Ananta Toer 1925- 134
Prance, Claude A(nnett) 1906- CANR-43
Earlier sketches in CA 89-92, CANR-20
Prance, Ghillean Tolmie 1937- 145
Prance, June E(lizebeth) 1929- 69-72
Prandy, K(enneth) 1938- CANR-45
Earlier sketch in CA 117
Prange, Erwin (Edward) 1917- 113
Prange, Gordon W(illiam) 1910-1980 158
Obituary 97-100
Pranger, Robert J(ohn) 1931- CANR-10
Earlier sketch in CA 25-28R
Prantera, Amanda 1942- 130
Brief entry 126
Prasad, S(rinivas) Benjamin 1929- CANR-5
Earlier sketch in CA 53-56
Prassel, Frank Richard 1937- CANR-1
Earlier sketch in CA 49-52
Pratchett, Terry 1948- 143
See also AAYA 19
See also SATA 82
Prater, Donald A(rthur) 1918- CANR-60
Earlier sketch in CA 128
Prater, John 1947- .... SATA 72
Prathap, G(angan) 1951- 148
Prather, Hugh 1938- CANR-2
Earlier sketch in CA 45-48
Prather, Richard S(cott) 1921- CANR-58
Earlier sketches in CA 1-4R, CANR-5
Pratley, Gerald 1923- 112
Pratney, William Alfred 1944- 124
Pratney, Winkie
See Pratney, William Alfred
Pratolini, Vasco 1913-1991 .... DLB 177
Pratson, Frederick John 1935- 101
Pratt, Allan D(aniel) 1933- 112
Pratt, Charles 1926-1976 .... CANR-21
Obituary 65-68
Earlier sketch in CA 69-72
Pratt, Chris (James) 1950- 118
Pratt, (Mildred) Claire 1921- 103
Pratt, Dallas 1914-1994 106
Obituary 145
Pratt, E(dwin) J(ohn) 1883(?)-1964 141
Obituary 93-96
See also CLC 19
See also DAC
See also DAM POET
See also DLB 92
Pratt, (Murray) Fletcher 1897-1956 161
Brief entry 113
See also SATA 102
Pratt, J(oseph) Gaither 1910-1979 .... CANR-6
Obituary 89-92
Earlier sketch in CA 9-12R
Pratt, James Norwood 1942- 112
Pratt, Jane 1963(?)- 138
See also AAYA 9
Pratt, John 1931- CANR-1
Earlier sketch in CA 1-4R
Pratt, John Clark 1932- CANR-40
Earlier sketches in CA 13-16R, CANR-17
Pratt, John Lowell 1906-1968 .... CANR-3
Earlier sketch in CA 1-4R
Pratt, Julius W(illiam) 1888- CAP-1
Earlier sketch in CA 11-12
Pratt, Keith L(eslie) 1938- 29-32R
Pratt, Kristin Joy 1976- .... SATA 87
Pratt, Norman T(wombly), Jr. 1911- 118
Pratt, Pierre 1962- 160
See also SATA 95
Pratt, Robert Cranford 1926- 101
Pratt, Samuel Jackson 1749-1814 .... DLB 39
Pratt, Theodore 1901-1969 .... CANR-4
Earlier sketch in CA 1-4R
Pratt, William C(rouch, Jr.) 1927- CANR-6
Earlier sketch in CA 13-16R
Pratt, Willis Winslow 1908- Brief entry 105
Pratt-Butler, Grace Kipp 1916- 103
Pratte, Richard (Norman) 1929- 93-96
Prattis, Percival L. 1895-1980 Obituary 97-100
Prawer, Joshua 1917- 41-44R
Prawer, S(iegbert) S(alomon) 1925- CANR-54
Earlier sketches in CA 103, CANR-29
Pray, Lawrence M. 1947- 113
Praz, Mario 1896-1982 101
Obituary 106
Prchal, Mildred 1895-1983 Obituary 109
Prebble, John Edward Curtis 1915- CANR-64
Earlier sketches in CA 5-8R, CANR-3
Prebble, Marjorie Mary Curtis 1912- CANR-15
Earlier sketch in CA 17-20R
Prebish, Charles S(tuart) 1944- 57-60
Preble, Duane 1936- 61-64
Preble, Robert Curtis 1897-1983 Obituary 111
Predmore, Michael P. 1938- CANR-34
Earlier sketch in CA 45-48
Predmore, Richard L. 1911- 17-20R
Preece, Harold 1906- 5-8R
Preece, Rod(ney John) 1939- 113
Preedy, George
See Campbell, (Gabrielle) Margaret (Vere)
Preeg, Ernest H. 1934- 33-36R
Prefontaine, Yves 1937- .... DLB 53
Pregel, Boris 1893-1976 Obituary 106
Preger, Paul D(aniel), Jr. 1926- 49-52
Preheim, Marion Keeney 1934- 25-28R
Preil, Gabriel (Joshua) 1911-1993 .... CANR-1
Obituary 141
Earlier sketch in CA 49-52
Preiser, Wolfgang F(riedrich) E(rnst) 1941- CANR-7
Earlier sketch in CA 57-60
Preiss, Byron (Cary) CANR-14
Earlier sketch in CA 69-72
See also SATA 47
See also SATA-Brief 42
Preiss, David (Lee) 1935- 69-72
Prejean, Helen 1939(?)- 147
Prelinger, Ernst 1926- 9-12R
Preller, James 1961- 152
See also SATA 88
Prelutsky, Jack 1940- CANR-38
Earlier sketch in CA 93-96
See also CLR 13
See also DLB 61
See also MAICYA
See also SATA 22, 66
Prem, Dhani 1904(?)-1979 Obituary 93-96
Prem, Hanns J(uergen) 1941- 153
Premacanda
See Srivastava, Dhanpat Rai
Premack, Ann J(ames) 1929- 57-60
Premack, David 1925- 126
Premchand
See Srivastava, Dhanpat Rai
See also TCLC 21
Premchand, Munshi
See Srivastava, Dhanpat Rai
Prem Chand, Munshi
See Srivastava, Dhanpat Rai
Preminger, Alex 1915- 13-16R
Preminger, Erik Lee 1944- 132
Preminger, Marion Mill 1913-1972 Obituary . 33-36R
Preminger, Otto (Ludwig) 1906(?)-1986 134
Obituary 119
Brief entry 110
Premont, Brother Jeremy
See Willett, Brother Franciscus
Prendergast, Alan 1956- 124
Prendergast, Curtis 1915- 154
Prendergast, John 1958- 150
Prendergast, Karen A(nn) 1951- 117
Prentice, Amy
See Kaler, James Otis
Prentice, Ann E(thelynd) 1933- CANR-6
Earlier sketch in CA 57-60
Prentice, Charlotte
See Platt, Charles
Prentice, George D. 1802-1870 .... DLB 43
Prentice, P(ierrepont) I(sham) 1899-1989 Obituary 127
Prenting, Theodore O(tto) 1933- 57-60
Prentis, Steve (?)-1987 Obituary 122
Prentiss, Augustin M. 1890-1977 Obituary 69-72
Presberg, Miriam Goldstein 1919-1978 .... CANR-3
Earlier sketch in CA 1-4R
See also SATA-Brief 38
Prescott, Allen 1904(?)-1978 Obituary 73-76
Prescott, Caleb
See Bingley, David Ernest
Prescott, Casey
See Morris, Chris(topher Crosby)
Prescott, David M(arshall) 1926- 127
Brief entry 113
Prescott, J(ohn) R(obert) V(ictor) 1931- .. CANR-23
Earlier sketch in CA 107
Prescott, Jack
See Preston, John
Prescott, John Brewster 1919- CANR-64
Earlier sketch in CA 5-8R
Prescott, Kenneth W(ade) 1920- CANR-8
Earlier sketch in CA 57-60
Prescott, Orville 1906-1996 .... 41-44R
Obituary 152
See also DLBY 96
Prescott, Peter S(herwin) 1935- CANR-14
Earlier sketch in CA 37-40R
Interview in CANR-14
Prescott, William Hickling 1796-1859 . DLB 1, 30, 59
Preseren, France 1800-1849 .... DLB 147
Preshing, W(illiam) A(nthony) 1929- 85-88
Preslan, Kristina 1945- 106
Presland, John
See Bendit, Gladys Williams
Presley, Delma E(ugene) 1939- CANR-31
Earlier sketch in CA 112
Presley, James (Wright) 1930- CANR-10
Earlier sketch in CA 21-24R
Presley, Priscilla Ann (Beaulieu) 1945- 166
Presnall, Judith (Ann) Janda 1943- 161
See also SATA 96
Presnell, Robert (Jr.) 1915(?)-1986 Obituary 119
Presner, Lewis A. 1945- 142
Press, (Otto) Charles 1922- CANR-6
Earlier sketch in CA 13-16R
Press, Frank 1924- 130
Press, John (Bryant) 1920- CANR-3
Earlier sketch in CA 9-12R
Press, Simone Juda 1943- 111
Press, Toni 1949- 108
Pressau, Jack Renard 1933- 77-80
Pressburger, Emeric 1902-1988 104
Obituary 124
Presseisen, Ernst L(eopold) 1928- 13-16R
Presser, (Gerrit) Jacob 1899-1970 .... CAP-2
Earlier sketch in CA 25-28
Presser, Janice 1946- CANR-24
Earlier sketch in CA 107
Presser, Stephen B. 1946- 139
Pressly, Thomas J(ames) 1919- 17-20R
Pressman, David 1937- 89-92
Pressman, Jeffrey L(eonard) 1943- CANR-3
Earlier sketch in CA 45-48
Prest, Alan Richmond 1919-1985 93-96
Obituary 115
Prest, Wilfred 1907-1985 111
Obituary 117
Prest, Wilfrid R(obertson) 1940- 112
Prestbo, John A(ndrew) 1941- CANR-2
Earlier sketch in CA 49-52
Prestera, Hector A(nthony) 1932- 65-68
Presthus, Robert 1917- CANR-20
Earlier sketches in CA 1-4R, CANR-5
Prestidge, Pauline 1922- 103
Preston, Dickson J(oseph) 1914-1985 .... CANR-8
Obituary 114
Earlier sketch in CA 61-64
Preston, Douglas 1956- 141
Preston, Edna Mitchell 111
See also SATA 40
Preston, Edward
See Guess, Edward Preston
Preston, Florence (Margaret) 1905- 103
Preston, Frances I(sabella) 1898- 61-64
Preston, Harry 1923- CANR-48
Earlier sketches in CA 57-60, CANR-23
Preston, Ivan L. 1931- 57-60
Preston, Ivy (Alice) Kinross 1914- CANR-58
Earlier sketches in CAP-1, CA 9-10, CANR-12, 30
Preston, James
See Unett, John
Preston, James 1913- CAP-1
Earlier sketch in CA 9-10
Preston, James J(ohn) 1941- CANR-27
Earlier sketch in CA 109
Preston, John 1945-1994 130
Obituary 145
Preston, John Hyde 1906-1980 Obituary 102
Preston, Lee E. 1930- CANR-11
Earlier sketch in CA 21-24R
Preston, Lillian Elvira 1918- 108
See also SATA 47
Preston, May Wilson 1873-1949 .... DLB 188
Preston, Michael B. 1933- 126
Preston, Nathaniel Stone 1928- 29-32R
Preston, Ralph C(lausius) 1908- CANR-6
Earlier sketch in CA 13-16R
Preston, Richard
See Lindsay, Jack
Preston, Richard (McCann) 1954- CANR-66
Earlier sketch in CA 128
Preston, Richard Arthur 1910- CANR-18
Earlier sketches in CA 5-8R, CANR-3
Preston, Thomas 1537-1598 .... DLB 62
Preston, Thomas A(rthur) 1933- 112
Preston, Thomas R(onald) 1936- Brief entry ... 109
Preston, William L(ee) 1949- 105
Preston-Mafham, Rod(ney Arthur) 1942- 146
Prestwich, Menna 1917- 21-24R
Prestwich, Michael (Charles) 1943- 134
Preti, Luigi 1914- 154
Pretorius, Hertha
See Kouts, Hertha Pretorius
Preto-Rodas, Richard (Anthony) 1936- 49-52
Prettyman, E(lijah) Barrett, Jr. 1925- 9-12R
Preus, Anthony 1936- 49-52
Preus, Herman Amberg 1896- 85-88
Preus, Jacob A(all) O(ttesen) 1920- 33-36R
Preus, Johan Carl Keyser 1881-1983 Obituary . 111
Preus, Robert 1924- 33-36R
Preuss, Paul 1942- 130
Preussler, Otfried 1923- 77-80
See also CLC 17
See also SATA 24
Prevelakis, Pandelis 1909-1986 Obituary 118
Prevert, Jacques (Henri Marie) 1900-1977 .... CANR-61
Obituary 69-72
Earlier sketches in CA 77-80, CANR-29
See also CLC 15
See also MTCW 1
See also SATA-Obit 30
Previn, Andre (George) 1929- 115
Previn, Dor(oth)y (Langan) 1929(?)- 111
Prevost, Alain 1930(?)-1971 Obituary 33-36R
Prevost, Marcel 1862-1941 Brief entry 116
Prevots, Naima 1935- 135
Prewitt, Kenneth 1936- CANR-12
Earlier sketch in CA 29-32R
Preziosi, Donald 1941- 93-96
Prezzolini, Giuseppi 1882-1982 Obituary 107
Pribam, Karl 1878(?)-1973 Obituary 41-44R
Pribichevich, Stoyan 1905(?)-1976 Obituary .. 65-68
Price, A(lice) Lindsay 1927- 152
Price, Alan 1943- 149
Price, Alfred 1936- CANR-24
Earlier sketches in CA 21-24R, CANR-9
Price, Anthony 1928- CANR-61
Earlier sketches in CA 77-80, CANR-15, 33
Price, Archibald Grenfell 1892-1977 .... 9-12R
Obituary 125
Price, Arnold H(ereward) 1912- 45-48
Price, Barbara Anne Ellvinger 1946(?)-1987 Obituary 122
Price, Barbara Pradal 1946- 103
Price, Beverley Joan 1931- CANR-49
Earlier sketches in CA 106, CANR-24
See also SATA 98
Price, Bruce D(eitrick) 1941- 25-28R
Price, Byron 1891-1981 Obituary 104

Price, Cecil (John Layton) 1915- 21-24R
Price, Charles 1925- 9-12R
Price, Charles C(oale) 1913- 107
Price, Charles P(hilip) 1920- 115
Price, Christine (Hilda) 1928-1980 CANR-4
Obituary 93-96
Earlier sketch in CA 5-8R
See also SATA 3
See also SATA-Obit 23
Price, Daniel O('Haver) 1918- 21-24R
Price, (Paul) David 1940- 130
Price, David Deakins 1902-1983 Obituary 110
Price, Deb 1958- 152
Price, Derek (John) de Solla 1922-1983 CANR-3
Obituary 110
Earlier sketch in CA 1-4R
Price, Don C(ravens) 1937- 81-84
Price, Don K(rasher, Jr.) 1910-1995 73-76
Obituary 149
Price, E(dgar) Hoffmann (Trooper) 1898-1988 CANR-10
Obituary 125
Earlier sketch in CA 61-64
Price, Emerson 1902(?)-1977 Obituary 104
Price, Eugenia 1916-1996 CANR-18
Obituary 152
Earlier sketches in CA 5-8R, CANR-2
See also BEST 89:4
See also DAM POP
Price, Evadne 1896-1985 Obituary 116
Price, Frances Brown 1895- 49-52
Price, Francis Wilson 1895-1974 CAP-1
Earlier sketch in CA 13-14
Price, Frank James 1917- 104
Price, Frank W.
See Price, Francis Wilson
Price, Garrett 1896-1979 Obituary 85-88
See also SATA-Obit 22
Price, George 1901-1995 103
Obituary 147
Price, George (Henry) 1910-(?) CAP-1
Earlier sketch in CA 13-14
Price, George R(ennie) 1909- CANR-4
Earlier sketch in CA 1-4R
Price, Glanville 1928- 132
Price, Glenn W(arren) 1918- 21-24R
Price, Harry 1881-1948 Brief entry 119
Price, Henry Habberley 1899-1984 Obituary 114
Price, J(oseph) H(enry) 1924- 25-28R
Price, Jacob M(yron) 1925- CANR-1
Earlier sketch in CA 45-48
Price, James Ligon, Jr. 1915- 1-4R
Price, Jennifer
See Hoover, Helen (Drusilla Blackburn)
Price, Jimmie
See White, John I(rwin)
Price, Joan 1931- CANR-54
Earlier sketch in CA 111
Price, John A(ndrew) 1933- CANR-7
Earlier sketch in CA 57-60
Price, John Valdimir 1937- 17-20R
Price, Jonathan (Reeve) 1941- CANR-19
Earlier sketches in CA 45-48, CANR-3
See also SATA 46
Price, Kenneth M(arsden) 1954- CANR-38
Earlier sketch in CA 115
Price, Kingsley Blake 1917- 21-24R
Price, Larkin B(url) 1927- Brief entry 112
Price, Leo 1941- 77-80
Price, Lucie Locke
See Locke, Lucie
Price, Margaret (Evans) 1888-1973 Obituary 109
See also SATA-Brief 28
Price, Marion E(lizabeth) 1947- 111
Price, Marjorie 1929- 53-56
Price, Martin 1920- CANR-13
Earlier sketch in CA 17-20R
Price, Miles O(scar) 1890-1968 CAP-1
Earlier sketch in CA 13-16
Price, Molly 1903(?)-1984 Obituary 114
Price, Morgan Philips 1885-1973 CAP-1
Earlier sketch in CA 13-14
Price, (Lilian) Nancy (Bache) 1880-1970 Obituary 111
Price, Nelson Lynn 1931- CANR-24
Earlier sketches in CA 61-64, CANR-8
Price, Olive 1903- 41-44R
See also SATA 8
Price, Paul 1912(?)-1985 Obituary 116
Price, R(onald) F(rancis) 1926- CANR-26
Earlier sketch in CA 29-32R
Price, R(ichard) G(eoffrey) G(eorge) 1910- CAP-1
Earlier sketch in CA 13-14
Price, Ray(mond John) 1931- 25-28R
Price, Ray Glenn 1903- CANR-2
Earlier sketch in CA 5-8R
Price, Raymond (Kissam, Jr.) 1930- 105
Price, (Edward) Reynolds 1933- CANR-57
Earlier sketches in CA 1-4R, CANR-1, 37
Interview in CANR-37
See also CLC 3, 6, 13, 43, 50, 63
See also DAM NOV
See also DLB 2
See also SSC 22
Price, Rhys
See Price, George (Henry)
Price, Richard 1723-1791 DLB 158
Price, Richard 1941- CANR-27
Earlier sketch in CA 105
Price, Richard 1949- CANR-3
Earlier sketch in CA 49-52
See also CLC 6, 12
See also DLBY 81
Price, Robert 1900- 33-36R
Price, Robert M. 1941- 139
Price, Robert W. 1925(?)-1979 Obituary 89-92
Price, Roger 1921- 9-12R
Price, Roger (David) 1944- CANR-35
Earlier sketch in CA 107
Price, S(eymour) Stephen 1919- 25-28R
Price, Sally 1943- CANR-27
Earlier sketch in CA 106
Price, Stanley 1931- 13-16R
Price, Steven D(avid) 1940- CANR-37
Earlier sketches in CA 49-52, CANR-1, 16
Price, Susan 1955- 105
See also SATA 25, 85
Price, V(incent) B(arrett) 1940- 69-72
Price, Victor 1930- 9-12R
Price, Vincent (Leonard) 1911-1993 89-92
Obituary 143
Price, Walter K(leber) 1924- CANR-7
Earlier sketch in CA 17-20R
Price, Willadene Anton 1914- 5-8R
Price, Willard 1887-1983 CANR-1
Earlier sketch in CA 1-4R
See also SATA 48
See also SATA-Brief 38
Price, William 1938- 37-40R
Price, Wilson T(itus) 1931- 37-40R
Priceman, Marjorie SATA 81
Price-Mars, Jean 1875-1969 153
Obituary 112
See also BW 2
Prichard, Caradog 1904-1980 103
Obituary 97-100
Prichard, Doris (Smith) 1947- 116
Prichard, James W(illiam) 1925- 13-16R
Prichard, Katharine Susannah 1883-1969 CANR-33
Earlier sketches in CAP-1, CA 11-12
See also CLC 46
See also MTCW 1
See also SATA 66
Prichard, Nancy S(awyer) 1924- 29-32R
Prichard, Peter S. 1944- 139
Prichard, Robert Williams 1923- 89-92
Prichard, Susan Perez 1953- 108
Prickett, (Alexander Thomas) Stephen 1939- CANR-29
Earlier sketch in CA 29-32R
Priddy, Fran(ces Rosaleen) 1931- CANR-17
Earlier sketch in CA 1-4R
Priddy, Laurance L. 1941- 144
Pride, Cletis 1925- 41-44R
Pride, J(ohn) B(ernard) 1929- Brief entry 110
Prideaux, James 1935- 138
Prideaux, Tom 1908-1993 108
Obituary 141
See also SATA 37
See also SATA-Obit 76
Pridham, Geoffrey 1942- CANR-38
Earlier sketches in CA 97-100, CANR-17
Pridham, Radost 1922- 21-24R
Pries, Nancy R(uth) 1944- 118
Priesand, Sally J(ane) 1946- 65-68
Priest, Alice L. 1931- 102
Priest, Christopher 1943- 33-36R
See also DLB 14
Priest, Harold Martin 1902- 73-76
Priest, John Michael 1949- 150
Priest, Lisa 1964- 140
Priest, Robert 1951- 118
Priest, Stephen 1954- 140
Priestley, Alice 1962- SATA 95
Priestley, Barbara 1937- 33-36R
Priestley, Brian 1946- 129
Priestley, F(rancis) E(thelbert) L(ouis) 1905- 21-24R
Priestley, Harold E(dford) 1901- 73-76
Priestley, J(ohn) B(oynton) 1894-1984 CANR-33
Obituary 113
Earlier sketch in CA 9-12R
See also CDBLB 1914-1945
See also CLC 2, 5, 9, 34
See also DAM DRAM, NOV
See also DLB 10, 34, 77, 100, 139
See also DLBY 84
See also MTCW 1
Priestley, Lee (Shore) 1904- CANR-2
Earlier sketch in CA 5-8R
See also SATA 27
Priestley, Mary 1925- 61-64
Priestley, Philip 1939- 123
Priestly, Mark
See Albert, Harold A.
Priestman, Martin 1949- 135
Prieto, Mariana Beeching 1912- CANR-5
Earlier sketch in CA 5-8R
See also SATA 8
Prigmore, Charles S(amuel) 1919- CANR-25
Earlier sketch in CA 45-48
Prigogine, Ilya 1917- 131
Priley, Margaret Hubbard 1909- 1-4R
Prill, Felician 1904- 103
Primack, Alice Lefler 1939- 143
Primack, Joel (Robert) 1945- 61-64
Primack, Richard B. 1950- 153
Primavera, Elise 1954- SATA 58
See also SATA-Brief 48
Prime, Benjamin Young 1733-1791 DLB 31
Prime, C(ecil) T(homas) 1909-1979 CANR-3
Earlier sketch in CA 49-52
Prime, Derek (James) 1931- CANR-50
Earlier sketches in CA 108, CANR-25
See also SATA 34
Primeau, Ronald 1946- 108
Primeaux, Walter J(oseph) Jr. 1928- 41-44R
Primm, Brother Orrin
See Willett, Brother Franciscus
Primm, James Neal 1918- 45-48
Primmer, Phyllis (Cora Griesbach) 1926- 5-8R
Primo, Albert T. 1935- 73-76
Primrose, Diana fl. 1630- DLB 126
Primrose, William 1904-1982 116
Obituary 106
Prince 1958(?)- CLC 35
Prince, Alison (Mary) 1931- CANR-52
Earlier sketches in CA 29-32R, CANR-26
See also SATA 28, 86
Prince, Carl E. 1934- CANR-14
Earlier sketch in CA 21-24R
Prince, (Peter) Derek 1915- CANR-34
Earlier sketch in CA 113
Prince, Don 1905(?)-1983 Obituary 110
Prince, F(rank) T(empleton) 1912- CANR-43
Earlier sketch in CA 101
See also CLC 22
See also DLB 20
Prince, Gary Michael 1948- 89-92
Prince, Gerald (Joseph) 1942- 57-60
Prince, J(ack) H(arvey) 1908- 81-84
See also SATA 17
Prince, Maggie SATA 102
Prince, Melvin 1932- 116
Prince, Morton 1854-1929 Brief entry 121
Prince, Peter (Alan) 1942- 139
Prince, Suzan D(enise) 1957- 111
Prince, Thomas 1687-1758 DLB 24, 140
Prince, Thomas Richard 1934- 13-16R
Prince Charming
See Thomas, Rosanne Daryl
Prince Ibis
See Randi, James
Prince Kropotkin
See Kropotkin, Peter (Aleksieevich)
Princess Anne
See Anne (Elizabeth Alice Louise Windsor), Princess
Princess Grace
See Kelly, Grace (Patricia)
Princeton, Michael
See Spencer, David
Prindl, A(ndreas) R(obert) 1939- 69-72
Prindle, David F. 1948- 147
Pring, Julian Talbot 1913- 5-8R
Pring, Martin J(ohn) 1943- 111
Pringle, David (William) 1950- 134
Pringle, J(ohn) M(artin) Douglas 1912- 13-16R
Pringle, Laurence (Patrick) 1935- CANR-60
Earlier sketches in CA 29-32R, CANR-14
See also CLR 4
See also MAICYA
See also SAAS 6
See also SATA 4, 68
Pringle, Mia (Lilly) Kellmer 1920(?)-1983 65-68
Obituary 109
Pringle, Peter 1940- CANR-27
Earlier sketch in CA 69-72
Pringle, Terrence Michael 1947- 136
Pringle, Terry
See Pringle, Terrence Michael
Pring-Mill, Robert D(uguid) F(orrest) 1924- 9-12R
Prins, Harald E. L. 1951- 164
Printz, Peggy 1945- 73-76
Printz, Wolfgang Caspar 1641-1717 DLB 168
Prinz, Joachim 1902- CAP-1
Earlier sketch in CA 11-12
Priolo, Pauline Pizzo 1907- 1-4R
Prior, A(rthur) N(orman) 1914-1969 CANR-3
Earlier sketch in CA 1-4R
Prior, Allan 1922- CANR-10
Earlier sketch in CA 65-68
Prior, Andrew 1940- 112
Prior, Ann 1949- 25-28R
Prior, Kenneth Francis William 1926- 17-20R
Prior, Matthew 1664-1721 DLB 95
Prior, Natalie Jane 1963- 168
Prisco, Michele 1920- 53-56
Prisco, Michele 1920- DLB 177
Prisco, Salvatore III 1943- CANR-12
Earlier sketch in CA 61-64
Prishvin, Mikhail 1873-1954 TCLC 75
Prising, Robin 1933- 57-60
Pritchard, Allan (Duncan) 1928- 157
Pritchard, Arnold 1949- 97-100
Pritchard, J(ohn) Harris 1923- 21-24R
Pritchard, James Bennett 1909-1997 5-8R
Obituary 156
Pritchard, John Paul 1902-1976 9-12R
Obituary 126
Pritchard, John Wallace 1912- 81-84
Pritchard, Leland J(ames) 1908- CAP-1
Earlier sketch in CA 11-12
Pritchard, Melissa 1948- CANR-64
Earlier sketch in CA 128
Pritchard, Norman Henry II 1939- 77-80
Pritchard, R(onald) E(dward) 1936- 37-40R
Pritchard, R(obert) John 1945- 116
Pritchard, Ray 1952- 162
Pritchard, Sheila (Edwards) 1909- CAP-1
Earlier sketch in CA 13-16
Pritchard, William H(arrison) 1932- CANR-23
Earlier sketch in CA 65-68
See also CLC 34
See also DLB 111
Pritchett, C(harles) Herman 1907- CANR-18
Earlier sketches in CA 1-4R, CANR-3
Pritchett, Elaine H(illyer) 1920- 108
See also SATA 36
Pritchett, John Perry 1902- 1-4R
Pritchett, Kay 1946- 135
Pritchett, Price 1941- 123
Pritchett, V(ictor) S(awdon) 1900-1997 CANR-63
Obituary 157
Earlier sketches in CA 61-64, CANR-31
See also CLC 5, 13, 15, 41
See also DAM NOV
See also DLB 15, 139
See also MTCW 1
See also SSC 14
Pritchett, W(illiam) Kendrick 1909- 97-100
Pritikin, Nathan 1915-1985 CANR-27
Obituary 114
Earlier sketch in CA 89-92
Pritikin, Robert C(harles) 1929- 104
Prittie, Terence Cornelius Farmer 1913-1985 CANR-4
Obituary 116
Earlier sketch in CA 1-4R
Pritts, Kim Derek 1953- 150
See also SATA 83
Private 19022
See Manning, Frederic
Privateer, Paul Michael 1946- 135
Priyamvada, Usha
See Nilsson, Usha Saksena
Prizzia, Ross 1942- 119
Probert, Lowri
See Jones, R(obert) M(aynard)
Probert, Walter 1925- 77-80
Probst, Leonard 1921-1982 65-68
Obituary 106
Probst, Mark 1925- 130
See also CLC 59
Probyn, Clive T. 1944- 145
Probyn, May 1856(?)-1909 DLB 199
Prochazkova, Iva 1953- 135
See also SATA 68
Prochnau, William W. 1937- CANR-55
Earlier sketch in CA 33-36R
Prochnow, Herbert V(ictor), Jr. 1931- 110
Prochnow, Herbert V. 1897- CANR-4
Earlier sketch in CA 1-4R
Procktor, Richard (Edward Christopher) 1933- 53-56
Procopio, Mariellen
See Grutz, Mariellen Procopio
Procter, Adelaide Anne 1825-1864 DLB 32, 199
Procter, Adelaide Anne 1825-1864 DLB 199
Procter, Ben H. 1927- CANR-9
Earlier sketch in CA 5-8R
Procter, Bryan Waller 1787-1874 DLB 96, 144
Procter, Maurice 1906-1973 CANR-62
Obituary 122
Earlier sketch in CA 5-8R
Proctor, Charles S(heridan) 1925- 29-32R
Proctor, (Philip) Dennis 1905-1983 Obituary 110
Proctor, Dorothea Hardy 1910- 61-64
Proctor, E(velyn) E(mma) S(tefanos) 1897-1980 103
Obituary 97-100
Proctor, Elsie 1902- 29-32R
Proctor, Everitt
See Montgomery, Rutherford George
Proctor, Lillian Cummins 1900- CAP-2
Earlier sketch in CA 23-24
Proctor, Priscilla 1945- 65-68
Proctor, Raymond L(ambert) 1920- 45-48
Proctor, Robert 1868-1903 DLB 184
Proctor, Robert N. 1954- 138
Proctor, Samuel 1919- CANR-3
Earlier sketch in CA 9-12R
Proctor, Samuel D(eWitt) 1921-1997 133
Obituary 158
Brief entry 118
Proctor, Thelwall 1912- 29-32R
Proctor, William (Gilbert, Jr.) 1941- CANR-16
Earlier sketch in CA 37-40R
Prodan, Mario 1911- 9-12R
Proeysen, Alf 1914-1970 136
See also Proysen, Alf
See also CLR 24
Proface, Dom
See Sheehy, Maurice S(tephen)
Professor Scribbler
See Hollingsworth, Mary
Proffer, Carl R(ay) 1938-1984 41-44R
Obituary 113
Proffer, Ellendea 1944- CANR-1
Earlier sketch in CA 45-48
Proffitt, Charles G. 1896-1982 Obituary 108
Proffitt, Nicholas (Charles) 1943- 139
Brief entry 131
Interview in 139
Profumo, David 1955- 137
Proger, Samuel (Herschel) 1906- Brief entry 106
Progoff, Ira 1921-1997 133
Obituary 163
Prohias, Antonio 1921-1998 104
Obituary 165
Prokasy, William F(rederick) 1930- 49-52
Prokes, Mary T(imothy) 1931- 163
Prokhorov, Aleksandr Mikhailovich 1916- 157
Prokhovnik, Simon Jacques 1920- 107
Prokofiev, Aleksandr Andreyevich 1900-1971 Obituary 33-36R
Prokofiev, Camilla Gray 1938(?)-1971 Obituary 33-36R
Prokofiev, Sergei (Sergeevich) 1891-1953 166
Brief entry 112
Prokop, Phyllis Stillwell 1922- CANR-9
Earlier sketch in CA 21-24R
Prokopczyk, Czeslaw 1935- 108
Prokopovich, Feofan 1681(?)-1736 DLB 150
Prokosch, Frederic 1908-1989 73-76
Obituary 128
See also CLC 4, 48
See also DLB 48

Prole, Lozania
See Bloom, Ursula (Harvey)
Promis, Jose 1940- 143
Pronin, Alexander 1927- 49-52
Pronko, Leonard Cabell 1927- CANR-1
Earlier sketch in CA 1-4R
Pronko, N(icholas) Henry 1908- 9-12R
Pronzini, Bill 1943- CANR-59
Earlier sketches in CA 49-52, CANR-1, 14, 32
Proosdii, Cornelis Van
See Van Proosdy, Cornelis
Propes, Stephen Charles 1942- CANR-1
Earlier sketch in CA 49-52
Propes, Steve
See Propes, Stephen Charles
Prophet, The
See Dreiser, Theodore (Herman Albert)
Propper, Dan 1937- 104
See also DLB 16
Prosch, Harry 1917- 13-16R
Prose, Francine 1947- CANR-46
Brief entry 109
Earlier sketch in CA 112
See also CLC 45
See also SATA 101
Prosek, James 1975- 166
Proske, Beatrice (Irene) Gilman 1899- CAP-1
Earlier sketch in CA 9-10
Proskouriakoff, Tatiana (Avenivovna)
1909-1985 Obituary 117
Prosper, John (joint pseudonym)
See Farrar, John C(hipman)
Prosper, Lincoln
See Cannon, Helen
Prosser, Eleanor 1922- 1-4R
Prosser, H(arold) L(ee) 1944- CANR-57
Earlier sketches in CA 77-80, CANR-15, 33
Prosser, Michael H. 1936- CANR-17
Earlier sketch in CA 25-28R
Prostano, Emanuel Theodore, Jr. 1931- 29-32R
Prostano, Joyce S. 126
Prosterman, Roy L. 1935- 57-60
Protagoras c. 490B.C.-420B.C. .... DLB 176
Prothero, R(alph) Mansell 1924- 41-44R
Prothero, Stephen (Richard) 1960- 162
Prothro, Edwin Terry 1919- 53-56
Prothro, James W(arren) 1922- CANR-8
Earlier sketch in CA 5-8R
Protopapas, George 1917- 57-60
Prou, Suzanne (Marcelle Henriette) 1920- ....
CANR-20
Earlier sketch in CA 33-36R
Proud, Robert 1728-1813 .... DLB 30
Proudfoot, J(ohn) J(ames) 1918- 21-24R
Proudfoot, Lindsay 1950- 153
Proudhon
See Cunha, Euclides (Rodrigues Pimenta) da
Proujan, Carl 1929- 81-84
Proulx, Annie
See Proulx, E(dna) Annie
Proulx, E(dna) Annie 1935- CANR-65
Earlier sketch in CA 145
See also CLC 81
See also DAM POP
Proussis, Costas M(ichael) 1911- CANR-15
Earlier sketch in CA 41-44R
Proust, (Valentin-Louis-George-Eugene-) Marcel
1871-1922 120
Brief entry 104
See also DA
See also DAB
See also DAC
See also DAM MST, NOV
See also DLB 65
See also MTCW 1
See also TCLC 7, 13, 33
See also WLC
Prout, W(illiam) Leslie 1922- 9-12R
Prouty, L. Fletcher 1917- 45-48
Prouty, Morton D(ennison), Jr. 1918- CANR-28
Earlier sketch in CA 1-4R
Prouty, Olive Higgins 1882(?)-1974 .... 9-12R
Obituary 49-52
Prouvost, Jean 1885-1978 Obituary 89-92
Provan, Jill E(llen) 1948- 117
Provence, Marcel
See Jouhandeau, Marcel Henri
Provence, Sally
See Provence, Sally A(nn)
Provence, Sally A(nn) 1916- 128
Provensen, Alice 1918- CANR-44
Earlier sketches in CA 53-56, CANR-5
See also CLR 11
See also MAICYA
See also SATA 9, 70
Provensen, Martin (Elias) 1916-1987 .... CANR-44
Obituary 122
Earlier sketches in CA 53-56, CANR-5
See also CLR 11
See also MAICYA
See also SATA 9, 70
See also SATA-Obit 51
Provenzo, Eugene (F., Jr.) 1949- 135
See also SATA 78
Provist, d'Alain
See Diop, Birago (Ismael)
Provo, Frank 1913(?)-1975 Obituary 61-64
Provost, Gail Levine 1944- 127
See also SATA 65
Provost, Gary (Richard) 1944- 133
See also SATA 66
Provus, Malcolm M. 1928- Brief entry 108
Prowe, Diethelm (Manfred-Hartmut) 1941- 57-60
Prowell, Sandra West 162
Prowler, Don(ald) 1950- 121
Prowler, Harley
See Masters, Edgar Lee
Prown, Jonathan 167
Prown, Jules David 1930- 29-32R
Proxmire, William 1915- CANR-31
Earlier sketch in CA 29-32R
Proysen, Alf
See Proeysen, Alf
See also SATA 67
Prozan, Charlotte (Krause) 1936- 167
Prpic, George J(ure) 1920- CANR-38
Earlier sketches in CA 25-28R, CANR-17
Prucha, Francis Paul 1921- CANR-38
Earlier sketches in CA 5-8R, CANR-2, 17
Prudden, Bonnie 1914- CANR-14
Earlier sketch in CA 77-80
Prude, Agnes George de Mille 1905-1993 ....
CANR-30
Obituary 142
Earlier sketch in CA 65-68
Pruden, (James) Wesley, Jr. 1935- 17-20R
Prueitt, Melvin L(ewis) 1932- 118
Pruessen, Ronald W. 1944- 158
Pruett, John H(aywood) 1947- 102
Pruett, Kyle D(ean) 1943- 131
Prugh, Jeff(ery Douglas) 1939- 41-44R
Pruitt, Evelyn L(ord) 1918- 5-8R
Pruitt, Ida 1888-1985 155
Obituary 116
Pruitt, William O(badiah), Jr. 1922- 21-24R
Pruner, Leonora 1931- 114
Prunty, Merle C(harles) 1917-1983 .... 37-40R
Obituary 109
Prunty, (Eugene) Wyatt 1947- 110
Prus, Boleslaw 1845-1912 .... TCLC 48
Prusek, Jaroslav 1906- 129
Brief entry 117
Prusina, Katica 1935- 69-72
Pruter, Robert 1944- 137
Pruthi, Surinder P(aul) S(ingh) 1934- 61-64
Pruyser, Paul W(illem) 1916- CANR-9
Earlier sketch in CA 21-24R
Prybyla, Jan S(tanislaw) 1927- 21-24R
Pryce, Roy 1928- 29-32R
Pryce-Jones, David 1936- CANR-71
Earlier sketches in CA 13-16R, CANR-14, 45
Pryde, Philip Rust 1938- 61-64
Pryer, Pauline
See Roby, Mary Linn
Prymak, Thomas M. 1948- 167
Prynne, J(eremy) H(alvard) 1936- CANR-39
Earlier sketch in CA 97-100
See also DLB 40
Pryor, Adel
See Wasserfall, Adel
Pryor, Bonnie H. 1942- 130
See also SATA 69
Pryor, Frederic L(eRoy) 1933- CANR-2
Earlier sketch in CA 5-8R
Pryor, Helen Brenton 1897-1972 .... CAP-2
Earlier sketch in CA 33-36
See also SATA 4
Pryor, Karen 1932- 119
Pryor, Larry
See Pryor, Lawrence A(lderdice)
Pryor, Lawrence A(lderdice) 1938- 85-88
Pryor, Margo (Browne) Tupper 1919-1995 .... 17-20R
Obituary 148
Pryor, Richard (Franklin Lenox Thomas) 1940- Brief
entry 122
See also CLC 26
Pryor, Vanessa
See Yarbro, Chelsea Quinn
Prys-Jones, Arthur Glyn 1888- 104
Przybyszewski, Stanislaw 1868-1927 160
See also DLB 66
See also TCLC 36
Psathas, George 1929- 21-24R
Pseudo-Dionysius the Areopagite .... DLB 115
Pteleon
See Grieve, C(hristopher) M(urray)
See also DAM POET
Puccetti, Roland (Peter) 1924- 93-96
Pucci, Albert John 1920- .... SATA 44
Pucci, Pietro 1927- 146
Pucciani, Oreste F(rancesco) 1916- 21-24R
Puche, Jose Luis Castillo
See Castillo Puche, Jose Luis
Puck, Wolfgang 1949- 124
Puck, Y. U.
See Andre, (Kenneth) Michael
Puckett, Lute
See Masters, Edgar Lee
Puckett, Robert Hugh 1935- 41-44R
Puckett, (William) Ronald 1936- 33-36R
Puckett, Ruby Parker 1932- 57-60
Puckey, Walter (Charles) 1899-1983 .... CAP-2
Obituary 111
Earlier sketch in CA 29-32
Pudaite, Rochunga 1927- 120
Puddepha, Derek (Noel) 1930- 61-64
Pudney, John (Sleigh) 1909-1977 .... CANR-5
Obituary 77-80
Earlier sketch in CA 9-12R
See also SATA 24
Pudovkin, V(sevolod) I(llarionovich) 1893-1953 Brief
entry 112
Puechner, Ray 1935- 25-28R
Pueckler-Muskau, Hermann von 1785-1871 .... DLB
133
Puette, William J(oseph) 1946- 77-80
Pufendorf, Samuel von 1632-1694 .... DLB 168
Puffer, K(enneth) Hart 1910- 5-8R
Pugh, Anthony (Roy) 1931- 53-56
Pugh, Charles 1948- 81-84
Pugh, Dianne G. 167
Pugh, Edwin William 1874-1930 .... DLB 135
Pugh, Ellen (Tiffany) 1920- 49-52
See also SATA 7
Pugh, Griffith T(hompson) 1908- 5-8R
Pugh, J(ohn) W(ilbur) 1912- 21-24R
Pugh, John Charles 1919- 110
Pugh, L(eslie) P(enrhys) 1895-1983 Obituary 110
Pugh, Ralph B(ernard) 1910-1982 .... CANR-28
Obituary 108
Earlier sketch in CA 25-28R
Pugh, Rod(erick) W(ellington) 1919- 45-48
Pugh, Samuel F(ranklin) 1904- CAP-1
Earlier sketch in CA 13-14
Pugh, Sheenagh 1950- 154
Pugh, (Virginia) Wynette 1942-1998 Obituary 165
Brief entry 111
Pugin, A. Welby 1812-1852 .... DLB 55
Pugliese, Anthony J(ulian) 1912-1985 Obituary 117
Pugsley, Alex 154
Pugsley, Clement H. 1908- CAP-1
Earlier sketch in CA 13-14
Pugsley, John A. 1934- CANR-19
Earlier sketch in CA 103
Puharich, Henry (Andrija) Karl 1918- 85-88
Puhvel, Jaan 1932- CANR-31
Earlier sketch in CA 29-32R
Puig, Manuel 1932-1990 .... CANR-63
Earlier sketches in CA 45-48, CANR-2, 32
See also CLC 3, 5, 10, 28, 65
See also DAM MULT
See also DLB 113
See also HLC
See also HW
See also MTCW 1
Pulaski, Mary Ann Spencer 1916-1992 .... CANR-10
Obituary 137
Earlier sketch in CA 25-28R
Pulay, George 1923-1981 45-48
Obituary 135
Puleo, Nicole
See Miller, Nicole Puleo
Pulgram, Ernst 1915- 49-52
Puligandla, Ramakrishna 1930- CANR-7
Earlier sketch in CA 61-64
Pulis, Clifford A(lton) 1916- 116
Pulitzer, Joseph, Jr. 1885-1955 .... DLB 29
Pulitzer, Joseph 1847-1911 Brief entry 114
See also DLB 23
See also TCLC 76
Pulitzer, Roxanne 1951- CANR-60
Earlier sketch in CA 128
Pulkingham, Betty Carr 1928- CANR-51
Earlier sketches in CA 61-64, CANR-8, 26
Pulkingham, W(illiam) Graham 1926- 53-56
Pullapilly, Cyriac K(alapura) 1932- 61-64
Pullar, Philippa 1935-1997 Obituary 161
Brief entry 116
Pullein-Thompson, Christine
See Popescu, Christine
See also SATA 3
Pullein-Thompson, Denis
See Cannan, Denis
Pullein-Thompson, Diana
See Farr, Diana (Pullein-Thompson)
See also SATA 3
Pullein-Thompson, Joanna Maxwell 1898-1961 106
See also Cannan, Joanna
Pullein-Thompson, Josephine (Mary Wedderburn) ....
CANR-43
Earlier sketches in CA 5-8R, CANR-7, 20
See also SATA 3, 82
Pullen, John James 1913- 17-20R
Puller, Lewis B(urwell), Jr. 1945(?)-1994 142
Obituary 145
Pulliam, Eugene C(ollins)
1889-1975 Obituary 89-92
See also AITN 2
See also DLB 127
Pulliam, H(oward) Ronald 1945- 114
Pulliam, Myrta 1947- 97-100
Pullias, Earl V(ivon) 1907- CAP-1
Earlier sketch in CA 11-12
Pulling, Albert Van Siclen 1891-1980 53-56
Obituary 135
Pulling, Christopher Robert Druce 1893- CAP-1
Earlier sketch in CA 13-14
Pulling, Pierre
See Pulling, Albert Van Siclen
Pullman, Philip (Nicholas) 1946- CANR-50
Earlier sketch in CA 127
See also AAYA 15
See also CLR 20
See also JRDA
See also MAICYA
See also SAAS 17
See also SATA 65
Pullum, Geoffrey K(eith) 1945- 138
Pulman, Jack 1928(?)-1979 Obituary 85-88
Pulman, Michael Barraclough 1933- 33-36R
Pulos, William L(eroy) 1920- 45-48
Pulsford, Petronella 1946- 133
Pulsipher, Gerreld L(ewis) 1939- 101
Pulver, Mary Monica
See Kuhfeld, Mary Pulver
Pulver, Robin 1945- 143
See also SATA 76
Pulzer, Peter George Julius 1929- 13-16R
Pumphrey, H(enry) George 1912- 13-16R
Pumroy, Donald K(eith) 1925- 49-52
Punch, Maurice 1941- 65-68
Pundeff, Marin 1921- 9-12R
Pundt, Helen Marie 1903(?)-1995 .... 5-8R
Obituary 149
Punekar, Shankar Mokashi
See Mokashi-Punekar, Shankar
Puner, Helen W(alker) 1915-1989 .... CANR-2
Obituary 129
Earlier sketch in CA 5-8R
See also SATA 37
See also SATA-Obit 63
Puner, Morton 1921- 73-76
Punnett, R(obert) M(alcolm) 1936- 25-28R
Purcal, John T(homas) 1931- 33-36R
Purcell, Anne G. 1932- 139
Purcell, Arthur Henry 1944- 102
Purcell, Ben(jamin H.) 1928- 139
Purcell, Donald 1916- 122
Purcell, Gillis Philip 1904-1987 Obituary 124
Purcell, H(ugh) D(ominic) 1932- CANR-17
Earlier sketch in CA 25-28R
Purcell, Mary 1906- CANR-2
Earlier sketch in CA 5-8R
Purcell, Roy E(verett) 1936- CANR-6
Earlier sketch in CA 57-60
Purcell, Sally 1944- 49-52
Purcell, Susan Kaufman 1942- Brief entry 114
Purcell, Theodore V(incent) 1911-1984 .... 41-44R
Obituary 112
Purcell, Victor 1896-1965 .... 5-8R
Purchas, Samuel 1577(?)-1626 .... DLB 151
Purdom, Charles B(enjamin) 1883-1965 .... CAP-1
Earlier sketch in CA 9-10
Purdom, P(aul) Walton 1917- 57-60
Purdom, Thomas E. 1936- 13-16R
Purdom, Tom
See Purdom, Thomas E.
Purdon, Eric (Sinclaire) 1913-1989 93-96
Obituary 130
Purdue, A(rthur) W(illiam) 1941- 124
Purdue, Bill
See Purdue, A(rthur) W(illiam)
Purdy, A(lfred) W(ellington) 1918- CANR-66
Earlier sketches in CA 81-84, CANR-42
See also CAAS 17
See also CLC 3, 6, 14, 50
See also DAC
See also DAM MST, POET
See also DLB 88
Purdy, Alexander 1890-1976 Obituary 65-68
Purdy, Anne S. 1902(?)-1987 Obituary 122
Purdy, (Charles) Anthony 1932- 17-20R
Purdy, Captain Jim
See Gillelan, G(eorge) Howard
Purdy, Carol 1943- 136
See also SATA 66
Purdy, Dwight H(illiard) 1941- 131
Purdy, James (Amos) 1923- CANR-51
Earlier sketches in CA 33-36R, CANR-19
Interview in CANR-19
See also CAAS 1
See also CLC 2, 4, 10, 28, 52
See also DLB 2
See also MTCW 1
Purdy, John David 1946- 122
Purdy, Ken W(illiam) 1913-1972 155
Obituary 37-40R
See also DLB 137
Purdy, Laura M. 1946- 137
Purdy, Richard Little 1904-1990 Obituary 132
Purdy, Susan Gold 1939- CANR-10
Earlier sketch in CA 13-16R
See also SATA 8
Purdy, Theodore Martindale
1903-1979 Obituary 89-92
Pure, Simon
See Swinnerton, Frank Arthur
Puri, Shamlal 1951- 130
Purkey, Roy (Delbert) 1905- CAP-2
Earlier sketch in CA 23-24
Purkey, William Watson 1929- 29-32R
Purkis, John 1933- 97-100
Purkiser, W(estlake) T(aylor) 1910- CAP-1
Earlier sketch in CA 13-16
Purl, Sandy M. 1953- 122
Purnell, Idella 1901- 61-64
Purpel, David E(dward) 1932- 49-52
Purpura, Lia 1964- 161
Purrington, Robert Daniel 1936- CANR-48
Earlier sketch in CA 122
Purscell, Phyllis 1934- 25-28R
See also SATA 7
Pursell, Carroll W(irth), Jr. 1932- 77-80
Purser, John Whitley 1942- 103
Purser, Philip John 1925- CANR-44
Earlier sketches in CA 104, CANR-21
Purtill, Richard L. 1931- CANR-29
Earlier sketch in CA 37-40R
See also SATA 53
Purton, Rowland W(illiam Crisby) 1925- CANR-4
Earlier sketch in CA 53-56
Purves, Alan C(arroll) 1931- CANR-9
Earlier sketch in CA 21-24R
Purves, Libby 1950- 130
Purvis, Charles C. 1902(?)-1985 Obituary 115
Puryear, Alvin N(elson) 1937- Brief entry 115
Puryear, Edgar F., Jr. 1930- 115
Pusey, Edward Bouverie 1800-1882 .... DLB 55
Pusey, Merlo John 1902-1985 .... 9-12R
Obituary 117
Pusey, Nathan Marsh 1907- 109
Pushkarev, Boris S. 1929- CANR-6
Earlier sketch in CA 5-8R
Pushkarev, Sergei Germanovich 1888- CANR-6
Earlier sketch in CA 5-8R
Pushker, Gloria (Teles) 1927- 142
See also SATA 75

Pushkin, Alexander (Sergeyevich) 1799-1837 ... DA
See also DAB
See also DAC
See also DAM DRAM, MST, POET
See also PC 10
See also SATA 61
See also SSC 27
See also WLC
Pustay, John S(tephen) 1931- ... 17-20R
P'u Sung-ling 1640-1715 ... SSC 31
Putcamp, Luise jr. 1924- ... 29-32R
Puthoff, Harold E(dward) 1936- Brief entry ... 113
Putnam, Alice 1916- ... CANR-45
Earlier sketch in CA 112
See also SATA 61
Putnam, Arnold Oscar 1922- ... 9-12R
Putnam, Arthur Lee
See Alger, Horatio, Jr.
Putnam, Carleton 1901-1998 ... 65-68
Obituary ... 167
Putnam, Constance E(lizabeth) 1943- ... 140
Putnam, Donald F(ulton) 1903- ... CAP-2
Earlier sketch in CA 29-32
Putnam, George Palmer 1814-1872 ... DLB 3, 79
Putnam, George Palmer 1887-1950 Brief entry . 109
Putnam, Hilary 1926- ... 61-64
Putnam, J. Wesley
See Drago, Harry Sinclair
Putnam, Jackson K(eith) 1929- ... 29-32R
Putnam, John
See Beckwith, Burnham Putnam
Putnam, John Fay 1924(?)-1982 Obituary ... 106
Putnam, Michael Courtney Jenkins 1933- ... 105
Putnam, Peter B(rock) 1920- ... 85-88
See also SATA 30
Putnam, Robert D(avid) 1941- ... CANR-10
Earlier sketch in CA 65-68
Putnam, Robert E. 1933- ... CANR-41
Earlier sketches in CA 53-56, CANR-5, 19
Putnam, Roy Clayton 1928- ... 69-72
Putnam, Samuel Whitehall 1892-1950 Brief entry ... 107
See also DLB 4
Putnam, William L(owell) 1924- ... 148
Putney, Gail J.
See Fullerton, Gail Jackson
Putney, Martha S. 1916- ... 143
Putney, Mary Jo ... 164
Putra, Kerala
See Panikkar, K(avalam) Madhava
Putt, Robert C. 1938- ... 120
Putt, S(amuel) Gorley 1913- ... CANR-6
Earlier sketch in CA 5-8R
Putter, Ad 1967- ... 149
Putter, Irving 1917- ... 65-68
Putter, Polly
See Adomeit, Ruth E(lizabeth)
Putterman, Louis (G.) 1952- ... 147
Putterman, Ron 1946- ... 108
Puttfarken, Thomas 1943- ... 122
Putz, Louis J. 1909- ... CAP-1
Earlier sketch in CA 13-14
Putzar, Edward (David) 1930- ... 41-44R
Putzel, Max 1910- ... 9-12R
Putzel, Michael 1942- ... 73-76
Puxley, Ray 1948- ... 142
Puxon, Grattan 1939- ... 81-84
Puzo, Mario 1920- ... CANR-65
Earlier sketches in CA 65-68, CANR-4, 42
See also CLC 1, 2, 6, 36, 107
See also DAM NOV, POP
See also DLB 6
See also MTCW 1
Pybrum, Steven 1951- ... 164
Pybus, Rodney 1938- ... 107
Pye, (John) David 1932- ... 25-28R
Pye, Jack
See Morton, James (Severs)
Pye, Lloyd (Anthony, Jr.) 1946- ... 77-80
Pye, Lucian W(ilmot) 1921- ... 21-24R
Pye, Michael (Kenneth) 1946- ... 149
Pye, Norman 1913- ... 109
Pyenson, Lewis (Robert) 1947- ... 146
Pygge, Edward
See Barnes, Julian (Patrick)
Pyk, Ann Phillips 1937- ... 77-80
Pykare, Nina 1932- ... CANR-60
Earlier sketch in CA 130
Pykare, Nina Coombs
See Pykare, Nina
Pyke, David (Alan) 1921- ... 138
Pyke, Helen Godfrey 1941- ... 29-32R
Pyke, Magnus 1908- ... CANR-6
Earlier sketch in CA 13-16R
Pyle, A(lbert) M(offett) 1945- ... 123
Pyle, Ernest Taylor 1900-1945 ... 160
Brief entry ... 115
See also Pyle, Ernie
Pyle, Ernie 1900-1945
See Pyle, Ernest Taylor
See also DLB 29
See also TCLC 75
Pyle, (William) Fitzroy 1907- ... CAP-2
Earlier sketch in CA 29-32
Pyle, Gerald F. 1937- ... 148
Pyle, Hilary 1936- ... 77-80
Pyle, Howard 1853-1911 ... 137
Brief entry ... 109
See also CLR 22
See also DLB 42, 188
See also DLBD 13
See also MAICYA
See also SATA 16, 100
See also TCLC 81
Pyle, Katharine 1863-1938 ... SATA 66
Pyle, Robert Michael 1947- ... 142
Pyles, Aitken
See McDavid, Raven I(oor), Jr.
Pyles, Thomas 1905-1980 ... 13-16R
Obituary ... 133
Pylyshyn, Zenon W(alter) 1937- ... 29-32R
Pym, Barbara (Mary Crampton) 1913-1980 ... CANR-34
Obituary ... 97-100
Earlier sketches in CAP-1, CA 13-14, CANR-13
See also CLC 13, 19, 37, 111
See also DLB 14
See also DLBY 87
See also MTCW 1
Pym, Christopher 1929- ... 13-16R
Pym, Denis 1936- ... 25-28R
Pym, Dora Olive (Ivens) 1890- ... CAP-1
Earlier sketch in CA 13-14
Pym, Michael 1890(?)-1983 Obituary ... 109
Pym, Peter and Delores
See Sandlin, Tim
Pynchon, Thomas (Ruggles, Jr.) 1937- .. CANR-46
Earlier sketches in CA 17-20R, CANR-22
See also BEST 90:2
See also CLC 2, 3, 6, 9, 11, 18, 33, 62, 72
See also DA
See also DAB
See also DAC
See also DAM MST, NOV, POP
See also DLB 2, 173
See also MTCW 1
See also SSC 14
See also WLC
Pyne, Mable Mandeville 1903-1969 ... 1-4R
Obituary ... 103
See also SATA 9
Pyne, Stephen J(oseph) 1949- ... CANR-54
Earlier sketch in CA 106
Pynn, Ronald 1942- ... 85-88
Pyrnelle, Louise-Clarke 1850-1907 ... DLB 42
Pyros, John 1931- ... 77-80
Pytchely, R. F. St. B.
See Cowie, Donald
Pythagoras c. 570B.C.-c. 500B.C. ... DLB 176

Q

Q
See Quiller-Couch, SirArthur (Thomas)
Qadar, Basheer
See Alexander, (Charles) K(halil)
Qazzaz, Ayad (Sayyid Ali) Al
See Al-Qazzaz, Ayad (Sayyid Ali)
Qian Hao 1925- ... 111
Qian Zhongshu
See Ch'ien Chung-shu
Qoboza, Percy 1938-1988 Obituary ... 124
Qroll
See Dagerman, Stig (Halvard)
Quackenbush, Margery (Carlson) 1943- ... 73-76
Quackenbush, Robert M(ead) 1929- ... CANR-38
Earlier sketches in CA 45-48, CANR-2, 17
See also MAICYA
See also SAAS 7
See also SATA 7, 70
Quad, M.
See Lewis, Charles Bertrand
Quade, E(dward) S(chaumberg) 1908-1988 Obituary ... 125
Quade, Quentin Lon 1933- Brief entry ... 106
Quaife, Darlene Barry 1948- ... 137
Quaife, Milo Milton 1880-1959 Brief entry ... 114
Quain, Edwin A. 1906(?)-1975 Obituary ... 61-64
Quale, G(ladys) Robina 1931- ... 21-24R
Qualey, Carlton C(hester) 1904- ... 77-80
Qualey, Marsha 1953- ... 148
See also SATA 79
Qualter, Terence H(all) 1925- ... 37-40R
Quammen, David 1948- ... CANR-28
Earlier sketch in CA 29-32R
See also SATA 7
Quanbeck, Philip A. 1927- ... 25-28R
Quandt, B. Jean 1932- ... 33-36R
Quandt, Richard E(meric) 1930- ... CANR-29
Earlier sketch in CA 45-48
Quandt, William B. 1941- ... CANR-35
Earlier sketch in CA 29-32R
Quantic, Diane Dufva 1941- ... 152
Quantrill, Malcolm 1931- ... CANR-35
Earlier sketch in CA 13-16R
Quaritch, Bernard 1819-1899 ... DLB 184
Quarles, Benjamin (Arthur) 1904-1996 ... CANR-16
Obituary ... 154
Earlier sketches in CA 1-4R, CANR-1
See also BW 1
See also SATA 12
Quarles, Francis 1592-1644 ... DLB 126
Quarles, John R(hodes), Jr. 1935- ... CANR-15
Earlier sketch in CA 65-68
Quarm, Daisy 1948- ... 122
Quarmby, Arthur 1934- ... 45-48
Quarrie, Bruce (Roy Bryant) 1947- ... 103
Quarrington, Paul (Lewis) 1953- ... CANR-62
Earlier sketch in CA 129
See also CLC 65
Quarry, Nick
See Albert, Marvin H(ubert)
Quartermain, James
See Lynne, James Broom
Quartermain, Peter (Allan) 1934- ... CANR-40
Earlier sketch in CA 117
Quasimodo, Salvatore 1901-1968 ... CAP-1
Obituary ... 25-28R
Earlier sketch in CA 13-16
See also CLC 10
See also DLB 114
See also MTCW 1
Quastel, J. H.
See Quastel, Juda Hirsch
Quastel, Juda Hirsch 1899-1987 Obituary ... 123
Quasten, Johannes 1900- ... 9-12R
Quatermass, Martin
See Carpenter, John (Howard)
Quattlebaum, Mary 1958- ... 152
See also SATA 88
Quay, Herbert C. 1927- ... CANR-33
Earlier sketch in CA 13-16R
Quay, Stephen 1947- ... CLC 95
Quay, Timothy 1947- ... CLC 95
Quaye, Cofie 1947(?)- ... 143
See also BW 2
Quaye, Kofi
See Quaye, Cofie
Quayle, (John) Anthony 1913-1989 Obituary ... 130
Quayle, (James) Dan(forth) 1947- ... 148
Quayle, Eric 1921- ... CANR-36
Earlier sketch in CA 21-24R
Qubain, Fahim I(ssa) 1924- ... 1-4R
Quebedeaux, Richard (Anthony) 1944- .. CANR-30
Earlier sketches in CA 73-76, CANR-12
Queen, Ellery
See Dannay, Frederic
and Davidson, Avram
and Lee, Manfred B(ennington)
and Marlowe, Stephen
and Sturgeon, Theodore (Hamilton)
and Vance, John Holbrook
See also CLC 3, 11
Queen, Ellery, Jr.
See Dannay, Frederic
and Holding, James (Clark Carlisle, Jr.)
and Lee, Manfred B(ennington)
Queen, Stuart Alfred 1890- ... 21-24R
Queenan, Joe 1950- ... 140
Queen Wilhelmina
See Nassau, Wilhelmina Helena Pauline Maria
Quelch, John A(nthony) 1951- ... CANR-53
Earlier sketches in CA 112, CANR-29
Queller, Donald E(dward) 1925- ... CANR-4
Earlier sketch in CA 53-56
Queneau, Raymond 1903-1976 ... CANR-32
Obituary ... 69-72
Earlier sketch in CA 77-80
See also CLC 2, 5, 10, 42
See also DLB 72
See also MTCW 1
Quenelle, Gilbert 1914- ... 25-28R
Quennell, Marjorie Courtney 1884-1972 ... 73-76
See also SATA 29
Quennell, Peter (Courtney) 1905-1993 ... CANR-69
Obituary ... 143
Brief entry ... 113
Earlier sketch in CA 115
See also DLB 155, 195
Quentin, Brad
See Bisson, Terry (Ballantine)
Quentin, Patrick
See Wheeler, Hugh (Callingham)
Querry, Ronald B(urns) 1943- ... 117
Query, William T(heodore), Jr. 1929- ... 41-44R
Quesnel, Joseph 1746-1809 ... DLB 99
Quesnell, John G(eorge) 1936- ... CANR-1
Earlier sketch in CA 45-48
Quesnell, Quentin 1927- ... 120
Quest, Linda (Gerber) 1935- ... 77-80
Quest, (Edna) Olga W(ilbourne) Hall
See Hall-Quest, (Edna) Olga W(ilbourne)
Quest, Rodney ... CAP-2
Earlier sketch in CA 29-32
Quester, George H. 1936- ... CANR-34
Earlier sketches in CA 25-28R, CANR-10
Quezada, Abel 1920(?)-1991 ... 5-8R
Obituary ... 133
Quiatt, Duane 1929- ... 149
Quichot, Dona
See Tomkiewicz, Mina
Quick, Amanda
See Krentz, Jayne Ann
Quick, Annabelle 1922- ... 21-24R
See also SATA 2
Quick, Armand James 1894-1978 Obituary ... 73-76
Quick, Barbara 1954- ... 133
Quick, Philip
See Strage, Mark
Quick, Richard (John Worth) 1944- ... 127
Quick, Thomas L(ee) 1929- ... CANR-34
Earlier sketch in CA 41-44R
Quick, William K(ellon) 1933- ... 137
Quickel, Stephen (Woodside) 1936- ... 73-76
Quie, Gretchen 1927- ... 117
Quiery, William H. 1926- ... 21-24R
Quigg, Jane (Hulda) (?)-1986 Obituary ... 120
See also SATA-Obit 49
Quigg, Philip W. 1920- ... CANR-35
Earlier sketch in CA 9-12R
Quigless, Helen Gordon 1944- Brief entry ... 105
Quigley, Aileen 1930- ... 124
Brief entry ... 104
Quigley, Austin E(dmund) 1942- ... 101
Quigley, Carroll 1910-1977 ... CANR-27
Obituary ... 69-72
Earlier sketch in CA 37-40R
Quigley, Declan 1956- ... 146
Quigley, Eileen Elliott
See Vivers, Eileen Elliott
Quigley, Ellen 1955- ... 111
Quigley, Harold Scott 1889-1968 ... 1-4R
Obituary ... 103
Quigley, Joan 1927- ... CANR-43
Earlier sketch in CA 29-32R
See also BEST 90:3
Quigley, John 1927- ... 17-20R
Quigley, John M(ichael) 1942- ... 110
Brief entry ... 107
Quigley, Kevin F. F. 1952- ... 166
Quigley, Martin (Schofield), Jr. 1917- ... CANR-38
Earlier sketches in CA 1-4R, CANR-17
Quigley, Martin (Peter) 1913- ... CANR-18
Earlier sketch in CA 17-20R
Quilici, Folco 1930- ... 105
Quill
See Grange, Cyril
Quill, Barnaby
See Brandner, Gary (Phil)
Quill, Monica
See McInerny, Ralph
Quiller, Andrew
See Bulmer, (Henry) Kenneth
Quiller-Couch, SirArthur (Thomas) 1863-1944 ... 166
Brief entry ... 118
See also DLB 135, 153, 190
See also TCLC 53
Quilligan, Maureen 1944- ... CANR-16
Earlier sketch in CA 89-92
Quilter, Deborah 1950- ... 147
Quilty, Rafe
See Witcombe, R(ick) T(rader)
Quimber, Mario
See Alexander, (Charles) K(halil)
Quimby, George Irving 1913- ... CANR-34
Earlier sketch in CA 57-60
Quimby, Myron J. ... 25-28R
Quimby, Myrtle 1891- ... CAP-2
Earlier sketch in CA 25-28
Quin, Ann (Marie) 1936-1973 ... 9-12R
Obituary ... 45-48
See also CLC 6
See also DLB 14
Quin, Mike
See Ryan, Paul William
Quinan, Jack
See Quinan, John F.
Quinan, John F. 1939- ... 125
Quince, Peter
See Day, George Harold
Quince, Peter Lum
See Ritchie, (Harry) Ward
Quincunx, Ramona J.
See Borgmann, Dmitri A(lfred)
Quincy, Samuel ... DLB 31
Quincy, Samuel 1734-1789 ... DLB 31
Quindlen, Anna 1953- ... 138
Quine, Judith Balaban 1932- ... 140
Quine, W. V.
See Quine, Willard Van Orman
Quine, Willard V.
See Quine, Willard Van Orman
Quine, Willard Van Orman 1908- ... CANR-37
Earlier sketches in CA 1-4R, CANR-1, 16
Quin-Harkin, Janet 1941- ... CANR-59
Earlier sketches in CA 81-84, CANR-15, 33
See also AAYA 6
See also SATA 18, 90
Quinlan, David 1942- ... 147
Quinlan, Red
See Quinlan, Sterling C(arroll)
Quinlan, Sterling C(arroll) 1916- ... CANR-8
Earlier sketch in CA 5-8R
Quinlan, Susan E(lizabeth) 1954- ... 152
See also SATA 88
Quinley, Harold E(arl) 1942- ... 61-64
Quinn, A(lexander) James 1932- ... 29-32R
Quinn, Anthony (Rudolph Oaxaca) 1915- ... 155
Brief entry ... 111
See also DLB 122
See also HW
Quinn, Arthur 1942- ... 110
Quinn, (Mary) Bernetta 1915- ... 105
Quinn, C(osmas) Edward 1926-1989 Obituary ... 129
Quinn, Charles (Nicholas) 1930- ... 123
Brief entry ... 110
Interview in ... 123
Quinn, D. Michael 1944- ... 155
Quinn, Daniel 1935- ... 137
Quinn, David B(eers) 1909- ... CANR-15
Earlier sketch in CA 77-80
Quinn, Edward 1932- ... 77-80
Quinn, Elisabeth 1881-1962 ... SATA 22
Quinn, Esther Casier 1922- ... CANR-35
Earlier sketch in CA 5-8R
Quinn, Francis X. 1932- ... CANR-4
Earlier sketch in CA 9-12R
Quinn, Herbert F(urlong) 1910- ... CAP-1
Earlier sketch in CA 19-20
Quinn, James 1919- ... 13-16R
Quinn, James Brian 1928- ... CANR-35
Earlier sketch in CA 13-16R
Quinn, Jane Bryant 1939- ... 93-96
Quinn, John 1870-1924 ... DLB 187
Quinn, John Francis 1925- Brief entry ... 115
Quinn, John M(ichael) 1922- ... 45-48
Quinn, John Paul 1943- ... 33-36R
Quinn, John R. 1938- ... 97-100
Quinn, Kenneth (Fleming) 1920- ... CANR-17
Earlier sketch in CA 25-28R
Quinn, Martin
See Smith, Martin Cruz
Quinn, Michael A(lan) 1945- ... CANR-25
Earlier sketch in CA 45-48
Quinn, Niall 1943- ... CANR-37
Earlier sketch in CA 108
Quinn, Patrick 1950- ... SATA 73

Quinn, Peter 1947- .... CLC 91
Quinn, R(obert) M(acLean) 1920- 21-24R
Quinn, Sally 1941- CANR-27
Earlier sketch in CA 65-68
Interview in CANR-27
See also AITN 2
Quinn, Seabury (Grandin) 1889-1969 108
Obituary 104
Quinn, Simon
See Smith, Martin Cruz
Quinn, Sister Bernetta
See Quinn, (Mary) Bernetta
Quinn, Sunny 1949- 165
Quinn, Susan 1940- 103
See also Jacobs, Susan
Quinn, Terry 1945- CANR-18
Earlier sketch in CA 101
Quinn, Theodora K.
See Kroeber, Theodora (Kracaw)
See also SATA 1
Quinn, Vernon
See Quinn, Elisabeth
Quinn, Vincent 1926- 21-24R
Quinn, William Arthur 1920- 5-8R
Quinn, Zdenka (Hodbodova) 1942- 33-36R
Quinnell, A. J. 1939- 144
Quinnett, Paul G(uthrie) 1939- 114
Quinney, Richard 1934- CANR-9
Earlier sketch in CA 57-60
Quinones, Ricardo J(oseph) 1935- 153
Brief entry 112
Quinsey, Mary Beth 1948- 132
Quint, Barbara Gilder 1928- 103
Quint, Bert 1930- 69-72
Quint, Howard H. 1917- 97-100
Quint, Jeanne
See Benoliel, Jeanne Quint
Quintal, Claire 1930- 13-16R
Quintana, Bertha B(eatrice) 1924- Brief entry .. 113
Quintana, Frances
See Swadesh, Frances Leon
Quintana, Leroy V. 1944- CANR-65
Earlier sketch in CA 131
See also DAM MULT
See also DLB 82
See also HLC
See also HW
Quintana, Ricardo (Beckwith) 1898- 25-28R
Quintana Ranck, Katherine 1942- .... DLB 122
Quintanilla, (Maria) Aline (Griffith y Dexter) 1921- ... CANR-50
Earlier sketch in CA 9-12R
Quintero, Jose (Benjamin) 1924- 153
See also HW
Quintero, Ruben 1949- 143
Quintilian
See Quintilianus, Marcus Fabius
Quinto, Leon 1926- 37-40R
Quinton, Anthony Meredith 1925- CANR-10
Earlier sketch in CA 21-24R
Quirarte, Jacinto 1931- CANR-32
Earlier sketch in CA 45-48
See also HW
Quirin, G(eorge) David 1931- CANR-9
Earlier sketch in CA 21-24R
Quirin, William L(ouis) 1942- 93-96
Quirk, Anne (E.) 1956- 167
See also SATA 99
Quirk, James P(atrick) 1926- CANR-7
Earlier sketch in CA 57-60
Quirk, John E(dward) 1920- 5-8R
Quirk, Lawrence J. 1923- CANR-52
Earlier sketches in CA 25-28R, CANR-12, 27
Quirk, Paul J. 1949- 108
Quirk, Randolph 1920- CANR-2
Earlier sketch in CA 5-8R
Quirk, Robert E. 1918- 1-4R
Quirk, Thomas Vaughan 1946- CANR-48
Earlier sketch in CA 122
Quirk, Tom
See Quirk, Thomas Vaughan
Quirk, William J. 1933- 154
Quiroga, Horacio (Sylvestre) 1878-1937 131
Brief entry 117
See also DAM MULT
See also HLC
See also HW
See also MTCW 1
See also TCLC 20
Quispel, Gilles 1916- 89-92
Quist, Susan 1944- 57-60
Quitslund, Sonya A(ntoinette) 1935- CANR-1
Earlier sketch in CA 49-52
Quixley, Jim 1931- .... SATA 56
Quoirez, Francoise 1935- CANR-39
Earlier sketches in CA 49-52, CANR-6
See also Sagan, Francoise
See also CLC 9
See also MTCW 1
Quoist, Michel 1921- 65-68
Quong, Rose Lanu 1879(?)-1972 Obituary .. 37-40R
Qureshi, Hazel 1949- 138
Qureshi, Ishtiaq Husain 1903- CAP-1
Earlier sketch in CA 11-12

R

Ra, Carol F. 1939- 143
See also SATA 76
Ra, Jong Oh 1945- 85-88
Raab, Lawrence 1946- 65-68
Raab, Menachem 1923- 114
Raab, Robert Allen 1924- 29-32R
Raab, Selwyn 1934- 73-76
Raabe, Wilhelm (Karl) 1831-1910 167
See also DLB 129
See also TCLC 45
Raack, R(ichard) C(harles) 1928- 41-44R
Raad, Virginia 1925- 154
Ra'Anan, Gavriel D. 1954(?)-1983 Obituary 110
Ra'Anan, H. F. Frischwasser
See Ra'Anan, Uri
Ra'Anan, Uri 1926- CANR-25
Earlier sketch in CA 108
Raat, W(illiam) Dirk 1939- CANR-48
Earlier sketches in CA 106, CANR-23
Rabalais, Maria 1921- 61-64
Raban, Jonathan 1942- CANR-65
Earlier sketches in CA 61-64, CANR-17
Rabassa, Gregory 1922- CANR-51
Earlier sketches in CA 45-48, CANR-2, 26
See also CAAS 9
See also HW
Rabasseire, Henri
See Pachter, Henry M(aximillian)
Rabate, Jean-Michel 1949- 139
Rabb, Jane M. 1938- 152
Rabb, Theodore K. 1937- CANR-10
Earlier sketch in CA 21-24R
Rabbie
See Towers, Maxwell
Rabbitt, Thomas 1943- 57-60
Rabdau, Marianne
See Bakker-Rabdau, Marianne K(atherine)
Rabe, Berniece (Louise) 1928- CANR-1
Earlier sketch in CA 49-52
See also SAAS 10
See also SATA 7, 77
Rabe, David (William) 1940- CANR-59
Earlier sketch in CA 85-88
See also CABS 3
See also CLC 4, 8, 33
See also DAM DRAM
See also DLB 7
Rabe, Olive H(anson) (?)-1968 .... CAP-2
Earlier sketch in CA 19-20
See also SATA 13
Rabe, Stephen G(eorge) 1948- 108
Rabelais, Francois 1483-1553 .... DA
See also DAB
See also DAC
See also DAM MST
See also WLC
Raben, Joseph 1924- CANR-12
Earlier sketch in CA 69-72
Rabi, I(sidor) I(saac) 1898-1988 Obituary 125
Rabie, Jan 1920- 29-32R
Rabie, Mohamed 1940- 151
Rabikovitz, Dalia 1936- Brief entry 108
Rabikovitz, Dalyah
See Rabikovitz, Dalia
Rabil, Albert, Jr. 1934- CANR-10
Earlier sketch in CA 25-28R
Rabin, A(lbert) I(srael) 1912- CANR-41
Earlier sketches in CA 53-56, CANR-4, 19
Rabin, Chaim 1915- 105
Rabin, Edward H(arold) 1937- 49-52
Rabin, Leah 1927(?)- 160
Rabin, Robert L. 1939- 148
Rabin, Staton 1958- .... SATA 84
Rabin, Yitzhak 1922-1995 149
Brief entry 111
Rabinbach, Anson (Gilbert) 1945- 142
Rabinovich, Abraham 1933- 61-64
Rabinovich, Isaiah 1904-1972 .... CAP-2
Earlier sketch in CA 25-28
Rabinovitch, Sholem 1859-1916 Brief entry 104
See also Aleichem, Sholom
Rabinovitz, Rubin 1938- 21-24R
Rabinow, Paul 1944- CANR-13
Earlier sketch in CA 61-64
Rabinowich, Ellen 1946- 106
See also SATA 29
Rabinowicz, Mordka Harry 1919- 5-8R
Rabinowitch, Alexander 1934- 21-24R
Rabinowitch, Eugene 1901-1973 77-80
Obituary 41-44R
Rabinowitz, Alan 1927- CANR-27
Earlier sketch in CA 29-32R
Rabinowitz, Ezekiel 1892- 25-28R
Rabinowitz, Howard Neil 1942- 105
Rabinowitz, Isaac 1909-1988 Obituary 126
Rabinowitz, Louis Isaac 1906-1984 Obituary 113
Rabinowitz, Paula 1951- CANR-55
Earlier sketch in CA 127
Rabinowitz, Peter MacGarr 1956- 104
Rabinowitz, Sandy 1954- 103
See also SATA 52
See also SATA-Brief 39
Rabinowitz, Solomon
See Rabinovitch, Sholem
Rabins, Peter V(incent) 1947- 109
Rabkin, Brenda 1945- 101
Rabkin, Eric S. 1946- CANR-4
Earlier sketch in CA 49-52
Rabkin, Gerald Edward 1930- Brief entry 105
Rabkin, Norman C. 1930- CANR-4
Earlier sketch in CA 1-4R
Rabkin, Richard 1932- 33-36R
Rable, George C(alvin) 1950- 116
Raboff, Ernest Lloyd .... SATA-Brief 37
Raboni, Giovanni 1932- .... DLB 128
Raborg, Frederick A(shton), Jr. 1934- ... CANR-20
Earlier sketch in CA 103
Raboteau, Albert J(ordy) 1943- 151
Rabow, Gerald 1928- 25-28R
Raboy, Marc 1948- 135
Rabushka, Alvin 1940- Brief entry 116
Rabuzzi, Kathryn Allen 1938- 113
Raby, Derek Graham 1927- 103
Raby, William L(ouis) 1927- CANR-23
Earlier sketches in CA 17-20R, CANR-8
Race, Jeffrey 1943- 37-40R
Race, Robert Russell 1907-1984 Obituary 113
Racevskis, Karlis 1939- 117
Rachilde 1860-1953 .... DLB 123, 192
See also TCLC 67
Rachleff, Owen S(pencer) 1934- CANR-40
Earlier sketches in CA 21-24R, CANR-14
Rachleff, Peter (J.) 1951- 141
Rachlin, Carol K(ing) 1919- 57-60
See also SATA 64
Rachlin, Harvey (Brant) 1951- CANR-26
Earlier sketch in CA 107
See also SATA 47
Rachlin, Nahid CANR-14
Earlier sketch in CA 81-84
See also CAAS 17
See also SATA 64
Rachlis, Eugene (Jacob) 1920-1986 .... 5-8R
Obituary 121
See also SATA-Obit 50
Rachman, David Jay 1928- 57-60
Rachman, Stanley Jack 1934- 89-92
Rachow, Louis A(ugust) 1927- 57-60
Racin, Koco 1908-1943 .... DLB 147
Racina, Thom
See Raucina, Thomas Frank
Racine, Jean 1639-1699 .... DAB
See also DAM MST
Racine, Michel 1942- 136
Racine, Philip N. 1941- 148
Rack, Henry D(enman) 1931- 13-16R
Racker, Efraim 1913- 89-92
Rackham, Arthur 1867-1939 .... DLB 141
See also MAICYA
See also SATA 15, 100
Rackham, John
See Phillifent, John Thomas
Rackham, Thomas W(illiam) 1919- 25-28R
Rackin, Phyllis 1933- 85-88
Rackman, Emanuel 1910- 29-32R
Rackowe, Alec 1897- 25-28R
Rad, Gerhard von
See von Rad, Gerhard
Radakovich, Anka 1957- 152
Radan, G. T.
See Radan, George T(ivadar)
Radan, George T(ivadar) 1923- CANR-39
Earlier sketch in CA 116
Radano, Ronald M. 1956- 149
Radbill, Samuel X. 1901- 49-52
Radcliff, Alan L(awrence) 1920- 49-52
Radcliff, Peter (Edward, Jr.) 1932- 21-24R
Radcliffe, Ann (Ward) 1764-1823 .... DLB 39, 178
Radcliffe, Donnie
See Radcliffe, Redonia
Radcliffe, George L. 1878(?)-1974 Obituary .. 53-56
Radcliffe, Janette
See Roberts, Janet Louise
Radcliffe, Lynn J. 1896- 1-4R
Radcliffe, Philip (Fitzhugh) 1905-1986 Obituary . 120
Radcliffe, Redonia 132
Radcliffe, Virginia
See Hurst, Virginia Radcliffe
Radcliffe-Brown, A(lfred) R(eginald) 1881-1955 Brief entry 114
Radcliff-Umstead, Douglas 1944- CANR-13
Earlier sketch in CA 33-36R
Radclyffe-Hall, Marguerite
See Hall, (Marguerite) Radclyffe
Raddall, Thomas Head 1903- CANR-28
Earlier sketch in CA 1-4R
See also DLB 68
Radden, Jennifer H. 1943- 168
Raddysh, Garry
See Radison, Garry
Radel, John J(oseph) 1934- 29-32R
Radelet, Louis A(ugust) 1917- 89-92
Radelet, Michael L. 1950- 140
Radencich, Marguerite C. 1952- 148
See also SATA 79
Rader, Benjamin G(ene) 1935- 21-24R
Rader, Dotson 1942- CANR-11
Earlier sketch in CA 61-64
Rader, Melvin (Miller) 1903-1981 .... CANR-5
Earlier sketch in CA 13-16R
Rader, Ralph Wilson 1930- 13-16R
Rader, Randall R(ay) 1949- 121
Rader, Rosemary 1931- 112
Rader, (John) Trout (III) 1938- 37-40R
Radest, Howard B(ernard) 1928- 41-44R
Radford, Edwin Isaac 1891- 104
Radford, Irene 1950- 152
Radford, John 1901-1967 .... CAP-2
Earlier sketch in CA 21-22
Radford, Richard F(rancis), Jr. 1939- CANR-20
Earlier sketch in CA 104
Radford, Ruby L(orraine) 1891-1971 .... CANR-4
Earlier sketch in CA 1-4R
See also SATA 6
Radha, Sivananda 1911- CANR-36
Earlier sketch in CA 114
Radha, Swami Sivananda
See Radha, Sivananda
Radhakrishnan, C(hakkorayil) 1939- 57-60
Radhakrishnan, Sarvepalli 1888-1975 .... CAP-1
Obituary 57-60
Earlier sketch in CA 13-16
Radice, Barbara 133
Radice, Betty 1912-1985 .... CANR-12
Obituary 115
Earlier sketch in CA 25-28R
Radice, Giles 1936- CANR-17
Earlier sketch in CA 25-28R
Radichkov, Yordan 1929- .... DLB 181
Radiguet, Raymond 1903-1923 162
See also DLB 65
See also TCLC 29
Radimsky, Ladislaw 1898-1970 Obituary ... 29-32R
Radin, Edward D(avid) 1909-1966 Obituary 114
Radin, George 1896-1981 Obituary 102
Radin, Paul 1883-1959 Brief entry 120
Radin, Ruth Yaffe 1938- 124
See also SATA 56
See also SATA-Brief 52
Radishchev, Aleksandr Nikolaevich 1749-1802 . DLB 150
Radison, Garry 1949- 117
Radji, Parviz C(amran) 1936- 131
Radke, Don 1940- 57-60
Radl, Shirley L(ouise) 1935- CANR-12
Earlier sketch in CA 69-72
Radlauer, David 1952- 106
See also SATA 28
Radlauer, Edward 1921- CANR-30
Earlier sketches in CA 69-72, CANR-13
See also SATA 15
Radlauer, Ruth Shaw 1926- CANR-30
Earlier sketches in CA 81-84, CANR-13
See also SATA 15, 98
Radler, D(on) H. 1926- 13-16R
Radley, Eric John 1917- 109
Radley, Gail 1951- CANR-16
Earlier sketch in CA 89-92
See also SATA 25
Radley, Paul John 1962- 121
Radley, Sheila
See Robinson, Sheila Mary
Radley, Virginia L. 1927- 25-28R
Radner, Gilda 1946-1989 129
Obituary 128
See also BEST 89:4
Radner, Joan Newlon 167
Radner, Roy 1927- 49-52
Radnoti, Miklos 1909-1944 Brief entry 118
See also TCLC 16
Rado, Alexander
See Rado, Sandor
Rado, James 1939- 105
See also CLC 17
Rado, Sandor 1900-1981 109
Obituary 105
Radoff, Morris L(eon) 1905-1978 85-88
Obituary 81-84
Radom, Matthew 1905- 57-60
Radosh, Ronald 1937- CANR-57
Earlier sketch in CA 101
Radtke, Guenter 1920- 110
Radtke, Gunter
See Radtke, Guenter
Radvanyi, Janos 1922- 41-44R
Radvanyi, Netty 1900-1983 85-88
Obituary 110
See also Seghers, Anna
Radwanski, Pierre A(rthur) 1903- CAP-2
Earlier sketch in CA 23-24
Radwanski-Szinagel, Dr. Pierre A.
See Radwanski, Pierre A(rthur)
Radway, Ann
See Geis, Richard E(rwin)
Radway, Janice A(nne) 1949- 121
Radyr, Tomos
See Haldane-Stevenson, James Patrick
Radzinowicz, Leon 1906- CANR-26
Earlier sketch in CA 106
Radzinsky, Edvard (Stanislavovich) 1936- CANR-72
Earlier sketch in CA 142
Rae, Ben
See Griffiths, Trevor
Rae, Daphne 1933- 109
Rae, (Margaret) Doris 1907- CANR-15
Earlier sketches in CAP-1, CA 11-12
Rae, Douglas W(hiting) 1939- 77-80
Rae, Evonne 1928-1974 Obituary 104
Rae, Gwynedd 1892-1977 65-68
See also SATA 37
Rae, Hugh C(rauford) 1935- CANR-55
Earlier sketches in CA 17-20R, CANR-8, 29
Rae, John B(ell) 1911- 13-16R
Rae, John Malcolm 1931- CANR-4
Earlier sketch in CA 1-4R
Rae, Milford Andersen 1946- CANR-8
Earlier sketch in CA 61-64
Rae, Nicol C(ursiter) 1960- 131
Rae, Rusty
See Rae, Milford Andersen
Rae, Walter 1916- 57-60
Rae, Wesley D(ennis) 1932- 21-24R
Raebeck, Lois 1921- 13-16R
See also SATA 5
Raeburn, Antonia 1934- 101
Raeburn, John (Hay) 1941- 57-60
See also CLC 34
Raeburn, Michael 1940- 107
Raeburn, Michael 1943- 103
Raef, Laura (Gladys) C(auble) CANR-11
Earlier sketch in CA 29-32R
Raeff, Marc 1923- 61-64
Rael, Leyla 1948- 106
Raelin, Joseph A(lan) 1948- 125
Raeper, William 1959- 131
Raeschild, Sheila 1936- CANR-22
Earlier sketch in CA 105
Raetsch, Christian 1957- 144
Rafael, Gideon 1913- 129
Brief entry 106

RAF Casualty
See Gleave, T(homas) P(ercy)
Rafe, Stephen C. 1937- 132
Rafelson, Bob 128
Brief entry 112
Raffa, Frederick Anthony 1944- 53-56
Raffaele, Joseph A(ntonio) 1916- CANR-8
Earlier sketch in CA 5-8R
Raffel, Burton 1928- CANR-30
Earlier sketches in CA 9-12R, CANR-7
See also CAAS 9
Raffelock, David 1897- CAP-2
Earlier sketch in CA 25-28
See also AITN 1
Rafferty, Kathleen Kelly 1915-1981 Obituary 103
Rafferty, Max L. 1917-1982 .... CANR-1
Obituary 107
Earlier sketch in CA 1-4R
Rafferty, Milton 1932- 101
Rafferty, S. S.
See Hurley, John J(erome)
Raffi
See Cavoukian, Raffi
Raffini, James O. 1941- CANR-40
Earlier sketch in CA 117
Rafroidi, Patrick (Pierre) 1930-1989 132
Raftery, B(arry Joseph) 1944- 149
Raftery, Gerald (Bransfield) 1905- CAP-1
Earlier sketch in CA 13-14
See also SATA 11
Ragan, David 1925- 65-68
Ragan, Sam(uel Talmadge) 1915-1996 .... 13-16R
Obituary 152
Ragan, William Burk 1896-1973 .... CANR-2
Earlier sketch in CA 1-4R
Ragan-Reid, Gale 1956- 155
See also SATA 90
Ragaway, Martin A(rnold) 1928(?)-1989 .. CANR-12
Obituary 128
Earlier sketch in CA 61-64
Ragen, Joseph E(dward) 1897-1971 .... CAP-2
Obituary 33-36R
Earlier sketch in CA 21-22
Ragen, Naomi 1949- 130
Raghavan, Manayath D. 1892- CAP-2
Earlier sketch in CA 19-20
Ragins, Sanford 117
Raglan, Baron
See Raglan, FitzRoy
Raglan, FitzRoy 1885-1964 .... 5-8R
Ragni, Gerome 1942-1991 105
Obituary 134
See also CLC 17
Rago, Henry Anthony 1915-1969 .... CAP-2
Earlier sketch in CA 25-28
Rago, Louis J(oseph von) 1924- 9-12R
Ragone, Helena 1955- 150
Ragosta, Millie J(ane) 1931- CANR-12
Earlier sketch in CA 73-76
Ragsdale, Ray W(aldo) 1909- 45-48
Ragsdale, W(arner) B(ernice) 1898-1986 73-76
Obituary 121
Raguin, Yves (Emile) 1912- 81-84
Ragusa, Olga (M.) 1922- 122
Raham, (R.) Gary 1946- 136
Rahaman, Vashanti 1953- .... SATA 98
Rahe, Paul A. 1948- 145
Rahill, Peter J(ames) 1910- 5-8R
Rahim, Enayetur 1938- 107
Rahl, James A(ndrew) 1917- 77-80
Rahm, David A. 1931- 57-60
Rahman, Abdul
See Wayman, Tony Russell
Rahman, F.
See Rahman, Fazlur
Rahman, Fazlur 1919-1988 Obituary 126
Rahman, Matiur 1940- 141
Rahn, Joan Elma 1929- CANR-13
Earlier sketch in CA 37-40R
See also SATA 27
Rahner, Karl 1904-1984 109
Obituary 112
Rahner, Raymond M. 101
Rahsepar
See Yar-Shater, Ehsan O(llah)
Rahtjen, Bruce D(onald) 1933- 21-24R
Rahtz, Philip (Arthur) 1921- 149
Rahv, Betty T(homas) 1931- 105
Rahv, Philip 1908-1973
See Greenberg, Ivan
See also CLC 24
See also DLB 137
Rai, Kul B(husan) 1937- 105
Rai, Navab
See Srivastava, Dhanpat Rai
Raia, Anthony P(aul) 1928- 61-64
Raible, Alton (Robert) 1918- .... SATA 35
Raickovic, Stevan 1928- .... DLB 181
Raiff, Stan 1930- 61-64
See also SATA 11
Railton, Esther P(auline) 1929- 101
Raimi, Sam(uel M.) 1959- CANR-55
Earlier sketch in CA 123
Raimond, C. E.
See Robins, Elizabeth
Raimund, Ferdinand Jakob 1790-1836 .... DLB 90
Raimy, Eric 1942- 93-96
Raimy, Victor 1913- 81-84
Rainbird, George (Meadus) 1905-1986 133
Obituary 120
Rainbolt, William 1946- 152
Rainbow-Wind, Shandor
See Weiss, (Paul) Shandor
Raine, Craig 1944- CANR-51
Earlier sketches in CA 108, CANR-29
See also CLC 32, 103
See also DLB 40
Raine, Jerry 1955- 161
Raine, Kathleen (Jessie) 1908- CANR-46
Earlier sketch in CA 85-88
See also CLC 7, 45
See also DLB 20
See also MTCW 1
Raine, Norman Reilly 1895-1971 Obituary .. 33-36R
Raine, Richard
See Forbes, Colin
Rainer, George
See Greenburger, Ingrid Elisabeth
Rainer, Julia
See Goode, Ruth
Rainer, Yvonne 1934- 133
Raines, Howell (Hiram) 1943- 73-76
Raines, Jeff 1958- 127
Raines, John C. 1933- 73-76
Raines, Robert A(rnold) 1926- CANR-7
Earlier sketch in CA 13-16R
Raines, Shirley (Carol) 1945- 113
Raines, Theron 1925- 127
Rainey, Bill G. 1926- 89-92
Rainey, Buck
See Rainey, Bill G.
Rainey, Gene E(dward) 1934- 25-28R
Rainey, Homer Price 1896-1985 Obituary 118
Rainey, Patricia Ann 1937- 49-52
Rainey, W. B.
See Blassingame, Wyatt Rainey
Rainham, Thomas
See Barren, Charles (MacKinnon)
Rainis, Janis 1865-1929 .... TCLC 29
Rains, Rob 1956- 138
Rainsberger, Todd J(effrey) 1951- 106
Rainsford, George Nichols 1928- 49-52
Raintree, Lee
See Sellers, Con(nie Leslie, Jr.)
Rainwater, (Mary) Catherine 1953- 119
Rainwater, Dorothy T(hornton) 1918- CANR-1
Earlier sketch in CA 45-48
Rainwater, Lee 1928- 53-56
Raistrick, Arthur 1896- CANR-3
Earlier sketch in CA 9-12R
Raisz, Erwin J(osephus) 1893-1968 .... 1-4R
Obituary 103
Raitt, A(lan) W(illiam) 1930- 29-32R
Raizen, Senta A. 1924- 148
Raizis, M(arios) Byron 1931- 41-44R
Raizner, Bernard I. 1945- 127
Rajan, Balachandra 1920- 69-72
Rajan, M(annarswamighala) S(reeranga) 1920- ....
CANR-13
Earlier sketch in CA 13-16R
Rajan, Tilottama 1951- 107
Rajanen, Aini 109
Rajaram
See Iyengar, K(odaganallur) R(amaswami)
Srinivasa
Rajasekharaiah, T(umkur) R(udraradhya)
1926- 33-36R
Rajec, Elizabeth M(olnar) 1931- 109
Rajic, Negovan 1923- 130
Rajneesh, Acharya 1931-1990 93-96
Obituary 130
Rajneesh, Bhagwan Shree
See Rajneesh, Acharya
Rajski, Raymond B. 1917- 21-24R
Rajtar, Steve 1951- 160
Raju, Poolla Tirupati 1904- 33-36R
Rake, Alan 1933- 142
Rakel, Robert E(dwin) 1932- CANR-54
Earlier sketches in CA 107, CANR-26
Rakic, Milan 1876-1938 .... DLB 147
Raknes, Ola 1887-1975 .... CAP-2
Earlier sketch in CA 29-32
Rako, Susan Mandell 1939- 117
Rakoff, Alvin 1927- 102
Rakosi, Carl 1903-
See Rawley, Callman
See also CAAS 5
See also CLC 47
See also DLB 193
Rakosi, Matyas 1892-1971 Obituary 29-32R
Rakove, Jack N(orman) 1947- 93-96
Rakove, Milton L(eon) 1918-1983 .... CANR-15
Obituary 111
Earlier sketch in CA 65-68
Rakowski, James Peter 1945- 105
Rakowski, John 1922- 106
Rakstis, Ted J(ay) 1932- 101
Ralbovsky, Martin Paul 1942- 49-52
Rale, Nero
See Burgess, Michael (Roy)
Raleigh, Donald J(oseph) 1949- CANR-51
Earlier sketch in CA 125
Raleigh, John Henry 1920- CANR-3
Earlier sketch in CA 1-4R
Raleigh, Michael 1947- CANR-70
Earlier sketch in CA 141
Raleigh, Richard
See Lovecraft, H(oward) P(hillips)
Raleigh, Sir Walter 1554(?)-1618 .... CDBLB Before
1660
See also DLB 172
Raley, Harold (Cecil) 1934- 41-44R
Raley, Patricia E(ward) 1940- 73-76
Raley, Rowena
See McCulley, Johnston
Ralin, Radoy 1923- .... DLB 181
Rallentando, H. P.
See Sayers, Dorothy L(eigh)
Ralph, David Clinton 1922- CANR-2
Earlier sketch in CA 5-8R
Ralph, Elizabeth K(ennedy) 1921- 33-36R
Ralph, James R., Jr. 1960- 145
Ralph, Julian 1853-1903 .... DLB 23
Ralph, Margaret Nutting 1941- CANR-47
Earlier sketch in CA 121
Ralphs, Sheila 1923- 106
Ralston, Alma (Smith Payne) CANR-11
Earlier sketch in CA 17-20R
Ralston, Anthony 1930- 144
Ralston, Gilbert A(lexander) 1912- CANR-2
Earlier sketch in CA 45-48
Ralston, James Kenneth 1896- 49-52
Ralston, Jan
See Dunlop, Agnes M. R.
Ralston, Leonard F. 1925- 45-48
Ralston, Melvin B. 1937- 49-52
Ram, Immanuel
See Velikovsky, Immanuel
Rama
See Gupta, Ram Chandra
Rama
See Lenz, Frederick (P.), (Jr.)
Rama, Swami
See Swami Rama
Ramacharaka, Yogi
See Atkinson, William Walker
Ramage, Edwin S(tephen) 1929- 65-68
Ramage, James A(lfred) 1940- 61-64
Ramal, Walter
See de la Mare, Walter (John)
Ramamurty, K(otamraju) Bhaskara 1924- 53-56
Raman, Chandrasekhara Venkata
1888-1970 Obituary 113
Ramana Maharshi 1879-1950 .... TCLC 84
Ramanujan, A(ttipat) K(rishnaswami) 1929-1993 ...
CANR-24
Obituary 141
Earlier sketches in CA 17-20R, CANR-8
See also SATA 86
Ramanujan, Molly 1932- CANR-24
Earlier sketch in CA 29-32R
Ramanujan, Shouri
See Ramanujan, Molly
Ramapryia
See Gaulden, Albert Clayton
Rama Rau, Dhanvanthi (Handoo)
1893-1987 Obituary 123
Brief entry 106
Rama Rau, Santha
See Wattles, Santha Rama Rau
Ramaswamy, Mysore 1902- CAP-1
Earlier sketch in CA 13-14
Ramat, Silvio 1939- .... DLB 128
Ramati, Alexander D. 1921- CANR-44
Earlier sketches in CA 13-16R, CANR-7
Ramati, Yohanan (Joseph) 1921- 111
Ramazani, Jahan 1960- 150
Ramazani, Rouhollah K(aregar) 1928- CANR-26
Earlier sketches in CA 13-16R, CANR-10
Rambam, Cyvia
See Rambert, Marie
Rambam, Myriam
See Rambert, Marie
Rambeau, James (Morris) 1938- 117
Ramberg, Bennett 1946- 111
Rambert, Marie 1888-1982 103
Obituary 107
Rambo, Lewis Ray 1943- 109
Rambuss, Richard 145
Ramdin, Ron(ald Andrew) 1942- 131
Rame, David
See Divine, Arthur Durham
Rameh, Clea 1927- 53-56
Ramenofsky, Ann F. 1942- 125
Ramey, James W(alter) 1928- 112
Ramey, Mary Ann 1947- 125
Ramge, Sebastian Victor 1930- 9-12R
Ramien, Th.
See Hirschfeld, Magnus
Ramirez, Carolyn H(olmes) 1933- CANR-2
Earlier sketch in CA 5-8R
Ramirez, Sergio 1942- .... DLB 145
Ramirez, Susan E(lizabeth) 1946- 130
See also HW
Ramirez de Arellano, Diana (T. Clotilde) 1919- ....
CANR-32
Earlier sketch in CA 45-48
See also HW
Ramirez de Arellano, Rafael W(illiam) 1884- ... HW
Ramis, Harold (Allen) 1944- 128
Brief entry 124
See also AAYA 14
Ramke, Bin 1947- CANR-31
Earlier sketches in CA 81-84, CANR-14
See also DLB 120
Ramler, Karl Wilhelm 1725-1798 .... DLB 97
Ramm, Bernard L(awrence) 1916- Brief entry .. 112
Rammelkamp, Julian S(turtevant) 1917- 17-20R
Ramo, Simon 1913- Brief entry 111
Ramon, Juan
See Jimenez (Mantecon), Juan Ramon
Ramond, Charles K(night) 1930- 101
Ramon Ribeyro, Julio 1929- .... DLB 145
Ramos, Graciliano 1892-1953 167
See also TCLC 32
Ramos, Joseph R(afael) 1938- 139
Ramos, Suzanne 1942- 101
Ramos-Oliveira, Antonio 1907-1973 Obituary .. 104
Ramous, Mario 1924- .... DLB 128
Ramp, Eugene A(ugust) 1942- 49-52
Rampa, Tuesday Lobsang
See Hoskin, Cyril Henry
Rampersad, Arnold 1941- 133
Brief entry 127
Interview in 133
See also BW 2
See also CLC 44
See also DLB 111
Ramphal, Shridath (Surendranath) 1928- 141
Rampling, Anne
See Rice, Anne
Ramquist, Grace (Bess) Chapman 1907- .. CANR-3
Earlier sketch in CA 9-12R
Ramras-Rauch, Gila 147
Ramrus, Al 1930- 105
Rams, Edwin M(arion) 1922- 17-20R
Ramsaur, Ernest Edmondson, Jr. 1915- 41-44R
Ramsay, Allan 1684(?)-1758 .... DLB 95
Ramsay, David 1749-1815 .... DLB 30
Ramsay, J(ames) A(rthur) 1909-1988 Obituary . 124
Ramsay, Jay 1958- 135
Ramsay, Martha Laurens 1759-1811 .... DLB 200
Ramsay, Raylene L(ammas) 1945- 145
Ramsay, Raymond (Henry) 1927- 77-80
Ramsay, William M(cDowell) 1922- CANR-12
Earlier sketch in CA 13-16R
Ramsbottom, John 1885-1974 Obituary 53-56
Ramsdell, Kristin (Romeis) 1940- 125
Ramsden, E. H. 102
Ramsden, Herbert 1927- CANR-25
Earlier sketch in CA 108
Ramsden, John Andrew 1947- 108
Ramsell, Donald 1926(?)-1983 Obituary 110
Ramsett, David E. 1942- 29-32R
Ramsey, Charles E(ugene) 1923- 13-16R
Ramsey, Dan(ny Clarence) 1945- 101
Ramsey, Doug(las A.) 1934- 132
Ramsey, Eric
See Hagberg, David J(ames)
Ramsey, Frank Plumpton 1903-1930 158
Ramsey, (Charles) Frederic, Jr. 1915- 5-8R
Ramsey, G(ordon) C(lark) 1941- CANR-9
Earlier sketch in CA 21-24R
Ramsey, George Wilson 1937- 113
Ramsey, Ian T(homas) 1915-1972 .... CANR-4
Earlier sketch in CA 5-8R
Ramsey, Jackson E. 1938- 122
Ramsey, Jarold 1937- 33-36R
Ramsey, John F(raser) 1907- 49-52
Ramsey, Lee C(arter) 1935- 120
Ramsey, (Arthur) Michael 1904-1988 .... CANR-14
Obituary 125
Earlier sketch in CA 77-80
Ramsey, (Robert) Paul 1913-1988 .... CANR-1
Obituary 124
Earlier sketch in CA 1-4R
Ramsey, Paul 1924- 41-44R
Ramsey, Paul W. 1905-1976 Obituary 69-72
Ramsey, Robert D. 1934- 25-28R
Ramsey, Roy S. 1920(?)-1976 Obituary 65-68
Ramsey, Russell W. 1935- 124
Ramseyer, John A(lvin) 1908-1968 .... CANR-4
Earlier sketch in CA 5-8R
Ramseyer, Lloyd L. 1899- CAP-2
Earlier sketch in CA 19-20
Ramskill, Valerie Patricia Roskams CAP-1
Earlier sketch in CA 9-10
Ramsland, Katherine 1953- 136
Ramson, W(illiam) S(tanley) 1933- 45-48
Ramundo, Bernard A. 1925- 21-24R
Ramuz, Charles-Ferdinand 1878-1947 165
See also TCLC 33
Rana, Indi
See Rana, Indira Higham
Rana, Indira Higham 1944- 149
See also SATA 82
Rana, J.
See Bhatia, Jamunadevi
Ranadive, Gail 1944- 53-56
See also SATA 10
Rance, Joseph
See Hoyle, Trevor
Rance, Patrick 1918- 138
Rancour-Laferriere, Daniel 138
Rand, Ann (Binkley) 106
See also SATA 30
Rand, Austin Loomer 1905- 89-92
Rand, Ayn 1905-1982 .... CANR-27
Obituary 105
Earlier sketch in CA 13-16R
See also AAYA 10
See also CLC 3, 30, 44, 79
See also DA
See also DAC
See also DAM MST, NOV, POP
See also MTCW 1
See also WLC
Rand, Brett
See Norwood, Victor G(eorge) C(harles)
Rand, Christopher 1912-1968 77-80
Rand, Clayton (Thomas) 1891-1971 .... 5-8R
Obituary 29-32R
Rand, Earl (James) 1933- 21-24R
Rand, Frank Prentice 1889- CAP-1
Earlier sketch in CA 11-12
Rand, Gloria 1925- 168
See also SATA 101
Rand, Harry 1947- 137
Rand, J. H.
See Holland, James R.
Rand, James S.
See Attenborough, Bernard George
Rand, Paul 1914-1996 .... CANR-61
Obituary 154
Earlier sketch in CA 21-24R
See also SATA 6
Rand, Peter 1942- CANR-62
Earlier sketch in CA 77-80

Rand, Willard J., Jr. 1913- 9-12R
Randal, Beatrice (a pseudonym) 1916- 61-64
Randal, Vera 1922- 9-12R
Randall, Belle 1940- 118
Randall, Bob 1937-1995 106
Obituary 148
Randall, Carrie
See Ransom, Candice F.
Randall, Charles Edgar 1897- 41-44R
Randall, Charles H(enry) 1920- 133
Randall, Clarence Belden 1891-1967 .... CAP-1
Earlier sketch in CA 13-14
Randall, Clay
See Adams, Clifton
Randall, Dale B(ertrand) J(onas) 1929- ... CANR-2
Earlier sketch in CA 5-8R
Randall, David A(nton) 1905-1975 Obituary .. 57-60
See also DLB 140
Randall, Deborah 1957- 131
Randall, Diane
See Ross, W(illiam) E(dward) D(aniel)
Randall, Donald A. 1933- 61-64
Randall, Dudley (Felker) 1914- CANR-23
Earlier sketch in CA 25-28R
See also BLC 3
See also BW 1
See also CLC 1
See also DAM MULT
See also DLB 41
Randall, Florence Engel 1917- 41-44R
See also SATA 5
Randall, Francis Ballard 1931- 9-12R
Randall, Henry S. 1811-1876 .... DLB 30
Randall, J. G.
See Randall, James Garfield
Randall, James G.
See Randall, James Garfield
See also DLB 17
Randall, James Garfield 1881-1953 Brief entry . 118
See also Randall, James G.
Randall, Janet
See Young, Janet Randall
and Young, Robert W(illiam)
Randall, Jo Anne Yarus 1942- 118
Randall, John E(rnest, Jr.) 1924- 65-68
Randall, John Herman, Jr. 1899-1980 .... CANR-1
Obituary 102
Earlier sketch in CA 1-4R
Randall, John L(eslie) 1933- 107
Randall, Joseph Hungerford 1897- 1-4R
Randall, Joshua
See Randisi, Robert J(oseph)
Randall, Julia (Sawyer) 1923- 33-36R
Randall, Laura 1935- 37-40R
Randall, Lillian M. C. 1931- 21-24R
Randall, Margaret 1936- 41-44R
Randall, Marta 107
Randall, Mary
See Colver, Alice Mary (Ross)
Randall, Mercedes M. 1895-1977 .... 13-16R
Obituary 69-72
Randall, Monica 1944- 97-100
Randall, Randolph C. 1900- 17-20R
Randall, Richard H(arding), Jr. 1926-1997 148
Obituary 159
Randall, Robert
See Garrett, (Gordon) Randall (Phillip)
and Silverberg, Robert
Randall, Ruth (Elaine) Painter 1892-1971 ..... 1-4R
Obituary 103
See also SATA 3
Randall, Steven
See Andrews, Clarence A(delbert)
Randall, Tony 1 1920- 156
Randall, Willard Sterne 1942- 69-72
Randall, William Lowell 1950- 158
Randall-Mills, Elizabeth West 1906- 13-16R
Randazzo, Mary Callahan 1950- 127
Randazzo, Renee
See Randazzo, Mary Callahan
Randel, William (Peirce) 1909- 13-16R
Randell, Beverley
See Price, Beverley Joan
Randell, John Bulmer 1918-1982 109
Obituary 106
Randers-Pehrson, Justine Davis 1910- 111
Randhawa, M(ohinder) S(ingh) 1909-1986 .... CANR-28
Earlier sketch in CA 29-32R
Randi, James 1928- 117
Randisi, Robert J(oseph) 1951- CANR-60
Earlier sketch in CA 116
Randle, Kristen D(owney) 1952- 156
See also SAAS 24
See also SATA 92
Randles, Anthony V(ictor), Jr. 1942- 65-68
Randles, Jennifer Christine 1951- 142
Randles, Jenny
See Randles, Jennifer Christine
Randles, Slim
See Randles, Anthony V(ictor), Jr.
Randoll, Anthony
See Blacking, John (Anthony Randoll)
Randolph, A(sa) Philip 1889-1979 125
Obituary 85-88
See also BW 2
Randolph, Arthur C.
See Greene, A(lvin) C(arl)
Randolph, Boynton M.D.
See Ellis, Edward S(ylvester)
Randolph, David James 1934- CANR-3
Earlier sketch in CA 49-52
Randolph, (Mary) Elizabeth 1930- 135
Randolph, Ellen
See Ross, W(illiam) E(dward) D(aniel)
Randolph, Geoffrey
See Ellis, Edward S(ylvester)
Randolph, Georgiana Ann 1908-1957 Brief entry 116
Randolph, Gordon
See von Block, Bela W(illiam)
and von Block, Sylvia
Randolph, J. H.
See Ellis, Edward S(ylvester)
Randolph, John 1915- 45-48
Randolph, Lieutenant J. H.
See Ellis, Edward S(ylvester)
Randolph, Marion
See Rodell, Marie F(reid)
Randolph, Melanie
See Ragosta, Millie J(ane)
Randolph, Nancy
See Robb, Inez (Callaway)
Randolph, Ruth Elizabeth 1964- 162
Randolph, Thomas 1605-1635 .... DLB 58, 126
Randolph, Vance 1892- 105
Random, Alan
See Kay, Ernest
Random, Alex
See Rowland, D(onald) S(ydney)
Rands, William Brighty 1823-1882 .... SATA 17
Randsborg, Klavs 1944- 142
Ranelagh, John (O'Beirne) 1947- 128
Raney, Ken 1953- .... SATA 74
Ranga (Nayakulu), N(idubrolu) G(ogineni) 1900-1995 .... 29-32R
Obituary 148
Ranganathan, S(hiyali) R(amamrita) 1892-1972 .... CANR-5
Earlier sketch in CA 5-8R
Range, Willard Edgar Allen 1910- 1-4R
Rangel, Carlos 1929-1988 104
Obituary 124
Rangell, Leo 1913- 105
Ranger, Ken
See Creasey, John
Ranger, Paul 1933- 37-40R
Ranger, T(erence) O(sborn) 1929- CANR-19
Earlier sketch in CA 25-28R
Ranis, Gustav 1929- CANR-3
Earlier sketch in CA 9-12R
Ranis, Peter 1935- 41-44R
Ranjee
See Shahani, Ranjee
Rank, Benjamin (Keith) 1911- 109
Rank, Hugh (Duke) 1932- CANR-12
Earlier sketch in CA 73-76
Rank, Maureen Joy 1947- 117
Ranke-Heinemann, Uta (Johanna Ingrid) 1927- . 137
Ranki, Gyoergy 1930-1988 Obituary 124
Rankin, Daniel S(tanislaus) 1895-1972 ..... CAP-1
Earlier sketch in CA 13-16
Rankin, David J. 1945- 108
Rankin, Herbert David 1931- 103
Rankin, Hugh F(ranklin) 1913- CANR-1
Earlier sketch in CA 1-4R
Rankin, Ian (James) 1960- 148
Rankin, Jeannette 1880-1973 Obituary 41-44R
Rankin, Joan 1940- .... SATA 88
Rankin, Judith Torluemke 1945- Brief entry 107
Rankin, Judy
See Rankin, Judith Torluemke
Rankin, Karl Lott 1898- CAP-1
Earlier sketch in CA 13-16
Rankin, Paula C(lark) 1945- CANR-21
Earlier sketch in CA 104
Rankin, Robert 1915- 126
Brief entry 108
Rankin, Robert Harry 1909-1990 Obituary 131
Rankin, Robert P(arks) 1912- 77-80
Rankin, Ruth (DeLone) I(rvine) 1924- 61-64
Rankine, John
See Mason, Douglas R(ankine)
Rankine, Paul Scott 1909(?)-1983 Obituary 109
Ranly, Ernest W. 1930- 37-40R
Rann, Sheila 1952- 152
Rann, Shelly
See Rann, Sheila
Ranney, Agnes V. 1916- 5-8R
See also SATA 6
Ranney, (Joseph) Austin 1920- 77-80
Rannit, Aleksis 1914-1985 Obituary 114
Brief entry 109
Ranous, Charles A. 1912- 13-16R
Ransel, David L(orimer) 1939- 73-76
Ransford, Oliver (Neil) 1914-1993 .... CANR-10
Obituary 142
Earlier sketch in CA 21-24R
Ransley, Peter 1931- CANR-21
Earlier sketch in CA 69-72
Ransohoff, Paul M(artin) 1948- 103
Ransom, Bill 1945- CANR-44
Earlier sketches in CA 101, CANR-19
Ransom, Candice F. 1952- CANR-47
Earlier sketch in CA 121
See also SATA 52, 89
See also SATA-Brief 49
Ransom, Daniel
See Gorman, Edward
Ransom, Harry 1908-1976 .... DLB 187
Ransom, Harry Howe 1922- 9-12R
Ransom, Jane (Reavill) 1958- 158
Ransom, Jay Ellis 1914- CANR-44
Earlier sketches in CA 9-12R, CANR-3, 20
Ransom, John Crowe 1888-1974 .... CANR-34
Obituary 49-52
Earlier sketches in CA 5-8R, CANR-6
See also CLC 2, 4, 5, 11, 24
See also DAM POET
See also DLB 45, 63
See also MTCW 1
Ransom, William Michael 1945- Brief entry 108
Ransom, William R. 1876-1973 Obituary ... 37-40R
Ransome, Arthur (Michell) 1884-1967 73-76
See also CLR 8
See also DLB 160
See also MAICYA
See also SATA 22
Ransome, Eleanor 1915- 93-96
Ransome, James E. 1961- .... SATA 76
Ransome, Stephen
See Davis, Frederick C(lyde)
Ransome-Davies, Basil
See Colley, Iain
Ransone, Coleman B(ernard), Jr. 1920- 45-48
Rant, Tol E.
See Longyear, Barry Brookes
Ranum, Orest Allen 1933- CANR-8
Earlier sketch in CA 9-12R
Ranum, Patricia M(cGroder) 1932- 45-48
Ranz, James 1921- 9-12R
Ranz, Jim
See Ranz, James
Ranzini, Addis Durning 1909-1983 Obituary 110
Rao, Aruna P. 1955- 141
Rao, B. Shiva 1900(?)-1975 Obituary 61-64
Rao, C. H. Hanumantha 1929- CANR-7
Earlier sketch in CA 17-20R
Rao, K(oneru) Ramakrishna 1932- 130
Rao, R(anganatha) P(admanabha) 1924- ... 13-16R
Rao, Raja 1909- CANR-51
Earlier sketch in CA 73-76
See also CLC 25, 56
See also DAM NOV
See also MTCW 1
Raoul, Anthony
See Wilmot, Anthony
Rapaport, Herman 1947- CANR-35
Earlier sketch in CA 114
Rapaport, Ionel F. 1909(?)-1972 Obituary .. 37-40R
Rapaport, Stella F(read) 1-4R
Raper, Arthur F(ranklin) 1899-1979 ...... CANR-12
Obituary 89-92
Earlier sketch in CA 61-64
Raper, J(ulius) R(owan) 1938- 33-36R
Raper, Jack
See Raper, J(ulius) R(owan)
Raphael, Bertram 1936- 97-100
Raphael, Beverley 1934- 117
Raphael, Chaim 1908-1994 .... CANR-16
Obituary 146
Earlier sketch in CA 85-88
Raphael, Dan 1952- 104
Raphael, Dana 61-64
Raphael, David D(aiches) 1916- CANR-20
Earlier sketches in CA 5-8R, CANR-2
Raphael, Elaine
See Bolognese, Elaine (Raphael Chionchio)
See also SATA 23
Raphael, Frederic (Michael) 1931- CANR-1
Earlier sketch in CA 1-4R
See also CLC 2, 14
See also DLB 14
Raphael, Jay
See Josephs, Ray
Raphael, Lev 1954- CANR-72
Earlier sketch in CA 134
Raphael, Marc Lee 1942(?)- Brief entry 113
Raphael, Phyllis 1940- 45-48
Raphael, Rick 1919- CANR-10
Earlier sketch in CA 21-24R
Raphael, Robert 1927- 45-48
Raphael, Sandra (Joan) 1939- 104
Raphaelson, Elliot 1937- 124
Raphaelson, Samson 1896-1983 65-68
Obituary 110
See also DLB 44
Rapkin, Chester 1918- 17-20R
Rapoport, Alan M. 1942- 134
Rapoport, Amos 1929- 65-68
Rapoport, Anatol 1911- 41-44R
Rapoport, Janis 1946- CANR-40
Earlier sketches in CA 101, CANR-18
Rapoport, Judith L. .... BEST 89:3
Rapoport, Louis (Harvey) 1942- 117
Rapoport, Rhona (Ross) 1927- CANR-8
Earlier sketch in CA 61-64
Rapoport, Robert Norman 1924-1996 ... CANR-39
Obituary 154
Earlier sketches in CA 5-8R, CANR-2, 17
Rapoport, Roger 1946- 33-36R
Rapoport, Ron 1940- 89-92
Raposo, Joseph Guilherme 1938-1989 Obituary 127
See also SATA-Obit 61
Rapp, Doris Jean 1929- CANR-21
Earlier sketch in CA 37-40R
Rapp, George (Robert), Jr. 1930- 130
Rapp, Joel .... AITN 1
Rapp, Lynn .... AITN 1
Rappaport, Alfred 1932- Brief entry 110
Rappaport, Armin H. 1916- Brief entry 111
Rappaport, David 1907- CAP-2
Earlier sketch in CA 19-20
Rappaport, Eva 1924- 29-32R
See also SATA 6
Rappaport, Julian 1942- Brief entry 112
Rappaport, Roy A(braham) 1926-1997 ..... 41-44R
Obituary 161
Rappaport, Sheldon R(aphael) 1926- 29-32R
Rappaport, Steve 1948- 134
Rappole, John H(ilton) 1946- 123
Rappoport, David Steven 1957- 133
Rappoport, Ken 1935- CANR-42
Earlier sketches in CA 53-56, CANR-4, 20
See also SATA 89
Rappoport, Leon 1932- 41-44R
Rappoport, Shloyme Zanul 1863-1920 144
Rapson, Richard L(awrence) 1937- CANR-10
Earlier sketch in CA 21-24R
Rarick, Carrie 1911- 115
See also SATA 41
Rasberry, Robert W. 1945- 110
Rasberry, Salli 1940- CANR-46
Earlier sketches in CA 107, CANR-23
Rasch, Sunna Cooper 1925- 105
Raschka, Chris
See Raschka, Christopher
Raschka, Christopher 1959- .... SATA 80
Raschke, Carl A(llan) 1944- 104
Rascoe, Jesse Ed
See Bartholomew, Ed(ward Ellsworth)
Rascoe, Judith 1941(?)- 107
Rascovich, Mark 1918(?)-1976 Obituary 69-72
Rasey, Ruth M.
See Simpson, Ruth Mary Rasey
Rash, Dora Eileen Agnew (Wallace) 1897- CANR-2
Earlier sketch in CA 5-8R
Rash, J(esse) Keogh 1906- 93-96
Rash, Nancy 1940- CANR-37
Rashad, Johari M(ahasin) 1951- 138
See also BW 2
Rashidof, Sharif Rashidovich
See Rashidov, Sharaf Rashidovich
Rashidov, Sharaf Rashidovich 1917(?)-1983 Obituary 111
Rashke, Richard L. 1936- CANR-24
Earlier sketch in CA 107
Raskin, A(braham) H(enry) 1911-1993 104
Obituary 143
Raskin, Barbara 1935- 129
Brief entry 126
Raskin, Edith Lefkowitz 1908- CANR-3
Earlier sketch in CA 9-12R
See also SATA 9
Raskin, Ellen 1928-1984 .... CANR-37
Obituary 113
Earlier sketch in CA 21-24R
See also CLR 1, 12
See also DLB 52
See also MAICYA
See also SATA 2, 38
Raskin, Eugene 1909- 33-36R
Raskin, Herbert A(lfred) 1919-1979 .... 29-32R
Obituary 122
Raskin, Jonah (Seth) 1942- CANR-64
Earlier sketch in CA 81-84
Raskin, Joseph 1897-1982 .... CANR-13
Obituary 105
Earlier sketch in CA 33-36R
See also SATA 12
See also SATA-Obit 29
Raskin, Marcus G. 1934- 37-40R
Rasky, Frank (John) 1923- Brief entry 107
Rasky, Harry 1928- CANR-31
Earlier sketch in CA 105
Rasmussen, Henry N(eil) 1909- 5-8R
Rasmussen, Alis A. 1958- 148
Rasmussen, David (William) 1942- 53-56
Rasmussen, Douglas B(ruce) 1948- 119
Rasmussen, John Peter 1933- Brief entry 110
Rasmussen, Knud Johan Victor 1879-1933 Brief entry 113
See also SATA-Brief 34
Rasmussen, Larry L. 1939- 118
Rasmussen, Louis J(ames, Jr.) 1921- 73-76
Rasmussen, R. Kent 1943- 93-96
Rasmussen, Steen Eiler 1898-1990 Obituary ... 132
Rasmussen, Wayne D(avid) 1915- 33-36R
Raso, Jack 1954- 148
Rasof, Henry 1946- 113
Rasor, Eugene L(atimer) 1936- 89-92
Raspberry, William J(ames) 1935- 122
Brief entry 110
Interview in 122
See also BW 2
Rasponi, Lanfranco 1914-1983 .... 17-20R
Obituary 109
Rasputin, Maria
See Bern, Maria Rasputin Soloviev
Rasputin, Valentin (Grigorevich) 1937- 127
Brief entry 108
Rass, Rebecca 1936- 105
Rast, Walter E(mil) 1930- 73-76
Rastell, John fl. 1509(?)-1536(?) .... DLB 170
Ratch, Jerry 1944- 118
Ratcliff, Carter 1941- CANR-64
Earlier sketches in CA 61-64, CANR-13
Ratcliff, John Drury 1903-1973 108
Obituary 106
Ratcliff, Ruth 1905- 121
Ratcliffe, Barrie M(ichael) 1940- 114
Ratcliffe, F(rederick) W(illiam) 1927- CANR-52
Earlier sketch in CA 125
Ratcliffe, James M(axwell) 1925- 21-24R
Ratcliffe, James P.
See Mencken, H(enry) L(ouis)
Ratcliffe, T(om) A(rundel) 1910- CAP-2
Earlier sketch in CA 25-28
Ratermanis, J(anis) B(ernhards) 1904- 9-12R
Ratey, John J(oseph) 1948- 146
Rath, Frederick L(ouis), Jr. 1913- 41-44R
Rath, Patricia M(ink) 17-20R
Rath, R. John 1910- 37-40R
Rath, Sara 1941- 108
Rathbone, Belinda 1950- 151
Rathbone, Julian 1935- CANR-34
Earlier sketch in CA 101
See also CLC 41
Rathbone, Lucy 1896- 5-8R
Rathbone, Ouida Bergere 1886(?)-1974 Obituary 53-56

Rathbone, Richard 1942- 144
Rathbone, Robert Reynolds 1916- 21-24R
Rathe, Alex W(erner) 1912- 17-20R
Rathe, Gustave 1921- 138
Rathenau, Walther 1867-1922 Brief entry 121
Rather, Dan (Irvin) 1931- CANR-9
Earlier sketch in CA 53-56
Interview in CANR-9
See also AITN 1
Rather, L(elland) J(oseph) 1913- 77-80
Rathje, William (Laurens) 1945- 143
Rathjen, Carl Henry 1909- CANR-2
Earlier sketch in CA 5-8R
See also SATA 11
Rathjen, Frederick W(illiam) 1929- 41-44R
Rathlesberger, James (H.) 1948- Brief entry 114
Rathmann, Peggy (Margaret Crosby) 1953- 159
See also SATA 94
Rathmell, J(ohn) C. A. 1935- 9-12R
Rathmell, Neil 1947- 104
Ratigan, Eleanor Eldridge 1916- 5-8R
Ratigan, William 1910- 29-32R
Ratiu, Ion 1917- 5-8R
Ratliff, Charles Edward, Jr. 1926- CANR-1
Earlier sketch in CA 1-4R
Ratliff, Gerald Lee 1944- 107
Ratliff, Richard C(harles) 1922- 65-68
Ratliff, William 1937- 144
Ratliffe, Sharon A(nn) 1939- 61-64
Ratner, Joseph 1901(?)-1979 Obituary 85-88
Ratner, Leonard G(ilbert) 1916- 21-24R
Ratner, Lorman 1932- CANR-10
Earlier sketch in CA 25-28R
Ratner, Marc L. 1926- 45-48
Ratner, Rochelle 1948- CANR-12
Earlier sketch in CA 33-36R
Ratner, Sidney 1908-1996 .... 21-24R
Obituary 151
Ratner, Stanley C(harles) 1925- 13-16R
Ratsch, Christian
See Raetsch, Christian
Rattenbury, Arnold (Foster) 1921- 29-32R
Rattenbury, Ken(neth Miller) 1920- 134
Ratti, John 1933- 73-76
Ratti, Oscar 41-44R
Rattigan, Jama Kim 1951- 167
See also SATA 99
Rattigan, Terence (Mervyn) 1911-1977 85-88
Obituary 73-76
See also CDBLB 1945-1960
See also CLC 7
See also DAM DRAM
See also DLB 13
See also MTCW 1
Rattner, David S(amuel) 1916- 69-72
Ratto, Linda Lee 1952- 148
See also SATA 79
Rattray, Everett T(ennant) 1932-1980 89-92
Obituary 97-100
Rattray, Simon
See Trevor, Elleston
Ratushinskaya, Irina 1954- CANR-68
Earlier sketch in CA 129
See also CLC 54
Ratzan, Scott C. 1962- 124
Ratz de Tagyos, Paul 1958- 143
See also SATA 76
Rau, Dana Meachen 1971- 159
See also SATA 94
Rau, Dhanvanthi (Handoo) Rama
See Rama Rau, Dhanvanthi (Handoo)
Rau, Margaret 1913- CANR-8
Earlier sketch in CA 61-64
See also CLR 8
See also SATA 9
Rauch, Basil 1908-1986 .... CAP-2
Obituary 119
Earlier sketch in CA 19-20
Rauch, Constance 1937- 57-60
Rauch, Earl Mac 1950(?)- Brief entry 118
Rauch, Georg Von
See Von Rauch, Georg
Rauch, Gila Ramras
See Ramras-Rauch, Gila
Rauch, Irmengard 1933- CANR-11
Earlier sketch in CA 21-24R
Rauch, Jonathan (Charles) 1960- 144
Rauch, Joseph B(rian) 1965- 131
Rauch, Leo 1927- 110
Rauch, Mabel Thompson 1888-1972 .... 5-8R
Obituary 103
See also SATA-Obit 26
Rauch, Rufus William, Jr. 1929-1977 Obituary 113
Rauch, William 1950- 144
Raucher, Alan R(ichard) 1939- 118
Raucher, Herman 1928- CANR-29
Earlier sketch in CA 29-32R
See also SATA 8
Raucina, Thomas Frank 1946- CANR-29
Earlier sketches in CA 73-76, CANR-12
Raudive, Konstantin 1909-1974 .... 29-32R
Obituary 126
Rauf, Abdur 1924- CANR-42
Earlier sketches in CA 73-76, CANR-13
Rauf, Muhammad Abdul
See Abdul-Rauf, Muhammad
Raulston, J(ames) Leonard 1905- 89-92
Rault, Walter
See Gorham, Maurice Anthony Coneys
Rauner, Robert M(cKenzie) 1925- CANR-1
Earlier sketch in CA 1-4R
Raunikar, Robert 1931- 124
Raup, H(allock) F(loyd) 1901- 37-40R
Raup, Robert 1888(?)-1976 Obituary 65-68
Rausch, Edward N. 1919- CANR-7
Earlier sketch in CA 13-16R
Rausch, Jane M(eyer) 1940- 119
Rauschenberg, Roy A(nthony) 1929- 45-48
Rauscher, Donald J. 1921- 9-12R
Rauschning, Hermann 1887-1982 Obituary 109
Raush, Harold L(ester) 1921- Brief entry 110
Raushenbush, Esther (Mohr) 1898- CAP-1
Earlier sketch in CA 13-16
Ravel, Aviva 1928- CANR-45
Earlier sketch in CA 119
Raven, Daniel
See Lazuta, Gene
Raven, Frithjof Andersen 1907-1966 .... CAP-1
Earlier sketch in CA 13-16
Raven, J(ohn) E(arle) 1914-1980 103
Obituary 97-100
Raven, Ninette Helene Jeanty
1903-1990 Obituary 132
Raven, Ronald William 1904-1991 .... CANR-23
Obituary 136
Earlier sketch in CA 107
Raven, Simon (Arthur Noel) 1927- 81-84
See also CLC 14
Ravenal, Earl C(edric) 1931- 33-36R
Ravenel, Shannon 1938- CANR-27
Earlier sketch in CA 108
Ravenna, Michael
See Welty, Eudora
Ravenna, Roger
See Horbach, Michael
Ravenscroft, Arthur 1924- CANR-29
Earlier sketch in CA 110
Ravetch, Irving 1915(?)- Brief entry 110
Ravetz, Alison 1930- 116
Ravetz, Jerome R(aymond) 1929- 97-100
Ravetz, Jerry
See Ravetz, Jerome R(aymond)
Ravi, Bison
See Vian, Boris
Ravich, Robert A(lan) 1920- Brief entry 113
Ravielli, Anthony 1916-1997 .... CANR-11
Obituary 156
Earlier sketch in CA 29-32R
See also SATA 3
See also SATA-Obit 95
Ravikovitch, Dahlia
See Rabikovitz, Dalia
Ravikovitz, Dalia
See Rabikovitz, Dalia
Ravilious, Robin 1944- 145
See also SATA 77
Ravin, Neil 1947- 105
Ravindra, Ravi 1939- CANR-35
Earlier sketch in CA 114
Ravitch, Diane 1938- CANR-65
Earlier sketches in CA 53-56, CANR-4, 31
See also MTCW 1
Ravitch, Mark M(itchell) 1910-1989 Obituary 128
Ravitch, Norman 1936- 37-40R
Ravitz, Abe Carl 1927- 9-12R
Ravitz, Shlomo 1885-1980 Obituary 103
Raviv, Dan 1954- 140
Ravvin, Norman 1963- 138
Raw, Isaias 1927- 57-60
Rawcliffe, (John) Michael 1934- 115
Rawding, F(rederick) W(illiam) 1930- .... SATA 55
Rawford, W. C.
See Crawford, William (Elbert)
Rawick, George P(hilip) 1929- 61-64
Rawitch, Robert Joe 1945- 133
Rawlence, Christopher 1945- 136
Rawles, Beverly A(rcher) 1930- 107
Rawley, Callman 1903- CANR-32
Earlier sketches in CA 21-24R, CANR-12
See also Rakosi, Carl
Rawley, James A. 1916- 21-24R
Rawling, Thomas Jackson 1916- 114
Rawling, Tom
See Rawling, Thomas Jackson
Rawlings, Hunter Ripley III 1944- 103
Rawlings, John 1930(?)-1981(?) Obituary 102
Rawlings, Louisa
See Baumgarten, Sylvia
Rawlings, Marjorie Kinnan 1896-1953 137
Brief entry 104
See also AAYA 20
See also DLB 9, 22, 102
See also DLBD 17
See also JRDA
See also MAICYA
See also SATA 100
See also TCLC 4
See also YABC 1
Rawlings, Maurice S(kaggs) 1922- 108
Rawlins, Clive Leonard 1940- CANR-22
Earlier sketch in CA 105
Rawlins, Dennis 1937- 45-48
Rawlins, Eustace Robert
See Barton, Eustace Robert
Rawlins, Jack P. 1946- 57-60
Rawlins, Jennie Brown 1910- CAP-2
Earlier sketch in CA 23-24
Rawlins, Winifred 1907- 9-12R
Rawlinson, A(rthur) R(ichard)
1894-1984 Obituary 113
Rawlinson, Dick
See Rawlinson, A(rthur) R(ichard)
Rawlinson, Jane 1947- 138
Rawls, Eugene S. 1927- 9-12R
Rawls, James J(abus) 1945- 112
Rawls, John (Bordley) 1921- 147
Rawls, John Bordley 1921- Brief entry 114
Rawls, Philip
See Levinson, Leonard
Rawls, Walter Cecil, Jr. 1928- 111
Rawls, Walton (Hendry) 1933- CANR-48
Earlier sketch in CA 121
Rawls, Wendell L(ee), Jr. 1941- CANR-22
Earlier sketch in CA 73-76
Rawls, (Woodrow) Wilson 1913- CANR-5
Earlier sketch in CA 1-4R
See also AAYA 21
See also AITN 1
See also JRDA
See also SATA 22
Rawlyk, George Alexander 1935- CANR-51
Earlier sketches in CA 109, CANR-26
See also SATA 64
Rawn, Melanie (Robin) 1954- 157
See also SATA 98
Raworth, Thomas Moore 1938- CANR-46
Earlier sketch in CA 29-32R
See also Raworth, Tom
Raworth, Tom
See Raworth, Thomas Moore
See also CAAS 11
See also DLB 40
Rawski, Conrad H(enry) 1914- 73-76
Rawski, Evelyn S(akakida) 1939- 89-92
Rawson, Beryl 1933- 121
Rawson, C(laude) J(ulien) 1935- 25-28R
Rawson, Clayton 1906-1971 .... CANR-4
Obituary 29-32R
Earlier sketch in CA 5-8R
Rawson, Elizabeth (Donata) 1934-1988 Brief
entry 115
Rawson, Margaret B(yrd) 1899- 25-28R
Rawson, Philip Stanley 1924-1995 .... CANR-21
Obituary 150
Earlier sketches in CA 5-8R, CANR-6
Rawson, Wyatt Trevelyan Rawson 1894-1980 .... 5-8R
Obituary 103
Ray, Ann 1937- 114
Ray, Arthur J. 1941- 127
Ray, Carl 1943-1978 .... SATA 63
Ray, Clyde H. 1938- 157
Ray, Cyril 1908-1991 .... CANR-21
Obituary 135
Earlier sketches in CA 5-8R, CANR-5
Ray, D(avid) Michael 1935- CANR-9
Earlier sketch in CA 17-20R
Ray, Daryll E. 1943- 149
Ray, David (E.) 1932- CANR-47
Earlier sketches in CA 9-12R, CANR-5
See also CAAS 7
See also DLB 5
Ray, Deborah
See Kogan Ray, Deborah
See also SATA 8
Ray, Delia 1963- 138
See also SATA 70
Ray, Dixy Lee 1914-1994 134
Obituary 143
Ray, Dorothy Jean 1919- CANR-12
Earlier sketch in CA 25-28R
Ray, George McNeill 1910- 1-4R
Ray, Gordon N(orton) 1915-1986 57-60
Obituary 121
See also DLB 103, 140
Ray, H(enrietta) Cordelia 1849(?)-1916 124
Brief entry 122
See also BW 1
See also DLB 50
Ray, Irene
See Sutton, Margaret Beebe
Ray, Jane 1960- .... SATA 72
Ray, JoAnne 1935- 61-64
See also SATA 9
Ray, John (Philip) 1929- CANR-11
Earlier sketch in CA 25-28R
Ray, John B(ernard) 1930- 61-64
Ray, John R(obert) 1921- 37-40R
Ray, Joseph M(alchus) 1907- 41-44R
Ray, (Suzanne) Judy 1939- 111
Ray, Karen 1956- 108
Ray, Kenneth Clark 1901- CAP-2
Earlier sketch in CA 19-20
Ray, Man 1890-1976 .... CANR-29
Obituary 69-72
Earlier sketch in CA 77-80
Ray, Mary (Eva Pedder) 1932- CANR-12
Earlier sketch in CA 29-32R
See also SATA 2
Ray, Mary Lyn 1946- CANR-59
See also SATA 90
Ray, Michele S. 1938- 25-28R
Ray, N(ancy) L(ouise) 1918- CANR-51
Earlier sketches in CA 109, CANR-26
Ray, Oakley S(tern) 1931- 45-48
Ray, Paul C(harles) 1926- 104
Ray, Philip A(lexander) 1911-1970 .... CAP-2
Earlier sketch in CA 23-24
Ray, Robert H. 1940- 135
Ray, Robert J. 1935- 126
Ray, Russell
See Strait, Raymond
Ray, Satyajit 1921-1992 114
Obituary 137
See also CLC 16, 76
See also DAM MULT
Ray, Sibnarayan 1921- CANR-15
Earlier sketch in CA 21-24R
Ray, Talton F. 1939- 29-32R
Ray, Trevor 1934- 107
Ray, Wesley
See Gaulden, Ray
Ray, Wilbert S(cott) 1901- CAP-2
Earlier sketch in CA 25-28
Rayback, Joseph G(eorge) 1914- 5-8R
Rayburn, James Chalmers III 1945- 121
Rayburn, Jim III
See Rayburn, James Chalmers III
Rayburn, Robert G(ibson) 1915- 25-28R
Raycraft, Donald R(obert) 1942- 41-44R
Raycraft, Stan
See Shaver, Richard S(harpe)
Rayevsky, Robert 1955- .... SATA 81
Rayfiel, David 1923- 139
Rayfield, David 1940- 45-48
Rayfield, (Patrick) Donald 1942- 103
Rayfield, Stanley C. 1901(?)-1983(?) Obituary 108
Raygor, Alton Lamon 1922- 49-52
Rayman, Paula Marian 1947- 107
Raymond, Agnes G. 1916- 25-28R
Raymond, Alex(ander Gillespie) 1909-1956 Brief
entry 112
Raymond, C. Elizabeth 1953- 139
Raymond, Charles
See Koch, Charlotte
and Koch, Raymond
Raymond, Diana (Joan) 1916- 89-92
Raymond, E. V.
See Gallun, Raymond Z(inke)
Raymond, Ellsworth (Lester) 1912-1996 .... 37-40R
Obituary 153
Raymond, Ernest 1888-1974 Obituary 89-92
See also DLB 191
Raymond, Father M.
See Flanagan, Joseph David Stanislaus
Raymond, G. Alison
See Lanier, Alison Raymond
Raymond, Harold 1887-1975 Obituary 104
Raymond, Henry J. 1820-1869 .... DLB 43, 79
Raymond, James (Charles) 1940- 119
Raymond, James Crossley
1917-1981 Obituary 105
See also SATA-Obit 29
Raymond, Janice G. 1943- 89-92
Raymond, John
See Brosnan, John
Raymond, Joseph H.
See Le Fontaine, Joseph (Raymond)
Raymond, Laurie W(atson) 1951- 166
Raymond, Lee
See Hill, Mary Raymond
Raymond, Margaret E(lmendorf) 1912- 104
Raymond, Mary
See Keegan, Mary Heathcott
Raymond, P. L.
See Gibson, Walter B(rown)
Raymond, Patrick (Ernest) 1924- 102
Raymond, Rene (Brabazon) 1906-1985 .... CANR-61
Obituary 115
Earlier sketch in CA 126
Raymond, Robert
See Alter, Robert Edmond
Raymond, Steve 1940- 49-52
Raymond, Walter J(ohn) 1930- 53-56
Raymond, William O. 1880-1970 .... CAP-2
Earlier sketch in CA 19-20
Raymond de Jesus, Mother
See Dion, Sister Anita
Raynal, Paul 1885(?)-1971 Obituary 33-36R
Rayne, Alan
See Tobin, James Edward
Rayner, Claire (Berenice) 1931- CANR-70
Earlier sketches in CA 21-24R, CANR-13
Rayner, E(dgar) G(eoffrey) 1927- CANR-10
Earlier sketch in CA 21-24R
Rayner, John Desmond 1924- 103
Rayner, Mary 1933- CANR-52
Earlier sketches in CA 69-72, CANR-12, 29
See also CLR 41
See also SATA 22, 87
Rayner, Ray
See Rahner, Raymond M.
Rayner, Richard
See McIlwain, David
Rayner, William 1929- CANR-64
Earlier sketch in CA 77-80
See also SATA 55
See also SATA-Brief 36
Raynor, David R(alph) 1948- 111
Raynor, Dorka 106
See also SATA 28
Raynor, Henry (Broughton) 1917- 85-88
Rayside, Betty 1931- 57-60
Rayson, Paul
See Jennings, Leslie Nelson
Rayson, Steven 1932- 106
See also SATA 30
Rayward, W(arden) Boyd 1939- 102
Raywid, Mary Anne 5-8R
Raz, Joseph 1939- 125
Raz, Simcha 1931- 157
Razaf, Andy 1895-1973 Obituary 41-44R
Razik, Taher A. 1924- CANR-19
Earlier sketch in CA 25-28R
Razin, Assaf 1941- 136
Razor Saltboy
See Louis, Ray Baldwin
Razran, Gregory 1901-1973 .... 41-44R
Obituary 45-48
Razzell, Arthur (George) 1925- 85-88
See also SATA 11
Razzell, Mary (Catherine) 1930- 160
See also SATA 102
Razzi, James 1931- CANR-5
Earlier sketch in CA 53-56
See also SATA 10
Re, Edward D(omenic) 1920- CANR-12
Earlier sketch in CA 21-24R
Rea, Frederick B(eatty) 1908- 9-12R
Rea, Gardner 1892-1966 Obituary 93-96
Rea, K(enneth) J(ohn) 1932- Brief entry 107
Rea, Kenneth Wesley 1944- 107
Rea, Michael M. 1927-1996 .... DLBY 97
Rea, Robert R(ight) 1922- CANR-28
Earlier sketch in CA 1-4R

Reach, Angus 1821-1856 ... DLB 70
Reach, James 1910(?)-1970 Obituary ... 29-32R
Read, Al 1919-1987 Obituary ... 123
Read, Anthony 1935- ... 107
Read, Bill 1917- ... 13-16R
Read, Brian (Ahier) 1927- ... 108
Read, Cecil B(yron) 1901-1972 ... CAP-1
Earlier sketch in CA 13-16
Read, David Haxton Carswell 1910- ... CANR-3
Earlier sketch in CA 1-4R
Read, Donald 1930- ... CANR-1
Earlier sketch in CA 1-4R
Read, Elfreida 1920- ... CANR-25
Earlier sketches in CA 21-24R, CANR-9
See also SATA 2
Read, Forrest 1926-1980 Obituary ... 112
Read, Gardner 1913- ... CANR-6
Earlier sketch in CA 13-16R
Read, Hadley 1918- ... 81-84
Read, Helen Appleton
1887(?)-1974 Obituary ... 53-56
Read, Herbert Edward 1893-1968 ... 85-88
Obituary ... 25-28R
See also CLC 4
See also DLB 20, 149
Read, Jan
See Read, John Hinton
Read, John Hinton 1917- ... CANR-32
Earlier sketches in CA 77-80, CANR-15
Read, Kenneth E(yre) 1917- ... 101
Read, Leonard Edward 1898-1983 ... CANR-11
Obituary ... 109
Earlier sketch in CA 17-20R
Read, Martha Meredith ... DLB 200
Read, Maureen Hay 1937- ... 113
Read, Opie 1852-1939 ... DLB 23
Read, Peter G. 1927- ... 141
Read, Piers Paul 1941- ... CANR-38
Earlier sketch in CA 21-24R
See also CLC 4, 10, 25
See also DLB 14
See also SATA 21
Read, R. B. 1916-1982 ... CANR-13
Earlier sketch in CA 61-64
Read, Ritchard 1914- ... 57-60
Read, Sylvia Joan ... 103
Read, William M(erritt) 1901- ... 33-36R
Reade, B(rian) Edmund 1913- ... 21-24R
Reade, Charles 1814-1884 ... DLB 21
Reade, Deborah 1949- ... SATA 69
Reade, Hamish
See Gray, Simon (James Holliday)
Reade, Lang
See Carter, David C(harles)
Reader, Dennis 1929- ... SATA 71
Reader, Dennis Joel 1939- ... 106
Reader, Desmond H. 1920- ... 21-24R
Reader, W(illiam) J(oseph) 1920-1990 ... CANR-39
Obituary ... 132
Earlier sketches in CA 37-40R, CANR-16
Reading, Peter 1946- ... CANR-46
Earlier sketch in CA 103
See also CLC 47
See also DLB 40
Readings, Bill 1960- ... 139
Readman, Jo 1958- ... 155
See also SATA 89
Ready, Kirk L(ewis) 1943- ... 114
See also SATA 39
Ready, William B(ernard) 1914-1981 ... CANR-22
Earlier sketch in CA 25-28R
Reagan, Charles E(llis) 1942- ... 53-56
Reagan, Michael D(aniel) 1927- ... 49-52
Reagan, Nancy (Davis) 1923- ... CANR-33
Earlier sketch in CA 110
See also BEST 90:1
Reagan, Patricia Ann
See Davis, Patti
Reagan, Ronald (Wilson) 1911- ... CANR-47
Earlier sketch in CA 85-88
See also BEST 90:1
Reagan, Sydney C(handler) 1916- ... 41-44R
Reagan, Thomas (James) B(utler) 1916- ... 37-40R
Reagen, Edward P(aul) 1924- ... 49-52
Reagen, Michael V. 1942- ... 81-84
Reagin, Ewell Kerr 1900- ... 41-44R
Reagon, Bernice Johnson 1942- ... 147
Real, Terrence 1950(?)- ... 167
Reaman, George Elmore 1889-1969 ... CAP-1
Earlier sketch in CA 11-12
Reamer, Judy 1940- ... 125
Reams, Bernard D(insmore), Jr. 1943- ... CANR-16
Earlier sketch in CA 93-96
Reamy, Tom 1935-1977 ... 81-84
Reaney, James 1926- ... CANR-42
Earlier sketch in CA 41-44R
See also CAAS 15
See also CLC 13
See also DAC
See also DAM MST
See also DLB 68
See also SATA 43
Rearden, Jim 1925- ... CANR-40
Earlier sketch in CA 65-68
Reardon, B(ernard) M(orris) G(arvin) 1914- ... CANR-2
Earlier sketch in CA 5-8R
Reardon, Dennis J(oseph) 1944- ... 113
Brief entry ... 110
Interview in ... 113
Reardon, Joan 1930- ... 116
Reardon, John J(oseph) 1926- ... 45-48
Reardon, William R. 1920- ... CANR-2
Earlier sketch in CA 1-4R
Rearick, Charles Walter 1942- ... 102
Reaske, Christopher R(ussell) 1941- ... 21-24R
Reason, James T(ootle) 1938- ... 104
Reasoner, Harry 1923-1991 ... 111
Obituary ... 135
See also AITN 1
Reat, N(oble) Ross 1951- ... 139
Reaver, Chap 1935-1993 ... 137
Obituary ... 142
See also SATA 69
See also SATA-Obit 77
Reaver, Herbert R.
See Reaver, Chap
Reaver, J(oseph) Russell 1915- ... 33-36R
Reaves, J. Michael
See Reaves, (James) Michael
Reaves, (James) Michael 1950- ... 158
See also SATA 99
Reaves, Philip
See Kiester, Edwin, Jr.
Reaves, Wendy Wick 1950- ... 114
Reavey, George 1907-1976 Obituary ... 69-72
Reavey, Jean (Bullowa) 1917(?)-1987 Obituary . 123
Reavis, Dick J. 1945- ... 133
Reay, Barry 1950- ... 144
Reb, Paul 1924- ... 49-52
Rebatet, Lucien 1903-1972 Obituary ... 37-40R
Rebay, Luciano 1928- ... 45-48
Rebbot, Olivier 1951(?)-1981 Obituary ... 103
Rebelsky, Freda Gould 1931- ... 41-44R
Rebert, M. Charles 1920- ... 53-56
Rebeta-Burditt, Joyce ... 81-84
Rebholz, Ronald A(lexander) 1932- ... 111
Rebhun, Paul c. 1500-1546 ... DLB 179
Rebischung, James A. 1928- ... 53-56
Rebora, Clemente 1885-1957 ... DLB 114
Rebreanu, Liviu 1885-1944 ... 165
See also TCLC 28
Rebuffat, Gaston (Louis Simon) 1921-1985 . 21-24R
Obituary ... 116
Receveur, Betty Layman 1930- ... 130
Rechcigl, Miloslav, Jr. 1930- ... CANR-12
Earlier sketch in CA 17-20R
Rechy, John (Francisco) 1934- ... CANR-64
Earlier sketches in CA 5-8R, CANR-6, 32
Interview in ... CANR-6
See also CAAS 4
See also CLC 1, 7, 14, 18, 107
See also DAM MULT
See also DLB 122
See also DLBY 82
See also HLC
See also HW
Reck, Alma Kehoe 1901- ... 1-4R
Reck, Andrew J(oseph) 1927- ... CANR-6
Earlier sketch in CA 13-16R
Reck, David 1935- ... 73-76
Reck, Franklin Mering 1896-1965 Obituary ... 109
See also SATA-Brief 30
Reck, Rima Drell 1933- ... 21-24R
Reck, W(aldo) Emerson 1903- ... 61-64
Recker, Colane 1940- ... 113
Reckless, Walter Cade 1899- ... 37-40R
Reckord, Barry ... 77-80
Record, Cy Wilson 1916- ... 9-12R
Record, Jane Cassels 1915-1981 ... CANR-5
Earlier sketch in CA 13-16R
Rector, Frank ... 106
Reday, Ladislaw 1913- ... 112
Red Bird
See Bonnin, Gertrude
Red Butterfly
See Lauritsen, John (Phillip)
Redcam, Tom 1870-1933 ... TCLC 25
Redcliffe-Maud, John
See Redcliffe-Maud, John Primatt
Redcliffe-Maud, John Primatt 1906-1982 ... 129
Obituary ... 108
Redcliffe-Maud, Lord
See Redcliffe-Maud, John Primatt
Redd, (Newton) Lawrence 1941- ... 57-60
Redd, Louise 1967- ... 153
Reddan, Harold J. 1926- ... 13-16R
Reddaway, (Arthur Frederick) John
1916-1990 Obituary ... 132
Reddaway, Peter (Brian) 1939- ... CANR-10
Earlier sketch in CA 21-24R
Reddaway, W(illiam) Brian 1913- ... 17-20R
Redden, James Erskine 1928- ... 41-44R
Redder, George
See Drummond, Jack
Reddick, DeWitt Carter 1904- ... 5-8R
Reddick, L(awrence) D(unbar) 1910-1995 ... 61-64
Obituary ... 149
Reddin, Keith ... CLC 67
Reddin, W(illiam) J(ames) 1930- ... 29-32R
Redding, Bud
See Redding, Edward C.
Redding, David A. 1923- ... CANR-3
Earlier sketch in CA 1-4R
Redding, Edward C. 1917-1984 Obituary ... 113
Redding, Robert Hull 1919- ... CANR-28
Earlier sketches in CA 21-24R, CANR-11
See also SATA 2
Redding, (Jay) Saunders 1906-1988 ... CANR-26
Obituary ... 124
Earlier sketches in CA 1-4R, CANR-5
See also BW 1
See also DLB 63
Reddy, John F. X. 1912(?)-1975 Obituary ... 53-56
Reddy, Maureen T. 1955- ... 136
Reddy, Michael 1933- ... 61-64
Reddy, T. J. 1945- ... 45-48
Reddy, T(hammaiahgari) Ramakrishna 1937- . 45-48
Redekop, Calvin Wall 1925- ... CANR-51
Earlier sketches in CA 25-28R, CANR-10, 26
Redekop, John Harold 1932- ... 21-24R
Redekopp, Elsa ... 127
See also SATA 61
Reder, Philip 1924-1983 Obituary ... 110
Redfern, George B. 1910- ... 9-12R
Redfern, W(alter) D(avid) 1936- ... 21-24R
Redfield, Alden 1941- ... 77-80
Redfield, Alfred Clarence 1890-1983 Obituary .. 109
Redfield, Clark
See McMorrow, Fred
Redfield, James 195(?)- ... 158
Redfield, James M. 1935- ... 155
Redfield, Jennifer
See Hoskins, Robert
Redfield, Malissa
See Elliott, Malissa Childs
Redfield, Margaret Park
1899(?)-1977 Obituary ... 69-72
Redfield, Robert 1897-1958 Brief entry ... 121
Redfield, William 1927-1976 Obituary ... 69-72
Redford, Donald B(ruce) 1934- ... 149
Redford, Emmette Shelburn 1904- ... 112
Redford, Kent H(ubbard) 1955- ... 141
Redford, Polly 1925-1972 ... CAP-2
Earlier sketch in CA 33-36
Redford, (Charles) Robert (Jr.) 1937- ... 107
See also AAYA 15
Red Fox, William 1871(?)-1976 Obituary ... 65-68
Redgate, John
See Kennedy, Adam
Redgrave, Corin 1939- ... 154
Redgrave, Deirdre 1939-1997 ... 157
Obituary ... 161
Redgrave, Lady
See Kempson, Rachel
Redgrave, Lynn (Rachel) 1943- ... 157
Redgrave, Michael (Scudamore) 1908-1985 ... 143
Obituary ... 115
Redgrave, Paul 1920- ... 5-8R
Redgrave, Vanessa 1937- ... 148
Redgrove, Peter (William) 1932- ... CANR-39
Earlier sketches in CA 1-4R, CANR-3
See also CLC 6, 41
See also DLB 40
Redhead, Brian 1929-1994 ... 128
Obituary ... 143
Red Hog
See Martin, Dannie M.
Redinger, Ruby V(irginia) 1915-1981 ... 65-68
Obituary ... 120
Redish, Bessie Braid 1905-1974 ... CAP-2
Earlier sketch in CA 25-28
Redkey, Edwin S(torer) 1931- ... 29-32R
Redlich, Frederick Carl 1910- Brief entry ... 106
Redman, Ben Ray 1896-1961 Obituary ... 93-96
Redman, Eric 1948- ... 49-52
Redman, L(ister) A(ppleton) 1933- ... 108
Redmayne, John
See Wood, Herbert Fairlie
Redmayne, Paul (Brewis) 1900- ... 5-8R
Redmon, Anne
See Nightingale, Anne Redmon
See also CLC 22
See also DLBY 86
Redmond, Eugene B. 1937- ... CANR-25
Earlier sketches in CA 25-28R, CANR-12
See also BW 2
See also DLB 41
Redmond, Gerald 1934- ... 37-40R
Redmond, Howard A(lexander) 1925- ... 13-16R
Redmond, Ian (Michael) 1954- ... 147
Redmond, Juanita
See Hipps, Juanita Redmond
Redmond, Layne ... 165
Redmont, Bernard Sidney 1918- ... 73-76
Redmont, Dennis Foster 1942- ... 77-80
Redner, Harry 1937- ... 110
Redon, Joel 1961- ... 131
Redonnet, Marie 1948- ... 154
Redpath, Alan (Ogle) 1907-1989 Obituary ... 128
Redpath, (Robert) Theodore (Holmes) 1913- ... 104
Redpath, William 1893(?)-1985 Obituary ... 116
Redshaw, Peggy A(nn) 1948- ... 168
Redstone, Louis G(ordon) 1903- ... CANR-2
Earlier sketch in CA 49-52
Redway, Ralph
See Hamilton, Charles (Harold St. John)
Redway, Ridley
See Hamilton, Charles (Harold St. John)
Redwood, Alec
See Milkomane, George Alexis Milkomanovich
Redwood, John (Alan) 1951- ... CANR-41
Earlier sketches in CA 102, CANR-19
Ree, Jonathan 1948- ... 57-60
Reece, Benny R(amon) 1930- ... 41-44R
Reece, Gabrielle 1970- ... 161
Reece, Jack Eugene 1941- ... 101
Reece, Robert D(enton) 1939- ... 128
Reeck, Darrell (Lauren) 1939- ... 104
Reed, A(lfred) H(amish) 1875-1975 ... CANR-4
Obituary ... 57-60
Earlier sketch in CA 9-12R
Reed, A(lexander) W(yclif) 1908-1979 ... CANR-4
Earlier sketch in CA 9-12R
Reed, Alison Touster 1952- ... 105
Reed, Barry
See Reed, Barry C(lement)
Reed, Barry C(lement) 1927- ... CANR-23
Earlier sketch in CA 29-32R
Reed, Betty Jane 1921- ... 29-32R
See also SATA 4
Reed, Bobbie (Butler) 1944- ... 77-80
Reed, Carroll E(dward) 1914- ... 103
Reed, Christopher (G.) 1961- ... 163
Reed, Daniel 1892(?)-1978 Obituary ... 77-80
Reed, David 1946- ... 167
Reed, Don C(harles) 1945- ... 106
Reed, Donald A(nthony) 1935- ... 103
Reed, Douglas 1895-1976 ... 103
Obituary ... 89-92
Reed, E.
See Evans, Mari
Reed, Edward W(ilson) 1913- ... 29-32R
Reed, Eliot
See Ambler, Eric
Reed, Elizabeth Liggett 1895-1978 ... 77-80
Obituary ... 133
Reed, Elizabeth Stewart 1914- ... 1-4R
Reed, Emmett X.
See King, Florence
Reed, Evelyn 1905-1979 ... 102
Reed, Graham 1923- ... CANR-24
Earlier sketch in CA 45-48
Reed, Gwendolyn E(lizabeth) 1932- ... 25-28R
See also SATA 21
Reed, H(erbert) Owen 1910- ... CANR-42
Earlier sketches in CA 53-56, CANR-4, 19
Reed, Harold W(illiam) 1909- ... 118
Reed, Harrison Merrick, Jr. 1898-(?) ... 1-4R
Obituary ... 134
Reed, Henry 1808-1854 ... DLB 59
Reed, Henry 1914-1986 ... 104
Obituary ... 121
See also DLB 27
Reed, Henry Clay 1899-1972 Obituary ... 111
Reed, Howard Alexander 1920- ... 13-16R
Reed, Ishmael 1938- ... CANR-48
Earlier sketches in CA 21-24R, CANR-25
See also BLC 3
See also BW 2
See also CLC 2, 3, 5, 6, 13, 32, 60
See also DAM MULT
See also DLB 2, 5, 33, 169
See also DLBD 8
See also MTCW 1
Reed, J(ames) D(onald) 1940- ... 33-36R
Reed, James 1922- ... 102
Reed, James F(red) 1909- ... CAP-1
Earlier sketch in CA 11-12
Reed, James Wesley 1944- ... 112
Reed, Jeremy 1951- ... 154
Reed, John (Silas) 1887-1920 Brief entry ... 106
See also TCLC 9
Reed, John 1909- ... 125
Reed, John F(ord) 1911- ... 13-16R
Reed, John L(incoln) 1938- ... 57-60
Reed, John P(lume) 1921- ... 65-68
Reed, John Q(uincy) 1918-1978 ... 45-48
Obituary ... 103
Reed, John R(obert) 1938- ... CANR-8
Earlier sketch in CA 17-20R
Reed, John Shelton (Jr.) 1942- ... CANR-5
Earlier sketch in CA 53-56
Reed, Joseph Verner 1902-1973 Obituary ... 45-48
Reed, Joseph W(ayne), Jr. 1932- ... 37-40R
Reed, Kenneth 1944- ... 57-60
Reed, Kenneth T(errence) 1937- ... 73-76
Reed, Kit ... CANR-36
Earlier sketches in CA 1-4R, CANR-1, 16
See also SATA 34
Reed, Lawrence
See Reday, Ladislaw
Reed, Linda 1955- ... 137
Reed, Lou
See Firbank, Louis
See also CLC 21
Reed, Louis S(chultz) 1902-1975 Obituary ... 61-64
Reed, Luther D(otterer) 1873- ... 5-8R
Reed, M(athilda) N(ewman) 1905-(?) ... 1-4R
Obituary ... 134
Reed, Macon, Jr. 1911(?)-1986 Obituary ... 121
Reed, Marcia 1929- ... 120
Reed, Mark D(ouglas) Morrison
See Morrison-Reed, Mark D(ouglas)
Reed, Mark L(afayette) III 1935- ... 93-96
Reed, Mary Jane (Pobst) 1920- ... 25-28R
Reed, Michael 1930- ... CANR-50
Earlier sketch in CA 123
Reed, (Fred) Mort(on) 1912- ... 61-64
Reed, Neil 1961- ... SATA 99
Reed, Nelson A. 1926- ... 9-12R
Reed, Paul 1956- ... 113
Reed, Peter J. 1935- ... 53-56
Reed, Philip (Chandler) 1952- ... 159
Reed, Philip G. 1908- ... SATA-Brief 29
Reed, Rex (Taylor) 1938- ... CANR-68
Earlier sketches in CA 53-56, CANR-9, 27
See also AITN 1
See also DLB 185
Reed, Robert 1956- ... 127
Reed, Robert C(arroll) 1937- ... CANR-10
Earlier sketch in CA 65-68
Reed, Robert Rentoul, Jr. 1911- ... 33-36R
Reed, Ronald F. 1945- ... 116
Reed, S(amuel) Kyle 1922- ... 41-44R
Reed, Sampson 1800-1880 ... DLB 1
Reed, Talbot Baines 1852-1893 ... DLB 141
Reed, Thomas (James) 1947- ... 103
See also SATA 34
Reed, Thomas Harrison 1881-1971 Obituary ... 110
Reed, Thomas Thornton 1902- ... 107
Reed, Victor (Brenner) 1926- ... 33-36R
Reed, Walter Logan 1943- ... 102
Reed, William Maxwell 1871-1962 ... SATA 15
Reed, Willis 1942- ... 104
Reeder, Carolyn 1937- ... 135
See also SATA 66, 97
Reeder, Colin (Dawson) 1938- ... 141
See also SATA 74
Reeder, Colonel Red
See Reeder, Russell P(otter), Jr.
Reeder, John P., Jr. 1937- ... 101
Reeder, Ray 1931- ... 158

Reeder, Russell P(otter), Jr. 1902-1998 ... CANR-5
Obituary ... 165
Earlier sketch in CA 1-4R
See also SATA 4
See also SATA-Obit 101
Reeder, Stephanie Owen 1951- ... SATA 102
Reedstrom, Ernest Lisle 1928- ... 89-92
Reedy, George E(dward) 1917- ... 29-32R
Reedy, Jerry Edward 1936- ... 119
Reedy, John Louis 1925-1983 Obituary ... 111
Reedy, William A. 1916(?)-1975 Obituary ... 61-64
Reedy, William James 1921- ... 13-16R
Reedy, William Marion 1862-1920 ... DLB 91
Reef, Catherine 1951- ... SATA 73
Reefe, Thomas Q(uentin) 1943- ... 123
Brief entry ... 116
Reel, A(dolf) Frank 1907- ... 93-96
Reeman, Douglas Edward 1924- ... CANR-59
Earlier sketches in CA 1-4R, CANR-3
See also SATA 63
See also SATA-Brief 28
Reems, Harry 1947- ... 61-64
Reens, Mary
See Singleton, Betty
Reep, Edward 1918- ... 33-36R
Rees, Alan M(axwell) 1929- ... 106
Rees, Albert (Everett) 1921-1992 ... CANR-12
Obituary ... 139
Earlier sketch in CA 29-32R
Rees, Barbara (Elizabeth) 1934- ... CANR-9
Earlier sketch in CA 53-56
Rees, Brian 1929- ... 133
Rees, C. Roger 1946- ... 146
Rees, Clair (Francis) 1938- ... 117
Rees, David 1928- ... CANR-11
Earlier sketch in CA 9-12R
Rees, David Bartlett 1936-1993 ... CANR-47
Obituary ... 141
Earlier sketch in CA 105
See also MAICYA
See also SAAS 5
See also SATA 36, 69
See also SATA-Obit 76
Rees, David Morgan 1904- ... 104
Rees, Dilwyn
See Daniel, Glyn (Edmund)
Rees, Ennis (Samuel, Jr.) 1925- ... CANR-2
Earlier sketch in CA 1-4R
See also SATA 3
Rees, (Morgan) Goronwy 1909- ... CANR-3
Earlier sketch in CA 45-48
Rees, Helen Christina Easson (Evans)
1903-1970 ... 5-8R
Obituary ... 89-92
Rees, Henry 1916- ... 107
Rees, Ioan Bowen 1929- ... 29-32R
Rees, Jean A(nglin) 1912- ... CANR-1
Earlier sketch in CA 1-4R
Rees, Joan 1927- ... CANR-29
Earlier sketches in CA 25-28R, CANR-12
Rees, Joan Alice Gladys
See Rees, Joan
Rees, (George) Leslie (Clarence) 1905- .. CANR-26
Earlier sketch in CA 104
Rees, Lucy 1943- ... 107
Rees, Margaret A(nn) 1933- ... CANR-39
Earlier sketches in CA 101, CANR-18
Rees, Meriel
See Lambot, Isobel
Rees, Nigel (Thomas) 1944- ... 132
Rees, Paul Stromberg 1900- ... 5-8R
Rees, Richard (Lodowick Edward Montagu)
1900-1970 ... CANR-4
Obituary ... 89-92
Earlier sketch in CA 5-8R
Rees, Richard-Lewis 1950- ... 142
Rees, Robert A(lvin) 1935- ... 81-84
Rees, Roberta ... 166
Rees, (Margaret) Una 1920- ... 124
Rees, William 1887-1978(?) ... 5-8R
Obituary ... 104
Reesby, Ralph (Harold) 1911- ... 154
Reese, Alexander 1881-1969 ... 97-100
Reese, Algernon B(everly) 1896-1981 Obituary . 105
Reese, Bob
See Reese, Robert A.
Reese, Carolyn Johnson 1938- ... 112
See also Reese, Lyn
Reese, Curtis W(illiford) 1887-1961 Obituary ... 110
Reese, Edward, Jr. 1928- ... 113
Reese, Francesca Gardner 1940- ... 65-68
Reese, Gustave 1899-1977 Obituary ... 73-76
Reese, Heloise (Bowles) 1919-1977 ... 9-12R
Obituary ... 73-76
Reese, Jim E(anes) 1912-1976 ... 13-16R
Obituary ... 134
Reese, John (Henry) 1910-1981 ... CANR-66
Earlier sketch in CA 102
Reese, Laura 1950- ... 156
Reese, Lizette Woodworth 1856-1935 ... DLB 54
Reese, Lyn
See Reese, Carolyn Johnson
See also SATA 64
Reese, M(ax) M(eredith) 1910-1987 ... CANR-3
Obituary ... 123
Earlier sketch in CA 9-12R
Reese, Mason 1966- ... 97-100
Reese, Robert A. 1938- ... 114
See also SATA 60
See also SATA-Brief 53
Reese, Roger R(oi) 1959- ... 159
Reese, Sammy
See Reese, Samuel Pharr
Reese, Samuel Pharr 1930-1985 ... 49-52
Obituary ... 117
Reese, (John) Terence 1913-1996 ... 109
Obituary ... 151
See also SATA 59
Reese, Thomas 1742-1796 ... DLB 37
Reese, Thomas J(oseph) 1945- ... 106
Reese, Thomas R. 1890(?)-1974 Obituary ... 53-56
Reese, Trevor Richard 1929- ... 9-12R
Reese, William Lewis 1921- ... CANR-8
Earlier sketch in CA 17-20R
Reese, William S(herman) 1955- ... 111
Reese, Willis L(ivingston) M(esier) 1913- ... 57-60
Reesink, Maryke 1919- ... CANR-45
Earlier sketch in CA 25-28R
Rees-Mogg, William 1928- ... 142
Reeve, Agnesa B. 1927- ... 138
Reeve, Clara 1729-1807 ... DLB 39
Reeve, F(ranklin) D(olier) 1928- ... 77-80
Reeve, Frank D(river) 1899-1967 ... CAP-1
Earlier sketch in CA 11-12
Reeve, G. Joan (Price) 1901- ... 13-16R
Reeve, Joel
See Cox, William R(obert)
Reeve, Richard M(ark) 1935- ... 37-40R
Reeve, Wilfred D. 1895- ... CAP-1
Earlier sketch in CA 13-14
Reeve, William Charles 1943- ... 93-96
Reeves, Alexander Stuart Frere
See Frere-Reeves, Alexander Stuart
Reeves, Amber
See Blanco White, Amber
Reeves, (Richard) Ambrose
1899-1980 Obituary ... 105
Reeves, Bruce Douglas 1940- ... CANR-11
Earlier sketch in CA 21-24R
Reeves, Charles Everand 1889- ... 5-8R
Reeves, Diane Lindsey 1959- ... 145
Reeves, Donald 1952- ... 37-40R
Reeves, Dorothea D(resser) 1901- ... CAP-1
Earlier sketch in CA 11-12
Reeves, Earl J(ames, Jr.) 1933- ... 61-64
Reeves, Elton T(raver) 1912- ... 29-32R
Reeves, Faye Couch 1953- ... 143
See also SATA 76
Reeves, Fionnuala 1943- ... 112
Reeves, Floyd (Wesley) 1890-1979 Obituary . 89-92
Reeves, Gareth 1947- ... 119
Reeves, Gene (Arthur) 1933- ... 61-64
Reeves, Gregory Shaw 1950- ... 77-80
Reeves, Hubert 1932- ... 132
Reeves, James
See Reeves, John Morris
See also DLB 161
See also SATA 15
Reeves, Joan Wynn 1910-1972 ... CAP-2
Earlier sketch in CA 21-22
Reeves, John 1926- ... 113
See also DLB 88
Reeves, John K(night) 1907- ... CAP-2
Earlier sketch in CA 25-28
Reeves, John Morris 1909-1978 ... CANR-44
See also Reeves, James
See also SATA 87
Reeves, Joyce 1911- ... CANR-12
Earlier sketch in CA 73-76
See also SATA 17
Reeves, Lawrence F. 1926- ... 105
See also SATA 29
Reeves, Marjorie E(thel) 1905- ... CANR-42
Earlier sketches in CA 13-16R, CANR-5, 20
Reeves, Martha (Rose) 1941- ... 147
Reeves, Martha Emilie 1941- ... 65-68
Reeves, Mavis Mann 1921- ... CANR-25
Earlier sketch in CA 45-48
Reeves, Nancy 1913- ... 33-36R
Reeves, Paschal 1917-1976 ... 81-84
Reeves, Patricia Houts 1947- ... 126
Reeves, Richard 1936- ... CANR-28
Earlier sketch in CA 69-72
Reeves, Rosser 1910-1984 ... 89-92
Obituary ... 111
Reeves, Ruth Ellen
See Ranney, Agnes V.
Reeves, Thomas C(harles) 1936- ... CANR-9
Earlier sketch in CA 57-60
Reeves, Thomas Carl 1939- ... 33-36R
Reeves, Trish
See Reeves, Patricia Houts
Reff, Theodore Franklin 1930- ... 89-92
Refregier, Anton 1905- ... 5-8R
Regalado, Nancy Freeman 1935- ... 17-20R
Regan, Brad
See Norwood, Victor G(eorge) C(harles)
Regan, Cronan 1925- ... 45-48
Regan, Dian Curtis 1950- ... 142
See also SATA 75
Regan, Donald T(homas) 1918- ... 127
Brief entry ... 106
Regan, Geoffrey 1946- ... 129
Regan, John J. 1929-1995 ... 131
Obituary ... 149
Regan, Milton C., Jr. 1952- ... 145
Regan, Richard Joseph 1930- ... 5-8R
Regan, Robert (Charles) 1930- ... 17-20R
Regan, Stephen 1957- ... 142
Regan, Thomas Howard 1938- ... 104
Regan, Tom
See Regan, Thomas Howard
Regardie, (Francis) Israel 1907- ... 85-88
Regehr, Lydia 1903- ... 45-48
See also SATA 37
Regehr, T. D. 1937- ... 168
Regelski, Thomas A(dam) 1941- ... 57-60
Regenstein, Lewis 1943- ... 57-60
Regensteiner, Else (Friedsam) 1906- Brief
entry ... 111
Reger, Gary 1954- ... 150
Reger, Roger 1933- ... 21-24R
Reggiani, Renee 1925- ... CANR-36
Earlier sketch in CA 85-88
See also SATA 18
Reghaby, Heydar 1932- ... 29-32R
Regin, Deric (Wagenvort) ... 37-40R
Reginald
See Burgess, Michael (Roy)
Reginald, R(obert)
See Burgess, Michael (Roy)
Reginald, Robert
See Burgess, Michael (Roy)
Region, Oscar
See Trimpey, John P.
Regis, Ed
See Regis, Edward, Jr.
Regis, Edward, Jr. 1944- ... 132
Regis, Sister Mary 1908- ... CAP-1
Earlier sketch in CA 13-14
Register, Cheri
See Register, Cheryl Lynn
Register, Cheryl Lynn 1945- ... 126
Register, Willie Raymond 1937- ... 45-48
Regnery, Henry 1912- ... 101
Interview in ... 101
Regoli, Robert M. 1950- ... 116
Regosin, Richard L(loyd) 1937- Brief entry ... 109
Regueiro, Helen 1943- ... 104
Regulus, Evelyn Judy
See Buehler, Evelyn Judy
Rehak, Peter (Stephen) 1936- ... 77-80
Rehbein, Edna Aguirre 1955- ... 145
Rehberg, Hans 1901-1963 ... DLB 124
Rehder, Helmut 1905-1977 ... CANR-4
Earlier sketch in CA 5-8R
Rehder, Jessie Clifford 1908-1967 ... CAP-1
Earlier sketch in CA 9-10
Rehfeld, Barry J. 1946- ... 132
Rehfisch, Hans Jose 1891-1960 ... DLB 124
Rehfuss, John Alfred 1934- ... 85-88
Rehg, William (Richard) 1952- ... 149
Rehm, Karl M. 1935- ... SATA 72
Rehnquist, William H(ubbs) 1924- ... 140
Rehrauer, George 1923- ... 53-56
Reibel, Paula
See Schwartz, Paula
Reich, Ali
See Katz, Bobbi
Reich, Bernard 1941- ... CANR-32
Earlier sketches in CA 81-84, CANR-14
Reich, Charles Alan 1928- ... CANR-64
Earlier sketch in CA 108
Interview in ... 108
Reich, Deborah 1960- ... 130
Reich, Edward 1903(?)-1983 Obituary ... 109
Reich, Howard 1954- ... 143
Reich, Ilse Ollendorff 1909- ... 49-52
Reich, John Theodore 1906-1988 Obituary ... 124
Reich, Kenneth 1938- ... 69-72
Reich, Lee 1947- ... 142
Reich, Nancy B(assen) ... CANR-55
Earlier sketch in CA 126
Reich, Peter M(aria) 1929- ... 85-88
Reich, Robert B. 1946(?)- ... 141
Reich, Sheldon 1931- ... 112
Reich, Simon (F.) 1959- ... 162
Reich, Steve 1936- ... CANR-8
Earlier sketch in CA 61-64
Reich, Tova Rachel 1942- ... CANR-66
Earlier sketch in CA 103
Reich, Walter 1943- ... CANR-65
Earlier sketch in CA 129
Reich, Wilhelm 1897-1957 ... TCLC 57
Reichard, Gary Warren 1943- ... CANR-26
Earlier sketches in CA 61-64, CANR-10
Reichard, Robert S. 1923- ... 21-24R
Reichardt, Jasia 1933- ... CANR-2
Earlier sketch in CA 5-8R
Reichardt, Mary R. 1956- ... 167
Reichart, Elisabeth 1953- ... 132
Reichart, Walter A(lbert) 1903- ... 5-8R
Reiche, Reimut 1941- ... 41-44R
Reichek, Morton A(rthur) 1924- ... 85-88
Reichel, Aaron I(srael) 1950- ... 130
Reichel, Mary 1946- ... 125
Reichel, O. Asher 1921- ... 45-48
Reichel, Sabine 1946- ... 132
Reichenbach, Bruce R. 1943- ... 33-36R
Reichenberger, Arnold G(ottfried) 1903- ... 17-20R
Reichert, Edwin C(lark) 1909-1988 Obituary ... 126
See also SATA-Obit 57
Reichert, Herbert W(illiam) 1917-1978 ... CANR-24
Earlier sketch in CA 45-48
Reichert, Mickey Zucker
See Zucker, Miriam S.
Reichert, Victor Emanuel 1897- ... 13-16R
Reichl, Ernst 1900-1980 Obituary ... 102
Reichl, Ruth 1948- ... 61-64
Reichler, Joseph Lawrence 1915-1988 ... 103
Obituary ... 127
Reichley, (Anthony) James 1929- ... 1-4R
Reichmann, Felix 1899- ... 104
Reicke, Bo I(var) 1914- ... 13-16R
Reid, Alan 1915(?)-1987 Obituary ... 123
Reid, Alastair 1926- ... CANR-3
Earlier sketch in CA 5-8R
See also DLB 27
See also SATA 46
Reid, Albert Clayton 1894- ... 53-56
Reid, Alfred S(andlin) 1924-1976 ... CANR-2
Earlier sketch in CA 45-48
Reid, Anthony 1916- ... 29-32R
Reid, B(enjamin) L(awrence) 1918-1990 ... 17-20R
Obituary ... 133
See also DLB 111
Reid, Barbara 1922- ... CANR-12
Earlier sketch in CA 25-28R
See also SATA 21
Reid, Barbara 1957- ... SATA 93
Reid, Charles (Stuart) 1900-1987 ... 101
Obituary ... 121
Reid, Charles K(er) II 1912-(?) ... CAP-1
Earlier sketch in CA 19-20
Reid, Charles L(loyd) 1927- ... 37-40R
Reid, Charles R(obert) 1926- ... 114
Reid, Christopher (John) 1949- ... 140
See also CLC 33
See also DLB 40
Reid, Clyde H. 1928- ... CANR-12
Earlier sketch in CA 25-28R
Reid, Constance (Bowman) 1918- ... 148
Reid, Daniel P. (Jr.) 1948- ... 125
Reid, David 1940- ... 147
Reid, Desmond
See McNeilly, Wilfred (Glassford)
and Moorcock, Michael (John)
Reid, Donald (Matthew) 1952- ... 124
Reid, Dorothy M(arion) (?)-1974 Obituary ... 109
See also SATA-Brief 29
Reid, E. Emmet 1872-1973 Obituary ... 45-48
Reid, Ela 1907-1982 Obituary ... 107
Reid, Escott (Meredith) 1905- ... CANR-20
Earlier sketch in CA 101
Reid, Esmond 1945- ... 123
Reid, Eugenie Chazal 1924- ... 13-16R
See also SATA 12
Reid, Forrest 1875-1947 ... DLB 153
Reid, Frances P(ugh) 1910- ... CANR-2
Earlier sketch in CA 5-8R
Reid, H. 1925- ... 17-20R
Reid, Helen Rogers 1882-1970 Obituary ... 115
See also DLB 29
Reid, Hilda (Stewart) 1898-1982 Obituary ... 106
Reid, Ian 1915-1984 Obituary ... 113
Reid, Inez Smith ... 49-52
Reid, J(ohn) C(owie) 1916-1972 ... 9-12R
Obituary ... 103
Reid, James ... DLB 31
Reid, James Macarthur 1900-1970 ... CAP-1
Earlier sketch in CA 9-10
Reid, James Malcolm 1902-1982 ... 5-8R
Obituary ... 107
Reid, James W. 1912-197(?) ... CAP-2
Earlier sketch in CA 25-28
Reid, Jan 1945- ... 61-64
Reid, Jim 1929- ... 61-64
Reid, John Calvin ... CANR-11
Earlier sketch in CA 25-28R
See also SATA 21
Reid, John Kelman Sutherland 1910- ... CANR-3
Earlier sketch in CA 1-4R
Reid, John Phillip 1930- ... CANR-41
Earlier sketches in CA 25-28R, CANR-19
Reid, John T(urner) 1908-1978 ... 81-84
Reid, Leslie Hartley 1895- ... CAP-1
Earlier sketch in CA 13-14
Reid, Loren (Dudley) 1905- ... CANR-1
Earlier sketch in CA 1-4R
Reid, Louis Arnaud 1895- ... CAP-1
Earlier sketch in CA 13-14
Reid, Malcolm 1941- ... 53-56
Reid, Margaret (Isabel) 1925-1992 ... 130
Obituary ... 139
Reid, (Thomas) Mayne 1818-1883 ... DLB 21
See also SATA 24
Reid, Mayne 1818-1883 ... DLB 163
Reid, Meta Mayne ... 13-16R
See also SATA 58
See also SATA-Brief 36
Reid, Michaela (Ann) 1933- ... 128
Reid, Mildred I. 1908- ... 21-24R
Reid, P(atrick) R(obert) 1910-1990 Obituary ... 131
Reid, Pat
See Reid, P(atrick) R(obert)
Reid, Philip
See Ingrams, Richard (Reid)
and Osmond, Andrew
Reid, R(obert) W(illiam) 1933-1990(?) ... 29-32R
Obituary ... 132
Reid, Randall 1931- ... 25-28R
Reid, Robert G(eorge) B(urnside) 1939- ... 119
Reid, Seerley 1909(?)-1972 Obituary ... 37-40R
Reid, Sue Titus 1939- ... CANR-58
Earlier sketches in CA 37-40R, CANR-14, 31
Reid, Tim
See Reid, Timothy E. H.
Reid, Timothy E. H. 1936- ... 17-20R
Reid, Vic(tor Stafford) 1913- ... CANR-16
Earlier sketch in CA 65-68
See also BW 1
See also DLB 125
Reid, W(illiam) Stanford 1913- ... CANR-18
Earlier sketches in CA 49-52, CANR-1
Reid, Whitelaw 1837-1912 ... DLB 23
Reid, William 1926- ... 85-88
Reid, William H(oward) 1945- ... CANR-37
Earlier sketches in CA 93-96, CANR-16
Reid, William J(ames) 1928- ... CANR-39
Earlier sketches in CA 77-80, CANR-17
Reida, Bernice 1915- ... 93-96
Reid Banks, Lynne 1929- ... CANR-38
Earlier sketches in CA 1-4R, CANR-6, 22
See also Banks, Lynne Reid
See also CLR 24
See also JRDA
See also MAICYA
See also SATA 22, 75
Reidel, Carl Hubert 1937- ... 107
Reidel-Geubtner, Virginia 1921- ... 116
Reidenbaugh, Lowell (Henry) 1919- ... CANR-48
Earlier sketch in CA 121

Reid Jenkins, Debra 1955- ... SATA 87
Reidy, John Patrick 1930- ... 17-20R
Reidy, Joseph 1920- ... 53-56
Reierson, Gary B(ruce) 1948- ... CANR-36
Earlier sketch in CA 114
Reif, Rita 1929- ... 41-44R
Reife, Abraham 1931- ... 163
Reifen, David 1911- ... 93-96
Reiff, Henry 1899-1983 Obituary ... 110
Reiff, Robert (Frank) 1918-1982 ... 17-20R
Obituary ... 135
Reiff, Stephanie Ann 1948- ... 93-96
See also SATA 47
See also SATA-Brief 28
Reiffel, Leonard 1927- ... 101
Reifler, Samuel 1939- ... 93-96
Reifsnyder, William E(dward) 1924- ... 65-68
Reig, June 1933- ... 105
See also SATA 30
Reigelman, Milton Monroe 1942- ... 65-68
Reiger, George (Wesley) 1939- ... CANR-18
Earlier sketch in CA 101
Reiger, John F(ranklin) 1943- ... 57-60
Reiger, Kurt (Edward) 1956- ... 116
Reigot, Betty Polisar 1924- ... 111
See also SATA 55
See also SATA-Brief 41
Reigstad, Paul (Matthew) 1921- ... 81-84
Reik, Theodor 1888-1969 ... CANR-5
Obituary ... 25-28R
Earlier sketch in CA 5-8R
Reile, Louis 1925- ... 29-32R
Reill, Peter Hanns 1938- ... 101
Reilly, Bernard F. 1925- ... 142
Reilly, Catherine W(inifred) 1925- ... 118
Reilly, Christopher T(homas) 1924- ... 101
Reilly, D(avid) Robin 1928- ... CANR-8
Earlier sketch in CA 5-8R
Reilly, Edward R(andolph) 1929- ... 93-96
Reilly, Edwin David, Jr. 1932- ... 111
Reilly, Esther H(untington) 1917- ... 33-36R
Reilly, Francis E(agan) 1922- ... 29-32R
Reilly, Harold J. 1895(?)-1987 Obituary ... 123
Reilly, John H(urford) 1934- ... 77-80
Reilly, John M(arsden) 1933- ... CANR-48
Earlier sketch in CA 104
Reilly, Judith G(ladding) 1935- ... 61-64
Reilly, Mary 1920- ... 128
Brief entry ... 114
Reilly, Mary Lonan 1926- ... 33-36R
Reilly, Michael (Francis)
1910(?)-1973 Obituary ... 41-44R
Reilly, Patrick 1932- ... CANR-37
Earlier sketch in CA 115
Reilly, Patrick D.
See Rogers, Peter D(amien)
Reilly, Paul 1912-1990 ... 125
Obituary ... 132
Reilly, Robert Thomas 1922- ... CANR-2
Earlier sketch in CA 5-8R
Reilly, Robin 1928- ... CANR-5
Earlier sketch in CA 53-56
Reilly, William J(ohn) 1899- ... CAP-2
Earlier sketch in CA 19-20
Reilly, William K.
See Creasey, John
Reiman, Donald H(enry) 1934- ... CANR-31
Earlier sketches in CA 33-36R, CANR-14
Reiman, Jeffrey H. 1942- ... 93-96
Reimann, Brigitte 1933-1973 ... DLB 75
Reimann, Guenter Hans 1904- ... 25-28R
Reimann, Katya 1965- ... 168
Reimann, Lewis C. 1890-1961 Obituary ... 113
Reimann, Viktor 1915- ... 69-72
Reimer, Bennett 1932- ... CANR-3
Earlier sketch in CA 45-48
Reimers, David 1931- ... 115
Rein, Irving J. 1937- ... CANR-28
Earlier sketch in CA 25-28R
Rein, Martin 1928- ... 93-96
Rein, Mercedes ... 131
See also HW
Rein, Raanan 1960- ... 146
Rein, Richard
See Smith, Richard Rein
Reina, Ruben E. 1924- ... 49-52
Reinach, Jacquelyn (Krasne) 1930- ... CANR-22
Earlier sketch in CA 105
See also SATA 28
Reincheld, Bill 1946- ... 57-60
Reindorp, George E(dmund) 1911- ... CANR-5
Earlier sketch in CA 5-8R
Reindorp, Reginald C(arl) 1907- ... 25-28R
Reinecke, Ian 1945- ... 117
Reinemer, Vic 1923- ... 21-24R
Reiner, Carl 1922- ... 138
Brief entry ... 112
Reiner, Joseph H. 1912(?)-1983 Obituary ... 111
Reiner, Laurence E(rwin) ... 102
Reiner, Max
See Caldwell, (Janet Miriam) Taylor (Holland)
Reiner, Rob(ert) 1945- ... 138
See also AAYA 13
Reiner, William B(uck) 1910-1976 ... CANR-3
Obituary ... 61-64
Earlier sketch in CA 45-48
See also SATA 46
See also SATA-Obit 30
Reinerman, Alan J(erome) 1935- ... 114
Reinert, Paul C(lare) 1910- ... 85-88
Reines, Alvin J. 1926- ... 53-56
Reinfeld, Fred 1910-1964 ... CAP-1
Earlier sketch in CA 9-10
See also SATA 3
Reinfeld, Linda M. 1940- ... 141
Reingold, Nathan 1927- ... 140
Reinhard, David W(illiam) 1952- ... 118
Reinhard, Ernst
See Frank, Rudolf
Reinhardt, Ad(olph Frederick)
1913-1967 Obituary ... 111
Reinhardt, Gottfried 1913-1994 ... 93-96
Obituary ... 146
Reinhardt, James Melvin 1894-1974 ... CANR-4
Obituary ... 49-52
Earlier sketch in CA 1-4R
Reinhardt, Jon M(c Ewen) 1936- ... 41-44R
Reinhardt, Kurt F(rank) 1896- ... CANR-1
Earlier sketch in CA 1-4R
Reinhardt, Richard W. 1927- ... CANR-31
Earlier sketches in CA 25-28R, CANR-13
Reinhart, Bruce Aaron 1926- ... 5-8R
Reinhart, Charles (Franklin) 1946- ... 104
Reinhart, Peter 1950- ... 136
Reinhart, Theodore R(ussell) 1938- ... 125
Reinhartz, Dennis 1944- ... 123
Reinharz, Jehuda 1944- ... CANR-49
Earlier sketches in CA 65-68, CANR-9, 24
Reinharz, Shulamit 1946- ... 138
Reinhold, Meyer 1909- ... CANR-51
Earlier sketches in CA 5-8R, CANR-5, 26
Reinhold, Robert 1941-1996 ... 133
Obituary ... 153
Reinicke, Wolfgang H. 1955- ... 154
Reiniger, Lotte 1899-1981 Obituary ... 108
See also SATA 40
See also SATA-Obit 33
Reining, Conrad C(opeland) 1918-1984 ... 21-24R
Obituary ... 114
Reinisch, June M(achover) 1943- ... 138
Reinitz, Richard (Martin) 1934- ... 89-92
Reinke, William A(ndrew) 1928- ... CANR-49
Earlier sketches in CA 45-48, CANR-24
Reinmar der Alte c. 1165-c. 1205 ... DLB 138
Reinmar von Zweter c. 1200-c. 1250 ... DLB 138
Reinmuth, Oscar William 1900- ... 37-40R
Reinsma, Carol 1949- ... 155
See also SATA 91
Reinsmith, Richard
See Smith, Richard Rein
Reinstedt, Randall A. 1935- ... 168
See also SATA 101
Reinstedt, Randy
See Reinstedt, Randall A.
Reis, Claire Raphael 1889-1978 Obituary ... 77-80
Reis, Ricardo
See Pessoa, Fernando (Antonio Nogueira)
Reis, Richard H(erbert) 1930- ... 41-44R
Reisberg, Mira 1955- ... SATA 82
Reisch, Walter 1903-1983 Obituary ... 109
See also DLB 44
Reischauer, August Karl 1879-1971 ... CAP-2
Earlier sketch in CA 19-20
Reischauer, Edwin O(ldfather) 1910-1990 ... 17-20R
Obituary ... 132
Reischauer, Haru Matsukata 1915- ... 145
Reiser, Lynn (Whisnant) 1944- ... SATA 81
Reiser, Martin 1927- ... 53-56
Reiser, Morton F(rancis) 1919- ... 124
Reiser, Oliver Leslie 1895-1974 ... CANR-4
Obituary ... 49-52
Earlier sketch in CA 1-4R
Reiser, Paul 1957- ... 153
Reiser, William (Edward) 1943- ... 114
Reisfeld, Bert 1906- ... 112
Reisgies, Teresa (Maria) 1966- ... SATA 74
Reising, Robert W(illiam) 1933- ... 89-92
Reisinger, William M. 1957- ... 138
Reisman, Arnold 1934- ... CANR-12
Earlier sketch in CA 33-36R
Reisman, George Gerald 1937- ... 104
Reisman, John M(ark) 1930- ... CANR-8
Earlier sketch in CA 21-24R
Reisner, George
See Ben-Ephraim, Gavriel
Reisner, Marc P. 1948- ... 144
Reisner, Robert George 1921-1974 ... 9-12R
Obituary ... 135
Reisner, Thomas Andrew 1935- ... 113
Reiss, Albert J(ohn), Jr. 1922- ... CANR-49
Earlier sketches in CA 21-24R, CANR-9, 24
Reiss, Alvin 1932- ... 61-64
Reiss, Alvin H(erbert) 1930- ... 81-84
Reiss, Barbara Eve 1941- ... CANR-15
Earlier sketch in CA 41-44R
Reiss, David S. 1953- ... 108
Reiss, Edmund (Allan) 1934- ... CANR-10
Earlier sketch in CA 21-24R
Reiss, Edward 1964- ... 146
Reiss, Ira L(eonard) 1925- ... 13-16R
Reiss, James 1941- ... 33-36R
Reiss, Johanna (de Leeuw) 1929(?)- ... 85-88
See also CLR 19
See also JRDA
See also SATA 18
Reiss, John J. ... 106
See also SATA 23
Reiss, Kathryn 1957- ... 143
See also SATA 76
Reiss, Mitchell 1957- ... 152
Reiss, Oscar 1925- ... 167
Reiss, Stephen (Charles) 1918- ... 57-60
Reiss, Timothy James 1942- ... 107
Reissig, Herman F. 1899(?)-1985 Obituary ... 116
Reissig, Julio Herrera y
See Herrera y Reissig, Julio
Reissman, Leonard 1921-1975 ... CANR-4
Obituary ... 53-56
Earlier sketch in CA 5-8R
Reister, Floyd Nester 1919- ... 69-72
Reit, Seymour (V.) 1918- ... CANR-16
Earlier sketch in CA 93-96
See also SATA 21
Reit, Sy
See Reit, Seymour (V.)
Reitan, E(arl) A(aron) 1925- ... 17-20R
Reitci, John G(eorge) 1922-1983 Obituary ... 109
Reitci, Rita Krohne 1930- ... 5-8R
Reitemeyer, John Reinhart
1898-1979 Obituary ... 85-88
Reiter, Charles Jules 1928- ... 25-28R
Reiter, Robert E. 1932- ... 25-28R
Reiter, Seymour 1921- ... 101
Reiter, Victoria (Kelrich) ... 139
Reiterman, Carl 1921- ... 49-52
Reiterman, Tim 1947- ... 109
Reith, Charles C. 1953- ... 122
Reith, J. C. W.
See Reith, John Charles Walsham
Reith, John Charles Walsham
1889-1971 Obituary ... 113
Reither, Joseph 1903- ... 109
Reitlinger, Gerald R. 1900(?)-1978 Obituary ... 104
Reitman, Judith 1951- ... 142
Reitmeister, Louis Aaron 1903-1975 ... 49-52
Obituary ... 61-64
Reitsch, Hanna 1912(?)-1979 Obituary ... 89-92
Reitz, Donald J(oseph) 1932- ... 25-28R
Reitz, Miriam 1935- ... 143
Reitze, Arnold W(infred), Jr. 1938- ... 49-52
Rejai, Mostafa 1931- ... CANR-13
Earlier sketch in CA 37-40R
Rejali, Darius M. 1959- ... 153
Rejaunier, Jeanne 1934- ... 29-32R
Rekai, Kati 1921- ... 105
Rekers, George A(lan) 1948- ... 119
Relf, Patricia 1954- ... SATA 71
Relgis, Eugene 1895- ... 81-84
Relis, Harry
See Endore, (Samuel) Guy
Rella, Ettore 1907(?)-1988 Obituary ... 126
Relyea, Suzanne 1945- ... 77-80
Remak, Henry H. H. 1916- ... 17-20R
Remak, Joachim 1920- ... CANR-3
Earlier sketch in CA 1-4R
Remarque, Erich Maria 1898-1970 ... 77-80
Obituary ... 29-32R
See also AAYA 27
See also CLC 21
See also DA
See also DAB
See also DAC
See also DAM MST, NOV
See also DLB 56
See also MTCW 1
Rembar, Charles 1915- ... 25-28R
Remen, (Rachelle) Naomi 1938- ... 122
Brief entry ... 118
Remenih, Maurine 1916(?)-1985 Obituary ... 118
Remer, Gary 1957- ... 157
Remer, Theodore G. 1899- ... CAP-1
Earlier sketch in CA 13-16
Remi, Georges 1907-1983 ... CANR-31
Obituary ... 109
Earlier sketch in CA 69-72
See also Herge
See also SATA 13
See also SATA-Obit 32
Remington, Ella-Carrie 1914- ... 69-72
Remington, Frederic 1861-1909 Brief entry ... 108
See also DLB 12, 186, 188
See also SATA 41
Remington, Mark
See Bingley, David Ernest
Remington, Robin Alison 1938- ... CANR-12
Earlier sketch in CA 33-36R
Remini, Robert V(incent) 1921- ... CANR-44
Earlier sketches in CA 9-12R, CANR-3, 20
Remizov, A.
See Remizov, Aleksei (Mikhailovich)
Remizov, A. M.
See Remizov, Aleksei (Mikhailovich)
Remizov, Aleksei (Mikhailovich) 1877-1957 ... 133
Brief entry ... 125
See also TCLC 27
Remkiewicz, Frank 1939- ... 145
See also SATA 77
Remley, David A. 1931- ... 45-48
Remley, Mary L(ouise) 1930- ... 102
Remmers, H(ermann) H(enry) 1892-1969 ... 1-4R
Obituary ... 103
Remmling, Gunter W(erner) 1929- ... 41-44R
Remnick, David J. 1958- ... 154
Remoff, Heather T(rexler) 1938- ... 117
Remonda-Ruibal, Jorge Silvestre 1928- ... 108
Rempel, William C. 1947- ... 141
Remsberg, Bonnie K(ohn) 1937- ... 69-72
Remsberg, Charles A(ndruss) 1936- ... CANR-7
Earlier sketch in CA 57-60
Remson, Irwin 1923- ... 53-56
Remy
See Renault, Gilbert (Leon Etienne Theodore)
Remy, Georges
See Remi, Georges
Remy, Pierre-Jean
See Angremy, Jean-Pierre
Remy, Richard C. 1942- ... CANR-29
Earlier sketch in CA 111
Rena, Sally
See Rena, Sarah Mary
Rena, Sarah Mary 1941- ... 103
Renan, Sheldon (Jackson) 1941- ... CANR-14
Earlier sketch in CA 21-24R
Renard, Alexandre Charles
1906-1983 Obituary ... 111
Renard, Jules 1864-1910 Brief entry ... 117
See also TCLC 17
Renard, Maurice 1875-1939 ... 162
Renaud, Bernadette 1945- ... 134
See also SATA 66
Renaud, Jacques 1943- ... DLB 60
Renauer, Albin (J.) 1959- ... 133
Renault, Gilbert (Leon Etienne Theodore)
1904-1984 Obituary ... 113
Renault, Mary
See Challans, Mary
See also CLC 3, 11, 17
See also DLBY 83
Renault, Rick
See Wallmann, Jeffrey M(iner)
Renaut, Alain 1948- ... 156
Renaux, Sigrid 1938- ... 148
Renay, Liz 1926- ... 33-36R
Rendall, Steven 1939- ... 139
Rendall, Ted S. ... 101
Rendel, George William 1889-1979 ... 5-8R
Obituary ... 103
Rendel, John 1906(?)-1978 Obituary ... 104
Rendell, Joan ... CANR-23
Earlier sketches in CA 61-64, CANR-7
See also SATA 28
Rendell, Ruth (Barbara) 1930- ... CANR-52
Earlier sketches in CA 109, CANR-32
Interview in ... CANR-32
See also Vine, Barbara
See also CLC 28, 48
See also DAM POP
See also DLB 87
See also MTCW 1
Render, Sylvia Lyons 1913- ... CANR-15
Earlier sketch in CA 41-44R
Rendina, Laura (Jones) Cooper 1902- ... 9-12R
See also SATA 10
Rendleman, Danny L(ee) 1945- ... 65-68
Rendon, Armando B. 1939- ... 37-40R
Rendon, Marcie R. 1952- ... 164
See also SATA 97
Rene, Leon (T.) 1902-1982 Obituary ... 107
Rene, Natalia 1908(?)-1977 Obituary ... 69-72
Renehan, Edward J(ohn), Jr. 1956- ... 140
Renehan, Robert (Francis Xavier) 1935- Brief
entry ... 108
Renetzky, Alvin 1940- ... 101
Renfield, Richard L. 1932- ... 29-32R
Renfrew, (Andrew) Colin 1937- ... 158
Renfrew, Jane Margaret 1942- ... 49-52
Renfro, Ed 1924- ... SATA 79
Renfroe, Martha Kay 1938- ... CANR-9
Earlier sketch in CA 65-68
Rengert, George F. 1940- ... 158
Renich, Fred C. 1916-1979 ... 115
Renich, Jill 1916- ... 25-28R
Renick, Marion (Lewis) 1905- ... CANR-1
Earlier sketch in CA 1-4R
See also SATA 1
Renier, Elizabeth
See Baker, Betty D(oreen Flook)
Renken, Aleda 1907- ... CANR-12
Earlier sketch in CA 21-24R
See also SATA 27
Renker, Elizabeth 1961- ... 158
Renkiewicz, Frank 1935- ... CANR-26
Earlier sketch in CA 45-48
Renlie, Frank H. 1936- ... SATA 11
Renn, Casey
See Crim, Keith R(enn)
Renn, Ludwig
See Vieth von Golssenau, Arnold Friedrich
Renn, Thomas E(dward) 1939- ... 29-32R
Renne, Roland Roger 1905- ... 1-4R
Renner, Al G. 1912- ... 89-92
Renner, Beverly Hollett 1929- ... 85-88
Renner, Bruce 1944- ... 33-36R
Renner, John Wilson 1924- ... 41-44R
Renner, K(enneth) Edward 1936- ... 101
Renner, Thomas C(hoate) 1928-1990 ... 73-76
Obituary ... 130
Renner, Tom
See Renner, Thomas C(hoate)
Rennert, Maggie 1922- ... CANR-13
Earlier sketch in CA 61-64
Rennert, Richard Scott 1956- ... 135
See also SATA 67
Rennick, Robert M(orris) 1932- ... CANR-48
Earlier sketch in CA 122
Rennie, Christopher
See Ambrose, Eric (Samuel)
Rennie, Eric 1947- ... 45-48
Rennie, James Alan 1899-1969 ... CAP-1
Earlier sketch in CA 11-12
Rennie, Ysabel Fisk 1918- ... CANR-2
Earlier sketch in CA 5-8R
Reno, Clint
See Ballard, (Willis) Todhunter
Reno, Dawn E. 1953- ... 125
Reno, Marie R(oth) ... CANR-10
Earlier sketch in CA 65-68
Reno, Mark
See Keevill, Henry J(ohn)
Reno, Ottie W(ayne) 1929- ... 41-44R
Reno, Philip 1913-1981 Obituary ... 111
Renoir, Alain 1921- ... 77-80
Renoir, Jean 1894-1979 ... 129
Obituary ... 85-88
See also CLC 20
Renouf, Alan 1919- ... 108
Rensberger, Boyce 1942- ... CANR-66
Earlier sketch in CA 81-84
Rensch, Bernhard (Carl Emmanuel) 1900- ... 102
Renshaw, Corrine 1929- ... 156
Renshaw, Domeena C(ynthia) 1929- ... 89-92

Renshaw, Patrick (Richard George) 1936- .. 21-24R
Renshaw, Samuel 1892-1981 77-80
Obituary 133
Renshon, Stanley Allen 1943- Brief entry 109
Rensie, Willis
See Eisner, Will(iam Erwin)
Renton, Cam
See Armstrong, Richard
Renton, Julia
See Cole, Margaret Alice
Rentschler, Eric 1949- CANR-42
Earlier sketch in CA 118
Renvoize, Jean 41-44R
See also SATA 5
Renwick, Ethel Hulbert 1910- 5-8R
Renwick, Fred B(lackwell) 1930- 33-36R
Renzi, Thomas C. 1948- 143
Renzulli, L(ibero) Marx, Jr. 1934- Brief entry ... 108
Repetto, Robert C. 129
Replansky, Naomi 1918- CANR-68
Earlier sketch in CA 33-36R
Repp, Arthur C(hristian) 1906- CAP-1
Earlier sketch in CA 13-16
Repp, Ed Earl 1900(?)-1979 Obituary 85-88
Repp, William 1936- 110
Reps, John W(illiam) 1921- CANR-39
Earlier sketches in CA 45-48, CANR-1, 18
Reps, (Saladin) Paul 1895-1990 .... CANR-6
Obituary 132
Earlier sketch in CA 5-8R
ReQua, Eloise Gallup 1902- CAP-1
Earlier sketch in CA 13-16
Resch, John Phillips 1940- Brief entry 108
Rescher, Nicholas 1928- CANR-55
Earlier sketches in CA 21-24R, CANR-12
Resciniti, Angelo G. 1952- .... SATA 75
Rescoe, A(ntoine) Stan(ley) 1910- 5-8R
Reshetar, John S(tephen) Jr. 1924- 5-8R
Reshevsky, Samuel Herman 1911- 65-68
Resick, Matthew C(larence) 1916- 57-60
Resis, Albert 1921- 145
Reske, Hermann 1911- 45-48
Reskind, John
See Wallmann, Jeffrey M(iner)
Resnais, Alain 1922- .... CLC 16
Resnick, H(arvey) L(ewis) P(aul) 1930- 21-24R
Resnick, Marvin D. 1933- 21-24R
Resnick, Michael D(iamond) 1942- CANR-24
Earlier sketch in CA 107
See also SATA 38
Resnick, Mike
See Resnick, Michael D(iamond)
Resnick, Nathan 1910-1977 .... CAP-2
Obituary 73-76
Earlier sketch in CA 19-20
Resnick, Patricia 1953- 135
Resnick, Rose 61-64
Resnick, Seymour 1920- 73-76
See also SATA 23
Resnick, Sylvia (Safran) 1927- CANR-30
Earlier sketch in CA 93-96
Resnik, H(arvey) L(ewis) P(aul) 1930- ... CANR-10
Earlier sketch in CA 21-24R
Resnik, Hank
See Resnik, Henry S.
Resnik, Henry S. 1940- CANR-29
Earlier sketch in CA 29-32R
Resnik, Michael D(avid) 1938- 116
Resposo, Epifania R. Castro
1922-1974 Obituary 113
Ressler, Alice 1918- 53-56
Ressner, Phil(ip) 1922- 13-16R
Rest, Friedrich Otto 1913- CANR-38
Earlier sketches in CA 5-8R, CANR-2, 17
Rest, Karl H(einrich) A(lbert) 1908- 5-8R
Restak, Richard M(artin) 1942- CANR-24
Earlier sketches in CA 61-64, CANR-8
Restany, Pierre 1930- 130
Restivo, Sal 1940- 112
Restle, Frank (Joseph) 1927-1982(?) 41-44R
Obituary 133
Reston, James (Barrett) 1909-1995 ..... CANR-58
Obituary 150
Earlier sketches in CA 65-68, CANR-31
See also AITN 1, 2
Reston, James B(arrett), Jr. 1941- CANR-60
Earlier sketches in CA 37-40R, CANR-31
Reston, Jody .... AITN 2
Reston, Richard .... AITN 2
Reston, Scotty
See Reston, James (Barrett)
Retamar, Roberto Fernandez
See Fernandez Retamar, Roberto
Retla, Robert
See Alter, Robert Edmond
Retner, Beth A.
See Brown, Beth
Rettenbacher, Simon 1634-1706 .... DLB 168
Rettie, Dwight F. 1930- 153
Rettig, Edward B(ertram) 1940- 57-60
Rettig, Jack L(ouis) 1925- 57-60
Reuben, Bryan G. 1934- 160
Reuben, David 1933- 41-44R
See also AITN 1
Reuben, Shelly 1945- 127
Reubens, Paul 1952- 165
Reuber, Grant L(ouis) 1927- CANR-3
Earlier sketch in CA 49-52
Reuchlin, Johannes 1455-1522 .... DLB 179
Reul, R(ose) Myrtle 1919- 21-24R
Reuman, Robert E(verett) 1923- 37-40R
Reumann, John 1927- CANR-5
Earlier sketch in CA 1-4R
Reuss, Carl F(rederick) 1915- 41-44R
Reuss, Frederick G(ustav) 1904- CAP-1
Earlier sketch in CA 11-12
Reuss, Henry S(choellkopf) 1912- CANR-6
Earlier sketch in CA 9-12R
Reuss-Ianni, Elizabeth 1946- 130
Reuter, Bjarne (B.) 1950- 137
See also SATA 68
Reuter, Carol (Joan) 1931- 21-24R
See also SATA 2
Reuter, Christian 1665-1712(?) .... DLB 168
Reuter, Frank T. 1926- 21-24R
Reuter, Fritz 1810-1874 .... DLB 129
Reuter, Gabriele 1859-1941 .... DLB 66
Reuther, David L(ouis) 1946- CANR-57
Earlier sketches in CA 112, CANR-31
Reuther, Ruth E. 1917- CANR-12
Earlier sketch in CA 33-36R
Reuther, Victor G(eorge) 1912- 77-80
Reutter, Mark 1950- 129
Rev, B.
See Eisner, Betty Grover
Reval, Jacques
See Laver, James
Revankar, Ratna G. 1937- 33-36R
Revard, Carter (Curtis) 1931- 144
See also NNAL
Revard, Stella Purce 1933- 97-100
Reve, Karel van het
See van het Reve, Karel
Revel, Jean-Francois 1924- CANR-55
Brief entry 109
Earlier sketch in CA 127
Reveley, Edith 1930- 123
Reveley, W(alter) Taylor III 1943- 126
Revell, Donald 1954- CANR-39
Earlier sketch in CA 116
Revell, J(ohn) R(obert) S(tephen) 1920- . CANR-51
Earlier sketches in CA 25-28R, CANR-11, 26
Revell, Jack
See Revell, J(ohn) R(obert) S(tephen)
Revell, Peter 1929-1983 .... CANR-13
Earlier sketch in CA 29-32R
ReVelle, Charles S. 1938- 45-48
ReVelle, Penelope 1941- 49-52
Revena
See Wright, Betty Ren
Reventlow, Franziska Graefin zu 1871-1918 ... DLB 66
Reverdy, Pierre 1889-1960 97-100
Obituary 89-92
See also CLC 53
Revere, Michael Rigsby 1951- 163
Reverend Mandju
See Su, Chien
Reves, Emery 1904-1981 Obituary 105
Revsbech, Vicki
See Liestman, Vicki
Rewald, John 1912-1994 .... CANR-44
Obituary 144
Earlier sketches in CA 9-12R, CANR-5
Rewoldt, Stewart H(enry) 1922- 37-40R
Rex, Barbara (Clayton) 1904- 77-80
Rex, John A(rderne) 1925- CANR-24
Earlier sketches in CA 5-8R, CANR-6
Rex, Walter E(dwin) 1927- 45-48
Rexine, John E(fstratios) 1929-1993 ..... CANR-46
Obituary 146
Earlier sketches in CA 37-40R, CANR-15
Rex-Johnson, Braiden 1956- 139
Rexroth, Kenneth 1905-1982 .... CANR-63
Obituary 107
Earlier sketches in CA 5-8R, CANR-14, 34
Interview in CANR-14
See also CDALB 1941-1968
See also CLC 1, 2, 6, 11, 22, 49, 112
See also DAM POET
See also DLB 16, 48, 165
See also DLBY 82
See also MTCW 1
See also PC 20
Rey, H(ans) A(ugusto) 1898-1977 .... CANR-6
Obituary 73-76
Earlier sketch in CA 5-8R
See also CLR 5
See also DLB 22
See also MAICYA
See also SATA 1, 26, 69, 100
Rey, Margret (Elisabeth) 1906-1996 ..... CANR-38
Obituary 155
Earlier sketch in CA 105
See also CLR 5
See also MAICYA
See also SATA 26, 86
See also SATA-Obit 93
Rey, Michael Stephan 1946- 113
Reyam
See Mayer, Charles Leopold
Reybold, Malcolm 1911(?)-1988 Obituary 124
Reyburn, Wallace (Macdonald) 1913- CANR-1
Earlier sketch in CA 49-52
Reyes, Alfonso 1889-1959 131
See also HW
See also TCLC 33
Reyes, Carlos 1935- CANR-3
Earlier sketch in CA 49-52
Reyes, Carlos Jose 1941- .... HW
Reyes y Basoalto, Ricardo Eliecer Neftali
See Neruda, Pablo
Reyher, Becky
See Reyher, Rebecca Hourwich
Reyher, Rebecca Hourwich
1897-1987 Obituary 121
See also SATA 18
See also SATA-Obit 50
Reyhner, Jon (Allan) 1944- 139
Reyles, Carlos 1868-1938 153
See also HW
Reymont, Wladyslaw (Stanislaw) 1868(?)-1925 Brief entry 104
See also TCLC 5
Reynolds, Alan 1942- 61-64
Reynolds, Ann
See Bly, Carol(yn)
Reynolds, Anne
See Steinke, Ann E(lizabeth)
Reynolds, Arlene 1947- 148
Reynolds, Barbara 1914- CANR-54
Earlier sketches in CA 9-12R, CANR-29
Reynolds, Barbara (Ann) 1942- 73-76
Reynolds, Barrie (Gordon Robert) 1932- 13-16R
Reynolds, Bart
See Emblen, D(onald) L(ewis)
Reynolds, Bede 1893(?)-1989 Obituary 130
Reynolds, Bertha Capen 1885- CAP-2
Earlier sketch in CA 19-20
Reynolds, Bill 1945- 166
Reynolds, Charles O. 1921- 9-12R
Reynolds, (Alfred) Christopher 1911- 104
Reynolds, Clark G(ilbert) 1939- CANR-56
Earlier sketches in CA 25-28R, CANR-12, 27
Reynolds, Clark Winton 1934- CANR-8
Earlier sketch in CA 21-24R
Reynolds, (Richard) Clay 1949- 139
Reynolds, Dallas McCord 1917- CANR-9
Earlier sketch in CA 5-8R
See also Reynolds, Mack
Reynolds, David 1952- 148
Reynolds, David K(ent) 1940- CANR-25
Earlier sketches in CA 65-68, CANR-9
Reynolds, David S(pencer) 1948- 124
Reynolds, Dickson
See Reynolds, Helen Mary Greenwood Campbell
Reynolds, Donald E. 1931- 33-36R
Reynolds, Elizabeth
See Steinke, Ann E(lizabeth)
Reynolds, Ernest (Randolph) 1910- CANR-6
Earlier sketch in CA 3-16R
Reynolds, Frank 1923-1983 114
Obituary 109
Reynolds, G. Scott 1925- 29-32R
Reynolds, G. W. M. 1814-1879 .... DLB 21
Reynolds, (Arthur) Graham 1914- CANR-17
Earlier sketch in CA 13-16R
Reynolds, Graham 1944- 138
Reynolds, Harry W., Jr. 1924- 13-16R
Reynolds, Helen Mary Greenwood Campbell
1884-1969 .... 5-8R
Obituary 103
See also SATA-Obit 26
Reynolds, Jack
See Jones, Jack
Reynolds, Jan 1925- 145
Reynolds, Joe
See Steward, Samuel M(orris)
Reynolds, John
See Whitlock, Ralph
Reynolds, John 1901- 9-12R
Reynolds, John Hamilton 1794-1852 .... DLB 96
Reynolds, John J(oseph) 1924- 37-40R
Reynolds, Jonathan 1942- CANR-28
Earlier sketch in CA 65-68
See also CLC 6, 38
Reynolds, Joshua 1723-1792 .... DLB 104
Reynolds, Julia Louise 1883(?)-1980 Obituary .. 102
Reynolds, Kenyon L.
See Reynolds, Bede
Reynolds, Kevin 1952- 160
Reynolds, Kimberley (Griffith) 1955- 135
Reynolds, Larry T(homas) 1938- 134
Brief entry 107
Reynolds, Lloyd George 1910- CANR-15
Earlier sketch in CA 21-24R
Reynolds, Louis B. 1917- 41-44R
Reynolds, Mack
See Reynolds, Dallas McCord
See also DLB 8
Reynolds, Madge
See Whitlock, Ralph
Reynolds, Malvina 1900-1978 114
Obituary 105
See also SATA 44
See also SATA-Obit 24
Reynolds, Marie E. 1912- 17-20R
Reynolds, Marilyn 1935- .... SAAS 23
Reynolds, Marilynn 1940- .... SATA 80
Reynolds, Marjorie Harris 1903- 5-8R
Reynolds, Mary Trackett 1914- 109
Reynolds, Michael Shane 1937- CANR-9
Earlier sketch in CA 65-68
See also CLC 44
Reynolds, (Marjorie) Moira Davison 1915- CANR-45
Earlier sketches in CA 105, CANR-21
Reynolds, Morgan O(wen) 1942- 117
Reynolds, Pamela 1923- 103
See also SATA 34
Reynolds, Paul Davidson 1938- CANR-12
Earlier sketch in CA 33-36R
Reynolds, Paul R(evere) 1904-1988 102
Obituary 125
Reynolds, Peter C(arlton) 1943- 105
Reynolds, Philip Alan 1920- CANR-3
Earlier sketch in CA 5-8R
Reynolds, Quentin (James) 1902-1965 73-76
Reynolds, Robert Leonard 1902-1966 .... 1-4R
Obituary 103
Reynolds, Roger 1934- 53-56
Reynolds, Ruth Sutton
1890(?)-1977 Obituary 69-72
Reynolds, Sheri 1967- 147
Reynolds, Susan (Mary Grace) 1929- 117
Reynolds, Terry S(cott) 1946- CANR-43
Earlier sketch in CA 117
Reynolds, Theodore (Andrus) 1938- 158
Reynolds, Timothy (Robin) 1936- CANR-8
Earlier sketch in CA 9-12R
Reynolds, Valrae 1944- 93-96
Reynolds, Vernon 1935- 132
Reynolds, William Howard 1922-1972 Obituary . 107
Reynolds, William J. 1956- CANR-62
Earlier sketch in CA 123
Reynolds, William Jensen 1920- CANR-7
Earlier sketch in CA 5-8R
Rey-Rosa, Rodrigo 1958- 131
Rezits, Joseph 1925- 107
Rezler, Julius 1911- 25-28R
Rezmerski, John Calvin 1942- CANR-27
Earlier sketch in CA 29-32R
Rezneck, Samuel 1897-1983 .... CANR-24
Obituary 110
Earlier sketch in CA 45-48
Reznikoff, Charles 1894-1976 .... CAP-2
Obituary 61-64
Earlier sketch in CA 33-36
See also CLC 9
See also DLB 28, 45
Rezny, Arthur A(dolph) 1910- CAP-2
Earlier sketch in CA 19-20
Rezzori (d'Arezzo), Gregor von 1914-1998 136
Obituary 167
Brief entry 122
See also CLC 25
Rhea, Claude H(iram), Jr. 1927- 103
Rhea, Gordon Campbell 1945- 146
Rhea, Nicholas
See Walker, Peter N.
Rhees, Rush 1905(?)-1989(?) Obituary 129
Rheims, Maurice 1910- 153
Rhein, Francis Bayard 1915- 17-20R
Rhein, Phillip H(enry) 1923- 81-84
Rheingold, Howard (E.) 1947- 147
Rheinstein, Max 1899-1977 Obituary 73-76
Rhenisch, Harold (Arthur) 1958- 113
Rhett, Robert Barnwell 1800-1876 .... DLB 43
Rhie, Schi-Zhin 1936- 77-80
Rhine, J(oseph) B(anks) 1895-1980 ...... CANR-4
Obituary 93-96
Earlier sketch in CA 5-8R
Rhine, Louisa (Weckesser) E. 1891- CANR-4
Earlier sketch in CA 1-4R
Rhine, Richard
See Silverstein, Alvin
Rhinehart, Luke
See Cockcroft, George Powers
Rhinehart, Marilyn D. 1948- 139
Rhinehart, Susan Oneacre 1938- 1-4R
Rhoades, Diane 1952- 155
See also SATA 90
Rhoades, Jonathan
See Olsen, John Edward
Rhoades, Judith G(rubman) 1935- 97-100
Rhoads, Dorothy M(ary) 1895- CAP-2
Earlier sketch in CA 19-20
Rhoads, Edward J(ohn) M(ichael) 1938- 33-36R
Rhoads, Jonathan E(vans) 1907- 104
Rhode, Austen
See Francis, Basil (Hoskins)
Rhode, Eric 1934- 21-24R
Rhode, Irma 1900-1982 Obituary 106
Rhode, John 1884-1964 .... DLB 77
Rhode, Robert B(artlett) 1916- 17-20R
Rhode, Robert D(avid) 1911- 93-96
Rhode, Winslow
See Roe, F(rederic) Gordon
Rhodehamel, Josephine DeWitt 1901- 61-64
Rhodes, Albert 1916-1977 .... CANR-14
Earlier sketch in CA 21-24R
Rhodes, Anthony (Richard Ewart) 1916- 9-12R
Rhodes, Arnold Black 1913- 13-16R
Rhodes, Bennie (Loran) 1927- 108
See also SATA 35
Rhodes, Carolyn Hodgson 1925- 122
Rhodes, Clifford Oswald 1911-1985 65-68
Obituary 118
Rhodes, Colin 1963- 153
Rhodes, David 1946- 57-60
Rhodes, Dennis Everard 1923- 13-16R
Rhodes, Donna McKee 1962- 152
See also SATA 87
Rhodes, Ernest Lloyd 1915- 119
Rhodes, Eugene Manlove 1869-1934 ...... TCLC 53
Rhodes, Evan H. 1929- CANR-10
Earlier sketch in CA 57-60
Rhodes, Frank Harold Trevor 1926- 107
See also SATA 37
Rhodes, Ginger 1955- 160
Rhodes, Hari 1932- 17-20R
Rhodes, Irwin Seymour 1901- 73-76
Rhodes, James Allen 1909- Brief entry 105
Rhodes, James Ford 1848-1927 .... DLB 47
Rhodes, James M. 1940- 89-92
Rhodes, John J(acob) 1916- 103
Rhodes, Laura
See Robinson, Lisa
Rhodes, Leland
See Paine, Lauran (Bosworth)
Rhodes, Margaret 1915- 45-48
Rhodes, Norman (L.) 1942- 152
Rhodes, Olin E(ugene), Jr. 1960- 158
Rhodes, Philip 1922- 107
Rhodes, R. A. W. 1944- 139
Rhodes, Richard (Lee) 1937- CANR-58
Earlier sketches in CA 45-48, CANR-1, 20
See also BEST 90:1
See also DLB 185
Rhodes, Robert E(dward) 1927- 122
Rhodes, Robert Hunt 1937- 136
Rhodes, Robert I. 1942- 69-72
Rhodes, William C(onley) 1918- 81-84

Rhodes, Zandra (Lindsey) 1940- 153
Rhodes James, Robert (Vidal) 1933- CANR-14
Earlier sketch in CA 101
Rhodin, Eric Nolan 1916- CANR-3
Earlier sketch in CA 1-4R
Rhodius, Apollonius c. 3rd cent. B.C.- ..... DLB 176
Rhone, Trevor (Dave) 1940- 127
See also BW 1
R'hoone
See Balzac, Honore de
Rhue, Morton
See Strasser, Todd
Rhydderch, Ieuan
See Jones, Evan David
Rhymer, Joseph 1927- CANR-9
Earlier sketch in CA 21-24R
Rhyne, Nancy 1926- 133
See also SATA 66
Rhys, Frank
See Rees, Clair (Francis)
Rhys, Ioan
See Rees, Ioan Bowen
Rhys, J(ohn) Howard W(inslow) 1917- 17-20R
Rhys, Jean 1890(?)-1979 .... CANR-62
Obituary 85-88
Earlier sketches in CA 25-28R, CANR-35
See also CDBLB 1945-1960
See also CLC 2, 4, 6, 14, 19, 51
See also DAM NOV
See also DLB 36, 117, 162
See also MTCW 1
See also SSC 21
Rhys, Kate
See Donald, Anabel
Rhys, Keidrych 1915-1987 Obituary 122
Riach, Alan 1957- 141
Riad, Mahmoud 1917-1992 131
Obituary 136
Riahi-Belkaoui, Ahmed 1943- 140
Riasanovsky, Nicholas V(alentine) 1923- .. CANR-3
Earlier sketch in CA 5-8R
Ribal, Joseph E(dward) 1931- 61-64
Ribalow, Harold U(riel) 1919-1982 .... CANR-2
Obituary 108
Earlier sketch in CA 5-8R
Ribalow, Meir Z(vi) 1948- 144
Ribar, Joe 1943- 77-80
Ribbons, Ian 1924- 108
See also SAAS 3
See also SATA 37
See also SATA-Brief 30
Ribeiro, Aileen 1944- 124
Ribeiro, Darcy 1922-1997 .... 33-36R
Obituary 156
See also CLC 34
Ribeiro, Joao Ubaldo (Osorio Pimentel)
1941- 81-84
See also CLC 10, 67
Ribera Chevremont, Evaristo 1896-1976 ...... HW
Ribicoff, Abraham (Alexander) 1910-1998 108
Obituary 167
Ribman, Ronald (Burt) 1932- CANR-46
Earlier sketch in CA 21-24R
See also CLC 7
Ribner, Irving 1921-1972 .... CANR-3
Obituary 37-40R
Earlier sketch in CA 1-4R
Riboud, Barbara (Dewayne Tosi) Chase
See Chase-Riboud, Barbara (Dewayne Tosi)
Ribowsky, Mark 1951- 146
Ribuffo, Leo P(aul) 1945- 118
Ricapito, Joseph V. 1933- 158
Ricardo, David 1772-1823 .... DLB 107, 158
Ricardo, Harry R(alph) 1885-1974 Obituary 114
Ricardo, Jack 1940- 140
Ricardo-Campbell, Rita CANR-26
Earlier sketches in CA 57-60, CANR-8
Ricardou, Jean 1932- .... DLB 83
Ricart, Josep Gudiol i
See Gudiol i Ricart, Josep
Riccards, Michael P(atrick) 1944- 61-64
Ricchiuti, Paul B(urton) 1925- 107
Ricci, David M. 1940- 143
Ricci, Larry J. 1948- 109
Ricci, Nino 1959- 137
See also CLC 70
Ricciardi, Lorenzo 1930- 109
Ricciuti, Edward R(aphael) 1938- 41-44R
See also SATA 10
Rice, A(lbert) Kenneth 1908- 5-8R
Rice, Albert
See Leventhal, Albert Rice
Rice, Albert R(ichard) 1951- 142
Rice, Alice (Caldwell) Hegan 1870-1942 .. SATA 63
Rice, Allan Lake 1905-1984 .... CANR-27
Earlier sketch in CA 37-40R
Rice, Anne 1941- CANR-53
Earlier sketches in CA 65-68, CANR-12, 36
See also AAYA 9
See also BEST 89:2
See also CLC 41
See also DAM POP
Rice, Arnold Sanford 1928- 113
Rice, Bebe Faas 1932- 155
See also SATA 89
Rice, Berkeley 1937- 21-24R
Rice, C(harles) David 1941- CANR-41
Earlier sketch in CA 118
Rice, C(harles) Duncan 1942- CANR-10
Earlier sketch in CA 57-60
Rice, Charles D(uane) 1910-1971 Obituary 104
See also SATA-Obit 27
Rice, Charles E. 1931- CANR-1
Earlier sketch in CA 1-4R
Rice, Charles L(ynvel) 1936- 65-68
Rice, Condoleezza 1954- 154
Rice, Craig
See Randolph, Georgiana Ann
Rice, Cy 1905-1971 .... CAP-1
Obituary 33-36R
Earlier sketch in CA 11-12
Rice, Dale R(ichard) 1948- 116
See also SATA 42
Rice, David G(ordon) 1938- 101
Rice, David Talbot 1903-1972 .... CANR-5
Earlier sketch in CA 9-12R
Rice, Desmond Charles 1924- CANR-21
Earlier sketches in CA 9-12R, CANR-5
Rice, Donald L. 1938- CANR-14
Earlier sketch in CA 37-40R
Rice, Dorothy Mary 1913- 9-12R
Rice, Earle, Jr. 1928- 156
See also SATA 92
Rice, Edmund C. 1910(?)-1982 Obituary 106
Rice, Edward 1918- CANR-47
Earlier sketches in CA 49-52, CANR-1
See also BEST 90:4
See also SATA 47
See also SATA-Brief 42
Rice, Edward E(arl) 1909- 41-44R
Rice, Elinor
See Hays, Elinor Rice
Rice, Elizabeth 1913- 21-24R
See also SATA 2
Rice, Elmer (Leopold) 1892-1967 .... CAP-2
Obituary 25-28R
Earlier sketch in CA 21-22
See also CLC 7, 49
See also DAM DRAM
See also DLB 4, 7
See also MTCW 1
Rice, Eugene F(ranklin), Jr. 1924- 29-32R
Rice, Eve (Hart) 1951- CANR-4
Earlier sketch in CA 53-56
See also SATA 34, 91
Rice, Frank M(artin) 1908- 45-48
Rice, George H(all), Jr. 1923- 53-56
Rice, Grantland 1880-1954 Brief entry 114
See also DLB 29, 171
Rice, Helen Steiner 1900(?)-1981 133
Rice, Homer C(ranston) 1927- 73-76
Rice, Inez 1907- 29-32R
See also SATA 13
Rice, James 1934- CANR-65
Earlier sketches in CA 61-64, CANR-8
See also SATA 22, 93
Rice, John F. 1958- .... SATA 82
Rice, John R(ichard) 1895-1980 .... CANR-5
Earlier sketch in CA 5-8R
Rice, Joseph Peter 1930- 29-32R
Rice, Julius 1923- 41-44R
Rice, Keith A(lan) 1954- 109
Rice, Lawrence D. 1929- 33-36R
Rice, Linda Lightsey 1950- 166
Rice, Luanne 1955- 139
Rice, Martin P(aul) 1938- 57-60
Rice, Max M(cGee) 1928- 93-96
Rice, Michael 1928- 137
Rice, Mitchell F. 1948- 138
See also BW 2
Rice, Otis K(ermit) 1919- CANR-27
Earlier sketch in CA 29-32R
Rice, R. B.
See Chapman, Frank M(onroe)
Rice, Ross R(ichard) 1922- 45-48
Rice, Stan 1942- CANR-36
Earlier sketch in CA 77-80
Rice, Tamara (Abelson) Talbot 1904- Brief
entry 111
Rice, Thomas Jackson 1945- CANR-18
Earlier sketch in CA 101
Rice, Tim(othy Miles Bindon) 1944- CANR-46
Earlier sketch in CA 103
See also CLC 21
Rice, Wayne 1945- 89-92
Rice, William (Edward) 1938- 118
Rice, William C(arroll) 1911- 9-12R
Rich, Adrienne (Cecile) 1929- CANR-53
Earlier sketches in CA 9-12R, CANR-20
See also CLC 3, 6, 7, 11, 18, 36, 73, 76
See also DAM POET
See also DLB 5, 67
See also MTCW 1
See also PC 5
Rich, Alan 1924- 9-12R
Rich, Barbara
See Graves, Robert (von Ranke)
Rich, Bennett M(ilton) 1909-1984 134
Rich, Daniel Catton 1904-1976 73-76
Obituary 69-72
Rich, Doris L. 1920- 138
Rich, Edwin Ernest 1904-1979 Obituary 89-92
Rich, Elaine Sommers 1926- CANR-49
Earlier sketches in CA 17-20R, CANR-9, 24
See also SATA 6
Rich, Elizabeth 1935- 29-32R
Rich, (Ora) Everett 1900- CAP-1
Earlier sketch in CA 11-12
Rich, Frank 1949- 73-76
Rich, Gerry
See Brandon, Johnny
Rich, (David) Gibson 1936- 57-60
Rich, Joe 1935- 57-60
Rich, John H., Jr. 1917- 81-84
Rich, John Martin 1931- 21-24R
Rich, Josephine Bouchard 1912- 5-8R
See also SATA 10
Rich, Louise Dickinson 1903-1991 73-76
Obituary 134
See also SATA 54
See also SATA-Obit 67
Rich, Mark J. 1948- .... SATA-Brief 53
Rich, Matty 1971- 140
See also BW 2
Rich, Michael B(enjamin) 1935- 29-32R
Rich, Norman 1921- 45-48
Rich, Paul B(enjamin) 1950- 124
Rich, Robert
See Trumbo, Dalton
Rich, Russell R(ogers) 1912- 101
Richard, Adrienne 1921- 29-32R
See also SAAS 9
See also SATA 5
Richard, Arthur Windsor
See Windsor-Richards, Arthur (Bedlington)
Richard, Betty Byrd 1922- 106
Richard, Carl J(ohn) 1962- 150
Richard, James Robert
See Bowen, Robert Sydney
Richard, John 1954- 106
Richard, Keith
See Richards, Keith
See also CLC 17
Richard, Lee
See Le Pelley, Guernsey
Richard, Lionel (Camille Paul) 1938- 93-96
Richard, Lucien J(oseph) 1931- 105
Richard, Mark 1955- 145
Richard, Marthe 1889-1982 Obituary 110
Richard, Michel Paul 1933- 45-48
Richard, Olga 1914- 103
Richard, Susan
See Ellis, Julie
Richard-Amato, Patricia (Abbott) 1940- 126
Richards, Alayna
See Posner, Richard
Richards, Alfred (Luther) 1939- 45-48
Richards, Allen
See Rosenthal, Richard A.
Richards, Alun 1929- CANR-17
Earlier sketch in CA 65-68
Richards, Arlene Kramer 1935- CANR-11
Earlier sketch in CA 65-68
Richards, Audrey I(sabel) 1899-1984 .... CANR-27
Obituary 113
Earlier sketch in CA 21-24R
Richards, Beah 153
See also BW 2
Richards, Blair P(atton) 1940- 69-72
Richards, Cara E(lizabeth) 1927- CANR-1
Earlier sketch in CA 49-52
Richards, Carl Edward, Jr. 1933- CANR-24
Earlier sketch in CA 45-48
Richards, Caroline 1939- 77-80
Richards, Charles
See Marvin, John T.
Richards, Clare
See Titchener, Louise
Richards, Clay
See Crossen, Kendell Foster
Richards, David
See Bickers, Richard (Leslie) Townshend
Richards, David 1940- 166
Richards, David A. J. 1944- 167
Richards, David Adams 1950- CANR-60
Earlier sketch in CA 93-96
See also CLC 59
See also DAC
See also DLB 53
Richards, David P. 1950- 166
Richards, Denis (George) 1910- 9-12R
Richards, Dennis L(ee) 1938- 102
Richards, Dorothy B(urney) 1894- 85-88
Richards, Duane
See Hurley, Vic
Richards, E. B.
See Bayley, Edwin Richard
Richards, Eric 1940- 148
Richards, Eugene 1944- 154
Richards, Francis
See Lockridge, Frances Louise
and Lockridge, Richard
Richards, Frank
See Hamilton, Charles (Harold St. John)
Richards, Fred
See Richards, Alfred (Luther)
Richards, George 1760(?)-1814 .... DLB 37
Richards, Guy 1905-1979 .... CANR-11
Obituary 81-84
Earlier sketch in CA 61-64
Richards, H(arold) M(arshall) S(ylvester)
1894-1985 .... CAP-2
Obituary 116
Earlier sketch in CA 23-24
Richards, Hilda
See Hamilton, Charles (Harold St. John)
Richards, Horace G(ardiner) 1906- 5-8R
Richards, Hubert J. 1921- CANR-67
Earlier sketch in CA 128
Richards, I(vor) A(rmstrong) 1893-1979 .. CANR-34
Obituary 89-92
Earlier sketch in CA 41-44R
See also CLC 14, 24
See also DLB 27
Richards, J(ohn) Howard 1916- CANR-18
Earlier sketches in CA 45-48, CANR-2
Richards, J(ames) M(aude) 1907- CANR-25
Earlier sketches in CA 5-8R, CANR-5
Richards, Jack W(esley) 1933- 33-36R
Richards, Jackie 1925- .... SATA 102
Richards, James O(lin) 1936- 37-40R
Richards, Jane 1934- 33-36R
Richards, Janet Radcliffe 1944- 133
Richards, Jeffrey (Michael) 1945- CANR-13
Earlier sketch in CA 73-76
Richards, Jock 1918- 107
Richards, Joe 1909-1992 .... CAP-1
Obituary 136
Earlier sketch in CA 9-10
Richards, John 1939- 57-60
Richards, John F(olsom) 1938- 115
Richards, John Marvin 1929- 13-16R
Richards, Kathleen
See Dale, Kathleen
Richards, Kay
See Baker, Susan (Catherine)
Richards, Keith 1943- 107
See also Richard, Keith
Richards, Kenny
See Broderick, Richard L(awrence)
Richards, Kent David 1938- 104
Richards, Larry
See Richards, Lawrence O.
Richards, Laura E(lizabeth Howe) 1850-1943 ... 137
Brief entry 120
See also DLB 42
See also MAICYA
See also YABC 1
Richards, Lawrence O. 1931- CANR-42
Earlier sketches in CA 29-32R, CANR-20
Richards, Lewis A(lva) 1925- 45-48
Richards, M(ary) C(aroline) 1916- 108
Richards, Mark
See Ra'Anan, Uri
Richards, Martin P(aul) M(eredith) 1940- . CANR-49
Earlier sketches in CA 61-64, CANR-8, 23
Richards, Matt 1968- 162
Richards, Max D(eVoe) 1923- CANR-16
Earlier sketch in CA 21-24R
Richards, Nat
See Richardson, James Nathaniel
Richards, Norman 1932- CANR-31
Earlier sketch in CA 112
See also SATA 48
Richards, Owain Westmacott
1901-1984 Obituary 114
Richards, Pamela Spence 1941- 111
Richards, Peter
See Monger, (Ifor) David
Richards, Peter Godfrey 1923-1987 108
Obituary 123
Richards, Phyllis
See Auty, Phyllis
Richards, R(onald) C(harles) W(illiam) 1923- ....
CANR-26
Earlier sketches in CA 21-24R, CANR-10
See also SATA 59
See also SATA-Brief 43
Richards, Robert J. 144
Richards, Stanley 1918-1980 .... 25-28R
Obituary 101
Richards, Susan 1948- 135
Richards, Todd
See Sutphen, Richard Charles
Richards, Victor 1918- 57-60
Richards, Walter Alden (Jr.)
1907-1988 Obituary 125
See also SATA-Obit 56
Richards, William Carey 1818-1892 .... DLB 73
Richardson, Alan 1923- 29-32R
Richardson, Ann 1942- CANR-45
Earlier sketch in CA 119
Richardson, Anne
See Roiphe, Anne (Richardson)
Richardson, Arleta 1923- CANR-36
Earlier sketches in CA 93-96, CANR-16
Richardson, Beth
See Gutcheon, Beth R(ichardson)
Richardson, Betty 1935- 53-56
Richardson, Beulah
See Richards, Beah
Richardson, Beulah
See Richards, Beah
Richardson, Bonham C. 1939- 135
Richardson, Bradley M. 1928- 49-52
Richardson, C.
See Munsey, Cecil (Richard, Jr.)
Richardson, Carl 1950- 143
Richardson, Carol 1932- .... SATA 58
Richardson, Cecil Antonio 1928-1991 121
Obituary 136
Brief entry 115
Interview in 121
Richardson, Charles E(verett) 1928- 57-60
Richardson, Charles F. 1851-1913 .... DLB 71
Richardson, Cyril Charles 1909-1976 .... 37-40R
Obituary 69-72
Richardson, Don(ald MacNaughton) 1935- ....
CANR-9
Earlier sketch in CA 65-68
Richardson, Donald P(orter) 1932- CANR-44
Earlier sketch in CA 119
Richardson, Dorothy Lee 1900-1986 106
Obituary 121
Richardson, Dorothy Miller 1873-1957 Brief
entry 104
See also DLB 36
See also TCLC 3
Richardson, Dorsey 1896-1981 Obituary 105
Richardson, (Robert) Douglas
1893-1989 Obituary 128
Richardson, Edgar Preston 1902-1985 110
Obituary 115
Richardson, Elliot L(ee) 1920- Brief entry 111
Richardson, Elmo (R.) 1930- CANR-11
Earlier sketch in CA 13-16R
Richardson, Ethel Florence (Lindesay)
1870-1946 Brief entry 105
See also Richardson, Henry Handel
Richardson, Evelyn M(ay Fox) 1902- CAP-1
Earlier sketch in CA 13-14

Richardson, Frank Howard
1882-1970 Obituary 104
See also SATA-Obit 27
Richardson, Frank McLean 1904-....... CANR-20
Earlier sketch in CA 103
Richardson, Gayle E(lwin) 1911-............9-12R
Richardson, George Barclay 1924-...........1-4R
Richardson, Gladwell 1903-1980............. 123
Richardson, Grace Lee
See Dickson, Naida
Richardson, H(arold) Edward 1929-..... CANR-15
Earlier sketch in CA 29-32R
Richardson, Harry V(an Buren) 1901-........69-72
Richardson, Harry W(ard) 1938-....... CANR-27
Earlier sketch in CA 29-32R
Richardson, Henrietta
See Richardson, Ethel Florence (Lindesay)
Richardson, Henry Handel
See Richardson, Ethel Florence (Lindesay)
See also DLB 197
See also TCLC 4
Richardson, Henry V(okes) M(ackey) 1923-. 25-28R
Richardson, Howard (Dixon) 1917-1984.... 41-44R
Obituary 114
Richardson, Isla Paschal 1886-1971....... CAP-1
Earlier sketch in CA 9-10
Richardson, Ivan L(eRoy) 1920-.............. 101
Richardson, Ivor Lloyd Morgan 1930-....... 9-12R
Richardson, J. G.
See Richardson, Jacques (Gabriel)
Richardson, Jack (Carter) 1935-.............5-8R
See also DLB 7
Richardson, Jacques (Gabriel) 1924-..........125
Richardson, James 1950-..................77-80
Richardson, James F(rancis) 1931-........29-32R
Richardson, James L(ongden) 1933-........21-24R
Richardson, James Nathaniel 1942-.........53-56
Richardson, James R. 1911-.................1-4R
Richardson, James T. 1941-................. 139
Richardson, Jean (Mary)...................... 127
See also SATA 59
Richardson, Jeremy John 1942-........ CANR-27
Earlier sketch in CA 29-32R
Richardson, Joanna CANR-51
Earlier sketches in CA 13-16R, CANR-10, 26
Richardson, Joe M(artin) 1934-......... CANR-26
Earlier sketch in CA 45-48
Richardson, John 1796-1852.................DAC
See also DLB 99
Richardson, John 1924-.....................140
Richardson, John Adkins 1929-.............57-60
Richardson, John Martin, Jr. 1938-....... CANR-12
Earlier sketch in CA 33-36R
Richardson, Judith Benet 1941-..........SATA 77
Richardson, Justin 1900(?)-1975 Obituary... 61-64
Richardson, Kenneth Ridley 1934-.........29-32R
Richardson, Laurel 1938-.....................111
Richardson, Laurence E(aton) 1893-....... CAP-1
Earlier sketch in CA 11-12
Richardson, (Stewart) Lee (Jr.) 1940-..... CANR-9
Earlier sketch in CA 21-24R
Richardson, Leopold John Dixon
1893-1979(?) Obituary..................... 104
Richardson, Malcolm 1947-...................120
Richardson, Midge Turk 1930-.............33-36R
Richardson, Miles (Edward) 1932-..........33-36R
Richardson, Mozelle Groner 1914-.........33-36R
Richardson, Neil R(yan) 1944-................. 103
Richardson, Nola 1936-.................... 57-60
See also BW 1
Richardson, (George) Peter 1935-...... CANR-43
Earlier sketch in CA 114
Richardson, R. C. 1944-.......................162
Richardson, R(alph) Daniel 1931-.............109
Richardson, Richard C(olby), Jr. 1933-... CANR-13
Earlier sketch in CA 77-80
Richardson, Richard Judson 1935-........ 29-32R
Richardson, Robert 1940-..................... 149
Richardson, Robert D(ale), Jr. 1934-.... CANR-29
Earlier sketches in CA 29-32R, CANR-12
Richardson, Robert Galloway 1926-...... CANR-7
Earlier sketch in CA 13-16R
Richardson, Robert S(hirley) 1902-..........49-52
See also SATA 8
Richardson, Rupert Norval 1891-..........17-20R
Richardson, Ruth 1951-...................... 136
Richardson, S(tanley) D(ennis) 1925-.... CANR-28
Earlier sketches in CA 21-24R, CANR-10
Richardson, Samuel 1689-1761 . CDBLB 1660-1789
See also DA
See also DAB
See also DAC
See also DAM MST, NOV
See also DLB 39
See also WLC
Richardson, Stephen A. 1920-..............61-64
Richardson, Thomas Dow 1887-.............5-8R
Richardson, Tony
See Richardson, Cecil Antonio
Richardson, Vokes
See Richardson, Henry V(okes) M(ackey)
Richardson, W(alter) C(ecil) 1902-....... CANR-1
Earlier sketch in CA 1-4R
Richardson, William John 1920-...........21-24R
Richardson, Willis 1889-1977............... 124
See also BW 1
See also DLB 51
See also SATA 60
Richason, Benjamin F(ranklin, Jr.) 1922-....41-44R
Richberg, Donald R(andall)
1881-1960 Obituary.........................113
Riche, Pierre 1921-.........................123
Riche, Robert 1925-........................ 108
Riche, William Harding le
See le Riche, William Harding
Richelieu, Peter
See Robinson, P. W.
Richelson, Geraldine 1922-................. 106
See also SATA 29
Richelson, Jeffrey T(albot) 1949-........ CANR-43
Earlier sketch in CA 119
Richemont, Enid 1940-.......................149
See also SATA 82
Richens, Richard Hook 1919-1984 Obituary... 114
Richepin, Jean 1849-1926.............. DLB 192
Riches, David 1947-........................ 128
Riches, John (Kenneth) 1939-................117
Riches, Pierre 1927-................. CANR-44
Earlier sketch in CA 118
Richette, Lisa Aversa 1928-.............. 25-28R
Richetti, John J(oseph) 1938-................ 110
Richey, David 1939-................... CANR-10
Earlier sketch in CA 57-60
Richey, Dorothy Hilliard CANR-6
Earlier sketch in CA 9-12R
Richey, Elinor 1920-...................... 45-48
Richey, Margaret Fitzgerald
1883(?)-1974 Obituary....................53-56
Richey, Robert W(illiam) 1912-1978..... CANR-17
Obituary....................................116
Earlier sketch in CA 25-28R
Richey, Russell Earle 1941-................69-72
Richie, Donald (Steiner) 1924-........... CANR-49
Earlier sketches in CA 17-20R, CANR-8, 24
See also CAAS 20
Richland, W(ilfred) Bernard 1909-............102
Richler, Daniel 1956-.........................137
Richler, Mordecai 1931-................. CANR-62
Earlier sketches in CA 65-68, CANR-31
See also AITN 1
See also CLC 3, 5, 9, 13, 18, 46, 70
See also CLR 17
See also DAC
See also DAM MST, NOV
See also DLB 53
See also MAICYA
See also MTCW 1
See also SATA 44, 98
See also SATA-Brief 27
Richman, Barry M(artin) 1936-1978..... CANR-17
Earlier sketch in CA 21-24R
Richman, Irwin 1937-...................... 165
Richman, Milton (Saul) 1922-1986.......... 69-72
Obituary.....................................119
Richman, Phyllis C(hasanow) 1939-...... CANR-66
Earlier sketch in CA 89-92
Richman, Robert (Maxwell)
1914-1987 Obituary.........................124
Richman, Saul 1917(?)-1979 Obituary....... 85-88
Rich-McCoy, Lois
See McCoy, Lois (Rich)
Richmond, Al 1913-1987...................41-44R
Obituary.................................... 124
Richmond, Anthony H(enry) 1925-.........21-24R
Richmond, Cindy Packard 1948-..............112
Richmond, Claire
See Titchener, Louise
Richmond, Dick 1933-.......................61-64
Richmond, Douglas W(ertz) 1946-............ 111
Richmond, Grace
See Marsh, John
Richmond, H(ugh) M(acrae) 1932-....... CANR-3
Earlier sketch in CA 9-12R
Richmond, Ian Archibald 1902-1965 Obituary.. 111
Richmond, John C(hristopher) B(lake) 1909- Brief entry......................................106
Richmond, Julius B(enjamin) 1916-........ 29-32R
Richmond, Lee 1943-...................... 49-52
Richmond, Lee J(oyce) 1934-................ 113
Richmond, Leigh (Tucker) 1911-...........21-24R
Richmond, Peter 1953-........................147
Richmond, Roaldus Frederick 1910-(?).. CANR-64
Earlier sketch in CA 114
Richmond, Robert P. 1914-................21-24R
Richmond, Robert W(illiam) 1927-...........53-56
Richmond, Robin 1951-...................... 142
See also SATA 75
Richmond, Rod
See Glut, Donald F(rank)
Richmond, Roe
See Richmond, Roaldus Frederick
Richmond, Samuel B(ernard) 1919-.........41-44R
Richmond, Sandra 1948-.......................117
Richmond, (John) Stanley 1906-.............45-48
Richmond, Velma E. B(ourgeois) 1931-...... 61-64
Richmond, W(illiam) Kenneth 1910-...... CANR-10
Earlier sketch in CA 25-28R
Richmond, Walt(er F.) 1922-1977.........21-24R
Obituary......................................117
Richoux, Pat(ricia) 1927-................ 25-28R
See also SATA 7
Richstatter, Thomas 1939-....................112
Richter, Alice 1941-..........................105
See also SATA 30
Richter, C(harles) F(rancis)
1900-1985 Obituary..........................117
Richter, Conrad (Michael) 1890-1968.... CANR-23
Obituary.................................25-28R
Earlier sketch in CA 5-8R
See also AAYA 21
See also CLC 30
See also DLB 9
See also MTCW 1
See also SATA 3
Richter, Daniel K(arl) 1954-................ 143
Richter, David H. 1945-..................... 101
Richter, Derek 1907-.........................101
Richter, Dorothy 1906-....................29-32R
Richter, Gerard R(ichard) 1905-............ 5-8R
Richter, Gisela M(arie) A(ugusta) 1882-1972......
CANR-4
Earlier sketch in CA 5-8R
Richter, Gregory C. 1955-.................... 146
Richter, Hans 1888-1976.............. CANR-30
Obituary...................................65-68
Earlier sketch in CA 73-76
Richter, Hans Peter 1925-............... CANR-2
Earlier sketch in CA 45-48
See also CLR 21
See also MAICYA
See also SAAS 11
See also SATA 6
Richter, Hans Werner 1908-.............. 97-100
See also DLB 69
Richter, Harvena 1919-................. CANR-3
Earlier sketch in CA 5-8R
Richter, Horst-Eberhard 1923-......... CANR-20
Earlier sketches in CA 53-56, CANR-5
Richter, Irving 1911-..................... 57-60
Richter, J. H(ans) 1901-.................. CAP-1
Earlier sketch in CA 13-16
Richter, Joan 1930-..........................101
Richter, Johann Paul Friedrich 1763-1825.. DLB 94
Richter, Lin 1936-..........................73-76
Richter, Linda K. 1942-.......................117
Richter, Maurice N(athaniel), Jr. 1930-.......49-52
Richter, Melvin 1921- Brief entry............. 110
Richter, Valentin
See Pick, Robert
Richter, Vernon
See Hutchcroft, Vera
Richter, W(alter) D(uch) 1945-................156
Richter, William L. 1942-............... CANR-52
Earlier sketch in CA 126
Rickard, Bob
See Rickard, Robert J(ohn) M(oberley)
Rickard, Graham 1949-..................SATA 71
Rickard, Robert J(ohn) M(oberley) 1945-...... 106
Rickards, Colin (William) 1937-............25-28R
Rickards, Maurice 1919-.......................103
Rickel, Annette U. 1941-..................... 123
Rickels, Karl 1924-...................... CANR-1
Earlier sketch in CA 45-48
Rickels, Milton H. 1920-.....................5-8R
Rickenbacker, Eddie
See Rickenbacker, Edward Vernon
Rickenbacker, Edward Vernon 1890-1973..... 101
Obituary...................................41-44R
Ricker, George Marvin 1922-........... CANR-20
Earlier sketch in CA 89-92
Rickert, Corinne Holt
See Sawyer, Corinne Holt
Rickert, John E(arl) 1923-............. CANR-24
Earlier sketch in CA 45-48
Rickett, Frances 1921-...................... 107
Rickett, Harold William 1896-............. 17-20R
Ricketts, C(arl) E(verett) 1906-............ 57-60
Ricketts, Mac Linscott 1930-.................130
Ricketts, Ralph Robert 1902-................. 116
Ricketts, Viva Leone (Harris) 1900-........ CAP-1
Earlier sketch in CA 11-12
Rickey, Don, Jr. 1925-.................. CANR-9
Earlier sketch in CA 5-8R
Rickey, George Warren 1907-.............. 65-68
Rickey, Mary Ellen 1929-.................21-24R
Rickford, John R(ussell) 1949-.............. 126
Ricklefs, Roger 1940-........................127
Rickman, Geoffrey (Edwin) 1932-..........29-32R
Rickman, H(ans) P(eter) 1918-......... CANR-68
Earlier sketches in CA 17-20R, CANR-14, 32
Rickman, Thomas.............................165
Rickover, H. G.
See Rickover, Hyman G(eorge)
Rickover, Hyman G(eorge) 1900-1986........156
Obituary.....................................119
Ricks, Chip
See Ricks, Nadine
Ricks, Christopher (Bruce) 1933-........ CANR-47
Earlier sketches in CA 9-12R, CANR-7, 23
Ricks, David F(rank) 1927-............. CANR-10
Earlier sketch in CA 21-24R
Ricks, David Trulock 1936-............... 25-28R
Ricks, Don(ald) M(ax) 1936-.............. 25-28R
Ricks, James 1975-...........................168
Ricks, Nadine 1925-...................... CANR-53
Earlier sketches in CA 77-80, CANR-13, 29
Rickword, (John) Edgell 1898-1982..... CANR-36
Obituary.....................................106
Earlier sketch in CA 101
See also DLB 20
Rico, Don(ato) 1917-1985.............. CANR-28
Obituary......................................115
Earlier sketch in CA 81-84
See also SATA-Obit 43
Rico, Gabriele Lusser 1937-................. 110
Ricoeur, Paul 1913-.................... CANR-10
Earlier sketch in CA 61-64
Ricostranza, Tom
See Ellis, Trey
Ricou, Laurence (Rodger) 1944-........ CANR-50
Earlier sketches in CA 61-64, CANR-8, 25
Riday, George E(mil) 1912-................13-16R
Ridd, Stephen (John) 1948-....................149
Riddel, Frank S(tephen) 1940-..............85-88
Riddel, Joseph N(eill) 1931-............. CANR-5
Earlier sketch in CA 9-12R
Riddell, Alan 1927-......................... 104
Riddell, Charlotte 1832-1906................ 165
See also DLB 156
See also TCLC 40
Riddell, Edwina 1955-.................. SATA 82
Riddell, Elizabeth (Richmond) 1907-.......... 154
Riddell, J. H. 1832-1906
See Riddell, Charlotte
Riddell, John 1942-..........................142
Ridder, Bernard J. 1913-1983 Obituary........110
Ridder, Joseph B(ernard) 1920-1989 Obituary. 127
Ridder, Marie 1925-........................73-76
Ridderbos, Herman N(icolaas) 1909-........ 57-60
Riddle, Donald H(usted) 1921-............. 9-12R
Riddle, Jean
See Weihs, Jean
Riddle, John M(arion) 1937-.................45-48
Riddle, Kenneth Wilkinson 1920-............ 1-4R
Riddle, Maxwell 1907-.................. CANR-3
Earlier sketch in CA 5-8R
Riddle, Thomas Wilkinson 1886-1983 Obituary.110
Riddle, Tohby 1965-........................SATA 74
Riddleberger, Patrick Williams 1915-....... 21-24R
Riddy, Felicity (Jacqueline) 1940-............ 128
Ride, Sally (Kristen) 1951-.................... 158
Rideau, Wilbert 1942-.........................144
Ridenour, Fritz 1932-.................. CANR-50
Earlier sketches in CA 108, CANR-25
Ridenour, George M(eyer) 1928-............93-96
Ridenour, Ron 1939-........................69-72
Rider, Alice Damon 1895-...................69-72
Rider, (Arthur) Fremont 1885-1962 Obituary. 89-92
Rider, J. W.
See Stevens, Shane
Rider, John R. 1923-......................25-28R
Ridge, Antonia (Florence) (?)-1981......... 9-12R
Obituary.....................................104
See also SATA 7
See also SATA-Obit 27
Ridge, George Ross 1931-................. 1-4R
Ridge, John Rollin 1827-1867.................144
See also DAM MULT
See also DLB 175
See also NNAL
Ridge, Julie 1956-...........................120
Ridge, Lola 1873-1941....................DLB 54
Ridge, Martin 1923-.................... CANR-47
Earlier sketch in CA 121
See also SATA 43
Ridge, William Pett c. 1859-1930.........DLB 135
Ridgely, Beverly S(ellman) 1920-....... CANR-17
Earlier sketch in CA 25-28R
Ridgely, Joseph Vincent 1921-.............. 5-8R
Ridgeway, James Fowler 1936-............... 106
Ridgeway, Jason
See Marlowe, Stephen
Ridgeway, Marian E(lizabeth) 1913-........33-36R
Ridgeway, Rick 1949-.......................93-96
Ridgway, Brunilde Sismondo 1929-....... CANR-1
Earlier sketch in CA 45-48
Ridgway, John M. 1938-...................25-28R
Ridgway, Judith 1939-.................. CANR-26
Earlier sketch in CA 109
Ridgway, Judy
See Ridgway, Judith
Ridgway, Ronald S(idney) 1923-............45-48
Ridgway, Whitman H(awley) 1941-.............101
Riding, Alan 1943-...........................122
Riding, Laura
See Jackson, Laura (Riding)
See also CLC 3, 7
Ridington, Robin 1939-.......................139
Ridle, Julia Brown 1923-.....................1-4R
Ridler, Anne Barbara 1912-............... CANR-3
Earlier sketch in CA 5-8R
See also DLB 27
Ridley, Anthony 1933-........................107
Ridley, Arnold 1896-1984 Obituary........... 112
Ridley, B(rian) K(idd) 1931-................. 104
Ridley, Charles P(rice) 1933-...............73-76
Ridley, Elizabeth J(ayne) 1966-...............142
Ridley, Jane 1953-...........................149
Ridley, Jasper (Godwin) 1920-.......... CANR-45
Earlier sketches in CA 13-16R, CANR-6, 22
Ridley, Mark 1956-........................... 133
Ridley, Matt(hew White) 1958-................ 149
Ridley, Nat, Jr. CANR-26
Earlier sketches in CAP-2, CA 19-20
Ridley, Nicholas 1929-....................... 141
Ridley, Philip................................ 140
See also SATA 88
Ridley, Ronald T(homas) 1940-...............143
Ridlington, Sandy 1944-...................... 162
Ridlon, Marci
See Balterman, Marcia Ridlon
See also SATA 22
Ridout, Albert K(ilburn) 1905-.............. CAP-2
Earlier sketch in CA 19-20
Ridout, Ronald 1916-1994............... CANR-20
Obituary.....................................147
Earlier sketch in CA 103
Ridpath, Ian (William) 1947-................77-80
Ridpath, M(ichael) G(errans) 1926-........... 139
Ridpath, Michael 1961-.......................151
Ridruejo, Dionisio 1913(?)-1975 Obituary.... 57-60
See also DLB 108
Rieber, Alfred J(oseph) 1931-..............9-12R
Rieber, R(obert) W(olff) 1932-........... CANR-3
Earlier sketch in CA 45-48
Riede, David G(eorge) 1951-..................131
Riedel, Eunice 1931(?)-1986 Obituary.........120
Riedel, Richard Langham 1908-1988....... CAP-2
Obituary.....................................127
Earlier sketch in CA 29-32
Riedel, Walter E(rwin) 1936-........... CANR-24
Earlier sketch in CA 45-48
Rieder, Marge.................................143
Riedesel, C(lark) Alan 1930-..............25-28R
Riedl, John O(rth) 1905-.................. CAP-2
Earlier sketch in CA 21-22
Riedman, Sarah R(egal) 1902-.......... CANR-37
Earlier sketches in CA 1-4R, CANR-1
See also SATA 1
Riefe, Alan 1925-....................... CANR-9
Earlier sketch in CA 61-64

Riefe, Barbara
See Riefe, Alan
Riefenstahl, Berta Helene Amalia 1902- ... 108
See also Riefenstahl, Leni
Riefenstahl, Leni
See Riefenstahl, Berta Helene Amalia
See also CLC 16
Rieff, Philip 1922- ... 49-52
Riegel, Robert Edgar 1897- ... 5-8R
Rieger, James H(enry) 1936- ... 93-96
Rieger, Shay 1929- ... 29-32R
Riegert, Eduard Richard 1932- ... 69-72
Riegert, Ray 1947- ... 105
Riegle, Donald W(ayne), Jr. 1938- ... CANR-43
Earlier sketch in CA 61-64
Riel, Louis 1844-1885 ... DLB 99
Riely, John (Cabell) 1945- ... CANR-32
Earlier sketch in CA 113
Riemer, George 1920-1973 ... CAP-2
Obituary ... 41-44R
Earlier sketch in CA 25-28
Riemer, Johannes 1648-1714 ... DLB 168
Riemer, Neal 1922- ... 21-24R
Rienits, Rex 1909-1971 ... CAP-1
Obituary ... 29-32R
Earlier sketch in CA 13-14
Rienow, Leona Train 1903(?)-1983 ... 111
Rienow, Robert 1909-1989 ... CANR-36
Earlier sketch in CA 21-24R
Rienstra, Ellen Walker 1940- ... CANR-49
Earlier sketch in CA 123
Riepe, Dale (Maurice) 1918- ... 37-40R
Ries, Al 1926- ... CANR-45
Earlier sketch in CA 120
Ries, Estelle H. 1896- ... 25-28R
Ries, John C(harles) 1930- ... 13-16R
Ries, Lawrence R(obert) 1940- ... 65-68
Riese, Walther 1890- ... 49-52
Rieseberg, Harry E(arl) 1892- ... 5-8R
Rieselbach, Leroy N(ewman) 1934- ... CANR-24
Earlier sketches in CA 21-24R, CANR-9
Riesenberg, Felix, Jr. 1913-1962 ... 101
See also SATA 23
Riesenberg, Peter 1925- ... 145
Riesenberg, Saul H(erbert) 1911- ... 49-52
Rieser, Dolf 1898-1983 Obituary ... 109
Riesman, David 1909- ... CANR-34
Earlier sketch in CA 5-8R
Riesman, Evelyn Thompson 1912- ... 21-24R
Riesner, Rainer 1950- ... 148
Riess, Claudia 1937- ... 110
Riess, Oswald George Lorenz 1896- ... 5-8R
Riess, Steven A(llan) 1947- ... 112
Riess, Walter 1925- ... 17-20R
Riessen, Martin Clare 1941- ... 41-44R
Riessman, Frank 1924- ... CANR-6
Earlier sketch in CA 1-4R
Riesterer, Berthold P(hillip) 1935- ... 41-44R
Rieth, Marian
See Amft, M(arian) J(anet)
Rietz, Sandra A. 1943- ... 123
Rieu, E(mile) V(ictor) 1887-1972 ... CANR-15
Obituary ... 103
Earlier sketch in CA 1-4R
See also SATA 46
See also SATA-Obit 26
Riewald, J(acobus) G(erhardus) 1910- ... CANR-44
Earlier sketches in CA 57-60, CANR-6, 21
Rifaat, Alifa
See Rifaat, Fatma Abdalla
Rifaat, Fatma Abdalla 1930- ... CANR-50
Earlier sketch in CA 123
Rifbjerg, Klaus (Thorvald) 1931- ... 137
Brief entry ... 124
Rife, J(ohn) Merle 1895- ... 61-64
Rife, Joanne 1932- ... 110
Rife, Rosemary
See Nusbaum, Rosemary
Riffaterre, Michael 1924- ... DLB 67
Riffe, Ernest
See Bergman, (Ernst) Ingmar
Riffel, Herman H(arold) 1916- ... 112
Rifkin, Adam 1972(?)- ... 157
Rifkin, Jeremy 1945- ... CANR-50
Brief entry ... 121
Earlier sketch in CA 129
Interview in ... 129
Rifkin, Paul 1942- ... 127
Rifkin, Shepard 1918- ... CANR-64
Earlier sketches in CA 1-4R, CANR-1
Rifkind, Carole 1935- ... 85-88
Rifkind, Simon H(irsch) 1901-1995 ... 109
Obituary ... 150
Rift, Valerie
See Bartlett, Marie (Swan)
Riga, Frank P(eter) 1936- ... 89-92
Riga, Peter J(ohn) 1933- ... CANR-37
Earlier sketch in CA 5-8R
Rigault, Andre 1922- ... 45-48
Rigbey, Liz 1960(?)- ... 156
Rigby, Andrew 1944- ... 61-64
Rigby, Ida Katherine 1944- ... CANR-10
Earlier sketch in CA 65-68
Rigby, Paul H(erbert) 1924- ... 17-20R
Rigby, T(homas) H(enry Richard) 1925- ... CANR-36
Earlier sketches in CA 17-20R, CANR-10
Rigden, John S. 1934- ... 127
Rigdon, Raymond M. 1919- ... 29-32R
Rigdon, Walter 1930- ... 13-16R
Rigelhof, T(errance) F(rederick) 1944- ... 112
Rigg, A(rthur) G(eorge) 1937- ... 37-40R
Rigg, H(enry Hemmingway) K(ilburn) 1911-1980 ... 29-32R
Obituary ... 93-96
Rigg, John Linton 1894- ... 5-8R
Rigg, Robinson P(eter) 1918- ... 33-36R
Rigg, Sharon
See Creech, Sharon
Riggan, (John) Rob(inson) 1943- ... 115
Riggan, William (Edward, Jr.) 1946- ... 103
Riggio, Anita 1952- ... SATA 73
Riggio, Thomas P(asquale) 1943- ... 109
Riggs, David (Ramsey) 1941- ... 133
Riggs, Dionis Coffin 1898- ... CAP-2
Earlier sketch in CA 29-32
Riggs, Fred(erick) W(arren) 1917- ... CANR-16
Earlier sketch in CA 25-28R
Riggs, James (Lear) 1929- ... 33-36R
Riggs, John R(aymond) 1945- ... CANR-37
Earlier sketch in CA 115
Riggs, (Rolla) Lynn 1899-1954 ... 144
See also DAM MULT
See also DLB 175
See also NNAL
See also TCLC 56
Riggs, Paula Detmer 1944- ... 162
Riggs, Robert E. 1927- ... CANR-8
Earlier sketch in CA 13-16R
Riggs, Sidney Noyes 1892-1975 ... 1-4R
Obituary ... 103
See also SATA-Obit 28
Riggs, Webster, Jr. 1934- ... 168
Riggs, William (George) 1938- ... 61-64
Righter, Anne
See Barton, Anne
Righter, Carroll (Burch) 1900-1988 ... 93-96
Obituary ... 125
Righter, James H(aslam) 1916-1984 Obituary ... 113
Righter, Robert Willms 1933- ... 108
Right Honourable Lord Denning
See Denning, Alfred Thompson
Rightmire, G. Philip 1942- ... 135
Rigney, James Oliver, Jr. 1948- ... CANR-62
Earlier sketch in CA 140
See also Jordan, Robert
See also SATA 95
Rigoni, Orlando (Joseph) 1897- ... CANR-11
Earlier sketch in CA 13-16R
Rigsby, Howard 1909-1975 ... CANR-70
Earlier sketch in CA 9-12R
Rigutti, Mario 1926- ... 131
Riha, Thomas 1929- ... 9-12R
Riis, Jacob A(ugust) 1849-1914 ... 168
Brief entry ... 113
See also DLB 23
See also TCLC 80
Riis, Sharon 1947- ... 136
Rijkens, Rein 1913- ... 143
Riker, John H. 1943- ... 111
Riker, Leigh 1941- ... CANR-45
Earlier sketch in CA 119
Riker, Tom L. 1936- ... 104
Riker, William H(arrison) 1920-1993 ... CANR-24
Obituary ... 141
Earlier sketch in CA 1-4R
Rikhoff, James C. 1931- ... 13-16R
Rikhoff, Jean 1928- ... 61-64
See also SATA 9
Rikhye, Indar Jit 1920- ... CANR-17
Earlier sketch in CA 93-96
Rikki
See Ducornet, Erica
Rikon, Irving 1931- ... 29-32R
Riley, Barry 1942- ... 136
Riley, Carroll L(averne) 1923- ... CANR-70
Earlier sketches in CA 25-28R, CANR-10
Riley, Charles A. II 1958- ... 150
Riley, Clara (Mae Deatherage) 1931- ... 25-28R
Riley, Dan 1946- ... 135
Riley, Dawn 1964- ... 150
Riley, Dick 1946- ... 101
Riley, E(dward) C(alverley) 1923- ... 9-12R
Riley, G. Micheal 1934- ... 45-48
Riley, Georgia
See Cooper, Carolyn (Joy)
Riley, Glenda 1938- ... CANR-46
Earlier sketches in CA 106, CANR-23
Riley, James 1777-1840 ... DLB 183
Riley, James A. 1939- ... 149
See also SATA 97
Riley, James C. 1943- ... 133
Riley, James F(rederic) 1912-1985 ... 29-32R
Obituary ... 134
Riley, James Whitcomb 1849-1916 ... 137
Brief entry ... 118
See also DAM POET
See also MAICYA
See also SATA 17
See also TCLC 51
Riley, Jeannie C(arolyn Stephenson) 1945- ... 129
Riley, Joan 1958- ... 143
Riley, Jocelyn (Carol) 1949- ... CANR-39
Earlier sketch in CA 115
See also SATA 60
See also SATA-Brief 50
Riley, John 1937-1978 ... DLB 40
Riley, Judith (Astria) Merkle 1942- ... CANR-35
Earlier sketch in CA 105
See also Merkle, Judith A(stria)
Riley, Lawrence 1897(?)-1975 Obituary ... 61-64
Riley, Lee
See Vare, Ethlie Ann
Riley, Linda Capus 1950- ... SATA 85
Riley, Madeleine 1933- ... 25-28R
Riley, Martin 1948- ... 149
See also SATA 81
Riley, Matilda White 1911- ... 132
Brief entry ... 114
Riley, Miles O'Brien 1937- ... CANR-21
Earlier sketch in CA 104
Riley, (Thomas) Nord 1914- ... 13-16R
Riley, Pat(rick James) 1945- ... 147
Riley, R. David 1944(?)-1983 Obituary ... 111
Riley, (Hugh) Ridge(ly, Jr.) 1907-1976 ... 101
Riley, Roy, Jr. 1943(?)-1977 Obituary ... 73-76
Riley, Sam G. 1939- ... 136
Riley, Sandra 1938- ... 104
Riley, Tex
See Creasey, John
Riley, Thomas J. 1901(?)-1977 Obituary ... 73-76
Riley, Tim 1960- ... 129
Riley-Smith, Jonathan (Simon Christopher) 1938- ... 21-24R
Riling, Raymond L. J. 1896(?)-1974 Obituary ... 53-56
Rilke, Rainer Maria 1875-1926 ... CANR-62
Brief entry ... 104
Earlier sketch in CA 132
See also DAM POET
See also DLB 81
See also MTCW 1
See also PC 2
See also TCLC 1, 6, 19
Rilla, Wolf 1925- ... 49-52
Rils
See Bohr, R(ussell) L(eRoi)
Rima, I(ngrid) H(ahne) 1925- ... 21-24R
Rimanelli, Giose 1925- ... DLB 177
Rimanoczy, Richard Stanton 1902- ... 73-76
Rimbaud, (Jean Nicolas) Arthur 1854-1891 ... DA
See also DAB
See also DAC
See also DAM MST, POET
See also PC 3
See also WLC
Rimberg, John 1929- ... 57-60
Rimel, Duane (Weldon) 1915- ... 29-32R
Rimer, Barbara K. 1949- ... 136
Rimer, J. Thomas ... 130
Rimington, Critchell 1907-1976 Obituary ... 61-64
Rimland, Bernard 1928- ... CANR-6
Earlier sketch in CA 13-16R
Rimland, Ingrid 1936- ... 61-64
Rimler, Walter 1946- ... 139
Rimlinger, Gaston V. 1926- ... 37-40R
Rimmer, C(harles) Brandon 1918- ... CANR-12
Earlier sketch in CA 61-64
Rimmer, Douglas 1927- ... 111
Rimmer, Robert H(enry) 1917- ... CANR-20
Earlier sketches in CA 9-12R, CANR-4
See also CAAS 10
Rimmer, W. J.
See Rowland, D(onald) S(ydney)
Rimmington, Gerald T(horneycroft) 1930- ... 17-20R
Rinaldi, Ann 1934- ... 111
See also AAYA 15
See also CLR 46
See also JRDA
See also SATA 51, 78
See also SATA-Brief 50
Rinaldi, Nicholas M. 1934- ... CANR-22
Earlier sketch in CA 104
Rinaldini, Angiolo
See Battisti, Eugenio
Rinard, Judith E(llen) 1947- ... 97-100
See also SATA 44
Rinchen, Byambyn 1905(?)-1977 Obituary ... 69-72
Rinder, Lenore 1949- ... 156
See also SATA 92
Rinder, Walter (Murray) 1934- ... CANR-11
Earlier sketch in CA 69-72
Rinderle, Walter 1940- ... 140
Rindfleisch, Norval (William) 1930- ... 65-68
Rindo, Ron(ald J.) 1959- ... 155
Rinehart, Frederick Roberts 1903(?)-1981 Obituary ... 104
Rinehart, Mary Roberts 1876-1958 ... 166
Brief entry ... 108
See also TCLC 52
Rinehart, Stanley Marshall, Jr. 1897-1969 Obituary ... 29-32R
Ring, Alfred A. 1905- ... 29-32R
Ring, Daniel F(rank) 1945- ... 113
Ring, Douglas
See Prather, Richard S(cott)
Ring, Elizabeth 1912- ... 103
Ring, Elizabeth 1920- ... SATA 79
Ring, Jennifer 1948- ... 140
Ring, Malvin E. 1919- ... 120
Ring, Nancy G. 1956- ... 157
Ring, Raymond H. 1949- ... 128
Ringdalh, Mark
See Longyear, Barry Brookes
Ringe, Donald A(rthur) 1923- ... 1-4R
Ringenbach, Paul T(homas) 1936- ... CANR-25
Earlier sketch in CA 45-48
Ringer, Alexander L(othar) 1921- ... CANR-49
Earlier sketches in CA 45-48, CANR-24
Ringer, Barbara Alice 1925- ... 9-12R
Ringer, Fritz (Franz) K(laus) 1934- ... 73-76
Ringer, R. Jeffrey 1957- ... 147
Ringer, Robert J. ... 81-84
Ringgold, Faith 1930- ... 154
See also AAYA 19
See also CLR 30
See also SATA 71
Ringgold, Gene 1918- ... 25-28R
Ringgren, (Karl Vilhelm) Helmer 1917- ... CANR-3
Earlier sketch in CA 5-8R
Ringi, Kjell (Arne Soerensen) 1939- ... CANR-1
Earlier sketch in CA 45-48
See also SATA 12
Ringkamp, Jonathan 1929-1986 ... 153
Obituary ... 120
Ringler, William A(ndrew), Jr. 1912-1987(?) ... 5-8R
Obituary ... 121
Ringmaster, The
See Mencken, H(enry) L(ouis)
Ringo, Johnny
See Keevill, Henry J(ohn)
Ringold, Clay
See Hogan, (Robert) Ray
Ringold, May Spencer 1914- ... 21-24R
Ringquist, Evan J. 1962- ... 146
Ringrose, David R. 1938- ... 53-56
Ringuet
See Panneton, Philippe
See also DLB 68
Ringwald, Donald C(harles) 1917-1987 ... CANR-36
Obituary ... 122
Earlier sketch in CA 21-24R
Ringwood, Gwen(dolyn Margaret) Pharis 1910-1984 ... 148
Obituary ... 112
See also CLC 48
See also DLB 88
Rinhart, Floyd (Lincoln) 1915- ... CANR-10
Earlier sketch in CA 25-28R
Rinhart, Marion (Hutchinson) 1916- ... CANR-10
Earlier sketch in CA 25-28R
Rink, Oliver A(lbert) 1947- ... 125
Rinker, Rosalind Beatrice 1906- ... CANR-5
Earlier sketch in CA 5-8R
Rinkoff, Barbara Jean (Rich) 1923-1975 ... CAP-2
Obituary ... 57-60
Earlier sketch in CA 19-20
See also SATA 4
See also SATA-Obit 27
Rinpoche
See Chogyam Trungpa
Rinser, Luise 1911- ... DLB 69
Rintels, David 1939- ... 73-76
Rinvolucri, Mario (Francesco Giuseppe) 1940- ... CANR-53
Earlier sketches in CA 21-24R, CANR-10, 26
Rinvolucri, Mina Josephine Moore
See Moore-Rinvolucri, Mina Josephine
Rinzema, Jakob 1931- ... 102
Rinzler, Alan 1938- ... CANR-12
Earlier sketch in CA 21-24R
Rinzler, Carol Ann 1937- ... 135
Rinzler, Carol Eisen (Gene) 1941-1990 ... 49-52
Obituary ... 133
Rio, Michel 19(?)- ... CLC 43
Riols, Noreen 1926- ... 124
Riopelle, Arthur J. 1920- ... 37-40R
Riordan, J. W.
See Feist, Gene
Riordan, James 1936- ... CANR-69
Earlier sketches in CA 69-72, CANR-11
See also SATA 95
Riordan, James 1949- ... 111
Riordan, Mary Marguerite 1931- ... 106
Riordan, Michael 1946- ... CANR-37
Earlier sketch in CA 106
Riordon, Michael 1944- ... 133
Rios, Alberto (Alvaro) 1952- ... CANR-34
Earlier sketch in CA 113
See also DLB 122
Rios, Francisco Giner de los
See Giner de los Rios, Francisco
Rios, Isabella
See Lopez, Diana
Rios, Julian 1941- ... 154
Rios, Tere
See Versace, Marie Teresa Rios
Riotte, Louise 1909- ... 57-60
Riotto, Guy Michael 1943- ... 73-76
Riou, Roger 1909- ... 61-64
Ripa, Karol 1895-1983 Obituary ... 109
Ripken, Cal(vin Edward), Jr. 1960- ... 160
Ripley, Alexandra 1934- ... CANR-58
Earlier sketches in CA 119, CANR-38
See also DAM POP
Ripley, Arthur 1895-1961 ... DLB 44
Ripley, Catherine 1957- ... 149
See also SATA 82
Ripley, (Sidney) Dillon 1913- ... 57-60
Ripley, Elizabeth Blake 1906-1969 ... CANR-3
Earlier sketch in CA 1-4R
See also SATA 5
Ripley, Francis Joseph 1912- ... CANR-39
Earlier sketches in CA 1-4R, CANR-3, 18
Ripley, George 1802-1880 ... DLB 1, 64, 73
Ripley, Jack
See Wainwright, John
Ripley, Michael David 1952- ... CANR-70
Earlier sketch in CA 130
Ripley, Mike
See Ripley, Michael David
Ripley, Randall B(utler) 1938- ... CANR-41
Earlier sketches in CA 53-56, CANR-5, 19
Ripley, Sheldon N(ichols) 1925- ... 5-8R
Ripley, Stephens 1901(?)-1984 Obituary ... 111
Ripley, Theresa M(argaret) 1944- ... 85-88
Ripley, (William Young) Warren 1921- ... CANR-33
Earlier sketches in CA 33-36R, CANR-15
Rippa, S(ol) Alexander 1925- ... 53-56
Ripper, Charles L(ewis) 1929- ... CANR-1
Earlier sketch in CA 1-4R
See also SATA 3
Ripper, Chuck
See Ripper, Charles L(ewis)
Ripperger, Helmut Lothar 1897-1974 Obituary ... 53-56
Ripperger, Henrietta
See Hawley, Henrietta Ripperger
Rippey, Mari 1939- ... 112
Rippey, Robert (Max) 1926- ... 45-48
Ripple, Paula ... 112
Ripple, Richard E. 1931- ... CANR-22
Earlier sketch in CA 33-36R
Rippley, La Vern J. 1935- ... 33-36R
Rippon, Angela 1944- ... 126

Rippon, Marion E(dith) 1921- ... CANR-1
Earlier sketch in CA 49-52
Rippy, Frances (Marguerite) Mayhew 1929- .. 89-92
Rips, Ervine M(ilton) 1921- ... 101
Rips, Geoffrey 1950- ... 108
Rips, Rae Elizabeth 1914-1970 Obituary ... 104
Riq
See Atwater, Richard (Tupper)
Riquelme, John Paul 1946- ... 119
Risatti, Howard A(nthony) 1943- ... 49-52
Rischin, Moses 1925- ... CANR-3
Earlier sketch in CA 9-12R
Rise, Eric W. 1963- ... 151
Risebero, Bill 1938- ... 130
Riseley, Jerry B(urr, Jr.) 1920- ... CANR-13
Earlier sketch in CA 21-24R
Riseling, John J. W. 1888(?)-1977 Obituary .. 73-76
Risenhoover, Morris 1940- ... 65-68
Riser, Wayne H. 1909- ... CAP-1
Earlier sketch in CA 13-14
Rishell, Lyle 1927- ... 144
Risjord, Norman K(urt) 1931- ... CANR-47
Earlier sketches in CA 17-20R, CANR-7, 22
Riskin, Mary (Winifred) Walters 1949- ... 163
Riskin, Robert 1897-1955 ... DLB 26
Riskind, Mary 1944- ... CANR-26
Earlier sketch in CA 108
See also SATA 60
Risley, Albert G. 1915- ... 168
Riss, Richard 1952- ... 81-84
Risse, Heinz 1898- ... DLB 69
Rissi, Mathias 1920- ... 45-48
Rissinger, Matt 1956- ... 159
See also SATA 93
Rissman, Art
See Sussman, Susan
Rissman, Susan
See Sussman, Susan
Rissover, Fredric 1940- ... 33-36R
Rist, Johann 1607-1667 ... DLB 164
Rist, John M(ichael) 1936- ... CANR-18
Earlier sketch in CA 101
Rist, Ray C(harles) 1944- ... CANR-3
Earlier sketch in CA 49-52
Ristaino, Marcia R. 1939- ... 127
Rist Arnold, Elisabeth 1950- ... 65-68
Riste, Olav 1933- ... CANR-12
Earlier sketch in CA 29-32R
Ristic, Dragisha N. 1909- ... CAP-2
Earlier sketch in CA 21-22
Ristow, Walter W(illiam) 1908- ... 17-20R
Rit, Jean Qui
See Arkell, David
Ritcheson, Charles R(ay) 1925- Brief entry ... 112
Ritchey, John A(rthur) 1919- ... 21-24R
Ritchie, (John) Andrew 1943- ... 85-88
Ritchie, Andrew Carnduff
1907-1978 Obituary ... 81-84
Ritchie, Anna Cora (Ogden) Mowatt
1819-1870 ... DLB 3
Ritchie, Anne Thackeray 1837-1919 ... DLB 18
Ritchie, Barbara Gibbons ... 73-76
See also SATA 14
Ritchie, Bill
See Edgar, Frank Terrell Rhoades
Ritchie, C(icero) T(heodore) 1914- ... 9-12R
Ritchie, Daniel E. 1955- ... 162
Ritchie, Dennis (MacAlistair) 1941- ... 158
Ritchie, Donald A(rthur) 1945- ... CANR-48
Brief entry ... 106
Earlier sketch in CA 122
Ritchie, Donald D(irk) 1914- ... 112
Ritchie, Edwin 1921- ... CANR-35
Earlier sketch in CA 29-32R
Ritchie, Elisavietta (Yurievna Artamonoff) ... CANR-2
Earlier sketch in CA 49-52
Ritchie, G(eorge) Stephen 1914- ... 13-16R
Ritchie, Harry 1958- ... 143
Ritchie, Jack
See Reitci, John G(eorge)
Ritchie, James A. 1953- ... 151
Ritchie, James McPherson 1927- ... 25-28R
Ritchie, James T. R. 1908- ... CAP-2
Earlier sketch in CA 19-20
Ritchie, John C(ollins) 1927- ... 49-52
Ritchie, M(iller) A(lfred) F(ranklin) 1909- ... CAP-2
Earlier sketch in CA 29-32
Ritchie, Paul 1923- ... 21-24R
Ritchie, Rita
See Reitci, Rita Krohne
Ritchie, Ruth 1900- ... CANR-2
Earlier sketch in CA 1-4R
Ritchie, Simon
See Fodden, Simon R.
Ritchie, Thomas 1778-1854 ... DLB 43
Ritchie, (Harry) Ward 1905-1996 ... CANR-46
Obituary ... 151
Earlier sketches in CA 57-60, CANR-7, 22
Ritchie, William A(ugustus) 1903- ... CANR-24
Earlier sketch in CA 45-48
Ritchie-Calder, Peter Ritchie 1906-1982 . CANR-72
Obituary ... 105
Earlier sketches in CA 1-4R, CANR-4
Ritner, Peter Vaughn 1927(?)-1976 ... 77-80
Obituary ... 69-72
Ritschl, Dietrich 1929- ... CANR-24
Earlier sketches in CA 21-24R, CANR-9
Ritsos, Giannes
See Ritsos, Yannis
Ritsos, Yannis 1909-1990 ... CANR-61
Obituary ... 133
Earlier sketches in CA 77-80, CANR-39
See also CLC 6, 13, 31
See also MTCW 1
Rittenhouse, Mignon 1904- ... 41-44R
Ritter, Alan 1937- ... 117
Brief entry ... 113
Ritter, Ed 1917- ... 17-20R
Ritter, Erika 1948(?)- ... CLC 52
Ritter, Felix
See Kruess, James
Ritter, Gerhard 1888-1967 Obituary ... 111
Ritter, Henry, Jr. 1920- ... 93-96
Ritter, Jess(e P., Jr.) 1930- ... 37-40R
Ritter, Lawrence S(tanley) 1922- ... CANR-22
Earlier sketch in CA 21-24R
See also SATA 58
Ritter, Naomi 1937- ... 138
Ritterbush, Philip C. 1936- ... CANR-6
Earlier sketch in CA 9-12R
Ritthaler, Shelly 1955- ... 155
See also SATA 91
Ritts, Paul 1920(?)-1980 Obituary ... 102
See also SATA-Obit 25
Ritvala, M.
See Waltari, Mika (Toimi)
Ritvo, Harriet 1946- ... 124
Ritz, Charles 1891-1976 Obituary ... 65-68
Ritz, David 1943- ... CANR-40
Earlier sketch in CA 85-88
Ritz, Jean-Georges 1906- ... 5-8R
Ritz, Joseph P. 1929- ... 21-24R
Ritz, Karen 1957- ... SATA 80
Ritzenthaler, Pat 1914- ... 25-28R
Ritzer, George 1940- ... CANR-20
Earlier sketches in CA 53-56, CANR-5
Riva, Maria 1925(?)- ... 144
Rivard, Adjutor 1868-1945 ... DLB 92
Rivard, David 1953- ... 159
Rivas, Gilberto Lopez y
See Lopez Y Rivas, Gilberto
Rive, Richard (Moore) 1931-1989 ... CANR-27
Obituary ... 128
Earlier sketch in CA 13-16R
See also BW 2
See also DLB 125
Rivel, Isade
See Cuevas, Clara
Rivele, Stephen J. 1949- ... 142
Rivenburgh, Viola K(leinke) 1897- ... 17-20R
Rivera, Feliciano (Moreno) 1932- ... CANR-24
Earlier sketch in CA 45-48
Rivera, Geraldo (Miguel) 1943- ... CANR-32
Earlier sketch in CA 108
See also HW
See also SATA 54
See also SATA-Brief 28
Rivera, Jose Eustasio 1889-1928 ... 162
See also HW
See also TCLC 35
Rivera, Marina 1942- ... DLB 122
Rivera, Tomas 1935-1984 ... CANR-32
Earlier sketch in CA 49-52
See also DLB 82
See also HW
Rivere, Alec
See Nuetzel, Charles (Alexander)
Rivero, Eliana Suarez 1942- ... 41-44R
Rivers, Caryl 1937- ... CANR-22
Earlier sketches in CA 49-52, CANR-4
Rivers, Clarence Joseph 1931- ... 77-80
Rivers, Conrad Kent 1933-1968 ... 85-88
See also BW 1
See also CLC 1
See also DLB 41
Rivers, Elfrida
See Bradley, Marion Zimmer
Rivers, Elias L(ynch) 1924- ... 17-20R
Rivers, Francine (Sandra) 1947- ... CANR-58
Earlier sketch in CA 130
Rivers, Joan
See Molinsky, Joan Sandra
Rivers, Julian Alfred Pitt
See Pitt-Rivers, Julian Alfred
Rivers, Larry 1923- ... 124
Brief entry ... 117
Rivers, Patrick 1920- ... 131
Rivers, William L. 1925- ... CANR-7
Earlier sketch in CA 17-20R
Rivers-Coffey, Rachel 1943- ... 73-76
Riverside, John
See Heinlein, Robert A(nson)
Rives, Leigh
See Seward, William W(ard), Jr.
Rives, Stanley G(ene) 1930- ... CANR-11
Earlier sketch in CA 21-24R
Rives, William T. 1911(?)-1983 Obituary ... 111
Rivet, A(lbert) L(ionel) F(rederick) 1915-1993 ...
CANR-24
Obituary ... 142
Earlier sketches in CA 21-24R, CANR-9
Rivett, Carol
See Rivett, Edith Caroline
Rivett, Edith Caroline 1894-1958 Brief entry ... 110
Rivett, Rohan (Deakin) 1917-1977 ... 25-28R
Obituary ... 135
Rivett-Carnac, Charles Edward 1901- ... CAP-2
Earlier sketch in CA 19-20
Rivette, Marc 1916- ... 5-8R
Riviere, Bill
See Riviere, William Alexander
Riviere, Claude 1932- ... 102
Riviere, Peter Gerard 1934- ... 103
Riviere, William Alexander 1916- ... CANR-8
Earlier sketch in CA 5-8R
Rivington, James 1724(?)-1802 ... DLB 43
Rivkin, Allen (Erwin) 1903-1990 ... CANR-28
Obituary ... 130
Earlier sketches in CA 65-68, CANR-11
See also DLB 26
Rivkin, Ann 1920- ... 112
See also SATA 41
Rivkin, Arnold 1919-1968 ... CANR-3
Earlier sketch in CA 1-4R
Rivkin, Ellis 1918- ... 33-36R
Rivlin, Alice M(itchell) 1931- ... 33-36R
Rivlin, Gary 1958- ... 139
Rivlin, Harry N. 1904- ... 17-20R
Rivlin, Paul Anthony 1952- ... 144
Rivoire, Jean 1929- ... CANR-21
Earlier sketches in CA 9-12R, CANR-5
Rivoli, Mario 1943- ... SATA 10
Rix, Donna
See Rowland, D(onald) S(ydney)
Rizkalla, John 1935- ... 129
Rizzo, Betty 1926- ... 111
Rizzo, Mario 1948- ... 124
Rizzoli, Andrea 1914-1983 Obituary ... 109
Rizzoli, Angelo 1889-1970 Obituary ... 104
Rizzuto, Anthony 1937- ... 106
Rizzuto, James J(oseph) 1939- ... 107
Rizzuto, Jim
See Rizzuto, James J(oseph)
Roa (y Garcia), Raul 1908-1982 Obituary ... 107
Roa Bastos, Augusto (Antonio) 1917- ... 131
See also CLC 45
See also DAM MULT
See also DLB 113
See also HLC
See also HW
Roach, Helen P(auline) 1903- ... CAP-1
Earlier sketch in CA 11-12
Roach, Hildred 1937- ... 57-60
Roach, Jack L. 1925- Brief entry ... 109
Roach, James P. 1907-1978 Obituary ... 77-80
Roach, Joyce Gibson 1935- ... CANR-40
Earlier sketches in CA 101, CANR-18
Roach, Marilynne K(athleen) 1946- ... CANR-12
Earlier sketch in CA 57-60
See also SATA 9
Roach, Marion 1956- ... 120
Roach, Mary Ellen 1921- ... 17-20R
Roach, Portia
See Takakjian, Portia
Roadarmel, Gordon 1932-1972 Obituary ... 104
Roadarmel, Paul 1942- ... 93-96
Roaden, Arliss L. 1930- ... 37-40R
Roadstrum, William H(enry) 1915- ... 25-28R
Roalfe, William R(obert) 1896- ... 93-96
Roam, Pearl (Sovern) 1920- ... 1-4R
Roark, Albert E(dward) 1933- ... 85-88
Roark, Dallas M(organ) 1931- ... 37-40R
Roark, Garland 1904-1985 ... CANR-63
Obituary ... 115
Earlier sketches in CA 1-4R, CANR-1
Roark, James L. 1941- ... CANR-19
Earlier sketch in CA 85-88
Roarke, Mike
See Kosser, Mike
Roazen, Paul 1936- ... 25-28R
Roback, A(braham) A(aron) 1890-1965 ... 5-8R
Robacker, Earl Francis 1904- ... CANR-37
Earlier sketch in CA 53-56
Robana, Abderrahman 1938- ... 65-68
Robard, Jackson
See Wallmann, Jeffrey M(iner)
Robards, Karen 1954- ... CANR-42
Earlier sketch in CA 122
Robards, Sherman M(arshall) 1939- ... CANR-37
Earlier sketch in CA 61-64
Robards, Terry
See Robards, Sherman M(arshall)
Robathan, Dorothy M(ae) 1898- ... 41-44R
Robb, Brian 1913-1979 ... 113
Robb, David M(etheny) 1903-1990 Obituary ... 131
Brief entry ... 113
See also AITN 1
Robb, (George) Douglas 1899-1974 Obituary .. 114
Robb, Frank Thomson 1908- ... 57-60
Robb, Graham 1958- ... 136
Robb, Inez (Callaway) 1901(?)-1979 ... 97-100
Obituary ... 85-88
Robb, J(ohn) Wesley 1919- ... 5-8R
Robb, James H(arding) 1920- ... 9-12R
Robb, James Willis 1918- ... 41-44R
Robb, Kenneth
See Phipps, Joe (Kenneth)
Robb, Laura 1937- ... 160
See also SATA 95
Robb, Mary K(unkle) 1908- ... CAP-2
Earlier sketch in CA 19-20
Robb, Nesca A(deline) 1905- ... 9-12R
Robbe-Grillet, Alain 1922- ... CANR-65
Earlier sketches in CA 9-12R, CANR-33
See also CLC 1, 2, 4, 6, 8, 10, 14, 43
See also DLB 83
See also MTCW 1
Robben, John 1930- ... 93-96
Robbert, Louise Buenger 1925- ... 41-44R
Robbin, (Jodi) Luna 1936- ... 103
Robbin, Tony 1943- ... 142
Robbins, Anthony J. 1960- ... 126
Robbins, Brother Gerald 1940- ... 13-16R
Robbins, Caroline 1903- ... 107
Robbins, Ceila Dame 1943- ... 118
Robbins, Daniel 1933-1995 ... CANR-3
Obituary ... 147
Earlier sketch in CA 45-48
Robbins, Frank 1917- ... 109
See also SATA 42
See also SATA-Brief 32
Robbins, Glaydon Donaldson 1908- ... 5-8R
Robbins, Harold 1916-1997 ... CANR-54
Obituary ... 162
Earlier sketches in CA 73-76, CANR-26
See also CLC 5
See also DAM NOV
See also MTCW 1
Robbins, Henry 1928(?)-1979 Obituary ... 89-92
Robbins, Horace 1909-1982 Obituary ... 107
Robbins, Ira A(braham) 1954- ... 123
Robbins, J(ohn) Albert 1914- ... 17-20R
Robbins, Jane (Borsch) 1939- ... CANR-38
Robbins, Jane Marla 1943- ... 134
Robbins, June ... 61-64
Robbins, Kay
See Hooper, Kay
Robbins, Keith (Gilbert) 1940- ... CANR-28
Earlier sketches in CA 25-28R, CANR-11
Robbins, Ken ... SATA 94
See also SATA-Brief 53
Robbins, Kenneth 1944- ... 128
Robbins, Lawrence H. 1938- ... 140
Robbins, Lionel (Charles) 1898-1984 Obituary . 112
Robbins, Martin 1931- ... CANR-12
Earlier sketch in CA 29-32R
Robbins, Marty
See Robinson, Martin David
Robbins, Matthew ... 129
Brief entry ... 110
Robbins, Mildred Brown ... CAP-2
Earlier sketch in CA 33-36
Robbins, Millie
See Robbins, Mildred Brown
Robbins, Paul R(ichard) 1930- ... CANR-35
Earlier sketch in CA 114
Robbins, Raleigh
See Hamilton, Charles (Harold St. John)
Robbins, Richard (H.) 1922- ... 163
Robbins, Richard G., Jr. 1939- ... 53-56
Robbins, Rossell Hope 1912-1990 ... CANR-2
Obituary ... 131
Earlier sketch in CA 45-48
Robbins, Roy M(arvin) 1904-1981 ... CANR-36
Earlier sketch in CA 65-68
Robbins, Ruth 1917(?)- ... 73-76
See also SATA 14
Robbins, S(allie) A(nn) 1940- ... 21-24R
Robbins, Sam
See Potter, Carole A.
Robbins, Thomas Eugene 1936- ... CANR-59
Earlier sketches in CA 81-84, CANR-29
See also Robbins, Tom
See also DAM NOV, POP
See also MTCW 1
Robbins, Tom
See Robbins, Thomas Eugene
See also BEST 90:3
See also CLC 9, 32, 64
See also DLBY 80
Robbins, Tony
See Pashko, Stanley
Robbins, Trina 1938- ... 128
See also CLC 21
Robbins, Vesta O(rdelia) 1891- ... 53-56
Robbins, Wayne
See Cox, William R(obert)
Robbins-Carter, Jane
See Robbins, Jane (Borsch)
Robe, Stanley L(inn) 1915- ... CANR-6
Earlier sketch in CA 5-8R
Robeck, Mildred C(oen) 1915- ... 57-60
Robel, S. L.
See Fraustino, Lisa Rowe
Roberge, Earl 1918- ... 85-88
Roberson, (Charles) Ed(win) 1939- ... 77-80
Roberson, Jennifer 1953- ... CANR-41
Earlier sketch in CA 117
See also SATA 72
Roberson, John R(oyster) 1930- ... 129
See also SATA 53
Roberson, Marie
See Hamm, Marie Roberson
Roberson, Ricky James 1956- ... 101
Roberson, William H(oward) 1952- ... 110
Robert, Adrian
See St. John, Nicole
Robert, Dana L. 1956- ... 168
Robert, Marc 1927- ... 114
Robert, Marika Barna ... 9-12R
Robert, Paul 1911(?)-1980 Obituary ... 101
Robert, Paul A.
See Roubiczek, Paul (Anton)
Robertiello, Richard C. 1923- ... CANR-3
Earlier sketch in CA 9-12R
Roberto, Brother
See Mueller, Gerald F(rancis)
Roberts, (Edward) Adam 1940- ... CANR-9
Earlier sketch in CA 21-24R
Roberts, Allen 1914- ... 29-32R
Roberts, Andrew 1963- ... 135
Roberts, Anthony
See Watney, John B(asil)
Roberts, Archibald Edward 1915- ... CANR-6
Earlier sketch in CA 57-60
Roberts, Arthur O. 1923- ... 25-28R
Roberts, Arthur Sydney 1905(?)-1978 ... 85-88
Obituary ... 81-84
Roberts, Barrie 1939- ... 151
Roberts, Ben
See Eisenberg, Benjamin
Roberts, Benjamin Charles 1917- ... 102
Roberts, Bill 1914(?)-1978 Obituary ... 81-84
Roberts, Bleddyn J(ones) 1906- ... CAP-1
Earlier sketch in CA 13-14
Roberts, Brian 1930- ... CANR-12
Earlier sketch in CA 29-32R

Roberts, Bruce (Stuart) 1930- ... CANR-6
Earlier sketch in CA 9-12R
See also SATA 47
See also SATA-Brief 39
Roberts, C(atherine) 1917- ... 21-24R
Roberts, Carey 1935- ... 106
Roberts, Carlos A.
See Avila, Charles
Roberts, Carol A. 1933- ... 37-40R
Roberts, Cecil (Edric Mornington) 1892-1976 ... CAP-2
Obituary ... 69-72
Earlier sketch in CA 29-32
Roberts, Chalmers M(cGeagh) 1910- ... 41-44R
Roberts, Charles G(eorge) D(ouglas) 1860-1943 Brief entry ... 105
See also CLR 33
See also DLB 92
See also SATA 88
See also SATA-Brief 29
See also TCLC 8
Roberts, Charles Wesley 1916-1992 ... 17-20R
Obituary ... 136
Roberts, (Ray) Clayton, (Jr.) 1923- ... 159
Roberts, Clete 1910(?)-1984 Obituary ... 113
Roberts, Cokie 1943- ... 167
Roberts, Colette Jacqueline 1910-1971 Obituary ... 115
Roberts, Colin H(enderson) 1909-1990 ... 132
Roberts, Dan
See Ross, W(illiam) E(dward) D(aniel)
Roberts, Daniel (Frank) 1922- ... CANR-6
Earlier sketch in CA 9-12R
Roberts, David
See Cox, John Roberts
Roberts, David Arthur 1924-1987 ... 134
Obituary ... 122
Roberts, David D(ion) 1943- ... 101
Roberts, David S(tuart) 1943- ... 33-36R
Roberts, Dell
See Fendell, Bob
Roberts, Dennis W(ayne) 1947- ... 109
Roberts, Denys (Tudor Emil) 1923- ... CAP-1
Earlier sketch in CA 9-10
Roberts, Denys Kilham 1904(?)-1976 Obituary ... 65-68
Roberts, Derrell C(layton) 1927- ... 29-32R
Roberts, Donald Alfred 1897-1978 Obituary ... 77-80
Roberts, Donald Frank, Jr. 1939- ... 107
Roberts, Doreen 1922- ... 145
Earlier sketch in CA 108
Roberts, Dorothy 1906- ... DLB 88
Roberts, Dorothy James 1903-1990 ... CAP-1
Obituary ... 131
Earlier sketch in CA 13-14
Roberts, Edgar V. 1928- ... 21-24R
Roberts, Edward B(aer) 1935- ... CANR-9
Earlier sketch in CA 21-24R
Roberts, Edward Barry 1900-1972 ... CAP-2
Earlier sketch in CA 19-20
Roberts, Edward Dryhurst 1904-1989 Obituary ... 129
Roberts, Edwin A(lbert), Jr. 1932- ... 21-24R
Roberts, Elfed Vaughan 1946- ... 143
Roberts, Elizabeth 1944- ... 148
See also SATA 80
Roberts, Elizabeth H. 1913- ... 61-64
Roberts, Elizabeth Madox 1886-1941 ... 166
Brief entry ... 111
See also DLB 9, 54, 102
See also SATA 33
See also SATA-Brief 27
See also TCLC 68
Roberts, Elizabeth (Allan) Mauchline 1936- Brief entry ... 114
Roberts, Ellen Elizabeth Mayhew 1946- ... CANR-26
Earlier sketch in CA 108
Roberts, Elliott B. 1899-1988 ... 1-4R
Obituary ... 126
Roberts, Eric 1914- ... 5-8R
Roberts, Estelle (Wills) 1889-1970 Obituary ... 112
Roberts, Eugene (L., Jr.) 1932- ... 97-100
Interview in ... 97-100
Roberts, Evelyn Lutman 1917- ... 65-68
Roberts, F(rederick) David 1923- ... 5-8R
Roberts, Florence Bright 1941- ... 65-68
Roberts, Frances C(abaniss) 1916- ... 9-12R
Roberts, Francis Warren 1916- ... 13-16R
Roberts, Geoffrey R(ansford) 1924- ... 101
Roberts, Grant
See Wallmann, Jeffrey M(iner)
Roberts, Harold 1896(?)-1982 Obituary ... 108
Roberts, Harold S(elig) 1911-1970 ... CAP-2
Earlier sketch in CA 23-24
Roberts, Henry L(ithgow) 1916-1972 Obituary ... 37-40R
Roberts, Hortense Roberta ... 89-92
Roberts, Howard R(adclyffe) 1906- ... 109
Roberts, I.
See Roberts, Irene
Roberts, I(olo) F(rancis) 1925- ... 29-32R
Roberts, I. M.
See Roberts, Irene
Roberts, Irene 1925- ... CANR-21
Earlier sketches in CA 13-16R, CANR-6
Roberts, Ivor
See Roberts, Irene
Roberts, J(ohn) A(lexander) Fraser 1899-1987 Obituary ... 121
Roberts, J(ohn) Kimberley 1935- ... 117
Roberts, J. R.
See Randisi, Robert J(oseph)
Roberts, James Deotis 1927- ... CANR-15
Earlier sketch in CA 33-36R
Roberts, James Hall
See Duncan, Robert L(ipscomb)
Roberts, Jane
See Butts, Jane Roberts
Roberts, Janet Louise 1925- ... CANR-13
Earlier sketch in CA 61-64
Roberts, Jason
See Bock, Fred
Roberts, Jeanne Addison ... 89-92
Roberts, Jim
See Bates, Barbara S(nedeker)
Roberts, Joan Ila 1935- ... 29-32R
Roberts, Joe
See Saltzman, Joseph
Roberts, John
See Bingley, David Ernest
Roberts, John G(aither) 1913- ... 49-52
See also SATA 27
Roberts, John M(ilton) 1916- ... 37-40R
Roberts, John M(orris) 1928- ... CANR-16
Earlier sketch in CA 85-88
Roberts, John R. 1934- ... CANR-12
Earlier sketch in CA 33-36R
Roberts, John Storm 1936- ... CANR-12
Earlier sketch in CA 25-28R
Roberts, Joseph B(oxley), Jr. 1918- ... 41-44R
Roberts, Judy I. 1957- ... SATA 93
Roberts, Julian
See Bardens, Dennis (Conrad)
Roberts, K.
See Lake, Kenneth R(obert)
Roberts, K(enneth) B(ryson) 1923- ... 139
Roberts, Kate 1891-1985 ... 107
Obituary ... 116
See also CLC 15
Roberts, Keith (John Kingston) 1935- ... CANR-46
Earlier sketch in CA 25-28R
See also CLC 14
Roberts, Keith 1937(?)-1979 Obituary ... 85-88
Roberts, Ken
See Lake, Kenneth R(obert)
Roberts, Kenneth (Lewis) 1885-1957 Brief entry ... 109
See also DLB 9
See also TCLC 23
Roberts, Kenneth H(arris) 1930- ... 33-36R
Roberts, Kevin E(rnest) A(lbert) 1940- ... 113
Roberts, Lawrence
See Fish, Robert L(loyd)
Roberts, Lee
See Martin, Robert (Lee)
Roberts, Leigh
See Smith, Lora R(oberts)
Roberts, Len
See Roberts, Leonard
See also CAAS 27
Roberts, Leonard 1947- ... CANR-32
Earlier sketch in CA 113
See also Roberts, Len
Roberts, Leonard W(ard) 1912-1983 ... CANR-28
Earlier sketch in CA 33-36R
Roberts, Les 1937- ... CANR-62
Earlier sketch in CA 128
Roberts, Leslie 1896-1980 ... 103
Roberts, Lionel
See Fanthorpe, R(obert) Lionel
Roberts, Lisa
See Turner, Robert (Harry)
Roberts, Lora
See Smith, Lora R(oberts)
Roberts, MacLennan
See Terrall, Robert
Roberts, Madge Thornall 1929- ... 152
Roberts, Marguerite 1905(?)-1989 Obituary ... 128
Roberts, Mary D(uffy) 1925- ... 1-4R
Roberts, Mervin F(rancis) 1922- ... CANR-24
Earlier sketches in CA 65-68, CANR-9
Roberts, Michael 1945- ... 69-72
Roberts, Michele (B.) 1949- ... CANR-58
Earlier sketch in CA 115
See also CLC 48
Roberts, Monty 1935- ... 164
Roberts, Myron 1923-1992 ... CANR-31
Obituary ... 139
Earlier sketch in CA 29-32R
Roberts, Nancy Correll 1924- ... CANR-6
Earlier sketch in CA 9-12R
See also SATA 52
See also SATA-Brief 28
Roberts, Nancy N(orma) 1957- ... 150
Roberts, Nora 1950- ... CANR-45
Earlier sketch in CA 123
Roberts, Oral 1918- ... 41-44R
Roberts, (Thomas) Patrick 1920- ... 61-64
Roberts, Paul Craig 1939- ... CANR-22
Earlier sketch in CA 33-36R
Roberts, Paul McHenry 1917-1967 ... 1-4R
Obituary ... 103
Roberts, Paul William 1950- ... 141
Roberts, Percival R(udolph) III 1935- ... 41-44R
Roberts, Philip Davies 1938- ... CANR-26
Earlier sketch in CA 109
Roberts, Phyllis Barzillay 1932- ... 41-44R
Roberts, Rachel 1927-1980 Obituary ... 115
Roberts, Rand
See Parham, Robert Randall
Roberts, Randy (W.) 1951- ... 134
Roberts, Richard J(erome) 1928- ... 5-8R
Roberts, Richard W. 1935-1978 Obituary ... 73-76
Roberts, Rinalda
See Cudlipp, Edythe
Roberts, Robert B. 1911- ... 117
Roberts, Robert C(ampbell) 1942- ... CANR-31
Earlier sketches in CA 69-72, CANR-14
Roberts, Ron E. 1939- ... 33-36R
Roberts, Roy Allison 1887-1967 Obituary ... 89-92
Roberts, Rufus Putnam 1926- ... 1-4R
Roberts, Sally
See Jones, Sally Roberts
Roberts, Sheila 1942- ... 102
Roberts, Spencer Eugene 1920- ... 89-92
Roberts, Steven V(ictor) 1943- ... 61-64
Roberts, Susan F. 1919- ... 104
Roberts, Suzanne 1931- ... 106
Roberts, Sydney (Castle) 1887-1966 ... CAP-1
Earlier sketch in CA 13-16
Roberts, Terence
See Sanderson, Ivan T(erence)
Roberts, Theodore Goodridge 1877-1953 ... DLB 92
Roberts, Thom(as Sacra) 1940- ... CANR-15
Earlier sketch in CA 81-84
Roberts, Thomas J(ohn) 1925- ... 41-44R
Roberts, Tom
See Thomas, R(obert) Murray
Roberts, Trev
See Trevathan, Robert E(ugene)
Roberts, Vera Mowry 1918- ... 17-20R
Roberts, Virginia
See Dean, Nell Marr
Roberts, Walter Orr 1915- ... 131
Roberts, Walter R(onald) 1916- ... CANR-1
Earlier sketch in CA 49-52
Roberts, Warren (Errol) 1933- ... 73-76
Roberts, Warren Aldrich 1901- ... CAP-1
Earlier sketch in CA 11-12
Roberts, Wayne
See Overholser, Wayne D.
Roberts, Wesley K. 1946- ... 147
Roberts, Wess
See Roberts, Wesley K.
Roberts, William 1767-1849 ... DLB 142
Roberts, William 1868-1959 Brief entry ... 122
Roberts, William P(utnam) 1931- ... CANR-66
Earlier sketches in CA 113, CANR-32
Roberts, Willo Davis 1928- ... CANR-47
Earlier sketches in CA 49-52, CANR-3, 19
See also AAYA 13
See also JRDA
See also MAICYA
See also SAAS 8
See also SATA 21, 70
Roberts, Willow
See Powers, Willow Roberts
Robertshaw, (James) Denis 1911- ... 65-68
Robertson, Alec
See Robertson, Alexander Thomas Parke Anthony Cecil
Robertson, Alexander Thomas Parke Anthony Cecil 1892-1982 ... 104
Obituary ... 105
Robertson, Andrew (Beaumont) 1921-1986 ... 134
Obituary ... 120
Robertson, Arthur Henry 1913-1984 ... 9-12R
Obituary ... 113
Robertson, Barbara (Anne) 1931- ... 25-28R
See also SATA 12
Robertson, Brian 1951- ... 101
Robertson, Carol P. 1934- ... 123
Robertson, Charles L(angner) 1927- ... 21-24R
Robertson, Charles Martin 1911- ... 104
Robertson, Colin 1906- ... 9-12R
Robertson, Constance (Pierrepont Noyes) 1896(?)-1985 ... 29-32R
Obituary ... 116
Robertson, Cordelia Biddle 1898(?)-1984 Obituary ... 114
Robertson, D(onald) J(ames) 1926-1970 ... CANR-10
Earlier sketch in CA 5-8R
Robertson, D(urant) W(aite), Jr. 1914-1992 ... CANR-9
Obituary ... 139
Earlier sketch in CA 61-64
Robertson, Dale 1923- Brief entry ... 107
Robertson, David (Allan, Jr.) 1915- ... 81-84
Robertson, Dede 1927- ... 114
Robertson, Don 1929- ... CANR-23
Earlier sketches in CA 9-12R, CANR-7
See also SATA 8
Robertson, Donald S. 1918- ... 123
Robertson, Dorothy Lewis 1912- ... 25-28R
See also SATA 12
Robertson, Dougal 1924-1991 ... 61-64
Obituary ... 135
Robertson, E(smonde) M(anning) 1923-1987 ... 29-32R
Obituary ... 121
Robertson, Edith Anne (Stewart) 1883-(?) ... CAP-1
Earlier sketch in CA 11-12
Robertson, Edwin (Hanton) 1912- ... 130
Robertson, Elizabeth Chant 1899- ... 49-52
Robertson, Ellis
See Ellison, Harlan (Jay)
and Silverberg, Robert
Robertson, Eric Desmond 1914-1987 Obituary ... 122
Robertson, Frank C(hester) 1890-1969 ... CANR-64
Earlier sketches in CA 1-4R, CANR-4
Robertson, Geoffrey R. 1946- ... 147
Robertson, H(ector) M(enteith) 1905-1984 Obituary ... 113
Robertson, Heather Margaret 1942- ... CANR-37
Earlier sketches in CA 93-96, CANR-17
Robertson, Howard Stephen 1931- ... 41-44R
Robertson, Ian (Campbell) 1928- ... 132
Robertson, James (Irvin), Jr. 1930- ... CANR-6
Earlier sketch in CA 9-12R
Robertson, James 1911- ... 5-8R
Robertson, James Douglas 1904- ... 5-8R
Robertson, James Louis 1907-1994 ... CAP-2
Obituary ... 144
Earlier sketch in CA 29-32
Robertson, James Oliver 1932- ... 111
Brief entry ... 106
Robertson, James Wilson 1899-1983 ... 109
Obituary ... 110
Robertson, Janet (E.) 1935- ... 137
See also SATA 68
Robertson, Jean (K.) 1913-1990 Obituary ... 132
Robertson, Jennifer Sinclair 1942- ... CANR-5
Earlier sketch in CA 53-56
See also SATA 12
Robertson, Jenny
See Robertson, Jennifer Sinclair
Robertson, Joel C. 1952- ... 154
Robertson, John (Charles) 1951- ... 124
Robertson, Keith (Carlton) 1914-1991 ... CANR-37
Obituary ... 135
Earlier sketch in CA 9-12R
See also MAICYA
See also SAAS 15
See also SATA 1, 85
See also SATA-Obit 69
Robertson, Leon S(purgeon) 1936- ... 41-44R
Robertson, M(arion) G(ordon) 1930- ... CANR-58
Earlier sketch in CA 111
Robertson, Marian 1921- ... 111
Robertson, Martin
See Robertson, Charles Martin
Robertson, Mary D(emmond) 1927- ... 102
Robertson, Mary Elsie 1937- ... CANR-33
Earlier sketches in CA 81-84, CANR-15
Robertson, Nan 1926- ... 121
Robertson, Olivia (Melian) 1917- ... 9-12R
Robertson, Pat
See Robertson, M(arion) G(ordon)
Robertson, Patrick 1940- ... 61-64
Robertson, Priscilla (Smith) 1910-1989 ... CAP-2
Obituary ... 130
Earlier sketch in CA 23-24
Robertson, Roland 1938- ... 29-32R
Robertson, Stephen
See Walker, Robert W(ayne)
Robertson, Thomas Anthony 1897- ... CAP-1
Earlier sketch in CA 13-16
Robertson, Thomas William 1829-1871 ... DAM DRAM
Robertson, Wally
See Robertson, Walter
Robertson, Walter 1892-1983 Obituary ... 109
Robertson, Wilfrid 1892- ... 5-8R
Robertson, William 1721-1793 ... DLB 104
Roberts-Wray, Kenneth (Owen) 1899- ... CAP-2
Earlier sketch in CA 25-28
Robertus, Polly M. 1948- ... SATA 73
Robeson, Eslanda Cardoza Goode 1896-1965 ... 141
Robeson, Gerald B(yron) 1938- ... 65-68
Robeson, Kenneth
See Dent, Lester
and Goulart, Ron(ald Joseph)
Robeson, Paul, Jr. 1927- ... 143
Robeson, Paul (Leroy Bustill) 1898-1976 ... 124
Obituary ... 109
See also BW 1
Robey, Daniel 1944- ... 111
Robey, Edward George (Haydon) 1900-1983 Obituary ... 109
Robey, Harriet 1900- ... 107
Robey, Ralph W(est) 1899-1972 Obituary ... 37-40R
Robhs, Dwight
See Monaco, Richard
Robichaud, Gerald A(laric) 1912-1979 Obituary ... 85-88
Robichaud, Gerard 1908- ... CAP-2
Earlier sketch in CA 17-18
Robichon, Jacques 1920- ... 101
Robie, Bill
See Robie, William A., Jr.
Robie, Edward H(odges) 1886- ... CAP-2
Earlier sketch in CA 19-20
Robie, William A., Jr. 1947- ... 146
Robilliard, Eileen Dorothy 1921- ... 21-24R
Robilliard, St. John Anthony 1953- ... 124
Robin
See Roberts, Eric
Robin, Arthur de Quetteville 1929- ... 104
Robin, Harry 1915- ... 147
Robin, Leo 1900(?)-1984 Obituary ... 114
Robin, Ralph 1914- ... 65-68
Robin, Richard S(hale) 1926- ... 21-24R
Robinet, Harriette Gillem 1931- ... CANR-42
Earlier sketch in CA 69-72
See also BW 2
See also SATA 27
Robinett, Betty Wallace 1919- ... 41-44R
Robinett, Stephen (Allen) 1941- ... 101
Robinette, Joseph A. 1939- ... 131
Robinowitz, Carolyn B. 1938- ... 136
Robins, Corinne 1934- ... 118
Robins, Denise (Naomi) 1897(?)-1985 ... CANR-70
Obituary ... 116
Earlier sketches in CA 65-68, CANR-10, 19
Robins, Dorothy B.
See Robins-Mowry, Dorothy B(ernice)
Robins, Eli 1921-1994 ... 109
Obituary ... 147
Robins, Elizabeth 1862(?)-1952 Brief entry ... 116
See also DLB 197
Robins, Harry Franklin 1915- ... 5-8R
Robins, Lee N(elken) 1922- ... CANR-14
Earlier sketch in CA 21-24R
Robins, Michael H(arvey) 1941- ... 133
Robins, Natalie S. 1938- ... 17-20R
Robins, Patricia
See Lorrimer, Claire
Robins, Robert Henry 1921- ... 5-8R
Robins, Robert S. 1938- ... 144
Robins, Rollo, Jr.
See Ellis, Edward S(ylvester)

Robins, Seelin
See Ellis, Edward S(ylvester)
Robins-Mowry, Dorothy B(ernice) 1921- 25-28R
Robinson, A(ntony) M(eredith) Lewin 1916- CANR-9
Earlier sketch in CA 21-24R
Robinson, A(rthur) N(apoleon) R(aymond) 1926- 33-36R
Robinson, Abby 1947- 117
Robinson, Adjai 1932- 45-48
See also SATA 8
Robinson, Alan R(onald) 1920- CAP-1
Earlier sketch in CA 11-12
Robinson, Albert J(ohn) 1926- 53-56
Robinson, Alice Gram 1896(?)-1984 Obituary .. 111
Robinson, Alice M(erritt) 1920-1983 108
Obituary 109
Robinson, Aminah Brenda Lynn 1940- .... SATA 77
Robinson, Andrew 1957- 146
Robinson, Anthony (Christopher) 1931- ... CANR-1
Earlier sketch in CA 1-4R
Robinson, Archie W. 1906(?)-1987 Obituary ... 123
Robinson, B(asil) W(illiam) 1912- CANR-3
Earlier sketch in CA 5-8R
Robinson, Barbara Webb 1927- 1-4R
See also SATA 8, 84
Robinson, Barry (James) 1938- 25-28R
Robinson, Betsy Julia 1951- 109
Robinson, Bill
See Robinson, William Wheeler
Robinson, Blackwell P(ierce) 1916- CANR-24
Earlier sketch in CA 45-48
Robinson, Blake 1932- 143
Robinson, Brooks (Calbert, Jr.) 1937- 116
Robinson, Bruce 1946- 131
Robinson, Budd
See Robinson, David
Robinson, C(harles) A(lexander), Jr. 1900-1965 .... CANR-4
Earlier sketch in CA 1-4R
See also SATA 36
Robinson, Casey 1903-1979 .... DLB 44
Robinson, Cecil 1921- 13-16R
Robinson, Cervin 1928- 61-64
Robinson, Chaille Howard (Payne) 13-16R
Robinson, Charles 1870-1937 .... SATA 17
Robinson, Charles 1931- CANR-2
Earlier sketch in CA 49-52
See also SATA 6
Robinson, Charles E(dward) 1941- CANR-13
Earlier sketch in CA 77-80
Robinson, Charles Knox (Jr.) 1909-1980 103
Obituary 97-100
Robinson, Charles M. III 1949- CANR-46
Earlier sketch in CA 120
Robinson, Charles P. III 1950- 156
Robinson, Chuck
See Robinson, Charles P. III
Robinson, Corinne H(ogden) 1909- 93-96
Robinson, Daniel N. 1937- 33-36R
Robinson, Daniel Sommer 1888-1977 .... 29-32R
Obituary 125
Robinson, David 1915- 81-84
Robinson, David A. 1925- 17-20R
Robinson, Dean (Stewart) 1946- CANR-36
Earlier sketch in CA 114
Robinson, Debbie
See Robinson, Deborah A.
Robinson, Deborah A. 1958- 156
Robinson, Derek 1932- 77-80
Robinson, Donald 1913-1991 .... 25-28R
Obituary 135
Robinson, Donald H(oy) 1910- CAP-2
Earlier sketch in CA 33-36
Robinson, Donald L(eonard) 1936- 41-44R
Robinson, Donald W(ittmer) 1911-1980 .. CANR-12
Earlier sketch in CA 21-24R
Robinson, Dorothy W. 1929- .... SATA 54
Robinson, Douglas Hill 1918- CANR-8
Earlier sketch in CA 5-8R
Robinson, Earl (Hawley) 1910-1991 .... CANR-43
Obituary 135
Earlier sketches in CA 45-48, CANR-2
Robinson, Edgar Eugene
1887-1977 Obituary 73-76
Robinson, Edward G. 1893-1973 Obituary 45-48
Robinson, Edward L(ouis) 1921- 41-44R
Robinson, Edwin Arlington 1869-1935 133
Brief entry 104
See also CDALB 1865-1917
See also DA
See also DAC
See also DAM MST, POET
See also DLB 54
See also MTCW 1
See also PC 1
See also TCLC 5
Robinson, Elwyn B(urns) 1905- CAP-2
Earlier sketch in CA 19-20
Robinson, Eric 1924- 49-52
Robinson, Forrest G(len) 1940- 41-44R
Robinson, Francis (Arthur)
1910-1980 Obituary 97-100
Robinson, Francis (Christopher Rowland)
1944- 112
Robinson, Frank M(elvin), Jr. 1928- 57-60
Robinson, Frank M(alcolm) 1926- CANR-19
Earlier sketches in CA 49-52, CANR-3
Robinson, Frank S(teven) 1947- 97-100
Robinson, Fred Colson 1930- 37-40R
Robinson, Fred Miller 1942- 107
Robinson, Glen(dal P.) 1953- 156
See also SATA 92
Robinson, Godfrey Clive 1913- 13-16R
Robinson, Gustavus H.
1881-1972 Obituary 37-40R
Robinson, H(enry) Basil 1919- 131
Robinson, Haddon W. 1931- 73-76
Robinson, Halbert B(enefiel) 1925-1981 ... CANR-9
Earlier sketch in CA 17-20R
Robinson, Harlow (Loomis) 1950- 128
Robinson, Helen Caister 1899- CANR-16
Earlier sketch in CA 93-96
Robinson, Helen Mansfield 1906- 13-16R
Robinson, Helene M. 13-16R
Robinson, Henry Crabb 1775-1867 .... DLB 107
Robinson, Henry Morton 1898-1961 Obituary .. 116
Robinson, Herbert Spencer 93-96
Robinson, Horace W(illiam) 1909- 93-96
Robinson, Howard 1885- CAP-1
Earlier sketch in CA 13-14
Robinson, Hubbell 1905-1974 Obituary 53-56
Robinson, Ira E(dwin) 1927- 81-84
Robinson, J(ohn) Lewis 1918- 107
Robinson, J(ohn) W(illiam) 1934- 17-20R
Robinson, James A(rthur) 1932- 17-20R
Robinson, James Harvey 1863-1936 .... DLB 47
Robinson, James K(eith) 1916- 17-20R
Robinson, James L. 1945- 149
Robinson, James M(cConkey) 1924- 13-16R
Robinson, Jan M. 1933- 61-64
See also SATA 6
Robinson, Jancis (Mary) 1950- CANR-60
Earlier sketch in CA 128
Robinson, Janet O(live) 1939- 33-36R
Robinson, Janice S(tevenson) 1941- 111
Robinson, Jay (Luke) 1932- 41-44R
Robinson, Jean O. 1934- 29-32R
See also SATA 7
Robinson, Jeffrey 1945- CANR-37
Earlier sketch in CA 121
Robinson, Jerry 1922- Brief entry 112
See also SATA-Brief 34
Robinson, Jill 1936- 102
Interview in 102
See also CLC 10
Robinson, Jo Ann Ooiman 1942- 111
Robinson, Joan (Violet) 1903-1983 .... CANR-6
Obituary 110
Earlier sketch in CA 9-12R
See also MTCW 1
Robinson, Joan (Mary) G(ale Thomas) 1910- CANR-5
Earlier sketch in CA 5-8R
See also SATA 7
Robinson, John A(rthur) T(homas) 1919-1983 .... CANR-6
Obituary 111
Earlier sketch in CA 5-8R
Robinson, John W(esley) 1929- CANR-2
Earlier sketch in CA 49-52
Robinson, Joseph 1927- 45-48
Robinson, Joseph Frederick 1912- 13-16R
Robinson, Joseph William 1908- CAP-2
Earlier sketch in CA 25-28
Robinson, Karl Frederic 1904-1967 .... CANR-5
Earlier sketch in CA 5-8R
Robinson, Kathleen
See Robinson, Chaille Howard (Payne)
Robinson, Kenneth Ernest 1914- 5-8R
Robinson, Kevin 1951- 145
Robinson, Kim Stanley 1952- 126
See also AAYA 26
See also CLC 34
Robinson, L(eonard) W(allace) 1912- 69-72
Robinson, (Esme Stuart) Lennox 1886-1958 Brief entry 120
See also DLB 10
Robinson, Leonard A. 1904(?)-1980 97-100
Robinson, Linda 1960- 143
Robinson, Lisa 1936- 93-96
Robinson, Lloyd
See Silverberg, Robert
Robinson, Logan Gilmore 1949- 108
Robinson, Louie, Jr. 1926- 107
Robinson, Lynda S(uzanne) 1951- CANR-71
Earlier sketch in CA 145
Robinson, Lytle W(ebb) 1913- 61-64
Robinson, Mabel Louise 1874-1962 Obituary .. 113
See also DLB 22
Robinson, Mairi 1945- 123
Robinson, Margaret A(twood) 1937- 107
Robinson, Marguerite S. 1935- 49-52
Robinson, Marileta 1942- 101
See also SATA 32
Robinson, Marilynne 1944- 116
See also CLC 25
Robinson, Martin David 1925-1982 Obituary ... 108
Robinson, Mary 1758-1800 .... DLB 158
Robinson, Matt(hew) 1937- 45-48
Robinson, Maudie Millian Oller 1914- CANR-8
Earlier sketch in CA 61-64
See also SATA 11
Robinson, Maurice R(ichard)
1895-1982 Obituary 106
See also SATA-Obit 29
Robinson, Max (C.) 1939-1988 124
Obituary 127
Brief entry 110
Interview in 124
See also BW 1
Robinson, Michael J(ay) 1945- 113
Robinson, Nancy K(onheim) 1942-1994 .. CANR-24
Obituary 144
Earlier sketch in CA 106
See also SATA 32, 91
See also SATA-Brief 31
See also SATA-Obit 79
Robinson, Nancy (Lou) M(ayer) 1930- 61-64
Robinson, Norman H(amilton) G(alloway)
1912- 13-16R
Robinson, O(liver) Preston 1903- 13-16R
Robinson, (Frances) Olvis 1923- 53-56
Robinson, P. W. 1893- 103
Robinson, Patricia
See Goedicke, Patricia (McKenna)
Robinson, Patricia Colbert 1923- 77-80
Robinson, Patrick 1940- 154
Robinson, Paul 1940- 81-84
Robinson, Peter 1950- CANR-67
Earlier sketch in CA 147
Robinson, Peter (Mark) 1957- 149
Robinson, Phil Alden 1950- 139
Robinson, Philip (Bedford) 1926- CANR-16
Earlier sketch in CA 21-24R
Robinson, Philip (Samuel) 1946- 129
Robinson, Phyllis C(umins) 1924- 148
Robinson, Ras 1935- 105
Robinson, Ray(mond Kenneth) 1920- 77-80
See also SATA 23
Robinson, Ray Charles 1932- Brief entry 115
Robinson, Raymond Henry 1927- 41-44R
Robinson, Richard c. 1545-1607 .... DLB 167
Robinson, Richard 1945- CANR-13
Earlier sketch in CA 57-60
Robinson, Richard Dunlop 1921- 5-8R
Robinson, Robert 1886-1975 Obituary 113
Robinson, Robert (Reginald) 1922- CANR-14
Earlier sketch in CA 41-44R
Robinson, Robert 1927- 9-12R
Robinson, Robert H(ouston) 1936- CANR-6
Earlier sketch in CA 5-8R
Robinson, Roland Inwood 1907- CANR-1
Earlier sketch in CA 1-4R
Robinson, Rollo S(mith) 1915- 41-44R
Robinson, Rose 77-80
Robinson, Roxana (Barry) CANR-58
Earlier sketch in CA 128
Robinson, Sally 1933- 145
Robinson, Selma 1899(?)-1977 Obituary 73-76
Robinson, Shari
See McGuire, Leslie (Sarah)
Robinson, Sharon 1950- 154
Robinson, Sheila Mary 1928- CANR-62
Brief entry 126
Earlier sketch in CA 131
Interview in 131
Robinson, Sidney K. 1943- CANR-33
Earlier sketch in CA 113
Robinson, Sister Marian Dolores 1916- 9-12R
Robinson, Smokey
See Robinson, William, Jr.
See also CLC 21
Robinson, Sondra Till 1931- CANR-7
Earlier sketch in CA 53-56
Robinson, Spider 1948- CANR-11
Earlier sketch in CA 65-68
Robinson, Suzanne
See Robinson, Lynda S(uzanne)
Robinson, T(homas) H(eath) 1869-1950 .. SATA 17
Robinson, T(homas) M(ore) 1936- 29-32R
Robinson, Terry 1916- 108
Robinson, Therese 1797-1870
See Talvj
See also DLB 59
Robinson, Thomas W. 1935- 33-36R
Robinson, Trevor 1929- 53-56
Robinson, Vaughan 1957- 132
Robinson, (Wanda) Veronica 1926- 105
See also SATA 30
Robinson, Vince
See Newton, Michael
Robinson, Virgil E. 1908- 21-24R
Robinson, W(illiam) Gordon 1903-1977 ... CANR-5
Earlier sketch in CA 5-8R
Robinson, W(illiam) Heath 1872-1944 .... SATA 17
Robinson, W(illiam) R(onald) 1927- 21-24R
Robinson, W. Stitt
See Robinson, W(alter) Stitt, Jr.
Robinson, W(alter) Stitt, Jr. 1917- CANR-53
Brief entry 105
Earlier sketch in CA 126
Robinson, Wayne 1916- 1-4R
Robinson, Wayne A(ustin) 1937- 73-76
Robinson, Wayne C. 1955- 156
Robinson, Wilhelmena S(impson) 1912- 25-28R
Robinson, Willard B(ethurem) 1935- 57-60
Robinson, William, Jr. 1940- Brief entry 116
See also Robinson, Smokey
Robinson, William Childs 1897-1982 .... 1-4R
Obituary 116
Robinson, William F(rank) 1946- 118
Robinson, William H. 1912-1984 Obituary 111
Robinson, William H(enry) 1922- CANR-25
Earlier sketch in CA 37-40R
See also BW 1
Robinson, William I. 1959- 127
Robinson, William P(owell) 1910- 5-8R
Robinson, William Wheeler 1918- CANR-18
Earlier sketches in CA 5-8R, CANR-3
Robison, Bonnie 1924- 57-60
See also SATA 12
Robison, David V. 1911(?)-1978 93-96
Obituary 81-84
Robison, Mabel Otis 1891- CAP-1
Earlier sketch in CA 11-12
Robison, Mary 1949- 116
Brief entry 113
Interview in 116
See also CLC 42, 98
See also DLB 130
Robison, Nancy L(ouise) 1934- 93-96
See also SATA 32
Robison, Sophia Moses 1888-1969 .... 5-8R
Obituary 103
Robitscher, Jonas B(ondi, Jr.) 1920-1981 .... CANR-19
Obituary 103
Earlier sketch in CA 21-24R
Robles, Emmanuel 1914-1995 81-84
Obituary 148
See also DLB 83
Robles, Harold E. 1948- 151
See also SATA 87
Robles, Mireya 1934- 81-84
See also HW
Robley, Grace 1918- 61-64
Robley, Rob
See Robley, Wendell
Robley, Wendell 1916- 61-64
Robo, Etienne 1879- CAP-1
Earlier sketch in CA 11-12
Robock, Stefan H. 1915- 17-20R
Robottom, John 1934- CANR-38
Earlier sketches in CA 29-32R, CANR-16
See also SATA 7
Robsjohn-Gibbings, Terence Harold
1905-1976 Obituary 69-72
Robson, B(rian) T(urnbull) 1939- 29-32R
Robson, D(erek) I(an) 1935- 25-28R
Robson, Dirk
See Robinson, Derek
Robson, E(manuel) W(alter) 1897- 65-68
Robson, Elizabeth 1942- 101
Robson, Eric 1939- .... SATA 82
Robson, Ernest (Mack) 1902- CANR-24
Earlier sketch in CA 45-48
Robson, James 1890- 5-8R
Robson, Jeremy 1939- CANR-4
Earlier sketch in CA 5-8R
Robson, John M(ercel) 1927- CANR-28
Earlier sketch in CA 29-32R
Robson, L(eslie) L(loyd) 1931-1990 132
Robson, Lucia St. Clair 1942- CANR-51
Earlier sketches in CA 108, CANR-27
Robson, Marion M. 1908- 89-92
Robson, Roy R(aymond) 1963- 162
Robson, Ruthann 1956- 139
Robson, W(illiam) W(allace) 1923- 158
Robson, William Alexander 1895-1980 103
Obituary 97-100
Robson, William N. .... AITN 1
Roby, Kinley E. 1929- 77-80
Roby, Mary Linn CANR-7
Earlier sketch in CA 13-16R
Roby, Pamela A. 1942- 29-32R
Roby, Robert C(urtis) 1922- 5-8R
Robyns, Gwen 1917- 93-96
Roca-Pons, Josep 1914- 49-52
Roccapriore, Marie 1933- 115
Roccatagliata Ceccardi, Ceccardo 1871-1919 .. DLB 114
Roch, John H(enry) 1916- 102
Rocha, Adolfo 1907-1995 141
Obituary 147
Rocha, Guy Louis 1951- 128
Rocha, Rina Garcia
See Garcia Rocha, Rina
Rochard, Henri
See Charlier, Roger H(enri)
Rochberg-Halton, Eugene 1950- 111
Roche, A. K.
See Abisch, Roslyn Kroop
and Kaplan, Boche
Roche, Alex F. 1921- 144
Roche, Alphonse Victor 1895- 104
Roche, Daniel(-Robert) 1935- 128
Roche, Denis (Mary) 1967- 167
See also SATA 99
Roche, Douglas J. 1929- 101
Roche, George Charles III 1935- 29-32R
Roche, J. Jeffrey 1916(?)-1975 Obituary 61-64
Roche, John
See Le Roi, David (de Roche)
Roche, John P(earson) 1923- 69-72
Roche, Kennedy Francis 1911- 61-64
Roche, Orion 1948- 61-64
Roche, Owen I. A. 1911(?)-1973 Obituary .. 41-44R
Roche, P(atricia) K. 1935- 158
Brief entry 112
See also SATA 57
See also SATA-Brief 34
Roche, Paul 1928- CANR-4
Earlier sketch in CA 5-8R
Roche, T(homas) W(illiam) E(dgar) 1919-197(?) CAP-2
Earlier sketch in CA 21-22
Roche, Terry
See Poole, Peggy
Roche, Thomas P(atrick), Jr. 1931- 106
Rochelle, Jay C. 1938- 53-56
Rochelle, Mercedes 1955- 140
Rocher, Guy 1924- CANR-49
Earlier sketches in CA 45-48, CANR-24
Rocher, Ludo 1926- Brief entry 106
Rochester, Devereaux 1917- 105
Rochester, Harry A(rthur)
1897(?)-1983 Obituary 109
Rochester, J. Martin 1945- 37-40R
Rochester, Jack B. 1944- 122
Rochlin, Doris 1932- CANR-67
Earlier sketch in CA 128
Rochlin, Gregory 1912- 49-52
Rochlin, Harriet 1924- 117
Rochlitz, Rainer 1946- 162
Rochman, Hazel 1938- 144
Rochmis, Lyda N(onne) 1912- 29-32R
Rock, David (Peter) 1945- CANR-19
Earlier sketch in CA 101
Rock, Gail Brief entry 111
See also SATA-Brief 32

Rock, Howard 1911-1976 ... DLB 127
Rock, Howard B. 1944- ... 139
Rock, Irvin 1922- ... CANR-10
Earlier sketch in CA 21-24R
Rock, James M(artin) 1935- ... 102
Rock, John 1890-1984 ... 156
Obituary ... 114
Rock, Maxine 1940- ... 113
Rock, Milton L(ee) 1921- ... 49-52
Rock, Phillip 1927- ... 101
Rock, Richard
See Mainprize, Don
Rock, Stanley A(rthur) 1937- ... 101
Rock, William R(ay) 1930- ... 41-44R
Rockas, Leo 1928- ... 13-16R
Rockcastle, Verne N(orton) 1920- ... 73-76
Rocke, Russell 1945- ... 33-36R
Rockefeller, John D(avison Sr.) 1839-1937 Brief entry ... 116
Rockefeller, John Davison III 1906-1978 ... 81-84
Obituary ... 77-80
Rockefeller, John William, Jr. 1899(?)-1987 Obituary ... 122
Rocker, Fermin 1907- ... SATA 40
Rockfern, Danielle
See Nolan, Frederick William
Rockingham, Montague
See Nye, Nelson C(oral)
Rockland, Mae Shafter 1937- ... 65-68
Rockland, Michael Aaron 1935- ... CANR-64
Earlier sketches in CA 37-40R, CANR-32
Rockley, L(awrence) E(dwin) 1916- ... CANR-27
Earlier sketch in CA 29-32R
Rocklin, Joanne 1946- ... 151
See also SATA 86
Rocklin, Ross Louis 1913- ... 61-64
Rocklynne, Ross
See Rocklin, Ross Louis
Rockmore, Tom 1942- ... 127
Rockne, Dick 1939- ... 61-64
Rockowitz, Murray 1920- ... 25-28R
Rocks, Lawrence 1933- ... 85-88
Rockwell, Anne F(oote) 1934- ... CANR-45
Earlier sketches in CA 21-24R, CANR-22
See also MAICYA
See also SAAS 19
See also SATA 33, 71
Rockwell, Bart
See Pellowski, Michael (Joseph)
Rockwell, F(rederick) F(rye) 1884-1976 ... 49-52
Obituary ... 103
Rockwell, Gail ... SATA-Brief 36
Rockwell, Harlow 1910-1988 ... CANR-45
Obituary ... 125
Earlier sketches in CA 109, CANR-22
See also SATA 33
See also SATA-Obit 56
Rockwell, Jane 1929- ... 65-68
Rockwell, John (Sargent) 1940- ... 126
Brief entry ... 114
Interview in ... 126
Rockwell, Kiffin Ayres 1917- ... 37-40R
Rockwell, Matt
See Rowland, D(onald) S(ydney)
Rockwell, Norman (Percevel) 1894-1978 ... 89-92
Obituary ... 81-84
See also DLB 188
See also SATA 23
Rockwell, Theodore (III) 1922- ... 140
Rockwell, Thomas 1933- ... CANR-44
Earlier sketch in CA 29-32R
See also CLR 6
See also MAICYA
See also SATA 7, 70
Rockwell, Wilson (Miller) 1909- ... CAP-2
Earlier sketch in CA 19-20
Rockwood, Joyce 1947- ... CANR-6
Earlier sketch in CA 57-60
See also SATA 39
Rockwood, Louis G. 1925- ... 45-48
Rockwood, Roy ... CANR-27
Earlier sketches in CAP-2, CA 19-20
See also Stratemeyer, Edward L.
See also SATA 1, 67
Rod, Edouard 1857-1910 ... TCLC 52
Rodahl, Kaare 1917- ... 9-12R
Rodale, J(erome) I(rving) 1898-1971 Obituary ... 29-32R
Rodale, Robert (David) 1930-1990 ... 53-56
Obituary ... 132
Rodan, Paul N. Rosenstein
See Rosenstein-Rodan, Paul N.
Rodari, Gianni 1920-1980 ... CLR 24
Rodarmor, William 1942- ... 140
Rodaway, Angela 1918- ... 120
Rodberg, Leonard S(idney) 1932- ... CANR-24
Earlier sketch in CA 45-48
Rodberg, Lillian 1936- ... 29-32R
Rodd, Kathleen Tennant
See Rodd, Kylie Tennant
See also SATA 57
See also SATA-Obit 55
Rodd, Kylie Tennant 1912-1988 ... CANR-26
Obituary ... 124
Earlier sketches in CA 5-8R, CANR-5
See also Rodd, Kathleen Tennant
and Tennant, Kylie
See also MTCW 1
Rodda, Charles 1891- ... 5-8R
Rodda, Emily 1948(?)- ... 164
See also CLR 32
See also SATA 97
Rodda, Peter (Gordon) 1937- ... 81-84
Rodden, John (Gallagher) 1956- ... 131
Roddenberry, Eugene Wesley 1921-1991 ... CANR-37
Obituary ... 135
Earlier sketch in CA 110
See also Roddenberry, Gene
See also SATA 45
See also SATA-Obit 69
Roddenberry, Gene
See Roddenberry, Eugene Wesley
See also AAYA 5
See also CLC 17
See also SATA-Obit 69
Roddick, Alan (Melven) 1937- ... CANR-15
Earlier sketch in CA 77-80
Roddick, Anita (Lucia) 1942- ... 140
Roddick, Ellen 1936- ... 41-44R
See also Meade, Ellen
Roddis, Louis Harry 1887- ... 5-8R
Roddis, Roland J. 1908- ... 5-8R
Rodd-Marling, Yvonne 1912-1982 Obituary ... 107
Roddy, Lee 1921- ... 123
See also SATA 57
Rodefer, Stephen 1940- ... CANR-23
Earlier sketch in CA 107
Rodell, Fred 1907-1980 Obituary ... 97-100
Rodell, Marie F(reid) 1912-1975 Obituary ... 61-64
Roden, Claudia ... 159
Roden, Michael 1962- ... 156
Rodenas, Paula ... SATA 73
Rodenberg, Julius 1884-1970 Obituary ... 104
Roder, Wolf 1932- ... 17-20R
Roderus, Frank 1942- ... CANR-38
Earlier sketches in CA 89-92, CANR-17
Rodes, John E(dward) 1923- ... 13-16R
Rodes, Robert Emmet, Jr. 1927- ... 112
Rodewyk, Adolf 1894- ... 65-68
Rodger, Alec
See Rodger, Thomas Alexander
Rodger, Anne 1910-1983 Obituary ... 111
Rodger, Ian (Graham) 1926- ... CANR-4
Earlier sketch in CA 5-8R
Rodger, Richard 1947- ... 143
Rodger, Thomas Alexander 1907-1982 Obituary ... 106
Rodgers, Alan (Paul) 1959- ... 168
Rodgers, Audrey T(ropauer) 1923- ... 148
Rodgers, Betsy (Aikin-Sneath) 1907- ... CAP-1
Earlier sketch in CA 13-14
Rodgers, Betty June (Flint) 1921- ... 9-12R
Rodgers, Brian 1910- ... 29-32R
Rodgers, Buck
See Rodgers, Francis G.
Rodgers, Carolyn M(arie) 1945- ... CANR-70
Earlier sketches in CA 45-48, CANR-2, 27
See also CAAS 13
See also BW 2
See also DLB 41
Rodgers, Daniel T(racy) 1942- ... 124
Rodgers, Dorothy F(einer) 1909-1992 ... 89-92
Obituary ... 139
Rodgers, Eugene 1939- ... 132
Rodgers, Francis G. 1926- ... 123
Rodgers, Frank
See Infield, Glenn (Berton)
Rodgers, Frank 1944- ... 137
See also SATA 69
Rodgers, Frank P(eter) 1924- ... 9-12R
Rodgers, Franklin C. 1931- ... 133
Rodgers, Harrell R(oss), Jr. 1939- ... CANR-50
Earlier sketches in CA 53-56, CANR-7, 25
Rodgers, Joann Ellison 1941- ... 77-80
Rodgers, John (Charles) 1906- ... CAP-1
Earlier sketch in CA 11-12
Rodgers, Mary 1931- ... CANR-55
Earlier sketches in CA 49-52, CANR-8
Interview in ... CANR-8
See also CLC 12
See also CLR 20
See also JRDA
See also MAICYA
See also SATA 8
Rodgers, Pepper
See Rodricks, Daniel J.
Rodgers, Raboo 1945- ... 119
Rodgers, Richard (Charles) 1902-1979 ... 89-92
Rodgers, Stanley 1928-1977 Obituary ... 106
Rodgers, W(illiam) R(obert) 1909-1969 ... 85-88
See also CLC 7
See also DLB 20
Rodgers, William H. 1918- ... 17-20R
Rodgers, William Henry 1947- ... 101
Rodham Clinton, Hillary
See Clinton, Hillary Rodham
Rodick, Burleigh Cushing 1889- ... 5-8R
Rodimer, Eva 1895- ... CAP-2
Earlier sketch in CA 21-22
Rodimstev, Aleksandr 1905(?)-1977 Obituary 69-72
Rodin, Alvin E(li) 1926- ... CANR-44
Earlier sketch in CA 119
Rodin, Arnold W. 1917- ... 89-92
Rodini, Robert J(oseph) 1936- ... 29-32R
Rodinson, Maxime 1915- ... CANR-4
Earlier sketch in CA 53-56
Roditi, Edouard Herbert 1910-1992 ... CANR-50
Obituary ... 137
Earlier sketch in CA 101
See also CAAS 14
Rodli, Agnes Sylvia 1921- ... 9-12R
Rodman, Bella (Kashin) 1903- ... CAP-2
Earlier sketch in CA 19-20
Rodman, Dennis (Keith) 1961- ... 155
Rodman, Emerson
See Ellis, Edward S(ylvester)
Rodman, Eric
See Silverberg, Robert
Rodman, F(rancis) Robert 1934- ... 122
Brief entry ... 117
Rodman, Howard 1920(?)-1985 Obituary ... 118
See also CLC 65
Rodman, Hyman 1931- ... CANR-25
Earlier sketches in CA 17-20R, CANR-8
Rodman, Maia
See Wojciechowska, Maia (Teresa)
Rodman, Selden 1909- ... CANR-51
Earlier sketches in CA 5-8R, CANR-5, 25
See also SATA 9
Rodney, Bob
See Rodrigo, Robert
Rodney, Howard
See Koch, Howard
Rodney, Robert M(orris) 1911- ... 77-80
Rodney, Walter 1942-1980 ... 125
Rodney, William 1923- ... 25-28R
Rodnick, David 1908- ... 33-36R
Rodnitzky, Jerome Leon 1936- ... 41-44R
Rodolph, Utto
See Ouologuem, Yambo
Rodowsky, Colby (F.) 1932- ... CANR-23
Earlier sketch in CA 69-72
Interview in ... CANR-23
See also AAYA 23
See also SAAS 22
See also SATA 21, 77
Rodricks, Daniel J. 1954- ... 133
Rodrigo, Robert 1928- ... 13-16R
Rodrigues, Jose Honorio 1913- ... CANR-13
Earlier sketch in CA 29-32R
Rodriguez, Alejo 1941- ... 150
See also SATA 83
Rodriguez, Alfred 1932- ... 145
Rodriguez, Ana 1938- ... 150
Rodriguez, Andres 1955- ... 151
Rodriguez, Claudio 1934- ... CLC 10
See also DLB 134
Rodriguez, Judith Green 1936- ... CANR-23
Earlier sketch in CA 107
Rodriguez, Luis J. 1954- ... 142
See also CAAS 29
Rodriguez, Mario 1922- ... 17-20R
Rodriguez, Richard 1944- ... CANR-66
Earlier sketch in CA 110
See also DAM MULT
See also DLB 82
See also HLC
See also HW
Rodriguez, Walter 1948- ... 142
Rodriguez-Alcala, Hugo (Rosendo) 1917- ... CANR-14
Earlier sketch in CA 21-24R
See also HW
Rodriguez-Alcala, Sally 1938- ... 21-24R
Rodriguez Cepeda, Enrique 1939- ... 45-48
Rodriguez Delgado, Jose M(anuel)
See Delgado, Jose Manuel R(odriguez)
Rodriguez Julia, Edgardo 1946- ... DLB 145
Rodriguez Monegal, Emir 1921-1985 ... 131
Obituary ... 117
Brief entry ... 115
See also HW
Rodriguez O(rdonez), Jaime E(dmundo) 1940- . 110
See also HW
Rodway, Allan 1919- ... 13-16R
Rodwin, Lloyd 1919- ... CANR-42
Earlier sketches in CA 5-8R, CANR-4, 19
Rodwin, Victor G(eorge) 1950- ... 120
Rodzinski, Halina 1904-1993 ... 69-72
Obituary ... 141
Roe, Anne 1904- ... 17-20R
Roe, Barbara L(ouise) 1947- ... 141
Roe, Caroline ... 165
Roe, Daphne A(nderson) 1923-1993 ... 93-96
Obituary ... 142
Roe, Derek A(rthur) 1937- ... CANR-23
Earlier sketch in CA 107
Roe, Dorothy
See Lewis, Dorothy Roe
Roe, E. P. 1838-1888 ... DLB 202
Roe, F(rederic) Gordon 1894-1985 ... 9-12R
Obituary ... 115
Roe, Gerald 1940- ... 117
Roe, Harry Mason ... CANR-26
Earlier sketches in CAP-2, CA 19-20
Roe, JoAnn ... 143
Roe, SirJohn 1581-1608 ... DLB 121
Roe, Kathleen Robson 1910- ... 93-96
Roe, Keith E. 1937- ... 127
Roe, Richard L(ionel) 1936- ... CANR-15
Earlier sketch in CA 65-68
Roe, W(illiam) G(ordon) 1932- ... 21-24R
Roe, William Henry 1918- ... 5-8R
Roeber, Edward C(harles) 1913-1969 ... CANR-5
Earlier sketch in CA 5-8R
Roebuck, Carl Angus 1914- Brief entry ... 105
Roebuck, Derek 1935- ... CANR-54
Earlier sketches in CA 111, CANR-29
Roebuck, Janet 1943- ... 49-52
Roebuck, Julian B(aker) 1920- ... 101
Roebuck, Peter (Michael) 1956- ... 119
Roeburt, John 1909(?)-1972 Obituary ... 33-36R
Roecker, W(illiam) A. 1942- ... 61-64
Roeder, Bill 1922-1982 Obituary ... 107
Roeder, George H., Jr. 1944- ... 147
Roeder, Ralph Leclerq 1890-1969 Obituary ... 104
Roeder, Virginia Marsh 1926- ... SATA 98
Roediger, David R(andall) 1952- ... 142
Roehr, George L. 1931(?)-1983 Obituary ... 110
Roehrig, Catharine H. 1949- ... 134
See also SATA 67
Roehrs, Walter R(obert) 1901- ... 103
Roeiker, Nancy Lyman 1915- ... 9-12R
Roelofs, H. Mark 1923- ... 111
Roelvaag, O(le) E(dvart) 1876-1931 Brief entry . 117
See also DLB 9
See also TCLC 17
Roemer, Joan (Phylis Akre) 1933- ... 132
Roemer, Kenneth Morrison 1945- ... CANR-32
Earlier sketch in CA 112
Roemer, Lawrence John 1916(?)-1989 Obituary ... 129
Roemer, Michael 1937- ... 111
Roemer, Milton I(rwin) 1916- ... CANR-47
Earlier sketches in CA 57-60, CANR-6, 21
Roemer, Norma H. 1905-1973 ... CAP-2
Earlier sketch in CA 19-20
Roemer, William F., Jr. 1926- ... 132
Roeming, Robert Frederick 1911- ... 29-32R
Roennfeldt, Robert 1953- ... SATA 78
Roepke, Wilhelm (Theodor) 1899-1966 ... CAP-1
Earlier sketch in CA 9-10
Roer, Berniece Marie ... 9-12R
Roes, Nicholas 1926- ... 29-32R
Roes, Nicholas A. 1952- ... 124
Roesch, Roberta F(leming) 1919- ... CANR-2
Earlier sketch in CA 5-8R
Roesch, Ronald 1947- ... 106
Roeseler, Robert O. 1882- ... CAP-2
Earlier sketch in CA 17-18
Roeseler, W(olfgang) G(uenter) 1925- ... 111
Roeske, Paulette 1945- ... 153
Roesler, Robert Harry 1927- ... 120
Roessel-Waugh, C. C.
See Waugh, Carol-Lynn Rossel
and Waugh, Charles G(ordon)
Roessler, Carl (Fred) 1933- ... 117
Roessner, Michaela(-Marie) 1950- ... 155
Roethenmund, Robert 1956- ... 103
Roethke, Theodore (Huebner) 1908-1963 ... 81-84
See also CABS 2
See also CDALB 1941-1968
See also CLC 1, 3, 8, 11, 19, 46, 101
See also DAM POET
See also DLB 5
See also MTCW 1
See also PC 15
Roets, Lois F. 1937- ... SATA 91
Roett, Riordan Joseph Allenby III 1938- ... 57-60
Roetter, Charles Frederick 1919- ... 61-64
Roetzel, Calvin J. 1931- ... 112
Roever, J(oan) M(arilyn) 1935- ... 105
See also SATA 26
Rofe, (Fevzi) Husein 1922- ... CAP-1
Earlier sketch in CA 9-10
Rofes, Eric Edward 1954- ... 106
See also SATA 52
Roff, William R(obert) 1929- ... 57-60
Roffey, Maureen 1936- ... 108
See also SATA 33
Roffman, Howard 1953- ... 61-64
Roffman, Roger A. 1942- ... 110
Roffman, Sara
See Hershman, Morris
Rofheart, Martha 1925- ... 149
Rogak, Lisa Angowski 1962- ... 148
See also SATA 80
Rogal, Samuel J. 1934- ... CANR-39
Earlier sketches in CA 25-28R, CANR-17
Rogaly, (Henry) Joseph 1935- ... 104
Rogan, Barbara 1951- ... 124
Rogan, Donald L(ynn) 1930- ... 29-32R
Rogan, Johnny 1953- ... 130
Rogan, Josh
See Mathison, Melissa
Rogasky, Barbara 1933- ... CANR-51
Earlier sketch in CA 130
See also SATA 86
Roger
See Sanchez Flores, Daniel
Roger, Mae Durham ... 57-60
Rogers, A(mos) Robert 1927- ... CANR-8
Earlier sketch in CA 61-64
Rogers, Agnes
See Allen, Agnes Rogers
Rogers, Alan 1933- ... CANR-28
Earlier sketches in CA 21-24R, CANR-11
Rogers, (Thomas) Alan (Stinchcombe) 1937- ... CANR-18
Earlier sketch in CA 25-28R
See also SATA 2, 81
Rogers, Annie G. ... 156
Rogers, Augustus James III 1929- ... 33-36R
Rogers, Barbara 1945- ... CANR-17
Earlier sketch in CA 65-68
Rogers, Berto 1903-1974 ... CAP-2
Earlier sketch in CA 29-32
Rogers, Bruce 1870-1957 Brief entry ... 123
Rogers, Carl R(ansom) 1902-1987 ... CANR-18
Obituary ... 121
Earlier sketches in CA 1-4R, CANR-1
See also MTCW 1
Rogers, (Grenville) Cedric (Harry) 1915- ... CANR-1
Earlier sketch in CA 1-4R
Rogers, Charles B. 1911- ... 89-92
Rogers, Cindy 1950- ... 155
See also SATA 89
Rogers, Clara Coltman
See Vyvyan, C(lara) C(oltman Rogers)
Rogers, Colin D(arlington) 1936- ... 155
Rogers, Cyril A(lfred) 1923-1993 ... 5-8R
Obituary ... 141
Rogers, Cyril H(arold) 1907- ... CANR-20
Earlier sketches in CA 9-12R, CANR-5
Rogers, Dale Evans 1912- ... 103
Interview in ... 103
Rogers, David 1930- ... 29-32R
Rogers, David C(harles) D(rummond) 1931- ... CANR-5
Earlier sketch in CA 9-12R

Rogers, Donald I(rwin) 1918-1980 57-60
Obituary 102
Rogers, Dorothy 1914-1986 .... CANR-1
Obituary 118
Earlier sketch in CA 1-4R
Rogers, Douglass Marcel 1925- 127
Rogers, Edith R(andam) 1924- 117
Rogers, Elizabeth F(rances) 1892-1974 .... 5-8R
Obituary 53-56
Rogers, Elyse M(acFadyen) 1932- 102
Rogers, Emma 1951- .... SATA 74
Rogers, Evelyn 1935- 165
Rogers, Florence K(atherine) 1936- 101
Rogers, Floyd
See Spence, William John Duncan
Rogers, Frances 1888-1974 .... 5-8R
See also SATA 10
Rogers, Francis M(illet) 1914- CANR-1
Earlier sketch in CA 1-4R
Rogers, Franklin R(obert) 1921- 1-4R
Rogers, Fred B(aker) 1926- 109
Rogers, Fred McFeely 1928- 107
See also SATA 33
Rogers, Garet 1-4R
Rogers, Gayle 1923- 69-72
Rogers, George Calvin, Jr. 1922- CANR-1
Earlier sketch in CA 1-4R
Rogers, George W(illiam) 1917- CANR-1
Earlier sketch in CA 1-4R
Rogers, H(ugh) C(uthbert) Basset 1905- . CANR-14
Earlier sketch in CA 73-76
Rogers, Helen Spelman 1913(?)-1990 Obituary 132
Rogers, Henry C. 1914-1995 102
Obituary 148
Rogers, Ingrid 1951- 116
Rogers, Jack 1934- 93-96
Rogers, James Allen 1929- 13-16R
Rogers, James T(racy) 1921- 45-48
Rogers, Jane 1952- 113
See also DLB 194
Rogers, Jean 1919- 115
See also SATA 55
See also SATA-Brief 47
Rogers, Jeanne F. 1926(?)-1984 Obituary 113
Rogers, JoAnn V. 1940- 89-92
Rogers, Joel Augustus 1880(?)-1966 153
See also BW 2
Rogers, Joel Townsley 1896-1984 Obituary 114
Rogers, John 1906- 5-8R
Rogers, Josephine 1925- 61-64
Rogers, Kate Ellen 1920- 13-16R
Rogers, Katharine M(unzer) 1932- CANR-8
Earlier sketch in CA 21-24R
Rogers, Kenneth Paul 1940- 53-56
Rogers, Kenneth Ray 85-88
Rogers, Kenny
See Rogers, Kenneth Ray
Rogers, Linda (Hall) 1944- 77-80
Rogers, Marian H. 1932- 140
Rogers, Matilda 1894-1976 .... CAP-2
Earlier sketch in CA 29-32
See also SATA 5
See also SATA-Obit 34
Rogers, Max Gray 1932- 53-56
Rogers, Michael (A.) 1950- CANR-28
Earlier sketches in CA 49-52, CANR-1
Rogers, Mick
See Glut, Donald F(rank)
Rogers, Millard F(oster), Jr. 1932- 101
Rogers, Neville William 1908- 108
Rogers, Pamela 1927- CANR-4
Earlier sketch in CA 49-52
See also SATA 9
Rogers, Pat 1938- 85-88
Rogers, Pattiann 1940- CANR-26
Earlier sketch in CA 109
See also DLB 105
Rogers, Paul (Patrick) 1900- 41-44R
Rogers, Paul 1950- 123
See also SATA 54, 98
Rogers, Paul T(aylor) 1936-1984 119
Obituary 113
Rogers, Peter 1934- 101
Rogers, Peter D(amien) 1942- CANR-38
Earlier sketch in CA 116
Rogers, Raymond A(rthur) 1911- 21-24R
Rogers, Robert
See Hamilton, Charles (Harold St. John)
Rogers, Robert F. 1930- 150
Rogers, Rolf E(rnst) 1931- 57-60
Rogers, Rosemary 1932- CANR-23
Earlier sketches in CA 49-52, CANR-3
Interview in CANR-23
See also AITN 1
See also DAM POP
See also MTCW 1
Rogers, Roy 1912- 112
Rogers, Rutherford D(avid) 1915- Brief entry ... 109
Rogers, Samuel 1763-1855 .... DLB 93
Rogers, Sarah F. 1923(?)-1976 Obituary 69-72
Rogers, Thomas Hunton 1927- 89-92
Interview in 89-92
See also CLC 57
Rogers, Timothy (John Godfrey) 1927- ... CANR-1
Earlier sketch in CA 45-48
Rogers, (George) Truett 1931- 69-72
Rogers, Tyler Stewart 1895-1967 .... 5-8R
Obituary 134
Rogers, Vincent R(obert) 1926- Brief entry 115
Rogers, W(illiam) G(arland) 1896-1978 .... 9-12R
Obituary 77-80
See also SATA 23
Rogers, Wade
See Madlee, Dorothy (Haynes)
Rogers, Warren
See Brucker, Roger W(arren)
Rogers, Warren (Joseph, Jr.) 1922- CANR-13
Earlier sketch in CA 77-80
Rogers, Will(iam Penn Adair) 1879-1935 144
Brief entry 105
See also DAM MULT
See also DLB 11
See also NNAL
See also TCLC 8, 71
Rogers, William C(ecil) 1919- 17-20R
Rogers, William D(ill) 1927- 41-44R
Rogers, William Elford 1944- 113
Rogers, William R(aymond) 1932- 104
Rogers, William Warren 1929- 127
Brief entry 112
Rogerson, J(ohn) W(illiam) 1935- CANR-38
Earlier sketch in CA 115
Rogerson, John
See Rogerson, J(ohn) W(illiam)
Rogg, Eleanor H(ertha) Meyer 1942- 57-60
Rogg, Sanford G. 1917-1976 .... 17-20R
Obituary 134
Rogge, Oetje John 1903-1981 .... 1-4R
Obituary 103
Rogin, Gilbert 1929- CANR-15
Earlier sketch in CA 65-68
See also CLC 18
Rogin, Michael Paul 1937- CANR-43
Earlier sketch in CA 101
Roginski, J(ames) W. 1945- 119
Roginski, Jim
See Roginski, J(ames) W.
Rogler, Lloyd H(enry) 1930- 17-20R
Roglieri, John Louis 1939- 105
Rogness, Alvin N. 1906- CANR-8
Earlier sketch in CA 21-24R
Rogness, Michael 1935- 101
Rogo, D. Scott 1950- CANR-28
Earlier sketches in CA 33-36R, CANR-13
Rogoff, Barbara 1950- CANR-42
Earlier sketch in CA 118
Rogoff, Harry 1882-1971 Obituary 33-36R
Rogosin, (William) Donn 1947- 123
Rogovin, Anne 1918- 97-100
Rogow, Arnold Austin 1924- CANR-1
Earlier sketch in CA 1-4R
Rogow, Roberta 1942- 140
Rogow, Zack 1952- 146
See also CAAS 28
Rogowski, Ronald (Lynn) 1944- CANR-58
Earlier sketch in CA 125
Roh, Jae Min 1927- 117
Rohan, Koda
See Koda Shigeyuki
See also TCLC 22
Rohan, Michael Scott 1951- 157
See also Scot, Michael
See also SATA 98
Rohan, Mike Scott
See Rohan, Michael Scott
Rohan, Zina 1946- 137
Rohatyn, Dennis 1949- 69-72
Rohatyn, Felix G(eorge) 1928- 118
Rohde, David S. 1967- 167
Rohen, Edward 1931- CANR-4
Earlier sketch in CA 53-56
Rohlen, Tom 1940- 85-88
Rohlfs, Anna Katharine Green
See Green, Anna Katharine
Rohmer, Eric
See Scherer, Jean-Marie Maurice
See also CLC 16
Rohmer, Harriet 1938- .... SATA 56
Rohmer, Richard 1924- CANR-19
Earlier sketch in CA 103
Rohmer, Sax
See Ward, Arthur Henry Sarsfield
See also DLB 70
See also TCLC 28
Rohn, Arthur H(enry, Jr.) 1929- CANR-25
Earlier sketch in CA 45-48
Rohner, Ronald P(reston) 1935- CANR-32
Earlier sketch in CA 37-40R
Rohr, John A. 1934- 33-36R
Rohrbach, Peter Thomas 1926- CANR-1
Earlier sketch in CA 1-4R
Rohrbaugh, Joanna Bunker 1943- 101
Rohrberger, Mary 1929- CANR-1
Earlier sketch in CA 45-48
Rohrbough, Malcolm J(ustin) 1932- 29-32R
Rohrer, Alyce Stevens 1922- 123
Rohrer, Daniel M(organ) 1941- 33-36R
Rohrer, Doug 1962- 155
See also SATA 89
Rohrer, Norman B(echtel) 1929- CANR-16
Earlier sketch in CA 93-96
Rohrer, Wayne C(urry) 1920- 21-24R
Rohrl, Vivian J. (Lober) 110
Rohrlich, Chester 1900(?)-1974 Obituary 53-56
Rohrlich, George F(riedrich) 1914- CANR-14
Earlier sketch in CA 37-40R
Rohrlich, Ruby CANR-5
Earlier sketch in CA 53-56
Rohrlich-Leavitt, Ruby
See Rohrlich, Ruby
Rohrlick, Paula 1955- 111
Rohrman, Nicholas L(eroy) 1937- 29-32R
Rohwer, Juergen 1924- 65-68
Rohwer, Jurgen
See Rohwer, Juergen
Roider, Karl A(ndrew), Jr. 1943- 111
Roiphe, Anne (Richardson) 1935- CANR-45
Earlier sketch in CA 89-92
Interview in 89-92
See also CLC 3, 9
See also DLBY 80
Roiphe, Katie 1968(?)- 145
Rojan
See Rojankovsky, Feodor Stepanovich
Rojankovsky, Feodor Stepanovich
1891-1970 77-80
See also SATA 21
Rojany, Lisa 159
See also SATA 94
Rojas, A. R.
See Rojas, Arnold R.
Rojas, Arnold R. 1896(?)-1988 153
See also DLB 82
See also HW
Rojas, Carlos 1928- CANR-49
Earlier sketches in CA 17-20R, CANR-7, 22
Rojas, Guillermo 1938- 153
See also HW
Rojas (Sepulveda), Manuel 1896-1973 153
See also HW
Rojko, Anthony J. 1918(?)-1978 Obituary 77-80
Rojo, Ricardo 1923- 25-28R
Rokeach, Milton 1918-1988 .... CANR-5
Obituary 127
Earlier sketch in CA 1-4R
Rokeby-Thomas, Anna E(lma) 1911- 77-80
See also SATA 15
Rokes, Willis Park 1926- 25-28R
Rokkan, Elizabeth 1925- 140
Roland, Albert 1925- 61-64
See also SATA 11
Roland, Betty 1903- 103
Roland, Charles G. 1933- 146
Roland, Charles P(ierce) 1918- 41-44R
Roland, Mary
See Lewis, Mary (Christianna)
Roland, Nicholas
See Walmsley, Arnold Robert
Roland Smith, Gordon 1931- 102
Rolant, Rene
See Fanthorpe, R(obert) Lionel
Rolde, Neil 1931- 148
Roldos Aguilera, Jaime 1940-1981 Obituary ... 108
Roleder, George 1928- CANR-21
Earlier sketch in CA 105
Rolerson, Darrell A(llen) 1946- 49-52
See also SATA 8
Rolf, David 1938- 130
Rolfe, Bari 1916- CANR-32
Earlier sketch in CA 113
Rolfe, Eugene (Edward Musgrave) 1914- ... 13-16R
Rolfe, Franklin P(rescott) 1902-1985 Obituary .. 117
Rolfe, Frederick (William Serafino Austin Lewis
1860-1913 Brief entry 107
See also DLB 34, 156
See also TCLC 12
Rolfe, Lionel (Menuhin) 1942- CANR-28
Earlier sketch in CA 110
Rolfe, Sheila Constance 1935- 102
Rolfe, Sidney 1921-1976 69-72
Obituary 65-68
Rolfsrud, Erling Nicolai 1912- 65-68
Roll, Charles W(eissert), Jr. 1928- CANR-1
Earlier sketch in CA 45-48
Roll, Eric 1907- 102
Roll, Richard J(effrey) 1952- 124
Roll, Samuel 1942- 124
Roll, William George, Jr. 1926- 81-84
Roll, Winifred 1909- 49-52
See also SATA 6
Rolland, Barbara J(une) 1929- 77-80
Rolland, Romain 1866-1944 Brief entry 118
See also DLB 65
See also TCLC 23
Rolle, Andrew Frank 1922- CANR-3
Earlier sketch in CA 1-4R
Rolle, Richard c. 1300-c. 1349 .... DLB 146
Roller, David C(harles) 1937- 107
Roller, Duane H(enry) D(uBose) 1920- 61-64
Rolleston, James Lancelot 1939- 85-88
Rollin, Bernard Elliot 1943- 108
Rollin, Betty 1936- CANR-22
Earlier sketches in CA 13-16R, CANR-7
Interview in CANR-22
Rollin, Roger Best 1930- CANR-8
Earlier sketch in CA 17-20R
Rollini, Arthur 1912- 127
Rollins, Alden M(ilton) 1946- 139
Rollins, Alfred Brooks, Jr. 1921- 5-8R
Rollins, Bryant 1937- 49-52
Rollins, C(alvin) D(wight) 1918- 41-44R
Rollins, Charlemae Hill 1897-1979 .... 9-12R
Obituary 104
See also BW 1
See also SATA 3
See also SATA-Obit 26
Rollins, Ed(ward J.) 1943(?)- 156
Rollins, Henry 1961- 154
Rollins, Judith 122
Rollins, Kelly (a pseudonym) 1924- 106
Rollins, Peter C(ushing) 1942- CANR-26
Earlier sketch in CA 108
Rollins, Richard M(eryl) 1945- 121
Rollins, Royce
See Pepper, Choral
Rollins, Steed 1916-1985 Obituary 118
Rollins, Wayne G(ilbert) 1929- CANR-3
Earlier sketch in CA 9-12R
Rollison, William D(ewey) 1897-1971 .... CAP-2
Earlier sketch in CA 19-20
Rollo, Vera Foster 1924- 81-84
Rollock, Barbara T(herese) 1924- .... SATA 64
Rolls, Anthony
See Vulliamy, Colwyn Edward
Rolls, Charles J(ubilee) 1887- 107
Rolls, Eric C(harles) 1923- CANR-13
Earlier sketch in CA 33-36R
Rollyson, Carl
See Rollyson, Carl E(dmund), Jr.
Rollyson, Carl E(dmund), Jr. 1948- CANR-65
Earlier sketch in CA 129
See also DLBY 97
Rolo, Charles J(acques) 1916-1982 101
Obituary 108
Rolo, Paul Jacques Victor 1917- 21-24R
Roloff, Leland Harold 1927- 49-52
Roloff, Michael 1937- 130
Rolph, C. H.
See Hewitt, Cecil Rolph
Rolph, Earl R(obert) 1910- CAP-2
Earlier sketch in CA 23-24
Rolston, Holmes III 1932- CANR-32
Earlier sketch in CA 113
Rolston, Holmes 1900-1977 .... CANR-3
Earlier sketch in CA 1-4R
Rolt, Francis 1955- 127
Rolt, L(ionel) T(homas) C(aswall) 1910-1974 ......
CANR-1
Earlier sketch in CA 1-4R
Rolt-Wheeler, Francis William
1876-1960 Obituary 89-92
Rolvaag, O(le) E(dvart)
See Roelvaag, O(le) E(dvart)
Rom, M. Martin 1946- 81-84
Romack, Janice Reed
See LeNoir, Janice
Romagnoli, G(ian) Franco 1926- 73-76
Romagnoli, Margaret O'Neill 1922- 73-76
Romain Arnaud, Saint
See Aragon, Louis
Romaine, Lawrence B. 1900- CAP-1
Earlier sketch in CA 13-14
Romaine, Paul
See Bleamer, Burton
Romaine-Davis, Ada 1929- 142
Romains, Jules 1885-1972 .... CANR-34
Earlier sketch in CA 85-88
See also CLC 7
See also DLB 65
See also MTCW 1
Roman, Daniel (David) 1921- 41-44R
Roman, Eric 1926- CANR-1
Earlier sketch in CA 1-4R
Roman, Howard (Edgar)
1916(?)-1988 Obituary 127
Roman, Murray 1920-1984 Obituary 112
Roman, Nancy Grace 1925- 161
Roman, Stephen B(oleslav) 1921- Brief entry .. 112
Romanell, Patrick 1912- 21-24R
Romanelli, Charles S. 1930- 13-16R
Romanelli, Giandomenico 1945- 168
Romanenko, Vitaliy 1962- .... SATA 101
Romano, Clare 1922- CANR-24
Earlier sketch in CA 41-44R
See also Ross, Clare
Romano, Deane Louis 1927- 25-28R
Romano, Don
See Turner, Robert (Harry)
Romano, Enotrio
See Carducci, Giosue (Alessandro Giuseppe)
Romano, John 1948- 133
Romano, Lalla 1906- .... DLB 177
Romano, Louis G. 1921- CANR-8
Earlier sketch in CA 17-20R
See also SATA 35
Romano, Octavio I. 1932- 153
See also DLB 122
See also HW
Romanoff, Alexis Lawrence 1892-1980 ... CANR-5
Earlier sketch in CA 9-12R
Romanoff, Harry 1892(?)-1970 Obituary 104
Romanow, Roy (John) 1939- 132
Romanowski, Patricia
See Bashe, Patricia Ann Romanowski
Romans, J(ohn) Thomas 1933- 13-16R
Romanucci-Ross, Lola 1928- CANR-18
Earlier sketch in CA 101
Romanus, Charles Franklin 1915-1983 ..... 21-24R
Obituary 111
Romanyshyn, Robert Donald 1942- 108
Romasco, Albert U(go) 1930- 110
Romberger, Judy 1940- 106
Rome, Anthony
See Albert, Marvin H(ubert)
Rome, Beatrice K(aufman) 1913- 13-16R
Rome, David 1910- 142
Rome, Elaine
See Barbieri, Elaine
Rome, Florence 1910- 33-36R
Romein, J. M.
See Romein, Jan (Marius)
Romein, Jan (Marius) 1893-1962 Obituary 111
Romer, Alfred 1906- 37-40R
Romer, (Louis) John 1941- 110
Romer, Stephen 1957- 125
Romero, George A. 1940(?)- 147
Brief entry 116
Romero, Gerry
See Neyland, James (Elwyn)
Romero, Jose Ruben 1890-1952 131
Brief entry 114
See also HW
See also TCLC 14
Romero, Leo 1950- .... DLB 122
Romero, Lin 1947- .... DLB 122
Romero, Luis 1916- Brief entry 111
Romero, Orlando 1945- 69-72
See also DLB 82
See also HW
Romero, Patricia W. 1935- CANR-31
Romerstein, Herbert 1931- 9-12R
Romey, Bill
See Romey, William D(owden)

Romey, William D(owden) 1930- ... 57-60
Romig, Edna Davis 1889-1978 ... 45-48
Obituary ... 103
Romig, Walter 1903-1977 Obituary ... 110
Romijn, Johanna Maria Kooyker
See Kooyker-Romijn, Johanna Maria
Romm, Ethel Grodzins 1925- ... 33-36R
Romm, Sharon 1942- ... 118
Rommel, (Mimi) Dayton ... 5-8R
Rommetveit, Ragnar 1924- ... 57-60
Romney, George W(ilcken)
1907-1995 Obituary ... 149
Brief entry ... 106
Romney, Rodney Ross 1931- ... 102
Romney, Ronna 1943- ... 116
Romney, Steve
See Bingley, David Ernest
Romo, Ricardo 1943- ... 111
Romoser, George K(enneth) 1929- ... 41-44R
Rompkey, Ronald (George) 1943- ... CANR-37
Earlier sketch in CA 118
Romtvedt, David 1950- ... 125
Romulo, Carlos P(ena) 1899(?)-1985 ... CANR-10
Obituary ... 118
Earlier sketch in CA 13-16R
Romyn, Johanna Maria Kooyker
See Kooyker-Romijn, Johanna Maria
Rona, Peter A(rnold) 1934- ... 108
Ronald, Ann 1939- ... 124
Ronald, David William 1937- ... 65-68
Ronald, Hugh 1912(?)-1983 Obituary ... 109
Ronalds, Mary Teresa 1946- ... 25-28R
Ronaldson, Agnes S. 1916- ... 17-20R
Ronan, Colin A(listair) 1920-1995 ... CANR-6
Obituary ... 148
Earlier sketch in CA 5-8R
Ronan, Frank 1963- ... 138
Ronan, Georgia
See Crampton, Georgia Ronan
Ronan, Margaret 1918- ... 102
Ronan, Thomas Matthew 1907- ... CAP-1
Earlier sketch in CA 9-10
Ronan, Tom
See Ronan, Thomas Matthew
Ronan, William W. 1917- ... 33-36R
Ronay, Gabriel Ernest 1930- ... 85-88
Roncalli, Angelo Giuseppe
See John XXIII, Pope
Ronck, Ronn 1946- ... 121
Ronda, James P(aul) 1943- ... 134
Brief entry ... 113
Rondell, Florence 1907- ... 57-60
Ronder, Paul 1940(?)-1977 Obituary ... 73-76
Rondinelli, Dennis A(ugust) 1943- ... 111
Rondthaler, Edward 1905- ... 13-16R
Ronell, Avital 1956- ... 133
Ronen, Dov 1933- ... CANR-28
Earlier sketches in CA 57-60, CANR-10
Roney, Ruth Anne
See McMullin, Ruth R(oney)
Rongen, Bjoern 1906- ... CAP-2
Earlier sketch in CA 29-32
See also SATA 10
Rongen, Bjorn
See Rongen, Bjoern
Rongione, Louis Anthony 1912- ... 57-60
Ronk, Martha C(lare) 1940- ... 152
Ronken, Harriet
See Lynton, Harriet Ronken
Ronne, Finn 1899-1980 ... CANR-1
Obituary ... 97-100
Earlier sketch in CA 1-4R
Ronnie, Art(hur William) 1931- ... 41-44R
Ronning, C. Neale 1927- ... 5-8R
Ronning, Chester A. 1894-1984 Obituary ... 114
Ronns, Edward
See Aarons, Edward S(idney)
Ronsard, Pierre de 1524-1585 ... PC 11
Ronsheim, Sally B(ober) 1917(?)-1990 ... 57-60
Obituary ... 133
Ronsin, Jean
See Rodinson, Maxime
Ronsley, Joseph 1931- ... CANR-10
Earlier sketch in CA 25-28R
Ronsman, M. M.
See Nowak, Mariette
Ronson, Mark
See Alexander, Marc
Rood, Allan 1894- ... CAP-1
Earlier sketch in CA 13-14
Rood, John (Hiram) 1902-1974 ... 5-8R
Obituary ... 120
Rood, Karen Lane 1946- ... 102
Rood, Robert Thomas 1942- ... 107
Rood, Ronald (N.) 1920- ... CANR-50
Earlier sketches in CA 21-24R, CANR-9, 24
See also SATA 12
Roodenburg, Nancy McKee
1909-1972 Obituary ... 104
Roof, Wade Clark 1939- ... 114
Rook, (William) Alan 1909- ... 97-100
Rook, Clarence 1863-1915 ... DLB 135
Rook, Earnest Robert 1917- ... 104
Rook, Tony 1932- ... 69-72
Rooke, Constance 1942- ... 126
Rooke, Daphne (Marie) 1914- ... 53-56
See also SATA 12
Rooke, Leon 1934- ... CANR-53
Earlier sketches in CA 25-28R, CANR-23
See also CLC 25, 34
See also DAM POP
Rooke, P(atricia) T. 1938- ... 127
Rookmaaker, Hendrik Roelof 1922-1977 ... CANR-26
Earlier sketch in CA 57-60
Rooks, George (M.) 1951- ... CANR-22
Earlier sketch in CA 105
Rooks, Judith P. 1941- ... 168
Rooksby, Rikky 1958- ... 144
Room, Adrian 1933- ... CANR-16
Earlier sketch in CA 97-100
Roome, Katherine Ann Davis 1952- ... 85-88
Rooney, Andrew A(itken) 1919- ... CANR-65
Earlier sketches in CA 5-8R, CANR-9, 45
Interview in ... CANR-9
See also Rooney, Andy
See also MTCW 1
Rooney, Andy ... CANR-9
See also Rooney, Andrew A(itken)
Rooney, David Douglas 1924- ... CANR-11
Earlier sketch in CA 21-24R
Rooney, Elmo
See Perry, Charles
Rooney, James 1938- ... 101
Rooney, James R(owell) 1927- ... 61-64
Rooney, Jim
See Rooney, James
Rooney, John F(rancis), Jr. 1939- ... 101
Rooney, Lucy 1926- ... 135
Rooney, Miriam Theresa ... 81-84
Rooney, Patrick C. 1937- ... 29-32R
Rooney, William Richard 1938- ... 102
Roop, Connie
See Roop, Constance Betzer
Roop, Constance Betzer 1951- ... CANR-49
Earlier sketch in CA 122
See also SATA 54
See also SATA-Brief 49
Roop, Peter (G.) 1951- ... CANR-48
Earlier sketch in CA 122
See also SATA 54
See also SATA-Brief 49
Roorbach, Bill 1953- ... 137
Roos, Audrey (Kelley) 1912-1982 ... 128
Obituary ... 108
Roos, Charles A. 1914(?)-1974 Obituary ... 53-56
Roos, Hans
See Meissner, Hans-Otto
Roos, Hans Dietrich 1919- ... 17-20R
Roos, Johan 1961- ... 145
Roos, Kelley
See Roos, Audrey (Kelley)
Roos, Leslie L(eon), Jr. 1940- ... 33-36R
Roos, Murphre (joint pseudonym)
See Mele, Jim
Roos, Noralou P(reston) 1942- ... 33-36R
Roos, Stephen (Kelley) 1945- ... CANR-31
Earlier sketch in CA 112
See also JRDA
See also SATA 47, 77
See also SATA-Brief 41
Roosa, Robert V(incent) 1918-1993 ... 25-28R
Obituary ... 143
Roose, Ronald 1945- ... 81-84
Roose-Evans, James 1927- ... CANR-35
Earlier sketch in CA 29-32R
See also SATA 65
Roosen, William (James) 1940- ... 117
Roosenburg, Henriette 1920-1972 Obituary ... 37-40R
Roosevelt, Archibald Bulloch, Jr. 1918-1990 ... 127
Obituary ... 131
Roosevelt, Archie
See Roosevelt, Archibald Bulloch, Jr.
Roosevelt, Edith Kermit 1926- ... 69-72
Roosevelt, (Anna) Eleanor
1884-1962 Obituary ... 89-92
See also SATA 50
Roosevelt, Elliott 1910-1990 ... 105
Obituary ... 132
See also AITN 1
Roosevelt, Felicia Warburg 1927- ... 57-60
Roosevelt, Franklin Delano 1882-1945 Brief
entry ... 116
Roosevelt, James 1907-1991 ... CANR-12
Obituary ... 135
Earlier sketch in CA 69-72
Roosevelt, Nicholas 1893-1982 Obituary ... 106
Roosevelt, Selwa 1929- ... 134
Roosevelt, Theodore 1858-1919 Brief entry ... 115
See also DLB 47, 186
See also TCLC 69
Root, Betty ... SATA 84
Root, Deane L(eslie) 1947- ... CANR-47
Earlier sketches in CA 107, CANR-23
Root, Deborah 1953- ... 164
Root, E(dward) Merrill 1895-1973 ... CAP-1
Earlier sketch in CA 13-16
Root, Franklin Russell 1923- ... 5-8R
Root, Judith C(arol) ... 65-68
Root, Lin (Segal) ... 69-72
Root, Oren 1911- ... 85-88
Root, Phyllis 1949- ... CANR-50
Earlier sketch in CA 123
See also SATA 55, 94
See also SATA-Brief 48
Root, Shelton L., Jr. 1923-1986 ... SATA-Obit 51
Root, Waverley (Lewis) 1903-1982 ... CANR-29
Obituary ... 108
Earlier sketch in CA 25-28R
See also DLB 4
Root, William Pitt 1941- ... CANR-12
Earlier sketch in CA 25-28R
See also CAAS 11
See also DLB 120
Root-Bernstein, Michele 1953- ... 167
Root-Bernstein, Robert Scott 1953- ... 132
Rooth, Gerhard Theodore
1898(?)-1983 Obituary ... 110
Rootham, Jasper (St. John) 1910-1990 ... CANR-41
Earlier sketches in CA 5-8R, CANR-4, 19
Roots, Clive (George) 1935- Brief entry ... 111
Roots, Ivan Alan 1921- ... 9-12R
Roots, John McCook 1904(?)-1988 Obituary ... 126
Rooze, Gene E(dward) 1934- ... 120
Rope, Henry Edward George 1880-1978 ... 5-8R
Obituary ... 103
Roper, Gayle G(ordinier) 1940- ... 97-100
Roper, H(ugh) R(edwald) Trevor
See Trevor-Roper, H(ugh) R(edwald)
Roper, John Herbert 1948- ... 128
Roper, John Stephen 1924(?)-1980 Obituary ... 102
Roper, Lanning 1912-1983 Obituary ... 109
Roper, Laura Wood 1911- ... 57-60
See also SATA 34
Roper, Robert 1946- ... 73-76
See also SATA 78
Roper, Ronnalie J. 1936- ... 41-44R
Roper, Steve 1941- ... 103
Roper, Susan Bonthron 1948- ... 81-84
Roper, William L(eon) 1897-1990 ... 33-36R
Obituary ... 130
Ropes, Linda Brubaker 1942- ... 140
Ropke, Wilhelm (Theodor)
See Roepke, Wilhelm (Theodor)
Ropp, Theodore 1911- ... 5-8R
Roppolo, Joseph Patrick 1913- ... 13-16R
Rops, Daniel
See Petiot, Henri Jules Charles
Roquebrune, Robert (Laroque) de 1889-1978 ... 148
See also DLB 68
Roquelaure, A. N.
See Rice, Anne
Roquemore, Kathleen (Ann) 1941- ... 61-64
Rorabaugh, William Joseph 1945- ... 101
Rorby, Ginny 1944- ... 159
See also SATA 94
Rorem, Ned 1923- ... CANR-32
Earlier sketch in CA 17-20R
Rorer, Abigail 1949- ... SATA 85
Roripaugh, Robert A(lan) 1930- ... CANR-64
Earlier sketch in CA 13-16R
Rorke, Margaret (Curry) 1915- ... 110
Rorty, Amelie Oksenberg 1932- ... 107
Rorty, James 1891(?)-1973 Obituary ... 41-44R
Rorty, Richard M(cKay) 1931- ... CANR-9
Earlier sketch in CA 21-24R
Rorty, Winifred Raushenbush
1894(?)-1979 Obituary ... 93-96
Rorvik, David M(ichael) 1946- ... CANR-38
Earlier sketch in CA 85-88
Rosa, Alexis Gomez
See Gomez Rosa, Alexis
See also HW
Rosa, Alfred F(elix) 1942- ... 41-44R
Rosa, Joao Guimaraes 1908-1967 Obituary ... 89-92
See also CLC 23
See also DLB 113
Rosa, Joseph G. 1932- ... 13-16R
Rosa, Nicholas 1926- ... 110
Rosage, David E. 1913- ... CANR-21
Earlier sketches in CA 13-16R, CANR-6
Rosaldo, Michelle Z(imbalist) 1944-1981 ... 101
Obituary ... 108
Rosaldo, Renato I(gnacio), Jr. 1941- ... 89-92
Rosaler, Robert C. 1920- ... 155
Rosales, Francisco A(rturo) 1942- ... 131
See also HW
Rosales, Luis 1910-1992 ... DLB 134
Rosand, David 1938- ... 111
Rosa-Nieves, Cesareo 1901-1974 ... 57-60
See also HW
Rosario Green (de Heller), Maria del 1941- ... 130
See also HW
Rosato, Dominick V. 1921- ... 166
Rosbottom, Ronald C(arlisle) 1942- ... 61-64
Rosca, Ninotchka ... 127
Roscoe, A(drian) A(lan) 1939- ... 49-52
Roscoe, Charles
See Rowland, D(onald) S(ydney)
Roscoe, D(onald) T(homas) 1934- ... 113
See also SATA 42
Roscoe, Edwin Scott 1896-1978 ... 5-8R
Obituary ... 103
Roscoe, George B(oggs) 1907-1996 ... 65-68
Obituary ... 152
Roscoe, Patrick 1962- ... 151
Roscoe, Will 1955- ... 148
Roscoe, William 1753-1831 ... DLB 163
Rosdail, Jesse Hart 1914(?)-1977 Obituary ... 73-76
Rose, A(rthur) James 1927- ... 17-20R
Rose, Ada Campbell 1902(?)-1976 Obituary ... 65-68
Rose, Al 1916- ... 97-100
Rose, Alan Henry 1938- ... 93-96
Rose, Albert H(enry) 1903- ... 41-44R
Rose, Alvin E(manuel) 1903-1983 Obituary ... 109
Rose, Andrew (Wyness) 1944- ... 136
Rose, Anna Perrott
See Wright, Anna (Maria Louisa Perrott) Rose
Rose, Anne ... CANR-2
Earlier sketch in CA 49-52
See also SATA 8
Rose, Anthony Lewis 1939- ... 101
Rose, Arnold 1916-1983 Obituary ... 109
Rose, Arnold M(arshall) 1918-1968 ... 5-8R
Rose, Barbara E. 1937- Brief entry ... 111
Rose, Betsy
See Rose, Elizabeth
Rose, Billy 1899-1966 Obituary ... 116
Rose, Brian Waldron 1915- ... 97-100
Rose, Camille Davied 1893- ... CAP-2
Earlier sketch in CA 21-22
Rose, Carl 1903-1971 Obituary ... 29-32R
See also SATA-Brief 31
Rose, Clarkson 1890-1968 ... 5-8R
Rose, Clive (Martin) 1921- ... 121
Rose, Constance Hubbard 1934- ... CANR-16
Earlier sketch in CA 29-32R
Rose, Daniel M. 1940- ... 33-36R
Rose, David S. 1947- ... 121
Rose, Deborah Lee 1955- ... SATA 71
Rose, Elinor K(iess) 1920- ... 29-32R
Rose, Elizabeth 1915- ... 73-76
Rose, Elizabeth (Jane Pretty) 1933- ... CANR-9
Earlier sketch in CA 5-8R
See also SATA 68
See also SATA-Brief 28
Rose, (Edward) Elliot 1928- ... 65-68
Rose, Ernst A(ndreas) G(ottlieb) 1899- ... CANR-4
Earlier sketch in CA 5-8R
Rose, Florella
See Carlson, Vada F.
Rose, Frank 1949- ... 103
Rose, Gerald (Hembdon Seymour) 1935- ...
CANR-42
Earlier sketches in CA 65-68, CANR-9
See also SATA 68
See also SATA-Brief 30
Rose, Gilbert J(acob) 1923- ... 103
Rose, (Arthur) Gordon 1920-1975 ... CANR-4
Earlier sketch in CA 1-4R
Rose, Grace B(erne) 1914- ... 108
Rose, Hannah T. 1909(?)-1976 Obituary ... 69-72
Rose, Harold 1921-1967 ... 5-8R
Obituary ... 103
Rose, Harold Wickliffe 1896- ... CAP-1
Earlier sketch in CA 9-10
Rose, Helen 1904(?)-1985 Obituary ... 117
Rose, Hilary
See Mackinnon, Charles Roy
Rose, Homer C. 1909-1967 ... CAP-1
Earlier sketch in CA 13-16
Rose, James M. 1941- ... 102
Rose, Jeanne 1940- ... CANR-16
Earlier sketch in CA 93-96
Rose, Jennifer
See Weber, Nancy
Rose, Jerome G. 1926- ... CANR-8
Earlier sketch in CA 13-16R
Rose, Jerry D. 1933- ... 33-36R
Rose, Joel 1948- ... CANR-66
Earlier sketch in CA 129
Rose, Kenneth (Vivian) 1924- ... 128
Brief entry ... 123
Rose, Kenneth Jon 1954- ... CANR-38
Earlier sketch in CA 115
Rose, Laurel L. 1952- ... 144
Rose, Lawrence F.
See Fearn, John Russell
Rose, Leo E. 1926- ... 85-88
Rose, Lisle A(bbott) 1936- ... CANR-10
Earlier sketch in CA 65-68
Rose, Lynn Edmondson 1934- Brief entry ... 105
Rose, Marcia
See Kamien, Marcia
and Novak, Rose
Rose, Margaret A. 1947- ... 138
Rose, Marilyn Gaddis 1930- ... 33-36R
Rose, Mark 1939- ... CANR-10
Earlier sketch in CA 25-28R
Rose, Michael (Simon) 1937- ... 133
Rose, Nancy (Ann) 1934- ... 37-40R
Rose, Nancy A.
See Sweetland, Nancy A(nn)
Rose, Norman Anthony 1934- ... 104
Rose, Paul (Bernard) 1935- ... 103
Rose, Pete(r Edward) 1942- Brief entry ... 113
Rose, Peter I(saac) 1933- ... CANR-5
Earlier sketch in CA 13-16R
Rose, Phyllis
See Thompson, Phyllis Hoge
Rose, Phyllis 1942- ... CANR-45
Earlier sketch in CA 135
Rose, R(obert) B(arrie) 1929- ... 61-64
Rose, Ralph 1911(?)-1984 Obituary ... 112
Rose, Reginald 1920- ... CANR-42
Earlier sketch in CA 73-76
See also DLB 26
Rose, Richard 1933- ... CANR-27
Earlier sketches in CA 21-24R, CANR-10
Rose, Stephen C. 1936- ... 129
Rose, Steven 1938- ... 168
Rose, Stuart 1899(?)-1975 Obituary ... 61-64
Rose, Susan (Phyllida) 1938- ... 111
Rose, Ted 1940- ... SATA 93
Rose, Thomas 1938- ... 33-36R
Rose, Wendy 1948- ... CANR-51
Earlier sketches in CA 53-56, CANR-5
See also CLC 85
See also DAM MULT
See also DLB 175
See also NNAL
See also PC 13
See also SATA 12
Rose, Will(iam Palen) 1889-1977 ... 57-60
Obituary ... 134
Rose, William 1920(?)-1987 Obituary ... 121
Rose, Willie Lee (Nichols) 1927- ... 13-16R
Rose-Ackerman, Susan 1942- ... 111
Roseberry, Cecil R. 1902- ... 21-24R
Roseboom, Eugene Holloway 1892- ... 5-8R
Roseboro, John 1933- ... 102
Rosebrock, Ellen Fletcher 1947- ... CANR-10
Earlier sketch in CA 57-60
Rosebury, Theodor 1904-1976 ... CAP-2
Obituary ... 69-72
Earlier sketch in CA 25-28
Rosecrance, Francis Chase 1897- ... 5-8R
Rosecrance, Richard (Newton) 1930- Brief
entry ... 111
Rosedale, Valerie
See Harron, Don(ald)
Rosefielde, Steven 1942- ... CANR-25
Earlier sketch in CA 45-48
Rosegger, Peter 1843-1918 ... DLB 129
Rosegrant, Susan 1954- ... 144

Rosei, Peter 1946- DLB 85
Roseliep, Raymond 1917- CANR-6
Earlier sketch in CA 9-12R
Roselle, Daniel 1920- 13-16R
Roseller, David
See Timms, E(dward) V(ivian)
Roseman, Ellen Barbara 1947- 124
Roseman, Kenneth David 1939- 110
See also SATA-Brief 52
Rosemeyer, Nita (Mary) 1907- 119
Rosemond, John K(irk) 1947- 110
Rosemont, Henry, Jr. 1934- 41-44R
Rosen, Barbara 1929- 37-40R
Rosen, Barry 1944- 136
Rosen, Benson 1942- 120
Rosen, Carol (Cynthia) 1950- 119
Rosen, Charles (Welles) 1927- CANR-50
Earlier sketch in CA 126
Rosen, Corey 1948- 138
Rosen, Dorothy 1916- CANR-43
Earlier sketch in CA 119
Rosen, Edward 1906-1985 21-24R
Obituary 115
Rosen, Elliot A(lfred) 1928- 93-96
Rosen, Frederick 1938- CANR-45
Earlier sketch in CA 120
Rosen, George 1910-1977 CANR-31
Obituary 73-76
Earlier sketch in CA 81-84
Rosen, George 1920- 57-60
Rosen, Gerald 1938- 33-36R
See also CAAS 29
Rosen, Haiim B(aruch) 1922- CANR-49
Earlier sketches in CA 1-4R, CANR-20
Rosen, Hjalmar 1922- 17-20R
Rosen, Ira 1954- 114
Rosen, James Alan 1908(?)-1972 Obituary 37-40R
Rosen, Joe
See Rosen, Joseph
Rosen, Joseph 1937- CANR-9
Earlier sketch in CA 65-68
Rosen, Laura 1948- 116
Rosen, Lawrence R(onald) 1938- 57-60
Rosen, Leonard 1954- 125
Rosen, Leora N(adine) 1950- 159
Rosen, Lillian (Diamond) 1928- 108
See also SATA 63
Rosen, Martin Meyer
See Rosen, Moishe (Martin)
Rosen, Marvin J(erold) 1929- 69-72
Rosen, Michael 1946- CANR-32
Earlier sketches in CA 25-28R, CANR-15
See also SATA 48
See also SATA-Brief 40
Rosen, Michael (Wayne) 1946- CANR-52
See also CLR 45
See also SATA 84
Rosen, Michael J(oel) 1954- CANR-49
Earlier sketch in CA 132
See also SATA 86
Rosen, Moishe (Martin) 1932- CANR-4
Earlier sketch in CA 49-52
Rosen, Mortimer (Gilbert) 1931- 101
Rosen, Norma (Gangel) 1925- 33-36R
See also DLB 28
Rosen, Paul L(yon) 1939- 61-64
Rosen, R. D.
See Rosen, Richard (Dean)
Rosen, Richard (Dean) 1949- CANR-62
Earlier sketch in CA 77-80
Interview in CANR-30
See also CLC 39
Rosen, Robert C(harles) 1947- 106
Rosen, Robert H. 1955- 139
Rosen, Ruth (E.) 1945- 125
Rosen, S. McKee 1902(?)-1978 Obituary 77-80
Rosen, Sam 1920- 5-8R
Rosen, Samuel 1897-1981 Obituary 108
Rosen, Seymour Michael 1924- 33-36R
Rosen, Sheldon 1943- 109
Rosen, Shirley 1933- 105
Rosen, Sidney 1916- 9-12R
See also SATA 1
Rosen, Stanley H. 1929- 25-28R
Rosen, Stephen 1934- 65-68
Rosen, Trix 1947- 116
Rosen, Winifred 1943- CANR-32
Earlier sketch in CA 29-32R
See also SATA 8
Rosenak, Charles B. 1927- 134
Rosenak, Chuck
See Rosenak, Charles B.
Rosenak, Jan(ice M.) 1930- 134
Rosenast, Eleanor S(trauss) 1929- 97-100
Rosenau, Helen 101
Rosenau, James N(athan) 1924- CANR-18
Earlier sketches in CA 1-4R, CANR-2
Rosenau, Pauline Vaillancourt 1943- 144
Rosenauer, Johnnie L(ee) 1951- 110
Rosenbach, A. S. W. 1876-1952 DLB 140
Rosenbaum, Alan S(helby) 1941- 124
Brief entry 106
Rosenbaum, Alvin 1945- 113
Rosenbaum, Bernard L. 1937- 107
Rosenbaum, Edward E. 1915- 139
Rosenbaum, Eileen 1936- 21-24R
Rosenbaum, Ernest H. 1929- 97-100
Rosenbaum, H. Jon 1941- 41-44R
Rosenbaum, Jean 1927- 17-20R
Rosenbaum, Jonathan 1943- 130
Rosenbaum, Kurt 1926- 13-16R
Rosenbaum, Maurice 1907- 17-20R
See also SATA 6
Rosenbaum, Max 1923- 41-44R
Rosenbaum, Nathan 1897- CAP-2
Earlier sketch in CA 23-24
Rosenbaum, Patricia L(eib) 1932- 105
Rosenbaum, Peter S. 1940- CANR-14
Earlier sketch in CA 21-24R
Rosenbaum, Ron 1946- DLB 185
Rosenbaum, S(tanford) P(atrick) 1929- 13-16R
Rosenbaum, Samuel R(awlins)
1888-1972 Obituary 37-40R
Rosenbaum, Veryl 1936- CANR-1
Earlier sketch in CA 49-52
Rosenbaum, Walter A(nthony) 1937- 21-24R
Rosenberg, Alexander 1946- 132
Rosenberg, Amye 1950- SATA 74
Rosenberg, Arthur D(onald) 1939- 61-64
Rosenberg, Betty 1916- 113
Rosenberg, Blanca 1913- 143
Rosenberg, Bruce A(lan) 1934- 29-32R
Rosenberg, Charles E(rnest) 1936- 97-100
Rosenberg, Claude N(ewman), Jr. 1928- CANR-5
Earlier sketch in CA 1-4R
Rosenberg, David 1943- 147
Rosenberg, David A(aron) 1940- 93-96
Rosenberg, Dorothy 1906- CANR-18
Earlier sketches in CA 45-48, CANR-2
See also SATA 40
Rosenberg, Edgar 1925- 13-16R
Rosenberg, Emily S(chlaht) 1944- 108
Rosenberg, Ethel (Clifford) 1915- CANR-57
Earlier sketches in CA 29-32R, CANR-16
See also Clifford, Eth
See also SATA 3
Rosenberg, George S(tanley) 1930- 29-32R
Rosenberg, Harold 1906-1978 CANR-39
Obituary 77-80
Earlier sketch in CA 21-24R
Rosenberg, Harry E. 1932- 57-60
Rosenberg, Isaac 1890-1918 Brief entry 107
See also DLB 20
See also TCLC 12
Rosenberg, Israel 1909- 49-52
Rosenberg, J(ehiol) Mitchell 1906- 37-40R
Rosenberg, Jakob 1893-1980 Obituary 97-100
Rosenberg, James L. 1921- 13-16R
Rosenberg, Jane 1949- CANR-47
Earlier sketch in CA 121
See also SATA 58
Rosenberg, Janet 1930- 117
Rosenberg, Jerome Roy 1926- 104
Rosenberg, Jerry M. 1935- CANR-24
Earlier sketches in CA 21-24R, CANR-9
Rosenberg, Jessie 1941- 21-24R
Rosenberg, Joel 1954- 115
Rosenberg, John D(avid) 1929- CANR-5
Earlier sketch in CA 1-4R
Rosenberg, John J.
See Ramati, Yohanan (Joseph)
Rosenberg, Joseph
See Ramati, Yohanan (Joseph)
Rosenberg, Judith K(aren) 1945- 57-60
Rosenberg, Kenyon Charles 1933- 57-60
Rosenberg, Liz 1958- 142
See also SATA 75
Rosenberg, Marvin 1912- 1-4R
Rosenberg, Maurice 1919- 81-84
Rosenberg, Maxine B(erta) 1939- CANR-65
Earlier sketches in CA 117, CANR-41
See also SATA 55, 93
See also SATA-Brief 47
Rosenberg, Morris 1922- CANR-2
Earlier sketch in CA 5-8R
Rosenberg, Nancy (Sherman) 1931- CANR-22
Earlier sketches in CA 1-4R, CANR-5
See also SATA 4
Rosenberg, Nancy Taylor 1946- CANR-62
Earlier sketch in CA 140
Rosenberg, Nathan 1927- 147
Brief entry 113
Rosenberg, Neil V. 1939- 122
Rosenberg, Norman J(ack) 1930- 57-60
Rosenberg, Norman L(ewis) 1942- CANR-48
Earlier sketch in CA 122
Rosenberg, Philip 1942- 103
Interview in 103
Rosenberg, Robert 1951- 160
Rosenberg, Rosalind 1946- 108
Rosenberg, Samuel 1912-1996 53-56
Obituary 151
Rosenberg, Sharon 1942- CANR-10
Earlier sketch in CA 57-60
See also SATA 8
Rosenberg, Shirley Sirota 1925- CANR-12
Earlier sketch in CA 21-24R
Rosenberg, Stephen N(icholas) 1941- 111
Rosenberg, Stuart E. 1922-1990 CANR-9
Obituary 131
Earlier sketch in CA 5-8R
Rosenberg, Tina 1960- CANR-53
Earlier sketch in CA 136
Rosenberg, William Gordon 1938- 61-64
Rosenberg, Wolfgang 1915- CANR-9
Earlier sketch in CA 65-68
Rosenberger, Francis Coleman 1915- CANR-15
Earlier sketch in CA 41-44R
Rosenberger, Harleigh M. 1913- 21-24R
Rosenberger, Homer Tope 1908- CANR-8
Earlier sketch in CA 17-20R
Rosenberry, Vera 1948- SATA 83
Rosenblatt, Arthur
See Rosenblatt, Arthur S.
Rosenblatt, Arthur S. 1938- 134
See also SATA 68
See also SATA-Brief 45
Rosenblatt, Bernard A. 1886- CAP-1
Earlier sketch in CA 13-14
Rosenblatt, Fred 1914- 41-44R
Rosenblatt, Gary 1947- 77-80
Rosenblatt, Jason P. 1941- 137
Rosenblatt, Joe
See Rosenblatt, Joseph
See also CLC 15
Rosenblatt, Jon M(ichael) 1947- 89-92
Rosenblatt, Joseph 1933- 89-92
Interview in 89-92
See also Rosenblatt, Joe
Rosenblatt, Lily 1956- SATA 90
Rosenblatt, Louise M(ichelle) 1904- 49-52
Rosenblatt, Milton B. 1908(?)-1975 Obituary 53-56
Rosenblatt, Roger 1940- CANR-34
Earlier sketch in CA 85-88
Rosenblatt, Samuel 1902- 53-56
Rosenblatt, Stanley M. 1936- 29-32R
Rosenblatt, Suzanne Maris 1937- 69-72
Rosenblith, Judy F(rancis) 1921- 25-28R
Rosenbloom, Bert 1944- 109
Rosenbloom, David H(arry) 1943- 73-76
Rosenbloom, David L. 1944- 45-48
Rosenbloom, Jerry S(amuel) 1939- 129
Brief entry 110
Rosenbloom, Joseph 1928- CANR-21
Earlier sketches in CA 57-60, CANR-6
See also SATA 21
Rosenbloom, Joseph R. 1928- 29-32R
Rosenbloom, Noah H. 1915- CANR-14
Earlier sketch in CA 37-40R
Rosenblum, Art 1927- 57-60
Rosenblum, Davida 1927- 93-96
Rosenblum, Gershen 1924- 41-44R
Rosenblum, Helen Faye 1941- 121
Rosenblum, Joseph 1947- 111
Rosenblum, Leonard A. 1936- CANR-11
Earlier sketch in CA 57-60
Rosenblum, Marc J. 1936- 29-32R
Rosenblum, Martin J(ack) 1946- CANR-40
Earlier sketches in CA 45-48, CANR-2, 18
See also CAAS 11
Rosenblum, Mort 1943- 73-76
Rosenblum, Nancy L. 1947- 133
Rosenblum, Richard 1928- CANR-9
Earlier sketch in CA 65-68
See also SATA 11
Rosenblum, Robert H. 1927- CANR-5
Earlier sketch in CA 1-4R
Rosenbluth, Gideon 1921- 61-64
Rosenburg, Ellis Howard
1936(?)-1986 Obituary 121
Rosenburg, John M. 1918- 21-24R
See also SATA 6
Rosenburg, Robert K(emper) 1920- CANR-4
Earlier sketch in CA 5-8R
Rosendall, Betty 1916- 49-52
Rosenfarb, Chawa 1923- 53-56
Rosenfeld, Albert (Hyman) 1920- CANR-11
Earlier sketch in CA 65-68
Rosenfeld, Alvin (Z.) 1919-1992 73-76
Obituary 139
Rosenfeld, Alvin H(irsch) 1938- CANR-24
Earlier sketches in CA 49-52, CANR-4
Rosenfeld, Arnold (Solomon) 1933- 65-68
Rosenfeld, Dina 1962- 167
See also SATA 99
Rosenfeld, Edward J(ulius) 1943- 41-44R
Rosenfeld, Harry M(orris) 1929- 69-72
Rosenfeld, Harvey 1939- 110
Rosenfeld, Isaac 1918-1956 DLB 28
Rosenfeld, Isadore 1926- CANR-40
Earlier sketch in CA 81-84
Rosenfeld, Jeffrey P(hilip) 1946- 115
Rosenfeld, Lulla 1914- 85-88
Rosenfeld, Marthe 1928- 45-48
Rosenfeld, Nancy (G.) 1941- 148
Rosenfeld, Sam 1920- 9-12R
Rosenfeld, Samuel
See Tzara, Tristan
Rosenfeld, Sybil (Marion) 1903-1996 119
Obituary 154
Rosenfield, Isadore 1893-1980 Obituary 97-100
Rosenfield, Israel 1939- 128
Rosenfield, James A(lexander) 1943- 49-52
Rosenfield, John M(ax) 1924- CANR-14
Earlier sketch in CA 21-24R
Rosenfield, Leonora Cohen 1909-1982 41-44R
Obituary 105
Rosenfield, Paul 1948- 139
Rosengart, Oliver A. 1941- 49-52
Rosengarten, Frank 1927- 73-76
Rosengarten, Frederic (Jr.) 1916- 118
Rosengarten, Herbert (J.) 1940- 138
Rosengarten, Theodore 1944- 103
Rosengren, William R(udolph) 1929- Brief entry 114
Rosenhaupt, Hans 1911-1985 Obituary 116
Rosenheim, Andrew 1955- 139
Rosenheim, Edward W(eil), Jr. 1918- 25-28R
Rosenheim, Lucile G. 1902-1990 Obituary 132
Rosenhouse, Archie 1878- CAP-2
Earlier sketch in CA 21-22
Rosenkrantz, Linda 1934- CANR-11
Earlier sketch in CA 25-28R
Rosenkranz, E. Joshua 1961- 159
Rosenkranz, Richard S. 1942- 37-40R
Rosenman, John B(rown) 1941- 106
Rosenman, Ray H(arold) 1920- 97-100
Rosenman, Samuel I(rving)
1896-1973 Obituary 41-44R
Rosenmeyer, Patricia A. 1958- 142
Rosenmeyer, Thomas Gustav 1920- 111
Rosenn, Keith S(amuel) 1938- 111
Rosenof, Theodore 1943- CANR-10
Earlier sketch in CA 65-68
Rosenow, John E(dward) 1949- 97-100
Rosenquist, Carl M(artin) 1895-1973 CAP-2
Earlier sketch in CA 29-32
Rosenrauch, Heinz Erich
See Rosen, Haiim B(aruch)
Rosensaft, Menachem Z. 1948- 21-24R
Rosenstein-Rodan, Paul N. 1902-1985 107
Obituary 116
Rosenstiel, Annette 1911- 115
Rosenstiel, Leonie 1947- 85-88
Rosenstiel, Tom 1956- 142
Rosenstock, (Patricia) Janet (Stearns) 1933- 108
Rosenstock, Sami
See Tzara, Tristan
Rosenstock, Samuel
See Tzara, Tristan
Rosenstock-Huessy, Eugen 1888-1973 CAP-1
Obituary 41-44R
Earlier sketch in CA 13-16
Rosenstone, Robert A(llan) 1936- CANR-52
Earlier sketches in CA 29-32R, CANR-28
Rosenstone, Steven J(ay) 1952- 104
Rosenthal, A(braham) M(ichael) 1922- CANR-27
Earlier sketch in CA 21-24R
Rosenthal, Alan 1936- 105
Rosenthal, Albert H(arold) 1914- 21-24R
Rosenthal, Andrew 1918(?)-1979 Obituary 89-92
Rosenthal, Bernard G(ordon) 1922-1993 CANR-11
Obituary 141
Earlier sketch in CA 29-32R
Rosenthal, Bernice (Glatzer) 1938- 121
Rosenthal, David 1916- 41-44R
Rosenthal, Donald B. 1937- CANR-14
Earlier sketch in CA 37-40R
Rosenthal, Douglas E(urico) 1940- 57-60
Rosenthal, Earl E(dgar) 1921- 41-44R
Rosenthal, Edwin Stanley 1914- 77-80
Rosenthal, Eric 1905- CANR-6
Earlier sketch in CA 9-12R
Rosenthal, Erwin Isak Jacob 1904- 102
Rosenthal, F(rank) F(ranz)
1911(?)-1979 Obituary 89-92
Rosenthal, Harold 1914- 111
See also SATA 35
Rosenthal, Harold (David) 1917-1987 5-8R
Obituary 122
Rosenthal, Harry F(rederick) 1927- 65-68
Rosenthal, Harry Kenneth 1941- 57-60
Rosenthal, Henry Moses
1906-1977 Obituary 73-76
Rosenthal, Jack
See Rosenthal, Jacob
Rosenthal, Jack (Morris) 1931- 140
Rosenthal, Jacob 1935- 161
Rosenthal, Joe
See Rosenthal, Joseph J.
Rosenthal, Joel T(homas) 1934- 57-60
Rosenthal, Joseph J. 1911- 69-72
Rosenthal, Jules M. 1924- 17-20R
Rosenthal, Lucy (Gabrielle) 1933- 144
Rosenthal, M(acha) L(ouis) 1917-1996 CANR-51
Obituary 152
Earlier sketches in CA 1-4R, CANR-4
See also CAAS 6
See also CLC 28
See also DLB 5
See also SATA 59
Rosenthal, Mark 1945- 130
Rosenthal, Mark A(lan) 1946- SATA 64
Rosenthal, Mitchell S(tephen) 1935- 104
Rosenthal, Odeda 1934- 161
Rosenthal, Peggy 1944- 121
Rosenthal, Renee (?)-1975 Obituary 57-60
Rosenthal, Richard A. 1925- 1-4R
Rosenthal, Ricky 1930(?)-1984 Obituary 114
Rosenthal, Robert 1933- CANR-42
Earlier sketches in CA 41-44R, CANR-16
Rosenthal, Shirley Lord 1934- CANR-57
Earlier sketches in CA 65-68, CANR-11, 27
Rosenthal, Stuart 1934- 117
Rosenthal, Sylvia 1911- CANR-27
Earlier sketch in CA 109
Rosenus, Alan (Harvey) 1940- 73-76
Rosenwald, Henry M(artin) 1905- 33-36R
Rosenwald, Lessing J. 1891-1979 DLB 187
Rosenwasser, Dorothy Eckmann 1917- 1-4R
Rosenzweig, Michael L(eo) 1941- 101
Rosenzweig, Norman 1924- CANR-6
Earlier sketch in CA 57-60
Rosenzweig, Peter M. 1949- 139
Rosenzweig, Robert Myron 1931- 113
Rosenzweig, Roy 1950- CANR-35
Earlier sketch in CA 113
Rosenzweig, Saul 1907- 141
Roses, Lorraine Elena 1943- 166
Rosett, Arthur (Irwin) 1934- 69-72
Rosette, Bennetta Jules
See Jules-Rosette, Bennetta (Washington)
Roseveare, Helen Margaret 1925- 73-76
Rosewell, Paul Truman 1926- 17-20R
Roseyear, John 1936- 21-24R
Roshco, Bernard 1929- 5-8R
Rosher, Grace (?)-1980 Obituary 111
Roshwalb, Irving 1924- 45-48
Roshwald, Aviel 1962- 145
Roshwald, Mordecai Marceli 1921- 1-4R
Rosi, Eugene J(oseph) 1931- 61-64
Rosichan, Richard H(arry) 1941- 45-48
Rosie, George 1941- 120
Rosier, Bernard 1931- CANR-12
Earlier sketch in CA 29-32R
Rosier, James L(ouis) 1932-1992 CANR-22
Obituary 145
Earlier sketch in CA 1-4R
Rosillo-Calle, Francisco 1945- 121
Rosis, Brendan
See Tilly, Chris
Rositzke, Harry A(ugust) 1911- CANR-29
Earlier sketch in CA 45-48

Roskamp, Karl Wilhelm 1923-........13-16R
Roske, Ralph Joseph 1921-........122
Roskies, David G(regory) 1948-........120
Roskies, Ethel 1933-........CANR-25
Earlier sketch in CA 45-48
Roskill, Mark W(entworth) 1933-........CANR-6
Earlier sketch in CA 5-8R
Roskill, Stephen W(entworth) 1903-1982..CANR-6
Obituary........108
Earlier sketch in CA 13-16R
Rosko, Milt 1930-........41-44R
Roskolenko, Harry 1907-1980........CANR-17
Obituary........101
Earlier sketch in CA 13-16R
Roslavleva, Natalia
See Rene, Natalia
Rosman, Abraham 1930-........89-92
Rosman, Steven M(ichael) 1956-........149
See also SATA 81
Rosmond, Babette 1921-........CANR-6
Earlier sketch in CA 5-8R
Rosner, Bob 1956-........166
Rosner, David K(arl) 1947-........112
Rosner, Fred 1935-........CANR-32
Earlier sketch in CA 113
Rosner, Joseph 1914-........57-60
Rosner, Lisa 1958-........140
Rosner, Lynn 1944-........61-64
Rosner, Stanley 1928-........41-44R
Rosnow, Ralph L(eon) 1936-........CANR-28
Earlier sketches in CA 21-24R, CANR-10
Rosochacki, Daniel 1942-........45-48
Rosoff, Sidney D. 1924-........1-4R
Rosovsky, Henry 1927- Brief entry........105
Rosow, Irving 1921-........85-88
Rosow, Jerome M(orris) 1919-........81-84
Rosowski, Susan J(ean) 1942-........CANR-54
Earlier sketches in CA 111, CANR-29
Ross, Alan
See Warwick, Alan R(oss)
Ross, Alan 1922-........CANR-44
Earlier sketches in CA 9-12R, CANR-6, 21
Ross, Alan O(tto) 1921-1993........41-44R
Obituary........143
Ross, Alan Strode Campbell 1907-1980........9-12R
Obituary........102
Ross, Albert
See Jarrett, Philip (Martin)
Ross, Alec 1926-........29-32R
Ross, Alex(ander) 1909-........SATA-Brief 29
Ross, Alexander 1591-1654........DLB 151
Ross, Alf (Niels Christian Hansen) 1899-........53-56
Ross, Angus
See Giggal, Kenneth
Ross, Angus 1911-........21-24R
Ross, Barnaby
See Dannay, Frederic
Ross, Becki L. 1959-........153
Ross, Bernard H(arvey) 1934-........102
Ross, Bernard L.
See Follett, Ken(neth Martin)
Ross, Bette M. 1932-........106
Ross, Betty........69-72
Ross, Bill D. 1921-1994........123
Obituary........146
Ross, Billy I(rvan) 1925-........57-60
Ross, Brian (Elliot) 1948-........126
Brief entry........119
Interview in........126
Ross, Caroline
See Nicolson, Catherine
Ross, Catherine
See Beaty, Betty
Ross, Charles (Derek) 1924(?)-1986 Obituary..118
Ross, Charlotte (Brand) 1921-........117
Ross, Christine 1950-........SATA 83
Ross, Clare
See Romano, Clare
See also SATA 48
Ross, Clarissa
See Ross, W(illiam) E(dward) D(aniel)
Ross, Colin
See Roskolenko, Harry
Ross, Corinne Madden 1931-........106
Ross, Dallas
See Reynolds, Dallas McCord
Ross, Dan
See Ross, W(illiam) E(dward) D(aniel)
Ross, Dana
See Ross, W(illiam) E(dward) D(aniel)
Ross, Dana Fuller
See Gerson, Noel Bertram
Ross, Dave
See Ross, David
See also SATA 32
Ross, David 1896-1975........65-68
Obituary........61-64
See also SATA 49
See also SATA-Obit 20
Ross, David 1949-........111
See also Ross, Dave
Ross, David O(liver), Jr. 1936- Brief entry........117
Ross, David P(reston), Jr. 1908-1984 Obituary..112
Ross, Davis R. B. 1934-........33-36R
Ross, Diana
See Denney, Diana
Ross, Diana 1944-........146
Ross, Donald H. 1928-........159
Ross, Donald K. 1943-........49-52
Ross, Dorothy 1936-........137
Ross, Edward S(hearman) 1915-........SATA 85
Ross, Elizabeth Irvin 1942-........121
Ross, Ellen 1942-........147
Ross, Emory 1887-1973 Obituary........41-44R
Ross, Eric (De Witt) 1929-........29-32R
Ross, Eulalie Steinmetz 1910-1975........17-20R
Obituary........134
Ross, Eva J(eany) 1903-1969........CAP-2
Earlier sketch in CA 23-24
Ross, Floyd H(iatt) 1910-........73-76
Ross, Frances Aileen 1909-........CAP-1
Earlier sketch in CA 9-10
Ross, Frank (Xavier), Jr. 1914-........CANR-16
Earlier sketch in CA 93-96
See also SATA 28
Ross, Frank E. 1925-........17-20R
Ross, Gary 1948-........CANR-38
Earlier sketch in CA 115
Ross, George
See Morgan-Grenville, Gerard (Wyndham)
Ross, H(ugh) Laurence 1934-........CANR-13
Earlier sketch in CA 77-80
Ross, Hal 1941-........65-68
Ross, Harold Raymond 1904-........CAP-2
Earlier sketch in CA 19-20
Ross, Harold W(allace) 1892-1951 Brief entry..119
See also DLB 137
Ross, Helaine
See Daniels, Dorothy
Ross, Helen 1890(?)-1978........85-88
Obituary........81-84
Ross, Ian
See Rossmann, John F(rancis)
Ross, Ian Simpson 1930-........CANR-3
Earlier sketch in CA 45-48
Ross, Irwin 1919-........97-100
Ross, Ishbel 1897-1975........93-96
Obituary........61-64
Ross, Ivan T.
See Rossner, Robert
Ross, J. H.
See Lawrence, T(homas) E(dward)
Ross, James Davidson 1924-........49-52
Ross, James F(rancis) 1931-........CANR-11
Earlier sketch in CA 21-24R
Ross, James Frederick Stanley 1886-........9-12R
Ross, James R(odman) 1950-........145
Ross, James S(tiven) 1892-1975 Obituary...57-60
Ross, Jane 1961-........SATA 79
Ross, Janet 1914-........37-40R
Ross, Joel E(lmore, Jr.) 1922-........29-32R
Ross, John 1921-........108
See also SATA 45
Ross, John A(ddison) 1919-........17-20R
Ross, John Hume
See Lawrence, T(homas) E(dward)
Ross, John Munder 1945-........127
Ross, John O'C(onnell) 1916-........25-28R
Ross, Jonathan
See Rossiter, John
Ross, Joseph
See Wrzos, Joseph Henry
Ross, Judith Wilson 1937-........114
Ross, Judy 1942-........SATA 54
Ross, K. G. M. (?)-1985 Obituary........116
Ross, Katharine (Reynolds) 1948-........SATA 89
Ross, Katherine
See Walter, Dorothy Blake
Ross, Kenneth (Michael Andrew) 1941-........107
Ross, Kenneth Lynn 1940-........125
Ross, Kenneth N(eedham) 1908-1970........CANR-5
Earlier sketch in CA 5-8R
Ross, Kent 1956-........155
See also SATA 91
Ross, Lanson Clifford, Jr. 1936-........120
Ross, Laura
See Mincieli, Rose Laura
Ross, Leah
See Webb, Mary H(aydn)
Ross, Leonard
See Rosten, Leo C(alvin)
Ross, Leonard M(ichael) 1945-1985........CANR-29
Obituary........116
Earlier sketch in CA 29-32R
Ross, Leonard Q.
See Rosten, Leo C(alvin)
Ross, Lillian 1927-........CANR-68
Earlier sketches in CA 9-12R, CANR-46
See also DLB 185
Ross, Lillian Hammer 1925-........140
See also SATA 72
Ross, Lola Romanucci
See Romanucci-Ross, Lola
Ross, Lynne Nannen
See Ross-Robertson, Lynne Nannen
Ross, Mabel (Irene) H(ughes) 1909-........81-84
Ross, Malcolm
See Ross-Macdonald, Malcolm J(ohn)
Ross, Marc H(ansen) 1928-........114
Ross, Marilyn
See Ross, W(illiam) E(dward) D(aniel)
Ross, Marilyn (Ann) Heimberg 1939-........CANR-57
Earlier sketches in CA 81-84, CANR-14, 31
Ross, Marjorie Drake Rhoades 1901-........1-4R
Ross, Martha 1951-........103
Ross, Martin
See Martin, Violet Florence
See also DLB 135
Ross, Martin J. 1912-........53-56
Ross, Marvin C(hauncey) 1904-1977........CAP-2
Obituary........69-72
Earlier sketch in CA 19-20
Ross, Mary Adelaide Eden
See Phillpotts, (Mary) Adelaide Eden
Ross, Michael 1905-........85-88
Ross, Michael Elsohn 1952-........148
See also SATA 80
Ross, Michael W(allis) 1952-........118
Ross, Mitchell S(cott) 1953-........81-84
Ross, Murray George 1912-........17-20R
Ross, Nancy
See DeRoin, Nancy
Ross, Nancy Wilson 1910-1986........97-100
Obituary........118
Ross, Nathaniel 1904-........21-24R
Ross, Pat(ricia Kienzle) 1943-........128
See also SATA 53
See also SATA-Brief 48
Ross, Patricia
See Baxter, Patricia E. W.
Ross, Paul
See Crawford, William (Elbert)
Ross, Philip 1939-........69-72
Ross, Phyllis (Freedman) 1926-1970........CAP-2
Earlier sketch in CA 17-18
Ross, Prudence Leith
See Leith-Ross, Prudence
Ross, Ralph 1911-........13-16R
Ross, Ramon R(oyal) 1930-........SATA 62
Ross, Raymond S(amuel) 1925-........CANR-27
Earlier sketches in CA 21-24R, CANR-8
Ross, Richard 1944-........163
Ross, Robert H(enry), Jr. 1916-........13-16R
Ross, Robert Horace........106
Ross, Robert S(amuel) 1940-........57-60
Ross, Robert W.
See Power-Ross, Robert W.
Ross, Ronald 1857-1932........157
Ross, Russell M. 1921-........21-24R
Ross, Ruth 1930(?)-1986 Obituary........119
Ross, Sam 1912-1998........13-16R
Obituary........166
Ross, Sheila Muriel 1925-........106
Ross, (James) Sinclair 1908-........73-76
See also CLC 13
See also DAC
See also DAM MST
See also DLB 88
See also SSC 24
Ross, Stanley R(obert) 1921-........CANR-7
Earlier sketch in CA 17-20R
Ross, Stanley Ralph 1940-........CANR-20
Earlier sketch in CA 97-100
Ross, Stephen David 1935-........CANR-39
Earlier sketches in CA 41-44R, CANR-17
Ross, Steven Thomas 1937-........41-44R
Ross, Stewart 1947-........156
See also SAAS 23
See also SATA 92
Ross, Stewart Halsey 1928-........162
Ross, Stuart 1950-........155
Ross, Sutherland
See Callard, Thomas Henry
Ross, T(heodore) J(ohn) 1924-........57-60
Ross, Terrence 1947-........103
Ross, Thomas B. 1929-........29-32R
Ross, Thomas W(ynne) 1923-........41-44R
Ross, Timothy A(rrowsmith) 1936-........57-60
Ross, Tom 1958-........SATA 84
Ross, Tony 1938-........CANR-35
Earlier sketch in CA 77-80
See also MAICYA
See also SATA 17, 65
Ross, Veronica 1946-........113
Ross, W(illiam) E(dward) D(aniel) 1912-..CANR-32
Earlier sketches in CA 81-84, CANR-14
Ross, W(illiam) Gordon 1900-........45-48
Ross, W. W. E. 1894-1966........DLB 88
Ross, Wilda 1915-........85-88
See also SATA 51
See also SATA-Brief 39
Ross, William
See Dewart, Leslie
Ross, William B. 1915-........25-28R
Ross, Z. H.
See Ross, Zola Helen
Ross, Zola Helen 1912-1989........CANR-64
Obituary........130
Earlier sketch in CA 53-56
Rossabi, Morris 1941-........102
Rossant, Murray J(oseph) 1923-1988 Obituary..125
Rossbach, Richard M. 1915(?)-1987 Obituary..123
Rossbacher, Lisa A(nn) 1952-........117
Rossberg, Robert H. 1926-........45-48
Rosse, Ian
See Straker, J(ohn) F(oster)
Rosse, Susanna
See Connolly, Vivian
Rossel, Seymour 1945-........CANR-21
Earlier sketches in CA 53-56, CANR-5
See also SATA 28
Rossel, Sven H(akon) 1943-........CANR-22
Earlier sketch in CA 105
Rosselli, Amelia 1930-........DLB 128
Rossellini, Isabella 1952-........162
Rossellini, Roberto 1906-1977 Obituary........69-72
Rossel-Waugh, C. C.
See Waugh, Carol-Lynn Rossel
Rossen, Robert 1908-1966 Obituary........113
See also DLB 26
Rosser, Neill A(lbert) 1916-1973........CAP-1
Earlier sketch in CA 13-16
Rosser, Sue V(ilhauer) 1947-........156
Rosset, B(enjamin) C(harles) 1910-1974........9-12R
Obituary........103
Rosset, Barnet Lee, Jr. 1922-........97-100
Interview in........97-100
Rosset, Barney
See Rosset, Barnet Lee, Jr.
Rossetti, Christina (Georgina) 1830-1894........DA
See also DAB
See also DAC
See also DAM MST, POET
See also DLB 35, 163
See also MAICYA
See also PC 7
See also SATA 20
See also WLC
Rossetti, Dante Gabriel 1828-1882........CDBLB 1832-1890
See also DA
See also DAB
See also DAC
See also DAM MST, POET
See also DLB 35
See also WLC
Rossetti, Minerva
See Rowland, D(onald) S(ydney)
Rossi, Aga
See Agarossi, Elena
Rossi, Alfred 1935-........29-32R
Rossi, Alice S(chaerr) 1922-........CANR-17
Earlier sketches in CA 45-48, CANR-1
Rossi, Bruno
See Levinson, Leonard
Rossi, Cristina Peri
See Peri Rossi, Cristina
Rossi, Ernest Lawrence 1933-........CANR-14
Earlier sketch in CA 37-40R
Rossi, Ino........89-92
Rossi, John V. 1955-........152
Rossi, Lino 1923-........104
Rossi, Mario 1916-........CANR-8
Earlier sketch in CA 5-8R
Rossi, Nicholas Louis, Jr. 1924-........CANR-6
Earlier sketch in CA 13-16R
Rossi, Nick
See Rossi, Nicholas Louis, Jr.
Rossi, Paul A. 1929- Brief entry........110
Rossi, Peter Henry 1921-........CANR-41
Earlier sketches in CA 1-4R, CANR-4, 19
Rossi, Philip Joseph 1943-........115
Rossi, Roxanne 1962-........152
Rossi, Sanna Morrison Barlow 1917-........93-96
Rossi, William A(nthony) 1916-........65-68
Rossie, Jonathan Gregory 1935- Brief entry...106
Rossi-Landi, Ferruccio 1921-........114
Rossini, Frederick A(nthony) 1939-........CANR-12
Earlier sketch in CA 73-76
Rossit, Edward A. 1921-........17-20R
Rossiter, Clare
See Dawson, Janis
Rossiter, Clinton (Lawrence)
1917-1970 Obituary........25-28R
Rossiter, Frank R(aymond) 1937-........61-64
Rossiter, Ian
See Ross Williamson, Hugh
Rossiter, Jane
See Ross, W(illiam) E(dward) D(aniel)
Rossiter, John 1916-........CANR-59
Earlier sketch in CA 33-36R
Rossiter, Margaret W(alsh) 1944-........CANR-13
Earlier sketch in CA 77-80
Rossiter, Sarah 1942-........136
Rossiter, (Percival) Stuart (Bryce) 1923-........85-88
Rosskam, Edwin 1903(?)-1985 Obituary........115
Rosskopf, Myron Frederick 1907-1973........CANR-5
Obituary........41-44R
Earlier sketch in CA 5-8R
Ross-Macdonald, Malcolm J(ohn) 1932-..CANR-48
Earlier sketches in CA 65-68, CANR-13
Rossman, Charles Raymond 1938-........CANR-34
Earlier sketch in CA 113
Rossman, Evelyn
See Rothchild, Sylvia
Rossman, Jack E(ugene) 1936-........49-52
Rossman, Marlene L. 1948-........124
Rossman, Michael Dale 1939-........101
Rossman, (George) Parker 1919-........69-72
Rossmann, John F(rancis) 1942-........101
Rossner, Judith (Perelman) 1935-........CANR-51
Earlier sketches in CA 17-20R, CANR-18
Interview in........CANR-18
See also AITN 2
See also BEST 90:3
See also CLC 6, 9, 29
See also DLB 6
See also MTCW 1
Rossner, Robert 1932-........CANR-1
Earlier sketch in CA 1-4R
Rosso, Julee 1944-........139
Rossoff, Martin 1910-........9-12R
Rossol, Monona 1936-........140
Rossomando, Frederic William 1924-........49-52
Rossotti, Hazel Swaine 1930-........142
See also SATA 95
Ross-Robertson, Lynne Nannen 1936-..CANR-25
Earlier sketch in CA 107
Ross Williamson, Hugh 1901-1978........CANR-8
Earlier sketch in CA 17-20R
Rostand, Edmond (Eugene Alexis) 1868-1918..126
Brief entry........104
See also DA
See also DAB
See also DAC
See also DAM DRAM, MST
See also DLB 192
See also MTCW 1
See also TCLC 6, 37
Rostand, J.
See Rostand, Jean
Rostand, Jean 1894-1977........126
Brief entry........124
Rostand, Robert
See Hopkins, Robert S(ydney)

Rosten, Leo C(alvin) 1908-1997 .... CANR-6
Obituary 156
Earlier sketch in CA 5-8R
Interview in CANR-6
See also DLB 11
Rosten, Norman 1914-1995 .... CANR-21
Obituary 147
Earlier sketch in CA 77-80
Rostenberg, Leona 1908- CANR-5
Earlier sketch in CA 5-8R
See also DLB 140
Rostkowski, Margaret I. 1945- CANR-54
Earlier sketch in CA 127
See also AAYA 22
See also SATA 59
Roston, Murray 1928- CANR-5
Earlier sketch in CA 53-56
Rostovsky, Dimitrii 1651-1709 .... DLB 150
Rostow, Eugene Victor 1913- 5-8R
Rostow, Walt W(hitman) 1916- CANR-8
Earlier sketch in CA 13-16R
Interview in CANR-8
Rostvold, Gerhard N(orman) 1919- CANR-10
Earlier sketch in CA 21-24R
Roszak, Betty 1933- 29-32R
Roszak, Theodore 1933- CANR-45
Earlier sketch in CA 77-80
Rota, Bertram 1903-1966 .... DLB 201
Rota, Gian-Carlo 1932- 126
Rotarius
See Kerekes, Tibor
Rotberg, Robert I. 1935- CANR-21
Earlier sketches in CA 13-16R, CANR-6
Rotblat, Joseph 1908- CANR-26
Earlier sketch in CA 109
Rotchstein, Janice 1944- CANR-25
Earlier sketch in CA 106
Rote, Kyle 1928- 21-24R
Rotella, Guy Louis 1947- 115
Rotelle, John E. 1939- 158
Rotenstreich, Nathan 1914- CANR-23
Earlier sketches in CA 61-64, CANR-8
Roth, Alexander
See Dunner, Joseph
Roth, Andrew 1919- 53-56
Roth, Arlen 1952- 103
Roth, Arnold 1929- 21-24R
See also SATA 21
Roth, Arthur 1920- 1-4R
Roth, Arthur J(oseph) 1925-1993 .... CANR-7
Obituary 140
Earlier sketch in CA 53-56
See also SAAS 11
See also SATA 43
See also SATA-Brief 28
See also SATA-Obit 75
Roth, Audrey J. 1927- 21-24R
Roth, Cecil 1899-1970 .... CANR-13
Obituary 25-28R
Earlier sketch in CA 9-12R
Roth, Charles E(dmund) 1934- 111
Roth, Claire Jarett 1923- 5-8R
Roth, Darlene R(ebecca) 1941- 149
Roth, David 1940- 106
See also SATA 36
Roth, David F(rancisco) 1939- 41-44R
Roth, David Lee 1954- 166
Roth, David M. 1874(?)-1971 Obituary 104
Roth, David M(orris) 1935- 57-60
Roth, Don A. 1927- 25-28R
Roth, Ernst 1896-1971 .... CAP-2
Earlier sketch in CA 25-28
Roth, Eugen 1895-1976 Obituary 65-68
Roth, Geneen 1951- CANR-42
Earlier sketch in CA 111
Roth, Gerhard (Jurgen) 1942- 159
See also DLB 85, 124
Roth, Hal 1927- 37-40R
Roth, Harold .... SATA-Brief 49
Roth, Harold L(eo) 1919-1982 Obituary 108
Roth, Harry 1903(?)-1976 Obituary 65-68
Roth, Henry 1906-1995 .... CANR-63
Obituary 149
Earlier sketches in CAP-1, CA 11-12, CANR-38
See also CLC 2, 6, 11, 104
See also DLB 28
See also MTCW 1
Roth, Herbert (Otto) 1917- 61-64
Roth, Herrick S. 1916- 77-80
Roth, Holly 1916-1964 .... CANR-61
Earlier sketches in CA 1-4R, CANR-6
Roth, Jack J(oseph) 1920- 21-24R
Roth, John K(ing) 1940- CANR-51
Earlier sketches in CA 25-28R, CANR-10, 26
Roth, Julius A(lfred) 1924- 21-24R
Roth, June (Doris Spiewak) 1926-1990 .. CANR-19
Obituary 132
Earlier sketches in CA 9-12R, CANR-5
Roth, Klaus 1939- 150
Roth, Leland M(artin) 1943- CANR-16
Earlier sketch in CA 93-96
Roth, (Hyam) Leon 1896-1963 Obituary 106
Roth, Lillian 1910-1980 Obituary 97-100
Roth, Mark J(oseph) 1941- 77-80
Roth (Vanceburg), Martha 1938- 137
Roth, Martin 1924- 134
Roth, Marty
See Roth, Martin
Roth, Mary Jane 21-24R
Roth, Michael S. 1957- 127
Roth, Moira 1933- 121
Roth, Norman 1938- 150
Roth, Peggy (Meehan) (?)-1973 Obituary 104
Roth, Philip (Milton) 1933- CANR-55
Earlier sketches in CA 1-4R, CANR-1, 22, 36
See also BEST 90:3
See also CDALB 1968-1988
See also CLC 1, 2, 3, 4, 6, 9, 15, 22, 31, 47, 66, 86
See also DA
See also DAB
See also DAC
See also DAM MST, NOV, POP
See also DLB 2, 28, 173
See also DLBY 82
See also MTCW 1
See also SSC 26
See also WLC
Roth, Richard H(enry) 1949- 77-80
Roth, Robert Howard 1933- CANR-14
Earlier sketch in CA 41-44R
Roth, Robert J. 1920- 17-20R
Roth, Robert Paul 1919- 61-64
Roth, Samuel 1894-1974 Obituary 49-52
Roth, Sister Mary Augustine 1926- CANR-3
Earlier sketch in CA 9-12R
Roth, Sol 1927- 65-68
Roth, Theodore W(illiam) 1916- 57-60
Roth, William 1942- 101
Roth, Wolfgang M(ax) W(ilhelm) 1930- 41-44R
Rotha, Paul 1907-1984 .... 9-12R
Obituary 112
Rothafel, Roxy
See Rothafel, Samuel L(ionel)
Rothafel, Samuel L(ionel) 1881(?)-1936(?) Brief entry 123
Rothbard, Murray N(ewton) 1926-1995 .. CANR-22
Obituary 148
Earlier sketches in CA 5-8R, CANR-6
Rothbart, Harold A(rthur) 1917- 111
Rothbaum, Melvin 1926- 5-8R
Rothberg, Abraham 1922- 33-36R
See also SATA 59
Rothblatt, Ben 1924- 25-28R
Rothblatt, Donald N(oah) 1935- CANR-23
Earlier sketches in CA 61-64, CANR-8
Rothblatt, Henry B(arnett) 1916-1985 .... CANR-19
Obituary 117
Earlier sketch in CA 25-28R
Rothchild, Donald (Sylvester) 1928- CANR-14
Earlier sketches in CA 41-44R, CANR-31
Rothchild, Sylvia 1923- 77-80
Rothel, David 1936- CANR-10
Earlier sketch in CA 65-68
Rothenberg, Alan B(aer) 1907-1977 Obituary 73-76
Rothenberg, Albert 1930- CANR-51
Earlier sketches in CA 57-60, CANR-8, 25
Rothenberg, B(arbara) Annye 1940- 107
Rothenberg, Diane Brodatz 1932- 115
Rothenberg, Gunther Eric 1923- CANR-8
Earlier sketch in CA 21-24R
Rothenberg, Jerome 1924- 29-32R
Rothenberg, Jerome 1931- CANR-1
Earlier sketch in CA 45-48
See also CLC 6, 57
See also DLB 5, 193
Rothenberg, Joshua 1911- 37-40R
Rothenberg, Lillian 1922- 9-12R
Rothenberg, Marc 1949- 115
Rothenberg, Polly 1916- 85-88
Rothenberg, Randall 1956- 118
Rothenberg, Robert E(dward) 1908- 37-40R
Rothenstein, John K(newstub) M(aurice) 1901- CANR-1
Earlier sketch in CA 1-4R
Rothermere, Viscount
See Harmsworth, Esmond Cecil
Rothery, Brian 1934- CANR-1
Earlier sketch in CA 49-52
Rothfork, John 1946- 110
Roth-Hano, Renee 1931- 151
See also SATA 85
Rothkopf, Carol Z. 1929- 25-28R
See also SATA 4
Rothman, Barbara Katz 1948- CANR-29
Earlier sketch in CA 111
Rothman, Charles Warren 1952- 120
Rothman, Chuck
See Rothman, Charles Warren
Rothman, David B. 1956- 111
Rothman, David J. 1937- CANR-57
Earlier sketch in CA 33-36R
Rothman, Esther P. 1919- 37-40R
Rothman, Hal (K.) 1958- 130
Rothman, Joel 1938- 37-40R
See also SATA 7
Rothman, Judith
See Peters, Maureen
Rothman, Milton A. 1919- 41-44R
Rothman, Stanley 1927- 93-96
Rothman, Theodore 1907- CAP-2
Earlier sketch in CA 29-32
Rothman, Tony 1953- CANR-33
Earlier sketches in CA 85-88, CANR-15
Rothmiller, Mike 1950- 143
Rothmuller, Aron Marko 1908- 73-76
Rothrock, George A(bel) 1932- 61-64
Rothschild, Alfred 1894(?)-1972 .... 37-40R
Rothschild, Fritz A(lexander) 1919- Brief entry . 106
Rothschild, Guy de
See de Rothschild, Guy (Edouard Alphonse Paul)
Rothschild, J(acquard) H(irshorn) 1907- CAP-2
Earlier sketch in CA 17-18
Rothschild, Joseph 1931- CANR-3
Earlier sketch in CA 9-12R
Rothschild, Kurt Wilhelm 1914- CANR-47
Earlier sketches in CA 102, CANR-23
Rothschild, Lincoln 1902-1983 .... CANR-12
Obituary 109
Earlier sketch in CA 45-48
Rothschild, Miriam (Louisa) 1908- 145
Rothschild, Nathaniel Mayer Victor 1910-1990 Obituary 131
Rothschild, Norman 1913- 103
Rothschild, Richard Charles 1895-1986 Obituary 118
Rothschild Family .... DLB 184
Rothstein, Arthur 1915-1985 .... CANR-6
Obituary 117
Earlier sketch in CA 57-60
Rothstein, Edward 1952- 136
Rothstein, Eric 1936- 73-76
Rothstein, Samuel 1902(?)-1978 Obituary 77-80
Rothstein, Samuel 1921- 61-64
Rothstein, Stanley William 1929- 120
Rothstein, William G(ene) 1937- 73-76
Rothweiler, Paul Roger 1931- CANR-10
Earlier sketch in CA 65-68
Rothwell, Bruce 1923(?)-1984 Obituary 114
Rothwell, Kenneth J(ames) 1925- CANR-14
Earlier sketch in CA 21-24R
Rothwell, Kenneth S(prague) 1921- 33-36R
Rothwell, Talbot (Nelson Conn) 1916-1981 Obituary 103
Rothwell, V(ictor) H(oward) 1945- 37-40R
Rothwell, William J. 1951- 158
Rotimi, E. G. O.
See Rotimi, (Emmanuel Gladstone) Ola(wale)
Rotimi, (Emmanuel Gladstone) Ola(wale) 1938(?)- 124
See also BW 2
See also DLB 125
Rotimi, Olawale
See Rotimi, (Emmanuel Gladstone) Ola(wale)
Rotkin, Charles E. 1916- 5-8R
Rotmans, Elmer A. 1896- 5-8R
Rotner, Shelley 1951- 143
See also SATA 76
Rotondi, Cesar 1926- 97-100
Rotsler, William 1926- CANR-4
Earlier sketch in CA 53-56
Rotstein, Abraham 1929- 104
Rotten, Johnny
See Lydon, John (Joseph)
Rottenberg, Dan(iel) 1942- CANR-40
Earlier sketches in CA 102, CANR-19
Rottenberg, Isaac C. 1925- 13-16R
Rottensteiner, Franz 1942- CANR-33
Earlier sketches in CA 81-84, CANR-15
Rotter, Julian B(ernard) 1916- 33-36R
Rotter, Marion 1940(?)-1973 Obituary 104
Rotundo, Louis C. 1949- 146
Roubiczek, Paul (Anton) 1898-1972 Obituary .. 115
Roubinek, Darrell L(eRoy) 1935- 57-60
Roucek, Joseph S(labey) 1902- CANR-32
Earlier sketch in CA 9-12R
Roud, Richard 1929-1989 Obituary 127
Roudiez, Leon S(amuel) 1917- 37-40R
Roudinesco, Elisabeth 1944- 142
Roudybush, Alexandra (Brown) 1911- 65-68
Roueche, Berton 1911-1994 .... CANR-48
Obituary 145
Earlier sketches in CA 1-4R, CANR-1
See also SATA 28
Roueche, John E(dward) 1938- 49-52
Rougemont, Denis de
See de Rougemont, Denis (Louis)
Roughsey, Dick 1921(?)-1985 109
See also CLR 41
See also SATA 35
Rougier, Louis (Auguste Paul) 1889-1982 .... CANR-13
Earlier sketch in CA 29-32R
Rougier, Nicole 1929- 29-32R
Rouhani, Fuad 1907- 37-40R
Roukes, Nicholas 1925- 25-28R
Roulac, Stephen E. 1945- 104
Rouleau, Raymond (Edgard Marie) 1904-1981 Obituary 108
Roulston, Marjorie Hillis 1890-1971 Obituary 104
Roumain, Jacques (Jean Baptiste) 1907-1944 .. 125
Brief entry 117
See also BLC 3
See also BW 1
See also DAM MULT
See also TCLC 19
Rounds, David 1930-1983 Obituary 111
Rounds, David 1942- 143
Rounds, Glen (Harold) 1906- CANR-44
Earlier sketches in CA 53-56, CANR-7, 22
See also MAICYA
See also SATA 8, 70
Rouner, Arthur A(cy), Jr. 1929- CANR-5
Earlier sketch in CA 9-12R
Rouner, Leroy S(tephens) 1930- 73-76
Rountree, Owen
See Krauzer, Steven M(ark)
Rountree, Owen
See Kittredge, William
and Krauzer, Steven M(ark)
Rountree, Thomas J. 1927- 25-28R
Rourke, Constance (Mayfield) 1885-1941 Brief entry 107
See also TCLC 12
See also YABC 1
Rourke, Francis E(dward) 1922- CANR-6
Earlier sketch in CA 1-4R
Rous, Stanley (Ford) 1895- 108
Rous, Stephen N. 1931- 141
Rousculp, Charles G(ene) 1923- 29-32R
Rouse, Anne (Barrett) 1954- 149
Rouse, (Hubert) Blair 1912- 1-4R
Rouse, (Benjamin) Irving, (Jr.) 1913- 9-12R
Rouse, John E(dward), Jr. 1942- 89-92
Rouse, John E(vans) 1892- 73-76
Rouse, Mary A(mes) 1934- 141
Rouse, Parke (Shepherd), Jr. 1915- 17-20R
Rouse, Richard H(unter) 1933- 29-32R
Rouse, Russell 1913(?)-1987 Obituary 123
Rouse Jones, Lewis 1907- CAP-1
Earlier sketch in CA 13-14
Roush, Barbara 1940- 109
Roush, John H., Jr. 1923- 37-40R
Rousmaniere, John 1944- CANR-38
Earlier sketches in CA 93-96, CANR-17
Rousseau, George Sebastian 1941- CANR-11
Earlier sketch in CA 29-32R
Rousseau, Jean-Jacques 1712-1778 .... DA
See also DAB
See also DAC
See also DAM MST
See also WLC
Rousseau, Richard W(ilfred) 1924- 110
Rousseau, Victor 1879-1960 165
Roussel, Raymond 1877-1933 Brief entry 117
See also TCLC 20
Rousselle, Aline 1939- 130
Rousset, (Elisee) David 1912-1997 144
Obituary 163
Roussin, Andre (Jean Paul Marie) 1911-1987 Obituary 124
Rout, Leslie B(rennan), Jr. 1936-1987 57-60
Obituary 122
Routh, C(harles) R(ichard) N(airne) 1896- ... CAP-1
Earlier sketch in CA 13-14
Routh, Donald K(ent) 1937- 57-60
Routh, Francis John 1927- 13-16R
Routh, Jonathan 110
Routh, Porter W(roe) 1911- 77-80
Routhier, Adolphe-Basile 1839-1920 .... DLB 99
Routier, Simone 1901-1987 153
See also DLB 88
Routley, Erik (Reginald) 1917-1982 .... CANR-5
Obituary 108
Earlier sketch in CA 1-4R
Routley, (Bernarra) Jane 1962- 158
Routsong, Alma 1924- 49-52
Routt, Mary Patterson 1890(?)-1986 Obituary .. 119
Routtenberg, Max Jonah 1909- 77-80
Rouverol, Jean
See Butler, Jean Rouverol
Roux, Edward R(udolph) 1903- 13-16R
Roux, Georges 1914- 17-20R
Roux, Willan Charles 1902- CAP-2
Earlier sketch in CA 17-18
Rover, Constance (Mary) 1910- 21-24R
Rovere, Richard H(alworth) 1915-1979 ... CANR-3
Obituary 89-92
Earlier sketch in CA 49-52
Roversi, Roberto 1923- .... DLB 128
Rovin, Ben
See Clevenger, Ernest Allen, Jr.
Rovin, Jeff 1951- 77-80
Rovit, Earl (Herbert) 1927- CANR-12
Earlier sketch in CA 5-8R
See also CLC 7
Rowan, Andrew N(icholas) 1946- 124
Rowan, Carl T(homas) 1925- CANR-46
Earlier sketch in CA 89-92
See also BW 2
Rowan, Dan (Hale) 1922-1987 Obituary 125
Rowan, Deirdre
See Williams, Jeanne
Rowan, Ford 1943- CANR-29
Earlier sketch in CA 69-72
Rowan, Helen 1927(?)-1972 Obituary 37-40R
Rowan, Hester
See Robinson, Sheila Mary
Rowan, Richard Lamar 1931- 9-12R
Rowan, Roy 1920- 156
Rowan, Stephen A(nthony) 1928- 45-48
Rowan, Steven William 1943- 116
Rowans, Virgina
See Tanner, Edward Everett III
Rowat, Donald C(ameron) 1921- CANR-42
Earlier sketches in CA 9-12R, CANR-5, 20
Rowatt, G(eorge) Wade, Jr. 1943- 126
Rowbotham, David (Harold) 1924- 149
Brief entry 112
Rowbotham, Sheila 1943- CANR-59
Earlier sketch in CA 101
Rowdon, Maurice 1922- Brief entry 110
Rowe, A(lbert) W(ard) 1915- CANR-14
Earlier sketch in CA 21-24R
Rowe, C(hristopher) J(ames) 1944- 132
Rowe, Clarence J(ohn), Jr. 1916- 104
Rowe, David C. 1949- 147
Rowe, David Knox 1924(?)-1989 77-80
Obituary 129
Rowe, David Nelson 1905- CANR-2
Earlier sketch in CA 5-8R
Rowe, Elizabeth Singer 1674-1737 .... DLB 39, 95
Rowe, Erna (Dirks) 1926- 93-96
Rowe, Frank (A.) 1921-1985 130
Obituary 115
Rowe, Frederick William 1912- 101
Rowe, G(ail) S(tuart) 1936- 112
Rowe, George E(rnest), Jr. 1947- 93-96
Rowe, H. Edward 1927- 69-72
Rowe, James L(ester), Jr. 1948- 69-72
Rowe, James N(icholas) 1938-1989 .... 37-40R
Obituary 128
Rowe, Jeanne A. 1938- 29-32R
Rowe, Jennifer
See Rodda, Emily
Rowe, John (Seymour) 1936- CANR-28
Earlier sketch in CA 109
Rowe, John Carlos 1945- CANR-36
Earlier sketch in CA 114

Rowe, John L(eroy) 1914-1975(?) ... 17-20R
Obituary ... 135
Rowe, Margaret (Kevin) 1920- ... 13-16R
Rowe, Mary Budd 1925- ... 113
Rowe, Nicholas 1674-1718 ... DLB 84
Rowe, Robert 1920- ... 17-20R
Rowe, Terry ... AITN 2
Rowe, Viola Carson 1903-1969 ... 1-4R
Obituary ... 103
See also SATA-Obit 26
Rowe, Vivian C(laud) 1902-1978 ... CANR-2
Earlier sketch in CA 1-4R
Rowe, William (Neil) 1942- ... 131
Rowe, William D(avid) 1930- ... 114
Rowe, William L. 1931- Brief entry ... 108
Rowell, Galen 1940- ... CANR-55
Earlier sketches in CA 65-68, CANR-18
Rowell, (Douglas) Geoffrey 1943- ... 129
Rowell, George (Rignall) 1923- ... CANR-39
Earlier sketches in CA 5-8R, CANR-2, 18
Rowell, Henry T(hompson) 1904- ... CAP-1
Earlier sketch in CA 13-14
Rowell, John W(illiam) 1914- ... 33-36R
Rowen, Betty (Jane Rose) 1920- ... 127
Brief entry ... 109
Rowen, Henry S(tanislaus) 1925- ... 123
Brief entry ... 118
Rowen, Herbert H(arvey) 1916- ... CANR-3
Earlier sketch in CA 9-12R
Rowen, Hobart 1918-1995 ... 9-12R
Obituary ... 148
Rowen, Lilian 1925- ... 108
Rowen, Ruth Halle 1918- ... 33-36R
Rowes, Barbara Gail ... 101
Rowett, Colin 1952- ... 128
Rowh, Mark 1952- ... 155
See also SATA 90
Rowland, Arthur R(ay) 1930- ... CANR-21
Earlier sketches in CA 13-16R, CANR-6
Rowland, Benjamin, Jr.
1904-1972 Obituary ... 37-40R
Rowland, Beryl ... 89-92
Rowland, Christopher (Charles) 1947- ... 116
Rowland, Claude K. 1943- ... 112
Rowland, D(onald) S(ydney) 1928- ... CANR-65
Earlier sketch in CA 21-24R
Rowland, Diana 1950- ... 122
Rowland, Edna 1922- ... 139
Rowland, Florence Wightman 1900- ... CANR-5
Earlier sketch in CA 5-8R
See also SATA 8
Rowland, Iris
See Roberts, Irene
Rowland, J(ohn) R(ussell) 1925- ... 101
Rowland, Judith 1944- ... 124
Rowland, Laura Joh 1954(?)- ... 156
Rowland, Lawrence S. 1942- ... 166
Rowland, Peter (Kenneth) 1938- ... 25-28R
Rowland, Robin F. 1950- ... 136
Rowland, Stanley J., Jr. 1928- ... 13-16R
Rowland, Virgil K(enneth) 1909- ... 5-8R
Rowland-Entwistle, (Arthur) Theodore (Henry)
1925- ... CANR-49
Earlier sketches in CA 107, CANR-24
See also SATA 31, 94
Rowlands, John Robert 1947- ... 109
Rowlands, Peter
See Lovell, Mark
Rowlands, Samuel 1570(?)-1630 ... DLB 121
Rowlandson, Mary 1637(?)-1711 ... DLB 24, 200
Rowlatt, Mary 1908- ... 5-8R
Rowley, Ames Dorrance
See Lovecraft, H(oward) P(hillips)
Rowley, Anthony 1939- ... 61-64
Rowley, Brian A(lan) 1923- ... 5-8R
Rowley, Charles (Dunford) 1906-1985 ... 103
Obituary ... 117
Rowley, Charles K(ershaw) 1939- ... 143
Rowley, Hazel 1951- ... 149
Rowley, Peter 1934- ... 65-68
Rowley, Peter T(empleton) 1929- Brief entry ... 112
Rowley, (Richard) Trevor 1942- ... 131
Rowley, William 1585(?)-1626 ... DLB 58
Rowley, William Dean 1939- ... 112
Rowling, Marjorie A(lice Thexton) 1900- ... 5-8R
Rowlingson, Donald T(aggart) 1907- ... CANR-6
Earlier sketch in CA 1-4R
Rowlinson, Matthew 1956- ... 150
Rowney, Don Karl 1936- ... 108
Rowny, Edward L. 1917- ... 145
Rowse, A(lfred) L(eslie) 1903-1997 ... CANR-45
Obituary ... 161
Earlier sketches in CA 1-4R, CANR-1
See also CAAS 8
See also DLB 155
Rowsome, Frank (Howard), Jr. 1914-1983 ... 112
See also SATA 36
Rowson, Susanna Haswell 1762(?)-1824 .. DLB 37, 200
Rowthorn, Anne W(heeler) 1939- ... 113
Roxas, Savina A. ... 37-40R
Roxborough, Henry Hall 1891- ... 5-8R
Roxon, Lillian 1933(?)-1973 Obituary ... 111
Roy, Archibald Edmiston 1924- ... 102
Roy, Archie E.
See Roy, Archibald Edmiston
Roy, Arundhati 1960(?)- ... 163
See also CLC 109
See also DLBY 97
Roy, Camille 1870-1943 ... DLB 92
Roy, David Tod 1933- ... 41-44R
Roy, Donald H. 1944- ... 163
Roy, Emil L. 1933- ... 25-28R
Roy, Ewell Paul 1929- ... 9-12R
Roy, F. Hampton 1937- ... 144
Roy, G(eorge) Ross 1924- ... 77-80
Roy, Gabrielle 1909-1983 ... CANR-61
Obituary ... 110
Earlier sketches in CA 53-56, CANR-5
See also CLC 10, 14
See also DAB
See also DAC
See also DAM MST
See also DLB 68
See also MTCW 1
Roy, Gregor 1929- ... 21-24R
Roy, Jack
See Dangerfield, Rodney
Roy, Jacqueline 1954- ... 153
See also BW 2
See also SATA 74
Roy, James A(lexander) 1884- ... CAP-1
Earlier sketch in CA 11-12
Roy, Jessie Hailstalk 1895-1986 Obituary ... 121
See also SATA-Obit 51
Roy, Joaquin 1943- ... 77-80
Roy, John (Flint) 1913- ... 93-96
Roy, Jules 1907- ... DLB 83
Roy, Katherine (Morris) 1906- ... 1-4R
Roy, Liam
See Scarry, Patricia (Murphy)
Roy, Lucinda (H.) ... 168
Roy, Michael 1913-1976 ... CANR-10
Obituary ... 65-68
Earlier sketch in CA 61-64
Roy, Mike
See Roy, Michael
Roy, Patricia E. ... 137
Roy, Reginald H(erbert) 1922- ... 49-52
Roy, Robert L(ouis) 1947- ... 106
Roy, Robin 1946- ... CANR-36
Earlier sketch in CA 114
Roy, Ron(ald) 1940- ... 114
See also SATA 40
See also SATA-Brief 35
Roy, Rustum 1924- ... 113
Royal, Claudia Smith 1904- ... 5-8R
Royal, D.
See Du Breuil, (Elizabeth) L(or)inda
Royal, Denise 1935- ... 25-28R
Royal, Rosamond
See Hines, Jeanne
Royal, William Robert 1905- ... 101
Royale, A.
See Gibson, Arthur
Royall, Anne 1769-1854 ... DLB 43
Royall, Vanessa
See Hinkemeyer, Michael T(homas)
Royalton-Kisch, Martin (Bruce) 1952- ... CANR-60
Earlier sketch in CA 128
Roybal, Laura (Husby) 1956- ... 152
See also SATA 85
Royce, Anya Peterson 1940- ... 101
Royce, James E(mmet) 1914-1996 ... CANR-34
Obituary ... 151
Earlier sketch in CA 1-4R
Royce, Kenneth
See Gandley, Kenneth Royce
Royce, Patrick M(ilan) 1922- ... 13-16R
Royce, R(ussell) Joseph 1921- ... CANR-9
Earlier sketch in CA 21-24R
Royde-Smith, Naomi 1875-1964 ... DLB 191
Royds, Caroline 1953- ... 123
See also SATA 55
Royer, Fanchon 1902- ... 5-8R
Royko, Mike 1932-1997 ... CANR-26
Obituary ... 157
Earlier sketch in CA 89-92
See also CLC 109
Roylance, William H(erbert) 1927- ... 61-64
Royle, Edward 1944- ... 61-64
Royle, Nicholas 1957- ... 151
Royle, Selena 1904-1983 Obituary ... 109
Royle, Trevor 1945- ... CANR-31
Earlier sketch in CA 112
Royster, Charles 1944- ... 101
Royster, Philip M. 1943- ... CANR-13
Earlier sketch in CA 65-68
Royster, Salibelle 1895-1975 ... CAP-2
Earlier sketch in CA 25-28
Royster, Vermont (Connecticut) 1914-1996 . 21-24R
Obituary ... 152
See also DLB 127
Royston, Angela 1945- ... CANR-67
Earlier sketch in CA 128
Royston, Olive 1904- ... 102
Royston, Richard fl. 1628-1686 ... DLB 170
Rozakis, Gregory 1943(?)-1989 Obituary ... 129
Rozakis, Laurie E. 1952- ... 150
See also SATA 84
Rozan, S. J. ... 165
Rozeboom, William W(arren) 1928- ... 17-20R
Rozek, Evalyn Robillard 1941- ... 61-64
Rozell, Mark J. 1959- ... 154
Rozensztroch, Daniel 1944- ... 128
Rozental, Alek A(ron) 1920- ... 33-36R
Rozewicz, Tadeusz 1921- ... CANR-66
Earlier sketches in CA 108, CANR-36
See also CLC 9, 23
See also DAM POET
See also MTCW 1
Rozhdestvensky, Vsevolod A.
1895(?)-1977 Obituary ... 73-76
Rozier, John W(iley) 1918- ... 107
Rozin, Skip 1941- ... 89-92
Roziner, Felix (Yakovlevich) 1936- ... 142
Rozman, Deborah 1949- ... 115
Rozman, Gilbert Friedell 1943- ... CANR-51
Earlier sketches in CA 109, CANR-26
Rozovsky, Lorne Elkin 1942- ... CANR-24
Earlier sketch in CA 108
Rozwenc, Edwin C(harles) 1915-1974 ... CAP-1
Earlier sketch in CA 13-14
Ruan, Fang-fu 1937- ... 156
Ruane, Gerald P(atrick) 1934- ... 69-72
Ruano, Argimiro 1924- ... 33-36R
Ruano, Nazario
See Ruano, Argimiro
Ruark, Gibbons 1941- ... CANR-57
Earlier sketches in CA 33-36R, CANR-14, 31
See also CAAS 23
See also CLC 3
See also DLB 120
Ruark, Robert (Chester) 1915-1965 ... CAP-2
Obituary ... 25-28R
Earlier sketch in CA 19-20
Ruas, Charles (Edward) 1938- ... 124
Rubadeau, Duane O. 1927- ... 29-32R
Ruban, Vasilii Grigor'evich 1742-1795 ... DLB 150
Rubashov, Schneor Zalman
See Shazar, (Schneor) Zalman
Rubashov, Zalman
See Shazar, (Schneor) Zalman
Rubbra, Edmund 1901-1986 Obituary ... 119
Rubel, Arthur J. 1924- ... CANR-15
Earlier sketch in CA 41-44R
Rubel, Marc (Reid) 1949- ... CANR-54
Earlier sketch in CA 123
Rubel, Maximilien 1905- ... CAP-1
Earlier sketch in CA 11-12
Rubel, Nicole 1953- ... CANR-69
Earlier sketch in CA 125
See also SATA 18, 95
Rubel, Paula G(licksman) 1933- ... 89-92
Ruben, Brent David 1944- ... 41-44R
Ruben, Harvey L. 1941- ... 119
Rubens, Bernice (Ruth) 1923- ... CANR-65
Earlier sketches in CA 25-28R, CANR-33
See also CLC 19, 31
See also DLB 14
See also MTCW 1
Rubens, Jeff(rey Peter) 1941- ... CANR-39
Earlier sketches in CA 25-28R, CANR-17
Rubenson, Sven (Abel) 1921- ... 115
Rubenstein, Boris B. 1907(?)-1974 Obituary .. 53-56
Rubenstein, Joshua 1949- ... 103
Rubenstein, Richard E(dward) 1938- ... CANR-32
Earlier sketch in CA 29-32R
Rubenstein, Richard L(owell) 1924- ... CANR-17
Earlier sketch in CA 21-24R
Interview in ... CANR-17
Rubenstein, (Clarence) Robert 1926- ... 21-24R
Rubenstein, Roberta 1944- ... 89-92
Rubenstein, William B(ruce) 1960- ... 147
Rubenstone, Jessie 1912- ... 69-72
Rubia Barcia, Jose 1914-1997 ... CANR-41
Obituary ... 157
Earlier sketches in CA 103, CANR-19
Rubicam, Harry Cogswell, Jr. 1902- ... CAP-2
Earlier sketch in CA 17-18
Rubicon
See Lunn, Arnold
Rubin, Alan (Michael) 1936- ... 113
Rubin, Amy Kateman 1945- ... 106
Rubin, Arnold P(erry) 1946- ... 69-72
Rubin, Barnett R(ichard) 1950- ... 154
Rubin, Barry (M.) 1950- ... CANR-32
Earlier sketch in CA 108
Rubin, Benny 1899-1986 Obituary ... 119
Rubin, Bruce Joel 1943(?)- ... 140
Rubin, Charles 1953- ... 168
Rubin, Charles J. 1950- ... 101
Rubin, Cynthia Elyce 1944- ... 97-100
Rubin, David Lee 1939- ... CANR-33
Earlier sketches in CA 41-44R, CANR-15
Rubin, David M. 1945- ... 77-80
Rubin, Dorothy 1932- ... CANR-41
Earlier sketches in CA 101, CANR-19
Rubin, Duane R(oger) 1931- ... 57-60
Rubin, Eli Z(under) 1922- ... 17-20R
Rubin, Ernest 1915-1978 Obituary ... 81-84
Rubin, Eva Johanna 1925- ... SATA 38
Rubin, Eva R(edfield) 1926- ... 113
Rubin, Frederick 1926- ... 33-36R
Rubin, Hank 1916- ... 165
Rubin, Harold
See Robbins, Harold
Rubin, Ida Ely 1923- ... 107
Rubin, Isadore 1912-1970 ... CAP-1
Obituary ... 29-32R
Earlier sketch in CA 13-16
Rubin, Israel 1923- ... 37-40R
Rubin, Jacob A. 1910-1972 ... CAP-1
Obituary ... 37-40R
Earlier sketch in CA 11-12
Rubin, James Henry 1944- ... 106
Rubin, Jerry (C.) 1938-1994 ... 69-72
Obituary ... 147
Rubin, Joan 1932- ... 102
Rubin, Joan Shelley 1947- ... 139
Rubin, Julia Danielle 1944- ... 113
Rubin, Larry (Jerome) 1930- ... CANR-47
Earlier sketch in CA 5-8R
Rubin, Leona G(reenstone) 1920- ... 49-52
Rubin, Lillian B(reslow) 1924- ... CANR-37
Earlier sketch in CA 65-68
Rubin, Louis D(ecimus), Jr. 1923- ... CANR-47
Earlier sketches in CA 1-4R, CANR-6, 21
Rubin, Mann 1927- ... 119
Rubin, Mark 1946- ... CANR-9
Earlier sketch in CA 53-56
Rubin, Michael 1935- ... CANR-1
Earlier sketch in CA 1-4R
Rubin, Morris H(arold) 1911-1980 Obituary ... 101
Rubin, Morton 1923- ... 41-44R
Rubin, Nancy 1944- ... 129
Rubin, Patricia Lee 1951- ... 152
Rubin, Stanley 1928- ... 107
Rubin, Steven Jay 1951- ... 110
Rubin, Steven Joel 1943- ... 107
Rubin, Susan Goldman 1939- ... 150
See also SATA 84
Rubin, Theodore Isaac 1923- ... 110
Brief entry ... 108
Interview in ... 110
See also AITN 1
Rubin, Vera (Dourmashkin)
1911-1985 Obituary ... 115
Rubin, Vitalii 1923-1981 ... 69-72
Obituary ... 105
Rubin, William 1927- ... 77-80
Rubin, Zick 1944- ... CANR-1
Earlier sketch in CA 49-52
Rubin-Dorsky, Jeffrey 1947- ... 158
Rubinetti, Donald 1947- ... 156
See also SATA 92
Rubinfeld, William A. 1914(?)-1984 Obituary ... 113
Rubington, Earl 1923- ... 73-76
Rubino, Jane ... 166
Rubinoff, (M.) Lionel 1930- ... 25-28R
Rubinow, Sol (Isaac) 1923-1981 Obituary ... 103
Rubins, Harriett 1942- ... 120
Rubins, Jack L(awrence) 1916-1982 ... 85-88
Obituary ... 107
Rubinstein, Alvin Zachary 1927- ... CANR-39
Earlier sketches in CA 9-12R, CANR-3, 18
Rubinstein, Amnon 1931- ... CANR-7
Earlier sketch in CA 13-16R
Rubinstein, Arthur 1887(?)-1982 ... 113
Obituary ... 108
Rubinstein, Daryl Reich 1938(?)-1981 Obituary . 102
Rubinstein, David H(ugh) 1915- ... 109
Rubinstein, David M(ichael) 1942- ... 93-96
Rubinstein, E(lliott) 1936- ... 41-44R
Rubinstein, Edwin S. 1946- ... 166
Rubinstein, Erna F(erber) 1922- ... 120
Rubinstein, Gillian (Margaret) 1942- ... 136
See also AAYA 22
See also CLR 35
See also SATA 68
Rubinstein, H(arold) F(rederick)
1891-1975 Obituary ... 115
Rubinstein, Helena 1871(?)-1965 Obituary ... 113
Rubinstein, Helge 1929- ... 134
Rubinstein, Hilary 1926- ... 57-60
Rubinstein, Isaak 1949- ... 150
Rubinstein, Lev (I.) 1914- ... 149
Rubinstein, Moshe F(ajwel) 1930- ... 57-60
Rubinstein, Paul (Arthur) ... CANR-7
Earlier sketch in CA 61-64
Rubinstein, Robert E(dward) 1943- ... 106
See also SATA 49
Rubinstein, Ruth P. ... 149
Rubinstein, S(amuel) Leonard 1922- ... 45-48
Rubinstein, Stanley (Jack) 1890-1975 ... CAP-2
Earlier sketch in CA 29-32
Rubinstein, W(illiam) D(avid) 1946- ... 114
Rublowsky, John M(artin) 1928- ... 17-20R
See also SATA 62
Rubsamen, Walter H. 1911- ... 13-16R
Rubulis, Aleksis 1922- ... 37-40R
Ruby, Jay 1935- ... 136
Ruby, Kathryn 1947- ... 65-68
Ruby, Lois (F.) 1942- ... CANR-69
Earlier sketches in CA 97-100, CANR-18, 39
See also SATA 35, 95
See also SATA-Brief 34
Ruby, Robert Holmes 1921- ... CANR-7
Earlier sketch in CA 17-20R
Ruchames, Louis 1917-1976 ... CANR-2
Obituary ... 65-68
Earlier sketch in CA 1-4R
Ruchelman, Leonard I. 1933- ... CANR-28
Earlier sketch in CA 29-32R
Ruchlis, Hy(man) 1913-1992 ... CANR-47
Earlier sketches in CA 1-4R, 139, CANR-2
See also SATA 3
See also SATA-Obit 72
Ruchwarger, Gary 1949- ... 128
Ruck, Amy Roberta 1878-1978 ... CANR-69
Earlier sketches in CA 5-8R, CANR-5
Ruck, Berta
See Ruck, Amy Roberta
Ruck, Carl A(nton) P(aul) 1935- ... 25-28R
Ruck, Peter F(rederick) Carter
See Carter-Ruck, Peter F(rederick)
Rucker, Bryce W(ilson) 1921- ... 9-12R
Rucker, (Egbert) Darnell 1921- ... 41-44R
Rucker, Frank Warren 1886-1975 ... 1-4R
Obituary ... 103
Rucker, Helen (Bornstein) ... 1-4R
Rucker, Mike 1940- ... 155
See also SATA 91
Rucker, Rudolf v(on) B(itter) 1946- ... 124
Brief entry ... 119
Interview in ... 124
Rucker, Rudy
See Rucker, Rudolf v(on) B(itter)
Rucker, W(infred) Ray 1920- ... 13-16R
Ruckman, Ivy 1931- ... CANR-61
Earlier sketch in CA 111
See also SATA 37, 93
Ruck-Pauquet, Gina 1931- ... 122
Brief entry ... 116
See also SATA 40
See also SATA-Brief 37
Rudd, Anthony 1963- ... 146
Rudd, Enid ... 108
Rudd, Hughes (Day) 1921-1992 ... 73-76
Obituary ... 139
Rudd, Margaret
See Newlin, Margaret Rudd
Rudd, Margaret T(homas) 1907- ... 17-20R

Rudd, Robert D(ean) 1924- 93-96
Rudd, Robert L. 1921- 117
Rudd, Steele
See Davis, Arthur Hoey
Ruddell, Robert B(yron) 1937- 93-96
Rudder, Robert S(ween) 1937- CANR-5
Earlier sketch in CA 53-56
Rudder, Virginia L. 1941- 65-68
Ruddick, Nicholas 1952- 142
Ruddick, Sara 1935- 77-80
Ruddock, Ralph 1913- 53-56
Ruddock, Ted 1930- 139
Ruddy, Frank C.
See Frank, Rudolf
Ruddy, T(homas) Michael 1946- 124
Rude, George F(rederick) E(lliot) 1910-1993 CANR-24
Obituary 140
Earlier sketches in CA 5-8R, CANR-5
Rudeen, Kenneth Brief entry 117
See also SATA-Brief 36
Rudel, Hans-Ulrich 1916-1982 Obituary 110
Rudelius, William 1931- CANR-29
Earlier sketch in CA 45-48
Rudensky, Morris "Red"
See Friedman, Max Motel
Rudenstine, Neil Leon 1935- Brief entry 105
Ruder, William 1921- 17-20R
Rudhart, Alexander 1930- 61-64
Rudhyar, Dane 1895-1985 CANR-21
Obituary 117
Earlier sketch in CA 29-32R
Rudin, Jacob Philip 1902-1982 Obituary 107
Rudin, Marcia Ruth 1940- 102
Rudinsky, Joseph F(rancis) 1891- 5-8R
Rudis, Al 1943- 77-80
Rudisill, D(orus) P(aul) 1902-1978 45-48
Obituary 135
Rudkin, (James) David 1936- 89-92
See also CLC 14
See also DLB 13
Rudley, Stephen 1946- 106
See also SATA 30
Rudloe, Jack 1943- 97-100
Rudman, Mark 1948- CANR-45
Earlier sketch in CA 119
Rudman, Masha Kabakow 1933- CANR-27
Earlier sketch in CA 110
Rudnick, Hans H(einrich) 1935- 41-44R
Rudnick, Lois Palken 1944- 121
Rudnick, Milton Leroy 1927- CANR-3
Earlier sketch in CA 1-4R
Rudnick, Paul 1957- 139
Rudnik, Raphael 1933- 29-32R
See also CLC 7
Rudofsky, Bernard 1905-1988 17-20R
Obituary 125
Rudolf, Anthony 1942- CANR-24
Earlier sketches in CA 61-64, CANR-9
Rudolf von Ems c. 1200-c. 1254 DLB 138
Rudolph, Albert
See Frank, Rudolf
Rudolph, Donna Keyse 1934- 33-36R
Rudolph, Erwin Paul 1916- 33-36R
Rudolph, Frederick 1920- 9-12R
Rudolph, Kurt 1929- 158
Rudolph, L(avere) C(hristian) 1921- CANR-2
Earlier sketch in CA 5-8R
Rudolph, Lee (Norman) 1948- CANR-7
Earlier sketch in CA 57-60
Rudolph, Lloyd I(rving) 1927- 57-60
Rudolph, Marguerita 1908- CANR-13
Earlier sketch in CA 33-36R
See also SATA 21
Rudolph, Nancy 1923- 57-60
Rudolph, Richard (H.) 1940- 128
Rudolph, Robert S. 1937- 41-44R
Rudolph, Susanne Hoeber 1930- 25-28R
Rudomin, Esther
See Hautzig, Esther Rudomin
Rudrum, Alan (William) 1932- CANR-36
Earlier sketch in CA 25-28R
Rudwick, Elliot M. 1927-1986(?) 104
Obituary 118
Rudy, Ann 1927- 101
Rudy, Kathy 1956- 164
Rudy, Peter 1922- 53-56
Rudy, Willis 1920- 37-40R
Rudyerd, SirBenjamin 1572-1658 DLB 121
Rue, John E. 1924- 21-24R
Rue, Leonard Lee III 1926- CANR-1
Earlier sketch in CA 1-4R
See also SATA 37
Rue, Leslie W(aits) 1944- 110
Rue, Loyal D. 1944- 145
Rue, Nancy Naylor 1951- 122
Ruebsaat, Helmut J(ohannes) 1920- 61-64
Ruechelle, Randall C(ummings) 1920- 41-44R
Rueckert, William H(owe) 1926- 21-24R
Ruedi, Norma Paul
See Ainsworth, Norma
Ruedy, John 1927- 145
Ruef, John S. 1927- 37-40R
Rueff, Jacques (Leon) 1896-1978 CANR-12
Obituary 77-80
Earlier sketch in CA 65-68
Ruege, Klaus 1934- CANR-11
Earlier sketch in CA 65-68
Ruehle, Juergen 1924- 25-28R
Ruehlmann, William 1946- 105
Ruell, Patrick
See Hill, Reginald (Charles)
Ruelle, Karen Gray 1957- SATA 84
Ruemmler, John D(avid) 1948- 146
See also SATA 78
Ruesch, Hans 1913- 13-16R
Ruesch, Jurgen 1909- 73-76
Rueschemeyer, Dietrich 1930- 146
Rueschemeyer, Marilyn 1938- CANR-49
Earlier sketch in CA 122
Rueschhoff, Phil H. 1924- 29-32R
Ruether, Rosemary Radford 1936- CANR-39
Earlier sketch in CA 97-100
Rueveni, Uri 1933- 102
Ruff, Ann 1930-1993 120
Obituary 145
Ruff, Howard J. CANR-36
Earlier sketch in CA 93-96
Ruffell, Ann 1941- CANR-23
Earlier sketch in CA 107
See also SATA 30
Ruffell, Thomas
See Laslett, Peter
Ruffian, M.
See Hasek, Jaroslav (Matej Frantisek)
Ruffin, C(aulbert) Bernard III 1947- CANR-27
Earlier sketch in CA 109
Ruffin, Josephine St. Pierre 1842-1924 DLB 79
Ruffini, (Jacopo) Remo 1942- 57-60
Ruffins, Reynold 1930- CANR-46
Earlier sketch in CA 112
See also MAICYA
See also SATA 41
Ruffle, The
See Tegner, Henry (Stuart)
Ruffner, Budge
See Ruffner, Lester Ward
Ruffner, Lester Ward 1918- 89-92
Ruffo, Vinnie 25-28R
Ruganda, John 1941- DLB 157
Rugel, Miriam 1911- 101
Rugg, Dean S(prague) 1923- 41-44R
Ruggiero, Guido 1944- 118
Ruggiers, Paul G(eorge) 1918- CANR-24
Earlier sketch in CA 25-28R
Ruggles, Eleanor 1916- 5-8R
Ruggles, Henry Joseph 1813-1906 DLB 64
Ruggles, Joanne Beaule 1946- 73-76
Ruggles, Philip (Kent) 1944- 73-76
Rugh, Belle Dorman 1908- CAP-1
Earlier sketch in CA 13-16
Rugh, Roberts 1903-1978 93-96
Obituary 81-84
Rugoff, Milton 1913- CANR-49
Earlier sketch in CA 21-24R
See also SATA 30
Ruhen, Olaf 1911- CANR-20
Earlier sketches in CA 1-4R, CANR-5
See also SATA 17
Ruhlen, Merritt 1944- CANR-48
Earlier sketch in CA 122
Ruibal, Jorge Silvestre Remonda
See Remonda-Ruibal, Jorge Silvestre
Ruihley, Glenn Richard 107
Ruitenbeek, Hendrik M(arinus) 1928-1983 CANR-8
Obituary 109
Earlier sketch in CA 5-8R
Ruiz, Jose Martinez
See Martinez Ruiz, Jose
See also CLC 11
Ruiz, Ramon Eduardo 1921- CANR-11
Earlier sketch in CA 25-28R
See also HW
Ruiz, Ricardo Navas
See Navas-Ruiz, Ricardo
Ruiz, Roberto 1925- 41-44R
Ruiz, Vicki Lynn 1955- 127
Ruiz-De-Conde, Justina (Malaxechevarria) 1909- 73-76
Ruiz-Fornells, Enrique 1925- CANR-36
Earlier sketch in CA 33-36R
Ruja, Harry 1912- 41-44R
Rukeyser, Louis 1933- CANR-36
Earlier sketch in CA 65-68
Rukeyser, Merryle Stanley 1897-1988 CAP-2
Obituary 127
Earlier sketch in CA 23-24
Rukeyser, Muriel 1913-1980 CANR-60
Obituary 93-96
Earlier sketches in CA 5-8R, CANR-26
See also CLC 6, 10, 15, 27
See also DAM POET
See also DLB 48
See also MTCW 1
See also PC 12
See also SATA-Obit 22
Rukeyser, William Simon 1939- CANR-37
Earlier sketch in CA 69-72
Ruksenas, Algis 1942- 49-52
Ruland, Richard (Eugene) 1932- CANR-36
Earlier sketch in CA 21-24R
Ruland, Vernon Joseph 1931- 17-20R
Rule, Ann 1935- CANR-65
Earlier sketch in CA 145
See also BEST 90:2
See also DAM POP
Rule, Gordon Wade 1906-1982 Obituary 107
Rule, James B(ernard) 1943- CANR-47
Earlier sketch in CA 73-76
Rule, Jane (Vance) 1931- CANR-12
Earlier sketch in CA 25-28R
See also CAAS 18
See also CLC 27
See also DLB 60
Rulfo, Juan 1918-1986 CANR-26
Obituary 118
Earlier sketch in CA 85-88
See also CLC 8, 80
See also DAM MULT
See also DLB 113
See also HLC
See also HW
See also MTCW 1
See also SSC 25
Rulon, Philip Reed 1934- CANR-14
Earlier sketch in CA 37-40R
Rumaker, Michael 1932- CANR-2
Earlier sketch in CA 1-4R
See also DLB 16
Rumanes, George N(icholas) 1925- 45-48
Rumbaut, Hendle 1949- 150
See also SATA 84
Rumbelow, Donald 1940- 49-52
Rumberger, Russell W(illiam) 1949- CANR-26
Earlier sketch in CA 109
Rumble, Adrian 1945- 137
Rumble, Thomas C(lark) 1919- 13-16R
Rumble, Wilfrid E., Jr. 1931- 25-28R
Rumbold-Gibbs, Henry St. John Clair 1913- CANR-3
Earlier sketch in CA 1-4R
Rumens, Carol(-Ann) 1944- 131
See also DLB 40
Rumer, Boris 156
Rummel, J(osiah) Francis 1911- CANR-45
Earlier sketch in CA 17-20R
Rummel, (Louis) Jack(son) 1950- 132
Rummel, R(udolph) J(oseph) 1932- 65-68
Rumpleforeskin
See Krassner, Paul
Rumscheidt, H(ans) Martin 1935- CANR-36
Earlier sketch in CA 57-60
Rumsey, Marian (Barritt) 1928- 21-24R
See also SATA 16
Runcie, Robert (Alexander Kennedy) 1921- CANR-28
Earlier sketch in CA 108
Runcie, Robert A. K.
See Runcie, Robert (Alexander Kennedy)
Runciman, (James Cochran) Steven(son) 1903- CANR-3
Earlier sketch in CA 1-4R
Rundell, Walter, Jr. 1928- CANR-3
Earlier sketch in CA 9-12R
Rundle, Anne CANR-12
Earlier sketch in CA 57-60
Runes, Dagobert D(avid) 1902-1982 CANR-26
Obituary 108
Earlier sketch in CA 25-28R
Runge, C(arlisle) Ford 1953- 122
Runge, William H(arry) 1927- 1-4R
Runia, Klaas 1926- CANR-45
Earlier sketches in CA 5-8R, CANR-5, 20
Runkel, Philip J(ulian) 1917- CANR-11
Earlier sketch in CA 29-32R
Runkle, Gerald 1924- CANR-14
Earlier sketch in CA 37-40R
Runnels, Curtis 1950- 126
Runnerstroem, Bengt Arne 1944- SATA 75
Running, Leona Glidden 1916- 89-92
Runte, Alfred 1947- CANR-41
Earlier sketches in CA 102, CANR-19
Runyan, Harry (John) 1913-(?) CAP-2
Earlier sketch in CA 23-24
Runyan, John
See Palmer, Bernard
Runyan, Thora J. 1931- 69-72
Runyon, A(lfred) Milton 1905-1983 Obituary 109
Runyon, Catherine 1947- 61-64
See also SATA 62
Runyon, Charles W. 1928- 17-20R
Runyon, (Alfred) Damon 1884(?)-1946 165
Brief entry 107
See also DLB 11, 86, 171
See also TCLC 10
Runyon, Daniel V. 1954- 120
Runyon, John H(arold) 1945- 33-36R
Runyon, Randolph Paul 1947- 148
Runyon, Richard P(orter) 1925- CANR-3
Earlier sketch in CA 45-48
Ruoff, A. LaVonne Brown 1930- 143
See also SATA 76
Ruoff, James E. 1925- 41-44R
Ruokanen, Miikka 1953- 146
Ruotolo, Andrew K(eogh) 1926(?)-1979 103
Obituary 89-92
Ruotolo, Lucio P(eter) 1927- 41-44R
RuPaul 1960- 155
Rupert, Hoover 1917- CANR-3
Earlier sketch in CA 1-4R
Rupert, James C(layton) II 1957- 136
Rupert, Raphael Rudolph 1910- CAP-2
Earlier sketch in CA 19-20
Ruple, Wayne Douglas 1950- 53-56
Rupp, E. G.
See Rupp, E(rnest) Gordon
Rupp, E(rnest) Gordon 1910-1986 124
Brief entry 113
Rupp, Gordon
See Rupp, E(rnest) Gordon
Rupp, James M. 1952- 142
Rupp, Leila J(ane) 1950- 81-84
Rupp, Richard H(enry) 1934- 29-32R
Ruppenthal, Karl M. 1917- 17-20R
Ruppersburg, Hugh Michael 1950- 124
Ruppli, Michel 1934- 101
Ruprecht, Mary M(argaret Wyant) 1934- 118
Rus, Vladimir 1931- 17-20R
Rusalem, Herbert 1918- 41-44R
Rusbridger, Alan 1953- 125
Rusbridger, James 1928-1994 CANR-39
Obituary 144
Earlier sketch in CA 134
Rusch, Hermann G. 1907- 61-64
Rusch, John J(ay) 1942- 106
Rusch, Kris
See Rusch, Kristine Kathryn
Rusch, Kristine Kathryn 1960- 157
Rusco, Elmer R(itter) 1928- 65-68
Ruscoe, (Steuart) James (Bailey) 1947- 116
Ruse, Gary Alan 1946- CANR-12
Earlier sketch in CA 61-64
Ruse, Michael E. 1940- 107
Rush, Alison 1951- 115
See also SATA 41
Rush, Anne Kent 1945- CANR-8
Earlier sketch in CA 61-64
Rush, Benjamin 1746-1813 DLB 37
Rush, Christopher 1944- 122
Rush, Elizabeth 1918- 115
Rush, James J. 1929- 120
Rush, Joseph H(arold) 1911- 5-8R
Rush, Joshua
See Pearlstein, Howard J.
Rush, Michael (David) 1937- 61-64
Rush, Myron 1922- 45-48
Rush, N(ixon) Orwin 1907- CANR-25
Earlier sketch in CA 45-48
Rush, Norman 1933- 126
Brief entry 121
Interview in 126
See also CLC 44
Rush, Peter 1937- 111
See also SATA 32
Rush, Philip
See Lardner, Ring(gold Wilmer), Jr.
Rush, Philip 1908- 104
Rush, Ralph E(ugene) 1903-1965 5-8R
Rush, Rebecca 1779-(?) DLB 200
Rush, Richard Henry 1915- CANR-6
Earlier sketch in CA 5-8R
Rush, Robert
See Barber, D(ulan) F(riar Whilberton)
Rush, Theressa Gunnels 1945- 104
Rushbrook Williams, L(aurence) F(rederic) 1890-1978 97-100
Rushdie, (Ahmed) Salman 1947- CANR-56
Brief entry 108
Earlier sketches in CA 111, CANR-33
Interview in 111
See also BEST 89:3
See also CLC 23, 31, 55, 100
See also DAB
See also DAC
See also DAM MST, NOV, POP
See also DLB 194
See also MTCW 1
See also WLCS
Rushdoony, R(ousas) J(ohn) 1916- 93-96
Rusher, William A(llen) 1923- CANR-28
Earlier sketch in CA 103
Rushford, Patricia H(elen) 1943- CANR-37
Earlier sketch in CA 115
Rushforth, Peter (Scott) 1945- 101
See also CLC 19
Rushing, Francis W(illard) 1939- CANR-31
Earlier sketch in CA 112
Rushing, Jane Gilmore 1925- CANR-64
Earlier sketch in CA 49-52
Rushing, William A. 1930- 81-84
Rushkoff, Douglas 1961- 164
Rushmer, Robert F(razer) 1914- 134
Brief entry 111
Rushmore, Helen 1898- 25-28R
See also SATA 3
Rushmore, Robert (William) 1926-1986 25-28R
Obituary 120
See also SATA 8
See also SATA-Obit 49
Rusholm, Peter
See Powell, Eric F(rederick) W(illiam)
Rushton, J(ohn) Philippe 1943- CANR-66
Earlier sketch in CA 111
Rushton, Julian (Gordon) 1941- 132
Rushton, William Faulkner 1947- CANR-22
Earlier sketch in CA 101
Rusi, Alpo M. 1949- 167
Rusinek, Alla 1949- 45-48
Rusinko, Susan 1922- 133
Rusinow, Dennison I. 1930- 85-88
Rusk, (David) Dean 1909-1994 141
Obituary 147
Rusk, Howard A(rchibald) 1901-1989 103
Obituary 130
Rusk, Ralph Leslie 1888-1962 5-8R
See also DLB 103
Rusk, Richard (Geary) 1946- 138
Ruskay, Joseph A. 1910- CAP-2
Earlier sketch in CA 29-32
Ruskay, Sophie 1887-1980 69-72
Obituary 97-100
Ruskin, Ariane
See Batterberry, Ariane Ruskin
Ruskin, John 1819-1900 129
Brief entry 114
See also CDBLB 1832-1890
See also DLB 55, 163, 190
See also SATA 24
See also TCLC 63
Ruskin, Ronald 1944- 115
Ruslanov, Sviatoslav
See Krasnov, Vladislav Georgievich

Russ, Joanna 1937- ... CANR-65
Earlier sketch in CANR-11, 31
See also CLC 15
See also DLB 8
See also MTCW 1
Russ, Laurence 1943- ... 114
Russ, Lavinia (Faxon) 1904-1992 ... 25-28R
Obituary ... 137
See also SATA 74
Russ, Martin 1931- ... 106
Russ, William Adam, Jr. 1903- ... 1-4R
Russak, Ben 1912-1988 Obituary ... 127
Russek, Henry I(rving) 1911-1990 Obituary ... 131
Russel, Myra T(eicher) 1920- ... 145
Russel, Robert R(oyal) 1890- ... 13-16R
Russell, Alan 1956- ... 168
Russell, Albert
See Bixby, Jerome Lewis
Russell, Allan Melvin 1930- ... 122
Russell, Amanda
See Feldman, Ellen (Bette)
Russell, Andy 1915- ... CANR-26
Earlier sketches in CA 21-24R, CANR-10
Russell, Annie V(est) 1880(?)-1974 Obituary ... 49-52
Russell, Arthur (Wolseley) 1908- ... CANR-16
Earlier sketches in CAP-1, CA 13-14
Russell, (Muriel) Audrey
1906(?)-1989(?) Obituary ... 129
Russell, Benjamin 1761-1845 ... DLB 43
Russell, Bertrand (Arthur William) 1872-1970 ...
CANR-44
Obituary ... 25-28R
Earlier sketches in CAP-1, CA 13-16
See also DLB 100
See also MTCW 1
Russell, Bill
See Russell, William Felton
Russell, C(harles) Allyn 1920- ... 65-68
Russell, Carroll Mason 1898(?)-1983 Obituary ... 111
Russell, Charles 1944- ... 111
Russell, Charles Edward 1860-1941 ... DLB 25
Russell, Charles M. 1864-1926 ... DLB 188
Russell, Charlotte
See Rathjen, Carl Henry
Russell, Cheryl 1953- ... 150
Russell, Claude Vivian 1919- ... 17-20R
Russell, Clifford S(pringer) 1938- ... CANR-12
Earlier sketch in CA 73-76
Russell, Colin Archibald 1928- ... 45-48
Russell, Conrad 1937- ... 33-36R
Russell, D(avid) S(yme) 1916- ... 13-16R
Russell, Daniel 1937- ... 41-44R
Russell, Diana E(lizabeth) H(amilton) 1938- ...
CANR-34
Earlier sketches in CA 61-64, CANR-8
Russell, Diarmuid 1902(?)-1973 Obituary ... 45-48
Russell, Dick 1947- ... 152
Russell, Don(ald Bert) 1899-1986 ... CANR-1
Obituary ... 118
Earlier sketch in CA 1-4R
See also SATA-Obit 47
Russell, Donald Andrew (Frank Moore) 1920- ... 110
Russell, Dora (Winifred Black) 1894-1986 ... 125
Obituary ... 119
Russell, Douglas A(ndrew) 1927- ... CANR-16
Earlier sketch in CA 41-44R
Russell, E(nid) S(herry) 1924- ... 139
Russell, Edward (Frederick Langley)
1895-1981 ... 107
Obituary ... 103
Russell, Eric Frank 1905-1978 ... 124
Obituary ... 102
Russell, Foster Meharry 1907- ... 111
Russell, Francis 1910-1989 ... 25-28R
Obituary ... 128
Russell, Frank
See Fearn, John Russell
Russell, Frank D. 1923- ... 126
Russell, Franklin (Alexander) 1926- ... CANR-11
Earlier sketch in CA 17-20R
See also SATA 11
Russell, Frederick S(tratten) 1897-1984 ... 157
Obituary ... 113
Russell, George 1923- ... 166
Russell, George William 1867-1935 ... 153
Brief entry ... 104
See also Baker, Jean H.
See also CDBLB 1890-1914
See also DAM POET
Russell, Gertrude Barrer
See Barrer-Russell, Gertrude
Russell, (Sydney) Gordon 1892- ... CAP-2
Earlier sketch in CA 29-32
Russell, Gordon 1930(?)-1981 Obituary ... 102
Russell, H. Diane 1936- ... 110
Russell, Harold (John) 1914- ... 129
Russell, Helen Ross 1915- ... 33-36R
See also SATA 8
Russell, Howard Lewis 1962- ... 136
Russell, Howard S(ymmes) 1887-1980 ... 105
Russell, I(saac) Willis 1903-1985 ... 118
Russell, Ivy E(thel Southern) 1909- ... 5-8R
Russell, J.
See Bixby, Jerome Lewis
Russell, J(effrey) P(eter) 1954- ... 112
Russell, James
See Harknett, Terry
Russell, James 1933- ... SATA 53
Russell, James E. 1916-1975 Obituary ... 57-60
Russell, Jeffrey Burton 1934- ... CANR-52
Earlier sketches in CA 25-28R, CANR-11, 28
Russell, Jeremy Longmore 1935- ... 110
Russell, Jim
See Russell, James
Russell, Joan Mercedes 1921- ... 102
Russell, John
See Fearn, John Russell
Russell, John 1919- ... CANR-34
Earlier sketch in CA 13-16R
Russell, John David 1928- ... 9-12R
Russell, John L(owry), Jr. 1921- ... 9-12R
Russell, John L(eonard) 1906- ... 13-16R
Russell, John Malcolm 1953- ... 149
Russell, Josiah Cox 1900- ... 41-44R
Russell, (Henry) Ken(neth Alfred) 1927- ... 105
See also CLC 16
Russell, Ken(neth Victor) 1929- ... CANR-11
Earlier sketch in CA 25-28R
Russell, Letty M(andeville) 1929- ... CANR-8
Earlier sketch in CA 57-60
Russell, Lois Ann 1931- ... 113
Russell, Mariann Barbara 1935- ... 109
Russell, Mark 1932- ... 113
Brief entry ... 108
Interview in ... 113
Russell, Martin 1934- ... CANR-61
Earlier sketch in CA 73-76
Russell, CountessMary Annette Beauchamp
1866-1941 ... 167
See also Author of Elizabeth and Her German
Garden
and Cholmondeley, Alice
and Elizabeth
and von Arnim, Elizabeth
Russell, Mary D(oria) 1950- ... 162
Russell, Maud 1893(?)-1989 Obituary ... 130
Russell, Maurin
See Russell, Maurine (Fletcher)
Russell, Maurine (Fletcher) 1899- ... CAP-1
Earlier sketch in CA 9-10
Russell, Norma Hull Lewis 1902- ... 5-8R
Russell, Norman H(udson), Jr. 1921- ... CANR-45
Earlier sketch in CA 49-52
Russell, O(live) Ruth 1897-1979 ... 57-60
Obituary ... 133
Russell, P. Craig 1951- ... 148
See also SATA 80
Russell, P(eggy) J(ean) 1934- ... 97-100
Russell, Pamela Redford 1950- ... 81-84
Russell, Patrick
See Sammis, John
Russell, Paul (Gary) 1942- ... SATA 57
Russell, Paul 1956- ... 133
Russell, (Irwin) Peter 1921- ... CANR-44
Earlier sketch in CA 97-100
Russell, Ray 1924- ... CANR-6
Earlier sketch in CA 1-4R
Russell, Rinaldina 1934- ... 167
Russell, Robert W(allace) 1912-1992 ... 160
Russell, Robert W(illiam) 1924- ... CANR-34
Earlier sketch in CA 1-4R
Russell, Ronald (Stanley) 1904-1974 ... CAP-1
Earlier sketch in CA 11-12
Russell, Ronald 1924- ... 102
Russell, Rosalind 1911-1976 ... 116
Obituary ... 111
Russell, Ross 1909- ... CANR-34
Earlier sketch in CA 1-4R
Russell, Roy 1918- ... CANR-26
Earlier sketch in CA 107
Russell, Russell
See Meades, Jonathan (Turner)
Russell, Sarah
See Laski, Marghanita
Russell, Shane
See Norwood, Victor G(eorge) C(harles)
Russell, Sharman Apt 1954- ... 142
Russell, Solveig Paulson 1904- ... CANR-5
Earlier sketch in CA 1-4R
See also SATA 3
Russell, Thomas 1902(?)-1984 Obituary ... 114
Russell, Victor L. 1948- ... 117
Russell, William F(rank) 1945- ... CANR-67
Earlier sketch in CA 126
Russell, William Felton 1934- ... 108
Russell, William H. 1911- ... 61-64
Russell, William Martin 1947- ... 164
See also CLC 60
Russell, Willy
See Russell, William Martin
Russell-Smith, Enid (Mary Russell)
1903-1989 Obituary ... 129
Russell Taylor, Elisabeth 1930- ... CANR-34
Earlier sketches in CA 81-84, CANR-15
Russell-Wood, A(nthony) J(ohn) R(ussell) 1939- ...
CANR-7
Earlier sketch in CA 57-60
Russett, Bruce M(artin) 1935- ... CANR-2
Earlier sketch in CA 5-8R
Russett, Cynthia Eagle 1937- ... 21-24R
Russman, Thomas A. 1944- ... 128
Russo, Anthony 1933- ... 61-64
Russo, Giuseppe Luigi 1884- ... CAP-1
Earlier sketch in CA 9-10
Russo, John Paul 1944- ... 41-44R
Russo, Joseph Louis
See Russo, Giuseppe Luigi
Russo, Monica J. 1950- ... SATA 83
Russo, Richard 1949- ... 133
Brief entry ... 127
Russo, Richard Paul 1954- ... 129
Russo, Sarett Rude 1918(?)-1976 Obituary ... 65-68
Russo, Susan 1947- ... 106
See also SATA 30
Russo, Vito 1946- ... 107
Russon, Allien R. 1905- ... 105
Russon, L(eslie) J(ohn) 1907- ... 17-20R
Rust, Brian Arthur Lovell 1922- ... CANR-2
Earlier sketch in CA 45-48
Rust, Claude 1916- ... 109
Rust, Doris (Dibblin) ... 13-16R
Rust, Eric C(harles) 1910- ... 13-16R
Rust, Marina (Marshall) 1964- ... 141
Rust, Richard Dilworth 1937- ... 29-32R
Rusticus
See Martin, Brian P(hilip)
Rustin, Bayard 1910(?)-1987 ... CANR-25
Obituary ... 123
Earlier sketch in CA 53-56
See also BW 1
Rustomji, Nari Kaikhosru 1919- ... 101
Rustow, Dankwart A(lexander) 1924-1996 . CANR-1
Obituary ... 153
Earlier sketch in CA 1-4R
Ruta, Suzanne 1940- ... 127
Rutan, Dick 1938- ... 149
Rutan, J. Scott 1940- ... 142
Rutan, Richard Glenn
See Rutan, Dick
Rutberg, Sidney 1924- ... 69-72
Rutenber, Culbert G(erow) 1909- ... CAP-2
Earlier sketch in CA 17-18
Rutgers, Leonard Victor 1964- ... 152
Rutgers van der Loeff, An
See Rutgers van der Loeff-Basenau, An(na) Maria
Margaretha
Rutgers van der Loeff-Basenau, An(na) Maria
1910- ... CANR-7
Earlier sketch in CA 9-12R
See also SATA 22
Ruth, Babe
See Ruth, George Herman (Jr.)
Ruth, Claire (Merritt) 1900-1976 Obituary ... 69-72
Ruth, George Herman (Jr.) 1895-1948 Brief
entry ... 116
Ruth, John L(andis) 1930- ... 73-76
Ruth, Kent Ringelman 1916- ... CANR-2
Earlier sketch in CA 5-8R
Ruth, Rod 1912- ... SATA 9
Ruthchild, Rochelle Goldberg 1940- ... 152
Rutherford, Andrew 1929-1998 ... CANR-9
Obituary ... 165
Earlier sketch in CA 5-8R
Rutherford, Douglas
See McConnell, James Douglas Rutherford
Rutherford, Edward
See Wintle, Francis Edward
Rutherford, Ernest 1871-1937 ... 156
Rutherford, Malcolm 1939- ... 119
Rutherford, Margaret 1882-1972 Obituary ... 33-36R
Rutherford, Mark
See White, William Hale
See also DLB 18
See also TCLC 25
Rutherford, Meg 1932- ... 29-32R
See also SATA 34
Rutherford, Michael (Andrew) 1946- ... CANR-26
Earlier sketch in CA 45-48
Rutherford, Phillip Roland 1939- ... 37-40R
Rutherford, Ward 1927- ... CANR-14
Earlier sketch in CA 77-80
Ruthin, Margaret ... SATA 4
Ruthstrom, Dorotha 1936- ... 107
Ruthven, Beverly (M.) 1953- ... 149
Ruthven, K(enneth) K(nowles) 1936- ... CANR-51
Earlier sketches in CA 25-28R, CANR-26
Rutkoff, Peter M. 1942- ... CANR-39
Earlier sketch in CA 116
Rutkowski, Edwin H(enry) 1923- ... 37-40R
Rutland, Dodge
See Singleton, Betty
Rutland, Robert A(llen) 1922- ... CANR-2
Earlier sketch in CA 45-48
Rutledge, Aaron L(eslie) 1919- ... 45-48
Rutledge, Albert J(ohn) 1934- ... 33-36R
Rutledge, Archibald (Hamilton) 1883-1973 CANR-5
Obituary ... 45-48
Earlier sketch in CA 5-8R
Rutledge, Brett
See Paul, Elliot (Harold)
Rutledge, Dom Denys
See Rutledge, Edward William
Rutledge, Edward William 1906- ... 5-8R
Rutledge, Harley Dean 1926- ... 107
Rutledge, Howard Elmer
1929(?)-1984 Obituary ... 113
Rutledge, Leigh W. 1957- ... 151
Rutman, Darrett B(ruce) 1929- ... CANR-6
Earlier sketch in CA 13-16R
Rutman, Gilbert L(ionel) 1935- ... 25-28R
Rutman, Leo 1935- ... 45-48
Rutsala, Vern 1934- ... CANR-43
Earlier sketches in CA 9-12R, CANR-6, 20
Rutstein, David D(avis) 1909-1986 ... 33-36R
Obituary ... 118
Rutstein, Harry Sidney 1929- ... 109
Rutstein, Nat(han) 1930- ... 53-56
Rutstrum, Calvin 1895-1982 ... CANR-1
Obituary ... 106
Earlier sketch in CA 1-4R
Rutt, M. E.
See Shah, Amina
Rutt, Richard 1925- ... CANR-6
Earlier sketch in CA 9-12R
Ruttan, Vernon W(esley) 1924- ... 41-44R
Ruttenberg, Joseph 1889-1983 Obituary ... 109
Ruttenberg, Stanley H(arvey) 1917- ... 33-36R
Rutter, Barbara A. 1943- ... 118
Rutter, Eileen Joyce 1945- ... CANR-10
Earlier sketch in CA 61-64
Rutter, Jeremy B. 1946- ... 163
Rutter, Michael (Llewellyn) 1933- ... CANR-53
Earlier sketches in CA 109, CANR-29
Ruttkowski, Wolfgang Victor 1935- ... CANR-15
Earlier sketch in CA 41-44R
Ruttle, Lee 1909- ... 81-84
Rutz, Viola Larkin 1932- ... 21-24R
See also SATA 12
Rutzebeck, Hjalmar 1889- ... 9-12R
Ruud, Charles A(rthur) 1933- ... CANR-48
Earlier sketch in CA 121
Ruud, Josephine Bartow 1921- ... 73-76
Ruurs, Margriet 1952- ... 164
See also SATA 97
Ruuth, Marianne 1937- ... CANR-21
Earlier sketches in CA 57-60, CANR-6
Ruxin, Robert H(arris) 1953- ... 110
Ruxton, George Frederick 1821-1848 ... DLB 186
Ruyerson, James Paul
See Rothweiler, Paul Roger
Ruyslinck, Ward 1929-
See Belser, Reimond Karel Maria de
See also CLC 14
Ruz, Fidel Castro
See Castro (Ruz), Fidel
Ruzic, Neil P. 1930- ... CANR-39
Earlier sketches in CA 17-20R, CANR-8
Ruzicka, Rudolph 1883-1978 Obituary ... 81-84
See also SATA-Obit 24
R-va, Zeneida
See Gan, Elena Andreevna
Ryall, Edward W(illiam) 1902- ... 61-64
Ryall, George (Francis Trafford) 1887(?)-1979 .. 103
Obituary ... 89-92
Ryalls, Alan 1919- ... 102
Ryals, Clyde de L(oache) 1928- ... 21-24R
Ryan, Alan 1940- ... CANR-49
Earlier sketch in CA 29-32R
Ryan, Allan A(ndrew), Jr. 1945- ... 124
Ryan, Alvan Sherman 1912- ... 17-20R
Ryan, Bernard, Jr. 1923- ... CANR-6
Earlier sketch in CA 5-8R
Ryan, Betsy
See Ryan, Elizabeth (Anne)
Ryan, Bob 1946- ... CANR-4
Earlier sketch in CA 49-52
Ryan, Bryce F(inley) 1911- ... 81-84
Ryan, Charles W(illiam) 1929- ... 57-60
Ryan, Charles W(illiam) 1932- ... 93-96
Ryan, Cheli Duran ... 102
See also SATA 20
Ryan, Claude 1925- Brief entry ... 111
Ryan, Cornelius (John) 1920-1974 ... CANR-38
Obituary ... 53-56
Earlier sketch in CA 69-72
See also CLC 7
Ryan, Craig 1953- ... 153
Ryan, Desmond 1893-1964 Obituary ... 113
Ryan, Desmond 1943- ... 130
Ryan, Dorothy (Barger) 1942- ... CANR-13
Earlier sketch in CA 73-76
Ryan, Edwin 1916- ... 5-8R
Ryan, Elizabeth (Anne) 1943- ... CANR-7
Earlier sketch in CA 61-64
See also SATA 30
Ryan, Frank 1944- ... 145
Ryan, Gig (Elizabeth) 1956- ... 154
Ryan, Herbert J(oseph) 1931- ... 41-44R
Ryan, James G(ilbert) 1947- ... 165
Ryan, James H(erbert) 1928- ... 53-56
Ryan, Jeanette Mines
See Mines, Jeanette (Marie)
Ryan, Jessica Cadwalader
1915(?)-1972 Obituary ... 33-36R
Ryan, Joan 1960(?)- ... 158
Ryan, John (Gerald Christopher) 1921- ... CANR-16
Earlier sketches in CA 49-52, CANR-1
See also SATA 22
Ryan, John Barry 1933- ... CANR-7
Earlier sketch in CA 57-60
Ryan, John Fergus 1931- ... 73-76
Ryan, John J. 1922(?)-1977 Obituary ... 69-72
Ryan, John Julian 1898- ... 73-76
Ryan, John K(enneth) 1897-1981 ... CANR-16
Earlier sketch in CA 13-16R
Ryan, Joseph A. 1920- ... 138
Ryan, Joseph J. 1910(?)-1976 Obituary ... 69-72
Ryan, Juanita 1949- ... 120
Ryan, Kathryn Morgan 1925-1993 ... 102
Obituary ... 140
Interview in ... 102
Ryan, Kevin 1932- ... CANR-12
Earlier sketch in CA 29-32R
Ryan, Lawrence Vincent 1923- ... 5-8R
Ryan, Leonard Eames 1930- ... 9-12R
Ryan, Marah Ellis 1866(?)-1934 Brief entry ... 122
Ryan, Margaret 1950- ... 146
See also SATA 78
Ryan, Marleigh Grayer 1930- ... 17-20R
Ryan, Mary E(lizabeth) 1953- ... SATA 61
Ryan, Mary P(atricia) 1945- ... 134
Brief entry ... 113
Ryan, Maureen Jones
See Jones-Ryan, Maureen
Ryan, Michael 1946- ... 49-52
See also CLC 65
See also DLBY 82
Ryan, Milo 1907- ... 5-8R
Ryan, Neil Joseph 1930- ... 13-16R
Ryan, Oscar 1904- ... DLB 68
Ryan, Pat M(artin) 1928- ... CANR-13
Earlier sketch in CA 33-36R
Ryan, Patrick J. 1902- ... CAP-1
Earlier sketch in CA 11-12
Ryan, Paul B(rennan) 1913- ... CANR-15
Earlier sketch in CA 81-84
Ryan, Paul William 1906-1947 Brief entry ... 114
Ryan, Peter (Charles) 1939- ... 61-64
See also SATA 15
Ryan, Peter Allen 1923- ... 109
Ryan, Rachel
See Brown, Sandra

Ryan, Regina (Claire) 1938- 118
Ryan, Regina S(ara) 1945- 119
Ryan, Robert Michael 1934- 29-32R
Ryan, Sister Joseph Eleanor 61-64
Ryan, T. Antoinette 1924- 41-44R
Ryan, Thomas Arthur 1911- 41-44R
Ryan, Thomas Richard 1897-1981 ..... 29-32R
Obituary 122
Ryan, Tim
See Dent, Lester
Ryan, Tom 1938- CANR-10
Earlier sketch in CA 57-60
Ryan, William (Howard) 1914- 104
Ryan, William (Michael) 1948- 122
Ryan, William H. 1928(?)-1986 Obituary 121
Ryan, William M(artin) 1918- 33-36R
Ryang, Sonia 1960- 165
Ryan-Lush, Geraldine 1949- ..... SATA 89
Ryans, David Garriott 1909- 5-8R
Ryans, John K(elley), Jr. 1932- 61-64
Ryavec, Karl W(illiam) 1936- 137
Ryback, Eric 1952- 37-40R
Rybak, Nathan 1913-1978(?) Obituary 81-84
Rybakov, Anatoli (Naumovich) 1911- 135
Brief entry 126
See also CLC 23, 53
See also SATA 79
Rybalka, Michel 1933- 41-44R
Rybczynski, Witold (Marian) 1943- CANR-29
Earlier sketch in CA 110
Rybka, Edward F(rank) 1928- 33-36R
Rybolt, Thomas R(oy) 1954- ..... SATA 62
Rybot, Doris
See Ponsonby, D(oris) A(lmon)
Rychlak, Joseph F(rank) 1928- CANR-14
Earlier sketch in CA 37-40R
Ryckmans, Pierre 1935- CANR-16
Earlier sketch in CA 85-88
Rycroft, Charles (Frederick) 1914- CANR-11
Earlier sketch in CA 21-24R
Ryczek, William J. 1953- 143
Rydberg, Ernest E(mil) 1901- 13-16R
See also SATA 21
Rydberg, Lou(isa Hampton) 1908- 69-72
See also SATA 27
Rydel, Christine A(nn) 1944- 118
Rydell, Forbes
See Forbes, DeLoris (Florine) Stanton
Rydell, Katy 1942- 155
See also SATA 91
Rydell, Robert W(illiam) 1952- CANR-52
Earlier sketch in CA 126
Rydell, Wendell
See Rydell, Wendy
Rydell, Wendy 33-36R
See also SATA 4
Ryden, Ernest Edwin 1886-1981 Obituary 102
Ryden, Hope CANR-59
Earlier sketches in CA 33-36R, CANR-14
See also SATA 8, 91
Rydenfelt, Sven 1911- 132
Ryder, A(rthur) J(ohn) 1913- 21-24R
Ryder, Eileen 1908- 117
Ryder, Ellen 1913- 29-32R
Ryder, Frank G(lessner) 1916- 5-8R
Ryder, Joanne (Rose) 1946- 133
Brief entry 112
See also CLR 37
See also MAICYA
See also SATA 65
See also SATA-Brief 34
Ryder, John 1917- CANR-5
Earlier sketch in CA 5-8R
Ryder, Jonathan
See Ludlum, Robert
Ryder, M(ichael) L(awson) 1927- 102
Ryder, Meyer S. 1909- 21-24R
Ryder, Norman B(urston) 1923- 37-40R
Ryder, Pamela
See Lamb, Nancy
Ryder, Richard D. 1940- 139
Ryder, Ron 1904- 61-64
Ryder, Rowland (Vint) 1914- 85-88
Ryder, T(homas) A(rthur) 1902- 5-8R
Ryder, Thom
See Harvey, John (Barton)
Ryding, William W. 1924- 77-80
Rye, Anthony
See Youd, (Christopher) Samuel
Rye, Bjoern Robinson 1942- 61-64
Ryerson, Margery (Austin) 1886-1989 Obituary . 128
Ryerson, Martin 1907- CANR-8
Earlier sketch in CA 13-16R
Ryf, Robert S. 1918-1985 ..... 17-20R
Obituary 117
Ryga, George 1932-1987 ..... CANR-43
Obituary 124
Earlier sketch in CA 101
See also CLC 14
See also DAC
See also DAM MST
See also DLB 60
Ryken, Leland 1942- CANR-52
Earlier sketches in CA 29-32R, CANR-12, 28
Rykwert, Joseph 1926- CANR-11
Earlier sketch in CA 69-72
Ryland, Lee
See Arlandson, Leone
Rylands, Enriqueta Augustina Tennant
1843-1908 ..... DLB 184
Rylands, John 1801-1888 ..... DLB 184
Rylands, Philip 1950- 144
Rylant, Cynthia 1954- 136
See also AAYA 10
See also CLR 15
See also JRDA
See also MAICYA
See also SAAS 13
See also SATA 50, 76
See also SATA-Brief 44
Ryle, Anthony 1927- 107
Ryle, Gilbert 1900-1976 73-76
Obituary 69-72
Ryle, Martin (H.) 1918-1984 133
Ryle, Michael 1927- 133
Rylski, Aleksander Scibor
See Scibor-Rylski, Aleksander
Ryman, Geoff(rey Charles) 1951- 134
Rymer, Alta May 1925- CANR-1
Earlier sketch in CA 49-52
See also SATA 34
Rymer, Thomas 1643(?)-1713 ..... DLB 101
Rymes, Thomas Kenneth 1932- 37-40R
Ryn, Claes G. 1943- 129
Rynearson, Edward H(arper)
1901-1987 Obituary 121
Rynew, Arden N. 1943- 37-40R
Rynne, Xavier
See Murphy, Francis X(avier)
Ryrie, Charles C(aldwell) 1925- CANR-39
Earlier sketches in CA 9-12R, CANR-3, 18
Ryskamp, Charles (Andrew) 1928- 104
Ryskind, Morrie 1895-1985 Obituary 117
Brief entry 109
See also DLB 26
Rystrom, Kenneth 1932- 110
Rywell, Martin 1905-1971 ..... CAP-2
Earlier sketch in CA 19-20
Rywkin, Michael 1925- 13-16R
Ryzl, Milan 1928- 29-32R
Rzepka, Charles J(ulian) 1949- 127
Rzhevsky, Aleksai Andreevich 1737-1804 . DLB 150
Rzhevsky, Leonid 1905- CANR-14
Earlier sketch in CA 41-44R
Rzhevsky, Nicholas 1943- 115

S

S. H.
See Hartmann, Sadakichi
S. L. C.
See Clemens, Samuel Langhorne
S. S.
See Sassoon, Siegfried (Lorraine)
S. S. E.
See Sperry, (Sally) Baxter
S., Svend Otto
See Soerensen, Svend Otto
Saab, E(velyn) Ann Pottinger 1934- 107
Saab, Edouard 1929-1976 Obituary 65-68
Saadawi, Nawal El
See El Saadawi, Nawal
Saal, Jocelyn
See Sachs, Judith
Saalman, Howard 1928- CANR-1
Earlier sketch in CA 1-4R
Saar, James 1949- 131
Saari, Carolyn 1939- 140
Saarikoski, Pentti (Ilmari) 1937-1983 162
Saarinen, Aline B(ernstein Louchheim)
1914-1972 Obituary 37-40R
Saarinen, Eero 1910-1961 Obituary 113
Saatkamp, Herman J(oseph), Jr. 1942- CANR-53
Earlier sketch in CA 126
Saaty, Thomas L(orie) 1926- CANR-8
Earlier sketch in CA 57-60
Saavedra, Luis Spota
See Spota (Saavedra), Luis
Saba, Umberto 1883-1957 144
See also DLB 114
See also TCLC 33
Sabais, Heinz Winfried 1922-1981 Obituary 114
Sabaliunas, Leonas 1934- 61-64
Saban, Cheryl (Lynn) 1951- 144
Sabar, Yona 1939- CANR-30
Earlier sketch in CA 112
Sabaroff, Rose Epstein 1918- 85-88
Sabatier, Paul 1854-1941 156
Sabatier, Robert 1923- CANR-39
Earlier sketches in CA 102, CANR-18
Sabatine, Jean A. 1941- 158
Sabatini, Rafael 1875-1950 162
See also TCLC 47
Sabato, Ernesto (R.) 1911- CANR-65
Earlier sketches in CA 97-100, CANR-32
See also CLC 10, 23
See also DAM MULT
See also DLB 145
See also HLC
See also HW
See also MTCW 1
Sabato, Larry (J.) 1952- CANR-27
Earlier sketch in CA 108
Sabbag, Robert 1946- 101
Sabbah, Hassan i
See Butler, William Huxford
Sabe, Quien
See Bates, Harry
Sabel, Charles F(rederick) 1947- 129
Saberhagen, Fred(erick Thomas) 1930- CANR-64
Earlier sketches in CA 57-60, CANR-7, 27, 33
See also DLB 8
See also MTCW 1
See also SATA 37, 89
Sabiad
See White, Stanhope
Sabin, Albert B(ruce) 1906-1993 156
Sabin, Arthur J. 1930- 144
Sabin, Edwin L(egrand) 1870-1952 ..... YABC 2
Sabin, Florence Rena 1871-1953 156
Sabin, Francene CANR-11
Earlier sketch in CA 69-72
See also SATA 27
Sabin, Joseph 1821-1881 ..... DLB 187
Sabin, Katharine Cover 1910- 57-60
Sabin, Lou
See Sabin, Louis
Sabin, Louis 1930- CANR-11
Earlier sketch in CA 69-72
See also SATA 27
Sabin, Mark
See Fox, Norman A(rnold)
Sabin, Thomas D. 1936- 147
Sabine, B(asil) E. V. 1914- CANR-28
Earlier sketch in CA 97-100
Sabine, Ellen S. (Borcherding) 1908- CAP-1
Earlier sketch in CA 17-18
Sabine, Gordon Arthur 1917- CANR-41
Earlier sketch in CA 117
Sabine, Waldo
See Sabine, William H(enry) W(aldo)
Sabine, William H(enry) W(aldo) 1903- CANR-4
Earlier sketch in CA 53-56
Sabines, Jaime 1925(?)- 153
See also HW
Sabini, John Anthony 1921- 9-12R
Sabisch, Christian 1955- 129
Sabki, Hisham M. 1934- Brief entry 106
Sable, Martin Howard 1924- CANR-29
Earlier sketches in CA 33-36R, CANR-12
Sableman, Mark (Stephen) 1951- 163
Sabloff, Jeremy A(rac) 1944- CANR-8
Earlier sketch in CA 61-64
Sablosky, Irving L. 1924- 124
Sabom, Michael Bruce 1944- 109
Sabourin, Anne Winifred 1910- 101
Sabourin, Justine
See Sabourin, Anne Winifred
Sabourin, Leopold 1919- CANR-11
Earlier sketch in CA 65-68
Sabre, Dirk
See Laffin, John (Alfred Charles)
Sabri-Tabrizi, Gholam-Reza 1934- 61-64
Sabuda, Robert (James) 1965- 149
See also SATA 81
Sa-Carniero, Mario de 1890-1916 ..... TCLC 83
Sacastru, Martin
See Bioy Casares, Adolfo
Saccio, Peter (Churchill) 1941- 61-64
Sacer, Gottfried Wilhelm 1635-1699 ..... DLB 168
Sach, Nathan
See Zach, Nathan
Sachar, Abram Leon 1899-1993 97-100
Obituary 142
Sachar, Emily 1958- 135
Sachar, Howard Morley 1928- CANR-6
Earlier sketch in CA 5-8R
Sachar, Louis 1954- CANR-33
Earlier sketches in CA 81-84, CANR-15
See also CLR 28
See also JRDA
See also SATA 63
See also SATA-Brief 50
Sacharoff, Shanta Nimbark 1945- 61-64
Sachdev, Paul 115
Sachem, E. B.
See Creel, Stephen Melville
Sacher, Jack, Jr. 1931- 57-60
Sacher-Masoch, Alexander
1902(?)-1972 Obituary 37-40R
Sachs, Albert Louis 1935- CANR-14
Earlier sketch in CA 21-24R
Sachs, Albie
See Sachs, Albert Louis
Sachs, Alexander 1893-1973 Obituary 41-44R
Sachs, Elizabeth-Ann 1946- 111
See also SATA 48
Sachs, Georgia
See Adams, Georgia Sachs
Sachs, Hans 1494-1576 ..... DLB 179
Sachs, (Stewart) Harvey 1946- 85-88
Sachs, Herbert L. 1929- 25-28R
Sachs, Judith 1947- CANR-48
Earlier sketch in CA 122
See also SATA 52
See also SATA-Brief 51
Sachs, Lewis Benjamen 1938- 61-64
Sachs, Margaret 1948- Brief entry 115
Sachs, Marianne 1945- 114
Sachs, Marilyn (Stickle) 1927- CANR-47
Earlier sketches in CA 17-20R, CANR-13
See also AAYA 2
See also CLC 35
See also CLR 2
See also JRDA
See also MAICYA
See also SAAS 2
See also SATA 3, 68
Sachs, Mary P(armly) K(oues)
1882(?)-1973 Obituary 45-48
Sachs, Mendel 1927- CANR-12
Earlier sketch in CA 29-32R
Sachs, Michael L(eo) 1951- CANR-37
Earlier sketch in CA 115
Sachs, Murray 1924- CANR-14
Earlier sketch in CA 37-40R
Sachs, Nelly 1891-1970 ..... CAP-2
Obituary 25-28R
Earlier sketch in CA 17-18
See also CLC 14, 98
Sachs, Wolfgang 1946- 143
Sachse, William L(ewis) 1912- 25-28R
Sack, James J(ohn) 1944- 101
Sack, John 1930- CANR-68
Earlier sketches in CA 21-24R, CANR-14, 50
See also DLB 185
Sack, Saul 1912- 53-56
Sackerman, Henry
See Kahm, H(arold) S.
Sackett, L(eyland) H(ugh) 1928- 119
Sackett, S(amuel) J(ohn) 1928- CANR-6
Earlier sketch in CA 1-4R
See also SATA 12
Sackett, Susan 1943- CANR-22
Earlier sketch in CA 106
Sackett, Theodore Alan 1940- 89-92
Sackett, Walter W(allace), Jr. 1905-1985 ..... 5-8R
Obituary 117
Sackheim, Maxwell 1890-1982 Obituary 108
Sackler, Howard (Oliver) 1929-1982 ..... CANR-30
Obituary 108
Earlier sketch in CA 61-64
See also CLC 14
See also DLB 7
Sackman, Harold 1927- CANR-12
Earlier sketch in CA 21-24R
Sackrey, Charles 1936- 77-80
Sacks, Benjamin 1903- CAP-2
Earlier sketch in CA 23-24
Sacks, Claire
See Sprague, Claire S(acks)
Sacks, David Harris 1942- 139
Sacks, Howard L. 1949- 147
Sacks, Judith Rose 1952- 152
Sacks, Karen 1941- CANR-26
Earlier sketch in CA 109
Sacks, Norman P(aul) 1914- 45-48
Sacks, Oliver (Wolf) 1933- CANR-50
Earlier sketches in CA 53-56, CANR-28
Interview in CANR-28
See also CLC 67
See also MTCW 1
Sacks, Peter
See Sacks, Peter M.
Sacks, Peter M. 1950- 124
Sacks, Sheldon 1930-1979 ..... 17-20R
Obituary 122
Sackson, Sid 1920- CANR-12
Earlier sketch in CA 69-72
See also SATA 16
Sackton, Alexander H(art) 1911- 37-40R
Sackville, Charles 1643-1706 ..... DLB 131
Sackville, Thomas 1536-1608 ..... DAM DRAM
See also DLB 62, 132
Sackville-West, Edward 1901-1965 ..... DLB 191
Sackville-West, V(ictoria Mary) 1892-1962 .....
CANR-60
Obituary 93-96
Earlier sketches in CA 104, CANR-40
See also DLB 34, 195
See also MTCW 1
Sadakichi
See Hartmann, Sadakichi
(el-)Sadat, Anwar 1918-1981 101
Obituary 104
Sadd, Susan 1951- 103
Saddhatissa, Hammalawa 1914- CANR-17
Earlier sketch in CA 97-100
Saddlemyer, E(leanor) Ann 1932- 17-20R
Saddler, Allen
See Richards, R(onald) C(harles) W(illiam)
Saddler, K. Allen
See Richards, R(onald) C(harles) W(illiam)
Sadecky, Petr Milos 1943- 41-44R
Sadeh, Pinhas 1929-1994 ..... CANR-34
Obituary 143
Earlier sketches in CA 25-28R, CANR-13
Sader, Emir 1943- 142
Sadick, Neil (S.) 1951- 138
Sadie, Stanley (John) 1930- CANR-9
Earlier sketch in CA 17-20R
See also SATA 14
Sadiq, Muhammad 1898-1984 ..... CANR-18
Earlier sketch in CA 17-20R
Sadiq, Nazneen 1944- 160
See also SATA 101
Sadker, Myra Pollack 1943-1995 ..... CANR-46
Obituary 148
Earlier sketches in CA 53-56, CANR-5, 22
Sadler, Arthur Lindsay 1882- 5-8R
Sadler, Barry 1940- 129
Sadler, Catherine Edwards 1952- 154
See also SATA 60
See also SATA-Brief 45
Sadler, Christine 1908-1983 ..... CAP-1
Obituary 110
Earlier sketch in CA 11-12
Sadler, Ella Jo 1942- 57-60
Sadler, Glenn Edward 1935- 97-100
Sadler, Julius Trousdale, Jr. 1923- 65-68
Sadler, Marilyn 1950- ..... SATA 79
Sadler, Mark
See Lynds, Dennis
Sadler, William A(lan), Jr. 1931- 25-28R
Sadlier, Darlene J. 1950- 139
Sadlier, Mary Anne 1820-1903 ..... DLB 99
Sadock, Benjamin James 1933- Brief entry 105

Sadoff, Ira 1945- ... CANR-21
Earlier sketches in CA 53-56, CANR-5
See also CLC 9
See also DLB 120
Sadri, Ahmad 1953- ... 145
Sadrin, Anny 1935- ... 150
Sadun, Elvio H. 1918(?)-1974 Obituary ... 49-52
Saenz, Benjamin Alire ... 159
Saenz, Dalmiro
See Saenz, Dalmiro A.
Saenz, Dalmiro A. 1926- ... HW
Saenz, Jaime 1921-1986 ... DLB 145
Saerchinger, Cesar 1884-1971 Obituary ... 33-36R
Saetone
See Camus, Albert
Safa, Helen M. Icken 1930- ... CANR-57
Earlier sketches in CA 45-48, CANR-1, 30
Safarian, Albert Edward 1924- ... 105
Safarik, Allan 1948- ... 114
Safdie, Moshe 1938- ... 69-72
Safer, Daniel J. 1934- ... CANR-11
Earlier sketch in CA 69-72
Safer, Elaine Berkman 1937- ... 41-44R
Safer, Morley 1931- ... 93-96
See also AITN 2
Saffell, David C(lyde) 1941- ... CANR-11
Earlier sketch in CA 61-64
Saffin, John 1626(?)-1710 ... DLB 24
Saffle, Michael 1946- ... 139
Saffron, Morris Harold 1905- ... 45-48
Saffron, Robert 1918(?)-1985 Obituary ... 114
Safian, Jill
See Bharti, Ma Satya
Safilios-Rothschild, Constantina 1936- ... CANR-31
Earlier sketch in CA 45-48
Safir, Leonard 1921-1992 ... 109
Obituary ... 140
Safire, William 1929- ... CANR-54
Earlier sketches in CA 17-20R, CANR-31
See also CLC 10
Safran, Claire 1930- ... 101
Safran, Nadav 1925- ... 5-8R
Safran, William 1930- ... CANR-64
Earlier sketches in CA 113, CANR-32
Safransky, Sy 1945- ... 145
Sagall, Elliot L. 1918- ... 29-32R
Sagalyn, Lynne B. 1947- ... 134
Sagan, Carl (Edward) 1934-1996 ... CANR-36
Obituary ... 155
Earlier sketches in CA 25-28R, CANR-11
See also AAYA 2
See also CLC 30, 112
See also MTCW 1
See also SATA 58
See also SATA-Obit 94
Sagan, Dorion 1959- ... 131
Sagan, Eli 1927- ... 124
Sagan, Francoise
See Quoirez, Francoise
See also CLC 3, 6, 9, 17, 36
See also DLB 83
Sagan, Leonard A. 1928- ... 49-52
Sagan, Miriam 1954- ... 77-80
Sagar, Keith (Milsom) 1934- ... CANR-45
Earlier sketches in CA 21-24R, CANR-14
Sagarin, Edward 1913- ... CANR-4
Earlier sketch in CA 5-8R
Sagarin, Mary 1903- ... 81-84
Sagarra, Eda 1933- ... CANR-11
Earlier sketch in CA 65-68
Sage, George Harvey 1929- ... 61-64
Sage, Joe
See Sage, Joseph
Sage, Jonathan 1953- ... 129
Sage, Joseph 1921-1987 Obituary ... 122
Sage, Juniper
See Brown, Margaret Wise
and Hurd, Edith (Thacher)
Sage, Leland L(ivingston) 1899- ... 61-64
Sage, (Frank) Norman 1910- ... 150
Sage, Robert 1899-1962 ... 106
See also DLB 4
Sagel, Jim 1947-1998 ... 131
Obituary ... 166
See also DLB 82
See also HW
Sagendorf, Bud
See Sagendorf, Forrest C(owles)
Sagendorf, Forrest C(owles) 1915- Brief entry ... 112
Sagendorph, Robb Hansell 1900-1970 ... CANR-7
Obituary ... 29-32R
Earlier sketch in CA 5-8R
See also DLB 137
Sager, Carole Bayer 1947- ... 146
Sager, Clifford J. 1916- ... CANR-12
Earlier sketch in CA 29-32R
Sager, Ruth 1918- ... 158
Sager, Samuel 1923- ... 123
Sageser, A(delbert) Bower 1902- ... 29-32R
Saggs, Henry W(illiam) F(rederick) 1920- ... 5-8R
Saghir, Marcel T(awfic) 1937- ... 49-52
Sagnier, Thierry (Bright) 1946- ... 53-56
Sagola, Mario J.
See Kane, Henry
Sagsoorian, Paul 1923- ... SATA 12
Sagstetter, Karen 1941- ... 105
Sahagun, Carlos 1938- ... DLB 108
Sahakian, Lucille 1894- ... 53-56
Sahakian, Mabel Lewis 1921- ... 21-24R
Sahakian, William S(ahak) 1921- ... CANR-8
Earlier sketch in CA 17-20R
Sahgal, Nayantara (Pandit) 1927- ... CANR-11
Earlier sketch in CA 9-12R
See also CLC 41
Sahihi, Ashkan 1963- ... 141
Sahl, Hans 1902-1993 ... 144
See also DLB 69
Sahl, Mort(on Lyon) 1927- ... 148
Brief entry ... 113
Sahlins, Marshall
See Sahlins, Marshall D(avid)
Sahlins, Marshall D(avid) 1930- ... 133
Brief entry ... 114
Sahn, Seung 1927- ... 113
Sahni, Balbir S. 1934- ... CANR-3
Earlier sketch in CA 45-48
Sahni, Chaman L. 1933- ... 128
Sahota, Gian Singh 1924- ... 142
Said, Abdul Aziz 1930- ... 81-84
Said, Edward W. 1935- ... CANR-45
Earlier sketch in CA 21-24R
See also DLB 67
Said, Laila
See Abou-Saif, Laila
Saida
See LeMair, H(enriette) Willebeek
Saidel, Rochelle G. 1942- ... 121
Sa'Idi, Ghulam Husayn 1936-1985 Obituary ... 119
Saidman, Anne 1952- ... 142
See also SATA 75
Saidy, Anthony Fred 1937- ... 89-92
Saidy, Fareed Milhem 1907-1982 Obituary ... 106
Saidy, Fred M.
See Saidy, Fareed Milhem
Saiki, Jessica K(awasuna) 1928- ... 138
Saiko, George 1892-1962 ... DLB 85
Sail, Lawrence (Richard) 1942- ... 132
Saille, Davydd ap
See Seals, David
Sailor, Charles 1947- ... 97-100
Sailor, Merlin F(orrest) 1906- ... CAP-1
Earlier sketch in CA 13-16
Saine, Thomas P(rice) 1941- ... 41-44R
Sainer, Arthur 1924- ... CANR-3
Earlier sketch in CA 49-52
Saini, B(alwant) S(ingh) 1930- ... 107
Sainsbury, Eric (Edward) 1925- ... CANR-13
Earlier sketch in CA 33-36R
Sainsbury, John A. 1946- ... 127
Sainsbury, Maurice Joseph 1927- ... 108
Saint, Andrew (John) 1946- ... 65-68
Saint, Dora Jessie 1913- ... CANR-46
Earlier sketches in CA 13-16R, CANR-7, 22
See also SATA 10
Saint, H(arry) F. 1941- ... 127
See also CLC 50
Saint, Phil(ip) 1912- ... 61-64
St. Andre, Lucien
See Mott, Vincent Valmon
St. Angelo, Douglas 1931- ... 45-48
St. Antoine, Sara L. 1966- ... 150
See also SATA 84
St. Antoine, Theodore J(oseph) 1929- ... 41-44R
St. Aubin de Teran, Lisa 1953- ... 126
Brief entry ... 118
Interview in ... 126
See also Teran, Lisa St. Aubin de
St. Aubyn, F(rederic) C(hase) 1921- ... 25-28R
St. Aubyn, Fiona 1952- ... CANR-23
Earlier sketch in CA 106
St. Aubyn, Giles 1925- ... CANR-19
Earlier sketches in CA 5-8R, CANR-4
St. Bruno, Albert Francis 1909- ... CAP-1
Earlier sketch in CA 9-10
St. Clair, (Howard) Barry 1945- ... CANR-46
Earlier sketch in CA 120
St. Clair, Byrd Hooper 1905-1976 ... 1-4R
Obituary ... 103
See also SATA-Obit 28
St. Clair, Clovis
See Skarda, Patricia Lyn
St. Clair, David 1932- ... 33-36R
St. Clair, Elizabeth
See Cohen, Susan (Lois)
St. Clair, Katherine
See Huff, T(om) E.
St. Clair, Leonard 1916-1986 ... 101
Obituary ... 118
St. Clair, Margaret 1911- ... 49-52
See also CAAS 8
St. Clair, Philip
See Howard, Munroe
St. Clair, Robert James 1925- ... 9-12R
St. Clair, William ... 77-80
St. Claire, Erin
See Brown, Sandra
St. Cyr, Cyprian
See Berne, Eric (Lennard)
St. Cyr, Margaret 1920- ... 29-32R
Saint-Denis, Michel Jacques 1897-1971 ... CAP-2
Obituary ... 33-36R
Earlier sketch in CA 19-20
Saint Dorliae
See Dorliae, Peter Gondro
Saint-Eden, Dennis
See Foster, Don(ald)
Sainte-Marie, Beverly 1941- ... 107
Sainte-Marie, Buffy
See Sainte-Marie, Beverly
Saint-Exupery, Antoine (Jean Baptiste Marie Roger) 1900-1944 ... 132
Brief entry ... 108
See also CLR 10
See also DAM NOV
See also DLB 72
See also MAICYA
See also MTCW 1
See also SATA 20
See also TCLC 2, 56
See also WLC
Saint-Gall, Auguste Amedee de
See Strich, Christian
St. George, Andrew 1962- ... 146
St. George, Arthur
See Paine, Lauran (Bosworth)
St. George, David
See Markov, Georgi
St. George, Edith
See Delatush, Edith G.
St. George, George 1904- ... 25-28R
St. George, Judith 1931- ... CANR-14
Earlier sketch in CA 69-72
See also AAYA 7
See also JRDA
See also SAAS 12
See also SATA 13, 99
St. George, Margaret
See Osborne, Margaret Ellen
St. George, Noel
See Green, Jonathon
St. Germain, Gregory
See Wallmann, Jeffrey M(iner)
St. Hereticus
See Brown, Robert McAfee
Saint-Jacques, Bernard 1928- ... CANR-37
Earlier sketches in CA 41-44R, CANR-16
St. James, Bernard
See Treister, Bernard W(illiam)
St. James, Blakely
See Gottfried, Theodore Mark
and Platt, Charles
Saint James, Synthia 1949- ... SATA 84
St. Jean, Yanick ... 166
St. John, Beth
See John, Elizabeth Beaman
St. John, Bob J. 1937- ... 146
Brief entry ... 122
St. John, Bruce (Carlisle) 1923- ... 107
St. John, David
See Hunt, E(verette) Howard, (Jr.)
St. John, David 1949- ... 148
St. John, Elizabeth
See John, Elizabeth Beaman
St. John, Henry 1678-1751 ... DLB 101
St. John, J. Allen 1872-1957 ... DLB 188
St. John, John 1917-1988 ... CANR-5
Obituary ... 127
Earlier sketch in CA 5-8R
St. John, Leonie
See Bayer, William
and Jenkins, Nancy (Harmon)
St. John, Lisa
See Sanford, Annette
St. John, Nicole ... CANR-32
See also Johnston, Norma
See also CLR 46
See also SAAS 7
See also SATA 89
St. John, Patricia Mary 1919-1993 ... CANR-3
Obituary ... 142
Earlier sketch in CA 5-8R
See also SATA-Obit 79
St. John, Philip
See del Rey, Lester
St. John, Primus 1939- ... 113
See also BW 1
St. John, Robert 1902- ... CANR-5
Earlier sketch in CA 1-4R
St. John, Ronald Bruce 1943- ... 141
St. John, Wylly Folk 1908-1985 ... 21-24R
Obituary ... 117
See also SATA 10
See also SATA-Obit 45
Saint-John Perse
See Leger, (Marie-Rene Auguste) Alexis Saint-Leger
St. Johns, Adela Rogers 1894-1988 ... 108
Obituary ... 126
Interview in ... 108
See also AITN 1
See also DLB 29
St. John-Stevas, Norman Anthony Francis 1929- ... CANR-4
Earlier sketch in CA 49-52
St. John Thomas, David
See Thomas, David St. John
St. Martin, Hardie 1924- ... 153
St. Max, E. S.
See Ellis, Edward S(ylvester)
St. Meyer, Ned
See Stratemeyer, Edward L.
St. Mox, E. A.
See Ellis, Edward S(ylvester)
St. Myer, Ned
See Stratemeyer, Edward L.
St. Omer, Garth ... 73-76
See also BW 2
See also DLB 117
St. Onge, Keith R. 1920- ... 139
Saint Phalle, Thibaut de
See de Saint Phalle, Thibaut
St. Pierre, Dorothy
See Nyren, Dorothy Elizabeth
Saint Pierre, Michel de 1916-1987 ... DLB 83
St. Pierre, Paul 1923- ... 113
Saintsbury, George (Edward Bateman) 1845-1933 ... 160
See also DLB 57, 149
See also TCLC 31
St. Tamara
See Kolba, St. Tamara
St. Vincent, Paul
See Markham, E(dward) A(rchibald)
St. Vivant, M.
See Bixby, Jerome Lewis
Sainty, John Christopher 1934- ... 93-96
Sainz, Gustavo 1940- ... 131
See also HW
Sainz de la Maza, Regino 1896-1981 Obituary ... 108
Saisselin, Remy G(ilbert) 1925- ... 9-12R
Sait Faik
See Abasiyanik, Sait Faik
See also TCLC 23
Saito, Fred
See Saito, Hiroyuki
Saito, Hiroyuki 1917- ... 61-64
Saito, Michiko
See Fujiwara, Michiko
Sajdak, Bruce T. 1945- ... 142
Sajna, Mike 1950- ... 141
Sakamaki, Shunzo 1906-1973 ... 1-4R
Obituary ... 103
Sakamoto, Yoshikazu 1927- ... 133
Sakell, Achilles Nicholas 1906-1987 ... 1-4R
Obituary ... 123
Sakers, Don 1958- ... 127
See also SATA 72
Sakers, George 1950- ... 108
Sakharnov, S.
See Sakharnov, Svyatoslav (Vladimirovich)
Sakharnov, Svyatoslav (Vladimirovich) 1923- ... 133
See also SATA 65
Sakharov, Andrei D(mitrievich) 1921-1989 ... 157
Obituary ... 130
Brief entry ... 105
Saki
See Munro, H(ector) H(ugh)
See also SSC 12
See also TCLC 3
Saklatvala, Beram 1911-1976 ... 89-92
Sakoian, Frances 1912- ... 65-68
Sakol, Jeannie 1928- ... CANR-11
Earlier sketch in CA 5-8R
Sakran, Frank Charles 1895(?)-1983 Obituary ... 111
Saks, Elmer Eliot
See Fawcett, F(rank) Dubrez
Saks, Katia 1939- ... 29-32R
Saks, Mike 1952- ... 140
Sakurai, Gail 1952- ... 152
See also SATA 87
Sakutaro, Hagiwara 1886-1942 ... 154
Sala, Charles 1924- ... 116
Salaam, Kalamu ya 1947- ... 126
See also CAAS 21
See also BW 2
See also DLB 38
Saladino, Salvatore 1922- ... 33-36R
Salaff, Janet W. 1940- ... 112
Salam, Abdus 1926- ... 157
Salama, Hannu 1936- ... CLC 18
Salaman, Esther 1900- ... 61-64
Salaman, Nicholas 1936- ... 146
Brief entry ... 116
Salamanca, J(ack) R(ichard) 1922- ... 25-28R
See also CLC 4, 15
Salamanca, Lucy
See del Barco, Lucy Salamanca
Salamatullah
See Ullah, Salamat
Salamon, Julie 1953- ... 136
Salamon, Lester M(ilton) 1943- ... 89-92
Salamon, Sonya 1939- ... 146
Salamun, Tomaz 1941- ... DLB 181
Salant, Nathan N(athaniel) 1955- ... 106
Salant, Walter S. 1911- ... CANR-2
Earlier sketch in CA 5-8R
Salarrue
See Salazar Arrue, Salvador
Salas, Floyd Francis 1931- ... CANR-44
Earlier sketch in CA 119
See also CAAS 27
See also DAM MULT
See also DLB 82
See also HLC
See also HW
Salas, Rafael M(ontinola) 1928-1987 ... 129
Obituary ... 121
Salassi, Otto R(ussell) 1939-1993 ... 106
Obituary ... 142
See also SATA 38
See also SATA-Obit 77
Salat, Cristina ... 149
See also SATA 82
Salazar, Antonio de Oliveira 1889-1970 Obituary ... 113
Salazar, Carles 1961- ... 162
Salazar, Dixie 1947- ... 149
Salazar, Fred A. 1942- ... 21-24R
Salazar, Rachel 1954- ... 123
Salazar, Ruben 1928-1970 Obituary ... 115
Salazar Bondy, Sebastian 1924-1965 ... HW
Salaz-Marquez, Ruben 1935- ... DLB 122
Salber, Eva J. 1916- ... 125
Saldana, Theresa 1955- ... 158
Saldutti, Denise 1953- ... SATA 39
Sale, J. Kirkpatrick
See Sale, Kirkpatrick
Sale, Kirkpatrick 1937- ... CANR-10
Earlier sketch in CA 13-16R
See also CLC 68
Sale, Larry L(owell) 1939- Brief entry ... 113
Sale, Richard (Bernard) 1911-1993 ... CANR-61
Obituary ... 140
Earlier sketch in CA 9-12R
Sale, Roger 1932- ... CANR-33
Earlier sketch in CA 21-24R
Sale, William (Merritt III) 1929- ... 45-48
Saleh, Dennis 1942- ... CANR-13
Earlier sketch in CA 33-36R
Salem, Elie Adib 1930- ... 49-52
Salem, James M. 1937- ... 21-24R
Salem, Kay 1952- ... SATA 92

Salem, Sema'an I. 1927- 142
Salemme, Lucia (Autorino) 1919- 89-92
Salemson, Harold J(ason) 1910-1988 110
Obituary 126
Brief entry 108
Interview in 110
See also DLB 4
Salerno, Lynn M(cCormick) 1926- 119
Sales, Grover 1919- 65-68
Sales, Jane M(agorian) 1931- 49-52
Sales, M(ary) E(ileen) 1936- 29-32R
Sales, M(illard) Vance 1929- 53-56
Saletore, Bhasker Anand 1900- 5-8R
Salgado, Gamini 1929- 102
Salgado, Maria Antonia 1933- 41-44R
Saliba, George 1939- 149
Saliba, John A. 1937- CANR-35
Earlier sketch in CA 114
Saliers, Don E(arl) 1937- 119
Salih, H(alil) Ibrahim 1939- 93-96
Salin, Mary Wolff
See Wolff-Salin, Mary
Salinas, Luis Omar 1937- 131
See also CLC 90
See also DAM MULT
See also DLB 82
See also HLC
See also HW
Salinas (y Serrano), Pedro 1891(?)-1951 Brief entry 117
See also DLB 134
See also TCLC 17
Saline, Carol 1939- 128
Salinger, Herman 1905- CAP-1
Earlier sketch in CA 13-14
Salinger, J(erome) D(avid) 1919- CANR-39
Earlier sketch in CA 5-8R
See also AAYA 2
See also CDALB 1941-1968
See also CLC 1, 3, 8, 12, 55, 56
See also CLR 18
See also DA
See also DAB
See also DAC
See also DAM MST, NOV, POP
See also DLB 2, 102, 173
See also MAICYA
See also MTCW 1
See also SATA 67
See also SSC 2, 28
See also WLC
Salinger, Margaretta 1908(?)-1985 Obituary 115
Salinger, Pierre (Emil George) 1925- CANR-14
Earlier sketch in CA 17-20R
Salisbury, Carola (Isobel Julien) 1943- 89-92
Salisbury, Charlotte Y. 1914- 129
Salisbury, Dorothy (Kendall Cleveland) 1891(?)-1976 Obituary 69-72
Salisbury, Edward J(ames) 1886- CAP-1
Earlier sketch in CA 13-14
Salisbury, Frank 1930- 108
Salisbury, Frank B(oyer) 1926- CANR-8
Earlier sketch in CA 17-20R
Salisbury, Graham 1944- 143
See also AAYA 26
See also SATA 76
Salisbury, Harrison E(vans) 1908-1993 CANR-30
Obituary 141
Earlier sketches in CA 1-4R, CANR-3
Interview in CANR-30
See also CAAS 15
See also MTCW 1
Salisbury, John
See Caute, (John) David
Salisbury, Joyce E(llen) 1944- 135
Salisbury, Mike 1942- 136
Salisbury, Ralph 1926- CANR-15
Earlier sketch in CA 41-44R
Salisbury, Ray(mond Eric) 1942- CANR-31
Earlier sketch in CA 110
Salisbury, Richard Frank 1926- CANR-9
Earlier sketch in CA 5-8R
Salisbury, Robert H(olt) 1930- 9-12R
Salisbury, Ruth 1921- 73-76
Salisbury-Jones, Guy 1896-1985 Obituary 115
Salitan, Laurie P. 146
Salivarova, Zdena
See Skvorecka, Zdena Salivarova
Salk, Erwin Arthur 1918- 81-84
Salk, Jonas Edward 1914- 49-52
Salk, Lee 1926-1992 104
Obituary 137
See also AITN 1
Salkeld, Robert J(ohn) 1932- CANR-31
Earlier sketch in CA 29-32R
Salkever, Louis R(omov) 1914- 17-20R
Salkey, (Felix) Andrew (Alexander) 1928-1995 CANR-27
Obituary 148
Earlier sketches in CA 5-8R, CANR-13
See also BW 1
See also DLB 125
See also SATA 35
Sallada, Logan Henry 1942-1987 Obituary 123
Sallaska, Georgia 1933- 25-28R
Sallaway, George H(enry) 1930- 21-24R
Sallis, James 1944- CANR-58
Earlier sketch in CA 33-36R
Sallis, John C(leveland) 1938- 41-44R
Sallis, Susan (Diana) 1929- SATA 55
Sallnow, Michael (Julian) 1949-1990 Obituary 131
Salls, Betty Ruth 1926- 49-52
Sallust
See Crispus, Gaius Sallustius
Salm, Peter 1919-1990 41-44R
Obituary 132
Salma, Abu
See Karmi, Abdul Karim
Salmansohn, Karen 1960- 148
Salmen, Walter (Heinrich) 1926- 132
Salmon, Annie Elizabeth 1899- CANR-12
Earlier sketch in CA 69-72
See also SATA 13
Salmon, Charles Gerald 1930- 49-52
Salmon, Edward T(ogo) 1905- CANR-2
Earlier sketch in CA 5-8R
Salmon, H. Morrey 1892(?)-1985 Obituary 116
Salmon, J(ohn) B(rynmor) 1942- 118
Salmon, J(ohn) H(earsey) M(cMillan) 1925- 25-28R
Salmon, Jacqueline L. 1957- 156
Salmon, James F(rancis) 1925- 111
Salmon, John Tenison 1910- 13-16R
Salmon, Margaret Belais 1921- CANR-8
Earlier sketch in CA 17-20R
Salmon, Nathan Ucuzoglu 1951- CANR-27
Earlier sketch in CA 109
Salmon, Tim(othy) 1942- 128
Salmon, Wesley C(harles) 1925- CANR-23
Earlier sketches in CA 17-20R, CANR-8
Salmond, John A(lexander) 1937- CANR-53
Earlier sketch in CA 114
Salmond, Mary Anne 1945- 142
Salmonson, Jessica Amanda 1950- CANR-58
Earlier sketches in CA 114, CANR-36
Salmonson, R(oland) F(rank) 1922- CANR-17
Earlier sketch in CA 25-28R
Salom, Philip 1950- 154
Saloma, John S. III 1935(?)-1983 Obituary 110
Salomon, Albert 1891-1966 5-8R
Salomon, Herman Prins 1930- 41-44R
Salomon, I(sidore) L(awrence) 1899-1985 73-76
Obituary 116
Salomon, Irving 1897-1979 Obituary 85-88
Salomon, Janet Lynn (Nowicki) 1953- 61-64
Salomon, Julian Harris 1896-1987 Obituary 123
Salomon, Roger Blaine 1928- 1-4R
Salomon, Sir Walter
See Salomon, Walter (Hans)
Salomon, Walter (Hans) 1906-1987 Obituary 123
Salomone, A(rcangelo) William 1915-1989 13-16R
Obituary 127
Salop, Lynne
See Hawes, Lynne Gusikoff Salop
Salot, Lorraine 1914- 17-20R
Saloutos, Theodore 1910- 9-12R
Salper, Roberta Linda 1940- 105
Salpeter, Eliahu (Arnost) 1927- 93-96
Salpukas, Agis 1939- 128
Salsbury, Barbara G(race) 1937- 121
Brief entry 118
Salsbury, Edith Colgate 1907-1971 CAP-2
Earlier sketch in CA 17-18
Salsbury, Kathryn H(errick) 1924- 107
Salsbury, Stephen 1931- CANR-11
Earlier sketch in CA 21-24R
Salsini, Paul E(dward) 1935- 77-80
Salt, Beryl (Winifred) 1931- 110
Salt, Waldo 1914-1987 111
Obituary 121
Interview in 111
See also DLB 44
Salten, Felix
See Salzmann, Siegmund
Salter, Cedric
See Knight, Francis Edgar
Salter, Charles A. 1947- 127
Salter, Donald P. M. 1942- 93-96
Salter, Elizabeth 1918-1981 CANR-9
Obituary 103
Earlier sketch in CA 53-56
Salter, Elizabeth 1925-1980 105
Obituary 97-100
Salter, James 1925- 73-76
See also CLC 7, 52, 59
See also DLB 130
Salter, Lionel (Paul) 1914- CANR-3
Earlier sketch in CA 5-8R
Salter, Margaret Lennox
See Donaldson, Margaret
Salter, Mary D.
See Ainsworth, Mary D(insmore) Salter
Salter, Mary Jo 1954- CANR-45
Earlier sketch in CA 119
See also DLB 120
Salter, Paul Sanford 1926- 61-64
Salter, Robbie
See Salter, Robina
Salter, Robina 123
Salter, Stefan 1908(?)-1985 Obituary 115
Salter, W(illiam) H(enry) 1880-1970 Obituary 112
Salter-Mathieson, Nigel Cedric Stephen 1932- 1-4R
Salthe, Stanley N(orman) 1930- 53-56
Saltman, Jack 1936- 129
Saltman, Judith 1947- CANR-53
Earlier sketch in CA 126
See also SATA 64
Saltman, Juliet 1923- 101
Saltonstall, Richard, Jr. 1937-1981 33-36R
Obituary 103
Saltonstall, William G(urdon) 1905(?)-1989 Obituary 130
Saltus, Edgar (Everton) 1855-1921 Brief entry 105
See also DLB 202
See also TCLC 8
Saltz, Donald 1933- 102
Saltz, Eli 1926- Brief entry 108
Saltzgaber, Jan M. 1933- 115
Saltzman, Arthur M(ichael) 1953- 136
Saltzman, David (Charles Laertes) 1967-1990 SATA 86
Saltzman, Joe
See Saltzman, Joseph
Saltzman, Joseph 1939- 81-84
Saltzman, Marvin L(ouis) 1922- 85-88
Salu, Mary 1919- 93-96
Salusinszky, Imre 1955- 126
Salutin, Rick 1942- 131
Salvadori, Joyce
See Lussu, Joyce (Salvadori)
Salvadori, Mario (George) 1907-1997 108
Obituary 159
See also CAAS 25
See also SATA 40, 97
Salvadori, Massimo
See Salvadori-Paleotti, Massimo
Salvadori, Max (William)
See Salvadori-Paleotti, Massimo
Salvadori-Paleotti, Massimo 1908-1992 CANR-7
Obituary 138
Earlier sketch in CA 9-12R
Salvaggio, John 1933- 144
Salvan, Jacques-Leon 1898- 1-4R
Salvato, Larry 1948- 118
Salvato, Sharon 1938- CANR-15
Earlier sketch in CA 65-68
Salvatore, Diane 1960- 139
Salvatore, Nicholas 1943- CANR-65
Earlier sketches in CA 109, CANR-32
Salvatore, Nick
See Salvatore, Nicholas
Salvatore, R(obert) A(nthony) 1959- 166
Salvendy, Gavriel 1938- 49-52
Salverson, Laura Goodman 1890-1970 153
See also DLB 92
Salwak, Dale (Francis) 1947- 137
Salway, Peter 1932- 148
Salwen, Michael B(rian) 1954- 142
Salwolke, Scott 1964- 146
Salwood, F. K.
See Kilworth, Garry (D.)
Salyer, Lucy E. 1956- 159
Salzano, F(rancisco) M(auro) 1928- CANR-45
Earlier sketches in CA 29-32R, CANR-12
Salzberg, Allen 1953- 137
Salzer, Felix 1904-1986 109
Obituary 120
Salzer, L. E.
See Wilson, Lionel
Salzer, Linda P(arsons) 1951- 122
Salzinger, Kurt 1929- 134
Brief entry 107
Salzman, Eric 1933- CANR-13
Earlier sketch in CA 25-28R
Salzman, Eva (Frances) 1960- 139
Salzman, Jack 1937- CANR-11
Earlier sketch in CA 25-28R
Salzman, Marian 1959- 146
See also SATA 77
Salzman, Mark (Joseph) 1959- 136
Salzman, Neil 1940- 139
Salzman, Paul 1953- CANR-58
Earlier sketch in CA 125
Salzman, Yuri SATA-Brief 42
Salzmann, Siegmund 1869-1945 137
Brief entry 108
See also MAICYA
See also SATA 25
Salzmann, Zdenek 1925- CANR-36
Earlier sketches in CA 97-100, CANR-16
Samachson, Dorothy (Mirkin) 1914- 9-12R
See also SATA 3
Samachson, Joseph 1906-1980 17-20R
Obituary 122
See also SATA 3
See also SATA-Obit 52
Samarakis, Antonis 1919- CANR-36
Earlier sketch in CA 25-28R
See also CAAS 16
See also CLC 5
Samarin, William J. 1926- 93-96
Samartha, S(tanley) J(edidiah) 1920- CAP-1
Earlier sketch in CA 11-12
Samay, Sebastian 1926- 37-40R
Sambrook, Arthur James 1931- CANR-40
Earlier sketch in CA 13-16R
Sambrot, William 1920- 25-28R
Samek, Hana 1953- 126
Samelson, William 1928- CANR-37
Earlier sketches in CA 25-28R, CANR-17
Samenow, Stanton E(than) 1941- 129
Sametz, Arnold W(illiam) 1919- CANR-1
Earlier sketch in CA 1-4R
Samford, Clarence D(ouglas) 1905- CAP-2
Earlier sketch in CA 19-20
Samford, Doris E. 1923- 21-24R
Samhaber, Ernst Marzell 1901-1974 9-12R
Obituary 122
Samigli, E.
See Schmitz, Aron Hector
Samkange, S. J. T.
See Samkange, Stanlake (John Thompson)
Samkange, Stanlake (John Thompson) 1922-1988 CANR-28
Obituary 125
Earlier sketch in CA 29-32R
See also BW 2
Samli, A. Coskun 1931- CANR-22
Earlier sketch in CA 105
Sammartino, Peter 1904-1992 CANR-7
Obituary 137
Earlier sketch in CA 57-60
Sammis, John 1942- 29-32R
See also SATA 4
Sammons, David 1938- 73-76
Sammons, Jeffrey L(eonard) 1936- CANR-19
Earlier sketch in CA 21-24R
Samoiloff, Louise Cripps
See Cripps, L(ouise) L(ilian)
Samolin, William 1911- 61-64
Samora, Julian 1920-1996 37-40R
Obituary 151
See also HW
Samore, Theodore 1924- Brief entry 108
Sampedro, Jose Luis 1917- CANR-11
Earlier sketch in CA 21-24R
Sampford, Michael 1924(?)-1983 Obituary 109
Sampley, Arthur M(cCullough) 1903-1975 41-44R
Sampley, J(ohn) Paul 1935- 105
Sampson, A(ylwin) A(rthur) 1926- 117
Sampson, Anthony (Terrell Seward) 1926- CANR-63
Earlier sketches in CA 1-4R, CANR-3
Sampson, Curt 1952- 139
Sampson, Edward C(oolidge) 1920- 57-60
Sampson, Edward E. 1934- CANR-14
Earlier sketch in CA 37-40R
Sampson, Emma (Keats) Speed 1868-1947 135
See also SATA 68
Sampson, Fay (Elizabeth) 1935- CANR-40
Earlier sketches in CA 101, CANR-18
See also SATA 42
See also SATA-Brief 40
Sampson, Geoffrey 1944- 97-100
Sampson, H(erbert) Grant 1932- 45-48
Sampson, Henry T(homas) 1934- 117
See also BW 2
Sampson, Michael 1952- 160
See also SATA 95
Sampson, R(obert) Neil 1938- CANR-58
Earlier sketches in CA 106, CANR-31
Sampson, R(onald) V(ictor) 1918- CANR-5
Earlier sketch in CA 9-12R
Sampson, Richard Henry
See Hull, Richard
Sampson, Robert C. 1909- 21-24R
Sampson, Roy J(ohnson) 1919- CANR-1
Earlier sketch in CA 1-4R
Samra, Cal 1931- 37-40R
Sams, David R. 1958- 138
Sams, Eric 1926- CANR-49
Earlier sketch in CA 123
Sams, Ferrol, (Jr.) 1922- 146
Sams, Jonathan Carter 1942- Brief entry 110
Samsell, R(ay) L(ane) 1925- 69-72
Samson, Anne S(tringer) 1933- 25-28R
See also SATA 2
Samson, Jack
See Samson, John G(adsden)
Samson, (Thomas) Jim 1946- 129
Samson, Joan 1937-1976 73-76
See also SATA 13
Samson, John G(adsden) 1922- 134
Brief entry 109
Samson, Suzanne M. 1959- 155
See also SATA 91
Samsonov, Leon
See Maximov, Vladimir (Yemelyanovich)
Samstag, Nicholas 1903-1968 5-8R
Obituary 25-28R
Samter, Linda Bantel
See Bantel, Linda
Samtur, Susan J(oy) 1944- 97-100
Samuel, Alan E(douard) 1932- CANR-37
Earlier sketches in CA 73-76, CANR-17
Samuel, Athanasius Y.
See Samuel, Yeshue
Samuel, Dorothy T(ucker) 1918- 45-48
Samuel, Edwin Herbert 1898-1978 CANR-2
Earlier sketch in CA 1-4R
Samuel, Irene 1915-1991 17-20R
Obituary 134
Samuel, Maurice 1895-1972 102
Obituary 33-36R
Samuel, Sealhenry Olumide
See Seal
Samuel, Yeshue 1907-1995 CAP-2
Obituary 148
Earlier sketch in CA 21-22
Samuels, Charles 1902-1982 CANR-5
Obituary 106
Earlier sketch in CA 1-4R
See also SATA 12
Samuels, Charles Thomas 1936-1974 41-44R
Obituary 49-52
Samuels, Cynthia K(alish) 1946- 135
See also SATA 79
Samuels, E. A.
See Tiffany, E. A.
Samuels, Ernest 1903-1996 CANR-43
Obituary 151
Earlier sketches in CAP-1, CA 11-12
See also DLB 111
Samuels, Gertrude CANR-6
Earlier sketch in CA 9-12R
See also SATA 17
Samuels, Harold 1917- 93-96
Samuels, Harry 1893- 13-16R
Samuels, Jayne Newcomer 1914- 150
Samuels, Lesser 1894(?)-1980 Obituary 102
Samuels, M(ichael) L(ouis) 1920- 41-44R
Samuels, Peggy 1922- 97-100
Samuels, Shirley 1957- 144
Samuels, Warren J. 1933- CANR-14
Earlier sketch in CA 21-24R
Samuelson, Arnold 1912(?)-1981 Obituary 116
Samuelson, Hyman 1919- 154
Samuelson, Paul A(nthony) 1915- CANR-40
Earlier sketch in CA 5-8R
Samuelson, Robert J(acob) 1945- 155
Samuelsson, Bengt Ingemar 1934- 168
Samway, Patrick H(enry) 1939- CANR-71
Earlier sketches in CA 105, CANR-21
Sanborn, B. X.
See Ballinger, William Sanborn

Sanborn, Duane 1914- CANR-1
Earlier sketch in CA 1-4R
See also SATA 38
Sanborn, Franklin Benjamin 1831-1917 ..... DLB 1
Sanborn, Margaret 1915- CANR-4
Earlier sketch in CA 53-56
Sanborn, Patricia F. 1937- 25-28R
Sanborn, Ruth Cummings 1917- 29-32R
Sancha, Sheila 1924- CANR-11
Earlier sketch in CA 69-72
See also SATA 38
Sanchez, David A. 1933- 157
Sanchez, Federico
See Semprun, Jorge
Sanchez, Florencio 1875-1910 153
See also HW
See also TCLC 37
Sanchez (y Sanchez), George I(sidore)
1906-1972 153
See also HW
Sanchez, Jose M(ariano) 1932- 9-12R
Sanchez, Luis Rafael 1936- 128
See also CLC 23
See also DLB 145
See also HW
Sanchez, Oscar Arias
See Arias Sanchez, Oscar
Sanchez, Philomeno "Phil" 1917- .... DLB 122
Sanchez, Ramiro Guerra y
See Guerra y Sanchez, Ramiro
Sanchez, Ricardo 1941-1995 .... CANR-32
Obituary 149
Earlier sketch in CA 73-76
See also DAM MULT
See also DLB 82
See also HW
Sanchez, Sonia 1934- CANR-49
Earlier sketches in CA 33-36R, CANR-24
See also BLC 3
See also BW 2
See also CLC 5
See also CLR 18
See also DAM MULT
See also DLB 41
See also DLBD 8
See also MAICYA
See also MTCW 1
See also PC 9
See also SATA 22
Sanchez, Thomas 1944- CANR-32
Earlier sketches in CA 45-48, CANR-2
See also BEST 90:1
See also HW
Sanchez, Trinidad, Jr. 167
Sanchez Albornoz (y Mediuna), Claudio
1893-1984 127
Obituary 113
Sanchez Flores, Daniel 1960(?)-1990 Obituary . 132
Sanchez-Hidalgo, Efrain Sigisfredo
1918-1974 57-60
Sanchez-Korrol, Virginia 131
See also HW
Sanchez-Scott, Milcha 131
See also HW
Sanchez-Silva, Jose Maria 1911- 73-76
See also CLR 12
See also MAICYA
See also SATA 16
Sanctuary, Gerald 1930- CANR-12
Earlier sketch in CA 29-32R
Sand, George 1804-1876 .... DA
See also DAB
See also DAC
See also DAM MST, NOV
See also DLB 119, 192
See also WLC
Sand, George X. 13-16R
See also SATA 45
Sand, Margaret 1932- 85-88
Sand, Richard E(ugene) 1924- 33-36R
Sandage, Allan R(ex) 1926- 167
Sandak, Cass R(obert) 1950- 108
See also SATA 51
See also SATA-Brief 37
Sandars, N(ancy) K(atharine) 1914- 61-64
Sanday, Peggy Reeves 1937- 157
Sandbach, Francis Henry 1903-1991 93-96
Obituary 135
Sandbach, Mary (Warburton) 1901- 25-28R
Sandberg, (Karin) Inger 1930- CANR-52
Earlier sketches in CA 65-68, CANR-11, 26
See also SATA 15
Sandberg, John H(ilmer) 1930- 49-52
Sandberg, Karl C. 1931- 49-52
See also SATA 35
Sandberg, Larry 1944- 77-80
Sandberg, Lars G(unnarsson) 1939- 53-56
Sandberg, Lasse (E. M.) 1924- .... SATA 15
Sandberg, Margaret M(ay) 1919- 61-64
Sandberg, Peter Lars 1934- CANR-24
Earlier sketches in CA 61-64, CANR-9
Sandbrook, K(eith) R(ichard) J(ames) 1943- ....
CANR-36
Earlier sketches in CA 97-100, CANR-16
Sandburg, Carl (August) 1878-1967 .... CANR-35
Obituary 25-28R
Earlier sketch in CA 5-8R
See also AAYA 24
See also CDALB 1865-1917
See also CLC 1, 4, 10, 15, 35
See also DA
See also DAB
See also DAC
See also DAM MST, POET
See also DLB 17, 54
See also MAICYA
See also MTCW 1
See also PC 2
See also SATA 8
See also WLC
Sandburg, Charles
See Sandburg, Carl (August)
Sandburg, Charles A.
See Sandburg, Carl (August)
Sandburg, Helga 1918- CANR-5
Earlier sketch in CA 1-4R
See also SAAS 10
See also SATA 3
Sande, Theodore Anton 1933- CANR-12
Earlier sketch in CA 65-68
Sandeen, Ernest (Emanuel) 1908-1997 .... 13-16R
Obituary 159
Sandeen, Ernest Robert 1931- CANR-1
Earlier sketch in CA 45-48
Sandelowski, Margarete J. 1946- 116
Sander, (Jane) Ellen 1944- 41-44R
Sander, Joseph Lincoln 1926- Brief entry 108
Sander, Volkmar 1929- 113
Sanderlin, David 1943- 123
Sanderlin, George 1915- 13-16R
See also SATA 4
Sanderlin, Owenita (Harrah) 1916- CANR-7
Earlier sketch in CA 17-20R
See also SATA 11
Sanders, Albert
See Davidson, David
Sanders, Andrew 1946- 145
Sanders, Ann(a Pearl Goodman) 1935- 5-8R
Sanders, Arthur 1955- 143
Sanders, Bill 1951- 137
Sanders, Buck
See Frentzen, Jeffrey
Sanders, Byrne Hope
See Sperry, Byrne Hope
Sanders, Charles 1935- 25-28R
Sanders, Charles L. 1932(?)-1990 Obituary 132
Sanders, Clinton R. 1944- 139
Sanders, Coyne Steven 1956- 142
Sanders, D(onald) G(len) 1899- 85-88
Sanders, Daphne
See Randolph, Georgiana Ann
Sanders, David (Scott, Jr.) 1926- 25-28R
Sanders, (Franklin) David 1934- 41-44R
Sanders, Dennis 1949- 108
Sanders, Donald 1915(?)-1979 Obituary 89-92
Sanders, Donald H. 1932- CANR-10
Earlier sketch in CA 25-28R
Sanders, Dorothy Lucie 1917- 33-36R
Sanders, (James) Ed(ward) 1939- CANR-44
Earlier sketches in CA 13-16R, CANR-13
See also CAAS 21
See also CLC 53
See also DLB 16
Sanders, Ed 1939- .... DAM POET
Sanders, Ed Parish 1937- 105
Sanders, Frederick K(irkland) 1936- 65-68
Sanders, Gerald D(eWitt) 1895- CAP-1
Earlier sketch in CA 13-14
Sanders, Gladys (Shultz)
1919(?)-1988 Obituary 125
Sanders, Harland 1890-1980 114
Obituary 102
Sanders, Herbert H(arvey) 1909- 13-16R
Sanders, Ivan 1944- CANR-44
Earlier sketch in CA 119
Sanders, J(ohn) Oswald 1902- CANR-21
Earlier sketches in CA 13-16R, CANR-6
Sanders, Jack T(homas) 1935- 37-40R
Sanders, Jacquin 1922- 1-4R
Sanders, James A(lvin) 1927- CANR-14
Earlier sketch in CA 21-24R
Sanders, James Bernard 1924- 41-44R
Sanders, James Edward 1911- 103
Sanders, Jeanne
See Rundle, Anne
Sanders, Jennings B(ryan) 1901- CAP-2
Earlier sketch in CA 25-28
Sanders, Joan Allred 1924- 9-12R
Sanders, John H. 1941- 162
Sanders, Joseph Lee 1940- 105
Sanders, Kent
See Wilkes-Hunter, R(ichard)
Sanders, Lawrence 1920-1998 .... CANR-62
Obituary 165
Earlier sketches in CA 81-84, CANR-33
See also BEST 89:4
See also CLC 41
See also DAM POP
See also MTCW 1
Sanders, Leonard 1929- CANR-3
Earlier sketch in CA 9-12R
Sanders, Leslie Catherine 1944- 129
Sanders, Margaret 5-8R
Sanders, Marion K. 1905-1977 .... 33-36R
Obituary 73-76
Sanders, Marlene 1931- 65-68
Sanders, Nancy I. 1960- 155
See also SATA 90
Sanders, Noah
See Blount, Roy (Alton), Jr.
Sanders, Norman (Joseph) 1929- 9-12R
Sanders, Peter B(asil) 1938- 105
Sanders, Pieter 1912- CANR-12
Earlier sketch in CA 29-32R
Sanders, (Charles) Richard 1904- 53-56
Sanders, Ronald 1932-1991 .... CANR-20
Obituary 133
Earlier sketch in CA 21-24R
Sanders, Scott Russell 1945- CANR-35
Earlier sketches in CA 85-88, CANR-15
See also SATA 56
Sanders, Sol (Witner) 1926- CANR-2
Earlier sketch in CA 49-52
Sanders, Stephen (Jesse, Jr.) 1919- 29-32R
Sanders, Thomas E. 1926- 21-24R
Sanders, Thomas Griffin 1932- 9-12R
Sanders, Tobi Gillian
See Hammes, Tobi Gillian Sanders
Sanders, William B(rauns) 1944- CANR-10
Earlier sketch in CA 65-68
Sanders, William T(imothy) 1926- CANR-3
Earlier sketch in CA 45-48
Sanders, Winston P.
See Anderson, Poul (William)
Sanderson, Irma 1912- 135
See also SATA 66
Sanderson, Isabel S(aunders)
1913-1987 Obituary 123
Sanderson, Ivan T(erence) 1911-1973 .... 37-40R
Obituary 41-44R
See also SATA 6
Sanderson, James L(ee) 1926- Brief entry 111
Sanderson, Jayne 1943- 21-24R
Sanderson, Lennox, Jr.
See Slide, Anthony
Sanderson, Margaret Love
See Keats, Emma
and Sampson, Emma (Keats) Speed
Sanderson, (John) Michael 1939- 127
Sanderson, Milton W(illiam) 1910- CANR-9
Earlier sketch in CA 9-12R
Sanderson, Peter (Crawshaw) 1929- 33-36R
Sanderson, Ruth (L.) 1951- .... SATA 41
Sanderson, Sabina W(arren) 1931- CANR-3
Earlier sketch in CA 9-12R
Sanderson, Stewart (Forson) 1924- 108
Sanderson, Warren 1931- 105
Sandford, Cedric Thomas 1924- CANR-68
Earlier sketches in CA 113, CANR-32
Sandford, Christopher 1902-1983 Obituary 109
Sandford, John
See Camp, John
Sandford, John Loren 1929- CANR-36
Earlier sketch in CA 101
Sandford, Nell Mary 1936- 81-84
See also Dunn, Nell (Mary)
Sandford, Paula 1931- CANR-36
Earlier sketch in CA 101
Sandford, William P(hillips) 1896-1975 .... CAP-2
Earlier sketch in CA 17-18
Sandhaus, Paul 1923- 25-28R
Sandifer, Durward Valdamir
1900-1981 Obituary 108
Sandifer, Linda P(rophet) 1951- 120
Sandin, Joan 1942- 159
See also SATA 12, 94
Sandin, Robert T(heodore) 1927- 111
Sandison, Alan 1932- 21-24R
Sandison, Janet
See Cameron, Elizabeth Jane
Sandle, Floyd Leslie 1913- Brief entry 106
Sandler, Benjamin P. 1902(?)-1979 Obituary . 85-88
Sandler, Irving (Harry) 1925- CANR-31
Earlier sketch in CA 29-32R
Sandler, Kevin s. 1969- 168
Sandler, Lucy Freeman 1930- CANR-31
Brief entry 113
Sandler, Stanley Lawrence 1937- CANR-56
Earlier sketch in CA 113
Sandlin, Joann S(chepers) De Lora 1935- . CANR-4
Earlier sketch in CA 53-56
Sandlin, John L(ewis) 1908- CANR-4
Earlier sketch in CA 1-4R
Sandlin, Tim 1950- 126
Sandman, Peter M(ark) 1945- 25-28R
Sandmel, Samuel 1911-1979 .... CANR-2
Earlier sketch in CA 1-4R
Sando, Joe S. 1923- 123
Sandom, J. Gregory 1956- 137
Sandon, Henry 1928- 81-84
Sandon, J. D.
See Harvey, John (Barton)
Sandon, J. D.
See Wells, Angus
Sandor, Bela I(mre) 1935- 102
Sandor, Gyorgy 108
Sandoz, (George) Ellis (Jr.) 1931- CANR-14
Earlier sketch in CA 37-40R
Sandoz, Mari(e Susette) 1896-1966 .... CANR-64
Obituary 25-28R
Earlier sketches in CA 1-4R, CANR-17
See also CLC 28
See also DLB 9
See also MTCW 1
See also SATA 5
Sandrof, Ivan 1912(?)-1979 93-96
Obituary 85-88
Sandroff, Ronni 1943- 102
Sandrow, Edward T. 1906-1975 Obituary 61-64
Sands, Donald B. 1920- 13-16R
Sands, Dorothy 1893-1980 Obituary 102
Sands, Edith Sylvia (Abeloff) 1912- 21-24R
Sands, John Edward 1930- 13-16R
Sands, Kathleen M.
See Sands, Kathleen Mullen
Sands, Kathleen Mullen CANR-41
Earlier sketch in CA 118
Sands, Leo G(eorge) 1912-1984 .... CANR-29
Obituary 114
Earlier sketch in CA 17-20R
See also Craig, Lee A(llen)
Sands, Martin
See Burke, John (Frederick)
Sands, Melissa 1949- 109
Sandstroem, Yvonne L. 1933- 140
Sandstrom, Alan R(ussell) 1945- 139
Sandstrom, Eve K. 1936- 141
Sandstrom, Pamela Effrein 1954- 139
Sandu, Gabriel 1954- 141
Sandusky, Annie Lee 1900(?)-1976 Obituary . 69-72
Sandved, Arthur O. 1931- 33-36R
Sandweiss, Martha A(nn) 1954- 136
Sandwell, B. K. 1876-1954 .... DLB 92
Sandy, Max
See Saunders, Carl Maxon
Sandy, Stephen 1934- CANR-22
Earlier sketches in CA 49-52, CANR-5
See also CAAS 29
See also DLB 165
Sandys, Celia 1943- 152
Sandys, Elspeth (Somerville) 1940- CANR-26
Earlier sketch in CA 108
Sandys, George 1578-1644 .... DLB 24, 121
Saner, Reg(inald Anthony) 1931- 65-68
See also CLC 9
Sanfield, Steve 1937- 124
Sanfilip, Thomas 1952- 57-60
Sanford, Abigail
See Foster, Jeannette Howard
Sanford, Agnes (White) 1897-1976 .... 17-20R
See also SATA 61
Sanford, Annette 1929- 130
Sanford, Charles B(elding) 1920- 113
Sanford, Charles Le Roy 1920- 5-8R
Sanford, David (Boyer) 1943- Brief entry 114
Sanford, Doris 1937- 138
See also SATA 69
Sanford, Fillmore H(argrave) 1914-1967 .... 1-4R
Obituary 103
Sanford, George 1943- 118
Sanford, Harry Allen 1929- 1-4R
Sanford, Jack D(onald) 1925- 5-8R
Sanford, John 1904- CANR-50
Brief entry 117
Earlier sketch in CA 123
Interview in 123
Sanford, John A. 1929- CANR-50
Earlier sketches in CA 25-28R, CANR-10
Sanford, John B.
See Sanford, John
Sanford, Kate
See Sanford, Kathleen (D.)
Sanford, Kathleen (D.) 1952- 163
Sanford, Kathy
See Sanford, Kathleen (D.)
Sanford, Leda 1933- CANR-12
Earlier sketch in CA 65-68
Sanford, Richard 1950- 152
Sanford, Terry 1917-1998 .... 17-20R
Obituary 167
Sanford, Thomas K(yle), Jr. 1921-1977 73-76
Sanger, Andrew 1948- 123
Sanger, Clyde 1928- CANR-36
Earlier sketch in CA 114
Sanger, David E. 1960- 136
Sanger, Elliott M(axwell) 1897-1989 Obituary .. 129
Sanger, Margaret (Higgins)
1883-1966 Obituary 89-92
Sanger, Marjory Bartlett 1920- 37-40R
See also SATA 8
Sanger, Richard H. 1905(?)-1979 Obituary ... 85-88
Sangiuliano, Iris (Agatha) 1923- Brief entry 114
Sangrey, Dawn 1942- CANR-15
Earlier sketch in CA 85-88
Sangster, Charles 1822-1893 .... DLB 99
Sangster, Ian 1934- 61-64
Sangster, Jimmy 1927- CANR-14
Earlier sketch in CA 21-24R
Sangster, Margaret E(lizabeth)
1894-1981 Obituary 105
Sanguineti, Edoardo 1930- .... DLB 128
Sanguinetti, Elise Ayers 1926- CANR-1
Earlier sketch in CA 1-4R
Sang Ye
See Shen Dajun
Saniel, Josefa M. 1925- 13-16R
Sanjek, David 1952- 163
Sanjian, Avedis K(rikor) 1921-1995 .... 33-36R
Obituary 149
San Juan, Epifanio, Jr. 1938- CANR-44
Earlier sketches in CA 25-28R, CANR-10
Sankar, Andrea (Patrice) 1948- 139
Sankar, D(evarakonda) V(enkata) Siva 1927- . 53-56
Sankey, Alice (Ann-Susan) 1910- 61-64
See also SATA 27
Sankhala, Kailash S. 1925- 101
San Martin, Marta 1942- 102
Sann, Paul 1914-1986 .... CANR-5
Obituary 120
Earlier sketch in CA 13-16R
Sannebeck, Norvelle 1909- 97-100
Sano, Furumi
See Mallett, Daryl F(urumi)
Sanoff, Alvin P. 1941- 136
Sansay, Leonora (?)-1823(?) .... DLB 200
Sansom, Arthur B(aldwin) 1920-1991 112
Obituary 134
Sansom, Clive 1910- 104
Sansom, Peter 1958- 133

Sansom, William 1912-1976 ... CANR-42
Obituary ... 65-68
Earlier sketch in CA 5-8R
See also CLC 2, 6
See also DAM NOV
See also DLB 139
See also MTCW 1
See also SSC 21
Sansone, Sam J(ohn) 1915- ... 115
San Souci, Daniel ... 161
See also SATA 96
San Souci, Robert D. 1946- ... CANR-46
Earlier sketch in CA 108
See also CLR 43
See also SATA 40, 81
Sansweet, Stephen Jay 1945- ... 61-64
Sant, Thomas 1948- ... 136
Santa Cruz (Gamarra), Nicomedes 1925- ... HW
Santa Maria
See Powell-Smith, Vincent (Walter Francis)
Santas, Joan Foster 1930- ... 17-20R
Santayana, George 1863-1952 Brief entry ... 115
See also DLB 54, 71
See also DLBD 13
See also TCLC 40
Sant Cassia, Paul 1954- ... 143
Sante, Luc 1954- ... 147
Santee, Ross 1889(?)-1965 ... CANR-64
Earlier sketch in CA 108
Santesson, Hans Stefan 1914(?)-1975 ... 93-96
Obituary ... 57-60
See also SATA-Obit 30
Santi, Enrico Mario 1950- ... 116
Santiago, Danny
See James, Daniel (Lewis)
See also CLC 33
See also DLB 122
Santini, Rosemarie ... 81-84
Santmire, H(arold) Paul 1935- ... 53-56
Santmyer, Helen Hoover 1895-1986 ... CANR-33
Obituary ... 118
Earlier sketches in CA 1-4R, CANR-15
See also CLC 33
See also DLBY 84
See also MTCW 1
Santoka, Taneda 1882-1940 ... TCLC 72
Santoli, Al 1949- ... 105
Santoni, Georges V. 1938- ... 103
Santoni, Ronald E(rnest) 1931- ... 5-8R
Santoro, Carlo Maria 1935- ... 143
Santos, Bienvenido N(uqui) 1911-1996 ... CANR-46
Obituary ... 151
Earlier sketches in CA 101, CANR-19
See also CLC 22
See also DAM MULT
Santos, Eduardo 1888-1974 Obituary ... 89-92
Santos, Helen
See Griffiths, Helen
Santos, Sherod (A.) 1948- ... 132
Santostefano, Sebastiano 1929- ... 41-44R
Santrey, Louis
See Sabin, Louis
Sanville, Jean 1918- ... 89-92
Sanvitale, Francesca 1928- ... DLB 196
Sanwal, B(hairava) D(at) 1917- ... 17-20R
Saperstein, Alan ... 103
Saperstein, David 1937- ... 130
Saphier, Michael 1911- ... 25-28R
Saphire, Saul 1896(?)-1974 Obituary ... 53-56
Sapia, Yvonne (V.) 1946- ... CANR-56
Earlier sketch in CA 126
Sapidus, Joannes 1490-1561 ... DLB 179
Sapiets, Janis 1921-1983(?) Obituary ... 109
Sapieyevski, Anne Lindbergh 1940-1993 ... 115
Obituary ... 143
Brief entry ... 113
See also Feydy, Anne Lindbergh
and Lindbergh, Anne
See also SATA 35, 78
Sapinsley, Alvin 1921- ... CANR-21
Earlier sketch in CA 104
Sapinsley, Barbara ... 137
Sapir, Edward 1884-1939 ... DLB 92
Sapir, Richard (Ben) 1936-1987 ... CANR-13
Obituary ... 121
Earlier sketch in CA 69-72
Sapiro, Virginia 1951- ... CANR-53
Earlier sketch in CA 126
Sapori, Armando 1892- ... 33-36R
Saporta, Marc(el) 1923- ... 21-24R
Saporta, Sol 1925- ... 17-20R
Saposnik, Irving Seymour 1936- ... 97-100
Saposs, David Joseph 1886-1968 ... CANR-15
Obituary ... 103
Earlier sketch in CA 1-4R
Sapp, Phyllis Woodruff 1908- ... CANR-1
Earlier sketch in CA 1-4R
Sappell, Joel 1953- ... 133
Sapper
See McNeile, Herman Cyril
See also TCLC 44
Sapper, Laurence Joseph 1922-1989 Obituary ... 129
Sapphire 1950- ... CLC 99
Sappho fl. 6th cent. B.C.- ... DAM POET
See also DLB 176
See also PC 5
Sappington, Roger E(dwin) 1929- ... 13-16R
Sara
See Blake, Sally Mirliss
Sara, Dorothy 1897(?)-1976 Obituary ... 69-72
Sarac, Roger
See Caras, Roger A(ndrew)
Saracevic, Tefko 1930- ... 37-40R
Sarah, Duchess of York
See Ferguson, Sarah (Margaret)
Sarah, Edith 1921- ... 149
Sarah, Robyn 1949- ... CANR-31
Earlier sketch in CA 112
Saramago, Jose 1922- ... 153
Saran, Parmatma 1943- ... 129
Sarano, Jacques 1920- ... 29-32R
Sarant, P(eter) C. 1933(?)-1979 Obituary ... 89-92
Sarasin, Jennifer
See Sachs, Judith
Sarason, Seymour Bernard 1919- ... 120
Sarasy, Phyllis Powell 1930- ... 13-16R
Sarat, Austin Dean 1947- ... 106
Sarban
See Wall, John W.
SarDesai, D(amodar) R. 1931- ... CANR-11
Earlier sketch in CA 25-28R
Sardeson, Charles T. 1921- ... 5-8R
Sardi, Jan 1953- ... 164
Sardou, Victorien 1831-1908 ... DLB 192
Sarducci, Father Guido
See Novello, Don
Sarduy, Severo 1937-1993 ... CANR-58
Obituary ... 142
Earlier sketch in CA 89-92
See also CLC 6, 97
See also DLB 113
See also HW
Sarett, Alma (Johnson) 1908- ... CAP-2
Earlier sketch in CA 17-18
Sarett, Morton R(euben) 1916- ... 93-96
Sarewitz, Daniel 1955- ... 158
Sareyan, Alex 1913- ... 149
Sarf, Wayne M(ichael) 1957- ... 114
Sarfoh, Joseph A. 1936- ... 145
Sarg, Anthony Frederick
See Sarg, Tony
Sarg, Tony 1880-1942 ... YABC 1
Sargant, Norman 1909-1982 Obituary ... 107
Sargant, William (Walters) 1907- ... 65-68
Sargeant, Howland H(ill) 1911-1984 Obituary ... 112
Sargeant, Winthrop 1903-1986 ... 29-32R
Obituary ... 120
Sargent, Alice G(oldstein) 1939-1988 ... 110
Obituary ... 125
Sargent, Alvin 1927- ... CANR-48
Brief entry ... 111
Earlier sketch in CA 121
Sargent, Ben 1948- ... 118
Brief entry ... 113
Interview in ... 118
Sargent, Brian (Lawrence) 1927- ... 97-100
Sargent, Daniel 1890-1987 Obituary ... 121
Sargent, David R(utledge) 1920- ... 93-96
Sargent, Frederic O(berlin) 1919- ... 41-44R
Sargent, Inge 1932- ... 147
Sargent, Jean Vieth 1918- ... 106
Sargent, John Richard 1925- ... 13-16R
Sargent, Lyman Tower 1940- ... CANR-15
Earlier sketch in CA 29-32R
Sargent, Pamela 1948- ... CANR-41
Earlier sketches in CA 61-64, CANR-8
See also CAAS 18
See also AAYA 18
See also DLB 8
See also SATA 29, 78
Sargent, Ralph M(illard) 1904-1985 ... 37-40R
Obituary ... 116
Sargent, Robert 1933- ... 21-24R
See also SATA 2
Sargent, Ruth (Sexton) 1920- ... 112
Sargent, Sarah 1937- ... 106
See also SATA 44
See also SATA-Brief 41
Sargent, Shirley 1927- ... CANR-2
Earlier sketch in CA 1-4R
See also SATA 11
Sargent, (Francis) William (Jr.) 1946- ... 106
Sargent, Wyn ... 49-52
Sargeson, Frank 1903-1982 ... CANR-38
Obituary ... 106
Earlier sketch in CA 25-28R
See also CLC 31
Sarhan, Samir 1941- ... 103
Sari
See Fleur, Anne
Saricks, Ambrose 1915- ... 17-20R
Sariego, Patricia Treece
See Treece, Patricia
Sariola, Sakari 1919- ... 41-44R
Sarjeant, William A(ntony) S(within) 1935- ... 105
Sarkar, Asoke 1911(?)-1983 Obituary ... 109
Sarkar, (Anvil) Kumar 1912- ... 37-40R
Sarkesian, Sam C(harles) 1927- ... 57-60
Sarlos, Robert Karoly 1931- ... 109
Sarma, G. V. L. N. 1925- ... 17-20R
Sarmiento, Felix Ruben Garcia
See Dario, Ruben
Sarna, Jonathan D(aniel) 1955- ... CANR-59
Earlier sketches in CA 109, CANR-27
Sarna, Nahum M(attathias) 1923- ... 17-20R
Sarnat, Marshall 1929- ... CANR-26
Earlier sketches in CA 21-24R, CANR-10
Sarndal, Carl Erik 1937- ... 105
Sarner, Harvey 1934- ... 17-20R
Sarno, Arthur D. 1921(?)-1982 Obituary ... 106
Sarno, Ronald A(nthony) 1941- ... CANR-27
Earlier sketches in CA 29-32R, CANR-12
Sarnoff, David 1891-1971 Obituary ... 113
Sarnoff, Dorothy 1917- ... 33-36R
Sarnoff, Irving 1922- ... CANR-8
Earlier sketch in CA 17-20R
Sarnoff, Jane 1937- ... CANR-9
Earlier sketch in CA 53-56
See also SATA 10
Sarnoff, Paul 1918- ... CANR-40
Earlier sketches in CA 5-8R, CANR-2, 18
Sarnoff, Stanley Jay 1917-1990 Obituary ... 131
Sarnoff, Suzanne 1928- ... 97-100
Saro-Wiwa, Ken(ule Beeson) 1941-1995 ... CANR-60
Obituary ... 150
Earlier sketch in CA 142
See also BW 2
See also DLB 157
Saroyan, Aram 1943- ... CANR-30
Earlier sketch in CA 21-24R
See also CAAS 5
Saroyan, Arshalyus 1923-1974 Obituary ... 53-56
Saroyan, William 1908-1981 ... CANR-30
Obituary ... 103
Earlier sketch in CA 5-8R
See also CLC 1, 8, 10, 29, 34, 56
See also DA
See also DAB
See also DAC
See also DAM DRAM, MST, NOV
See also DLB 7, 9, 86
See also DLBY 81
See also MTCW 1
See also SATA 23
See also SATA-Obit 24
See also SSC 21
See also WLC
Sarrantonio, Al 1952- ... CANR-70
Earlier sketch in CA 120
Sarratt, Reed 1918(?)-1986 Obituary ... 118
Sarraute, Nathalie 1900- ... CANR-66
Earlier sketches in CA 9-12R, CANR-23
See also CLC 1, 2, 4, 8, 10, 31, 80
See also DLB 83
See also MTCW 1
Sarrazin, Albertine 1937-1967 ... DLB 83
Sarre, Winifred Turner 1931- ... 29-32R
Sarri, Rosemary C(onzemius) 1926- ... 111
Sarris, Andrew 1928- ... 21-24R
Sarris, Greg 1952- ... DLB 175
Sarsfield, C. P.
See Marshner, Connaught Coyne
Sartain, Aaron Quinn 1905- ... 1-4R
Sarti, Roland 1937- ... 37-40R
Sarti, Ron 1947- ... 154
Sarto, Ben
See Fawcett, F(rank) Dubrez
Sarton, (Eleanor) May 1912-1995 ... CANR-55
Obituary ... 149
Earlier sketches in CA 1-4R, CANR-1, 34
Interview in ... CANR-34
See also CLC 4, 14, 49, 91
See also DAM POET
See also DLB 48
See also DLBY 81
See also MTCW 1
See also SATA 36
See also SATA-Obit 86
Sartor, Margaret 1959- ... CANR-51
Earlier sketch in CA 125
Sartori, Giovanni 1924- ... CANR-38
Earlier sketches in CA 5-8R, CANR-2, 17
Sartre, Jean-Paul 1905-1980 ... CANR-21
Obituary ... 97-100
Earlier sketch in CA 9-12R
See also CLC 1, 4, 7, 9, 13, 18, 24, 44, 50, 52
See also DA
See also DAB
See also DAC
See also DAM DRAM, MST, NOV
See also DC 3
See also DLB 72
See also MTCW 1
See also WLC
Sartwell, Crispin 1958- ... 168
Sarvepalli, Gopal 1923- ... 81-84
Sarver, Hannah
See Nielsen, Jean Sarver
Sasaki, R. A. 1952- ... 136
Sasaki, Tazu 1932- ... CANR-10
Earlier sketch in CA 25-28R
Saseen, Sharon (Dillon) 1949- ... SATA 59
Sasek, Lawrence A(nton) 1923- ... CANR-1
Earlier sketch in CA 1-4R
Sasek, Miroslav 1916-1980 ... 73-76
Obituary ... 101
See also CLR 4
See also SATA 16
See also SATA-Obit 23
Saslow, Helen 1926- ... 105
Sasnett, Martena T(enney) 1908- ... 53-56
Saso, Michael R. 1930- ... 112
Sass, Lorna Janet 1945- ... 102
Sass, Stephen L. 1940- ... 167
Sass, Steven A(rthur) 1949- ... 116
Sassen, Saskia 1949- ... 154
Sasser, Charles W(ayne) 1942- ... CANR-48
Earlier sketch in CA 122
Sasso, Sandy Eisenberg 1947- ... 151
See also SATA 86
Sasson, Jean P. 1947- ... 144
Sasson, Sarah Diane Hyde 1946- ... 125
Sassoon, Beverly Adams ... 65-68
Sassoon, Rosemary 1931- ... CANR-48
Earlier sketch in CA 118
Sassoon, Siegfried (Lorraine) 1886-1967 ... CANR-36
Obituary ... 25-28R
Earlier sketch in CA 104
See also CLC 36
See also DAB
See also DAM MST, NOV, POET
See also DLB 20, 191
See also DLBD 18
See also MTCW 1
See also PC 12
Sassoon, Vidal 1928- ... CANR-15
Earlier sketch in CA 65-68
Sasuly, Richard 1913- ... 109
Sata Ineko 1904- ... DLB 180
Satchidananda, Swami
See Dharmi, Santana
Satchwell, John ... SATA-Brief 49
Sater, William F(rederick) 1937- ... 118
Sateren, Leland B. 1913- ... 141
Sather, Julia Coley Duncan 1940- ... 103
Sathre, Vivian 1952- ... SATA 79
Satiafa
See Gordon, Vivian V(erdell)
Satin, Joseph 1922- ... 9-12R
Satin, Mark 1946- ... 41-44R
Satir, Virginia (Mildred) 1916-1988 Obituary ... 126
Satiricus
See Roetter, Charles Frederick
Sato, Esther Masako Tateishi 1915- ... 108
Sato, Hiroaki 1942- ... 145
Satprem 1923- ... CANR-35
Earlier sketches in CA 85-88, CANR-15
Satran, Pamela Redmond 1953- ... 110
Sattelmeyer, Robert 1946- ... 125
Satter, Ellyn 1942- ... 145
Satter, Robert 1919- ... 139
Satterfield, Archie 1933- ... CANR-14
Earlier sketch in CA 57-60
Satterfield, Charles
See del Rey, Lester
and Pohl, Frederik
Satterlund, Donald R(obert) 1928- ... 53-56
Satterly, Weston
See Sunners, William
Satterthwait, Walter 1946- ... CANR-62
Earlier sketch in CA 127
Sattgast, L. J.
See Sattgast, Linda J.
Sattgast, Linda J. 1953- ... 155
See also SATA 91
Sattin, Anthony (Neil) 1956- ... 126
Sattler, Helen Roney 1921-1992 ... CANR-31
Earlier sketches in CA 33-36R, CANR-14
See also CLR 24
See also SATA 4, 74
Sattler, Henry V(ernon) 1917- ... CANR-7
Earlier sketch in CA 5-8R
Sattler, Jerome M(urray) 1931- ... 49-52
Sattler, Warren 1934- ... 65-68
Sattley, Helen R(owland) ... 1-4R
Satyamurti, Carole 1939- ... CANR-55
Earlier sketch in CA 127
Satz, Paul 1932- ... 61-64
Satz, Ronald Norman 1944- ... CANR-8
Earlier sketch in CA 61-64
Saucy, Robert L(loyd) 1930- ... 123
Brief entry ... 118
Sauder, Robert A(lden) 1943- ... 148
Sauer, Carl Ortwin 1889-1975 ... CANR-9
Earlier sketch in CA 61-64
Sauer, Elizabeth M. 1964- ... 164
Sauer, Julia Lina 1891-1983 ... 81-84
See also SATA 32
See also SATA-Obit 36
Sauer, Muriel Stafford ... 13-16R
Sauer, Peter 1937- ... 139
Sauer, Val John, Jr. 1938- ... 107
Sauerhaft, Stan 1926- ... 85-88
Sauerlaender, Willibald 1924- ... 118
Sauerlander, Willibald
See Sauerlaender, Willibald
Sauers, Richard A(llen) 1954- ... 164
Sauers, Richard James 1930- ... 53-56
Sauers, Wendy 1958- ... 116
Saul, Carol P. 1947- ... SATA 78
Saul, George Brandon 1901-1986 ... CANR-6
Obituary ... 120
Earlier sketch in CA 13-16R
Saul, John (W. III) 1942- ... CANR-40
Earlier sketches in CA 81-84, CANR-16
See also AAYA 10
See also BEST 90:4
See also CLC 46
See also DAM NOV, POP
See also SATA 98
Saul, John Ralston 1947- ... 133
Saul, Leon J(oseph) 1901- ... CANR-10
Earlier sketch in CA 21-24R
Saul, Mary ... 105
Saul, Nigel Edward 1952- ... 117
Saul, Norman E(ugene) 1932- ... 53-56
Saul, Oscar
See Halpern, Oscar Saul
Saul, (Ellen) Wendy 1946- ... 114
See also SATA 42
Saulnier, Karen Luczak 1940- ... 148
See also SATA 80
Saulnier, Raymond Joseph 1908- ... CANR-65
Earlier sketch in CA 5-8R
Sauls, Roger 1944- ... 33-36R
Saum, Karen 1935- ... 137
Saumarez Smith, Charles Robert 1954- ... 144
Saunders, Allen 1899-1986 ... 69-72
Obituary ... 118
Saunders, Ann Loreille 1930- ... 103
Saunders, Aretas (Andrews) 1884- ... CAP-1
Earlier sketch in CA 11-12
Saunders, B(ernard) C(harles)
1903-1983 Obituary ... 115
Saunders, Beatrice ... 49-52
Saunders, Blanche 1906- ... CAP-1
Earlier sketch in CA 13-14
Saunders, Caleb
See Heinlein, Robert A(nson)
Saunders, Carl Maxon 1890-1974 Obituary ... 89-92
Saunders, Charles B(askerville), Jr. 1928- ... 61-64
Saunders, Christopher T(homas) 1907- ... 119
Saunders, Dave 1939- ... SATA 85

Saunders, David
  See Sontup, Dan(iel)
Saunders, Doris E(vans) 1921- ... 77-80
Saunders, E. Dale 1919- ... 5-8R
Saunders, Ernest 1901(?)-1983 Obituary ... 109
Saunders, Francis J. 1927- ... 131
Saunders, Frank
  See Saunders, Francis J.
Saunders, Gail 1944- ... 145
Saunders, George 1958- ... 164
Saunders, Helen E(lizabeth) 1912- ... 25-28R
Saunders, Hilary Aidan St. George 1898-1951 Brief entry ... 121
Saunders, Ione
  See Cole, Margaret Alice
Saunders, J(ohn) W(hiteside) 1920- ... CANR-39
  Earlier sketch in CA 116
Saunders, James (Arthur) 1925- ... 139
  Brief entry ... 124
  See also DLB 13
Saunders, James Robert 1953- ... 153
Saunders, Jason Lewis 1922- Brief entry ... 106
Saunders, Jean 1932- ... CANR-19
  Earlier sketch in CA 102
Saunders, John Monk 1897-1940 ... DLB 26
Saunders, John Turk 1929-1974 ... CAP-2
  Earlier sketch in CA 21-22
Saunders, Julie 1939- ... SATA 85
Saunders, Keith 1910- ... 57-60
  See also SATA 12
Saunders, Margaret Marshall 1861-1947 ... DLB 92
Saunders, Max 1957- ... 164
Saunders, Peter 1950- ... CANR-36
  Earlier sketch in CA 114
Saunders, Richard 1947- ... CANR-21
  Earlier sketch in CA 105
Saunders, Roy 1911- ... CAP-1
  Earlier sketch in CA 11-12
Saunders, Rubie (Agnes) 1929- ... 49-52
  See also SATA 21
Saunders, Sally Love 1940- ... 125
Saunders, Susan 1945- ... CANR-68
  Earlier sketch in CA 106
  See also SATA 46, 96
  See also SATA-Brief 41
Saunders, Thomas 1909- ... CANR-12
  Earlier sketch in CA 73-76
Saura (Atares), Carlos 1932- ... 131
  Brief entry ... 114
  See also CLC 20
  See also HW
Sauro, Regina Calderone 1924- ... 9-12R
Sause, George G(abriel) 1919- ... 41-44R
Sauser-Hall, Frederic 1887-1961 ... CANR-62
  Obituary ... 93-96
  Earlier sketches in CA 102, CANR-36
  See also Cendrars, Blaise
  See also CLC 18
  See also MTCW 1
Saussure, Eric de
  See de Saussure, Eric
Saussure, Ferdinand de 1857-1913 ... TCLC 49
Sautel, Maureen Ann 1951- ... 61-64
Sauter, Edwin Charles Scott, Jr. 1930- ... 13-16R
Sauter, Eric 1948- ... CANR-62
  Earlier sketch in CA 117
Sauter, Van Gordon 1935- ... 73-76
Sautet, Claude 1924- ... 143
Sautter, Udo 1934- ... 144
Sauvage, Franck
  See Horn, Maurice
Sauvage, Leo 1913(?)-1988 Obituary ... 127
Sauvage, Roger 1917-1977 Obituary ... 73-76
Sauvageau, Juan 1917- ... CANR-11
  Earlier sketch in CA 65-68
Sauvain, Philip Arthur 1933- ... CANR-49
  Earlier sketches in CA 104, CANR-21
Sauvant, Karl P(eter) 1944- ... 77-80
Sauvy, Jean (Maurice Paul) 1916- ... 65-68
Sauvy, Simonne 1922- ... 65-68
Sava, George
  See Milkomane, George Alexis Milkomanovich
Savacool, John K(enneth) 1917- ... 45-48
Savadier, Elivia 1950- ... SATA 79
Savage, Alan
  See Nicole, Christopher (Robin)
Savage, Blake
  See Goodwin, Harold L(eland)
Savage, Brian 1933- ... 41-44R
Savage, Candace (M.) 1949- ... 123
Savage, Carlton Raymond 1897-1990 Obituary ... 131
Savage, Catharine
  See Brosman, Catharine Savage
Savage, Charles 1918- ... 53-56
Savage, Christina
  See Newcomb, Kerry
  and Schaefer, Frank
Savage, Christopher I(vor) 1924-1969 ... CANR-6
  Earlier sketch in CA 5-8R
Savage, D(ouglas) J(oseph) 1950- ... 118
Savage, D(erek) S(tanley) 1917- ... 104
Savage, Deborah 1955- ... 143
  See also SATA 76
Savage, Elizabeth Fitzgerald 1918-1989 ... CANR-69
  Earlier sketches in CA 1-4R, CANR-1
Savage, Ernest 1918- ... 112
Savage, Frances Higginson (Fuller) 1898- ... CAP-1
  Earlier sketch in CA 19-20
Savage, (Leonard) George (Gimson) 1909- ... CANR-5
  Earlier sketch in CA 9-12R
Savage, Georgia ... 138
Savage, Helen 1915- ... 97-100
Savage, Henry, Jr. 1903- ... CAP-2
  Earlier sketch in CA 25-28
Savage, Herbert
  See Picot, Derek
Savage, James 1784-1873 ... DLB 30
Savage, James F(rancis) 1939- ... 73-76
Savage, Jeff 1961- ... 164
  See also SATA 97
Savage, Jon
  See Sage, Jonathan
Savage, Joseph P. 1895(?)-1977 Obituary ... 69-72
Savage, Katharine James 1905-1989 ... 13-16R
  Obituary ... 128
  See also SATA-Obit 61
Savage, Lee 1928- ... 101
Savage, Leonard J(immie) 1917-1971 ... CAP-2
  Obituary ... 33-36R
  Earlier sketch in CA 17-18
Savage, Marc 1945- ... 65-68
Savage, Marmion 1803(?)-1872 ... DLB 21
Savage, Michael D(onald) 1946- ... 101
Savage, Mildred (Spitz) 1919- ... 9-12R
Savage, Minot Judson 1841-1918 Brief entry ... 115
Savage, Richard 1697(?)-1743 ... DLB 95
Savage, Robert L(ynn) 1939- ... CANR-46
  Earlier sketch in CA 109
Savage, Roth
  See Kehrer, Daniel M(ark)
Savage, Sean J. 1964- ... 161
Savage, Teresa 1950- ... 113
Savage, Thomas 1915- ... 132
  Brief entry ... 126
  Interview in ... 132
  See also CAAS 15
  See also CLC 40
Savage, Thomas Gerard 1926- ... 49-52
Savage, W(illiam) Sherman 1890- ... 69-72
Savage, William W(oodrow), Jr. 1943- ... 57-60
Savage, William W(oodrow) 1914- ... 37-40R
Savageau, Cheryl 1950- ... 152
  See also SATA 96
Savain, Petion (?)-1973 Obituary ... 41-44R
Savan, Bruce (Sheldon) 1927-1987 ... 5-8R
  Obituary ... 122
Savan, Glenn 19(?)- ... CLC 50
Savard, Felix-Antoine 1896-1982 ... 148
  See also DLB 68
Savarese, Julia ... 37-40R
Savarin
  See Courtine, Robert
Savary, Louis M(ichael) 1936- ... CANR-49
  Earlier sketches in CA 21-24R, CANR-9, 24
Savas, E(manuel) S(tephen) 1931- ... 17-20R
Saveland, Robert N(elson) 1921- ... 41-44R
Savell, Don P(atrick) 1939- ... 119
Savelle, Max(well) 1896- ... 21-24R
Savery, Constance (Winifred) 1897- ... CANR-7
  Earlier sketch in CA 9-12R
  See also SATA 1
Savery, Ranald 1903(?)-1974 Obituary ... 104
Saveson, John E(dward) 1923- ... 41-44R
Saveth, Edward N(orman) 1915- ... 21-24R
Saville, Diana 1943- ... 160
Saville, Eugenia (Curtis) 1913- ... 41-44R
Saville, Lloyd (Blackstone) 1913- ... 21-24R
Saville, (Leonard) Malcolm 1901-1982 ... 101
  Obituary ... 107
  See also DLB 160
  See also SATA 23
  See also SATA-Obit 31
Savin, Marc 1948- ... 106
Saviozzi, Adriana
  See Mazza, Adriana
Savitch, Jessica 1948-1983 ... 108
  Obituary ... 110
Savitt, Ronald 1939- ... 33-36R
Savitt, Sam ... CANR-17
  Earlier sketches in CA 1-4R, CANR-1
  See also SATA 8
Savitt, Todd Lee 1943- ... 102
Savitz, Harriet May 1933- ... CANR-64
  Earlier sketches in CA 41-44R, CANR-14, 32
  See also MAICYA
  See also SAAS 9, 26
  See also SATA 5, 72
Savitz, Leonard D. 1926- ... CANR-8
  Earlier sketch in CA 21-24R
Savoie, Donald J(oseph) 1947- ... 112
Savoie, Paul 1946- ... 113
Savory, Alan Forsyth 1905- ... 9-12R
Savory, Hubert Newman 1911- ... CANR-26
  Earlier sketches in CA 25-28R, CANR-10
Savory, Jerold 1933- ... CANR-10
  Earlier sketch in CA 25-28R
Savory, Teo 1907-1989 ... CANR-31
  Earlier sketch in CA 29-32R
Savory, Theodore Horace 1896-1980 ... CANR-6
  Earlier sketch in CA 5-8R
Savours, Ann (Margaret) 1927- ... 57-60
Savoy, Lauret E. ... 139
Savoy, Mark
  See Turner, Robert (Harry)
Sawai, Gloria Ostrem ... 113
Saward, Dudley 1913- ... 147
Saward, Michael 1932- ... 97-100
Sawatsky, Harry Leonard 1931- ... 89-92
Sawatsky, John 1948- ... 144
Sawer, Geoffrey 1910- ... 17-20R
Sawey, Orlan (Lester) 1920- ... CANR-12
  Earlier sketch in CA 29-32R
Sawhill, Isabel V(an Devanter) 1937- ... 130
Sawicki, Marianne 1950- ... CANR-36
  Earlier sketch in CA 114
Sawicki, Mary 1950- ... SATA 90
Sawin, Martica 1927- ... 124
Sawin, Philip 1933- ... 137
Sawkins, Raymond H(arold) ... 103
  See also Forbes, Colin
Sawley, Petra
  See Marsh, John
Sawrey, Robert D. 1948- ... 144
Sawyer, Albert E(rnest) 1898- ... 5-8R
Sawyer, Charles 1887-1979 ... CAP-2
  Obituary ... 85-88
  Earlier sketch in CA 25-28
Sawyer, Corinne Holt ... 17-20R
Sawyer, Diane K. 1946(?)- ... 115
  Brief entry ... 109
  Interview in ... 115
Sawyer, (Frederick) Don(ald) 1947- ... 133
  See also SATA 72
Sawyer, Jack 1931- ... 61-64
Sawyer, Jesse O. 1918- ... 17-20R
Sawyer, John
  See Foley, (Cedric) John
Sawyer, Kem Knapp 1953- ... 150
  See also SATA 84
Sawyer, Mark
  See Greenhood, (Clarence) David
Sawyer, Mary R. 1944- ... 148
Sawyer, P(eter) H(ayes) 1928- ... CANR-6
  Earlier sketch in CA 9-12R
Sawyer, R(obert) McLaran 1929- ... 45-48
Sawyer, Ralph Alanson 1895-1978 Obituary ... 81-84
Sawyer, Robert J(ames) 1960- ... 149
  See also SATA 81
Sawyer, Roger 1931- ... 123
Sawyer, Ruth 1880-1970 ... CANR-37
  Earlier sketch in CA 73-76
  See also CLR 36
  See also DLB 22
  See also MAICYA
  See also SATA 17
Sawyer, W(alter) W(arwick) 1911- ... 53-56
Sawyer-Laucanno, Christopher 1951- ... CANR-36
  Earlier sketch in CA 114
Sawyerr, Harry (Alphonso Ebun) 1909-1986 ... 37-40R
  Obituary ... 120
Sax, Gilbert 1930- ... 21-24R
Sax, Joseph L. 1936- ... 33-36R
Sax, Karl 1892-1973 Obituary ... 45-48
Sax, Richard 1949-1995 ... 125
  Obituary ... 149
Sax, Saville 1924- ... 97-100
Saxberg, Borje O(svald) 1928- ... 41-44R
Saxby, H. M.
  See Saxby, (Henry) Maurice
Saxby, (Henry) Maurice 1924- ... SATA 71
Saxe, Isobel
  See Rayner, Claire (Berenice)
Saxe, Richard W(arren) 1923- ... 49-52
Saxe, Thomas E., Jr. 1903-1975 Obituary ... 61-64
Saxon, A(rthur) H(artley) 1935- ... CANR-37
  Earlier sketches in CA 25-28R, CANR-16
Saxon, Alex
  See Pronzini, Bill
  and Quennell, Peter (Courtney)
Saxon, Antonia
  See Sachs, Judith
Saxon, Bill
  See Wallmann, Jeffrey M(iner)
Saxon, Charles D(avid) 1920-1988 Obituary ... 127
  Brief entry ... 118
Saxon, Gladys Relyea ... 5-8R
Saxon, Grant Tracy
  See Raucina, Thomas Frank
Saxon, John
  See Rumbold-Gibbs, Henry St. John Clair
Saxon, Lyle 1891-1946 Brief entry ... 119
Saxon, Peter
  See McNeilly, Wilfred (Glassford)
Saxon, Van
  See Henderson, M(arilyn) R(uth)
Saxon, William
  See Mayleas, William
Saxton, Alexander P(laisted) 1919- ... 105
Saxton, Josephine (Mary) 1935- ... CANR-56
  Earlier sketch in CA 29-32R
Saxton, Judith 1936- ... 105
Saxton, Lloyd 1919- ... 29-32R
Saxton, Mark 1914-1988 ... 93-96
  Obituary ... 124
Saxton, Martha 1945- ... 81-84
Saxton, Ruth O. 1941- ... 150
Say, Allen 1937- ... CANR-30
  Earlier sketch in CA 29-32R
  See also CLR 22
  See also JRDA
  See also MAICYA
  See also SATA 28, 69
Saya, Peter
  See Peterson, Robert E(ugene)
Sayce, Richard Anthony 1917- ... 61-64
Saydah, J. Roger 1939-1976 ... 25-28R
  Obituary ... 120
Saye, Albert B(erry) 1912- ... CANR-5
  Earlier sketch in CA 5-8R
Sayeed, Khalid B. 1926- ... 25-28R
Sayegh, Fayez A(bdullah) 1922-1980 ... 9-12R
  Obituary ... 102
Sayer, Angela 1935- ... 89-92
Sayer, Ian (Keith Terence) 1945- ... 139
Sayer, Karen (Anne) 1967- ... 153
Sayer, Paul 1955- ... 132
Sayers, Dorothy L(eigh) 1893-1957 ... CANR-60
  Brief entry ... 104
  Earlier sketch in CA 119
  See also CDBLB 1914-1945
  See also DAM POP
  See also DLB 10, 36, 77, 100
  See also MTCW 1
  See also TCLC 2, 15
Sayers, Frances Clarke 1897-1989 ... 17-20R
  Obituary ... 129
  See also SATA 3
  See also SATA-Obit 62
Sayers, Gale 1943- ... 73-76
Sayers, Janet 1945- ... 134
Sayers, Peig 1873-1958 Brief entry ... 113
Sayers, Raymond S. 1912- ... CANR-10
  Earlier sketch in CA 25-28R
Sayers, Richard Sidney 1908-1989 Obituary ... 128
Sayers, Valerie 1952- ... CANR-61
  Earlier sketch in CA 134
  See also CLC 50
Sayle, Charles Edward 1864-1924 ... DLB 184
Sayles, E(dwin) B(ooth) 1892- ... CAP-2
  Earlier sketch in CA 25-28
Sayles, George O(sborne) 1901-1994 ... CANR-4
  Obituary ... 144
  Earlier sketch in CA 53-56
Sayles, John (Thomas) 1950- ... CANR-41
  Earlier sketch in CA 57-60
  See also CLC 7, 10, 14
  See also DLB 44
Sayles, Leonard Robert 1926- ... CANR-1
  Earlier sketch in CA 1-4R
Sayles, Nettie Leitch Major 1903(?)-1984 Obituary ... 113
Sayles, Ted
  See Sayles, E(dwin) B(ooth)
Saylor, David J(onathan) 1945- ... 89-92
Saylor, Irene 1932- ... 33-36R
Saylor, J(ohn) Galen 1902- ... CANR-9
  Earlier sketch in CA 17-20R
Saylor, Neville 1922- ... 61-64
Saylor, Steven 1956- ... CANR-67
  Earlier sketch in CA 142
Saylor-Marchant, Linda 1963- ... 149
  See also SATA 82
Sayre, Anne 1923-1998 ... 61-64
  Obituary ... 167
Sayre, April Pulley 1966- ... 152
  See also SATA 88
Sayre, Eleanor Axson 1916- ... 25-28R
Sayre, Gordon M. 1964- ... 168
Sayre, Henry M(arshall) 1948- ... 119
Sayre, J(ohn) Woodrow 1913- ... CANR-5
  Earlier sketch in CA 9-12R
Sayre, Joel 1900-1979 Obituary ... 89-92
Sayre, John L(eslie) 1924- ... 53-56
Sayre, Kenneth Malcolm 1928- ... CANR-3
  Earlier sketch in CA 9-12R
Sayre, Leslie C. 1907- ... CAP-1
  Earlier sketch in CA 11-12
Sayre, Nora ... CANR-55
  Earlier sketch in CA 118
Sayre, Robert F(reeman) 1933- ... 9-12R
Sayre, Wallace S. 1905-1972 Obituary ... 33-36R
Sayres, Alfred Nevin 1893-(?) ... CAP-1
  Earlier sketch in CA 17-18
Sayres, William C(ortlandt) 1927-1993 ... 17-20R
  Obituary ... 140
Sayrs, Henry John 1904- ... 5-8R
Saywell, John T(upper) 1929- ... 13-16R
Sazer, Nina 1949- ... 69-72
  See also SATA 13
Sbarbaro, Camillo 1888-1967 ... DLB 114
Scabrini, Janet 1953- ... SATA 13
Scacco, Anthony M., Jr. 1939- ... 109
Scaduto, Anthony ... 104
Scaduto, Tony
  See Scaduto, Anthony
Scaer, David P(aul) 1936- ... CANR-12
  Earlier sketch in CA 33-36R
Scaglione, Aldo D(omenico) 1925- ... CANR-21
  Earlier sketches in CA 13-16R, CANR-6
Scaglione, Cecil F(rank) 1934- ... 81-84
Scagnetti, Jack 1924- ... CANR-4
  Earlier sketch in CA 49-52
  See also SATA 7
Scala, James 1934- ... 124
Scalapino, Leslie 1947- ... CANR-67
  Earlier sketch in CA 123
  See also DLB 193
Scalapino, Robert A(nthony) 1919- ... CANR-40
  Earlier sketches in CA 1-4R, CANR-2, 18
Scales, Barbara 1926- ... 140
Scales, James Ralph 1919- ... 120
Scales, Junius Irving 1920- ... 126
Scales, Pat(sy) R. 1944- ... 122
Scales-Trent, Judy 1940- ... 158
Scali, John (Alfred) 1918- ... 65-68
Scalia, Antonin 1936- ... 168
Scalia, Toni 1939- ... 133
Scally, M. A.
  See Scally, Sister (Mary) Anthony
Scally, Robert James 1937- ... 61-64
Scally, Sister (Mary) Anthony 1905- ... 110
Scally, Sister Mary Anthony
  See Scally, Sister (Mary) Anthony
Scalzo, Joe 1941- ... 49-52
Scamehorn, H(oward) Lee 1926- ... 69-72
Scamell, Ragnhild 1940- ... 145
  See also SATA 77
Scammell, Michael 1935- ... 156
  See also CLC 34
Scammell, William McConnell 1920- ... CANR-6
  Earlier sketch in CA 5-8R
Scammon, John H(umphrey) 1905- ... 53-56
Scammon, Richard M(ontgomery) 1915- ... 61-64
Scandura, Joseph M(ichael) 1931- ... CANR-5
  Earlier sketch in CA 53-56
Scanlan, James P(atrick) 1927- ... 9-12R
Scanlan, Michael 1931- ... CANR-23
  Earlier sketches in CA 57-60, CANR-7
Scanlan, Patrick F. 1895(?)-1983 Obituary ... 109
Scanlan, Thomas J. 1934- ... 114

Scanlon, David G. 1921-1990 .... 13-16R
Obituary 132
Scanlon, James Edward 1940- 125
Scanlon, Kathryn I(da) 1909- CAP-1
Earlier sketch in CA 11-12
Scanlon, Marion Stephany 5-8R
See also SATA 11
Scannell, Francis P. 1915-1988 Obituary 125
Scannell, Frank
See Scannell, Francis P.
Scannell, Vernon 1922- CANR-57
Earlier sketches in CA 5-8R, CANR-8, 24
See also CLC 49
See also DLB 27
See also SATA 59
Scanzoni, John H. 1935- CANR-24
Earlier sketches in CA 21-24R, CANR-9
Scanzoni, Letha Dawson 1935- CANR-14
Earlier sketch in CA 57-60
Scarberry, Alma Sioux 1899-1990 Obituary 131
Scarborough, Alma May C. 1913- 5-8R
Scarborough, Elizabeth (Ann) 1947- CANR-58
Earlier sketch in CA 120
See also SATA 98
Scarborough, John 1940- CANR-15
Earlier sketch in CA 41-44R
Scarborough, Ruth 1904- 115
Scarborough, Vernon L(ee) 1950- 139
Scarborough, William Kauffman 1933- 17-20R
Scarbrough, George (Addison) 1915- CANR-38
Earlier sketches in CA 77-80, CANR-16
Scardino, Albert (James) 1948- 129
Brief entry 119
Scaretti, Marjorie (?)-1982 Obituary 107
Scarf, Maggi
See Scarf, Maggie
Scarf, Maggie 1932- CANR-53
Earlier sketches in CA 29-32R, CANR-22
See also SATA 5
Scarfe, Allan (John) 1931- CANR-13
Earlier sketch in CA 25-28R
Scarfe, Francis Harold 1911-1986 Obituary 118
Scarfe, Wendy (Elizabeth) 1933- CANR-13
Earlier sketch in CA 25-28R
Scargall, Jeanne Anna 1928- 93-96
Scargill, (David) Ian 1935- CANR-12
Earlier sketch in CA 61-64
Scariano, Margaret M. 1924- 151
See also SATA 86
Scarisbrick, J(ohn) J(oseph) 1928- CANR-18
Earlier sketch in CA 25-28R
Scarlett, Elizabeth 1961- 150
Scarlett, Roger
See Page, Evelyn
Scarlett, Susan
See Streatfeild, (Mary) Noel
Scarne, John 1903-1985 159
Obituary 116
Scarpitti, Frank R(oland) 1936- CANR-14
Earlier sketch in CA 41-44R
Scarr, Dee 1948- 122
Scarr, Deryck (Antony) 1939- 132
Scarr(-Salapatek), Sandra (Wood) 1936- 126
Scarrott, Michael
See Fisher, A(rthur) Stanley T(heodore)
Scarrow, Howard A(lbert) 1928- 110
Scarry, Elaine (Margaret) 1946- 137
Scarry, Huck
See Scarry, Richard McClure, Jr.
Scarry, Patricia (Murphy) 1924- 17-20R
See also SATA 2
Scarry, Patsy
See Scarry, Patricia (Murphy)
Scarry, Richard (McClure) 1919-1994 .... CANR-39
Obituary 145
Earlier sketches in CA 17-20R, CANR-18
See also CLR 3, 41
See also DLB 61
See also MAICYA
See also SATA 2, 35, 75
See also SATA-Obit 90
Scarry, Richard McClure, Jr. 1953- 130
See also SATA 35
Scavullo, Francesco 1929- CANR-43
Earlier sketch in CA 102
Schaaf, C(arl) Hart 1912- 5-8R
Schaaf, Martha Eckert 1911- CANR-1
Earlier sketch in CA 1-4R
Schaaf, Peter 1942- 106
Schaafsma, David 1953- 149
Schaafsma, Polly 1935- 57-60
Schaal, John H. 1908- 73-76
Schaap, Dick
See Schaap, Richard J(ay)
Schaap, James C(alvin) 1948- CANR-41
Earlier sketch in CA 118
Schaap, Richard J(ay) 1934- CANR-5
Earlier sketch in CA 9-12R
Schaar, John H(omer) 1928- CANR-31
Earlier sketch in CA 1-4R
Schaarwaechter, Georg 1929- 25-28R
Schabert, Kyrill S. 1909(?)-1983 Obituary 109
Schach, Paul 1915- 142
Schachner, Judith Byron 1951- .... SATA 88
Schachner, Nathan(iel) 1895-1955 156
Brief entry 120
Schacht, Al(exander) 1894(?)-1984 Obituary 113
Schacht, Hjalmar (Horace Greeley)
1877-1970 Obituary 113
Schacht, Richard (Lawrence) 1941- CANR-31
Earlier sketch in CA 29-32R
Schachtel, Ernest G(eorge) 1903-1975 .... 37-40R
Schachtel, Hyman Judah 1907- 49-52
Schachtel, Roger (Bernard) 1949- 106
See also SATA 38
Schachter, Gustav 1926- 17-20R
Schachter, Michael 1941- 102
Schachter, Oscar 1915- 65-68
Schachter, Stanley 1922-1997 .... 37-40R
Obituary 159
Schachterle, Nancy (Lange) 1925- 101
Schachtman, Max 1903-1972 Obituary 37-40R
Schack, William 1898-1988 Obituary 128
Schackne, Stewart 1905-1975 Obituary 61-64
Schad, Jasper G(ripper) 1932- 110
Schad, Wilhelm
See Reichert, Herbert W(illiam)
Schaechter, Elio
See Schaechter, Moselio
Schaechter, Mordkhe 1927- 41-44R
Schaechter, Moselio 1928- 164
Schaedel, Richard P. 1920- 45-48
Schaef, Anne Wilson 1934- 118
Schaefer, Charles E. 1933- 37-40R
Schaefer, Claude 1913- 33-36R
Schaefer, Claudia 1949- 162
Schaefer, Frank 1936- CANR-10
Earlier sketch in CA 65-68
Schaefer, Jack (Warner) 1907-1991 .... CANR-64
Obituary 133
Earlier sketches in CAP-1, CA 19-20R, CANR-15
See also SATA 3, 66
See also SATA-Obit 65
Schaefer, John 1958- 126
Schaefer, John H(arrison) 1937- 57-60
Schaefer, Josephine O'Brien 1929- 37-40R
Schaefer, Leah Cahan 1920- 49-52
Schaefer, Lola M. 1950- 155
See also SATA 91
Schaefer, Nicola Caroline 1939- 104
Schaefer, Ted 1939- 77-80
Schaefer, Vincent J(oseph) 1906-1993 .... CANR-46
Obituary 142
Earlier sketch in CA 120
Schaefer, Walter Erich 1901-1982(?) Obituary 106
Schaefer, William D. 1928- 134
Schaeffer, Albrecht 1885-1950 .... DLB 66
Schaeffer, Claude Frederic Armand
1898-1982 Obituary 108
Schaeffer, Edith (Seville) 1914- 77-80
Schaeffer, Elizabeth 1939- 45-48
Schaeffer, Francis A(ugust) 1912-1984 77-80
Obituary 112
Schaeffer, Frank 1952- 140
Schaeffer, K(laus) H(eymann) 1921- 61-64
Schaeffer, Mark 1956- 140
Schaeffer, Mead 1898- .... SATA 21
Schaeffer, Neil 1940- 107
Schaeffer, Norma 1924-1985 119
Schaeffer, Susan Fromberg 1941- CANR-65
Earlier sketches in CA 49-52, CANR-18
See also CLC 6, 11, 22
See also DLB 28
See also MTCW 1
See also SATA 22
Schaeffer-Forrer, Claude F. A.
See Schaeffer, Claude Frederic Armand
Schaeling, Marianne
See Amft, M(arian) J(anet)
Schaeper, Thomas J(erome) 1948- 109
Schaeren, Beatrix 1941- 29-32R
Schaerf, Carlo 1935- 133
Schaetzel, J(oseph) Robert 1917- 65-68
Schaetzel, Wendy 1950- 136
Schafer, Charles (Louis) 1916- 61-64
Schafer, Edward Hetzel 1913- CANR-1
Earlier sketch in CA 1-4R
Schafer, Elisabeth 1945- 166
Schafer, Grant C. 1926- 21-24R
Schafer, R(aymond) Murray 1933- 77-80
Schafer, Robert 1942- 108
Schafer, Stephen 1911-1976 .... 37-40R
Schafer, Violet (Christine) 1910- 61-64
Schafer, William J. 1937- 49-52
Schaff, Adam 1913- CANR-12
Earlier sketch in CA 25-28R
Schaff, David 1943- 33-36R
Schaff, Philip 1819-1893 .... DLBD 13
Schaffer, (Benjamin) Bernard
1925-1984 Obituary 113
Schaffer, Daniel 1950- 114
Schaffer, Frank 1910- 103
Schaffer, Jeff(rey P.) 1943- CANR-22
Earlier sketch in CA 105
Schaffer, Lewis A(dam) 1934- 101
Schaffer, Marion 1931- 111
Schaffer, Ulrich 1942- CANR-31
Earlier sketch in CA 69-72
Schaffner, Bradley L(ewis) 1959- 152
Schaffner, Cynthia V. A. 1947- 121
Schaffner, Kenneth 1939- 45-48
Schaffner, Nicholas 1953-1991 .... CANR-15
Obituary 135
Earlier sketch in CA 85-88
Schaffner, Val(entine) 1951- 107
Schaflander, Gerald M(aurice) 1920- 37-40R
Schagrin, Morton L(ouis) 1930- 25-28R
Schaie, K(laus) Warner 1928- CANR-34
Earlier sketches in CA 41-44R, CANR-15
Schakne, Robert 1926-1989 65-68
Obituary 129
Schakovskoy, Zinaida 1908- CANR-8
Earlier sketch in CA 17-20R
Schaldenbrand, Mary 1922- 49-52
Schaleben, Arville Orman 1907- CANR-1
Earlier sketch in CA 1-4R
Schalk, Adolph F(rancis) 1923- 33-36R
Schalk, David L(ouis) 1936- 89-92
Schall, James V(incent) 1928- CANR-42
Earlier sketches in CA 9-12R, CANR-6, 20
Schaller, George B(eals) 1933- CANR-9
Earlier sketch in CA 5-8R
See also SATA 30
Schaller, Lyle E(dwin) 1923- 131
Schaller, Michael 1947- 126
Brief entry 110
Schaller, Susan 1957(?)- 145
Schally, Andrew V(ictor) 1926- 156
Schalm, Bernard 1928-1974 .... 1-4R
Obituary 103
Scham, Alan (Myron) 1937- 29-32R
Schama, Simon (Michael) 1945- CANR-39
Earlier sketch in CA 105
See also BEST 89:4
Schanberg, Sydney H(illel) 1934- 69-72
Schanche, Don(ald) A(rthur) 1926-1994 .... CANR-6
Obituary 147
Earlier sketch in CA 5-8R
Schandler, Herbert Y(ale) 1928- 69-72
Schang, Frederick C. 1893- CANR-13
Earlier sketch in CA 33-36R
Schank, Roger C(arl) 1946- 132
Schanke, Robert A(nders) 1940- 141
Schanz, John P(hilip) 1924- 107
Schanzer, George O(swald) 1914- 41-44R
Schanzer, Ros
See Schanzer, Rosalyn
Schanzer, Rosalyn 1942- .... SATA 77
Schanzer, Roz
See Schanzer, Rosalyn
Schaper, Edzard 1908-1984 .... DLB 69
Schapiro, Barbara 1952- 145
Schapiro, J(acob) Salwyn 1879-1973 .... CANR-5
Obituary 45-48
Earlier sketch in CA 5-8R
Schapiro, Leonard (Bertram) 1908-1983 .... CANR-13
Obituary 111
Earlier sketch in CA 65-68
Schapiro, Meyer 1904-1996 97-100
Obituary 151
Schapper, Beatrice Aronson 1906-1974 .... 9-12R
Obituary 45-48
Schappes, Morris U(rman) 1907- 49-52
Schapsmeier, Edward L(ewis) 1927- 29-32R
Schapsmeier, Frederick H(erman) 1927- 29-32R
Schara, Ron 1942- 69-72
Scharbach, (John) Alexander 1909- 114
Scharbach, J. Alexander
See Scharbach, (John) Alexander
Scharf, Bertram 1931- 53-56
Scharf, J. Thomas 1843-1898 .... DLB 47
Scharfenberg, Doris 1925- 108
Scharff, Edward E. 1946- 123
Scharfstein, Ben-Ami 1919- 101
Scharfstein, Zevi 1884-1972 Obituary 37-40R
Scharine, Richard (G.) 1938- Brief entry 118
Scharine, Richard G. 1938- 123
Scharlatt, Hal 1936(?)-1974 Obituary 104
Scharlemann, Dorothy Hoyer 1912- 65-68
Scharlemann, Martin H(enry) 1910- 13-16R
Scharlemann, Robert Paul 1929- 9-12R
Scharnhorst, Gary (Francis) 1950- 119
Scharper, Phillip (Jenkins) 1919-1985 73-76
Obituary 116
Scharrer, Berta (Vogel) 1906- 158
Schary, Dore 1905-1980 .... CANR-1
Obituary 101
Earlier sketch in CA 1-4R
Schary, Jill
See Robinson, Jill
Schatell, Brian 124
See also SATA 66
See also SATA-Brief 47
Schatkin, Margaret 1944- 118
Schatkin, Sidney B. 1903- 25-28R
Schatt, Stanley 1943- CANR-26
Earlier sketch in CA 69-72
Schatten, Fritz (Max Robert) 1930- 13-16R
Schatten, Robert 1911-1977 Obituary 73-76
Schatz, Mark N(orton) 1929- 113
Schatz, Ronald W. 1949- 125
Schatz, Sayre P(erry) 1922- 41-44R
Schatzki, Walter 1899- .... SATA-Brief 31
Schau, Michael 1945- 85-88
Schaub, Marilyn McNamara 1928- 17-20R
Schaub, Mary H(unter) 1943- 140
Schaub, Thomas Hill 1947- 105
Schauensee, Rodolphe Meyer de
See De Schauensee, Rodolphe Meyer
Schauer, Frederick Franklin 1946- CANR-42
Earlier sketch in CA 112
Schauf, George Edward 1925- 41-44R
Schaufele, William E., Jr. 1923- 111
Schawlow, Arthur L(eonard) 1921- 157
Scheader, Catherine 1932- 85-88
Schealer, John M(ilton) 1920- 5-8R
Schechner, Richard 1934- CANR-17
Earlier sketches in CA 45-48, CANR-1
Schechter, A(bel) A(lan) 1907-1989 Obituary 128
Schechter, Alan H(enry) 1936- 9-12R
Schechter, Betty (Goodstein) 1921- 5-8R
See also SATA 5
Schechter, Harold 1948- 108
Schechter, Ruth Lisa 1927- CANR-49
Earlier sketch in CA 33-36R
Schechter, William 1934- 21-24R
Schechtman, Joseph B. 1891-1970 .... CANR-3
Earlier sketch in CA 1-4R
Schecter, Darrow 1961- 143
Schecter, Ellen 1944- .... SATA 85
Schecter, Jerrold L. 1932- CANR-49
Earlier sketch in CA 21-24R
Schede, Paul Melissus 1539-1602 .... DLB 179
Scheel, J(oergen) D(itlev) 1918- 9-12R
Scheele, Adele M. 1938- CANR-18
Earlier sketch in CA 97-100
Scheele, Carl H(arry) 1928- 85-88
Scheer, George F(abian) 1917-1996 .... 13-16R
Obituary 151
Scheer, Julian (Weisel) 1926- 49-52
See also SATA 8
Scheer, Robert 1936- 106
Scheer, Wilbert E. 1909- CANR-17
Earlier sketch in CA 25-28R
Scheff, Thomas Joel 1929- 105
Scheffel, Joseph Viktor von 1826-1886 .... DLB 129
Scheffer, Nathalie P. 1890(?)-1981 Obituary 105
Scheffer, Victor B(lanchard) 1906- CANR-11
Earlier sketch in CA 29-32R
See also SATA 6
Scheffler, Harold W(alter) 1932- 17-20R
Scheffler, Israel 1923- CANR-1
Earlier sketch in CA 1-4R
Scheffler, Johann 1624-1677 .... DLB 164
Scheffler, Ursel 1938- 149
See also SATA 81
Scheffrin-Falk, Gladys 1928- .... SATA 76
Scheflen, Albert E. 1920-1980 .... CANR-3
Obituary 101
Earlier sketch in CA 45-48
Schefter, Jim 1940- 89-92
Scheibe, Karl E(dward) 1937- CANR-11
Earlier sketch in CA 29-32R
Scheiber, Harry N(oel) 1935- CANR-1
Earlier sketch in CA 1-4R
Scheiber, Jane L(ang) 1937- 93-96
Scheibla, Shirley 1919- 41-44R
Scheick, William J(oseph) 1941- CANR-38
Earlier sketches in CA 49-52, CANR-1, 17
Scheid, Francis J(ames) 1920- 17-20R
Scheidl, Gerda Marie 1913- 152
See also SATA 85
Scheidler, Joseph M. 1927- 122
Scheier, Ivan Henry 1926- CANR-7
Earlier sketch in CA 5-8R
Scheier, Libby 1946- 136
Scheier, Michael 1943- CANR-36
Earlier sketch in CA 115
See also SATA 40
See also SATA-Brief 36
Scheimann, Eugene 1897-1993 .... 33-36R
Obituary 140
Schein, Clarence J(acob) 1918- 65-68
Schein, James Arns 1920(?)-1983 Obituary 110
Schein, Jerome D(aniel) 1923- 118
Schein, Lorraine 1953- 149
Schein, Muriel
See Dimen, Muriel
Scheindlin, Raymond P. 1940- 146
Scheiner, Seth M(ordecai) 1933- 17-20R
Scheinfeld, Aaron 1899-1970 .... CAP-2
Earlier sketch in CA 29-32
Scheinfeld, Amram 1897-1979 .... 17-20R
Obituary 89-92
Scheingold, Stuart A(llen) 1931- 53-56
Scheleen, Joseph C(arl) 1904-1985 Obituary 116
Schell, Bunny
See Schell, Rolfe F(inch)
Schell, Edgar T(homas) 1931- 45-48
Schell, Herbert S(amuel) 1899- CANR-21
Earlier sketch in CA 1-4R
Schell, Jim 1936- 142
Schell, Jonathan 1943- CANR-12
Earlier sketch in CA 73-76
See also CLC 35
Schell, Maximilian 1930- Brief entry 116
Schell, Mildred 1922- 113
See also SATA 41
Schell, Orville H. 1940- 25-28R
See also SATA 10
Schell, Rolfe F(inch) 1916- CANR-7
Earlier sketch in CA 57-60
Schellenberg, Helene Chambers 13-16R
Schellenberg, James A. 1932- 37-40R
Schellenberg, Theodore R. 1903-(?) CAP-1
Earlier sketch in CA 17-18
Scheller, Melanie 1953- .... SATA 77
Schellie, Don 1932- 101
See also SATA 29
Schelling, Andrew 1953- 158
Schelling, Friedrich Wilhelm Joseph von
1775-1854 .... DLB 90
Schelling, Thomas Crombie 1921- CANR-49
Earlier sketch in CA 1-4R
Schelly, William 1951- 114
Schembechler, Bo 1929- 139
Schemering, (Crien) Christopher 1956- 123
Schemm, Mildred Walker 1905- CANR-1
Earlier sketch in CA 1-4R
See also SATA 21
Schemmer, Benjamin Franklin 1932- 61-64
Schemmer, Kenneth E(dwin) 1936- 110
Schenck, Anita A(llen) 1909- 89-92
Schenck, Hilbert (van Nydeck) 1926- 166
Schenck, Janet Daniels
1883(?)-1976 Obituary 69-72
Schendel, Arthur van 1874-1946 .... TCLC 56
Schendel, Dan 1934- 148
Schendler, Sylvan 1925- 25-28R
Schenk, George (Walden) 1929- 139
Schenk, H(ans) G(eorg) 1912- 21-24R
Schenkar, Joan 1946- 133
Schenken, Howard 1904(?)-1979 93-96
Obituary 85-88
Schenker, Alexander M(arian) 1924- 33-36R
Schenker, Dona 1947- 135
See also SATA 68
Schenker, Eric 1931- 37-40R
Schenkkan, Robert (Frederic, Jr.) 1953- 132
Scheper, Nancy
See Scheper-Hughes, Nancy
Scheper-Hughes, Nancy 1944- 89-92

Schepers, Maurice B. 1928- ... 13-16R
Scheps, Clarence 1915- ... 33-36R
Scher, Helene L(enz) 1935- ... 123
Scher, Helene Lenz 1935- Brief entry ... 118
Scher, Les 1946- ... 101
Scher, Paula 1948- ... 115
See also SATA 47
Scher, Steven Paul 1936- ... CANR-3
Earlier sketch in CA 49-52
Schere, Monroe 1913- ... 85-88
Scherer, F(rederic) M(ichael) 1932- ... CANR-12
Earlier sketch in CA 29-32R
Scherer, Frances Schlosser 1912- ... 69-72
Scherer, Jack F(ranklin) 1939- ... 69-72
Scherer, Jacqueline Rita 1931- ... 53-56
Scherer, Jean-Marie Maurice 1920- ... 110
See also Rohmer, Eric
Scherer, Joanna Cohan 1942- ... 107
Scherer, Klaus R(ainer) 1943- ... 101
Scherer, Lester B(uryl) 1931- ... 132
Scherer, Migael 1947- ... 144
Scherer, Paul (Ehrman) 1892-1969 ... 5-8R
Obituary ... 134
Scherer, Priscilla 1948- ... 119
Scherer, Raymond Lewis 1919- ... 104
Scherer, Wilhelm 1841-1886 ... DLB 129
Scherer, William F(rederick) 1939- ... 41-44R
Scherf, Kathleen D. 1960- ... 142
Scherf, Margaret 1908-1979 ... CANR-62
Earlier sketches in CA 5-8R, CANR-6
See also SATA 10
Scherle, Victor 1935- ... 25-28R
Scherman, Bernadine Kielty
1890(?)-1973 Obituary ... 45-48
Scherman, David E(dward) 1916-1997 ... 102
Obituary ... 158
Scherman, Katharine 1915- ... CANR-27
Earlier sketches in CA 5-8R, CANR-11
Scherman, Thomas K(ielty)
1917-1979 Obituary ... 106
Schermbrucker, Bill
See Schermbrucker, William (Gerald)
Schermbrucker, William (Gerald) 1938- ... 155
Schermer, Judith (Denise) 1941- ... 106
See also SATA 30
Schermerhorn, Richard A(lonzo) 1903- ... 37-40R
Scherr, George Harry 1920- ... 114
Scherr, Max 1916(?)-1981 Obituary ... 105
Schertenleib, Charles 1905-1972 Obituary ... 37-40R
Schertle, Alice 1941- ... CANR-59
Earlier sketches in CA 107, CANR-23
See also SATA 36, 90
Scherzer, Carl John 1901- ... 1-4R
Scheub, Harold 1931- ... 61-64
Scheuer, Joseph F(rancis)
1918-1975 Obituary ... 61-64
Scheuer, Philip K(atz) 1902-1985 Obituary ... 115
Scheuerle, William H(oward) 1930- ... 33-36R
Scheuerman, Richard D(ean) 1951- ... CANR-27
Earlier sketch in CA 57-60
Scheuring, Lyn 1937- ... 73-76
Scheuring, Tom 1942- ... 73-76
Schevill, James (Erwin) 1920- ... 5-8R
See also CAAS 12
See also CLC 7
Schevill, Maqrgot Blum 1931- ... 150
Schevitz, Jeffrey M(orrie) 1941- ... 65-68
Scheyer, Ernst 1900- ... 13-16R
Schiaparelli, Elsa 1890-1973 Obituary ... 113
Schiappa, Barbara D(ublin) 1943- ... 109
Schiappa, (Anthony) Edward (Jr.) 1954- ... 141
Schiavone, Giuseppe 1938- ... 146
Schiavone, James 1933- ... CANR-9
Earlier sketch in CA 5-8R
Schick, Alice 1946- ... CANR-15
Earlier sketch in CA 81-84
See also SATA 27
Schick, Eleanor 1942- ... CANR-41
Earlier sketches in CA 49-52, CANR-4, 19
See also SATA 9, 82
Schick, Frank L(eopold) 1918- ... 132
Schick, George B(aldwin Powell) 1903- ... 41-44R
Schick, Joel 1945- ... 107
See also SATA 31
See also SATA-Brief 30
Schick, Lawrence 1955- ... 139
Schick, Renee 1919- ... 149
Schickel, Julia Whedon 1936- ... 49-52
Schickel, Richard (Warren) 1933- ... CANR-34
Earlier sketches in CA 1-4R, CANR-1
See also AITN 1
Schickele, Peter 1935- ... 85-88
Schickele, Rene 1883-1940 ... DLB 66
Schiddel, Edmund 1909-1982 ... 5-8R
Obituary ... 107
Schiefelbusch, Richard L. 1918- ... CANR-11
Earlier sketch in CA 25-28R
Schieffer, Bob 1937- ... 69-72
Schields, Gretchen 1948- ... SATA 75
Schier, Donald (Stephen) 1914- ... 29-32R
Schier, Ernest L. 1918- ... 77-80
Schier, Flint 1954(?)-1988 Obituary ... 126
Schiff, Dorothy 1903-1989 ... 121
Obituary ... 129
Brief entry ... 114
Interview in ... 121
See also DLB 127
Schiff, Harold (Irvin) 1923- ... 89-92
Schiff, Irwin A(llan) 1928- ... CANR-25
Earlier sketch in CA 65-68
Schiff, Isaac 1944- ... 153
Schiff, Jacqui Lee 1934- ... 37-40R
Schiff, James A(ndrew) 1958- ... 143
Schiff, Ken(neth Roy) 1942- ... 49-52
See also SATA 7
Schiff, Michael 1915- ... 13-16R
Schiff, Ze'ev 1932- ... 144
Schiffer, Irvine 1917- Brief entry ... 114
Schiffer, Michael 1948- ... 106
Schiffer, Michael B(rian) 1947- ... CANR-52
Earlier sketches in CA 110, CANR-27
Schifferes, Justus J(ulius) 1907-1997 ... CANR-5
Obituary ... 156
Earlier sketch in CA 5-8R
Schiffhorst, Gerald J. 1940- ... CANR-38
Earlier sketch in CA 17-20R
Schiffman, Jack 1921- ... 49-52
Schiffman, Joseph Harris 1914- ... 17-20R
Schiffrin, Harold Z. 1922- ... 29-32R
Schiler, Marc (Eugene) 1951- ... 106
Schillaci, Anthony
See Schillaci, Peter Paul
Schillaci, Peter Paul 1929- ... 29-32R
Schillebeeckx, Edward (Cornelis Florentius Alfons)
1914- ... 127
Brief entry ... 111
Schiller, A. Arthur 1902-1977 ... CANR-28
Obituary ... 73-76
Earlier sketch in CA 37-40R
Schiller, Andrew 1919- ... 41-44R
See also SATA 21
Schiller, Barbara (Heyman) 1928- ... 17-20R
See also SATA 21
Schiller, Bob
See Schiller, Robert Achille
Schiller, Bradley R(obert) 1943- ... 57-60
Schiller, Craig 1951- ... 81-84
Schiller, Dan(iel T.) 1951- ... 131
Schiller, Dorothea E. 1898(?)-1987 Obituary ... 123
Schiller, Friedrich 1759-1805 ... DAM DRAM
See also DLB 94
Schiller, Greta 1954- ... 158
Schiller, Herbert I(rving) 1919- ... 29-32R
Schiller, Jerome P(aul) 1934- ... 25-28R
Schiller, JoAnn 1949- ... 140
Schiller, Justin G. 1943- Brief entry ... 110
See also SATA-Brief 31
Schiller, Lawrence 1936- ... 163
Schiller, Lee Virginia Chambers
See Chambers-Schiller, Lee Virginia
Schiller, Mayer
See Schiller, Craig
Schiller, Robert Achille 1918- ... 123
Brief entry ... 118
Interview in ... 123
Schiller, Rose Leiman
See Goldemberg, Rose Leiman
Schilling, Betty 1925- ... 106
Schilling, S. Paul 1904- ... CANR-16
Earlier sketches in CA 1-4R, CANR-1
Schilling, Warner R(oller) 1925- Brief entry ... 112
Schilpp, Madelon Golden ... 117
Schilpp, Paul A(rthur) 1897-1993 ... CANR-19
Obituary ... 142
Earlier sketches in CA 1-4R, CANR-4
Schilz, Thomas F. 1950- ... 125
Schimel, John L(ouis) 1916- ... 25-28R
Schimmel, Annemarie (Brigitte) 1922- ... 132
Brief entry ... 120
Schimmel, Herbert D(avid) 1927- ... 117
Schimmel, Solomon 1941- ... 139
Schimmels, Cliff 1937- ... 115
Schimpf, Ann L.
See Linnea, Ann
Schimpff, Jill Wagner 1945- ... 135
Schinagl, Mary S(onora) 1914- ... 17-20R
Schindel, John 1955- ... SATA 77
Schindeler, Fred(erick) Fernand 1934- ... 41-44R
Schindelman, Joseph 1923- ... SATA 67
See also SATA-Brief 32
Schindler, Marvin Samuel 1932- Brief entry ... 106
Schindler, S(teven) D. 1952- ... SATA 75
See also SATA-Brief 50
Schine, Cathleen 1953- ... 149
Schinhan, Jan Philip 1887-1975 ... CAP-2
Obituary ... 61-64
Earlier sketch in CA 23-24
Schinto, Jeanne 1951- ... CANR-69
Earlier sketch in CA 133
See also SATA 93
Schioetz, Aksel 1906-1975 Obituary ... 111
Schiotz, Aksel
See Schioetz, Aksel
Schipf, Robert G(eorge) 1923- ... 61-64
Schipper, Mineke
See Schipper de Leeuw, W(ilhelmina) J(anneke)
J(osepha)
Schipper de Leeuw, W(ilhelmina) J(anneke)
1938- ... 156
Schirmer, Daniel B(oone) 1915- ... 41-44R
Schirmer, Gregory A(lan) 1944- ... 117
Schirmer, Henry W. 1922- ... 107
Schirmer, Jennifer G(ay) 1947- ... 113
Schirmerhorn, Clint
See Riemer, George
Schirokauer, Conrad M(ax) 1929- ... 107
Schisgal, Murray (Joseph) 1926- ... CANR-48
Earlier sketch in CA 21-24R
See also CLC 6
Schisgall, Oscar 1901-1984 ... CANR-9
Obituary ... 112
Earlier sketch in CA 53-56
See also SATA 12
See also SATA-Obit 38
Schivelbusch, Wolfgang 1941- ... CANR-45
Earlier sketch in CA 105
Schjeldahl, Peter 1942- Brief entry ... 113
Schkade, Lawrence L. 1930- ... CANR-7
Earlier sketch in CA 17-20R
Schlabach, Theron F(rederick) 1933- ... 25-28R
Schlabrendorff, Fabian von
See von Schlabrendorff, Fabian
Schlachter, Gail Ann 1943- ... CANR-60
Earlier sketches in CA 77-80, CANR-14, 31
Schlachter, Susan
See Thaler, Susan
Schlaf, Johannes 1862-1941 ... DLB 118
Schlafly, Phyllis 1924- ... CANR-52
Earlier sketches in CA 25-28R, CANR-26
See also AITN 1
See also MTCW 1
Schlain, Bert H(oward) 1898- ... 17-20R
Schlamm, William S(iegmund) 1904-1978 ... 93-96
Obituary ... 81-84
Schlanger, Henry 1918(?)-1984 Obituary ... 113
Schlant, Ernestine 1935- ... 81-84
Schlapbach-Oberhansli, Trudi 1944- ... 21-24R
Schlatter, Richard 1912-1987 ... 21-24R
Obituary ... 123
Schlauch, Margaret 1898-1986 ... CAP-1
Obituary ... 119
Earlier sketch in CA 13-14
Schlayer, Mary Elizabeth 1915-1987 ... 129
Schlebecker, John T(homas) 1923- ... 9-12R
Schleck, Charles A. 1925- ... CANR-6
Earlier sketch in CA 5-8R
Schlee, Ann 1934- ... CANR-29
Earlier sketch in CA 101
See also CLC 35
See also SATA 44
See also SATA-Brief 36
Schlee, Guenther 1951- ... 135
Schlee, Gunther
See Schlee, Guenther
Schlee, Susan
See Baur, Susan
Schlegel, August Wilhelm von 1767-1845 ... DLB 94
Schlegel, Dorothea 1763-1839 ... DLB 90
Schlegel, Dorothy B(adders) 1910- ... 37-40R
Schlegel, Friedrich 1772-1829 ... DLB 90
Schlegel, John Henry 1942- ... 154
Schlegel, Richard 1913- ... 65-68
Schlegel, Stuart A(llen) 1932- ... 61-64
Schlegelmann, V. E.
See Hartz, Fred R.
Schleh, Eugene 1939- ... 137
Schleicher, Charles P. 1907- ... 9-12R
Schleichert, Elizabeth 1945- ... 145
See also SATA 77
Schleier, Curt 1944- ... 89-92
Schleier, Gertrude 1933- ... 1-4R
Schleiermacher, Friedrich 1768-1834 ... DLB 90
Schleifer, James T(homas) 1942- ... 97-100
Schleifer, Ronald 1948- ... CANR-43
Earlier sketch in CA 118
Schlein, Miriam 1926- ... CANR-52
Earlier sketches in CA 1-4R, CANR-2
See also CLR 41
See also SATA 2, 87
Schleiner, Winfried 1938- ... 29-32R
Schlem
See Prevost, Marcel
Schlender, William E(lmer) 1920- ... CANR-14
Earlier sketch in CA 17-20R
Schlenker, Elizabeth D. (Wallace) 1912- ... 17-20R
Schlenther, Boyd (Stanley) 1936- ... 41-44R
Schlepp, Wayne Allen 1931- ... 29-32R
Schlereth, Howard (Hewitt) 1936- ... 57-60
Schlereth, Thomas J(ohn) 1941- ... 97-100
Schlesinger, Alfred Cary 1900- ... CAP-1
Earlier sketch in CA 13-14
Schlesinger, Allen B(rian) 1924- ... 149
Schlesinger, Arthur M(eier), Jr. 1917- ... CANR-58
Earlier sketches in CA 1-4R, CANR-1, 28
Interview in ... CANR-28
See also AITN 1
See also CLC 84
See also DLB 17
See also MTCW 1
See also SATA 61
Schlesinger, Arthur Meier 1888-1965 ... CANR-5
Obituary ... 25-28R
Earlier sketch in CA 5-8R
Schlesinger, Benjamin 1928- ... CANR-46
Earlier sketches in CA 17-20R, CANR-7, 22
Schlesinger, Bruno Walter 1876-1962 ... 116
Obituary ... 111
Schlesinger, Elizabeth Bancroft
1886-1977 Obituary ... 69-72
Schlesinger, Hilde S(tephanie) ... CANR-6
Earlier sketch in CA 53-56
Schlesinger, Joseph A(braham) 1922- ... 61-64
Schlesinger, Lawrence E(rwin) 1921- ... 41-44R
Schlesinger, Leonard A. 1952- ... 126
Schlesinger, Marian Cannon 1912- ... 89-92
Schlesinger, Roger 1943- ... 126
Schlesinger, Stephen C(annon) 1942- ... CANR-28
Earlier sketch in CA 57-60
Schlesinger, Thomas O(tto) 1925- ... 41-44R
Schlessinger, Laura 1947(?)- ... 152
Schlessinger, Philip J. 1914- ... 5-8R
Schleunes, Karl A(lbert) 1937- ... 29-32R
Schley, Jim 1956- ... 118
Schlichting, Harold E(ugene, Jr.) 1926- ... 112
Schlicke, Priscilla 1945- ... 146
Schlimbach, Alice (Paula) 1898- ... CAP-1
Earlier sketch in CA 13-16
Schlink, Basilea
See Schlink, Klara
Schlink, Bernhard 1944- ... 163
Schlink, Frederick John 1891-1995 ... 65-68
Obituary ... 147
Schlink, Klara 1904- ... CANR-49
Earlier sketch in CA 101
Schlink, M. Basilea
See Schlink, Klara
Schlink, Mother Basilea
See Schlink, Klara
Schlissel, Lillian 1930- ... CANR-53
Earlier sketches in CA 25-28R, CANR-13, 29
Schlitzer, Albert Lawrence 1902- ... 1-4R
Schloat, G. Warren, Jr. 1914- ... 21-24R
See also SATA 4
Schlobin, Roger Clark 1944- ... CANR-18
Earlier sketch in CA 102
Schlosberg, H. J.
See May, H(enry) J(ohn)
Schloss, Arthur David
See Waley, Arthur (David)
Schlossberg, Dan 1948- ... CANR-19
Earlier sketch in CA 101
Schlossberg, Edwin (Arthur) 1945- Brief entry ... 112
Schlossberg, Herbert 1935- ... 111
Schlossman, Beryl 1955- ... 124
Schlossman, Steven L(awrence) 1947- ... CANR-16
Earlier sketch in CA 81-84
Schlossstein, Steven 1941- ... 122
Schlueter, June 1942- ... CANR-32
Earlier sketch in CA 101
Schlueter, Paul (George) 1933- ... CANR-32
Earlier sketches in CA 13-16R, CANR-11
Schlumberger, Daniel 1904-1972 Obituary ... 37-40R
Schlumberger, Jean 1877-1968 ... 155
Obituary ... 116
See also DLB 65
Schmacher, Evelyn A(nn) 1919- ... 130
Schmalenbach, Werner 1920- ... CANR-53
Earlier sketches in CA 73-76, CANR-13, 29
Schmalz, Rosemary 1940- ... 148
Schmandt, Henry J. 1918- ... CANR-9
Earlier sketch in CA 5-8R
Schmandt, Jurgen 1929- ... 144
Schmandt, Raymond H(enry, Jr.) 1925- ... 9-12R
Schmandt-Besserat, Denise 1933- ... CANR-42
Earlier sketches in CA 69-72, CANR-20
Schmeck, Harold M(arshall), Jr. 1923- ... 17-20R
Schmeidler, Gertrude Raffel 1912- ... 37-40R
Schmeiser, Douglas Albert 1934- ... CANR-3
Earlier sketch in CA 9-12R
Schmeling, Gareth L(on) 1940- ... 73-76
Schmeling, Marianne 1930- ... 101
Schmeltz, Susan Alton ... 111
Schmeltz, Susan M.
See Schmeltz, Susan Alton
Schmeltz, William Frederick 1924- ... 41-44R
Schmemann, Alexander 1921-1983 ... 117
Obituary ... 111
Schmemann, Serge 1945- ... 136
Schmertz, Herb(ert) 1930- ... 120
Schmid, A. Allan 1935- ... 37-40R
Schmid, Carlo 1896-1979 Obituary ... 97-100
Schmid, Carol L(ouise) 1946- ... 105
Schmid, Claus-Peter 1942- ... 61-64
Schmid, Eduard 1890-1966 Obituary ... 113
See also Edschmid, Kasimir
Schmid, Elenore 1939- ... CANR-21
Earlier sketches in CA 53-56, CANR-5
See also SATA 12, 84
Schmid, John 1926- ... 133
Schmid, Mark J(oseph) 1901-(?) ... CAP-1
Earlier sketch in CA 13-14
Schmid, Walter T(homas) 1946- ... 145
Schmid, Wolfram George 1930- ... 143
Schmiderer, Dorothy 1940- ... 85-88
See also SATA 19
Schmidgall, Gary 1945- ... 77-80
Schmidhauser, John R(ichard) 1922- ... CANR-1
Earlier sketch in CA 45-48
Schmidt, Albert J(ohn) 1925- ... 37-40R
Schmidt, Alice M(ahany) 1925- ... 65-68
Schmidt, Alvin J(ohn) 1932- ... CANR-1
Earlier sketch in CA 45-48
Schmidt, Annie M. G. 1911-1995 ... 135
Obituary ... 152
See also CLR 22
See also SATA 67
See also SATA-Obit 91
Schmidt, Arno (Otto) 1914-1979 ... 128
Obituary ... 109
See also CLC 56
See also DLB 69
Schmidt, Arthur 1943- ... 158
Schmidt, Charles T., Jr. 1934- ... 25-28R
Schmidt, Claire Harman 1957- ... 109
Schmidt, Dana Adams 1915- ... 9-12R
Schmidt, Diane 1953- ... SATA 70
Schmidt, Dolores Barracano 1931- ... 41-44R
Schmidt, Dorothea
See Wender, Dorothea
Schmidt, Elizabeth 1915- ... SATA 15
Schmidt, Emerson Peter 1899-1976 Obituary ... 111
Schmidt, Fred H(artz) 1918- ... 85-88
Schmidt, Frederick G. 1924- ... 49-52
Schmidt, Gary D. 1957- ... 158
See also SATA 93
Schmidt, George P. 1894(?)-1989 Obituary ... 130
Schmidt, Hans 1938- ... 61-64
Schmidt, Helmut Dan 1915- ... 9-12R
Schmidt, Hubert (Glasgow)
1905-1980 Obituary ... 112
Schmidt, J(akob) E(dward) 1906- ... 13-16R
Schmidt, James Norman 1912- ... CANR-1
Earlier sketch in CA 1-4R
See also SATA 21
Schmidt, James W. 1947- ... 121
Schmidt, Jerry A(rthur) 1945- ... CANR-28
Earlier sketch in CA 69-72
Schmidt, Joel (Paul Armand) 1937- ... 130
Schmidt, John 1905-1969 ... CAP-1
Earlier sketch in CA 19-20
Schmidt, Karen Lee 1953- ... SATA 94
Schmidt, Karl H. 1955- ... 168
Schmidt, Karl M. (Jr.) 1917- ... 13-16R

Schmidt, Laura M(arie) 1952- CANR-16
Earlier sketch in CA 65-68
Schmidt, Leigh Eric 1961- 133
Schmidt, Lyle D(arrel) 1933- 61-64
Schmidt, Lynette 1952- SATA 76
Schmidt, Margaret Fox 1925-1979 65-68
Obituary 125
Schmidt, Marlene 133
Schmidt, Michael Jack 1949- 126
Schmidt, Michael Norton 1947- CANR-2
Earlier sketch in CA 49-52
See also DLB 40
Schmidt, Mike
See Schmidt, Michael Jack
Schmidt, Nancy Jeanne 1936- CANR-7
Earlier sketch in CA 57-60
Schmidt, Paul Frederic 1925- CANR-1
Earlier sketch in CA 1-4R
Schmidt, Peggy Jeanne 1951- 109
Schmidt, Rick
See Schmidt, William R(ichard) III
Schmidt, Robert Milton 1930- 5-8R
Schmidt, Royal Jae (Jr.) 1915- 41-44R
Schmidt, Samuel 1950- 141
Schmidt, Sandra
See Oddo, Sandra (Schmidt)
Schmidt, Sarah 1934- 152
Schmidt, Stanley (Albert) 1944- CANR-24
Earlier sketches in CA 61-64, CANR-8
Schmidt, Steven (Thomas) 1927- 33-36R
Schmidt, Warren H(arry) 1920- CANR-1
Earlier sketch in CA 45-48
Schmidt, Werner Felix 1935- 9-12R
Schmidt, Werner H. 1935- 131
Schmidt, William E. 1947- 73-76
Schmidt, William R(ichard) III 1949- 110
Schmidt, Wilson Emerson 1927- 103
Schmidt, Winsor C. Jr. 1949- 156
Schmidtbonn, Wilhelm August 1876-1952 . DLB 118
Schmidt-Nielsen, Knut 1915- 106
Schmiechen, James A. 1940- 126
Schmiechen, Peter 1938- 159
Schmieding, Holger 1958- 144
Schmier, Louis Eugene 1940- 112
Schmit, Patricia Brady
See Brady, Patricia
Schmithals, Walter 1923- CANR-9
Earlier sketch in CA 65-68
Schmitt, Abraham 1927- CANR-17
Earlier sketch in CA 97-100
Schmitt, Albert R(ichard) 1929- 73-76
Schmitt, Bernadotte Everly 1886-1969 1-4R
Obituary 103
Schmitt, Charles 1934(?)-1986 Obituary 119
Schmitt, David (Edward) 1940- 53-56
Schmitt, Gladys 1909-1972 CANR-2
Obituary 37-40R
Earlier sketch in CA 1-4R
Schmitt, Hans A. 1921- CANR-5
Earlier sketch in CA 1-4R
Schmitt, Heinrich 1894-1976 Obituary 115
Schmitt, Karl Michael 1922- 41-44R
Schmitt, Marshall L. 1919- 13-16R
Schmitt, Martin (Ferdinand) 1917-1978 ... CANR-9
Earlier sketch in CA 53-56
Schmitt, Raymond L(ouis) 1936- 93-96
Schmitt, Richard 1927- 118
Schmitter, Dean Morgan 1917- 41-44R
Schmitter, Phillipe Charles 1936- 115
Schmitthoff, Clive M(acmillan) 1903-1990
CANR-18
Obituary 132
Earlier sketches in CA 5-8R, CANR-3
Schmittroth, John (William), Jr. 1949- CANR-19
Earlier sketch in CA 97-100
Schmittroth, John 1924-1988 49-52
Obituary 125
Schmitz, Aron Hector 1861-1928 122
Brief entry 104
See also Svevo, Italo
See also MTCW 1
Schmitz, Carl August 1920-1966 Obituary 116
Schmitz, Cecilia M. 1960- 154
Schmitz, Charles Henry 1904- 5-8R
Schmitz, David F. 1956- 132
Schmitz, Dennis 1937- 29-32R
Schmitz, James H(enry) 1911-1981 CANR-58
Earlier sketch in CA 103
See also DLB 8
Schmitz, Joseph William 1905-1966 5-8R
Schmitz, Michael J. 1934- 21-24R
Schmitz, Robert L(enzen) 1914- 145
Schmitz, Virginia
See Pasley, Virginia Schmitz
Schmoeller, David (Lee) 1947- 144
Schmokel, Wolfe W(illiam) 1933- 9-12R
Schmoller, Hans 1916-1985 Obituary 117
Schmook, Kathy Grizzard 1947- 127
Schmookler, Andrew Bard 1946- 135
Schmuck, Richard A(llen) 1936- 13-16R
Schmucke, Anne
See Strich, Christian
Schmuhl, Robert (Philip) 1948- 135
Schmuller, Aaron 1910- 53-56
Schmurz, Adolph
See Vian, Boris
Schnabel, Billie H(agen)
1944(?)-1980 Obituary 101
Schnabel, Johann Gottfried 1692-c. 1760 . DLB 168
Schnabel, Julian 1951- 156
Schnabel, Truman Gross, Jr. 1919- 105
Schnacke, Dick
See Schnacke, Richard N(ye)
Schnacke, Richard N(ye) 1919- 61-64
Schnackenberg, Gjertrud 1953- Brief entry 116
See also CLC 40
See also DLB 120
Schnackenburg, Rudolf 1914- CANR-45
Earlier sketches in CA 29-32R, CANR-12
Schnall, Maxine (Swartz) 1934- 17-20R
Schnapper, Dominique 1934- 130
Schnarch, David M(orris) 1946- 160
Schnaubelt, Franz Joseph 1914- 65-68
Schneck, Jerome M. 1920- 17-20R
Schneck, Stephen 1933-1996 CANR-10
Obituary 155
Earlier sketch in CA 13-16R
Schneebaum, Tobias 1921- CANR-15
Earlier sketch in CA 29-32R
Schneede, Uwe M(ax) 1939- Brief entry 111
Schneemann, Carolee 1939- 155
Schneewind, Elizabeth Hughes 1940- CANR-2
Earlier sketch in CA 45-48
Schneewind, J(erome) B(orges) 1930- 25-28R
Schneidau, Herbert N. 1935- 29-32R
Schneider, Abram Leopoldovich
See Schneider, Alan (Leo)
Schneider, Alan (Leo) 1917-1984 145
Schneider, Andrew (J.) 1942- 132
Brief entry 127
Interview in 132
Schneider, Anna
See Sequoia, Anna
Schneider, Antonie 1954- SATA 89
Schneider, Ben Ross, Jr. 1920- 37-40R
Schneider, Benjamin 1938- 41-44R
Schneider, Carl D(avid) 1942- 69-72
Schneider, Clement J(oseph) 1927-1972 ... 41-44R
Schneider, Daniel J(ohn) 1927- 61-64
Schneider, David 1918- 114
Schneider, David M(urray) 1918- Brief entry ... 112
Schneider, Deborah Lucas 1943- 168
Schneider, Delwin Byron 1926- 37-40R
Schneider, Dick
See Schneider, Richard H(enry)
Schneider, Duane 1937- 103
Schneider, Elisa
See Kleven, Elisa
Schneider, Elisabeth Wintersteen 1897- CAP-1
Earlier sketch in CA 11-12
Schneider, Elizabeth (Susan) 1943- CANR-36
Earlier sketches in CA 93-96, CANR-16
Schneider, Fred B. 1953- 150
Schneider, Hans J(uergen) 1935- 73-76
Schneider, Harold K(enneth) 1925- 33-36R
Schneider, Herbert Wallace 1892-1984 13-16R
Obituary 114
Schneider, Herman 1905- CANR-16
Earlier sketch in CA 29-32R
See also SATA 7
Schneider, Howie AITN 2
Schneider, Isidor 1896-1977 CAP-1
Obituary 73-76
Earlier sketch in CA 13-14
Schneider, Jo Anne 1959- 149
Schneider, John C(harles) 1945- 102
Schneider, Joyce Anne 1942- 107
Schneider, Karen 1948- 168
Schneider, Kenneth Ray 1927- 49-52
Schneider, Lambert 1900-1970 Obituary 104
Schneider, Laurence Allen 1937- 81-84
Schneider, Laurie
See Adams, Laurie
Schneider, Leo 1916- 5-8R
Schneider, Leonard Alfred 1925-1966 89-92
See also Bruce, Lenny
Schneider, Louis 1915-1979 CANR-13
Earlier sketch in CA 57-60
Schneider, Martina
See Duettmann, Martina (Friederike)
Schneider, Myles J(ay) 1943- 116
Schneider, Myra 1936- CANR-24
Earlier sketch in CA 107
Schneider, Nicholas A. 1930- 25-28R
Schneider, Nina 1913- CANR-15
Earlier sketch in CA 29-32R
See also SATA 2
Schneider, Rex 1937- 122
See also SATA 44
Schneider, Richard H(enry) 1922- 97-100
Schneider, Robert G. 1930- 112
Schneider, Robert T(homas) 1925- 5-8R
Schneider, Robert W. 1933- 13-16R
Schneider, Rolf 1932- 130
Brief entry 112
Schneider, Ronald M(ilton) 1932- 53-56
Schneider, Sara K. 1962- 150
Schneider, Sherrie 1959- 161
Schneider, Stanley D(ale) 1921- 17-20R
Schneider, Stephen H(enry) 1945- CANR-66
Earlier sketches in CA 69-72, CANR-12
Schneider, Steven A. 1952- 120
Schneider, Susan Weidman 1944- 118
Schneider, William, Jr. 1941- CANR-19
Earlier sketch in CA 29-32R
Schneiderman, Beth Kline 97-100
Schneiderman, Harry 1885-1975 Obituary ... 61-64
Schneiderman, L(awrence) J(erome) 1932- ... 57-60
Schneiderman, Stuart (Alan) 1943- CANR-66
Earlier sketch in CA 114
Schneiders, Alexander A(loysius) 1909-1968
CAP-1
Earlier sketch in CA 17-18
Schneier, Edward V(incent), Jr. 1939- 29-32R
Schneir, Miriam 1933- 77-80
Schnell, George A(dam) 1931- CANR-57
Earlier sketches in CA 29-32R, CANR-12, 27
Schnell, R(odolph) L(eslie) 1931- 113
Schnell, William J(acob) 5-8R
Schnelle, Kenneth E(dward) 1914- 21-24R
Schnepper, Jeff A(lan) 1947- CANR-21
Earlier sketch in CA 85-88
Schneps, Maurice 1917- 1-4R
Schnessel, S. Michael 1947- CANR-14
Earlier sketch in CA 73-76
Schneyder, J. F.
See Taylor, (Frank Herbert) Griffin
Schnirel, James R. 1931- 69-72
See also SATA 14
Schnitter, Jane T. 1958- 152
See also SATA 88
Schnitter, Nicholas J. 1927- 148
Schnitzer, Martin C(olby) 1925- 134
Brief entry 110
Schnitzler, Arthur 1862-1931 Brief entry 104
See also DLB 81, 118
See also SSC 15
See also TCLC 4
Schnore, Leo F(rancis) 1927- 17-20R
Schnur, Steven 1952- 140
See also SATA 95
Schnurre, Wolfdietrich 1920-1989 Obituary 129
See also DLB 69
See also SATA-Obit 63
Schob, David Eugene 1941- 61-64
Schoberle, Cecile 1949- SATA 80
Schochet, Gordon J(oel) 1937- 45-48
Schochet, J(acob) Immanuel 1935- CANR-1
Earlier sketch in CA 45-48
Schock, Pauline 1928- 111
See also SATA 45
Schocken, Theodore 1914-1975 Obituary 104
Schodek, Daniel L(ewis) 1941- 127
Schoder, Raymond V(ictor) 1916-1987 CANR-1
Obituary 122
Earlier sketch in CA 1-4R
Schodt, Frederick L(owell) 1950- 132
Schoeck, Richard J(oseph) 1920- CANR-5
Earlier sketch in CA 1-4R
Schoeffler, Oscar E(dmund) 1899-1979 73-76
Obituary 85-88
Schoeman, Karel 1939- 101
Schoemperlen, Diane 1954- CANR-60
Earlier sketch in CA 133
Schoen, Barbara (Taylor) 1924-1993 21-24R
Obituary 142
See also SATA 13
Schoen, Elin 1945- 101
Schoen, Juliet P. 1923- 69-72
Schoenbach, Carrie 1928- 120
Schoenbaum, S(amuel) 1927-1996 CANR-28
Obituary 151
Earlier sketch in CA 107
Schoenbaum, Thomas John 1939- 104
Schoenberg, Arnold 1874-1951 Brief entry 109
See also TCLC 75
Schoenberg, B(ernhardt) Mark 1928- 97-100
Schoenberg, Bernard 1927-1979 CANR-2
Obituary 85-88
Earlier sketch in CA 45-48
Schoenberg, Robert J. 1933- 141
Schoenberg, Ronald 1942- 126
Schoenberg, Wilfred Paul 1915- 9-12R
Schoenberger, Guido L. 1891-1974 Obituary . 53-56
Schoenberger, Nancy 1950- 126
Schoenberger, Walter Smith 1920- 29-32R
Schoenberner, Franz 1892-1970 Obituary 104
Schoenbohm, Wilko B. 1913- 17-20R
Schoenbrod, David 1942- 146
Schoenbrun, Amy
See Glazer, Ellen Sarasohn
Schoenbrun, David (Franz) 1915-1988 CANR-3
Obituary 125
Earlier sketch in CA 49-52
Schoendoerffer, Pierre 1928- Brief entry 111
Schoener, Allon 1926- 144
Schoenewolf, Gerald 1941- 136
Schoenfeld, Clarence Albert 1918- CANR-6
Earlier sketch in CA 1-4R
Schoenfeld, David 1923- CANR-12
Earlier sketch in CA 17-20R
Schoenfeld, Eugene 1935- Brief entry 118
Schoenfeld, Hanns Martin W(alter) 1928- . CANR-6
Earlier sketch in CA 57-60
Schoenfeld, Maxwell Philip 1936- 33-36R
Schoenfield, Allen 1896(?)-1979 Obituary 85-88
Schoenherr, John (Carl) 1935- 136
See also MAICYA
See also SAAS 13
See also SATA 37, 66
Schoenherr, Karl 1867-1943 DLB 118
Schoenherr, Richard Anthony 1935-1996
CANR-21
Obituary 151
Earlier sketch in CA 29-32R
Schoenholtz, Larry 1948- 57-60
Schoenman, Ralph 1935- 25-28R
Schoenstein, Paul 1902-1974 Obituary 89-92
Schoenstein, Ralph 1933- 13-16R
Schoenwald, Richard L. 1927- 17-20R
Schoep, Arthur Paul 1920- 53-56
Schoepfer, Virginia B. 1934- 33-36R
Schoepflin, George A. 1939- 29-32R
Schoeps, Hans-Joachim 1909- Brief entry 106
Schoeps, Karl-Heinz 1935- CANR-50
Earlier sketches in CA 107, CANR-24
Schoer, Lowell A(ugust) 1931- 29-32R
Schoeser, Mary 1950- 133
Schoettle, Lynn 49-52
Schofer, Lawrence 1940- 77-80
Schoffman, Nachum 1930- 137
Schofield, B(rian) B(etham) 1895-1984 21-24R
Obituary 114
Schofield, Carey 1955- 130
Schofield, (Edward) Guy 1902-1990 Obituary 131
Schofield, J(ohn) N(oel) 1899-1986 Obituary 120
Schofield, Jonathan
See Streib, Dan(iel Thomas)
Schofield, Mary Anne 1948- 124
Schofield, Michael 1919- CANR-14
Earlier sketch in CA 41-44R
Schofield, Paul
See Tubb, E(dwin) C(harles)
Schofield, Robert E(dwin) 1923- 162
Schofield, Sandy
See Rusch, Kristine Kathryn
Schofield, Sylvia Anne 1918- CANR-13
Earlier sketch in CA 73-76
Schofield, W(ilfred) B(orden) 1927- 134
Schofield, William 1921- 9-12R
Schofield, William G(reenough) 1909- CANR-2
Earlier sketch in CA 5-8R
Schogt, Henry G(ilius) 1927- 154
Scholastica, Sister Mary
See Jenkins, Marie M(agdalen)
Scholberg, Henry 1921- 77-80
Scholderer, Victor 1880-1971 Obituary 104
See also DLB 201
Scholefield, A. T.
See Scholefield, Alan
Scholefield, Alan 1931- CANR-34
Earlier sketch in CA 97-100
See also SATA 66
Scholefield, Edmund O.
See Butterworth, W(illiam) E(dmund III)
Scholem, Gershom (Gerhard) 1897-1982
CANR-39
Obituary 106
Earlier sketch in CA 45-48
Scholer, David M(ilton) 1938- 101
Scholes, Katherine 1959- 123
Scholes, Marie V(ielmetti) 1916- 29-32R
Scholes, Robert (Edward) 1929- CANR-46
Earlier sketches in CA 9-12R, CANR-14
Scholes, Walter V(inton) 1916-1975 CAP-2
Earlier sketch in CA 29-32
Scholey, Arthur 1932- 93-96
See also SATA 28
Scholl, John 1922- 9-12R
Scholl, Lisette 1945- 89-92
Scholl, Sharon L. 1932- 41-44R
Scholl, William M(athias) 1882-1968 Obituary 113
Scholt, Grayce 1925- 104
Scholz, Albert A(ugust) 1899-(?) CAP-2
Earlier sketch in CA 29-32
Scholz, Carter 1953- 119
Scholz, Jackson Volney 1897-1986 5-8R
Obituary 120
See also SATA-Obit 49
Scholz, William 1916- 5-8R
Schom, Alan (Morris) 1937- CANR-52
Earlier sketch in CA 128
Schomaker, Mary Zimmeth 1928- 108
Schomp, Gerald 1937- 29-32R
Schon, Donald A(lan) 1930- 17-20R
Schon, Isabel 1940- 110
See also HW
Schonberg, Arnold
See Schoenberg, Arnold
Schonberg, Harold C(harles) 1915- 112
Schonberg, Leonard A. 1935- 164
Schonberg, Rosalyn Krokover
1913(?)-1973 Obituary 41-44R
Schonberger, Richard J. 1937- 110
Schonborg, Virginia 1913- 77-80
Schone, Virginia 97-100
See also SATA 22
Schonell, Fred(erick) Joyce 1900-1969 CANR-2
Earlier sketch in CA 1-4R
Schonfeld, William R(ost) 1942- CANR-17
Earlier sketch in CA 37-40R
Schonfield, Hugh J(oseph) 1901-1988 CANR-46
Obituary 124
Earlier sketch in CA 9-12R
Schongut, Emanuel 1936- SATA 52
See also SATA-Brief 36
Schoolcraft, Jane Johnston 1800-1841 ... DLB 175
Schooler, Carmi 1933- 114
Schooler, (Seward) Dean, Jr. 1941- 73-76
Schoolfield, George C(larence) 1925- CANR-6
Earlier sketch in CA 1-4R
Schoolland, Marian M(argaret) 1902- CANR-2
Earlier sketch in CA 5-8R
Schoonhoven, Calvin R(obert) 1931- 21-24R
Schoonmaker, Alan N. 1936- 25-28R
Schoonmaker, Ann 1928- 73-76
Schoonmaker, Frank 1905-1976 Obituary 61-64
Schoonover, Frank (Earle) 1877-1972 106
See also SATA 24
Schoonover, Jason 1946- 129
Schoonover, Lawrence Lovell 1906-1980 . CANR-4
Obituary 97-100
Earlier sketch in CA 1-4R
Schoonover, Melvin E(ugene) 1926- Brief
entry 114
Schoonover, Shirley 1936- 77-80
Schoonover, Thelma I(rene) 1907- 41-44R
Schoonover, Thomas D(avid) 1936- CANR-45
Earlier sketch in CA 120
Schoor, Gene 1921- CANR-29
Earlier sketch in CA 29-32R
See also SATA 3
Schopenhauer, Arthur 1788-1860 DLB 90
Schopenhauer, Johanna 1766-1838 DLB 90
Schopf, J(ames) William 1941- 133
Schopflin, George A.
See Schoepflin, George A.
Schor, Amy 1954- 105
Schor, Juliet B. 1955- 140
Schor, Lynda 1938- 73-76
Schor, Naomi 1943- CANR-16
Earlier sketch in CA 89-92

Schor, Sandra (M.) 1932(?)-1990 Obituary ... 132
See also CLC 65
Schorb, E(dwin) M(arsh) 1940- ... 61-64
Schorer, Mark 1908-1977 ... CANR-7
Obituary ... 73-76
Earlier sketch in CA 5-8R
See also CLC 9
See also DLB 103
Schorr, Alan Edward 1945- ... 85-88
Schorr, Alvin L. 1921- ... CANR-15
Earlier sketch in CA 29-32R
Schorr, Daniel (Louis) 1916- ... 65-68
See also AITN 2
Schorr, Jerry 1934- ... 29-32R
Schorr, Lisbeth B. 1931- ... 136
Schorr, Mark 1953- ... CANR-62
Earlier sketch in CA 122
Schorsch, Ismar 1935- Brief entry ... 115
Schorsch, Laurence 1960- ... 149
Schorske, Carl E(mil) 1915- ... 85-88
Schosberg, Paul A. 1938- ... 13-16R
Schossberger, Emily Maria
1905-1979 Obituary ... 104
Schott, Jeffrey J. 1949- ... 126
Schott, John R(obert) 1936- ... CANR-7
Earlier sketch in CA 57-60
Schott, Penelope Scambly 1942- ... 77-80
Schott, Richard Lockwood 1939- ... 117
Schott, Webster 1927- ... 49-52
Schottelius, Justus Georg 1612-1676 ... DLB 164
Schottenfeld, Barbara ... 134
Schotter, Roni ... 160
Schottland, Charles Irwin 1906-1995 ... 13-16R
Obituary ... 149
Schouler, James 1839-1920 ... DLB 47
Schouvaloff, Alexander 1934- ... 143
Schowalter, John E(rwin) 1936- ... 109
Schoyer, B. Preston 1912(?)-1978 Obituary ... 77-80
Schrader, Constance 1933- ... CANR-18
Earlier sketch in CA 101
Schrader, George A(lfred), Jr. 1917- ... 21-24R
Schrader, Paul (Joseph) 1946- ... CANR-41
Earlier sketch in CA 37-40R
See also CLC 26
See also DLB 44
Schrader, Richard James 1941- ... 85-88
Schrader, Robert F(ay) 1931- ... 119
Schraepler, Hans-Albrecht 1934- ... 157
Schraff, Anne E(laine) 1939- ... CANR-59
Earlier sketches in CA 49-52, CANR-1, 17, 39
See also SATA 27, 92
Schraff, Francis Nicholas 1937- ... 101
Schraffenberger, Nancy 1933- ... CANR-16
Earlier sketch in CA 93-96
Schrag, Adele Frisbie 1921- ... 105
Schrag, Calvin Orville 1928- ... CANR-1
Earlier sketch in CA 1-4R
Schrag, Oswald O. 1916- ... 49-52
Schrag, Peter 1931- ... CANR-8
Earlier sketch in CA 13-16R
Schrag, Philip G(ordon) 1943- ... 102
Schrager, Jeanne Hart 1919- ... 127
Schram, Martin 1942- ... CANR-13
Earlier sketch in CA 69-72
Schram, Stuart R(eynolds) 1924- ... 97-100
Schramm, David N(orman) 1945-1997 ... 135
Obituary ... 163
Schramm, Laurier L. 1954- ... 146
Schramm, Percy Ernst 1894-1970 Obituary ... 104
Schramm, Richard (Howard) 1934- ... 41-44R
Schramm, Sarah Slavin 1942- ... 93-96
Schramm, Wilbur (Lang) 1907-1987 ... CANR-22
Obituary ... 124
Earlier sketch in CA 105
Schrank, Jeffrey 1944- ... 29-32R
Schrank, Joseph 1900-1984 ... CANR-20
Obituary ... 112
Earlier sketch in CA 5-8R
See also SATA-Obit 38
Schreck, Alan (Edward) 1951- ... 124
Schreck, Everett M. 1897- ... CAP-2
Earlier sketch in CA 33-36
Schrecker, John (Ernest) 1937- Brief entry ... 112
Schrecker, Judie 1954- ... 155
See also SATA 90
Schreiber, Daniel 1909-1981 ... CAP-1
Obituary ... 103
Earlier sketch in CA 13-14
Schreiber, Elizabeth Anne (Ferguson) 1947- ... 69-72
See also SATA 13
Schreiber, Flora Rheta 1918-1988 ... CANR-11
Obituary ... 127
Earlier sketch in CA 53-56
Interview in ... CANR-11
See also AITN 1
Schreiber, Georges 1904-1977 Obituary ... 109
See also SATA-Brief 29
Schreiber, Hermann (Otto Ludwig) 1920- ... CANR-36
Earlier sketch in CA 25-28R
Schreiber, Jan 1941- ... 65-68
Schreiber, Jean-Jacques Servan
See Servan-Schreiber, Jean-Jacques
Schreiber, Joseph 1969- ... 147
Schreiber, Le Anne 1945- ... 140
See also BEST 90:2
Schreiber, Mark 1960- ... 116
Schreiber, Michael 1937- ... 116
Schreiber, Ralph W(alter) 1942- ... 69-72
See also SATA 13
Schreiber, Ron 1934- ... 41-44R
Schreiber, Roy E. 1941- ... 142
Schreiber, Ted
See Schreiber, V. Theodore
Schreiber, V. Theodore 1905-1986 ... 124
Schreiber, Vernon R(oy) 1925- ... 61-64
Schreiber-Wicke, Edith 1943- ... 123
Schreider, Frank(lin David) 1924-1994 ... 5-8R
Obituary ... 145
Schreiner, George F(rederic) 1949- ... 117
Schreiner, Lee
See Schreiner, George F(rederic)
Schreiner, Olive (Emilie Albertina) 1855-1920 ... 154
Brief entry ... 105
See also DLB 18, 156, 190
See also TCLC 9
Schreiner, Samuel A(gnew), Jr. 1921- ... CANR-52
Earlier sketches in CA 65-68, CANR-9, 26
See also SATA 70
Schreiner-Mann, Joan 1939- ... 45-48
Schreiter, Rick 1936- ... 21-24R
Schreivogl, Paul A. 1930- ... 25-28R
Schrepfer, Susan R(ita) 1941- ... 117
Schreuder, D(eryck) M(arshall) 1942- ... 120
Schreyer, George M(aurice) 1913- ... 5-8R
Schriber, Mary Suzanne 1938- ... 126
Schrier, Arnold 1925- ... 49-52
Schrier, Nettie Vander
See Vander-Schrier, Nettie
Schrier, William 1900-1973 ... 41-44R
Schrift, Shirley 1922(?)- ... 113
Brief entry ... 110
Schriftgiesser, Karl (John) 1903-1988 ... CAP-1
Obituary ... 126
Earlier sketch in CA 11-12
Schrire, Theodore 1906- ... 21-24R
Schrock, Simon 1938- ... 113
Schroder, Amund A. Schulze 1925- ... CANR-5
Earlier sketch in CA 13-16R
Schroder, John Henry Erle 1895- ... CAP-1
Earlier sketch in CA 13-14
Schroder, Walter K. 1928- ... 149
Schrodinger, Erwin
See Schroedinger, Erwin
Schrodt, Philip A(ndrew) 1951- ... 111
Schroedel, Jean Reith 1951- ... 122
Schroeder, Alan 1961- ... 133
See also SATA 66, 98
Schroeder, Albert H(enry) 1914- ... CANR-14
Earlier sketch in CA 41-44R
Schroeder, Andreas (Peter) 1946- ... CANR-37
Earlier sketches in CA 93-96, CANR-16
See also DLB 53
Schroeder, Barbet 1941- ... 143
Schroeder, Binette
See Nickl, Barbara (Elisabeth)
See also SATA 56
Schroeder, David 1924- ... 21-24R
Schroeder, Eric 1904- ... CAP-1
Earlier sketch in CA 13-14
Schroeder, Fred E(rich) H(arald) 1932- ... 41-44R
Schroeder, Frederick W(illiam) 1896- ... 1-4R
Schroeder, Glenna R.
See Schroeder-Lein, Glenna R(uth)
Schroeder, Henry A(lfred) 1906-1975 ... CAP-2
Earlier sketch in CA 25-28
Schroeder, Joan V(annorsdall) 1951- ... 153
Schroeder, John H(erman) 1943- ... 49-52
Schroeder, Manfred (Robert) 1926- ... 138
Schroeder, Mary 1903- ... 73-76
Schroeder, Oliver Charles, Jr. 1916- ... CANR-30
Earlier sketch in CA 110
Schroeder, Paul Walter 1927- ... 5-8R
Schroeder, Ted 1931(?)-1973 ... SATA-Obit 20
Schroeder, W(illiam) Widick 1928- Brief entry ... 111
Schroeder-Lein, Glenna R(uth) 1951- ... 147
Schroedinger, Erwin 1887-1961 Obituary ... 113
Schroeter, James 1927- ... 21-24R
Schroeter, Louis C(larence) 1929- ... 29-32R
Schroetter, Hilda Noel 1917- ... 29-32R
Schroll, Herman T(heodore III) 1946- ... 33-36R
Schruben, Francis W(illiam) 1918- ... 45-48
Schruth, Peter Elliott 1917-1979 Obituary ... 89-92
Schubart, Christian Friedrich Daniel 1739-1791 DLB 97
Schubart, Mark Allen 1918- ... 105
Schubel, J(erry) R(obert) 1936- ... 126
Schubel, Vernon James ... 152
Schubert, Delwyn George 1919- ... 9-12R
Schubert, Dieter 1947- ... CANR-28
Earlier sketch in CA 111
See also SATA 62, 101
Schubert, Frank N. 1943- ... 154
Schubert, Glendon 1918- ... CANR-44
Earlier sketches in CA 5-8R, CANR-6, 21
Schubert, Gotthilf Heinrich 1780-1860 ... DLB 90
Schubert, Kurt 1923- ... 5-8R
Schubert-Gabrys, Ingrid 1953- ... CANR-28
Earlier sketch in CA 111
See also SATA 62, 101
Schuberth, Christopher J. 1933- ... CANR-18
Earlier sketch in CA 25-28R
Schuchman, Joan 1934- ... 101
Schuck, Peter H. 1940- ... 129
Schudson, Charles B(enjamin) 1950- ... 130
Schudson, Michael 1946- ... CANR-42
Earlier sketches in CA 101, CANR-19
Schuecking, Levin 1814-1883 ... DLB 133
Schueler, Donald G(ustave) 1929- ... 106
Schueler, G(eorge) F(rederick) 1944- ... 154
Schuerer, Ernst 1933- ... CANR-37
Earlier sketches in CA 45-48, CANR-1, 17
Schuessler, Hermann E.
1929(?)-1975 Obituary ... 61-64
Schuessler, Karl F(rederick) 1915- ... 105
Schuett, Stacey 1960- ... SATA 75
Schuettinger, Robert Lindsay 1936- ... 33-36R
Schuetz, John Howard 1933- ... 97-100
Schuetze, Armin William 1917- ... 57-60
Schug, Willis E(rvin) 1924- ... 49-52
Schuh, Dwight R(aymond) 1945- ... 101
Schuh, G(eorge) Edward 1930- ... CANR-30
Earlier sketch in CA 29-32R
Schuker, Stephen Alan 1939- ... 69-72
Schul, Bill D(ean) 1928- ... CANR-8
Earlier sketch in CA 61-64
Schulberg, Budd (Wilson) 1914- ... CANR-19
Earlier sketch in CA 25-28R
See also CLC 7, 48
See also DLB 6, 26, 28
See also DLBY 81
Schulberg, Herbert C(harles) 1934- ... CANR-8
Earlier sketch in CA 61-64
Schulberg, Stuart 1922-1979 Obituary ... 89-92
Schulder, Diane Blossom 1937- ... 37-40R
Schulenberg, David 1955- ... 145
Schuler, Carol Ann 1946- ... 106
Schuler, Edgar A(lbert) 1905- ... CAP-2
Earlier sketch in CA 23-24
Schuler, Stanley Carter 1915- ... CANR-5
Earlier sketch in CA 5-8R
Schulian, John 1945- ... 129
Schulke, Flip Phelps Graeme 1930- ... CANR-22
Earlier sketch in CA 105
See also SATA 57
Schulkind, Eugene (Walter) 1923- ... 97-100
Schull, (John) Joseph 1916-1980 ... CANR-8
Earlier sketch in CA 53-56
Schuller, Gunther 1925- ... CANR-28
Earlier sketch in CA 69-72
Schuller, Robert (Harold) 1926- ... CANR-46
Earlier sketches in CA 9-12R, CANR-14
Schullery, Paul (David) 1948- ... CANR-57
Earlier sketches in CA 111, CANR-30
Schulman, Arnold 1925- ... 103
Schulman, Audrey 1963- ... 146
Schulman, Bob
See Schulman, Robert
Schulman, Grace ... 65-68
Schulman, Helen 1961- ... 128
Schulman, Ivan A(lbert) 1931- ... 131
Schulman, J(oseph) Neil 1953- ... 89-92
Schulman, Janet 1933- ... 101
See also SATA 22
Schulman, L(ester) M(artin) 1934- ... CANR-12
Earlier sketch in CA 33-36R
See also SATA 13
Schulman, Michael D. 1948- ... 137
Schulman, Robert 1916- ... 77-80
Schulman, Rosalind 1914- ... 41-44R
Schulman, Sam 1924- ... 45-48
Schulman, Sarah 1958- ... CANR-72
Earlier sketch in CA 118
Schulman, Tom 1951(?)- ... 133
Schulmerich, Alma 1902(?)-1985 Obituary ... 115
Schulte, Elaine L(ouise) 1934- ... CANR-28
Earlier sketches in CA 73-76, CANR-12
See also SATA 36
Schulte, Henry F(rank) 1924- ... 25-28R
Schulte, Paul C(larence) 1890-1984 Obituary ... 112
Schulte, Rainer ... 21-24R
Schultes, Richard Evans 1915- ... CANR-50
Earlier sketches in CA 108, CANR-25
Schultheis, Rob 1943- ... 111
Schulthess, Emil 1913- ... 65-68
Schults, Raymond L. 1926- ... 105
Schultz, Alfred W. 1920- ... 162
Schultz, Barbara 1923- ... 21-24R
Schultz, Barbara A. ... 117
Schultz, (Reynolds) Bart(on) 1951- ... 142
Schultz, Dodi 1930- ... CANR-36
Earlier sketches in CA 45-48, CANR-1, 16
Schultz, Donald O. 1939- ... CANR-17
Earlier sketch in CA 25-28R
Schultz, Duane P(hilip) 1934- ... 29-32R
Schultz, Ed 1933- ... 45-48
Schultz, Edna Moore 1912- ... 13-16R
Schultz, Edward W(illiam) 1936- ... CANR-1
Earlier sketch in CA 45-48
Schultz, George F(ranklin) 1908- ... CAP-2
Earlier sketch in CA 19-20
Schultz, George J(oseph) 1932- Brief entry ... 109
Schultz, Gerard 1902-1974 Obituary ... 110
Schultz, Gladys Denny 1896(?)-1984 Obituary ... 113
Schultz, Gwendolyn ... 65-68
See also SATA 21
Schultz, Harold John 1923- ... 103
Schultz, Harry D. ... CANR-14
Earlier sketch in CA 21-24R
Schultz, James Willard 1859-1947 Brief entry ... 121
See also YABC 1
Schultz, John (Ludwig) 1932- ... CANR-15
Earlier sketch in CA 41-44R
Schultz, Joseph P(enn) 1928- ... 113
Schultz, Mark 1935- ... 116
Schultz, Mort(on) J(oel) 1930- ... CANR-28
Earlier sketches in CA 73-76, CANR-12
Schultz, Pearle Henriksen 1918- ... CANR-1
Earlier sketch in CA 49-52
See also SATA 21
Schultz, Philip 1945- ... 104
Schultz, Samuel J(acob) 1914- ... CANR-12
Earlier sketch in CA 25-28R
Schultz, Sigrid (Lillian) 1893-1980 Obituary ... 97-100
Schultz, Stanley K(enton) 1938- Brief entry ... 116
Schultz, Terri 1946- ... CANR-10
Earlier sketch in CA 65-68
Schultz, Theodore William 1902-1998 ... 85-88
Obituary ... 165
Schultz, Vernon B(urdette) 1924- ... 9-12R
Schultz, Ward
See Schultz, (Reynolds) Bart(on)
Schultze, Charles L(ouis) 1924- Brief entry ... 114
Schultze, William Andrew 1937- ... 37-40R
Schulz, Ann Tibbitts 1938- ... 116
Schulz, Anne Markham 1938- ... 121
Schulz, Bruno 1892-1942 ... 123
Brief entry ... 115
See also SSC 13
See also TCLC 5, 51
Schulz, Charles M(onroe) 1922- ... CANR-6
Earlier sketch in CA 9-12R
Interview in ... CANR-6
See also CLC 12
See also SATA 10
Schulz, Clare Elmore 1924- ... 13-16R
Schulz, David A. 1933- ... CANR-30
Earlier sketch in CA 29-32R
Schulz, Ernst B(ernhard) 1896- ... 73-76
Schulz, Florence 1908- ... CAP-2
Earlier sketch in CA 21-22
Schulz, James Henry 1936- ... 89-92
Schulz, John E. 1939- ... 29-32R
Schulz, Juergen 1927- ... 41-44R
Schulz, Max F(rederick) 1923- ... 5-8R
Schulz, Phillip Stephen 1946- ... CANR-50
Earlier sketch in CA 123
Schulz-Behrend, George 1913- ... 45-48
Schulze, Dallas ... 164
Schulze, Franz 1927- ... 125
Schulze, Gene 1912- ... 85-88
Schulze, Hertha 1935- ... 122
Schulze, Ingo 1962- ... 168
Schulzinger, Robert D(avid) 1945- ... 61-64
Schumacher, Alvin J. 1928- ... 13-16R
Schumacher, E(rnst) F(riedrich) 1911-1977 ... CANR-34
Obituary ... 73-76
Earlier sketch in CA 81-84
See also CLC 80
Schumacher, Evelyn A(nn) 1919- ... 130
Schumacher, John N(orbert, Jr.) 1927- ... 131
Schumaker, Paul 1946- ... 139
Schumaker, Ward 1943- ... 161
See also SATA 96
Schuman, Ben N. 1923- ... 17-20R
Schuman, David Feller 1942- ... CANR-17
Earlier sketch in CA 97-100
Schuman, Frederick Lewis 1904-1981 ... 45-48
Obituary ... 135
Schuman, Howard 1928- ... 124
Schuman, Michael A. 1953- ... 152
See also SATA 85
Schuman, Patricia Glass 1943- ... CANR-14
Earlier sketch in CA 33-36R
Schumann, Elizabeth Creighton 1907- ... CAP-1
Earlier sketch in CA 11-12
Schumann, Paul L. 1955- ... 112
Schumer, Fran 1953- ... 148
Schumm, Ruth Frances 1921-1988 Obituary ... 125
Schuon, Frithjof 1907- ... CANR-13
Earlier sketch in CA 73-76
Schuon, Karl Albert 1913-1984 ... 13-16R
Obituary ... 114
Schupp, Johann Balthasar 1610-1661 ... DLB 164
Schur, Edwin M(ichael) 1930- ... CANR-7
Earlier sketch in CA 13-16R
Schur, Maxine
See Schur, Maxine Rose
Schur, Maxine Rose 1948- ... 129
See also SATA 53, 98
See also SATA-Brief 49
Schur, Norman W(arren) 1907- ... CANR-37
Earlier sketches in CA 41-44R, CANR-17
Schurer, Ernst
See Schuerer, Ernst
Schurer, Leopold (Sidney) Launitz, Jr.
See Launitz-Schurer, Leopold (Sidney), Jr.
Schurfranz, Vivian 1925- ... 61-64
See also SATA 13
Schurke, Paul 1955- ... 126
Schurmacher, Emile C.
1903(?)-1976 Obituary ... 69-72
Schurman, D(onald) M. 1924- ... 37-40R
Schurr, Cathleen ... 9-12R
Schurz, Carl 1829-1906 ... DLB 23
Schuschnigg, Kurt von
See von Schuschnigg, Kurt
Schusky, Ernest L(ester) 1931- ... CANR-8
Earlier sketch in CA 17-20R
Schuster, George 1873-1972 Obituary ... 37-40R
Schuster, George 1881-1982 Obituary ... 107
Schuster, Louis A. 1916- ... 13-16R
Schuster, Marilyn R. 1943- ... 148
Schuster, Max Lincoln 1897-1970 Obituary ... 29-32R
Schutte, Anne Jacobson 1940- ... 139
Schutte, William Metcalf 1919- ... 5-8R
Schutz, Anton Friedrich Joseph 1894-1977 ... 81-84
Obituary ... 73-76
Schutz, Benjamin Merrill 1949- ... 107
Schutz, John Adolph 1919- ... 5-8R
Schutz, John Howard
See Schuetz, John Howard
Schutz, Susan Polis 1944- ... 105
Schutz, Wallace J. 1908- ... 135
Schutz, Wilhelm Wolfgang 1911- ... 25-28R
Schutz, William C(arl) 1925- ... CANR-10
Earlier sketch in CA 25-28R
Schutze, Gertrude 1917- ... 17-20R
Schutze, Jim 1946- ... 123
Schutzer, A. I. 1922- ... 25-28R
See also SATA 13
Schutzman, Steven 1947- ... 114
Schuyler, David 1950- ... CANR-52
Earlier sketch in CA 126
Schuyler, George Samuel 1895-1977 ... CANR-42
Obituary ... 73-76
Earlier sketch in CA 81-84
See also BW 2
See also DLB 29, 51

Schuyler, James Marcus 1923-1991 101
Obituary 134
Interview in 101
See also CLC 5, 23
See also DAM POET
See also DLB 5, 169
Schuyler, Jane 1943- 65-68
Schuyler, Joseph B(ernard) 1921- 1-4R
Schuyler, Judy
See Eshbach, Lloyd Arthur
Schuyler, Keith C. 1919- CANR-12
Earlier sketch in CA 29-32R
Schuyler, Pamela R. 1948- 106
See also SATA 30
Schuyler, Philippa Duke 1934-1967 .... 5-8R
See also BW 1
Schuyler, Robert Livingston 1883-1966 ..... CAP-1
Earlier sketch in CA 11-12
Schvaneveldt, Jay D. 1937- 103
Schvey, Henry I(van) 1948- 133
Schwab, Arnold T. 1922- 9-12R
Schwab, George 1931- CANR-37
Earlier sketches in CA 45-48, CANR-1, 16
Schwab, James C. 1949- 128
Schwab, Jim
See Schwab, James C.
Schwab, John J. 1923- 85-88
Schwab, Joseph J(ackson) 1909- CANR-5
Earlier sketch in CA 5-8R
Schwab, Paul Josiah 1894-1966 .... 5-8R
Obituary 103
Schwab, Peter 1940- CANR-14
Earlier sketch in CA 41-44R
Schwabacher, Ethel K(remer)
1903-1984 Obituary 114
Schwabe, William
See Cassidy, William L(awrence Robert)
Schwaber, Paul 1936- 13-16R
Schwadron, Abraham A(be)
1925-1987 Obituary 123
Schwager, Raymund 1935- 165
Schwalberg, Carol(yn Ernestine Stein) 1930- . 69-72
Schwaller, John Frederick 1948- 126
Schwamm, Ellen 1934- 122
Schwandt, Stephen (William) 1947- 126
See also SATA 61
Schwantes, Carlos A(rnaldo) 1945- 150
Schwarberg, Guenther 1926- 130
Schwarcz, Vera 1947- 152
Schwark, Mary Beth 1954- .... SATA 51
Schwartau, Winn 1952- 151
Schwartz, Al(bert) 1911(?)-1988 Obituary 125
Schwartz, Alfred 1922- 17-20R
Schwartz, Alvin 1927-1992 .... CANR-49
Obituary 137
Earlier sketches in CA 13-16R, CANR-7, 24
See also CLR 3
See also MAICYA
See also SATA 4, 56
See also SATA-Obit 71
Schwartz, Amy 1954- CANR-57
Earlier sketches in CA 110, CANR-29
Interview in CANR-29
See also CLR 25
See also SAAS 18
See also SATA 47, 83
See also SATA-Brief 41
Schwartz, Anna J(acobson) 1915- 125
Schwartz, Anne Powers 1913- CANR-1
Earlier sketch in CA 1-4R
See also SATA 10
Schwartz, Arthur Nathaniel 1922- CANR-28
Earlier sketches in CA 61-64, CANR-8
Schwartz, Audrey James 1928- 89-92
Schwartz, Barry 1938- 77-80
Schwartz, Barry N. 1942- 33-36R
Schwartz, Benjamin I. 1916- 13-16R
Schwartz, Bernard 1923-1997 Obituary 163
Brief entry 117
Schwartz, Bernard (Sherman) 1945- 106
Schwartz, Bertie G. 1901(?)-1976 Obituary ... 69-72
Schwartz, Betty 1927- 93-96
Schwartz, Carol 1954- .... SATA 77
Schwartz, Charles 73-76
Schwartz, Charles W(alsh) 1914- 13-16R
See also SATA 8
Schwartz, Cheryl (A.) 1965- 154
Schwartz, Daniel (Bennet) 1929- .... SATA-Brief 29
Schwartz, David (E.) 1916-1989 Obituary 130
Schwartz, David B. 1948- 165
Schwartz, David C. 1939- 37-40R
Schwartz, David J(oseph), Jr. 1927- CANR-13
Earlier sketch in CA 17-20R
Schwartz, David M(artin) 1951- 118
See also SATA 59
Schwartz, Delmore (David) 1913-1966 ... CANR-35
Obituary 25-28R
Earlier sketches in CAP-2, CA 17-18
See also CLC 2, 4, 10, 45, 87
See also DLB 28, 48
See also MTCW 1
See also PC 8
Schwartz, Donald E(dward)
1930-1988 Obituary 127
Schwartz, Douglas W(right) 1929- CANR-17
Earlier sketch in CA 25-28R
Schwartz, Eleanor Brantley 1937- 57-60
Schwartz, Eli 1921- CANR-34
Earlier sketch in CA 1-4R
Schwartz, Elias 1923- 41-44R
Schwartz, Elizabeth Reeder 1912- 13-16R
See also SATA 8
Schwartz, Elkanah 1937- 21-24R
Schwartz, Elliott S. 1936- 13-16R
Schwartz, Emanual K. 1912-1973 .... 37-40R
Obituary 41-44R
Schwartz, Ernst
See Ozu, Yasujiro
Schwartz, Eugene M. 1927-1995 .... 13-16R
Obituary 149
Schwartz, Gail Garfield 117
Schwartz, Gary (David) 1940- 145
Schwartz, George 1908-1974 Obituary 104
Schwartz, George Leopold
1891-1983 Obituary 109
Schwartz, George R. 1942- CANR-17
Earlier sketch in CA 97-100
Schwartz, Gerald 1932- 120
Schwartz, Harry W. 1903(?)-1984 Obituary 114
Schwartz, Helen 1935- 111
Schwartz, Helene E(nid) 1941- 65-68
Schwartz, Hillel 1948- CANR-43
Earlier sketches in CA 102, CANR-20
Schwartz, Howard 1945- CANR-22
Earlier sketches in CA 49-52, CANR-5
Schwartz, Israel J(acob)
1885-1971 Obituary 33-36R
Schwartz, Jerome L.
See Lawrence, Jerome
Schwartz, Joan 1938- 144
Schwartz, Joel 1942- 144
Schwartz, Joel L. 1940- 121
See also SATA 54
See also SATA-Brief 51
Schwartz, John Burnham 1965- 132
See also CLC 59
Schwartz, Jonathan 1938- 97-100
See also DLBY 82
Schwartz, Joseph 1925- 33-36R
Schwartz, Joyce R. 1950- 159
See also SATA 93
Schwartz, Julius 1907- 109
See also SATA 45
Schwartz, K(arlene) V. 1936- 104
Schwartz, Kessel 1920- CANR-6
Earlier sketch in CA 1-4R
Schwartz, Larry 1922- 53-56
Schwartz, Laurens R. 1951- 127
Schwartz, Leon 1922- 113
Schwartz, Lester J(erome) 1927- 113
Schwartz, Lewis M(arvin) 1935- 45-48
Schwartz, Lita Linzer 1930- 29-32R
Schwartz, Lloyd 1941- 112
Schwartz, Lois C. 1935- 33-36R
Schwartz, Loretta 1943- 97-100
Schwartz, Louis B. 1913- 21-24R
Schwartz, Lynne Sharon 1939- CANR-44
Earlier sketch in CA 103
See also CLC 31
Schwartz, Martin D(avid) 1945- 118
Schwartz, Melvin 1932- 168
Schwartz, Michael 1942- 113
Schwartz, Mildred A(nne) 1932- CANR-9
Earlier sketch in CA 21-24R
Schwartz, Morris S. 1916- 17-20R
Schwartz, Mortimer (Donald) 1922- 116
Schwartz, Muriel A.
See Eliot, T(homas) S(tearns)
Schwartz, Murray M. 1942- 116
Schwartz, Nancy Lynn 1952-1978 107
Schwartz, Norman B(oris) 1932- 111
Schwartz, Paula 1925- CANR-41
Earlier sketches in CA 85-88, CANR-18
Interview in CANR-18
Schwartz, Pedro 1935- CANR-24
Earlier sketch in CA 107
Schwartz, Pepper 1945- 33-36R
Schwartz, Perry 1942- 142
See also SATA 75
Schwartz, Richard Alan 1951- 165
Schwartz, Richard B. 1941- CANR-15
Earlier sketch in CA 85-88
Schwartz, Richard D(erecktor) 1925- CANR-6
Earlier sketch in CA 1-4R
Schwartz, Ronald 1937- 65-68
Schwartz, S.
See Starr, S(tephen) Frederick
Schwartz, Samuel M. 1929- 144
Schwartz, Selwyn S. 1907(?)-1988 Obituary ... 125
Schwartz, Sheila (Ruth) 1929- CANR-30
Earlier sketches in CA 25-28R, CANR-11
See also SATA 27
Schwartz, Shloime
See Schwartz, Selwyn S.
Schwartz, Stephan A(ndrew) 1942- 130
Schwartz, Stephen (Lawrence) 1948- 85-88
See also CAAS 26
See also SATA 19
Schwartz, Stephen (Alfred) 1948- CANR-68
Earlier sketch in CA 144
Schwartz, Steven 1950- 118
Schwartz, Stuart B. 1940- 126
Brief entry 108
Schwartz, William 1916-1982 Obituary 107
Schwartzberg, Julie 1943- 29-32R
Schwartzman, Aaron 1900(?)-1981 Obituary ... 102
Schwartzman, David 1924- 41-44R
Schwartzman, Edward 1927- 73-76
Schwartzman, Simon 1939- 143
Schwartzman, Sylvan D(avid) 1913- CANR-21
Earlier sketch in CA 41-44R
Schwartzmann, Mischa 1919- 29-32R
Schwarz, Adam 1961- 152
Schwarz, Adele Aron
See Greenspun, Adele Aron
Schwarz, Alfred 1925- Brief entry 118
Schwarz, Arturo (Samuele) 1924- 166
Schwarz, Boris 1906-1983 .... CANR-29
Obituary 111
Earlier sketch in CA 37-40R
Schwarz, Daniel R(oger) 1941- 131
Schwarz, Egon 1922- 57-60
Schwarz, Fred(erick) Charles 1913- CANR-69
Earlier sketches in CA 1-4R, CANR-32
Schwarz, Hans 1939- 41-44R
Schwarz, Henry G(uenter) 1928- 37-40R
Schwarz, Jack
See Schwarz, Jacob
Schwarz, Jacob 1924- 103
Schwarz, Jordan A(braham) 1937- CANR-45
Earlier sketch in CA 105
Schwarz, Karen 1957- 138
Schwarz, Leo W(alder) 1906-1967 .... 5-8R
Schwarz, Liese O'Halloran 1963- 133
Schwarz, Richard W(illiam) 1925- CANR-12
Earlier sketch in CA 29-32R
Schwarz, Robert 1921- 77-80
Schwarz, Sibylle 1621-1638 .... DLB 164
Schwarz, Solomon M. 1882(?)-1973 Obituary 45-48
Schwarz, Ted
See Schwarz, Theodore R., Jr.
Schwarz, Theodore R., Jr. 1945- CANR-26
Earlier sketches in CA 65-68, CANR-10
Schwarz, Vera 1947- 152
Schwarz, Walter 1930- 13-16R
Schwarz, Wilhelm Johannes 1929- 65-68
Schwarz-Bart, Andre 1928- 89-92
See also CLC 2, 4
Schwarz-Bart, Simone 1938- 97-100
See also BLCS
See also BW 2
See also CLC 7
Schwarzenberger, Georg 1908- 13-16R
Schwarzenegger, Arnold 1947- CANR-21
Earlier sketch in CA 81-84
See also AAYA 19
Schwarzkopf, H. Norman 1934- 145
Schwarzkopf, LeRoy C(arl) 1920- CANR-38
Earlier sketch in CA 115
Schwarzkopf-Legge, Elisabeth 1915- 109
Schwarzschild, Bettina 1925- 29-32R
Schwarzschild, Stuart 1918- 5-8R
Schwarzweller, Harry K(arl) 1929- 37-40R
Schwebel, Milton 1914- 17-20R
Schwebel, Stephen M(yron) 1929- 77-80
Schwebell, Gertrude C(lorius) 9-12R
Schwed, Peter 1911- CANR-56
Earlier sketches in CA 57-60, CANR-13, 31
Schweickart, Patrocinio P. 1942- 138
Schweid, Eliezer 1929- CANR-18
Earlier sketches in CA 45-48, CANR-1
Schweid, Richard M. 1946- 106
Schweik, Robert C(harles) 1927- CANR-57
Earlier sketches in CA 45-48, CANR-31
Schweikart, Larry (Earl) 1951- 134
Schweitzer, Albert 1875-1965 Obituary 93-96
Schweitzer, Arthur 1905- 9-12R
Schweitzer, Byrd Baylor
See Baylor, Byrd
Schweitzer, Christoph E(ugen) 1922- Brief
entry 107
Schweitzer, Darrell 1952- CANR-39
Earlier sketch in CA 116
Schweitzer, George K(eene) 1924- 17-20R
Schweitzer, Gertrude 1909- 85-88
Schweitzer, Iris 156
Brief entry 117
See also SATA 59
See also SATA-Brief 36
Schweitzer, Jerome William 1908- 41-44R
Schweitzer, John C. 1934- 17-20R
Schweizer(-Hanhart), Eduard 1913- CANR-20
Earlier sketches in CA 13-16R, CANR-5
Schweizer, Karl W. 1946- 136
Schwendeman, J(oseph) R(aymond) 1897- ... 81-84
Schweninger, Ann 1951- 107
See also SATA 29, 98
Schweninger, Loren (Lance) 1941- 101
Schwerin, Doris H(alpern) 1922- CANR-9
Earlier sketch in CA 65-68
See also SATA 64
Schwerin, Jules 1919- 144
Schwerin, Kurt 1902- 45-48
Schwerner, Armand 1927- CANR-50
Earlier sketch in CA 9-12R
See also DLB 165
Schwertfeger, Ruth 1941- 132
Schwichtenberg, Cathy 1953- 142
Schwiebert, Ernest G(eorge) 1895- CAP-1
Earlier sketch in CA 13-16
Schwieder, Dorothy 1933- 89-92
Schwimmer, Walter 1903-1989 Obituary 129
Schwitters, Kurt (Hermann Edward Karl Julius)
1887-1948 158
Schwitzgebel, Robert L. 1934- 41-44R
Schwob, Marcel (Mayer Andre) 1867-1905 168
Brief entry 117
See also DLB 123
See also TCLC 20
Schwoerer, Lois G(reen) 1927- CANR-15
Earlier sketch in CA 77-80
Schydlowsky, Daniel M(oses) 1940- CANR-27
Earlier sketch in CA 45-48
Sciabarra, Chris Matthew 1960- 155
Scialiano, Robert (G.) 1925- 9-12R
Sciascia, Leonardo 1921-1989 .... CANR-35
Obituary 130
Earlier sketch in CA 85-88
See also CLC 8, 9, 41
See also DLB 177
See also MTCW 1
Scibetta, Barbara Smith 1949- 129
Scibor-Rylski, Aleksander
1927(?)-1983 Obituary 109
Scicluna, Hannibal Publius
1880-1981(?) Obituary 106
Scieszka, Jon 1954- 135
See also AAYA 21
See also CLR 27
See also SATA 68
Scifres, Bill(y N.) 1925- 103
Scimecca, Joseph A. 1940- 129
Scioscia, Mary (Hershey) 1926- .... SATA 63
Scipes, Kim 1951- 162
Scipio
See Watson, (John Hugh) Adam
Scire
See Gardner, G(erald) B(rosseau)
Scism, Carol K. 1931- 41-44R
Scithers, George H(arry) 1929- 57-60
Scitovsky, Tibor 1910- 104
Scivener, Michael (Henry) 1948- 130
Scliar, Moacyr 1937- 136
Scoales, William 1933- 33-36R
Scobel, Donald N. 1929- 122
Scobey, Joan 1927- CANR-46
Earlier sketches in CA 57-60, CANR-7
Scobey, Mary-Margaret 1915- CANR-1
Earlier sketch in CA 1-4R
Scobie, James R(alston) 1929-1981 ...... CANR-6
Obituary 104
Earlier sketch in CA 9-12R
Scobie, Stephen 1943- 111
Scoby, Donald R(ay) 1931- 33-36R
Scofield, Jonathan
See Levinson, Leonard
and Rothweiler, Paul Roger
and Toombs, John
Scofield, Martin (Paul) 1945- 132
Scofield, Norma Margaret Cartwright 1924- 103
Scofield, Penrod 1933- .... SATA 62
See also SATA-Obit 78
Scofield, Sandra (Jean) 1943- 146
Scofield, William H. 1915- 17-20R
Scoggin, Margaret C(lara) 1905-1968 ..... SATA 47
See also SATA-Brief 28
Scoggins, James (Lawrence) 1934- 21-24R
Scoles, Eugene F(rancis) 1921- CANR-15
Earlier sketch in CA 37-40R
Scollan, E. A.
See O'Grady, Anne
Scolnick, Sylvan 1930(?)-1976 Obituary 69-72
Scoltock, Jack 1942- .... SATA 72
Scopes, John T. 1900-1970 Obituary 29-32R
Scoppettone, Sandra 1936- CANR-41
Earlier sketch in CA 5-8R
See also AAYA 11
See also CLC 26
See also SATA 9, 92
Scorer, Richard 1919- 77-80
Scorsese, Martin 1942- CANR-46
Brief entry 110
Earlier sketch in CA 114
See also CLC 20, 89
Scortia, Thomas N(icholas) 1926-1986 .... CANR-6
Obituary 119
Earlier sketch in CA 1-4R
Scorza, Manuel 1928-1983 131
Obituary 113
See also HW
Scorza, Thomas J. 1948- 132
Scot, Chesman
See Bulmer, (Henry) Kenneth
Scot, Michael
See Rohan, Michael Scott
Scotellaro, Rocco 1923-1953 .... DLB 128
Scotford, John Ryland 1888-1976 .... 5-8R
Obituary 103
Scotland, Andrew 1905- 5-8R
Scotland, James 1917-1983 .... CANR-36
Obituary 110
Earlier sketch in CA 33-36R
Scotland, Jay
See Jakes, John (William)
Scotson, John L(loyd) 1928-1980 .... 21-24R
Obituary 134
Scotson, Linda 1945- 128
Scott
See Charlier, Roger H(enri)
Scott, A(dolphe) C(larence) 1909- CANR-2
Earlier sketch in CA 5-8R
Scott, Alan (B.) 1957- 141
Scott, Alastair
See Allen, Kenneth S.
Scott, Alexander 1920- 105
Scott, Allan
See Shiach, Allan G.
Scott, Allen John 1938- 97-100
Scott, Amoret (Scudamore) 1930- CANR-10
Earlier sketch in CA 21-24R
Scott, Andrew M(acKay) 1922- 17-20R
Scott, Ann Herbert 1926- CANR-68
Earlier sketch in CA 21-24R
See also SATA 56, 94
See also SATA-Brief 29
Scott, Anne Firor 1921- 33-36R
Scott, Anthony
See Dresser, Davis
Scott, Anthony Dalton 1923- CANR-29
Earlier sketches in CA 65-68, CANR-11
Scott, Arthur Finley 1907- CANR-41
Earlier sketches in CA 5-8R, CANR-2, 18
Scott, Arthur L(incoln) 1914- 21-24R
Scott, Austin (Wakeman)
1885(?)-1981 Obituary 103
Scott, Beth (Bailey) 1922- 132
Scott, Bill
See Scott, William N(eville)
Scott, Bill 1920(?)-1985 Obituary 117
See also SATA-Obit 46
Scott, Bonnie Kime 1944- CANR-43
Earlier sketch in CA 119

Scott, C(atharine) A(my) Dawson
See Dawson-Scott, C(atharine) A(my)
Scott, C(ecil) Winfield 1905- 5-8R
Scott, Casey
See Kubis, Pat
Scott, Cecil Alexander 1902(?)-1981 Obituary .. 104
Scott, Charles R(alph), Jr. 1914- CANR-16
Earlier sketch in CA 89-92
Scott, Charles T. 1932- 21-24R
Scott, Charles W(esley) 1932- 116
Scott, Christopher 1930- 21-24R
Scott, Claudia 1948-1979 Obituary 114
Scott, Clinton Lee 1890- CAP-2
Earlier sketch in CA 19-20
Scott, Cora Annett (Pipitone) 1931- 17-20R
See also SATA 11
Scott, Cyril (Meir) 1879-1970 Obituary 111
Scott, Dan CANR-27
Earlier sketches in CAP-2, CA 19-20
Scott, Dan
See Barker, S(quire) Omar
Scott, Dana
See Robertson, Constance (Pierrepont Noyes)
Scott, Daryl Michael 1958- 166
Scott, David (Aubrey) 1919- 109
Scott, David (Henry Tudor) 1948- 127
Scott, David A. 1949- 168
Scott, David L. 1942- 167
Scott, David W(infield) 1916- 109
Scott, Denise 114
Scott, Dennis (Courtney) 1939-1991 143
See also BW 2
See also DLB 125
Scott, Derek B. 1950- 137
Scott, Dixon 1881-1915 .... DLB 98
Scott, Donald F(letcher) 1930- 89-92
Scott, Dorothea Hayward 93-96
Scott, Duncan Campbell 1862-1947 153
Brief entry 104
See also DAC
See also DLB 92
See also TCLC 6
Scott, Edward M. 1919- 33-36R
Scott, Elaine 1940- CANR-50
Earlier sketches in CA 105, CANR-21
See also SATA 36, 90
Scott, Eleanor 1921- 61-64
Scott, Ellis L(averne) 1915- 49-52
Scott, Eve
See Rodgers, Joann Ellison
Scott, Evelyn 1893-1963 .... CANR-64
Obituary 112
Earlier sketch in CA 104
See also CLC 43
See also DLB 9, 48
Scott, F(rancis) R(eginald) 1899-1985 101
Obituary 114
Interview in 101
See also CLC 22
See also DLB 88
Scott, Frances V.
See Wing, Frances (Scott)
Scott, Frank
See Scott, F(rancis) R(eginald)
Scott, Frank 1949- 141
Scott, Franklin D(aniel) 1901-1994 .... CANR-5
Obituary 146
Earlier sketch in CA 5-8R
Scott, Frederick George 1861-1944 .... DLB 92
Scott, Gail 1945- 127
Scott, Gavin 1936- 77-80
Scott, Geoffrey 1884-1929 .... DLB 149
Scott, Geoffrey 1952- 106
Scott, George (Edwin) 1925-1988 .... 29-32R
Obituary 127
Scott, George Walton 1921- 21-24R
Scott, Grant F. 1961- 151
Scott, (Peter) Hardiman 1920- 144
Scott, Harold George 1925- 61-64
Scott, Harold Richard 1887- 5-8R
Scott, Harold W(illiam) 1906- 118
Scott, Harvey W. 1838-1910 .... DLB 23
Scott, Helen G. 1915(?)-1987 Obituary 124
Scott, Herbert 1931- CANR-6
Earlier sketch in CA 53-56
Scott, Hilda 1915- 124
Scott, Ira O(scar), Jr. 1918- 17-20R
Scott, J(ohn) D(ick) 1917-1980 77-80
Obituary 97-100
Scott, J(ames) M(aurice) 1906-1986 105
Obituary 118
Scott, Jack B(rown) 1928- 77-80
Scott, Jack Denton 1915-1995 .... CANR-48
Earlier sketch in CA 108
See also CLR 20
See also MAICYA
See also SAAS 14
See also SATA 31, 83
Scott, Jack S.
See Escott, Jonathan
Scott, James A. 1946- 123
Scott, James B(urton) 1926- 85-88
Scott, James C(ampbell) 1936- 29-32R
Scott, James F(razier) 1934- CANR-47
Earlier sketches in CA 77-80, CANR-22
Scott, Jane
See McElfresh, (Elizabeth) Adeline
Scott, Jane (Harrington) 1931- .... SATA 55
Scott, Jay 1949-1993 133
Obituary 142
Scott, Jean
See Muir, Marie
Scott, Jeffrey
See Usher, Shaun
Scott, Jeremy
See Dick, Kay
Scott, Joanna 1960- CANR-53
Earlier sketch in CA 126
See also CLC 50
Scott, Jody 81-84
Scott, John 1912-1976 .... CANR-6
Obituary 69-72
Earlier sketch in CA 5-8R
See also SATA 14
Scott, John (Peter) 1949- 126
Scott, John A. 1948- 135
Scott, John Anthony 1916- CANR-23
Earlier sketches in CA 9-12R, CANR-6
See also SATA 23
Scott, John Irving E(lias) (?)-1981 73-76
Obituary 133
Scott, John M(artin) 1913- CANR-50
Earlier sketches in CA 65-68, CANR-10, 25
See also SATA 12
Scott, Johnie Harold 1946- CANR-14
Earlier sketch in CA 33-36R
Scott, Jonathan 1958- 132
Scott, (Henry) Joseph 1917- 57-60
Scott, Joseph Reid 1926- 41-44R
Scott, Judith Unger 1916- 5-8R
Scott, Justin CANR-26
Earlier sketch in CA 104
Scott, Kenneth 1900-1993 .... CANR-26
Obituary 143
Earlier sketches in CA 69-72, CANR-11
Scott, Kenneth J. 1933(?)-1983 Obituary 111
Scott, Lalla (McIntosh) 1893- CAP-2
Earlier sketch in CA 21-22
Scott, Latayne Colvett 1952- CANR-17
Earlier sketch in CA 97-100
Scott, Lauren
See Frentzen, Jeffrey
Scott, Laurence Prestwich 1909-1983 Obituary . 110
Scott, Leonard B. III 1948- 143
Scott, Lloyd
See Turner, George E(ugene)
Scott, Lloyd F. 1926- 21-24R
Scott, Louise Binder 1910- CANR-4
Earlier sketch in CA 1-4R
Scott, Marcia (Adele Morse) 1943- 97-100
Scott, Margaret (Allan Bennett) 1928- 145
Scott, Margaret B(rodie) (?)-1976 Obituary ... 61-64
Scott, Martin
See Gehman, Richard (Boyd)
Scott, Marvin B(ailey) 1944- Brief entry 118
Scott, Mary Jane W(ittstock) 1949- 129
Scott, Mel(lier Goodin) 1906- 29-32R
Scott, Melissa 1960- 161
Scott, (Guthrie) Michael 1907-1983 130
Obituary 110
Scott, Michael 1924(?)-1989 Obituary 129
Scott, (Robert James) Munroe 1927- 130
Scott, Natalie Anderson 1906- CAP-2
Earlier sketch in CA 23-24
Scott, Nathan A(lexander), Jr. 1925- CANR-20
Earlier sketches in CA 9-12R, CANR-5
See also BW 2
Scott, Nerissa
See Ring, Elizabeth
Scott, Nina M. 1937- 146
Scott, Norford
See Rowland, D(onald) S(ydney)
Scott, Otto J. 1918- 85-88
Scott, Owen Le Grand 1898-1985 Obituary 117
Scott, P(aul) H(enderson) 1920- 142
Scott, P. T.
See Poage, Scott T(abor)
Scott, Patrick (Greig) 1945- 112
Scott, Paul (Mark) 1920-1978 .... CANR-33
Obituary 77-80
Earlier sketch in CA 81-84
See also CLC 9, 60
See also DLB 14
See also MTCW 1
Scott, Peter (Markham) 1909-1989 101
Obituary 129
Scott, Peter Dale 1929- CANR-9
Earlier sketch in CA 21-24R
Scott, Peter Graham
See Graham Scott, Peter
Scott, R(obert) B(algarnie) Y(oung)
1899-1987 Obituary 124
Scott, Rachel (Ann) 1947- 103
Scott, Ralph S(amuel) 1927- 41-44R
Scott, Rebecca J(arvis) 1950- 128
Scott, Richard
See Rennert, Richard Scott
Scott, Richard A(llen) 1931- 25-28R
Scott, Ridley 1937- .... AAYA 13
Scott, Robert A. 1936- 89-92
Scott, Robert Adrian
1901(?)-1972 Obituary 37-40R
Scott, Robert E(dwin) 1923- CANR-1
Earlier sketch in CA 1-4R
Scott, Robert F(alcon) 1868-1912 Brief entry .. 115
Scott, Robert Garth 1957- 137
Scott, Robert Haney 1927- 17-20R
Scott, Robert Ian 1931- 106
Scott, Robert Lee, Jr. 1908- CAP-1
Earlier sketch in CA 11-12
Scott, Robert Lee 1928- CANR-3
Earlier sketch in CA 5-8R
Scott, Robin
See Wilson, Robin Scott
Scott, Roger (Dennis) 1939- 97-100
Scott, Ronald Bodley 1906-1982 109
Obituary 106
Scott, Ronald Guthrie McNair
See McNair Scott, Ronald (Guthrie)
Scott, Roney
See Gault, William Campbell
Scott, Roy Vernon 1927- CANR-1
Earlier sketch in CA 1-4R
Scott, Sally 1909-1978 116
See also SATA 43
Scott, Sally (Elisabeth) 1948- 125
See also SATA 44
Scott, Sarah 1723-1795 .... DLB 39
Scott, Sheila (Christine) 1927-1988 53-56
Obituary 126
Scott, Stanley
See Fagerstrom, Stan
Scott, Stephen E. 1948- CANR-43
Earlier sketch in CA 119
Scott, Steve
See Crawford, William (Elbert)
Scott, Stuart
See Aitken, W(illiam) R(ussell)
Scott, Tirsa Saavedra 1920- 13-16R
Scott, Tom 1918- 9-12R
See also DLB 27
Scott, Valerie
See Rowland, D(onald) S(ydney)
Scott, Virgil (Joseph) 1914- CANR-2
Earlier sketch in CA 5-8R
Scott, Virginia M(uhleman) 1945- 121
Scott, W(illiam) E(dgar), Jr. 1929- 49-52
Scott, W. N.
See Scott, William N(eville)
Scott, W(illiam) Richard 1932- 17-20R
Scott, Walter 1771-1832 .... AAYA 22
See also CDBLB 1789-1832
See also DA
See also DAB
See also DAC
See also DAM MST, NOV, POET
See also DLB 93, 107, 116, 144, 159
See also PC 13
See also WLC
See also YABC 2
Scott, Warwick
See Trevor, Elleston
Scott, Whitney
See Nelson, P.
Scott, Willard H., Jr. 1934- 109
Scott, William Abbott 1926- CANR-9
Earlier sketch in CA 5-8R
Scott, William B(utler) 1945- 126
Scott, William Bell 1811-1890 .... DLB 32
Scott, William C(lyde) 1937- 119
Scott, William G(eorge) 1926- CANR-11
Earlier sketch in CA 21-24R
Scott, William Henry 1921- 132
Scott, William L.
See Finley, Joseph E(dwin)
Scott, William N(eville) 1923- CANR-52
Earlier sketch in CA 132
See also SATA 87
Scott, William R(eese) 1907- 77-80
Scott, William R(alph) 1918-1992 101
Obituary 136
Scott, Wilson L(udlow) 1909-1983 .... CANR-34
Obituary 111
Earlier sketch in CA 45-48
Scott, Winfield H(arker) 1932-1992 .... 21-24R
Obituary 136
Scott, Winfield Townley 1910-1968 .... CANR-7
Obituary 25-28R
Earlier sketch in CA 5-8R
Scott-Giles, C(harles) W(ilfred)
1893-1982(?) Obituary 106
Scott-Heron, Gil 1949- CANR-24
Earlier sketch in CA 45-48
See also BW 1
See also DLB 41
Scotti, Anna
See Coates, Anna
Scotti, Anna
See Coates, Anna
Scotti, Paul C(arl) 1943- 118
Scotti, R. A. 1946- CANR-48
Earlier sketch in CA 122
Scott-James, Anne Eleanor 1913- 105
Scott-Moncrieff, David (William Hardy)
1907-1987 Obituary 123
Scott-Moncrieff, George (Irving) 1910- CAP-1
Earlier sketch in CA 11-12
Scott Moncrieff, Martha Christian 1897- 61-64
Scotto, Robert M(ichael) 1942- 57-60
Scott-Stokes, Henry J. M. 128
Brief entry 117
Scott-Taggart, John 1897-1979 Obituary 104
Scott Thorn, Ronald
See Wilkinson, Ronald
Scouten, Arthur Hawley 1910-1995 .... CANR-11
Obituary 148
Earlier sketches in CAP-1, CA 13-14
Scovel, Myra (Scott) 1905- CANR-2
Earlier sketch in CA 5-8R
Scovell, Brian (Souter) 1935- 130
Scovell, E(dith) J(oy) 1907- 136
Scovell, Jane (Frances) 1934- 136
Scoville, Herbert, Jr. 1915-1985 .... CANR-43
Obituary 116
Earlier sketch in CA 29-32R
Scoville, James G(riffin) 1940- 29-32R
Scoville, Warren Candler 1913-1969 .... CANR-2
Earlier sketch in CA 1-4R
Scowcroft, Richard P(ingree) 1916- 9-12R
Scraton, Phil 1949- 128
Screech, M(ichael) A(ndrew) 1926- 140
Scriabine, Helene (A. Gorstrine) 1906- ... CANR-45
Earlier sketches in CA 21-24R, CANR-14
Scribe, (Augustin) Eugene 1791-1861 .. DAM DRAM
See also DC 5
See also DLB 192
Scribner, Charles, Jr. 1921-1995 69-72
Obituary 150
See also DLBD 17
See also DLBY 95
See also SATA 13
See also SATA-Obit 87
Scribner, Charles III 1951- 126
Scribner, Joanne L. 1949- .... SATA 33
Scribner, Kimball 1917- .... SATA 63
Scribner, Sylvia 1923- 133
Scrimgeour, Gary J(ames) 1934- 108
Scrimshaw, Nevin Stewart 1918- 89-92
Scrimsher, Lila Gravatt 1897-1974 .... 1-4R
Obituary 103
See also SATA-Obit 28
Scripps, E(dward) W(yllis) 1854-1926 Brief
entry 118
See also DLB 25
Scripps, James G. 1911-1986 Obituary 121
Scriven, Michael (John) 1928- CANR-14
Earlier sketch in CA 21-24R
Scrivener, Michael (Henry) 1948- 130
Scriver, Bob
See Scriver, Robert MacFie
Scriver, Robert MacFie 1914- 115
Scrivner, Wilma Possien 1915- 107
Scroder, Walter K. 1928- .... SATA 82
Scroggins, Daniel C(oy) 1937- 33-36R
Scroggs, Robin (Jerome) 1930- 116
Scruggs, C(harles) Eugene 1937- 113
Scruggs, Sandy 1961- 155
See also SATA 89
Scrum, R.
See Crumb, R(obert)
Scruton, Roger 1944- CANR-39
Earlier sketches in CA 89-92, CANR-16
Scudamore, Pauline 1936- 129
Scudder, C(leo) W(ayne) 1915- CANR-3
Earlier sketch in CA 1-4R
Scudder, Horace E(lisha) 1838-1902 Brief
entry 119
See also DLB 42, 71
Scudder, Kenyon J. 1890-1977 Obituary 73-76
Scudder, Mildred Lee 1908- 9-12R
See also Lee, Mildred
Scudder, Rogers V(aughn) 1912- 17-20R
Scudder, Thayer 1930- 126
Brief entry 106
Scudder, Townsend (III) 1900-1988 Obituary 126
Scudder, Vida Dutton 1861-1954 .... DLB 71
Sculatti, (Eu)Gene 1947- 110
Scull, Andrew 1947- CANR-33
Earlier sketches in CA 81-84, CANR-15
Scull, Florence Doughty 1905- CAP-1
Earlier sketch in CA 11-12
Scull, Marie-Louise 1943-1993 .... SATA 77
Scullard, Howard Hayes 1903-1983 .... CANR-3
Obituary 109
Earlier sketch in CA 9-12R
Sculley, John 1939- 127
Scully, Frank 1892-1964 .... 5-8R
Scully, Gerald William 1941- 65-68
Scully, James 1937- CANR-11
Earlier sketch in CA 25-28R
See also CAAS 30
Scully, Julia S(ilverman) 1929- 103
Scully, Vincent (Joseph, Jr.) 1920- Brief entry .. 113
Scully, Vincent (Joseph, Jr.) 1920- 147
Scum
See Crumb, R(obert)
Scumbag, Little Bobby
See Crumb, R(obert)
Scuorzo, Herbert E(rnest) 1928- 21-24R
Scupham, John Peter 1933- CANR-9
Earlier sketch in CA 65-68
See also DLB 40
Scuro, Vincent 1951- CANR-40
Earlier sketches in CA 53-56, CANR-5
See also SATA 21
Scutt, Ronald 1916- 97-100
Seaberg, Stanley 1929- 21-24R
Seaborg, Glenn T(heodore) 1912- CANR-2
Earlier sketch in CA 49-52
Seabough, Ed(ward Ellis) 1932- 29-32R
Seabrook, Jeremy 1939- 108
Seabrook, John
See Hubbard, L(afayette) Ron(ald)
Seabrook, Mike 1950- 147
Seabrook, William B(uehler) 1886-1945 Brief
entry 107
See also DLB 4
Seabrooke, Brenda 1941- 107
See also SATA 30, 88
Seabury, Paul 1923-1990 Obituary 132
Brief entry 115
Seabury, Samuel 1729-1796 .... DLB 31
Seacole, Mary Jane Grant 1805-1881 .... DLB 166
Seagears, Clayton B. 1902(?)-1983 Obituary 110
Seager, Allan 1906-1968 .... 5-8R
Obituary 25-28R
Seager, Ralph William 1911- CANR-6
Earlier sketch in CA 9-12R
Seager, Robert II 1924- CANR-6
Earlier sketch in CA 5-8R
Seager, Stephen B. 1950- 139
Seager, Walter H(arold) T(ennant) 1938- 120
Seagle, Janet 1924- 102
Seagle, William 1898-1977 .... 5-8R
Obituary 73-76
Seagoe, May V(iolet) 1906-1980 .... CANR-10
Earlier sketch in CA 13-16R
Seagrave, Sterling 1937- 135
Brief entry 125
Interview in 135
Seagraves, Margaret 1920- CANR-13
Earlier sketch in CA 73-76

Seagull, Louis Martin 1941- 112
Seal 1963- 156
Seal, Anil 1938- 25-28R
Seal, Basil
See Kavanagh, Dan(iel)
Seale, Alan 1955- 164
Seale, Bobby
See Seale, Robert George
Seale, Ervin 1910(?)-1990 Obituary 130
Seale, Patrick 1930- 97-100
Seale, Robert George 1936- 110
See also BW 1
Seale, William 1939- CANR-7
Earlier sketch in CA 17-20R
Sealey, Bruce
See Sealey, D(onald) Bruce
Sealey, D(onald) Bruce 1929- 121
Sealey, Danguole 1931- 33-36R
Sealey, Leonard (George William) 1923- 103
Sealey, (Bertram) Raphael (Izod) 1927- 65-68
Sea-Lion
See Bennett, Geoffrey (Martin)
Sealock, Richard Burl 1907- CAP-2
Earlier sketch in CA 23-24
Seals, David 1947- 145
Sealsfield, Charles 1793-1864 DLB 133, 186
Sealts, Merton M(iller), Jr. 1915- 13-16R
Sealy, I. Allan 1951- CLC 55
Sealy, I(rwin) Allan 1951- 136
Seaman, Augusta Huiell 1879-1950 Brief entry 110
See also SATA 31
Seaman, Barbara 1935- 29-32R
Seaman, (A.) Barrett 1945- 73-76
Seaman, Don F(erris) 1935- 77-80
Seaman, Donald (Peter) 1922-1997 155
Obituary 161
Brief entry 114
Seaman, Elizabeth Cochrane
See Cochrane, Elizabeth
Seaman, Gerald Roberts 1934- 25-28R
Seaman, John E(ugene) 1932- 89-92
Seaman, L(ewis) C(harles) B(ernard) 1911- 57-60
Seaman, P. David 1932- 143
Seaman, Sylvia S(ybil Bernstein) 1901(?)-1995 CAP-2
Obituary 147
Earlier sketch in CA 23-24
Seaman, William M(illard) 1907- 41-44R
Seamands, John Thompson 1916- 9-12R
Seamands, Ruth 1916- 45-48
See also SATA 9
Sear, Frank 1944- 121
Seara Vazquez, M(odesto) 1931- CANR-14
Earlier sketch in CA 17-20R
Search, Alexander
See Pessoa, Fernando (Antonio Nogueira)
Search-Light
See Frank, Waldo (David)
Searcy, Margaret Zehmer 1926- 81-84
See also SATA 54
See also SATA-Brief 39
Seare, Nicholas
See Whitaker, Rod(ney)
Seare, Nicholas
See Whitaker, Rod(ney)
Searight, Mary W(illiams) 1918- 29-32R
See also SATA 17
Searing, Donald D. 1942- 148
Searing, Helen E. 1933- 111
Searing, Susan Ellis 1950- 122
Searle, Elizabeth 1962- 164
Searle, Humphrey 1915-1982 9-12R
Obituary 106
Searle, John R(ogers) 1932- CANR-51
Earlier sketches in CA 25-28R, CANR-26
Searle, Kathryn Adrienne 1942- 29-32R
See also SATA 10
Searle, Leroy F(rank) 1942- 73-76
Searle, Mark 1941- 114
Searle, Ronald (William Fordham) 1920- CANR-50
Earlier sketches in CA 9-12R, CANR-25
See also MAICYA
See also SATA 42, 70
Searle, Verna (Ruth) 1919- 132
Searles, (William) Baird 1934- 123
Searles, Herbert L(eon) 1891- 45-48
Searles, P. D(avid) 1933- 164
Searles, Richard B. 1936- 139
Searls, Hank
See Searls, Henry Hunt, Jr.
Searls, Henry Hunt, Jr. 1922- CANR-28
Earlier sketch in CA 13-16R
Sears, Barry 1947- 154
Sears, David O'Keefe 1935- 29-32R
Sears, Deane
See Rywell, Martin
Sears, Donald A(lbert) 1923- CANR-6
Earlier sketch in CA 5-8R
Sears, Edward I. 1819(?)-1876 DLB 79
Sears, Francis W. 1898-1975 Obituary 61-64
Sears, Hal D(on) 1942- 122
Sears, James T(homas) 1951- 164
Sears, Joe 1949- 160
Sears, Paul Bigelow 1891- 17-20R
Sears, Paul M(cCutcheon) 1920- 1-4R
Sears, Pauline Snedden 1908- 29-32R
Sears, Peter 1937- 110
Sears, Robert R(ichardson) 1908-1989 17-20R
Obituary 128
Sears, Sallie 1932- 41-44R
Sears, Stephen W. 1932- CANR-45
Earlier sketch in CA 33-36R
See also SATA 4
Sears, Val 1927- 73-76
Sears, William P(aul), Jr. 1902-1976 Obituary 61-64
Sears, William P. 1939- 160
Seary, E(dgar) R(onald) 1908- 41-44R
Seashore, Stanley E. 1915- CANR-24
Earlier sketch in CA 33-36R
Seasoltz, R(obert) Kevin 1930- 9-12R
Seasongood, Murray 1878-1983 Obituary 109
Seat, William R(obert), Jr. 1920- 13-16R
Seaton, Beryl
See Platts, Beryl
Seaton, Don Cash(ius) 1902- CAP-1
Earlier sketch in CA 9-10
Seaton, Douglas P(aul) 1947- 107
Seaton, Frederick Andrew
1909-1974 Obituary 89-92
Seaton, George 1911-1979 105
Obituary 89-92
Interview in 105
See also DLB 44
Seaton, J(erome) P. 1941- 166
Seaton, Mary Ethel (?)-1974 Obituary 53-56
Seaton, William Winston 1785-1866 DLB 43
Seaver, George (Fenn) 1890- CAP-1
Earlier sketch in CA 13-14
Seaver, Paul S(iddall) 1932- 29-32R
Seay, James 1939- 29-32R
Seay, Thomas A(ustin) 1942- 97-100
Sebag Montefiore, Simon
See Sebag-Montefiore, Simon
Sebag-Montefiore, Simon 1965- 136
Sebald, Hans 1929- 73-76
Sebald, W(infried) G(eorg) 1944- 159
Sebald, William J(oseph) 1901-1980 CAP-1
Obituary 101
Earlier sketch in CA 13-16
Sebastian, Jeanne
See Newsome, Arden J(eanne)
Sebastian, Lee
See Silverberg, Robert
Sebastian, Margaret
See Gladstone, Arthur M.
Sebastian, Tim 1952- 139
Sebastian Owl
See Thompson, Hunter S(tockton)
Sebba, Anne (Marietta) 1951- CANR-55
Earlier sketch in CA 127
Sebenthall, R(oberta) E(lizabeth) 1917- 33-36R
Sebeok, Thomas A(lbert) 1920- CANR-46
Earlier sketch in CA 9-12R
Seberg, Jean 1938-1979 Obituary 89-92
Sebes, Joseph (Schobert) 1915-1990 Obituary 131
Sebesta, Sam L(eaton) 1930- 85-88
Sebestyen, Gyorgy 1930- CANR-6
Earlier sketch in CA 9-12R
Sebestyen, Ouida 1924- CANR-40
Earlier sketch in CA 107
See also AAYA 8
See also CLC 30
See also CLR 17
See also JRDA
See also MAICYA
See also SAAS 10
See also SATA 39
Seboldt, Roland H(enry) A(ugust) 1924- 5-8R
Sebree, Charles 1914-1985 Obituary 117
Sebrey, Mary Ann 1951- 116
See also SATA 62
Secher, Bjorn 1929- 33-36R
Sechrest, Lee 1929- 17-20R
Sechrist, Elizabeth Hough 1903- 5-8R
See also SATA 2
Seckel, Al 1958- 122
Seckler, David William 1935- 115
Secombe, Harry (Donald) 1921- 57-60
Secondari, John Hermes 1919-1975 61-64
Obituary 57-60
Second Duke of Buckingham
See Villiers, George
Secor, Robert 1939- CANR-15
Earlier sketch in CA 89-92
Secrest, Meryle
See Doman, June
Secretan, Lance H. K. 1939- 130
Secrist, Margaret C(rystal) 1905- 111
Secunda, Sholom 1894-1974 Obituary 49-52
Secunda, Victoria (H.) 1939- 141
Secundus, H. Scriblerus
See Fielding, Henry
Secundus, Petrus Lotichius 1528-1560 DLB 179
Sedaitis, Judith B. 165
Sedaka, Neil 1939- 103
Sedaris, David 1957(?)- CANR-68
Earlier sketch in CA 147
Seddon, Andrew M. 1959- 155
Sederberg, Arelo Charles 1930- 37-40R
Sederberg, Peter C(arl) 1943- 65-68
Sedges, John
See Buck, Pearl S(ydenstricker)
Sedgewick, Ellery 1872-1960 Obituary 89-92
See also DLB 91
Sedgwick, Alexander 1930- 17-20R
Sedgwick, Arthur George 1844-1915 DLB 64
Sedgwick, Catharine Maria 1789-1867 DLB 1, 74
Sedgwick, Eve Kosofsky 1950- 145
Sedgwick, Fred 1945- 154
Sedgwick, Jeffrey Leigh 1951- 116
Sedgwick, John 1954- 145
Sedgwick, Michael Carl 1926-1983 89-92
Obituary 111
Sedgwick, Peter 1934-1983 Obituary 110
Sedgwick, Walter (Bradbury) 1885- CAP-1
Earlier sketch in CA 13-14
Sedlacek, William E(dward) 1939- 69-72
Sedlar, Jean W. 1935- 147
Sedler, Robert Allen 1935- 41-44R
Sedley, Charles 1639-1701 DLB 131
Sed-Rajna, Gabrielle 1927- 168
Seduro, Vladimir 1910- 41-44R
Sedwick, B(enjamin) Frank 1924- 9-12R
Sedych, Andrei
See Zwibak, Jacques
See, Carolyn (Penelope) 1934- CANR-50
Earlier sketches in CA 29-32R, CANR-25
Interview in CANR-25
See also CAAS 22
See, (Nadine) Ingram 1904- 112
See, Lisa
See Kendall, Lisa See
See, Ruth Douglas 1910- CANR-35
Earlier sketches in CA 1-4R, CANR-1
Seeber, Edward Derbyshire 1904- 13-16R
Seeber, Gerd Christian 1941- 113
Seebohm, Caroline 1940- 102
Seebord, G. R.
See Soderberg, Percy Measday
Seed, Cecile Eugenie 1930- CANR-51
Earlier sketches in CA 21-24R, CANR-26
See also Seed, Jenny
See also SATA 86
Seed, David 1946- 150
Seed, Jenny
See Seed, Cecile Eugenie
See also SATA 8
Seed, Sheila Turner 1937(?)-1979 Obituary 89-92
See also SATA-Obit 23
Seedman, Albert A. 1918- Brief entry 112
Seefeldt, Carol 1935- 146
Seeger, Alan 1888-1916 DLB 45
Seeger, Charles Louis 1886-1979 101
Obituary 85-88
Seeger, Elizabeth 1889-1973 Obituary 45-48
See also SATA-Obit 20
Seeger, Murray (Amsdell) 1929- 152
Seeger, Pete(r R.) 1919- CANR-33
Earlier sketch in CA 69-72
See also SATA 13
Seegers, Kathleen Walker 1915- 21-24R
Seeley, John R(onald) 1913- 25-28R
Seeley, Laura L. 1958- SATA 71
Seelhammer, Ruth 1917- 41-44R
Seelig, Sharon Cadman 1941- 119
Seely, Gordon M. 1930- 37-40R
Seely, Norma 1942- 113
Seely, Rebecca Z(ahm) 1935- 104
Seelye, H(ugh) Ned 1934- 102
Seelye, John (Douglas) 1931- CANR-70
Earlier sketch in CA 97-100
Interview in 97-100
See also CLC 7
Seeman, Bernard 1911- 21-24R
Seeman, Elizabeth (Brickel) 1904- CAP-1
Earlier sketch in CA 19-20
Seeman, Ernest Albright 1887- 85-88
Seers, Dudley 1920-1983 129
Obituary 109
Seese, Ethel Gray 1903- 89-92
Seese, June Akers 1935- 134
Seever, R.
See Reeves, Lawrence F.
Seferiades, Giorgos Stylianou 1900-1971 CANR-36
Obituary 33-36R
Earlier sketches in CA 5-8R, CANR-5
See also Seferis, George
See also MTCW 1
Seferis, George
See Seferiades, Giorgos Stylianou
See also CLC 5, 11
Sefler, George Francis 1945- 81-84
Sefozo, Mary 1925- SATA 82
Sefton, Catherine
See Waddell, Martin
Sefton, James E(dward) 1939- 21-24R
Segal, Abraham 1911(?)-1977 Obituary 69-72
Segal, Alan F(ranklin) 1945- CANR-44
Earlier sketch in CA 119
Segal, Bernice G. 1929-1989 Obituary 128
Segal, Charles Paul 1936- CANR-39
Earlier sketches in CA 41-44R, CANR-16
Segal, David I. 1928(?)-1970 Obituary 104
Segal, David R(obert) 1941- CANR-52
Earlier sketches in CA 111, CANR-28
Segal, Elliot A(lan) 1938- 93-96
Segal, Erich (Wolf) 1937- CANR-65
Earlier sketches in CA 25-28R, CANR-20, 36
Interview in CANR-20
See also BEST 89:1
See also CLC 3, 10
See also DAM POP
See also DLBY 86
See also MTCW 1
Segal, Fred 1924(?)-1976 69-72
Obituary 65-68
Segal, Gerald 1953- 117
Segal, Geraldine R(osenbaum) 1908- 113
Segal, Hanna M(aria) 1918- 101
Segal, Harold S. 1903- 29-32R
Segal, Harriet 1931- CANR-50
Earlier sketch in CA 123
Segal, Harvey H(irst) 1922-1994 1-4R
Obituary 144
Segal, Henry 1901(?)-1985 Obituary 116
Segal, Howard P. 1948- 144
Segal, Jeanne (Sandra) 1939- 108
Segal, Joyce 1940- 101
See also SATA 35
Segal, Julia (Clare) 1950- 145
Segal, Julius 1924- Brief entry 112
Segal, Lore (Groszmann) 1928- CANR-5
Earlier sketch in CA 13-16R
See also SAAS 11
See also SATA 4, 66
Segal, Lynne 1943- 133
Segal, Marilyn 1927- CANR-23
Earlier sketches in CA 17-20R, CANR-8
Segal, Martin CANR-1
Earlier sketch in CA 1-4R
Segal, Melvin J(ames) 1910- 37-40R
Segal, Mendel 1914- 49-52
Segal, Muriel 1913- 121
Segal, Naomi (Dinah) 1949- 128
Segal, Robert M(ilton) 1925- CANR-32
Earlier sketch in CA 29-32R
Segal, Ronald (Michael) 1932- CANR-14
Earlier sketch in CA 21-24R
Segal, S(tanley) S. 1919- 25-28R
Segalen, Martine 1940- 130
Segalman, Ralph 1916- 106
Segar, E(lzie) C(risler) 1894-1938 SATA 61
Segedin, Petar 1909- DLB 181
Segel, Harold B(ernard) 1930- 21-24R
Segel, Thomas D(onald) 1931- 93-96
Seger, Bob 1945- CLC 35
Segerberg, Osborn, Jr. 1924- 115
Segger, Sydney Walter 1902-(?) CAP-1
Earlier sketch in CA 13-16
Seghers
See Radvanyi, Netty
Seghers, Anna
See Radvanyi, Netty
See also CLC 7
See also DLB 69
Segler, Franklin Morgan 1907- 17-20R
Segovia, Andres 1893(?)-1987 147
Obituary 122
Brief entry 111
See also SATA-Obit 52
Segrave, Edmond 1904-1971 Obituary 29-32R
Segrave, Elisa 1949- 150
Segraves, Kelly L(ee) 1942- CANR-13
Earlier sketch in CA 61-64
Segre, Claudio Giuseppe 1937- 53-56
Segre, Dan V(ittorio) 1922- 104
Segre, Emilio (Gino) 1905-1989 CANR-13
Obituary 128
Earlier sketch in CA 33-36R
Segriff, Larry 1960- 153
Seguin, Marilyn W(eymouth) 1951- 155
See also SATA 91
Segundo, Bart
See Rowland, D(onald) S(ydney)
Segy, Ladislas 1904- CANR-30
Earlier sketch in CA 45-48
Seib, Kenneth Allen 1938- 29-32R
Seib, Philip 1949- 129
Seibel, C(lifford) W(inslow) 1890- CAP-2
Earlier sketch in CA 25-28
Seibel, Hans Dieter 1941- CANR-29
Earlier sketches in CA 65-68, CANR-11
Seibold, J. Otto 1960- SAAS 22
See also SATA 83
Seid, Ruth 1913-1995 5-8R
Obituary 148
See also Sinclair, Jo
Seide, Diane 1930- CANR-31
Earlier sketches in CA 73-76, CANR-14
Seide, Michael 1911- 111
Seidel, Frederick (Lewis) 1936- CANR-8
Earlier sketch in CA 13-16R
See also CLC 18
See also DLBY 84
Seidel, George J(oseph) 1932- 13-16R
Seidel, Ina 1885-1974 Obituary 116
See also DLB 56
Seidel, Kathleen G(illes) 1951- 112
Seidel, Michael Alan 1943- 93-96
Seidel, Ross 160
See also SATA 95
Seidelman, James Edward 1926- 25-28R
See also SATA 6
Seiden, Art(hur) SATA-Brief 42
Seiden, Martin H. 1934- 13-16R
Seiden, Morton Irving 1921- 17-20R
Seidenbaum, Art(hur David) 1930-1990 29-32R
Obituary 132
Seidenberg, Robert 1920- 25-28R
Seidenberg, Roderick 1890(?)-1973 Obituary 45-48
Seidensticker, Edward G. 1921- 89-92
Seidick, Kathryn A(melia) 1943- 108
Seidler, Ann (G.) 1925- 25-28R
Seidler, Grzegorz Leopold 1913- CANR-28
Earlier sketches in CA 29-32R, CANR-12
Seidler, Lee J. 1935- 73-76
Seidler, Murray Benjamin 1924- 5-8R
Seidler, Tor 1952- 123
See also SATA 52, 98
See also SATA-Brief 46
Seidlin, Oskar 1911- 41-44R
Seidman, Ann (Willcox) 1926- 81-84
Seidman, Harold 1911- 29-32R
Seidman, Hugh 1940- CANR-35
Earlier sketch in CA 29-32R
Seidman, Jerome M(artin) 1911- 45-48
Seidman, Joel 1906- CANR-9
Earlier sketch in CA 5-8R
Seidman, L. William 1921- 144
Seidman, Laurence Ivan 1925- 77-80
See also SATA 15
Seidman, Robert J(erome) 1941- 73-76
Seidmann, Ginette
See Spanier, Ginette
Seidner, Diane
See Seide, Diane
Seiferheld, Alfredo M. 1950-1988 Obituary 125
Seiferle, Rebecca 1951- 150
Seifert, Anne 1943- 105
Seifert, Elizabeth
See Gasparotti, Elizabeth Seifert

Seifert, Harvey (J.D.) 1911- CANR-3
Earlier sketch in CA 9-12R
Seifert, Jaroslav 1901-1986 127
See also CLC 34, 44, 93
See also MTCW 1
Seifert, Shirley L(ouise) 1888-1971 ..... CANR-2
Obituary 33-36R
Earlier sketch in CA 1-4R
Seifman, Eli 1936- 37-40R
Seifrid, Thomas 1956- 139
Seigel, Catharine F. 1933- 146
Seigel, Jerrold (Edward) 1936- 85-88
Seigel, Jules 1931- 93-96
Seigel, Kalman 1917- 25-28R
See also SATA 12
Seigenthaler, John (Lawrence) 1927- Brief entry 113
See also DLB 127
Seignobosc, Francoise 1897-1961 73-76
See also SATA 21
Seignolle, Claude 1917- 21-24R
Seiho
See Sullivan, M(ichael) J(ustin)
Seiler, John A(ndrew) 1927- 21-24R
Seiler, Robert E. 1925- 17-20R
Seilhamer, Frank Henry 1933- 85-88
Seim, Richard K(nudt) 1928- 102
Seimer, Stanley J(ames) 1918- CANR-28
Earlier sketch in CA 1-4R
Seinfel, Ruth
See Goode, Ruth
Seinfeld, Jerry 1954- 140
See also AAYA 11
Seip, Terry Lee 1944- 113
Seitlin, Charlotte 1907(?)-1979 Obituary 89-92
Seitz, Frederick 1911- 167
Seitz, Georg J(osef) 1920- 13-16R
Seitz, Jacqueline 1931- ..... SATA 50
Seitz, Nick 1939- 97-100
Seitz, William Chapin 1914-1974 ..... CANR-2
Obituary 53-56
Earlier sketch in CA 1-4R
Seixas, Judith S. 1922- 85-88
See also SATA 17
Sejima, Yoshimasa 1913- 33-36R
See also SATA 8
Sejour, Victor 1817-1874 ..... DLB 50
Sejour Marcou et Ferrand, Juan Victor
See Sejour, Victor
Sekaxsu, Petakwonexnajunkis 1950- 133
Sekers, Simone 1945- 119
Sekler, Eduard F(ranz) 1920- 69-72
Sekora, John 1939- Brief entry 106
Sekowski, Jozef-Julian
See Senkovsky, Osip Ivanovich
Selavy, Rrose
See Duchamp, (Henri-Robert) Marcel
Selberg, Ingrid (Maria) 1950- 136
See also SATA 68
Selbourne, David 1937- CANR-38
Earlier sketches in CA 89-92, CANR-16
Selby, Bettina 1934- CANR-41
Earlier sketch in CA 117
Selby, Curt
See Piserchia, Doris (Elaine)
Selby, Donald Joseph 1915- CANR-24
Earlier sketch in CA 1-4R
Selby, Edward B(urford), Jr. 1938- 45-48
Selby, Elliot
See Nicholson, Hubert
Selby, Hazel Barrington 1889-1972 ..... CAP-2
Earlier sketch in CA 17-18
Selby, Henry A. 1934- 37-40R
Selby, Hubert, Jr. 1928- CANR-33
Earlier sketch in CA 13-16R
See also CLC 1, 2, 4, 8
See also DLB 2
See also SSC 20
Selby, James Winford III 1947- 108
Selby, John (Allen) 1897-1980 ..... 1-4R
Obituary 97-100
Selby, John M(illin) 1905- 25-28R
Selcamm, George
See Machlis, Joseph
Selcer, Richard F. 1950- 139
Selcher, Wayne A(lan) 1942- CANR-10
Earlier sketch in CA 65-68
Selden, George
See Thompson, George Selden
See also CLR 8
See also DLB 52
Selden, Mark 1938- 81-84
Selden, Neil R(oy) 1931- 106
See also SATA 61
Selden, Raman 1937-1991 127
Obituary 134
Selden, Samuel 1899-1979 ..... CANR-3
Earlier sketch in CA 1-4R
Selden, William K(irkpatrick) 1911- 1-4R
Seldes, George (Henry) 1890-1995 ..... CANR-2
Obituary 149
Earlier sketch in CA 5-8R
Seldes, Gilbert (Vivian) 1893-1970 ..... 5-8R
Obituary 29-32R
Seldes, Marian (Hall) 1928- CANR-19
Earlier sketch in CA 85-88
Seldin, Maury 1931- CANR-34
Earlier sketches in CA 29-32R, CANR-15
Seldis, Henry 1925-1978 Obituary 77-80
Seldon, Anthony 1953- 136
Seldon, James R(alph) 1944- 112
Seldon, Mary Elisabeth 1921- 37-40R
Seldon, W(endell) Lynn, Jr. 1961- 167
Seldon-Truss, Leslie 1892- 5-8R
Selegen, Galina V(assily) 1899- 41-44R
Selement, George Joseph 1946- 113
Selenic, Slobodan 1933-1995 ..... DLB 181
Self, Carolyn Shealy 1931- CANR-16
Earlier sketch in CA 93-96
Self, Edwin F(orbes) 1920- 69-72
See also DLB 137
Self, Huber 1914- 73-76
Self, Jerry M(arvin) 1938- 61-64
Self, Margaret Cabell 1902- CANR-3
Earlier sketch in CA 5-8R
See also SATA 24
Self, Peter J(ohn) O(tter) 1919- CANR-47
Earlier sketch in CA 120
Self, Will 1961- 143
Self, William L(ee) 1932- 122
Selg, Herbert 1935- 69-72
Selig, Elaine Booth 1935- 104
Selig, Robert L. 1932- 152
Selig, Sylvie 1942- ..... SATA 13
Seligman, Barnard 1923- 113
Seligman, Ben B(aruch) 1912-1970 ..... CANR-2
Obituary 29-32R
Earlier sketch in CA 1-4R
Seligman, Daniel 1924- Brief entry 113
Seligman, Edwin R. A. 1861-1939 ..... DLB 47
Seligman, Eustace 1889(?)-1976 Obituary 69-72
Seligman, Germain 1893-1978 Obituary 77-80
Seligman, Lester George 1918- 13-16R
Seligman, Linda H(elen Goldberg) 1944- 114
Seligman, Martin E. P. 1942- 150
Seligman, Susan Meilach 1950- 105
Seligmann, G(ustav) L(eonard) Jr. 1934- 45-48
Seligmann, Herbert J(acob) 1891-1984 Obituary 112
Seligmann, Nancy 1948- 57-60
Seligson, Mitchell A(llan) 1945- 119
Seligson, Tom 1946- 33-36R
Selimovic, Mehmed 1910-1982 Obituary 108
See also Selimovic, Mesa
Selimovic, Mesa
See Selimovic, Mehmed
See also DLB 181
Selke, William L(ee) 1947- 144
Selkirk, Jane
See Chapman, John Stanton Higham
Sell, Betty (Marie) H(aas) 1928- 102
Sell, Charles M(urray) 1933- 113
Sell, DeWitt E(llsworth) 1915- 1-4R
Sell, Francis Edmund 1902- 5-8R
Sell, Henry Blackman 1889-1974 Obituary 89-92
Sell, Joseph
See Haley, William (John)
Sell, Kenneth D(aniel) 1928- 102
Sell, Roger D(avid) 1944- 116
Sell, Ted 1928-1989 69-72
Obituary 128
Sellars, Jane 1951- 149
Sellars, Wilfrid Stalker 1912-1989 Obituary 129
Sellen, Robert W(alker) 1930- 45-48
Seller, Maxine Schwartz 1935- 104
Sellerberg, Ann-Mari 1943- 154
Sellers, Bettie M(ixon) 1926- 77-80
Sellers, Charles Coleman 1903-1980 ..... CANR-11
Earlier sketch in CA 17-20R
Sellers, Christopher C. 1958- 166
Sellers, Con(nie Leslie, Jr.) 1922-1992 ..... CANR-37
Obituary 136
Earlier sketch in CA 97-100
Sellers, James Earl 1926- 113
Sellers, Naomi
See Flack, Naomi John White
Sellers, Robert Victor 1894-1973 ..... CAP-1
Obituary 89-92
Earlier sketch in CA 13-14
Sellers, Ronnie 1948- 115
Sellery, C. Morley 1894- CAP-2
Earlier sketch in CA 21-22
Sellew, Gladys 1887- CAP-1
Earlier sketch in CA 11-12
Sellin, Eric 1933- CANR-22
Earlier sketches in CA 17-20R, CANR-7
Sellin, Paul R(oland) 1930- 45-48
Sellings, Arthur
See Ley, Arthur Gordon
Sellman, Hunton Dade 1900- 5-8R
Sellman, Roger R(aymond) 1915- CANR-1
Earlier sketch in CA 1-4R
Sells, Arthur Lytton 1895- CANR-6
Earlier sketch in CA 5-8R
Sells, Iris (Esther) Lytton
See Lytton-Sells, Iris (Esther)
Sells, S(aul) B. 1913- CANR-19
Earlier sketches in CA 1-4R, CANR-4
Selltiz, Claire (Alice) 1914- 5-8R
Selman, LaRue W. 1927- ..... SATA 55
Selman, Robyn 1959- 152
Selmark, George
See Seldon-Truss, Leslie
Selness, Craig A(lan) 1955- 119
Selormey, Francis 1927- 21-24R
See also BW 1
Selous, Frederick Courteney 1851-1917 ..... DLB 174
Selous, Trista 142
Selsam, Howard 1903-1970 Obituary 29-32R
Selsam, Millicent Ellis 1912-1996 ..... CANR-38
Obituary 154
Earlier sketches in CA 9-12R, CANR-5
See also CLR 1
See also MAICYA
See also SATA 1, 29
See also SATA-Obit 92
Seltzer, Alvin J(ay) 1939- 65-68
Seltzer, Chester E. 1915-1971 131
See also Muro, Amado (Jesus)
See also HW
Seltzer, Daniel 1933-1980 89-92
Obituary 97-100
Seltzer, David 1920(?)- Brief entry 110
Seltzer, George 1924- 73-76
Seltzer, Leon E(ugene) 1918-1988 89-92
Obituary 124
Seltzer, Leon F(rancis) 1940- 33-36R
Seltzer, Louis B(enson) 1897-1980 Obituary 97-100
Seltzer, Meyer 1932- ..... SATA 17
Seltzer, Richard (Warren, Jr.) 1946- 105
See also SATA 41
Selvadurai, Shyam 1965- 167
Selver, (Percy) Paul 1888-1970 ..... CAP-2
Earlier sketch in CA 29-32
Selvidge, Marla J(ean) 1948- 162
Selvin, David F(rank) 1913- 25-28R
Selvin, Hanan C(harles) 1921- 9-12R
Selvin, Joel 1950- 133
Selvon, Sam
See Selvon, Samuel (Dickson)
See also DLB 125
Selvon, Samuel (Dickson) 1923-1994 128
Obituary 146
Brief entry 117
See also Selvon, Sam
See also BW 2
See also MTCW 1
Selway, Martina 1940- ..... SATA 74
Selwyn-Clarke, Selwyn 1893-1976 Obituary 65-68
Selwyn-Lloyd, John S. B. 1904-1978 Obituary 110
Selye, Hans 1907-1982 ..... CANR-2
Obituary 108
Earlier sketch in CA 5-8R
Selz, Peter (Howard) 1919- CANR-53
Earlier sketches in CA 1-4R, CANR-29
Selzer, Joae Graham 1926- 53-56
Selzer, Michael (I.) 1940- CANR-9
Earlier sketch in CA 53-56
Selzer, Richard 1928- CANR-14
Earlier sketch in CA 65-68
See also CLC 74
Selznick, Brian 1966- ..... SATA 79
Selznick, David O(liver) 1902-1965 Obituary 110
Selznick, Irene Mayer 1907-1990 Obituary 132
Semaan, Khalil I. H. 1920- 37-40R
Sembene, Ousmane
See Ousmane, Sembene
Semchyshyn, Stefan 1940- 134
Semeiks, Jonna Gormely 1944- 109
Semenov, Julian
See Lyandres, Yulian Semenovich
Semenov, Julian Semenovich
See Lyandres, Yulian Semenovich
Semenov, Nikolai N(ikolaevich) 1896-1986 157
Semenov, Yulian
See Lyandres, Yulian Semenovich
Semkiw, Virlyana
See Bishop, Tania Kroitor
Semler, H. Eric 1965- 125
Semler, Ricardo 1959- 149
Semloh
See Holmes, Peggy
Semmel, Bernard 1928- 77-80
Semmelroth, Otto 1912-1979 ..... CANR-10
Earlier sketch in CA 13-16R
Semmens, James P(ike) 1919- 61-64
Semmes, Raphael 1809-1877 ..... DLB 189
Semmler, Clement (William) 1914- CANR-45
Earlier sketches in CA 21-24R, CANR-14
Semonche, John E(rwin) 1933- CANR-30
Earlier sketch in CA 45-48
Sempell, Charlotte 1909- 41-44R
Semple, Gordon
See Neubauer, William Arthur
Semple, Lorenzo, Jr. 129
Brief entry 125
Semprun, Jorge 1923- 158
Brief entry 111
Semyonov, Julian
See Lyandres, Yulian Semenovich
Semyonov, Moshe 1946- 139
Semyonov, Yulian
See Lyandres, Yulian Semenovich
Sen, Amartya K. 1933- 147
Sen, Ela
See Reid, Ela
Sen, Sudhir 1906-1989 ..... 33-36R
Obituary 129
Sen, Zekai 1947- 153
Sena, John F(rancis) 1940- 110
Senancour, Etienne Pivert de 1770-1846 ..... DLB 119
Senarens, Luis P(hilip) 1865-1939 164
Sencourt, Robert
See George, Robert Esmonde Gordon
Sencourt, Robert Esmonde
See George, Robert Esmonde Gordon
Sendak, Jack 1924(?)-1995 77-80
Obituary 147
See also SATA 28
Sendak, Maurice (Bernard) 1928- CANR-39
Earlier sketches in CA 5-8R, CANR-11
Interview in CANR-11
See also CLR 1, 17
See also DLB 61
See also MAICYA
See also MTCW 1
See also SATA 1, 27
Sender, Ramon (Jose) 1902-1982 ..... CANR-8
Obituary 105
Earlier sketch in CA 5-8R
See also CLC 8
See also DAM MULT
See also HLC
See also HW
See also MTCW 1
Sender, Ruth M(insky) 1926- ..... SATA 62
Sender Barayon, Ramon 1934- 130
See also HW
Sendler, David A. 1938- 65-68
Sendrey, A(ladar) Alfred 1884- 13-16R
Sendy, Jean 1910-1978 ..... CANR-12
Earlier sketch in CA 53-56
Seneca, Lucius Annaeus 4B.C.-65 ..... DAM DRAM
See also DC 5
Senecal, Eva 1905- ..... DLB 92
Senelick, Laurence P(hilip) 1942- CANR-47
Earlier sketches in CA 106, CANR-22
Senesh, Hannah 1921-1944 Brief entry 119
Senesi, Mauro 1931- 17-20R
Seng, Peter J. 1922- 17-20R
Senghor, Leopold Sedar 1906- CANR-47
Brief entry 116
Earlier sketch in CA 125
See also BLC 3
See also BW 2
See also CLC 54
See also DAM MULT, POET
See also MTCW 1
Sengler, Johanna 1924- ..... SATA 18
Sengstacke, John H(erman Henry) 1912-1997 101
Obituary 158
See also BW 1
See also DLB 127
Sen Gupta, Pranati 1938- 102
Sen Gupta, Rajeswar 1908- CAP-1
Earlier sketch in CA 9-10
Senick, Gerard J(oseph) 1953- 97-100
Senie, Harriet F. 1943- 146
Senior, Clarence (Ollson) 1903-1974 65-68
Obituary 53-56
Senior, Donald 1940- CANR-53
Earlier sketches in CA 77-80, CANR-13, 29
Senior, Isabel J(anet Couper Syme) CANR-9
Earlier sketch in CA 5-8R
Senior, Michael 1940- 103
Senior, Nancy 1941- 119
Senior, Olive (Marjorie) 1941- 154
See also DLB 157
Senior, W(illiam) A. 1953- 155
Senkevitch, Anatole, Jr. 1942- CANR-19
Earlier sketch in CA 101
Senkovsky, Osip Ivanovich 1800-1858 ..... DLB 198
Senn, Alfred Erich 1932- 134
Brief entry 112
Senn, Bryan 1962- 145
Senn, Frank C(olvin) 1943- CANR-39
Earlier sketch in CA 115
Senn, Fritz 1928- 41-44R
Senn, Milton J(ohn) E(dward) 1902- 81-84
Senn, Peter R(ichard) 1923- 33-36R
Senn, Steve 1950- 105
See also SATA 60
See also SATA-Brief 48
Senna, Carl 1944- CANR-19
Earlier sketches in CA 49-52, CANR-4
Sennett, Richard 1943- 73-76
Sennett, Ted 1928- CANR-38
Earlier sketch in CA 33-36R
Sennholz, Hans F. 1922- CANR-47
Brief entry 118
Earlier sketch in CA 120
Senoa, August 1838-1881 ..... DLB 147
Sensabaugh, George Frank 1906- CAP-1
Earlier sketch in CA 13-14
Senser, Robert A(nton) 1921- 5-8R
Sensibar, Judith L(evin) 1941- 144
Senter, Florence H.
See Ellis, Florence Hawley
Senter, Sylvia 1921- 113
Sentner, David P. 1898-1975 Obituary 57-60
Sentner, Mary Steele 1900(?)-1983 Obituary 110
Seoane, Rhoda 1905- CAP-2
Earlier sketch in CA 25-28
Sepamla, (Sydney) Sipho 1932- 154
See also DLB 157
Sepetys, Jonas 1901- 57-60
Sepheriades, Georgios
See Seferiades, Giorgos Stylianou
Sepia
See Holmvik, Oyvind
Sequoia, Anna 109
Serafian, Michael
See Martin, Malachi
Serafini, Anthony Louis 1945- 112
Serage, Nancy 1924- 65-68
See also SATA 10
Serb, Ann Toland 1937- 81-84
Serban, George 1926- 129
Serban, William M(ichael) 1949- 102
Serebriakoff, Victor 1912- 148
Serebryakova, Galina Iosifovna 1905-1980 Obituary 102
Seredy, Kate 1899-1975 ..... 5-8R
Obituary 57-60
See also CLR 10
See also DLB 22
See also MAICYA
See also SATA 1
See also SATA-Obit 24
Serels, M. Mitchell 1948- 144
Sereni, Vittorio 1913-1983 Obituary 109
See also DLB 128
Sereny, Gitta
See Serenyi, Gitta
Serenyi, Gitta 1923- CANR-58
Earlier sketch in CA 119
Serenyi, Peter 1931- 61-64
Seres, William fl. 1546(?)-1579(?) ..... DLB 170
Seret, Roberta 1945- 146
Serfaty, Simon 1940- CANR-26
Earlier sketches in CA 25-28R, CANR-10
Serfozo, Mary 1925- 149

Sergeant, Harriet 1954- 132
Sergeant, (Herbert) Howard 1914-1987 .. CANR-20
Obituary 121
Earlier sketches in CA 5-8R, CANR-5
Sergel, Ruth
See Perry, Ruth (Fuller)
Sergent, Bernard 1946- 133
Sergievsky, Orest 1911-1984 Obituary 114
Sergio, Elisa 1905-1989 61-64
Obituary 129
Sergio, Lisa
See Sergio, Elisa
Sergios, Paul A. 1961- 145
Seriel, Jerome
See Vallee, Jacques F.
Serif, Med 1924- 17-20R
Serig, Beverly J. 1934- 101
Serjeant, Robert Bertram 1915- 139
Serle, (Alan) Geoffrey 1922- 13-16R
Serling, Carol 1929- 140
Serling, Robert J(erome) 1918- CANR-1
Earlier sketch in CA 45-48
Serling, (Edward) Rod(man) 1924-1975 162
Obituary 57-60
See also AAYA 14
See also AITN 1
See also CLC 30
See also DLB 26
Serna, Ramon Gomez de la
See Gomez de la Serna, Ramon
Serna-Maytorena, Manuel Antonio 1932- .. CANR-3
Earlier sketch in CA 45-48
Sernett, Milton C(harles) 1942- 61-64
Sernine, Daniel 1955- 156
Seroff, Victor I(ilyitch) 1902-1979 .... 25-28R
Obituary 85-88
See also SATA 12
See also SATA-Obit 26
Seroka, James H. 1950- 124
Seroka, Jim
See Seroka, James H.
Serote, Mongane Wally 1944- 142
See also BW 2
See also DLB 125
Serpieres
See Guillevic, (Eugene)
Serra, Diana
See Cary, Peggy-Jean Montgomery
Serraillier, Ian (Lucien) 1912-1994 .... CANR-1
Obituary 147
Earlier sketch in CA 1-4R
See also CLR 2
See also DLB 161
See also MAICYA
See also SAAS 3
See also SATA 1, 73
See also SATA-Obit 83
Serrano, Lucienne J. 1936- 131
Serrano, Miguel 1917- 132
Serrano, Napoleon Diestro Valeriano
See Valeriano, Napoleon D(iestro)
Serrano, Nina 1934- .... DLB 122
Serrano Plaja, Arturo 1909-1979 .... CANR-13
Earlier sketch in CA 29-32R
Serrifile, F. O. O.
See Holmes, William Kersley
Serron, Luis A(ugusto) 1930- 102
Serry, Victor
See Serebriakoff, Victor
Sert, Josep Lluis 1902-1983 Obituary 109
Servadio, Gaia 1938- CANR-11
Earlier sketch in CA 25-28R
Servan-Schreiber, Jean-Jacques 1924- 102
Servello, Joe 1932- .... SATA 10
Serventy, Vincent (Noel) CANR-27
Earlier sketches in CA 65-68, CANR-10
Server, Lee 146
Service, Alastair (Stanley Douglas) 1933- 130
Service, Elman Rogers 1915- 112
Service, Grace 1879-1954 142
Service, John S(tewart) 1909- 142
Brief entry 113
Service, Pamela F. 1945- CANR-47
Earlier sketch in CA 120
See also AAYA 20
See also SATA 64
Service, Robert
See Service, Robert W(illiam)
See also DAB
See also DLB 92
Service, Robert W(illiam) 1874(?)-1958 140
Brief entry 115
See also Service, Robert
See also DA
See also DAC
See also DAM MST, POET
See also SATA 20
See also TCLC 15
See also WLC
Servin, Manuel P(atrick) 1920- 37-40R
Serviss, Garrett P(utnam) 1851-1929 160
Brief entry 119
Serwadda, W(illiam) Moses 1931- 107
See also SATA 27
Serwer, Blanche L. 1910- 65-68
See also SATA 10
Serwicher, Kurt 1912-1979 Obituary 89-92
Seshadri, Vijay 1954- 156
Seskin, Eugene P(aul) 1948- 89-92
Sesonske, Alexander 1917- 13-16R
Sessions, Kyle Cutler 1934- Brief entry 106
Sessions, Roger Huntington 1896-1985 93-96
Obituary 115
Sessions, Will 1905- 1-4R
Sessler, Charles 1854-1935 .... DLB 187
Sessoms, H(anson) Douglas 1931- 41-44R
Sesti, Giuseppe Maria 1942- 137
Seth, Ronald (Sydney) 1911-1985 106
Obituary 115
Seth, Vikram 1952- CANR-50
Brief entry 121
Earlier sketch in CA 127
Interview in 127
See also CLC 43, 90
See also DAM MULT
See also DLB 120
Sethi, Narendra Kumar 1935- CANR-14
Earlier sketch in CA 37-40R
Sethi, S. Prakash 1934- 41-44R
Sethna, Jehangir Minocher 1941- 37-40R
Sethna, Minocher Jehangirji 1911- 9-12R
Seth-Smith, Elsie K.
See Murrell, Elsie Kathleen Seth-Smith
Seth-Smith, Leslie James 1923- 104
Seth-Smith, Michael 1928- CANR-16
Earlier sketch in CA 29-32R
Setien, Miguel Delibes
See Delibes Setien, Miguel
Seton, Anya 1904(?)-1990 .... CANR-69
Obituary 133
Earlier sketch in CA 17-20R
See also SATA 3
See also SATA-Obit 66
Seton, Cynthia Propper 1926-1982 .... CANR-7
Obituary 108
Earlier sketch in CA 5-8R
See also CLC 27
Seton, Elizabeth Ann 1774-1821 .... DLB 200
Seton, Ernest (Evan) Thompson 1860-1946 Brief entry 109
See also DLB 92
See also DLBD 13
See also JRDA
See also SATA 18
See also TCLC 31
Seton, Marie 1910- 105
Seton-Thompson, Ernest
See Seton, Ernest (Evan) Thompson
Seton-Watson, Christopher 1918- CANR-11
Earlier sketch in CA 21-24R
Seton-Watson, (George) Hugh (Nicholas) 1916-1984 117
Obituary 114
Setouchi, Harumi 1922- .... DLB 182
Settanni, Harry 1945- 146
Settel, Gertrude S. 17-20R
Settel, Irving 1916- 17-20R
Settel, Trudy S.
See Settel, Gertrude S.
Setterberg, Fred 1951- 144
Settle, Edith
See Andrews, (William) Linton
Settle, Mary Lee 1918- CANR-44
Earlier sketch in CA 89-92
Interview in 89-92
See also CAAS 1
See also CLC 19, 61
See also DLB 6
Setton, Kenneth M. 1914- CANR-39
Earlier sketches in CA 9-12R, CANR-3, 18
Setzekorn, William David 1935- 65-68
Setzer, (Cynthia) Lynn 1955- 167
Setzler, Frank M(aryl) 1902-1975 Obituary 57-60
Seufert, Karl Rolf 1923- CANR-28
Earlier sketch in CA 9-12R
Seuling, Barbara 1937- CANR-52
Earlier sketches in CA 61-64, CANR-8, 26
See also SAAS 24
See also SATA 10, 98
Seume, Johann Gottfried 1763-1810 .... DLB 94
Seung, Thomas Kaehao 1930- CANR-36
Earlier sketch in CA 108
Seuphor, Michel
See Arp, Jean
Seuren, Pieter A. M. 1934- 49-52
Seuse, Heinrich c. 1295-1366 .... DLB 179
Seuss, Dr.
See Geisel, Theodor Seuss
Sevareid, (Arnold) Eric 1912- 69-72
See also AITN 1
Sevela, Efraim 1928- CANR-30
Earlier sketch in CA 69-72
Seventeenth Earl of Oxford
See de Vere, Edward
Severance, Carol (Ann Wilcox) 1944- 155
Severance, John B(ridwell) 1935- 164
Severin, Mark (Fernand) 1906- 107
Severin, (Giles) Timothy 1940- CANR-10
Earlier sketch in CA 21-24R
Severino, Alexandrino E(usebio) 1931- 41-44R
Severino, Carol (J.) 1949- 168
Severn, Bill
See Severn, William Irving
Severn, David
See Unwin, David S(torr)
Severn, Donald
See Nolan, Frederick William
Severn, Sue 1918- 5-8R
Severn, William Irving 1914- CANR-36
Earlier sketches in CA 1-4R, CANR-1, 16
See also SATA 1
Severo, Richard 1932- 73-76
Severs, Jerome
See Wooley, John (Steven)
Severs, Vesta-Nadine 1935- CANR-15
Earlier sketch in CA 89-92
Severson, John H(ugh) 1933- 13-16R
Sewall, Joseph 1688-1769 .... DLB 24
Sewall, Marcia 1935- CANR-18
Earlier sketches in CA 45-48, CANR-1
See also MAICYA
See also SATA 37, 69
Sewall, Mary Franklin 1884-(?) CAP-2
Earlier sketch in CA 21-22
Sewall, Richard B(enson) 1908- 93-96
Interview in 93-96
See also DLB 111
Sewall, Samuel 1652-1730 .... DLB 24
Seward, Desmond 1935- 158
Brief entry 114
Seward, Jack
See Seward, John Neil
Seward, James H(odson) 1928- 65-68
Seward, John Neil 1924- CANR-8
Earlier sketch in CA 21-24R
Seward, Prudence 1926- .... SATA 16
Seward, William W(ard), Jr. 1913- 9-12R
Sewart, Alan 1928- CANR-25
Earlier sketch in CA 108
Sewel, John 1946- 103
Sewell, Anna 1820-1878 .... CLR 17
See also DLB 163
See also JRDA
See also MAICYA
See also SATA 24, 100
Sewell, Brocard 1912- 107
Sewell, (Margaret) Elizabeth 1919- 49-52
Sewell, Helen (Moore) 1896-1957 137
Brief entry 123
See also MAICYA
See also SATA 38
Sewell, J. Leslie 1923- 21-24R
Sewell, James Patrick 1930- 73-76
Sewell, Marilyn 166
Sewell, Richard H(erbert) 1931- Brief entry 117
Sewell, W. R. Derrick 1931- CANR-9
Earlier sketch in CA 21-24R
Sewell, William H(amilton) 1909- 45-48
Sewell, Winifred 1917- 102
Sewny, Kathryn Wiehe 1909- CAP-1
Earlier sketch in CA 13-16
Sewter, Albert Charles 1912- 89-92
Sexton, A(da) Jeanette 1924- 65-68
Sexton, Adam 1962- 142
Sexton, Anne (Harvey) 1928-1974 .... CANR-36
Obituary 53-56
Earlier sketches in CA 1-4R, CANR-3
See also CABS 2
See also CDALB 1941-1968
See also CLC 2, 4, 6, 8, 10, 15, 53
See also DA
See also DAB
See also DAC
See also DAM MST, POET
See also DLB 5, 169
See also MTCW 1
See also PC 2
See also SATA 10
See also WLC
Sexton, James D(ean) 1942- 113
Sexton, Linda Gray 1953- CANR-36
Earlier sketch in CA 101
Sexton, Michael J(oseph) 1939- 45-48
Sexton, Patricia Cayo 1924- 141
Sexton, Richard J(oseph) 1912- 45-48
Sexton, Virgil Wesley 1918- 33-36R
Sexton, Virginia Staudt 1916- 29-32R
Sexton, William C(ottrell) 1928- 133
Seybolt, Peter J(ordan) 1934- CANR-35
Earlier sketch in CA 53-56
Seydel, Mildred Woolley 1890(?)-1988 .... 37-40R
Obituary 124
Seydell, Mildred
See Seydel, Mildred Woolley
Seydor, Paul 1947- 97-100
Seyer, Philip C. 1941- 119
Seyersted, Brita Lindberg
See Lindberg-Seyersted, Brita
Seyersted, Per 1921- CANR-15
Earlier sketch in CA 29-32R
Seyfert, Carl K(eenan) 1938- 57-60
Seyler, Dorothy U(pton) 1938- 109
Seymour, A(rthur) J(ames) 1914- CANR-29
Earlier sketch in CA 97-100
See also BW 2
Seymour, Alan
See Wright, S(ydney) Fowler
Seymour, Alan 1927- 53-56
Seymour, Alta Halverson CAP-1
Earlier sketch in CA 11-12
See also SATA 10
Seymour, Anne
See Morton, Phyllis Digby
Seymour, Charles, Jr. 1912-1977 .... 9-12R
Obituary 69-72
Seymour, Digby G. 1923- 17-20R
Seymour, Dorothy Jane Z(ander) 1928- 89-92
Seymour, Emery W. 1921- 13-16R
Seymour, Forrest W. 1905-1983 Obituary 111
Seymour, (William Herschel Kean) Gerald 1941- ... CANR-68
Earlier sketches in CA 101, CANR-45
Seymour, Harold 1910- 138
Seymour, Henry
See Hartmann, Helmut Henry
Seymour, James D. 1935- 162
Seymour, John 1914- CANR-9
Earlier sketch in CA 13-16R
Seymour, Miranda
See Sinclair, Miranda
Seymour, Raymond B(enedict) 1912-1991 .... CANR-44
Earlier sketches in CA 73-76, CANR-13
Seymour, Rogers James 1942- 110
Seymour, Stephan A(ndrew) 1920- 21-24R
Seymour, Tres 1966- 149
See also SATA 82
Seymour, W(illiam) Douglas 1910- 49-52
Seymour, Whitney North, Jr. 1923- CANR-14
Earlier sketch in CA 81-84
Seymour, William Kean 1887-1975 .... 9-12R
Obituary 126
Seymour, William Napier 1914- 77-80
Seymour-Smith, Martin 1928- CANR-54
Earlier sketch in CA 5-8R
See also DLB 155
Seymour-Ure, Colin K. 1938- CANR-18
Earlier sketch in CA 25-28R
Seyton, Marion
See Saxon, Gladys Relyea
Seznec, Jean J. 1905-1983 Obituary 111
Sgorlon, Carlo 1930- .... DLB 196
Sgroi, Peter Philip 1936- 57-60
Sgroi, Suzanne M(ary) 1943- 108
Shaaban, Bouthaina 1953- 137
Shaaber, M. A.
See Shaaber, Matthias A(dam)
Shaaber, Matthias A(dam) 1897-1979 Obituary 111
Shaara, Jeff 1952- 163
Shaara, Michael (Joseph, Jr.) 1929-1988 .... CANR-52
Obituary 125
Earlier sketch in CA 102
See also AITN 1
See also CLC 15
See also DAM POP
See also DLBY 83
Shabad, Theodore 1922-1987 .... CANR-10
Obituary 122
Earlier sketch in CA 25-28R
Shachtman, Tom 1942- 89-92
See also SATA 49
Shack, William A(lfred) 1923- 113
Shackelford, Jean A. 1946- CANR-43
Earlier sketch in CA 105
Shacket, Sheldon R(ubin) 1941- 102
Shackford, Martha Hale 1875-1963 .... 1-4R
Shackford, R(oland) H(erbert) 1908-1998 .... 1-4R
Obituary 165
Shackle, G(eorge) L(ennox) S(harman) 1903-1992 .... CANR-2
Obituary 137
Earlier sketch in CA 5-8R
Shackleford, Bernard L. 1889-1975 .... CAP-2
Earlier sketch in CA 29-32
Shackleford, Ruby P(aschall) 1913- 57-60
Shackleton, C. C.
See Aldiss, Brian W(ilson)
Shackleton, Doris (Cavell) 1918- 93-96
Shackleton, Edward Arthur Alexander 1911- 13-16R
Shackleton, Ernest Henry 1874-1922 Brief entry 118
Shackleton, Keith Hope 1923- 5-8R
Shackleton, Philip 1923- 101
Shackleton, Robert 1919-1986 .... 1-4R
Obituary 120
Shackleton Bailey, D(avid) R(oy) 1917- .. CANR-19
Earlier sketches in CA 5-8R, CANR-3
Shackley, Myra (Lesley) 1949- 115
Shackley, Theodore (George, Jr.) 1927- Brief entry 117
Shacochis, Bob
See Shacochis, Robert G.
See also CLC 39
Shacochis, Robert G. 1951- 124
Brief entry 119
Interview in 124
See also Shacochis, Bob
Shadbolt, Maurice (Francis Richard) 1932- CANR-5
Earlier sketch in CA 13-16R
See also CAAS 3
Shade, Rose (Marian) 1927- 57-60
Shade, William G(erald) 1939- 41-44R
Shade, William L(eonard) 1945- Brief entry 113
Shadegg, Stephen C. 1909-1990 .... 13-16R
Obituary 131
Shader, Rachel
See Sofer, Barbara
Shadi, Dorothy Clotelle Clarke 1908- 13-16R
Shadily, Hassan 1920- 105
Shadlick, Harold (Ernest) 1902- 41-44R
Shadoian, Jack 1940- 105
Shadowitz, Albert 1915- 69-72
Shadwell, Thomas
See Cover, Arthur Byron
Shadwell, Thomas 1641(?)-1692 .... DLB 80
Shaevitz, Marjorie Hansen 1943- 101
Shaevitz, Morton H(erbert) 1935- 102
Shafarevich, Igor Rostislavovich 1923- 105
Shafer, Boyd Carlisle 1907- 17-20R
Shafer, Byron E. 1947- 165
Shafer, D. Michael 1953- 134
Shafer, Glenn (Ray) 1946- 168
Shafer, Neil 1933- 33-36R
Shafer, Robert E(ugene) 1925- CANR-10
Earlier sketch in CA 57-60
See also SATA 9
Shafer, Robert Jones 1920- 37-40R
Shafer, Ronald G. 1939- CANR-10
Earlier sketch in CA 65-68
Shafer, Thomas 1910(?)-1986 Obituary 119
Shaff, Albert L(averne) 1937- 29-32R
Shaffer, Anthony (Joshua) 1926- 116
Brief entry 110
See also CLC 19
See also DAM DRAM
See also DLB 13
Shaffer, Betty
See Shaffer, Elizabeth (Nickerson)
Shaffer, Dale Eugene 1929- 37-40R
Shaffer, Elizabeth (Nickerson) 1925- 113
Shaffer, Harry George 1919- CANR-6
Earlier sketch in CA 5-8R

Shaffer, Helen B. 1909(?)-1978 ... 85-88
Obituary ... 81-84
Shaffer, Jeffrey 1953- ... 151
Shaffer, Jerome A(rthur) 1929- ... 37-40R
Shaffer, K(atherine) Stevenson 1902- ... CAP-2
Earlier sketch in CA 17-18
Shaffer, Karen A. 1947- ... CANR-57
Earlier sketch in CA 127
Shaffer, Kenneth R(aymond) 1914- ... 5-8R
Shaffer, Laurance Frederic
1903-1976 Obituary ... 65-68
Shaffer, Louise ... 152
Shaffer, Peter (Levin) 1926- ... CANR-47
Earlier sketches in CA 25-28R, CANR-25
See also CDBLB 1960 to Present
See also CLC 5, 14, 18, 37, 60
See also DAB
See also DAM DRAM, MST
See also DC 7
See also DLB 13
See also MTCW 1
Shaffer, Rosalind Keating 1896-1990 Obituary . 131
Shaffer, Samuel 1910- ... 104
Shaffer, Terea 1968- ... SATA 79
Shaffer, Thomas Lindsay 1934- ... 37-40R
Shaffer, Wilma L. 1916- ... 17-20R
Shafir, Michael 1944- ... 129
Shafquat, Sofia 1959- ... 141
Shafritz, Jay M(ichael) 1944- ... 117
Shaftel, Oscar 1912- ... 57-60
Shaftner, Dorothy 1918- ... 25-28R
Shagan, Steve 1927- ... CANR-6
Earlier sketch in CA 53-56
Shaginyan, Marietta (Sergeyevna) 1888-1982 .. 129
Obituary ... 106
Shah, A(ruind) M(anilal) 1931- ... 73-76
Shah, Amina 1918- ... 49-52
Shah, Diane K(iver) 1945- ... 73-76
Shah, (Sayed) Idries 1924-1996 ... CANR-47
Obituary ... 154
Earlier sketches in CA 17-20R, CANR-7, 22
Shah, Jami J. 1950- ... 159
Shah, Krishna B. 1933- ... 17-20R
Shaha, Rishikesh 1925- ... CANR-47
Earlier sketch in CA 69-72
Shahan, Lynn 1941- ... 106
Shahan, Sherry 1949- ... 156
See also SATA 92
Shahane, Vasant Anant 1923- ... CANR-12
Earlier sketch in CA 25-28R
Shahani, Ranjee 1904-1968 ... CANR-2
Earlier sketch in CA 1-4R
Shahar, David 1926- ... 65-68
Shaheen, Jack G(eorge) 1935- ... 124
Shaheen, Naseeb 1931- ... CANR-34
Earlier sketch in CA 65-68
Shahn, Ben(jamin) 1898-1969 ... 121
Obituary ... 89-92
See also SATA-Obit 21
Shahn, Bernarda Bryson
See Bryson, Bernarda
Shah of Iran
See Pahlevi, Mohammed Riza
Shain, Henry 1941- ... 57-60
Shain, Merle 1935- ... 61-64
See also AITN 1
Shain, Milton 1949- ... 149
Shain, Yossi 1956- ... 131
Shainberg, Lawrence 1936- ... 137
Brief entry ... 131
Interview in ... 137
Shainmark, Eliezer L. 1900-1976 Obituary ... 104
Shainmark, Lou
See Shainmark, Eliezer L.
Shairp, (Alexander) Mordaunt 1887-1939 Brief
entry ... 110
See also DLB 10
Shakabpa, Tsepon W(angchuk) D(eden)
1907-1989 ... CAP-2
Obituary ... 128
Earlier sketch in CA 23-24R
Sha'Ked, Ami 1945- ... 101
Shaked, Gershon 1929- ... 131
Shaked, Haim 1939- ... 130
Shakeri, Khosrow 1938- ... 154
Shakesby, Paul S(tewart) 1946- ... 57-60
Shakespeare, Geoffrey (Hithersay)
1893-1980 Obituary ... 105
Shakespeare, (William Richmond) Nicholas
1957- ... 145
Shakespeare, William 1564-1616 ... CDBLB Before
1660
See also DA
See also DAB
See also DAC
See also DAM DRAM, MST, POET
See also DLB 62, 172
See also WLC
Shakey, Bernard
See Young, Neil
Shakhovskoi, Aleksandr Aleksandrovich
1777-1846 ... DLB 150
Shakow, David 1901-1981 Obituary ... 108
Shakur, Sanyika 1963- ... 148
Shakur, Tupac (Amaru) 1971-1996 ... 156
Shalamov, Varlam (Tikhonovich) 1907(?)-1982 . 129
Obituary ... 105
See also CLC 18
Shale, Richard 1947- ... 89-92
Shales, Thomas William 1948- ... 112
Brief entry ... 110
Interview in ... 112
Shales, Tom
See Shales, Thomas William
Shalett, Anita Effron 1917(?)-1984 Obituary ... 112
Shalhope, Robert E. 1941- ... 85-88
Shalit, Beatrice 1945- ... 142
Shallcrass, John James 1922- ... CANR-20
Earlier sketch in CA 103
Shallenberger, David 1950- ... 166
Shallit, Jeffrey (Outlaw) 1957- ... 164
Shallow, Robert
See Atkinson, Frank
Shaloff, Stanley 1939- ... CANR-43
Earlier sketch in CA 29-32R
Shalom, Stephen Rosskamm 1948- ... 112
Shalvey, Thomas (Joseph) 1937- ... 105
Shambaugh, David L. 1953- ... 142
Shamburger, (Alice) Page ... 9-12R
Shames, Laurence 1951- ... 124
Shamir, Yitzhak 1915- ... 150
Shamlu, Ahmad 1925- ... CLC 10
Shammas, Anton 1951- ... CLC 55
Shamon, Albert Joseph 1915- ... 13-16R
Shan, Yeh
See Wang, C(hing) H(sien)
Shanahan, Daniel (A.) 1947- ... 139
Shanahan, Eileen 1924- ... 102
Shanahan, William J. 1935- ... 29-32R
Shands, Harley Cecil 1916-1981 ... 109
Obituary ... 105
Shane, Alex M(ichael) 1933- ... 45-48
Shane, Bart
See Rowland, D(onald) S(ydney)
Shane, C(harles) Donald 1895-1983 Obituary .. 109
Shane, Don (Graves) 1933- ... 53-56
Shane, Harold Gray 1914-1993 ... CANR-21
Obituary ... 141
Earlier sketches in CA 9-12R, CANR-3
See also SATA 36
See also SATA-Obit 76
Shane, John
See Durst, Paul
Shane, Mark
See Norwood, Victor G(eorge) C(harles)
Shane, Maxwell 1905(?)-1983 Obituary ... 111
Shane, Rhondo
See Norwood, Victor G(eorge) C(harles)
Shane, Scott 1954- ... 146
Shaner, Madeleine 1932- ... 73-76
Shanes, Eric 1944- ... 134
Shanet, Howard (Stephen) 1918- ... 130
Shange, Ntozake 1948- ... CANR-48
Earlier sketches in CA 85-88, CANR-27
See also CABS 3
See also AAYA 9
See also BLC 3
See also BW 2
See also CLC 8, 25, 38, 74
See also DAM DRAM, MULT
See also DC 3
See also DLB 38
See also MTCW 1
Shank, Alan 1936- ... 53-56
Shank, David Arthur 1924- ... 29-32R
Shank, Joseph E(lmer) 1892- ... CAP-2
Earlier sketch in CA 25-28
Shank, Margarethe Erdahl 1910- ... CAP-2
Earlier sketch in CA 19-20
Shank, Theodore
See Shank, Theodore J(unior)
Shank, Theodore J(unior) 1929- ... CANR-65
Earlier sketch in CA 129
Shankel, George Edgar 1894- ... CAP-2
Earlier sketch in CA 23-24
Shankland, Peter Macfarlane 1901- ... CANR-16
Earlier sketches in CAP-1, CA 11-12
Shankle, Ralph O(tis) 1933- ... 9-12R
Shanklin, William L(eslie) 1941- ... 120
Shankman, Arnold M(ichael) 1945- ... 129
Shankman, Florence V(ogel) 1912- ... 41-44R
Shankman, Paul (Andrew) 1943- ... 93-96
Shanks, Ann Zane (Kushner) ... 53-56
See also SATA 10
Shanks, Bob 1932- ... 101
Shanks, Bruce ... AITN 1
Shanks, Hershel 1930- ... CANR-52
Brief entry ... 106
Earlier sketch in CA 126
Shanks, Michael (James) 1927-1984 ... CANR-8
Obituary ... 111
Earlier sketch in CA 5-8R
Shanley, John Patrick 1950- ... 133
Brief entry ... 128
See also CLC 75
Shanley, Mary L(yndon) 1944- ... 163
Shann, Renee 1907(?)-1979 Obituary ... 89-92
Shannon, Claude (Elwood) 1916- ... 162
Shannon, David Allen 1920- ... CANR-43
Earlier sketch in CA 1-4R
Shannon, Dell
See Linington, (Barbara) Elizabeth
Shannon, Doris 1924- ... CANR-62
Earlier sketches in CA 61-64, CANR-8, 23
Shannon, Edgar F(inley), Jr. 1918- ... 9-12R
Shannon, Elizabeth (McNelly) 1937- ... 147
Shannon, Ellen 1927- ... 77-80
Shannon, Foster (Houts) 1930- ... 106
Shannon, Fred Albert 1893-1963 Obituary ... 111
Shannon, George (William Bones) 1952- . CANR-69
Earlier sketches in CA 106, CANR-23
See also SATA 35, 94
Shannon, Jacqueline ... SATA 63
Shannon, Jasper Berry 1903-1984 ... 1-4R
Obituary ... 114
Shannon, John 1943- ... 57-60
Shannon, Lyle William 1920- ... 61-64
Shannon, M.
See Geddie, John
Shannon, Margaret
See Silverwood, Margaret Shannon
Shannon, Mike 1951- ... 127
Shannon, Monica 1905(?)-1965 Obituary ... 109
See also SATA 28
Shannon, Richard 1945- ... 73-76
Shannon, Robert
See Wieder, Robert S(hannon)
Shannon, Robert C. 1930- ... 13-16R
Shannon, Robert L(eroy) 1926- ... 93-96
Shannon, Terry
See Mercer, Jessie
See also SATA 21
Shannon, Thomas A(nthony) 1940- ... CANR-42
Earlier sketches in CA 53-56, CANR-5, 20
Shannon, William H(enry) 1917- ... 45-48
Shannon, William V(incent) 1927-1988 ... CANR-6
Obituary ... 126
Earlier sketch in CA 9-12R
Shanor, Donald Read 1927- ... CANR-30
Earlier sketches in CA 61-64, CANR-12
Shanwa
See Haarer, Alec Ernest
Shao, Stephen P(inyee) 1924- ... CANR-11
Earlier sketch in CA 21-24R
Shapard, Robert (Perry) 1942- ... 126
Shapcott, Jo 1958- ... 135
Shapcott, Thomas W(illiam) 1935- ... CANR-49
Earlier sketch in CA 69-72
See also CLC 38
Shapell, Nathan 1922- ... 49-52
Shapera, Robert J.
See Evans, Robert
Shapere, Dudley 1928- ... 17-20R
Shapin, Steven 1943- ... 164
Shapiro, Alan 1952- ... 125
See also CAAS 23
Shapiro, Alan E(lihu) 1942- ... 128
Shapiro, Barbara J(une) 1934- ... 130
Shapiro, Barry M. 1944- ... 146
Shapiro, Bonnie L. ... 150
Shapiro, Cecile ... 85-88
Shapiro, Charles K. 1926- ... 5-8R
Shapiro, Dani (J.) ... 167
Shapiro, David (Joel) 1947- ... CANR-45
Earlier sketch in CA 13-16R
Shapiro, David S(idney) 1923-1983 ... CANR-1
Obituary ... 109
Earlier sketch in CA 1-4R
Shapiro, Deborah 1923- ... 106
Shapiro, Dolph
See Sharp, Dolph
Shapiro, Edward 1920- ... 17-20R
Shapiro, Edward S. 1938- ... 148
Shapiro, Eileen C. ... 152
Shapiro, Elizabeth Klein
See Klein, Elizabeth
Shapiro, Fred(eric) C(harles) 1931-1993 ... 17-20R
Obituary ... 143
Shapiro, Fred R(ichard) 1954- ... 145
Shapiro, Harold I(srael) 1931- ... 45-48
Shapiro, Harold T(afler) 1935- ... 132
Shapiro, Harry L(ionel) 1902- ... 49-52
Shapiro, Harvey 1924- ... CANR-34
Earlier sketches in CA 41-44R, CANR-15
Shapiro, Henry D(avid) 1937- ... CANR-3
Earlier sketch in CA 9-12R
Shapiro, Herbert 1929- ... 37-40R
Shapiro, Herman 1922- ... 13-16R
Shapiro, Howard I(ra) 1937- ... 73-76
Shapiro, Irving 1917- ... 29-32R
Shapiro, Irwin 1911-1981 ... CANR-45
Earlier sketch in CA 81-84
See also SATA 32
Shapiro, James E(arnest) 1946- ... 108
Shapiro, Jane ... CLC 76
Shapiro, Jane P.
See Zacek, Jane Shapiro
Shapiro, Jerrold Lee 1943- ... 144
Shapiro, Jim
See Shapiro, James E(arnest)
Shapiro, Joan Hatch 1928- ... 33-36R
Shapiro, Judith 1953- ... 144
Shapiro, Julian L.
See Sanford, John
Shapiro, Karl (Jay) 1913- ... CANR-66
Earlier sketches in CA 1-4R, CANR-1, 36
See also CAAS 6
See also CLC 4, 8, 15, 53
See also DLB 48
See also MTCW 1
Shapiro, Kenneth A(llan) 1942- ... 118
Shapiro, Laura 1946- ... 145
Shapiro, Lillian L(adman) 1913- ... 102
Shapiro, Linda Gaye 1953- ... 65-68
Shapiro, Marianne (Goldner) 1940- ... 123
Brief entry ... 118
Shapiro, Martin M(athew) 1933- ... 102
Shapiro, Max 1912(?)-1981 Obituary ... 105
Shapiro, Mel 1937- ... 101
Shapiro, Milton J. 1926- ... 81-84
See also SATA 32
Shapiro, Nat(haniel M.) 1922-1983 ... CANR-15
Obituary ... 111
Earlier sketch in CA 29-32R
Shapiro, Norman R(ichard) 1930- ... 93-96
Shapiro, Paulett
See Tumay, Paulett
Shapiro, Robert 1935- ... 113
Shapiro, Robert L(eslie) 1942- ... 156
Shapiro, Robert Y. 1953- ... 142
Shapiro, Samuel 1927- ... CANR-1
Earlier sketch in CA 1-4R
Shapiro, Sidney 1915- ... 136
Shapiro, Stanley 1925-1990 Obituary ... 132
Shapiro, Stuart C(harles) 1944- ... 127
Shapiro, Sue A. 1947- ... 109
Shapiro, William E. 1934- ... CANR-20
Earlier sketch in CA 25-28R
Shaplen, June Herman 1924(?)-1982 Obituary . 108
Shaplen, Robert (Modell) 1917-1988 ... 9-12R
Obituary ... 125
Shapley, Fern Rusk 1890-1984 ... 41-44R
Obituary ... 114
Shapley, Harlow 1885-1972 Obituary ... 37-40R
Shapley, John 1890(?)-1978 Obituary ... 81-84
Shapo, Marshall S(chambelan) 1936- ... CANR-15
Earlier sketch in CA 41-44R
Shapp, Charles M(orris) 1906-1989 ... 57-60
Obituary ... 127
See also SATA-Obit 61
Shapp, Martha Glauber 1910- ... CANR-2
Earlier sketch in CA 1-4R
See also SATA 3
Shappiro, Herbert (Arthur) 1899(?)-1975 . CANR-68
Obituary ... 57-60
Earlier sketches in CAP-2, CA 21-22
Sharabi, H(isham) B(ashir) 1927- ... CANR-2
Earlier sketch in CA 5-8R
Sharat Chandra, G(ubbi) S(hankara Chetty)
1938- ... 53-56
Sharfman, Amalie ... 73-76
See also SATA 14
Sharif, M(ohammad) Nawaz 1942- ... CANR-36
Earlier sketch in CA 114
Sharif, Omar
See Chalhoub, Michael
Sharkansky, Ira 1938- ... 29-32R
Sharkawi, A(bdel)-R(ahman)
1920-1987 Obituary ... 125
Sharkey, Bernarda 1934- ... 33-36R
Sharkey, Jack
See Sharkey, John Michael
Sharkey, Joe 1946- ... 146
Sharkey, John Michael 1931- ... CANR-3
Earlier sketch in CA 1-4R
Sharkey, Olive (Margaret Mary) 1954- ... 128
Sharkey, (Neil) Owen 1917- ... 61-64
Sharlet, Robert (Stewart) 1935- ... 37-40R
Sharlin, Harold I(ssadore) 1925- ... 9-12R
Sharma, Arvind 1940- ... 152
Sharma, Chandradhar 1920- ... 13-16R
Sharma, Govind Narain 1927- ... 45-48
Sharma, Jagdish Prasad 1934- ... 81-84
Sharma, Partap 1939- ... CANR-14
Earlier sketch in CA 77-80
See also SATA 15
Sharma, Rashmi
See Singh, Rashmi Sharma
Sharma, Ravindra N(ath) 1944- ... 110
Sharma, Shripad Rama 1879- ... CAP-2
Earlier sketch in CA 29-32
Sharma, Sohan L(al) 1927- ... 128
Sharman, Alison
See Leonard, Alison
Sharman, Maisie
See Bolton, Maisie Sharman
Sharman, Miriam
See Bolton, Maisie Sharman
Sharmat, Marjorie Weinman 1928- ... CANR-39
Earlier sketches in CA 25-28R, CANR-12
See also JRDA
See also MAICYA
See also SATA 4, 33, 74
Sharmat, Mitchell 1927- ... CANR-46
Earlier sketch in CA 104
See also SATA 33
Sharon, Donna Haye
See Scharlemann, Dorothy Hoyer
Sharon, Rose
See Merril, Judith
Sharon, Sylvia
See Little, Paul H(ugo)
Sharot, Stephen 1943- ... 109
Sharouni, Yusuf
See Al Sharouni, Youssef
Sharp, Aaron John 1904-1997 ... 9-12R
Obituary ... 162
Sharp, Alan 1934- ... 13-16R
Sharp, Andrew 1906-1974 ... CANR-3
Earlier sketch in CA 1-4R
Sharp, Ann Margaret 1942- ... 81-84
Sharp, Ansel M(iree) 1924- ... 77-80
Sharp, Buchanan 1942- ... 105
Sharp, Clifford Henry 1922- ... 108
Sharp, Daniel A(sher) 1932- ... 49-52
Sharp, Dolph 1914- ... 29-32R
Sharp, Donald Bruce 1938- ... 29-32R
Sharp, Doreen Maud 1920- ... CANR-25
Earlier sketch in CA 108
Sharp, Dorothea Elizabeth ... 21-24R
Sharp, Edith Lambert 1917- ... 5-8R
Sharp, Ernest Jack
See Sharpsteen, Ernest Jack
Sharp, Francis Michael 1941- ... 106
Sharp, Hal
See Sharp, Harold W(ilson)
Sharp, Harold S(pencer) 1909- ... CANR-3
Earlier sketch in CA 9-12R
Sharp, Harold W(ilson) 1914- ... 93-96
Sharp, Helen
See Paine, Lauran (Bosworth)
Sharp, James
See Kinghorn, A(lexander) M(anson)
Sharp, James Roger 1936- ... 29-32R
Sharp, John Kean 1892-1979 Obituary ... 93-96
Sharp, John R. 1921- ... 17-20R
Sharp, Laure M(etzger) 1921- ... 29-32R

Sharp, Margery 1905-1991 .... CANR-18
Obituary 134
Earlier sketch in CA 21-24R
See also CLR 27
See also DLB 161
See also MAICYA
See also SATA 1, 29
See also SATA-Obit 67
Sharp, Martin 1900(?)-1987 Obituary 124
Sharp, Maurice L. 1933- 145
Sharp, Paula 1957- 128
Sharp, Robert P(hillip) 1911- 168
Sharp, Roger (William) 1935-1986 73-76
Obituary 119
Sharp, Ronald A(lan) 1945- CANR-49
Earlier sketch in CA 123
Sharp, Saundra 1942- 45-48
See also BW 1
Sharp, Shirley I. 1934- 45-48
Sharp, Sister Mary Corona 1922- 13-16R
Sharp, William 1855-1905 160
See also DLB 156
See also TCLC 39
Sharp, Zerna A. 1889-1981 Obituary 104
See also SATA-Obit 27
Sharpe, Genell J(ackson) Subak
See Subak-Sharpe, Genell J(ackson)
Sharpe, Grant W(illiam) 1925- 69-72
Sharpe, J(ames) A(nthony) 1946- 117
Sharpe, Jon
See Knott, William C(ecil, Jr.)
Sharpe, Kevin 1949- 136
Sharpe, Lawrence A(lbright) 1920- 49-52
Sharpe, Lucretia
See Burgess, Michael (Roy)
Sharpe, Mitchell R(aymond) 1924- 29-32R
See also SATA 12
Sharpe, Myron E(manuel) 1928- 136
Sharpe, Roger Carter 1948- 93-96
Sharpe, Susan 1946- .... SATA 71
Sharpe, Thomas Ridley 1928- 122
Brief entry 114
Interview in 122
See also Sharpe, Tom
Sharpe, Tom
See Sharpe, Thomas Ridley
See also CLC 36
See also DLB 14
Sharpe, William Chapman 1951- 139
Sharpe, William D(onald) 1927- 17-20R
Sharpes, Donald K(enneth) 1934- CANR-1
Earlier sketch in CA 45-48
Sharples, Win(ston S.), Jr. 1932- 45-48
Sharpless, F(rancis) Parvin 1929- 25-28R
Sharpsteen, Ernest Jack 1880-1976 Obituary .. 110
Sharpton, Robert E(arl) 1936- 104
Sharrock, Roger (Ian) 1919-1991(?) CANR-2
Obituary 133
Earlier sketch in CA 5-8R
Sharwood Smith, Bryan Evers 1899-1983 ... CAP-2
Obituary 111
Earlier sketch in CA 29-32
Shasha, Dennis (E.) 1955- 143
Shasha, Mark 1961- .... SATA 80
Shatner, William 1931- 146
Shatto, Gloria M. 1931- 41-44R
Shattock, Ernest (Henry) 1904- 102
Shattuck, Charles H(arlen) 1910-1992 ... CANR-47
Obituary 139
Earlier sketches in CA 5-8R, CANR-2
Shattuck, George C. 1927- 137
Shattuck, Roger (Whitney) 1923- CANR-71
Earlier sketches in CA 5-8R, CANR-7, 47
See also SATA 64
Shatzkin, Leonard 1919- 109
Shaughnessy, Alfred (James) 1916- 134
Shaughnessy, Edward J(oseph, Jr.) 1934- 110
Shaughnessy, Edward L(awrence) 1932- 130
Shaughnessy, Mary Alice 1951- 141
Shaul, Frank
See Rowland, D(onald) S(ydney)
Shaull, (Millard) Richard 1919- CANR-11
Earlier sketch in CA 21-24R
Shave, Gordon A(shton) 1922- 101
Shavelson, Lonny 1952- 147
Shavelson, Melville 1917- CANR-4
Earlier sketch in CA 53-56
Shaver, James P. 1933- CANR-7
Earlier sketch in CA 17-20R
Shaver, Phillip (Robert) 1944- 130
Shaver, Richard S(harpe) 1907-1975 166
Shaver-Crandell, Anne (Elizabeth) 1941- 113
Shaver-Crandell, Annie
See Shaver-Crandell, Anne (Elizabeth)
Shavin, Norman 1926- 81-84
Shaw, Alan George Lewers 1916- CANR-9
Earlier sketch in CA 21-24R
Shaw, Albert 1857-1947 .... DLB 91
Shaw, Alison 1957- 130
Shaw, Arnold 1909-1989 .... CANR-44
Obituary 129
Earlier sketches in CA 1-4R, CANR-1
See also SATA 4
See also SATA-Obit 63
Shaw, Artie 1910- 144
Shaw, B(iswanath) N. 1923- 37-40R
Shaw, Barton C(arr) 1947- 123
Shaw, Bernard
See Shaw, George Bernard
See also BW 1
See also TCLC 45
Shaw, Bernard 1940- 119
Brief entry 109
Interview in 119
See also BW
Shaw, Bob 1931-1996 .... CANR-41
Obituary 151
Earlier sketches in CA 49-52, CANR-1, 19
Shaw, Brian
See Tubb, E(dwin) C(harles)
Shaw, Bruce 1941- 119
Shaw, Bruno 1905-1984 Obituary 114
Shaw, Bryan
See Fearn, John Russell
Shaw, Bynum (Gillette) 1923- CANR-4
Earlier sketch in CA 1-4R
Shaw, Carleton Ford 1908- CAP-1
Earlier sketch in CA 13-16
Shaw, Carlos M. Fernandez
See Fernandez-Shaw, Carlos M(anuel)
Shaw, Carolyn Hagner
1903(?)-1977 Obituary 69-72
Shaw, Carolyn V. 1934- 155
See also SATA 91
Shaw, Charles (Green) 1892-1974 .... CAP-1
Earlier sketch in CA 17-18
See also SATA 13
Shaw, Charles R(aymond) 1921- CANR-14
Earlier sketch in CA 21-24R
Shaw, Chester Lee 1898(?)-1985 Obituary 118
Shaw, Christine 1952- 146
Shaw, David 1943- 49-52
Shaw, David W. 1961- 167
Shaw, Dawn
See Shaw, Thelma
Shaw, Donald Lewis 1936- 61-64
Shaw, Earl Bennett 1889- CAP-1
Earlier sketch in CA 17-18
Shaw, Edward P(ease) 1911-1986 .... 21-24R
Obituary 118
Shaw, Elizabeth
See Prance, June E(lizebeth)
Shaw, Ellen Torgerson
See Torgerson Shaw, Ellen
Shaw, Evelyn S. 1927- 104
See also SATA 28
Shaw, Felicity 1918-1989 .... CANR-61
Earlier sketch in CA 104
Shaw, Flora Louisa
See Lugard, Flora Louisa Shaw
Shaw, Fred (?)-1972 Obituary 104
Shaw, Frederick 1912- CANR-1
Earlier sketch in CA 45-48
Shaw, Frederick W. 1916(?)-1983 Obituary 111
Shaw, G. Bernard
See Shaw, George Bernard
Shaw, Gaylord 1942- 81-84
Shaw, George
See Bickham, Jack M(iles)
Shaw, George Bernard 1856-1950 128
Brief entry 104
See also Shaw, Bernard
See also CDBLB 1914-1945
See also DA
See also DAB
See also DAC
See also DAM DRAM, MST
See also DLB 10, 57, 190
See also MTCW 1
See also TCLC 3, 9, 21
See also WLC
Shaw, Graham 1944- 118
Shaw, Harold 1916(?)-1986 Obituary 118
Shaw, Harry (Lee, Jr.) 1905- 81-84
Shaw, Harry Edmund 1946- 114
Shaw, Helen 1913-1985 .... CANR-20
Earlier sketch in CA 103
Shaw, Henry I(var), Jr. 1926- 33-36R
Shaw, Henry Wheeler 1818-1885 .... DLB 11
Shaw, Howard 1934- 106
Shaw, Irene
See Roberts, Irene
Shaw, Irwin 1913-1984 .... CANR-21
Obituary 112
Earlier sketch in CA 13-16R
See also AITN 1
See also CDALB 1941-1968
See also CLC 7, 23, 34
See also DAM DRAM, POP
See also DLB 6, 102
See also DLBY 84
See also MTCW 1
Shaw, J(oseph) Thomas 1919- 17-20R
Shaw, Janet 1937- 127
See also SATA 61
Shaw, Janet Beeler
See Shaw, Janet
Shaw, John Bennett 1913- 21-24R
Shaw, John Mackay 1897-1984 .... CANR-13
Earlier sketch in CA 29-32R
Shaw, Joseph M(inard) 1925- 140
Shaw, Joseph T. 1874-1952 .... DLB 137
Shaw, Lau
See Shu, Ch' ing-ch'un
Shaw, Lawrence H(ugh) 1940- 69-72
Shaw, Leroy R(obert) 1923- 13-16R
Shaw, Linda 1938- CANR-46
Earlier sketches in CA 106, CANR-23
Shaw, Luci N(orthcote) 1928- CANR-39
Earlier sketches in CA 101, CANR-17
Shaw, Malcolm Edwin 1926- CANR-1
Earlier sketch in CA 1-4R
Shaw, Margret 1940- 136
See also SATA 68
Shaw, Mark 1945- 147
Shaw, Martin 1947- 143
Shaw, Marvin E(vert) 1919- 21-24R
Shaw, Maxine 1945- 57-60
Shaw, Murray 1908- 134
Shaw, Nancy 1946- .... SATA 71
Shaw, Nancy Stoller 1942- 57-60
Shaw, Patrick W. 1938- 143
Shaw, Peter 1936-1995 .... CANR-9
Obituary 149
Earlier sketch in CA 65-68
Shaw, Priscilla Washburn 1930- 13-16R
Shaw, Ralph R(obert) 1907-1972 Obituary .. 37-40R
Shaw, Ray 33-36R
See also SATA 7
Shaw, Richard 1923- 37-40R
See also SATA 12
Shaw, Robert (H.) 1916- 167
Shaw, Robert 1927-1978 .... CANR-4
Obituary 81-84
Earlier sketch in CA 1-4R
See also AITN 1
See also CLC 5
See also DLB 13, 14
Shaw, Robert B. 1947- 137
See also DLB 120
Shaw, Robert Byers 1916- 37-40R
Shaw, Ron W. 1951- 145
Shaw, Ronald D. M. 1883- CAP-1
Earlier sketch in CA 13-14
Shaw, Ronald E. 1923- 17-20R
Shaw, Russell B(urnham) 1935- CANR-3
Earlier sketch in CA 1-4R
Shaw, Simon 166
Shaw, Sophia 1969- 152
Shaw, Stanford Jay 1930- CANR-6
Earlier sketch in CA 5-8R
Shaw, Steven John 1918- 17-20R
Shaw, T. D. W.
See Shaw, Thelma
Shaw, T. E.
See Lawrence, T(homas) E(dward)
Shaw, Thelma 25-28R
Shaw, Thurstan 1914- 103
Shaw, Timothy Milton 1945- CANR-30
Earlier sketch in CA 112
Shaw, Vivian
See Seldes, Gilbert (Vivian)
Shaw, W. David 1937- 29-32R
Shaw, (Harold) Watkins 1911- 1-4R
Shaw, Wayne E(ugene) 1932- 53-56
Shaw, William 1959- 143
Shaw, William Harlan 1922- CANR-15
Earlier sketch in CA 41-44R
Shawchuck, Norman 1935- 126
Shawcross, John T. 1924- 13-16R
Shawcross, William 1946- 105
Shawhan, Ralph 1903(?)-1990 Obituary 130
Shawn, Edwin Meyers 1891-1972 Obituary . 33-36R
Shawn, Frank S.
See Goulart, Ron(ald Joseph)
Shawn, Ted
See Shawn, Edwin Meyers
Shawn, Wallace 1943- 112
See also CLC 41
Shawn, William 1907-1992 108
Obituary 140
See also DLB 137
Shawver, Lois 1939- 150
Shay, Arthur 1922- CANR-46
Earlier sketch in CA 33-36R
See also SATA 4
Shay, Lacey
See Shebar, Sharon Sigmond
Shayne, Gordon
See Winter, Bevis (Peter)
Shaynoux, Bucky
See Landau, Paul Stuart
Shayon, Robert Lewis 49-52
Shayon, Samuel 1904(?)-1984 Obituary 112
Shazar, Rachel
See Katznelson-Shazar, Rachel
Shazar, (Schneor) Zalman 1889-1974 101
Obituary 53-56
Shea, Donald F(rancis) 1925- 73-76
Shea, George 1940- CANR-49
Earlier sketch in CA 108
See also SATA 54
See also SATA-Brief 42
Shea, George E., Jr. 1902-1980 Obituary ... 97-100
Shea, James J. 1890(?)-1977 Obituary 69-72
Shea, John 1941- 73-76
Shea, John Gerald 1906- 9-12R
Shea, John Gilmary 1824-1892 .... DLB 30
Shea, John S. 1933- 21-24R
Shea, Lisa 1953- 147
See also CLC 86
Shea, Michael (Sinclair MacAuslan) 1938- 130
Shea, Michael 1946- 112
Shea, Patrick 1908- 130
Shea, Pegi Deitz 1960- 145
See also SATA 77
Shea, Robert (Joseph) 1933-1994 101
Obituary 144
Shea, Shirley 1924- 121
Sheaffer, Louis 1912-1993 Obituary 142
See also DLB 103
Sheaffer, Robert M(errill) 1949- 106
Sheagren, Thomas G(eorge) 1949- 118
Sheahan, John 1923- 17-20R
Sheahan, Richard T(homas) 1942- CANR-15
Earlier sketch in CA 65-68
Shealy, C(lyde) Norman 1932- CANR-7
Earlier sketch in CA 57-60
Shean, Glenn (Daniel) 1939- 53-56
Shear, Jeff 1947- 147
Sheard, Kevin 1916- 41-44R
Sheard, Sarah 1953- 141
Shearer, Harry (Julius) 1943- 165
Shearer, John 1947- 125
See also CLR 34
See also SATA 43
See also SATA-Brief 27
Shearer, Ronald A(lexander) 1932- 77-80
Shearer, Ted 1919- .... SATA 43
Shearing, Joseph
See Campbell, (Gabrielle) Margaret (Vere)
See also DLB 70
Shearman, Hugh (Francis) 1915- 13-16R
Shearman, John 1931- 13-16R
Shears, Billie
See Watson, O(scar) Michael
Sheats, Mary Boney 1918- 13-16R
Sheats, Paul Douglas 1932- 101
Shebar, Sharon Sigmond 1945- CANR-41
Earlier sketches in CA 103, CANR-19
See also SATA 36
Shebbeare, John 1709-1788 .... DLB 39
Shebl, James M(ichael) 1942- CANR-23
Earlier sketches in CA 61-64, CANR-8
Shechner, Mark E. 1940- 124
Sheckley, Robert 1928- CANR-2
Earlier sketch in CA 1-4R
See also DLB 8
Shecter, Ben 1935- 81-84
See also SATA 16
Shecter, Leonard 1926-1974 Obituary 45-48
Shedd, Charlie W. 1915- 17-20R
Shedd, Clarence Prouty 1887-1973 Obituary . 45-48
Shedd, Margaret Cochran 1900-1986 Obituary . 118
Shedd, Warner 1934- 151
See also SATA 87
Shedd, William G. T. 1820-1894 .... DLB 64
Shedley, Ethan I.
See Beizer, Boris
Sheean, Diana 1915(?)-1987 Obituary 124
Sheean, (James) Vincent 1899-1975 61-64
Sheed, F. J.
See Sheed, Francis Joseph
Sheed, Francis J.
See Sheed, Francis Joseph
Sheed, Francis Joseph 1897-1981 129
Obituary 105
Sheed, Frank
See Sheed, Francis Joseph
Sheed, Frank J.
See Sheed, Francis Joseph
Sheed, Wilfrid (John Joseph) 1930- CANR-66
Earlier sketches in CA 65-68, CANR-30
See also CLC 2, 4, 10, 53
See also DLB 6
See also MTCW 1
Sheedy, Alexandra Elizabeth 1962- 85-88
See also SATA 19, 39
Sheehan, Arthur 1910(?)-1975 Obituary 61-64
Sheehan, Aurelie 1963- 147
Sheehan, Bernard W(illiam) 1934- 41-44R
Sheehan, Donald Henry 1917-1974 .... CANR-2
Earlier sketch in CA 1-4R
Sheehan, Ethna 1908- 61-64
See also SATA 9
Sheehan, George (Augustine) 1918-1993 ....
CANR-13
Obituary 143
Earlier sketch in CA 73-76
Sheehan, Helen E(lizabeth) 1944- 146
Sheehan, James J(ohn) 1937- CANR-11
Earlier sketch in CA 17-20R
Sheehan, John F(rancis) X(avier) 1933- 122
Brief entry 118
Sheehan, Joseph Green 1918-1983 Obituary .. 111
Sheehan, Margaret A(nne) 1956- 111
Sheehan, Neil 1936- CANR-40
Earlier sketch in CA 29-32R
See also BEST 89:2
Sheehan, Patrick Augustine
See O Siochain, P(adraig) A(ugustine)
Sheehan, Patty 1945- 145
See also SATA 77
Sheehan, Paul V(incent) 1904- 33-36R
Sheehan, Sean 1951- 151
See also SATA 86
Sheehan, Sister Helen 1904- CAP-1
Earlier sketch in CA 17-18
Sheehan, Susan 1937- CANR-40
Earlier sketches in CA 21-24R, CANR-12
Sheehan, Thomas 1941- 122
Sheehan, Valerie Harms
See Harms, Valerie
Sheehan, William 1954- 139
Sheehy, Eugene P(aul) 1922- 9-12R
Sheehy, Gail 1937- CANR-55
Earlier sketches in CA 49-52, CANR-1, 33
See also MTCW 1
Sheehy, Helen 1948- 133
Sheehy, Jeanne 1939- 110
Sheehy, Maurice S(tephen)
1898-1972 Obituary 111
Sheekman, Arthur 1901-1978 81-84
Obituary 73-76
Sheen, Fulton J(ohn) 1895-1979 .... CANR-5
Obituary 89-92
Earlier sketch in CA 5-8R
See also MTCW 1
Sheeran, James Jennings 1932- 65-68
Sheerin, John Basil 1906-1992 .... CANR-4
Obituary 136
Earlier sketch in CA 1-4R
Sheerman, Barry 1940- 144
Sheets, Elva (Darah) 1898- 57-60
Sheets, John R(ichard) 1922- 25-28R
Sheets, Kenneth Ray 1936- 136
Sheets, Millard (Owen) 1907-1989 Obituary 128
Sheets, Robin Lauterbach 1943- 131
Sheets-Pyenson, Susan 163
Sheetz, Ann Kindig 1934- 101
Shefelman, Janice Jordan 1930- CANR-45
Earlier sketch in CA 120
See also SATA 58

Shefelman, Tom (Whitehead) 1927- SATA 58
Sheffer, H. R.
See Abels, Harriette S(heffer)
Sheffer, Isaiah 1935- 17-20R
Sheffield, Charles 1935- 162
Sheffield, James Rockwell 1936- Brief entry 106
Sheffield, Janet N. 1926- 65-68
See also SATA 26
Sheffy, Lester Fields 1887- CAP-1
Earlier sketch in CA 13-14
Sheftel, Victor O. 1936- 152
Sheftell, Fred D. 1941- 137
Shefter, Harry 1910- 9-12R
Shefter, Martin 1943- 136
Shefts, Joelle SATA-Brief 49
Shehadeh, Raja 1951- 141
Shehadi, Fadlou 1926- 162
Shehan, Lawrence Joseph 1898-1984 117
Sheikh, Nazneen
See Sadiq, Nazneen
Shein, Brian 1947- 110
Shein, Louis J(ulius) 1914- 25-28R
Sheiness, (Lee) Marsha 1940- CANR-15
Earlier sketch in CA 89-92
Sheinin, David (M. K.) 1960- 154
Sheinwold, Alfred 1912-1997 61-64
Obituary 157
Sheinwold, Patricia
See Fox-Sheinwold, Patricia
Shek, Ben-Zion 1927- 110
Shekerjian, Regina Tor SATA 16
Shelbourne, Cecily
See Goodwin, Suzanne
Shelby, Anne 1948- 151
See also SAAS 26
See also SATA 85
Shelby, Brit
See Grady, James (Thomas)
Shelby, Carroll Hall 1923- 17-20R
Shelby, Graham 1940- 102
Shelby, Susan
See Kinnicutt, Susan Sibley
Shelden, Michael 1951- 141
Sheldon, Alan 1933- 114
Sheldon, Alice Hastings Bradley 1915(?)-1987
CANR-34
Obituary 122
Earlier sketch in CA 108
Interview in 108
See also Tiptree, James, Jr.
See also MTCW 1
Sheldon, Ann CANR-27
Earlier sketches in CAP-2, CA 19-20
See also SATA 1, 67
Sheldon, Ann
See Antle, Nancy
Sheldon, Aure 1917-1976 61-64
See also SATA 12
Sheldon, Charles Harvey 1929- 107
Sheldon, Charles S(tuart) II
1917-1981 Obituary 105
Sheldon, Deyan 53-56
Sheldon, Edward 1886-1946 DLB 7
Sheldon, Eleanor Bernert 1920- 85-88
Sheldon, Esther K. 1906- 37-40R
Sheldon, Garrett Ward 1954- 139
Sheldon, George E.
See Stahl, Le Roy
Sheldon, John
See Bloch, Robert (Albert)
Sheldon, Joseph K(enneth) 1943- 143
Sheldon, Lee
See Lee, Wayne C.
Sheldon, Michael 1918- 17-20R
Sheldon, Muriel 1926- CANR-18
Earlier sketch in CA 101
See also SATA 45
See also SATA-Brief 39
Sheldon, Peter 1922- 25-28R
Sheldon, Raccoona
See Sheldon, Alice Hastings Bradley
Sheldon, Richard (Robert) 1932- 33-36R
Sheldon, Roy AITN 1
Sheldon, Roy
See Tubb, E(dwin) C(harles)
Sheldon, Scott
See Wallmann, Jeffrey M(iner)
Sheldon, Sidney 1917- CANR-33
Earlier sketch in CA 29-32R
See also AITN 1
See also BEST 89:1
See also DAM NOV, POP
See also MTCW 1
Sheldon, Suzanne Eaton
1928(?)-1985 Obituary 117
Sheldon, Walt
See Sheldon, Walter J.
Sheldon, Walter J. 1917- CANR-10
Earlier sketch in CA 25-28R
See also AITN 1
Sheldon, William (Herbert) 1898-1977 25-28R
Obituary 116
Sheldon, William Denley 1915- 17-20R
Sheldrake, Rupert 1942- CANR-55
Earlier sketch in CA 127
Sheldrick, Daphne 1934- CANR-3
Earlier sketch in CA 49-52
Shelemay, Kay Kaufman 1948- 142
Shell, Ellen Ruppel 1952- 138
Shell, Robert C(arl)-H(einz) 1949- 152
Shell, Virginia Law 1923- 21-24R
Shellabarger, Samuel 1888-1954 163
Shelley, Bruce L(eon) 1927- CANR-9
Earlier sketch in CA 21-24R
Shelley, Dolores 1937- 122
Shelley, Florence D(ubroff) 1921- 65-68
Shelley, Frances
See Wees, Frances Shelley
Shelley, Lillian
See Koppel, Lillian
and Koppel, Shelley R(uth)
Shelley, Louise I(sabel) 1952- 108
Shelley, Mack Clayton II 1950- CANR-56
Earlier sketch in CA 126
Shelley, Mary Wollstonecraft (Godwin)
1797-1851 AAYA 20
See also CDBLB 1789-1832
See also DA
See also DAB
See also DAC
See also DAM MST, NOV
See also DLB 110, 116, 159, 178
See also SATA 29
See also WLC
Shelley, Noreen 1920- 104
Shelley, Percy Bysshe 1792-1822 CDBLB
1789-1832
See also DA
See also DAB
See also DAC
See also DAM MST, POET
See also DLB 96, 110, 158
See also PC 14
See also WLC
Shelley, Rebecca 1887(?)-1984 Obituary 111
Shelly, (Michael) Bruce 1929- 57-60
Shelly, Judith A(llen) 1944- CANR-38
Earlier sketch in CA 115
Shelly, Maynard W(olfe) 1928- CANR-7
Earlier sketch in CA 13-16R
Shelly, Peter
See Dresser, Davis
Shelmerdine, Cynthia Wright 1949- 117
Shelnutt, Eve (Brown) 1941- 132
See also CAAS 14
See also DLB 130
Shelp, Earl E(dward) 1947- 116
Shelton, Barrett C(linton)
1903(?)-1984 Obituary 112
Shelton, Beth Anne 1957- 143
Shelton, Hal T(erry) 1935- 150
Shelton, (Austin) Jess(e), Jr. 1926- CANR-25
Earlier sketch in CA 1-4R
Shelton, Kathleen J. 1946-1990 Obituary 131
Shelton, Lola
See Klaue, Lola Shelton
Shelton, Mark L(ogan) 1958- 135
Shelton, Regina Maria 1927- 112
Shelton, Richard 1933- CANR-13
Earlier sketch in CA 33-36R
Shelton, Ron(ald W.) 1945- 166
Shelton, Suzanne
See Buckley, Suzanne Shelton
Shelton, William Roy 1919- CANR-11
Earlier sketch in CA 5-8R
See also AITN 1
See also SATA 5
Shem, Samuel 1944- 144
Shemesh, Haim 1954- 142
Shemie, Bonnie (Jean Brenner) 1949- CANR-70
Earlier sketch in CA 133
See also SATA 96
Shemin, Margaretha (Hoeneveld) 1928- 13-16R
See also SATA 4
Shen, Congwen 1902-1988 Obituary 125
Shen, James C. H. 1909- 126
Shen, Peter 110
Shen, Tong 1968- 135
Shen Dajun 1955- 168
Shengold, Leonard 1925- 136
Shenk, David 1967(?)- 167
Shenk, David W(itmer) 1937- 106
Shenk, Lois (Landis) 1944- 114
Shenk, Marcia Ann 1953- 73-76
Shenk, Wilbert R. 1935- 21-24R
Shenkin, Elizabeth Shoemaker
(?)-1975 Obituary 61-64
Shenkman, Richard (Bennett) 1954- 144
Shennan, Joseph Hugh 1933- 103
Shenon, Philip 1959- 136
Shenoy, B(ellikoth) R(aghunath) 1905- 77-80
Shenstone, William 1714-1763 DLB 95
Shenton, Edward 1895-1977 SATA 45
Shenton, Edward H(eriot) 1932- CANR-17
Earlier sketch in CA 25-28R
Shenton, James P(atrick) 1925- CANR-2
Earlier sketch in CA 5-8R
Shepard, Aaron 1950- 142
See also SATA 75
Shepard, Alan B., Jr. 1923- 158
Shepard, Charles E. 1954- 145
Shepard, David W. 1922- 93-96
Shepard, Elaine (Elizabeth) 1923- 21-24R
Shepard, Ernest Howard 1879-1976 CANR-23
Obituary 65-68
Earlier sketch in CA 9-12R
See also CLR 27
See also DLB 160
See also MAICYA
See also SATA 3, 33, 100
See also SATA-Obit 24
Shepard, Francis P(arker) 1897- 13-16R
Shepard, Gary 1939- 97-100
Shepard, Jean H(eck) 1930- 49-52
Shepard, Jim 1956- CANR-59
Earlier sketch in CA 137
See also CLC 36
See also SATA 90
Shepard, Jon M(ax) 1939- CANR-7
Earlier sketch in CA 57-60
Shepard, Leslie (Alan) 1917- CANR-8
Earlier sketch in CA 17-20R
Shepard, Leslie Albert 1929- 29-32R
Shepard, Lucius 1947- 141
Brief entry 128
See also CLC 34
Shepard, Martin 1934- 33-36R
Shepard, Mary
See Knox, (Mary) Eleanor Jessie
Shepard, Neil 1951- 140
Shepard, Odell 1884-1967 CANR-3
Obituary 25-28R
Earlier sketch in CA 5-8R
Shepard, Paul (Howe) 1925-1996 CANR-10
Obituary 152
Earlier sketch in CA 21-24R
Shepard, Richard F. 1922-1998 115
Obituary 167
Shepard, Richmond 1929- 29-32R
Shepard, Sam 1943- CANR-22
Earlier sketch in CA 69-72
See also CABS 3
See also AAYA 1
See also CLC 4, 6, 17, 34, 41, 44
See also DAM DRAM
See also DC 5
See also DLB 7
See also MTCW 1
Shepard, Thomas I 1604(?)-1649 DLB 24
Shepard, Thomas II 1635-1677 DLB 24
Shepard, Thomas Rockwell, Jr. 1918- 105
Shepardson, Mary (Thygeson) 1906- 29-32R
Shephard, Esther 1891-1975 CAP-2
Obituary 57-60
Earlier sketch in CA 25-28
See also SATA 5
See also SATA-Obit 26
Shephard, John (Brownlow) 1900- CAP-1
Earlier sketch in CA 13-14
Shephard, Roy J(esse) 1929- CANR-11
Earlier sketch in CA 29-32R
Shepherd, (Richard) David 1931- 65-68
Shepherd, David Gwynne 1924- 5-8R
Shepherd, Donald (Lee) 1932- 61-64
Shepherd, Donna Walsh
See Walsh Shepherd, Donna
Shepherd, Elizabeth 33-36R
See also SATA 4
Shepherd, Geoffrey (Seddon) 1898- CANR-20
Earlier sketch in CA 1-4R
Shepherd, George W., Jr. 1926- CANR-6
Earlier sketch in CA 1-4R
Shepherd, Gordon
See Brook-Shepherd, (Frederick) Gordon
Shepherd, J(ohn) Barrie 1935- CANR-29
Earlier sketch in CA 111
Shepherd, Jack 1937- CANR-43
Earlier sketch in CA 57-60
Shepherd, James L(eftwich) III 1921- 21-24R
Shepherd, Jean (Parker) 1929- 77-80
See also AITN 2
Shepherd, Joan
See Buchanan, Betty (Joan)
Shepherd, John
See Ballard, (Willis) Todhunter
Shepherd, L. P. 53-56
Shepherd, Massey H., Jr.
See Shepherd, Massey Hamilton, Jr.
Shepherd, Massey Hamilton
See Shepherd, Massey Hamilton, Jr.
Shepherd, Massey Hamilton, Jr. 1913- 122
Shepherd, Michael
See Ludlum, Robert
Shepherd, Nan 1893- 105
Shepherd, Neal
See Morland, Nigel
Shepherd, Robert 1949- 136
Shepherd, Robert Henry Wishart 1888-1971
CAP-1
Earlier sketch in CA 13-14
Shepherd, Simon 1951- 120
Shepherd, Walter Bradley 1904- 105
Shepherd, William C(hauncey) 1942- CANR-18
Earlier sketch in CA 25-28R
Shepley, James R(obinson)
1917-1988 Obituary 127
Brief entry 112
Sheppard, Alice 1945- 152
Sheppard, Anne
See Sheppard, Anne D(eborah) R(aphael)
Sheppard, Anne D(eborah) R(aphael) 1951- 128
Sheppard, Barry 1937- 61-64
Sheppard, Cynthia A(nne) 1955- 108
Sheppard, David Stuart 1929- 103
Sheppard, Don(ald D.) 1930- 138
Sheppard, Eugenia (Benbow) 1900(?)-1984 103
Obituary 114
Sheppard, Francis Henry Wollaston 1921- 21-24R
Sheppard, Harold L(loyd) 1922-1997 CANR-1
Obituary 159
Earlier sketch in CA 45-48
Sheppard, Joseph 1930- CANR-23
Earlier sketches in CA 61-64, CANR-8
Sheppard, Lancelot C(apel) 1906- CANR-5
Earlier sketch in CA 5-8R
Sheppard, Lila (Brooks) 1906- CAP-1
Earlier sketch in CA 13-14
Sheppard, Mary 29-32R
Sheppard, Roger 1939- 77-80
Sheppard, Sally 1917- 69-72
Sheppard, Stephen 1945- 105
Sheppard, Thomas F(rederick) 1935- 73-76
Sheppard, Walter Lee, Jr. 1911- 69-72
Sheppard-Jones, Elisabeth 1920- 13-16R
Shepperson, Wilbur Stanley 1919- CANR-6
Earlier sketch in CA 1-4R
Sheps, Cecil G(eorge) 1913- 9-12R
Sheps, Mindel (Cherniack)
1913-1973 Obituary 37-40R
Sher, Barbara 1935- 132
Sher, Eva CAP-2
Earlier sketch in CA 23-24
Sher, Gerson S(amuel) 1947- 81-84
Sher, Gila 142
Sher, Jack 1913-1988 Obituary 126
Sher, Zelig 1888-1971 Obituary 104
Shera, Jesse Hauk 1903-1982 CANR-2
Obituary 106
Earlier sketch in CA 5-8R
Sherar, Mariam G(hose) 1924- 45-48
Sherashevski, Boris
See Brown, John J.
Sheraton, Mimi 1926- 126
Sheraton, Neil
See Smith, Norman Edward Mace
Sheratsky, Rodney E(arl) 1933- 25-28R
Sherblom, Liz 1942- 154
Sherbo, Arthur 1918- Brief entry 113
Sherburne, Donald W(ynne) 1929- 1-4R
Sherburne, Edward 1616-1702 DLB 131
Sherburne, James (Robert) 1925- 33-36R
Sherburne, Zoa (Morin) 1912- CANR-37
Earlier sketches in CA 1-4R, CANR-3
See also AAYA 13
See also CLC 30
See also MAICYA
See also SAAS 18
See also SATA 3
Sherby, Linda B(arbara) 1946- 108
Shercliff, Jose 1902(?)-1985 Obituary 115
Sherdeman, Ted 1910(?)-1987 Obituary 123
Shere, Dennis 1940- 77-80
Sherek, Henry 1900-1967 CAP-1
Earlier sketch in CA 13-16
Sherer, Mary Louise 1901- 101
Sherer, Michael W. 1952- 127
Sherer, Robert G(lenn, Jr.) 1940- 69-72
Sheret, Rene (Dundee) 1933- 29-32R
Sherfey, Mary Jane 1933-1983 Obituary 109
Shergold, N(orman) D(avid) 1925- 25-28R
Sheridan, Adora
See Hong, Jane Fay
and Pavlik, Evelyn Marie
Sheridan, Anne-Marie 1948- 85-88
Sheridan, Dorothy Elizabeth 1948- 116
Sheridan, Eugene Robert 1945- CANR-23
Earlier sketch in CA 107
Sheridan, Frances 1724-1766 DLB 39, 84
Sheridan, James E(dward) 1922- 21-24R
Sheridan, James F(rancis), Jr. 1927- 29-32R
Sheridan, Jane
See Winslow, Pauline Glen
Sheridan, John V. 1915- CANR-3
Earlier sketch in CA 9-12R
Sheridan, L(ionel) A(stor) 1927- CANR-9
Earlier sketch in CA 21-24R
Sheridan, Lane
See Winslow, Pauline Glen
Sheridan, Lee
See Lee, Elsie
Sheridan, Marion Campbell 17-20R
Sheridan, Martin 1914- 104
Sheridan, Polly
See Oates, Jeannette
Sheridan, Richard B. 1918- 45-48
Sheridan, Richard Brinsley 1751-1816 CDBLB
1660-1789
See also DA
See also DAB
See also DAC
See also DAM DRAM, MST
See also DC 1
See also DLB 89
See also WLC
Sheridan, Thomas 1938- 61-64
Sheridan, Thomas L. 1926- 37-40R
Sherif, Carolyn W(ood) 1922- 17-20R
Sherif, Muzafer 1906-1988 CAP-1
Obituary 126
Earlier sketch in CA 13-14
Sheriff, John K(eith) 1944- CANR-47
Earlier sketch in CA 120
Sherlock, John 1932- CANR-3
Earlier sketch in CA 9-12R
Sherlock, Patti SATA 71
Sherlock, Philip Manderson 1902- CANR-6
Earlier sketch in CA 5-8R
Sherlock, Richard 1947- 126
Sherman, A(lan) Robert 1942- 57-60
Sherman, Allan 1924-1973 101
Obituary 45-48
Sherman, Arnold 1932- CANR-14
Earlier sketch in CA 33-36R
Sherman, Arthur W(esley), Jr. 1917- CANR-21
Earlier sketch in CA 1-4R
Sherman, Barbara H(ayes) 1942- 25-28R
Sherman, Bernard 1929- 29-32R
Sherman, Cecil E(dwin) 1927- 127
Brief entry 110
Sherman, Charles Bezalel 1896-1971 1-4R
Obituary 103
Sherman, Charlotte A.
See Sherman, Jory (Tecumseh)
Sherman, Charlotte Watson 1958- 143
See also BW 2
Sherman, Claire Richter 1930- 106
Sherman, Constance D(enise) 1909- 45-48
Sherman, D(enis) R(onald) 1934- CANR-8
Earlier sketch in CA 13-16R
See also SATA 48
See also SATA-Brief 29
Sherman, Dan(iel Michael) 1950- 77-80

Sherman, Diane (Finn) 1928- ... CANR-5
Earlier sketch in CA 9-12R
See also SATA 12
Sherman, Edmund 1927- ... 139
Sherman, Eileen Bluestone 1951- ... CANR-45
Earlier sketch in CA 119
Sherman, Eleanor Rae 1929- ... 13-16R
Sherman, Elizabeth
See Friskey, Margaret (Richards)
Sherman, Eric 1947- ... 69-72
Sherman, Francis 1871-1926 ... DLB 92
Sherman, Franklin (Eugene) 1928- ... 57-60
Sherman, G(eorge) W(itters) 1903- ... 117
Sherman, Harold (Morrow) 1898- ... 77-80
See also SATA 37
Sherman, (Marcus) Harvey 1917-1985 ... 21-24R
Obituary ... 114
Sherman, Howard J. 1931- ... CANR-10
Earlier sketch in CA 13-16R
Sherman, Ingrid 1919- ... 103
Sherman, James E(dward) 1939- ... 25-28R
Sherman, Jane 1908- ... CANR-12
Earlier sketch in CA 73-76
Sherman, Jason 1962- ... 165
Sherman, Jerry 1924- ... 97-100
Sherman, Joan
See Dern, Erolie Pearl Gaddis
Sherman, Joe 1945- ... 137
Sherman, Jonathan Marc ... CLC 55
Sherman, Jory (Tecumseh) 1932- ... CANR-53
Earlier sketches in CA 69-72, CANR-11, 28
Sherman, Josepha ... 127
See also SATA 75
Sherman, Julia A(nn) 1934- ... 37-40R
Sherman, Kenneth 1950- ... CANR-40
Earlier sketch in CA 117
Sherman, L. L.
See Armentrout, Fred S(herman)
Sherman, Lawrence W(illiam) 1949- ... CANR-7
Earlier sketch in CA 57-60
Sherman, Lynn
See Obrecht, Jaŝ
Sherman, Martin 1941(?)- ... 123
Brief entry ... 116
See also CLC 19
Sherman, Michael
See Lowndes, Robert A(ugustine) W(ard)
Sherman, Michele 1945- ... CANR-36
Earlier sketch in CA 114
Sherman, Murray H(erbert) 1922- ... 17-20R
Sherman, Nancy
See Rosenberg, Nancy (Sherman)
Sherman, Patrick 1928- ... 103
Sherman, Peter Michael
See Lowndes, Robert A(ugustine) W(ard)
Sherman, Philip M(artin) 1930- ... 29-32R
Sherman, Ray W(esley)
1884-1971 Obituary ... 33-36R
Sherman, Richard B. 1929- ... 29-32R
Sherman, Richard M(orton) 1928- Brief entry ... 107
Sherman, Robert 1928- ... 142
Sherman, Robert B(ernard) 1925- Brief entry ... 108
Sherman, Roger 1930- ... 37-40R
Sherman, Spencer E. 1936- ... 112
Sherman, Steve (Barry) 1938- ... 37-40R
Sherman, Susan Jean 1939- ... 1-4R
Sherman, T. P. 1917-1976 ... CAP-2
Earlier sketch in CA 29-32
Sherman, Theodore A(llison) 1901-1981 ... 17-20R
Obituary ... 134
Sherman, Vincent 1906- ... 159
Sherman, William David 1940- ... CANR-21
Earlier sketch in CA 105
Sherman, William H. 1966- ... 150
Sherman, William Lewis 1927- ... 105
Shero, Fred (Alexander) 1925- ... 105
Sherover, Charles M. ... 25-28R
Sherr, Lynn B(eth) 1942- ... 165
Brief entry ... 109
Sherr, Paul C(linton) 1920- ... 77-80
Sherraden, Michael (Wayne) 1948- ... 137
Sherrard, Philip (Owen Arnould) 1922-1995 ... CANR-7
Obituary ... 148
Earlier sketch in CA 13-16R
Sherred, T(homas) L. 1915-1985 ... 153
Sherrer, Quin(ton M.) 1933- ... 163
Sherriff, R(obert) C(edric) 1896-1975 ... 85-88
Obituary ... 61-64
See also DLB 10, 191
Sherriffs, Ronald E(verett) 1934- Brief entry ... 112
Sherrill, Dorothy 1901- ... 69-72
Sherrill, Elizabeth 1928- ... 110
Sherrill, Henry Knox 1890-1980 Obituary ... 97-100
Sherrill, John L. 1923- ... 110
Sherrill, Kenneth S. 1942- ... 145
Sherrill, Robert G(lenn) 1925- ... CANR-15
Earlier sketch in CA 21-24R
Sherrill, Suzanne
See Woods, Sherryl
Sherrin, Edward George 1931- ... CANR-15
Earlier sketch in CA 21-24R
Sherrin, Ned
See Sherrin, Edward George
Sherrington, Richard (Wallace) 1940-1977 ... 108
Sherrod, Blackie ... AITN 2
Sherrod, Drury 1943- ... 109
Sherrod, Jane
See Singer, Jane Sherrod
Sherrod, Robert (Lee) 1909- ... 77-80
Sherry, Clifford J. 1943- ... 150
See also SATA 84
Sherry, James (Terence) 1946- ... CANR-41
Earlier sketch in CA 112
Sherry, John (Olden) 1923- ... 119
Sherry, John E(rnest) H(orwath) 1932- ... CANR-37
Earlier sketches in CA 89-92, CANR-16
Sherry, Michael S(tephen) 1945- ... 73-76
Sherry, Norman 1925- ... CANR-34
Earlier sketch in CA 49-52
See also BEST 89:4
See also DLB 155
Sherry, Patrick 1938- ... 138
Sherry, Pearl Andelson 1899- ... 109
Sherry, Suzanna 1954- ... 167
Sherry, (Dulcie) Sylvia 1932- ... CANR-34
Earlier sketch in CA 49-52
See also SATA 8
Sherry, Vincent B(ernard), Jr. 1948- ... CANR-39
Earlier sketch in CA 116
Shershow, Scott Cutler 1953- ... 123
Shertzer, Bruce E(ldon) 1928- ... CANR-3
Earlier sketch in CA 9-12R
Sherwan, Earl 1917- ... 5-8R
See also SATA 3
Sherwin, Byron L(ee) 1946- ... CANR-49
Earlier sketch in CA 123
Sherwin, Judith Johnson 1936- ... CANR-34
Earlier sketch in CA 25-28R
See also CLC 7, 15
Sherwin, Martin J(ay) 1937- Brief entry ... 110
Sherwin, Oscar 1902-1976 ... 1-4R
Obituary ... 65-68
Sherwin, Richard E(lliott) 1933- ... 69-72
Sherwin, Sidney 1920- ... 65-68
Sherwin, Sterling
See Hagen, John Milton
Sherwin-White, A(drian) N(icholas) 1911-1993 ... 119
Obituary ... 143
Sherwood, Debbie
See Sherwood, Deborah
Sherwood, Deborah ... 25-28R
Sherwood, Dolly ... 138
Sherwood, Frances 1940- ... 146
See also CLC 81
Sherwood, Frank Persons 1920- ... CANR-9
Earlier sketch in CA 5-8R
Sherwood, Hugh C. 1928- ... 29-32R
Sherwood, John (Herman Mulso) 1913- ... CANR-61
Earlier sketches in CA 5-8R, CANR-6, 21
Sherwood, John C(ollingwood) 1918- ... 13-16R
Sherwood, John J(oseph) 1933- ... 29-32R
Sherwood, Jonathan
See London, Jonathan (Paul)
Sherwood, Martin (Anthony) 1942- ... CANR-19
Earlier sketch in CA 102
Sherwood, Mary Martha 1775-1851 ... DLB 163
Sherwood, Michael 1938-1976 ... CAP-2
Earlier sketch in CA 29-32
Sherwood, Morgan B(ronson) 1929- ... CANR-6
Earlier sketch in CA 13-16R
Sherwood, Nelson
See Bulmer, (Henry) Kenneth
Sherwood, Robert D(an) 1949- ... 118
Sherwood, Robert E(mmet) 1896-1955 ... 153
Brief entry ... 104
See also DAM DRAM
See also DLB 7, 26
See also TCLC 3
Sherwood, Tom 1946- ... 147
Sherwood, Valerie
See Hines, Jeanne
Sherwood, William Robert 1929- ... 21-24R
Shesgreen, Sean N(icholas) 1939- ... 45-48
Shestack, Alan 1938- ... 33-36R
Shestack, Jerome J(oseph) 1925- ... 118
Shestack, Melvin (Bernard) 1931- ... 120
Shestov, Lev 1866-1938 ... TCLC 56
Sheth, Jagdish N(anchand) 1938- ... CANR-11
Earlier sketch in CA 61-64
Shetter, William Z(eiders, Jr.) 1927- ... 81-84
Shetterly, Will(iam Howard) 1955- ... 119
See also SATA 78
Shettles, Landrum Brewer 1909- ... CANR-13
Earlier sketch in CA 77-80
Shetty, C(handrashekar) M(ajur) 1927- ... CANR-10
Earlier sketch in CA 13-16R
Shetty, Manohar 1953- ... 154
Shetty, Sharat 1940- ... 73-76
Shev, Edward E(lmer) 1919- ... 93-96
Shevchenko, A. N.
See Shevchenko, Arkady N(ikolaevich)
Shevchenko, Arkady N(ikolaevich) 1930-1998 ... 129
Obituary ... 165
Shevchuk, Tetiana
See Bishop, Tania Kroitor
Shevelove, Burt 1915-1982 Obituary ... 106
Shevin, David (Avram) 1951- ... 77-80
Shevrin, Aliza 1931- ... 129
Shew, E(dward) Spencer 1908-1977 ... CANR-3
Obituary ... 69-72
Earlier sketch in CA 1-4R
Shewbridge, Edythe A(nne) 1943- ... 41-44R
Shewell-Cooper, W(ilfred) E(dward) 1900- ... CANR-7
Earlier sketch in CA 9-12R
Shewmaker, Kenneth E. 1936- ... 33-36R
Shewring, Walter Hayward (Francis)
1906(?)-1990 Obituary ... 132
Shi, David Emory 1951- ... CANR-28
Earlier sketch in CA 106
Shiach, Allan G. 1941- ... 136
Shiarella, Robert 1936- ... 57-60
Shibles, Warren 1933- ... CANR-12
Earlier sketch in CA 29-32R
Shibutani, Tamotsu 1920- ... 17-20R
Shideler, John C(lement) 1949- ... 118
Shideler, Mary McDermott 1917- ... 25-28R
Shidle, Norman G(lass) 1895- ... 17-20R
Shiefman, Vicky 1942- ... 57-60
See also SATA 22
Shieh, Francis S(hih-hoa) 1926- ... 37-40R
Shiel, M(atthew) P(hipps) 1865-1947 ... 160
Brief entry ... 106
See also Holmes, Gordon
See also DLB 153
See also TCLC 8
Shield, Renee Rose 1948- ... 115
Shields, Allan (Edwin) 1919- ... 65-68
Shields, Brenda Desmond (Armstrong) 1914- ... 5-8R
See also SATA 37
Shields, Carol 1935- ... CANR-51
Earlier sketch in CA 81-84
See also CLC 91, 113
See also DAC
Shields, Charles 1944- ... SATA 10
Shields, Currin Vance 1918- ... 1-4R
Shields, David 1956- ... CANR-48
Earlier sketch in CA 124
See also CLC 97
Shields, Donald J(ames) 1937- ... 53-56
Shields, Gerald R. 1925- ... 110
Shields, John M(ackie) 1954- ... 147
Shields, Joyce Farley 1930- Brief entry ... 109
Shields, Laurie 1922(?)-1989 Obituary ... 128
Shields, Nancy E. 1928- ... 146
Shiels, Barbara
See Adams, Barbara Johnston
Shiels, Frederick L(ambert) 1949- ... 118
Shiels, George 1886-1949 Brief entry ... 111
See also DLB 10
Shiels, W(illiam) Eugene 1897- ... CAP-1
Earlier sketch in CA 9-10
Shiers, George 1908- ... 73-76
Shiff, Nathan A. 1914- ... 25-28R
Shiffert, Edith (Marcombe) 1916- ... CANR-6
Earlier sketch in CA 13-16R
Shifflett, Crandall A(vis) 1938- ... 135
Shiffman, Lena 1957- ... SATA 101
Shiffrin, Nancy 1944- ... 81-84
Shiflet, Kenneth E(lwood) 1918-1978 ... CANR-2
Obituary ... 81-84
Earlier sketch in CA 1-4R
Shiflett, Lee
See Shiflett, Orvin Lee
Shiflett, Orvin Lee 1947- ... 115
Shiga, Naoya 1883-1971 ... 101
Obituary ... 33-36R
See also CLC 33
See also DLB 180
See also SSC 23
Shigley, Forrest Dwight 1930- ... 1-4R
Shih, Chih-yu 1958- ... 143
Shih, Chung-wen ... 81-84
Shih, Vincent Y(u) C(hung) 1903- ... 77-80
Shih Hsio-Yen 1933- ... 119
Shiina, Makoto 1944- ... 150
See also SATA 83
Shiina, Rinzo 1911-1973 ... DLB 182
Shikes, Ralph E. 1912-1992 ... CANR-12
Obituary ... 137
Earlier sketch in CA 29-32R
Shillaber, Benjamin Penhallow 1814-1890 ... DLB 1, 11
Shiller, Jack G(erald) 1928- ... 73-76
Shiller, Robert J. 1946- ... 136
Shilling, Dana 1953- ... CANR-29
Earlier sketch in CA 109
Shilling, N(ed) 1924- ... 29-32R
Shillinglaw, Gordon 1925- ... CANR-7
Earlier sketch in CA 17-20R
Shillingsburg, Miriam J.
See Shillingsburg, Miriam (Carolyn) Jones
Shillingsburg, Miriam (Carolyn) Jones 1943- ... 130
Shillingsburg, Peter L(eRoy) 1943- ... 139
Shillony, Ben-Ami 1937- ... 73-76
Shiloah, Amnon 1928- ... 158
Shiloh, Ailon 1924- ... 33-36R
Shils, Edward B. 1915- ... CANR-6
Earlier sketch in CA 5-8R
Shilton, Lance(lot) R(upert) 1921- ... 5-8R
Shilts, Randy 1951-1994 ... CANR-45
Obituary ... 144
Brief entry ... 115
Earlier sketch in CA 127
Interview in ... 127
See also AAYA 19
See also CLC 85
Shim, Jae K. 1943- ... 142
Shimada, Masahiko 1961- ... 143
Shimao, Toshio 1917-1986 ... DLB 182
Shimazaki, Haruki 1872-1943 ... 134
Brief entry ... 105
See also Shimazaki Toson
Shimazaki Toson 1872-1943
See Shimazaki, Haruki
See also DLB 180
See also TCLC 5
Shimberg, Benjamin 1918- ... 45-48
Shimberg, Elaine Fantle 1937- ... CANR-31
Earlier sketch in CA 112
Shimer, Dorothy Blair 1911- ... 45-48
Shimin, Symeon 1902- ... 81-84
See also MAICYA
See also SATA 13
Shimkin, Michael B(oris) 1912-1989 Obituary ... 127
Shi Mo
See Bei, Dao
Shimomura, Tsutomu 1965(?)- ... 155
Shimoni, Yaacov 1915- ... 141
Shimoniak, Wasyl 1923- Brief entry ... 108
Shimota, Helen
See Gross, Helen Shimota
Shinagel, Michael 1934- ... 25-28R
Shindell, Sidney 1923- ... 13-16R
Shinder, Jason (Scott) 1955- ... 133
Shine, Deborah 1932- ... CANR-44
Earlier sketch in CA 110
See also SATA 71
Shine, Frances L(ouise) 1927- ... 25-28R
Shine, Richard 1950- ... 139
Shine, Ted 1931- ... CANR-24
Earlier sketches in CA 77-80, CANR-13
See also BW 1
See also DLB 38
Shiner, Larry (Ernest) 1934- ... 21-24R
Shiner, Lewis 1950- ... CAAS 30
Shiner, Roger A(lfred) 1940- Brief entry ... 109
Shingleton, John D. ... CANR-37
Earlier sketch in CA 115
Shingleton, Royce (Gordon Sr.) 1935- ... CANR-12
Earlier sketch in CA 29-32R
Shinichi, Kano
See Jackson, G. Mark
Shinkle, James D. 1897(?)-1973 Obituary ... 104
Shinkle, Tex
See Shinkle, James D.
Shinn, Everett 1876-1953 ... SATA 21
Shinn, Larry Dwight 1942- ... 107
Shinn, Roger L(incoln) 1917- ... CANR-40
Earlier sketches in CA 1-4R, CANR-18
Shinn, Sharon 1957- ... 155
Shinnie, Peter Lewis 1915- ... 103
Shinoda, Minoru 1915- ... 5-8R
Shinwell, Emanuel 1884-1986 Obituary ... 119
Ship, Reuben 1915-1975 ... 148
See also DLB 88
Shipler, David K(arr) 1942- ... CANR-21
Earlier sketch in CA 103
Shiplett, June Lund 1930- ... CANR-36
Earlier sketches in CA 81-84, CANR-16
Shipley, David
See Holden, David (Shipley)
Shipley, David O. 1925- ... 37-40R
Shipley, Joseph T(wadell) 1893-1988 ... CANR-9
Obituary ... 125
Earlier sketch in CA 13-16R
Shipley, Nan (Sommerville) ... 9-12R
Shipley, Peter (Samuel) 1946- ... CANR-20
Earlier sketch in CA 103
Shipley, (Howard) Thorne 1927- ... 5-8R
Shipman, David 1932-1996 ... CANR-30
Obituary ... 152
Earlier sketches in CA 29-32R, CANR-12
Shipman, Harry L(ongfellow) 1948- ... CANR-32
Earlier sketches in CA 65-68, CANR-10
Shipman, Pat 1949- ... 141
Shipp, Nelson 1892- ... 57-60
Shipp, Steve 1937- ... 160
Shipp, Thomas J. 1918- ... 13-16R
Shippen, Katherine B(inney) 1892-1980 ... 5-8R
Obituary ... 93-96
See also CLR 36
See also SATA 1
See also SATA-Obit 23
Shipper, Frank M(artin) 1945- ... 119
Shippey, Frederick Alexander 1908- ... CAP-1
Earlier sketch in CA 13-14
Shippey, (Henry) Lee 1884-1969 Obituary ... 89-92
Shippey, Thomas Alan 1943- ... 108
Shipps, Jan (Barnett) 1929- ... 127
Shippy, Richard W. 1927- ... 81-84
Shipton, Clifford K(enyon) 1902-1973 ... CAP-2
Earlier sketch in CA 17-18
Shipton, Eric Earle 1907-1977 ... 65-68
Obituary ... 69-72
See also SATA 10
Shipway, George 1908- ... 25-28R
Shirakawa, Yoshikazu 1935- ... CANR-14
Earlier sketch in CA 73-76
Shiras, Wilmar H(ouse) 1908-1990 ... 160
Shiratori, Rei 1937- ... 133
Shire, Helena (Mary) Mennie 1912-1991 ... CANR-27
Obituary ... 136
Earlier sketch in CA 29-32R
Shirer, William L(awrence) 1904-1993 ... CANR-55
Obituary ... 143
Earlier sketches in CA 9-12R, CANR-7
See also DLB 4
See also MTCW 1
See also SATA 45
See also SATA-Obit 78
Shires, Henry M(illis) 1913-1980 ... 17-20R
Obituary ... 134
Shires, Linda M(arguerite) 1950- ... 118
Shirinsky-Shikhmatov, Sergii Aleksandrovich
1783-1837 ... DLB 150
Shirk, Evelyn Urban 1918- ... 17-20R
Shirk, George H(enry) 1913- ... 17-20R
Shirk, Susan L(ee) 1945- ... 108
Shirkey, Albert P(atterson) 1904-1990 ... CAP-2
Obituary ... 133
Earlier sketch in CA 17-18
Shirley, Dennis 1955- ... 137
Shirley, Frances A(nn) 1931- ... CANR-2
Earlier sketch in CA 5-8R
Shirley, Gayle C(orbett) 1955- ... 161
See also SATA 96
Shirley, Glenn 1916- ... 89-92
Shirley, Hardy L(omax) 1900- ... 37-40R
Shirley, James 1596-1666 ... DLB 58
Shirley, Jean 1919- ... 138
See also SATA 70
Shirley, John 1953- ... 126
Shirley, John William 1908- ... 126
Brief entry ... 114
Shirley, Ralph 1865-1946 Brief entry ... 117
Shirley, Shirley 1934- ... 162
Shirley-Smith, Hubert 1901-1981 Obituary ... 113
Shirreffs, Gordon D(onald) 1914- ... CANR-49
Earlier sketches in CA 13-16R, CANR-6, 21
See also SATA 11

Shirts, Morris A(lpine) 1922- 73-76
See also SATA 63
Shishkov, Aleksandr Semenovich 1753-1841 .. DLB 150
Shissler, Barbara Johnson
See Nosanow, Barbara Shissler
Shivanandan, Mary 1932- CANR-12
Earlier sketch in CA 73-76
Shively, Donald H(oward) 1921- Brief entry 115
Shively, George Jenks
1893(?)-1980 Obituary 97-100
Shivers, Alfred Samuel 1929- 41-44R
Shivers, Frank R(emer), Jr. 1924- 130
Shivers, Jay S(anford) 1930- CANR-52
Earlier sketches in CA 33-36R, CANR-12, 27
Shivers, Louise 1929- 136
Shivers, Samuel A.
See Shivers, Alfred Samuel
Shivpuri, Gopi Krishna 1903-1984 CANR-42
Obituary 113
Earlier sketch in CA 101
Shklovsky, Iosif Samuilovitch
1916-1985 Obituary 115
Shklovsky, Viktor Borisovich 1893-1984 144
Obituary 114
Shlaim, Avi 1945- 136
Shlechter, Theodore M. 1952- 144
Shlemon, Barbara Leahy 1936- CANR-31
Earlier sketch in CA 112
Shlichta, Joe 1968- SATA 84
Shlonsky, Abraham 1898(?)-1973 Obituary . 41-44R
Shmanske, Stephen 1954- 139
Shmeruk, Chone 1921-1997 166
Shmueli, Adi 1941- CANR-1
Earlier sketch in CA 45-48
Shnayerson, Michael 1954- 132
Shneerson, Grigory Mikhailovich
1901-1982 Obituary 106
Shneiderman, Ben A. 1947- 115
Shneiderman, Samuel L(oeb) 1906- 97-100
Shneidman, Conalee Levine
See Levine-Shneidman, Conalee
Shneidman, Edwin S. 1918- CANR-36
Earlier sketch in CA 29-32R
Shneidman, J(erome) Lee 1929- 37-40R
Shneidman, N(oah) N(orman) 1924- 136
Shneour, Elie A(lexis) 1925- 37-40R
Shoaf, Richard Allen 1948- CANR-45
Earlier sketch in CA 119
Shoales, Ian
See Kessler, Merle (Bruce)
Shoben, Edward Joseph, Jr. 1918- 21-24R
Shober, Joyce Lee 1932- 1-4R
Shoberg, Lore 1949- 33-36R
Shobin, David 1945- CANR-20
Earlier sketch in CA 104
Shoblad, Richard H(anson) 1937- 41-44R
Shock, Julian
See Williamson, Gerald Neal
Shock, Nathan W(etherill) 1906-1989 5-8R
Obituary 130
Shockley, Ann Allen 1927- CANR-59
Earlier sketches in CA 49-52, CANR-1
See also BW 1
See also DLB 33
Shockley, Donald G(rady) 1937- 103
Shockley, William (Bradford)
1910-1989 Obituary 129
Brief entry 113
Shoe, Lucy T.
See Meritt, Lucy Shoe
Shoemaker, Bill
See Shoemaker, William
Shoemaker, Don(ald) C(leavenger) 1912- ... 97-100
Shoemaker, Donald J(ay) 1927- 37-40R
Shoemaker, Leonard Calvin 1881- CAP-1
Earlier sketch in CA 13-16
Shoemaker, Lloyd R. 1921- 133
Shoemaker, Lynn Henry 1939- CANR-9
Earlier sketch in CA 65-68
Shoemaker, Richard H(eston) 1907-1970 ... CAP-1
Earlier sketch in CA 11-12
Shoemaker, Robert B(rink) 1956- 142
Shoemaker, Robert G(ardner) 1941- 142
Shoemaker, Robert John 1919- 13-16R
Shoemaker, Robin 1949- 108
Shoemaker, Sarah
See Wolf, Sarah (Elizabeth)
Shoemaker, William 1931- 154
Shoemaker, William H(utchinson) 1902- 13-16R
Shoemaker, William Lee 1931- Brief entry 115
Shoemaker, Willie
See Shoemaker, William Lee
Shoenight, Aloise 1914- 77-80
Shoesmith, Kathleen A(nne) 1938- CANR-17
Earlier sketches in CA 49-52, CANR-1
Shofner, Jerrell H(arris) 1929- 57-60
Shofner, Robert D(ancey) 1933- 57-60
Shogan, Robert 1930- 153
Shokeid, Moshe 1936- CANR-16
Earlier sketch in CA 41-44R
Sholinsky, Jane 1943- 89-92
Sholokhov, Mikhail (Aleksandrovich)
1905-1984 101
Obituary 112
See also CLC 7, 15
See also MTCW 1
See also SATA-Obit 36
Shomaker, Dianna 1934- 109
Shomer, Enid 143
Shomon, Joseph James 1914- 73-76
Shomroni, Reuven
See von Block, Bela W(illiam)
Shone, Anna
See Shone, Bridget Ann
Shone, Bridget Ann 1947- 150
Shone, Patric
See Hanley, James
Shone, Richard (N.) 1949- 141
Shone, Robert 1906- 109
Shone, Ronald 1946- CANR-20
Earlier sketch in CA 103
Shonfield, Andrew (Akiba) 1917-1981 105
Obituary 102
Shono, Junzo 1921- DLB 182
Shontz, Franklin C(urtis) 1926- 17-20R
Shook, Karel 1920-1985 Obituary 117
Shook, Laurence K(ennedy) 1909- 73-76
Shook, Robert L. 1938- CANR-46
Earlier sketches in CA 61-64, CANR-8, 23
Shookman, Ellis 1957- 166
Shoolbred, C(laude) F(rederick) 1901- CAP-2
Earlier sketch in CA 25-28
Shooter, James (Charles) 1951- 136
Shooter, Jim
See Shooter, James (Charles)
Shor, Elizabeth N(oble) 1930- 110
Shor, Franc(is Marion Luther)
1914-1974 Obituary 111
Shor, Ira 1945- CANR-55
Earlier sketch in CA 126
Shor, Joel 1919- 89-92
Shor, Pekay 1923- 45-48
Shor, Ronald (Edwin) 1930- 61-64
Shorb, Wil(bert Hanson, Jr.) 1938- 45-48
Shore, Anne
See Sanford, Annette
Shore, Arabella 1820(?)-1901 DLB 199
Shore, Bernard (Alexander Royle)
1896-1985 Obituary 116
Shore, Jane 1947- CANR-66
Earlier sketch in CA 77-80
Shore, June Lewis 105
See also AITN 1
See also SATA 30
Shore, Louisa 1824-1895 DLB 199
Shore, Norman
See Smith, Norman Edward Mace
Shore, Paul J(ohn) 1956- 118
Shore, Philippa
See Holbeche, Philippa Jack
Shore, Robert 1924- SATA 39
Shore, Sidney 1921-1981 Obituary 103
Shore, William B(urton) 1925- 53-56
Shore, Wilma 1913- 13-16R
Shores, David L(ee) 1933- 123
Brief entry 118
Shores, Louis 1904-1981 CANR-8
Obituary 104
Earlier sketch in CA 13-16R
Shorris, Earl 1936- CANR-34
Earlier sketches in CA 65-68, CANR-10
Shorrock, William I(rwin) 1941- 65-68
Short, Alan Lennox
See Lennox-Short, Alan
Short, Alison 1920- 61-64
Short, Bobby
See Short, Robert Waltrip
Short, Brian (Michael) 1944- 136
Short, Bryan C. 139
Short, (Charles) Christopher (Dudley) (?)-1978 .....
CANR-2
Earlier sketch in CA 1-4R
Short, Clarice 1910-1977 45-48
Obituary 103
Short, Edmund C(oen) 1931- 25-28R
Short, Howard E(lmo) 1907- 61-64
Short, Jackson 53-56
Short, James F(ranklin, Jr.) 1924- CANR-25
Earlier sketches in CA 5-8R, CANR-8
Short, James R. 1922(?)-1980 Obituary 103
Short, K(enneth) R(ichard) M(acDonald) 1936- . 131
Short, Kathy G(nagey) 1952- 150
Short, Luke
See Glidden, Frederick D(illey)
Short, Michael 1937- CANR-42
Earlier sketch in CA 117
See also SATA 65
Short, Peter fl. 1589-1603 DLB 170
Short, Philip 1945- 105
Short, Robert L(ester) 1932- 77-80
Short, Robert Stuart 1938- 29-32R
Short, Robert Waltrip 1924(?)- Brief entry 107
Short, Roger
See Arkin, Alan (Wolf)
Short, Roger, Jr.
See Eyen, Tom
Short, Roy Hunter 1902- 120
Short, Ruth Gordon CANR-6
Earlier sketch in CA 1-4R
Short, Thayne R(edford) 1929- 108
Short, Wayne 1926- 9-12R
Shortall, Leonard W. 81-84
See also SATA 19
Shorter, Aylward 1932- 81-84
Shorter, Carl
See Schwalberg, Carol(yn Ernestine Stein)
Shorter, Edward 1941- CANR-46
Earlier sketch in CA 73-76
Shorter, Frank C(harles) 1947- 132
Shorthouse, Joseph Henry 1834-1903 164
Brief entry 121
See also DLB 18
Shorto, Harry L(eonard) 1919- 5-8R
Shortridge, James R. 1944- 136
Shortt, Terence Michael 1911- 77-80
Shortt, Tim(othy Donald) 1961- 161
See also SATA 96
Shostak, Arthur B. 1937- 108
Shostak, Jerome 1913- CANR-7
Earlier sketch in CA 17-20R
Shostak, Stanley 1938- 117
Shostakovich, Dmitri (Dmitrievich) 1906-1975 .. 148
Obituary 113
Shosteck, Robert 1910-1979 CANR-11
Obituary 85-88
Earlier sketch in CA 61-64
Shott, James R. 1925- 139
Shotwell, Louisa Rossiter 1902- CANR-4
Earlier sketch in CA 1-4R
See also SATA 3
Shouksmith, George A. 1931- 49-52
Shoumatoff, Alex(ander) 1946- CANR-48
Earlier sketches in CA 53-56, CANR-9
Shoup, Barbara 1947- 151
See also SAAS 24
See also SATA 86
Shoup, Carl S(umner) 1902- 49-52
Shoup, Laurence H(enry) 1943- CANR-43
Earlier sketch in CA 102
Shoup, Paul Snedden 1929- 106
Shover, John L. 1927- 21-24R
Showalter, Dennis 1942- 89-92
Showalter, Elaine 1941- CANR-58
Earlier sketch in CA 57-60
See also DLB 67
Showalter, English, Jr. 1935- 53-56
Showalter, Jean B(reckinridge) 21-24R
See also SATA 12
Showalter, Ronda Kerr 1942- 37-40R
Showell, Ellen Harvey 1934- 85-88
See also SATA 33
Showers, Paul C. 1910- CANR-59
Earlier sketches in CA 1-4R, CANR-4, 38
See also CLR 6
See also MAICYA
See also SAAS 7
See also SATA 21, 92
Showers, Renald E(dward) 1935- CANR-13
Earlier sketch in CA 77-80
Showers, Victor 1910- 53-56
Shoy, Lee Ang
See Sheridan, L(ionel) A(stor)
Shpakow, Tanya 1959(?)- 159
See also SATA 94
Shpitalnik, Vladimir 1964- SATA 83
Shrader, Charles R. 1943- 153
Shrady, Maria 1924- 49-52
Shragin, Boris 1926-1990 102
Obituary 132
Shrake, Bud
See Shrake, Edwin
Shrake, Edwin 1931- 144
Brief entry 116
Shreffler, Philip A. 1948- 138
Shreve, Anita 1947- 139
Shreve, L(evin) G(ale) 1910- 101
Shreve, Susan Richards 1939- CANR-69
Earlier sketches in CA 49-52, CANR-5, 38
See also CAAS 5
See also CLC 23
See also MAICYA
See also SATA 46, 95
See also SATA-Brief 41
Shriber, Ione Sandberg 1911-1987 Obituary ... 121
Shrimpton, Gordon Spencer 1941- 115
Shrimsley, Anthony 1934-1984 Obituary 114
Shrimsley, Bernard 1931- 103
Shrivastava, Paul 1951- 133
Shriver, Donald W(oods), Jr. 1927- CANR-1
Earlier sketch in CA 45-48
Shriver, George H(ite), Jr. 1931- 21-24R
Shriver, Harry C(lair) 1904- CANR-10
Earlier sketch in CA 65-68
Shriver, Jean Adair 1932- 142
See also SATA 75
Shriver, Lionel 1957- CANR-72
Earlier sketch in CA 134
Shriver, Peggy (Ann) L(eu) 1931- 107
Shriver, Phillip Raymond 1922- 13-16R
Shriver, Rosalia (Oliver) 1927-1987 115
Obituary 135
Shrode, Mary
See Hollingsworth, Mary
Shroder, Maurice Z(orensky) 1933- 1-4R
Shrodes, Caroline 1908- CANR-4
Earlier sketch in CA 1-4R
Shropshire, Kenneth (L.) 1955- 160
Shropshire, W(alter), Jr. 1932- 118
Shrosbree, Colin (John) 1938- 130
Shrout, Richard Neil 1931- 144
Shrout, Thomas R(euben) 1919- 41-44R
Shroyer, Frederick B(enjamin) 1916-1983 .....
CANR-13
Earlier sketch in CA 13-16R
Shryock, (Edwin) Harold 1906- CANR-8
Earlier sketch in CA 21-24R
Shryock, Richard Harrison 1893-1972 CAP-2
Obituary 33-36R
Earlier sketch in CA 17-18
Shtainmets, Leon 105
See also SATA 32
Shtemenko, Sergei Matveyevich 1907-1976 103
Shternfeld, Ari A(bramovich)
1905-1980 Obituary 105
Shtromas, Alexander 1931- 132
Shu, Austin Chi-wei 1915- 29-32R
Shu, Ch' ing-ch'un 1899-1966 Obituary 109
Shub, Beth
See Pessen, Beth
Shub, David 1887-1973 Obituary 41-44R
Shub, Elizabeth CANR-15
Earlier sketch in CA 41-44R
See also SATA 5
Shubik, Martin 1926- CANR-2
Earlier sketch in CA 5-8R
Shubin, Seymour 1921- 1-4R
Shucard, Alan R(obert) 1935- CANR-51
Earlier sketches in CA 61-64, CANR-26
Shuchman, Abraham 1919-1978 Obituary ... 77-80
Shue, Larry 1946-1985 145
Obituary 117
See also CLC 52
See also DAM DRAM
Shuffelton, Frank 1940- CANR-38
Earlier sketch in CA 115
Shuford, Cecil Eugene 1907- 13-16R
See also AITN 1
Shuford, Gene
See Shuford, Cecil Eugene
Shugart, Herman H(enry, Jr.) 1944- 145
Shughart, William F. (II) 1947- 154
Shugrue, Michael F(rancis) 1934- 21-24R
Shu-Jen, Chou 1881-1936 Brief entry 104
See also Lu Hsun
Shuken, Julia 1948- 150
See also SATA 84
Shukert, Elfrieda Berthiaume 1948- 129
Shukman, Harold 1931- CANR-66
Earlier sketch in CA 53-56
Shukshin, V.
See Shukshin, Vasily (Makarovich)
Shukshin, V. M.
See Shukshin, Vasily (Makarovich)
Shukshin, Vasily (Makarovich) 1929-1974 135
Shula
See Reinharz, Shulamit
Shula, Don(ald Francis) 1930- Brief entry 106
Shulberg, Alan
See Wilkes-Hunter, R(ichard)
Shuldinger, Herbert 1929- 130
Shuler, Linda Lay 128
Shulevitz, Uri 1935- CANR-3
Earlier sketch in CA 9-12R
See also CLR 5
See also DLB 61
See also MAICYA
See also SATA 3, 50
Shull, Fremont Adam, Jr. 1924- CANR-1
Earlier sketch in CA 1-4R
Shull, Margaret Anne Wyse 1940- 77-80
Shull, Peg
See Shull, Margaret Anne Wyse
Shull, Steven A. 1943- 147
Shulman, Albert M(aimon) 1902- 49-52
Shulman, Alix Kates 1932- CANR-43
Earlier sketch in CA 29-32R
See also CLC 2, 10
See also SATA 7
Shulman, Arnold 1914- 29-32R
Shulman, Bernard H. 1922- 108
Shulman, Charles E. 1904-1968 CAP-1
Earlier sketch in CA 13-14
Shulman, David Dean 1949- 102
Shulman, Fay Grissom Stanley
1925(?)-1990 Obituary 133
Shulman, Frank Joseph 1943- CANR-60
Earlier sketches in CA 29-32R, CANR-12, 30
Shulman, Harry 1903-1955 Brief entry 112
Shulman, Harry Manuel 1899- 1-4R
Shulman, Irving 1913-1995 CANR-6
Obituary 148
Earlier sketch in CA 1-4R
See also SATA 13
Shulman, Mark R(ussell) 1963- 147
Shulman, Marshall Darrow 1916- 1-4R
Shulman, Max 1919-1988 89-92
Obituary 126
See also DLB 11
See also SATA-Obit 59
Shulman, Milton 1913- 103
Shulman, Morton 1925- CANR-14
Earlier sketch in CA 21-24R
See also AITN 1
Shulman, Neil B(arnett) 1945- CANR-53
Earlier sketches in CA 65-68, CANR-9, 26
See also SATA 89
Shulman, Sandra (Dawn) 1944- CANR-9
Earlier sketch in CA 21-24R
Shultz, George P(ratt) 1920- CANR-49
Earlier sketch in CA 104
Shultz, Gladys Denny 1895- 49-52
Shultz, Suzanne M. 1947- 144
Shultz, William J(ohn) 1902-1970 CANR-16
Obituary 103
Earlier sketch in CA 1-4R
Shulvass, Moses A. 1909- 13-16R
Shumaker, Peggy 1952- 154
Shumaker, Wayne 1910- 5-8R
Shuman, Bruce A(lan) 1941- 110
Shuman, James B(urrow) 1932- 61-64
Shuman, Nicholas R(oman) 1921- 109
Shuman, R(obert) Baird 1929- CANR-4
Earlier sketch in CA 1-4R
Shuman, Samuel I(rving) 1925- CANR-3
Earlier sketch in CA 9-12R
Shumsky, Zena
See Collier, Zena
Shumway, Floyd M(allory, Jr.) 1917-1997 ....
CANR-29
Obituary 162
Earlier sketch in CA 29-32R
Shumway, George (Alfred, Jr.) 1928- 9-12R
Shumway, Mary L. 1926- CANR-7
Earlier sketch in CA 17-20R
Shupe, Anson 1948- CANR-67
Earlier sketch in CA 129
Shupp, Mike 1946- 121
Shura, Mary Francis
See Craig, Mary (Francis) Shura
Shurden, Walter B(yron) 1937- CANR-21
Earlier sketch in CA 69-72

Shurkin, Joel N. 1938- ... CANR-14
Earlier sketch in CA 69-72
Shurr, Emily Grey 1972- ... 147
Shurr, William H(oward) 1932- ... CANR-18
Earlier sketch in CA 41-44R
Shurter, Robert L(e Fevre) 1907-1974 ... CANR-2
Earlier sketch in CA 1-4R
Shurtleff, Malcolm C., Jr. 1922- ... 5-8R
Shurtleff, Michael 1930- ... 41-44R
Shurtleff, William 1941- ... CANR-16
Earlier sketch in CA 93-96
Shusaku, Endo 1923-1996 ... DLB 182
Shuseki, Hayashi
See Hubbell, Lindley Williams
Shuster, Albert H., Jr. 1917- ... 17-20R
Shuster, Alvin 1930- Brief entry ... 113
Shuster, Bud
See Shuster, E. G.
Shuster, E. G. 1932- ... 138
Shuster, George Nauman 1894-1977 ... 77-80
Obituary ... 69-72
Shuster, Joe 1914- ... CLC 21
Shuster, Ronald L(owell) 1927- ... 45-48
Shusterman, David 1912- ... 25-28R
Shusterman, Neal 1962- ... 133
See also AAYA 21
See also SATA 85
Shusterman, Richard (M.) 1949- ... 136
Shute, Alberta V(an Horn) 1906- ... CANR-7
Earlier sketch in CA 57-60
Shute, Gary Brana
See Brana-Shute, Gary
Shute, Henry A. 1856-1943 ... DLB 9
Shute, Jenefer 1956- ... 138
Shute, Nerina ... 101
Shute, Nevil
See Norway, Nevil Shute
See also CLC 30
Shute, R(eginald) Wayne 1933- ... 29-32R
Shute, Wallace B. 1911- ... 29-32R
Shute, Wilfred Eugene 1907- ... 105
Shuter, Jane Margaret 1955- ... 155
See also SATA 90
Shuttle, Penelope (Diane) 1947- ... CANR-39
Earlier sketch in CA 93-96
See also CLC 7
See also DLB 14, 40
Shuttlesworth, Dorothy Edwards ... CANR-4
Earlier sketch in CA 1-4R
See also SATA 3
Shuttleworth, John 1937- ... AITN 1
Shuval, Judith T(annenbaum) 1925- ... CANR-25
Earlier sketch in CA 45-48
Shuy, Roger W(ellington) 1931- ... CANR-13
Earlier sketch in CA 61-64
Shvarts, Elena 1948- ... 147
Shvets, Yuri B. 1953- ... 147
Shvidkovsky, Dimitri 1959- ... 157
Shwadran, Benjamin 1907- ... CANR-20
Earlier sketches in CA 13-16R, CANR-5
Shwartz, Susan (Martha) 1949- ... CANR-56
Earlier sketch in CA 109
See also SATA 94
Shwayder, David S(amuel) 1926- ... 106
Shy, John W(illard) 1931- ... CANR-3
Earlier sketch in CA 5-8R
Shyer, Charles (Richard) 1941- ... 138
Shyer, Christopher 1961- ... 157
See also SATA 98
Shyer, Marlene Fanta ... CANR-11
Earlier sketch in CA 69-72
See also SATA 13
Shyne, Ann W(entworth) 1914- ... 115
Shyre, Paul 1929(?)-1989 ... 103
Obituary ... 130
Siano, Mary M(artha) 1924- ... 77-80
Sibbes, Richard 1577-1635 ... DLB 151
Siberell, Anne ... 104
See also SATA 29
Siberry, (Jane) Elizabeth 1957- ... 122
Sibley, Agnes M(arie) 1914- ... 61-64
Sibley, Celestine 1917- ... 85-88
Sibley, Don 1922- ... SATA 12
Sibley, Elbridge 1903- ... CAP-1
Earlier sketch in CA 13-14
Sibley, Katherine A. S. 1961- ... 156
Sibley, Marilyn McAdams 1923- ... 21-24R
Sibley, Mulford Quickert 1912- ... CANR-6
Earlier sketch in CA 5-8R
Sibley, Patricia (Hayles) 1928- ... 97-100
Sibley, Susan
See Kinnicutt, Susan Sibley
Sibly, John 1920- ... 1-4R
Sibson, Caroline
See Dracup, Angela
Sices, David 1933- ... 25-28R
Sichel, Peter M(ax) F(erdinand) 1922- ... 65-68
Sichel, Pierre (Laugier) 1915- ... 1-4R
Sichel, Werner 1934- ... CANR-47
Earlier sketches in CA 21-24R, CANR-8, 23
Sicherman, Carol 1937- ... 135
Sichol, Marcia W. 1940- ... 135
Sichov, Vladimir 1945- ... 108
Sichrovsky, Peter 1947- ... 148
Sicignano, Robert 1946- ... 116
Siciliano, Enzo 1934- ... 147
Siciliano, Vincent Paul 1911- ... CAP-2
Earlier sketch in CA 29-32
Sicinski, Andrzej 1924- ... CANR-40
Earlier sketch in CA 115
Sick, Gary G(ordon) 1935- ... 144
Sickels, Noelle 1945- ... 153
Sickels, Robert J(udd) 1931- ... 41-44R
Sicker, Martin 1931- ... 146
Sicker, Philip 1951- ... 103
Sickles, William Russell 1913- ... 57-60
Sickman, Laurence C(halfant) S(tevens)
1906-1988 ... CAP-1
Obituary ... 125
Earlier sketch in CA 11-12
Siculan, Daniel 1922- ... SATA 12
Sidahmed, Abdel Salam 1956- ... 159
Sidak, J. Gregory 1955- ... 148
Siddal, Elizabeth Eleanor 1829-1862 ... DLB 199
Siddall, William R(ichard) 1928- ... 41-44R
Siddiqi, Akhtar Husain 1925- ... 61-64
Siddiqui, Ashraf (Hossain) 1927- ... CANR-2
Earlier sketch in CA 5-8R
Siddons, (Sybil) Anne Rivers 1936- ... CANR-53
Earlier sketches in CA 101, CANR-33
See also BEST 89:2
See also DAM POP
See also MTCW 1
Siddons, Robert 1952- ... 119
Sidel, Victor W(illiam) 1931- ... CANR-9
Earlier sketch in CA 65-68
Sider, Don 1933- ... 77-80
Sider, Robert Dick 1932- ... CANR-16
Earlier sketch in CA 37-40R
Sider, Ronald J(ames) 1939- ... CANR-39
Earlier sketches in CA 93-96, CANR-17
Siders, Ellis L(eroy) 1920- ... 17-20R
Sides, W(ade) Hampton 1962- ... 139
Sidetracked Home Executives
See Jones, Peggy
and Young, Pam
Sidey, Hugh (Swanson) 1927- ... 124
Brief entry ... 111
Sidgwick, Ethel 1877-1970 ... DLB 197
Sidgwick, Henry 1838-1900 Brief entry ... 120
Sidhwa, Bapsy (N.) 1938- ... CANR-57
Earlier sketches in CA 108, CANR-25
Sidhwa, Keki R(attanshah) 1926- ... 69-72
Sidjakov, Nicolas 1924- ... SATA 18
Sidley, Nathan T(heodore) 1929- ... 113
Sidnell, Michael John 1935- ... 113
Sidney, Frank
See Warwick, Alan R(oss)
Sidney, Jonathan
See Cooper, Emmanuel
Sidney, Kathleen M(arion) 1944- ... 103
Sidney, Margaret
See Lothrop, Harriet Mulford Stone
Sidney, Neilma
See Gantner, Neilma
Sidney, Sir Philip 1554-1586 ... CDBLB Before 1660
See also DA
See also DAB
See also DAC
See also DAM MST, POET
See also DLB 167
Sidney-Fryer, Donald 1934- ... CANR-46
Earlier sketch in CA 45-48
Sidney Herbert, Mary 1561-1621 ... DLB 167
Sidowski, Joseph B(oleslaus) 1925- ... 21-24R
Sidran, Ben H. 1943- ... 102
Sidransky, Ruth 1929- ... 135
Siebel, Fritz (Frederick) 1913- ... SATA-Brief 44
Siebenheller, Norma 1937- ... 107
Siebenschuh, William R(obert) 1942- ... 89-92
Sieber, Joan E. 1937- ... CANR-35
Earlier sketch in CA 114
Sieber, Roy 1923- ... 102
Sieber, Sam Dixon 1931- ... 13-16R
Siebert, Fred(rick) Seaton 1901- ... 21-24R
Siebold, Cathy 1951- ... 145
Siedel, Frank 1914- ... 25-28R
Siedel, James M. 1937- ... 25-28R
Siegal, Aranka 1930- ... 112
See also AAYA 5
See also SATA 88
See also SATA-Brief 37
Siegal, Diana Laskin 1931- ... 127
Siegal, Harvey A. 1945- ... 127
Siegal, Mordecai 1934- ... 102
Siegal, Sanford (Sherwin) 1928- ... 105
Siegan, Bernard H(erbert) 1924- ... CANR-45
Earlier sketch in CA 65-68
Siegbahn, Kai M. 1918- ... 161
Siegbahn, Karl M(anne) G(eorg) 1886-1978 ... 161
Siegel, Adrienne 1936- ... CANR-12
Earlier sketch in CA 61-64
Siegel, Beatrice ... CANR-40
Earlier sketches in CA 101, CANR-18
See also SATA 36
Siegel, Ben 1925- ... 77-80
Siegel, Benjamin 1914-1991 ... CANR-4
Obituary ... 135
Earlier sketch in CA 1-4R
Siegel, Bernie S(hepard) 1932- ... CANR-49
Earlier sketch in CA 123
See also BEST 89:4
Siegel, Bertram M. 1936- ... 25-28R
Siegel, Daniel M. 1939- ... 144
Siegel, Dorothy (Schainman) 1932- ... 9-12R
Siegel, Eli 1902-1978 ... CANR-9
Obituary ... 81-84
Earlier sketch in CA 17-20R
Siegel, Ernest 1922- ... 73-76
Siegel, Esther 1949- ... 102
Siegel, Fred 1941- ... 167
Siegel, Frederick F(ein) 1945- ... 133
Siegel, Gonnie McClung 1928- ... 110
Siegel, Helen
See Siegl, Helen
Siegel, Irving H(erbert) 1914-1988 ... CANR-9
Obituary ... 125
Earlier sketch in CA 21-24R
Siegel, Jack
See Siegel, Jacob
Siegel, Jacob 1913- ... 17-20R
Siegel, James T. 1937- Brief entry ... 113
Siegel, Jerome 1914-1996 Obituary ... 151
Brief entry ... 116
See also CLC 21
Siegel, Jerry
See Siegel, Jerome
Siegel, June 1929- ... 77-80
Siegel, Katherine A. S.
See Sibley, Katherine A. S.
Siegel, Lee 1945- ... CANR-71
Earlier sketch in CA 126
Siegel, Marcia B. 1932- ... CANR-37
Earlier sketch in CA 69-72
Siegel, Mark Richard 1949- ... CANR-29
Earlier sketch in CA 110
Siegel, Martin 1933- ... 33-36R
Siegel, Mary-Ellen (Kulkin) 1932- ... CANR-40
Earlier sketch in CA 116
Siegel, Max 1904-1972 Obituary ... 104
Siegel, Maxwell E(dward) 1933- ... 101
Siegel, Paul N. 1916- ... 37-40R
Siegel, Rachel Josefowitz 1924- ... 163
Siegel, Richard L(ewis) 1940- ... 73-76
Siegel, Robert (Harold) 1939- ... CANR-50
Earlier sketches in CA 53-56, CANR-5, 21
See also SATA 39
Siegel, Seymour 1927-1988 Obituary ... 124
Siegel, Stanley E(lliott) 1928- ... 41-44R
Siegelbaum, Lewis H. 1949- ... 144
Siegel-Gorelick, Bryna 1954- ... 115
Siegelman, James Howard 1951- ... 81-84
Siegelman, Jim
See Siegelman, James Howard
Siegener, Ray(mond) 1931- ... 123
Brief entry ... 118
Sieghart, (Henry Laurence) Paul (Alexander)
1927-1988 Obituary ... 127
Siegl, Helen 1924- ... SATA 34
Siegle, Bernard A(ndrew) 1914- ... 89-92
Siegler, Frederick Adrian 1932- ... 49-52
Siegler, Ilene C. 1946- ... 114
Siegman, Gita 1939- ... CANR-31
Earlier sketch in CA 112
Siegmeister, Elie 1909-1991 ... CANR-46
Obituary ... 133
Earlier sketches in CA 1-4R, CANR-1
Siegner, C(larence) Vernon, Jr. 1920- ... 1-4R
Sielaff, Theodore J. 1920- ... 13-16R
Sieller, William Vincent 1917- ... 29-32R
Siemanowski, Richard F.
1922(?)-1981 Obituary ... 104
Siemens, Alfred H. 1932- ... 139
Siemens, Reynold Gerrard 1932- ... 41-44R
Siemon, James Ralph 1948- ... 121
Siemon, Jeff 1950- ... 103
Sienkiewicz, Henryk (Adam Alexander Pius)
1846-1916 ... 134
Brief entry ... 104
See also TCLC 3
Sienkiewicz-Mercer, Ruth 1950- ... 136
Sienko, Michell J. 1923-1983 Obituary ... 111
Siepmann, Charles Arthur 1899-1985 ... 1-4R
Obituary ... 115
Sierpinski, Waclaw 1882-1969 ... 161
Sierra, Gregorio Martinez
See Martinez Sierra, Gregorio
Sierra, Judy 1945- ... 128
Sierra, Maria (de la O'LeJarraga) Martinez
See Martinez Sierra, Maria (de la O'LeJarraga)
Sierra, Patricia ... 166
Sierra, Ruben 1946- ... DLB 122
Sies, Luther F(rank) 1927- ... 111
Siev, Asher 1913- ... 57-60
Sievers, Allen M. 1918- ... 89-92
Sievers, Harry J(oseph) 1920-1977 ... 25-28R
Obituary ... 73-76
Sievers, W(ieder) David 1919-1966 ... 1-4R
Obituary ... 103
Sievert, Philipp 1970- ... 150
Siewert, Frances E. (Cornelius) 1881- ... CAP-1
Earlier sketch in CA 11-12
Sifakis, G(regory) M(ichael) 1935- ... 25-28R
Siffert, Robert S(pencer) 1918- ... 109
Sifford, (Charles) Darrell 1931- ... CANR-15
Earlier sketch in CA 77-80
Sifton, Claire 1897(?)-1980 Obituary ... 93-96
Sifton, Paul F. 1893(?)-1972 Obituary ... 33-36R
Sigal, Clancy 1926- ... 1-4R
See also CLC 7
Sigal, Leon V(ictor) 1942- Brief entry ... 114
Sigband, Norman Bruce 1920- ... CANR-17
Earlier sketches in CA 5-8R, CANR-2
Sigel, Efrem 1943- ... 121
Sigelschiffer, Saul 1902- ... 81-84
Siger of Brabant 1240(?)-1284(?) ... DLB 115
Siggins, Maggie 1942- ... 165
Sigler, Jay A(drian) 1933- ... 25-28R
Sigler, John W(illiam) 1946- ... 127
Sigler, William F. ... 128
Sigmund, Paul E(ugene) 1929- ... CANR-39
Earlier sketches in CA 5-8R, CANR-2, 18
Signoret, Simone 1921-1985 ... 135
Obituary ... 117
Sigourney, Andre R. ... 132
Sigourney, Lydia Howard (Huntley) 1791-1865 . DLB 1, 42, 73
Sigurjonsson, Johann 1880-1919 ... TCLC 27
Sigworth, Oliver F(rederic) 1921- ... 13-16R
Sihanouk, Norodom
See Norodom Sihanouk (Varman), Samdech Preah
Siirala, Aarne 1919- ... 13-16R
Sik, Endre 1891-1978 Obituary ... 77-80
Sikelianos, Angelos 1884-1951 ... TCLC 39
Sikes, Herschel Moreland 1928- ... 17-20R
Sikes, Melvin P. 1917- ... 146
Sikes, Walter W(allace) 1925- ... 57-60
Sikora, Frank J(oseph) 1936- ... CANR-40
Earlier sketch in CA 115
Sikora, Joseph (John) 1932-1967 ... CAP-2
Earlier sketch in CA 17-18
Sikora, Stefan
See Rey, Michael Stephan
Sikorski, Radek (Tomasz) 1963- ... 164
Sikorsky, Igor I(van) 1889-1972 ... 157
Obituary ... 113
Siks, Geraldine Brain 1912- ... 25-28R
Sikula, Andrew F(rank) 1944- ... CANR-2
Earlier sketch in CA 49-52
Silangan, Manuel
See Yabes, Leopoldo Y(abes)
Silard, Bela (A.) 1900- ... 140
Silbajoris, Frank
See Silbajoris, Rimvydas
Silbajoris, Rimvydas 1926- ... 25-28R
Silber, Diana 1936- ... 134
Silber, Evelyn (Ann) 1949- ... 124
Silber, Irwin 1925- ... 9-12R
Silber, Joan 1945- ... CANR-20
Earlier sketch in CA 104
Silber, Kate 1902- ... 77-80
Silber, Mark 1946- ... CANR-43
Earlier sketch in CA 45-48
Silber, Nina 1959- ... 140
Silber, Norman I. 1951- ... 114
Silber, William L. 1942- ... CANR-29
Earlier sketch in CA 29-32R
Silberberg, R(ein) 1932- ... 149
Silberg, Moshe 1900-1975 Obituary ... 61-64
Silberg, Richard 1942- ... 21-24R
Silberger, Julius 1929- ... CANR-21
Earlier sketch in CA 105
Silberkleit, Louis Horace 1905-1986 Obituary .. 118
Silberman, Arlene ... 133
Silberman, Charles E(liot) 1925- ... CANR-7
Earlier sketch in CA 9-12R
Silberman, James H(enry) 1927- ... 133
Silberman, Jerome
See Wilder, Gene
Silberman, Marc (D.) 1948- ... 162
Silberman, Neil Asher 1950- ... 108
Silbermann, Eileen Z(ieget) 1925- ... 114
Silbersack, John (Walter) 1954- ... CANR-33
Earlier sketch in CA 107
Silberschlag, Eisig 1903- ... CANR-17
Earlier sketches in CA 1-4R, CANR-1
Silberschmidt, Max 1899- ... 65-68
Silberstang, Edwin 1930- ... CANR-3
Earlier sketch in CA 49-52
Silberstein, Gerard Edward 1926- ... 37-40R
Silberstein, Howard E. 1907(?)-1984 Obituary ... 112
Silberstein, Warren P(aul) 1948- ... 110
Silberstein-Storfer, Muriel (Rosoff) ... 111
Silbey, Joel H. 1933- ... 21-24R
Silbiger, Alexander 1935- ... 136
Silcock, Sara Lesley 1947- ... SATA 12
Silcock, Thomas H(enry) 1910- ... 9-12R
Silcox, David Phillips 1937- ... 109
Silen, Juan Angel 1938- ... 33-36R
Silesky, Barry 1949- ... 135
See also CAAS 29
Silet, Charles L(oring) P(rovine) 1942- ... CANR-17
Earlier sketch in CA 93-96
Silex, Edgar Gabriel 1958- ... 150
Silinsh, Edgar A. 1927- ... 152
Silitch, Clarissa MacVeagh 1930- ... CANR-31
Earlier sketch in CA 112
Silk, Andrew 1953(?)-1981 Obituary ... 106
Silk, Dennis (Peter) 1928- ... 161
Silk, Gerald 1947- ... 133
Silk, Joseph (Ivor) 1942- ... 149
Silk, Leonard S(olomon) 1918-1995 ... CANR-46
Obituary ... 147
Earlier sketches in CA 1-4R, CANR-4
Silkin, Jon 1930- ... 5-8R
See also CAAS 5
See also CLC 2, 6, 43
See also DLB 27
Silko, Leslie (Marmon) 1948- ... CANR-65
Brief entry ... 115
Earlier sketches in CA 122, CANR-45
See also AAYA 14
See also CLC 23, 74
See also DA
See also DAC
See also DAM MST, MULT, POP
See also DLB 143, 175
See also NNAL
See also WLCS
Sill, Cathryn 1953- ... SATA 74
Sill, Geoffrey M(ichael) 1944- ... 111
Sill, Gertrude Grace ... 69-72
Sill, John 1947- ... SATA 74
Sill, Sterling Welling 1903- ... CANR-6
Earlier sketch in CA 57-60
Sillanpaa, Frans Eemil 1888-1964 ... 129
Obituary ... 93-96
See also CLC 19
See also MTCW 1
Sillem, Edward 1916-1964 ... 5-8R
Sillen, Samuel 1911(?)-1973 Obituary ... 41-44R
Sillery, Anthony 1903-1976 ... CANR-5
Obituary ... 65-68
Earlier sketch in CA 5-8R
Silliman, Benjamin 1779-1864 ... DLB 183
Silliman, Ron(ald Glenn) 1946- ... CANR-46
Earlier sketch in CA 45-48
See also CAAS 29
See also DLB 169
Silliphant, Stirling (Dale) 1918-1996 ... CANR-42
Obituary ... 152
Earlier sketches in CA 73-76, CANR-14
See also DLB 26

Sillitoe, Alan 1928- ... CANR-55
Earlier sketches in CA 9-12R, CANR-8, 26
See also CAAS 2
See also AITN 1
See also CDBLB 1960 to Present
See also CLC 1, 3, 6, 10, 19, 57
See also DLB 14, 139
See also MTCW 1
See also SATA 61
Sillitoe, Linda 1948- ... 152
Sillman, Leonard (Dexter) 1908-1982 Obituary . 105
Sills, Beverly 1929- ... 89-92
Sills, David Lawrence 1920- ... 33-36R
Sills, Frank D(reyer) 1914- ... 1-4R
Sills, Jennifer
See Lewis, Stephen
Sills, Judith 1948(?)- ... 144
Sills, Leslie (Elka) 1948- ... 130
Sills, Ruth C(urtis) ... 29-32R
Silly, E. S.
See Kraus, (Herman) Robert
Silman, Roberta 1934- ... 101
See also DLB 28
Silone, Ignazio 1900-1978 ... CANR-34
Obituary ... 81-84
Earlier sketches in CAP-2, CA 25-28
See also CLC 4
See also MTCW 1
Silsbe, Brenda 1953- ... SATA 73
Siluriensis, Leolinus
See Jones, Arthur Llewellyn
Silva, Beverly 1935- ... 131
See also DLB 122
See also HW
Silva, Eduardo Neale
See Neale-Silva, Eduardo
Silva, Jose Asuncion
See da Silva, Antonio Jose
Silva, Joseph
See Goulart, Ron(ald Joseph)
Silva, Julian 1927- ... 115
Silva, Julio A(lberto) 1933- ... 17-20R
Silva, Ruth C(aridad) 1920-1995 ... 13-16R
Obituary ... 148
Silvanus
See Strasser, Bernard Paul
Silvaroli, Nicholas J. 1930- ... CANR-12
Earlier sketch in CA 29-32R
Silver, A(aron) David 1941- ... 124
Silver, A(aron) Henry 1891-1986 Obituary ... 121
Silver, Abba Hillel 1893-1963 ... 1-4R
Silver, Alain (Joel) 1947- ... CANR-10
Earlier sketch in CA 57-60
Silver, Alfred 1951- ... CANR-15
Earlier sketch in CA 85-88
Silver, Carole G(reta) 1937- ... 132
Silver, Daniel Jeremy 1928-1989 ... CANR-3
Obituary ... 130
Earlier sketch in CA 5-8R
Silver, Gary (Thomas) 1944- ... 89-92
Silver, Gerald A(lbert) 1932- ... CANR-58
Earlier sketches in CA 33-36R, CANR-13, 30
Silver, Harold 1928- ... CANR-10
Earlier sketch in CA 21-24R
Silver, Isidore 1934- ... 53-56
Silver, James W(esley) 1907-1988 ... 9-12R
Obituary ... 126
Silver, Joan Micklin 1935- ... 121
Brief entry ... 114
Interview in ... 121
See also CLC 20
Silver, Jody 1942- ... 109
Silver, Marjorie A. 1948- ... 93-96
Silver, Nathan 1936- ... CANR-11
Earlier sketch in CA 21-24R
Silver, Nicholas
See Faust, Frederick (Schiller)
Silver, Philip Warnock 1932- ... 106
Silver, Richard
See Bulmer, (Henry) Kenneth
Silver, Rollo G(abriel) 1909- ... CAP-1
Earlier sketch in CA 19-20
Silver, Roy R. 1918-1979 Obituary ... 89-92
Silver, Ruth
See Chew, Ruth
Silver, Samuel 1915(?)-1976 Obituary ... 69-72
Silver, Samuel M. 1912- ... CANR-11
Earlier sketch in CA 21-24R
Silver, Warren A. 1914- ... 65-68
Silvera, Alain 1930- ... 21-24R
Silverberg, Ira 1962- ... 139
Silverberg, Robert 1935- ... CANR-36
Earlier sketches in CA 1-4R, CANR-1, 20
Interview in ... CANR-20
See also CAAS 3
See also AAYA 24
See also CLC 7
See also DAM POP
See also DLB 8
See also MAICYA
See also MTCW 1
See also SATA 13, 91
Silverburg, Sanford R. 1940- ... 143
Silverlock, Anne
See Titchener, Louise
Silverman, Al 1926- ... 9-12R
Silverman, Alvin Michaels 1912- ... 9-12R
Silverman, Burt(on Philip) 1928- ... 103
Silverman, Corinne 1930- ... 5-8R
Silverman, David 1907- ... CAP-2
Earlier sketch in CA 21-22
Silverman, Erica 1955- ... SATA 78
Silverman, Gerry 1938- ... 133
Silverman, Harold M(artin) 1945- ... 112
Silverman, Hillel E. 1924- ... CANR-11
Earlier sketch in CA 21-24R
Silverman, Hirsch Lazaar 1915- ... 45-48
Silverman, Hugh J(erald) 1945- ... 118
Silverman, Jason H(oward) 1952- ... 110
Silverman, Jerry 1931- ... CANR-7
Earlier sketch in CA 13-16R
Silverman, Jonathan 1955- ... 138
Silverman, Joseph H(erman) 1924- ... 104
Silverman, Judith 1933- ... 103
Silverman, Kaja 1947- ... 132
Silverman, Kenneth 1936- ... CANR-71
Earlier sketches in CA 57-60, CANR-17
See also DLB 111
Silverman, Mark Philip 1945- ... 147
Silverman, Mel(vin Frank) 1931-1966 ... 5-8R
See also SATA 9
Silverman, Milton (M.) 1910- ... 152
Silverman, Milton J. 1944- ... 108
Silverman, Morris 1894-1972 Obituary ... 33-36R
Silverman, Oscar Ansell 1903-1977 Obituary . 69-72
Silverman, Robert A(llan) 1943- ... 57-60
Silverman, Robert E(ugene) 1924- ... 41-44R
Silverman, Robert J(ay) 1940- ... 101
Silverman, Robin L(andew) 1954- ... 161
See also SATA 96
Silverman, Rose
See Millstein, Rose Silverman
Silverman, S(ol) Richard 1911- ... 107
Silverman, Samuel ... AITN 1
Silverman, Stephen M. 1951- ... 135
Silverman, Sydel 1933- ... 77-80
Silverman, Sylvia W. 1907-1992 ... 139
Silverman, Willa Z. 1959- ... 155
Silverman, William B. 1913- ... 49-52
Silvern, Leonard C. 1919- ... CANR-7
Earlier sketch in CA 17-20R
Silvers, Phil
See Silversmith, Philip
Silvers, Robert B. 1929- ... 165
Silvers, Vicki 1941- ... 93-96
Silversmith, Philip 1912-1985 Obituary ... 117
Brief entry ... 111
Silverstein, Alvin 1933- ... CANR-2
Earlier sketch in CA 49-52
See also CLC 17
See also CLR 25
See also JRDA
See also MAICYA
See also SATA 8, 69
Silverstein, Charles 1935- ... 73-76
Silverstein, Josef 1922- ... CANR-58
Earlier sketches in CA 37-40R, CANR-14, 31
Silverstein, Mel(vin Jerome) 1940- ... 101
Silverstein, Norman 1922-1974 ... 37-40R
Obituary ... 49-52
Silverstein, Robert Alan 1959- ... SATA 77
Silverstein, Shel(by) 1932- ... CANR-47
Earlier sketch in CA 107
See also CLR 5
See also JRDA
See also MAICYA
See also SATA 33, 92
See also SATA-Brief 27
Silverstein, Theodore 1904- ... 106
Silverstein, Virginia B(arbara Opshelor) 1937- ... CANR-2
Earlier sketch in CA 49-52
See also CLC 17
See also CLR 25
See also JRDA
See also MAICYA
See also SATA 8, 69
Silverstone, Lou 1928- ... 108
Silverstone, Paul H. 1931- ... 21-24R
Silvert, Kalman H(irsch) 1921-1976 ... CANR-6
Obituary ... 65-68
Earlier sketch in CA 13-16R
Silverthorn, J(ames) E(dwin) 1906- ... CAP-1
Earlier sketch in CA 13-16
Silverthorne, Elizabeth 1930- ... 89-92
See also SATA 35
Silverton, Michael 1935- ... 65-68
Silverton, Nancy 1954- ... 164
Silverwood, Jane
See Titchener, Louise
Silverwood, Margaret Shannon 1966- ... 150
See also SATA 83
Silvester, Christopher (Paul Victor) 1959- ... 167
Silvester, Frank
See Bingley, David Ernest
Silvester, P(eter) P. 1935- ... 135
Silvester, Peter (John) 1934- ... 133
Silvester, Victor ... CAP-1
Earlier sketch in CA 13-14
Silvestri, Richard 1944- ... 81-84
Silving, Helen 1906- ... 41-44R
Silvis, Randall 1950- ... 136
Silvius, G(eorge) Harold 1908-1981 ... CANR-3
Obituary ... 104
Earlier sketch in CA 5-8R
Sim, Dorrith M. 1931- ... 161
See also SATA 96
Sim, Georges
See Simenon, Georges (Jacques Christian)
Sim, John Cameron 1911-1990 ... 25-28R
Obituary ... 132
Sim, Katharine (Thomasset) 1913- ... 13-16R
Sim, Myre 1915- ... 61-64
Sim, Yawsoon 1937- ... 108
Simak, Clifford D(onald) 1904-1988 ... CANR-35
Obituary ... 125
Earlier sketches in CA 1-4R, CANR-1
See also CLC 1, 55
See also DLB 8
See also MTCW 1
See also SATA-Obit 56
Simard, Real 1951- ... 129
Simbari, Nicola 1927- ... CANR-1
Earlier sketch in CA 1-4R
Simckes, L(azarre) S(eymour) 1937- ... 9-12R
Simcoe, Elizabeth 1762-1850 ... DLB 99
Simcox, Carroll E(ugene) 1912- ... 132
Simcox, Edith Jemima 1844-1901 ... DLB 190
Simcox, George Augustus 1841-1905 ... DLB 35
Sime, Jessie Georgina 1868-1958 ... DLB 92
Sime, Mary 1911- ... 53-56
Simecka, Martin M. 1957- ... 151
Simenon, Georges (Jacques Christian) 1903-1989 . CANR-35
Obituary ... 129
Earlier sketch in CA 85-88
See also CLC 1, 2, 3, 8, 18, 47
See also DAM POP
See also DLB 72
See also DLBY 89
See also MTCW 1
Simeon, Mother Mary 1888- ... CAP-1
Earlier sketch in CA 13-14
Simeon, Richard 1943- ... CANR-9
Earlier sketch in CA 61-64
Simeone, Diane A. 1953(?)-1983 Obituary ... 109
Simeti, Mary Taylor 1941- ... 144
Simic, Andrei 1930- ... 93-96
Simic, Charles 1938- ... CANR-61
Earlier sketches in CA 29-32R, CANR-12, 33, 52
See also CAAS 4
See also CLC 6, 9, 22, 49, 68
See also DAM POET
See also DLB 105
Simic, Goran 1952- ... 168
Simini, Joseph Peter 1921- ... CANR-8
Earlier sketch in CA 17-20R
Simirenko, Alex 1931- ... 13-16R
Simis, Konstantin 1919- ... 130
Simister, Florence Parker 1913- ... CANR-2
Earlier sketch in CA 5-8R
Simkin, C(olin) G(eorge) F(rederick) 1915- .. 29-32R
Simkin, Penny 1938- ... 116
Simkin, Tom 1933- ... 132
Simkin, William E(dward) 1907- ... 45-48
Simkins, Lawrence D(avid) 1933- ... 41-44R
Simley, Anne 1891- ... 5-8R
Simmel, Edward C(lemens) 1932- ... CANR-31
Earlier sketch in CA 45-48
Simmel, Georg 1858-1918 ... 157
See also TCLC 64
Simmel, Johannes M(ario) 1924- ... 81-84
See also DLB 69
Simmel, Marianne L(enore) 1923- ... 21-24R
Simmes, Valentine fl. 1589(?)-1623(?) ... DLB 170
Simmie, James Martin 1941- ... CANR-38
Earlier sketch in CA 115
Simmie, Lois (Ann) 1932- ... 165
Simmonds, A(ndrew) J(effrey) 1943- ... 81-84
Simmonds, George W. 1929- ... 21-24R
Simmonds, James D(udley) 1933- ... 104
Simmonds, John 1942- ... 135
Simmonds, Posy ... CLR 23
Simmonds, Walter H(enry) C(live) 1917- ... 118
Simmons, A(lan) John 1950- ... 106
Simmons, Anthony 1922- ... 103
Simmons, Billy E. 1931- ... CANR-10
Earlier sketch in CA 21-24R
Simmons, Blake
See Wallmann, Jeffrey M(iner)
Simmons, Charles (Paul) 1924- ... 89-92
Interview in ... 89-92
See also CLC 57
Simmons, D(avid) R(oy) 1930- ... CANR-56
Earlier sketches in CA 110, CANR-28
Simmons, Dan 1948- ... CANR-53
Earlier sketch in CA 138
See also AAYA 16
See also CLC 44
See also DAM POP
Simmons, David
See Gold, Alan R(obert)
Simmons, Dawn Langley ... 29-32R
Simmons, Edwin Howard 1921- ... 89-92
Simmons, Ernest J(oseph) 1903-1972 ... CANR-3
Earlier sketch in CA 1-4R
See also DLB 103
Simmons, Geoffrey 1943- ... 104
Simmons, Gloria Mitchell 1932-1993 ... 37-40R
Obituary ... 143
Simmons, Henry T. 1927(?)-1986 Obituary ... 120
Simmons, Herbert A(lfred) 1930- ... 1-4R
See also BW 1
See also DLB 33
Simmons, Ian 1937- ... 106
Simmons, J(oseph) Edgar (Jr.) 1921-1979 ... CANR-49
Earlier sketch in CA 21-24R
Simmons, J(erry) L(aird) 1933- ... 29-32R
Simmons, Jack 1915- ... CANR-38
Earlier sketches in CA 5-8R, CANR-2
Simmons, James (Stewart Alexander) 1933- ... 105
See also CAAS 21
See also CLC 43
See also DLB 40
Simmons, James C(oleman) 1939- ... 144
Simmons, James E(dwin) 1923- ... 41-44R
Simmons, James W(illiam) 1936- ... CANR-12
Earlier sketch in CA 17-20R
Simmons, Jerold L. 1941- ... 129
Simmons, John Edwards 1918-1986 Obituary .. 121
Simmons, Joseph Larry 1935- ... 65-68
Simmons, Judy Dothard 1944- ... 77-80
Simmons, Mabel Clark 1899-1988 Obituary ... 124
Simmons, Marc 1937- ... CANR-51
Earlier sketches in CA 25-28R, CANR-10, 26
Simmons, Mary Kay 1933- ... 81-84
Simmons, Matty 1926- ... 29-32R
Simmons, Merle Edwin 1918- ... CANR-2
Earlier sketch in CA 5-8R
Simmons, Michael 1935- ... CANR-66
Earlier sketch in CA 128
Simmons, Otis D(avis) 1928- ... 57-60
Simmons, Ozzie Gordon 1919-1988 ... 9-12R
Obituary ... 127
Simmons, Patricia A. 1930- ... 93-96
Simmons, Paul D(ewayne) 1936- ... CANR-58
Earlier sketches in CA 45-48, CANR-31
Simmons, Robert R. 1940- ... 97-100
Simmons, S. H.
See Simmons, Sylvia
Simmons, Sylvia ... 49-52
Simmons, Thomas 1956- ... 150
Simmons, William S(cranton) 1938- ... 121
Simms, D(enton) Harper 1912- ... 29-32R
Simms, Eric Arthur 1921- ... 101
Simms, George (Otto) 1910-1991 ... CANR-25
Obituary ... 136
Earlier sketch in CA 108
Simms, Peter (F. J.) 1925- ... 21-24R
Simms, Ruth P. 1937- ... 17-20R
Simms, Willard S. 1943- ... 29-32R
Simms, William Gilmore 1806-1870 .. DLB 3, 30, 59, 73
Simon, Alfred (Edward) 1907-1991 ... 41-44R
Obituary ... 134
Simon, Andre (Louis) 1877-1970 Obituary .. 29-32R
Simon, Anne W(ertheim) 1914-1996 ... 105
Obituary ... 152
Simon, Arthur 1930- ... 33-36R
Simon, Bennett 1933- ... 101
Simon, Boris-Jean 1913(?)-1972 Obituary .. 33-36R
Simon, Carl P(aul) 1945- ... 107
Simon, Carly 1945- ... 105
See also CLC 26
Simon, Charlie May
See Fletcher, Charlie May Hogue
Simon, Christopher Fitz
See Fitz-Simon, Christopher
Simon, Claude 1913-1984 ... CANR-33
Earlier sketch in CA 89-92
See also CLC 4, 9, 15, 39
See also DAM NOV
See also DLB 83
See also MTCW 1
Simon, Daniel (Martin) 1957- ... 147
Simon, David 1960- ... 136
Simon, Disney 1927- ... 21-24R
Simon, Eckehard 1939- ... 61-64
Simon, Edith 1917- ... 13-16R
Simon, Fritz B(ernhard) 1948- ... 156
Simon, George T(homas) 1912- ... CANR-17
Earlier sketch in CA 25-28R
Simon, Henry W(illiam) 1901-1970 ... CANR-4
Obituary ... 29-32R
Earlier sketch in CA 5-8R
Simon, Herbert 1898(?)-1974 Obituary ... 53-56
Simon, Herbert A(lexander) 1916- ... CANR-49
Earlier sketches in CA 13-16R, CANR-9
Simon, Hilda Rita 1921- ... 77-80
See also CLR 39
See also SATA 28
Simon, Howard 1903-1979 ... 33-36R
Obituary ... 89-92
See also SATA 32
See also SATA-Obit 21
Simon, Hubert K. 1917- ... 13-16R
Simon, James E(dward) 1954- ... CANR-44
Earlier sketch in CA 119
Simon, James F. 1939- ... 134
Simon, Jo Ann 1946- ... 106
Simon, Joan L. 1921- ... 13-16R
Simon, Joe
See Simon, Joseph H.
Simon, John (Ivan) 1925- ... 21-24R
Simon, John G. 1928- ... 37-40R
Simon, John Y. 1933- ... CANR-53
Earlier sketches in CA 25-28R, CANR-12, 29
Simon, Joseph H. 1913- ... 29-32R
See also SATA 7
Simon, Julian L(incoln) 1932-1998 ... CANR-45
Obituary ... 165
Earlier sketch in CA 33-36R
Simon, Kate (Grobsmith) 1912-1990 ... CANR-61
Obituary ... 130
Brief entry ... 115
Earlier sketch in CA 127
Interview in ... 127
See also MTCW 1
Simon, Leonard 1922- ... 9-12R
Simon, Linda 1946- ... CANR-13
Earlier sketch in CA 73-76
Simon, Lorena Cotts 1897- ... 5-8R
Simon, Louis M(ortimer) 1906-1996 ... 77-80
Obituary ... 154
Simon, Marcia L. 1939- ... 93-96
Simon, Martin P(aul William) 1903-1969 ... CAP-1
Earlier sketch in CA 11-12
See also SATA 12
Simon, Mary of the Angels 1897(?)-1985 Obituary ... 116
Simon, Matila 1908- ... 17-20R
Simon, Michael A(rthur) 1936- ... CANR-13
Earlier sketch in CA 33-36R
Simon, Mina Lewiton
See Lewiton, Mina
Simon, Morton J. 1913- ... 17-20R
Simon, (Marvin) Neil 1927- ... CANR-54
Earlier sketches in CA 21-24R, CANR-26
See also AITN 1
See also CLC 6, 11, 31, 39, 70
See also DAM DRAM
See also DLB 7
See also MTCW 1

Simon, Norma (Feldstein) 1927- CANR-44
Earlier sketches in CA 5-8R, CANR-6, 21
See also MAICYA
See also SATA 3, 68
Simon, Paul 1928- CANR-43
Earlier sketch in CA 81-84
Simon, Paul (Frederick) 1941(?)- 153
Brief entry 116
See also CLC 17
Simon, Pierre-Henri 1903-1972 Obituary 37-40R
Simon, Rita James 1931- CANR-8
Earlier sketch in CA 21-24R
Simon, Robert
See Musto, Barry
Simon, Robert A. 1897(?)-1981 Obituary 103
Simon, Robin (John Hughes) 1947- 128
Simon, Roger David 1943- 109
Simon, Roger L(ichtenberg) 1943- CANR-63
Earlier sketch in CA 137
Simon, Samuel A(lan) 1945- 117
Simon, Seymour 1931- CANR-29
Earlier sketches in CA 25-28R, CANR-11
See also CLR 9
See also MAICYA
See also SATA 4, 73
Simon, Sheldon W(eiss) 1937- CANR-51
Earlier sketches in CA 25-28R, CANR-10, 26
Simon, Shirley (Schwartz) 1921- CANR-16
Earlier sketches in CA 1-4R, CANR-1
See also SATA 11
Simon, Sidney B(lair) 1927- 101
Simon, Solomon 1895-1970 Obituary 104
See also SATA 40
Simon, (Edward) Ted 1931- 105
Simon, Tony 1921- 5-8R
Simon, Ulrich E(rnst) 1913-1997 29-32R
Obituary 159
Simon, Uriel 1929- 168
Simon, Walter G(old) 1924- 17-20R
Simon, William 1927- 9-12R
Simon, William E(dward) 1927- 81-84
Simonds, John Ormsbee 1913- 77-80
Simonds, Roger (Tyrrell) 1929- 93-96
Simonds, Rollin Head 1910- 1-4R
Simonds, William Adams 1887-(?) CAP-1
Earlier sketch in CA 11-12
Simone
See Porche, Simone (Benda)
Simone, Albert Joseph 1935- 17-20R
Simone, Charles B(rian) 1949- 116
Simonelli, Maria Picchio 1921- 49-52
Simonet, Thomas Solon 1942- 116
Simonetta, Linda 1948- 77-80
See also SATA 14
Simonetta, Sam 1936- 77-80
See also SATA 14
Simonhoff, Harry 1891- 5-8R
Simoni, John Peter 1911- Brief entry 106
Simonin, Albert (Charles) 1905-1980 Obituary 104
Simonini, R(inaldo) C(harles), Jr. 1922-1967 CAP-1
Earlier sketch in CA 11-12
Simonon, Paul 1956(?)- CLC 30
Simonov, Konstantin (Kirill) Mikhailovich
1915-1979 Obituary 89-92
Simons, Barbara B(rooks) 1934- 108
See also SATA 41
Simons, Beverley 1938- 104
Simons, David G(oodman) 1922- 17-20R
Simons, Donald L. 1945- 138
Simons, Elwyn LaVerne 1930- CANR-22
Earlier sketch in CA 105
Simons, Eric N(orman) 1896- 13-16R
Simons, Hans 1893-1972 Obituary 33-36R
Simons, Harry 1912- 1-4R
Simons, Howard 1929-1989 65-68
Obituary 128
Simons, James Marcus 1939- 106
Simons, Jim
See Simons, James Marcus
Simons, John D(onald) 1935- 41-44R
Simons, Joseph 1933- 81-84
Simons, Katherine Drayton Mayrant
1892(?)-1969 9-12R
Obituary 112
See also DLBY 83
Simons, Lewis M(artin) 1939- 128
Brief entry 123
Interview in 128
Simons, Margaret A. 1946- 157
Simons, Myron (Bud) 1920- 113
Simons, Rita Dandridge
See Dandridge, Rita B(ernice)
Simons, Robin 1951- 65-68
Simons, Thomas G(erald) 1950- 111
Simons, Thomas W(inston), Jr. 1938- 134
Simons, William Edward 1927- 17-20R
Simonsen, Thordis 1944- 145
Simonson, Conrad 1931- 49-52
Simonson, Harold P(eter) 1926- 33-36R
Simonson, Lee 1888-1967 9-12R
Simonson, Mary Jane
See Wheeler, Mary Jane
Simonson, Solomon S. 1914- 21-24R
Simont, Marc 1915- CANR-38
Earlier sketch in CA 61-64
See also MAICYA
See also SATA 9, 73
Simontacchi, Carol 1947- 165
Simonton, Dean Keith 1948- CANR-43
Earlier sketch in CA 119
Simonton, Stephanie
See Matthews-Simonton, Stephanie
Simoons, Frederick J. 1922- CANR-23
Earlier sketch in CA 1-4R
Simos, Miriam 1951- 104
Simper, Robert 1937- CANR-46
Earlier sketches in CA 61-64, CANR-8, 23
Simpich, Frederick, Jr. 1911-1975 61-64
Obituary 57-60
Simpkin, Richard E(velyn) 1921-1986 124
Simpson, A(lfred) W. Brian 1931- CANR-46
Earlier sketch in CA 5-8R
Simpson, Alan 1912- CANR-30
Earlier sketch in CA 1-4R
Simpson, Cedric Keith 1907-1985 111
Obituary 117
Simpson, Claude M(itchell), Jr. 1910-1976 5-8R
Obituary 65-68
Simpson, Colin 1908- CANR-5
Earlier sketch in CA 53-56
See also SATA 14
Simpson, Craig M(ichael) 1942- 119
Simpson, D(avid) P(enistan) 1917- 9-12R
Simpson, Dick 1940- CANR-30
Earlier sketches in CA 33-36R, CANR-13
Simpson, Doris 1913- CANR-68
Simpson, Dorothy 1933- CANR-62
Earlier sketches in CA 107, CANR-30
Interview in CANR-30
See also MTCW 1
Simpson, E(rvin) P(eter) Y(oung) 1911- 17-20R
Simpson, Eileen B. 139
Simpson, Elizabeth 1947- 163
Simpson, Elizabeth Alice Hilts
1921-1989 Obituary 130
Simpson, Elizabeth Leonie 33-36R
Simpson, Ethel 1937- 117
Simpson, (John) Evan 1940- 97-100
Simpson, George E(dward) 1944- 101
Simpson, George Eaton 1904- 77-80
Simpson, George Gaylord 1902-1984 CANR-61
Obituary 114
Earlier sketches in CAP-1, CA 19-20, CANR-16
See also MTCW 1
Simpson, Harold Brown 1917- CANR-4
Earlier sketch in CA 9-12R
Simpson, Harriette
See Arnow, Harriette (Louisa) Simpson
Simpson, Hassell A(lgernon) 1930- 41-44R
Simpson, Helen (De Guerry) 1897-1940 Brief
entry 109
See also DLB 77
Simpson, Helen 1957- CANR-56
Earlier sketch in CA 134
Simpson, Hilary 1954- 131
Simpson, Howard Russell 1925- CANR-1
Earlier sketch in CA 1-4R
Simpson, Ian J(ames) 1895- CAP-1
Earlier sketch in CA 13-14
Simpson, Ida Harper 1928- 17-20R
Simpson, Jacqueline (Mary) 1930- CANR-5
Earlier sketch in CA 13-16R
Simpson, Jacynth Hope
See Hope Simpson, Jacynth
Simpson, James B(easley) 1926- CANR-9
Earlier sketch in CA 5-8R
Simpson, Jean I(rwin) 1896- 5-8R
Simpson, Jeffrey (Carl) 1949- 153
Simpson, Jerry H(oward, Jr.) 1925- 138
Simpson, Joan Murray 1918-1977 Obituary 89-92
Simpson, John (Cody Fidler) 1944- 140
Simpson, John (Andrew) 1953- CANR-48
Earlier sketch in CA 122
Simpson, John E(dwin) 1951- 140
Simpson, John L(iddle) 9-12R
Simpson, Judith H(olroyd) 1941- 110
Simpson, Kemper 1893- CAP-1
Earlier sketch in CA 11-12
Simpson, Kirke L(arue)
1882(?)-1972 Obituary 37-40R
Simpson, Leo 1934- 101
See also AITN 2
Simpson, Lewis P(earson) 1916- CANR-8
Earlier sketch in CA 17-20R
Simpson, Louis (Aston Marantz) 1923- CANR-61
Earlier sketches in CA 1-4R, CANR-1
See also CAAS 4
See also CLC 4, 7, 9, 32
See also DAM POET
See also DLB 5
See also MTCW 1
Simpson, Matt(hew William) 1936- 131
Simpson, Michael Andrew 1944- 89-92
Simpson, Mona (Elizabeth) 1957- CANR-68
Brief entry 122
Earlier sketch in CA 135
See also CLC 44
Simpson, Myrtle L(illias) 1931- CANR-11
Earlier sketch in CA 21-24R
See also SATA 14
Simpson, N(orman) F(rederick) 1919- 13-16R
See also CLC 29
See also DLB 13
Simpson, Norman T. 1919(?)-1988 Obituary 125
Simpson, O(renthal) J(ames) 1947- CANR-50
Earlier sketch in CA 103
Simpson, R(onald) A(lbert) 1929- CANR-14
Earlier sketch in CA 77-80
Simpson, Ray H. 1907- 1-4R
Simpson, Richard L(ee) 1929- 9-12R
Simpson, Robert (Wilfred Levick) 1921- 103
Simpson, Robert 1924- 49-52
Simpson, Robert H. 1912- 108
Simpson, Ruth 1926- 73-76
Simpson, Ruth Mary Rasey 1902- CANR-1
Earlier sketch in CA 1-4R
Simpson, (Robert) Smith 1906- CAP-2
Earlier sketch in CA 21-22
Simpson, Stanhope Rowton 1903- 73-76
Simpson, Thomas W(illiam) 1957- 137
Simpson, W. W.
See Simpson, William Wynn
Simpson, William Hays 1903- 41-44R
Simpson, William Kelly 1928- 105
Simpson, William Wynn 1907-1987 Obituary 123
Sims, Bernard John 1915- 13-16R
Sims, Blanche (L.) SATA 75
Sims, Bobbi 1931- 117
Sims, Charles A(ugustus) 1901-1983 Obituary 111
Sims, Edward H. 1923- CANR-6
Earlier sketch in CA 1-4R
Sims, Edward J(ames) 1927- 41-44R
Sims, George (Frederick Robert) 1923- CANR-58
Earlier sketches in CA 25-28R, CANR-12
See also DLB 87
Sims, George R. 1847-1922 DLB 35, 70, 135
Sims, Harold D(ana) 1935- 41-44R
Sims, Henry P. Jr. 1939- 156
Sims, James H(ylbert) 1924- CANR-46
Earlier sketch in CA 1-4R
Sims, Janet L.
See Sims-Wood, Janet L(ouise)
Sims, Lois Dorothy Lang
See Lang-Sims, Lois Dorothy
Sims, Mary Sophia Stephens
1886-1976 Obituary 65-68
Sims, Naomi (Ruth) 1949- CANR-26
Earlier sketch in CA 69-72
Sims, Norman (Howard) 1948- 132
Sims, Patsy 1938- 135
Brief entry 110
Sims, Patterson 1947- 124
Sims, Phillip L(eon) 1940- 105
Simson, Eve 1937- 73-76
Simsova, Sylva 1931- CANR-12
Earlier sketch in CA 29-32R
Sims-Wood, Janet L(ouise) 1945- 108
Simundsson, Elva 1950- SATA 63
Sinai, I(saac) Robert 1924- CANR-10
Earlier sketch in CA 21-24R
Sinan, Rogelio 1904- DLB 145
Sinclair, Andrew (Annandale) 1935- CANR-38
Earlier sketches in CA 9-12R, CANR-14
See also CAAS 5
See also CLC 2, 14
See also DLB 14
See also MTCW 1
Sinclair, Bennie Lee 1939- CANR-1
Earlier sketch in CA 49-52
Sinclair, Bertrand William 1881-1972 148
See also DLB 92
Sinclair, Brett J(ason) 1942- 141
Sinclair, Bruce A. 1929- 126
Brief entry 106
Sinclair, Carla 160
Sinclair, Catherine 1800-1864 DLB 163
Sinclair, Clive (John) 1948- CANR-56
Earlier sketch in CA 127
Sinclair, Clover
See Gater, Dilys
Sinclair, Donna 1943- CANR-46
Earlier sketches in CA 106, CANR-23
Sinclair, Elizabeth
See Smith, Marguerite
Sinclair, Emil
See Hesse, Hermann
Sinclair, (Allan) Gordon 1900-1984 102
Obituary 112
Interview in 102
See also AITN 1
Sinclair, Grace
See Wallmann, Jeffrey M(iner)
Sinclair, Grant
See Drago, Harry Sinclair
Sinclair, Harold (Augustus) 1907-1966 5-8R
Sinclair, Heather
See Johnston, William
Sinclair, Iain 1943- 132
See also CLC 76
Sinclair, Iain MacGregor
See Sinclair, Iain
Sinclair, Ian
See Foley, (Cedric) John
Sinclair, Irene
See Griffith, D(avid Lewelyn) W(ark)
Sinclair, James
See Staples, Reginald Thomas
Sinclair, Jeff 1958- SATA 77
Sinclair, Jo
See Seid, Ruth
See also DLB 28
Sinclair, John L(eslie) 1902-1993 105
Obituary 143
Sinclair, Julian
See Sinclair, Mary Amelia St. Clair
Sinclair, Keith 1922-1993 17-20R
Obituary 142
Sinclair, Lister (Shedden) 1921- 105
See also DLB 88
Sinclair, Marjorie (Jane) 1913- 132
Sinclair, Mary Amelia St. Clair 1865(?)-1946 Brief
entry 104
See also Sinclair, May
Sinclair, Max 1945- 113
Sinclair, May 1863-1946 166
See also Sinclair, Mary Amelia St. Clair
See also DLB 36, 135
See also TCLC 3, 11
Sinclair, Michael
See Shea, Michael (Sinclair MacAuslan)
Sinclair, Miranda 1948- 77-80
Sinclair, Murray 1950- 108
Sinclair, Olga 1923- CANR-51
Earlier sketches in CA 61-64, CANR-11, 26
Sinclair, Rose
See Smith, Susan Vernon
Sinclair, Roy
See Griffith, D(avid Lewelyn) W(ark)
Sinclair, Sandra 1940- 120
Sinclair, Sonia 1928- 126
Sinclair, Upton (Beall) 1878-1968 CANR-7
Obituary 25-28R
Earlier sketch in CA 5-8R
Interview in CANR-7
See also CDALB 1929-1941
See also CLC 1, 11, 15, 63
See also DA
See also DAB
See also DAC
See also DAM MST, NOV
See also DLB 9
See also MTCW 1
See also SATA 9
See also WLC
Sinclair-Stevenson, Christopher 1939- 102
Sincoff, Michael Z(olman) 1943- 85-88
Sinden, Donald (Alfred) 1923- 132
Sindermann, Carl J(ames) 138
Sindler, Allan Paul 1928- 97-100
Sinel, Allen 1936- 45-48
Siner, Howard W(alter) 1946- 117
Sinfield, Alan 1941- CANR-68
Earlier sketches in CA 113, CANR-32
Singal, Daniel Joseph 1944- 129
Singe, (Edmund) J(ohn) M(illington)
1871-1909 WLC
Singer, A. L.
See Lerangis, Peter
Singer, Adam
See Karp, David
Singer, Alan 1948- 156
Singer, Amanda
See Brooks, Janice Young
Singer, Armand Edwards 1914- CANR-14
Earlier sketch in CA 41-44R
Singer, Arthur 1917-1990 SATA 64
Singer, Barry 1957- 144
Singer, Benjamin D. 1931- 37-40R
Singer, Beth J(udith) 1927- 113
Singer, Burns
See Singer, James Hyman
Singer, C(harles) Gregg 1910- CANR-12
Earlier sketch in CA 73-76
Singer, David L(in) 1937- 73-76
Singer, Fred J. 1931- 21-24R
Singer, Irving 1925- 21-24R
Singer, Isaac
See Singer, Isaac Bashevis
Singer, Isaac Bashevis 1904-1991 CANR-39
Obituary 134
Earlier sketches in CA 1-4R, CANR-1
See also AITN 1, 2
See also CDALB 1941-1968
See also CLC 1, 3, 6, 9, 11, 15, 23, 38, 69, 111
See also CLR 1
See also DA
See also DAB
See also DAC
See also DAM MST, NOV
See also DLB 6, 28, 52
See also DLBY 91
See also JRDA
See also MAICYA
See also MTCW 1
See also SATA 3, 27
See also SATA-Obit 68
See also SSC 3
See also WLC
Singer, Israel Joshua 1893-1944 TCLC 33
Singer, J(oel) David 1925- CANR-49
Earlier sketches in CA 1-4R, CANR-6
Singer, Jack W(olfe) 1942- 104
Singer, James Hyman 1928-1964 102
Obituary 89-92
Singer, Jane Sherrod 1917-1985 CANR-17
Obituary 115
Earlier sketch in CA 25-28R
See also SATA 4
See also SATA-Obit 42
Singer, Jerome L(eonard) 1924- 132
Singer, Joe
See Singer, Joseph
Singer, Joseph 1923-(?) CANR-2
Earlier sketch in CA 45-48
Singer, Joseph I.
See Singer, Joseph
Singer, Joy Daniels 1928- 29-32R
Singer, Judith 1926- 61-64
Singer, Julia 1917- 65-68
See also SATA 28
Singer, June (Kurlander) 1918- CANR-10
Earlier sketch in CA 41-44R
Interview in CANR-10
Singer, June Flaum 1933- 106
Singer, Kurt D(eutsch) 1911- CANR-2
Earlier sketch in CA 49-52
See also SATA 38
Singer, Marcus George 1926- CANR-3
Earlier sketch in CA 1-4R
Singer, Marilyn 1948- CANR-39
Earlier sketches in CA 65-68, CANR-9
See also CLR 48
See also JRDA
See also MAICYA
See also SAAS 13
See also SATA 48, 80
See also SATA-Brief 38
Singer, Mark 1950- CANR-68
Earlier sketch in CA 138
See also DLB 185
Singer, Marshall R. 1932- 41-44R
Singer, Max 1931- 145

Singer, Maxine 1931- 160
Singer, Michael A(lan) 1947- 57-60
Singer, Milton Borah 1912-1994 .... CANR-49
Obituary 147
Earlier sketches in CA 105, CANR-23
Singer, Neil M(ichael) 1939- 93-96
Singer, Norman 1925- 41-44R
Singer, Peter (Albert David) 1946- CANR-51
Earlier sketches in CA 57-60, CANR-8
Singer, Phylis
See Morrison, Phylis
Singer, Ray (Eleazer) 1916-1992 105
Obituary 140
Singer, Richard G. 1943- 89-92
Singer, (Dennis) Robert 1931- 49-52
Singer, Robert N. CANR-50
Earlier sketches in CA 53-56, CANR-5, 25
Singer, Rochelle 1939- CANR-20
Earlier sketch in CA 104
Singer, S(iegfried) Fred 1924- Brief entry 118
Singer, Samuel L(oewenberg) 1911- 65-68
Singer, Sarah 1915- 81-84
Singer, Shelley
See Singer, Rochelle
Singer, Sholom A. 1924-1987 Obituary 123
Singer, Susan (Mahler) 1941- 61-64
See also SATA 9
Singerman, Robert 1942- 110
Singh, Ajit 1940- 109
Singh, Amritjit 1945- 102
Singh, Arjan 1917- 49-52
Singh, Avtar 1929- 65-68
Singh, Baljit 1929-1980 .... CANR-49
Earlier sketch in CA 41-44R
Singh, Bawa Satinder 1932- 101
Singh, Chetan 1955- 138
Singh, D(asharath) 1937- 167
Singh, Darshan 1921- 133
Singh, G(han Shyam) 1929- CANR-43
Earlier sketches in CA 9-12R, CANR-5, 20
Singh, Harbans 1921- 17-20R
Singh, Karan 1931- 13-16R
Singh, Khushwant 1915- CANR-6
Earlier sketch in CA 9-12R
See also CAAS 9
See also CLC 11
Singh, Lalita Prasad 1936- 21-24R
Singh, Madanjeet 1924- 17-20R
Singh, Nagendra 1914- CANR-7
Earlier sketch in CA 17-20R
Singh, Patwant 1925- 150
Singh, R. K. Janmeja 1932- 37-40R
Singh, Rashmi Sharma 1952- .... SATA 90
Singh, St. Nihal 1884- 105
Singh, Simon 1964- 166
Singh, Surender 1932- 49-52
Singh, Surendra Nihal
See Nihal Singh, Surendra
Singh, Vijai Pratap 1939- Brief entry 106
Singhal, D(amodar) P(rasad) 1925- 49-52
Singher, Martial (Jean-Paul)
1904-1990 Obituary 131
Singing Nun, The
See Deckers, Jeanine
Singletary, Otis Arnold, Jr. 1921- 45-48
Singleton, Ann
See Benedict, Ruth (Fulton)
Singleton, Betty 1910- CAP-2
Earlier sketch in CA 25-28
Singleton, Charles S(outhward) 1909-1985 155
Obituary 117
Brief entry 113
Singleton, Frederick Bernard 1926- 89-92
Singleton, Ira C(uster) 1920- 5-8R
Singleton, Jack 1911- 13-16R
Singleton, John 1930- 21-24R
Singleton, John 1968(?)- CANR-67
Earlier sketch in CA 138
See also BW 2
See also DAM MULT
Singleton, Linda Joy 1957- .... SATA 88
Singleton, M(arvin) K(enneth) 1933- 1-4R
Singleton, Mary Ann 1934- 57-60
Singleton, Ralph Herbert 1900- 13-16R
Singleton, Rebecca (Jane) 1948- 121
Singleton, Rupert
See Pitt-Kethley, Fiona
Singleton, V(ernon) L(eRoy) 1923- 25-28R
Singmaster, Elsie 1879-1958 Brief entry 110
See also DLB 9
Sington, Philip 1962- 161
Singular, Stephen 1950- 139
Sinha, Krishna N(andan) 1924- 13-16R
Sinha, Phulgenda 1924- 130
Sinha, Sasadhar 1901- 17-20R
Sinibaldi, Fosco
See Kacew, Romain
Sinick, Daniel 1913- CANR-45
Earlier sketch in CA 45-48
Sinicropi, Giovanni Andrea 1924- CANR-42
Earlier sketch in CA 45-48
Sinisgalli, Leonardo 1908-1981 Obituary 103
See also DLB 114
Sinjohn, John
See Galsworthy, John
Sinjun
See John, Elizabeth Beaman
Sinkankas, John 1915- CANR-6
Earlier sketch in CA 1-4R
Sinkler, George 1927- 85-88
Sinnema, John R(alph) 1911- 41-44R
Sinnen, Jeanne 1926-1976 Obituary 104
Sinnette, Elinor Des Verney 1925- 132
Sinnigen, William G. 1928- 13-16R
Sinning, Wayne E. 1931- 77-80
Sinofsky, Esther R. 1951- 126
Sinopoli, Carla M. 1956- 141
Sinopoli, Richard C. 1956-1997 138
Obituary 158
Sinor, Denis 1916- CANR-6
Earlier sketch in CA 1-4R
Sinor, John 1930-1996 .... CANR-11
Obituary 153
Earlier sketch in CA 69-72
Sinyavsky, Andrei (Donatevich) 1925-1997 85-88
Obituary 159
See also CLC 8
Sinykin, Sheri Cooper 1950- .... SATA 72
Siodmak, Curt 1902- 113
Brief entry 111
See also DLB 44
Sion, Mari
See Jones, R(obert) M(aynard)
Sionil Jose, F(rancisco) 1924- CANR-60
Earlier sketches in CA 21-24R, CANR-10
Sions, Harry 1906-1974 Obituary 104
Siotis, Jean 1931- 25-28R
Sipherd, Ray 1935- 144
Sipiera, Paul P., (Jr.) 1948- 155
See also SATA 89
Siple, Molly 1942- 156
Siporin, Steve 1947- 139
Sippl, Charles J. 1924- CANR-18
Earlier sketch in CA 21-24R
Sipress, David 1947- 130
Siracusa, Catherine (Jane) 1947- 149
See also SATA 82
Siracusa, Joseph 1929- CANR-1
Earlier sketch in CA 45-48
Siracusa, Joseph M(arcus) 1944- CANR-12
Earlier sketch in CA 73-76
Sirageldin, Ismail A(bdel-Hamid) 1930- CANR-16
Earlier sketch in CA 29-32R
Sirc, Ljubo 1920- 103
Sire, H. J. A. 1949- 146
Sire, James W(alter) 1933- CANR-52
Earlier sketches in CA 29-32R, CANR-11, 28
Sirett, Dawn (Karen) 1966- .... SATA 88
Siri, Giuseppe 1906-1989 Obituary 128
Sirica, John J(oseph) 1904- 110
Sirin, V.
See Nabokov, Vladimir (Vladimirovich)
Siringo, Charles A. 1855-1928 .... DLB 186
Siris, Peter 1944- 117
Sirius
See Beuve-Mery, Hubert
Sirjamaki, John 1911- 13-16R
Sirkin, Gerald 1920- 25-28R
Sirkis, Nancy 1936- 102
Sirluck, Ernest 1918- 25-28R
Sirof, Harriet 1930- CANR-43
Earlier sketches in CA 104, CANR-20
See also SATA 37, 94
Sirois, Allen L. 1950- 143
See also SATA 76
Sirrom, Wes
See Weiss, Morris S(amuel)
Sirvaitis (Chernyaev), Karen (Ann) 1961- 148
See also SATA 79
Sis, Peter 1949- 128
See also CLR 45
See also SATA 67
Sisco, John I(sodore) 1931- 41-44R
Sisk, Dorothy Poole 1897-1983 Obituary 111
Sisk, Frank A., Jr. 1915-1985 Obituary 115
Sisk, Henry L(ybran) 1914- 49-52
Sisk, John P(aul) 1914- 29-32R
Siskel, Eugene Kal 1946- 113
Brief entry 110
Siskel, Gene
See Siskel, Eugene Kal
Sisler, Harry Hall 1917- 109
Sisler, Rebecca 1932- 104
Sisley, Emily L(ucretia) 1930- Brief entry 113
Sissle, Noble 1889-1975 Obituary 112
Sissman, L(ouis) E(dward) 1928-1976 .... CANR-13
Obituary 65-68
Earlier sketch in CA 21-24R
See also CLC 9, 18
See also DLB 5
Sisson, A(lbert) F(ranklin) 1901- 5-8R
Sisson, C(harles) H(ubert) 1914- CANR-48
Earlier sketches in CA 1-4R, CANR-3
See also CAAS 3
See also CLC 8
See also DLB 27
Sisson, Rosemary Anne 1923- CANR-29
Earlier sketches in CA 13-16R, CANR-12
See also SATA 11
Sister Carol Anne O'Marie
See O'Marie, Carol Anne
Sister Luc-Gabrielle
See Deckers, Jeanine
Sister M. Victoria
See Maria Del Rey, Sister
Sister Magdeleine de Jesus
See Hutin, Magdeleine
Sister Mary Annette
See Buttimer, Anne
Sister Mary Jeremy
See Finnegan, Mary Jeremy
Sister Mary Terese
See Donze, Mary Terese
Sister Maura
See Eichner, Maura
Sister Smile
See Deckers, Jeanine
Sister Teresa Margaret
See Rowe, Margaret (Kevin)
Sisyphus
See Barthelmes, (Albert) Wes(ley, Jr.)
Sita, Lisa 1962- 151
See also SATA 87
Sitaram, K(ondavagil) S(urya) 1935- 69-72
Sitarz, Paula (Gaj) 1955- CANR-48
Earlier sketch in CA 122
Sitchin, Zecharia 1920- CANR-22
Earlier sketch in CA 69-72
Sites, James N(eil) 1924- 1-4R
Sites, Paul 1926- 53-56
Sithole, Ndabaningi 1920- Brief entry 110
Sitomer, Harry 1903- 101
See also SATA 31
Sitomer, Mindel 1903- 101
See also SATA 31
Sitter, John E(dward) 1944- 130
Brief entry 114
Sitterly, Charlotte Emma Moore
See Moore, Charlotte E(mma)
Sitting Bull 1831(?)-1890 .... DAM MULT
See also NNAL
Sittler, Joseph 1904-1987 Obituary 124
Sitton, Claude (Fox) 1925- Brief entry 122
Sitton, Claude (Fox) 1925- 154
Sittser, Gerald L. 1950- 166
Sitwell, Dame Edith 1887-1964 .... CANR-35
Earlier sketch in CA 9-12R
See also CDBLB 1945-1960
See also CLC 2, 9, 67
See also DAM POET
See also DLB 20
See also MTCW 1
See also PC 3
Sitwell, (Francis) Osbert (Sacheverell) 1892-1969 .. CAP-2
Obituary 25-28R
Earlier sketch in CA 21-22
See also DLB 100, 195
Sitwell, Sacheverell 1897-1988 .... 21-24R
Obituary 126
Sitzfleisch, Vladimir
See Spirer, Herbert F(rederick)
Siu, Helen 1950- 114
Siu, R(alph) G(un) H(oy) 1917- CANR-10
Earlier sketch in CA 25-28R
Sive, Helen R(obinson) 1951- 107
See also SATA 30
Sive, Mary Robinson 1928- CANR-10
Earlier sketch in CA 65-68
Siverson, Randolph M. 1940- 138
Siviero, Rodolpho 1912(?)-1983 Obituary 111
Sivulich, Sandra (Jeanne) Stroner 1941- 61-64
See also SATA 9
Siwaarmill, H. P.
See Sharp, William
Siwek, Manuel 1908-1976 Obituary 65-68
Siwundhla, Alice Msumba 1928- 45-48
Sixsmith, Eric Keir Gilborne 1904-1986 .... 33-36R
Obituary 118
Siy, Robert Y(oung), Jr. 1955- CANR-45
Earlier sketch in CA 119
Sizemore, Burlan A. 1933- 45-48
Sizemore, Chris(tine) Costner 1927- 81-84
Sizemore, Christine Wick 1945- 134
Sizemore, Deborah Lightfoot 1956- 138
Sizemore, Margaret D(avidson) CAP-2
Earlier sketch in CA 19-20
Sizer, John 1938- CANR-12
Earlier sketch in CA 29-32R
Sizer, Mona Young 1934- 146
Sizer, Nancy F(aust) 1935- 45-48
Sizer, Theodore R(yland) 1932- CANR-13
Earlier sketch in CA 33-36R
Sjoeberg, Leif 1925- 65-68
Sjoestrand, Sven-Erik 1945- 147
Sjoewall, Maj 1935- 65-68
See also CLC 7
Sjostrand, Sven-Erik
See Sjoestrand, Sven-Erik
Sjowall, Maj
See Sjoewall, Maj
Skaar, Grace Brown 1903- 69-72
Skaer, Peter M(acKall) 1953- 103
Skagen, Kiki
See Munshi, Kiki Skagen
Skaggs, David Curtis (Jr.) 1937- 41-44R
Skaggs, Jimmy M(arion) 1940- CANR-39
Earlier sketches in CA 45-48, CANR-1
Skaggs, Merrill Maguire 1937- CANR-45
Earlier sketch in CA 45-48
Skala, John J. 1923- 17-20R
Skaldaspillir, Sigfridur
See Broxon, Mildred Downey
Skallerup, Harry R(obert) 1927- 73-76
Skard, Sigmund 1903- CANR-22
Earlier sketches in CA 17-20R, CANR-7
Skarda, Patricia Lyn 1946- 106
Skardal, Dorothy Burton 1922- 61-64
Skardon, Alvin W(ilson, Jr.) 1912- 53-56
Skarmeta, Antonio 1940- 131
See also DLB 145
See also HW
See also SATA 57
Skarsaune, Oskar 1946- 136
Skarsten, Malvin O. 1892- CAP-1
Earlier sketch in CA 13-16
Skartvedt, Dan (L.) 1945- 77-80
Skates, John R(ay) 1934- 97-100
Skeaping, John Rattenbury 1901-1980 108
Obituary 97-100
Skeaping, Mary 1902-1984 Obituary 112
Skeat, Walter W. 1835-1912 .... DLB 184
Skedgell, Marian Jay 1921- CANR-14
Earlier sketch in CA 17-20R
Skeel, Dorothy J(une) 1932- CANR-8
Earlier sketch in CA 61-64
Skeen, Carl Edward 1937- 113
Skeet, Ian 1928- 145
Skegg, P(eter) D(onald) G(raham) 1944- 127
Skehan, James W(illiam) 1923- 57-60
Skei, Allen B(ennet) 1935-1985 .... CANR-31
Earlier sketch in CA 108
Skellings, Edmund 1932- 77-80
Skelly, James R(ichard) 1927- 85-88
See also SATA 17
Skelly, Madge 1903- 41-44R
Skelton, Barbara 1918-1996 136
Obituary 151
Skelton, Eugene (Lamar) 1914- CANR-1
Earlier sketch in CA 45-48
Skelton, Geoffrey (David) 1916- CANR-40
Earlier sketches in CA 49-52, CANR-1, 18
Skelton, John E. 1934- 37-40R
Skelton, Peter 1928- 13-16R
Skelton, Red 1913-1997 104
Obituary 161
Skelton, Richard
See Skelton, Red
Skelton, Robin 1925-1997 .... CANR-28
Obituary 160
Earlier sketch in CA 5-8R
See also CAAS 5
See also AITN 2
See also CLC 13
See also DLB 27, 53
Skelton, Roger
See Horn, Peter (Rudolf Gisela)
Skelton, William B(arott) 1939- 140
Skemp, Joseph Bright 1910-1992 106
Obituary 140
Skemp, Richard R(owland) 1919- 107
Skendi, Stavro 1906- 25-28R
Skene-Melvin, Ann (Patricia) 1936- 108
Skene-Melvin, (Lewis) David (St. Columb)
1936- 108
Skerpan, Elizabeth (Penley) 1955- 142
Skibbe, Eugene M(oritz) 1930- 21-24R
Skidelsky, Robert 1939- CANR-70
Earlier sketches in CA 25-28R, CANR-11
Skidmore, David (G. II) 1958- 161
Skidmore, Ian 1929- CANR-10
Earlier sketch in CA 61-64
Skidmore, Max J(oseph Sr.) 1933- CANR-12
Earlier sketch in CA 29-32R
Skidmore, Rex A(ustin) 1914- 13-16R
Skidmore, Thomas E. 1932- 21-24R
Skiles, Jacqueline D(ean) 1937- 108
Skilken, Patricia S(tout) 1943- 119
Skilling, H(arold) Gordon 1912- CANR-7
Earlier sketch in CA 13-16R
Skillings, R(oger) D(eering) 1937- 61-64
Skilliter, S(usan) A. 1931(?)-1985 Obituary 117
Skilton, John H. 1906- 37-40R
Skimin, Robert (Elwayne) 1929- 108
Skinner, Ainslie
See Gosling, Paula
Skinner, B(urrhus) F(rederic) 1904-1990 .. CANR-42
Obituary 132
Earlier sketches in CA 9-12R, CANR-18
See also MTCW 1
Skinner, Charles Edward 1891- CAP-1
Earlier sketch in CA 17-18
Skinner, Constance Lindsay 1882-1939 .... DLB 92
See also YABC 1
Skinner, Cornelia Otis 1901-1979 .... 17-20R
Obituary 89-92
See also SATA 2
Skinner, Elliott P(ercival) 1924- 13-16R
Skinner, G(eorge) William 1925- CANR-2
Earlier sketch in CA 49-52
Skinner, Gloria Dale 1951- 167
Skinner, Gordon S(weetland) 1924- 13-16R
Skinner, Jeffrey 1949- CANR-52
Earlier sketch in CA 126
Skinner, John Emory 1925- 5-8R
Skinner, John Stuart 1788-1851 .... DLB 73
Skinner, June O'Grady 1922- 5-8R
Skinner, Knute (Rumsey) 1929- CANR-49
Earlier sketches in CA 17-20R, CANR-9, 24
Skinner, Margaret 1942- 147
Skinner, Michael 1953- 134
Skinner, Rulon Dean 1931- 61-64
Skinner, Thomas Edward 1909- 109
Skinner, Tom 1942-1994 .... 25-28R
Obituary 145
Skiold, Birgit (?)-1982 Obituary 107
Skipp, Victor (Henry Thomas) 1925- 123
Brief entry 118
Skipper, Betty
See Barr, Betty
Skipper, G. C. 1939- CANR-14
Earlier sketch in CA 77-80
See also SATA 46
See also SATA-Brief 38
Skipper, James K(inley), Jr. 1934-1993 .. CANR-12
Obituary 140
Earlier sketch in CA 17-20R
Skipsey, Joseph 1832-1903 .... DLB 35
Skipwith, Sofka 1907-1994 .... 29-32R
Obituary 144
Skira, Albert 1904-1973 Obituary 104
Skirpa, Kazys 1895(?)-1979 Obituary 89-92
Skjei, Eric William 1947- 97-100
Sklansky, Morris Aaron 1919- 17-20R
Sklar, Dusty 1928- 65-68
Sklar, George 1908-1988 .... 1-4R
Obituary 125
Sklar, Kathryn Kish 1939- CANR-40
Earlier sketches in CA 45-48, CANR-3, 18
Sklar, Lawrence 1938- 105
Sklar, Michael Joel 1945(?)-1984 Obituary 112
Sklar, Morty 1935- CANR-13
Earlier sketch in CA 77-80

Sklar, Richard L(awrence) 1930- ... 9-12R
Sklar, Robert 1936- ... CANR-8
Earlier sketch in CA 21-24R
Sklar, Scott 1950- ... 131
Sklare, Arnold B(eryl) 1924- ... 17-20R
Sklare, Marshall 1921-1992 ... CANR-12
Obituary ... 137
Earlier sketch in CA 21-24R
Sklarew, Myra 1934- ... CANR-30
Earlier sketch in CA 109
Sklarewitz, Norman 1924- ... 69-72
Skocpol, Theda (Ruth) 1947- ... 154
Skocpol, Theda Ruth 1947- Brief entry ... 105
Skofield, James ... 156
See also SATA 95
See also SATA-Brief 44
Skoglund, Elizabeth 1937- ... CANR-34
Earlier sketches in CA 41-44R, CANR-15
Skoglund, Goesta 1904- ... 65-68
Skoglund, John Egnar 1912- ... 9-12R
Skold, Betty Westrom 1923- ... 112
See also SATA 41
Skolimowski, Jerzy 1938- ... 128
See also CLC 20
Skolnick, Jerome H(erbert) 1931- Brief entry ... 114
Skolnik, Alfred 1920(?)-1977 Obituary ... 69-72
Skolnik, Peter L(aurence) 1944- ... 57-60
Skolnikoff, Eugene B. 1928- ... 21-24R
Skolsky, Sidney 1905-1983 ... 103
Obituary ... 109
Skoog, Folke Karl 1908- ... 162
Skornia, Harry J(ay) 1910- ... CAP-2
Earlier sketch in CA 17-18
Skorpen, Liesel Moak 1935- ... 25-28R
See also SATA 3
Skorupski, John 1946- ... 146
Skotheim, Robert Allen 1933- ... 21-24R
Skou-Hansen, Tage 1925- ... CANR-6
Earlier sketch in CA 13-16R
Skousen, Mark ... 104
Skousen, W(illard) Cleon 1913- ... CANR-5
Earlier sketch in CA 5-8R
Skover, David M. 1951- ... 152
Skowronek, Stephen 1951- ... 146
Skowronski, JoAnn ... 108
Skoyles, John 1949- ... 104
Skrade, Carl 1935- ... 65-68
Skram, Amalie (Bertha) 1847-1905 ... 165
See also TCLC 25
Skramstad, Susan 1942- ... 139
Skrivanek, John M(arion) 1913- ... 49-52
Skrzynecki, Peter 1945- ... 128
Skulicz, Matthew V. 1944- ... 37-40R
Skulsky, Harold Lawrence 1935- ... 107
Skura, Meredith Anne 1944- ... 117
Skurdenis, Juliann V.
See Skurdenis-Smircich, Juliann V(eronica)
Skurdenis-Smircich, Juliann V(eronica) 1942- ... 77-80
Skurnik, W. A. E. 1926- ... 41-44R
Skurzynski, Gloria (Joan) 1930- ... CANR-58
Earlier sketches in CA 33-36R, CANR-13, 30
See also SAAS 9
See also SATA 8, 74
Skutch, Alexander F(rank) 1904- ... CANR-49
Earlier sketches in CA 33-36R, CANR-21
Skutch, Margaret F. 1932- ... 105
Skutch, Robert 1925- ... 155
See also SATA 89
Skutsch, Otto 1906- ... 126
Skvorecka, Zdena Salivarova 1933- ... 41-44R
Skvorecky, Josef (Vaclav) 1924- ... CANR-63
Earlier sketches in CA 61-64, CANR-10, 34
See also CAAS 1
See also CLC 15, 39, 69
See also DAC
See also DAM NOV
See also MTCW 1
Sky, Kathleen
See Goldin, Kathleen Mckinney
Sky, Michael 1951- ... 144
Skye, Maggie
See Werner, Herma
Skynner, (Augustus Charles) Robin 1922- ... 141
Skyrms, Brian 1938- ... CANR-26
Earlier sketch in CA 108
Slaatte, Howard A(lexander) 1919- ... CANR-31
Earlier sketches in CA 41-44R, CANR-14
Slabbert, F(rederik) Van Zyl 1940- ... 133
Slaby, Andrew Edmund 1942- ... CANR-7
Earlier sketch in CA 57-60
Slack, Adrian (Charles) ... 104
Slack, Charles W(illiam) 1929- ... 61-64
Slack, Kenneth 1917-1987 Obituary ... 123
Slack, Robert C(harles) 1914- ... 81-84
Slack, Walter H. 1932- ... 21-24R
Slackman, Charles B. 1934- ... SATA 12
Slade, Afton J. 1919-1993 ... 89-92
Obituary ... 140
Slade, Bernard
See Newbound, Bernard Slade
See also CAAS 9
See also CLC 11, 46
See also DLB 53
Slade, Caroline (Beach) 1886-1975 Obituary ... 61-64
Slade, Jack
See Ballard, (Willis) Todhunter
and Germano, Peter B.
and Haas, Ben(jamin) L(eopold)
Slade, Joseph W(arren) 1941- ... 89-92
Slade, Leonard A., Jr. 1942- ... 148
Slade, Madeleine 1892-1982 Obituary ... 115
Slade, Peter 1912- ... 13-16R
Slade, Richard 1910-1971 ... CAP-2
Earlier sketch in CA 23-24
See also SATA 9
Slade, Tony 1936- ... 33-36R
Sladek, John 1937- ... 25-28R
Sladen, Kathleen 1904- ... 69-72
Sladen, Norman St. Barbe (?)-1969 ... CAP-1
Earlier sketch in CA 13-14
Slader, John M. 1924- ... 154
Slaght, Lawrence T(ownsend) 1912- ... 73-76
Slakter, Malcolm J(ulian) 1929- ... 41-44R
Slamecka, Vladimir 1928- ... 5-8R
Slamnig, Ivan 1930- ... DLB 181
Slaney, George Wilson 1884- ... CAP-1
Earlier sketch in CA 13-14
Slapikoff, Saul A(braham) 1931- ... 141
Slappey, Sterling G(reene) 1917- ... 65-68
Slate, Joseph 1927- ... 45-48
Slate, Joseph (Frank) 1928- ... 110
See also SATA 38
Slate, Sam J(ordan) 1909- ... 49-52
Slaten, Yeffe Kimball 1914(?)-1978 Obituary ... 77-80
Slater, Charlotte (Wolpers) 1944- ... 65-68
Slater, Eliot (Trevor Oakeshott) 1904- ... 53-56
Slater, Ian 1941- ... CANR-34
Earlier sketch in CA 85-88
Slater, James (Derrick)
See Slater, Jim
Slater, Jerome N(orman) 1935- ... 17-20R
Slater, Jim 1929- ... 144
Brief entry ... 112
See also SATA-Brief 34
Slater, John Clarke 1900-1976 ... 156
Slater, Layton Ernest Alfred
1916-1984 Obituary ... 114
Slater, Leonard 1920- ... 13-16R
Slater, Lydia (Elizabeth) Pasternak
1902-1989 Obituary ... 128
Slater, Mariam K(reiselman) 1922- ... 123
Brief entry ... 118
Slater, Mary Louise 1923- ... 29-32R
Slater, Maya 1941- ... 119
Slater, Miriam 1931- ... 120
Slater, Niall W. 1954- ... 126
Slater, Nigel 1944- ... CANR-18
Earlier sketch in CA 102
Slater, Patrick 1880-1951 ... DLB 68
Slater, Peter Gregg 1940- ... 81-84
Slater, Philip E(lliot) 1927- ... CANR-40
Earlier sketch in CA 21-24R
Slater, Ralph P(hipps) 1915- ... 21-24R
Slater, Robert 1943- ... CANR-43
Earlier sketch in CA 119
Slater, Robert (Henry) Lawson 1896- ... CAP-1
Earlier sketch in CA 13-14
Slater, Thomas J. 1955- ... 140
Slater, Veronica
See Sullivan, Victoria
Slatin, John M. 1952- ... 126
Slatkin, Charles Eli 1907-1977 Obituary ... 73-76
Slatoff, Walter J(acob) 1922-1991 ... 9-12R
Obituary ... 133
Slatta, Richard W(ayne) 1947- ... 133
Slattery, Marty 1938- ... 134
Slattery, Timothy Patrick 1911- ... 25-28R
Slattery, William J(ames) 1930- ... 101
Slatzer, Robert F(ranklin) 1927- Brief entry ... 113
Slaughter, Carolyn 1946- ... 85-88
See also CLC 56
Slaughter, Eugene Edward 1909- ... 37-40R
Slaughter, Frank G(ill) 1908- ... CANR-5
Earlier sketch in CA 5-8R
Interview in ... CANR-5
See also AITN 2
See also CLC 29
Slaughter, Guy 1919- ... 151
Slaughter, Hope 1940- ... SATA 84
Slaughter, Howard K(ey) 1927- ... 45-48
Slaughter, Jane M(undy) 1908- ... 73-76
Slaughter, Jean
See Doty, Jean Slaughter
Slaughter, Jim
See Paine, Lauran (Bosworth)
Slaughter, M(ary) M(artina) 1940- ... 131
Slavens, Thomas P(aul) 1928- ... CANR-46
Earlier sketches in CA 104, CANR-22
Slavet, Joseph S. 1920- ... 61-64
Slaveykov, Pencho 1866-1912 ... DLB 147
Slavic, Rosalind Welcher
See Welcher, Rosalind
Slavicek, Milivoj 1929- ... DLB 181
Slavick, William H(enry) 1927- ... 104
Slavin, Arthur Joseph 1933- ... CANR-3
Earlier sketch in CA 9-12R
Slavin, Bill 1959- ... SATA 76
Slavin, Morris 1913- ... CANR-41
Earlier sketch in CA 118
Slavin, Robert E(dward) 1950- ... 146
Slavin, Stephen L(eron) 1939- ... 111
Slavitt, David R(ytman) 1935- ... CANR-41
Earlier sketch in CA 21-24R
See also CAAS 3
See also CLC 5, 14
See also DLB 5, 6
Slavson, Samuel R(ichard) 1891- ... 17-20R
Slavutych, Yar 1918- ... CANR-38
Earlier sketches in CA 45-48, CANR-2, 17
Slawson, Ron(ald L.) 1932- ... 128
Slawson, William David 1931- ... 110
Slaymaker, R(edsecker) Samuel II 1923- ... 65-68
Slayton, Donald K(ent) 1924-1993 ... 159
Slayton, Mariette (Elizabeth) Paine 1908- ... 65-68
Sleator, William (Warner III) 1945- ... CANR-46
Earlier sketch in CA 29-32R
See also AAYA 5
See also CLR 29
See also JRDA
See also MAICYA
See also SATA 3, 68
Sledd, James Hinton 1914- ... 17-20R
Sledge, Linda Ching 1944- ... 108
Sledge, Michael 1962- ... 151
Slee, Debora A. 1949- ... 146
Slee, Vergil N(elson) 1917- ... 146
Sleeper, James A. 1947- ... 133
Sleeper, Jim
See Sleeper, James A.
Sleigh, Barbara 1906-1982 ... CANR-51
Obituary ... 106
Earlier sketches in CA 13-16R, CANR-6
See also SATA 3, 86
See also SATA-Obit 30
Sleigh, Burrows Willcocks Arthur 1821-1869 ... DLB 99
Sleigh, (Brocas) Linwood 1902- ... 5-8R
Sleigh, Robert Collins, Jr. 1932- ... 37-40R
Sleight, Robert B(enton) 1922- ... 41-44R
Slepian, Jan(ice B.) 1921- ... 136
See also AAYA 20
See also JRDA
See also MAICYA
See also SAAS 8
See also SATA 51, 85
See also SATA-Brief 45
Slesar, Henry 1927- ... CANR-61
Earlier sketches in CA 1-4R, CANR-1
Slesin, Suzanne 1944- ... 123
Slesinger, Doris P(eyser) 1927- ... 113
Slesinger, Reuben E. 1916- ... 5-8R
Slesinger, Tess 1905-1945 Brief entry ... 107
See also DLB 102
See also TCLC 10
Slesinger, Warren 1933- ... 33-36R
Slesser, Malcolm 1926- ... 17-20R
Slessor, Kenneth 1901-1971 ... 102
Obituary ... 89-92
See also CLC 14
Slethaug, Gordon E. 1940- ... 140
Sletholt, Erik 1919- ... 77-80
Slezak, Walter 1902-1983 Obituary ... 109
Slicer, Margaret O. 1920- ... 25-28R
See also SATA 4
Slide, Anthony 1944- ... CANR-53
Earlier sketches in CA 33-36R, CANR-12, 29
Slier, Debby
See Shine, Deborah
Slim, William Joseph 1891-1970 Obituary ... 107
Slimming, John 1927-1979 ... 25-28R
Obituary ... 89-92
Slinger, Joey 1943(?)- ... 164
Slitor, Richard Eaton 1911- ... CANR-32
Earlier sketch in CA 45-48
Slive, Seymour 1920- ... 103
Sliwa, Curtis 1954- ... 111
Sljivic-Simsic, Biljana 1933- ... 41-44R
Sloan, Alfred P(ritchard), Jr.
1875-1966 Obituary ... 113
Sloan, Allan 1944- ... 118
Sloan, Anthony
See Feist, Gene
Sloan, Carolyn 1937- ... CANR-55
Earlier sketch in CA 127
See also SATA 58
Sloan, Don 1928- ... 142
Sloan, Edward William III 1931- ... 37-40R
Sloan, Harold Stephenson 1887- ... CAP-1
Earlier sketch in CA 17-18
Sloan, Irving J. 1924- ... CANR-7
Earlier sketch in CA 17-20R
Sloan, James Park (Jr.) 1944- ... CANR-63
Earlier sketch in CA 29-32R
Sloan, Jane 1946- ... 145
Sloan, John 1871-1951 ... DLB 188
Sloan, John 1948- ... 153
Sloan, Kay 1951- ... 108
Sloan, Michael 1946- ... 130
Sloan, Pat(rick Alan) 1908-1978 ... CANR-43
Earlier sketch in CA 65-68
Sloan, Phillip R(eid) 1938- ... 109
Sloan, Raymond Paton 1893-1983 ... CAP-1
Obituary ... 109
Earlier sketch in CA 19-20
Sloan, Ruth Catherine
1898(?)-1976 Obituary ... 65-68
Sloan, Stephen 1936- ... 33-36R
Sloan, Thomas 1928- ... 93-96
Sloan, Tod (Stratton) 1952- ... 140
Sloan, William Wilson 1901- ... 1-4R
Sloane, Arthur A(llan) 1931- ... 33-36R
Sloane, Eric 1910(?)-1985 ... 108
Obituary ... 115
See also SATA 52
See also SATA-Obit 42
Sloane, Eugene A(nthony) 1926- ... 65-68
Sloane, Howard N(orman) 1932- ... 81-84
Sloane, Joseph C(urtis) 1909- ... CAP-1
Earlier sketch in CA 11-12
Sloane, Leonard 1932- ... 21-24R
Sloane, Martin 1940- ... 132
Sloane, Peter J(ames) 1942- ... 108
Sloane, R(obert) Bruce 1923- ... 53-56
Sloane, Sara
See Bloom, Ursula (Harvey)
Sloane, Thomas O. 1929- ... 37-40R
Sloane, Todd 1955- ... SATA 88
Sloane, William M. 1906-1974 Obituary ... 53-56
Sloat, Teri 1948- ... 138
See also SATA 70
Sloate, Daniel 1931- ... CANR-32
Earlier sketch in CA 113
Slobin, Dan Isaac 1939- ... CANR-11
Earlier sketch in CA 65-68
Slobin, Mark 1943- ... 93-96
Slobodin, Richard 1915- ... 102
Slobodkin, Florence Gersh 1905- ... 1-4R
See also SATA 5
Slobodkin, Lawrence (B.) 1928- ... 137
Slobodkin, Louis 1903-1975 ... 13-16R
Obituary ... 57-60
See also MAICYA
See also SATA 1, 26
Slobodkina, Esphyr 1908- ... CANR-1
Earlier sketch in CA 1-4R
See also SAAS 8
See also SATA 1
Slochower, Harry 1900-1991 ... CANR-2
Obituary ... 134
Earlier sketch in CA 49-52
Slocum, Bill
See Slocum, William J(oseph Michael), Jr.
Slocum, Donald Barclay 1911-1983 Obituary ... 110
Slocum, Frank 1925-1997 ... 136
Obituary ... 158
Slocum, John W(esley), Jr. 1940- ... 112
Slocum, Michael
See Slocum, William J(oseph Michael), Jr.
Slocum, Milton Jonathan 1905-1993 ... 126
Obituary ... 140
Slocum, Robert Bigney 1922- ... 9-12R
Slocum, Walter L(ucius) 1910- ... 21-24R
Slocum, William J(oseph Michael), Jr.
1912(?)-1974 Obituary ... 53-56
Sloggatt, Arthur H(astings)
1917(?)-1975 Obituary ... 61-64
Sloggett, Nellie 1851-1923 ... SATA 44
Sloma, Richard Stanley 1929- ... CANR-19
Earlier sketch in CA 103
Sloman, Albert Edward 1921- ... 5-8R
Sloman, Larry 1948- ... CANR-20
Earlier sketch in CA 81-84
Slomovitz, Philip 1896- ... 81-84
Slone, Dennis 1930-1982 Obituary ... 106
Slone, Verna Mae 1914- ... 89-92
Slonim, Marc 1894-1976 Obituary ... 65-68
Slonim, Morris J(ames) 1909- ... 1-4R
Slonim, Reuben 1914- ... 97-100
Slonim, Ruth 1918- ... 17-20R
Slonimski, Antoni 1895-1976 Obituary ... 65-68
Slonimsky, Nicolas 1894-1995 ... 17-20R
Obituary ... 150
Slonimsky, Yuri 1902-1978 Obituary ... 77-80
Slosberg, Mike 1934- ... 69-72
Slosberg, Myron
See Slosberg, Mike
Sloss, Lesley Lord 1965- ... SATA 72
Slosser, Bob G(ene) 1929- ... CANR-10
Earlier sketch in CA 65-68
Slosson, Preston (William) 1892- ... CANR-8
Earlier sketch in CA 61-64
Slote, Alfred 1926- ... CLR 4
See also JRDA
See also MAICYA
See also SAAS 21
See also SATA 8, 72
Slote, Bernice D. 1915(?)-1983 Obituary ... 109
Slote, Elizabeth 1956- ... SATA 80
Slote, Michael A(nthony) 1941- ... 61-64
Slote, Stanley J(ames) 1917- ... 61-64
Slotkin, Richard S(idney) 1942- ... CANR-41
Earlier sketch in CA 102
Slotnick, Daniel L(eonid) 1931-1985 Obituary ... 117
Slouka, Mark ... 156
Slovenko, Ralph 1926- ... 17-20R
Slovo, Joe 1926-1995 ... 161
Slowikowski, M. Z. Rygor
1896-1989(?) Obituary ... 129
Sloyan, Gerard Stephen 1919- ... CANR-40
Earlier sketches in CA 5-8R, CANR-2, 18
Sluckin, W(ladyslaw) 1919-1985 ... 21-24R
Obituary ... 116
Slung, Louis Sheaffer
See Sheaffer, Louis
Slung, Michele (Beth) 1947- ... 102
Slusher, Howard S. 1937- ... 25-28R
Slusser, Dorothy M. 1922- ... 33-36R
Slusser, George Edgar 1939- ... CANR-13
Earlier sketch in CA 69-72
Slusser, Gerald H(erbert) 1920- ... 13-16R
Slusser, Robert M(elville) 1916- ... CANR-3
Earlier sketch in CA 1-4R
Slye, Leonard
See Rogers, Roy
Smale, Stephen 1930- ... 162
Small, Bertrice 1937- ... CANR-53
Earlier sketches in CA 77-80, CANR-13, 29
Small, David 1937- ... CANR-39
Earlier sketch in CA 108
Small, David 1945- ... SATA 50, 95
See also SATA-Brief 46
Small, Dwight Hervey 1919- ... CANR-8
Earlier sketch in CA 61-64
Small, Ernest
See Lent, Blair
Small, Gary W. 1951- ... 127
Small, George L(eroy) 1924- ... 85-88
Small, George Raphael 1918- ... 57-60
Small, Kenneth A(lan) 1945- ... CANR-43
Earlier sketch in CA 112
Small, Melvin 1939- ... CANR-58
Earlier sketches in CA 29-32R, CANR-12, 30
Small, Miriam Rossiter 1899- ... 1-4R
Small, Norman M. 1944- ... 41-44R
Small, Terry 1942- ... 142
See also SATA 75
Small, William
See Eversley, D(avid) E(dward) C(harles)
Smallenburg, Harry W. 1907- ... CAP-1
Earlier sketch in CA 13-14
Smalley, Barbara Martin 1926- ... 105
Smalley, Beryl 1905-1984 ... 103
Obituary ... 112
Smalley, Donald (Arthur) 1907- ... 17-20R

Smalley, Ruth E(lizabeth) 1903- ... CAP-2
Earlier sketch in CA 21-22
Smalley, Stephen Stewart 1931- ... 103
Smalley, William A. 1923-1997 ... CANR-1
Obituary ... 163
Earlier sketch in CA 45-48
Smallman, Basil 1921- ... 150
Smalls-Hector, Irene 1950- ... SATA 73
Smallwood, Carol 1939- ... CANR-45
Earlier sketch in CA 122
Smallwood, Frank(lin) 1927- ... 123
Brief entry ... 118
Smallwood, James (Milton) 1944- ... 115
Smallwood, Joseph R(oberts) 1900-1991 ... CANR-43
Earlier sketch in CA 105
Smallwood, Norah (Evelyn) 1910(?)-1984 Obituary ... 114
See also SATA-Obit 41
Smaridge, Norah (Antoinette) 1903- ... 37-40R
See also SATA 6
Smart, (Peter) Alastair (Marshall) 1922- ... 37-40R
Smart, Albert Davis 1931(?)-1989 Obituary ... 130
Smart, Barry 1946- ... 117
Smart, Carol 1948- ... CANR-37
Earlier sketches in CA 73-76, CANR-16
Smart, Carolyn (Alexandra) 1952- ... CANR-38
Earlier sketch in CA 116
Smart, Charles Allen 1904-1967 ... CAP-1
Earlier sketch in CA 11-12
Smart, Christopher 1722-1771 ... DAM POET
See also DLB 109
See also PC 13
Smart, David A. 1892-1952 ... DLB 137
Smart, Elizabeth 1913-1986 ... 81-84
Obituary ... 118
See also CLC 54
See also DLB 88
Smart, Graydon F. 1906(?)-1984 Obituary ... 111
Smart, Harold R(obert) 1892- ... CAP-1
Earlier sketch in CA 9-10
Smart, Ian Isidore 1944- ... 142
See also BW 2
Smart, J(ohn) J(amieson) C(arswell) 1920- ... CANR-36
Earlier sketches in CA 13-16R, CANR-7
Smart, James D(ick) 1906-1982 ... CANR-8
Obituary ... 105
Earlier sketch in CA 57-60
Smart, Mary (Spencer Simpson) 1915- ... 159
Smart, Mollie S(tevens) 1916- ... 61-64
Smart, (Roderick) Ninian 1927- ... CANR-56
Earlier sketches in CA 29-32R, CANR-12, 30
Smart, S(tephen) Bruce, Jr. 1923- ... 142
Smart, William (Edward, Jr.) 1933- ... CANR-7
Earlier sketch in CA 13-16R
Smartt, J(oseph) 1931- ... 138
Smead, (Edwin) Howard 1953- ... 124
Smedes, Lewis B. 1921- ... CANR-36
Earlier sketches in CA 69-72, CANR-11
Smedley, Agnes 1892-1950 ... 154
Smedley, Audrey ... 147
Smedley, Hester Marsden
See Marsden-Smedley, Hester
Smedley, Menella Bute 1820(?)-1877 ... DLB 199
Smedley, Philip Marsden
See Marsden-Smedley, Philip
Smeds, Dave 1955- ... 118
Smee, John (Charles) Odling
See Odling-Smee, John (Charles)
Smee, Nicola 1948- ... SATA 76
Smeed, J. W. 1926- ... CANR-55
Earlier sketch in CA 127
Smeeton, Miles (Richard) 1906-1988 ... 13-16R
Obituary ... 126
Smellie, Jim 1955- ... 133
Smellie, K.
See Smellie, Kingsley Bryce (Speakman)
Smellie, K. B.
See Smellie, Kingsley Bryce (Speakman)
Smellie, Kingsley Bryce (Speakman) 1897-1987 ... 5-8R
Obituary ... 124
Smelser, Marshall 1912-1978 ... 17-20R
Obituary ... 135
Smelser, Neil J(oseph) 1930- ... CANR-8
Earlier sketch in CA 17-20R
Smelser, William T. 1924- ... 29-32R
Smeltzer, C(larence) H(arry) 1900-(?) ... CANR-15
Earlier sketch in CA 1-4R
Smelyakov, Yaroslav 1913(?)-1972 Obituary ... 37-40R
Smerk, George M(artin) 1933- ... 107
Smertenko, Johan J. 1897(?)-1983 Obituary ... 109
Smerud, Warren D(ouglas) 1928- ... 49-52
Smetana, Josette 1928- ... 93-96
Smethurst, Mae J. 1935- ... 133
Smethurst, William (Knowles) 1945- ... 117
Smidt, Kristian 1916- ... 17-20R
Smigel, Erwin O. 1917-1973 ... 41-44R
Obituary ... 45-48
Smil, Vaclav 1943- ... CANR-30
Earlier sketch in CA 112
Smiles, Samuel 1812-1904 ... DLB 55
Smiley, Charles W(esley) 1940- ... 113
Smiley, David L(eslie) 1921- ... 5-8R
Smiley, Jane (Graves) 1949- ... CANR-50
Earlier sketches in CA 104, CANR-30
Interview in ... CANR-30
See also CLC 53, 76
See also DAM POP
Smiley, Sam Max 1931- ... 105
Smiley, Virginia Kester 1923- ... CANR-28
Earlier sketches in CA 29-32R, CANR-12
See also SATA 2
Smirnov, Sergei Sergeevich 1915-1976 Obituary ... 65-68
Smith, A(nthony) C(harles) H(ockley) 1935- ... CANR-44
Brief entry ... 116
Earlier sketch in CA 119
Smith, A(lexander) G(raham) Cairns
See Cairns-Smith, A(lexander) G(raham)
Smith, A(lbert) H(ugh) 1903- ... 5-8R
Smith, A(lbert) J(ames) 1924-1991 ... 65-68
Obituary ... 136
Smith, A(rthur) J(ames) M(arshall) 1902-1980 ... CANR-4
Obituary ... 102
Earlier sketch in CA 1-4R
See also CLC 15
See also DAC
See also DLB 88
Smith, A. Robert 1925- ... 73-76
Smith, A. Weston 1900(?)-1975 Obituary ... 57-60
Smith, Abbot E(merson) 1906-1983 Obituary ... 109
Smith, Ada Beatrice Queen Victoria Louisa Virginia 1894-1984 Obituary ... 111
Smith, Adam
See Goodman, George J(erome) W(aldo)
Smith, Adam 1723-1790 ... DLB 104
Smith, Alan M(cKinley) 1937- ... 41-44R
Smith, Alexander 1829-1867 ... DLB 32, 55
Smith, Alfred Edward 1895-1969 ... CAP-1
Earlier sketch in CA 11-12
Smith, Alfred G(oud) 1921- ... CANR-4
Earlier sketch in CA 9-12R
Smith, Ali 1962- ... 150
Smith, Alice K(imball) 1907- ... 138
Smith, Alice Upham 1908- ... 45-48
Smith, Allen William 1938- ... 61-64
Smith, Alson Jesse 1908-1965 ... 1-4R
Obituary ... 103
Smith, Alton E. 1917- ... 17-20R
Smith, Angel
See Masterton, Graham
Smith, Anna Deavere 1950- ... 133
See also CLC 86
Smith, Anna H(ester) 1912- ... CANR-6
Earlier sketch in CA 57-60
Smith, Anna Piszczan-Czaja 1920- ... 110
Smith, Anne Mollegen 1940- ... 81-84
Smith, Anne Warren 1938- ... 111
See also SATA 41
See also SATA-Brief 34
Smith, Annick 1936- ... 149
Smith, Anthony (John Francis) 1926- ... CANR-45
Earlier sketches in CA 9-12R, CANR-3
Smith, Anthony 1938- ... CANR-10
Earlier sketch in CA 53-56
Smith, Anthony D(avid) 1939- ... 101
Smith, Anthony Peter 1912-1980 Obituary ... 105
Smith, April 1949- ... 151
Smith, Arnold Cantwell 1915- ... 109
Smith, Arthur 1948- ... 120
Smith, Arthur C. 1916- ... 21-24R
Smith, Arthur L(ee)
See Asante, Molefi K(ete)
Smith, Arthur L(ee), Jr. 1927- ... 37-40R
Smith, Arthur M(umford) 1903- ... CAP-2
Earlier sketch in CA 17-18
Smith, Audrey D(owling) 1930- ... 119
Smith, Barbara 1946- ... 142
See also BW 2
Smith, Barbara Clark 1951- ... 124
Smith, Barbara Herrnstein 1932- ... 13-16R
Smith, Bardwell L(eith) 1925- ... 41-44R
Smith, Barry (Edward Jervis) 1943- ... SATA 75
Smith, Barry D(ecker) 1940- ... 29-32R
Smith, Beatrice S(chillinger) ... CANR-10
Earlier sketch in CA 57-60
See also SATA 12
Smith, Ben A(rwood) 1916- ... 1-4R
Smith, Benjamin Franklin 1902- ... 41-44R
Smith, Bernard (William) 1916- ... CANR-17
Earlier sketches in CA 1-4R, CANR-1
Smith, Bert Kruger 1915- ... CANR-11
Earlier sketch in CA 13-16R
Smith, Betsy Covington 1937- ... 111
See also SATA 43, 55
Smith, Betty (Wehner) 1896-1972 ... 5-8R
Obituary ... 33-36R
See also CLC 19
See also DLBY 82
See also SATA 6
Smith, Beulah Fenderson 1915- ... 13-16R
Smith, Bobbi
See Walton, Bobbi Smith
Smith, Bonnie G(ene) 1940- ... CANR-50
Earlier sketches in CA 108, CANR-25
Smith, Boyd M. 1888(?)-1973 Obituary ... 41-44R
Smith, Bradford 1909-1964 ... CANR-16
Earlier sketch in CA 1-4R
See also SATA 5
Smith, Bradley 1910-1997 ... CANR-19
Obituary ... 160
Earlier sketches in CA 5-8R, CANR-2
Smith, Bradley F. 1931- ... CANR-43
Earlier sketch in CA 108
Smith, Brenda 1946- ... 149
See also SATA 82
Smith, Brian 1949- ... 139
Smith, Brian C(live) 1938- ... CANR-30
Earlier sketch in CA 110
Smith, Brian R. 1939- ... CANR-70
Earlier sketch in CA 129
Smith, Bromley K(eables) 1911-1987 Obituary ... 121
Smith, Bruce 1949- ... 108
Smith, Bruce L. R. 1936- ... 141
Smith, Bruce R. 1946- ... 139
Smith, Bryan Evers Sharwood
See Sharwood Smith, Bryan Evers
Smith, C. Busby
See Smith, John (Charles)
Smith, C. Pritchard
See Hoyt, Edwin P(almer), Jr.
Smith, C. Ray 1929-1988 ... CANR-28
Obituary ... 126
Earlier sketch in CA 109
Smith, C(lifford) T(horpe) 1924- ... 21-24R
Smith, C. U. 1901- ... 41-44R
Smith, C(hristopher) U(pham) M(urray) 1930- ... 33-36R
Smith, C(harles) W(illiam) 1940- ... 61-64
Smith, C. Willard 1899(?)-1979 Obituary ... 89-92
Smith, Caesar
See Trevor, Elleston
Smith, Cameron Mitchell 1935- ... 133
Smith, Carleton 1910-1984 Obituary ... 112
Smith, Carlton
See Rocklin, Ross Louis
Smith, Carmichael
See Linebarger, Paul M(yron) A(nthony)
Smith, Carol H(ertzig) 1929- ... 5-8R
Smith, Carol Sturm 1938- ... CANR-25
Earlier sketch in CA 25-28R
See also DLBY 81
Smith, Carole 1935- ... 101
Smith, (Charles) Carter (Jr.) 1930- ... 107
Smith, Catherine C. 1929- ... 29-32R
Smith, Cecil (Howard III) 1917- ... 69-72
Smith, Celina Janson
See Janson-Smith, Celina
Smith, Chard Powers 1894-1977 ... 5-8R
Obituary ... 73-76
Smith, Charles E(dward) 1904-1970 Obituary ... 29-32R
Smith, Charles Harvard Gibbs
See Gibbs-Smith, Charles Harvard
Smith, Charles Henry 1826-1903 Brief entry ... 119
See also DLB 11
Smith, Charles Merrill (?)-1985 Obituary ... 115
Smith, Charles W(illiam) (Frederick) 1905-1993 ... 13-16R
Obituary ... 142
Smith, Charlie 1947- ... 143
Smith, Charlotte (Turner) 1749-1806 ... DLB 39, 109
Smith, Cherry 1931- ... 120
Smith, Chet 1899-1973 ... DLB 171
Smith, Christine 1945- ... 143
Smith, Clagett G. 1930- ... 37-40R
Smith, Clark Ashton 1893-1961 ... 143
See also CLC 43
Smith, Clifford Neal 1923- ... 41-44R
Smith, Clodus R(ay) 1928- ... CANR-8
Earlier sketch in CA 21-24R
Smith, (Christopher) Colin 1927- ... 102
Smith, Constance Babington
See Babington Smith, Constance
Smith, Cordelia Titcomb 1902- ... CAP-1
Earlier sketch in CA 11-12
Smith, Cordwainer
See Linebarger, Paul M(yron) A(nthony)
See also DLB 8
Smith, Cornelius C(ole, Jr.) 1913- ... CANR-22
Earlier sketch in CA 21-24R
Smith, Courtland L(ester) 1939- ... 81-84
Smith, Craig 1955- ... SATA 81
Smith, Craig R(alph) 1944- ... 81-84
Smith, Curt 1951- ... 81-84
Smith, Curtis C. 1939- ... 127
Smith, Cynthia S. 1924- ... 106
Smith, Cyril 1928- ... 109
Smith, Cyril James 1909-1974 Obituary ... 53-56
Smith, D(avid) Howard 1900-1987 ... 25-28R
Obituary ... 123
Smith, D. MacLeod
See Smith, David MacLeod
Smith, D(wight) Moody, Jr. 1931- ... CANR-42
Earlier sketches in CA 41-44R, CANR-20
Smith, D(onald) V(incent) 1933-1978 ... 25-28R
Obituary ... 117
Smith, D(avid) W(arner) 1932- ... CANR-12
Earlier sketch in CA 17-20R
Smith, Dale L. 1953- ... 146
Smith, Dale O(rville) 1911- ... 73-76
Smith, Dan Throop 1908-1982 Obituary ... 106
Smith, Dana Prom 1927- ... 49-52
Smith, Daniel M(alloy) 1922-1976 ... CANR-8
Earlier sketch in CA 17-20R
Smith, Daniel S(omers) 1961- ... 147
Smith, Darren L. 1958- ... 124
Smith, Datus C(lifford), Jr. 1907- ... CANR-11
Earlier sketches in CAP-1, CA 11-12
See also SATA 13
Smith, Dave
See Smith, David (Jeddie)
See also CAAS 7
See also CLC 22, 42
See also DLB 5
Smith, David 1906-1965 Obituary ... 113
Smith, David (Jeddie) 1942- ... CANR-59
Earlier sketches in CA 49-52, CANR-1
See also Smith, Dave
See also DAM POET
Smith, David (Anthony) 1943- ... 128
Smith, David A(lden) 1956- ... 162
Smith, David Alexander 1953- ... 143
Smith, David C(layton) 1929- ... 49-52
Smith, David C. 1931- ... 69-72
Smith, David C. 1952- ... 120
Smith, David Elvin 1939- ... 29-32R
Smith, David Fay 1939- ... 112
Smith, David H. 1939- ... 93-96
Smith, David Horton 1939- ... CANR-7
Earlier sketch in CA 57-60
Smith, David L(awrence) 1963- ... 149
Smith, David M(arshall) 1936- ... CANR-12
Earlier sketch in CA 29-32R
Smith, David MacLeod 1920- ... CANR-5
Earlier sketch in CA 53-56
Smith, David Osmond
See Osmond-Smith, David
Smith, David Shiverick 1918- ... 108
Smith, David T. 1935- ... 53-56
Smith, David W. 1921-1981 ... 110
Obituary ... 108
Smith, Dean E(llis) 1923- ... CANR-4
Earlier sketch in CA 9-12R
Smith, Deborah 1955- ... 143
Smith, Debra 1955- ... SATA 89
Smith, Delia ... 149
Smith, Delos Owen 1905-1973 Obituary ... 41-44R
Smith, Denison Langley 1924- ... 13-16R
Smith, Dennis 1940- ... CANR-10
Earlier sketch in CA 61-64
Smith, Desmond 1927- ... 103
Smith, Dian G. 1946- ... 120
Smith, Diana Kappel
See Kappel-Smith, Diana
Smith, Dick 1908-1974 ... CAP-1
Earlier sketch in CA 19-20
Smith, Dick King
See King-Smith, Dick
Smith, Dinitia 1945- ... 136
Smith, Dodie
See Smith, Dorothy Gladys
Smith, Don(ald Taylor) 1909- ... 49-52
Smith, Don Ian 1918- ... 45-48
Smith, Donal Ian Bryce 1934- ... 41-44R
Smith, Donald Eugene 1927- ... 9-12R
Smith, Donald G. 1927- ... 13-16R
Smith, Doris Buchanan 1934- ... CANR-11
Earlier sketch in CA 69-72
See also DLB 52
See also JRDA
See also MAICYA
See also SAAS 10
See also SATA 28, 75
Smith, Doris E(dna Elliott) 1919- ... CANR-18
Earlier sketch in CA 25-28R
Smith, Dorothy Gladys 1896-1990 ... CANR-37
Obituary ... 133
See also MAICYA
See also SATA 82
See also SATA-Obit 65
Smith, Dorothy Stafford 1905- ... 21-24R
See also SATA 6
Smith, Dorothy Valentine 1908- ... 29-32R
Smith, Douglas 1918- ... 73-76
Smith, Douglas 1949- ... 113
Smith, Douglas K. 1949- ... 160
Smith, Duane A(llan) 1937- ... CANR-47
Earlier sketches in CA 21-24R, CANR-8, 23
Smith, Dwight C(hichester), Jr. 1930- ... 77-80
Smith, Dwight L. 1918- ... CANR-49
Earlier sketches in CA 33-36R, CANR-24
Smith, Dwight R. 1921- ... 106
Smith, E(lmer) Boyd 1860-1943 ... YABC 1
Smith, E(dric) Brooks 1917- ... 5-8R
See also SATA 40
Smith, E(ric) D(avid) 1923- ... CANR-41
Earlier sketch in CA 118
Smith, E. E.
See Smith, Edward Elmer
Smith, E. E. "Doc"
See Smith, Edward Elmer
Smith, Edgar H(erbert) 1934- ... 25-28R
Smith, Edna Hopkins 1932(?)-1979 Obituary ... 89-92
Smith, Edward Conrad 1891- ... 45-48
Smith, Edward E.
See Smith, Edward Elmer
Smith, Edward E. "Doc"
See Smith, Edward Elmer
Smith, Edward Ellis 1921- ... 25-28R
Smith, Edward Elmer 1890-1965 ... 118
Obituary ... 102
See also DLB 8
Smith, Edward W(illiam) 1920-1975 Obituary ... 57-60
Smith, Edwin H. 1920- ... 13-16R
Smith, Elbert B(enjamin) 1920- ... 21-24R
Smith, Eleanor Touhey 1910- ... 25-28R
Smith, Elihu Hubbard 1771-1798 ... DLB 37
Smith, Elinor Goulding 1917- ... CANR-3
Earlier sketch in CA 1-4R
Smith, Eliot Fremont
See Fremont-Smith, Eliot
Smith, Elizabeth A(ngele) T(aft) 1958- ... 133
Smith, Elizabeth Oakes (Prince) 1806-1893 ... DLB 1
Smith, Elliott Dunlap 1890(?)-1976 Obituary ... 61-64
Smith, Elsdon C(oles) 1903- ... CANR-6
Earlier sketch in CA 1-4R
Smith, Elske v(an)P(anhuys) 1929- ... 77-80
Smith, Elton E(dward) 1915- ... CANR-14
Earlier sketch in CA 13-16R
Smith, Elva Sophronia 1871-1965 Obituary ... 107
See also SATA-Brief 31
Smith, Elwyn Allen 1919- ... CANR-9
Earlier sketch in CA 5-8R
Smith, Emma 1923- ... 73-76
See also SATA 52
See also SATA-Brief 36
Smith, Eric Ledell 1949- ... 144
Smith, Ernest A(llyn) 1911-1977 ... 1-4R
Obituary ... 103
Smith, Ethel Sabin 1887- ... CAP-1
Earlier sketch in CA 13-16
Smith, Eugene L(ewis) 1912-1986 ... 21-24R
Obituary ... 118
Smith, Eugene Waldo 1905- ... CAP-1
Earlier sketch in CA 9-10
Smith, Eunice 1757-1823 ... DLB 200

Smith, (Katherine) Eunice (Young) 1902- ... CANR-2
Earlier sketch in CA 5-8R
See also SATA 5
Smith, Evelyn E. 1927- Brief entry ... 113
Smith, F(rederick) G(eorge) Walton 1909-1989 ... CANR-44
Obituary ... 130
Earlier sketch in CA 45-48
Smith, F. Hopkinson 1838-1915 ... DLBD 13
Smith, F. Joseph 1925- ... CANR-2
Earlier sketch in CA 45-48
Smith, F. Todd 1957- ... 152
Smith, Fay Jackson 1912- ... 25-28R
Smith, Faye McDonald 1950- ... 157
Smith, Florence Margaret 1902-1971 ... CANR-35
Obituary ... 29-32R
Earlier sketches in CAP-2, CA 17-18
See also Smith, Stevie
See also DAM POET
See also MTCW 1
Smith, Frances C(hristine) 1904- ... CANR-1
Earlier sketch in CA 1-4R
See also SATA 3
Smith, Frances Scott Fitzgerald Lanahan 1921-1986 Obituary ... 119
Smith, Frank (Arthur) 1917- ... 69-72
Smith, Frank E(llis) 1918-1997 ... 17-20R
Obituary ... 160
Smith, Frank E. 1919-1984 Obituary ... 114
Smith, Frank Kingston 1919- ... CANR-18
Earlier sketch in CA 102
Smith, Frank O. M. (?)-1983 Obituary ... 109
Smith, Frank Seymour 1898-1972 ... 9-12R
Obituary ... 89-92
Smith, (David) Fred(erick) 1898(?)-1976 Obituary ... 69-72
Smith, Frederick E(screet) 1922- ... CANR-44
Earlier sketches in CA 5-8R, CANR-3, 19
Smith, Frederick W(illiam) 1920- ... 73-76
Smith, Frederick William Robin 1936-1985 Obituary ... 115
Smith, Frederick Winston Furneaux 1907-1975 ... 65-68
Obituary ... 57-60
Smith, Fredrika Shumway 1877-1968 Obituary . 109
See also SATA-Brief 30
Smith, G(eorge) E(verard) Kidder 1913-1997 . 9-12R
Obituary ... 162
Smith, Gaddis 1932- ... 21-24R
Smith, Garry (Van Dorn) 1933- ... 5-8R
Smith, Gary (Milton) 1943- ... 97-100
Smith, Gary R. 1932- ... 69-72
See also SATA 14
Smith, Gary V(incent) 1943- ... 101
Smith, Gavin D. 1960- ... 144
Smith, Gene 1924- ... 77-80
Smith, Gene 1929- ... 81-84
Smith, Genevieve Love 1917- ... 21-24R
Smith, Geof 1969- ... SATA 102
Smith, Geoffrey (John) 1943- ... 120
Smith, Geoffrey (Francis) Hattersley
See Hattersley-Smith, Geoffrey (Francis)
Smith, Geoffrey Sutton 1941- ... 49-52
Smith, George (Henry) 1922- ... 103
Smith, George D. 1870-1920 ... DLB 140
Smith, George E. 1938- ... 37-40R
Smith, George Harmon 1920- ... 49-52
See also SATA 5
Smith, George Ivan 1915-1995 ... 121
Obituary ... 150
Smith, George O(liver) 1911-1981 ... CANR-28
Obituary ... 103
Earlier sketch in CA 97-100
See also DLB 8
Smith, George P(atrick) II 1939- ... 131
Smith, Gerald A(lfred) 1921- ... 37-40R
Smith, Gerald B. 1909- ... CAP-2
Earlier sketch in CA 25-28
Smith, Gerald L(yman) K(enneth) 1898-1976 Obituary ... 65-68
Smith, Gerald Stanton 1938- ... 123
Smith, Glenn C. 1924- ... 123
Smith, Glenn Robert 1952- ... 145
Smith, Godfrey 1926- ... 9-12R
Smith, Goldwin 1823-1910 ... DLB 99
Smith, Goldwin (Albert) 1912- ... 41-44R
Smith, Gordon Roland
See Roland Smith, Gordon
Smith, Gordon Ross 1917- ... 5-8R
Smith, Grahame 1933- ... 25-28R
Smith, Gregory Blake 1951- ... 141
Smith, Gregory White 1951- ... 144
Smith, Gretchen L. (?)-1972 Obituary ... 104
Smith, Grover C(leveland) 1923- ... 33-36R
Smith, Gudmund J(ohn) W(ilhelm) 1920- ... 102
Smith, Guy-Harold 1895- ... CAP-2
Earlier sketch in CA 19-20
Smith, H(arry) Allen 1907-1976 ... CANR-5
Obituary ... 65-68
Earlier sketch in CA 5-8R
See also AITN 2
See also DLB 11, 29
See also SATA-Obit 20
Smith, H. Jeff 1957- ... 150
Smith, H(arold) Wendell 1923- ... 111
Smith, Hale G(illiam) 1918- ... 61-64
Smith, Hallett (Darius) 1907-1996 ... 21-24R
Obituary ... 153
Smith, Harmon L. 1930- ... 29-32R
Smith, Harold Ivan 1947- ... 121
Smith, Harold L(ester) 1942- ... 125
Smith, Harris (Gordon) 1921- ... 49-52
Smith, (Oliver) Harrison 1888-1971 Obituary ... 29-32R
Smith, Harry 1936- ... CANR-29
Earlier sketches in CA 77-80, CANR-13
Smith, Harry B. 1860-1936 ... DLB 187
Smith, Harry E(dmund) 1928- ... 25-28R
Smith, Harry W(illiam) 1937- ... 112
Smith, Harvey K(ennedy) 1904-1968 ... CAP-1
Earlier sketch in CA 13-14
Smith, Hazel Brannon 1914- ... DLB 127
Smith, Hedrick (Laurence) 1933- ... CANR-41
Earlier sketches in CA 65-68, CANR-11
Smith, Helen Zenna
See Price, Evadne
Smith, Henry
See Smith, Henry DeWitt II
Smith, Henry 1560-1591 ... DLB 136
Smith, Henry 1905-1988 Obituary ... 124
Smith, Henry Clay 1913- ... 1-4R
Smith, Henry DeWitt II 1940- ... 119
Smith, Henry Lee, Jr. 1913-1972 Obituary .. 37-40R
Smith, Henry Nash 1906-1986 ... CANR-2
Obituary ... 119
Earlier sketch in CA 1-4R
Smith, Henry Peter 1910-1968 ... 1-4R
Obituary ... 103
Smith, Herbert F(rancis) 1922- ... CANR-58
Earlier sketches in CA 77-80, CANR-13, 30
Smith, Herbert F. A. 1915-1969 ... CAP-1
Earlier sketch in CA 13-16
Smith, Hermon Dunlap 1900-1983 Obituary ... 109
Smith, Hilda Worthington 1889(?)-1984 Obituary ... 112
Smith, Hobart M(uir) 1912- ... CANR-9
Earlier sketch in CA 65-68
Smith, Hope M(ayhew) 1916- ... 1-4R
Smith, Horatio (Horace) 1779-1849 ... DLB 96, 116
Smith, Howard E(verett), Jr. 1927- ... CANR-21
Earlier sketch in CA 25-28R
See also SATA 12
Smith, Howard K(ingsbury) 1914- ... CANR-71
Earlier sketches in CA 45-48, CANR-2
Smith, Howard R(oss) 1917- ... 1-4R
Smith, Howard Van 1910(?)-1986 ... 5-8R
Obituary ... 120
Smith, Hubert Shirley
See Shirley-Smith, Hubert
Smith, Hugh L(etcher) 1921-1968 ... CAP-2
Earlier sketch in CA 25-28
See also SATA 5
Smith, Huston (Cummings) 1919- ... 61-64
Smith, Hyrum W. 1943- ... 145
Smith, I(rving) Norman 1909- ... 107
Smith, Iain Crichton 1928- ... 21-24R
See also CLC 64
See also DLB 40, 139
Smith, Imogene Henderson 1922- ... 5-8R
See also SATA 12
Smith, Irene 1903- ... 73-76
Smith, Irving H(arold) 1932- ... 49-52
Smith, Irwin 1892-1977 ... 5-8R
Obituary ... 73-76
Smith, Isadore Leighton Luce 1901-1985 ... 101
Obituary ... 118
Smith, J. Allen 1860-1924 ... DLB 47
Smith, J. C. S.
See Smith, Jane S.
Smith, J(ohn) Holland 1932- ... 17-20R
Smith, J(ames) L(eonard) B(rierley) 1897-1968 ... CAP-1
Earlier sketch in CA 13-14
Smith, J(ohn) Malcolm 1921- ... 49-52
Smith, J(oseph) Russell 1874-1966 ... CAP-1
Earlier sketch in CA 13-14
Smith, J(oe) W(illiam) Ashley 1914- ... 5-8R
Smith, Jack (Clifford) 1916-1996 ... CANR-12
Obituary ... 151
Earlier sketch in CA 69-72
Smith, Jack Prescott 1945- ... 127
Smith, Jackie M. 1930- ... 93-96
Smith, Jackson Algernon 1917- Brief entry ... 105
Smith, Jacqueline B. 1937- ... SATA 39
Smith, James 1775-1839 ... DLB 96
Smith, James 1904-1972 ... 85-88
Smith, James A. 1914-1983(?) ... CANR-39
Earlier sketch in CA 21-24R
Smith, James D(ale) 1940- ... 121
Smith, James L(eslie Clarke) 1936- ... 25-28R
Smith, James Monroe 1975- ... 164
Smith, James Morton 1919- ... 103
Smith, James R. 1941- ... 101
Smith, James Roy 1920- ... 21-24R
Smith, Jane F(rances) 1916- ... 123
Brief entry ... 117
Smith, Jane I(dleman) 1937- ... 107
Smith, Jane S. 1947- ... 118
Smith, Janet (Buchanan) Adam
See Adam Smith, Janet (Buchanan)
Smith, Janet L. ... 167
Smith, Janice Lee 1949- ... SATA 54
Smith, Janna M(alamud) 1952- ... 164
Smith, Jean
See Smith, Frances C(hristine)
Smith, Jean DeMouthe 1949- ... 65-68
Smith, Jean Edward 1932- ... 37-40R
Smith, Jean Pajot 1945- ... 53-56
See also SATA 10
Smith, Jeff(rey Alan) 1958- ... CANR-66
Earlier sketch in CA 132
See also SATA 93
Smith, Jeff Allen
See Smith, Jeff(rey Alan)
Smith, Jenny 1963- ... SATA 90
Smith, Jerome F(ranken) 1928- ... 107
Smith, Jessica 1895- ... CANR-2
Earlier sketch in CA 49-52
Smith, Jessie
See Kunhardt, Edith
Smith, Jessie Carney 1930- ... CANR-39
Earlier sketches in CA 89-92, CANR-17
See also BW 2
Smith, Jessie Willcox 1863-1935 ... DLB 188
See also MAICYA
See also SATA 21
Smith, Jim 1920- Brief entry ... 115
See also SATA-Brief 36
Smith, Joan (Mary) 1933- ... SATA 54
See also SATA-Brief 46
Smith, Joan 1935- ... 61-64
Smith, Joan Gerarda 1932- ... 145
Smith, Joan K(aren) 1939- ... 93-96
Smith, Joanmarie 1932- ... CANR-16
Earlier sketch in CA 85-88
Smith, Jody Brant 1943- ... 113
Smith, John
See Herrick, Marvin Theodore
Smith, John 1580(?)-1631 ... DLB 24, 30
Smith, John (Charles) 1924- ... 103
Smith, John Chabot 1915- ... 69-72
Smith, John Coventry 1903-1984 ... 115
Smith, John David 1949- ... CANR-60
Earlier sketches in CA 111, CANR-30
Smith, John Edwin 1921- ... 103
Smith, John F(erris) 1934- ... 81-84
Smith, John H(azel) 1928- ... 9-12R
Smith, John M. 1942- ... 139
Smith, John Norton
See Norton-Smith, John
Smith, Johnston
See Crane, Stephen (Townley)
Smith, Jon R(ichard) 1946- ... 77-80
Smith, Jonathan 1942- ... 144
Smith, Jonathan M(ark) 1957- ... 165
Smith, Jordan 1954- ... 110
Smith, Jos(eph) A. 1936- ... SATA 73
Smith, Joseph B(urkholder) 1921- ... 65-68
Smith, Joseph Fielding 1876-1972 Obituary .37-40R
Smith, Joseph H(enry) 1913-1981 Obituary ... 105
Smith, Josiah 1704-1781 ... DLB 24
Smith, Judie R. 1936- ... 148
See also SATA 80
Smith, Julia Floyd 1914- ... 85-88
Smith, Julia Frances 1911-1989 Obituary ... 128
Smith, Julian 1937- ... 61-64
Smith, Julian C(leveland, Jr.) 1919- ... 144
Smith, Julian W. 1901- ... 13-16R
Smith, Julie 1944- ... CANR-63
Earlier sketches in CA 112, CANR-32
Smith, K(ermit) Wayne 1938- ... 29-32R
Smith, Karl U(lrich) 1907-1994 ... CANR-46
Earlier sketches in CA 61-64, CANR-9
Smith, Kate
See Smith, Kathryn Elizabeth
Smith, Kathleen J(oan) 1929- ... 103
Smith, Kathryn Elizabeth 1907(?)-1986 Obituary ... 119
Smith, Kay
See Smith, Catherine C.
Smith, Kay Nolte 1932-1993 ... CANR-66
Obituary ... 142
Earlier sketches in CA 101, CANR-18, 43
Smith, Keith V(an) 1937- ... 112
Smith, Ken(neth Danforth) 1902- ... CANR-1
Earlier sketch in CA 45-48
Smith, Ken(neth John) 1938- ... CANR-39
Earlier sketch in CA 33-36R
See also DLB 40
Smith, Kenneth Lee 1925- ... 77-80
Smith, Kenneth M(anley) 1892-1981 Obituary ... 108
Smith, Kerri S. 1960- ... 139
Smith, Kevin 1970- ... 166
Smith, Kurtis 1958- ... 163
Smith, L(eonard) Glenn 1939- ... 93-96
Smith, L(ester) Neil 1946- ... 144
Smith, Lacey Baldwin 1922- ... CANR-6
Earlier sketch in CA 5-8R
Smith, Lafayette
See Higdon, Hal
Smith, Lane 1959- ... 143
See also AAYA 21
See also CLR 47
See also SATA 76
Smith, Larry 1940- ... 49-52
Smith, Laura I(vory) 1902- ... 17-20R
Smith, Laura J. ... 144
Smith, Laurence D. 1950- ... 123
Smith, Lavon B(enson) 1921- ... 21-24R
Smith, Lawrence Berk 1939- ... CANR-13
Earlier sketch in CA 73-76
Smith, Lawrence R(ichard) 1945- ... 117
Smith, Lee
See Albion, Lee Smith
Smith, Lee 1937- ... 73-76
Smith, Lee 1944- ... CANR-46
Brief entry ... 114
Earlier sketch in CA 119
Interview in ... 119
See also CLC 25, 73
See also DLB 143
See also DLBY 83
Smith, Lee L. 1930- ... 29-32R
Smith, Lena (Kennedy) 1914- ... 93-96
Smith, Lendon H(oward) 1921- ... 81-84
See also SATA 64
Smith, LeRoi Tex 1934- ... 29-32R
Smith, Leslie F(rancis) 1901- ... CAP-1
Earlier sketch in CA 19-20
Smith, Leslie James Seth
See Seth-Smith, Leslie James
Smith, Leslie R(aymond) 1904- ... 1-4R
Smith, Lew
See Floren, Lee
Smith, Lillian (Eugenia) 1897-1966 ... CANR-72
Obituary ... 25-28R
Earlier sketches in CAP-2, CA 17-18
Smith, Lillian H(elena) 1887-1983 Obituary ... 111
See also SATA-Obit 32
Smith, Linell Nash 1932- ... 5-8R
See also SATA 2
Smith, Liz 1923- ... 65-68
Smith, Logan Pearsall 1865-1946 ... DLB 98
Smith, Lora R(oberts) 1949- ... 153
Smith, Lou 1918- ... 73-76
Smith, Louis
See Barzini, Luigi (Giorgio, Jr.)
Smith, Louis M(ilde) 1929- ... 17-20R
Smith, Lucia B. 1943- ... 108
See also SATA 30
Smith, Lynnette 1951- ... 116
Smith, M(ahlon) Brewster 1919- ... 61-64
Smith, M. Estellie 1935- ... CANR-8
Earlier sketch in CA 61-64
Smith, M. Weston
See Weston-Smith, M.
Smith, Malcolm 1938- ... 97-100
Smith, Malcom N(orman) 1919(?)-1985 Obituary ... 116
Smith, Manuel (Juan) 1934- ... 105
Smith, Marcus J(oel) 1918- ... 73-76
Smith, Margaret (Middleton) 1931- ... 162
Smith, Margaret (Madeline) Chase 1897-1995 ... 73-76
Obituary ... 148
Smith, Margaret Emily Noel Nuttall
See Nuttall-Smith, Margaret Emily Noel
Smith, Margaret F(oltz) 1915- ... 102
Smith, Margaret Mary 1916- ... 108
Smith, Margaret Ruth 1902- ... CAP-1
Earlier sketch in CA 19-20
Smith, Margarita G. 1923(?)-1983 Obituary ... 109
Smith, Marguerite 1940- ... 162
Smith, Marie D. ... 13-16R
Smith, Marilyn Cochran
See Cochran-Smith, Marilyn
Smith, Marion Hagens 1913- ... 17-20R
See also SATA 12
Smith, Marion Jaques 1899- ... CANR-11
Earlier sketch in CA 69-72
See also SATA 13
Smith, Marisa 1956- ... 147
Smith, Mark (Richard) 1935- ... CANR-44
Earlier sketches in CA 13-16R, CANR-10
See also DLBY 82
Smith, Marny 1932- ... 108
Smith, Martin
See Smith, Martin Cruz
Smith, Martin Cruz 1942- ... CANR-65
Earlier sketches in CA 85-88, CANR-6, 23, 43
Interview in ... CANR-23
See also BEST 89:4
See also CLC 25
See also DAM MULT, POP
See also NNAL
Smith, Martin R. 1934- ... 144
Smith, Mary Ann 1934- ... 126
Smith, Mary Benton 1903- ... CAP-2
Earlier sketch in CA 17-18
Smith, Mary Elizabeth 1932- ... 41-44R
Smith, Mary Ellen ... 69-72
See also SATA 10
Smith, Marya 1945- ... 146
See also SATA 78
Smith, Mary-Ann Tirone 1944- ... 136
Brief entry ... 118
See also CLC 39
Smith, Mason McCann 1952- ... 108
Smith, Maxwell A(ustin) 1894- ... 37-40R
Smith, (Albert) Merriman 1913-1970 ... CANR-2
Obituary ... 29-32R
Earlier sketch in CA 1-4R
Smith, Merritt Roe 1940- ... 77-80
Smith, Michael 1698-1771(?) ... DLB 31
Smith, Michael (Townsend) 1935- ... CANR-11
Earlier sketch in CA 21-24R
Smith, Michael 1946- ... 132
Smith, Michael A(nthony) 1942- ... 102
Smith, Michael Marshall 1965- ... 162
Smith, Michael P(eter) 1942- ... 65-68
Smith, Michael R(obert) 1946- ... 144
Smith, Michael Stephen 1944- ... 103
Smith, Michael W(hitaker) 1958- ... 166
Smith, Mike
See Smith, Mary Ellen
Smith, Mildred C(atharine) 1891-1973 ... 101
Obituary ... 45-48
Smith, Mildred Nelson 1918- ... 69-72
Smith, Mitchell 1935- ... 136
Smith, Morris 1928- ... 164
Smith, Mortimer B(rewster) 1906-1981 ... 107
Obituary ... 104
Smith, Morton 1915-1991 ... CANR-6
Obituary ... 134
Earlier sketch in CA 5-8R
Smith, Morton Howison 1923- ... 45-48
Smith, Murphy D(e Witt) 1920- ... CANR-42
Earlier sketches in CA 37-40R, CANR-13
Smith, Murray G(ordon) 1952- ... 120
Smith, Myron J(ohn), Jr. 1944- ... CANR-38
Earlier sketches in CA 45-48, CANR-1, 16
Smith, N(orman) J(ames) 1930- ... CANR-20
Earlier sketch in CA 103
Smith, N. V.
See Smith, Neil(son Voyne)
Smith, Nancy Covert 1935- ... CANR-10
Earlier sketch in CA 57-60
See also SATA 12
Smith, Nancy Taylor ... 57-60
Smith, Neil(son Voyne) 1939- ... 133

Smith, Neil Homer 1909(?)-1972 Obituary .. 37-40R
Smith, Nicholas D. 1949- ... 137
Smith, Nigel J(ohn) H(arwood) 1949- ... 109
Smith, Nila Banton 1890-1976 ... 21-24R
Obituary ... 120
Smith, Nina Slingsby 1928- ... 119
Smith, Noel W. 1933- ... 144
Smith, Norman Edward Mace 1914- ... 103
Smith, Norman F. 1920- ... CANR-44
Earlier sketch in CA 29-32R
See also SATA 5, 70
Smith, Norman Lewis 1941- ... 77-80
Smith, Norris Kelly 1917- ... 21-24R
Smith, Ophia D(elilah) Smith 1891- ... 5-8R
Smith, Oswald J(effrey) 1889-1986 Obituary ... 119
Smith, (Charles) Page 1917-1995 ... CANR-2
Obituary ... 149
Earlier sketch in CA 1-4R
Smith, Patricia Clark 1943- ... 161
See also SATA 96
Smith, Patricia Jean Adam
See Adam-Smith, Patricia Jean
Smith, Patrick 1936- ... 77-80
Smith, Patrick D(avis) 1927- ... 77-80
Smith, Patrick J(ohn) 1932- ... 41-44R
Smith, Patrick Wykeham Montague
See Montague-Smith, Patrick Wykeham
Smith, Patti 1946- ... CANR-63
Earlier sketch in CA 93-96
See also CLC 12
Smith, Pattie Sherwood
1909(?)-1974 Obituary ... 53-56
Smith, Paul ... CANR-2
Earlier sketch in CA 1-4R, 144
Smith, Paul B(rainerd) 1921- ... CANR-28
Earlier sketches in CA 13-16R, CANR-10
Smith, Paul C. 1908-1976 Obituary ... 65-68
Smith, Paul F. 1919- ... 57-60
Smith, Paul H(ubert) 1931- ... 89-92
Smith, Paul Jordan
See Jordan-Smith, Paul
Smith, Paul Julian 1956- ... 138
Smith, Pauline (Urmson) 1882-1959 ... TCLC 25
Smith, Pauline C(oggeshall) 1908- ... 29-32R
See also SATA 27
Smith, Percival Gardner
See Gardner-Smith, Percival
Smith, Perry McCoy 1934- ... 29-32R
Smith, Peter 1897-1982 Obituary ... 107
Smith, Peter C(harles Horstead) 1940- ... CANR-56
Earlier sketches in CA 57-60, CANR-7, 30
Smith, Peter H(opkinson) 1940- ... 41-44R
Smith, Peter J(ohn) 1931- ... 114
Smith, Philip Chadwick Foster 1939- ... 77-80
Smith, Philip E(dward II) 1943- ... 25-28R
Smith, Philip L. 1943- ... 108
Smith, Philip Warren 1936- ... SATA 46
Smith, R(ichard) A(lbert) N(ewton) 1908- ... 9-12R
Smith, R(eginald) C(harles) 1907- ... 65-68
Smith, R(eginald) D(onald) 1914-1985 ... 117
Obituary ... 140
Smith, R(obert) Philip 1907- ... 81-84
Smith, R(ichard) Selby 1914- ... 108
Smith, Ralph (Bernard) 1939- ... 33-36R
Smith, Ralph Alexander 1929- ... 77-80
Smith, Ralph B. 1894(?)-1985 Obituary ... 115
Smith, Ralph Carlisle 1910- ... 124
Smith, Ralph Lee 1927- ... CANR-1
Earlier sketch in CA 1-4R
Smith, Ray 1915- ... CANR-11
Earlier sketch in CA 13-16R
Smith, Ray 1941- ... CANR-18
Earlier sketch in CA 101
Smith, Ray Winfield 1897-1982 Obituary ... 110
Smith, Red
See Smith, Walter W(ellesley)
See also DLB 29, 171
Smith, Rex Alan 1921- ... 61-64
Smith, Rhea Marsh 1907- ... CAP-1
Earlier sketch in CA 17-18
Smith, Richard 1941- ... 81-84
Smith, Richard A(ustin) 1911- ... 17-20R
Smith, Richard C(hristopher) 1948- ... 81-84
Smith, Richard Harris 1946- ... 41-44R
Smith, Richard Joseph 1944- ... CANR-42
Earlier sketches in CA 97-100, CANR-20
Smith, Richard K(ent) 1936- ... 41-44R
Smith, Richard L. 1950- ... 152
Smith, Richard M(ills) 1946- ... 73-76
Smith, Richard N. 1937- ... 21-24R
Smith, Richard P(aul) 1949- ... CANR-56
Earlier sketches in CA 111, CANR-30
Smith, Richard Rein 1930- ... 97-100
See also Davis, Jim
Smith, Robert A(rthur) 1944- ... 69-72
Smith, Robert Allan 1909-1980 Obituary ... 105
Smith, Robert C(hester) 1912-1975 Obituary ... 114
Smith, Robert C(harles) 1947- ... 111
Smith, Robert Charles 1938- ... 65-68
Smith, Robert D. 1937- ... 37-40R
Smith, Robert Dickie 1928- ... 9-12R
Smith, Robert Eliot 1899- ... 37-40R
Smith, Robert Ellis 1940- ... CANR-16
Earlier sketch in CA 89-92
Smith, Robert Freeman 1930- ... CANR-1
Earlier sketch in CA 1-4R
Smith, Robert G(illen) 1913- ... CANR-42
Earlier sketch in CA 45-48
Smith, Robert G(ordon) 1947- ... 102
Smith, Robert Griffin, Jr. 1920- ... 41-44R
Smith, Robert Houston 1931- ... 105
Smith, Robert J(ohn) 1927- ... 53-56
Smith, Robert Kimmel 1930- ... CANR-42
Earlier sketches in CA 61-64, CANR-8
See also JRDA
See also SATA 12, 77
Smith, Robert Lee 1928- ... 111
Smith, Robert Paul 1915-1977 ... 73-76
Obituary ... 69-72
See also SATA 52
See also SATA-Obit 30
Smith, Robert S(idney) 1904-1969 ... CAP-1
Earlier sketch in CA 13-16
Smith, Robert W(illiam) 1926- ... 13-16R
Smith, Robert W(ayne) 1926- ... 45-48
Smith, Robin Baird
See Baird-Smith, Robin
Smith, Rockwell Carter 1908- ... 53-56
Smith, Rodney P(ennell), Jr. 1930- ... 29-32R
Smith, Roger H(askell) 1932-1980 ... 69-72
Obituary ... 101
Smith, Roger Montgomery
1915(?)-1975 Obituary ... 57-60
Smith, Rogers M(ood) 1953- ... 120
Smith, Roland B(eatcher) 1909- ... 1-4R
Smith, Rolando (R.) Hinojosa
See Hinojosa(-Smith), Rolando (R.)
Smith, Rollin 1942- ... 144
Smith, Ronald Gregor 1913-1968 ... CAP-1
Earlier sketch in CA 9-10
Smith, Ronald L(ande) 1952- ... CANR-36
Earlier sketch in CA 110
Smith, Rosamond
See Oates, Joyce Carol
Smith, Rosemary 1942- ... 150
Smith, Rosie 1954- ... 139
Smith, Roswell 1829-1892 ... DLB 79
Smith, Rowland (James) 1938- ... CANR-43
Earlier sketch in CA 45-48
Smith, Roy C(yrus) 1896- ... 124
Smith, Roy H(armon) III 1936- ... 25-28R
Smith, Russell E. 1932- ... 77-80
Smith, Russell F. W. 1915(?)-1975 Obituary .. 61-64
Smith, Ruth Leslie 1902- ... CAP-2
Earlier sketch in CA 29-32
See also SATA 2
Smith, Ruth Schluchter 1917- ... CANR-26
Earlier sketches in CA 69-72, CANR-11
Smith, S(idney) G(erald) Denis 1932- ... 103
Smith, Sally Bedell 1948- ... 140
Smith, Sally Liberman 1929- ... CANR-11
Earlier sketch in CA 21-24R
Smith, Sam(uel Frederic Houston) 1937- ... 73-76
Smith, Sam 1948- ... 141
Smith, Samantha 1972-1985 Obituary ... 117
See also SATA-Obit 45
Smith, Samuel 1904- ... CANR-11
Earlier sketch in CA 29-32R
Smith, Samuel Harrison 1772-1845 ... DLB 43
Smith, Samuel Stanhope 1751-1819 ... DLB 37
Smith, Sandra 1940- ... 122
Smith, Sandra Lee 1945- ... 142
See also SATA 75
Smith, Sarah 1832-1911 Brief entry ... 112
See also Stretton, Hesba
See also DLB 190
Smith, Sarah (Winthrop) 1947- ... 147
Smith, Sarah Pogson 1774-1870 ... DLB 200
Smith, Sarah Stafford
See Smith, Dorothy Stafford
Smith, Scott 1965(?)- ... 145
Smith, Scottie
See Smith, Frances Scott Fitzgerald Lanahan
Smith, Scottie Fitzgerald
See Smith, Frances Scott Fitzgerald Lanahan
Smith, Seba 1792-1868 ... DLB 1, 11
Smith, Sharon 1947- ... 77-80
See also SATA 82
Smith, Sheila Kaye
See Kaye-Smith, Sheila
Smith, Shelley
See Bodington, Nancy H(ermione)
and Shelley, Dolores
and Smith, Sandra
Smith, Sherry L. 1951- ... 133
Smith, Sherwin 1924(?)-1985 Obituary ... 116
Smith, Sherwood 1951- ... 149
See also SATA 82
Smith, Shirley M(ae) 1923- ... CANR-42
Earlier sketches in CA 53-56, CANR-4
Smith, Stan(ley William) 1943- ... 120
Smith, Stan(ley Roger) 1946- ... 85-88
Smith, Stanley H. 1920- ... 138
Smith, Stephen Murray
See Murray-Smith, Stephen
Smith, Steve(n R.) 1947- ... 118
Smith, Steven A(lbert) 1939- ... 57-60
Smith, Steven G(arry) 1953- ... 139
Smith, Steven Phillip 1943- ... CANR-10
Earlier sketch in CA 57-60
Smith, Stevie
See Smith, Florence Margaret
See also CLC 3, 8, 25, 44
See also DLB 20
See also PC 12
Smith, Susan Carlton 1923- ... SATA 12
Smith, Susan M. 1942- ... 137
Smith, Susan Mathias 1950- ... 114
See also SATA 43
See also SATA-Brief 35
Smith, Susan Vernon 1950- ... CANR-19
Earlier sketch in CA 102
See also Mendonca, Susan
See also SATA 48
Smith, Susy 1911- ... CANR-6
Earlier sketch in CA 5-8R
Smith, Sydney 1771-1845 ... DLB 107
Smith, Sydney Goodsir 1915-1975 ... 101
Obituary ... 57-60
See also DLB 27
Smith, T(ed) C. 1915- ... 49-52
Smith, T(homas) E(dward) 1916- ... 13-16R
Smith, T(homas) Lynn 1903- ... CANR-42
Earlier sketch in CA 5-8R
Smith, Talbot 1899- ... CAP-1
Earlier sketch in CA 11-12
Smith, Terence (Fitzgerald) 1938- ... 73-76
Smith, Terrence L(ore) 1942-1988 Obituary ... 127
Smith, Terri McFerrin 1954- ... 129
Smith, Thomas 1513-1577 ... DLB 132
Smith, Thomas B(ell) 1923- ... 122
Smith, Thomas G. 1945- ... 123
Smith, Thomas Malcolm 1921- Brief entry ... 106
Smith, Thorne 1893-1934 ... 162
Smith, Tilman R(ay) 1903- ... 113
Smith, Timothy Dudley
See Dudley-Smith, Timothy
Smith, Timothy L(awrence) 1924- ... 116
Smith, Timothy Wilson
See Wilson-Smith, Timothy
Smith, Toby 1946- ... CANR-43
Earlier sketch in CA 119
Smith, Tony
See Smith, Anthony Peter
Smith, Tony ... 93-96
Smith, Ursula 1934- ... SATA 54
Smith, V(incent) Kerry 1945- ... 111
Smith, Varrel Lavere 1925- ... 29-32R
Smith, Verla Lee 1927(?)-1982 Obituary ... 106
Smith, Vernon Lomax 1927- ... CANR-6
Earlier sketch in CA 1-4R
Smith, Vesta (Henderson) 1933- ... 5-8R
Smith, Vian (Crocker) 1920-1969 ... CANR-3
Earlier sketch in CA 1-4R
See also SATA 11
Smith, Victor C(lyde) 1902- ... 5-8R
Smith, Vincent E(dward)
1915-1972 Obituary ... 33-36R
Smith, Virginia Carlson 1944- ... 49-52
Smith, Virginia Masterman
See Masterman-Smith, Virginia
Smith, Vivian (Brian) 1933- ... CANR-23
Earlier sketches in CA 61-64, CANR-8
Smith, Vivian Bickford
See Bickford-Smith, Vivian
Smith, W(illiam) David 1928- ... 77-80
Smith, W. Eugene 1918(?)-1978 Obituary ... 81-84
Smith, W(illiam) Eugene 1918-1978 ... 142
Smith, Walter W(ellesley) 1905-1982 ... CANR-62
Obituary ... 105
Earlier sketches in CA 77-80, CANR-36
See also Smith, Red
Smith, Wanda VanHoy 1926- ... 133
See also SATA 65
Smith, Ward
See Goldsmith, Howard
Smith, Warren L(ounsbury) 1914-1972 ... CAP-2
Earlier sketch in CA 21-22
Smith, Warren Sylvester 1912- ... 21-24R
Smith, Warren T(homas) 1923-1986 ... 117
Obituary ... 119
Smith, Webster
See Coleman, Clayton W(ebster)
Smith, Wendell 1914-1972 Obituary ... 104
See also DLB 171
Smith, Wendell I(rving) 1921- ... 13-16R
Smith, Wendy 1956- ... 138
Smith, Wesley D(ale) 1930- Brief entry ... 111
Smith, Wesley E. 1938- ... 29-32R
Smith, Wesley J. 1949- ... 160
Smith, Whitney, Jr. 1940- ... 97-100
Smith, Wilbur (Addison) 1933- ... CANR-66
Earlier sketches in CA 13-16R, CANR-7, 46
See also CLC 33
See also MTCW 1
Smith, Wilbur M(oorehead) ... 17-20R
Smith, Wilda M(axine) 1924- ... 137
Smith, Wilford E(mery) 1916- ... 49-52
Smith, Wilfred Cantwell 1916- ... CANR-7
Earlier sketch in CA 13-16R
Smith, Wilfred R(obert) 1915- ... 13-16R
Smith, Will(ard) 1968- ... 166
Smith, Willard L(aurence) 1927- ... 5-8R
Smith, William 16th cent. - ... DLB 136
Smith, William 1727-1803 ... DLB 31
Smith, William 1728-1793 ... DLB 30
Smith, William A. 1918- ... SATA 10
Smith, William A. 1929- ... 45-48
Smith, William Allen 1904- ... 45-48
Smith, William C(harles) 1881-1972 Obituary ... 111
Smith, William Dale 1929- ... 49-52
Smith, William E(rnest) 1892- ... 5-8R
Smith, William Frank 1925- ... 103
Smith, William Gardner 1926-1974 ... 65-68
Obituary ... 53-56
See also BW 1
See also DLB 76
Smith, William Henry 1808-1872 ... DLB 159
Smith, William I. 1932- ... 29-32R
Smith, William J. 1907(?)-1986 Obituary ... 118
Smith, William Jay 1918- ... CANR-44
Earlier sketch in CA 5-8R
See also CLC 6
See also DLB 5
See also MAICYA
See also SAAS 22
See also SATA 2, 68
Smith, William Martin 1911- ... 105
Smith, William S. 1917- ... 13-16R
Smith, William Scott 1926- ... 117
Smith, William Stevenson 1907-1969 ... CAP-2
Earlier sketch in CA 21-22
Smith, (Francis) Wilson 1922- ... 81-84
Smith, Winsome 1935- ... 115
See also SATA 45
Smith, Woodrow Wilson
See Kuttner, Henry
Smith, Woodruff D(onald) 1946- ... 85-88
Smith, Z. Z.
See Westheimer, David
Smith-Ayala, Emilie 1964- ... 155
Smith Brindle, Reginald 1917- ... 89-92
Smith-Brown, Fern 1939- ... 168
Smithdas, Robert Joseph 1925- ... 17-20R
Smithells, Roger (William) 1905- ... CAP-1
Earlier sketch in CA 13-14
Smither, Elizabeth (Edwina) 1941- ... CANR-44
Earlier sketch in CA 107
Smitherman, Geneva 1940- ... 130
Smitherman, P(hilip) H(enry) 1910- ... 21-24R
Smithers, Don LeRoy 1933- ... 45-48
Smithers, Peter Henry Berry Otway 1913- .. 29-32R
Smithgall, Elizabeth
See Watts, Elizabeth (Bailey) Smithgall
Smith-Griswold, Wendy 1955- ... SATA 88
Smithies, Arthur 1907-1981 Obituary ... 104
Smithies, Edward (Draper) 1941- ... 132
Smithies, Richard H(ugo) R(ipman) 1936- ... 21-24R
Smith-Rex, Susan J. 1950- ... 159
See also SATA 94
Smithsen, Richard
See Pellowski, Michael (Joseph)
Smithson, Alison (Margaret) 1928- ... CANR-5
Earlier sketch in CA 25-28R
Smithson, Norman 1931- ... 33-36R
Smithson, Peter (Denham) 1923- ... CANR-5
Earlier sketch in CA 53-56
Smithson, Rulon N(ephi) 1927- ... 45-48
Smithyman, (William) Kendrick 1922- ... 101
Smits, Teo
See Smits, Theodore R(ichard)
Smits, Theodore R(ichard) 1905- ... 77-80
See also SATA 45
See also SATA-Brief 28
Smitten, Jeffrey Roger 1941- ... 105
Smitten, Richard 1940- ... 136
Smoke, Jim ... 109
Smoke, Richard 1944- ... CANR-10
Earlier sketch in CA 65-68
Smolansky, Oles M. 1930- ... CANR-1
Earlier sketch in CA 45-48
Smolar, Boris (Ber) 1897-1986 ... 41-44R
Obituary ... 118
Smolens, John (Harrison), (Jr.) 1949- ... 125
Smolich, Yurik K. 1899(?)-1976 Obituary ... 69-72
Smolin, C. Roger 1948- ... 110
Smolinski, Dick 1932- ... SATA 86
Smoll, Frank L(ouis) 1941- ... 115
Smolla, Rodney A(lan) 1953- ... 121
Smoller, Bruce M. 1944- ... 113
Smoller, Sanford J(erome) 1937- ... 57-60
Smollett, Tobias (George) 1721-1771 ... CDBLB 1660-1789
See also DLB 39, 104
Smoluchowski, Louise 1922- ... 126
Smoodin, Roberta 1952- ... 147
Smooha, Sammy 1941- ... 101
Smoot, Dan 1913- ... CANR-1
Earlier sketch in CA 1-4R
Smothers, Ethel Footman 1944- ... 143
See also SATA 76
Smothers, Frank A(lbert) 1901-1981 Obituary .. 104
Smout, T(homas) C(hristopher) 1933- ... CANR-9
Earlier sketch in CA 21-24R
Smucker, Barbara (Claassen) 1915- ... CANR-23
Earlier sketch in CA 106
See also CLR 10
See also JRDA
See also MAICYA
See also SAAS 11
See also SATA 29, 76
Smucker, Donovan E(bersole) 1915- ... 149
Smucker, Leonard 1928- ... 21-24R
Smullyan, Arthur Francis 1912- ... 1-4R
Smullyan, Raymond
See Smullyan, Raymond M(errill)
Smullyan, Raymond M(errill) 1919- ... 125
Brief entry ... 120
Interview in ... 125
Smurl, James F(redrick) 1934- ... 45-48
Smurr, John Welling 1922- ... 1-4R
Smurthwaite, Ronald 1918-1975 ... CAP-2
Earlier sketch in CA 21-22
Smyer, Richard 1935- ... 102
Smykay, Edward W(alter) 1924- ... CANR-12
Earlier sketch in CA 17-20R
Smylie, James H(utchinson) 1925- ... CANR-14
Earlier sketch in CA 37-40R
Smylie, Mark A. 1954- ... 111
Smyllie, J. S.
See Smellie, Jim
Smyrl, Frank H(erbert) 1938- ... 113
Smyser, Adam A(lbert) 1920- ... 77-80
Smyser, H(amilton) M(artin) 1901- ... CAP-1
Earlier sketch in CA 13-16
Smyser, Jane Worthington 1914-1975 ... 65-68
Obituary ... 61-64
Smyth, Alice M.
See Hadfield, Alice M(ary)
Smyth, David 1929- ... CANR-12
Earlier sketch in CA 61-64
Smyth, H. D.
See Smyth, Henry DeWolf
Smyth, H(arriet) Rucker (Crowell) 1926- ... 1-4R
Smyth, Henry DeWolf 1898-1986 Obituary ... 120
Smyth, Howard McGaw 1901-1975 Obituary . 61-64
Smyth, Jacqui (Marie) 1960- ... 124
Smyth, John (George) 1893-1983 ... CANR-11
Obituary ... 109
Earlier sketch in CA 61-64
Smyth, Paul 1944- ... CANR-8
Earlier sketch in CA 61-64
Smyth, R(obert) L(eslie) 1922- ... CANR-10
Earlier sketch in CA 9-12R

Smyth, William J. 1949- ... 135
Smythe, Colin 1942- ... CANR-16
Earlier sketch in CA 97-100
Smythe, Daniel Webster 1908- ... 13-16R
Smythe, David Mynders 1915- ... 1-4R
Smythe, Donald 1927- ... 41-44R
Smythe, Francis Sydney 1900-1949 ... DLB 195
Smythe, Hugh H(eyne) 1913-1977 ... 9-12R
Obituary ... 69-72
Smythe, Mabel M(urphy) 1918- ... 37-40R
Smythe, Reginald 1918(?)- ... AITN 1
Smythe, Ted Curtis 1932- ... 101
Smythies, J(ohn) R(aymond) 1922- ... 37-40R
Snadowsky, Alvin M. 1938- ... 61-64
Snailham, (George) Richard 1930- ... 37-40R
Snaith, Norman Henry 1898-1982 Obituary ... 106
Snaith, William Theodore 1908-1974 ... 110
Obituary ... 106
Snape, H(enry) Currie 1902- ... 9-12R
Snape, R(ichard) H(al) 1936- ... 29-32R
Snapes, Joan 1925- ... 107
Snavely, Adam A. 1930- ... 25-28R
Snavely, Ellen Bartow 1910- ... CAP-2
Earlier sketch in CA 21-22
Snavely, Guy Everett 1881-1974 ... 5-8R
Obituary ... 49-52
Snavely, Tipton Ray 1890- ... 17-20R
Snavely, William P(ennington) 1920- ... 17-20R
Snead, Rodman Eldredge 1931- ... 73-76
Snead, Sam(uel Jackson) 1912- Brief entry ... 114
Snedeker, Bonnie 1947- ... 119
Snedeker, Caroline Dale (Parke) 1871-1956 .. YABC 2
Sneed, Joseph Donald 1938- ... 49-52
Sneed, Joseph Tyree 1920- ... 21-24R
Sneider, Vern(on) John 1916-1981 ... CANR-13
Obituary ... 103
Earlier sketch in CA 5-8R
Snell, Bruno 1896- ... CAP-1
Earlier sketch in CA 13-16
Snell, Daniel C. 1947- ... 166
Snell, David 1936- ... 77-80
Snell, Foster Dee 1898-1980 Obituary ... 108
Snell, Frank 1920- ... 1-4R
Snell, George Davis 1903-1996 ... 106
Obituary ... 152
Snell, John Leslie, Jr. 1923-1972 ... CANR-3
Obituary ... 33-36R
Earlier sketch in CA 5-8R
Snell, John Nicholas Blashford
See Blashford-Snell, John (Nicholas)
Snell, Michael 1945- ... 140
Snell, Nigel (Edward Creagh) 1936- ... 111
See also SATA 57
See also SATA-Brief 40
Snell, Tee Loftin 1922- ... 105
Sneller, Delwyn Lee 1945- ... 111
Snellgrove, David L(lewellyn) 1920- ... 147
Brief entry ... 115
Snellgrove, L(aurence) E(rnest) 1928- ... CANR-23
Earlier sketches in CA 9-12R, CANR-3
See also SATA 53
Snellgrove, Louis 1928- ... 45-48
Snelling, Dennis (Wayne) 1958- ... 150
See also SATA 84
Snelling, Lois ... 5-8R
Snelling, O(swald) F(rederick) 1916- ... 17-20R
Snelling, W(illiam) Rodman 1931- ... 93-96
Snelling, William Joseph 1804-1848 ... DLB 202
Snellings, Rolland
See Toure, Askia Muhammad Abu Bakr el
Snepp, Frank (Warren III) 1943- ... 105
Interview in ... 105
Snetsinger, John (Goodall) 1941- ... 73-76
Snetsinger, Robert 1928- ... 107
Sneve, Virginia Driving Hawk 1933- ... CANR-68
Earlier sketches in CA 49-52, CANR-3
See also CLR 2
See also SATA 8, 95
Snider, Delbert A(rthur) 1914- ... 1-4R
Snider, Jim ... 141
Snider, Lewis W. ... 119
Sniderman, Florence (Lama) 1915- ... 33-36R
Snipes, Wilson Currin 1924- ... 29-32R
Snively, Susan 1945- ... 117
Snively, W(illiam) D(aniel), Jr. 1911- ... 29-32R
Snoddy, Theo 1922- ... 168
Snodgrass, A(nthony) M(cElrea) 1934- ... CANR-10
Earlier sketch in CA 21-24R
Snodgrass, Donald R(ay) 1935- ... 112
Snodgrass, Joan Gay 1934- ... 77-80
Snodgrass, Jon 1941- ... 113
Snodgrass, Mary Ellen 1944- ... 142
See also SATA 75
Snodgrass, Milton M(oore) 1931- ... 29-32R
Snodgrass, Quentin Curtius
See Clemens, Samuel Langhorne
Snodgrass, Thomas Jefferson
See Clemens, Samuel Langhorne
Snodgrass, W(illiam) D(e Witt) 1926- ... CANR-65
Earlier sketches in CA 1-4R, CANR-6, 36
See also CLC 2, 6, 10, 18, 68
See also DAM POET
See also DLB 5
See also MTCW 1
Snoek, J(aap) Diedrick 1931- ... 49-52
Snoke, Albert W(aldo) 1907- ... 125
Snook, Barbara (Lillian) 1913-1976 ... 109
See also SATA 34
Snook, I(van) A(ugustine) 1933- ... CANR-14
Earlier sketch in CA 77-80
Snook, Jean M(cGregor) 1952- ... 150
Snook, John B. 1927- ... 106
Snortum, Niel K(lendenon) 1928- ... 21-24R
Snow, C(harles) P(ercy) 1905-1980 ... CANR-28
Obituary ... 101
Earlier sketch in CA 5-8R
See also CDBLB 1945-1960
See also CLC 1, 4, 6, 9, 13, 19
See also DAM NOV
See also DLB 15, 77
See also DLBD 17
See also MTCW 1
Snow, Charles Ernest 1910-1967 Obituary ... 116
Snow, D(avid) W(illiam) 1924- ... 65-68
Snow, Davis W. 1913(?)-1975 Obituary ... 61-64
Snow, Donald 1951- ... 138
Snow, Donald Clifford 1917- ... 85-88
See also SATA 16
Snow, Donald M(erritt) 1943- ... CANR-52
Earlier sketches in CA 106, CANR-27
Snow, Dorothea J(ohnston) 1909- ... CANR-27
Earlier sketches in CA 1-4R, CANR-3
See also SATA 9
Snow, Dorothy Mary Barter 1897- ... CAP-1
Earlier sketch in CA 13-14
Snow, Edgar Parks 1905-1972 ... CANR-38
Obituary ... 33-36R
Earlier sketch in CA 81-84
Snow, Edward Rowe 1902-1982 ... CANR-6
Obituary ... 106
Earlier sketch in CA 9-12R
Snow, Frances Compton
See Adams, Henry (Brooks)
Snow, George (D'Oyly) 1903- ... 5-8R
Snow, Helen Foster 1907-1997 ... CANR-46
Obituary ... 156
Earlier sketch in CA 57-60
Snow, John Hall 1924- ... 37-40R
Snow, Karen (a pseudonym) 1923- ... 120
Snow, Kathleen 1944- ... 81-84
Snow, Keith Ronald 1943- ... 110
Snow, Lois Wheeler 1920- ... 57-60
Snow, Lucy
See Aubert, Rosemary
Snow, Peter G(ordon) 1933- ... 21-24R
Snow, Philip (Albert) 1915- ... CANR-54
Earlier sketches in CA 9-12R, CANR-28
Snow, Philip 1952- ... 130
Snow, Richard F(olger) 1947- ... 106
See also SATA 52
See also SATA-Brief 37
Snow, Roslyn 1936- ... CANR-9
Earlier sketch in CA 21-24R
Snow, Russell E(lwin) 1938- ... 65-68
Snow, Sinclair 1909-1972 ... CAP-2
Earlier sketch in CA 25-28
Snow, Vernon F. 1924- ... 37-40R
Snow, (Charles) Wilbert 1884-1977 ... 9-12R
Obituary ... 73-76
Snow, William George Sinclair 1908- ... 5-8R
Snowden, Frank M(artin), Jr. 1911- ... 41-44R
Snowdon
See Armstrong-Jones, Antony (Charles Robert)
Snowman, Daniel 1938- ... CANR-33
Earlier sketches in CA 53-56, CANR-4
Snukal, Robert (Martin) 1942- ... 45-48
Snyder, Anne 1922- ... CANR-14
Earlier sketch in CA 37-40R
See also SATA 4
Snyder, Bernadette McCarver 1930- ... CANR-37
Earlier sketch in CA 115
See also SATA 97
Snyder, Carl Dean 1921- Brief entry ... 113
Snyder, Carol 1941- ... 85-88
See also SATA 35
Snyder, Cecil K., Jr. 1927- ... 29-32R
Snyder, Charles M. 1909- ... 49-52
Snyder, Charles Royce 1924- ... 105
Snyder, Chuck 1933- ... 122
Snyder, Don J. 1950- ... 126
Snyder, E(ugene) V(incent) 1943- ... 41-44R
Snyder, Eldon E. 1930- ... 49-52
Snyder, Eloise C(olleen) 1928- ... 29-32R
Snyder, Francis Gregory 1942- ... CANR-22
Earlier sketches in CA 17-20R, CANR-7
Snyder, Fred A. 1931- ... 37-40R
Snyder, Gary (Sherman) 1930- ... CANR-60
Earlier sketches in CA 17-20R, CANR-30
See also CLC 1, 2, 5, 9, 32
See also DAM POET
See also DLB 5, 16, 165
See also PC 21
Snyder, George Sergeant 1952- ... 122
Snyder, Gerald S(eymour) 1933- ... CANR-12
Earlier sketch in CA 61-64
See also SATA 48
See also SATA-Brief 34
Snyder, Glenn Herald 1924- ... CANR-18
Earlier sketch in CA 1-4R
Snyder, Graydon F. 1930- ... 13-16R
Snyder, Guy (Eugene, Jr.) 1951- ... 57-60
Snyder, Henry Leonard 1929- ... 41-44R
Snyder, Howard A(lbert) 1940- ... CANR-34
Earlier sketch in CA 113
Snyder, James E(dward) 1928-1990 ... 123
Obituary ... 132
Brief entry ... 117
Snyder, Jane McIntosh 1943- ... 130
Snyder, Jerome 1916-1976 Obituary ... 65-68
See also SATA-Obit 20
Snyder, Joan 1943- ... 41-44R
Snyder, John P(arr) 1926-1997 ... CANR-31
Obituary ... 157
Earlier sketch in CA 41-44R
Snyder, John William 1924- ... 1-4R
Snyder, Keith 1966- ... 164
Snyder, Laura (Lillie) 1940- ... 120
Snyder, Leslie 1945- ... 114
Snyder, Louis L(eo) 1907-1993 ... CANR-34
Obituary ... 143
Earlier sketches in CA 1-4R, CANR-2
Snyder, Marilyn 1936- ... 120
Snyder, Midori 1954- ... 167
Snyder, (Donald) Paul 1933- ... CANR-1
Earlier sketch in CA 45-48
Snyder, Rachel 1924- ... 9-12R
Snyder, Richard C(arlton) 1916-1997 ... 61-64
Obituary ... 163
Snyder, Robert Edward 1943- ... CANR-46
Earlier sketch in CA 120
Snyder, Robert L. 1928- ... 25-28R
Snyder, Solomon H(albert) 1938- ... CANR-14
Earlier sketch in CA 37-40R
Snyder, Susan 1934- ... 93-96
Snyder, Tom 1936- ... 121
Brief entry ... 109
Interview in ... 121
Snyder, William 1951- ... 104
Snyder, William P(aul) 1928- ... 13-16R
Snyder, William S(tover) 1927- ... 123
Brief entry ... 118
Snyder, Zilpha Keatley 1927- ... CANR-38
Earlier sketch in CA 9-12R
See also AAYA 15
See also CLC 17
See also CLR 31
See also JRDA
See also MAICYA
See also SAAS 2
See also SATA 1, 28, 75
Snyderman, Reuven K. 1922- ... 29-32R
See also SATA 5
Soames, Jane
See Nickerson, Jane Soames (Bon)
Soames, Mary 1922- ... 111
Soares, Anthony T(homas) 1923- ... 45-48
Soares, Bernardo
See Pessoa, Fernando (Antonio Nogueira)
Sobacos, Juan, Jr.
See Mallett, Daryl F(urumi)
Sobczak, A(ndrew) J(ames) 1962- ... 163
Sobel, B. Z. 1933- ... 77-80
Sobel, Bernard 1887-1964 ... 5-8R
Sobel, Brian M. 1954- ... 107
Sobel, Dava 1947- ... 154
Sobel, Harold W(illiam) 1933- ... 61-64
Sobel, Irwin Philip 1901-1991 ... 45-48
Obituary ... 134
Sobel, Lester A(lbert) 1919- ... CANR-9
Earlier sketch in CA 21-24R
Sobel, Michael I. 1939- ... 128
Sobel, Robert 1931- ... CANR-31
Earlier sketches in CA 5-8R, CANR-8
Sobell, Morton 1917- ... 53-56
Sober, Elliott (Reuben) 1948- ... 132
Soberman, Richard M. 1937- ... CANR-10
Earlier sketch in CA 25-28R
Sobh, A.
See Shamlu, Ahmad
Sobieski, Carol (O'Brien) 1939-1990 ... 129
Obituary ... 132
Brief entry ... 124
Interview in ... 129
Sobiloff, Hy(man J.) 1912-1970 Obituary ... 29-32R
See also DLB 48
Sobin, A. G.
See Sobin, Anthony
Sobin, Anthony 1944- ... 116
Sobin, Gustaf 1935- ... CANR-38
Earlier sketch in CA 115
Sobin, Julian M(elvin) 1920- ... 132
Soble, Alan 1947- ... 122
Soble, Jennie
See Cavin, Ruth (Brodie)
Sobol, Donald J. 1924- ... CANR-38
Earlier sketches in CA 1-4R, CANR-1, 18
See also CLR 4
See also JRDA
See also MAICYA
See also SATA 1, 31, 73
Sobol, Harriet Langsam 1936- ... CANR-8
Earlier sketch in CA 61-64
See also SATA 47
See also SATA-Brief 34
Sobol, Joshua ... CLC 60
Sobol, Louis 1896-1986 ... CAP-2
Obituary ... 118
Earlier sketch in CA 29-32
Sobol, Rose 1931- ... 101
See also SATA 76
Sobolev, Leonid (Sergeevich)
1898-1971 Obituary ... 29-32R
Sobosan, Jeffrey G. 1946- ... CANR-52
Earlier sketch in CA 126
Sobott-Mogwe, Gaele 1956- ... 152
See also SATA 97
Soboul, Albert Marius 1914-1982 Obituary ... 107
Sobre, Judith Berg 1941- ... 139
Sobrino, Josephine 1915- ... CANR-36
Earlier sketch in CA 45-48
Soby, James Thrall 1906-1979 ... 103
Socarides, Charles W(illiam) 1922- Brief entry .. 118
Sochen, June 1937- ... CANR-43
Earlier sketches in CA 41-44R, CANR-14
Sockman, Ralph W(ashington) 1889-1970 ... 5-8R
Obituary ... 89-92
Socolofsky, Homer E(dward) 1922- ... CANR-1
Earlier sketch in CA 1-4R
Socolow, Robert H(arry) 1937- ... 37-40R
Sodaro, Craig 1948- ... CANR-40
Earlier sketches in CA 101, CANR-18
Soddy, Frederick 1877-1956 ... 167
Soderberg, Hjalmar 1869-1941 ... TCLC 39
Soderberg, Paul Stephen 1949- ... CANR-19
Earlier sketch in CA 103
Soderberg, Percy Measday 1901-1969 ... CAP-1
Earlier sketch in CA 9-10
Sodergran, Edith (Irene)
See Soedergran, Edith (Irene)
Soderholm, Marjorie Elaine 1923- ... 13-16R
Soderlind, Arthur E(dwin) 1920- ... 69-72
See also SATA 14
Soderlund, Jean Ruth 1947- ... 127
Soderstrom, Edward Jonathan 1954- ... CANR-30
Earlier sketch in CA 111
Sodowsky, Roland (E.) 1938- ... 134
Soedergran, Edith (Irene) 1892-1923 ... TCLC 31
Soedjatmoko 1922-1989 Obituary ... 130
Soekarno
See Sukarno, (Ahmed)
Soelle, Dorothee 1929- ... CANR-11
Earlier sketch in CA 69-72
Soentpiet, Chris K. 1970- ... SATA 97
Soerensen, Svend Otto 1916- ... 132
See also SATA 67
Soeur Sourire
See Deckers, Jeanine
Sofen, Edward 1919- ... 9-12R
Sofer, Barbara 1949- ... 163
Sofer, Cyril 1921- ... 5-8R
Sofer, Rachel q
See Sofer, Barbara
Soffer, Reba N(usbaum) 1934- ... 85-88
Soffici, Ardengo 1879-1964 ... DLB 114
Sofola, 'Zulu 1938- ... 163
See also DLB 157
Softly, Barbara Frewin 1924- ... CANR-2
Earlier sketch in CA 5-8R
See also SATA 12
Softly, Edgar
See Lovecraft, H(oward) P(hillips)
Softly, Edward
See Lovecraft, H(oward) P(hillips)
Soglow, Otto 1900-1975 ... 93-96
Obituary ... 57-60
See also SATA-Obit 30
Sogolow, Rosalie (K.) 1939- ... 153
Sohl, Frederic J(ohn) 1916- ... 21-24R
See also SATA 10
Sohl, Jerry 1913- ... CANR-15
Earlier sketch in CA 81-84
Sohl, Robert (Allen) 1941- ... 103
Sohn, David A. 1929- ... CANR-6
Earlier sketch in CA 9-12R
Sohn, Louis B(runo) 1914- ... 101
Sokel, Walter H(erbert) 1917- ... CANR-6
Earlier sketch in CA 5-8R
Sokil, Ya.
See Sokolyszyn, Aleksander
Sokol, Anthony E. 1897- ... 37-40R
Sokol, Bill
See Sokol, William
Sokol, David M(artin) 1942- ... CANR-16
Earlier sketches in CA 49-52, CANR-1
Sokol, William 1923- ... SATA 37
Sokoloff, Alice Hunt 1912- ... 25-28R
Sokoloff, Boris Theodore 1889- ... 89-92
Sokoloff, Kiril 1947- ... 108
Sokoloff, Naomi B. 1953- ... 144
Sokoloff, Natalie B.
See Scott, Natalie Anderson
Sokoloff, Natalie J(ean) 1944- ... CANR-44
Earlier sketch in CA 113
Sokolov, Alexander V(sevolodovich) 1943- ... 73-76
Sokolov, Kirill 1930- ... SATA 34
Sokolov, Raymond 1941- ... 85-88
See also CLC 7
Sokolov, Sasha
See Sokolov, Alexander V(sevolodovich)
Sokolov, Valentin 1925(?)-1984 Obituary ... 114
Sokolow, Jayme Aaron 1946- ... 113
Sokolowski, Robert (Stanley) 1934- ... 89-92
Sokolski, Alan 1931- ... 13-16R
Sokolsky, George Ephraim
1893-1962 Obituary ... 89-92
Sokolyszyn, Aleksander 1914- ... 132
Solano, Solita 1888-1975 ... 117
Obituary ... 61-64
See also DLB 4
Solaun, Mauricio 1935- ... 138
Brief entry ... 106
Solberg, Carl 1915- ... CANR-12
Earlier sketch in CA 73-76
Solberg, Carl Edward 1940- ... 61-64
Solberg, Gunard 1932- ... 29-32R
Solberg, Richard W. 1917- ... CANR-3
Earlier sketch in CA 9-12R
Solberg, S(ammy) E(dward) 1930- ... 21-24R
Solberg, Winton U(dell) 1922- ... 41-44R
Solbert, Romaine G. 1925- ... 29-32R
See also SATA 2
Solbert, Ronni
See Solbert, Romaine G.
Solbrig, Dorothy J. 1945- ... 146
Solbrig, Otto T(homas) 1930- ... CANR-9
Earlier sketch in CA 21-24R
Soldati, Mario 1906- ... 108
See also DLB 177
Soldo, John J(oseph) 1945- ... CANR-14
Earlier sketch in CA 77-80
Soldofsky, Robert Melvin 1920- ... CANR-1
Earlier sketch in CA 1-4R
Sole, Carlos A(lberto) 1938- ... 53-56
Solecki, Ralph S(tefan) 1917- Brief entry ... 109
Solem, (George) Alan 1931- ... 57-60
Solensten, John M(artin) 1929- ... CANR-28
Earlier sketch in CA 110
Soleri, Paolo 1919- ... 106
Soley, Lawrence C(harles) 1949- ... 150

Soliday, Gerald Lyman 1939- CANR-12
Earlier sketch in CA 61-64
Solinger, Dorothy J(ane) 1945- CANR-66
Earlier sketches in CA 113, CANR-32
Soljan, Antun 1932-1993 DLB 181
Solkoff, Joel 1947- 133
Soll, Ivan 1938- 29-32R
Sollberger, Edmond (Albert)
1920-1989 Obituary 129
Solle, Dorothee
See Soelle, Dorothee
Sollers, Philippe 1936- DLB 83
Solley, Charles Marion, Jr. 1925- 1-4R
Sollogub, Vladimir Aleksandrovich 1813-1882 DLB 198
Sollors, Werner 1943- CANR-45
Earlier sketch in CA 119
Sollosy, Judith 1946- 149
Solman, Paul 1944- 148
Brief entry 119
Solmi, Sergio 1899-1981 DLB 114
Solmon, Lewis C(alvin) 1942- 41-44R
Solmsen, Friedrich (Rudolf Heinrich)
1904-1989 53-56
Obituary 127
Solmssen, Arthur R(obert) G(eorge) 1928- 143
Solnick, Bruce B. 1933- 29-32R
Solnit, Albert J. 1919- 103
Solo, Jay
See Ellison, Harlan (Jay)
Solo, Robert A(lexander) 1916- CANR-37
Earlier sketches in CA 45-48, CANR-1, 17
Sologub, Fyodor
See Teternikov, Fyodor Kuzmich
See also TCLC 9
Solomon, Andrew 1963- 140
Solomon, Barbara H. 1936- CANR-42
Earlier sketches in CA 73-76, CANR-13
Solomon, Barbara Probst 1928- 5-8R
Solomon, Barry D. 1955- 141
Solomon, Bernard S(imon) 1924- 61-64
Solomon, Brad 1945- 101
Solomon, (Neal) Brad(ley) 1945- 103
Solomon, Carl 1928- 21-24R
See also DLB 16
Solomon, Charles J. 1906(?)-1975 Obituary 61-64
Solomon, Daniel 1933- 9-12R
Solomon, David J. 1925- 17-20R
Solomon, Deborah 1957- 127
Solomon, Dorothy Allred 1949- 119
Solomon, Esther Riva 1921-1969 5-8R
Obituary 135
Solomon, Ezra 1920- CANR-17
Earlier sketch in CA 85-88
Solomon, Flora 1895(?)-1984 Obituary 114
Solomon, George 1940- 45-48
Solomon, Goody L(ove) 57-60
Solomon, Henry A. 1937- 123
Solomon, Irving I. 1922- CANR-16
Earlier sketch in CA 21-24R
Solomon, Janis Little 1938- CANR-15
Earlier sketch in CA 41-44R
Solomon, Jay 1960- 135
Solomon, Joan 1930- CANR-28
Earlier sketch in CA 109
See also SATA 51
See also SATA-Brief 40
Solomon, Kenneth Ira 1942- 49-52
Solomon, Leonard 1930- 45-48
Solomon, Margaret C(laire) 1918- 29-32R
Solomon, Marion F. 1935- 146
Solomon, Maynard (Elliott) 1930- 41-44R
Solomon, Michael M(aurice) 1909- 97-100
Solomon, Morris J. 1919- 13-16R
Solomon, Neil 1932- CANR-27
Earlier sketch in CA 65-68
Solomon, Norman 1951- CANR-9
Earlier sketch in CA 57-60
Solomon, Richard H(arvey) 1937- 103
Solomon, Robert 1921- 108
Solomon, Robert C(harles) 1942- CANR-32
Earlier sketches in CA 41-44R, CANR-15
Solomon, Ruth (Freeman) 1908- 21-24R
Solomon, Samuel 1904-1988 53-56
Obituary 126
Solomon, Shirl 1928- 93-96
Solomon, Stanley J. 1937- 41-44R
Solomon, Stephen D(avid) 1950- 69-72
Solomon, Steve 1942- 117
Solomon, Susan 1956- 158
Solomons, David 1912-1995 13-16R
Obituary 148
Solomons, Ikey Esquir
See Thackeray, William Makepeace
Solon, Gregory Kent 1923(?)-1985 Obituary 117
Solonevich, George 1915- SATA 15
Solorzano, Carlos 1922- 153
See also HW
Solot, Mary Lynn 1939- 49-52
See also SATA 12
Solotaroff, Robert David 1937- 57-60
Solotaroff, Ted
See Solotaroff, Theodore
See also CAAS 2
Solotaroff, Theodore 1928- CANR-8
Earlier sketch in CA 9-12R
Interview in CANR-8
See also Solotaroff, Ted
Soloukhin, Vladimir (Alekseevich) 1924- Brief entry 111
Solow, Martin 1920-1991 81-84
Obituary 135
Soloway, Richard Allen 1934- 118
Solsona, S.
See Schwartz, Stephen (Alfred)
Solt, Mary Ellen (Bottom) 1920- 17-20R
Soltau, T(heodore) Stanley 1890- 5-8R
Solter, Aletha J(auch) 1945- 166
Soltis, Andrew (Eden, Jr.) 1947- CANR-4
Earlier sketch in CA 49-52
Soltis, Andy
See Soltis, Andrew (Eden, Jr.)
Soltis, Jonas F(rancis) 1931- CANR-31
Earlier sketches in CA 37-40R, CANR-14
Soltow, James H(arold) 1924- 109
Soltow, Lee 1923- 108
Soltow, Martha-Jane 1924- 110
Solum, John 1935- 145
Solway, David 1941- 112
See also DLB 53
Solway, Diane 1958- 147
Solwoska, Mara
See French, Marilyn
Solyn, Paul 1951- 77-80
Solzhenitsyn, Aleksandr I(sayevich) 1918- CANR-65
Earlier sketches in CA 69-72, CANR-40
See also AITN 1
See also CLC 1, 2, 4, 7, 9, 10, 18, 26, 34, 78
See also DA
See also DAB
See also DAC
See also DAM MST, NOV
See also MTCW 1
See also WLC
Soma, Daniel
See Lange, Martin
Soman, Alfred 1934- CANR-36
Earlier sketch in CA 45-48
Soman, Jean Powers 1949- 122
Soman, Shirley Camper CANR-3
Earlier sketch in CA 9-12R
Some, Malidoma Patrice 1956- 145
Somekh, Emile 1915- 53-56
Somer, John (Laddie) 1936- 37-40R
Somerlott, Robert 1928- 105
See also SATA 62
Somers, Albert B(ingham) 1939- 115
Somers, Bart
See Fox, G(ardner) F(rancis)
Somers, Gerald G(eorge) 1922-1977 CANR-5
Earlier sketch in CA 13-16R
Somers, Herman Miles 1911-1991 CANR-1
Obituary 134
Earlier sketch in CA 1-4R
Somers, Jane
See Lessing, Doris (May)
Somers, Paul
See Winterton, Paul
Somers, Robert H(ough) 1929- 45-48
Somers, Suzanne 1946- 139
See also Daniels, Dorothy
Somerset, Anne 1955- 145
Somerset, FitzRoy Richard
See Raglan, FitzRoy
Somerset, Henry Hugh Arthur FitzRoy
1900-1984 Obituary 112
Somerset Fry, (Peter George Robin) Plantagenet
1931- 104
Somerville, Edith 1858-1949 DLB 135
See also TCLC 51
Somerville, (James) Hugh (Miller) 1922-1992 9-12R
Obituary 137
Somerville, James 1947- 128
Somerville, John (P. M.) 1905-1994 CANR-29
Obituary 143
Earlier sketch in CA 45-48
Somerville, (Henry) Lee 1915- 69-72
Somerville, Mollie CANR-12
Earlier sketch in CA 29-32R
Somerville, Rose M(aurer)
1908- 45-48SOMERVILLE
Somerville & Ross
See Martin, Violet Florence
and Somerville, Edith
Somerville-Large, Peter 1928- CANR-20
Earlier sketch in CA 97-100
Somit, Albert 1919- 81-84
Somkin, Fred 1924- 25-28R
Somkin, Steven 1941- 149
Sommer, Angela
See Sommer-Bodenburg, Angela
Sommer, Elyse 1929- CANR-2
Earlier sketch in CA 49-52
See also SATA 7
Sommer, Joellen 1957- 45-48
Sommer, John 1941- 29-32R
Sommer, Mark 1945- 140
Sommer, Richard J(erome) 1934- CANR-1
Earlier sketch in CA 45-48
Sommer, Robert 1929- CANR-18
Earlier sketches in CA 9-12R, CANR-3
See also SATA 12
Sommer, Scott 1951- 106
See also CLC 25
Sommer-Bodenburg, Angela 1948- 132
See also SATA 63
Sommerfeld, Ray(nard) M(atthias) 1933- CANR-28
Earlier sketch in CA 105
Sommerfeld, Richard Edwin 1928- 13-16R
Sommerfeldt, John R(obert) 1933- CANR-3
Earlier sketch in CA 49-52
Sommerfelt, Aimee 1892- 37-40R
See also SATA 5
Sommerness, Martin David 1954- 116
Sommers, Christina Hoff 153
Sommers, David
See Smith, Howard Van
Sommers, Fred(eric Tamler) 1923- 113
Sommers, Jay 1917(?)-1985 Obituary 117
Sommers, Joseph 1924-1979 CANR-29
Earlier sketch in CA 25-28R
Sommers, Lawrence M(elvin) 1919- CANR-53
Earlier sketch in CA 126
Sommers, Robert (Thomas) 1926- 151
Sommers, Tish 1914(?)-1985 Obituary 117
Sommerville, C(harles) John 1938- 137
Somorjai, Gabor Arpad 1935- 105
Somov, Orest Mikhailovich 1793-1833 DLB 198
Somtow, S. P.
See Sucharitkul, Somtow
Sondak, Norman E(dward) 1931- 112
Sondermann, Fred A. 1923- 49-52
Sonders, Scott (Alejandro) 1953- CANR-56
Earlier sketch in CA 132
Sondheim, Stephen (Joshua) 1930- CANR-68
Earlier sketches in CA 103, CANR-47
See also AAYA 11
See also CLC 30, 39
See also DAM DRAM
Sondrup, Steven P(reece) 1944- 103
Sonenberg, Maya 1960- 131
Sonenblick, Jerry 1931- 104
Sonenblum, Sidney 1924- 29-32R
Sonenscher, Michael 1947- 118
Sonero, Devi
See Pelton, Robert W(ayne)
Song, Ben (Chunho) 1937- 37-40R
Song, Cathy 1955- 154
See also DLB 169
See also PC 21
Song, C(hoan-)S(eng) 1929- 115
Songe, Alice Heloise 1914- 102
Sonkin, Robert 1911(?)-1980 Obituary 97-100
Sonn, Richard D. 144
Sonneborn, Harry L(ee) 1919- 77-80
Sonneborn, Ruth (Cantor) 1899-1974 CAP-2
Obituary 49-52
Earlier sketch in CA 21-22
See also SATA 4
See also SATA-Obit 27
Sonneborn, Tracy Morton 1905-1981 Obituary 108
Sonnenberg, Ben 1936- 139
Sonnenfeld, Barry AAYA 26
Sonnenfeld, Marion (Wilma) 1928- 37-40R
Sonnenmark, Laura A. 1958- SATA 73
Sonnenschein, Allan 1941- 133
Sonneveld, A.
See Stolk, Anthonie
Sonnichsen, C. L. 1901-1991 CANR-39
Earlier sketches in CA 1-4R, CANR-2, 17
Sonntag, Jacob 1905-1984 Obituary 113
Sono, Ayako
See Miura, Chizuko
See also DLB 182
Son of the Soil
See Fletcher, J(oseph) S(mith)
Sons, Raymond W(illiam) 1926- 136
Sonstegard, Manford Aldrich 1911- CANR-2
Earlier sketch in CA 49-52
Sonstroem, David 1936- 29-32R
Sontag, Alan 1946- 85-88
Sontag, Frederick (Earl) 1924- CANR-1
Earlier sketch in CA 1-4R
Sontag, Frederick H(erman) 1924- 81-84
Sontag, Raymond J(ames)
1897-1972 Obituary 37-40R
Sontag, Susan 1933- CANR-51
Earlier sketches in CA 17-20R, CANR-25
See also CLC 1, 2, 10, 13, 31, 105
See also DAM POP
See also DLB 2, 67
See also MTCW 1
Sontheimer, Morton 101
Sontup, Dan(iel) 1922- 1-4R
Soong, Ching-ling 1890-1981 Obituary 108
Soos, Troy 1957- 164
Soper, Alexander Coburn 1904-1993 105
Obituary 140
Soper, Donald Oliver 1903- 109
Soper, Eileen A(lice) 1905-1990(?) 9-12R
Obituary 131
Soper, Eileen Louise 1900- 103
Soper, Fred L. 1894(?)-1977 Obituary 69-72
Soper, Paul L(eon) 1906- 5-8R
Soper, Tony 1939- CANR-22
Earlier sketch in CA 105
Sopher, Sharon Isabel 1945- 101
Sophocles 496(?)B.C.-406(?)B.C. DA
See also DAB
See also DAC
See also DAM DRAM, MST
See also DC 1
See also DLB 176
See also WLCS
Sopko, Eugen 1949- SATA 58
Sopov, Aco 1923-1982 DLB 181
Sorauf, Francis Joseph 1928- 9-12R
Sorauf, Frank J.
See Sorauf, Francis Joseph
Sorden, L(eland) G(eorge) 1898- CANR-1
Earlier sketch in CA 1-4R
Sorel, Byron
See Yatron, Michael
Sorel, Edward 1929- CANR-33
Earlier sketch in CA 9-12R
See also SATA 65
See also SATA-Brief 37
Sorel, Georges 1847-1922 Brief entry 118
Sorel, Julia
See Drexler, Rosalyn
Sorel, Nancy Caldwell 1934- 37-40R
Sorel-Cameron, James (Robert) 1948- 136
Sorell, Walter 1905-1997 21-24R
Obituary 156
Sorensen, Andrew Aaron 1938- 65-68
Sorensen, Chris 1942- 107
Sorensen, Georg 1948- 145
Sorensen, Henri 1950- SATA 77
Sorensen, Jacki 1942- 110
Sorensen, Robert C(haikin) 1923- 45-48
Sorensen, Roy A. 1957- 139
Sorensen, Svend Otto
See Soerensen, Svend Otto
Sorensen, Theodore C(haikin) 1928- CANR-2
Earlier sketch in CA 45-48
Sorensen, Thomas C. 1926- 21-24R
Sorensen, Virginia 1912-1991 CANR-22
Earlier sketch in CA 13-16R, 139
See also MAICYA
See also SAAS 15
See also SATA 2
See also SATA-Obit 72
Sorensen, W. Conner 1942- 155
Sorenson, Herbert 1898- 21-24R
Sorenson, Jane 1926- SATA 63
Sorenson, Margo 1946- 161
See also SATA 96
Sorenson, Marian 1925-1968 CAP-1
Earlier sketch in CA 11-12
Sorescu, Marin 1936-1996 147
Obituary 155
Sorestad, Glen (Allan) 1937- CANR-57
Earlier sketches in CA 112, CANR-31
Sorge, Reinhard Johannes 1892-1916 DLB 118
Sorgman, Mayo 1912- 13-16R
Soria, Regina 1911- CANR-55
Earlier sketch in CA 126
Sorin, Gerald 1940- CANR-57
Earlier sketches in CA 77-80, CANR-31
Sorine, Stephanie Riva 1954- 105
Sorkin, Adam J. 1943- 143
Sorkin, Alan Lowell 1941- CANR-57
Earlier sketches in CA 41-44R, CANR-14, 31
Sorley, Lewis 1934- 117
Sorley Walker, Kathrine CANR-6
Earlier sketch in CA 5-8R
See also SATA 41
Sorokin, Boris 1922- 116
Sorokin, Elena 1894(?)-1975 Obituary 61-64
Sorokin, Pitirim A(lexandrovitch) 1889-1968 CANR-5
Obituary 25-28R
Earlier sketch in CA 5-8R
Sorrell, Alan 1904-1974 93-96
Sorrell, J(ohn) E(dward) 1954- 137
Sorrells, Dorothy C. 9-12R
Sorrells, Helen 1908- 37-40R
Sorrells, Robert T. 1932- 127
Sorrentino, Gilbert 1929- CANR-33
Earlier sketches in CA 77-80, CANR-14
Interview in CANR-14
See also CLC 3, 7, 14, 22, 40
See also DLB 5, 173
See also DLBY 80
Sorrentino, Joseph N. 1937- CANR-3
Earlier sketch in CA 49-52
See also SATA 6
Sorret, Ludovico
See Noonan, Tom
Sorrow, Barbara Head 1945- 147
Sorsby, Arnold 1900- 85-88
Sortor, June Elizabeth 1939- 61-64
See also SATA 12
Sortor, Toni
See Sortor, June Elizabeth
Sorum, Paul Clay 1943- 103
Sosa, Ernest 1940- 53-56
Sosa, Roberto 1930- 131
See also HW
Sosa de Quesada, Aristides V. 1908- 53-56
Soskice, Janet Martin 1951- 124
Soskin, V. H.
See Ellison, Virginia H(owell)
Sosna, Morton 1945- 102
Sosnick, Stephen H(oward) 1930- 45-48
Sosnow, Eric 1910-1987 Obituary 121
Sosnowski, David (J.) 1959- 159
Sossaman, Stephen 1944- 77-80
Soth, Lauren (Kephart) 1910-1998 CAP-1
Obituary 165
Earlier sketch in CA 17-18
Sotheby, William 1757-1833 DLB 93
Soto, Gary 1952- CANR-50
Brief entry 119
Earlier sketch in CA 125
Interview in 125
See also AAYA 10
See also CLC 32, 80
See also CLR 38
See also DAM MULT
See also DLB 82
See also HLC
See also HW
See also JRDA
See also SATA 80
Soto, Pedro Juan 1928- 131
Brief entry 114
See also HW
Soto, Shirlene A(nn) 1947- 131
See also HW
Sotomayor, Antonio 1902- 73-76
See also SATA 11
Sotter, Fred
See Lake, Kenneth R(obert)
Souci, Robert D. San
See San Souci, Robert D.
Soucie, Gary (Arnold) 1937- 127
Soucy, Robert J(oseph) 1933- CANR-30
Earlier sketch in CA 45-48
Soudley, Henry
See Wood, James Playsted
Soueif, Ahdaf 1950- 168

Souerwine, Andrew H(arry) 1924- CANR-19
Earlier sketch in CA 81-84
Souhami, Diana 1940- 130
Soukup, James R(udolph) 1928- 9-12R
Soule, Gardner (Bosworth) 1913- CANR-2
Earlier sketch in CA 5-8R
See also SATA 14
Soule, George (Henry, Jr.) 1887-1970 .... CAP-2
Obituary 29-32R
Earlier sketch in CA 21-22
Soule, George (Alan) 1930- 57-60
Soule, Isabel Walker
1898(?)-1972 Obituary 37-40R
Soule, Jean Conder 1919- 5-8R
See also SATA 10
Soule, Sandra W(olf) 1946- 137
Souljah, Sister 1964- 154
Soupault, Philippe 1897-1990 147
Obituary 131
Brief entry 116
See also CLC 68
Soupcoff, Murray 1943- 101
Souper, Patrick Charles 1928- 110
Sour, Robert B(andler) 1905-1985 Obituary 115
Sourian, Peter 1933- 1-4R
Souritz, Elizabeth 1923- 135
Sourkes, Theodore L(ionel) 1919- 17-20R
Sours, John Appling 1931-1983 .... CANR-9
Obituary 110
Earlier sketch in CA 21-24R
Sourvinou-Inwood, Christiane 1945- 143
Sousa, Marion 1941- 65-68
Sussloff, Catherine M. 1951- 165
Soustelle, Jacques (Emile)
1912-1990 Obituary 132
Souster, (Holmes) Raymond 1921- CANR-53
Earlier sketches in CA 13-16R, CANR-13, 29
See also CAAS 14
See also CLC 5, 14
See also DAC
See also DAM POET
See also DLB 88
See also SATA 63
South, Clark
See Swain, Dwight V(reeland)
South, Cris 1950- 118
South, Grace
See Clark, Gail
South, Malcolm Hudson 1937- 107
South, Sheri Cobb 1959- 149
See also SATA 82
Southall, Aidan (William) 1920- 77-80
Southall, Ivan (Francis) 1921- CANR-47
Earlier sketches in CA 9-12R, CANR-7
See also AAYA 22
See also CLR 2
See also JRDA
See also MAICYA
See also SAAS 3
See also SATA 3, 68
Southam, B(rian) C(harles) 1931- CANR-26
Earlier sketches in CA 13-16R, CANR-10
Southard, Frank Allan, Jr. 1907- 107
Southard, Helen Fairbairn 1906- 5-8R
Southard, Samuel 1925- CANR-3
Earlier sketch in CA 1-4R
Southerington, F(rank) R(odney) 1938- 57-60
Southerland, Ellease 1943- 107
Interview in 107
See also BW 1
See also DLB 33
Southern, David W. 1938- 25-28R
Southern, Eileen 1920- CANR-31
Earlier sketches in CA 37-40R, CANR-14
Southern, Richard 1903-1989 Obituary 129
Southern, Richard William 1912- 9-12R
Southern, Terry 1924(?)-1995 .... CANR-55
Obituary 150
Earlier sketches in CA 1-4R, CANR-1
See also CLC 7
See also DLB 2
Southerne, Thomas 1660-1746 .... DLB 80
Southey, Caroline Anne Bowles 1786(?)-1854 . DLB 116
Southey, Robert 1774-1843 .... DLB 93, 107, 142
See also SATA 54
Southgate, Minoo S. 132
Southgate, Vera 109
See also SATA 54
Southgate, W(yndham) M(ason) 1910- CAP-2
Earlier sketch in CA 23-24
Southwell, Eugene A. 1928- 17-20R
Southwell, Robert 1561(?)-1595 .... DLB 167
Southwell, Samuel B(eall) 1922- 17-20R
Southwick, Charles H(enry) 1928- 65-68
Southworth, Herbert Rutledge 1908- 85-88
Southworth, Horton C. 1926- 17-20R
Southworth, James G(ranville) 1896- CAP-2
Earlier sketch in CA 33-36
Southworth, John Van Duyn 1904-1986 ... CANR-6
Obituary 118
Earlier sketch in CA 5-8R
Southworth, Louis
See Grealey, Thomas Louis
Southworth, Warren H(ilbourne) 1912- 37-40R
Soutter, Fred
See Lake, Kenneth R(obert)
Souvarine, Boris
See Lifchitz, Boris
Souza, Ernest
See Scott, Evelyn
Souza, Marcio 1946- 145
See also DAM MULT
Souza, Raymond D(ale) 1936- CANR-30
Earlier sketches in CA 69-72, CANR-13
See also HW
Souza, Steven M. 1953- 49-52
Souza Filho, Henrique de
1945(?)-1988 Obituary 124
Sovik, E(dward) A(nders) 1918- Brief entry 112
Sowande, Bode 1948- .... DLB 157
Sowards, J(esse) K(elley) 1924- 73-76
Sowden, Lewis 1905-1974 .... CAP-1
Earlier sketch in CA 9-10
Sowell, David (Lee) 1952- 139
Sowell, Mike 1948- 131
Sowell, Thomas 1930- CANR-61
Earlier sketches in CA 41-44R, CANR-26
See also BW 2
Sowerby, A(rthur) L(indsay) M(cRae) 1899- . CAP-1
Earlier sketch in CA 9-10
Sowerby, E(mily) Millicent 1883-1977 .... CAP-2
Obituary 73-76
Earlier sketch in CA 25-28
Sowers, Miriam R. 1922- 89-92
Sowers, Robert (Watson) 1923- 17-20R
Sowers, Sidney Gerald, Jr. 1935- 17-20R
Sowle, Tace fl. 1691-1749 .... DLB 170
Sowls, Lyle K. 1916- 165
Sowter, Nita .... SATA 69
Sox, (Harold) David 1936- 124
Soyer, Raphael 1899-1987 81-84
Obituary 124
Soyfer, Jura 1912-1939 .... DLB 124
Soyinka, Wole 1934- CANR-39
Earlier sketches in CA 13-16R, CANR-27
See also BLC 3
See also BW 2
See also CLC 3, 5, 14, 36, 44
See also DA
See also DAB
See also DAC
See also DAM DRAM, MST, MULT
See also DC 2
See also DLB 125
See also MTCW 1
See also WLC
Spaak, Paul-Henri 1899-1972 Obituary 37-40R
Spaatz, Carl A(ndrew) 1891-1974 Obituary ... 49-52
Spach, John Thom 1928- 29-32R
Spache, Evelyn B(ispham) 1929- CANR-30
Earlier sketch in CA 29-32R
Spache, George D(aniel) 1909- CANR-6
Earlier sketch in CA 5-8R
Spackman, Doc
See Spackman, Robert R., Jr.
Spackman, Robert R., Jr. 1917-1984 .... 13-16R
Obituary 111
Spackman, W(illiam) M(ode) 1905-1990 81-84
Obituary 132
See also CLC 46
Spacks, Barry (Bernard) 1931- CANR-33
Earlier sketch in CA 154
See also CLC 14
See also DLB 105
Spacks, Patricia Meyer 1929- CANR-1
Earlier sketch in CA 1-4R
Spada, James 1950- CANR-28
Earlier sketches in CA 57-60, CANR-7
Interview in CANR-28
Spade, Mark
See Balchin, Nigel (Marlin)
Spade, Rupert
See Pawley, Martin Edward
Spaeth, Anthony 1955- 133
Spaeth, David A(nthony) 1941- 119
Spaeth, Eloise O'Mara 1904- 104
Spaeth, Gerold 1939- CANR-24
Earlier sketches in CA 65-68, CANR-9
See also Spath, Gerold
See also DLB 75
Spaeth, Harold J(oseph) 1930- CANR-32
Earlier sketch in CA 45-48
Spaeth, Robert L(ouis) 1935- 119
Spaeth, Sigmund 1885-1965 .... 5-8R
Spagnoli, Cathy 1950- .... SATA 79
Spahn, Mary Attea 1929- CANR-7
Earlier sketch in CA 57-60
Spain, Daphne 1949- 111
Spain, David H. 1939- 57-60
Spain, James W(illiam) 1926- 5-8R
Spain, John
See Adams, Cleve F(ranklin)
Spain, Rufus B(uin) 1923- 21-24R
Spake, Amanda 1947- 77-80
Spalatin, Christopher 1909- 49-52
Spalding, Andrea 1944- 160
See also SATA 101
Spalding, Frances 1950- CANR-26
Earlier sketch in CA 104
See also DLB 155
Spalding, Graydon (Edward) 1911- 89-92
Spalding, Henry D(aniel) 1915- CANR-11
Earlier sketch in CA 25-28R
Spalding, Jack 1913- 69-72
Spalding, Linda 1943- CANR-62
Earlier sketch in CA 128
Spalding, Lucile
See Spalding, Ruth
Spalding, P(hilip) A(nthony) 1911- 5-8R
Spalding, (Billups) Phinizy 1930-1994 .... CANR-39
Obituary 144
Earlier sketches in CA 41-44R, CANR-16
Spalding, R(onald) W(olcott) 1904- 81-84
Spalding, Ruth 104
Spalek, John M. 1928- 104
Spallone, Patricia 1951- 144
Spalter, Max 1929- 21-24R
Spanbauer, Tom 142
Spanfeller, James J(ohn) 1930-
See Spanfeller, Jim
See also MAICYA
See also SATA 19
Spanfeller, Jim
See Spanfeller, James J(ohn)
See also SAAS 8
Spangenberg, Judith Dunn 1942- CANR-12
Earlier sketch in CA 29-32R
See also SATA 5
Spanger, Hans-Joachim 1953- 145
Spangler, Earl 1920- CANR-5
Earlier sketch in CA 5-8R
Spanidou, Irini 1946- .... CLC 44
Spanier, David 1932- CANR-39
Earlier sketches in CA 101, CANR-18
Spanier, Ginette 1904-1987 Obituary 125
Spanier, John W(inston) 1930- CANR-2
Earlier sketch in CA 1-4R
Spanier, Sandra Whipple 1951- 141
Spann, Edward K(enneth) 1931- 45-48
Spann, Gloria Carter 1926-1990 77-80
Obituary 131
Spann, Meno H. 1903-1991 .... CANR-21
Obituary 136
Earlier sketch in CA 1-4R
Spann, Philip O. 1941- 128
Spann, Weldon O(rna) 1924- 17-20R
Spano, Charles 1948- 93-96
Spanos, William V(aios) 1925- CANR-11
Earlier sketch in CA 21-24R
Spar, Jerome 1918- 25-28R
See also SATA 10
Sparano, Vin(cent) T(homas) 1934- CANR-22
Earlier sketch in CA 45-48
Sparer, Joyce
See Adler, Joyce Sparer
Spargo, John 1876-1966 Obituary 89-92
Spark, Debra (Alison) 1962- CANR-45
Earlier sketch in CA 122
Spark, Muriel (Sarah) 1918- CANR-36
Earlier sketches in CA 5-8R, CANR-12
Interview in CANR-12
See also CDBLB 1945-1960
See also CLC 2, 3, 5, 8, 13, 18, 40, 94
See also DAB
See also DAC
See also DAM MST, NOV
See also DLB 15, 139
See also MTCW 1
See also SSC 10
Sparke, (George) Archibald 1871-1970 .... CAP-2
Earlier sketch in CA 21-22
Sparke, Michael fl. 1607-1653 .... DLB 170
Sparke, Penny 1948- 146
Sparkes, Ivan G(eorge) 1930- CANR-38
Earlier sketch in CA 115
Sparkia, Roy (Bernard) 1924- 77-80
Sparkman, Brandon B(uster) 1929- CANR-13
Earlier sketch in CA 61-64
Sparkman, G(rady) Temp 1932- CANR-15
Earlier sketch in CA 89-92
Sparkman, William
See Roper, William L(eon)
Sparks, Allister (Haddon) 1933- 150
Sparks, Asa H(oward) 1937- CANR-19
Earlier sketch in CA 97-100
Sparks, Barbara 1942- .... SATA 78
Sparks, Beatrice Mathews 1918- 97-100
See also SATA 44
See also SATA-Brief 28
Sparks, Bertel M(ilas) 1918- 21-24R
Sparks, Donald B. 1931- 124
Sparks, Donald L. 1953- 143
Sparks, Edgar H(erndon) 1908- 13-16R
Sparks, Fred 1916(?)-1981 Obituary 103
Sparks, Jack Norman 1928- 102
Sparks, James Allen 1933- 109
Sparks, Jared 1789-1866 .... DLB 1, 30
Sparks, John 1939- CANR-44
Earlier sketch in CA 103
Sparks, Mary W. 1920- .... SATA 15
Sparks, Merla Jean
See McCormick, Merla Jean
Sparks, Merrill 1922- 21-24R
Sparks, Will (R.) 1924-1987 .... 37-40R
Obituary 124
Sparrow, (John Walter) Gerald 1903- 49-52
Sparrow, John (Hanbury Angus) 1906- 103
Sparrow, Phil
See Steward, Samuel M(orris)
Sparrow, Philip
See Steward, Samuel M(orris)
Sparse Grey Hackle
See Miller, Alfred W.
Sparshott, F. E.
See Sparshott, Francis (Edward)
Sparshott, Francis (Edward) 1926- CANR-51
Earlier sketches in CA 25-28R, CANR-10, 26
See also CAAS 15
See also DLB 60
Spartacus, Deutero
See Fanthorpe, R(obert) Lionel
Spartacus, Tertius
See Burgess, Michael (Roy)
Spash, Clive L(aurence) 1962- 153
Spate, O(skar) H(ermann) K(hristian) 1911- CANR-29
Earlier sketches in CA 25-28R, CANR-10
Spater, George (Alexander) 1909-1984 145
Obituary 113
Spath, Gerold
See Spaeth, Gerold
See also DLB 75
Spatola, Adriano 1941-1988 .... DLB 128
Spatz, (Kenneth) Chris(topher, Jr.) 1940- ... 37-40R
Spatz, Jonas 1935- 29-32R
Spaulding, Dayton M(athewson) 1922- 61-64
Spaulding, Douglas
See Bradbury, Ray (Douglas)
Spaulding, Leonard
See Bradbury, Ray (Douglas)
Spaulding, Robert K(ilburn) 1898- 5-8R
Spaulding, William E(llsworth)
1898-1979 Obituary 93-96
Spaull, Hebe (Fanny Lily) 1893- 9-12R
Spaziani, Maria Luisa 1924- .... DLB 128
Speaight, George Victor 1914- CANR-12
Earlier sketch in CA 29-32R
Speaight, Robert (William) 1904-1976 ... CANR-12
Earlier sketch in CA 13-16R
Speakes, Larry (Melvin) 1939- 137
Speakwell, Justus
See Humez, Nicholas (David)
Spear, Allan Henry 1937- 21-24R
Spear, Benjamin
See Henisch, Heinz K.
Spear, George E(lliott) 1925- 102
Spear, Hilda D(oris) 1926- CANR-47
Earlier sketches in CA 107, CANR-23
Spear, (Thomas George) Percival 1901-1982 ... 106
Obituary 108
Spear, Richard E(dmund) 1940- 45-48
Spear, Roberta 1948- 113
Speare, Elizabeth George 1908-1994 .... 1-4R
Obituary 147
See also CLR 8
See also JRDA
See also MAICYA
See also SATA 5, 62
See also SATA-Obit 83
Spearing, Judith (Mary Harlow) 1922- CANR-3
Earlier sketch in CA 49-52
See also SATA 9
Spearman, Arthur Dunning 1899- CAP-2
Earlier sketch in CA 21-22
Spearman, Walter (Smith) 1908- CAP-2
Earlier sketch in CA 29-32
Spears, Betty (Mary) 1918- CANR-6
Earlier sketch in CA 1-4R
Spears, Dorothea (Johnson) 1901- CAP-1
Earlier sketch in CA 13-14
Spears, Edward (Louis) 1886-1974 .... CAP-2
Obituary 45-48
Earlier sketch in CA 23-24
Spears, Jack 1919- 29-32R
Spears, Monroe K(irk) 1916-1998 .... CANR-2
Obituary 167
Earlier sketch in CA 5-8R
Spears, Richard A(lan) 1939- CANR-21
Earlier sketch in CA 104
Spears, Ross 1947- 122
Spears, Woodridge 1913- 13-16R
Spear-Swerling, Louise 1954- 158
Specht, Ernst Konrad 1926- 29-32R
Specht, Harry 1929-1995 .... CANR-8
Obituary 148
Earlier sketch in CA 53-56
Specht, Robert 1928- 103
Specht, Walter F(rederick) 1912- 97-100
Speck, Bruce W. 1948- 145
Speck, Gordon 1898- CAP-2
Earlier sketch in CA 17-18
Speck, Ross V(ictor) 1927- 125
Brief entry 107
Specking, Inez 1890-196(?) 5-8R
See also SATA 11
Spectator
See Popovic, Nenad D(ushan)
Spector, Debra 1953- 109
Spector, Irwin 1916- 45-48
Spector, Ivar 1898- 1-4R
Spector, Jack J. 1925- 29-32R
Spector, Leonard S. 1945- 122
Spector, Marshall 1936- 45-48
Spector, Robert Donald 1922- 13-16R
Spector, Ronald (Harvey) 1943- 57-60
Spector, Samuel I(ra) 1924- 77-80
Spector, Sherman David 1927- CANR-22
Earlier sketch in CA 1-4R
Spector, Shushannah 1903- 9-12R
Spector, Stanley 1924- 9-12R
Spector, Stephen 1946- 134
Spectorsky, A(uguste) C(omte) 1910-1972 .. CAP-2
Obituary 33-36R
Earlier sketch in CA 17-18
Spedding, (Alison Louise) 1962- 155
Spedding, C(olin) R(aymond) W(illiam) 1925- . 53-56
Spedding, Frank Harold 1902-1984 162
Spedding, James 1808-1881 .... DLB 144
Speed, Eric CANR-27
Earlier sketches in CAP-2, CA 19-20
Speed, F(rederick) Maurice 1912- 107
Speed, Frank Warren 104
Speed, (Herbert) Keith 1934- 115
Speed, Nell
See Keats, Emma
and Sampson, Emma (Keats) Speed
Speed, Nell (Ewing) 1878-1913 135
See also SATA 68
Speelman, Arlene 1916- 41-44R
Speer, Albert 1905-1981 .... CANR-40
Obituary 104
Earlier sketch in CA 65-68
Speer, David G(ordon) 1913- 45-48
Speer, Laurel 1940- 132
Speer, Michael L. 1934- 93-96
Speer-Lyon, Tammie L. 1965- .... SATA 89
Speeth, Kathleen Riordan 1937- 89-92
Speght, Rachel 1597-c. 1630 .... DLB 126
Spehar, Betty M. 1924- 45-48
Spehr, Paul C(hristopher) 1931- 163

Speicher, Helen Ross S(mith) 1915- ... CANR-4
Earlier sketch in CA 5-8R
See also SATA 8
Speicher, John 1934(?)-1986 Obituary ... 119
Speidel, Hans 1897-1984 ... 133
Obituary ... 114
Speidel, Michael P(aul) 1937- ... 108
Speier, Hans 1905-1990 ... CANR-9
Obituary ... 131
Earlier sketch in CA 21-24R
Speight, Harold 1916- ... 5-8R
Speight, Johnny 1921(?)- Brief entry ... 117
Speir, Nancy 1958- ... SATA 81
Speirs, John (Hastie) 1906- ... 61-64
Speirs, Logan 1938- ... 37-40R
Speirs, Russell 1901-1975 ... CANR-4
Obituary ... 61-64
Earlier sketch in CA 45-48
Speiser, Jean ... 69-72
Speiser, Stuart Marshall 1923- Brief entry ... 106
Speitel, H. H.
See Speitel, Hans(-Henning)
Speitel, Hans(-Henning) 1937- ... 123
Speizman, Morris 1905- ... 77-80
Speke, John Hanning 1827-1864 ... DLB 166
Spekke, Arnolds 1887-1972 Obituary ... 37-40R
Spelios, Thomas 1930- ... 25-28R
Spellman, Alfred B. 1935- ... 97-100
See also BW 1
See also DLB 41
Spellman, Cathy Cash 1941- ... 121
Spellman, Francis (Joseph)
1889-1967 Obituary ... 113
Spellman, Francis Cardinal
See Spellman, Francis (Joseph)
Spellman, Frank R. 1944- ... 165
Spellman, John W(illard) 1934- ... 13-16R
See also SATA 14
Spellman, Roger G.
See Cox, William R(obert)
Spellman, W. M. 1956- ... 141
Spelman, Cornelia 1946- ... 161
See also SATA 96
Spelman, Mary 1934- ... CANR-13
Earlier sketch in CA 77-80
See also SATA 28
Spelvin, George
See Phillips, David Atlee
Spemann, Hans 1869-1941 ... 162
Spence, Bill
See Spence, William John Duncan
Spence, Clark C(hristian) 1923- ... CANR-6
Earlier sketch in CA 1-4R
Spence, Cynthia
See Eble, Diane
Spence, Donald P(ond) 1926- Brief entry ... 109
Spence, Donald P(ond) 1926- ... 154
Spence, Duncan
See Spence, William John Duncan
Spence, Eleanor (Rachel) 1928- ... CANR-3
Earlier sketch in CA 49-52
See also CLR 26
See also SATA 21
Spence, Gerald Leonard 1929- ... CANR-71
Earlier sketch in CA 118
Spence, Geraldine 1931- ... SATA 47
Spence, Gerry
See Spence, Gerald Leonard
Spence, Gordon William 1936- ... 25-28R
Spence, Hartzell 1908- ... 5-8R
Spence, J. A. D.
See Eliot, T(homas) S(tearns)
Spence, J(ohn) E(dward) 1931- ... 25-28R
Spence, James R(obert) 1927- ... 25-28R
Spence, Jonathan D(ermot) 1936- ... CANR-54
Earlier sketches in CA 21-24R, CANR-23
See also BEST 90:4
Spence, (James) Lewis (Thomas Chalmers)
1874-1955 Brief entry ... 115
Spence, Mary Lee 1927- ... 45-48
Spence, Piers 1959- ... 149
Spence, Thomas 1750-1814 ... DLB 158
Spence, Vernon Gladden 1924- ... 37-40R
Spence, William John Duncan 1923- ... CANR-43
Earlier sketches in CA 103, CANR-20
Spencer
See Herz, Jerome Spencer
Spencer, Ann 1918- ... 29-32R
See also SATA 10
Spencer, Anne 1882-1975 ... 161
See also BW 2
See also DLB 51, 54
Spencer, Benjamin T(ownley) 1904- ... 124
Spencer, (Charles) Bernard
1909-1963 Obituary ... 115
Spencer, Bonnell 1909- ... 106
Spencer, Brent 1952- ... 149
Spencer, Catherine (Marie-Louise) 1960- ... 144
Spencer, Charles 1920- ... 49-52
Spencer, Christopher 1930- ... 13-16R
Spencer, Colin 1933- ... CANR-12
Earlier sketch in CA 21-24R
Spencer, Cornelia
See Yaukey, Grace S(ydenstricker)
Spencer, Dale R(ay) 1925- ... 57-60
Spencer, David 1954- ... 149
Spencer, Donald D(ean) 1931- ... 108
See also SATA 41
Spencer, Duncan 1940- ... 144
Spencer, Edgar Winston 1931- ... 41-44R
Spencer, Elizabeth 1921- ... CANR-65
Earlier sketches in CA 13-16R, CANR-32
See also CLC 22
See also DLB 6
See also MTCW 1
See also SATA 14
Spencer, Frank 1941- ... 139
Spencer, George John 1758-1834 ... DLB 184
Spencer, Harold (Edwin) 1920- ... CANR-23
Earlier sketch in CA 45-48
Spencer, Herbert 1820-1903 ... DLB 57
Spencer, J(oseph) E(arle) 1907-1984 ... CANR-22
Earlier sketch in CA 45-48
Spencer, James 1932- ... 109
Spencer, Jean E(lizabeth) 1933- ... 17-20R
Spencer, Jeffry Withers B(urress) 1927- ... 45-48
Spencer, John (Walter) 1922- ... 9-12R
Spencer, John Hall 1928- ... 5-8R
Spencer, John Hathaway 1907- ... 112
Spencer, Jon Michael ... 159
Spencer, LaVyrle 1943- ... CANR-34
Earlier sketch in CA 102
See also BEST 89:3
See also DAM POP
Spencer, Leonard G.
See Garrett, (Gordon) Randall (Phillip)
and Silverberg, Robert
Spencer, Lloyd Neville 1955- ... 121
Spencer, Margaret 1916- ... 21-24R
Spencer, Mark 1956- ... 154
Spencer, Metta Wells 1931- ... 69-72
Spencer, Michael (Clifford) 1936- ... 57-60
Spencer, Milton Harry 1926- ... CANR-6
Earlier sketch in CA 1-4R
Spencer, Raine ... 132
Spencer, Robert Allan 1920- ... 5-8R
Spencer, Robert F(rancis) 1917- Brief entry ... 108
Spencer, Ross (Harrison) 1921- ... 101
Spencer, Scott 1945- ... CANR-51
Earlier sketch in CA 113
See also CLC 30
See also DLBY 86
Spencer, Sharon Dougherty 1933- ... CANR-13
Earlier sketch in CA 5-8R
Spencer, Sidney ... 5-8R
Spencer, Steven M. 1905- ... CAP-1
Earlier sketch in CA 13-14
Spencer, Stewart 1949- ... 121
Spencer, Terence (John Bew)
1915-1978 Obituary ... 77-80
Spencer, Warren F(rank) 1923- ... 29-32R
Spencer, William 1922- ... CANR-23
Earlier sketches in CA 17-20R, CANR-8
See also SATA 9
Spencer, William Browning 1946- ... CANR-60
Earlier sketch in CA 133
Spencer, Zane A(nn) 1935- ... 89-92
See also SATA 35
Spencer-Churchill, Laura 1915-1990 Obituary ... 131
Spender, Dale 1943- ... 125
Brief entry ... 120
Interview in ... 125
Spender, J. A. 1862-1942 ... DLB 98
Spender, Lynne 1946- ... 119
Spender, Stephen (Harold) 1909-1995 ... CANR-54
Obituary ... 149
Earlier sketches in CA 9-12R, CANR-31
See also CDBLB 1945-1960
See also CLC 1, 2, 5, 10, 41, 91
See also DAM POET
See also DLB 20
See also MTCW 1
Spener, Philipp Jakob 1635-1705 ... DLB 164
Spengemann, William Charles 1932- ... 102
Spengler, Edwin H(arold) 1906-1981 Obituary ... 104
Spengler, Oswald (Arnold Gottfried)
1880-1936 Brief entry ... 118
See also TCLC 25
Spenser, Edmund 1552(?)-1599 ... CDBLB Before 1660
See also DA
See also DAB
See also DAC
See also DAM MST, POET
See also DLB 167
See also PC 8
See also WLC
Sperber, A(nn) M. ... 126
Sperber, Al E(lias) 1916- ... 65-68
Sperber, Manes 1905-1984 ... 124
Obituary ... 112
Sperber, Murray A(rnold) 1940- ... CANR-12
Earlier sketch in CA 61-64
Sperber, Perry Arthur 1907- ... 37-40R
Sperber, Philip 1944- ... CANR-26
Earlier sketch in CA 109
Speregen, Devra Newberger 1964- ... 150
See also SATA 84
Sperelakis, Nicholas Sr. 1930- ... 162
Spergel, Irving A. 1924- ... CANR-11
Earlier sketch in CA 21-24R
Sperka, Joshua S. 1905- ... 49-52
Sperlich, Peter W. 1934- ... 37-40R
Sperling, Dan(iel Lee) 1949- ... 112
See also SATA 65
Sperling, John G(len) 1921- ... 49-52
Sperling, Milton M. 1912-1988 Obituary ... 126
Spero, Sterling D. 1896-1976 ... 65-68
Obituary ... 61-64
Speroni, Charles 1911-1984 ... 93-96
Obituary ... 113
Sperr, Martin 1944- ... DLB 124
Sperry, Armstrong W. 1897-1976 ... CAP-1
Obituary ... 107
Earlier sketch in CA 9-10
See also MAICYA
See also SATA 1
See also SATA-Obit 27
Sperry, (Sally) Baxter 1914- ... CANR-16
Earlier sketches in CA 49-52, CANR-1
Sperry, Byrne Hope 1902- ... 69-72
Sperry, J. E.
See Eisenstat, Jane Sperry
Sperry, Kip 1940- ... CANR-19
Earlier sketch in CA 101
Sperry, Len 1943- ... CANR-12
Earlier sketch in CA 61-64
Sperry, Margaret 1905- ... 37-40R
Sperry, Ralph A(ddison) 1944- ... 106
Sperry, Raymond
See Garis, Howard R(oger)
Sperry, Raymond, Jr. ... CANR-26
Earlier sketches in CAP-2, CA 19-20
See also SATA 1
Sperry, Roger W(olcott) 1913- ... 157
Sperry, Stuart M(ajor) 1929- ... 49-52
Speshock, Phyllis (Nieboer) 1925- ... 17-20R
Spewack, Bella 1899-1990 Obituary ... 131
Spewack, Samuel 1899-1971 Obituary ... 33-36R
Spice, Marjorie Davis 1924- ... 9-12R
Spicehandler, Daniel 1923- ... 1-4R
Spicer, Bart 1918- ... CANR-61
Earlier sketch in CA 103
Spicer, Dorothy Gladys ... CANR-4
Earlier sketch in CA 1-4R
See also SATA 32
Spicer, Jack 1925-1965 ... 85-88
See also CLC 8, 18, 72
See also DAM POET
See also DLB 5, 16, 193
Spicer, James 1928(?)-1979 Obituary ... 85-88
Spicer, Michael 1943- ... 135
Spicer, Ron
See Kelly, Ronald
Spicher, Julia
See Kasdorf, Julia
Spicker, Stuart Francis 1937- ... CANR-30
Earlier sketch in CA 65-68
Spidle, Jake Wilton, Jr. 1941- ... 127
Spiegel, Allen D(avid) 1927- ... 139
Spiegel, Don(ald Elwin) 1926- ... 41-44R
Spiegel, Henry William 1911- ... 1-4R
Spiegel, John P(aul) 1911-1991 ... 103
Obituary ... 135
Spiegel, Joseph 1928- ... 9-12R
Spiegel, Richard Alan 1947- ... CANR-58
Earlier sketches in CA 104, CANR-30
Spiegel, Robert H. 1922- ... 81-84
Spiegel, Shalom 1899-1984 Obituary ... 112
Spiegel, Steven L(ee) 1941- ... 77-80
Spiegel, Ted 1934- Brief entry ... 105
Spiegelberg, Herbert 1904-1990 ... 9-12R
Obituary ... 132
Spiegelman, Art 1948- ... CANR-55
Earlier sketches in CA 125, CANR-41
See also AAYA 10
See also CLC 76
Spiegelman, J(oseph) Mavvin 1926- ... 57-60
Spiegelman, Judith 1942- ... 101
Spiegelman, Judith M. ... 21-24R
See also SATA 5
Spiegelman, Katia 1959- ... 143
Spiegler, Charles G. 1911- ... CANR-3
Earlier sketch in CA 9-12R
Spiegler, Michael D(avid) 1943- ... 61-64
Spiel, Hilde (Maria) 1911-1990 ... CANR-14
Obituary ... 133
Earlier sketches in CAP-1, CA 9-10
Spielberg, Peter 1929- ... CANR-48
Earlier sketches in CA 5-8R, CANR-4
See also CLC 6
See also DLBY 81
Spielberg, Steven 1947- ... CANR-32
Earlier sketch in CA 77-80
See also AAYA 8, 24
See also CLC 20
See also SATA 32
Spielberger, Charles D(onald) 1927- ... 102
Spielberger, Walter Jakob 1925- ... CANR-16
Earlier sketch in CA 21-24R
Spielhagen, Friedrich 1829-1911 ... DLB 129
Spielman, John P. 1930- ... 144
Spielman, Patrick E. 1936- ... CANR-22
Earlier sketches in CA 13-16R, CANR-7
Spielmann, Peter James 1952- ... 97-100
Spier, Peter (Edward) 1927- ... CANR-41
Earlier sketch in CA 5-8R
See also CLR 5
See also DLB 61
See also MAICYA
See also SATA 4, 54
Spier, Robert F(orest) G(ayton) 1922- ... 41-44R
Spier, William H. 1907(?)-1973 Obituary ... 41-44R
Spierenburg, Pieter (Cornelis) 1948- ... 132
Spiering, Frank 1938- ... CANR-10
Earlier sketch in CA 25-28R
Spiers, Edward M(ichael) 1947- ... CANR-43
Earlier sketch in CA 119
Spies, Werner 1937- ... 37-40R
Spigel, Irwin M(yron) 1926- ... 17-20R
Spigelgass, Leonard 1908-1985 ... 103
Obituary ... 115
Spike, John T(homas) 1951- ... 140
Spike, Paul 1947- ... 120
Spikes, Brian S. J. ... 101
Spikes, Daniel 1953- ... 149
Spilhaus, Athelstan (Frederick) 1911-1998 ... CANR-31
Obituary ... 165
Earlier sketch in CA 17-20R
See also SATA 13
See also SATA-Obit 102
Spilka, Arnold 1917- ... 49-52
See also SATA 6
Spilka, Mark 1925- ... CANR-58
Earlier sketches in CA 81-84, CANR-31
Spilke, Francine S. ... 101
Spillane, Frank Morrison 1918- ... CANR-63
Earlier sketches in CA 25-28R, CANR-28
See also Spillane, Mickey
See also MTCW 1
See also SATA 66
Spillane, John D(avid) 1909(?)-1985 Obituary ... 117
Spillane, Mickey
See Spillane, Frank Morrison
See also CLC 3, 13
Spillard, Anne 1932- ... 128
Spiller, Burton L(owell) 1886- ... 5-8R
Spiller, Earl A(lexander), Jr. 1934- ... 21-24R
Spiller, Gene A(lan) 1927- ... 133
Spiller, Robert E. 1896- ... CANR-4
Earlier sketch in CA 5-8R
Spillmann, Betty Evelyn 1920- ... 53-56
Spilman, Richard 1946- ... 132
Spilsbury, Richard J(oy) 1919-1984 ... 104
Obituary ... 113
Spina, Tony 1914- ... 69-72
Spinage, Clive A(lfred) 1933- ... 13-16R
Spindler, Arthur 1918- ... 104
Spindler, George Dearborn 1920- ... 21-24R
Spindler, Konrad 1939- ... 147
Spindler, Louise Schaubel 1917- ... 49-52
Spindler, Michael (James) 1948- ... 116
Spinelli, Altiero 1907-1986 ... CANR-16
Obituary ... 119
Earlier sketch in CA 21-24R
Spinelli, Eileen 1942- ... 107
See also SATA 38, 101
Spinelli, Jerry 1941- ... CANR-45
Earlier sketches in CA 111, CANR-30
See also AAYA 11
See also CLR 26
See also JRDA
See also MAICYA
See also SATA 39, 71
Spinelli, Marcos 1904-1970 Obituary ... 29-32R
Sping, Dan
See Spalding, Henry D(aniel)
Spingarn, Lawrence P(erreira) 1917- ... CANR-46
Earlier sketches in CA 1-4R, CANR-6, 23
Spingarn, Natalie Davis 1922- ... 85-88
Spinifex
See Martin, David
Spink, Ian 1932- Brief entry ... 113
Spink, John Stephenson 1909-1985 Obituary ... 116
Spink, Reginald (William) 1905- ... CANR-41
Earlier sketches in CA 53-56, CANR-4, 19
See also SATA 11
Spink, Walter M. 1928- ... 61-64
Spinka, Matthew 1890-1972 ... CANR-2
Obituary ... 37-40R
Earlier sketch in CA 1-4R
Spinka, Penina Keen 1945- ... SATA 72
Spinks, G(eorge) Stephens 1903- ... CAP-2
Earlier sketch in CA 23-24
Spinks, John William Tranter 1908- ... 109
Spinner, Stephanie 1943- ... CANR-59
Earlier sketches in CA 45-48, CANR-32
See also SATA 38, 91
Spinner, Thomas J(ohn), Jr. 1929- ... 45-48
Spinney, David
See Spinney, J(ohn) D(avid)
Spinney, J(ohn) D(avid) 1912- ... 29-32R
Spinossimus
See White, William, Jr.
Spinrad, Norman (Richard) 1940- ... CANR-20
Earlier sketch in CA 37-40R
Interview in ... CANR-20
See also CAAS 19
See also CLC 46
See also DLB 8
Spinrad, William 1917- ... 29-32R
Spira, Ruth Rodale 1928- ... 61-64
Spirer, Herbert F(rederick) 1925- ... CANR-16
Earlier sketch in CA 93-96
Spires, Elizabeth 1952- ... CANR-52
Earlier sketches in CA 106, CANR-28
See also DLB 120
See also SATA 71
Spires, Robert C(ecil) 1936- ... 125
Spirin, Gennady 1948- ... SATA 95
Spiro, Edward 1908- ... 25-28R
Spiro, Herbert J(ohn) 1924- ... CANR-6
Earlier sketch in CA 1-4R
Spiro, Herzl Robert 1935- ... 104
Spiro, Howard M(arget) 1924- ... CANR-58
Earlier sketch in CA 125
Spiro, Jack D. 1933- ... CANR-6
Earlier sketch in CA 9-12R
Spiro, Melford E(lliot) 1920- ... CANR-1
Earlier sketch in CA 45-48
Spirt, Diana L(ouise) 1925- ... 17-20R
Spisak, James W(illiam) 1951- ... 117
Spit, Sam
See Schneck, Stephen
Spittel, Richard Lionel 1881-1969 ... CAP-1
Earlier sketch in CA 13-14
Spitteler, Carl (Friedrich Georg) 1845-1924 Brief entry ... 109
See also DLB 129
See also TCLC 12
Spitz, A. Edward 1923- ... 73-76
Spitz, Allan A(ugust) 1928- ... 13-16R
Spitz, David 1916-1979 ... 41-44R
Obituary ... 85-88
Spitz, Ellen Handler 1939- ... 147
Spitz, Lewis W(illiam) 1922- ... CANR-64
Earlier sketches in CA 1-4R, CANR-6, 32
Spitz, Mark (Andrew) 1950- Brief entry ... 115
Spitz, Reuben T. 1954- ... 165
Spitzer, Abe 1912(?)-1984 Obituary ... 112
Spitzer, E(rwin) E(dwin) 1910- ... CAP-2
Earlier sketch in CA 21-22

Spitzer, Herbert Frederick 1906- ... CAP-1
Earlier sketch in CA 13-14
Spitzer, John 1956- ... CANR-18
Earlier sketch in CA 102
Spitzer, Leo 1939- ... 61-64
Spitzer, Lyman (Jr.) 1914-1997 ... 116
Obituary ... 157
Spitzer, Morton Edward ... 41-44R
Spitzer, Nicholas R. 1950- ... 142
Spitzer, Robert J(ames) 1953- ... CANR-56
Earlier sketches in CA 112, CANR-30
Spitzer, Robert S(idney) 1926- ... 61-64
Spivack, Charlotte K(esler) 1926- ... 21-24R
Spivack, Ellen Sue 1937- ... 106
Spivack, George 1927- Brief entry ... 109
Spivack, Kathleen (Romola Drucker) 1938- ... 49-52
See also CLC 6
Spivack, Robert (Gerald) 1915-1970 Obituary ... 104
Spivak, Dawnine ... 168
See also SATA 101
Spivak, Gayatri Chakravorty 1942- ... 154
Brief entry ... 110
Spivak, John L(ouis) 1897-1981 Obituary ... 105
Spivak, Lawrence E. 1900- ... DLB 137
Spivak, Mel 1937- ... 57-60
Spivak, Talbot 1937- ... 77-80
Spivakovsky, Erika 1909- ... 49-52
Spivey, Nigel
See Spivey, Nigel Jonathon
Spivey, Nigel Jonathon 1958- ... 139
Spivey, Richard L. 1937- ... 115
Spivey, Robert Atwood 1931- Brief entry ... 106
Spivey, Ted R(ay) 1927- ... 105
Splane, Richard B. 1916- ... 17-20R
Splaver, Sarah ... 85-88
See also SATA-Brief 28
Spletter, Mary 1946- ... 111
Splichal, Joachim 1954- ... 153
Spock, Benjamin (McLane) 1903-1998 ... CANR-65
Obituary ... 166
Earlier sketches in CA 21-24R, CANR-35
Interview in ... CANR-35
See also AITN 1
See also MTCW 1
Spodek, Bernard 1931- ... CANR-49
Earlier sketches in CA 17-20R, CANR-7, 22
Spoehr, Alexander 1913-1992 ... 109
Obituary ... 139
Spoelstra, Nyle (Ray) 1939- ... 29-32R
Spofford, Harriet Prescott 1835-1921 ... DLB 74
Spofford, Walter O(smon), Jr. 1936- ... 107
Spohn, David 1948- ... SATA 72
Spohn, Kate 1962- ... SATA 87
Spollen, Christopher 1952- ... SATA 12
Spolsky, Bernard 1932- ... CANR-45
Earlier sketches in CA 45-48, CANR-1
Spolsky, Ellen 1943- ... CANR-45
Earlier sketch in CA 119
Spolter, Pari (Dokht) 1930- ... 163
Spong, John Shelby 1931- ... 104
Spooner, Frank (Clyffurde) 1924- ... 85-88
Spooner, Frederick Percy 1898- ... CAP-1
Earlier sketch in CA 13-14
Spooner, Jane R(oss) 1922- ... 5-8R
Spooner, John D. 1937- ... 21-24R
Spooner, Mary Helen 1951- ... 150
Spooner, Michael (Tim) 1954- ... 156
See also SATA 92
Spooner, (Glenda) Victoria Maude (Graham) 1897- . CAP-1
Earlier sketch in CA 9-10
Spores, Ronald 1931- ... 21-24R
Spot, Ryhen
See Post, Henry
Spota, Luis
See Spota (Saavedra), Luis
Spota (Saavedra), Luis 1925-1985 ... 153
Obituary ... 114
See also HW
Spotnitz, Hyman 1908- ... CANR-6
Earlier sketch in CA 1-4R
Spoto, Donald 1941- ... CANR-57
Earlier sketches in CA 65-68, CANR-11
See also CLC 39
Spotte, Stephen 1942- ... CANR-1
Earlier sketch in CA 45-48
Spottiswoode, Raymond J.
1913-1970 Obituary ... 104
Spotts, Charles D(ewey) 1899-1974(?) ... CAP-2
Earlier sketch in CA 19-20
Spotts, Frederic 1930- ... 101
Spowart, Robin 1947- ... SATA 82
Spradley, James P(hillip) 1933-1982 ... CANR-13
Earlier sketch in CA 29-32R
Spradling, Mary Elizabeth Mace 1911- ... 104
Spragens, Thomas A(rthur), Jr. 1942- ... 85-88
Spragens, William C(lark) 1925- ... 41-44R
Spraggett, Allen (Frederick) 1932- ... CANR-18
Earlier sketch in CA 25-28R
Sprague, Arthur Colby 1895- ... 89-92
Sprague, Carter
See Merwin, Sam(uel Kimball), Jr.
Sprague, Charles Arthur 1887-1969 Obituary . 89-92
Sprague, Claire S(acks) 1926- ... 25-28R
Sprague, Gretchen (Burnham) 1926- ... 13-16R
See also SATA 27
Sprague, Howard B(ennet) 1898- ... 41-44R
Sprague, Irvine H(enry, Jr.) 1921- ... CANR-51
Earlier sketch in CA 123
Sprague, Ken 1945- ... 108
Sprague, Marshall 1909-1994 ... CANR-1
Obituary ... 146
Earlier sketch in CA 1-4R
Sprague, Richard E. 1921- ... 29-32R
Sprague, Rosamond Kent 1922- ... CANR-2
Earlier sketch in CA 5-8R
Sprague, Rosemary ... 17-20R
Sprague, Stuart Seely 1937- ... 161
Sprague, W. D.
See von Block, Bela W(illiam)
and von Block, Sylvia
Spraos, John 1926- ... 5-8R
Spratt, Hereward Philip 1902- ... 5-8R
Spray, Pauline 1920- ... CANR-10
Earlier sketch in CA 25-28R
Spray, Sherrad L(ee) 1935- ... 104
Spreiregen, Paul D. 1931- ... 21-24R
Sprengel, Donald P(hilip) 1938- ... 53-56
Spretnak, Charlene 1946- ... 145
Spriegel, William R(obert) 1893- ... 5-8R
Sprigel, Olivier
See Avice, Claude (Pierre Marie)
Sprigg, C(hristopher) St. John 1907-1937 Brief entry ... 120
Sprigg, June 1953- ... 65-68
Sprigge, Elizabeth (Miriam Squire)
1900-1974 ... 13-16R
See also SATA 10
Sprigge, Timothy L(auro) S(quire) 1932- ... 57-60
Sprinchorn, Evert Manfred 1923- ... 107
Spring, Bob
See Spring, Robert W(alton)
Spring, David 1918- ... 81-84
Spring, Eileen 1923- ... 147
Spring, Gerald M(ax) 1897- ... 61-64
Spring, (Robert) Howard 1889-1965 ... CAP-1
Earlier sketch in CA 9-10
See also SATA 28
Spring, Howard 1889-1965 ... DLB 191
Spring, Ira L. 1918- ... CANR-7
Earlier sketch in CA 57-60
Spring, Joel Henry 1940- ... CANR-3
Earlier sketch in CA 49-52
Spring, Norma 1917- ... 61-64
Spring, Robert W(alton) 1918- ... CANR-7
Earlier sketch in CA 57-60
Springborg, Robert 1944- ... 119
Springer, Axel 1912-1985 Obituary ... 117
Springer, Bernhard J.
1907(?)-1970 Obituary ... 29-32R
Springer, Claudia 1956- ... 159
Springer, E(ustace) Laurence 1903- ... 21-24R
Springer, Haskell S(aul) 1939- ... CANR-29
Earlier sketch in CA 111
Springer, John 1916- ... 53-56
Springer, John L(awrence) 1915- ... CANR-25
Earlier sketch in CA 1-4R
Springer, L(ois) Elsinore 1911- ... 69-72
Springer, Margaret 1941- ... 146
See also SATA 78
Springer, Marilyn Harris 1931- ... CANR-9
Earlier sketch in CA 21-24R
See also SATA 47
Springer, Marlene Ann 1937- ... 107
Springer, Mary Doyle 1918- ... 116
Springer, Nancy 1948- ... CANR-41
Earlier sketches in CA 101, CANR-18
See also SATA 65
Springer, Nelson P(aul) 1915- ... 115
Springer, Nesha Bass 1930-1990 ... 81-84
Obituary ... 132
Springer, Otto 1905- ... CAP-1
Earlier sketch in CA 13-14
Springer, Sally P(earl) 1947- ... 108
Springfield
See Kelly, Maurice Anthony
Springfield, David
See Lewis, (John) Roy(ston)
Springs, Nadia
See Obrecht, Jas
Springsted, Eric Osmon 1951- ... 113
Springsteen, Bruce (F.) 1949- ... 111
See also CLC 17
Springstubb, Tricia 1950- ... CANR-46
Earlier sketches in CA 105, CANR-21
See also SATA 46, 78
See also SATA-Brief 40
Sprinkel, Beryl W(ayne) 1923- ... 9-12R
Sprinker, Michael 1950- ... 129
Sprinkle, Patricia Houck 1943- ... 133
Sprinthall, Richard C(lark) 1930- ... 45-48
Sprinzak, Ehud 1940- ... 139
Sproat, Iain (MacDonald) 1938- ... 152
Sproat, John G(erald) 1921- ... 25-28R
Sproat, Robert 1944- ... 144
Sproston, John
See Scott, Peter Dale
Sprott, Duncan 1952- ... 158
Sprott, W(alter) John Herbert 1897-1971 . CANR-16
Obituary ... 103
Earlier sketch in CA 1-4R
Sproul, Barbara Chamberlain 1945- ... 105
Sproul, Dorothy Noyes
See Noyes-Kane, Dorothy
Sproul, R(obert) C(harles) 1939- ... CANR-30
Earlier sketch in CA 111
Sprouse, Mary L. 1948- ... 108
Sprout, Harold 1901-1980 ... CANR-6
Obituary ... 102
Earlier sketch in CA 1-4R
Spruch, Grace Marmor 1926- ... 57-60
Spruch, Larry 1923- ... 102
Sprug, Joseph W(illiam) 1922- ... 21-24R
Spruill, Charles R(ay) 1946- ... 117
Spruill, Steven G(regory) 1946- ... CANR-59
Earlier sketch in CA 73-76
Sprunger, Keith L(a Verne) 1935- ... 41-44R
Sprunt, Alexander, Jr. 1898-1973 Obituary . 37-40R
Spry, Irene Mary 1907- ... 163
Spudvilas, Anne 1951- ... SATA 94
Spuhler, J(ames) N(orman) 1917- ... CANR-3
Earlier sketch in CA 1-4R
Spulber, Nicolas 1915- ... CANR-3
Earlier sketch in CA 9-12R
Spuler, Bertold 1911- ... 81-84
Spungen, Deborah 1937- ... 119
Spungin, Charlotte I(sabelle) 1929- ... 158
Spurling, Hilary 1940- ... CANR-52
Earlier sketches in CA 104, CANR-25
See also CLC 34
Spurling, John 1936- ... CANR-50
Earlier sketches in CA 45-48, CANR-1, 25
Spurll, Barbara 1952- ... SATA 78
Spurr, Clinton
See Rowland, D(onald) S(ydney)
Spurr, David Anton 1949- ... 118
Spurr, Russell 1922- ... 144
Spurr, Stephen Hopkins 1918- ... 81-84
Spurr, William A(lfred) 1905- ... 5-8R
Spurrier, William A(twell) 1916- ... 53-56
Spycket, Jerome 1928- ... 145
Spyers-Duran, Peter 1932- ... CANR-23
Earlier sketches in CA 17-20R, CANR-8
Spyker, John Howland
See Elman, Richard (Martin)
Spykman, E(lizabeth) C(hoate) 1896-1965 ... 101
See also CLR 35
See also SATA 10
Spyri, Johanna (Heusser) 1827-1901 ... 137
See also CLR 13
See also MAICYA
See also SATA 19, 100
Spyridakis, Stylianos 1937- ... 89-92
Squibob
See Derby, George Horatio
Squier, Charles L(a Barge) 1931- ... 17-20R
Squier, E(phraim) G(eorge) 1821-1888 ... DLB 189
Squier, Susan Merrill 1950- ... 120
Squire, Elizabeth 1919- ... 13-16R
Squire, Elizabeth Daniels 1926- ... 164
Squire, Jason E(dward) 1948- ... CANR-23
Earlier sketch in CA 45-48
Squire, Norman 1907- ... CANR-3
Earlier sketch in CA 9-12R
Squire, Robin 1937- ... 105
Squire, Russel Nelson 1908- ... 1-4R
Squire, Susan 1950- ... 112
Squires, Eric
See Ball, Sylvia Patricia
Squires, James (David) 1943- ... 119
Squires, James Duane 1904- ... 5-8R
Squires, Michael (George) 1941- ... 61-64
Squires, Patricia
See Ball, Sylvia Patricia
Squires, Phil
See Barker, S(quire) Omar
Squires, (James) Radcliffe 1917-1993 ... CANR-21
Obituary ... 140
Earlier sketches in CA 1-4R, CANR-6
See also CLC 51
Squires, Richard D(onald) 1957- ... 150
Sraffa, Piero 1898-1983 ... CANR-27
Obituary ... 110
Earlier sketch in CA 45-48
Srba, Lynne ... SATA 98
Sreenivasan, Jyotsna 1964- ... 156
See also SATA 101
Srere, Benson M. 1928- ... 77-80
S-Ringi, Kjell
See Ringi, Kjell (Arne Soerensen)
Srivastava, C(handrika) P(rasad) 1920- ... 153
Srivastava, Dhanpat Rai 1880(?)-1936 Brief entry ... 118
See also Premchand
Srivastava, Jane Jonas 1941- ... 119
See also SATA-Brief 37
Srivastava, Ramesh K(umar) 1940- ... CANR-55
Earlier sketch in CA 127
Srole, Leo 1908- ... 125
Brief entry ... 107
Staaf, Robert J(ames) 1939- ... 93-96
Staal, Cyril 1912- Brief entry ... 113
Staal, J(ohan) F(rederik) 1930- ... 45-48
Staal, Julius D(irk) W(illem)
1917-1986 Obituary ... 120
Staar, Richard F(elix) 1923- ... CANR-38
Earlier sketches in CA 1-4R, CANR-1, 16
Staats, Arthur (Wilbur) 1924- ... 13-16R
Staats, Marilyn Dorn 1939- ... 139
Stabb, Martin S(anford) 1928- ... 21-24R
Stabenow, Dana 1952- ... 164
Stabile, Donald R(obert) 1944- ... 149
Stabile, Toni ... 85-88
Stableford, Brian (Michael) 1948- ... CANR-55
Earlier sketches in CA 57-60, CANR-29
Stablein, Marilyn 1946- ... 120
Stabler, Arthur P(hillips) 1919- ... CANR-14
Earlier sketch in CA 41-44R
Stabley, Fred(erick) W(illiam) 1915- ... 112
Stace, Christopher 1942- ... 97-100
Stace, Walter Terence 1886-1967 ... CANR-2
Earlier sketch in CA 1-4R
Stacey, C(harles) P(erry) 1906- ... CANR-19
Earlier sketch in CA 101
Stacey, Cherylyn 1945- ... 161
See also SATA 96
Stacey, Frank Arthur 1923-1977 ... 57-60
Obituary ... 135
Stacey, Judith 1943- ... CANR-56
Earlier sketch in CA 125
Stacey, Kathryn
See Fenton, Kate
Stacey, Margaret 1922- ... CANR-38
Earlier sketches in CA 29-32R, CANR-17
Stacey, Michelle 1959- ... 150
Stacey, Nicholas Anthony Howard 1920- ... 5-8R
Stacey, Roy 1919- ... 9-12R
Stacey, Susannah
See Staynes, Jill
Stacey, Thomas Charles Gerard 1930- ... CANR-47
Earlier sketches in CA 9-12R, CANR-21
Stacey, Tom
See Stacey, Thomas Charles Gerard
Stach, Patricia Burgess
See Burgess, Patricia
Stachow, Hasso G(ert) 1924- ... 109
Stachys, Dimitris
See Constantelos, Demetrios J.
Stack, Edward M(acGregor) 1919- ... CANR-28
Earlier sketch in CA 1-4R
Stack, Frank H(untington) 1937- ... CANR-9
Earlier sketch in CA 61-64
Stack, George J. 1931- ... 37-40R
Stack, Herbert James 1893-1967 ... CANR-3
Earlier sketch in CA 1-4R
Stack, Nicolete Meredith 1896- ... 13-16R
Stackhouse, Max L. 1935- ... 21-24R
Stackhouse, Reginald 1925- ... 21-24R
Stackpole, Edouard Alexander 1903-1993 ... CANR-16
Obituary ... 142
Earlier sketches in CA 1-4R, CANR-1
Stackpole, Edward J(ames) 1894-1967 ... 1-4R
Obituary ... 103
Stackpole, Michael A(ustin) 1957- ... 153
Stacks, John F(ultz) 1942- ... 113
Stacpoole, H. de Vere 1863-1951 ... DLB 153
Stacton, David (Derek) 1925-1968 ... CANR-6
Obituary ... 25-28R
Earlier sketch in CA 5-8R
Stacy, Bruce
See Elliott, Bruce (Walter Gardner Lively Stacy)
Stacy, Donald
See Pohl, Frederik
Stacy, Donald L. 1925- ... 29-32R
Stacy, Jan 1948(?)-1989 Obituary ... 129
Stacy, Pat(ricia A.) 1941- ... 118
Stacy, R(obert) H(arold) 1919- ... 73-76
Stacy, Walter
See Elliott, Bruce (Walter Gardner Lively Stacy)
Staddon, John (E. R.) 1937- ... 148
Stade, George 1933- ... CANR-46
Earlier sketch in CA 29-32R
Stadelman, S(ara) L(ee) 1917- ... 81-84
Stadler, Karl R(udolph) 1913- ... 21-24R
Stadler, Matthew 1959- ... 140
Stadley, Pat (Anna May Gough) 1918- Brief entry ... 114
Stadt, Ronald W(ilmer) 1935- ... CANR-16
Earlier sketch in CA 93-96
Stadter, Philip A(ustin) 1936- ... 104
Stadtfeld, Curtis K(arl) 1935- ... 49-52
Stadtler, Bea 1921- ... 65-68
See also SATA 17
Stadtman, Verne A. 1926- ... 29-32R
Staebler, Edna ... 101
Staebler, Neil 1905- ... 77-80
Staebler, Warren 1912- ... 45-48
Staehle, Albert 1899-1974 ... AITN 1
Stael, Germaine de 1766-1817
See Stael-Holstein, Anne Louise Germaine Necker Baronn
See also DLB 119
Stael-Holstein, Anne Louise Germaine Necker
1766-1817
See Stael, Germaine de
See also DLB 192
Staender, Gilbert F(rank) 1930- ... 104
Staender, Vivian 1923- ... 97-100
Staff, Adrienne 1947- ... 123
Staff, Frank 1908- ... 25-28R
Staffel, Megan 1952- ... 128
Stafford, Barbara Maria 1941- ... 149
Stafford, Caroline
See Watjen, Carolyn L. T.
Stafford, David (Christopher) 1943- ... 103
Stafford, David Alexander Tetlow 1942- ... CANR-21
Earlier sketch in CA 104
Stafford, Edward Peary 1918- ... 135
Stafford, Fiona (Jane) 1960- ... 131
Stafford, Gilbert Wayne 1938- ... CANR-56
Earlier sketches in CA 112, CANR-31
Stafford, Irvin G. 1936- ... 114
Stafford, Jean 1915-1979 ... CANR-65
Obituary ... 85-88
Earlier sketches in CA 1-4R, CANR-3
See also CLC 4, 7, 19, 68
See also DLB 2, 173
See also MTCW 1
See also SATA-Obit 22
See also SSC 26
Stafford, Kenneth R(ay) 1922- ... 17-20R
Stafford, Kim R(obert) 1949- ... CANR-46
Earlier sketches in CA 69-72, CANR-22
Stafford, Linda (Crying Wind) 1943- ... 108
Stafford, Muriel
See Sauer, Muriel Stafford
Stafford, Peter
See Tabori, Paul
Stafford, Robert A(ndrew) 1953- ... 133
Stafford, Tim ... 135
Stafford, William (Edgar) 1914-1993 ... CANR-22
Obituary ... 142
Earlier sketches in CA 5-8R, CANR-5
Interview in ... CANR-22
See also CAAS 3
See also CLC 4, 7, 29
See also DAM POET
See also DLB 5
Stafford, William B(utler) 1931- ... 53-56
Stafford, William T(almadge) 1924- ... CANR-25
Earlier sketch in CA 1-4R
Stafford-Clark, David 1916- ... 21-24R

Stafford-Deitsch, Jeremy 1958- 141
Staffordshire Knot
See Wrottesley, A(rthur) J(ohn) F(rancis)
Stageberg, Norman C(lifford) 1905- CAP-1
Earlier sketch in CA 11-12
Stage Door Jimmy
See Starr, James (A.)
Stagg, Albert 1903- 85-88
Stagg, Evelyn 1914- 85-88
Stagg, Frank 1911- CANR-18
Earlier sketches in CA 1-4R, CANR-1
Stagg, James Martin 1900-1975 Obituary 61-64
Stagg, Paul L. 1914- 21-24R
Stagge, Jonathan
See Wheeler, Hugh (Callingham)
Staggenborg, Suzanne 1955- 140
Stagner, Lloyd Ernest 1923- 101
Stagner, Ross 1909- CANR-5
Earlier sketch in CA 5-8R
Stahl, Ben(jamin) 1910-1987 .... 29-32R
Obituary 123
See also SATA 5
See also SATA-Obit 54
Stahl, Donald 1935- 25-28R
Stahl, Fred Alan 1944- 45-48
Stahl, Gustav Richard 1888(?)-1978 Obituary 81-84
Stahl, Hilda 1938-1993 .... CANR-40
Obituary 142
Earlier sketch in CA 116
See also SATA 48
See also SATA-Obit 77
Stahl, J(ohn) D(aniel) 1952- 149
Stahl, Le Roy 1908- CAP-1
Earlier sketch in CA 11-12
Stahl, Lesley R(ene) 1941- 107
Interview in 107
See also AITN 2
Stahl, Nancy 1937- 104
Stahl, Norman 1931- 85-88
Stahl, O(scar) Glenn 1910- CANR-14
Earlier sketch in CA 41-44R
Stahl, Saul 1942- 165
Stahl, William Harris 1908-1969 Obituary 111
Stahlecker, Lotar V(ictor) 1915- 21-24R
Stahlman, James Geddes
1893-1976 Obituary 89-92
Stahnke, Arthur A(llan) 1935- 65-68
Stahnke, Astrida B. 1935- 123
Stahr, John W. 1904-1981 Obituary 104
Staib, Bjorn O. 1938- 17-20R
Staicar, Thomas Edward 1946- 108
Staicar, Tom
See Staicar, Thomas Edward
Staiger, Janet 1946- 123
Stainback, Berry 1935- 161
Stainback, Susan Bray 1947- CANR-31
Earlier sketches in CA 57-60, CANR-7, 14
Stainback, William (Clarence) 1943- CANR-31
Earlier sketches in CA 77-80, CANR-14
Stainer, Pauline 1941- 154
Staines, David 1946- CANR-52
Earlier sketch in CA 125
Staines, Trevor
See Brunner, John (Kilian Houston)
Stainsby, Charles 1925-1985 Obituary 118
Stair, Gobin (John) 1912- .... SATA 35
Stairs, Dennis (Winfield) 1939- Brief entry 114
Stairs, Gordon
See Austin, Mary (Hunter)
Stalder, Valerie 41-44R
See also SATA 27
Staley, Allen (Percival Green) 1935- 146
Brief entry 115
Staley, Charles E(arl) 1927- 45-48
Staley, (Alvah) Eugene 1906- 77-80
Staley, Lynn 1947- 151
Staley, Thomas F(abian) 1935- CANR-60
Earlier sketches in CA 77-80, CANR-13, 30
Stalheim, O(le) H. V. 1917- 149
Stalker, John 1939- 127
Stall, Katharine 1950- 127
Stallaerts, Robert 1947- 151
Stallard, John (Richard) 1935-1985 49-52
Obituary 116
Stalley, Rodney E(dward) 1930- 116
Stalley, Roger 1945- 101
Stallibrass, (Helen) Alison 1916- 104
Stallings, Constance L(ee) 1932- CANR-17
Earlier sketch in CA 97-100
Stallings, James O. 1938- CANR-19
Earlier sketch in CA 103
Stallings, Laurence 1894-1968 Obituary 89-92
See also DLB 7, 44
Stallman, Robert Wooster 1911- CANR-3
Earlier sketch in CA 1-4R
Stallone, Sylvester (Enzio) 1946- 77-80
Stallwood, Veronica 162
Stallworth, Anne Nall 1935- 85-88
Stallworthy, Jon (Howie) 1935- CANR-8
Earlier sketch in CA 9-12R
See also DLB 40
Stallybrass, Oliver (George Weatherhead)
1925-1978 .... CANR-24
Earlier sketch in CA 29-32R
Stalvey, Lois Mark 1925- CANR-14
Earlier sketch in CA 29-32R
Stam, James H(enry) 1937- 49-52
Stam, Robert 1941- 115
Stamaty, Mark Alan 1947- CANR-15
Earlier sketch in CA 61-64
See also SATA 12
Stambaugh, Joan 1932- 89-92
Stambaugh, Sara 1936- CANR-43
Earlier sketch in CA 119
Stamberg, Susan 1938- 103
Interview in 103
Stambler, Helen
See Latner, Helen (Stambler)
Stambler, Irwin 1924- CANR-2
Earlier sketch in CA 5-8R
See also SATA 5
Stambolian, George 1938-1991 .... CANR-72
Obituary 136
Earlier sketch in CA 41-44R
Stambuk, George 1927- 5-8R
Stames, Ward
See Steward, Samuel M(orris)
Stamey, Sara (Lucinda) 1953- 126
Stamford Krause, Shari 1961- 157
Stamm, Keith R(oman) 1941- 116
Stamm, Martin L. 1917- CANR-19
Earlier sketch in CA 37-40R
Stammers, Neil 1950- 119
Stamp, L(aurence) Dudley 1898-1966 .... CAP-1
Earlier sketch in CA 13-14
Stamp, Robert M(iles) 1937- 126
Stamper, Alexander
See Kent, Arthur William Charles
Stampfer, Judah (Leon) 1923-1996 .... 25-28R
Obituary 154
Stampfle, Felice 1912- 105
Stampp, Kenneth M. 1912- 13-16R
See also DLB 17
Stanbury, David 1933- 104
Stanbury, Walter A. 1910-1976 Obituary 65-68
Stancliffe, Michael (Staffurth) 1916-1987 124
Stancu, Zaharia 1902-1974 97-100
Obituary 53-56
Standard, William L. 1900(?)-1978 Obituary .. 77-80
Stander, Siegfried 1935- CANR-19
Earlier sketches in CA 9-12R, CANR-4
Standiford, Lester A(lan) 1945- 77-80
Standiford, Natalie 1961- 149
See also SATA 81
Standing, Edwin (Mortimer) 1887- CAP-1
Earlier sketch in CA 9-10
Standing, Sue 1952- 119
Standing Bear, Luther 1868(?)-1939(?) 144
Brief entry 113
See also DAM MULT
See also NNAL
Standish, Buck
See Paine, Lauran (Bosworth)
Standish, Carole
See Koehler, Margaret (Hudson)
Standish, Robert 1898(?)-1981 Obituary 105
Standley, Fred L(loyd) 1932- 41-44R
Standon, Anna (Slater) 1929- 17-20R
Standring, Gillian 1935- 69-72
Stands In Timber, John 1884-1967 154
Stanek, Carolyn 1951- 107
Stanek, Lou Willett 1931- .... SATA 63
Stanek, Muriel (Novella) 1915- Brief entry 112
See also SATA-Brief 34
Stanev, Emilian
See Stanev, Nikola (Stoyanov)
See also DLB 181
Stanev, Nikola (Stoyanov) 1907-1979 108
See also Stanev, Emilian
Stanfield, Nancy Fisher Clay 1905- CAP-1
Earlier sketch in CA 9-10
Stanfield, Vernon Latrelle 1920- 97-100
Stanford, Alfred (Boller) 1900-1985 .... CAP-1
Obituary 115
Earlier sketch in CA 17-18
Stanford, Ann 1916-1987 .... CANR-32
Obituary 123
Earlier sketches in CA 9-12R, CANR-4
See also DLB 5
Stanford, Barbara Dodds 1943- 37-40R
Stanford, Derek 1918- CANR-45
Earlier sketch in CA 9-12R
Stanford, Don
See Stanford, Donald E(lwin)
Stanford, Don(ald Kent) 1918- 53-56
Stanford, Donald E(lwin) 1913- CANR-28
Earlier sketches in CA 13-16R, CANR-5
Stanford, Edward V(alentine) 1897-1966 .... 5-8R
Stanford, Gene 1944- 37-40R
Stanford, J(ohn) K(eith) 1892- 5-8R
Stanford, Melvin Joseph 1932- CANR-16
Earlier sketch in CA 89-92
Stanford, Miles J(oseph) 1914- 65-68
Stanford, Neal 1906(?)-1988 Obituary 127
Stanford, Quentin Hunt 1935- 45-48
Stanford, Sally 1903-1982 Obituary 105
Stanford, William Bedell 1910-1984 85-88
Obituary 115
Stanforth, Deirdre 1924- 102
Stang, Ivan 1949- 129
Stang, Judit 1921-1977 .... CANR-8
Earlier sketch in CA 5-8R
See also SATA 29
Stang, Judy
See Stang, Judit
Stang, Sondra J. 1928- 131
Stange, G(eorge) Robert 1919- 21-24R
Stanger, Frank Bateman 1914- 109
Stanger, Ila (Ann) 1940- 65-68
Stangerup, Helle 1939- 132
Stangerup, Henrik 1937- 147
Stangl, (Mary) Jean 1928- 136
See also SATA 67
Stangos, Nicolas 1936- 146
Stangos, Nikos
See Stangos, Nicolas
Stanhope, Eric
See Hamilton, Charles (Harold St. John)
Stanhope, Philip Dormer 1694-1773 .... DLB 104
Stanier, Maida Euphemia Kerr 1909- 101
Staniforth, (John Hamilton) Maxwell 1893- .. CAP-2
Earlier sketch in CA 25-28
Stanislavsky, Constantin (Sergeivich)
1863(?)-1938 Brief entry 118
Stanislawski, Dan 1903- CANR-3
Earlier sketch in CA 5-8R
Stanislawski, Michael 1952- 119
Stanke, Alain 1934- 81-84
Stanke, Don E(dward) 1929- 61-64
Stankevich, Boris 1928- 21-24R
See also SATA 2
Stankevich, Nikolai Vladimirovich 1813-1840 ... DLB 198
Stankiewicz, Edward 1920- CANR-43
Earlier sketch in CA 45-48
Stankiewicz, Marketa Goetz
See Goetz-Stankiewicz, Marketa
Stankiewicz, W(ladyslaw) J(ozef) 1922- ... CANR-1
Earlier sketch in CA 45-48
Stanko, Elizabeth Anne 1950- CANR-38
Earlier sketch in CA 116
Stankovic, Borisav 1876-1927 .... DLB 147
Stanley, Alexander O. 1910- 5-8R
Stanley, Autumn 144
Stanley, Bennett
See Hough, S(tanley) B(ennett)
Stanley, C(laude) Maxwell 1904-1984 114
Stanley, Carol
See White, Carol
Stanley, Dave
See Dachs, David
Stanley, David 1944- CANR-39
Earlier sketch in CA 115
Stanley, David T(aylor) 1916- Brief entry 107
Stanley, Diana 1909- .... SATA-Brief 30
Stanley, Diane 1943- CANR-64
Earlier sketches in CA 112, CANR-32
See also CLR 46
See also SAAS 15
See also SATA 37, 80
See also SATA-Brief 32
Stanley, Fay Grissom
See Shulman, Fay Grissom Stanley
Stanley, George 1934- Brief entry 114
Stanley, George Edward 1942- CANR-39
Earlier sketches in CA 97-100, CANR-17
See also SATA 53
Stanley, George F(rancis) G(ilman) 1907- ....
CANR-15
Earlier sketch in CA 41-44R
Stanley, Henry M. 1841-1904 .... DLB 189
See also DLBD 13
Stanley, Jerry 1941- 148
See also SATA 79
Stanley, John 1940- 21-24R
Stanley, John L(angley) 1937-1998 45-48
Obituary 167
Stanley, Julian C(ecil), Jr. 1918- CANR-8
Earlier sketch in CA 21-24R
Stanley, Leo Leonidas 1886- 69-72
Stanley, Liz 1947- CANR-45
Earlier sketch in CA 119
Stanley, Marge
See Weinbaum, Stanley Grauman
Stanley, Nora Kathleen Begbie Strange 1885- ....
CAP-1
Earlier sketch in CA 11-12
Stanley, Patricia H. 138
Stanley, Peter (Alan) 1956- 118
Stanley, Peter W(illiam) 1940- 143
Stanley, Phil
See Ind, Allison
Stanley, Richard P. 1944- 161
Stanley, Robert
See Hamilton, Charles (Harold St. John)
Stanley, Robert Henry 1940- 101
Stanley, Roy M. II 1936- 114
Stanley, Steven M(itchell) 1941- 109
Stanley, Thomas 1625-1678 .... DLB 131
Stanley, Timothy Wadsworth 1927-1997 77-80
Obituary 161
Stanley, Warwick
See Hilton, John Buxton
Stanley, William O(liver), Jr. 1902- CANR-1
Earlier sketch in CA 1-4R
Stanley-Brown, Katherine (Oliver)
1893(?)-1972 Obituary 33-36R
Stanley-Jones, D(ouglas) 1905- 9-12R
Stanley-Wrench, Margaret 1916- 9-12R
Stanli, Sue
See Meilach, Dona Z(weigoron)
Stanlis, Peter J(ames) 1919- 101
Stanmeyer, William A(nthony) 1934- 118
Stann, Francis E. 1912(?)-1987 Obituary 124
Stannard, David E(dward) 1941- 65-68
Stannard, Martin 1947- 142
See also CLC 44
See also DLB 155
Stannard, Neville (George) 1949- 118
Stannard, Richard M. 1925- 141
Stannard, Una 1927- 73-76
Stanner, W(illiam) E(dward) H(anley)
1905-1981 Obituary 108
Stannus, (James) Gordon (Dawson)
1902-1989 65-68
Obituary 129
Stanovich, Betty Jo 1954- 118
See also SATA-Brief 51
Stans, Maurice H(ubert) 1908-1998 Obituary ... 167
Brief entry 113
Stansberger, Richard 1950- CANR-18
Earlier sketch in CA 101
Stansberry, Domenic (Joseph) 1952- 149
Stansbury, Donald L. 1929- 37-40R
Stansby, William fl. 1597-1636 .... DLB 170
Stansfield, Richard Habberton 1921- 107
Stansky, Peter (David Lyman) 1932- CANR-12
Earlier sketch in CA 17-20R
Stanstead, John
See Groom, Arthur William
Stanton, Dorothy
See Lamour, Dorothy
Stanton, Edward F(eagler) 1942- CANR-56
Earlier sketches in CA 89-92, CANR-42
Stanton, Elizabeth Cady 1815-1902 .... DLB 79
See also TCLC 73
Stanton, Frank L. 1857-1927 .... DLB 25
Stanton, Gerald B(arry) 1918- 9-12R
Stanton, Graham N(orman) 1940- 61-64
Stanton, Jessie Earl 1887-1976 Obituary 65-68
Stanton, Marietta (P.) 1948- 134
Stanton, Mary 1947- 150
Stanton, Maura 1946- CANR-15
Earlier sketch in CA 89-92
See also CLC 9
See also DLB 120
Stanton, Paul
See Beaty, (Arthur) David
Stanton, Peggy Smeeton 1939- 61-64
Stanton, Phoebe B(aroody) 1914- 37-40R
Stanton, Royal (Waltz) 1916- 37-40R
Stanton, Schuyler
See Baum, L(yman) Frank
Stanton, Shelby L(ee) 1948- 147
Stanton, Vance
See Avallone, Michael (Angelo, Jr.)
Stanton, Will 1918- 85-88
Stanton, William 1925- 1-4R
Stanton, William J(ohn, Jr.) 1919- Brief entry ... 115
Stanwood, Brooks
See Kaminsky, Howard
and Kaminsky, Susan Stanwood
Stanwood, Brooks
See Kaminsky, Susan Stanwood
Stanwood, P(aul) G(rant) 1933- 49-52
Stanyer, Jeffrey 1936- 61-64
Staph, C. C.
See Carroll, Bob
Stapledon, (William) Olaf 1886-1950 162
Brief entry 111
See also DLB 15
See also TCLC 22
Stapler, Harry (Bascom) 1919- CANR-13
Earlier sketch in CA 61-64
Staples, Brent 1951- 153
Staples, Mary Jane
See Staples, Reginald Thomas
Staples, Reginald Thomas 1911- CANR-43
Earlier sketches in CA 69-72, CANR-14
Staples, Robert (Eugene) 1942- CANR-2
Earlier sketch in CA 49-52
Staples, Suzanne Fisher 1945- 132
See also AAYA 26
See also SATA 70
Stapleton, Amy 1959- 154
Stapleton, Constance 1930- 104
Stapleton, G(eorge) Brian 1922- 25-28R
Stapleton, Jean 1942- 69-72
Stapleton, Katherine
See Kane, Henry
Stapleton, (Katharine) Laurence 1911- 17-20R
Stapleton, Margaret (Lucy) 1903- 57-60
Stapleton, Marjorie (Winifred) 1932- 106
See also SATA 28
Stapleton, Richard John 1940- 89-92
Stapleton, Richard M. 1942- 147
Stapleton, Ruth Carter 1929-1983 81-84
Obituary 110
Stapp, Arthur D(onald) 1906-1972 .... CANR-2
Obituary 33-36R
Earlier sketch in CA 1-4R
See also SATA 4
Stapp, William B. 1929- CANR-48
Earlier sketches in CA 45-48, CANR-2, 22
Stappenbeck, Herb(ert) Louis (Jr.) 1935- 65-68
Star, Angel
See Quigley, Joan
Star, Cima 1939- 110
Star, Jack 1920- 73-76
Star, Max 1890(?)-1986 Obituary 121
Star, Shirley A(nn) 1918-1976 .... 41-44R
Obituary 65-68
Starbird, Kaye 1916- CANR-38
Earlier sketch in CA 17-20R
See also MAICYA
See also SATA 6
Starbuck, George (Edwin) 1931-1996 .... CANR-23
Obituary 153
Earlier sketch in CA 21-24R
See also CLC 53
See also DAM POET
Starbuck, William H(aynes) 1934- CANR-7
Earlier sketch in CA 57-60
Starch, Daniel 1883-1979 .... 37-40R
Obituary 133
Starchild, Adam (Aristotle) 1946- 123
Starchuk, Orest 1915- 5-8R
Stardust, Alvin 1942- 123
Stare, Fredrick J(ohn) 1910- 132
Starenko, Ronald C(harles) 1930- 93-96
Starer, Daniel 1954- 144
Starer, Robert 1924- 125
Stargell, Willie
See Stargell, Wilver Dornel
Stargell, Wilver Dornel 1941- 146
Brief entry 118
Starhawk
See Simos, Miriam
Starita, Joe 1948- 150
Stark, Bradford 1948-1979 .... CANR-3
Earlier sketch in CA 49-52
Stark, Claude Alan 1935-1980 57-60
Obituary 134
Stark, Cruce 1942- 137

Stark, Evan 1942- ... 146
See also SATA 78
Stark, Freya (Madeline) 1893-1993 ... CANR-47
Obituary ... 141
Earlier sketches in CA 5-8R, CANR-5
See also DLB 195
Stark, Gary Duane 1948- ... CANR-21
Earlier sketch in CA 105
Stark, George Washington
1884-1966 Obituary ... 89-92
Stark, Harry 1895- ... 1-4R
Stark, Irwin 1912-1994 ... 9-12R
Obituary ... 145
Stark, Jack
See Stark, John H.
Stark, James
See Goldston, Robert (Conroy)
Stark, John
See Godwin, John
Stark, John H. 1914- ... 49-52
Stark, John Olsen 1939- ... CANR-5
Earlier sketch in CA 53-56
Stark, Joshua
See Olsen, T(heodore) V(ictor)
Stark, Lucien 1929- ... 156
Stark, Michael
See Lariar, Lawrence
Stark, Paul C. 1891(?)-1974 Obituary ... 53-56
Stark, R. J.
See Kikel, Rudy (John)
Stark, Raymond 1919- ... 73-76
Stark, Richard
See Westlake, Donald E(dwin)
Stark, Stephen (Edward) 1958- ... 140
Stark, Steven D. 1951- ... 163
Stark, Werner 1909- ... CANR-10
Earlier sketch in CA 21-24R
Starke, Aubrey (Harrison)
1905(?)-1972 Obituary ... 37-40R
Starke, Catherine Juanita 1913- ... 37-40R
Starke, J(oseph) G(abriel) 1911- ... 115
Starke, Roland ... 53-56
Starkey, David ... 164
Starkey, Lycurgus M(onroe), Jr. 1928- ... 5-8R
Starkey, Marion L(ena) 1901- ... CANR-1
Earlier sketch in CA 1-4R
See also SATA 13
Starkey, Thomas c. 1499-1538 ... DLB 132
Starkie, Enid 1903(?)-1970 ... CANR-2
Obituary ... 29-32R
Earlier sketch in CA 1-4R
Starkie, Walter F(itzwilliam) 1894-1976 ... 77-80
Obituary ... 69-72
See also DLB 195
Starkins, Edward 1946- ... 120
Starkloff, Carl F. 1933- ... 53-56
Starkman, Miriam K(osh) 1916- ... 65-68
Starkman, Moshe 1906-1975 Obituary ... 57-60
Starks, Richard 1947- ... 113
Starkweather, David 1935- ... 97-100
See also DLB 7
Starling, Thomas
See Hayton, Richard Neil
Star-Man's Padre
See Patrick, Johnstone G(illespie)
Starn, Randolph 1939- ... CANR-67
Earlier sketches in CA 45-48, CANR-32
Starnes, Richard 1922- Brief entry ... 114
Starobin, Joseph R(obert) 1913-1976 ... 45-48
Obituary ... 69-72
Starobin, Rosalind Gould
1912(?)-1983 Obituary ... 111
Starobinski, Jean 1920- ... 131
Starr, Anne
See Sanford, Annette
Starr, Cecile 1921- ... 65-68
Starr, Chauncey 1912- ... 109
Starr, Chester G. 1914- ... CANR-36
Earlier sketches in CA 1-4R, CANR-1, 16
Starr, Edward Caryl 1911- ... 13-16R
Starr, Frank 1938- ... 69-72
Starr, Henry
See Bingley, David Ernest
Starr, Herbert F(rederick) 1932- ... 116
Starr, Isidore 1911- ... CANR-7
Earlier sketch in CA 13-16R
Starr, James (A.) 1904(?)-1990 Obituary ... 132
Starr, Jerold M. 1941- ... 77-80
Starr, Jimmy
See Starr, James (A.)
Starr, John
See Counselman, Mary Elizabeth
Starr, John 1914(?)-1980 Obituary ... 101
Starr, John A.
See Gillese, John Patrick
Starr, John Bryan 1939- ... 77-80
Starr, Judy
See Gelfman, Judith S(chlein)
Starr, June (O.) ... 140
Starr, Kevin 1940- ... CANR-72
Earlier sketch in CA 120
Starr, Larry 1946- ... 143
Starr, Louis M(orris) 1917-1980 ... 53-56
Obituary ... 97-100
Starr, Mark 1894-1985 Obituary ... 116
See also AITN 1
Starr, Martin Kenneth 1927- ... CANR-8
Earlier sketch in CA 17-20R
Starr, Patricia 1943- ... 145
Starr, Patti
See Starr, Patricia
Starr, Paul (Elliot) 1949- ... 127
Brief entry ... 123
Starr, Penelope
See Gelles-Cole, Sandi
Starr, Raymond 1937- ... 65-68
Starr, Roger 1918- ... CANR-11
Earlier sketch in CA 21-24R
Starr, Roland
See Rowland, D(onald) S(ydney)
Starr, S(tephen) Frederick 1940- ... CANR-17
Earlier sketch in CA 85-88
Starr, Stephen Z. 1909-1985 ... CANR-17
Earlier sketch in CA 37-40R
Starr, Ward
See Manes, Stephen
Starr, William Thomas 1910- ... 41-44R
Starr, Wilmarth Holt 1913- ... 17-20R
Starratt, Alfred B(yron) 1914- ... 17-20R
Starret, William
See McClintock, Marshall
Starrett, (Charles) Vincent (Emerson) 1886-1974 ...
CANR-62
Obituary ... 45-48
Earlier sketches in CA 73-76, CANR-31
See also DLB 187
Starrs, James E(dward) 1930- ... 118
Starr Taylor, Bridget 1959- ... SATA 99
Starry, Donn Albert 1925- ... 109
Start, Clarissa
See Lippert, Clarissa Start
Starzl, Thomas E(arl) 1926- ... 140
Stasch, Stanley F. 1931- ... 41-44R
Stasheff, Christopher 1944- ... CANR-58
Earlier sketches in CA 65-68, CANR-10, 26
Stasheff, (Adolph) Edward 1909- ... 5-8R
Stashower, Daniel (Meyer) 1960- ... 131
Stasiak, Krystyna ... SATA 49
Stasio, Marilyn L(ouise) 1940- ... 33-36R
Stassinopoulos, Arianna
See Huffington, Arianna Stassinopoulos
Stasz, Clarice ... CANR-7
Earlier sketch in CA 61-64
Staten, Patricia S. 1945- ... 53-56
Statera, Gianni 1943- ... CANR-8
Earlier sketch in CA 57-60
States, Bert O(len) 1929- ... 73-76
Statham, E. Robert 1963- ... 152
Statham, Frances P(atton) 1931- ... 101
Statham, Jane 1917- ... 13-16R
Statius
See Statius, Publius Papinius
Statler, Oliver Hadley 1915- ... 5-8R
Staton, Knofel L. 1934- ... CANR-35
Earlier sketch in CA 114
Staton, Thomas Felix 1917- ... 5-8R
Statten, Vargo
See Fearn, John Russell
Staub, August W(illiam) 1931- ... CANR-2
Earlier sketch in CA 45-48
Staub, Ervin 1938- ... 133
Staubach, Charles N(eff) 1906- ... CANR-4
Earlier sketch in CA 5-8R
Staubach, Roger (Thomas) 1942- ... 104
Staudacher, Joseph M. 1914- ... 25-28R
Staudacher, Rosemarian V(alentiner) 1918- ... 5-8R
Staudenraus, P(hilip) J(ohn) 1928-1971 ... 1-4R
Obituary ... 103
Stauder, Jack 1939- ... 37-40R
Stauderman, Albert P(hilip) 1910- ... CANR-39
Earlier sketches in CA 77-80, CANR-18
Staudinger, Hermann 1881-1965 ... 162
Obituary ... 113
Staudt, Virginia
See Sexton, Virginia Staudt
Stauffer, Don
See Berkebile, Fred D(onovan)
Stauffer, Donald Barlow 1930- ... 57-60
Stauffer, Helen Winter 1922- ... CANR-30
Earlier sketch in CA 109
Staum, Martin Sheldon 1943- ... 103
Staunton, Schuyler
See Baum, L(yman) Frank
Staunton, Ted 1956- ... 163
Staupers, Mabel Keaton 1890-1989 Obituary ... 129
Stauter, (Justin) Jay 1907-1986 Obituary ... 118
Stavans, Ilan 1961- ... 151
Stave, Bruce M(artin) 1937- ... CANR-12
Earlier sketch in CA 29-32R
Staveacre, Tony 1942- ... 130
Staveley, Gaylord L(ee) 1931- ... 37-40R
Stavenhagen, Lee 1933- ... 104
Stavenhagen, Rodolfo 1932- ... CANR-12
Earlier sketch in CA 29-32R
Stavis, Barrie 1906- ... 49-52
Stavis, Ben(edict) 1941- ... 29-32R
Stavrianos, Leften Stavros 1913- ... CANR-6
Earlier sketch in CA 5-8R
Stavros, Niko
See King, Florence
Stavrou, Theofanis G(eorge) 1934- ... CANR-48
Earlier sketch in CA 45-48
Stayer, James M(entzer) 1935- ... CANR-26
Earlier sketch in CA 45-48
Staynes, Jill ... 133
Stead, C(hristian) K(arlson) 1932- ... CANR-44
Earlier sketches in CA 57-60, CANR-6
Stead, Christina (Ellen) 1902-1983 ... CANR-40
Obituary ... 109
Earlier sketches in CA 13-16R, CANR-33
See also CLC 2, 5, 8, 32, 80
See also MTCW 1
Stead, Philip John 1916- ... 108
Stead, Robert J. C. 1880-1959 ... DLB 92
Stead, Thistle Yolette 1902- ... 107
Stead, William Thomas 1849-1912 ... 167
See also TCLC 48
Steadman, David (Wilton) 1936- ... 107
Steadman, John M(arcellus III) 1918- ... 25-28R
Steadman, Mark 1930- ... 37-40R
See also DLB 6
Steadman, Ralph (Idris) 1936- ... CANR-29
Earlier sketch in CA 107
See also SATA 32
Steahly, Vivian Eugenia Emrick 1915- ... 61-64
Steakley, John 1951- ... 120
Stealingworth, Slim
See Wesselmann, Tom
Steamer
See Nason, Leonard H(astings)
Steamer, Robert J(ulius) 1920- ... 41-44R
Steane, J(ohn) B(arry) 1928- ... 9-12R
Steans, Jill A. 1961- ... 167
Steanson, Karen E(lizabeth) 1942- ... 116
Stearn, Gerald E. 1934(?)-1982 Obituary ... 108
Stearn, Jess ... 97-100
Stearn, William T(homas) 1911- ... 158
Stearns, Harold Edmund 1891-1943 Brief
entry ... 107
See also DLB 4
Stearns, Marshall Winslow 1908-1966 Obituary 110
Stearns, Martha Genung 1886- ... 9-12R
Stearns, Monroe (Mather) 1913-1987 ... CANR-2
Obituary ... 124
Earlier sketch in CA 5-8R
See also SATA 5
See also SATA-Obit 55
Stearns, Pamela Fujimoto 1935- ... 65-68
Stearns, Peter N. 1936- ... CANR-55
Earlier sketches in CA 21-24R, CANR-10, 28
Stearns, Raymond Phineas 1904-1970 ... CAP-1
Earlier sketch in CA 11-12
Stebbins, G(eorge) Ledyard 1906- ... 45-48
Stebbins, Richard P(oate) 1913- ... CANR-2
Earlier sketch in CA 5-8R
Stebbins, Robert A(lan) 1938- ... CANR-30
Earlier sketches in CA 29-32R, CANR-12
Stebbins, Robert C(yril) 1915- ... 49-52
Stebbins, Theodore Ellis, Jr. 1938- ... 89-92
Stebel, S(idney) L(eo) 1924- ... 29-32R
Stebenne, David 1960- ... 154
Steber, A. R.
See Palmer, Raymond A.
Steber, Rick 1946- ... 128
Stecher, Miriam B(rodie) 1917- ... 106
Stechow, Wolfgang 1896-1974 ... CANR-9
Obituary ... 53-56
Earlier sketch in CA 65-68
Steck, James S(perow) 1911- ... 41-44R
Steckel, William Reed 1915- ... 17-20R
Stecker, Ann Page 1942- ... 149
Steckler, Arthur 1921-1985 ... 108
See also SATA 65
Steckler, Doug(las) 1948- ... 107
Steckler, Phyllis B. (Schwartzbard) 1933- ... 9-12R
Stedman, Edmund Clarence 1833-1908 ... DLB 64
Stedman, James Murphy 1938- ... 77-80
Stedman, Jane W(inifred) 1920- ... 37-40R
Stedman, Murray S(alisbury), Jr. 1917- ... 17-20R
Stedman, R(aymond) William 1930- ... 29-32R
Stedman, Ray C. 1917- ... 104
Stedman Jones, Gareth 1942- ... CANR-31
Earlier sketch in CA 45-48
Stedmond, John Mitchell 1916- ... 103
Stedwell, Paki 1945- ... 103
Steed, Gitel P. 1914-1977 ... 41-44R
Steed, Thomas Jefferson 1904-1983 Obituary ... 110
Steed, Tom
See Steed, Thomas Jefferson
Steedman, Carolyn (Kay) 1947- ... 152
Steedman, Marguerite Couturier 1908- ... CANR-1
Earlier sketch in CA 1-4R
Steefel, Lawrence D. 1894- ... CAP-2
Earlier sketch in CA 21-22
Steeger, Henry 1903-1990 ... 41-44R
Obituary ... 133
Steeger, Henry 1929(?)-1978 Obituary ... 77-80
Steegmuller, Francis 1906- ... CANR-2
Earlier sketch in CA 49-52
See also DLB 111
Steel, Anthony Bedford 1900-1973 ... 5-8R
Obituary ... 89-92
Steel, Byron
See Steegmuller, Francis
Steel, Danielle (Fernande) 1947- ... CANR-65
Earlier sketches in CA 81-84, CANR-19, 36
Interview in ... CANR-19
See also AAYA 23
See also BEST 89:1, 90:4
See also DAM POP
See also MTCW 1
See also SATA 66
Steel, David 1938- ... 145
Steel, Dawn 1946-1997 ... 151
Obituary ... 163
Steel, Edward M(arvin), Jr. 1918- ... 9-12R
Steel, Eric M. 1904- ... 89-92
Steel, Flora Annie (Webster) 1847-1929 Brief
entry ... 116
See also DLB 153, 156
Steel, Gayla R(uth) 1933- ... 149
Steel, Joyce 1937- ... 164
Steel, Nigel 1962- ... 147
Steel, Ronald (Lewis) 1931- ... CANR-7
Earlier sketch in CA 9-12R
Steel, Tex
See Ross, W(illiam) E(dward) D(aniel)
Steele, A(rchibald) T(rojan) 1903-1992 ... CAP-2
Obituary ... 137
Earlier sketch in CA 19-20
Steele, Addison II
See Lupoff, Richard A(llen)
Steele, Alan 1905-1985 Obituary ... 115
Steele, Allen 1958- ... 136
Steele, Arthur R(obert) 1916- ... 9-12R
Steele, Chester K. ... CANR-26
Earlier sketches in CAP-2, CA 19-20
Steele, Colin Robert 1944- ... 104
Steele, Curtis
See Davis, Frederick C(lyde)
Steele, Cynthia 1951- ... 156
Steele, Dale
See Glut, Donald F(rank)
Steele, Dirk
See Plawin, Paul
Steele, Elizabeth 1921- ... CANR-43
Earlier sketch in CA 45-48
Steele, Erskine
See Henderson, Archibald
Steele, Fletcher 1885-1971 ... CAP-1
Earlier sketch in CA 13-14
Steele, Frank 1935- ... 37-40R
Steele, Fred I(rving) 1938- ... CANR-17
Earlier sketches in CA 45-48, CANR-2
Steele, Fritz
See Steele, Fred I(rving)
Steele, George P(eabody II) 1924- ... 1-4R
Steele, Gordon (Charles) 1892-1981 ... 105
Obituary ... 102
Steele, Harwood E(lmes Robert) 1897- ... CANR-64
Earlier sketches in CAP-1, CA 13-16
Steele, Henry 1931- ... 41-44R
Steele, I(an) K(enneth) 1937- ... 45-48
Steele, Jack 1914-1980 ... 109
Obituary ... 102
Steele, James B(ruce, Jr.) 1943- ... 115
Brief entry ... 110
Interview in ... 115
Steele, Mary 1930- ... 159
See also SATA 94
Steele, Mary Q(uintard Govan) 1922-1992 ...
CANR-22
Obituary ... 139
Earlier sketches in CA 1-4R, CANR-6
See also MAICYA
See also SATA 3, 51
See also SATA-Obit 72
Steele, (Henry) Max(well) 1922- ... 25-28R
See also DLBY 80
See also SATA 10
Steele, Michael Rhoads 1945- ... 111
Steele, Peter (R.) 1935- ... 108
Steele, Philip 1948- ... 149
See also SATA 81
Steele, Phillip W(ayne) 1934- ... 61-64
Steele, R. David 1931- ... 135
Steele, Richard 1672-1729 ... CDBLB 1660-1789
See also DLB 84, 101
Steele, Richard W(illiam) 1934- ... 134
Brief entry ... 107
Steele, Robert (Scott) 1917- ... 49-52
Steele, Shelby 1946- ... 155
Steele, Thomas J(oseph) 1933- ... 61-64
Steele, Timothy (Reid) 1948- ... CANR-50
Earlier sketches in CA 93-96, CANR-16
See also CLC 45
See also DLB 120
Steele, Tommy
See Hicks, Thomas
Steele, Valerie (Fahnestock) 1955- ... 138
Steele, Wilbur Daniel 1886-1970 ... 109
Obituary ... 29-32R
See also DLB 86
Steele, William O(wen) 1917-1979 ... CANR-64
Earlier sketches in CA 1-4R, CANR-2
See also MAICYA
See also SATA 1, 51
See also SATA-Obit 27
Steelhammer, Ilona 1952- ... SATA 98
Steelman, Robert J(ames) 1914- ... CANR-28
Earlier sketches in CA 69-72, CANR-11
Steelsmith, Shari 1962- ... SATA 72
Steely, John E(dward) 1922- ... 37-40R
Steen, Edwin B. 1901- ... 101
Steen, Frank
See Felstein, Ivor
Steen, John Warren, Jr. 1925- ... 13-16R
Steen, Malcolm Harold 1928-1983 ... 29-32R
Obituary ... 135
Steen, Marguerite 1894-1975 ... 97-100
Obituary ... 61-64
Steen, Mike
See Steen, Malcolm Harold
Steen, Sara Jayne 1949- ... 106
Steenberg, Sven 1905- ... 37-40R
Steene, Birgitta 1928- ... 85-88
Steensma, Robert Charles 1930- ... 41-44R
Steenson, Gary P(aul) 1944- ... 107
Steer, Alfred G(ilbert), Jr. 1913- ... 45-48
Steer, Charlotte
See Hunter, Maud L(ily)
Steere, Daniel C(onrad) 1938- ... 93-96
Steere, Douglas V(an) 1901-1995 ... 13-16R
Obituary ... 147
Steere, Richard 1643(?)-1721 ... DLB 24
Steers, J(ames) A(lfred) 1899-1987 ... 124
Steese, Edward 1902-1981 Obituary ... 105
Steese, Peter B(echler) 1933- ... 17-20R
Steeves, Frank Leslie 1921- ... 13-16R
Steeves, Harrison R(oss) 1881-1981 Obituary ... 104
Stefan, Verena 1947- ... 154
Stefanelli, Vladimir Clain
See Clain-Stefanelli, Vladimir
Stefanics, Charlotte L(ouise) 1927- ... 116
Stefanik, Alfred T. 1939- ... SATA 55
Stefanile, Felix 1920- ... CANR-1
Earlier sketch in CA 45-48
Stefanovski, Goran 1952- ... DLB 181
Stefansson, Evelyn
See Nef, Evelyn Stefansson
Stefansson, Thorsteinn 1912- ... CANR-29
Earlier sketch in CA 77-80
Steffan, Alice Kennedy 1907- ... 5-8R

Steffan, Jack
See Steffan, Alice Kennedy
Steffan, Siobhan R.
See Goulart, Frances Sheridan
Steffan, Truman Guy 1910- 29-32R
Steffanson, Con
See Cassiday, Bruce (Bingham)
and Goulart, Ron(ald Joseph)
Steffek, Edwin F(rancis) 1912-1985 89-92
Obituary 118
Steffen, Albert 1884-1963 Obituary 93-96
Steffen, Jerome O(rville) 1942- 112
Steffen, Jonathan 1958- 135
Steffens, Bradley 1955- 146
See also SATA 77
Steffens, (Joseph) Lincoln 1866-1936 Brief entry 117
See also TCLC 20
Steffensmeier, Darrell J. 1942- 123
Stefferud, Alfred (Daniel) 1903- CAP-1
Earlier sketch in CA 13-16
Steffler, John 1947- CANR-33
Earlier sketch in CA 110
Stefflre, Buford 1916- 5-8R
Steffy, J. Richard 1924- 151
Stegall, Carrie Coffey 1908- CAP-2
Earlier sketch in CA 25-28
Stegeman, Janet Allais 1923- 128
See also Britton, Kate
See also SATA 53
See also SATA-Brief 49
Stegeman, John F(oster) 1918- 17-20R
Stegenga, James A. 1937- 25-28R
Steger, Shelby 1906- 49-52
Steglich, W(infred) G(eorge) 1921- CANR-30
Earlier sketch in CA 45-48
Stegman, Michael A(llen) 1940- 41-44R
Stegner, Page 1937- CANR-10
Earlier sketch in CA 21-24R
Stegner, Wallace (Earle) 1909-1993 CANR-46
Obituary 141
Earlier sketches in CA 1-4R, CANR-1, 21
See also CAAS 9
See also AITN 1
See also BEST 90:3
See also CLC 9, 49, 81
See also DAM NOV
See also DLB 9
See also DLBY 93
See also MTCW 1
See also SSC 27
Stehling, Kurt R(ichard) 1919-1997 162
Obituary 157
Brief entry 110
Stehr, Hermann 1864-1940 DLB 66
Steible, Daniel J(oseph) 1912-1976 45-48
Obituary 103
Steichen, Edward 1879-1973 Obituary 41-44R
Steichen, Joanna T(aub) 1933- 132
Steichen, Paula 1943- 25-28R
Steig, Irwin 1901-1977 Obituary 73-76
Steig, William (H.) 1907- CANR-44
Earlier sketches in CA 77-80, CANR-21
Interview in CANR-21
See also AITN 1
See also CLR 2, 15
See also DLB 61
See also MAICYA
See also SATA 18, 70
Steiger, Andrew Jacob 1900- 5-8R
Steiger, Brad (E.) 1936- CANR-21
Earlier sketch in CA 33-36R
Steiger, Paul E(rnest) 1942- 77-80
Steigman, Benjamin 1889(?)-1974 Obituary 53-56
Steiman, Sidney 1922- 5-8R
Steimle, Edmund A(ugustus) 1907- 121
Stein, Aaron Marc 1906-1985 CANR-63
Obituary 117
Earlier sketches in CA 9-12R, CANR-6
Stein, Arnold (Sidney) 1915- Brief entry 114
Stein, Arthur (Benjamin) 1937- 29-32R
Stein, Ben
See Stein, Benjamin
Stein, Benjamin 1944- 106
Interview in 106
Stein, Bob 1920- 37-40R
Stein, Bruno 1930-1996 37-40R
Obituary 151
Stein, Calvert 1903-1982 29-32R
Obituary 125
Stein, Charles
See Schwalberg, Carol(yn Ernestine Stein)
Stein, Charles S. 1940- 21-24R
Stein, Charles W(arner) 1918- 116
Stein, Dan J(oseph) 1962- 166
Stein, Dona 77-80
Stein, Edith Sarah
See Sarah, Edith
Stein, Edward D. 1965- 162
Stein, Edward V(incent) 1920- 13-16R
Stein, Emanuel 1908-1985 Obituary 114
Stein, Eugene 1960- 149
Stein, George P(hilip) 1917- 65-68
Stein, Gertrude 1874-1946 132
Brief entry 104
See also CDALB 1917-1929
See also DA
See also DAB
See also DAC
See also DAM MST, NOV, POET
See also DLB 4, 54, 86
See also DLBD 15
See also MTCW 1
See also PC 18
See also TCLC 1, 6, 28, 48
See also WLC

Stein, Harry 1938- 61-64
Stein, Harry 1948- 128
Brief entry 120
Interview in 128
Stein, Harve 1904- SATA-Brief 30
Stein, Herb 1928- 65-68
Stein, Herbert 1916- 106
Stein, Herman D(avid) 1917- CANR-30
Earlier sketch in CA 1-4R
Stein, Jack M(adison) 1914-1976 CANR-15
Obituary 103
Earlier sketch in CA 1-4R
Stein, Jan
See Hegeler, Sten
Stein, Jane Jacobson 1937- 97-100
Stein, Janice Gross 1943- CANR-55
Earlier sketch in CA 127
Stein, Jerome L(eon) 1928- 81-84
Stein, Jess 1914-1984 Obituary 113
Stein, Joseph 1912- CANR-61
Earlier sketches in CA 13-16R, CANR-31
Stein, Kevin 1954- 159
Stein, Leo Daniel 1872-1947 Brief entry 107
See also DLB 4
Stein, Leon 1910- 17-20R
Stein, Leon 1912-1990 CANR-7
Obituary 130
Earlier sketch in CA 17-20R
Stein, Louis 1917- 138
Stein, M(eyer) L(ewis) 1920- CANR-13
Earlier sketch in CA 17-20R
See also SATA 6
Stein, Mark (Avrum) 1951- 118
Stein, Martha L(inda) 1942- 53-56
Stein, Maurice Robert 1926- 49-52
Stein, Michael B. 1940- CANR-32
Earlier sketch in CA 45-48
Stein, Mini 29-32R
See also SATA 2
Stein, Morris I(saac) 1921- CANR-1
Earlier sketch in CA 1-4R
Stein, Peter (Gonville) 1926- 21-24R
Stein, Philip L(awrence) 1939- 61-64
Stein, R(ichard) Conrad 1937- CANR-22
Earlier sketch in CA 41-44R
See also SATA 31, 82
Stein, Rita F. 1922- Brief entry 106
Stein, Robert 1924- 49-52
Stein, Robert H(arry) 1935- 101
Stein, Roger B(reed) 1932- CANR-2
Earlier sketch in CA 45-48
Stein, Sandra Kovacs 1939- 106
Stein, Sara Bonnett SATA-Brief 34
Stein, Sherman K. 1926- 151
Stein, Sol 1926- CANR-2
Earlier sketch in CA 49-52
See also AITN 1
Stein, Stanley J. 1920- Brief entry 108
Stein, Susan M. 1942- CANR-14
Earlier sketch in CA 37-40R
Stein, Thomas A. 1924- 45-48
Stein, Toby 1935- 5-8R
Stein, Walter 1924- 25-28R
Stein, Wendy 1951- 145
See also SATA 77
Stein, William B. 1915- 104
Stein, William W(arner) 1921- 1-4R
Steinbach, Alexander Alan 1894-1978 85-88
Obituary 81-84
Steinbach, Meredith 1949- 107
Steinbeck, John (Ernst) 1902-1968 CANR-35
Obituary 25-28R
Earlier sketches in CA 1-4R, CANR-1
See also AAYA 12
See also CDALB 1929-1941
See also CLC 1, 5, 9, 13, 21, 34, 45, 75
See also DA
See also DAB
See also DAC
See also DAM DRAM, MST, NOV
See also DLB 7, 9
See also DLBD 2
See also MTCW 1
See also SATA 9
See also SSC 11
See also WLC
Steinberg, Aaron Zacharovich
1891-1975 Obituary 61-64
Steinberg, Alfred 1917-1995 CANR-9
Obituary 147
Earlier sketch in CA 5-8R
See also SATA 9
Steinberg, Blema S. 1934- 163
Steinberg, Charles S(ide) 1913-1978 CANR-4
Earlier sketch in CA 49-52
Steinberg, Clarence B. 1929- 153
Steinberg, Danny D(avid Charles) 1931- CANR-14
Earlier sketch in CA 37-40R
Steinberg, David Joel 1937- 25-28R
Steinberg, Eleanor B(usick) 1936- 65-68
Steinberg, Erwin R(ay) 1920- CANR-12
Earlier sketch in CA 29-32R
Steinberg, Fannie 1899- 115
See also SATA 43
Steinberg, Fred J. 1933- 37-40R
See also SATA 4
Steinberg, Harriet 1954- 127
Steinberg, Israel 1903(?)-1983 Obituary 109
Steinberg, J(ay) Leonard 1930- 57-60
Steinberg, Jacob 1915- 141
Steinberg, Jeffrey 1947(?)-1981 Obituary 104
Steinberg, Jonathan 1934- 21-24R
Steinberg, Joseph L(awrence) 1928- 25-28R
Steinberg, Judah 1861-1908 Brief entry 106
Steinberg, Laurence 1952- 146

Steinberg, Leo 1920- CANR-17
Earlier sketches in CA 45-48, CANR-1
Steinberg, M. W. 1918- 127
Steinberg, Mark D(avid) 1953- 153
Steinberg, Neil 1960- 139
Steinberg, Norman 1939- 159
Steinberg, Phillip Orso 1921- CANR-2
Earlier sketch in CA 5-8R
See also SATA 34
Steinberg, Rafael (Mark) 1927- CANR-9
Earlier sketch in CA 61-64
See also SATA 45
Steinberg, Rolf 1929- 132
Steinberg, S(igrid) H(enry) 1899-1969 CAP-1
Earlier sketch in CA 9-10
Steinberg, Saul 1914- 89-92
See also SATA 67
Steinberg, Warren 1944- 147
Steinberg, Wendy 1952- 146
Steinbergh, Judith W(olinsky) 1943- CANR-1
Earlier sketch in CA 45-48
Steinbicker, Paul G(eorge) 1906- CAP-2
Earlier sketch in CA 19-20
Steinbreder, Harry John, Jr.
1930-1985 Obituary 117
Steinbreder, Sandy
See Steinbreder, Harry John, Jr.
Steinbrook, Gordon L. 1942- 149
Steinbrueck, Victor 1911- 13-16R
Steinbruner, John David 1941- 77-80
Steinbrunner, (Peter) Chris(tian) 1933-1993 CANR-1
Obituary 141
Earlier sketch in CA 45-48
Steincrohn, Peter J(oseph)
1899-1986 Obituary 118
Brief entry 112
Steinem, Gloria 1934- CANR-51
Earlier sketches in CA 53-56, CANR-28
See also CLC 63
See also MTCW 1
Steiner, Barbara A(nnette) 1934- CANR-30
Earlier sketches in CA 73-76, CANR-13
See also SAAS 13
See also SATA 13, 83
Steiner, Barry H(oward) 1942- 137
Steiner, Barry R(aymond) 115
Steiner, Charlotte 1900-1981 SATA 45
Steiner, Claude 1935- 97-100
Steiner, Frederick 1949- CANR-39
Earlier sketch in CA 116
Steiner, Gary A(lbert) 1931-1966 9-12R
Obituary 103
Steiner, George 1929- CANR-67
Earlier sketches in CA 73-76, CANR-31
See also CLC 24
See also DAM NOV
See also DLB 67
See also MTCW 1
See also SATA 62
Steiner, George A(lbert) 1912- CANR-7
Earlier sketch in CA 13-16R
Steiner, Gerolf 1908- 29-32R
Steiner, Gilbert Yale 1924- 160
Brief entry 115
Steiner, H. Arthur 1905- 5-8R
Steiner, Irene Hunter 1920- 97-100
Steiner, Joerg 1930- CANR-56
Earlier sketches in CA 108, CANR-29
See also SATA 35
Steiner, Jorg
See Steiner, Joerg
Steiner, K. Leslie
See Delaney, Samuel R(ay, Jr.)
Steiner, K. Leslie
See Delany, Samuel R(ay, Jr.)
Steiner, Kurt 1912- CANR-7
Earlier sketch in CA 17-20R
Steiner, Lee R. 1901- CAP-1
Earlier sketch in CA 13-14
Steiner, Michael C. 1947- 149
Steiner, Paul CANR-37
Earlier sketches in CA 9-12R, CANR-4
Steiner, Peter O(tto) 1922- CANR-14
Earlier sketch in CA 37-40R
Steiner, Ralph 1899-1986 148
Obituary 119
Brief entry 113
Steiner, Roger J(acob) 1924- CANR-32
Earlier sketch in CA 45-48
Steiner, Rudolf 1861-1925 Brief entry 107
See also TCLC 13
Steiner, Shari 1941- 73-76
Steiner, Stan(ley) 1925-1987 CANR-39
Obituary 121
Earlier sketches in CA 45-48, CANR-1, 16
See also SATA 14
See also SATA-Obit 50
Steiner, Susan Clemmer 1947- 115
Steiner, Thomas R(obert) 1934- 45-48
Steiner, Vera P(olgar) John
See John-Steiner, Vera P(olgar)
Steiner, Wendy 1949- CANR-61
Earlier sketches in CA 81-84, CANR-14
Steiner, Zara S(hakow) 1928- 129
Steiner-Prag, Hugo 1880-1945 SATA-Brief 32
Steinert, Marlis G(ertrud) 81-84
Steinfels, Peter (Francis) 1941- Brief entry 116
Steingold, Fred S(aul) 1936- 109
Steinhardt, Anne Elizabeth 1941- 104
Steinhardt, Herschel S. 1910- CANR-40
Earlier sketches in CAP-2, CA 23-24
Steinhardt, Milton 1909- 77-80
Steinhardt, Nancy Shatzman 1954- 135
Steinhart, Carol E(lder) 1935- 57-60
Steinhart, Peter 1943- 148

Steinhauer, Harry 1905- CANR-1
Earlier sketch in CA 1-4R
Steinhaus, Arthur H. 1897-1970 CAP-1
Earlier sketch in CA 19-20
Steinhaus, John Edward 1917- 127
Steinheimer, Richard (V.) 1929- CANR-50
Earlier sketch in CA 123
Steinhoff, Dan 1911- 77-80
Steinhoff, William (Richard) 1914- 85-88
Steinhowel, Heinrich c. 1411-1479 DLB 179
Steinitz, Kate T(rauman) 1889-1975 CAP-2
Earlier sketch in CA 23-24
Steinitz, Paul 1909- 104
Steinke, Ann E(lizabeth) 1946- CANR-32
Earlier sketch in CA 113
Steinke, Peter L(ouis) 1938- 29-32R
Steinkraus, Warren E(dward) 1922- 21-24R
Steinlauf, Michael C. 1947- 167
Steinle, John G(erard) 1916-1990 9-12R
Obituary 132
Steinle, Paul (Michael) 1939- 77-80
Steinman, David 1958- 153
Steinman, Lisa Malinowski 1950- 69-72
Steinman, Louise 1951- 147
Steinman, Michael 1952- 134
Steinmann, Anne G. 1906(?)-1987 Obituary 121
Steinmann, Martin, Jr. 1915- CANR-26
Earlier sketch in CA 1-4R
Steinmetz, Eulalie
See Ross, Eulalie Steinmetz
Steinmetz, Lawrence L(eo) 1938- CANR-11
Earlier sketch in CA 21-24R
Steinmetz, Leon 136
Steinmetz, Paul B. 1928- 135
Steinmetz, Rollin C. 1912(?)-1986 Obituary 121
Steinmetz, Urban G. 1920- CANR-10
Earlier sketch in CA 25-28R
Steins, Richard 1942- 148
See also SATA 79
Steintrager, James A(lvin) 1936- 93-96
Steinwedel, Louis William 1943- 37-40R
Steirman, Hy 1921- 29-32R
Steiss, Alan Walter 1937- CANR-28
Earlier sketches in CA 29-32R, CANR-12
Steitz, Edward S(tephen) 1920-1990 69-72
Obituary 131
Stekert, Ellen J(ane) 1935- 33-36R
Stekler, Herman O. 1932- 17-20R
Stell, Aaron 1911- 57-60
Stell, Elizabeth P(arker) 1958- 166
Stell, Geoffrey (Percival) 1944- 124
Stellingwerf, Steve(n Lee) 1962- 138
Stellman, Jeanne M(ager) 1947- 102
Stellman, Steven D(ale) 1945- 85-88
Steloff, Frances 1887-1989 DLB 187
Steltenkamp, Michael F(rancis) 1950- 112
Stelter, Gilbert Arthur 1933- CANR-15
Earlier sketch in CA 41-44R
Steltzer, Ulli 1923- 104
Stelzer, Dick 1950- 107
Stelzig, Eugene Louis 1943- 81-84
Stem, Thad(deus Garland), Jr. 1916-1980 97-100
Obituary 101
Stember, Charles Herbert 1916-1982 21-24R
Obituary 135
Stemp, Isay 1922- 29-32R
Stemp, Robin (Jenniver Pamela) 1944- 107
Stempel, Guido H(ermann) III 1928- 77-80
Stempel, John Dallas 1938- 110
Stempel, Thomas Ritter 1941- 110
Stempel, Tom
See Stempel, Thomas Ritter
Sten, Christopher (W.) 1944- 137
Stenberger, Marten 1898- CANR-5
Earlier sketch in CA 5-8R
Stendahl, Krister 1921- CANR-12
Earlier sketch in CA 17-20R
Stendhal 1783-1842 DA
See also DAB
See also DAC
See also DAM MST, NOV
See also DLB 119
See also SSC 27
See also WLC
Stendhal, Renate (Neumann) 1944- 148
Stene, Edwin O(tto) 1900- CAP-2
Earlier sketch in CA 21-22
Steneck, Nicholas H. 1940- 106
Steneman, Shep 1945- 107
Stenerson, Douglas C. 1920- 37-40R
Stengel, Richard 1955- 136
Stenhouse, David 1932- 89-92
Stenius, George
See Seaton, George
Stensboel, Ottar 1930- 69-72
Stenson, Frederick 1951- 113
Stent, Gunther S(iegmund) 1924- 29-32R
Stenton, Doris Mary (Parsons)
1894-1971 Obituary 104
Stenus
See Huxley, Herbert H(enry)
Stenzel, Anne K(atherine) 1911- 57-60
Stenzel, George 1910- 45-48
Stepanchev, Stephen 1915- CANR-7
Earlier sketch in CA 17-20R
Stepanian, Michael 1939- 45-48
Stephan, John J(ason) 1941- CANR-45
Earlier sketch in CA 41-44R
Stephan, Leslie (Bates) 1933- CANR-24
Earlier sketches in CA 21-24R, CANR-9
Stephan, Ruth 1910-1974 5-8R
Obituary 145
Stephen, Adeline Virginia
See Woolf, (Adeline) Virginia
Stephen, David 1910- 106

Stephen, Felix N. 1925- ... 153
See also BW 2
Stephen, George 1926- ... 102
Stephen, Jan 1933- ... 1-4R
Stephen, SirLeslie 1832-1904 Brief entry ... 123
See also DLB 57, 144, 190
See also TCLC 23
Stephen, Martin 1949- ... 135
Stephen, Parel Lukose 1898- ... CAP-1
Earlier sketch in CA 9-10
Stephen, R. J.
See Barrett, Norman (S.)
Stephen, Sid 1942- ... 105
Stephen, Sir Leslie
See Stephen, SirLeslie
Stephen, Virginia
See Woolf, (Adeline) Virginia
Stephens, A. Ray 1932- ... CANR-13
Earlier sketch in CA 77-80
Stephens, Alan 1925- ... 17-20R
Stephens, Alexander H. 1812-1883 ... DLB 47
Stephens, Alice Barber 1858-1932 ... DLB 188
See also SATA 66
Stephens, Andy 1956- ... 146
Stephens, Ann Sophia (Winterbotham)
1810-1886 ... DLB 3, 73
Stephens, C(harles) Ralph 1943- ... CANR-48
Earlier sketch in CA 122
Stephens, Casey
See Wagner, Sharon B.
Stephens, Charles
See Goldin, Stephen
Stephens, Charles Asbury 1844(?)-1931 ... DLB 42
Stephens, Donald G. 1931- ... 21-24R
Stephens, Edna Buell 1903- ... CANR-14
Earlier sketch in CA 37-40R
Stephens, Edward Carl 1924- ... 21-24R
Stephens, Eve
See Ward-Thomas, Evelyn Bridget Patricia
Stephens
Stephens, Evelyne Huber 1950- ... 145
Stephens, Frances
See Bentley, Margaret
Stephens, Henrietta Henkle 1909-1983 ... CANR-6
Obituary ... 109
Earlier sketch in CA 9-12R
See also Buckmaster, Henrietta
Stephens, Ian Melville 1903-1984 Obituary ... 112
Stephens, J(ohn) M(ortimer) 1901- ... 13-16R
Stephens, Jack Edward (Jr.) 1955- ... 133
Stephens, James 1882(?)-1950 Brief entry ... 104
See also DLB 19, 153, 162
See also TCLC 4
Stephens, James Charles 1915- ... CANR-3
Earlier sketch in CA 5-8R
Stephens, Jeanne
See Hager, Jean
Stephens, John D(avid) 1947- ... 145
Stephens, John Lloyd 1805-1852 ... DLB 183
Stephens, Joyce 1941- ... 69-72
Stephens, Lester D(ow) 1933- ... CANR-32
Earlier sketch in CA 45-48
Stephens, Martha (Thomas) 1937- ... 77-80
Stephens, Mary Jo 1935- ... 37-40R
See also SATA 8
Stephens, Meic 1938- ... 65-68
Stephens, Michael (Gregory) 1946- ... CANR-43
Earlier sketches in CA 49-52, CANR-3
Stephens, Michael D(awson) 1936- ... CANR-22
Earlier sketches in CA 57-60, CANR-7
Stephens, Mitchell 1949- ... 136
Stephens, Otis H(ammond), Jr. 1936- ... 65-68
Stephens, Reed
See Donaldson, Stephen R.
Stephens, Robert O(ren) 1928- ... 25-28R
Stephens, Rockwell R(ittenhouse) 1900- ... 53-56
Stephens, Rosemary 1924- ... 77-80
Stephens, Thomas M. 1931- ... 29-32R
Stephens, W(illiam) P(eter) 1934- ... CANR-52
Earlier sketches in CA 29-32R, CANR-12, 28
Stephens, W(illiam) Richard 1932- ... 29-32R
Stephens, Wade C. 1932- ... 21-24R
Stephens, Will Beth 1918- ... 37-40R
Stephens, William M(cLain) 1925- ... 57-60
See also SATA 21
Stephens, William N(ewton) 1927- ... CANR-1
Earlier sketch in CA 1-4R
Stephensen, A. M.
See Manes, Stephen
Stephenson, Alan M. G. (?)-1984 Obituary ... 113
Stephenson, Andrew M(ichael) 1946- ... 124
Brief entry ... 118
Stephenson, Crocker 1956- ... 142
Stephenson, David 1947- ... 118
Stephenson, Gilbert T(homas) 1884-1972 ... CAP-1
Obituary ... 37-40R
Earlier sketch in CA 17-18
Stephenson, Howard 1893-1978 ... 37-40R
Stephenson, Jean 1892-1979 Obituary ... 85-88
Stephenson, John B(ell) 1937- ... 61-64
Stephenson, John Edward Drayton 1928- Brief
entry ... 112
Stephenson, Matthew A(rnold) 1935- ... 45-48
Stephenson, Maureen 1927- ... CANR-38
Earlier sketches in CA 85-88, CANR-16
Stephenson, Neal 1959- ... 122
Stephenson, (William) Ralph (Ewing) 1910- . 17-20R
Stephenson, Richard M(anning) 1918- ... 109
Stephenson, Wendell Holmes 1899-1970 . CANR-3
Earlier sketch in CA 1-4R
Stepka, Milan
See Benes, Jan
Stepp, Ann 1935- ... 106
See also SATA 29
Stepto, Michele 1946- ... 128
See also SATA 61
Stepto, Robert B(urns) 1945- ... 101
See also BW 1
Steptoe, Andrew (P. A.) ... 162
Steptoe, John (Lewis) 1950-1989 ... CANR-26
Obituary ... 129
Earlier sketches in CA 49-52, CANR-3
See also BW 1
See also CLR 2, 12
See also MAICYA
See also SATA 8, 63
Steptoe, Lydia
See Barnes, Djuna
Steptoe, Patrick Christopher 1913-1988 ... 163
Obituary ... 125
Sterba, Gunther Hans Wenzel 1922- ... 5-8R
Sterba, Richard F(rancis) 1898- ... 124
Sterchi, Beat 1949- ... CLC 65
Stercho, Peter George 1919- ... 49-52
Sterken, Christiaan (L.) 1946- ... 142
Sterland, E(rnest) G(eorge) 1919- ... 65-68
Sterling, Anna Kate
See Slide, Anthony
Sterling, Anthony
See Caesar, (Eu)Gene (Lee)
Sterling, Brett
See Bradbury, Ray (Douglas)
and Hamilton, Edmond
and Samachson, Joseph
Sterling, Bruce 1954- ... CANR-44
Earlier sketch in CA 119
See also CLC 72
Sterling, Bryan B. 1922- ... 164
Sterling, Chandler W(infield) 1911- ... 21-24R
Sterling, Claire 1919-1995 ... 123
Obituary ... 148
Sterling, David L. 1929- ... 139
Sterling, Donald J(ustus), Jr. 1927- ... 77-80
Sterling, Dorothy 1913- ... CANR-28
Earlier sketches in CA 9-12R, CANR-5
See also CLR 1
See also JRDA
See also MAICYA
See also SAAS 2
See also SATA 1, 83
Sterling, George 1869-1926 ... 165
Brief entry ... 117
See also DLB 54
See also TCLC 20
Sterling, Helen
See Watts, Helen L. Hoke
Sterling, James 1701-1763 ... DLB 24
Sterling, John 1806-1844 ... DLB 116
Sterling, Maria Sandra
See Floren, Lee
Sterling, Philip 1907-1989 ... 49-52
Obituary ... 129
See also SATA 8
See also SATA-Obit 63
Sterling, Richard W(hitney) 1922- ... 45-48
Sterling, Robert R. 1931- ... CANR-28
Earlier sketch in CA 29-32R
Sterling, Sandra
See Floren, Lee
Sterling, Shirley (Anne) 1948- ... 160
See also SATA 101
Sterling, Susan Fisher 1955- ... 147
Sterling, Theodor D(avid) 1923- ... 25-28R
Stermer, Bill 1947- ... 110
Stern, Alfred 1899- ... 53-56
Stern, Barbara L.
See Lang, Barbara
Stern, Bill 1907-1971 Obituary ... 89-92
Stern, Boris 1892-1984 ... CAP-2
Obituary ... 113
Earlier sketch in CA 17-18
Stern, Carl 1937- ... 97-100
Stern, Catherine B(rieger)
1894-1973 Obituary ... 37-40R
Stern, Clarence A. 1913- ... 17-20R
Stern, Curt 1902-1981 Obituary ... 105
Stern, Daniel 1928- ... CANR-5
Earlier sketch in CA 5-8R
Stern, Daniel N. 1934- ... 136
Stern, David 1949- ... 138
Stern, Donald A. 1928(?)-1975 Obituary ... 57-60
Stern, E. Mark 1929- ... 37-40R
Stern, Edith Mendel 1901-1975 Obituary ... 57-60
Stern, Edward Severin 1924- ... 53-56
Stern, Elizabeth
See Uhr, Elizabeth
Stern, Ellen Norman 1927- ... CANR-14
Earlier sketch in CA 37-40R
See also SATA 26
Stern, Frances Meritt 1938- ... 112
Stern, Frederick Curtis 1929- ... 108
Stern, Frederick M. 1890(?)-1977 Obituary ... 69-72
Stern, Fritz 1926- ... CANR-1
Earlier sketch in CA 1-4R
Stern, G(ladys) B(ertha) 1890-1973 Obituary . 45-48
See also DLB 197
Stern, George G(ordon) 1923-1974 ... CAP-2
Earlier sketch in CA 29-32
Stern, Gerald 1925- ... CANR-28
Earlier sketch in CA 81-84
See also CLC 40, 100
See also DLB 105
Stern, Gerald M(ann) 1937- ... 69-72
Stern, Geraldine 1907- ... 101
Stern, Gerd Jacob 1928- Brief entry ... 106
Stern, Guy 1922- ... 41-44R
Stern, Harold P. 1922-1977 Obituary ... 69-72
Stern, Harold S. 1923(?)-1976 ... 153
Obituary ... 65-68
See also BW 2
Stern, Harry Joshua 1897- ... 69-72
Stern, Henry L. 1899- ... 97-100
Stern, Howard 1954- ... 146
Stern, J(ulius) David 1886-1971 Obituary ... 104
Stern, J(oseph) P(eter Maria) 1920-1991 . CANR-10
Obituary ... 136
Earlier sketch in CA 21-24R
Stern, Jacqueline Lee
See Marten, Jacqueline (Lee)
Stern, James (Andrew) 1904-1993 ... 21-24R
Obituary ... 143
Stern, Jane 1946- ... CANR-10
Earlier sketch in CA 61-64
Stern, Jay B(enjamin) 1929- ... CANR-18
Earlier sketch in CA 25-28R
Stern, Jean Gordon 1904(?)-1985 Obituary ... 117
Stern, Jerome H(illel) 1938-1996 ... 163
Stern, Judith M. 1951- ... 142
See also SATA 75
Stern, Karl 1906-1975 ... CANR-12
Obituary ... 61-64
Earlier sketch in CA 9-12R
Stern, Kenneth S. 1953- ... 154
Stern, Laurence (Marcus) 1929-1979 ... 85-88
Obituary ... 89-92
Stern, Louis William 1935- ... CANR-18
Earlier sketch in CA 25-28R
Stern, Madeleine B(ettina) 1912- ... CANR-46
Earlier sketches in CA 17-20R, CANR-7, 22
See also DLB 111, 140
See also SATA 14
Stern, Malcolm H(enry) 1915-1994 ... 73-76
Obituary ... 143
Stern, Marie 1909- ... 45-48
Stern, Martha Eccles Dodd
1908-1990 Obituary ... 132
Stern, Michael 1910- ... CAP-2
Earlier sketch in CA 23-24
Stern, Milton R(alph) 1928- ... CANR-15
Earlier sketch in CA 41-44R
Stern, Nancy (B.) 1944- ... CANR-56
Earlier sketches in CA 110, CANR-28
Stern, Paul C(linton) 1944- ... 143
Stern, Paula 1945- ... 102
Stern, Philip M(aurice) 1926-1992 ... 104
Obituary ... 137
Stern, Philip Van Doren 1900-1984 ... CANR-6
Obituary ... 113
Earlier sketch in CA 5-8R
See also SATA 13
See also SATA-Obit 39
Stern, Richard (Gustave) 1928- ... CANR-52
Earlier sketches in CA 1-4R, CANR-1, 25
Interview in ... CANR-25
See also CLC 4, 39
See also DLBY 87
Stern, Richard Martin 1915- ... CANR-70
Earlier sketches in CA 1-4R, CANR-2, 18, 40
Stern, Robert ... 168
Stern, Robert A. M. 1939- ... CANR-50
Earlier sketches in CA 29-32R, CANR-25
Stern, Robert M. 1927- ... CANR-10
Earlier sketch in CA 21-24R
Stern, Rudi 1936- Brief entry ... 115
Stern, S. M.
See Stern, Samuel Miklos
Stern, Samuel Miklos 1920-1969 Obituary ... 111
Stern, Sheila (Frances) 1922- ... 136
Stern, Simon 1943- ... 89-92
See also SATA 15
Stern, Steve 1947- ... 132
Brief entry ... 126
Interview in ... 132
Stern, Stewart 1922- Brief entry ... 113
See also DLB 26
Stern, Stuart
See Rae, Hugh C(rauford)
Stern, Susan (Tanenbaum)
1943-1976 Obituary ... 65-68
Stern, Sydney Ladensohn 1947- ... 134
Stern, Tracy 1953- ... 129
Stern, William B(ernhard) 1910-1972 ... CAP-1
Earlier sketch in CA 13-16
Stern, Wilma 1940- ... 138
Stern, Zelda 1949- ... 116
Sternau, Cynthia 1956- ... 150
Sternberg, Cecilia 1908-1983 ... CANR-39
Obituary ... 111
Earlier sketch in CA 73-76
Sternberg, Jacques 1923- Brief entry ... 111
Sternberg, Josef von 1894-1969 ... 81-84
See also CLC 20
Sternberg, Martin L(eo) A(ltar) 1925- ... 107
Sternberg, Patricia 1930- ... 118
Sternberg, Robert J(effrey) 1949- ... 126
Brief entry ... 119
Interview in ... 126
Sternberg, Vernon (Arthur)
1915-1979 Obituary ... 104
Sternberger, Dolf 1907- ... 104
Sterne, Colin C(hase) 1921- ... 144
Sterne, Emma Gelders 1894- ... CANR-5
Earlier sketch in CA 5-8R
See also SATA 6
Sterne, Laurence 1713-1768 ... CDBLB 1660-1789
See also DA
See also DAB
See also DAC
See also DAM MST, NOV
See also DLB 39
See also WLC
Sterne, Richard Clark 1927- ... 150
Sterne, Richard S(tephen) 1921- ... 13-16R
Sterner, Jerry (Joseph) 1938- ... 161
Sterner, Lewis George 1894- ... 5-8R
Sterner, R. Eugene 1912- ... CANR-3
Earlier sketch in CA 9-12R
Sternfeld, Robert 1917- ... 81-84
Sternfield, Allen 1930- ... 53-56
Sterngold, James (S.) 1954- ... 140
Sternheim, (William Adolf) Carl 1878-1942 Brief
entry ... 105
See also DLB 56, 118
See also TCLC 8
Sternhold, Thomas (?)-1549 ... DLB 132
Sternlicht, Sanford 1931- ... CANR-51
Earlier sketches in CA 25-28R, CANR-10, 26
Sternlieb, George 1928- ... CANR-25
Earlier sketches in CA 21-24R, CANR-8
Sternsher, Bernard 1925- ... 9-12R
Sterrett, Cliff 1883-1964 ... 155
Sterry, Rick 1938- ... 25-28R
Stertz, Eda 1921- ... 104
Stessin, Lawrence 1911- ... 9-12R
Stetler, Charles E(dward) 1927- ... 65-68
Stetler, Russell (Dearnley, Jr.) 1945- ... 41-44R
Stetson, Charlotte Perkins
See Gilman, Charlotte (Anna) Perkins (Stetson)
Stetson, Damon 1915- ... 85-88
Stetson, Erlene ... 108
Stettler, Howard Frederic 1919- ... 5-8R
Stettner, Irving 1922- ... CANR-37
Earlier sketches in CA 77-80, CANR-16
Steuerle, C. Eugene 1946- ... 143
Steurt, Marjorie Rankin 1888- ... 13-16R
See also SATA 10
Steven, Hugh 1931- ... CANR-14
Earlier sketch in CA 41-44R
Stevens, Ana Maria Diaz
See Diaz-Stevens, Ana Maria
Stevens, Anita 1911- Brief entry ... 110
Stevens, Anthony (George) 1933- ... CANR-71
Earlier sketch in CA 110
Stevens, April 1963- ... 154
Stevens, Ardis 1921- ... 45-48
Stevens, Art 1935- ... 124
Stevens, (John) Austin ... 53-56
Stevens, Austin N(eil) 1930- ... 104
Stevens, Bernice A. ... 37-40R
Stevens, Blaine
See Whittington, Harry (Benjamin)
Stevens, Bryna 1924- ... 136
See also SATA 65
Stevens, Carl
See Obstfeld, Raymond
Stevens, Carla M(cBride) 1928- ... CANR-12
Earlier sketch in CA 69-72
See also SATA 13
Stevens, Cat
See Georgiou, Steven Demetre
Stevens, Charles W. 1955- ... 136
Stevens, Christopher
See Tabori, Paul
Stevens, Christopher 1948- ... 119
Stevens, Clifford 1926- ... CANR-6
Earlier sketch in CA 9-12R
Stevens, Clysle
See Wade, John Stevens
Stevens, Dan J.
See Overholser, Wayne D.
Stevens, David Harrison 1884-1980 ... 77-80
Obituary ... 93-96
Stevens, Denis William 1922- ... CANR-3
Earlier sketch in CA 9-12R
Stevens, Diane 1939- ... 159
See also SATA 94
Stevens, Diane 1944- ... 65-68
Stevens, Dick 1928- ... 143
Stevens, E. S.
See Drower, E(thel) S(tefana May)
Stevens, Edmund William 1910-1992 ... 109
Obituary ... 137
Stevens, Edward 1928- ... CANR-11
Earlier sketch in CA 29-32R
Stevens, Edwin L(ockwood) 1913-1987 ... 21-24R
Obituary ... 122
Stevens, Eleanour V(irginia) 1926- ... 29-32R
Stevens, Elisabeth (Goss) 1929- ... 110
Stevens, Fae Hewston
See Stevens, Frances Isted
Stevens, Frances Isted 1907- ... CAP-1
Earlier sketch in CA 9-10
Stevens, Franklin 1933- ... 29-32R
See also SATA 6
Stevens, George (Cooper), Jr. 1932- ... 125
Brief entry ... 118
Interview in ... 125
Stevens, George 1904(?)-1985 Obituary ... 116
Stevens, George Putnam 1918- ... 45-48
Stevens, Georgiana G(erlinger) 1904- ... CAP-1
Earlier sketch in CA 17-18
Stevens, Gerald 1909- ... 5-8R
Stevens, Graeme R(oy) 1932- ... 118
Stevens, Greg
See Cook, Glen (Charles)
Stevens, Gwendolyn 1944- ... 104
See also SATA 33
Stevens, Halsey 1908-1989 ... 25-28R
Obituary ... 127
Stevens, Harold 1917- ... 89-92
Stevens, Harvey A(lonzo) 1913- ... 89-92
Stevens, Henry 1819-1886 ... DLB 140
Stevens, Holly 1924-1992 ... 25-28R
Obituary ... 137
Stevens, J. D.
See Rowland, D(onald) S(ydney)
Stevens, James (Richard) 1940- ... CANR-16
Earlier sketch in CA 93-96
Stevens, James F. 1892-1971 Obituary ... 33-36R
Stevens, Jan Romero 1953- ... 160
See also SATA 95
Stevens, Jane Greengold 1945- ... 108
Stevens, Janet 1953- ... SATA 90
Stevens, Jay (Karl) 195(?)- ... 166

Stevens, Joan 1908- ... CANR-2
Earlier sketch in CA 5-8R
Stevens, John
See Tubb, E(dwin) C(harles)
Stevens, Joseph C(harles) 1929- ... 17-20R
Stevens, Joseph E. 1956- ... 128
Stevens, Kathleen 1936- ... CANR-39
Earlier sketch in CA 116
See also SATA 49
Stevens, L(ewell) Robert 1932- ... 111
Stevens, Laird 1953- ... 128
Stevens, Lauren R(ogers) 1938- ... 5-8R
Stevens, Lawrence L.
See London, Lawrence Steven
Stevens, Lee
See Leigh, Stephen (W.)
Stevens, Leonard A. 1920- ... CANR-12
Earlier sketch in CA 17-20R
See also SATA 67
Stevens, Leonie 1962- ... 167
Stevens, Lucile Vernon 1899- ... 61-64
See also SATA 59
Stevens, Mark 1951- ... 122
See also CLC 34
Stevens, Martin 1927- ... 13-16R
Stevens, Michael 1919- ... 53-56
Stevens, Norma Young 1927- ... 21-24R
Stevens, Pam
See Gilbert, George
Stevens, Patricia Bunning 1931- ... 53-56
See also SATA 27
Stevens, Paul 1946- ... 123
Stevens, Peter
See Geis, Darlene Stern
Stevens, Peter 1927- ... 93-96
Stevens, Peter S(mith) 1936- ... 53-56
Stevens, R(obert) B(ocking) 1933- ... CANR-9
Earlier sketch in CA 21-24R
Stevens, R. L.
See Hoch, Edward D(entinger)
Stevens, Richard P. 1931- ... CANR-10
Earlier sketch in CA 21-24R
Stevens, Robert D(avid) 1921- ... 112
Stevens, Robert E(llis) 1942- ... 142
Stevens, Robert Tyler
See Staples, Reginald Thomas
Stevens, Robert Warren 1918-1987 ... CANR-1
Obituary ... 122
Earlier sketch in CA 45-48
Stevens, Roger (Bentham)
1906-1980 Obituary ... 105
Stevens, Rolland E(lwell) 1915- ... 81-84
Stevens, Rosemary (Anne) 1935- ... 85-88
Stevens, S. P.
See Palestrant, Simon S.
Stevens, S(tanley) S(mith) 1906-1973 Obituary . 116
Stevens, Serita (Deborah) 1949- ... CANR-44
Earlier sketch in CA 119
See also SATA 70
Stevens, Shane 1941- ... CANR-43
Earlier sketch in CA 21-24R
Stevens, Sharon 1949- ... 77-80
Stevens, Shira
See Stevens, Serita (Deborah)
Stevens, Stuart ... 162
Stevens, Suzanne H. 1938- ... 136
Stevens, Sylvester K(irby) 1904-1974 ... CAP-1
Obituary ... 45-48
Earlier sketch in CA 13-16
Stevens, Thomas Terry Hoar
1911-1990 Obituary ... 130
Stevens, Tricia
See Pearl, Jacques Bain
Stevens, Trisha
See Pearl, Jacques Bain
Stevens, Wallace 1879-1955 ... 124
Brief entry ... 104
See also CDALB 1929-1941
See also DA
See also DAB
See also DAC
See also DAM MST, POET
See also DLB 54
See also MTCW 1
See also PC 6
See also TCLC 3, 12, 45
See also WLC
Stevens, William 1925- ... 21-24R
Stevens, William W(ilson) 1914- ... 37-40R
Stevens-Arroyo, Antonio M. 1941- ... 120
Stevenson, Adlai E(wing) 1900-1965 ... CAP-1
Earlier sketch in CA 13-16
Stevenson, Anna (M.) 1905- ... SATA 12
Stevenson, Anne (Katharine) 1933- ... CANR-33
Earlier sketches in CA 17-20R, CANR-9
See also CAAS 9
See also CLC 7, 33
See also DLB 40
See also MTCW 1
Stevenson, Augusta 1869(?)-1976 ... 1-4R
Obituary ... 65-68
See also SATA 2
See also SATA-Obit 26
Stevenson, (William) Bruce 1906- ... 49-52
Stevenson, Burton Egbert 1872-1962 ... 102
Obituary ... 89-92
See also SATA 25
Stevenson, Carol Dornfeld 1931- ... 5-8R
Stevenson, Charles 1908(?)-1979 Obituary ... 85-88
Stevenson, Christopher Sinclair
See Sinclair-Stevenson, Christopher
Stevenson, David 1942- ... CANR-28
Earlier sketch in CA 109
Stevenson, David Lloyd 1910-1975 ... CAP-2
Obituary ... 57-60
Earlier sketch in CA 23-24
Stevenson, Dorothy E(mily) 1892-1973 ... CAP-1
Obituary ... 49-52
Earlier sketch in CA 13-16
See also DLB 191
Stevenson, Drew 1947- ... SATA 60
Stevenson, Dwight E(shelman) 1906- ... CANR-1
Earlier sketch in CA 1-4R
Stevenson, Elizabeth 1919- ... CANR-26
Earlier sketch in CA 1-4R
Stevenson, Florence ... CANR-16
Earlier sketch in CA 97-100
Stevenson, Garth 1943- ... 148
Stevenson, George J(ames) 1924- ... 9-12R
Stevenson, Gloria 1945- ... 61-64
Stevenson, Grace Thomas 1900- ... 37-40R
Stevenson, Harold W(illiam) 1921- ... 25-28R
Stevenson, Harvey 1960- ... SATA 80
Stevenson, Henry M(iller) 1914- ... 77-80
Stevenson, Herbert Frederick 1906- ... CANR-2
Earlier sketch in CA 5-8R
Stevenson, Hugh A(lexander) 1935- ... 112
Stevenson, Ian (Pretyman) 1918- ... 158
Brief entry ... 115
Stevenson, Ian Ralph 1943- ... 102
Stevenson, J. P.
See Haldane-Stevenson, James Patrick
Stevenson, James 1929- ... CANR-47
Earlier sketch in CA 115
See also CLR 17
See also MAICYA
See also SATA 42, 71
See also SATA-Brief 34
Stevenson, James Patrick
See Haldane-Stevenson, James Patrick
Stevenson, Janet 1913- ... CANR-29
Earlier sketch in CA 13-16R
See also SATA 8
Stevenson, John (Edward) 1952- ... 160
Stevenson, John Albert
1890(?)-1979 Obituary ... 89-92
Stevenson, John P.
See Grierson, Edward
Stevenson, Jonathan 1956- ... 151
Stevenson, L(eland) W(ells) 1916- ... 107
Stevenson, Laura Caroline 1946- ... 120
Stevenson, Leslie (Forster) 1943- ... 65-68
Stevenson, (Arthur) Lionel 1902-1973 ... 103
Obituary ... 45-48
See also DLB 155
Stevenson, Louise L. 1948- ... 143
Stevenson, Mary Lou K.
See Kohfeldt, Mary Lou (Stevenson)
Stevenson, Michael Ian 1953- ... 103
Stevenson, Randall 1953- ... 128
Stevenson, Richard
See Lipez, Richard
Stevenson, Robert 1905-1986 Obituary ... 120
Stevenson, Robert (Murrell) 1916- ... CANR-1
Earlier sketch in CA 1-4R
Stevenson, Robert G. 1945- ... 148
Stevenson, Robert Louis (Balfour)
1850-1894 ... AAYA 24
See also CDBLB 1890-1914
See also CLR 10, 11
See also DA
See also DAB
See also DAC
See also DAM MST, NOV
See also DLB 18, 57, 141, 156, 174
See also DLBD 13
See also JRDA
See also MAICYA
See also SATA 100
See also SSC 11
See also WLC
See also YABC 2
Stevenson, Sucie 1956- ... 162
Stevenson, Suzanne Silvercruys
1898(?)-1973 Obituary ... 41-44R
Stevenson, T(homas) H(ulbert) 1919- ... 61-64
Stevenson, Tom 1899(?)-1982 Obituary ... 106
Stevenson, Vera Kemp 1920- ... 57-60
Stevenson, Victoria F.
1878(?)-1973 Obituary ... 41-44R
Stevenson, W(illiam) Taylor 1928- ... CANR-18
Earlier sketch in CA 25-28R
Stevenson, (Stanley) Warren 1933- ... 41-44R
Stevenson, William Henri 1924- ... CANR-41
Earlier sketch in CA 13-16R
Stevermer, C. J.
See Stevermer, Caroline
Stevermer, Caroline 1955- ... 136
Stevick, Philip T. 1930- ... 132
Steward, F(rederick) C(ampion) 1904-1993 . 41-44R
Obituary ... 142
Steward, Hal D(avid) 1922- ... 69-72
Steward, Julian H. 1902-1972 Obituary ... 33-36R
Steward, Samuel M(orris) 1909-1993 ... 112
Obituary ... 143
Stewart, A(gnes) C(harlotte) ... 77-80
See also SATA 15
Stewart, A(nthony) T(erence) Q(uincey)
1929- ... 25-28R
Stewart, (John) Allan 1939- ... 1-4R
Stewart, Allegra 1899- ... 45-48
Stewart, Angus (J. M.) 1936- ... 106
Stewart, Bertie Ann Gardner 1912- ... 5-8R
Stewart, Bill 1942(?)-1979 Obituary ... 89-92
Stewart, Charles
See Zurhorst, Charles (Stewart, Jr.)
Stewart, Charles J(oseph) 1936- ... 41-44R
Stewart, Charles T(odd), Jr. 1922- ... 101
Stewart, Christina Duff 1926- ... 65-68
Stewart, Cochrane
See Stewart, Kenneth
Stewart, D(avid) H(ugh) 1926- ... 21-24R
Stewart, Daniel Blair 1951- ... 153
Stewart, Daniel K(enneth) 1925- ... 29-32R
Stewart, David
See Politella, Dario
Stewart, David W. 1929- ... 146
Stewart, Desmond (Stirling) 1924-1981 ... CANR-30
Obituary ... 104
Earlier sketch in CA 37-40R
Stewart, Donald Charles 1930- ... 37-40R
Stewart, Donald H(enderson) 1911- ... 29-32R
Stewart, Donald Ogden 1894-1980 ... CANR-43
Obituary ... 101
Earlier sketch in CA 81-84
See also DLB 4, 11, 26
Stewart, Dorothy Mary 1917-1965 Obituary ... 104
Stewart, Douglas (Alexander) 1913- ... 81-84
Stewart, Douglas Day 1940- ... 166
Stewart, Edgar I(rving) 1900- ... 5-8R
Stewart, Edith Hamilton 1883- ... CAP-1
Earlier sketch in CA 11-12
Stewart, Elbert Wilton 1916- ... 37-40R
Stewart, Eleanor
See Porter, Eleanor H(odgman)
Stewart, Elisabeth J(ane) 1927- ... 158
See also SATA 93
Stewart, Elizabeth Grey
See Reed, Elizabeth Stewart
Stewart, Elizabeth Laing 1907- ... 49-52
See also SATA 6
Stewart, Ella Winter 1898-1980 Obituary ... 101
Stewart, Eve
See Napier, Priscilla
Stewart, Frank 1946- ... CANR-42
Earlier sketches in CA 104, CANR-20
Stewart, Fred Mustard 1936- ... CANR-42
Earlier sketch in CA 37-40R
Stewart, Garrett (Fitzgerald) 1945- ... 93-96
Stewart, Gary 1944- ... 145
Stewart, George, Jr. 1848-1906 ... DLB 99
Stewart, George 1892-1972 Obituary ... 33-36R
Stewart, George Rippey 1895-1980 ... CANR-3
Obituary ... 101
Earlier sketch in CA 1-4R
See also DLB 8
See also SATA 3
See also SATA-Obit 23
Stewart, Hal D(ouglas) 1899- ... CAP-1
Earlier sketch in CA 13-16
Stewart, Harold C. 1891(?)-1976 Obituary ... 69-72
Stewart, Harold Frederick 1916- ... CANR-48
Earlier sketch in CA 69-72
Stewart, Harris B(ates), Jr. 1922- ... CANR-35
Earlier sketch in CA 45-48
Stewart, Harry E. 1931- ... 150
Stewart, Hilary 1924- ... CANR-16
Earlier sketch in CA 93-96
Stewart, Horace Floyd, Jr. 1928- ... 49-52
Stewart, Ian (Nicholas) 1945- ... 139
Stewart, J(ohn) I(nnes) M(ackintosh) 1906-1994 ...
CANR-47
Obituary ... 147
Earlier sketch in CA 85-88
See also CAAS 3
See also CLC 7, 14, 32
See also MTCW 1
Stewart, James Alexander 1948- ... 113
Stewart, James B. 1957(?)- ... 146
Stewart, James Brewer 1940- ... CANR-32
Earlier sketch in CA 29-32R
Stewart, James S(tuart) 1896-1990 ... 9-12R
Obituary ... 132
Stewart, Jean
See Newman, Mona Alice Jean
Stewart, Jeffrey C. 1950- ... 152
Stewart, Jim
See Stewart, James Alexander
Stewart, John 1904(?)-1985 Obituary ... 116
Stewart, John (William) 1920- ... 33-36R
See also SATA 14
Stewart, John 1933- ... CANR-37
Earlier sketches in CA 97-100, CANR-16
Stewart, John 1941- ... 97-100
Stewart, John 1952- ... 142
Stewart, John B(enjamin) 1924- ... 9-12R
Stewart, John G(ilman) 1935- Brief entry ... 112
Stewart, Judith
See Polley, Judith (Anne)
Stewart, Judith Anne
See Maciel, Judi(th Anne)
Stewart, K(athleen) Alison Clarke
See Clarke-Stewart, K(athleen) Alison
Stewart, Katharine Jeanne (Dark) 1914- ... 9-12R
Stewart, Kaye
See Howe, Doris Kathleen
Stewart, Kenneth 1918-1985 Obituary ... 118
Stewart, Kenneth L. 1949- ... 147
Stewart, Kenneth N. 1901-1978 Obituary ... 77-80
Stewart, Kerry
See Stewart, Linda
Stewart, Lawrence D(elbert) 1926- ... 89-92
Stewart, Lawrence H(oyle) 1922- ... 17-20R
Stewart, Linda ... 101
Stewart, Margaret 1912- ... CANR-18
Earlier sketch in CA 25-28R
Stewart, Marie M(cCaffery) 1899- ... 5-8R
Stewart, Mark Armstrong 1929- ... 89-92
Stewart, Mart A. 1947- ... 167
Stewart, Martha 1942(?)- ... 152
Stewart, Mary (Florence Elinor) 1916- ... CANR-59
Earlier sketches in CA 1-4R, CANR-1
See also CLC 7, 35
See also DAB
See also SATA 12
Stewart, Mary Rainbow
See Stewart, Mary (Florence Elinor)
Stewart, Maxwell S(lutz) 1900-1990 Obituary ... 131
Stewart, Melville Y. 1935- ... 146
Stewart, (Robert) Michael (Maitland) 1906-1990 ...
CANR-22
Obituary ... 131
Earlier sketch in CA 106
Stewart, Michael 1924(?)-1987 Obituary ... 123
Stewart, Michael 1933- ... 116
Stewart, Michael 1945- ... 138
Stewart, Natacha
See Ullman, Natacha
Stewart, Oliver 1895-1980 ... CANR-5
Earlier sketch in CA 5-8R
Stewart, Omer C(all) 1908- ... 127
Stewart, Pat(ricia) 1944- ... 97-100
Stewart, Paul (James), (Jr.) 1929- ... 151
Stewart, Paul D(ekker) 1918- ... 1-4R
Stewart, Philip Robert 1940- ... 29-32R
Stewart, Phyllis Langton 1933- Brief entry ... 106
Stewart, Ramona 1922- ... CANR-6
Earlier sketch in CA 1-4R
Stewart, Randall 1896-1964 ... CANR-1
Earlier sketch in CA 1-4R
See also DLB 103
Stewart, Rex William 1907-1967 Obituary ... 110
Stewart, Rhea Talley 1915- ... 41-44R
Stewart, Robert G(ordon) 1931- ... 65-68
Stewart, Robert Neil 1891- ... 9-12R
See also SATA 7
Stewart, Robert T. 1920(?)-1977 Obituary ... 73-76
Stewart, Robert Wilson 1935- ... 49-52
Stewart, Ron(nie) 1956- ... 142
Stewart, Rosemary (Gordon) ... CANR-15
Earlier sketch in CA 37-40R
Stewart, Sam
See Stewart, Linda
Stewart, Scott
See Zaffo, George J.
Stewart, (Michael) Sean 1965- ... 148
Stewart, Seumas 1919- ... 61-64
Stewart, Shelia 1928- ... 21-24R
Stewart, Stanley N(ordahl) 1931- ... 17-20R
Stewart, Susan 1952- ... 168
Stewart, Suzanne ... 61-64
Stewart, Vincent (Astor, Jr.) 1939- ... 29-32R
Stewart, W(illiam) A(lexander) Campbell
1915- ... 13-16R
Stewart, W(alter) P. 1924- ... SATA 53
Stewart, Walter 1931- ... 129
Stewart, Walter Bingham 1913- ... CANR-16
Earlier sketch in CA 85-88
Stewart, Whitney 1959- ... 156
See also SATA 92
Stewart, Will
See Williamson, John Stewart
Stewart, William Stanley 1938- ... 89-92
Stewart, William T(homas) 1934- ... 127
Stewart, Wynn 1934-1985 Obituary ... 116
Stewart, Wynn 1934-1985 ... 154
Stewart, Zeph 1921- ... 41-44R
Stewig, John Warren 1937- ... CANR-69
Earlier sketches in CA 81-84, CANR-14, 32, 56
See also SATA 26
Steyaert, Thomas A(dolph) 1930- ... 37-40R
Steyer, Wesley W. 1923- ... 29-32R
Steyermark, Julian A(lfred) 1909-1988 ... CANR-17
Obituary ... 126
Earlier sketches in CAP-1, CA 13-14
Stibbe, Mark W. G. 1960- ... 143
Stibbs, Alan M(arshall) 1901- ... CANR-2
Earlier sketch in CA 1-4R
Stich, Stephen P(eter) 1943- ... 41-44R
Stick, David 1919- ... CANR-17
Earlier sketch in CA 97-100
Stickells, Austin T. 1914- ... 41-44R
Stickgold, Bob 1945- ... 104
Stickland, Caroline (Amanda) 1955- ... 127
Stickney, Benjamin D. 1940- ... 135
Stickney, Trumbull 1874-1904 ... DLB 54
Stidworthy, John 1943- ... SATA 63
Stieber, Jack 1919- ... CANR-6
Earlier sketch in CA 1-4R
Stiebing, William H(enry), Jr. 1940- ... 141
Stiehm, Judith 1935- ... 61-64
Stieler, Caspar 1632-1707 ... DLB 164
Sterlin, Helm 1926- ... 29-32R
Stierwell, Jay
See Swicegood, Thomas L. P.
Stiff, Robert M(artin) 1931- ... 132
Stiffel, Frank 1916- ... 117
Stifle, June
See Campbell, Maria
Stifter, Adalbert 1805-1868 ... DLB 133
See also SSC 28
Stigger, Judith A. 1949- ... 111
Stigler, George J(oseph) 1911-1991 ... 41-44R
Obituary ... 136
Stigler, Stephen M(ack) 1941- ... 125
Stigum, Marcia (Lee) 1934- ... CANR-8
Earlier sketch in CA 61-64
Stigwood, Robert C. 1934- ... 102
Stiles, Ezra 1727-1795 ... DLB 31
Stiles, John R. 1916(?)-1976 Obituary ... 65-68
Stiles, Joseph 1903- ... CAP-2
Earlier sketch in CA 17-18
Stiles, Lindley Joseph 1913- ... CANR-3
Earlier sketch in CA 5-8R
Stiles, Martha Bennett ... 37-40R
See also SATA 6
Stiles, Merritt N. 1899-1975 Obituary ... 57-60
Stiles, Ned B. 1932- ... 17-20R
Stiles, Norman B. 1942- ... 114
See also SATA-Brief 36
Stiles, T(imothy) J(udd) 1964- ... 152
Stilgoe, John R. ... 109
Still, C. Henry 1920- ... 9-12R

Still, Edgar
See Garber, Joseph R(ene)
Still, James 1906- CANR-26
Earlier sketches in CA 65-68, CANR-10
See also CAAS 17
See also CLC 49
See also DLB 9
See also SATA 29
Still, Richard R(alph) 1921- CANR-1
Earlier sketch in CA 1-4R
Still, William N(orwood), Jr. 1932- CANR-18
Earlier sketch in CA 25-28R
Stille, Alexander 159
Stiller, Brian C(arl) 1942- CANR-41
Earlier sketch in CA 117
Stillerman, Robbie 1947- .... SATA 12
Stilley, Frank 1918- 61-64
See also SATA 29
Stillinger, Jack 1931- CANR-1
Earlier sketch in CA 1-4R
Stillman, Damie 1933- CANR-36
Earlier sketch in CA 45-48
Stillman, Edmund O. 1924-1983 Obituary 111
Stillman, Frances (Jennings) 1910-1975 .... CAP-1
Obituary 57-60
Earlier sketch in CA 13-16
Stillman, Irwin M(axwell) 1895-1975 49-52
Obituary 61-64
Stillman, Myra Stephens 1915- CANR-6
Earlier sketch in CA 5-8R
Stillman, Nathan 1914- 5-8R
Stillman, Noam
See Stillman, Norman A(rthur)
Stillman, Norman A(rthur) 1945- 136
Stillman, Richard J. 1917- CANR-34
Earlier sketches in CA 37-40R, CANR-14
Stillman, (John) Whit(ney) 1952(?)- 153
Stillwell, Margaret Bingham 1887-1984 ..... 41-44R
Obituary 112
Stillwell, Norma Jamieson 1894- CAP-1
Earlier sketch in CA 13-16
Stillwell, Paul (Lewis) 1944- 126
Stillwell, Richard 1899-1982 Obituary 111
Stilson, Max 1919- 9-12R
Stilwell, William E(arle) III 1936- 107
Stimmel, Barry 1939- CANR-11
Earlier sketch in CA 69-72
Stimpson, Catherine R(oslyn) 1936- 41-44R
Stimson, Dorothy 1890-1988 Obituary 126
Stimson, Robbe Pierce 1948- 136
Stimson, William 1946- 122
Stinchcombe, Arthur L. 1933- CANR-23
Earlier sketches in CA 13-16R, CANR-8
Stinchcombe, William 1937- 105
Stinchecum, Amanda Mayer 1941- 139
Stine, G(eorge) Harry 1928- CANR-30
Earlier sketches in CA 65-68, CANR-9
See also SATA 10
Stine, Hank
See Stine, Henry Eugene
Stine, Henry Eugene 1945- 133
Stine, Jovial Bob
See Stine, R(obert) L(awrence)
Stine, R(obert) L(awrence) 1943- CANR-53
Earlier sketches in CA 105, CANR-22
See also AAYA 13
See also CLR 37
See also JRDA
See also SATA 31, 76
Stine, Whitney Ward 1930- CANR-7
Earlier sketch in CA 57-60
See also AITN 1
Stineman, Esther F. 1947- CANR-17
Earlier sketch in CA 97-100
Stinetorf, Louise (Allender) 1900- 9-12R
See also SATA 10
Sting 1951- 167
See also Sumner, Gordon Matthew
Stinger, Charles L(ewis) 1944- 77-80
Stini, William A(rthur Anthony) 1930- 127
Brief entry 107
Stinnett, Caskie 1911- 5-8R
Stinnett, Nick 1942- 110
Stinnett, Ronald F. 1929- 21-24R
Stinnett, Tim Moore 1901-1985 .... CANR-13
Obituary 115
Earlier sketch in CA 17-20R
Stinnette, Charles R(oy), Jr. 1914- 77-80
Stinson, James Emerson, Jr. 1937- CANR-45
Earlier sketch in CA 119
Stinson, Jim
See Stinson, James Emerson, Jr.
Stinson, Kathy 1952- 113
See also SATA 98
Stinson, Robert William 1941- 111
Stinton, T(homas) C(harles) W(arren)
1925-1985 Obituary 117
Stipe, Robert Edwin 1928- 49-52
Stirling, Alfred (Thorpe) 1902-1981 110
Obituary 108
Stirling, Anna Maria Diana Wilhelmina (Pickering)
1865-1965 .... CAP-1
Earlier sketch in CA 9-10
Stirling, Arthur
See Sinclair, Upton (Beall)
Stirling, Betty Rutledge 1923- 9-12R
Stirling, (Thomas) Brents 1904- CAP-2
Earlier sketch in CA 25-28
Stirling, Ian 1941- 145
See also SATA 77
Stirling, Jessica
See Coghlan, Margaret M.
and Rae, Hugh C(rauford)
Stirling, Lilla (May Elderkin) 1902- 107
Stirling, Matthew Williams
1896-1975 Obituary 53-56
Stirling, Monica 1916-1983 81-84
Obituary 111
Stirling, Nora B(romley) 1900- CANR-3
Earlier sketch in CA 5-8R
See also SATA 3
Stirling, S(tephen) M(ichael) 1953- 140
Stirner, Max 1806-1856 .... DLB 129
Stirnweis, Shannon 1931- .... SATA 10
Stirt, Joseph A. 1948- 140
Stitelman, Leonard (Arnold) 1932- 41-44R
Stites, Francis N(oel) 1938- 41-44R
Stites, Raymond S(omers) 1899-1974 65-68
Obituary 53-56
Stith, John E(dward) 1947- CANR-40
Earlier sketch in CA 117
Stith, William 1707-1755 .... DLB 31
Stitskin, Leon D. 1910-1978 .... CANR-1
Earlier sketch in CA 1-4R
Stitt, Milan 1941- 69-72
See also CLC 29
Stitt, Peter 1940- CANR-52
Earlier sketch in CA 123
Stitz, Aline M. Stomfay
See Stomfay-Stitz, Aline M.
Stitzel, Thomas E(dward) 1936- 93-96
Stivender, Ed 1946- 141
Stivens, Dal(las George) 1911- CANR-14
Earlier sketch in CA 69-72
Stiver, Mary Weeden 1909- CAP-1
Earlier sketch in CA 13-14
Stivers, Robert L(loyd) 1940- 69-72
Stjernberg, Lloyd A(rmand) 1937- 25-28R
St-John Nevill, Barry
See Nevill, Barry St-John
Stoan, Stephen K(uzman) 1942- 111
Stob, Ralph 1894-1965 .... 1-4R
Obituary 103
Stobart, Thomas Ralph 1914- 13-16R
Stobaugh, Robert B. (Jr.) 1927- 101
Stobbs, John L(ouis) N(ewcombe) 1921- ... 13-16R
Stobbs, William 1914- 81-84
See also SATA 17
Stock, A(my) G(eraldine) 1902-1988 Obituary .. 126
Stock, Alfred 1876-1946 158
Stock, Barbara R(uth) 1942- CANR-19
Earlier sketch in CA 112
Stock, Brian 1939- 41-44R
Stock, Carolmarie 1951- .... SATA 75
Stock, Catherine 1952- 119
See also SATA 65
Stock, Claudette 1934- 65-68
Stock, Ernest 1924- 21-24R
Stock, Guy 1933- 124
Stock, Irvin 1920- 25-28R
Stock, Phyllis H(artman) 1930- 85-88
Stock, R(obert) D(ouglas) 1941- CANR-43
Earlier sketches in CA 41-44R, CANR-14
Stockanes, Anthony E(dward) 1935- 109
Stockard, James Wright, Jr. 1935- 13-16R
Stockard, Jimmy
See Stockard, James Wright, Jr.
Stockbridge, Grant
See Page, Norvell W(ooten)
Stockdale, Eric 1929- 25-28R
Stockdale, James B(ond) 1923- 143
Stockdale, Jim
See Stockdale, James B(ond)
Stockdale, Susan 1954- 166
See also SATA 98
Stockel, H. Henrietta 1938- 139
Stockenberg, Antoinette 1943- 167
Stocker, Jeffrey D. 1958- 162
Stocker, Margarita 1955- 121
Stocker, Mark (Andrew) 1956- 131
Stockham, Peter (Alan) 1928- .... SATA 57
Stockhammer, Morris 1904- 13-16R
Stocking, David M(ackenzie) 1919- 25-28R
Stocking, George W(ard), Jr. 1928- CANR-44
Earlier sketch in CA 73-76
Stocking, George Ward 1892-1975 Obituary . 61-64
Stocking, Hobart E(bey) 1906- 101
Stocking, Kathleen 1945- 135
Stocking, Marion Kingston 1922- 25-28R
Stocking, S(usan) Holly 1945- 117
Stockley, Grif 1944- CANR-70
Earlier sketch in CA 140
Stockman, David A(llen) 1946- 123
Stocks, Mary (Danvers Brinton) 1891-1975 . 13-16R
Obituary 118
Stockton, Adrian James 1935-1981 .... 29-32R
Obituary 134
Stockton, Bayard 1930- 134
Stockton, Francis Richard 1834-1902 137
Brief entry 108
See also Stockton, Frank R.
See also MAICYA
See also SATA 44
Stockton, Frank R.
See Stockton, Francis Richard
See also DLB 42, 74
See also DLBD 13
See also SATA-Brief 32
See also TCLC 47
Stockton, J. Roy 1893(?)-1972 Obituary 37-40R
Stockton, Jim
See Stockton, Adrian James
Stockton, John R(obert) 1903- 13-16R
Stockton, Ronald R. 1940- 118
Stockwell, Edward G(rant) 1933- 21-24R
Stockwell, John R(obert) 1937- 104
Stockwell, Robert P(aul) 1925- 17-20R
Stockwin, (James) Arthur (Ainscow) 1935- 103
Stockwood, (Arthur) Mervyn 1913- Brief entry .. 117
Stoddard, Charles
See Kuttner, Henry
Stoddard, Charles Warren 1843-1909 ..... DLB 186
Stoddard, Edward G. 1923- 9-12R
See also SATA 10
Stoddard, Elizabeth Drew 1823-1902 ..... DLB 202
Stoddard, Ellwyn R(eed) 1927- CANR-38
Earlier sketches in CA 45-48, CANR-1, 17
Stoddard, George Dinsmore
1897-1981 Obituary 106
Stoddard, Hope 1900- 49-52
See also SATA 6
Stoddard, Richard 1942- 102
Stoddard, Richard Henry 1825-1903 Brief
entry 114
See also DLB 3, 64
See also DLBD 13
Stoddard, Robert H. 1928- 133
Stoddard, Sandol 1927- CANR-8
Earlier sketch in CA 5-8R
See also Warburg, Sandol Stoddard
See also SATA 98
Stoddard, Solomon 1643-1729 .... DLB 24
Stoddard, Tom 1933- 37-40R
Stoddard, Whitney Snow 1913- 109
Stoddart, Brian 1946- 152
Stoddart, Jack Elliott 1916-1988 Obituary 124
Stodelle, Ernestine 1912- 117
Stoeckle, John D(uane) 1922- 128
Stoehr, C(arl) Eric 1945- 65-68
Stoehr, Shelley 168
See also AAYA 27
Stoeke, Janet Morgan 1957- .... SATA 90
Stoekl, Allan 1951- 144
Stoessinger, John G. 1927- CANR-9
Earlier sketch in CA 13-16R
Stoett, Peter J. 1963- 153
Stoetzer, O(tto) Carlos (Enrique) 1921- .. CANR-28
Earlier sketch in CA 109
Stoff, Joshua 1958- 136
Stoff, Sheldon (Ptaschevitch) 1930- 21-24R
Stoffel, Albert Law 1909- 65-68
Stoffel, Betty W. 1922- 17-20R
Stoffel, Ernest Lee 1923- 114
Stoffel, Lester L(enneth, Jr.) 1920- 45-48
Stoffle, Carla J(oy) 1943- CANR-7
Earlier sketch in CA 61-64
Stofflet, Mary 1942- 127
Stogdill, Ralph M(elvin) 1904- CANR-1
Earlier sketch in CA 1-4R
Stohl, Michael (Steven) 1947- CANR-25
Earlier sketch in CA 107
Stohlman, Martha Lou Lemmon 1913- 65-68
Stoianovich, Trajan 1921- 21-24R
Stoiber, Rudolph M(aria) 1925- 1-4R
Stoiko, Michael 1919- 9-12R
See also SATA 14
Stoil, Michael Jon 1950- 53-56
Stojanovic, Svetozar 1931- 134
Brief entry 112
Stok, T.
See Stolk, Anthonie
Stokely, James R(orex), Jr. 1913-1977 ...... 9-12R
Obituary 69-72
Stoker, Abraham 1847-1912 150
Brief entry 105
See also Stoker, Bram
See also DA
See also DAC
See also DAM MST, NOV
See also SATA 29
Stoker, Alan 1930- CANR-24
Earlier sketches in CA 21-24R, CANR-9
Stoker, Bram 1847-1912
See Stoker, Abraham
See also AAYA 23
See also CDBLB 1890-1914
See also DAB
See also DLB 36, 70, 178
See also TCLC 8
See also WLC
Stoker, H(oward) Stephen 1939- CANR-8
Earlier sketch in CA 61-64
Stoker, Richard 1938- 164
Stokes, Adrian Durham 1902-1972 .... CANR-5
Obituary 89-92
Earlier sketch in CA 13-16R
Stokes, Alec 1925- 144
Stokes, Bob
See Wilkening, Howard (Everett)
Stokes, Bruce 1948- 130
Stokes, Carl B(urton) 1927-1996 69-72
Obituary 152
Stokes, Cedric
See Beardmore, George
Stokes, Charles (Herbert) 1932- 103
Stokes, Charles J(unius) 1922- CANR-10
Earlier sketch in CA 25-28R
Stokes, Daniel M. J. 1950- 57-60
Stokes, Donald (Hubert) 1913-1986 Obituary .. 119
Stokes, Donald Elkinton 1927-1997 ...... CANR-1
Obituary 156
Earlier sketch in CA 1-4R
Stokes, Donald W. 1947- 132
Stokes, Doris 1919-1987 Obituary 122
Brief entry 115
Stokes, Edward 1922- 128
Stokes, Eric (Thomas) 1924-1981 107
Obituary 103
Stokes, Gale 1933- 146
Stokes, Geoffrey 1940-1995 .... CANR-36
Obituary 149
Earlier sketch in CA 69-72
Stokes, Henry J. M. Scott
See Scott-Stokes, Henry J. M.
Stokes, Jack (Tilden) 1923- 29-32R
See also SATA 13
Stokes, Martin 1958- 127
Stokes, Olivia Pearl 1916- 37-40R
See also SATA 32
Stokes, Peg (Lee Ewing) 1-4R
Stokes, Robert
See Wilkening, Howard (Everett)
Stokes, Roy 1915- 17-20R
Stokes, Roy Eliot CANR-26
Earlier sketches in CAP-2, CA 19-20
Stokes, Simpson
See Fawcett, F(rank) Dubrez
Stokes, Thomas L. 1898-1958 .... DLB 29
Stokes, William Lee 1915- CANR-42
Earlier sketches in CA 41-44R, CANR-20
Stokesbury, James L(awton) 1934- CANR-38
Earlier sketches in CA 93-96, CANR-17
Stokesbury, Leon 1945- CANR-21
Earlier sketch in CA 69-72
See also DLB 120
Stokke, Baard Richard 1937- 25-28R
Stokoe, William C(larence), Jr. 1919- 41-44R
Stokstad, Marilyn 1929- CANR-15
Earlier sketch in CA 37-40R
Stolberg, Christian Graf zu 1748-1821 .... DLB 94
Stolberg, Friedrich Leopold Graf zu 1750-1819 . DLB 94
Stoler, Ann Laura 1949- 119
Stoler, Peter (Robert) 1935- CANR-44
Earlier sketch in CA 97-100
Stolk, Anthonie 1916- 131
Stoll, Clarice Stasz
See Stasz, Clarice
Stoll, Clifford 1950- 136
See also BEST 90:3
Stoll, Dennis G(ray) 1912-1987 .... 13-16R
Obituary 124
Stoll, Irma 1929- 135
Stoll, John E(dward) 1933- 49-52
Stoller, Robert J(esse) 1924-1991 Obituary 135
Brief entry 117
Stollnitz, Fred 1939- 45-48
Stoloff, Carolyn 1927- CANR-9
Earlier sketch in CA 65-68
Stolorow, Robert D(avid) 1942- 102
Stolper, Wolfgang F(riedrich) 1912- 21-24R
Stolten, Jane (Henry) 97-100
Stoltenberg, Donald Hugo 1927- 89-92
Stoltenberg, John (Vincent) 1944- 146
Stoltzfus, Ben Franklin 1927- 103
Stoltzfus, (Mary) Louise 1952- 138
Stolz, Lois Meek 1891- CAP-2
Earlier sketch in CA 21-22
Stolz, Mary (Slattery) 1920- CANR-41
Earlier sketches in CA 5-8R, CANR-13
See also AAYA 8
See also AITN 1
See also CLC 12
See also JRDA
See also MAICYA
See also SAAS 3
See also SATA 10, 71
Stolzenbach, Norma Frizzell 1904- 41-44R
Stolzenberg, Mark 1950- 102
Stomfay-Stitz, Aline M. 147
Stommel, Henry Melson 1920-1992 155
Stonberg, Selma F(ranks) 69-72
Stone, Alan
See Svenson, Andrew E(dward)
See also SATA 1
Stone, Alan A(braham) 1929- 17-20R
Stone, Albert E., Jr.
See Stone, Albert E(dward)
Stone, Albert E(dward) 1924- CANR-50
Earlier sketches in CA 17-20R, CANR-8
Stone, Alfred R. 1926- 17-20R
Stone, Alma 1908- 77-80
Stone, Barbara Haskins
1924(?)-1979 Obituary 89-92
Stone, Betty E. 1926- 9-12R
Stone, Bonnie (M.) Domrose 1941- 133
Stone, Brian 1919- 13-16R
Stone, Charles Sumner, Jr. 1924- 77-80
See also BW 2
Stone, Christopher D(avid) 1937- 53-56
Stone, Chuck
See Stone, Charles Sumner, Jr.
Stone, Clarence N. 1935- CANR-30
Earlier sketch in CA 112
Stone, Clifford A. 1951-1986 Obituary 118
Stone, David (Anthony) 1929- 5-8R
Stone, David K(arl) 1922- 85-88
See also SATA 9
Stone, David U. 1927- CANR-7
Earlier sketch in CA 17-20R
Stone, Deborah
See Navas, Deborah
Stone, Del, Jr. 1958(?)- 167
Stone, Donald (Adelbert), Jr. 1937- 29-32R
Stone, Donald D(avid) 1942- 81-84
Stone, Doris (Zemurray) 1909- 105
Stone, Doris (Mary) 1918- 117
Stone, Edward 1913- 37-40R
Stone, Elaine Murray 1922- CANR-38
Earlier sketches in CA 89-92, CANR-17
Stone, Elizabeth W(enger) 1918- CANR-25
Earlier sketch in CA 107
Stone, Ellery W(heeler) 1894-1981 Obituary ... 105
Stone, Elna CANR-5
Earlier sketch in CA 13-16R
Stone, Eugenia 1879-1971 .... 9-12R
See also SATA 7
Stone, Ferdinand Fairfax 1908-1989 Obituary .. 129
Stone, Frank A(ndrews) 1929- CANR-8
Earlier sketch in CA 61-64
Stone, G. H.
See Lynds, Gayle (Hallenbeck)

Stone, Gayle
See Lynds, Gayle (Hallenbeck)
Stone, Gene
See Stone, Eugenia
Stone, George Winchester, Jr. 1907- ... CANR-6
Earlier sketch in CA 5-8R
Stone, Gerald (Charles) 1932- ... 104
Stone, Glenn D(avis) 1954- ... 164
Stone, Grace Zaring 1891-1991 ... CAP-2
Obituary ... 135
Earlier sketch in CA 25-28
Stone, Gregory P(rentice) 1921-1981 ... CANR-1
Obituary ... 116
Earlier sketch in CA 49-52
Stone, Hampton
See Stein, Aaron Marc
Stone, Harris B. 1934- ... 57-60
Stone, Harry 1926- ... 130
Stone, Harry 1928- ... 13-16R
Stone, Helen V(irginia) ... 25-28R
See also SATA 6
Stone, Howard W. 1942- ... 124
Stone, Hoyt E(dward) 1935- ... 101
Stone, I(sidor) F(einstein) 1907-1989 ... CANR-40
Obituary ... 129
Earlier sketch in CA 61-64
Stone, Idella Purnell
See Purnell, Idella
Stone, Ikey
See Purnell, Idella
Stone, Irving 1903-1989 ... CANR-23
Obituary ... 129
Earlier sketches in CA 1-4R, CANR-1
Interview in ... CANR-23
See also CAAS 3
See also AITN 1
See also CLC 7
See also DAM POP
See also MTCW 1
See also SATA 3
See also SATA-Obit 64
Stone, James Champion 1916- ... 17-20R
Stone, James H(erbert) 1918- ... 41-44R
Stone, James S(tuart) 1919- ... 151
Stone, Jeanne C. Fawtier 1920- ... 144
Stone, Jennifer 1933- ... CAAS 30
Stone, Jerry 1942(?)-1987 Obituary ... 124
Stone, Joan 1930- ... CANR-13
Earlier sketch in CA 77-80
Stone, Joel 1931- ... 138
Stone, John (Timothy, Jr.) 1933- ... 102
Stone, John H(enry) 1936- ... 89-92
Stone, Jon 1931-1997 ... 107
Obituary ... 157
See also SATA 39
See also SATA-Obit 95
Stone, Josephine Rector
See Dixon, Jeanne
Stone, Judith F. 1946- ... 162
Stone, Julius 1907-1985 ... CANR-5
Obituary ... 117
Earlier sketch in CA 53-56
Stone, Justin (Federman) 1916- ... 116
Stone, L(awrence) Joseph
1912-1975 Obituary ... 61-64
Stone, Laurie 1946- ... 163
Stone, Lawrence 1919- ... 13-16R
Stone, Lesley
See Trevor, Elleston
Stone, Louis 1910(?)-1985 Obituary ... 115
Stone, Lucy 1818-1893 ... DLB 79
Stone, Margaret N.
See Dresser, Norine
Stone, Marvin Lawrence 1924- ... 69-72
Stone, Matt(hew) 1971- ... 168
See also AAYA 27
Stone, Melville 1848-1929 ... DLB 25
Stone, Merlin 1931- ... CANR-39
Earlier sketches in CA 101, CANR-17
Stone, Michael E(dward) 1938- ... 132
Stone, Mildred Fairbanks 1902- ... CAP-1
Earlier sketch in CA 11-12
Stone, Nancy (Young) 1925- ... 49-52
Stone, Natalie
See Goldenbaum, Sally
and Staff, Adrienne
Stone, Oliver (William) 1946- ... CANR-55
Earlier sketch in CA 110
See also AAYA 15
See also CLC 73
Stone, Patti 1926- ... 5-8R
Stone, Peter 1930- ... CANR-7
Earlier sketch in CA 9-12R
See also SATA 65
Stone, Peter B(ennet) 1933- ... 143
Stone, Philip James III 1936- ... 21-24R
Stone, Ralph A. 1934- ... 37-40R
Stone, Raymond ... CANR-26
Earlier sketches in CAP-2, CA 19-20
See also SATA 1
Stone, Reynolds 1909-1979 Obituary ... 89-92
Stone, Richard
See Delaney, Jack J(ames)
Stone, Richard H. ... CANR-26
Earlier sketches in CAP-2, CA 19-20
Stone, Robert (Anthony) 1937- ... CANR-66
Earlier sketches in CA 85-88, CANR-23
Interview in ... CANR-23
See also CLC 5, 23, 42
See also DLB 152
See also MTCW 1
Stone, Robert B. 1916- ... CANR-31
Earlier sketch in CA 29-32R
Stone, Rodney 1932- ... 140
Stone, Roger D. 1934- ... CANR-43
Earlier sketch in CA 119
Stone, Ronald H. 1939- ... CANR-40
Earlier sketches in CA 77-80, CANR-16
Stone, Rosetta
See Geisel, Theodor Seuss
Stone, Rufus
See Cowie, Donald
Stone, Ruth 1915- ... CANR-2
Earlier sketch in CA 45-48
See also DLB 105
Stone, Samuel 1602-1663 ... DLB 24
Stone, Scott C(linton) S(tuart) 1932- ... CANR-40
Earlier sketches in CA 25-28R, CANR-18
Stone, Shelley C(lyde, Jr.) 1928- ... 61-64
Stone, Shepard 1908-1990 Obituary ... 131
Stone, Susan Berch 1944- ... 61-64
Stone, Thomas H.
See Harknett, Terry
Stone, Todd 1957- ... 140
Stone, Vernon A(lfred) 1929- ... 65-68
Stone, Wilfred (Healey) 1917- ... 21-24R
Stone, William F(rank) 1931- ... 41-44R
Stone, William Leete 1792-1844 ... DLB 202
Stone, William Sidney 1928- ... 13-16R
Stone, Zachary
See Follett, Ken(neth Martin)
Stoneburner, (Charles Joseph) Tony 1926- ... 41-44R
Stonehouse, Bernard 1926- ... CANR-42
Earlier sketches in CA 49-52, CANR-2, 19
See also SATA 13, 80
Stonehouse, John (Thomson) 1925- ... 112
Stonehouse, Merlin 1911- ... 13-16R
Stoneman, Elvyn Arthur 1919- ... 17-20R
Stoneman, Paul 1947- ... 115
Stoneman, Richard (John) 1951- ... 130
Stoneman, William H(arlan)
1904-1987 Obituary ... 122
Stonequist, Everett Verner
1901-1979 Obituary ... 85-88
Stoner, Carol Hupping 1949- ... 53-56
Stoner, K. Lynn 1946- ... 143
Stones, (Cyril) Anthony 1934- ... SATA 72
Stones, E(dgar) 1922- ... CANR-15
Earlier sketch in CA 37-40R
Stones, E(dward) L(ionel) G(regory)
1914-1987 Obituary ... 121
Stonesifer, Richard James 1922- ... 13-16R
Stong, Clair L. 1902(?)-1975 Obituary ... 61-64
Stong, Phil(ip Duffield) 1899-1957 ... SATA 32
Stong, Red
See Stong, Clair L.
Stonier, Tom (Ted) 1927- ... 5-8R
Stonor, Oliver 1903- ... CAP-1
Earlier sketch in CA 13-16
Stonov (Vlodavsky), Dmitry 1898-1962 ... 154
Stonov, Natasha 1932- ... 154
Stonum, Gary Lee 1947- ... 89-92
Stoodley, Bartlett Hicks 1907-1978 ... 1-4R
Obituary ... 103
Stookey, Richard 1938- ... 93-96
Stookey, Robert W(ilson) 1917- ... CANR-14
Earlier sketch in CA 81-84
Stoop, David 1937- ... 119
Stoop, Norma McLain ... 65-68
Stoops, Emery 1902- ... CANR-17
Earlier sketches in CA 1-4R, CANR-1
Stoops, Erik D. 1966- ... 146
See also SATA 78
Stoops, John A(lbert) 1925- ... 29-32R
Stopelman, Francis
See Stoppelman, Frans
Stopes, M. C.
See Stopes, Marie (Charlotte) Carmichael
Stopes, Marie (Charlotte) 1880-1958 ... 154
Stopes, Marie C.
See Stopes, Marie (Charlotte) Carmichael
Stopes, Marie (Charlotte) Carmichael
1880-1958 Brief entry ... 115
Stopford, John M(orton) 1939- ... 140
Stopford, Robert Wright 1901- ... CAP-1
Earlier sketch in CA 13-14
Stopp, Elisabeth (Charlotte Vellar-Etscheit)
1911- ... 5-8R
Stoppard, Miriam 1937- ... 120
Stoppard, Tom 1937- ... CANR-67
Earlier sketches in CA 81-84, CANR-39
See also CDBLB 1960 to Present
See also CLC 1, 3, 4, 5, 8, 15, 29, 34, 63, 91
See also DA
See also DAB
See also DAC
See also DAM DRAM, MST
See also DC 6
See also DLB 13
See also DLBY 85
See also MTCW 1
See also WLC
Stoppelman, Francis
See Stoppelman, Frans
Stoppelman, Frans 1921- ... CAP-1
Earlier sketch in CA 9-10
Stops, Sue 1936- ... 151
See also SATA 86
Storch, Margaret 1941- ... 137
Storer, Doug(las) 1899-1985 ... 57-60
Obituary ... 118
Storer, J(ames) D(onald) 1928- ... CANR-23
Earlier sketch in CA 107
Storer, Norman W(illiam) 1930- ... 41-44R
Storer, Tracy I(rwin) 1889-1973 ... 13-16R
Obituary ... 126
Stores, Teresa (T.) 1958- ... 154
Storey, Anthony 1928- ... CANR-2
Earlier sketch in CA 49-52
See also DLB 14
Storey, Arthur 1915- ... 45-48
Storey, David (Malcolm) 1933- ... CANR-36
Earlier sketch in CA 81-84
See also CLC 2, 4, 5, 8
See also DAM DRAM
See also DLB 13, 14
See also MTCW 1
Storey, Dee
See Storey, Denise Carol
Storey, Denise Carol 1950- ... 146
Storey, Edward 1930- ... 97-100
Storey, Edward J. 1901- ... 89-92
Storey, Gail Donohue 1947- ... 140
Storey, John W(oodrow) 1938- ... 121
Storey, Margaret 1926- ... CANR-1
Earlier sketch in CA 49-52
See also SATA 9
Storey, Mark ... 167
Storey, R(obin) L(indsay) 1927- ... CANR-11
Earlier sketch in CA 21-24R
Storey, Richard
See Gold, H(orace) L(eonard)
Storey, Robert F(ranklin) 1945- ... 85-88
Storey, Victoria Carolyn 1945- ... 33-36R
See also SATA 16
Storey, W(illiam) George 1923- ... CANR-6
Earlier sketch in CA 5-8R
Storfer, Muriel (Rosoff) Silberstein
See Silberstein-Storfer, Muriel (Rosoff)
Storing, Herbert James 1928-1977 Obituary ... 73-76
Storke, Thomas More 1876-1971 Obituary ... 89-92
Storlie, Erik Fraser 1940- ... 168
Storm, Christopher
See Olsen, T(heodore) V(ictor)
Storm, Elizabeth
See Sandstrom, Eve K.
Storm, Hester G(lory) 1903- ... 9-12R
Storm, Hyemeyohsts 1935- ... CANR-45
Earlier sketch in CA 81-84
See also CLC 3
See also DAM MULT
See also NNAL
Storm, Lesley
See Clark, Mabel Margaret (Cowie)
Storm, Mallory
See Fairman, Paul W.
Storm, Marian 1892(?)-1975 Obituary ... 61-64
Storm, Russell
See Williams, Robert Moore
Storm, (Hans) Theodor (Woldsen) 1817-1888 ... DLB 129
See also SSC 27
Storm, Virginia
See Swatridge, Irene Maude (Mossop)
Stormcrow
See Talifero, Gerald
Storme, Peter
See Stern, Philip Van Doren
Stormer, John A. 1928- ... 25-28R
Storni, Alfonsina 1892-1938 ... 131
Brief entry ... 104
See also DAM MULT
See also HLC
See also HW
See also TCLC 5
Storr, Anthony 1920- ... CANR-41
Earlier sketches in CA 97-100, CANR-17
Storr, Catherine (Cole) 1913- ... CANR-52
Earlier sketches in CA 13-16R, CANR-23
See also SATA 9, 87
Storrer, Carol Marchal 1949- ... 112
Storrer, William Allin 1936- ... 156
Storrow, H(ugh) A(lan) 1926- ... 21-24R
Storrow, James J., Jr. 1917-1984 Obituary ... 111
Storry, Richard 1914(?)-1982 Obituary ... 106
Storsve, LaVaughn (Ernestine Kipena) 1921- ... 1-4R
Story, E(ugenia) Macer
See Macer-Story, E(ugenia)
Story, Edward M. 1921- ... 29-32R
Story, G(eorge) M(orley) 1927- ... CANR-9
Earlier sketch in CA 21-24R
Story, Gertrude 1929- ... 129
Story, Jack Trevor 1917-1991 ... CANR-49
Obituary ... 136
Earlier sketch in CA 29-32R
Story, Josephine
See Loring, Emilie (Baker)
Story, Ronald (D.) 1946- ... CANR-11
Earlier sketch in CA 65-68
Story, Thomas 1670(?)-1742 ... DLB 31
Story, William Wetmore 1819-1895 ... DLB 1
Stoskopf, Neal C. 1934- ... 148
Stotland, Ezra 1924- ... 17-20R
Stott, D(enis) H(erbert) 1909-1988 ... CANR-8
Obituary ... 124
Earlier sketch in CA 13-16R
Stott, Dorothy (M.) 1958- ... 134
See also SATA 67, 99
Stott, Dot
See Stott, Dorothy (M.)
Stott, Douglas W(ayne) 1948- ... 109
Stott, Jane 1940- ... 85-88
Stott, John R. W. 1921- ... CANR-40
Earlier sketches in CA 5-8R, CANR-2, 18
Stott, Leland H. 1897- ... 25-28R
Stott, Mary 1907- ... 104
Stott, Mike 1944- ... 104
Stott, Raymond Toole
See Toole Stott, Raymond
Stott, William (Merrell) 1940- ... 61-64
Stotts, Herbert Edward 1916- ... CANR-1
Earlier sketch in CA 1-4R
Stotts, Jack L. 1932- ... 49-52
Stotz, Charles Morse 1898-1985 Obituary ... 115
Stouck, David (Hamilton) 1940- ... 61-64
Stoudemire, Sterling A(ubrey) 1902-1992 ... 37-40R
Obituary ... 137
Stoudt, John Joseph 1911- ... 49-52
Stouffer, Allen P. 1937- ... 143
Stough, Furman C(harles) 1928- Brief entry ... 107
Stoughton, Clarence Charles
1895-1975 Obituary ... 61-64
Stoughton, Gertrude K. 1901- ... CAP-2
Earlier sketch in CA 25-28
Stoughton, William 1631-1701 ... DLB 24
Stout, Alan Ker 1900-1983 Obituary ... 110
Stout, Chris E. 1959- ... 154
Stout, David 1942- ... 136
Stout, Gardner Dominick 1903-1984 Obituary ... 111
Stout, George L(eslie) 1897-1978 ... 81-84
Obituary ... 77-80
Stout, Glenn 1958- ... 138
Stout, Irving Wright 1903-1972 ... CANR-3
Earlier sketch in CA 1-4R
Stout, James (Harvey) 1954- ... 119
Stout, Janis P. 1939- ... 139
Stout, Jeffrey Lee 1950- ... 106
Stout, Joseph A(llen), Jr. 1939- ... CANR-2
Earlier sketch in CA 45-48
Stout, Nancy 1942- ... 137
Stout, Neil Ralph 1932- ... 97-100
Stout, Rex (Todhunter) 1886-1975 ... CANR-71
Earlier sketch in CA 61-64
See also AITN 2
See also CLC 3
Stout, Robert Joe 1936- ... 65-68
Stout, Russell, Jr. 1932- ... CANR-18
Earlier sketch in CA 101
Stout, Ruth 1884-1980 ... 33-36R
Obituary ... 120
Stout, Wesley Winans 1889-1971 Obituary ... 89-92
Stout, William 1949- ... 126
Stoutamire, Albert 1921- ... 41-44R
Stoutenburg, Adrien (Pearl) 1916- ... CANR-45
Earlier sketch in CA 5-8R
See also SATA 3
Stovall, Floyd 1896- ... 9-12R
Stovall, Tyler 1954- ... 163
Stove, D. C.
See Stove, David (Charles)
Stove, David (Charles) 1927- ... 136
Stover, Allan C(arl) 1938- ... CANR-12
Earlier sketch in CA 69-72
See also SATA 14
Stover, Bill
See Stover, W(illiam) H(arrison) M(owbray)
Stover, Jill (Griffin) 1958- ... SATA 82
Stover, Jo Ann 1931- ... 37-40R
Stover, John F(ord) 1912- ... CANR-1
Earlier sketch in CA 1-4R
Stover, Leon E(ugene) 1929- ... CANR-43
Earlier sketches in CA 49-52, CANR-2
Stover, Marjorie Filley 1914- ... CANR-31
Earlier sketch in CA 45-48
See also SATA 9
Stover, W(illiam) H(arrison) M(owbray)
1898-1980 ... 103
Obituary ... 97-100
Stover, Webster 1902- ... 53-56
Stow, John 1525-1605 ... DLB 132
Stow, (Julian) Randolph 1935- ... CANR-33
Earlier sketch in CA 13-16R
See also CLC 23, 48
See also MTCW 1
Stowe, Charles E(dwin) Hambrick
See Hambrick-Stowe, Charles E(dwin)
Stowe, Cynthia 1944- ... 146
Stowe, David M. 1919- ... 9-12R
Stowe, Harriet (Elizabeth) Beecher
1811-1896 ... CDALB 1865-1917
See also DA
See also DAB
See also DAC
See also DAM MST, NOV
See also DLB 1, 12, 42, 74, 189
See also JRDA
See also MAICYA
See also WLC
See also YABC 1
Stowe, James L(ewis) 1950- ... 89-92
Stowe, Leland 1899-1994 ... CANR-53
Obituary ... 143
Earlier sketch in CA 77-80
See also DLB 29
See also SATA 60
See also SATA-Obit 78
Stowe, Noel James 1942- ... 106
Stowe, Richard S(cribner) 1925- ... 73-76
Stowe, Rosetta
See Ogan, George F.
and Ogan, Margaret E. (Nettles)
Stowe, William McFerrin 1913- ... 5-8R
Stowe, William W. 1946- ... 145
Stowell, Joseph M(ishael) 1944- ... 119
Stowers, Carlton 1942- ... CANR-14
Earlier sketches in CA 81-84, CANR-31
Stoy, R(ichard) H(ugh) 1910- ... 57-60
Strabo c. 64B.C.-c. 25 ... DLB 176
Strabolgi, Bartolomeo
See Tucci, Niccolo
Strachan, Hew (Francis Anthony) 1949- ... 61-64
Strachan, Ian 1938- ... 151
See also SATA 85
Strachan, J(ohn) George 1910- ... 107
Strachan, Margaret Pitcairn 1908- ... 5-8R
See also SATA 14
Strachan, T(ony) S(impson) 1920- ... 13-16R
Strachan, W. J.
See Strachan, Walter John
Strachan, Walter John 1903- ... 120
Strachan, Winona Peacock 1918- ... 5-8R
Strachey, Alix 1892-1973 ... 133

Strachey, Barbara
See Halpern, Barbara Strachey
Strachey, Isobel 1907-1987 Obituary ... 122
Strachey, James 1888-1967 ... 128
Brief entry ... 124
Strachey, (Evelyn) John (St. Loe)
1901-1963 Obituary ... 93-96
Strachey, (Giles) Lytton 1880-1932 Brief entry . 110
See also DLB 149
See also DLBD 10
See also TCLC 12
Strackbein, O(scar) R(obert) 1900-1993 ... 21-24R
Obituary ... 143
Straczynski, J(oseph) Michael 1954- ... 109
Strader, June (Sellers) 1925- ... 97-100
Stradley, Mark
See Smith, Richard Rein
Stradling, Leslie Edward 1908-1998 ... 104
Obituary ... 165
Stradling, R. A. 1942- ... 144
Strage, Mark 1927- ... 81-84
Strahan, Randall (W.) 1954- ... 136
Strahinich, H. C.
See Strahinich, Helen C.
Strahinich, Helen C. 1949- ... 146
See also SATA 78
Strahl, Leonard E. 1926- ... 29-32R
Strahlem, Richard E(arl) 1909- ... 37-40R
Strahler, Arthur N(ewell) 1918- ... 139
Straight, Michael Whitney 1916- ... CANR-7
Earlier sketch in CA 5-8R
Straight, Susan 1960- ... 145
Strain, Dudley 1909- ... CAP-1
Earlier sketch in CA 11-12
Strain, Frances Bruce (?)-1975 ... CAP-2
Earlier sketch in CA 29-32
Strain, Lucille Brewton ... 69-72
Strainchamps, Ethel (Reed) 1912- ... 53-56
Strait, Raymond 1924- ... CANR-4
Earlier sketch in CA 53-56
Strait, Treva Adams 1909- ... 97-100
See also SATA 35
Straiton, E(dward) C(ornock) 1917- ... CANR-42
Earlier sketches in CA 45-48, CANR-3, 19
Straiton, Eddie
See Straiton, E(dward) C(ornock)
Straiton, John S(eal) 1922- ... 136
Straka, Gerald Milton 1931- ... CANR-2
Earlier sketch in CA 5-8R
Straker, J(ohn) F(oster) 1904- ... CANR-11
Earlier sketch in CA 13-16R
Strakosch, Avery
See Denham, Avery Strakosch
Straley, John ... 166
Straley, John A(lonzo) 1894-1966 ... 1-4R
Obituary ... 103
Strand, Kenneth A(lbert) 1927- ... CANR-3
Earlier sketch in CA 9-12R
Strand, Mark 1934- ... CANR-65
Earlier sketches in CA 21-24R, CANR-40
See also CLC 6, 18, 41, 71
See also DAM POET
See also DLB 5
See also SATA 41
Strand, Paul 1890-1976 Obituary ... 65-68
Strand, Paul E.
See Palestrant, Simon S.
Strand, Thomas 1944- ... 65-68
Strand, William K. 1931- ... 29-32R
Strandberg, Victor H(ugo) 1935- ... CANR-16
Earlier sketch in CA 89-92
Strane, Susan 1944- ... 136
Strang, Barbara M(ary) H(ope) 1925-1982 .. 37-40R
Obituary ... 106
Strang, Gerald 1908- ... CAP-2
Earlier sketch in CA 25-28
Strang, Ruth May 1895-1971 ... CANR-2
Earlier sketch in CA 1-4R
Strange, Dillon
See Norwood, Victor G(eorge) C(harles)
Strange, Jack Roy 1921- ... 17-20R
Strange, James F(rancis) 1938- ... CANR-42
Earlier sketch in CA 117
Strange, K(athleen) H(aidee) 1904- ... 113
Strange, Maureen 1948- ... 89-92
Strange, N. Blair
See Sargent, Brian (Lawrence)
Strange, Nora K.
See Stanley, Nora Kathleen Begbie Strange
Strange, Philippa
See Coury, Louise Andree
Strange, Susan 1923- ... 49-52
Stranger, Joyce 1921-
See Wilson, Joyce M(uriel Judson)
See also SAAS 24
Strankay, Sam J(ames) 1905- ... 57-60
Strannigan, Shawn (Alyne) 1956- ... 158
See also SATA 93
Strasberg, Lee 1901-1982 ... CANR-29
Obituary ... 106
Earlier sketch in CA 13-16R
Strasberg, Susan (Elizabeth) 1938- Brief entry . 120
Strasburger, Victor C. 1949- ... 112
Strassels, Paul N. ... 109
Strasser, Bernard Paul 1895- ... CAP-1
Earlier sketch in CA 9-10
Strasser, Marland K(eith) 1915- ... CANR-6
Earlier sketch in CA 5-8R
Strasser, Otto (Johann Maximilian)
1897-1974 Obituary ... 53-56
Strasser, Stephan 1905- ... 133
Strasser, Susan 1948- ... CANR-24
Earlier sketch in CA 107
Strasser, Todd 1950- ... CANR-47
Brief entry ... 117
Earlier sketch in CA 123
See also AAYA 2
See also CLR 11
See also JRDA
See also MAICYA
See also SATA 41, 45, 71
Strassfeld, Michael J. 1950- ... 120
Strassfeld, Sharon M(arcia) 1950- ... 107
Strassmann, W(olfgang) Paul 1926- ... 41-44R
Strassova, Helena 1924- ... 49-52
Stratemeyer, Edward L. 1862-1930 ... CANR-27
Earlier sketches in CAP-2, CA 19-20
See also DLB 42
See also MAICYA
See also SATA 1, 67, 100
Stratford, H. Philip
See Bulmer, (Henry) Kenneth
Stratford, Michael
See Cassiday, Bruce (Bingham)
Stratford, Philip 1927- ... CANR-5
Earlier sketch in CA 9-12R
See also SATA 47
Strathern, Andrew (Jamieson) 1939- ... CANR-19
Earlier sketches in CA 49-52, CANR-2
Strathern, Ann Marilyn 1941- ... CANR-3
Earlier sketch in CA 49-52
Strati, Saverio 1924- ... CANR-48
Earlier sketches in CA 17-20R, CANR-7, 23
See also DLB 177
Stratman, Carl J(oseph) 1917-1972 ... CAP-2
Earlier sketch in CA 19-20
Straton, Hillyer H(awthorne) 1905- ... CAP-1
Earlier sketch in CA 9-10
Stratton, Arthur M. 1910(?)-1975 Obituary ... 61-64
Stratton, George Malcolm 1865-1957 Brief
entry ... 112
Stratton, Henry
See Nelson, Michael Harrington
Stratton, J. M.
See Whitlock, Ralph
Stratton, J(ohn) T(heodore) ... 61-64
Stratton, John R(ay) 1935- ... 45-48
Stratton, Porter Andrew 1918- ... 37-40R
Stratton, Rebecca Brief entry ... 115
Stratton, Roy (Olin) ... CAP-2
Earlier sketch in CA 21-22
Stratton, Ted
See Stratton, J(ohn) T(heodore)
Stratton, Thomas
See Coulson, Robert S(tratton)
and DeWeese, Thomas Eugene
Stratton, William David 1896- ... CAP-1
Earlier sketch in CA 9-10
Stratton-Porter, Gene(va Grace) 1863-1924 ... 137
See also DLBD 14
See also MAICYA
See also SATA 15
Stratyner, Barbara Naomi Cohen
See Cohen-Stratyner, Barbara Naomi
Straub, Gerard Thomas 1947- ... 126
Straub, Peter (Francis) 1943- ... CANR-65
Earlier sketches in CA 85-88, CANR-28
See also BEST 89:1
See also CLC 28, 107
See also DAM POP
See also DLBY 84
See also MTCW 1
Straubing, Harold (Elk) 1918- ... 126
Strauch, Carl F(erdinand) 1908- ... 41-44R
Strauch, Judith V(ivian) 1942- ... 107
Strauch, Katina (Parthemos) 1946- ... 105
Straughan, Robert P(aul) L(ouis) 1924- ... 49-52
Straughn, Charles (Thomas II) 1933- ... 117
Straumann, Heinrich 1902- ... 13-16R
Straus, Dennis ... CANR-23
Earlier sketch in CA 105
Straus, Dorothea 1916- ... CANR-72
Earlier sketch in CA 37-40R
Straus, Murray A(rnold) 1926- ... CANR-10
Earlier sketch in CA 21-24R
Straus, Nathan 1889-1961 Obituary ... 89-92
Straus, Richard 1925-1986 ... CANR-22
Earlier sketch in CA 1-4R
Straus, Robert 1923- ... CANR-6
Earlier sketch in CA 57-60
Straus, Roger A(ustin) 1948- ... 109
Strauss, Albrecht B(enno) 1921- ... 37-40R
Strauss, Anselm L(eonard)
1916-1996 Obituary ... 153
Brief entry ... 114
Strauss, Bert(ram) Wiley 1901- ... 13-16R
Strauss, Botho 1944- ... 157
See also CLC 22
See also DLB 124
Strauss, David 1937- ... 89-92
Strauss, David Frederick 1808-1874 ... DLB 133
Strauss, Diane Wheeler 1943- ... 128
Strauss, Elaine Mandle 1916(?)-1982 Obituary . 107
Strauss, Erich 1911-1981 ... 13-16R
Obituary ... 135
Strauss, Frances Goetzmann 1904-1991 ... CAP-2
Obituary ... 134
Earlier sketch in CA 29-32
Strauss, Gerald 1922- ... CANR-33
Earlier sketch in CA 9-12R
Strauss, Gwen 1963- ... 145
See also SATA 77
Strauss, Hans 1898(?)-1977 Obituary ... 69-72
Strauss, Harold 1907-1975 Obituary ... 104
Strauss, Helen M(arion) 1904(?)-1987 Obituary . 122
Strauss, Herbert A(rthur) 1918- ... 133
Brief entry ... 121
Strauss, Jennifer 1933- ... 154
Strauss, Joyce 1936- ... 93-96
See also SATA 53
Strauss, Leo 1899-1973 ... 101
Obituary ... 45-48
Strauss, Lewis Lichtenstein
1896-1974 Obituary ... 45-48
Strauss, (Mary) Lucille Jackson 1908- ... CAP-1
Earlier sketch in CA 11-12
Strauss, Maurice B(enjamin) 1904-1974 ... CAP-2
Earlier sketch in CA 25-28
Strauss, Patricia (Frances O'Flynn)
1909-1987 Obituary ... 123
Strauss, Richard (Georg) 1864-1949 Brief
entry ... 118
Strauss, Richard L(ehman) 1933- ... CANR-36
Earlier sketches in CA 49-52, CANR-1, 16
Strauss, Susan (Elizabeth) 1954- ... 142
See also SATA 75
Strauss, Victor 1907(?)-1979 Obituary ... 89-92
Strauss, W(allace) Patrick 1923- ... 41-44R
Strauss, Walter A(dolf) 1923- ... 81-84
Strauss, Walter L(eopold) 1922-1988 ... CANR-28
Obituary ... 124
Earlier sketch in CA 81-84
Strauss, Werner 1930- ... 29-32R
Strauss, William 1947- ... 145
Strauss, William Louis 1914- ... 61-64
Strausz-Hupe, Robert 1903- ... 9-12R
Stravinski, Igor Fedorovich
See Stravinsky, Igor Fedorovich
Stravinsky, Igor Fedorovich 1882-1971 ... 107
Obituary ... 29-32R
Stravinsky, Vera 1888-1982 ... 106
Obituary ... 107
Strawinsky, Igor Fedorovich
See Stravinsky, Igor Fedorovich
Strawson, Galen 1952- ... 133
Strawson, John 1921- ... CANR-12
Earlier sketch in CA 29-32R
Strawson, P(eter) F(rederick) 1919- ... 25-28R
Strax, Philip 1909- ... 61-64
Stray, Christopher 1943- ... 142
Strayer, Barry L. 1932- ... 29-32R
Strayer, E. Ward
See Stratemeyer, Edward L.
Strayer, Joseph Reese 1904-1987 ... 103
Obituary ... 123
Strayer, Sara Barker 1896(?)-1986 Obituary ... 118
Strean, Herbert S(amuel) 1931- ... CANR-19
Earlier sketch in CA 103
Streano, Vince(nt Catello) 1945- ... 53-56
See also SATA 20
Streatfeild, (Mary) Noel 1895(?)-1986 ... CANR-31
Obituary ... 120
Earlier sketch in CA 81-84
See also CLC 21
See also CLR 17
See also DLB 160
See also MAICYA
See also SATA 20
See also SATA-Obit 48
Streebeck, Nancy 1934- ... 118
Street, Alicia (Kumpula) 1911- ... 5-8R
Street, Arthur George 1892-1966 ... CAP-1
Earlier sketch in CA 13-14
Street, Brian Jeffrey 1955- ... 133
Street, Cecil John Charles
See Rhode, John
Street, G. S. 1867-1936 ... DLB 135
Street, Harry 1919-1984 Obituary ... 112
Street, James H(arry) 1915-1988 ... CANR-4
Obituary ... 125
Earlier sketch in CA 53-56
Street, Janet Travell 1959- ... SATA 84
Street, Jay
See Slesar, Henry
Street, Julia Montgomery 1898- ... CANR-2
Earlier sketch in CA 5-8R
See also SATA 11
Street, Lee
See Hampton, Kathleen
Street, Leslie
See Freemantle, Brian (Harry)
Street, Lucie ... 13-16R
Street, Margaret M(ary) 1907- ... 65-68
Street, Mattie (Waters) 1896- ... CAP-1
Earlier sketch in CA 13-16
Street, Pamela 1921- ... CANR-52
Earlier sketches in CA 45-48, CANR-27
Streeten, Paul Patrick 1917- ... CANR-53
Earlier sketches in CA 25-28R, CANR-11, 28
Streeter, Edward 1891-1976 ... CANR-2
Obituary ... 65-68
Earlier sketch in CA 1-4R
See also DLB 11
Streeter, Herbert Andrus 1918- ... 5-8R
Streeter, James (Jr.) ... 61-64
Streeter, Thomas Winthrop 1883-1965 ... DLB 140
Strehlow, Theodor (George Heinrich) 1908- Brief
entry ... 106
Strehlow, Theodor George Henry
See Strehlow, Theodor (George Heinrich)
Streib, Dan(iel Thomas) 1928-1996 ... 106
Obituary ... 151
Streib, Gordon F(ranklin) 1918- ... 112
Streiker, Lowell D(ean) 1939- ... 49-52
Streisand, Barbra 1942- ... 144
Streit, Clarence Kirshman 1896-1986 ... 1-4R
Obituary ... 119
Streithorst, Tom 1932(?)-1981 Obituary ... 103
Strelka, Joseph P(eter) 1927- ... CANR-51
Earlier sketches in CA 61-64, CANR-8, 26
Strelkoff, Tatiana 1957- ... 155
See also SATA 89
Strelsky, Katharine (Anderson) ... 108
Strempek, Carol Campbell ... 37-40R
Stren, Patti 1949- ... 124
Brief entry ... 117
See also CLR 5
See also SATA 88
See also SATA-Brief 41
Streng, Frederick J(ohn) 1933-1993 ... CANR-27
Obituary ... 141
Earlier sketch in CA 21-24R
Streng, William D(ietrich) 1909- ... CANR-1
Earlier sketch in CA 1-4R
Streng, William Paul 1937- Brief entry ... 108
Streshinsky, Shirley G. 1934- ... CANR-45
Earlier sketches in CA 85-88, CANR-20
Strete, Craig Kee 1950- ... CANR-69
Earlier sketch in CA 161
See also SATA 44, 96
Stretton, Barbara (Humphrey) 1936- ... CANR-39
Earlier sketch in CA 116
See also SATA 43
See also SATA-Brief 35
Stretton, Charles
See Dyer, Charles (Raymond)
Stretton, Hesba
See Smith, Sarah
See also DLB 163
Stretton, Hugh 1924- ... 104
Stribling, T(homas) S(igismund)
1881-1965 Obituary ... 107
See also CLC 23
See also DLB 9
Strich, Christian 1930- ... 109
Strick, Ivy 1952- ... 85-88
Strick, Philip 1939- Brief entry ... 109
Strick, Wesley 1954- ... 164
Stricker, Der c. 1190-c. 1250 ... DLB 138
Stricker, George 1936- ... CANR-14
Earlier sketch in CA 37-40R
Strickland, Arvarh E(unice) 1930- ... 21-24R
Strickland, (William) Brad(ley) 1947- ... 130
See also SATA 83
Strickland, Charles E(verett) 1930- ... 77-80
Strickland, Cowles 1903(?)-1971 Obituary ... 33-36R
Strickland, Craig (A.) 1956- ... SATA 102
Strickland, D. A.
See Strickland, Donald A(llen)
Strickland, Donald A(llen) 1934- Brief entry ... 109
Strickland, Dorothy S(alley) 1933- ... CANR-59
Earlier sketch in CA 108
See also SATA 89
Strickland, Glenn G. 1917- ... 97-100
Strickland, Joshua 1896- ... 81-84
Strickland, Margaret 1930- ... 116
Strickland, Margot 1927- ... CANR-10
Earlier sketch in CA 65-68
Strickland, Michael R. 1965- ... SATA 83
Strickland, Phil D. 1941- ... 29-32R
Strickland, Rennard (James) 1940- ... CANR-43
Earlier sketch in CA 21-24R
Strickland, Rex W(allace) 1897- ... 45-48
Strickland, Ron(ald Gibson) 1943- ... 122
Strickland, Ruth Gertrude 1898- ... CANR-5
Earlier sketch in CA 5-8R
Strickland, Samuel 1804-1867 ... DLB 99
Strickland, Stephen P(arks) 1933- ... CANR-3
Earlier sketch in CA 45-48
Strickler, Susan (Elizabeth) 1952- ... 124
Strickon, Arnold 1930- ... 127
Brief entry ... 108
Strieber, (Louis) Whitley 1945- ... CANR-43
Earlier sketches in CA 81-84, CANR-12
Interview in ... CANR-12
Strieby, Irene Macy 1894- ... CAP-1
Earlier sketch in CA 11-12
Strieder, Peter (Adolf) 1913- ... 131
Strier, Karen B. 1959- ... 145
Strietelmeier, John (Henry) 1920- ... 25-28R
Stright, Hayden Leroy 1898-1975 ... 37-40R
Strike, Jeremy
See Renn, Thomas E(dward)
Striker, Cecil Leopold 1932- ... 109
Striker, Susan 1942- ... SATA 63
Strimple, Earl O. 1938- ... 97-100
Strindberg, (Johan) August 1849-1912 ... 135
Brief entry ... 104
See also DA
See also DAB
See also DAC
See also DAM DRAM, MST
See also TCLC 1, 8, 21, 47
See also WLC
Stringer, Arthur 1874-1950 ... 161
See also DLB 92
See also TCLC 37
Stringer, Christopher 1947- ... 165
Stringer, David
See Roberts, Keith (John Kingston)
Stringer, Lorene A(dair) 1908- ... 37-40R
Stringer, Ruth M(arjorie) Pearson 1905- ... 5-8R
Stringer, William Henry 1908-1976 Obituary ... 65-68
Stringfellow, (Frank) William 1928-1985 ... CANR-9
Obituary ... 115
Earlier sketch in CA 5-8R
Stringfield, Leonard H(arry) 1920- ... 85-88
Stripp, Alan 1924- ... 144
Stritch, Elaine 1926(?)- ... 158
Strittmatter, Erwin 1912- ... DLB 69
Strnisa, Gregor 1930-1987 ... DLB 181
Strobel, Margaret 1946- ... 124
Strober, Gerald S. 1935- ... 85-88
Strobos, Robert Julius 1921- ... 102
Strobridge, Truman R(ussell) 1927- ... 41-44R
Strodach, George Kleppinger 1905- ... 5-8R
Strode, Hudson 1892-1976 ... CANR-8
Obituary ... 69-72
Earlier sketch in CA 13-16R
Strode, William 1603-1645 ... DLB 126

Strodtbeck, Fred L(ouis) 1919- 5-8R
Stroeyer, Poul 1923- CANR-14
Earlier sketch in CA 77-80
See also SATA 13
Stroh, Guy W(eston) 1931- 49-52
Stroh, Thomas F. 1924- CANR-11
Earlier sketch in CA 21-24R
Stroheim, Erich von 1885-1957 TCLC 71
Strohm, John
See Strohm, John L(ouis)
Strohm, John L(ouis) 1912-1987 Obituary 124
Strohmeyer, John 1924- 128
Brief entry 125
Interview in 128
Strom, Deborah 1947- 123
Strom, Ingrid Mathilda 1912- 13-16R
Strom, Leslie Winter
See Winter, Leslie
Strom, Robert D(uane) 1935- CANR-10
Earlier sketch in CA 25-28R
Strom, Yale 1957- 142
Stroman, Duane F(rederick) 1934- 104
Stromberg, Gustaf (Benjamin)
1882-1962 Obituary 112
Stromberg, Peter G. 1952- 145
Stromberg, Roland N(elson) 1916- CANR-46
Earlier sketches in CA 5-8R, CANR-6, 21
Strommen, Merton P. 1919- CANR-5
Earlier sketch in CA 9-12R
Stronach, Bruce 1950- 146
Strong, Anna Louise 1885-1970 Obituary 29-32R
Strong, Charles
See Epstein, Beryl (M. Williams)
and Epstein, Samuel
Strong, Charles Olen 1925- 5-8R
Strong, David
See McGuire, Leslie (Sarah)
Strong, Donald Stuart 1912- 41-44R
Strong, Douglas H(illman) 1935- 117
Brief entry 111
Strong, Douglas M. 1956- 167
Strong, Eithne 1923- 97-100
Strong, Harrington
See McCulley, Johnston
Strong, J. J.
See Strong, Jeremy
Strong, Jeremy 1949- 108
See also SATA 36
Strong, John S. 1956- 138
Strong, John W. 1930- 37-40R
Strong, John William 1935- 37-40R
Strong, Jonathan 1944- 37-40R
Strong, June 1928- 126
Strong, Kenneth William Dobson 1900-1982 104
Obituary 105
Strong, L. A. G. 1896-1958 DLB 191
Strong, Leah A(udrey) 1922- 21-24R
Strong, Lennox
See Grier, Barbara G(ene Damon)
Strong, Pat
See Hough, Richard (Alexander)
Strong, Patience
See Cushing, Winifred
Strong, Philip Nigel Warrington 1899-1983 109
Obituary 110
Strong, Roy (Colin) 1935- CANR-21
Earlier sketches in CA 49-52, CANR-1
Strong, Rupert 1911- 13-16R
Strong, Solange
See Hertz, Solange (Strong)
Strong, Stacie 1965- 141
See also SATA 74
Strong, Susan
See Rees, Joan
Strong, Terence 1946- 145
Strong, Tracy B(urr) 1943- 93-96
Strong, William S. 1951- 124
Strongblood, Casper
See Webster, David Endicott
Stronge, James H. 1945- 146
Strongin, Lynn 1939- CANR-44
Earlier sketches in CA 49-52, CANR-1
Strongman, K(enneth) T(homas) 1940- CANR-10
Earlier sketch in CA 61-64
Strong Man of the Pen, The
See Olisah, Sunday Okenwa
Stroop, Helen E.
See Witty, Helen E. S(troop)
Strother, David B(oyd) 1928- 25-28R
Strother, David Hunter 1816-1888 DLB 3
Strother, Elsie (Frances Warmoth Weitzel) 1912-
CANR-28
Earlier sketches in CA 65-68, CANR-11
Strother, Horatio Theodore 1930- 5-8R
Strother, Pat Wallace 1929- CANR-29
Earlier sketches in CA 65-68, CANR-9
Strother, Patricia
See Strother, Pat Wallace
Stroube, Hal 1921(?)-1983 Obituary 110
Stroud, Bettye 1939- 161
See also SATA 96
Stroud, Carsten 1946- 165
Stroud, Dorothy Nancy 1910- 144
Stroud, Joe H(inton) 1936- 103
Stroud, Jonathan 1970- SATA 102
Stroud, Kandy (Andrea) 108
Stroud, Patricia Tyson 1932- 138
Strouhal, Eugen 1931- 140
Stroup, Herbert H(ewitt) 1916- 13-16R
Stroup, Thomas B(radley) 1903- 25-28R
Strouse, Jean 1945- 103
See also DLB 111
Strousse, Flora G. 1897(?)-1974 Obituary 49-52
Strout, (Sewall) Cushing (Jr.) 1923- 13-16R
Strout, Richard L(ee) 1898-1990 69-72
Obituary 132
Strover, Dorothea 9-12R
Strow, Mary R. 1946- 148
Stroyen, William Basil 1925- 25-28R
Stroyer, Poul
See Stroeyer, Poul
Stroynowski, Juliusz 1919- 132
Strozier, Charles B(urnett) 1944- CANR-50
Earlier sketches in CA 107, CANR-24
Struble, Mitch 1945- 93-96
Struble, Virginia
See Burlingame, Virginia (Struble)
Struever, Stuart McKee 1931- 104
Strugatskii, Arkadii (Natanovich) 1925-1991 106
Obituary 135
See also CLC 27
Strugatskii, Boris (Natanovich) 1933- 106
See also CLC 27
Struglia, Erasmus Joseph 1915- 13-16R
Struik, Dirk Jan 1894- CANR-6
Earlier sketch in CA 5-8R
Struk, Danylo H(usar) 1940- CANR-55
Earlier sketch in CA 57-60
Strum, Philippa 1938- 61-64
Strummer, Joe 1953(?)- CLC 30
Strumpen-Darrie, Robert L. 1912- 13-16R
Strung, Norman 1941- CANR-14
Earlier sketch in CA 41-44R
Strunk, Oliver 1901-1980 Obituary 97-100
Strunk, (William) Oliver 1901-1980 105
Strunk, Orlo, Jr. 1925- CANR-1
Earlier sketch in CA 1-4R
Strunk, William, Jr. 1869-1946 164
Brief entry 118
Strupp, Hans H(ermann) 1921- CANR-2
Earlier sketch in CA 1-4R
Strutt, Malcolm 1936- 115
Strutton, William Harold 1918- 77-80
Strutz, Henry 1932- CANR-50
Earlier sketches in CA 5-8R, CANR-7, 24
Struve, Walter 1935- 49-52
Struyk, Raymond J(ay) 1944- 134
Brief entry 107
Stryjkowski, Julian 1905-1996 CANR-30
Obituary 153
Earlier sketches in CA 49-52, CANR-3
Stryk, Dan 1951- 120
Stryk, Lucien 1924- CANR-55
Earlier sketches in CA 13-16R, CANR-10, 28
Stryker, Daniel
See Morris, Chris(topher Crosby)
and Stump, Jane Barr
Stryker, (Philip) David 1916- 45-48
Stryker, Perrin 1908- 5-8R
Stryker, Sheldon 1924- 9-12R
Stryker-Rodda, Harriet 1905- 81-84
Stryker-Rodda, Kenn 1903-1990 73-76
Obituary 132
Stuart, Aimee 1886(?)-1981 Obituary 103
Stuart, Alex
See Stuart, (Violet) Vivian (Finlay)
Stuart, Alice V(andockum) 1899- 13-16R
Stuart, Anthony
See Hale, Julian A(nthony) S(tuart)
Stuart, Charles
See Mackinnon, Charles Roy
and Reid, Charles (Stuart)
Stuart, Clay
See Whittington, Harry (Benjamin)
Stuart, Colin 1910- 104
Stuart, Dabney 1937- CANR-68
Earlier sketches in CA 17-20R, CANR-8
See also DLB 105
Stuart, David
See Hoyt, Edwin P(almer), Jr.
Stuart, Derek
See Foster, John L(ouis)
Stuart, Don A.
See Campbell, John W(ood, Jr.)
Stuart, Douglas (Keith) 1943- 115
Stuart, Forbes 1924- 69-72
See also SATA 13
Stuart, Francis 1902- CANR-44
Earlier sketch in CA 13-16R
Stuart, Graham H. 1887- CAP-1
Earlier sketch in CA 13-14
Stuart, Ian
See MacLean, Alistair (Stuart)
Stuart, Ian 1927- CANR-30
Earlier sketches in CA 73-76, CANR-13
Stuart, Irving R. 1916- CANR-14
Earlier sketch in CA 41-44R
Stuart, (Jessica) Jane 1942- CANR-31
Earlier sketch in CA 41-44R
Stuart, Jay Allison
See Tait, Dorothy
Stuart, Jesse (Hilton) 1906-1984 CANR-31
Obituary 112
Earlier sketch in CA 5-8R
See also CLC 1, 8, 11, 14, 34
See also DLB 9, 48, 102
See also DLBY 84
See also SATA 2
See also SATA-Obit 36
See also SSC 31
Stuart, Kenneth
See Cox, P(atrick) Brian
See also DLB 9
Stuart, Leslie
See Marlowe, Kenneth
Stuart, Lyle 1922- 81-84
Stuart, Margaret
See Paine, Lauran (Bosworth)
Stuart, Monroe
See Shapiro, Max
Stuart, Reginald (Charles) 1943- CANR-38
Earlier sketch in CA 116
Stuart, Richard Bernard 1933- 41-44R
Stuart, Ruth McEnery 1849(?)-1917 DLB 202
Stuart, Sally E(lizabeth) 1940- 152
Stuart, Sarah Payne 1952- 136
Stuart, Sheila
See Baker, Mary Gladys Steel
Stuart, Sidney
See Avallone, Michael (Angelo, Jr.)
Stuart, Simon (Walter Erskine) 1930- 29-32R
Stuart, V. A.
See Stuart, (Violet) Vivian (Finlay)
Stuart, Virginia (Elaine) 1953- 128
Stuart, (Violet) Vivian (Finlay) 1914- CANR-12
Earlier sketch in CA 13-16R
Stuart, W. J.
See MacDonald, Philip
Stuart, Warren
See MacDonald, Philip
Stuart-Clark, Christopher (Anthony) 1940-
CANR-24
Earlier sketch in CA 107
See also SATA 32
Stuart-Jones, Edwyn Henry 1895-(?) CAP-1
Earlier sketch in CA 13-16
Stub, Holger R(ichard) 1922- 41-44R
Stubbings, Hilda Uren
See U'Ren-Stubbings, Hilda
Stubblebine, Donald J(ames) 1925- 139
Stubblebine, James H(arvey) 1920-1987 97-100
Obituary 121
Stubblefield, Harold W. 1934- 17-20R
Stubbs, Harry C(lement) 1922- CANR-26
Earlier sketches in CA 13-16R, CANR-7
See also Clement, Hal
Stubbs, Jean 1926- CANR-43
Earlier sketch in CA 5-8R
Stubbs, Joanna 1940- SATA-Brief 53
Stubbs, John C(aldwell) 1936- 29-32R
Stubbs, P(eter) C(harles) 1937- 117
Stuber, Florian (Cy) 1947- CANR-24
Earlier sketch in CA 106
Stuber, Stanley I(rving) 1903-1985 CAP-1
Obituary 116
Earlier sketch in CA 13-14
Stubis, Talivaldis 1926- SATA 5
Stubley, Trevor (Hugh) 1932- SATA 22
Stuckenschmidt, H(ans) H(einz) 1901-1988
CANR-18
Obituary 126
Earlier sketch in CA 25-28R
Stuckey, Elma 1907(?)-1988 Obituary 126
Stuckey, Gilbert B. 1912- 65-68
Stuckey, Sterling 1932- 101
Stuckey, William Joseph 1923- 41-44R
Stucki, Curtis W(illiam) 1928- 13-16R
Stucky, Naomi R. 1922- SATA 72
Stucky, Solomon 1923-1988 117
Obituary 140
Stucky, Steven 1949- 109
Stucley, Elizabeth
See Northmore, Elizabeth Florence
Studd, Stephen (Allen) 1946- 116
Studdert-Kennedy, (William) Gerald 1933- 131
Studebaker, J. W.
See Studebaker, John W(ard)
Studebaker, John W(ard) 1887-1989 Obituary 129
Studer, Gerald C. 1927- 65-68
Studlar, Donley T(rent) 1947- 120
Studwell, William E. 1936- 152
Stueart, Robert D. 1935- 105
Stuebing, (Arthur) Douglas 1913- 25-28R
Stueck, William Whitney, Jr. 1945- 105
Stuempke, Harald
See Steiner, Gerolf
Stuermann, Walter E(arl) 1919-1965 5-8R
Stuermer, Nina Roberta 1933- 104
Stuerup, Georg Kristoffer 1905- 25-28R
Stuetzle, Walther 1941- 147
Stuewe, Paul 1943- 130
Stuhlmann, Gunther (Andrew) 1927- CANR-44
Earlier sketch in CA 25-28R
Stuhlmueller, Carroll 1923-1994 CANR-24
Obituary 144
Earlier sketches in CA 13-16R, CANR-9
Stuhr(-Rommereim), Rebecca (Ann) 1958- 168
Stulman, Julius 1906- 118
Stultifer, Morton
See Curtis, Richard (Alan)
Stultz, Newell M(aynard) 1933- 29-32R
Stump, Al 1917(?)- 149
Stump, Jane Barr 1936- 133
Stumpf, Samuel Enoch 1918- 41-44R
Stumpf, Stephen A(lan) 1949- CANR-34
Earlier sketch in CA 111
Stumpke, Harald
See Steiner, Gerolf
Stunkard, Albert J(ames) 1922- 117
Stunkel, Kenneth Reagan 1931- 127
Stuntz, Albert Edward 1902-1976 Obituary 65-68
Stuntz, Laurance F(itzhugh) 1908- 61-64
Stupak, Ronald J(oseph) 1934- 29-32R
Stupples, Peter (Cecil) 1936- 133
Sturcken, Frank 1929- 135
Sturdivant, Frederick D(avid) 1937- 41-44R
Sture-Vasa, Mary
See Alsop, Mary O'Hara
Sturgeon, Foolbert
See Stack, Frank H(untington)
Sturgeon, Theodore (Hamilton) 1918-1985
CANR-32
Obituary 116
Earlier sketch in CA 81-84
See also Queen, Ellery
See also CLC 22, 39
See also DLB 8
See also DLBY 85
See also MTCW 1
Sturgeon, Wina 85-88
Sturges, Patricia P(atterson) 1930- 69-72
Sturges, Preston 1898-1959 149
Brief entry 114
See also DLB 26
See also TCLC 48
Sturges, Robert S(tuart) 1953- 138
Sturgess, Philip J. M. 1946- 141
Sturgill, Claude C(arol) 1933- CANR-9
Earlier sketch in CA 13-16R
Sturgis, James L(averne) 1936- 37-40R
Sturm, Douglas E. 1929- 145
Sturm, Ernest 1932- 65-68
Sturm, John E. 1927- 37-40R
Sturm, Rudolf 1912- Brief entry 109
Sturm, Sara
See Sturm-Maddox, Sara Higgins
Sturmey, S(tanley) G(eorge) 1924- 9-12R
Sturm-Maddox, Sara Higgins 1938- Brief entry 108
Sturmthal, Adolf F(ox) 1903-1986 9-12R
Obituary 119
Sturrock, Jeremy
See Healey, Ben (James)
Stursberg, Peter 1913- 101
Sturt, Mary 1896- CAP-2
Earlier sketch in CA 23-24
Sturtevant, A(lfred) H(enry) 1891-1970 158
Sturtevant, Catherine (?)-1970 Obituary 104
Sturtevant, David Reeves 1926- 104
Sturtevant, Peter M(ann), Jr. 1943- 69-72
Sturton, Hugh
See Johnston, H(ugh) A(nthony) S(tephen)
Sturtzel, Jane Levington 1903- CANR-6
Earlier sketch in CA 1-4R
See also SATA 1
Sturup, Georg Kristoffer
See Stuerup, Georg Kristoffer
Stutler, Boyd B. 1889-1970 CAP-2
Earlier sketch in CA 23-24
Stutz, Bruce 1950- 139
Stutz, Robert Michael 1941- Brief entry 110
Stutzle, Walther
See Stuetzle, Walther
Stutzman, Christian
See Mallett, Daryl F(urumi)
Stutzman, Linford L. 1950- 139
Styan, J(ohn) L(ouis) 1923- CANR-6
Earlier sketch in CA 5-8R
Stychin, Carl F. 1964- 162
Stycos, J(oseph) Mayone 1927- 13-16R
Styles, Jimmie C(arter) 1931- 41-44R
Styles, (Frank) Showell 1908- CANR-60
Earlier sketches in CA 1-4R, CANR-6, 21
See also SATA 10
Stylla, Joanne
See Branden, Victoria (Fremlin)
Styron, Rose (Burgunder) 1928- 17-20R
Styron, William 1925- CANR-33
Earlier sketches in CA 5-8R, CANR-6
Interview in CANR-6
See also BEST 90:4
See also CDALB 1968-1988
See also CLC 1, 3, 5, 11, 15, 60
See also DAM NOV, POP
See also DLB 2, 143
See also DLBY 80
See also MTCW 1
See also SSC 25
Styx, Marguerite (Salzer)
1908(?)-1975 Obituary 53-56
Su, Chien 1884-1918 Brief entry 123
See also Su Man-shu
Suares, Guy 1932- 103
Suarez, Mario 1925- DLB 82
Suarez, Virgil 1962- 131
See also HW
Suarez Lynch, B.
See Bioy Casares, Adolfo
and Borges, Jorge Luis
Suba, Susanne 29-32R
See also SATA 4
Subak-Sharpe, Genell J(ackson) 1936- CANR-31
Earlier sketch in CA 112
Subbiah, B(ommireddi) V(enkata)
1917-1975 41-44R
Subilia, Vittorio 1911- CANR-4
Earlier sketch in CA 9-12R
Sublette, Edith Blanche 1909- 17-20R
Sublette, Walter (Edwards) 1940- 124
Brief entry 117
Subond, Valerie
See Grayland, Valerie (Merle Spanner)
Subotnik, Rena F. 1948- 153
Such, David G. 1954- 154
Such, Peter 1939- DLB 60
Sucharitkul, Somtow 1952- CANR-51
Earlier sketch in CA 118
Sucher, Dorothy 1933- 128
Sucher, Harry V(ictor) 1915- 89-92
Suchlicki, Jaime 1939- CANR-53
Earlier sketches in CA 29-32R, CANR-29
Suchman, Edward A(llen) 1915-197(?) CAP-1
Earlier sketch in CA 13-14
Suchocki, Marjorie Hewitt 1933- 109
Suchoff, Benjamin 1918- CANR-11
Earlier sketch in CA 69-72
Suchting, W. A. 1931- 142

Suckiel, Ellen Kappy 1943- CANR-55
Earlier sketch in CA 127
Suckling, John 1609-1642 DAM POET
See also DLB 58, 126
Suckow, Ruth 1892-1960 Obituary 113
See also DLB 9, 102
See also SSC 18
Sucre, Guillermo 1933- HW
Suda, Zdenek (Ludvik) 1920- CANR-31
Earlier sketch in CA 29-32R
Sudbery, Rodie 1943- 104
See also SATA 42
Sudermann, Hermann 1857-1928 Brief entry 107
See also DLB 118
See also TCLC 15
Sudhalter, Richard M(errill) 1938- 101
Sudman, Seymour 1928- CANR-15
Earlier sketch in CA 41-44R
Sue, Eugene 1804-1857 DLB 119
Sue, Judy
See Epstein, Judith Sue
Suedfeld, Peter 1935- 41-44R
Suelflow, August R(obert) 1922- 9-12R
Sueltz, Arthur Fay 1928- CANR-2
Earlier sketch in CA 49-52
Suenens, Leon Joseph 1904-1996 61-64
Obituary 152
Sueskind, Patrick 1949-
See Suskind, Patrick
See also CLC 44
Suetonius
See Morris, Roger
Sueyoshi, Akiko 1942- 132
Suffling, Mark
See Rowland, D(onald) S(ydney)
Sufrin, Mark 1925- 143
See also SATA 76
Sufrin, Sidney Charles 1910-1997 CANR-17
Obituary 159
Earlier sketches in CA 5-8R, CANR-2
Sugano, Takuo 1931- CANR-51
Earlier sketch in CA 123
Sugar, Bert Randolph 1937- CANR-9
Earlier sketch in CA 65-68
Sugarman, Daniel A(rthur) 1931- 21-24R
Sugarman, Joan G. 1917- SATA 64
Sugarman, Karlene A. 1969- 168
Sugarman, Tracy 1921- 21-24R
See also SATA 37
Sugden, John 1947- CANR-51
Earlier sketch in CA 120
Sugden, Mark 1902-1990 CAP-1
Obituary 130
Earlier sketch in CA 13-14
Sugerman, Danny 1954- 137
Sugerman, Shirley 1919- 65-68
Sugg, Joyce (Marie) 1926- 131
Sugg, Redding S(tancill), Jr. 1922- CANR-2
Earlier sketch in CA 45-48
Sugg, Richard P(eter) 1941- 131
Suggs, George G(raham), Jr. 1929- 41-44R
Suggs, M(arion) Jack 1924- CANR-3
Earlier sketch in CA 1-4R
Suggs, Robert Carl 1932- 9-12R
Suggs, Willie Kathryn 1950- 77-80
Sugimoto, Yoshio 1939- 130
Sugita, Yutaka 1930- 115
See also SATA 36
Sugiyama, Shinya 1949- 132
Sugnet, Charles (Joseph) 1944- 109
Suh, Dae-Sook 1931- 21-24R
Suhl, Benjamin 49-52
Suhl, Yuri (Menachem) 1908-1986 CANR-38
Obituary 121
Earlier sketches in CA 45-48, CANR-2
See also CLR 2
See also MAICYA
See also SAAS 1
See also SATA 8
See also SATA-Obit 50
Suhor, Charles 1935- CANR-10
Earlier sketch in CA 25-28R
Suhr, Elmer George 1902-1976 9-12R
Obituary 65-68
Su Hsuan-ying
See Su, Chien
Su Hsuean-ying
See Su, Chien
Suid, Lawrence Howard 1938- 101
Suid, Murray 1942- CANR-30
Earlier sketch in CA 97-100
See also SATA 27
Suinn, Richard M(ichael) 1933- 29-32R
Sui Sin Far
See Eaton, Edith Maude
Suits, Daniel B(urbidge) 1918- 29-32R
Sujata, Anagarika 1948- 65-68
Suk, Julie CANR-38
Earlier sketch in CA 115
Sukarno, (Ahmed) 1901-1970 Obituary 113
Sukenick, Ronald 1932- CANR-32
Earlier sketch in CA 25-28R
See also CAAS 8
See also CLC 3, 4, 6, 48
See also DLB 173
See also DLBY 81
Sukhotin-Tolstoy, Tatyana
See Tolstoy, Tatyana (Sukhotin)
Sukhwal, Bheru Lal 1929- 57-60
Sukiennik, Adelaide Weir 1938- 126
Suknaski, Andrew 1942- 101
See also CLC 19
See also DLB 53
Suleiman, Ezra N. 1941- 85-88
Suleiman, Michael W(adie) 1934- CANR-42
Earlier sketches in CA 21-24R, CANR-9
Suleiman, Susan Rubin CANR-28
Earlier sketch in CA 109
Suleri, Sara 1953- 136
Sulimirski, Tadeusz Joseph
1898-1983 Obituary 110
Sulitzer, Paul-Loup 1946- 126
Brief entry 122
Sulkin, Sidney 1918-1995 CANR-17
Obituary 149
Earlier sketches in CA 5-8R, CANR-2
Sullens, Idelle 1921- 21-24R
Sullivan, A(loysius) M(ichael) 1896-1980 CAP-2
Obituary 97-100
Earlier sketch in CA 29-32
Sullivan, Alan 1868-1947 DLB 92
Sullivan, (Edward) Alan 1868-1947 162
Sullivan, Alvin 1942- 29-32R
Sullivan, Andrew 1963- 154
Sullivan, Anita T. 1942- 123
Sullivan, Barry
See Sullivan, Matthew Barry
Sullivan, Brian R. 1945- 141
Sullivan, C(harles) Gardner
1886(?)-1965 Obituary 113
See also DLB 26
Sullivan, C(harles) W(illiam) III 1944- 139
Sullivan, Chester L(amar) 1939- 53-56
Sullivan, Clara K(atherine) 1915- 21-24R
Sullivan, Colleen (M.) 1950-1991 117
Obituary 133
Sullivan, D(ale) H(owill) 1936- 61-64
Sullivan, Dan(iel Joseph) 1935- 135
Sullivan, Dean A(lan) 1963- 156
Sullivan, Denis G(artland) 1929- 103
Sullivan, Dolores P. 1925- 148
Sullivan, Donald 1942(?)-1989 Obituary 130
Sullivan, Dulcie Turner 1895-1969 CAP-2
Earlier sketch in CA 25-28
Sullivan, Earl L. 1942- 124
Sullivan, Ed(ward Vincent)
1902(?)-1974 Obituary 89-92
Sullivan, Edmund V(incent) 1938- 61-64
Sullivan, Edward A(nthony) 1936- 115
Sullivan, Edward Daniel 1913-1995 5-8R
Obituary 150
Sullivan, Eleanor (Regis) 1928-1991 139
Brief entry 112
Sullivan, Elizabeth L. 1904(?)-1985 Obituary 115
Sullivan, Evelin 1947- 142
Sullivan, Faith 1933- 134
Sullivan, Francis (Patrick) 1929- CANR-7
Earlier sketch in CA 57-60
Sullivan, Francis John 1892-1976 CAP-2
Obituary 65-68
Earlier sketch in CA 25-28
See also Sullivan, Frank
Sullivan, Frank
See Sullivan, Francis John
See also DLB 11
Sullivan, Frank 1912-1975 65-68
Obituary 61-64
Sullivan, George (Edward) 1927- CANR-44
Earlier sketch in CA 13-16R
See also SATA 4, 89
Sullivan, Henry W(ells) 1942- 149
Sullivan, J(ohn) P(atrick) 1930- CANR-26
Earlier sketches in CA 25-28R, CANR-10
Sullivan, Jack 1946- 119
Sullivan, James L(enox) 1910- 29-32R
Sullivan, Jerry 1938- 115
Sullivan, John L. 1908- 21-24R
Sullivan, Judy 1936- 53-56
See also AITN 1
Sullivan, Kevin 1918(?)-1987 CANR-34
Obituary 122
Earlier sketch in CA 1-4R
Sullivan, Larry E. 1944- 136
Sullivan, Louis (Graydon) 1951- 134
Sullivan, M(ichael) J(ustin) 1940- 142
Sullivan, Marion F. 1899- 37-40R
Sullivan, Mark W(ilbur) 1927- 25-28R
Sullivan, Martin (Gloster) 1910-1980 107
Obituary 104
Sullivan, Martin (Richard Preece) 1934- 29-32R
Sullivan, Mary Ann 1954- 125
See also SATA 63
Sullivan, Mary B(arrett) 1918- 13-16R
Sullivan, Mary W(ilson) 1907- CANR-12
Earlier sketch in CA 73-76
See also SATA 13
Sullivan, Matthew Barry 1915- 132
Sullivan, Maurice William 1925- CANR-2
Earlier sketch in CA 5-8R
Sullivan, (Donovan) Michael 1916- CANR-3
Earlier sketch in CA 5-8R
Sullivan, Michael B. 1938- 77-80
Sullivan, Nancy 1929- 17-20R
Sullivan, Navin 1929- 5-8R
Sullivan, Pat
See Messmer, Otto
Sullivan, Paul (Robert) 1951- 133
Sullivan, Peggy (Anne) 1929- CANR-12
Earlier sketch in CA 29-32R
Sullivan, Prescott 1904(?)-1985 Obituary 116
Sullivan, Randall 1951- 154
Sullivan, Richard 1908-1981 77-80
Obituary 104
Sullivan, Richard E(ugene) 1921- Brief entry 112
Sullivan, Robert E(rtel) 1947- 135
Sullivan, Roger J. 1928- 132
Sullivan, Rosemary 1947- CANR-54
Earlier sketch in CA 97-100
Sullivan, Ruth Christ 1924- 57-60
Sullivan, Sean Mei
See Sohl, Jerry
Sullivan, Sheila 1927- CANR-14
Earlier sketch in CA 77-80
Sullivan, Silky
See Makowski, Silvia Ann
Sullivan, Sister Bede 1915- 25-28R
Sullivan, Stanislaus 1930- 127
Sullivan, Thomas (William) 1940- 127
Sullivan, Thomas Joseph, Jr. 1947- 81-84
See also SATA 16
Sullivan, Tom
See Sullivan, Thomas Joseph, Jr.
Sullivan, Tony
See Sullivan, Stanislaus
Sullivan, Vernon
See Vian, Boris
Sullivan, Victoria 1943- 65-68
Sullivan, Vincent F. 1899- CAP-2
Earlier sketch in CA 29-32
Sullivan, Walter 1906- 13-16R
Sullivan, Walter (Laurence) 1924- 41-44R
Sullivan, Walter Seager 1918-1996 CANR-2
Obituary 151
Earlier sketch in CA 1-4R
Sullivan, William H(ealy) 1922- 133
Sullivan, William M. 1945- CANR-43
Earlier sketch in CA 109
Sullivan, Winona 1942- 141
Sullivan Harper, Akiba
See Sullivan Harper, Donna Akiba
Sullivan Harper, Donna Akiba 1954- 151
Sullivant, Robert S(cott) 1925- 1-4R
Sulloway, Alison G. 1917- Brief entry 111
Sulloway, Frank J(ones) 1947- 124
Brief entry 118
Interview in 124
Sully, (Lionel Henry) Francois 1927-1971 CAP-2
Obituary 29-32R
Earlier sketch in CA 25-28
Sully, Kathleen M. 1910- 13-16R
Sully, Nina (Rosemary) 1948- 110
Sully Prudhomme 1839-1907 TCLC 31
Sultan, Alan 1948- 145
Sultan, Arne 1925-1986 Obituary 118
Sultan, Stanley 1928- CANR-26
Earlier sketches in CA 13-16R, CANR-10
Sultana, Donald Edward 1924- 103
Sulte, Benjamin 1841-1923 DLB 99
Sulzberger, Arthur Hays 1891-1968 Obituary 89-92
See also DLB 127
Sulzberger, Arthur Ochs 1926- DLB 127
Sulzberger, C(yrus) L(eo II) 1912-1993 CANR-23
Obituary 142
Earlier sketches in CA 53-56, CANR-7
Sulzberger, Iphigene (Bertha) Ochs
1892-1990 Obituary 131
Sulzberger, Marina Tatiana
1919(?)-1976 Obituary 111
Sum, Ngai-Ling 1952- 146
Su Man-shu
See Su, Chien
See also TCLC 24
Sumarokov, Aleksandr Petrovich 1717-1777 DLB 150
Sumarsam 1944- 159
Sumichrast, Jozef 1948- SATA 29
Sumichrast, Michael M. 1921- CANR-21
Earlier sketch in CA 104
Sumida, Jon Tetsuro 1949- 124
Sumiko
See Davies, Sumiko
Summer, Brian
See Du Breuil, (Elizabeth) L(or)inda
Summer, Charles Edgar 1923- 81-84
Summerfield, Harry L. 1940- 37-40R
Summerfield, Jack
See Summerfield, John D(udley)
Summerfield, Joanne 1940- 117
Summerfield, John D(udley) 1927- 21-24R
Summerfield, Lin(da Victoria) 1952- 132
Summerfield, Margie 1949- 89-92
Summerfield, Penny 1951- 119
Summerforest, Ivy B.
See Kirkup, James
Summerhayes, Victor Samuel
1897(?)-1974 Obituary 53-56
Summerhill, J. K.
See Schere, Monroe
Summerlin, Sam(uel A.) 1928- CANR-34
Earlier sketch in CA 45-48
Summerlin, Vernon 168
Summers, Andrew James 1942- CLC 26
Summers, Andy
See Summers, Andrew James
Summers, Anthony (Bruce) 1942- CANR-23
Earlier sketch in CA 69-72
Summers, Clyde Wilson 1918- 109
Summers, Essie
See Summers, Ethel Snelson
Summers, Ethel Snelson 1912- Brief entry 116
Summers, Festus P(aul) 1895- CAP-1
Earlier sketch in CA 11-12
Summers, Gene F(ranklin) 1936- CANR-12
Earlier sketch in CA 29-32R
Summers, Gordon
See Hornby, John (Wilkinson)
Summers, Hal
See Summers, Henry Forbes
Summers, Harrison B(oyd) 1894- 13-16R
Summers, Harry G(lenn), Jr. 1932- 123
Summers, Henry Forbes 1911- 109
Summers, Hollis (Spurgeon, Jr.) 1916- CANR-3
Earlier sketch in CA 5-8R
See also CLC 10
See also DLB 6
Summers, Ian 1939- 105
Summers, James L(evingston) 1910-1973 13-16R
See also SATA 57
See also SATA-Brief 28
Summers, JoAn 1943- 106
Summers, John A.
See Lawson, H(orace) L(owe)
Summers, Joseph H(olmes) 1920- 41-44R
Summers, Lionel M(organ) 1905-1975 45-48
Obituary 103
Summers, Merna 1933- 131
Summers, (Alphonsus Joseph-Mary Augustus)
1880-1948 163
Brief entry 118
See also TCLC 16
Summers, Ray 1910- 13-16R
Summers, Robert 1922- 77-80
Summers, Robert E. 1918- 25-28R
Summers, Robert S(amuel) 1933- CANR-11
Earlier sketch in CA 69-72
Summers, Rowena
See Saunders, Jean
Summerscales, William 1921- 29-32R
Summersell, Charles Grayson 1908- CANR-19
Earlier sketches in CA 1-4R, CANR-3
Summerskill, Edith 1901-1980 Obituary 93-96
Summerson, John (Newenham) 1904- Brief entry 117
Summerson, Rachel (Elizabeth) 1944- 107
Summertree, Katonah
See Windsor, Patricia
Summerville, James 1947- CANR-45
Earlier sketch in CA 119
Sumner, Cid Ricketts 1890-1970 5-8R
Obituary 29-32R
Sumner, Colin 1949- 111
Sumner, David (W. K.) 1937- 57-60
Sumner, David E. 1946- 163
Sumner, Eldon
See Bruno, James Edward
Sumner, Gordon Matthew
See Sting
See also CLC 26
Sumner, Lloyd Quinton 1943- 103
Sumner, Richard (William) 1949- 69-72
Sumption, Jonathan (Philip Chadwick) 1948- 136
Sumrall, Amber Coverdale 1945- 147
Sumwalt, Martha Murray 1924- 69-72
Sun, Annalise
See Maxwell, Ann (Elizabeth)
Sun, Chyng Feng 1959- 155
See also SATA 90
Sun, Ruth Q(uinlan) 1907- 57-60
Sunagel, Lois A(nn) 1926- 93-96
Sund, Robert B(ruce) 1926- CANR-36
Earlier sketch in CA 29-32R
Sundahl, Daniel James 1947- 146
Sundarananda
See Nakashima, George Katsutoshi
Sunday, Billy
See Sunday, William Ashley
Sunday, William Ashley 1862(?)-1935 Brief entry 120
Sundberg, Trudy James 1925- 17-20R
Sundell, Roger H(enry) 1936- 21-24R
Sundelson, David 1946- 152
Sunder, Shyam 1944- 118
Sunderland, Eric 1930- CANR-21
Earlier sketch in CA 103
Sunderland, Glenn W. 1925- 25-28R
Sunderland, Lane V(on) 1945- 97-100
Sunderlin, Sylvia (S.) 1911-1997 73-76
Obituary 162
See also SATA 28
See also SATA-Obit 99
Sunderman, James F. 1919- 17-20R
Sunderman, Lloyd Frederick
1905-1983 Obituary 109
Sundgaard, Arnold (Olaf) 1909- CANR-2
Earlier sketch in CA 45-48
Sundiata, Ibrahim K. 1944- 158
Sundman, Per Olof 1922- Brief entry 111
Sundquist, Eric J. 1952- 129
Sundquist, James L(loyd) 1915- 29-32R
Sundquist, Ralph Roger, Jr. 1922- Brief entry 106
Sung, Betty Lee CANR-10
Earlier sketch in CA 25-28R
See also SATA 26
Sung, P. M.
See Chun, Jinsie K(yung) S(hien)
Sungolowsky, Joseph 1931- 41-44R
Sunley, Margaret 1921-1990 134
Sunners, William 1903-1988 CAP-1
Obituary 125
Earlier sketch in CA 9-10
Sunoo, Harold Hak-Won 1918- 41-44R
Sunseri, Alvin R(aymond) 1925- 93-96
Sunshine, John 1897(?)-1987 Obituary 123
Sunshine, Linda 1948- 154
Sunstein, Emily W(eisberg) 1924- 53-56
Suny, Ronald Grigor 1940- CANR-55
Earlier sketches in CA 111, CANR-29
Sun Yat-sen, Madame
See Soong, Ching-ling
Sun Yefang 1908-1983 Obituary 109
Suomi, Verner E(dward) 1915- 161
Super, Donald E(dwin) 1910- CANR-3
Earlier sketch in CA 1-4R
Super, R(obert) H(enry) 1914- 13-16R
Super Santa
See Berman, Ed
Supervielle, Jules 1884-1960 Obituary 114
Suponev, Michael 1923- 65-68
Suppe, Frederick (Roy) 1940- 41-44R
Suppes, Patrick 1922- CANR-42
Earlier sketches in CA 1-4R, CANR-4, 20
Suppon, Charles 1949-1989 Obituary 128

Supraner, Robyn 1930- ... CANR-51
Earlier sketches in CA 69-72, CANR-26
See also SATA 20, 101
Supree, Burt(on) 1941-1992 ... 65-68
Obituary ... 137
See also SATA 73
Surace, Samuel J. 1919- ... 21-24R
Suran, Bernard G(regory) 1939- ... 81-84
Suransky, Valerie Polakow
See Polakow, Valerie (Suransky)
Suret-Canale, Jean 1921- ... CANR-1
Earlier sketch in CA 49-52
Surette, (Philip) Leon 1938- ... 110
Surface, Bill
See Surface, William E.
Surface, William E. 1935-1980(?) ... CANR-13
Earlier sketch in CA 5-8R
Surge, Frank 1931- ... 69-72
See also SATA 13
Suria, Violeta Lopez
See Lopez Suria, Violeta
Surkin, Marvin 1938- ... 61-64
Surkov, Alexei Aleksandrovich
1899-1983 Obituary ... 110
Surles, Lynn 1917- ... 13-16R
Surman, Charles Edward 1901- ... 5-8R
Surmelian, Leon (Zaven) 1907- ... CAP-2
Earlier sketch in CA 25-28
Surplus, Robert W. 1923- ... 5-8R
Surrey, (Arthur) John 1933- ... 117
Surrey, Peter J. 1928- ... 106
Surrey, Stanley Sterling 1910-1984 Obituary ... 113
Surtees, Robert Smith 1803-1864 ... DLB 21
Surtz, Edward 1910(?)-1973 Obituary ... 41-44R
Susac, Andrew 1929- ... 49-52
See also SATA 5
Susan
See Graham, (Maude Fitzgerald) Susan
Susann, Jacqueline 1921-1974 ... 65-68
Obituary ... 53-56
See also AITN 1
See also CLC 3
See also MTCW 1
Susi, Geraldine Lee 1942- ... 165
Susi, Geraldine Lee 1942- ... SATA 98
Suskind, Patrick ... 145
See also Sueskind, Patrick
Suskind, Richard 1925- ... CANR-9
Earlier sketch in CA 13-16R
Suslov, Alexander 1950- ... 105
Suslov, Mikhail Andreyevich
1902-1982 Obituary ... 105
Susman, Gerald I. 1941- ... 139
Susman, Warren (Irving) 1927-1985 Obituary ... 116
Suss, Elaine ... 102
Susser, Mervyn (Wilfred) 1921- ... CANR-1
Earlier sketch in CA 45-48
Susser, Samuel S. 1910- ... 97-100
Sussex, Lucy (Jane) 1957- ... 159
Susskind, Charles 1921- ... CANR-15
Earlier sketch in CA 85-88
Sussman, Aaron 1903- Brief entry ... 116
Sussman, Barry 1934- ... 53-56
Sussman, Cornelia Silver 1914- ... CANR-13
Earlier sketch in CA 5-8R
See also SATA 59
Sussman, Gerald 1933(?)-1989 Obituary ... 130
Sussman, Henry 1947- ... CANR-43
Earlier sketch in CA 111
Sussman, Herbert L. 1937- ... 25-28R
Sussman, Irving 1908- ... CANR-13
Earlier sketch in CA 77-80
See also SATA 59
Sussman, Leonard R(ichard) 1920- ... CANR-4
Earlier sketch in CA 53-56
Sussman, Marvin B(ernard) 1918- ... CANR-19
Earlier sketches in CA 9-12R, CANR-4
Sussman, Peter Y. 1941- ... 144
Sussman, Susan 1942- ... CANR-58
Earlier sketches in CA 111, CANR-30
See also SATA 48
Sutch, Richard C(harles) 1942- ... CANR-34
Earlier sketch in CA 107
Sutcliff, Rosemary 1920-1992 ... CANR-37
Obituary ... 139
Earlier sketch in CA 5-8R
See also AAYA 10
See also CLC 26
See also CLR 1, 37
See also DAB
See also DAC
See also DAM MST, POP
See also JRDA
See also MAICYA
See also SATA 6, 44, 78
See also SATA-Obit 73
Sutcliffe, Anthony (Richard) 1942- ... CANR-34
Earlier sketch in CA 106
Suter, Ronald 1930- ... 41-44R
Sutermeister, Robert Arnold 1913- ... 5-8R
Suther, Marshall E(dward), Jr. 1918- ... 1-4R
Sutherland, Allan T(homas) 1950- ... 132
Sutherland, Arthur Eugene, Jr. 1902-1973 ... CAP-1
Obituary ... 41-44R
Earlier sketch in CA 19-20
Sutherland, C(arol) Humphrey V(ivian)
1908- ... 13-16R
Sutherland, Colleen 1944- ... SATA 79
Sutherland, Daniel E(llyson) 1946- ... CANR-63
Earlier sketches in CA 109, CANR-26
Sutherland, Donald 1915- ... 37-40R
Sutherland, Donald W(ayne) 1931- ... 9-12R
Sutherland, Douglas 1919- ... 21-24R
Sutherland, Earl Wilbur 1915-1974 ... 163
Obituary ... 49-52
Sutherland, Efua (Theodora Morgue) 1924- ... 105
See also BW 1
See also DLB 117
See also SATA 25
Sutherland, Elizabeth
See Martinez, Elizabeth Sutherland
Sutherland, Elizabeth 1926- ... 85-88
Sutherland, Fraser 1946- ... 102
Sutherland, Gordon (Brims Black McIvor)
1907-1980 Obituary ... 108
Sutherland, H(erbert) W(arren) 1917-1981 ... 13-16R
Obituary ... 134
Sutherland, Ivan (Edward) 1938- ... 161
Sutherland, James (Edward) 1948- ... CANR-2
Earlier sketch in CA 49-52
Sutherland, John 1919-1956 ... DLB 68
Sutherland, John (Patrick) 1920-1988 Obituary ... 125
Sutherland, John (Anthony) 1933- ... CANR-16
Earlier sketch in CA 93-96
Sutherland, John P(atrick) 1920-1988 ... 21-24R
Sutherland, Jon Nicholas 1941-1977 ... CANR-32
Earlier sketch in CA 41-44R
Sutherland, Lucy Stuart 1903-1980 ... CAP-1
Obituary ... 105
Earlier sketch in CA 13-14
Sutherland, Margaret 1941- ... CANR-14
Earlier sketch in CA 77-80
See also SATA 15
Sutherland, N(icola) M(ary) 1925- ... 49-52
Sutherland, R(ussell) Galbraith 1924- ... CAP-1
Earlier sketch in CA 9-10
Sutherland, Robert D(onald) 1937- ... 37-40R
Sutherland, Roger
See Hicks, Roger W(illiam)
Sutherland, Ronald 1933- ... 25-28R
Sutherland, (Norman) Stuart 1927- ... 65-68
Sutherland, (William) Temple (Gairdner) 1906- ...
CAP-1
Earlier sketch in CA 9-10
Sutherland, Zena Bailey 1915- ... 102
See also SATA 37
Suthinee
See Ambhanwong, Suthilak
Suthren, Victor (James Henry) 1942- ... CANR-23
Earlier sketch in CA 107
Sutin, Lawrence 1951- ... 135
Sutnar, Ladislav 1897-1976 Obituary ... 104
Su Tong
See Tong, Zhong Gui
Sutphen, Dick
See Sutphen, Richard Charles
Sutphen, Richard Charles 1937- ... CANR-53
Earlier sketches in CA 25-28R, CANR-11, 28
Sutphin, Winfield Blair 1919(?)-1990 Obituary ... 131
Sutphin, Wyn Blair
See Sutphin, Winfield Blair
Sutro, Alfred 1863-1933 Brief entry ... 105
See also DLB 10
See also TCLC 6
Sutro, John 1903(?)-1985 Obituary ... 117
Sutryn, Barbara M(ay) 1927- ... 120
Sutter, Franz
See Strich, Christian
Sutter, Frederic Koehler 1938- ... 107
Sutter, Ruth E(laine) 1935- ... 45-48
Suttles, Gerald 1932- ... 85-88
Suttles, Shirley (Smith) 1922- ... 13-16R
See also SATA 21
Suttmeier, Richard Peter 1942- ... CANR-6
Earlier sketch in CA 57-60
Sutton, Allan 1952- ... 163
Sutton, Ann (Livesay) 1923- ... CANR-10
Earlier sketch in CA 5-8R
See also SATA 31
Sutton, Antony C. 1925- ... 97-100
Sutton, Barry 1919-1988 Obituary ... 125
Sutton, Carol 1933-1985 Obituary ... 115
Sutton, Caroline 1953- ... 106
Sutton, Christine 1950- ... 120
Sutton, Dana F. 1942- ... 145
Sutton, David (John) 1944- ... 116
Sutton, David 1947- ... 101
Sutton, Denys (Miller) 1917-1991 ... CANR-20
Obituary ... 133
Earlier sketches in CA 53-56, CANR-5
Sutton, Eve(lyn Mary) 1906- ... CANR-10
Earlier sketch in CA 65-68
See also SATA 26
Sutton, Felix 1910(?)- ... 77-80
See also SATA 31
Sutton, George Miksch 1898-1982 ... 107
Obituary ... 109
Sutton, Gordon 1910- ... 21-24R
Sutton, Henry
See Slavitt, David R(ytman)
Sutton, Horace (Ashley) 1919-1991 ... CANR-10
Obituary ... 135
Earlier sketch in CA 13-16R
Sutton, Howard 1930- ... 65-68
Sutton, Jane 1950- ... 89-92
See also SATA 52
See also SATA-Brief 43
Sutton, Jeff
See Sutton, Jefferson (Howard)
Sutton, Jefferson (Howard) 1913-1979 ... CANR-10
Earlier sketch in CA 21-24R
Sutton, John L(awrence) 1917- ... 105
Sutton, L(aurence) P(aul) Elwell
See Elwell-Sutton, L(aurence) P(aul)
Sutton, Larry M(atthew) 1931- ... CANR-14
Earlier sketch in CA 37-40R
See also SATA 29
Sutton, Margaret Beebe 1903- ... 1-4R
See also SATA 1
Sutton, Maurice Lewis 1927- ... CANR-64
Earlier sketch in CA 13-16R
Sutton, Max Keith 1937- ... 93-96
Sutton, Myron Daniel 1925- ... 107
See also SATA 31
Sutton, Penny
See Wood, Christopher (Hovelle)
Sutton, Peter C. 1949- ... 132
Sutton, R. Anderson 1949- ... 142
Sutton, Remar 1941- ... 126
Sutton, Robert M(ize) 1915- ... 77-80
Sutton, Robert P. 1940- ... 150
Sutton, Roberta Briggs 1899- ... 5-8R
Sutton, Roger 1956- ... 159
See also SATA 93
Sutton, S(tephanne) B(arry) 1940- ... 29-32R
Sutton, Stack
See Sutton, Maurice Lewis
Sutton, Tony C.
See Sutton, Antony C.
Sutton, Walter 1916- ... 85-88
Sutton, William A(lfred) 1915- ... 61-64
Sutton-Smith, Brian 1924- ... CANR-17
Earlier sketch in CA 29-32R
Sutton-Vane, Vane Hunt
See Vane, (Vane Hunt) Sutton
Suttor, T(imothy) L(achlan) 1926- ... 21-24R
Suvin, Darko (Ronald) 1932- ... CANR-38
Earlier sketches in CA 89-92, CANR-16
Suvorov, Viktor (a pseudonym) ... 116
Suyin, Han
See Han Suyin
Su Yuan-ying
See Su, Chien
Su Yuean-ying
See Su, Chien
Suzanne, Jamie
See Hawes, Louise
and Singleton, Linda Joy
and Zach, Cheryl (Byrd)
Suzman, Helen 1917- ... 145
Suzuki, D. T.
See Suzuki, Daisetz Teitaro
Suzuki, Daisetz T.
See Suzuki, Daisetz Teitaro
Suzuki, Daisetz Teitaro 1870-1966 ... 121
Obituary ... 111
See also MTCW 1
Suzuki, Teitaro
See Suzuki, Daisetz Teitaro
Suzuki, Tessa Morris
See Morris-Suzuki, Tessa
Suzuki, Yoshio 1931- ... 143
Svajian, Stephen G. 1906(?)-1977 Obituary ... 73-76
Svanstrom, Ragnar 1904(?)-1988 Obituary ... 127
Svareff, Count Vladimir
See Crowley, Edward Alexander
Svarlien, Oscar 1906- ... CAP-1
Earlier sketch in CA 13-16
Svartvik, Jan 1931- ... 21-24R
Svedberg, Theodor 1884-1971 ... 167
Svejda, George J. 1927- ... 41-44R
Svendsen, Hanne Marie 1933- ... 134
Svendsen, Linda 1954- ... 139
Svenson, Andrew E(dward) 1910-1975 ... CANR-27
Obituary ... 61-64
Earlier sketch in CA 5-8R
See also Stone, Alan
See also SATA 2
See also SATA-Obit 26
Svensson, Arne 1929- ... 49-52
Sverdlin, Hannah Grad 1911(?)-1989 Obituary ... 127
Svestka, Oldrich 1922-1983 Obituary ... 110
Svevo, Italo 1861-1928
See Schmitz, Aron Hector
See also SSC 25
See also TCLC 2, 35
Svirsky, Grigori (Tsezarevich) 1921- ... CANR-42
Earlier sketch in CA 69-72
Svoboda, Frederic Joseph 1949- ... 116
Svoboda, Terese 1950- ... 147
Svoray, Yaron 1954(?)- ... 158
Swaan, Wim 1927-1995 ... CANR-18
Obituary ... 149
Earlier sketch in CA 25-28R
Swabey, Marie Collins 1890-1966 ... CANR-16
Earlier sketch in CA 1-4R
Swadesh, Frances Leon 1917- ... 120
Swadley, Elizabeth 1929- ... 21-24R
Swados, Elizabeth (A.) 1951- ... CANR-49
Earlier sketch in CA 97-100
Interview in ... 97-100
See also CLC 12
Swados, Harvey 1920-1972 ... CANR-6
Obituary ... 37-40R
Earlier sketch in CA 5-8R
See also CLC 5
See also DLB 2
Swaffer, Hannen 1879-1962 Obituary ... 112
Swafford, Jan Johnson 1946- ... 167
Swaim, Alice Mackenzie 1911- ... CANR-6
Earlier sketch in CA 9-12R
Swaim, Joan (Hewatt) 1934- ... 138
Swaim, Lawrence 1942- ... 69-72
Swain, Bruce M(cArthur) 1943- ... 101
Swain, Charles 1801-1874 ... DLB 32
Swain, Donald C(hristie) 1931- ... 29-32R
Swain, Dwight V(reeland) 1915- ... CANR-37
Earlier sketches in CA 17-20R, CANR-7
Swain, Frank G. 1893(?)-1975 Obituary ... 53-56
Swain, Gwenyth 1961- ... 150
See also SATA 84
Swain, James E(dgar) 1897-1975 ... CAP-2
Earlier sketch in CA 25-28
Swain, Joseph P(eter) 1955- ... 136
Swain, Joseph Ward 1891-1971 ... CAP-2
Earlier sketch in CA 21-22
Swain, Margaret (Helen) 1909- ... 53-56
Swain, Mark
See Latimer, Dean
Swain, Marshall (William) 1940- ... 124
Brief entry ... 117
Swain, Martha H(elen) 1929- ... 85-88
Swain, Olive 1896- ... 5-8R
Swain, Raymond Charles 1912- ... 9-12R
Swain, Roger (Bartlett) 1949- ... CANR-41
Earlier sketch in CA 102
Swain, Su Zan (Noguchi) 1916- ... CANR-6
Earlier sketch in CA 5-8R
See also SATA 21
Swainson, Donald 1938- ... CANR-56
Earlier sketches in CA 109, CANR-30
Swainson, Eleanor Frances ... 111
Swale, Rose 1947- Brief entry ... 116
Swale, Rosie
See Swale, Rose
Swales, Martin 1940- ... 81-84
Swallow, Alan 1915-1966 ... CANR-16
Obituary ... 25-28R
Earlier sketch in CA 1-4R
Swallow, Mark (Richard Crawley) 1963- ... 134
Swallow, Norman 1921- ... 21-24R
Swami Rama 1925- ... 119
Swamp, Jake 1941- ... SATA 98
Swamp, Jake 1941- ... 165
Swamy, Subramanian 1939- ... 49-52
Swan, Berta W(aterhouse) 1928- ... 29-32R
Swan, Bradford Fuller 1908(?)-1976 Obituary ... 65-68
Swan, Carroll J. 1914-1984 Obituary ... 112
Swan, Christopher C(ushing) 1946- ... 103
Swan, Gladys 1934- ... CANR-39
Earlier sketches in CA 101, CANR-17
See also CLC 69
Swan, James H. 1946- ... 144
Swan, Jon 1929- ... 89-92
Swan, Marie
See Bartlett, Marie (Swan)
Swan, Susan 1944- ... SATA 22
Swan, Thomas 1926- ... 162
Swanberg, W(illiam) A(ndrew) 1907-1992 ... CANR-8
Obituary ... 139
Earlier sketch in CA 5-8R
See also CAAS 13
See also DLB 103
Swander, Mary 1950- ... CANR-48
Earlier sketch in CA 122
Swanger, David 1940- ... 49-52
Swann, Brian (Stanley Frank) 1940- ... CANR-56
Earlier sketches in CA 37-40R, CANR-31
Swann, Donald (Ibrahim) 1923-1994 ... CANR-41
Obituary ... 144
Earlier sketches in CA 21-24R, CANR-16
Swann, Francis 1913- ... CANR-4
Earlier sketch in CA 9-12R
Swann, Ingo 1933- ... 57-60
Swann, Lois 1944- ... CANR-12
Earlier sketch in CA 65-68
Swann, Peggy
See Geis, Richard E(rwin)
Swann, Peter C(harles) 1921- ... 5-8R
Swann, Ruth Rice 1920- ... SATA 84
Swann, Thomas Burnett, Jr. 1928-1976 ... CANR-4
Earlier sketch in CA 5-8R
Swansea, Charleen 1932- ... CANR-16
Earlier sketch in CA 103
Swansen, Vern 1916- ... 49-52
Swanson, Arlene Collyer 1913- ... 5-8R
Swanson, Austin D. 1930- ... 25-28R
Swanson, Bert E(lmer) 1924- ... 29-32R
Swanson, Carl P(ontius) 1911- ... 45-48
Swanson, David 1935- ... 146
Swanson, Don R(ichard) 1924- ... 13-16R
Swanson, Donald Roland 1927- ... 41-44R
Swanson, Doug J. 1953- ... 160
Swanson, Edward I. 1923- ... 29-32R
Swanson, Gerald J. 1940- ... 147
Swanson, Gloria 1899(?)-1983 ... 142
Obituary ... 109
Swanson, Gloria Borseth 1927- ... 77-80
Swanson, Gustav A(dolph) 1910- ... CANR-14
Earlier sketch in CA 77-80
Swanson, H(arold) N(orling) 1899- ... 132
Swanson, Harold B(urdette) 1917- ... 37-40R
Swanson, Heather (Crichton) 1949- ... 135
Swanson, Helen M(cKendry) 1919- ... 159
See also SATA 94
Swanson, Judith A(nn) 1957- ... 139
Swanson, June 1931- ... 143
See also SATA 76
Swanson, Neil H(armon) 1896-1983 Obituary ... 109
Swanson, Roy Arthur 1925- ... 17-20R
Swanson, (Karl) Thor (Waldemar) 1922- ... CANR-22
Earlier sketch in CA 45-48
Swanson, Walter S. J. 1917- ... 29-32R
Swanson, Wayne 1951- ... 130
Swanton, Ernest William 1907- ... CANR-18
Earlier sketches in CA 5-8R, CANR-2
Swanwick, Michael 1950- ... CANR-55
Earlier sketch in CA 119
Swarbrick, Andrew 1955- ... 120
Sward, Robert (Stuart) 1933- ... CANR-23
Earlier sketches in CA 5-8R, CANR-5
See also CAAS 13
Swardson, Harold Roland, Jr. 1925- ... 1-4R
Swarthout, Doris L(ouise) 1931- ... 77-80
Swarthout, Glendon (Fred) 1918-1992 ... CANR-47
Obituary ... 139
Earlier sketches in CA 1-4R, CANR-1
See also CLC 35
See also SATA 26
Swarthout, Kathryn 1919- ... 41-44R
See also SATA 7
Swartley, David Warren 1950- ... 102

Swartley, Willard M(yers) 1936- CANR-41
Earlier sketch in CA 117
Swartz, Harry (Felix) 1911- CANR-6
Earlier sketch in CA 57-60
Swartz, Jon D(avid) 1934- CANR-39
Earlier sketch in CA 69-72
Swartz, Marc J(erome) 1931- 21-24R
Swartz, Marvin 1941- 101
Swartz, Mary I(sabelle) 1942- 97-100
Swartz, Melvin Jay 1930- 97-100
Swartz, Norman (Manuel) 1939- 127
Swartz, Paul 1927- 5-8R
Swartz, Robert D(avid) 1937- 41-44R
Swartz, Robert J(ason) 1936- 17-20R
Swartz, Willis George 1902-1965 1-4R
Swartzlow, Ruby Johnson 1903- CAP-1
Earlier sketch in CA 13-16
Swarzenski, Hanns (Peter Theophil)
1903-1985 Obituary 116
Swasy, Alecia 1963- 145
Swatridge, Charles (John) (?)-1964 CANR-34
Earlier sketches in CA 13-16R, CANR-7
Swatridge, Irene Maude (Mossop) CANR-34
Earlier sketches in CA 29-32R, CANR-7
Swatuk, Larry A(nthony) 1957- 167
Sway, Marlene 1950- 129
Swaybill, Roger E(lliot) 1943-1991 105
Obituary 133
Swayne, Geoffrey
See Campion, Sidney R(onald)
Swayne, Sam(uel F.) 1907- SATA 53
Swayne, Zoa (Lourana) 1905- SATA 53
Swayze, (Sarah) Beulah G(arland) 1907- 5-8R
Swayze, Carolyn (Norma) 1945- 127
Swayze, E(rnest) Harold 1930- 1-4R
Swayze, John Cameron 1906-1995 102
Obituary 149
Swearengen, Thomas F. 1924- 17-20R
Swearer, Donald K(eeney) 1934- 37-40R
Swearingen, Arthur Rodger 1923- CANR-10
Earlier sketch in CA 5-8R
Sweat, Lynn 1934- SATA 57
Sweazey, George E. 1905- CANR-4
Earlier sketch in CA 1-4R
Swedberg, Richard 1948- 139
Swedburg, Wilma Adeline 5-8R
Swede, George 1940- CANR-64
Earlier sketches in CA 113, CANR-32
See also SATA 67
Sweeney, Amin 1938- 105
Sweeney, Barry
See Hand, G(eoffrey) J(oseph Philip Macaulay)
Sweeney, (Roderick) Charles (Hinton) 1922- CANR-16
Earlier sketch in CA 21-24R
Sweeney, Earl M. 1937- 112
Sweeney, Francis 1916- 5-8R
Sweeney, Henry Whitcomb 1898-1967 CAP-2
Earlier sketch in CA 17-18
Sweeney, James B(artholomew) 1910- CANR-12
Earlier sketch in CA 29-32R
See also SATA 21
Sweeney, James Johnson 1900-1986 CANR-6
Obituary 119
Earlier sketch in CA 5-8R
Sweeney, Joyce (Kay) 1955- CANR-35
Earlier sketch in CA 116
See also AAYA 26
See also SATA 65, 68
Sweeney, Julia 1960(?)- 160
Sweeney, Karen O'Connor
See O'Connor, Karen
Sweeney, (Charles) Leo 1918- CANR-34
Earlier sketches in CA 37-40R, CANR-15
Sweeney, R. C. H.
See Sweeney, (Roderick) Charles (Hinton)
Sweeney, Robert Dale 1939- 45-48
Sweeney, Terrance (Allen) 1945- 142
Sweeney, Thomas J(ohn) 1936- 41-44R
Sweeney, William J(oseph) III 1922- CANR-33
Obituary 161
Earlier sketch in CA 45-48
Sweeny, Mary K. 1923- 126
Sweet, Donald H(erbert) 1925- 112
Sweet, Franklyn Haley 1916- 9-12R
Sweet, Frederick A(rnold) 1903- CAP-2
Earlier sketch in CA 17-18
Sweet, George Elliott 1904-1997 45-48
Obituary 156
Sweet, J(ohn) P(hilip) M(cMurdo) 1927- 119
Sweet, James Stouder 1918- 41-44R
Sweet, Jeffrey 1950- CANR-43
Earlier sketch in CA 81-84
Sweet, Leonard Ira 1947- 97-100
Sweet, Muriel W. 1888-1977 106
Sweet, O. Robin 1952- 139
Sweet, Paul R(obinson) 1907- 77-80
Sweet, Robert Burdette 1930- 85-88
Sweet, Sarah C.
See Jewett, (Theodora) Sarah Orne
Sweet, Waldo Earle 1912- 1-4R
Sweeting, George 1924- CANR-11
Earlier sketch in CA 65-68
Sweetkind, Morris 1898- 13-16R
Sweetland, Nancy A(nn) 1934- SATA 48
Sweetland, Richard C. 1931- 119
Sweetman, David 1943- 141
Sweetman, Jack 1940- CANR-26
Earlier sketches in CA 25-28R, CANR-10
Sweetman, Rosita (Anne) 1948- 124
Brief entry 118
Sweets, John Frank 1945- 89-92
Sweetser, Mary (Chisholm) 1894- 41-44R
Sweetser, Ted
See Sweetser, Mary (Chisholm)
Sweetser, Thomas P(atrick) 1939- 112
Sweetser, Wesley D(uaine) 1919- 37-40R
Sweezy, Alan Richardson 1907- 41-44R
Sweezy, Paul M(arlor) 1910- CANR-5
Earlier sketch in CA 1-4R
Sweigard, Lulu E. (?)-1974 Obituary 53-56
Swell, Lila 97-100
Sweney, Fredric 1912- 1-4R
Swenson, Allan A(rmstrong) 1933- 77-80
See also SATA 21
Swenson, Clifford H(enrik) Jr. 1926- 45-48
Swenson, Judy Harris 1947- 120
Swenson, Karen 1936- 53-56
See also CAAS 13
Swenson, Loyd S(ylvan), Jr. 1932- CANR-15
Earlier sketch in CA 41-44R
Swenson, May 1919-1989 CANR-61
Obituary 130
Earlier sketches in CA 5-8R, CANR-36
See also CLC 4, 14, 61, 106
See also DA
See also DAB
See also DAC
See also DAM MST, POET
See also DLB 5
See also MTCW 1
See also PC 14
See also SATA 15
Swenson, Peggy
See Geis, Richard E(rwin)
Swenson, Peggye 1933- 73-76
Swensson, Paul S. 1907- 77-80
Swentzell, Rina 1939- SATA 79
Swerdlow, Amy (Miriam) G(alstuck) 1923- 105
Swerling, Jo 1897- DLB 44
Swetman, Glenn R(obert) 1936- CANR-4
Earlier sketch in CA 53-56
Swetnam, Evelyn (Frances) 1919- 93-96
Swets, John A(rthur) 1928- CANR-9
Earlier sketch in CA 21-24R
Swetz, Frank J. 1937- 135
Swezey, Kenneth M.
1905(?)-1972 Obituary 33-36R
Swicegood, Thomas L. P. 1930- 53-56
Swick, Clarence 1883(?)-1979 Obituary 89-92
Swick, Kevin J(ames) 1943- 111
Swick, Marly 1949- CANR-60
Earlier sketch in CA 135
Swick, Thomas 1952- 138
Swidler, Ann 1944- 132
Swidler, Arlene (Anderson) 1929- CANR-12
Earlier sketch in CA 61-64
Swidler, Leonard 1929- CANR-7
Earlier sketch in CA 17-20R
Swierenga, Robert P. 1935- 25-28R
Swift, Augustus
See Lovecraft, H(oward) P(hillips)
Swift, Benjamin
See McKimmey, James
Swift, Bryan
See Knott, William C(ecil, Jr.)
Swift, Carolyn Ruth 1928- 107
Swift, Clive 1936- 129
Swift, David
See Kaufmann, John
Swift, Donald C. 1937- 166
Swift, E(dward) M(cKelvy) 1951- 107
Swift, Edd
See Swift, Edward
Swift, Edward 1943- 37-40R
Swift, George B. 1902(?)-1983 Obituary 110
Swift, Graham (Colin) 1949- CANR-71
Brief entry 117
Earlier sketches in CA 122, CANR-46
See also CLC 41, 88
See also DLB 194
Swift, Helen C(ecilia) 1920- 117
Swift, Helen Miller 1914- 1-4R
Swift, Hildegarde Hoyt
1890(?)-1977 Obituary 69-72
See also SATA-Obit 20
Swift, Howard W. 1908- CAP-1
Earlier sketch in CA 9-10
Swift, Joan 1926- 115
Swift, Jonathan 1667-1745 CDBLB 1660-1789
See also DA
See also DAB
See also DAC
See also DAM MST, NOV, POET
See also DLB 39, 95, 101
See also PC 9
See also SATA 19
See also WLC
Swift, Kate 1923- 69-72
Swift, Marshall S(tefan) 1936- 53-56
Swift, Mary Grace 1927- 29-32R
Swift, Merlin
See Leeming, Joseph
Swift, Patrick 1927-1983 Obituary 110
Swift, Richard N(ewton) 1924- CANR-34
Earlier sketch in CA 1-4R
Swift, W. Porter 1914- 29-32R
Swigart, Rob 1941- CANR-28
Earlier sketches in CA 69-72, CANR-11
Swiger, Elinor Porter 1927- 37-40R
See also SATA 8
Swigg, Richard 1938- 103
Swihart, Altman K 1903- 1-4R
Swihart, Thomas L(ee) 1929- 107
Swinburne, Algernon Charles 1837-1909 140
Brief entry 105
See also CDBLB 1832-1890
See also DA
See also DAB
See also DAC
See also DAM MST, POET
See also DLB 35, 57
See also TCLC 8, 36
See also WLC
Swinburne, Laurence (Joseph) 1924- CANR-15
Earlier sketch in CA 61-64
See also SATA 9
Swinburne, Richard 1934- CANR-52
Earlier sketches in CA 25-28R, CANR-10, 28
Swindell, Larry (Nolan) 1929- 25-28R
Swindells, Madge 157
Swindells, Robert (Edward) 1939- CANR-21
Earlier sketch in CA 97-100
See also AAYA 20
See also JRDA
See also MAICYA
See also SAAS 14
See also SATA 50, 80
See also SATA-Brief 34
Swinden, Patrick 1941- 49-52
Swindler, William F(inley) 1913-1984 13-16R
Obituary 112
Swindoll, Luci 1932- 112
Swineford, Ada 1917- 61-64
Swineshead, Richard DLB 115
Swinfen, Ann CLC 34
Swinfen, D(avid) B(erridge) 1936- 37-40R
Swinford, Betty (June Wells) 1927- CANR-7
Earlier sketch in CA 5-8R
See also SATA 58
Swinford, Bob
See Swinford, Betty (June Wells)
Swing, Raymond Gram 1887-1968 Obituary 89-92
Swing, Thomas Kaehao 1930- 9-12R
Swingle, Paul G(eorge) 1937- 41-44R
Swinglehurst, Edmund 1917- CANR-28
Earlier sketches in CA 57-60, CANR-8
Swinnerton, A(rnold) R(eber) 1912- 106
Swinnerton, Frank Arthur 1884-1982 Obituary 108
See also CLC 31
See also DLB 34
Swinnerton, James Guilford
1875-1974 Obituary 93-96
Swinson, Arthur 1915-1970 CAP-2
Earlier sketch in CA 17-18
Swint, Henry L(ee) 1909- 37-40R
Swinton, Elizabeth de Sabato 1937- 153
Swinton, George 1917- 85-88
Swinton, John 1939- 111
Swinton, Stanley M(itchell)
1919-1982 Obituary 107
Swinton, William E(lgin) 1900-1994 13-16R
Obituary 145
Swinyard, Alfred W(ilbur) 1915- 9-12R
Swire, Otta F(lora Macdonald Lois) 1898-1973 CAP-1
Earlier sketch in CA 13-14
Swisher, Carl Brent 1897-1968 CANR-16
Obituary 103
Earlier sketch in CA 1-4R
Swisher, (Frank) Earl 1902- CAP-2
Earlier sketch in CA 29-32
Swisher, Robert K., Jr. 1947- 61-64
Swisher, Viola Hegyi 1904(?)-1990 Obituary 131
Swisshelm, Jane Grey 1815-1884 DLB 43
Swithen, John
See King, Stephen (Edwin)
Switzer, Barry 1937- 143
Switzer, David Karl 1925- 57-60
Switzer, Ellen 1923- CANR-2
Earlier sketch in CA 45-48
See also SATA 48
Switzer, Les 1935- 147
Switzer, (Perry) Richard 1925-1995 CANR-18
Obituary 161
Earlier sketch in CA 25-28R
Swivett, R. G. O.
See Trippett, Frank
Swomley, John M., Jr. 1915- 9-12R
Swope, George S(teel) 1915- 29-32R
Swope, Herbert Bayard 1882-1958 DLB 25
Swor, Chester E(ugene) 1907- 9-12R
Sword, Randall S(tanford) 1942- 114
Sword, Wiley 1937- 85-88
Swords, James (?)-1844 DLB 73
Swords, Thomas 1763-1843 DLB 73
Swortzell, Lowell (Stanley) 1930- CANR-1
Earlier sketch in CA 49-52
Swycaffer, Jefferson P(utnam) 1956- 119
Swyhart, Barbara Ann DeMartino 1942- 61-64
Syal, Meera 1962(?)- 160
Syberberg, Hans-Juergen 1935- 93-96
Sybesma, Jetske
See Ironside, Jetske
Syburg, Jane 1927- 29-32R
Sydenham, Michael J(ohn) 1923- 17-20R
Sydney, Cynthia
See Tralins, S(andor) Robert
Sydney, Frank
See Warwick, Alan R(oss)
Sydnor, Charles W(right), Jr. 1943- 77-80
Sydnor, James Rawlings 1911- 5-8R
Sydnor, (Charles) William 1911- 112
Syed, Anwar H(ussain) 1926- 102
Syers, Ed
See Syers, William Edward
Syers, William Edward 1914- CANR-4
Earlier sketch in CA 1-4R
Sykes, (Richard) Adam 1940- 29-32R
Sykes, Alrene 77-80
Sykes, Charles J. 153
Sykes, Christopher (Hugh) 1907-1986 29-32R
Obituary 121
Sykes, Ella C. (?)-1939 DLB 174
Sykes, Gerald 1903-1984 134
Obituary 113
Sykes, Jay G(ilbert) 1922- 45-48
Sykes, John 1918- 17-20R
Sykes, Roosevelt 1906-1983 Obituary 110
Syktus, Jozef 1959- 155
Sylva, Carmen
See Elisabeth (Ottilie Luise), Queen (Pauline)
Sylvander, Carolyn W(edin) 1939- 117
Sylvester, A(lbert) J(ames) 1889- 101
Sylvester, Arline 1914- 65-68
Sylvester, Bob
See Sylvester, Robert (McPherson)
Sylvester, (Anthony) David (Bernard) 1924- 168
Sylvester, Dorothy 1906- 29-32R
Sylvester, Edward J(oseph) 1942- CANR-44
Earlier sketch in CA 118
Sylvester, Janet 1950- 162
Sylvester, Janet Hart 1917-1987 Obituary 123
Sylvester, Josuah 1562(?)-1618 DLB 121
Sylvester, Kathryn F. 1901(?)-1983 Obituary 111
Sylvester, Natalie G(abry) 1922- 97-100
See also SATA 22
Sylvester, Richard Standish 1926-1978 CANR-2
Obituary 77-80
Earlier sketch in CA 1-4R
Sylvester, Robert (McPherson) 1907-1975 61-64
Obituary 57-60
Sylvester, William (Arthur) 1918- CANR-34
Earlier sketch in CA 45-48
Sylvestre, (Joseph Jean) Guy 1918- 61-64
Sylvia
See Ashton-Warner, Sylvia (Constance)
Sylvin, Francis
See Seaman, Sylvia S(ybil Bernstein)
Symanski, Richard 1941- 111
Symcox, Geoffrey Walter 1938- 112
Syme, Ronald 1903-1989 Obituary 129
Syme, (Neville) Ronald 1913- CANR-6
Earlier sketch in CA 9-12R
See also SATA 2, 87
Symeonoglou, Sarantis 1937- 126
Symes, R. F. SATA 77
Symington, David 1904-1984 CAP-2
Obituary 113
Earlier sketch in CA 29-32
Symmes, Robert Edward
See Duncan, Robert (Edward)
Symmons-Symonolewicz, Konstantin 1909- 37-40R
Symonds, Craig L. 1946- CANR-52
Earlier sketch in CA 126
Symonds, Deborah A(nn) 1951- 164
Symonds, Emily Morse
See Paston, George
Symonds, Helen Sanford 1899- 5-8R
Symonds, John 105
Symonds, John Addington 1840-1893 DLB 57, 144
Symonds, (John) Richard (Charters) 1918- 21-24R
Symons, A. J. A. 1900-1941 DLB 149
Symons, Allene 1944- 110
Symons, Arthur 1865-1945 Brief entry 107
See also DLB 19, 57, 149
See also TCLC 11
Symons, (Dorothy) Geraldine 1909- 85-88
See also SATA 33
Symons, Julian (Gustave) 1912-1994 CANR-59
Obituary 147
Earlier sketches in CA 49-52, CANR-3, 33
See also CAAS 3
See also CLC 2, 14, 32
See also DLB 87, 155
See also DLBY 92
See also MTCW 1
Symons, Leslie John 1926- CANR-26
Earlier sketch in CA 109
Symons, R(obert) D(avid) 1898-1973 41-44R
Symons, (Hugh Brennan) Scott 1933- CANR-70
Earlier sketch in CA 77-80
See also DLB 53
Symynkywicz, Jeffrey B(ruce) 1954- 151
See also SATA 87
Synan, Edward A(loysius) 1918- 17-20R
Synan, (Harold) Vinson 1934- CANR-14
Earlier sketch in CA 37-40R
Synge, Allen 1930- 142
Synge, (Edmund) J(ohn) M(illington) 1871-1909 141
Brief entry 104
See also CDBLB 1890-1914
See also DAM DRAM
See also DC 2
See also DLB 10, 19
See also TCLC 6, 37
Synge, (Phyllis) Ursula 1930- CANR-1
Earlier sketch in CA 49-52
See also SATA 9
Synnestvedt, Sig(fried T.) 1924-1977 37-40R
Syntax, John
See Dennett, Herbert Victor
Sypher, Francis Jacques, Jr. 1941- CANR-10
Earlier sketch in CA 57-60
Sypher, Lucy Johnston 1907- CANR-2
Earlier sketch in CA 45-48
See also SATA 7
Sypher, Wylie 1905- CANR-3
Earlier sketch in CA 1-4R
Syracuse, Marcella Pfeiffer 1930- 21-24R
Syrdal, Rolf A(rthur) 1902- 25-28R
Syred, Celia 1911- CANR-12
Earlier sketch in CA 29-32R
Syrett, David 1939- Brief entry 106
Syrett, Harold Coffin 1913-1984 Obituary 113
Syrett, Netta 1865-1943 DLB 135, 197

Syrkin, Marie 1899-1989 ... CANR-6
Obituary ... 127
Earlier sketch in CA 9-12R
Syrop, Konrad 1914- ... CANR-5
Earlier sketch in CA 9-12R
Syruc, J.
See Milosz, Czeslaw
Sysyn, Frank E. 1946- ... 126
Syvertsen, Edythe 1921- ... 73-76
Syverud, Genevieve Wold 1914- ... 21-24R
Szabo, Denis 1929- ... CANR-43
Earlier sketches in CA 89-92, CANR-20
Szabo, Istvan 1938- ... 144
Szabo, Sandor 1954- ... 153
Szabolcsi, Bence 1899-1973 Obituary ... 116
Szajkowski, Zosa
See Frydman, Szajko
Szakolczai, A'rpa'd 1958- ... 147
Szancer, Henryk (?)-1976 Obituary ... 61-64
Szaniawski, Jerzy 1886-1970 Obituary ... 29-32R
Szanto, George H. 1940- ... 41-44R
Szanton, Andrew (Emlew) 1963- ... 140
Szanton, Peter L(oeb) 1930- ... CANR-11
Earlier sketch in CA 69-72
Szasz, Ferenc Morton 1940- ... CANR-56
Earlier sketch in CA 125
Szasz, Kathleen 1912- ... 25-28R
Szasz, Margaret Connell 1935- ... 97-100
Szasz, Suzanne (Shorr) 1915-1997 ... CANR-18
Obituary ... 159
Earlier sketches in CA 5-8R, CANR-3
See also SATA 13
See also SATA-Obit 99
Szasz, Thomas (Stephen) 1920- ... CANR-9
Earlier sketch in CA 17-20R
Szathmary, Louis (Istvan) II 1919- ... 81-84
Szaz, Zoltan Michael 1930- ... CANR-3
Earlier sketch in CA 1-4R
Szczesniak, Boleslaw (B.) 1908- ... 9-12R
Szczypiorski, Andrzej 1928- ... CANR-60
Earlier sketch in CA 133
Sze, Arthur C. 1950- ... 152
Szechter, Szymon 1920(?)-1983 Obituary ... 110
Szekely, Endre 1922- ... 17-20R
Szekely, Istvan P(al) 1959- ... 151
Szekeres, Cyndy 1933- ... 137
See also MAICYA
See also SAAS 13
See also SATA 5, 60
Szekessy, Tanja ... 166
See also SATA 98
Szenberg, Michael 1934- ... 144
Szent-Gyoergyi, Albert (von Nagyrapolt)
1893-1986 Obituary ... 120
Brief entry ... 112
Szent-Gyorgyi, Albert (von Nagyrapolt)
See Szent-Gyoergyi, Albert (von Nagyrapolt)
Szep
See Szep, Paul (Michael)
Szep, Paul (Michael) 1941- ... 128
Brief entry ... 110
Interview in ... 128
Szeplaki, Joseph 1932- ... 73-76
Szerlip, Barbara 1949- ... CANR-3
Earlier sketch in CA 49-52
Szigeti, Joseph 1892-1973 ... CAP-1
Earlier sketch in CA 9-10
Szilard, Leo 1898-1964 ... 158
Obituary ... 113
Szirtes, George 1948- ... CANR-61
Earlier sketches in CA 109, CANR-27
See also CLC 46
Szittya, Ruth Outland 1910- ... 112
Szoeverffy, Joseph 1920- ... CANR-40
Earlier sketches in CA 65-68, CANR-17
Szogyi, Alex 1929- ... CANR-35
Earlier sketch in CA 45-48
Szostak, Rick 1959- ... 139
Szporluk, Roman 1933- ... CANR-1
Earlier sketch in CA 45-48
Szpur, Mary 1956- ... 128
Szpura, Beata 1961- ... SATA 93
Sztompka, Piotr 1944- ... 141
Szudek, Agnes S(usan) P(hilomena) ... SATA 57
See also SATA-Brief 49
Szulc, Tad 1926- ... CANR-23
Earlier sketches in CA 9-12R, CANR-4
Interview in ... CANR-23
See also SATA 26
Szumigalski, Anne 1922- ... CANR-36
Earlier sketches in CA 49-52, CANR-1, 16
Szumski, Bonnie 1958- ... 122
Szwajger, Adina Blady 1917-1993 ... 140
Obituary ... 141
Szwarc, Josef 1947- ... 118
Szydlow, Jarl
See Szydlowski, Mary Vigliante
Szydlowski, Mary Vigliante 1946- ... CANR-65
Earlier sketch in CA 104
See also SATA 94
Szydlowski, Roman 1918(?)-1983 Obituary ... 111
Szyliowicz, Joseph S. 1931- ... 41-44R
Szymanski, Albert (John)
1942(?)-1985 Obituary ... 115
Szymanski, Leszek 1933- ... 146
Szymanski, Lois 1957- ... 155
See also SATA 91
Szymanski, Richard
See Symanski, Richard
Szymborska, Wislawa 1923- ... 154
See also CLC 99
See also DLBY 96
Szymczak, Leonard K. 1947- ... 159

T

T. B. D.
See James, William Milbourne
T. O., Nik
See Annensky, Innokenty (Fyodorovich)
Ta, Van Tai 1938- ... 133
Taaffe, Edward James 1921- ... 85-88
Taaffe, James G. 1932- ... 17-20R
Taaffe, Michael
See Maguire, R(obert) A(ugustine) J(oseph)
Taagepera, Rein 1933- ... 109
Tabachnik, Abraham B(er)
1902-1970 Obituary ... 29-32R
Taback, Simms 1932- Brief entry ... 115
See also SATA 40
See also SATA-Brief 36
Tabak, Israel 1904- Brief entry ... 105
Taban lo Liyong
See Liyong, Taban lo
See also DLB 125
Tabard, Geoffrey
See McNelly, Willis E(verett)
Tabard, Peter
See Blake, L(eslie) J(ames)
Tabb, Jay Yanai 1907-1976 ... CAP-2
Earlier sketch in CA 29-32
Taber, Anthony Scott 1944- ... 105
Taber, George M(cCaffrey) 1942- ... 65-68
Taber, Gladys (Bagg) 1899-1980 ... CANR-4
Obituary ... 97-100
Earlier sketch in CA 5-8R
See also SATA-Obit 22
Taber, Julian Ingersoll 1929- Brief entry ... 106
Taber, Robert ... 17-20R
Taber, Robert W(illiam) 1921- ... 73-76
Tabler, Edward C. 1916- ... 5-8R
Tablet, Hilda
See Swann, Donald (Ibrahim)
Tabor, Nancy Maria Grande 1949- ... SATA 89
Tabor, Paul
See Tabori, Paul
Tabor, Stephen 1951- ... 127
Tabori, George 1914- ... CANR-69
Earlier sketches in CA 49-52, CANR-4
See also CLC 19
Tabori, Paul 1908-1974 ... CANR-5
Obituary ... 53-56
Earlier sketch in CA 5-8R
Taborsky, Edward (Joseph) 1910- ... CANR-3
Earlier sketch in CA 1-4R
Tabouis, Genevieve 1892-1985 Obituary ... 117
Tabrah, Ruth Milander 1921- ... CANR-52
Earlier sketches in CA 13-16R, CANR-10, 28
See also SATA 14
Tabucchi, Antonio 1943- ... DLB 196
Tacey, William S(anford) 1904- ... 37-40R
Tachau, Frank 1929- ... CANR-55
Brief entry ... 111
Earlier sketch in CA 127
Tachau, Mary K(atherine) Bonsteel 1926- ... 85-88
Tache, Joseph-Charles 1820-1894 ... DLB 99
Tacheron, Donald Glen 1928-1996 ... 21-24R
Obituary ... 152
Tachihara, Masaaki 1926-1980 ... DLB 182
Tacitus
See Cornelius, Tacitus
Tack, Alfred 1906- ... 104
Tadijanovic, Dragutin 1905- ... DLB 181
Tadlock, Max R. 1919- ... 17-20R
Tadrack, Moss
See Caryl, Warren
Taegel, William S(tephens) 1940- ... 45-48
Taetzsch, Lyn 1941- ... CANR-8
Earlier sketch in CA 57-60
Taeuber, Alma Ficks 1933- ... 17-20R
Taeuber, Conrad 1906- ... CANR-28
Earlier sketch in CA 45-48
Taeuber, Cynthia M. 1947- ... 161
Taeuber, Irene Barnes 1906-1974 Obituary ... 106
Taeuber, Karl E(rnst) 1936- ... CANR-28
Earlier sketch in CA 17-20R
Tae-yong, Ro
See Rutt, Richard
Tafel, Edgar Allen 1912- ... 89-92
Taffy
See Llewellyn, D(avid) W(illiam) Alun
Tafolla, (Mary) Carmen 1951- ... 131
See also DLB 82
See also HW
Taft, Charles P(helps II) 1897-1983 Obituary ... 110
Brief entry ... 105
Taft, John (Thomas) 1950- ... 133
Taft, Pauline Dakin 1891- ... CAP-1
Earlier sketch in CA 13-16
Taft, Philip 1902-1976 Obituary ... 69-72
Taft, Ronald 1920- ... 21-24R
Taft, William H(oward) 1915- ... 13-16R
Tafti, H. B. Dehqani
See Dehqani-Tafti, H. B.
Tafuri, Manfredo 1935- ... CANR-26
Earlier sketch in CA 69-72
Tafuri, Nancy 1946- ... CANR-44
Earlier sketch in CA 118
See also MAICYA
See also SAAS 14
See also SATA 39, 75
Tager, Jack 1936- ... 118
Tager-Flusberg, Helen 1951- ... 145
Tageson, Carroll W(illiam) 1925- ... 53-56
Taggard, Genevieve 1894-1948 ... 166
See also DLB 45
Taggard, Mindy Nancarrow 1951- ... 143
Taggart, Dorothy T(rekell) 1917- ... 102
Taggart, (Paul) John 1942- ... CANR-1
Earlier sketch in CA 45-48
See also DLB 193
Taggart, John Scott
See Scott-Taggart, John
Taggart, Joseph Herman 1902-1984 Obituary ... 112
Taggart, Robert (III) 1945- Brief entry ... 111
Tagiuri, Renato 1919- ... 77-80
Tagliabue, John 1923- ... 21-24R
Tagliaferri, Aldo 1931- ... 77-80
Tagliavia, Sheila 1936- ... 104
Tagore, Amitendranath 1922- ... 61-64
Tagore, Rabindranath 1861-1941 ... 120
Brief entry ... 104
See also DAM DRAM, POET
See also MTCW 1
See also PC 8
See also TCLC 3, 53
Taha, Hamdy A(bdelaziz) 1937- ... 37-40R
Taha, Karen T(erry) 1942- ... 120
See also SATA 71
Tahara, Mildred Machiko 1941- ... 104
Taheri, Amir 1942- ... 136
Tahir, Abe M(ahmoud), Jr. 1931- ... 69-72
Tahir, Kemal 1910(?)-1973 Obituary ... 45-48
Tahlaquah, David
See LeMond, Alan
Tahtinen, Dale R(udolph) 1945- ... 65-68
Tai, Hung-chao 1929- ... 73-76
Taibo, Paco Ignacio II 1949- ... CANR-58
Earlier sketch in CA 131
See also HW
Taichert, Louise C(ecile) 1925- ... 89-92
Taikeff, Stanley 1940- ... 109
Taine, John
See Bell, Eric Temple
Taines, Beatrice (Green) 1923- ... CANR-14
Earlier sketch in CA 73-76
Tainter, Frank H(ugh) 1941- ... 159
Taira, Koji 1926- ... 41-44R
Taishoff, Sol J(oseph) 1904-1982 ... 73-76
Obituary ... 107
Tait, Alan A(nderson) 1934- ... CANR-10
Earlier sketch in CA 21-24R
Tait, Dorothy 1902(?)-1972 Obituary ... 33-36R
Tait, Douglas 1944- ... SATA 12
Tait, George E(dward) 1910- ... 5-8R
Tait, Katharine 1923- ... 65-68
Tait, L(eslie) Gordon 1926- ... 45-48
Taitz, Emily 1937- ... 85-88
Takacs, Carol Addison 1926- ... 124
Takagi, Akimitsu 1920- Brief entry ... 108
Takagi, Dana Y. 1954- ... 141
Takahashi, Akira 1932- ... 29-32R
Takahashi, Yasundo 1912- ... CANR-14
Earlier sketch in CA 41-44R
Takaki, Ronald T(oshiyuki) 1939- ... 37-40R
Takakjian, Portia 1930- ... SATA 15
Takashima, Shizuye 1928- ... 45-48
See also SATA 13
Takayama, Akira 1932- ... CANR-2
Earlier sketch in CA 49-52
Takei, George (Hosato) 1937- ... 147
Takenaka, Heizo 1951- ... 142
Takeshita, Thomas Kohachiro
1891(?)-1973 Obituary ... 45-48
Takeuchi, Yoshinori 1913- ... 132
Taki
See Theodoracopulos, Taki
Taktsis, Costas 1927-1988 ... 21-24R
Obituary ... 126
Talafous, Don (Francis) 1926- ... 113
Talalay, Kathryn M(arguerite) 1949- ... 154
Talamantes, Florence Williams 1931- ... CANR-6
Earlier sketch in CA 57-60
Talamini, John T(homas) 1940- ... 126
Brief entry ... 113
Talarico, Ross 1945- ... 73-76
Talayesva, Don C. 1890-(?) ... NNAL
Talbert, Ansel Edward (McLaurine)
1912-1987 Obituary ... 124
Talbert, Charles Gano 1912- ... 5-8R
Talbert, Charles H(arold) 1934- ... CANR-58
Earlier sketches in CA 41-44R, CANR-14, 31
Talbert, Marc 1953- ... 136
See also AAYA 25
See also SATA 68, 99
Talbot, Alice-Mary 1939- ... 112
Talbot, Allan R. 1934- ... CANR-10
Earlier sketch in CA 21-24R
Talbot, Carol Terry 1913- ... 13-16R
Talbot, Charlene Joy 1928- ... CANR-8
Earlier sketch in CA 17-20R
See also SATA 10
Talbot, Edward Hugh Frederick Chetwynd
See Chetwynd-Talbot, Edward Hugh Frederick
Talbot, Emile J. 1941- ... 145
Talbot, Godfrey (Walker) 1908- ... 107
Talbot, Gordon (Gray) 1928- ... CANR-14
Earlier sketch in CA 69-72
Talbot, Hugh
See Chetwynd-Talbot, Edward Hugh Frederick
Talbot, Kay
See Rowland, D(onald) S(ydney)
Talbot, Lawrence
See Bryant, Edward (Winslow, Jr.)
Talbot, Michael 1953-1992 ... 119
Obituary ... 137
Talbot, Nathan B(ill) 1909- ... 104
Talbot, Norman (Clare) 1936- ... CANR-9
Earlier sketch in CA 21-24R
Talbot, Ross B. 1919- ... 17-20R
Talbot, Toby 1928- ... CANR-29
Earlier sketch in CA 21-24R
See also Josephs, Rebecca
See also SATA 14
Talbot Rice, David
See Rice, David Talbot
Talbot Rice, Tamara (Abelson)
See Rice, Tamara (Abelson) Talbot
Talbott, Basil 1899-1985 Obituary ... 117
Talbott, Hudson 1949- ... 128
See also SATA 84
Talbott, John E(dwin) 1940- ... 25-28R
Talbott, Robert D(ean) 1928- ... 57-60
Talbott, Strobe 1946- ... CANR-42
Earlier sketch in CA 93-96
See also AITN 1
Talcott, Dudley Vaill 1899-1986 Obituary ... 119
Talese, Gay 1932- ... CANR-58
Earlier sketches in CA 1-4R, CANR-9
Interview in ... CANR-9
See also AITN 1
See also CLC 37
See also DLB 185
See also MTCW 1
Talev, Dimitur 1898-1966 ... DLB 181
Taliaferro, H. E. 1811-1875 ... DLB 202
Talifero, Gerald 1950- ... SATA 75
Talker, T.
See Rands, William Brighty
Talkin, Gil
See Rosenthal, Alan
Talkington, Virginia Savage
See McAlester, Virginia
Tall, Deborah 1951- ... CANR-47
Earlier sketches in CA 105, CANR-22
Tall, Stephen
See Crook, Compton Newby
Talland, George A(lexander) 1917-(?) ... CAP-2
Earlier sketch in CA 25-28
Tallcott, Emogene ... 29-32R
See also SATA 10
Tallent, Elizabeth (Ann) 1954- ... CANR-72
Earlier sketch in CA 117
See also CLC 45
See also DLB 130
Tallent, Norman 1921- ... 17-20R
Talleur, Richard W(iley) 1931- ... 97-100
Talley-Morris, Neva B(ennett) 1909- ... 57-60
Tallis, Robyn
See Macdonald, James D.
and Zambreno, Mary Frances
Tallman, Albert 1902- ... 53-56
Tallmountain, Mary 1918-1997 ... 146
Obituary ... 161
See also DLB 193
See also NNAL
Tallon, Robert 1939- ... CANR-8
Earlier sketch in CA 9-12R
See also SATA 43
See also SATA-Brief 28
Tally, Ted 1952- ... 124
Brief entry ... 120
Interview in ... 124
See also CLC 42
Talmadge, Marian ... SATA 14
Talmage, Anne
See Powell, Talmage
Talmage, Frank (Ephraim) 1938- ... 97-100
Talmey, Allene
See Plaut, Allene Talmey
Talmon, Jacob L(aib) 1916-1980 ... 13-16R
Obituary ... 101
Talmon, Shemaryahu 1920- ... CANR-55
Earlier sketches in CA 29-32R, CANR-12, 28
Talpalar, Morris 1900- ... 73-76
Talvi
See Robinson, Therese
Talvj
See Robinson, Therese
See also DLB 133
Tamaki, Norio 1940- ... CANR-65
Earlier sketch in CA 128
Tamar, Erika 1934- ... 168
See also SATA 62, 101
Tamari, Meier 1927- ... 127
Tamarin, Alfred H. 1913-1980 ... CANR-4
Obituary ... 102
Earlier sketch in CA 29-32R
See also SATA 13
Tamasi, Aron 1897-1966 Obituary ... 114
Tambasco, Anthony J(oseph) 1939- ... CANR-41
Earlier sketch in CA 117
Tambi
See Tambimuttu, Thurairajah
Tambiah, S. J.
See Tambiah, Stanley Jeyaraja
Tambiah, Stanley Jeyaraja 1929- ... 123
Tambimuttu, Thurairajah
1915(?)-1983 Obituary ... 110
Tambling, Jeremy (Charles Richard) 1948- ... 128
Tambs, Lewis Arthur 1927- ... CANR-4
Earlier sketch in CA 53-56
Tamburine, Jean 1930- ... 9-12R
See also SATA 12
Tamburri, Anthony Julian 1949- ... 138
Tamedly, Elisabeth L. 1931- ... 29-32R
Tames, Richard (Lawrence) 1946- ... 103
See also SATA 67, 102
Tamir, Max Mordecai 1912- ... 29-32R
Tamir, Vicki 1924- ... 29-32R
Tamm, Igor (Evgenievich) 1895-1971 ... 162
Tamm, Igor Yevgenyevich
See Tamm, Igor (Evgenievich)
Tammaro, Thom(as Michael) 1951- ... 109
Tammeus, William David 1945- ... 136
Tamminga, Frederick W(illiam) 1934- ... 135
See also SATA 66
Tammsaare, A(nton) H(ansen) 1878-1940 ... 164
See also TCLC 27

Tammuz, Benjamin 1919-1989 CANR-36
Obituary 129
Earlier sketch in CA 85-88
See also SATA-Obit 63
Tamny, Martin 1941- 37-40R
Tampion, John 1937- 73-76
Tam'si, Tchicaya U
See Tchicaya, Gerald Felix
Tamsin
See Summers, Ethel Snelson
Tamulaitis, Vytas 1913- 17-20R
Tamuno, Tekena N. 1932- 21-24R
Tamura, Linda 1949- 152
Tan, Amy (Ruth) 1952- CANR-54
Earlier sketch in CA 136
See also AAYA 9
See also BEST 89:3
See also CLC 59
See also DAM MULT, NOV, POP
See also DLB 173
See also SATA 75
Tan, Fred 1955(?)-1990 Obituary 131
Tana, Tomoe (Hayashima) 1913- 21-24R
Tanahashi, Kazuaki 1933- 122
Tanaka, Beatrice 1932- 115
See also SATA 76
Tanaka, Hideyuki 1940- 132
Tanaquil, Paul
See Le Clercq, Jacques Georges Clemenceau
Tanay, Emanuel 1928- 93-96
Tanchuck, Nathaniel 1912- 13-16R
Tancock, John (Leon) 1942- 105
Tancredi, Laurence R(ichard) 1940- CANR-39
Earlier sketch in CA 116
Tandem, Felix
See Spitteler, Carl (Friedrich Georg)
Tandon, Prakash 1911- 93-96
Tandy, Clifford Ronald Vivien
1919(?)-1981 Obituary 104
Taneda, Santoka 1882-1940 166
Tanenbaum, Jan Karl 1936- 61-64
Tanenbaum, Robert K. CANR-60
Brief entry 116
Earlier sketch in CA 128
Tanenhaus, Sam 163
Tang, Charles 1948- SATA 81
Tang, Peter Shen-Hao 1919- 1-4R
Tang, Victor 1942- 138
Tang, You-Shan 1946- SATA 53
Tang, Yungmei 1940- 129
Tangerman, Elmer John 1907- CANR-46
Earlier sketches in CA 106, CANR-23
Tangri, Shanti S. 1928- 25-28R
Tangye, Nigel (Trevithick) 1909-1988 Obituary 125
Brief entry 117
Tanham, George K(ilpatrick) 1922- CANR-1
Earlier sketch in CA 1-4R
Tania B.
See Blixen, Karen (Christentze Dinesen)
Taniguchi, Kazuko 1946- 93-96
Taniguchi, Masaharu 1893-1985 Obituary 116
Tanikawa, Shuntaro 1931- CANR-49
Earlier sketch in CA 121
Tanis, James (Robert) 1928- 118
Tanis, Norman Earl 1929- 110
Tanizaki, Jun'ichiro 1886-1965 93-96
Obituary 25-28R
See also CLC 8, 14, 28
See also DLB 180
See also SSC 21
Tank, Herbert 1922(?)-1982 Obituary 108
Tank, Ronald W(arren) 1929- 49-52
Tankard, Alice (Doumanian) 1926- 117
Tankard, James William, Jr. 1941- 73-76
Tanksley, Perry 1928- 37-40R
Tann, Jennifer 1939- 103
Tannahill, Reay 1929- CANR-59
Earlier sketches in CA 49-52, CANR-2
Tannehill, Robert C(ooper) 1934- CANR-51
Earlier sketches in CA 45-48, CANR-26
Tannen, Deborah F(rances) 1945- 118
Tannen, Jack 1907-1991 114
Obituary 136
Tannen, Mary 1943- CANR-51
Earlier sketch in CA 105
See also SATA 37
Tannenbaum, Arnold S(herwood) 1925- 17-20R
Tannenbaum, Arthur C. 1941- 123
Tannenbaum, Beulah Goldstein 1916- CANR-7
Earlier sketch in CA 5-8R
See also SATA 3
Tannenbaum, D(onald) Leb 1948- 115
See also SATA 42
Tannenbaum, Edward R(obert) 1921- 17-20R
Tannenbaum, Frank 1893-1969 9-12R
Tannenbaum, Harold E. 1914- 5-8R
Tannenbaum, Percy Hyman 1927- Brief entry 106
Tannenbaum, Robert 1915- 21-24R
Tannenbaum, Stanley I. 1928- 144
Tanner, Adam 1964- 127
Tanner, C(harles) Kenneth 1938- 53-56
Tanner, Clara L(ee) 1905- 41-44R
Tanner, Daniel 1926- 17-20R
Tanner, Edward Everett III 1921-1976 73-76
Obituary 69-72
Tanner, Helen Hornbeck 1916- 61-64
Tanner, Henry 1918-1998 73-76
Obituary 167
Tanner, James M(ourilyan) 1920- CANR-5
Earlier sketch in CA 13-16R
Tanner, James T(homas) F(ontenot) 1937- 41-44R
Tanner, Jane 1946- SATA 74
Tanner, Jo A. 145
Tanner, John
See Matcha, Jack
Tanner, John (Ian) 1927- 103
Tanner, John S. 1950- 138
Tanner, Karen Holliday (Olson) 1940- 168
Tanner, Louise S(tickney) 1922- 69-72
See also SATA 9
Tanner, Michael (K.) 1935- 168
Tanner, Nancy Makepeace
1933-1989 Obituary 129
Tanner, Paul O(ra) W(arren) 1917- 61-64
Tanner, Roy L(ynn) 1947- 118
Tanner, Stephen L. 1938- 123
Tanner, Terence A(rthur) 1948- 135
Tanner, Thomas 1936- 128
Tanner, Tony 1935- 85-88
Tanner, William
See Amis, Kingsley (William)
Tanner-Rutherford, C.
See Winchester, Clarence
Tanobe, Miyuki 1937- 69-72
See also SATA 23
Tanous, Peter (Joseph) 1938- CANR-7
Earlier sketch in CA 61-64
Tanselle, G(eorge) Thomas 1934- CANR-52
Earlier sketches in CA 21-24R, CANR-11, 28
Tansill, Charles Callan 1890-1964 1-4R
Tanter, Raymond 1938- CANR-25
Earlier sketch in CA 45-48
Tantrist
See Cox, P(atrick) Brian
Tanyzer, Harold Joseph 1929- 9-12R
Tanzer, Lester 1929- 17-20R
Tanzer, Michael David 1935- 57-60
Tanzi, Vito 1935- CANR-5
Earlier sketch in CA 53-56
Tao Lao
See Storni, Alfonsina
Tao Mulian
See Totten, George Oakley III
Tapahonso, Luci 1953- CANR-72
Earlier sketch in CA 145
See also DLB 175
See also NNAL
Tapia, Ralph J(ohn) 1925- 41-44R
Tapia, Richard A(lfred) 1939- 161
Tapio, Pat Decker
See Kines, Pat Decker
Tapley, Caroline 1934- 97-100
Taplin, Glen W(illiam) 1917- 107
Taplin, Oliver 1943- 102
Taplin, Walter 1910- CAP-1
Earlier sketch in CA 9-10
Taplinger, Cecily Lent 1943-1983 Obituary 110
Taplinger, Richard Jacques
1911-1973 Obituary 41-44R
Taplinger, Terry
See Taplinger, Cecily Lent
Tapp, Jack Thomas 1934- 49-52
Tapp, June Louin 1929- 41-44R
Tapp, Kathy Kennedy 1949- CANR-39
Earlier sketch in CA 116
See also SATA 88
See also SATA-Brief 50
Tapp, Robert B(erg) 1925- 41-44R
Tappan, Paul Wilbur 1911-1964 5-8R
Tapper, Nancy
See Lindisfarne, Nancy
Tappert, Theodore G(erhardt) 1904-1973 CANR-2
Earlier sketch in CA 1-4R
Tapply, H(orace) G(ardner) 1910- 13-16R
Tapply, William G(eorge) 1940- CANR-72
Earlier sketches in CA 118, CANR-41
Tapscott, Stephen (J.) 1948- CANR-17
Earlier sketch in CA 89-92
Tapsell, R(obert) F(rederick) 1936- 21-24R
Taraborrelli, J. Randy 1956- 142
Taradash, Daniel 1913- CANR-71
Earlier sketch in CA 101
Interview in 101
See also DLB 44
Taragano, Martin 1959- 139
Taranovsky, Kiril 1911- 114
Taranow, Gerda 37-40R
Taras, Raymond (C.) 1946- 139
Tarascio, Vincent J(oseph) 1930- 45-48
Tarassoff, Lev
See Troyat, Henri
Tarassuk, Leonid (Ilyich) 1925-1990 130
Obituary 132
Tarazaga, Santiago Genoves
See Genoves Tarazaga, Santiago
Tarbell, Ida M(inerva) 1857-1944 Brief entry 122
See also DLB 47
See also TCLC 40
Tarbell, Roberta K. 1944- 139
Tarbert, Gary C(harles) 1937- 101
Tarcher, Martin 1921- 17-20R
Tardat, Claude 1949- 136
Tardieu, Jean 1903- Brief entry 116
Tardiff, Olive 1916- 73-76
Tardivel, Jules-Paul 1851-1905 DLB 99
Tardy, Gaye 1929(?)-1982 Obituary 108
Targ, Harry R. 1940- 118
Targ, Russell 1934- 104
Targ, William 1907- 61-64
Targan, Barry 1932- CANR-71
Earlier sketches in CA 73-76, CANR-17
See also DLB 130
Targ Brill, Marlene
See Brill, Marlene Targ
Target, G(eorge) W(illiam) 1924- CANR-7
Earlier sketch in CA 5-8R
Targetti, Ferdinando 1945- 146
Tarica, Ralph 1932- 113
Tarkenton, Fran(cis Asbury) 1940- 103
Tarkington, (Newton) Booth 1869-1946 143
Brief entry 110
See also DLB 9, 102
See also SATA 17
See also TCLC 9
Tarkovsky, Andrei (Arsenyevich) 1932-1986 127
See also CLC 75
Tarling, (Peter) Nicholas 1931- 21-24R
Tarlock, A(nthony) Dan 1940- CANR-37
Earlier sketches in CA 97-100, CANR-16
Tarlov, I. M. 1905(?)-1977 Obituary 69-72
Tarlow, Nora
See Cohen, Nora
Tarlton, Gillian Leigh 1953- 119
Tarn, John Nelson 1934- 41-44R
Tarn, Nathaniel 1928- CANR-70
Earlier sketches in CA 9-12R, CANR-5, 30
See also CAAS 16
Tarnawski, Wit(old) 1894-1988 Obituary 126
Tarnawsky, Maxim 1955- 150
Tarnawsky, Ostap 1917- 73-76
Tarnopol, Lester 1913- 77-80
Tarnopolsky, Yuri 1936- 153
Tarnower, Herman 1910-1980 89-92
Obituary 97-100
Tarpey, Lawrence Xavier 1928- 21-24R
Tarpley, Fred 1932- 41-44R
Tarpley, Natasha A(nastasia) 1971- 147
Tarpy, Roger M(aynard) 1941- 93-96
Tarr, Herbert 1929-1993 CANR-54
Obituary 143
Earlier sketch in CA 13-16R
Tarr, Joel A(rthur) 1934- CANR-38
Earlier sketches in CA 37-40R, CANR-14
Tarr, Judith 1955- CANR-52
Earlier sketch in CA 120
See also SATA 64
Tarr, Rodger L(eRoy) 1941- 110
Tarr, Yvonne Young 1929- CANR-8
Earlier sketch in CA 61-64
Tarrance, V(ernon) Lance, Jr. 1940- 37-40R
Tarrant, Desmond 1924- 21-24R
Tarrant, John
See Egleton, Clive (Frederick)
Tarrant, John J(oseph) 1924- CANR-41
Earlier sketches in CA 53-56, CANR-4, 19
Tarrant, Wilma
See Sherman, Jory (Tecumseh)
Tarrok, Peer
See Zwerenz, Gerhard
Tarry, Ellen 1906- CANR-69
Earlier sketch in CA 73-76
See also BW 1
See also CLR 26
See also SAAS 16
See also SATA 16
Tarsaidze, Alexandre 1901-1978 37-40R
Obituary 77-80
Tarshis, Jerome 1936- 61-64
See also SATA 9
Tarsis, Valery Yakovlevich 1906-1983 Obituary 109
Tarski, Alfred 1901(?)-1983 157
Obituary 111
Tarsky, Sue 1946- CANR-31
Earlier sketch in CA 112
See also SATA 41
Tart, Charles T(heodore) 1937- 29-32R
Tarter, Donald E(dward) 1938- 112
Tartikoff, Brandon 1949-1997 166
Tartre, Raymond S. 1901-1975 CAP-2
Earlier sketch in CA 21-22
Tartt, Donna 1964(?)- 142
See also CLC 76
Tarver, Ben 1927- 113
Tasca, Henry J. 1912-1979 Obituary 89-92
Tasca, Jules 1938- CANR-26
Earlier sketch in CA 109
See also AITN 1
Tasch, Peter A(nthony) 1933- 73-76
Taschdjian, Claire L(ouise) 1914- 73-76
Tashjian, Dickran (Levon) 1940- 61-64
Tashjian, Janet 1956- SATA 102
Tashjian, Virginia A. 1921- 29-32R
See also SATA 3
Tashlin, Frank 1913-1972 CANR-69
Obituary 110
Earlier sketch in CA 113
See also DLB 44
Tasker, James 1908- 49-52
See also SATA 9
Tasker, Joe 1948-1982 129
Obituary 108
Tassin, Myron Jude 1933- 61-64
Tassin, Ray(mond Jean) 1926- 53-56
Tatalovich, Raymond 1943- 152
Tatar, Maria M. 1945- 85-88
Tatarka, Dominik 1913-1989 Obituary 128
Tatarkiewicz, Wladyslaw 1886-1980 103
Obituary 97-100
Tatchell, Peter 1952- CANR-52
Earlier sketch in CA 125
Tate, (John Orley) Allen 1899-1979 CANR-32
Obituary 85-88
Earlier sketch in CA 5-8R
See also CLC 2, 4, 6, 9, 11, 14, 24
See also DLB 4, 45, 63
See also DLBD 17
See also MTCW 1
Tate, B. H.
See Boyer, Bruce Hatton
Tate, Carolyn E. 1952- 144
Tate, Claudia C. 1946- 121
Tate, Edward
See Dransfield, Michael (John Pender)
Tate, Eleanora E(laine) 1948- CANR-43
Earlier sketches in CA 105, CANR-25
See also AAYA 25
See also BW 2
See also CLR 37
See also JRDA
See also SATA 38, 94
Tate, Ellalice
See Hibbert, Eleanor Alice Burford
Tate, Gary 1930- 21-24R
Tate, George T(homas) 1931- 21-24R
Tate, Jackson R. 1899(?)-1978 Obituary 81-84
Tate, James (Vincent) 1943- CANR-57
Earlier sketches in CA 21-24R, CANR-29
See also CLC 2, 6, 25
See also DLB 5, 169
Tate, Joan 1922- CANR-54
Earlier sketches in CA 49-52, CANR-1, 48
See also SAAS 20
See also SATA 9, 86
Tate, Marilyn Freeman 1921- 13-16R
Tate, Mary Anne
See Hale, Arlene
Tate, Merle W(esley) 1903- CAP-1
Earlier sketch in CA 17-18
Tate, Merze 1905-1996 17-20R
Obituary 152
Tate, Nahum 1652(?)-1715 DLB 80
Tate, Peter 1940- 161
Tate, Richard
See Masters, Anthony
Tate, Robin
See Fanthorpe, R(obert) Lionel
Tate, Suzanne 1930- SATA 91
Tate, Velma 1913- 21-24R
Tatelbaum, Judith Ann 1938- 104
Tatelbaum, Judy
See Tatelbaum, Judith Ann
Tatem, Moira (Phillips) 1928- 133
Tatford, Brian F(rederick) B(arrington) 1927-
CAP-1
Earlier sketch in CA 9-10
Tatford, Frederick Albert 1901- CANR-10
Earlier sketch in CA 13-16R
Tatgenhorst, John 1938- 65-68
Tatham, Andrew Francis 1949- 125
Tatham, C. Ernest 1905- CAP-1
Earlier sketch in CA 9-10
Tatham, Campbell
See Elting, Mary
Tatham, Campbell
See Elting, Mary
Tatham, David 1932- 138
Tatham, Julie
See Tatham, Julie Campbell
Tatham, Julie Campbell 1908- 148
See also SATA 80
Tatham, Laura (Esther) 1919- 13-16R
Tati, Jacques
See Tatischeff, Jacques
Tatischeff, Jacques 1908-1982 Obituary 108
Tatlow, Antony 1935- CANR-48
Earlier sketch in CA 122
Taton, Rene 1915- 9-12R
Tatray, Istvan
See Rupert, Raphael Rudolph
Tattersall, Ian (Michael) 1945- 115
Tattersall, (Honor) Jill 1931- CANR-10
Earlier sketch in CA 25-28R
Tattersall, Lawrence H(olmes) 1933- 29-32R
Tattersall, M(uriel Joyce) 1931- CAP-1
Earlier sketch in CA 9-10
Tatu, Michel 1933- 25-28R
Tatum, Arlo 1923- 25-28R
Tatum, Billy Joe 1933- 61-64
Tatum, Charles M(ichael) 1943- CANR-29
Earlier sketch in CA 111
Tatum, Edward Lawrie 1909-1975 Obituary 113
Tatum, Jack
See Tatum, John David
Tatum, John David 1948- 104
Taub, Harald (Jay) 1918- 110
Taube, Evert 1890-1976 Obituary 61-64
Taube, Lester S. 1920- 69-72
Taubenfeld, Howard J(ack) 1924- 13-16R
Tauber, Abraham 1915(?)-1977 Obituary 69-72
Tauber, Edward S(anford) 1908-1988 Obituary 124
Tauber, Gerald E(rich) 1922- 89-92
Tauber, Gilbert 1935- CANR-9
Earlier sketch in CA 21-24R
Tauber, Kurt P(hilip) 1922- 21-24R
Tauber, Maurice F(alcolm) 1908-1980 105
Obituary 102
Tauber, Peter 1947- 37-40R
Taubert, Sigfred 1914- 120
Taubert, William H(owland) 1934- 103
Taubes, Frederic 1900-1981 CANR-9
Obituary 104
Earlier sketch in CA 17-20R
Taubes, Susan
See Feldmann, Susan Judith
Taubes, Timothy 1955- 148
Taubman, Bruce 1947- 141
Taubman, Jane A. 1942- 130
Taubman, William 1941- 21-24R
Taubr, Paul Raymond 1937- 29-32R
Taufer, Veno 1933- DLB 181
Taulbert, Clifton L(emoure) 1945- 143
See also BW 2
Tauler, Johannes c. 1300-1361 DLB 179
Taunton, Eric
See Westcott-Jones, K(enneth)
Tauranac, John 1939- 124
Taussig, Helen Brooke 1898-1986 163
Tavard, George H(enry) 1922- CANR-37
Earlier sketches in CA 1-4R, CANR-1, 16

Tavcar, Ivan 1851-1923 ... DLB 147
Tave, Stuart M(alcolm) 1923- ... 104
Tavel, Ronald 1940- ... CANR-33
Earlier sketch in CA 21-24R
See also CLC 6
Taverne, Dick 1928- ... 85-88
Tavernier, Bertrand 1941- ... 123
Tavernor, Robert (William) 1954- ... 168
Taves, Ernest H(enry) 1916- ... 93-96
Taves, Isabella 1915- ... CANR-8
Earlier sketch in CA 21-24R
See also SATA 27
Taviani, Paolo 1931- ... 153
Taviani, Vittorio 1929- ... 153
Taviss, Irene
See Thomson, Irene Taviss
Tavo, Gus
See Ivan, Martha Miller Pfaff
Tavor, Eve
See Bannet, Eve Tavor
Tavris, Carol (Anne) 1944- ... 143
Tavuchis, Nicholas 1934- ... 57-60
Tavy, Peter
See Hemery, Eric
Tawa, Nicholas E. 1923- ... 136
Tawney, R(ichard) H(enry)
1880-1962 Obituary ... 93-96
Tax, Meredith (Jane) 1942- ... 144
Tax, Sol 1907- ... 5-8R
Taydo
See McDonald, Erwin L(awrence)
Tayler, Irene ... 136
Taylor, A(lan) J(ohn) P(ercivale) 1906-1990 ...
CANR-32
Obituary ... 132
Earlier sketch in CA 5-8R
See also MTCW 1
Taylor, Alan Carey 1905-1975 Obituary ... 114
Taylor, Alan R(os) 1926-1992 ... 109
Obituary ... 139
Taylor, Alastair M(acDonald) 1915- ... 17-20R
Taylor, Albert E(dward) 1908- ... 89-92
Taylor, Alec Clifton
See Clifton-Taylor, Alec
Taylor, Alfred 1896-1973 ... 105
Taylor, Alice J. 1909-1969 ... CAP-2
Earlier sketch in CA 25-28
Taylor, Alice L(ouise) 1911-1985 ... 61-64
Obituary ... 116
Taylor, Alison 1927- ... 21-24R
Taylor, Alix 1921- ... 5-8R
Taylor, Allegra 1940- ... 136
Taylor, Andrew (McDonald) 1940- ... CANR-51
Earlier sketches in CA 69-72, CANR-11, 27
Taylor, Andrew 1944-1988 ... 126
Taylor, Andrew (John Robert) 1951- ... CANR-52
Earlier sketches in CA 110, CANR-28
See also SATA 70
Taylor, Anique 1946- ... 109
Taylor, Ann
See Smith, Richard Rein
Taylor, Ann 1782-1866 ... DLB 163
See also SATA 41
See also SATA-Brief 35
Taylor, Anna 1944- ... 25-28R
Taylor, Anne 1934- ... 140
Taylor, Anne (Gary) Pannell
1910-1984 Obituary ... 112
Taylor, Apirana 1956- ... 128
Taylor, Archer 1890-1973 Obituary ... 107
Taylor, Arnold H. 1929- ... 33-36R
Taylor, Art(hur Stephen, Jr.) 1929-1995 ... 122
Obituary ... 148
Taylor, Arthur Samuel 1894-1963 ... 1-4R
Obituary ... 103
Taylor, Audilee Boyd 1931- ... SATA 59
Taylor, Barbara G. 1942- ... 25-28R
Taylor, Barbara J. 1927- ... 53-56
See also SATA 10
Taylor, Bayard 1825-1878 ... DLB 3, 189
Taylor, Ben
See Strachan, Ian
Taylor, Benjamin J. 1934- ... 21-24R
Taylor, Bernard 1934- ... CANR-24
Earlier sketch in CA 69-72
Taylor, Bert Leston 1866-1921 Brief entry ... 117
See also DLB 25
Taylor, Betty Jo 1933- ... 13-16R
Taylor, Beverly (White) 1947- ... 132
Taylor, Bob L(eslie) 1923- ... 33-36R
Taylor, Brad
See Smith, Richard Rein
Taylor, Bron Raymond 1955- ... 138
Taylor, C(ecil) P(hilip) 1929-1981 ... CANR-47
Obituary ... 105
Earlier sketch in CA 25-28R
See also CLC 27
Taylor, Carl 1937- ... 69-72
See also SATA 14
Taylor, Carl S. 1949- ... 146
Taylor, Carol MacKenzie 1957- ... 167
Taylor, Charlene M(ae) 1938- ... 33-36R
Taylor, Charles 1931- ... CANR-27
Earlier sketches in CA 13-16R, CANR-11
Taylor, Charles Alfred 1922- ... 109
Taylor, Charles D(oonan) 1938- ... CANR-37
Earlier sketches in CA 101, CANR-17
Taylor, Charles Henry 1846-1921 ... 166
See also DLB 25
Taylor, Charles Lewis 1935- ... CANR-13
Earlier sketch in CA 77-80
Taylor, Cheryl Munro 1957- ... SATA 96
Taylor, Clyde R(ussell) 1931- ... 45-48
Taylor, Clyde Willis 1904-1988 Obituary ... 125
Taylor, Constance Lindsay 1907- ... 106
Taylor, Cora (Lorraine) 1936- ... 124
See also SATA 64
Taylor, Cora Sibal 1941(?)-1987 Obituary ... 123
Taylor, D. J. 1960- ... 122
Taylor, Dallas 1948- ... 157
Taylor, Dalmas A(rnold) 1933-1998 ... 57-60
Obituary ... 164
Taylor, Daniel (William) 1948- ... 154
Taylor, Dave 1948- ... 146
See also SATA 78
Taylor, David
See Taylor, Dave
Taylor, David 1900-1965 ... 1-4R
See also SATA 10
Taylor, David (Conrad) 1934- ... 105
Taylor, David Alan 1943- ... 108
Taylor, Dawson 1916- ... CANR-50
Earlier sketches in CA 13-16R, CANR-25
Taylor, Day
See Parkinson, Cornelia M.
and Salvato, Sharon
Taylor, Dayna
See Parkinson, Cornelia M.
Taylor, (Joseph) Deems 1885-1966 Obituary . 89-92
Taylor, Delores ... 138
Taylor, Demetria 1903-1977 Obituary ... 73-76
Taylor, (Edmund) Dennis 1940- ... CANR-43
Earlier sketch in CA 119
Taylor, Desmond 1930- ... CANR-45
Earlier sketch in CA 37-40R
Taylor, Don(ald) 1910- ... 13-16R
Taylor, Donald L(avor) 1916- ... 17-20R
Taylor, Donald Stewart 1924- Brief entry ... 106
Taylor, Donna June 1949- ... 37-40R
Taylor, Duncan (Burnett) 1912- ... 25-28R
Taylor, Duncan Norton
See Norton-Taylor, Duncan
Taylor, Dwight 1902-1986(?) Obituary ... 121
Taylor, Earl Aulick 1904-1965 ... CAP-1
Earlier sketch in CA 13-14
Taylor, Edith 1913- ... 45-48
Taylor, Edward 1642(?)-1729 ... DA
See also DAB
See also DAC
See also DAM MST, POET
See also DLB 24
Taylor, Eleanor Ross 1920- ... CANR-70
Earlier sketch in CA 81-84
See also CLC 5
Taylor, Elisabeth (D.) 1931- ... 135
Taylor, Elisabeth Russell
See Russell Taylor, Elisabeth
Taylor, Elizabeth 1912-1975 ... CANR-70
Earlier sketches in CA 13-16R, CANR-9
See also CLC 2, 4, 29
See also DLB 139
See also MTCW 1
See also SATA 13
Taylor, Elizabeth Atwood 1936- ... 142
Taylor, Elizabeth Tebbetts ... 101
Taylor, Ethel Stoddard
1895(?)-1975 Obituary ... 57-60
Taylor, Eugene Jackson 1913-1978 Obituary . 81-84
Taylor, Florance Walton ... 37-40R
See also SATA 9
Taylor, Florence M(arian Tompkins) 1892- .. 13-16R
See also SATA 9
Taylor, Frank J. 1894-1972 ... CAP-1
Obituary ... 37-40R
Earlier sketch in CA 13-14
Taylor, Fred James 1919- ... 107
Taylor, (George) Frederick 1928- ... 77-80
Taylor, Frederick Winslow 1856-1915 ... TCLC 76
Taylor, G(eorge) Jeffrey 1944- ... 116
Taylor, Gage 1942- ... SATA 87
Taylor, Gary 1953- ... 154
Taylor, George
See Parulski, George R(ichard), Jr.
Taylor, George A(lbert) 1942- ... 102
Taylor, George E(dward) 1905- ... CANR-22
Earlier sketch in CA 1-4R
Taylor, Gordon O(verton) 1938- ... 25-28R
Taylor, Gordon Rattray 1911-1981 ... 85-88
Obituary ... 105
Taylor, (Frank Herbert) Griffin 1917- ... 65-68
Taylor, H. Baldwin
See Waugh, Hillary Baldwin
Taylor, H. Kerr 1891(?)-1977 Obituary ... 73-76
Taylor, Harold 1914-1993 ... 25-28R
Obituary ... 140
Taylor, Harold L(awrence) 1934- ... 110
Taylor, Harold McCarter 1907-1995 ... 109
Obituary ... 150
Taylor, Harold S. 1901(?)-1985 Obituary ... 116
Taylor, Harry
See Granick, Harry
Taylor, Harry H. 1926- ... 57-60
Taylor, Helen 1947- ... 133
Taylor, Henry 1800-1886 ... DLB 32
Taylor, Henry (Splawn) 1942- ... CANR-31
Earlier sketch in CA 33-36R
See also CAAS 7
See also CLC 44
See also DLB 5
Taylor, Henry J(unior) 1902-1984 ... CAP-2
Obituary ... 112
Earlier sketch in CA 23-24
Taylor, Herb(ert Norman, Jr.) 1942-1987 ... 97-100
Obituary ... 123
See also SATA 22
See also SATA-Obit 54
Taylor, Howard F(rancis) 1939- ... 110
Taylor, Hugh 1917(?)-1987 Obituary ... 123
Taylor, Hugh A(lexander) 1920- ... 115
Taylor, Ian 1944- ... 77-80
Taylor, Ina (Margaret Kathleen) 1949- ... 119
Taylor, Irving A. 1925- ... 61-64
Taylor, J. David
See Taylor, Dave
Taylor, J. Thomas 1930- ... 107
Taylor, Jack W(ilson) 1915- ... 9-12R
Taylor, James A. 1925- ... 147
Taylor, James B(entley) 1930- ... 37-40R
Taylor, James C(hapman) 1937- ... 77-80
Taylor, James R(owe) 1907- ... CAP-2
Earlier sketch in CA 17-18
Taylor, James Spear 1897(?)-1979 Obituary . 85-88
Taylor, James Stephen 1935- ... 121
Taylor, Jane 1783-1824 ... DLB 163
See also SATA 41
See also SATA-Brief 35
Taylor, Janelle (Diane Williams) 1944- ... CANR-67
Brief entry ... 118
Earlier sketches in CA 124, CANR-43
Interview in ... 124
Taylor, (Samuel) Jared 1951- ... CANR-64
Earlier sketch in CA 122
Taylor, Jayne
See Krentz, Jayne Ann
Taylor, Jean 1947- ... 151
Taylor, Jed H(arbottle) 1902- ... CAP-1
Earlier sketch in CA 13-16
Taylor, Jennifer (Evelyn) 1935- ... 128
Taylor, Jenny 1910- ... 105
Taylor, Jeremy c. 1613-1667 ... DLB 151
Taylor, Jeremy F. 1952- ... 137
Taylor, Jeremy James 1948- ... 128
Taylor, Jerome 1918- ... CANR-1
Earlier sketch in CA 1-4R
Taylor, Jerry D(uncan) 1938- ... 115
See also SATA 47
Taylor, Jesse
See Amidon, Bill (Vincent)
Taylor, Jim 1937- ... 119
Taylor, Joan du Plat (?)-1983 Obituary ... 109
Taylor, Joan E(lizabeth) 1958- ... 163
Taylor, Joe 1949- ... 159
Taylor, Joe Gray 1920- ... CANR-6
Earlier sketch in CA 57-60
Taylor, John 1577(?)-1653 ... DLB 121
Taylor, John 1916- ... 93-96
Taylor, John 1921- ... CANR-16
Earlier sketch in CA 21-24R
Taylor, John 1925- ... 81-84
Taylor, John (Alfred) 1931- ... 61-64
Taylor, John 1955- ... 124
Taylor, John F(rank) A(dams) 1915- ... 17-20R
Taylor, John G(erald) 1931- ... 29-32R
Taylor, John H(ilton) 1958- ... 138
Taylor, John Laverack 1937- ... CANR-1
Earlier sketch in CA 45-48
Taylor, John M(axwell) 1930- ... 25-28R
Taylor, John Randolph 1929- ... 1-4R
Taylor, John Robert
See Taylor, Andrew (John Robert)
Taylor, John Russell 1935- ... CANR-37
Earlier sketch in CA 5-8R
Taylor, John Vernon 1914- ... CANR-44
Earlier sketches in CA 9-12R, CANR-5, 21
Taylor, John W(illiam) R(ansom) 1922- ... 49-52
Taylor, Joshua Charles 1917-1981 ... 104
Taylor, Judy
See Hough, Judy Taylor
Taylor, Kamala (Purnaiya) 1924- ... 77-80
See also Markandaya, Kamala
Taylor, Karen
See Malpede, Karen (Sophia)
Taylor, Karl K. 1938- ... 41-44R
Taylor, Katharine Whiteside 1897- ... CAP-2
Earlier sketch in CA 25-28
Taylor, Kathy 1950- ... 154
Taylor, Keith Weller 1946- ... 111
Taylor, Ken 1922- ... 108
Taylor, Kenneth N(athaniel) 1917- ... CANR-8
Earlier sketch in CA 17-20R
See also AITN 2
See also SATA 26
Taylor, (Paul) Kent 1940- ... CANR-9
Earlier sketch in CA 17-20R
Taylor, L(aurie) A(ylma) 1939- ... CANR-30
Earlier sketch in CA 111
Taylor, L(ester) B(arbour), Jr. 1932- ... CANR-26
Earlier sketches in CA 57-60, CANR-11
See also SATA 27
Taylor, Larissa J(uliet) 1952- ... 138
Taylor, Laurie
See Taylor, L(aurie) A(ylma)
Taylor, Lawrence 1942- ... 105
Taylor, (M.) Lee 1930- ... 41-44R
Taylor, Lester D(ean) 1938- ... 17-20R
Taylor, Lisa (Suter) 1933-1991 ... 128
Obituary ... 134
Taylor, Liz McNeill
See Taylor, Elisabeth (D.)
Taylor, Liza Pennywitt 1955- ... 140
Taylor, Lloyd A(ndrew) 1921- ... 41-44R
Taylor, Lloyd C(hamberlain), Jr. 1923- ... 57-60
Taylor, Lois Dwight Cole
See Cole, Lois Dwight
Taylor, Lord
See Taylor, Stephen James Lake
Taylor, Louis 1900- ... CANR-2
Earlier sketch in CA 5-8R
Taylor, Louise Todd 1939- ... 115
See also SATA 47
Taylor, M(artin) J. 1952- ... 143
Taylor, Malcolm Gordon 1915- ... 109
Taylor, Margaret
See Burroughs, Margaret Taylor (Goss)
Taylor, Margaret
See Burroughs, Margaret Taylor (Goss)
Taylor, Margaret Stewart ... 89-92
Taylor, Marion Ansel 1904- ... 13-16R
Taylor, Mark 1927- ... 108
See also SATA 32
See also SATA-Brief 28
Taylor, Mark C. 1945- ... CANR-56
Earlier sketch in CA 125
Taylor, Mary Ann 1912- ... 97-100
Taylor, Maxwell D(avenport)
1901-1987 Obituary ... 122
Brief entry ... 111
Taylor, Michael J. 1924- ... CANR-7
Earlier sketch in CA 17-20R
Taylor, Michael J(ohn) H(addrick) 1949- . CANR-34
Earlier sketches in CA 77-80, CANR-14
Taylor, Michael M. 1944- ... 97-100
Taylor, Michael Ray 1959- ... 160
Taylor, Mildred D. ... CANR-25
Earlier sketch in CA 85-88
See also AAYA 10
See also BW 1
See also CLC 21
See also CLR 9
See also DLB 52
See also JRDA
See also MAICYA
See also SAAS 5
See also SATA 15, 70
Taylor, Moddie Daniel 1912-1976 ... 168
Taylor, Morris F. 1915- ... 37-40R
Taylor, Nick 1945- ... 146
Taylor, Norman 1883-1967 ... CAP-2
Earlier sketch in CA 23-24
Taylor, Owen Reece 1912(?)-1983 Obituary ... 111
Taylor, P(hilip) A. M. 1920- ... 136
Taylor, Pat Ellis 1941- ... 111
Taylor, Paul 1948- ... 121
Taylor, Paul B(eekman) 1930- ... 81-84
Taylor, Paul F. 1927- ... 146
Taylor, Paul S(chuster) 1895-1984 ... CANR-29
Obituary ... 112
Earlier sketch in CA 81-84
Taylor, Paul W(arren) 1923- ... CANR-21
Earlier sketch in CA 1-4R
Taylor, Paula (Wright) 1942- ... 122
Brief entry ... 111
See also SATA 48
See also SATA-Brief 33
Taylor, Peggy 1946- ... 120
Taylor, Peter (Hillsman) 1917-1994 ... CANR-50
Obituary ... 147
Earlier sketches in CA 13-16R, CANR-9
Interview in ... CANR-9
See also CLC 1, 4, 18, 37, 44, 50, 71
See also DLBY 81, 94
See also MTCW 1
See also SSC 10
Taylor, Philip Elbert 1908-1975 Obituary ... 61-64
Taylor, Phoebe Atwood 1909-1976 Obituary . 61-64
Taylor, Phoebe Jean 1921(?)-1979 Obituary . 89-92
Taylor, Quintard 1948- ... 168
Taylor, Ransom Theodore 1913- ... 45-48
Taylor, Ray J. 1918(?)-1977 Obituary ... 69-72
Taylor, Ray Ward 1908- ... CAP-2
Earlier sketch in CA 19-20
Taylor, Rebe Prestwich 1911- ... 13-16R
Taylor, Rex 1921- ... 13-16R
Taylor, Richard 1919- ... 17-20R
Taylor, Richard K(night) 1933- ... CANR-39
Earlier sketches in CA 101, CANR-18
Taylor, Richard S(helley) 1912- ... CANR-38
Earlier sketch in CA 115
Taylor, Richard W(arren) 1924- ... CANR-19
Earlier sketches in CA 5-8R, CANR-3
Taylor, Robert, Jr. 1941- ... 118
Taylor, Robert 1925- ... 81-84
Taylor, Robert B(artley) 1926- ... 81-84
Taylor, Robert Brown 1936- ... CANR-12
Earlier sketch in CA 61-64
Taylor, Robert Lewis 1912- ... CANR-64
Earlier sketches in CA 1-4R, CANR-3
See also CLC 14
See also SATA 10
Taylor, Robert Martin 1909- ... CAP-2
Earlier sketch in CA 25-28
Taylor, Robert R(atcliffe) 1939- ... 53-56
Taylor, Rogan 1945- ... CANR-65
Earlier sketch in CA 152
Taylor, Roger ... 155
Taylor, Roland 1907- ... CAP-1
Earlier sketch in CA 13-14
Taylor, Ron(ald) W(illiam) 1922- ... CAP-1
Earlier sketch in CA 11-12
Taylor, Ronald (Jack) 1924- ... CANR-26
Earlier sketch in CA 93-96
Taylor, Ronald B. 1930- ... 142
Taylor, Ronald J. 1932- ... 143
Taylor, Ronald L(ee) 1938- ... 77-80
Taylor, Ross McLaury 1909(?)-1977 Obituary 69-72
Taylor, Rupert (Maurice) 1946- ... 45-48
Taylor, Ruth Mattson 1922- ... 101
Taylor, Samuel (Woolley) 1907-1997 ... CANR-28
Obituary ... 161
Earlier sketch in CA 73-76
Taylor, Samuel (Albert) 1912- ... 25-28R
Taylor, Sandra C. 1936- ... 123
Taylor, Stephen
See Taylor, Stephen James Lake
Taylor, Stephen 1948- ... 133
Taylor, Stephen James Lake
1910-1988 Obituary ... 124
Taylor, Sybil (Renee) 1933- ... 122

Taylor, Sydney (Brenner) 1904(?)-1978 ... CANR-4
Obituary ... 77-80
Earlier sketch in CA 5-8R
See also MAICYA
See also SATA 1, 28
See also SATA-Obit 26
Taylor, T(homas) F(is) 1913- ... 136
Taylor, T. G.
See Taylor, T(homas) Geoffrey
Taylor, T(homas) Geoffrey 1918-1987 Obituary . 123
Taylor, Telford 1908- ... CANR-16
Earlier sketch in CA 25-28R
Interview in ... CANR-16
See also MTCW 1
Taylor, Theodore 1921- ... CANR-50
Earlier sketches in CA 21-24R, CANR-9, 25, 38
See also AAYA 2, 19
See also CLR 30
See also JRDA
See also MAICYA
See also SAAS 4
See also SATA 5, 54, 83
Taylor, Theodore Brewster 1925- ... 102
Taylor, Theodore W(alter) 1913- ... 119
Taylor, Thomas 1934- ... 21-24R
Taylor, Thomas Lowe 1938- ... CAAS 26
Taylor, Tim 1920-1974 ... 45-48
Obituary ... 53-56
Taylor, Tom
See Taylor, J. Thomas
Taylor, Valerie
See Tate, Velma
Taylor, Vernon L. 1922- ... 33-36R
Taylor, Verta 1948- ... 114
Taylor, W(illiam) H(odge) 1904-1984 Obituary .. 113
Taylor, Walter Fuller 1900-1966 ... 1-4R
Taylor, Walter W(illard) 1913- ... 61-64
Taylor, Warren 1903- ... 21-24R
Taylor, Weldon J. 1908- ... 1-4R
Taylor, Welford Dunaway 1938- ... 37-40R
Taylor, Wendell H(ertig) 1905- ... 102
Taylor, William 1930- ... CANR-15
Earlier sketch in CA 81-84
Taylor, William 1938- ... 146
See also SATA 78
Taylor, William C. 1959- ... 142
Taylor, William David, Jr. 1902-1975 Obituary .. 107
Taylor, William E(dwards) 1920- ... CANR-10
Earlier sketch in CA 25-28R
Taylor, William Ewart, Jr. 1927-1994 ... 126
Obituary ... 152
Taylor, William L. 1937- ... 29-32R
Taylor, William N(athaniel), (Jr.) 1952- ... 153
Taylor, William R(obert) 1922- ... 138
Taylor, Zack 1927- ... 65-68
Taylor-Gooby, Peter 1947- ... CANR-41
Earlier sketch in CA 118
Taylor-Hall, Mary Ann 1937- ... 147
Taylor-Olson, Clara Mae
1899(?)-1988 Obituary ... 124
Taze, James E. 1938- ... 166
Tazewell, Charles 1900-1972 Obituary ... 37-40R
See also SATA 74
Tazieff, Haroun 1914-1998 Obituary ... 165
Brief entry ... 113
Tchaadaieff
See Sorokin, Pitirim A(lexandrovitch)
Tchekhov, Anton
See Chekhov, Anton (Pavlovich)
Tchernichovski, Saul (Gutmanovich)
1875-1943 Brief entry ... 116
Tchicaya, Gerald Felix 1931-1988 ... 129
Obituary ... 125
See also CLC 101
Tchicaya U Tam'si
See Tchicaya, Gerald Felix
Tchividjian, Gigi Graham 1945- ... 108
Tchobanoglous, George 1935- ... 102
Tchudi, Stephen N. 1942- ... CANR-22
Earlier sketch in CA 89-92
See also SATA 55
Teachout, Terry 1956- ... 133
Tead, Ordway 1891-1973 Obituary ... 45-48
Teaford, Jon C(hristian) 1946- ... CANR-10
Earlier sketch in CA 65-68
Teague, Bob
See Teague, Robert
Teague, Frances 1949- ... 139
Teague, Kathleen 1937- ... 97-100
Teague, Mark (Christopher) 1963- ... 136
See also SATA 68, 99
Teague, Michael 1932- ... 109
Teague, Robert 1929- ... 106
See also BW 2
See also SATA 32
See also SATA-Brief 31
Teahan, Sheila 1961- ... 153
Teal, G. Donn 1932- ... 33-36R
Teal, John J(erome), Jr. 1921-1982 Obituary ... 110
Teal, Val(entine M.) 1903- ... 61-64
See also SATA 10
Teale, Edwin Way 1899-1980 ... CANR-2
Obituary ... 102
Earlier sketch in CA 1-4R
See also SATA 7
See also SATA-Obit 25
Tearle, John L. 1917- ... 140
Teasdale, Sara 1884-1933 ... 163
Brief entry ... 104
See also DLB 45
See also SATA 32
See also TCLC 4
Teasdale, Wayne (Q.) 1945- ... 158
Te Awekotuku, Ngahuia ... 154
Tebbel, John (William) 1912- ... CANR-29
Earlier sketch in CA 85-88
See also SATA 26
Tebbel, Robert E(verett) 1924- ... 5-8R
Tebbetts-Taylor, Elizabeth
See Taylor, Elizabeth Tebbetts
Tebbit, Norman 1931- ... 138
Tebeau, Charlton Watson 1904- ... 110
Tebelak, John-Michael 1949(?)-1985 Obituary .. 115
Tec, Leon 1919- ... 97-100
Tec, Nechama 1931- ... CANR-48
Earlier sketches in CA 9-12R, CANR-23
Techine, Andre 1943- ... 146
Teck, Alan 1934- ... 25-28R
Tecumseh 1768-1813 ... DAM MULT
See also NNAL
Tedder, Arthur William 1890-1967 ... CAP-2
Earlier sketch in CA 23-24
Tedder, Lord
See Tedder, Arthur William
Teddy, Paul
See Aldrich, Jonathan
Tedeschi, (Theodore) James, Jr. 1928- ... 41-44R
Tedlock, E(rnest) W(arnock), Jr. 1910- ... CAP-2
Earlier sketch in CA 17-18
Tedone, David A. 1953- ... 132
Tedrow, John C. F. 1917- ... 142
Tedrow, R. L.
See Tedrow, Richard L(ove)
Tedrow, Richard L(ove) 1913(?)-1987 Obituary . 121
Tee, John
See Meades, Jonathan (Turner)
Teece, David J(ohn) 1948- ... 138
Teed, Peter (Litterland) 1924- ... 143
Teegen, Otto John 1899-1983 Obituary ... 109
Teensma, Lynne Bertrand
See Bertrand, Lynne
Teer, Frank 1934- ... 53-56
Teeter, Don E(l) 1934- ... 73-76
Teeter, Karl V(an Duyn) 1929- ... 17-20R
Teeters, Negley K(ing) 1896-1971 ... CAP-2
Obituary ... 33-36R
Earlier sketch in CA 23-24
Teetor, Paul R(aymond) 1919- ... 113
Teets, Bruce E. 1914- ... 37-40R
Teets, John Phillip 1948- ... 132
Tee-Van, Helen Damrosch 1893-1976 ... 49-52
Obituary ... 65-68
See also SATA 10
See also SATA-Obit 27
Teevan, Richard C(ollier) 1919- ... CANR-4
Earlier sketch in CA 1-4R
Tefertiller, Casey (Orie) 1952- ... 165
Teffeteller, Gordon Lamar 1931- ... 115
Tefft, Bess H(agaman) 1915(?)-1977 Obituary .. 110
Tega, Vasile 1921- ... CANR-18
Earlier sketch in CA 102
Tegenfeldt, Herman G(ustaf) 1913- ... 73-76
Tegerdine, Maria
See Morsy, Magali
Tegethoff, Wolf W. 1953- ... 144
Tegner, Bruce 1928- ... CANR-8
Earlier sketch in CA 61-64
See also SATA 62
Tegner, Henry (Stuart) 1901- ... CANR-12
Earlier sketch in CA 13-16R
Tehan, Arline Boucher 1930- ... 130
Teich, Albert H(arris) 1942- ... CANR-50
Earlier sketches in CA 45-48, CANR-25
Teicher, Morton I(rving) 1920- ... CANR-11
Earlier sketch in CA 69-72
Teichgraeber, Richard F., III III 1950- ... CANR-56
Earlier sketch in CA 125
Teichman, Jenny 1930- ... CANR-55
Earlier sketch in CA 127
Teichman, Judith A. 1947- ... 163
Teichmann, Howard (Miles) 1916-1987 ... CANR-17
Obituary ... 123
Earlier sketch in CA 69-72
Teikmanis, Arthur L. 1914- ... 13-16R
Teilhard de Chardin, (Marie Joseph) Pierre
1881-1955 Brief entry ... 105
See also TCLC 9
Teiser, Ruth 1915- ... 109
Teish, Luisah 1948- ... 141
See also BW 2
Teissier du Cros, Janet 1906- ... CAP-2
Earlier sketch in CA 17-18
Teitelbaum, Harry 1930- ... 21-24R
Teitelbaum, Matthew 1956- ... 144
Teitelbaum, Michael 1953- ... 121
See also SATA 59
Teitelbaum, Myron 1929- ... 13-16R
Teitelman, Robert 1954- ... 135
Teiwes, Helga 1930- ... 140
Teixeira, Bernardo 1926- ... 108
Teixeira da Mota, Avelino (?)-1982 Obituary ... 106
Teja, Jesus F(rancisco) de la 1956- ... 154
Tejima 1931- ... CLR 20
Tekahionwake
See Johnson, E. Pauline
Tekeyan, Charles 1927- ... 29-32R
Telander, Richard F(orster) 1948- ... 65-68
Telander, Todd (G.) 1967- ... SATA 88
Teleki, Geza 1943- ... CANR-19
Earlier sketches in CA 49-52, CANR-3
See also SATA 45
Telemaque, Eleanor Wong 1934- ... 104
See also SATA 43
Telescope, Tom
See Newbery, John
Telfer, Dariel (Doris) 1905-1987 ... CAP-2
Obituary ... 122
Earlier sketch in CA 25-28
Telfer, R(oss) 1937- ... 106
Telfer, William 1886-1968 ... CAP-1
Earlier sketch in CA 13-14
Telford, Charles W(itt) 1903- ... 65-68
Tell, Jack 1909(?)-1979 Obituary ... 89-92
Teller, Edward 1908- ... CANR-65
Earlier sketches in CAP-1, CA 13-14, CANR-33
See also MTCW 1
Teller, James D(avid) 1906- ... 41-44R
Teller, Judd L. 1912-1972 Obituary ... 33-36R
Teller, Neville 1931- ... CANR-49
Earlier sketches in CA 103, CANR-23
Teller, Walter (Magnes) 1910-1993 ... CANR-2
Obituary ... 140
Earlier sketch in CA 5-8R
Telles, Lygia Fagundes 1923- ... 157
See also DLB 113
Tello, Carlos 1938- ... 112
Telser, Lester G(reenspan) 1931- ... 33-36R
Tem, Melanie ... 165
Tem, Steve
See Tem, Steve Rasnic
Tem, Steve R.
See Tem, Steve Rasnic
Tem, Steve Rasnic 1950- ... 165
Temerson, Catherine 1944- ... 147
Temianka, Dan(iel) 1948- ... 152
Temianka, Henri 1906- ... 45-48
Temin, Peter 1937- ... 13-16R
Temkin, Pauline B. 1919- ... 25-28R
Temkin, Sara Anne Schlossberg 1913- ... 1-4R
See also SATA 26
Temko, Allan 1924- ... 136
Temko, Florence ... CANR-37
Earlier sketches in CA 49-52, CANR-1, 17
See also SATA 13
Temmer, Mark J. 1922- Brief entry ... 107
Temp, George (Edward) 1929- ... 45-48
Temperley, Howard 1932- ... 85-88
Temperley, Nicholas 1932- ... 107
Tempest, Jan
See Swatridge, Irene Maude (Mossop)
Tempest, Margaret Mary 1892-1982 Obituary .. 108
See also SATA-Obit 33
Tempest, Sarah
See Ponsonby, D(oris) A(lmon)
Tempest, Theresa
See Kent, Louise Andrews
Tempest, Victor
See Philipp, Elliot Elias
Templar, Maurice
See Groom, Arthur William
Temple, Ann
See Mortimer, Penelope (Ruth)
Temple, Arthur
See Northcott, (William) Cecil
Temple, Charles 1947- ... 148
See also SATA 79
Temple, Cliff 1947-1994 ... 111
Obituary ... 143
Temple, Dan
See Newton, D(wight) B(ennett)
Temple, Frances (Nolting) 1945-1995 ... 151
See also AAYA 19
See also SATA 85
Temple, Herbert 1919- ... SATA 45
Temple, Joe 1917- ... 97-100
Temple, Nigel (Hal Longdale) 1926- ... 29-32R
Temple, Norman J. 1947- ... 148
Temple, Paul
See Durbridge, Francis (Henry)
Temple, Paul
See McConnell, James Douglas Rutherford
Temple, Philip (Robert) 1939- ... CANR-22
Earlier sketch in CA 104
Temple, Robert (Kyle Grenville) 1945- ... CANR-40
Earlier sketches in CA 89-92, CANR-16
Temple, Robert M(ickler), Jr. 1935- Brief entry . 107
Temple, Ruth Z(abriskie) 1908- ... 61-64
Temple, Wayne C(alhoun) 1924- ... CANR-17
Earlier sketches in CA 1-4R, CANR-1
Temple, Willard H. 1912- ... 1-4R
Temple, William 1628-1699 ... DLB 101
Temple, William 1881-1944 Brief entry ... 120
Temple, William F(rederick) 1914-1989 ... 166
Templeman, Eleanor Lee (Reading)
1906-1990 Obituary ... 131
Templeton, Charles B. 1915- ... 101
Templeton, Edith 1916- ... 53-56
Templeton, Janet
See Hershman, Morris
Templeton, John J(oseph), Jr. 1928- ... 25-28R
Tenax
See Lean, Garth Dickinson
ten Boom, Corrie 1892-1983 ... 111
Obituary ... 109
Tendryakov, Vladimir Fyodorovich
1923-1984(?) ... 104
Obituary ... 113
Tenenbaum, Frances 1919- ... CANR-12
Earlier sketch in CA 73-76
Tenenbaum, Shea 1910- ... CANR-1
Earlier sketch in CA 49-52
Tenenbaum, Shelly 1955- ... 146
Tener, Robert L(awrence) 1924- ... 110
Teng, S(su)-Y(u) 1906-1988 ... CANR-22
Obituary ... 145
Earlier sketch in CA 13-16R
Tengbom, Mildred 1921- ... CANR-39
Earlier sketches in CA 97-100, CANR-17
Tenggren, Gustaf 1896-1970 ... SATA 18
See also SATA-Obit 26
Ten Harmsel, Henrietta 1921- ... 106
Ten Hoor, Elvie (Marie Mortensen)
1900-1984 ... 9-12R
Obituary ... 112
TenHouten, Warren David 1939- Brief entry ... 108
Tenhula, John 1951- ... 135
Tenison, Marika Hanbury
See Hanbury-Tenison, Marika
Tenison, Robin Hanbury
See Hanbury-Tenison, (Airling) Robin
Tenn, William 1919- ... DLB 8
Tennant, Alan 1943- ... 108
Tennant, Emma (Christina) 1937- ... CANR-59
Earlier sketches in CA 65-68, CANR-10, 38
See also CAAS 9
See also CLC 13, 52
See also DLB 14
Tennant, Ivo (S.) 1955- ... 128
Tennant, Kylie
See Rodd, Kylie Tennant
See also SATA 6
Tennant, Nora Jackson 1915- ... CANR-4
Earlier sketch in CA 9-12R
Tennant, (Charles) Roger 1919- ... 106
Tennant, Stephen (James Napier)
1906-1987 Obituary ... 122
Tennant, Veronica 1947- ... 103
See also SATA 36
Tennen, Howard 1948- ... 138
Tennenbaum, Silvia 1928- ... CANR-21
Earlier sketch in CA 77-80
Tenner, Edward 1944- ... 155
Tenneshaw, S. M.
See Beaumont, Charles
and Garrett, (Gordon) Randall (Phillip)
and Silverberg, Robert
Tenness, George
See Delk, Robert Carlton
Tenney, H(orace) Kent 1892-1982 Obituary ... 107
Tenney, Merrill C(hapin) 1904-1985 ... CANR-4
Obituary ... 115
Earlier sketch in CA 1-4R
Tenney, Tabitha Gilman 1762-1837 ... DLB 37, 200
Tenniel, John 1820-1914 Brief entry ... 111
See also CLR 18
See also MAICYA
See also SATA 74
See also SATA-Brief 27
Tennien, Mark A. 1900(?)-1983 Obituary ... 108
Tennies, Arthur C(ornelius) 1931- ... 53-56
Tennison, Patrick Joseph 1928- ... CANR-23
Earlier sketch in CA 106
Tennissen, Anthony C(ornelius) 1920-1982 ... 114
Tennov, Dorothy 1928- ... 41-44R
Tennyson, Alfred 1809-1892 ... CDBLB 1832-1890
See also DA
See also DAB
See also DAC
See also DAM MST, POET
See also DLB 32
See also PC 6
See also WLC
Tennyson, Charles (Bruce Locker) 1879-1977 ...
CANR-29
Obituary ... 73-76
Earlier sketch in CA 81-84
Tennyson, Frederick 1807-1898 ... DLB 32
Tennyson, G(eorg) B(ernhard) 1930- ... CANR-9
Earlier sketch in CA 21-24R
Tenpas, Margaret (Susan Lyon) 1923- ... 85-88
Tensen, Ruth M(arjorie) ... 5-8R
Tent, Ned
See Dennett, Herbert Victor
Tenzin, Gyatso
See Gyatso, Tenzin
TePaske, John J(ay) 1929- ... CANR-40
Earlier sketch in CA 117
Teplitz, Paul V(ictor) 1940- ... 111
Tepper, Albert 1928- ... 25-28R
Tepper, Ellen Jean
See Glazer, Ellen Sarasohn
Tepper, Michael 1941- ... CANR-12
Earlier sketch in CA 73-76
Tepper, Sheri S. 1929- ... 137
Tepper, Terri P(atricia) 1942- ... 107
Terada, Alice M. 1928- ... 155
See also SATA 90
Teran, Lisa St. Aubin de
See St. Aubin de Teran, Lisa
See also CLC 36
Terayama, Shuji 1936-1983 Obituary ... 109
Terban, Marvin 1940- ... SATA 54
See also SATA-Brief 45
Terborgh, George (Willard) 1897-1989 ... CAP-2
Obituary ... 128
Earlier sketch in CA 23-24
Terbovich, John B. 1933-1969 ... CAP-2
Earlier sketch in CA 21-22
Terchek, Ronald John 1936- ... 49-52
Terdiman, Richard 1941- ... 73-76
Terence 195(?)B.C.-159B.C. ... DC 7
Terenzio, Stephanie 1932- ... 118
Teresi, Judith M.
See Goldberger, Judith M.
Ter Haar, B. J. 1958- ... 144
ter Haar, Jaap 1922- ... 37-40R
See also Haar, Jaap ter
See also SATA 6
terHorst, J(erald) F(ranklin) 1922- ... 107
Interview in ... 107
See also AITN 1
ter Horst, Robert 1929- ... 116
Terhune, Albert Payson 1872-1942 ... 136
Brief entry ... 111
See also DLB 9
See also MAICYA
See also SATA 15
Terhune, Mary Virginia 1830-1922 ... DLBD 13
Terhune, William B(arclay) 1893-1987 ... 61-64
Obituary ... 122
Terich, Thomas A. 1943- ... 125

Terkel, Louis 1912- CANR-67
Earlier sketches in CA 57-60, CANR-18, 45
See also Terkel, Studs
See also MTCW 1
Terkel, Studs
See Terkel, Louis
See also AITN 1
See also CLC 38
Terkel, Susan N(eiburg) 1948- CANR-38
Earlier sketch in CA 115
See also SATA 59
Terlecki, Tymon Tadeusz J(ulian) 1905- 132
Terlouw, Jan (Cornelis) 1931- 108
See also SATA 30
Terman, Douglas 1933- 136
Brief entry 112
Terman, Sibyl 1902(?)-1975 Obituary 57-60
Terme, Hilary
See Hay, Jacob
Terner, Janet 1938- 102
Terni-Cialente, Fausta 1900- CANR-5
Earlier sketch in CA 5-8R
Terpstra, Vern 1927- CANR-11
Earlier sketch in CA 21-24R
Terr, Lenore (C.) 1936- 134
Terr, Leonard B(rian) 1946- 73-76
Terrace, Edward L. B. 1936(?)-1973 Obituary 45-48
Terrace, Herbert S(ydney) 1936- CANR-43
Earlier sketch in CA 102
Terrace, Vincent 1948- CANR-50
Earlier sketches in CA 65-68, CANR-9, 25
Terraine, John (Alfred) 1921- CANR-13
Earlier sketch in CA 5-8R
Terrall, Robert 1914- 102
Terranova, Elaine 1939- 139
Terras, Victor 1921- 128
Brief entry 113
Terrell, Carroll F(ranklin) 1917- CANR-20
Earlier sketch in CA 102
Terrell, Donna McManus 1908- 57-60
Terrell, John Upton 1900-1988 29-32R
Obituary 127
See also SATA-Obit 60
Terrell, Robert L(ouis) 1943- CANR-17
Earlier sketch in CA 41-44R
Terres, John K(enneth) 1905- CANR-5
Earlier sketch in CA 5-8R
Terrien, Samuel Lucien 1911- 81-84
Terrill, Marshall 1963- 145
Terrill, Ross 1938- CANR-35
Earlier sketch in CA 25-28R
Interview in CANR-35
Terrill, Tom E(dward) 1935- 41-44R
Terris, Susan 1937- CANR-12
Earlier sketch in CA 29-32R
See also JRDA
See also SATA 3, 77
Terris, Virginia R(inaldy) 1917- 65-68
Terry, Arthur 1927- 85-88
Terry, Bill 1931- 118
Terry, C. V.
See Slaughter, Frank G(ill)
Terry, Carol
See Talbot, Carol Terry
Terry, Charles S. 1926(?)-1982 Obituary 107
Terry, Doug(las) 1950- 120
Terry, Edith (Buchanan) 1952- 120
Terry, Edward D(avis) 1927- 29-32R
Terry, Irwin J. 1960- 150
Terry, John V(erlin) 1920- 144
Terry, Luther L(eonidas) 1911-1985 CAP-2
Obituary 115
Earlier sketch in CA 33-36
See also SATA 11
See also SATA-Obit 42
Terry, Margaret
See Dunnahoo, Terry Janson
Terry, Mark 1947- 37-40R
Terry, Marshall 1931- 1-4R
Terry, Megan 1932- CANR-43
Earlier sketch in CA 77-80
See also CABS 3
See also CLC 19
See also DLB 7
Terry, Michael 1899-1981 104
Terry, Robert H(arold) 1935- 29-32R
Terry, Robert Meredith 1939- 41-44R
Terry, Robert W(illiam) 1937- 37-40R
Terry, Sarah Meiklejohn 1937- 111
Terry, Saralee
See Kaye, Marvin (Nathan)
Terry, Walter 1913-1982 CANR-10
Obituary 107
Earlier sketch in CA 21-24R
See also SATA 14
Terry, William
See Harknett, Terry
Terry-Thomas
See Stevens, Thomas Terry Hoar
Terson, Peter 1932- CANR-70
Earlier sketch in CA 104
See also DLB 13
Terstegge, Mabel Alice 1905- 93-96
Tertis, Lionel 1876-1975 93-96
Obituary 57-60
Tertz, Abram
See Sinyavsky, Andrei (Donatevich)
Tervalon, Jervey 1958- 157
Terwilliger, Robert E(lwin) 1917-1991 65-68
Obituary 134
Terzani, Tiziano 1938- CANR-14
Earlier sketch in CA 77-80
Terzian, James P. 1915- 13-16R
See also SATA 14
Terzian, Kathryn
See Cramer, Kathryn
Terzian, Pierre 1948- 136
Terzian, Yervant 1939- 125
TeSelle, Eugene (Arthur, Jr.) 1931- 37-40R
TeSelle, Sallie McFague
See McFague, Sallie
Tesich, Steve 1943(?)-1996 105
Obituary 152
See also CLC 40, 69
See also DLBY 83
Teske, Paul Eric 1958- 152
Tesla, Nikola 1856-1943 157
Teslik, Kennan Lee 1952- 113
Tessa, Delio 1886-1939 DLB 114
Tessendorf, K(enneth) C(harles) 1925- 142
See also SATA 75
Tessier, (Ernst) M(aurice) 1885-1973 CANR-3
Earlier sketch in CA 5-8R
Tessler, Mark A(rnold) 1941- CANR-37
Earlier sketches in CA 45-48, CANR-1, 16
Tessler, Stephanie Gordon 1940- CANR-59
Earlier sketch in CA 124
See also SAAS 26
See also SATA 64, 89
Tester, S. J(im) 1924-1986 140
Tester, Sylvia Root 1939- CANR-8
Earlier sketch in CA 9-12R
See also SATA 64
See also SATA-Brief 37
Testori, Giovanni 1923-1993 DLB 128, 177
Teta, Jon (Anthony) 1933- 25-28R
Tetel, Julie 1950- CANR-42
Earlier sketch in CA 118
Tetel, Marcel 1932- 21-24R
Tetens, Tete Harens 1899(?)-1976 Obituary 65-68
Teternikov, Fyodor Kuzmich 1863-1927 Brief entry 104
See also Sologub, Fyodor
Tether, (Cynthia) Graham 1950- CANR-6
Earlier sketch in CA 57-60
See also SATA 46
See also SATA-Brief 36
Tetlow, Edwin 1905- 17-20R
Tetreault, Wilfred F. 1927- 106
Teubal, Savina J. 1926- 132
Teune, Henry 1936- CANR-3
Earlier sketch in CA 49-52
Teunissen, John James 1933- 112
Teuscher, Robert H(erman) 1934- 77-80
Teveth, Shabtai (Amotz) 1926(?)- 156
Brief entry 117
Tevis, Walter 1928-1984 113
See also CLC 42
Tewkesbury, Joan 1936- 101
Interview in 101
Texon, Meyer 1909- 124
Tey, Josephine
See Mackintosh, Elizabeth
See also DLB 77
See also TCLC 14
Teyber, Edward C. 1950- 141
Teynac, Francoise (Dolores Dupuis) 123
Teyte, Maggie 1888-1976 Obituary 65-68
Tezla, Albert 1915- CANR-57
Earlier sketches in CA 37-40R, CANR-14, 31
Thacher, Alida McKay 1951- CANR-11
Earlier sketch in CA 69-72
Thacher, James 1754-1844 DLB 37
Thacher, John Boyd 1847-1909 DLB 187
Thacher, Mary McGrath 1933- SATA 9
Thacher, Russell 1919(?)-1990 Obituary 132
Thackara, James 1944- 129
Thacker, Eric (Lee) 1923- Brief entry 107
Thacker, Ernest W(ichman) 1914- 13-16R
Thacker, Jonathan W(illiam) 1967- 143
Thacker, Thomas William 1911-1984 Obituary 113
Thackeray, Frank W. 1943- 146
Thackeray, Milton G. 1914- 13-16R
Thackeray, William Makepeace 1811-1863 CDBLB 1832-1890
See also DA
See also DAB
See also DAC
See also DAM MST, NOV
See also DLB 21, 55, 159, 163
See also SATA 23
See also WLC
Thackray, Arnold 1939- 49-52
Thackray, Derek V(incent) 1926- 103
Thackrey, Russell I. 1904- 37-40R
Thackrey, Ted, Jr. 1918- 132
Thaddeus, Janice Farrar 1933- 13-16R
Thaden, Edward Carl 1922- 17-20R
Thagard, Paul 1950- 149
Thain, Chris 1937- 127
Thain, Donald H(ammond) 1928- CANR-25
Earlier sketch in CA 1-4R
Thakur, Shivesh Chandra 1936- 29-32R
Thakura, Ravindranatha
See Tagore, Rabindranath
Thalacker, Donald W(illiam) 1939-1987 127
Brief entry 108
Thalberg, Irving (Grant, Jr.) 1930-1987 41-44R
Obituary 123
Thale, Jerome 1927- 13-16R
Thaler, Alwin 1891- CAP-1
Earlier sketch in CA 11-12
Thaler, M. N.
See Kerner, Fred
Thaler, Michael C. 1936- CANR-61
Earlier sketch in CA 124
See also SATA 56, 93
See also SATA-Brief 47
Thaler, Mike
See Thaler, Michael C.
Thaler, Shmuel 1958- SATA 72
Thaler, Susan 1939- 21-24R
Thalheimer, Ross 1905-1977 41-44R
Thalia
See Bokum, Fanny Butcher
Thalmann, Rita Renee Line 1926- CANR-19
Earlier sketches in CA 53-56, CANR-4
Thamer, Katie
See Treherne, Katie Thamer
Thamer, Katie 1955- SATA 42
Thames, C. H.
See Marlowe, Stephen
Thames, Jack
See Ryan, John Fergus
Thames, Susan 1947- 158
Thamm, Robert 1933- 89-92
Thampi, Parvathi (Menon) 1925- 5-8R
Thane, (Lillian) Adele 1904- 25-28R
Thane, Elswyth 1900-(?) CANR-60
Earlier sketch in CA 5-8R
See also SATA 32
Thanet, Neil
See Fanthorpe, R(obert) Lionel
Thant, U 1909-1974 Obituary 108
Thapar, Romesh 1922- 133
Thapar, Valmik 1952- 139
Tharaud, Lucien Rostaing, Jr. 1953- 69-72
Tharaud, Ross
See Tharaud, Lucien Rostaing, Jr.
Tharoor, Shashi 1956- 141
See also CLC 70
Tharp, Louise (Marshall) Hall 1898- CANR-33
Earlier sketch in CA 1-4R
See also SATA 3
Tharpe, Jac Lyndon 1928-1985 CANR-7
Obituary 117
Earlier sketch in CA 57-60
't Hart, Maarten
See Hart, Martin
t'Hart, Marjolein C. 1955- 146
Tharu, Susie Jacob 1943- 142
Thass-Thienemann, Theodore 1900- 25-28R
Thatcher, David 1922- 77-80
Thatcher, Dora (Fickling) 1912- 13-16R
Thatcher, Dorothy Southwell 1903- CAP-1
Earlier sketch in CA 13-14
Thatcher, Floyd W(ilson) 1917- 102
Thatcher, Joan (Claire) 1934- 106
Thatcher, Julia
See Bensen, Donald R.
Thatcher, Margaret (Hilda) 1925- 147
Thaxton, John 1949- 127
Thaxton, Ralph 1944- 114
Thayer, Caroline Matilda Warren 1785-1844 DLB 200
Thayer, Charles Wheeler 1910-1969 CANR-26
Obituary 103
Earlier sketch in CA 1-4R
Thayer, Emma R(edington) Lee 1874-1973 CAP-1
Obituary 45-48
Earlier sketch in CA 9-10
Thayer, Ernest Lawrence 1865-1940 168
Brief entry 119
See also SATA 60
Thayer, Frederick C(lifton), Jr. 1924- CANR-12
Earlier sketch in CA 73-76
Thayer, George (Chapman, Jr.) 1933-1973 CAP-2
Obituary 45-48
Earlier sketch in CA 25-28
Thayer, Geraldine
See Daniels, Dorothy
Thayer, H(orace) S(tandish) 1923- CANR-27
Earlier sketch in CA 45-48
Thayer, James Stewart 1949- 73-76
Thayer, Jane
See Woolley, Catherine
Thayer, Lee
See Thayer, Emma R(edington) Lee
Thayer, Lee (Osborne) 1927- CANR-18
Earlier sketches in CA 49-52, CANR-3
Thayer, Marjorie -1992 Brief entry 116
See also SATA 74
See also SATA-Brief 37
Thayer, Mary Van Rensselaer 1903(?)-1983 97-100
Obituary 111
Thayer, Molly
See Thayer, Mary Van Rensselaer
Thayer, Nathaniel B(owman) 1929- 45-48
Thayer, Peter
See Wyler, Rose
Thayer, Theodore 1904-1981 Obituary 103
Thayer, V(ivian) T(row) 1886-1979 CAP-2
Obituary 89-92
Earlier sketch in CA 17-18
Thayler, Carl 1933- CANR-69
Earlier sketch in CA 37-40R
See also CAAS 11
Thayne, Emma Lou 1924- 65-68
Thayne, Miria Greenwood 1907- 21-24R
Theakston, Kevin 1958- 127
Theall, Donald Francis 1928- 105
Thebaud, Jo 1914- 49-52
Theberge, James D.
See Theberge, James Daniel
Theberge, James Daniel 1930-1988 25-28R
Obituary 124
Thede, Marion Draughon 1903- CAP-2
Earlier sketch in CA 25-28
Thee, Marek 1918- 101
Theen, Rolf H(einz) W(ilhelm) 1937- 41-44R
Thegan and the Astronomer fl. c. 850- DLB 148
Theil, Henri 1924- CANR-22
Earlier sketches in CA 17-20R, CANR-7
Theiler, Max 1899-1972 164
Theiner, George (Fredric) 1927-1988 CANR-27
Earlier sketch in CA 29-32R
Theis, John William 1911- Brief entry 109
Theis, Paul A(nthony) 1923- 41-44R
Theisen, Jerome Paul 1930- 113
Theissen, Gerd 1943- CANR-41
Earlier sketch in CA 117
Theisz, R. D. 1941- 150
Thekaekara, Matthew P(othen) 1914-1976 77-80
Obituary 69-72
Thelen, David P(aul) 1939- 134
Brief entry 110
Thelen, Gil 1938- 73-76
Thelen, Herbert Arnold 1913- 108
Thelin, John R(obert) 1947- CANR-11
Earlier sketch in CA 69-72
Thelle, Notto R(eidar) 1941- CANR-51
Earlier sketch in CA 125
Thelwall, John 1764-1834 DLB 93, 158
Thelwell, Michael Miles 1939- 101
See also BW 2
See also CLC 22
Thelwell, Norman 1923- CANR-4
Earlier sketch in CA 5-8R
See also SATA 14
Themerson, Stefan 1910-1988 CANR-28
Obituary 126
Earlier sketches in CA 65-68, CANR-9
See also SATA 65
Theo, Ion
See Theodorescu, Ion N.
Theobald, Lewis, Jr.
See Lovecraft, H(oward) P(hillips)
Theobald, Robert 1929- 37-40R
Theobald, William F. 1934- 156
Theocharis, Reghinos D(emetrios) 1929- CANR-11
Earlier sketch in CA 13-16R
Theocritus c. 300B.C.-c. 260B.C. DLB 176
Theodoracopulos, Taki 1937- 129
Theodorakis, Michalis 1925- Brief entry 105
Theodorakis, Mikis
See Theodorakis, Michalis
Theodorakopoulos, Ioannis 1900-1981 Obituary 108
Theodoratus, Robert J(ames) 1928- 41-44R
Theodore, Athena 1919- 41-44R
Theodore, Chris A(thanasios) 1920- 13-16R
Theodore, Sister Mary 1907- 5-8R
Theodorescu, Ion N. 1880-1967 Obituary 116
See also Arghezi, Tudor
Theodorson, George A. 1924- 29-32R
Theodulf c. 760-c. 821 DLB 148
Theoharis, Athan G(eorge) 1936- CANR-56
Earlier sketches in CA 29-32R, CANR-12, 30
Theophrastus c. 371B.C.-287B.C. DLB 176
Theorell, (Per Gunnar) Toeres 1942- 139
Theorell, (Per Gunnar) Tores
See Theorell, (Per Gunnar) Toeres
Theriault, Albert A(ugustine), Jr. 1928- 53-56
Theriault, Joseph-Adrien
See Therio, Adrien
Theriault, Yves 1915-1983 102
See also CLC 79
See also DAC
See also DAM MST
See also DLB 88
Therio, Adrien 1925- 160
See also DLB 53
Thernstrom, Abigail M. 1936- 127
Thernstrom, Stephan (Albert) 1934- 13-16R
Theron, Johan 1924- 140
Theroux, Alexander (Louis) 1939- CANR-63
Earlier sketches in CA 85-88, CANR-20
See also CLC 2, 25
Theroux, Joseph (Peter) 1953- 133
Theroux, Paul (Edward) 1941- CANR-45
Earlier sketches in CA 33-36R, CANR-20
See also BEST 89:4
See also CLC 5, 8, 11, 15, 28, 46
See also DAM POP
See also DLB 2
See also MTCW 1
See also SATA 44
Theroux, Peter (Christopher Sebastian) 1956- 132
Theroux, Phyllis 1939- 110
Thersites
See Bram, Christopher
Thesen, Hjalmar Peter 1925- 107
Thesen, Sharon 1946- 163
See also CLC 56
Thesiger, Wilfred (Patrick) 1910- CAP-2
Earlier sketch in CA 17-18
Thesing, William B(arney) 1947- CANR-32
Earlier sketch in CA 113
Thesman, Jean AAYA 16
See also JRDA
See also SATA 74
Theunissen, Michael 1932- 132
Thevenin, Denis
See Duhamel, Georges
Thevoz, Michel 1936- 132
Thewlis, P(eter) J(ohn) 1944- 127
Thibaudeau, Colleen 1925- 113
See also DLB 88
Thibaudeau, May Murphy 1908- 131
Thibault, Jacques Anatole Francois 1844-1924 127
Brief entry 106
See also France, Anatole
See also DAM NOV
See also MTCW 1
Thibault, John C(rowell) 1922- 77-80
Thibeaud, Wayne 1920- 45-48
Thiebaux, Marcelle 1931- 122
Brief entry 110
Thieda, Shirley Ann 1943- 69-72
See also SATA 13
Thiede, Carsten Peter 1952- 156

Thiele, Colin (Milton) 1920- ... CANR-53
Earlier sketches in CA 29-32R, CANR-12, 28
See also CLC 17
See also CLR 27
See also MAICYA
See also SAAS 2
See also SATA 14, 72
Thiele, Edwin R(ichard) 1895- ... CAP-1
Earlier sketch in CA 19-20
Thiele, Leslie Paul 1959- ... 166
Thiele, Margaret Rossiter 1901- ... 21-24R
Thielen, Benedict 1903-1965 ... DLB 102
Thielen, Thoraf Theodore 1921- ... 5-8R
Thielens, Wagner P., Jr. 1925- ... 1-4R
Thielicke, Helmut 1908-1986 ... CANR-11
Obituary ... 118
Earlier sketch in CA 69-72
Thielman, Jeff(rey D.) 1963- ... 139
Thiem, E(zra) George 1897-1987 ... 134
Obituary ... 123
Thiem, George
See Thiem, E(zra) George
Thiemann, Ronald F. 1946- ... 159
Thien-An, Thich 1926- ... 57-60
Thier, Herbert D(avid) 1932- ... 29-32R
Thierauf, Robert J(ames) 1933- ... CANR-12
Earlier sketch in CA 29-32R
Thiering, Barbara (Elizabeth) 1930- ... 140
Thiesenhusen, William C. 1936- ... 21-24R
Thiesing, Lisa 1958- ... SATA 95
Thiessen, Jack 1931- ... CANR-34
Earlier sketches in CA 41-44R, CANR-15
Thiessen, John
See Thiessen, Jack
Thiessen, John C(aldwell) 1890- ... 5-8R
Thiher, Allen 1941- ... CANR-57
Earlier sketches in CA 41-44R, CANR-14, 31
Thiman, Eric Harding 1900- ... CAP-1
Earlier sketch in CA 13-14
Thimblethorpe, June Sylvia 1926- Brief entry ... 117
Thimm, Alfred L. 1923- ... CANR-8
Earlier sketch in CA 61-64
Thimmesch, Nicholas Palen 1927-1985 .. CANR-28
Obituary ... 116
Earlier sketch in CA 13-16R
Thimmesch, Nick
See Thimmesch, Nicholas Palen
Thirgood, J(ack) V(incent) 1924- ... 127
Thirion, Andre 1907- ... 101
Thirkell, Angela (Margaret) 1890-1961 ... 140
Obituary ... 93-96
Thirkell, John Henry 1913- ... CANR-10
Earlier sketch in CA 13-16R
Thirlwall, John C(onnop, Jr.) 1904- ... 69-72
Thirsk, (Irene) Joan 1922- ... 25-28R
Thiry, Joan (Marie) 1926- ... 121
See also SATA 45
Thisby
See Turner, Dona M.
Thiselton, Anthony C(harles) 1937- ... 145
Thistle, Mel(ville William) 1914- ... 53-56
Thistlethwaite, Miles 1945- ... SATA 12
Thistlethwaite, Susan (Brooks) 1948- ... 127
Thoby-Marcelin, (Emile) Philippe 1904-1975 ... 125
Obituary ... 61-64
See also BW 1
Thody, Philip 1928- ... CANR-9
Earlier sketch in CA 5-8R
Thoene, Alma E(vans) 1903- ... 49-52
Thoene, (William) Brock 1952- ... 167
Thoene, Peter
See Bihalji-Merin, Oto
Thoene, William Brock
See Thoene, (William) Brock
Thoger, Marie 1923- ... CANR-11
Earlier sketch in CA 25-28R
Tholfsen, Trygve R(ainone) 1924- ... 134
Brief entry ... 108
Thollander, Earl 1922- ... CANR-18
Earlier sketch in CA 101
See also SATA 22
Thom, Alexander 1894-1985 ... 133
Thom, James Alexander 1933- ... CANR-64
Earlier sketches in CA 77-80, CANR-15
Thom, Mary 1944- ... 128
Thom, Paul 1941- ... 139
Thom, Rene Frederic 1923- ... 161
Thom, Robert 1929-1979 ... 21-24R
Obituary ... 85-88
Thom, Robert Anderson 1915- ... 61-64
Thom, Valerie M(acLaren) 1929- ... 124
Thoma, Henry F. 1909(?)-1983 Obituary ... 110
Thoma, Ludwig 1867-1921 ... DLB 66
Thoma, Richard 1902- ... 167
See also DLB 4
Thomae, Betty Kennedy 1920- ... 61-64
Thoman, Richard S(amuel) 1919- ... 65-68
Thomaneck, J(uergen) K. A. 1941- ... 132
Thomas, A(rthur) J(oshua), Jr. 1918-1982 ... CANR-10
Earlier sketch in CA 5-8R
Thomas, A(ndrew) R(owland) B(enedick) 1904- ... 65-68
Thomas, Abraham V(azhayil) 1934- ... 61-64
Thomas, Alan (Cedric) 1933- ... 81-84
Thomas, Alan G. 1911- ... 25-28R
Thomas, Alexander 1914- ... 103
Thomas, Andrea
See Hill, Margaret (Ohler)
Thomas, Ann Van Wynen 1919- ... CANR-10
Earlier sketch in CA 5-8R
Thomas, Anna (Irena) 1948- ... CANR-24
Earlier sketch in CA 41-44R
Thomas, Annabel 1929- ... 106
Thomas, Arline 1913-1989 ... 49-52
Obituary ... 128
Thomas, Armstrong 1909(?)-1975 Obituary .. 57-60
Thomas, Art(hur Lawrence) 1952- ... 105
See also SATA 48
See also SATA-Brief 38
Thomas, Audrey (Callahan) 1935- ... CANR-58
Earlier sketches in CA 21-24R, CANR-36
See also CAAS 19
See also AITN 2
See also CLC 7, 13, 37, 107
See also DLB 60
See also MTCW 1
See also SSC 20
Thomas, Barbara L(ee) 1939- ... 145
Thomas, Ben Bowen 1899-1977 Obituary ... 108
Thomas, Bill 1934- ... CANR-8
Earlier sketch in CA 61-64
Thomas, Bob
See Thomas, Robert J(oseph)
Thomas, Brook 1947- ... 139
Thomas, Bruce ... 134
Thomas, Bruce
See Paine, Lauran (Bosworth)
Thomas, Carl H.
See Doerffler, Alfred
Thomas, (Antony) Charles 1928- ... 119
Thomas, Charles W. 1903-1973 Obituary ... 41-44R
Thomas, Charles W(ellington) 1943- ... 65-68
Thomas, Claire Sherman 1923- ... 108
Thomas, Clara (McCandless) 1919- ... 25-28R
Thomas, Clarence 1948- ... 166
Thomas, Conrad Ward 1914- ... 37-40R
Thomas, Cornell 1955- ... 145
Thomas, Craig (David) 1942- ... 112
Brief entry ... 108
Interview in ... 112
Thomas, Cullen
See Kimes, Beverly Rae
Thomas, D(onald) M(ichael) 1935- ... CANR-45
Earlier sketches in CA 61-64, CANR-17
Interview in ... CANR-17
See also CAAS 11
See also CDBLB 1960 to Present
See also CLC 13, 22, 31
See also DLB 40
See also MTCW 1
Thomas, D(avid) O(swald) 1924- ... CANR-41
Earlier sketch in CA 117
Thomas, Dan
See Sanders, Leonard
Thomas, Daniel B.
See Bluestein, Daniel Thomas
Thomas, Daniel H(arrison) 1904- ... 13-16R
Thomas, Danny 1912(?)-1991 ... 143
Thomas, Dante 1922- ... 53-56
Thomas, Dave 1949- ... 152
Brief entry ... 115
Thomas, David 1931- ... 103
Thomas, David 1959- ... 143
Thomas, David A(rthur) 1925- ... 13-16R
Thomas, David H(urst) 1945- ... 108
Thomas, David St. John 1929- ... CANR-30
Earlier sketch in CA 112
Thomas, David Winton 1901-1970 ... CAP-1
Earlier sketch in CA 9-10
Thomas, Denis 1922- ... CANR-34
Earlier sketches in CA 77-80, CANR-15
Thomas, Dian 1945- ... CANR-10
Earlier sketch in CA 65-68
Thomas, Diane Renee 1946(?)-1985 Obituary .. 117
Thomas, Donald 1926- ... 49-52
Thomas, Donald F. 1913- ... 29-32R
Thomas, Donald Roff 1924-1979 Obituary ... 111
Thomas, Dorothy Swaine 1899-1977 ... CAP-2
Obituary ... 69-72
Earlier sketch in CA 17-18
Thomas, Dwight (Rembert) 1944- ... 127
Thomas, Dylan (Marlais) 1914-1953 ... CANR-65
Brief entry ... 104
Earlier sketch in CA 120
See also CDBLB 1945-1960
See also DA
See also DAB
See also DAC
See also DAM DRAM, MST, POET
See also DLB 13, 20, 139
See also MTCW 1
See also PC 2
See also SATA 60
See also SSC 3
See also TCLC 1, 8, 45
See also WLC
Thomas, E(ric) H(ubert) Gwynne
See Gwynne-Thomas, E(ric) H(ubert)
Thomas, Earl W(esley) 1915- ... 53-56
Thomas, Edison H(ugh) 1912- ... 85-88
Thomas, (Philip) Edward 1878-1917 ... 153
Brief entry ... 106
See also DAM POET
See also DLB 19
See also TCLC 10
Thomas, Edward 1878-1917 ... DLB 156
Thomas, Edward Llewellyn
See Llewellyn-Thomas, Edward
Thomas, Edwin J(ohn) 1927- ... 21-24R
Thomas, Egbert S.
See Ellis, Edward S(ylvester)
Thomas, Elizabeth Ann 1952- ... 85-88
Thomas, Elizabeth Marshall 1931- ... 17-20R
Thomas, Emory M. 1939- ... 97-100
Thomas, Ernest Lewys 1904- ... CANR-1
Earlier sketch in CA 1-4R
Thomas, Estelle Webb 1899- ... 21-24R
See also SATA 26
Thomas, Evangeline 1904- ... 117
Thomas, F(ranklin) Richard 1940- ... CANR-55
Earlier sketches in CA 77-80, CANR-13, 29
Thomas, Frances 1943- ... CANR-59
Earlier sketch in CA 130
See also SATA 92
Thomas, Frank P(atrick) 1916- ... 119
Thomas, Frederick William 1806-1866 ... DLB 202
Thomas, G. K.
See Davies, L(eslie) P(urnell)
Thomas, G(regory) Scott 1955- ... 151
Thomas, (Thomas) George 1909- ... 126
Thomas, George Finger 1899-1977 Obituary . 73-76
Thomas, George I. 1915- ... 25-28R
Thomas, George Leicester, Jr. 1907- ... CAP-1
Earlier sketch in CA 11-12
Thomas, Gilbert (Oliver) 1891- ... 5-8R
Thomas, Gordon 1933- ... CANR-40
Earlier sketch in CA 9-12R
Thomas, Gordon L. 1914- ... 37-40R
Thomas, Graham Stuart 1909- ... CANR-41
Earlier sketches in CA 9-12R, CANR-4, 19
Thomas, Gwyn 1913-1981 ... CANR-9
Obituary ... 103
Earlier sketch in CA 65-68
See also DLB 15
Thomas, H. C.
See Keating, Lawrence A.
Thomas, H(ubert) Nigel 1947- ... 148
Thomas, Harold Becken 1888-1971 Obituary .. 104
Thomas, Heather Smith 1944- ... CANR-6
Earlier sketch in CA 57-60
Thomas, Helen A. 1920- ... 101
Thomas, Helen Shirley 1931-1968 ... 5-8R
Obituary ... 103
Thomas, Henri (Joseph Marie) 1912- ... CAP-1
Earlier sketch in CA 9-10
Thomas, Henry 1886-1970 Obituary ... 29-32R
Thomas, Hugh Swynnerton 1931- ... CANR-5
Earlier sketch in CA 9-12R
Thomas, I(saac) D(avid) E(llis) 1921- ... 65-68
Thomas, Ianthe 1951- ... CLR 8
See also SATA-Brief 42
Thomas, Isaiah 1750-1831 ... DLB 43, 73, 187
Thomas, Ivo Herbert Christopher 1912- ... 5-8R
Thomas, J(eremy) A(mbler) 1947- ... 118
Thomas, J. C. ... 57-60
Thomas, J(ames) D(avid) 1910- ... CANR-57
Earlier sketches in CA 57-60, CANR-6, 31
Thomas, J. James 1933- ... 53-56
Thomas, J. W. 1917- ... 101
Thomas, Jack Ray 1931- ... 41-44R
Thomas, Jack W(illiam) 1930- ... CANR-16
Earlier sketches in CA 49-52, CANR-1
Thomas, James H(arold) 1943- ... 119
Thomas, Jane Resh 1936- ... CANR-59
Earlier sketches in CA 106, CANR-24
See also SATA 38, 90
Thomas, Jeannette Grise 1935- ... 101
Thomas, Jerry D. 1959- ... SATA 91
Thomas, Jim
See Reagan, Thomas (James) B(utler)
Thomas, Joan Gale
See Robinson, Joan (Mary) G(ale Thomas)
Thomas, Johann 1624-1679 ... DLB 168
Thomas, John 1890- ... 49-52
Thomas, John Allen Miner 1900-1932 Brief entry ... 107
See also DLB 4
Thomas, John Clayton 1944- ... 139
Thomas, John Hunter 1928- ... 57-60
Thomas, John Lawrence 1910-1991 ... 5-8R
Obituary ... 134
Thomas, Joyce Carol 1938- ... CANR-48
Brief entry ... 113
Earlier sketch in CA 116
Interview in ... 116
See also AAYA 12
See also BW 2
See also CLC 35
See also CLR 19
See also DLB 33
See also JRDA
See also MAICYA
See also MTCW 1
See also SAAS 7
See also SATA 40, 78
Thomas, Julian (Stewart) 1959- ... 143
Thomas, June Manning 1950- ... 166
Thomas, K. H.
See Kirk, T(homas) H(obson)
Thomas, Keith (Vivian) 1933- ... CANR-34
Earlier sketches in CA 37-40R, CANR-15
Thomas, Kenneth Bryn (?)-1978 Obituary ... 81-84
Thomas, Kurt 1956- Brief entry ... 114
Thomas, Kurt 1956- ... 154
Thomas, Latta R(oosevelt) 1927- ... 65-68
Thomas, Lawrence L(eslie) 1924- ... 45-48
Thomas, Lee
See Floren, Lee
Thomas, Lee 1918- ... CANR-1
Earlier sketch in CA 1-4R
Thomas, Leslie (John) 1931- ... CANR-22
Earlier sketch in CA 13-16R
Thomas, Lewis 1913-1993 ... CANR-60
Obituary ... 143
Earlier sketches in CA 85-88, CANR-38
See also CLC 35
See also MTCW 1
Thomas, Lewis H(erbert) 1917-1983 ... CANR-13
Earlier sketch in CA 73-76
Thomas, Lionel H(ugh) C(hristopher) 1922(?)-1978 Obituary ... 104
Thomas, Liz
See Thomas, Elizabeth Ann
Thomas, Lorenzo 1944- ... CANR-25
Earlier sketch in CA 73-76
See also BW 1
See also DLB 41
Thomas, Lowell (Jackson) 1892-1981 ... CANR-3
Obituary ... 104
Earlier sketch in CA 45-48
See also AITN 1, 2
Thomas, Lowell Jackson, Jr. 1923- ... 85-88
See also SATA 15
Thomas, M(ilton) Halsey 1903-1977 ... 25-28R
Obituary ... 73-76
Thomas, Mack
See Womack, Thomas Hale
Thomas, Mack 1928- ... 9-12R
Thomas, Maria
See Worrick, Roberta
Thomas, Marlo 1938- ... 165
Thomas, Mary Martha Hosford 1927- ... 53-56
Thomas, Mason P(age), Jr. 1928- ... CANR-22
Earlier sketch in CA 25-28R
Thomas, Mervyn
See Curran, Mona (Elisa)
Thomas, Michael
See Wilks, Michael Thomas
Thomas, Michael M(ackenzie) 1936- ... 139
Thomas, (William) Miles (Webster) 1897-1980 Obituary ... 105
Thomas, Nicholas (Jeremy) 1960- ... 135
Thomas, Norman (Mattoon) 1884-1968 ... 101
Obituary ... 25-28R
Thomas, Norman C(arl) 1932- ... 17-20R
Thomas, Norman L(ee) 1925- ... 41-44R
Thomas, Owen Clark 1922- ... 9-12R
Thomas, Patricia J. 1934- ... 37-40R
See also SATA 51
Thomas, Paul
See Mann, (Paul) Thomas
Thomas, Paul 1908- ... CANR-22
Earlier sketches in CAP-1, CA 9-10
Thomas, Peter 1928- ... 37-40R
Thomas, Peter Wynne
See Wynne-Thomas, Peter
Thomas, Phillip Drennon 1938- ... 124
Thomas, Phyllis 1935- ... 119
Thomas, Piri 1928- ... 73-76
See also CLC 17
See also HW
Thomas, R. George 1914- ... 146
Thomas, R(ichard) Hinton 1912-1983 ... CANR-5
Obituary ... 110
Earlier sketch in CA 5-8R
Thomas, R(obert) Murray 1921- ... CANR-22
Earlier sketches in CA 17-20R, CANR-7
Thomas, R(onald) S(tuart) 1913- ... CANR-30
Earlier sketch in CA 89-92
See also CAAS 4
See also CDBLB 1960 to Present
See also CLC 6, 13, 48
See also DAB
See also DAM POET
See also DLB 27
See also MTCW 1
Thomas, Richard (Earl) 1951- ... 107
Thomas, Rob ... 164
See also AAYA 25
See also SATA 97
Thomas, Robert 1930- ... 25-28R
Thomas, Robert C(harles) 1925-1993 ... 101
Obituary ... 141
Thomas, Robert J(oseph) 1922- ... CANR-13
Earlier sketch in CA 77-80
Thomas, Rollin G. 1896-(?) ... CAP-1
Earlier sketch in CA 13-16
Thomas, Rosalind 1959- ... 132
Thomas, Rosanne Daryl 1956- ... 143
Thomas, Rosie 1947- ... 133
Brief entry ... 126
Interview in ... 133
Thomas, Ross (Elmore) 1926-1995 ... CANR-63
Obituary ... 150
Earlier sketches in CA 33-36R, CANR-22
See also CLC 39
Thomas, S(idney) Claudewell 1932- ... 17-20R
Thomas, Sara (Sally) 1911(?)-1982 Obituary ... 106
Thomas, Sewell 1884- ... CAP-1
Earlier sketch in CA 9-10
Thomas, Sherilyn 1948- ... CANR-13
Earlier sketch in CA 73-76
Thomas, Sherry
See Thomas, Sherilyn
Thomas, Shirley ... 5-8R
Thomas, Stanley 1933- ... 21-24R
Thomas, Stephen N(aylor) 1942- ... 89-92
Thomas, Sue
See Thomas, Susan-Jane
Thomas, Susan-Jane 1951- ... 143
Thomas, T. M(athai) 1933- ... 53-56
Thomas, Ted
See Thomas, Theodore L.
Thomas, Theodore L. 1920- ... 29-32R
Thomas, Thom 1940- ... 108
Thomas, (Philip) Thomas 1878-1917 ... DLB 98
Thomas, Tony 1947- ... 61-64
Thomas, Vaughan 1934- ... 81-84
Thomas, Vernon (Arthur) 1934- ... SATA 56
Thomas, Victoria
See DeWeese, Thomas Eugene and Kugi, Constance Todd
Thomas, Virginia Castleton
See Castleton, Virginia
Thomas, W(illiam) A(rthur) 1937- ... 127
Thomas, W(alter) Ian 1914- ... 17-20R
Thomas, William 1906- ... 73-76
Thomas, William E(dward) 1942- ... 111
Thomas, William F. 1924- ... 69-72
Thomas, William G(ordan) 1931- ... 93-96
Thomas, William L(eRoy, Jr.) 1920- ... 41-44R
Thomasin von Zerclaere c. 1186-c. 1259 .. DLB 138
Thomasius, Christian 1655-1728 ... DLB 168

Thomasma, David Charles 1939- CANR-44
Earlier sketches in CA 104, CANR-21
Thomasma, Kenneth R. 1930- 155
See also SATA 90
Thomason, A(lan) Mims 1910-1985 Obituary ... 117
Thomason, Burke C(urtis) 1943- 113
Thomason, Tommy 1949- 73-76
Thomassie, Tynia 1959- 156
See also SATA 92
Thometz, Carol Estes 1938- 9-12R
Thomey, Tedd 1920- CANR-2
Earlier sketch in CA 5-8R
Thomis, Malcolm I(an) 1936- Brief entry 118
Thomis, Wayne 1907-1988 Obituary 126
Thomison, Dennis 1937- 53-56
Thomlinson, Ralph 1925- 41-44R
Thommen, George S. 1896- CAP-1
Earlier sketch in CA 13-16
Thompson, A(lbert) Gray 1928- 41-44R
Thompson, A(rthur) L(eonard) B(ell) 1917-1975 ....
CANR-5
Obituary 61-64
Earlier sketch in CA 53-56
Thompson, Alan Eric 1924- 109
Thompson, Anne Armstrong 1939- 85-88
Thompson, Anne Hall Whitt 1930-1996 119
Obituary 155
Thompson, Arthur A., Jr. 1940- 85-88
Thompson, Arthur W(illiam) 1920-1966 .... 1-4R
Thompson, Bard 1925-1987 .... CANR-1
Obituary 123
Earlier sketch in CA 1-4R
Thompson, Betty A(nne) 1926- 111
Thompson, Blanche Jennings 5-8R
Thompson, Brenda 1935- 106
See also SATA 34
Thompson, Brian 1935- 109
Thompson, Buck
See Paine, Lauran (Bosworth)
Thompson, C(lara) Mildred
1881-1975 Obituary 57-60
Thompson, Carol 1951- .... SATA 85
Thompson, Caroline 1956- 110
Thompson, Charles Lowell 1937- CANR-3
Earlier sketch in CA 49-52
Thompson, Charles P. 1933- 147
Thompson, Charles Waters, Jr.
See Thompson, Toby
Thompson, China
See Lewis, Mary (Christianna)
Thompson, Claude Holmes 1908- CAP-1
Earlier sketch in CA 11-12
Thompson, Claudia G(reig) 1953- 142
Thompson, Colin (Edward) 1942- 160
See also SATA 95
Thompson, Corrie 1887- 61-64
Thompson, Craig 1907-1986 Obituary 121
Thompson, Daniel (Calbert) 1916- 13-16R
Thompson, Daniel P(ierce) 1795-1868 .... DLB 202
Thompson, Darcy Wentworth 1860-1948 164
Thompson, David 1770-1857 .... DLB 99
Thompson, David (Bradford) 1938- 57-60
Thompson, David 1953- 127
Thompson, David H(ugh) 1941- 81-84
See also SATA 17
Thompson, Dennis F(rank) 1940- 53-56
Thompson, Dennis L. 1935- 41-44R
Thompson, (Arthur) Denys (Halstead) 1907-1988 ..
CANR-4
Obituary 124
Earlier sketch in CA 9-12R
Thompson, Don(ald Arthur) 1935- 53-56
Thompson, Donald 1928- 140
Thompson, Donald Eugene 1913- 109
Thompson, Donald L(ambert) 1930- 49-52
Thompson, Donald Neil 1939- 37-40R
Thompson, Donnis Stark 1928- 21-24R
Thompson, Dorothy 1894-1961 Obituary 89-92
See also DLB 29
Thompson, Dorothy (Katherine) 1923- 142
Thompson, Duane G(len) 1933- 73-76
Thompson, Earl 1931(?)-1978 85-88
Obituary 81-84
Thompson, Edgar T(ristram) 1900- 17-20R
Thompson, Edward Thorwald 1928- CANR-21
Earlier sketch in CA 105
Thompson, Eileen
See Panowski, Eileen Thompson
Thompson, Elizabeth Allen 1914-1984 119
Thompson, Emma 1959(?)- 154
Thompson, Era Bell 1905-1986 89-92
Obituary 121
See also BW 2
Thompson, Eric
See Thompson, J(ohn) Eric S(idney)
Thompson, (Richard) Ernest 1949- 123
Brief entry 115
Thompson, Ernest Trice 1894-1985 .... 1-4R
Obituary 115
Thompson, Eugene Allen 1924- CANR-26
Earlier sketch in CA 104
Thompson, Evelyn Wingo 1921- 21-24R
Thompson, Ewa M(ajewska) 1937- 49-52
Thompson, Flora (Jane Timms) 1877(?)-1947 Brief
entry 123
Thompson, Frances C(lements) 1906- CAP-1
Earlier sketch in CA 9-10
Thompson, Francis Clegg
See Mencken, H(enry) L(ouis)
Thompson, Francis George 1931- CANR-23
Earlier sketch in CA 106
Thompson, Francis Joseph 1859-1907 Brief
entry 104
See also CDBLB 1890-1914
See also DLB 19
See also TCLC 4
Thompson, Frank H., Jr. 1926- 25-28R
Thompson, Fred 1900-1987 Obituary 121
Thompson, Fred Dalton 1942- 69-72
Thompson, Fred P(riestly), Jr. 1917- 89-92
Thompson, G(ary) R(ichard) 1937- CANR-2
Earlier sketch in CA 45-48
Thompson, Gene
See Thompson, Eugene Allen
Thompson, George Clifford 1920- 104
Thompson, George G(reene) 1914- 21-24R
Thompson, George H(yman) 1923- 125
Brief entry 117
Thompson, George Malcolm
1899-1996 Obituary 152
Thompson, George Selden 1929-1989 ... CANR-37
Obituary 130
Earlier sketches in CA 5-8R, CANR-21
Interview in CANR-21
See also Selden, George
See also MAICYA
See also SATA 4, 73
See also SATA-Obit 63
Thompson, Gerald E(verett) 1924- 53-56
Thompson, Gertrude Caton
See Caton-Thompson, Gertrude
Thompson, Glenda
See Goss, Glenda Dawn
Thompson, Grant P(helps) 1940- 111
Thompson, Gregory Lee 1946- 154
Thompson, Harlan (Howard) 1894-1987 .... CAP-1
Obituary 123
Earlier sketch in CA 9-10
See also SATA 10
See also SATA-Obit 53
Thompson, Harry 1960- 164
Thompson, Harry C. 1921(?)-1980 Obituary . 97-100
Thompson, (Harry) Harwood 1894- 65-68
Thompson, Helen M. (Smith) 1903- CAP-1
Earlier sketch in CA 13-14
Thompson, Henry O(rrin) 1931- CANR-25
Earlier sketch in CA 45-48
Thompson, Henry Yates 1838-1928 ..... DLB 184
Thompson, Hilary 1943- 127
See also SATA 56
See also SATA-Brief 49
Thompson, Hildegard (Steerstedter) 1901- .. 17-20R
Thompson, Hunter S(tockton) 1939- CANR-46
Earlier sketches in CA 17-20R, CANR-23
See also BEST 89:1
See also CLC 9, 17, 40, 104
See also DAM POP
See also DLB 185
See also MTCW 1
Thompson, Ian B(entley) 1936- 37-40R
Thompson, Irene 1919- 110
Thompson, Isabel
See Kelsay, Isabel Thompson
Thompson, J(ohn) Eric S(idney) 1898-1975 .. 65-68
Obituary 61-64
Thompson, J(esse) J(ackson) 1919- 5-8R
Thompson, Jack Maynard 1924- 41-44R
Thompson, Jacqueline 1945- CANR-38
Earlier sketches in CA 97-100, CANR-17
Thompson, James 1902-1983 Obituary 109
Thompson, James 1932- 73-76
Thompson, James Clay 1943- 127
Thompson, James D(avid) 1920-1973 .... CAP-2
Earlier sketch in CA 21-22
Thompson, James H.
See Freeman, G(raydon) L(a Verne)
Thompson, James Myers
See Thompson, Jim (Myers)
Thompson, James W. 1935- 105
Thompson, Janet A(nn) 1944- 150
Thompson, Jean 1950- 136
Thompson, Jeanie 1952- .... CAAS 28
Thompson, Jewel Taylor 1935- 148
Thompson, Jim (Myers) 1906-1977(?) 140
See also CLC 69
Thompson, Joan 1943- 97-100
Thompson, Joan Berengild 1915- 17-20R
Thompson, Joanna Maxwell Pullein
See Pullein-Thompson, Joanna Maxwell
Thompson, Joe Allen 1936- 37-40R
Thompson, Joel A. 1950- 146
Thompson, John (Anderson) 1918- 5-8R
Thompson, John 1938-1976 148
See also DLB 60
Thompson, John Leslie 1917- 5-8R
Thompson, John M(eans) 1926- 129
Thompson, John N. 1951- 154
Thompson, John Reuben 1823-1873 .... DLB 3, 73
Thompson, Josiah 1935- CANR-48
Earlier sketch in CA 41-44R
Thompson, Judith .... CLC 39
Thompson, Judith (Clare Francesca) 1954- 143
Thompson, Julian F(rancis) 1927- CANR-56
Earlier sketches in CA 111, CANR-30
See also AAYA 9
See also CLR 24
See also JRDA
See also MAICYA
See also SAAS 13
See also SATA 55, 99
See also SATA-Brief 40
Thompson, Julius Eric 1946- 49-52
Thompson, K(athryn Carolyn) Dyble 1952- ... SATA
82
Thompson, Karl F. 1917- 37-40R
Thompson, Kay 1912(?)- 85-88
See also CLR 22
See also MAICYA
See also SATA 16
Thompson, Ken D(avid) 1926- 65-68
Thompson, Kenneth W(infred) 1921- CANR-54
Earlier sketches in CA 9-12R, CANR-5, 29
Thompson, Kent 1936- 49-52
Thompson, Kristin 1950- CANR-25
Earlier sketch in CA 108
Thompson, Laura (Maud) 1905- 53-56
Thompson, Laurence C(assius) 1926- CANR-7
Earlier sketch in CA 5-8R
Thompson, Laurence G(raham) 1920- 37-40R
Thompson, Lawrance (Roger) 1906-1973 ....
CANR-10
Obituary 41-44R
Earlier sketch in CA 5-8R
See also DLB 103
Thompson, Lawrence Sidney 1916-1986 .. CANR-5
Obituary 121
Earlier sketch in CA 9-12R
Thompson, Leon (Whitey) 1923- 145
Thompson, Leonard Monteath 1916- CANR-16
Earlier sketches in CA 1-4R, CANR-1
Thompson, Lewis 1915(?)-1972 Obituary ... 37-40R
Thompson, Lloyd A(rthur) 1932-1997 137
Obituary 160
Thompson, Loring M(oore) 1918- 45-48
Thompson, Luther Joe 1918- 21-24R
Thompson, M(ichael) W(elman) 1928- CANR-65
Earlier sketch in CA 128
Thompson, Marian Spitzer
1899(?)-1983 Obituary 110
Thompson, Mark 1952- 142
Thompson, Mark L. 1945- 137
Thompson, Mary Wolfe 1886- 107
Thompson, Maurice 1844-1901 .... DLB 71, 74
Thompson, Mel(vin R.) 1929- 73-76
Thompson, Morris Mordecai 1912- 109
Thompson, Neil 1929- 108
Thompson, Neville 1938- 37-40R
Thompson, Noel W. 1951- 123
Thompson, Paul (Richard) 1935- CANR-38
Earlier sketches in CA 21-24R, CANR-16
Thompson, Paul 1943- CANR-32
Earlier sketches in CA 77-80, CANR-14
Thompson, Phyllis Hoge 1926- CANR-36
Earlier sketches in CA 29-32R, CANR-13
Thompson, Ralph 1904-1979 Obituary 89-92
Thompson, (William) Ralph 1910- 53-56
Thompson, Randall 1899-1984 Obituary 113
Thompson, Richard 1924- 9-12R
Thompson, Richard A(rlen) 1930- 61-64
Thompson, Robert (Grainger Ker) 1916- 49-52
Thompson, Robert Elliott 1921- 77-80
See also AITN 2
Thompson, Robert Farris 1932- 103
Thompson, Robert Norman 1914- 106
Thompson, Robert Sidney 1918- 111
Thompson, Roger Francis 1933- CANR-13
Earlier sketch in CA 73-76
Thompson, Roy Anton 1897- CAP-2
Earlier sketch in CA 29-32
Thompson, Russ
See Paine, Lauran (Bosworth)
Thompson, Ruth Plumly 1891-1976 134
Obituary 113
See also DLB 22
See also SATA 66
Thompson, Samuel M(artin)
1902-1983 Obituary 110
Thompson, Sandra (Jean) 1943- 121
Thompson, Stanbury Dugard 1905- CAP-1
Earlier sketch in CA 11-12
Thompson, Steven L(ynn) 1948- 114
Thompson, Stith 1885-1976 .... CANR-5
Obituary 61-64
Earlier sketch in CA 5-8R
See also SATA 57
See also SATA-Obit 20
Thompson, Susan (Ayers) 1946- 132
Thompson, Susan L. 1945- 114
Thompson, Susan O(tis) 1931- 85-88
Thompson, Sylvia
See Thompson, Sylvia (Vaughn Sheekman)
Thompson, Sylvia (Vaughn Sheekman) 1935- .....
CANR-51
Earlier sketches in CA 5-8R, CANR-26
Thompson, Thomas 1933-1982 .... CANR-14
Obituary 108
Earlier sketch in CA 65-68
Thompson, Thomas Kirkland 1914- 13-16R
Thompson, Thomas L. 1939- 146
Thompson, Thomas Phillips 1843-1933 .... DLB 99
Thompson, Toby 1944- 65-68
Thompson, Tracy 1955(?)- 152
Thompson, Travis I. 1937- 37-40R
Thompson, Victor A(lexander) 1912- 25-28R
Thompson, Virginia
See Adloff, Virginia Thompson
Thompson, Virginia 1937- 108
Thompson, Vivian L(aubach) 1911- CANR-1
Earlier sketch in CA 1-4R
See also SATA 3
Thompson, W. Grant 1935- 146
Thompson, W(illard) Scott 1942- CANR-12
Earlier sketch in CA 25-28R
Thompson, Wayne C(urtis) 1943- 109
Thompson, Wayne N. 1914- 21-24R
Thompson, Wilbur R(ichard) 1923- 13-16R
Thompson, Willa 1916- 9-12R
Thompson, Willard Mead 1913- 5-8R
Thompson, William 1775-1833 .... DLB 158
Thompson, William A(ncker) 1931- 77-80
Thompson, William Bernard 1914- CAP-1
Earlier sketch in CA 9-10
Thompson, William C. L.
See Edwards, William B(ennett)
Thompson, William D. 1929- 17-20R
Thompson, William E(llison), Jr. 1923- 13-16R
Thompson, William Fletcher, Jr. 1929- 1-4R
Thompson, William Irwin 1938- CANR-66
Earlier sketches in CA 21-24R, CANR-9
Thompson, William J. 1939- 146
Thompson, William N. 1940- 135
Thompson, William Tappan 1812-1882 .. DLB 3, 11
Thompson, Wolfe
See Thompson, Mary Wolfe
Thompson-Frey, Nancy 1955- 127
Thoms, Herbert 1885-1972 Obituary 110
Thomsen, Harry 1928- 5-8R
Thomsen, Moritz 1915- 29-32R
Thomsen, Robert 1915(?)-1983 Obituary 117
Thomsen, Russel J(ohn) 1941- 37-40R
Thomsett, Michael C. 1948- 119
Thomson, Alistair 1960- 151
Thomson, Arthur Alexander (Malcolm) 1894-1969 ..
CAP-1
Earlier sketch in CA 11-12
Thomson, Basil (Home) 1861-1939 Brief entry . 110
Thomson, Beatrix 1900-1986 Obituary 120
Thomson, Betty Flanders 1913- 9-12R
Thomson, C(harles) Leslie 1914- 9-12R
Thomson, Daisy H(icks) 1918- CANR-20
Earlier sketch in CA 103
Thomson, Dale C(airns) 1923- 25-28R
Thomson, David 1912-1970 .... CANR-2
Obituary 29-32R
Earlier sketch in CA 1-4R
Thomson, David (Robert Alexander) 1914-1988 ....
CANR-24
Obituary 124
Earlier sketch in CA 107
See also SATA 40
See also SATA-Obit 55
Thomson, Derick S(mith) 1921- CANR-12
Earlier sketch in CA 25-28R
Thomson, Douglas Ferguson Scott 1919- ... 41-44R
Thomson, Edward
See Tubb, E(dwin) C(harles)
Thomson, Edward William 1849-1924 ...... DLB 92
Thomson, Elizabeth
See Thomson, Elizabeth M.
Thomson, Elizabeth M. 1957- 127
Thomson, F(rancis) P(aul) 1914- 21-24R
Thomson, Frank S(elee) 1881-1975 57-60
Thomson, Garry 1925- 109
Thomson, George Derwent
1903-1987 Obituary 121
Thomson, George H(enry) 1924- 21-24R
Thomson, George Malcolm 1899- 9-12R
Thomson, George Paget 1892-1975 ...... CANR-4
Obituary 61-64
Earlier sketch in CA 5-8R
Thomson, (George) Ian F(alconer)
1912-1987 .... 9-12R
Obituary 122
Thomson, Irene Taviss 1941- 29-32R
Thomson, James 1700-1748 .... DAM POET
See also DLB 95
Thomson, James 1834-1882 .... DAM POET
See also DLB 35
Thomson, James C(laude), Jr. 1931- CANR-32
Earlier sketch in CA 29-32R
Thomson, James C(utting) 1909- 61-64
Thomson, James Miln 1921- 109
Thomson, Joan
See Charnock, Joan
Thomson, John (Edward Palmer) 1936- 109
Thomson, John A(idan) F(rancis) 1934- 132
Thomson, John W(illiam) 1940- 125
Thomson, Jonathan H.
See Thomson, Daisy H(icks)
Thomson, Joseph 1858-1895 .... DLB 174
Thomson, June (Valerie) 1930- CANR-44
Earlier sketches in CA 81-84, CANR-21
Interview in CANR-21
Thomson, Keith 1912- 29-32R
Thomson, Liz
See Thomson, Elizabeth M.
Thomson, Mortimer 1831-1875 .... DLB 11
Thomson, Pat 1939- 146
See also SATA 77
Thomson, Peggy 1922- 85-88
See also SATA 31
Thomson, Peter 1913- 5-8R
Thomson, Peter (William) 1938- 108
Thomson, Randall J(oseph) 1946- 109
Thomson, Robert 1921- 25-28R
Thomson, Robert 1943- 122
Thomson, Robert (James) 1961- 127
Thomson, Robert W(illiam) 1934- CANR-21
Earlier sketch in CA 104
Thomson, Ronald William 1908- 25-28R
Thomson, Roy Herbert 1894-1976 Obituary .. 69-72
Thomson, S(amuel) Harrison 1895-1975 ... 41-44R
Obituary 61-64
Thomson, Virgil (Garnett) 1896-1989 .... 41-44R
Obituary 129
Thomson, William 1927- 141
Thomson, William A. 1879-1971 Obituary .. 33-36R
Thomson, William A(rchibald) R(obson)
1906-1983 103
Obituary 111
Thomy, Al(fred Marshall) 69-72
Thon, Melanie Rae 1957- CANR-72
Earlier sketch in CA 134
Thondup, Tulku 1939- 159
Thonssen, Lester 1904- 5-8R
Thorat, Sudhakar S. 1935- CANR-29
Earlier sketch in CA 45-48
Thorburn, David 1940- CANR-7
Earlier sketch in CA 53-56
Thorburn, Hugh G(arnet) 1924- 13-16R
Thorburn, John
See Goldsmith, John Herman Thorburn

Thoreau, Henry David 1817-1862 ... CDALB 1640-1865
See also DA
See also DAB
See also DAC
See also DAM MST
See also DLB 1
See also WLC
Thorelli, Hans B(irger) 1921- ... CANR-6
Earlier sketch in CA 13-16R
Thoren, Arne 1927- ... 69-72
Thoresen, Carl E. 1933- ... 57-60
Thorez, Maurice 1900-1964 Obituary ... 113
Thorlby, Anthony K. 1928- ... 25-28R
Thormaehlen, Marianne 1949- ... 143
Thormahlen, Marianne
See Thormaehlen, Marianne
Thorman, Donald J. 1924-1977 ... 17-20R
Obituary ... 73-76
Thorman, Richard 1924- ... 105
Thorn, Barbara
See Paine, Lauran (Bosworth)
Thorn, John 1947- ... CANR-17
Earlier sketch in CA 97-100
See also SATA 59
Thorn, Richard S(emour) 1929- ... 17-20R
Thorn, Ronald Scott
See Wilkinson, Ronald
Thorn, William E. 1923- ... 9-12R
Thornber, Jean H(ewitt) 1919- ... 61-64
Thornbrook, Bill
See Turnbaugh, William A(rthur)
Thornbrough, Emma Lou ... 25-28R
Thornburg, Hershel D(ean) 1936-1987 ... CANR-14
Obituary ... 121
Earlier sketch in CA 37-40R
Thornburg, Newton K(endall) 1930- ... CANR-71
Earlier sketches in CA 21-24R, CANR-9
Thorndike, A.
See Thorndike, A(nthony) E(dward)
Thorndike, A(nthony) E(dward) 1941- ... 117
Thorndike, E. L.
See Thorndike, Edward L(ee)
Thorndike, Edward L(ee) 1874-1949 Brief entry ... 121
Thorndike, John 1942- ... 153
Thorndike, Joseph J(acobs), Jr. 1913- Brief entry ... 117
Thorndike, (Everett) Lynn 1882-1965 Obituary ... 111
Thorndike, Robert Ladd 1910-1990 ... CANR-1
Obituary ... 132
Earlier sketch in CA 1-4R
Thorndike, (Arthur) Russell 1885-1972 Obituary ... 37-40R
Thorndike, Susan 1944- ... 41-44R
Thorndike, Tony
See Thorndike, A(nthony) E(dward)
Thorndyke, Helen Louise ... CANR-27
Earlier sketches in CAP-2, CA 19-20
See also Benson, Mildred (Augustine Wirt)
See also SATA 1, 67
Thorne, Alice Dunn 1910-1973 Obituary ... 45-48
Thorne, Barrie 1942- ... 143
Thorne, Bliss K(irby) 1916- ... 17-20R
Thorne, Bradley D.
See Glut, Donald F(rank)
Thorne, Christopher 1934-1992 ... CANR-29
Obituary ... 137
Earlier sketches in CA 21-24R, CANR-11
Thorne, Florence Calvert 1878(?)-1973 Obituary ... 41-44R
Thorne, Hart
See Carhart, Arthur Hawthorne
Thorne, Hooper
See Sage, (Frank) Norman
Thorne, Ian
See May, Julian
Thorne, Jean Wright
See May, Julian
Thorne, Jim 1922- ... CANR-1
Earlier sketch in CA 1-4R
Thorne, John (H.) 1943- ... 136
Thorne, Kip S. 1940- ... 144
Thorne, Nicola
See Ellerbeck, Rosemary (Anne L'Estrange)
Thorne, Ramsay
See Cameron, Lou
Thorne, Ron
See Thorne-Finch, Ron(ald Barry)
Thorne, Sabina 1927- ... 106
Thorne, Sterling
See Fuller, Dorothy Mason
Thorne, William James 1898- ... 5-8R
Thorne-Finch, Ron(ald Barry) 1958- ... 146
Thornhill, Alan 1907(?)-1988 Obituary ... 127
Thornhill, Jan 1955- ... SATA 77
Thorning, Joseph F(rancis) 1896-1985 ... CAP-1
Obituary ... 115
Earlier sketch in CA 9-10
Thornley, Diann 1957- ... 164
Thornley, Richard 1950- ... 117
Thornley, Stew 1955- ... 139
Thornton, Big Mama
See Thornton, Willie Mae
Thornton, Billy Bob 1955- ... 168
Thornton, Bruce S. 1953- ... 165
Thornton, Emma Shore 1908- ... 114
Thornton, Francis John 1938- ... 85-88
Thornton, Gene ... 93-96
Thornton, Hall
See Silverberg, Robert
Thornton, Ian 1926- ... 154
Thornton, J(onathan) Mills III 1943- ... 77-80
Thornton, James W., Jr. 1908- ... CANR-1
Earlier sketch in CA 1-4R
Thornton, Jerry
See Thornton, Emma Shore
Thornton, John Leonard 1913- ... CANR-4
Earlier sketch in CA 9-12R
Thornton, John W(illiam), Jr. 1948- ... 106
Thornton, John W(illiam) 1922- ... 106
Thornton, Lawrence 1937- ... 132
Thornton, Lee 1944- ... 73-76
Thornton, Margaret ... 139
Thornton, Mark 1960- ... 141
Thornton, Martin (Stuart Farrin) 1915- ... 9-12R
Thornton, Michael 1941- ... 105
Thornton, Peter (Kai) 1925- ... CANR-43
Earlier sketches in CA 102, CANR-20
Thornton, R(obert) K(elsey) R(ought) 1938- ... 119
Thornton, Ralph 1922(?)-1989 Obituary ... 129
Thornton, Richard C. 1936- ... 81-84
Thornton, Robert J(ames) 1949- ... 148
Thornton, Thomas Perry 1931- ... 9-12R
Thornton, W. B.
See Burgess, Thornton Waldo
Thornton, Weldon 1934- ... 25-28R
Thornton, Willie Mae 1926-1984 Obituary ... 113
Thornton, Willis 1900- ... CAP-1
Earlier sketch in CA 13-16
Thornton, Yvonne S(hirley) 1947- ... 153
See also SATA 96
Thorp, Duncan Roy 1914- ... 13-16R
Thorp, Edward O. 1932- ... 21-24R
Thorp, John 1947- ... 133
Thorp, Margaret Farrand 1891-1970 Obituary ... 104
Thorp, Roderick Mayne, Jr. 1936- ... CANR-46
Earlier sketches in CA 1-4R, CANR-6
Thorp, Willard 1899-1990 ... CANR-3
Obituary ... 130
Earlier sketch in CA 5-8R
Thorp, Willard Long 1899-1992 ... CANR-28
Obituary ... 137
Earlier sketch in CA 1-4R
Thorpe, Adam 1956- ... 129
Thorpe, D. R. 1943- ... CANR-68
Earlier sketch in CA 129
Thorpe, Donald W(illiam) 1928- ... 29-32R
Thorpe, E(ustace) G(eorge) 1916- ... 9-12R
See also SATA 21
Thorpe, Earl(ie) E(ndris) 1924- ... 61-64
Thorpe, Elliott R(aymond) 1897-1989 ... 65-68
Obituary ... 129
Thorpe, George P. 1913(?)-1983 Obituary ... 110
Thorpe, J. K.
See Nathanson, Laura Walther
Thorpe, James 1915- ... CANR-17
Earlier sketches in CA 5-8R, CANR-2
Thorpe, Lewis (Guy Melville) 1913-1977 ... CANR-10
Earlier sketch in CA 9-12R
Thorpe, Louis P(eter) 1893- ... CANR-20
Earlier sketch in CA 1-4R
Thorpe, Michael 1932- ... CANR-55
Earlier sketches in CA 21-24R, CANR-8
Thorpe, Peter 1932- ... 57-60
Thorpe, Sylvia
See Thimblethorpe, June Sylvia
Thorpe, Thomas Bangs 1815-1878 ... DLB 3, 11
Thorpe, Trebor
See Fanthorpe, R(obert) Lionel
Thorpe, Trevor
See Fanthorpe, R(obert) Lionel
Thorpe, William Homan 1902-1986 ... CANR-2
Obituary ... 119
Earlier sketch in CA 5-8R
Thorsell, Richard Lawrence 1938- ... 89-92
Thorsley, Peter L(arsen), Jr. 1929- ... 5-8R
Thorson, John E. 1946- ... 150
Thorson, Thomas Landon 1934- ... 17-20R
Thorstad, David 1941- ... 57-60
Thorstein, Eric
See Merril, Judith
Thorup, Kirsten 1942- ... 127
Brief entry ... 125
Thorvall, Kerstin 1925- ... CANR-13
Earlier sketch in CA 17-20R
See also SATA 13
Thorvall-Falk, Kerstin
See Thorvall, Kerstin
Thorwald, Juergen 1916- ... CANR-21
Earlier sketches in CA 49-52, CANR-1
Thouless, Robert H(enry) 1894-1984 ... 77-80
Obituary ... 114
Thrapp, Dan Lincoln 1913-1994 ... CANR-4
Obituary ... 145
Earlier sketch in CA 9-12R
Thrasher, Crystal (Faye) 1921- ... CANR-8
Earlier sketch in CA 61-64
See also SATA 27
Threadgall, Colin 1941- ... SATA 77
Threlkeld, Richard 1937- ... 65-68
Thresher, B(rainard) Alden 1896-1984 Obituary ... 111
Thribb, E. J.
See Fantoni, Barry (Ernest)
Thring, M(eredith) W(ooldridge) 1915- ... 130
Throckmorton, Burton Hamilton, Jr. 1921- ... 5-8R
Throckmorton, Peter 1928-1990 ... 17-20R
Obituary ... 131
Throneberry, Jimmy B. 1933- ... 89-92
Throneburg, James ... 5-8R
Thrower, Norman J(oseph) W(illiam) 1919- ... 41-44R
Thrower, Percy John 1913-1988 ... CANR-4
Obituary ... 125
Earlier sketch in CA 9-12R
Thruelsen, Richard (Delmar) 1908-1989 Obituary ... 129
Thubron, Colin (Gerald Dryden) 1939- ... CANR-59
Earlier sketches in CA 25-28R, CANR-12, 29
Thubten, Sigme Norbu 1922- Brief entry ... 109
Thucydides c. 455B.C.-399B.C. ... DLB 176
Thuemmel, Moritz August von 1738-1817 ... DLB 97
Thuery, Jacques (H. A.) 1951- ... 143
Thuesen, Gerald J(organ) 1938- ... 37-40R
Thuillier, Jacques 1928- ... CANR-7
Earlier sketch in CA 9-12R
Thulstrup, Niels 1924- ... CANR-26
Earlier sketches in CA 21-24R, CANR-10
Thum, Gladys 1920- ... 41-44R
See also SATA 26
Thum, Marcella ... CANR-49
Earlier sketches in CA 9-12R, CANR-6, 21
See also SATA 3, 28
Thumann, Albert 1942- ... 139
Thumm, Garold W(esley) 1915- ... 13-16R
Thuna, Lee
See Thuna, Leonora
Thuna, Leonora 1929- ... CANR-16
Earlier sketch in CA 21-24R
Thundercloud, Katherine
See Witt, Shirley Hill
Thunder-Traveling-Over-The-Mountains
See Chief Joseph
Thundy, Zacharias Pontian 1936- ... 102
Thundyil, Zacharias Pontian
See Thundy, Zacharias Pontian
Thurber, Helen (Wismer) 1902(?)-1986 ... 152
Obituary ... 121
Thurber, James (Grover) 1894-1961 ... CANR-39
Earlier sketches in CA 73-76, CANR-17
See also CDALB 1929-1941
See also CLC 5, 11, 25
See also DA
See also DAB
See also DAC
See also DAM DRAM, MST, NOV
See also DLB 4, 11, 22, 102
See also MAICYA
See also MTCW 1
See also SATA 13
See also SSC 1
Thurber, Walter A(rthur) 1908- ... CANR-12
Earlier sketch in CA 21-24R
Thurian, Max 1921- ... 129
Thurkettle, James 1929- ... 69-72
Thurley, Geoffrey John 1936- ... CANR-13
Earlier sketch in CA 61-64
Thurley, Jon (Mark) ... CANR-42
Earlier sketch in CA 118
Thurley, Simon 1962- ... 146
Thurlow, David (Michael) 1932- ... 134
Thurm, Marian ... 168
Thurman, Christa C(harlotte) Mayer 1934- ... CANR-2
Earlier sketch in CA 49-52
Thurman, Howard 1900-1981 ... CANR-25
Obituary ... 103
Earlier sketch in CA 97-100
See also BW 1
Thurman, Judith 1946- ... CANR-1
Earlier sketch in CA 49-52
See also SATA 33
Thurman, Kelly 1914- ... 57-60
Thurman, Mark (Gordon Ian) 1948- ... 131
See also SATA 63
Thurman, Wallace (Henry) 1902-1934 ... 124
Brief entry ... 104
See also BLC 3
See also BW 1
See also DAM MULT
See also DLB 51
See also TCLC 6
Thurman, Wayne L(averne) 1923- ... 49-52
Thurmond, Nancy Moore 1946- ... 132
Brief entry ... 114
Thurmond, (J.) Strom 1902- ... 89-92
Thurow, Lester C(arl) 1938- ... CANR-45
Earlier sketch in CA 81-84
Thursby, Vincent Victor 1918- ... 41-44R
Thurstan, Violetta ... CAP-1
Earlier sketch in CA 13-16
Thurston, Carol (M.) ... 126
Thurston, David B. 1918- ... CANR-6
Earlier sketch in CA 5-8R
Thurston, Elliott Ladd 1895-1975 Obituary ... 89-92
Thurston, H. D.
See Thurston, H. David
Thurston, H. David 1927- ... 143
Thurston, Harry 1950- ... CANR-32
Earlier sketch in CA 113
Thurston, Hazel (Patricia) 1906- ... 57-60
Thurston, Jarvis 1914- ... 13-16R
Thurston, Lorrin P. 1900(?)-1984 Obituary ... 114
Thurston, Robert (Donald) 1936- ... CANR-15
Earlier sketch in CA 85-88
Thut, I(saac) N(oah) ... CAP-1
Earlier sketch in CA 13-16
Thwaite, Ann (Barbara Harrop) 1932- ... CANR-41
Earlier sketch in CA 5-8R
See also SATA 14
Thwaite, Anthony (Simon) 1930- ... CANR-41
Earlier sketch in CA 5-8R
See also DLB 40
Thwaite, M(ary) F. (Austin) ... 21-24R
Thwaites, Michael 1915- ... 77-80
Thwaites, Reuben Gold 1853-1913 ... 159
See also DLB 47
Thwing, Leroy (L.) 1879- ... 5-8R
Thybony, Scott 1948- ... 146
Thygerson, Alton L(uie) 1940- ... CANR-39
Earlier sketches in CA 45-48, CANR-1, 18
Thynn, Alexander (George) 1932- ... 132
Thynne, Alexander
See Thynn, Alexander (George)
Tiant, Luis 1940- ... 73-76
(al-)Tibawi, A(bdul-)L(atif) 1910-1981 ... CANR-24
Obituary ... 105
Earlier sketch in CA 25-28R
Tibber, Robert
See Friedman, (Eve) Rosemary (Tibber)
Tibber, Rosemary
See Friedman, (Eve) Rosemary (Tibber)
Tibbets, Albert B. 1888- ... 5-8R
Tibbetts, Arnold M(acLean) 1927- ... CANR-16
Earlier sketch in CA 93-96
Tibbetts, Charlene 1921- ... 93-96
Tibbetts, John C(arter) 1946- ... 89-92
Tibbetts, John W(esley) 1928- ... 25-28R
Tibbetts, Norris L. 1892(?)-1983 Obituary ... 108
Tibbetts, Orlando L(ailer), Jr. 1919- ... CANR-11
Earlier sketch in CA 29-32R
Tibbetts, William
See Brannon, William T.
Tibble, Anne 1912-1980 ... CANR-10
Obituary ... 102
Earlier sketch in CA 9-12R
Tibbs, Ben 1907- ... 61-64
Tibbs, Virginia M.
See Scott, Virginia M(uhleman)
Tiber, Elliot 1935- ... 129
Tibi, Bassam 1944- ... 130
Tibo, Gilles 1951- ... 136
See also SATA 67
Tiburzi, Bonnie 1948- ... 136
See also SATA 65
Tice, George A(ndrew) 1938- ... CANR-12
Earlier sketch in CA 61-64
Ticheburn, Cheviot
See Ainsworth, William Harrison
Tichenor, Tom 1923- ... 29-32R
See also SATA 14
Tichi, Cecelia 1942- ... 104
Tichnor, Richard 1959- ... SATA 90
Tichy, H(enrietta) J. 1912- ... 21-24R
Tichy, Susan (Elizabeth) 1952- ... 123
Tichy, William 1924- ... 107
See also SATA 31
Tickell, Renee Oriana Haynes
See Haynes, Renee (Oriana Tickell)
Tickle, P(hyllis) A(lexander) 1934- ... CANR-49
Earlier sketches in CA 65-68, CANR-9, 24
Tickner, Fred(erick James) 1902- ... CAP-1
Earlier sketch in CA 9-10
Tickner, Lisa 1944- ... 128
Ticknor, George 1791-1871 ... DLB 1, 59, 140
Tidball, Derek J(ohn) 1948- ... 120
Tidy, Michael 1943- ... 113
Tidyman, Ernest 1928-1984 ... CANR-29
Obituary ... 113
Earlier sketch in CA 73-76
Tieck, (Johann) Ludwig 1773-1853 ... DLB 90
See also SSC 31
Tiede, Tom (Robert) 1937- ... 25-28R
Tiedt, Iris M(cClellan) 1928- ... CANR-49
Earlier sketches in CA 13-16R, CANR-7, 24
Tiedt, Sidney W(illis) 1927- ... CANR-24
Earlier sketch in CA 13-16R
Tiegreen, Alan F. 1935- ... SATA 94
See also SATA-Brief 36
Tiempo, Edith (Lopez) 1919- ... 104
Tien, H. Yuan 1926- ... 49-52
Tien, Hung-Mao 1938- ... 73-76
Tierney, Brian 1922- ... 103
Tierney, Frank M. 1930- ... SATA 54
Tierney, Gene 1920- Brief entry ... 116
Tierney, Helen 1928- ... 142
Tierney, John Lawrence 1892-1972 ... CAP-2
Earlier sketch in CA 21-22
Tierney, Kevin (Hugh) 1942- ... CANR-26
Earlier sketch in CA 29-32R
Tierney, M. Leo 1932(?)-1986 Obituary ... 118
Tierney, Michael 1894-1975 Obituary ... 114
Tierney, Neil 1913- ... 145
Tierney, Paul Ambrose 1895(?)-1979 Obituary ... 85-88
Tierney, Richard L(ouis) 1936- ... 111
Tierney, Ronald 1944- ... 140
Tierney, Tom 1928- ... CANR-47
Earlier sketches in CA 57-60, CANR-8, 23
Tiersky, Ronald S. 1944- ... 118
Tietenberg, T(homas) H(arry) 1942- ... 143
Tietjens, Eunice 1884-1944 ... DLB 54
Tietze, Andreas 1914- ... 49-52
Tietze, Christopher 1908-1984 Obituary ... 112
Tiffany, Donald Wayne 1930- Brief entry ... 108
Tiffany, E. A. 1911- ... 103
Tiffany, Phyllis G. 1932- ... 37-40R
Tiffany, William R(obert) 1920- ... 5-8R
Tiffault, Benette W. 1955- ... SATA 77
Tiffin, Joseph 1905- ... 17-20R
Tifft, Ellen ... CANR-1
Earlier sketch in CA 49-52
Tifft, Susan E. 1951- ... 135
Tifton, Leo
See Page, Gerald W(ilburn)
Tigar, Michael E(dward) 1941- ... 77-80
Tigay, Alan M(errill) 1947- ... 124
Tiger, Derry
See Ellison, Harlan (Jay)
Tiger, Jack
See Puechner, Ray
Tiger, John
See Wager, Walter H(erman)
Tiger, Lionel 1937- ... CANR-14
Earlier sketch in CA 25-28R
Tiger, Madeline 1934- ... CANR-42
Tiger, Virginia Marie 1940- Brief entry ... 106
Tigerman, Stanley 1930- ... CANR-36
Earlier sketch in CA 114
Tiger of the Snows
See Norgay, Tenzing
Tighe, Donald J. 1928- ... 29-32R
Tighe, Thomas B. 1907(?)-1983 Obituary ... 109

Tignor, Robert L(ee) 1933- 134
Brief entry 109
Tigue, Ethel Erkkila 1918- 21-24R
Tikhonov, Nikolai Semyonovich
1896-1979 Obituary 85-88
Tikhonov, Valentin
See Payne, (Pierre Stephen) Robert
Tikku, Girdhari L(al) 1925- 45-48
Tiktin, Carl 1930- CANR-13
Earlier sketch in CA 73-76
Tilden, Freeman 1884(?)-1980 97-100
Tildon, J(ames) Tyson 1931- 159
Tiles, J. E. 1944- 128
Tilford, Earl H., Jr. 1945- 142
Tilghman, Benjamin R(oss) 1927- 134
Brief entry 107
Tilghman, Christopher 1948(?)- 159
See also CLC 65
Till, Barry 1923- 49-52
Till, Geoffrey 1945- 132
Till, Nicholas 1955- 141
Tillard, Jean-M(arie) Roger 1927- CANR-28
Earlier sketch in CA 45-48
Tillema, Herbert K(endall) 1942- 45-48
Tilleman, William Arthur 1932- 53-56
Tiller, Carl W(illiam) 1915- 108
Tiller, Ruth L. 1949- 150
See also SATA 83
Tiller, Ted
See Tiller, Theodore II
Tiller, Terence (Rogers) 1916-1987 101
Obituary 124
Tiller, Theodore II 1913(?)-1988 Obituary 126
Tilles, Solomon 1932- Brief entry 108
Tillett, Bill G(lenn) 1942- 118
Tillett, Gregory J. 1950- 110
Tilley, Ethel 1894- CAP-1
Earlier sketch in CA 9-10
Tilley, Patrick 1928- CANR-55
Earlier sketch in CA 106
Tilley, (William) Roger (Montgomerie) 1905-1971
CAP-2
Earlier sketch in CA 25-28
Tillich, Hannah 1896-1988 73-76
Obituary 127
Tillich, Paul (Johannes) 1886-1965 CANR-33
Obituary 25-28R
Earlier sketch in CA 5-8R
See also MTCW 1
Tillinghast, B(urette) S(tinson), Jr. 1930- 65-68
Tillinghast, Pardon E(lisha) 1920- 9-12R
Tillinghast, Richard (Williford) 1940- CANR-51
Earlier sketches in CA 29-32R, CANR-26
See also CAAS 23
See also CLC 29
Tillion, Diana (Rutzebeck) 1928- Brief entry 110
Tillion, Germaine Marie Rosine 1907- 104
Tillman, Barrett 1948- 132
Tillman, Rollie, Jr. 1933- 21-24R
Tillman, Seth Phillip 1930- 1-4R
Tillman, Stephen Frederick
1900(?)-1977 Obituary 69-72
Tillotson, G(iles) H(enry) R(upert) 1960- 126
Tillotson, Geoffrey 1905-1969 CAP-1
Earlier sketch in CA 13-14
Tillson, Albert H., Jr. 1948- 139
Tilly, Charles 1929- CANR-20
Earlier sketch in CA 103
Tilly, Chris 1955- 159
Tilly, Louise A(udino) 1930- CANR-47
Earlier sketch in CA 120
Tilly, Meg 1960- 149
Tilly, Nancy 1935- 120
See also SATA 62
Tilly, Richard H(ugh) 1932- 17-20R
Tillyard, E(ustace) M(andeville) W(etenhall)
1889-1962 Obituary 93-96
Tillyard, Stella 164
Tilman, Harold William 1898-1978 103
Tilman, Robert O(liver) 1929- CANR-1
Earlier sketch in CA 45-48
Tilson, Everett 1923- 41-44R
Tiltman, Hessell 1897(?)-1976 Obituary 69-72
Tiltman, Ronald Frank 1901- CAP-1
Earlier sketch in CA 9-10
Tilton, Alice
See Taylor, Phoebe Atwood
Tilton, Eleanor M(arguerite) 1913- Brief entry 110
Tilton, John W(ightman) 1928-1983 122
Brief entry 118
Tilton, Madonna Elaine 1929- CANR-36
Earlier sketch in CA 114
See also SATA 41
Tilton, Rafael
See Tilton, Madonna Elaine
Tilton, Timothy Alan 1942- 61-64
Timasheff, Nicholas S. 1886-1970 1-4R
Obituary 29-32R
Timberlake, Carolyn
See Dresang, Eliza (Carolyn Timberlake)
Timberlake, Charles E(dward) 1935- 41-44R
Timberlake, Richard Henry, Jr. 1922- 21-24R
Timberman, David G. 1955- 139
Timbrell, Charles 1942- 143
Timerman, Jacobo 1923- CANR-32
Brief entry 109
Earlier sketch in CA 120
See also HW
Timko, Michael 1925- 17-20R
Timlett, Peter Valentine 1933- Brief entry 111
Timm, Uwe 1940- 130
Timmen, Fritz 1918- 53-56
Timmerman, Joan 1938- 118
Timmerman, John H(ager) 1945- CANR-56
Earlier sketches in CA 111, CANR-29
Timmerman, John Johnson 1908- 111
Timmerman, Kenneth R. 1953- 141
Timmermans, Claire 1938- 104
Timmermans, Tricia 1946- 167
Timmers, J(an) Joseph M(arie) 1907- CAP-1
Earlier sketch in CA 13-14
Timmins, Lois Fahs 1914- CANR-27
Earlier sketch in CA 45-48
Timmins, William F(rederick) SATA 10
Timmis, John Henry III 1934- 104
Timmons, Bascom N(olly) 1890-1987 104
Obituary 122
Timmons, Bonnie 1951- 120
Timmons, Jeffry A. 1941- 108
Timms, Arthur W(arren) 1940- 120
Timms, David 1946- 109
Timms, E(dward) V(ivian) 1895-1960 Brief
entry 112
Timms, Edward 1937- 143
Timms, Kathleen 1943- 122
Timms, Noel 1927- CANR-16
Earlier sketch in CA 13-16R
Timoney, Francis 1938- 61-64
Timoshenko, Stephen P.
1878-1972 Obituary 33-36R
Timothy, Hamilton B(aird) 1913- 102
Timothy, Peter 1725(?)-1782 DLB 43
Timpe, Eugene Frank 1926- 77-80
Timperley, Rosemary Kenyon 1920- CANR-17
Earlier sketch in CA 97-100
Timrod, Henry 1828-1867 DLB 3
Tinbergen, Jan 1903-1994 CANR-2
Obituary 145
Earlier sketch in CA 5-8R
Tinbergen, Niko(laas) 1907-1988 108
Obituary 127
See also SATA-Obit 60
Tindal, Henrietta 1818(?)-1879 DLB 199
Tindall, George Brown 1921- 85-88
Tindall, Gillian (Elizabeth) 1938- CANR-65
Earlier sketches in CA 21-24R, CANR-11
See also CLC 7
Tindall, Kenneth (Thomas) 1937- CANR-42
Earlier sketch in CA 29-32R
Tindall, P(eggy) E(leanor) N(ancy) 1927- 29-32R
Tindall, William York 1903-1981 CANR-16
Obituary 104
Earlier sketch in CA 1-4R
Tiner, John Hudson 1944- CANR-40
Earlier sketches in CA 101, CANR-18
See also SATA 32
Tiner, Ralph W., Jr. 1948- 124
Ting
See Tingley, Merle R(andolph)
Ting, Jan C(hing-an) 1948- 37-40R
Ting, Samuel C. C. 1936- 157
Ting, Walasse 1929- 21-24R
Tingay, Lance 1915-1990 101
Obituary 131
Tingle, Dolli 1920- CANR-10
Earlier sketch in CA 25-28R
Tingley, Donald F(red) 1922- CANR-10
Earlier sketch in CA 25-28R
Tingley, Elizabeth 1955- 114
Tingley, Merle R(andolph) 1921- 129
Tingsten, Herbert 1896-1973 Obituary 45-48
Tingum, Janice 1958- 155
See also SATA 91
Tinic, Seha M(ehmet) 1941- 37-40R
Tinkelman, Murray 1933- SATA 12
Tinker, Beamish
See Jesse, F(ryniwyd) Tennyson
Tinker, Ben (Hill) 1903- 102
Tinker, Chauncey Brewster 1876-1963 DLB 140
Tinker, Edward Larocque 1881-1968 CAP-1
Earlier sketch in CA 13-14
Tinker, Grant A(lmerin) 1926- 147
Tinker, Hugh (Russell) 1921- CANR-3
Earlier sketch in CA 5-8R
Tinker, Jack (Samuel) 1938-1996 132
Obituary 154
Tinker, Miles Albert 1893-1977 CANR-4
Earlier sketch in CA 5-8R
Tinker, Spencer Wilkie 1909- 41-44R
Tinkham, Ace
See Tinkham, Harley
Tinkham, Harley 1923-1990 Obituary 132
Tinkle, (Julien) Lon 1906-1980 104
See also SATA 36
Tinling, Marion (Rose) 1904- 142
Tinling, Ted 1910-1990 Obituary 131
Tinling, Teddy
See Tinling, Ted
Tinne, Dorothea
See Strover, Dorothea
Tinne, E. D.
See Strover, Dorothea
Tinnin, David B(ruce) 1930- 49-52
Tinniswood, Peter 1936- CANR-43
Earlier sketch in CA 25-28R
Tinsley, Ernest John 1919- 5-8R
Tinsley, James Robert 1921- 13-16R
Tinsley, Jim Bob
See Tinsley, James Robert
Tinsley, (John) Russell 1932- 17-20R
Tinterow, Gary 1953- 109
Tintner, Adeline R. 1912- CANR-50
Earlier sketch in CA 123
Tio (y Nazario de Figueroa), Aurelio 1907- HW
Tiomkin, Dimitri 1899-1979 Obituary 93-96
Tipler, Frank J(ennings III) 1947- 157
Tippett, James S(terling) 1885-1958 135
See also SATA 66
Tippett, Michael (Kemp) 1905-1998 CANR-27
Obituary 164
Earlier sketch in CA 109
Tippette, Giles 1934- CANR-37
Earlier sketches in CA 65-68, CANR-17
Tipping, Marjorie Jean 1917- 122
Tippit, Sammy 1947- 104
Tipple, John Ord 1916- 9-12R
Tipton, Charles Leon 1932- 41-44R
Tipton, David 1934- Brief entry 111
Tipton, James (Sherwood) 1942- CANR-50
Earlier sketches in CA 57-60, CANR-8
Tiptree, James, Jr.
See Sheldon, Alice Hastings Bradley
See also CLC 48, 50
See also DLB 8
Tirbutt, Honoria CANR-22
Earlier sketch in CA 106
Tirion, Wil 1943- 143
Tirro, Frank (Pascale) 1935- 81-84
Tiryakian, Edward A(shod) 1929- CANR-19
Earlier sketches in CA 5-8R, CANR-2
Tischler, Barbara L. 1949- 123
Tischler, Hans 1915- CANR-6
Earlier sketch in CA 1-4R
Tischler, Nancy Marie (Patterson) 1931- 5-8R
Tischner, Rudolf (E.) 1879-1961 Obituary 112
Tisdale, Celes 1941- 57-60
Tisdale, Sallie 1957- 142
Tisdell, Clement Allan 1939- CANR-15
Earlier sketch in CA 25-28R
Tise, Larry Edward 1942- 102
Tish-Tash
See Tashlin, Frank
Tisma, Aleksandar 1924- 160
See also DLB 181
Tisserand, Jacques
See Barnes, Jim
Titamgim, R. Dirk
See Dietrich, Richard V(incent)
Titan, Earl
See Fearn, John Russell
Titchener, James Lampton 1922- 45-48
Titchener, Louise 1941- CANR-48
Earlier sketch in CA 122
Titcomb, Margaret 1891- CANR-5
Earlier sketch in CA 5-8R
Titler, Dale M(ilton) 1926- 81-84
See also SATA 35
See also SATA-Brief 28
Titley, David Paul 1929- 110
Titley, E. Brian 1945- 128
Titley, Norah M(ary) 1920- 118
Titmarsh, Michael Angelo
See Thackeray, William Makepeace
Titmuss, Richard M(orris) 1907-1973 109
Obituary 107
Tito, Josip Broz 1892-1980 Obituary 97-100
Tito, Marshal
See Tito, Josip Broz
Titon, Jeff Todd 1943- CANR-37
Earlier sketches in CA 89-92, CANR-16
Titra, Stephen Andrew 1945- 97-100
Titterton, Ernest William 1916- 109
Tittle, Charles R(ay) 1939- CANR-15
Earlier sketch in CA 41-44R
Tittler, Jonathan (Paul) 1945- CANR-43
Earlier sketch in CA 119
Tittler, Robert 1942- CANR-15
Earlier sketch in CA 81-84
Tittmann, George Fabian 1915-1978 5-8R
Obituary 81-84
Titunik, Irwin R(obert) 1929- 126
Titus, A(lice) Costandina 1950- 127
Titus, Barry J(oseph) 1938- 1-4R
Titus, Charles 1942- 45-48
Titus, David Anson 1934- 97-100
Titus, Edward William 1870-1952 DLB 4
See also DLBD 15
Titus, Eve 1922- CANR-30
Earlier sketch in CA 29-32R
See also SATA 2
Titus, Harold H(opper) 1896- 5-8R
Titus, Warren Irving 1921- 17-20R
Tiusanen, Timo 1936-1985 85-88
Obituary 117
Tizard, Henry Thomas 1885-1959 161
Tjader, Marguerite 1901- 17-20R
Tjepkema, Sandra L(ynn) 1953- 114
Tjernagel, Neelak S(erawlook) 1906- 17-20R
Tjong Khing, The 1933- SATA 76
Tjosvold, Dean 1948- 142
Tkacik, Arnold J(ohn) 1919- 81-84
Tlali, Miriam 1933- 164
See also DLB 157
Toan, Arthur B(enjamin), Jr. 1915- 25-28R
Tobach, Ethel 1921- 81-84
Toback, James 1944- 41-44R
Tobe, John Harold 1907-1979 CANR-1
Earlier sketch in CA 1-4R
Tobey, George B., Jr. 1917- 49-52
Tobey, Kathrene McLandress 1908- CAP-2
Earlier sketch in CA 29-32
Tobey, Mark 1890-1976 Obituary 65-68
Tobey, Ronald C(harles) 1942- 73-76
Tobias, Andrew P. 1947- CANR-14
Earlier sketch in CA 37-40R
Tobias, Henry J(ack) 1925- 41-44R
Tobias, J(ohn) J(acob) 1925- 53-56
Tobias, Katherine
See Gottfried, Theodore Mark
Tobias, Michael (Charles) 1951- 140
Tobias, Phillip V. 1925- CANR-15
Earlier sketch in CA 37-40R
Tobias, Richard C(lark) 1925- 29-32R
Tobias, Ronald B(enjamin) 1948- CANR-28
Earlier sketch in CA 111
Tobias, Sheila 1935- CANR-65
Earlier sketch in CA 93-96
Tobias, Tobi 1938- CANR-16
Earlier sketch in CA 29-32R
See also CLR 4
See also SATA 5, 82
Tobin, James 1918- CANR-5
Earlier sketch in CA 53-56
Interview in CANR-5
Tobin, James Edward 1905-1968 CAP-2
Earlier sketch in CA 23-24
Tobin, Jean Holloway 1917(?)-1989 Obituary 130
Tobin, Juanita Brown 1915- 156
Tobin, Kay 1930- 37-40R
Tobin, Richard J. 1946- 137
Tobin, Richard Lardner 1910-1995 CANR-1
Obituary 149
Earlier sketch in CA 1-4R
Tobin, Sheldon S(idney) 1931- 134
Brief entry 110
Tobin, Terence 1938- 53-56
Toby, Liz
See Minsky, Betty Jane (Toebe)
Toby, Mark 1913(?)-1972 Obituary 37-40R
Toch, Hans (Herbert) 1930- CANR-49
Earlier sketches in CA 17-20R, CANR-7, 23
Toch, Henry 1923- CANR-21
Earlier sketches in CA 9-12R, CANR-6
Toch, Thomas 1954- 145
Toczek, Nick 1950- 106
Tod, Ian J. 1945- 103
Tod, Osma Gallinger 1898-1982(?) CAP-1
Obituary 108
Earlier sketch in CA 9-10
Todd, Alden 1918- CANR-6
Earlier sketch in CA 1-4R
Todd, Alexander (Robertus) 1907-1997 146
Obituary 156
Todd, Ann 1909- 129
Todd, Anne Ophelia
See Dowden, Anne Ophelia
Todd, Barbara Euphan 1890-1976 104
See also DLB 160
Todd, Barbara K(eith) 1917- 61-64
See also SATA 10
Todd, Burbank L. CANR-26
Earlier sketches in CAP-2, CA 19-20
Todd, Clark 1945(?)-1983 Obituary 110
Todd, Edgeley W(oodman) 1914- Brief entry 109
Todd, Edward N. 1931- 53-56
Todd, Frances 1910- 13-16R
Todd, Frederick Porter 1903-1977 Obituary 73-76
Todd, Galbraith Hall 1914- 1-4R
Todd, H(erbert) E(atton) 1908-1988 CANR-53
Earlier sketches in CAP-1, CA 9-10, CANR-12, 30
See also SATA 11, 84
Todd, Hollis N(elson) 1914- 57-60
Todd, Ian A(lexander) 1941- CANR-31
Earlier sketch in CA 112
Todd, Ian Menzies 1923- 69-72
Todd, Janet M(argaret) 1942- CANR-53
Earlier sketches in CA 49-52, CANR-1, 28
Todd, Jerry D(ale) 1941- 53-56
Todd, John M(urray) 1918-1993 CANR-47
Obituary 141
Earlier sketch in CA 9-12R
Todd, Karen (Iris) Rohne (Pritchett) 1936- Brief
entry 111
Todd, Leonard 1940- 65-68
Todd, Loreto 1942- 107
See also SATA 30
Todd, Louise
See Sandweiss, Martha A(nn)
Todd, Malcolm 1939- 101
Todd, Olivier 1929- 168
Todd, Paul
See Posner, Richard
Todd, Peter
See Hamilton, Charles (Harold St. John)
Todd, R. Larry 1952- CANR-60
Earlier sketch in CA 128
Todd, Richard (Killingworth) 1949- 125
Todd, Ruth Van Dorn 1889(?)-1976 Obituary 65-68
Todd, Ruthven 1914- 81-84
Todd, Virgil H. 1921- Brief entry 106
Todd, Vivian Edmiston 1912- 17-20R
Todd, William Burton 1919- 41-44R
Todd, William Mills III 1944- 65-68
Todman, Bill
See Todman, William S.
Todman, William S. 1916-1979 Obituary 89-92
Todorov, Nikolai (Todorov) 1921- 132
Todorov, Tzvetan 1939- CANR-64
Earlier sketch in CA 73-76
Todrank, Gustave H(erman) 1924- 41-44R
Todrin, Boris 1915- 61-64
Toekes, Rudolf L(eslie) 1935- 21-24R
Toepfer, Ray Grant 1923- 21-24R
Toeplitz, Jerzy 1909-1995 65-68
Obituary 149
Toernqvist, (Per) Egil 1932- 29-32R
Tofani, Loretta 1953- 116
Brief entry 113
Interview in 116
Toffler, Alvin 1928- CANR-67
Earlier sketches in CA 13-16R, CANR-15, 46
See also DAM POP
See also MTCW 1
Toffler, Heidi 1929- 146
Toft, (Eric) John 1933- 103
Tofte, Arthur 1902-1980 73-76
Obituary 103
Tofte, Robert c. 1561-c. 1619 DLB 172
Togliatti, Palmiro 1893(?)-1964 133
Obituary 113
Tohata, Seiichi 1899-1983 Obituary 110
Toibin, Colm 1955- 142

Toka, Salchak Kalbakkhoreviich
1901-1973 Obituary 41-44R
Tokarczyk, Michelle M. 1953- 144
Tokayer, Marvin 1936- 102
Toker, Franklin K(arl) B(enedict) S(erchuk) 1944- .. CANR-15
Earlier sketch in CA 81-84
Tokes, Rudolf L(eslie) 1935- Brief entry 114
Toklas, Alice B(abette) 1877-1967 81-84
Obituary 25-28R
See also DLB 4
Tokmakoff, George 1928- 123
Tokuda Shusei 1872-1943 .... DLB 180
Tolan, Stephanie S. 1942- CANR-34
Earlier sketches in CA 77-80, CANR-15
See also JRDA
See also SATA 38, 78
Toland, John (Willard) 1912- CANR-46
Earlier sketches in CA 1-4R, CANR-6, 23
See also MTCW 1
See also SATA 38
Tolbert, E(lias) L(ake) 1915- CANR-3
Earlier sketch in CA 1-4R
Tolbert, Francis Xavier 1912-1984 .... CANR-71
Obituary 111
Earlier sketches in CA 1-4R, CANR-16
Tolbert, Frank X.
See Tolbert, Francis Xavier
Tolbert, Malcolm O(liver) 1924- 65-68
Tolbert, Mary Ann 1947- 116
Tolby, Arthur
See Infield, Glenn (Berton)
Tolchin, Martin 1928- CANR-46
Earlier sketch in CA 120
Tolchin, Susan J(ane) 1941- 141
Toldson, Ivory L. 1943- 114
Toledano, Ralph de 1916- CANR-31
Earlier sketch in CA 9-12R
See also AITN 1
Toledano, Roulhac (Bunkley) 1938- 101
Tolegian, Aram 1909- CANR-6
Earlier sketch in CA 1-4R
Toles, Thomas G. 1951- 126
Toles, Tom
See Toles, Thomas G.
Tolf, Robert W(alter) 1929- 73-76
Tolischus, Otto D(avid) 1890-1967 Obituary .. 93-96
Toliver, George
See Masselink, Ben
Toliver, Harold E(arl) 1932- CANR-34
Earlier sketch in CA 21-24R
Toliver, Raymond F. 1914- CANR-35
Earlier sketch in CA 17-20R
Tolkien, J(ohn) R(onald) R(euel) 1892-1973 .... CANR-36
Obituary 45-48
Earlier sketches in CAP-2, CA 17-18
See also AAYA 10
See also AITN 1
See also CDBLB 1914-1945
See also CLC 1, 2, 3, 8, 12, 38
See also DA
See also DAB
See also DAC
See also DAM MST, NOV, POP
See also DLB 15, 160
See also JRDA
See also MAICYA
See also MTCW 1
See also SATA 2, 32, 100
See also SATA-Obit 24
See also WLC
Tolkin, Michael 1950- 137
Toll, Nelly S. 1935- 146
See also SATA 78
Toll, Robert C(harles) 1938- 53-56
Toll, Seymour I. 1925- 29-32R
Toll, William 1941- 114
Tolland, W. R.
See Heitzmann, William Ray
Tollefson, James W(illiam) 1950- 144
Toller, Ernst 1893-1939 Brief entry 107
See also DLB 124
See also TCLC 10
Toller, Kate Caffrey
See Caffrey, Kate
Tollers, Vincent L(ouis) 1939- 57-60
Tolles, Frederick B(arnes) 1915-1975 .... 5-8R
Obituary 103
Tolles, Martha 1921- 49-52
See also SATA 8, 76
Tollet, Elizabeth 1694-1754 .... DLB 95
Tolley, A(rnold) T(revor) 1927- CANR-50
Earlier sketch in CA 123
Tolley, Howard B(oyd), Jr. 1943- 53-56
Tolley, Kemp 1908- 45-48
Tolley, William Pearson 1900-1996 93-96
Obituary 151
Tolliver, Ruby C(hangos) 1922- 111
See also SATA 55
See also SATA-Brief 41
Tolman, Newton F. 1908-1986 .... 1-4R
Obituary 120
Tolmie, Kenneth Donald 1941- 69-72
See also SATA 15
Tolmie Prance, Ghillean
See Prance, Ghillean Tolmie
Tolnai, Karoly
See De Tolnay, Charles Erich
Tolnai, Vagujhelyi Karoly
See De Tolnay, Charles Erich
Tolson, Jay 1948- 141
Tolson, M. B.
See Tolson, Melvin B(eaunorus)
Tolson, Melvin B(eaunorus) 1898(?)-1966 124
Obituary 89-92
See also BLC 3
See also BW 1
See also CLC 36, 105
See also DAM MULT, POET
See also DLB 48, 76
Tolstaya, Tatyana 1951- 130
Tolstoi, Aleksei Nikolaevich
See Tolstoy, Alexey Nikolaevich
Tolstoy, Alexandra L(vovna) 1884-1979 .. CANR-42
Obituary 89-92
Earlier sketch in CA 65-68
Tolstoy, Alexey Nikolaevich 1882-1945 158
Brief entry 107
See also TCLC 18
Tolstoy, Count Leo
See Tolstoy, Leo (Nikolaevich)
Tolstoy, Dimitry 1912- 29-32R
Tolstoy, Leo (Nikolaevich) 1828-1910 123
Brief entry 104
See also DA
See also DAB
See also DAC
See also DAM MST, NOV
See also SATA 26
See also SSC 9, 30
See also TCLC 4, 11, 17, 28, 44, 79
See also WLC
Tolstoy, Mary Koutouzov
1884(?)-1976 Obituary 69-72
Tolstoy (-Miloslavsky), Nikolai (Dimitrievich) 1935- .. CANR-45
Earlier sketch in CA 81-84
Tolstoy, Tatyana (Sukhotin) 1864-1950 Brief entry 117
Tolzmann, Don Heinrich 1945- CANR-38
Earlier sketches in CA 49-52, CANR-2, 17
Toma, David 1933- CANR-42
Earlier sketch in CA 118
Tomajczyk, S. F. 1960- 157
Tomalin, Claire 1933- CANR-52
Earlier sketch in CA 89-92
See also DLB 155
Tomalin, Nicholas 1931-1973 Obituary 45-48
Tomalin, Ruth CANR-29
Earlier sketches in CA 13-16R, CANR-13
See also SATA 29
Toman, Walter 1920- 5-8R
Tomas, Andrew Paul 73-76
Tomasek, Robert D(ennis) 1928- 17-20R
Tomaselli, Sylvana 1957- 137
Tomasevic, Nebojsa 1929- 81-84
Tomashevich, George Vid 1927- 133
Tomasi, Silvano M(ario) 1940- 115
Tomasi, Thomas E(dward) 1955- 139
Tomasic, D(inko) A(nthony) 1902- CAP-1
Earlier sketch in CA 19-20
Tomasi di Lampedusa, Giuseppe 1896-1957 Brief entry 111
See also Lampedusa, Giuseppe (Tomasi) di
Tomasson, Katherine 1895- CAP-1
Earlier sketch in CA 9-10
Tomasson, Richard F(inn) 1928- CANR-1
Earlier sketch in CA 45-48
Tomb, David A(lan) 1944- CANR-40
Earlier sketch in CA 117
Tomek, Ivan 1939- 120
Tomes, Margot (Ladd) 1917-1991 .... MAICYA
See also SATA 36, 70
See also SATA-Brief 27
See also SATA-Obit 69
Tomeski, Edward Alexander 1930- 37-40R
Tomey, Ingrid 1943- 145
See also SATA 77
Tomfool
See Farjeon, Eleanor
Tomikel, John 1928- CANR-4
Earlier sketch in CA 53-56
Tomin, Zdena 1941- 123
Tomkiewicz, Mina 1917-1975 .... CAP-2
Earlier sketch in CA 29-32
Tomkins, Calvin 1925- CANR-8
Earlier sketch in CA 13-16R
Interview in CANR-8
Tomkins, Jasper
See Batey, Tom
Tomkins, Mary E(ileen) 1914- 61-64
Tomkinson, Constance
See Weeks, Constance Tomkinson
Tomkinson, Michael 1940- CANR-22
Earlier sketch in CA 93-96
Tomlan, Michael A. 1947- 137
Tomlin, E(ric) W(alter) F(rederick) 1913-1988(?) CANR-3
Obituary 124
Earlier sketch in CA 5-8R
Tomlin, Lily
See Tomlin, Mary Jean
See also CLC 17
Tomlin, Mary Jean 1939(?)- Brief entry 117
See also Tomlin, Lily
Tomlins, Jack E(dward) 1929- 25-28R
Tomlinson, (Alfred) Charles 1927- CANR-33
Earlier sketch in CA 5-8R
See also CLC 2, 4, 6, 13, 45
See also DAM POET
See also DLB 40
See also PC 17
Tomlinson, Edward 1891(?)-1973 Obituary ... 45-48
Tomlinson, Gerald (Arthur) 1933- 85-88
Tomlinson, H(enry) M(ajor) 1873-1958 161
Brief entry 118
See also DLB 36, 100, 195
See also TCLC 71
Tomlinson, Harry 1943- 135
Tomlinson, Jill 1931-1976 .... CAP-2
Earlier sketch in CA 29-32
See also SATA 3
See also SATA-Obit 24
Tomlinson, Kenneth Y(oung) 1944- 65-68
Tomlinson, Reginald R(obert)
1885-1979(?) Obituary 104
See also SATA-Obit 27
Tomlinson, T(homas) B(rian) 1925- 9-12R
Tomlinson-Keasey, Carol 1942- 101
Tommasini, Anthony 166
Tommeraasen, Miles 1923- 21-24R
Tompert, Ann 1918- CANR-59
Earlier sketches in CA 69-72, CANR-11
See also SATA 14, 89
Tompkins, C(linton) David 1937- 41-44R
Tompkins, Dorothy (Campbell) 1908- 17-20R
Tompkins, E(dwin) Berkeley 1935- 29-32R
Tompkins, Everett Thomas 1931- 107
Tompkins, J(oyce) M(arjorie) S(anxter)
1897-1986 Obituary 121
Tompkins, Jane P(arry) 1940- CANR-39
Earlier sketches in CA 29-32R, CANR-17
Tompkins, Jerry R(obert) 1931- 17-20R
Tompkins, Julia (Marguerite Hunter Manchee)
1909- 29-32R
Tompkins, Kathleen Burns 1934- 93-96
Tompkins, Peter 1919- CANR-12
Earlier sketch in CA 9-12R
Tompkins, Ptolemy (Christian) 1962(?)- 168
Tompkins, Richard A. 1896(?)-1977 Obituary . 73-76
Tompkins, Stuart R(amsay) 1886-1977 .... 37-40R
Tompkins, Tom
See Tompkins, Everett Thomas
Tompkins, Walker A. 1909-1990(?) CANR-66
Earlier sketch in CA 5-8R
Tompson, Benjamin 1642-1714 .... DLB 24
Toms, Bernard 1931- 17-20R
Tomson, Bernard 1909-1978 Obituary 77-80
Ton, Mary Ellen 1933- 112
Tonashi
See Harrington, Mark Raymond
Tondelli, Pier Vittorio 1955-1991 .... DLB 196
Tone, John Lawrence 1959- 151
Tone, Teona 1944- 112
Toner, Raymond John 1908- 5-8R
See also SATA 10
Toney, Albert (Livingston, Jr.) 1933- 120
Toney, Anthony 1913- CANR-9
Earlier sketch in CA 17-20R
Tong, Gary S. 1942- 135
See also SATA 66
Tong, Raymond 1922- CANR-2
Earlier sketch in CA 5-8R
Tong, Te-kong 1920- CANR-8
Earlier sketch in CA 9-12R
Tong, Zhong Gui 1963- 144
Tongren, Sally S(tetson) 1926- 118
Tonkin, Elizabeth 1934- 140
Tonkin, Humphrey 1939- CANR-38
Earlier sketches in CA 41-44R, CANR-16
Tonkin, Peter (Francis) 1950- 101
Tonkinson, Carole 1964- 150
Tonkinson, Robert 1928- 77-80
Tonks, A. Ronald 1934- 125
Tonks, Rosemary (D. Boswell) 89-92
See also DLB 14
Tonn, Martin H. 1921- 5-8R
Tonna, Charlotte Elizabeth 1790-1846 .... DLB 163
Tonquedec, Joseph de 1868-1962 Obituary ... 112
Tonson, Jacob
See Bennett, (Enoch) Arnold
Tonson, Jacob fl. 1677-1718 .... DLB 170
Tonsor, Stephen (John) 1923- Brief entry 114
Too, Yun Lee 1965- 149
Toobin, Jerome 1920(?)-1984 Obituary 111
Toohey, Catherine 1949- 109
Toohey, Robert E(ugene) 1935- 89-92
Took, Belladonna
See Chapman, Vera (Ivy May)
Tooke, Ann (Mary Margaret) Hales
See Hales-Tooke, Ann (Mary Margaret)
Tooke, Louise Mathews 1950- 105
See also SATA 38
Tooke, Thomas (Renshaw) 1947- 73-76
Tooker, Elisabeth (Jane) 1927- 49-52
Toole, John Kennedy 1937-1969 104
See also CLC 19, 64
See also DLBY 81
Toole, K(enneth) Ross 1920- Brief entry 112
Toole, Rex
See Tralins, S(andor) Robert
Toole, William Bell III 1930- 21-24R
Toole Stott, Raymond 1910-1982 Obituary 105
Tooley, M. J.
See Tooley, Michael J(ohn)
Tooley, Michael J(ohn) 1942- CANR-24
Earlier sketch in CA 106
Tooley, R(onald) Vere 1898-1986 .... 9-12R
Obituary 120
Toomay, Patrick J(ay) 1948- 65-68
Toombs, John 1927- 106
Toombs, Lawrence Edmund 1919- CANR-8
Earlier sketch in CA 5-8R
Toomer, Derek 1946- 65-68
Toomer, Jean 1894-1967 85-88
See also BLC 3
See also BW 1
See also CDALB 1917-1929
See also CLC 1, 4, 13, 22
See also DAM MULT
See also DLB 45, 51
See also MTCW 1
See also PC 7
See also SSC 1
See also WLCS
Toon, Peter 1939- CANR-30
Earlier sketch in CA 112
Toona, Elin(-Kai) 1937- CANR-15
Earlier sketch in CA 81-84
Toonder, Martin
See Groom, Arthur William
Toothaker, Roy Eugene 1928- 65-68
See also SATA 18
Tooze, Ruth (Anderson) 1892- 5-8R
See also SATA 4
Topaz, Jacqueline
See Hyman, Jackie (Diamond)
Topek, Susan Remick 1955- 146
See also SATA 78
Topel, L(ouis) John 1934- 118
Toperoff, Sam 1933- CANR-30
Earlier sketch in CA 45-48
Topitsch, Ernst 1919- 136
Topkins, Katharine 1927- 49-52
Topkins, Richard 1925- 25-28R
Toplin, Robert Brent 1940- CANR-15
Earlier sketch in CA 77-80
Topol, Allan 1941- 93-96
Topol, Edward 1938- 139
Topolski, Daniel 1945- CANR-28
Earlier sketch in CA 110
Topolski, Feliks 1907- Brief entry 112
Topor, Tom 1938- 105
Topper, Suzanne 1939- 128
Toppin, Edgar A(llan) 1928- 21-24R
Topping, Anne Marie 25-28R
Topping, Audrey R(onning) 1928- 41-44R
See also SATA 14
Topping, C(oral) W(esley) 1889- 41-44R
Topping, Donald M(edley) 1929- 53-56
Topping, Seymour 1921- 49-52
Topping, Wesley
See Topping, C(oral) W(esley)
Topsfield, L(eslie) T(homas) 1920-1981 ... CANR-9
Obituary 105
Earlier sketch in CA 61-64
Tor, Regina
See Shekerjian, Regina Tor
Torack, Richard M(aurice) 1927- 106
Torberg, Friedrich
See Kantor-Berg, Friedrich
See also DLB 85
Torbert, Floyd James 1922- 105
See also SATA 22
Torbert, William Rockwell 1944- 41-44R
Torbet, Laura 1942- CANR-16
Earlier sketch in CA 69-72
Torbet, Robert G(eorge) 1912- 9-12R
Torbett, Harvey Douglas Louis 1921- 9-12R
Torchiana, Donald T(hornhill) 1923- 17-20R
Torchio, Menico 1932- 61-64
Torday, Ursula 1888- CANR-58
Earlier sketches in CA 97-100, CANR-28
See also CABS 28
Tordoff, William 1925- 120
Toren, Heller 77-80
Torga, Miguel
See Rocha, Adolfo
Torgersen, Don Arthur 1934- 111
See also SATA 55
See also SATA-Brief 41
Torgersen, Eric 1943- 37-40R
Torgersen, Paul Ernest 1931- 81-84
Torgerson, Dial 1928- 53-56
Torgerson Shaw, Ellen 1929(?)-1983 Obituary . 109
Torgoff, Martin 1952- 109
Torgov, Morley 1927- 162
Torgovnick, Marianna 1949- CANR-44
Earlier sketch in CA 115
Torgovnick, Marianna DeMarco
See Torgovnick, Marianna
Torley, Luke
See Blish, James (Benjamin)
Torme, Mel(vin Howard) 1925- 143
Brief entry 118
Tormey, John Connolly 1942- 61-64
Tornabene, Lyn 1930- 69-72
Tornatore, Giuseppe 1956- 143
Torney, Judith V.
See Torney-Purta, Judith V(ollmar)
Torney-Purta, Judith V(ollmar) 1937- CANR-10
Earlier sketch in CA 65-68
Tornimparte, Alessandra
See Ginzburg, Natalia
Tornqvist, Egil 1932- 149
Torok, Lou 1927- 49-52
Torok, Lou 1927- 154
Torr, Iain
See Mackinnon, Charles Roy
Torrance, E. Paul 1915- CANR-40
Earlier sketches in CA 1-4R, CANR-3, 18
Torrance, Thomas F(orsyth) 1913- CANR-55
Earlier sketches in CA 9-12R, CANR-5, 29
Torre, Jose de la
See de la Torre, Jose
Torre, Raoul della
See Mencken, H(enry) L(ouis)
Torre-Bueno, Lillian de la
See McCue, Lillian Bueno
Torregian, Sotere 1941- CANR-3
Earlier sketch in CA 45-48
Torrence, Ridgely 1874-1950 .... DLB 54
Torrens, Duncan
See Ripley, Michael David
Torrens, Robert George (?)-1981 Obituary 105
Torrents, Nissa 1937- 128
Torres, Andres Segovia
See Segovia, Andres
Torres, Daniel 1958- .... SATA 102
Torres, Edwin 111
Torres, Emmanuel 1932- 97-100

Torres, John A(lbert) 1965- 159
See also SATA 94
Torres, Jose Acosta 1925- CANR-32
Earlier sketch in CA 57-60
See also HW
Torres, Laura 1967- 151
See also SATA 87
Torres, Sergio
See Torres Gonzalez, Sergio A(ntonio)
Torres, Tereska
See Torres-Levin, Tereska (Szwarc)
Torres Bodet, Jaime 1902-1974 CANR-32
Obituary 49-52
Earlier sketch in CA 101
See also HW
See also MTCW 1
Torres Gonzalez, Sergio A(ntonio) 1929- 117
Torres-Levin, Tereska (Szwarc) CANR-15
Earlier sketch in CA 5-8R
Torres-Metzgar, Joseph V. 1933- DLB 122
Torres-Rioseco, Arturo 1897-1971 CAP-1
Earlier sketch in CA 9-10
Torrey, E(dwin) Fuller 1937- CANR-71
Earlier sketch in CA 119
See also CLC 34
Torrey, Gordon H(oward) 1919- 9-12R
Torrey, Norman Lewis 1894-1980 1-4R
Obituary 102
Torrey, Therese von Hohoff
1898(?)-1974 Obituary 45-48
Torrey, Volta (Wray) 1905- 69-72
Torrie, James H(iram) 1908- 73-76
Torrie, Malcolm
See Mitchell, Gladys (Maude Winifred)
Torrington, Jeff 144
Torro, Pel
See Fanthorpe, R(obert) Lionel
Tors, Ivan (Lawrence) 1916-1983 103
Obituary 110
Torsney, Cheryl B. 1955- 135
Torsvan, Ben Traven
See Traven, B.
Torsvan, Benno Traven
See Traven, B.
Torsvan, Berick Traven
See Traven, B.
Torsvan, Berwick Traven
See Traven, B.
Torsvan, Bruno Traven
See Traven, B.
Torsvan, Traven
See Traven, B.
Tortolano, William 1930- 77-80
Tortora, Daniel F(rancis) 1947- CANR-13
Earlier sketch in CA 73-76
Tory, Avraham 1909- 140
Toscano, Peter Ralph 1920- 45-48
Tosches, Nick 1949- CANR-45
Earlier sketch in CA 81-84
Tosi, Henry L(ouis), Jr. 1936- 125
Tosics, Ivan 1952- 138
Toson
See Shimazaki, Haruki
Tosti, Donald Thomas 1935- 49-52
Toten, Teresa 1955- 160
See also SATA 99
Toth, Charles W(illiam) 1919- CANR-10
Earlier sketch in CA 65-68
Toth, Emily 1944- 101
Toth, Endre
See de Toth, Andre
Toth, Jennifer 1967- 152
Toth, Lazlo
See Novello, Don
Toth, Robert Charles 1928- 102
Toth, Stephen, Jr. 1950- 69-72
Toth, Susan Erickson Allen 1940- 105
See also DLBY 86
Totham, Mary
See Breinburg, Petronella
Totman, Conrad 1934- CANR-38
Earlier sketches in CA 101, CANR-17
Tottell, Richard fl. 1550-1593 DLB 170
Totten, George Oakley III 1922- CANR-48
Earlier sketches in CA 9-12R, CANR-5, 21
Totten, Martha Wescoat 1957- 118
Totten, Sam(uel) 1949- 118
Totten, W. Fred 1905- 37-40R
Tough, Allen (MacNeill) 1936- 108
Touliatos, John 1944- 93-96
Toulmin, Stephen Edelston 1922- CANR-20
Earlier sketches in CA 9-12R, CANR-5
Toulouse-Lautrec, Marie-Pierre (Mapie) de
1901-1972 Obituary 37-40R
Toulson, Shirley 1924- CANR-38
Earlier sketches in CA 101, CANR-17
Touraine, Alain 1925- 85-88
Toure, Askia Muhammad
See Toure, Askia Muhammad Abu Bakr el
See also DLB 41
Toure, Askia Muhammad Abu Bakr el 1938- 124
See also Toure, Askia Muhammad
See also BW 2
Tourevski, Mark 1952- 142
Tourgee, Albion W. 1838-1905 DLB 79
Tourneur, Cyril 1580(?)-1626 DAM DRAM
See also DLB 58
Tourneur, Dina-Kathelijn 1934- 108
Tourney, Garfield 1927- 57-60
Tournier, Michel (Edouard) 1924- CANR-36
Earlier sketches in CA 49-52, CANR-3
See also CLC 6, 23, 36, 95
See also DLB 83
See also MTCW 1
See also SATA 23
Tournier, Paul 1898-1986 CANR-29
Obituary 120
Earlier sketch in CA 81-84
Tournimparte, Alessandra
See Ginzburg, Natalia
Tours, Hugh Berthold 1910- CAP-1
Earlier sketch in CA 9-10
Tourtellot, Arthur Bernon 1913-1977 CANR-4
Obituary 73-76
Earlier sketch in CA 5-8R
Tourtellot, Jonathan B. 1946- 111
Tourville, Elsie A(lma) 1926- 57-60
Tousley, Clare M. 1889(?)-1985 Obituary 114
Toussaint, Stanley D. 1928- 115
Toussaint-Samat, Maguelonne 1926- 156
Touster, Alison
See Reed, Alison Touster
Touval, Saadia E. 1932- CANR-35
Earlier sketch in CA 45-48
Touw, Kathleen 1949- 109
Tovey, Doreen Evelyn 1918- 104
Tovo, Jerome 1936- 45-48
Towber, Chaim 1902(?)-1972 Obituary 33-36R
Towell, Julie E. 1953- 122
Tower, Ann
See Straubing, Harold (Elk)
Tower, Diana
See Smith, Richard Rein
Tower, Don
See Bower, Donald E(dward)
Tower, John G(oodwin) 1925- Brief entry 106
Tower, Margene 1939- 37-40R
Towers, Ivar
See Kornbluth, C(yril) M.
Towers, Maxwell 1909- 57-60
Towers, Regina
See Pykare, Nina
Towers, (Augustus) Robert 1923-1995 CANR-51
Obituary 148
Earlier sketch in CA 132
Towey, Cyprian 1912- 21-24R
Towle, Joseph W(alter) 1909- CAP-1
Earlier sketch in CA 13-14
Towle, Philip 1945- 117
Towle, Tony 1939- 37-40R
Towle, Wendy 1963- SATA 79
Towler, Juby Earl 1913- 13-16R
Town, Glenn P(atrick) 1949- 118
Town, Harold (Barling) 1924- CANR-15
Earlier sketch in CA 41-44R
Towne, Anthony 1928-1980 25-28R
Obituary 117
Towne, Benjamin 1740(?)-1793 DLB 43
Towne, Marian K(leinsasser) 1933- 154
Towne, Mary
See Spelman, Mary
Towne, Peter
See Nabokov, Peter (Francis)
Towne, Robert (Burton) 1936(?)- 108
See also CLC 87
See also DLB 44
Towne, Stuart
See Rawson, Clayton
Towner, Donald (Chisholm) 1903-1985 CAP-1
Obituary 117
Earlier sketch in CA 19-20
Towner, Jason
See Smith, Harold Ivan
Towner, W. Sibley
See Towner, Wayne Sibley
Towner, Wayne Sibley 1933- Brief entry 118
Townes, Charles H(ard) 1915- 154
Townley, Ralph 1923- 21-24R
Townley, Rod
See Townley, Roderick
Townley, Roderick 1942- CANR-29
Earlier sketches in CA 57-60, CANR-12
Towns, Elmer L(eon) 1932- CANR-2
Earlier sketch in CA 45-48
Towns, James E(dward) 1942- CANR-23
Earlier sketches in CA 61-64, CANR-8, 21
Towns, Jim
See Towns, James E(dward)
Townsend, Brad W. 1962- 155
See also SATA 91
Townsend, Charles Bud 1929- 53-56
Townsend, Charles E(dward) 1932- 41-44R
Townsend, Charles R(ay) 1929- 69-72
Townsend, Doris McFerran 1914- CANR-19
Earlier sketch in CA 103
Townsend, Elsie Doig 1908- 29-32R
Townsend, Harry 1925- 25-28R
Townsend, Irving 1920- 101
Townsend, J(ames) Benjamin 1918-1993 21-24R
Obituary 143
Townsend, J(acob) David 1888- 5-8R
Townsend, James B(arclay) J(ermain) 1910- 49-52
Townsend, Janet (Elizabeth) 1925- 107
Townsend, John Rowe 1922- CANR-41
Earlier sketch in CA 37-40R
See also AAYA 11
See also CLR 2
See also JRDA
See also MAICYA
See also SAAS 2
See also SATA 4, 68
Townsend, Larry 1935- 136
Townsend, Lindsay 1960- 154
Townsend, Mark
See Wallmann, Jeffrey M(iner)
Townsend, Peter (Wooldridge) 1914- CANR-28
Earlier sketch in CA 29-32R
Townsend, Ralph M. 1901(?)-1976 Obituary 65-68
Townsend, Reginald T. 1890-1977 Obituary 73-76
Townsend, Richard (Fraser) 1938- 140
Townsend, Richard E.
1897(?)-1975 Obituary 61-64
Townsend, Robert 1920-1998 45-48
Obituary 164
Townsend, Robert 1957- AAYA 24
Townsend, Robert 1957- 162
Townsend, Sue
See Townsend, Susan Elaine
See also CLC 61
See also SATA 55, 93
See also SATA-Brief 48
Townsend, Susan Elaine 1946- CANR-65
Brief entry 119
Earlier sketch in CA 127
See also Townsend, Sue
See also DAB
See also DAC
See also DAM MST
Townsend, Thomas L. 1944- 127
See also SATA 59
Townsend, Tom
See Townsend, Thomas L.
Townsend, William Cameron
1896-1982 Obituary 106
Townsend, William H(enry)
1890-1964 Obituary 111
Townshend, Aurelian 1583(?)-1651(?) DLB 121
Townshend, Peter (Dennis Blandford) 1945- 107
See also CLC 17, 42
Townshend, Richard
See Bickers, Richard (Leslie) Townshend
Townson, Hazel CANR-18
Earlier sketch in CA 97-100
Towry, Peter
See Piper, David (Towry)
Towse, Ruth 1943- 150
Toy, Henry, Jr. 1915- 37-40R
Toy, Maggie 1964- 162
Toye, Clive 1933(?)- SATA-Brief 30
Toye, John Francis 1883-1964 CAP-1
Earlier sketch in CA 9-10
Toye, William Eldred 1926- CANR-4
Earlier sketch in CA 1-4R
See also SATA 8
Toynbee, Arnold J(oseph) 1889-1975 CANR-36
Obituary 61-64
Earlier sketch in CA 5-8R
See also AITN 2
Toynbee, Jocelyn M(ary) C(atherine)
1897-1985 37-40R
Obituary 118
Toynbee, (Theodore) Philip 1916-1981 CANR-4
Obituary 104
Earlier sketch in CA 1-4R
Toynbee, Polly (Mary Louisa) 1946- CANR-9
Earlier sketch in CA 21-24R
Tozer, Mary (Christine) 1947- 101
Tozzi, Federigo 1883-1920 160
See also TCLC 31
Traba, Marta 1930-1983 154
Trabasso, Tom 1935- CANR-11
Earlier sketch in CA 21-24R
Trace, Arther Storrey, Jr. 1922- CANR-20
Earlier sketch in CA 1-4R
Tracey, Hugh (Travers) 1903-1977 CAP-2
Obituary 77-80
Earlier sketch in CA 29-32
Tracey, Lindalee 1957- 145
Tracey, Patricia Cleland 1932- 5-8R
Trachman, Muriel Karlin CANR-15
Earlier sketch in CA 85-88
Trachte, Don(ald) 1915- 89-92
Trachtenberg, Alan 1932- 157
Trachtenberg, Inge 1923- 77-80
Trachtenberg, Marvin (Lawrence) 1939- 65-68
Trachtenberg, Paul 1948- 112
Trachtenberg, Stanley 119
Traci, Philip (Joseph) 1934-1984 41-44R
Obituary 133
Tracy, Aloise
See Shoenight, Aloise
Tracy, Ann B(laisdell) 1941- 107
Tracy, Charles (William) 1938- 128
Tracy, Clarence 1908- 9-12R
Tracy, David W. 1939- 101
Tracy, Don(ald Fiske) 1905-197(?) CANR-2
Earlier sketch in CA 1-4R
Tracy, Doris 1925- 61-64
Tracy, Honor (Lilbush Wingfield) 1913-1989
CANR-24
Obituary 128
Earlier sketches in CA 61-64, CANR-8
See also DLB 15
Tracy, Hugh
See Evans, (Edwin) Stuart (Gomer)
Tracy, Jack W. 1945- 105
Tracy, James 1961- 164
Tracy, James D. 1938- 102
Tracy, John A(lvin) 1934- 53-56
Tracy, L(ee) Jack 1926- 9-12R
Tracy, Leland
See Tralins, S(andor) Robert
Tracy, Lorna 1934- 132
Tracy, Louise Treadwell 1896-1983 Obituary 114
Tracy, Michael 1932- 13-16R
Tracy, (John) Nicholas 1944- 141
Tracy, Powers
See Ward, Don(ald G.)
Tracy, Robert E. 1928- 89-92
Tracy, Susan
See Marino, Carolyn Fitch
Tracy, Theodore J(ames) 1916- 29-32R
Tracy, Thomas F. 1948- 156
Tracy, Thomas Henry 1900- CAP-2
Earlier sketch in CA 17-18
Tracz, Richard Francis 1944- CANR-17
Earlier sketch in CA 29-32R
Trader Vic
See Bergeron, Victor (Jules, Jr.)
Traeder, Tamara 1960- 166
Traer, James Frederick 1938- 102
Trafford, F. G.
See Riddell, Charlotte
Trafzer, Clifford Earl 1949- CANR-26
Earlier sketch in CA 109
Trager, Frank N(ewton) 1905-1984 CANR-9
Obituary 113
Earlier sketch in CA 17-20R
Trager, George L(eonard) 1906- 41-44R
Trager, Helen G. 1910- 69-72
Trager, James 1925- CANR-34
Earlier sketches in CA 37-40R, CANR-15
Tragle, Henry Irving 1914- 37-40R
Trahan, Ronald 1950- 106
Traherne, Michael
See Watkins-Pitchford, Denys James
Traherne, Thomas 1637(?)-1674 DLB 131
Trahey, Jane 1923- CANR-17
Earlier sketch in CA 17-20R
See also SATA 36
Traill, Catharine Parr 1802-1899 DLB 99
Train, Arthur (Cheney) 1875-1945 159
Brief entry 112
See also DLB 86
See also DLBD 16
Train, Arthur K(issam) 1902(?)-1981 Obituary 104
Train, John 1928- CANR-30
Earlier sketch in CA 106
Traina, Richard P(aul) 1937- 25-28R
Trainer, David 1947- CANR-20
Earlier sketch in CA 25-28R
Trainer, Jennifer 1956- 108
Trainer, Orvel 1925- 45-48
Trainor, Bernard E. 1928- 153
Trainor, Richard
See Tralins, S(andor) Robert
Traister, Aaron 1904(?)-1976 Obituary 65-68
Trakas, Pedro N(icholas) 1923- 104
Trakl, Georg 1887-1914 165
Brief entry 104
See also PC 20
See also TCLC 5
Tralbaut, Mark-Edo 1902-1976 CAP-2
Earlier sketch in CA 29-32
Tralins, Bob
See Tralins, S(andor) Robert
Tralins, Robert S.
See Tralins, S(andor) Robert
Tralins, S(andor) Robert 1926- CANR-40
Earlier sketches in CA 21-24R, CANR-14
See also Miles, Keith
Trambley, Estela Portillo 1936- 77-80
Trani, Eugene P(aul) 1939- CANR-29
Earlier sketch in CA 25-28R
Transtroemer, Tomas (Goesta) 1931- 129
Brief entry 117
See also CAAS 17
See also CLC 52, 65
See also DAM POET
Transtromer, Tomas Gosta
See Transtroemer, Tomas (Goesta)
Transue, Jacob
See Matheson, Joan (Transue)
Transue, Joan
See Matheson, Joan (Transue)
Tranter, John Ernest 1943- 110
Tranter, Nigel (Godwin) 1909- CANR-59
Earlier sketches in CA 9-12R, CANR-5, 20
Tran Thi Nga 1927- 148
Trantino, Tommy 1938- 65-68
Trapani, Iza 1954- SATA 80
Trapido, Barbara 1941- 123
Trapier, Elizabeth du Gue
1893(?)-1974 Obituary 53-56
Trapp, E(dward) Philip 1923- 45-48
Trapp, Frank Anderson 1922- 57-60
Trapp, (Kerwin) Kenneth R(aymond Stephen)
1943- 145
Trapp, Maria Augusta von
See von Trapp, Maria Augusta
See also SATA 16
Trapp, Stefan (Alfred Josef) 1962- 152
Traschen, Isadore 1915- 25-28R
Trask, David F(rederic) 1929- CANR-17
Earlier sketches in CA 1-4R, CANR-1
Trask, John Jacquelin 1904(?)-1977 Obituary 69-72
Trask, Jonathan
See Levinson, Leonard
Trask, Margaret Pope 1907- 1-4R
Trask, Roger R(eed) 1930- 41-44R
Trask, Willard (Ropes) 1900(?)-1980 Obituary 101
Trasko, Mary 1959- 144
Trasler, Gordon (Blair) 1929- CANR-3
Earlier sketch in CA 1-4R
Trattner, Walter I(rwin) 1936- CANR-13
Earlier sketch in CA 37-40R
Traube, Ruy
See Tralins, S(andor) Robert
Traube, Shepard 1907-1983 Obituary 111
Traubel, Horace
See Traubel, Horace L(ogo)
Traubel, Horace L(ogo) 1858-1919 Brief entry 123
Traudl
See Flaxman, Traudl
Trauger, Wilmer K(ohl) 1898- CAP-1
Earlier sketch in CA 9-10
Traugott, Elizabeth Closs 1939- 41-44R
Traupman, John C. 1923- 41-44R
Traut, Dennis 1953- 111
Trautman, Donald T. 1924- 37-40R
Trautman, Ray 1907- 45-48

Trautmann, Frederic 1936- 132
Trautmann, Thomas R(oger) 1940- 131
Travell, Janet (Graeme) 1901- CAP-2
Earlier sketch in CA 29-32
Traven, B. (?)-1969 CAP-2
Obituary 25-28R
Earlier sketch in CA 19-20
See also CLC 8, 11
See also DLB 9, 56
See also MTCW 1
Traven, Beatrice
See Goldemberg, Rose Leiman
Traver, Robert
See Voelker, John D(onaldson)
Travers, Ben 1886-1980 133
Obituary 102
See also DLB 10
Travers, Kenneth
See Hutchin, Kenneth Charles
Travers, Louise Allderdice 1891- CAP-1
Earlier sketch in CA 9-10
Travers, P(amela) L(yndon) 1906-1996 CANR-30
Obituary 152
Earlier sketch in CA 33-36R
See also CLR 2
See also DLB 160
See also MAICYA
See also SAAS 2
See also SATA 4, 54, 100
See also SATA-Obit 90
Travers, Paul J(oseph) 1951- 138
Travers, Robert J. 1911(?)-1974 Obituary 49-52
Travers, Robert M(orris) W(illiam) 1913- CANR-2
Earlier sketch in CA 5-8R
Travers, Scott A(ndrew) 1961- 125
Travers, Virginia
See Coigney, Virginia
Travers, Will
See Rowland, D(onald) S(ydney)
Traversi, Derek A(ntona) 1912- 77-80
Travis, Aaron
See Saylor, Steven
Travis, Anthony S(tewart) 1943- 147
Travis, Charles S. 1943- 37-40R
Travis, Dempsey J(erome) 1920- CANR-49
Earlier sketches in CA 85-88, CANR-15
Travis, Elizabeth (Frances Chandler) 1920- 134
Travis, Frederick F. 1942- 135
Travis, Gerry
See Trimble, Louis P(reston)
Travis, Gretchen A. 103
Travis, Jack 1952- 141
Travis, John T. 1935- 25-28R
Travis, Lucille 152
See also SATA 88
Travis, Neal 1939(?)- 103
Travis, Stephen H(enry) 1944- 106
Travis, Tony
See Travis, Anthony S(tewart)
Travis, Walter Earl 1926- 21-24R
Travis, Will
See Keevill, Henry J(ohn)
Travis, William 1924- 25-28R
Travisano, Thomas (J.) 1951- 164
Travlos, John 1908(?)-1985 Obituary 118
Trawick, Buckner Beasley 1914- 5-8R
Trawick, Leonard M. 1933- 137
Traxler, Arthur E(dwin) 1900- CAP-2
Earlier sketch in CA 21-22
Traxler, Patricia 1947- 147
Traylor, Ellen Gunderson 1946- 122
Traylor, W. L. 1929- 37-40R
Traynor, Alex
See Lagerwall, Edna
TRB
See Strout, Richard L(ee)
Treacy, William 1919- 61-64
Treadgold, Donald W(arren) 1922- 9-12R
Treadgold, Mary 1910- 13-16R
See also SATA 49
Treadway, John D(avid) 1950- 128
Treadway, Terry
See Treadway, Theresa
Treadway, Theresa 1941- 107
Treadwell, Sandy 1946- 124
Treahearne, Elizabeth
See Maxwell, Patricia
Treanor, John Holland
1903(?)-1978 Obituary 77-80
Treanor, Oliver 1949- 128
Trease, (Robert) Geoffrey 1909-1998 CANR-38
Obituary 165
Earlier sketches in CA 5-8R, CANR-7, 22
See also CLR 42
See also MAICYA
See also SAAS 6
See also SATA 2, 60
See also SATA-Obit 101
Treaster, Joseph B. 1941- 128
Treasure, G(eoffrey) R(ussell) R(ichards)
1929- 77-80
Treat, Ida
See Bergeret, Ida Treat
Treat, John Whittier 1953- 128
Treat, Lawrence 1903-1998 CANR-64
Obituary 164
Earlier sketch in CA 49-52
See also SATA 59
Treat, Payson J(ackson)
1879-1972 Obituary 37-40R
Trebach, Arnold S. 1928- CANR-12
Earlier sketch in CA 9-12R
Trebay, Guy 1952- 149
Trebing, Harry M(artin) 1926- CANR-31
Earlier sketch in CA 29-32R
Trecker, Harleigh B(radley) 1911- CANR-5
Earlier sketch in CA 5-8R
Trecker, Janice Law 1941- CANR-9
Earlier sketch in CA 65-68
Tredell, Nicolas (Samuel) 1950- 149
Tredennick, (George) Hugh (Percival Phair)
1899-1981 109
Obituary 105
Tredez, Alain 1926- 85-88
See also SATA 17
Tredez, Denise 1930- CANR-8
Earlier sketch in CA 5-8R
See also SATA 50
Tredgold, Nye
See Tranter, Nigel (Godwin)
Tredgold, Roger F(rancis) 1911-1975 CANR-5
Earlier sketch in CA 5-8R
Trediakovsky, Vasilii Kirillovich 1703-1769 DLB 150
Tree, Christina 1944- CANR-12
Earlier sketch in CA 73-76
Tree, Cornelia
See Nichols, Nina (Marianna) da Vinci
Tree, Gregory
See Bardin, John Franklin
Tree, Michael (John) 1926- 9-12R
Tree, Ronald 1897-1976 69-72
Obituary 65-68
Treece, Henry 1912-1966 CANR-60
Obituary 25-28R
Earlier sketches in CA 1-4R, CANR-6
See also CLR 2
See also DLB 160
See also MAICYA
See also SATA 2
Treece, Patricia 1938- 110
Trefethen, Florence 1921- 29-32R
Trefethen, James B(yron, Jr.) 1916-1976 CANR-11
Obituary 69-72
Earlier sketch in CA 21-24R
Treffert, Darold A(llen) 1933- 131
Trefflich, Henry (Herbert Frederick) 1908-1978
CAP-2
Obituary 77-80
Earlier sketch in CA 23-24
Trefftzs, Kenneth Lewis 1911- 13-16R
Trefil, James S. 1938- CANR-27
Earlier sketch in CA 101
Trefor, Eirlys
See Williams, Eirlys O(lwen)
Trefousse, Hans Louis 1921- CANR-14
Earlier sketch in CA 37-40R
Tregarthen, Enys
See Sloggett, Nellie
Tregaskis, Hugh 1905(?)-1983 Obituary 110
Tregaskis, Richard 1916-1973 CANR-2
Obituary 45-48
Earlier sketch in CA 1-4R
See also SATA 3
See also SATA-Obit 26
Tregear, Thomas R(efoy) 1897- 21-24R
Treger, Harvey 1924- 61-64
Treggiari, Susan (Mary) 1940- 61-64
Tregidgo, Philip Sillince 1926- 105
Treglown, Jeremy (Dickinson) 1946- 114
Brief entry 111
Interview in 114
Trego, Walter
See Smith, W(illiam) Eugene
Tregoe, Benjamin B., Jr. 1927- 125
Tregonning, Kennedy Gordon 1923- 9-12R
Treherne, Katie Thamer 1955- SATA 76
Trehey, Harold F. 1902(?)-1978 Obituary 77-80
Trehub, Arnold 1923- 140
Treichler, Jessie C(ambron)
1906(?)-1972 Obituary 37-40R
Treister, Bernard W(illiam) 1932- 101
Treitel, G(uenter) H(einz) 1928- 139
Treitel, Jonathan 1959- CLC 70
Trejo, Arnulfo D(uenes) 1922- CANR-32
Earlier sketch in CA 57-60
See also HW
Trejo, Ernesto 1950-1991 DLB 122
Trejos, Carlota 1920- 49-52
Trekell, Harold E(verett) 1910- 49-52
Trela, D(ale) J(ohn) 1958- 152
Trelawny, Edward John 1792-1881 DLB 110, 116,
144
Trelease, Allen William 1928- 108
Trelease, James J(oseph) 1941- 112
Trelease, Jim
See Trelease, James J(oseph)
Trelford, Donald Gilchrist 1937- 111
Trell, Bluma L(ee) 1903-1997 77-80
Obituary 159
Trell, Max 1900- 41-44R
See also SATA 14
Treloar, Dorothy 1920(?)-1983 Obituary 111
Treloar, James A(rthur) 1933- 45-48
Trelos, Tony
See Crechales, Anthony George
Tremain, Rose 1943- CANR-44
Earlier sketch in CA 97-100
See also CLC 42
See also DLB 14
Tremain, Ruthven 1922- 85-88
See also SATA 17
Tremaine, Jennie
See Chesney, Marion
Tremaine, Katherine
See Tremaine, Kit
Tremaine, Kit 1907-1997 139
Obituary 156
Tremayne, Jonathan
See Forrest-Webb, Robert
Tremayne, Ken(neth Eugene, Jr.) 1933- 17-20R
Tremayne, Peter
See Ellis, Peter Berresford
Tremayne, Sydney (Durward) 1912- CANR-5
Earlier sketch in CA 5-8R
Trembath, Don 1963- 161
See also SATA 96
Trembath, Kern R(obert) 1951- 144
Tremblay, Bill
See Tremblay, William (Andrew)
Tremblay, Marc-Adelard 1922- 41-44R
Tremblay, Michel 1942- 128
Brief entry 116
See also CLC 29, 102
See also DAC
See also DAM MST
See also DLB 60
See also MTCW 1
Tremblay, William (Andrew) 1940- CANR-59
Earlier sketch in CA 89-92
Tremble, Freda B. 1894- 73-76
Tremens, Del
See MacDonald, Amy
Treml, Vladimir G(uy) 1929- 25-28R
Tremlett, George (William) 1939- 142
Tremmel, William Calloley 1918- 97-100
Trench, (William Francis) Brinsley Le Poer
See Le Poer Trench, (William Francis) Brinsley
Trench, Charles (Pocklington) Chenevix 1914-
CANR-45
Trench, Richard 1949- 133
Trendall, Arthur Dale 1909-1995 CANR-46
Obituary 150
Earlier sketches in CA 53-56, CANR-5, 22
Treneer, Anne 1891- CAP-1
Earlier sketch in CA 9-10
Trenerry, Walter N. 1917- 135
Trengove, Alan Thomas 1929- 108
Trenhaile, John (Stevens) 1949- 110
Trenholm, Virginia Cole 1902- 13-16R
Trenker, Alois Franz 1892-1990 Obituary 131
Trenker, Luis
See Trenker, Alois Franz
Trennert, Robert A., Jr. 1937- 57-60
Trensky, Paul I. 1929- 93-96
Trent, James W(illiam) 1933- 21-24R
Trent, Jimmie Douglas 1933- 49-52
Trent, May Wong 1939- 57-60
Trent, Olaf
See Fanthorpe, R(obert) Lionel
Trent, Robbie 1894- CAP-1
Earlier sketch in CA 9-10
See also SATA 26
Trent, Timothy
See Malmberg, Carl
Trent, William 1919- CANR-3
Earlier sketch in CA 1-4R
Trent, William P(eterfield) 1862-1939 Brief
entry 122
See also DLB 47, 71
Trento, Joseph John 1947- 45-48
Trento, Salvatore Michael 1952- 101
Trepp, Leo 1913- CANR-40
Earlier sketches in CA 5-8R, CANR-2, 18
Trepper, Leopold Leib 1904-1982(?) Obituary 105
Tresch, John William, Jr. 1937- Brief entry 106
Trescot, William Henry 1822-1898 DLB 30
Trescott, Paul B(arton) 1925- CANR-2
Earlier sketch in CA 1-4R
Trese, Leo J(ohn) 1902- 5-8R
Treseder, Terry Walton 1956- SATA 68
Tresemer, David 1948- 108
Treshow, Michael 1926- 57-60
Tresidder, Argus John 1907- CANR-5
Earlier sketch in CA 5-8R
Tresilian, Liz
See Green, Elisabeth Sara
Tresilian, (Cecil) Stuart 1891-(?) SATA 40
Tress, Arthur 1940- 101
Tressell, Robert 1870-1911 DLB 197
Tresselt, Alvin 1916- CANR-1
Earlier sketch in CA 49-52
See also CLR 30
See also MAICYA
See also SATA 7
Tressidy, Jim
See Norwood, Victor G(eorge) C(harles)
Tressilian, Charles
See Atcheson, Richard
Tressler, Donald K(iteley) 1894-1981 CANR-4
Obituary 103
Earlier sketch in CA 45-48
Trethowan, K(enneth) Illtyd 1907- CANR-3
Earlier sketch in CA 1-4R
Tretick, Stanley 1921- 103
Trettel, (Mario) Efrem 1921- 69-72
Treuenfels, Peter 1926- 37-40R
Treuer, David 1970- 153
Treuer, Robert 1926- 69-72
Trevanian
See Whitaker, Rod(ney)
See also CLC 29
Trevaskis, G(erald) K(ennedy) N(icholas)
1915-1990 Obituary 131
Trevaskis, John 1911-1968 CAP-1
Earlier sketch in CA 9-10
Trevaskis, Sir Kennedy
See Trevaskis, G(erald) K(ennedy) N(icholas)
Trevathan, Robert E(ugene) 1925- CANR-64
Earlier sketches in CA 1-4R, CANR-6
Trevelyan, George Macaulay 1876-1962 89-92
Trevelyan, George Otto 1838-1928 DLB 144
Trevelyan, Humphrey 1905-1985 37-40R
Obituary 115
Trevelyan, Julian O(tto) 1910-1988 9-12R
Obituary 126
Trevelyan, Katharine 1908- CAP-1
Earlier sketch in CA 11-12
Trevelyan, (Walter) Raleigh 1923- CANR-47
Earlier sketches in CA 13-16R, CANR-6, 22
Trevelyan, Robert
See Forrest-Webb, Robert
Trever, John C(ecil) 1915- 17-20R
Treverton, Gregory F(rye) 1947- 118
Treves, Ralph 1906- 13-16R
Trevino, Elizabeth B(orton) de 1904- CANR-9
Earlier sketch in CA 17-20R
See also MAICYA
See also SAAS 5
See also SATA 1, 29
Trevino, Lee (Buck) 1939- 113
Trevisa, John c. 1342-c. 1402 DLB 146
Trevor, Elleston 1920-1995 CANR-59
Obituary 149
Earlier sketch in CA 5-8R
See also SATA 28
Trevor, Frances
See Teasdale, Sara
Trevor, Glen
See Hilton, James
Trevor, (Lucy) Meriol 1919- CANR-16
Earlier sketches in CA 1-4R, CANR-1
See also SATA 10
Trevor, William 1928-
See Cox, William Trevor
See also CLC 7, 9, 14, 25, 71
See also DLB 14, 139
See also SSC 21
Trevor-Roper, H(ugh) R(edwald) 1914- 101
Trew, Antony (Francis) 1906- CANR-2
Earlier sketch in CA 45-48
Trewin, Ion (Courtenay Gill) 1943- 69-72
Trewin, J(ohn) C(ourtenay)
1908-1990 Obituary 131
Brief entry 112
Treyz, Russell 1940- 132
Trez, Alain
See Tredez, Alain
Trez, Denise
See Tredez, Denise
Trezise, Percy (James) 1923- 132
See also CLR 41
Trezise, Philip Harold 1912- 109
Trezza, Alphonse F(iore) 1920- CANR-42
Earlier sketch in CA 118
Triana, Jose 1932(?)- 131
See also HW
Triandis, Harry C(haralambos) 1926- 41-44R
Tribbe, Frank C(alvert) 1914- 117
Tribble, Edwin 1907-1986 142
Obituary 119
Tribble, Harold Wayland 1899-1986 Obituary 121
Tribe, David (Harold) 1931- 25-28R
Tribe, Ivan M(athews) 1940- CANR-48
Earlier sketch in CA 122
Tribe, Laurence H(enry) 1941- 133
Tribich, Susan 1945(?)-1985 Obituary 115
Trible, Phyllis 1932- 154
Tribune
See Armstrong, Douglas Albert
Trice, Borough
See Allen, A(rthur) B(ruce)
Trice, Dawn Turner 166
Trice, Harrison M. 1920- 21-24R
Tricker, B(rian) J(ohn) K(ingsbury) 1937- 25-28R
Trickett, Joyce 1915- CANR-34
Earlier sketch in CA 105
Trickett, Mabel Rachel 1923- 101
Triegel, Linda (Jeanette) 1942- 117
Triem, Eve 1902- CANR-9
Earlier sketch in CA 17-20R
Triere, Lynette 1941- 108
Trieschman, Albert E(well) 1931-1984 29-32R
Obituary 113
Triffin, Robert 1911-1993 CANR-3
Obituary 140
Earlier sketch in CA 1-4R
Trifonov, Yuri (Valentinovich) 1925-1981 126
Obituary 103
See also CLC 45
See also MTCW 1
Trigg, George L. 1925- 139
Trigg, Harry Davis 1927- 61-64
Trigg, Joseph Wilson 1949- 118
Trigg, Roger (Hugh) 1941- 49-52
Trigg, Yolanda Lillian 1926- 61-64
Trigger, Bruce G(raham) 1937- CANR-29
Earlier sketches in CA 21-24R, CANR-9
Trigger, David S. 1953- 147
Triggs, Tony D. 1946- 138
See also SATA 70
Trigoboff, Joseph 1947- 81-84
Trillin, Calvin (Marshall) 1935- CANR-67
Earlier sketches in CA 85-88, CANR-20, 46
See also AITN 1
See also DLB 185
See also MTCW 1
Trilling, Diana (Rubin) 1905-1996 CANR-46
Obituary 154
Earlier sketches in CA 5-8R, CANR-10
Interview in CANR-10
See also MTCW 1
Trilling, Lionel 1905-1975 CANR-10
Obituary 61-64
Earlier sketch in CA 9-12R
Interview in CANR-10
See also CLC 9, 11, 24
See also DLB 28, 63
See also MTCW 1
Trilussa 1871-1950 DLB 114
Trimball, W. H.
See Mencken, H(enry) L(ouis)

Trimble, Barbara Margaret 1921- CANR-62
Earlier sketch in CA 132
Trimble, Jacquelyn W(hitney) 1927- 13-16R
Trimble, John F(elix) 1925- 97-100
Trimble, Louis P(reston) 1917- CANR-64
Earlier sketches in CA 13-16R, CANR-6
Trimble, Marshall I(ra) 1939- CANR-61
Earlier sketch in CA 77-80
See also SATA 93
Trimble, Martha Scott 1914- 29-32R
Trimble, Stephen 1950- 149
Trimble, Vance H(enry) 1913- 49-52
Trimble, William Raleigh 1913- 9-12R
Trimby, Elisa 1948- 122
See also SATA 47
See also SATA-Brief 40
Trimiew, Darryl M. 1952- 158
Trimingham, J(ohn) Spencer 1904- CANR-3
Earlier sketch in CA 1-4R
Trimmer, Ellen McKay 1915- 9-12R
Trimmer, Eric J. 1923- 9-12R
Trimmer, Joseph F(rancis) 1941- CANR-42
Earlier sketches in CA 77-80, CANR-13
Trimmer, Sarah 1741-1810 .... DLB 158
Trimpey, Jack
See Trimpey, John P.
Trimpey, John P. 1941- 139
Tring, A. Stephen
See Meynell, Laurence Walter
Trinh, T. Min-Ha 1952- 154
Trinidad, Corky
See Trinidad, Francisco D., Jr.
Trinidad, Francisco D., Jr. 1939- 69-72
Trinkaus, Charles (Edward) 1911- 29-32R
Trinkaus, Erik 1948- 140
Trinklein, Frederick E(rnst) 1924- 41-44R
Trinkner, Charles L. 1920- 29-32R
Trinquier, Roger Paul 1908- CANR-5
Earlier sketch in CA 9-12R
Triola, Mario F(rank) 1944- 57-60
Triolet, Elsa 1896-1970 Obituary 25-28R
See also DLB 72
Triplehorn, Charles A(lbert) 1927- 130
Triplett, Kenneth E(arl) 1926- 57-60
Triplett, Raymond (Francis) 1921- 117
Tripodi, Thomas Charles 1932- 141
Tripodi, Tom
See Tripodi, Thomas Charles
Tripodi, Tony 1932- CANR-12
Earlier sketch in CA 29-32R
Tripp, C(larence) A(rthur) 1919- 73-76
Tripp, Charles R(ees) H(oward) 1952- 158
Tripp, Eleanor B(aldwin) 1936- 29-32R
See also SATA 4
Tripp, John
See Moore, John Travers
Tripp, John 1927- 97-100
See also DLB 40
Tripp, Karen 1923-1993 .... CANR-47
Obituary 141
Earlier sketch in CA 53-56
Tripp, L(ouis) Reed 1913- 5-8R
Tripp, Miles (Barton) 1923- CANR-60
Earlier sketches in CA 13-16R, CANR-12, 28
Tripp, Nathaniel 1944- 161
See also SATA 101
Tripp, Paul 1916- 21-24R
See also SATA 8
Tripp, Valerie 1951- 146
See also SATA 78
Tripp, Wallace (Whitney) 1940- CANR-23
Earlier sketch in CA 106
See also SATA 31
Tripp, Wendell, Jr. 1928- 114
Trippett, Frank 1926- 21-24R
Trisco, Robert Frederick 1929- 41-44R
Triska, Jan Francis 1922- CANR-7
Earlier sketch in CA 5-8R
Trisler, Hank 1937- 121
Tristan
See Gomez de la Serna, Ramon
Tristram
See Housman, A(lfred) E(dward)
Tritel, Barbara
See Quick, Barbara
Trites, Roberta Seelinger 1962- 168
Triton, A. N.
See Barclay, Oliver R(ainsford)
Tritt, Robert E(arl) 1921- 21-24R
Trittschuh, Travis Edward 1920- 5-8R
Trivas, A(lexander) Victor 1894-1970 .... CAP-1
Obituary 29-32R
Earlier sketch in CA 19-20
Trivelpiece, Laurel 1926- 123
See also SATA 56
See also SATA-Brief 46
Trivers, Howard 1909-1987 73-76
Obituary 122
Trivett, Daphne Harwood 1940- 97-100
See also SATA 22
Trivizas, Eugene 1946- 150
See also SATA 84
Trnka, Jiri 1912-1969 Obituary 111
See also MAICYA
See also SATA 43
See also SATA-Brief 32
Trobian, Helen R(eed) 1918- 5-8R
Trobisch, Ingrid (Hult) 1926- CANR-28
Earlier sketch in CA 97-100
Trocchi, Alexander 1925-1984 .... CANR-72
Obituary 112
Earlier sketch in CA 9-12R
See also DLB 15
Troche, Rose 1964(?)- 147
Trocme, Etienne 1924- 49-52
Troeger, Thomas H(enry) 1945- CANR-34
Earlier sketches in CA 89-92, CANR-15
Troelstrup, Arch William 1901- 17-20R
Troen, Selwyn K. 1940- 104
Trofimenkoff, Susan Mann 1941- 73-76
Trogdon, William (Lewis) 1939- CANR-47
Brief entry 115
Earlier sketch in CA 119
Interview in 119
See also Heat-Moon, William Least
Trohan, Walter (Joseph) 1903- 81-84
Troiden, Richard (Russell) 1946- 89-92
Troise, Joe 1942- 103
Troisgros, Jean (Georges) 1926-1983 Obituary 110
Troisi, Dante 1920-1989 .... DLB 196
Troitsky, Artemy 1955- 136
Trojan, Judith 1947- 131
Trojanowicz, John M.
See Troyanovich, John M(ichael)
Trojanowicz, Robert C(hester) 1941-1994 .... CANR-31
Obituary 144
Earlier sketch in CA 45-48
Trojanski, John 1943- 45-48
Trolander, Judith Ann 1942- 61-64
Trollope, Anthony 1815-1882 ... CDBLB 1832-1890
See also DA
See also DAB
See also DAC
See also DAM MST, NOV
See also DLB 21, 57, 159
See also SATA 22
See also SSC 28
See also WLC
Trollope, Frances 1779-1863 .... DLB 21, 166
Trollope, Joanna 1943- CANR-58
Earlier sketch in CA 101
Troman, Morley 1918- 13-16R
Tromanhauser, Edward (Downer) 1932- 41-44R
Trombley, Charles C(yprian) 1928- 65-68
Trombley, Stephen 1954- 129
Trombold, Charles D(ickson) 1942- 143
Tromp, S. W.
See Tromp, Solco Walle
Tromp, Solco W.
See Tromp, Solco Walle
Tromp, Solco Walle 1909-1983 Obituary 116
Tronchin-James, (Robert) Nevil 1916- CAP-1
Earlier sketch in CA 9-10
Trooboff, Peter D(ennis) 1942- 65-68
Troop, Elizabeth 1931- 164
Brief entry 116
See also DLB 14
Troop, Miriam 1917- 13-16R
Tropman, John E. 1939- 154
Tropp, Martin 1945- 65-68
Trost, Cathy 1951- 125
Trost, Lucille W(ood) 1938- CANR-9
Earlier sketch in CA 61-64
See also SATA 12
Trotman, Jack H(arry) 129
Trotsky, Leon 1879-1940 167
Brief entry 118
See also TCLC 22
Trott, Betty 1933- 155
See also SATA 91
Trott, Susan 1937- 97-100
Trotta, John 1936- 45-48
Trotta, Maurice S. 1907-1976 Obituary 111
Trotter, Catharine (Cockburn), Catharine 1679-1749 .... DLB 84
Trotter, Grace V(iolet) 1900- CANR-1
Earlier sketch in CA 1-4R
See also SATA 10
Trotter, Jesse McLane (?)-1983 Obituary 110
Trotter, Michael H(amilton) 1936- 165
Trotter, Patrick C. 1935- 126
Trotter, Robert J(oseph) 1943- 120
Trotter, Sallie (W. B.) 1915- 29-32R
Trotter, William R., (Jr.) 1943- 141
Trotti, John H. 1936- 118
Trotti, Lamar 1898-1952 .... DLB 44
Trottier, Pierre 1925- .... DLB 60
Troughton, Joanna (Margaret) 1947- CANR-26
Earlier sketch in CA 109
See also SATA 37
Trouncer, Margaret (Lahey) 1903-1982 .... CANR-10
Obituary 108
Earlier sketch in CA 5-8R
Troup, Cornelius V. 1902- CAP-1
Earlier sketch in CA 9-10
Troupe, Quincy (Thomas, Jr.) 1943- CANR-43
Brief entry 113
Earlier sketch in CA 124
See also BW 2
See also DLB 41
Trout, Charles Hathaway 1935- 113
Trout, Kilgore
See Farmer, Philip Jose
Trout, Robert J(ay) 1947- 142
Troutman, Charles (Henry) 1914- 69-72
Trouve, Roger 1882(?)-1984 Obituary 112
Trow, George W. S. 1943- 126
See also CLC 52
Trow, M(eirion) J(ames) 1949- 120
Trow, Martin A. 1926- 112
Trow, W(illiam) Clark 1894- CANR-6
Earlier sketch in CA 5-8R
Trowbridge, Clinton W(hiting) 1928- CANR-10
Earlier sketch in CA 65-68
Trowbridge, John Townsend 1827-1916 .... DLB 202
Trowbridge, Keith W(ayne) 1937- 108
Trowbridge, Leslie Walter 1920- CANR-13
Earlier sketch in CA 77-80
Trowell, Kathleen Margaret 1904- 65-68
Troxell, Eugene A(nthony) 1937- 73-76
Troxell, Mary D(earborn) 1907- 37-40R
Troy, George F(rancis), Jr. 1909-1969 .... 1-4R
Obituary 103
Troy, Judy 1951- 143
Troy, Katherine
See Buxton, Anne (Arundel)
Troy, Lawrence M. 1928- 21-24R
Troy, Nancy J. 1952- CANR-37
Earlier sketch in CA 115
Troy, Una 1913- CANR-3
Earlier sketch in CA 1-4R
Troy, William 1903-1961 Obituary 89-92
Troyanovich, John M(ichael) 1936- CANR-57
Earlier sketches in CA 49-52, CANR-31
Troyat, Henri 1911- CANR-67
Earlier sketches in CA 45-48, CANR-2, 33
See also CLC 23
See also MTCW 1
Troyer, Byron L(eRoy) 1909- 65-68
Troyer, Johannes 1902-1969 .... SATA-Brief 40
Troyer, Warner 1932- 101
Interview in 101
Troyka, Lynn Quitman 1938- 37-40R
Troyna, Barry 1951- CANR-40
Earlier sketch in CA 117
Truax, Carol 1900- CANR-5
Earlier sketch in CA 5-8R
Truax, Charles B. 1933-197(?) CANR-13
Earlier sketches in CAP-2, CA 21-22
Truax, R. Hawley 1889(?)-1978 Obituary 81-84
Trubitt, Allen R(oy) 1931- 77-80
Trubo, Richard 1946- CANR-11
Earlier sketch in CA 61-64
Trubowitz, Sidney 1926- 21-24R
Truby, J(ohn) David 1938- CANR-24
Earlier sketches in CA 53-56, CANR-4
Truch, Stephen 1947- 115
Trudeau, G(arretson) B(eekman) 1948- CANR-31
Earlier sketch in CA 81-84
See also Trudeau, Garry B.
See also SATA 35
Trudeau, Garry B.
See Trudeau, G(arretson) B(eekman)
See also AAYA 10
See also AITN 2
See also CLC 12
Trudeau, Margaret (Joan) 1948- 93-96
Trudeau, Noah Andre 1949- 132
Trudeau, (Joseph Philippe) Pierre (Yves) Elliott 1919- CANR-3
Earlier sketch in CA 45-48
Trudel, Marcel 1917- 104
Trudix, Marty
See Truman, Ruth
True, Dan 1924- 117
True, Michael (D.) 1933- CANR-37
Earlier sketches in CA 41-44R, CANR-17
Trueblood, Alan Stubbs 1917- 103
Trueblood, D(avid) Elton 1900- 41-44R
Trueblood, Paul Graham 1905- CANR-12
Earlier sketches in CAP-1, CA 17-18
Trueblood, Ted Whitaker 1913-1982 Obituary 111
Trueheart, Charles 1951- 45-48
Truemper, David G(eorge) 1939- 112
Truesdale, C(alvin) W(illiam) 1929- CANR-30
Earlier sketch in CA 29-32R
Truesdell, Leon E. 1881(?)-1979 Obituary 85-88
Truesdell, Sue
See Truesdell, Susan G.
Truesdell, Susan G. .... SATA-Brief 45
Truett, Fred M(oore) 1899- CAP-2
Earlier sketch in CA 21-22
Truett, Joe C(lyde) 1941- 118
Truffaut, Francois 1932-1984 .... CANR-34
Obituary 113
Earlier sketch in CA 81-84
See also CLC 20, 101
Truillier-Lacombe, Joseph-Patrice 1807-1863 .. DLB 99
Truitt, Anne (Dean) 1921- 142
Truitt, Deborah H(unsberger) 1945- 45-48
Truitt, Evelyn Mack 1931- 57-60
Truitt, Gloria A(nn) 1939- CANR-56
Earlier sketches in CA 111, CANR-30
Truitt, John O(liver) 1934- 117
Truitt, Willis H(arrison) 1936- 57-60
Truman, Harry S 1884-1972 106
Obituary 37-40R
Truman, Jill 1934- 128
Truman, (Mary) Margaret 1924- CANR-54
Earlier sketches in CA 105, CANR-29
See also BEST 90:1
See also DAM POP
See also MTCW 1
Truman, Ruth 1931- 53-56
Trumbo, Dalton 1905-1976 .... CANR-10
Obituary 69-72
Earlier sketch in CA 21-24R
See also CLC 19
See also DLB 26
Trumbull, Benjamin 1735-1820 .... DLB 30
Trumbull, John 1750-1831 .... DLB 31
Trumbull, Robert 1912-1992 .... CANR-5
Obituary 139
Earlier sketch in CA 9-12R
Trump, Donald J.
See Trump, Donald J(ohn)
See also BEST 89:1
Trump, Donald J(ohn) 1946- 130
See also Trump, Donald J.
Trump, Fred(erick Leonard) 1924- 13-16R
Trump, Ivana M. 1949- 140
Trump, Richard F. 1912- 126
Trumpener, Ulrich 1930- 25-28R
Trumper, Hubert Bagster 1902- CAP-1
Earlier sketch in CA 9-10
Trundlett, Helen B.
See Eliot, T(homas) S(tearns)
Trungpa, Chogyam
See Chogyam Trungpa
Trunk, Isaiah Elezer 1905-1981 89-92
Obituary 108
Interview in 89-92
Truong, Thanh-Dam 1949- 136
Trupin, James E. 1940- 37-40R
Trupp, Beverly Ann 1937- 105
Truscott, Alan (Fraser) 1925- 25-28R
Truscott, Lucian K(ing) IV 1947- CANR-65
Earlier sketch in CA 89-92
Truscott, Robert Blake 1944- 77-80
Truse, Kenneth (Philip) 1946- 105
Truss, Jan 1925- 102
See also SATA 35
Truss, Seldon
See Seldon-Truss, Leslie
Trussell, C(harles) P(rescott) 1892-1968 Obituary 89-92
Trussler, Simon 1942- CANR-28
Earlier sketches in CA 25-28R, CANR-12
Trustman, Alan Robert 1930- Brief entry 111
Truumaa, Aare 1926- 49-52
Truzzi, Marcello 1935- 41-44R
Tryon, Darrell Trevor 1942- 111
Tryon, Georgiana Shick 1945- 116
Tryon, Ruth Wilson 1892(?)-1987 Obituary 123
Tryon, Thomas 1926-1991 .... CANR-32
Obituary 135
Earlier sketch in CA 29-32R
See also AITN 1
See also CLC 3, 11
See also DAM POP
See also MTCW 1
Tryon, Tom
See Tryon, Thomas
Tryon, W(arren) S(tenson) 1901-1989 .... CAP-1
Obituary 129
Earlier sketch in CA 11-12
Trypanis, C(onstantine) A(thanasius) 1909-1993 ... CANR-24
Obituary 140
Earlier sketches in CA 5-8R, CANR-7
Trythall, Anthony John 1927- 77-80
Trythall, J(ohn) W(illiam) D(onald) 1944- 29-32R
Trzebinski, Errol 1936- 143
Tsadick, Marta Gabre
See Gabre-Tsadick, Marta
Tsai, Shih-shan Henry 1940- 125
Tsaloumas, Dimitris 1921- 154
Tsambassis, Alexander N(icholas) 1919- 21-24R
Tsatsos, Jeanne 1909- CANR-13
Earlier sketch in CA 29-32R
Tschachbasov, Nahum 1899-1984 Obituary 112
Tschebotarioff, Gregory P. 1899- 13-16R
Tscherning, Andreas 1611-1659 .... DLB 164
Tschichold, Jan 1902(?)-1974 Obituary 53-56
Tschudy, James Jay 1925- 13-16R
Tschumi, Raymond Robert 1924- CANR-3
Earlier sketch in CA 5-8R
Tse, K. K. 1948- 125
Tsegaye, Gabre-Medhin (Kawessa)
See Gabre-Medhin, Tsegaye (Kawessa)
Tseng Wen-Shing 1935- CANR-35
Earlier sketch in CA 114
Tsernianski, Milos
See Crnjanski, Milos
Tshiamala, Kabasele (?)-1983(?) Obituary 109
Tsien, Tsuen-hsuin 1909- CANR-23
Earlier sketches in CA 17-20R, CANR-7
Tsiolkovsky, Konstantin Eduardovich 1857-1935 164
Brief entry 119
Tsipis, Kosta 1934- 110
Tso, Yiu-kam 1918(?)-1983 Obituary 110
Tsomo, Karma Lekshe 1944- 150
Tsongas, Paul Efthemios 1941-1997 108
Obituary 156
Tsou, Tang 1918- CANR-8
Earlier sketch in CA 5-8R
Tsubouchi Shoyo 1859-1935 .... DLB 180
Tsuji, Kunio 1925- 154
Tsuji, Shinichi
See Oiwa, Keibo
Tsukahira, Toshio George 1915- 21-24R
Tsukinabe, Isao
See Vermeule, Cornelius Clarkson III
Tsukui, Nobuko 1938- 133
Tsuneishi, Warren M(ichio) 1921- 17-20R
Tsurumi, Shunsuke 1922- 138
Tsurutani, Taketsugu 1935- 104
Tsushima, Satoko 1947- 154
Tsushima, Shuji 1909-1948 Brief entry 107
See also Dazai Osamu
Tsushima, Yuko
See Tsushima, Satoko
Tsutomu, Minakami 1919- .... DLB 182
Tsutsui, Yoriko 1945- 132
Tsuzuki, Chushichi 1926- CANR-3
Earlier sketch in CA 1-4R
Tsvetaeva (Efron), Marina (Ivanovna) 1892-1941 128
Brief entry 104
See also MTCW 1
See also PC 14
See also TCLC 7, 35
Tswett, Mikhail Semyonovich 1872-1919 162
Tu, Wei-ming 1940- 65-68
Tuan, Yi-Fu 1930- CANR-37
Earlier sketches in CA 93-96, CANR-16
Tuann, Lucy H(siu-mei) C(hen) 1938- 85-88
Tubb, E(dwin) C(harles) 1919- CANR-21
Earlier sketch in CA 101
Tubb, Ernest (Dale) 1914-1984 Obituary 114

Tubb, Jonathan N. 1951- ... 146
See also SATA 78
Tubbs, Stewart L(ee) 1943- ... CANR-6
Earlier sketch in CA 57-60
Tubby, I. M.
See Kraus, (Herman) Robert
Tucci, Giuseppe 1894-1984 Obituary ... 112
Tucci, Niccolo 1908- ... 81-84
Tucci, Stanley 1960- ... 165
Tuccille, Jerome 1937- ... CANR-12
Earlier sketch in CA 29-32R
Tuchinsky, Joseph S. 1937- ... CANR-10
Earlier sketch in CA 25-28R
Tuchman, Barbara W(ertheim) 1912-1989 ... CANR-24
Obituary ... 127
Earlier sketches in CA 1-4R, CANR-3
See also BEST 89:1
See also DAM POP
See also MTCW 1
Tuchman, Gaye 1943- ... 85-88
Tuchman, Maurice 1936- ... CANR-27
Earlier sketches in CA 49-52, CANR-4
Tuchman, Phyllis 1947- ... 114
Tuchock, Wanda 1898(?)-1985 Obituary ... 115
Tucholsky, Kurt 1890-1935 ... DLB 56
Tuck, (John) Anthony 1940- ... 124
Tuck, Dorothy
See McFarland, Dorothy Tuck
Tuck, James A(lexander) 1940- ... 37-40R
Tuck, Lily 1938- ... 139
See also CLC 70
Tuck, Lon 1938(?)-1987 ... 133
Obituary ... 122
Tuck, Susan H. 1947- ... 118
Tucker, Ann
See Giudici, Ann Couper
Tucker, Anne 1945- ... CANR-19
Earlier sketch in CA 102
Tucker, Anthony 1924- ... 104
Tucker, Archibald Norman 1904(?)-1980 Obituary ... 101
Tucker, Audrie Manley
See Manley-Tucker, Audrie
Tucker, Bob
See Tucker, (Arthur) Wilson
Tucker, Carll 1951- ... 133
Tucker, Caroline
See Nolan, Jeannette Covert
Tucker, Charlotte Maria 1 1821-1893 . DLB 163, 190
Tucker, Cynthia Grant 1941- ... 135
Tucker, David M(ilton) 1937- ... 101
Tucker, Edward L(lewellyn) 1921- ... 17-20R
Tucker, Ernest E(dward) 1916-1969 ... 61-64
Tucker, Eva 1929- ... 17-20R
Tucker, Frank H(ammond) 1923- ... CANR-10
Earlier sketch in CA 25-28R
Tucker, Gabe
See Tucker, Gaylord B(ob)
Tucker, Gaylord B(ob) 1915- ... 110
Tucker, Gene M(ilton) 1935- ... CANR-15
Earlier sketch in CA 37-40R
Tucker, George 1775-1861 ... DLB 3, 30
Tucker, Georgina P. 1911- ... 97-100
Tucker, Gina
See Tucker, Georgina P.
Tucker, Glenn (Irving) 1892-1976 ... 5-8R
Obituary ... 69-72
Tucker, Graham Harold 1925- ... 113
Tucker, Harry, Jr. 1921- ... 41-44R
Tucker, Helen 1926- ... CANR-11
Earlier sketch in CA 29-32R
Tucker, Irwin St. John 1886-1982 Obituary ... 105
Tucker, James 1929- ... CANR-9
Earlier sketch in CA 21-24R
Tucker, Jonathan B(rin) 1954- ... 109
Tucker, Karen ... 143
Tucker, Lael
See Wertenbaker, Lael (Tucker)
Tucker, Lael
See Wertenbaker, Lael (Tucker)
Tucker, Link
See Bingley, David Ernest
Tucker, Marcia 1940- ... 65-68
Tucker, Mark (D.) 1954- ... 155
Tucker, Martin 1928- ... 17-20R
Tucker, Melvin J(ay) 1931- ... 113
Tucker, Michael R(ay) 1941- ... CANR-12
Earlier sketch in CA 61-64
Tucker, Nathaniel Beverley 1784-1851 ... DLB 3
Tucker, Nicholas 1936- ... CANR-11
Earlier sketch in CA 65-68
Tucker, Patricia 1912- ... 65-68
Tucker, Paul Hayes 1950- ... 110
Tucker, Robert C(harles) 1918- ... CANR-3
Earlier sketch in CA 1-4R
Tucker, Robert W(arren) 1924- ... 134
Tucker, Robin 1950- ... 53-56
Tucker, Ruth A(nne) 1945- ... CANR-40
Earlier sketch in CA 117
Tucker, St. George 1752-1827 ... DLB 37
Tucker, Spencer C. 1937- ... 146
Tucker, Susan (Norris) 1950- ... 130
Tucker, Wallace H. 1939- ... 121
Tucker, William 1942- ... 163
Tucker, William E(dward) 1932- ... CANR-3
Earlier sketch in CA 9-12R
Tucker, William R(ayburn) 1923- ... 61-64
Tucker, (Arthur) Wilson 1914- ... 17-20R
Tucker-Fettner, Ann
See Giudici, Ann Couper
Tuckerman, Henry Theodore 1813-1871 ... DLB 64
Tuckey, John S(utton) 1921- ... CANR-7
Earlier sketch in CA 5-8R
Tuckman, Bruce W(ayne) 1938- ... CANR-11
Earlier sketch in CA 25-28R
Tuckman, Howard P(aul) 1941- ... CANR-10
Earlier sketch in CA 57-60
Tuckner, Howard 1932(?)-1980 Obituary ... 101
Tudge, Colin 1943- ... 154
Tudhope, Richard
See Rodda, Peter (Gordon)
Tudor, Andrew Frank 1942- ... 107
Tudor, Dean 1943- ... CANR-8
Earlier sketch in CA 61-64
Tudor, Henry 1937- ... 147
Tudor, Nancy (Patricia Rice) 1943- Brief entry ... 109
Tudor, Tasha 1915- ... 81-84
See also CLR 13
See also MAICYA
See also SATA 20, 69
Tudor-Craig, Pamela 1928- ... 124
Tudyman, Al 1914- ... 21-24R
Tuell, Jack Marvin 1923- ... 29-32R
Tueni, Nadia (Hamade) 1935-1983 Obituary ... 110
Tuerck, David G(eorge) 1941- ... CANR-14
Earlier sketch in CA 21-24R
Tuerk, Hanne 1951- ... CANR-45
Earlier sketch in CA 118
See also SATA 71
Tufail, Muhammad 1921(?)-1984 Obituary ... 113
Tuffs, J(ack) Elsden 1922- ... 5-8R
Tufte, Edward R(olf) 1942- ... CANR-1
Earlier sketch in CA 49-52
Tufte, Virginia J(ames) 1918- ... 125
Brief entry ... 106
Tufts, Eleanor (May) 1927-1991 ... 77-80
Obituary ... 136
Tufty, Barbara 1923- ... 37-40R
Tufty, Esther Van Wagoner 1896-1986 Obituary ... 119
Tu Fu 712-770 ... DAM MULT
See also PC 9
Tugay, Emine Foat
See Foat Tugay, Emine
Tugend, Harry 1898(?)-1989 Obituary ... 129
Tugendhat, Christopher Samuel 1937- ... 89-92
Tuggle, Ann Montgomery 1942- ... 125
Tuggle, Richard (Allan) 1948- ... 139
Tuggy, Joy Turner 1922- ... 21-24R
Tugwell, Franklin 1942- ... 57-60
Tugwell, Rexford Guy 1891-1979 ... 85-88
Obituary ... 89-92
Tulasiewicz, J(an) B(runo) 1913- ... 41-44R
Tulchin, Joseph S(amuel) 1939- ... 37-40R
Tulchin, Lewis 1905-1971 ... CAP-1
Earlier sketch in CA 19-20
Tuleja, Tad
See Tuleja, Thaddeus F(rancis)
Tuleja, Thaddeus F(rancis) 1944- ... 108
Tulis, Jeffrey K. 1950- ... CANR-56
Earlier sketches in CA 111, CANR-30
Tull, Charles Joseph 1931- ... 17-20R
Tull, Delena 1950- ... 125
Tull, Donald S(tanley) 1924- ... 81-84
Tull, James E. 1913- ... CANR-13
Earlier sketch in CA 77-80
Tuller, Lawrence W. 1933- ... 145
Tullett, James Stuart 1912- ... 106
Tullis, F. LaMond 1935- ... 81-84
Tulloch, G(ertrude) Janet 1924- ... 65-68
Tulloch, Richard (George) 1949- ... 143
See also SATA 76
Tullock, Gordon 1922- ... CANR-3
Earlier sketch in CA 1-4R
Tullos, Allen 1950- ... 132
Tully, Andrew (Frederick, Jr.) 1914-1993 ... 17-20R
Obituary ... 142
Tully, Gordon F(rederick) 1935- ... 106
Tully, Grace George 1900-1984 Obituary ... 113
Tully, John (Kimberley) 1923- ... CANR-53
Earlier sketches in CA 69-72, CANR-12, 28
See also SATA 14
Tully, (William) Mark 1935- ... 136
Tully, Mary Jo 1937- ... CANR-22
Earlier sketch in CA 105
Tuma, Elias H. 1928- Brief entry ... 115
Tuman, Myron C(hester) 1946- ... 139
Tumay, Paulett 1945- ... 128
Tumelty, James J. 1921(?)-1979(?) Obituary ... 104
Tumin, Melvin M(arvin) 1919-1994 ... 45-48
Obituary ... 144
Tumpson, Helen ... AITN 1
Tung, Ling
See Tung, William L(ing)
Tung, Shih-tsin (Shih-chin) 1900- ... 5-8R
Tung, William L(ing) 1907- ... 85-88
Tunick, Irve 1912-1987 Obituary ... 123
Tunick, Stanley B(loch) 1900- ... CAP-1
Earlier sketch in CA 17-18
Tunink, Wilfrid Bernard 1920- ... 5-8R
Tunis, Edwin (Burdett) 1897-1973 ... CANR-7
Obituary ... 45-48
Earlier sketch in CA 5-8R
See also CLR 2
See also MAICYA
See also SATA 1, 28
See also SATA-Obit 24
Tunis, John R(oberts) 1889-1975 ... CANR-62
Earlier sketch in CA 61-64
See also CLC 12
See also DLB 22, 171
See also JRDA
See also MAICYA
See also SATA 37
See also SATA-Brief 30
Tunley, Roul 1912- ... 13-16R
Tunnadine, Prudence 1928- ... 129
Tunnard, Christopher 1910-1979 ... CANR-6
Obituary ... 85-88
Earlier sketch in CA 5-8R
Tunnell, Doug(las Alan) 1949- ... 97-100
Tunner, William H(enry) 1906-1983 ... CAP-1
Obituary ... 109
Earlier sketch in CA 13-16
Tunney, Gene
See Tunney, James Joseph
Tunney, James Joseph 1898(?)-1978 Obituary . 111
Tunney, John V(arick) 1934- ... 61-64
Tunney, Kieran 1922- ... 117
Tunnicliffe, C(harles) F(rederick) 1901- ... 104
See also SATA 62
Tunstall, C. Jeremy 1934- ... CANR-42
Earlier sketches in CA 5-8R, CANR-4, 20
Tunstall, Cuthbert 1474-1559 ... DLB 132
Tunstall, Shana Barrett
See Tunstall, Velma
Tunstall, Velma 1914- ... 53-56
Tunyogi, Andrew C(sapo) 1907- ... CAP-2
Earlier sketch in CA 29-32
Tuohy, Frank
See Tuohy, John Francis
See also CLC 37
See also DLB 14, 139
Tuohy, John Francis 1925- ... CANR-47
Earlier sketches in CA 5-8R, CANR-3
See also Tuohy, Frank
Tuohy, William 1941- ... 37-40R
Tuohy, William Klaus 1926- ... 104
Tuohy, William S. 1938- ... 41-44R
Tupitsyn, Margarita 1955- ... 157
Tuplin, W(illiam) A(lfred) 1902-1975 Obituary ... 111
Tupper, Martin F. 1810-1889 ... DLB 32
Turabian, Kate L(arimore) 1893-1987 Obituary . 123
Turan, Kenneth 1946- ... 132
Turbayne, Colin Murray 1916- ... CANR-24
Earlier sketch in CA 1-4R
Turbet, Richard 1948- ... 141
Turbyfill, Mark 1896- ... 108
See also DLB 45
Turchin, Valentin F(yodorovich) 1931- ... 101
Turco, Lewis (Putnam) 1934- ... CANR-51
Earlier sketches in CA 13-16R, CANR-24
See also CAAS 22
See also CLC 11, 63
See also DLBY 84
Turco, Richard (Peter) 1943- ... 135
Turell, Saul J. 1921-1986 Obituary ... 120
Turetzky, Bertram Jay 1933- ... 57-60
Turgenev, Aleksandr Ivanovich 1784-1845 DLB 198
Turgenev, Ivan 1818-1883 ... DA
See also DAB
See also DAC
See also DAM MST, NOV
See also DC 7
See also SSC 7
See also WLC
Turgeon, Charlotte Snyder 1912- ... CANR-3
Earlier sketch in CA 5-8R
Turgeon, Lynn 1920- ... 5-8R
Turgeon, Pierre 1947- ... 163
Turiel, Isaac 1941- ... 122
Turing, John (Ferrier) 1908- ... CAP-2
Earlier sketch in CA 25-28
Turing, Penelope (Anne Tryon) 1925- ... 132
Turk, Frances (Mary) 1915- ... CAP-1
Earlier sketch in CA 9-10
Turk, Hanne
See Tuerk, Hanne
Turk, Herman 1929- ... 45-48
Turk, Laurel H(erbert) 1903- ... 21-24R
Turk, Midge
See Richardson, Midge Turk
Turk, Rudy H(enry) 1927- ... 97-100
Turk, Ruth 1917- ... 149
See also SATA 82
Turkel, Christopher 1955(?)-1983 Obituary ... 110
Turkel, Pauline
See Kesselman-Turkel, Judi
Turkel, Robin R. 1929(?)-1984 Obituary ... 113
Turkevich, Ludmilla Buketoff 1909-1995 ... 5-8R
Obituary ... 148
Turki, Fawaz 1940- ... 41-44R
Turkle, Brinton 1915- ... 25-28R
See also SATA 2, 79
Turkle, Sherry 1948- ... 102
Turkus, Burton B. 1902-1982 Obituary ... 108
Turley, Gerald H. 1931- ... 136
Turley, William S(tephen) 1943- ... CANR-21
Earlier sketch in CA 105
Turlington, Bayly 1919-1977 ... 29-32R
Obituary ... 122
See also SATA 5
See also SATA-Obit 52
Turlington, Catherine (Isabel) Hackett 1900(?)-1978 Obituary ... 77-80
Turlington, Henry E. 1918- ... 21-24R
Turnage, Anne Shaw 1927- ... 77-80
Turnage, Mac(lyn) N(eil) 1927- ... 77-80
Turnbaugh, William A(rthur) 1948- ... CANR-58
Earlier sketches in CA 112, CANR-31
Turnbull, Agnes Sligh 1888-1982 ... CANR-2
Obituary ... 105
Earlier sketch in CA 1-4R
See also SATA 14
Turnbull, Alexander H. 1868-1918 ... DLB 184
Turnbull, Andrew Winchester 1921-1970 .. CANR-3
Obituary ... 25-28R
Earlier sketch in CA 1-4R
See also DLB 103
Turnbull, Ann (Christine) 1943- ... 65-68
See also SATA 18
Turnbull, Bob 1936- ... CANR-14
Earlier sketch in CA 37-40R
Turnbull, Colin M(acmillan) 1924-1994 ... CANR-3
Obituary ... 146
Earlier sketch in CA 1-4R
See also AITN 1
Turnbull, Gael Lundin 1928- ... CANR-10
Earlier sketch in CA 65-68
See also CAAS 14
See also DLB 40
Turnbull, John G. 1913- ... 1-4R
Turnbull, Patrick Edward Xenophon 1908- . CANR-6
Earlier sketch in CA 5-8R
Turnbull, Peter (John) 1950- ... 130
Turnbull, Stephen (Richard) 1948- ... CANR-20
Earlier sketch in CA 104
Turnell, (George) Martin 1908-1979 ... 45-48
Obituary ... 103
Turner, A(lmon) Richard 1932- ... 17-20R
Turner, Alberta Tucker 1919- ... CANR-17
Earlier sketches in CA 49-52, CANR-1
Turner, Alice K. 1940- ... 53-56
See also SATA 10
Turner, Amedee E. 1929- ... 9-12R
Turner, Ann W(arren) 1945- ... CANR-58
Earlier sketches in CA 69-72, CANR-14, 31
See also SATA 14, 77
Turner, (Henry) Arlin 1909-1980 ... CANR-6
Obituary ... 97-100
Earlier sketch in CA 5-8R
See also DLB 103
Turner, Arnella K. 1917- ... 138
Turner, Arthur C(ampbell) 1918- ... 17-20R
Turner, B. L. II 1945- ... 142
Turner, Bessye Tobias 1917- ... 53-56
Turner, Bill
See Turner, W(illiam) Price
Turner, Bonnie 1932- ... 142
See also SATA 75
Turner, Brian (Lindsay) 1944- ... 154
Turner, Bruce (Malcolm) 1922- ... 132
Turner, Bryan S(tanley) 1945- ... 115
Turner, Charles (Tennyson) 1808-1879 ... DLB 32
Turner, Charles L. 1948- ... 167
Turner, Charles W(ilson) 1916- ... CANR-30
Earlier sketches in CA 37-40R, CANR-13
Turner, Clair (Elsmere) 1890- ... CAP-1
Earlier sketch in CA 9-10
Turner, Clay
See Ballard, (Willis) Todhunter
Turner, D(avid) Harold 1912- ... 117
Turner, Daniel F(rank) 1947- ... 97-100
Turner, Darwin T(heodore Troy) 1931-1991 ... CANR-11
Obituary ... 133
Earlier sketch in CA 21-24R
See also BW 1
Turner, David R(euben) 1915- ... 57-60
Turner, Dean (Edson) 1927- ... 29-32R
Turner, Dennis C(lair) 1948- ... 61-64
Turner, Dona M. 1951- ... 103
Turner, E(rnest) S(ackville) 1909- ... 113
Turner, Edward R(euben) A(rthur) 1924- ... 81-84
Turner, Elizabeth 1774-1846 ... YABC 2
Turner, Eloise Fain 1906- ... 5-8R
Turner, Eric Gardner 1911-1983 Obituary ... 109
Turner, Ethel (Sybil) 1872-1958 Brief entry ... 111
Turner, Florence (Hayes) 1919- ... 128
Turner, Francis Joseph (Michael) 1929- .. CANR-22
Earlier sketch in CA 69-72
Turner, Frederick (William III) 1937- ... CANR-34
Earlier sketches in CA 37-40R, CANR-15
Turner, Frederick 1943- ... CANR-56
Earlier sketches in CA 73-76, CANR-12, 30
See also CAAS 10
See also CLC 48
See also DLB 40
Turner, Frederick C(lair) 1938- ... CANR-28
Earlier sketch in CA 25-28R
Turner, Frederick Jackson 1861-1932 Brief entry ... 113
See also DLB 17, 186
Turner, George (Reginald) 1916- ... CANR-21
Earlier sketch in CA 103
Turner, George Allen 1908- ... CANR-10
Earlier sketch in CA 13-16R
Turner, George E(ugene) 1925- ... CANR-5
Earlier sketch in CA 53-56
Turner, George W(illiam) 1921- ... CANR-49
Earlier sketches in CA 104, CANR-24
Turner, Gladys T(ressia) 1935- ... CANR-13
Earlier sketch in CA 77-80
Turner, Glennette Tilley 1933- ... 133
See also SATA 71
Turner, Graham 1932- ... CANR-14
Earlier sketch in CA 21-24R
Turner, Guinevere 1968(?)- ... 147
Turner, Gwenda 1947- ... CANR-42
Earlier sketch in CA 118
Turner, H(arold) W(alter) 1911- ... CANR-10
Earlier sketch in CA 21-24R
Turner, Henry Andrew, Jr. 1919- ... 9-12R
Turner, Henry Ashby, Jr. 1932- ... 49-52
Turner, Henry Dicken 1919- ... 61-64
Turner, Henry Ernest William 1907-1995 ... CAP-1
Obituary ... 150
Earlier sketch in CA 9-10
Turner, Herbert Snipes 1891-1976 ... 41-44R
Turner, Howard M(oore), Jr. 1918- ... 13-16R
Turner, John Elliot 1917- ... CANR-3
Earlier sketch in CA 5-8R
Turner, John F(reeland) 1942- ... 97-100
Turner, John Frayn 1923- ... CANR-3
Earlier sketch in CA 9-12R
Turner, John H(enry) 1938- ... 77-80
Turner, Jonathan H. 1942- ... CANR-14
Earlier sketches in CA 37-40R, CANR-32
Turner, Joseph Addison 1826-1868 ... DLB 79
Turner, Josie
See Crawford, Phyllis
Turner, Judy
See Saxton, Judith

Turner, Justin G(eorge) 1898-1976 ... CANR-32
Earlier sketch in CA 41-44R
Turner, Katharine Charlotte 1910- ... CAP-2
Earlier sketch in CA 23-24
Turner, Kathleen J. 1952- ... 138
Turner, Kay 1932- ... 69-72
Turner, Kermit 1936- ... 104
Turner, L(eonard) C(harles) F(rederick) 1914- ... 29-32R
Turner, Len
See Floren, Lee
Turner, Lloyd 1924- ... 103
Interview in ... 103
Turner, Louis (Mark) 1942- ... CANR-34
Earlier sketches in CA 37-40R, CANR-15
Turner, Lowell 1947- ... 138
Turner, Lynn Warren 1906- ... 5-8R
Turner, Marjorie S. 1921- ... 145
Turner, Martha Anne (Bonner) 1904-1985 ... 134
Obituary ... 117
Turner, Martin 1948- ... 142
Turner, Mary
See Lambot, Isobel
Turner, Mason 1914- ... 123
Turner, Megan Whalen 1965- ... 156
See also SATA 94
Turner, Merfyn (Lloyd) 1915-1991 ... 104
Obituary ... 135
Turner, Morrie
See Turner, Morris
Turner, Morris 1923- ... CANR-15
Earlier sketch in CA 29-32R
Turner, Myron 1935- ... 112
Turner, Nancy J. 1947- ... 142
Turner, Paul Digby Lowry 1917- ... 105
Turner, Paul R(aymond) 1929- ... 45-48
Turner, Peter Paul
See Jeffery, Grant
Turner, Philip (William) 1925- ... CANR-27
Earlier sketches in CA 25-28R, CANR-11
See also SAAS 6
See also SATA 11, 83
Turner, Ralph 1936- Brief entry ... 107
Turner, Ralph H(erbert) 1919- ... 37-40R
Turner, Ralph Lilley 1888-1983 ... 5-8R
Obituary ... 109
Turner, Ralph V(ernon) 1939- ... 77-80
Turner, Richard Brent 1951- ... 165
Turner, Richard E(ugene) 1920- ... 29-32R
Turner, Robert (Harry) 1915- ... CANR-1
Earlier sketch in CA 45-48
Turner, Robert C(lemens) 1908- ... 77-80
Turner, Robert Edward III 1938(?)- ... 120
Turner, Robert F(oster) 1944- ... CANR-30
Earlier sketches in CA 77-80, CANR-13
Turner, Robert Kean, Jr. 1926- ... 17-20R
Turner, Robert Y(ongue) 1927- Brief entry ... 110
Turner, Robyn 1947- ... 145
See also SATA 77
Turner, Roger (Humphrey George) 1943- ... 123
Turner, Roland 1943- ... 106
Turner, Ronald Cordell 1939- ... 41-44R
Turner, Sheila
See Rowbotham, Sheila
Turner, Sheila 1906- ... CAP-1
Earlier sketch in CA 13-14
Turner, Sheila R.
See Seed, Sheila Turner
Turner, Silvie 1946- ... 117
Turner, Stansfield 1923- ... 124
Brief entry ... 118
Interview in ... 124
Turner, Stephen P. 1951- ... CANR-48
Earlier sketch in CA 122
Turner, Steve
See Turner, Stephen P.
Turner, (Clarence) Steven 1923- ... 29-32R
Turner, Susan 1952- ... 106
Turner, T. H. D. 1946- ... 122
Turner, Ted
See Turner, Robert Edward III
Turner, Thomas B(ourne) 1902- ... 41-44R
Turner, Thomas Coleman 1927- ... 5-8R
Turner, Thomas N(oel) 1940- ... 113
Turner, Tina 1939- ... 147
Turner, Tom
See Turner, T. H. D.
Turner, Tom 1942- ... 136
Turner, Victor Witter 1920-1983 ... CANR-3
Obituary ... 111
Earlier sketch in CA 5-8R
Turner, Violet Bender 1902(?)-1990 Obituary ... 130
Turner, W(illiam) Price 1927- ... CANR-16
Earlier sketch in CA 21-24R
Turner, Wallace 1921- ... 17-20R
Turner, William F. 1936(?)-1989 Obituary ... 130
Turner, William O(liver) 1914-1980 ... CANR-64
Earlier sketches in CA 1-4R, CANR-3
See also AITN 1
Turner, William W. 1927- ... CANR-12
Earlier sketch in CA 25-28R
Turney, Alfred (Walter) 1916- ... 73-76
Turney, Catherine 1906- ... 101
Turney, Denise
See Campbell, Rhonda
Turngren, Annette 1902(?)-1980 ... 9-12R
Obituary ... 101
See also SATA-Obit 23
Turngren, Ellen (?)-1964 ... 5-8R
See also SATA 3
Turnill, Reginald 1915- ... CANR-15
Earlier sketch in CA 37-40R
Turnock, David 1938- ... 109
Turock, Betty J(ane) ... CANR-30
Earlier sketch in CA 110
Turow, Joseph G(regory) 1950- ... CANR-57
Earlier sketches in CA 111, CANR-30
Turow, Rita P(astron) 1919- ... 101
Turow, Scott 1949- ... CANR-65
Earlier sketches in CA 73-76, CANR-40
See also BEST 90:3
See also DAM POP
Turpin, James W(esley) 1927- ... 21-24R
Turpin, Jennifer 1961- ... 148
Turpin, Lorna 1950- ... 107
Turpin, Waters Edward 1910-1968 ... 125
See also BW 1
See also DLB 51
Turrini, Peter 1944- ... DLB 124
Turska, Krystyna (Zofia) 1933- ... 106
See also SATA 31
See also SATA-Brief 27
Tursun-Zade, Mirzo 1911-1977 Obituary ... 104
Turtledove, Harry (Norman) 1949- ... 153
Turton, Godfrey (Edmund) 1901- ... 21-24R
Turton, James
See Crace, Jim
Turton-Jones, Edith Constance (Bradshaw) 1904-1968 ... CAP-1
Earlier sketch in CA 9-10
Turville-Petre, Edward Oswald Gabriel 1908-1978 ... 9-12R
Obituary ... 77-80
Turyn, Alexander 1900-1981 Obituary ... 104
Tusa, Ann ... 160
Tusa, John (Jr.) 1936- ... 127
Tusa, Michael C(harles) 1953- ... 142
Tusa, Tricia 1960- ... SATA 72
Tusan, Stan 1936- ... 105
Tushingham, A(rlotte) Douglas 1914- ... 41-44R
Tushnet, Leonard 1908-1973 ... CAP-1
Obituary ... 45-48
Earlier sketch in CA 13-16
Tushnet, Mark V. 1945- ... 126
Tusiani, Joseph 1924- ... CANR-43
Earlier sketches in CA 9-12R, CANR-5, 20
See also SATA 45
Tuska, Jon 1942- ... CANR-13
Earlier sketch in CA 73-76
Tussing, A(ubrey) Dale 1935- ... 17-20R
Tutaev, David 1916- ... 21-24R
Tute, Warren (Stanley) 1914- ... CANR-1
Earlier sketch in CA 1-4R
Tuten, Frederic 1936- ... 37-40R
Tuthill, John Wills 1910-1996 ... 108
Obituary ... 153
Tutin, Thomas Gaskell 1908-1987 Obituary ... 123
Tutko, Thomas A(rthur) 1931- ... 69-72
Tutorow, Norman E. 1934- ... CANR-29
Earlier sketch in CA 25-28R
Tuttle, Alva M(aurice) 1900- ... 5-8R
Tuttle, Day
See Tuttle, (Frank) Day, Jr.
Tuttle, (Frank) Day, Jr. 1902- ... 116
Tuttle, Frank W(aldo) 1896- ... 61-64
Tuttle, Howard Nelson 1935- ... 41-44R
Tuttle, Lisa 1952- ... 126
Tuttle, Russell (Howard) 1939- ... 77-80
Tuttle, W(ilbur) C(oleman) 1883-(?) ... CANR-64
Earlier sketches in CAP-2, CA 21-22
Tuttle, William M., Jr. 1937- ... CANR-11
Earlier sketch in CA 29-32R
Tuttleton, James Welsey 1934- ... 41-44R
Tutu, Desmond M(pilo) 1931- ... CANR-67
Earlier sketch in CA 125
See also BLC 3
See also BW 1
See also CLC 80
See also DAM MULT
Tutuola, Amos 1920-1997 ... CANR-66
Obituary ... 159
Earlier sketches in CA 9-12R, CANR-27
See also BLC 3
See also BW 2
See also CLC 5, 14, 29
See also DAM MULT
See also DLB 125
See also MTCW 1
Tuve, Merle Antony 1901-1982 Obituary ... 106
Tuve, Rosemond 1903-1964 ... CAP-1
Earlier sketch in CA 9-10
Tuveson, Ernest (Lee) 1915- ... 17-20R
Tuwhare, Hone 1922- ... 103
Tuzin, Donald F(rancis) 1945- ... 106
Tvardovsky, Alexandr Trifonovich 1910-1971 ... 102
Obituary ... 33-36R
Twaddell, Kristie
See Miller, Kristie
Twaddell, W(illiam) F(reeman) 1906-1982 ... CANR-32
Earlier sketch in CA 81-84
Twaddle, Andrew C. 1938- ... 120
Twain, Mark
See Clemens, Samuel Langhorne
See also AAYA 20
See also DLB 11, 12, 23, 64, 74
See also SSC 6, 26
See also TCLC 6, 12, 19, 36, 48, 59
See also WLC
Twark, Allan J(oseph) 1931- ... 49-52
Twedt, Dik Warren 1920-1985 ... CANR-14
Obituary ... 115
Earlier sketch in CA 37-40R
Tweed, Stephen C. 1949- ... 133
Tweed, Thomas A. 1954- ... 137
Tweedale, Douglas 1958(?)-1990 Obituary ... 132
Tweedale, J.
See Bickle, Judith Brundrett
Tweedale, Violet (Chambers) 1862-1936 Brief entry ... 116
Tweedie, Donald F(erguson), Jr. 1926- ... 13-16R
Tweedie, Ethel Brilliana c. 1860-1940 ... DLB 174
Tweeten, Luther 1931- ... 89-92
Tweit, Susan J(oan) 1956- ... 151
See also SATA 94
Twelveponies, Mary
See Cleveland, Mary
Twemlow, Stuart W(est) 1941- ... 128
Twersky, Isadore 1930-1997 ... 120
Obituary ... 162
Twersky, Jacob 1920- ... 49-52
Tweton, D. Jerome 1933- ... SATA 48
Twichell, Chase 1950- ... CANR-56
Earlier sketch in CA 127
Twigg, Alan (Robert) 1952- ... 125
Twiggy
See Hornby, Leslie
Twin, Stephanie L. 1948- ... 101
Twiname, Eric 1942(?)-1980 Obituary ... 102
Twinem, Neecy 1958- ... SATA 92
Twining, Nathan F(arragut) 1897-1982 Obituary ... 106
Twining, William (Lawrence) 1934- ... CANR-51
Earlier sketch in CA 123
Twisleton-Wykeham-Fiennes, Richard Nathaniel 1909- ... CANR-11
Earlier sketch in CA 21-24R
Twiss, Sumner B(arnes), Jr. 1944- Brief entry ... 114
Twist, Ananias
See Nunn, William Curtis
Twitchell, James B(uell) 1943- ... CANR-43
Earlier sketch in CA 118
Twitchell, Paul 1908(?)-1971 ... 132
Obituary ... 111
Twitchett, Carol Cosgrove 1943- ... CANR-26
Earlier sketch in CA 29-32R
Twitchett, Denis Crispin 1925- Brief entry ... 106
Twohig, Elizabeth Shee 1946- ... 132
Twohill, Maggie
See Gaberman, Judie Angell
Twohy, David ... 167
Twombly, Robert C(harles) 1940- ... 85-88
Twombly, Wells A. 1935-1977 ... 41-44R
Obituary ... 69-72
Tworkov, Jack 1900-1982 Obituary ... 107
See also SATA 47
See also SATA-Obit 31
Twyman, Gib
See Twyman, Gilbert Oscar III
Twyman, Gilbert Oscar III 1943- ... 109
Ty-Casper, Linda 1931- ... CANR-50
Earlier sketches in CA 107, CANR-24
Tyde, Eddie
See Meades, Jonathan (Turner)
Tydeman, William (Marcus) 1935- ... CANR-43
Earlier sketch in CA 119
Tydings, Joseph D(avies) 1928- ... 29-32R
Tye, Michael 1950- ... 158
Tyerman, Hugo 1880-1977 Obituary ... 77-80
Tyers, Jenny 1969- ... SATA 89
Tyers, Kathy 1952- ... 149
See also SATA 82
Tygiel, Jules 1949- ... 132
Tyl, Noel 1936- ... 93-96
Tylden-Wright, David 1923- ... 25-28R
Tyldesley, Joyce (Ann) 1960- ... 155
Tylecote, Mabel (Phythian) 1896-1987 ... CAP-1
Obituary ... 121
Earlier sketch in CA 13-14
Tylecote, R(onald) F(rank) 1916-1990 Obituary ... 132
Tyler, A. E.
See Armstrong, (Annette) Elizabeth
Tyler, Anne 1941- ... CANR-53
Earlier sketches in CA 9-12R, CANR-11, 33
See also AAYA 18
See also BEST 89:1
See also CLC 7, 11, 18, 28, 44, 59, 103
See also DAM NOV, POP
See also DLB 6, 143
See also DLBY 82
See also MTCW 1
See also SATA 7, 90
Tyler, Converse 1903(?)-1978 Obituary ... 81-84
Tyler, David B(udlong) 1899-1993 ... 77-80
Obituary ... 140
Tyler, Elias S. 1904(?)-1977 Obituary ... 73-76
Tyler, Gus 1911- ... 130
Tyler, Hamilton A(lden) 1917- ... CANR-5
Earlier sketch in CA 9-12R
Tyler, J. Allen 1924- ... 101
Tyler, John Ecclesfield (?)-1966 ... CAP-1
Earlier sketch in CA 9-10
Tyler, Leona E(lizabeth) 1906- ... 17-20R
Tyler, Linda
See Tyler, Linda W(agner)
Tyler, Linda W(agner) 1952- ... 136
See also SATA 65
Tyler, Mary Palmer 1775-1866 ... DLB 200
Tyler, Moses Coit 1835-1900 ... DLB 47, 64
Tyler, Parker 1907-1974 ... CANR-5
Obituary ... 49-52
Earlier sketch in CA 5-8R
Tyler, Patrick (Edward) 1951- ... 125
Tyler, (John) Poyntz 1907-1971 ... 1-4R
Obituary ... 103
Tyler, Ralph Winfred 1902-1994 ... 109
Obituary ... 144
Tyler, Richard W(illis) 1917- ... CANR-24
Earlier sketch in CA 41-44R
Tyler, Robert L(awrence) 1922- ... 13-16R
Tyler, Rodney 1943- ... 127
Tyler, Ron(nie) C(urtis) 1941- ... CANR-53
Earlier sketches in CA 29-32R, CANR-12, 28
Tyler, Royall 1757-1826 ... DLB 37
Tyler, S(amuel) Lyman 1920- ... 77-80
Tyler, Sandra 1963- ... 154
Tyler, Stephen A(lbert) 1932- ... 29-32R
Tyler, Tom R(ichard) 1950- ... 135
Tyler, Varro Eugene 1926- ... 110
Tyler, Vicki 1952- ... 121
See also SATA 64
Tyler, W. T.
See Hamrick, Samuel J., Jr.
Tyler, William R(oyall) 1910- ... 37-40R
Tyler, Zeke
See Marshall, Mel(vin D.)
Tyler-Whittle, Michael Sidney 1927- ... CANR-4
Earlier sketch in CA 5-8R
Tylor, Edward Burnett 1832-1917 Brief entry ... 123
See also DLB 57
Tymchuk, Alexander J(ames) 1942- ... 57-60
Tymeson, Mildred McClary
See Petrie, Mildred McClary
Tymieniecka, Anna-Teresa ... CANR-9
Earlier sketch in CA 61-64
Tymms, Ralph Vincent 1913-1987 Obituary ... 123
Tymn, Marshall (Benton) 1937- ... 107
Tymon, Dorothy ... 85-88
Tynan, Katharine 1861-1931 ... 167
Brief entry ... 104
See also DLB 153
See also TCLC 3
Tynan, Kathleen 1937(?)-1995 ... 97-100
Obituary ... 147
Tynan, Kenneth (Peacock) 1927-1980 ... CANR-63
Obituary ... 101
Earlier sketches in CA 13-16R, CANR-22
See also MTCW 1
Tyndale, William c. 1494-1536 ... DLB 132
Tyre, Nedra ... 104
Tyre, Peg 1960- ... 146
Tyrell, Donald J(ohn) 1929- Brief entry ... 110
Tyrmand, Leopold 1920-1985 ... CANR-5
Obituary ... 115
Earlier sketch in CA 49-52
Tyrone, Paul
See Norwood, Victor G(eorge) C(harles)
Tyrrell, Bernard (James) 1933- ... 57-60
Tyrrell, Francis M(artin) 1916- Brief entry ... 107
Tyrrell, Ian R(obert) 1947- ... 142
Tyrrell, Joseph M(orten) 1927- ... 41-44R
Tyrrell, R(obert) Emmett, Jr. 1943- ... CANR-25
Earlier sketch in CA 85-88
Interview in ... CANR-25
Tyrrell, Robert 1929- ... 41-44R
Tyrrell, William Blake 1940- ... 125
Tyrwhitt, (Mary) Jacqueline 1905-1983(?) Obituary ... 109
Tyrwhitt, Janice 1928- ... 97-100
Tysdahl, B(joern) J(ohan) 1933- ... 25-28R
Tysliava, Valerie 1914(?)-1984 Obituary ... 112
Tyson, Alan (Walker) 1926- ... 128
Tyson, James (Levering, Jr.) ... 151
Tyson, Joseph B(lake) 1928- ... CANR-38
Earlier sketches in CA 37-40R, CANR-14
Tyson, Lois (M.) ... 150
Tyson, Nancy Jane 1949- ... 117
Tyson, Remer (Hoyt) 1934- ... 131
Tyson, Richard 1944- ... 69-72
Tyson, Salinda 1952- ... 162
Tysse, Agnes N. 1904- ... 101
Tytell, John 1939- ... 29-32R
Tytler, Graeme (Douglas Colville) 1934- ... 117
Tzannes, Nicolaos S(tamatios) 1937- ... 57-60
Tzara, Tristan 1896-1963 ... 153
Obituary ... 89-92
See also CLC 47
See also DAM POET
Tzitsikas, Helene 1926- ... 45-48
Tzonis, Alexander 1937- ... 101

U

Ubbelohde, Carl (William, Jr.) 1924- ... CANR-6
Earlier sketch in CA 1-4R
Ubelaker, Douglas H. 1946- ... 146
Ubell, Earl 1926- ... 37-40R
See also SATA 4
Ucelay, Margarita 1916- ... 21-24R
Uchida, Tadao 1939- ... 65-68
Uchida, Yoshiko 1921-1992 ... CANR-61
Obituary ... 139
Earlier sketches in CA 13-16R, CANR-6, 22, 47
See also AAYA 16
See also CLR 6
See also JRDA
See also MAICYA
See also MTCW 1
See also SAAS 1
See also SATA 1, 53
See also SATA-Obit 72
Ucko, Barbara 1945- ... 136
Udall, Brady 1957(?)- ... 163
Udall, Jan Beaney 1938- ... CANR-35
Earlier sketch in CA 65-68
See also SATA 10
Udall, Morris K(ing) 1922- ... CANR-1
Earlier sketch in CA 45-48
Udall, Nicholas 1504-1556 ... DLB 62
Udall, Stewart L(ee) 1920- ... 69-72
Ude, Wayne (Richard) 1946- ... CANR-64
Earlier sketches in CA 77-80, CANR-13
Udell, Jon G(erald) 1935- ... CANR-37
Earlier sketches in CA 45-48, CANR-1, 16
Udelson, Joseph H. 1943- ... 125
Uden, (Bernard Gilbert) Grant 1910- ... 102
See also SATA 26
Uderzo, Albert 1927- ... CLR 37

Udo, Reuben Kenrick 1935- CANR-35
Earlier sketch in CA 77-80
Udoff, Yale M(aurice) 1935- CANR-12
Earlier sketch in CA 57-60
Udolf, Roy 1926- CANR-4
Earlier sketch in CA 53-56
Udovitch, Abraham Labe 1933- Brief entry 105
Udry, J(oe) Richard 1928- 33-36R
Udry, Janice May 1928- CANR-6
Earlier sketch in CA 5-8R
See also SATA 4
Udy, Stanley Hart, Jr. 1928- Brief entry 106
Ueda, Makoto 1931- CANR-34
Earlier sketch in CA 21-24R
Uehling, Carl Theodore 1927- 29-32R
Uehling, Theodore Edward, Jr. 1935- CANR-20
Earlier sketch in CA 104
Ueno, Noriko
See Nakae, Noriko
Uffelman, F. C.
See Gehman, Richard (Boyd)
Uffenbeck, Lorin A(rthur) 1924- 61-64
Ugama, LeRoi
See Smith, LeRoi Tex
Ugarte, Francisco 1910-1969 .... CAP-1
Earlier sketch in CA 9-10
Ugarte, Michael 1949- 114
Ugboajah, (Francis) Okwu 1945- 93-96
Ugent, Donald 1933- 141
Ugresic, Dubravka 1949- 136
See also DLB 181
Uhalley, Stephen, Jr. 1930- Brief entry 106
Uher, Lorna
See Crozier, Lorna
Uhl, Alexander H. 1899(?)-1976 Obituary 69-72
Uhl, Melvin John 1915- CANR-34
Earlier sketch in CA 5-8R
Uhlan, Edward 1912-1988 Obituary 127
Uhland, Ludwig 1787-1862 .... DLB 90
Uhlenbeck, Karen (Keskulla) 1942- 160
Uhlfelder, Myra L. 1923- Brief entry 109
Uhlin, Donald M(acbeth) 1930- 49-52
Uhlinger, Susan J. 1942-1980 .... CANR-34
Obituary 120
Earlier sketch in CA 57-60
Uhlman, Fred 1901-1985(?) CANR-34
Obituary 116
Earlier sketch in CA 105
Uhnak, Dorothy 1933- CANR-63
Earlier sketches in CA 81-84, CANR-29
See also AITN 1
Uhr, Carl George 1911- 81-84
Uhr, Elizabeth 1929- 25-28R
Uhr, Leonard (Merrick) 1927- CANR-7
Earlier sketch in CA 5-8R
Uhry, Alfred 1936- 133
Brief entry 127
Interview in 133
See also CLC 55
See also DAM DRAM, POP
Uitti, Karl David 1933- CANR-10
Earlier sketch in CA 17-20R
Ujevic, Augustin 1891-1955 .... DLB 147
Ujfalussy, Jozsef 1920- Brief entry 114
Ujse, Bodo 1904-1963 .... DLB 69
Ulack, Richard 1942- 140
Ulam, Adam B(runo) 1922- CANR-51
Earlier sketches in CA 13-16R, CANR-7, 26
Ulam, S(tanislaw) M(arcin) 1909-1984 ... CANR-34
Obituary 112
Earlier sketch in CA 61-64
See also SATA 51
Ulanoff, Stanley M(elvin) 1922- CANR-23
Earlier sketches in CA 17-20R, CANR-7
Ulanov, Ann Belford 1938- CANR-38
Earlier sketches in CA 49-52, CANR-16
Ulanov, Barry 1918- CANR-38
Earlier sketches in CA 1-4R, CANR-16
Ulasi, Adaora Lily 1932- 167
Ulbricht, Walter 1893-1973 Obituary 113
Ulc, Otto 1930- CANR-13
Earlier sketch in CA 77-80
Ulene, Art(hur Lawrence) 1936- CANR-30
Earlier sketch in CA 103
Ulenhart, Niclas fl. 1600- .... DLB 164
Ulett, George A(ndrew) 1918- 21-24R
Ulevich, Neal Hirsch 1946- 108
Ulf, Haerved
See Strindberg, (Johan) August
Ulf, Harved
See Strindberg, (Johan) August
Ulibarri, Sabine R(eyes) 1919- 131
See also CLC 83
See also DAM MULT
See also DLB 82
See also HW
Ulica, Jorge 1870-1926 .... DLB 82
Ulich, Robert 1890(?)-1977 Obituary 69-72
Ulivi, Ferruccio 1912- .... DLB 196
Ulizio, B. George 1889-1969 .... DLB 140
Ullah, Najib 1914- 13-16R
Ullah, Salamat 1913- 13-16R
Ulle, Robert F. 1948- 117
Ullendorff, Edward 1920- CANR-40
Earlier sketches in CA 1-4R, CANR-2, 18
Ullian, Joseph S(ilbert) 1930- 41-44R
Ullman, Allan 1909(?)-1982 Obituary 106
Ullman, Barbara
See Schwalberg, Carol(yn Ernestine Stein)
Ullman, Edward L(ouis) 1912-1976 45-48
Obituary 125
Ullman, Elwood 1903(?)-1985 Obituary 117
Ullman, James Ramsey 1907-1971 .... CANR-3
Obituary 29-32R
Earlier sketch in CA 1-4R
See also SATA 7
Ullman, Leslie 1947- 104
Ullman, Michael (Alan) 1945- 103
Ullman, Montague 1916- CANR-28
Earlier sketch in CA 41-44R
Ullman, Natacha 1929(?)-1986 Obituary 119
Ullman, Pierre L(ioni) 1929- 33-36R
Ullman, Richard Henry 1933- CANR-3
Earlier sketch in CA 1-4R
Ullmann, Christian 1942- 165
Ullmann, John E(manuel) 1923- CANR-34
Earlier sketch in CA 17-20R
Ullmann, Leonard P(aul) 1930- 17-20R
Ullmann, Liv 1939- 102
Ullmann, Owen 1947- 144
Ullmann, Stephen 1914-1976 .... CANR-4
Obituary 65-68
Earlier sketch in CA 5-8R
Ullmann, Walter 1910-1983 .... CANR-10
Obituary 108
Earlier sketch in CA 21-24R
Ullrich, Helen D(enning) 1922- CANR-28
Earlier sketch in CA 109
Ullstein, Hermann 1875(?)-1943 Brief entry 116
Ullyot, Joan 1940- 73-76
Ulm, Robert 1934-1977 .... SATA 17
Ulman, William A. 1908(?)-1979 103
Obituary 89-92
Ulmer, (Roland) Curtis 1923- 103
Ulmer, Diane K. 1943- 122
Ulmer, Gregory L(eland) 1944- 136
Ulmer, Louise 1943- 113
See also SATA 53
Ulmer, Melville J(ack) 1911- 21-24R
Ulmer, S(hirley) Sidney 1923- 41-44R
Ulph, Owen 1914- 133
Ulrich, Anton 1633-1714 .... DLB 168
Ulrich, Betty Garton 1919- 29-32R
Ulrich, Carolyn F. 1881(?)-1970 Obituary 104
Ulrich, Heinz 1927(?)-1980 Obituary 97-100
Ulrich, (John) Homer 1906-1987 .... CANR-36
Obituary 124
Earlier sketches in CA 5-8R, CANR-2
Ulrich, Laurel Thatcher 1938- 142
Ulrich, Louis E., Jr. 1918- 13-16R
Ulrich, Roger E(lwood) 1931- 41-44R
Ulrich von Liechtenstein c. 1200-c. 1275 .. DLB 138
Ulrich von Zatzikhoven c. 1194-c. 1214 ... DLB 138
Ultan, Lloyd 1929- 117
Ultee, (J.) Maarten 1949- 109
Ulyanov, V. I.
See Lenin
Ulyanov, Vladimir Ilyich
See Lenin
Ulyanov-Lenin
See Lenin
Ulyatt, Kenneth 1920- CANR-8
Earlier sketch in CA 61-64
See also SATA 14
Uman, Myron F. 1939- 149
Umen, Samuel 1917(?)-1990 Obituary 132
Umland, Craig (Owen) 1947- 61-64
Umphlett, Wiley Lee 1931- CANR-34
Earlier sketches in CA 49-52, CANR-1
Umpierre (Herrera), Luz Maria 1947- 153
See also HW
Umstatter, Jack 1950- 158
Umstead, William Lee 1921- 81-84
Unada
See Gliewe, Unada (Grace)
Unamuno (y Jugo), Miguel de 1864-1936 131
Brief entry 104
See also DAM MULT, NOV
See also DLB 108
See also HLC
See also HW
See also MTCW 1
See also SSC 11
See also TCLC 2, 9
Unbegaun, Boris Ottokar
1898-1973 Obituary 41-44R
Uncle Gordon
See Roe, F(rederic) Gordon
Uncle Gus
See Rey, H(ans) A(ugusto)
Uncle Mac
See McCulloch, Derek (Ivor Breashur)
Uncle Ray
See Coffman, Ramon Peyton
Uncle Shelby
See Silverstein, Shel(by)
Undercliffe, Errol
See Campbell, (John) Ramsey
Underdown, David (Edward) 1925- CANR-51
Earlier sketches in CA 5-8R, CANR-11, 26
Underhill, Alice Mertie (Waterman) 1900-1971 . 1-4R
Obituary 103
See also SATA 10
Underhill, Charles
See Hill, Reginald (Charles)
Underhill, Frank Hawkins 1889-1971 163
Underhill, Hal
See Underhill, Harold
Underhill, Harold 1926-1972 .... CAP-2
Earlier sketch in CA 25-28
Underhill, Hugh 1937- 145
Underhill, Liz 1948- 121
See also SATA 53
See also SATA-Brief 49
Underhill, Lois Beachy 151
Underhill, Miriam E. 1898(?)-1976 Obituary ... 61-64
Underhill, Peter
See Soderberg, Percy Measday
Underhill, Ruth Murray 1884-1984 .... CANR-39
Obituary 114
Earlier sketches in CA 1-4R, CANR-3
Underwood, Aggie
See Underwood, Agness May Wilson
Underwood, Agness May Wilson
1902-1984 Obituary 113
Underwood, Barbara 1952- 101
Underwood, Benton J. 1915- CANR-34
Earlier sketch in CA 101
Underwood, (Mary) Betty 1921- 37-40R
Underwood, Gary Neal 1940- Brief entry 113
Underwood, Helen 1914- 139
Underwood, Jane H(ammons) 1931- 61-64
Underwood, Jeffery S(cott) 1954- 137
Underwood, John Weeden 1932- CANR-35
Earlier sketch in CA 17-20R
Underwood, Lewis Graham
See Wagner, C(harles) Peter
Underwood, Mavis Eileen 1916- Brief entry 108
Underwood, Michael
See Evelyn, (John) Michael
Underwood, Miles
See Glassco, John
Underwood, Norman 1878(?)-1974 Obituary . 53-56
Underwood, Paul S(taats) 1915-1985 77-80
Obituary 118
Underwood, Peter 1923- CANR-44
Earlier sketches in CA 104, CANR-21
Underwood, Sam J(esse) 1922- CANR-2
Earlier sketch in CA 45-48
Underwood, Ted Leroy 1935- 115
Underwood, Tim (Edward) 1948- CANR-24
Earlier sketch in CA 105
Undine, P. F.
See Paine, Lauran (Bosworth)
Undset, Sigrid 1882-1949 129
Brief entry 104
See also DA
See also DAB
See also DAC
See also DAM MST, NOV
See also MTCW 1
See also TCLC 3
See also WLC
Undy, R(oger) 1938- 115
Unett, John 13-16R
Ungar, Frederick 1898-1988 Obituary 127
Ungar, Sanford J. 1945- CANR-71
Earlier sketches in CA 37-40R, CANR-13, 29
Ungar, Sheldon (B.) 1948- 144
Ungar, Steven (Ronald) 1945- 126
Ungaretti, Giuseppe 1888-1970 .... CAP-2
Obituary 25-28R
Earlier sketch in CA 19-20
See also CLC 7, 11, 15
See also DLB 114
Ungaro, Harold R(aymond) Mancusi, Jr.
See Mancusi-Ungaro, Harold R(aymond), Jr.
Ungaro, Susan Kelliher 1953- 103
Unger, Arthur 1924- 1-4R
Unger, Barbara 1932- CANR-40
Earlier sketches in CA 77-80, CANR-13
Unger, Craig 1949- 128
Unger, David 1950- 153
See also HW
Unger, Douglas 1952- 130
See also CLC 34
Unger, Friederike Helene 1741-1813 .... DLB 94
Unger, Hans 1915- 17-20R
Unger, Harlow G. 1931- 142
See also SATA 75
Unger, Henry F. 1912- 13-16R
Unger, Irwin 1927- CANR-7
Earlier sketch in CA 9-12R
Unger, J(ames) Marshall 1947- 126
Unger, Jim 1937- CANR-13
Earlier sketch in CA 61-64
See also SATA 67
Unger, Len
See Unger, Leonard
Unger, Leonard 1916- CANR-34
Earlier sketch in CA 5-8R
Unger, Leonard 1934- 69-72
Unger, Marion
See Thede, Marion Draughon
Unger, Marvin H. 1936- 29-32R
Unger, Maurice Albert 1917- CANR-3
Earlier sketch in CA 9-12R
Unger, Merrill F. 1909- CANR-6
Earlier sketch in CA 1-4R
Unger, Peter K(enneth) 1942- 136
Brief entry 109
Unger, Richard (Lawrence) 1939- CANR-15
Earlier sketch in CA 65-68
Unger, Richard W. 1942- 121
Unger, Walter P(eter) 1939- Brief entry 115
Ungerer, Jean Thomas 1931- 41-44R
See also Ungerer, Tomi
See also MAICYA
See also SATA 5, 33
Ungerer, Miriam 1929- 117
Ungerer, Tomi
See Ungerer, Jean Thomas
See also CLR 3
Unger-Hamilton, Clive (Wolfgang) 1942- . CANR-42
Earlier sketches in CA 101, CANR-19
Ungermann, Kenneth Armistead 1916- 9-12R
Ungs, Thomas D(ale) 1928- 81-84
Unkelbach, Kurt 1913- CANR-8
Earlier sketch in CA 21-24R
See also SATA 4
Unklesbay, A. G. 1914- 143
Unkovic, Charles M. 1922- 45-48
Unnerstad, Edith (Totterman) 1900- CANR-72
Earlier sketches in CA 5-8R, CANR-6
See also CLR 36
See also SATA 3
Uno, Chiyo 1897-1996 .... CANR-70
Earlier sketch in CA 154
See also DLB 180
Unrau, Ruth 1922- 61-64
See also SATA 9
Unrau, William E. 1929- 37-40R
Unrue, Darlene Harbour 1938- 139
Unruh, Fritz von
See Von Unruh, Fritz
See also DLB 118
Unruh, Glenys Grace (Green) 1910- 29-32R
Unruh, James A(rlen) 1941- 156
Unruh, John D., Jr. 1938(?)-1976 Obituary 105
Unser, Bobby
See Unser, Robert William
Unser, Robert William 1934- 97-100
Unstead, R(obert) J(ohn) 1915-1988 .... CANR-23
Obituary 125
Earlier sketches in CA 9-12R, CANR-7
See also SATA 12
See also SATA-Obit 56
Unsworth, Barry (Forster) 1930- CANR-54
Earlier sketches in CA 25-28R, CANR-30
See also CLC 76
See also DLB 194
Unsworth, Mair 1909- CANR-10
Earlier sketch in CA 25-28R
Unsworth, Walt(er) 1928- CANR-38
Earlier sketches in CA 29-32R, CANR-17
See also SATA 4
Unterberger, Betty Miller 1923- 25-28R
Unterbrink, Mary 1937- 113
Unterecker, John (Eugene) 1922-1989 ... CANR-34
Obituary 127
Earlier sketch in CA 17-20R
Untereiner, Raymond Edward
1898-1983 Obituary 110
Unterman, Alan 1942- 97-100
Unterman, Issar Y(ehuda)
1886-1976 Obituary 61-64
Untermeyer, Bryna Ivens 1909-1985 .... CANR-31
Earlier sketches in CA 5-8R, CANR-3
See also SATA 61
Untermeyer, Jean Starr
1886-1970 Obituary 29-32R
Untermeyer, Louis 1885-1977 .... CANR-31
Obituary 73-76
Earlier sketch in CA 5-8R
See also SATA 2, 37
See also SATA-Obit 26
Unthank, Luisa-Teresa 33-36R
Unthank, Tessa Brown
See Unthank, Luisa-Teresa
Unwalla, Darab B. 1928- 25-28R
Unwin, David S(torr) 1918- CANR-6
Earlier sketch in CA 9-12R
See also SATA 14
Unwin, Derick (James) 1931- 21-24R
Unwin, Nora S(picer) 1907-1982 .... 21-24R
Obituary 120
See also SATA 3
See also SATA-Obit 49
Unwin, Rayner S(tephens) 1925- 1-4R
Unwin, Stanley 1884-1968 .... 5-8R
Unzner, Christa 1958- .... SATA 80
Unzner-Fischer, Christa
See Unzner, Christa
Upchurch, Boyd (Bradfield) 1919- CANR-27
Earlier sketch in CA 25-28R
See also Boyd, John
Upchurch, Michael 1954- 155
Updike, David (H.) 1957- 128
Updike, John (Hoyer) 1932- CANR-51
Earlier sketches in CA 1-4R, CANR-4, 33
See also CABS 1
See also CDALB 1968-1988
See also CLC 1, 2, 3, 5, 7, 9, 13, 15, 23, 34, 43, 70
See also DA
See also DAB
See also DAC
See also DAM MST, NOV, POET, POP
See also DLB 2, 5, 143
See also DLBD 3
See also DLBY 80, 82, 97
See also MTCW 1
See also SSC 13, 27
See also WLC
Updike, L(eRoy) Wayne 1916- 49-52
Updyke, James
See Burnett, W(illiam) R(iley)
Upfield, Arthur W(illiam) 1888-1964 Obituary ... 114
Upgren, Arthur P. 1897-1986 Obituary 120
Uphaus, Robert W(alter) 1942- 57-60
Uphaus, Willard Edwin 1890-1983 .... CAP-1
Obituary 111
Earlier sketch in CA 19-20
Uphoff, Norman T(homas) 1940- CANR-11
Earlier sketch in CA 29-32R
Uphoff, Walter H. 1913- CANR-14
Earlier sketch in CA 25-28R
Upits, Andrejs 1877-1970 Obituary 104
Upjohn, Everard M(iller) 1903-1978 .... CAP-1
Obituary 81-84
Earlier sketch in CA 13-14
Uppal, Jogindar S. 1927- CANR-1
Earlier sketch in CA 45-48
Uppman, Jean Seward 1922- 136
Upright, Diane W(arner) 1947- 120
Upshaw, Margaret Mitchell
See Mitchell, Margaret (Munnerlyn)
Upson, Norma 1919- CANR-8
Earlier sketch in CA 61-64
Upson, William Hazlett 1891-1975 .... 5-8R
Obituary 57-60

Upton, Albert 1897- ... CAP-2
Earlier sketch in CA 23-24
Upton, Anthony F. 1929- ... 17-20R
Upton, Arvin 1914- ... 81-84
Upton, Bertha (Hudson) 1849-1912 Brief entry . 121
See also DLB 141
Upton, Charles 1948- Brief entry ... 116
See also DLB 16
Upton, Dell 1949- ... CANR-50
Earlier sketch in CA 123
Upton, Florence K. 1873-1922 ... DLB 141
Upton, Joseph C(heshire) N(ash) 1946- ... 81-84
Upton, L(eslie) F(rancis) S(tokes) 1931-1980 . 61-64
Obituary ... 125
Upton, Lee 1953- ... 123
Upton, Mark
See Sanders, Lawrence
Upton, Monroe 1898- ... CAP-2
Earlier sketch in CA 17-18
Upton, Robert ... CANR-55
Earlier sketches in CA 73-76, CANR-13, 29
Upward, Allen 1863-1926 Brief entry ... 117
See also DLB 36
Upward, Edward (Falaise) 1903- ... 77-80
Urakami, Hiroko 1937- ... 140
Urbach, Reinhard 1939- Brief entry ... 113
Urban, Michael E(dward) 1947- ... CANR-29
Earlier sketch in CA 111
Urban, Wilbur Marshall 1873-1952 Brief entry .. 119
Urban, William L(awrence) 1939- ... CANR-18
Earlier sketches in CA 45-48, CANR-2
Urbanek, Mae 1903- ... 77-80
Urbanek, Zdenek 1917- ... 140
Urbano, Victoria (Eugenia) 1926- ... CANR-2
Earlier sketch in CA 45-48
Urbanska, Wanda (Marie) 1956- ... 124
Urbanski, Edmund Stefan
See Urbanski, Edmund Stephen
Urbanski, Edmund Stephen 1909- ... CANR-23
Earlier sketch in CA 45-48
Urbanski, Marie M. Olesen 1922- ... 102
Urch, Elizabeth 1921- ... 103
Urda, Nicholas 1922- ... 21-24R
Urdang, Constance (Henriette) 1922- ... CANR-24
Earlier sketches in CA 21-24R, CANR-9
See also CLC 47
Urdang, Laurence 1927- ... CANR-40
Earlier sketches in CA 89-92, CANR-17
Ure, Jean 1943- ... CANR-48
Earlier sketch in CA 125
See also CLR 34
See also JRDA
See also MAICYA
See also SAAS 14
See also SATA 48, 78
Ure, John (Burns) 1931- ... 144
Ure, Peter 1919-1969 ... CAP-1
Earlier sketch in CA 11-12
Uren, Hilda
See U'Ren-Stubbings, Hilda
U'Ren, Hilda
See U'Ren-Stubbings, Hilda
U'Ren-Stubbings, Hilda 1914- ... CANR-49
Earlier sketch in CA 29-32R
Uretsky, Myron 1940- ... 53-56
Urey, Harold (Clayton) 1893-1981 ... 157
Obituary ... 102
Uri, Pierre (Emmanuel) 1911-1992 ... CANR-47
Obituary ... 138
Earlier sketch in CA 97-100
Uriel, Henry
See Faust, Frederick (Schiller)
Uris, Auren 1913- ... CANR-22
Earlier sketch in CA 17-20R
Uris, Dorothy ... CANR-9
Earlier sketch in CA 61-64
Uris, Leon (Marcus) 1924- ... CANR-65
Earlier sketches in CA 1-4R, CANR-1, 40
See also AITN 1, 2
See also BEST 89:2
See also CLC 7, 32
See also DAM NOV, POP
See also MTCW 1
See also SATA 49
Urista, Alberto H. 1947- ... CANR-2
Earlier sketches in CA 45-48, CANR-32
See also Alurista
See also HW
Urkowitz, Steven 1941- ... 111
Urmson, J(ames) O(pie) 1915- ... 25-28R
Urmuz
See Codrescu, Andrei
Urness, Carol 1936- Brief entry ... 111
Uroff, Margaret Dickie 1935- ... 93-96
Urofsky, Melvin I. 1939- ... CANR-31
Earlier sketches in CA 37-40R, CANR-14
Urquhart, Alvin W. 1931- ... 13-16R
Urquhart, Brian (Edward) 1919- ... CANR-51
Earlier sketches in CA 105, CANR-26
Urquhart, Caroline 1940- ... 118
Urquhart, Colin 1940- ... CANR-37
Earlier sketch in CA 115
Urquhart, Fred(erick Burrows) 1912-1995 ...
CANR-72
Obituary ... 150
Earlier sketches in CA 9-12R, CANR-6, 21
See also DLB 139
Urquhart, Guy
See McAlmon, Robert (Menzies)
Urquhart, Jane 1949- ... CANR-68
Earlier sketches in CA 113, CANR-32
See also CLC 90
See also DAC
Urquhart, Judy 1942- ... 123
Urrutia Lleo, Manuel 1901-1981 Obituary ... 104
Urry, David (Laurence) 1931- ... 85-88
Urry, John 1946- ... CANR-48
Earlier sketch in CA 122
Urry, W(illiam) G(eorge) 1913-1981 Obituary ... 103
Ursano, Robert J. 1947- ... 148
Ursell, Geoffrey 1943- ... 158
Ursini, James 1947- ... CANR-68
Earlier sketch in CA 61-64
Urvater, Michele 1946- ... 102
Urwick, Lyndall Fownes 1891-1983 ... CAP-1
Obituary ... 111
Earlier sketch in CA 13-14
Urwin, Derek W(illiam) 1939- ... 149
Urwin, Gregory J(ohn) W(illiam) 1955- ... CANR-36
Earlier sketch in CA 114
Ury, Allen B. 1954- ... 166
See also SATA 98
Ury, William L(anger) 1953- ... CANR-27
Earlier sketch in CA 109
Ury, Zalman F. 1924- ... CANR-17
Earlier sketch in CA 65-68
Urzidil, Johannes 1896-1970 Obituary ... 29-32R
See also DLB 85
Us
See Deal, Borden
Usborne, Cornelie 1942- ... 145
Usborne, Richard Alexander 1910- ... 104
Usco
See Stern, Gerd Jacob
Usdin, Gene (Leonard) 1922- ... 37-40R
Useem, Michael 1942- ... 61-64
Useni
See Perkins, (Useni) Eugene
Usher, Dan 1934- ... CANR-12
Earlier sketch in CA 29-32R
Usher, Frank (Hugh) 1909-1976 ... CANR-5
Earlier sketch in CA 5-8R
Usher, George 1930- ... 109
Usher, Margo Scegge
See McHargue, Georgess
Usher, Shaun 1937- ... 77-80
Usher, Stephen 1931- ... 29-32R
Usher-Wilson, Rodney N.
1908(?)-1983 Obituary ... 109
Usherwood, Elizabeth (Ada) 1923- ... CANR-51
Earlier sketch in CA 123
Usherwood, Stephen Dean 1907- ... CANR-41
Earlier sketches in CA 5-8R, CANR-3, 19
Usigli, Rodolfo 1905-1979 ... 131
See also HW
Usikota
See Brinitzer, Carl
Usk, Thomas (?)-1388 ... DLB 146
Uslaner, Eric M(ichael) 1947- ... 111
Uslar Pietri, Arturo 1906- ... 150
See also DAM MULT
See also DLB 113
See also HW
Usmiani, Renate 1931- ... 113
Usry, Becky (S.) 1949- ... 152
Usry, Milton F. 1931- ... 17-20R
Ussher, (Percival) Arland 1899-1980 ... CANR-10
Obituary ... 102
Earlier sketches in CAP-1, CA 13-14
Ussher, Jane M. 1961- ... 139
Ussher, Percy Arland
See Ussher, (Percival) Arland
Ustinov, D(mitri) F(edorovich) 1908-1984 ... 133
Obituary ... 114
Ustinov, Peter (Alexander) 1921- ... CANR-51
Earlier sketches in CA 13-16R, CANR-25
See also AITN 1
See also CLC 1
See also DLB 13
Uston, Ken(neth Senzo) 1935-1987 ... 108
Obituary ... 123
See also SATA 65
U Tam'si, Gerald Felix Tchicaya
See Tchicaya, Gerald Felix
U Tam'si, Tchicaya
See Tchicaya, Gerald Felix
Utechin, S(ergei) V(asilievich) 1921- ... 9-12R
Utgard, Russell O(liver) 1933- ... 49-52
Utke, Allen R(ay) 1936- ... 81-84
Utlee, (J.) Maarten 1949- ... CANR-37
Utley, Francis Lee 1907-1974 ... CANR-2
Obituary ... 49-52
Earlier sketch in CA 1-4R
Utley, Freda 1898-1978 ... 81-84
Obituary ... 77-80
Utley, (Clifton) Garrick 1939- ... 69-72
Utley, Jonathan G. 1942- ... 129
Utley, Ralph
See Cairns, Huntington
Utley, Robert M(arshall) 1929- ... CANR-2
Earlier sketch in CA 5-8R
Utley, T(homas) E(dwin) 1921-1988 Obituary ... 125
Utt, Richard H. 1923- ... CANR-7
Earlier sketch in CA 9-12R
Utt, Walter C(harles) 1921- ... 21-24R
Uttley, Alice Jane (Taylor) 1884-1976 ... CANR-52
Obituary ... 65-68
Earlier sketches in CA 53-56, CANR-7
See also Uttley, Alison
See also SATA 3
See also SATA-Obit 26
Uttley, Alice Jane (Taylor) 1884-1976 ... SATA 88
Uttley, Alison
See Uttley, Alice Jane (Taylor)
Uttley, Alison
See Uttley, Alice Jane (Taylor)
See also DLB 160
Uttley, John 1914- ... 21-24R
Utton, Albert Edgar 1931- ... CANR-1
Earlier sketch in CA 45-48
Utz, Lois (Marie) 1932-1986 ... 25-28R
Obituary ... 121
See also SATA 5
See also SATA-Obit 50
Utz, Robert T(homas) 1934- ... 53-56
Uu, David
See Harris, David W.
Uvalic, Milica 1952- ... 167
Uveges, Joseph A(ndrew), Jr. 1938- ... 41-44R
Uvezian, Sonia ... CANR-9
Earlier sketch in CA 57-60
Uviller, H. Richard 1929- ... CANR-65
Earlier sketch in CA 129
Uyl, Douglas J(ohn) Den
See Den Uyl, Douglas J(ohn)
Uys, Errol Lincoln 1943- ... 136
Uz, Johann Peter 1720-1796 ... DLB 97
Uzgiris, Ina Cepenas 1937- Brief entry ... 108
Uzodinma, E(dmund) C(hukuemeka) C(hieke)
1936- ... 153
See also BW 2
Uzzell, J(ohn) Douglas 1937- ... 93-96

V

V., Nina
See Vickers, Antoinette L.
Vac, Bertrand 1914- ... DLB 88
Vacca, Roberto 1927- ... CANR-1
Earlier sketch in CA 49-52
Vaccaro, Ernest B. 1905(?)-1979 Obituary ... 89-92
Vaccaro, Joseph P(ascal) 1935- ... 104
Vaccaro, Louis C(harles) 1930- ... CANR-1
Earlier sketch in CA 45-48
Vaccaro, Tony
See Vaccaro, Ernest B.
Vachek, Josef 1909- ... 132
Vachell, Horace Annesley 1861-1955 Brief
entry ... 120
Vachon, Brian 1941- ... 41-44R
Vachon, Mary L. S. 1945- ... 127
Vachss, Andrew (Henry) 1942- ... CANR-44
Earlier sketch in CA 118
See also CLC 106
Vachss, Andrew H.
See Vachss, Andrew (Henry)
Vaculik, Ludvik 1926- ... CANR-72
Earlier sketch in CA 53-56
See also CLC 7
Vaczek, Louis 1913-1983 ... CANR-21
Obituary ... 111
Earlier sketch in CA 9-12R
Vad, Poul 1927- ... 142
Vadakin, James C(harles) 1924-1981 ... 29-32R
Obituary ... 134
Vadianus, Joachim 1484-1551 ... DLB 179
Vadim, Roger 1928- ... 143
Vadney, Thomas E(ugene) 1939- ... 45-48
Vaeth, J(oseph) Gordon 1921- ... 5-8R
See also SATA 17
Vaggi, Gianni 1947- ... 127
Vago, Bela Adalbert 1922- ... 93-96
Vagts, Alfred (Hermann Friedrich) 1892- ... 5-8R
Vagts, Detlev F(rederick) 1929- ... 25-28R
Vagts, Miriam Beard 1901-1983 Obituary ... 110
Vahanian, Gabriel (Antoine) 1927- ... CANR-45
Earlier sketches in CA 1-4R, CANR-6, 22
Vaid, Krishna Baldev 1927- ... CANR-8
Earlier sketch in CA 61-64
Vaid, Urvashi 1958- ... 156
Vaidon, Lawdom
See Woolman, David S.
Vaihinger, Hans 1852-1933 ... 166
Brief entry ... 116
See also TCLC 71
Vail, (Marilyn) Elaine 1948- ... 109
Vail, Laurence 1891-1968 Obituary ... 112
See also DLB 4
Vail, Priscilla L. 1931- ... 101
Vail, Rachel 1966- ... 159
See also SATA 94
Vail, Robert William 1921- ... CANR-12
Earlier sketch in CA 17-20R
Vaill, George D. 1911(?)-1986 Obituary ... 119
Vaillancourt, Jean-Guy 1937- ... CANR-21
Earlier sketch in CA 105
Vaillancourt, Pauline M(ariette) ... 104
Vaillancourt, Pauline Marie
See Rosenau, Pauline Vaillancourt
Vailland, Roger (Francois) 1907-1965 ... CANR-70
Obituary ... 89-92
Earlier sketch in CA 103
See also DLB 83
Vaillant, George E. 1934- ... CANR-13
Earlier sketch in CA 77-80
Vaillant, Janet G. 1937- ... 136
Vainio, Pirkko 1957- ... SATA 76
Vairo, Philip Dominic 1933- ... 102
Vaizey, John 1929-1984 ... CANR-4
Obituary ... 113
Earlier sketch in CA 5-8R
Vaizey, Marina 1938- ... 116
Vajda, Ernest 1887-1954 Brief entry ... 122
See also DLB 44
Vajda, Stephan 1926-1987 ... CANR-27
Earlier sketch in CA 29-32R
Vajk, J(oseph) Peter 1942- ... 117
Vakar, N(icholas) P(latonovich) 1897-1970 ...
CANR-20
Obituary ... 103
Earlier sketch in CA 1-4R
Valaoritis, Nanos 1921- ... CAAS 26
Valaskakis, Kimon Plato 1941- ... 89-92
Valberg, J. J. 1936- ... 144
Valbonne, Jean
See Leprohon, Pierre
Valbuena-Briones, Angel (Julian) 1928- ... CANR-3
Earlier sketch in CA 45-48
Valcarcel, Emilio Diaz
See Diaz Valcarcel, Emilio
Valcoe, H. Felix
See Swartz, Harry (Felix)
Valdemi, Maria L. 1947- ... 114
Valder, Peter 1928- ... 153
Valdes, Donald M(anuel) 1922- ... 21-24R
Valdes, Gina 1943- ... DLB 122
Valdes, Ivy 1921- ... 105
Valdes, Joan 1931- ... 49-52
Valdes, Mario J. 1934- ... CANR-44
Earlier sketches in CA 13-16R, CANR-6, 21
Valdes, Nelson P. 1945- ... CANR-38
Earlier sketch in CA 33-36R
Valdez, Luis (Miguel) 1940- ... CANR-32
Earlier sketch in CA 101
See also CLC 84
See also DAM MULT
See also DLB 122
See also HLC
See also HW
Valdez, Paul
See Yates, A(lan) G(eoffrey)
Valdman, Albert 1931- ... 103
Valdombre
See Grignon, Claude-Henri
Valduga, Patrizia 1953- ... DLB 128
Vale, C(orwyn) P(hilip) 1921- ... 49-52
Vale, (Henry) Edmund (Theodoric) 1888-1969 ...
CAP-1
Earlier sketch in CA 9-10
Vale, Eugene 1916-1997 ... CANR-12
Obituary ... 158
Earlier sketch in CA 57-60
Vale, Juliet (Elizabeth) 1952- ... 132
Vale, Lewis
See Oglesby, Joseph
Vale, Malcolm Graham Allan 1942- Brief entry . 109
Valen, Nanine 1950- ... 65-68
See also SATA 21
Valencak, Hannelore
See Mayer, Hannelore Valencak
See also SATA 42
Valency, Maurice 1903-1996 ... CANR-26
Obituary ... 153
Earlier sketches in CA 25-28R, CANR-10
Valens, Amy 1946- ... 138
See also SATA 70
Valens, E(vans) G., Jr. 1920- ... CANR-3
Earlier sketch in CA 5-8R
See also SATA 1
Valens, Evans G. ... CANR-14
Earlier sketch in CA 81-84
Valenstein, Elliot S(piro) 1923- ... 132
Valenstein, Suzanne G(ebhart) 1928- ... 77-80
Valente, Jose Angel 1929- ... DLB 108
Valente, Michael F(eeney) ... 57-60
Valenti, Jack 1921- ... 73-76
Valentin, Thomas 1922-1981 Obituary ... 103
Valentine, Alan (Chester) 1901-1980 ... CANR-2
Obituary ... 101
Earlier sketch in CA 5-8R
Valentine, Charles A. 1929- ... 25-28R
Valentine, Charles Wilfrid 1879-1964 Obituary ... 107
Valentine, D(onald) G(raham) 1929- ... 5-8R
Valentine, David
See Ludovici, Anthony M(ario)
Valentine, Douglas 1949- ... 139
See also Williams, (George) Valentine
Valentine, Foy (Dan) 1923- ... CANR-10
Earlier sketch in CA 17-20R
Valentine, Helen
See Valentine, Sister Mary Hester
Valentine, Helen (Lachman)
1893-1986 Obituary ... 121
Valentine, James W(illiam) 1926- ... 126
Valentine, Jean 1934- ... CANR-34
Earlier sketch in CA 65-68
Valentine, Jo
See Armstrong, Charlotte
Valentine, Johnny ... SATA 72
Valentine, Lloyd Magnus 1922- Brief entry ... 110
Valentine, Mark 1959- ... 155
Valentine, Roger
See Duke, Donald Norman
Valentine, Sister Mary Hester 1909- ... CAP-2
Earlier sketch in CA 23-24
Valentine, Steven Richards 1956- ... 113
Valentine, Tom 1935- ... CANR-22
Earlier sketch in CA 45-48
Valentine, William Alexander 1905- ... 57-60
Valentis, Mary 1945- ... 148
Valenzuela, Arturo A. 1944- ... 101
Valenzuela, Luisa 1938- ... CANR-65
Earlier sketches in CA 101, CANR-32
See also CLC 31, 104
See also DAM MULT
See also DLB 113
See also HW
See also SSC 14
Valeo, Francis Ralph 1916- Brief entry ... 108
Valeran, A. B.
See Starr, S(tephen) Frederick
Valera y Alcala-Galiano, Juan 1824-1905 Brief
entry ... 106
See also TCLC 10
Valeri, Diego 1887-1976 ... DLB 128
Valeriani, Richard (Gerard) 1932- ... CANR-12
Earlier sketch in CA 65-68

Valeriano, Napoleon D(iestro)
1917(?)-1975 Obituary....................53-56
Valerio, Anthony 1940-....................165
Valery, Bernard 1913(?)-1984 Obituary........113
Valery, (Ambroise) Paul (Toussaint Jules)
1871-1945....................122
Brief entry....................104
See also DAM POET
See also MTCW 1
See also PC 9
See also TCLC 4, 15
Vales, Robert L(ee) 1933-.................. 53-56
Valesio, Paolo 1939-.................. DLB 196
Valett, Robert E. 1927-.............. CANR-22
Earlier sketches in CA 17-20R, CANR-7
Valette, Rebecca M(arianne Loose) 1938-. CANR-8
Earlier sketch in CA 21-24R
Valgardson, W(illiam) D(empsey) 1939-.. CANR-60
Earlier sketches in CA 41-44R, CANR-38
See also DAC
See also DAM MST
See also DLB 60
See also SATA 101
Valgemae, Mardi 1935-.................. 41-44R
Vali, Ferenc Albert 1905-1984.......... CANR-37
Obituary....................114
Earlier sketches in CA 1-4R, CANR-3
Valiani, Leo 1909-.................. CANR-18
Earlier sketch in CA 101
Valin, Jonathan Louis 1948-............ CANR-62
Earlier sketches in CA 101, CANR-38
Valin, Martial (Henry) 1898-1980 Obituary..... 105
Valis, Noel M(aureen Ritter) 1945-............110
Valkenier, Elizabeth Kridl 1926-.............. 119
Valko, Peter 1950-....................159
Vall, Seymour 1925(?)-1987 Obituary........ 124
Vallance, Elizabeth (Mary) 1945-........ CANR-40
Earlier sketch in CA 102
Vallbona, Rima-Gretel Rothe 1931-........... 146
Valle, Victor Manuel 1950-.............. DLB 122
Valleau, Emily 1925-.................. SATA 51
Vallee, Hubert P(rior) 1901-1986......... CANR-2
Obituary....................119
Earlier sketch in CA 1-4R
Vallee, Jacques F. 1939-.............. CANR-10
Earlier sketch in CA 17-20R
Vallee, Lillian (Bozenna) 1949-............... 135
Vallee, Rudy
See Vallee, Hubert P(rior)
Valle-Inclan, Ramon (Maria) del 1866-1936.... 153
Brief entry....................106
See also DAM MULT
See also DLB 134
See also HLC
See also TCLC 5
Vallejo, Antonio Buero
See Buero Vallejo, Antonio
Vallejo, Armando 1949-.................DLB 122
Vallejo, Boris 1941-....................167
See also AAYA 13
Vallejo, Cesar (Abraham) 1892-1938.......... 153
Brief entry....................105
See also DAM MULT
See also HLC
See also HW
See also TCLC 3, 56
Vallen, Jerome J(ay) 1928-.................93-96
Vallentine, John F(ranklin) 1931-........ CANR-41
Earlier sketches in CA 53-56, CANR-4, 19
Vallerand, April Hazard 1957-................ 168
Valles, Jules 1832-1885................ DLB 123
Vallette, Marguerite Eymery
See Rachilde
Valle Y Pena, Ramon del
See Valle-Inclan, Ramon (Maria) del
Vallinder, Torbjorn 1925-.................... 155
Vallone, Lynne 1962-........................ 150
Vallone, Ralph, Jr. 1947-..................... 147
Valmaggia, Juan S. 1895-1980 Obituary.... 97-100
Valsan, E. H. 1933-....................29-32R
Valtz, Robert C. K. 1936-..................13-16R
Value, Barbara Ann 1932-1986 Obituary....... 120
Valverde, Jose Maria 1926-.............. DLB 108
Vambe, Lawrence (Chinyani) 1917-........... 110
Vamos, Mara (Miriam) 1927- Brief entry....... 114
Vamplew, Wray 1943-................. CANR-20
Earlier sketch in CA 103
Van Abbe, Derek Maurice 1916-............57-60
Van Abbe, Salaman 1883-1955.......... SATA 18
Van Allen, James (Alfred) 1914-..............162
Van Allsburg, Chris 1949-.............. CANR-38
Brief entry....................113
Earlier sketch in CA 117
See also CLR 5, 13
See also DLB 61
See also MAICYA
See also SATA 37, 53
van Alphen, Ernst 1958-....................143
Van Alstyne, Richard W(arner) 1900-1983.........
CANR-39
Earlier sketch in CA 9-12R
Van Alstyne, William W. 1934-............... 145
Van Anda, Carr 1864-1945................ DLB 25
Van Anrooy, Francine 1924-............ 21-24R
See also SATA 2
Van Anrooy, Frans
See Van Anrooy, Francine
van Appledorn, Mary Jeanne 1927-...... CANR-51
Earlier sketches in CA 25-28R, CANR-10, 26
Vanardy, Varick
See Dey, Frederic (Merrill) Van Rensselaer
Van Arsdel, Rosemary T(horstenson) 1926-.......
CANR-43
Earlier sketch in CA 108
Van Ash, Cay 1918-.................... CLC 34
Van Atta, Winfred 1910-................ CANR-1
Earlier sketch in CA 1-4R
Vanauken, Sheldon 1914-.............. CANR-35
Earlier sketches in CA 85-88, CANR-15
Vanbalen, A.
See Stolk, Anthonie
van Beeck, Frans Jozef 1930-................115
van Belle, Gerald.......................... 146
Vanberg, Bent J(arl) 1915-..................118
van Beusekom, Janneke 1956-...............167
VanBibber, Max A(rnold)
1913(?)-1981 Obituary.................... 103
van Brabant, Jozef M(artin) 1942-............ 141
Van Briggle, Margaret F(rances) Jessup
1917-.................................. 9-12R
Van Brocklin, Norm(an Mack)
1926-1983 Obituary........................109
Vanbrugh, Sir John 1664-1726........DAM DRAM
See also DLB 80
Van Brunt, H. L.
See Van Brunt, (Howell) Lloyd
Van Brunt, (Howell) Lloyd 1936-........ CANR-35
Earlier sketch in CA 49-52
See also CAAS 15
Van Buitenen, J(ohannes) A(drian) B(ernard)
1928(?)-1979.............................103
Obituary................................ 89-92
Van Buren, Abigail
See Phillips, Pauline (Esther Friedman)
Van Buren, James G(eil) 1914-............. 57-60
van Buren, Paul (Matthews) 1924-....... CANR-11
Earlier sketch in CA 61-64
Van Buren, Raeburn 1891-1987........ CANR-39
Earlier sketch in CA 103
Van Caenegem, R(aoul) C(harles) 1927-. CANR-23
Earlier sketch in CA 45-48
Van Campen, Karl
See Campbell, John W(ood, Jr.)
Van Caspel, Venita 1922-....................104
Vance, A. D.
See Vane-Wright, R(ichard) I(rwin)
Vance, Adrian 1936-...................... 77-80
Vance, Barbara Jane 1934-............... 57-60
Vance, Bruce 1931-....................33-36R
Vance, Cyrus R(oberts) 1917-................121
Vance, Edgar
See Ambrose, Eric (Samuel)
Vance, Eleanor Graham 1908-............. 9-12R
See also SATA 11
Vance, Ethel
See Stone, Grace Zaring
Vance, Eugene 1934-...................... 126
Vance, Gerald
See Garrett, (Gordon) Randall (Phillip)
and Silverberg, Robert
Vance, Jack
See Kuttner, Henry
and Vance, John Holbrook
See also CLC 35
See also DLB 8
Vance, John Holbrook 1916-........... CANR-65
Earlier sketches in CA 29-32R, CANR-17
See also Queen, Ellery
and Vance, Jack
See also MTCW 1
Vance, Lawrence L(ee) 1911-1978...... CANR-39
Earlier sketch in CA 49-52
Vance, Louis Joseph 1879-1933 Brief entry....112
Vance, Marguerite 1889-1965 Obituary........109
See also SATA 29
Vance, (Robert) Norman (Colbert) 1950-. CANR-48
Earlier sketch in CA 122
Vance, Rupert B(ayless) 1899-1975 Obituary.61-64
Vance, Samuel 1939-....................29-32R
Vance, Sandra S. 1946-....................147
Vance, Stanley 1915-.................. CANR-3
Earlier sketch in CA 1-4R
Vance, William E. 1911-1986.......... CANR-64
Obituary....................119
Earlier sketch in CA 105
Vance, William L(ynn) 1934-................ 132
Vanceburg, Martha
See Roth (Vanceburg), Martha
Vance-Watkins, Lequita 1936-...............151
Vancil, Richard F(ranklin) 1931-1996.... CANR-40
Obituary....................151
Earlier sketches in CA 5-8R, CANR-8
Van Cise, Jerrold G(ordon) 1910-1996....... 114
Obituary....................153
VanCleave, Janice 1942-................... 142
See also SATA 75
Van Cleef, Eugene 1887-1973 Obituary....... 107
Van Cleve, John Walter 1950-.......... CANR-48
Earlier sketch in CA 122
Van Cleve, Thomas Curtis 1888-1976......41-44R
Obituary................................ 65-68
Van Coevering, Jack
See Van Coevering, Jan Adrian
Van Coevering, Jan Adrian 1900-.......... CAP-1
Earlier sketch in CA 9-10
van Corstanje, Auspicius
See van Corstanje, Charles
van Corstanje, Charles 1913-............... 107
van Croonenburg, Engelbert J(ohannes)
1909-..................................37-40R
Van Dahm, Thomas E(dward) 1924-.........65-68
Van Dalen, Deobold B(ertrude) 1911-... CANR-20
Earlier sketch in CA 1-4R
Van Dam, Ine 1947-........................ 109
van Dam, J.
See Presser, (Gerrit) Jacob
Van Deburg, William L. 1948-............... 139
See also BW 2
Vande Kieft, Ruth Marguerite 1925-........17-20R
Van D'Elden, Karl H. 1923-.................45-48
Vandeman, George E(dward) 1916- Brief entry.114
Van De Mieroop, Marc 1956-................ 139
Vandenberg, Arthur Hendrick 1884-1951 Brief
entry.....................................120
Vandenberg, Donald 1931-.............. 29-32R
Vandenberg, Philipp 1941-............. CANR-47
Earlier sketches in CA 61-64, CANR-8, 23
Vandenberg, T. F. 1941-................. 25-28R
Van Den Bergh, Nan 1947-....................140
van den Berghe, Pierre L. 1933-......... CANR-5
Earlier sketch in CA 9-12R
Van Den Bogarde, Derek Jules Gaspard Ulric Niven
1921-....................................77-80
See also Bogarde, Dirk
Vandenbosch, Amry 1894-.................61-64
Vandenbosch, Robert 1922-1978 Obituary.....107
Vanden Bossche, Chris R. 1950-............. 141
VandenBroeck, Andre 1923-.................. 128
Vandenbroucke, Lucien S. 1951-............. 148
Vandenburg, Mary Lou 1943-...............73-76
See also SATA 17
Vandenburgh, Jane......................... 168
See also CLC 59
Vandenburgh, Mildred 1898-............. 97-100
Vandenbusche, Duane (Lee) 1937-...... CANR-49
Earlier sketches in CA 45-48, CANR-24
van den Bussche, Henri O(mer) A(ntoine)
See Bussche, Henri O(mer) A(ntoine) Van den
van den Haag, Ernest 1914-........... CANR-26
Earlier sketches in CA 5-8R, CANR-6
van den Heuvel, Albert H(endrik) 1932-.... 17-20R
van den Heuvel, Cornelisz A. 1931-........13-16R
vanden Heuvel, Katrina 1959-................133
van den Hoven, Adrian T. 1939-..............141
Van De Pitte, Frederick P. 1932-.............45-48
Vander, Harry J(oseph) III 1913-(?).......... CAP-2
Earlier sketch in CA 25-28
VanDerBeets, Richard 1932-........... CANR-35
Earlier sketch in CA 29-32R
van der Bent, Ans J(oachim) 1924-........... 131
Vanderbilt, Amy 1908-1974.............. CANR-3
Obituary................................ 53-56
Earlier sketch in CA 1-4R
Vanderbilt, Arthur T. II 1950-................ 122
Vanderbilt, Cornelius, Jr. 1898-1974....... CAP-1
Obituary................................ 49-52
Earlier sketch in CA 9-10
See also AITN 1
Vanderbilt, Gloria (Laura Morgan) 1924-. CANR-60
Earlier sketches in CA 89-92, CANR-22
Interview in CANR-22
Vander Boom, Mae M.................... SATA 14
Vanderburgh, R(osamond) M(oate) 1926-......105
Vander-Els, Betty 1936-................. SATA 63
Vander Goot, Mary 1947-....................112
Vandergriff, (Lola) Aola 1920-1989...... CANR-18
Obituary....................128
Earlier sketch in CA 89-92
Interview in CANR-18
Vanderhaar, Gerard A(nthony) 1931-..........125
Vanderhaeghe, Guy 1951-............. CANR-72
Earlier sketch in CA 113
See also CLC 41
van der Heyden, A(ntonius) A(lphonsus) M(aria)
1922-............................. CANR-7
Earlier sketch in CA 57-60
Vander Hill, C(harles) Warren 1937-....... 33-36R
VanDerhoof, Jack W(arner) 1921-............53-56
Van der Horst, Brian 1944-............... 41-44R
VanderKam, James C(laire) 1946-........... 148
Van der kiste, John (Patrick Guy) 1954-....... 147
Vander Kooi, Ronald C(harles)............. CANR-2
Earlier sketch in CA 45-48
van der Kroef, Justus M(aria) 1925-...... CANR-14
Earlier sketch in CA 41-44R
van der Linde, Laurel 1952-..................146
See also SATA 78
Vanderlip, D(odava) George 1926-...... CANR-15
Earlier sketch in CA 77-80
Vander Lugt, Herbert 1920-............ CANR-18
Earlier sketch in CA 101
van der Marck, Jan 1929-.................... 119
van der Meer, Ron 1945-.....................152
See also SATA 98
van der Merwe, Nikolaas J(ohannes) 1940-.......
CANR-35
Earlier sketch in CA 41-44R
van der Meulen, Daniel 1894-..................117
VanderMolen, Robert 1947-............ CANR-36
Earlier sketch in CA 57-60
van der Plas, Rob(ert) 1938-................. 138
van der Ploeg, Johannes P(etrus) M(aria) 1909-...
CANR-42
Earlier sketches in CAP-1, CA 9-10, CANR-15
van der Poel, Cornelius J(ohannes) 1921-. CANR-4
Earlier sketch in CA 53-56
Vanderpool, Harold Y(oung) 1936-.......... 53-56
Vanderpool, James A(lbert)
1916-1983 Obituary........................109
van der Poorten, Alf(red J.) 1942-............ 163
van der Post, Laurens (Jan) 1906-1996.. CANR-35
Obituary....................155
Earlier sketch in CA 5-8R
See also CLC 5
Van Dersal, William R(ichard) 1907-1990.... 77-80
Obituary....................131
Vander-Schrier, Nettie 1922-................114
Vandersee, Charles (Andrew) 1938-..... CANR-29
Earlier sketch in CA 41-44R
Van Der Slik, Jack R(onald) 1936-...... CANR-65
Earlier sketches in CA 29-32R, CANR-30
van der Smissen, Betty
See van der Smissen, Margaret Elisabeth
van der Smissen, Margaret Elisabeth 1927-.......
CANR-9
Earlier sketch in CA 17-20R
van der Vat, Dan(iel Francis Jeroen) 1939-........
CANR-55
Earlier sketches in CA 109, CANR-28
Vanderveen, Bareld Harmannus 1932-........ 103
Vanderveen, Bart H.
See Vanderveen, Bareld Harmannus
Van der Veer, Judy 1912-1982............33-36R
Obituary................................ 108
See also SATA 4
See also SATA-Obit 33
Vandervelde, Marjorie (Mills) 1908-...... CANR-10
Earlier sketch in CA 21-24R
Van der Veldt, James 1893(?)-1977 Obituary.73-76
Van der Veur, Paul W. 1921-...............21-24R
Van Der Voort, Richard Lee 1936-.........37-40R
Vanderwall, Francis W(illiam) 1946-..... CANR-26
Earlier sketch in CA 108
Van der Wee, Herman (Frans Anna) 1928-.....133
Vanderwerken, David L(eon) 1945-............ 119
Vanderwerth, W(illiam) C(onnor) 1904-.......73-76
Vanderwood, Paul J(oseph) 1929-...... CANR-28
Earlier sketch in CA 29-32R
Vander Zanden, James Wilfrid 1930-.... CANR-19
Earlier sketches in CA 13-16R, CANR-5
van der Zee, Barbara (Blanche) 1932-.........146
van der Zee, Henri (Antony) 1934- Brief entry..114
Van Der Zee, James (Augustus Joseph)
1886-1983................................104
Obituary....................109
van der Zee, John 1936-.............. CANR-32
Earlier sketches in CA 21-24R, CANR-15
Vanderzell, John H. 1924-................. 45-48
VanderZwaag, Harold J. 1929-.......... CANR-23
Earlier sketch in CA 45-48
van Deurs, George 1901-................25-28R
van Deursen, A. Th. 1931-...................138
Van Deusen, Dayton G(roff) 1914-.......... 9-12R
Van Deusen, Glyndon Garlock 1897-..... CANR-1
Earlier sketch in CA 1-4R
Van Deusen, L. Marshall 1922-............. 61-64
Van Deusen, Ruth B(rown) 1907-............. 5-8R
Van De Vall, Mark 1923-............... CANR-30
Earlier sketches in CA 29-32R, CANR-12
Van Devander, Charles W(ood)
1902-1986 Obituary........................121
Van Devanter, Lynda (Margaret) 1947-........ 117
Van de Vate, Dwight, Jr. 1928-............. 61-64
Vande Velde, Vivian 1951-...................160
See also SATA 62, 95
Van Deventer, David E(arl) 1937- Brief entry...115
Van Deventer, Fred 1903-1971........... CAP-1
Earlier sketch in CA 13-16
VanDeventer, Robert........................ 105
Van de Water, Frederic F(ranklyn)
1890-1968 Obituary........................110
van de Wetering, Janwillem 1931-....... CANR-62
Earlier sketches in CA 49-52, CANR-4
See also CLC 47
Van Dine, S. S.
See Wright, Willard Huntington
See also TCLC 23
Vandiver, Edward P(inckney), Jr. 1902-..... CAP-1
Earlier sketch in CA 13-14
Vandiver, Frank E(verson) 1925-......... CANR-7
Earlier sketch in CA 5-8R
Vandivert, Rita (Andre) 1905-............ CANR-6
Earlier sketch in CA 5-8R
See also SATA 21
Van Domelen, John E(mory) 1935-........... 130
Van Dommelen, David B. 1929-........ CANR-35
Earlier sketch in CA 5-8R
van Dooren, Ingrid 1949-.................... 114
Van Dooren, L(eonard) A(lfred) T(heophile) 1912-..
CANR-19
Earlier sketches in CA 5-8R, CANR-3
Van Doren, Carl (Clinton) 1885-1950.......... 168
Brief entry....................111
See also TCLC 18
Van Doren, Charles L. 1926-............. CANR-4
Earlier sketch in CA 5-8R
Van Doren, Dorothy Graffe 1896-1993........1-4R
Obituary....................141
Van Doren, Irita 1891-1966 Obituary....... 89-92
Van Doren, Mark 1894-1972............ CANR-3
Obituary................................37-40R
Earlier sketch in CA 1-4R
See also CLC 6, 10
See also DLB 45
See also MTCW 1
Van Dorne, R.
See Wallmann, Jeffrey M(iner)
Vandour, Cyril
See Surmelian, Leon (Zaven)
Van Dover, J(ames) K(enneth) 1950-..........139
Van Druten, John (William) 1901-1957........ 161
Brief entry....................104
See also DLB 10
See also TCLC 2
Van Dusen, Albert E(dward) 1916-....... CANR-3
Earlier sketch in CA 5-8R
Van Dusen, Clarence Raymond 1907-........5-8R
Van Dusen, Henry P(itney) 1897-1975.... CANR-3
Obituary................................ 57-60
Earlier sketch in CA 1-4R
Van Dusen, Robert LaBranche 1929-...... 41-44R
Van Duyn, Janet 1910-.................. 69-72
See also SATA 18
Van Duyn, Mona (Jane) 1921-........... CANR-60
Earlier sketches in CA 9-12R, CANR-7, 38
See also CLC 3, 7, 63
See also DAM POET
See also DLB 5
Van Duzee, Mabel 1895-....................... 5-8R
Van Duzer, Chet A. 1966-.................... 153
Van Dyk, Jere
See Van Dyk, Wilmer Jerald

Van Dyk, Wilmer Jerald 1945- 131
Van Dyke, Carolynn 1947- 116
Van Dyke, Dick 1925- 166
  Brief entry 112
Van Dyke, Henry 1852-1933 ....DLB 71
  See also DLBD 13
Van Dyke, Henry 1928- CANR-25
  Earlier sketch in CA 49-52
  See also BW 1
  See also DLB 33
Van Dyke, John C. 1856-1932 ....DLB 186
Van Dyke, Jon M. 1943- 29-32R
Van Dyke, Lauren A. 1906- 29-32R
Van Dyke, Vernon Brumbaugh 1912- CANR-46
  Earlier sketches in CA 1-4R, CANR-23
Van Dyne, Edith
  See Baum, L(yman) Frank
  and Sampson, Emma (Keats) Speed
  and van Zantwijk, Rudolf (Alexander Marinus)
Vane, Brett
  See Kent, Arthur William Charles
Vane, John R(obert) 1927- 160
Vane, Michael
  See Humphries, Sydney Vernon
Vane, Roland
  See, McKeag, Ernest L(ionel)
Vane, (Vane Hunt) Sutton 1888-1963 Obituary . 113
  See also DLB 10
Van Eenwyk, John R. 1946- 164
Van Eerde, Katherine S(ommerlatte) 1920- ..61-64
Van Egmond, Peter (George) 1937- 61-64
Vanek, Jaroslav 1930- 103
Van Engen, John H. 1947- 117
Van Ermengem, Frederic
  1881-1972 Obituary 33-36R
Van Erven, Eugene 1955- 138
Van Ess, Dorothy 1885(?)-1975 Obituary . . 61-64
Van Ettinger, Jan 1902- CANR-21
  Earlier sketch in CA 1-4R
Van Every, Dale 1896-1976 ....CANR-3
  Earlier sketch in CA 1-4R
Van Ewijk, Casper 1953- 140
Vane-Wright, R(ichard) I(rwin) 1942- 121
Van Fossen, Richard W(aight) 1927- CANR-6
  Earlier sketch in CA 5-8R
van Fraassen, Bastiaan Cornelis CANR-14
  Earlier sketch in CA 37-40R
van Geert, Paul 1950- 132
Van Geil, Mercury E. C. L.
  See McGilvery, Laurence
van Gelder, Dora 1904- Brief entry 116
van Gelder, Lindsy 1944- 97-100
van Gelder, Richard George 1928- 73-76
Vangelisti, Paul 1945- CANR-31
  Earlier sketches in CA 77-80, CANR-14
Vangen, Roland Dean 1935- 105
Vanger, Milton Isadore 1925- CANR-34
  Earlier sketch in CA 13-16R
Van Ginneken, Jaap 1943- 142
Van Goethem, Larry 1934- 101
van Gulik, Robert Hans 1910-1967 ......CANR-62
  Obituary 25-28R
  Earlier sketches in CA 1-4R, CANR-3
  See also DLBD 17
VanGundy, Arthur B(oice), Jr. 1946- CANR-29
  Earlier sketch in CA 110
Van Haaften, Julia 1946- 109
Van Hassen, Amy
  See Wiles, Domini
Van Hattum, Rolland J(ames) 1924- CANR-21
  Earlier sketch in CA 105
Van Hecke, B(resee) C(oleman) 1926- ...29-32R
van Heerden, Etienne 143
Van Heijenoort, Jean 1912-1986 161
  Obituary 120
Van Helden, Albert 1940- 125
Van Herik, Judith 1947- 108
van Herk, Aritha 1954- 101
van het Reve, Karel 1921- 49-52
van Heyningen, Christina 1900- 17-20R
van Heyningen, William Edward 1911- 112
Van Hise, Della 1955- 121
Van Hoesen, Walter H.
  1898(?)-1972 Obituary 69-72
Van Hook, Beverly H. 1941- 167
Van Hook, Beverly H. 1941- ....SATA 99
Van Hook, Roger Eugene 1943- 29-32R
Van Hoose, William H. 1927- 89-92
Van Horn, Richard L. 1932- 53-56
Van Horn, William 1939- 115
  See also SATA 43
Van Horne, Harriet 1920-1998 Obituary . . . 164
  Brief entry 113
Van Houten, Lois 1918- CANR-34
  Earlier sketch in CA 77-80
Van Huss, Wayne D(aniel) 1917- 61-64
Van Hyning, Thomas E. 1954- 154
van Inwagen, Peter (Jan) 1942- CANR-39
  Earlier sketch in CA 116
van Itallie, Jean-Claude 1936- CANR-48
  Earlier sketches in CA 45-48, CANR-1
  See also CAAS 2
  See also CLC 3
  See also DLB 7
Van Itallie, Philip H. 1899- CAP-1
  Earlier sketch in CA 9-10
Van Iterson, S(iny) R(ose) 102
  See also SATA 26
van Jaarsveld, Floris Albertus 1922- ...CANR-7
  Earlier sketch in CA 5-8R
van Kaam, Adrian (L.) 1920- CANR-52
  Earlier sketches in CA 17-20R, CANR-10, 26
Van Kampen, Vlasta 1943- ....SATA 54
Van Kleek, Peter Eric 1929- CANR-35
  Earlier sketch in CA 53-56
Van Krevelen, Alice 1914- 45-48

van Lawick, Hugo 1937- 85-88
van Lawick-Goodall, Jane
  See Goodall, Jane
Vanleer, Jay
  See Williams, June Vanleer
Van Leeuwen, Jean 1937- CANR-52
  Earlier sketches in CA 25-28R, CANR-11, 28
  See also SAAS 8
  See also SATA 6, 82
van Lemmen, Hans 1946- 144
Van Lente, Charles R(obert) 1941- 65-68
van Lhin, Erik
  See del Rey, Lester
Van Lierde, John 1907- CAP-1
  Earlier sketch in CA 9-10
Van Lierde, Peter Canisius
  See Van Lierde, John
van Lint, June 1928- 65-68
Van Loan, Charles E. 1876-1919 ....DLB 171
van Loon, Gerard Willem 1911- 45-48
Van Loon, Hendrik Willem 1882-1944 Brief
  entry 117
  See also SATA 18
Van Meerhaeghe, M(arcel) A(lfons) G(ilbert) 1921- .
  CANR-13
  Earlier sketch in CA 77-80
Van Melsen, Andreas G(erardus) M(aria) 1912- ....
  CANR-34
  Earlier sketches in CA 1-4R, CANR-4
VanMeter, Vandelia 1934- 142
Vann, J(erry) Don 1938- 29-32R
Vann, James Allen 1939- 110
Vann, Richard T(ilman) 1931- 21-24R
Vann, Robert L. 1879-1940 ....DLB 29
Vannatta, Dennis 1946- 138
Vanneman, Reeve 1945- 127
Van Ness, Peter 1933- 29-32R
Van Niel, Cornelius B(ernardus)
  1897-1985 Obituary 115
Vannier, Maryhelen 1915- CANR-22
  Earlier sketches in CA 1-4R, CANR-6
van Nieuwenhuijze, C(hristoffel) A(nthonie) O(livier)
  1920- 25-28R
Van Nimmen, (Carol) Jane 1937- 125
Van Nooten, Barend A(drian) 1932- 45-48
Van Noppen, Ina (Faye) W(oestemeyer)
  1906-1980 ....5-8R
  Obituary 103
Vannorsdall, John Warren 1924- 113
Van Nostrand, A(lbert) D(ouglass) 1922- . CANR-16
  Earlier sketch in CA 41-44R
Vannoy, Russell (Columbus) 1933- 119
Vano, Gerard S. 1943- 112
Vanocur, Edith C. 1924(?)-1975 Obituary . 57-60
Vanocur, Sander 1928- 120
  Brief entry 109
  Interview in 120
van Onselen, Charles 1944- 154
van Oort, Jan 1921- CANR-31
  Earlier sketch in CA 29-32R
Van Orden, M(erton) D(ick) 1921- 37-40R
  See also SATA 4
Van Orman, Bonny 1939(?)-1987 Obituary 122
Van Orman, Richard A(lbert) 1936- CANR-34
  Earlier sketch in CA 21-24R
Van Osdol, William R(ay) 1927- 53-56
van Ostaijen, Paul 1896-1928 163
  See also TCLC 33
Van Over, Raymond 1934- Brief entry 112
van Overbeek, Johannes 1908- CAP-1
  Earlier sketch in CA 13-14
Van Parijs, Philippe 1951- 152
Van Peebles, Melvin 1932- CANR-67
  Earlier sketches in CA 85-88, CANR-27
  See also BW 2
  See also CLC 2, 20
  See also DAM MULT
van Pelt, Robert-Jan 1955- 139
van Peursen, Cornelius Anthonie 1920- ...53-56
Van Praagh, David 1931- 165
Van Praagh, Margaret 1910-1990 ....CAP-2
  Obituary 130
  Earlier sketch in CA 17-18
Van Praagh, Peggy
  See Van Praagh, Margaret
Van Proosdy, Cornelis 1919- CANR-5
  Earlier sketch in CA 9-12R
Van Proyen, Mark 1954- ....CAAS 25
Van Raden, Kristine 1953- 165
Van Ravenswaay, Charles 1911- 119
Van Rensselaer, Alexander (Taylor Mason)
  1892-1962 73-76
  See also SATA 14
van Rensselaer, Maria van Cortlandt
  1645-1689 ....DLB 200
Van Rensselaer, Mariana Griswold 1851-1934 . DLB
  47
Van Rensselaer, Mrs. Schuyler
  See Van Rensselaer, Mariana Griswold
Van Rheenen, Gailyn 1946- 69-72
van Rijn, Ignatius
  See Ingram, Forrest L(eo)
Van Riper, Francis A(lbert) 1946- CANR-11
  Earlier sketch in CA 69-72
Van Riper, Frank
  See Van Riper, Francis A(lbert)
Van Riper, Guernsey, Jr. 1909- CANR-6
  Earlier sketch in CA 5-8R
  See also SATA 3
Van Riper, Paul P(ritchard) 1916- CANR-31
  Earlier sketch in CA 1-4R
Van Riper, Robert 1921- 37-40R
van Rjndt, Philippe 1950- CANR-14
  Earlier sketch in CA 65-68
van Rooy, C(harles) A(ugust) 1923- 17-20R

van Ruler, Han
  See van Ruler, J. A.
van Ruler, J. A. 1963- 152
Van Rynbach, Iris 1952- ....SATA 102
Van Saher, Lilla 1912-1968 ....CAP-1
  Earlier sketch in CA 11-12
Vansant, Carl 1938- 37-40R
Van Sant, Gus 1952- 152
  See also AAYA 17
Vansant, Rhonda Joy Edwards 1950- .....SATA 92
Van Schaick, Frances L.
  1912(?)-1979 Obituary 89-92
Van Scyoc, Sydney J(oyce) 1939- CANR-33
  Earlier sketches in CA 89-92, CANR-15
Van See, John
  See Vance, John Holbrook
Van Sertima, Ivan 1935- CANR-42
  Earlier sketch in CA 104
  See also BW 2
Van Seters, John 1935- CANR-38
  Earlier sketch in CA 115
Van Sickle, Emily 1910- 140
Van Sickle, John V(alentine) 1892- CANR-35
  Earlier sketch in CA 5-8R
Van Sickle, Neil D(avid) 1915- 41-44R
VanSickle, V. A.
  See Carhart, Arthur Hawthorne
Vansina, Jan 1929- CANR-10
  Earlier sketch in CA 65-68
Vansittart, Jane
  See Moorhouse, Hilda Vansittart
Vansittart, Peter 1920- CANR-49
  Earlier sketches in CA 1-4R, CANR-3
  See also CLC 42
Van Slingerland, Peter 1929- 21-24R
Van Slooten, Henry 1916- 1-4R
Van Slyck, Abigail A(yres) 1959- 161
Van Slyck, Philip 1920- 13-16R
Van Slyke, Donald Dexter 1883-1971 Obituary . 104
Van Slyke, Helen (Lenore) 1919-1979 ...CANR-28
  Obituary 89-92
  Earlier sketch in CA 37-40R
Van Slyke, Lyman P(age) 1929- 21-24R
Van Smith, Howard
  See Smith, Howard Van
van Someren, Liesje
  See Lichtenberg, Elisabeth Jacoba
Van Staaveren, Jacob 1917- 153
Van Steenberghen, Fernand (Emmanuel)
  1904- 130
Van Steenwyk, Elizabeth (Ann) 1928- ...CANR-40
  Earlier sketches in CA 101, CANR-18
  See also SATA 34, 89
Van Stockum, Hilda 1908- CANR-5
  Earlier sketch in CA 9-12R
  See also SATA 5
van Straten, Florence W(ilhelmina)
  1913-1992 ....17-20R
  Obituary 137
Van Tassel, Alfred J. 1910- 41-44R
Van Tassel, David Dirck 1928- CANR-35
  Earlier sketch in CA 103
Van Tassel, Dennie L(ee) 1939- CANR-35
  Earlier sketch in CA 57-60, CANR-8
Van Tassel, George W. 1910-1978 Obituary . . 112
Van Tassel, Roger (Carleton) 1924- 45-48
van Thal, Herbert (Maurice) 1904-1983 . CANR-30
  Obituary 111
  Earlier sketch in CA 65-68
Van Til, Cornelius 1895- CANR-3
  Earlier sketch in CA 1-4R
Van Til, William 1911- CANR-10
  Earlier sketch in CA 25-28R
Van Tilburg, Jo Anne 1942- 151
Van Tine, Warren R(ussell) 1942- 53-56
Van Trump, James D(enholm) 1908- 41-44R
Van Tuyl, Barbara 1940- 53-56
  See also SATA 11
Van Valkenburg, Samuel 1891-1976 ....5-8R
  Obituary 103
Van Valkenburgh, Paul 1941- 89-92
Van Vechten, Benjamin D(avenport) 1935- ..110
Van Vechten, Carl 1880-1964 Obituary ...89-92
  See also CLC 33
  See also DLB 4, 9, 51
Van Vleck, David B. 1929- 101
Van Vleck, John Hasbrouck
  1899-1980 Obituary 102
Van Vleck, L(loyd) Dale 1933- 53-56
Van Vleck, Sarita 1933- 13-16R
Van Vlissingen, Arthur 1894-1986 Obituary . . 120
Van Vogt, A(lfred) E(lton) 1912- CANR-28
  Earlier sketch in CA 21-24R
  See also CLC 1
  See also DLB 8
  See also SATA 14
Van Vooren, Monique 1933- 107
Van Voorhis, Linda Lynn 1902-1989 Obituary . . 129
Van Voris, Jacqueline 1922- 57-60
Van Vuuren, Nancy 1938- CANR-35
  Earlier sketch in CA 49-52
Van Wagenen, Gertrude 1893-1978 Obituary . 77-80
Van Wageningen, J.
  See Presser, (Gerrit) Jacob
Van Wart, Alice 1948- 137
Van Waters, Miriam 1887-1974 Obituary . . . 45-48
Van Weddingen, Marthe 1924- CANR-14
  Earlier sketch in CA 81-84
Van Wert, William F(rancis) 1945- 105
Van Winckel, Nance 1951- 131
van Witsen, Leo 1912- 106
Van Woeart, Alpheus
  See Halloway, Vance
Van Woerkom, Dorothy (O'Brien) 1924- .. CANR-26
  Earlier sketches in CA 57-60, CANR-11
  See also SATA 21

Van Wormer, Joe
  See Van Wormer, Joseph Edward
Van Wormer, Joseph Edward 1913- CANR-5
  Earlier sketch in CA 9-12R
  See also SATA 35
Van Wormer, Laura (Eleanor) 1955- 127
Van Young, Eric (Julian) 1946- 122
Van Zandt, E. F.
  See Cudlipp, Edythe
Van Zandt, Roland 1918-1991 ....17-20R
  Obituary 134
Vanzant, Iyanla (Rhonda) 1952- 142
  See also BW 2
Van Zante, Helen Johnson 1906- 13-16R
Van Zanten, John W(illiam) 1913- 101
van Zantwijk, Rudolf (Alexander Marinus)
  1931- 133
van Zeller, Claud 1905-1984 ....CANR-6
  Obituary 113
  Earlier sketch in CA 1-4R
van Zeller, Hubert
  See van Zeller, Claud
Vanzi, Max (Bruno) 1934- 123
Van Zwienen, Ilse Charlotte Koehn 1929-1991 ....
  CANR-35
  Earlier sketch in CA 85-88
  See also SATA 34
  See also SATA-Brief 28
  See also SATA-Obit 67
van Zwoll, James A. 1909- CAP-1
  Earlier sketch in CA 13-14
Van Zyle, Jon 1942- ....SATA 84
Van Zyl Slabbert, F.
  See Slabbert, F(rederik) Van Zyl
Vaqar, Nasrollah 1920- 41-44R
Vara, Albert C. 1931- CANR-35
  Earlier sketch in CA 33-36R
Vara, Madeleine
  See Jackson, Laura (Riding)
Varah, Chad 1911- 57-60
Varandyan, Emmanuel P(aul) 1904- 65-68
Varas, Florencia
  See Olea, Maria Florencia Varas
Varda, Agnes 1928- 122
  Brief entry 116
  See also CLC 16
Vardaman, E. Jerry 1927- 17-20R
Vardaman, George T(ruett) 1920- CANR-4
  Earlier sketch in CA 1-4R
Vardaman, James M(oney) 1921- 104
Vardaman, Patricia B(lack) 1931- 37-40R
Vardamis, Alex A. 1934- 77-80
Vardamis, Frances (Diem) 1935- 149
Vardeman, Robert E(dward) 1947- 158
  See also Appleton, Victor
Varderi, Alejandro 1960- ....HW
Vardey, Lucinda 1949- 128
Vardre, Leslie
  See Davies, L(eslie) P(urnell)
Vardy, Steven Bela 1936- CANR-41
  Earlier sketches in CA 53-56, CANR-4, 19
Vardys, V(ytautas) Stanley 1924- CANR-5
  Earlier sketch in CA 13-16R
Vare, Daniele 1880-1956 Brief entry 119
Vare, Ethlie Ann 1953- CANR-49
  Earlier sketch in CA 127
Vare, Robert 1943- 103
Vareldzis, Georgia M. 1933- 149
Varenhorst, Barbara B(raden) 1928- 116
Varese, Louise 1890-1989 ....41-44R
  Obituary 129
Varey, Simon 1951- 135
Varg, Paul A(lbert) 1912-1994 118
  Obituary 144
  Brief entry 113
Varga, Andrew Charles 1917- 113
Varga, Balint Andras 1941- 132
Varga, Judy
  See Stang, Judit
Vargas, Julie S. 1938- CANR-34
  Earlier sketch in CA 57-60
Vargas, Margarita 1956- 149
Vargas Llosa, (Jorge) Mario (Pedro) 1936- .....
  CANR-67
  Earlier sketches in CA 73-76, CANR-18, 32, 42
  See also CLC 3, 6, 9, 10, 15, 31, 42, 85
  See also DA
  See also DAB
  See also DAC
  See also DAM MST, MULT, NOV
  See also DLB 145
  See also HLC
  See also HW
  See also MTCW 1
Vargish, Thomas 1939- CANR-14
  Earlier sketch in CA 37-40R
Varia, Radu 1940- 128
Varlamov, Aleksandr
  See Varlamoff, Nicolas
Varlar, Rene G. 1927- 1-4R
Varlay, Dimitry V. 1906- CAP-1
  Earlier sketch in CA 17-18
  See also SATA 10
Varley, Gloria 1939- 101
Varley, H(erbert) Paul 1931- 77-80
Varley, John (Herbert) 1947- CANR-25
  Earlier sketch in CA 69-72
  See also DLBY 81
Varley, John Philip
  See Mitchell, Langdon (Elwyn)
Varley, Susan 1961- ....SATA 63
Varma, Baidya Nath 1921- 41-44R
Varma, Devendra P. 1923-1994 144
  Obituary 147
  Brief entry 113
Varma, Monika 1916- 77-80
Varmus, Harold E(liot) 1939- 162

Varnac, d'Hugues
See Prevost, Alain
Varnado, Jewel Goodgame 1915- 9-12R
Varnalis, Costas 1884-1974 Obituary 53-56
Varner, Jeannette J.
See Varner, Jeannette Johnson
Varner, Jeannette Johnson 1909- 132
Varner, John Grier 1905-1978 .... 25-28R
Obituary 120
Varner, Velma V. 1916-1972 Obituary 37-40R
Varney, Carleton B(ates) 1937- CANR-16
Earlier sketch in CA 89-92
Varney, Philip 1943- 125
Varnhagen von Ense, Karl August 1785-1858 .. DLB 90
Varnhagen von Ense, Rahel 1771-1833 .... DLB 90
Varnum, Keith A. 1948- 1948
Vars, Gordon F(orrest) 1923- 21-24R
Varshavsky, Ilya 1909- 167
Vartan, Vartanig G(arabed) 1923-1988 61-64
Obituary 125
Vartanian, Aram 1922- CANR-3
Earlier sketch in CA 1-4R
Varzi, Achille C. 1958- 149
Vasconcelos (Calderon), Jose 1882-1959 Brief entry 118
Vas Dias, Robert (Leonard Michael) 1931- CANR-7
Earlier sketch in CA 17-20R
Vasey, Lloyd Roland 113
Vash, Carolyn L(ee) 1934- CANR-46
Brief entry 116
Earlier sketch in CA 121
Vasil, R(aj) K(umar) 1931- CANR-14
Earlier sketch in CA 37-40R
Vasiliev, Valery 1949- .... SATA 80
Vasiliu, Gheorghe 1881-1957 Brief entry 123
See also Bacovia, George
Vasiliu, Mircea 1920- 21-24R
See also SATA 2
Vaske, Martin O. 1915- CANR-2
Earlier sketch in CA 5-8R
Vasquez, John A(nthony) 1945- 108
Vasquez, Richard 1928- 131
See also HW
Vass, George 1927- 37-40R
See also SATA 57
See also SATA-Brief 31
Vass, Winifred Kellersberger 1917- 57-60
Vassa, Gustavus
See Equiano, Olaudah
Vassalli, Sebastiano 1941- .... DLB 128, 196
Vassanji, M(oyez) G. 1950- 136
Vassberg, David E(rland) 1936- 131
Vassi, Marco 1937- CANR-13
Earlier sketch in CA 61-64
Vassilikos, Vassilis 1933- 81-84
See also CLC 4, 8
Vassiliou, Yannis 1949- 117
Vasta, Edward 1928- 17-20R
Vasu, Nirmala-Kumara
See Bose, N(irmal) K(umar)
Vasvary, Edmund 1888-1977 Obituary 73-76
Vatikiotis, Michael R. J. 1957- 144
Vatikiotis, P(anayiotis) J(erasimos) 1928- . CANR-28
Earlier sketches in CA 13-16R, CANR-6
Vatsyayan, Sachchidanand Hiranand 1911-1987 158
Vatter, Harold Goodhue 1910- 5-8R
Vaucher, Andrea R. 1949- 142
Vauclair, Jacques 1947- 166
Vaudrin, Bill
See Vaudrin, William
Vaudrin, William 1943-1976 .... CAP-2
Earlier sketch in CA 29-32
Vaughan, Adrian 1941- 120
Vaughan, Agnes Carr 1887- CAP-1
Earlier sketch in CA 9-10
Vaughan, Alan 1936- 81-84
Vaughan, Alden T. 1929- CANR-7
Earlier sketch in CA 17-20R
Vaughan, Beatrice 1909(?)-1972 Obituary .. 37-40R
Vaughan, Bill
See Vaughan, William E(dward)
Vaughan, Carter A.
See Gerson, Noel Bertram
Vaughan, Clark (Alvord) 1924- 108
Vaughan, David 1924- 77-80
Vaughan, Denis 1920- 61-64
Vaughan, Donald S(hores) 1921- CANR-10
Earlier sketch in CA 17-20R
Vaughan, Frances E. 1935- CANR-51
Brief entry 107
Earlier sketch in CA 125
Vaughan, Frederick 1935- 120
Vaughan, Harold Cecil 1923- 29-32R
See also SATA 14
Vaughan, Henry 1621-1695 .... DLB 131
Vaughan, Hilda
See Morgan, Hilda Campbell
Vaughan, J(ohn) G(riffith) 1926- 168
Vaughan, James A(gnew) 1936- 49-52
Vaughan, John Edmund 1935- 61-64
Vaughan, Leo
See Lendon, Kenneth Harry
Vaughan, Marcia (K.) 1951- 160
See also SATA 60, 95
Vaughan, Paul 1925- 29-32R
Vaughan, Richard
See Thomas, Ernest Lewys
Vaughan, Richard 1947- .... SATA 87
Vaughan, Richard Patrick 1919- 13-16R
Vaughan, Robert (Richard) 1937- 103
Vaughan, Roger 1937- 85-88
Vaughan, Ronald G(eorge) 1952- 143
Vaughan, Sam(uel) 1928- 13-16R
See also DLBY 97
See also SATA 14
Vaughan, Sheila Marie 1930- 21-24R
Vaughan, Susan C. 1941- 167
Vaughan, Thomas 1621-1666 .... DLB 131
Vaughan, Virginia M(ason) 1947- 110
Vaughan, William E(dward) 1915-1977 .... 5-8R
Obituary 69-72
Vaughan-Thomas, (Lewis John) Wynford 1908-1987 130
Vaughan Williams, Ralph 1872-1958 Brief entry 115
Vaughan Williams, Ursula Wood 1911- .. CANR-24
Earlier sketches in CA 9-12R, CANR-6
Vaughn, Charles L(e Claire) 1911- 41-44R
Vaughn, Donald E(arl) 1932- 21-24R
Vaughn, Elizabeth Dewberry
See Dewberry, Elizabeth
Vaughn, Ellen Santilli 168
Vaughn, Jack A(lfred) 1935- 85-88
Vaughn, Jesse Wendell 1903-1968 .... 1-4R
Obituary 103
Vaughn, Lewis 1950- CANR-41
Earlier sketch in CA 111
Vaughn, Michael J(effery) 1943- 37-40R
Vaughn, Patrika 1933- 157
Vaughn, Richard C(lements) 1925- CANR-9
Earlier sketch in CA 21-24R
Vaughn, Robert (Francis) 1932- 61-64
Vaughn, Ruth 1935- CANR-15
Earlier sketch in CA 41-44R
See also SATA 14
Vaughn, Sally N(orthrop) 1939- 126
Vaughn, Sister Ann Carol 1922- 9-12R
Vaughn, Stephanie .... CLC 62
Vaughn, Stephen L. 1947- 101
Vaughn, Toni
See Du Breuil, (Elizabeth) L(or)inda
Vaughn, William Preston 1933- 73-76
Vaught, Jacque
See Brogan, Jacqueline Vaught
Vaupel, James W(alton) 1945- 111
Vaurie, Charles 1906-1975 .... CANR-4
Earlier sketch in CA 5-8R
Vause, L(aurence) Mikel 1952- 140
Vaussard, Maurice (Rene Jean Arthur Andre) 1888- 9-12R
Vautier, Ghislaine 1932- 112
See also SATA 53
Vaux, Thomas 1509-1556 .... DLB 132
Vavra, Robert James 1935- CANR-25
Earlier sketch in CA 25-28R
See also SATA 8
Vavra, Terry G. 1941- 143
Vawter, F(rancis) Bruce 1921- CANR-4
Earlier sketch in CA 1-4R
Vayda, Andrew P. 1931- 17-20R
Vayhinger, John Monroe 1916- 73-76
Vayle, Valerie
See Brooks, Janice Young
Vaz, Edmund (Winston) 1924- 108
Vazakas, Byron 1905- CAP-2
Earlier sketch in CA 25-28
Vazov, Ivan (Minchov) 1850-1921 167
Brief entry 121
See also DLB 147
See also TCLC 25
Vazquez, Carmen Inoa 1942- 154
Vazquez Amaral, Jose 1913-1987 153
See also HW
Vazquez Montalban, Manuel 1939- .... DLB 134
Vazsonyi, Nicholas 1963- 168
Veach, William B. Templeton 1896- CAP-1
Earlier sketch in CA 9-10
Veaner, Allen B(arnet) 1929- 41-44R
Veatch, Henry Babcock 1911- CANR-6
Earlier sketch in CA 5-8R
Veatch, Robert M(arlin) 1939- CANR-11
Earlier sketch in CA 69-72
Veber, Francis 1937- 135
Veblen, Thorstein B(unde) 1857-1929 165
Brief entry 115
See also TCLC 31
Vecoli, Rudolph J(ohn) 1927- CANR-51
Earlier sketches in CA 17-20R, CANR-10, 26
Vecsey, George S. 1909(?)-1984 Obituary 114
Vecsey, George Spencer 1939- CANR-10
Earlier sketch in CA 61-64
See also SATA 9
Vedavyasa
See Vyasa
Vedder, James S(herman) 1912- 117
Vedder, John K.
See Gruber, Frank
Vedder, Richard K(ent) 1940- 115
Vedeler, Harold C. 1903- 122
Veder, Bob 1940- 104
Vedral, Joyce L(auretta) 1943- CANR-41
Earlier sketch in CA 117
See also SATA 65
Veeck, Bill
See Veeck, William Louis, Jr.
Veeck, William Louis, Jr. 1914-1986 Obituary .. 118
Veedam, Voldemar 1912-1983 Obituary 109
Veenendaal, Cornelia 1924- 117
Vega, Janine Pommy 1942- CANR-2
Earlier sketch in CA 49-52
See also DLB 16
Vegh, Claudine 1934- 142
Veglahn, Nancy (Crary) 1937- CANR-7
Earlier sketch in CA 17-20R
See also SATA 5
Vehr, Bill 1940(?)-1988 Obituary 126
Veiga, Jose J(acinto da) 1915- CANR-33
Earlier sketches in CA 37-40R, CANR-15
Veiller, Anthony 1903-1965 .... DLB 44
Veillon, Lee 1942- 49-52
Veit, Fritz 1907- 111
Veit, Lawrence A. 1938- Brief entry 115
Veit, Stan(ley Stanford) 1929- 110
Vekemans, Roger 1921- 37-40R
Velasquez, Manuel G(onzales) 1942- 113
Velasquez-Trevino, Gloria 1949- .... DLB 122
Veler, Richard P(aul) 1936- 49-52
Veley, Margaret 1843-1887 .... DLB 199
Velez-Ibanez, Carlos G(uillermo) 1936- 118
See also HW
Velie, Alan R. 1937- CANR-1
Earlier sketch in CA 45-48
Velie, Lester 1908- CAP-2
Earlier sketch in CA 17-18
Velikovsky, Immanuel 1895-1979 .... CANR-15
Obituary 89-92
Earlier sketch in CA 69-72
Veliz, Claudio 1930- 25-28R
Veljanovski, (G.) Cento 1953- 128
Velkley, Richard L. 1949- 148
Vella, Walter F(rancis) 1924- CANR-24
Earlier sketch in CA 45-48
Vellacott, Jo 1922- CANR-56
Earlier sketch in CA 126
Vellela, Tony 1945- 65-68
Velleman, Daniel J. 1954- 150
Velleman, Ruth A(nn) 1921- 110
Veloz Maggiolo, Marcio E. 1936- .... DLB 145
See also HW
Velthuijs, Max 1923- 89-92
See also SATA 53
Vel'tman, Aleksandr Fomich 1800-1870 ... DLB 198
Veltman, Vera
See Panova, Vera (Fedorovna)
Veltri, George (M.) 1949- 150
Velvel, Lawrence R. 1939- 29-32R
Venable, Alan (Hudson) 1944- 45-48
See also SATA 8
Venable, Tom C(alvin) 1921- 29-32R
Venable, Vernon 1906-1996 .... CAP-2
Obituary 152
Earlier sketch in CA 21-22
Venables, Stephen 1954- 144
Venables, Terry 1943- 152
Venafro, Mark
See Pizzat, Frank J(oseph)
Venardos, Thomas J(oseph) 1945- 151
Vencent, Gabrielle (a pseudonym) 126
Venclova, Tomas 1937- 158
Vendler, Helen (Hennessy) 1933- CANR-72
Earlier sketches in CA 41-44R, CANR-25
See also MTCW 1
Vendler, Zeno 1921- 126
Brief entry 105
Vendrovskii, David Efimovich 1879-1971 Obituary 33-36R
Vendrovsky, David
See Vendrovskii, David Efimovich
Venegas, Daniel .... DLB 82
Veness, Molly 1900(?)-1985 Obituary 118
Veness, (Winifred) Thelma 1919-1971 .... 5-8R
Obituary 122
Vengroff, Richard 1945- CANR-10
Earlier sketch in CA 65-68
Venison, Alfred
See Pound, Ezra (Weston Loomis)
Veniste, Richard Ben
See Ben-Veniste, Richard
Venn, Cecilia
See Keenan, Sheila
Venn, Grant 1919-1979 .... 13-16R
Obituary 122
Vennard, Edwin 1902- CAP-2
Earlier sketch in CA 25-28
Vennema, Alje 1932- 101
Venner, J. G.
See Lewis, John (Noel Claude)
Vennewitz, Leila 148
Venning, Corey 1924- 49-52
Venning, Hugh
See van Zeller, Claud
Venning, Michael
See Randolph, Georgiana Ann
Venolia, Jan(et G.) 1928- 151
Venter, Al(bertus) J(ohannes) 1938- 117
Venton, W. B. 1898-1976 .... CAP-2
Earlier sketch in CA 25-28
Ventsel, Elena Sergeevna 1907- 154
Ventura, Jeffrey
See Feinman, Jeffrey
Ventura, Michael 1945- 146
Ventura, Piero (Luigi) 1937- CANR-39
Earlier sketch in CA 103
See also CLR 16
See also MAICYA
See also SATA 61
See also SATA-Brief 43
Venturi, Denise Scott Brown
See Brown, Denise Scott
Venturi, Franco 1914- 130
Venturi, Marcello 1925- CANR-42
Earlier sketches in CA 29-32R, CANR-13
Venturi, Robert 1925- 61-64
Venuti, Lawrence (Michael) 1953- CANR-48
Earlier sketch in CA 120
Vequin, Capini
See Quinn, Elisabeth
Vera, Yvonne 1964- 168
Verb, M. L.
See Tammeus, William David
Verba, Joan Marie 1953- 146
See also SATA 78
Verba, Sidney 1932- CANR-3
Earlier sketch in CA 1-4R
Verbeke, Gerard 1910- 131
Verbitsky, Bernardo 1907- .... HW
Vercors
See Bruller, Jean (Marcel)
Vercors, J. Bruller
See Bruller, Jean (Marcel)
Vercoutter, Jean 1911- 142
Verdecchia, Guillermo (Luis) 1962- 161
Verdelle, A. J. 1960- 152
Verdenius, W(illem) J(acob) 1913- 25-28R
Verdery, John D(uane) 1917- 9-12R
Verdi, Marie de
See Mencken, H(enry) L(ouis)
Verdi, Richard 1941- 128
Verdick, Mary (Peyton) 1923- CANR-4
Earlier sketch in CA 1-4R
Verdon, Dorothy
See Tralins, S(andor) Robert
verDorn, Bethea (Stewart) 1952- .... SATA 76
Verdu, Matilde
See Cela, Camilo Jose
Verduin, John R(ichard), Jr. 1931- CANR-49
Earlier sketches in CA 21-24R, CANR-9, 24
Verduin, Leonard 1897- 61-64
Verene, Donald Phillip 1937- CANR-45
Earlier sketches in CA 41-44R, CANR-15
Verey, David (Cecil Wynter) 1913-1984 .. CANR-15
Obituary 113
Earlier sketch in CA 65-68
Verey, Rosemary 1918- 130
Verga, Giovanni (Carmelo) 1840-1922 123
Brief entry 104
See also SSC 21
See also TCLC 3
Vergani, Luisa 1931- 21-24R
Vergara, Jose Manuel 1929- 97-100
Vergara, Joseph R. 1915- 29-32R
Vergara, Lisa 1948- 120
Vergara, William C(harles) 1923- 1-4R
Verghese, Abraham 1955- 150
Verghese, T. Paul
See Gregorios, Paulos Mar
Vergil 70B.C.-19B.C. .... DA
See also DAB
See also DAC
See also DAM MST, POET
See also PC 12
See also WLCS
Vergil, Polydore c. 1470-1555 .... DLB 132
Verhaeren, Emile (Adolphe Gustave) 1855-1916 Brief entry 109
See also TCLC 12
Verhalen, Philip A(ndrew) 1934- 69-72
Verheyen, Dirk 1957- 139
Verhoeven, Cornelis 1928- CANR-46
Earlier sketches in CA 61-64, CANR-8, 23
Verhoeven, Paul 1901-1975 Obituary 115
Verhonick, Phillis J. 1922(?)-1977 Obituary ... 73-76
Verhoogen, John 1912- 109
Verin, Velko
See Inkiow, (Janakiev) Dimiter
Verissimo, Erico (Lopes) 1905-1975 Obituary .. 115
See also DLB 145
Verlaine, Paul (Marie) 1844-1896 .... DAM POET
See also PC 2
Verluise, Pierre 1961- 154
Vermes, Geza 1924- 57-60
Vermes, Jean C(ampbell Pattison) 1907- 106
Vermes, Pamela 1918- 118
Vermeule, Cornelius Clarkson III 1925- 41-44R
Vermeule, E(mily) D. T. 1928- 17-20R
Vermillion, Robert 1915(?)-1987 Obituary 122
Vernadsky, George 1887-1973 Obituary 41-44R
Vernam, Glenn R. 1896-1980 .... CANR-10
Earlier sketch in CA 17-20R
Vernant, Jean-Pierre 1914- CANR-54
Earlier sketches in CA 109, CANR-29
Vernazza, Marcelle Wynn 1909- CANR-10
Earlier sketch in CA 17-20R
Verne, Jules (Gabriel) 1828-1905 131
Brief entry 110
See also AAYA 16
See also DLB 123
See also JRDA
See also MAICYA
See also SATA 21
See also TCLC 6, 52
Verner, Coolie 1917-1979 .... CANR-7
Earlier sketch in CA 53-56
Verner, Gerald 1897(?)-1980 Obituary 102
See also SATA-Obit 25
Vernerey, Denise 1947- 146
Verney, Douglas Vernon 1924- 13-16R
Verney, John 1913-1993 65-68
Obituary 140
See also SATA 14
See also SATA-Obit 75
Verney, Michael P(almer) 1923- CANR-6
Earlier sketch in CA 13-16R
Verney, Peter (Vivian Lloyd) 1930- CANR-19
Earlier sketch in CA 81-84
Verney, Sarah
See Holloway, Brenda W(ilmar)
Verney, Stephen Edmund 1919- 104
Vernon, Amelia Wallace 1926- 149
Vernon, Betty D(esiree) 1917- 146
Vernon, Eddie
See Stone, Hoyt E(dward)
Vernon, Edward
See Coleman, Vernon
Vernon, (Georgina) Frances 1963-1991 110
Obituary 135
Vernon, Glenn M(orley) 1920- 49-52
Vernon, James 1965- 146
Vernon, John 1943- 41-44R
Vernon, Judy 1945- 119

Vernon, Lee M.
See von Block, Bela W(illiam)
Vernon, Lorraine 1921- 113
Vernon, (Elda) Louise A(nderson) 1914- 53-56
See also SATA 14
Vernon, McCay 1928- 41-44R
Vernon, Philip Ewart 1905-1987 CANR-12
Obituary 133
Earlier sketch in CA 5-8R
Vernon, Raymond 1913- CANR-40
Earlier sketches in CA 5-8R, CANR-2, 18
Vernon, Rosemary
See Smith, Susan Vernon
Vernon, Thomas Bowater 1939- 118
Vernon, Thomas S. 1914- 25-28R
Vernon, Tom
See Vernon, Thomas Bowater
Vernon, Walter N(ewton), Jr. 1907- CANR-12
Earlier sketch in CA 17-20R
Vernon-Jackson, Hugh (Owen Hardinge)
1925- 21-24R
Vernor, D.
See Casewit, Curtis W(erner)
Verny, Tom 1936- 73-76
Verona, Stephen (Frederic) 1940- 154
Veronica, Sister Mary 1924-1977 17-20R
Obituary 134
Verplanck, Gulian C. 1786-1870 DLB 59
Verr, Harry Coe
See Kunhardt, Edith
Verral, Charles Spain 1904-1990 CANR-37
Obituary 131
Earlier sketches in CAP-1, CA 9-10, CANR-16
See also SATA 11
See also SATA-Obit 65
Verrette, Joyce 1939- 129
Verrier, Suzanne 1942- 153
Verrier, Suzy
See Verrier, Suzanne
Verrill, A(lpheus) Hyatt 1871-1954 Brief entry 111
Verrone, Robert J. 1935(?)-1984 Obituary 113
See also SATA-Obit 39
Versace, Marie Teresa Rios 1917- 17-20R
See also SATA 2
Verschuur, Gerrit L(aurens) 1937- 142
Versenyi, Adam 1957- 149
Ver Steeg, Clarence L(ester) 1922- 13-16R
Versteeg, Robert John 1930- 1-4R
Vertreace, Martha M. 1945- 143
See also BW 2
See also SATA 78
Verus, Marcus Annius
See Antoninus, Marcus Aurelius
Verval, Alain
See Lande, Lawrence (Montague)
Verwilghen, A(lbert-) Felix 1916- 25-28R
Verwoerdt, Adriaan 1927- 17-20R
Very, Alice (N.) 1894-1977 21-24R
Obituary 120
Very, Jones 1813-1880 DLB 1
Veryan, Patricia
See Bannister, Patricia Valeria
Vesaas, Tarjei 1897-1970 Obituary 29-32R
See also CLC 48
Vesely, Erik 1905(?)-1970 Obituary 57-60
Vesenyi, Paul E. 1911- 53-56
Veseth, Michael 1949- 135
Vesey, A(manda) 1939- 127
See also SATA 62
Vesey, Godfrey (Norman Agmondisham)
1923- 89-92
Vesey, Paul
See Allen, Samuel W(ashington)
Vesey-FitzGerald, Brian Seymour 1900-1981 104
Obituary 105
Vesper, Karl H(ampton) 1932- 115
Vess, David M(arshall) 1925- 89-92
Vessel, Matthew F. 1912- Brief entry 108
Vesselo, I(saac) Reginald 1903- CAP-2
Earlier sketch in CA 17-18
Vest, Herb D. 1944- 145
Vest, Hilda 1933- 148
Vestal, David 1924- 89-92
Vestal, Edith Ballard 1884-1970 CAP-2
Earlier sketch in CA 25-28
Vestdijk, Simon 1898-1971 Obituary 89-92
Vester, Frederic 1925- 120
Vester, Horatio 1906-1985 CAP-1
Obituary 117
Earlier sketch in CA 13-14
Vesterman, William 1942- 89-92
Vestly, Anne-Cath(arina) 1920- CANR-41
Earlier sketches in CA 85-88, CANR-18
See also SATA 14
Vet, T. V.
See Straiton, E(dward) C(ornock)
Vetch, John (Hamilton) 1911- 150
Vetere, Richard 1952- 104
Vetoe, Miklos 1936- 49-52
Vetter, Carole 1939- 25-28R
Vetter, Harold J. 1926- 29-32R
Vetterling-Braggin, Mary (Katherine) 1947- 124
Veverka, Frank B. 1923(?)-1985 Obituary 117
Vevers, (Henry) Gwynne 1916-1988 113
Obituary 126
See also SATA 45
See also SATA-Obit 57
Vexillum
See Banner, Hubert Stewart
Veysey, Arthur (Ernest) 1914-1997 133
Obituary 160
Veysey, Laurence R(uss) 1932- 21-24R
Vezhinov, Pavel
See Gougov, Nikola Delchev
Vial, Fernand (Louis) 1905- CANR-21
Earlier sketch in CA 1-4R
Vialis, Gaston
See Simenon, Georges (Jacques Christian)
Vian, Boris 1920-1959 164
Brief entry 106
See also DLB 72
See also TCLC 9
Viana, Javier de 1868-1926 HW
Viano, Emilio C. 1942- 107
Viansson-Ponte, Pierre 1920-1979 101
Obituary 85-88
Viator, Vacuus
See Hughes, Thomas
Viaud, (Louis Marie) Julien 1850-1923 Brief
entry 107
See also Loti, Pierre
Vicar, Henry
See Felsen, Henry Gregor
Vicary, Dorothy
See Rice, Dorothy Mary
Vicchio, Stephen (John) 1950- 138
Vice, Lisa 1951- 156
Vichas, Robert P. 1933- CANR-14
Earlier sketch in CA 29-32R
Vick, Helen Hughes 1950- 152
See also SATA 88
Vicker, Angus
See Felsen, Henry Gregor
Vicker, Ray 1917- 61-64
Vickers
See Kaufman, Wallace
Vickers, Antoinette L. 1942- 103
Vickers, Douglas 1924- CANR-11
Earlier sketch in CA 13-16R
Vickers, (Charles) Geoffrey 1894-1982 41-44R
Obituary 106
Vickers, Hugo (Ralph) 1951- 128
Brief entry 124
Vickers, Joanne F. 1941- 145
Vickers, John 1916-1976 9-12R
Obituary 134
Vickers, Roy 1888(?)-1965 DLB 77
Vickers, Sheena 1960- SATA 94
Vickery, Donald M(ichael) 1944- 101
Vickery, Florence E. 1906- 37-40R
Vickery, John B. 1925- 57-60
Vickery, Kate
See Kennedy, T(eresa) A.
Vickery, Olga W(estland) 1925-1970 CANR-3
Earlier sketch in CA 1-4R
Vickery, Robert L. (Jr.) 1932- 49-52
Vickery, Sukey 1779-1821 DLB 200
Vickery, Tom Rusk 1935- 53-56
Vickrey, William (Spencer) 1914-1996 41-44R
Obituary 154
Victor, Barbara 1946- 141
Victor, Charles B.
See Puechner, Ray
Victor, Daniel D(avid) 1944- 140
Victor, David 1910(?)-1989 Obituary 130
Victor, Edward 1914- CANR-3
Earlier sketch in CA 1-4R
See also SATA 3
Victor, George 168
Victor, Joan Berg 1942- 105
See also SATA 30
Victor, Sam
See Hershman, Morris
Victoria 1819-1901 DLB 55
Vicuna, Cecilia 1948- 157
Vida, Nina 1933- CANR-60
Earlier sketch in CA 117
Vidal, Gore 1925- CANR-65
Earlier sketches in CA 5-8R, CANR-13, 45
Interview in CANR-13
See also AITN 1
See also BEST 90:2
See also CLC 2, 4, 6, 8, 10, 22, 33, 72
See also DAM NOV, POP
See also DLB 6, 152
See also MTCW 1
Vidal, Nicole 1928- 25-28R
Vidaver, Doris 108
Vidger, Leonard P(erry) 1920- CANR-5
Earlier sketch in CA 9-12R
Vidich, Arthur J. 1922- 115
Vidler, Alec R.
See Vidler, Alexander Roper
Vidler, Alexander Roper 1899-1991 CANR-5
Obituary 135
Earlier sketch in CA 5-8R
Vidler, Virginia (Ellen) 1928-1986 69-72
Obituary 121
Vidor, King (Wallis) 1894(?)-1982 Obituary 108
Viebig, Clara 1860-1952 DLB 66
Vieg, John A.
See Vieg, John Albert
Vieg, John Albert 1904-1988 1-4R
Obituary 124
Vieira, Sergio 1941- 146
Vier, Gene 1926- 105
Viereck, Ellen K. 1928- 53-56
See also SATA 14
Viereck, George Sylvester 1884-1962 Obituary 116
See also DLB 54
Viereck, Peter (Robert Edwin) 1916- CANR-47
Earlier sketches in CA 1-4R, CANR-1
See also CLC 4
See also DLB 5
Viereck, Phillip 1925- CANR-8
Earlier sketch in CA 5-8R
See also SATA 3
Viertel, Janet 1915- 53-56
See also SATA 10
Viertel, Joseph 1915- 13-16R
Viertel, Peter 1920- CANR-52
Earlier sketch in CA 13-16R
Viessman, Warren, Jr. 1930- 53-56
Vieth, David M(uench) 1925- 5-8R
Vieth von Golssenau, Arnold Friedrich
1889-1979 89-92
Vietor, John A(dolf) 1914-1982 Obituary 108
Viets, Roger 1738-1811 DLB 99
Viets, Wallace T(rowbridge) 1919- 17-20R
Vig, Norman Joseph 1939- 25-28R
Vigee, Claude (Andre Strauss) 1921- 157
Vigeland, Carl A. 1947- 122
Vigeveno, H(enk) S. 1925- 108
Vigfusson, Robin 1949- 106
Viggiani
See Viggiani, Guy
Viggiani, Guy 1932- 123
Vighi, Marco 1945- 154
Vigil, Diego
See Vigil, James Diego
Vigil, James Diego 1938- 130
Vigil, Lawrence
See Finnin, (Olive) Mary
Vigil-Pinon, Evangelina 1949- DLB 122
Vigliante, Mary
See Szydlowski, Mary Vigliante
Viglini, Janelle (Therese) 1933- 57-60
Vigna, Judith 1936- CANR-56
Earlier sketches in CA 77-80, CANR-13, 29
See also SATA 15, 102
Vigneault, Gilles 1928- 160
See also DLB 60
Vigneras, Louis-Andre 1903- 65-68
Vigness, David M(artell) 1922- 13-16R
Vigness, Paul G. 1894- 41-44R
Vignoles, R. H.
See Ford, Boris
Vignone, Joseph A. 1939- 37-40R
Vigny, Alfred (Victor) de 1797-1863 DAM POET
See also DLB 119, 192
Vigolo, Giorgio 1894-1983 DLB 114
Viguers, Ruth Hill 1903-1971 CAP-1
Obituary 29-32R
Earlier sketch in CA 13-16
See also SATA 6
Vikis-Freibergs, Vaira 1937- 53-56
Viksnins, George J(uris) 1937- 105
Viktoria, Luise 1892-1980 Obituary 102
Vila, Bob
See Vila, Robert
Vila, Robert 1946- 106
Vilakazi, Benedict Wallet 1906-1947 168
See also TCLC 37
Vilar, Esther 1935- CANR-8
Earlier sketch in CA 49-52
Vilarino, Idea 1920- 153
See also HW
Vildrac, Charles
See Messager, Charles
Viljoen, Helen Gill 1899-1974 45-48
Obituary 103
Vilkitis, James R(ichard) 1941- 61-64
Villa, Jose Garcia 1904-1997 CANR-12
Earlier sketch in CA 25-28R
See also PC 22
Villa, Susie Hoogasian
See Hoogasian-Villa, Susie
Villada, Gene Harold Bell
See Bell-Villada, Gene Harold
Villafane, Eldin 1940- 146
Villa-Gilbert, Mariana 1937- 29-32R
Villamil, Victoria Etnier 1940- 149
Villanch, Bruce 1947- 167
Villanueva, Alma Luz 1944- 131
See also CAAS 24
See also DLB 122
See also HW
Villanueva, Tino 1941- CANR-1
Earlier sketch in CA 45-48
See also DLB 82
See also HW
Villard, Henry 1835-1900 DLB 23
Villard, Henry Hilgard 1911-1983 Obituary 111
Villard, Henry S(errano) 1900-1996 17-20R
Obituary 151
Villard, Oswald Garrison 1872-1949 162
Brief entry 113
See also DLB 25, 91
Villarejo, Mary (Holan) 1915- 9-12R
Villarejo, Oscar M(ilton) 1909- 17-20R
Villari, Rosario 1925- 147
Villarreal, Jose Antonio 1924- 133
See also DAM MULT
See also DLB 82
See also HLC
See also HW
Villars, Elizabeth
See Feldman, Ellen (Bette)
Villas Boas, Claudio 1916-1998 Obituary 166
Brief entry 117
Villas Boas, Orlando 1914- Brief entry 117
Villasenor, David V. 1913- 13-16R
Villasenor, Edmund
See Villasenor, Victor E(dmundo)
Villasenor, Victor
See Villasenor, Victor E(dmundo)
Villasenor, Victor E(dmundo) 1940- CANR-67
Earlier sketches in CA 45-48, CANR-32
See also DAM MULT
See also HW
Villaurrutia, Xavier 1903-1950 HW
See also TCLC 80
Villegas, Daniel Cosio 1898-1976 Obituary 65-68
Villegas de Magnon, Leonor 1876-1955 DLB 122
Villella, Edward 1936- 140
Villemaire, Yolande 1949- DLB 60
Villena, Luis Antonio de 1951- DLB 134
Villeneuve, Jocelyne 1941- 132
Villere, Sidney Louis 1900- 69-72
Villers, Raymond 1911- CAP-2
Earlier sketch in CA 25-28
Villers, Robert 1921-1980 Obituary 93-96
Villet, Barbara 1931- 85-88
Villiard, Paul 1910-1974 CANR-10
Obituary 53-56
Earlier sketches in CAP-2, CA 25-28
See also SATA 51
See also SATA-Obit 20
Villiers, Alan (John) 1903- CANR-1
Earlier sketch in CA 1-4R
See also SATA 10
Villiers, George 1628-1687 DLB 80
Villiers, Guy
See Goulding, Peter Geoffrey
Villiers, Marie de
See Routier, Simone
Villiers, Marjorie 1903-1982 Obituary 107
Villiers de l'Isle Adam, Jean Marie Mathias Philippe
Auguste, Comte de 1838-1889 DLB 123
See also SSC 14
Villoldo, Alberto Pedro 1949- 108
Villon, Francois 1431-1463(?) PC 13
Villum, Kjartan
See Floegstad, Kjartan
Vilmorin, Louise Leveque de
1902-1969 Obituary 104
Vilnay, Zev 1900-1988 Obituary 124
Vinacke, W(illiam) Edgar 1917- 5-8R
Vinal, Harold 1891-1965 Obituary 89-92
Vinas, D.
See Vinas, David
Vinas, David 1929(?)- HW
Vinaver, Eugene 1899- 13-16R
Vincent, Adrian 1917- 1-4R
Vincent, Andrew 1951- 141
Vincent, Charles 1945- 65-68
Vincent, Claire
See Allen, Charlotte Vale
Vincent, Clark E(dward) 1923- CANR-2
Earlier sketch in CA 1-4R
Vincent, E. Lee
See Vincent, Elizabeth Lee
Vincent, Elizabeth Lee 1897- CAP-2
Earlier sketch in CA 19-20
Vincent, Eric Douglas 1953- SATA 40
Vincent, Felix 1946- 118
See also SATA 41
Vincent, Gabrielle (a pseudonym) 126
See also CLR 13
See also MAICYA
See also SATA 61
Vincent, Howard Paton 1904- 65-68
Vincent, Jack 1904- 29-32R
Vincent, Jack E(rnest) 1932- CANR-19
Earlier sketch in CA 102
Vincent, Joan 1920- 21-24R
Vincent, John Carter 1900-1972 Obituary 37-40R
Vincent, John J(ames) 1929- CANR-51
Earlier sketches in CA 57-60, CANR-10, 26
Vincent, John R(ussell) 1937- 120
Vincent, K(enneth) Steven 1947- CANR-68
Earlier sketch in CA 128
Vincent, Leona
See Vincent, Elizabeth Lee
Vincent, Mary Keith
See St. John, Wylly Folk
Vincent, Peter 1944- 37-40R
Vincent, R(aymond) J(ohn) 1943-1990 77-80
Obituary 133
Vincent, Theodore G. 1936- CANR-13
Earlier sketch in CA 77-80
Vincent, William R.
See Heitzmann, William Ray
Vincent, William S(hafer) 1907- 41-44R
Vinciguerra, Mario 1887-1973 Obituary 104
Vincitorio, Gaetano L(eonard) 1921- 89-92
Vine, Barbara
See Rendell, Ruth (Barbara)
See also BEST 90:4
See also CLC 50
Vine, Louis L(loyd) 1922- CANR-3
Earlier sketch in CA 1-4R
Vine, Paul Ashley Laurence 1927- 21-24R
Vine, Phyllis 1945- 130
Vine, Sarah
See Rowland, D(onald) S(ydney)
Vineberg, Arthur (Martin) 1903-1988 104
Obituary 125
Vineberg, Ethel (Shane) 1902- 85-88
Vinegar, Tom
See Gregg, Andrew K.
Viner, George 1913(?)-1983 Obituary 109
Viner, Jacob 1892-1970 Obituary 104
Vines, Alice Gilmore 1923- 81-84
Vines, (Henry) Ellsworth (Jr.)
1911-1994 Obituary 144
Brief entry 109
Vines, Lois Davis 1939- 144
Vinest, Shaw
See Longyear, Barry Brookes
Viney, Ethna 166
Viney, Wayne 1932- 103
Vineyard, Edwin Earle 1926- 5-8R
Vineyard, Jerry D. 1935- 143
Vinge, Joan (Carol) D(ennison) 1948- CANR-72
Earlier sketch in CA 93-96
See also CLC 30
See also SATA 36
See also SSC 24
Vinge, Vernor (Steffen) 1944- 101
Vinikas, Vincent 1951- 161

Vining, Elizabeth Gray 1902- ... CANR-7
Earlier sketch in CA 5-8R
See also MAICYA
See also SATA 6
Vinograd, Julia 1943- ... CAAS 26
Vinogradov, Ivan M(atveyevich) 1891-1983 Obituary ... 109
Vinokur, Grigory
See Weinrauch, Herschel
Vinokurov, Yevgeny Mikhailovich 1925- Brief entry ... 116
Vinson, Elaine
See Rowland, D(onald) S(ydney)
Vinson, J(ohn) Chal(mers) 1919- ... 9-12R
Vinson, J(ohn) William 1916-1979 Obituary .. 89-92
Vinson, James (Albert) 1933- ... 120
Brief entry ... 118
Vinson, Jane 1927- ... 77-80
Vinson, Kathryn 1911- ... 5-8R
See also SATA 21
Vinson, Rex Thomas 1935- ... 101
Vinton, Bobby
See Vinton, Stanley Robert, Jr.
Vinton, Eleanor W(inthrop) 1899-1977 ... 61-64
Obituary ... 73-76
Vinton, Iris 1906(?)-1988 ... 77-80
Obituary ... 124
See also SATA 24
See also SATA-Obit 55
Vinton, John 1937- ... 73-76
Vinton, Stanley Robert, Jr. 1935(?)- Brief entry . 120
Vinyard, C. Dale 1932- ... 25-28R
Vinz, Mark 1942- ... 93-96
Viola, Herman J(oseph) 1938- ... CANR-48
Earlier sketches in CA 61-64, CANR-8, 23
Viola, Lynne 1955- ... 135
Violet, Ultra
See Dufresne, Isabelle
Violett, Ellen 1925- ... 73-76
Violi, Paul 1944- ... CANR-49
Earlier sketches in CA 45-48, CANR-24
Violis, G.
See Simenon, Georges (Jacques Christian)
Viorst, Judith 1931- ... CANR-59
Earlier sketches in CA 49-52, CANR-2, 26
Interview in ... CANR-26
See also BEST 90:1
See also CLR 3
See also DAM POP
See also DLB 52
See also MAICYA
See also SATA 7, 70
Viorst, Milton 1930- ... CANR-55
Earlier sketches in CA 9-12R, CANR-26
Vip
See Partch, Virgil Franklin II
Vipond, Don (Harry) 1932- ... 65-68
Vipond, Mary ... 152
Vipont, Charles
See Foulds, Elfrida Vipont
Vipont, Elfrida
See Foulds, Elfrida Vipont
See also DLB 160
Viramontes, Helena Maria 1954- ... 159
See also DLB 122
Virden, Jenel 1954- ... 156
Virga, Vincent 1942- ... 107
Virgil
See Vergil
Virgilio, Nicholas A(nthony) 1928-1989 Obituary ... 127
Virgines, George E. 1920- ... CANR-28
Earlier sketches in CA 25-28R, CANR-12
Virginius
See Connett, Eugene Virginius III
Virgo, Sean 1940- ... 161
Virtanen, A(rtturi) I(lmari) 1895-1973 ... 168
Virtanen, Reino 1910- ... CANR-4
Earlier sketch in CA 1-4R
Virtue, Noel 1947- ... 130
Vis, William Ryerson 1886-1969 Obituary ... 110
Viscardi, Henry, Jr. 1912- ... CANR-5
Earlier sketch in CA 5-8R
Vischer, Friedrich Theodor 1807-1887 .... DLB 133
Vischer, Helen (Cassin Lombard) Carusi 1905(?)-1986 Obituary ... 119
Vischer, Lukas 1926- ... 131
Visconti, Luchino 1906-1976 ... CANR-39
Obituary ... 65-68
Earlier sketch in CA 81-84
See also CLC 16
Viscott, David S(teven) 1938- ... CANR-26
Earlier sketch in CA 29-32R
See also AITN 1
See also SATA 65
Viscusi, W. Kip 1949- ... 138
Visher, Emily B. 1918- ... 109
Visher, Halene Hatcher 1909- ... 45-48
Visher, John Sargent 1921- ... 109
Vishniak, Mark 1883-1976 Obituary ... 69-72
Vishny, Michele 1932- ... 69-72
Visocchi, Mark 1938- ... CANR-16
Earlier sketch in CA 93-96
Visotzky, Burton L. 1951- ... 138
Visram, Rozina 1939- ... 133
Visscher, Maurice B(olks) 1901- ... 77-80
Visser, Margaret 1940- ... CANR-72
Earlier sketch in CA 123
Visser, W(illem) F(rederik) H(endrik) 1900-1968 .... CAP-2
Earlier sketch in CA 25-28
See also SATA 10
Visser 't Hooft, Willem Adolf 1900-1985 ..... 9-12R
Obituary ... 116
Visson, Lynn 1945- ... 134
Visson, Vladimir 1905(?)-1976 Obituary ... 69-72
Viswanathan, S(ubrahmanyam) 1933- ... 132
Visweswaran, Kamala 1962- ... 152
Vita-Finzi, Claudio 1936- ... 89-92
Vita-Finzi, Penelope (Jean) 1939- ... 133
Vital, David 1927- ... CANR-44
Earlier sketches in CA 29-32R, CANR-12
Vitale, Joseph T(homas) 1951- ... 107
Vitale, Philip H. 1913- ... 17-20R
Vitali, Julius 1952- ... 153
Vitek, Donna
See Vitek, Donna Kimel
Vitek, Donna Kimel 1947- ... 131
Vitek, John D(ennis) 1942- ... 124
Vitelli, James R(obert) 1920- ... 29-32R
Vitezovic, Tomislav
See Kuehnelt-Leddihn, Erik (Maria) Ritter von
Vitiello, Justin 1941- ... 139
Vitier, Cintio
See Vitier (y Bolanos), Cynthio
Vitier (y Bolanos), Cynthio 1921- ... HW
Vitola, Denise 1957- ... 159
Vittengl, Morgan John 1928- ... 5-8R
Vittitow, Mary L(ou) 1937- ... 139
Vittorini, Elio 1908-1966 ... 133
Obituary ... 25-28R
See also CLC 6, 9, 14
Vitz, Robert C. 1938- ... 136
Vitzthum, Hilda 1902-1993 ... 143
Vitzthum, Richard Carleton 1936- ... 103
Vivanco, Luis Felipe 1907-1975 ... DLB 108
Vivante, Arturo 1923- ... CANR-72
Earlier sketches in CA 17-20R, CANR-10
See also CAAS 12
Vivante, Paolo 1921- ... 29-32R
Vivas, Eliseo 1901- ... CANR-5
Earlier sketch in CA 5-8R
Vivas, Julie 1947- ... SATA 96
Vivas, Julie 1947- ... 163
Viveash, Cherry Jacqueline Lee 1929- ... CAP-1
Earlier sketch in CA 9-10
Vivelo, Jacqueline J. 1943- ... SATA 63
Vivers, Eileen Elliott 1905- ... 41-44R
Vivian, Cordy Tindell 1924- ... 49-52
Vivian, E. Charles
See Cannell, Charles (Henry)
Vivian, Evelyn C. H.
See Cannell, Charles (Henry)
Vivian, Francis
See Ashley, (Arthur) Ernest
Viviani, Cesare 1947- ... DLB 128
Viviano, Benedict T(homas) 1940- ... CANR-10
Earlier sketch in CA 21-24R
Vivienne
See Entwistle, Florence Vivienne
Vivion, Michael J. 1944- ... 140
Vizard, Stephen
See James, (David) Burnett (Stephen)
Vizedom, Monika B(asch) 1929- ... 69-72
Vizenor, Gerald Robert 1934- ... CANR-67
Earlier sketches in CA 13-16R, CANR-5, 21, 44
See also CAAS 22
See also CLC 103
See also DAM MULT
See also DLB 175
See also NNAL
Vizinczey, Stephen 1933- ... 128
Interview in ... 128
See also CLC 40
Vizzard, Jack
See Vizzard, John Anthony
Vizzard, John Anthony 1914- ... 29-32R
Vizzini, Salvatore 1926- ... 103
Vlach, John Michael 1948- ... 123
Vladeck, Bruce C. 1949- ... 101
Vladimirov, Leonid
See Finkelstein, Leonid Vladimirovitch
Vladimov, G.
See Vladimov, Georgii Nikolaevich
Vladimov, Georgii
See Vladimov, Georgii Nikolaevich
Vladimov, Georgii Nikolaevich 1931- ... 123
Vlahos, Olivia 1924- ... 21-24R
See also SATA 31
Vlasic, Bob
See Hirsch, Phil
Vlasic, Ivan Albert 1926- ... 9-12R
Vlasich, James A(nthony) 1944- ... 137
Vlastos, Gregory 1907-1991 ... 130
Obituary ... 135
Vliet, R(ussell) G(ordon) 1929-1984 ..... CANR-18
Obituary ... 112
Earlier sketch in CA 37-40R
See also CLC 22
Vlock, Laurel F(ox) ... 37-40R
Vloyantes, John P. 1918- ... 61-64
Voaden, Herman Arthur 1903- ... 103
See also DLB 88
Vo-Dinh, Mai 1933- ... CANR-53
Earlier sketches in CA 77-80, CANR-13, 29
See also SATA 16
Vodola, Thomas M(ichael) 1925- ... CANR-19
Earlier sketches in CA 49-52, CANR-3
Voegeli, V(ictor) Jacque 1934- ... 21-24R
Voegelin, Eric (Herman Wilhelm) 1901-1985 ... 132
Obituary ... 114
Voehringer, Erich F(rederick) 1905-1973 ... CANR-2
Obituary ... 41-44R
Earlier sketch in CA 1-4R
Voeks, Virginia (Wilna) 1921- ... 13-16R
Voelcker, Hunce 1940- ... 77-80
Voelkel, Robert T(ownsend) 1933- ... 25-28R
Voelker, John D(onaldson) 1903-1991 ... CANR-42
Obituary ... 134
Earlier sketch in CA 1-4R
See also DAM POP
Voellner, Louada McCaughen 1888(?)-1986 Obituary ... 119
Voermans, Paul 1960- ... 168
Vogan, Sara 1947-1991 ... 134
Vogau, Boris Andreyevich 1894-1937(?) Brief entry ... 123
See also Pilnyak, Boris
Vogel, Alfred T(ennyson) 1906- ... 104
Vogel, Arthur A(nton) 1924- ... CANR-10
Earlier sketch in CA 25-28R
Vogel, Carole Garbuny 1951- ... 138
See also SATA 70
Vogel, Dan 1927- ... 120
Vogel, David 1947- ... CANR-11
Earlier sketch in CA 65-68
Vogel, Donald Stanley 1917- ... 141
Vogel, Ezra F. 1930- ... CANR-30
Earlier sketch in CA 13-16R
Vogel, Frederick G. 1934- ... 153
Vogel, Helen Wolff 1918- ... 17-20R
Vogel, Hunter Bertram August 1903-1990 Obituary ... 131
Vogel, Ilse-Margret 1918- ... CANR-7
Earlier sketch in CA 13-16R
See also SATA 14
Vogel, Irving L. 1918- ... 122
Vogel, Jerry 1896(?)-1980 Obituary ... 101
Vogel, John H., Jr. 1950- ... 77-80
See also SATA 18
Vogel, Linda Jane 1940- ... 61-64
Vogel, Lucy E(laine) ... 49-52
Vogel, Morris J. 1945- ... 128
Vogel, Paula A(nne) 1951- ... 108
See also CLC 76
Vogel, Shawna 1964- ... 149
Vogel, Speed
See Vogel, Irving L.
Vogel, Stanley M(orton) 1921- ... 77-80
Vogel, Steve 1946- ... 132
Vogel, Steven 1940- ... 53-56
Vogel, Victor H(ugh) 1905-1978 ... CANR-3
Earlier sketch in CA 1-4R
Vogel, Virgil (Howard) J(oseph) 1918-1994 ... CANR-10
Obituary ... 143
Earlier sketch in CA 25-28R
Vogeler, Ingolf 1944- ... 107
Vogelgesang, Sandra Louise 1942- ... 57-60
Vogelgesang, Sandy
See Vogelgesang, Sandra Louise
Vogelman, Joyce 1936- ... 106
Vogelsang, Arthur 1942- ... 49-52
Vogelsinger, Hubert 1938- ... 25-28R
Vogenitz, David George 1930- ... 41-44R
Voget, Fred W. 1913- ... 61-64
Vogler, Roger E. 1938- ... 126
Vogt, Bill
See Vogt, William McKinley
Vogt, Esther Loewen 1915- ... CANR-7
Earlier sketch in CA 17-20R
See also SATA 14
Vogt, Evon Zartman, Jr. 1918- ... CANR-27
Earlier sketch in CA 69-72
Vogt, Gregory L. ... SATA-Brief 45
Vogt, Gregory L. ... 153
See also SATA 94
Vogt, Gregory Max 1949- ... 137
Vogt, Joseph 1895- Brief entry ... 112
Vogt, Marie Bollinger 1921- ... 57-60
See also SATA 45
Vogt, William McKinley 1935- ... 89-92
Voien, Steven 1954- ... 166
Voight, Virginia Frances 1909- ... CANR-18
Earlier sketches in CA 5-8R, CANR-2
See also SATA 8
Voigt, Cynthia 1942- ... CANR-40
Earlier sketches in CA 106, CANR-18, 37
Interview in ... CANR-18
See also AAYA 3
See also CLC 30
See also CLR 13,48
See also JRDA
See also MAICYA
See also SATA 48, 79
See also SATA-Brief 33
Voigt, David Quentin 1926- ... CANR-32
Earlier sketches in CA 41-44R, CANR-14
Voigt, Ellen Bryant 1943- ... CANR-55
Earlier sketches in CA 69-72, CANR-11, 29
See also CLC 54
See also DLB 120
Voigt, Erna 1925- ... SATA 35
Voigt, Karsten D. 1941- ... 113
Voigt, Lieselotte E. Kurth
See Kurth-Voigt, Lieselotte E.
Voigt, Melvin J(ohn) 1911- ... CANR-5
Earlier sketch in CA 13-16R
Voigt, Milton 1924- ... 9-12R
Voigt, Robert J(oseph) 1916- ... 93-96
Voigt, William, Jr. 1902- ... 73-76
Voigt-Rother, Erna
See Voigt, Erna
Voils, Jessie Wiley ... CAP-2
Earlier sketch in CA 29-32
Voinovich, Vladimir (Nikolaevich) 1932- .. CANR-67
Earlier sketches in CA 81-84, CANR-33
See also CAAS 12
See also CLC 10, 49
See also MTCW 1
Voitle, Robert (Brown, Jr.) 1919- ... 1-4R
Vojnovic, Ivo 1857-1929 ... DLB 147
Vojtech, Anna 1946- ... SATA 42
Volbach, Walther R(ichard) 1897-1996 ... 29-32R
Obituary ... 153
Volcker, Paul A(dolph) 1927- ... 129
Brief entry ... 114
Vole, Zenobia N.
See Douglas, Lauren Wright
Volente, Deo
See DeVincentes-Hayes, Nan
Volgyes, Ivan 1936- ... CANR-20
Earlier sketch in CA 104
Volin, Michael 1911- ... 101
Volk, Hannah Marie
See Wormington, Hannah Marie
Volk, Patricia (Gay) 1943- ... 140
Volk, Toni 1944- ... 155
Volkan, Vamik D(jemal) 1932- ... CANR-19
Earlier sketch in CA 102
Volkart, Edmund H(owell) 1919- ... 21-24R
Volkening, Henry T. 1902-1972 Obituary ... 37-40R
Volker, Roger 1934- ... 53-56
Volker, Roy 1924- ... 57-60
Volkman, Ernest 1940- ... 132
Volkoff, Vladimir 1932- ... 73-76
See also DLB 83
Volkogonov, Dmitri (A.) 1928-1995 ... 157
Volkov, Leon 1920(?)-1974 Obituary ... 45-48
Volkov, Solomon (Moiseevich) 1944- ... 168
Voll, John O(bert) 1936- ... CANR-67
Earlier sketch in CA 129
Vollbehr, Otto H. F. 1872(?)-1945(?) ... DLB 187
Vollenweider, Richard 1922- ... 160
Vollers, Maryanne 1955- ... 150
Vollert, Cyril (Oscar) 1901- ... 61-64
Vollmann, William T. 1959- ... CANR-67
Earlier sketch in CA 134
See also CLC 89
See also DAM NOV, POP
Vollmer, Howard M. 1928- ... CANR-13
Earlier sketch in CA 17-20R
Vollstedt, Maryana 1925- ... 149
Voloshinov, V. N.
See Bakhtin, Mikhail Mikhailovich
Volpe, E(rminio) Peter 1927- ... CANR-15
Earlier sketch in CA 37-40R
Volpe, Edmond L(oris) 1922- ... CANR-1
Earlier sketch in CA 1-4R
Volpe, Vernon L(ewis) 1955- ... 135
Volponi, Paolo 1924- ... DLB 177
Volta, Ornella 1927- ... 158
Voltaire 1694-1778 ... DA
See also DAB
See also DAC
See also DAM DRAM, MST
See also SSC 12
See also WLC
Voltz, Jeanne Appleton 1920- ... CANR-21
Earlier sketch in CA 104
Volz, Carl (Andrew) 1933- ... 29-32R
Volz, Marlin M(ilton) 1917- ... 37-40R
von Abele, Rudolph (Radama) 1922-1989 104
Obituary ... 127
Von Ahnen, Katherine 1922- ... 159
See also SATA 93
von Albertini, Rudolf 1923- ... 131
Vonarburg, Elisabeth 1947- ... 149
von Arnim, Elizabeth 1866-1941
See Russell, CountessMary Annette Beauchamp
See also DLB 197
von Baeyer, Hans Christian 1938- ... CANR-41
Earlier sketch in CA 117
von Balthasar, Hans U.
See von Balthasar, Hans Urs
von Balthasar, Hans Urs 1905-1988 ... 130
Obituary ... 125
Brief entry ... 106
Von Bencke, Matthew Justin 1972- ... 164
von Berg, J(ohan) F(riedrich) (?)-1983(?) Obituary ... 108
von Bertalanffy, Ludwig 1901-1972 ... CAP-2
Earlier sketch in CA 25-28
von Birken, Sigmund 1626-1681 ... DLB 164
von Block, Bela W(illiam) 1922- ... 104
von Block, Sylvia 1931- ... CANR-7
Earlier sketch in CA 53-56
von Bothmer, Dietrich Felix 1918- ... 106
von Brand, Theodor C. 1900(?)-1978 Obituary ... 81-84
von Braun, Wernher 1912-1977 ... CANR-9
Obituary ... 69-72
Earlier sketch in CA 5-8R
von Castlehun, Friedl
See Marion, Frieda
von Cube, Irmgard 1900(?)-1977 Obituary ... 73-76
von Daeniken, Erich 1935- ... CANR-44
Earlier sketches in CA 37-40R, CANR-17
See also AITN 1
See also CLC 30
von Daniken, Erich
See von Daeniken, Erich
von dem Werder, Diederich 1584-1657 ... DLB 164
von der Gruen, Max 1926- ... DLB 75
von der Mehden, Fred R. 1927- ... 9-12R
Vonderplanitz, Aajonus 1947- ... 156
von Doderer, Heimito 1896-1966 Obituary ... 25-28R
See also Doderer, Heimito von
Vondra, Josef Gert 1941- ... 104
von Dreele, W(illiam) H(enry) 1924- ... 93-96
von Eckardt, Ursula M(aria) 1925- ... 13-16R
Von Eckardt, Wolf 1918-1995 ... 5-8R
Obituary ... 149
von Elbe, Joachim 1902- ... 132
Von Elsner, Don Byron 1909- ... 1-4R
von Ende, Richard Chaffey 1907- ... 103
Von Erffa, Helmut (Hartmann) 1900-1979 ... 133
von Euler, Ulf (Svante) 1905-1983 ... 158
Obituary ... 109
von Eyb, Albrecht 1420-1475 ... DLB 179
von Frank, Albert J(ames) 1945- ... CANR-45
Earlier sketch in CA 120

von Franz, Marie-Louise 1915-1998 ..... CANR-65
Obituary 165
Earlier sketch in CA 85-88
von Frisch, Karl (Ritter)
See Frisch, Karl (Ritter) von
von Frisch, Otto 1929- 101
von Fuerer-Haimendorf, Christoph 1909- 131
von Furstenberg, Egon (Edvard) 1946- 102
von Furstenberg, George Michael 1941- . CANR-10
Earlier sketch in CA 65-68
von Glahn, Gerhard E(rnst) 1911- 13-16R
von Gronicka, Andre 1912- 25-28R
von Grumbach, Argula 1492-1563(?) ..... DLB 179
von Grunebaum, G(ustave) E(dmund) 1909-1972 ..
CANR-3
Earlier sketch in CA 1-4R
Von Gunden, Heidi Cecilia 1940- 125
Vo Nguyen, Giap 1912(?)- Brief entry 115
von Habsburg(-Lothringen), Geza Louis Eusebius
Gebhard Ralphael Albert Maria 1940- 161
von Hagen, Mark (L.) 168
Von Hagen, Victor Wolfgang 1908- 105
See also SATA 29
von Hassell, Fey 1918- 134
von Hayek, Friedrich August
See Hayek, F(riedrich) A(ugust von)
von Heidenstam, (Carl Gustaf) Verner
See Heidenstam, (Carl Gustaf) Verner von
von Heller, Marcus
See Zachary, Hugh
von Hertzen, Heikki 1913- 37-40R
von Heyse, Paul (Johann Ludwig)
See Heyse, Paul (Johann Ludwig von)
von Hildebrand, Alice 1923- 21-24R
von Hildebrand, Dietrich 1889-1977 ..... CANR-10
Obituary 69-72
Earlier sketch in CA 17-20R
Von Hilsheimer, George E(dwin III) 1934- 29-32R
Von Hippel, Frank 1937- 93-96
von Hirsch, Andrew 1934- CANR-14
Earlier sketch in CA 81-84
von Hofe, Harold 1912- CANR-4
Earlier sketch in CA 1-4R
von Hoffman, Nicholas 1929- CANR-34
Earlier sketch in CA 81-84
von Hofmannsthal, Hugo
See Hofmannsthal, Hugo von
von Horn, Carl 1903- CAP-2
Earlier sketch in CA 21-22
von Horvath, Odon
See Horvath, Oedoen von
von Horvath, Oedoen
See Horvath, Oedoen von
von Kalnein, Wend 1914- 153
von Kaschnitz-Weinberg, Marie Luise
1901-1974 127
Obituary 93-96
See also Kaschnitz, Marie Luise
von Kellenbach, Katharina 1960- 151
Von Klemperer, Klemens 1916- 21-24R
von Klopp, Vahrah
See Malvern, Gladys
von Koenigswald, (Gustav Heinrich) Ralph
1902-1982 Obituary 110
von Koerber, Hans Nordewin 1886- 41-44R
von Kuffstein, Hans Ludwig 1582-1656 ..... DLB 164
von Lang, Jochen
See von Lang-Piechocki, Joachim
von Langenfeld, Friedrich Spee 1591-1635 ..... DLB
164
von Lang-Piechocki, Joachim 1925- 101
von Laue, Max Theodor Felix
See Laue, Max Theodor Felix von
Von Laue, Theodore Herman 1916- 9-12R
von le Fort, Gertrud (Petrea)
See le Fort, Gertrud (Petrea) von
Von Leyden, Wolfgang Marius 1911- CANR-3
Earlier sketch in CA 5-8R
von Liliencron, (Friedrich Adolf Axel) Detlev
See Liliencron, (Friedrich Adolf Axel) Detlev von
von Logau, Friedrich 1605-1655 ..... DLB 164
von Maltitz, Horst 1905- 77-80
Von Manstein, Erich 1887-1973 Obituary 45-48
von Meck, Galina 1891-1985 Obituary 116
von Mehren, Arthur T(aylor) 1922- 17-20R
von Mendelssohn, Felix 1918- 13-16R
Von Mering, Otto Oswald, Jr. 1922- 1-4R
von Miklos, Josephine Bogdan
1900-1972 Obituary 37-40R
von Mises, Ludwig (Edler)
See Mises, Ludwig (Edler) von
von Mises, Margit
See Mises, Margit von
Von Mises, Richard (Martin Edler) 1883-1953 .. 162
Von Mohrenschildt, Dimitri Sergius 1902- Brief
entry 106
Von Molnar, Geza (Walter Elemer) 1932- 29-32R
von Moltke, Helmuth James 1907-1945 140
von Moltke, Konrad 1941- CANR-19
Earlier sketch in CA 101
Von Moschzisker, Michael 1918- 37-40R
von Nassau-Saarbrucken, Elisabeth c.
1393-1456 ..... DLB 179
Vonnegut, Kurt, Jr. 1922- CANR-49
Earlier sketches in CA 1-4R, CANR-1, 25
See also AAYA 6
See also AITN 1
See also BEST 90:4
See also CDALB 1968-1988
See also CLC 1, 2, 3, 4, 5, 8, 12, 22, 40, 60, 111
See also DA
See also DAB
See also DAC
See also DAM MST, NOV, POP
See also DLB 2, 8, 152
See also DLBD 3
See also DLBY 80
See also MTCW 1
See also SSC 8
See also WLC
Vonnegut, Mark 1947- 65-68
See also AITN 2
von Neumann, John 1903-1957 Brief entry 117
von Ost, Henry Lerner 1915-1994 101
Obituary 145
Von Rachen, Kurt
See Hubbard, L(afayette) Ron(ald)
von Rad, Gerhard 1901-1971 Obituary 104
von Rago, Louis J(oseph)
See Rago, Louis J(oseph von)
Von Rauch, Georg 1904- 73-76
von Rezzori (d'Arezzo), Gregor
See Rezzori (d'Arezzo), Gregor von
von Rhein, John (Richard) 1945- 120
von Riekhoff, Harald 1937- 89-92
Von Rosenstiel, Helene 1944- 105
Von Salis, Jean-R. 1901- 21-24R
von Salomon, Ernst 1902-1972 Obituary 37-40R
von Schilcher, Florian 1944- 118
von Schlabrendorff, Fabian
1907-1980 Obituary 105
von Schmidt, Eric 1931- CANR-13
Earlier sketch in CA 17-20R
See also SATA 50
See also SATA-Brief 36
Von Schmidt, Harold 1896(?)-1982 Obituary 107
von Schoenhoff, Ulrike
See Frank, Rudolf
von Schuschnigg, Kurt 1897-1977 103
von Schwarzenfeld, Gertrude
See Cochrane de Alencar, Gertrude E. L.
von Staden, Heinrich 1939- 37-40R
von Staden, Wendelgard 1925- 110
von Stark, G.
See le Fort, Gertrud (Petrea) von
von Sternberg, Josef
See Sternberg, Josef von
von Storch, Anne B. 1910- CAP-2
Earlier sketch in CA 29-32
See also SATA 1
von Stubenberg, Johann Wilhelm 1619-1663 .. DLB
164
von Tepl, Johannes c. 1350-c. 1414 ..... DLB 179
von Trapp, Maria Augusta 1905-1987 81-84
Obituary 122
See also Trapp, Maria Augusta von
von Trier, Lars 1956- 167
von Trotta, Margarethe 1942- 126
von Tunzelmann, G(eorge) N(icholas) 1943- 156
Von Unruh, Fritz 1885-1970 Obituary 29-32R
See also Unruh, Fritz von
See also DLB 56
von Wangenheim, Chris 1942-1981 Obituary 103
von Weizsaecker, Carl Friedrich 1912- 105
von Wiegand, Charmion
1898(?)-1983 Obituary 110
Von Wiren-Garczynski, Vera 1931- 41-44R
von Wodtke, Charlotte Buel Johnson
1918-1982 112
See also Johnson, Charlotte Buel
von Wohl-Musciny, Ludwig
See de Wohl, Louis
von Wolkenstein, Oswald c. 1376-1445 ... DLB 179
von Wright, G(eorg) H(enrik)
See Wright, G(eorg) H(enrik) von
von Wuthenau, Alexander 1900- 65-68
von Wyle, Niklas c. 1415-1479 ..... DLB 179
Von Zelewsky, Alexander 1936- 159
Von Zesen, Philipp 1619-1689 ..... DLB 164
von Zuehlsdorff, Volkmar J(ohannes) 1912- .....
CANR-20
Earlier sketch in CA 5-8R
Vooren, Monique Van
See Van Vooren, Monique
Voorhees, Richard J(oseph) 1916- 5-8R
Voorhies, Barbara 1939- 104
Voorhis, Horace Jeremiah 1901-1984 ..... CANR-6
Obituary 113
Earlier sketch in CA 1-4R
Voorhis, Jerry
See Voorhis, Horace Jeremiah
Voos, Henry 1928- 25-28R
Voos, Paula B. 1949- 150
Voranc, Prezihov 1893-1950 ..... DLB 147
Vorhees, Melvin B. 1904(?)-1977 Obituary 69-72
Vorobeva, Maria 1892-1984 Obituary 113
Vorpahl, Ben Merchant 1937- 41-44R
Vorspan, Albert 1924- CANR-13
Earlier sketch in CA 21-24R
Vorster, Gordon 1924- 133
See also CLC 34
Vorzimmer, Peter J. 1937- 93-96
Vos, Clarence J(ohn) 1920- 45-48
Vos, Ida 1931- 137
See also SATA 69
Vos, Nelvin (LeRoy) 1932- 17-20R
Vosburgh, Leonard (W.) 1912- ..... SATA 15
Vosce, Trudie
See Ozick, Cynthia
Vose, Clement E(llery) 1923-1985 ..... 41-44R
Obituary 115
Vose, Ruth Hurst 1944- CANR-26
Earlier sketch in CA 109
Voskovec, George 1905-1981 Obituary 104
Voskuil, Dennis N(eal) 1944- 112
Voslensky, M(ichael) S(ergeevich) 1920- 128
Voss, Carl Hermann 1910- CANR-10
Earlier sketch in CA 21-24R
Voss, E(rnst) Theodore 1928- 37-40R
Voss, Earl H. 1922- 9-12R
Voss, George L. 1922- 57-60
Voss, James F(rederick) 1930- 41-44R
Voss, Johann Heinrich 1751-1826 ..... DLB 90
Voss, Ralph F. 1943- 137
Voss, Sarah (Lou) 1945- 167
Voss, Thomas M(ichael) 1945- 105
vos Savant, Marilyn 1946- 154
Vosteen, Thomas R(aymond) 1944- 152
Votaw, Dow 1920- 17-20R
Voureka, Amalia
See Fleming, Amalia
Vournakis, John N(icholas) 1939- 57-60
Voute, J. Peter 1906- 125
Vowles, Richard B(eckman) 1917- 25-28R
Voyageur
See Allen, Cecil J(ohn)
Voyce, Arthur 1889- CAP-1
Earlier sketch in CA 13-14
Voyle, Mary
See Manning, Rosemary (Joy)
Voynich, Ethel Lillian (Boole)
1864-1960 Obituary 104
See also DLB 197
Voysey, Margaret 1945- 108
Voysey, Michael 1920-1987 Obituary 123
Vozenilek, Helen S. 1958- 140
Voznesensky, Andrei (Andreievich) 1933- .....
CANR-37
Earlier sketch in CA 89-92
See also CLC 1, 15, 57
See also DAM POET
See also MTCW 1
Vranich, Joseph 1945- 138
Vrba, Rudolf 1924- 21-24R
Vrbovska, Anca 1905- 81-84
Vredenburg, Harvey L. 1921- 25-28R
Vreeland, Diana (Dalziel) 1903(?)-1989 111
Obituary 129
Vreeland, Jane D. 1915- 21-24R
Vrettos, Theodore 1919- CANR-27
Earlier sketch in CA 13-16R
Vreuls, Diane 57-60
Vries, Anne de
See de Vries, Anne
Vries, Leonard de 1919- 113
Vroman, Leo 1915- 49-52
Vroman, Mary Elizabeth (Gibson) 1923-1967 ... 125
Obituary 109
See also BW 1
See also DLB 33
Vroom, Victor H(arold) 1932- 9-12R
Vrooman, Jack Rochford 1929- 45-48
Vryonis, Speros (P.), Jr. 1928- 85-88
Vucinich, Alexander S. 1914- 156
Brief entry 109
Vucinich, Wayne S. 1913- 13-16R
Vugteveen, Verna Aardema 1911- CANR-39
Earlier sketches in CA 5-8R, CANR-3, 18
See also Aardema, Verna
Vuilleumier, Marion 1918- 81-84
Vujica, Stanko M(irko) 1909-1976 ..... 41-44R
Vulliamy, Colwyn Edward
1886-1971 Obituary 89-92
Vulture, Elizabeth T.
See Gilbert, Suzie
Vuong, Lynette Dyer 1938- CANR-46
Earlier sketch in CA 117
See also SATA 60
Vuong g(ia) Thuy 1938- 69-72
Vyn, Kathleen 1949- 89-92
Vyverberg, Henry (Sabin) 1921- 109
Vyvyan, C(lara) C(oltman Rogers) 1885- CAP-1
Earlier sketch in CA 9-10
Vyvyan, Nigel
See Nevill, Barry St-John

W

Waage, Frederick 1943- 104
Waagenaar, Sam 1908- 57-60
Waas, Uli
See Waas-Pommer, Ulrike
Waas-Pommer, Ulrike 1949- ..... SATA 85
Waber, Bernard 1924- CANR-68
Earlier sketches in CA 1-4R, CANR-2, 38
See also MAICYA
See also SATA 47, 95
See also SATA-Brief 40
Wabun
See James, Marlise Ann
Wace, Robert c. 1100-c. 1175 ..... DLB 146
Wach, Kenneth 1944- 163
Wacher, J(ohn) S(tewart) 1927- 125
Brief entry 105
Wachhorst, Wyn 1938- 106
Wachs, Mark Marshall 1933- 25-28R
Wachs, Saul P(hilip) 1931- CANR-56
Earlier sketches in CA 112, CANR-30
Wachsberger, Ken(neth) 1949- 138
Wachsmann, Klaus Philipp 1907- Brief entry ... 106
Wachsmann, Shelley 1950- 150
Wachtel, Albert 1939- CANR-50
Earlier sketch in CA 123
Wachtel, Eleanor 1947- 134
Wachtel, Howard M(artin) 1938- 49-52
Wachtel, Isidore H. 1909(?)-1979 Obituary ... 89-92
Wachtel, Paul L(awrence) 1940- 115
Wachtel, Paul Spencer 1947- 133
Wachtel, Shirley Russak 1951- 152
See also SATA 88
Wachter, Kenneth W. 1947- 139
Wachter, Oralee (Roberts) 1935- 122
See also SATA 61
See also SATA-Brief 51
Wachter, Susan M. 1943- 120
Wachtler, Sol 1930- 163
Wachtman, John B. 1928- 145
Waciuma, Wanjohi 1938- 77-80
Wackenroder, Wilhelm Heinrich 1773-1798 . DLB 90
Wacker, Charles H(enry), Jr. 1925- 73-76
Wackerbarth, Marjorie CAP-1
Earlier sketch in CA 13-14
Wackernagel, Wilhelm 1806-1869 ..... DLB 133
Wadbrook, William P. 1933- 45-48
Waddams, Herbert Montague
1911-1972 Obituary 107
Waddell, D(avid) A(lan) G(ilmour) 1927- .. CANR-23
Earlier sketch in CA 1-4R
Waddell, Eric (Wilson) 1939- 45-48
Waddell, Evelyn Margaret 1918- 53-56
See also SATA 10
Waddell, Helen (Jane) 1889-1965 102
Waddell, Jack O('Brien) 1933- 33-36R
Waddell, Martin 1941- CANR-56
Earlier sketches in CA 113, CANR-34
See also AAYA 23
See also CLR 31
See also SAAS 15
See also SATA 43, 81
Waddell, Thomas F. 1937-1987 154
Wadden, Marie 1955- 139
Waddington, C(onrad) H(al) 1905-1975 ... CANR-6
Obituary 61-64
Earlier sketch in CA 13-16R
Waddington, Miriam 1917- CANR-30
Earlier sketches in CA 21-24R, CANR-12
See also CLC 28
See also DLB 68
Waddington, Patrick (Haynes) 1934- 149
Waddington, Raymond B(ruce) 1935- 53-56
Waddy, Charis 1909- 69-72
Waddy, Lawrence (Heber) 1914- CANR-59
Earlier sketches in CA 13-16R, CANR-7
See also SATA 91
Wade, Alan
See Vance, John Holbrook
Wade, Bob
See Wade, Robert (Allison)
Wade, Carlson 1928- 29-32R
Wade, David 1929- 103
Wade, Donald W(illiam) 1904-1988 Obituary ... 128
Wade, E(ileen) K(irkpatrick)
1892(?)-1985 Obituary 117
Wade, Edwin L. 1940- 126
Wade, Francis C(larence) 1907- CAP-1
Earlier sketch in CA 13-14
Wade, Graham 1940- CANR-25
Earlier sketch in CA 107
Wade, Harry Vincent 1894-1973 Obituary 89-92
Wade, Henry
See Aubrey-Fletcher, Henry Lancelot
See also DLB 77
Wade, Herbert
See Wales, Hugh Gregory
Wade, Hugh Mason 1913-1986 Obituary 118
Wade, Ira Owen 1896-1983 73-76
Obituary 109
Wade, Jack Warren, Jr. 1948- 131
Wade, Jennifer
See Wehen, Joy DeWeese
Wade, Jerry L(ee) 1941- 53-56
Wade, Jewel Millsap 1937- Brief entry 107
Wade, Joanna
See Berckman, Evelyn Domenica
Wade, John Stevens 1927- CANR-6
Earlier sketch in CA 13-16R
Wade, Kit
See Carson, Xanthus
Wade, L(arry) L(ee) 1935- 33-36R
Wade, Lawrence 1949(?)-1990 Obituary 131
Wade, Mary Dodson 1930- ..... SATA 79
Wade, Mason 1913- 9-12R
Wade, Nicholas (Michael Landon) 1942- . CANR-16
Earlier sketch in CA 77-80
Wade, Rex A(rvin) 1936- 61-64
Wade, Richard Clement 1922- 17-20R
Wade, Robert
See McIlwain, David
Wade, Robert (Allison) 1920- CANR-62
Earlier sketch in CA 108
Wade, Rosalind Herschel 1909-1989(?) CAP-1
Obituary 127
Earlier sketch in CA 9-10
Wade, Sidney 1951- 136
Wade, Terence (L. B.) 1930- 141
Wade, Theodore E., Jr. 1936- ..... SATA 37
Wade, (Sarah) Virginia 1945- 132
Wade, (Henry) William (Rawson) 1918- ... CANR-4
Earlier sketch in CA 1-4R
Wade, Wyn Craig 1944- 103
Wade-Gayles, Gloria Jean 1938- 142
See also BW 2
Wadekin, Karl-Eugen
See Waedekin, Karl-Eugen
Wadell, Paul J(oseph) 1951- 145
Wadepuhl, Walter 1895- 61-64

Wadia, Maneck S(orabji) 1931- CANR-13
Earlier sketch in CA 17-20R
Wadinasi, Sedeka
See Nall, Hiram Abiff
Wadley, Susan S(now) 1943- 77-80
Wadlington, Walter 1931- 33-36R
Wadlington, Warwick 1938- 73-76
Wadsworth, Barry James 1935- 37-40R
Wadsworth, Frank W(hittemore) 1919- 9-12R
Wadsworth, Ginger 1945- 134
Wadsworth, James J(eremiah) 1905-1984 .. CAP-2
Obituary 112
Earlier sketch in CA 19-20
Wadsworth, Jerry
See Wadsworth, James J(eremiah)
Wadsworth, M(arshall) D. 1936- 45-48
Wadsworth, Michael E(dwin) J(ohn) 1942- .. 93-96
Wadsworth, Nelson B(ingham) 1930- 65-68
Waedekin, Karl-Eugen 1921- 73-76
Waehrer, Helen (Youngelson) 1938- 53-56
Waelder, Robert 1900-1967 .... CAP-1
Earlier sketch in CA 13-14
Waelti-Walters, Jennifer 1942- 136
Waengler, Hans-Heinrich B. 1921- CANR-20
Earlier sketch in CA 41-44R
Waffle, Harvey W(illiam) 1904- 5-8R
Wagamese, Richard 1955- 163
Wagar, W(alter) Warren 1932- CANR-3
Earlier sketch in CA 5-8R
Wagatsuma, Hiroshi 1927- 21-24R
Wagemaker, Herbert, Jr. 1929- 93-96
Wagenaar, Theodore C(larence) 1948- 111
Wagener, Hans 1940- CANR-1
Earlier sketch in CA 45-48
Wagenheim, Kal 1935- CANR-26
Earlier sketch in CA 29-32R
See also SATA 21
Wagenknecht, Edward (Charles) 1900- .. CANR-46
Earlier sketches in CA 1-4R, CANR-6, 22
See also DLB 103
Wagenvoord, James 1937- 41-44R
Wager, Walter H(erman) 1924- CANR-33
Earlier sketches in CA 5-8R, CANR-8
Wager, Willis Joseph 1911- 37-40R
Waggaman, William Henry
1884(?)-1978 Obituary 77-80
Waggner, George 1894-1984 Obituary 114
Waggoner, Glen 1940- CANR-46
Earlier sketch in CA 121
Waggoner, Hyatt H(owe) 1913-1988 ...... CANR-9
Obituary 126
Earlier sketch in CA 21-24R
Waggoner, Lawrence W. 1937- 128
Wagley, Charles (Walter) 1913-1991 .... CANR-10
Obituary 136
Earlier sketch in CA 13-16R
Waglow, Irving Frederick 1915- 1-4R
Wagman, Fredrica 1937- 97-100
Interview in 97-100
See also CLC 7
Wagman, Morton 1925- 141
Wagman, Naomi 1937- 57-60
Wagman, Robert John 1942- 93-96
Wagner, Anthony Richard 1908- CANR-42
Earlier sketches in CA 1-4R, CANR-5, 20
Wagner, Bruce 1954- 140
Wagner, C(harles) Peter 1930- CANR-49
Earlier sketches in CA 21-24R, CANR-9, 24
Wagner, Charles Abraham 1901- 5-8R
Wagner, David 1950- 148
Wagner, David G(eorge) 1949- 114
Wagner, Denson
See Iannelli, Richard
Wagner, Doc
See Wagner, Edward J. Sr.
Wagner, Edward J. Sr. 1908(?)-1986 Obituary .. 118
Wagner, Edwin E(ric) 1930- 45-48
Wagner, Elaine 1939- 45-48
Wagner, Eliot 1917- 105
Wagner, Erica 1967- 166
Wagner, Francis S(tephen) 1911- CANR-8
Earlier sketch in CA 61-64
Wagner, Frederick (Reese, Jr.) 1928- 5-8R
Wagner, Geoffrey (Atheling) 1927- CANR-2
Earlier sketch in CA 1-4R
Wagner, Gillian (Mary Millicent) 1927- 141
Wagner, Gordon Parsons 1915-1987 Obituary . 124
Wagner, Harvey M. 1931- CANR-6
Earlier sketch in CA 13-16R
Wagner, Heinrich Leopold 1747-1779 ...... DLB 94
Wagner, Helmut R(udolf) 1904- CANR-19
Earlier sketches in CA 53-56, CANR-4
Wagner, Henry R. 1862-1957 .... DLB 140
Wagner, Jack Russell 1916- 49-52
Wagner, Jane CANR-42
Earlier sketch in CA 109
Wagner, Jean Pierre 1919- 21-24R
Wagner, Jon G(regory) 1944- 109
Wagner, Joseph Frederick
1900(?)-1974 Obituary 53-56
Wagner, Karl Edward 1945-1994 .... CANR-51
Earlier sketches in CA 49-52, CANR-3
Wagner, Ken(neth) 1911- 37-40R
Wagner, Kenneth A. 1919- 53-56
Wagner, Lilya 1940- 112
Wagner, Linda W.
See Wagner-Martin, Linda (C.)
Wagner, Linda Welshimer
See Wagner-Martin, Linda (C.)
Wagner, Linda Welshimer 1936- CANR-3
Earlier sketch in CA 9-12R
Wagner, Margaret D. 1949- 5-8R
Wagner, (Griegg) Marsden 1930- 69-72
Wagner, Michael G. 1951- 133
Wagner, Nathaniel N(ed) 1930- 57-60
Wagner, Peggy
See Wagner, Margaret D.
Wagner, Philip L(aurence) 1921- 41-44R
Wagner, Philip Marshall 1904-1996 102
Obituary 155
Wagner, Ray(mond) David 1924- CANR-41
Earlier sketches in CA 5-8R, CANR-3, 19
Wagner, Ray Jay 1931- 77-80
Wagner, Richard 1813-1883 .... DLB 129
Wagner, Richard Vansant 1935- Brief entry 105
Wagner, Roy 1938- 41-44R
Wagner, Rudolph F(red) 1921- 37-40R
Wagner, Ruth H(ortense) 1909- 29-32R
Wagner, Sharon B. 1936- CANR-10
Earlier sketch in CA 25-28R
See also SATA 4
Wagner, Stanley P(aul) 1923- 29-32R
Wagner, Walter 1927(?)-1983(?) Obituary 109
Wagner, Walter F(rederick), Jr. 1926-1985 ....
CANR-26
Obituary 116
Earlier sketch in CA 69-72
Wagner, Wenceslas Joseph 1917- 37-40R
Wagner-Martin, Linda (C.) 1936- 159
See also CLC 50
Wagoner, David (Russell) 1926- CANR-71
Earlier sketches in CA 1-4R, CANR-2
See also CAAS 3
See also CLC 3, 5, 15
See also DLB 5
See also SATA 14
Wagoner, Harless D. 1918-1973 .... 29-32R
Obituary 134
Wagoner, Jay J. 1923- 25-28R
Wagoner, John L(eonard) 1927-1984 69-72
Obituary 112
Wagoner, Walter D. 1918- 21-24R
Wagonseller, Bill R(oss) 1933- 107
Wagschal, Harry 1939- 108
Wagschal, Peter H(enry) 1944- CANR-19
Earlier sketch in CA 102
Wagstaff, (John) Malcolm 1940- CANR-28
Earlier sketch in CA 109
Wah, Fred(erick James) 1939- 141
Brief entry 107
See also CLC 44
See also DLB 60
Wahking, Harold L(eroy) 1931- 29-32R
Wahl, Jan (Boyer) 1933- CANR-38
Earlier sketches in CA 25-28R, CANR-12
See also MAICYA
See also SAAS 3
See also SATA 2, 34, 73
Wahl, Jean 1888-1974 Obituary 49-52
Wahl, Paul 1922- 9-12R
Wahl, Robert (Charles) 1948- CANR-1
Earlier sketch in CA 49-52
Wahl, Thomas (Peter) 1931- 9-12R
Wahlberg, Rachel Conrad 1922- 93-96
Wahler, Robert G(ordon) 1936- Brief entry 109
Wahlke, John C(harles) 1917- CANR-11
Earlier sketch in CA 21-24R
Wahloo, Per 1926-1975 61-64
See also CLC 7
Wahloo, Peter
See Wahloo, Per
Wahlroos, Sven 1931- 57-60
Wahtera, John (Edward) 1929-1985 61-64
Obituary 117
Waiblinger, Wilhelm 1804-1830 .... DLB 90
Waide, Jan 1952- 105
See also SATA 29
Waidson, H(erbert) Morgan 1916- 5-8R
Waife, Marie
See Waife-Goldberg, Marie
Waife-Goldberg, Marie 1892-1985 .... CAP-2
Obituary 118
Earlier sketch in CA 25-28
Wailey, Anthony Paul 1947- 126
Wailey, Tony
See Wailey, Anthony Paul
Wain, Barry 1944- 122
Wain, John (Barrington) 1925-1994 ..... CANR-54
Obituary 145
Earlier sketches in CA 5-8R, CANR-23
See also CAAS 4
See also CDBLB 1960 to Present
See also CLC 2, 11, 15, 46
See also DLB 15, 27, 139, 155
See also MTCW 1
Waine, Anthony 1946- 113
Wainer, Cord
See Dewey, Thomas B(lanchard)
Wainhouse, David Walter 1900-1976 .... 17-20R
Obituary 65-68
Wainscott, John Milton 1910-1981 .... SATA 53
Wainscott, Ronald H(arold) 1948- 131
Wainwright, A(lfred) 1907-1991 140
Wainwright, Arthur William 1925- 114
Wainwright, Charles Anthony 1933- 37-40R
Wainwright, David
See Stansfield, Richard Habberton
Wainwright, Geoffrey 1939- CANR-34
Earlier sketches in CA 37-40R, CANR-15
Wainwright, Gordon Ray 1937- 113
Wainwright, Hilary 1949- 131
Wainwright, J(oseph) Allan 1921- 13-16R
Wainwright, Jeffrey 1944- 142
Brief entry 122
See also DLB 40
Wainwright, John 1921- CANR-64
Brief entry 108
Earlier sketch in CA 110
Interview in 110
Wainwright, Loudon (Snowden)
1925(?)-1988 Obituary 127
Wainwright, Nicholas Biddle 1914- 65-68
Wainwright, Richard M. 1935- .... SATA 91
Wainwright, William J(udson) 1935- 120
Waisanen, F(rederick) B(rynolf) 1923- 45-48
Waisman, Sergio Gabriel 1967- 152
Waite, A. E.
See Waite, Arthur Edward
Waite, Arthur Edward 1857-1942 Brief entry ... 121
Waite, Helen Elmira 1903- 1-4R
Waite, Michael P(hillip) 1960- 168
See also SATA 101
Waite, P(eter) B(usby) 1922- 9-12R
See also SATA 64
Waite, Robert G(eorge) L(eeson) 1919- 9-12R
Waite, William W(iley) 1903- CAP-1
Earlier sketch in CA 13-16
Waith, Eugene M(ersereau) 1912- CANR-5
Earlier sketch in CA 5-8R
Waitley, Douglas 1927- CANR-9
Earlier sketch in CA 21-24R
See also SATA 30
Waitman, Katharine Lura 1956- 168
Waitman, Katie
See Waitman, Katharine Lura
Waitzkin, Howard 1945- 141
Waitzmann, Dorothea 1915- 13-16R
Wajcman, Judy 1950- 140
Wajda, Andrzej 1926- 102
See also CLC 16
Wakefield, Celia 1910- 164
Wakefield, Connie LaVon 1948- 65-68
Wakefield, Dan 1932- 21-24R
See also CAAS 7
See also CLC 7
Wakefield, David 1950- 145
Wakefield, Donam Hahn 1927- 37-40R
Wakefield, Herbert Russell 1888-1965 .... 5-8R
Wakefield, Hubert George 1915-1984 Obituary . 112
Wakefield, Hugh
See Wakefield, Hubert George
Wakefield, Jean L.
See Laird, Jean E(louise)
Wakefield, R. I.
See White, Gertrude M(ason)
Wakefield, Robert A. 1916- 13-16R
Wakefield, Sherman Day
1894-1971 Obituary 29-32R
Wakefield, Tom 1935-1996 101
Obituary 152
Wakefield, Walter Leggett 1911- 81-84
Wakeford, John 1936- Brief entry 112
Wakeham, Irene 1912- 29-32R
Wakeley, John H(albert) 1932- 41-44R
Wakelin, Martyn Francis 1935- 65-68
Wakelyn, Jon L(ouis) 1938- CANR-1
Earlier sketch in CA 45-48
Wakeman, Carolyn 1943- 126
Wakeman, Frederic (Evans), Jr. 1937- CANR-1
Earlier sketch in CA 49-52
Wakeman, Geoffrey 1926- CANR-15
Earlier sketch in CA 37-40R
Wakeman, John 1928- 124
Wakeman, Robert Parker
1914(?)-1981 Obituary 104
Wakeman, Stephen H. 1859-1924 .... DLB 187
Wakerman, Elyce 1947- 128
Wakil, S(heikh) P(arvez) 1935- 85-88
Wakin, Daniel (Joseph) 1961- .... SATA 84
Wakin, Edward 1927- CANR-17
Earlier sketches in CA 5-8R, CANR-2
See also SATA 37
wa Kinyatti, Maina 1944- 132
Wako, Mdogo
See Nazareth, Peter
Wakoski, Diane 1937- CANR-60
Earlier sketches in CA 13-16R, CANR-9
Interview in CANR-9
See also CAAS 1
See also CLC 2, 4, 7, 9, 11, 40
See also DAM POET
See also DLB 5
See also PC 15
Wakoski-Sherbell, Diane
See Wakoski, Diane
Waksman, Selman A(braham) 1888-1973 ... CAP-1
Obituary 45-48
Earlier sketch in CA 13-16
Wakstein, Allen M. 1931- 29-32R
Walahfrid Strabo c. 808-849 .... DLB 148
Walbank, F. W.
See Walbank, Frank William
Walbank, F(rank) W(illiam) 1909- 142
Walbank, Frank William 1909- Brief entry 111
Walberg, Herbert J(ohn) 1937- 61-64
Walch, Timothy (George) 1947- CANR-21
Earlier sketch in CA 105
Walchars, John 1912- 81-84
Walck, Henry Z. 1908(?)-1984 Obituary 114
See also SATA-Obit 40
Walcott, Charles E(liot) 1943- 152
Walcott, Derek (Alton) 1930- CANR-47
Earlier sketches in CA 89-92, CANR-26
See also BLC 3
See also BW 2
See also CLC 2, 4, 9, 14, 25, 42, 67, 76
See also DAB
See also DAC
See also DAM MST, MULT, POET
See also DC 7
See also DLB 117
See also DLBY 81
See also MTCW 1
Walcott, Fred G. 1894- 37-40R
Walcott, John 1949- 126
Walcott, Robert 1910- CAP-1
Earlier sketch in CA 13-14
Walcutt, Charles Child 1908-1989 .... CANR-3
Obituary 128
Earlier sketch in CA 1-4R
Wald, Alan M(aynard) 1946- 129
Wald, Carol 1935- 65-68
Wald, George 1906- 159
Wald, Kenneth D. 1949- 129
Wald, Malvin (Daniel) 1917- CANR-1
Earlier sketch in CA 45-48
Wald, Richard C(harles) 108
Waldbauer, Gilbert (P.) 1928- 157
Walde, Ralph E(ldon) 1943- 53-56
Waldeck, Peter Bruce 1940- 41-44R
Waldegrave, Robert fl. 1578-1603 .... DLB 170
Walden, Amelia Elizabeth CANR-2
Earlier sketch in CA 1-4R
See also SATA 3
Walden, Becky
See Usry, Becky (S.)
Walden, Daniel 1922- 25-28R
Walden, Howard T(albot) II 1897-1981 45-48
Obituary 103
Walden, John C(layton) 1928- 53-56
Waldenfels, Hans 1931- 131
Walder, (Alan) David 1928-1978 .... CANR-17
Obituary 81-84
Earlier sketch in CA 65-68
Walder, Dennis 1943- 117
Walders, Joe 1948- 85-88
Waldheim, Kurt 1918- 89-92
Waldherr, Kris 1963- .... SATA 76
Waldhorn, Arthur 1918- CANR-3
Earlier sketch in CA 1-4R
Waldinger, Ernst 1896-1970 Obituary 104
Waldinger, Roger (David) 1953- 165
Waldis, Burkhard c. 1490-1556(?) .... DLB 179
Waldman, Anne (Lesley) 1945- CANR-69
Earlier sketches in CA 37-40R, CANR-34
See also CAAS 17
See also CLC 7
See also DLB 16
Waldman, Bruce 1949- .... SATA 15
Waldman, Diane 1936- CANR-26
Earlier sketch in CA 33-36R
Waldman, Eric 1914- 17-20R
Waldman, Harry 1945- 148
Waldman, Max 1919-1981 105
Obituary 103
Waldman, Milton 1895-1976 69-72
Obituary 65-68
Waldman, Neil 1947- CANR-67
Earlier sketch in CA 128
See also SATA 51, 94
Waldmeir, Joseph John 1923- 9-12R
Waldo, Anna Lee 1925- CANR-64
Earlier sketch in CA 85-88
Waldo, Dave
See Clarke, D(avid) Waldo
Waldo, E. Hunter
See Sturgeon, Theodore (Hamilton)
Waldo, Edward Hamilton
See Sturgeon, Theodore (Hamilton)
Waldo, Kay Cronkite 1938- 107
Waldo, Myra 93-96
Waldo, Ralph Emerson III 1944- 102
Waldo, Terry
See Waldo, Ralph Emerson III
Waldo, Willis H. 1920- 13-16R
Waldock, (Claud) Humphrey (Meredith)
1904-1981 Obituary 108
Waldorf, Paul D(ouglass) 1908- CAP-1
Earlier sketch in CA 13-16
Waldrep, Christopher (Reef) 1951- 146
Waldrep, (Alvis) Kent (II) 1954- 150
Waldrip, Louise B. 1912- 37-40R
Waldron, Ann Wood 1924- CANR-45
Earlier sketches in CA 13-16R, CANR-7
See also SATA 16
Waldron, Arthur (Nelson) 1948- 135
Waldron, D'Lynn
See Waldron-Shah, Diane Lynn
Waldron, Eli 1916(?)-1980 Obituary 101
Waldron, Ingrid 1939- 53-56
Waldron, Martin O. 1925-1981 Obituary 103
Waldron-Shah, Diane Lynn 1936- 9-12R
Waldrop, Howard 1946- CANR-41
Earlier sketch in CA 118
Waldrop, Keith 1932- 117
See also CAAS 30
Waldrop, M(orris) Mitchell 1947- 143
Waldrop, Rosmarie 1935- CANR-67
Earlier sketches in CA 101, CANR-18, 39
See also CAAS 30
See also DLB 169
Waldrop, W. Earl 1910- 5-8R
Wale, Michael 81-84
Walen, Harry L(eonard) 1915- 41-44R
Wales, Hugh Gregory 1910- CANR-2
Earlier sketch in CA 5-8R
Wales, Nym
See Snow, Helen Foster
Wales, Robert 1923- 93-96
Wales, William
See Ambrose, David (Edwin)
Walesa, Lech 1943- 128
Waley, Arthur (David) 1889-1966 85-88
Obituary 25-28R
Walford, Christian
See Dilcock, Noreen
Walford, Lionel Albert 1905-1979 Obituary ... 85-88
Walford, Roy L(ee, Jr.) 1924- 111
Walgenbach, Paul H(enry) 1923- 53-56
Walhout, Donald 1927- CANR-2
Earlier sketch in CA 5-8R
Walicki, Andrzej 1930- 101

Walinsky, Louis J(oseph) 1908- CAP-2
Earlier sketch in CA 17-18
Walinsky, Ossip J. 1887(?)-1973 Obituary 41-44R
Waliullah, Syed 1922-1971 21-24R
Obituary 134
Walkden, (George) Brian 1923- CANR-10
Earlier sketch in CA 13-16R
Walkenstein, Eileen 1923- CANR-14
Earlier sketch in CA 69-72
Walker, Addison
See Walker, (Addison) Mort
Walker, Alan 1911- CANR-26
Earlier sketches in CA 13-16R, CANR-7
Walker, Alan 1949- 129
Walker, Albert L(yell) 1907- 41-44R
Walker, Alexander 1930- 142
Brief entry 116
Walker, Alice 1900-1982 DLB 201
Walker, Alice (Malsenior) 1944- CANR-66
Earlier sketches in CA 37-40R, CANR-9, 27, 49
Interview in CANR-27
See also AAYA 3
See also BEST 89:4
See also BLC 3
See also BW 2
See also CDALB 1968-1988
See also CLC 5, 6, 9, 19, 27, 46, 58, 103
See also DA
See also DAB
See also DAC
See also DAM MST, MULT, NOV, POET, POP
See also DLB 6, 33, 143
See also MTCW 1
See also SATA 31
See also SSC 5
See also WLCS
Walker, Anne Collins 1939- 141
Walker, Ardis Manly 1901- CANR-22
Earlier sketch in CA 37-40R
Walker, Augusta 1914- 21-24R
Walker, Barbara G(oodwin) 1930- 73-76
Walker, Barbara (Jeanne) K(erlin) 1921- CANR-38
Earlier sketches in CA 33-36R, CANR-16
See also SATA 4, 80
Walker, Barbara M(uhs) 1928- SATA 57
Walker, Benjamin 1923- CANR-10
Earlier sketch in CA 25-28R
Walker, Bessie
See Henry, Bessie Walker
Walker, Betty A. 140
Walker, (James) Braz(elton) 1934-1983 69-72
See also SATA 45
Walker, Brooks R. 1935- 9-12R
Walker, Bruce (James) 1944- 85-88
Walker, Bryce S(tewart) 1934- 117
Walker, C(larence) Eugene 1939- CANR-52
Earlier sketches in CA 61-64, CANR-10, 28
Walker, Charles
See Gettings, Fred
Walker, Charles 1911- 17-20R
Walker, Charles R(umford) 1893-1974 CAP-2
Obituary 53-56
Earlier sketch in CA 17-18
Walker, Cheryl 1947- 111
Walker, Claxton 1924- 101
Walker, Clive (Phillip) 1954- 124
Walker, D(aniel) P(ickering) 1914-1985 85-88
Obituary 116
Walker, Dale L(ee) 1935- CANR-49
Earlier sketches in CA 57-60, CANR-8, 24
Walker, Daniel Downing 1915- CANR-2
Earlier sketch in CA 1-4R
Walker, Danton (MacIntyre)
1899-1960 Obituary 93-96
Walker, David 1950- CANR-28
Earlier sketch in CA 104
Walker, David Clifton 1942- 69-72
Walker, David G(ordon) 1926- 110
See also SATA 60
Walker, David Harry 1911-1992 CANR-1
Obituary 137
Earlier sketch in CA 1-4R
See also CLC 14
See also SATA 8
See also SATA-Obit 71
Walker, David M(axwell) 1920- CANR-46
Earlier sketches in CA 9-12R, CANR-5, 22
Walker, Deward E(dgar), Jr. 1935- CANR-43
Earlier sketches in CA 25-28R, CANR-19
Walker, Diana 1925- CANR-4
Earlier sketch in CA 49-52
See also SATA 9
Walker, Dianne Marie Catherine 1950-
See Walker, Kate
See also SATA 82
Walker, Dick
See Pellowski, Michael (Joseph)
Walker, Donald E(dwin) 1941- 152
Walker, Donald Smith 1918- 9-12R
Walker, Doreen 1920- 135
Walker, Earl Thomas 1891- 105
Walker, Edward Joseph 1934- CANR-53
Earlier sketches in CA 21-24R, CANR-12, 28
See also Walker, Ted
Walker, Edward L(ewis) 1914- CANR-11
Earlier sketch in CA 25-28R
Walker, Elinor 1911- 13-16R
Walker, Eric Anderson 1886-1976 CAP-2
Obituary 65-68
Earlier sketch in CA 13-14
Walker, Ethel Valerie 1944- 53-56
Walker, Evan 1933(?)-1982 Obituary 107
Walker, Everett 1906-1983 Obituary 109
Walker, Frank 1930- 69-72
See also SATA 36
Walker, Frank B. 1916(?)-1985 Obituary 117
Walker, Franklin (Dickerson) 1900-1979 21-24R
Obituary 85-88
Walker, Geoffrey de Q(uincey) 1940- 131
Walker, Geoffrey James 1936- 93-96
Walker, George F. 1947- CANR-59
Earlier sketches in CA 103, CANR-21, 43
See also CLC 44, 61
See also DAB
See also DAC
See also DAM MST
See also DLB 60
Walker, Gerald 1928- 9-12R
Walker, Gilbert James 1907-1982 Obituary 107
Walker, Glen 1937- 108
Walker, Graham S. 1956- 122
Walker, Gregory P(iers) M(ountford) 1942- 73-76
Walker, Greta 1927- 77-80
Walker, Harold Blake 1904- 17-20R
Walker, Harry
See Waugh, Hillary Baldwin
Walker, Helen M(ary) 1891-1983 Obituary 109
Walker, Henry M(acKay) 1947- 151
Walker, Hill M(ontague) 1939- 93-96
Walker, Holly Beth
See Bond, Gladys Baker
Walker, Ira
See Walker, Irma Ruth (Roden)
Walker, Irma Ruth (Roden) 1921- CANR-46
Earlier sketches in CA 5-8R, CANR-6, 21
Walker, J.
See Crawford, John Richard
Walker, J(ohn) Ingram 1944- 112
Walker, Jack
See Thayer, Frederick C(lifton), Jr.
Walker, James Lynwood 1940- 37-40R
Walker, James R(obert) 1950- 164
Walker, Janet A(nderson) 1942- 119
Walker, Jeanne 1924- 61-64
Walker, Jeanne Murray 1944- 111
Walker, Jeremy D(esmond) B(romhead)
1936- 21-24R
Walker, Joan 5-8R
Walker, John 1906- CANR-6
Earlier sketch in CA 5-8R
Walker, John 1933- 113
Walker, John (Bruce) 1938- 120
Walker, John 1947- 127
Walker, John Brisben 1847-1931 DLB 79
Walker, Joseph 1892-1985 Obituary 117
Walker, Joseph A. 1935- CANR-26
Earlier sketch in CA 89-92
See also BW 1
See also CLC 19
See also DAM DRAM, MST
See also DLB 38
Walker, Joseph E(rdman) 1911- 37-40R
Walker, Kate 1950- 149
See also Walker, Dianne Marie Catherine
Walker, Kathrine Sorley
See Sorley Walker, Kathrine
Walker, Keith 1934- 121
Walker, Kenneth Francis 1924- 33-36R
Walker, Kenneth Macfarlane 1882-1966 5-8R
Walker, Kenneth R(oland) 1928- 37-40R
Walker, Kenneth Richard 1931-1989 17-20R
Obituary 129
Walker, Laurence C(olton) 1924- 53-56
Walker, Lawrence David 1931- 53-56
Walker, Lenore E(lizabeth) 1942- 97-100
Walker, Leo 13-16R
Walker, Leslie 1953- 139
Walker, Lou Ann 1952- CANR-53
Earlier sketch in CA 126
See also SATA 66
See also SATA-Brief 53
Walker, Louise Jean 1891-1976 Obituary 110
See also SATA-Obit 35
Walker, Lucy
See Sanders, Dorothy Lucie
Walker, Mack 1929- 9-12R
Walker, Margaret (Abigail) 1915- CANR-54
Earlier sketches in CA 73-76, CANR-26
See also BLC
See also BW 2
See also CLC 1, 6
See also DAM MULT
See also DLB 76, 152
See also MTCW 1
See also PC 20
Walker, Margaret Pope 1901(?)-1980 Obituary 101
Walker, Marianne (Cascio) 1933- 144
Walker, Mark 1953- 117
Walker, Marshall (John) 1912- 17-20R
Walker, Martin 1947- 101
Walker, Martin 1949- 146
Walker, Mary Alexander 1927- 104
See also SATA 61
Walker, Mary Willis 1942- 161
Walker, Matthew
See Mewhinney, Bruce
Walker, Michael John 1932-1989(?) Obituary 129
Walker, Mickey 1901-1981 Obituary 108
Walker, Mildred
See Schemm, Mildred Walker
Walker, (Addison) Mort 1923- CANR-25
Earlier sketches in CA 49-52, CANR-3
See also SATA 8
Walker, Morton 1929- CANR-22
Earlier sketch in CA 85-88
Walker, Nancy A. 1942- 136
Walker, Nicolette (Daisy) Milnes 1943- 41-44R
Walker, Nigel (David) 1917- 61-64
Walker, Pamela 1948- 69-72
See also SATA 24
Walker, Paul E(rnest) 1941- 147
Walker, Peter F(ranklin) 1931- 13-16R
Walker, Peter N. 1936- CANR-14
Earlier sketch in CA 77-80
Walker, Philip (Doolittle) 1924- 133
Walker, Philip Mitchell 1943- 29-32R
Walker, R. B. J. 1947- 145
Walker, Raymond Myerscough
See Myerscough-Walker, Raymond
Walker, Rebecca 1970- 154
Walker, Richard (John) 1952- 132
Walker, Richard L(ouis) 1922- CANR-7
Earlier sketch in CA 9-12R
Walker, Robert H(arris) 1924- CANR-48
Earlier sketches in CA 13-16R, CANR-7, 23
Walker, Robert Newton 1911- 53-56
Walker, Robert W(ayne) 1948- CANR-48
Earlier sketches in CA 93-96, CANR-23
See also SATA 66
Walker, Roger W(illiams) 1931- 45-48
Walker, Ronald G(ary) 1945- CANR-39
Earlier sketches in CA 93-96, CANR-16
Walker, Ruth
See Walker, Irma Ruth (Roden)
Walker, Samuel 1942- 85-88
Walker, Scott 1950- 120
Walker, Sheila S(uzanne) 1944- 127
Walker, Shel
See Sheldon, Walter J.
Walker, Stanley 1898-1962 Obituary 93-96
Walker, Stella Archer 1907- 61-64
Walker, Stephen (Francis) 1941- 131
Walker, Stephen J. 1951- SATA 12
Walker, Stuart (Armstrong) 1880(?)-1941 Brief entry 120
Walker, Stuart H(odge) 1923- CANR-24
Earlier sketch in CA 45-48
Walker, Sydney III 1931- 21-24R
Walker, T. Michael 1937- 77-80
Walker, Ted
See Walker, Edward Joseph
See also CLC 13
See also DLB 40
Walker, Theodore J. 1922- 102
Walker, Thomas W(illiam) 1940- 142
Walker, Walter (Colyear) 1912- 117
Walker, Walter (Herbert III) 1949- CANR-42
Earlier sketch in CA 117
Walker, Warren S(tanley) 1921- CANR-38
Earlier sketches in CA 9-12R, CANR-3, 16
Walker, Wendy (Alison) 1951- 131
Walker, Willard (Brewer) 1926- CANR-23
Earlier sketch in CA 45-48
Walker, William Edward 1925- 9-12R
Walker, William G(eorge) 1928- 77-80
Walker, William H. 1913- 17-20R
Walker, William Otis 1896-1981 Obituary 105
Walker, Wyatt Tee 1929- 127
Walker-Blondell, Becky 1951- 155
See also SATA 89
Walkerdine, Valerie 1947- 164
Walkerley, Rodney Lewis (de Burgh) 1905- CAP-1
Earlier sketch in CA 9-10
Walkinshaw, Colin
See Reid, James Macarthur
Walkinshaw, Lawrence H(arvey) 1904- 45-48
Walkland, S(tuart) A(lan)
1925(?)-1989 Obituary 128
Walkowicz, Chris 1943- 135
Walkowitz, Daniel J(ay) 1942- 81-84
Wall, A(rthur) E(dward) P(atrick) 1925- 119
Wall, Barbara 1911- 97-100
Wall, Bennett H(arrison) 1914- 77-80
Wall, C. Edward 1942- 37-40R
Wall, Elizabeth S(pooner) 1924- 93-96
Wall, James M(cKendree) 1928- 134
Brief entry 113
Wall, John Nelson, Jr. 1945- 114
Wall, John W. 1910-1989 166
Wall, Joseph Barrye 1899(?)-1985 Obituary 117
Wall, Joseph Frazier 1920-1995 CANR-13
Obituary 149
Earlier sketch in CA 29-32R
Wall, Maggie 1937- 65-68
Wall, Margaret
See Wall, Maggie
Wall, Martha 1910- CAP-2
Earlier sketch in CA 25-28
Wall, Mervyn 1908- 129
Wall, Michael Morris 1942- 53-56
Wall, Mike
See Wall, Michael Morris
Wall, Patrick (Henry Bligh) 1916- 104
Wall, Patrick D(avid) 1925- 17-20R
Wall, Richard 1944- 41-44R
Wall, Robert Emmet, Jr. 1937- CANR-23
Earlier sketch in CA 45-48
Wall, Stephen D. 1948- 140
Wall, T. D.
See Wall, Toby (Douglas)
Wall, Toby (Douglas) 1946- 119
Wall, Toby D.
See Wall, Toby (Douglas)
Wall, Wendy Somerville 1942- 49-52
Wallace, Alexander Fielding 1918-1991 33-36R
Obituary 135
Wallace, Alexander Ross 1891-1982 Obituary 107
Wallace, Alfred Russel 1823-1913 Brief entry 123
See also DLB 190
Wallace, Amy 1955- CANR-27
Earlier sketch in CA 81-84
Wallace, Andrew 1930- 37-40R
Wallace, Anthony F(rancis) C(larke) 1923-
CANR-13
Earlier sketch in CA 61-64
Wallace, B. Alan 1950- 158
Wallace, Barbara Brooks CANR-28
Earlier sketches in CA 29-32R, CANR-11
See also SAAS 17
See also SATA 4, 78
Wallace, Ben J. 1937- 45-48
Wallace, Beverly Dobrin 1921- 101
See also SATA 19
Wallace, Bill 1947-
See Wallace, William Keith
and Wallace, William N.
See also SATA 101
See also SATA-Brief 47
Wallace, Bronwen 1945- 112
Wallace, Bruce 1920- CANR-15
Earlier sketch in CA 85-88
Wallace, Claire 1956- 138
Wallace, Daisy
See Cuyler, Margery S(tuyvesant)
Wallace, David Foster 1962- CANR-59
Earlier sketch in CA 132
See also CLC 50
Wallace, David H(arold) 1926- 25-28R
Wallace, David J. 1954- 124
Wallace, David Rains 1945- CANR-14
Earlier sketches in CA 81-84, CANR-31
Wallace, Deborah 1945- 138
Wallace, DeWitt 1889-1981 Obituary 103
See also DLB 137
Wallace, Dexter
See Masters, Edgar Lee
Wallace, Doreen
See Rash, Dora Eileen Agnew (Wallace)
Wallace, Earl W. 1942- 164
Wallace, Ed(ward Tatum)
1906-1976 Obituary 69-72
Wallace, (Richard Horatio) Edgar 1875-1932 Brief entry 115
See also DLB 70
See also TCLC 57
Wallace, Edward C. 1946- 143
Wallace, Ernest 1906-1985 CANR-25
Earlier sketch in CA 13-16R
Wallace, Francis 1894(?)-1977 Obituary 73-76
Wallace, G(erald) L. 1938- 97-100
Wallace, George C(orley) 1919- 150
Brief entry 114
Wallace, Helen Kingsbury 1897- CAP-2
Earlier sketch in CA 25-28
Wallace, Helen M(argaret) 1913- CANR-12
Earlier sketch in CA 61-64
Wallace, Henry A(gard) 1888-1965 105
Obituary 89-92
Wallace, Ian 1950- CANR-50
Earlier sketches in CA 107, CANR-25, 38
See also CLR 37
See also MAICYA
See also SATA 53, 56
Wallace, Irving 1916-1990 CANR-27
Obituary 132
Earlier sketches in CA 1-4R, CANR-1
Interview in CANR-27
See also CAAS 1
See also AITN 1
See also CLC 7, 13
See also DAM NOV, POP
See also MTCW 1
Wallace, James 1947- 138
Wallace, James D. 1937- 162
Wallace, James Donald 1937- 108
Wallace, Joanne (M.) 1938- 117
Wallace, John A(dam) 1915- 5-8R
See also SATA 3
Wallace, John Malcolm 1928- 25-28R
Wallace, K(ay) K. 1949- 111
Wallace, Karen 1951- 150
See also SATA 83
Wallace, Karl R(ichards) 1906-1973 101
Wallace, Lew(is) 1827(?)-1905 Brief entry 120
See also DLB 202
Wallace, Lewis Grant 1910- CAP-2
Earlier sketch in CA 23-24
Wallace, Lila Bell Acheson
1889-1984 Obituary 112
Brief entry 105
See also DLB 137
Wallace, Lillian Parker 1890-1971 1-4R
Obituary 103
Wallace, Luther T(ompkins) 1928- 13-16R
Wallace, Marc J., Jr. 1944- 114
Wallace, Marjorie 101
Wallace, Michael David 1943- 77-80
Wallace, Michele Faith 1952- CANR-58
Earlier sketch in CA 108
Wallace, Mike 1918- 65-68
Wallace, Myron Leon
See Wallace, Mike
Wallace, Naomi (French) 1960- 163
Wallace, Nigel
See Hamilton, Charles (Harold St. John)
Wallace, Pamela 1949- 105
Wallace, Pat
See Strother, Pat Wallace
Wallace, Paul 1931- 61-64
Wallace, Paul A(nthony) W(ilson) 1891- CAP-1
Earlier sketch in CA 13-16
Wallace, Philip (Adrian) Hope
See Hope-Wallace, Philip (Adrian)
Wallace, Phyllis Ann 105
Wallace, Richard
See Ind, Allison
Wallace, Robert 1932- CANR-10
Earlier sketch in CA 13-16R
See also SATA 47
See also SATA-Brief 37
Wallace, Robert Ash 1921- 1-4R
Wallace, Robert Kimball 1944- 69-72

Wallace, Robert M. 1947- 141
Wallace, Robin 1955- 128
Wallace, Roger
See Charlier, Roger H(enri)
Wallace, Ronald (William) 1945- CANR-42
Earlier sketches in CA 57-60, CANR-6, 20
Wallace, Ronald S(tewart) 1911- CANR-5
Earlier sketch in CA 9-12R
Wallace, Ruby Ann 1923(?)- CANR-26
Earlier sketch in CA 112
See also Dee, Ruby
See also BW 1
Wallace, Samuel E(ugene) 1935- 41-44R
Wallace, Sarah Leslie 1914- 9-12R
Wallace, Sister M. Jean
See Paxton, Mary Jean Wallace
Wallace, Sylvia CANR-27
Earlier sketch in CA 73-76
Wallace, Tom 1874-1961 Obituary 93-96
Wallace, Vesna A. 1952- 158
Wallace, Walter L. 1927- 81-84
Wallace, Willard M(osher) 1911- 13-16R
Wallace, William A(ugustine) 1918- 41-44R
Wallace, William A(lan) 1935- 49-52
Wallace, William Keith 1947- 124
See also Wallace, Bill
See also SATA 53
Wallace, William N. 1924- 13-16R
See also Wallace, Bill
Wallace, William Stewart 1884-1970 Obituary .. 116
Wallace-Brodeur, Ruth 1941- 107
See also SATA 51, 88
See also SATA-Brief 41
Wallace-Clarke, George 1916- 117
Wallace-Crabbe, Chris(topher Keith) 1934- CANR-14
Earlier sketch in CA 77-80
Wallace-Hadrill, Andrew (Frederic) 1951- . CANR-40
Earlier sketch in CA 117
Wallace-Hadrill, D(avid) S(utherland) 1920- . 29-32R
Wallace-Hadrill, John Michael 1916-1985 ..... 5-8R
Obituary 118
Wallach, Alan 1942- 147
Wallach, Erica Glaser 1922-1993 .... 21-24R
Obituary 143
Wallach, Ira 1913-1995 .... 9-12R
Obituary 150
Wallach, Janet 1942- CANR-38
Earlier sketch in CA 106
Wallach, John P. 1943- 139
Wallach, Mark I(rwin) 1949- 69-72
Wallach, Michael A(rthur) 1933- CANR-51
Earlier sketches in CA 13-16R, CANR-11, 26
Wallach, Paul I. 1927- CANR-8
Earlier sketch in CA 17-20R
Wallach, Robert Charles 1935- 107
Wallach, Sidney 1905-1979 103
Obituary 89-92
Wallance, Gregory Joseph 1948- 109
Wallant, Edward Lewis 1926-1962 ...... CANR-22
Earlier sketch in CA 1-4R
See also CLC 5, 10
See also DLB 2, 28, 143
See also MTCW 1
Wallechinsky, David 1948- CANR-55
Earlier sketches in CA 61-64, CANR-27
Wallek, Lee
See Johnson, Curt(is Lee)
Wallen, Carl J(oseph) 1931- 93-96
Wallenstein, Barry J(ay) 1940- CANR-11
Earlier sketch in CA 45-48
Wallenstein, Meir 1903- CAP-1
Earlier sketch in CA 13-16
Waller, Altina L(aura) 1940- 112
Waller, Brown
See Fraser, W(aller) B(rown)
Waller, Charles T(homas) 1934- 61-64
Waller, Douglas C. 1949- 146
Waller, Edmund 1606-1687 .... DAM POET
See also DLB 126
Waller, G(ary) F(redric) 1944- CANR-31
Earlier sketch in CA 112
Waller, Gary
See Waller, G(ary) F(redric)
Waller, George Macgregor 1919- 9-12R
Waller, Gregory A(lbert) 1950- 127
Waller, Irene Ellen 1928- 109
Waller, J(ames) Irvin 1944- CANR-14
Earlier sketch in CA 61-64
Waller, Jane (Ashton) 1944- 132
Waller, John Stanier 1917-1995 45-48
Obituary 147
Waller, Leslie 1923- CANR-2
Earlier sketch in CA 1-4R
See also SATA 20
Waller, P(hilip) J(ohn) 1946- 143
Waller, Peter Louis 1935- 106
Waller, Robert J(ames) 1939- 117
Waller, Robert James 1939- CANR-65
Earlier sketch in CA 147
See also DAM POP
Waller, Susan (Stewart) 1948- 139
Wallerstein, Immanuel 1930- CANR-49
Earlier sketches in CA 21-24R, CANR-9, 24
Wallerstein, Judith (Hannah) S(aretsky) 1921- .. 124
Brief entry 105
See also BEST 89:3
Wallerstein, Mitchel B(ruce) 1949- 105
Wallerstein, Robert S(olomon) 1921- CANR-12
Earlier sketch in CA 33-36R
Walley, Byron
See Card, Orson Scott
Walley, David G. 1945- CANR-37
Earlier sketch in CA 41-44R
Wallhauser, Henry T. 1930- 29-32R
Wallich, Henry C(hristopher) 1914-1988 ... CANR-6
Obituary 126
Earlier sketch in CA 1-4R
Wallich-Clifford, Anton 1923- 61-64
Wallig, Gaird (Elizabeth) 1942- 106
Wallin, Luke 1943- 130
Walling, William (Herbert) 1926- 103
Wallingford, Lee 1947- 142
Wallis, Charles L(angworthy) CANR-8
Earlier sketch in CA 5-8R
Wallis, Diz 1949- 145
See also SATA 77
Wallis, G. McDonald
See Campbell, Hope
Wallis, George A. 1892- 17-20R
Wallis, Hal B.
See Wallis, Harold Brent
Wallis, Harold Brent 1898(?)-1986 153
Obituary 120
Wallis, Jim 1948- CANR-50
Earlier sketch in CA 102
Wallis, Keith 1930- 25-28R
Wallis, Kenneth F(rank) 1938- CANR-24
Earlier sketch in CA 45-48
Wallis, Michael 1945- 139
Wallis, R(ichard) T(yrrell) 1941- 45-48
Wallis, Redmond Frankton 1933- 5-8R
Wallis, Robert 1900- CAP-2
Earlier sketch in CA 29-32
Wallis, Roy 1945- CANR-17
Earlier sketch in CA 97-100
Wallis, Ruth O(tis) S(awtell) 1895-1978 Obituary 73-76
Wallis, Velma 167
Wallis, W(ilson) Allen 1912- 41-44R
Wallmann, Jeffrey M(iner) 1941- CANR-35
Earlier sketches in CA 77-80, CANR-14
Wallmeyer, Dick
See Wallmeyer, Richard
Wallmeyer, Richard 1931- 133
Wallner, Alexandra 1946- CANR-13
Earlier sketch in CA 73-76
See also SATA 51, 98
See also SATA-Brief 41
Wallner, John C. 1945- .... MAICYA
See also SATA 10, 51
Wallop, (John) Douglass III 1920-1985 ... CANR-13
Obituary 115
Earlier sketch in CA 73-76
Wallop, Lucille Fletcher 1912- CANR-62
Earlier sketch in CA 13-16R
Wallower, Lucille CANR-9
Earlier sketch in CA 21-24R
See also SATA 11
Wallraff, Charles Fredric 1909- 1-4R
Walls, David Stuart 1941- CANR-14
Earlier sketch in CA 37-40R
Walls, Dwayne E(stes) 1932- CANR-14
Earlier sketch in CA 41-44R
Walls, H(enry) J(ames) 1907-1988 .... 9-12R
Obituary 126
Walls, Ian G(ascoigne) 1922- 104
Walls, Ronald 1920- 103
Walls, William J(acob) 1885-1975 81-84
Wallsten, Robert 1912- 101
Wallwork, Ernest (Edward) 1937- 41-44R
Walman, Jerome 1937- 125
Walmsley, Arnold Robert 1912- 41-44R
Walmsley, Buck
See Walmsley, Haines
Walmsley, (Ronald) Charles 1910-1983 Obituary 110
Walmsley, Haines 1930(?)-1983 Obituary 111
Walmsley, Jane 128
Walmsley, Leo 1892-1966 .... CAP-1
Earlier sketch in CA 11-12
Walmsley, Lewis C(alvin) 1897- 61-64
Walmsley, Robert 1905-1976 .... CAP-2
Earlier sketch in CA 29-32
Walmsley, Tom 1948- 126
Waln, Nora 1895-1964 Obituary 89-92
Walpole, Horace 1717-1797 .... DLB 39, 104
Walpole, Hugh (Seymour) 1884-1941 165
Brief entry 104
See also DLB 34
See also TCLC 5
Walpole, Ronald Noel 1903- 106
Walrath, Douglas Alan 1933- 120
Walrath, Jane Dwyer 1939- 97-100
Walrond, Eric (Derwent) 1898-1966 125
See also BW 1
See also DLB 51
Walschap, Gerard 1898- 103
Walsdorf, John J(oseph) 1941- 115
Walser, Martin 1927- CANR-46
Earlier sketches in CA 57-60, CANR-8
See also CLC 27
See also DLB 75, 124
Walser, Richard (Gaither) 1908- CANR-2
Earlier sketch in CA 5-8R
Walser, Robert 1878-1956 165
Brief entry 118
See also DLB 66
See also SSC 20
See also TCLC 18
Walsh, Ann 1942- .... SATA 62
Walsh, Annmarie Hauck 1938- 25-28R
Walsh, Bren(dan) 1921- 121
Walsh, Chad 1914-1991 .... CANR-6
Obituary 133
Earlier sketch in CA 1-4R
Walsh, Clune J(oseph), Jr. 1928- 114
Walsh, Des 1954- 116
Walsh, Donald Devenish 1903-1980 ...... CANR-3
Obituary 97-100
Earlier sketch in CA 49-52
Walsh, Edward J(oseph) 1937- 37-40R
Walsh, Edward N. 1925- 144
Walsh, Edward Warren 1930(?)-1986 Obituary . 118
Walsh, Elizabeth M(iller) 1937- 120
Walsh, Ellen Stoll 1942- 104
See also SATA 49, 99
Walsh, Ernest 1895-1926 165
Brief entry 109
See also DLB 4, 45
Walsh, George (Vincent) 1923- 109
Walsh, George (William) 1931- 118
Brief entry 114
Walsh, George B. 1947(?)-1989 Obituary 127
Walsh, George Johnston 1889-1981 ..... SATA 53
Walsh, Gillian Paton
See Paton Walsh, Gillian
Walsh, Jack 1919(?)-1984 Obituary 114
Walsh, James
See Robinson, Frank M(alcolm)
Walsh, James 1920-1986(?) Obituary 119
Walsh, James Edward 1891-1981 Obituary 104
Walsh, James J(erome) 1924- 9-12R
Walsh, James P(atrick) 1937- 111
Walsh, Jill Paton
See Paton Walsh, Gillian
See also AAYA 11
See also CLC 35
See also CLR 2
See also DLB 161
See also SAAS 3
Walsh, John (Dixon) 1927- 17-20R
Walsh, John Evangelist 1927- CANR-44
Earlier sketch in CA 85-88
Walsh, Justin E(arl) 1933- CANR-10
Earlier sketch in CA 25-28R
Walsh, Lawrence Edward 1912- 167
Walsh, M. M. B. 101
Walsh, Marcus 1947- CANR-41
Earlier sketch in CA 118
Walsh, Marnie
See Walsh, M. M. B.
Walsh, Mary Williams 1955- 136
Walsh, Maurice 1879-1964 133
Brief entry 124
Walsh, Michael J. 1937- 106
Walsh, Myles E(ugene) 1937- 109
Walsh, P(atrick) G(erard) 1923- CANR-52
Earlier sketches in CA 25-28R, CANR-28
Walsh, Patricia L(ouise) 1942- 109
Walsh, Raoul 1887-1980 Obituary 102
Walsh, (Walter) Richard 1923- 25-28R
Walsh, Richard 1941- CANR-46
Earlier sketch in CA 120
Walsh, Robb 1952- 167
Walsh, Robert 1784-1859 .... DLB 59
Walsh, Ronald A. 1934- 149
Walsh, Sheila 1928- 115
Walsh, (Michael) Stephen 1942- 37-40R
Walsh, (Richard) Taylor 1947- 73-76
Walsh, Thomas (Francis Morgan) 1908-1984 Obituary 114
Walsh, Timothy J(ames) 1927- 41-44R
Walsh, W(alter) Bruce 1936- 93-96
Walsh, Warren Bartlett 1909- CAP-2
Earlier sketch in CA 13-14
Walsh, William 1916-1996 .... CANR-11
Obituary 152
Earlier sketch in CA 65-68
Walsh, William B(ertalan) 1920-1996 ..... CANR-4
Obituary 155
Earlier sketch in CA 49-52
Walsh, William Henry 1913-1986 Obituary 119
Walshe, M(aurice) O'C(onnell) 1911- 5-8R
Walshe, Peter (Aubrey) 1934- 130
Walshe, R(obert) D(aniel) 1923- CANR-21
Earlier sketch in CA 104
Walsh Shepherd, Donna 1948- 146
See also SATA 78
Walster, Elaine Hatfield
See Hatfield, Elaine (Catherine)
Walster, G. William 1941- 85-88
Walston, Joseph
See Walston, Marie
Walston, Marie 1925- 41-44R
Walt, Lewis W(illiam) 1913-1989 .... 33-36R
Obituary 128
Waltari, Mika (Toimi) 1908-1979 .... 9-12R
Obituary 89-92
Waltch, Lilla M. 1932- 128
Walter, Bruno
See Schlesinger, Bruno Walter
Walter, Claire 1943- 81-84
Walter, Dorothy Blake 1908- CAP-1
Earlier sketch in CA 11-12
Walter, Elizabeth CANR-38
Earlier sketches in CA 97-100, CANR-17
Walter, Eugene (Ferdinand) 1927(?)-1998 ... 9-12R
Obituary 166
Walter, Eugene Victor 1925- 25-28R
Walter, Frances V. 1923- .... SATA 71
Walter, Gladys Mae 1901-1973 .... 41-44R
Walter, Hartmut 1940- 89-92
Walter, Ingo 1940- CANR-22
Earlier sketches in CA 17-20R, CANR-7
Walter, J(ulian) A(nthony) 1948- CANR-46
Earlier sketch in CA 120
Walter, John 1948- 134
Walter, Mildred Pitts 1922- 138
See also BW 2
See also CLR 15
See also JRDA
See also MAICYA
See also SAAS 12
See also SATA 69
See also SATA-Brief 45
Walter, Nancy
See Holmgren, Norah
Walter, Nina Willis 1900- 5-8R
Walter, Otis M. 1921- 5-8R
Walter, Richard 1944- 128
Walter, Robert H(enry) K(eamer, Jr.) 1922- ... 5-8R
Walter, Samuel 1916- 5-8R
Walter, Tony
See Walter, J(ulian) A(nthony)
Walter, Villiam Christian
See Andersen, Hans Christian
Walter, William Grey 1910-1977 103
Walters, A(lan) A(rthur) 1926- CANR-26
Earlier sketch in CA 29-32R
Walters, Anna L. 1946- 73-76
See also NNAL
Walters, Audrey 1929- .... SATA 18
Walters, Barbara 1931- 65-68
See also AITN 2
Walters, Basil L(eon) 1896-1975 Obituary 89-92
Walters, C(harles) Glenn 1929- 81-84
Walters, Chad
See Smith, Richard Rein
Walters, D(avid) Gareth 1948- 128
Walters, Derek 1936- 128
Walters, Dorothy 1928- 65-68
Walters, Dorothy Mae Wells 1924- CANR-2
Earlier sketch in CA 5-8R
Walters, Dottie
See Walters, Dorothy Mae Wells
Walters, Eleanor 1955- 108
Walters, Eric (Robert) 1957- .... SATA 99
Walters, Helen B. (?)-1987 133
Obituary 121
See also SATA-Obit 50
Walters, Henry 1848-1931 .... DLB 140
Walters, Hugh
See Hughes, Walter (Llewellyn)
Walters, J. Donald 1926- 132
Walters, Jack Edward 1896-1967 .... 5-8R
Obituary 134
Walters, James E. 1922- 144
Walters, James W. 1945- 144
Walters, Janet Lane 1936- 49-52
Walters, Jennifer Waelti
See Waelti-Walters, Jennifer
Walters, John Beauchamp 1906- CANR-6
Earlier sketch in CA 5-8R
Walters, John Bennett, Jr. 1912- 105
Walters, Kenneth D. 1941- 132
Walters, LeRoy (B., Jr.) 1940- 108
Walters, Minette 1949- 160
Walters, Nell
See Muse, Patricia (Alice)
Walters, Richard P(aul) 1935- 107
Walters, Rick
See Rowland, D(onald) S(ydney)
Walters, Robert Mark 1938- 69-72
Walters, Robert S(tephen) 1941- 29-32R
Walters, Ronald 139
See also BW 2
Walters, Ronald G(ordon) 1942- 85-88
Walters, Roy W(ashington) 1918- 93-96
Walters, Shelly
See Sheldon, Walter J.
Walters, Sister Annette 1910- 37-40R
Walters, Stanley D(avid) 1931- 53-56
Walters, Thomas N(oble) 1935- 65-68
Walters, Vernon A(nthony) 1917- 122
Waltham, Antony Clive 1942- CANR-51
Earlier sketches in CA 65-68, CANR-10, 26
Walther, Eric H(arry) 1960- 140
Walther, Fritz R(udolf) 1921- 132
Walther, R(ichard) E(rnest) 1921- 41-44R
Walther, Regis (Hills) 1917-1983 .... CANR-8
Obituary 111
Earlier sketch in CA 17-20R
Walther, Thomas A. 1950- 107
See also SATA 31
Walther, Tom
See Walther, Thomas A.
Walther don der Vogelweide c. 1170-c. 1230 .. DLB 138
Waltman, Jerold (Lloyd) 1945- 117
Waltman, John L. 1946- 120
Waltner, Elma 1912- 17-20R
See also SATA 40
Waltner, Willard H. 1909- .... SATA 40
Walton, Alfred Grant 1887-1970 .... CAP-1
Earlier sketch in CA 13-14
Walton, Bobbi Smith 1949- 137
Walton, Bryce 1918- 21-24R
Walton, Chelle Koster 1954- 167
Walton, Clarence C. 1915- CANR-3
Earlier sketch in CA 1-4R
Walton, Clyde C(ameron) 1925- 29-32R
Walton, Craig 1934- 41-44R
Walton, Donald William 1917- 112
Walton, Douglas N(eil) 1942- CANR-40
Earlier sketch in CA 117
Walton, Ed(ward Hazen) 1931- CANR-45
Earlier sketches in CA 105, CANR-22
Walton, Elizabeth Cheatham 5-8R
Walton, Evangeline
See Ensley, Evangeline
Walton, Fiona L. M. 1959- .... SATA 89
Walton, George (H.) 1904- 17-20R
Walton, Hanes, Jr. 1942- 41-44R
Walton, Henry J(ohn) 1924- CANR-35
Earlier sketch in CA 53-56
Walton, Izaak 1593-1683 ..... CDBLB Before 1660
See also DLB 151
Walton, J(ohn) Michael 1939- 117
Walton, John 1910- CANR-5
Earlier sketch in CA 1-4R

Walton, John (Nicholas) 1922- ... CANR-55
Earlier sketch in CA 127
Walton, John 1937- ... 89-92
Walton, John K(immons) 1948- ... 124
Walton, Kendall L(ewis) 1939- ... 136
Walton, Luke
See Henderson, William Charles
Walton, Mary 1941- ... 166
Walton, Ortiz Montaigne 1933- ... CANR-26
Earlier sketch in CA 45-48
Walton, Priscilla L. 1957- ... 150
Walton, Richard Eugene 1931- ... 81-84
Walton, Richard J. 1928- ... 25-28R
See also SATA 4
Walton, Rick 1957- ... 168
See also SATA 101
Walton, Robert Cutler 1932- ... 73-76
Walton, Ronald (Gordon) 1936- ... 65-68
Walton, Sam (Moore) 1920(?)-1992 ... 144
Walton, Su 1944- ... 25-28R
Walton, Vicki (Elizabeth) 1949- ... 65-68
Walton, W. Robert 1902- ... 69-72
Walton, William 1909- ... 125
Waltrip, Lela (Kingston) 1904- ... 5-8R
See also SATA 9
Waltrip, Mildred 1911- ... SATA 37
Waltrip, Robert
See Short, Robert Waltrip
Waltrip, Rufus (Charles) 1898- ... 5-8R
See also SATA 9
Waltz, Jon R(ichard) 1929- ... 17-20R
Waltz, Kenneth N(eal) 1924- ... 37-40R
Waltzer, Herbert 1930- ... 41-44R
Walvin, James 1942- ... CANR-37
Earlier sketches in CA 49-52, CANR-1, 17
Walvoord, John F(lipse) 1910- ... CANR-6
Earlier sketch in CA 9-12R
Walwik, Theodore J. 1937- ... 25-28R
Walworth, Alice
See Graham, Alice Walworth
Walworth, Arthur 1903- ... 21-24R
Walworth, Nancy Zinsser 1917- ... CANR-3
Earlier sketch in CA 5-8R
See also SATA 14
Walz, Audrey Boyers 1907(?)-1983 Obituary ... 109
Walz, Edgar 1914- ... 29-32R
Walz, Jay (Franklin) 1907-1991 ... 49-52
Obituary ... 135
Walz, Marjorie A. 1939- ... 153
Walzer, Michael (Laban) 1935- ... CANR-48
Earlier sketches in CA 37-40R, CANR-15
Walzer, Norman 1943- ... CANR-53
Earlier sketches in CA 111, CANR-29
Wambaugh, Joseph (Aloysius, Jr.) 1937- ... CANR-65
Earlier sketches in CA 33-36R, CANR-42
See also AITN 1
See also BEST 89:3
See also CLC 3, 18
See also DAM NOV, POP
See also DLB 6
See also DLBY 83
See also MTCW 1
Wamble, Gaston Hugh 1923- ... 5-8R
Wamble, Thelma 1916- Brief entry ... 106
Wamsley, Gary L(ee) 1935- ... CANR-3
Earlier sketch in CA 49-52
Wanamaker, A(llison) Temple 1918- ... 17-20R
Wand, (John) William (Charles) 1885-(?) ... 103
Wandel, Joseph 1918- ... 93-96
Wanderer, Zev W(illiam) 1932- ... 105
Wandesforde-Smith, Geoffrey Albert 1943- ... 29-32R
Wandor, Michelene (Dinah) 1940- ... 142
Wandro, Mark 1948- ... 106
Wandycz, Piotr Stefan 1923- ... CANR-2
Earlier sketch in CA 1-4R
Wang, An 1920-1990 ... 132
Wang, C(hing) H(sien) 1940- ... CANR-8
Earlier sketch in CA 61-64
Wang, (Fred) Fang Yu 1913-1997 ... 37-40R
Obituary ... 162
Wang, Hao 1921- ... 65-68
Wang, Hui-Ming 1922- ... 33-36R
Wang, J(en) Y(u) 1918- ... CANR-25
Earlier sketch in CA 45-48
Wang, John Ching-yu 1934- ... 41-44R
Wang, Julie C(aroline) 1947- ... 114
Wang, Leonard J(udah) 1926- ... 33-36R
Wang, Sabine E(isenberg) 1925- ... 37-40R
Wang, Yi Chu 1916- ... 61-64
Wang, Zhongshu 1925- ... CANR-41
Earlier sketch in CA 117
Wangenheim, Chris von
See von Wangenheim, Chris
Wangensteen, Owen Harding 1898-1981 ... 103
Wangensteen, Sarah (Anne) D(avidson) 1908- ... 120
Wangerin, Theodora Scharffenberg 1888- ... 5-8R
Wangerin, Walter, Jr. 1944- ... CANR-34
Earlier sketch in CA 108
Interview in ... 108
See also SATA 45, 98
See also SATA-Brief 37
Wangermann, Ernst 1925- ... 103
Wang Gungwu 1930- ... CANR-10
Earlier sketch in CA 65-68
Wang Wei 699(?)-761(?) ... PC 18
Wangyal, Geshe 1901(?)-1983 Obituary ... 108
Waniek, Marilyn Nelson 1946- ... CANR-15
Earlier sketch in CA 89-92
See also DLB 120
See also SATA 60
Wankowicz, Melchoir 1892(?)-1974 Obituary ... 53-56
Wanlass, Stanley G(len) 1941- ... 61-64
Wann, Kenneth D(ouglass) 1915- ... 5-8R
Wannamaker, Bruce
See Moncure, Jane Belk
Wannan, Bill
See Wannan, William Fielding
Wannan, William Fielding 1915- ... CANR-10
Earlier sketch in CA 21-24R
Wanniski, Jude 1936- ... 133
Wanrooy, Willem F(rederik) 1925- ... 118
Wansell, (Stephen) Geoffrey 1945- ... 143
Wanshel, Jeff(rey Mark) 1947- ... CANR-13
Earlier sketch in CA 57-60
Wantland, William C(harles) 1934- ... 111
Wantling, William 1933-1974 ... 105
Obituary ... 89-92
Waples, Douglas 1893-1978 Obituary ... 77-80
Wapshott, Nicholas (Henry) 1952- ... 135
Warbler, J. M.
See Cocagnac, Augustin Maurice(-Jean)
Warbridge, C. W.
See Woods, Clee
Warburg, Fredric (John) 1898-1981 ... 105
Warburg, James Paul 1896-1969 ... CAP-2
Obituary ... 25-28R
Earlier sketch in CA 21-22
Warburg, Otto (Heinrich) 1883-1970 ... 158
Warburg, Sandol Stoddard
See Stoddard, Sandol
See also SATA 14
Warburton, Amber Arthun
1898(?)-1976 Obituary ... 61-64
Warburton, Clark (Abram) 1896-1979 ... 73-76
Obituary ... 89-92
Warburton, Minnie 1949- ... 101
Warburton, William 1698-1779 ... DLB 104
Warch, Richard 1939- ... 105
Warcollier, Rene 1881-1962 Obituary ... 112
Ward, Aileen 1919- ... 5-8R
See also DLB 111
Ward, Alan Joseph 1936- ... 73-76
Ward, Allen M(ason) 1942- ... 89-92
Ward, Andrew (Spencer) 1946- ... 81-84
Ward, Anne G. 1932- ... 77-80
Ward, Artemus
See Browne, Charles Farrar
Ward, Arthur Henry Sarsfield 1883-1959 Brief entry ... 108
See also Rohmer, Sax
Ward, Barbara
See Jackson, Barbara (Ward)
Ward, Benedicta 1933- ... CANR-56
Earlier sketches in CA 65-68, CANR-12, 28
Ward, Brendan Noel 1947- ... 129
Ward, Burt 1945- ... 167
Ward, Charles D(uane) 1935- ... 33-36R
Ward, Charles Dexter
See Taylor, John (Alfred)
Ward, Charlotte
See Chesney, Marion
Ward, Chester 1907-1977 Obituary ... 69-72
Ward, Colin 1924- ... 57-60
Ward, Craig 1892-1979 Obituary ... 85-88
Ward, David 1938- ... 29-32R
Ward, Dennis 1924- ... 13-16R
Ward, Diane (Lee) 1956- ... 154
Ward, Don(ald G.) 1911- ... 17-20R
Ward, Donald 1909- ... 109
Ward, Donald 1930- ... 37-40R
Ward, Douglas Turner 1930- ... CANR-27
Earlier sketch in CA 81-84
See also BW 1
See also CLC 19
See also DLB 7, 38
Ward, E. D.
See Gorey, Edward (St. John)
Ward, Ed
See Stratemeyer, Edward L.
Ward, Ed(mund O.) 1948- ... 114
Ward, Elizabeth 1952- ... 110
Ward, Elizabeth Campbell 1936- ... 45-48
Ward, Elizabeth Honor (Shedden) 1926- ... 9-12R
Ward, Eric
See Ebon, Martin
Ward, Evelyn
See Everett-Green, Evelyn
Ward, Fred 1935- ... 85-88
Ward, Geoffrey C(hampion) 1940- ... 141
Ward, Harry Merrill 1929- ... CANR-2
Earlier sketch in CA 1-4R
Ward, Helen 1962- ... SATA 72
Ward, Herman Matthew 1914- ... CANR-39
Earlier sketches in CA 5-8R, CANR-2, 18
Ward, Hiley Henry 1929- ... CANR-2
Earlier sketch in CA 1-4R
Ward, J. Alan 1937- ... 114
Ward, J(oseph) Neville 1915- ... 77-80
Ward, J(ohn) P(owell) 1937- ... CANR-27
Earlier sketch in CA 109
Ward, James A(rthur) 1941- ... 49-52
Ward, James Myron 1919-1984 Obituary ... 112
Ward, Jay 1920-1989 ... SATA-Obit 63
Ward, John (Stanton) 1917- ... SATA 42
Ward, John M(anning) 1919- ... 21-24R
Ward, John Owen 1919- ... 13-16R
Ward, John Towers 1930-1987 ... CANR-7
Obituary ... 122
Earlier sketch in CA 109
Ward, John William 1922-1985 ... 5-8R
Obituary ... 116
Ward, Jonas
See Ard, William (Thomas)
and Cox, William R(obert)
and Garfield, Brian (Wynne)
Ward, Jonathon
See Stine, Whitney Ward
Ward, Joseph A(nthony, Jr.) 1931- ... 1-4R
Ward, Justine Bayard Cutting
1879-1975 Obituary ... 61-64
Ward, (John Stephen) Keith 1938- ... CANR-37
Earlier sketches in CA 29-32R, CANR-16
Ward, Ken 1949- ... 136
Ward, Lynd (Kendall) 1905-1985 ... 17-20R
Obituary ... 116
See also DLB 22
See also MAICYA
See also SATA 2, 36
See also SATA-Obit 42
Ward, Maisie 1889-1975 ... 69-72
Obituary ... 53-56
Ward, Margaret 1950- ... 168
Ward, Martha (Eads) ... 17-20R
See also SATA 5
Ward, Mary Augusta
See Ward, Mrs. Humphry
Ward, Mary Josephine
See Ward, Maisie
Ward, Matthew 1951(?)-1990 Obituary ... 132
Ward, Maurine Carr 1939- ... 157
Ward, Melanie
See Curtis, Richard (Alan)
and Lynch, Marilyn
Ward, Michael 1939- ... 37-40R
Ward, Mrs. Humphry 1851-1920 ... DLB 18
See also TCLC 55
Ward, Nathaniel 1578(?)-1652 ... DLB 24
Ward, Norman 1918- ... 41-44R
Ward, Olivia Tucker 1927- ... 57-60
Ward, Patricia A(nn) 1940- ... 57-60
Ward, Paul W. 1905-1976 Obituary ... 69-72
Ward, Pearl L(ewis) 1920- ... 107
Ward, Peter
See Faust, Frederick (Schiller)
Ward, (William) Peter 1943- ... 134
Ward, Philip 1938- ... CANR-56
Earlier sketches in CA 25-28R, CANR-12, 30
Ward, Philip C. 1932- ... 21-24R
Ward, R(ichard) H(eron) 1910-1969 ... CAP-1
Earlier sketch in CA 11-12
Ward, R. Patrick
See Holzapfel, Rudolf Patrick
Ward, Ralph Gerard 1933- ... 107
Ward, Ralph T(homas) 1927- ... 49-52
Ward, Richard J(oseph) 1921- ... 41-44R
Ward, Ritchie R(unyan) 1906- ... 29-32R
Ward, Robert 1943- ... CANR-44
Earlier sketch in CA 104
Ward, Robert E(rnest) 1927- ... 49-52
Ward, Robert Elmer 1937- ... 49-52
Ward, Ronald A(rthur) 1908- ... 53-56
Ward, Russel (Braddock) 1914- ... CANR-22
Earlier sketch in CA 103
Ward, Russell A(very) 1947- ... 110
Ward, Stephen R(alph) 1938- ... 65-68
Ward, Ted (Warren) 1930- ... CANR-16
Earlier sketch in CA 97-100
Ward, Theodora 1890-1974 ... CAP-2
Obituary ... 53-56
Earlier sketch in CA 33-36
Ward, Theodore (James) 1902-1983 ... 125
Obituary ... 109
See also BW
See also DLB 76
Ward, Tom
See Stratemeyer, Edward L.
Ward, Virgil S(cott) 1916- ... 1-4R
Ward, W. R. 1925- ... 146
Ward, Waylon O. 1942- ... 114
Ward, Willa
See Ward-Royster, Willa
Ward, William Alan Heaton
See Heaton-Ward, William Alan
Ward, William Arthur 1921- ... 29-32R
Ward, William B(ethea) 1912- ... 5-8R
Ward, William Ernest Frank 1900- ... CANR-19
Earlier sketches in CA 9-12R, CANR-4
Ward, William G. 1929- ... 21-24R
Ward, William R(eed) 1918- ... 61-64
Ward, Winfred O('Neil) 1933- ... 106
Warddel, Nora Helen
See Heron-Allen, Edward
Warde, Alan 1949- ... CANR-67
Earlier sketches in CA 112, CANR-31
Warde, William F.
See Novack, George (Edward)
Wardell, Dean
See Prince, J(ack) H(arvey)
Wardell, Phyl(lis Robinson) 1909- ... CAP-1
Earlier sketch in CA 11-12
Wardell, Steven (William) 1971- ... 148
Warden, G(erard) B(ryce) 1939- ... 29-32R
Warden, John 1936- ... 41-44R
Warden, Lewis (Christopher) 1913- ... 13-16R
Warden, Rob 1940- ... 142
Wardhaugh, Ronald 1932- ... 37-40R
Wardlaw, Lee 1955- ... 148
See also SATA 79
Wardle, David 1930- ... 69-72
Wardle, (John) Irving 1929- ... 77-80
Wardle, Lynn D(ennis) 1947- ... 109
Wardle, Ralph Martin 1909- ... CANR-5
Earlier sketch in CA 1-4R
See also DLB 103
Wardman, Alan (Edgar) 1926-1986 ... 77-80
Obituary ... 120
Wardman, Gordon 1948- ... 136
Ward-Perkins, John Bryan 1912-1981 ... 93-96
Obituary ... 108
Wardroper, John (Edmund) 1923- ... 29-32R
Wardropper, Bruce W(ear) 1919- ... 13-16R
Wardropper, Ian (Bruce) 1951- ... 137
Ward-Royster, Willa 1922- ... 162
Ward-Thomas, Evelyn Bridget Patricia Stephens
1928- ... CANR-58
Earlier sketches in CA 9-12R, CANR-5, 26
Wardwell, Allen 1935- ... 151
Ware, Caroline F. 1899-1990 Obituary ... 131
Ware, Cheryl 1963- ... 158
See also SATA 101
Ware, Ciji 1942- ... 103
Ware, Clyde 1932- ... 33-36R
Ware, Emma 1896(?)-1975 Obituary ... 57-60
Ware, George W(hitaker) 1902- ... 13-16R
Ware, Gilbert 1933- ... 65-68
Ware, Jane (O.) 1936- ... 133
Ware, Jean (Jones) 1914- ... CAP-1
Earlier sketch in CA 11-12
Ware, John
See Mabley, Edward (Howe)
Ware, Kallistos (Timothy Richard) 1934- ... CANR-24
Earlier sketches in CA 9-12R, CANR-7
Ware, Leon (Vernon) 1909-1976 ... CANR-2
Earlier sketch in CA 1-4R
See also SATA 4
Ware, Leonard 1900(?)-1976 Obituary ... 69-72
Ware, Monica
See Marsh, John
Ware, Runa Erwin ... CAP-2
Earlier sketch in CA 29-32
Ware, Timothy
See Ware, Kallistos (Timothy Richard)
Ware, W. Porter 1904- ... 105
Ware, Wallace
See Karp, David
Ware, William 1797-1852 ... DLB 1
Wareham, John 1940- ... 101
Warenski, Marilyn L(iston) 1931- ... 117
Warfel, Harry R(edcay) 1899-1971 ... CAP-1
Earlier sketch in CA 13-14
Warfield, (A.) Gallatin 1946- ... 140
Warfield, Gerald (Alexander) 1940- ... 117
Warford, Jeremy J(ames) 1938- ... 37-40R
Warga, Wayne 1937- ... 152
Wargo, Dan M. 1920- ... 21-24R
Warhaft, Sidney 1921- ... 61-64
Warhol, Andy 1928(?)-1987 ... CANR-34
Obituary ... 121
Earlier sketch in CA 89-92
See also AAYA 12
See also BEST 89:4
See also CLC 20
Warhol, Robyn R. 1955- ... 135
Wark, David M(ayer) 1934- ... 33-36R
Wark, Ian W(illiam) 1899- ... CAP-2
Earlier sketch in CA 29-32
Wark, Robert R(odger) 1924- ... CANR-8
Earlier sketch in CA 61-64
Wark, Wesley K. 1952- ... CANR-50
Earlier sketch in CA 123
Warkentin, Germaine (Therese) 1933- ... 109
Warkentin, John 1928- ... 9-12R
Warland, John
See Buchanan-Brown, John
Warlick, Ashley 1972- ... 154
Warlimont, Walter 1894- ... CAP-1
Earlier sketch in CA 13-16
Warlum, Michael Frank 1940- ... 37-40R
Warman, (William) Eric 1904- ... CAP-1
Earlier sketch in CA 13-14
Warman, Henry J(ohn) 1907-1982 ... 41-44R
Obituary ... 133
Warmbrand, Max 1896(?)-1976 Obituary ... 65-68
Warmbrunn, Werner 1920- ... 21-24R
Warmington, Brian Herbert 1924- ... 65-68
Warmington, E(ric) H(erbert) 1898-1987 ... 124
Warmington, William Allan 1922- ... 5-8R
Warmke, Roman F. 1929- ... CANR-9
Earlier sketch in CA 17-20R
Warnath, Charles F. 1925- ... 37-40R
Warne, Clinton L. 1921- ... 13-16R
Warne, Colston Estey 1900-1987 Obituary ... 122
Warne, Randi R(uth) 1952- ... 152
Warne, William E(lmo) 1905-1996 ... 41-44R
Obituary ... 151
Warneke, Sara ... 167
Warner, Alan 1912- ... 104
Warner, Anne 1869-1913 ... DLB 202
Warner, B. F.
See Bowers, Warner Fremont
Warner, Bob
See Warner, Robert
Warner, Charles Dudley 1829-1900 ... DLB 64
Warner, Daniel 1946- ... 141
Warner, Daniel S(umner) 1906-1983 ... CANR-16
Earlier sketch in CA 1-4R
Warner, Deborah Jean 1941- ... 108
Warner, Denis Ashton 1917- ... CANR-3
Earlier sketch in CA 5-8R
Warner, Edythe Records 1916-1980 ... 5-8R
Obituary ... 134
Warner, Emily S(mith)
1902(?)-1980 Obituary ... 97-100
Warner, Esther S.
See Dendel, Esther (Sietmann Warner)
Warner, Francis (Robert le Plastrier) 1937- ...
CANR-11
Earlier sketch in CA 53-56
See also CLC 14
Warner, Frank
See Richardson, Gladwell
Warner, Frank A. ... CANR-26
Earlier sketches in CAP-2, CA 19-20
See also SATA 1, 67
Warner, Gary 1936- ... 21-24R
Warner, (George) Geoffrey John 1923- ... 1-4R
Warner, Gertrude Chandler 1890-1979 ... CANR-3
Earlier sketch in CA 1-4R
See also SATA 9
See also SATA-Obit 73
Warner, Glen 1947- ... CANR-46
Earlier sketch in CA 121

Warner, H(oyt) Landon 1911- 13-16R
Warner, Harry, Jr. 1922- 29-32R
Warner, J(ohn) F. 1929- 142
See also SATA 75
Warner, Jack 1896-1981 Obituary 108
Warner, Jack L(eonard) 1892-1978 Obituary 108
Warner, James A(loysius) 1918- CANR-24
Earlier sketch in CA 45-48
Warner, John Harley 1953- 127
Warner, Judith 1965- 142
Warner, Ken(neth Wilson, Jr.) 1928- CANR-10
Earlier sketch in CA 65-68
Warner, Kenneth (Lewis) 1915- CAP-1
Earlier sketch in CA 9-10
Warner, Langdon 1881-1955 Brief entry 112
Warner, Lucien (Hynes) 1900-1963 Obituary 112
Warner, Lucille Schulberg CANR-11
Earlier sketch in CA 69-72
See also SATA 30
Warner, Malcolm 1953- 167
Warner, Margaret
See Humphreys, Margaret
Warner, Marina 1946- CANR-55
Earlier sketches in CA 65-68, CANR-21
See also CLC 59
See also DLB 194
Warner, Martin 1940- 137
Warner, Matt
See Fichter, George S.
Warner, Oliver (Martin Wilson) 1903-1976 CANR-3
Obituary 69-72
Earlier sketch in CA 1-4R
See also SATA 29
Warner, Penny 1947- 165
Warner, Philip 1914- CANR-40
Earlier sketches in CA 101, CANR-18
Warner, Rex (Ernest) 1905-1986 89-92
Obituary 119
See also CLC 45
See also DLB 15
Warner, Richard 1943- 120
Warner, Robert 1905- 53-56
Warner, Robert M(ark) 1927- CANR-7
Earlier sketch in CA 9-12R
Warner, Sam Bass, Jr. 1928- CANR-39
Earlier sketches in CA 5-8R, CANR-2, 17
Warner, Seth 1927- 53-56
Warner, Sharon Oard 1952- 138
Warner, Susan (Bogert) 1819-1885 DLB 3, 42
Warner, Sylvia (Constance) Ashton
See Ashton-Warner, Sylvia (Constance)
Warner, Sylvia Townsend 1893-1978 CANR-60
Obituary 77-80
Earlier sketches in CA 61-64, CANR-16
See also CLC 7, 19
See also DLB 34, 139
See also MTCW 1
See also SSC 23
Warner, Val 1946- CANR-23
Earlier sketch in CA 49-52
Warner, Virginia
See Brodine, Virginia Warner
Warner, W(illiam) Lloyd 1898-1970 CANR-2
Obituary 29-32R
Earlier sketch in CA 1-4R
Warner, Wayne E(arl) 1933- CANR-3
Earlier sketch in CA 49-52
Warner, William 1558-1609 DLB 172
Warner, William W(hitesides) 1920- 134
Brief entry 114
Warner-Crozetti, R(uth G.) 1913- 101
Warnick, Barbara 1946- 120
Warnock, G(eoffrey) J(ames) 1923-1995 21-24R
Obituary 150
Warnock, Mary (Wilson) 1924- CANR-8
Earlier sketch in CA 5-8R
Warr, Bertram 1917-1943 DLB 88
Warr, Peter B(ryan) 1937- 25-28R
Warrack, Graeme Matthew
1913-1985 Obituary 115
Warrack, John 1928- CANR-5
Earlier sketch in CA 13-16R
Warre, Michael 1922-1987 Obituary 121
Warren, Andrea 1946- 165
Warren, Andrea 1946- SATA 98
Warren, Andrew
See Tute, Warren (Stanley)
Warren, Austin 1899-1986 17-20R
Obituary 120
Warren, Betsy
See Warren, Elizabeth Avery
Warren, Bill 1943- 118
Warren, Billy
See Warren, William Stephen
Warren, Cathy 1951- 159
See also SATA 62
See also SATA-Brief 46
Warren, Charles 1948- 147
Warren, Charles Marquis
1913(?)-1990 Obituary 132
Warren, Dave
See Wiersbe, Warren W(endell)
Warren, David 1943- 77-80
Warren, Donald Irwin 1935-1997 CANR-1
Obituary 158
Earlier sketch in CA 45-48
Warren, Donald R. 1933- 111
Warren, Doug(las) 1935- CANR-34
Earlier sketch in CA 61-64
Warren, E(ugene) H(oward), Jr. 1943- 111
Warren, Earl 1891-1974 123
Obituary 49-52
Warren, Elizabeth
See Supraner, Robyn
Warren, Elizabeth Avery 1916- CANR-8
Earlier sketch in CA 5-8R
See also SATA 46
See also SATA-Brief 38
Warren, (Francis) Eugene 1941- CANR-1
Earlier sketch in CA 49-52
Warren, Frank A. III 1933- Brief entry 115
Warren, Gordon Harris 1944- 114
Warren, Harold Ostrander, Jr.
1910-1985 Obituary 116
Warren, Harris G(aylord) 1906- CANR-5
Earlier sketch in CA 1-4R
Warren, Harry
See Guaragna, Salvatore
Warren, James E(dward), Jr. 1908- CANR-24
Earlier sketch in CA 21-24R
Warren, James Francis 1942- 146
Warren, James Hugo, Jr.
1928(?)-1983 Obituary 110
Warren, James Vaughn 1915-1990 Obituary 130
Warren, Jefferson T(rowbridge) 1912- 41-44R
Warren, (William) John 1937- 138
Warren, John Byrne Leicester
See De Tabley, Lord
Warren, Joyce W(illiams) 1935- 77-80
See also SATA 18
Warren, Karen J. 1947- 168
Warren, Kenneth 1931- 109
Warren, Kenneth W. 1957- 147
Warren, Lansing 1894-1987 Obituary 124
Warren, Lella 1899-1982 Obituary 113
See also DLBY 83
Warren, Louis Austin 1885-1983 CANR-21
Obituary 110
Earlier sketch in CA 5-8R
Warren, Louise 1909(?)-1981 Obituary 104
Warren, Lucian (Crissey) 1913-1988 101
Obituary 126
Warren, Mary Bondurant 1930- CANR-52
Earlier sketches in CA 73-76, CANR-12, 27
Warren, Mary Douglas
See Greig, Maysie
Warren, Mary Phraner 1929- CANR-5
Earlier sketch in CA 53-56
See also SATA 10
Warren, Matthew Madison 1907-1986 Obituary 119
Warren, Mercy Otis 1728-1814 DLB 31, 200
Warren, Michael 1935- 138
Warren, Patricia Nell 1936- CANR-1
Earlier sketch in CA 45-48
Warren, Peter Whitson 1941- CANR-5
Earlier sketch in CA 53-56
Warren, Richard (Andrew) 1961- 146
Warren, Richard M. 1925- 112
Warren, Robert Penn 1905-1989 CANR-47
Obituary 129
Earlier sketches in CA 13-16R, CANR-10
Interview in CANR-10
See also AITN 1
See also CDALB 1968-1988
See also CLC 1, 4, 6, 8, 10, 13, 18, 39, 53, 59
See also DA
See also DAB
See also DAC
See also DAM MST, NOV, POET
See also DLB 2, 48, 152
See also DLBY 80, 89
See also MTCW 1
See also SATA 46
See also SATA-Obit 63
See also SSC 4
See also WLC
Warren, Roland L(eslie) 1915- CANR-51
Earlier sketches in CA 57-60, CANR-10, 26
Warren, Rosanna 1953- 145
Warren, Samuel 1807-1877 DLB 190
Warren, Sandra K. 1944- 138
Warren, Scott S. 1957- SATA 79
Warren, Sidney 1916- 25-28R
Warren, Thomas (Bratton) 1920- 103
Warren, Thomas L(eo) 1937- 111
Warren, Vernon
See Chapman, G(eorge) W(arren) Vernon
Warren, Virginia Burgess 1913- 13-16R
Warren, W(ilfred) Lewis 1929- CANR-21
Earlier sketch in CA 1-4R
Warren, W(illiam) Preston 1901- 37-40R
Warren, William Stephen 1882-1968 CAP-2
Earlier sketch in CA 21-22
See also SATA 9
Warrender, James Howard
1922-1985 Obituary 116
Warrick, Patricia Scott 1925- CANR-25
Earlier sketches in CA 61-64, CANR-8
See also SATA 35
Warrigal, Jack
See Furphy, Joseph
Warriner, Charles K(ing) 1920- 41-44R
Warriner, John 1907(?)-1987 Obituary 123
See also SATA-Obit 53
Warrner, Thomas W(endell) 1955- 118
Warry, J(ohn) G(ibson) 1916- 5-8R
Warsaw, Irene CAP-1
Earlier sketch in CA 13-16
Warsh
See Warshaw, Jerry
Warsh, David (Lewis) 1944- 118
Warsh, Lewis 1944- CANR-24
Earlier sketches in CA 61-64, CANR-9
Warshaw, Jerry 1929- CANR-14
Earlier sketch in CA 37-40R
See also SATA 30
Warshaw, Leon J(oseph) 1917- 107
Warshaw, Mary 1931- SATA 89
Warshofsky, Fred 1931- CANR-45
Earlier sketch in CA 9-12R
See also SATA 24
Warshofsky, Isaac
See Singer, Isaac Bashevis
Wartels, Nat(han) 1902-1990 Obituary 130
Warth, Robert D(ouglas) 1921- 9-12R
Wartofsky, Marx W(illiam) 1928-1997 41-44R
Obituary 157
Wartofsky, (William) Victor 1931- 29-32R
Warton, Joseph 1722-1800 DLB 104, 109
Warton, Thomas 1728-1790 DAM POET
See also DLB 104, 109
Wartski, Maureen (Ann Crane) 1940- 89-92
See also SATA 50
See also SATA-Brief 37
Waruk, Kona
See Harris, (Theodore) Wilson
Warung, Price 1855-1911 TCLC 45
Warwick, Alan R(oss) 1900-1973 112
See also SATA 42
Warwick, Christopher 1949- 110
Warwick, Dennis 1930- 73-76
Warwick, Dolores
See Frese, Dolores Warwick
Warwick, Donald P(hillip) 1934- 118
Warwick, Granville
See Griffith, D(avid Lewelyn) W(ark)
Warwick, Jack 1930- 29-32R
Warwick, James 1894(?)-1983 Obituary 110
Warwick, Jarvis
See Garner, Hugh
Warwick, Ray 1911(?)-1983 Obituary 109
Warwick, Roger 1912-1991 109
Obituary 135
Warzeski, Walter C. 1929- 37-40R
Wasby, Stephen L(ewis) 1937- 139
Wa-Sha-Quon-Asin
See Belaney, Archibald Stansfeld
Wa-sha-quon-asin
See Belaney, Archibald Stansfeld
Washburn, (Henry) Bradford (Jr.) 1910- CANR-3
Earlier sketch in CA 49-52
See also SATA 38
Washburn, Charles 1890(?)-1972 Obituary 104
Washburn, Dorothy K(oster) 1945- CANR-24
Earlier sketch in CA 106
Washburn, Jan(ice) 1926- 93-96
See also SATA 63
Washburn, Mark 1948- 77-80
Washburn, O(swell) A(aron) 1914- 57-60
Washburn, Patrick S(cott) 1941- 145
Washburn, Sherwood L(arned) 1911- Brief
entry 105
Washburn, Stan 1943- 146
Washburn, Wilcomb Edward 1925-1997 41-44R
Obituary 156
Washburne, Carleton W(olsey) 1889- CAP-1
Earlier sketch in CA 13-16
Washburne, Carolyn Kott 1944- 151
See also SATA 86
Washburne, Heluiz Chandler 1892-1970 CAP-1
Obituary 104
Earlier sketch in CA 11-12
See also SATA 10
See also SATA-Obit 26
Washington, Alex
See Harris, Mark
Washington, Booker T(aliaferro) 1856-1915 125
Brief entry 114
See also BLC 3
See also BW 1
See also DAM MULT
See also SATA 28
See also TCLC 10
Washington, Chester Lloyd
1902-1983 Obituary 110
Washington, Donna L. 1967- 166
See also SATA 98
Washington, George 1732-1799 DLB 31
Washington, Gladys J(oseph) 1931- 29-32R
Washington, Harold R(obert) 1935- 112
Washington, Ida Harrison 1924- CANR-35
Earlier sketch in CA 107
Washington, James Melvin 1948-1997 149
Obituary 158
Washington, Joseph R(eed), Jr. 1930- 9-12R
Washington, (Catherine) Marguerite Beauchamp
1892-1972 CAP-1
Earlier sketch in CA 9-10
Washington, Mary Helen 1941- CANR-51
Earlier sketches in CA 65-68, CANR-26
See also BW 2
Washington, Pat Beauchamp
See Washington, (Catherine) Marguerite
Beauchamp
Washington, Warren M(orton) 1936- 168
Washton, Nathan S(eymour) 1916- 53-56
Wasiolek, Edward 1924- CANR-6
Earlier sketch in CA 1-4R
Waskin, Yvonne 1923- 21-24R
Waskow, Arthur I(rwin) 1933- CANR-4
Earlier sketch in CA 5-8R
Wasley, Robert S(echrist) 1918- 17-20R
Wasmuth, William J. 1925- CANR-24
Earlier sketch in CA 45-48
Wason, Betty
See Wason, Elizabeth
Wason, Elizabeth 1912- CANR-2
Earlier sketch in CA 1-4R
Wason, P(eter) C(athcart) 1924- 45-48
Wasow, Mona 1933- 110
Wass, Sir Douglas (William Gretton) 1923- 138
Wassenbergh, Henri Abraham 1924- 21-24R
Wasser, Henry H. 1919- CANR-8
Earlier sketch in CA 21-24R
Wasserfall, Adel 1918- CANR-6
Earlier sketch in CA 1-4R
Wasserman, Aaron O(sias) 1927- 53-56
Wasserman, Burton 1929- 53-56
Wasserman, Dale 1917- 49-52
Wasserman, Earl R(eeves) 1913-1973 CAP-2
Earlier sketch in CA 17-18
Wasserman, Gary 1944- 69-72
Wasserman, Harriet 167
Wasserman, Harvey 1945- CANR-27
Earlier sketch in CA 45-48
Wasserman, Jack 1921- 61-64
Wasserman, John L. 1938- 77-80
Wasserman, Mark 1946- CANR-56
Earlier sketch in CA 125
Wasserman, Max Judd 1895-1977 CANR-4
Earlier sketch in CA 5-8R
Wasserman, Paul 1924- CANR-25
Earlier sketches in CA 1-4R, CANR-1
Wasserman, Pauline 1943- CANR-24
Earlier sketch in CA 110
Wasserman, Selma (Ginsberg) 1929- 5-8R
Wasserman, Sheldon 1940-1992 CANR-24
Obituary 137
Earlier sketches in CA 65-68, CANR-9
Wassermann, (Karl) Jakob 1873-1934 Brief
entry 104
See also DLB 66
See also TCLC 6
Wassermann, (Karl) Jakob 1873-1934 163
Wasserstein, Abraham 1921- 109
Wasserstein, Bernard (Mano Julius) 1948- 143
Wasserstein, Bruce 1947- 37-40R
Wasserstein, Susan 1952- 107
Wasserstein, Wendy 1950- CANR-53
Brief entry 121
Earlier sketch in CA 129
Interview in 129
See also CABS 3
See also CLC 32, 59, 90
See also DAM DRAM
See also DC 4
See also SATA 94
Wasserstrom, Richard Alan 1936- CANR-6
Earlier sketch in CA 1-4R
Wasserstrom, (Jacob) William 1922-1985 9-12R
Obituary 115
Wassersug, Joseph D. 1912- 17-20R
Wassil, Aly 1930- 17-20R
Wassmer, Arthur C(harles) 1947- 103
Wassmo, Herbjorg 1942- 164
Wassner, Selig O. 1923- 25-28R
Wasson, Ben 1899(?)-1982 Obituary 114
Wasson, Chester R(eynolds) 1906- CANR-10
Earlier sketch in CA 13-16R
Wasson, David Atwood 1823-1887 DLB 1
Wasson, Donald 1914(?)-1976 Obituary 69-72
Wasson, John M. 1928- 45-48
Wasson, R(obert) Gordon 1898-1986 153
Brief entry 116
Wasti, Syed R(azi) 1929- CANR-7
Earlier sketch in CA 13-16R
Waswo, Richard 1939- 53-56
Watada, Terry 1951- 164
Watanabe, Hitoshi 1919- 73-76
Watanabe, Ruth T(aiko) 1916- 37-40R
Watanabe, Shigeo 1928- CANR-45
Earlier sketch in CA 112
See also CLR 8
See also MAICYA
See also SATA 39
See also SATA-Brief 32
Waten, Judah Leon 1911- 101
Water, Silas
See Loomis, Noel M(iller)
Waterfield, Gordon 1903-1987 61-64
Obituary 124
Waterfield, Robin (Everard) 1914- 49-52
Waterford, Van
See Wanrooy, Willem F(rederik)
Waterhouse, Charles 1924- 29-32R
Waterhouse, Ellis K(irkham) 1905-1985 65-68
Obituary 117
Waterhouse, Keith (Spencer) 1929- CANR-67
Earlier sketches in CA 5-8R, CANR-38
See also CLC 47
See also DLB 13, 15
See also MTCW 1
Waterhouse, Larry G(ene) 1944- 37-40R
Waterhouse, Roger 1940- 129
Waterlow, Charlotte 1915- 25-28R
Waterman, Andrew (John) 1940- CANR-57
Earlier sketches in CA 109, CANR-31
See also DLB 40
Waterman, Arthur E. 1926- 17-20R
Waterman, Bic
See Joseph, Stephen M.
Waterman, Cary (Martha) 1942- 103
Waterman, Charles F(rederick) 1913- 49-52
Waterman, Guy 1932- 97-100
Waterman, John Thomas 1918- CANR-8
Earlier sketch in CA 5-8R
Waterman, Jonathan 1956- 151
Waterman, Laura 1939- 97-100
Waterman, Leroy 1875-1972 CAP-1
Obituary 33-36R
Earlier sketch in CA 19-20
Waterman, Margaret 1909- 37-40R
Waterman, Richard Alan 1914-1971 Obituary 111
Watermeier, Daniel J(ude) 1940- 73-76
Water Rat
See Jones, Stephen (Phillip)
Waters, Bob 1921(?)-1987 Obituary 122
Waters, Brian Power
See Power-Waters, Brian

Waters, Catherine C.
See Cash, Catherine
Waters, Chocolate 1949- 77-80
Waters, Chris
See Waters, Harold A(rthur)
Waters, D(avid) W(atkin) 1911- 25-28R
Waters, Enoch P. 1910(?)-1987 134
Obituary 122
Waters, Ethel 1896-1977 81-84
Obituary 73-76
Waters, Frank (Joseph) 1902-1995 .... CANR-63
Obituary 149
Earlier sketches in CA 5-8R, CANR-3, 18
See also CAAS 13
See also CLC 88
See also DLBY 86
Waters, Harold A(rthur) 1926- 53-56
Waters, John 1946- 130
Brief entry 126
Interview in 130
See also AAYA 16
Waters, John F(rederick) 1930- CANR-46
Earlier sketches in CA 37-40R, CANR-23
See also SATA 4
Waters, K(enneth) H(ugh) 1912- 120
Waters, Marianne
See Waters, Chocolate
Waters, Mary-Alice 1942- CANR-9
Earlier sketch in CA 61-64
Waters, Michael 1949- CANR-56
Earlier sketches in CA 65-68, CANR-10, 27
See also DLB 120
Waters, Roger 1944- .... CLC 35
Waters, Thomas F(rank) 1926- 81-84
Waters, Tony 1958- 142
See also SATA 75
Waters, William R(oland) 1920- 49-52
Waterston, Albert 1907- CAP-1
Earlier sketch in CA 13-14
Waterston, Alisse 1951- 146
Waterston, Barbara Johns 1940- 25-28R
Waterston, (Margaret) Elizabeth (Hillman) 1922- 69-72
Waterton, Betty (Marie) 1923- CANR-56
Earlier sketches in CA 111, CANR-28
See also SATA 37, 99
See also SATA-Brief 34
Wathen, Richard B. 1917- 37-40R
Wathern, Peter 1947- 105
Watjen, Carolyn L. T. 85-88
Watkin, David (John) 1941- CANR-51
Earlier sketches in CA 29-32R, CANR-26
Watkin, Edward Ingram 1888-1981 Obituary 103
Watkin, Lawrence Edward 1901- 81-84
Watkins, A(rthur) M(artin) 1924- CANR-7
Earlier sketch in CA 9-12R
Watkins, Alan (Rhun) 1933- 104
Watkins, Arthur Rich 1916- 41-44R
Watkins, Arthur Thomas Levi 1907-1965 .... 5-8R
Watkins, Arthur V(ivian) 1886-1973 Obituary 111
Watkins, Evan Paul 1946- 104
Watkins, Floyd C. 1920- CANR-18
Earlier sketches in CA 1-4R, CANR-2
Watkins, Frances Ellen
See Harper, Frances Ellen Watkins
Watkins, Gerrold
See Malzberg, Barry N(athaniel)
Watkins, Glenn (Elson) 1927- Brief entry 117
Watkins, Gloria 1955(?)- 143
See also hooks, bell
See also BW 2
Watkins, Gordon R(onald) 1930- 37-40R
Watkins, Grace F. 1927- 21-24R
Watkins, Graham 1944- 150
Watkins, Gwen(doline Mary) 1923- 116
Watkins, J(ohn) W(illiam) N(evill) 1924- 21-24R
Watkins, Jane 1929- 77-80
Watkins, Joan C.
See Casale, Joan T(herese)
Watkins, John C(umming), Jr. 1935- 113
Watkins, John G(oodrich) 1913- CANR-38
Earlier sketches in CA 1-4R, CANR-1, 17
Watkins, Keith 1931- 106
Watkins, Lois 1930- .... SATA 88
Watkins, Mark Hanna 1903-1976 Obituary 65-68
Watkins, Mary M. 1950- CANR-44
Earlier sketches in CA 104, CANR-20
Watkins, Mel 1940- 89-92
Watkins, Nicholas 1946- 148
Watkins, Paul 1964- CANR-62
Earlier sketch in CA 132
See also CLC 55
Watkins, Peter 1934- 109
See also SATA 66
Watkins, Ralph J(ames) 1896-1984 45-48
Obituary 113
Watkins, (Arthur) Ronald (Dare) 1904- 53-56
Watkins, Ronald J(oseph) 1945- 133
Watkins, Stephen Hulme 1954- 165
Watkins, Steve
See Watkins, Stephen Hulme
Watkins, T(homas) H(enry) 1936- CANR-57
Earlier sketches in CA 37-40R, CANR-14, 31
Watkins, Tobias 1780-1855 .... DLB 73
Watkins, Vernon Phillips 1906-1967 .... CAP-1
Obituary 25-28R
Earlier sketch in CA 9-10
See also CLC 43
See also DLB 20
Watkins, William John 1942- CANR-58
Earlier sketches in CA 41-44R, CANR-56
Watkins, Yoko Kawashima 1933- 158
See also SATA 93
Watkinson, John 1950- 143
Watkinson, Sandra
See Haarsager, Sandra (L.)
Watkinson, Valerie
See Elliston, Valerie Mae (Watkinson)
Watkins-Pitchford, Denys James 1905-1990 .... CANR-38
Obituary 132
Earlier sketches in CA 9-12R, CANR-4
See also SAAS 4
See also SATA 6, 87
See also SATA-Obit 66
Watkyn, Arthur
See Watkins, Arthur Thomas Levi
Watland, Charles D(unton) 1913-1972 .... CAP-2
Earlier sketch in CA 25-28
Watling, James 1933- .... SATA 67
Watlington, Patricia (Sue) 1933- 37-40R
Watmough, David 1926- CANR-33
Earlier sketches in CA 85-88, CANR-15
See also DLB 53
Watney, John B(asil) 1915-1995 .... CANR-5
Obituary 148
Earlier sketch in CA 9-12R
Watney, Sanders (?)-1983 Obituary 109
Watrous, James Scales 1908- 141
Watrous, Livingston Vance 1943- 165
Watson, (John Hugh) Adam 1914- CANR-17
Earlier sketch in CA 25-28R
Watson, Alan
See Watson, William Alexander Jardine
Watson, Alan D(ouglas) 1942- CANR-6
Earlier sketch in CA 57-60
Watson, Aldren A(uld) 1917- CANR-39
Earlier sketches in CA 81-84, CANR-4
See also SATA 42
See also SATA-Brief 36
Watson, Amy Zakrzewski 1965- 143
See also SATA 76
Watson, Andrew Samuel 1920- 45-48
Watson, Anthony I. 1926-1990 Obituary 132
Watson, B. S.
See Teitelbaum, Michael
Watson, Barbara Bellow 77-80
Watson, Ben 1956- 146
Watson, Bernard B(ennett) 1911-1977 Obituary 69-72
Watson, Billy 1938- 77-80
Watson, Burton (DeWitt) 1925- CANR-18
Earlier sketches in CA 5-8R, CANR-3
Watson, Carol 1949- 146
See also SATA 78
Watson, Charles N(elles, Jr.) 1939- 113
Watson, Charles S(t. Denis), Jr. 1934- 61-64
Watson, Clarissa 69-72
Watson, Clyde 1947- CANR-39
Earlier sketches in CA 49-52, CANR-4
See also CLR 3
See also MAICYA
See also SATA 5, 68
Watson, Colin 1920-1983 .... CANR-60
Obituary 108
Earlier sketches in CA 1-4R, CANR-2
Watson, Cynthia 1957- 137
Watson, David 1934- CANR-49
Earlier sketches in CA 45-48, CANR-24
Watson, David Christopher Knight 1934(?)-1984 Obituary 112
Watson, David Robin 1935- 109
Watson, Derek 1948- 129
Watson, Donald Stevenson 1909- CAP-1
Earlier sketch in CA 13-14
Watson, E(lliot) L(ovegood) Grant 1885-1970 .... CAP-1
Earlier sketch in CA 11-12
Watson, Elaine 1921- 115
Watson, Ernest W(illiam) 1884-1969 .... 5-8R
Obituary 134
Watson, Eunice L. 1932- 65-68
Watson, F. J. B.
See Watson, Francis John Bagott
Watson, Fletcher Guard (Jr.) 1912-1997 .... 5-8R
Obituary 158
Watson, Francis (Leslie) 1907-1988 Obituary 127
Watson, Francis John Bagott 1907- Brief entry 116
Watson, Francis M(arion) 1921- 105
Watson, Frank
See Ames, Francis H.
Watson, Gayle Hudgens
See Hudgens, A(lice) Gayle
Watson, George (Grimes) 1927- CANR-42
Earlier sketches in CA 13-16R, CANR-5, 20
Watson, George (Henry) 1936- 77-80
Watson, Goodwin 1899(?)-1976 Obituary 69-72
Watson, Graham (Angus) 1913- 104
Watson, Harold M. 1924- 37-40R
Watson, Harry Legare 1949- 111
Watson, Helen Orr 1892-1978 .... 5-8R
Obituary 77-80
See also SATA-Obit 24
Watson, (George) Hugh (Nicholas) Seton
See Seton-Watson, (George) Hugh (Nicholas)
Watson, Ian 1943- CANR-54
Earlier sketches in CA 61-64, CANR-24
Watson, Irving S.
See Mencken, H(enry) L(ouis)
Watson, J. R. 1934- CANR-39
Earlier sketches in CA 97-100, CANR-18
Watson, J(ohn) Steven 1916- 5-8R
Watson, J(ames) Wreford 1915-1990 .... CANR-19
Obituary 132
Earlier sketch in CA 25-28R
Watson, Jack Brierley 1927- 104
Watson, James 1936- CANR-4
Earlier sketch in CA 53-56
See also SATA 10
Watson, James B(ennett) 1918- 41-44R
Watson, James D(ewey) 1928- CANR-46
Earlier sketch in CA 25-28R
Watson, James Gray 1939- 29-32R
Watson, Jane Werner 1915- CANR-8
Earlier sketch in CA 5-8R
See also SATA 3, 54
Watson, Janet Lynch
See Lynch-Watson, Janet
Watson, Jean 1936- CANR-41
Earlier sketches in CA 89-92, CANR-16
Watson, John 1850-1907 .... DLB 156
Watson, John A(rthur) F(ergus) 1903- 65-68
Watson, John H.
See Farmer, Philip Jose
Watson, Julia 1943- CANR-15
Earlier sketch in CA 41-44R
Watson, Ken 1925(?)-1984 Obituary 114
Watson, Larry 1947- 160
Watson, Leland Hale 1926-1989 Obituary 130
Watson, Lyall 1939- CANR-62
Earlier sketches in CA 57-60, CANR-8, 24
Watson, Margaret Goodrich 1913- 13-16R
Watson, Mark Skinner 1887-1966 Obituary 89-92
Watson, Mary Ann 1944- 144
Watson, Mary Gordon
See Gordon-Watson, Mary
Watson, Michael (C.) 1958- 161
Watson, N. Cameron 1955- .... SATA 81
Watson, Nan Marriott
See Marriott-Watson, Nan
Watson, Nancy Dingman CANR-4
Earlier sketch in CA 49-52
See also SATA 32
Watson, O(scar) Michael 1936- 33-36R
Watson, Patricia Seets 1930- 121
Watson, Patrick 1929- 97-100
Watson, Patty Jo (Andersen) 1932- CANR-13
Earlier sketch in CA 77-80
Watson, Pauline 1925- CANR-29
Earlier sketches in CA 69-72, CANR-11
See also SATA 14
Watson, Peter 1943- 147
Watson, Peter L(eslie) 1944- 53-56
Watson, Philip S(aville) 1909- 104
Watson, Richard A(bernethy) 1923- CANR-25
Earlier sketch in CA 45-48
Watson, Richard A(llan) 1931- 77-80
Watson, Richard F.
See Silverberg, Robert
Watson, Richard Jesse 1951- .... SATA 62
Watson, Richard L(yness), Jr. 1914- 17-20R
Watson, Robert (Winthrop) 1925- CANR-4
Earlier sketch in CA 1-4R
Watson, Robert I(rving) 1909-1980 Obituary 111
Watson, Robert N(athaniel) 1953- 118
Watson, Roderick (Bruce) 1943- 102
Watson, Russell 1939- 77-80
Watson, Sally (Lou) 1924- CANR-3
Earlier sketch in CA 5-8R
See also SATA 3
Watson, Sara Ruth 1907- 37-40R
Watson, Sheila 1909- 155
See also AITN 2
See also DAC
See also DLB 60
Watson, Sophia 1962- 158
Watson, Steven 1947- 135
Watson, Thomas 1545(?)-1592 .... DLB 132
Watson, Thomas J(ohn), Jr. 1914-1993 138
Obituary 143
See also BEST 90:4
Watson, Thomas J(oel) 1948- 109
Watson, Tom, Jr. 1918- 21-24R
Watson, Wendy (McLeod) 1942- CANR-39
Earlier sketches in CA 49-52, CANR-4
See also MAICYA
See also SATA 5, 74
Watson, Wilfred 1911-1998 164
See also DLB 60
Watson, Will
See Floren, Lee
Watson, William 1917- 9-12R
Watson, William Alexander Jardine 1933- CANR-12
Earlier sketch in CA 13-16R
Watson Taylor, Elizabeth 1915- .... SATA 41
Watson-Watt, Robert A(lexander) 1892-1973 .... CAP-1
Obituary 45-48
Earlier sketch in CA 13-14
Watstein, Esther 1928- 57-60
Watt, (John) David (Henry) 1932-1987 133
Obituary 122
Watt, David Harrington 1957- 141
Watt, Donald 1938- 41-44R
Watt, Donald Beates 1893-1977 Obituary 73-76
Watt, Donald Cameron
See Cameron Watt, Donald
Watt, Donley 1940- 154
Watt, Douglas (Benjamin) 1914- 69-72
Watt, Frank Hedden 1889-1981 Obituary 105
Watt, Frederick B. 1901- 129
Watt, George Steven Harvie
See Harvie-Watt, George Steven
Watt, (Raymond Egerton) Harry 1906-1987 Obituary 122
Watt, Ian 1917- 13-16R
Watt, James G(aius) 1938- 144
Watt, John Robertson 1934- 37-40R
Watt, Kenneth E(dmund) F(erguson) 1929- 61-64
Watt, Richard M(artin) 1930- 5-8R
Watt, Ruth M. 1919- CANR-10
Earlier sketch in CA 57-60
Watt, Thomas 1935- 37-40R
See also SATA 4
Watt, W(illiam) Montgomery 1909- CANR-44
Earlier sketches in CA 1-4R, CANR-6, 21
Wattel, Harold Louis 1921- 126
Watten, Barrett 1948- .... DLB 193
Wattenbarger, James L(orenzo) 1922- 106
Wattenberg, Ben J. 1933- CANR-33
Earlier sketch in CA 57-60
Wattenberg, Martin P(aul) 1956- 142
Wattenberg, William W(olff) 1911- 21-24R
Wattenmaker, Richard J. 1941- 104
Watters, Barbara H(unt) 1907-1984 .... CANR-3
Obituary 111
Earlier sketch in CA 5-8R
Watters, (Walter) Pat(terson) 1927- CANR-8
Earlier sketch in CA 21-24R
Watters, R(eginald) E(yre) 1912- 25-28R
Watterson, Bill 1958- 134
See also AAYA 9
See also SATA 66
Watterson, Henry 1840-1921 .... DLB 25
Watterson, Joseph 1900-1972 .... CAP-2
Obituary 33-36R
Earlier sketch in CA 25-28
Watt-Evans, Lawrence 1954-
See Evans, Lawrence Watt
See also SATA 75
Wattie, Margaret
See 'Espinasse, Margaret
Wattles, Santha Rama Rau 1923- CANR-1
Earlier sketch in CA 1-4R
Watts, A. J.
See Watts, Anthony J(ohn)
Watts, Al(bert) L. 1934- 85-88
Watts, Alan (Wilson) 1915-1973 .... CANR-32
Obituary 45-48
Earlier sketch in CA 41-44R
See also DLB 16
Watts, Alan (James) 1925- 108
Watts, Ann Chalmers 1938- 53-56
Watts, Anthony J(ohn) 1942- CANR-11
Earlier sketch in CA 25-28R
Watts, (Anna) Bernadette 1942- CANR-31
Earlier sketch in CA 29-32R
See also SATA 4
Watts, Charles Edwin 1929- CANR-2
Earlier sketch in CA 5-8R
Watts, David 1935- 53-56
Watts, Elizabeth (Bailey) Smithgall 1941- CANR-12
Earlier sketch in CA 73-76
Watts, Emily Stipes 1936- 81-84
Watts, Ephraim
See Horne, Richard Henry
Watts, Franklin (Mowry) 1904-1978 .... CANR-9
Obituary 89-92
Earlier sketches in CAP-2, CA 25-28
See also SATA 46
See also SATA-Obit 21
Watts, George W(illiam) 1952- 139
Watts, Harold H(olliday) 1906- CAP-2
Earlier sketch in CA 13-14
Watts, Harriet M(ayor) 1933- 45-48
Watts, Helen L. Hoke 1903-1990 .... CANR-43
Obituary 131
See also Hoke, Helen
Watts, Irene N(aemi) 1931- .... SATA 56
Watts, Isaac 1674-1748 .... DLB 95
See also SATA 52
Watts, J(ames) Wash(ington) 1896-197(?) CANR-20
Earlier sketch in CA 1-4R
Watts, James K(ennedy) M(offitt) 1955- .... SATA 59
Watts, John (Francis) 1926- CANR-21
Earlier sketch in CA 25-28R
Watts, John D. W. 1921- 21-24R
Watts, Lew 1922- 41-44R
Watts, Mabel Pizzey 1906- CANR-3
Earlier sketch in CA 1-4R
See also SATA 11
Watts, May Theilgaard 1893-1975 .... 41-44R
Watts, Meredith W(ayne, Jr.) 1941- CANR-24
Earlier sketch in CA 45-48
Watts, Michael J(ohn) 1951- CANR-48
Earlier sketch in CA 122
Watts, Nigel 1957- 130
Watts, Peter Christopher 1919- CANR-12
Earlier sketch in CA 69-72
Watts, Reginald John 1931- CANR-30
Earlier sketch in CA 29-32R
Watts, Richard (Jr.) 1898-1981 Obituary 102
Watts, Ronald L(ampman) 1929- 21-24R
Watts, Sarah Miles 1934- 65-68
Watts, Stephen 1910- 5-8R
Watts, Thomas D(ale) 1941- CANR-41
Earlier sketch in CA 117
Watts, Timothy 1957- 141
Watts, William 1930- CANR-1
Earlier sketch in CA 45-48
Watzlawick, Paul 1921- CANR-4
Earlier sketch in CA 9-12R
Waud, Alfred Rudolph 1828-1891 .... DLB 188
Waud, Elizabeth
See Tattersall, M(uriel Joyce)
Waugh, Albert E(dmund) 1902-1985 .... 37-40R
Obituary 115
Waugh, Alec
See Waugh, Alexander Raban
Waugh, Alexander Raban 1898-1981 .... CANR-22
Obituary 104
Earlier sketch in CA 17-20R
See also DLB 191
Waugh, Auberon (Alexander) 1939- CANR-22
Earlier sketches in CA 45-48, CANR-6
See also CLC 7
See also DLB 14, 194
Waugh, C. C. Roessel
See Waugh, Carol-Lynn Rossel
and Waugh, Charles G(ordon)

Waugh, Carol-Lynn Rossel 1947- CANR-44
Earlier sketch in CA 107
See also SATA 41
Waugh, Charles
See Waugh, Charles G(ordon)
Waugh, Charles G(ordon) 1943- 123
Brief entry 118
Interview in 123
Waugh, Coulton 1896(?)-1973 Obituary 41-44R
Waugh, Dorothy CANR-1
Earlier sketch in CA 1-4R
See also SATA 11
Waugh, Evelyn (Arthur St. John) 1903-1966 ....
CANR-22
Obituary 25-28R
Earlier sketch in CA 85-88
See also CDBLB 1914-1945
See also CLC 1, 3, 8, 13, 19, 27, 44, 107
See also DA
See also DAB
See also DAC
See also DAM MST, NOV, POP
See also DLB 15, 162, 195
See also MTCW 1
See also WLC
Waugh, Harriet 1944- CANR-22
Earlier sketch in CA 85-88
See also CLC 6
Waugh, Harry 1904- 21-24R
Waugh, Hillary Baldwin 1920- CANR-2
Earlier sketch in CA 1-4R
Waugh, John C(linton) 1929- 150
Waugh, Linda R(uth) 1942- CANR-16
Earlier sketch in CA 89-92
Waugh, Nancy Collier 1930- 45-48
Waugh, Teresa (Lorraine) 1940- 158
Waugh, Virginia
See Sorensen, Virginia
Waughburton, Richard
See Sykes, Christopher (Hugh)
Wauthier, Claude Rene 1923- 73-76
Wauzzinski, Robert A. 1950- 143
Wavell, Stewart Brooke 1921- 13-16R
Wax, Emmanuel 1911-1983 Obituary 109
Wax, Jimmy
See Wax, Emmanuel
Wax, Judith 1932(?)-1979 101
Obituary 85-88
Wax, Murray L(ionel) 1922- 37-40R
Wax, Rosalie (Amelia) H. 1911- 45-48
Wax, Sheldon 1928(?)-1979 Obituary 85-88
Wax, Wendy A. 1963- .... SATA 73
Wax, William Edward 1956- 133
Waxberg, Joseph David 1922- 108
Waxman, Chaim I(saac) 1941- CANR-19
Earlier sketch in CA 103
Waxman, Ruth B(ilgray) 1916-1996 93-96
Obituary 154
Waxman, Wayne 1956- 150
Way, Irene 1924- 93-96
Way, Margaret 162
Way, Peter (Howard) 1936- 163
Brief entry 115
Way, Robert E(dward) 1912- 57-60
Way, Walter L. 1931- 57-60
Way, Wayne
See Humphries, Adelaide M.
Wayans, Keenen Ivory 1958(?)- 140
See also AAYA 11
See also BW 2
See also DAM MULT, POP
Wayburn, Peggy 1921- CANR-24
Earlier sketch in CA 45-48
Waycott, Edon 1943- 149
Waylan, Mildred
See Harrell, Irene B(urk)
Wayland, April Halprin 1954- 146
See also SAAS 26
See also SATA 78
Wayland, Patrick
See O'Connor, Richard
Waymack, W(illiam) W(esley)
1888-1960 Obituary 93-96
Wayman, Alex 1921- 104
Wayman, Dorothy G. 1893-1975 65-68
Obituary 61-64
Wayman, Norbury Lansing 1912- 41-44R
Wayman, Thomas Ethan 1945- 101
See also Wayman, Tom
Wayman, Tom
See Wayman, Thomas Ethan
See also DLB 53
Wayman, Tony Russell 1929- 25-28R
Wayne, Alice
See Ressler, Alice
Wayne, Anderson
See Dresser, Davis
Wayne, David
See Balsiger, David (Wayne)
Wayne, Donald
See Dodd, Wayne (Donald)
Wayne, Doreen 29-32R
Wayne, Frances
See Wedge, Florence
Wayne, Jane Ellen 1936- CANR-42
Earlier sketches in CA 49-52, CANR-4, 20
Wayne, (Anne) Jenifer 1917-1982 105
Obituary 108
See also SATA 32
Wayne, Jerry 1919- 29-32R
Wayne, John 1907-1979 85-88
Wayne, Joseph
See Overholser, Wayne D.
Wayne, Kyra Petrovskaya 1918- CANR-4
Earlier sketch in CA 1-4R
See also SATA 8
Wayne, Mary Collier 1913- 57-60
Wayne, Michael 1947- 112
Wayne, Philip
See Powell, Philip Wayne
Wayne, Richard
See Decker, Duane
Wayne, Stephen J(ay) 1939- CANR-44
Earlier sketches in CA 53-56, CANR-5, 20
Wayne, Valerie 1945- 137
Wayre, Philip 1921- 89-92
Ways, C. R.
See Blount, Roy (Alton), Jr.
Ways, Max 1905-1985 Obituary 116
Waystaff, Simon
See Swift, Jonathan
Wazyk, Adam 1905-1982 Obituary 114
Wead, R(oy) Douglas 1946- CANR-20
Earlier sketch in CA 69-72
Weaks, Mary Louise 1961- 136
Weal, Michele 1936- 61-64
Weales, Gerald (Clifford) 1925- CANR-3
Earlier sketch in CA 5-8R
See also SATA 11
Wear, Ted Graham
See Wear, Theodore G(raham)
Wear, Theodore G(raham) 1902- CAP-1
Earlier sketch in CA 9-10
Weare, Ralston B.
See La Barre, Weston
Weare, Walter B(urdette) 1938- 73-76
Wearin, Otha D(onner) 1903-1990 .... CANR-5
Obituary 131
Earlier sketch in CA 13-16R
Wearing, J. P. CANR-41
Earlier sketches in CA 102, CANR-19
Wearne, Alan (Richard) 1948- 126
Weart, Edith L. 1898(?)-1977 Obituary 69-72
Weart, Spencer R(ichard) 1942- CANR-53
Earlier sketches in CA 25-28R, CANR-29
Weary, Ogdred
See Gorey, Edward (St. John)
Weatherall, Norman Leigh 1902- CAP-1
Earlier sketch in CA 11-12
Weatherby, Harold L(erow), Jr. 1934- 45-48
Weatherby, W(illiam) J(ohn) 1930(?)-1992 ....
CANR-47
Obituary 139
Earlier sketches in CA 17-20R, CANR-12
Weathercock, The
See Romaine, Lawrence B.
Weatherford, J. McIver
See Weatherford, Jack McIver
Weatherford, Jack
See Weatherford, Jack McIver
Weatherford, Jack McIver 1946- CANR-56
Earlier sketches in CA 111, CANR-30
Weatherford, Richard M(orris) 1939- 53-56
Weatherford, Willis Duke, Jr. 1916- 5-8R
Weatherhead, A(ndrew) Kingsley 1923- ... CANR-3
Earlier sketch in CA 5-8R
Weatherhead, Leslie D(ixon) 1893-1976 .. CANR-4
Obituary 61-64
Earlier sketch in CA 5-8R
Weatherly, Edward H(owell) 1905- 5-8R
Weatherly, (John) Max 1921- 13-16R
Weatherly, Owen M. 1915- 5-8R
Weatherly, Tom 1942- CANR-25
Earlier sketch in CA 45-48
See also BW 1
See also DLB 41
Weathers, Wesley Wayne 1942- 111
Weathers, Winston 1926- CANR-8
Earlier sketch in CA 21-24R
Weatherwax, Rudd (B.) 1908(?)-1985 Obituary . 115
Weatherwise, Abe
See Sagendorph, Robb Hansell
Weaver, Anthony Frederick 1913- 13-16R
Weaver, Bertrand 1908-1973 .... CAP-1
Obituary 45-48
Earlier sketch in CA 13-16
Weaver, Carl H(arold) 1910- 73-76
Weaver, Charley
See Arquette, Cliff(ord)
Weaver, David H(ugh) 1946- 111
Weaver, Denis 1906-1984 Obituary 114
Weaver, Earl S(idney) 1930- 116
Weaver, Earle
See Willets, Walter E.
Weaver, Frank Parks 1904- 104
Weaver, Frederick S(tirton) 1939- 156
Weaver, Gordon (Allison) 1937- CANR-26
Earlier sketches in CA 25-28R, CANR-10
See also DLB 130
Weaver, Harriett E. 1908- CANR-20
Earlier sketches in CA 5-8R, CANR-5
See also SATA 65
Weaver, Herbert 1905- 61-64
Weaver, Horace R. 1915- 13-16R
Weaver, James H. 1933- 17-20R
Weaver, Jerry L(ee) 1939- 69-72
Weaver, John D(owning) 1912- CANR-4
Earlier sketch in CA 9-12R
Weaver, John L. 1949- 112
See also SATA 42
Weaver, Katherine Grey Dunlap 1910- 37-40R
Weaver, Kitty
See Weaver, Katherine Grey Dunlap
Weaver, Leon Hiram 1913- 5-8R
Weaver, Mateman
See Greene, A(lvin) C(arl)
Weaver, Michael D. 1961- 126
Weaver, Michael S. 1951- 149
Weaver, Pat
See Weaver, Sylvester L(aflin), Jr.
Weaver, Peter 1925- CANR-15
Earlier sketch in CA 85-88
Weaver, Peter Malcolm 1927- 13-16R
Weaver, R(obert) Kent 1953- 138
Weaver, Richard L. II 1941- CANR-46
Earlier sketches in CA 106, CANR-23
Weaver, Robert 1921- .... DLB 88
Weaver, Robert C(lifton) 1907-1997 .... 9-12R
Obituary 159
Weaver, Sylvester L(aflin), Jr. 1908- 146
See also Weaver, Sylvester L(aflin), Jr.
Weaver, Thomas 1929- CANR-13
Earlier sketch in CA 61-64
Weaver, Ward
See Mason, F(rancis) van Wyck
Weaver, Warren, Jr. 1923-1997 .... 41-44R
Obituary 156
Weaver, Warren 1894-1978 89-92
Obituary 81-84
Weaver, Will(iam Weller) 1950- 143
See also SATA 88
Weaver, William 1923- 116
Brief entry 112
Interview in 116
Weaver, William Woys 1947- CANR-51
Earlier sketch in CA 123
Weaver-Gelzer, Charlotte 1950- 148
See also SATA 79
Webb, Alex 1952- 161
Webb, Anthony
See Wilson, N(orman) Scarlyn
Webb, Barbara (Helen) 1929- 103
Webb, (Stephen) Barry 1947- 135
Webb, (Martha) Beatrice (Potter) 1858-1943 Brief
entry 117
See also Potter, (Helen) Beatrix
See also TCLC 22
Webb, Beatrice (Martha Potter) 1858-1943 162
Webb, Beatrice 1858-1943 .... DLB 190
Webb, Bernice Larson CANR-15
Earlier sketch in CA 37-40R
Webb, Bob
See Forrest-Webb, Robert
Webb, C(harles) R(ichard), Jr. 1919- 5-8R
Webb, Charles (Richard) 1939- 25-28R
See also CLC 7
Webb, Christopher
See Wibberley, Leonard (Patrick O'Connor)
Webb, Clifford (Cyril) 1895-1972 105
Webb, Eugene 1938- 29-32R
Webb, Forrest
See Forrest-Webb, Robert
Webb, Francis Charles 1925-1973 101
Webb, Frank J. .... DLB 50
Webb, George Ernest 1952- 113
Webb, Harri 1920- 104
Webb, Harry 1887-1984 Obituary 113
Webb, Henry J(ameson) 1915- 17-20R
Webb, Herschel (F.) 1924-1983 .... 5-8R
Obituary 109
Webb, Holmes 1904- CAP-2
Earlier sketch in CA 25-28
Webb, Igor 1941- 109
Webb, Jack (Randolph) 1920-1982 Obituary ... 108
Brief entry 106
Webb, James (C. N.) 1946-1980 103
Webb, James H(enry), Jr. 1946- 81-84
See also CLC 22
Webb, James Watson 1802-1884 .... DLB 43
Webb, Jean Francis 1910- CANR-21
Earlier sketches in CA 5-8R, CANR-6
See also SATA 35
Webb, Jon (Edgar) 1905(?)-1971 Obituary 104
Webb, Karl (Eugene) 1938- 105
Webb, Kaye 1914- .... SATA 60
Webb, Kempton E. 1931- 13-16R
Webb, Kenneth B(eals) 1902- 97-100
Webb, Lance 1909- CANR-10
Earlier sketch in CA 13-16R
Webb, Lionel
See Hershman, Morris
Webb, Lois Sinaiko 1922- 149
See also SATA 82
Webb, Lucas
See Burgess, Michael (Roy)
Webb, Margot 1934- 134
See also SATA 67
Webb, Margot S. 1914- 77-80
Webb, Martha G.
See Wingate, (Martha) Anne (Guice)
Webb, Mary (Gladys Meredith)
1881-1927 Obituary 123
See also DLB 34
See also TCLC 24
Webb, Mary H(aydn) 1938- CANR-28
Earlier sketch in CA 61-64
Webb, Melody Rae 1946- 126
Webb, Mena 1915- 127
Webb, Michael (Dennis Puzey) 1937- 124
Webb, Michael (Jack) 1953- 137
Webb, Michael Gordon 1940- 109
Webb, Mrs. Sidney
See Webb, (Martha) Beatrice (Potter)
Webb, Muriel S(chlosberg) 1913-1977 ... CANR-36
Obituary 134
Earlier sketch in CA 17-20R
Webb, Nancy (Bukeley) 1915- CANR-21
Earlier sketch in CA 1-4R
Webb, Neil
See Rowland, D(onald) S(ydney)
Webb, Pauline M(ary) 1927- CANR-49
Earlier sketches in CA 61-64, CANR-8, 24
Webb, Peggy (Elaine Hussey) 1942- 123
Webb, Peter B(randram) 1941- CANR-24
Earlier sketch in CA 106
Webb, Phyllis 1927- CANR-23
Earlier sketch in CA 104
See also CLC 18
See also DLB 53
Webb, R(obert) K(iefer) 1922- 25-28R
Webb, Richard 1915-1993 .... CANR-47
Obituary 141
Earlier sketch in CA 37-40R
Webb, Robert 1947- 118
Webb, Robert Forrest-
See Forrest-Webb, Robert
Webb, Rodman B. 1941- CANR-28
Earlier sketch in CA 110
Webb, Ross A. 1923- 37-40R
Webb, Rozana 1908- 29-32R
Webb, Ruth Enid Borlase Morris 1926- 9-12R
Webb, Samuel C(lement) 1934- 69-72
Webb, Sharon 1936- CANR-32
Earlier sketch in CA 113
See also SATA 41
Webb, Sidney (James) 1859-1947 163
Brief entry 117
See also DLB 190
See also TCLC 22
Webb, Spider
See Gohman, Fred Joseph
Webb, Stephen S(aunders) 1937- CANR-70
Earlier sketch in CA 104
Webb, Walter Prescott 1888-1963 Obituary 113
See also DLB 17
Webb, Willard 1903-1978 Obituary 77-80
Webb, William (Griffin) 1919- 25-28R
Webb, Wilse B(ernard) 1920- CANR-3
Earlier sketch in CA 1-4R
Webbe, Gale D(udley) 1909- 5-8R
Webbe, William (?)-1591 .... DLB 132
Webber, Andrew Lloyd
See Lloyd Webber, Andrew
See also CLC 21
Webber, Bert
See Webber, Ebbert T(rue)
Webber, Charles Wilkins 1819-1856(?) .... DLB 202
Webber, Ebbert T(rue) 1921- CANR-39
Earlier sketches in CA 45-48, CANR-2, 17
Webber, George J(ulius)
1899-1982(?) Obituary 108
Webber, Gordon 1912-1986 89-92
Obituary 120
Webber, Irma E(leanor Schmidt) 1904- 69-72
See also SATA 14
Webber, Joan Malory 1930-1978 .... CANR-7
Earlier sketch in CA 5-8R
Webber, Robert (Eugene) 1933- CANR-37
Earlier sketches in CA 89-92, CANR-16
Webber, (Edwin) Ronald 1915- CANR-4
Earlier sketch in CA 53-56
Webber, Ross A. 1934- 29-32R
Webber, Sabra J. 1945- 141
Webber, Thomas L(ane) 1947- 85-88
Weber, Alfons 1921- 29-32R
See also SATA 8
Weber, Brom 1917- 13-16R
Weber, Bruce 1942- CANR-49
Earlier sketches in CA 97-100, CANR-21
See also SATA 73
Weber, Burton Jasper 1934- 103
Weber, C(larence) A(dam) 1903- CANR-37
Earlier sketches in CA 37-40R, CANR-13
Weber, Carl J(efferson) 1894-1966 .... CANR-3
Earlier sketch in CA 5-8R
Weber, David J. 1940- CANR-14
Earlier sketch in CA 37-40R
Weber, David R(yder) 1943- 89-92
Weber, Debora 1955- .... SATA 58
Weber, Doron 1955- 138
Weber, Eric 1942- CANR-15
Earlier sketch in CA 101
Interview in CANR-15
Weber, Eugen 1925- CANR-2
Earlier sketch in CA 5-8R
Weber, Eugene 1939- 41-44R
Weber, Francis J. 1933- CANR-69
Earlier sketches in CA 9-12R, CANR-4
Weber, Frank George 1932- 45-48
Weber, Gerard Peter 1918- 9-12R
Weber, Hans H. 1935- 61-64
Weber, Hans-Ruedi 1923- CANR-2
Earlier sketch in CA 5-8R
Weber, J(ohn) Sherwood 1918-1978 .... 37-40R
Obituary 77-80
Weber, James A(mbrose) 1932- 102
Weber, Janice CANR-46
Earlier sketch in CA 121
Weber, Jean-Paul 1917- 45-48
Weber, Jerome C(harles) 1938- 73-76
Weber, Joe 1945- 141
Weber, Judith E(ichler) 1938- .... SATA 64
Weber, Katharine 1955- 157
Weber, Ken(neth J.) 1940- .... SATA 90
Weber, Ken(neth J.) 1940- CANR-59
Earlier sketches in CA 116, CANR-39
Weber, Lenora Mattingly 1895-1971 .... CAP-1
Obituary 29-32R
Earlier sketch in CA 19-20
See also CLC 12
See also SATA 2
See also SATA-Obit 26
Weber, Marc 1950- CANR-1
Earlier sketch in CA 49-52
Weber, Max 1864-1920 Brief entry 109
See also TCLC 69
Weber, Michael 1945- 151
See also SATA 87
Weber, Michael P. 127
Weber, Nancy 1942- 101
Weber, Nathan 1942- 111

Weber, Nicholas F(ox) 1947- 120
Weber, Paul J. 1937- 137
Weber, R. David 1941- 127
Weber, Ralph Edward 1926- CANR-2
Earlier sketch in CA 5-8R
Weber, Robert J(ohn) 1936- 139
Weber, Robert L(emmerman) 1913- 53-56
Weber, Ronald 1934- CANR-43
Earlier sketch in CA 115
Weber, Rubin
See Rubinstein, S(amuel) Leonard
Weber, Sarah Appleton
See Appleton, Sarah
Weber, Simon 1910(?)-1987 Obituary 124
Weber, Thomas 1950- 159
Weber, William A(lfred) 1918- 77-80
Weber, William J(ohn) 1927- CANR-25
Earlier sketch in CA 69-72
See also SATA 14
Weberman, Ben(jamin) 1923- 77-80
Webster, Alice Jane Chandler 1876-1916 Brief entry 116
See also SATA 17
Webster, Anthony 1923(?)-1987 Obituary 123
Webster, Augusta 1837-1894 .... DLB 35
Webster, Brenda 1946- .... CAAS 30
Webster, Brenda S. 1936- 53-56
Webster, C(onstance) Muriel 1906- 49-52
Webster, Cyril Charles 1909- CAP-2
Earlier sketch in CA 25-28
Webster, David 1930- 29-32R
See also SATA 11
Webster, David Endicott 1929- 25-28R
Webster, Donald 1926- 118
Webster, Donald Blake, Jr. 1933- 37-40R
Webster, Douglas 1920-1986 .... 13-16R
Obituary 118
Webster, Edna Robb 1896- 69-72
Webster, Elizabeth 1918- CANR-40
Earlier sketch in CA 117
Webster, Ernest 1923- 132
Webster, Frank V. CANR-27
Earlier sketches in CAP-2, CA 19-20
See also SATA 1, 67
Webster, Frederick E., Jr. 1937- CANR-14
Earlier sketch in CA 37-40R
Webster, Gary
See Garrison, Webb B(lack)
Webster, Graham 1915- 49-52
Webster, Grant T. 1933- 104
Webster, Harvey (Curtis) 1906- 41-44R
Webster, J(ames) Carson 1905- 45-48
Webster, James 1925-1981 .... CANR-29
Obituary 104
Earlier sketch in CA 73-76
See also SATA 17
See also SATA-Obit 27
Webster, Jan 1924- CANR-14
Earlier sketch in CA 77-80
Webster, Jean
See Webster, Alice Jane Chandler
Webster, John 1579(?)-1634(?) .... CDBLB Before 1660
See also DA
See also DAB
See also DAC
See also DAM DRAM, MST
See also DC 2
See also DLB 58
See also WLC
Webster, John 1925- 152
Webster, Josh (Lew) 1949- 113
Webster, Margaret 1905-1972 Obituary 37-40R
Webster, Noah
See Knox, William
Webster, Noah 1758-1843 ... DLB 1, 37, 42, 43, 73
Webster, Norman William 1920- 104
Webster, Paul 1916- 41-44R
Webster, Paul Francis 1907-1984 Obituary 112
Webster, Randolph Wyatt 1900- CAP-1
Earlier sketch in CA 19-20
Webster, Richard A. 1928- 21-24R
Webster, S(tanley) Eric 1919-1971 .... CAP-1
Earlier sketch in CA 17-18
Webster, Sally 1938- 140
Webster, Staten Wentford 1928- 21-24R
Webster, Thomas Bertram Lonsdale 1905-1974 105
Obituary 107
Webster, Tony
See Webster, Anthony
Wechman, Robert Joseph 1939- CANR-49
Earlier sketches in CA 45-48, CANR-24
Wechsberg, Joseph 1907-1983 .... CANR-34
Obituary 109
Earlier sketch in CA 105
Wechsler, David 1896-1981 Obituary 103
Wechsler, Harold S(tuart) 1946- 110
Wechsler, Henry 1932- CANR-7
Earlier sketch in CA 17-20R
Wechsler, Herbert 1909- CANR-24
Earlier sketch in CA 1-4R
Wechsler, Herman J. 1904-1976 65-68
Obituary 61-64
See also SATA-Obit 20
Wechsler, James A(rthur) 1915-1983 101
Obituary 110
Wechsler, Judith Glatzer 1940- CANR-42
Earlier sketches in CA 57-60, CANR-8
Wechsler, Louis K. 1905- 65-68
Wechter, Nell Wise 1913- 57-60
See also SATA 60
Weck, Thomas L. 1942- 128
See also SATA 62
Wecker, David 1950- 148
Weckesser, Elden C(hristian) 1910- 139
Weckherlin, Georg Rodolf 1584-1653 .... DLB 164
Weckmann, Luis 1923- 143
Weckstein, Richard (Selig) 1924- 49-52
Wedberg, Anders 1913-1978 Obituary 77-80
Wedd, Kate
See Gregory, Philippa
Wedda, John A. 1911- 17-20R
Wedde, Ian 1946- 104
Wedderburn, Dorothy (Enid Cole) 1925- Brief entry 113
Wedderburn, K(enneth) W(illiam) 1927- 77-80
Wedding, Dan 1949- 93-96
Wedding, Donald Keith 1934- 41-44R
Weddington, Sarah (Ragle) 1945- 156
Weddle, Ethel Harshbarger 1897- CANR-4
Earlier sketch in CA 9-12R
See also SATA 11
Weddle, Ferris 1922- 17-20R
Weddle, Robert S(amuel) 1921- 9-12R
Wedeck, Harry E(zekiel) 1894-1996 .... CANR-4
Obituary 152
Earlier sketch in CA 1-4R
Wedeen, Richard Peter 1934- 146
Wedeen, Shirley Ullman 1926-1992 .... 17-20R
Obituary 137
Wedekind, (Benjamin) Frank(lin) 1864-1918 153
Brief entry 104
See also DAM DRAM
See also DLB 118
See also TCLC 7
Wedel, Alfred R(aphael) 1934- 117
Wedel, Alton F. 21-24R
Wedel, Cynthia Clark 1908-1986 Obituary 120
Wedel, Janine (R.) 1957- 132
Wedel, Leonard E. 1909- 21-24R
Wedel, Theodore Otto 1892-1970 .... CANR-4
Earlier sketch in CA 5-8R
Wedel, Waldo R(udolph) 1908- 126
Brief entry 105
Wedell, Eberhard (Arthur Otto) George 1927- 104
Wedemeyer, Albert C(oady) 1897-1989 Obituary 130
Wedemeyer, Maria von 1924(?)-1977 148
Wedge, Bryant (Miner) 1921- CANR-10
Earlier sketch in CA 13-16R
Wedge, Florence 1919- 5-8R
Wedgwood, C(icely) V(eronica) 1910-1997 .... CANR-67
Obituary 157
Earlier sketches in CA 105, CANR-21
See also MTCW 1
Wedgwood, Pamela
See Tudor-Craig, Pamela
Wedlock, Eldon D(yment), Jr. 1942- 128
Weed, Florence C(ollins) 1897(?)-1983 Obituary 109
Weed, Joseph J(ohn) 1901- 25-28R
Weeden, Robert B(arton) 1933- 85-88
Weedon, Chris 1952- 121
Weegee 1899-1968 145
Weekes, Mark Kinkead
See Kinkead-Weekes, Mark
Weekes, Richard V. 1924- 13-16R
Weekley, Ian George 1933- 113
Weekly, William G(eorge) 1890(?)-1983 Obituary 111
Weeks, Albert L. 1923- 13-16R
Weeks, Brigitte 1943- 132
Weeks, Christopher 1930- 21-24R
Weeks, Constance Tomkinson 1915- 17-20R
Weeks, David (Joseph) 1944- 156
Weeks, (Norman) Donald CANR-25
Earlier sketch in CA 45-48
Weeks, Edward (Augustus) 1898-1989 ... CANR-36
Obituary 128
Earlier sketch in CA 85-88
See also DLB 137
Weeks, Edward J(oseph) 1902- CAP-1
Earlier sketch in CA 13-14
Weeks, Francis W(illiam) 1916- Brief entry 111
Weeks, Grace E(zell) 1923- 49-52
Weeks, H(erbert) Ashley 1903- 45-48
Weeks, Jeffrey 1945- 108
Weeks, John (Stafford) 1928- 77-80
Weeks, John F. 1941- 141
Weeks, Kent M(cCuskey) 1937- Brief entry 112
Weeks, Lewis G(eorge) 1893-1977 Obituary 69-72
Weeks, Philip 1949- 110
Weeks, Robert Lewis 1924- 13-16R
Weeks, Robert P(ercy) 1915- 13-16R
Weeks, Sheldon G. 1931- CANR-30
Earlier sketches in CA 21-24R, CANR-13
Weeks, Stephen B. 1865-1918 .... DLB 187
Weeks, Thelma E(vans) 1921- 57-60
Weems, David B(urnola) 1922- 148
See also SATA 80
Weems, J. Eddie, Jr.
See Weems, John Edward
Weems, John Edward 1924- CANR-19
Earlier sketches in CA 1-4R, CANR-4
Weems, Mason Locke 1759-1825 .. DLB 30, 37, 42
Weenolsen, Hebe CANR-60
Earlier sketches in CA 111, CANR-34
Weenolsen, Patricia 1930- 157
Weer, William
See Kaufman, I(sadore)
Weerth, Georg 1822-1856 .... DLB 129
Weertman, Julia 1926- 160
Weerts, Richard Kenneth 1928- 49-52
Wees, Frances Shelley 1902-1982 .... CANR-3
Earlier sketch in CA 5-8R
See also SATA 58
Wees, W(ilfred) R(usk) 1899- 61-64
Weesner, Theodore 105
Weevers, Peter 1944- .... SATA 59
Wegela, Karen Kissel 1945- 168
Wegelin, Christof 1911- 45-48
Wegen, Ron(ald) .... SATA-Brief 44
Wegen, Ronald 1946-1985 154
See also SATA 99
Wegener, Alfred 1880-1930 161
Weglyn, Michi(ko Nishiura) 1926- 85-88
Wegman, William (George) 1943- 148
See also AAYA 15
See also SATA 78
Wegmann, Peter 1957- 146
Wegner, Fritz 1924- .... SATA 20
Wegner, Robert E. 1929- 17-20R
Wehen, Joy DeWeese CANR-3
Earlier sketch in CA 5-8R
Wehlitz, (Annie) Lou(ise) Rogers 1906- 5-8R
Wehmeyer, Lillian (Mabel) Biermann 1933- CANR-8
Earlier sketch in CA 61-64
Wehringer, Cameron K(ingsley) 1924- 25-28R
Wehrle, Edmund S(heridan) 1930- 65-68
Wehrli, Eugene S(tanley) 1923- 45-48
Wehrwein, Austin C(arl) 1916- 77-80
Wei, Yung 1937- 49-52
Weichel, Kim 1951- 107
Weida, Bill
See Weida, William J.
Weida, William J. 1942- 135
Weideger, Paula 1939- 65-68
Weideman, Ryan 1941- 137
Weidenbaum, Murray L(ew) 1927- CANR-14
Earlier sketch in CA 37-40R
Weidenfeld, (Arthur) George 1919- 153
Weidenfeld, Sheila Rabb 1943- 89-92
Weidenreich, Franz 1873-1948 164
Weider, Ben 1923- 108
Weidhorn, Manfred 1931- 53-56
See also SATA 60
Weidlein, Edward R(ay) 1887-1983 Obituary 110
Weidman, Jerome 1913- CANR-1
Earlier sketch in CA 1-4R
See also AITN 2
See also CLC 7
See also DLB 28
Weidman, John 1946- 109
Weidman, Judith L(ynne) 1941- CANR-25
Earlier sketch in CA 107
Weidner, Edward William 1921- 13-16R
Weidt, Maryann N. 1944- 151
See also SATA 85
Weiers, Ronald M. 1941- CANR-19
Earlier sketch in CA 25-28R
Weigand, George R(obert) J(oseph) 1917- 13-16R
Weigand, Hermann J(ohn) 1892-1985 .... CAP-1
Obituary 117
Earlier sketch in CA 13-14
Weigel, George 1951- 125
Weigel, Gustave 1906-1964 Obituary 107
Weigel, John A(rthur) 1912- 57-60
Weiger, John George 1933- CANR-20
Earlier sketch in CA 104
Weigert, Andrew J(oseph) 1934- 109
Weigert, Edith 1894- CAP-2
Earlier sketch in CA 29-32
Weigert, Hans Werner 1902(?)-1983 Obituary 111
Weightman, Gavin 1945- 120
Weightman, J(ohn) G(eorge) 1915- CANR-5
Earlier sketch in CA 9-12R
Weigl, Bruce 1949- CANR-30
Earlier sketch in CA 110
See also DLB 120
Weigle, Luther Allan 1880-1976 77-80
Obituary 69-72
Weigle, Marta 1944- CANR-26
Earlier sketches in CA 69-72, CANR-11
Weigley, Russell F(rank) 1930- CANR-19
Earlier sketches in CA 5-8R, CANR-2
Weihofen, Henry 1904- 37-40R
Weihs, Erika 1917- 93-96
See also SATA 15
Weihs, Jean 1930- 153
Weihs, Jean Riddle
See Weihs, Jean
Wei Jingsheng 1951(?)- 162
Weik, Mary Hays 1898(?)-1979 .... 21-24R
Obituary 93-96
See also SATA 3
See also SATA-Obit 23
Weil, Andre 1906- 161
Weil, Andrew (Thomas) 1942- CANR-43
Earlier sketches in CA 73-76, CANR-20
Weil, Ann Yezner 1908-1969 .... 5-8R
Obituary 103
See also SATA 9
Weil, Dorothy 1929- 93-96
Weil, Gordon L(ee) 1937- CANR-12
Earlier sketch in CA 73-76
Weil, Herbert S., Jr. 1933- 21-24R
Weil, Irwin 1928- 21-24R
Weil, James L(ehman) 1929- CANR-36
Earlier sketches in CA 93-96, CANR-16
Weil, Jerry 1928- 1-4R
Weil, Jiri 1900-1959 141
Weil, Joseph 1875-1976 Obituary 65-68
Weil, Lisl 1910- CANR-2
Earlier sketch in CA 49-52
See also SATA 7
Weil, Mildred 45-48
Weil, Robert 1955- 125
Weil, Roman L(ee) 1940- CANR-44
Earlier sketches in CA 37-40R, CANR-14
Weil, Simone (Adolphine) 1909-1943 159
Brief entry 117
See also TCLC 23
Weil, Ulric Henry 113
Weilbacher, William Manning 1928- 108
Weilerstein, Sadie Rose 1894-1993 .... 5-8R
Obituary 141
See also SATA 3
See also SATA-Obit 75
Weill, Gus 1933- CANR-7
Earlier sketch in CA 53-56
Weiman, Eiveen 1925- 108
Weimann, Gabriel 1950- 149
Weimann, Jeanne Madeline 1943- 108
Weimar, Karl S(iegfried) 1916- 5-8R
Weimer, Arthur M(artin) 1909-1987 .... 1-4R
Obituary 122
Weimer, Ferne 1950- 137
Weimer, Joan 1936- 144
Weimer, Maryellen 1947- 135
Wein, Elizabeth E(ve) 1964- 149
See also SATA 82
Wein, Jacqueline 1938- 93-96
Weinbaum, Marvin G. 1935- 150
Weinbaum, Raquel
See Vinas, David
Weinbaum, Stanley Grauman 1902(?)-1935 168
Brief entry 110
See also DLB 8
Weinberg, Arthur 1915-1989 .... CANR-15
Obituary 127
Earlier sketch in CA 25-28R
Weinberg, Bernard 1909-1973 Obituary 106
Weinberg, Daniel H. 1949- 120
Weinberg, Daniela 1936- 104
Weinberg, David Henry 1945- 89-92
Weinberg, Edgar 1917-1985 Obituary 117
Weinberg, Florence M(ay) 1933- 37-40R
Weinberg, Gerald M(arvin) 1933- CANR-18
Earlier sketch in CA 89-92
Weinberg, Gerhard L(udwig) 1928- CANR-3
Earlier sketch in CA 9-12R
Weinberg, H. Barbara 134
Weinberg, Helen A(rnstein) 1927- 73-76
Weinberg, Herman G(ershon) 1908-1983 CANR-29
Obituary 111
Earlier sketch in CA 45-48
Weinberg, Ian 1938-1969 .... CAP-2
Earlier sketch in CA 21-22
Weinberg, Janet Hopson
See Hopson, Janet L(ouise)
Weinberg, Julius 1922- 37-40R
Weinberg, Julius R(udolph) 1908-1971 .... CAP-1
Earlier sketch in CA 17-18
Weinberg, Kenneth G. 1920- 41-44R
Weinberg, Kerry 29-32R
Weinberg, Kurt 1912- 41-44R
Weinberg, Larry
See Weinberg, Lawrence (E.)
Weinberg, Lawrence (E.) .... SATA 92
See also SATA-Brief 48
Weinberg, Lila (Shaffer) 25-28R
Weinberg, Martin S(tephen) 1939- CANR-15
Earlier sketch in CA 41-44R
Weinberg, Meyer 1920- CANR-4
Earlier sketch in CA 1-4R
Weinberg, Nathan Gerald 1945- 104
Weinberg, Robert Charles 1901-1974 Obituary 45-48
Weinberg, Robert E(dward) 1946- 97-100
Weinberg, Samuel Kirson 1912- CANR-1
Earlier sketch in CA 1-4R
Weinberg, Sanford Bruce 1950- 109
Weinberg, Steve 1948- 142
Weinberg, Steven 1933- CANR-36
Earlier sketches in CA 53-56, CANR-5
Weinberg, Thomas S(tephen) 1943- 151
Weinberg, Werner 1915- CANR-16
Earlier sketch in CA 41-44R
Weinberger, Betty Kiralfy 1932- 65-68
Weinberger, Caspar W(illard) 1917- 133
Weinberger, Eliot 1949- CANR-40
Earlier sketch in CA 117
Weinberger, Everett 1964- 148
Weinberger, Leon J. 1926- 77-80
Weinberger, Marvin I(rvin) 1954- 113
Weinberger, Miro (Leonard) 1970- 135
Weinberger, Paul E. 1931-1983(?) 29-32R
Obituary 134
Weinberger, Tanya 1939- .... SATA 84
Weinbrot, Howard D. 1936- Brief entry 107
Weiner, Andrew 1949- 161
Weiner, Andrew D(avid) 1943- Brief entry 111
Weiner, Annette B. 1933-1997 93-96
Obituary 163
Weiner, Bernard 1935- 57-60
Weiner, Bernard 1940- .... CAAS 29
Weiner, Charles 1931- 134
Brief entry 109
Weiner, Dora B(ierer) 1924- 25-28R
Weiner, Edith M. 1948- 127
Weiner, Edmund (Simon Christopher) 1950- 139
Weiner, Egon 1906-1987 97-100
Obituary 123
Weiner, Elliot 1943- 122
Weiner, Florence 1931- 25-28R
Weiner, Henri
See Longstreet, Stephen
Weiner, Herbert 5-8R
Weiner, Howard L. 1944- CANR-55
Earlier sketch in CA 127
Weiner, Hyman J(oseph) 1926- 49-52
Weiner, Irving B(ernard) 1933- CANR-27
Earlier sketch in CA 29-32R
Weiner, J(oseph) S(idney) 1915-1982 114
Weiner, Jonathan (David) 1953- 123
Weiner, Kay Bain 1932- 136
Weiner, Leonard 1927- 21-24R
Weiner, Linda 1943- 114
Weiner, Marc A. 1955- 146
Weiner, Marcella Bakur 1925- Brief entry 105

Weiner, Myron 1931- CANR-4
Earlier sketch in CA 1-4R
Weiner, Neal (Orlove) 1942- 118
Weiner, Neil S(herman) 1936- 119
Weiner, Richard 1927- 89-92
Weiner, Sandra 1922- 49-52
See also SATA 14
Weiner, Shelley 1949- 139
Weiner, Skip
See Weiner, Stewart
Weiner, Stephen 1955- 155
Weiner, Steven
See Weiner, Stephen
Weiner, Stewart 1945- CANR-16
Earlier sketch in CA 89-92
Weiner, Susan 1946- 145
Weiner, Tim 1956- 135
Weiner-Davis, Michele 1952- 149
Weinerman, Lisa 1967- 149
Weinfield, Henry 1949- 37-40R
Weingand, Darlene E. 1937- 115
Weingarden, Lauren S. 1948- 128
Weingart, L(aurence) O. 1931- 17-20R
Weingarten, Henry 57-60
Weingarten, Roger 1945- CANR-10
Earlier sketch in CA 61-64
Weingarten, Violet (Brown) 1915-1976 .... CANR-7
Obituary 65-68
Earlier sketch in CA 9-12R
See also SATA 3
See also SATA-Obit 27
Weingartner, Charles 1922- 49-52
See also SATA 5
Weingartner, Herbert J. 1935- 148
Weingartner, James J(oseph) 1940- 93-96
Weingartner, Rudolph H(erbert) 1927- 13-16R
Weingast, David E(lliott) 1912- 5-8R
Weinhaus, Carol L. 1947- 137
Weinhouse, Beth (R) 1957- CANR-68
Earlier sketch in CA 128
Weinig, Jean Maria 1920- CANR-12
Earlier sketch in CA 29-32R
Weinig, Sister Mary Anthony
See Weinig, Jean Maria
Weininger, Benjamin Isaac
1905-1988 Obituary 126
Weininger, Otto 1880-1903 .... TCLC 84
Weininger, Richard 1887(?)-1979 Obituary 89-92
Weinkauf, Mary S(tanley) 1938- 150
Weinland, James D(avid) 1894- 57-60
Weinman, Benzion 1897-1987 Obituary 121
Weinman, Irving 1937- 122
Weinman, Paul 1940- CANR-29
Earlier sketches in CA 77-80, CANR-13
Weinrauch, Herschel 1905- CAP-1
Earlier sketch in CA 13-16
Weinreb, Lloyd L(obell) 1936- 69-72
Weinreich, Beatrice Silverman 1928- 129
Weinrich, A(nna) K(atharina) H(ildegard) 1933- CANR-37
Earlier sketches in CA 37-40R, CANR-16
Weinroth, Michelle 1959- 158
Weinryb, Bernard D(ov) 1905- CANR-25
Earlier sketch in CA 45-48
Weinstein, Allen 1937- CANR-26
Earlier sketch in CA 41-44R
Weinstein, Arnold 1927- 9-12R
Weinstein, Bernard L(ee) 1942- 111
Weinstein, Bob 1941- 120
Weinstein, Brian 1937- 21-24R
Weinstein, Cindy 1960- 149
Weinstein, Donald 1926- 13-16R
Weinstein, Fred 1931- 65-68
Weinstein, Gerald 1930- 25-28R
Weinstein, Grace W(ohlner) CANR-51
Earlier sketches in CA 61-64, CANR-10, 26
Weinstein, Howard 1954- CANR-23
Earlier sketch in CA 107
Weinstein, Jacob Joseph 1902-1974 110
Obituary 108
Weinstein, James 1926- 21-24R
Weinstein, Leo 1921- Brief entry 110
Weinstein, Mark A. 1937- 25-28R
Weinstein, Marlene 1946- 45-48
Weinstein, Martin E. 1934- 85-88
Weinstein, Michael 1898- CAP-1
Earlier sketch in CA 13-14
Weinstein, Michael A(lan) 1942- CANR-65
Earlier sketch in CA 129
Weinstein, Nathan
See West, Nathanael
Weinstein, Nathan von Wallenstein
See West, Nathanael
Weinstein, Nina 1951- .... SATA 73
Weinstein, Norman Charles 1948- CANR-31
Earlier sketch in CA 37-40R
Weinstein, Philip M. 1940- 165
Weinstein, Robert A. 1914- 29-32R
Weinstein, Sol 1928- 13-16R
Weinstein, Warren 1941- 93-96
Weinstock, Herbert 1905-1971 .... CANR-2
Obituary 33-36R
Earlier sketch in CA 1-4R
Weinstock, John M(artin) 1936- 81-84
Weinstock, M(oshe) D(avid) 1922- 131
Weinstone, William W. 1898(?)-1985 Obituary 117
Weinswig, Melvin H. 1935- Brief entry 107
Weintal, Edward 1901-1973 Obituary 41-44R
Weintraub, David 1949- 167
Weintraub, Dov 1926-1985 .... CANR-36
Earlier sketch in CA 109
Weintraub, Karl Joachim 1924- 25-28R
Weintraub, Linda 1942- 135
Weintraub, Robert E. 1925-1983 Obituary 110
Weintraub, Rodelle (Selma) 1933- 97-100
Weintraub, Sidney 1914-1983 .... CANR-6
Obituary 110
Earlier sketch in CA 1-4R
Weintraub, Sidney 1922- CANR-26
Earlier sketch in CA 108
Weintraub, Stanley 1929- CANR-22
Earlier sketches in CA 1-4R, CANR-2
See also CAAS 20
See also DLB 111
Weintraub, Wiktor 1908-1988 .... CANR-3
Obituary 126
Earlier sketch in CA 5-8R
Weintraub, William 1926- 1-4R
Weinwurm, George F(elix) 1935- 33-36R
Weinzweig, Helen 1915- 106
Weir, Alice M.
See McLaughlin, Emma Maude
Weir, Ben(jamin M.) 1923- 144
Weir, Bob 1947- 143
See also SATA 76
Weir, Carol S. 1924- 125
Weir, Charlene 1937- 153
Weir, David (A.) 1947- 147
Weir, Gary E. 1951(?)- 145
Weir, J(ohn) E(dward) 1935- 118
Weir, Joan S(herman) 1928- CANR-58
Earlier sketches in CA 112, CANR-31
See also SATA 99
Weir, John
See Cross, Colin (John)
Weir, LaVada CANR-9
Earlier sketch in CA 21-24R
See also SATA 2
Weir, Molly 1920- CANR-12
Earlier sketch in CA 29-32R
Weir, Nancie MacCullough 1933- 65-68
Weir, Peter (Lindsay) 1944- 123
Brief entry 113
See also CLC 20
Weir, Robert M(cColloch) 1933- 93-96
Weir, Rosemary (Green) 1905- CANR-10
Earlier sketch in CA 13-16R
See also SATA 21
Weir, Thomas R(obert) 1912- 41-44R
Weir, Walter 1909- 5-8R
Weir, Wendy 1949- 143
See also SATA 76
Weis, Elisabeth 1944- 112
Weis, Jack 1932- 105
Weis, Margaret (Edith) 1948- CANR-59
Earlier sketches in CA 111, CANR-34
See also SATA 38, 92
Weis, Norman D(wight) 1923- 61-64
Weis, Rene (Jean Alphonse) 1953- 127
Weisberg, Barry 33-36R
Weisberg, Gabriel P(aul) 1942- 73-76
Weisberg, Harold 1913- 41-44R
Weisberg, Herbert F. 1941- 151
Weisberg, Joseph Gotland
1911-1984 Obituary 112
Weisberg, Joseph S(impson) 1937- 107
Weisberg, Richard H(arvey) 1944- 128
Weisberger, Bernard A(llen) 1922- CANR-7
Earlier sketch in CA 5-8R
See also SATA 21
Weisberger, Eleanor (Burt) 1920- 97-100
Weisbord, Albert 1900(?)-1977 Obituary 69-72
Weisbord, Marvin R(oss) 1931- CANR-9
Earlier sketch in CA 65-68
Weisbord, Robert G. 1933- Brief entry 109
Weisbord, Vera Buch 1895-1987 73-76
Obituary 123
Weisbrod, Burton Allen 1931- CANR-21
Earlier sketches in CA 45-48, CANR-1
Weisbrot, Robert (S.) 1951- 131
Weisbuch, Robert 1946- 104
Weisburd, Martin Harold
1940(?)-1978 Obituary 77-80
Weise, Christian 1642-1708 .... DLB 168
Weise, R. Eric 1933- 41-44R
Weisenborn, Guenther 1902-1969 Obituary 114
See also Weisenborn, Gunther
See also DLB 69, 124
Weisenborn, Gunther
See Weisenborn, Guenther
See also DLB 69, 124
Weisenburger, Francis Phelps 1900- CAP-1
Earlier sketch in CA 17-18
Weisenfeld, Murray 1923- 104
Weiser, David K. 1944- 127
Weiser, Eric 1907- 17-20R
Weiser, Marjorie P(hillis) K(atz) 1934- 103
See also SATA 33
Weisgal, Meyer W(olf) 1894-1977 Obituary 89-92
Weisgall, Jonathan M. 1949- 154
Weisgard, Leonard (Joseph) 1916- 9-12R
See also MAICYA
See also SAAS 19
See also SATA 2, 30, 85
Weisgerber, Charles A(ugust) 1912-1977 .... 41-44R
Weisgerber, Jean 1924- 65-68
Weisgerber, Robert A(rthur) 1929- 49-52
Weisheipl, James A(thanasius) 1923- CANR-15
Earlier sketch in CA 41-44R
Weisheit, Eldon 1933- CANR-14
Earlier sketch in CA 29-32R
Weisinger, Mort 1915- 9-12R
Weiskopf, Bob
See Weiskopf, Robert J.
Weiskopf, Robert J. 1914- 123
Brief entry 118
Interview in 123
Weisman, Alan H. 1947- 127
Weisman, Avery Danto 1913- 156
Weisman, Brent Richards 1952- 142
Weisman, Herman M. 1916- 9-12R
Weisman, John 1942- CANR-40
Earlier sketches in CA 45-48, 145, CANR-1
Weisman, Marilee 1939- 65-68
Weisman, Mary-Lou 1937- 109
Weismann, Donald L(eroy) 1914- 33-36R
Weismiller, Edward Ronald 1915- CANR-1
Earlier sketch in CA 1-4R
Weiss, Abraham 1895-1971 Obituary 104
Weiss, Adelle 1920- 81-84
See also SATA 18
Weiss, Allen 1918- 109
Weiss, Andrea 1956- 154
Weiss, Ann E(dwards) 1943- CANR-28
Earlier sketches in CA 45-48, CANR-1, 11
See also MAICYA
See also SAAS 13
See also SATA 30, 69
Weiss, Arthur 1912- 25-28R
Weiss, Bennet A., Jr. 1926(?)-1983 Obituary 109
Weiss, Beno 1933- 123
Weiss, Bernard J(acob) 1936- 109
Weiss, Brian L(eslie) 1944- 165
Weiss, Dale Eugene 1947- 114
Weiss, Daniel Evan 1953- 147
Weiss, David
See Halivni, David Weiss
Weiss, David 1909- CANR-12
Earlier sketch in CA 13-16R
Weiss, Edna
See Barth, Edna
Weiss, Edna Smith 1916- 5-8R
Weiss, Elizabeth S(chwartz) 1944- CANR-11
Earlier sketch in CA 61-64
Weiss, Ellen 1953- 113
See also SATA 44
Weiss, Ernst 1882-1940 .... DLB 81
Weiss, Francis Joseph
1899(?)-1975 Obituary 53-56
Weiss, G(ustav) A(dolf) M(ichael) 1922- 41-44R
Weiss, Gaea (Laughingbird) 1941- 119
Weiss, Harry B(ischoff) 1883-1972 45-48
Weiss, Harvey 1922- CANR-38
Earlier sketches in CA 5-8R, CANR-6
See also CLR 4
See also MAICYA
See also SAAS 19
See also SATA 1, 27, 76
Weiss, Herbert F. 1930- 21-24R
Weiss, Irving J. 1921- CANR-10
Earlier sketch in CA 17-20R
Weiss, Jaqueline Shachter 1926- 119
See also SATA 65
Weiss, Jess E(dward) 1926- CANR-38
Earlier sketch in CA 49-52
Weiss, Joan Talmage 1928- CANR-2
Earlier sketch in CA 5-8R
Weiss, John 1818-1879 .... DLB 1
Weiss, John 1927- CANR-66
Earlier sketch in CA 17-20R
Weiss, Jonathan A(rthur) 1939- 93-96
Weiss, Kenneth M(onrad) 1941- 101
Weiss, Leatie 1928- 65-68
See also SATA-Brief 50
Weiss, Leonard W(inchell) 1925- CANR-6
Earlier sketch in CA 5-8R
Weiss, Lillian (?)-1972 Obituary 104
Weiss, Louise 1893-1983 Obituary 109
Weiss, M(orton) Jerome 1926- CANR-9
Earlier sketch in CA 17-20R
Weiss, M. Jerry
See Weiss, M(orton) Jerome
Weiss, Malcolm E. 1928- CANR-11
Earlier sketch in CA 25-28R
See also SATA 3
Weiss, Margaret R. 1923(?)-1992 57-60
Obituary 137
Weiss, Melford Stephen 1937- 53-56
Weiss, Michael
See Weiss, Mike
Weiss, Mike 1942- 141
Weiss, Miriam
See Schlein, Miriam
Weiss, Miriam (Strauss) 1905- CAP-2
Earlier sketch in CA 29-32
Weiss, Morris S(amuel) 1915- 89-92
Weiss, Nancy J(oan) 1944- CANR-13
Earlier sketch in CA 77-80
Weiss, Nicki 1954- CANR-26
Earlier sketch in CA 108
See also SATA 33, 86
Weiss, Paul
See Weiss, Paul A(lfred)
Weiss, Paul 1901- CANR-3
Earlier sketch in CA 5-8R
See also CAAS 12
Weiss, Paul A(lfred) 1898-1989 Obituary 129
Weiss, Peg 1933(?)-1996 125
Obituary 152
Weiss, Peter (Ulrich) 1916-1982 .... CANR-3
Obituary 106
Earlier sketch in CA 45-48
See also CLC 3, 15, 51
See also DAM DRAM
See also DLB 69, 124
Weiss, Raymond L. 1930- 142
Weiss, Renee Karol 1923- 41-44R
See also SATA 5
Weiss, Robert M. 1929- 37-40R
Weiss, Robert S(tuart) 1925- 25-28R
Weiss, Roger W(illiam) 1930- 45-48
weiss, ruth 1928- 122
See also CAAS 24
Weiss, Samuel A(bba) 1922- 41-44R
Weiss, Sanford 1927- 25-28R
Weiss, (Paul) Shandor 1954- 120
Weiss, Theodore (Russell) 1916- CANR-46
Earlier sketch in CA 9-12R
See also CAAS 2
See also CLC 3, 8, 14
See also DLB 5
Weiss, Thomas Fischer 1934- 162
Weiss, Thomas G. 1946- 142
Weiss, Thomas J(oseph) 1942- 105
Weiss, Timothy F. 1949- 146
Weiss, Winfried (Ferdinand) 1937-1991 117
Obituary 140
Weissberg, Michael P. 1942- 126
Weissberger, L. Arnold 1907-1981 Obituary 103
Weissbort, Daniel 1935- CANR-2
Earlier sketch in CA 45-48
Weissbourd, Bernice (Targ) 1923- 153
Weissbourd, Richard 167
Weisse, Christian Felix 1726-1804 .... DLB 97
Weissenborn, Hellmuth 1898-1982 Obituary 107
See also SATA-Obit 31
Weisser, Michael R. 1944- 143
Weisskopf, Kurt 1907- 25-28R
Weisskopf, Thomas E. 1940- 130
Weisskopf, Victor Frederick 1908- 107
Weisskopf, Walter A(lbert) 1904- 37-40R
Weissman, Benjamin M(urry) 1917- 73-76
Weissman, Dick
See Weissman, Richard
Weissman, Jack 1921- 13-16R
Weissman, Paul 1932- 45-48
Weissman, Philip 1911(?)-1972 Obituary 33-36R
Weissman, Richard 1935- 81-84
Weissman, Rozanne 1942- 101
Weissman, Stephen R(ichard) 1941- CANR-11
Earlier sketch in CA 57-60
Weissman, Steve
See Weissman, Stephen R(ichard)
Weissmann, Ann B. 1934- 139
Weissmann, Gerald 1930- CANR-52
Earlier sketch in CA 126
Weissmuller, Johnny
See Weissmuller, Peter John
Weissmuller, Peter John 1904-1984 Obituary 111
Weisstein, Ulrich W(erner) 1925- 21-24R
Weisstub, D(avid) N(orman) 1944- CANR-44
Earlier sketch in CA 29-32R
Weist, Dwight 1910- 132
Weith, Warren 1926- 114
Weithorn, Stanley S(tephen) 1924- 13-16R
Weitling, Wilhelm 1808-1871 .... DLB 129
Weitz, Henry 1911- 41-44R
Weitz, John 1923- 29-32R
Weitz, Martin Mishli 1909- CANR-13
Earlier sketches in CAP-2, CA 17-18
Weitz, Morris 1916-1981 .... CANR-7
Obituary 102
Earlier sketch in CA 5-8R
Weitz, Raanan 1913- CANR-1
Earlier sketch in CA 45-48
Weitzel, Edwin A(nthony) 1905-1988 Obituary 127
Weitzel, Eugene Joseph 1927- 5-8R
Weitzel, Tony
See Weitzel, Edwin A(nthony)
Weitzel, William (Frederick) 1936- 143
Weitzenhoffer, Andre M(uller) 1921- 5-8R
Weitzman, Alan 1933- 29-32R
Weitzman, Arthur J(oshua) 1933- 53-56
Weitzman, Elliot D. 1929-1983 Obituary 110
Weitzman, Martin L(awrence) 1942- 117
Weitzmann, Kurt 1904-1993 .... CANR-35
Obituary 141
Earlier sketch in CA 41-44R
Weixlmann, Joe
See Weixlmann, Joseph Norman
Weixlmann, Joseph Norman 1946- 109
Weizenbaum, Joseph 1923- Brief entry 113
Weizman, Ezer 1924- 111
Weizman, Savine Gross 1929- 131
Weizsaecker, Carl Friedrich von
See von Weizsaecker, Carl Friedrich
Wekesser, Carol A. 1963- 143
See also SATA 76
Welber, Robert 104
See also SATA 26
Welbourn, F(rederick) B(urkewood) 1912- 21-24R
Welburn, Ron(ald Garfield) 1944- CANR-17
Earlier sketches in CA 45-48, CANR-1
See also BW 1
Welch, Amanda (Jane) 1945- .... SATA 75
Welch, Ann Courtenay (Edmonds) 1917- CANR-18
Earlier sketches in CA 9-12R, CANR-3
Welch, Bob
See Welch, Robert Lynn
Welch, Charles Scott
See Smith, LeRoi Tex
Welch, Claude E(merson), Jr. 1939- CANR-32
Earlier sketches in CA 41-44R, CANR-14
Welch, Cyril 1939- 118
Welch, D. Don, (Jr.) 148
Welch, D'Alte Aldridge 1907-1970 Obituary 104
See also SATA-Obit 27
Welch, David 1950- 130
Welch, (Maurice) Denton 1915-1948 148
Brief entry 121
See also TCLC 22
Welch, Don(ovan LeRoy) 1932- CANR-43
Earlier sketches in CA 104, CANR-20
Welch, Finis R. 1938- 118
Welch, George Patrick 1901-1976 .... CAP-1
Obituary 65-68
Earlier sketch in CA 13-14
Welch, Gita (Bernardo) Honwana 1948- 138
Welch, Herbert 1862-1969 .... CAP-1
Earlier sketch in CA 13-16
Welch, Holmes (Hinkley) 1921- 21-24R
Welch, J(oseph) Edmund 1922- 57-60

Welch, James 1940- CANR-66
Earlier sketches in CA 85-88, CANR-42
See also CLC 6, 14, 52
See also DAM MULT, POP
See also DLB 175
See also NNAL
Welch, Jean-Louise
See Kempton, Jean Welch
Welch, Jerome A. 1933- 65-68
Welch, June Rayfield 1927- 41-44R
Welch, Kathleen E(thel) 1951- 136
Welch, Kenneth Frederick 1917- 105
Welch, Lew(is Barrett, Jr.) 1926-1971(?) 153
Obituary 113
See also DLB 16
Welch, Liliane 1937- CANR-27
Earlier sketch in CA 110
Welch, Martha McKeen 1914- Brief entry 114
See also SATA-Brief 45
Welch, Mary Ross 1918- 53-56
Welch, Mary-Scott (Stewart) 1919-1995 104
Obituary 149
Welch, Michael Irene 1940- 97-100
Welch, Patrick
See Welch, George Patrick
Welch, Pauline
See Bodenham, Hilda Morris
Welch, Richard Edwin, Jr. 1924- 85-88
Welch, Robert 1947- 159
Welch, Robert H(enry) W(inborne), Jr. 1899-1985 Obituary 114
Welch, Robert Lynn 1956- 112
Welch, Ronald
See Felton, Ronald Oliver
Welch, Rowland
See Davies, L(eslie) P(urnell)
Welch, Stuart Cary 1928- 103
Welch, Timothy L. 1935- 85-88
Welch, William 1917- Brief entry 115
Welch, William 1917-1981(?) 154
Welch, William A. 1915(?)-1976 Obituary 65-68
Welch, Willy 1952- 159
See also SATA 93
Welcher, Jeanne K. 1922- Brief entry 116
Welcher, Rosalind 1922- CANR-25
Earlier sketch in CA 45-48
Welchman, Gordon 1906(?)-1985 Obituary 117
Welcome, John
See Brennan, John N(eedham) H(uggard)
Weld, John 1905- 147
Weld, Philip S(altonstall Sr.) 1914-1984 Obituary 114
Welding, Patsy Ruth 1924- 61-64
Weldon, Fay 1931- CANR-63
Earlier sketches in CA 21-24R, CANR-16, 46
Interview in CANR-16
See also CDBLB 1960 to Present
See also CLC 6, 9, 11, 19, 36, 59
See also DAM POP
See also DLB 14, 194
See also MTCW 1
Weldon, John 1890(?)-1963 Obituary 115
See also MacNamara, Brinsley
Weldon, John F(rederick Stover) 1948- 113
Weldon, Lynn Leroy 1930- 97-100
Weldon, Michael J(ames) 1952- 117
Weldon, Rex
See Rimel, Duane (Weldon)
Weldon, (Nathaniel) Warren (Jr.) 1919- 29-32R
Weldt-Basson, Helene Carol 1958- 145
Welfare, Humphrey 1950- 124
Welfare, Simon 1946- 133
Welfle, Richard A. 1901- CAP-1
Earlier sketch in CA 13-14
Welfling, Weldon 1912-1978 Obituary 111
Welford, A(lan) T(raviss) 1914- CANR-5
Earlier sketch in CA 13-16R
Welford, Sue 1942- 142
See also SATA 75
Welk, Lawrence 1903- 134
Brief entry 105
Welke, Elton 1941- 65-68
Welker, David 1917- 57-60
Welker, Robert Henry 1917- 89-92
Welker, Robert L(ouis) 1924- 9-12R
Welkowitz, Joan 1929- 53-56
Well, Alan Stewart
See Sewart, Alan
Welland, Colin
See Williams, Colin
Welland, Dennis (Sydney Reginald) 1919- CANR-2
Earlier sketch in CA 5-8R
Wellard, James (Howard) 1909-1987 CANR-3
Obituary 122
Earlier sketch in CA 5-8R
Wellborn, Charles 1923- 29-32R
Wellborn, Fred W(ilmot) 1894- 9-12R
Wellborn, Grace Pleasant 1906-(?) CAP-2
Earlier sketch in CA 17-18
Wellek, Rene 1903-1995 CANR-8
Obituary 150
Earlier sketch in CA 5-8R
Interview in CANR-8
See also CAAS 7
See also CLC 28
See also DLB 63
Wellen, Edward (Paul) 1919- 85-88
Weller, Allen Stuart 1907- CANR-24
Earlier sketch in CA 1-4R
Weller, Charles 1911- 21-24R
Weller, George (Anthony) 1907- 65-68
See also SATA 31
Weller, Michael 1942- 85-88
See also CLC 10, 53
Weller, Paul 1958- CLC 26
Weller, Robert P(aul) 1953- 118
Weller, Sheila 1945- 77-80
Weller, Vann K. 166
Wellershoff, Dieter 1925- CANR-37
Earlier sketches in CA 89-92, CANR-16
See also CLC 46
Welles, Margery Miller 1923-1985 Obituary 115
Welles, (George) Orson 1915-1985 93-96
Obituary 117
See also CLC 20, 80
Welles, Samuel Gardner 1913(?)-1981 Obituary 105
Welles, Winifred 1893-1939 Brief entry 112
See also SATA-Brief 27
Wellesbourne, Peter
See Williams, P(eter) F(airney)
Wellesley, Gerald 1885-1972 Obituary 104
Wellesley, Kenneth 1911- 106
Wellesz, Egon Joseph 1885-1974 Obituary 53-56
Wellford, Harrison 1940- Brief entry 111
Wellford, Lin(da) 1951- 165
Wellham, John W(alter) G(eorge) 1919- 150
Welling, Kathryn M. 1952- 127
Welling, William 1924- 81-84
Wellington, C(harles) Burleigh 1920- 1-4R
Wellington, Harry H(illel) 1926- 25-28R
Wellington, Jean Willett 1922- 1-4R
Wellington, John H. 1892- CAP-2
Earlier sketch in CA 25-28
Wellington, Kate
See Schulze, Hertha
Wellington, Monica 1957- 136
See also SATA 67, 99
Wellington, R(ichard) A(nthony) 1919- 61-64
Wellisch, Hans H(anan) 1920- 102
Wellisz, Leopold T. 1882-1972 Obituary 37-40R
Wellman, Alice 1900-1984 89-92
See also SATA 51
See also SATA-Brief 36
Wellman, Carl (Pierce) 1926- 37-40R
Wellman, Frederick L(ovejoy) 1897- 77-80
Wellman, Henry Q. 1945- 37-40R
Wellman, John McDowell 1945- 166
See also Wellman, Mac
Wellman, Mac 1945-
See Wellman, John McDowell
and Wellman, John McDowell
See also CLC 65
Wellman, Manly Wade 1903-1986 CANR-44
Obituary 118
Earlier sketches in CA 1-4R, CANR-6, 16
See also CLC 49
See also SATA 6
See also SATA-Obit 47
Wellman, Paul I(selin) 1898-1966 CANR-64
Obituary 25-28R
Earlier sketches in CA 1-4R, CANR-16
See also SATA 3
Wellman, William A(ugustus) 1896-1975 Obituary 61-64
Wellner, Alison S(tein) 1974- 163
Wells, Allen 1951- CANR-56
Earlier sketch in CA 125
Wells, Angus 1943- 167
Wells, Anna Mary 1906- CANR-2
Earlier sketch in CA 5-8R
Wells, Arvin Robert 1927- 1-4R
Wells, Bella Fromm 1901(?)-1972 Obituary 104
Wells, C(olin) M(ichael) 1933- 41-44R
Wells, Carolyn 1869(?)-1942 Brief entry 113
See also DLB 11
See also TCLC 35
Wells, Catherine 1952- 164
Wells, Charles Jeremiah 1800-1879 DLB 32
Wells, David Franklin 1928- Brief entry 108
Wells, Dee (Alberta) 1925- 85-88
See also AITN 1
Wells, (William) Dicky 1910- 61-64
Wells, Donald A(rthur) 1917- 21-24R
Wells, Edward
See Wellsted, W. Raife
Wells, Ellen B(aker) 1934- 103
Wells, Evelyn 53-56
Wells, Gabriel 1862-1946 DLB 140
Wells, George A(lbert) 1926- CANR-32
Earlier sketches in CA 81-84, CANR-15
Wells, George Philip 1901-1985 Obituary 117
Wells, H(erbert) G(eorge) 1866-1946 121
Brief entry 110
See also AAYA 18
See also CDBLB 1914-1945
See also DA
See also DAB
See also DAC
See also DAM MST, NOV
See also DLB 34, 70, 156, 178
See also MTCW 1
See also SATA 20
See also SSC 6
See also TCLC 6, 12, 19
See also WLC
Wells, Harold P(hilmore) 1925- CANR-10
Earlier sketch in CA 65-68
Wells, Harry Kohlsaat 1911-1976 5-8R
Obituary 65-68
Wells, Helen
See Campbell, Hope
Wells, Helen 1910-1986 CANR-37
Earlier sketch in CA 29-32R
See also MAICYA
See also SATA 2, 49
Wells, Helena 1758(?)-1824 DLB 200
Wells, Henry W(illis) 1895-1978 CANR-28
Obituary 77-80
Earlier sketch in CA 81-84
Wells, Hondo
See Whittington, Harry (Benjamin)
Wells, J. Wellington
See de Camp, L(yon) Sprague
Wells, James B(uchanan) 1909- 45-48
Wells, James M. 1917- 17-20R
Wells, Jane 1961- 155
Wells, Jerome C(ovell) 1936- 41-44R
Wells, Jessica
See Buckland, Raymond
Wells, Joel F(reeman) 1930- CANR-23
Earlier sketch in CA 13-16R
Wells, John Campbell 1936-1998 104
Obituary 164
Wells, John Jay
See Coulson, Juanita (Ruth)
Wells, John Warren 1938- CANR-4
Earlier sketch in CA 49-52
Wells, June
See Swinford, Betty (June Wells)
Wells, Kenneth McNeill 1905- CAP-1
Earlier sketch in CA 13-14
Wells, Lawrence 1941- 120
Wells, Leon W. 1925- 17-20R
Wells, Linton 1893-1976 97-100
Obituary 61-64
Wells, Lisa
See Raucina, Thomas Frank
Wells, Louis T(ruitt), Jr. 1937- 65-68
Wells, M. Gawain 1942- 101
Wells, Marian (Louise Bradfield) 1931- 113
Wells, Martha 1964- 142
Wells, Mary Ann 1944- 155
Wells, Merle William 1918- CANR-37
Earlier sketches in CA 85-88, CANR-16
Wells, Nigel 1944- 118
Wells, Patricia 1946- 132
Wells, Peter D. 1936- 25-28R
Wells, Robert
See Welsch, Roger L(ee)
Wells, (Frank Charles) Robert 1929- 97-100
Wells, Robert 1947- 155
See also DLB 40
Wells, Robert Vale 1943- CANR-12
Earlier sketch in CA 73-76
Wells, Robert W(ayne) 1918- CANR-2
Earlier sketch in CA 49-52
Wells, Roger 1947- 136
Wells, Ronald Vale 1913- CANR-14
Earlier sketch in CA 37-40R
Wells, Rosemary 1943- CANR-48
Earlier sketch in CA 85-88
See also AAYA 13
See also CLC 12
See also CLR 16
See also MAICYA
See also SAAS 1
See also SATA 18, 69
Wells, Samuel F(ogle, Jr.) 1935- 104
Wells, Samuel J(ames III) 1936- 123
Wells, Stanley W(illiam) 1930- CANR-29
Earlier sketches in CA 21-24R, CANR-10
Wells, Susan (Mary) 1951- 146
See also SATA 78
Wells, Theodora (Westmont) 1926- 134
Brief entry 113
Wells, Tim 1954- 129
Wells, Tobias
See Forbes, DeLoris (Florine) Stanton
Wells, Tom H. 1917- 21-24R
Wells, Walter 1937- 25-28R
Wells, William D(eWitt) 1926- CANR-13
Earlier sketch in CA 61-64
Wells, William Thomas 1908-1990(?) Obituary 130
Wells-Barnett, Ida B. 1862-1931 DLB 23
Wellsted, W. Raife 1929- 125
Wellstone, Paul David 1944- 107
Wellwarth, George E(manuel) 1932- CANR-3
Earlier sketch in CA 9-12R
Welmers, William Evert 1916- 104
Wels, Alena 1938(?)-1985 Obituary 115
Wels, Byron G(erald) 1924- CANR-8
Earlier sketch in CA 61-64
See also SATA 9
Welsbacher, Anne 1955- 155
See also SATA 89
Welsby, Paul A(ntony) 1920- 129
Welsch, Erwin Kurt 1935- 17-20R
Welsch, Glenn Albert 1915- CANR-10
Earlier sketch in CA 13-16R
Welsch, Roger L(ee) 1936- CANR-9
Earlier sketch in CA 21-24R, 149
See also SATA 82
Welsh, Alexander 1933- CANR-6
Earlier sketch in CA 5-8R
Welsh, Andrew 1937- 110
Welsh, Anne 1922- 101
Welsh, David
See Hills, C(harles) A(lbert) R(eis)
Welsh, David J(ohn) 1920- 17-20R
Welsh, Frank (Reeson) 1931- 135
Welsh, George Schlager 1918- 17-20R
Welsh, James Michael 1938- CANR-20
Earlier sketches in CA 53-56, CANR-4
Welsh, John R(ushing) 1916-1974 37-40R
Welsh, Ken 1941- CANR-13
Earlier sketch in CA 77-80
Welsh, Marion E. 1910- 118
Welsh, Mary
See Hemingway, Mary Welsh
Welsh, Mary Flynn 1910(?)-1984 Obituary 112
See also SATA-Obit 38
Welsh, Paul 1911- 104
Welsh, Peter C(orbett) 1926- 25-28R
Welsh, Stanley L. 1928- 103
Welsh, Susan
See Collins, Margaret (Brandon James)
Welsh, William A(llen) 1940- CANR-25
Earlier sketch in CA 45-48
Welsing, Frances Cress 1935- 142
See also BW 2
Welsman, Ernest 1912- 5-8R
Welt, Elly 127
Welt, Louis G(ordon) 1913-1974 Obituary 45-48
Welter, Erich 1900-1982 Obituary 107
Welter, Paul (R.) 1928- 121
Welter, Rush (Eastman) 1923- CANR-2
Earlier sketch in CA 5-8R
Weltge, Ralph (William) 1930- 21-24R
Weltge, Sigrid W(ortmann) 1935- 145
Weltge-Wortmann, Sigrid
See Weltge, Sigrid W(ortmann)
Welthy, Soni Halstead 1933- 13-16R
Weltmann, Lutz 1901- CAP-1
Earlier sketch in CA 11-12
Weltner, Linda R(iverly) 1938- 105
See also SATA 38
Weltner, Peter (Nissen) 1942- 160
Welton, Jude 1955- 148
See also SATA 79
Weltsch, Robert 1891-1982 Obituary 108
Welty, Eudora 1909- CANR-65
Earlier sketches in CA 9-12R, CANR-32
See also CABS 1
See also CDALB 1941-1968
See also CLC 1, 2, 5, 14, 22, 33, 105
See also DA
See also DAB
See also DAC
See also DAM MST, NOV
See also DLB 2, 102, 143
See also DLBD 12
See also DLBY 87
See also MTCW 1
See also SSC 1, 27
See also WLC
Welty, Joel Carl 1901- CANR-2
Earlier sketch in CA 5-8R
Welty, S. F.
See Welty, Susan F.
Welty, Susan F. 1905- CAP-2
Earlier sketch in CA 17-18
See also SATA 9
Welwood, John 1943- CANR-46
Earlier sketch in CA 120
Welzenbach, Lanora F.
See Miller, Lanora
Wemple, Suzanne Fonay 1927- 106
Wen, Chihua 1958- 147
Wenar, Charles 1922- 93-96
Wende, Philip 1939- 29-32R
Wendel, Francois Jean 1905-(?) CAP-1
Earlier sketch in CA 13-14
Wendel, Natalja Rose 1900- 61-64
Wendel, Thomas H(arold) 1924- 53-56
Wendel, Tim 1956- 105
Wendelin, Rudolph 1910- SATA 23
Wendell, Barrett 1855-1921 DLB 71
Wender, Dorothea 1934- CANR-24
Earlier sketch in CA 45-48
Wender, Paul H. 1934- CANR-51
Earlier sketches in CA 109, CANR-26
Wenderoth, Joe 1966- 150
Wenders, Wim 1945- 93-96
Wendland, Michael F(letcher) 1946- CANR-9
Earlier sketch in CA 65-68
Wendland, Mike
See Wendland, Michael F(letcher)
Wendling, Ronald C(harles) 1939- 152
Wendorf, Patricia 1928- 113
Wendorf, Richard (Harold) 1948- CANR-36
Earlier sketch in CA 114
Wendover, Robert W(arren) 1955- 145
Wendroff, Zalman
See Vendrovskii, David Efimovich
Wendrowsky, Zalman
See Vendrovskii, David Efimovich
Wendt, Albert 1939- 57-60
Wendt, Gerald L(ouis) 1891-1973 Obituary 45-48
Wendt, Ingrid 1944- 117
Wendt, Jo Ann 1935- 109
Wendt, Lloyd 1908- CANR-25
Earlier sketch in CA 102
Wendt, Viola (Sophia) 1907- 104
Wendzel, Robert L. 1938- 112
Weng, Byron S. J. 1934- CANR-16
Earlier sketch in CA 41-44R
Weng, Hsing Ching
See Weng, Wan-go
Weng, Wan-go 1918- 97-100
Wengenroth, Edith Flack Ackley 1887-1970 Obituary 104
Wengenroth, Stow 1906-1978 Obituary 104
Wenger, (Anna) Grace 1919- 13-16R
Wenger, J(ohn) C(hristian) 1910- CANR-21
Earlier sketches in CA 1-4R, CANR-6
Wengert, Norman Irving 1916- 85-88
Wengrov, Charles 1925- CANR-7
Earlier sketch in CA 5-8R
Wenham, David 1945- 152
Wenham, John W(illiam) 1913- 57-60
Wenhe, Mary B. 1910- 65-68
Wen I-to 1899-1946 TCLC 28
Wenk, Edward, Jr. 1920- 53-56
Wenkam, Robert 1920- CANR-4
Earlier sketch in CA 53-56
Wenkart, Heni
See Wenkart, Henny
Wenkart, Henny 1928- 9-12R
Wennblom, Ralph D. 1922(?)-1986 Obituary 121
Wenner, Jann S(imon) 1946- 101
Interview in 101
Wenner, Kate 1947- 77-80

Wenner, Lettie McSpadden 1937- 65-68
Wenner, Manfred W. 1936- 29-32R
Wenner, Sim 1922- 1-4R
Wennerstrom, Mary H(annah) 1939- 134
Brief entry 110
Wensing, Michael G. 1950- 118
Wensinger, Arthur S(tevens) 1926- CANR-33
Earlier sketches in CA 37-40R, CANR-15
Wentink, Andrew Mark 1948- 105
Wentworth, Barbara
See Pitcher, Gladys
Wentworth, Elise H(ughes) 1931- 77-80
Wentworth, Harold 1904- CAP-1
Earlier sketch in CA 13-14
Wentworth, Michael J(ustin) 1938- 118
Wentworth, Patricia 1878-1961 DLB 77
Wentworth, Robert
See Hamilton, Edmond
Wentz, Frederick K(uhlman) 1921- 9-12R
Wentz, Walter B. 1929- CANR-10
Earlier sketch in CA 25-28R
Wenzel, Siegfried 1928- 21-24R
Weores, Sandor 1913-1989 Obituary 127
Wepman, Dennis 1933- CANR-46
Earlier sketch in CA 120
Wepman, Joseph M. 1907- 45-48
Weppner, Robert S. 1936- 121
Werblow, Dorothy N. 1908-1972 Obituary 37-40R
Werckmeister, O(tto) K(arl) 1934- 140
Were, Gideon S(aulo) 1934- CANR-11
Earlier sketch in CA 65-68
Werenskiold, Marit 1942- 130
Werfel, Franz (Viktor) 1890-1945 161
Brief entry 104
See also DLB 81, 124
See also TCLC 8
Werich, Jan 1905(?)-1980 Obituary 102
Werking, Richard Hume 1943- Brief entry 113
Werkley, Caroline E(lsea) 29-32R
Werkman, Sidney L(ee) 1927- 49-52
Werkmeister, Lucyle (Thomas) 1908- 5-8R
Werkmeister, W(illiam) H(enry) 1901- 21-24R
Werlich, David P(atrick) 1941- 81-84
Werlich, Robert (O'Donnell) 1924-1994 9-12R
Obituary 145
Werlin, Herbert Holland 1932- 61-64
Werlin, Nancy 1961- 151
See also SATA 87
Werlock, Abby Holmes P(otter) 1942- 137
Werman, Golda 1930- 158
Werman, Robert 1929- 139
Wermuth, Paul C(harles Joseph) 1925- 13-16R
Wernblad, Annette 1958- 144
Werne, Benjamin 1904-1978 Obituary 77-80
Wernecke, Herbert Henry 1895- 5-8R
Werner, Alfred 1911-1979 Obituary 89-92
Werner, D. Michael 1950- 120
Werner, Elsa Jane
See Watson, Jane Werner
Werner, Emmy Elizabeth 1929- 57-60
Werner, Eric 1901-1988 13-16R
Obituary 126
Werner, Flora
See Gonzalez (Mandri), Flora
Werner, Hans 1946- 131
Werner, Hazen G. 1895- 17-20R
Werner, Herma 1926- CANR-34
Earlier sketches in CA 85-88, CANR-15
See also SATA 47
See also SATA-Brief 41
Werner, Jane
See Watson, Jane Werner
Werner, Jayne S(usan) 1944- 112
Werner, John R(oland) 1930- 41-44R
Werner, K.
See Casewit, Curtis W(erner)
Werner, Karl Ferdinand 1924- 131
Werner, M(orris) R(obert) 1897-1981 107
Obituary 104
Werner, Peter Howard 1944- CANR-4
Earlier sketch in CA 53-56
Werner, Victor (Emile) 1894-1980 29-32R
Obituary 93-96
Werner, Vivian 1921- 105
Werner, Zacharias 1768-1823 DLB 94
Wernette, J(ohn) Philip 1903- 5-8R
Wernher der Gartenaere fl. 1265-1280 DLB 138
Wernick, Andrew (Lee) 1945- 142
Wernick, Robert 1918- 97-100
Wernick, Saul 1921- 81-84
Werning, Waldo J. 1921- CANR-10
Earlier sketch in CA 13-16R
Wernstedt, Frederick L(age) 1921- 21-24R
Werr, Donald F. 1920- 21-24R
Werry, Richard R. 1916- 9-12R
Wersba, Barbara 1932- CANR-38
Earlier sketches in CA 29-32R, CANR-16
See also AAYA 2
See also CLC 30
See also CLR 3
See also DLB 52
See also JRDA
See also MAICYA
See also SAAS 2
See also SATA 1, 58
Wershoven, Carol Jean 1947- 112
Werstein, Irving 1914(?)-1971 73-76
Obituary 29-32R
See also SATA 14
Wert, Lynette L(emon) 1938- 106
Wertenbaker, Lael (Tucker) 1909-1997 CANR-18
Obituary 157
Earlier sketches in CA 5-8R, CANR-3
Wertenbaker, Thomas Jefferson 1879-1966 5-8R
Wertenbaker, Timberlake 1951- 165
Wertenbaker, William 1938- 97-100
Werth, Alexander 1901-1969 CAP-1
Obituary 25-28R
Earlier sketch in CA 13-16
Werth, Kurt 1896- 81-84
See also SATA 20
Wertham, Fredric 1895-1981 5-8R
Obituary 105
Wertheim, Arthur Frank 1935- 97-100
Wertheim, Bill 1944- 37-40R
Wertheim, Stanley 1930- 41-44R
Wertheimer, Barbara M(ayer) 1926(?)-1983 129
Obituary 110
Wertheimer, Jack 1948- 144
Wertheimer, Leonard 1914- 116
Wertheimer, Linda Brief entry 123
Wertheimer, Marilyn L(ou) 1928- 102
Wertheimer, Max 1880-1943 Brief entry 123
Wertheimer, Michael (Matthew) 1927- CANR-2
Earlier sketch in CA 1-4R
Wertheimer, Richard F(rederick) II 1943- 29-32R
Wertheimer, Roger 1942- 37-40R
Werther, William B(lanchfield), Jr. 1947- CANR-21
Earlier sketch in CA 105
Werthman, Michael S(cott) 1939- 89-92
Wertime, Theodore A(llen) 1919-1982 109
Obituary 106
Wertmueller, Lina 1928- CANR-39
Earlier sketch in CA 97-100
See also CLC 16
Werts, Margaret F. 1915- 102
Wertsman, Vladimir (F.) 1929- CANR-50
Earlier sketches in CA 61-64, CANR-8, 20, 31
Wertz, Richard W(ayne) 1933- 45-48
Wertz, S. K.
See Wertz, Spencer K.
Wertz, Spencer K. 1941- 125
Wesander, Bioern Kenneth
See Cox, P(atrick) Brian
Wesberry, James Pickett 1906- 85-88
Weschcke, Carl L(ouis) 1930- 61-64
Wesche, L(ilburn) E(dgar) 1929- 93-96
Wesche, Percival A. 1912- 49-52
Weschler, Lawrence 1952- CANR-69
Earlier sketch in CA 135
Weschler, Louis F(redrick) 1933- 41-44R
Wescott, Glenway 1901-1987 CANR-70
Obituary 121
Earlier sketches in CA 13-16R, CANR-23
See also CLC 13
See also DLB 4, 9, 102
Wescott, Roger W. 1925- 25-28R
Wesencraft, Charles Frederick 1928- 61-64
Wesker, Arnold 1932- CANR-33
Earlier sketches in CA 1-4R, CANR-1
See also CAAS 7
See also CDBLB 1960 to Present
See also CLC 3, 5, 42
See also DAB
See also DAM DRAM
See also DLB 13
See also MTCW 1
Weslager, C(linton) A(lfred) 1909-1994 CANR-24
Obituary 146
Earlier sketches in CA 21-24R, CANR-9
Wesley, Alison
See Barnes, Michael
Wesley, Charles 1707-1788 DLB 95
Wesley, Charles H(arris) 1891-1987 101
Obituary 123
Wesley, Elizabeth
See McElfresh, (Elizabeth) Adeline
Wesley, George R(andolph) 1931- 41-44R
Wesley, James
See Rigoni, Orlando (Joseph)
Wesley, John 1703-1791 DLB 104
Wesley, Mary 1912- CANR-66
Earlier sketch in CA 49-52
See also MTCW 1
See also SATA 66
Wesley, Patricia Jabbeh 167
Wesley, Richard (Errol) 1945- CANR-27
Earlier sketch in CA 57-60
See also BW 1
See also CLC 7
See also DLB 38
Wesley, Valerie Wilson 1947- 167
Wesling, Donald 1939- 101
Wesner, Maralene 1935- 112
Wesner, Miles 1933- 112
Wess, Jane A. 1953- 150
Wess, Martin 1906(?)-1975 Obituary 104
Wessel, Andrew E(rnest) 1925- 73-76
Wessel, Carl John 1911-1984 Obituary 113
Wessel, Helen (Strain) 1924- CANR-11
Earlier sketch in CA 13-16R
Wessel, Milton R(alph) 1923- 89-92
Wessel, Robert H. 1921- 1-4R
Wesselman, Hank (Henry Barnard) 1941- 153
Wesselmann, Tom 1931- 108
Wessels, William L. 1889- 5-8R
Wesser, Robert F. 1933- 21-24R
Wessler, Ruth Ann 1938- 29-32R
Wessman, Alden E(benhart) 1930- 21-24R
Wesson, Joan
See Pittock, Joan (Hornby)
Wesson, Robert G(ale) 1920-1991 CANR-18
Obituary 134
Earlier sketches in CA 9-12R, CANR-3
West, Allan M(orrell) 1910- 109
West, Anna 1938- 106
See also SATA 40
West, Anthony (Panther) 1914-1987 CANR-19
Obituary 124
Earlier sketches in CA 45-48, CANR-3
See also CLC 50
See also DLB 15
West, Anthony C(athcart Muir) 1910- CANR-31
Earlier sketch in CA 69-72
West, Barbara
See Price, Olive
West, Betty 1921- CANR-7
Earlier sketch in CA 5-8R
See also SATA 11
West, Beverly Henderson 1939- 119
West, Bill
See West, William G.
West, Bonnie 1946- 114
West, Bruce 1951- SATA 63
West, C. P.
See Wodehouse, P(elham) G(renville)
West, Charles Converse 1921- 81-84
West, Colin 1951- 136
West, Cornel (Ronald) 1953- 144
See also BLCS
West, D(onald) J(ames) 1924- CANR-42
Earlier sketches in CA 13-16R, CANR-5, 20
West, Darrell M. 1954- 145
West, David (Alexander) 1926- 21-24R
West, Delno C(loyde), Jr. 1936- 57-60
West, Dick Sheppard 1920-1989 Obituary 130
West, Don 1928- 57-60
West, Dorothy
See Benson, Mildred (Augustine Wirt)
West, Dorothy 1907- 143
See also BW 2
See also DLB 76
West, E(dwin) G(eorge) 1922- CANR-29
Earlier sketch in CA 25-28R
West, Earle H(uddleston) 1925- 53-56
West, Edward Nason 1909- CAP-2
Earlier sketch in CA 19-20
West, Edwin G.
See West, E(dwin) G(eorge)
West, Elliot 1924- 17-20R
West, Elmer D(alton) 1907-1991 CAP-1
Obituary 135
Earlier sketch in CA 13-14
West, Emily Govan 1919- 109
See also SATA 38
West, Emmy
See West, Emily Govan
West, Eugenia Lovett 85-88
West, Ewan (D.) 1960- 142
West, Francis (James) 1927- CANR-3
Earlier sketch in CA 5-8R
West, Francis Horner 1909- 118
West, Frank H.
See West, Francis Horner
West, Fred 1918- 5-8R
West, G(eorge) Allen, Jr. 1915- 17-20R
West, George Algernon
1893-1980 Obituary 97-100
West, Gertrude 110
West, Gordon 1896- CAP-1
Earlier sketch in CA 13-14
West, Henry Woolliscroft 1925- 41-44R
West, Herbert B(uell) 1916- 53-56
West, Herbert Faulkner 1898-1974 CAP-2
Obituary 53-56
Earlier sketch in CA 19-20
West, J. B.
See West, J. Bernard
West, J. Bernard 1913(?)-1983 120
Obituary 110
West, James
See Withers, Carl A.
West, James King 1930- 45-48
West, James L(emuel) W(ills III) 1946- 131
West, James W. 1914(?)- 162
West, (Mary) Jane 1939(?)-1981 Obituary 104
West, Jerry
See Svenson, Andrew E(dward)
West, (Mary) Jessamyn 1902-1984 CANR-27
Obituary 112
Earlier sketch in CA 9-12R
See also CLC 7, 17
See also DLB 6
See also DLBY 84
See also MTCW 1
See also SATA-Obit 37
West, John Anthony 1932- 81-84
West, John Foster 1918- 13-16R
West, John Frederick 1929- 103
West, John G(ilbert) 1941- 142
West, Joyce (Tarlton) 106
West, Kirkpatrick
See Harris, F(rank) Brayton
West, Leonard J(ordan) 1921- 41-44R
West, Lindsay
See Weber, Nancy
West, M(artin) L(itchfield) 1937- 147
West, Mae 1893-1980 89-92
Obituary 102
See also DLB 44
West, Marion B(ond) 1936- 101
West, Mark
See Runyon, Charles W.
West, Morris L(anglo) 1916- CANR-64
Earlier sketches in CA 5-8R, CANR-24, 49
See also CLC 6, 33
See also MTCW 1
West, Muriel (Leitzell) 1903-(?) CAP-1
Earlier sketch in CA 13-16
West, Nancy Richard
See Westphal, Wilma Ross
West, Nathanael 1903-1940 125
Brief entry 104
See also CDALB 1929-1941
See also DLB 4, 9, 28
See also MTCW 1
See also SSC 16
See also TCLC 1, 14, 44
West, Owen
See Koontz, Dean R(ay)
West, Pat
See Strother, Pat Wallace
West, Paul 1930- CANR-53
Earlier sketches in CA 13-16R, CANR-22
Interview in CANR-22
See also CAAS 7
See also CLC 7, 14, 96
See also DLB 14
West, Ray B(enedict), Jr. 1908- CANR-3
Earlier sketch in CA 1-4R
West, Rebecca 1892-1983 CANR-19
Obituary 109
Earlier sketch in CA 5-8R
See also CLC 7, 9, 31, 50
See also DLB 36
See also DLBY 83
See also MTCW 1
West, Richard 1941- DLB 185
West, Richard 1941- DLB 185
West, Richard S(edgewick), Jr. 1902-1968 CAP-1
Earlier sketch in CA 13-16
West, Richard Samuel 1955- 130
West, Robert C(raig) 1947- 89-92
West, Robert Frederick 1916- 5-8R
West, Robert H(unter) 1907- 37-40R
West, Thomas R(eed) 1936- 124
Brief entry 118
West, Token
See Humphries, Adelaide M.
West, Trudy
See West, Gertrude
West, Uta 1928- 85-88
West, V(ictoria Mary) Sackville
See Sackville-West, V(ictoria Mary)
West, Ward
See Borland, Harold Glen
West, William G. 1930- CANR-14
Earlier sketch in CA 37-40R
Westall, Robert (Atkinson) 1929-1993 CANR-68
Obituary 141
Earlier sketches in CA 69-72, CANR-18
See also AAYA 12
See also CLC 17
See also CLR 13
See also JRDA
See also MAICYA
See also SAAS 2
See also SATA 23, 69
See also SATA-Obit 75
Westberg, Granger E(llsworth) 1913- CANR-6
Earlier sketch in CA 1-4R
Westbie, Constance 1910- 85-88
Westbrook, Adele 41-44R
Westbrook, Max (Roger) 1927- 37-40R
Westbrook, Perry D(ickie) 1916- CANR-21
Earlier sketches in CA 1-4R, CANR-6
Westbrook, Peter (J.) 1952- 164
Westbrook, Robert 1945- 25-28R
Westbrook, Wayne W(illiam) 1939- 97-100
Westbury, Ian Douglas 1939- Brief entry 106
Westby, David L. 1929- 45-48
Westby-Gibson, Dorothy Pauline 1920- 17-20R
Westcott, Cynthia 1898-1983 5-8R
Obituary 109
Westcott, Edward Noyes 1846-1898 DLB 202
Westcott, Jan Vlachos 1912- CANR-2
Earlier sketch in CA 1-4R
Westcott, Kathleen
See Abrahamsen, Christine Elizabeth
Westcott, W(illiam) F(ranklin) 1949- 113
Westcott-Jones, K(enneth) 1921- CANR-4
Earlier sketch in CA 53-56
Westebbe, Richard (Manning) 1925- 45-48
Westell, Anthony 1926- 101
Westerberg, Christine 1950- 61-64
See also SATA 29
Westergaard, John (Harald) 1927- CANR-43
Earlier sketches in CA 69-72, CANR-11
Westerhoff, John H(enry) III 1933- CANR-17
Earlier sketches in CA 45-48, CANR-1
Westerink, Leendert Gerrit 1913- 93-96
Westerman, Percy F(rancis) 1876-1959 Brief
entry 110
Westermann, Claus 1909- CANR-15
Earlier sketch in CA 81-84
Westermeier, Clifford P(eter) 1910- 45-48
Westermeyer, Joseph John 1937- 109
Western, J(ohn) R(andle) 1928-1971 CAP-2
Earlier sketch in CA 21-22
Western, John (Charles) 1947- 105
Western, Mark
See Crisp, Anthony Thomas
Western Spy, The
See Dillon, John M(yles)
Westervelt, Virginia Veeder 1914- CANR-10
Earlier sketch in CA 61-64
See also SATA 10
Westfall, David 1927- 117
Westfall, Don C. 1928-1973 CAP-2
Earlier sketch in CA 17-18
Westfall, Ralph (Libby) 1917- 5-8R
Westfall, Richard S(amuel) 1924-1996 21-24R
Obituary 153
Westfeldt, Lulie 1896- CAP-1
Earlier sketch in CA 13-14
Westheimer, David 1917- CANR-2
Earlier sketch in CA 1-4R
See also SATA 14
Westhues, Kenneth 1944- CANR-11
Earlier sketch in CA 25-28R
Westin, Alan F(urman) 1929- CANR-10
Earlier sketch in CA 13-16R
Westin, Av(ram) 1929- 77-80
Westin, Jeane Eddy 1931- 85-88

Westin, Richard A(xel) 1945- ... CANR-37
Earlier sketch in CA 115
Westing, Arthur H(erbert) 1928- ... CANR-38
Earlier sketches in CA 41-44R, CANR-17
Westing, John Howard 1911- ... 9-12R
Westlake, Aubrey Thomas 1893-1985 Obituary . 119
Westlake, Donald E(dwin) 1933- ... CANR-65
Earlier sketches in CA 17-20R, CANR-16, 44
Interview in ... CANR-16
See also CAAS 13
See also CLC 7, 33
See also DAM POP
Westlake, Helen Gum 1927- ... 41-44R
Westlake, Michael 1942- ... 127
Westland, Lynn
See Joscelyn, Archie L.
Westley, Bruce H(utchinson) 1915- ... CANR-2
Earlier sketch in CA 1-4R
Westley, Dick
See Westley, Richard John
Westley, Richard John 1928- ... 112
Westley, William A. 1920- ... 37-40R
Westling, Louise (Hutchings) 1942- ... 133
Westlund, Joseph 1936- ... 118
Westmacott, Mary
See Christie, Agatha (Mary Clarissa)
Westmacott, Richard 1941- ... 141
Westman, Barbara ... 105
See also SATA 70
Westman, Daniel P. 1956- ... 139
Westman, Jack C(onrad) 1927- ... 93-96
Westman, Paul (Wendell) 1956- ... 106
See also SATA 39
Westman, Wesley C(harles) 1936- ... 29-32R
Westmeier, Karl-Wilhelm 1939- ... 151
Westminster, Aynn
See Mundis, Hester
Westmore, Ann 1953- ... 109
Westmore, Frank 1923(?)-1985 Obituary ... 116
Westmoreland, Reg(inald Conway) 1926- ... 29-32R
Westmoreland, William C(hilds) 1914- ... 101
See also SATA 63
Westoff, Charles Francis 1927- ... 81-84
Westoff, Leslie Aldridge 1928- ... 77-80
Weston, Alan J(ay) 1940- ... 73-76
Weston, Allen
See Hogarth, Grace (Weston Allen)
and Norton, Andre
Weston, Ann
See Pitcher, Gladys
Weston, Burns H. 1933- ... 29-32R
Weston, Carolyn 1921- ... 107
Weston, Christine (Goutiere)
1904-1989 Obituary ... 128
Weston, Cole
See Randisi, Robert J(oseph)
Weston, Corinne Comstock 1919- ... CANR-21
Earlier sketch in CA 1-4R
Weston, Elizabeth Jane c. 1582-1612 ... DLB 172
Weston, Glen E(arl) 1922- ... 49-52
Weston, Helen Gray
See Daniels, Dorothy
Weston, J(ohn) Fred(erick) 1916- ... CANR-1
Earlier sketch in CA 1-4R
Weston, John
See Davies, John Evan Weston
Weston, John (Harrison) 1932- ... 17-20R
See also SATA 21
Weston, Joseph H(arry) 1911(?)-1983 Obituary . 111
Weston, Martha 1947- ... 129
See also SATA 53
Weston, Michael 1931- ... 154
Weston, Paul B(rendan) 1910- ... 13-16R
Weston, Rubin Francis 1921- ... 104
Weston, Susan B(rown) 1943- ... 81-84
Weston-Smith, M. 1956- ... 93-96
Westphal, Arnold Carl 1897- ... SATA 57
Westphal, Barbara Osborne 1907- ... CAP-1
Earlier sketch in CA 11-12
Westphal, Clarence 1904- ... CAP-2
Earlier sketch in CA 17-18
Westphal, Siegfried 1902-1982 Obituary ... 107
Westphal, Wilma Ross 1907- ... 21-24R
Westphall, Victor 1913- ... 119
Westrum, Dexter 1944- ... 139
Westrup, Hugh ... SATA 102
Westrup, J(ack) A(llan) 1904-1975 Obituary ... 115
Westsmith, Kim 1945- ... 57-60
Westwater, Sister Agnes Martha 1929- ... 21-24R
Westwood, Gordon
See Schofield, Michael
Westwood, Gwen 1915- ... CANR-19
Earlier sketch in CA 25-28R
Westwood, J(ohn) N(orton) 1931- ... CANR-20
Earlier sketches in CA 13-16R, CANR-5
Westwood, Jennifer 1940- ... CANR-29
Earlier sketches in CA 65-68, CANR-9
See also SATA 10
Westwood, Richard E. 1921- ... 137
Wetcheek, J. L.
See Feuchtwanger, Lion
Wetenhall, John 1957- ... 136
Wetering, Janwillem van de
See van de Wetering, Janwillem
Wetherald, Agnes Ethelwyn 1857-1940 ... DLB 99
See also TCLC 81
Wetherbee, Winthrop (III) 1938- ... CANR-28
Earlier sketches in CA 73-76, CANR-12
Wetherby, Terry (Lynne) 1943- ... 102
Wetherell, Elizabeth
See Warner, Susan (Bogert)
Wetherell, W(alter) D(avid) 1948- ... 138
Wetherell-Pepper, Joan Alexander 1920- ... 9-12R
Wetherill, Peter Michael 1932- ... CANR-12
Earlier sketch in CA 61-64

Wethey, Harold E(dwin) 1902-1984 ... CANR-2
Obituary ... 113
Earlier sketch in CA 1-4R
Wetmore, Alexander 1886-1978 ... 85-88
Obituary ... 81-84
Wetmore, Ruth Y. 1934- ... 57-60
Wetmore, Thomas Hall 1915- ... 25-28R
Wetmore, William T. 1930- ... 9-12R
Wettenhall, Roger (Llewellyn) 1931- ... CANR-51
Earlier sketches in CA 109, CANR-26
Wetter, Gustav A(ndreas) 1911- ... 9-12R
Wettig, Gerhard 1934- ... 143
Wettlaufer, George 1935- ... 57-60
Wettlaufer, Nancy 1939- ... 57-60
Wettstein, Howard K(enneth) 1943- ... 105
Wetzel, (Earl) Donald 1921- ... 25-28R
Wetzel, Elizabeth 1930- ... 114
Wetzel, Friedrich Gottlob 1779-1819 ... DLB 90
Wetzel, James (Richard) 1959- ... 139
Wetzel, Richard D(ean) 1935- ... 85-88
Weverka, Robert 1926- ... CANR-2
Earlier sketch in CA 49-52
Wevers, Richard Franklin 1933- Brief entry ... 106
Wevill, David 1937- ... 13-16R
Wexler, Alan 1947- ... 146
Wexler, Alice (Ruth) 1942- ... 144
Wexler, Jean Stewart 1921- ... 65-68
Wexler, Jerome (LeRoy) 1923- ... 73-76
See also SATA 14
Wexler, Jerry 1917- ... 142
Wexler, Joyce Piell 1947- ... 97-100
Wexler, Nancy (Sabin) 1945- ... 161
Wexler, Norman 1926- ... 154
Brief entry ... 116
Wexler, Richard 1953- ... 135
Wexley, John 1907-1985 Obituary ... 115
Wexley, Kenneth N. ... 93-96
Weyand, Alexander Mathias 1892- ... 5-8R
Weybright, Victor 1903-1978 Obituary ... 89-92
Weyermann, Debra 1954- ... 147
Weygant, Noemi ... CANR-2
Earlier sketch in CA 45-48
Weyl, (Claus Hugo) Hermann 1885-1955 ... 157
Weyl, Joachim 1915-1977 Obituary ... 73-76
Weyl, Nathaniel 1910- ... CANR-5
Earlier sketch in CA 9-12R
Weyl, Woldemar A. 1901(?)-1975 Obituary ... 61-64
Weyland, Jack 1940- ... 149
See also SATA 81
Weyler, Rex 1947- ... 110
Weyman, Stanley J. 1855-1928 ... DLB 141, 156
Weyn, Suzanne 1955- ... 168
See also SATA 63, 101
Weyr, Thomas 1927- ... 142
Weyrauch, Walter O(tto) 1919- ... CANR-10
Earlier sketch in CA 13-16R
Weyrich, Paul M(ichael) 1942- ... 118
Wezel, Johann Karl 1747-1819 ... DLB 94
Wezeman, Frederick Hartog 1915-1981 ... CANR-6
Obituary ... 106
Earlier sketch in CA 9-12R
Wezyk, Joanna 1966- ... SATA 82
Whale, James 1889-1957 ... TCLC 63
Whale, John (Hilary) 1931- ... 101
Whalen, Barbara G. 1928- ... 120
Whalen, Charles William, Jr. 1920- ... 105
Whalen, Edward L. 1936- ... 139
Whalen, George J. 1939- ... CANR-16
Earlier sketch in CA 89-92
Whalen, Philip 1923- ... CANR-39
Earlier sketches in CA 9-12R, CANR-5
See also CLC 6, 29
See also DLB 16
Whalen, Richard J(ames) 1935- ... CANR-32
Earlier sketch in CA 13-16R
Whalen, Terry (Anthony) 1944- ... 127
Whalen, William Joseph 1926- ... CANR-4
Earlier sketch in CA 1-4R
Whaley, Barton Stewart 1928- ... 41-44R
Whaley, Donald L. 1934- ... 33-36R
Whaley, Joyce Irene 1923- ... SATA 61
Whaley, Russell Francis 1934- ... 57-60
Whalin, W. Terry 1953- ... 158
Whalin, W. Terry 1953- ... SATA 93
Whaling, Frank 1934- ... CANR-67
Earlier sketches in CA 113, CANR-32
Whalley, Dorothy 1911- ... CAP-1
Earlier sketch in CA 9-10
Whalley, George 1915-1983 ... 101
See also DLB 88
Whalley, Janet 1945- ... 117
Whalley, Joyce Irene ... 103
Whalon, Marion K(elley) 1913- ... 119
Wharf, Michael
See Weller, George (Anthony)
Wharmby, Margot ... CANR-49
Earlier sketches in CA 17-20R, CANR-8, 24
See also SATA 63
Wharton, Annabel (Jane) ... CANR-50
Earlier sketch in CA 123
Wharton, Anthony
See McAllister, Alister
Wharton, Anthony P.
See McAllister, Alister
Wharton, Clifton R(eginald), Jr. 1926- ... 41-44R
Wharton, David B(ailey) 1914- ... 73-76

Wharton, Edith (Newbold Jones) 1862-1937 ... 132
Brief entry ... 104
See also AAYA 25
See also CDALB 1865-1917
See also DA
See also DAB
See also DAC
See also DAM MST, NOV
See also DLB 4, 9, 12, 78, 189
See also DLBD 13
See also MTCW 1
See also SSC 6
See also TCLC 3, 9, 27, 53
See also WLC
Wharton, Elizabeth Austin 1920-1985 Obituary . 116
Wharton, Gary C(harles) 1940- ... 45-48
Wharton, George Frederick III 1952- ... 109
Wharton, James
See Mencken, H(enry) L(ouis)
Wharton, Joanna
See Hamel Peifer, Kathleen
Wharton, John Franklin 1894-1977 ... 81-84
Obituary ... 73-76
Wharton, William (a pseudonym) ... 93-96
Interview in ... 93-96
See also CLC 18, 37
See also DLBY 80
Whateley, Leslie Violet Lucy Evelyn Mary
1899-1987 Obituary ... 123
Whately, Mary Louisa 1824-1889 ... DLB 166
Whately, Richard 1787-1863 ... DLB 190
Whatmore, Leonard Elliott 1912- ... 13-16R
Whatmough, Joshua 1897- ... 5-8R
Whealey, Robert 1930- ... 127
Wheat, Carolyn 1946- ... 152
Wheat, Cathleen Hayhurst 1904- ... CAP-1
Earlier sketch in CA 17-18
Wheat, (Marcus) Ed(ward, Jr.) 1926- ... CANR-42
Earlier sketch in CA 118
Wheat, Gilbert Collins, Jr. 1927- ... 1-4R
Wheat, Joe Ben 1916-1997 ... 41-44R
Obituary ... 159
Wheat, Leonard F. 1931- ... 29-32R
Wheat, Patte 1935- ... CANR-19
Earlier sketch in CA 101
Wheatcroft, Andrew (Jonathan Maclean) 1944- . 110
Wheatcroft, Geoffrey 1945- ... 124
Wheatcroft, John 1925- ... CANR-14
Earlier sketch in CA 37-40R
Wheatcroft, Stephen F(rederick) 1921- ... 5-8R
Wheatley, Arabelle 1921- ... SATA 16
Wheatley, Dennis (Yeats) 1897-1977 ... CANR-72
Obituary ... 73-76
Earlier sketches in CA 5-8R, CANR-9
See also DLB 77
See also MTCW 1
Wheatley, Jon 1931- ... 29-32R
Wheatley (Peters), Phillis 1754(?)-1784 ... BLC 3
See also CDALB 1640-1865
See also DA
See also DAC
See also DAM MST, MULT, POET
See also DLB 31, 50
See also PC 3
See also WLC
Wheatley, Richard C(harles) 1904- ... CAP-1
Earlier sketch in CA 11-12
Wheatley, Ronald 1923(?)-1985 Obituary ... 115
Wheatley, Vera (Semple) ... CAP-1
Earlier sketch in CA 13-16
Wheat-Lieber, Patte
See Wheat, Patte
Wheaton, Anne (Williams)
1892-1977 Obituary ... 69-72
Wheaton, Barbara Ketcham 1931- ... 146
Wheaton, Bruce R. 1944- ... CANR-22
Earlier sketch in CA 104
Wheaton, Philip D(amon) 1916- ... 104
Wheaton, William L. C. 1913-1978 ... CANR-3
Earlier sketch in CA 1-4R
Whedon, Julia
See Schickel, Julia Whedon
Whedon, Margaret B(runssen) 1926- ... 105
Whedon, Peggy
See Whedon, Margaret B(runssen)
Wheeler, Allen 1903-1984 Obituary ... 111
Wheeler, Anna Doyle 1785-1848(?) ... DLB 158
Wheeler, Bayard O. 1905- ... 41-44R
Wheeler, Bonnie G(rant) 1943- ... 109
Wheeler, Burton K(endall)
1882-1975 Obituary ... 53-56
Wheeler, Charles (Thomas) 1892-1974 ... CAP-2
Obituary ... 53-56
Earlier sketch in CA 29-32
Wheeler, Charles Stearns 1816-1843 ... DLB 1
Wheeler, Cindy 1955- ... CANR-57
Earlier sketches in CA 110, CANR-31
See also SATA 49
See also SATA-Brief 40
Wheeler, David L. 1934- ... 37-40R
Wheeler, David Raymond 1942- ... 73-76
Wheeler, Deborah (Jean Ross) 1947- ... 150
See also SATA 83
Wheeler, Douglas L. 1937- ... 29-32R
Wheeler, (Charles) Gidley 1938- ... CANR-24
Earlier sketch in CA 107
Wheeler, (John) Harvey 1918- ... CANR-17
Earlier sketches in CA 45-48, CANR-1
Wheeler, Helen Rippier ... CANR-14
Earlier sketches in CA 17-20R, CANR-31
Wheeler, Hugh (Callingham) 1912-1987 ... CANR-59
Obituary ... 123
Earlier sketch in CA 89-92
Interview in ... 89-92
Wheeler, J(oseph) Clyde 1910- ... 1-4R

Wheeler, Janet D. ... CANR-26
Earlier sketches in CAP-2, CA 19-20
See also SATA 1
Wheeler, Jesse H(arrison), Jr. 1918- ... 45-48
Wheeler, Jill 1964- ... 151
See also SATA 86
Wheeler, Jody 1952- ... SATA 84
Wheeler, John Archibald 1911- ... 160
Wheeler, Kate 1955- ... 155
Wheeler, Keith 1911- ... CANR-7
Earlier sketch in CA 5-8R
Wheeler, Leslie A. 1945- ... CANR-11
Earlier sketch in CA 65-68
Wheeler, Lora Jeanne 1923- ... 33-36R
Wheeler, Margaret 1916- ... CAP-2
Earlier sketch in CA 25-28
Wheeler, Mary Jane ... 29-32R
Wheeler, Michael 1943- ... CANR-9
Earlier sketch in CA 65-68
Wheeler, Molly 1920- ... 29-32R
Wheeler, Monroe 1900-1988 Obituary ... 126
See also DLB 4
Wheeler, (Robert Eric) Mortimer 1890-1976 ...
CANR-32
Obituary ... 65-68
Earlier sketch in CA 77-80
Wheeler, Opal 1898- ... SATA 23
Wheeler, Paul 1934- ... 25-28R
Wheeler, Penny Estes 1943- ... 33-36R
Wheeler, Raymond Milner 1919-1982 Obituary . 106
Wheeler, Richard 1922- ... CANR-50
Earlier sketches in CA 17-20R, CANR-8, 25
Wheeler, Richard Paul 1943- ... 108
Wheeler, Richard S(eabrook) 1928- ... 45-48
Wheeler, Robert C(ordell) 1913- ... 61-64
Wheeler, Ron 1954- ... 136
Wheeler, Ruth Carr 1899- ... 5-8R
Wheeler, Sessions S(amuel) 1911- ... CANR-25
Earlier sketch in CA 17-20R
Wheeler, Thomas C. 1927- ... 104
Wheeler, Thomas H(utchin) 1947- ... CANR-40
Earlier sketch in CA 93-96
Wheeler, Tom
See Wheeler, Thomas H(utchin)
Wheeler, W(illiam) Lawrence 1925- ... 13-16R
Wheeler-Bennett, John 1902-1975 ... 65-68
Obituary ... 61-64
Wheelis, Allen B. 1915- ... 17-20R
Wheelock, Arthur Kingsland, Jr. 1943- ... 107
Wheelock, (Kinch) Carter 1924- ... 61-64
Wheelock, David C. 1960- ... 143
Wheelock, Frederic M(elvin) 1902-1987 ... 97-100
Obituary ... 124
Wheelock, John Hall 1886-1978 ... CANR-14
Obituary ... 77-80
Earlier sketch in CA 13-16R
See also CLC 14
See also DLB 45
Wheelock, Martha E. 1941- ... 25-28R
Wheelwright, Edward Lawrence 1921- ... CANR-50
Earlier sketches in CA 103, CANR-21
Wheelwright, John 1592(?)-1679 ... DLB 24
Wheelwright, John 1897-1940 ... DLB 45
Wheelwright, Julie (Diana) 1960- ... 130
Wheelwright, Philip (Ellis) 1901-1970 ... CAP-2
Earlier sketch in CA 23-24
Wheelwright, Richard 1936- ... 33-36R
Wheelwright, Steven C. 1943- ... 119
Whelan, Elizabeth M(urphy) 1943- ... CANR-24
Earlier sketches in CA 57-60, CANR-8
See also SATA 14
Whelan, G(eraldine) V(alerie) 1952- ... 160
Whelan, Gloria (Ann) 1923- ... 101
See also SATA 85
Whelan, James Robert 1933- ... 102
Whelan, Joseph P(aul) 1932- ... 41-44R
Whelan, Richard 1946- ... 144
Whelan, Tensie 1960- ... 141
Wheldon, David 1950- ... 146
Wheldon, Huw (Pyrs) 1916-1986 ... 107
Obituary ... 118
Whelehan, Imelda 1960- ... 153
Whelpton, (George) Eric 1894-1981 ... CANR-5
Obituary ... 103
Earlier sketch in CA 9-12R
Whelpton, Pascal K(idder) 1893-1964 ... CANR-16
Earlier sketch in CA 1-4R
Whelton, Clark 1937- ... 69-72
Whenham, (Ernest) John 1946- ... 127
Whetstone, Colonel Pete
See Noland, C. F. M.
Whetten, Lawrence L. 1932- ... CANR-27
Earlier sketches in CA 61-64, CANR-11
Whetten, Nathan Laselle 1900- ... 1-4R
Whicher, John F. 1919- ... 17-20R
Whicher, Stephen E. 1915-1961 ... DLB 111
Whicker, Alan (Donald) 1925- ... 130
Whidden, Mary Bess 1936- ... 126
Whiffen, Marcus 1916- ... CANR-12
Earlier sketch in CA 61-64
Whigham, Peter (George) 1925-1987 ... CANR-28
Obituary ... 123
Earlier sketch in CA 25-28R
Whinnery, John R(oy) 1916- ... 162
Whinney, Margaret Dickens
1897-1975 Obituary ... 61-64
Whinnom, Keith 1927-1986 Obituary ... 118
Whipkey, Kenneth Lee 1932- ... CANR-4
Earlier sketch in CA 53-56
Whipple, A(ddison) B(eecher) C(olvin) 1918- ... 125
See also SATA 64
Whipple, Beverly 1941- ... CANR-56
Earlier sketches in CA 109, CANR-30
Whipple, Cal
See Whipple, A(ddison) B(eecher) C(olvin)
Whipple, Chandler (Henry) 1905- ... 25-28R

Whipple, Dorothy 1893- CAP-1
Earlier sketch in CA 13-14
Whipple, Edwin Percy 1819-1886 DLB 1, 64
Whipple, Fred Lawrence 1906- CAP-1
Earlier sketch in CA 11-12
Whipple, George 1927- 119
Whipple, George Hoyt 1878-1976 158
Whipple, James B. 1913- 29-32R
Whipple, Maurine 1910- 5-8R
Whisenand, Paul M. 1935- CANR-22
Earlier sketch in CA 69-72
Whisenhunt, Donald W(ayne) 1938- CANR-9
Earlier sketch in CA 57-60
Whisler, John A(lbert) 1951- 109
Whisler, Thomas L(ee) 1920- 154
Brief entry 115
Whisnant, Charleen
See Swansea, Charleen
Whisnant, David E(ugene) 1938- 41-44R
Whisnant, Luke 1957- 144
Whistler, Laurence 1912- CANR-19
Earlier sketches in CA 9-12R, CANR-3
Whistler, Reginald John 1905-1944 SATA 30
Whistler, Rex
See Whistler, Reginald John
Whiston, Lionel (Abney) 1895- 69-72
Whitacre, Donald (DuMont) 1920- 69-72
Whitaker, Alexander 1585-1617 DLB 24
Whitaker, Arthur Preston 1895-1979 Obituary 112
Whitaker, Ben(jamin Charles George) 1934- 53-56
Whitaker, C(leophaus) S(ylvester), Jr. 1935- CANR-28
Earlier sketch in CA 29-32R
Whitaker, Carl A(lanson) 1912-1995 Obituary 148
Brief entry 114
Whitaker, Daniel K. 1801-1881 DLB 73
Whitaker, David 1930-1980 21-24R
Obituary 134
Whitaker, Dorothy Stock 1925- 13-16R
Whitaker, Frederic 1891-1980 CANR-4
Obituary 97-100
Earlier sketch in CA 5-8R
Whitaker, Gilbert R(iley), Jr. 1931- 9-12R
Whitaker, Haddon 1908(?)-1982 Obituary 105
Whitaker, James 1931- 154
Whitaker, James W. 1936- 102
Whitaker, John O(gden), Jr. 1935- 105
Whitaker, Malachi Taylor 1895-1976 Obituary 104
Whitaker, Mary 1896(?)-1976 Obituary 65-68
Whitaker, Peter 1952- 124
Whitaker, Rod(ney) 1925- CANR-45
Earlier sketch in CA 29-32R
Whitaker, Rogers E(rnest) M(alcolm) 1899-1981 Obituary 103
Whitaker, Shelagh (Dunwoody) 1930- 125
Whitaker, T(ommy) J(ames) 1949- 53-56
Whitaker, Thomas R(ussell) 1925- 25-28R
Whitaker, Urban George, Jr. 1924- 9-12R
Whitaker, W(illiam) Denis 1915- 128
Whitbeck, George W(alter) 1932- 73-76
Whitbourn, John 1958- 155
Whitbread, Jane
See Levin, Jane Whitbread
Whitbread, Leslie George 1917- 37-40R
Whitbread, Thomas (Bacon) 1931- 13-16R
Whitburn, Joel (Carver) 1939- CANR-67
Earlier sketches in CA 33-36R, CANR-15, 32
Whitby, Henry Augustus Morton 1898-1969 CAP-1
Earlier sketch in CA 11-12
Whitby, Sharon
See Peters, Maureen
Whitby, Thomas J. 1919- 126
Whitcher, Frances Miriam 1812-1852 DLB 11, 202
Whitcher, Susan (Godsil) 1952- 161
See also SATA 96
Whitcomb, Edgar D(oud) 1918- 21-24R
Whitcomb, Hale C(hristy) 1907- CAP-2
Earlier sketch in CA 29-32
Whitcomb, Helen Hafemann CANR-6
Earlier sketch in CA 13-16R
Whitcomb, Ian 1941- CANR-8
Earlier sketch in CA 57-60
Whitcomb, John C(lement) 1924- CANR-4
Earlier sketch in CA 1-4R
Whitcomb, Jon 1906-1988 CAP-1
Obituary 125
Earlier sketch in CA 13-16
See also SATA 10
See also SATA-Obit 56
Whitcomb, Meg W. 1930- CANR-50
Earlier sketch in CA 123
Whitcomb, Noel 1918(?)-1993 134
Obituary 141
Whitcomb, Philip W(right) 1891- 73-76
White, A(drian) N(icholas) Sherwin
See Sherwin-White, A(drian) N(icholas)
White, Alan CANR-60
Earlier sketches in CA 45-48, CANR-3
White, Alan R(ichard) 1922-1992 25-28R
Obituary 137
White, Alex Sandri 1916(?)-1983(?) Obituary 108
White, Alice Violet 1922- CANR-13
Earlier sketch in CA 61-64
White, Alicen 77-80
White, Allon (H.) 1951-1988 128
White, Amber Blanco
See Blanco White, Amber
White, Andrea 1942- 144
White, Andrew 1579-1656 DLB 24
White, Andrew Dickson 1832-1918 DLB 47
White, Anne Hitchcock 1902-1970 Obituary 108
See also SATA-Brief 33
White, Anne S(hanklin) 93-96
White, Anne Terry 1896-1980 9-12R
Obituary 135
See also SATA 2
White, Anthony Gene 1946- CANR-12
Earlier sketch in CA 73-76
White, Antonia 1899-1980 104
Obituary 97-100
White, Augustus A(aron III) 1936- 168
White, Babington
See Braddon, Mary Elizabeth
White, Bailey 1950- 141
White, Barbara A(nne) 1942- CANR-56
Earlier sketches in CA 109, CANR-29
White, Barbara Ehrlich 1936- 136
White, Beatrice (Mary Irene) 1902-1986 Obituary 119
White, Benjamin V(room) 1908- 101
White, Benton R. 1949- 124
White, Bessie (Felstiner) 1892(?)-1986 Obituary 121
See also SATA-Obit 50
White, Betty 1917- 5-8R
White, Brian Terence 1927- 105
White, Burton L(eonard) 1929- CANR-4
Earlier sketch in CA 45-48
White, Carl M(ilton) 1903-1983 13-16R
Obituary 111
White, Carol 1946- 111
White, Carol Hellings 1939- 81-84
White, Carolinne 1955- 142
White, (Edwin) Chappell 1920- 25-28R
White, Claire Nicolas 1925- CANR-25
Earlier sketch in CA 108
White, Curtis 1951- CANR-27
Earlier sketch in CA 110
White, Cynthia L(eslie) 1940- 37-40R
White, Dale
See Place, Marian T(empleton)
White, Dan S(eligsberger) 1939- 97-100
White, Dana
See Larsen, Anita
White, David Gordon 1953- 165
White, David Manning 1917-1993 CANR-4
Obituary 143
Earlier sketch in CA 1-4R
White, David Omar 1927- 17-20R
White, Dori 1919- 37-40R
See also SATA 10
White, Dorothy Shipley CAP-1
Earlier sketch in CA 13-14
White, Douglas M(alcolm) 1909- CANR-4
Earlier sketch in CA 1-4R
White, E(lwyn) B(rooks) 1899-1985 CANR-37
Obituary 116
Earlier sketches in CA 13-16R, CANR-16
See also AITN 2
See also CLC 10, 34, 39
See also CLR 1, 21
See also DAM POP
See also DLB 11, 22
See also MAICYA
See also MTCW 1
See also SATA 2, 29, 100
See also SATA-Obit 44
White, Edgar (B.) 1947- CANR-27
Earlier sketch in CA 61-64
See also BW 1
See also DLB 38
White, Edmund (Valentine III) 1940- CANR-62
Earlier sketches in CA 45-48, CANR-3, 19, 36
See also AAYA 7
See also CLC 27, 110
See also DAM POP
See also MTCW 1
White, Edward M. 1933- 37-40R
White, Elijah (Brockenborough III) 1938- 69-72
White, Eliza Orne 1856-1947 YABC 2
White, Elizabeth H(erzog) 1901(?)-1972 Obituary 37-40R
White, Elizabeth Wade 1906- 97-100
White, Elliott 1936- CANR-55
Earlier sketch in CA 127
White, Elmer G. 1926-1979 21-24R
Obituary 134
White, Emmons E(aton) 1891-1982 73-76
Obituary 133
White, Eric Walter 1905-1985 CAP-1
Obituary 117
Earlier sketch in CA 11-12
White, Ethel Lina 1887-1944 167
Brief entry 108
See also DLB 77
White, Eugene E. 1919- 13-16R
White, Evelyn C. 1954- 164
White, F(rederick) Clifton 1918-1993 113
Obituary 140
White, Florence M(eiman) 1910- 41-44R
See also SATA 14
White, Frank 1944- 126
White, G(eorge) Edward 1941- CANR-62
Earlier sketches in CA 69-72, CANR-12
White, Geoffrey M. 1949- 143
White, George Abbott 1943- 143
White, Gerald Taylor 1913- CANR-2
Earlier sketch in CA 5-8R
White, Gertrude M(ason) 1915- 81-84
White, Gillian Mary 1936- 17-20R
White, Glenn M. 1918(?)-1978 93-96
Obituary 81-84
White, Gordon Eliot 1933- 101
White, H. T.
See Engh, Rohn
White, Harrison C(olyar) 1930- 45-48
White, Harry
See Whittington, Harry (Benjamin)
White, Hayden V. 1928- 128
White, Helen Constance 1896- 5-8R
White, Henry Kirke 1785-1806 DLB 96
White, Hilda Crystal 1917- 5-8R
White, Horace 1834-1916 Brief entry 119
See also DLB 23
White, Howard 1945- 164
White, Howard Ashley 1913-1991 29-32R
Obituary 133
White, Howard B. 1912(?)-1974 Obituary 53-56
White, Hugh Clayton 1936- 45-48
White, Hugh Vernon 1889- 5-8R
White, Irvin L(inwood) 1932- CANR-8
Earlier sketch in CA 57-60
White, Jack Joseph 1954- 149
White, Jack McBride
See White, Jack Joseph
White, James 1913- 109
White, James 1928- CANR-4
Earlier sketch in CA 53-56
White, James Boyd 1938- CANR-30
Earlier sketch in CA 111
White, James Dillon
See White, Stanley
White, James F(loyd) 1932- CANR-49
Earlier sketches in CA 107, CANR-24
White, James L. (?)-1981 Obituary 115
White, James P(atrick) 1940- CANR-42
Earlier sketches in CA 69-72, CANR-11
White, Jane
See Brady, Jane
White, Jane Neal 1918- 110
White, Jerry E(ugene) 1937- 129
White, Jerry S. 1946- 130
White, John 1924- CANR-20
White, John Albert 1910- CAP-2
Earlier sketch in CA 23-24
White, John Baker
See Baker White, John
White, John H(enry) 1945- 124
Brief entry 117
White, John Hoxland, Jr. 1933- CANR-42
Earlier sketch in CA 25-28R
White, John I(rwin) 57-60
White, John K(enneth) 1952- CANR-39
Earlier sketch in CA 116
White, John W. 1939- CANR-13
Earlier sketch in CA 37-40R
White, John Wesley 1928- CANR-31
Earlier sketch in CA 29-32R
White, Jon (Ewbank) Manchip 1924- CANR-67
Earlier sketches in CA 13-16R, CANR-15, 32
See also CAAS 4
White, Jonathan 1956- 146
White, Joseph B. 1958- 147
White, Joyce C(arol) 1952- 112
White, Jude Gilliam 1947- CANR-41
Earlier sketches in CA 106, CANR-23
See also Deveraux, Jude
See also DAM POP
White, K(enneth) D(ouglas) 1908- CANR-12
Earlier sketch in CA 69-72
White, K(enneth) Owen 1902- CAP-2
Earlier sketch in CA 17-18
White, Karol Koenigsberg 1938- 5-8R
White, Katharine Sergeant 1892-1977 Obituary 104
White, Kenneth 1936- 25-28R
White, Kenneth Steele 1922- 93-96
White, Kevin 1959- 144
White, Laurence B(arton), Jr. 1935- CANR-24
Earlier sketches in CA 65-68, CANR-9
See also SATA 10
White, Lawrence 1942- 115
White, Lawrence H(enry) 1954- 118
White, Lawrence J. 1943- CANR-31
Earlier sketches in CA 37-40R, CANR-14
White, Lee A. 1886-1971 Obituary 115
White, Leslie A(lvin) 1900-1975 CANR-3
Obituary 57-60
Earlier sketch in CA 1-4R
White, Leslie Turner 1903-(?) CAP-1
Earlier sketch in CA 13-14
White, Lionel 1905- CANR-58
Earlier sketch in CA 103
White, Lonnie J(oe) 1931- 13-16R
White, Lucia 123
White, Lynn (Townsend), Jr. 1907-1987 CANR-2
Obituary 122
Earlier sketch in CA 5-8R
White, M(ary) E(llen) 1938- 21-24R
White, Margaret B(lackburn) 1936- 115
White, Martin 1943- SATA 51
White, Mary Alice 1920- 9-12R
White, Mary Wheeling 1965- 167
White, Matthew (Hagy) 1956- 129
White, Maurine
See Miller (Riis), Maurine
White, Maury 1919- 77-80
White, Melvin R(obert) 1911- CANR-40
Earlier sketches in CA 21-24R, CANR-18
White, Merry (I.) 1941- 141
White, Michael C(harles) 167
White, Mimi 1953- 145
White, Minor (Martin) 1908-1976 CANR-10
Obituary 65-68
Earlier sketch in CA 17-20R
White, Morton Gabriel 1917- CANR-35
Earlier sketches in CA 5-8R, CANR-7
White, Nancy Bean 1922- 13-16R
White, Ned 1946- 129
White, Nicholas P. 1942- 73-76
White, Norval (Crawford) 1926- 77-80
White, Orion F(orrest) 1938- 53-56
White, Osmar (Egmont Dorkin) 1909- 130
Brief entry 105
White, Owen R(oberts) 1945- 41-44R
White, Patricia (Ann) 1937- CANR-43
Earlier sketch in CA 117
White, Patrick (Victor Martindale) 1912-1990 CANR-43
Obituary 132
Earlier sketch in CA 81-84
See also CLC 3, 4, 5, 7, 9, 18, 65, 69
See also MTCW 1
White, Patrick C. T. 1924- 85-88
White, Paul Dudley 1886-1973 Obituary 45-48
White, Paul Hamilton Hume 1910- CANR-23
Earlier sketches in CA 5-8R, CANR-7
White, Paulette Childress 1948- 111
White, Percival 1887-1970 CANR-2
Earlier sketch in CA 1-4R
White, Peter (O. G.) 1932- 139
White, Philip L(loyd) 1923- 81-84
White, Phillip M. 1950- 152
White, Phyllis Dorothy James 1920- CANR-65
Earlier sketches in CA 21-24R, CANR-17, 43
See also James, P. D.
See also DAM POP
See also MTCW 1
White, Poppy Cannon 1906(?)-1975 65-68
Obituary 57-60
White, R. S. 1948- 127
White, Ramy Allison CANR-26
Earlier sketches in CAP-2, CA 19-20
See also SATA 1, 67
White, Randall 1945- 121
White, Randy Wayne 1950- 161
White, Ray Lewis 1941- CANR-9
Earlier sketch in CA 21-24R
White, Reginald E(rnest) O(scar) 1914- CANR-44
Earlier sketches in CA 5-8R, CANR-5, 21
White, Reginald James 1905-1971 108
Obituary 104
White, Rhea A(melia) 1931- 77-80
White, Richard 1931- 110
White, Richard Alan 1944- 97-100
White, Richard C(lark) 1926- 45-48
White, Richard Grant 1821-1885 DLB 64
White, Richard W(eddington), Jr. 1936- 142
White, Robb 1909- CANR-1
Earlier sketch in CA 1-4R
See also CLR 3
See also SAAS 1
See also SATA 1, 83
White, Robert B(enjamin), Jr. 1930- Brief entry 118
White, Robert I. 1908- 1-4R
White, Robert Lee 1928- 17-20R
White, Robert Mitchell II 1915- 73-76
White, Robert R(ankin) 1942- 123
White, (William) Robin(son) 1928- CANR-20
Earlier sketches in CA 9-12R, CANR-4
White, Ronald C(edric), Jr. 1939- 93-96
White, Ruth C. 1942- 111
See also SATA 39
White, Ruth M(argaret) 1914- 17-20R
White, Ruth Morris 1902(?)-1978 Obituary 81-84
White, Ryan 1971-1990 141
White, Sarah Harriman 1929- 9-12R
White, Sheldon Harold 1928- 105
White, Stanhope 1913- 21-24R
White, Stanley 1913- CANR-6
Earlier sketch in CA 9-12R
White, Stephanie F(rances) T(hirkell) 1942- 17-20R
White, Stephen (Leonard) 1945- 134
White, Stephen D(aniel) 1945- 93-96
White, Stephen E. 1947- 145
White, Stephen K. 1949- 146
White, Steve
See McGarvey, Robert
White, Steven F(orsythe) 1955- CANR-56
Earlier sketches in CA 112, CANR-30
White, Susan J. 1949- 126
White, Suzanne 1938- 77-80
White, Sybille
See Pearson, Sybille
White, T(erence) H(anbury) 1906-1964 CANR-37
Earlier sketch in CA 73-76
See also AAYA 22
See also CLC 30
See also DLB 160
See also JRDA
See also MAICYA
See also SATA 12
White, Ted
See White, Theodore Edwin
White, Terence de Vere 1912-1994 CANR-3
Obituary 145
Earlier sketch in CA 49-52
See also CLC 49
White, Teri 1946- CANR-66
Brief entry 127
Earlier sketch in CA 132
Interview in 132
White, Theo Ballou 1903-1978 Obituary 111
White, Theodore Edwin 1938- CANR-12
Earlier sketch in CA 21-24R
White, Theodore H(arold) 1915-1986 CANR-64
Obituary 118
Earlier sketches in CA 1-4R, CANR-3, 33
See also MTCW 1
White, Thomas Justin, Jr. 1919-1987 Obituary 122
White, Tim D. 1950- 143
White, Timothy (Thomas Anthony) 1952- SATA 60
White, W. D. 1926- 37-40R
White, W(illiam) J(ohn) 1920-1980 13-16R
Obituary 97-100
White, Walter BLC 3
See also DAM MULT
White, Walter F(rancis) 1893-1955 124
Brief entry 115
See also White, Walter
See also BW 1
See also DLB 51
See also TCLC 15

White, William, Jr. 1934-.... CANR-31
Earlier sketches in CA 37-40R, CANR-14
See also SATA 16
White, William 1910-.... CANR-29
Earlier sketch in CA 21-24R
White, William A(nthony) P(arker) 1911-1968.... CANR-67
Obituary.... 25-28R
Earlier sketches in CAP-1, CA 11-12
See also Boucher, Anthony
White, William Allen 1868-1944 Brief entry.... 108
See also DLB 9, 25
White, William D. 1945-.... 146
White, William F(rancis) 1928-.... CANR-1
Earlier sketch in CA 45-48
White, William Hale 1831-1913 Brief entry.... 121
See also Rutherford, Mark
White, William J(oseph) 1926-.... 97-100
White, William L(indsay) 1900-1973.... 101
Obituary.... 41-44R
White, William L. 1937-1985 Obituary.... 114
White, William Luther 1931-.... 29-32R
White, William S(mith) 1907-1994.... 5-8R
Obituary.... 145
White, Zita
See Denholm, Therese Mary Zita White
Whitebird, J(oanie) 1951-.... CANR-25
Earlier sketch in CA 69-72
White-Bowden, Susan 1939-.... 120
Whitechurch, Victor L(orenzo) 1868-1933.... 160
Brief entry.... 116
See also DLB 70
Whited, Charles 1929-.... 141
White Elk, Michael
See Walker, T. Michael
Whitefield, Ann
See Stone, Susan Berch
Whiteford, Andrew H(unter) 1913-.... CANR-51
Earlier sketches in CA 45-48, CANR-26
Whitefriar
See Hiscock, Eric
Whitehall, Harold 1905-1986.... CAP-2
Obituary.... 118
Earlier sketch in CA 21-22
Whitehead, Alfred North 1861-1947.... 165
Brief entry.... 117
See also DLB 100
Whitehead, Barbara (Maude) 1930-.... 97-100
Whitehead, Barbara Dafoe 1944-.... 164
Whitehead, Catherine Sarah 1960-.... 131
Whitehead, Don(ald) F. 1908-1981.... 9-12R
Obituary.... 102
See also SATA 4
Whitehead, E(dward) A(nthony) 1933-.... CANR-58
Earlier sketch in CA 65-68
See also CLC 5
Whitehead, (Walter) Edward 1908-1978.... 81-84
Obituary.... 77-80
Whitehead, Evelyn Annette Eaton 1938-.... 104
Whitehead, Frank S. 1916-.... 37-40R
Whitehead, G(eorge) Kenneth 1913-.... CANR-8
Earlier sketch in CA 61-64
Whitehead, James 1936-.... 77-80
See also DLBY 81
Whitehead, James D(ouglas) 1939-.... 105
Whitehead, John (Randolph) 1924-.... 120
Whitehead, John W. 1946-.... 117
Whitehead, Kate
See Whitehead, Catherine Sarah
Whitehead, Raymond Leslie 1933-.... 77-80
Whitehead, Robert J(ohn) 1928-.... CANR-13
Earlier sketch in CA 37-40R
Whitehead, William 1715-1785.... DLB 84, 109
Whitehead, William Grant 1943-1987 Obituary. 124
Whitehill, Arthur M(urray, Jr.) 1919-.... CANR-13
Earlier sketch in CA 77-80
Whitehill, Walter Muir 1905-1978.... CANR-6
Obituary.... 77-80
Earlier sketch in CA 13-16R
Whitehorn, Alan (James) 1946-.... 138
Whitehorn, Katharine
See Lyall, Katharine Elizabeth
Whitehouse, Arch
See Whitehouse, Arthur George Joseph
Whitehouse, Arthur George Joseph 1895-1979.... CANR-4
Obituary.... 89-92
Earlier sketch in CA 5-8R
See also SATA 14
See also SATA-Obit 23
Whitehouse, David (Bryn) 1941-.... 131
Whitehouse, Elizabeth S(cott) 1893-1968.... CAP-1
Earlier sketch in CA 13-14
See also SATA 35
Whitehouse, Franklin S., Jr. 1934-1985 Obituary.... 117
Whitehouse, Jack E(dward) 1933-.... 111
Whitehouse, Jeanne 1939-.... 103
See also SATA 29
Whitehouse, Roger 1939-.... 57-60
Whitehouse, Ruth D(elamain) 1942-.... 118
Whitehouse, W(alter) A(lexander) 1915-.... CANR-3
Earlier sketch in CA 1-4R
Whitelaw, Nancy 1933-.... 143
See also SATA 76
Whitelaw, William Menzies 1890(?)-1974 Obituary.... 45-48
Whiteley, Denys Edward Hugh 1914-1987 Obituary.... 123
Whiteley, George 1909(?)-1990 Obituary.... 132
Whiteley, Peter 1928-.... 165
Whitelock, Dorothy 1901-1982.... 129
Obituary.... 107
Whiteman, (David) Bruce 1952-.... 132
Whiteman, Maxwell 1914-.... CANR-10
Earlier sketch in CA 21-24R
Whiteman, Paul 1890(?)-1967 Obituary.... 113
Whiteman, Roberta J. Hill 1947-.... 146
See also NNAL
Whiteman, Robin 1944-.... 167
Whitemore, Hugh (John) 1936-.... 132
Interview in.... 132
See also CLC 37
White-Parks, Annette 1935-.... 156
Whitesell, (James) Edwin 1909-.... 41-44R
Whitesell, Faris Daniel 1895-1984.... 5-8R
Obituary.... 146
Whiteside, Lynn W. 1908-.... 25-28R
Whiteside, Robert L(eo) 1907-.... 53-56
Whiteside, Thomas 1918(?)-1997.... 161
Brief entry.... 109
Whitesitt, Linda (Marie) 1951-.... 129
Whiteson, Leon 1930-.... CANR-69
Earlier sketches in CA 21-24R, CANR-16
Whiteway, Doug(las) Alfred 1951-.... 164
Whitfield, George J(oshua) N(ewbold) 1909-.... CAP-1
Earlier sketch in CA 11-12
Whitfield, James Monroe 1822-1871.... DLB 50
Whitfield, John Humphreys 1906-.... 9-12R
Whitfield, Phil(ip John) 1944-.... 97-100
Whitfield, Raoul 1897(?)-1945 Brief entry.... 109
Whitfield, Sarah 1942-.... 141
Whitfield, Shelby 1935-.... 49-52
Whitfield, Stephen J(ack) 1942-.... 61-64
Whitford, Bessie 1885(?)-1977 Obituary.... 69-72
Whitford, Frank 1941-.... CANR-50
Earlier sketch in CA 97-100
Whitgift, John c. 1533-1604.... DLB 132
Whitin, Thomson McLintock 1923-.... CANR-3
Earlier sketch in CA 1-4R
Whiting, Allen S(uess) 1926-.... 125
Brief entry.... 105
Whiting, Beatrice Blyth 1914-.... 5-8R
Whiting, Charles E. 1914(?)-1980 Obituary.... 97-100
Whiting, Frank M. 1907-.... 101
Whiting, John (Robert) 1917-1963.... 102
Obituary.... 89-92
See also DLB 13
Whiting, Kenneth R. 1913-.... CANR-5
Earlier sketch in CA 5-8R
Whiting, Nathan 1946-.... 41-44R
Whiting, Percy H(ollister) 1880-.... CAP-1
Earlier sketch in CA 13-16
Whiting, Robert 1942-.... 102
Whiting, Robert L(ouis) 1918-.... 17-20R
Whiting, Samuel 1597-1679.... DLB 24
Whiting, Thomas A. 1917-.... CANR-3
Earlier sketch in CA 1-4R
Whitinger, R. D.
See Place, Marian T(empleton)
Whitington, R(ichard) S. 1912-.... 77-80
Whitlam, (Edward) Gough 1916-.... 109
Whitley, George
See Chandler, A(rthur) Bertram
Whitley, Mary Ann
See Sebrey, Mary Ann
Whitley, Oliver R. 1918-.... 77-80
Whitlock, Baird W(oodruff) 1924-.... 112
Whitlock, Brand 1869-1934.... 162
Brief entry.... 110
See also DLB 12
Whitlock, Glenn E(verett) 1917-.... 21-24R
Whitlock, Pamela 1921(?)-1982 Obituary.... 107
See also SATA-Obit 31
Whitlock, Quentin A(rthur) 1937-.... 109
Whitlock, Ralph 1914-1995.... CANR-45
Obituary.... 150
Earlier sketches in CA 101, CANR-20
See also SATA 35
Whitlock, Virginia Bennett (?)-1972 Obituary.... 37-40R
Whitlow, Roger 1940-.... 41-44R
Whitman, Albery Allson 1851-1901.... DLB 50
Whitman, Alden 1913-1990.... CANR-29
Obituary.... 132
Earlier sketch in CA 17-20R
See also DLBY 91
Whitman, Alice
See Marker, Sherry
Whitman, (Evelyn) Ardis 1905(?)-1990.... 9-12R
Obituary.... 131
Whitman, Bertha Yerex 1892-1984 Obituary.... 114
Whitman, Cedric H(ubbell) 1916-1979.... CANR-27
Obituary.... 120
Earlier sketch in CA 17-20R
Whitman, David (deFreudiger) 1955-.... 113
Whitman, Edmund Spurr 1900-.... 17-20R
Whitman, Howard 1915(?)-1975 Obituary.... 53-56
Whitman, John 1944-.... CANR-11
Earlier sketch in CA 61-64
Whitman, Marina von Neumann 1935-.... 17-20R
Whitman, Martin J. 1924-.... 104
Whitman, Robert Freeman 1925-.... 81-84
Whitman, Ruth (Bashein) 1922-.... CANR-31
Earlier sketches in CA 21-24R, CANR-12
Whitman, Sarah Helen (Power) 1803-1878.... DLB 1
Whitman, Sylvia (Choate) 1961-.... 151
See also SATA 85
Whitman, T(orrey) Stephen 1950-.... 164
Whitman, Virginia Bruner 1901-.... CANR-4
Earlier sketch in CA 5-8R
Whitman, W(illiam) Tate 1909-.... CAP-1
Earlier sketch in CA 11-12
Whitman, Walt(er) 1819-1892.... CDALB 1640-1865
See also DA
See also DAB
See also DAC
See also DAM MST, POET
See also DLB 3, 64
See also PC 3
See also SATA 20
See also WLC
Whitman, Wanda (?)-1976 Obituary.... 65-68
Whitmarsh, Anne (Mary Gordon) 1933-.... 106
Whitmont, Edward C. 1912-.... 115
Whitmore, Charles (Stanleigh) 1949-.... 117
Whitmore, Cilla
See Gladstone, Arthur M.
Whitmore, Eugene 1895-.... 5-8R
Whitmore, George 1945-1989.... CANR-30
Obituary.... 128
Earlier sketch in CA 102
Whitnah, Donald R(obert) 1925-.... 9-12R
Whitnah, Dorothy L. 1926-.... CANR-16
Earlier sketch in CA 93-96
Whitnell, Barbara
See Hutton, Ann
Whitney, Alec
See White, Alan
Whitney, Alex(andra) 1922-.... 53-56
See also SATA 14
Whitney, Byrl A(lbert) 1901-.... CAP-1
Earlier sketch in CA 13-14
Whitney, Charles Allen 1929-.... 81-84
Whitney, Cornelius Vanderbilt 1899-.... 85-88
Whitney, Craig Richard 1943-.... 131
Whitney, Dallas (Cole) 1952-.... 117
Whitney, David
See Malick, Terrence
Whitney, David C(harles) 1921-.... CANR-5
Earlier sketch in CA 9-12R
See also SATA 48
See also SATA-Brief 29
Whitney, Eleanor Noss 1938-.... CANR-6
Earlier sketch in CA 13-16R
Whitney, Elizabeth Dalton 1906-.... 21-24R
Whitney, George D(ana) 1918-.... 93-96
Whitney, Hallam
See Whittington, Harry (Benjamin)
Whitney, J(ohn) D(enison) 1940-.... CANR-3
Earlier sketch in CA 49-52
Whitney, J. L. H.
See Trimble, Jacquelyn W(hitney)
Whitney, John Hay 1904-1982 Obituary.... 106
See also DLB 127
Whitney, John Raymond 1920-.... 105
Whitney, Leon F(radley) 1894-1973.... CANR-5
Earlier sketch in CA 5-8R
Whitney, Malika Lee 1946-.... 133
Whitney, Marie Louise (Schroeder) Hosford 1925(?)- Brief entry.... 113
Whitney, Marylou
See Whitney, Marie Louise (Schroeder) Hosford
Whitney, Peter Dwight 1915-.... 9-12R
Whitney, Phyllis A(yame) 1903-.... CANR-60
Earlier sketches in CA 1-4R, CANR-3, 25, 38
See also AITN 2
See also BEST 90:3
See also CLC 42
See also DAM POP
See also JRDA
See also MAICYA
See also SATA 1, 30
Whitney, Polly 1948-.... 152
Whitney, Robert Frost 1906(?)-1986 Obituary.... 119
Whitney, Ruth Reinke 1928-.... 133
Whitney, Sharon 1937-.... SATA 63
Whitney, Steve(n) 1946-.... 81-84
Whitney, Thomas P(orter) 1917-.... 104
See also SATA 25
Whiton, James Nelson 1932-.... 13-16R
Whitridge, Arnold 1891-1989.... 9-12R
Obituary.... 127
Whitrow, Gerald James 1912-.... CANR-3
Earlier sketch in CA 5-8R
Whitson
See Warren, Peter Whitson
Whitson, Skip 1944-.... 118
Whitt, Anne Hall
See Thompson, Anne Hall Whitt
Whitt, Richard 1944-.... 81-84
Whittaker, C(harles) R(ichard) 1929-.... 131
Whittaker, Kathryn Putnam 1931-.... 13-16R
Whittaker, Otto (Jr.) 1916-.... 25-28R
Whittaker, Robert Harding 1920-.... 105
Whittemore, Charles P(ark) 1921-.... 9-12R
Whittemore, Don.... 69-72
Whittemore, L(ouis) H(enry) 1941-.... 45-48
Whittemore, Mildred 1946-.... 9-12R
Whittemore, (Edward) Reed (Jr.) 1919-.... CANR-4
Earlier sketch in CA 9-12R
See also CAAS 8
See also CLC 4
See also DLB 5
Whittemore, Robert Clifton 1921-.... 9-12R
Whitten, Jamie L(loyd) 1910-.... CAP-2
Earlier sketch in CA 23-24
Whitten, Leslie H(unter), Jr. 1928-.... CANR-53
Earlier sketches in CA 17-20R, CANR-29
Whitten, Mary Evelyn 1922-.... 17-20R
Whitten, Norman E(arl), Jr. 1937-.... 17-20R
Whittet, G(eorge) S(orley) 1918-.... 21-24R
Whittet, T. D.
See Whittet, Thomas Douglas
Whittet, Thomas Douglas 1915-1987 Obituary. 122
Whittick, Arnold 1898-.... CAP-1
Earlier sketch in CA 11-12
Whittier, John Greenleaf 1807-1892.... DLB 1
Whitting, Philip (David) 1903-.... 97-100
Whittingham, Harry E(dward), Jr. 1918-.... 5-8R
Whittingham, Jack 1910-1972 Obituary.... 37-40R
Whittingham, Richard 1939-.... CANR-36
Earlier sketch in CA 37-40R
Whittington, Geoffrey 1938-.... CANR-42
Earlier sketches in CA 104, CANR-20
Whittington, H(orace) G(reeley) 1929-.... 21-24R
Whittington, Harry (Benjamin) 1915-1989 CANR-58
Earlier sketches in CA 21-24R, CANR-5
Interview in.... CANR-5
Whittington, Mary K(athrine) 1941-.... SATA 75
Whittington, Peter
See Mackay, James (Alexander)
Whittington-Egan, Richard 1924-.... CANR-42
Earlier sketches in CA 9-12R, CANR-5, 20
Whittle, Amberys R(ayvon) 1935-.... 45-48
Whittle, Frank 1907-.... 162
Whittle, Tyler
See Tyler-Whittle, Michael Sidney
Whittlebot, Hernia
See Coward, Noel (Peirce)
Whittlesey, E(unice) S. 1907-.... 93-96
Whittlesey, Susan 1938-.... 29-32R
Whitton, Charlotte (Elizabeth) 1896-1975 Obituary.... 89-92
Whitton, David 1947-.... 149
Whitton, John Boardman 1892-.... CAP-2
Earlier sketch in CA 23-24
Whitton, Kenneth S(tuart) 1925-.... 131
Whittow, J. B.
See Whittow, John B(yron)
Whittow, John B(yron) 1929-.... CANR-46
Earlier sketch in CA 120
Whitworth, John 1945-.... 131
Whitworth, John McKelvie 1942-.... 77-80
Whitworth, Reginald Henry 1910-.... 109
Whitworth, Rex (Henry) 1916-.... 144
Whitworth, William 1937-.... 37-40R
Whitzman, Carolyn 1963-.... 152
Whiz, Walter
See Johnson, Curt(is Lee)
Wholey, Dennis 1938-.... 127
Whone, Herbert 1925-.... CANR-49
Earlier sketches in CA 108, CANR-24
Whorton, James C(lifton) 1942-.... 77-80
Whorton, M. Donald 1946-.... CANR-43
Earlier sketch in CA 117
Whozis, S. F.
See Bates, Harry
Whritner, John Alden 1935-.... 45-48
Whyard, Florence 1917-.... 129
Whyatt, Frances
See Boyd, Shylah
Whybray, Roger Norman 1923-1998.... 89-92
Obituary.... 166
Whynott, Douglas (Vernon) 1950-.... 137
Whyte, Fredrica (Harriman) 1905-.... CAP-1
Earlier sketch in CA 11-12
Whyte, Henry Malcolm 1920-.... CANR-3
Earlier sketch in CA 5-8R
Whyte, Iain Boyd 1947-.... 132
Whyte, James Huntington 1909-.... 5-8R
Whyte, John D. 1940-.... 129
Whyte, Lancelot Law 1896-1972.... CAP-1
Earlier sketch in CA 13-16
Whyte, Lewis (Gilmour) 1906-1986 Obituary.... 121
Whyte, Mal(colm Kenneth, Jr.) 1933-.... 106
See also SATA 62
Whyte, Martin King 1942-.... 81-84
Whyte, Mary 1953-.... 159
See also SATA 94
Whyte, (Harry Archibald) Maxwell 1908-.... 105
Whyte, Robert Orr 1903- Brief entry.... 106
Whyte, Ron 1942(?)-1989.... 132
Obituary.... 129
See also SATA-Obit 63
Whyte, Sibly
See Stine, Henry Eugene
Whyte, William Foote 1914-.... CANR-40
Earlier sketches in CA 1-4R, CANR-3, 18
Whyte, William H(ollingsworth) 1917-.... 9-12R
Wiarda, Howard J(ohn) 1939-.... CANR-21
Earlier sketches in CA 53-56, CANR-4
Wiat, Philippa
See Ferridge, Philippa
Wiater, Stanley 1953-.... 150
See also SATA 84
Wibbelsman, Charles J(oseph) 1945-.... 128
See also SATA 59
Wibberley, Leonard (Patrick O'Connor) 1915-1983. CANR-3
Obituary.... 111
Earlier sketch in CA 5-8R
See also CLR 3
See also SATA 2, 45
See also SATA-Obit 36
Wiber, Melanie G(ay) 1954-.... 151
Wiberg, Harald (Albin) 1908-.... SATA 93
See also SATA-Brief 40
Wicclair, Mark R. 1944-.... 149
Wice, Aubrey (Agnew) 1913(?)-1985 Obituary.... 119
Wice, Paul B(ernard) 1942-.... 57-60
Wick, Carter
See Wilcox, Collin
Wick, John W(illiam) 1935-.... CANR-15
Earlier sketch in CA 41-44R
Wick, Steve 1951-.... 159
Wick, Stuart Mary
See Freeman, Kathleen
Wick, Wendy
See Reaves, Wendy Wick
Wicke, Charles R(obinson) 1928-.... 37-40R
Wicke, Edith Schreiber
See Schreiber-Wicke, Edith
Wickenden, Elizabeth 1909-.... 1-4R
Wickenden, Leonard Daniel 1913(?)-1989 Obituary.... 130
Wickens, Delos D(onald) 1909-.... CAP-1
Earlier sketch in CA 13-16
Wickens, Elaine.... SATA 86
Wickens, James F. 1933-.... 57-60
Wicker, Brian 1929-.... 17-20R

Wicker, Ireene 1905(?)-1987 69-72
Obituary 124
See also SATA-Obit 55
Wicker, Randolfe Hayden 1938- 45-48
Wicker, Thomas Grey 1926- CANR-46
Earlier sketches in CA 65-68, CANR-21
See also Wicker, Tom
Wicker, Tom
See Wicker, Thomas Grey
See also CLC 7
Wickers, David 1944- 77-80
Wickersham, Edward Dean 1927-1966 .... 5-8R
Wickersham, Joan Barrett 1957- 105
Wickert, Erwin 1915- 132
Wickert, Frederic R(obinson) 1912- 21-24R
Wickes, George 1923- 9-12R
Wickes, Kim 1947- 109
Wickett, Ann 1942- 122
Wickett, William Harold, Jr. 1919- 108
Wickey, Gould 1891- 25-28R
Wickham, Christopher J. 1950- 144
Wickham, David 1944- 141
Wickham, Edward Ralph 1911- 5-8R
Wickham, Glynne (William Gladstone) 1922- CANR-7
Earlier sketch in CA 5-8R
Wickham, Jean 1903- 69-72
Wickham, Mary Fanning
See Bond, Mary Fanning Wickham
Wickham, Thomas Frederick 1926- 13-16R
Wickham-Crowley, Timothy P. 1951- 155
Wicklein, John (Frederick) 1924- 106
Wicklund, Robert A. 1941- 144
Wickram, Georg c. 1505-c. 1561 .... DLB 179
Wickremasinghe, Esmond
1920(?)-1985 Obituary 117
Wickremasinghe, S(ugiswara) A(beywardena)
1901-1981 Obituary 108
Wicks, Ben 1926- 73-76
Wicks, Harold Vernon, Jr. 1931- 102
Wicks, Harry
See Wicks, Harold Vernon, Jr.
Wicks, Jared 1929- CANR-21
Earlier sketch in CA 25-28R
Wicks, John H. 1936- 17-20R
Wicks, Robert J(ohn) 1946- 113
Wicks, Robert Stewart 1923- 17-20R
Wickstrom, Lois 1948- 106
Wickwar, (William) Hardy 1903- 57-60
Wickwire, Franklin B(acon) 1931- 21-24R
Wickwire, Mary Botts 1935- 104
Wicomb, Zoe 1948- 127
Widdemer, Mabel Cleland 1902-1964 .... 5-8R
See also SATA 5
Widdemer, Margaret 18(?)-1978 .... CANR-4
Obituary 77-80
Earlier sketch in CA 5-8R
Widder, (John) Arthur, (Jr.) 1928- 5-8R
Widder, Milton 1907(?)-1985 Obituary 118
Widdicombe, Richard Toby 1955- 150
Widdifield, Stacie G(raham) 1953- 168
Widdows, P(aul) F. 1918- 143
Widell, Helene 1912- 37-40R
Wideman, John Edgar 1941- CANR-67
Earlier sketches in CA 85-88, CANR-14, 42
See also BLC 3
See also BW 2
See also CLC 5, 34, 36, 67
See also DAM MULT
See also DLB 33, 143
Widener, Alice 1905(?)-1985 Obituary 114
Widener, Don(ald) 1930- 37-40R
Widener, Harry Elkins 1885-1912 .... DLB 140
Widenor, William C(ramer) 1937- 102
Widerberg, Siv 1931- 53-56
See also SATA 10
Widgery, Alban G(regory) 1887- 5-8R
Widgery, David 1947-1992 .... CANR-47
Obituary 139
Earlier sketch in CA 69-72
Widgery, Jan 1920- 17-20R
Widick, B. J. 1910- 9-12R
Widicus, Wilbur W(ilson), Jr. 1932- 53-56
Widman, F. Lisle 1919(?)-1983 Obituary 111
Widmer, Eleanor (Rackow) 1925- 17-20R
Widmer, Emmy Louise 1925- 29-32R
Widmer, Kingsley 1925- CANR-3
Earlier sketch in CA 1-4R
Widner, Jennifer A(nne) 1958- 144
Widutis, Florence 1912(?)-1989 128
Wiebe, Katie Funk 1924- 132
Wiebe, M(elvin) G(eorge) 1939- 114
Wiebe, Robert H(uddleston) 1930- 5-8R
Wiebe, Rudy (Henry) 1934- CANR-67
Earlier sketches in CA 37-40R, CANR-42
See also CLC 6, 11, 14
See also DAC
See also DAM MST
See also DLB 60
Wiebenson, Dora (Louise) 1926- 37-40R
Wiecek, William Michael 1938- 37-40R
Wiechert, Ernst 1887-1950 .... DLB 56
Wieck, Fred D(ernburg) 1910-1973 Obituary 104
Wieckert, Jeanne E. (Lentz) 1939- 89-92
Wiecking, Anna M. 1887-1973 .... CAP-1
Earlier sketch in CA 13-14
Wieczynski, Joseph L. 1934- 37-40R
Wied, Martina 1882-1957 .... DLB 85
Wiedemann, Thomas (E. J.) 1950- 138
Wieder, Laurance 1946- CANR-8
Earlier sketch in CA 57-60
Wieder, Robert S(hannon) 1944- 85-88
Wiederumb, Trotzhard
See Steiner, Gerolf
Wiedner, Donald L(awrence) 1930- 13-16R
Wiegand, Charmion von
See von Wiegand, Charmion
Wiegand, G(uenther) Carl 1906- 21-24R
Wiegand, Wayne A. 1946- 164
Wiegand, William G(eorge) 1928- 9-12R
Wieghart, James G. 1933- 77-80
Wiegner, Kathleen K(napp) 1938- 93-96
Wiehl, Andrew (M.) 1904- 89-92
Wieland, Christoph Martin 1733-1813 .... DLB 97
Wieland, George F(red) 1936- 89-92
Wieland, Heinrich Otto 1877-1957 167
Wieland, Liza 1960- 139
Wieler, Diana (Jean) 1961- 163
Wiells, Helen
See Cameron, (Barbara) Anne
Wieman, Harold F(rancis) 1917- 61-64
Wieman, Henry N(elson) 1884-1975 61-64
Obituary 57-60
Wiemer, Rudolf Otto 1905- CANR-53
Earlier sketches in CA 21-24R, CANR-9, 25
Wienandt, Elwyn A(rthur) 1917- 41-44R
Wienbarg, Ludolf 1802-1872 .... DLB 133
Wiene, Robert 1881-1938 .... TCLC 56
Wiener, Alexander (Solomon) 1907-1976 158
Wiener, Allen J. 1943- CANR-53
Earlier sketch in CA 125
Wiener, Daniel N(orman) 1921- 37-40R
Wiener, Harvey Shelby 1940- 102
Wiener, Joan
See Bordow, Joan (Wiener)
Wiener, Joel H. 1937- CANR-14
Earlier sketches in CA 37-40R, CANR-31
Wiener, Jon
See Wiener, Jonathan M.
Wiener, Jonathan B(aert) 1962- 158
Wiener, Jonathan M. 1944- 115
Wiener, Joshua M(ark) 1949- 133
Wiener, Leigh Auston 1929-1993 .... CANR-47
Obituary 141
Earlier sketch in CA 108
Wiener, Lori 1956- .... SATA 84
Wiener, M. Jean 1896-1982 Obituary 107
Wiener, Martin J. 1941- 85-88
Wiener, Norbert 1894-1964 157
Obituary 107
Wiener, Philip P(aul) 1905-1992 .... CAP-1
Obituary 137
Earlier sketch in CA 9-10
Wiener, Sally Dixon 1926- 101
Wiener, Sam
See Dolgoff, Sam
Wiener, Solomon 1915- CANR-7
Earlier sketch in CA 17-20R
Wieners, John 1934- 13-16R
See also CLC 7
See also DLB 16
Wieniewska, Celina
See Janson-Smith, Celina
Wienpahl, Paul D(e Velin) 1916- 9-12R
Wier, Allen 1946- 77-80
Wier, Dara 1949- CANR-53
Earlier sketches in CA 77-80, CANR-27
Wier, Ester (Alberti) 1910- 9-12R
See also DLB 52
See also SATA 3
Wiersbe, Warren W(endell) 1929- CANR-46
Earlier sketches in CA 5-8R, CANR-7, 23
Wiersma, Stanley M(arvin) 1930- CANR-11
Earlier sketch in CA 29-32R
Wiersma, William, Jr. 1931- CANR-1
Earlier sketch in CA 45-48
Wierwille, Victor Paul 1916-1985 .... CANR-2
Obituary 116
Earlier sketch in CA 5-8R
Wierzynski, Gregory H(ieronim) 1939- 73-76
Wierzynski, Kazimierz 1894-1969 Obituary 115
Wiese, Arthur E(dward) 1946- 73-76
Wiese, Kurt 1887-1974 .... 9-12R
Obituary 49-52
See also MAICYA
See also SATA 3, 36
See also SATA-Obit 24
Wiesel, Elie(zer) 1928- CANR-65
Earlier sketches in CA 5-8R, CANR-8, 40
Interview in CANR-8
See also CAAS 4
See also AAYA 7
See also AITN 1
See also CLC 3, 5, 11, 37
See also DA
See also DAB
See also DAC
See also DAM MST, NOV
See also DLB 83
See also DLBY 87
See also MTCW 1
See also SATA 56
See also WLCS 2
Wiesen, Allen E. 1939- 29-32R
Wiesenfarth, Joseph (John) 1933- CANR-8
Earlier sketch in CA 5-8R
Wiesenfeld, Joe 1947- 131
Wiesenthal, Simon 1908- CANR-13
Earlier sketch in CA 21-24R
Wiesner, David 1956- .... CLR 43
See also SATA 72
Wiesner, Jerome B(ert) 1915-1994 .... 13-16R
Obituary 147
Wiesner, Merry E. 1952- 148
Wiesner, Portia
See Takakjian, Portia
Wiesner, William 1899- 41-44R
See also SATA 5
Wiest, Claire (Johnson) 1930- CANR-34
Earlier sketch in CA 113
Wigal, Donald 1933- CANR-14
Earlier sketch in CA 81-84
Wigan, Anthony (?)-1983 Obituary 110
Wigan, Bernard (John) 1918- 13-16R
Wigan, Christopher
See Bingley, David Ernest
Wigan, Tony
See Wigan, Anthony
Wigforss, Ernst 1882(?)-1977 Obituary 69-72
Wigg, George (Edward Cecil)
1900-1983 Obituary 115
Wiggers, Raymond 1952- 149
See also SATA 82
Wiggin, Eric E(llsworth) 1939- 152
See also SATA 88
Wiggin, Kate Douglas 1856-1923 Brief entry 111
See also DLB 42
See also YABC 1
Wiggin, Kate Douglas (Smith) 1856-1923 137
See also CLR 52
See also MAICYA
Wiggin (Riggs), Kate Douglas (Smith)
1856-1923 160
Wiggin, Maurice (Samuel) 1912- CANR-5
Earlier sketch in CA 9-12R
Wiggin, Paul 1934- 25-28R
Wiggins, Arthur W. 1938- 53-56
Wiggins, Charles W(illiam) 1937- 41-44R
Wiggins, David 1933- 118
Wiggins, Jack G(illmore) 1926- 41-44R
Wiggins, James B(ryan) 1935- 37-40R
Wiggins, James Russell 1903- 133
See also AITN 2
Wiggins, James Wilhelm 1914- 17-20R
Wiggins, Jerry S. 1931- 163
Wiggins, Marianne 1947- CANR-60
Earlier sketch in CA 130
See also BEST 89:3
See also CLC 57
Wiggins, Melanie 1934- 159
Wiggins, Robert A. 1921- 13-16R
Wiggins, Sam P. 1919- 21-24R
Wiggins, VeraLee (Chesnut) 1928-1995 155
See also SATA 89
Wigginton, Eliot 1942- 101
See also AITN 1
Wigglesworth, Michael 1631-1705 .... DLB 24
Wigglesworth, Vincent B(rian) 1899-1994 157
Wigham, Eric Leonard 1904- 109
Wight, Frederick S.
See Wight, Frederick Stallknecht (Van Buren)
Wight, Frederick Stallknecht (Van Buren)
1902-1986 Obituary 120
Wight, James Alfred 1916-1995 77-80
See also Herriot, James
See also SATA 55
See also SATA-Brief 44
Wight, (Robert James) Martin 1913-1972 .... CAP-2
Earlier sketch in CA 21-22
Wightman, Edith Mary
1939(?)-1983(?) Obituary 111
Wightman, George Brian Hamilton 1933- 107
Wighton, Charles Ernest 1913- 5-8R
Wighton, Rosemary Neville 1925- 9-12R
Wigmore
See Fabricius, Johan (Johannes)
Wignall, Anne 1912- 97-100
Wignell, Edel 1936- 137
See also SATA 69
Wigner, Eugene Paul 1902-1995 .... CAP-2
Obituary 147
Earlier sketch in CA 25-28
Wigoder, Geoffrey Bernard 1922- 105
Wihl, Gary 120
Wiig, Howard (Calvert) 1940- 61-64
Wijasuriya, D(onald) E(arlian) K(ingsley)
1934- 81-84
Wijnberg, Ellen 151
See also SATA 85
Wik, Reynold M. 1910- CANR-14
Earlier sketch in CA 81-84
Wikan, Unni 1944- 147
Wikander, Matthew H. 1950- 125
Wikberg, Ron 1943(?)-1994 144
Obituary 147
Wike, Edward L. 1922- 37-40R
Wikland, Ilon 1930- Brief entry 111
See also SATA 93
See also SATA-Brief 32
Wikler, Madeline 1943- 117
Wikramanayake, Marina 1938- 45-48
Wiksell, Milton J. 1910- 5-8R
Wiksell, Wesley 1906- CAP-1
Earlier sketch in CA 17-18
Wilber, Charles G(rady) 1916- CANR-21
Earlier sketch in CA 41-44R
Wilber, Charles K. 1935- 134
Brief entry 113
Wilber, Cynthia J. 1951- 140
Wilber, Donald N(ewton) 1907- CANR-2
Earlier sketch in CA 5-8R
See also SATA 35
Wilberforce, William 1759-1833 .... DLB 158
Wilbers, Stephen 1949- 106
Wilbert, Johannes 1927- 124
Brief entry 118
Wilbourn, Carole C(ecile) 1940- CANR-14
Earlier sketch in CA 81-84
Wilbrandt, Adolf von 1837-1911 .... DLB 129
Wilbur, C. Keith 1923- CANR-57
Earlier sketches in CA 25-28R, CANR-11, 28
See also SATA 27
Wilbur, C(larence) Martin 1908-1997 85-88
Obituary 159
Wilbur, Crane 1887(?)-1973 Obituary 45-48
Wilbur, James B(enjamin) III 1924- CANR-41
Earlier sketches in CA 37-40R, CANR-14
Wilbur, Marguerite Eyer 1889- CAP-1
Earlier sketch in CA 11-12
Wilbur, Richard (Purdy) 1921- CANR-29
Earlier sketches in CA 1-4R, CANR-2
Interview in CANR-29
See also CABS 2
See also CLC 3, 6, 9, 14, 53, 110
See also DA
See also DAB
See also DAC
See also DAM MST, POET
See also DLB 5, 169
See also MTCW 1
See also SATA 9
Wilbur, William H(ale) 1888- CAP-1
Earlier sketch in CA 13-14
Wilburn, Jean Alexander 1915- 21-24R
Wilburn, Kathy 1948- .... SATA 68
Wilburn, Ralph G(lenn) 1909- CAP-1
Earlier sketch in CA 17-18
Wilby, Basil Leslie 1930- CANR-41
Earlier sketches in CA 103, CANR-19
Wilcher, Robert 1942- 121
Wilcken, Lois 1949- 145
Wilckens, Ulrich 1928- Brief entry 114
Wilcock, Donald E. 1944- 151
Wilcock, John 1927- CANR-2
Earlier sketch in CA 1-4R
Wilcocks, Julie 1943- 110
Wilcox, Charlotte 1948- .... SATA 72
Wilcox, Clair 1898-1970 .... CANR-4
Earlier sketch in CA 5-8R
Wilcox, (William) Clyde 1953- 154
Wilcox, Collin 1924-1996 .... CANR-59
Obituary 152
Earlier sketches in CA 21-24R, CANR-14, 31
Wilcox, Daniel 1941- 53-56
Wilcox, Dennis L. 1941- CANR-14
Earlier sketch in CA 37-40R
Wilcox, Desmond (John) 1931- CANR-21
Earlier sketch in CA 69-72
Wilcox, Donald J(ames) 1938-1991 109
Obituary 134
Wilcox, Earl J(unior) 1933- 111
Wilcox, Francis (Orlando) 1908-1985 .... 37-40R
Obituary 115
Wilcox, Fred A(llen) 1940- 129
Wilcox, Helen (Elizabeth) 1955- 136
Wilcox, Herbert 1891-1977 57-60
Obituary 118
Wilcox, Howard 1913(?)-1987 Obituary 122
Wilcox, James (P.) 1949- CANR-72
Brief entry 125
Earlier sketch in CA 129
Interview in 129
Wilcox, Jess
See Hershman, Morris
Wilcox, John T(homas) 1933- 45-48
Wilcox, Laird (M.) 1942- 140
Wilcox, Michael (Denys) 1943- 77-80
Wilcox, Paul L(orentus) 1899- 69-72
Wilcox, R(uth) Turner 1888-1970 .... 5-8R
Obituary 29-32R
See also SATA 36
Wilcox, Richard L. 1918-1978 Obituary 77-80
Wilcox, Robert K(alleen) 1943- CANR-24
Earlier sketch in CA 77-80
Wilcox, Roger P. 1916- 21-24R
Wilcox, Stephen F. 1951- 141
Wilcox, Tamara 1940- CANR-19
Earlier sketch in CA 97-100
Wilcox, Virginia Lee 1911- 37-40R
Wilcox, Walter 1920-1983 Obituary 110
Wilcox, Wayne Ayres 1932-1974 .... CANR-4
Obituary 49-52
Earlier sketch in CA 5-8R
Wilcoxon, George Dent, Jr. 1913- 93-96
Wild, (Robert) David (Fergusson) 1910-1995 139
Obituary 150
Wild, Jocelyn 1941- 116
See also SATA 46
Wild, John D(aniel) 1902-1972 Obituary 37-40R
Wild, Peter 1940- 37-40R
See also CLC 14
See also DLB 5
Wild, Robert A(nthony) 1940- 111
Wild, Robin (Evans) 1936- 116
See also SATA 46
Wild, Rolf H(einrich) 1927- 81-84
Wildavsky, Aaron (B.) 1930-1993 .... CANR-30
Obituary 142
Earlier sketches in CA 1-4R, CANR-2
Wilde, Alan 1929- CANR-31
Earlier sketch in CA 110
Wilde, D. Gunther
See Hurwood, Bernhardt J.
Wilde, Daniel U(nderwood) 1937- 57-60
Wilde, Jean T(oeplitz) 1898-1973 Obituary 45-48
Wilde, Jennifer
See Huff, T(om) E.
Wilde, Jocelyn
See Toombs, John
Wilde, Kathey
See King, Patricia
Wilde, Kelley (Cotter) 1947(?)- 168
Wilde, Lady Jane Francesca 1821-1896 .... DLB 199
Wilde, Larry 1928- CANR-51
Earlier sketches in CA 25-28R, CANR-10, 26, 40
Wilde, Meta Carpenter (Doherty) 1907-1994 81-84
Obituary 147

Wilde, Oscar (Fingal O'Flahertie Wills)
1854(?)-1900...119
Brief entry...104
See also CDBLB 1890-1914
See also DA
See also DAB
See also DAC
See also DAM DRAM, MST, NOV
See also DLB 10, 19, 34, 57, 141, 156, 190
See also SATA 24
See also SSC 11
See also TCLC 1, 8, 23, 41
See also WLC
Wilde, Richard Henry 1789-1847...DLB 3, 59
Wilde, W(illiam) H(enry) 1923-...CANR-11
Earlier sketch in CA 69-72
Wildeblood, Peter 1923-...65-68
Wildeman, Marlene 1948-...141
Wilden, Anthony 1935-...CANR-28
Earlier sketch in CA 37-40R
Wildenhain, Marguerite 1896-...77-80
Wilder, Alec
See Wilder, Alexander Lafayette Chew
Wilder, Alexander Lafayette Chew 1907-1980...104
Obituary...102
Wilder, Amos Niven 1895-1993...CANR-47
Obituary...141
Earlier sketch in CA 81-84
Wilder, Billy
See Wilder, Samuel
See also CLC 20
See also DLB 26
Wilder, Charlotte Elizabeth
1898(?)-1980 Obituary...97-100
Wilder, Cherry
See Grimm, Cherry Barbara
Wilder, Effie Leland 1909-...149
Wilder, Gene 1935-...142
Wilder, John Bunyan 1914-...5-8R
Wilder, Joseph 1895-1976 Obituary...116
Wilder, Laura (Elizabeth) Ingalls 1867-1957...137
Brief entry...111
See also AAYA 26
See also CLR 2
See also DLB 22
See also JRDA
See also MAICYA
See also SATA 15, 29, 100
Wilder, Robert (Ingersoll) 1901-1974...CAP-2
Obituary...53-56
Earlier sketch in CA 13-14
Wilder, Robert D. 1916-...41-44R
Wilder, Roy (E.), Jr. 1914-...121
Wilder, Samuel 1906-...89-92
See also Wilder, Billy
Wilder, Stephen
See Marlowe, Stephen
Wilder, Thornton (Niven) 1897-1975...CANR-40
Obituary...61-64
Earlier sketch in CA 13-16R
See also AITN 2
See also CLC 1, 5, 6, 10, 15, 35, 82
See also DA
See also DAB
See also DAC
See also DAM DRAM, MST, NOV
See also DC 1
See also DLB 4, 7, 9
See also DLBY 97
See also MTCW 1
See also WLC
Wilders, John (Simpson) 1927-...21-24R
Wilder-Smith, A(rthur) E(rnest) 1915-...CANR-27
Earlier sketches in CA 57-60, CANR-11
Wildes, Harry Emerson 1890-...57-60
Wildgans, Anton 1881-1942...DLB 118
Wild Horse Annie
See Johnston, Velma B.
Wilding, Ann
See Budd, Mavis
Wilding, Michael 1942-...CANR-49
Earlier sketches in CA 104, CANR-24
See also CLC 73
Wildman, Allan K. 1927-...105
Wildman, Eugene 1938-...25-28R
Wildman, John Hazard 1911-...37-40R
Wildman, Louis Robert 1941-...CANR-5
Earlier sketch in CA 13-16R
Wildman, Steven S. 1948-...139
Wildmon, Donald E(llis) 1938-...CANR-13
Earlier sketch in CA 61-64
Wildrick, Stanley B. 1894-1984 Obituary...112
Wilds, Nancy Alexander 1926-...13-16R
Wildsmith, Alan 1937-...97-100
Wildsmith, Brian 1930-...CANR-35
Earlier sketch in CA 85-88
See also CLR 2, 52
See also MAICYA
See also SAAS 5
See also SATA 16, 69
Wile, Mary Lee 1947-...151
Wilenski, Peter Stephen 1939-...109
Wilenski, R(eginald) H(oward) 1887-1975...61-64
Obituary...57-60
Wilensky, Harold L. 1923-...CANR-34
Earlier sketches in CA 41-44R, CANR-15
Wilentz, Gay (A.) 1950-...138
Wilentz, Joan Steen 1930-...25-28R
Wilentz, Ted
See Wilentz, Theodore
Wilentz, Theodore 1915-...29-32R
Wiles, David K(imball) 1942-...CANR-7
Earlier sketch in CA 53-56
Wiles, Domini 1942-...102
Wiles, Gordon Pitts 1909-...108
Wiles, John 1924-...9-12R
Wiles, Kimball 1913-1969...CANR-4
Earlier sketch in CA 5-8R
Wiles, Maurice Frank 1923-...108
Wiles, Peter John de la Fosse 1919-1997...5-8R
Obituary...159
Wiles, Roy McKeen 1903-(?)...CAP-1
Earlier sketch in CA 19-20
Wiley, Bell
See Strauss, Frances Goetzmann
Wiley, Bell I(rvin) 1906-1980...CANR-4
Obituary...97-100
Earlier sketch in CA 5-8R
See also DLB 17
Wiley, David Sherman 1935-...CANR-29
Earlier sketches in CA 61-64, CANR-12
Wiley, Farida A(nna) 1887(?)-1986 Obituary...121
Wiley, Jack 1936-...CANR-8
Earlier sketch in CA 61-64
Wiley, James (Milton) 1920-...154
Wiley, Jay Wilson 1913-...5-8R
Wiley, John P., Jr. 1936-...89-92
Wiley, Karla H(ummel) 1918-...61-64
Wiley, Margaret L.
See Marshall, Margaret Wiley
Wiley, Paul L(uzon) 1914-1979...CANR-10
Earlier sketch in CA 5-8R
Wiley, Peter (Booth) 1942-...131
Wiley, Ralph 1952-...136
Wiley, Raymond A(loysius) 1923-...37-40R
Wiley, Richard 1944-...CANR-71
Brief entry...121
Earlier sketch in CA 129
See also CLC 44
Wiley, Stan
See Hill, John S(tanley)
Wiley, Tom 1906-...25-28R
Wiley, William Leon 1903-...111
Wilf, Alexander 1905(?)-1981 Obituary...103
Wilford, Allen 1948-...128
Wilford, Hugh 1965-...151
Wilford, John Noble 1933-...CANR-44
Earlier sketches in CA 29-32R, CANR-15
Wilford, Walton T. 1937-...49-52
Wilgus, A(lva) Curtis 1897-...CANR-3
Earlier sketch in CA 5-8R
Wilgus, D(onald) K(night) 1918-1989...37-40R
Obituary...130
Wilhelm, Hans 1945-...CANR-48
Earlier sketch in CA 119
See also CLR 46
See also SAAS 21
See also SATA 58
Wilhelm, Hellmut 1905-...5-8R
Wilhelm, James Jerome 1932-...CANR-32
Earlier sketch in CA 17-20R
Wilhelm, John R(emsen) 1916-1994...5-8R
Obituary...145
Wilhelm, Kate
Interview in...CANR-17
See also Wilhelm, Katie Gertrude
See also CAAS 5
See also AAYA 20
See also CLC 7
See also DLB 8
Wilhelm, Kathryn Stephenson 1915-...13-16R
Wilhelm, Katie Gertrude 1928-...CANR-60
Earlier sketches in CA 37-40R, CANR-17, 36
See also Wilhelm, Kate
See also MTCW 1
Wilhelm, Paul A. 1916-...61-64
Wilhelm, Walt 1893-...29-32R
Wilhelm II
See Hohenzollern, Friedrich Wilhelm (Victor Albert)
Wilhelmina
See Cooper, Wilhelmina (Behmenburg)
Wilhelmsen, Frederick D(aniel) 1923-...CANR-3
Earlier sketch in CA 1-4R
Wilhoit, Francis M(arion) 1920-...126
Brief entry...109
Wilk, David 1951-...CANR-4
Earlier sketch in CA 53-56
Wilk, Gerard H(ermann) 1902-...69-72
Wilk, Max 1920-...CANR-37
Earlier sketches in CA 1-4R, CANR-1, 16
Wilk, Richard R(alph) 1953-...120
Wilke, Ekkehard-Teja 1941-...65-68
Wilke, Harold H(enry) 1914-...132
Wilke, Ulfert (Stephan) 1907-...CAP-1
Earlier sketch in CA 13-16
Wilken, Robert L(ouis) 1936-...CANR-16
Earlier sketch in CA 29-32R
Wilkening, Howard (Everett) 1909-1995...89-92
Obituary...150
Wilkens, Emily 1917-...103
Wilkerson, Cynthia
See Levinson, Leonard
Wilkerson, David R(ay) 1931-...41-44R
Wilkerson, Hugh 1939-...104
Wilkerson, Loree A. R(andleman) 1923-...17-20R
Wilkerson, Rich(ard Preston) 1952-...123
Wilkes, Charles 1798-1877...DLB 183
Wilkes, Edward T. 1889-1983 Obituary...111
Wilkes, George 1817-1885...DLB 79
Wilkes, Glenn Newton 1928-...CANR-17
Earlier sketch in CA 1-4R
Wilkes, Ian (Henry) 1932-...41-44R
Wilkes, John W(illiam) 1924-...25-28R
Wilkes, Maurice (Vincent) 1913-...158
Wilkes, Paul 1938-...CANR-42
Earlier sketches in CA 81-84, CANR-15
Wilkes, Peter 1937-...125
Wilkes, William Alfred 1910-...45-48
Wilkes-Hunter, R(ichard)...13-16R
Wilkie, Angus 1958-...128
Wilkie, Brian 1929-...13-16R
Wilkie, James W. 1936-...21-24R
Wilkie, Jane 1917-...102
Wilkie, Katharine E(lliott) 1904-1980...21-24R
Obituary...125
See also SATA 31
Wilkie, Kenneth 1942-...85-88
Wilkin, Eloise (Burns) 1904-1987...124
See also MAICYA
See also SATA 49
See also SATA-Obit 54
Wilkins, Alfred T., Jr. 1949-...129
Wilkins, Arnold J(onathan) 1946-...157
Wilkins, Beatrice (Brunson) 1928-...61-64
Wilkins, Burleigh Taylor 1932-...105
Wilkins, Ernest J. 1918-...53-56
Wilkins, Frances 1923-...73-76
See also SATA 14
Wilkins, H. Ford 1901(?)-1983 Obituary...111
Wilkins, Kathleen Sonia 1941-...104
Wilkins, Kay S.
See Wilkins, Kathleen Sonia
Wilkins, Kirby L. 1936-...127
Wilkins, Leslie T. 1915-...CANR-22
Earlier sketches in CA 17-20R, CANR-7
Wilkins, Marilyn (Ruth) 1926-...105
See also SATA 30
Wilkins, Marne
See Wilkins, Marilyn (Ruth)
Wilkins, Mary
See Freeman, Mary Eleanor Wilkins
Wilkins, Mary Huiskamp 1926-...CANR-18
Earlier sketches in CA 5-8R, CANR-2
See also Calhoun, Mary
See also SATA 84
Wilkins, Mesannie 1891-...CAP-2
Earlier sketch in CA 25-28
Wilkins, Mira 1931-...156
Brief entry...112
Wilkins, Roger (Wood) 1932-...117
Brief entry...109
See also BW 1
Wilkins, Ronald J(ohn) 1916-...CANR-16
Earlier sketch in CA 93-96
Wilkins, Roy 1901-1981...104
See also BW 1
Wilkins, Skip
See Wilkins, Alfred T., Jr.
Wilkins, Thurman 1915-...5-8R
Wilkins, (William) Vaughan 1890-1959...165
Wilkins, William R(ichard) 1933-...61-64
Wilkinson, Alec 1952-...CANR-44
Earlier sketch in CA 109
Wilkinson, Anne (Cochran Boyd) 1910-1961...148
See also DLB 88
Wilkinson, (Thomas) Barry 1923-...SATA 50
See also SATA-Brief 32
Wilkinson, Bertie 1898-...9-12R
Wilkinson, Beth 1925-...148
See also SATA 80
Wilkinson, Bonaro
See Overstreet, Bonaro (Wilkinson)
Wilkinson, Brenda 1946-...CANR-51
Earlier sketches in CA 69-72, CANR-26
See also BW 2
See also CLR 20
See also JRDA
See also SATA 14, 91
Wilkinson, Bud
See Wilkinson, Charles B(urnham)
Wilkinson, (John) Burke 1913-...CANR-49
Earlier sketch in CA 9-12R
See also SATA 4
Wilkinson, C. E. 1948-...109
Wilkinson, Charles B(urnham) 1916-1994...105
Obituary...144
Wilkinson, Charlotte Jefferson...69-72
Wilkinson, Clyde Winfield 1910-...1-4R
Wilkinson, David...93-96
Wilkinson, Doris Yvonne 1936-...29-32R
Wilkinson, Eliza Yonge 1757-1813(?)...DLB 200
Wilkinson, Elizabeth C. 1926-...123
Wilkinson, Ernest Leroy 1899-1978...CANR-3
Earlier sketch in CA 49-52
Wilkinson, G(eoffrey) K(edington) 1907-...1-4R
Wilkinson, J(oseph) F. 1925-...105
Wilkinson, James Hardy 1919-1986 Obituary...120
Wilkinson, James Harvie III 1944-...101
Wilkinson, John (Donald) 1929-...CANR-42
Earlier sketch in CA 9-12R
Wilkinson, John Thomas 1893-1980...107
Obituary...104
Wilkinson, L(ancelot) P(atrick) 1907-1985
CANR-20
Obituary...116
Earlier sketches in CA 5-8R, CANR-3
Wilkinson, Lorna Hilda Kathleen 1909-...CAP-1
Earlier sketch in CA 13-14
Wilkinson, Louis (Umfreville)
1881-1966 Obituary...116
Wilkinson, Maxwell Penrose
1905(?)-1985 Obituary...116
Wilkinson, Norman Beaumont 1910-1983...37-40R
Obituary...126
Wilkinson, Patrick
See Wilkinson, L(ancelot) P(atrick)
Wilkinson, Paul 1937-...CANR-14
Earlier sketch in CA 77-80
Wilkinson, Richard Gerald 1943-...45-48
Wilkinson, Richard H(erbert) 1951-...144
Wilkinson, (William) Roderick 1917-...13-16R
Wilkinson, Ronald 1920-1996...5-8R
Obituary...152
Wilkinson, Rosemary C(halloner) 1924-...CANR-42
Earlier sketches in CA 49-52, CANR-1, 17
Wilkinson, Rupert Hugh 1936-...9-12R
Wilkinson, Sylvia 1940-...CANR-47
Earlier sketch in CA 17-20R
See also AITN 1
See also DLBY 86
See also SATA 56
See also SATA-Brief 39
Wilkinson, Walter 1888-1970 Obituary...104
Wilkinson, (Arthur) Warren (Jr.) 1945-...132
Wilkinson, William Cleaver 1833-1920...DLB 71
Wilkinson, Winifred
See Hausmann, Winifred
Wilkomirski, Binjamin...167
Wilkon, Jozef 1930-...107
See also MAICYA
See also SATA 31, 71
Wilks, Brian 1933-...69-72
Wilks, Ed 1928(?)-1984 Obituary...114
Wilks, John 1922-...73-76
Wilks, Michael Thomas 1947-...110
See also SATA 44
Wilks, Mike
See Wilks, Michael Thomas
Wilks, Yorick 1939-...73-76
Will
See Lipkind, William
Will, Clifford M(artin) 1946-...136
Will, Frederic 1928-...CANR-16
Earlier sketches in CA 49-52, CANR-1
Will, Frederick L(udwig) 1909-...13-16R
Will, George F(rederick) 1941-...CANR-67
Earlier sketches in CA 77-80, CANR-32
See also BEST 90:3
See also MTCW 1
Will, Lawrence Elmer 1893-...CAP-2
Earlier sketch in CA 17-18
Will, Lester J. 1908(?)-1984 Obituary...111
Will, Robert E(rwin) 1928-...17-20R
Will, W(ilbur) Marvin 1937-...118
Willan, Anne 1938-...CANR-6
Earlier sketch in CA 57-60
Willan, Thomas Stuart 1910-...9-12R
Willans, Jean Stone 1924-...CANR-57
Earlier sketch in CA 65-68
Willard, Barbara (Mary) 1909-1994...CANR-15
Obituary...144
Earlier sketch in CA 81-84
See also CLR 2
See also DLB 161
See also MAICYA
See also SAAS 5
See also SATA 17, 74
Willard, Beatrice E(lizabeth) 1925-...41-44R
Willard, Charles
See Armstrong, John Byron
Willard, Charlotte 1914-1977...81-84
Obituary...73-76
Willard, Dallas (Albert) 1935-...116
Willard, Mildred Wilds 1911-1978...21-24R
Obituary...135
See also SATA 14
Willard, Nancy 1936-...CANR-68
Earlier sketches in CA 89-92, CANR-10, 39
See also CLC 7, 37
See also CLR 5
See also DLB 5, 52
See also MAICYA
See also MTCW 1
See also SATA 37, 71
See also SATA-Brief 30
Willard, Portman
See Norwood, Victor G(eorge) C(harles)
Willard, Samuel 1640-1707...DLB 24
Willcock, M(alcolm) M(aurice) 1925-...65-68
Willcox, A(lexander) R(obert) 1911-1993...118
Obituary...142
Willcox, Donald J. 1933-...49-52
Willcox, Isobel 1907-...111
See also SATA 42
Willcox, Sheila 1936-...73-76
Willcox, William Bradford 1907-1985...CANR-3
Obituary...117
Earlier sketch in CA 5-8R
Wille, Janet Neipris 1936-...CANR-55
Earlier sketches in CA 109, CANR-30
Wille, Lois 1931-...163
Willee, Albert William 1916-1982...109
Willeford, Betsy Ann 1939-...132
Willeford, Charles (Ray III) 1919-1988...CANR-48
Obituary...125
Earlier sketches in CA 33-36R, CANR-15
See also DAM POP
Willeford, William 1929-...25-28R
Willem, John M. 1909-1979...CAP-1
Obituary...93-96
Earlier sketch in CA 17-18
Willemen, Paul 1944-...156
Willems, Emilio 1905-...105
Willems, J. Rutherford 1944-...CANR-23
Earlier sketch in CA 45-48
Willen, Diane 1943-...117
Willens, Doris 1924-...127
Willens, Harold 1914-...132
Willensky, Elliot 1933-1990...29-32R
Obituary...131
Willenson, Kim Jeremy 1937-...103
Willenz, June A. 1924-...121
Willerding, Margaret F(rances) 1919-...57-60
Willes, Mary (Janette) 1927-...120
Willets, F(rederick) W(illiam) 1930-...21-24R
Willets, Walter E. 1924-...25-28R
Willett, Brother Franciscus 1922-...13-16R
Willett, Edward R(ice) 1923-...CANR-21
Earlier sketches in CA 5-8R, CANR-2
Willett, Frank 1925-...25-28R
Willett, Jincy 1946-...127

Willett, John (William Mills) 1917- CANR-4
Earlier sketch in CA 9-12R
Willett, Ralph 1935- 161
Willett, T(erence) C(harles) 1918- 37-40R
Willett, Thomas D(unaway) 1942- 108
Willetts, R(onald) F(rederick) 1915- CANR-2
Earlier sketch in CA 5-8R
Willey, Basil 1897-1978 .... 9-12R
Obituary 135
Willey, Darrell S. 1925- 41-44R
Willey, F. T.
See Willey, Frederick Thomas
Willey, Fred
See Willey, Frederick Thomas
Willey, Frederick Thomas 1910-1987 Obituary . 124
Willey, Gordon R(andolph) 1913- CANR-2
Earlier sketch in CA 5-8R
Willey, John C(offin) 1914-1990 Obituary 131
Willey, Keith (Greville) 1930- CANR-9
Earlier sketch in CA 21-24R
Willey, Margaret 1950- CANR-51
Earlier sketches in CA 117, CANR-40
See also AAYA 27
See also SATA 86
Willey, Peter (Robert Everard) 1922- 13-16R
Willey, R(oy) DeVerl 1910-197(?) CAP-2
Earlier sketch in CA 19-20
Willey, Richard J(ames) 1934- 41-44R
Willey, Robert
See Ley, Willy
Willgoose, Carl E(dward) 1916- CANR-6
Earlier sketch in CA 13-16R
Wilhelm, Sidney M(clarty) 1934- 9-12R
Willhoite, Michael A. 1946- .... SATA 71
William, Maurice 1882(?)-1973 Obituary 45-48
William II
See Hohenzollern, Friedrich Wilhelm (Victor Albert)
William of Auvergne 1190(?)-1249 .... DLB 115
William of Conches 1090(?)-1154(?) .... DLB 115
William of Sherwood 1200(?)-1266(?) .... DLB 115
Williams, Alan F. 1933- 49-52
Williams, Alan L(arson) 1947- 139
Williams, (Timothy) Alden 1932- 41-44R
Williams, Alice Cary 1892-1983 65-68
Obituary 111
Williams, Alice Davis 1901- 113
Williams, Amanda Kyle 1957- 138
Williams, Ann, Jr. 1951-1985 Obituary 117
Williams, (Elisabeth) Ann 1937- 154
Williams, Anne
See Steinke, Ann E(lizabeth)
Williams, Aston R. 1912- 21-24R
Williams, Aubrey L(ake) 1922- CANR-6
Earlier sketch in CA 1-4R
Williams, Barbara 1925- CANR-17
Earlier sketches in CA 49-52, CANR-1
See also CLR 48
See also SAAS 16
See also SATA 11
Williams, Barbara 1937- .... SATA 62
Williams, Barry 1932- 29-32R
Williams, Ben A(mes), Jr. 1915- 116
Williams, Ben Ames 1889-1953 .... DLB 102
Williams, Benjamin Buford 1923- 113
Williams, Benjamin H(arrison) 1889-1974 CANR-29
Earlier sketch in CA 37-40R
Williams, Bernard (Arthur Owen) 1929- 130
Brief entry 112
Williams, Bert Nolan 1930- 103
Williams, Beryl
See Epstein, Beryl (M. Williams)
Williams, Bill
See Crawford, William (Elbert)
Williams, Brad 1918- CANR-1
Earlier sketch in CA 1-4R
Williams, Brian (Peter) 1943- .... SATA 54
Williams, Bronwyn
See Browning, Dixie Burrus
Williams, Bruce R(odda) 1919- 13-16R
Williams, Burton John 1927- 41-44R
Williams, Byron (Leigh) 1934- 29-32R
Williams, C(hester) Arthur, Jr. 1924- CANR-2
Earlier sketch in CA 1-4R
Williams, C(lifford) Glyn 1928- 29-32R
Williams, C(hristopher) J(ohn) F(ardo) 1930- ... 103
Williams, C(harles) K(enneth) 1936- CANR-57
Earlier sketch in CA 37-40R
See also CAAS 26
See also CLC 33, 56
See also DAM POET
See also DLB 5
Williams, Carl C(arnelius) 1903- 45-48
Williams, Carol M. 1917- 65-68
Williams, Carol T(raynor) 1935- 112
Williams, Catharine M(elissa) 1903- 37-40R
Williams, Cecil B(rown) 1901-1966 .... CAP-1
Earlier sketch in CA 11-12
Williams, Chancellor 1905(?)- 142
See also BW 2
See also DLB 76
Williams, Charles
See Collier, James L(incoln)
Williams, Charles (Walter Stansby) 1886-1945 .. 163
Brief entry 104
See also DLB 100, 153
See also TCLC 1, 11
Williams, Charles 1933- 150
Williams, Chester
See Schechter, William
Williams, Christian 1943- 130
Williams, Cicely 1907-1985 57-60
Obituary 117
Williams, Claerwen 1938- 102
Williams, Clayton (Wheat) 1895-1983 125
Williams, Clyde C. 1881-1974 .... CAP-2
Earlier sketch in CA 23-24
See also SATA 8
See also SATA-Obit 27
Williams, Coe
See Harrison, C(hester) William
Williams, Colin 1934- 109
Interview in 109
Williams, Colin W(ilbur) 1921- CANR-19
Earlier sketch in CA 25-28R
Williams, Cris
See De Cristoforo, R(omeo) J(ohn)
Williams, Cyril Glyndwr 1921- CANR-15
Earlier sketch in CA 37-40R
Williams, D.
See Ronald, David William
Williams, (Walter) Dakin 1919- Brief entry 116
Williams, Daniel Day 1910-1973 .... CANR-1
Obituary 45-48
Earlier sketch in CA 1-4R
Williams, David (Frank) 1909-1983 Obituary ... 109
Williams, David 1926- CANR-48
Earlier sketch in CA 122
Williams, David (Eliot) 1939- 123
Williams, David 1939- 73-76
Williams, David 1945- 97-100
Williams, David A. 1922- 29-32R
Williams, David Glenwood 1918- 5-8R
Williams, David L. 1940- CANR-10
Earlier sketch in CA 25-28R
Williams, David Rhys 1890- 5-8R
Williams, David Ricardo 1923- CANR-51
Earlier sketches in CA 101, CANR-26
Williams, Denis (Joseph Ivan) 1923- CANR-41
Earlier sketches in CA 93-96, CANR-17
See also BW 2
See also DLB 117
Williams, Donna 1963- 143
Williams, Donna Reilly 1945- 150
See also SATA 83
Williams, Dorian 1914- CANR-3
Earlier sketch in CA 9-12R
Williams, Dorothy
See Williams, (Marcia) Dorothy
Williams, (Marcia) Dorothy 1945- 164
See also SATA 71, 97
Williams, Duncan 1927- 41-44R
Williams, Dwight 1966- 156
Williams, E(ric) C(yril) 1918- 97-100
Williams, E(rnest) N(eville) 1917- 9-12R
Williams, Edward Ainsworth
1907-1976 Obituary 65-68
Williams, Edward Bennett 1920-1988 .... 1-4R
Obituary 126
Williams, Edward Francis
1903-1970 Obituary 29-32R
Williams, Edward G. 1929- 29-32R
Williams, Edward J(erome) 1935- CANR-10
Earlier sketch in CA 21-24R
Williams, Edward K. 1923-1966 .... CAP-1
Earlier sketch in CA 13-16
Williams, Edward V(inson) 1935- 121
Williams, Edwin B(ucher) 1891-1975 .... 5-8R
Obituary 57-60
Williams, Edwin E(veritt) 1913- 45-48
Williams, Edwina Dakin
1885(?)-1980 Obituary 97-100
Williams, Eirlys O(lwen) CAP-1
Earlier sketch in CA 9-10
Williams, Elizabeth
See Dohen, Dorothy M.
Williams, (George) Emlyn 1905-1987 .... CANR-36
Obituary 123
Earlier sketch in CA 104
See also CLC 15
See also DAM DRAM
See also DLB 10, 77
See also MTCW 1
Williams, Emmett 1925- CANR-2
Earlier sketch in CA 45-48
Williams, Eric (Eustace) 1911-1981 125
Obituary 103
See also BW 2
Williams, Eric (Ernest) 1911-1983 .... CANR-28
Obituary 111
Earlier sketch in CA 9-12R
See also SATA 14
See also SATA-Obit 38
Williams, Ernest Wells
1896(?)-1980 Obituary 97-100
Williams, Estelle S. 1908- 123
Williams, Ethel L. 37-40R
Williams, F(rederick) Winston 1935- 103
Williams, Ferelith Eccles
See Eccles Williams, Ferelith
See also SATA 22
Williams, Forman A. 1934- 145
Williams, Frances 1935- 25-28R
Williams, Frances B.
See Browin, Frances Williams
Williams, Frances Leigh 1909- 13-16R
Williams, Frances Marion 1919- 57-60
Williams, Francis 1903-1970 Obituary 104
Williams, Francis Stewart 1921-1974 .... 37-40R
Williams, Frank B(royles), Jr. 1913- 118
Williams, Frederick (Dowell) 1933- 136
Williams, Frederick D(eForrest) 1918- 65-68
Williams, G(erhard) Mennen
1911-1988 Obituary 124
Williams, G. Robert 1948- 108
Williams, Garth (Montgomery) 1912-1996 134
Obituary 152
See also DLB 22
See also MAICYA
See also SAAS 7
See also SATA 18, 66
See also SATA-Obit 90
Williams, Geoffrey (John) 1943- 29-32R
Williams, Geoffrey J(ames) 1936- 118
Williams, George (Joseph) III 1949- 125
Williams, George (Guion) 1902- 13-16R
Williams, George C(hristopher) 1926- 73-76
Williams, George Huntston 1914- CANR-16
Earlier sketches in CA 1-4R, CANR-1
Williams, George M(ason, Jr.) 1940- 61-64
Williams, George W(alton) 1922- 9-12R
Williams, George Washington 1849-1891 ... DLB 47
Williams, Geraint 1942- 124
Williams, Gertrude 1897-1983 Obituary 109
Williams, Gilbert M. 1917- 61-64
Williams, Glanmor 1920- 5-8R
Williams, Glanville Llewelyn 1911-1997 106
Obituary 157
Williams, Gluyas 1888-1982 Obituary 108
See also AITN 2
Williams, Gordon
See Williams, Gordon M(aclean)
Williams, Gordon
See Venables, Terry
Williams, Gordon Leslie 1933- 110
Williams, Gordon M(aclean) 1934(?)- 130
Brief entry 116
Williams, Greer 1909- CANR-10
Earlier sketch in CA 13-16R
Williams, Greg(ory) Alan 167
Williams, Gregory 1952- 109
Williams, Gregory Howard 1943- 155
Williams, Griffith Wynne 1897-1972 .... CAP-2
Earlier sketch in CA 25-28
Williams, Gurney III 1941- CANR-30
Earlier sketch in CA 69-72
Williams, Guy Neal 1953- 77-80
Williams, Guy R(ichard) 1920- CANR-31
Earlier sketch in CA 13-16R
See also SATA 11
Williams, (David) Gwyn 1904- 103
Williams, Hank, Jr. 1949- Brief entry 117
Williams, Hank 1923-1953 .... TCLC 81
Williams, Harold (Claude Noel)
1914-1990 Obituary 131
Williams, Harold A(nthony) 1916- 37-40R
Williams, Harold R(oger) 1935- 53-56
Williams, Harold S(tannett) 1898- CANR-20
Earlier sketches in CA 9-12R, CANR-5
Williams, Harold Workman
See Wilson, Halsey William
Williams, Hawley
See Heyliger, William
Williams, Hazel Pearson 1914- 57-60
Williams, Heathcote 1941- CANR-49
Earlier sketch in CA 21-24R
See also DLB 13
Williams, Helen 1948- 145
See also SATA 77
Williams, Helen Maria 1761-1827 .... DLB 158
Williams, Henry
See Manville, W(illiam) H(enry)
Williams, Henry Lionel 1895-1974 Obituary .. 45-48
Williams, Herbert (Lloyd) 1932- CANR-12
Earlier sketch in CA 29-32R
Williams, Herbert Lee 1918- CANR-29
Earlier sketch in CA 1-4R
Williams, Hermann Warner, Jr. 1908-1974 .... 5-8R
Obituary 53-56
Williams, Hiram D. 1917- 13-16R
Williams, Hosea L(orenzo) 1926- 49-52
Williams, Howard L(loyd) 1950- CANR-41
Earlier sketch in CA 117
Williams, Howard Russell 1915- 13-16R
Williams, Hugh (Anthony Glanmor) 1904-1969 .....
CAP-2
Earlier sketch in CA 25-28
Williams, Hugh Aldersey
See Aldersey-Williams, Hugh
Williams, Hugh Steadman 1935- 132
Williams, Hugo 1942- CANR-45
Earlier sketch in CA 17-20R
See also CLC 42
See also DLB 40
Williams, Ioan Miles 1941- CANR-11
Earlier sketch in CA 25-28R
Williams, Ira E., Jr. 1926- 53-56
Williams, Irving G(regory) 1915- 41-44R
Williams, Isaac 1802-1865 .... DLB 32
Williams, J(ames) David Lewis
See Lewis-Williams, J(ames) David
Williams, J(ames) Earl 1922- 41-44R
Williams, J(ohn) H(argreaves) Harley 9-12R
Williams, J. R.
See Williams, Jeanne
Williams, J(ohn) Rodman 1918- 81-84
Williams, J. Walker
See Wodehouse, P(elham) G(renville)
Williams, J. X.
See Ludwig, Myles Eric
and Offutt, Andrew J(efferson V)
Williams, Jacqueline (B.) 1934- 145
Williams, James G. 1936- 165
Williams, Jay 1914-1978 .... CANR-39
Obituary 81-84
Earlier sketches in CA 1-4R, CANR-2
See also CLR 8
See also MAICYA
See also SATA 3, 41
See also SATA-Obit 24
Williams, Jay G(omer) 1932- 41-44R
Williams, Jeanne 1930- CANR-67
Earlier sketches in CA 25-28R, CANR-64
See also SATA 5
Williams, (Edward) Jeffery 1920- 132
Williams, Jenny 1939- 112
See also SATA 60
Williams, Jeremy (Napier) Howard
See Howard-Williams, Jeremy (Napier)
Williams, Jerome 1926- CANR-1
Earlier sketch in CA 49-52
Williams, Joan 1928- CANR-48
Earlier sketch in CA 1-4R
See also DLB 6
Williams, Joel
See Jennings, John (Edward, Jr.)
Williams, John (Herbert) 1908-1976 .... CANR-10
Earlier sketch in CA 13-16R
Williams, John (Edward) 1922-1994 .... CANR-2
Obituary 144
Earlier sketch in CA 1-4R
See also DLB 6
Williams, John 1954- 129
Williams, John A(lfred) 1925- CANR-51
Earlier sketches in CA 53-56, CANR-6, 26
Interview in CANR-6
See also CAAS 3
See also BLC 3
See also BW 2
See also CLC 5, 13
See also DAM MULT
See also DLB 2, 33
Williams, John Alden 1928- CANR-2
Earlier sketch in CA 1-4R
Williams, John B. 1919- 93-96
Williams, John Burr 1900-1989 Obituary 129
Williams, John D(elane) 1938- 57-60
Williams, John Edwin 1928- 93-96
Williams, John G(ordon) 1906- CAP-2
Earlier sketch in CA 23-24
Williams, John G. 1915- 120
Williams, John Hartley 1942- 130
Williams, John Henry 1887-1980 Obituary 105
Williams, John Hoyt 1940- 128
Williams, John R(yan) 1919- 37-40R
Williams, John Stanley 1925- CAP-1
Earlier sketch in CA 9-10
Williams, John Stuart 1920- 65-68
Williams, Jon
See Williams, Walter Jon
Williams, Jonathan (Chamberlain) 1929- .. CANR-8
Earlier sketch in CA 9-12R
See also CAAS 12
See also CLC 13
See also DLB 5
Williams, Joy 1944- CANR-48
Earlier sketches in CA 41-44R, CANR-22
See also CLC 31
Williams, Joyce E(layne) 1937- 104
Williams, Juan 1954- 125
See also BW 2
Williams, Juanita da Lomba Jones 1925- ... 37-40R
Williams, June Vanleer 131
Williams, Justin Sr. 1906- 101
Williams, Karen Lynn 1952- 133
See also SATA 66, 99
Williams, Kate
See Flynn, Donald R(obert)
Williams, Kenneth 1926-1988 Obituary 125
Williams, Kim 1924(?)-1986 Obituary 120
Williams, Kimmika L(yvette Hawes) 1959- 153
See also BW 2
Williams, Kit 1946(?)- 107
See also CLR 4
See also SATA 44
Williams, Kyffin 1918- 145
Williams, L(aurence) F(rederic) Rushbrook
See Rushbrook Williams, L(aurence) F(rederic)
Williams, L(eslie) Pearce 1927- 65-68
Williams, Lady
See Williams, Gertrude
Williams, Lawrence 1916(?)-1983 Obituary 108
Williams, Lawrence K(enneth) 1930- 29-32R
Williams, Lee E(rskine) II 1946- 41-44R
Williams, LeRoy T. 1944- 120
Williams, Leslie 1941- 107
See also SATA 42
Williams, Linda 1946- 110
Williams, Linda 1948- .... SATA 59
Williams, Liza 1928- 102
Williams, Loring G. 1924-1974 .... CAP-2
Earlier sketch in CA 29-32
Williams, Louise Bonino 1904(?)-1984 Obituary 114
See also SATA-Obit 39
Williams, Lovett E(dward), Jr. 1935- 109
Williams, Lynn
See Hale, Arlene
Williams, M(artin) A(nthony) J(ames) 1941- 141
Williams, Marcia 1932- 123
Williams, Margaret (Anne) 1902- 21-24R
Williams, Margaret (Vyner) 1914- 25-28R
Williams, Margery
See Bianco, Margery (Williams)
Williams, Marie S(heppard) 1931- 164
Williams, Mark 1951- 138
Williams, Martha E(thelyn) 1934- 125
Williams, Martin 1924-1992 49-52
Obituary 137
Williams, Mary Alice 1949- Brief entry 123
Williams, Mary C(ameron) 1923- 57-60
Williams, Mary Elizabeth 1909-1976 Obituary . 65-68
Williams, Mary McGee 1925- 25-28R
Williams, Mary Pat 1946- 112
Williams, Mason 1938- 25-28R
Williams, Maureen 1951- 85-88
See also SATA 12
Williams, Melvin D(onald) 1933- 73-76

Williams, Merryn 1944- ... CANR-15
Earlier sketch in CA 41-44R
Williams, Michael
See St. John, Wylly Folk
Williams, Michael 1935- ... 133
Williams, Miller 1930- ... CANR-67
Earlier sketch in CA 13-16R
See also CAAS 20
See also DLB 105
Williams, Mona (Goodwyn) 1916- ... 81-84
Williams, Nancy M(argaret) 1929- ... 122
Williams, Ned 1909- ... 13-16R
Williams, Neville (John) 1924-1977 Obituary ... 111
Williams, Niall 1958- ... 167
Williams, Nigel 1948- ... 147
Williams, Noel Trevor St. John 1918- ... 41-44R
Williams, Norman 1952- ... 118
See also CLC 39
Williams, Oliver F(ranklin) 1939- ... CANR-35
Earlier sketch in CA 114
Williams, Oliver P(erry) 1925- ... 37-40R
Williams, Ora (Ruby) 1926- ... 73-76
Williams, Oscar 1900-1964 ... CANR-6
Earlier sketch in CA 1-4R
Williams, Otis (C.) 1941- ... 130
Williams, P(eter) F(airney) 1931- ... 121
Williams, Patricia J(oyce) 1951- ... 154
Williams, Patrick 1950- ... 129
Williams, Patrick J.
See Butterworth, W(illiam) E(dmund III)
Williams, Patti 1936- ... 73-76
Williams, Paul (Revere) 1894-1980 Obituary ... 93-96
Williams, Paul (Hamilton) 1940- ... 121
Williams, Paul (Steven) 1948- ... 81-84
Williams, Paul O(sborne) 1935- ... CANR-24
Earlier sketch in CA 106
Williams, Penry (Herbert) 1925- ... 128
Williams, Pete
See Faulknor, Cliff(ord Vernon)
Williams, Peter 1937- ... 138
Williams, Peter W(illiam) 1944- ... CANR-30
Earlier sketch in CA 112
Williams, Philip F. (C.) 1956- ... 146
Williams, Philip Lee 1950- ... CANR-65
Earlier sketch in CA 129
Williams, Philip Maynard 1920-1984 Obituary ... 114
Williams, Philip Middleton 1952- ... 145
Williams, Philip W(alter) 1941- ... CANR-11
Earlier sketch in CA 69-72
Williams, Phyllis S(awyer) 1931- ... 65-68
Williams, R(obert) D(eryck) 1917-1986 ... CANR-45
Obituary ... 120
Earlier sketch in CA 103
Williams, R(obert) J(oseph) P(aton) 1926- ... 143
Williams, Ralph Mehlin 1911- ... 5-8R
Williams, Ralph Vaughan
See Vaughan Williams, Ralph
Williams, Randall Herbert Monier
See Monier-Williams, Randall Herbert
Williams, Raymond (Henry) 1921-1988 ... CANR-44
Obituary ... 124
Earlier sketches in CA 21-24R, CANR-33
See also DLB 14
See also MTCW 1
Williams, Raymond (Brady) 1935- ... 132
Williams, Rebecca (Yancy)
1899-1976 Obituary ... 65-68
Williams, Richard Hays 1912- ... CANR-2
Earlier sketch in CA 1-4R
Williams, Richard Lippincott 1910- ... 101
Williams, Robert C. 1938- ... CANR-14
Earlier sketch in CA 37-40R
Williams, Robert Coleman 1940- ... 21-24R
Williams, Robert G. 1948- ... 125
Williams, Robert Hugh 1907(?)-1983 Obituary ... 109
Williams, Robert L(ewis) 1903- ... CANR-10
Earlier sketch in CA 13-16R
Williams, Robert Moore 1907-1977 Obituary ... 102
Williams, Robert P. 1906(?)-1977 Obituary ... 69-72
Williams, Robin M(urphy), Jr. 1914- ... 13-16R
Williams, Robyn 1944- ... 165
Williams, Roger 1603(?)-1683 ... DLB 24
Williams, Roger J(ohn) 1893-1988 ... CANR-7
Obituary ... 124
Earlier sketch in CA 17-20R
Williams, Roger L(awrence) 1923- Brief entry ... 112
Williams, Roger M(iller) 1934- ... 37-40R
Williams, Roger Neville 1943- ... 37-40R
Williams, Ronald Ralph 1906-1979 ... CANR-7
Earlier sketch in CA 13-16R
Williams, Rosalind
See Fergusson, Rosalind (Joyce)
Williams, Rosalind H. 1944- ... 109
Williams, Rose
See Ross, W(illiam) E(dward) D(aniel)
Williams, Rowan (Douglas) 1950- ... 128
Williams, Rowland 1817-1870 ... DLB 184
Williams, Russell J(ohn) 1944- ... 104
Williams, S. P.
See Hart, Virginia
Williams, Samm-Art
See Williams, Samuel Arthur
See also DLB 38
Williams, Samuel Arthur 1946- ... 123
Brief entry ... 117
See also Williams, Samm-Art
See also BW 1
Williams, Selma R(uth) 1925- ... CANR-1
Earlier sketch in CA 49-52
See also SATA 14
Williams, Sherley Anne 1944- ... CANR-25
Earlier sketch in CA 73-76
Interview in ... CANR-25
See also BLC 3
See also BW 2
See also CLC 89
See also DAM MULT, POET
See also DLB 41
See also SATA 78
Williams, Sheron 1955- ... 145
See also SATA 77
Williams, Shirley
See Williams, Sherley Anne
Williams, Shirley (Vivien Teresa Brittain) 1930- . 158
Williams, Simon 1943- ... 133
Williams, Slim
See Williams, Clyde C.
Williams, Stanley W. 1917- ... 17-20R
Williams, Stephen 1926- Brief entry ... 114
Williams, Stirling B(acot), Jr. 1943- ... 29-32R
Williams, Strephon Kaplan 1934- ... CANR-20
Earlier sketch in CA 102
Williams, Susan 1960- ... 141
Williams, Suzanne (Bullock) 1953- ... SATA 71
Williams, T(erence) C(harles) 1925- ... 29-32R
Williams, T(homas) David 1929- ... 123
Williams, T(homas) Harry 1909-1979 ... CANR-3
Earlier sketch in CA 1-4R
See also DLB 17
Williams, (Robert Paul) Tad 1957- ... 146
Williams, Tennessee 1911-1983 ... CANR-31
Obituary ... 108
Earlier sketch in CA 5-8R
See also CABS 3
See also AITN 1, 2
See also CDALB 1941-1968
See also CLC 1, 2, 5, 7, 8, 11, 15, 19, 30, 39, 45, 71, 111
See also DA
See also DAB
See also DAC
See also DAM DRAM, MST
See also DC 4
See also DLB 7
See also DLBD 4
See also DLBY 83
See also MTCW 1
See also WLC
Williams, Terry Tempest 1959(?)- ... 153
Williams, Theodore C(urtis) 1930- ... 69-72
Williams, Thomas (Alonzo) 1926-1990 ... CANR-2
Obituary ... 132
Earlier sketch in CA 1-4R
See also CLC 14
Williams, Thomas (Andrew) 1931- ... 49-52
Williams, Thomas Howard 1935- ... 13-16R
Williams, Tina
See Wiles, Domini
Williams, Tony 1946- ... 147
Williams, Trevor Illtyd 1921-1996 ... 109
Obituary ... 154
Williams, Ursula Moray
See Moray Williams, Ursula
See also DLB 160
See also SATA 3
Williams, (George) Valentine 1883-1946 Brief entry ... 111
See also Valentine, Douglas
See also DLB 77
Williams, Vera B. 1927- ... CANR-38
Earlier sketch in CA 123
See also CLR 9
See also MAICYA
See also SATA 53, 102
See also SATA-Brief 33
Williams, Vergil L(ewis) 1935- ... CANR-9
Earlier sketch in CA 57-60
Williams, Vernon J(ohnson, Jr.) 1948- ... 159
Williams, W. S. C. 1929- ... 139
Williams, Wallace Edward 1926- Brief entry ... 105
Williams, Walter
See Williams, Walter E(dward)
Williams, Walter E(dward) 1936- ... 154
Brief entry ... 123
Williams, Walter G(eorge) 1903- ... CAP-1
Earlier sketch in CA 13-16
Williams, Walter Jon 1953- ... 152
See also DAM POP
Williams, Walter L(ee) 1948- ... 127
Williams, (Margaret) Wetherby ... CANR-3
Earlier sketch in CA 45-48
Williams, Willard F(orest) 1921- ... 13-16R
Williams, William Appleman 1921-1990 ... CANR-3
Obituary ... 131
Earlier sketch in CA 1-4R
See also DLB 17
Williams, William C.
See Williams, William Carlos
Williams, William Carlos 1883-1963 ... CANR-34
Earlier sketch in CA 89-92
See also CDALB 1917-1929
See also CLC 1, 2, 5, 9, 13, 22, 42, 67
See also DA
See also DAB
See also DAC
See also DAM MST, POET
See also DLB 4, 16, 54, 86
See also MTCW 1
See also PC 7
See also SSC 31
Williams, William David 1917- ... 5-8R
Williams, William H(enry) 1936- ... CANR-36
Earlier sketch in CA 69-72
Williams, William P(roctor) 1939- ... CANR-47
Earlier sketches in CA 45-48, CANR-23
Williams, Wirt (Alfred, Jr.) 1921-1986 ... 9-12R
Obituary ... 119
See also DLB 6
Williams-Andriani, Renee 1963- ... SATA 98
Williams-Ellis, (Mary) Amabel (Nassau Strachey)
1894-1984 ... 105
Obituary ... 114
See also SATA 29
See also SATA-Obit 41
Williams-Ellis, Clough 1883- ... 13-16R
Williams-Garcia, Rita ... 159
See also AAYA 22
See also CLR 36
See also SATA 98
Williamson, Alan (Bacher) 1944- ... 57-60
Williamson, Anthony George 1932- ... 101
Williamson, Audrey (May) 1913-1986(?) ... CANR-3
Obituary ... 118
Earlier sketch in CA 49-52
Williamson, Bruce 1893-1984 Obituary ... 111
Williamson, Bruce 1930- ... 101
Williamson, Chet 1948- ... 156
Williamson, Chilton, Jr. 1947- ... 102
Williamson, Chilton 1916- ... 13-16R
Williamson, Claude C(harles) H. 1891-(?) ... CAP-1
Earlier sketch in CA 17-18
Williamson, Craig (Burke) 1943- ... CANR-16
Earlier sketch in CA 29-32R
Williamson, David (Geoffrey) 1927- ... 134
Williamson, David (Keith) 1942- ... CANR-41
Earlier sketch in CA 103
See also CLC 56
Williamson, David L(ouis) 1937- ... 111
Williamson, Donald I. 1922- ... 145
Williamson, Doug 1944- ... 136
Williamson, Duncan 1928- ... 123
Williamson, Edward 1908-1984 Obituary ... 113
Williamson, Ellen Douglas 1905-1984 ... CANR-39
Obituary ... 114
Earlier sketch in CA 17-20R
See also Douglas, Ellen
Williamson, Eugene L. (Jr.) 1930- ... 9-12R
Williamson, Geoffrey 1897- ... 9-12R
Williamson, Gerald Neal 1932- ... CANR-34
Earlier sketch in CA 112
Williamson, Glen 1909- ... CANR-9
Earlier sketch in CA 57-60
Williamson, Greg 1964- ... 154
Williamson, H(enry) D(arvall) 1907- ... 65-68
Williamson, Harold Francis 1901- ... 5-8R
Williamson, Henry 1895-1977 ... CANR-36
Obituary ... 73-76
Earlier sketch in CA 81-84
See also DLB 191
See also MTCW 1
See also SATA 37
See also SATA-Obit 30
Williamson, J. N.
See Williamson, Gerald Neal
Williamson, J. Peter 1929- ... CANR-6
Earlier sketch in CA 1-4R
Williamson, J(erry) W(ayne) 1944- ... 148
Williamson, Jack
See Williamson, John Stewart
See also CAAS 8
See also CLC 29
See also DLB 8
Williamson, Jeffrey G(ale) 1935- ... CANR-39
Earlier sketches in CA 85-88, CANR-18
Williamson, Joanne Small 1926- ... 13-16R
See also SATA 3
Williamson, Joel (Roudolph) 1929- ... 144
Williamson, John 1937- ... 149
Williamson, John (Gordon) 1949- ... 138
Williamson, John Butler 1943- ... 89-92
Williamson, John G(rant) 1933- ... 45-48
Williamson, John Stewart 1908- ... CANR-70
Earlier sketches in CA 17-20R, CANR-23
See also Williamson, Jack
Williamson, Joseph 1895-1988 ... CAP-1
Obituary ... 125
Earlier sketch in CA 11-12
Williamson, Juanita V. 1917- ... 37-40R
Williamson, Karina 1928- ... 127
Williamson, Lamar, Jr. 1926- ... 89-92
Williamson, Margaret 1947- ... 153
Williamson, Marianne 1952- ... 141
Williamson, Moncrieff 1915- ... 102
Williamson, Norma (Goff) 1934- ... 65-68
Williamson, Oliver E(aton) 1932- ... 81-84
Williamson, Philip G. 1955- ... 157
Williamson, Porter B(eyers) 1916- ... CANR-28
Earlier sketch in CA 110
Williamson, Rene de Visme 1908- ... CANR-13
Earlier sketches in CAP-1, CA 17-18
Williamson, Richard 1930- ... 37-40R
Williamson, Richard 1935- ... 109
Williamson, Robert C(lifford) 1916- ... 21-24R
Williamson, Robin (Martin Eyre) 1938- ... 29-32R
Williamson, Robin (Duncan Harry) 1943- ... 102
Williamson, Stanford Winfield 1916- ... 5-8R
Williamson, Tony
See Williamson, Anthony George
Williamson, William Bedford 1918- ... CANR-6
Earlier sketch in CA 1-4R
Williamson, William Landram 1920- ... 9-12R
Willie, Charles V(ert) 1927- ... CANR-58
Earlier sketches in CA 41-44R, CANR-14, 31
Willie, Frederick
See Lovecraft, H(oward) P(hillips)
Williford, Lex 1954- ... 145
Willig, George 1949- ... 102
Willig, John M. 1913-1982 Obituary ... 107
Willig, Rosette F. 1950- ... 114
Willimon, William H(enry) 1946- ... CANR-56
Earlier sketch in CA 106, 151
Willing, Jules Z. 1914-1981 ... 108
Willing, Martha Kent 1920- ... 37-40R
Willingham, Calder (Baynard, Jr.) 1922-1995 ...
CANR-3
Obituary ... 147
Earlier sketch in CA 5-8R
See also CLC 5, 51
See also DLB 2, 44
See also MTCW 1
Willingham, John J. 1935- ... 37-40R
Willingham, John R(obert) 1919- ... 17-20R
Willings, David 1932- ... 111
Williram of Ebersberg c. 1020-1085 ... DLB 148
Willis, (George) Anthony Armstrong
1897-1976 ... 69-72
Willis, Arthur J(ames) 1895-1983 ... CANR-5
Obituary ... 111
Earlier sketch in CA 5-8R
Willis, Barry 1952- ... 148
Willis, Charles
See Clarke, Arthur C(harles)
Willis, Cleve E(dward) 1942- ... 123
Brief entry ... 118
Willis, Connie 1945- ... CANR-35
Earlier sketch in CA 114
Willis, Corinne Denneny ... 21-24R
Willis, Donald C(halmers) 1947- ... CANR-15
Earlier sketch in CA 41-44R
Willis, Donald J. 1919- ... 127
Willis, E(dward) David 1932- ... 37-40R
Willis, Edgar E(rnest) 1913- ... 5-8R
Willis, Edward Henry 1918-1992 ... CANR-65
Obituary ... 140
Earlier sketches in CA 9-12R, CANR-7, 23
Willis, Ellen Jane 1941- ... 106
Willis, F(rank) Roy 1930- ... 13-16R
Willis, Irene 1929- ... CANR-10
Earlier sketch in CA 65-68
Willis, James 1928- ... 109
Willis, Jeanne (Mary) 1959- ... 128
See also SATA 61
Willis, Jerry W. 1943- ... 85-88
Willis, John A(lvin) 1916- ... 17-20R
Willis, John H(oward), Jr. 1929- ... 37-40R
Willis, John Ralph 1938- ... 121
Willis, Margaret 1899- ... CANR-19
Earlier sketches in CA 5-8R, CANR-3
Willis, Maud
See Lottman, Eileen
Willis, Meredith Sue 1946- ... CANR-16
Earlier sketch in CA 85-88
See also SATA 101
Willis, Nancy Carol 1952- ... SATA 93
Willis, Nathaniel Parker 1806-1867 ... DLB 3, 59, 73, 74
See also DLBD 13
Willis, Resa 1949- ... 138
Willis, Roy (Geoffrey) 1927- ... CANR-17
Earlier sketch in CA 77-80
Willis, Samuel
See Parker, Hershel
Willis, Sharon O(zell) 1938- ... 37-40R
Willis, Stanley E. II 1923- ... 21-24R
Willis, Ted
See Willis, Edward Henry
Willis, Val 1946- ... 130
Willis, Wayne 1942- ... 29-32R
Willison, George F(indlay) 1896-1972 ... CAP-1
Obituary ... 37-40R
Earlier sketch in CA 13-14
Willison, Marilyn Murray 1948- ... 105
Willke, John Charles 1925- ... CANR-24
Earlier sketches in CA 65-68, CANR-9
Willkens, William H(enry) R(obert) 1919- ... 21-24R
Willkomm, Ernst Adolf 1810-1886 ... DLB 133
Willmington, Harold L. 1932- ... 49-52
Willmott, H(edley) P(aul) 1945- ... 157
Willmott, Peter 1923- ... 21-24R
Willmott, Phyllis ... CANR-40
Earlier sketch in CA 117
Willms, Russ ... SATA 95
Willner, Ann Ruth 1924- ... 21-24R
Willner, Dorothy 1927-1993 ... 53-56
Obituary ... 140
Willnow, Ronald D. 1933- ... 77-80
Willock, Colin 1919- ... CANR-10
Earlier sketch in CA 13-16R
Willock, Ruth ... 13-16R
Willocks, Tim 1958(?)- ... 156
Willoughby, Cass
See Olsen, T(heodore) V(ictor)
Willoughby, Charles Andrew
1892-1972 Obituary ... 104
Willoughby, David P(atrick) 1901- ... 37-40R
Willoughby, Elaine Macmann 1926- ... 101
Willoughby, Glynn
See Allentuck, Andrew
Willoughby, Hugh
See Harvey, Nigel
Willoughby, Lee Davis
See Avallone, Michael (Angelo, Jr.)
and Brandner, Gary (Phil)
and DeAndrea, William L(ouis)
and Streib, Dan(iel Thomas)
and Toombs, John
and Webb, Jean Francis
Willoughby, William Reid 1910- ... 1-4R
Willrich, Mason 1933- ... 77-80
Willrich, Ted L. 1924- ... 29-32R
Wills, A(lfred) J(ohn) 1927- ... 21-24R
Wills, Christopher 1938- ... 132
Wills, David Hilary 1904-1985 Obituary ... 117
Wills, Garry 1934- ... CANR-1
Earlier sketch in CA 1-4R
Wills, Geoffrey
See Staal, Cyril

Wills, Jean 1929- CANR-22
Earlier sketch in CA 105
Wills, John E(lliot), Jr. 1936- CANR-44
Earlier sketch in CA 45-48
Wills, Jonathan 1947- 69-72
Wills, Maurice Morning 1932- Brief entry 105
Wills, Maury
See Wills, Maurice Morning
Wills, Millicent A(gatha) 1901(?)-1988 Obituary . 125
Wills, Philip Aubrey 1907-1978 81-84
Wills, Thomas
See Ard, William (Thomas)
Willson, A(mos) Leslie, Jr. 1923- CANR-44
Earlier sketch in CA 9-12R
Willson, Leslie
See Willson, A(mos) Leslie, Jr.
Willson, Mary F(rances) 1938- 129
Willson, Meredith 1902-1984 49-52
Obituary 113
Willson, Robina Beckles
See Beckles Willson, Robina (Elizabeth)
See also SATA 27
Willstaetter, Richard (Martin) 1872-1942 161
Willstatter, Richard
See Willstaetter, Richard (Martin)
Willumsen, Dorrit (Kirsten) 1940- 131
Willumson, Glenn G(ardner) 1949- 146
Willwerth, James 1943- 57-60
Willy
See Colette, (Sidonie-Gabrielle)
Willy, Colette
See Colette, (Sidonie-Gabrielle)
Willy, Margaret (Elizabeth) 1919- 9-12R
Wilma, Dana
See Faralla, Dana
Wilmer, Clive 1945- 130
Brief entry 122
See also DLB 40
Wilmer, Dale
See Miller, (H.) Bill(y)
and Wade, Robert (Allison)
Wilmer, Valerie (Sybil) 1941- 85-88
Wilmerding, John 1938- 111
Wilmeth, Don B(urton) 1939- CANR-41
Earlier sketches in CA 102, CANR-19
Wilmore, Gayraud S(tephen, Jr.) 1921- 134
Brief entry 114
Wilmore, Jack H(arrison) 1938- 129
Wilmore, Sylvia (Joan) Bruce 1914- 89-92
Wilmot, Anthony 1933- 77-80
Wilmot, John 1647-1680 .... DLB 131
Wilmot, William (Wallace) 1943- CANR-7
Earlier sketch in CA 57-60
Wilms, Barbara 1941- 57-60
Wilmshurst, Rea 1941- 127
Wilmut, Roger (Francis) 1942- CANR-19
Earlier sketch in CA 102
Wilner, Eleanor 1937- CANR-37
Earlier sketches in CA 93-96, CANR-16
Wilner, Herbert 1925-1977 .... CANR-3
Earlier sketch in CA 45-48
Wiloch, Thomas 1953- 164
Wilroy, Mary Edith (Farr) 1910-1987 Obituary .. 122
Wilsford, David 1956- 140
Wilsher, Ann
See Henisch, Bridget Ann
Wilshire, Bruce W(ithington) 1932- 77-80
Wilson, A(lfred) Jeyaratnam 1928- CANR-12
Earlier sketch in CA 61-64
Wilson, A(ndrew) N(orman) 1950- 122
Brief entry 112
See also CLC 33
See also DLB 14, 155, 194
Wilson, Abraham 1899(?)-1983 Obituary 110
Wilson, Adrian 1923-1988 132
Obituary 125
Wilson, Alison M. 1932- 120
Wilson, Alton H(orace) 1925- 61-64
Wilson, Andrew 1923- 29-32R
Wilson, Angus (Frank Johnstone) 1913-1991 ....
CANR-21
Obituary 134
Earlier sketch in CA 5-8R
See also CLC 2, 3, 5, 25, 34
See also DLB 15, 139, 155
See also MTCW 1
See also SSC 21
Wilson, April .... SATA 80
Wilson, Arthur 1595-1652 .... DLB 58
Wilson, Arthur M(cCandless) 1902-1979 61-64
Obituary 89-92
Wilson, August 1945- CANR-54
Brief entry 115
Earlier sketches in CA 122, CANR-42
See also AAYA 16
See also BLC 3
See also BW 2
See also CLC 39, 50, 63
See also DA
See also DAB
See also DAC
See also DAM DRAM, MST, MULT
See also DC 2
See also MTCW 1
See also WLCS
Wilson, Augusta Jane Evans 1835-1909 ... DLB 42
Wilson, Barbara
See Janifer, Laurence M(ark)
Wilson, Barbara Ker
See Ker Wilson, Barbara
Wilson, Beth P(ierre) CANR-1
Earlier sketch in CA 49-52
See also SATA 8
Wilson, Betty 1923- 97-100
Wilson, Brian 1942- .... CLC 12
Wilson, Bryan R(onald) 1926- CANR-41
Earlier sketches in CA 5-8R, CANR-3, 19
Wilson, Budge 1927- 121
See also Wilson, Marjorie
See also SATA 55
Wilson, Callie C(oe) 1917- 124
Wilson, Camilla Jeanne 1945- 61-64
Wilson, Cammy
See Wilson, Camilla Jeanne
Wilson, Cara 1944- 150
Wilson, Carletta 1951- 141
See also BW 2
See also SATA 81
Wilson, Carlos 1941- 61-64
Wilson, Carole
See Wallmann, Jeffrey M(iner)
Wilson, Carolyn 1938- 21-24R
Wilson, Carroll L(ouis) 1910-1983 89-92
Obituary 109
Wilson, Carter 1941- 17-20R
See also SATA 6
Wilson, Catherine 1951- 132
Wilson, (Lindsay) Charles 1932- 65-68
Wilson, Charles (P.) 1939- 135
Wilson, Charles McMoran 1882-1977 .... CAP-2
Obituary 69-72
Earlier sketch in CA 21-22
Wilson, Charles Morrow 1905-1977 .... CANR-4
Earlier sketch in CA 5-8R
See also SATA 30
Wilson, Charles Reagan 1948- 105
Wilson, Chris(topher Paul) 1949- 125
Wilson, Christine
See Geach, Christine
Wilson, Christopher B. 1910(?)-1985 Obituary .. 117
See also SATA-Obit 46
Wilson, Clifford (Allan) 1923- 93-96
Wilson, Clifton E. 1919- 21-24R
Wilson, Clyde N(orman, Jr.) 1941- CANR-40
Earlier sketch in CA 116
Wilson, Colin 1931- CANR-33
Earlier sketches in CA 1-4R, CANR-1, 22
See also CAAS 5
See also CLC 3, 14
See also DLB 14, 194
See also MTCW 1
Wilson, Craig R. 1947- 57-60
Wilson, Crane
See O'Brien, Cyril C(ornelius)
Wilson, Cynthia 145
Wilson, D. A.
See Wilson, Derek (Alan)
Wilson, D(udley) B(utler) 1923- 21-24R
Wilson, Dagmar 1916- .... SATA-Brief 31
Wilson, Dale 1894-1987 .... CAP-1
Obituary 121
Earlier sketch in CA 13-14
Wilson, Daniel J(oseph) 1949- 117
Wilson, Darryl B(abe) 1939- 155
See also SATA 90
Wilson, Dave
See Floren, Lee
Wilson, David
See MacArthur, D(avid) Wilson
Wilson, (Anthony) David 1927- CANR-43
Earlier sketch in CA 97-100
Wilson, David 1942- CANR-38
Earlier sketches in CA 93-96, CANR-16
Wilson, David Allen 1926- CANR-7
Earlier sketch in CA 5-8R
Wilson, David Henry 1937- CANR-32
Earlier sketch in CA 113
Wilson, David L(ee) 1943- 112
Wilson, David M(ackenzie) 1931- 146
Wilson, David Scofield 1931- 106
Wilson, Deirdre (Susan Moir) 1941- 97-100
Wilson, Derek (Alan) 1935- 123
Brief entry 115
Interview in 123
Wilson, Derek A.
See Wilson, Derek (Alan)
Wilson, Dick
See Wilson, Richard Garratt
Wilson, Dirk
See Pohl, Frederik
Wilson, Don(ald) 1932- 81-84
Wilson, Don W(hitman) 1942- 61-64
Wilson, (Alan) Doric 1939- 129
Wilson, Dorothy Clarke 1904- CANR-6
Earlier sketch in CA 1-4R
See also SATA 16
Wilson, Douglas L. 1935- 37-40R
Wilson, (Archibald) Duncan 1911- 103
Wilson, E(dward) Raymond 1896-1987 61-64
Obituary 122
Wilson, (Harvey) Earl 1907-1987 69-72
Obituary 121
Wilson, Earl (Dean) 1939- 118
Wilson, Edmund 1895-1972 .... CANR-46
Obituary 37-40R
Earlier sketches in CA 1-4R, CANR-1
See also CLC 1, 2, 3, 8, 24
See also DLB 63
See also MTCW 1
Wilson, Edmund Beecher 1856-1939 159
Wilson, Edward A(rthur) 1886-1970 Obituary ... 116
See also SATA 38
Wilson, Edward M(eryon) 1906-1977 Obituary .. 114
Wilson, Edward O(sborne), (Jr.) 1929- CANR-58
Earlier sketches in CA 61-64, CANR-16
See also CAAS 16
See also MTCW 1
Wilson, Edward T(homas) 1941- 129
Wilson, Elena 1907(?)-1979 Obituary 89-92
Wilson, Elizabeth 1947- 149
Wilson, Elizabeth Z. 1951- 123
Wilson, Ellen (Janet Cameron) (?)-1976 49-52
Obituary 103
See also SATA 9
See also SATA-Obit 26
Wilson, Eric (H.) 1940- CANR-20
Earlier sketch in CA 101
See also SATA 34
See also SATA-Brief 32
Wilson, Erica CANR-23
Earlier sketches in CA 53-56, CANR-7
See also SATA 51
Wilson, Erle (Alexander Mann) 1898- 5-8R
Wilson, Ernest Charles 1896- 29-32R
Wilson, Ethel Davis (Bryant) 1888(?)-1980 102
See also CLC 13
See also DAC
See also DAM POET
See also DLB 68
See also MTCW 1
Wilson, Eugene E. 1887(?)-1974 Obituary 49-52
Wilson, Eugene Smith 1905-1981 Obituary 103
Wilson, Eva 1925- 146
Wilson, Evan M(orris) 1910-1984 129
Obituary 112
Wilson, Everett K(eith) 1913- 93-96
Wilson, F(rank) P(ercy) 1889-1963 .... CANR-1
Earlier sketch in CA 1-4R
See also DLB 201
Wilson, F(rancis) Paul 1946- CANR-71
Earlier sketch in CA 138
Wilson, Forbes (Kingsbury) 1910- 126
Brief entry 112
Wilson, Forrest 1918- CANR-7
Earlier sketch in CA 53-56
See also SATA 27
Wilson, Fran
See Wilson, Frances Engle
Wilson, Frances Engle 1922- 130
Wilson, Francesca Mary 1888-1981 Obituary .. 103
Wilson, Francis Graham 1901-1976 Obituary . 65-68
Wilson, Frank (Avray) 1914- CAP-1
Earlier sketch in CA 11-12
Wilson, Frank J. 1887-1970 .... CAP-1
Earlier sketch in CA 13-16
Wilson, Frank L(eondus) 1941- 57-60
Wilson, Fred 1937- 37-40R
Wilson, G(eorge) B(ulkeley) L(aird) 1908-1984 .. 111
Obituary 114
Wilson, Gahan 1930- CANR-19
Earlier sketch in CA 25-28R
See also SATA 35
See also SATA-Brief 27
Wilson, Garff B(ell) 1909- 45-48
Wilson, George C. 1927- 124
Wilson, George M(acklin) 1937- 25-28R
Wilson, George W(ilton) 1928- CANR-7
Earlier sketch in CA 17-20R
Wilson, Gina 1943- CANR-53
Earlier sketch in CA 106
See also SATA 36, 85
See also SATA-Brief 34
Wilson, Glenn Daniel 1942- CANR-46
Earlier sketches in CA 104, CANR-21
Wilson, (Leslie) Granville 1912- CANR-11
Earlier sketch in CA 69-72
See also SATA 14
Wilson, Gregory
See DeLamotte, Roy Carroll
Wilson, Gretchen 1956- 165
Wilson, H. W.
See Wilson, Halsey William
Wilson, Halsey William 1868-1954 Brief entry .. 118
Wilson, (James) Harold 1916-1995 .... CANR-16
Obituary 148
Earlier sketch in CA 53-56
Wilson, Harold Stacy 1935- 41-44R
Wilson, Harriet E. Adams 1828(?)-1863(?) ... BLC 3
See also DAM MULT
See also DLB 50
Wilson, Harriett (Charlotte) 1916- CANR-16
Earlier sketch in CA 1-4R
Wilson, Harris W(ard) 1919- 21-24R
Wilson, Harry Leon 1867-1939 160
Brief entry 108
See also DLB 9
Wilson, Hazel (Hutchins) 1898-1992 .... CANR-6
Obituary 139
Earlier sketch in CA 1-4R
See also SATA 3
See also SATA-Obit 73
Wilson, Helen Helga (Mayne) CANR-4
Earlier sketch in CA 9-12R
Wilson, Helen Van Pelt 1901- 105
Wilson, Howard Allan 1927- Brief entry 106
Wilson, Howard Hazen 1908-1978 Obituary ... 77-80
Wilson, Ian (William) 1941- 85-88
Wilson, Iris Higbie
See Engstrand, Iris (H.) Wilson
Wilson, Isaiah Herbert 1909-1990 Obituary 131
Wilson, Ivor (Arthur) 1924- CAP-1
Earlier sketch in CA 11-12
Wilson, J(anice) J. 1936- 97-100
Wilson, J(ohn) Tuzo 1908-1993 .... CANR-47
Obituary 141
Earlier sketch in CA 45-48
Wilson, Jack 1937- 21-24R
Wilson, Jacqueline 1945- CANR-38
Earlier sketches in CA 45-48, CANR-1, 17
See also SATA 61, 102
See also SATA-Brief 52
Wilson, Jacques M(arcel) P(atrick) 1920- 49-52
Wilson, James C(lyde) 1948- 111
Wilson, James Orville 1895- CAP-1
Earlier sketch in CA 11-12
Wilson, James Q(uinn) 1931- CANR-65
Brief entry 116
Earlier sketch in CA 128
Wilson, James Robert 1917- 1-4R
Wilson, James Vernon 1881- CAP-1
Earlier sketch in CA 9-10
Wilson, Jaye 1938- 104
Wilson, Jeanne (Patricia Pauline) 1920- .. CANR-12
Earlier sketch in CA 69-72
Wilson, Jerry V(ernon) 1928- CANR-7
Earlier sketch in CA 57-60
Wilson, Jim
See Wilson, James Vernon
Wilson, Joan Hoff 1937- 134
Brief entry 105
Wilson, Joe
See Wilson, Joseph T(homas)
Wilson, John 1588-1667 .... DLB 24
Wilson, John 1785-1854 .... DLB 110
Wilson, John 1922- .... SATA 22
Wilson, (Richard) John (McMoran) 1924- 117
Wilson, John A. 1900(?)-1976 Obituary 69-72
Wilson, John A(braham) R(oss) 1911- 41-44R
Wilson, John Boyd 1928- CANR-5
Earlier sketch in CA 9-12R
Wilson, John (Anthony) Burgess 1917-1993 ....
CANR-46
Obituary 143
Earlier sketches in CA 1-4R, CANR-2
See also Burgess, Anthony
See also DAC
See also DAM NOV
See also MTCW 1
Wilson, John C.
See Morrow, Felix
Wilson, John Dover 1881-1969 102
Obituary 93-96
See also DLB 201
Wilson, John F(rederick) 1933- Brief entry 117
Wilson, John Foster 1919- 109
Wilson, John Harold 1900-1982 Obituary 107
Wilson, John Oliver 1938- 129
Wilson, John R. M. 1944- 69-72
Wilson, John Stuart Gladstone 1916- CANR-11
Earlier sketch in CA 13-16R
Wilson, John T(odd) 1914-1990 Obituary 132
Wilson, Johnniece Marshall 1944- 142
See also SATA 75
Wilson, Jonathan 1950- 152
Wilson, Joseph T(homas) 1936- 117
Wilson, Joyce M(uriel Judson) CANR-51
Earlier sketches in CA 17-20R, CANR-12
See also Stranger, Joyce
See also SATA 21, 84
Wilson, Julia 1927- 21-24R
Wilson, Jussem
See Wilson, Nelly
Wilson, Justin 116
Wilson, Katharine M(argaret) 1895- 89-92
Wilson, Keith 1927- CANR-9
Earlier sketch in CA 21-24R
See also CAAS 5
Wilson, Keith 1929- CANR-49
Earlier sketch in CA 121
Wilson, Ken 1943- 168
Wilson, Kenneth G(eorge) 1923- 5-8R
Wilson, Kenneth L. 1897(?)-1979 Obituary ... 85-88
Wilson, Kenneth L(ee) 1916- 29-32R
Wilson, L(eland) Craig 1925- 37-40R
Wilson, Lanford 1937- CANR-45
Earlier sketch in CA 17-20R
See also CABS 3
See also CLC 7, 14, 36
See also DAM DRAM
See also DLB 7
Wilson, Larman C. 1930- CANR-14
Earlier sketch in CA 37-40R
Wilson, Leigh Allison 1957- 117
Wilson, Leonard G(ilchrist) 1928- CANR-7
Earlier sketch in CA 57-60
Wilson, Libby
See Wilson, Elizabeth Z.
Wilson, Lionel 1924- 105
See also SATA 33
See also SATA-Brief 31
Wilson, Logan 1907- 45-48
Wilson, Lois (M.) 1927- 134
Wilson, Louis D(oull) 1917- 93-96
Wilson, Louis E. 1939- 143
Wilson, Louis Round 1876-1980 Obituary 93-96
Wilson, M(orris) Emett 1894- 5-8R
Wilson, Major L(oyce) 1926- 57-60
Wilson, Margaret (Wilhemina)
1882-1973 Obituary 113
See also DLB 9
Wilson, Margaret Gibbons 1943- 101
Wilson, Margery
See Strayer, Sara Barker
Wilson, Margo 1942- CANR-31
Earlier sketch in CA 110
Wilson, Marie B(eatrice) 1922- 53-56
Wilson, Marjorie
See Wilson, Budge
See also SATA-Brief 51
Wilson, Mary
See Roby, Mary Linn
Wilson, Mary C(hristina) 1950- 128
Wilson, Maurice (Charles John) 1914- .... SATA 46
Wilson, Melba (Jean) 1947- 164
Wilson, (Daphne) Merna 1930- 109
Wilson, Michael 1914-1978 85-88
Obituary 77-80
See also DLB 44
Wilson, Miles (Scott, Jr.) 1943- 139

Wilson, Mitchell 1913-1973 ... CANR-3
Obituary ... 41-44R
Earlier sketch in CA 1-4R
Wilson, Mona 1872-1954 ... DLB 149
Wilson, Monica Hunter 1908-1982 ... CANR-6
Obituary ... 108
Earlier sketch in CA 1-4R
Wilson, N(igel) G(uy) 1935- ... 127
Wilson, N(orman) Scarlyn 1901- ... CANR-5
Earlier sketch in CA 5-8R
Wilson, Nancy Hope 1947- ... 149
See also SATA 81
Wilson, Neil 1944- ... 133
Wilson, Neill C(ompton) 1889- ... 5-8R
Wilson, Nelly 1930- ... 106
Wilson, Nick
See Ellis, Edward S(ylvester)
Wilson, Noel Avon 1914- ... 73-76
Wilson, Pat 1910- ... CANR-12
Earlier sketch in CA 29-32R
Wilson, Paul C(arroll) 1944- ... 77-80
Wilson, Paul R(ichard) 1942- Brief entry ... 109
Wilson, Penelope Coker
See Hall, Penelope C(oker)
Wilson, Peter (Cecil) 1913-1984 Obituary ... 113
Wilson, Peter N. 1928- ... 25-28R
Wilson, Phillip (John) 1922- ... 57-60
Wilson, Phoebe Rous 1924(?)-1980 Obituary .. 101
Wilson, Phyllis Starr 1928- ... 69-72
Wilson, R(oger) H(arris) L(ebus) 1920- ... 13-16R
Wilson, R. Michael 1944- ... 166
Wilson, Raymond 1925-1995 ... CANR-17
Obituary ... 148
Earlier sketch in CA 97-100
Wilson, Richard Garratt 1928- ... 106
Wilson, Richard Guy 1940- ... CANR-45
Earlier sketches in CA 93-96, CANR-21
Wilson, Richard Lawson 1905-1981 Obituary .. 102
Wilson, Richard Trevor 1938- ... 118
Wilson, Richard W(hittingham) 1933- ... 73-76
Wilson, Robert (Edward) 1951- ... 124
Wilson, Robert Anton 1932- ... CANR-52
Earlier sketches in CA 65-68, CANR-18
Wilson, Robert C. 1951- ... 166
Wilson, Robert Charles 1953- ... 159
Wilson, Robert L. 1925-1991 ... CANR-9
Obituary ... 134
Earlier sketch in CA 57-60
Wilson, Robert M(ills) 1929- ... CANR-25
Earlier sketches in CA 21-24R, CANR-9
Wilson, Robert M. 1944- ... CANR-41
Earlier sketches in CA 49-52, CANR-2
See also CLC 7, 9
See also MTCW 1
Wilson, Robert McLachlan 1916- ... 109
Wilson, Robert McLiam 1964- ... 132
See also CLC 59
Wilson, Robert N(eal) 1924- ... 17-20R
Wilson, Robert R(athbun) 1914- ... 162
Wilson, Robert Renbert 1898-1975 ... CANR-23
Earlier sketch in CA 45-48
Wilson, Robert W. 1917- ... 145
Wilson, Robin Scott 1928- ... 101
Wilson, Robley (Conant), Jr. 1930- ... CANR-14
Earlier sketch in CA 77-80
Wilson, Rodney N. Usher
See Usher-Wilson, Rodney N.
Wilson, Roger Burdett 1919- ... 45-48
Wilson, Romer 1891-1930 ... DLB 191
Wilson, Ron(ald William) 1941- ... 112
See also SATA 38
Wilson, Ronald E(merson) 1932- ... 105
Wilson, Rosalind Baker 1923- ... 132
Wilson, (Edward) Ross (Armitage) 1914- ... 5-8R
Wilson, Rudy 1950- ... 136
Wilson, Sam 1946- ... 152
Wilson, Samuel, Jr. 1911- ... CANR-6
Earlier sketch in CA 53-56
Wilson, Sandra 1944- ... 102
Wilson, Sarah 1934- ... 127
See also SATA 50
Wilson, Sharon Rose 1941- ... 152
Wilson, Sloan 1920- ... CANR-44
Earlier sketches in CA 1-4R, CANR-1
See also CLC 32
Wilson, Snoo 1948- ... 69-72
See also CLC 33
Wilson, Steve 1943- ... 73-76
Wilson, Susan 1951- ... 156
Wilson, Theodore A(llen) 1940- ... 37-40R
Wilson, Thomas 1523(?)-1581 ... DLB 132
Wilson, Thomas C(ave) 1907-1984 Obituary ... 112
Wilson, Thomas Williams, Jr. 1912-1997 .. CANR-3
Obituary ... 162
Earlier sketch in CA 5-8R
Wilson, Tom 1931- ... 106
See also SATA 33
See also SATA-Brief 30
Wilson, Trevor (Gordon) 1928- ... 156
Wilson, W(illiam) Harmon 1905- ... 37-40R
Wilson, Walt(er N.) 1939- ... 69-72
See also SATA 14
Wilson, Wayne 1946- ... 136
Wilson, Wesley M. 1927- ... 9-12R
Wilson, Wilfrid George 1910- ... CAP-2
Earlier sketch in CA 21-22
Wilson, William A(lbert) 1933- ... 105
Wilson, William E(dward) 1906-1988 ... CANR-2
Obituary ... 125
Earlier sketch in CA 5-8R
Wilson, William H(enry) 1935- ... 13-16R
Wilson, William J. 1935- ... CANR-1
Earlier sketch in CA 45-48
Wilson, William P. 1922- ... 124
Wilson, William Ritchie 1911- ... 41-44R
Wilson, William S(mith) 1932- ... 81-84
See also CLC 49
Wilson, (Thomas) Woodrow 1856-1924 ... 166
See also DLB 47
See also TCLC 79
Wilson, Z. Vance 1950- ... 120
Wilson-Kastner, Patricia 1944- ... 126
Wilson-Max, Ken 1965- ... SATA 93
Wilson-Smith, Timothy 1936- ... 141
Wilt, David (Edward) 1955- ... 137
Wilt, Fred(erick Loren) 1920- ... CANR-9
Earlier sketch in CA 57-60
Wilt, Judith 1941- ... CANR-12
Earlier sketch in CA 57-60
Wiltenburg, Robert 1947- ... 139
Wiltgen, Ralph M(ichael) 1921- ... CANR-11
Earlier sketch in CA 25-28R
Wilton, (James) Andrew (Rutley) 1942- ... 97-100
Wilton, Elizabeth 1937- ... CANR-28
Earlier sketch in CA 69-72
See also SATA 14
Wilton, Hal
See Pepper, Frank S.
Wilton-Ely, John 1937- ... 128
Wiltse, Charles M(aurice) 1907-1990 ... CANR-3
Obituary ... 131
Earlier sketch in CA 1-4R
Wiltse, David 1940- ... CANR-22
Earlier sketch in CA 105
Wiltsee, Joseph L. 1920- ... 110
Wiltshire, Susan Ford 1941- ... 140
Wiltz, Chris(tine) 1948- ... CANR-24
Earlier sketch in CA 106
Wiltz, John Edward 1930- ... 9-12R
Wilwerding, Walter Joseph 1891-1966 ... CAP-1
Earlier sketch in CA 13-16
See also SATA 9
Wimmer, Larry T(urley) 1935- ... 101
Wimmer, Mike 1961- ... SATA 70
Wimpfeling, Jakob 1450-1528 ... DLB 179
Wimsatt, James I(rving) 1927- ... CANR-13
Earlier sketch in CA 61-64
Wimsatt, W(illiam) K(urtz), Jr. 1907-1975 .. CANR-3
Obituary ... 61-64
Earlier sketch in CA 1-4R
See also DLB 63
Winans, A(llan) D(avis, Jr.) 1936- ... CANR-12
Earlier sketch in CA 57-60
See also CAAS 28
Winans, Christopher 1950- ... 133
Winans, Edgar Vincent 1930- ... 5-8R
Winant, Fran 1943- ... CANR-70
Earlier sketch in CA 53-56
Winawer, Bonnie P. (Josephs) 1938- ... 17-20R
Winborn, Marsha (Lynn) 1947- ... SATA 75
Wincelberg, Shimon 1924- ... CANR-46
Earlier sketch in CA 45-48
Winch, D(avid) M(onk) 1933- ... 45-48
Winch, Donald N. 1935- ... 123
Winch, John
See Campbell, (Gabrielle) Margaret (Vere)
Winch, Julie 1953- ... 159
Winch, Michael Bluett 1907- ... CAP-1
Earlier sketch in CA 11-12
Winch, Peter G(uy) 1926-1997 ... 29-32R
Obituary ... 157
Winch, Robert F(rancis) 1911-1977 ... CANR-24
Earlier sketch in CA 25-28R
Winch, Terence 1945- ... 93-96
Winchell, Carol Ann 1936- ... CANR-7
Earlier sketch in CA 61-64
Winchell, Constance M(abel) 1896-1983 ... CAP-1
Obituary ... 109
Earlier sketch in CA 9-10
Winchell, Donna Haisty 1952- ... 145
Winchell, Wallace 1914- ... 53-56
Winchell, Walter 1897-1972 ... 101
Obituary ... 33-36R
See also DLB 29
Winchester, A(lbert) M(cCombs) 1908- ... 41-44R
Winchester, Clarence 1895-1981 Obituary ... 104
Winchester, Jack
See Freemantle, Brian (Harry)
Winchester, James H(ugh) 1917-1985 ... 17-20R
Obituary ... 117
See also SATA 30
See also SATA-Obit 45
Winchester, Otis 1933- ... 21-24R
Winchester, Simon 1944- ... 107
Winchilsea, Anne (Kingsmill) Finch Counte 1661-1720
See Finch, Anne
Winckelmann, Johann Joachim 1717-1768 . DLB 97
Winckler, Paul 1630-1686 ... DLB 164
Winckler, Paul A(lbert) 1926- ... 102
Wind, Barry 1942- ... 140
Wind, Edgar 1900-1971 Obituary ... 104
Wind, Herbert Warren 1916- ... CANR-62
Earlier sketches in CA 1-4R, CANR-6
See also DLB 171
Windal, Floyd W(esley) 1930- ... 9-12R
Windchy, Eugene G. 1930- ... 41-44R
Windeler, Robert 1944- ... 102
Winder, Alvin E. 1923- ... 93-96
Winder, George Herbert 1895- ... CAP-1
Earlier sketch in CA 11-12
Winder, Mavis Areta 1907- ... 21-24R
Winder, R(ichard) Bayly 1920-1988 ... 17-20R
Obituary ... 126
Winders, Gertrude Hecker ... CANR-6
Earlier sketch in CA 1-4R
See also SATA 3
Windet, John fl. 1554-1610 ... DLB 170
Windham, Basil
See Wodehouse, P(elham) G(renville)
Windham, Donald 1920- ... CANR-6
Earlier sketch in CA 1-4R
See also DLB 6
Windham, Douglas M(acArthur) 1943- ... CANR-43
Earlier sketch in CA 29-32R
Windham, Joan 1904- ... 21-24R
Windham, Kathryn T(ucker) 1918- ... CANR-11
Earlier sketch in CA 69-72
See also SATA 14
Windle, Janice Woods ... 164
Windle, William Frederick 1898-1985 ... 108
Obituary ... 115
Windley, Carol 1947- ... 159
Windley, Charles Ellis 1942- ... 65-68
Windling, Terri ... 163
Windmiller, Marshall 1924- ... 21-24R
Windmuller, John P. 1923- ... CANR-10
Earlier sketch in CA 25-28R
Windolph, F(rancis) Lyman 1889-1978 ... 41-44R
Windrich, Elaine 1921- ... 131
Windrow, Martin
See Windrow, Martin Clive
Windrow, Martin C.
See Windrow, Martin Clive
Windrow, Martin Clive 1944- ... 134
Brief entry ... 110
See also SATA 68
Windsor, Alan 1931- ... 127
Windsor, Annie
See Shull, Margaret Anne Wyse
Windsor, Claire
See Hamerstrom, Frances
Windsor, Duane 1947- ... 111
Windsor, Duke of
See Edward VIII
Windsor, Gerard (Charles) 1944- ... 124
Windsor, Merrill C(ranston, Jr.) 1924-1990 ... 113
Obituary ... 133
Windsor, Patricia 1938- ... CANR-42
Earlier sketches in CA 49-52, CANR-4, 19
See also AAYA 23
See also SAAS 19
See also SATA 30, 78
Windsor, Philip 1935- ... CANR-8
Earlier sketch in CA 5-8R
Windsor, Rex
See Armstrong, Douglas Albert
Windsor, Rudolph R. 1935- Brief entry ... 107
Windsor, (Bessie) Wallis Warfield (Spencer) 1896-1986 Obituary ... 119
Windsor-Liscombe, Rhodri 1946- ... 129
Windsor-Richards, Arthur (Bedlington) 1904- ... CAP-1
Earlier sketch in CA 11-12
Wine, Dick
See Posner, Richard
Wine, Sherwin T. 1928- ... 93-96
Wineapple, Brenda 1949- ... CANR-69
Earlier sketch in CA 133
Winearls, Jane 1908- ... 103
Winearls, Joan 1937- ... 139
Wineberg, Henry J. 1905(?)-1983 Obituary ... 109
Winebrenner, D(aniel) Kenneth 1908- ... CAP-1
Earlier sketch in CA 9-10
Winebrenner, Hubert W., Jr. 1937- ... 127
Winebrenner, Hugh
See Winebrenner, Hubert W., Jr.
Winecoff, Charles 1960- ... 162
Winegardner, Mark 1961- ... CANR-68
Earlier sketch in CA 127
Winegarten, Renee 1922- ... 65-68
Winehouse, Irwin 1922- ... 9-12R
Winek, Charles L(eone) 1936- ... 65-68
Wineman-Marcus, Irene 1952- ... SATA 81
Winer, Bart 1919(?)-1989 Obituary ... 127
Winer, Deborah Grace 1961- ... 136
Winer, Elihu 1914- Brief entry ... 111
Winer, Richard 1929- ... CANR-12
Earlier sketch in CA 73-76
Winerip, Michael ... 160
Wines, Roger (Andrew) 1933- ... 21-24R
Winetrout, Kenneth 1912- ... 21-24R
Winfield, Arthur M.
See Stratemeyer, Edward L.
Winfield, Edna
See Stratemeyer, Edward L.
Winfield, Fairlee E(lizabeth) 1929- ... 118
Winfield, Gerald Freeman 1908-1984 Obituary . 113
Winfield, Julia
See Armstrong, Jennifer
Winfield, Leigh
See Youngberg, Norma Ione (Rhoads)
Winford, Donald C. 1945- ... 137
Winfrey, Dorman H(ayward) 1924- ... 17-20R
Winfrey, John Crawford 1935- ... 57-60
Winfrey, Lee 1932- ... 69-72
Wing, Betsy 1936- ... 140
Wing, Cliff W(aldron), Jr. 1922- ... 49-52
Wing, Donald G(oddard) 1904-1972 Obituary ... 37-40R
See also DLB 187
Wing, Elizabeth Nelson
See Wing, Betsy
Wing, Frances (Scott) 1907- ... CAP-1
Earlier sketch in CA 17-18
Wing, George Douglas 1921- ... 17-20R
Wing, J(ohn) K(enneth) 1923- ... CANR-54
Earlier sketches in CA 29-32R, CANR-28
Wing, Jennifer Patai 1942- ... 57-60
Wing, John M. 1844-1917 ... DLB 187
Wing, Natasha (Lazutin) 1960- ... 149
See also SATA 82
Wing, R. L.
See Aero, Rita
Wing, Willis Kingsley 1899-1985 Obituary ... 116
Wingate, (Martha) Anne (Guice) 1943- ... 116
Wingate, Gifford W(endel) 1925- ... 65-68
Wingate, Isabel B(arnum) 1901-1987 ... 21-24R
Obituary ... 122
Wingate, John (Allan) 1920- ... CANR-24
Earlier sketch in CA 77-80
Wingate, John Williams 1899- ... 9-12R
Wingenbach, Charles E.
See Wingenbach, Gregory C(harles)
Wingenbach, Gregory C(harles) 1938- ... 13-16R
Winger, Fred E. 1912- ... 13-16R
Winger, Howard W(oodrow) 1914- ... CANR-7
Earlier sketch in CA 17-20R
Wingert, Paul S. 1900(?)-1974 Obituary ... 53-56
Wingfield, Paul 1961- ... 140
Wingfield, Sheila (Claude) 1906-1992 ... 130
Obituary ... 136
Brief entry ... 108
Wingfield Digby, George (Frederick) 1911-1989 ... CAP-1
Obituary ... 127
Earlier sketch in CA 11-12
Wingler, Hans M(aria) 1920- ... CANR-14
Earlier sketch in CA 29-32R
Wingo, E(lvis) Otha 1934- ... 37-40R
Wingo, Glenn Max 1913- ... 5-8R
Wingo, T(ullius) Lowdon, Jr. 1923- ... 21-24R
Wingo, Walter (Scott) 1931- ... 81-84
Wingrave, Anthony
See Wright, S(ydney) Fowler
Wingren, Gustaf F(redrik) 1910- ... 13-16R
Wingrove, David (John) 1954- ... 133
See also CLC 68
Wings, Mary 1949- ... CANR-70
Earlier sketch in CA 145
Winick, Bruce J. 1944- ... 147
Winick, Charles 1922- ... 134
Brief entry ... 109
Winick, Myron 1929- ... 107
Winick, Steven 1944- ... 61-64
Wink, Richard L(ee) 1930- ... 93-96
Wink, Walter Philip 1935- ... CANR-36
Earlier sketches in CA 37-40R, CANR-15
Winkelman, Donald M. 1934- ... 41-44R
Winkler, Allan M(ichael) 1945- ... 81-84
Winkler, Anthony C. 1942- ... 123
Winkler, Bee (Finkelberg) 1919- ... 13-16R
Winkler, Erhard M(ario) 1921- ... 89-92
Winkler, Franz E. 1907- ... 5-8R
Winkler, Henry R(alph) 1916- ... CANR-10
Earlier sketch in CA 17-20R
Winkler, John J(oseph) 1943-1990 Obituary ... 131
Winkler, Paul 1898-1982 Obituary ... 107
Winkler, Win Ann 1935- ... 73-76
Winkless, Nels(on Brock) III 1934- ... 57-60
Winks, Donald 1928- ... 25-28R
Winks, Robin William 1930- ... CANR-30
Earlier sketches in CA 5-8R, CANR-3
See also SATA 61
Winkworth, Stephen 1939- ... 127
Winn, Albert Curry 1921- ... 106
Winn, Alison
See Wharmby, Margot
Winn, Bob
See Seuling, Barbara
Winn, Charles S. 1932- ... CANR-23
Earlier sketch in CA 69-72
Winn, Chris 1952- ... 117
See also SATA 42
Winn, Ira Jay 1929- ... 57-60
Winn, James Anderson 1947- ... 120
Winn, Janet Bruce 1928- ... 105
See also SATA 43
Winn, Laura Rocke 1902- ... CAP-1
Earlier sketch in CA 13-14
Winn, Marie 1936(?)- ... 111
See also SATA 38
Winn, Ralph Bubrich 1895- ... 5-8R
Winn, Rowland (Denys Guy) 1916-1984 Obituary ... 114
Winn, Wilkins B(owdre) 1928- ... 49-52
Winnegrad, Mark Harris 1948- ... 77-80
Winnemucca, Sarah 1844-1891 ... DAM MULT
See also DLB 175
See also NNAL
Winner, Anna K(ennedy) 1900- ... 29-32R
Winner, Irene P(ortis) 1923- ... CANR-14
Earlier sketch in CA 41-44R
Winner, Michael Robert 1935- ... 137
Winner, Percy 1899-1974 Obituary ... 45-48
Winner, Thomas G(ustav) 1917- ... CANR-15
Earlier sketch in CA 37-40R
Winner, Viola Hopkins 1928- ... CANR-4
Earlier sketch in CA 53-56
Winnett, Fred Victor 1903- ... 37-40R
Winnett, Thomas 1921- ... CANR-22
Earlier sketches in CA 61-64, CANR-7
Winnick, Karen B(eth) B(inkoff) 1946- ... 73-76
See also SATA 51
Winnick, R. H. 1947- ... 144
Winnicott, Donald (Woods) 1896-1971 ... CAP-1
Earlier sketch in CA 13-14
Winnifrith, Thomas John 1938- ... CANR-50
Earlier sketches in CA 108, CANR-25
See also DLB 155
Winnikoff, Albert 1930- ... 29-32R
Winnington, Alan 1910(?)-1983 Obituary ... 111
Winnington-Ingram, R(eginald) P(epys) 1904-1993 ... 129
Obituary ... 140
Winograd, Terry (Allen) 1946- ... CANR-67
Earlier sketch in CA 128
Winokur, Joan Gelman 1935- ... 41-44R
Winokur, Jon 1947- ... 132
Winokur, Stephen 1941- ... 89-92
Winold, Allen 1929- ... 17-20R
Winsberg, Morton D. 1930- ... 13-16R

Winsborough, Hal (Liman) H. 1932- 9-12R
Winsett, Marvin Davis 1902- 1-4R
Winsey, Valentine Rossilli 145
Winship, Elizabeth 1921- 41-44R
Winship, Laurence Leathe 1890-1975 Obituary 104
Winslade, William J(oseph) 1941- 118
Winsloe, Christa 1888-1944 DLB 124
Winslow, Anna Green 1759-1780 DLB 200
Winslow, Barbara 1947- 155
See also SATA 91
Winslow, Dean Hendricks, Jr. 1934-1972 37-40R
Obituary 41-44R
Winslow, Don 1953- 145
Winslow, Donald
See Zoll, Donald Atwell
Winslow, Gerald A. 109
Winslow, John Hathaway 1932- 37-40R
Winslow, Martha
See Rickett, Frances
Winslow, Ola Elizabeth 1885(?)-1977 CANR-3
Obituary 73-76
Earlier sketch in CA 1-4R
Winslow, Pauline Glen CANR-69
Earlier sketches in CA 101, CANR-18, 41
Winslow, Pete
See Winslow, Dean Hendricks, Jr.
Winslow, Richard E(lliott) III 1934- 129
Winslow, Robert W(allace) 1940- Brief entry 108
Winslow, Ron(ald A.) 1949- 103
Winslow, Thyra Samter 1893-1961 Obituary 89-92
Winslowe, John
See Richardson, Gladwell
Winslowe, John R.
See Richardson, Gladwell
Winsor, Justin 1831-1897 DLB 47
Winsor, Kathleen 1919- CANR-62
Earlier sketch in CA 97-100
Winsor, Mary P(ickard) 1943- 69-72
Winsor, Phil 1938- 142
Winsor, Roy (William) 1912-1987 65-68
Obituary 122
Winspear, Alban Dewes 1899- 45-48
Winspear, Violet 1928-1989 CANR-64
Earlier sketch in CA 122
Winstanley, Michael J. 1949- 129
Winstanley, (Jane) Rita 1955- 128
Winston, Alexander 1909- CAP-2
Earlier sketch in CA 25-28
Winston, Carl H. 1-4R
Winston, Clara 1921-1983 CANR-44
Obituary 113
Earlier sketch in CA 25-28R
See also SATA 54
See also SATA-Obit 39
Winston, Daoma 1922- CANR-61
Earlier sketches in CA 45-48, CANR-1
Winston, Douglas Garrett 41-44R
Winston, Eric V(on) A(rthur) 1942- 29-32R
Winston, Henry 1911-1986 Obituary 121
Winston, Kenneth I(rwin) 1940- CANR-48
Earlier sketch in CA 117
Winston, Krishna 1944- 104
Winston, Mark L. 1950- 141
Winston, Martin Bradley 1948- 118
Winston, Michael R(ussell) 1941- 113
Winston, Mike
See King, Florence
Winston, R(obert) A(lexander) 1907-1974 CAP-2
Obituary 49-52
Earlier sketch in CA 25-28
Winston, Richard 1917-1979 25-28R
Obituary 93-96
See also SATA 54
Winston, Sarah 1912- 29-32R
Winstone, H(arry) V(ictor) F(rederick) 1926- CANR-44
Earlier sketches in CA 104, CANR-21
Wint, Guy 1910-1969 CANR-3
Earlier sketch in CA 1-4R
Winter, Abigail
See Schere, Monroe
Winter, Alice 1919- 13-16R
Winter, Bevis (Peter) 1918- CANR-8
Earlier sketch in CA 5-8R
Winter, Caryl 1944- 117
Winter, Colin O'Brien 1928-1981 Obituary 105
Winter, David Brian 1929- CANR-20
Earlier sketch in CA 103
Winter, David G(arrett) 1939- 57-60
Winter, Denis 1940- 118
Winter, Douglas E. 1950- CANR-45
Earlier sketch in CA 118
Winter, Edward H(enry) 1923- 1-4R
Winter, Elmer L(ouis) 1912- 13-16R
Winter, Gibson 1916- 49-52
Winter, Ginny Linville 1925- CANR-1
Earlier sketch in CA 1-4R
Winter, Gordon 1912-1993 CANR-14
Obituary 141
Earlier sketch in CA 77-80
Winter, H. G. Winter
See Bates, Harry
Winter, Herbert R(einhold) 1928- 45-48
Winter, J(erry) Alan 1937- 41-44R
Winter, J. M. 1945- 73-76
Winter, John F. 1913- 104
Winter, Kari J. 1960- 137
Winter, Keith 1906-1983 Obituary 109
Winter, Klaus 1928- 29-32R
Winter, Leslie 1940- CANR-6
Earlier sketch in CA 1-4R
Winter, Michael Morgan 1930- CAP-1
Earlier sketch in CA 11-12
Winter, Milo (Kendall) 1888-1956 SATA 21
Winter, Nathan H. 1926- 21-24R
Winter, Paula Cecelia 1929- 107
See also SATA 48
Winter, R. R.
See Winterbotham, R(ussell) R(obert)
Winter, Ralph K(arl, Jr.) 1935- 122
Brief entry 118
Winter, Roger 1931- 37-40R
Winter, Ruth (Nancy G.) 1930- 37-40R
Winter, William D(avid) 1927- 25-28R
Winter, William O(rville) 1918- 49-52
Winterbotham, F(rederick) W(illiam) 1897-1990 57-60
Obituary 130
Winterbotham, R(ussell) R(obert) 1904-1971 1-4R
Obituary 103
See also SATA 10
Winterbotham, Russ
See Winterbotham, R(ussell) R(obert)
Winterfeld, Henry 1901- 77-80
See also SATA 55
Wintergreen, Jane
See Duncan, Sara Jeannette
Wintergreen, John P.
See Ryskind, Morrie
Wintergreen, Warren
See Adamson, Joseph III
Winterich, John 1891-1970 Obituary 29-32R
Winteringham, F. Peter W. 1918- 144
Winternitz, Emanuel 1898-1983 CANR-20
Obituary 110
Earlier sketch in CA 25-28R
Winterowd, W. Ross 1930- 17-20R
Winters, Anne 1939- 122
Winters, Bayla 1921- 21-24R
Winters, Bernice
See Winters, Bayla
Winters, Catherine (Mary) 1951- 118
Winters, Donald L(ee) 1935- 29-32R
Winters, Francis Xavier 1933- 61-64
Winters, J. C.
See Cross, Gilbert B.
Winters, Janet Lewis
See Lewis, Janet
See also CLC 41
See also DLBY 87
Winters, John D(avid) 1917- 9-12R
Winters, Jon
See Cross, Gilbert B.
Winters, Marian 1924-1978 101
Obituary 81-84
Winters, Marjorie
See Henri, Florette
Winters, Mike 1930- 119
Winters, Nina 1944- SATA 62
Winters, Rosemary
See Breckler, Rosemary
Winters, Shelley
See Schrift, Shirley
Winters, (Arthur) Yvor 1900-1968 CAP-1
Obituary 25-28R
Earlier sketch in CA 11-12
See also CLC 4, 8, 32
See also DLB 48
See also MTCW 1
Winterson, Jeanette 1959- CANR-58
Earlier sketch in CA 136
See also CLC 64
See also DAM POP
Winterton, Gayle
See Adams, William Taylor
Winterton, Paul 1908- CANR-58
Earlier sketches in CA 5-8R, CANR-6
See also Garve, Andrew
Winther, Barbara 1926- CANR-17
Earlier sketch in CA 97-100
Winther, Oscar Osburn 1903-1970 CANR-2
Earlier sketch in CA 1-4R
Winther, Sophus Keith 1893-1983 CANR-66
Earlier sketch in CA 5-8R
Winthrop, Elizabeth
See Mahony, Elizabeth Winthrop
See also SATA 76
Winthrop, Henry 1910- 73-76
Winthrop, John, Jr. 1606-1676 DLB 24
Winthrop, John 1588-1649 DLB 24, 30
Winthrop, Margaret Tyndal 1591(?)-1647 DLB 200
Winthrop, Theodore 1828-1861 DLB 202
Wintle, Anne 29-32R
Wintle, Francis Edward 1948- 139
Wintle, Justin (Beecham) 1949- CANR-13
Earlier sketch in CA 77-80
Winton, Calhoun 1927- 9-12R
Winton, Chester Allen 1941- 89-92
Winton, Harry N(athaniel) M(cQuillian) 1907-1977(?) CANR-29
Earlier sketch in CA 41-44R
Winton, Ian (Kenneth) 1960- SATA 76
Winton, John
See Pratt, John
Winton, Kate Barber 1882(?)-1974 Obituary 53-56
Winton, Tim 1960- 152
See also SATA 98
Wintrobe, Maxwell M(yer) 1901-1986 133
Obituary 121
Wintterle, John F(rancis) 1927- 29-32R
Wintz, Cary D. 1943- 137
Wintz, Jack 1936- 109
Winwar, Frances 1900- 89-92
Winward, Stephen Frederick 1911- 9-12R
Winward, (Richard) Walter 1938- 105
Wippel, John Francis 1933- 114
Wippler, Migene Gonzalez
See Gonzalez-Wippler, Migene
Wirkus, Tom E(dward) 1933- 37-40R
Wirnt von Grafenberg 1170(?)-1235(?) DLB 138
Wirsing, Marie E(milia) 1931- 45-48
Wirt, Ann
See Benson, Mildred (Augustine Wirt)
Wirt, Frederick Marshall 1924- CANR-31
Earlier sketch in CA 112
Wirt, Mildred A.
See Benson, Mildred (Augustine Wirt)
Wirt, Sherwood Eliot 1911- CANR-33
Earlier sketches in CA 41-44R, CANR-15
Wirt, William 1772-1834 DLB 37
Wirt, Winola Wells 1905(?)-1986 93-96
Obituary 120
Wirtenberg, Patricia Z(arrella) 1932- 61-64
See also SATA 10
Wirth, Arthur G. 1919- CANR-10
Earlier sketch in CA 21-24R
Wirth, Beverly 1938- 118
See also SATA 63
Wirth, John D(avis) 1936- CANR-51
Earlier sketches in CA 29-32R, CANR-26
Wirth, Niklaus 1934- CANR-21
Earlier sketch in CA 105
Wirth, Thomas 1941- 117
Wirths, Claudine (Turner) G(ibson) 1926- CANR-53
Earlier sketch in CA 126
See also SATA 64
Wirtz, (William) Willard 1912- 101
Wisberg, Aubrey 1909(?)-1990 97-100
Obituary 131
Wisberg, Marian Aline 1923- 109
Wisbeski, Dorothy (Gross) 1929- 9-12R
Wisbey, Herbert Andrew, Jr. 1919- 13-16R
Wischnitzer, Rachel 1885(?)-1989 Obituary 130
Wisdom, (Arthur) John (Terence Dibben) 1904-1993 25-28R
Obituary 143
Wisdom, Kenny
See Grogan, Emmett
Wisdome, Thomas
See Dunbar, Charles Stuart
Wise, Arthur 1923- 9-12R
Wise, Charles C(onrad), Jr. 1913- CANR-9
Earlier sketch in CA 21-24R
Wise, David 1930- CANR-42
Earlier sketches in CA 1-4R, CANR-2
Wise, Ernie
See Wiseman, Ernest
Wise, Gene 1936- 93-96
Wise, Helen Dickerson 1928- Brief entry 106
Wise, Herbert H(erschel) 1928- 108
Wise, James Waterman 1901-1983 Obituary 111
Wise, Joe 1939- 163
Wise, John 1652-1725 DLB 24
Wise, John E(dward) 1905-1974 CAP-1
Obituary 49-52
Earlier sketch in CA 13-16
Wise, Leonard 77-80
Wise, Nancy B(aker) 1921- 147
Wise, Raymond L. 1895- 21-24R
Wise, S(ydney) F(rancis) 1924- CANR-16
Earlier sketch in CA 21-24R
Wise, Stephen S(amuel) 1874-1949 Brief entry 117
Wise, Steven W. 1948- 163
Wise, Terence 1935- 89-92
Wise, Thomas James 1859-1937 DLB 184
Wise, Victoria (Jenanyan) 1944- 148
Wise, William 1923- CANR-6
Earlier sketch in CA 13-16R
See also SATA 4
Wise, Winifred E. 25-28R
See also SATA 2
Wisely, Rae 1938- 106
Wiseman, Adele 1928- 77-80
See also DLB 88
Wiseman, Ann (Sayre) 1926- CANR-9
Earlier sketch in CA 65-68
See also SATA 31
Wiseman, Anne Marie (Murray) 1932- 5-8R
Wiseman, B(ernard) 1922- CANR-24
Earlier sketches in CA 5-8R, CANR-8
See also SATA 4
Wiseman, Christopher S(tephen) 1936- CANR-44
Earlier sketch in CA 113
Wiseman, David 1916- CANR-30
Earlier sketch in CA 109
See also SATA 43
See also SATA-Brief 40
Wiseman, Donald John 1918- 89-92
Wiseman, Ernest 1925- 129
Wiseman, Francis Jowett 1905- CAP-1
Earlier sketch in CA 13-14
Wiseman, Frederick 1930- 159
See also CLC 20
Wiseman, James R(ichard) 1934- CANR-1
Earlier sketch in CA 45-48
Wiseman, John A. 1945- 139
Wiseman, Robert F(rederick) 1935- 77-80
Wiseman, T(imothy) P(eter) 1940- CANR-40
Earlier sketches in CA 45-48, CANR-1, 18
Wiseman, Thomas 1931- 25-28R
Wisenthal, J. L. 1940- 126
Wiser, William 37-40R
Wish, Harvey 1909-1968 CANR-3
Earlier sketch in CA 1-4R
Wishard, Armin 1941- 37-40R
Wishart, David J(ohn) 1946- 124
Brief entry 118
Wishart, E(rnest) E(dward) 1902-1987 Obituary 123
Wishart, Henry
See Shepherd, Robert Henry Wishart
Wishinsky, Frieda 1948- 138
See also SATA 70
Wiskemann, Elizabeth (?)-1971 Obituary 111
Wisker, Gina 1951- 145
Wisler, G(ary) Clifton 1950- 129
See also SATA 58
See also SATA-Brief 46
Wisler, Gene C(harles) 1920- 9-12R
Wisloff, Carl Johan Fredrik 1908- CAP-1
Earlier sketch in CA 13-14
Wismer, Donald (Richard) 1946- CANR-28
Earlier sketch in CA 109
See also SATA 59
Wisner, Bill
See Wisner, William L.
Wisner, George 1812-1849 DLB 43
Wisner, William L. 1914(?)-1983 111
Obituary 110
See also SATA 42
Wisneski, Henry 1940- 57-60
Wisniewski, David 1953- 160
See also CLR 51
See also SATA 95
Wisse, Ruth R(oskies) 1936- 37-40R
Wissmann, Ruth Leslie CANR-2
Earlier sketch in CA 5-8R
Wister, John C(aspar) 1887-1982 Obituary 109
Wister, Owen 1860-1938 162
Brief entry 108
See also DLB 9, 78, 186
See also SATA 62
See also TCLC 21
Wister, Sarah 1761-1804 DLB 200
Wistrich, Robert Solomon 1945- 107
Wiswall, F(rank) L(awrence), Jr. 1939- 29-32R
Wiswell, Ella Lury 1909- 111
Wiswell, Thomas George 1910- CANR-2
Earlier sketch in CA 5-8R
Wiswell, Tom
See Wiswell, Thomas George
Witchel, Alex 159
Witchel, Dinah B(rown) 1936- 105
Witcombe, R(ick) T(rader) 1943- 132
Witcover, Jules (Joseph) 1927- CANR-48
Earlier sketch in CA 25-28R
Witcutt, William Purcell 1907- CAP-1
Earlier sketch in CA 11-12
Witemeyer, Hugh 1939- 25-28R
Witham, (Phillip) Ross 1917- 105
See also SATA 37
Witham, W(illiam) Tasker 1914- 13-16R
Witheford, Hubert 1921- 102
Wither, George 1588-1667 DLB 121
Witheridge, Elizabeth P(lumb) 1907- 97-100
Witherington, Ben III 1951- 168
Withers, Audrey
See Kennett, Audrey
Withers, Carl A. 1900-1970 CANR-30
Earlier sketch in CA 73-76
See also SATA 14
Withers, Charles W. J. 1954- 128
Withers, E. L.
See Potter, G(eorge) W(illiam, Jr.)
Withers, Josephine 1938- 101
Withers, Sara Cook 1924- 17-20R
Withers, William 1905-1987 13-16R
Obituary 121
Witherspoon, Frances 1887(?)-1973 Obituary 45-48
Witherspoon, Irene Murray 1913- CANR-1
Earlier sketch in CA 1-4R
Witherspoon, John 1723-1794 DLB 31
Witherspoon, Mary Elizabeth 1919- 77-80
Witherspoon, Naomi Long
See Madgett, Naomi Long
Witherspoon, Thomas E. 1934- 81-84
Witherup, William 1935- 133
Withey, J(oseph) A(nthony) 1918- 25-28R
Withim, Gloria 1929- 112
Withington, William Adriance 1924- CANR-14
Earlier sketch in CA 41-44R
Withorn, Ann 1947- 125
Withrow, Dorothy E. 1910- 21-24R
Withrow, William Henry 1839-1908 DLB 99
Witkacy
See Witkiewicz, Stanislaw Ignacy
Witke, Roxane 1938- 69-72
Witker, Kristi 77-80
Witkiewicz, Stanislaw Ignacy 1885-1939 162
Brief entry 105
See also TCLC 8
Witkin, Erwin 1926- 37-40R
Witkin, Herman A. 1916-1979 CANR-1
Earlier sketch in CA 1-4R
Witkin, Lee D(aniel) 1935-1984 Obituary 114
Witkin-Lanoil, Georgia Hope 1943- 120
Witmer, Helen L(eland) 1898-1979 CAP-2
Obituary 89-92
Earlier sketch in CA 25-28
Witt, Dick 1948- SATA 80
Witt, Harold (Vernon) 1923- CANR-39
Earlier sketches in CA 1-4R, CANR-1, 17
Witt, Howell Arthur John 1920- 109
Witt, Hubert 1935- CANR-28
Earlier sketches in CA 65-68, CANR-12
Witt, James F. 1937- 89-92
Witt, John (Clermont) 1907-1982 Obituary 106
Witt, Reginald Eldred 1907-1980 37-40R
Obituary 97-100
Witt, Ronald Gene 1932- 126
Witt, Shirley Hill 1934- CANR-5
Earlier sketch in CA 53-56
See also SATA 17
Wittanen, Etolin 1907- SATA 55
Wittcoff, Harold A. 1918- 160
Witte, Ann Dryden 1942- CANR-26
Earlier sketch in CA 107
Witte, Glenna Finley 1925- CANR-26
Earlier sketches in CA 13-16R, CANR-10
See also AITN 1
Witte, John 1948- 93-96
Wittels, Harriet Joan 1938- 107
See also SATA 31
Witten, Herbert F. 1920- 5-8R

Witten, Ian H(ugh) 1947- ... CANR-28
Earlier sketch in CA 111
Wittenberg, Judith Bryant 1938- ... 102
Wittenberg, Philip 1895-1987 ... CAP-2
Obituary ... 122
Earlier sketch in CA 23-24
Wittenberg, Rudolph M. 1906-1986 ... CANR-22
Earlier sketch in CA 69-72
Wittenwiler, Heinrich c. 1387-c. 1414 ... DLB 179
Wittermans, Elizabeth (Pino) ... 17-20R
Witters, Weldon L. 1929- ... 93-96
Wittfogel, Karl A(ugust) 1896-1988 Obituary ... 125
Wittgenstein, Ludwig (Josef Johann) 1889-1951 ... 164
Brief entry ... 113
See also TCLC 59
Wittich, Claus 1932- ... 113
Wittich, Walter A(rno) 1910- ... 49-52
Wittig, Alice J(osephine) 1929- ... 101
Wittig, Monique 1935(?)- ... 135
Brief entry ... 116
See also CLC 22
See also DLB 83
Witting, Amy 1918- ... 140
Witting, Clifford 1907- ... 1-4R
Wittke, Carl (Frederick) 1892-1971 Obituary ... 29-32R
Wittkofski, Joseph Nicholas 1912- ... 9-12R
Wittkower, Rudolf 1901-1971 Obituary ... 33-36R
Wittkowski, Wolfgang 1925- ... CANR-24
Earlier sketches in CA 61-64, CANR-8
Wittliff, William D. 1940- ... CANR-54
Earlier sketch in CA 123
Wittlin, Alma S(tephanie) ... 45-48
Wittlin, Jozef 1896-1976 ... CANR-3
Obituary ... 65-68
Earlier sketch in CA 49-52
See also CLC 25
Wittlin, Thaddeus (Andrew) 1909- ... CANR-2
Earlier sketch in CA 45-48
Wittlinger, Ellen 1948- ... 150
See also SATA 83
Wittman, Sally (Anne Christensen) 1941- ... 107
See also SATA 30
Wittmer, Joe 1937- ... 45-48
Wittmer, Pierre (Jean) 1942- ... 139
Wittner, Lawrence S(tephen) 1941- ... CANR-33
Earlier sketch in CA 25-28R
Witton, Dorothy ... 73-76
Witton-Davies, Carl(yle) 1913-1993 ... 9-12R
Obituary ... 141
Wittreich, Joseph Anthony, Jr. 1939- ... CANR-28
Earlier sketches in CA 29-32R, CANR-12
Wittrock, M(erlin) C(arl) 1931- ... CANR-2
Earlier sketch in CA 49-52
Wittwer, Sylvan Harold 1917- ... CANR-35
Earlier sketch in CA 114
Witty, Helen E. S(troop) 1921- ... 105
Witty, Paul 1898-1976 ... 73-76
Obituary ... 65-68
See also SATA 50
See also SATA-Obit 30
Witty, Robert G(ee) 1906- ... CAP-2
Earlier sketch in CA 23-24
Witucke, Virginia 1937- ... 37-40R
Witwer, Andrew S. 1920(?)-1990 Obituary ... 132
Witze, Claude 1909(?)-1977 Obituary ... 73-76
Witzel, Michael Karl 1960- ... 154
Wixman, Ronald 1947- ... 122
Wixom, Hartt 1933- ... 120
Wixson, Douglas 1933- ... 147
Wizard, Mariann G(arner) 1946- ... 37-40R
Wobbe, R(oland) A(rthur) 1938- ... 102
Woddis, Hillel Chayim Keith 1914- Brief entry ... 114
Woddis, Jack
See Woddis, Hillel Chayim Keith
Wodehouse, Lawrence 1934- ... CANR-41
Earlier sketches in CA 53-56, CANR-4, 19
Wodehouse, P(elham) G(renville) 1881-1975 ... CANR-33
Obituary ... 57-60
Earlier sketches in CA 45-48, CANR-3
See also AITN 2
See also CDBLB 1914-1945
See also CLC 1, 2, 5, 10, 22
See also DAB
See also DAC
See also DAM NOV
See also DLB 34, 162
See also MTCW 1
See also SATA 22
See also SSC 2
Woden, George
See Slaney, George Wilson
Wodge, Dreary
See Gorey, Edward (St. John)
Wodhams, (Herbert) Jack 1931- ... 115
Woebcke, Mary-Jane 1933- ... 25-28R
Woehr, Richard (Arthur) 1942- ... 57-60
Woehrlin, William F(rederick) 1928- ... 45-48
Woelfel, James W(arren) 1937- ... 41-44R
Woelfl, Paul A(loysius) 1913- ... 17-20R
Woerner, Karl Heinrich 1910-1969 Obituary ... 110
Woessner, Nina C. 1933- ... 29-32R
Woessner, Warren (Dexter) 1944- ... CANR-14
Earlier sketch in CA 37-40R
Woestemeyer, Ina Faye
See Van Noppen, Ina (Faye) W(oestemeyer)
Woestendiek, (William) John (Jr.) 1953- ... 133
Brief entry ... 127
Interview in ... 133
Woetzel, Robert K(urt) 1930-1991 ... CANR-6
Obituary ... 135
Earlier sketch in CA 5-8R
Woffinden, Bob 1948- ... 135
Wofford, Azile (May) 1896- ... 5-8R
Wofford, Harris (Llewellyn) 1926- ... 129
Wofsey, Marvin M(ilton) 1913- ... 105
Wogaman, J(ohn) Philip 1932- ... CANR-62
Earlier sketches in CA 25-28R, CANR-20
Wogaman, Philip
See Wogaman, J(ohn) Philip
Wohl, Gerald 1934- ... 17-20R
Wohl, James P(aul) 1937- ... 77-80
Wohl, Paul 1901(?)-1985 Obituary ... 115
Wohl, Robert 1936- ... 104
Wohlberg, Meg 1905-1990 Obituary ... 133
See also SATA 41
See also SATA-Obit 66
Wohlfeld, Valerie (Robin) 1956- ... 155
Wohlgelernter, Maurice 1921- ... CANR-6
Earlier sketch in CA 13-16R
Wohl-Musciny, Ludwig von
See de Wohl, Louis
Wohlmuth, Ed 1935- ... 124
Wohlrabe, Raymond A. 1900-1977 ... CANR-3
Earlier sketch in CA 1-4R
See also SATA 4
Wohlstetter, Albert J(ames) 1913-1997 ... 129
Obituary ... 156
Wohmann, Gabriele 1932- ... DLB 75
Woirol, Gregory R. 1948- ... 144
Woititz, Janet G(eringer) 1938-1994 ... CANR-19
Obituary ... 145
Earlier sketch in CA 101
Woito, Robert (Severin) 1937- ... 120
Woiwode, L.
See Woiwode, Larry (Alfred)
Woiwode, Larry (Alfred) 1941- ... CANR-16
Earlier sketch in CA 73-76
Interview in ... CANR-16
See also CLC 6, 10
See also DLB 6
Wojahn, David (Charles) 1953- ... 136
Wojciechowska, Maia (Teresa) 1927- ... CANR-41
Earlier sketches in CA 9-12R, CANR-4
See also AAYA 8
See also CLC 26
See also CLR 1
See also JRDA
See also MAICYA
See also SAAS 1
See also SATA 1, 28, 83
Wojciechowski, Susan ... 146
See also SATA 78
Wojtyla, Karol
See John Paul II, Pope
Wolberg, Arlene Robbins 1907-1989 Obituary ... 130
Wolberg, Lewis Robert 1905-1988 ... CANR-19
Obituary ... 124
Earlier sketches in CA 45-48, CANR-2
Wolcot, John 1738-1819 ... DLB 109
Wolcott, Harry F(letcher) 1929- ... 65-68
Wolcott, Leonard Thompson ... CANR-28
Earlier sketches in CA 13-16R, CANR-11
Wolcott, Patty 1929- ... 57-60
See also SATA 14
Wolcott, Roger 1679-1767 ... DLB 24
Wold, Allen L. 1943- ... CANR-22
Earlier sketch in CA 105
See also SATA 64
Wold, Jo Anne 1938- ... 61-64
See also SATA 30
Wold, Ruth 1923- ... 37-40R
Woldendorp, R(ichard) 1927- ... CANR-12
Earlier sketch in CA 29-32R
Woldin, Beth Weiner 1955- ... 102
See also SATA 34
Woldin, (Edwin) Judd 1925- ... 141
Brief entry ... 122
Wolf, Adolf Hungry
See Hungry Wolf, Adolf
Wolf, Arnold Jacob 1924- ... 29-32R
Wolf, Arnold Veryl 1916-1975 Obituary ... 104
Wolf, Barbara Herrman 1932- ... 57-60
Wolf, Bernard 1930- Brief entry ... 115
See also SATA 102
See also SATA-Brief 37
Wolf, Charlotte (Elizabeth) 1926- ... 29-32R
Wolf, Christa 1929- ... CANR-45
Earlier sketch in CA 85-88
See also CLC 14, 29, 58
See also DLB 75
See also MTCW 1
Wolf, Daniel 1955- ... 136
Wolf, Deborah Goleman 1938- ... 97-100
Wolf, Dick
See Wolf, Richard A.
Wolf, Donald J(oseph) 1929- ... 13-16R
Wolf, Edwin II 1911-1991 ... CANR-4
Obituary ... 133
Earlier sketch in CA 1-4R
Wolf, Eric R(obert) 1923- ... 17-20R
Wolf, Frank 1940- ... 57-60
Wolf, Frank L(ouis) 1924- ... 57-60
Wolf, Fred Alan 1934- ... 115
Wolf, Frederick
See Dempewolff, Richard F(rederic)
Wolf, Friedrich 1888-1953 ... DLB 124
Wolf, Gary K. 1941- ... 160
Wolf, George 1890(?)-1980 Obituary ... 97-100
Wolf, George D(ugan) 1923- ... 29-32R
Wolf, Gita 1956- ... 168
See also SATA 101
Wolf, Harold A. 1923- ... 13-16R
Wolf, Harvey 1935- ... 57-60
Wolf, Hazel Catharine 1907- ... 5-8R
Wolf, Herbert C(hristian) 1923- ... 13-16R
Wolf, Jack C(lifford) 1922- ... 57-60
Wolf, Jacqueline 1928- ... 109
Wolf, Janet 1957- ... SATA 78
Wolf, John B(aptist) 1907- ... 9-12R
Wolf, Karl E(verett) 1921- ... 17-20R
Wolf, Kirsten 1959- ... 137
Wolf, Leonard 1923- ... CANR-3
Earlier sketch in CA 49-52
Wolf, Margery 1933- ... 138
Wolf, Marguerite Hurrey 1914- ... 53-56
Wolf, Markus 1923- ... 162
Wolf, Marvin J(ules) 1941- ... 117
Wolf, Michael D(avid) 1953- ... 121
Wolf, Miriam Bredow 1895- ... CAP-1
Earlier sketch in CA 9-10
Wolf, Naomi 1962- ... 141
Wolf, Peter (Michael) 1935- ... 53-56
Wolf, Ray 1948- ... 107
Wolf, Richard A. 1946- ... 139
Wolf, Robert Charles 1955- ... 109
Wolf, S. K.
See Wolf, Sarah (Elizabeth)
Wolf, Sallie 1950- ... SATA 80
Wolf, Sarah (Elizabeth) 1936- ... 132
Wolf, Stewart (George, Jr.) 1914- ... 143
Wolf, Thomas H(oward) 1916-1996 ... 69-72
Obituary ... 152
Wolf, William ... 103
Wolf, William B. 1920- ... CANR-26
Earlier sketches in CA 17-20R, CANR-10
Wolf, William C(harles), Jr. 1933- ... 41-44R
Wolf, William J(ohn) 1918- ... CANR-29
Earlier sketch in CA 111
Wolfbein, Seymour L(ouis) 1915- ... CANR-6
Earlier sketch in CA 13-16R
Wolfe, Alan 1942- ... 108
Wolfe, Alvin William 1928- ... CANR-28
Earlier sketch in CA 1-4R
Wolfe, Art 1952- ... 143
See also SATA 76
Wolfe, Barbara (Lea) 1943- ... 149
Wolfe, Bernard 1915-1985 ... CANR-3
Obituary ... 117
Earlier sketch in CA 1-4R
Wolfe, Bertram D(avid) 1896-1977 ... CANR-40
Obituary ... 69-72
Earlier sketch in CA 5-8R
Wolfe, Burton H. 1932- ... 25-28R
See also SATA 5
Wolfe, Charles Keith 1943- ... CANR-34
Earlier sketches in CA 77-80, CANR-15
Wolfe, Christopher (F.) 1949- ... CANR-51
Earlier sketch in CA 123
Wolfe, Don Marion 1902-1976 Obituary ... 65-68
Wolfe, (George) Edgar 1906- ... CAP-2
Earlier sketch in CA 25-28
Wolfe, Elizabeth
See Lederer, Paul Joseph
Wolfe, Gary K(ent) 1946- ... 129
Wolfe, Gene (Rodman) 1931- ... CANR-60
Earlier sketches in CA 57-60, CANR-6, 32
See also CAAS 9
See also CLC 25
See also DAM POP
See also DLB 8
Wolfe, George C. 1954- ... 149
See also BLCS
See also CLC 49
Wolfe, George Willoughby (Hooper) 1894(?)-1983 Obituary ... 111
Wolfe, Gerard R(aymond) 1926- ... CANR-11
Earlier sketch in CA 69-72
Wolfe, Harry Deane 1901-1975 ... 41-44R
Wolfe, Harvey 1938- ... 45-48
Wolfe, Henry C. 1898(?)-1976 Obituary ... 69-72
Wolfe, Herbert S(now) 1898- ... CAP-1
Earlier sketch in CA 13-16
Wolfe, J(ames) N(athan) 1927-1988 Obituary ... 124
Wolfe, James H(astings) 1934- ... 93-96
Wolfe, Jane 1957- ... 133
Wolfe, John fl. 1576-1600 ... DLB 170
Wolfe, John N. 1910(?)-1974 Obituary ... 53-56
Wolfe, Josephine Brace 1917- ... 5-8R
Wolfe, Linda 1935- ... 138
Brief entry ... 129
See also BEST 90:1
Wolfe, Louis 1905- ... CANR-3
Earlier sketch in CA 5-8R
See also SATA 8
Wolfe, Margaret Ripley 1947- ... 128
Wolfe, Martin 1920- ... 37-40R
Wolfe, Michael
See Williams, Gilbert M.
Wolfe, Michael 1945- ... 123
Wolfe, Peter (Bernard) 1929-1986 Obituary ... 121
Wolfe, Peter 1933- ... CANR-8
Earlier sketch in CA 21-24R
Wolfe, Reyner (Reginald) fl. 1543-1573 ... DLB 170
Wolfe, Richard J(ames) 1928- ... CANR-56
Earlier sketches in CA 110, CANR-30
Wolfe, Rinna (Evelyn) 1925- ... 105
See also SATA 38
Wolfe, Ron 1945- ... 109
Wolfe, Roy I. 1917- ... 13-16R
Wolfe, Sidney M(anuel) 1937- ... 127
Wolfe, Thomas (Clayton) 1900-1938 ... 132
Brief entry ... 104
See also CDALB 1929-1941
See also DA
See also DAB
See also DAC
See also DAM MST, NOV
See also DLB 9, 102
See also DLBD 2, 16
See also DLBY 85, 97
See also MTCW 1
See also TCLC 4, 13, 29, 61
See also WLC
Wolfe, Thomas Kennerly, Jr. 1930- ... CANR-70
Earlier sketches in CA 13-16R, CANR-9, 33
Interview in ... CANR-9
See also Wolfe, Tom
See also DAM POP
See also DLB 185
See also MTCW 1
Wolfe, Thomas W. 1914- ... 93-96
Wolfe, Tom
See Wolfe, Thomas Kennerly, Jr.
See also AAYA 8
See also AITN 2
See also BEST 89:1
See also CLC 1, 2, 9, 15, 35, 51
See also DLB 152
Wolfe, (William) Willard 1936- ... 93-96
Wolfe, Winifred 1929-1981 ... CANR-10
Obituary ... 105
Earlier sketch in CA 17-20R
Wolfenden, George
See Beardmore, George
Wolfenden, John Frederick 1906-1985 ... 106
Obituary ... 114
Wolfenstein, E. Victor 1940- ... 21-24R
Wolfenstein, Martha 1911(?)-1976 Obituary ... 69-72
Wolferman, Kristie C(arlson) 1948- ... 154
Wolfers, Michael 1938- ... 136
Wolfert, Helen 1904- ... CAP-2
Earlier sketch in CA 17-18
Wolff, Alexander 1957- ... SATA 63
Wolff, Anthony 1938- ... 49-52
Wolff, (Jenifer) Ashley 1956- ... CANR-56
Earlier sketch in CA 118
See also SATA 50, 81
Wolff, Charlotte 1904-1986 ... CANR-15
Obituary ... 120
Earlier sketch in CA 37-40R
Wolff, Cynthia Griffin 1936- ... 49-52
Wolff, David
See Maddow, Ben
Wolff, Diane 1945- ... 77-80
See also SATA 27
Wolff, Edward N(athan) 1946- ... 132
Wolff, Egon 1926- ... 153
See also HW
Wolff, Ernst 1910- ... 73-76
Wolff, Ferida 1946- ... SATA 79
Wolff, Geoffrey (Ansell) 1937- ... CANR-43
Earlier sketches in CA 29-32R, CANR-29
See also CLC 41
Wolff, Hans Walter 1911- ... 130
Wolff, Helen 1906-1994 ... 117
Obituary ... 144
Brief entry ... 113
Interview in ... 117
See also DLBY 94
Wolff, Janet 1943- ... 77-80
Wolff, Janet L(oeb) 1924- ... 5-8R
Wolff, John U(lrich) 1932- ... CANR-18
Earlier sketch in CA 102
Wolff, Jurgen M(ichael) 1948- ... 57-60
Wolff, Konrad (Martin) 1907-1989 ... 37-40R
Obituary ... 130
Wolff, Kurt H(einrich) 1912- ... CANR-39
Earlier sketches in CA 49-52, CANR-1, 17
Wolff, Maritta 1918- ... 17-20R
Wolff, Mary Evaline 1887-1964 Obituary ... 116
Wolff, Michael 1930- ... CANR-19
Earlier sketch in CA 25-28R
Wolff, Miles 1945- ... CANR-14
Earlier sketch in CA 73-76
Wolff, Milton 1915- ... 146
Wolff, Richard D(avid) 1942- ... 73-76
Wolff, Robert Jay 1905-1977 ... 25-28R
Obituary ... 73-76
See also SATA 10
Wolff, Robert Lee 1915-1980 Obituary ... 102
Wolff, Robert Paul 1933- ... 103
Wolff, Ruth 1909(?)-1972 Obituary ... 37-40R
Wolff, Ruth (Rehrer) 1932- ... 165
Wolff, Sally 1954- ... 166
Wolff, Sonia
See Levitin, Sonia (Wolff)
Wolff, Theodore F. 1926- ... 162
Wolff, Tobias (Jonathan Ansell) 1945- ... CANR-54
Brief entry ... 114
Earlier sketch in CA 117
Interview in ... 117
See also CAAS 22
See also AAYA 16
See also BEST 90:2
See also CLC 39, 64
See also DLB 130
Wolff, Victoria 1910- ... 111
Wolff, Virginia Euwer 1937- ... 107
See also AAYA 26
See also SATA 78
Wolffe, B. P.
See Wolffe, Bertram (Percy)
Wolffe, Bertram (Percy) 1923(?)-1988 Obituary ... 124
Wolff-Salin, Mary 1932- ... 122
Wolfgang, Marvin E(ugene) 1924-1998 ... 5-8R
Obituary ... 167
Wolfinger, Raymond E(dwin) 1931- ... 156
Brief entry ... 112
Wolfle, Dael (Lee) 1906- ... 49-52
Wolfman, Augustus 1908(?)-1974 Obituary ... 53-56
Wolfman, Bernard 1924- ... 41-44R
Wolf-Phillips, Leslie 1929- ... 21-24R
Wolfram, Walter A. 1941- ... 29-32R
Wolfram von Eschenbach c. 1170-c. 1220 ... DLB 138
Wolfskill, George 1921- ... CANR-1
Earlier sketch in CA 1-4R
Wolfson, Evelyn 1937- ... SATA 62

Wolfson, Harry Austryn 1887-1974 .... CAP-2
Obituary 53-56
Earlier sketch in CA 19-20
Wolfson, Max
See Rosenberg, Robert
Wolfson, Murray 1927- 17-20R
Wolfson, P(incus) J. 1903- 5-8R
Wolfson, Randy M(eyers) 1952- 120
Wolfson, Robert J(oseph) 1925- 93-96
Wolfson, Susan 1947- 120
Wolfson, Victor 1910-1990 .... 33-36R
Obituary 131
Wolfthal, Diane (Bette) 1949- 135
Wolgast, Elizabeth H(ankins) 1929- 113
Wolgensinger, Bernard 1935- 37-40R
Wolin, Steven J. 1940- 143
Wolin, Sybil 143
Wolins, Leroy 1927- 107
Woliston, Jack 1916(?)-1990 Obituary 131
Wolitzer, Hilma 1930- CANR-40
Earlier sketches in CA 65-68, CANR-18
Interview in CANR-18
See also CLC 17
See also SATA 31
Wolitzer, Meg 1959- CANR-18
Earlier sketch in CA 107
See also AAYA 6
Wolk, Allan 1936- 77-80
Wolken, Jerome J(ay) 1917- 154
Wolkers, Jan (Hendrik) 1925- Brief entry 116
Wolkoff, Judie (Edwards) 159
Brief entry 115
See also SATA 93
See also SATA-Brief 37
Wolkstein, Diane 1942- CANR-32
Earlier sketches in CA 37-40R, CANR-14
See also SATA 7, 82
Woll, Peter 1933- 13-16R
Wollaston, Nicholas 1926- 25-28R
Wolle, Muriel Sibell 1898- CAP-1
Earlier sketch in CA 13-14
Wollheim, Donald A(llen) 1914-1990 ..... CANR-19
Obituary 135
Earlier sketches in CA 1-4R, CANR-1
See also SATA-Obit 69
Wollheim, Richard Arthur 1923- 101
Wollman, Nathaniel 1915- Brief entry 106
Wollstonecraft, Mary 1759-1797 . CDBLB 1789-1832
See also DLB 39, 104, 158
Wolman, Abel 1892-1989 168
Wolman, Benjamin B. 1908- CANR-11
Earlier sketch in CA 13-16R
Wolman, Harold L. 1942- 37-40R
Wolman, William 1927- 1-4R
Wolny, P.
See Janeczko, Paul B(ryan)
Wolny, P.
See Janeczko, Paul B(ryan)
Woloch, Isser 1937- CANR-12
Earlier sketch in CA 29-32R
Woloszynowski, Julian 1898-1978 Obituary .. 85-88
Wolozin, Harold 1920- 37-40R
Wolpe, Berthold (Ludwig) 1905-1989 Obituary . 129
Wolpe, David J. 1958- 140
Wolpe, Hilda Morley
See Morley (Wolpe), Hilda
Wolpe, Joseph 1915-1997 .... 17-20R
Obituary 163
Wolpert, Stanley A(lbert) 1927- CANR-15
Earlier sketch in CA 21-24R
Wolrige Gordon, Anne 1936- 103
Wolsch, Robert Allen 1925- 57-60
Wolseley, Roland E. 1904- CANR-39
Earlier sketches in CA 1-4R, CANR-1, 17
Wolsk, David 1930- 21-24R
Wolstein, Benjamin 1922- 9-12R
Wolter, Allan B(ernard) 1913- 106
Wolters, O(liver) W(illiam) 1915- 21-24R
Wolters, Raymond 1938- 29-32R
Wolters, Richard A. 1920-1993 .... CANR-18
Obituary 143
Earlier sketches in CA 5-8R, CANR-3
See also SATA 35
Wolterstorff, Nicholas (Paul) 1932- CANR-44
Earlier sketch in CA 69-72
Woltman, Frederick (Enos)
1905-1970 Obituary 89-92
Wolton, Thierry 1951- 166
Wolverton, Dave 1957- 166
Wolverton, Robert E(arl) 1925- 37-40R
Wolverton, Terry 1954- CANR-70
Earlier sketch in CA 150
Wolz, Henry G(eorge) 1905- 106
Womack, Brantly 1947- 114
Womack, David A(lfred) 1933- CANR-7
Earlier sketch in CA 53-56
Womack, Don (L.) 1922- 25-28R
Womack, Jack 1956- 141
Womack, John, Jr. 1937- 45-48
Womack, Peter 1952- CANR-60
Earlier sketch in CA 128
Womack, Steven (James) 1952- CANR-72
Earlier sketch in CA 133
Womack, Thomas Hale 1952- 133
Womble, Vernon G. 1942(?)-1979 Obituary .. 89-92
Womer, Frank B(urton) 1921- 45-48
Womersley, Peter (John Walter) 1941- 118
Won, Ko
See Ko, Won
Wonder, Alvin
See Lourie, Dick
Wonder, Stevie
See Morris, Steveland Judkins
See also CLC 12
Wonders, Anne
See Passel, Anne W(onders)
Wonders, William C(lare) 1924- 41-44R
Wondratschek, Wolf 1943- .... DLB 75
Wondriska, William 1931- CANR-4
Earlier sketch in CA 1-4R
See also SATA 6
Wong, Baoswan Dzung
See Dzung Wong, Baoswan
Wong, Bing W. 1922- 73-76
Wong, J(ohn) Y(ue-Wo) 1946- 126
Wong, Jade Snow 1922- 109
See also CLC 17
Wong, Janet S. 1962- 166
See also SATA 98
Wong, Lin Ken 1931- 13-16R
Wong, May 1944- 25-28R
Wong, Molly 1920- 93-96
Wong, Norman 1963- 168
Wong, Roderick 1932- 65-68
Wong, Shawn (Hsu) 1949- 162
Wonnacott, Paul 1933- 21-24R
Wonnacott, Ronald J(ohnston) 1930- CANR-14
Earlier sketch in CA 29-32R
Wonnacott, Thomas H(erbert) 1935- CANR-14
Earlier sketch in CA 45-48
Wood, A(rthur) Skevington 1916- CANR-40
Earlier sketches in CA 9-12R, CANR-3, 18
Wood, Abigail
See Marks, Jane (A. Steinberg)
Wood, Addie Robinson
See Wiggin, Eric E(llsworth)
Wood, Allen Tate 1947- 97-100
Wood, Allen W(illiam) 1942- CANR-37
Earlier sketches in CA 29-32R, CANR-17
Wood, Ann
See Douglas, Ann
Wood, Ann Douglas
See Douglas, Ann
Wood, Anne (Savage) 1937- .... SATA 64
Wood, Audrey 137
See also CLR 26
See also MAICYA
See also SATA 50, 81
See also SATA-Brief 44
Wood, Audrey 1905-1985 .... CANR-56
Obituary 118
Earlier sketch in CA 153
Wood, Barbara 1947- CANR-44
Earlier sketches in CA 85-88, CANR-15
Wood, Bari 1936- CANR-50
Earlier sketches in CA 81-84, CANR-13
Interview in CANR-13
Wood, Barry 1940- CANR-36
Earlier sketch in CA 29-32R
Wood, Benjamin 1820-1900 Brief entry 120
See also DLB 23
Wood, Bridget 1947- 155
Wood, Bruce 1943- 57-60
Wood, Bryce 1909-1985(?) CANR-19
Earlier sketch in CA 1-4R
Wood, Catherine
See Etchison, Birdie L(ee)
Wood, Charles Gerald 1932- 106
See also DLB 13
Wood, Charles Monroe 1944- 125
Wood, Charles Osgood III 1933- 109
Interview in 109
Wood, Charles T(uttle) 1933- CANR-30
Earlier sketch in CA 17-20R
Wood, Chauncey 1935- 37-40R
Wood, Christopher (Hovelle) 1935- CANR-43
Earlier sketch in CA 29-32R
Wood, Christopher 1941- CANR-36
Earlier sketch in CA 103
Wood, Clement Biddle 1925-1994 .... 21-24R
Obituary 147
Wood, Curtis W(illiam), Jr. 1941- 167
Wood, David 1944- CANR-52
Earlier sketch in CA 97-100
See also SATA 87
Wood, David (Bowne) 1945- 93-96
Wood, David G. 1919- 126
Wood, David M(ichael) 1934- Brief entry 109
Wood, Dennis (Michael) 1947- 143
Wood, Derek Harold 1930- CANR-16
Earlier sketch in CA 93-96
Wood, Don 1945- 136
See also CLR 26
See also MAICYA
See also SATA 50
See also SATA-Brief 44
Wood, Donald 1926- 45-48
Wood, Donna (Marie) 1949- CANR-41
Earlier sketches in CA 97-100, CANR-18
Wood, Dorothy Adkins 1912-1975 .... CANR-6
Earlier sketch in CA 13-16R
Wood, Douglas (Eric) 1951- 149
See also SATA 81
Wood, E(dward) Rudolf 1907- CANR-3
Earlier sketch in CA 9-12R
Wood, Edgar A(llardyce) 1907- 77-80
See also SATA 14
Wood, Edward John 1931- CANR-68
Earlier sketch in CA 141
Wood, Elizabeth A(rmstrong) 1912- CANR-30
Earlier sketch in CA 25-28R
Wood, Esther
See Brady, Esther Wood
Wood, Forrest G(len) 1931- 25-28R
Wood, Frances Elizabeth 107
See also SATA 34
Wood, Frances M. 1951- 164
See also SATA 97
Wood, Fred M. 1921- CANR-26
Earlier sketches in CA 13-16R, CANR-10
Wood, Frederic C(onger), Jr. 1932-1970 .... CAP-2
Earlier sketch in CA 25-28
Wood, Frederick Thomas 1905- CANR-5
Earlier sketch in CA 5-8R
Wood, G(eorge) R(obert) Harding 1878-1968 ......
CAP-1
Earlier sketch in CA 9-10
Wood, Gordon R(eid) 1913- 77-80
Wood, Gordon S(tewart) 1933- 25-28R
Wood, Harley Weston 1911- 109
Wood, Harold A(rthur) 1921- 17-20R
Wood, (Elizabeth) Harriet Harvey
See Harvey Wood, (Elizabeth) Harriet
Wood, Herbert Fairlie 1914-1967 110
Obituary 108
Wood, Ian N(icholas) 1950- 145
Wood, (David) Ira 1950- 142
Wood, J(ohn) Howard 1901-1988 Obituary 127
Wood, James 1889(?)-1975 Obituary 57-60
Wood, James (Alexander Fraser) 1918-1984 ......
CANR-16
Earlier sketches in CA 1-4R, CANR-1
Wood, James E(dward), Jr. 1922- CANR-28
Earlier sketches in CA 29-32R, CANR-12
Wood, James L(eslie) 1941- CANR-8
Earlier sketch in CA 57-60
Wood, James Playsted 1905- CANR-3
Earlier sketch in CA 9-12R
See also SATA 1
Wood, Janet L(ouise) Sims
See Sims-Wood, Janet L(ouise)
Wood, Jenny 1955- .... SATA 88
Wood, Joanna E. 1867-1927 .... DLB 92
Wood, John 1947- 136
Wood, John A(rmstead, Jr.) 1932- 125
Brief entry 108
Wood, John C(unningham) 1952- 133
Wood, John Norris 1930- .... SATA 85
Wood, John Thomas 1939- 77-80
Wood, Jonathan 1945- 128
Wood, Joyce 1928- 25-28R
Wood, June Rae 1946- .... SATA 79
Wood, June S(mallwood) 1931- 61-64
Wood, Kenneth 1922- CANR-26
Earlier sketches in CA 69-72, CANR-11
Wood, Kerry
See Wood, Edgar A(llardyce)
Wood, Kirk
See Stahl, Le Roy
Wood, Lana 1946- 139
Wood, Larry
See Wood, Marylaird
Wood, Laura N.
See Roper, Laura Wood
Wood, Lee Blair 1893-1982 Obituary 106
Wood, Leland Foster 1885- 1-4R
Wood, Leon J(ames) 1918-1976 .... CANR-26
Earlier sketch in CA 29-32R
Wood, Leonard C(lair) 1923- 37-40R
Wood, Leslie A(lfred) 1930- 29-32R
Wood, (James) Lew(is) 1928- 65-68
Wood, Linda C(arol) 1945- 110
See also SATA 59
Wood, Lorna 1913- 69-72
Wood, Marcia (Mae) 1956- 148
See also SATA 80
Wood, Margaret (Lucy Elizabeth) 1910- .. CANR-42
Earlier sketch in CA 13-16R
Wood, Margaret I(sabel) 1926- 97-100
Wood, Marion N(ewman) 1909- 61-64
Wood, Mary 1915- 21-24R
Wood, Marylaird CANR-21
Earlier sketch in CA 81-84
Wood, Maurice Arthur Ponsonby 1916- 109
Wood, Michael 1936- CANR-53
Earlier sketch in CA 37-40R
Wood, Monica 1953- 141
Wood, Mrs. Henry 1814-1887 .... DLB 18
Wood, N. Lee 167
Wood, Nancy 1936- CANR-9
Earlier sketch in CA 21-24R
See also SATA 6
Wood, Neal (Norman) 1922- 1-4R
Wood, Nuria
See Nobisso, Josephine
Wood, Owen 1929- .... SATA 64
Wood, Pat
See Baxter, Patricia E. W.
Wood, Paul W(inthrop) 1922- 61-64
Wood, Peggy 1892-1978 Obituary 77-80
Wood, Peter 1930- 93-96
Wood, Peter Weston 1953- 125
Wood, Phyllis Anderson 1923- CANR-43
Earlier sketches in CA 37-40R, CANR-14
See also SATA 33
See also SATA-Brief 30
Wood, R(ichard) Coke 1905-1979 .... CANR-7
Earlier sketch in CA 53-56
Wood, Ralph C. 1942- 145
Wood, Ramsay 1943- 103
Wood, Raymund F(rancis) 1911- 61-64
Wood, Robert Chapman 1949- 139
Wood, Robert Coldwell 1923- CANR-43
Earlier sketch in CA 1-4R
Wood, Robert L. 1925- 21-24R
Wood, Robert Paul 1931- CANR-5
Earlier sketch in CA 53-56
Wood, Robert S(tephen) 1938- CANR-7
Earlier sketch in CA 57-60
Wood, Robin
See Wood, Robert Paul
Wood, Ruth C. 37-40R
Wood, Ruzena (Alenka Valda) 1937- 135
Wood, Sally Sayward Barrell Keating
1759-1855 .... DLB 200
Wood, Sara
See Bowen-Judd, Sara (Hutton)
Wood, Serry
See Freeman, G(raydon) L(a Verne)
Wood, Susan 1946- 108
Wood, Susan Macduff 1941- 132
Wood, Sydney (Herbert) 1935- CANR-60
Earlier sketches in CA 112, CANR-31
Wood, Ted
See Wood, Edward John
Wood, Thomas W(esley), Jr. 1920- 81-84
Wood, Tim(othy William Russell) 1946- ... SATA 88
Wood, Ursula
See Vaughan Williams, Ursula Wood
Wood, W(illiam) J. 1917- 135
Wood, Wallace 1927-1981 Obituary 108
See also SATA-Obit 33
Wood, Walter Hunt Sr. 1916(?)-1987 Obituary .. 124
Wood, William .... DLB 24
Wood, William P(reston) 1951- CANR-42
Earlier sketch in CA 118
Woodall, Corbet 1929(?)-1982 Obituary 106
Woodall, Mary 1901-1988 Obituary 125
Woodall, Ronald 1935- 73-76
Woodard, Bronte 1941(?)-1980 Obituary 101
Woodard, Carol 1929- 73-76
See also SATA 14
Woodard, Christopher R. 1913- 13-16R
Woodard, Gloria (Jean) H(iner) 1937- 45-48
Woodberry, George Edward 1855-1930 165
See also DLB 71, 103
See also TCLC 73
Woodberry, Joan (Merle) 1921- CANR-6
Earlier sketch in CA 9-12R
Woodbridge, Benjamin 1622-1684 .... DLB 24
Woodbridge, Hensley Charles 1923- CANR-3
Earlier sketch in CA 9-12R
Woodbridge, Kenneth 1910- 127
Woodbridge, Linda 1945- 118
Woodbridge, Sally
See Woodbridge, Sally B(yrne)
Woodbridge, Sally B(yrne) 1930- CANR-67
Earlier sketch in CA 129
Woodburn, Arthur 1890-1978 Obituary 108
Woodburn, John Henry 1914- CANR-4
Earlier sketch in CA 1-4R
See also SATA 11
Woodbury, David Oakes 1896-1981 ...... SATA 62
Woodbury, Frank
See Chapman, Frank M(onroe)
Woodbury, Lael J(ay) 1927- 81-84
Woodbury, Marda 1925- CANR-17
Earlier sketch in CA 97-100
Woodbury, Mildred Fairchild
1894-1975 Obituary 57-60
Woodbury, Richard B(enjamin) 1917- Brief
entry 109
Woodcock, Bruce 1948- 119
Woodcock, George 1912-1995 .... CANR-1
Obituary 147
Earlier sketch in CA 1-4R
See also CAAS 6
See also DLB 88
Woodcott, Keith
See Brunner, John (Kilian Houston)
Wooden, Kenneth 1935- 81-84
Wooden, Warren W(alter) 1941-1983 132
Wooden, Wayne S(tanley) 1943- 109
Woodfield, William Read 1928- 9-12R
Woodford, Arthur M(acKinnon) 1940- CANR-7
Earlier sketch in CA 53-56
Woodford, Bruce P(owers) 1919- 57-60
Woodford, Frank B(ury) 1903-1967 .... CAP-1
Earlier sketch in CA 13-16
Woodford, Jack
See Woolfolk, Josiah Pitts
Woodford, Peggy 1937- 104
See also SATA 25
Woodford, Susan 1938- 128
Woodforde, John 1925- CANR-10
Earlier sketch in CA 25-28R
Woodgate, Mildred Violet 9-12R
Woodham-Smith, Cecil (Blanche Fitzgerald)
1896-1977 77-80
Obituary 69-72
Woodhead, Leslie 1937- 128
Woodhead, Peter 1944- 124
Woodhouse, Barbara (Blackburn) 1910-1988 ......
CANR-30
Obituary 126
Earlier sketches in CA 5-8R, CANR-13
See also SATA 63
Woodhouse, C(hristopher) M(ontague) 1917- ... 155
Brief entry 108
Woodhouse, Charles Platten 1915- 105
Woodhouse, Edward J(ames) 1946- 117
Woodhouse, Emma
See Harrod-Eagles, Cynthia
Woodhouse, Martin (Charlton) 1932- CANR-16
Earlier sketch in CA 21-24R
Woodhouse, Sarah 160
Woodhull, Victoria C. 1838-1927 .... DLB 79
Woodhull, Winifred 1950- 146
Woodin, Ann Snow 1926- 13-16R
Woodin, Noel 1929- 1-4R
Wooding, Dan 1940- 102
Wooding, Sharon
See Wooding, Sharon L(ouise)
Wooding, Sharon L(ouise) 1943- 136
See also SATA 66
Woodiwiss, Kathleen E(rin) 1939- CANR-41
Earlier sketches in CA 89-92, CANR-23
Interview in CANR-23
See also BEST 90:1
See also DAM POP
See also MTCW 1
Wood-Legh, Kathleen Louise
1901-1981 Obituary 105

Woodley, Winifred
See Hedden, Worth Tuttle
Woodman, Allen 1954- ... 143
See also SATA 76
Woodman, Anthony John 1945- ... CANR-23
Earlier sketches in CA 61-64, CANR-8
Woodman, Bill
See Woodman, William
Woodman, David C(harles) 1956- ... 141
Woodman, Harold D. 1928- ... CANR-9
Earlier sketch in CA 21-24R
Woodman, James Monroe 1931- ... 17-20R
Woodman, Jim
See Woodman, James Monroe
Woodman, John E. 1932(?)-1983 Obituary ... 109
Woodman, Loring 1942- ... 45-48
Woodman, Marion (Boa) 1928- ... 162
Woodman, Richard 1944- ... 132
Woodman, William 1936- ... 125
Woodmason, Charles 1720(?)-(?) ... DLB 31
Woodrell, Daniel 1953- ... CANR-46
Earlier sketch in CA 121
Woodress, James (Leslie, Jr.) 1916- ... CANR-3
Earlier sketch in CA 5-8R
See also DLB 111
Woodrew, Greta 1930- ... 106
Woodrich, Mary Neville 1915- ... 25-28R
See also SATA 2
Woodring, Carl (Ray) 1919- ... 5-8R
Woodring, Paul (Dean) 1907- ... 17-20R
Woodrock, R. A.
See Cowlishaw, Ranson
Woodroffe, John
See Woodroffe, John George
Woodroffe, John George 1865-1936 Brief entry ... 121
Woodroof, Horace M(alcolm) 1906- ... CAP-2
Earlier sketch in CA 29-32
Woodruff, Archibald Mulford, Jr. 1912-1984 ... 105
Obituary ... 113
Woodruff, Asahel D(avis) 1904- ... 1-4R
Woodruff, Elvira 1951- ... 138
See also SATA 70
Woodruff, J(ohn) Douglas 1897-1978 ... 107
Woodruff, John Douglas 1897-1978 Obituary ... 104
Woodruff, Judy (Carline) 1946- ... CANR-13
Earlier sketch in CA 73-76
Woodruff, Marian
See Goudge, Eileen
Woodruff, Marian
See Goudge, Eileen
Woodruff, Noah 1977- ... SATA 86
Woodruff, Philip
See Mason, Philip
Woodruff, Robert W.
See Mencken, H(enry) L(ouis)
Woodruff, Sue (Carolyn) 1943- ... 117
Woodruff, William 1916- ... 101
Woodrum, Lon 1901- ... 104
Woods, B(obby) W(illiam) 1930- ... CANR-19
Earlier sketch in CA 25-28R
Woods, Clee 1893- ... 108
Woods, Constance
See McComb, K(atherine Woods)
Woods, Donald 1933- ... 121
Brief entry ... 114
Interview in ... 121
Woods, Donald H. 1933- ... 25-28R
Woods, Earl 1932- ... 161
Woods, Elizabeth 1940- ... 101
Woods, Frederick 1932- ... CANR-7
Earlier sketch in CA 17-20R
Woods, George A(llan) 1926-1988 ... 29-32R
Obituary ... 126
See also SATA 30
See also SATA-Obit 57
Woods, Geraldine 1948- ... 97-100
See also SATA 56
See also SATA-Brief 42
Woods, Gerard
See Bosch, Henry G(erard)
Woods, Gregory 1953- ... 129
Woods, Harold 1945- ... 97-100
See also SATA 56
See also SATA-Brief 42
Woods, James M. 1952- ... 125
Woods, Jeannie Marlin 1947- ... 145
Woods, Joan (LeSueur) 1932- ... 9-12R
Woods, John 1926- ... CANR-23
Earlier sketch in CA 13-16R
Woods, John (Hayden) 1937- ... CANR-11
Earlier sketch in CA 57-60
Woods, John A(ubin) 1927- ... 13-16R
Woods, John B(arrie) 1933- Brief entry ... 107
Woods, John David 1939- ... 37-40R
Woods, John E(dmund) 1938- ... 104
Woods, Kenneth F. 1930- ... 13-16R
Woods, L. B. 1938- ... 112
Woods, L(awrence) Milton 1932- ... 127
Woods, Lawrence
See Lowndes, Robert A(ugustine) W(ard)
Woods, Lawrence T(imothy) 1960- ... 147
Woods, Margaret 1921- ... 21-24R
See also SATA 2
Woods, Margaret S(taeger) 1911- ... CANR-44
Earlier sketch in CA 81-84
Woods, Michael 1952- ... 137
Woods, Nat
See Stratemeyer, Edward L.
Woods, Oliver (Frederick John Bradley) 1911-1972 Obituary ... 114
Woods, P. F.
See Bayley, Barrington J(ohn)
Woods, Pamela 1938- ... 106
Woods, Paula L. 1953- ... 146
Woods, Ralph L(ouis) 1904- ... CANR-2
Earlier sketch in CA 5-8R
Woods, Randall Bennett 1944- Brief entry ... 106
Woods, Richard (John) 1941- ... CANR-4
Earlier sketch in CA 53-56
Woods, Richard G(lenn) 1933- ... 109
Woods, Samuel H(ubert), Jr. 1926- ... 25-28R
Woods, Sara
See Bowen-Judd, Sara (Hutton)
Woods, Shadrach 1923-1973 Obituary ... 45-48
Woods, Sharon 1949- ... 125
Woods, Sherryl 1944- ... CANR-65
Earlier sketch in CA 120
Woods, Shirley E(dwards), Jr. 1934- ... 119
Woods, Sister Frances Jerome 1913- ... 21-24R
Woods, Stockton
See Forrest, Richard (Stockton)
Woods, Stuart 1938- ... CANR-72
Earlier sketch in CA 93-96
Woods, William 1916- ... CANR-43
Earlier sketch in CA 77-80
Woods, William Crawford 1944- ... 29-32R
Woodside, Alexander Barton 1938- ... CANR-51
Earlier sketch in CA 123
Woodson, Carter G(odwin) 1875-1950 ... 141
See also BW 2
See also DLB 17
Woodson, Jack
See Woodson, John Waddie Jr.
Woodson, Jacqueline 1964- ... 159
See also CLR 49
Woodson, Jeff
See Oglesby, Joseph
Woodson, John Waddie Jr. 1913- ... SATA 10
Woodson, Leslie H(arold) 1929- ... 41-44R
Woodson, Meg
See Baker, Elsie
Woodson, Robert L. 1937- ... 127
Woodson, Thomas (Miller) 1931- ... 104
Woodson, Wesley E(dward) 1918- ... 37-40R
Woodstone, Arthur ... 69-72
Woodstra, Christopher 1969- ... 145
Woodtor, Dee Parmer ... 158
See also SATA 93
Woodward, Bob
See Woodward, Robert Upshur
Woodward, C. Hendrika
See Woodward, Caroline (Hendrika)
Woodward, C(omer) Vann 1908- ... CANR-44
Earlier sketches in CA 5-8R, CANR-2, 17
See also DLB 17
Woodward, Carl Raymond 1890-1974 ... 41-44R
Woodward, Caroline (Hendrika) 1952- ... 146
Woodward, (Landon) Cleveland 1900-1986 .. SATA 10
See also SATA-Obit 48
Woodward, Daniel Holt 1931- ... 37-40R
Woodward, David 1909-1986 Obituary ... 120
Woodward, David B(rainerd) 1918- ... 65-68
Woodward, David Reid 1939- ... 114
Woodward, Douglas P. 1954- ... 135
Woodward, E. L.
See Woodward, Ernest Llewellyn
Woodward, Ernest Llewellyn 1890-1971 Obituary ... 111
Woodward, G(eorge) W(illiam) O(tway) 1924- ... CANR-3
Earlier sketch in CA 5-8R
Woodward, Grace Steele 1899- ... CAP-1
Earlier sketch in CA 9-10
Woodward, Helen Beal 1914(?)-1982 Obituary . 108
Woodward, Helen Rosen 1882- ... 5-8R
Woodward, Herbert N(orton) 1911- ... 65-68
Woodward, Hildegard 1898- ... 5-8R
Woodward, James B(rian) 1935- ... CANR-2
Earlier sketch in CA 49-52
Woodward, John (William) 1920- ... 21-24R
Woodward, John (O.) 1922(?)-1988 Obituary ... 125
Woodward, John 1945- ... 113
Woodward, John Forster
See Woodward, Sandy
Woodward, Kenneth L. 1935- ... 141
Woodward, Lilian
See Marsh, John
Woodward, Llewellyn
See Woodward, Ernest Llewellyn
Woodward, Margaret E. 1950- ... 150
Woodward, Ralph Lee, Jr. 1934- ... 21-24R
Woodward, Robert B(urns) 1917-1979 ... 161
Woodward, Robert H(anson) 1925- ... 17-20R
Woodward, Robert Upshur 1943- ... CANR-67
Earlier sketches in CA 69-72, CANR-31
See also MTCW 1
Woodward, Sandy 1932- ... 143
Woodward, Stanley (Wingate) 1890- ... 5-8R
See also DLB 171
Woodward, Thomas B. 1937- ... 114
Woodward, W. Mary 1921- ... 45-48
Woodwell, George M. 1928- ... 142
Woodworth, Constance 1911-1983 Obituary ... 109
Woodworth, David (Perrin) 1932- ... 37-40R
Woodworth, G(eorge) Wallace 1902-1969 .. CAP-1
Earlier sketch in CA 13-16
Woodworth, G(eorge) Walter 1903- ... CAP-1
Earlier sketch in CA 19-20
Woodworth, Hugh (MacCallum) 1906-1978 Obituary ... 107
Woodworth, Steven E(dward) 1961- ... 135
Woody, Elizabeth 1959- ... 152
Woody, Regina Jones 1894- ... CANR-3
Earlier sketch in CA 5-8R
See also SATA 3
Woody, Robert H(enley) 1936- ... 93-96
Woody, Russell O(wen), Jr. 1934- ... 17-20R
Woodyard, David O. 1932- ... 21-24R
Woodyard, George 1934- ... 81-84
Woog, Adam 1953- ... 150
See also SATA 84
Woog, Dan 1953- ... 167
Woolard, Edgar 1899(?)-1978 Obituary ... 77-80
Wooldridge, Adrian 1959- ... 152
Wooldridge, Connie Nordhielm 1950- ... 156
See also SATA 92
Wooldridge, Rhoda 1906- ... 77-80
See also SATA 22
Wooldridge, William C(harles) 1943- ... CANR-25
Earlier sketch in CA 45-48
Wooler, Thomas 1785(?)-1853 ... DLB 158
Woolery, George W(illiam) 1931- ... CANR-49
Earlier sketch in CA 122
Wooley, John (Steven) 1949- ... 109
Woolf, Daniel J(ames) 1916- ... 5-8R
Woolf, Douglas 1922- ... CANR-2
Earlier sketch in CA 1-4R
Woolf, F. X.
See Engel, Howard
Woolf, Harry 1923- ... CANR-1
Earlier sketch in CA 1-4R
Woolf, James Dudley 1914- ... 37-40R
Woolf, Leonard S(idney) 1880-1969 ... CANR-39
Obituary ... 25-28R
Earlier sketch in CA 5-8R
See also DLB 100
See also DLBD 10
Woolf, Robert G(ary) 1928- ... 73-76
Woolf, S. J.
See Woolf, Stuart J(oseph)
Woolf, Stuart J(oseph) 1936- ... 153
Brief entry ... 118
Woolf, (Adeline) Virginia 1882-1941 ... CANR-64
Brief entry ... 104
Earlier sketch in CA 130
See also CDBLB 1914-1945
See also DA
See also DAB
See also DAC
See also DAM MST, NOV
See also DLB 36, 100, 162
See also DLBD 10
See also MTCW 1
See also SSC 7
See also TCLC 1, 5, 20, 43, 56
See also WLC
Woolf, Virginia Adeline
See Woolf, (Adeline) Virginia
Woolfe, H(arold) Geoffrey 1902- ... CAP-1
Earlier sketch in CA 11-12
Woolfe, Jennifer A(nne) 1944- ... 144
Woolfe, Sue 1950- ... 165
Woolfenden, John R(ichards) 1904- ... 113
Woolfolk, Joanna Martine 1940- ... 110
Woolfolk, Josiah Pitts 1894-1971 Obituary .. 29-32R
Woolfolk, Robert L(ee IV) 1947- Brief entry ... 112
Woolfolk, William 1917- ... 113
Woolgar, (George) Jack 1894- ... 17-20R
Woollam, William Gifford 1921- ... 9-12R
Woollcott, Alexander (Humphreys) 1887-1943 .. 161
Brief entry ... 105
See also DLB 29
See also TCLC 5
Woollen, Geoff 1945- ... 142
Woolley, A(lban) E(dward, Jr.) 1926- ... CANR-14
Earlier sketch in CA 41-44R
Woolley, (Lowell) Bryan 1937- ... CANR-4
Earlier sketch in CA 49-52
Woolley, Catherine 1904- ... CANR-6
Earlier sketch in CA 1-4R
See also SATA 3
Woolley, Davis Collier 1908-1971 Obituary ... 116
Woolley, Geoffrey Harold 1892-1968 ... CAP-1
Earlier sketch in CA 11-12
Woolley, Herbert B(allantyne) 1917-1978 Obituary ... 81-84
Woolley, Paul 1948- ... 146
Woolley, Richard van der Riet 1906-1986 Obituary ... 121
Woolley, Robert (C.) 1944- ... 152
Woolley, (Alfred) Russell 1899- ... 5-8R
Woolls, (Esther) Blanche 1935- ... CANR-39
Earlier sketch in CA 126
Woolman, David S. 1916- ... 29-32R
Woolman, John 1720-1772 ... DLB 31
Woolman, Steven 1969- ... SATA 90
Woolner, Frank 1916- ... 53-56
Woolner, Thomas 1825-1892 ... DLB 35
Woolrich, Cornell 1903-1968
See Hopley-Woolrich, Cornell George
See also CLC 77
Woolrych, Austin (Herbert) 1918- ... CANR-42
Earlier sketch in CA 1-4R
Woolsey, Arthur (Wallace) 1906- ... 45-48
Woolsey, Janette 1904- ... CANR-2
Earlier sketch in CA 1-4R
See also SATA 3
Woolsey, Sarah Chauncy 1835(?)-1905 Brief entry ... 115
See also DLB 42
Woolson, Constance Fenimore 1840-1894 . DLB 12, 74, 189
Woolson, Roland S., Jr. 1930(?)-1977 Obituary . 104
Woolverton, John F(rederick) 1926- ... 158
Woon, Basil 1894(?)-1974 Obituary ... 49-52
Wooster, Claire 1942- ... 101
Wooster, Ralph A(ncil) 1928- ... CANR-2
Earlier sketch in CA 5-8R
Wooster, Robert 1956- ... 124
Wooten, James (Terrell) 1937- Brief entry ... 112
Wootten, Morgan 1931- ... 101
Wootters, John (Henry, Jr.) 1928- ... CANR-43
Earlier sketch in CA 113
Wootton, Anthony 1935- ... 129
Wootton, Barbara (Frances Adam) 1897-1988 Obituary ... 126
Wootton, (Devere) Gareth 1937- ... 117
Wootton, (John) Graham (George) 1917- CANR-10
Earlier sketch in CA 5-8R
Worblefister, Petunia
See Gribbin, Lenore S.
Worboys, Anne(tte Isobel) Eyre ... CANR-60
Earlier sketches in CA 65-68, CANR-9
Worcester, Dean A(mory), Jr. 1918- ... 21-24R
Worcester, Donald E(mmet) 1915- ... CANR-19
Earlier sketches in CA 1-4R, CANR-4
See also SATA 18
Worcester, Gurdon Saltonstall 1897- ... CAP-1
Earlier sketch in CA 11-12
Worcester, Joseph Emerson 1784-1865 ... DLB 1
Worcester, Kent 1959- ... 157
Worcester, Robert (Milton) 1933- ... 134
Worchel, Stephen 1946- ... CANR-37
Earlier sketches in CA 89-92, CANR-16
Worden, Alfred M(errill) 1932- ... 101
Worden, J. William ... 168
Worden, William L. 1910- ... CAP-1
Earlier sketch in CA 13-16
Wordsworth, Christopher 1807-1885 ... DLB 166
Wordsworth, Dorothy 1771-1855 ... DLB 107
Wordsworth, Elizabeth 1840-1932 ... DLB 98
Wordsworth, Jonathan 1932- ... CANR-20
Earlier sketch in CA 29-32R
Wordsworth, William 1770-1850 . CDBLB 1789-1832
See also DA
See also DAB
See also DAC
See also DAM MST, POET
See also DLB 93, 107
See also PC 4
See also WLC
Worell, Judith 1928- ... CANR-7
Earlier sketch in CA 57-60
Work, Alison R. 1956- ... 128
Work, Robert E. 1928(?)-1986 Obituary ... 121
Work, Virginia 1946- ... 113
See also SATA 57
See also SATA-Brief 45
Working, Russell (Craig) 1959- ... 124
Workman, Fanny Bullock 1859-1925 ... DLB 189
Workman, Samuel K(linger) 1907- ... CAP-2
Earlier sketch in CA 23-24
Workman, William D(ouglas), Jr. 1914- ... 5-8R
Works, John 1949- ... 123
Worland, Stephen T. 1923- ... 21-24R
Worley, Robert Cromwell 1929- Brief entry ... 108
Worline, Bonnie Bess 1914- ... 69-72
See also SATA 14
Worlock, Derek John Harford 1920-1996 ... 103
Obituary ... 151
Worm, Piet 1909- ... 81-84
Wormald, Francis 1904(?)-1972 Obituary ... 104
Wormald, Jenny 1942- ... CANR-32
Earlier sketch in CA 112
Wormald, (Charles) Patrick 1947- ... 132
Worman, Charles G(ordon) 1933- ... 119
Worman, Eli
See Weil, Roman L(ee)
Wormell, Deborah 1946-1979 Obituary ... 114
Wormell, Mary 1959- ... 148
See also SATA 96
Wormington, Hannah Marie 1914-1994 ... CANR-3
Obituary ... 145
Earlier sketch in CA 45-48
Wormley, Cinda
See Kornblum, Cinda
Wormley, Stanton Lawrence 1909-1993 . CANR-12
Obituary ... 142
Earlier sketch in CA 73-76
Wormser, Baron Chesley 1948- ... 110
Wormser, Rene A(lbert) 1896-1981 ... CANR-11
Obituary ... 104
Earlier sketch in CA 13-16R
Wormser, Richard 1933- ... SAAS 26
Wormser, Sophie 1897- ... 65-68
See also SATA 22
Worner, Karl Heinrich
See Woerner, Karl Heinrich
Woroniak, Alexander 1920- ... 41-44R
Woronoff, Jon 1938- ... CANR-29
Earlier sketches in CA 29-32R, CANR-11
Woronov, Mary 1946- ... 149
Woronov, Naomi 1938- ... 132
Worrall, Ambrose A(lexander) 1899-1972 ... CAP-2
Earlier sketch in CA 29-32
Worrall, Olga (Nathalie) 1906- ... 29-32R
Worrell, Albert C(adwallader) 1913- ... 37-40R
Worrell, Eric 1924-1987 Obituary ... 123
Worrell, Rupert DeLisle 1945- ... 146
Worrick, Roberta 1941-1989 Obituary ... 129
Worsley, Dale 1948- ... 104
Worsley, Gump
See Worsley, Lorne (John)
Worsley, Lorne (John) 1929- Brief entry ... 111
Worster, Donald E(ugene) 1941- ... CANR-42
Earlier sketches in CA 57-60, CANR-12
Worsthorne, Peregrine 1923- ... 45-48
Worswick, Clark 1940- ... CANR-43
Earlier sketch in CA 104
Worswick, G(eorge) D(avid) N(orman) 1916- ... 142
Worth, C. Brooke 1908- ... 101
Worth, Dean S(toddard) 1927- Brief entry ... 112
Worth, Douglas 1940- ... CANR-9
Earlier sketch in CA 65-68
Worth, Fred L. 1943- ... 97-100
Worth, Helen 1913- ... 13-16R
Worth, Katharine (Joyce) 1922- ... 161
Worth, Katherine J.
See Worth, Katharine (Joyce)

Worth, Margaret
See Strickland, Margot
Worth, Richard 156
Worth, Richard
See Wiggin, Eric E(llsworth)
Worth, Richard 1945- .... SATA 59
See also SATA-Brief 46
Worth, Sol 1922(?)-1977 81-84
Obituary 73-76
Worth, Valerie
See Bahlke, Valerie Worth
See also CLR 21
See also MAICYA
See also SATA 8, 70
Wortham, John David 1941- 37-40R
Worthen, Blaine Richard 1936- CANR-15
Earlier sketch in CA 85-88
Worthington, Edgar Barton 1905- 109
Worthington, Janet Evans 1942- 115
Worthington, Marjorie (Muir) 1898(?)-1976 . CANR-2
Obituary 65-68
Earlier sketch in CA 1-4R
Worthington, Phoebe 1910- .... SATA-Brief 52
Worthington, Robin (Ann) 1932- 114
Worthley, Jean Reese 1925- 77-80
Worthy, James C(arson) 1910- 117
Worthy, Morgan 1936- 65-68
Worthylake, Mary Moore 1904- CANR-4
Earlier sketch in CA 1-4R
Wortis, Avi 1937- CANR-42
Earlier sketches in CA 69-72, CANR-12
See also Avi
See also JRDA
See also MAICYA
See also SATA 14
Wortley, Ben Atkinson 1907-1989 57-60
Obituary 129
Wortman, Marlene Stein 1937- 112
Wortman, Max S(idones), Jr. 1932- CANR-16
Earlier sketch in CA 21-24R
Wortman, Richard 1938- CANR-9
Earlier sketch in CA 21-24R
Wortman, (Leo) Sterling 1923-1981 Obituary ... 108
Worton, Stanley N(elson) 1923- 57-60
Wortsman, Peter 1952- 137
Woshinsky, Oliver H(anson) 1939- CANR-55
Brief entry 109
Earlier sketch in CA 127
Wosmek, Frances 1917- CANR-51
Earlier sketches in CA 29-32R, CANR-11, 26
See also SATA 29
Wotton, SirHenry 1568-1639 .... DLB 121
Woudenberg, Paul Richard 1927- 69-72
Woudhuysen, Jan Frank 1942- 107
Woudstra, Marten H. 1922- CANR-19
Earlier sketch in CA 25-28R
Wouil, George
See Slaney, George Wilson
Wouk, Herman 1915- CANR-67
Earlier sketches in CA 5-8R, CANR-6, 33
Interview in CANR-6
See also CLC 1, 9, 38
See also DAM NOV, POP
See also DLBY 82
See also MTCW 1
Woutat, Donald 1944- 136
Woy, James Bayly 1927- 13-16R
Woychuk, Denis 1953- .... SATA 71
Woychuk, N(icholas) A(rthur) 1915- 13-16R
Woytinsky, Emma S(hadkhan) 1893-1969 ... CAP-1
Earlier sketch in CA 17-18
Woznicki, Andrew N(icholas) 1931- CANR-49
Earlier sketches in CA 45-48, CANR-24
Wrage, Ernest J. 1911-1965 .... 1-4R
Wragg, David William 1946- CANR-4
Earlier sketch in CA 53-56
Wragg, E(dward) C(onrad) 1938- CANR-47
Earlier sketches in CA 57-60, CANR-8, 23
Wragg, Joanna DiCarlo 1941- 133
Wraight, A(aron) Joseph 1913- 21-24R
Wrede, Patricia C(ollins) 1953- 134
See also AAYA 8
See also SATA 67
Wreen, Michael 1950- 117
Wreford, James
See Watson, J(ames) Wreford
Wreggitt, Andrew 1955- 138
Wren, Chris (?)-1982 Obituary 108
Wren, Christopher S. 1936- 21-24R
Wren, Daniel Alan 1932- 41-44R
Wren, Ellaruth
See Elkins, Ella Ruth
Wren, M. K.
See Renfroe, Martha Kay
Wren, Melvin C(larence) 1910- 37-40R
Wren, Percival Christopher 1885-1941 Brief entry 123
See also DLB 153
Wren, Robert Meriwether 1928- 106
Wren, Thomas Edward 1938- 77-80
Wren, Wilfrid John 1930- 109
Wrench, David F(razer) 1932- 41-44R
Wrench, (John) Evelyn (Leslie) 1882-1966 .... 5-8R
Wrench, Sara J. 1961- 163
Wrench, Sarah
See Wrench, Sara J.
Wrenn, John H(aughton) 1920- 1-4R
Wrenn, John Henry 1841-1911 .... DLB 140
Wrenn, Lynette Boney 1928- 158
Wrenn, Robert L. 1933- 29-32R
Wrenn, Tony P(entecost) 1938- 89-92
Wrenn, Winnie Holden
1886(?)-1979 Obituary 89-92
Wreszin, Michael 1926- 145
Wriggins, Sally Hovey 1922- 97-100
See also SATA 17
Wriggins, W(illiam) Howard 1918- 61-64
Wright, A(nthony) Colin 1938- 120
Wright, A. D. 1947- CANR-68
Earlier sketch in CA 129
Wright, A(mos) J(asper) 1952- 93-96
Wright, Alice E(dwards) 1905-1980 104
Wright, Andrew (Howell) 1923- 17-20R
Wright, Anna (Maria Louisa Perrott) Rose
1890-1968 Obituary 109
See also SATA-Brief 35
Wright, Arthur Frederick 1913-1976 .... CANR-33
Obituary 69-72
Earlier sketch in CA 77-80
Wright, Austin 1904- 61-64
Wright, Austin (McGiffert) 1922- CANR-52
Earlier sketches in CA 1-4R, CANR-4
Wright, Barbara 1951- 149
Wright, Barton A(llen) 1920- CANR-8
Earlier sketch in CA 61-64
Wright, Basil Charles 1907-1987 105
Obituary 123
Wright, Beatrice A(nn) 1917- CANR-12
Earlier sketch in CA 21-24R
Wright, Benjamin Fletcher 1900-1976 77-80
Obituary 69-72
Wright, Betty Ren 147
See also JRDA
See also SATA 63
See also SATA-Brief 48
Wright, Brooks 1922- 25-28R
Wright, Bruce S(tanley) 1912-1975 .... CAP-2
Earlier sketch in CA 19-20
Wright, Burton 1917- 81-84
Wright, C(arolyn) D. 1949- 142
See also CAAS 22
See also DLB 120
Wright, Carolyne L(ee) 1949- 111
Wright, (Julia) Celeste Turner 1906- CAP-1
Earlier sketch in CA 9-10
Wright, Charles (Penzel, Jr.) 1935- CANR-62
Earlier sketches in CA 29-32R, CANR-23, 36
See also CAAS 7
See also CLC 6, 13, 28
See also DLB 165
See also DLBY 82
See also MTCW 1
Wright, Charles Alan 1927- CANR-37
Earlier sketches in CA 45-48, CANR-1, 16
Wright, Charles David 1932-1978 104
Wright, Charles H(oward) 1918- 61-64
Wright, Charles R(obert) 1927- CANR-1
Earlier sketch in CA 45-48
Wright, Charles Stevenson 1932- CANR-26
Earlier sketch in CA 9-12R
See also BLC 3
See also BW 1
See also CLC 49
See also DAM MULT, POET
See also DLB 33
Wright, Christopher 1926- 9-12R
Wright, Cliff 1963- 143
See also SATA 76
Wright, Clifford A. 1951- 149
Wright, Cobina (?)-1970 Obituary 115
Wright, (Charles) Conrad 1917- 21-24R
Wright, Constance Choate 1897-1987 .... 13-16R
Obituary 121
Wright, Courtni C(rump) 1950- 150
See also SATA 84
Wright, Cynthia Challed 1953- CANR-41
Earlier sketch in CA 77-80
Wright, D(avid) G(ordon) 1937- 65-68
Wright, D(onald) I(an) 1934- CANR-3
Earlier sketch in CA 49-52
Wright, Daphne 1951- 157
Wright, Dare 1926(?)- 93-96
See also SATA 21
Wright, David (John Murray) 1920-1994 ... CANR-3
Obituary 146
Earlier sketch in CA 9-12R
See also CAAS 5
Wright, David K. 1943- .... SATA 73
Wright, David McCord 1909-1968 .... CAP-2
Earlier sketch in CA 17-18
Wright, Deil S(pencer) 1930- 13-16R
Wright, Denis (Arthur Hepworth) 1911- 81-84
Wright, Derek 1947- 144
Wright, Don(ald Conway) 1934- CANR-20
Earlier sketch in CA 104
Wright, Donald R(ichard) 1944- 160
Wright, Dorothy 1910- 13-16R
Wright, Edward A(rlington) 1906- 29-32R
Wright, Elizabeth Atwell 1919-1976 Obituary . 65-68
Wright, Enid Meadowcroft (LaMonte) 1898-1966 ... CAP-2
Earlier sketch in CA 17-18
See also SATA 3
Wright, Eric 1929- CANR-63
Brief entry 127
Earlier sketch in CA 132
Interview in 132
Wright, Esmond 1915- CANR-44
Earlier sketches in CA 1-4R, CANR-6
See also SATA 10
Wright, F(rank) J(oseph) 1905- 9-12R
Wright, Frances 1795-1852 .... DLB 73
Wright, Frances Fitzpatrick 1897- CAP-1
Earlier sketch in CA 13-14
See also SATA 10
Wright, Frances J.
See Crothers, J(essie) Frances
Wright, Francesca
See Robins, Denise (Naomi)
Wright, Frank Cookman, Jr.
1904-1982 Obituary 107
Wright, Frank Gardner 1931- 136
Wright, Franz 1953- 139
Wright, G(eorge) Ernest 1909-1974 .... CANR-2
Obituary 53-56
Earlier sketch in CA 1-4R
Wright, G(eorg) H(enrik) von 1916- 157
Brief entry 112
Wright, Gavin Peter 1943- CANR-15
Earlier sketch in CA 89-92
Wright, George B(urton) 1912- 21-24R
Wright, George Nelson 1921- CANR-1
Earlier sketch in CA 45-48
Wright, George T(haddeus, Jr.) 1925- 5-8R
Wright, Gordon 1912- 9-12R
Wright, Grahame 1947-1977 103
Wright, H(arold) Bunker 1907- 5-8R
Wright, H(ugh) Elliott 1937- CANR-14
Earlier sketch in CA 37-40R
Wright, H(arry) Norman 1937- CANR-32
Earlier sketches in CA 57-60, CANR-8
Wright, Harold Bell 1872-1944 Brief entry 110
See also DLB 9
Wright, Harrison M(orris) 1928- 41-44R
Wright, (Mary) Helen Greuter 1914-1997 .... 9-12R
Obituary 162
Wright, Helen L(ouise) 1932- 116
Wright, Helena (Rosa Lowenfeld)
1887-1982 Obituary 110
Wright, Herbert Curtis 1928- 105
Wright, Howard W(ilson) 1915-1992 .... CANR-3
Obituary 136
Earlier sketch in CA 5-8R
Wright, Ione Stuessy 1905- CAP-1
Earlier sketch in CA 13-14
Wright, Irene Aloha 1879-1972 Obituary 33-36R
Wright, J. B.
See Barkan, Joanne
Wright, J(ames) Leitch, Jr. 1929- 21-24R
Wright, J(oseph) Patrick (Jr.) 1941- 103
Wright, J(ohn) Robert 1936- 111
Wright, J(ohn) Stafford 1905- CANR-11
Earlier sketch in CA 57-60
Wright, Jack R.
See Harris, Mark
Wright, James (Arlington) 1927-1980 .... CANR-64
Obituary 97-100
Earlier sketches in CA 49-52, CANR-4, 34
See also AITN 2
See also CLC 3, 5, 10, 28
See also DAM POET
See also DLB 5, 169
See also MTCW 1
Wright, James Bowers 1950- 127
Wright, James C(laud), Jr. 1922- 49-52
Wright, James D(avid) 1947- 156
Wright, Jay 1935- 73-76
See also BW 2
See also DAM MULT
See also DLB 41
Wright, Jim
See Wright, James Bowers
and Wright, James C(laud), Jr.
Wright, John D(ean), Jr. 1920- 117
Wright, John Eugene, Jr. 1931- 112
Wright, John J(oseph) 1909-1979 .... CANR-2
Earlier sketch in CA 1-4R
Wright, John L. 1937- 131
Wright, John S(hup) 1910- 37-40R
Wright, John S(herman) 1920- CANR-6
Earlier sketch in CA 5-8R
Wright, Judith (Arandell) 1915- CANR-31
Earlier sketch in CA 13-16R
See also CLC 11, 53
See also MTCW 1
See also PC 14
See also SATA 14
Wright, Katrina
See Gater, Dilys
Wright, Keith 1963- 136
Wright, Kenneth
See del Rey, Lester
Wright, Kit 1944- 151
See also SATA 87
Wright, L(afayette) Hart 1917-1983 .... CANR-32
Obituary 109
Earlier sketch in CA 41-44
Wright, L(aurali) R. 1939- 138
See also CLC 44
Wright, Larry 1940- 140
Brief entry 122
Wright, Lawrence 1906-1983 162
Wright, Lawrence 1947- 93-96
Wright, Leigh Richard 1925- 93-96
Wright, Leonard M(arshall), Jr. 1923- CANR-13
Earlier sketch in CA 61-64
Wright, Leslie B(ailey) 1959- 155
See also SATA 91
Wright, Linda Raney 1945- CANR-11
Earlier sketch in CA 69-72
Wright, Louis Booker 1899-1984 .... CANR-1
Obituary 112
Earlier sketch in CA 1-4R
See also DLB 17
Wright, M(aureen) R(osemary) 131
Wright, Mary Clabaugh 1917-1970 Obituary 109
Wright, Mary Pamela Godwin 1917- CAP-1
Earlier sketch in CA 9-10
Wright, Michael J(ohn) 1944- 144
Wright, Michael R(obert) 1901- CAP-1
Earlier sketch in CA 13-16
Wright, Monte Duane 1930- 41-44R
Wright, Muriel H(azel) 1889-1975 Obituary ... 57-60
Wright, N. T(om) 1948- 162
Wright, Nancy Means 104
See also SATA 38
Wright, Nathalia 1913- 120
Wright, Nathan, Jr. 1923- 37-40R
Wright, Nathaniel, Jr.
See Wright, Nathan, Jr.
Wright, Norman Edgar 1927- 101
Wright, Olgivanna Lloyd 1900(?)-1985 Obituary 115
Wright, (Mary) Patricia 1932- CANR-51
Earlier sketches in CA 65-68, CANR-10, 26
Wright, Peter (Maurice) 1916-1995 128
Obituary 148
Wright, Philip Arthur 1908- CAP-1
Earlier sketch in CA 11-12
Wright, (Philip) Quincy 1890-1970 .... CANR-5
Obituary 29-32R
Earlier sketch in CA 5-8R
Wright, R(obert) Glenn 1932- 111
Wright, R(obert) H(amilton) 1906- CANR-7
Earlier sketch in CA 17-20R
See also SATA 6
Wright, R(ichard) I(rwin) Vane
See Vane-Wright, R(ichard) I(rwin)
Wright, Rayburn B. 1922-1990 Obituary 131
Wright, Rebecca 1942- 105
Wright, Richard (Nathaniel) 1908-1960 ... CANR-64
Earlier sketch in CA 108
See also AAYA 5
See also BLC 3
See also BW 1
See also CDALB 1929-1941
See also CLC 1, 3, 4, 9, 14, 21, 48, 74
See also DA
See also DAB
See also DAC
See also DAM MST, MULT, NOV
See also DLB 76, 102
See also DLBD 2
See also MTCW 1
See also SSC 2
See also WLC
Wright, Richard A(lan) 1953- 156
Wright, Richard B(ruce) 1937- 85-88
See also CLC 6
See also DLB 53
Wright, Richard J. 1935- 89-92
Wright, Rick 1945- .... CLC 35
Wright, Robert (Alan) 1957- 129
Wright, Robert Lee 1920- CANR-13
Earlier sketch in CA 17-20R
Wright, Robert Roy 1917- 9-12R
Wright, Robin (B.) 1948- 131
Brief entry 119
Wright, Ronald 1948- 139
Interview in 139
Wright, Ronald (William Vernon) Selby 1908- CANR-6
Earlier sketch in CA 1-4R
Wright, Rosalie Muller 1942- 77-80
Wright, Rosalind 1952- 61-64
Wright, Rosemary Muir 1943- 158
Wright, Rowland
See Wells, Carolyn
Wright, Russel 1904-1976 Obituary 69-72
Wright, Russel O(wen) 1936- 155
Wright, S(ydney) Fowler 1874-1965 156
Wright, Sarah E(lizabeth) 1928- 37-40R
See also BW 2
See also DLB 33
Wright, Sewall 1889-1988 Obituary 125
Wright, Stephen 1922- CANR-1
Earlier sketch in CA 49-52
Wright, Stephen 1946- .... CLC 33
Wright, Stephen Caldwell 1946- 142
See also BW 2
Wright, Susan Kimmel 1950- 151
See also SATA 97
Wright, Sylvia 1917-1981 .... 29-32R
Obituary 104
Wright, T. M. 1947- 120
Wright, T(erence) R(oy) 1951- 125
Wright, Theodore P(aul), Jr. 1926- CANR-9
Earlier sketch in CA 13-16R
Wright, Theon 1904- Brief entry 109
Wright, Walter Francis 1912- 5-8R
Wright, Willard Hull 1894-1982 Obituary 107
Wright, Willard Huntington 1888-1939 Brief entry 115
See also Van Dine, S. S.
See also DLBD 16
Wright, William 1829-1898 .... DLB 186
Wright, William 1930- CANR-23
Earlier sketches in CA 53-56, CANR-7
See also CLC 44
Wright, William C(ook) 1939- 41-44R
Wright, William E(dward) 1926- 21-24R
Wrightfrierson
See Wright-Frierson, Virginia
Wright-Frierson, Virginia 1949- .... SATA 58
Wrightsman, Lawrence S(amuel), Jr. 1931- CANR-11
Earlier sketch in CA 21-24R
Wrightson, (Alice) Patricia 1921- CANR-36
Earlier sketches in CA 45-48, CANR-3, 19
See also AAYA 5
See also CLR 4, 14
See also JRDA
See also MAICYA
See also SAAS 4
See also SATA 8, 66
Wrigley, Chris (John) 1947- 129
Wrigley, E(dward) A(nthony) 1931- 129
Wrigley, Elizabeth S(pringer) 1915-1997 .... 41-44R
Obituary 157
Wriston, Henry M(erritt) 1889-1978 .... CAP-1
Obituary 77-80
Earlier sketch in CA 11-12
Wriston, Walter B(igelow) 1919- 154
Wrobel, David M. 1964- 139
Wrobel, Sylvia (Burroughs) 1941- 65-68

Wroblewski, Sergius C(harles) 1918- CANR-8
Earlier sketch in CA 5-8R
Wrone, David R(ogers) 1933- CANR-6
Earlier sketch in CA 57-60
Wrong, Dennis H(ume) 1923- 81-84
Wronker, Lili
See Wronker, Lili Cassel
Wronker, Lili Cassel 1924- ..... SATA 10
Wronski, Stanley P(aul) 1919- 13-16R
Wroth, Lawrence Counselman
1884-1970 Obituary 29-32R
See also DLB 187
Wroth, LadyMary 1587-1653(?) ..... DLB 121
Wrottesley, A(rthur) J(ohn) F(rancis) 1908- 45-48
Wryde, Dogear
See Gorey, Edward (St. John)
Wrzos, Joseph Henry 1929- 49-52
Wu, Chien-Shiung 1912(?)- 159
Wu, David Y(en) H(o) 1940- 140
Wu, Duncan 1961- 142
Wu, Edna
See Wu, Qingyun
Wu, Harry 1937- 145
Wu, Hsiu-Kwang 1935- 17-20R
Wu, John C(hing) H(siung) 1899-1986 104
Obituary 118
Wu, Joseph S. 1934- 97-100
Wu, K(uo) C(heng) 1903-1984 ..... 1-4R
Obituary 113
Wu, Nelson I(kon) 1919- 9-12R
Wu, Norbert 1961- 168
See also SATA 101
Wu, Qingyun 1950- 154
Wu, Silas H. L. 1929- 37-40R
Wu, William F(ranking) 1951- 109
Wu, Yenna 1957- 164
Wu, Yuan-li CANR-12
Earlier sketch in CA 17-20R
Wuamett, Victor 1941- 134
Wubbels, Lance 1952- 150
Wubben, Hubert H(ollensteiner) 1928- 102
Wubben, John 1938- 65-68
Wucherer, Ruth Marie 1948- CANR-8
Earlier sketch in CA 61-64
Wu Ching-hsiung
See Wu, John C(hing) H(siung)
WuDunn, Sheryl 1959- 132
Wuellner, Flora Slosson 1928- 53-56
Wuerpel, Charles E(dward) 1906- 105
Wuerthner, George 1952- 168
Wuerzbach, Natascha 1933- 154
Wu Hung 1945- 163
Wul, Stefan
See Pairault, Pierre
Wulf, Helen Harlan 1913- 53-56
Wulfekoetter, Gertrude 1895- 1-4R
Wulff, Lee 1905-1991 61-64
Obituary 134
Wulff, Robert M. 1926- 49-52
Wulffson, Don L. 1943- CANR-42
Earlier sketches in CA 102, CANR-19
See also SATA 32, 88
Wulforst, Harry David 1923- 125
Wuliger, Betty 1921- 65-68
Wullstein, L(eroy) H(ughes) 1931- 29-32R
Wulstan, David 1937- 127
Wunder, John Remley 1945- CANR-37
Earlier sketch in CA 107
Wunderli, Richard (M.) 1940- 140
Wunderli, Stephen 1958- ..... SATA 79
Wunderlich, Ray C., Jr. 1929- 37-40R
Wunderlich, Roger 1914- 144
Wundt, Wilhelm
See de Mille, Richard
Wundt, Wilhelm (Max) 1832-1920 Brief entry 121
Wunnakyawhtin U Ohn Ghine
See Maurice, David (John Kerr)
Wunsch, James S(tevenson) 1946- 136
Wunsch, Josephine (McLean) 1914- CANR-34
Earlier sketches in CA 1-4R, CANR-15
See also SATA 64
Wuorinen, John H(enry) 1897-1969 Obituary 111
Wuorio, Eva-Lis 1918- CANR-40
Earlier sketch in CA 77-80
See also SATA 34
See also SATA-Brief 28
Wurdemann, Audrey
See Auslander, Audrey (May) Wurdemann
Wurfel, Seymour W(alter) 1907- 73-76
Wurlitzer, Rudolph 1938(?)- 85-88
See also CLC 2, 4, 15
See also DLB 173
Wurm, Franz (Herbert) 1926- 150
Wurman, Richard Saul 1935- 162
Wurmbrand, Heinrich Richard 1909- CANR-27
Earlier sketch in CA 61-64
Wurmser, Leon 1931- 106
Wurtman, Judith J(oy) 1937- 113
Wurts, Janny 1953- 157
See also SATA 98
Wurtzel, Elizabeth (Leigh) 1967- 149
Wurzburger, Walter S. 1920- 151
Wuthnow, Robert 1946- CANR-15
Earlier sketch in CA 65-68
Wu Tien-wei 1922- 118
Wyandotte, Steve
See Thomas, Stanley
Wyant, William K(eblinger) 1913-1995 108
Obituary 150
Wyatt, Arthur R(amer) 1927- 1-4R
Wyatt, B. D.
See Robinson, Spider
Wyatt, Clarence R. 1956- 142
Wyatt, David K(ent) 1937- 29-32R
Wyatt, David M. 1948- 132
Wyatt, Don J. 1953- 166
Wyatt, Dorothea E(dith) 1909- CAP-2
Earlier sketch in CA 23-24
Wyatt, James
See Robinson, Louie, Jr.
Wyatt, Jane
See Bradbury, Bianca (Ryley)
Wyatt, Joan 1934- 97-100
Wyatt, John 1925- CANR-45
Earlier sketches in CA 105, CANR-22
Wyatt, Rachel 1929- 101
Wyatt, Richard Jed 1939- 115
Wyatt, Robert John 1931- 73-76
Wyatt, Robert Lee III 1940- 163
Wyatt, Stanley P(orter, Jr.) 1921-1980 ..... 9-12R
Obituary 120
Wyatt, Stephen (John) 1948- CANR-34
Earlier sketches in CA 81-84, CANR-15
Wyatt, Thomas c. 1503-1542 ..... DLB 132
Wyatt, Wesley Butler
See Torme, Mel(vin Howard)
Wyatt, (Alan) Will 1942- 101
Wyatt, William F., Jr. 1932- 37-40R
Wyatt, Wilson (Watkins) (Sr.) 1905-1996 153
Wyatt, Woodrow Lyle 1918-1997 ..... CANR-40
Obituary 163
Earlier sketch in CA 103
Wyatt-Brown, Anne M(arbury) 1939- 139
Wyatt-Brown, Bertram 1932- CANR-21
Earlier sketch in CA 25-28R
Wycherley, R(ichard) E(rnest) 1909- 77-80
Wycherley, William 1641-1715 .. CDBLB 1660-1789
See also DAM DRAM
See also DLB 80
Wyckoff, Charlotte Chandler 1893-1966 ..... CAP-2
Earlier sketch in CA 17-18
Wyckoff, D(onald) Daryl 1936-1985 ..... CANR-7
Obituary 114
Earlier sketch in CA 57-60
Wyckoff, Edith Hay 1916- 107
Wyckoff, James M. 1918- CANR-39
Earlier sketch in CA 17-20R
Wyckoff, (Gregory) Jerome 1911- 9-12R
Wyckoff, Peter (Gerritsen) 1914- 41-44R
Wyckoff, Ralph W(alter) G(raystone)
1897-1994 73-76
Obituary 147
Wyckoff, Russell L. 1916(?)-1984 Obituary 112
Wyclif, John c. 1335-1384 ..... DLB 146
Wycliffe, John
See Bedford-Jones, H(enry James O'Brien)
Wycoff, Mary Elizabeth Jordon 1932- 13-16R
Wyden, Peter H. 1923- 105
Wyer, Robert S., (Jr.) 1935- 153
Wyeth, Betsy James 1921- 89-92
See also SATA 41
Wyeth, N(ewell) C(onvers) 1882-1945 ..... DLB 188
See also DLBD 16
See also MAICYA
See also SATA 17
Wyeth, Paul James Logan 1920-1982 Obituary 107
Wykes, Alan 1914-1993 ..... CANR-47
Obituary 141
Earlier sketches in CA 1-4R, CANR-2
Wykstra, Ronald A. 1935- Brief entry 106
Wyld, Lionel D(arcy) 1925- CANR-4
Earlier sketch in CA 1-4R
Wylder, Delbert E(ugene) 1923- CANR-12
Earlier sketch in CA 29-32R
Wylder, Edith (Perry) 1925- 29-32R
Wylder, Robert C. 1921- 9-12R
Wyler, Rose 1909- 93-96
See also SATA 18
Wyler, William 1902-1981 Obituary 108
Wylie, Betty Jane CANR-21
Earlier sketch in CA 105
See also SATA 48
Wylie, C(larence) Ray(mond), Jr. 1911- CANR-36
Earlier sketch in CA 45-48
Wylie, Craig 1908-1976 Obituary 69-72
Wylie, Elinor (Morton Hoyt) 1885-1928 162
Brief entry 105
See also DLB 9, 45
See also PC 23
See also TCLC 8
Wylie, Francis E(rnest) 1905- CANR-37
Earlier sketch in CA 73-76
Wylie, Jeff
See Wylie, Francis E(rnest)
Wylie, Joanne 1928- 118
Wylie, John Anthony Hamilton
1919-1987 Obituary 123
Wylie, Jonathan 1945- 120
Wylie, Laura
See Matthews, Patricia (Anne)
Wylie, Laurence William 1909- 21-24R
Wylie, Laurie
See Matthews, Patricia (Anne)
Wylie, Max (Melville) 1904-1975 97-100
Obituary 61-64
Wylie, Philip (Gordon) 1902-1971 ..... CAP-2
Obituary 33-36R
Earlier sketch in CA 21-22
See also CLC 43
See also DLB 9
Wylie, Ruth C(arol) 1920- 89-92
Wylie, Turrell V(erl) 1927- 41-44R
Wylie, William P(ercy) 1898- 5-8R
Wyllie, Eugene D(onald) 1929- 123
Brief entry 118
Wyllie, John (Vectis Carew) 1914- CANR-5
Earlier sketch in CA 9-12R
Wyllie, John Cook 1908-1968 ..... DLB 140
Wyllie, Peter J(ohn) 1930- CANR-5
Earlier sketch in CA 53-56
Wyllie, Stephen ..... SATA 86
Wyly, Rachel Lumpkin 1892- CAP-2
Earlier sketch in CA 25-28
Wyman, Andrea 142
See also SATA 75
Wyman, Bill 1936- 146
Wyman, Bruce C. 1947- 139
Wyman, Carolyn 1956- 150
See also SATA 83
Wyman, David S. 1929- 25-28R
Wyman, Donald 1903- CANR-2
Earlier sketch in CA 5-8R
Wyman, Leland C(lifton) 1897-1988 Obituary 124
Wyman, Lillie Buffum Chace 1847-1929 ..... DLB 202
Wyman, Marc
See Howith, Harry
Wyman, Mark 1938- CANR-36
Earlier sketch in CA 101
Wyman, Mary Alice 1889(?)-1976 Obituary 61-64
Wyman, Max 1939- 140
Wyman, Oliver
See Holmes, Olive
Wyman, Walker D(e Marquis) 1907- CANR-36
Earlier sketch in CA 17-20R
Wymark, Olwen Margaret 1932- 104
Wymelenberg, Suzanne 1929- 140
Wymer, Norman (George) 1911- 104
See also SATA 25
Wymer, Thomas L(ee) 1938- 105
Wynand, Derk 1944- CANR-17
Earlier sketch in CA 77-80
Wynants, Miche 1934- ..... SATA-Brief 31
Wynar, Bohdan S(tephen) 1926- CANR-66
Earlier sketches in CA 17-20R, CANR-10, 27
Wynar, Christine L(oraine) 1933- 73-76
Wynar, Lubomyr R(oman) 1932- CANR-64
Earlier sketches in CA 73-76, CANR-14, 31
Wynard, Talbot
See Hamilton, Charles (Harold St. John)
Wynd, Oswald Morris 1913- CANR-39
Earlier sketches in CA 1-4R, CANR-1
Wynder, Mavis Areta
See Winder, Mavis Areta
Wyndham, Esther
See Lutyens, Mary
Wyndham, Everard Humphrey 1888- CAP-1
Earlier sketch in CA 13-14
Wyndham, Francis (Guy Percy) 1924- 131
Brief entry 126
Interview in 131
Wyndham, Joan 1921- 144
Wyndham, John
See Harris, John (Wyndham Parkes Lucas)
Beynon
See also CLC 19
Wyndham, Lee
See Hyndman, Jane Andrews Lee
Wyndham, Robert
See Hyndman, Robert Utley
Wynes, Charles E. 1929- 9-12R
Wyness, (James) Fenton 1903- CAP-1
Earlier sketch in CA 11-12
Wynette, Tammy
See Pugh, (Virginia) Wynette
Wynia, Gary W. 1942- 133
Wynkoop, Mildred Bangs 1905- CANR-40
Earlier sketch in CA 57-60
Wynkoop, Sally 1944- 41-44R
Wynkoop, William M. 1916- 21-24R
Wynn, Alfred
See Brewer, Fredric (Aldwyn)
Wynn, Allan 1920-1987 Obituary 123
Wynn, Charles M. 1939- 163
Wynn, D(ale) Richard 1918- CANR-43
Earlier sketches in CA 1-4R, CANR-4
Wynn, Daniel Webster 1919-1983 ..... 25-28R
Obituary 133
Wynn, Graeme 1946- 127
Wynn, John Charles 1920- CANR-2
Earlier sketch in CA 1-4R
Wynn, (Francis Xavier Aloysius James Jeremiah)
1916-1986 Obituary 120
Wynn, Neil A(lan) 1947- 113
Wynn, Tracey Keenan 1945- 144
Wynne, Brian
See Garfield, Brian (Wynne)
Wynne, Edward A. 1928- 130
Wynne, Frank
See Garfield, Brian (Wynne)
Wynne, Greville (Maynard)
1919-1990 Obituary 131
Wynne, John (Stewart) 149
Wynne, Lewis Nicholas 1943- 128
Wynne, May
See Knowles, Mabel Winifred
Wynne, Nancy Blue 1931- 85-88
Wynne, Paul 1943(?)-1990 Obituary 132
Wynne, Ronald D(avid) 1934- CANR-42
Earlier sketch in CA 102
Wynne, Thorne D. 1908- 5-8R
Wynne-Davies, Marion 1958- 133
Wynne-Jones, Tim(othy) 1948- CANR-39
Earlier sketch in CA 105
See also CLR 21
See also SATA 67, 96
Wynne-Thomas, Peter 1934- 118
Wynne-Tyson, Esme 1898-1972 ..... 21-24R
See also DLB 191
Wynne-Tyson, (Timothy) Jon (Lyden) 1924- 17-20R
Wynn-Jones, Michael 1941- CANR-14
Earlier sketch in CA 69-72
Wynot, Edward D(avis), Jr. 1943- 105
Wynter, Edward (John) 1914- 69-72
See also SATA 14
Wynter, Sylvia 1928- 153
See also BW 2
Wynyard, Talbot
See Hamilton, Charles (Harold St. John)
Wyon, Olive 1890-(?) CAP-1
Earlier sketch in CA 11-12
Wyrick, V(ictor) Neil, Jr. 1928- 13-16R
Wyschogrod, Edith 1930- Brief entry 111
Wyschogrod, Michael 1928- 89-92
Wyse, Lois (Helene) 1926- CANR-46
Earlier sketch in CA 108
See also BEST 89:3
Wyse, Marion 1952- 123
Wysor, Bettie 1928- CANR-13
Earlier sketch in CA 77-80
Wyss, Johann David Von 1743-1818 ..... JRDA
See also MAICYA
See also SATA 29
See also SATA-Brief 27
Wyss, Max Albert 1908-1977 106
Wyss, Thelma Hatch 1934- 29-32R
See also SATA 10
Wyss, Wallace A(lfred) 1944- 124
Brief entry 107
Wyszynski, Stefan 1901-1981 Obituary 108
Wyvis, Ben
See Munro, (Macfarlane) Hugh
Wyzanski, Charles E(dward), Jr. 1906-1986 . CAP-1
Obituary 120
Earlier sketch in CA 17-18

X

Xaveria, M. Barton
See Barton, M. Xaveria
Xaveria, Sister
See Barton, M. Xaveria
Xavier I
See Horne, Frank (Smith)
Xeno
See Lake, Kenneth R(obert)
Xenophon c. 430B.C.-c. 354B.C. ..... DLB 176
Xiang, Lanxin 1956- 152
Ximenes, Ben Cuellar, Jr. 1911- 5-8R
Xixx, Jezebel Q.
See Borgmann, Dmitri A(lfred)

Y

Yaari, Ehud 1945- 37-40R
Yabes, Leopoldo Y(abes) 1912- 101
Yablokoff, Herman 1903-1981 Obituary 108
Yablonsky, Lewis 1924- 21-24R
Yablonsky, Linda 1948- 166
Yabsley, Suzanne 1949- 124
Yabuki, Susumu 1938- 152
Yacine, Kateb 1929- 9-12R
Yacorzynski, George Kassimer 1907- 1-4R
Yacowar, Maurice 1942- CANR-43
Earlier sketch in CA 41-44R
Yadin, (Rav-Aloof) Yigael 1917-1984 ..... CANR-6
Obituary 113
Earlier sketch in CA 9-12R
See also SATA 55
Yaeger, Bart
See Strung, Norman
Yaeger, Don 1962- 144
Yafa, Stephen H. 1941- 21-24R
Yaffe, Alan
See Yorinks, Arthur
Yaffe, Barbara 1953- 85-88
Yaffe, James 1927- CANR-12
Earlier sketch in CA 5-8R
Yaffe, Richard 1903- 69-72
Yager, Jan 1948- CANR-30
Yager, Rosemary 1909- 1-4R
Yaggy, Duncan 1938- 116
Yaggy, Elinor 1907- 89-92
Yagoda, Ben 1954- 145
Yahil, Leni 29-32R
Yahraes, Herbert 1905- 81-84
Yahuda, Joseph 1900- CAP-1
Earlier sketch in CA 11-12
Yaker, Henri (Marc) 1922- Brief entry 109
Yakobson, Helen B(ates) 1913- 17-20R
Yakobson, Sergius O. 1901-1979 Obituary 89-92
Yakovenko, L.
See Kopelev, Lev (Zinovievich)
Yakovetic, (Joseph Sandy) 1952- ..... SATA 59
Yakovetic, Joe
See Yakovetic, (Joseph Sandy)
Yakovlev, Alexander 1923- 145
Yakumo Koizumi
See Hearn, (Patricio) Lafcadio (Tessima Carlos)
Yalden, Derek William 1940- 69-72
Yale, Kathleen Betsko 1939- 158
Yale, Wesley W(oodworth) 1900- CAP-2
Earlier sketch in CA 29-32
Yale, William 1888(?)-1975 Obituary 57-60
Yalem, Ronald J(oseph) 1926- 17-20R
Yalman, Ahmet Emin 1888-1972 Obituary 37-40R
Yalom, Irvin D(avid) 1931- 140
See also BEST 90:1
Yalom, Marilyn K. 1932- CANR-40
Earlier sketch in CA 117
Yalow, Rosalyn Sussman 1921- 157
Yamada, Mitsuye (May) 1923- 77-80

Yamada, Nanako 1939- … 143
Yamaguchi, J(ohn) Tohr 1932- … 17-20R
Yamaguchi, Marianne (Illenberger) 1936- … 29-32R
See also SATA 7
Yamaguchi, Yoji 1963- … 165
Yamaka, Sara 1978- … 156
See also SATA 92
Yamamoto, Hisaye 1921- … DAM MULT
Yamamoto, J(erry) Isamu 1947- … 77-80
Yamamoto, Kaoru 1932- … CANR-12
Earlier sketch in CA 25-28R
Yamamoto, Michiko 1936- … 132
Yamanaka, Lois-Ann 1961- … 161
Yamanouchi, Hisaaki 1934- … 93-96
Yamasaki, Minoru 1912-1986 … 155
Obituary … 118
Yamashita, Karen Tei 1951- … 166
Yamauchi, Edwin M(asao) 1937- … CANR-41
Earlier sketches in CA 45-48, CANR-3, 19
Yamba, C(hristian) Bawa 1944- … 163
Yan, Chiou-Shuang Jou 1934- Brief entry … 105
Yanaga, Chitoshi 1903- … CAP-2
Earlier sketch in CA 25-28
Yanagimura, Shimpu
See Verwilghen, A(lbert-) Felix
Yancey, Diane 1951- … 149
See also SATA 81
Yancey, Philip D(avid) 1949- … CANR-40
Earlier sketches in CA 101, CANR-18
Yancey, William L(ayton) 1938- … 21-24R
Yancy, Robert J(ames) 1944- … 57-60
Yandell, Keith E. 1938- … 37-40R
Yanev, Peter (Ivanov) 1946- … 77-80
Yaney, George L(evings) 1930- … 104
Yaney, Joseph P(aul) 1939- … CANR-9
Earlier sketch in CA 65-68
Yanez, Agustin 1904-1980 … 131
See also HW
Yanez, Jose Donoso
See Donoso (Yanez), Jose
Yang, Belle 1960- … 149
Yang, C(hing) K(un) 1911- … 5-8R
Yang, Chen Ning 1922- … 157
Yang, Cunzhong
See Ruan, Fang-fu
Yang, Dali L. … 139
Yang, Jay 1941- … SATA 12
Yang, Linda (Gureasko) 1937- … 57-60
Yang, Mingyi 1943- … SATA 72
Yang, Richard F. S. 1918- … CANR-10
Earlier sketch in CA 25-28R
Yang, Sung Chul 1939- … 117
Yang-Jen
See Shu, Austin Chi-wei
Yang Zhong Mei 1945- … 132
Yanikian, Gourgen Migirdic
1895-1984 Obituary … 112
Yaniv, Avner 1942- … 126
Yankelovich, Daniel 1924- … 105
Yanker, Gary 1947- … 37-40R
Yankowitz, Susan 1941- … CANR-39
Earlier sketches in CA 45-48, CANR-1, 17
Yannarella, Philip A(nthony) 1942- … 73-76
Yannatos, James 1929- … 102
Yannella, Donald 1934- … CANR-25
Earlier sketches in CA 57-60, CANR-8
Yanoff, Morris 1907- … 108
Yanouzas, John N(icholas) 1928- … 41-44R
Yanovsky, Basile S.
See Yanovsky, V(assily) S(emenovich)
Yanovsky, V(assily) S(emenovich)
1906-1989 … 97-100
Obituary … 129
See also CLC 2, 18
Yans-McLaughlin, Virginia 1943- … 89-92
Yant, Martin 1949- … 134
Yao, Esther Lee 1944- … CANR-56
Earlier sketches in CA 111, CANR-29
Yap, Arthur 1945- … 154
Yarber, Robert Earl 1929- … 49-52
Yarborough, Betty Hathaway 1927- … 45-48
Yarbro, Chelsea Quinn 1942- … CANR-25
Earlier sketches in CA 65-68, CANR-9
Yarbrough, Camille 1938- … 125
Brief entry … 105
See also BW 2
See also CLR 29
See also SATA 79
Yarbrough, Ira 1910(?)-1983 Obituary … 110
See also SATA-Obit 35
Yarbrough, Stephen R. 1950- … 138
Yarbrough, Tinsley E(ugene) 1941- … 109
Yarde, Jeanne Betty Frances 1925- … CANR-47
Earlier sketches in CA 105, CANR-23
Yardley, Alice 1913- Brief entry … 106
Yardley, Herbert O(sborn) 1889-1958 Brief
entry … 121
Yardley, Jonathan 1939- … 73-76
Yardley, Richard Q(uincy)
1903-1979 Obituary … 89-92
Yared, Nazek Saba 1928- … 168
Yaremko, Michael 1914-1970 … CAP-2
Earlier sketch in CA 25-28
Yarmey, A(lexander) Daniel 1938- … CANR-17
Earlier sketch in CA 101
Yarmolinsky, Adam 1922- … 37-40R
Yarmolinsky, Avrahm (Abraham) 1890-1975 …
CANR-7
Obituary … 61-64
Earlier sketch in CA 5-8R
Yarmon, Morton 1916- … 9-12R
Yarn, David H(omer), Jr. 1920- … 17-20R
Yarnall, Sophia
See Jacobs, Sophia Yarnall
Yarnell, Allen 1942- … 101
Yaroshinskaya, Alla 1953- … 153
Yaroslava
See Mills, Yaroslava Surmach
Yarrow, Arnold 1920- … 106
Yarrow, Marian J(eanette Radke) 1918- Brief
entry … 105
Yarrow, P(hilip) J(ohn) 1917- … 13-16R
Yarry, Mark Robert 1940- … 110
Yar-Shater, Ehsan O(llah) 1920- … 37-40R
Yartz, Frank Joseph … 65-68
Yarwood, Doreen 1918- … CANR-18
Earlier sketch in CA 101
Yaseen, Leonard C(layton)
1912-1989 Obituary … 129
Yashima, Taro
See Iwamatsu, Jun Atsushi
See also CLR 4
Yasouka, Shotaro 1920- … DLB 182
Yastrzemski, Carl (Michael, Jr.) 1939- … 104
Yates, A(lan) G(eoffrey) 1923-1985 … CANR-60
Obituary … 116
Earlier sketches in CA 1-4R, CANR-3
Yates, Alan
See Yates, A(lan) G(eoffrey)
Yates, Alayne 1929- … 81-84
Yates, Alfred 1917- … 21-24R
Yates, Aubrey J(ames) 1925- … 9-12R
Yates, Brock W(endel) 1933- … 9-12R
Yates, David O.
See Womack, David A(lfred)
Yates, Donald A(lfred) 1930- … 41-44R
Yates, Dornford
See Mercer, Cecil William
See also DLB 77, 153
Yates, Elizabeth 1905- … CANR-21
Earlier sketches in CA 1-4R, CANR-6
See also JRDA
See also MAICYA
See also SAAS 6
See also SATA 4, 68
Yates, Frances A(melia) 1899-1981 … CANR-30
Obituary … 105
Earlier sketch in CA 57-60
Yates, Gerard Francis 1907-1979 Obituary … 89-92
Yates, J. Michael 1938- … 21-24R
See also DLB 60
Yates, Janelle K(aye) 1957- … 145
See also SATA 77
Yates, John 1939- … SATA 74
Yates, Madeleine 1937- … 109
Yates, Norris W(ilson) 1923- … 9-12R
Yates, Paul 1954- Brief entry … 117
Yates, Peter Bertram 1909-1976 Obituary … 65-68
Yates, Philip 1956- … SATA 92
Yates, Raymond F(rancis) 1895-1966 Obituary … 110
See also SATA 31
Yates, Richard 1926-1992 … CANR-43
Obituary … 139
Earlier sketches in CA 5-8R, CANR-10
Interview in … CANR-10
See also CLC 7, 8, 23
See also DLB 2
See also DLBY 81, 92
Yates, W(illiam) E(dgar) 1938- … 49-52
Yatron, Michael 1921- … 37-40R
Yau, John 1950- … 154
Yau, Shing-Tung 1949- … 158
Yauch, Wilbur Alden 1904-1982 Obituary … 106
Yaukey, David (William) 1927- … 61-64
Yaukey, Grace S(ydenstricker) 1899-1994 . CANR-1
Obituary … 145
Earlier sketch in CA 1-4R
See also SATA 5, 80
Yavetz, Zvi 1925- … CANR-16
Earlier sketch in CA 29-32R
Yavitz, Boris 1923- … 114
Yavorov, Peyo 1878-1914 … DLB 147
Yaw, Yvonne 1936- … 65-68
Yawetz, Zwy
See Yavetz, Zvi
Yazdanfar, Farzin 1953- … 167
Yazijian, Harvey Z. 1948- … 107
Yeadon, David 1942- … 104
Yeager, Allan Edward 1943- … 101
Yeager, Chuck 1923- … 154
Yeager, Jeana 1952- … 158
Yeager, Leland B(ennett) 1924- … 125
Yeager, Peter C(leary) 1949- … 131
Yeager, Randolph O. 1912- … 130
Yeager, Robert Cushing 1942- … 102
Yeager, W(illard) Hayes 1897- … CAP-2
Earlier sketch in CA 19-20
Yeakley, Marjory Hall 1908- … CANR-2
Earlier sketch in CA 1-4R
See also SATA 21
Yeargers, Edward C. 1938- … 144
Yearley, Clifton K(rebs), Jr. 1925- … 13-16R
Yearns, W(ilfred) Buck 1918- … 134
Yearsley, Ann 1753-1806 … DLB 109
Yearwood, Richard M(eek) 1934- … 37-40R
Yeates, Mabel
See Pereira, Harold Bertram
Yeates, Maurice 1938- … CANR-14
Earlier sketch in CA 41-44R
Yeatman, Linda 1938- … 117
See also SATA 42
Yeats, W. B.
See Yeats, William Butler
Yeats, William Butler 1865-1939 … CANR-45
Brief entry … 104
Earlier sketch in CA 127
See also CDBLB 1890-1914
See also DA
See also DAB
See also DAC
See also DAM DRAM, MST, POET
See also DLB 10, 19, 98, 156
See also MTCW 1
See also PC 20
See also TCLC 1, 11, 18, 31
See also WLC
Yeats-Brown, F(rancis Charles Claypon)
1886-1944 Brief entry … 119
Yeazell, Ruth Bernard 1947- … CANR-52
Earlier sketches in CA 102, CANR-28
Yeck, John D(avid) 1912- … 13-16R
Yee, Albert H(oy) 1929- … CANR-1
Earlier sketch in CA 49-52
Yee, Chiang
See Chiang Yee
Yee, Herbert Wong 1953- … SATA 78
Yee, Min S. 1938- … 101
Yee, Paul (R.) 1956- … 135
See also AAYA 24
See also CLR 44
See also JRDA
See also SATA 67, 96
Yee, Shirley J. 1959- … 141
Yefremov, Ivan (Antonovich) 1907-1972 … 156
Yeganeh, Mohammed 1923- … 5-8R
Yegul, Fikret K. 1942- … 146
Yeh, Chun-Chan 1914- … 148
See also SATA 79
Yeh, George K(ung)-C(hao)
1904-1981 Obituary … 108
Yeh, Wei-lien
See Yip, Wai-lim
Yehiya, Eliezer Don
See Don-Yehiya, Eliezer
Yehoshua, A(braham) B. 1936- … CANR-43
Earlier sketch in CA 33-36R
See also CLC 13, 31
Yelin, Shulamis S. … 121
Yellen, Samuel 1906- … 1-4R
Yellen, Sherman 1932- … 29-32R
Yellin, Carol Lynn (Gilmer) 1920- … 17-20R
Yellin, David G(ilmer) 1916- … 158
Brief entry … 115
Yellin, Jean Fagan 1930- … 41-44R
Yellow Bird
See Ridge, John Rollin
Yellowitz, Irwin 1933- … CANR-4
Earlier sketch in CA 45-48
Yellow Robe, William S., (Jr.) 1950- … 148
Yelton, Donald Charles 1915- … 106
Yeltsin, Boris (Nikolayevich) 1931- … 140
Yelverton, Eric Esskildsen 1888-1964 … CAP-1
Earlier sketch in CA 9-10
Yen, Ching-hwang 1937- … 136
Yenawine, Philip 1942- … 151
See also SATA 85
Yen-Ping, Shen 1896(?)-1981 Obituary … 103
Yenser, Stephen 1941- … CANR-36
Earlier sketch in CA 114
Yensid, Retlaw
See Disney, Walt(er Elias)
Yeo, Cedric Arnold 1905- … CAP-1
Earlier sketch in CA 17-18
Yeo, Wilma (Lethem) 1918-1994 … 25-28R
Obituary … 146
See also SATA 24, 81
Yeoman, John 1934- … 106
See also CLR 46
See also SATA 28, 80
Yeomans, Patricia Henry 1917- … 97-100
Yep, Laurence Michael 1948- … CANR-46
Earlier sketches in CA 49-52, CANR-1
See also AAYA 5
See also CLC 35
See also CLR 3, 17
See also DLB 52
See also JRDA
See also MAICYA
See also SATA 7, 69
Yepsen, Roger B(ennet), Jr. 1947- … CANR-35
Earlier sketch in CA 114
See also SATA 59
Yerbury, Grace D. 1899- … 37-40R
Yerby, Frank G(arvin) 1916-1991 … CANR-52
Obituary … 136
Earlier sketches in CA 9-12R, CANR-16
Interview in … CANR-16
See also BLC 3
See also BW 1
See also CLC 1, 7, 22
See also DAM MULT
See also DLB 76
See also MTCW 1
Yergin, Daniel H. … 103
Yerian, Cameron John … 73-76
See also SATA 21
Yerian, Margaret A. … 73-76
See also SATA 21
Yermakov, Nicholas 1951- … 118
Yerushalmi, Yosef Hayim 1932- … 160
Brief entry … 112
Yerxa, Donald A(llan) 1950- … 139
Yesalis, Charles E(dward) 1946- … 144
Yeselson, Abraham 1921-1978 Obituary … 77-80
Yesenin, Sergei Alexandrovich
See Esenin, Sergei (Alexandrovich)
Yeshayahu, Yisrael 1910-1979 Obituary … 89-92
Yeshurun, Avot 1904-1992 … 132
Obituary … 136
Yessian, Mark R(obert) 1942- … CANR-10
Earlier sketch in CA 25-28R
Yetman, Norman R(oger) 1938- … 29-32R
Yetska
See Ironside, Jetske
Yette, Samuel F(rederick) 1929- … 102
Yeung Yue-man 1938- … 110
Yevtushenko, Yevgeny (Alexandrovich) 1933- …
CANR-54
Earlier sketches in CA 81-84, CANR-33
See also CLC 1, 3, 13, 26, 51
See also DAM POET
See also MTCW 1
Yezierska, Anzia 1885(?)-1970 … 126
Obituary … 89-92
See also CLC 46
See also DLB 28
See also MTCW 1
Yezzo, Dominick 1947- … 53-56
Yglesias, Helen 1915- … CANR-65
Earlier sketches in CA 37-40R, CANR-15
Interview in … CANR-15
See also CAAS 20
See also CLC 7, 22
See also MTCW 1
Yglesias, Jose 1919-1995 … CANR-32
Obituary … 150
Earlier sketch in CA 41-44R
See also HW
Yglesias, Rafael 1954- … 37-40R
Yiannopoulos, A(thanassios) N(ikolaos) 1928- …
CANR-27
Earlier sketch in CA 1-4R
Yick, Joseph K(ong) S(ang) 1953- … 157
Yiesla, Sharon A. 1960- … 142
Yim, Kwan Ha 1929- … 101
Yin, Robert K(uo-zuir) 1941- … CANR-1
Earlier sketch in CA 49-52
Yinger, J(ohn) Milton 1916- … 89-92
Yinon, Jehuda 1935- … 150
Yip, Wai-lim 1937- … 33-36R
Yllo, Kersti 1953- … CANR-44
Earlier sketch in CA 119
Ylvisaker, Paul 1921-1992 … CANR-16
Obituary … 137
Earlier sketches in CA 1-4R, CANR-1
Yngve, Victor H(use) 1920- … 57-60
Yntema, Theodore O(tte) 1900-1985 Obituary … 117
Y.O.
See Russell, George William
Yoakum, Robert 1922- … 77-80
Yochelson, Samuel 1906(?)-1976 Obituary … 69-72
Yochim, Louise Dunn 1909- … 37-40R
Yockey, Hubert P(almer) 1916- … 146
Yocom, Charles Frederick 1914- … CANR-7
Earlier sketch in CA 17-20R
Yoder, Dale 1901- … CANR-2
Earlier sketch in CA 1-4R
Yoder, Don 1921- … 85-88
Yoder, Dorothy Meenen 1921- … 163
See also SATA 96
Yoder, Dot
See Yoder, Dorothy Meenen
Yoder, Glee 1916- … CANR-9
Earlier sketch in CA 21-24R
Yoder, J(ames) Willard 1902- … 37-40R
Yoder, Janice D(ana) 1952- … 114
Yoder, Jess 1922- … 45-48
Yoder, John C. 1942- … 145
Yoder, John H(oward) 1927-1997 … 13-16R
Obituary … 163
Yoder, Marie Angeline 1914- … 5-8R
Yoder, Norman M. 1915- … 21-24R
Yoder, Paton 1912- … 93-96
Yoder, Sanford Calvin 1879- … CAP-1
Earlier sketch in CA 13-16
Yoder, Walter D. 1933- … SATA 88
Yoffe, Elkhonon (Hona) 1928- … 126
Yoggy, Gary A. 1938- … 152
Yogiji, Harbhajan Singh Khalsa 1929- … 93-96
Yogman, Michael W. 1947- … 126
Yohe, W(illiam) Frederick 1943- … 49-52
Yohn, David Waite 1933- … 41-44R
Yohn, Rick 1937- … CANR-8
Earlier sketch in CA 61-64
Yoingco, Angel Q. 1921- … CANR-11
Earlier sketch in CA 25-28R
Yoken, Melvin B(arton) 1939- … 65-68
Yokomitsu Riichi 1898-1947 … TCLC 47
Yokoyama, Toshio 1947- … 136
Yola, Yerima
See Kirk-Greene, Anthony (Hamilton Millard)
Yolen, Jane (Hyatt) 1939- … CANR-56
Earlier sketches in CA 13-16R, CANR-11, 29
Interview in … CANR-29
See also AAYA 4,22
See also CLR 4, 44
See also DLB 52
See also JRDA
See also MAICYA
See also SAAS 1
See also SATA 4, 40, 75
Yolen, Steven H. 1942- … 73-76
Yolen, Will(iam Hyatt) 1908-1985 … CANR-29
Obituary … 118
Earlier sketches in CA 5-8R, CANR-5
Yolton, John W(illiam) 1921- … CANR-14
Earlier sketch in CA 37-40R
Yone, Edward Michael Law
See Law Yone, Edward Michael
Yonemura, Margaret V. S. 1928- … 29-32R
Yonge, Charlotte (Mary) 1823-1901 … 163
Brief entry … 109
See also DLB 18, 163
See also SATA 17
See also TCLC 48

Yonge, (Charles) Maurice 1899-1986 Obituary . 118
Yonker, Nicholas J(unior) 1927- 117
Yoo, Grace S.
See Yoo, Young H(yun)
Yoo, Young H(yun) 1927- 41-44R
Yoo, Yushin 1940- CANR-2
Earlier sketch in CA 45-48
Yooll, Andrew M(ichael) Graham
See Graham-Yooll, Andrew M(ichael)
Yoors, Jan 1922(?)-1977 81-84
Obituary 73-76
Yorburg, Betty 1926- CANR-16
Earlier sketch in CA 29-32R
Yorck, Ruth (Landshoff)
1909-1966 Obituary 25-28R
Yordan, Philip 1913(?)- 129
Brief entry 116
Yorick, A. P.
See Tindall, William York
Yorinks, Arthur 1953- CANR-38
Earlier sketch in CA 106
See also CLR 20
See also MAICYA
See also SATA 33, 49, 85
York, Alison
See Nicole, Christopher (Robin)
York, Amanda
See Dial, Joan
York, Andrew
See Nicole, Christopher (Robin)
York, Carol Beach 1928- CANR-6
Earlier sketch in CA 1-4R
See also JRDA
See also SATA 6, 77
York, Elizabeth
See York, Margaret Elizabeth
York, Georgia
See Hoffman, Lee
York, Helen 1918- CANR-4
Earlier sketch in CA 53-56
York, Herbert (Frank) 1921- 29-32R
York, Jeremy
See Creasey, John
York, Lorraine (M.) 1958- CANR-66
Earlier sketch in CA 129
York, Margaret Elizabeth 1927- 103
York, Pauline
See Howl, Marcia (Yvonne Hurt)
York, Phyllis 1937- 132
York, Rebecca
See Buckholtz, Eileen (Garber)
and Glick, Ruth (Burtnick)
York, Reginald O(scar) 1942- 117
York, Simon
See Heinlein, Robert A(nson)
York, Susannah 1941- 130
York, Thomas (Lee) 1940- 73-76
York, William 1950- 107
Yorke, Amanda 1954- 139
Yorke, Henry Vincent 1905-1974 85-88
Obituary 49-52
See also Green, Henry
See also CLC 13
Yorke, Katherine
See Ellerbeck, Rosemary (Anne L'Estrange)
Yorke, Malcolm 1938- 131
Yorke, Margaret
See Larminie, Margaret Beda
Yorke, Ritchie 1944- 77-80
Yorke, Roger
See Bingley, David Ernest
Yorke, Susan 1915- CANR-1
Earlier sketch in CA 1-4R
Yorkist
See Morrah, Dermot (Michael Macgregor)
Yosano Akiko 1878-1942 161
See also PC 11
See also TCLC 59
Yoseloff, Martin 1919- 45-48
Yoseloff, Thomas 1913- 77-80
Yoshida, (Katsumi) Jim 1921- 41-44R
Yoshida, Shigeru 1878-1967 Obituary 113
Yoshida, Toshi 1911- .... SATA 77
Yoshikichi, Furui 1937- .... DLB 182
Yoshimasu, Gozo 1939- 126
Yoshimoto, Banana
See Yoshimoto, Mahoko
See also CLC 84
Yoshimoto, Mahoko 1964- 144
See also Yoshimoto, Banana
Yoshimura, Akira 1927- 156
Yoskowitz, Irving
See Younger, Irving
Yost, Charles W(oodruff) 1907-1981 ...... CANR-3
Obituary 104
Earlier sketch in CA 9-12R
Yost, Edna 1889-1971 .... 1-4R
Obituary 103
See also SATA-Obit 26
Yost, Elwy McMurran 1925- 126
Yost, F(rank) Donald 1927- 29-32R
Yost, Graham 1959- 129
Yost, Nellie Snyder 1905- CANR-16
Earlier sketch in CA 29-32R
Yost, Stanley K. 1924- 9-12R
Youcha, Geraldine 1925- CANR-51
Earlier sketch in CA 93-96
Youd, C. S.
See Youd, (Christopher) Samuel
See also SAAS 6
Youd, (Christopher) Samuel 1922- CANR-37
Earlier sketch in CA 77-80
See also Christopher, John
and Youd, C. S.
See also JRDA
See also MAICYA
See also SATA 47
See also SATA-Brief 30
Youdale, Peter J. 1928- 45-48
Youman, Roger J(acob) 1932- 65-68
Youmans, E(lmer) Grant 1907- CAP-2
Earlier sketch in CA 23-24
Youmans, Marlene 1953- 77-80
Young, Agatha
See Young, Agnes Brooks
Young, Agnes Brooks 1898-1974 Obituary 109
Young, Ahdele Carrine 1923- CANR-41
Earlier sketch in CA 107
Young, Al(bert James) 1939- CANR-65
Earlier sketches in CA 29-32R, CANR-26
See also BLC 3
See also BW 2
See also CLC 19
See also DAM MULT
See also DLB 33
Young, Alan 1930- CANR-6
Earlier sketch in CA 57-60
Young, Alan R(oger) 1941- 89-92
Young, Alison 1922- CANR-29
Earlier sketch in CA 53-56
Young, Allan Edward 1939- 125
Young, Allen 1941- CANR-39
Earlier sketches in CA 101, CANR-18
Young, Andre Ramelle
See Dre, Dr.
Young, Andrew (John) 1885-1971 .... CANR-29
Earlier sketches in CA 5-8R, CANR-7
See also CLC 5
Young, Andrew (J.) 1932- 160
Young, Angela
See Yardley, Alice
Young, Anne P(atricia) 1921- 65-68
Young, Anne Steele 1923- 129
Young, Arthur 1741-1820 .... DLB 158
Young, Arthur C(lements) 1923- 25-28R
Young, Arthur N(ichols) 1890-1984 .... 9-12R
Obituary 113
Young, Axel
See McDowell, Michael
Young, Barbara 1952- 141
Young, Bernice Elizabeth 1931- 37-40R
Young, Bertram Alfred 1912- 105
Young, Bette Roth 1937- 149
Young, Billie 1936- 53-56
Young, Bob
See Young, James Robert
and Young, Robert W(illiam)
Young, Brittany
See Young, Sandra
Young, Carol 1945- .... SATA 102
Young, Carrie
See Young, Ahdele Carrine
Young, Carter Travis
See Charbonneau, Louis (Henry)
Young, Catherine
See Olds, Helen Diehl
Young, Catherine Alicia 1963- 136
Young, Cathy
See Young, Catherine Alicia
Young, Charles M(atthew) 1951- 93-96
Young, Charles R(obert) 1927- 13-16R
Young, Chesley Virginia 1919- 33-36R
Young, Chic
See Young, Murat Bernard (Chic)
Young, Clarence CANR-27
Earlier sketches in CAP-2, CA 19-20
See also Stratemeyer, Edward L.
See also SATA 1, 67
Young, Coleman A(lexander) 1918-1997 156
Obituary 162
Young, Collier
See Bloch, Robert (Albert)
Young, Collier 1908(?)-1980 Obituary 103
Young, Dallas M. 1914- 17-20R
Young, David C(harles) 1937- 41-44R
Young, David P(ollock) 1936- CANR-50
Earlier sketches in CA 21-24R, CANR-9, 24
Young, David S(amuel D'arcy) 1946- 113
Young, Dean (Wayne) 1938- 130
Young, Delbert Alton 1907-1975 105
Young, Dennis R(alph) 1943- Brief entry 107
Young, Dianne 1959- 152
See also SATA 88
Young, Dick 1918(?)-1987 Obituary 123
See also DLB 171
Young, Donald (Richard) 1933- CANR-46
Earlier sketches in CA 13-16R, CANR-12
Young, Donald Ramsey 1898-1977 Obituary . 69-72
Young, Dorothea Bennett 1924- CANR-13
Earlier sketch in CA 13-16R
See also SATA 31
Young, Douglas (Cuthbert Colquhoun) 1913-1973 ..
CAP-1
Obituary 45-48
Earlier sketch in CA 17-18
Young, Ed (Tse-chun) 1931- 130
Brief entry 116
See also CLR 27
See also MAICYA
See also SATA 10, 74
Young, Edgar Berryhill 1908- 104
Young, Edith 49-52
Young, Edward
See Reinfeld, Fred
Young, Edward 1683-1765 .... DLB 95
Young, Edward J(oseph) 1907-1968 .... CAP-1
Earlier sketch in CA 11-12
Young, (Cecil) Edwyn 1913-1988 Obituary 124
Young, Elaine L.
See Schulte, Elaine L(ouise)
Young, Eleanor R. 1918- 37-40R
Young, Elisabeth Larsh 1910- 81-84
Young, Elizabeth 108
Young, Ellin Dodge 1932- 106
Young, Everett
See Cosby, Yvonne Shepard
Young, Ezra P(orter) 1902- 113
Young, Francis A(lfred) 1907- 130
Young, Francis Brett 1884-1954 Brief entry 122
See also DLB 191
Young, Frank Carl 1907- CAP-1
Earlier sketch in CA 13-14
Young, Frank Wilbur 1928- Brief entry 108
Young, Fred(erick) L(ee) 1922- 25-28R
Young, G(eorge) M(alcolm) 1882-1959 Brief
entry 120
Young, Gary 1951- CANR-40
Earlier sketch in CA 117
Young, Gavin (David) 1928- 143
Young, George Berkeley 1913-1988 Obituary .. 124
Young, George F(rederick) W(illiam) 1937- ... 57-60
Young, George Kennedy 1911-1990 Obituary .. 131
Young, Glennys 1959- 163
Young, Gregory G. 1929- Brief entry 110
Young, Harold Chester 1932- 129
Brief entry 109
Young, Harold H(erbert) 1903- CAP-2
Earlier sketch in CA 19-20
Young, Howard Thomas 1926- 9-12R
Young, Hugo (John Smelter) 1938- CANR-28
Earlier sketch in CA 25-28R
Young, I(sador) S. 1902- 102
Young, Ian (George) 1945- CANR-52
Earlier sketches in CA 29-32R, CANR-11, 27
Young, J(ames) Harvey 1915- CANR-6
Earlier sketch in CA 1-4R
Young, J(ohn) Michael 1944- 143
Young, J(ack) P. 1929- 157
Young, J(ohn) Z(achary) 1907-1997 ..... CANR-19
Obituary 159
Earlier sketch in CA 101
Young, James Allan 1934- 116
Young, James D(ean) 1925- Brief entry 111
Young, James Douglas 1921- 25-28R
Young, James E. 1951- 159
Young, James J(oseph) 1940- CANR-16
Earlier sketch in CA 93-96
Young, James O(wen) 1943- 49-52
Young, James Robert 1921- 93-96
Young, James V(an) 1936- 69-72
Young, Jan
See Young, Janet Randall
Young, Janet Randall 1919- CANR-5
Earlier sketch in CA 5-8R
See also SATA 3
Young, Jessica (Hankinson) Brett
See Brett-Young, Jessica (Hankinson)
Young, Jim 1930- 109
Young, Jock 1942- 104
Young, John
See Macintosh, Brownie
Young, John 1920- CANR-1
Earlier sketch in CA 45-48
Young, John 1934- 134
Young, John K(arl) 1951- 135
Young, John Orr 1886-1976 Obituary 65-68
Young, John Parke 1895- 5-8R
Young, John Sacret 1947- 144
Young, John V. 1909- 121
Young, John Wesley 1951- 135
Young, John Wray 1907- 45-48
Young, Jordan Marten 1920- 21-24R
Young, Judy (Elaine) Dockrey 1949- ...... SATA 72
Young, K(enneth) C. 1941- 155
Young, Karen M. 1942- 138
Young, Ken 1956- 151
See also SATA 86
Young, Kenneth 1916-1985 .... CANR-3
Obituary 118
Earlier sketch in CA 9-12R
Young, Kenneth Ray 1939- 150
Young, Kenneth T(odd)
1916-1972 Obituary 37-40R
Young, Leontine R(uth) 1910-1988 .... CAP-1
Obituary 126
Earlier sketch in CA 11-12
Young, Lesley 1949- 110
Young, Lois Horton 1911-1981 .... 9-12R
See also SATA 26
Young, Louise B. 1919- CANR-10
Earlier sketch in CA 25-28R
See also SATA 64
Young, Louise Merwin 1903-1992 .... CAP-1
Obituary 139
Earlier sketch in CA 11-12
Young, M(erwin) Crawford 1931- 13-16R
Young, Mahonri (Sharp) 1911-1996 81-84
Obituary 152
Young, Margaret B(uckner) 1922- 21-24R
See also SATA 2
Young, Margaret Labash 1926- 134
Brief entry 110
Young, Marguerite (Vivian) 1909-1995 ...... CAP-1
Obituary 150
Earlier sketch in CA 13-16
See also CLC 82
Young, Marjorie W(illis) 85-88
Young, Mark 1960- 139
Young, Martin 1947- 127
Young, Mary 1940- 155
See also SATA 89
Young, Mary Elizabeth 1929- 37-40R
Young, Mary Elizabeth Reardon
1901(?)-1981 Obituary 105
Young, Mary Lou Daves 1918-1991 126
Obituary 135
Young, Michael (Dunlop) 1915- 101
Young, Miriam 1913-1974 .... 37-40R
Obituary 53-56
See also SATA 7
Young, Morris N. 1909- 33-36R
Young, Murat Bernard (Chic)
1901-1973 Obituary 41-44R
Young, Nacella
See Tate, Velma
Young, Neil 1945- 110
See also CLC 17
Young, Noel 1922- 57-60
Young, Noela 1930- .... SATA 89
Young, Norman J(ames) 1930- 77-80
Young, Oran R(eed) 1941- 112
Brief entry 109
Young, Otis E., Jr. 1925- 53-56
Young, Pam 1943- 109
Young, (Rodney Lee) Patrick (Jr.) 1937- 69-72
See also SATA 22
Young, Paul Thomas 1892-1978 .... CANR-3
Earlier sketch in CA 1-4R
Young, Pauline Vislick 1896- 5-8R
Young, Percy M(arshall) 1912- CANR-31
Earlier sketch in CA 13-16R
See also SATA 31
Young, Perry Deane 1941- 57-60
Young, Peter 1915- 13-16R
Young, Peter Alan 1934- 107
Young, Philip
See Steward, Samuel M(orris)
Young, Philip 1918-1991 .... CANR-6
Obituary 135
Earlier sketch in CA 9-12R
Young, R(obert) V(aughan) 1947- 127
Young, Ralph Aubrey
1902(?)-1980 Obituary 97-100
Young, Richard Alan 1946- .... SATA 72
Young, Richard E(merson) 1932- 29-32R
Young, Richard Knox 1913- 13-16R
Young, Richard Phillip 1940- 29-32R
Young, Robert
See Payne, (Pierre Stephen) Robert
Young, Robert 1944- 123
Young, Robert A. 1950- 153
Young, Robert Doran 1928- CANR-17
Earlier sketch in CA 29-32R
Young, Robert F(ranklin) 1915-1986 166
Young, Robert J(ohn) 1942- 101
Young, Robert W(illiam) 1916-1969 ...... CANR-5
Earlier sketch in CA 5-8R
See also SATA 3
Young, Rosamond M. 1912- 154
Young, Rose
See Harris, Marion Rose (Young)
Young, Ruth 1884-1983 Obituary 111
Young, Ruth 1946- 136
See also SATA 67
Young, Sandra 1952- 124
Young, Scott A(lexander) 1918- CANR-20
Earlier sketches in CA 9-12R, CANR-5
See also SATA 5
Young, Seymour Dilworth 1897- CAP-2
Earlier sketch in CA 29-32
Young, Stanley (Preston)
1906-1975 Obituary 57-60
Young, Stark 1881-1963 .... CANR-60
Obituary 89-92
Earlier sketch in CA 105
See also DLB 9, 102
See also DLBD 16
Young, Stephen M(arvin)
1889(?)-1984 Obituary 114
Young, T(heron) Kue 1948- 149
Young, Thomas
See Yoseloff, Thomas
Young, Thomas Daniel 1919-1997 ...... CANR-14
Obituary 156
Earlier sketch in CA 37-40R
Young, Vernon 1912-1986 45-48
Obituary 120
Young, Virginia Brady 1921- 61-64
Young, Virginia G(arton) 1919- 13-16R
Young, Vivien
See Gater, Dilys
Young, Waldemar 1880-1938 .... DLB 26
Young, Warren C(ameron) 1913- 13-16R
Young, Warren R(ichard) 1926- 21-24R
Young, Wayland 1923- 13-16R
Young, Whitney M(oore), Jr. 1921-1971 .. CANR-25
Earlier sketches in CAP-1, CA 13-14
See also BW 1
Young, William 1918- 45-48
Young, William C(urtis) 1928- 45-48
Young, William H(enry) 1912- 21-24R
Young, William J. 1938- 109
Young Bear, Ray A. 1950- 146
See also CLC 94
See also DAM MULT
See also DLB 175
See also NNAL
Youngberg, Norma Ione (Rhoads) 1896- 9-12R
Youngberg, Ruth Tanis 1915- 107
Youngblood, Denise J. 1952- 139
Youngblood, Ila Dell 1926- 125
Youngblood, Ronald F. 1931- CANR-54
Earlier sketches in CA 37-40R, CANR-14, 30
Youngblood, Shay 1959- 168
Young-Bruehl, Elisabeth 1946- 131
Youngdahl, Benjamin E(manuel) 1897-1970 . CAP-2
Earlier sketch in CA 21-22

Youngdahl, Reuben K(enneth Nathaniel)
1911-1968 ... 5-8R
Obituary ... 103
Younge, Sheila 1945(?)-1977 Obituary ... 73-76
Young-Eisendrath, Polly 1947- ... 143
Younger, Edward Eugene
1909-1979 Obituary ... 89-92
Younger, George Colman the 1762-1836 ... DLB 89
Younger, Irving 1932-1988 Obituary ... 125
Younger, Paul 1935- ... 101
Younger, R(onald) M(ichel) 1917- ... CANR-10
Earlier sketch in CA 17-20R
Younger, Richard D(avis) 1921- ... 9-12R
Youngholm, Thomas 1949- ... 164
Younghusband, Eileen (Louise)
1902-1981 Obituary ... 108
Younghusband, Francis (Edward) 1863-1942 Brief
entry ... 113
Youngman, Henny 1906(?)- ... 134
Brief entry ... 107
Youngquist, Walter 1921- ... 61-64
Youngren, J(ohn) Alan 1937- ... 108
Youngs, Betty 1934-1985 ... 117
See also SATA 53
See also SATA-Obit 42
Youngs, Betty F(errell) 1928- ... 33-36R
Youngs, Frederic A., Jr. 1936- Brief entry ... 112
Youngs, J. William T., Jr. 1941- ... CANR-10
Earlier sketch in CA 65-68
Youngs, Robert W(ells) 1913- ... 13-16R
Younie, William John 1932- ... 21-24R
Younin, Wolf 1908(?)-1984 Obituary ... 112
Younker, Lucas 1942- ... 65-68
Younkin, Paula 1942- ... 145
See also SATA 77
Yount, John A(lonzo) 1935- ... CANR-47
Earlier sketches in CA 45-48, CANR-5
Yount, Lisa 1944- ... 141
See also SATA 74
Yount, Steven 1948- ... 146
Yourcenar, Marguerite 1903-1987 ... CANR-60
Earlier sketches in CA 69-72, CANR-23
See also CLC 19, 38, 50, 87
See also DAM NOV
See also DLB 72
See also DLBY 88
See also MTCW 1
Youree, Gary 1931- ... CANR-2
Earlier sketch in CA 49-52
Yousaf, Muhammad 1937- ... 141
Youssef, Edwar Kolta Faltas
See al-Kharrat, Edwar
Youst, Lionel 1934- ... 167
Yousuf, Ahmed
See Essop, Ahmed
Youtie, Herbert Chayyim
1904-1980 Obituary ... 97-100
Yovkov, Yordan 1880-1937 ... DLB 147
Yowa
See McMurray, Nancy A(rmistead)
Yoxall, Harry W(aldo) 1896-1984 ... 13-16R
Obituary ... 113
Yoxen, Edward (John) 1950- ... 123
Yu, Anthony C. 1938- ... 158
Brief entry ... 110
Yu, Beongcheon 1925- Brief entry ... 108
Yu, Charles
See Targ, William
Yu, David C. 1918- ... 37-40R
Yu, Elena S. H. 1947- ... 125
Brief entry ... 109
Yu, Frederick T. C. 1921- ... 9-12R
Yu, George T(zuchiao) 1931- ... 17-20R
Yu, Pauline (Ruth) 1949- ... 122
Brief entry ... 118
Yu, Sui
See Chou, Eric
Yu, Ying-shih 1930- ... CANR-43
Earlier sketch in CA 25-28R
Yu, Zhuoyun 1918- ... 132
Yuan, Lei Chen
See De Jaegher, Raymond-Joseph
Yuan, T'ung-li 1895-1965 ... CAP-1
Earlier sketch in CA 9-10
Yudell, Lynn D. 1943- ... 29-32R
Yudelman, David 1944- ... 140
Yudewitz, Hyman 1906- ... 93-96
Yuditskaya, Tatyana 1964- ... SATA 75
Yudkin, John 1910- ... 13-16R
Yudkin, Leon Israel 1939- ... CANR-12
Earlier sketch in CA 29-32R
Yudkin, Michael D(avid) 1938- ... 29-32R
Yudof, Mark G(eorge) 1944- ... 109
Yu-ho, Tseng
See Ecke, Betty Tseng Yu-ho
Yuill, Nicola M. 1965- ... 140
Yuill, P. B.
See Williams, Gordon M(aclean)
Yuill, P. D.
See Venables, Terry
Yuill, Phyllis Jean (Marquart) 1941- ... 65-68
Yuill, William Edward 1921- ... CANR-2
Earlier sketch in CA 1-4R
Yukawa, Hideki 1907-1981 ... 163
Obituary ... 108
Yuki
See Inoue, Yukitoshi
Yule, Andrew 1936- ... 129
Yuma, Dan
See Dunham, Robert
Yun, Tan
See Lin, Adet J(usu)
Yunck, John A(dam) III 1917- ... 9-12R
Yungblut, John R(ichard) 1913-1995 ... 41-44R
Obituary ... 149
Yunkel, Ramar
See Martin (Montes), Jose L(uis)
Yunkel, Ramar
See Martin (Montes), Jose L(uis)
Yurchenco, Henrietta 1916- ... 37-40R
Yurick, Sol 1925- ... CANR-25
Earlier sketch in CA 13-16R
See also CLC 6
Yurieff, Zoya I(osifovna) 1922- Brief entry ... 109
Yurka, Blanche 1887-1974 ... 9-12R
Obituary ... 120
Yusko, A(aron) A(llen) 1935- ... 65-68
Yuzyk, Paul 1913- ... CANR-18
Earlier sketch in CA 101
Yzermans, Vincent Arthur 1925- ... 13-16R

Z

Z
See Malia, Martin (Edward)
Zabaneh, Natalia (Shefka) 1946- ... 105
Zabeeh, Farhana 1919- ... 41-44R
Zabel, Diane 1957- ... 151
Zabih, Sepehr 1925- ... CANR-9
Earlier sketch in CA 21-24R
Zabilka, Gladys M. 1917- ... 5-8R
Zablocki, Benjamin 1941- ... 37-40R
Zablocki, Clement J(ohn) 1912-1983 Obituary ... 111
Zabolotsky, Nikolai Alekseevich 1903-1958 ... 164
Brief entry ... 116
See also TCLC 52
Zabor, Rafi 1946- ... 165
Zaborowska, Magdalena J. 1963- ... 150
Zabriskie, George 1919(?)-1989 Obituary ... 128
Zaccaria, Jerry A. 1945- ... 164
Zacek, Jane Shapiro 1938- ... 109
Zacek, Joseph Frederick 1930- ... 37-40R
Zach, Cheryl (Byrd) 1947- ... CANR-69
Earlier sketch in CA 124
See also AAYA 21
See also SAAS 24
See also SATA 58, 98
See also SATA-Brief 51
Zach, Natan
See Zach, Nathan
Zach, Nathan 1930- ... 156
Brief entry ... 105
Zachariae, Friedrich Wilhelm 1726-1777 ... DLB 97
Zacharias, Lee
See Zacharias, Lela Ann
Zacharias, Lela Ann 1944- ... CANR-27
Earlier sketch in CA 85-88
Zacharis, John C. 1936- ... 73-76
Zachary, Elizabeth 1928- ... 109
Zachary, Hugh 1928- ... CANR-47
Earlier sketches in CA 21-24R, CANR-13
Zachary, Saul 1934- ... 129
Zacher, Christian Keeler 1941- ... 105
Zacher, Mark W. 1938- ... 85-88
Zacher, Robert Vincent 1917- ... 1-4R
Zack, Arnold M(arshall) 1931- ... CANR-42
Earlier sketches in CA 9-12R, CANR-3, 19
Zack, Bill 1956- ... 141
Zack, Naomi 1944- ... 147
Zacks, Shelemyahu 1932- ... 141
Zade, Mirzo Tursun
See Tursun-Zade, Mirzo
Zadeh, Lotfi Asker 1921- ... 163
Zadeh, Norman 1950- ... 61-64
Zadravec, Katharine E. 1933(?)-1989 Obituary ... 128
Zaehner, Robert Charles 1913-1974 Obituary ... 109
Zaffo, George J. (?)-1984 ... SATA 42
Zaffuto, Anthony A(ngelo) 1926- ... 101
Zafren, Herbert C(ecil) 1925- ... CANR-50
Earlier sketches in CA 45-48, CANR-25
Zagar, J. Janko 1921- ... 121
Zagarell, Sandra A(belson) 1943- ... 118
Zagat, Arthur Leo 1895(?)-1949 Brief entry ... 110
Zagona, Salvatore Vincent 1920- Brief entry ... 108
Zagoren, Marc Alan 1940- ... 132
Zagoren, Ruby 1922-1974 ... CAP-1
Earlier sketch in CA 17-18
Zagoria, Donald S. 1928- ... CANR-16
Earlier sketch in CA 21-24R
Zagorin, Perez 1920- ... CANR-36
Earlier sketch in CA 53-56
Zagorski, Paul W. 1946- ... 144
Zagoskin, Mikhail Nikolaevich 1789-1852 ... DLB 198
Zagst, Michael (Sidney) 1950- ... 121
Zagwyn, Deborah Turney 1953- ... SATA 78
Zaharias, Babe Didrikson
See Zaharias, Mildred Ella Didrikson
Zaharias, Mildred Ella Didrikson 1914(?)-1956 Brief
entry ... 117
Zaharopoulos, George K. 1933- ... 41-44R
Zahava, Irene 1951- ... 57-60
Zaheer, Hasan 1930- ... 149
Zahl, Paul Arthur 1910-1985 Obituary ... 117
Zahler, Helene S. 1911-1981 Obituary ... 104
Zahn, Curtis 1912- ... CANR-5
Earlier sketch in CA 5-8R
Zahn, Frank 1936- ... 97-100
Zahn, Gordon C(harles) 1918- ... 9-12R
Zahn, Muriel 1894- ... 5-8R
Zahn, Timothy 1951- ... CANR-63
Earlier sketches in CA 123, CANR-59
See also AAYA 14
See also DAM POP
See also SATA 91
Zahniser, Marvin R(alph) 1934- ... 21-24R
Zahorchak, Michael G(eorge) 1929- ... CANR-15
Earlier sketch in CA 41-44R
Zahorski, Kenneth J. 1939- ... 123
Zaid, Barry 1938- ... SATA 51
Zaidenberg, Arthur 1908(?)-1990 ... 108
Obituary ... 131
See also SATA 34
See also SATA-Obit 66
Zaidi, S(yed) M(ohammad) Hafeez 1929- ... CANR-25
Earlier sketch in CA 45-48
Zaillian, Steven 1953- ... 152
Zainu'ddin, Ailsa
See Zainu'ddin, Ailsa G(wennyth) Thomson
Zainu'ddin, Ailsa G(wennyth) Thomson 1927- ...
CANR-12
Earlier sketch in CA 29-32R
Zajc, Dane 1929- ... DLB 181
Zajonc, Robert Boleslaw 1923- Brief entry ... 106
Zak, William F. 1945- ... 161
Zakaria, Haji Ahmad 1947- ... 138
Zakarian, John J. 1937- ... 132
Zakarian, Richard H(achadoor) 1925- ... 41-44R
Zakia, Richard D(onald) 1925- ... CANR-9
Earlier sketch in CA 65-68
Zaknic, Ivan 1938- ... 138
Zakon, Alan J. 1935- ... 17-20R
Zakrzewski, Sigmund F. 1919- ... 142
Zakuta, Leo 1925- ... 17-20R
Zalamea, Luis 1921- ... 17-20R
Zalan, Magda 1936- ... 112
Zalben, Jane Breskin 1950- ... CANR-4
Earlier sketch in CA 49-52
See also SATA 7, 79
Zald, Mayer N(athan) 1931- ... CANR-28
Earlier sketches in CA 17-20R, CANR-8
Zaldivar, Fulgencio Batista y
See Batista y Zaldivar, Fulgencio
Zaleski, Eugene 1918- ... 77-80
Zaleznik, Abraham 1924- ... CANR-37
Earlier sketch in CA 73-76
Zali, Paul M. 1922- Brief entry ... 108
Zalis, Paul 1952- ... 138
Zalkind, Sheldon S(tanley) 1922- ... 65-68
Zall, Paul M. 1922- ... CANR-20
Earlier sketches in CA 1-4R, CANR-6
Zallen, Doris Teichler 1941- ... 162
Zaller, Angelika Bita ... CANR-36
Earlier sketches in CA 77-80, CANR-13
Zaller, Robert 1940- ... CANR-64
Earlier sketches in CA 77-80, CANR-13, 32
Zallinger, Jean (Day) 1918- ... SATA 14, 80
Zallinger, Peter Franz 1943- ... 108
See also SATA 49
Zaloga, Steven J(oseph) 1952- ... 150
Zalon, Jean E(ugenia) 1919- ... 102
Zaltkovich, Charles T(heodore) 1917- ... 5-8R
Zaltman, Gerald 1938- ... CANR-7
Earlier sketch in CA 17-20R
Zalzanick, Sheldon 1928- ... 77-80
Zamble, Edward 1942- Brief entry ... 108
Zambrano, Myrna M. 1958- ... 165
Zambreno, Mary Frances 1954- ... 142
See also SATA 75
Zamiatin, Yevgenii
See Zamyatin, Evgeny Ivanovich
Zamir, Israel 1929- ... 154
Zamonski, Stanley W. 1919- ... 9-12R
Zamora, Bernice (B. Ortiz) 1938- ... 151
See also CLC 89
See also DAM MULT
See also DLB 82
See also HLC
See also HW
Zamoyski, Adam (Stefan Jan Maria Sariusz)
1949- ... 103
Zamoyta, Vincent C. 1921- ... 21-24R
Zampa, Luigi 1905-1991 ... 157
Zampaglione, Gerardo 1917- ... CANR-14
Earlier sketch in CA 77-80
Zamyatin, Evgeny Ivanovich 1884-1937 ... 166
Brief entry ... 105
See also TCLC 8, 37
Zancanella, Don 1954- ... 166
Zand, Dale Ezra 1926- ... 111
Zand, Herbert 1923-1970 ... DLB 85
Zand, Roxanne 1952- ... 138
Zander, Alvin Frederick 1913- ... CANR-19
Earlier sketch in CA 1-4R
Zanderbergen, George
See May, Julian
Zaner, Richard M(orris) 1933- ... CANR-16
Earlier sketch in CA 29-32R
Zanetti, J(oaquin) Enrique
1885-1974 Obituary ... 45-48
Zang, David W(illiam) 1950- ... 148
Zangeneh, Hamid 1945- ... 141
Zangger, Eberhard 1958- ... 138
Zangrando, Robert L. 1932- ... 25-28R
Zangwill, Israel 1864-1926 ... 167
Brief entry ... 109
See also DLB 10, 135, 197
See also TCLC 16
Zangwill, Oliver Louis 1913- ... 109
Zanjani, Sally Springmeyer ... 120
Zants, Emily 1937- ... 37-40R
Zanuck, Daryl F(rancis) 1902-1979 Obituary ... 93-96
Zanussi, Krzysztof 1939- ... 149
Zanzotto, Andrea 1921- ... DLB 128
Zapata Olivella, Manuel 1920- ... 153
See also DLB 113
See also HW
Zappa, Francis Vincent, Jr. 1940-1993 ... CANR-57
Obituary ... 143
Earlier sketch in CA 108
See also Zappa, Frank
Zappa, Frank
See Zappa, Francis Vincent, Jr.
See also CLC 17
Zappler, Lisbeth 1930- ... CANR-4
Earlier sketch in CA 49-52
See also SATA 10
Zar, Rose 1923- ... 117
Zara, Louis 1910- ... CAP-2
Earlier sketch in CA 13-14
Zarb, Janet M. 1941- ... 144
Zarchy, Harry 1912- ... CANR-2
Earlier sketch in CA 1-4R
See also SATA 34
Zarcone, Vincent P(eter), Jr. 1937- ... 61-64
Zarefsky, David (Harris) 1946- Brief entry ... 109
Zaremba, Eve 1930- ... 133
Zaremba, Joseph 1923- Brief entry ... 112
Zaretsky, Eli 1940- ... CANR-37
Earlier sketch in CA 85-88
Zarifopol-Johnston, Ilinca Marina ... 139
Zaring, Jane (Thomas) 1936- ... 108
See also SATA 40
Zarins, Joyce Audy
See dos Santos, Joyce Audy
See also SATA 57
Zariski, Raphael 1925- ... 49-52
Zarnecki, George 1915- ... CANR-10
Earlier sketch in CA 57-60
Zarnecki, Jerzy
See Zarnecki, George
Zarnow, Teryl 1951- ... 135
Zarnowitz, Victor 1919- ... 21-24R
Zarro, Richard A(llen) 1946- ... 33-36R
Zartman, I(ra) William 1932- ... CANR-5
Earlier sketch in CA 9-12R
Zarucchi, Jeanne Morgan 1955- ... 138
Zaslavskaya, T. I.
See Zaslavskaya, Tatyana (Ivanovna)
Zaslavskaya, Tatyana (Ivanovna) 1924- ... 138
Zaslavsky, Claudia 1917- ... CANR-1
Earlier sketch in CA 49-52
See also SATA 36
Zasloff, J. J.
See Zasloff, Joseph J(ermiah)
Zasloff, Joseph J(ermiah) 1925- ... 129
Brief entry ... 116
Zaslow, Morris 1918- ... CANR-24
Earlier sketch in CA 45-48
Zassenhaus, Hiltgunt 1916- ... 49-52
See also AITN 1
Zastrow, Charles (H.) 1942- ... CANR-71
Earlier sketch in CA 127
Zastrow, Erika
See Massey, Erika
Zatlin, Phyllis 1938- ... CANR-36
Earlier sketches in CA 41-44R, CANR-15
Zatlin Boring, Phyllis
See Zatlin, Phyllis
Zatlin-Boring, Phyllis
See Zatlin, Phyllis
Zatsiorsky, Vladimir M. 1932- ... 156
Zatuchni, Gerald I. 1935- ... 37-40R
Zaturenska, Marya 1902-1982 ... CANR-22
Obituary ... 105
Earlier sketch in CA 13-16R
See also CLC 6, 11
Zauberman, Alfred 1903-1984 Obituary ... 112
Zavala, Albert 1930- Brief entry ... 117
Zavala, Iris M(ilagros) 1936- ... CANR-32
Earlier sketches in CA 45-48, CANR-1
See also HW
Zavarzadeh, Mas'ud 1938- ... 106
Zavatsky, Bill
See Zavatsky, William Alexander
Zavatsky, William Alexander 1943- ... CANR-1
Earlier sketch in CA 49-52
Zavattini, Cesare 1902-1989 ... 130
Zavin, Benjamin B. 1920(?)-1981 Obituary ... 103
Zavin, Theodora 1922- ... 53-56
Zavrian, Suzanne (Ostro) 1928- ... 113
Zawadsky, Patience 1927- ... CANR-49
Earlier sketches in CA 21-24R, CANR-9, 24
Zawadzki, Edward S. 1914-1967 ... CAP-2
Earlier sketch in CA 17-18
Zawadzki, Marek 1958- ... SATA 97
Zawodny, J(anusz) K(azimierz) 1921- ... CANR-11
Earlier sketch in CA 13-16R
Zax, Melvin 1928- ... CANR-36
Earlier sketch in CA 37-40R
Zayas-Bazan, Eduardo 1935- ... CANR-37
Earlier sketch in CA 53-56
Zazove, Philip 1951- ... 149
Zdenek, Marilee 1934- ... 102
Zea, Leopoldo 1912- ... CANR-16
Earlier sketch in CA 29-32R
Zeami 1363-1443 ... DC 7
Zeavin, Edna A. 1930- ... 138
Zebel, Sydney H. 1914- ... 1-4R
Zebot, Cyril A. 1914-1989 Obituary ... 128
Zebouni, Selma A(ssir) 1930- ... 17-20R
Zebra, A.
See Scoltock, Jack
Zebrowski, George (T.) 1945- ... CANR-30
Earlier sketch in CA 41-44R
See also CAAS 19
See also DLB 8
See also SATA 67
Zec, Philip 1910(?)-1983 Obituary ... 110
Zech, Paul 1881-1946 ... DLB 56
Zeck, Gerald Anthony 1939- ... 114
See also SATA 40
Zeck, Gerry
See Zeck, Gerald Anthony
Zeckendorf, William 1905- ... 73-76
Zeckhauser, Richard J(ay) 1940- ... CANR-56
Earlier sketch in CA 126

Zed, Dr.
See Penrose, Gordon
Zedler, Beatrice H(ope) 1916- CANR-36
Earlier sketch in CA 41-44R
Zedler, Empress Young 1908- 41-44R
Zedric, Lance Q. 1961- 153
Zee, A. 138
Zeeveld, W(illiam) Gordon 1902-1975 41-44R
Zeff, Stephen A(ddam) 1933- CANR-19
Earlier sketches in CA 9-12R, CANR-3
Zegart, Arthur 1917(?)-1989 Obituary 127
Zegger, Robert Elie 1932- 41-44R
Zegura, Elizabeth Chesney 1949- 144
Zehna, Peter W(illiam) 1925- CANR-1
Earlier sketch in CA 1-4R
Zehnle, Richard F(rederick) 1933- 29-32R
Zehnpfennig, Gladys Burandt 1910- CANR-5
Earlier sketch in CA 5-8R
Zehring, John William 1947- 117
Zei, Alki 77-80
See also CLR 6
See also SATA 24
Zeidenstein, Harvey 1932- 57-60
Zeidman, Irving 1908- CAP-2
Earlier sketch in CA 21-22
Zeidner, Lisa 1955- 110
See also CAAS 24
See also DLB 120
Zeidner, Moshe 1948- 152
Zeier, Joan T(heresa) 1931- 149
See also SATA 81
Zeiger, Henry A(nthony) 1930- 9-12R
Zeiger, Larry
See King, Larry
Zeigerman, Gerald 1939- 21-24R
Zeigfreid, Karl
See Fanthorpe, R(obert) Lionel
Zeigler, L(uther) Harmon 1936- CANR-10
Earlier sketch in CA 13-16R
Zeilik, Michael 1946- CANR-36
Earlier sketch in CA 65-68
Zeiller, Warren 1929- 145
Zeinert, Karen 1942- 148
See also SATA 79
Zeisel, Hans 1905-1992 CANR-6
Obituary 137
Earlier sketch in CA 1-4R
Zeisler, Zvi
See Wachsmann, Shelley
Zeit, Calvin
See Barasch, Marc Ian
Zeitlin, Irving M. 1928- CANR-37
Earlier sketch in CA 21-24R
Zeitlin, Jonathan (Hart) 1955- 121
Zeitlin, Joseph 1906- 49-52
Zeitlin, Maurice 1935- CANR-51
Earlier sketches in CA 13-16R, CANR-10, 26
Zeitlin, Patty 1936- CANR-12
Earlier sketch in CA 25-28R
Zeitlin, Solomon 1888(?)-1976 77-80
Obituary 69-72
Zeitz, James (Victor) 1940- 110
Zeka, Valentin
See Sokolov, Valentin
Zekman, Pamela (Lois) 1944- 106
Interview in 106
Zekowski, Arlene 1922- CANR-1
Earlier sketch in CA 45-48
Zelazny, Roger (Joseph) 1937-1995 CANR-60
Obituary 148
Earlier sketches in CA 21-24R, CANR-26
See also AAYA 7
See also CLC 21
See also DLB 8
See also MTCW 1
See also SATA 57
See also SATA-Brief 39
Zeldin, Jesse 1923- 49-52
Zeldin, Theodore 1933- 147
Zeldis, Chayym 1927- CANR-6
Earlier sketch in CA 1-4R
Zeldis, Malcah 1931- SATA 86
Zelditch, Morris, Jr. 1928- 53-56
Zeldner, Max 1907- CAP-1
Earlier sketch in CA 13-14
Zeldovich, Ia(kov) B(orisovich)
1914-1987 Obituary 124
Zeleny, Jindrich 1922- 132
Zeleny, Lawrence 1904- 61-64
Zeleny, Leslie D(ay) 1898- 45-48
Zelermyer, William 1914- CANR-28
Earlier sketch in CA 1-4R
Zeligs, Meyer A(aron) 1909-1978 CAP-2
Obituary 77-80
Earlier sketch in CA 23-24
Zeligs, Rose 57-60
Zelikow, Philip 1954- 152
Zelinka, Sydney 1906(?)-1981 Obituary 102
Zelinsky, Paul O. 1953- CANR-38
Earlier sketch in CA 121
See also MAICYA
See also SATA 49, 102
See also SATA-Brief 33
Zelinsky, Wilbur 1921- 13-16R
Zelizer, Barbie 1954- 146
Zelizer, Viviana A. 1946- 125
Zelk, Zoltan 1906-1981 Obituary 103
Zelko, Harold Philip 1908- CANR-1
Earlier sketch in CA 1-4R
Zell, Hans M(artin) 1940- CANR-64
Earlier sketches in CA 113, CANR-32
Zellan, Audrey Penn
See Penn, Audrey
See also SATA 22
Zeller, Belle 1903- 57-60
Zeller, Frederic 1924- 132
Zeller, Frederick A. 1931- 21-24R
Zellerbach, Merla 1930- 1-4R
Zellers, Parker 1927- 37-40R
Zellmann-Finkbeiner, Peter 1942- 49-52
Zellner, Arnold 1927- 41-44R
Zelman, Aaron S(hepard) 1946- 101
Zelman, Anita 1924- 101
Zelman, Leon 1928- 164
Zelmer, A(dam) C(harles) Lynn 1943- CANR-16
Earlier sketch in CA 89-92
Zelomek, A. Wilbert 1900-1980 Obituary 97-100
Zelver, Patricia (Farrell) 1923- 29-32R
Zemach, Harve
See Fischtrom, Harvey
See also SATA 3
Zemach, Kaethe 1958- CANR-8
Earlier sketch in CA 57-60
See also SATA 49
See also SATA-Brief 39
Zemach, Margot 1931-1989 CANR-38
Obituary 128
Earlier sketch in CA 97-100
See also MAICYA
See also SATA 21, 70
See also SATA-Obit 59
Zeman, Jarold Knox 1926- 101
Zeman, Zbynek Anthony Bohuslav 1928-
CANR-44
Earlier sketch in CA 69-72
Zemansky, Mark W(aldo) 1900-1981 Obituary 105
Zemeckis, Robert 1952- 151
See also AAYA 16
Zenani, Nongenile Masithathu 1905(?)- 146
Zencey, Eric 1954(?)- 152
Zend, Robert 1929- 115
Zender, Karl F(rancis) 1937- 110
Zenger, John Peter 1697-1746 DLB 24, 43
Zenith, Richard 1956- 139
Zenkovsky, Serge A. 1907- CANR-2
Earlier sketch in CA 1-4R
Zen Master Rama
See Lenz, Frederick (P.), (Jr.)
Zenowich, Christopher 1954- 134
Zens, Patricia Martin 1926-1972 5-8R
Obituary 120
See also SATA-Brief 50
Zentner, Carola 1927- 65-68
Zentner, Peter 1932- 29-32R
Zepeda, Ofelia 1954- 114
Zephaniah, Benjamin (Obadiah Iqbal) 1958- 147
See also SATA 86
Zephir, Flore 1958- 162
Zephir, Jacques J(oseph) 1925- 45-48
Zepke, Brent Eric 1943- CANR-13
Earlier sketch in CA 69-72
Zepp, Ira G(ilbert), Jr. 1929- 135
Brief entry 114
Zerafa, Judy 1941- 113
Zerbe, Jerome (B.) 1904-1988 CANR-37
Obituary 126
Earlier sketch in CA 17-20R
Zerby, Lewis Kenneth 1916- 49-52
Zerden, Sheldon 1924- CANR-10
Earlier sketch in CA 25-28R
Zerin, Edward 1920- 5-8R
Zerman, Melvyn Bernard 1930- CANR-14
Earlier sketch in CA 77-80
See also SATA 46
Zernov, Nicolas (Michael) 1898-1980 CANR-6
Earlier sketch in CA 9-12R
Zerof, Herbert G. 1934- 85-88
Zesmer, David M(ordecai) 1924- 65-68
Zeta
See Cope, (Vincent) Zachary
Zetford, Tully
See Bulmer, (Henry) Kenneth
Zetkin, Clara 1857-1933 154
Zetler, Robert L. 1908- 1-4R
Zettel, Sarah 1965- 165
Zetterling, Mai (Elisabeth) 1925-1994 126
Obituary 144
Brief entry 111
Zettl, Herbert (Lorenz) 1929- 41-44R
Zettler, Howard G. 1926- Brief entry 113
Zettner, Pat 1940- 138
See also SATA 70
Zeuner, Frederick E(verard) 1905-1963 5-8R
Zeveloff, Samuel I. 1950- 140
Zevi, Bruno 1918- CANR-18
Earlier sketch in CA 101
Zevin, Ben David 1896(?)-1984 Obituary 114
Zevin, Jack 1940- 93-96
Zevin, Robert B(rooke) 1936- 117
Zeydel, Edwin H(ermann) 1893-1973 5-8R
Obituary 103
Zeyher, Lewis R. 1906- 25-28R
Zgusta, Ladislav 1924- 41-44R
Zhang, Christopher Zhong-Yuan 1954- SATA 91
Zhang, Jie 1937- 133
Zhang, Song Nan 1942- 151
See also SATA 85
Zhang, Xinxin 1953- 134
Zhdanov, Andrei Alexandrovich 1896-1948 167
Brief entry 117
See also TCLC 18
Zheludkov, Sergei 1909(?)-1984 Obituary 111
Zhenkai, Zhao 1949- CANR-69
See also Bei, Dao
Zhivkova, Lyudmila (Todorova)
1942-1981 Obituary 108
Zholkovsky, Alexander K(onstantinovich) 1937- 133
Zhu, Hong 1933- 139
Zhukov, Georgi K(onstantinovich)
1896(?)-1974 Obituary 110
Ziadeh, Farhat Jacob 1917- CANR-14
Earlier sketch in CA 25-28R
Ziadeh, Nicola A(bdo) 1907- 29-32R
Ziavras, Charles E.
See Jarvis, Charles E(fthemios)
Zibart, Carl F. 1907- 73-76
Zicree, Mark Scott 1955- 149
Zidek, Anthony 1936- 17-20R
Zidek, Tony
See Zidek, Anthony
Ziedonis, Arvids, Jr. 1931- 57-60
Ziefert, Harriet 1941- 168
See also SATA 101
Ziefle, Helmut W(ilhelm) 1939- 130
Zieg, Joan (Gallina) 116
Ziegel, Vic 1938(?)- Brief entry 122
Ziegelmueller, George (William) 1930- 45-48
Ziegenhagen, Eduard A(rthur) 1935- CANR-25
Earlier sketch in CA 45-48
Ziegenhagen, Eric CLC 55
Zieger, Robert H. 1938- 29-32R
Ziegfeld, Edwin Henry 1905-1987 Obituary 123
Ziegfeld, Richard E(van) 1948- 109
Ziegler, Alan 1947- CANR-3
Earlier sketch in CA 49-52
Ziegler, Arthur P(aul), Jr. 1937- 57-60
Ziegler, Bette 1940- 81-84
Ziegler, Charles E. 1953- 126
Ziegler, Donald J(enks) 1924- 25-28R
Ziegler, Edward K(rusen) 1903- 57-60
Ziegler, Elsie Reif 1910- 1-4R
Ziegler, Isabelle 1904- 25-28R
Ziegler, Jack (Denmore) 1942- 109
See also SATA 60
Ziegler, Jean 1934- 97-100
Ziegler, Jesse H(unsberger) 1913- CANR-19
Earlier sketch in CA 25-28R
Ziegler, Philip (Sandeman) 1929- 49-52
Ziegler, Raymond J. 1922- 13-16R
Ziegler, Richard S. 1931- 101
Ziegler, Ronald M(elvin) 1935- 102
Ziegler, (Karl Reinhart Ludwig) Theobald
1846-1918 Brief entry 119
Ziel, Ron 1939- 21-24R
Zielinski, David 1953- 132
Ziemer, Gregor (Athalwin) 1899-198(?) CANR-26
Earlier sketches in CAP-1, CA 13-14
Ziemer, Paul 1921(?)-1985 Obituary 117
Ziemian, Joseph 1922-1971 65-68
Ziemienski, Dennis (Theodore) 1947- SATA 10
Ziemke, Donald C(harles) 1929- 5-8R
Ziemke, Earl F(rederick) 1922- 37-40R
Zierold, Norman (John) 1927- 17-20R
Zieroth, Dale 1946- 117
See also DLB 60
Ziesler, J(ohn) A(nthony) 1930- CANR-1
Earlier sketch in CA 45-48
Zietlow, E(dward) R. 1932- CANR-7
Earlier sketch in CA 17-20R
Zietlow, Paul Nathan 1935- 93-96
Zietz, Karyl Lynn 151
Ziewacz, Lawrence E. 1942- 125
Zif, Jay Jehiel 1936- 37-40R
Ziff, Gil 1938- 106
Ziff, Larzer 1927- CANR-50
Earlier sketches in CA 13-16R, CANR-7, 25
Ziffrin, Marilyn J. 1926- 148
Zigal, Thomas 1948- 153
Zigler, Edward F(rank) 1930- CANR-33
Earlier sketches in CA 41-44R, CANR-15
Zigler und Kliphausen, Heinrich Anshelm von
1663-1697 DLB 168
Zigrosser, Carl 1891-1975 Obituary 111
Zijderveld, Anton C(ornelis) 1937- CANR-12
Earlier sketch in CA 29-32R
Zikmund, Barbara Brown 1939- 117
Zikmund, Joseph II 1937- CANR-15
Earlier sketch in CA 65-68
Zilahy, Lajos 1891(?)-1974 165
Obituary 53-56
Zilbergeld, Bernie 1939- 112
Zilbert, Edward R(udolph) 1925- 118
Zilboorg, Caroline (Crawford) 1948- 137
Zilg, Gerard Colby 1945- 57-60
Ziliox, Marc
See Fichter, George S.
Zillah
See Macdonald, Zillah K(atherine)
Zilmer, Bertram G. 1899(?)-1976 Obituary 65-68
Zilversmit, Arthur 1932- 25-28R
Zim, Herbert S(pencer) 1909-1994 CANR-17
Obituary 147
Earlier sketch in CA 13-16R
See also CLR 2
See also JRDA
See also MAICYA
See also SAAS 2
See also SATA 1, 30
See also SATA-Obit 85
Zim, Sonia Bleeker 1909-1971 CANR-3
Obituary 33-36R
Earlier sketch in CA 1-4R
See also Bleeker, Sonia
Zima, Gordon 1920- 155
See also SATA 90
Ziman, H(erbert) D(avid) 1902-1983 Obituary 110
Ziman, John M(ichael) 1925- CANR-29
Earlier sketch in CA 25-28R
Zimbalist, Andrew 1947- 142
Zimbardo, Philip G(eorge) 1933- 85-88
Zimbardo, Rose (Abdelnour) 1932- 17-20R
Zimdars-Swartz, Sandra L. 1949- 141
Zimelman, Nathan 1921- 133
See also SATA 65
See also SATA-Brief 37
Zimet, Melvin 1913- 73-76
Zimet, Sara (Florence) Goodman 1929- 25-28R
Zimiles, Martha Rogers 1946- 41-44R
Zimiles, Murray 1941- 41-44R
Zimin, Alexander 1920-1980 Obituary 97-100
Zimmer, A(rno) B. 1945- 105
Zimmer, Anne Y(oung) 1920- 85-88
Zimmer, Basil G(eorge) 1920- 13-16R
Zimmer, Dirk 1943- SATA 65
Zimmer, Eric 1932- 61-64
Zimmer, Herbert 1924- 1-4R
Zimmer, Jill Schary
See Robinson, Jill
Zimmer, Maude Files 1905- 25-28R
Zimmer, Paul J. 1934- CANR-56
Earlier sketches in CA 21-24R, CANR-27
See also DLB 5
Zimmer, Timothy W. L. 1947- 29-32R
Zimmerli, Walther Theodor
1907-1983 Obituary 111
Zimmerman, Bill
See Zimmerman, William
Zimmerman, Bill 1940- 69-72
Zimmerman, Bruce 1952- CANR-70
Earlier sketch in CA 131
Zimmerman, Carle C(lark) 1897-1983 CANR-21
Earlier sketch in CA 25-28R
Zimmerman, Cynthia (Diane) 1943- 154
Zimmerman, Dale A. 1928- 124
Zimmerman, David R(adoff) 1934- 57-60
Zimmerman, Deirdre A. 1959- 120
Zimmerman, Donald E(dward) 1944- 151
Zimmerman, Ed 1933(?)-1972 Obituary 37-40R
Zimmerman, Eleanor (Goedeke) 1916- 61-64
Zimmerman, Everett (Lee) 1936- 110
Zimmerman, Franklin B(ershir) 1923- CANR-12
Earlier sketch in CA 13-16R
Zimmerman, Fred W(esley) 1921- CANR-2
Earlier sketch in CA 1-4R
Zimmerman, Gary 1951- 107
Zimmerman, Gordon G(lenn) 1922- 13-16R
Zimmerman, H(einz) Werner 1951- 168
See also SATA 101
Zimmerman, Irene 1907- 37-40R
Zimmerman, Irla Lee 1923- 57-60
Zimmerman, Isidore 1917(?)-1983 Obituary 111
Zimmerman, Joseph Francis 1928- CANR-37
Earlier sketches in CA 5-8R, CANR-2, 17
Zimmerman, Mary K. 1945- 81-84
Zimmerman, Michael E(dward) 1946- 108
Zimmerman, Muriel L. 1938- 166
Zimmerman, Naoma 1914- 1-4R
See also SATA 10
Zimmerman, Paul A(lbert) 1918- Brief entry 109
Zimmerman, Paul D. 1938-1993 115
Obituary 141
Zimmerman, Paul Lionel 1932- CANR-10
Earlier sketch in CA 25-28R
Zimmerman, R(obert) D(ingwall) 163
Zimmerman, Robert
See Dylan, Bob
Zimmerman, Shirley L(ee) 1925- 144
Zimmerman, Velma E. 1902- 29-32R
Zimmerman, William 1936- 53-56
Zimmerman, William 1940- 69-72
Zimmermann, Arnold E. 1909- 101
See also SATA 58
Zimmermann, Caroline A(nna) 1944- 102
Zimmermann, Ethel Agnes 1909-1984 129
Obituary 112
Zimmermann, Jon E(mil) 1933- 101
Zimmeth, Mary
See Schomaker, Mary Zimmeth
Zimmy
See Stratemeyer, Edward L.
Zimnik, Reiner 1930- 77-80
See also CLR 3
See also SATA 36
Zimpel, Lloyd 1929- 37-40R
Zimring, Franklin E(ster) 1942- 93-96
Zimroth, Evan 1943- 93-96
Zimroth, Peter L. 1943- 93-96
Zimunya, (Bonas) Musaemura 1949- 133
Zinbarg, Edward D(onald) 1934- 21-24R
Zinberg, Norman E(arl) 1921-1989 CANR-16
Obituary 128
Earlier sketch in CA 85-88
Zincgref, Julius Wilhelm 1591-1635 DLB 164
Zindel, Bonnie 1943- CANR-31
Earlier sketch in CA 105
See also SATA 34
Zindel, Paul 1936- CANR-65
Earlier sketches in CA 73-76, CANR-31
See also AAYA 2
See also CLC 6, 26
See also CLR 3, 45
See also DA
See also DAB
See also DAC
See also DAM DRAM, MST, NOV
See also DC 5
See also DLB 7, 52
See also JRDA
See also MAICYA
See also MTCW 1
See also SATA 16, 58, 102
Zinder, Norton (David) 1928- 158
Ziner, Feenie
See Ziner, Florence
Ziner, Florence 1921- CANR-1
Earlier sketch in CA 1-4R
See also SATA 5
Zines, Leslie 1930- 137
Zingara, Professor
See Leeming, Joseph
Zingg, Paul J(oseph) 1945- 157
Zink, Zinovy 1945- 139
Zink, David D(aniel) 1927- CANR-3
Earlier sketch in CA 45-48

Zink, Lubor Jan 1920- CANR-9
Earlier sketch in CA 65-68
Zinke, George William 1904- 5-8R
Zinkin, Taya (Nathalie) Ettinger 1918- CANR-2
Earlier sketch in CA 1-4R
Zinn, Howard 1922- CANR-33
Earlier sketches in CA 1-4R, CANR-2
Zinner, Paul E(rnest) 1922- 1-4R
Zinner, Stephen H. 1939- 119
Zinnes, Harriet 1919- CANR-46
Earlier sketches in CA 45-48, CANR-1, 21
See also DLB 193
Zinov'Ev, A. A.
See Zinoviev, Alexander (Aleksandrovich)
Zinoviev, Alexander (Aleksandrovich) 1922- 133
Brief entry 116
See also CAAS 10
See also CLC 19
Zinsser, Caroline 1930- 141
Zinsser, Hans 1878-1940 159
Zinsser, Judith P. 1943- 146
Zinsser, William (Knowlton) 1922- CANR-58
Earlier sketches in CA 17-20R, CANR-12, 31
Zintz, Miles V(ernon) 1918- 29-32R
Zinzendorf, Nikolaus Ludwig von 1700-1760 ... DLB 168
Ziolkowski, Eric J(ozef) 1958- 139
Ziolkowski, Theodore (Joseph) 1932- CANR-12
Earlier sketch in CA 13-16R
Ziomek, Henryk 1922- CANR-57
Earlier sketches in CA 45-48, CANR-1, 30
Zion, Eugene 1913-1975 81-84
Obituary 61-64
See also SATA 18
Zion, Gene
See Zion, Eugene
Zionts, Stanley 1937- 49-52
Zipes, Jack (David) 1937- CANR-9
Earlier sketch in CA 65-68
Zipser, Arthur 1909- 113
Ziring, Lawrence 1928- CANR-53
Earlier sketches in CA 73-76, CANR-13, 29
Zisfein, Melvin Bernard 1926- 108
Zisk, Betty H(ershberger) 1930- CANR-25
Earlier sketch in CA 45-48
Ziskin, Harriet 1933- 153
Ziskind, Sylvia 1906- 29-32R
Zistel, Era CANR-41
Earlier sketches in CA 25-28R, CANR-19
Zitkala-Sa
See Bonnin, Gertrude
See also DLB 175
Zitkala Sa
See Bonnin, Gertrude
Zito, George V(incent) 1923- 113
Zitta, Victor 1926- 21-24R
Zivkovic, Peter D(ragi) 1929- 53-56
Zjawin, Dorothy 1945- 111
Zmijewsky, Boris 1946- CANR-20
Earlier sketch in CA 69-72
Zmora, Nurith 1950- 150
Zneimer, John (Nicolas) 1925- 29-32R
Zobel, Hiller B(ellin) 1932- 21-24R
Zobel, Louise Purwin 1922- 110
Zober, Martin 1918- 37-40R
Zochert, Donald (Paul, Jr.) 1938- 81-84
Zodhiates, Spiros 1922- CANR-10
Earlier sketch in CA 21-24R
Zodikoff, David H(yman) 1933- 37-40R
Zodrow, John 1944- 77-80
Zoellner, Robert 1926- 57-60
Zoffer, Gerald R. 1926(?)-1982 Obituary 107
Zohar, Danah 1944- 124
Brief entry 118
Zohn, Arnold 1924-1985 Obituary 116
Zohn, Harry 1923- CANR-50
Earlier sketches in CA 25-28R, CANR-10, 25
Zoilus
See Lovecraft, H(oward) P(hillips)
Zola, Emile (Edouard Charles Antoine) 1840-1902 138
Brief entry 104
See also DA
See also DAB
See also DAC
See also DAM MST, NOV
See also DLB 123
See also TCLC 1, 6, 21, 41
See also WLC
Zola, Irving Kenneth 1935- 107
Zola, Marion (Joy) 1945- 108
Zolar
See King, Bruce
Zolberg, Aristide R(odolphe) 1931- 21-24R
Zolberg, Vera L. 1932- 139
Zolbrod, Leon M(ax) 1930- 57-60
Zolbrod, Paul G(eyer) 1932- CANR-10
Earlier sketch in CA 21-24R
Zolf, Larry 1934- 101
Zoline, Pamela 1941- 161
See also CLC 62
Zoll, Donald Atwell 1927- 5-8R
Zolla, Elemire 1926- CANR-6
Earlier sketch in CA 9-12R
See also DLB 196
Zollinger, Gulielma 1856-1917 Brief entry 109
See also SATA-Brief 27
Zollinger, Norman 1921- 81-84
Zollitsch, Herbert G(eorge) 1916- 13-16R
Zollschan, George K(arl) 1930- 13-16R
Zolo, Danilo 1936- 141
Zolotas, Xenophon
See Zolotas, Xenophon E(uthymiou)
Zolotas, Xenophon E(uthymiou) 1904- 133
Zolotow, Charlotte S(hapiro) 1915- CANR-38
Earlier sketches in CA 5-8R, CANR-3, 18
See also CLR 2
See also DLB 52
See also MAICYA
See also SATA 1, 35, 78
Zolotow, Maurice 1913-1991 .... CANR-1
Obituary 133
Earlier sketch in CA 1-4R
Zolynas, Al(girdas Richard) 1945- 105
Zonderman, Jon 1957- 156
See also SATA 92
Zonia, Dhimitri 1921- .... SATA 20
Zonik, Eleanor Dorothy 1918- 13-16R
Zonis, Marvin 1936- 37-40R
Zonker, Patricia 85-88
Zook, David H(artzler), Jr. 1930-(?) 1-4R
Obituary 103
Zook, Deborah
See Green, Deborah
Zook, Paul D(avid) 1912- 5-8R
Zopf, Paul E(dward), Jr. 1931- 37-40R
Zophy, Jonathan Walter 1945- 104
Zopi
See Keys, Kerry Shawn
Zopilote
See Keys, Kerry Shawn
Zorach, William 1887-1966 .... CAP-1
Earlier sketch in CA 13-16
Zorn, Eric 1958- 134
Zorn, Robert L. 1938- 115
Zornes, Jeanne Doering 1947- 113
Zornow, William Frank 1920- 41-44R
Zoshchenko, Mikhail (Mikhailovich) 1895-1958 . 160
Brief entry 115
See also SSC 15
See also TCLC 15
Zosky, Brenda 1942- 89-92
Zoss, Joel 1944- 142
Zotos, Stephanos 21-24R
Zschokke, Heinrich 1771-1848 .... DLB 94
Zsoldos, Laszlo 1925- 37-40R
Zubek, John P(eter) 1925- 37-40R
Zubin, Joseph 1900-1990 .... CANR-30
Obituary 133
Earlier sketch in CA 17-20R
Zubly, John Joachim 1724-1781 .... DLB 31
Zu-Bolton, Ahmos II 1935- .... DLB 41
Zubrow, Ezra B. W. 1945- CANR-10
Earlier sketch in CA 65-68
Zubrowski, Bernard 1939- CANR-59
Earlier sketch in CA 104
See also SATA 35, 90
Zubrowski, Bernie
See Zubrowski, Bernard
Zubrzycki, Jerzy (George) 1920- CANR-10
Earlier sketch in CA 21-24R
Zucchi, John E. 1955- 138
Zuccotti, Susan 1940- 139
Zuck, Lowell H(ubert) 1926- 65-68
Zucker, Adolf Eduard 1890-1971 Obituary 116
Zucker, David 1947- 138
Zucker, David Hard 1938- 37-40R
Zucker, Dolores Mae Bolton CANR-7
Earlier sketch in CA 17-20R
Zucker, Jack 1935- 29-32R
Zucker, Jerry 1950- 138
Zucker, Martin 1937- CANR-57
Earlier sketches in CA 112, CANR-30
Zucker, Miriam S. 1962- 128
See also SATA 85
Zucker, Moses 1902-1987 Obituary 123
Zucker, Norman L(ivingston) 1933- 158
Zucker, Paul 1888-1971 .... CAP-2
Obituary 29-32R
Earlier sketch in CA 23-24
Zuckerman, Alan S(aul) 1945- CANR-22
Earlier sketch in CA 105
Zuckerman, Arthur J(acob) 1907- 41-44R
Zuckerman, Edward (Ben) 1948- 123
Zuckerman, Harriet 1937- 136
Zuckerman, Marvin 1928- 141
Zuckerman, Mary Ellen 1954- 137
Zuckerman, Michael 1939- 37-40R
Zuckerman, Seth (Abram) 1961- 124
Zuckerman, Solly 1904- CANR-28
Earlier sketch in CA 65-68
Zuckerman, Yitzhak 1917-1981 Obituary 108
Zuckermann, George 1916- 53-56
Zuckermann, Wolfgang (Joachim) 1922- 139
Zuckert, Catherine H. 1942- 155
Zuckmayer, Carl 1896-1977 69-72
See also CLC 18
See also DLB 56, 124
Zudeck, Darryl 1961- .... SATA 61
Zuelke, Ruth E. 1924- 13-16R
Zuelzer, Wolf(gang) W(illiam) 1909-1987 110
Obituary 122
Zuercher, Erik Jan
See Zuercher, Erik-Jan
Zuercher, Erik-Jan 1953- 158
Zuesse, Evan M. 1940- 105
Zug, Margaret Philbrook 1945(?)-1976 69-72
Zugsmith, Leane 1903-1969 Obituary 115
Zuidervaart, Lambert 1950- 141
Zuk, Georges
See Skelton, Robin
Zukerman, Eugenia 1944- 110
Zukin, Sharon 131
Zukofsky, Louis 1904-1978 .... CANR-39
Obituary 77-80
Earlier sketch in CA 9-12R
See also CLC 1, 2, 4, 7, 11, 18
See also DAM POET
See also DLB 5, 165
See also MTCW 1
See also PC 11
Zulaika, Joseba 1948- 137
Zulauf, Sander W(illiam) 1946- 101
Zulawski, Marek 1908-1985 Obituary 116
Zulli, Floyd (Jr.) 1922-1980 .... 37-40R
Obituary 108
Zumbo, Jim 1940- 109
Zumoff, Barnett 1926- 149
Zumwalt, Elmo Russell, Jr. 1920- 85-88
Zumwalt, Elmo Russell III 1946(?)-1988 Obituary 126
Zumwalt, Eva 1936- CANR-9
Earlier sketch in CA 65-68
Zundel, Veronica (Elsa) 1953- 120
Zunder, William (Limbery) 1938- 117
Zuniga, Jose M. 1969- 146
Zunkel, Charles Edward 1905- 57-60
Zunkel, Cleda 1903- 57-60
Zunser, Jesse 1898-1985 Obituary 118
Zunz, Olivier J. 1946- 110
Zupa, G. Anthony
See Zeck, Gerald Anthony
Zupan, Vitomil 1914-1987 .... DLB 181
Zupancic, Oton 1878-1949 .... DLB 147
Zupko, Ronald Edward 1938- CANR-13
Earlier sketch in CA 37-40R
Zupnick, I(rving) L(awrence) 1920- 45-48
Zurbo, Matt(hew) 1967- 166
See also SATA 98
Zurcher, Arnold John 1903(?)-1974 Obituary . 49-52
Zurcher, Erik Jan
See Zuercher, Erik-Jan
Zurcher, Erik-Jan
See Zuercher, Erik-Jan
Zurcher, Louis A(nthony), Jr. 1936- CANR-15
Earlier sketch in CA 41-44R
Zurhorst, Charles (Stewart, Jr.) 1913- CANR-1
Earlier sketch in CA 45-48
See also SATA 12
Zuriff, G(erald) E(ugene) 1943- 123
Zurita (Canessa), Raul 1951- 131
See also HW
zur Muehlen, Hermynia 1883-1951
See zur Muhlen, Hermynia
See also DLB 56
zur Muhlen, Hermynia
See zur Muehlen, Hermynia
See also DLB 56
Zuroff, Efraim 1948- 149
Zuromskis, Diane
See Stanley, Diane
Zuromskis, Diane Stanley
See Stanley, Diane
Zusne, Leonard 1924- 81-84
Zuwaylif, Fadil H. 1932- CANR-25
Earlier sketch in CA 45-48
Zuwiyya, Jalal (Zakariya) 1932- 77-80
Zwaanstra, Henry 1936- Brief entry 105
Zwahlen, Diana 1947- 152
See also SATA 88
Zwar, Desmond L(aurence) G(audin) 1931- 107
Zwarensteyn, Hendrik 1913-1976 .... 5-8R
Obituary 103
Zwart, Pieter (Hendrik) 1938- 53-56
Zweifel, Frances W. 1931- CANR-12
Earlier sketch in CA 73-76
See also SATA 14
Zweig, Arnold 1887-1968 Obituary 115
See also DLB 66
Zweig, David 1950- 140
Zweig, Ferdynand 1896-1988 Obituary 125
Zweig, Friderike M(aria Burger Winternitz) 1882-1971 Obituary 114
Zweig, Paul 1935-1984 85-88
Obituary 113
See also CLC 34, 42
Zweig, Ronald W. 1949- 124
Zweig, Stefan 1881-1942 Brief entry 112
See also DLB 81, 118
See also TCLC 17
Zwerdling, Alex 1932- 57-60
Zwerenz, Gerhard 1925- 33-36R
Zwerger, Lisbeth 1954- .... CLR 46
See also MAICYA
See also SAAS 13
See also SATA 66
Zwerling, L. Steven 1938- 61-64
Zwibak, Jacques 1902-1994 77-80
Obituary 143
Zwick, Peter Ronald 1942- 116
Zwicky, (Julia) Fay 1933- 154
Zwicky, Fritz 1898-1974 Obituary 49-52
Zwiebach, Burton 1933- 57-60
Zwinger, Ann (H.) 1925- CANR-30
Earlier sketches in CA 33-36R, CANR-13
See also SATA 46
Zwingli, Huldreich 1484-1531 .... DLB 179
Zwirn, Jerrold 1943- 109
Zworykin, Vladimir Kosma 1889-1982 157
Obituary 107
Zygulski, Zdzislaw 1921- 145
Zyla, Wolodymyr T(aras) 1919- CANR-2
Earlier sketch in CA 45-48
Zylberberg, Michael 1907-1971 .... CAP-2
Earlier sketch in CA 29-32
Zylbercweig, Zalman 1894-1972 Obituary .. 37-40R
Zyskind, Harold 1917-1990 57-60
Obituary 130
Zysman, John 1946- 149
Zytaruk, George John 1927- 110
Zytowski, Donald G(lenn) 1929- 29-32R